COME VISIT OUR NEW YORK CITY SHOW
Y.)
S0-AGW-142
FOUR COLOR
COMICS
BUY
SELL
WHY YOU SHOULD CALL US BEFORE YOU SELL YOUR COLLECTION OF COMICS, ARTWORK OR MEMORABILIA:
We make it easy! No waiting for payment, No song and dance about grading. We'll come to you: Anywhere, Anytime! FOUR COLOR COMICS takes the risk out of selling. Treat yourself to an honest, straight-forward experience—Sell your collection to us and walk away with more money in your pocket and a smile on your face.
And if you're looking to buy comics, original artwork or memorabilia, give us a call first! We probably already have that elusive issue or object you've been searching for—and at a price you'll like!
CALL ROBERT ROGOVIN!
(212) 675-6990
THE JOKER © 1939, 1998 DC COMICS. ALL RIGHTS RESERVED
NEW!
NEW YORK SHOWROOM: 115 W. 27th St, NY, NY 10001 TEL: (212) 675-6990, FAX (212) 675-6145
Visit our on-line
SEARCHABLE DATABASE!
1000's of Golden and Silver Age comics available without scrolling thru endless listings!
www.fourcolorcomics.com
ORIGINAL COMIC ART
SEARCH COMICS!
MOVIE POSTERS

METROPOLIS
COLLECTIBLES
873 Broadway, Suite 201
New York, NY 10003

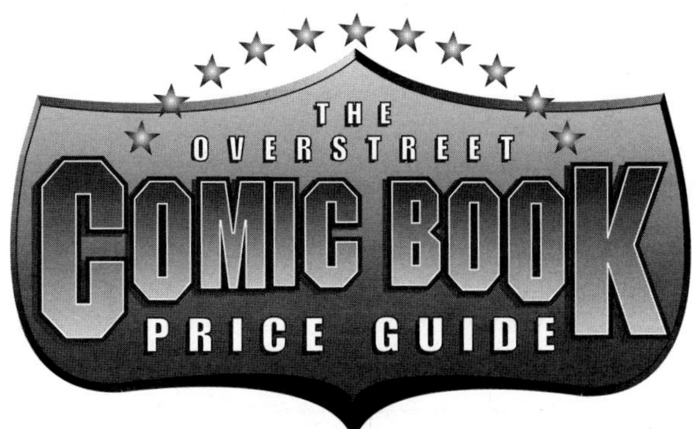

29th Edition

BOOKS FROM 1897 - PRESENT INCLUDED
CATALOGUE & EVALUATION GUIDE - ILLUSTRATED

by Robert M. Overstreet

GEMSTONE PUBLISHING:
Benn Ray • **Editor**
Arnold T. Blumberg • **Managing Editor**
Mark Huesman • **Pricing Coordinator**
Brenda Busick • **Art Director**
J. C. Vaughn • **Marketing Coordinator**

SPECIAL CONTRIBUTORS TO THIS EDITION:
Robert Beerbohm, Arnold T. Blumberg, Stephen Fishler, Mark Huesman, M. Thomas Inge, Richard D. Olson, Ph.D., Marc Patten, Benn Ray, J. C. Vaughn

SENIOR ADVISORS FOR OVER 20 YEARS:
Gary M. Carter • Steve Geppi • Bruce Hamilton • David R. Smith
John Snyder • Terry Stroud • Harry B. Thomas

SPECIAL ADVISORS TO THIS EDITION:
David T. Alexander • Dave Anderson • David J. Anderson, D.D.S. • Robert L. Beerbohm
Jon Berk • John Chruscinski • Gary Colabuono • Bill Cole • Larry Curcio • Gary Dolgoff
Joe Dungan • Conrad Eschenberg • Richard Evans • Stephen Fishler • Keif Fromm
Philip J. Gaudino • Steve Gentner • Michael Goldman • Jamie Graham
Daniel Greenhalgh • Eric Groves • Gary Guzzo • John Grasse • John Hone • John Hauser
Bill Hughes • Rob Hughes • Joseph Koch • Phil Levine • Joe Mannarino • Rick Manzella
Harry Matetsky • Jon McClure • Matt Nelson • Hugh O'Kennon • Richard Olson • Michael Naiman
James Payette • Ron Pussell • Todd Reznik • "Doc" Robinson • Robert Rogovin, • Rory Root
Robert Roter • Chuck Rozanski • Matt Schiffman • Dave Smith • Tony Starks • Doug Sulipa
Joel Thingvall • Raymond S. True • Joe Vereneault • John Verzyl • Rose Verzyl
Jerry Weist • Mark Wilson • Harley Yee • Vincent Zurzolo, Jr.

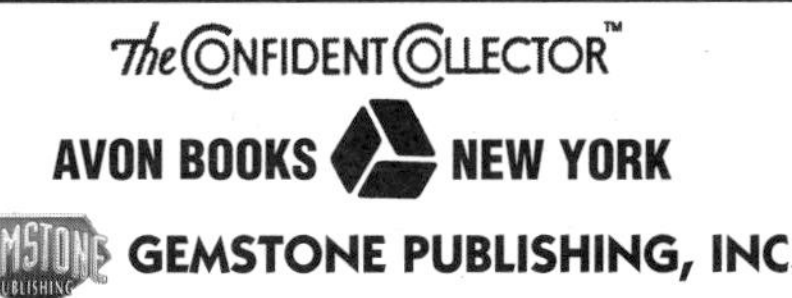
The Confident Collector™
AVON BOOKS NEW YORK
GEMSTONE PUBLISHING, INC.

Serious Comic Book Collectors, Also Look For
THE OVERSTREET COMIC BOOK GRADING GUIDE
By Robert M. Overstreet and Gary M. Carter
A Confident Collector Title from Avon Books

Important Notice. All of the information, including valuations, in this book has been compiled from the most reliable sources, and every effort has been made to eliminate errors and questionable data. Nevertheless, the possibility of error always exists in a work of such immense scope. The publisher will not be held responsible for losses which may occur in the purchase, sale, or other transaction of items because of information contained herein. Readers who feel they have discovered errors are invited to *write* and inform us so that the errors may be corrected in subsequent editions.

Cover Illustration by Alex Ross.

THE OVERSTREET COMIC BOOK PRICE GUIDE (29th Edition) is an original publication of Gemstone Publishing, Inc. and Avon Books, Inc. This edition has never before appeared in book form.

AVON BOOKS, INC.
1350 Avenue of the Americas
New York, New York 10019

Published by arrangement with Gemstone Publishing
ISBN: 0-380-80780-7

First Avon Books Trade Printing: April 1999
AVON TRADEMARK REG. U.S. PAT. OFF. AND IN OTHER COUNTRIES, MARCA REGISTRADA, HECHO EN U.S.A.

Printed in the U.S.A.
10 9 8 7 6 5 4 3 2 1

THE EARTH'S
MIGHTIEST
HEROES
THE WORLD'S
GREATEST
...COMICS
MARVEL COMICS

TABLE OF CONTENTS

ACKNOWLEDGEMENTS

Mark Arnold (Harvey data); Larry Bigman (Frazetta-Williamson data); Glenn Bray (Kurtzman data); Gary Carter (DC data); J. B. Clifford Jr. (EC data); Gary Coddington (Superman data); Wilt Conine (Fawcett data); Dr. S. M. Davidson (Cupples & Leon data); Al Dellinges (Kubert data); David Gerstein (Walt Disney Comics data); Kevin Hancer (Tarzan data); Charles Heffelfinger and Jim Ivey (March of Comics listing); R. C. Holland and Ron Pussell (Seduction and Parade of Pleasure data); Grant Irwin (Quality data); Richard Kravitz (Kelly data); Phil Levine (giveaway data); Dan Malan & Charles Heffelfinger (Classic Comics data); Fred Nardelli (Frazetta data); Michelle Nolan (love comics); Mike Nolan (MLJ, Timely, Nedor data); George Olshevsky (Timely data); Richard Olson (LOA & R. F. Outcault data); Scott Pell ('50s data); Greg Robertson (National data); Don Rosa (Late 1940s to 1950s data); Matt Schiffman (Bronze Age data); Frank Scigliano (Little Lulu data); Gene Seger (Buck Rogers data); Rick Sloane (Archie data); David R. Smith, Archivist, Walt Disney Productions (Disney data); Tony Starks (Silver and Bronze Age data); Don and Maggie Thompson (Four Color listing); Mike Tiefenbacher & Jerry Sinkovec (Atlas and National data); Raymond True (Classic Comics data); Jim Vadeboncoeur Jr. (Williamson and Atlas data); Kim Weston (Disney and Barks data); Cat Yronwode (Spirit data); Andrew Zerbe and Gary Behymer (M. E. data).

My appreciation must also be extended to Tom Gordon for providing Platinum Age books for photographing and to Dave Smith, Jerry Weist, Robert Roter, Joe Mannarino, Conrad Eschenberg, Eric Groves, Jon McClure, Matt Schiffman, Dave Anderson (OK), Gary Colabuono, Rod Dyke, Gary Guzzo, Harley Yee, John Snyder, Gary Dolgoff, Tony Starks, Matt Hawkins, Lou Bank, Jeff Mariotte, Donna Sava, Maureen McTigue, Marty Stever, Gale Young, Steve Geppi, Hugh O'Kennon and Don Maris, for their continued support and help; to Stephen Fishler and Marc Patten for their "How to Sell Your Comic Collection"; to Dr. Richard Olson for grading and Yellow Kid information; to Tom Inge for his "Chronology of the American Comic Book"; to Robert Beerbohm and & Richard Olson for their introductions to the Platinum Age and Golden Age sections; to Bill Blackbeard of the San Francisco Academy of Comic Art for his Platinum Age cover photos; to Bill Spicer and Zetta DeVoe (Western Publishing Co.) for their contribution of data; and especially to Bill for his kind permission to reprint portions of his and Jerry Bails' America's Four Color Pastime.

Thanks, Doug Sulipa for continuing to provide detailed data on Bronze Age books! Finally, several people including, Bruce Hamilton, Stephen Fishler, Jim Payette, Rob Rogovin, Joe Vereneault, Dave Anderson, and Mark Wilson supplied detailed pricing data, market reviews or other ideas included in this edition. Thanks is also given to Ron Pussell, John Verzyl and Terry Stroud for their year-long help and advice.

Special credit is due our talented staff for their assistance with this edition; to Benn Ray (Editor), Arnold T. Blumberg (Managing Editor), Mark Huesman (Pricing Coordinator), Brenda Busick (Art Director), and J. C. Vaughn (Marketing) for their valuable contributions to this edition and the continuing success of the Annual Price Guide. Thanks is also due my wife, Caroline, for her encouragement and support on such a tremendous project, and to all who placed ads in this edition.

Acknowledgement is also due to the following people who generously contributed much needed data for this edition:

Henrik Andreasen
Stephen Baer
Jonathan Bennett
Ivan Briggs
Mike Bromberg
Richard M. Brown
Quinton Clem
Jack Copley
Kyle Corbin
Timothy F. Craig
Josh Cudney
Joseph T. Farrell
Joseph Garner
Duncan Holmes
Soroh Huesman
H. Krissoff
Robert C. Kuhl
Rob Ledford
Mark Linder
Stefan Linz
Philipp Mahr
David W. Messer
Howard E. Michaels
Al Mindy
John Mlachnik
Bruce L. Moore
Ray Ossman
David Peattie
Gerry Rawlins
Jim Stangas
Barry Stephens
Jeff Walker
Timothy M. Walters
Murray R. Ward
M. Wayne Williams

INTRODUCTION

Congratulations! We at Gemstone welcome you to the hobby of comic books. This book is the most comprehensive reference work available on comics. It is also respected and used by dealers and collectors everywhere. The Overstreet price is the accepted price around the world, and we have not earned this privilege easily. Through hard work, diligence and constant contact with the market for decades, Overstreet has become the most trusted name in comics.

HOW TO USE THIS BOOK

This volume is an accurate, detailed alphabetical list of comic books and their retail values. Comic books are listed by title, regardless of company. Prices listed are shown in Good, Fine and Near Mint condition with many key books priced in an additional Very Fine grade. Comic books that fall in between the grades listed can be priced simply with the following procedure: Very Good is half way between Good and Fine; Very Fine is half way between Fine and Near Mint (unless a VF price is already shown). The older true Mint books usually bring a premium over the Near Mint price. Books in Fair bring 50 to 70% of the Good price. Some books only show a Very Fine price as the highest grade. The author has not been able to determine if these particular books exist in better than Very Fine condition, thus the omission of a Near Mint price. Most comic books are listed in groups, i.e., 11-20, 21-30, 31-50, etc. The prices listed opposite these groupings represent the value of each issue in that group. More detailed information is given for individual comic books. If you are looking for a particular character, consult the first appearance indexes which will help you locate the correct title and issue. This book also contains hundreds of ads covering all aspects of this hobby. Whether you are buying or selling, the advertising sections can be of tremendous benefit to you.

NEW COMIC BOOKS LISTED

New comic books usually enter the listings at their retail cover price. Since new listings have yet to become valuable on the secondary market, the listed cover price only represents what it costs to buy a reading copy at a retail store. These books are not yet collectors items and their value in the collector's market would be nil.

COMIC BOOK VALUES LISTED

All values listed in this book are in U.S. currency and are retail prices based on (but not limited to) reports from our extensive network of experienced advisors which include convention sales, mail order, auctions, unpublished personal sales and stores. Overstreet, with several decades of market experience, has developed a unique and comprehensive system for gathering, documenting, averaging and pricing data on comic books. The end result is a true fair market value for your use. We have earned the reputation for our cautious, conservative approach to pricing comic books. You, the collector, can be assured that the prices listed in this volume are the most accurate and useful in print.

IMPORTANT NOTE: This book is not a dealer's price list, although some dealers may base their prices on the values listed. The true value of any comic book is what you are willing to pay. Prices listed herein are an indication of what collectors (not dealers) would probably pay. For one reason or another, these collectors might want certain books badly, or else need specific issues to complete their runs and so are willing to pay more.

DEALERS' POSITION: Dealers are not in a position to pay the full prices listed, but work on a percentage depending largely on the amount of investment required and the quality of material offered. Usually they will pay from 20 to 70% of the list price depending on how long it will take them to sell the collection after making the investment; the higher the demand and better the condition, the more the percentage. Most dealers are faced with expenses such as advertising, travel, telephone and mailing, rent, employee salaries, plus convention costs. These costs all go in before the books are sold. The high demand books usually sell right away but there are many other titles that are difficult to sell due to low demand. Sometimes a dealer will have cost tied up in this type of material for several years before finally moving it. Remember, his position is that of handling, demand, and overhead. Most dealers are victims of these economics.

HOW COMIC BOOKS ARE LISTED

Comic books are listed alphabetically by title. The true title of a comic book can be found listed with the publisher's information, or indicia, usually found at the bottom of the first page. Titles that appear on the front cover can vary from the official title listed inside.

Comic book titles, sequence of issues, dates of first and last issues, publishing companies, origin and special issues are listed when known. Prominent and collectible artists are also pointed out (usually in footnotes). Page counts will always include covers. Most comic books began with a #1, but occasionally many titles began with an odd number. There is a reason for this. Publishers had to register new titles with the post office for 2nd class permits. The registration fee was expensive. To avoid this expense, many publishers would continue the numbering of new titles from old defunct titles. For instance, **Weird Science** #12 (1st issue) was continued from the defunct **Saddle Romances** #11 (the last issue). In doing this, the publishers hoped to avoid having to register new titles. However, the post office would soon discover the new title and force the publisher to pay the registration fee as well as to list the correct number. For instance, the previous title mentioned began with #12 (1st issue). Then #13 through #15 were published. The next issue became #5 after the Post Office correction. Now the sequence of published issues (see the listings) is #12-15, 5-on. This created a problem in early fandom for the collector because the numbers 12-15 in this title were duplicated.

WHAT COMIC BOOKS ARE LISTED

The Guide lists primarily American comic books due to space limitations. The earliest comic books date back to 1897 and are included in their own section under The Platinum Age. These books basically reprinted newspaper strips and were published in varying sizes, usually with cardboard covers, but sometimes as hardbacks. The format of **Funnies On Parade**, published in 1933 (saddle-stitched), soon became the standard for the modern comic book, although squarebound versions were also published. Most of these formats that appeared on newsstands will be included.

POLICY OF LISTING NEW COMIC BOOKS

The 1980s and '90s have experienced an explosion of publishers with hundreds of new titles appearing in black & white and color. Many of these comics are listed in this book, but not all due to space limitation. We will attempt to list complete information only on those titles that show some collector interest. The selection of titles to include is constantly being monitored by our board of advisors. Please do not contact us to list your new comic books. Listings are determined by the marketplace. However, we are interested in receiving review copies of all new comic books published.

THE NEXT REVOLUTION FOR COMIC BOOKS!

A NEW TEN-POINT GRADING SCALE AND A CERTIFICATION SERVICE TO GUARANTEE GRADING CONSISTENCY!

By Bruce Hamilton

History is being made, and by mid-1999, collecting comic books may never be the same. Victor Hugo once wrote that nothing is as powerful as an idea when its time has come, and now our hobby is about to be introduced to two new ideas! The first is a revised and simpler numerical grading scale for comics that retains all the familiar nomenclature (Good, Fine, Mint, etc.). The second is the establishment of a professionally consistent certification service to grade all of fandom's comic books. It sounds simple enough, but is it too tall an order? Certainly not—in fact, we predict it will stimulate fantastic growth in the next century.

Having enjoyed unprecedented advance support and advice from dozens of dealers and collectors around the country, Comics Guaranty Corporation will open for business this summer. They hope to do for comic books what their founders have already done for coins and sports cards. The process will also remain much the same; each comic to be graded will be evaluated by CGC using exacting standards and sealed in a special holder.

Here is what CGC has to say about itself:

"Comics Guaranty Corporation is based on the model of successful certification used by the leading grading service in rare coins, and the fastest growing grading service in sports cards. These companies have a proven and respected commitment to integrity, accuracy, consistency and impartiality in grading collectibles. Our team of dedicated professionals will apply this proven model of success to the unique challenges of grading comic books. CGC employees will not be permitted to engage in the commercial buying or selling of comic books. In this way CGC will remain completely impartial, having no interest other than a commitment to serving clients through accurate and consistent grading. We will release the names and background information on the management team and our grading people in a press release just prior to the company's official introduction in mid-1999."

No less an authority than Bob Overstreet commented recently that "almost no one is using our 100-point scale grading system." Even though that system can still be seen in the text headings of this year's edition, a new and simpler version will most likely be adopted by next year's Guide. This same system, which we believe will be the wave of the future, will also be used by CGC.

The major change in this new standard will be the conversion from a 100-point scale to a 10-point scale, as illustrated on the following page. The Guide is interested in hearing from any collectors or dealers. On the next several pages, we present answers to some of the most often asked and likeliest questions concerning this historic change:

NEW TEN POINT SCALE GRADING SYSTEM	
10.0	Mint
9.8	Near Mint/Mint
9.6	Near Mint +
9.4	Near Mint
9.2	Near Mint -
9.0	Very Fine/Near Mint
8.5	Very Fine +
8.0	Very Fine
7.5	Very Fine -
7.0	Fine/Very Fine
6.5	Fine +
6.0	Fine
5.5	Fine -
5.0	Very Good/Fine
4.5	Very Good +
4.0	Very Good
3.5	Very Good -
3.0	Good/Very Good
2.5	Good +
2.0	Good
1.5	Fair/Good
1.0	Fair
0.5	Poor

Q: ON THE 10-POINT SCALE, I SEE THAT NEAR MINT IS GOING TO BE NUMERICALLY HIGHER THAN IT HAS BEEN IN THE PAST. WHY IS THAT?

A. Research has determined that in the real marketplace, Very Fine/Near Mint is the highest grade usually found in most vintage comics. It therefore seems logical that this should be the beginning of 9 on a scale of 10.

Q: WOULDN'T A GRADING SERVICE ONLY BE GOOD FOR EXPENSIVE COMICS?

A. Definitely not. Experience in other fields has taught us that collectibles become more liquid and easily traded, as well as more valuable, after being graded and certified. And, incredibly, that extends to new product. In other words, the after-certification value of a comic book is likely to be higher than the total of its previous value plus the cost of certification.

Q: WHAT IF I WANT TO TAKE MY COMIC OUT OF THE SEALED HOLDER TO LOOK AT IT?

A. It's anticipated that many collectors will want to remove their comics from the holders, even though the certified grade will then no longer be applicable without re-certification. Remember, the process is designed primarily as a tool for buying and selling that establishes standards for consistency in the hobby. Nonetheless, it is also anticipated that many collectors will be content to leave a comic in its original CGC holder for protection and to enhance its liquidity when and if they decide to sell. This would eliminate any need for re-certification.

Q: WON'T MY COMICS BE DAMAGED IF I LEAVE THEM IN THE HOLDERS?

A. The CGC holder is designed to securely hold your comic book and provide many years of protection from most environmental hazards. All of the materials used have been tested for archival safety, a first line of defense that is a prudent storage plan for the collector.

Q: HOW DO I KNOW THE COMIC I'M BUYING OR HAVE SENT CGC IS THE SAME BOOK THAT'S BEEN CERTIFIED?

A. A number of scientifically advanced security measures have been built into the entire process. Once a comic is certified and encapsulated in its holder, any future attempt to open it will be visibly evident. CGC will also use digital imaging technology to randomly and selectively archive books it certifies, storing the information in its database.

Q: IF I BUY A COMIC THAT HAS BEEN CERTIFIED AT A HIGH GRADE, SAY VF/NM (VERY FINE TO NEAR MINT), HOW DO I KNOW I WILL BE SATISFIED WITH THE CONDITION WITHOUT BREAKING THE SEAL?

A. If you do break the seal you will find the comic's grade to have been determined by guidelines taken by CGC from a consensus of opinions as to books graded in similar condition by a 3-5 member advisory board--a dealer/collector committee appointed by Bob Overstreet. Neither Bob, nor any other Gemstone employee, however, will actually sit on the advisory board. Once you have bought a Comics Guaranty Corporation certified book and opened it, it's unlikely you will ever need to open another for grade verification. Though variations will exist between CGC grades and the standards of some collectors and dealers, one must remember that grading itself is not an exact science, but is a subjective art that develops from years of experience. Current disagreements in the uncertified market should diminish and will eventually be only a small over-all factor as collector confidence becomes widespread in buying books through almost any venue: by phone, mail, internet or at a convention.

Remember, the grading and certification of a comic book does not determine its value; only dealers and collectors can reach agreement on a price. What is important is to achieve the highest possible level of consistency in grading, so that you will know what you're getting when you put your money on the line. When a certified comic is offered to you by someone you don't know personally, you will no longer have doubts as to its condition.

Q: WHAT ASSURANCES AS A SUBMITTER DO I HAVE OF CONFIDENTIALITY AND ANONYMITY?

A. CGC will discuss the details of each transaction only with the original dealer who has made a submission. No information will be released concerning the certification of anyone's comics without written permission. *Complete anonymity is ensured by CGC's internal system of checks and balances, including bar-coding of submissions and a separate receiving department that does not convey information about the submitter to the people who do the grading.*

Q: WHAT MEASURES WILL BE TAKEN TO PROTECT MY COMICS WHILE THEY ARE IN CGC'S POSSESSION?

A. Protection includes vault storage, state-of-the-art security and surveillance equipment, multi-million dollar insurance against theft or damage, and the long-standing good reputation of CGC's founders backing up assurances that your comics will be handled only by professionals who understand the unique and delicate handling that is required.

Q: I'VE BOUGHT MANY HIGH GRADE BOOKS THAT HAVE COST ME A SUBSTANTIAL AMOUNT OF MONEY. I'M AFRAID IF I HAVE THEM CERTIFIED IT WILL BRING THEIR VALUES DOWN.

A. That could only happen if you've bought a lot of books that were badly overgraded. Nonetheless—and this is the beautiful part of certification—whether you have been intentionally or unintentionally sold an overgraded book, it's also possible (though less likely) that you may have bought one that was undergraded, in which case you would be pleasantly surprised to see the grade go up after it comes back from certification. The larger the percentage of your collection that has been certified, the more likely the total value of your books will offset initial losses. The inevitable end result will be in your favor in the atmosphere of an expanding marketplace.

Q: HOW REALISTIC IS IT THAT I CAN EXPECT THE TOTAL VALUE OF MY COLLECTION TO GO UP WITH THE ARRIVAL OF CGC'S GRADING AND CERTIFICATION SERVICE?

A. Very realistic indeed, if the history of comic certification repeats that of coins and sports cards. Both hobbies, on the whole, have benefited from tremendous price increases since certification began. The key, simply enough, is in the confidence of collectors.

To appreciate the full impact of certification in all arenas, it is useful to know and understand the thinking of collectors who have different goals from your own. First, there are the collectors who are pure fans and who do not care about grades or values. Certification means less to them, because they never intend to sell their collections. Due to a bad economy or other reasons beyond their control, they may change their minds, however, and fall into category two.

This category—the most populated group—is also made up of true fans, those who are involved in all aspects of the collecting game. These collectors upgrade their comics when they can, like to trade, and want to see a healthy market. They are the rocks around which the market prospers. Certification will usually make a lot of sense to them.

The investors make up group three. They often enter the hobby with totally different goals and without much information. Sometimes it is easy to take advantage of them, and they can quickly and easily become discouraged. The field benefits from their presence because of the money and the energy they invest. They perceive the value in certification and will now stay in the hobby longer because of the confidence it gives them. Dealers and other collectors will benefit greatly from offering them only certified books.

Q: HOW WILL I KNOW IF A COMIC HAS BEEN RESTORED?

A. As part of the certification process, CGC will check every comic for restoration, and a book that has been restored will be identified as such. Since it is not possible to accurately describe what grade a comic book was prior to restoration, CGC will assign books an apparent grade which includes a description of light, moderate or heavy restoration. Upon its official introduction, CGC will publish more specific guidelines of its restoration policies and standards, including the possibility that minuscule pinpricks of color repair, for instance, that are almost invisible to the naked eye, will not be identified specifically as having been restored.

Q: HOW WILL MAJOR DEFECTS BE DEALT WITH?

A. Comics with cumulative substantial defects will receive a grade no higher than Good or Very Good, with appropriate numerical grading. However, a single large defect, such as a coupon out of an otherwise Near Mint comic, would call for a specific description and a "qualified" grade, especially if the defect is hidden.

Q: WILL THE WHITENESS LEVEL OF PAPER BE NOTED?

A. No mention of paper color will be noted unless the quality is unusually high or low for a given grade. The original paper quality used to print a specific comic book will be taken into consideration, as will supple strength.

Q: DOES CGC ANTICIPATE SUBMISSION OF COMICS IN ALL CONDITIONS?

A. All comics submitted will be graded, though it is assumed that Fair or Poor condition books that have been severely trimmed or that have pages or covers missing will rarely justify the expense of certification. Their collector value will therefore remain low. Potentially, certification might add only a small amount to the value or marketability of such comics, the obvious exceptions being very rare or highly sought-after first issues.

Q: WILL I BE ABLE TO SUBMIT MY COMIC BOOKS DIRECTLY TO CGC?
A. Comics Guaranty Corporation will accept submissions through an international network of authorized, registered member dealers. Additionally, they will seek endorsements from national comic book collectors' organizations, authorizing them as submission centers in order to allow members to submit books for certification.

Q: HOW LONG WILL IT TAKE FOR MY ORDER TO BE PROCESSED, AND HOW MUCH WILL IT COST?
A. Prices will be publicized on or before the announced date certification is to begin in mid-1999, and will vary according to the turnaround time ordered and the value of the book or books submitted. CGC will establish four service levels:

1. Walk Through (same day).
2. Express (3-5 working days).
3. Standard (12-15 working days or less).
4. Economy (25-30 working days or less).

See Comics Guaranty Corporation's ad pages in this book and in other publications for more information.

GRADING COMIC BOOKS

GET THE TOOLS

For complete, detailed information on grading and restoration, consult the **Overstreet Comic Book Grading Guide**. Copies are available through all normal distribution channels or can be ordered direct from the publisher by sending $12 plus $2 postage and handling. You can also call Gemstone toll free at 1-888-375-9800.

The Overstreet Comic Book Grading Card, known as the **ONE** and **OWL Card** is also available. This card has two functions. The **ONE Card** (**O**verstreet's **N**umerical **E**quivalent) is used to convert grading condition terms to the new numerical grading system. The **OWL Card** (**O**verstreet's **W**hiteness **L**evel) is used for grading the whiteness of paper. The color scale on the **OWL Card** is simply placed over the interior comic book paper. The paper color is matched with the color on the card to get the **OWL** number. The **ONE/OWL Card** may be ordered direct from the publisher by sending $1.30 per card.

HOW TO GRADE

Before a comic book's true value can be assessed, its condition or state of preservation must be determined. In all comic books, the better the condition the more desirable and valuable the book. Comic books in **MINT** condition will bring several times the price of the same book in **POOR** condition. Therefore it is very important to be able to properly grade your books. Comics should be graded from the inside out, so the following comic book areas should be examined before assigning a final grade.

Check inside pages, inside spine and covers and outside spine and covers for any tears, markings, brittleness, tape, soiling, chunks out or other defects that would affect the grade. After all the above steps have been taken, then the reader can begin to consider an overall grade for his or her book. The grading of a comic book is done by simply looking at the book and describing its condition, which may range from absolutely perfect newsstand condition **MINT** to extremely worn, dirty, and torn **POOR**.

Numerous variables influence the evaluation of a comic book's condition and all must be considered in the final evaluation. As grading is the most subjective aspect of determining a comic's value, it is very important that the grader be careful not to allow wishful thinking to influence what the eyes see. It is also very important to realize that older comics in **MINT** condition are extremely scarce and are rarely advertised for sale; most of the higher grade comics advertised range from **VERY FINE** to **NEAR MINT**.

GRADING DEFINITIONS

Note: This edition uses both the traditional grade abbreviations and the **ONE** number throughout the listings. The **O**verstreet **N**umerical **E**quivalent (**ONE**) spread range is given with each grade.

MINT (MT) (ONE 100-98): Near perfect in every way. Only the most subtle bindery or printing defects are allowed. Cover is flat with no surface wear. Cover inks are bright with high reflectivity and minimal fading. Corners are cut square and sharp. Staples are generally centered, clean with no rust. Cover is generally well centered and firmly secured to interior pages. Paper is supple and fresh. Spine is tight and flat.

NEAR MINT (NM) (ONE 97-90): Nearly perfect with only minor imperfections allowed. This grade should have no corner or impact creases, stress marks should be almost invisible, and bindery tears must be less than 1/16 inch. A couple of very tiny color flecks, or a combination of the above that keeps the book from being perfect, where the overall eye appeal is less than Mint drops the book into this grade. Only the most subtle binding and/or printing defects allowed. Cover is flat with no surface wear. Cover inks are bright with high reflectivity and minimum of fading. Corners are cut square and sharp with ever so slight blunting permitted. Staples are generally centered, clean with no rust. Cover is well centered and firmly secured to interior pages. Paper is supple and like new. Spine is tight and flat.

VERY FINE (VF) (ONE 89-75): An excellent copy with outstanding eye appeal. Sharp, bright and clean with supple pages. Cover is relatively flat with almost no surface wear. Cover inks are generally bright with moderate to high reflectivity. Staples may show some discoloration. Spine may have a couple of almost insignificant transverse stress lines and is almost completely flat. A barely unnoticeable 1/4 inch crease is acceptable, if color is not broken. Pages and covers can be yellowish/tannish (at the least, but not brown and will usually be off-white to white).

FINE (FN) (ONE 74-55): An exceptional, above-average copy that shows minor wear but is still relatively flat and clean with no creasing or other serious defects. Eye appeal is somewhat reduced because of slight surface wear and possibly a very small defect such as a few very slight cross stress marks on spine. A Fine condition

See Next Page for Ordering Information →

comic book appears to have been read a few times and has been handled with moderate care. Compared to a VF, cover inks are beginning to show a significant reduction in reflectivity but it is still a highly collectible and desirable book.

VERY GOOD (VG) (ONE 54-35): The average used comic book. A comic in this grade shows some wear, can have a reading or center crease or a rolled spine, but has not accumulated enough total defects to reduce eye appeal to the point that it is not a desirable copy. Some discoloration, fading and even minor soiling is allowed. As much as a 1/4" triangle can be missing out of the corner or edge. A missing square piece (1/8" by 1/8") is also acceptable. Store stamps, name stamps, arrival dates, initials, etc. have no effect on this grade. Cover and interior pages can have one or two minor tears and folds and the centerfold may be loose or detached. One staple can be loose, but the cover is not completely detached. Common bindery and printing defects do not affect grade. Pages and inside covers may be brown but not brittle. Tape should never be used for comic book repair; however many VG condition comics have minor tape repair.

GOOD (GD) (ONE 34-15): A copy in this grade has all pages and covers, although there may be small pieces missing inside; the largest piece allowed from front or back cover is a 1/2" triangle or a square 1/4" by 1/4". Books in this grade are commonly creased, scuffed, abraded and soiled, but completely readable. Often paper quality is low but not brittle. Cover reflectivity is low and in some cases completely absent. Most collectors consider this the lowest collectible grade because comic books in lesser condition are usually incomplete and/or brittle. This grade can have a moderate accumulation of defects but still maintains its basic structural integrity.

FAIR (FR) (ONE 14-5): A copy in this grade has all pages and most of the covers, centerfold may be missing, if it does not affect the story, but price should be reduced; a book in this condition is soiled, ragged and unattractive. Creases and folds are prevalent and paper quality may be moderately low. Spine may be split up to 2/3 its entire length. Staples may be gone, and/or cover split up to 2/3 its length. Corners are commonly slightly rounded. If coupons are cut from front cover and/or back cover and/or interior pages the book will fall into this grade. Up to 1/12 of front cover may be missing. These books are mostly readable although soiling, staining, tears, markings or chunks missing may interfere with reading the complete story. Very often paper quality is low and may have slight brittleness around the edges but not in the central portion of the pages.

POOR (PR) (ONE 4-1): Most comic books in this grade have been sufficiently degraded to the point that there is no longer any collector value. Copies in this grade typically have pages and/or approximately 1/3 or more of the front cover missing. They may have extremely severe stains, mildew or heavy cover abrasion to the point that cover inks are indistinct/absent. They may have been defaced with paints, varnishes, glues, oil, indelible markers or dyes. Other defects often include severe rips, tears, folding and creasing. Another common defect in this grade is moderate to severe brittleness, often to the point that the comic book literally "falls apart" when examined.

from Bill Cole Enterprises, Inc.

DESIGNED FOR THE COMIC BOOK ARTIST

"ALL YOU NEED IS THE INSPIRATION"

Bill Cole Enterprises is pleased to present the famous Blue Line Art supplies. We are stocking items from sample packs to Pro Comic Book pages. Listed below are a few of our best selling items which are in stock for immediate delivery. For a complete catalog see us on the Internet at www.neponset.com/bcemylar and sign up for our email specials.

Designing Your Own Comic Book Pages

BL1001 COMIC BOOK PRO PAGES

11x17 3 ply Art Index board with 10x15 image area, designed to allow ink to dry quickly. Includes 1 #BL1007 Pro Comic Book Cover Sheet. 24 pages per pack

1-5pkg	6-11pkg	12+ pkg	Wt/pkg
$13.95	$13.00	$12.50	(3)

BL1003 COMIC BOOK PAGES

11x17 2 ply Bristol Board with 10x15 image area. Economical design allows ink to dry quickly. 24 pages per pack

1-5pkg	6-11pkg	12+ pkg	Wt/pkg
11.95	11.00	10.50	(2)

MA residents add 5% sales tax. 24 hour Toll Free Order Line for Mastercard, Visa, or Discover Orders Only

1-800-225-8249

This is a recorded tape and does not relay product information or messages.

24 hour Toll Free FAX Line for ordering only

1-800-FAX-BCE8
(1-800-329-2238)

Artists Kits

BL1012 INKERS ART KIT

Contains the following:

1 #102 inking pen, 1 1 oz. Black waterproof ink, 1 #1 round brush, 1 large kneaded eraser, 1 12" ruler, 1 protractor, 1 45/90 degree triangle, 1 60/30 degree triangle, 1 non-photo blue pencil, 2 penciled pages (ready to ink), travel box, and 20 Pro Comic Pages.

1-5pkg	6-11pkg	12+ pkg	Wt/pkg
29.95	27.95	27.00	(4)

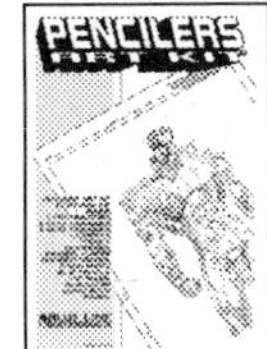

BL1013 PENCILERS ART KIT

Contains the following:

1 6" ruler, 2 protractors, 2 45/90 degree triangles, 2 60/30 degree triangles, 1 compass, 1 pencil sharpener, 1 eraser, 1 large kneaded eraser, 3 non-photo blue pencils, 1 12" ruler, travel box, 20 Pro Comic Book Pages.

1-5pkg	6-11pkg	12+ pkg	Wt/pkg
24.95	23.95	23.00	(3)

See shipping and handling charges on page 21

Bill Cole Enterprises, Inc.

P.O. Box 60, DEPT. 59, Randolph, MA 02368-0060
(781) 986-2653 FAX (781) 986-2656
e-mail: bcemylar@cwixmail.com
web site: http://www.neponset.com/bcemylar

Blue-Line™ is a trademark of Knight Entertainment

DUST JACKETS

Many of the early strip reprint comics were printed in hardback with dust jackets. Books with dust jackets are worth more. The value can increase from 20 to 50 percent depending on the rarity of book. Usually, the earlier the book, the greater the percentage. Unless noted, prices listed are without dust jackets. The condition of the dust jacket should be graded independently of the book itself.

RESTORED COMICS

Our board of advisors suggests that **professionally restored comic books** are an accepted component of the comic book market, but only if the following criteria are met: 1–Must be professional work. 2–Complete disclosure of the extent and type of restoration. 3–Both parties are informed. 4–Priced accordingly depending on availability and demand. **Note:** A professionally restored book, reasonably priced, while not worth as much as the same book unrestored, will increase in value at the same rate. However, if you pay the unrestored price for a restored book, you would be paying a premium, which of course may not be a good investment.

Initial indications on sales and auction results suggests the following: Unrestored key books in Fine or better condition may prove in the future to be better investments as their availability decreases and should not be restored to an apparent higher grade. Restoration should be concentrated on books in less than Fine condition. **Warning:** Before getting restoration done, seek advice from a professional and avoid doing it yourself.

Many rare and expensive books are being repaired and restored by professionals and amateurs alike. If the book is expensive, there is a strong likelihood that some type of repair, cleaning or restoration has been done. In most cases, after restoration, these books are not actually higher grades but are altered lower grade books. **Note:** Expert restoration is always preferable to amateur work and is sometimes very difficult to spot when grading. In some cases, the work is done so skillfully that it is impossible to spot. Depending upon the extent and type of restoration and the quality of what was done, you will have to decide whether the value has increased or decreased. In many cases we have observed in the market that the value has been increased on certain books that were originally in low grade before restoration where the appearance and structural integrity was greatly improved afterwards. Restoration on higher grade copies may or may not affect value depending on what is done. Of course, when a comic book is graded, everything must be taken into account in the final grade given.

To the novice grading will appear difficult at first, but as experience is gained accuracy will improve. Whenever in doubt (after using ***The Overstreet Comic Book Grading Guide***), consult with a reputable dealer or experienced collector in your area. The following grading information is given to further aid the collector:

SCARCITY OF COMIC BOOKS RELATED TO GRADE

1897-1933 Comics: Most of these books are bound with thick cardboard covers and are very rare to non-existent in VF or better condition. Due to their extreme age, paper browning is very common. Brittleness could be a problem.

1933-1940 Comics: There are many issues from this period that are very scarce in any condition, especially from the early to mid-1930s. Surviving copies of any particular issue range from a handful to several hundred. Near Mint to Mint copies are virtually non-existent with known examples of any particular issue limited to five or fewer copies. Most surviving copies are in FN-VF or less condition. Brittleness or browning of paper is fairly common and could be a problem.

1941-1952 Comics: Surviving comic books would number from less than 100 to several thousand copies of each issue. Near Mint to Mint copies are a little more common but are still relatively scarce with only a dozen or so copies in this grade existing of any particular issue. Exceptions would be recent warehouse finds of most Dell comics (6-100 copies, but usually 30 or less), and Harvey comics (1950s-1970s) surfacing. Due to low paper quality of the late 1940s and 1950s, many comics from this period are rare in Near Mint to Mint condition. Most remaining copies are VF or less. Browning of paper could be a problem.

1953-1959 Comics: As comic book sales continued to drop during the 1950s, production values were lowered resulting in cheaply printed comics. For this reason, high grade copies are extremely rare. Many Atlas and Marvel comics have chipping along the trimmed edges (Marvel chipping) which reduces even more the number of surviving high grade copies.

1960-1979 Comics: Early '60s comics are rare in Near Mint to Mint condition. Most copies of early '60s Marvels and DCs grade no higher than VF. Many early keys in NM or MT exist in numbers less than 10-20 of each. Mid-'60s to late-'70s books in high grade are more common due to the hoarding of comics that began in the mid-'60s.

1980-Present: Comics of today are common in high grade. VF to NM is the standard rather than the exception.

When you consider how few Golden and Silver Age books exist compared to the current market, you will begin to appreciate the true rarity of these early books. In many cases less than 5-10 copies exist of a particular issue in Near Mint to Mint condition, while most of the 1930s books do not exist in this grade at all.

COLLECTING COMIC BOOKS

HOW TO START COLLECTING

New comic books are available in many different kinds of stores. Grocery stores, drug stores, Wal-Mart, K-Mart, book stores, comic book stores and card and comics specialty shops are a few examples. Local flea markets and, of course, comic book conventions in your area are excellent sources for new and old comic books.

Most collectors begin by buying new issues in Mint condition directly off the newsstand or from their local comic store. (Subscription copies are available from several mail-order services, and often the publishers themselves.) Each week new comics appear on the stands that are destined to become true collectors' items. The trick is to locate a store that carries a complete line of comics. In several localities this may be difficult. Most collectors frequent several magazine stands in order not to miss something they want. Even then, it pays to keep in close contact with collectors in other areas. Sooner or later, nearly every collector has to rely upon a friend in Fandom or a dealer to obtain for him an item that is unavailable locally (see ads in this book).

Before you buy any comic to add to your collection, you should carefully inspect its condition. Unlike stamps and coins, defective comics are generally not highly prized. The cover should be properly cut and printed. Remember that every blemish or sign of wear depreciates the beauty and value of your comics.

The serious collector usually buys extra copies of popular titles. He may trade these multiples for items unavailable locally (for example, foreign comics), or he may store the multiples for resale at some future date. Such speculation is, of course, a gamble. Selecting the right investment books is tricky business that requires special knowledge. With experience, the beginner will improve his buying skills. Remember, if you play the new comics market, be prepared to buy and sell fast as values rise and fall rapidly.

COLLECTING IN THE 1990s

Today's comic books offer a wide variety of subjects, art styles and writers to satisfy even the most discriminating fan. Whether it's the latest new hot title or company, or one of many popular titles that have been around for a long time, the comic book fan has a broad range from which to pick. Print runs of many popular titles have dropped over the past few years, creating the possibility of a true rarity occurring when demand outstrips supply. Less "gimmicky" covers are seen these days, but occasionally an eye-catching specialty cover will appear, such as the Superman new costume issue (#123) that glows-in-the-dark. Some cover variants continue to appear as well. "Bad Girl" and horror titles have been popular along with the standard superhero fare. The collector should always stay informed about the new trends developing in this fast-moving market. Since the market fluctuates greatly, and there is a vast array of comics to choose from, it's recommended first and foremost that you collect what you enjoy reading; that way, despite any value changes, you will always maintain a sense of personal satisfaction with your collection.

POLYBAGGED COMICS: It is the official policy of this Guide to grade comics regardless of whether they are still sealed in their polybag or not. Sealed comics in bags are not always in MINT condition and could even be damaged. The value should not suffer as long as the bag (opened) and all of its original manufactured contents are preserved and kept together.

COLLECTING ON A BUDGET: Collectors check out their local newsstand or comic specialty store for the latest arrivals. Hundreds of brand new comic books are displayed each week for the collector, much more than anyone can afford to purchase. Today's reader must be careful and budget his money wisely in choosing what to buy.

COLLECTING ARTISTS: Many collectors enjoy favorite artists and follow their work from issue to issue, title to title, company to company. In recent years, some artists have achieved "star" status. Autograph signings occur at all major comic conventions as well as special promotions with local stores. Fans line up by the hundreds at such events to meet these superstars. Some of the current top artists of new comics are: Todd McFarlane, Alex Ross, Jim Lee, Michael Turner, Marc Silvestri, Rob Liefeld, Chris Bachalo, J. Scott Campbell, Humberto Ramos, and Adam and Andy Kubert. Original artwork from these artists have been bringing record prices at auctions and from dealers' lists.

COLLECTING BY COMPANIES: Some collectors become loyal to a particular company and only collect its titles. It's another way to specialize and collect in a market that expands faster than your pocket book.

COLLECTING #1 ISSUES: For decades, comic enthusiasts have always collected first (#1) issues. This is yet another way to control spending and build an interesting collection for the future. #1 issues have everything going for them--some introduce new characters, while others are under-printed, creating a rarity factor. #1 issues cross many subjects as well as companies, and make for an intriguing collection.

COLLECTING BACK ISSUES

A back issue is any comic currently not available on the stands. Collectors of current titles often want to find the earlier issues in order to complete the run. Thus a back issue collector is born. Comic books have been published and collected for over 100 years. However, the earliest known comic book dealers didn't appear until the late 1930s. But today, there are hundreds of dealers that sell old comic books (See ads in this book).

LOCATING BACK ISSUES: The first place to begin, of course, is with your collector friends who may have unwanted back issues or duplicates for sale. Look in the yellow pages, or call the Comic Shop Locator Service at 1-888-COMIC-BOOK, to see if you have a comic book store available. If you do, they would know of other collectors in your area. Advertising in local papers could get good results. Go to regional markets and look for comic book dealers. There are many trade publications in the hobby that would put you in touch with out-of-town dealers. This Annual Guide has ads buying and selling old comic books. Some dealers publish regular price lists of old comic books for sale. Get on their mailing list.

Putting a quality collection of old comics together takes a lot of time, effort and money. Many old comics are not easy to find. Persistence and luck play a big part in acquiring needed issues. Most quality collections are put together over a long period of time by placing mail orders with dealers and other collectors.

Comics of early vintage are extremely expensive if they are purchased through a regular dealer or collector. Unless you have unlimited funds to invest in your hobby, you will find it necessary to restrict your collecting in certain ways. However you define your collection, you should be careful to set your goals well within affordable limits.

PRESERVATION & STORAGE

PROPER HANDLING OF COMIC BOOKS

Comic books are fragile and easy to damage. Most dealers and collectors hesitate to let anyone personally handle their rare comics. It is common courtesy to ask permission before handling another person's comic book. Most dealers would prefer to remove the comic from its bag and show it to the customer themselves. In this way, if the book is damaged, it would be the dealer's responsibility–not the customer's. Remember, the slightest crease or chip could render an otherwise Mint book to Near Mint or even Very Fine.

Consult the **Overstreet Comic Book Grading Guide** and learn the proper way to hold a comic book. The following steps are provided to aid the novice in the proper handling of comic books: 1. Remove the comic from its protective sleeve or bag very carefully. 2. Gently lay the comic (unopened) in the palm of your hand so that it will stay relatively flat and secure. 3. You can now leaf through the book by carefully rolling or flipping the pages with the thumb and forefinger of your other hand. Caution: Be sure the book always remains relatively flat or slightly rolled. Avoid creating stress points on the covers with your fingers and be particularly cautious in bending covers back too far on Mint books. 4. After examining the book, carefully insert it back into the bag or protective sleeve. Watch corners and edges for folds or tears as you replace the book. Always keep tape completely away while inserting a comic in a bag.

STORAGE OF COMIC BOOKS

Comic books should be protected from the elements as well as the dangers of light, heat, and humidity. This can easily be achieved with proper storage. Improper storage methods will be detrimental to the "health" of your collection, and may even quicken its deterioration.

Store comic books away from direct light sources, especially florescent which contains high levels of ultraviolet (UV) radiation. UV lights are like sunlight, and will quickly fade the cover inks. Tungsten filament lighting is safer than florescent but should still be used at brief intervals. Remember, exposure to light accumulates damage, so store your collection in a cool, dark place away from windows.

Temperatures must also be carefully regulated. Fungus and mold thrives in higher temperatures, so the lower the temperature, the longer the life of your collection.

Atmospheric pollution is another problem associated with long term storage of paper. Sulfuric dioxide which can occur from automobile exhaust will cause paper to turn yellow over a period of time. For this reason, it is best not to store your valuable comics close to a garage. Some of the best preserved comic books known were protected from exposure to the air such as the Gaines EC collection. These books were carefully wrapped in paper at time of publication, and completely sealed from the air. Each package was then sealed in a box and stored in a closet in New York. After over 40 years of storage when the packages were opened, you could instantly catch the odor of fresh newsprint; the paper was snow white and supple, and the cover inks were as brilliant as the day they were printed. This illustrates how important it is to protect your comics from the atmosphere.

Like UV, high relative humidity (rh) can also be damaging to paper. Maintaining a low and stable relative humidity, around 50%, is crucial; varying humidity will only damage your collection.

Care must be taken when choosing materials for storing your comics. Many common items such as plastic bags, boards, and boxes may not be as safe as they seem. Some contain chemicals that will actually help to destroy your collection rather than save it. Always purchase materials designed for long-term storage, such as Mylar type "D" sleeves and acid-free boards and boxes. Polypropylene and polyethylene bags, while safe for temporary storage, should be changed every three to five years.

Comics are best stored vertically in boxes. For shelving, make sure that comics do not come into direct contact with the shelving surface. Use acid-free boards as a buffer between shelves comics. Also, never store comics directly on the floor; elevate them 6-10 inches to allow for flooding. Similarly, never store your collection directly against a wall, particularly an outside wall. Condensation and poor air circulation will encourage mold and fungus growth.

When handling your high grade comics, wash your hands first, eliminating harmful oils from the skin before coming into contact with the books. Lay the comic on a flat surface and slowly turn the pages. This will minimize the stress to the staples and spine. With these guidelines, your collection should enjoy a long life and maintain a reasonable condition and value.

BUYING & SELLING

HOW TO SELL YOUR COMIC COLLECTION

By purchasing this Guide, you have begun the long process necessary to successfully sell your comics. Before you can proceed, however, you must decide what category listed below best describes your collection. As a rule of thumb, the lower categories will need less detail provided in your inventory list. A collection of key late '30s DCs will require you to list exact titles, numbers, and grades, as well as possible restoration information. If, however, you have 20,000 miscellaneous '80s and '90s comics for sale, a rough list of the number of books and publishers should be enough. The categories are:

1. PLATINUM AGE (1897-1932): The supply is very scarce. More people are becoming interested in these early books due to comics passing their 100th birthday. Moderate interest among average dealers, but high interest with dealers that specialize in this material. A detailed list will be necessary paying attention to brittleness, damage and pages missing. Dealers will pay up to a high percentage of Guide list for key titles.

2. GOLDEN AGE, All Grades (1933 - pre-1956): The most desirable. A detailed inventory will be necessary. Key higher grade books are easier to sell, but lower grades in most titles show the best selling potential, due to the fact that many collectors cannot afford a $20,000 VF book but may be able to afford a GD for only $2,000. Highest demand is for the superhero titles such as **Batman**, **Superman**, **Human Torch**, etc. The percentage of Guide that dealers will pay for your collection will vary depending on condition and contents. A collection of low demand titles will not bring the same percentage as a collection of prime titles.

3. High Grade SILVER AGE (1956-mid 1960s): A detailed inventory will be necessary. There are always investors looking for VF or better books from this period. Dealers will usually pay a high percentage of Guide list for these high grade books. Silver Age below VF will fall into category #4.

4. Low Grade SILVER AGE: Spanning books lower than VF from the late '50s to 1970, this category exhibits the average grade of most collections. Consequently, the supply of this material is much more common than category #2. This means that you could be competing with many other similar collections being offered at the same time. You will have to shop this type of collection to get the best price, and be prepared to sell at a significant discount if you find a willing buyer with good references.

5. MODERN AGE (post-1970): Certain titles from the early 1970s in high grade are showing increasing demand. However, many books from the 1980s to the 1990s are in low demand with the supply for the most part always being of high grade books. These collections are typified by long runs of certain titles and/or publishers. A detailed inventory will not be necessary. Contact local comic stores or buyers first to gauge their level of interest. Dealing with buyers outside your area should be avoided if possible.

IMPORTANT: Many of the 1980s and 1990s books are listed at cover price. This indicates that these books have not established a collector's value. When selling books of this type, the true market value could be 20-50% of cover price or less.

6. BULK (post-1980 in quantities greater than 5,000): These collections usually contain multiple copies of the same issues. It is advisable to price on a per-book basis (2¢ and 20¢ each). Do NOT attempt an inventory list, and only contact buyers who advertise buying in bulk quantity.

You should never deal with a buyer without fully checking their references. For additional verification, consult The Better Business Bureau; the local BBB may be able to help you in establishing a buyer's credibility, as well as assisting in resolving any disputes. **The Overstreet Comic Book Price Guide** and **Comic Book Marketplace** are also recognized authorities. Advertised dealers will likely have a more established reputation.

Potential buyers will be most concerned with the retail value of your entire collection, which may be more or less than Guide depending what you have and their current demand. Some rare early books in VF or NM may bring a price over Guide list while other titles in lower grade may sell for a price under Guide list. Most vintage books, however, will sell for around the Guide price. However, 1980s or 1990s books that list at cover price may only be worth a percentage of that price. You must then decide on what percentage you would be willing to accept for your collection, taking into account how the collection breaks down into fast, moderate and slow moving books. To expect someone to pay full retail is unrealistic. You will have to be flexible in order to close a deal.

Many buyers may want to purchase only certain key or high grade books from your collection, almost always favoring the buyer. While you may be paid a high percentage of retail, you will find that "cherry-picked" collections are much more difficult to sell. Furthermore, the percentage of retail that you will receive for a "cherry-picked" collection will be much lower than if the collection had been left intact. Remember, key issues and/or high grade issues make or break a collection. Selling on consignment, another popular option in today's market, could become a breeding ground for cherry-pickers, so again, always check a dealer's references thoroughly.

Some collectors may choose to sell their comic books on a piecemeal basis, requiring much greater care and detail in preparing an inventory list and grading comics for sale. You will be able to realize a higher percentage of retail by selling your collection this way, but the key books will certainly sell first, leaving a significant portion of the collection unsold. You will need to keep repricing and discounting your books to encourage buyers.

You can advertise your collection in trade publications or through mass mailings. If you sell books through the mail, you must also establish a reasonable return policy, as some books will unquestionably be returned. Check the local post office and/or UPS regarding the various rates and services available for shipping your books. Marketing your books at conventions is another option. As a dealer, you will also incur overhead expenses such as postage, mailing and display supplies, advertising costs, etc.

In all cases, be willing to establish trust with a prospective buyer. By following the procedures outlined here, you will be able to sell your collection successfully, for a fair price, with both parties walking away satisfied. After all, collecting comic books is supposed to be fun; it only becomes a chore if you let it.

WHERE TO BUY AND SELL

Throughout this book you will find the advertisements of many reputable dealers who sell back-issue comics magazines. If you are an inexperienced collector, be sure to compare prices before you buy. When a dealer is selected (ask for references), send him a small order (under $100) first to check out his grading accuracy, promptness in delivery, guarantees of condition advertised, and whether he will accept returns when dissatisfied. Never send cash through the mail. Send money orders or checks for your personal protection. Beware of bargains, as the items advertised sometimes do not exist but are only a fraud to get your money.

The Price Guide is indebted to everyone who placed ads in this volume. Your mentioning this book when dealing with the advertisers would be greatly appreciated.

COMIC BOOK CONVENTIONS

The first comic book conventions, or cons, were originally conceived as the comic book counterpart to science fiction fandom conventions. There were many attempts to form successful national cons, but they were all stillborn. It is interesting that after only three relatively organized years of existence, the first comic con was held. Of course, its magnitude was nowhere near as large as most established cons held today.

What is a comic con? Dealers, collectors, fans, publishers, distributors, manufacturers, whatever they call themselves can be found trading, selling, and buying the adventures of their favorite characters for hours on end. Additionally most cons have guests of honor, usually professionals in the field of comic art, either writers, artists, or editors. The committees put together panels for the con attendees in which the assembled pros talk about certain areas of comics, most of the time fielding questions from the assembled audience. At cons one can usually find displays of various and sundry things, usually toys, thousands of comic books, original art, and more. There can be the showing of movies or videos. Of course there is always the chance to get together with friends at cons and just talk about comics. One also has a good opportunity to make new friends who have similar interests and with whom one can correspond after the con.

It is difficult to describe accurately what goes on at a con. The best way to find out is to go to one and see for yourself. The largest cons are WonderCon (April), Pittsburgh (April), San Diego (July), Chicago (July), and Atlanta (July). For accurate dates and addresses, consult ads in this edition as well as some of the adzines. Please remember when writing for convention information to include a self addressed, stamped envelope for reply.

COVER BAR CODES FOR NEW COMIC BOOKS

Today's comic books are cover-coded for the direct sales (comic shop, newsstand, and foreign markets). They are all first printings, with the special coding being the only difference. The comics sold to the comic shops have to be coded differently, as they are sold on a no-return basis while newsstand comics are not. The Price Guide has not detected any price difference between these versions. Currently, the difference is easily detected by looking at the front cover bar code (a box located at the lower left). The bar code used to be filled in for newsstand sales and left blank or contain a character for comic shop sales. Now, as you can see above, direct sale editions are clearly marked, both versions containing the bar code.

Newsstand

Direct Sales (DC)

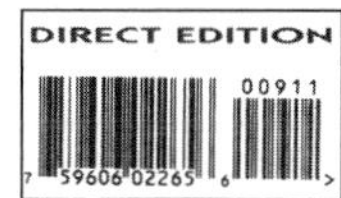

Direct Edition (Marvel)

MARVEL REPRINTS

In recent years Marvel has reprinted some of their comics. There has been confusion in identifying the reprints from the originals, but in 99% of the cases, the reprints have listed "reprint," or "2nd printing," etc. in the indicia, along with a later copyright date in some cases. Some Marvel 2nd printings have a gold logo. The only known exceptions are a few of the movie books such as **Star Wars**, the **Marvel Treasury Editions**, and tie-ins such as **G.I. Joe**. These books were reprinted and not identified as reprints. The **Star Wars** reprints have a large diamond with no date and a blank UPC symbol on the cover. Others had cover variations such as a date missing or different colors. Beginning in mid-1990, all Marvel 2nd printings have a gold logo.

Gold Key and other comics were also sold with a Whitman label. Even though collectors may prefer one label over the other, the Price Guide does not differentiate in the price. Beginning in 1980, all comics produced by Western carried the Whitman label.

COMIC BOOK PUBLISHERS' CODES The following abbreviations are used with the cover reproductions throughout the book for copyright credit purposes. The companies they represent are listed here:

AC-(Americomics)
ACE-Ace Periodicals
ACG-American Comics Group
AJAX-Ajax-Farrell
AP-Archie Publications
ATLAS-Atlas Comics (see below)
AVON-Avon Periodicals
BP-Better Publications
C & L-Cupples & Leon
CC-Charlton Comics
CEN-Centaur Publications
CCG-Columbia Comics Group
CG-Catechetical Guild
CHES-Harry 'A' Chesler
CLDS-Classic Det. Stories
CM-Comics Magazine
DC-DC Comics, Inc.
DEF-Defiant Comics
DELL-Dell Publishing Co.
DH-Dark Horse
DMP-David McKay Publishing
DS-D. S. Publishing Co.
EAS-Eastern Color Printing Co.
EC-E. C. Comics
ECL-Eclipse Comics
ENWIL-Enwil Associates
EP-Elliott Publications
ERB-Edgar Rice Burroughs
FAW-Fawcett Publications
FC-First Comics
FF-Famous Funnies
FH-Fiction House Magazines
FOX-Fox Features Syndicate
GIL-Gilberton
GK-Gold Key
GP-Great Publications
HARV-Harvey Publications
H-B-Hanna-Barbera
HILL-Hillman Periodicals
HOKE-Holyoke Publishing Co.
KING-King Features Syndicate
LEV-Lev Gleason Publications
MAL-Malibu Comics
MAR-Marvel Characters, Inc.
ME-Magazine Enterprises
MLJ-MLJ Magazines
MS-Mirage Studios
NOVP-Novelty Press
PG-Premier Group
PINE-Pines
PMI-Parents' Magazine Institute
PRIZE-Prize Publications
QUA-Quality Comics Group
REAL-Realistic Comics
RH-Rural Home
S & S-Street and Smith Publishers
SKY-Skywald Publications
STAR-Star Publications
STD-Standard Comics
STJ-St. John Publishing Co.
SUPR-Superior Comics
TC-Tower Comics
TM-Trojan Magazines
TOBY-Toby Press
TOPS-Tops Comics
UFS-United Features Syndicate
VAL-Valiant
VITL-Vital Publications
WDC-The Walt Disney Company
WEST-Western Publishing Co.
WHIT-Whitman Publishing Co.
WHW-William H. Wise
WMG-William M. Gaines (E. C.)
WP-Warren Publishing Co.
YM-Youthful Magazines
Z-D-Ziff-Davis Publishing Co.

TIMELY/MARVEL/ATLAS COMICS

"A Marvel Magazine" and "Marvel Group" was the symbol used between December 1946 and May 1947 (not used on all titles/issues during period). The Timely Comics symbol was used between July 1942 and September 1942 (not on all titles/issues during period). The round "Marvel Comic" symbol was used between February 1949 and June 1950. Early comics code symbol (star and bar) was used between April 1952 and February 1955. The Atlas globe symbol was used between December 1951 and September 1957. The M over C symbol (beginning of Marvel Comics) was used between July 1961 until the price increased to 12 cents in February 1962.

MARVEL/TIMELY/ATLAS PUBLISHERS' ABBREVIATION CODES

ACI-Animirth Comics, Inc.
AMI-Atlas Magazines, Inc.
ANC-Atlas News Co., Inc.
BPC-Bard Publishing Corp.
BFP-Broadcast Features Pubs.
CBS-Crime Bureau Stories
CLDS-Classic Detective Stories
CCC-Comic Combine Corp.
CDS-Current Detective Stories
CFI-Crime Files, Inc.
CmPI-Comedy Publications, Inc.
CmPS-Complete Photo Story
CnPC-Cornell Publishing Corp.
CPC-Chipiden Publishing Corp.
CPI-Crime Publications, Inc.
CPS-Canam Publishing Sales Corp.
CSI-Classics Syndicate, Inc.
DCI-Daring Comics, Inc.
EPC-Euclid Publishing Co.
EPI-Emgee Publications, Inc.
FCI-Fantasy Comics, Inc.
FPI-Foto Parade, Inc.
GPI-Gem Publishing, Inc.
HPC-Hercules Publishing Corp.
IPS-Interstate Publishing Corp.
JPI-Jaygee Publications, Inc.
LBI-Lion Books, Inc.
LCC-Leading Comic Corp.
LMC-Leading Magazine Corp.
MALE-Male Publishing Corp.
MAP-Miss America Publishing Corp.
MCI-Marvel Comics, Inc.
MgPC-Margood Publishing Corp.
MjMC-Marjean Magazine Corp.
MMC-Mutual Magazine Corp.
MPC-Medalion Publishing Corp.
MPI-Manvis Publications, Inc.
NPI-Newsstand Publications, Inc.
NPP-Non-Pareil Publishing Corp.
OCI-Official Comics, Inc.
OMC-Official Magazine Corp.
OPI-Olympia Publications, Inc.
PPI-Postal Publications, Inc.
PrPI-Prime Publications, Inc.
RCM-Red Circle Magazines, Inc.
SAI-Sports Actions, Inc.
SePI-Select Publications, Inc.
SnPC-Snap Publishing Co.
SPC-Select Publishing Co.
SPI-Sphere Publications, Inc.
TCI-Timely Comics, Inc.
TP-Timely Publications
20 CC-20th Century Comics Corp.
USA-U.S.A. Publications, Inc.
VPI-Vista Publications, Inc.
WFP-Western Fiction Publishing
WPI-Warwick Publications, Inc.
YAI-Young Allies, Inc.
ZPC-Zenith Publishing Co., Inc.

GLOSSARY

a-Story art; **a(i)**-Story art inks; **a(p)**-Story art pencils; **a(r)**-Story art reprint.
adult material–Contains story and/or art for "mature" readers. Re: sex, violence, strong language.
adzine-A magazine primarily devoted to the advertising of comic books and collectibles as its first publishing priority as opposed to written articles.
annual-A book that is published yearly.
arrival date-Markings on a comic book cover (usually in pencil) made by either the newsstand dealer or the distributor. These markings denote the date the book was placed on the newsstand. Usually the arrival date is one to two months prior to the cover date.
ashcan-A prepublication facsimile or dummy issue of an intended title usually prepared to show advertisers. Part or all of the pages may be blank or from a different book with a new cover. Black and white ashcans are common.
Atom Age- The period beginning in 1946 after the dropping of the first Atom bomb, continuing until the start of the Silver Age in 1956
B&W-Black and white art.
bad girl art (BGA)-A term coined in 1993 to describe an attitude as well as a style of art that portrays women in a sexually implicit way.
Baxter paper–A high quality, white, heavy paper used in the printing of some comic books.
bi-monthly-Published every two months.
bi-weekly-Published every two weeks.
bondage cover-Usually denotes a female in restraints.
brittleness-The final stage of paper deterioration.
c-Cover art; **c(i)**-Cover inks; **c(p)**-Cover pencils; **c(r)**-Cover reprint.
Bronze Age–(1) Non-specific term not in general acceptance by collectors which denotes comics published from approximately 1970 through 1980, (2) Term which describes "the Age" of comic books after the Silver Age.
browning-Paper aging between tanning and brittleness.
cameo-When a character appears briefly.
CCA-Comics Code Authority.
CCA seal-An emblem that was placed on the cover of all CCA approved comics beginning in April-May, 1955.
center crease– (see Subscription Crease)
centerfold-The stapled, four page middle sheet of a comic or magazine.
CFO–Abbreviation for "Centerfold out."
chromium cover–A special Chromium foil used on covers
Church, Edgar collection-A large high grade comic book collection discovered by Mile High Comics in Colorado (over 22,000 books).
classic cover–A cover highly prized by collectors as a prime or matchless example of its kind.
cleaning–A process in which dirt and dust is removed.
color touch–A restoration process by which colored ink is used to hide color flecks, flakes and larger areas
colorist-An artist who paints the color guides for comics. Many modern colorists use computer technology.
comic book dealer–(1) A seller of comic books. (2) One who makes a living buying and selling comic books.
comic book repair-When a tear, loose staple or centerfold has been mended without changing or adding to the original finish of the book. Repair may involve tape, glue or nylon gossamer and is easily detected. It is considered a defect
comic book restoration-Any attempt, whether professional or amateur, to enhance the appearance of a comic book. These procedures may include any or all of the following techniques: recoloring, adding missing paper, stain, ink, dirt, tape removal, whitening, pressing out wrinkles, staple replacement, trimming, re-glossing, etc. Note: Unprofessional work can lower the value of a book. In all cases, except for some simple cleaning procedures, a restored book can never be worth the same as an unrestored book in the same condition.
Comics Code Authority-In 1954 the major publishers joined together and formed a committee which set up guidelines for acceptable comic contents. It was their task to approve the contents of comics before publication.
complete run–All issues of a given title.
con-A Convention or public gathering of fans.
condition–The state of preservation of a comic book.
Cosmic Aeroplane-Refers to a large collectionof 1930s-1940s comics discovered by Cosmic Aeroplane Books.
costumed hero–A costumed crime fighter with "developed" powers instead of "super" powers.
coupon cut–Comic book missing a coupon.
cover loose–Cover is detached from staple or staples
cover trimmed–Cover has been reduced in size through trimming.
crease–A paper fold that occurs in comic books from misuse
crossover–When one character or characters appears briefly in another character's story.
deacidification–The process of reducing acid in paper.
debut-The first time that a character appears anywhere.
defect–Any fault or flaw that detracts from perfection.
Denver collection–A collection of early '40s high grade #1s bought at auction in Pennsylvania by a Denver, Colorado dealer.
die-cut cover–When areas of a cover are precut by a printer to a special shape or to create a desired effect.
distributor painted stripes–Color brushed or sprayed on the edges of comic book stacks as special coding by distributors (not a defect).
double–A duplicate copy.
double cover-An error in the binding process which results in two or more covers being bound to a single book. Multiple covers are not considered a defect.
drug propaganda story-Where comic makes an editorial stand about drug abuse.
drug use story-Shows the actual use of drugs: shooting, taking a trip, harmful effects, etc.
dust shadow–Usually the fore-edge of a comic cover exposed to the gathering of dust creating a dark stripe.
embossed cover–When a pattern is embossed onto the cover creating a

raised area.
eye appeal–A term used to describe the overall appeal of a comic's apparent condition.
fanzine-An amateur fan publication.
file copy-A comic originating from the publisher's file. Not all file copies are in pristine condition. **Note:** An arrival date on the cover of a comic indicates that it is not a file copy though a copyright date may.
first app.-Same as debut.
flashback-When a previous story is being recalled.
foil cover–A thin metallic foil that is hot stamped on comic covers.
four color-A printing process in which the three primary colors plus black are used. Also refers to the Four Color series published by Dell.
foxing-Tiny orange-brown spots on the cover or pages of a comic book caused by mold growth.
G. A.-Golden Age period.
gatefold cover–A double cover folded in itself.
genre–Categories of comic book subject matter grouped as to type.
giveaway–Type of comic book used as a premium for promotional purposes.
Golden Age (G.A.)-The period beginning with **Action** #1 (June, 1938) and ending with World War II in 1945.
good girl art (GGA)-A term coined in 1977 to describe a style of art that portrays women in a sexually implicit way.
headlights-Women's breasts, usually provocative.
hologram cover–True 3-D holograms are prepared and affixed to comic book covers and cards for special effect.
hot stamping–The process of pressing foil, prism paper and inks on cover stock.
i-Art inks.
indicia-Publishers title, issue number, date, copyright and general information statement usually located on the inside front facing pages or inside back cover.
infinity cover-Shows the same scene within a scene repeated into infinity.
inker-Artist that does the inking.
intro-Same as debut.
JLA-Justice League of America.
JLI-Justice League International.
JSA-Justice Society of America.
key issue–An important issue in a run.
Lamont Larson-Refers to a large high grade collection of 1940s comics. Many of the books have Lamont or Larson written on the cover.
lenticular covers (aka flicker covers)–Images move when viewed at different angles specially prepared and affixed to cover.
logo-The title of a strip or comic book as it appears on the cover or title page.
LSH-Legion of Super-Heroes.
Marvel chipping-A defect that occurred during the trimming process of 1950s and 1960s Marvels which produced a ragged edge around the comic cover. Usually takes the form of a tiny chip or chips along the right hand edge of the cover.
Mile High-Refers to a large NM-Mint collection of comics originating from Denver, Colorado (Edgar Church collection of 20,000+ copies).
Modern Age–Period from 1980 to the present.
Mylar ™–An inert, very hard, space age plastic used to make high quality protective bags and sleeves used for comic storage. Mylar ™ is a trademark of the DuPont Company.
nd-No date.
nn-No number.
N. Y. Legis. Comm.-New York Legislative Committee to Study the Publication of Comics (1951).
one-shot-When only one issue is published of a title or the title is published on an infrequent or irregular schedule, whether or not as part of a numbered series (such as Dell's Four Color).
origin-When the story of the character's creation is given.
over Guide-When a comic book is priced at a value over Guide list.
p-Art pencils.
painted cover–Cover taken from an actual painting instead of a line drawing.
paper cover–Comic book cover made from the same newsprint as interior pages (self cover). These books are extremely rare in high grade.
pedigree-A book from a famous collection, e.g. Allentown, Larson, Church/Mile High, Denver, San Francisco, Cosmic Aeroplane, etc. Note: Beware of non-pedigree collections being promoted as pedigree books. Only outstanding high grade collections similar to those listed qualify.
penciler-Artist that does the pencils.
photo cover–Made from a photograph instead of a line drawing or painting.
Platinum Age-First age of comics, beginning with newspaper strip reprint collections (**The Yellow Kid**) in 1897, and ending with 1933's **Detective Dan**, which contained original material.
POP-Parade of Pleasure, book about the censorship of comics.
post-Code-Comic books published with the CCA seal.
post-Golden Age-Comic books published between 1945 and 1950.
post-Silver Age-Comic books published from 1969 to present.
Poughkeepsie-Refers to a large collection of Dell Comics' "file copies" believed to have originated from the warehouse of Western Publishing in Poughkeepsie, N.Y.
pre-Code-Comic books published before the CCA seal.
pre-Golden Age-Comic books published prior to **Action** #1 (June, 1938).
pre-hero–A term that describes the issues in a run prior to a superhero entering the run.
pre-Silver Age-Comic books published between 1950 and **Showcase** #4 (1956).
printing defect-A defect caused by the printing process. Examples would include paper wrinkling, miscut edges, misfolded spine, untrimmed pages, off-registered color, off-centered trimming, misfolded and misbound pages. It should be noted that these are defects that lower the grade of the book.
prism cover–Special reflective foil material with 3-dimensional repeated designs. Used for special effect.
provenance-When the owner of a book is known and is stated for the purpose of authenticating and documenting the history of the book. Example: A book from the Stan Lee or Forrest Ackerman collection would be an example of a value-adding provenance.
quarterly-Published every three months (four times a year).
R or r-Reprint.
rare-10 to 20 copies estimated to exist.
rat chew–Damage caused by gnawing rats or mice.
reprint comics-Comic books that contain newspaper strip reprints.
restoration–The fine art of repairing a comic book to look as close as possible to its original condition.
rice paper-A thin, transparent paper commonly used by restorers to repair

tears and replace small pieces on covers and pages of comic books.
Reilly, Tom–A large high grade collection of 1939-1945 comics with 5000+ books.
rolled spine–A spine condition caused by folding back pages while reading.
S. A.-Silver Age.
Rockford–A high grade collection of 1940s comics with 2000+ books from Rockford, IL.
saddle stitch–The staple binding of comic books.
San Francisco Collection–(see Reilly, Tom)
S&K-Joe Simon and Jack Kirby (artists).
scarce-20 to 100 copies estimated to exist.
semi-monthly-Published twice a month, as distinguished from bi-weekly.
Silver Age-Officially begins with **Showcase** #4 in 1956 and ends in 1969.
silver proof-A black & white actual size print on thick glossy paper hand painted by an artist to indicate colors to the engraver.
SOTI-Seduction of the Innocent, book about the censorship of comics.
Refer to listing in this Guide.
spine-The area representing the folded and stapled part of a comic book.
spine roll-A defect caused by improper storage which results in uneven pages and the shifting or bowing of the spine.
splash panel-A large panel that usually appears at the front of a comic story.
squarebound-A comic book gluebound with a square spined cover, aka perfect bound.
store stamp–Store name stamped in ink on cover.
stress lines-Light, tiny wrinkles occuring along the spine, projecting from the staples or appearing anywhere on the covers of a comic book.
subscription crease-A center crease caused by the folding of comic books for mailing to subscribers. This is considered a defect.
sun shadow–A darkened strip along the fore-edge of a comic cover caused by prolonged exposure to light, unlike the dust shadow which can often be removed. A serious defect.
superhero–A costumed hero crime fighter with powers beyond those of mortal man.
supervillain–A costumed criminal with powers beyond those of mortal man.
swipe–A panel, sequence, or story obviously stolen or copied from previously published material.
3-D comic-Comic art that is drawn and printed in two mismatched colors, producing a 3-D effect when viewed through special glasses.
3-D effect comic-Comic art that is drawn to appear 3-D, but isn't.
title page–The first page showing the title of a story.
under Guide-When a comic book is priced at a value less than Guide list.
variant cover-a different cover image used on the same issue of a comic title.
very rare-1 to 10 copies estimated to exist.
warehouse copy-Originating from a publisher's warehouse; similar to file copy.
White Mountain–A large high grade collection of 1950s-1960s comics from New England.
x-over-When one character crosses over into another's strip.
zine-See Fanzine.

COMIC BOOK ARTISTS

COMIC BOOK ARTISTS LISTED: Many of the popular artists are pointed out in the listings. When more than one artist worked on a story, their names are separated by a (/). The first name did the pencil drawings and the second the inks. When two or more artists work on a story, only the most prominent will be noted in some cases. We wish all good artists could be listed, but due to space limitation, only the most popular can. The following list of artists are considered to be either the most collected in the comic field or are historically significant. Artists designated below with an (*) indicate that only their most noted work will be listed. The rest will eventually have all their work shown as the information becomes available. This list could change from year to year as new artists come into prominence.

Adams, Arthur
Adams, Neal
Bachalo, Chris
Bagley, Mark
Baker, Matt
Barks, Carl
Beck, C. C.
*Brunner, Frank
*Buscema, John
Byrne, John
Campbell, J. Scott
Capullo, Greg
*Check, Sid
Cole, Jack
Cole, L. B.
Craig, Johnny
Crandall, Reed
Darrow, Geof
Davis, Jack
Disbrow, Jayson
*Ditko, Steve
Eisner, Will
*Elder, Bill
Evans, George
Everett, Bill
Feldstein, Al
Fine, Lou
Foster, Harold
Fox, Matt
Frazetta, Frank
Gibbons, Dave
*Giffen, Keith
Golden, Michael
Gottfredson, Floyd
*Guardineer, Fred
Gustavson, Paul
*Heath, Russ
Howard, Wayne
*Infantino, Carmine
Ingels, Graham
Jones, Jeff
Kamen, Jack
Kane, Bob
*Kane, Gil
Kelly, Walt
Kieth, Sam
Kinstler, E. R.
Kirby, Jack
Krenkel, Roy
Krigstein, Bernie
Kubert, Adam
Kubert, Andy
*Kubert, Joe
Kurtzman, Harvey
Lapham, Dave
Larsen, Erik
Lee, Jae
Lee, Jim
Liefeld, Rob
Madureira, Joe
Manning, Russ
McFarlane, Todd
McWilliams, Al
Meskin, Mort
Mignola, Mike
Miller, Frank
Moreira, Ruben
*Morisi, Pete
*Newton, Don
Nostrand, Howard
Orlando, Joe
Pakula, Mac

*Palais, Rudy	Raymond, Alex	Siegel & Shuster	Steranko, Jim	Tuska, George	Wrightson, Bernie
*Perez, George	Ravielli, Louis	Silvestri, Marc	Stevens, Dave	Ward, Bill	Zeck, Mike
Portacio, Whilce	*Redondo, Nestor	Simon & Kirby (S&K)	Texeira, Mark	Williamson, Al	
Powell, Bob	Rogers, Marshall	*Simonson, Walt	Thibert, Art	Windsor-Smith, Barry	
Quesada, Joe	Ross, Alex	Smith, Paul	Torres, Angelo	Woggon, Bill	
Raboy, Mac	Schomburg, Alex	Stanley, John	Toth, Alex	Wolverton, Basil	
Ramos, Humberto	Sears, Bart	*Starlin, Jim	Turner, Michael	Wood, Wallace	

COMIC BOOK ARTISTS & THEIR FIRST WORK

Adams, Neal - (1 pg.) **Archie's Jokebook Mag.** #41, 9/59; (1st on Batman, cvr only) **Detective Comics** #370, 12/67; (1st Warren art) **Creepy** #14

Balent, Jim - **Sgt. Rock** #393, 10/84

Barks, Carl - (art only) **Donald Duck Four Color** #9, 8/42; (scripts only) **Large Feature Comic** #7, ca. Spring 1942

Broderick, Pat - (cover & art) **Planet of Vampires** #1, 2/75

Brunner, Frank - (fan club sketch) **Creepy** #10, 1965

Buckler, Rich - **Flash Gordon** #10, 11/67

Burnley, Jack - (cover & art) **NY World's Fair** nn, '40

Buscema, John - (1st at Marvel) **Strange Tales** #150, 11/66

Byrne, John - **Nightmare** #20, 8/74; (1st at DC) **Untold Legend of the Batman** #1, 7/80; (1st at Marvel) **Giant-Size Dracula** #5, 6/75

Capullo, Greg - (1st on X-Force) **X-Force Annual** #1, '92

Cole, Jack - (1 pg.) **Star Comics** #11, 4/38

Crandall, Reed - **Hit Comics** #10, 4/41

Davis, Jack - (cartoon) **Tip Top Comics** #32, 12/38

Ditko, Steve - (1st publ.) **Black Magic** V4#3, 11-12/53 (1st drawn story), **Fantastic Fears** #5, 1-2/54

Everett, Bill - **Amazing Mystery Funnies** V1#2, 9/38

Fine, Lou - (1st cvr) **Wonder Comics** #2, 6/39; **Jumbo Comics** #4, 12/38

Frazetta, Frank - **Tally-Ho Comics** nn, 12/44

Garney, Ron - **G. I. Joe, A Real American Hero** #110, 3/91

Giffen, Keith - (1 pg.) **Deadly Hands of Kung-Fu** #17, 11/75; (1st story) **Deadly Hands of Kung-Fu** #22, 4?/76; (tied w/Deadly Hands) **Amazing Adventures** #35, 3/76

Golden, Michael - **Marvel Classics Comics** #28, '77

Grell, Mike - **Adventure Comics** #435, 9-10/74

Hamner, Cully - **Green Lantern: Mosaic** #1, 6/92

Hughes, Adam - **Blood of Dracula** #1, 11/87

Ingels, Graham art at E.C. - **Saddle Justice** #4, Sum '48

Jurgens, Dan - **Warlord** #53, 1/82

Kaluta, Michael - **Teen Confessions** #59, 12/69

Kelly, Walt - **New Comics** #1, 12/35

Keown, Dale - **Samurai** #13, 1987; **Nth Man the Ultimate Ninja** #8, 1/90; (1st at Marvel); (1st on Hulk) **Incredible Hulk** #367, 3/90

Kieth, Sam - **Primer** #5, 11?/83

Kirby, Jack - **Jumbo Comics** #1, 9/38;

Kubert, Adam/Andy/Joe art - **Sgt. Rock** #422, 7/88

Kurtzman, Harvey - **Tip Top Comics** #36, 4/39; (1st at E.C.) **Lucky Fights It Through** nn, 1949

Larsen, Erik - **Megaton** #1, 11/83

Lee, Jae - **Marvel Comics Presents** #85, '91

Lee, Jim - (1st at Marvel) **Alpha Flight** #51, 10/87; (1st on X-Men) **X-Men** #248?, ?/89; (art on Punisher) **Punisher War Journal** #1, 11/88

Liefeld, Rob - (1st at DC) **Warlord** #131, 9/88; (1st at Marvel) **X-Factor** #40, 4?/89; (1st full story) **Megaton** #8, 8/87; (inside front cover only) **Megaton** #5, 6/86; (art on New Mutants) **New Mutants Annual** #5, '89

Lim, Ron - (art on Silver Surfer) **Silver Surfer Ann.** #1, '88

Matsuda, Jeff - **Brigade** #0, 9/93

Mayer, Sheldon - **New Comics** #1, 12/35

McFarlane, Todd - **Coyote** #11, ?/85; (1st full story) **All Star Squadron** #47, 7/85; (1st on Hulk) **Incredible Hulk** #330, 4/87

Medina, Angel - (pin-up only) **Megaton** #3, 2/86

Mignola, Mike - **Marvel Fanfare** #15, 5/83

Miller, Frank - (1st on Batman) **DC Special Series** #21, Spr '80; (1st on Daredevil) **Spectacular Spider-Man** #27, 2/79

Newton, Don - **Many Ghosts of Dr. Graves** #45, 5/74

Perez, George - (1st at DC) **Flash** #289, 9/80; (2 pgs.) **Astonishing Tales** #25, 8/74

Portacio, Whilce - (1st on X-Men) **X-Men** #201, 1/86

Pulido, Brian - **Evil Ernie** #1, 12/91

Quesada, Joe - (1st on X-Factor) **X-Factor Ann.** #7, '92

Raboy, Mac - (1st cover for Fawcett) **Master Comics** #21, 12/41

Ramos, Humberto - (1st U.S. work) **Hardwire** #15, 6/94

Romita, John - **Daredevil** #12, 1/66

Romita, John Jr. - (1st complete story) **Iron Man** #115, 10/78

Ross, Alex - **The Terminator: The Burning Earth** V2#1, 3/90

Shuster, Joe - (cover) **New Adv. Comics** #16, 6/37

Siegel & Shuster - **New Fun Comics** #6, 10/35

Simon & Kirby - **Blue Bolt** #2, 7/40

Simonson, Walter - **Magnus, Robot Fighter** #10, 5/65

Smith, Paul - (1 pg. pin-up) **King Conan** #7, 9/81; (1st full story) **Marvel Fanfare** #1, 3/82

Steranko, Jim - **Spyman** #1, Sep '66; (1st at Marvel) **Strange Tales** #151, 12/66

Swan, Curt - **Dick Cole** #1, 12-1/48-49

Talbot, Bryan - (1st U.S. work) **Hellblazer Annual** #1, Summer '89

Thomas, Roy - (scripts) **Son of Vulcan** #50, 1/66

Torres, Angelo - **Crime Mysteries** #13, 5/54

Turner, Mike - **Cyberforce Origins-Stryker**, 2/95

Weeks, Lee - **Tales of Terror** #5, 11/85

Weiss, Alan - (illo) **Blue Beetle** #5, 3-4/65

Williamson, Al - (1st at E.C.) **Tales From the Crypt** #31, 9/52; (text illos) **Famous Funnies** #169, 8/48

Windsor-Smith, Barry - **X-Men** #53, 2/69

Wood, Wally - (1st at E.C.) **Saddle Romances** #10, 1-2/50

Wrightson, Bernie - **House of Mystery** #179, 4/68; (1st at Marvel) **Chamber of Darkness** #7, 10/70; (1st cover) **Web of Horror** #3, 4/70; (fan club sketch) **Creepy** #9

Zeck, Mike - (illos) **Barney and Betty Rubble** #11, 2/75

KEY COMICS SOLD IN 1998

The following lists of sales were reported to Gemstone during the year and represent only a small portion of the total amount of important books that have sold.

GOLDEN-ATOM AGE SALES

Allentown (AT), Bethlehem (BH), Big Apple (BA), File (FC), Cosmic Aeroplane (CA), Denver (DEN), Gaines (GA), Green River (GR), Hawkeye (HK), Larson (LR), Mile High (MH), Mohawk Valley (MV), Oakland (OA), Pennsylvania (PA), Poughkeepsie File (PF), Restored (R), San Francisco (SF), Traded (T), White Mountain (WM); trade (tr)

Aces High #1 (GA)	$350
Action Comics #1FN/VF(r)	$57,000
Action Comics #12FN-	$1,300
Adventure Comics #51VF	$2,700
Adventure Comics #58VF+	$1,500
Adventure #72NM+ (MH)	$25,000
Adventure #74VF	$600
Adventure #87NM/MT (MH)	$4,705
Adventure #141NM/MT	$730
Adv. Into Darkness #5VF	$230
Adv. Into Terror #10VF+	$240
Avs. Into Darkness #8VF+	$300
Adventure Into Terror #9VF+	$255
Advs. Into Unknown #25NM	$280
Advs. Intro Unknown #38VF+ (WM)	$280
Advs. Into Weird Worlds #1NM	$1,100
Advs. Into Weird Worlds #18VF/NM	$300
All-American #16VG	$14,000
All American #19VG/FN	$2,000
All Flash #32FN/VF	$700
All Select #1VF+(r)	$3,700
All Star #8VG+	$4,750
All Star #10VF	$2,000
All Star #11NM+	$4,705
All Star #36NM-	$3,200
All Star #45NM+ (MH)	$4,480
All Star #56NM- (MH)	$1,120
All Winners #1VG/FN	$2,910
All Winners #21FN	$1,685
Amazing Man #5G/VG	$2,575
America's Best #8NM (MH)	$700
Astonishing #3VF-	$520
Astonishing #7VF/NM	$325
Astonishing #19NM-	$325
Atom-Age Combat #3NM	$300
Atomic War #1NM--	$1,125
Attack/Planet Mars VF+	$750
Authentic Police Cases #6NM (MH)	$1,600
Baffling Mysteries #9NM	$220
Batman #1FR	$6,000
Batman #1FR	$3,500
Batman #2FN-	$3,000
Batman 33VF-	$4,900
Batman #17NM-	$2,000
Batman #17NM	$2,800
Batman #22VF/NM	$1,475
Batman #27NM	$2,000
Batman #28NM	$1,570
Batman #30NM	$1,500
Batman #36NM	$1,200
Batman #40NM	$1,372
Batman #56VF/NM	$1,100
Batman #63NM	$1,000
Batman #71NM	$900
Batman #78NM-	$1,050
Beware Terror Tales #1NM-	$540
Beware Terror Tales #4NM	$400
Big 3 #1NM+ (MH)	$7,500
Big Town #4VF (MH)	$375
Blackhawk #9NM+ (MH)	$7,500
Black Hood #9NM (MH)	$1,993
Black Magic Vol.1/5VF/NM	$325
Blue Beetle #8NM (MH)	$1,125
Blue Bolt Weird #115NM	$1,000
Blue Bolt Weird #118NM-	$745
Bomber #2NM (MH)	$600
Boy Commandos #7NM+ (MH)	$1,850
Bulletman #3NM+ (MH)	$2,520
Canteen Kate #1NM- (MH)	$1,470
Captain America #3VF+(r)	$5,850
Captain America #7VF+	$3,940
Captain America #14VF+	$2,600
Captain America #28VF	$1,750
Captain Marvel Advs. #20VF	$2,700
Captain Mar.Advs. #28NM+ (MH)	$1,345
Captain Marv. Jr. #13MT (MH)	$2,015
Captain Marv. Jr. #13VF+ (PA)	$1,345
Catman #1NM	$4,500
Catman #1NM- (LR)	$4,800
City of Living Dead FN/VF	$325
Clue Comics #2NM (MH)	$920
Comic Calvacade #1VF (MH)	$8,050
Comic Calvacade #8NM (MH)	$1,840
Crime Does Not Pay #23VF	$835
Crusader From Mars #1VF+	$635
Crime Mysteries #15NM	$500
Dark Mysteries #15VF	$300
Dead Who Walk, The #1VF/NM	$675
Detective #9FN	$1,400
Detective #31VG/FN	$7,000
Detective #49VF+	$1,600
Detective #73NM	$2,000
Detective #106NM+ (MH)	$3,135
Detective #158VF	$375
Detective #176NM	$925
Detective #182NM	$750
Detective #190NM-	$1,000
Detective Eye #2NM+ (MH)	$4,500
Dynamic #17NM+ (MH)	$1,750
Eerie #7VF+	$550
Fantastic Comics #3FR/GD	$1,510
Fantastic Worlds #5VF/NM	$325
Feature Funnies #1NM+ (MH)	$9,000
Fight Comics #1FN/VF	$1,150
Fight Comics #3NM- (LR)	$1,100
Fight Comics #32VF	$300
Flame #1NM+ (MH)	$12,000
Flash Comics #86FN+	$900
Flying Saucers #1VF/NM	$750
Forbidden Worlds #1NM	$1,900
Forbidden Worlds #6NM	$500
Four Color #62FN+	$525
Ghost #1VF-	$350
Haunt of Fear #12NM	$300
Haunt of Fear #15NM+ (GA)	$840
Haunted Thrills #9NM-	$450
Heroic #8NM (MH)	$375
Hickory #1NM (MH)	$400
Horrors, The #13NM	$390
House of Mystery #2NM	$1,300
House of Mystery #7VF+	$500
Human Torch #3VF	$1,900
Human Torch #8NM	$6,000
Human Torch #10VF	$1,500
Journey Into Fear #7NM	$400
Journey Into Mystery #1NM-	$5,800
King #36VF- (MH)	$625
Mad #1VF/NM	$4,900
Mad #2NM-	$1,370
Mad #5NM-	$2,000
Mad #26NM	$420
Marvel Comics #1VF (LR)	$48,000
Marvel Comics #1vf(r)	$29,000
Marvel Mystery #4NM (LR)	$5,752
Marvel Mystery #5VG+	$4,480
Marvel Mystery #7VF (LR)	$6,662
Marvel Mystery #7 (Nova Scotia)	$7,200
Marvel Mystery #15NM-	$2,300
Marvel Mystery #24VF/NM	$2,600
Marvel Mystery #29FN/VF	$2,500
Marvel Mystery #47NM-	$1,425
Marvel Mystery #64NM-(CA)	$1,200
Marvel Tales #102NM-	$1,100
Marvel Tales #108NM	$620

GOLDEN-ATOM AGE SALES

Marvel Tales #114NM $513
Mask #2VG+ $650
Master #16NM-(AT) $1,300
Master #62VF/NM(MH) $1,300
Menace #2VF/NM (WM) $450
Men's Advs. #21VF/NM $500
Mister Mystery #2NM+ $500
Mister Mystery #5VF/NM $500
Monster #1NM- $515
More Fun #52FN- $10,000
More Fun #90NM+ (SF) $2,575
More Fun #101NM $17,920
Mysterious Advs. #1VF/NM $450
Mystery In Space #1VF+ $3,150
Mystery In Space #4NM $825
Mystery In Space #7NM+ $1,000
Mystery In Space #53VF+ $1,905
Mystery Tales #5NM $450
Mystic #1VF $9,240
Mystic #17NM $335
Night Of Mystery VF/NM $475
Nightmare (1st) #1NM- $575
O.K. #2NM+ (MH) $2,275
Outer Space #23NM+ (WM) $225
Out of the Shadows #5VF+ $425
Out of the Shadows #11NM $375
Pep Comics #3NM (LR) $1,500
Phantom Lady #17VG- $1,400
Phantom Stranger #5VF+ $650
Planet Comics #66VF/NM $455
Planet Comics #69NM+ $550
Punch #10NM (HK) $1,000
Punch #12VG- $1,150
Punch #12GD- $600
Racket Squad #14NM (MH) $300
Real Life #50NM (MH) $650
Red Ryder #3VF+ $975
Robotmen/Lost Planet VF- $700
Rocket to the Moon VF/NM $950
Rocketman #1VF/NM $400
Sensation #2VF/NM $3,700
Sensation #68NM+ (MH) $1,230
Sensation Mystery #113VF+ $375
Silver Streak #3NM+ (MH) $11,000
Silver Streak #6VG+(r) $4,300
Slam Bang #2NM (MH) $1,500
Son of Sinbad #1NM- (MH) $995
Space Action #3NM $525
Space Advs. #27NM+ (WM) $450
Space Busters #1VF/NM $735
Space Detective #1VF+ $800
Spaceman #1VF $600
Space Patrol #1VF $700
Space Squadron #2VF+ $480
Space Western #45NM- $600
Speed #42NM+ (MH) $1,050
Spellbound #4NM $400
Spook #24NM- $450
Star Spangled #37NM (MH) $1.850
Star Spangled #122NM- $525
Startling Terror Tales #11NM $2,500
Strange Advs. #3NM- $1,000
Strange Advs. #6NM- $800
Strange Advs. #10NM $1,150
Strange Advs. #18NM $875
Strange Advs. #26NM $850
Strange Fantasy #2VF+ $400
Strange Mysteries #3NM $388
Strange Sus. Stories #1NM- $725
Strange Sus. Stories #5VF+ $525
Strange Tales #1VF $4,700
Strange Tales #7VF/NM $690
Strange Terrors #1VF/NM $450
Strange Worlds #3NM- $2,200
Sub-Mariner #13NM (PA) $2,465
Superman #1 (r) $25,000
Superman #2FN- $2,690
Superman #2FN+ $5,040
Superman #3VF- $5,600
Superman #4FN/VF $3,700
Superman #5VF- $3,025
Superman #8NM (Recil Macon) $3,810
Superman #25NM- $1,200
Superman #31NM+ $1,230
Superman #33NM+ $1,345
Superman #53NM- $4,000
Superman #57VF+ $575
Superman #73NM+ $895
Super-Mystery #1NM+ (MH) $5,175
Tales F.T. Crypt #31NM+(GA) $1,125
Tales To Astonish #9NM+ $530
Target #7FN+ $1,500
Terrifying Tales #13NM- $775
Thing, The #3VF+ $750
Thing, The #7VF $800
Tim Holt #25NM (MH) $525
Tomahawk #2NM+ (MH) $1,345
Tomb of Terror #1VF/NM $255
Top Secrets #7VF (MH) $550
Torchy #6NM $840
True Crime #3VF $565
Uncanny Tales #1VF+ $775
Uncle Scrooge #10VF/NM (PF) $125
Vault of Horror #27NM/MT (GA) $670
Venus #16VF/NM $830
Voodoo #7VF/NM $450
Weird Fantasy #7NM/MT (GA) $895
Weird Fantasy #19NM (GA) $640
Weird Horrors #1NM $620
Weird Science/Fan.Ann. #1NM $2,000
Weird Tales/Future #2NM- $2,000
Weird Thrillers #1VF/NM $626
Western Crime Bus. #1NM- (MH) $725
Whiz #4VF+ (LR) $1950
Witchcraft #1VF+ $575
Wonder Woman #1NM+ $44,800
Wonder Woman #1VF+ $14,000
Wonder Woman #5NM+ (MH) $5,600
Wonder Woman #8NM+ (PA) $2,800
Wonder Woman #9MT (MH) $4,650
Wonder Woman #53NM (HK) $365
Wonderworld #7NM (MH) $6,460
Wonderworld #8NM- (MH) $6,460
Wonderworld #9NM- (MH) $4,800
Wonderworld #11NM (MH) $4,000
World's Best #1VF- $7,700
World's Best #1VF/NM (r) $7,750
World's Beyond #1NM $600
World's Finest #14VF/NM $1,200
World's Finest #17NM- $1,300
World's Finest #19NM+ (AT) $2,465
World's Finest #24NM $825
World's Finest #48NM $750
World's of Fear #3VF/NM $380
Yellowjacket #3NM+ (MH) $945
Zip-Jet #1VF/NM $530

SILVER-BRONZE AGE SALES

Adventure #214VF/NM (MV) $445
Adventure #220VF/NM (MV) $320
Adventure #253VF+ $250
Adventure #256NM- (MV) $1,190
Advs. Into/Unk. #135NM+ (WM) $130
Amazing Advs. #11 $125
Amazing Fantasy #15PR $380
Amazing Fantasy #15FR/GD $900
Amazing Fantasy #15GD/VG $1,510
Amaz. Spider-Man #1NM $25,000
Amaz. Spider-Man #1VF+ $6,500
Amaz.Spider-Man #2VF $2,400
Amaz. Spider-Man #2VF $1,500
Amaz. Spider-Man #3NM- $2,800
Amaz. Spider-Man #6VF/NM $1,050
Amaz. Spider-Man #8NM $1,050
Amaz. Spider-Man #13VF/NM $750
Amaz. Spider-Man #13NM- $925
Amaz. Spider-Man #14VG+ $250
Amaz. Spider-Man #15NM $900
Amaz. Spider-Man #19NM $450
Amaz. Spider-Man #26NM $375
Amaz. Spider-Man #39NM $350
Amaz. Spider-Man #50NM- $550
Amaz. Spider-Man #110NM (OA) $40
Avengers #1VF+ $1,200
Avengers #2NM- $750
Avengers #57NM-(OA) 115
Batlash #1NM (OA) $25
Batman #234NM (OA) $200
Brave & the Bold #1VF $1,200
Brave & The Bold #28VF+ $3,000
Captain America #100NM+ (OA) $425
Captain America #100NM+ $335
Conan #1NM (OA) $280
Daredevil #1FN+ $1,500

Daredevil #2VF/NM	$500
DC 100 PG. #4VF+	$285
Detective #395NM (OA)	$45
Fantastic Four #1VF+(r)	$3,100
Fantastic Four #2NM	$5,375
Fantastic Four #2VF/NM	$2,800
Fantastic Four #4FN-	$500
Fantastic Four #15NM	$475
Fantastic Four #48NM-	$750
Fear #1NM (OA)	$50
Flash #105NM-	$7,500
Forbidden Worlds #106NM+(WM)	$135
Forbidden Worlds #112NM(WM)	$107
Ghosts #1NM (WM)	$100
GI Combat #138NM (OA)	$150
Gorgo #5NM+ (WM)	$195
Gorgo #9NM+ (WM)	$195
Green Lantern #1VF+	$1,000
Green Lantern #1VF/NM	$3,000
Green Lantern #5NM	$535
Green Lantern #76NM-(OA)	$500
Increcible Hulk #1VF-	$5,550
Incredible Hulk #1FN-	$700
Incredible Hulk #3NM	$2,600
Incredible Hulk #3VF/NM	$1,700
Incredible Hulk #5VF/NM	$1,260
Incredible Hulk #181NM	$550
Incredible Hulk #181NM-	$475
Iron Man #1NM-(OA)	$533
Journey Into Mystery #83VF	$2,000
Journey Into Mystery #86NM	$575
Konga #5NM+ (WM)	$310
Marvel Spotlight #2NM	$350
My Love #1NM- (OA)	$100
Our Love Story #16NM (OA)	$48
Rawhide Kid #100NM (OA)	$20
Secret Hearts #141NM- (OA)	$50
Showcase #4FN+	$2,200
Showcase #15VF (MV)	$2,070
Showcase #18VF+ (MV)	$1,345
Showcase #19NM (WM)	$1,960
Showcase #22NM-	$7,920
Silver Surfer #3NM	$145
Showcase #60NM	$280
Star Sp. War #129NM	$102
Star Sp. War #151NM	$200
Super DC Giant #21NM+	$350
Superboy #158NM (OA)	$35
Superman #229NM (OA)	$60
Tales of Suspense #39VF+	$2,700
Tales of Suspense #46NM	$275
Tales To Astonish #52VF/NM (WM)	$247
Thor #155NM (OA)	$50
Two-Gun Kid #105NM (OA)	$10
X-Men #1NM	$9,000
X-Men #1GD+	$400
X-Men #1VF/NM	$8,000
X-Men #2NM	$2,300
X-Men #4NM	$800
X-Men #14NM	$335
X-Men Giant Size #1NM	$500
Witching Hour #2NM+ (OA)	$60

STRIP ART SALES

Original comic strip art is hot. As established and new collectors alike continue to become aware of the historical importance of newspaper comic strips, particularly in their relationship to comic books, prices realized continue to set records.

The connection between comic books, comic strips and the popularity of certain characters remains one of the most vital areas of exploration in our pop culture history. As enthusiasts and historians chronicle the important early events in comics and comic strips, they're finding more and more reason to view the two areas as parts of a whole rather than two individual art forms. For example, this is particularly true in the case of the Platinum Age comics which were, by and large, reprints of dailies and Sunday strips, but it is equally true of Superman, who started in comics but reached a much larger audience with his daily comic strip.

Auction Sales

Red Ryder daily 5/11/49	Fred Harmon	$1,155
Johnny Comet daily 1/23/53	Frank Frazetta	$1,980
Pogo daily strip 11/26/62	Walt Kelly	$1,540
Tarzan Sunday page 3/5/33	Hal Foster	$11,000
Tarzan Sunday page 7/31/49	Burne Hogarth	$10 450
Little Nemo in Slumberland 8/22/1909	Winsor McCay	$20,900
Thimble Theatre & 'Sappo' topper Sunday page 12i21/30	E.C. Segar	$9,900
Flash Gordon Sunday page 5/29/38	Alex Raymond	$13,200
Yellow Kid Sunday page 'Hogan's Alley' 7/12/1896	R.F. Outcault	$25,300
Donald Duck Sunday page 1936	Al Taliaferro	$20,000
Krazy Kat Specialty piece (watercolor) 1933	George Herriman	$41,250
Krazy Kat Sunday page handcolored by artist 1918	George Herriman	$40,000
KrazyKat daily1940	GeorgeHerriman	$2,000
Polly and Her Pals Sunday page w/matching Topper 1930.	Cliff Sterrett	$6,500
Mickey Mouse daily 1930	Floyd Gotffredson	$15,000

BY ROBERT M. OVERSTREET

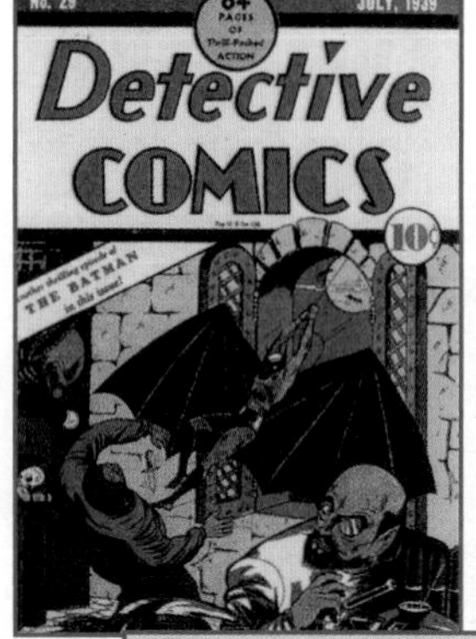

© DC

Detective Comics #29
VF/NM sold for $57,000!

MARKET BACK ON TRACK

With unemployment down and the continued rise of the stock market, the comic book marketplace's reaction to the 1998 Guide adjustments was mostly positive. Sales were definitely up at the major conventions last year. In fact, there was a buzz on the convention floor not seen for several years. Many dealers thought that the Guide's stand of lowering the prices last year had a very positive effect on the market. Dealers were noticing the return of collectors they hadn't seen for awhile buying books again. With the lower prices, these collectors could afford to collect once again.

1998 saw a tremendous increase in trading on the internet. More and more dealers are establishing their own web sites from Mile High Comics, to American Entertainment to Fantasy Illustrated to Four Color Comics (see ads in this book for web site info of all dealers) . But the site that has dominated the field is Ebay. Here, collectors and dealers are holding auctions constantly where thousands of books are being sold every week. Obviously, web sales will greatly impact prices listed in this book in the future as the web increases its domination of the market. Currently, most internet sales are well below $100 per item.

Price changes in this edition: The last Guide made numerous price adjustments that were needed to get this market back on track. This year's guide has taken a conservative approach to price increases with changes only in the areas indicated by our research and advisors.

Platinum, Golden and Atom Age books are still enjoying solid demand, while Silver Age books continued to recover from the price reductions of a year ago. Wider spreads were indicated for all Bronze Age books which continued to set records for high grade copies of specific isues.

Record sales still occurred throughout the year. A **Detective** #29 (Allentown copy) in VF/NM sold for $57,000. An **Action** #1FN+(restored) brought $57,000. The Mile High copy of **Silver Streak** #3NM+ sold for $11,000 and a **Wonder Woman** #1NM+ got $44,800! An **All-American** #16 in VG sold for $14,000!

GOLDEN AGE/ATOM AGE

Still the cornerstone of the hobby, collections continued to appear on the market for sale with no problem finding anxious buyers to snatch them up. Individual issues in all grades also sold well throughout the year. During the Summer conventions of 1997, some

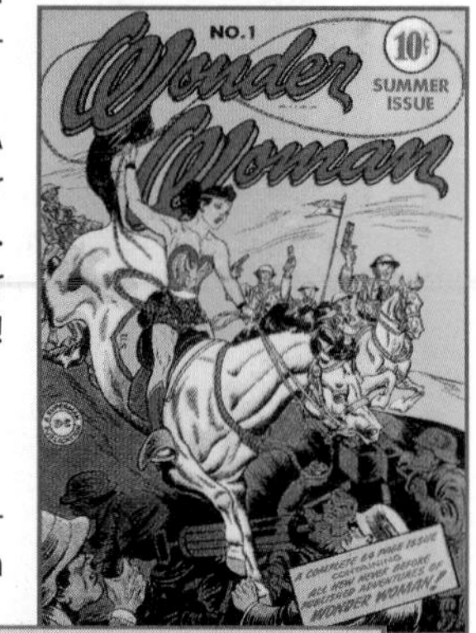

Wonder Woman #1 NM
brings $44,800!

© DC

of our advisors were complaining about a slowdown in Golden Age sales indicating wider spreads needed between Good and Near Mint. Due to this, last year's Guide began broadening the spreads for Golden Age books. However, while the 1998 Guide was at the printer, the market took a turn for the better. As 1998 progressed, it became more evident that the old 1997 spreads were correct and our advisors now strongly suggested that the 1999 Guide go back to the old spreads. To accomplish this, you will see above average increases for the Good and Fine prices in this edition for Golden Age. We sincerely hope that this will bring the Guide back into balance with what these books are bringing in the current market.

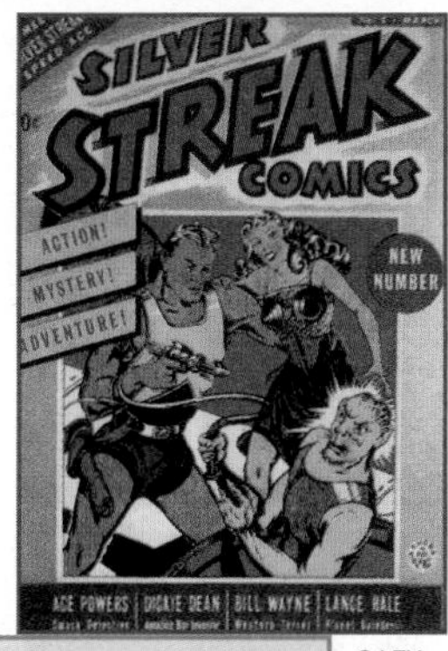

© LEV

Silver Streak #3 (Mile High) sells for $11,000!

Superhero books still dominate the market with DC and Timely on top, but the second tier companys such as MLJ, Quality, Gleason, Fawcett and Fox were in high demand. A **Wonderworld** #7 in Near Mint (Mile High) sold for $6,460 and a **Silver Streak** #3 in Near Mint plus (Mile High) brought $11,000!

© MAR

Wonderworld #7 NM (Mile High) brings $6,460!!

Many Atom Age books continued to sell at above Guide list in all grades. The Fox Love titles along with all the Good Girl Art books enjoyed high demand carrying over from the previous year.

All of the obscure companies' Horror titles sold very well, with some as much as 3 to 4 times Guide list. E.C. comics were in high demand when in high grade with Gaines File Copies continuing to break price records.

SILVER AGE

Internet sales in this area has been intense with thousands of books, mostly in the lower grades going to new collectors overseas as well as here at home. Web sales have had a tremendous impact on supply and demand for these books and will continue to play a major role in affecting prices in the future.

Otherwise, most books from this period are selling for around Guide list with the higher grade copies bringing just over Guide. With prices fairly stable now, this may be a good time for the investor to look at certain Silver Age books to buy before the market takes off again, and this could happen quickly as internet sales continue to skyrocket. At least for now, any increases in this edition have been very conservative.

© MAR

Amazing Spider-Man #1 in NM brings $25,000!

Key issues, when in high grade, still bring over-Guide prices! A **Spider-Man** #1 in NM sold for $25,000! We noticed that books from this period were still being dis-

X-Men #1 NM
sells for $9,000!

counted at the conventions but not to the extent of the previous year. Many dealers reported and increase in sales encouraged by the reduced 1998 Guide levels. Another high grade collection surfaced, dubbed the "Oakland Collection," which included virtually every Marvel and DC comic printed from 1966 to 1972. At the conventions we could see that interest in books of this quality was high, at and above current Guide levels.

BRONZE TO MODERN AGE

1970s books were again on the move during 1998 with more and more collectors geting involved. Condition was the key creating the need to expand the spreads from Good to Mint on all books from this period. Internet sales continue to make an impact in this area with thousands of copies going directly to the consumer. Web hits for comic books and related items are now numbering in the millions. Some notable sales include: **America's Best TV Comics** #1 NM $110; **DC 100-Page Super Spectacular** #14 VF/NM $20; **DC 100-Page Super Spectacular** #18 VF/NM $20; **Incredible Hulk** #181 NM-/NM $475; **Incredible Hulk** #181 VG $75; **Our Army at War** #168 VF $120; **Pizzazz** (set) VF/NM $174; **Sabrina** #1 FN/VF $49; **Scooby Doo** #1-#9 (set) NM $108; **X-Men** #94 NM $475; **X-Men Giant Size** #1 NM+ $600.

A COMIC BOOK GRADING SERVICE

Late in the year, NGC, one of the largest grading services in coins was approached about the possibility of grading and encapsulating comic books. Some dealers believe that if comic books could receive a professional guaranteed grade that everyone would accept, then more people would invest in this hobby. In fact, many coin collectors would be given the opportunity to include comic books in their investment portfolio. NGC was very interested and started investigating the possibility of doing this. In November of 1998 they met with several of the top dealers to explore how this could be done. At the meeting there was a discussion about changing the grading system. Most dealers agreed that the current 100 point system is too complicated. They further agreed that a simpler 10 point system should be devised that would serve the industry better. For more on this development, turn to page 17 for an exclusive special feature about the new grading and certification service.

REGIONAL MARKET REPORTS FROM OUR ADVISORS

For the first time ever in this book, we thought it would be interesting to include individual market reports by some of our advisors. The following reports are written by each submitter and do not necessarily represent the opinion of the publisher. We are providing these reports for your information only and also to show the diversity of ideas and sales trends that exists in our diverse market. Good luck to everyone and have a great 1999!

Bob Overstreet

CONTRIBUTORS

AVALON COMICS
LARRY CURCIO
P.O. Box 821
Medford, MA 02155
Phone: (617) 262-5544
Fax: (617) 948-2300

CLARENCE ROAD PRODUCTIONS
DALE & SHARI MOORE
612 N. Oaks #1
Tacoma, WA 98406
Phone: (253) 274-8274
E-Mail: crinc6@webtv.net

THE COMIC ART FOUNDATION
ERIC J. GROVES
P.O. Box 1414
Oklahoma City, OK 73101
Phone: (405) 236-5303
Fax: (405) 236-5309

COMICS INA FLASH
TONY STARKS
P.O. Box 3611
Evansville, IN 47735
Phone/Fax: (812) 867-1149

FLYING COLORS COMICS
& OTHER COOL STUFF
JOE FIELD
2980 Treat Blvd
Concord, CA 94518
Phone: (925) 825-5410
Fax: (925) 825-5412

GARY DOLGOFF COMICS
GARY DOLGOFF
116 Pleasant St.
Easthampton, MA 01027
Phone: (413) 529-0326
Fax: (413) 529-9824
E-Mail: gdcomics@javanet.com

METROPOLIS COLLECTIBLES
STEPHEN FISHLER
873 Broadway #201
New York, NY 10003
Phone: (212) 260-4147
E-Mail: comicbooks@earthlink.net

REDBEARD'S BOOK DEN
RON PUSSELL
P.O. Box 217
Crystal Bay, NV 89402-0217
Phone: (775) 831-4848
Fax: (775) 831-4483
Website: www.redbeardsbookden.com

RTS UNLIMITED, INC.
TIM COLLINS
P.O. Box 150412
Lakewood, CO 80215-0412
Phone: (303) 403-1840
Fax: (303) 403-1837

MATT SCHIFFMAN
4475 SW Scottie PL
Aloha, OR 97007
Phone: (503) 356-1124

SHOWCASE NEW ENGLAND
DANIEL GREENHALGH
67 Gail Drive
Northford, CT 06472
PHONE: (203) 484-4579
Fax: (203) 484-4837

DOUG SULIPA'S COMIC WORLD
DOUG SULIPA
Box # 21986
Steinbach, Manitoba
Canada R5G 1B5
Phone: (204) 346-3674

TERRY'S COMICS
TERRY O'NEILL
P.O. BOX 471
Atwood, CA 92811
Phone: (714) 288-8993

VINCENT'S COLLECTIBLES
VINCENT ZURZOLO, JR.
424 Beach 134th St.
Belle Harbor, NY 11694
Phone: (800) 974-2999
E-Mail: vincentcoll@earthlink.net
Website: www.vincentcollectibles.com

WANT LIST COMICS
DAVE ANDERSON
Box 701932
Tulsa, OK 74170-1932
Phone: (918) 299-0440

ANNUAL MARKET REPORT: 1999

INTRODUCTION

COMIC ART FOUNDATION

The collector market for old comic books remains relatively unchanged from a year ago. Demand is on a plateau, perhaps slightly increased. Prices, with a few exceptions, appear stable. Bargain hunters abound, but this is encouraging, denoting that such folks are still in the hobby.

GARY DOLGOFF COMICS "A Year Of Cautious Optimism"

Contrary to the "Nattering Nabobs of Negativity's" expectations, back issue selling has, for me, been stronger than it has been in a couple of years or more—very satisfactory indeed!

Hopefully we have all learned the lessons of the early '90s time of excess. Longterm thinking will guide us to further success, even expansion and respectability of our chosen passion of comics. Over-grade your comics, misrepresent them, and you may help to turn off a comics-loving collector forever. Grade them tightly and you will create a long-term base of happy collectors! And isn't that what it's all about?

FLYING COLORS COMICS

It seems the market is splintered into niche collectors...some love Pre-Code Horror, others love Silver Age Romance, etc. But over the last several months, we've seen a resurgence in back issue sales as readers/collectors now rule the market over the investors!!

METROPOLIS COLLECTIBLES

The market showed great strength and diversity this year. All publishers had their fans, and these fans collected in all grades.

REDBEARD'S BOOK DEN

Substantial gains were confined to specific areas in the collectible hobby. The emergence of internet trading has had a profound impact on comic book sales. Collectors previously denied an opportunity to purchase desired books through local retailers have found a new avenue to pursue.

RTS UNLIMITED, INC.

This year's San Diego ComiCon was my best ever.

The initial response to my catalog has been better than I

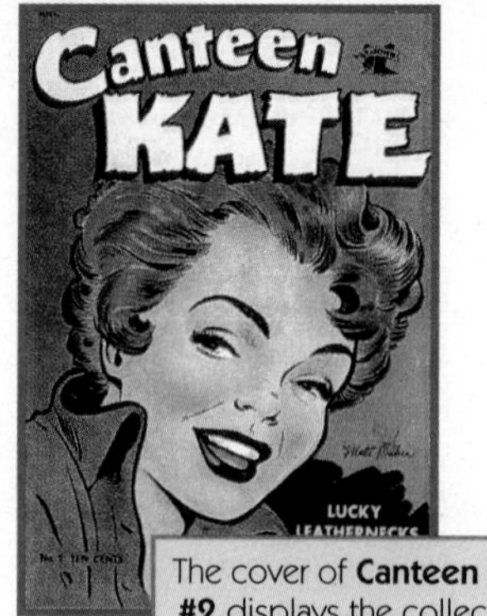

© STJ

The cover of **Canteen Kate #2** displays the collectible talents of Matt Baker.

expected. The market for oddball Silver and Golden Age stuff is especially strong. In my catalog I priced all Love comics at 1.5x Guide and they are still selling extremely well. Matt Baker stuff is really hot. War comics and TV-related comics are selling extremely well. Humor comics (eg. **Georgie**, **Nellie the Nurse**, **Gay**, etc) are, dare I say, "hot." Also, '70s horror comics are selling really well.

Disney stuff is dead, **Showcase** is dead, and The High End market is not doing well. Above $150.00 there is tremendous price resistance for most things. Unless the market changes dramatically, new comics are not going to survive. Two long time (20+ years) collectors that I know have stopped buying new comics completely. They say that comics have lost their sense of awe and wonder.

I've been thinking about the drop-off for new comics for quite sometime, and I don't buy the old argument that there's too much competition for comics (TV, movies, video games, computers, etc). There has always been competition for entertainment (radio, movies, and TV have been around since the '50s and earlier). Gold Key's **Tarzan** had a print run of 700,000 copies in the late-'60s/early-'70s. Also, there was a huge drop off in the mid-'70s when no new competition for entertainment dollars occurred. However, there was a series of price increases. Comics picked up again in the '80s as prices stabilized and then have been falling again partly due to the investors leaving the market and also price increases, among other things. Adjusted for inflation, a 1960's era 10¢ cover price should be less than $1.00 today. (Could this be explained by paper price increases alone?) Besides the loss of value, comics have gone collector, instead of reader, crazy. In the countries where comics are most successful (Europe and especially Japan), there is no collector/investor mentality. Comics are produced as cheaply as possible and are still disposable.

Lastly, the industry should be focusing on female readers. Girls generally have a higher propensity to read, are less involved with computers and sports than boys and don't really have an entertainment medium geared towards them.

© MAR

High grade Silver Age Marvels like **Captain America #109** rule the marketplace.

SHOWCASE NEW ENGLAND

"Trends in the Market"

The more things change the more they seem to stay the same.

As was true 5 years ago, 3 years ago, and still true today, high grade Silver Age Marvels rule the marketplace. In fact, I don't remember a time during this decade when this wasn't true.

Sure, different genres, publishers, periods, characters, etc. have had the spotlight from time to time, but this only disguised the advances in the only consistent generals in the marketplace: bonafide Near Mint Marvels. Demand for these gems is stronger than ever.

Admittedly, the pricier books like the keys have topped out and will likely not appreciate very much in value until the next cycle rolls around. However, there is still a lot of room for price growth in the books that are currently priced from $30-$150 in NM grades. Look for the early to mid-'70s Marvels (and DCs) to explode in the next few years.

After getting wacked in the past 18 months, prices for mid-grade Marvels appear to have bottomed and stabilized. These books sell well if priced properly and there seems to be much more consistency in the way they are priced on average. Mainstream DCs like **Action Comics**, **Batman** and **Detective**

Comics still sell well, particularly 10¢ copies. The lesser titles, however, like **Sea Devils** and **Rip Hunter**, move at an anemic rate—regardless of price. Again, in very high grades all books sell well and are still commanding premiums.

DOUG SULIPA'S COMIC WORLD

Last year an explosion of interest and demand began for traditionally non-collected titles! When it was discovered by many how scarce these titles can be, this fueled the fire. High grade? Forget it on many of the scarcer titles! For example, most Charltons, due to the cereal-box paper cover and general bad printing, would grade VF the initial day of release, much less now, after 25 years of being treated with disdain! Charltons are hot, or verging on it, for the first time ever in collectng history. Many traditionally non-collected titles are bringing record prices. But after the big price jumps in Guide #28, some collectors have returned to Superheroes. The biggest demand is for VF-NM Bronze Age key's, or on the flip side, reading copies of many now bargain priced titles.

TERRY'S COMICS

Generally speaking, 1997-1998 sales were steady in all areas. The 1998 **Overstreet Price Guide** was right on the money by adjusting the lower grades of comics slightly downward. Silver Age keys are still way over market price and should be adjusted downward again to reflect the true market. This won't upset collector confidence since most real collectors look forward to a corrected market just the way most investors look ahead to a stock market correction. They are both in to it for the long haul.

VINCENT'S COLLECTIBLES

In 1998, my New Year's resolution was to have my best year in business to date. I decided to go for it 100%. Several factors helped me to realize my goal. The acquisition of my first two pedigree collections, The Spokane Collection: an eight hundred book collection of super high grade Golden Age books and The Oakland Collection: a gorgeous collection of 3,500 books from the mid sixties to the early seventies. Also helping to revive the hobby was a healthy economy and though flawed in its sweeping price reform, the **Overstreet Guide's** lowering of prices.

GOLDEN/ ATOM AGE

CLARENCE ROAD PRODUCTIONS

Golden Age comics have been golden eggs of late. Low grade issues of any title prior to 1950 are swiftly gobbled at every turn. Restoration once considered a threat to collectibility is commonplace, making even scarcer the low grade item. Restoration (professional) has possibly aided the market in the sense that collectors are able to enhance the look of their prized items much like a restored classic vehicle or fixed-up house. The mid-range grades of Golden Age material also seem to move, but at a slower pace. We have not seen too much discounting in this area. The high grade record setting material is growing and pushing the price envelope further than ever. The five books likely to reach $1,000,000.00 by the year 2000: (1) **Action** #1 (2) **Superman** #1 (3) **Detective** #27 (4) **Whiz** #1 (5) **Marvel Comics** #1. We have seen lots of **Batman** #1's floating around; at least a different one every month. Prices and grades from GD ($6,700-$13,500) to VF ($33,000-$65,000). This is a good example of price challenges, of being in the right place at the right time, which is where Golden Age collectors need to be to find their books, in any grade. The only Golden Age books we've seen sit are amateur restored items, and eventually they sell!

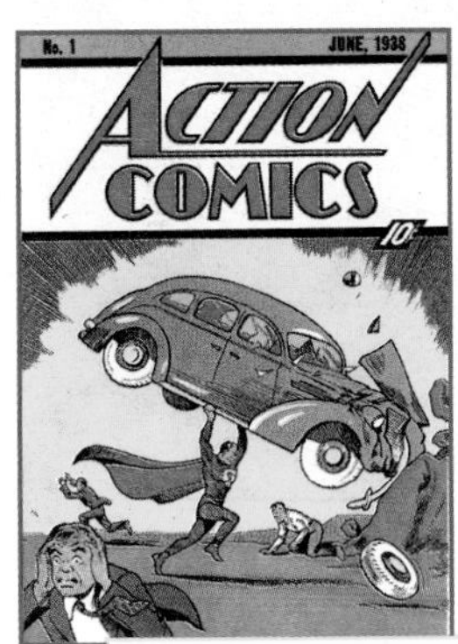

Will **Action Comics #1** be the first to reach $1,000,000?

COMIC ART FOUNDATION

Golden Age books sell across the board in all grades,

and price resistance can be eased with a slight discount. Some collectors will still pay premium prices for extraordinarily high grade copies.

COMICS INA FLASH

I seldom get Golden Age books. I find most '50s books (Sci-fi, Horror, Good Girl, Bad Girl, Jungle Girl, Western and even Archies) sell well when they are priced at $50 or less.

GARY DOLGOFF COMICS

Hero and superhero comics are still selling wonderfully! Last year I received a $73,000 collection of mostly Poors to Goods and even some coverless Golden Age (mostly superhero). They sold like hotcakes at 80-100% of guide or sometimes a bit over guide.

FLYING COLORS COMICS

Sales are definitely related to supply, and our supply has been relatively low for the last year or so. We've made no significant purchases, and sales seem to be from the bargain end of the spectrum, including mostly lower grade Romance, **Classics**, Funny Animal and Western stuff.

© AVON

A great cover can help sell any book. (**Strange Worlds #4**, cover by Wally Wood.)

METROPOLIS COLLECTIBLES

DC Golden Age was very strong, followed closely by Timely's. These books sold very strongly in all grades, though Timely collectors were a bit less picky than their DC counterparts. Fawcett collectors again favored books in lower grade.

Atomic Age books were on fire. We purchased many collections of extremely high-grade '50s material, including Science Fiction, Horror and Romance, and all of these sold easily for multiples of Guide. These genres sold above Guide in lower grades as well. Atlas, Avon, ACG, EC, St. John, Prize and DC: publisher did not matter, covers did.

For all of the above books, there has been a resurgence in the popularity of the Very Fine condition. This is certainly attributable to the increased spreads in prices; some collectors are finding it difficult to justify huge differences in price for books fractionally better than VF.

REDBEARD'S BOOK DEN

Collections are surfacing with a bit more frequency due to past price increases, but demand still outstrips supply; high grade copies are still in very short supply. The upcoming grading certification should drive the high grade copies to new record heights. Most of the mainline titles in less than FN sell for 85-145% of Guide. The decrease in FN or less has had the necessary impact. We are selling our lesser condition superhero books from this time frame at 100-145% of Guide. Sales remained consistent throughout the year at these prices. At 85-100% of Guide, these books fly for us if graded properly. Most dealers that state they can't sell superhero books from this time frame at the above listed percentages of guide simply can't grade the books properly!

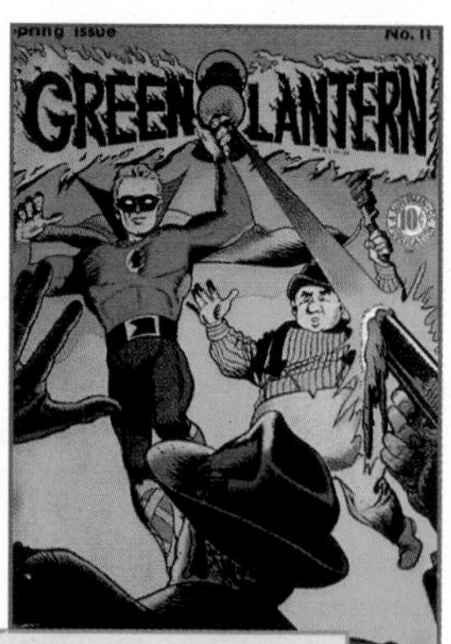

Golden Age books like **Green Lantern #11** sell well in all grades.

© DC

The Atom Age is a very hot area! One of the only areas in collecting where a few hundred dollars still buys a stack of books. The hottest publisher is still Fox. It should be remembered books from this time period sell very quickly in ALL grades.

MATT SCHIFFMAN

Golden Age can still be considered "hot" in certain segments. Low grade keys or Timely or DC still move very well and often in multiples. Books in VF or better still have an interest, but most sellers still ask for multiples of Guide prices and so the books often tend to sit. Key books still sell very well, if not just as fast as before. The price threshold seems to be a lower $750, but around $3,000 for icon books.

The Atom Age is still unbelievably hot for three reasons: (1) the low prices in the Guide allow an asking price of 2x-5x for books; (2) these books are really tough to find—especially in grade and most "larger" dealers don't find it worth their while to hunt these down yet (Pre-Code Horror, Crime and Romance are all experiencing huge demand); and (3) many of these books are not pictured in the **Gerber Photo-Journals**, nor have they been seen by most collectors, so there is an aura of mystique around them.

Matt Baker leads the way for Atom Age books, and these Romance books just cannot be found anywhere. Fox Romance or oddball titles are asked for quite often. Pre-Code Horror is still very popular and multiples are the norm. Even small publisher Western books are experiencing growth if it is Pre-Code.

TERRY'S COMICS

This material seems to always sell no matter what the title or subject. Most collections when eventually sold will average out about Guide value. Typically about a quarter of a collection goes quickly at slightly over Guide (around 125%). Then another half will trickle out at Guide. Then the remaining quarter will eventually go for around 75-80% of Guide.

Atom Age material is generally scarce in all conditions but extremely scarce in higher grade. The exception would be a large majority of Dell Comics. When I look at pre-1965 collections, about 70% of them are mostly or all Dell Comics. This is probably because there are far less sales being recorded on this material. This stuff usually sells very quickly especially in higher grade. (Above VG is considered higher grade for Atom Age.) There are certain issues from this period that seem to turn up quite often (mainly due to warehouse finds), and these usually sit unless priced very much below Guide.

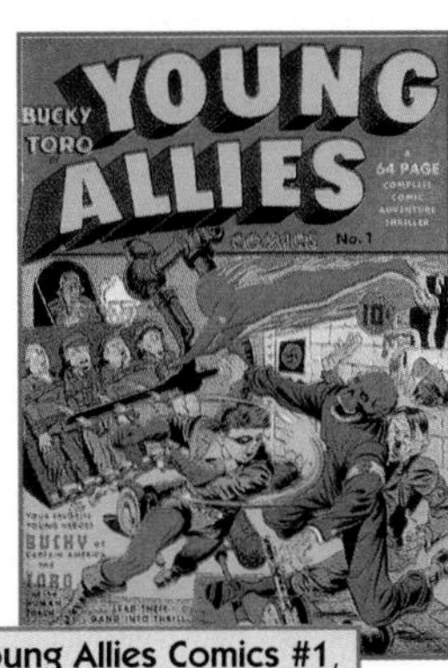

Young Allies Comics #1, a fun cover found in the **Gerber Photo-Journals**.

© MAR

VINCENT'S COLLECTIBLES

The Golden Age market has rebounded this year in most areas except for poorly restored books. There has been an influx of would-be restorers coming into the market over the last two years who really need to practice their craft on their own books before they work on unsuspecting collector's books. Please don't get me wrong, there are a handful of new restoration companies that do fine work, but the majority still needs to practice, practice, practice.

Areas where I have seen a sustained or increased demand have been in the Timely and DC mainstream Superhero titles. If you have a **Photo-Journal** you should take a look at some of these covers, they are truly fun and exciting works of art. Before you know it you too may find yourself collecting titles such as **Captain America**, **Wonder Woman**, **Superman**, **Batman**, **Detective**, **Young Allies**, **Sub-Mariner** and the like.

I have seen a decreased demand for Funny Animal books, Westerns and Crime.

Artists of particular popularity are Lou Fine, Wally Wood, Bill Everett, Jack Kirby and Frank Frazetta. Artists whose popularity have died down recently in comparison to several years ago are Alex Schomburg and L.B. Cole. While their books still sell well in high grade many collectors have sated their hunger for these masters' works.

GOLDEN/ ATOM AGE (by company)

ATLAS

AVALON COMICS

Still a good seller, and I usually sell through what I offer of these; but it should be noted, overall requests to buy are down. It should also be noted that I have sold several of the early Kirby/Ditko issues of **Journey Into Mystery** and **Strange Tales** for well over Guide prices and believe they are valued incorrectly, and I have held off stating so in this forum as I have had one or two issues of these, and wished no smack of manipulation or self-interest in my reports, but now I have none unlisted, so.... These should be valued higher, with the first issues, **Strange Tales** #67 and **Journey Into Mystery** #50 and #51 at 2x-3x current values. They came out the same months as **Tales of Suspense** #1 and **Tales to Astonish** #1, and like these titles, they began a fairly long and continuous run of pre-hero Kirby/Ditko monster material.

Strange Tales #1 and other Atlas Horror are scaring up higher prices!

© MAR

COMIC ART FOUNDATION

As you know, Atlas had a tremendous proliferation of titles in the late 1940s and early 1950s, and collectors are chasing just about all of them. Atlas Horror comics lead the pack, but fans will buy the Crime, War and even Romance titles. Prices on many of these issues are clearly bargains, and collectors know it.

REDBEARD'S BOOK DEN

This is a popular area for collectors. Horror/science fiction titles all sell very well at 100-150% of Guide in lesser condition, and 135-350% in higher grade. Crime titles sell well at 90-145% of Guide in lesser condition, and 125-350% in higher grade.

AVON

REDBEARD'S BOOK DEN

Good demand for all horror/science fiction titles. Sales at 110-165% of Guide in lesser condition, and 135-375% in higher grade. Western and War titles are slower for this publisher. Sales in lesser condition at 80-135% of Guide, and 100-225% in higher grade.

DC

AVALON COMICS

Golden Age DC is good with a slight tail-off overall. Better sellers have been **Action**, **Batman**, **Detective**, **Superman** and **Wonder Woman**.

COMIC ART FOUNDATION

The DC faithful continue their quest for all Golden Age titles. As we observed last year, they are nonetheless cautious in their spending. Demand for **More Fun** is noticeable, particularly those issues with Superboy. **Sensation** and **Wonder Woman** are doing well.

GARY DOLGOFF COMICS

Still very strong with **Superman**, **Flash** and **Green Lantern** leading in this group. **All-Stars** are very good sellers in almost any condition.

REDBEARD'S BOOK DEN

In higher grade all mainline superhero titles were selling at around 155-325% of Guide, in lesser grades the books were selling for approximately 85-145% of Guide. Key scarcer issues were, of course, selling at even higher percentages of Guide. Best sellers are **Batman**, **Superman**, **Flash**, **Green Lantern** and their related titles. Small gains were made by offbeat titles.

MATT SCHIFFMAN

Early **Actions**, **Detective** #28-66, and early **Superman** titles were very popular. The remaining books didn't move so quickly.

TERRY'S COMICS

DCs sell well in the $25-$100 range, but lower grade books over $100 are slow movers and generally have to be discounted.

© DC

All Star Comics are good sellers in almost any condition. (#2 shown)

DELLS

COMIC ART FOUNDATION

Last year, we reported the market to be awash with Dells, and that situation remains, but with some notable exceptions. We received requests for several early **Four Color** numbers, which appear quite scarce, particularly the first two **Porky Pigs FC** #16 and #48.

Also, collectors are on the prowl for **Roy Rogers FC** #38, which is becoming very hard to find, particularly in grade. We are still selling **Lulu, Felix** and **Looney Tunes** at Guide.

GARY DOLGOFF COMICS

Little LuLu and the ellusive **I Love Lucy** comics are among the top sellers in the Dell/Gold Key realm. Any Dell/Gold Key from 1942 or earlier will move. Goodies like **Four Color** #4, #9 and especially **Donald Duck Giveaways** are decent sellers. Generally, however, humor Dells from the late '40s (and some from the '50s and 60s) are slow sellers even at less than Guide. The exceptions could be NM copies, though my experience with these is limited.

REDBEARD'S BOOK DEN

Strong sales on lesser condition titles. Most collections of older books have large amounts of these lesser condition Dell/GK titles.

If reasonable, the giant annuals sell well in lower grade. Sales in higher grades are quite brisk due to their scarcity at 135-400% of Guide levels. Most collections of older books have large amounts of lesser condition Dell Giants that sell OK at 90% of Guide.

DISNEY

AVALON COMICS

Disney is steady. It was never a hot seller for me, but on the other hand I can't say I've experienced any tail-off in demand in this area as I have in many others. Quality Disney items usually find a buyer. Other cartoon character comics are generally sporadic sellers (and have always been so for me).

EC

REDBEARD'S BOOK DEN

Horror and SF titles are selling well at approximately 75-140% of Guide in lesser condition, and 100-350% in higher grade. **MAD** is still the hottest title selling quickly at approximately 90-140% of Guide in lesser condition, and 110-350% in higher grade. Gaines file copies are selling for record prices.

VINCENT'S COLLECTIBLES

The Christie's Auction did very well with the last set of Gaines File Copies this year. I sold many high grade E.C.s from The Spokane Collection but on average grade material the market has been relatively quiet this year. I have always said as far as stories are concerned there is not another company that can compete with E.C. Nobody does War, Crime, and Horror better. If you are simply looking for a good read that will not let you down, pick up some low grade copies of any E.C. title.

FAWCETT

COMIC ART FOUNDATION

During the last year, we probably sold more Fawcett books, in all grades, than any other Golden Age publisher. **Captain Marvel, Jr.** with Raboy covers, particularly during WWII, are very popular, as is **Captain Marvel**, **Bulletman** and **Marvel Family**. We do not recommend an increase in prices, but clearly Fawcetts are viewed as among the most reasonably priced Golden Agers.

GARY DOLGOFF COMICS

Captain Marvel Fawcetts are also solid sellers.

© FAW

Mac Raboy's **Captain Marvel, Jr.** covers are in demand. (#4 shown)

REDBEARD'S BOOK DEN

Sales of **Captain Marvel** and related titles were at approximately 75-135% of Guide in lesser condition, and sales of around 135-275% of Guide for higher grade copies. There were good sales for **Captain Midnight** and small gains by offbeat titles.

TERRY'S COMICS

These comics below $30 seem to be the best selling lower-priced superhero comics.

FICTION HOUSE

COMIC ART FOUNDATION

We can report steady demand for most Fiction House titles. We sold very high grade copies of **Jungle** and **Jumbo** over Guide prices, without complaint. Notably, there is collector desire for high-grade copies of Fiction House comics published toward the end of that company's tenure, including the obscure titles such as

Monster and **Ghost**. We even sold high grade **Kaanga** and **Wambi** comics this year, which are traditionally slow titles. Also, we acquired a single-owner collection of very high-grade Fiction House comics. Some were so pristine we felt justified in offering them at premium prices, approximately 1.25x Guide.

Fiction House's Good Girl art lead to sales of **Jumbo Comics.**(#20 shown) © FH

REDBEARD'S BOOK DEN

Continued demand from good-girl art collectors have lead to good sales for this publisher. Most popular is still **Planet** followed by **Jumbo**, **Jungle**, **Fight**, **Rangers** and **Wings**. These titles sell for approximately 75-130% over current Guide levels in lesser condition, and 125-250% in higher grade. Small gains were made by offbeat titles.

MATT SCHIFFMAN

Planets are very slow, with only slight interest in the **Jungle Jumbo** Matt Bakers. **Wings** are picking up, but **Fight** and **Rangers** lead the way as they have been perceived as under-valued for some time now.

FOX

COMIC ART FOUNDATION

Fox comics such as **Phantom Lady**, **Zoot**, **Rulah** and the like continue to be as hot as ever, and we sell them as soon as we offer them, at Guide or slightly above.

REDBEARD'S BOOK DEN

Good sales were realized for this publisher. Largest demand is for all superhero titles at prices 95-150% above current Guide levels in lesser grade, and approximately 155-325% in higher grade. There was a strong demand for early Lou Fine cover books.

MATT SCHIFFMAN

Still very hot, with a lot of growing interest in the Romance titles. Selling prices on the Romance books is about 2x-3x. If it has Matt Baker art in it or on the cover, it sells up to 4x.

LEV GLEASON

COMIC ART FOUNDATION

Lev Gleason titles sell only moderately, except for lower number B&W and **Daredevil Comics**, which are hot, especially the WWII covers.

GARY DOLGOFF COMICS

These are solid sellers. I sum it up this way: I've never met the Golden Age Superhero Comic that I couldn't sell!

REDBEARD'S BOOK DEN

Sales were at about 70-120% above current guide levels in lesser condition, and 105-255% in higher grade. Best sellers are still **Silver Streak**, **Daredevil Comics** and early issues of **Boy Comics**.

MLJ/ARCHIE

COMIC ART FOUNDATION

MLJ titles are in demand, but growing scarcer every year. We can sell them in any grade at Guide.

GARY DOLGOFF COMICS

A strong seller in all grades. Whether I reside in New York City (then) or Easthampton, MA (now), there is always a regular "happy to buy 'em" Archie collector who gratefully visits the warehouse. Early Archies reign supreme. I recently sold a **Jackpot** #4 (GD-, for 20-50% over Guide)! Where is that elusive **Archie** #1 or **Pep** #22? Archies are timeless; for many "lifers" in comicdom, Archie comics are our first love, the first true comics we enjoyed as kids.

REDBEARD'S BOOK DEN

Good demand for this publisher. Sales at about 95-150% of current Guide levels in lesser condition, and 150-300% in higher grade.

QUALITY

COMIC ART FOUNDATION

Interest is strong in several Quality titles. Collectors are looking for low number issues of **Hit**, **Crack** and **Smash**, and we see less and less of these copies. Interest in **Blackhawk** and **Plastic Man** remains moderate, but better than last year.

REDBEARD'S BOOK DEN

Good demand led by all Lou Fine titles selling at 75-135% in lesser condition, and 125-265% in higher grade.

Moderate sales of **Blackhawk** and all related titles at about 65-115% over current Guide levels in lesser grade, and 95-225% of guide in higher grade. Small gains were made by offbeat titles.

TIMELY

AVALON COMICS

The few Timelys I've been able to acquire usually sell quickly. This is pretty much the norm with these in recent years. Rarities in this area have been easy sells at over Guide prices.

COMIC ART FOUNDATION

Timelys are as popular and sought after as ever. Collectors frequently inquire for Good Girl titles such as **Blonde Phantom** and **Miss Fury** as well as the Superhero books. **Captain America** leads the field.

REDBEARD'S BOOK DEN

After years of large gains, prices stabilized for this publisher. High grade copies for most titles sell for around 145-315% of current Guide levels, lesser condition copies sell for approximately 80-140% of Guide. **Captain America**-related titles are still the most popular, but there's still solid demand for **Human Torch**, **Sub-Mariner** and their related titles. Small gains were made by offbeat titles.

MATT SCHIFFMAN

Icon covers and newly anointed icon covers lead the way. **All Select** still seems to be hugely popular in any grade up to issue #6. **Sub-Mariner** has beat out **H.T.** this year in demand, with **Cap** issues still very popular in higher grade and lower grade. **Marvel Mystery** issues were a bit slow except for the early issues in low grade.

GOLDEN/ ATOM AGE (by genre)

ART TITLES

REDBEARD'S BOOK DEN

Baker is very hot with sales in the 140-250% of Guide in lesser condition, and 175-450% in higher grade. L. B. Cole is selling well. Sales were 125-250% of Guide in lesser grade, and 150-400% in higher grade. There was also a good demand for Wolverton Horror/Science Fiction titles. Sales at 135-200% of Guide in lesser condition, and 150-450% in higher grade. Solid demand for Ditko and Kirby books continues. Prices at 135-185% of Guide in lesser condition, and 150-425% in higher grade. There was good demand for Kubert books, with sales in the 125-200% of Guide in lesser condition, and 150-400% in higher grade. There was another increase in demand for Frazetta work. Sales for lesser condition at approximately 135-200%, and 150%-400% in higher grade. Krigstein, Toth and Williamson were requested at a slower rate than the current biggies. Prices were around 120-175% of Guide in lesser condition, and 140%-385% in higher grade. Demand for Katz and Torres was slight in comparison to others. Prices were around 115-150% of Guide in lesser condition, and 135-325% in higher grade.

GOOD GIRL ART

REDBEARD'S BOOK DEN

This genre is still hot. Fox titles led by **Phantom Lady** remain the most popular. Atlas titles also have a solid following. There's a large demand for the recognized cover classics. Sales in the 125-250% of Guide in lesser condition, and approximately 135-400% in higher grade.

HORROR

COMIC ART FOUNDATION

Demand for these books is as strong or stronger than last year. Although collectors prefer high grade copies, we sold issues in the lower grades. Even the more obscure imprints, such as Ajax and Superior, are sought after.

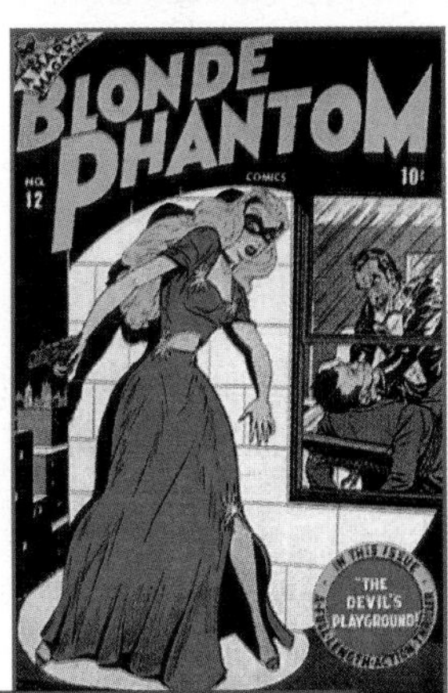

Blonde Phantom #12 is one of the popular Timelys of the Good Girl art genre.

GARY DOLGOFF COMICS

These are great. The collectors can't get enough of them no matter what the grade! A few months ago, I bought about 200+ ECs, most of them low grade. At least 2/3s of them are in other collectors' hands. High grade ECs always sell well.

REDBEARD'S BOOK DEN

Horror books have excellent sales and demand at approximately 110-165% over current Guide levels, and 140-425% in higher grade. DC Horror/Science Fiction titles have a solid following, but higher prices have slowed sales somewhat.

VINCENT'S COLLECTIBLES

Horror books have taken center stage. Fantastic, gory covers, astonishing artwork, graphic story lines and scarcity make these books fun to invest in and collect. It is definitely my favorite genre of collecting right now. I love to find a cover I have never seen before. The subject matter they drew and wrote about blows me away. Rather than specific companies being hot, the covers and titles dominate this part of the market.

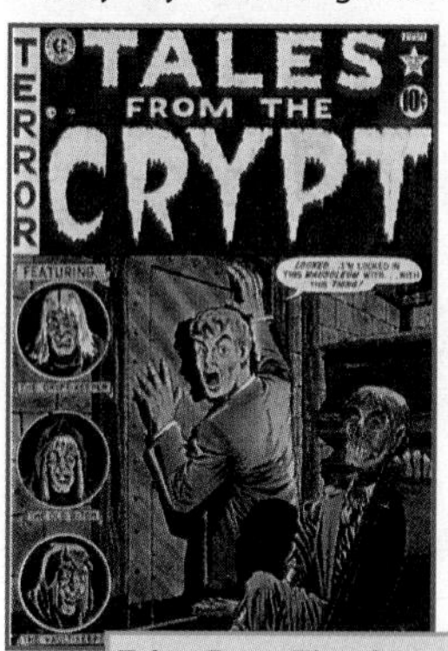

Tales From The Crypt #23 and other EC Horror books have taken center stage.

HUMOR/ FUNNY ANIMAL

COMIC ART FOUNDATION

We saw increased demand for certain titles, some of which may be considered bargains. DC issues of **Real Screen**, **Fox & Crow**, and **Flippity and Flop** are doing better. Interest in **Felix** has picked up, particularly the Toby issues. Sales of **Looney Tunes**, particularly lower numbers, are encouraging.

REDBEARD'S BOOK DEN

The biggest demand for Funny Animal books is in Timely and DC. Small gains were made for all publishers. Sales at around 75-125% of current Guide levels in lesser condition, and 85-200% of Guide in higher grade.

Humor books experienced marginal sales at about 75-135% of Guide in lesser condition, and 95-200% in high grade.

ROMANCE

REDBEARD'S BOOK DEN

Romance had a very strong demand, since one can spend a few hundred dollars in this area and still buy a sizeable stack of books. Sales at about 100-165% of Guide in lesser condition, and 125-350% in higher grade. Fox Romance titles are very hot. Sales in lesser condition are at approximately 125-200% of Guide, and 150-425% in higher grade.

SPORTS

REDBEARD'S BOOK DEN

Since I also deal in older sport cards, I will always have a strong demand for this area of comic collecting. We price at 135-200% of Guide in lower grade, and 175-450% in higher grade.

TV/MOVIE TIE-INS

AVALON COMICS

I might also have headed this as "photo cover" comics since that is unquestionably where the demand is. This area sells well and I've experienced an increase in demand for these, perhaps explainable by my attempts to branch out my business into other collectibles and advertising in publications like **Toy Shop**. Buyers of this type of comic refuse to go by our grading standards and price spread policy's, making many of my grades and prices look like bargains compared to what they are used to, which, of course, further helps sales. Generally though they like them cheap, and like to spend between $6-$12 per comic, with more expensive ones, no matter how popular or scarce, taking longer to sell. '60s TV shows are especially popular and '70s are starting to kick in. It should be noted that a chief concern of these buyers is to get a decent copy with an unmarked cover. Recently, I was offered a stack of photo cover comics that were glossy VF range condition except they had a name written fairly big on the cover of each. I ended up passing on buying them, even though they were valued at the VG to VG+, as I believed they were not what buyers of this stuff want and would be hard to sell.

COMIC ART FOUNDATION

After a slump of several years, we noticed renewed interest, of a nostalgic sort, in certain comics based on TV shows, mostly comedies, and with photo covers. Examples include **Bewitched** and **I Dream of Jeannie**. Also, **Three Stooges** is doing well. We sold Fawcett's **Pinhead & Foodini** quickly.

GARY DOLGOFF COMICS

These sell steadily; **Space Family Robinson**, **Three Stooges**, **Peanuts** and a few others are called for a bit more often. **Tarzans** and westerns climbed in popularity. A couple of years ago I had complete collections of **Gene Autry**, **Lone Ranger**, **Roy Rogers** and **Tarzan**. They are just about all gone.

WESTERNS

AVALON COMICS

Western comics sell pretty well, with the photo covers in greatest demand. This is a popular area and demand has slightly increased here for me. **Hoppy**, **Roy**, **Lone Ranger**, **Gene** and other '50s and '60s movies and TV shows are popular. Non-photo cover westerns are OK sellers, though Atlas has kicked in a bit with some increased sales.

Collectors remember their departed Western heroes with photo covers like **Gene Autry Comics #8.** © Gene Autry

SILVER AGE

COMICS INA FLASH

Silver is now selling for me in all grades, not just NM and not just at 50% off! This is great news for me, as I mostly buy complete sets and it's really nice to have the lower grade books selling well.

I don't set a lot of records with Silver, or move a lot of big keys. It's just consistent, steady sales that add up.

FLYING COLORS COMICS

Lots of action here, with key titles remaining **Amazing Spider-Man**, **Fantastic Four**, Neal Adams' **Batman** issues, and anything with Steranko art. Key issues, those with character first appearances or new title introductions have the most interest, while some collectors have returned to complete long runs of their favorite titles.

METROPOLIS COLLECTIBLES

The Silver Age was strong for us also. The problem here is not that the books move slowly; it is the over-availability that creates a sense of a glut of these books. As popular as they may be, Silver Age Marvels are still easier to buy than to sell.

REDBEARD'S BOOK DEN

This is the most impacted area from internet trading. There were very strong sales of lesser condition books via the internet. These same books are selling moderately from mail order catalogues or at conventions. Recent price decreases have had a positive impact in the lesser grade area. Most sales at prices over Guide are in the high grade area. The hottest Marvel title is still **Spider-Man**, followed by the **Fantastic Four**.

© MAR

Fantastic Four, one of the hot Silver Age titles (#7 shown).

Incredible Hulk #1-6 still remain very popular. There was also interest in offbeat Kirby Western titles. **Showcase** and key **Brave and the Bold** in high grade is still one of the better selling areas for DC. Very strong sales for the DC War titles were seen, led by **Our Army At War**.

TERRY'S COMICS

The Silver Age market picked up a little bit after the 1997 **The Guide #1: The Overstreet Comic Book Price Update** came out. Many dealers were already heavily discounting this material before The Update, but The Update and the 1998 **Price Guide** confirmed that these books were already at a lower market value than previous guides reflected. This correction was a healthy thing, but the lower grade keys are still too high. I had to sell many of my keys at or near cost in San Diego just to get them off the board. This is a good sign that the price is still too high and the supply still far exceeds the demand for these books at guide prices.

DC

AVALON COMICS

Silver Age DC is not bad with a general tail-off. Early **Showcase** and **Sgt. Rock** are the hottest. Other War and the five Horror/Mystery titles have become hard to sell for me. **Brave and the Bold**, **Challengers**, **Jimmy Olsen**, **Justice League** and **World's Finest** are titles that once sold well for me and are now only fair sellers. **Atom** and **Aquaman** have never been good sellers.

One of the most popular Sgt. Rock covers is **Our Army at War #112**

© DC

GARY DOLGOFF COMICS

It's tough to obtain strictly graded VFs or better. When I do get them in they are quickly gobbled up.

Low to mid-grades are decent, solid sellers. The best are **Batman** and **Superman** related titles. The worst: **House of Mystery** with "Dial H for Hero" and "Secret Six."

Flash, **JLA** and to some extent **Green Lanern** move very well while **Aquaman**, **Atom**, **Hawkman**, and a few others are relatively slow in mid-grade.

VINCENT'S COLLECTIBLES

This is a segment of the market I have watched blossom this year. When I grew up you were either a Marvel guy or a DC guy—I was a Marvel guy. This mentality carried over into my dealing and inventory. Luckily for me I hit some great DC collections this year that opened my eyes to all I had been missing. There is a wealth of great art and stories in the DC Silver Age books. From Science Fiction to War to straight Superhero comics, DC covered the gamut and covered it well. Artists of prominence and growing interest include Murphy Anderson, Gil Kane, Joe Kubert, and Alex Toth. **Green Lantern**, **Flash**, **Action**, **Superman**, **Wonder Woman**, **Detective**, and **Batman** are the best selling titles for me. Titles on the rise include **Our Army at War**, **Adventure**, **Mystery in Space**, **House of Mystery** and **Strange Adventures**. I have noticed an unfortunate slow-down in **Aquaman** (one of my favorites), **Atom**, **Hawkman**, and **Showcase**.

MARVEL

GARY DOLGOFF COMICS

1961-1964 high grades are relatively hard to find! When I find them they always move! A couple of years ago I sold a dealer **Amazing Spider-Man** #1 strict VF for $16,000! Other high-grade Marvels from that collection also sold well.

Medium to low grades are solid sellers. As long as I grade them with my usual strictness they move at 70-90% of Guide. Among the #1s, **Fantastic Four**, **Hulk**, and **X-Men** #1 as well **as Journey into Mystery** #83 (1st Thor) are the best, although the other early #1s move just fine. Many desire a **Sgt. Fury** #1, a relatively scarce Kirby Marvel #1 with more than reasonable price guide value.

1965-1971 (12 & 15¢ cover price Marvels) high grades—Yes Begorrah! Despite the warehouse copies that went from some of the oldest time dealers (Robert Bell, etc.) into the hands of other old hands (like yours truly), they are still (and rightfully so) solid sellers with ultra-high (VF/NMs) at the front of "the Conga Line" (the higher they grade the better they sell!). Best sellers here are **Amazing Spider-Man**, **Fantastic Four** and **X-Men**. Somewhat slower but still solid sellers in this grade are **Strange Tales**, **Tales of Suspense**, and **Tales to Astonish**; **Sub-Mariner** comics are middle of the road.

The Overstreet price reduction has helped mid-low grades. The titles that sell in high grade also sell well in this grade. **Iron Man** has become increasingly steady, bordering on a strong seller. Sometimes I get a decent size order for a goodly number of **Iron Man**s.

VINCENT'S COLLECTIBLES

This market is still a dichotomous part of the hobby. All titles are in demand in their respective grades and prices. NM- and better grade books sell well at premium prices to discerning customers who want nothing but the cream of the crop. However VF/NM down to FN move only when priced to sell and the lower grade books sell at slightly discounted prices. Overstreet's lowering of prices did help to refuel collector interests in the hobby, but it did not squelch their demand for lower prices regardless of what the Guide value is. As far as title interest is concerned **Fantastic Four**, **Amazing Spider-Man** and **X-Men** round out the top three. I noticed an increased interest in **Daredevil**, **Thor**, **Iron Man** and **Incredible Hulk**. The increase can be attributed to affordability, and dynamic art by Gil Kane, John Buscema and Gene Colan.

The DC Romance stories touched the teenager in all of us filled with campy lines like "Oh, I know he didn't bring me here just to watch a movie—Oh, why can't I grow up, boo, hoo, hoo!". **Falling in Love**, **Girl's Love**, **Young Romance** and **Heart Throbs** are several titles that may be of interest.

BRONZE AGE

COMICS INA FLASH

For the last couple of years, a lot of oddball, hard to find titles have driven the Bronze Age—titles like **Night Nurse** (#1 VF $45), **Secrets of Sinister House** (#1-#5 NM $165), **Dark Mansion of Forbidden Love** (#1 NM $75), **Vamp-irella Color Special** (sc NM $150), and **Vault of Evil** (#l NM $14). It's still these books, and many like them, that drive the market, but I see signs of the Superhero genre reemerging.

The chances of finding **Night Nurse**, **Peter the Pest** (#1 FN $30), **Dark Mansion of Forbidden Love** and any 100-page giant really cheap is all but gone. (There is still a chance to find Charlton Romance, Mystery and Horror cheap—be looking for it.) Collectors are taking a second look at the Superhero books of the 1970s because of the currently listed prices. I didn't notice it a first, but **Defenders**, **Luke Cage**, **Team-Up**, and **Two-In-One** below #30 have sold out, and I could sell more. **Red Wolf**, Adams or Smith **Avengers**, and Kirby's mid-'70s Marvel's are almost as hot. **Kamandi** and **Demon** are selling again, and **JLA** from the early '70s is selling great!

METROPOLIS COLLECTIBLES

The Bronze Age has been the most impressive of the ages. Even the die-hard Silver and Gold collectors who spurned the Bronze Age have changed their tunes. Bronze Age books have to be Near Mint to sell, but when they are, they sell for multiples of Guide very quickly: no title is too obscure. We purchased a collection of 3,000 Near Mint '70s books and though we were originally luke-warm about it, the response to it was phenomenal.

REDBEARD'S BOOK DEN

Sales in this area are mixed. Record prices are being realized for very high grade copies of mid-'70s books, but sales are much slower on lesser condition copies at conventions and mail order catalogues. Demand was solid via the internet. It seems this area of collecting will be showing some significant price growth in the coming years!

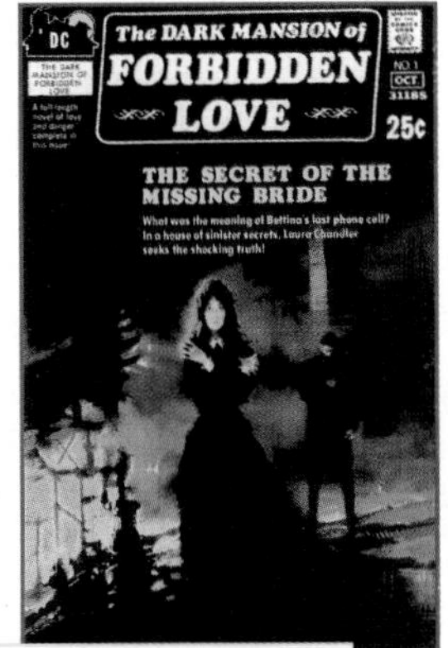

Dark Mansion of Forbidden Love #1 is one of the scarcer DC Bronze Age issues.

MATT SCHIFFMAN

Still a very hot market right now, but it is about to experience some growing pains from huge price run-ups. NM still rules the day and not many books are sellable even in VF condition. **DC Super Spectaculars** from #7 up experienced a lot of growth and interest. #5 is still popular, but the asking price between $350-$750 has cooled this issue somewhat.

TERRY'S COMICS

This is an area that I have avoided dealing for the past few years. This was mostly because I was getting tired of lugging these books to show after show and making $3 off of 4 long boxes of Bronze Age comics priced at $1-$2 each. I wholesaled what inventory I had to store dealers a few years ago. Then I started reading about record sales for different books, but I thought this was just some quirk. Then I started getting requests at shows, phone calls and even want lists looking for this stuff. I decided to buy some and bring it to San Diego this year. I brought a large collection with quite a lot of nice books in it and it sold very well and at or above Guide. This was especially true of Horror comics, Warren and Marvel Magazines.

VINCENT'S COLLECTIBLES

The Bronze Age, formerly known as bulk, back stock, or kindling has started to hit its mark. If you remember back in the late '80s and early '90s there was a growing demand and price on Silver Age books that were hitting their thirty year mark at the time. Now the Bronze Age books are turning thirty and demand is on the rise. I am twenty-seven years old so these books have a warm place in my heart, many can be included among the first books I ever read. Favorites like **Marvel Team-Up**, **Marvel Two-In-One**, and **Tomb of Dracula** are being scooped up in all grades. **Witching Hour**, **Phantom Stranger**, **Mr. Miracle**, **New Gods**, **Weird War Tales** and '70s mainstream Superhero books are being bought up as fast as bottled water at the local supermarket the day before Hurricane Pico is about to hit! Original artwork is also being sought after by diehard fans and investors alike. The most highly collected artist of this period is Neal Adams. He revolutionized comics and brought a truly realistic look to many characters who up until this period seemed mannequin-like and emotionless. When he drew Green Lantern weeping, you felt his sorrow as if it were your own. Other artists of high regard are Rich Buckler, Berni Wrightson, Jack Kirby, and Gil Kane.

ARCHIE

DOUG SULIPA'S COMIC WORLD

These have really picked up in sales! Most 1960-1980 issues are all selling briskly. Red hot are **Sabrina** and **Josie & the Pussycats**, likely because these were Hanna Barbera TV cartoons, and due to the recent **Sabrina** TV series! Also hot are all **Sonic the Hedgehog**, **Archie Band** (TV-related), **Little Sabrina in Little Archie**, many issues of **Life with Archie**, and other Sabrina appearances (**Archie's TV Laughout** & **Mad House**)! Red Circle titles are picking up steam, especially **Chilling Adventures in Sorcery**. The Spire titles are in demand. Digests are popular, with #1s and '70s being HOT! The '60s superheroes are also picking up, especially the teen ones. All giants are hot! Also look for Josie and Sabrina in **Archie Giant Series Magazine**. Many giants=150-200% of Guide! Sabrina and Josie appearances in **Archie Giant** series magazines=150-200% of Guide!

Life With Archie #50 presented the debut of the United Three. © AP

VINCENT'S COLLECTIBLES

Archie Comics are an area which will see a continued resurgence of interest. Everyone read at least one Archie as a child and anyone who has tried to turn their daughter into a "fanboy," pardon the expression, has started her off with an Archie.

CHARLTON

DOUG SULIPA'S COMIC WORLD

These are hard to find in high grades! Many are scarce in any condition. The red hot titles are: **Haunted Love**, **Scooby Doo**, **David Cassidy**, **Partridge Family**, **Hanna Barbera**, and **Wheelie & Chopper Bunch**! Also hot are **Bionic Woman**, **Bobby Sherman**, **Charlton Bullseye Magazine**, **Dudley Do-Right**, **Bugaloos**, **Emergency** (especially magazine), **Go-Go**, **Great Gazoo**, **Hanna Barbera Parade**, **Hong Kong Phooey**, **Kong** #2 (Byrne), **Ponytail**, **Ronald McDonald**, **Sarge Snorkel**, **Six Million Dollar Man** (especially magazine), **Space 1999** (especially magazine), **Speed Buggy**, **Time for Love**, and **Valley of Dinosaurs**. In demand are most artist issues; Glanzman, Byrne, Wayne Howard, Newton, Ditko, etc. & many Horror, Hot Rod, Cartoon, Superhero, Sci-Fi, obscure, and older War titles!

DC

COMICS INA FLASH

Weird War Tales # 1 has established itself as a legitimate key. I've had a high grade copy in three different auctions and each time the book brought $150. The **Young Love** and **Young Romance** 100-pagers are way over-priced, however. When they listed in Guide for $5, they sold in my auctions for $70-$95. Now that they list in Guide for $140 the demand is way down and they only bring about $50.

© DC

Jack Kirby's fans seek **Superman's Pal, Jimmy Olsen #133,** his first on this title.

Overall though, Romance is selling better than ever. **DC 100-Page Super Spectacular** #5 (Love Stories) is probably the scarcest and most sought after Bronze Age key (VG @ $150). Also in demand is the **House of Secrets** and **House of Mystery** books after the change to mystery format. The Guide has mostly caught up with the prices these books bring, with the exception of **House of Mystery** #174 and **House of Secrets** #81, these "first" issues still bring over-Guide (**House of Mystery** #174 VF @ $55, **House of Secrets** #81 FN @ $40). Any Wrightson cover on these books brings $10 in NM, which is also over-Guide on the later issues of **House of Mystery**.

GARY DOLGOFF COMICS

Runaway great sellers! I have a huge stock of '70s Marvels in my warehouse (not a bad thing really) but only a few shelving units of '70s DCs. They sell in all grades with high grades in the lead. Kirby books, **Wonder Woman**, '70s mystery titles, **Batman** and **Superman** titles (to some extent) and early **Jonah Hex** comics lead the pack of "Top Sellers!" Even the "oddball" titles are OK. I have recently sold multiples to dealers of some '70s DCs and sold them well.

MATT SCHIFFFMAN

Horror books are in high demand, with prices continuing to grow since they are tough to find in higher grade. 48-pg. and 52-pg. books, and 20¢ covers from **House Of Mystery** and **House Of Secrets** in NM are very hard to find and sell for about 40% above Guide.

Collectors are willing to pay high prices for Humor books, but I've found that this group is very small and not growing very quickly despite the fact that the books are tough to find in high grade.

Romance/Gothic is a very hot genre and seems to show no signs of slowing down

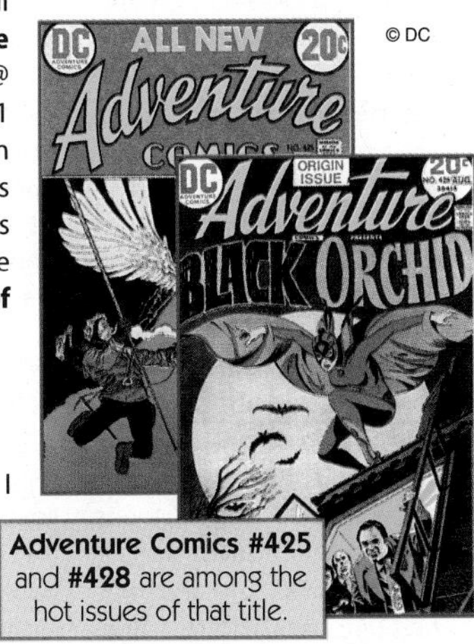

© DC

Adventure Comics #425 and **#428** are among the hot issues of that title.

given that it offers some collectibility beyond scarcity. Not many of these are found in the market due to high interest and great artwork. Pricing is well justified and interest is growing. **Young Love** and **Romance** still have interest but only in NM. The #107 still commands over $100 in NM, but only about $18 in FN. The other 100-page books sell for about $70 in NM and $12 FN.

Adventure #425-440 are very hot right now, with double Guide on #425. 48-pg and 52-pg Superhero books are hot right now and selling better than the 100-page books. 20¢ **Detective** and **Action** comics are doing very well as their print runs were low.

Westerns are doing very well and growing due to the lower Guide prices, but again, only a small group is paying these new market levels.

DOUG SULIPA'S COMIC WORLD

The best sellers are 100-pagers, 52-pagers, 68 pagers, "Dollar" Giants, 80-pagers, Mystery/Horror, Wrightson, Adams, Kirby, War titles, Teen, Cartoon, some Western, Digests, Treasurys, Mags, books, paperbacks, minor keys, Love, and 15¢/20¢ cover priced items!

DELL/GOLD KEY/ WHITMAN

DOUG SULIPA'S COMIC WORLD

In demand are: Hanna Barbera titles, Cult-TV shows, other TV animation based titles, obscure titles, giants, Horror (artist and keys), Kroft titles, Warner Bros Cartoons, Disney (non-duck, mouse titles), **Turok** (low and high numbers), etc! Hottest titles are: **Scooby Doo**, **Fun-In**, **Wacky Races**. Many are trying to complete their Whitman issue runs, but can't find the late 1980 issues, and post-1982 (non-dated) issues, which all likely came only in pre-packs!

MARVEL

GARY DOLGOFF COMICS

The top titles sell well: **Avengers** (especially #100-#148), **Amazing Spider-Man**, **Fantastic Four**, **X-Men**, etc. The other titles also sell well for the most part—they love VG/FNs for 75¢-$1 and GD/VGs for 50¢-75¢! '70s monster titles like **Dracula**, **Werewolf** and **Frankenstein** are all selling very well!

MATT SCHIFFMAN

Marvel Spotlight #2 is the book with the most interest. Large print runs and lots of interest at the time makes these books easy to find. **Conan** is gaining interest for NM examples and so are 20¢ cover **Amazing Spider-Man**s. **X-Men** #94 and **Giant Size** #1 still have a lot of interest around Guide levels, with good prices selling for a bit above Guide. **Avengers** and **Daredevil** are showing interest, but the title with growing interest and high prices is **Thor**. All three of these are have been bargain basement books for so long that they are perceived as collectible.

DOUG SULIPA'S COMIC WORLD

The best sellers are '70s reprint titles (Western, War, Love, Teen, Horror), odd format (magazines, Treasury's, books, fanzines, memorabilia, etc.) short series titles, all giants, minor & major keys for both non-Superhero and Superhero, Kirby and artist titles, all are scrambling to finish runs, and are having a hard time finding 15¢ and 20¢ cover priced issues. Also many want to upgrade issues with condition-sensitive covers (jet-black and deep red covers can especially be a problem). **Our Love Story** and **My Love** are often asked for. Marvel's Giant Size titles can be a real challenge.

Marvel Spotlight #2 is igniting a great deal of interest.

© MAR

MISC.

DOUG SULIPA'S COMIC WORLD

Parody magazines (**Mad**, **Cracked**, **Sick**, **Crazy**, **Goose**, **Thimk**, **Grin**, **Help**, **Humbug**, **International**, **Insanity**, **Apple Pie**, **Bananas**, **CarToons**, **Dynamite**, **Electric Co.**, **Harpoon**, **National Lampoon**, **Blast**, **Hot Rod Cartoons**, **Parody**, **Yell**) are on the move if you can find them. Many are under-valued and bring premium prices! But the hot ones, are the ones with collectible character covers and stories! A good character cover can bring 150-300% of Guide! The most sought after characters/personality covers are: Star Wars, Star Trek, Charlie's Angels, Partridge Family, John Travolta, Grease, Planet of the Apes, Snoopy/Peanuts, Superheroes, Hitler, KISS, Simpsons, Bruce Lee, Six Million Dollar Man/Bionic Woman, Beatles, rock stars, Michael Jackson, Space 1999, Battlestar Galactica, Wonder Woman, Spider-Man, Batman, TV Hulk, Osmonds, Fonz, Alien movies, Mork & Mindy, Sports, ET, etc! All of these can bring premiums, especially if sold in the non-comics collectibles and toy market!

Obscure Bronze Age (and Silver Age) titles are also in demand. Lower priced issues can bring premiums up to double Guide. Titles like the following bring 150-200% of Guide: **Captain Marvel**

Presents the Terrible Five, Fatman the Human Flying Saucer, **Henry Brewster**, **True Comics & Adventure Stories**, **Wham-O Giant Comics**, **Sojourn**, etc. Increase in activity is notable with Power Records and '70s alternatives. **Dennis the Menace** is selling. Keys, Giants, and Digests are the most popular and bring premium prices.

People are collecting by genre. Especially wanted from '50s-'70s are obscure War, Teen, Western, Cartoon, Horror, TV, Love, etc.

MODERN AGE

GARY DOLGOFF COMICS

There are selling slowly, even though I charge between 25%-40% (sometimes less) of Guide values. By the way, I feel that the reduced Overstreet '80s and '90s prices in many cases are justified and will help them sell better.

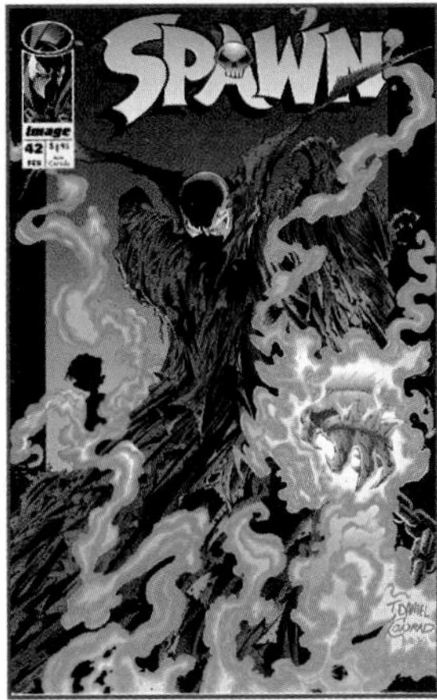

© Todd McFarlane Prod.

Later issues of **Spawn** are getting harder to find than the first 10.

FLYING COLORS COMICS

The last five years have taken a toll on the comics market, after the speculator binge and purge of '92-'94. Circulations on ALL comics have taken a tremendous hit since then, which leads to my most cogent point. It's bloody tough to put runs of nearly any title together from the last few years. I've had miscellaneous issues on my customer want list for a couple of years with no luck in finding them. New and returning readers/collectors are discovering a lot of books are impossible to find, whether it's something as innocuous as **Thunderstrike** #17, or something relatively popular like a **Starman** (1994) #3. While books from '92-'94 might be the most common comics from the last 25 years, some comics from '95-'98 are the toughest to find. It's much easier, for instance to find **Spawn** #1-#10 than it is to find **Spawn** #33-#50. So, fans, don't be surprised by seeing higher than expected prices on recent back issues that aren't necessarily reflected in the Guide. And, no, it's not endemic to just one or a handful of titles, it's almost across the board. Some of the most obvious titles in this are: **Spawn**, **Green Lantern**, **Spider-Man** "Clone Saga" tie-ins (believe it or not), **Astro City** (#3 particularly), **Nightwing** regular series issues under #18, and many, many more.

TERRY'S COMICS

I usually only deal in independents or high request books from this era. There were a couple of publishers from the early 1980s that did some great books. These usually sell well above Guide even though a diligent collector can find them in bargain boxes for $1 or less. The most poplular of these are **Twisted Tales** and **Alien Worlds** by Pacific Comics. A close second are **Tales of Terror** and **Alien Encounters** published by Eclipse.

VINCENT'S COLLECTIBLES

Although I do not consider myself a Modern Age comic dealer I still stay abreast of the Modern market. I have watched this market hit the bottom and start to rise up very, very slowly. The best material I have seen surface this year would have to be

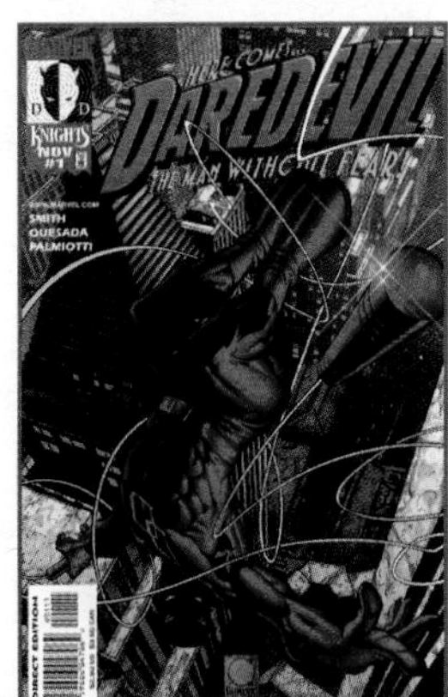

Kevin Smith's writing makes **Daredevil Vol. 2** a hot title!

© MAR

the Marvel Knights comic line. Under the direction of Jimmy Palmiotti and Joe Quesada, Marvel has taken several B and C class characters and given new life to them. From Kevin Smith's compelling writing on **Daredevil** to Mark Texeira's brilliant art on **Black Panther**, these titles stand out from the quagmire that has plagued the modern comic market. Praise should also be given to Mark Waid for his writing on **Captain America** and my favorite by far the combined talents of writer Paul Jenkins and artist Jae Lee on **The Inhumans**. The storyline is well crafted and Lee's art is mood altering. His art has always been a step above the rest, but with **The Inhumans** he has captured a feeling that is both eerie and haunting yet joyous and wise. David Quinn's gritty writing on **Lady Death** and Kevin Mack's intricate storytelling on **Kabuki** are two more reasons independent books should not be overlooked.

PEDIGREE COLLECTIONS

VINCENT'S COLLECTIBLES

"The Spokane Collection"

Nestled in the Heart of Spokane, Washington was an individual in his '70s living a quiet, secluded life. Over the course of the mid-'40s-mid-'50's he had amassed a hand-selected collection of comic books. So treasured was his collection he built a refrigerated steel meat locker in his basement where he kept them safe and sound. He knew his comic books had value, but not until friends made a detailed account of the collection did he realize what type of value. Steve Fishler of Metropolis and I were contacted and after a month of telephone negotiations and a day of viewing the collection we were able to come to a price and buy the prized collection.

This collection of ultra-high grades is even more unusual due to their impossibly snow white pages and extremely clean and glossy covers. The runs include **Batman**, **Detective**, **Strange Adventures**, **Mystery in Space**, **Worlds of Fear**, **Eerie**, **Blue Bolt/Weird Tales**, Avon one-shots, Atlas Horror titles, E.C.s and a tremendous amount of esoteric Horror and Science Fiction titles. The quality of these books as a group and individually is so impressive that we felt pedigreeing them was definitely warranted. There are many books here hardly seen above a VG and here they are in NM with white pages. Collectors who have purchased Spokane copies say the quality rivals that of The Mile High Collection.

"The Oakland Collection"

The Oakland Collection was purchased by Michael Carbonaro of Comic Box and myself from a man who began collecting comic books religiously at the age of seven. He became friendly with the proprietor of a local liquor store where they sold comic books. He made a deal wherein he would rack all the new books each week in exchange for getting the first pick. He methodically collected virtually every Marvel and DC comic printed from 1966-1972. When he took the books out of storage to view them, he had an almost neurotic step by step method of looking at them. First, one must wash his hands thoroughly with soap and water. Second, find a clean white towel, gently place the book on it and of course read. He stored the books carefully and unlike most children his age who shared and read each other's books he would not.

Exemplified by their unbelievably glossy covers, sharp corners and white pages, the books could almost be the Silver Age counterpart of The Spokane Collection. Apart from the mainstream Superhero titles included in this collection are '60s and '70s Marvel and DC Horror, War, and Romance in pristine condition. On a side note the original owner grew up to be—a cleaning consultant.

1998 CONVENTIONS

COMIC ART FOUNDATION

Some observations from the Chicago Convention are in order. Fan attendance was up. The crowd was overwhelmingly youthful; the number of older collectors (over 40 years old) was in the distinct minority. Dealers were numerous and presented excellent material. Competition for sales was intense. In an unusual move which annoyed several other major dealers, one particular dealer offered Golden Age DCs in all grades at 20% off the Guide. But discounting was not as widespread as a year ago, except, of course, for Bronze Age and Modern books.

VINCENT'S COLLECTIBLES

A market report would not be truly complete without an analysis of the national convention scene. This past San

Diego Comic Con was by far my best. It was so busy I did not even get a chance to enjoy it. The Chicago Wizard World was also extremely busy—kudos to Gareb Shamus and company for a job well done on their first show. The Oakland/San Francisco Bay area is home to one of my favorite conventions, The Wonder Con. This year's show was strong. The Big Apple Comic Con in New York City has also been doing very well. The Con draws thousands of collectors and dealers from all over the world on an almost monthly basis. I have seen certain recent trends that point to more difficult times ahead for the convention business though. An increase in internet use by customers who would rather bid on a comic on an online auction or shop on a dealer's website rather than trek to a show and wait on a line creates a big challenge for show promoters to overcome. I myself have built a website and it is definitely patronized by customers from all over the world who otherwise would have to travel long distances to attend a show.

CONCLUSIONS

COMIC ART FOUNDATION

The comic book market has not changed sufficiently during the last year. Downsizing of the number of retail stores has stabilized, but by the same token, very few, if any, new stores are opening. To an appreciable extent, our hobby is impacted by the intense competition for the entertainment dollar in America today. Consider, for example, the increasing number of local entertainment centers, where developers combine multiplex theaters with virtual reality, and other, forms of diversion, such as the enormously successful Spectrum at Irvine, California. On short, we think it behooves all of us in the comic arena not only to promote the art form we love, but to strive to keep the cost of collecting at manageable levels. All in color for a dime, so to speak.

FLYING COLOR COMICS

To close, it's a great time for comics, so invite your friends to join the fun and jump between the covers of your favorite title today!

METROPOLIS COLLECTIBLES

Finally, our philosophy is not to discount books; we feel that we grade and price reasonably and that enormous discounts should not be necessary to move material. Furthermore and without question—the huge discounts that some dealers offer affect the market adversely. Dealers who routinely offer 30%-50% blanket discounts undermine the value of all comics. Discounts should be more discretionary and limited. If a dealer's cashflow is so constricted that he has to flip books to make ends meet, perhaps he should consider another line of work.

VINCENT'S COLLECTIBLES

I believe the future is looking even better for the market in general and myself personally. The guiding forces in our industry must emphasize long term thinking if our hobby is to flourish in the next millennium. My advice to collectors and investors is to keep the fun of collecting a primary driving force in your mind and to always buy what you like.

© FAW © AP © ABC © DC © DAVID MACK

INVESTOR'S DATA

The following tables denote the rate of appreciation of the top Golden Age, Platinum Age, Silver Age and Bronze Age books, as well as selected genres over the past year. The retail value for a Near Mint copy of each book (or VF where a Near Mint copy is not known to exist) in 1999 is compared to its value in 1998. The rate of return for 1999 over 1998 is given. The place in rank is given for each comic by year, with its corresponding value in highest known grade. These tables can be very useful in forecasting trends in the market place. For instance, the investor might want to know which book is yielding the best dividend from one year to the next, or one might just be interested in seeing how the popularity of books changes from year to year. For instance, *All-American Comics* #16 was in 7th place in 1998 and has increased to 5th place in 1999. Premium books are also included in these tables and are denoted with an asterisk(*).

The following tables are meant as a guide to the investor. However, it should be pointed out that trends may change at anytime and that some books can meet market resistance with a slowdown in price increases, while others can develop into real comers from a presently dormant state. In the long run, if the investor sticks to the books that are appreciating steadily each year, he shouldn't go very far wrong.

TOP GOLDEN AGE BOOKS

1999 OVER 1998 GUIDE VALUES

ISSUE NO.	1999 RANK	1999 NM PRICE	1998 RANK	1998 NM PRICE	$ INCR.	% INCR.
Action Comics #1	1	$185,000	1	$180,000	$5,000	3%
Detective Comics #27	2	$165,000	2	$160,000	$5,000	3%
Superman #1	3	$130,000	3	$125,000	$5,000	4%
Marvel Comics #1	4	$115,000	4	$108,000	$7,000	6%
All-American Comics #16	5	$65,000	7	$60,000	$5,000	8%
Batman #1	6	$63,000	6	$62,000	$1,000	2%
Whiz Comics #2 (#1)	7	$63,000	5	$63,000	$0	0%
Flash Comics #1	8	$57,000	9	$55,000	$2,000	4%
Captain America Comics #1	9	$56,000	8	$56,000	$0	0%
Detective Comics #1	10	VF $50,000	10	VF $50,000	$0	0%
More Fun Comics #52	11	$48,000	11	$47,000	$1,000	2%
New Fun Comics #1	12	VF $38,000	12	VF $37,500	$500	1%
Detective Comics #33	13	$35,000	14	$32,000	$3,000	9%
Adventure Comics #40	14	$33,000	13	$32,000	$1,000	3%
More Fun Comics #53	15	$32,000	15	$32,000	$0	0%
All Star Comics #3	16	$31,000	16	$30,000	$1,000	3%
Detective Comics #38	17	$30,000	17	$28,000	$2,000	7%
Captain Marvel Adventures #1	18	$28,000	18	$27,000	$1,000	4%
Green Lantern #1	19	$27,000	19	$26,000	$1,000	4%
All Star Comics #8	20	$25,000	20	$24,000	$1,000	4%
Detective Comics #29	21	$25,000	22	$23,000	$2,000	9%
Detective Comics #31	22	$25,000	23	$23,000	$2,000	9%
New York World's Fair 1939	23	$24,000	21	$24,000	$0	0%
Famous Funnies-Series 1 #1	24	$22,000	24	$21,500	$500	2%
Human Torch #2 (#1)	25	$21,000	25	$21,000	$0	0%
Sensation Comics #1	26	$21,000	26	$21,000	$0	0%
Action Comics #2	27	$20,000	30	$19,000	$1,000	5%
Adventure Comics #48	28	$20,000	27	$20,000	$0	0%
Marvel Mystery Comics #2	29	$20,000	28	$20,000	$0	0%
Sub-Mariner Comics #1	30	$20,000	29	$20,000	$0	0%
New Fun Comics #6	31	VF $18,500	31	VF $18,000	$500	3%
Marvel Mystery Comics #9	32	$18,000	33	$17,000	$1,000	6%
Wonder Woman #1	33	$17,500	34	$17,000	$500	3%
* Century Of Comics nn	34	VF $17,000	32	VF $17,500	-$500	-3%
Daring Mystery Comics #1	35	$16,500	35	$16,500	$0	0%
Jumbo Comics #1	36	VF $16,500	36	VF $16,500	$0	0%
New Fun Comics #2	37	VF $16,500	37	VF $16,000	$500	3%
New Comics #1	38	VF $16,000	42	VF $15,000	$1,000	7%
Walt Disney's Comics & Stories #1	39	$16,000	38	$16,000	$0	0%
Famous Funnies #1	40	$15,500	40	$15,000	$500	3%

ISSUE NO.	1999 RANK	1999 NM PRICE	1998 RANK	1998 NM PRICE	$ INCR.	% INCR.
Detective Comics #28	41	$15,000	45	$14,300	$700	5%
Marvel Mystery Comics #5	42	$15,000	41	$15,000	$0	0%
* Motion Picture Funnies Weekly #1	43	$15,000	39	$15,000	$0	0%
All Winners #1	44	$14,500	46	$14,000	$500	4%
Amazing Man Comics #5	45	$14,500	43	$14,500	$0	0%
Detective Comics #2	46	VF $14,300	44	VF $14,300	$0	0%
Action Comics #3	47	$14,000	49	$13,000	$1,000	8%
World's Best Comics #1	48	$14,000	48	$13,500	$500	4%
Wonder Comics #1	49	$13,500	47	$13,500	$0	0%
Action Comics #7	50	$13,000	62	$11,000	$2,000	18%
New York World's Fair 1940	51	$13,000	50	$13,000	$0	0%
All-American Comics #17	52	$12,500	52	$12,000	$500	4%
All-American Comics #19	53	$12,500	53	$12,000	$500	4%
All Flash #1	54	$12,500	54	$12,000	$500	4%
Wow Comics #1	55	$12,500	51	$12,500	$0	0%
All Star Comics #1	56	$12,000	55	$12,000	$0	0%
Big Book of Fun Comics #1	57	VF $12,000	56	VF $12,000	$0	0%
Double Action #2	58	$12,000	66	$11,000	$1,000	9%
Mystic Comics #1	59	$12,000	57	$12,000	$0	0%
New Book Of Comics #1	60	VF $12,000	60	VF $11,500	$500	4%
Silver Streak #6	61	$12,000	68	$11,000	$1,000	9%
Archie Comics #1	62	$11,500	70	$10,500	$1,000	10%
More Fun Comics #14	63	VF $11,500	58	VF $11,500	$0	0%
More Fun Comics #55	64	$11,500	59	$11,500	$0	0%
Batman #2	65	$11,200	65	$11,000	$200	2%
Adventure Comics #61	66	$11,000	63	$11,000	$0	0%
Adventure Comics #73	67	$11,000	64	$11,000	$0	0%
* Funnies on Parade nn	68	$11,000	61	$11,000	$0	0%
Mickey Mouse Magazine #1	69	$11,000	67	$11,000	$0	0%
Big All-American #1	70	$10,800	69	$10,800	$0	0%
Four Color Ser. 1 (Donald Duck) #4	71	$10,500	71	$10,500	$0	0%
More Fun Comics #73	72	$10,500	72	$10,500	$0	0%
Silver Streak #1	73	$10,500	76	$10,000	$500	5%
Detective Comics #3	74	VF $10,200	73	VF $10,200	$0	0%
Adventure Comics #72	75	$10,000	74	$10,000	$0	0%
Captain America Comics #2	76	$10,000	75	$10,000	$0	0%
Looney Tunes and Merrie Melodies #1	77	$10,000	79	$9,500	$500	5%
Pep Comics #22	78	$10,000	87	$9,000	$1,000	11%
Red Raven Comics #1	79	$10,000	77	$9,600	$400	4%
Suspense Comics #3	80	$10,000	81	$9,500	$500	5%
Superman #2	81	$9,700	80	$9,500	$200	2%
Action Comics #10	82	$9,500	85	$9,000	$500	6%
Comics Magazine #1	83	VF $9,500	78	VF $9,500	$0	0%
Daredevil Comics #1	84	$9,500	86	$9,000	$500	6%
USA Comics #1	85	$9,500	84	$9,300	$200	2%
Young Allies Comics #1	86	$9,500	82	$9,500	$0	0%
Mystery Men Comics #1	87	$9,400	83	$9,400	$0	0%
Four Color Ser. 1 (Mickey Mouse) #16	88	VF $9,000	90	VF $8,500	$500	6%
Planet Comics #1	89	$9,000	88	$9,000	$0	0%
Marvel Mystery Comics #3	90	$8,600	89	$8,600	$0	0%
Green Giant Comics #1	91	$8,500	92	$8,200	$300	4%
More Fun Comics #54	92	$8,400	93	$8,200	$200	2%
Captain America Comics #3	93	$8,200	91	$8,200	$0	0%
Action Comics #4	94	$8,000	--	$7,500	$500	7%
Action Comics #5	95	$8,000	--	$7,500	$500	7%
Action Comics #6	96	$8,000	--	$7,500	$500	7%
All-American Comics #18	97	$8,000	94	$8,000	$0	0%
All-American Comics #25	98	$8,000	95	$8,000	$0	0%
Comic Cavalcade #1	99	$8,000	--	$8,000	$0	0%
Four Color Ser. 2 (Donald Duck) #9	100	$8,000	99	$7,500	$500	7%

TOP 10 PLATINUM AGE BOOKS

1999 OVER 1998 GUIDE VALUES

TITLE/ISSUE#	1999 RANK	1999 VF PRICE	1998 RANK	1998 VF PRICE	$ INCR.	% INCR.
Mickey Mouse Book (2nd printing)-variant	1	FN $12,000	--	--	--	--
Mickey Mouse Book (1st printing)	2	$11,000	1T	$10,000	$1,000	10%
Mickey Mouse Book (2nd printing)	3	$10,000	1T	$10,000	$0	0%
Yellow Kid in McFadden Flats	4	FN $8,000	2	FN $7,500	$500	7%
Buster Brown and His Resolutions 1903	5	$5,500	3	$4,500	$1,000	22%
Dreams of the Rarebit Fiend	6	$4,000	4	$3,600	$400	11%
Little Sammy Sneeze	7	$4,000	7	$3,300	$700	21%
Pore Li'l Mose	8	$4,000	10	$2,000	$2,000	100%
* Buster Brown's Blue Ribbon #1 1904	9	$3,600	5	$3,400	$200	6%
Little Nemo 1906	10	$3,500	6	$3,300	$200	6%

TOP 10 SILVER AGE BOOKS

1999 OVER 1998 GUIDE VALUES

TITLE/ISSUE#	1999 RANK	1999 NM PRICE	1998 RANK	1998 NM PRICE	$ INCR.	% INCR.
Amazing Fantasy #15	1	$27,000	1	$27,000	$0	0%
Showcase #4	2	$25,000	2	$25,000	$0	0%
Fantastic Four #1	3	$19,000	4	$18,400	$600	3%
Amazing Spider-Man #1	4	$18,000	3	$19,000	-$1,000	-5%
Incredible Hulk #1	5	$12,000	6	$11,000	$1,000	9%
Showcase #8	6	$12,000	5	$12,500	-$500	-4%
Showcase #9	7	$6,500	7	$6,000	$500	8%
X-Men #1	8	$6,000	8	$5,500	$500	9%
Detective Comics #225	9	$5,600	9	$5,200	$400	8%
Flash #105(#1)	10	$5,500	10	$5,200	$300	6%

TOP 10 BRONZE AGE BOOKS

1999 OVER 1998 GUIDE VALUES

TITLE/ISSUE#	1999 RANK	1999 NM PRICE	1998 RANK	1998 NM PRICE	$ INCR.	% INCR.
Star Wars #1 (35¢ cover price)	1	$510	1	$490	$20	4%
Giant-Size X-Men #1	2	$480	4	$440	$40	9%
House of Secrets #92	3	$470	2	$460	$10	2%
Incredible Hulk #181	4	$465	3	$450	$15	3%
X-Men #94	5	$440	5	$420	$20	5%
DC 100 Page Super Spectacular #5	6	$400	6	$375	$25	7%
X-Men #98 (30¢ cover price)	7	$280	7	$280	$0	0%
X-Men #99 (30¢ cover price)	8	$280	8	$280	$0	0%
Cerebus #1	9	$250	9	$250	$0	0%
Vampirella Annual #1	10	$250	10	$250	$0	0%

TOP 10 CRIME BOOKS

1999 OVER 1998 GUIDE VALUES

TITLE/ISSUE#	1999 RANK	1999 NM PRICE	1998 RANK	1998 NM PRICE	$ INCR.	% INCR.
Crime Does Not Pay #22	1	$1,650	1	$1,500	$150	10%
Crime Does Not Pay #23	2	$950	2	$900	$50	6%
Crimes By Women #1	3	$920	3	$840	$80	10%
Crime Does Not Pay #24	4	$750	4	$675	$75	11%
The Killers #1	5	$720	5	$650	$70	11%
The Killers #2	6	$630	7	$550	$80	15%
The Best of Crime Does Not Pay 1944	7	$600	6	$600	$0	0%
Crime Smashers #1	8	$575	8	$525	$50	10%
Crime Reporter #2	9	$510	9	$485	$25	5%
The Best of Crime Does Not Pay 1945	10	$450	10	$450	$0	0%

TOP 10 HORROR BOOKS

1999 OVER 1998 GUIDE VALUES

TITLE/ISSUE#	1999 RANK	1999 NM PRICE	1998 RANK	1998 NM PRICE	$ INCR.	% INCR.
Vault of Horror #12	1	$3,800	1	$3,600	$200	6%
Tales of Terror Annual #1	2	VF $3,200	2	VF $3,200	$0	0%
Journey into Mystery #1	3	$2,650	3	$2,450	$200	8%
Strange Tales #1	4	$2,500	4	$2,400	$100	4%
Eerie #1	5	$2,400	6	$2,000	$400	20%
Crypt of Terror #17	6	$2,200	5	$2,000	$200	10%
Haunt of Fear #15	7	$2,200	7	$2,000	$200	10%
Crime Patrol #15	8	$1,900	8	$1,800	$100	6%
House of Mystery #1	9	$1,650	9	$1,600	$50	3%
Tales to Astonish #1	10	$1,500	10	$1,450	$50	3%

TOP 10 ROMANCE BOOKS

1999 OVER 1998 GUIDE VALUES

TITLE/ISSUE#	1999 RANK	1999 NM PRICE	1998 RANK	1998 NM PRICE	$ INCR.	% INCR.
Giant Comics Edition #12	1	$750	1	$725	$25	3%
Intimate Confessions #1	2	$540	2	$525	$15	3%
Giant Comics Edition #9	3	$460	3	$450	$10	2%
Romance Trail #1	4	$440	5	$420	$20	5%
Giant Comics Edition #15	5	$430	4	$420	$10	2%
Young Lovers #18	6	$420	6	$400	$20	5%
DC 100 Page Super Spectacular #5	7	$400	8	$375	$25	7%
Giant Comics Edition #13	8	$395	7	$385	$10	3%
Secret Hearts #1	9	$390	9	$370	$20	5%
Women In Love nn - 1952	10	$365	10	$350	$15	4%

TOP 10 SCI-FI BOOKS

1999 OVER 1998 GUIDE VALUES

TITLE/ISSUE#	1999 RANK	1999 NM PRICE	1998 RANK	1998 NM PRICE	$ INCR.	% INCR.
Mystery In Space #1	1	$2,600	1	$2,600	$0	0%
Strange Adventures #1	2	$2,500	2	$2,300	$200	9%
Showcase (Adam Strange) #17	3	$2,100	3	$2,100	$0	0%
Showcase (Space Ranger) #15	4	$1,700	4	$1,650	$50	3%
Fawcett Movie (Man From Planet X) #15	5	$1,650	5	$1,600	$50	3%
Journey Into Unknown Worlds #36	6	$1,600	6	$1,500	$100	7%
Strange Adventures #9	7	$1,500	7	$1,400	$100	7%
Weird Fantasy #13 (#1)	8	$1,500	8	$1,400	$100	7%
Weird Science #12 (#1)	9	$1,500	9	$1,400	$100	7%
Weird Science-Fantasy Annual 1952	10	$1,500	10	$1,400	$100	7%

TOP 10 WESTERN BOOKS

1999 OVER 1998 GUIDE VALUES

TITLE/ISSUE#	1999 RANK	1999 NM PRICE	1998 RANK	1998 NM PRICE	$ INCR.	% INCR.
Gene Autry Comics #1	1	$7,000	1	$6,500	$500	8%
Hopalong Cassidy #1	2	$4,600	2	$4,200	$400	10%
* Lone Ranger Ice Cream 1939	3	VF $4,200	3	VF $4,000	VF $200	5%
Red Ryder Victory Patrol	4	$3,600	4	$3,400	$200	6%
Tom Mix Ralston #1	5	$2,700	5	$2,700	$0	0%
Red Ryder Comics #1	6	$2,500	6	$2,400	$100	4%
Roy Rogers Four Color #38	7	$2,000	7	$1,800	$200	11%
Western Picture Stories #1	8	$1,250	8	$1,250	$0	0%
Tomahawk #1	9	$1,200	9	$1,200	$0	0%
John Wayne Adventure Comics #1	10	$1,150	10	$1,100	$50	5%

THE OVERSTREET COMIC BOOK HALL OF FAME

For decades, historians, collectors and bibliofiles have tried to identify, list and document all the important, trend-setting comic books of the past century. This interesting topic continues to be debated and discussed by experts everywhere. In an attempt to answer these questions, Overstreet would like to nominate the following books to Overstreet's Hall Of Fame. The author invites your comments and ideas concerning the accuracy of this list for future editions. Remember, only the very top books will be considered for inclusion.

PLATINUM AGE
1897 - 1932

Yellow Kid in McFadden's Flats, The, 1897, Dillingham Co. (1st comic book)
Funny Folk, 1899, E.P. Dutton (2nd comic book)
Vaudeville and Other Things, 1900, Blandiard Co. (3rd comic book)
Blackberries, The, 1901, R.H. Russell (Ties as 4th comic book)
Foxy Grandpa, 1901, F.A. Stokes Co. (Ties as 4th comic book)
Pore Li'l Mose, 1902, Cupples & Leon (1st satire book) (1st Cupples & Leon book)
Alphonse & Gaston & Leon, 1903, Hearst's New York American
Buster Brown and His Resolutions, 1903, F.A. Stokes Co. (1st nationally distr. comic)
Happy Hooligan, 1903, Hearst's New York American (1st comic book app.)
Katzenjammer Kids, 1903, Hearst's New York American (1st comic book app.)
Brown's Blue Ribbon Book of Jokes and Jingles, 1904, Brown Shoe Co. (1st comic book premium)
Dreams of the Rarebit Fiend, 1905, Doffield & Co. (Ties as 1st Winsor McCay book)
Little Sammy Sneeze, 1905, New York Herald Co. (Ties as 1st Winsor McCay book)
Buster Brown, 1906, Cupples & Leon (1st C&L series comic)
Little Nemo, 1906, Doffield & Co. by Winsor McCay
3 Funmakers, 1908, Stokes (1st comic to feature more than one character)
Mutt & Jeff, 1910, Ball Publ. (1st comic book app.)
Comic Monthly, 1922, Embee Dist. Co. (1st monthly newsstand comic)
Funnies, The, 1929, Dell Publ. Co. (1st four-color comic newsstand publ.)
Mickey Mouse Book, 1930, Bibo & Lang (1st Disney licensed book)
Thimble Theatre Starring Popeye, 1931, Sonnet Publ. Co. (1st Popeye book)
Detective Dan, 1933, Humor Publ. Co. (1st comic w/original art & 1st on newsstand)
Adventures of Detective Ace King, 1933, Humor Publ. Co. (along with **Detective Dan**, helped bridge the gap between the PA and SA)

PRE-GOLDEN AGE
1933 - May, 1938

Funnies On Parade #nn, 1933, Eastern Color (1st GA comic book)
Century Of Comics #nn, 1933, Eastern Color (2nd GA comic book, 1st 100 pgs.)
Famous Funnies-Carnival Of Comics, nn, 1933, Eastern Color, (3rd GA comic book)
Famous Funnies-Series 1, 1934, Eastern Color, (1st 10 cent comic)
Famous Funnies #1, 7/34, Eastern Color (1st newsstand comic book)
New Fun Comics #1, 2/35, DC (1st DC comic book)
Big Book Of Fun Comics #1, Spr/35, DC, (1st annual in comics)
New Fun Comics #6, 10/35, DC (1st Siegel & Shuster work in comics)
More Fun Comics #14, 10/36, DC (1st Superman prototype at DC, 1st in color)
Detective Comics #1, 3/37, DC (1st issue of title that launched Batman)

GOLDEN AGE
June, 1938 - 1945

Action Comics #1, 6/38, DC (1st Superman and Lois Lane)
Funny Pages #V2#10, 9/38, Centaur (1st Arrow, 1st costumed hero)
Jumbo Comics #1, 9/38, Fiction House (1st Sheena, 1st Fiction House comic book)
Movie Comics #1, 4/39, DC (1st movie comic)
New York World's Fair 1939, 4/39, DC (1st published Sandman story)
Detective Comics #27, 5/39, DC (1st Batman)
Wonder Comics #1, 5/39, Fox (1st Wonderman, 1st Superman imitator)
Superman nn (#1), Summer/39, DC (1st issue, 1st hero to get his own book)
Adventure Comics #40, 7/39, DC (1st conceived Sandman story)
Marvel Comics #1, 10/39, Timely (1st newsstand Sub-Mariner, 1st Human Torch, 1st Marvel comic)
Silver Streak #1, 12/39, Lev Gleason (1st Gleason comic book, 1st Claw)
Flash Comics #1, 1/40, DC (1st Flash, Hawkman, & Johnny Thunder)
Pep Comics #1, 1/40, MLJ/Archie (1st app. Shield, 1st patriotic hero)
Planet Comics #1, 1/40, Fiction House (1st all science fiction comic book)
More Fun Comics #52, 2/40, DC (1st Spectre)
Whiz Comics #2 (#1), 2/40, Fawcett (1st Captain Marvel & Spy Smasher, 1st Fawcett comic book)
Adventure Comics #48, 3/40, DC (1st Hourman)

Pore L'il Mose © C&L

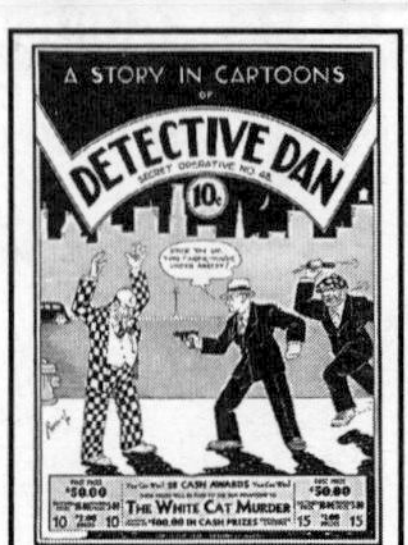

Detective Dan © Humor Publ. Co.

Superman nn (#1) © DC

Marvel Mystery Comics #9 ©MEG

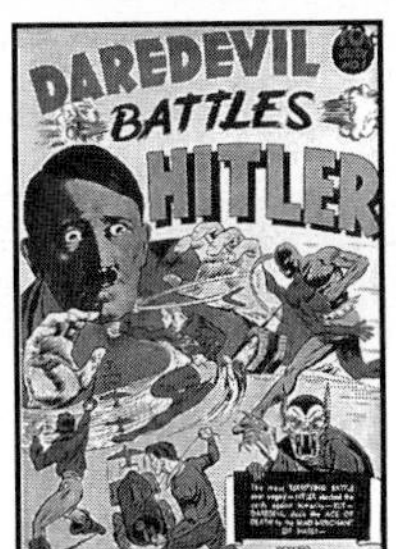
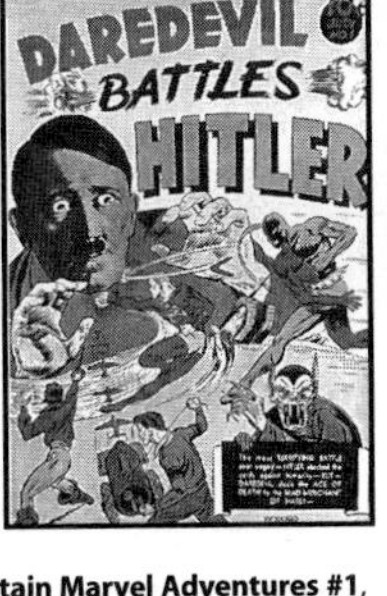

Daredevil Comics #1 © LEV

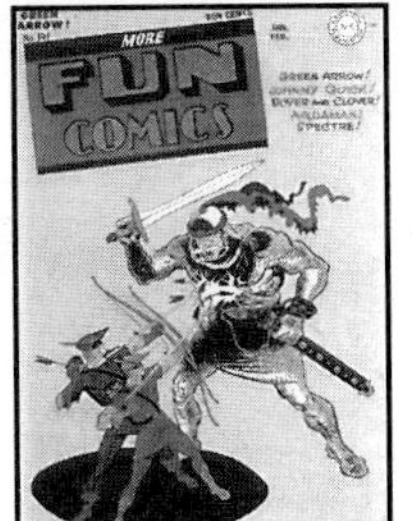

More Fun Comics #101 © DC

More Fun Comics #53, 3/40, DC (Part II of 1st Spectre story)
Four Color Ser. 1 #4 (Donald Duck), 3?/40, (1st four color Donald Duck)
Action Comics #23, 4/40, DC (1st Lex Luthor)
Detective Comics #38, 4/40, DC (1st Robin)
Batman #1, Spring/40, DC (1st issue of DC's 2nd most important character; 1st 2 Joker stories; 1st Catwoman)
More Fun Comics #55, 5/40, DC (1st Dr. Fate)
The Spirit #1, 6/2/40, Will Eisner (1st Spirit app. in weekly newspaper strip)
All American Comics #16, 7/40, DC (1st Green Lantern)
Blue Bolt #3, 7/40, Fox (1st Simon & Kirby story art)
Marvel Mystery Comics #9, 7/40, Timely (1st superhero battle; key battle issue)
Red Raven #1, 8/40, Timely (Early Kirby art)
Special Edition Comics #1, 8/40, Fawcett (1st comic book devoted to Captain Marvel)
Silver Streak #6, 9/40, Lev Gleason (1st Daredevil)
Batman #3, Fall/40, DC (1st Catwoman in costume)
Human Torch #2 (#1), Fall/40, Timely (1st issue of early Marvel star)
Walt Disney's Comics & Stories #1, 10/40, Dell (1st funny animal comic book series)
All American Comics #19, 10/40, DC (1st Atom)
All Star Comics #3, Winter/40-41, DC (1st superhero group)
Adventure Comics #72, 3/41, DC (1st Simon & Kirby Sandman)
Captain America Comics #1, 3/41, Timely (1st Captain America)

Captain Marvel Adventures #1, 3/41, Fawcett (1st issue of Fawcett's top character)
Sub-Mariner Comics #1, Spring/41, Timely (1st issue of Marvel's important character)
Adventure Comics #61, 4/41, DC (1st Starman)
All Flash #1, Summer/41, DC (1st issue of top DC character)
Daredevil #1, 7/41, Lev Gleason (1st issue of top character)
Military Comics #1, 8/41, Quality (1st Blackhawk)
Famous Funnies #100, 10/41, Eastern (1st comic book to reach issue #100)
Green Lantern #1, Fall/41, DC (1st issue of top DC character)
Looney Tunes #1, Fall/41, Dell (1st Bugs Bunny, Porky Pig & Elmer Fudd in comics)
More Fun Comics #73, 11/41, DC (1st Aquaman; 1st Green Arrow and Speedy)
Pep Comics #22, 12/41, MLJ/Archie (1st Archie)
Whiz Comics #25, 12/41, Fawcett (1st Captain Marvel Jr.)
Four Color Ser. 1 (Mickey Mouse) #16, 1941, (1st comic book devoted to Mickey Mouse)
All Star Comics #8, 12-1/41-42, DC (1st Wonder Woman)
Animal Comics #1, 12-1/41-42, Dell (1st Pogo by Walt Kelly)
Sensation Comics #1, 1/42, DC (1st series to star Wonder Woman)
Crime Does Not Pay #22, 6/42, Gleason (1st Crime comic series)
Sensation #6, June, 1942, DC, (1st app. Wonder Woman's magic lasso)
Wonder Woman #1, Summer/42, DC (1st issue of top DC character)
Four Color (Donald Duck) #9, 8/42 Dell (1st Barks work on Donald Duck)

Archie Comics #1, Winter/42-43, MLJ/ Archie, (1st Teenage comic)
Capt Marvel Adventures #22, 3/43, Fawcett, (Begins Mr. Mind serial)
Plastic Man #1, Summer/43, Quality (1st issue of top Quality character)
Big All-American Comic Book #1, 1944, DC, (1st annual of **All-American Comics**)
More Fun Comics #101, 1/2/45, DC (1st Superboy)
Molly O'Day #1, 2/45, Avon (1st Avon comic)
Terry Toones #38, 11/45, Timely (1st Mighty Mouse)

ATOM AGE 1946 - 1956

Romantic Picture Novelette #1, 1946, ME (one shot)(1st love comic theme)
All Winners #19, Fall/46, Timely (1st All Winners Squad, 1st Marvel group)
All Winners #21, Winter/46-47, Timely (2nd All Winners Squad)
Eerie #1, 1/47, Avon (1st horror comic)
Young Romance Comics #1, 9-10/47, Prize (1st romance series)
Four Color (Uncle Scrooge) #178, 12/47, Dell (1st Uncle Scrooge)
Phantom Lady #17, 4/48, Fox (Classic cover issue–good girl art)
Adventures Into The Unknown #1, Fall/48, ACG (1st horror series)
Moon Girl #5, Winter/48, EC (1st EC horror story)
Casper #1, 9/49, St John (1st Baby Huey)
Crime Patrol #15, 12-1/49-50, EC (1st Crypt Keeper)
War Against Crime #10, 12-1/49-50, EC (1st Vault Keeper)
Howdy Doody #1, 1/50, Dell (1st TV comic book)

All Star Comics #3 © DC

Four Color Series 2 #9 ©Disney

Howdy Doody #1 © California National Prod.

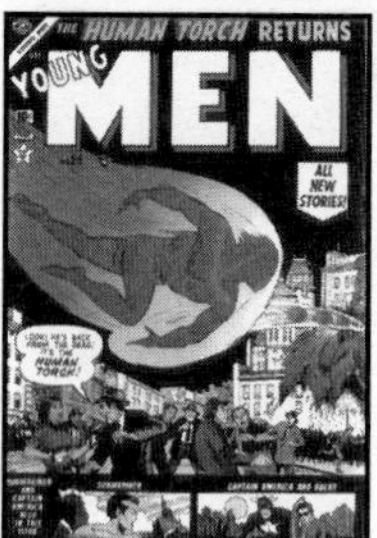

Young Men #24 © MEG

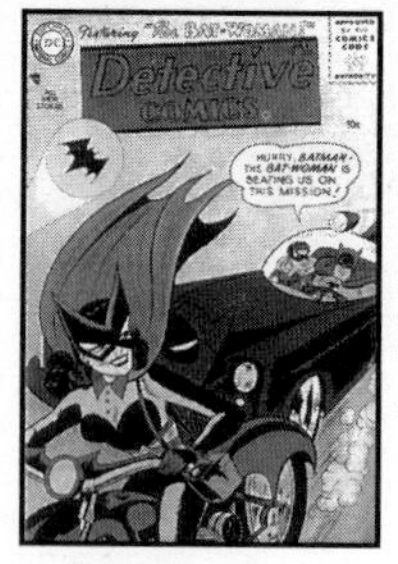

Detective Comics #233 © DC

Showcase #22 © DC

Archie Annual #1, 1950, Archie (1st **Archie** annual)
Crypt Of Terror #17, 4-5/50, EC (1st issue of Crypt Keeper tales, EC horror)
Haunt Of Fear #15 (#1), 5-6/50, EC (1st issue of EC horror, trend-setting)
Weird Fantasy #13 (#1), 5-6/50, EC (1st issue of EC science fiction, trend-setting)
Weird Science #12 (#1), 5-6/50, EC (1st issue of EC science fiction)
Strange Tales #1, 6/51, Marvel (1st issue of top Marvel title)
Mad #1, 10-11/52, EC (1st satire comic)
Journey Into Mystery #1, 6/52, Marvel (1st issue of top Marvel title)
Little Dot #1, 9/53, Harvey (1st Richie Rich)
Young Men #24, 12/53, Marvel (Revival of Capt. America, Human Torch & Sub-Mariner)
World's Finest Comics #71, 7-8/54, DC (1st Superman/Batman team issue)
Superman's Pal, Jimmy Olsen #1, 9-10/54, DC, (1st issue of top DC title)
My Greatest Adventure #1, 1-2/55, DC (1st issue of top DC fantasy title)
Brave And The Bold #1, 8-9/55, DC (1st issue of top DC showcase title)
Superman #100, 9-10/55, DC (Landmark issue)
Detective Comics #225, 11/55, DC (1st Martian Manhunter)
Tales Of The Unexpected #1, 2-3/56, DC (1st issue of top DC fantasy title)
Showcase #1, 3-4/56, DC (1st issue of top DC title)
Sugar & Spike #1, 4-5/56, DC (1st issue of top title by Sheldon Mayer)
Batman #100, 6/56, DC (Landmark issue)
Detective Comics #233, 7/56, DC (1st Batwoman)

SILVER AGE Sept, 1956 - 1969

Showcase #4, 9-10/56, DC (1st Silver Age book) (The Flash)
House Of Secrets #1, 11-12/56, DC (1st issue of top DC horror title)
Showcase #6, 1-2/57, DC (1st Silver Age group)(Challengers)
Showcase #9, 7-8/57, DC (1st Lois Lane book)
Superman's Girl Friend, Lois Lane #1, 3-4/58, DC (1st issue of top character)
Adventure Comics #247, 4/58, DC (1st Legion of Superheroes)
Challengers Of The Unknown #1, 4-5/58, DC, (1st issue of 1st Silver Age group)
Showcase #15, 7-8/58, DC (1st Space Ranger)
Showcase #17, 11-12/58, DC (1st Adam Strange)
Tales Of Suspense #1, 1/59, Marvel (1st issue of top fantasy title)
Tales To Astonish #1, 1/59, Marvel (1st issue of top fantasy title)
Flash #105 (#1), 2-3/59, DC (1st issue of top DC title)
Our Army At War #83, 6/59, DC (1st Sgt. Rock by Kubert/Kanigher)
Action Comics #252, 5/59, DC (1st Supergirl)
Showcase #20, 5-6/59, DC (1st Rip Hunter)
Double Life Of Private Strong #1, 6/59, Archie (1st Silver Age Shield, 1st Fly)
Mystery In Space #53, 8/59, DC (1st Adam Strange)
Tales Of The Unexpected #40, 8/59, DC (1st Space Ranger in own title)
Adventures of the Fly #1, 8/59, Archie (1st issue of top Archie title)
Showcase #22, 9-10/59, DC (1st Silver Age Green Lantern)
Flash #110, 12-1/59/60, DC (1st Kid Flash)
Brave And The Bold #28, 2/3/60, DC (1st Justice League of America)
Green Lantern #1, 7-8/60, DC (1st issue of top DC character)
Showcase #27, 7-8/60, DC (1st Sea Devils)
Brave And The Bold #31, 8-9/60, DC (1st Cave Carson)
Justice League Of America #1, 10-11/60, DC (1st issue of top DC title)
Showcase #30, 1-2/61, DC (1st Silver Age Aquaman)
Brave And The Bold #34, 2-3/61, DC (1st Silver Age Hawkman)
Amazing Adventures #1, 6/61, Marvel (1st Dr. Droom, the 1st Marvel-Age superhero)
Flash #123, 9/61, DC (1st G.A. Flash in Silver Age)
Showcase #34, 9-10/61, DC (1st Silver Age Atom)
Fantastic Four #1, 11/61, Marvel (1st Fantastic Four)
Amazing Adult Fantasy #7, 12/61, Marvel (1st issue of title that leads to Spider-Man)
Tales To Astonish #27, 1/62, Marvel (1st Antman)
Showcase #37, 3-4/62, DC (1st Metal Men)
Fantastic Four #4, 5/62, Marvel (1st Silver Age Sub-Mariner)
Incredible Hulk #1, 5/62, Marvel (1st Hulk)
Mystery In Space #75, 5/62, DC (Early JLA cross-over in Adam Strange story)
Fantastic Four #5, 7/62, Marvel (1st Dr. Doom)

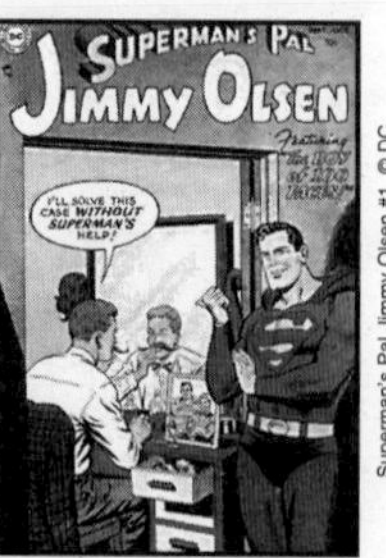

Superman's Pal Jimmy Olsen #1 © DC

The Double Life of Private Strong #1 © Archie Publ.

Fantastic Four #5 © MEG

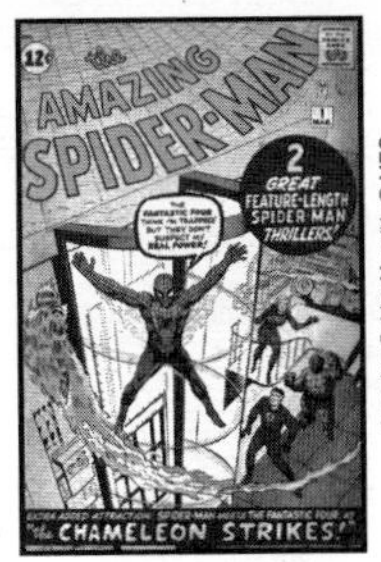

Amazing Spider-Man #1 © MEG

All-Star Western #10 © DC

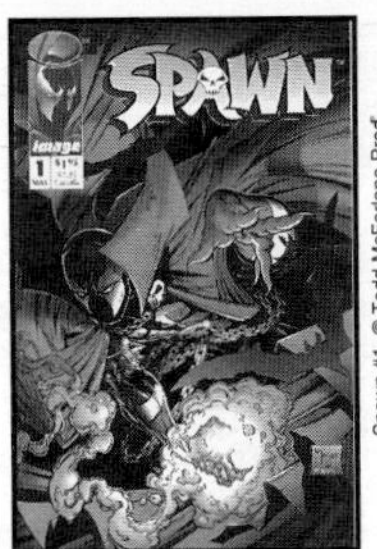

Spawn #1 © Todd McFarlane Prod.

Journey Into Mystery #83, 8/62, Marvel (1st Thor)
Amazing Fantasy #15, 8-9/62, Marvel (1st Spider-Man)
Tales To Astonish #35, 9/62, Marvel (2nd Antman, 1st in costume)
Strange Tales #101, 10/62, Marvel (1st S.A. Human Torch solo story)
Amazing Spider-Man #1, 3/63, Marvel (1st Spider-Man in own title)
Tales Of Suspense #39, 3/63, Marvel (1st Iron Man)
Strange Tales #110, 7/63, Marvel (1st Dr. Strange)
Justice League of America #21, 8/63, DC (1st JLA/JSA crossover)
Avengers #1, 9/63, Marvel (1st Avengers)
X-Men #1, 9/63, Marvel (1st X-Men)
Mystery In Space #87, 11/63, DC (1st Hawkman in title)
Avengers #4, 3/64, Marvel (1st Silver Age Captain America)
Daredevil #1, 4/64, Marvel (1st Daredevil)
Detective Comics #327, 5/64, DC (New Batman) (Silver Age/ Bronze)
Brave and the Bold #54, 6-7/64, DC (1st Teen Titans)
Amazing Spider-Man #14, 7/64, Marvel (1st Green Goblin)
Strange Tales #135, 7/65, Marvel (Origin & 1st app. Nick Fury)
Fantastic Four #48, 3/66, Marvel (1st Silver Surfer)
Our Army at War #168, 6/66, DC (1st Unknown Soldier)
Strange Adventures #205, 10/67, DC (1st Deadman)
Zap Comix#1, 11/67, Apex (Underground comic which instigated the direct sales market)

BRONZE AGE 1970 - 1979

Green Lantern #76, 4/70, DC (Begins Green Lantern/Green Arrow series by Denny O'Neil & Neal Adams)
Detective Comics #400, 6/70, DC (1st Man-Bat)
Superman's Pal, Jimmy Olsen #133, 10/70, DC (1st Silver Age Newsboy Legion)
Forever People #1, 2-3/71, DC (1st Forever People)
New Gods #1, 3/71, DC (1st New Gods)
Mister Miracle #1, 3/71, DC (1st Mister Miracle)
Savage Tales #1, 5/71, Marvel (1st Man-Thing)
House of Secrets #92, 6/71, DC (1st app. Swamp Thing by Bernie Wrightson)
Amazing Spider-Man #101, 10/71, Marvel (1st Morbius the Living Vampire)
Marvel Feature #1, 12/71, Marvel (Origin and 1st app. Defenders)
All Star Western #10, 2-3/72, DC (1st Jonah Hex)
Tomb of Dracula #1, 4/72, Marvel (1st app. Dracula)
Marvel Spotlight #2, 6/72, Marvel (1st app. Werewolf by Night)
Marvel Spotlight #5, 8/72, Marvel (Origin and 1st app. new Ghost Rider)
Kamandi: The Last Boy on Earth #1, 10/72, DC (Origin and 1st app. Kamandi)
Iron Man #55, 2/73, Marvel (1st. app. Thanos & Drax the Destroyer)
Shazam #1, 2/73, DC (1st revival of Captain Marvel since mid 50s)
Amazing Spider-Man #121, 6/73 Marvel (Death of Gwen Stacy)
Amazing Spider-Man #122, 7/73, Marvel (Death of Green Goblin I)
Amazing Spider-Man #129, 2/74, Marvel (1st Punisher)
Marvel Spotlight #12, 10/73, Marvel (1st solo Son of Satan)
Marvel Special Edition #15, 12/73, Marvel (1st Master of Kung Fu)
Amazing Spider-Man #129, 2/74, Marvel (1st Punisher)
Astonishing Tales #25, 8/74, Marvel (1st Deathlok)
Incredible Hulk #181, 11/74, Marvel (1st story app. of Wolverine)
Giant Size X-Men #1, Summer/75, Marvel (1st New X-Men; intro Nightcrawler, Storm, Colossus & Thunderbird)
X-Men #94, 8/75, Marvel (New X-Men team begins)
All Star Comics #58, 1-2/76, DC (1st Power Girl)
Marvel Spotlight #32, 2/77, Marvel (1st Spider-Woman)
Black Lightning #1, 4/77, DC (1st Black Lightning)
Cerebus #1, 12/77, Aardvark-Vanaheim (1st app. Cerebus)(B&W)
X-Men #108, 12/77, Marvel (1st important Byrne work)
Daredevil #158, 5/79, Marvel (Frank Miller begins work on Daredevil; his 1st important work)

MODERN AGE 1980 - PRESENT

X-Men #137, 9/80, Marvel (The story that started comicdom's "Death Craze")
Daredevil #168, 1/81, Marvel (1st Elektra)
Gobbledygook #1, pre 6/84; Mirage, (1st app. Teenage Mutant Ninja Turtles)
Crisis on Infinite Earths #1-12, 85/86, DC (1st appearance of revamped Modern Age DC universe) (#7, Death of Supergirl) (#8, Death of the Barry Allen Flash)
Batman: The Dark Knight #1, 3/86, DC (Beginning of Frank Miller's landmark revision of Batman)
Maus, 1986, Pantheon Books (1st comic book to win the Pulitzer Prize) (depicts the horrors of the Holocaust through the eyes of artist Art Spiegelman's father)
The Man of Steel #1, 6/86, DC (Beginning of John Byrne's update of the Superman mythos)
Watchmen #1, 10/87, DC (Beginning of Alan Moore's revisionist look at superheroes)
Amazing Spider-Man #300, 5/88, Marvel (1st Venom) (full app & story)
Sandman #1, 1/89, DC (1st app. new Sandman)
X-Men #1, 10/91, Marvel (1st comic to reach a print run of 8 million copies)
Youngblood #1, 4/92, Image (1st Image comic)
Spawn #1, 5/92, Image (1st app. Spawn)
Superman (2nd Series) #75, 1/93, DC (Death of Superman) (Huge Media Coverage)
Deathmate Black, 9/93, Valiant/ Image (1st Gen13 story)
Starman #0, 10/94, DC (1st app. of Modern Age Starman)
Strangers in Paradise #1, 11/94, Antarctic (1st issue of Terry Moore's series)
DC Vs. Marvel #1, 1996, DC (1st issue of landmark company crossover)
Kingdom Come #1-4, 1996, DC (Fully painted Elseworlds series about the future DC universe)
Final Night #4, 11/96, DC (Death of former Green Lantern Hal Jordan)
Superman: The Wedding Album, 12/96, DC (Marriage of Clark Kent and Lois Lane)

(First comic book of a genre, publisher, theme or type, etc.)

AVIATION COMIC–Wings Comics #1, 9/40
COMIC BOOK ANNUAL–Big Book of Fun Comics #1, Spr, 1936
COMIC BOOK–Funnies On Parade nn, 1933
COMIC BOOK TO GO INTO ENDLESS REPRINTS–Classic Comics #1, 10/41
COMIC BOOK TO KILL OFF A SUPERHERO–Pep Comics #17, 7/41 (The Comet)
COMIC BOOK WITH METALLIC LOGO–Silver Streak #1, 12/39
COMIC BOOK WITH ORIGINAL MATERIAL–New Fun Comics #1, 2/35
COSTUMED HERO BATTLE COMIC–Marvel Mystery #9, 7/40
COSTUMED HERO COMIC (STRIP)–Ace Comics #11, 2/38 (The Phantom)
COSTUMED HERO COMIC (Original material)–Funny Pages V2/10 9/38 (The Arrow)(3 months after Superman)
COSTUMED HERO SIDEKICK COMIC– Detective Comics #38, 4/40 (Robin)
CRIME–Crime Does Not Pay #22, 6/42
DETECTIVE COMIC–Detective Picture Stories #1, 12/36
DISNEY SINGLE CHARACTER COMIC BOOK–Donald Duck nn, 1938
DISNEY SINGLE CHARACTER COMIC BOOK IN COLOR–Donald Duck 4-Color #4, 3/40
EDUCATIONAL THEME COMIC–Classic Comics #1, 10/41
5 CENT COMIC–Nickel Comics #1, 1938
15 CENT COMIC–New York World's Fair, 1940
FLYING SAUCER COMIC–Spirit Section 9/28/47 (3 months after 1st alleged sighting in Idaho on 6/25/47)
FUNNY ANIMAL SERIES–Walt Disney's Comics & Stories #1, 10/40
FUNNY ANIMAL SINGLE CHARACTER COMIC–Donald Duck nn, 1938
GIVEAWAY COMIC–Funnies on Parade nn, 1933
GOLDEN AGE COMIC–Action Comics #1, 6/38
HEROINE SINGLE THEME COMIC–Sheena, Queen of the Jungle #1, Spr, 1942
HORROR COMIC (ONE SHOT)–Eerie Comics #1, 1/47
HORROR COMIC (SERIES)–Adventures into the Unknown #1, Fall, 1948
JUNGLE COMIC–Jumbo Comics #1, 9/38
LARGE SIZED COMIC–New Fun Comics #1, 2/35
LOVE COMIC (ONE SHOT)–Romantic Picture Novelettes #1, 1946 (Mary Worth strip-r)
LOVE COMIC (SERIES)–Young Romance Comics #1, 10/47
MAGICIAN COMIC–Super Magic Comics #1, 5/41
MAGICIAN COMIC SERIES–Super Magician Comics #2, 9/41
MASKED HERO–Funny Pages #6, 11/36 (The Clock)
MOVIE COMIC–Movie Comics #1, 4/39
NEGRO COMIC–Negro Heroes, Spr, 1947
NEWSSTAND COMIC–Famous Funnies #1, 7/34
#2 IN COMICS–Famous Funnies #2, 8/34
100 PAGE COMIC–Century of Comics nn, 1933
100TH ISSUE–Famous Funnies #100, 11/42
ONE SHOT SERIES–Feature Book nn, 1937
PATRIOTIC HERO COMIC–Pep Comics #1, 1/40 (The Shield)
PROTOTYPE COMIC–The Comics Magazine #1, 5/36 (Superman)
PUBLIC EVENT COMIC–New York World's Fair 1939
RELIGIOUS THEME SERIES–Topix Comics #1, 11/42
REPRINT COMIC–Funnies on Parade nn, 1933
SATIRE COMIC–Mad #1, 10-11/52
SCIENCE FICTION COMIC–Planet Comics #1, 1/40
SIDEKICK GROUP COMIC–Young Allies #1, Sum, 1941
SILVER AGE ARCHIE COMIC–Double Life of Private Strong #1, 6/59
SILVER AGE COMIC–Showcase #4, 9-10/56
SILVER AGE DC ANNUAL–Superman Annual #1, 10/60
SILVER AGE MARVEL ANNUAL–Strange Tales Annual #1, 1962
SILVER AGE MARVEL COMIC–Fantastic Four #1, 11/61
SINGLE CHARACTER COMIC–Skippy's Own Book of Comics, 1934
SINGLE ORIGINAL CHARACTER COMIC–Superman #1, Sum, 1939
SINGLE STRIP REPRINT CHARACTER COMIC–Mutt and Jeff #1, Sum, 1939
SINGLE THEME COMIC–Detective Picture Stories #1, 12/36
SINGLE THEME COMIC, THE FIRST IMPORTANT–Detective Comics #1, 3/37

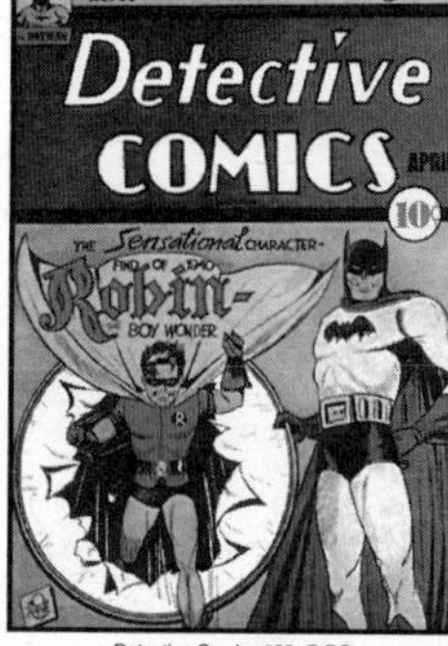

Detective Comics #38 © DC

SINGLE THEME REPRINT STRIP COMIC–Mutt and Jeff #1, Sum, 1939
SMALL-SIZED COMIC–Little Giant Comics #1, 7/38
SPORTS COMIC–Champion Comics #2, 12/39
SQUAREBOUND COMIC–New Book of Comics #1, 1937
SQUAREBOUND SERIES–World's Best #1, Spr, 1941
SUPER HERO COMIC–Action Comics #1, 6/38 (Superman)
SUPER HERO TEAM–All Star Comics #3, Wint, 1940-41
SUPER HEROINE COMIC–All Star Comics #8, 11-12/41
SUPER HEROINE COMIC SERIES–Sensation Comics #1, 1/42
SUPERMAN IMITATOR–Wonder Comics #1, 5/39 (Wonder Man)
TEEN-AGE COMIC–Pep Comics #22, 12/41
TEEN-AGE COMIC SERIES–Archie Comics #1, Wint, 1942-43
10 CENT COMIC–Famous Funnies Series 1, 3-5/34
3-D COMIC–Mighty Mouse 3-D #1, 9/53
T.V. COMIC–Howdy Doody #1, 1/50
25 CENT COMIC–New York World's Fair, 1939
TRUE LIFE COMIC–Sport Comics #1, 10/40
VILLAIN COVER (FU MANCHU)–Detective Comics #1, 3/37
VILLAIN STORY (FU MANCHU)–Detective Comics #17, 7/38
VILLAIN COVER/STORY (ORIGINAL TO COMICS)– Silver Streak #1, 12/39 (The Claw)
WAR COMIC–War Comics #1, 5/40
WEEKLY COMIC BOOK–The Spirit #1, 6/2/40
WESTERN COMIC–Western Picture Stories #1, 2/37 & Star Ranger #1, 2/37
WESTERN OF ONE CHARACTER–The Lone Ranger Comics nn, 1939
WESTERN RUN OF ONE CHARACTER (GIVEAWAY)–Tom Mix #1, 9/40
WESTERN NEWSSTAND RUN OF ONE CHARACTER–Red Ryder Comics #1, 8/41
WESTERN WITH PHOTO COVER–Roy Rogers Four Color #38, 4/44
X-OVER COMIC–Marvel Mystery #9, 7/40

A CHRONOLOGY OF THE DEVELOPMENT OF THE AMERICAN COMIC BOOK

BY M. THOMAS INGE

Precursors: The facsimile newspaper strip reprint collections constitute the earliest "comic books." The first of these was a collection of Richard Outcault's **Yellow Kid** from the **Hearst New York American** in March 1897. Commercial and promotional reprint collections, usually in cardboard covers, appeared through the 1920s and featured such newspaper strips as **Mutt and Jeff**, **Foxy Grandpa**, **Buster Brown**, and **Barney Google**. During 1922 a reprint magazine, **Comic Monthly**, appeared with each issue devoted to a separate strip, and from 1929 to 1930 George Delacorte published 36 issues of **The Funnies** in tabloid format with original comic pages in color, becoming the first four-color comic newsstand publication.

1933: The Ledger syndicate published a small broadside of their Sunday comics on 7" by 9" plates. Employees of Eastern Color Printing Company in New York, sales manager Harry I. Wildenberg and salesman Max C. Gaines, saw it and figured that two such plates would fit a tabloid page, which would produce a book about 7-1/2" x 10" when folded. Thus 10,000 copies of **Funnies on Parade**, containing 32 pages of Sunday newspaper reprints, was published for Proctor and Gamble to be given away as premiums. Some of the strips included were: **Joe Palooka**, **Mutt and Jeff**, **Hairbreadth Harry**, and **Reg'lar Fellas**. M. C. Gaines was very impressed with this book and convinced Eastern Color that he could sell a lot of them to such big advertisers as Milk-O-Malt, Wheatena, Kinney Shoe Stores, and others to be used as premiums and radio give-aways. So, Eastern Color printed **Famous Funnies: A Carnival of Comics**, and then **Century of Comics**, both as before, containing Sunday newspaper reprints. Mr. Gaines sold these books in quantities of 100,000 to 250,000. Although slightly larger in size than **Famous Funnies**, Humor Publications produced two one-issue magazines, **Detective Dan** and **The Adventures of Detective Ace King**, which contained original comic art and sold for ten cents per copy.

1934: The give-away comics were so successful that Mr. Gaines believed that youngsters would buy comic books for ten cents like the "Big Little Books" coming out at that time. So, early in 1934, Eastern Color ran off 35,000 copies of **Famous Funnies, Series 1**, 64 pages of reprints for Dell Publishing Company to be sold for ten cents in chain stores. Since it sold out promptly on the stands, Eastern Color, in May 1934, issued **Famous Funnies** No. 1 (dated July 1934) which became, with issue No. 2 in July, the first monthly comic magazine. The title continued for over 20 years through 218 issues, reaching a circulation peak of over 400,000 copies a month. At the same time, Mr. Gaines went to the sponsors of Percy Crosby's *Skippy*, which was on the radio, and convinced them to put out a Skippy book, advertise it on the air, and give away a free copy to anyone who bought a tube of Phillip's toothpaste. Thus 500,000 copies of **Skippy's Own Book of Comics** was run off and distributed through drug stores everywhere. This was the first four-color comic book of reprints devoted to a single character.

1935: Major Malcolm Wheeler-Nicholson's National Periodical Publications issued in

February a tabloid-sized comic publication called **New Fun**, which became **More Fun** after the sixth issue and was converted to the normal comic-book size after issue eight. **More Fun** was the first comic book of a standard size to publish original material, and it continued publication until 1947. **Mickey Mouse Magazine** began in the summer, to become **Walt Disney's Comics and Stories** in 1940, and combined original material with reprinted newspaper strips in most issues.

1936: In the wake of the success of **Famous Funnies**, other publishers, in conjunction with the major newspaper strip syndicates, inaugurated more reprint comic books: **Popular Comics** (News Tribune, February), **Tip Top Comics** (United Features, April), **King Comics** (King Features, April), and **The Funnies** (new series, NEA, October). Four issues of **Wow Comics**, from David McKay and Henle Publications, appeared, edited by S. M. Iger and including early art by Will Eisner, Bob Kane, and Alex Raymond. The first non-reprint comic book devoted to a single theme was **Detective Picture Stories** issued in December by The Comics Magazine Company.

1937: The second single theme title, **Western Picture Stories**, came in February from The Comics Magazine Company, and the third was **Detective Comics**, an offshoot of **More Fun**, which began in March to be published to the present. The book's initials, "D.C.," have long served to refer to National Periodical Publications, which was purchased from Major Nicholson by Harry Donenfeld late this year.

1938: "DC" copped a lion's share of the comic book market with the publication of **Action Comics** #1 in June which contained the first appearance of Superman by writer Jerry Siegel and artist Joe Shuster, a discovery of Max C. Gaines. The "man of steel" inaugurated the "Golden Era" in comic book history. Fiction House, a pulp publisher, entered the comic book field in September with **Jumbo Comics**, featuring Sheena, Queen of the Jungle, and appearing in over-sized format for the first eight issues.

1939: The continued success of "DC" was assured in May with the publication of **Detective Comics** #27 containing the first episode of Batman by artist Bob Kane and writer Bill Finger. **Superman Comics** appeared in the summer. Also, during the summer, a black and white premium comic titled **Motion Picture Funnies Weekly** was published to be given away at motion picture theatres. The plan was to issue it weekly and to have continued stories so that the kids would come back week after week not to miss an episode. Four issues were planned but only one came out. This book contains the first appearance and origin of the Sub-Mariner by Bill Everett (8 pages) which was later reprinted in **Marvel Comics**. In November, the first issue of **Marvel Comics** came out, featuring the Human Torch by Carl Burgos and the Sub-Mariner reprint with color added.

1940: The April issue of **Detective Comics** #38 introduced Robin the Boy Wonder as a sidekick to Batman, thus establishing the "Dynamic Duo" and a major precedent for later costumed heroes who would also have boy companions. **Batman Comics** began in the spring. Over 60 different comic book titles were being issued, including **Whiz Comics** begun in February by Fawcett Publications. A creation of writer Bill Parker and artist C. C. Beck, Whiz's Captain Marvel was the only superhero ever to surpass Superman in comic book sales. Drawing on their own popular pulp magazine heroes, Street and Smith Publications introduced **Shadow Comics** in March and **Doc Savage Comics** in May. A second trend was established with the summer appearance of the first issue of **All Star Comics**, which brought several superheroes together in one story and in its third issue that winter would announce the establishment of the Justice Society of America.

1941: Wonder Woman was introduced in the spring issue of **All Star Comics** #8, the creation of psychologist William Moulton Marston and artist Harry Peter. **Captain Marvel Adventures** began this year. By the end of 1941, over 160 titles were being published, including **Captain America** by Jack Kirby and Joe Simon, **Police Comics** with Jack Cole's Plastic Man and later Will Eisner's Spirit, **Military Comics** with Blackhawk by Eisner and Charles Cuidera, **Daredevil Comics** with the original character by Charles Biro, **Air Fighters** with Airboy also by Biro, and **Looney Tunes & Merrie Melodies** with Porky Pig, Bugs Bunny, and Elmer Fudd, reportedly created by Bob Clampett for the Leon Schlesinger Productions animated films and drawn for the comics by Chase Craig. Also, Albert Kanter's Gilberton Company initiated the **Classics Illustrated** series with **The Three Musketeers**.

1942: **Crime Does Not Pay** by editor Charles Biro and publisher Lev Gleason, devoted to factual accounts of criminals' lives, began a different trend in realistic crime stories. **Wonder Woman** appeared in the summer. John Goldwater's character Archie, drawn by Bob Montana, first published in **Pep Comics**, was given his own magazine **Archie Comics**, which has remained popular over 40 years. The first issue of **Animal Comics** contained Walt Kelly's "Albert Takes the Cake," featuring the new character of Pogo. In mid-1942, the undated Dell Four Color title, #9, **Donald Duck Finds Pirate Gold**, appeared with art by Carl Barks and Jack Hannah. Barks, also featured in **Walt Disney's Comics and Stories**, remained the most popular delineator of Donald Duck and later introduced his greatest creation, Uncle Scrooge, in **Christmas on Bear Mountain** (Dell Four Color #178). The fantasy work of George Carlson appeared in the first issue of **Jingle Jangle Comics**, one of the most imaginative titles for children ever to be published.

1945: The first issue of **Real Screen Comics** introduced the Fox and the Crow by James F. Davis, and John Stanley began drawing the **Little Lulu** comic book based on a popular feature in the **Saturday Evening Post** by Marjorie Henderson Buell from 1935 to 1944. Bill Woggon's Katy Keene appears in #5 of **Wilbur Comics** to be followed by appearances in **Laugh, Pep, Suzie** and her own comic book in 1950. The popularity of Dick Briefer's satiric version of the Frankenstein monster, originally drawn for **Prize Comics** in 1941, led to the publication of **Frankenstein Comics** by Prize publications.

1950: The son of Max C. Gaines, William M. Gaines, who earlier had inherited his father's firm Educational Comics (later Entertaining Comics), began publication of a series of well-written and masterfully drawn titles which would establish a "New Trend" in comics magazines: **Crypt of Terror** (later **Tales from the Crypt**, April), **The Vault of Horror** (April), **The Haunt of Fear** (May), **Weird Science** (May), **Weird Fantasy** (May), **Crime SuspenStories** (October), and **Two Fisted Tales** (November), the latter stunningly edited by Harvey Kurtzman.

1952: In October EC published the first number of **Mad** under Kurtzman's creative editorship, thus establishing a style of humor which would inspire other publications and powerfully influence the underground comic book movement of the 1960s.

1953: All Fawcett titles featuring Captain Marvel were ceased after many years of litigation in the courts during which National Periodical Publications claimed that the superhero was an infringement on the copyrighted Superman. In December, Captain America, Human Torch, and Sub-Mariner were revived by Atlas Comics. The first 3-D comic book, **Three Dimension Comics**, featuring **Mighty Mouse** and created by Joe Kubert and Norman Maurer, was issued in September by St. John

Publishing Co.

1954: The appearance of Fredric Wertham's book **Seduction of the Innocent** in the spring was the culmination of a continuing war against comic books fought by those who believed they corrupted youth and debased culture. The U. S. Senate Subcommittee on Juvenile Delinquency investigated comic books and in response the major publishers banded together in October to create the Comics Code Authority and adopted, in their own words, "the most stringent code in existence for any communications media." Before the Code took effect, more than 1,000,000,000 issues of comic books were being sold annually.

1955: In an effort to avoid the Code, EC launched a "New Direction" series of titles, such as **Impact**, **Valor**, **Aces High**, **Extra, M.D.**, and **Psychoanalysis**, none of which lasted beyond the year. **Mad** was changed into a larger magazine format with #24 in July to escape the Comics Code entirely, and EC closed down its line of comic books altogether.

1956: Beginning with the Flash in **Showcase** #4, Julius Schwartz began a popular revival of DC superheroes which would lead to the Silver Age in comic book history.

1957: Atlas reduced the number of titles published by two-thirds, with **Journey into Mystery** and **Strange Tales** surviving, while other publishers did the same or went out of business. Atlas would survive as a part of the Marvel Comics Group.

1960: After several efforts at new satire magazines (**Trump** and **Humbug**), Harvey Kurtzman, no longer with Gaines, issued in August the first number of another abortive effort, **Help!**, where the early work of underground cartoonists Jay Lynch, Skip Williamson, Gilbert Shelton, and Robert Crumb appeared.

1961: Stan Lee edited in November the first **Fantastic Four**, featuring Mr. Fantastic, the Human Torch, the Thing, and the Invisible Girl, and inaugurated an enormously popular line of titles from Marvel Comics featuring a more contemporary style of superhero.

1962: Lee introduced **The Amazing Spider-Man** in August, with art by Steve Ditko, **The Hulk** in May and **Thor** in August, the last two produced by Dick Ayers and Jack Kirby.

1963: Marvel's **The X-Men**, with art by Jack Kirby, began a successful run in November, but the title would experience a revival and have an even more popular reception in the 1980s.

1965: James Warren issued **Creepy**, a larger black and white comic book, outside Comics Code's control, which emulated the EC horror comic line. Warren's **Eerie** began in September and **Vampirella** in September 1969.

1967: Robert Crumb's **Zap** #1 appeared, the first underground comic book to achieve wide popularity, although the undergrounds had begun in 1962 with **Adventures of Jesus** by Foolbert Sturgeon (Frank Stack) and 1964 with **God Nose** by Jack Jackson.

1970: Editor Roy Thomas at Marvel begins **Conan the Barbarian** based on fiction by Robert E. Howard with art by Barry Smith, and Neal Adams began to draw for DC a series of **Green Lantern/Green Arrow** stories which would deal with relevant social issues such as racism, urban poverty, and drugs.

1972: **The Swamp Thing** by Berni Wrightson begins in November from DC.

1973: In February, DC revived the original **Captain Marvel** with new art by C. C. Beck and reprints in the first issue of **Shazam** and in October **The Shadow** with scripts by Denny O'Neil and art by Mike Kaluta.

1974: DC began publication in the spring of a series of over-sized facsimile reprints of the most valued comic books of the past under the general title of "Famous First Editions," beginning with a reprint of **Action** #1 and including afterwards **Detective Comics** #27, **Sensation Comics** #1, **Whiz Comics** #2, **Batman** #1, **Wonder Woman** #1, **All-Star Comics** #3, **Flash Comics** #1, and **Superman** #1. Mike Friedrich, an independent publisher, released **Star-Reach** with work by Jim Starlin, Neal Adams, and Dick Giordano, with ownership of the characters and stories invested in the creators themselves.

1975: In the first collaborative effort between the two major comic book publishers of the previous decade, Marvel and DC produced together an over-sized comic book version of MGM's **Marvelous Wizard of Oz** in the fall, and then the following year, in an unprecedented crossover, produced **Superman vs. the Amazing Spider-Man**, written by Gerry Conway, drawn by Ross Andru, and inked by Dick Giordano.

1976: Frank Brunner's Howard the Duck, who had appeared earlier in Marvel's **Fear** and **Man-Thing**, was given his own book in January, which because of distribution problems became an overnight collector's item. After decades of litigation, Jerry Siegel and Joe Shuster were given financial recompense and recognition by National Periodical Publications for their creation of Superman, after several friends of the team made a public issue of the case.

1977: Stan Lee's **Spider-Man** was given a second birth, fifteen years after his first, through a highly successful newspaper comic strip, which began syndication on January 3 with art by John Romita. This invasion of the comic strip by comic book characters continued with the appearance on June 6 of Marvel's **Howard the Duck**, with story by Steve Gerber and visuals by Gene Colan. In an unusually successful collaborative effort, Marvel began publication of the comic book adaption of the George Lucas film **Star Wars**, with script by Roy Thomas and art by Howard Chaykin, at least three months before the film was released nationally on May 25. The demand was so great that all six issues of **Star Wars** were reprinted at least seven times, and the installments were reprinted in two volumes of an over-sized Marvel Special Edition and a single paperback volume for the book trade. Dave Sim, with an issue dated December, began self-publication of his **Cerebus the Aardvark**, the success of which would help establish the independent market for non-traditional black-and-white comics.

1978: In an effort to halt declining sales, Warner Communications drastically cut back on the number of DC titles and overhauled its distribution process in June. The interest of the visual media in comic book characters reached a new high with the Hulk, Spider-Man, and Doctor Strange, the subjects of television shows; with various film versions produced of Flash Gordon, Dick Tracy, Popeye, Conan, The Phantom, and Buck Rogers; and with the movement reaching an outlandish peak of publicity with the release of **Superman** in December. Two significant applications of the comic book format to traditional fiction appeared this year: **A Contract with God and Other Tenement Stories** by Will Eisner and **The Silver Surfer** by Stan Lee and Jack Kirby. Eclipse Enterprises published Don McGregor and Paul Gulacy's **Sabre**, the first graphic album produced for the direct sales market, and initiated a policy of paying royalties and granting copyrights to comic book creators. Wendy and Richard Pini's **Elfquest**, a self-publishing project begun this year, eventually became so popular that it achieved bookstore distribution. The magazine **Heavy Metal** brought to American attention the avant-garde comic book work of European artists.

1980: Publication of the November premiere issue of **The New Teen Titans**, with art by George Perez and story by Marv Wolfman, brought back to widespread popularity a title originally published by DC in 1966.

1981: Distributor Pacific Comics began publishing titles for direct sales through comic shops with the first issue of Jack Kirby's **Captain Victory and the Galactic Rangers** and offered royalties to artists and writers on the basis of sales. DC would do the same for regular newsstand comics in November (with payments retroactive to July 1981), and Marvel followed suit by the end of the year. The first issue of **Raw**, irregularly published by Art Spiegelman and Francoise Mouly, carried comic book art into new extremes of experimentation and innovation with work by European and American artists. With #158, Frank Miller began to write and draw Marvel's **Daredevil** and brought a vigorous style of violent action to comic book pages.

1982: The first slick format comic book in regular size appeared, **Marvel Fanfare** #1, with a March date. Fantagraphics Books began publication in July of **Love and Rockets** by Mario, Gilbert, and Jaime Hernandez and brought a new ethnic sensibility and sophistication in style and content to comic book narratives for adults.

1983: More comic book publishers, aside from Marvel and DC, issued more titles than had existed in the past 40 years, most small independent publishers relying on direct sales, such as Americomics, Capital, Eagle, Eclipse, First, Pacific, and Red Circle, and with Archie, Charlton, and Whitman publishing on a limited scale. Frank Miller's mini-series **Ronin** demonstrated a striking use of sword play and martial arts typical of Japanese comic book art, and Howard Chaykin's stylish but controversial **American Flagg** appeared with an October date on its first issue.

1984: A publishing, media, film, and merchandising phenomenon began with the first issue of **Teenage Mutant Ninja Turtles** from Mirage Studios by Kevin Eastman and Peter Laird.

1985: Ohio State University's Library of Communication and Graphic Arts hosted the first major exhibition devoted to the comic book May 19 through August 2. In what was billed as an irreversible decision, the Silver Age superheroine Supergirl was killed in the seventh (October) issue of **Crisis on Infinite Earths**, a limited series intended to reorganize and simplify the DC universe on the occasion of their 50th anniversary.

1986: In recognition of its twenty-fifth anniversary, Marvel began publishing several new ongoing titles comprising Marvel's "New Universe", a self-contained fictional world. DC attracted extensive publicity and media coverage with its revisions of the character of **Superman** by John Byrne and of **Batman** in the **Dark Knight** series by Frank Miller. **Watchmen**, a limited-series graphic novel by Alan Moore and artist Dave Gibbons, began publication with a September issue from DC and Marvel's **The `Nam**, written by Vietnam veteran Doug Murray and penciled by Michael Golden, began with its December issue. DC issued guidelines in December for labelling their titles either for mature readers or for readers of all ages; in response, many artists and writers publicly objected or threatened to resign.

1987: Art Spiegelman's **Maus: A Survivor's Tale** was nominated for the National Book Critics Circle Award in biography, the first comic book to be so honored. A celebration of Superman's fiftieth Birthday began with the opening of an exhibition on his history at the Smithsonian's Museum of American History in Washington, D.C., in June and a symposium on "The Superhero in America" in October.

1988: Superman's birthday celebration continued with a public party in New York and a CBS television special in February, a cover story in **Time Magazine** in March (the first comic book character to appear on the cover), and an international exposition in Cleveland in June. With issue number 601 for May 24, **Action Comics** became the first modern weekly comic book, which ceased publication after 42 issues with the December 13 issue. In August, DC initiated a new policy of allowing creators of new characters to retain ownership of them rather than rely solely on work-for-hire.

1989: The fiftieth anniversary of Batman was marked by the release of the film **Batman**, starring Michael Keaton as Bruce Wayne and Jack Nicholson as the Joker; it grossed more money in its opening weekend than any other motion picture in film history to that time.

1990: The publication of a new **Classics Illustrated** series began in January from Berkley/First with adaptations of Poe's **The Raven and Other Poems** by Gahan Wilson, Dickens' **Great Expectations** by Rick Geary, Carroll's **Through the Looking Glass** by Kyle Baker, and Melville's **Moby Dick** by Bill Sienkiewicz, with extensive media attention. The adaptation of characters to film continued with the most successful in terms of popularity and box office receipts being **Teenage Mutant Ninja Turtles** and Warren Beatty's **Dick Tracy**. In November, the engagement of Clark Kent and Lois Lane was announced in **Superman** #50 which brought public fanfare about the planned marriage.

1991: One of the first modern comic books to appear in the former Soviet Union was a Russian version of **Mickey Mouse** published in Moscow on May 16 in a printing of 200,000 copies which were sold out within hours. The first issue of **Bone**, written, drawn, and published by Jeff Smith, appeared with a July cover date. Issue number one of a new series of Marvel's **X-Men**, with story and art by Chris Claremont and Jim Lee, was published in October in five different editions with a print run of eight million copies, the highest number in the history of the comic book. On December 18, Sotheby's of New York held its first auction of comic book material.

1992: In April, Image Comics debuted with **Youngblood** #1, changing the comic book industry by widening the playing field and legitimizing independent comics. Image Comics began publication of the first Todd McFarlane Productions title, **Spawn**, with a May cover date. The opening weekend for **Batman Returns** in June was the biggest in film box office history, bringing in over 46 million dollars, exceeding the record set by **Batman** in 1989, and not to be topped until the release of **Jurassic Park** a year later. At the second Sotheby auction in September, **Action Comics** #1 brought $82,500, a world record for a single comic book sold at auction. In November the death of Superman generated considerable media attention, with **Superman** #75 selling in excess of 4 million copies, the second best-selling issue in comic book history. A record number of over one hundred publishers of comic books and graphic albums issued titles this year.

1993: In April, for the first time since 1987, DC Comics surpassed Marvel in sales, primarily because of interest in the titles devoted to the return of Superman.

1994: Overproduction, changes in marketing practices, and publisher mergers and collapses triggered an apparent crisis in comic book publishing–which some have read as a sign of its influence and presence in American commerce and culture.

1995: **Batman Forever**, released in June with Val Kilmer in the lead role, grossed in its opening weekend over $53 million, the largest return in film box office history, exceeding the similar records set by the first two Batman films in 1989 and 1992. Writer Neil Gaiman decided after seven years to retire his popular and literate version of **Sandman**, the second revival of a Golden Age DC superhero first created in 1939.

1996: The longest-running give-away title ended after #467 of **The Adventures of the Big Boy** in September. In a long anticipated event coordinated between several comic book titles, the ABC television series **Lois & Clark: The New Adventures of Superman**, and the publication of **Superman: The Wedding Album**, Lois Lane and Clark Kent were married in October.

1997: Several Marvel Universe titles (**Fantastic Four, Avengers, Captain America, Iron Man**) ended their long runs and started over with new #1 issues under the umbrella title **Heroes Reborn**, a separate universe under the creative direction of Rob Liefeld and Jim Lee. They later returned, again with new #1s, in the **Heroes Return** crossover. Superman went through a startling metamorphosis at DC, complete with new powers and a new costume, eventually splitting into two beings, Superman Red & Superman Blue. The latest Batman film, **Batman & Robin**, was released to a tepid response, while the movie adaptation of Todd McFarlane's **Spawn** movie was moderately well received.

1998: Marvel continued to relaunch their popular titles, and Spider-Man was the focus. His titles were restarted with #1 issues, and John Byrne updated his origins with the start of the **Spider-Man: Chapter One** mini-series. Movie director Kevin Smith took over the reigns of **Daredevil**, and other titles were restarted under the **Marvel Knights** banner. DC bought Jim Lee's WildStorm properties, bringing into the fold popular titles like **Gen13, WildCATS**, and the highly successful new **Cliffhanger** titles **Battle Chasers, Danger Girl** and **Crimson**.

NEW COMIC BOOKS

This book lists all new comic books at cover price, regardless of their performance in the secondary market. In many cases, new comics are not worth their cover price in the secondary market, and collectors may pay pennies on the dollar for copies of these issues. Nevertheless, since these comics have yet to establish themselves as collectors' items, they are listed at full cover price. It should also be noted that regarding polybagged comics, it is the official policy of **The Overstreet Comic Book Price Guide** to grade comics regardless of whether they are still sealed in their polybag or not. If opened, the polybag and its contents should be preserved separately so that all components of the original package remain together.

FOREIGN COMIC BOOKS

One interesting and relatively inexpensive source of early vintage comics is the foreign market. Many American newspaper and magazine strips are reprinted abroad (in English and in other languages) months and even years after they appear in the States. By arranging trades with foreign collectors, one can obtain substantial runs of American comic book reprints and newspaper strips dating back years. These reprints are often in black and white, and sometimes the reproduction is poor. Once interest in foreign-published comics has been piqued, a collector might become interested in original strips from these countries.

COMIC BOOK FANDOM

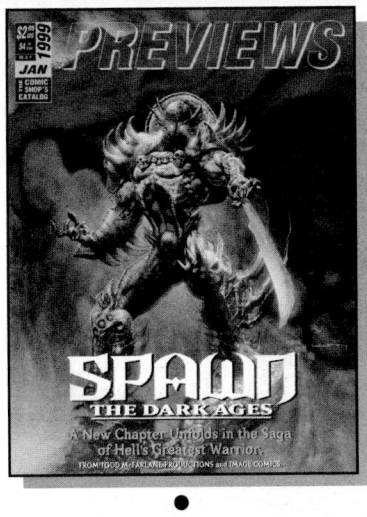

It's possible to discern two distinct and largely unrelated movements in the history of Comics Fandom. The first began around 1953 as a response to the the trend-

setting EC lines of comics. The first true comics fanzines of this movement were short-lived. Bob Stewart's **EC FAN BULLETIN** was a hectographed newsletter that ran two issues about six months apart; Jimmy Taurasi's **FANTASY COMICS**, a newsletter devoted to all science-fiction comics of the period, was a monthly that ran for about six months. These were followed by other newsletters such as Mike May's **EC FAN JOURNAL**, and George Jennings' **EC WORLD PRESS**. EC fanzines of a wider and more critical scope appeared somewhat later. Two of the finest were **POTRZEBIE**, from a number of fans, and Ron Parker's **HOOHAH**. Gauging from the response that **POTRZEBIE** received from an EC letter column plug, Ted White estimated the average age of EC fans at 9 to 13, while many were actually in their midteens. This was discouraging to many fanzine editors hoping to reach an older audience. Consequently, many gave up their efforts on behalf of Comics Fandom, especially with the demise of the EC groups, and turned to SF (science fiction) fandom with its longer tradition and older membership. While the flourish of fan activity in response to the EC comics was certainly noteworthy, it never developed into a full-fledged, independent, and self-sustaining movement.

The second movement began in 1960, largely as a response to (and later stimulus for) the reappearance of the costumed hero and the Second Heroic Age of Comics. Most historians date the Second Heroic Age from **Flash** #105, February 1959. The letter departments of Julius Schwartz (editor at National Periodicals), and later those of Stan Lee (Marvel Group) and Bill Harris (Gold Key) were influential in bringing comics readers into Fandom. Sparks were lit among SF fans first, when experienced fan writers, who were part of an established tradition, produced the first in a series of articles on '40s comics–ALL IN COLOR FOR A DIME. The series was introduced in **XERO** #1 (September 1960), a general SF fanzine edited and published by Dick Lupoff.

Meanwhile, outside SF fandom, Jerry Bails and Roy Thomas, two comics fans of long-standing, conceived the first true comics fanzine in response to the Second Heroic Age, **ALTER EGO**, appearing in March 1961. The first issues were widely circulated, and profoundly influenced the comics fan movement, attracting many fans in their twenties and thirties, unlike the earlier EC fan following. Many of these older fans had been collectors for years but were largely unknown to each other. Joined by scores of new, younger fans, this group formed the nucleus of a self-sustaining and still growing movement. Although it has borrowed a few appropriate SF terms, Comics Fandom of the '60s was an independent movement without the advantages and disadvantages of a longer tradition. What Comics Fandom did derive from SF fans was largely thanks to fanzines produced by so-called double fans, the most notable being **COMIC ART**, edited and published by Don and Maggie Thompson.

The **ROCKET'S BLAST COMIC COLLECTOR** by G.B. Love was the first sucessful adzine in the early 1960s and was instrumental in the development of the comics market. G.B. remembers beginning his fanzine **THE ROCKET'S BLAST** in late 1961. Only six copies of the first 4 page issue were printed. Soon after Mr. Love had a letter published in **MYSTERY IN SPACE**, telling all about his new fanzine. His circulation began to grow. Buddy Saunders, a well known comic book store owner, designed the first **ROCKET'S BLAST** logo and was an artist on the publication for many years thereafter. With issue #29 he took over **THE COMICOLLECTOR** fanzine from Biljo White and combined it with **ROCKET'S BLAST** to form the **RBCC**. He remembers that the **RBCC** hit its highest circulation of 2,500 around 1971. Many people who wrote, drew or otherwise contributed to the **RBCC** went on to become well known writers, artists, dealers and store-owners in the comics field.

COMIC-RELATED COLLECTIBLES

COLLECTING STRIPS

Collecting newspaper comic strips is somewhat different than collecting comic books, although it can be equally satisfying. Most strip collectors begin by clipping strips from their local paper, but soon branch out to out-of-town papers. Naturally this can become more expensive and more frustrating, as it is easy to miss out-of-town editions. Consequently, most strip collectors work out trade agreements with collectors in other cities. This usually means saving local strips for trade only.

Back issues of some newspaper comic strips are also occasionally available from dealers. Prices vary greatly depending on age, condition, and demand.

COLLECTING ORIGINAL ART

Some enthusiasts collect original comic book and strip art. These mostly black and white, inked drawings are usually done on illustration paper at about 30 percent larger than the original printed panels. Because original art is a one-of-a-kind article, it is highly prized and can be difficult to obtain.

Interest in original comic art has increased tremendously in the past few years because more current art is available now that companies return originals to the artists, who then either sell the work themselves at cons, or through agents and dealers. The best way to find the piece you want is to scour cons and get on as many art dealers' mailing lists as possible. Although the masters' works from the Golden and Silver Ages bring fine art prices, most current work is available at moderate prices, with something for everyone at various costs, from Kirby to McFarlane, Ditko to Bachalo.

COLLECTING COMIC-RELATED MERCHANDISE

In the past ten years or so, interest in collecting comic-related merchandise has soared. Comic book and toy shows are often dominated by toys and related products.

Action figures and limited edition statues based on comic characters are currently the most popular. Highly successful toy action figure lines based on Batman, Spawn, Spider-Man, and many others cram toy store shelves. Statues and figurines, either painted or in kit form, are very popular higher-end collectibles. Statues of characters like Witchblade, Sandman, Shi, and many more draw collector attention through print, web, and convention advertising.

Numerous other tie-in products based on comic characters are released every year and seem to represent a large percentage of the collectible market today. Books like **Hake's Price Guide to Character Toys**, and periodicals like **Collecting Figures** and **Toyfare** track the collectibility of these items.

Collector's Item!

CBM is your gateway to the nostalgic past and the exciting world of popular collectibles! Get the inside story on the rarest, the highest-demand and the most undervalued **Golden Age, Silver Age** and **Bronze Age** collectibles.

Comic Book Marketplace... the magazine for advanced collectors!

A GEMSTONE PUBLICATION

Available at your local comic shop!

Comic Book Marketplace • PO Box 180700 • Coronado • CA • 92178 • **(619) 437-1996**

Avenues of Collecting: A Walk Through the Comic Book Neighborhood

by J.C. Vaughn

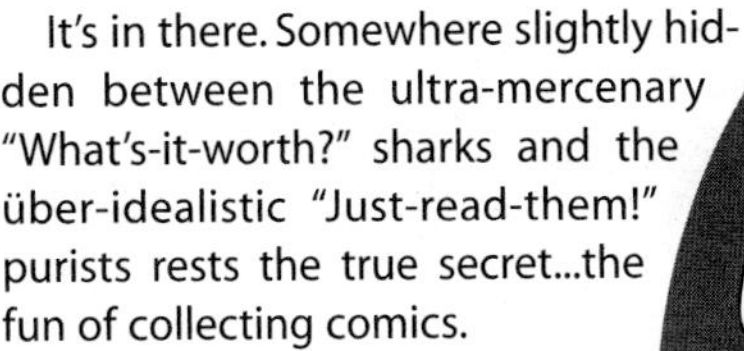

It's in there. Somewhere slightly hidden between the ultra-mercenary "What's-it-worth?" sharks and the über-idealistic "Just-read-them!" purists rests the true secret...the fun of collecting comics.

Comics, like any other type of collectible, are deeply personal to the true collector. They are best enjoyed when collected neither purely for monetary value nor strictly for entertainment. What interests you about your favorite title might be of little interest to some other collector, but so what? We're talking about what interests you, right?

If you're one of the top collectors in the business, you might take great pride in your copies of **Action Comics** #1 or **Detective Comics** #27. If you're new to the hobby, you might be just as enthusiastic about your copies of **Spawn** #1 or **Danger Girl** #1. If you started collecting in the '70s or '80s, maybe its **Cerebus** or **Love & Rockets** that gets you going.

You can like one book for its artistic merits and a different book for its financial value, or treasure the rare gems known for both. You can take pleasure from being the biggest collector of the best-known character in the hobby (**Superman**) or knowing more about questions. For instance, if you'll flip to the pricing section, you'll get the idea that neither of the two **Nathaniel Dusk** mini-series from DC Comics (1984, 1986) are worth a whole lot. What they're worth to me, though, is entirely different. They were my reintroduction to the work of Don McGregor and Gene Colan, and they serve as continual sources of good memories. My attachment to the title has only been furthered since I became friends with McGregor in the time I've worked here with Bob Overstreet. Sure, I'd sell you a set at double or triple guide, but only because I've got several others. That's because it has a specific worth to me beyond, oh, all reason.

My admiration for this character and his creative team not-withstanding, it shouldn't cost you very much to pick up a set. Again, it's supply and demand. There are a lot fewer copies of **Action Comics** #1, and it is by any reasonable standard one of the most important comics in history. The odds are very much against **Dusk** ever getting there.

But what makes collecting fun? Escapism? Adventure? Understanding? Fantasy? Have you ever thought about why you collect comics? If you haven't, don't worry. Most folks haven't really thought about why it's fun either. Thinking about it almost takes the fun out of it.

For just a few more minutes of your time, though, indulge the thought. What makes collecting fun? For some it's the escape offered by stories of heroes "with powers and abilities far beyond those of mortal men," but for others it's pure nostalgia.

We put the question to the visitors on the Gemstone Publishing website (**www.gemstonepub.com**): Why do you collect? The answers were insightful, but not all that surprising:

"Comic books have been responsible for igniting my imagination, widening my perspective, and showing me new ways to present a narrative," Jeffrey Schultz of Timonium, Maryland told the Gemstone website. "As an attorney, I am often faced with the job of relating the story of my client to a neutral party, so I must draw from the various elements highlighted in any good comic narrative: a story that the listener can relate to, understand and become interested in following. Collecting comic books allows me to appreciate the work of older artists and writers as a new reader, as well as gaining a better sense of the depth of history and development that has lead to the comic books that we read today."

Bill Stem, who has worked periodically in comic book retail, described comics as "a visual art form that can be picked up and enjoyed, not just for its intrinsic value, but also for its substance and content." He said it was nostalgia that got him back into comics, but now that he's back, there's a healthy measure of "just plain entertainment" thrown in.

C.J. Duggins of Monroe, Louisiana said "to follow a favorite artist, writer, or story," while Jonathan Keim of Pittsburgh, PA wrote, "...because when you cut through all the filler, these wonderful four-color comics are all about blacks and whites—good vs. evil, justice will prevail, the impact that one dedicated soul can make."

As collectors, we've all got something in common, but there are probably as many individual reasons to collect as there are collectors. Aside from the obvious advice ("collect what you like, not what someone tells you to like"), there are several methods you can use to make collecting fun.

COLLECTING BY THE NUMBERS

Comic books are unique. The broad catch-all term "comic character collectibles" includes roughly any item you can think of which features the likeness of a character or characters on it. Whether you're talking about action figures, movie posters, autographed photos, model kits, cereal boxes, or pin-backs, whether they be store-bought, giveaway or premium, other toys can feature intriguing visuals, exciting action or be just plain cool, but they don't identify themselves like comic books. The mind recognizes it right away: on comics, the issue number stands out—it's clearly printed on the cover. In magazines, one generally has to look in the indicia (if it's anywhere) to find a number.

It's simple, sure, but you know immediately if something has come before the issue in your hands. The numbering provides a natural collectibility. It offers an immediate reference point as to what you have and what you don't have.

COLLECTING BY CHARACTER

Captain America is the greatest character ever. And so is Cerebus. And Batman. And Devil Dinosaur. And the Master of Kung-fu, Aquaman, Casper, Katchoo and every other character who has graced the pages of a comic book. Each of them is the greatest to someone.

Collecting by character offers another fun way to collect, and it expands your collection in ways you might not imagine. If you're interested in, say, Spider-Man, then you've got to start with **Amazing Fantasy** #15 and then go on through **The Amazing Spider-Man**, but how could you stop there? There's so much more! Such past and present regular titles such as **Marvel Team-Up**, **Marvel Tales**, **Peter Parker**, **Spider-Man**, and **Web of Spider-Man** offer you more of the same excitement.

What about those great old **Marvel Treasury Editions** from the 1970s? What about the crossovers? Following Spider-Man would take you through almost every title in the Marvel Universe, from **Howard the Duck** to **Doctor Strange**, and then into other universes with such team-ups as **Spider-Man/Gen13**, **Spider-Man/Badrock** and **Superman Vs. The Amazing Spider-Man**.

This doesn't mean you have to get them all to collect Spider-Man, just that *you can if you want to*.

COLLECTING BY COMPANY

It used to be a reasonable statement to say "I collect Marvels" or "I collect DC titles." The major publishers now produce so many titles each month that it's no longer practical to try to keep up with all of them. Many fans have stepped away from collecting by company in favor of collecting by character or groups of characters (a large section of fandom, for instance, collects Marvel's **X-Men** class of titles, or DC's **Superman** group).

Collecting by company is far from impossible, though—in fact, it might be easier than ever. There are many small or medium-size publishers that offer a limited number of titles each month. There are also many publishers which are no longer in business and who only put out a relatively small number of books in total. In addition, several of the larger publishers now have sub-imprints.

Of the current publishers, Event Comics, Harris, Awesome and several others release an output well within the affordable range for most collectors. Of those publishers who have passed on from this plane of existence, Pacific Comics, First Comics, Eclipse, Comico, ACG, Tower, Defiant, Topps and a number of others represent a chance to acquire the entire output of a company for relatively small amounts of money.

DC's imprints, like Vertigo, Paradox Press, WildStorm, Cliffhanger, and America's Best Comics, offer comics from specific genres, styles or creators. While one might be hard-pressed to collect every DC title released in a month, most of the sub-imprints offer opportunities well within normal budgetary constraints. Other publishers continue to experiment with sub-imprints to varying degrees of success.

COLLECTING BY CREATOR

Collecting by creator means you follow the works of a particular creator instead of (or in addition to) collecting particular titles. For instance, you might collect covers by the great Golden Age cover artist Alex Schomburg or modern age painter Alex Ross. You might spotlight writer Mark Waid's work on **Flash** or **Captain America**, but not collect those titles otherwise. Just like any other method of collecting, it is a personal expression of what interests you—of what you like.

The best part of collecting by creator is that we have the most accessible creators of just about any creative enterprise one can think of. It's difficult for the average collector to meet the producers, directors, stars and technicians who make the most popular films or the recording artists with the biggest hit songs, but there isn't a similar problem meeting comic book creators. In fact, conventions are packed with them!

In the last few years it has not been at all odd to run into such legendary veterans as Stan Lee (Mr. Marvel Comics), Julie Schwartz (Mr. DC Comics), Will Eisner, (creator of **The Spirit**), Al Williamson (EC vet known to today's fans for **Daredevil**), Murphy Anderson (classic **JLA** and so much more) and many others.

These seasoned professionals could be seen signing autographs, chatting with fans, and exchanging trade talk with the hot stars of today's comics, like the aforementioned Alex Ross (who did this year's **Comic Book Price Guide** covers for us, among many other things), writer-artist Evan Dorkin (**Milk & Cheese**, **Space Ghost Coast to Coast**), or writer Jeph Loeb (**Superman For All Seasons**).

The accessibility of these creators and the ability to interact with them one-on-one or in a small group setting is unmatched. It makes collecting by creator one of the most dynamic ways to collect.

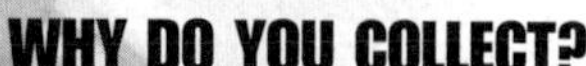

WHY DO YOU COLLECT?

There are probably as many reasons to collect as there are collectors, but underneath all of it should be a sense of fun. That doesn't mean it's not aggravating or frustrating at times, but it really should be something you enjoy.

So when next you scoff at the money-hungry hombre trying to sell you "the next big thing," or you're talking to the prig who refuses to take care of even his most cherished comics, smile. You know why you're doing this.

JUST ANOTHER JUSTICE LEAGUE?

EARTH'S MIGHTIEST HEROES DON'T THINK SO!!!

by J. C. Vaughn

Over the course of the past 36 years, their ranks have included Iron Man, Thor, Hulk, Giant Man, the Wasp, Captain America, Hawkeye, the Vision, and many others. They've saved the world from cer-

tain doom about as often as you've had lunch, and they've been tagged as everything from "Earth's Mightiest Heroes" to a rip-off of DC's Justice League of America.

The list of creators who worked on the title is as long as the team's membership roster. Stan Lee, Jack Kirby, Don Heck, Roy Thomas, John Buscema, Neal Adams, Tom Palmer, Steve Englehart, Jim Shooter, Roger Stern, and George Perez are among the many creators who have constructed the tales.

But were they just following the trail blazed by Superman and company, or were they putting their own unique footprints in the cement of comic book history?

The first & last issues of the Avengers' original run.

Created, or more precisely assembled, by Stan Lee and Jack Kirby in 1963, **The Avengers** latched onto the super-team concept that had recently been made popular again by DC's **Justice League of America**. (The JLA in turn owed their existence to the memory of the Golden Age Justice Society of America which appeared in **All-Star Comics**.)

The JLA had debuted in the pages of **Brave and the Bold** and quickly rocketed into its own title by bringing together DC's powerhouse characters: Flash, Green Lantern, Wonder Woman, Superman, Batman, and Aquaman. Each month they teamed up to defeat foes so powerful that none of the heroes could beat them individually. Their membership changed (mainstays like Martian Manhunter, Green Arrow and Black Canary joined), but that was the consistent formula for most of the next three decades.

"[Current **Avengers** writer] Kurt Busiek said comparing the Justice League and the Avengers is akin to comparing an All-Star team to a World Series team," said Tom Brevoort, Marvel's editor for the

FACE FRONT, AVENGERS!

THE BATTLE'S ABOUT TO BEGIN!

re-launch of **The Avengers** following the "Heroes Return" storyline in 1997. "A lot of people tend to think of them as the same thing, but that's really too simplistic."

While Lee and Kirby initially struck back at DC's JLA success with their own creation, **The Fantastic Four**, a team of brand new characters created specifically for the new comic, **The Avengers** followed the Justice League pattern of bringing together existing characters to form a team.

Justice League of America was definitely a hit, and there's no getting away from the fact that the Avengers were constituted from Marvel's existing base of heroes, but it's difficult to see Ant Man and the Wasp on par with Batman and Wonder Woman. Even the Hulk lasted only six issues in his original series. Though they're often tagged as copycats by JLA fans, the Avengers were different from the start.

Among other things, in **The Avengers** #1 (Volume I), Iron Man, Ant Man, Wasp, Thor and the Hulk came together to beat Loki, who Thor had taken care of several times by himself. Hardly a foe too powerful for one of them, obviously. Then, an issue later, Hulk quit.

By the third issue, Hulk had teamed up with the Sub-Mariner, a gray figure at best in those days, and fought the Avengers. It's impossible to imagine one of the JLA members doing that unless he or she was controlled by some alien or evil (or both) power. And if the first three issues were about changing the status quo of the nascent Marvel Universe, the fourth was about establishing a new one.

The Avengers #4 (under Kirby's energetic cover, one of two pieces re-created by Alex Ross as

the cover of this price guide) featured the return of *the* Captain America (like Sub-Mariner—a hold-over character from the Timely days), Marvel's Golden Age predecessor. He joined the team and in a short number of issues became the team's leader; the core of the Avengers, as most of fandom knows them, was formed.

It wasn't just the action in the comic itself that was different than its counterpart over at DC. The frame of reference for the reader was different, too.

"In the **Justice League of America**, the individual characters' titles were still clearly in their own little pocket universes," said former **Avengers** writer and former Marvel Editor-in-Chief Jim Shooter.

"They didn't interact very much. In **Green Lantern**, we were expected to worry about invading aliens, but we would really be thinking 'Why doesn't he call Superman?' or something similar. Yet when those characters were together as a team, they were portrayed as if they addressed every issue as a team," he said.

"With **The Avengers**, Stan took pains to keep things in continuity, but it was also dynamic and changing. The membership kept evolving. It had all of the things that were unique and revolutionary to Marvel back then going for it including better dialogue and more exciting stories. The **Justice League** stories in those days followed a very basic formula. Every story was basically constructed the same way.

The team would break up into small groups or act as individuals, they would be defeated, then they would get together as a team and then they would succeed. In **The Avengers**, you never knew what would happen."

If the Hulk, a founding member, becoming a hunted foe by the third issue wasn't proof enough of that, consider the career of Hank Pym, another of the team's founders. A scientist by trade, he became Ant Man. Ant Man became Giant Man, then became Goliath, then had a break down and became Yellow Jacket. He married Janet Van Dyne (The Wasp), got better, and then became Yellow Jacket, again. Then he had another breakdown. Then he got kicked off the team, and divorced. Then he got better. And along the way one of his many creations, the robot Ultron, became one of the team's most enduring and deadly foes. And now he's back.

Sound like a soap opera? In many ways it has been.

As the roster changed over the years, not all of the players involved were stars of their own titles. Characters like Scarlet Witch, Vision, Hawkeye, Falcon, Ms. Marvel, and others had **The Avengers** as their home comic

GREAT MILESTONES IN AVENGERS HISTORY

The Avengers

(Volume I, original series)

#1-8	Stan Lee & Jack Kirby
#1	Origin
#2	Hulk leaves
#3	First Sub-Mariner outside **Fantastic Four**
#4	Return of Captain America
#6	Intro—Masters of Evil
#9	Intro/death—Wonder Man
#16	Captain America, Scarlet Witch, Quicksilver, Hawkeye begin
#28	Giant Man becomes Goliath
#58	Origin of The Vision
#59	Intro—Yellowjacket
#60	Hank Pym and Janet Van Dyne marry
#87	Origin of Black Panther
#63	Goliath becomes Yellowjacket, Hawkeye becomes Goliath
#98	Goliath becomes Hawkeye
#144	Intro—Hellcat
#151	Wonder Man returns
#195	Intro—Taskmaster
#402	Last issue of original series

Avengers Annuals

#7	Warlock dies
#10	Intro—Rogue

THE AVENGERS IN PRINT

Avengers, The
Volume I
#1 (September 1963) – 402 (September 1996)

Avengers, The
Volume II
#1 (November 1996) – 13 (November 1997)

Avengers, The
Volume III
#1 (January 1998) – ongoing

WEST COAST AVENGERS

Volume I (mini-series)
#1 (September 1984) – 4 (December 1984)

West Coast Avengers
Volume II
#1 (October 1985) - #47 (August 1989)

Avengers West Coast
#48 (September 1989) - #102 (January 1994)

AVENGERS WEST COAST

(#1-47 **West Cost Avengers** and mini-series #1-4)

#1	mini-series intro of new team
#50 -	Re-intro—original Human Torch

SOLO AVENGERS

#1 (December 1987) – #20 (July 1989)

Avengers Spotlight
#21 (August 1989) – #40 (January 1991)

book. Their character development and back stories have been more likely to be revealed within the pages of **The Avengers**, while characters like Captain America, Thor and Iron Man were portrayed with more emphasis on action since they had their own comics and places to further explore their characters.

"Because the book was packed with so many important characters, Stan was forced to distill the characters and their action to the most essential elements," Shooter said.

"In The **Amazing Spider-Man**, for instance, you could have two pages of Peter Parker talking to Aunt May. In fact, that's part of what gave early Marvel its distinct flavor. I was working at DC at the time and the editors there would laugh and say kids wouldn't want to read that. Of course I was a kid at the time and I definitely wanted to read it. That said, there was a great value in the ability of a single line to crystallize a character for all time. In **The Avengers** #4, Captain America has a few lines which absolutely defined him for me," he said.

As much as the changing fortunes of characters within the stories, numerous writers and editors over the series' 36 years have struggled with the balance between "the big five" heroes (the founders plus Captain America minus the Hulk) and other heroes on the roster. In fact, even the roster changes themselves have become integral parts of the Avengers mythos.

"A lot of great Avengers stories have come about because of the interaction of the personalities, not because we've got the five most powerful Marvel characters together," Brevoort said. "You can look back to the 'Cap's Kooky Quartet' era [beginning in **Avengers** #16] with Captain America, Scarlet Witch, Quicksilver and Hawkeye. If you go back and read the letters columns in **Avengers #17-22**, the readers' opinions were definitely mixed. We had Captain America and three much lesser-known characters, but that's considered one of the best periods of the team now."

Through the many epochs of their history, the Avengers have often been considered the core of the Marvel Universe. In showing that an incident which occurred in **Iron Man** had effects in **The Avengers** and elsewhere, Stan Lee peppered the team with the same magic he was using elsewhere in the Marvel Universe. In doing so, he laid the groundwork for the creators who followed him, expanded on what he did, and even added their own concoctions to the mix. What no doubt began as a response to the success DC enjoyed with the JLA quickly took on a life of its own.

"I pity the guy who tries to beat us," the Hulk said at the end of **The Avengers** #1. The same still holds true.

ONE-SHOTS, MINI-SERIES & SPECIALS

Avengers Log, The
#1 (Feb 1994)

Avengers Strikefile
#1 (January 1994)

Avengers: The Crossing
#1 (July 1995)

Avengers: The Legend
#1 (October 1996)

Avengers: The Terminatrix Objective
#1 (September 1993) – 4 (December 1993)

Avengers: Timeslide
#1 (February 1996)

Avengers/Ultraforce
#1 (October 1995)

Avengers Unplugged
#1 (October 1995) – 6 (August 1996)

Marvel Graphic Novel #27
"Emperor Doom"

Ultraforce/Avengers
#1 (August 1995)

X-Men vs. The Avengers
#1 (April 1987) – 4 (July 1987)

REPRINTS

Kree/Skrull War Starring The Avengers, The Marvel Super Action Marvel Treasury Edition, Marvel Triple Action

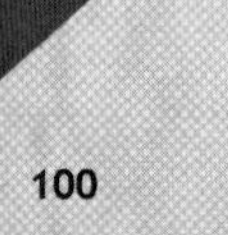

LEGIONDARY ADVENTURES

IF I COULD CROSS TIME IN A BUBBLE . . .

BY MARK HUESMAN

When you're 10 years old, and imagining yourself battling evil and saving the universe countless times, it can be a lonely task. It'd be more fun to have other kids, like yourself, sharing these adventures. You and your friends could form a club, adopt codenames, build a clubhouse, and defeat the forces of oppression while still having a good time. For 40 years, ten-year-olds of all ages have joined in the fun, following the futuristic adventures of the Legion of Super-Heroes.

The Legion was conceived as a 30th century super-hero club of teens from different planets, each with unique powers and abilities utilized to protect the universe from galactic evil or cosmic threats. Although many of their challenges were quite formidable, they were also fun reading. Battling a malevolent wizard, or trying to get a date with the new recruit, each challenge made a lasting impression with the countless, very devoted, fans of the Legion's lore.

The Legion members' cooperation and camaraderie was meant to serve as an example of how different people, or aliens from many worlds, could coexist in the 30th century in peace and friendship. The readers have also felt like members of this big family. No other title in comics has thrived for so long on the loyalty and devotion of its fans. The Legion may not have reached the widespread notoriety of other hero teams like the X-Men or the Justice League, but being the first Super-team of the Silver Age, and their 40 years of exciting adventures and teen drama, secures their special place in the history of comics.

It was Superboy who first introduced us to these super-hero clubmates, as the Legion's initial appearance was intended as a one-time guest-shot used simply to tell a good story. Longtime Superman editor Mort Weisinger and writer Otto Binder created this tale for the pages of **Adventure Comics** #247 (April 1958), a story not too different from the other offerings of those days: science fiction, time travel, flying belts, visitors from other worlds. The three teens from the 30th century visit Superboy to initiate him into their club–a Super Hero Club. The roster started with just 3 members: the telepathic Saturn Girl, Cosmic Boy, who had the power to control magnetism, and Lightning Boy, who could clap his hands together to produce lightning bolts.

Superboy was challenged to a contest against each of the three Legion heroes to earn his membership. Unbeknownst to Superboy, the Legion members had set up some distractions to sabotage his efforts, but Superboy's good sportsmanship in the face of the embarrassing failures and their subsequent "taunting" won him his membership.

The fans responded very favorably, so edi

Being one of the 3 founders has its perks, especially the of the Legion's first appear

COSMIC BOY

Rokk Krinn from the planet Braal, where all the inhabitants have magnetic powers. Level-headed, he was the obvious choice to be the Legion's first leader.

tor Weisinger and his staff brought the team back for more appearances in **Adventure Comics** and the various Superman titles also under Weisinger's reins. In those early days, the Legion benefitted from those close ties to the entire Super-family as Supergirl, Jimmy Olsen, which grew to around 20 members. New recruits, whose powers were easy to guess with names like Phantom Girl, Sun Boy, Shrinking Violet, Invisible Kid, Triplicate Girl, and the shape-shifting Chameleon Boy, gave the Legion a richer blend of characters to tell more interesting stories.

of the Legion of Super-Heroes one that gets you on the cover ance.

Lana Lang, and Pete Ross all became honorary members in one way or another. The continuing favorable response earned the Legion their first regular series in the pages of **Adventure Comics**, starting in issue #300.

As the number of stories increased, so did the roster, With so large a group, there was an opportunity for the writers to forge relationships, romances and rivalries in the tradition of the best soap operas. Adventure could take a back seat to human (or alien) interest tales, and it only served to enrich the mythos.

A wise man once said that God and thereby "the Good stuff" lies in the details, and the tapestry of Legion lore is woven with

SATURN GIRL

Imra Ardeen from Titan, one of Saturn's moons. Like all of her race, she could read minds and control the thoughts of others. She and Lightning Lad had been romantically linked, and they eventually married.

LIGHTNING LAD

(Lightning Boy)
(Live Wire)

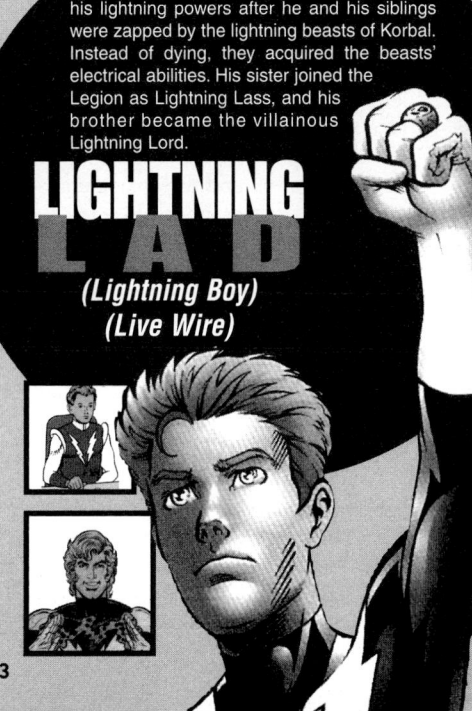

Garth Ranzz from the planet Winath gained his lightning powers after he and his siblings were zapped by the lightning beasts of Korbal. Instead of dying, they acquired the beasts' electrical abilities. His sister joined the Legion as Lightning Lass, and his brother became the villainous Lightning Lord.

both grand stories and the minutiae of alien and future facts. Each Legion character came with his or her own real name and home planet (usually with very complicated spellings), costume details, romantic interests and other data to be committed to memory and instantaneously accessed to the amazement of the reader's family and friends. The Legion's universe was full of a vast expanding history, and trying to keep track of all the details was addictive.

Despite the futuristic setting, young readers could relate to the adventures of these super-powered kids, especially when one of the writers was still a kid himself. Comics industry veteran Jim Shooter was one of those very young fans when he began his long and influential run scripting their adventures. Shooter remembers, "When I started writing Legion, I was 13 and the characters were 13-ish. No matter how old they were drawn, they behaved in a fairly childish manner. As I went from 13 to 18, the characters grew up as I did. So we all grew up together." One of the benefits of having a teenage writer scripting the adventures of teenagers was the true voice of youth that was not easily presented by the typical veteran writer of those days.

"One of the things I was doing was basing the characters on my friends. I thought I was cheating...because I was ripping off my friends' personalities and using them for Legion characters." The Legion readers could also identify these personalities in themselves and their own friends, so the close-knit feeling of family extended beyond the printed page.

The first clubhouse, the inverted rocket design, always looked MUCH bigger on the inside than it did from the outside.

Legion Flight rings. In 1997, DC finally sold gold-plated replicas, complete with the legalese warning that these rings didn't actually allow the wearer to fly (upwards, at least).

The Legion continued to team up with Superboy in **Adventure Comics** until the early 1970s, when they were all bounced out to make room for Supergirl. Mort Weisinger's retirement at that time meant that the Legion's most stalwart editor was no longer getting them prime exposure, so they subsisted mainly as backup stories in **Action Comics** and **Superboy**. This was the one time when the Legion was on the brink of oblivion. They had started as 13 year olds, but it was now time to grow up.

Artists Dave Cockrum, and later Mike Grell, updated the look of the Legion members, with new, fashionably slicker costumes and the latest 20th century hairstyles. Shaggy hair and sideburns became the rage. In a short span of time, the level of positive fan response for these back-up stories had moved the Legion from near-oblivion to their own title. In 1973 they once again took over the pages of Superboy's own title and it became **Superboy starring the Legion of Super-Heroes.** At this time, the Legion's fan base was becoming more organized, more vocal, and they made a lot of suggestions. For years, the fans were casting votes for a Legion leader, and the results went directly into the stories, as if decreed by the most exalted of editors. Now the fans were feeling more empowered and the editors were listening. More changes were made as some members died, some got new (and usually skimpier) costumes, some got married and left, some new members took their place. Popular heroes and villains from the past returned, and the Legion even got their long-overdue first black Legionnaire in 1976.

As the earlier architects of the Legion mythos moved on, their replacements were pulled from within the ranks of the Legion fandom. Like Jim Shooter before him, Paul Levitz (as long-time a fan as a 17 year old could be) took the scripting reins for a time, followed in later years by Tom and Mary Bierbaum, K.C. Carlson and Mark Waid. Under their direction, the Legion was headed towards a more serious tone. Now a Legion of young adults, their villains got nastier, the crises more terrible, and even the Earth was blown up. But no galactic force could match the destructiveness in the wake of John Byrne's 1986 revision of the Superman mythos.

The whole "John Byrne now says that Superman was never the Superboy who was the member of the Legion as well as its inspiration" tangle caused quite a few headaches for Legion editors and fans alike. A story was concocted that the Legion's longtime foe, the Time Trapper, had used his mastery of reality to secretly create a special dimension, home to the Superboy who joined the Legion (not the youthful version of the current Superman). EVERY time Superboy or the Legion crossed the Time

For a group of guys seemingly too young to grow mustaches, they sure had some full sideburns. DC has not yet announced plans to sell these to fans.

The Time Bubble has been the Legion's favorite method of time travel since their very first story. Never once did it roll over on its door, trapping the occupants inside.

There are certain images, both kitschy and cool, that warm the hearts of Legion fans.

Barrier to visit the other, the Time Trapper diverted them to each other's dimension, and this happened for several decades (even unbeknownst to the writers of the Legion), and he conveniently kept his mouth shut about this secret until 1987.

The current Superman and the old Superboy teamed with the Legion to save Superboy's Time Trapper-created reality after it began to destablize. Superboy died in the process, but his heroism was never forgotten. Much of the Legion's lore was tied to Superboy and events in his 20th century, so without that anchor, the sense of Legion history and tradition became unhinged. Throw in some youthful Legion clones (more of the Time Trapper's handiwork), and with two versions of each Legion member in action, you needed a very detailed map to find your way around the Legion's convoluted continuity.

DC had this and other continuity tangles to resolve in 1994 with its Zero Hour series, and the Legion was greatly affected. Recent storylines of alternate timelines, fractured realities, and other editorial indecisiveness left the Legion's reality at the bursting point, so with one great white *flash*, everything was restarted. The two Legion titles at that time began to chronicle the adventures from the very beginning, as the original members first met and started their Super-Hero club. The lightning shooting member was still Garth Ranzz, but now he was codenamed Live Wire instead of Lightning Lad. The irreplacable elements of Legion lore, like flight rings, Legion leader elections, and the Time Trapper returned. Aside from the absence of Superboy as an active member, most of the core elements of the mythology were retained, but new characters and a lighter tone made the series more accessible to new readers, who didn't have to be familiar with 30-some years of Legion history to enjoy the tales. Longtime readers can see old Legion moments given a polish and a new spin. Some of the past innocent, campy charm may be missing, but the creators are succeeding in bringing timeliness to the series – even though it's set one thousand years in the future.

After many years away from the original vision, the Legion of Super-Heroes is back to the adventures of generally upbeat, super-powered teens in an optimistic future. The mythos is flexible enough to survive for many years to come, even when the science-fiction starts to overlap today's science fact.

In 1998, the Legion made its television debut in an episode of **The New Superman Adventures** animated series. The familiar premise had three Legion members travel back in time to share an adventure with a teenage Clark Kent. Like Mort Weisinger 40 years earlier, the animated series' creators were probably intent on using the Legion just as a one-time guest strictly for the purpose of telling a good story. Perhaps a Legion of vocal fans shouting for more will help history repeat itself.

A BRIEF HISTORY OF SUPER-TEAMS

Arnold T. Blumberg

ALL FOR ONE...

Unlike some aspects of comic book history, the origin of super-teams is well-documented. Beginning with America's involvement in World War II, the super-team became an established mechanism for bringing multiple heroes together in one title to battle a common foe. The device was soon a familiar one for fans, and the super-team became a comic book staple.

The marketing punch is obvious—if the kids liked one hero, they should love a title with six or seven! And if one hero is a strong seller, he can boost sales for the other team members' own titles. From a financial standpoint, team books seemed like a pretty good bet (although these were not the methods used when the concept first took hold).

But there is a more fundamental psychology at work—superhero adventures were written with a youthful viewpoint in mind. Most old comic tales stand up to scrutiny only when seen as reflections of the world as seen through the eyes of a child. In this case, the superhero team was a brilliant concept that played off of several vital elements in most young readers' childhoods.

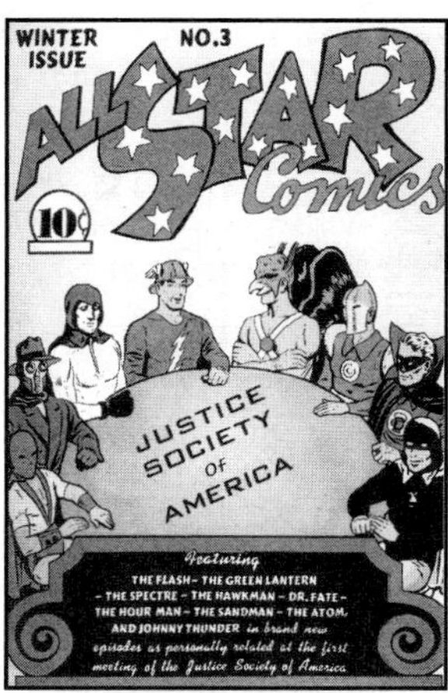

Socializing with your friends was incredibly important, for play and for reinforcing one's self-worth and identity. So it was comforting to see superheroes seeking out each other's company as well. And these super-teams weren't necessarily together for a

TOP 10 GREATEST SUPER-TEAMS

by

Benn Ray

The concept of the super-team, although seemingly a no-brainer, is not easy to deliver. How else would you explain all the teams that have come and gone over the years?

It's not as easy as taking a group of heroes, throwing them together and letting them save the world month after month. Their powers must be complimentary, there must be some sort of interpersonal dynamic between the heroes, and they must learn to function as a team. The creator must decide which characters to give the most panel time to, which character will become the leader, which ones will become romantically involved, who will be buddies, and who will be the mopey, angst-ridden loner who all the fans secretly wish would be killed off? All in all,it's not a very easy task.

The list that follows ranks the greatest teams in the history of comics, as selected by visitors to the Gemstone Website (**www.gemstonepub.com**). "No fair," you say? You don't have internet access? Well, it's time to catch up with the rest of the world. The millennium is almost over, you might want to get yourself one of them fancy computers all the kids are talking about. (And while your at it, 8 of these teams have had new comics out in the last year. Why not pick up something new to read too?)

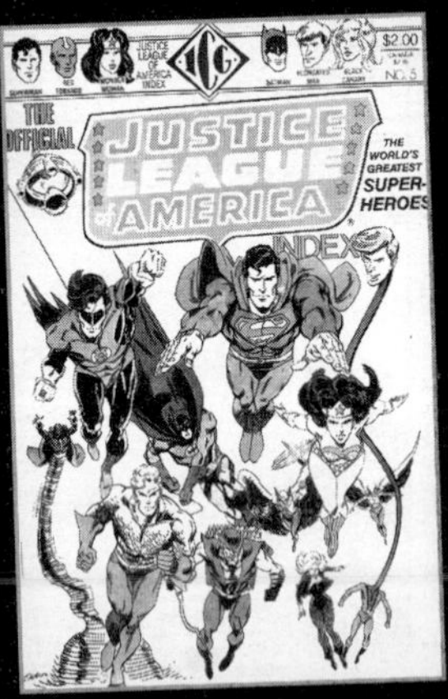

1. JLA

1st Appearance:
Brave and the Bold #28
Date: February 1960
About the team:
The Justice League was created in 1960 by Julius Schwartz. Containing comicdom's most powerful and experienced of heroes, specific mission—as far as young readers were concerned, they got together because it was more fun! The earliest super-teams adopted this "clubhouse" mentality, conducting their meetings with "minutes" and "motions" and even encouraging readers to join them (the many clubs built around super-teams were a valuable marketing tool for publishers while proving that the socializing aspect was the main focus for fans).

There have been dozens, if not hundreds, of super-teams created over the past sixty years by many publishers, so for the sake of brevity (and sanity), we will focus our brief historical survey on the teams published by the two largest comic book companies—DC and Marvel.

PATRIOT GAMES

The first superhero team was the Justice Society of America, founded in **All Star Comics** #3 in 1940-41. As America geared up for the ultimate team effort—WWII— there was also a subtle ramping up of youthful enthusiasm with super-team titles. And the most successful blend of entertainment and propaganda was the JSA, which not only spawned characters and stories that would influence the medium for the next sixty years, but also inspired a marketing bonanza of club-related premiums.

One of the quirks of the JSA was its rule preventing heroes with their own series from appearing in Justice Society adventures. Certainly this was not the norm with the teams that were to follow, most of which were deliberately comprised of the most popular characters from other titles. Originally, it was thought that a team book should bolster the popularity of lesser-known characters, but with the introduction of the JSA's successor, the Justice League of America, this theory was reversed.

By the end of the war, comic book readers had been inundated with wave after wave of superhero team books like the **All-Winners Squad**, **Young Allies**, and many others. But as the war came to a close, public attention slowly returned to matters domestic. Luckily for our champions, whose existence depended upon a foe to fight and a cause around which to rally, a new menace soon inspired additional adventures.

The Communist conspiracy was hard at work by the 1950s, dismantling our institutions and threatening our very existence—or so our own overzealous representatives would have us believe. America was obsessed with stamping out Communism, even if it meant persecuting segments of our own citizenry. Comics reflected this paranoia and supported the cause—they had been targeted as a medium themselves, and playing it safe was definitely the order of the day. Superhero teams that once defended liberty against the "Ratzis" and the "Japs" were now pummeling those ruthless "Reds" back into the dust.

As a tool to promote patriotism, super-teams did their job well. Characters like Superman, Captain America, the Flash, the Human Torch, and many more saw us through the turbulent times of the '40s and the more subtle paranoia of the '50s. But for all their efforts, they remained two-dimensional characters at best. In some cases, these teams seemed like nothing more than the same hero wearing different costumes. This button-down conformity was soon to pass.

FAMILY AFFAIR

Comics entered a stormy adolescence with the dawning of the Marvel Age in 1961. Stan Lee, Jack Kirby, Steve Ditko, and their cohorts not only brought superheroes into the next stage of development but portrayed their characters as a surrogate family for the reader, with parental and sibling figures. Typified by the **Fantastic Four** and the **X-Men**, this psychological dynamic may have been lost on adults, but it was very effective in drawing multitudes of young readers. DC characters such as the Legion of Super-

Superman, Batman, Wonder Woman, Flash, Green Lantern, Aquaman and Martian Manhunter came together to form the core around which other DC greats and second-stringers would revolve. Although this team has had its ups and downs, largely depending on the roster and the creative talent behind it, The Justice League of America will always be the greatest team of heroes ever assembled, and the model for every other super-team to copy.

Internet Comments:

Jonathan Keim: "By themselves,the most memorable super-heroes of all times. In the pages of comics, they represent everything a hero is, can be, and should be. It is simply a team composed of the greatest super-heroes in comics, to make the greatest super-hero team!"

2. FANTASTIC FOUR

1st Appearance:
Fantastic Four #1
Date: November 1961
About the team:
The FF, comics' first family, was created by Marvel largely in response to the success DC was having with the Justice League of America, but instead of a collection of great heroes, Stan Lee and Jack Kirby fired a family into space only to have them return with super-powers. Since then, Reed Richards, Sue, Johnny and Ben have been fighting on a monthly basis to save the planet and keep their family unit in tact.

Internet Comments:

Peter Meilinger: "First of all, they're a family and they always stuck together no matter what. And despite the fact that they're not as physically powerful as a lot of Marvel's characters I'd put my money on the FF vs. any other team, simply because they work together so well. Also, their arch-nemesis is Victor Von Doom. If it's true that a man and/or team is judged by their enemies, the FF are clearly the top of the heap."

3. X-MEN

1st Appearance: X-Men #1
Date: September 1963
About the team:
When you consider that the X-Men have been the most popular (in terms of circulation) super-team for years, it's hard to believe that Stan Lee's creation was one of his least popular back in 1963. But like the mutants that make up the team, **The X-Men** suffered through mass disfavor. The roster for this team has changed over the years, and the X-Men, in typical Marvel fashion, has spawned a series of related titles. With the most formidable mutant mind on the planet as their mentor (Professor X), the X-Men have formed an almost-familial unit that functions as a team better than most, when they are able to cast aside their angst.
Internet Comments:
Ryan Benjamin: "Even though they're not as powerful as other superteams, this particular group of X-Men were the most 'human' in terms of development and stories."

4. JUSTICE SOCIETY OF AMERICA

1st Appearance:
All Star Comics #3
Date: Winter 1940-41
About the team:
You have to give props to the first, and the JSA is the first, created by Sheldon Mayer and Gardner Fox. Although this "team" seemed more like a club, it did pose, by 1940s standards, a formidable force with a line-up that included: Atom, Dr. Fate, Flash, Green Lantern, Hawkman, Hourman, Sandman, and the Spectre. Bright and hokey in comparison to today's heroes, the JSA are fondly remembered and continue to pop up in the DC universe.
Internet Comments:
David Young: "This was the premier super-hero team. All future teams owe something to the JSA. And while the later JLA was arguably more powerful, the membership of the JSA included some of the most interesting heroes in comics...."

5. LEGION OF SUPER HEROES

1st Appearance:
Adventure Comics #247
Date: April 1958
About the team:
The LSH has amassed, over the years, a cult following as large as the ranks of the Legion itself. This futuristic, virtual army of teens, including Saturn Girl, Cosmic Boy, Lightning

Heroes would follow suit, showing the same signs of emotional maturation that would distinguish them from the more simplistic characterization of the '50s. For now, however, the realism of the Marvel heroes was unique.

Where did this shift in characterization come from? By the time the "Marvel Age of Comics" dawned in the early 1960s, America was facing some tough choices at home and abroad. The new breed of superheroes would come of age at a time when black and white gave way to shades of grey, and as a result, the Marvel heroes would exhibit as much personal angst as they would duty to their country.

A hero remains a hero, however, and in Marvel's formative years, many of their most celebrated superstars banded together to crusade against evil. The first Marvel heroes to debut were a tightly-knit team, and the first to have their own series before starring in solo titles. This team would also behave much more like a family than a club. With the birth of the Fantastic Four, the Marvel Age had begun.

Within three years, Marvel also rolled out the Avengers and the X-Men. In every case, these collections of heroes were more than just a brotherhood holding meetings and trouncing bad guys. They were people—extraordinary people certainly—but people nonetheless, with personality conflicts and personal lives caught in a whirlwind of fame and responsibility. There were romantic liaisons, unrequited loves among members, and friendships new and old... and they became our friends as well.

STORM FRONT

By the '70s, angst-ridden adolescence crept in as many super-teams grew up along with Marvel's initial audience. A new definition of teamwork emerged as Marvel introduced the first "non-team"—the Defenders. A loose collaboration between some of the company's more exiled heroes, such as the Hulk, the Gargoyle, and Valkyrie, the team's efforts were coordinated by Doctor Strange, and their adventures were understandably bizarre. Even short-lived teams like the Champions, also drawing on heroes that operated on the fringes of the Marvel Universe (including some erstwhile X-Men) had their share of success, as did oddball DC teams like the Metal Men and Doom Patrol. Perhaps Marvel's greatest team success at that point was the rebirth of the X-Men, ending a long-running reprint cycle with a landmark 1975 reintroduction.

Throughout the '80s an attention to social responsibility signaled the super-team concept's burgeoning adulthood, while new generations discovered the medium and inspired the introduction of other youthful teams like the New Mutants and the New Teen Titans. The superhero landscape had gotten far more complex, but nowhere was the change more prominent than in the pages of **The Avengers**.

These were clearly *not* your father's Avengers. In a controversial storyline that divided fandom, Henry "Hank" Pym, known variously as Ant-Man, Giant-Man, and now Yellowjacket, assaulted his wife, Janet Van Dyne (The Wasp) under the evil influence of his arch-enemy, Egghead. This tale of

Lad, Chameleon Boy, and Braniciac 5 to name a very few, could overwhelm any foe in sheer numbers alone. This is the earliest group of teen super-heroes and they led the way for the likes of the Titans and even the X-Men.

Internet Comments:
Lina Strickland: "The sheer quantity of characters gave it one of comics' earliest and best independent women characters: Saturn Girl. The futuristic, Sci-Fi settings provided a sense of wonder to spare. Smooth continuity (remember that?) with the rest of the DC universe, a plethora of cute guy characters (I was getting hooked on the series as I approached puberty), cool costumes, interesting and tightly-plotted stories, no-holds-barred tales of personal integrity, intelligent female characters...what more could you want? At least the new Legion's members still hold with being heroes and not anti-heroes!"

6. THE AVENGERS

1st Appearance:
The Avengers #1
Date: September 1963
About the team:
Here is yet another Stan Lee/Jack Kirby attempt to cash in on the success of the Justice League's popularity. By issue #4, they brought Captain America out of the history books and reintroduced him into the Marvel universe as a legend. Although always at his best when fighting Nazis, Cap became the heart and soul of the Avengers, leading the team to victory after victory. Over the years, just about every Marvel character answered to the unimaginative call, "Avengers Assemble," but under Cap's leadership, Marvel's JLA has become a formidable force for good.

Internet Comments:
Robert Bradley: "Diversity, interaction between characters, and big-name members...[make The Avengers] the greatest of super-teams."

7. WildC.A.T.S

1st Appearance: WildC.A.T.s: Covert Action Teams #1
Date: August 1992
About the team:
When Jim Lee left Marvel and helped form Image, one of his first creations was a super-team that seemed to many fans to parallel the X-Men. This team of super-powered refugees from an alien war and human outcasts, including Grifter, Voodoo, Void and Zealot, provided a tough modern take on the classic super-hero team formula.

Internet Comments:
Justin Freely: "The story arcs by Alan Moore and James Robinson and art by Travis Charest were really exciting. **WildC.A.T.s** modernized the concept of the super-team."

8. THE TITANS

1st Appearance:
Brave and the Bold #54
(as Teen Titans)
Date: June/July 1964
About the team:
So what are sidekicks to do when their mentors are off at a JLA meeting? If you're Robin, Kid Flash, Aqualad, Wonder Girl and Speedy, the answer is to start up your own team. This "JLA Junior" has been around in many incarnations, including The Teen Titans, The New Teen Titans, The Titans and even Young Justice. They formed a necessary peer group for each other and protected the Earth from threats that seemed to go without the JLA's notice.
Internet Comments:
Byron Whitley: "Typical mid-'60s story had hip lingo, groovy fashions, the mod scene, and conflicts between hippies and squares, portrayed somewhat clumsily by out-of-touch middle-aged writers...but it's still charming in an Austin Powers way. Plus when these kids grow up (if ever), they'll be the next generation of the Justice League."

9. THE INVADERS

1st Appearance:
The Avengers #71
Date: December 1969
About the team:
The Invaders is the Marvel Age's loose interpretation of Timely comics history, a retroactive WWII era super-team comprised of that era's heroes and their sidekicks. They were the best of the best for their time period, even though the comic was written about 30 years later. Think of The Invaders at Marvel's attempt to create the JSA decades late.
Internet Comments:
Greg Spiers: "The original Marvel superheroes and their sidekicks Captain America & Bucky, Sub-Mariner, Human Torch & Toro plus the Whizzer, Miss America, Union Jack and Spitfire make this powerhouse team one of the greatest."

10. SQUADRON SUPREME

1st Appearance:
Avengers #85 (as Squadron Supreme)
Date: February 1971
About the team:
Originally conceived as a team of villians, the Squadron Supreme became Marvel's most thinly-veiled attempt at their own JLA. Hyperion=Superman; Nighthawk=Batman, Power Princess= Wonder Woman, you get the point. Regardless of how unoriginal the concept was, the team was extremely powerful and continued to prove that the JLA was the model for all super-teams to come.
Internet Comments:
Bryan D. Tusick: "Not only were they the greatest heroes of their Earth by continually trouncing the bad guys, they took it upon themselves to make the Earth a better place by using their powers and abilities in humanitarian efforts...."

spousal abuse revealed a dark underside to a previously heroic character. While Hank later redeemed himself, this chapter in Avengers history was a turning point. There was no going back to the innocence of the past—our superheroes had grown up with us, and now they were facing a stormy adulthood, fraught with perils all too real and familiar.

SMELLS LIKE TEAM SPIRIT

The '90s have seen a further flowering of the super-team as many new publishers added their creativity and vitality to the mix. Marvel responded to the influx of new blood with **Generation X** and a plethora of other "X" mutant team titles, while DC has rededicated itself to bolstering and expanding the history established by both the **JLA** and **JSA** with current and forthcoming series.

And the myths continue to multiply into the 21st century, with names like the Suicide Squad, Young Justice, the Slingers, the Supermen of America, and even the Thunderbolts (villains posing as heroes!). In all of their guises, super-teams—like comics themselves—have grown up over the years, and will continue to do so.

...AND ONE FOR ALL

It's fashionable these days to look back on the past in light of the new millennium. Super-teams—and the medium that spawned them—will doubtless be in a very different place in the next twenty years, as our forms of expression develop in ways we can't possibly predict (or accept).

One truth remains: as long as we strive to be better than we are—to overcome the obstacles and face the challenges that lie ahead—we must cooperate with one another, and we must reflect it in our entertainment as well. We will always need our heroes to join forces and valiantly strive against impossible odds. Super-teams are more than a narrative device; they are our inspiration, and they preserve the hope that no matter what awaits us in the years ahead, we will be able to face it...together.

MARK HASPEL

Pre-1970 Comics Only!

art ©1999 Marvel Comics.

Website: http://members.aol.com/comxparade/index.html

Over 200 feedback!

• We run live **PHONE AUCTIONS** 3 to 4 times a year with the lowest consignment fees around. Over $50,000 of pre-Code horror and cool rare Golden Age sold last year through our auctions. Write or call to be placed on our free mailing list or to discuss consignment.

• We buy/sell **PRE-CODE HORROR**. This is one of our specialties. Comics On Parade unearthed the already famous Spokane collection early in 1998 and paid a 30% finder's fee. We have sold more books like Horrific, Mr. Mystery, Weird Terror, and all sorts of icon cover and in-demand pre-Code books than anyone!!! We also pay very competitive prices for this material.

• We are the top dealer in **MARVEL MASTERWORKS**. We have sold over 200 volumes. We consistently have the largest selection of Masterworks with over 100 in stock at all times. Call with your want lists!!! We are also consistently the biggest buyer of Masterworks.

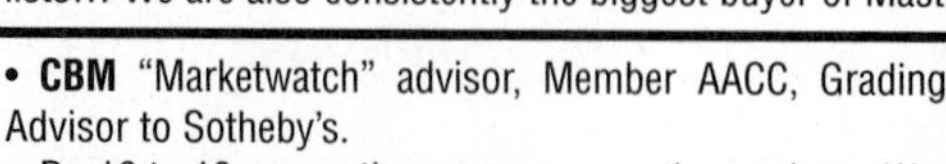

• **CBM** "Marketwatch" advisor, Member AACC, Grading Advisor to Sotheby's.
• Do 16 to 18 conventions a year – mostly as a buyer!!!
• I spend thousands a year traveling to shows to buy!!! Call to find out what I buy and look for!
• **BUYING** Pre-Code Horror/Crime, Early Golden Age, Timelys, Marvel Masterworks, non-pictured Gerber books, Rare & Esoteric Golden Age, Icon covers. Call or send list!

COMICS ON PARADE
Mark Haspel
1814 NE Miami Gardens Dr., Suite 701
N. Miami Beach, FL 33179
(305) 935-9981 • 10 am-8 pm est
comxparade@aol.com

Avengers #160

X-Men #121

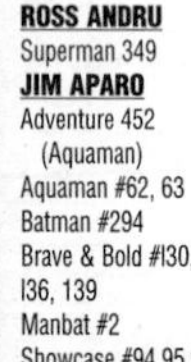

Adventure #452

Justice League #148

Showcase #94

Freedom Fighters #10

ORIGINAL ART

WANTED

Hulk #207

Godzilla #3

Iron Man #115

Superboy/Legion #228

Kamandi #55

Justice League #143

If you have any of these COVERS/some interiors (even if they are not for sale) please contact me so I can leave you with an offer (and I can stop looking for it). Cash Paid or will trade for other art or comics (Gold, Silver, Modern). PLEASE SAVE THIS LIST, it's good forever. Collector correspondence/other peoples' want lists welcome!!!

ALL ART LISTED IS FOR COVER ART UNLESS OTHERWISE NOTED!

Interior art indicated in italics.

NEAL ADAMS
Action #466
DC 1978 Calendar Cover - Disasters

ROSS ANDRU
Superman 349

JIM APARO
Adventure 452 (Aquaman)
Aquaman #62, 63
Batman #294
Brave & Bold #130, 136, 139
Manbat #2
Showcase #94,95,96 (Doom Patrol)

RICH BUCKLER
Action #478, 483
All Star Comics #69
Astonishing Tales #26, 27 (Deathlok)
DC Super Stars #10 (Strange Sports)
Freedom Fighters #9, 10, 14
Iron Man Annual #3
Justice League #148, 158
Kamandi #47, 50, 52, 56, 60
Secret Society Super Villians 6-8, 11-15
Secret Society Super Villains Spectacular (DC Special Series #6)
Superman #327
Super Team Family #8 (Challengers)
New Gods #14, 15
Teen Titans (Old) #50-53
X-Men #97

BOB BUDIANSKY
X-Men #120

JOHN BUSCEMA
Thor #262

SAL BUSCEMA
Hulk #207 *(Interior Pages)*
What If? #13

JOHN BYRNE
****Avengers #181 (*Interiors*), 186-190
****(no one will pay more for Byrne Avengers covers/interiors)
Capt. America #248
Champions #11 *(Pages 1-3)*
#12 *(Pages 2-3)*
Fantastic Four (ANY covers #211-267!)
Iron Man #109
Marvel Team-Up (ANY covers!)
Marvel 2-in-1 (ANY covers!)
Ints. #53-58
Secret Origins Annual #1 (Doom Patrol)
Spec. Spider-Man #17
Super Villian Team #Up #14
X-Men #108-142 (covers & *interiors*)

ERNIE CHAN (CHUA)
Batman #282
Champions #17
DC Super Stars #8 (of Space), 9 (Man Behind the Gun)
Flash #243
Invaders #29
Justice League #132
Kamandi #45, 48, 49
Secret Society Super Villains 1-5
Teen Titans (Old) #44

DAVE COCKRUM
Avengers #169, 175
Hulk #207
Human Fly #3
Iron Man #110
Star Wars #17
Super Villian Team-Up #12
X-Men - G.S. #1, 94- 126, 145-147 (ANY covers/pages)

GENE COLAN
Tomb of Dracula #62-64
What if #17 (Old) (Ghost Rider, Capt. Marvel, Spiderwoman)

DICK DILLIN
DC presents #13, 14
DC Superstars #10 (Strange Sports) *(Interior Pages)*
Justice League #143, 144, 147, 148 (Covers & *Interiors*), #168, 171, 173

STEVE DITKO
Shade #3, 7

KIETH GIFFEN
Defenders #44 (Interior Pages)

DICK GIORDANO
Batman #300
Superboy & Legion #253

MIKE GOLDEN
Micronauts #2-17

MIKE GRELL
Green Lantern #92, 100
Superboy + Legion #228, 230, 231

BOB HALL
Human Fly #17
Super Villian Team #Up #14 (*Interior pages*)

RICK HOBERG
Star Wars #2

CARMINE INFANTINO
Star Wars #14, 15, 19, 22

GIL KANE
Avengers #130. 141
Capt. America #216
Champions #11, 16
Jungle Action (Black Panther) #14
Star Wars #8

MIKE KALUTA
Batman Family #17

JACK KIRBY
Capt. America #202 (cover + *page 14*)
Defenders #44
Fantastic Four - 190
Invaders #14, 15
Kamandi (ANY cover!)
Weird Wonder Tales #18

ALAN KUPPERBERG
Invaders #37, 38

BOB LAYTON
Iron Man #121, 127, 135, 139
Marvel Premier #47 (Antman)

GARCIA LOPEZ
Action #481, 482, 484
DC Special Series #5 (Superman Spect.), 11 (Flash Spect.)
Untold Legend of Batman #2

PABLO MARCOS
Marvel Two In One #39

BOB McLEOD
Marvel Team #Up #86

AL MILGROM
All Star comics #70
Amazing Spiderman #194
Capt. Marvel #47
Defenders #74
Firestorm (Old) #2, 3
Flash #268
Invaders #41
Kamandi #53-55
Secret Society Super Villians #10
Shogun Warriors (ANY covers!)
Skull the Slayer #1

FRANK MILLER
Daredevil #158-181 *covers and splashes!*
Dark Knight (ANY pages)
X-Men Annual #3

MIKE NASSER
Kobra #6, 7
Spectacular Spiderman #37

DON NEWTON
Avengers Annual #9
New Gods #12 (Splash Page)

GEORGE PEREZ
****Avengers #160-168, 170-174, 181, 183-185, 191, 192, 194-201
Avengers Annual #8 (Especially #161,181), *Interiors wanted #167,*
Korvac TPBK cover
****(No one will pay/trade more for Perez Avengers covers!)
Batman/Outsiders #5,
Fantastic 4 (ANY cover!)
Infinity Gauntlet (ANY cover!)
Justice League #195 (cover & *centerfold*), 196, 197, 207, 209, 219, 220 (Any other covers considered)
Marvel Fanfare #10-12
Marvel Premiere #45-46 (Manwolf)
Marvel 2 In 1 #42, 50, 51, 57, 58, 61-63 *(Interiors #53-58)*
New Teen Titans #1-50
Annual #3,
New Titans (Baxter) #1-5,
War of the Gods #1,
X-Men #112, Annual #3 *(Interior Pages)*
Also looking for "odd-ball" titles Perez did from 1975-1987.

KEITH POLLARD
Iron Man #108, 111, 112
Marvel Two In One #55

FRANK ROBBINS
Human Fly #10

JOHN ROMITA JR.
Avengers #176
Defenders #62
Iron Man #114-117

ALEX ROSS
Marvels #0-4 (any splashes or nice panel pages)
Kingdom Come (various pages)

K. SCHAFFENBERGER
Action #474

MARSHALL ROGERS
Mr. Miracle (DC House ad page, 1977), 19-25

ALEX SCHOMBURG
Invaders annual #1 (also Human Torch pages)

JOE STATON
All Star Comics #71-73
"DC Explosion" (DC House ad pg 1978)
New Gods #19
Showcase #97, 99 (Power Girl) (*Splash to #94*)
Superboy + Legion #249

HERB TRIMPE
Godzilla #3

DAVE WENZEL
Avengers #177 (Interiors)

ALAN WEISS
Human Fly #7
Shazam (1977) #34

WALLY WOOD
All Star Comics #64

RON WILSON
Marvel Two in One #16, 37, 40

ARTISTS UNKNOWN
Marvel Spotlight #12 (Son of Satan)
Squadron Supreme #1-12
Super Villian Team-Up #15 (Doom Red Skull)

Please Contact: JONATHAN MANKUTA
75 Mc Arthur Lane, Smithtown, N.Y. 11787
Phone: 1-516-864-2281 (Leave message if no answer)
e-mail JONMANKUTA@AOL.COM

SEE MY OTHER ADS ON PAGES 178-179

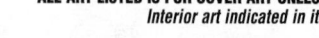

COMIC BOOKS WANTED

The following prices represent a small sample of the prices that we will pay for your comic books. Other dealers say that they will pay top dollar, but when it really comes down to it, they simply do not. If you have comics to sell, we invite you to contact every comic dealer in the country to get their offers. Then come to us to get your best offer. We can afford to pay the highest price for your Golden and Silver Age comics because that is all we sell. If you wish to sell us your comic books, please either ship us the books securely via Registered U.S. Mail or UPS. However, if your collection is too large to ship, kindly send us a detailed list of what you have and we will travel directly to you. The prices below are for NM copies, but we are interested in all grades. Thank You.

Action #1 .... $200,000
Action #242 .... $2,000
Adventure #40 .... $43,000
Adventure #48 .... $19,000
Adventure #210 .... $2,800
All-American #16 .... $65,000
All-American #19 .... $13,000
All-Star #3 .... $23,000
Amazing Fantasy #15 .... $25,000
Amaz.Spiderman #1 ..... $15,000
Arrow #1 .... $2,600
Batman #1 .... $55,000
Brave & the Bold #28 ..... $4,800
Captain America #1 ..... $45,000
Detective #1 .... $82,000
Detective #27 .... $180,000
Detective #38 .... $29,000
Detective #168 .... $4,200
Detective #225 .... $4,400
Detec. Picture Stories#1 .. $2,900
Donald Duck #9 .... $5,200
Fantastic Comics #3 ..... $15,000
Fantastic Four #1 .... $18,000
Fantastic Four #5 .... $2,200
Flash Comics #1 .... $72,000
Green Hornet #1 .... $2,900
Green Lantern #1 ...(GA)$23,000
Green Lantern #1 ....(SA)$3,000
Human Torch #2(#1) $18,000
Incredible Hulk #1 .... $10,000
Journey into Myst. #83 .... $4,000
Justice League #1 .... $3,000
Jumbo Comics #1 .... $12,000
Marvel Comics #1 .... $70,000
More Fun #52 .... $60,000
More Fun #54 .... $9,500
More Fun #55 .... $16,000
More Fun #73 .... $14,000
More Fun #101 .... $8,300
New Fun #6 .... $22,000
Pep Comics #22 .... $12,000
Showcase #4 .... $25,000
Showcase #8 .... $8,000
Superboy #1 .... $7,500
Superman #1 .... $140,000
Superman #14 .... $4,000
Suspense Comics #3 .... $16,000
Tales of Suspense #1 ..... $1,600
Tales of Suspense #39 .... $4,000
Tales to Astonish #27 ..... $3,700
Target Comics V1#7 ...... $3,800
Walt Disney C&S #1 ..... $12,000
Whiz #2 (#1) $40,000
Wonder Woman #1$ 13,500
Wow #1 (1936) $7,500
Young Allies #1 .... $7,500
X-Men #1 .... $7,500

The following is a sample of the books we are purchasing:

Action Comics .... #1-400
Adventure Comics ...... #32-400
Advs. Into Weird Worlds .... all
All-American Comics ..... #1-102
All-Flash Quarterly .... #1-32
All-Select .... #1-11
All-Star Comics .... #1-57
All-Winners .... #1-21
Amazing Spiderman ...... #1-150
Amazing Man .... #5-26
Amaz. Mystery Funnies .... #1
Avengers .... #1-100
Batman .... #1-300
Blackhawk .... #9-130
Boy Commandos .... #1-32
Brave & the Bold .... #1-100
Captain America .... #1-78
Captain Marvel Advs. ..... #1-150
Challengers .... #1-25
Classic Comics .... #1-169
Comic Cavalcade .... #1-63
Daredevil Comics .... #1-60
Daredevil (MCG) .... #1-50

COLLECTIBLES
873 BROADWAY, SUITE 201
NEW YORK, NY 10003
Phone: 212-260-4147
Fax: 212-260-4304
Email: comicbooks@earthlink.net
Web: www.metropoliscomics.com

Daring Mystery .... #1-8
Detective Comics .... #1-450
Donald Duck 4-Colors ..... #4-up
Fantastic Four .... #1-100
Fight Comics .... #1-86
Flash .... #105-150
Flash Comics .... #1-104
Funny Pages .... #6-42
Green Lantern (GA) .... #1-38
Green Lantern (SA) .... #1-90
Hit Comics .... #1-65
Human Torch .... #2(#1)-38
Incredible Hulk .... #1-6
Jimmy Olsen 1-150
Journey Into Mystery ..... #1-125
Jumbo Comics .... #1-167
Jungle Comics .... #1-163
Justice League .... #1-110
Mad .... #1-50
Marvel Mystery .... #1-92
Military Comics .... #1-43
More Fun Comics .... #7-127
Mystery in Space .... #1-75
Mystic Comics .... #1-up
National Comics .... #1-75
New Adventure .... #12-31
New Comics .... #1-11
New Fun Comics .... #1-6
Our Army at War .... #1-200
Our Fighting Forces ...... #1-180
Planet Comics .... #1-73
Rangers Comics .... #1-69
Reform School Girl
Sensation Comics .... #1-116
Shadow Comics .... all
Showcase .... #1-100
Star-Spangled Comics .... #1-130
Strange Tales .... #1-145
Sub-Mariner .... #1-42
Superboy .... #1-110
Superman .... #1-250
Tales From The Crypt ..... #20-46
Tales of Suspense .... #1-80
Tales to Astonish .... #1-80
Terrific Comics .... all
Thing .... #1-17
USA Comics .... #1-17
Weird Comics .... #1-20
Weird Mysteries .... #1-12
Weird Tales From The Future ... all
Wings Comics .... #1-124
Whiz Comics .... #1-155
Wonder Comics .... #1-20
Wonder Woman .... #1-200
Wonderworld .... #3-33
World's Finest .... #1-200
X-Men .... #1-30

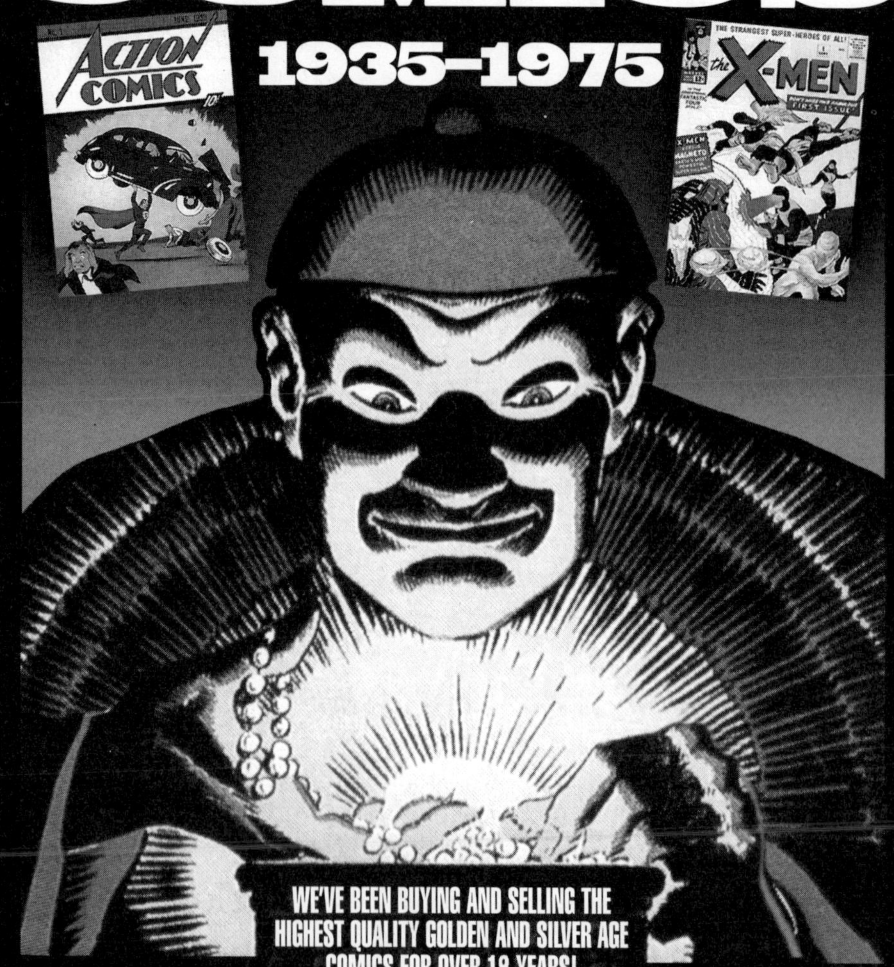

ACTION COMICS
1935–1975
THE STRANGEST SUPER-HEROES OF ALL!
the X-MEN
FIRST ISSUE!
WE'VE BEEN BUYING AND SELLING THE HIGHEST QUALITY GOLDEN AND SILVER AGE COMICS FOR OVER 18 YEARS!

DID YOU TURN INTO A
MONSTER
THE LAST TIME YOU RECEIVED
A MAIL ORDER?
If this looks familiar, treat yourself to honest grading and fair pricing by buying your Silver and Golden Age comics from us!
At FOUR COLOR COMICS, we specialize in treating the customer right and we unconditionally guarantee every book we sell!
Fantastic Four
10¢
FOUR COLOR
COMICS
NY SHOWROOM (By Appointment Only): 115 West 27th St, New York, NY 10001 (212) 675-6990 Fax:(212) 675-6145
DESIGN: ARNIE SAWYER All artwork: © DC COMICS, © MARVEL ENTERTAINMENT GROUP, INC

JUST IMAGINE!

AT YOUR FINGERTIPS...

one of the world's most amazing inventories of Golden and Silver Age comic books—in grades from strict Near Mint to collectible reading copies, single books and complete runs...

24 HOURS A DAY
7 DAYS A WEEK
and 365 DAYS A YEAR!!

All in a completely searchable database so you can locate a specific copy of the book you need without painfully scrolling through hundreds of titles and thousands of listings!!

FOUR COLOR COMICS

NY SHOWROOM: ,115 West 27th St, New York, NY 10001 (212) 675-6990 Fax:(212) 675-6145

www.fourcolorcomics.com

D.W. GRIFFITH'S
MIGHTY SPECTACLE
THE BIRTH OF A NATION
FOUNDED ON THOMAS DIXON'S THE CLANSMAN
THE DAY THE EARTH STOOD STILL
MICHAEL RENNIE · PATRICIA NEAL · HUGH MARLOWE
FRANKENSTEIN meets THE WOLF MAN
ILONA MASSEY
KING KONG
FAY WRAY · ROBT. ARMSTRONG
BRUCE CABOT
EDGAR WALLACE
FOUR COLOR COMICS
BUYING PRE-1955 POSTERS
I buy, sell, and collect movie posters and theater displays. I can and will pay you the highest price for your poster or collection of posters. Call me before you sell.
•
Of particular interest:
EARLY DISNEY
UNIVERSAL HORROR
1950's SCIENCE-FICTION
1930's POSTERS
•
115 West 27th St.
New York, NY 10001
Tel: (212) 675-6990
Fax: (212) 675-6145
Keybooks@aol.com
www.fourColorComics.com

FOUR COLOR
COMICS
BUYING PRE-1980 LINE-ART
I buy, sell, and collect original comic art. I can and will pay you the highest price for your art. Call me before you sell.
Of particular interest:
GOLDENAGE ART
DC SILVERAGE ART
MARVEL SILVERAGE ART
EC COVER ART
FRAZETTA, KIRBY, DITKO, BARKS
115 West 27th St.
New York, NY 10001
Tel: (212) 675-6990
Fax: (212) 675-6145
Keybooks@aol.com
www.fourColorComics.com
SPIDER-MAN NO MORE!
I BROUGHT THE ROC TO LIFE!
TALES CALCULATED TO DRIVE YOU MAD
"TO FREE A BRAIN SLAVE"

BUYING!

Consider The Following:

■Willing to pay up to 200% of Overstreet Price Guide(or more depending upon current market conditions). Do not settle for less.

■ Buying all comics 1900-1970 in all grades!Whether one book or 10,000. I can pay instantly!

■ Having been involved in collecting/selling for 22 years, I have built my reputation on courteous, professional service (I do not believe in high pressure transactions-I do believe in the seller being fully informed!)Please ask questions

■ Advisor to Overstreet.

■ Finders fee paid for information leading to purchase. I will travel to view large collections.

SELLING - TRADING

●Accurate Grading & Pricing●
●Dependable, Reputable Service●
●Large Selection of Golden Age & Silver Age●
●Marvel & DC●
●Constantly Acquiring New Collections●
●Satisfaction Guaranteed●

A-1 Comics

Brian Peets - Owner
5800 Madison Ave.
Sacramento, CA 95841
(916)331-9203 Fax(916)331-2141

"Serving The West Since 1974"

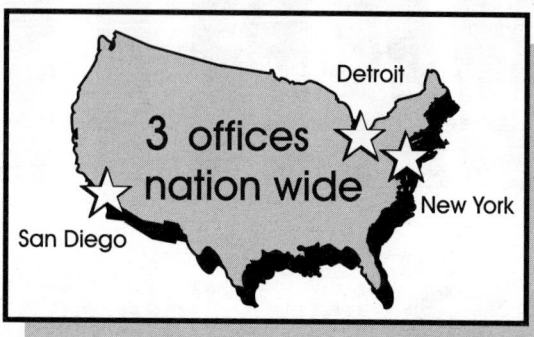

WHY?

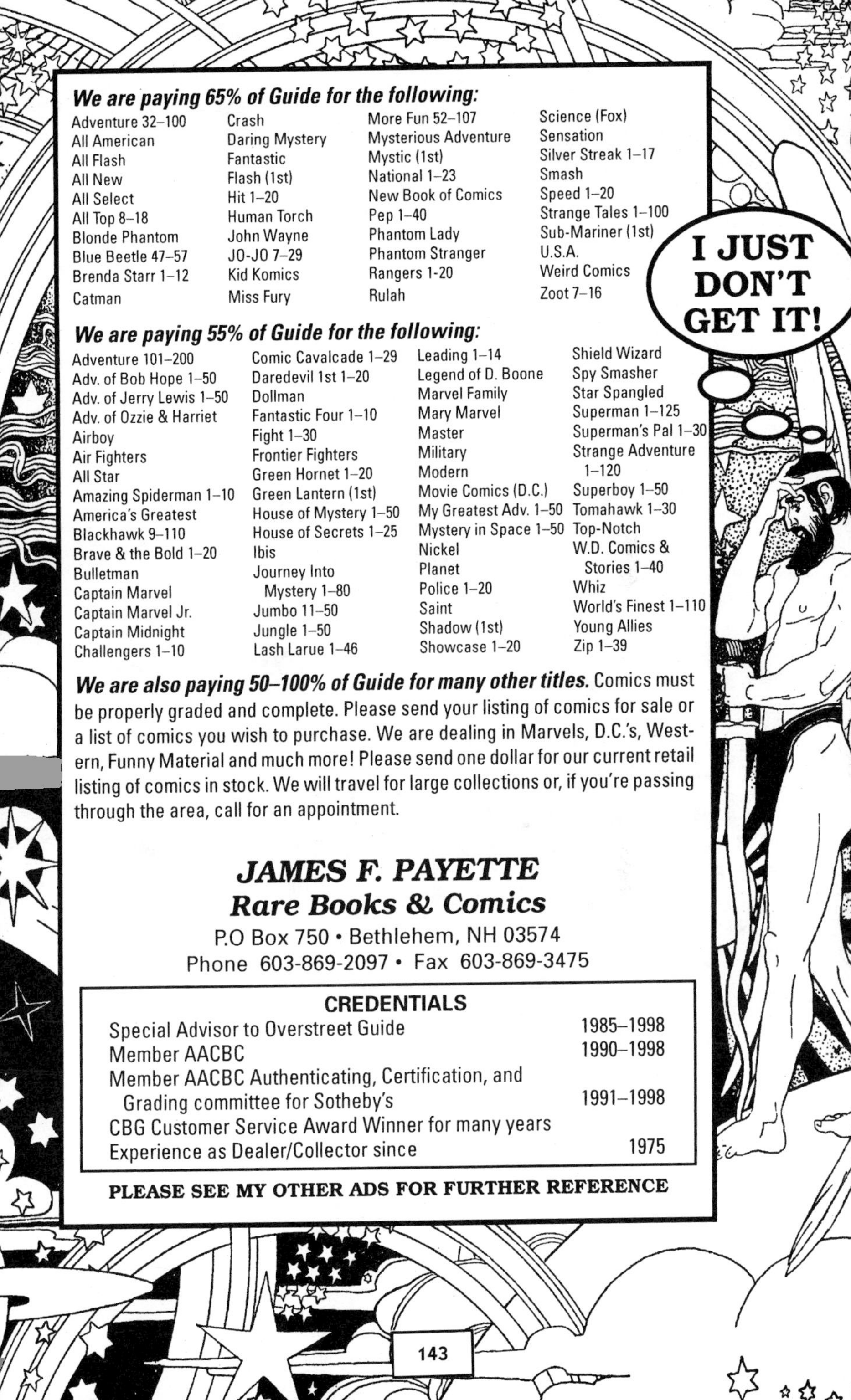

We are paying 65% of Guide for the following:
Adventure 32–100
All American
All Flash
All New
All Select
All Top 8–18
Blonde Phantom
Blue Beetle 47–57
Brenda Starr 1–12
Catman
Crash
Daring Mystery
Fantastic
Flash (1st)
Hit 1–20
Human Torch
John Wayne
JO-JO 7–29
Kid Komics
Miss Fury
More Fun 52–107
Mysterious Adventure
Mystic (1st)
National 1–23
New Book of Comics
Pep 1–40
Phantom Lady
Phantom Stranger
Rangers 1-20
Rulah
Science (Fox)
Sensation
Silver Streak 1–17
Smash
Speed 1–20
Strange Tales 1–100
Sub-Mariner (1st)
U.S.A.
Weird Comics
Zoot 7–16
I JUST DON'T GET IT!
We are paying 55% of Guide for the following:
Adventure 101–200
Adv. of Bob Hope 1–50
Adv. of Jerry Lewis 1–50
Adv. of Ozzie & Harriet
Airboy
Air Fighters
All Star
Amazing Spiderman 1–10
America's Greatest
Blackhawk 9–110
Brave & the Bold 1–20
Bulletman
Captain Marvel
Captain Marvel Jr.
Captain Midnight
Challengers 1–10
Comic Cavalcade 1–29
Daredevil 1st 1–20
Dollman
Fantastic Four 1–10
Fight 1–30
Frontier Fighters
Green Hornet 1–20
Green Lantern (1st)
House of Mystery 1–50
House of Secrets 1–25
Ibis
Journey Into Mystery 1–80
Jumbo 11–50
Jungle 1–50
Lash Larue 1–46
Leading 1–14
Legend of D. Boone
Marvel Family
Mary Marvel
Master
Military
Modern
Movie Comics (D.C.)
My Greatest Adv. 1–50
Mystery in Space 1–50
Nickel
Planet
Police 1–20
Saint
Shadow (1st)
Showcase 1–20
Shield Wizard
Spy Smasher
Star Spangled
Superman 1–125
Superman's Pal 1–30
Strange Adventure 1–120
Superboy 1–50
Tomahawk 1–30
Top-Notch
W.D. Comics & Stories 1–40
Whiz
World's Finest 1–110
Young Allies
Zip 1–39
We are also paying 50–100% of Guide for many other titles. Comics must be properly graded and complete. Please send your listing of comics for sale or a list of comics you wish to purchase. We are dealing in Marvels, D.C.'s, Western, Funny Material and much more! Please send one dollar for our current retail listing of comics in stock. We will travel for large collections or, if you're passing through the area, call for an appointment.
JAMES F. PAYETTE
Rare Books & Comics
P.O Box 750 • Bethlehem, NH 03574
Phone 603-869-2097 • Fax 603-869-3475
CREDENTIALS
Special Advisor to Overstreet Guide 1985–1998
Member AACBC 1990–1998
Member AACBC Authenticating, Certification, and Grading committee for Sotheby's 1991–1998
CBG Customer Service Award Winner for many years
Experience as Dealer/Collector since 1975
PLEASE SEE MY OTHER ADS FOR FURTHER REFERENCE

Follow the Leader in Golden and Silver Age Comics with
BEDROCK CITY
COMIC COMPANY
TM
6517 Westheimer
(at Hillcroft)
Houston, Texas 77057
(713) 780-0675
2204-D FM 1960 W.
(at Kuykendahl)
Houston, Texas 77090
(281) 444-9763
fax (713) 780-2366
www.bedrockcity.com
Shazam © 1997 D.C. Comics

The Following Sotheby's Catalogues are available, some in limited editions

1. SOTHEBY'S COMIC ART AUCTION, 1991 . . . . $75
   Hardcover with color cover. Special inaugural inserts with signed & numbered edition limited to 50 copies.
2. SOTHEBY'S COMIC ART AUCTION, 1991 . . . . $250
   Same package as no. 1 listing, in limited hand-made box. Limit of four.
3. SOTHEBY'S COMIC ART AUCTION, 1991 . . . . $50
   Regular hardcover.
4. SOTHEBY'S COMIC ART AUCTION, 1992 . . . . $250
   Regular softcover; this edition sold out before auction. SCARCE (3 available).
5. SOTHEBY'S COMIC ART AUCTION, 1993 . . . . $50
   Limited edition of 50 in hardcover boards. Signed.
6. SOTHEBY'S CATALOGUE FOR 1993 . . . . $35
   Regular softcover.
7. SOTHEBY'S COMIC ART AUCTION, 1994 . . . . $50
   Hardcover with color cover. Limited edition of 50 copies, signed with drawing.
8. SOTHEBY'S COMIC ART AUCTION, 1994 . . . . $40
   Regular release softcover edition. Limited numbers.
9. SOTHEBY'S COMIC ART AUCTION, 1995 . . . . $150
   Special Science Fiction Catalogue with original Hannes Bok drawing. Signed & numbered edition of 10.
10. SOTHEBY'S COMIC ART AUCTION, 1995 . . . . $50
    Science Fiction Catalogue, bound in boards with original drawing. Limited edition of 50.
11. SOTHEBY'S COMIC ART AUCTION, 1995 . . . . $40
    Both Comic Art and Science Fiction in regular softcover edition.
12. SOTHEBY'S COMIC ART AUCTION, 1996 . . . . $50
    Special hardcover edition, signed and bound in boards with drawing. Edition of 50.
13. SOTHEBY'S COMIC ART AUCTION, 1996 . . . . $35
    Regular softcover edition.
14. SOTHEBY'S COMIC ART AUCTION, 1997 . . . . $50
    Special hardcover edition, signed and bound in boards with drawing. Edition of 50.
15. SOTHEBY'S COMIC ART AUCTION, 1997 . . . . $30
    Regular softcover edition.
16. SOTHEBY'S COMIC ART AUCTION, 1998 . . . . $30
    Regular softcover edition.
17. SOTHEBY'S MASTERPIECES, 1998 . . . . $50
    Special hardcover edition, signed and bound in boards with drawing. Edition of 50.
18. SOTHEBY'S MAD ABOUT MAD $50
    MAD auction's special hardcover edition, signed and bound in boards with drawing. Edition of 50.
19. SOTHEBY'S MAD ABOUT MAD $30
    MAD auction's regular softcover edition.
20. SOTHEBY'S THE SCIENCE FICTION COLLECTION of SAM MOSKOWITZ, 1999 . . . . $75
    Special edition with signed insert; bound in boards. Edition of 100.

NOTE: Each catalogue will come with prices realized list enclosed.

For More Information

Please call Jerry Weist's in-house office at (212) 606-7862, his home office at (978) 283-1419, or call Dana Hawkes at (212) 606-7910. Or, write to Sotheby's, 1334 York Avenue, New York, NY, 10021. To inquire about consigning important property, Call Jerry Weist, Laura Woolley or Dana Hawkes at the above listed numbers.

To Order Catalogues

Write to Jerry Weist at
18 Edgemoor Road, Gloucester, MA 01930
or to order by phone, call
(978) 283-1419

BARRY WINDSOR-SMITH'S cover artwork for *X-Men* no. 186. From the Kevin Eastman Collection. Auction estimate: $800-$1,200.

SOTHEBY'S

...we've worked on preserving and restoring classic Golden Age and Silver Age comics for over 17 years. From a simple cleaning and pressing to a more detailed intervention, we'll add value and life to your collection.
ACTION COMICS
SHOWCASE
AMAZING FANTASY
SPIDER MAN

Who Can You TRUST?

Have you been searching through this guide and asking yourself "Who can I trust to sell my collection to?" and "Who can I trust to buy **GUARANTEED UNRESTORED BOOKS** from?" *The answer is clear!*

At Collectors Assemble, (previously known as Marnin Rosenberg and Scott Whaley), we've been buying and selling books through the pages of the Comics Buyer's Guide (CBG) since 1973, and never, we repeat, **NEVER** has that publication received a complaint about us! We've also advertised in various other major comic publications including Overstreet, with the same **SPOTLESS REPUTATION.**

Just how many other dealers in these pages can boast that claim along with such longevity? We believe in ourselves and you can too!

COLLECTORS ASSEMBLE!

Drew Friedman © 1996

To Sell Books	**To Buy Books**

(Buying books from 1933 to 1966)

Scott Whaley
507 Carlisle Drive
Alexandria, VA 22301-2709
phone/fax
(516) 466-8147
(703) 860-3633

Marnin Rosenberg
P.O. Box 222047
Great Neck, NY 11022-9998
phone/fax
(516) 466-8147

Overstreet Advisors • CBG Customer Service Award • Members A.C.C.

Visit our website at: www.collectorsassemble.com

OUR SPECIALTIES SINCE 1976...

BUYING OUT STORES WAREHOUSES, PUBLISHERS REMAINDERS, COLLECTIONS

GOT A FEW HUNDRED THOUSAND BOOKS? A **MILLION** BOOKS? WE ARE LOOKING FOR **LARGE LOTS** OF COMICS AND RELATED MATERIALS (Sci-Fi, Games, Cards, Records, etc.. etc.). **SMALLER STOCKS & COLLECTIONS** APPRECIATED AS WELL. **LOVE GOLD & SILVER AGE COMICS – WILL PAY FINDER'S FEE.**

THE MORE, THE MERRIER
WILL FLY, SWIM, SKATEBOARD
ANYWHERE IN THE WORLD

SUPPLYING DEALERS & INVESTORS STOCKING NEW STORES

THE MOST EXTENSIVE BACK ISSUE WHOLESALE LIST IN THE WORLD – BY FAR, WE HAVE BEEN SUPPLYING DEALERS IN THE U.S. & ABROAD FOR YEARS. OUR LISTS INCLUDE BACK-ISSUE LISTINGS, LOTS, COLLECTIONS, ETC. **OPENING A STORE? LOOKING FOR INVENTORY?** WE HAVE PROVIDED THE INITIAL STOCKS FOR DOZENS OF STORES OPENING IN THE LAST DECADE.

OVERSEAS ACCOUNTS A SPECIALTY

THE ENDLESS DEALER'S ONLY CONVENTION

OUR WAREHOUSE IS OPEN TO DEALERS BY INVITATION OR APPOINTMENT ONLY. IT'S A COMIC BOOK SUPERMARKET: OVER 400,000 PRICED, UNADVERTISED COMICS (IN ALPHA NUMERICAL ORDER) AVAILABLE AT ALL TIMES. WHEN YOU'RE IN TOWN GIVE US A CALL.

JOSEPH KOCH
208 41ST ST., BROOKLYN, NY 11232
718-768-8571

I Will Travel Anywhere
to View Your Collection
Highest Prices Paid
Immediate Cash
No Collection Too Big or Too Small
Complete Customer Satisfaction
Experienced, Professional Service
Buying
Call, Write or Fax:
Harley Yee
P.O. Box 51758
Livonia, MI 48151-5758
Phone: 800.731.1029 or 734.421.7921
Fax: 734.421.7928
©Better Publications

Spawn

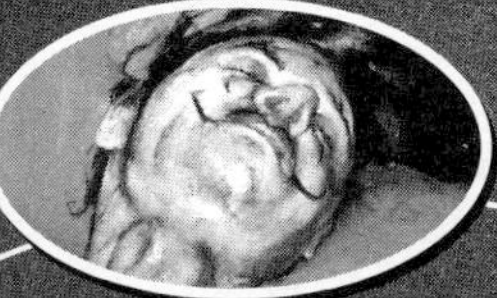

The Crow

Lady Pendragon

Witchblade

Savage Dragon

Darkness

THERE'S NEVER BEEN ANYTHING LIKE US BEFORE!

image® COMICS

Kiss

Fathom

Darkminds

The Tenth

Aria

Mage

Spider-Man tm & © 1999 Marvel Entertainment. All Rights Reserved.
America's Favorite Comic Convention
JRJR + JOHN ROMITA
HEROES CONVENTION CHARLOTTE™
'99
just a few of the confirmed guests include...
John Byrne • Harlan Ellison • Adam Hughes
Gil Kane • George Perez • John Romita, JR
...with hundreds more to be announced!!!
Comic Books • Toys • Gaming
Original Art • Workshops • Exhibits
FATHER'S DAY WEEKEND
JUNE 18-20, 1999
CHARLOTTE CONVENTION CENTER
Exhibitors, Professionals sign-up and for more information:
Heroes Aren't Hard To Find

DC
THE BEST IN COMICS READING
Jimmy Olsen

ANIMAL
COMICS

HERE'S YOUR
U.S. ROYAL
Middleweight
BIKE TIRE

DOC SAVAGE
MAGAZINE

The MARK of
ZORRO

P.A. POWERS
COMI COLOR
CARTOON
Brementown
Musicians

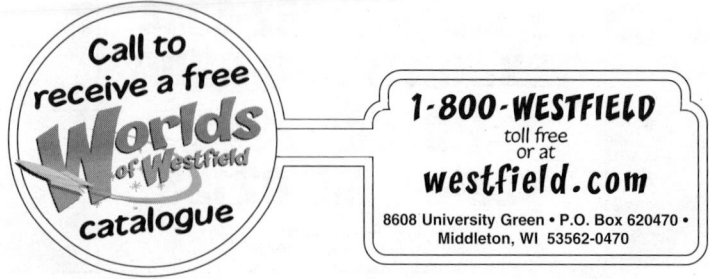

PACIFIC COMIC EXCHANGE, INC.

SELLERS: Please contact The Exchange if you would like to *consign* these or other books at full market value. See our catalog at our web site at www.pcei.com

CGSA	M	NM/M	++ + NM --	VFN/NM	++ + VFN --	FN/VFN	+ FN --	VG/FN	+ VG	G/VG	G	Fr/G	Fr	Pr
	100 - 91	90	88.85.80.75	70	68.65.63.60.55	50	45.40.35	30	25.20	15	10	8	6	3
OVERSTREET - 100		99	98.96.94.92	90	88.86.84.82.78	73	70.65.60	55	50.45	35	25	18	10	3

Action Comics 1

Detective Comics 27

Marvel Comics 1

	G 10	VG 20	FN 40	VFN 60	NM 80	NM/M 90
Action Comics 1	$30,000	$50,000	$100,000	$150,000	$300,000	$600,000
Detective Comics 27	$25,000	$45,000	$85,000	$125,000	$250,000	$450,000
Marvel Comics 1	$12,000	$20,000	$40,000	$60,000	$120,000	$300,000

Wanted Immediately in VFN 60 - NM/M 90

	VFN 60	NM 80	NM/M 90
Action Comics 1	$150,000	$300,000	$600,000
Adventure Comics 40	$30,000	$60,000	$120,000
Adventure Comics 210	$1,800	$4,000	$7,500
Adventure Comics 247	$2,000	$5,000	$10,000
All Star Comics 3	$20,000	$40,000	$120,000
All Star Comics 8	$18,000	$35,000	$100,000
All-American Comics 16	$40,000	$80,000	$175,000
Amazing Fantasy 15	$10,000	$25,000	$50,000
Amazing Spider-Man 1	$6,000	$20,000	$35,000
Batman 1	$40,000	$80,000	$160,000
Batman 100	$1,500	$3,000	$6,000
Captain America 1	$30,000	$60,000	$120,000
Detective Comics 1	$50,000	$100,000	$225,000
Detective Comics 27	$125,000	$250,000	$450,000
Detective Comics 33	$20,000	$45,000	$100,000
Detective Comics 38	$18,000	$35,000	$100,000
Fantastic Four 1	$7,000	$25,000	$50,000
Flash Comics 1	$30,000	$75,000	$150,000
Flash Comics 104	$4,000	$10,000	$20,000
Green Lantern 1 (SA)	$1,500	$4,000	$7,500
Green Lantern 1 (GA)	$12,500	$30,000	$75,000
Incredible Hulk 1	$5,000	$12,000	$24,000
Jimmy Olsen 1	$3,500	$10,000	$15,000
Journey Into Mystery 83	$1,500	$5,000	$10,000
Justice League 1	$1,500	$4,500	$9,000
Lois Lane 1	$2,000	$4,500	$8,500
Marvel Comics 1	$60,000	$120,000	$300,000
More Fun Comics 52	$35,000	$70,000	$140,000
More Fun Comics 55	$7,500	$15,000	$40,000
Sensation Comics 1	$10,000	$21,000	$60,000
Showcase 4	$15,000	$35,000	$70,000
Showcase 22	$2,000	$6,000	$12,000
Sub-Mariner Comics 1	$10,000	$20,000	$50,000
Superman 1	$75,000	$125,000	$250,000
Superman 100	$1,600	$3,000	$6,000
Suspense Comics 3	10,000	$25,000	$50,000
Wonder Woman 1	$9,000	$25,000	$50,000
X-Men 1	$2,500	$6,000	$12,000

Visit our web site at www.pcei.com

Corporate Office:
337 S. Robertson Blvd. Ste 203, Beverly Hills, CA 90211
Tel: (310) 836-7234 (PCEI), Fax: (310) 836-7127

Shipping Address:
P.O. Box 34849 Los Angeles, CA 90034
E-Mail: sales@pcei.com, www.pcei.com

VISA

Avengers #185

X-Men #100

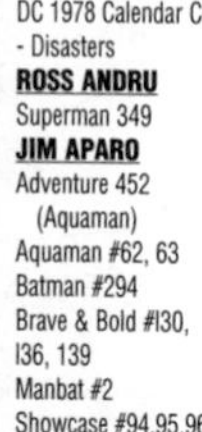

Justice League #207

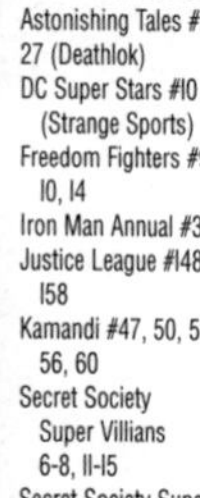

All-Star #70

Secret Society of Super Villains #8

Star Wars #15

Jungle Action #14

Green Lantern #92

Captain America #202

Brave/Bold #136

Human Fly #10

Flash #243

SILVER AGE
12¢
BUYING
COMICS
107
APR.
ALL COMICS, ALL GRADES
•WILL TRAVEL TO YOU!
•WILL PAY MORE!
•WILL PAY CASH!
©MARVEL COMICS
SELLING
the LARGEST SELECTION of SILVER AGE in N.Y.C. WITHOUT APPOINTMENT
• COMPETITIVE PRICING!
• STRICT GRADING!
• MAIL ORDER ANYWHERE
• WANT LIST SERVICE
• FREE CATALOGUE
• OPEN 7 DAYS
Silver Age Comics • 22-55 31 St. • Astoria, NY 11105
phone (800) 278-9691, (718) 721-9691 fax (718) 728-9691
www.silveragecomics.com/e-mail gus@silveragecomics.com

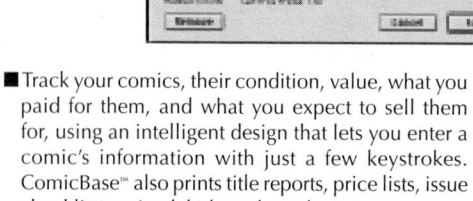

We Urgently Require Quality Golden-Age, Silver-Age Comics and related material for outright purchase or auction.

When it comes time to sell your comics (one book or an entire collection), nobody will get you more for it than GMAI. Our unparalleled knowledge, experience, and integrity means more money in your pocket.

Always Seeking:

Comic Books:
Platinum, Golden, and Silver-Age (1900-1970)

Movie Posters:
Animation, Comedy, Epic, Horror, Mystery, Western, Sci-Fi (1920-1970)

Related Material:
Original Comic Book Artwork, Production Cels, Pulps, Lithographs, Etc... (1920-Present)

We hold several major auctions each year and are always seeking quality Golden and Silver-Age comics and related material for consignment or purchase. Call us for details about our next major auction event!

Contact Bill Hughes - Senior Advisor to Overstreet Guide
800-221-0243

775 Passaic Avenue • West Caldwell • NJ • 07006
800-221-0243 • 973-882-0004 • 973-882-3499 fax • www.gregmanning.com

A publicly traded company. NASDAQ symbol GMAI

IN PREMIUM QUALITY GOLDEN & SILVER AGE COMIC BOOKS

Try us once and you'll be hooked!

19 Harrison Court • Toronto • CANADA • L1N 6E2
tel:905•666•0011 fax:905•839•0330

Nick Catros Steve Quinnell

Mail order/Want list specialists
GRADE GUARANTEED

VISA

TOP DOLLAR PAID FOR ALL COLLECTIONS

COMICS
GUARANTY
CORPORATION

TODD McFARLANE
PRODUCTIONS

Comic Heaven
John and Nanette Verzyl
P.O. Box 900
Big Sandy, TX 75755
1-903-636-5555

JOHN VERZYL AND DAUGHTER ROSE, "HARD AT WORK."

John Verzyl started collecting comic books in 1965, and within ten years he had amassed thousands of Golden and Silver Age comic books. In 1979, with his wife Nanette, he opened "COMIC HEAVEN," a retail store devoted entirely to the buying and selling of comic books.

Over the years, John Verzyl has come to be recognized as an authority in the field of comic books. He has served as a special advisor to the "Overstreet Comic Book Price Guide" for the last ten years. Thousands of his "mint" comics were photographed for Ernst Gerber's newly-released "Photo-Journal Guide To Comic Books." His tables and displays at the annual San Diego Comic Convention and the Chicago Comic Convention draw customers from all over the country.

The first COMIC HEAVEN AUCTION was held in 1987, and today his Auction Catalogs are mailed out to more than ten thousand interested collectors and dealers.

Comic Heaven
John and Nanette Verzyl
P.O. Box 900
Big Sandy, TX 75755
1-903-636-5555

The American Comic Book: 1897-1932

IN THE BEGINNING: THE PLATINUM AGE

by Robert L. Beerbohm & Richard D. Olson, PhD

© 1999

The story of the success of the comic strip as we know it today is tied closely to the companies who sponsored them and paid licenses to the copyright holder for the purpose of advertising products.

What keeps the Platinum Age from being collected as much as later era comics is simply the extreme rarity of these volumes, especially in any type of high grade. Many Platinum Age books are much rarer than Golden Age comic books, yet despite this

The first known cartoon, "The Burning of Mr. John Rogers," 1646.

rarity, **Mutt & Jeff**, **Bringing Up Father**, **The Katzenjammer Kids**, and many more were as popular if not more so than Superman and Batman when they were introduced. **Superman** #1 sold out three printings totaling 900,000 copies, yet on any given day in the same year (1939), over 100 million people were reading the adventures of Chic Young's **Blondie** in the funny pages. Recent research has come up with some more amazing rediscoveries. There is much that can be learned and applied to today's comics market by a simple historical examination of the medium's evolution.

The first known cartoon printed on paper in the New World was in a Puritan children's book first published in 1646. Titled simply **The Burning of Mr. John Rogers**, it showed in flaming graphic detail what happens to those who stray from the flock and have to be burned at the stake. The first cartoon published in a newspaper in America is generally credited to Benjamin Franklin's "God Helps Those Who Help Themselves," in his periodical **Plain Truth** (1747). Other panel cartoons soon followed all over America, many utilizing word balloons.

According to **The New York Times** (Sept. 3, 1904), the first American comic book was issued as a supplement to **Brother Jonathan** (New York, Sept. 14, 1842). It was a reprint of Rudolphe Töpffer's **The Adventures of Obadiah Oldbuck**—40 pages in length, side-stitched, printed on both sides of the paper with six to twelve panels per page, and measuring 8 1/2" x 11". One copy turned up in Oakland, California in late 1998, confirming its existence.

Töpffer, who was Swiss, created at least eight widely published comic books which might also be called "graphic novels." Jerry Robinson, in his authoritative 1974 history book **The Comics**, wrote that "Töpffer is considered by some historians the inventor of the picture story, as he called it, and consequently the father of today's comics." Many other comics historians of equal stature have written just as eloquently about the man who invented the modern comic strip in 1827. By 1841, Töpffer's picture stories had been translated into over half a dozen languages including rare British editions; the American one is a reprint of this reprint. Several more were printed in America in 1846. Töpffer's comic books remained in print in the USA until at least 1877. Over 100 years later, even though he is widely acknowledged in Europe as the father of the comic book, he remains obscure on the other side of the Atlantic.

As the second millennium comes to a close, we have discovered many other comic books printed, distributed and widely read in America throughout the 1800s which are little known today due to their rarity. In the last decade, serious collectors have begun looking into the dim past and are steadily expanding their awareness of these earlier comic books. As knowledge grows in this area, we hope to report more about what we tentatively dub "Victorian Age" comic books.

The first graphic advertising appeared several years after the Civil War, initially sponsored by the likes of cereal and tobacco companies. At first these ads contained young kids, then animals of all kinds. With the immigrant influx of the 1870s and '80s, fairies soon dominated the scene.

Palmer Cox's **The Brownies** were the first North American comics-type characters to be internationally merchandised. For over a quarter of a century, Cox deftly combined the popular advertising motifs of animals and fairies into a wonderful, whimsical world of society at its best and worst.

Cox's (1840-1924) first work in **St. Nicholas**, a magazine for children, was in the March 1879 issue, titled "The Wasp and the Bee." He began his famous creation, **The Brownies**, with his trademark verse and art, with a creation entitled **The Brownies' Ride** in the February 1883 issue. **The Brownies**' first book was issued by 1887, titled **The Brownies: Their Book**; many more followed. Cox also added a run of his hugely popular characters in **Ladies Home Journal** from October 1891 through February 1895, as well as a special on December 1910.

With the 1892-93 World's Fair, the merchandising exploded with a host of products, including pianos, paper dolls and other figurines, chairs, stoves, puzzles, cough drops, coffee, soap, boots, candy, and many more. **Brownies** material was being produced in Europe as well as the United States.

Cox ran **The Brownies** as a newspaper strip in the **San Francisco Examiner** during 1898 and in the **New York World** in 1900. It was syndicated from 1903 through 1907. He seems to have retired from regularly drawing **The Brownies** with the January 1914 issue of **St. Nicholas** when he was 74. A wealthy man, he lived to the ripe old age of

"Fourth Ward Brownies," artwork by Richard F. Outcault. Note the Yellow Kid, second from left.

84. Shortly before he died, he did a special commemorative **Brownies** for the October 1924 **St. Nicholas** issue, titled "The Wasp—a Rhyme."

By the mid-1890s, while keeping careful track of quickly rising circulations of magazines with graphic humor such as **Harper's**, **Puck**, **St. Nicholas**, **Judge**, **Life** and **Truth**, New York based newspaper publishers began to recognize that illustrated humor would sell extra papers. Thus was born the Sunday "comic supplement." Most of the regular favorites were under contract with these magazines; however, there was an artist working for **Truth** who wasn't. Roy L McCardell, then a staffer at **Puck**, informed Morrill Goddard, Sunday editor of **The New York World**, that he knew someone who could fit what was needed at the then largest newspaper in America.

THE WASP AND THE BEE.
BY PALMER COX.

Richard F. Outcault (1863-1928) first introduced his street children strip in the June 2, 1894 issue of **Truth**, somewhat inspired by Michael Angelo Woolf's slum kids single panel cartoons in **Life** which began in the mid 1880s. It's also possible that Outcault's **Hogan's Alley** cast, including the **Yellow Kid**, was possibly inspired by Charles W. Saalburg's **The Ting Ling Kids** which began in the **Chicago Inter-Ocean** by May 1894. By 1895 Saalburg was Art Director in charge of coloring for the new color printing press at the **New York World**. Edward Harrigan's play "O'Reilly and the Four Hundred," which had a song beginning with the words "Down in Hogan's Alley..." likely provided direct inspiration.

Top, "The Wasp and the Bee," the first Palmer Cox artwork, March 1879, Middle, The Brownies, Ride, February 1883. Bottom, Palmer Cox's ubiquitous Brownies

By the November 18, 1894 issue of the **World**, Outcault was working for Goddard and Saalburg. Outcault produced a successful Sunday newspaper sequential comic strip in color with **The Origin of a New Species** on the back page in the **World**'s first colored Sunday supplement. Walt McDougall, a famous cartoonist reputed to have turned the 1884 Presidential race with a single cartoon that ran in the **World**, handled the front page.

The **World** began running full page color single panels on May 21, 1893. McDougall did various other page panels during 1893, but it was January 28, 1894 when the first sequence of comic pictures in a newspaper appeared in panels in the same format as our comic strips today. It was a full page cut up into nine panels, and the sequence was drawn entirely in pantomime, with no words. This historic page was drawn by Mark Fenderson.

The second page to appear in panels was an eight panel strip, also lacking words except for the title. This page was a collaboration between Walt McDougall and Mark

Fenderson. From then on, many full page color strips by McDougall and Fenderson appeared; they were the first cartoonists to draw for the Sunday newspaper comic section.

It was Outcault, however, who soon became the most famous cartoonist featured. After first appearing in black and white in the **New York World** on February 17, 1895, **The Yellow Kid** was introduced to the public in color. The strip is widely recognized today as the first newspaper comic strip to demonstrate without a doubt that the general public was ready for full color comics. **The Yellow Kid** was the first to show that (1) comics could increase newspaper sales, and that (2) comic characters could be merchandised. **The Yellow Kid** was the headlining spark of what soon became dubbed by Hearst as "eight pages of polychromatic effulgence that makes the rainbow look like a lead pipe."

Ongoing research suggests that Palmer Cox's fabulous success with **The Brownies** was a direct inspiration for Richard Outcault's work. The ultimate proof lies in the fourth **Yellow Kid** cartoon, which appeared in the February 9, 1895 issue of **Truth**. It was reprinted in the **New York World** eight days later on February 17, 1895, becoming the first **Yellow Kid** cartoon in the newspapers. The caption read "FOURTH WARD BROWNIES. MICKEY, THE ARTIST (adding a finishing touch)—Dere, Chimmy! If Palmer Cox wuz t' see yer, he'd git yer copyrighted in a minute."

Happy Hooligan's Reception, ©Frederick A. Stokes

The Yellow Kid was widely licensed in the greater New York area for all kinds of products, including gum and cigarette cards, toys, pin backs, cookies, post cards, tobacco products, and appliances. There was also a short-lived humor magazine from Street & Smith named **The Yellow Kid**, featuring exquisite Outcault covers, plus a 196-page comic book from Dillingham & Co. known as **The Yellow Kid in McFadden's Flats**, dated to early 1897. In addition, there were several **Yellow Kid** plays produced, spawning other collectibles like show posters, programs and illustrated sheet music. (For those interested in more information regarding the Yellow Kid, it is available on the internet at **www.neponset.com/yellowkid**.)

Mickey Dugan burned brightly for a few years as Outcault secured a copyright on the character with the United States Government by Sept. 1896. By the time he completed the necessary paper work, however, hundreds of business people nationwide had pirated the image of **The Yellow Kid** and plastered it all over every product imaginable; mothers were even dressing their newborns to look like Dugan.

Outcault soon found himself in a maelstrom not of his choosing, which probably pushed him to eventually drop the character. Outcault's creation went back and forth between newspaper giants Pulitzer and Hearst until Bennett's **New York Herald** mercifully snatched the cartoonist away in 1900 to do a few short-run strips. Later, he did one particular strip for a year—a satire of rural black America—titled **Pore Li'l Mose**, and then his newer creation, **Buster Brown**, debuted May 4, 1902. **Mose** had a very rare comic book collection published in 1902 by Cupples & Leon, now highly sought after by today's savvy collectors. Outcault continued drawing him in the background of occasional **Buster Brown** strips for many years to come.

William Randolph Hearst loved the comic strip medium ever since he was a little boy growing up on **Max & Moritz** by Wilhelm Busch in American collected book editions translated from the original German (these collections were first published in book form in 1870, probably serving as the influence for **The Katzenjammer Kids**). One of the ways Hearst responded to losing Outcault in 1900 was by purchasing the highly successful humor magazine **Puck**, and within a year Hearst transformed this **National Lampoon** of its day into the colored Sunday comics section, **Puck-The Comic Weekly**. With **Puck** and its exclusive cartoonist contracts, he got Frederick Burr Opper's undivided attention. At first featuring Rudolph Dirk's **The Katzenjammer Kids** (1897), **Happy Hooligan** and other fine strips by the wildly popular Opper and a few others, the section steadily added more strips; for decades to come, there just wasn't anything else that could compete with **Puck**. Hearst hired the best of the best and made **Puck** into the most popular comics section anywhere.

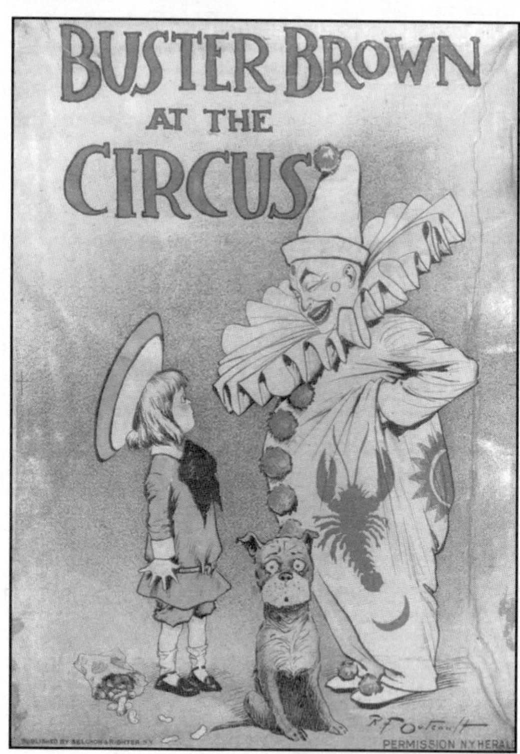

Buster Brown at the Circus, ©Cupples & Leon

Outcault followed in Palmer Cox's footprints a decade later by using the nexus of a World's Fair as a jumping off venue. **Buster Brown** was an instant sensation when he debuted as the new merchandising mascot of the Brown Shoe Company at the 1904 St. Louis World's Fair in a special Buster Brown Shoes pavilion. The character has the honor of being the first nationally licensed comic strip character in America. Many hundreds of different Buster Brown premiums have been issued. Comic books by Frederick A. Stokes Company featuring **Buster Brown & His Dog Tige** began as early as 1903 with **Buster Brown and His Resolutions**, simultaneously published in several different languages throughout the world.

After a few years **Buster** and Outcault returned to Hearst in late 1905, joining what soon became the flagship of the comics world. **Buster**'s popularity quickly spread all over the United States and then the world as he single-handedly spawned the first great comics licensing dynasty. For years there were little people traveling from town to town performing as **Buster Brown** and selling shoes while accompanied by small dogs named Tige. Many other highly competitive licensed strips would soon follow. We suggest checking out **Hake's Price Guide to Character Toys** for information on several hundred **Buster Brown** competitors, as well as several pages of the more fascinating Buster Brown material.

Within a few years, there were many comic strip syndicates not only offering hundreds of various comic strips but also offering to license the characters for any company interested in paying the fee. The history of the comic strips with wide popularity since **The Yellow Kid** has been intertwined with giveaway premiums and character-based, store-bought merchandise of all kinds. Since its infancy as a profitable art form unto itself with **The Yellow Kid**, the comic strip world has profited from selling all sorts of "stuff" to the public featuring their favorite character or strip as its motif. American business gladly responded to the desire for comic character memorabilia with thousands of fun items to enjoy and collect. Most of the early comics were not aimed specifically at kids, though children understandably enjoyed them as well.

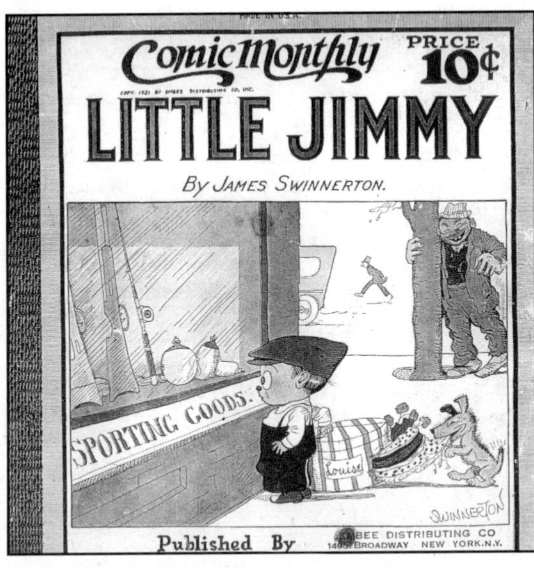

Top, Comic Monthly #7, 1922. ©Embee Dist. Co.
Below, Foxy Grandpa, 1905, ©Frederick A. Stokes

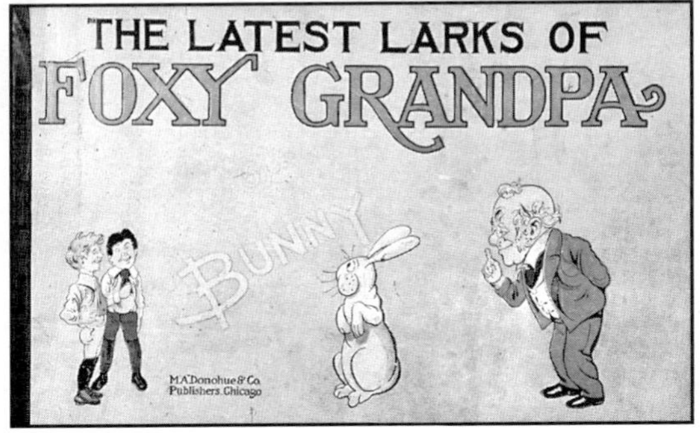

The comic book has generally been associated with almost all of the licensed merchandise in this century. In the Platinum Age section beginning right after this essay, you will find a great many comic books in varied formats and sizes published before the advent of the first successful monthly newsstand comic book, **Famous Funnies**. What drove each of these evolutionary format changes was the need by their producers to make money.

The first significant format was F. M. Howarth's **Funny Folks**, published in 1899 by E. P. Dutton and drawn from the black and white pages of **Puck**. This hardcover volume measured 16 1/2" wide by 12" tall. E. W. Kemble's **The Blackberries** had a color collection by 1901, published by R. H. Russell of New York.

Soon settling on a popular size of 17" wide by 11" tall, comic books were soon available that featured Charles "Bunny" Shultze's **Foxy Grandpa**, Rudolph Dirk's **The Katzenjammer Kids**, Winsor McCay's **Little Sammy Sneeze**, **Rarebit Fiend** and **Little**

Nemo, and Fred Opper's **Happy Hooligan** and **Maud**, in addition to dozens of **Buster Brown** comic books. For well over a decade, these large-size, full-color volumes were the norm, retailing for 50 cents. These collections offered Sunday comics at full-size with only one side printed on a page.

With the popularity of Bud Fisher's new daily strip sensation, **Mutt & Jeff**, a new format was created for reprinting daily strips in black and white—a hardcover book about 15" wide by 5" tall, published by Ball starting in 1910, for five volumes.

The next significant change occurred in 1919, when Cupples & Leon began issuing their black and white daily strip reprint books in a new format, about 10" wide by 10" tall, with four panels reprinted per page in a two by two matrix. These books were 52 pages for 25 cents, and the first editions featured **Bringing Up Father** and **Mutt & Jeff**.

In 1926 Cupples & Leon added a new 7" wide by 9" tall format with **Little Orphan Annie**, **Smitty**, and others. These books were issued in both softcover and hardcover editions with dust jackets, and became extremely popular at 60 cents per copy. The competition amongst publishers included Dell, McKay, Sonnet and Whitman. Even the extremely popular **Big Little Book**, introduced in 1932, can be viewed as a smaller version of the existing formats.

Of special historical interest, Embee issued the first 10 cent monthly comic book, **Comic Monthly**, with a first issue dated January 1922. A dozen 8 1/2" by 9" issues were published, each featuring solo adventures of popular King Features strips. The monthly 10 cent comic book had finally arrived, though it would be more than a decade before it became successful. Dell began publishing all original material in **The Funnies** in late 1929 in a larger tabloid format. At least three dozen issues were published before Delacorte threw in the towel.

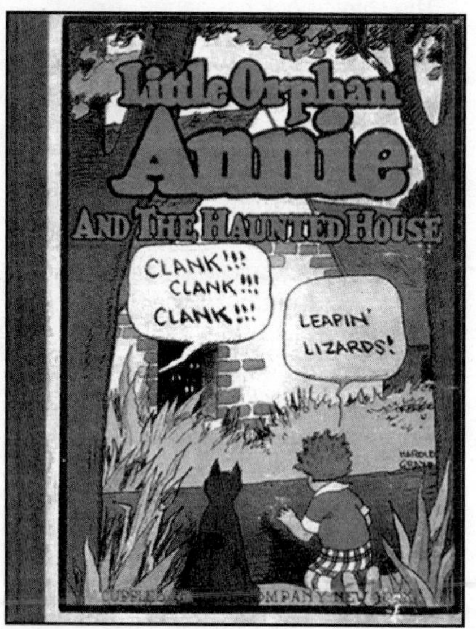

Little Orphan Annie #3, 1928. ©Cupples & Leon.

The 1930s saw a definite shift in merchandising comic strip material from adults to children. This was the decade when Kellogg's placed **Buck Rogers** on the map, and when Ovaltine issued tons of **Little Orphan Annie** material. Merchandising pioneers Sam Gold and Kay Kamen spearheaded this transformation.

Upwards of a thousand of these **Funnies On Parade** precursors, in all formats, were published through 1935 and were very popular. Toward the end of this era, beautiful collections of **Popeye**, **Mickey Mouse**, **Dick Tracy**, and many others were published.

Each year, this Platinum Age section grows as advanced collectors continue to report in with new finds. We encourage readers to help with this section of the book, as each new data entry is very important. For further information on this earlier fascinating era of American comic books, check out Robert L. Beerbohm's "The American Comic Book 1897-1932," originally printed in the 27th edition of **The Overstreet Comic Book Price Guide** and on Gemstone's website at **www.gemstonepub.com**.

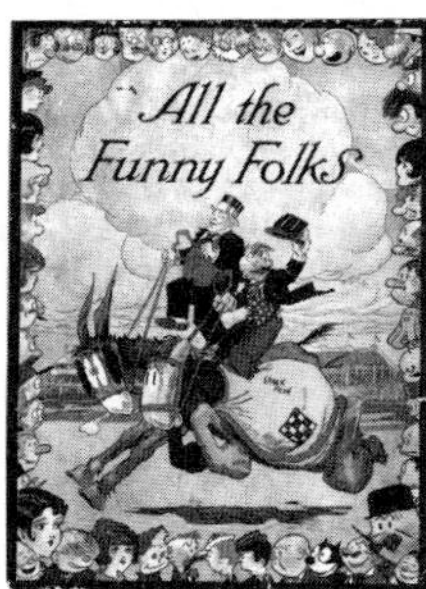

All the Funny Folks
© World Press Today, Inc.

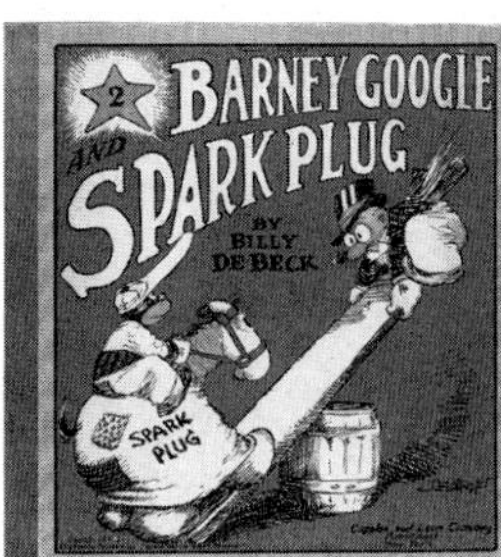

Barney Google and Spark Plug #2
© C&L

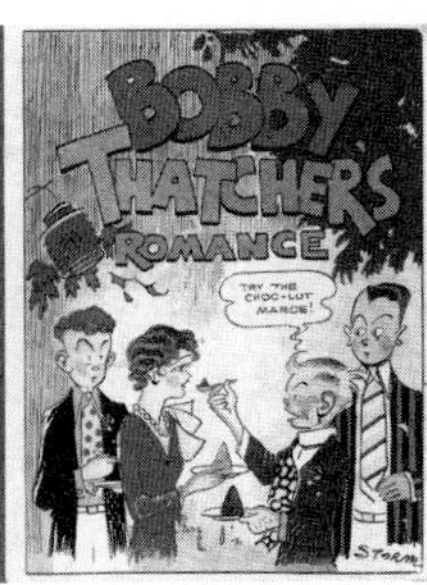

Bobby Thatcher's Romance
© Henry Altemus Co.

	GD25	FN65	VF82

ADVENTURES OF HAWKSHAW (See Hawkshaw The Detective)
The Saalfield Publishing Co.: 1917 (9-3/4x13-1/2", 48 pgs., Color & two-tone)
nn-By Gus Mager (only 24 pgs. of strips, reverse of each pg. is blank) 41.00 164.00 290.00
nn-1927 Reprints 1917 issue 36.00 144.00 250.00

ADVENTURES OF MICKEY MOUSE, THE
David McKay Co., Inc.: Book I, 1931 - Book II, 1932 (5-1/2"x8-1/2", 32 pgs.)
Book I-First Disney book, by strict definition (1st printing-50,000 copies)(see Mickey Mouse Book by Bibo & Lang). Illustrated text refers to Clarabelle Cow as "Carolyn" and Horace Horsecollar as "Henry". The name "Donald Duck" appears with a non-costumed generic duck on back cover & inside, not in the context of the character that later debuted in the Wise Little Hen.
Hardback w/characters on back-c 71.00 284.00 500.00
Softcover w/characters on back-c 36.00 144.00 250.00
Version without characters on back-c 43.00 172.00 300.00
Book II-Less common than Book I. Character development brought into conformity with the Mickey Mouse cartoon shorts and syndicated strips. Captain Church Mouse, Tanglefoot, Peg-Leg Pete and Pluto appear with Mickey & Minnie 18.00 72.00 125.00

ADVENTURES OF SLIM AND SPUD, THE
Prairie Farmer Publ. Co.: 1924 (3-3/4x 9-3/4", 104 pgs., B&W strip reprints)
nn 41.00 164.00 290.00

ADVENTURES OF WILLIE GREEN, THE
Frank M. Acton Co.: 1915 (50¢, 8-1/2X16", B&W, soft-c)
Book 1-By Harris Brown; strip-r 43.00 172.00 300.00

AIN'T IT A GRAND & GLORIOUS FEELING? (Also see Mr. & Mrs.)
Whitman Publishing Co.: 1922 (9x9-3/4", 52 pgs., stiff cardboard-c)
nn-1921 daily strip-r; B&W, color-c; Briggs-a 43.00 172.00 300.00
nn-(9x9-1/2", 28pgs., stiff cardboard-c)-Sunday strip-r in color (inside front-c says "More of the Married Life of Mr. & Mrs".) 32.00 128.00 225.00

ALL THE FUNNY FOLKS
World Press Today, Inc.: 1926 (11-1/2x8-1/2", 112 pgs., color, hard-c)
nn-Barney Google, Spark Plug, Jiggs & Maggie, Tillie The Toiler, Happy Hooligan, Hans & Fritz, Toots & Casper, etc. 90.00 360.00 635.00

ALONG THE FIRING LINE WITH ROGER BEAN
Chas. B. Jackson: 1916 (6x17", 66 pgs., B&W, hard-c)
3-By Chic Jackson (1915 daily strips) 50.00 200.00 350.00

ALPHONSE & GASTON & LEON
Hearst's New York American & Journal: 1902,1903 (15x10", Sunday strip reprints in color)
nn-(1902)By Fred Opper 280.00 840.00 1400.00
nn-(1903)-reprint 220.00 660.00 1100.00

ANGELIC ANGELINA
Cupples & Leon Company: 1909 (11-1/2x17", 30 pgs., 2 colors)
nn-By Munson Paddock 50.00 200.00 350.00

BANANA OIL
MS Publ. Co.: 1924 (52 pgs., B&W)
nn-Milt Gross-a; not reprints 57.00 228.00 400.00

BARNEY GOOGLE AND SPARK PLUG (See Comic Monthly & Giant Comic Album)
Cupples & Leon Co.: 1923 - No. 6, 1928 (52 pgs., B&W, daily strip-r)
1-By Billy DeBeck 55.00 220.00 385.00
2-6 43.00 172.00 300.00
NOTE: *Started in 1918 as newspaper strip; Spark Plug began 1922, 1923.*

BLACKBERRIES, THE
R. H. Russell: 1901 (9"x12", color, hard-c)
nn-By E. W. Kemble 180.00 540.00 900.00

BOBBY THATCHER & TREASURE CAVE
Altemus Co.: 1932 (7x9", 86 pgs., B&W, hard-c)
nn-Reprints; Storm-a 24.00 96.00 170.00

BOBBY THATCHER'S ROMANCE
The Bell Syndicate/Henry Altemus Co.: 1931 (7x8-3/4")
nn-By Storm 24.00 96.00 170.00

BRINGING UP FATHER
Star Co. (King Features): 1917 (16-1/2x5-1/2", 100 pgs., B&W, cardboard-c)
nn-(Rare)-Daily strip reprints by George McManus (no price on-c) 129.00 516.00 900.00

BRINGING UP FATHER
Cupples & Leon Co.: 1919 - No. 26, 1934 (10x10", 52 pgs., B&W, stiff cardboard-c) (No. 22 is 9-1/4x9-1/2")
1-Daily strip-r by George McManus in all 86.00 344.00 600.00
2-10 43.00 172.00 300.00
11-26 (Scarcer) 50.00 200.00 350.00
The Big Book 1(1926)-Thick book (hardcover); 10-1/4x10-1/4", 142 pgs. 121.00 484.00 850.00
The Big Book 2(1929) 96.00 384.00 675.00
NOTE: *The Big Books contain 3 regular issues rebound and probably w/dust jackets.*

BUDDY TUCKER & HIS FRIENDS (Also see Buster Brown)
Cupples & Leon Co.: 1906 (11x17", color)
nn-1905 Sunday strip-r by R. F. Outcault 121.00 484.00 850.00

BUDDY TUCKER VISITS THE HOUSE THAT JACK BUILT
Cupples & Leon Co.: 1907
nn 37.00 148.00 260.00

BUFFALO BILL'S PICTURE STORIES
Street & Smith Publications: 1909 (Soft cardboard cover)
nn 49.00 196.00 340.00

BUGHOUSE FABLES
Embee Distributing Co. (King Features): 1921 (10¢, 4x4-1/2", 48 pgs.)
1-Barney Google 39.00 156.00 275.00

BUG MOVIES
Dell Publishing Co.: 1931 (52 pgs., B&W)
nn-Not reprints; Stookie Allen-a 32.00 128.00 225.00

BUSTER BROWN (Also see Brown's Blue Ribbon Book of Jokes and Jingles & Buddy Tucker & His Friends)
Frederick A. Stokes Co.: 1903 - 1916 (Daily strip-r in color)
(1)...& His Resolutions (1903, 11-1/4x16", 66 pgs.) by R. F. Outcault (Rare)-1st nationally distributed comic. Distr. through Sears & Roebuck(Rare) 915.00 3200.00 5500.00
(2)...His Dog Tige & Their Troubles (1904, 11-1/4x16-1/4", 66 pgs.)(Rare) 315.00 1110.00 1900.00
(3)...Pranks (1905, 11-1/4x16-3/8", 66 pgs.)(Rare) 267.00 933.00 1600.00
(4)...Antics (1906, 11x16-3/8", 66 pgs.)(Rare) 267.00 933.00 1600.00
(5)...And Company (1906, 11x16-1/2", 66 pgs.)(Scarce) 186.00 744.00 1300.00
(6)...Mary Jane & Tige (1906, 11-1/4x16, 66 pgs.)(Scarce) 186.00 744.00 1300.00
(7) Collection of Buster Brown Comics (1908)(Scarce) 143.00 572.00 1000.00
(8)...Up to Date (1910, 10-1/8x15-3/4", 66 pgs.)(Rare) 157.00 628.00 1100.00
(9)... Fun And Nonsense (1911, 10-1/8x15-3/4", 62 pgs.) 143.00 572.00 1000.00
(10)...The Fun Maker (1912, 10-1/8x15-3/4", 66 pgs.)(Rare)-Yellow Kid (4 pgs.) 143.00 572.00 1000.00

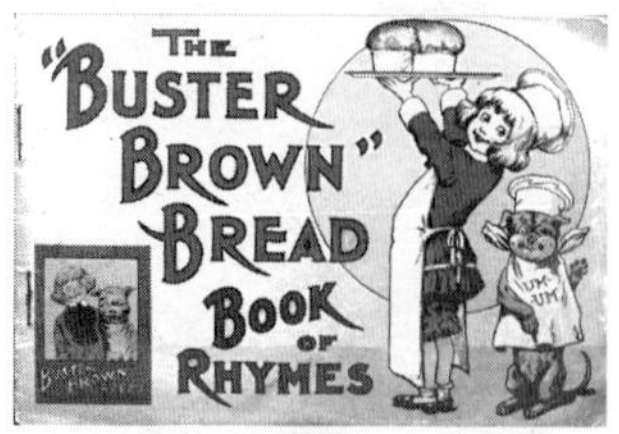

The Buster Brown Bread Book of Rhymes
© Buster Brown Bread Co.

Buster Brown Nuggets #2
© C&L

Charlie Chaplin Up In The Air
© Essaney

	GD25	FN65	VF82
(11)...At Home (1913, 10-1/8x15-3/4", 56 pgs.)	129.00	516.00	900.00
(12)...The Little Rogue (1916, 10-1/8x15-3/4", 62 pgs.) (Rare)	129.00	516.00	900.00
(13)...And Tige Here Again	121.00	484.00	850.00
(14)...The Real Buster Brown	121.00	484.00	850.00

NOTE: *Rarely found in fine or mint condition.*

BUSTER BROWN
Various Publishers: 1904 - 1912 (3x5" to 5x7"; sizes vary)(Advertising premium booklets)

The Brown Shoe Company, St. Louis, USA
Set of five books (5x7", 16 pgs., color)

	GD25	FN65	VF82
Brown's Blue Ribbon Book of Jokes and Jingles Book 1 (nn, 1904)-By R. F. Outcault; Buster Brown & Tige, Little Tommy Tucker, Jack & Jill, Little Boy Blue, Dainty Jane; The Yellow Kid app. on back-c (1st comic book premium)	514.00	2056.00	3600.00
Buster Brown's Blue Ribbon Book of Jokes and Jingles Book 2 (1905)-Original color art by Outcault	229.00	916.00	1600.00
Buster's Book of Jokes & Jingles Book 3 (1909)-r/Blue Ribbon post cards not signed by R.F. Outcault	229.00	916.00	1600.00
Buster's Book of Instructive Jokes and Jingles Book 4 (1910)-Original color art not signed by R.F. Outcault	229.00	916.00	1600.00
...Book of Travels nn (1912, 3x5")-Original color art not signed by Outcault	100.00	400.00	700.00

NOTE: *Estimated 5 to 6 known copies exist of books #1-4.*

The Buster Brown Bread Company

	GD25	FN65	VF82
"Buster Brown" Bread Book of Rhymes, The nn (1904, 4x6", 12 pgs.)-Original color art not signed by R.F. Outcault	136.00	544.00	950.00

The Buster Brown Stocking Company

	GD25	FN65	VF82
Buster Brown Drawing Book, The nn (nd, 5x6", 20 pgs.)-B&W reproductions of 1903 R.F. Outcault art to trace	68.00	272.00	475.00

Collins Baking Company

	GD25	FN65	VF82
Buster Brown Drawing Book nn (1904, 3x5", 12 pgs.)-Original B&W art to trace not signed by R.F. Outcault	68.00	272.00	475.00

C. H. Morton, St. Albans, VT

	GD25	FN65	VF82
Merry Antics of Buster Brown, Buddy Tucker & Tige nn (nd, 3-1/2x5-1/2", 16 pgs.)-Original B&W art by R.F. Outcault	68.00	272.00	475.00

Frederick A. Stokes Co.

	GD25	FN65	VF82
...Abroad (1904, 8x10-1/4, 86 pgs., B&W, hard-c)-R. F. Outcault-a (Rare)	143.00	572.00	1000.00
...Abroad (1904, B&W, 67 pgs.)-R. F. Outcault-a	143.00	572.00	1000.00
...My Resolutions (1906, 10x8", B&W, 68 pgs.)-R.F. Outcault-a (Rare)	171.00	684.00	1200.00

Ivan Frank & Company

	GD25	FN65	VF82
Buster Brown nn (1904, 3x5", 12 pgs.)-B&W repros of R. F. Outcault Sunday pages (First premium to actually reproduce Sunday comic pages – may be first premium comic book?)	64.00	256.00	450.00

Pond's Extract

	GD25	FN65	VF82
Buster Brown's Experiences With Pond's Extract nn (1904, 4-1/2x6-3/4", 28 pgs.)-Original color art by R.F. Outcault	129.00	516.00	900.00

Ringen Stove Company

	GD25	FN65	VF82
Quick Meal Steel Ranges nn (nd, 3x5", 16 pgs.)-Original B&W art not signed by R.F. Outcault	61.00	244.00	425.00

Saalfield Company Muslin Books

	GD25	FN65	VF82
(1)...Goes Fishing (1907, 6-7/8x6-1/8", 24 pgs., color)-r/1905 Sunday comics page by Outcault(Rare)	30.00	120.00	210.00
(2)...Plays Indian (1907, 6-7/8x6-1/8", 24 pgs., color)-r/1905 Sunday comics page by Outcault(Rare)	23.00	92.00	160.00
(3)...Plays Cowboy (1907, 6-3/4x6", 10 pgs., color)-r/1905 Sunday comics page by Outcault(Rare)	23.00	92.00	160.00
(4)...And The Donkey (1907, 6-7/8x6-1/8", 24 pgs., color)-r/1905 Sunday comics page by Outcault (Rare)	23.00	92.00	160.00

No Publisher Listed

	GD25	FN65	VF82
The Drawing Book nn (1906, 3-9/16x5", 8 pgs.)-Original B&W art to trace not signed by R.F. Outcault	61.00	244.00	425.00

BUSTER BROWN
Cupples & Leon Co./N. Y. Herald Co.: 1906 - 1917 (11x17", color, strip-r) (By R. F. Outcault)

	GD25	FN65	VF82
(1A)...His Dog Tige & Their Jolly Times (1906, 11x16, 46 pgs.)	214.00	856.00	1500.00
(1B)...His Dog Tige And Their Jolly Times (1906, 11-3/8x16-5/8", 68 pgs.)			
(2)...Latest Frolics (1906, 11-3/8x16-5/8", 66 pgs.)	121.00	484.00	850.00
(3)...Amusing Capers (1908, 58 pgs.)	93.00	372.00	650.00
(4)...The Busy Body (1909, 11-3/8x16-5/8", 62 pgs.)	93.00	372.00	650.00
(5)...On His Travels (1910, 11x16", 46 pgs.)	93.00	372.00	650.00
(6)...Happy Days (1911, 11-3/8x16-5/8", 58 pgs.)	93.00	372.00	650.00
(7)...In Foreign Lands (1912)	93.00	372.00	650.00
(8)...And His Pets (1913, 11x16", 46 pgs.)	93.00	372.00	650.00
(9)...Funny Tricks (1914, 11-3/8x16-5/8", 58 pgs.)	93.00	372.00	650.00
(10)...And the Cat (1917)	93.00	372.00	650.00

NOTE: *Rarely found in fine or mint condition.*

BUSTER BROWN NUGGETS
Cupples & Leon Co./N.Y.Herald Co.: 1907 (1905, 7-1/2x6-1/2", 36 pgs., color, strip-r, hard-c)(By R. F. Outcault)

	GD25	FN65	VF82
(1) Buster Brown Goes Fishing	33.00	134.00	235.00
(2) Buster Brown Goes Swimming	33.00	134.00	235.00
(3) Buster Brown Plays Indian	33.00	134.00	235.00
(4) Buster Brown Goes Shooting	33.00	134.00	235.00
(5) Buster Brown Plays Cowboy	33.00	134.00	235.00
(6) Buster Brown On Uncle Jack's Farm	33.00	134.00	235.00
(7) Buster Brown Tige And The Bull	33.00	134.00	235.00
(8) Buster Brown And Uncle Buster	33.00	134.00	235.00
(9) Buddy Tucker Meets Alice in Wonderland	33.00	134.00	235.00
(10) Buddy Tucker Visits The House That Jack Built	33.00	134.00	235.00

BUSTER BROWN'S AUTOBIOGRAPHY
Frederick A. Stokes Co.: 1907 (B&W, 10x8", 71 pgs.) (16 color plates & 36 B&W illos)

	GD25	FN65	VF82
nn	54.00	216.00	375.00

BUTTONS & FATTY IN THE FUNNIES
Whitman Publishing Co.: nd (1927)(10-1/4"x15-1/2", 28pg., color)

	GD25	FN65	VF82
W936-Signed "M.E.B.", probably Merrill Blosser; strips in color copyright The Brooklyn Daily Eagle; thought to be one of the first two western Publ. Co. books (very rare)	61.00	244.00	425.00

CHARLIE CHAPLIN
Essanay/M. A. Donohue & Co.: 1917 (9x16", B&W, large size soft-c)

	GD25	FN65	VF82
Series 1, #315-Comic Capers (9-3/4x15-3/4")-18pgs. by Segar; Series 1, #316-In the Movies	200.00	800.00	1400.00
Series 1, #317-Up in the Air, #318-In the Army	200.00	800.00	1400.00
Funny Stunts-(12-1/2x16-3/8", color)	164.00	656.00	1150.00

NOTE: *All contain **Segar** -a; pre-Thimble Theatre.*

CHASING THE BLUES
Doubleday Page: 1912 (7-1/2x10", 52 pgs., B&W, hard-c)

	GD25	FN65	VF82
nn-by Rube Goldberg	118.00	472.00	825.00

CLANCY THE COP
Dell Publishing Co.: 1930 - No. 2, 1931 (10x10", 52 pgs., B&W, cardboard-c) (not-r)

	GD25	FN65	VF82
1,2-Vep-a	40.00	162.00	285.00

Comic Monthly #1
© Embee Dist. Co.

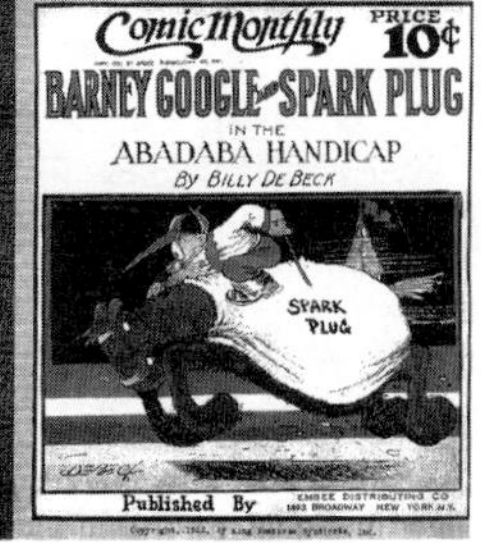

Comic Monthly #11
© KING

Foxy Grampa's Triumphs
© Bunny Publ.

GD25 FN65 VF82

CLIFFORD MCBRIDE'S IMMORTAL NAPOLEON & UNCLE ELBY
The Castle Press: 1932 (12x17"; soft-c cartoon book)

nn-Intro. by Don Herod 36.00 144.00 250.00

COMIC MONTHLY
Embee Dist. Co.: Jan, 1922 - No. 12, Dec, 1922 (10¢, 8-1/2"x9", 28 pgs., 2-color covers) (1st monthly newsstand comic publication) (Reprints 1921 B&W dailies)

1-Polly & Her Pals 193.00 772.00 1350.00
2-Mike & Ike by Rube Goldberg 114.00 456.00 800.00
3-S'Matter, Pop? 71.00 284.00 500.00
4-Barney Google 114.00 456.00 800.00
5-Tillie the Toiler 71.00 284.00 500.00
6-12: 6-Indoor Sports. 7-Little Jimmy. 8-Toots and Casper. 9,10-Foolish Questions. 11-Barney Google & Spark Plug in the Abadaba Handicap. 12-Polly & Her Pals 71.00 284.00 500.00

COMIC PAINTING AND CRAYONING BOOK
Saalfield Publ. Co.: 1917 (10x13-1/2", 32 pgs.) (No price on-c)

nn-Tidy Teddy by F. M. Follett, Clarence the Cop, Mr. & Mrs. Butt-In; regular comic stories to read or color 43.00 172.00 300.00

DAFFYDILS
Cupples & Leon Co.: 1911 (6x8", 52 pgs., B&W, hard-c)

nn-By Tad 43.00 172.00 300.00

DEADWOOD GULCH
Dell Publishing Co.: 1931 (52 pgs., B&W)

nn-By Charles "Boody" Rogers 25.00 100.00 175.00

DICK TRACY & DICK TRACY JR. CAUGHT THE RACKETEERS, HOW
Cupples & Leon Co.: 1933 (7x8-1/2", 88pgs., hard-c) (See Treasure Box of Famous Comics)

2-(Numbered on pg. 84)-Continuation of Stooge Viller book (daily strip reprints from 8/3/33 thru 11/8/33)(Rarer than #1) 79.00 316.00 550.00
With dust jacket... 118.00 472.00 825.00

DICK TRACY & DICK TRACY JR. AND HOW THEY CAPTURED "STOOGE" VILLER
Cupples & Leon Co.: 1933 (7x8-1/2", 100 pgs., hard-c, one-shot)
Reprints 1932 & 1933 Dick Tracy daily strips

nn(No.1)-1st app. of "Stooge" Viller 79.00 316.00 550.00
with dust jacket... 118.00 472.00 825.00

DOINGS OF THE DOO DADS, THE
Detroit News (Universal Feat. & Specialty Co.): 1922 (50¢, 7-3/4x7-3/4", 34 pgs, B&W, red & white-c, square binding)

nn-Reprints 1921 newspaper strip "Text & Pictures" given away as prize in the Detroit News Doo Dads contest; by Arch Dale 40.00 162.00 285.00

DOLLY DIMPLES & BOBBY BOONCE'
Cupples & Leon Co.: 1933

nn 24.00 96.00 165.00

DREAMS OF THE RAREBIT FIEND
Doffield & Co.?: 1905

nn-By Winsor McCay (Very Rare) (Three copies known to exist)
Estimated value.... 670.00 2680.00 4000.00

FELIX
Henry Altemus Company: 1931 (6-1/2"x8-1/4", 52 pgs., color, hard-c w/dust jacket)

1-3-Sunday strip reprints of Felix the Cat by Otto Messmer. Book No. 2 r/1931 Sunday panels mostly two to a page in a continuity format oddly arranged so each tier of panels reads across two pages, then drops to the next tier. (Books 1 & 3 have not been documented.)(Rare)
Each 100.00 400.00 700.00
With dust jacket 143.00 572.00 1000.00

FELIX THE CAT BOOK
McLoughlin Bros.: 1927 (8"x15-3/4", 52 pgs, half in color-half in B&W)

nn-Reprints 23 Sunday strips by Otto Messmer from 1926 & 1927, every other one in color, two pages per strip. (Rare) 200.00 800.00 1400.00
260-Reissued (1931), reformatted to 9-1/2"x10-1/4" (same color plates, but one strip per every three pages), retitled ("Book" dropped from title) and abridged (only eight strips repeated from first issue, 28 pgs.).(Rare) 79.00 316.00 550.00

FOXY GRANDPA (Also see The Funnies, 1st series)
N. Y. Herald/Frederick A. Stokes Co./M. A. Donahue & Co./Bunny Publ. (L. R. Hammersly Co.): 1901 - 1916 (Strip-r in color, hard-c)

1901-9x15" in color-N. Y. Herald 200.00 800.00 1200.00
1902- "Latest Larks of...", 32 pgs., 9-1/2x15-1/2" 125.00 500.00 750.00
1902- "The Many Advs. of...", 9x12", 148 pgs. (Hammersly) 133.00 532.00 800.00
1903- "Latest Advs.", 9x15", 24 pgs., Hammersly Co. 125.00 500.00 750.00
1903- "...'s New Advs.", 10x15", 32 pgs., Stokes 125.00 500.00 750.00
1904- "Up to Date", 10x15", 28 pgs., Stokes 125.00 500.00 750.00
1905- "& Flip Flaps", 9-1/2x15-1/2", 52 pgs. 125.00 500.00 750.00
1905- "The Latest Advs. of", 9x15", 28, 52, & 66 pgs, M.A. Donohue Co.; re-issue of 1902 issue 79.00 315.00 550.00
1905- "Merry Pranks of", 9-1/2x15-1/2", 52 pgs., Donahue 79.00 315.00 550.00
1905- "Latest Larks of", 9-1/2x15-1/2", 52 pgs., Donahue; re-issue of 1902 issue 79.00 315.00 550.00
1905- "Latest Larks of", 9-1/2x15-1/2", 24 pg. edition, Donahue; re-issue of 1902 issue 79.00 315.00 550.00
1906- "Frolics", 10x15", 30 pgs., Stokes 79.00 315.00 550.00
1907 79.00 315.00 550.00
1908?- "Triumphs", 10x15" 79.00 315.00 550.00
1908?- "...& Little Brother", 10x15" 79.00 315.00 550.00
1911- "Latest Tricks", r-1910,1911 Sundays-Stokes Co. 79.00 315.00 550.00
1914-(9-1/2x15-1/2", 24 pgs.)-6 color cartoons/page, Bunny Publ. 68.00 272.00 475.00
1916- "Merry Book", 10x15", Stokes 68.00 272.00 475.00

FOXY GRANDPA SPARKLETS SERIES
M. A. Donahue & Co.: 1908 (6-1/2x7-3/4"; 24 pgs., color)

"... Rides the Goat", "...& His Boys", "...Playing Ball", "...Fun on the Farm", "...Fancy Shooting", "...Show the Boys Up Sports",... "Plays Santa Claus" each.... 79.00 316.00 550.00
900- "Playing Ball"; Bunny illos; 8 pgs., linen like pgs., no date 62.00 248.00 435.00

FUNNIES, THE (Also see Comic Cuts)
Dell Publishing Co.: 1929 - No. 36, 10/18/30 (10¢; 5¢ No. 22 on) (16 pgs.)
Full tabloid size in color; not reprints; published every Saturday

1-My Big Brudder, Johnathan, Jazzbo & Jim, Foxy Grandpa, Sniffy, Jimmy Jams & other strips begin; first four-color comic newsstand publication; also contains magic, puzzles & stories 129.00 516.00 900.00
2-21 (1930, 30¢) 43.00 172.00 300.00
22(nn-7/12/30-5¢) 33.00 132.00 230.00
23(nn-7/19/30-5¢), 24(nn-7/26/30-5¢), 25(nn-8/2/30), 26(nn-8/9/30), 27(nn-8/16/30), 28(nn-8/23/30), 29(nn-8/30/30), 30(nn-9/6/30), 31(nn-9/13/30), 32(nn-9/20/30), 33(nn-9/27/30), 34(nn-10/4/30), 35(nn-10/11/30), 36(nn, no date-10/18/30) each.... 33.00 132.00 230.00

FUNNY FOLK
E. P. Dutton: 1899 (12"x16-1/2", half in color-half in B&W, hard-c) (Reprints cartoons from Puck)

nn 267.00 1067.00 1600.00

Hans Und Fritz #193
© Saalfield Publ.

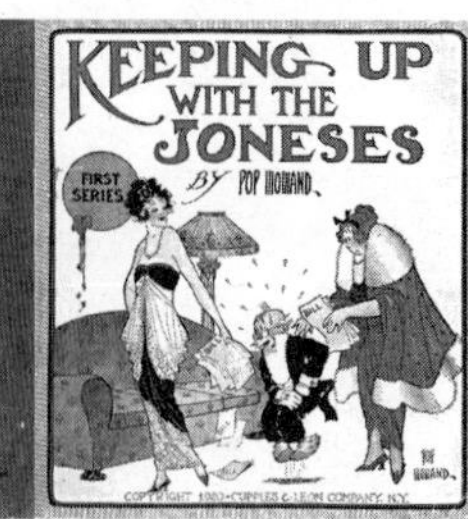

Keeping Up With The Jones #1
© C&L

Little Nemo 1906
© Doffield & Co.

	GD25	FN65	VF82
GASOLINE ALLEY (Also see Popular Comics & Super Comics) **Reilly & Lee Publishers:** 1929 (7x8-3/4", B&W daily strip-r, hard-c)			
nn-By King (96 pgs.)	46.00	184.00	320.00
GUMPS, THE **Landfield-Kupfer/Cupples & Leon No. 2:** No. 1, 1918 - No. 6, 1921; 1924 - No. 8, 1931 (10x10", 52 pgs., B&W)			
Book No. 1(1918)(Rare)-cardboard-c, 5-1/4x13-1/3", 64 pgs., daily strip-r by Sidney Smith	143.00	572.00	1000.00
Book No.2(1918)-(Rare); 5-1/4x13-1/3"; paper cover; 36 pgs. daily strip reprints by Sidney Smith	100.00	400.00	700.00
Book No. 3-6 (Rare)	57.00	228.00	400.00
nn(1924)-By Sidney Smith	61.00	244.00	425.00
2,3	39.00	156.00	270.00
4-7	33.00	132.00	230.00
8-(10x14"); 36 pgs.; B&W; National Arts Co.	33.00	132.00	230.00
GUMPS, ANDY AND MIN, THE **Landfield-Kupfer Printing Co., Chicago/Morrison Hotel:** nd (1920s) (Giveaway, 5-1/2"x14", 20 pgs., B&W, soft-c)			
nn-Strip-r by Sidney Smith; art & logo embossed on cover w/hotel restaurant menu on back-c or a hotel promo ad; 4 diff. issues known	43.00	172.00	300.00
HANS UND FRITZ **The Saalfield Publishing Co.:** 1929 (10x13-1/2", 28 pgs., B&W)			
193-(Rare)-By R. Dirks; contains 1916 Sunday strip reprints of Katzenjammer Kids & Hawkshaw the Detective	104.00	416.00	725.00
...The Funny Larks Of (1927) reprints 1916 strips; Halloween-c	82.00	328.00	575.00
...The Funny Larks Of 2(1929)	79.00	316.00	550.00
HAPPY HOOLIGAN (See Alphonse...) **Hearst's New York American-Journal:** 1902,1903 (18 pgs., Sunday strip reprints in color)			
Book 1-(1902)By Fred Opper	143.00	572.00	1000.00
50 Pg. Edition(1903)-10x15" in color	157.00	628.00	1100.00
HAPPY HOOLIGAN (Handy...) (See The Travels of...) **Frederick A. Stokes Co.:** 1908 (10x15", 32 pgs, color, cardboard-c)			
nn	86.00	344.00	600.00
HAPPY HOOLIGAN (Story of...) **McLoughlin Bros.:** No. 281, 1932 (9-1/2x12", 16 pgs., soft-c)			
281-Three-color text, pictures on heavy paper	64.00	193.00	450.00
HAROLD TEEN (Adventures of...) **Cupples & Leon Co.:** 1929-31 (52 pgs., cardboard-c)			
nn-B&W daily strip reprints by Carl Ed	41.00	164.00	290.00
HAWKSHAW THE DETECTIVE (See Advs. of..., Hans Und Fritz & Okay) **The Saalfield Publishing Co.:** 1917 (10-1/2x13-1/2", 24 pgs., B&W Sunday strip-r)			
nn-By Gus Mager	41.00	164.00	290.00
HENRY **David McKay Co.:** 1935 (25¢, soft-c)			
Book 1-By Carl Anderson	50.00	200.00	350.00
HOME, SWEET HOME **M.S. Publishing Co.:** 1925 (10-1/4x10")			
nn-By Tuthill	33.00	134.00	235.00
IT HAPPENS IN THE BEST FAMILIES **Powers Photo Engraving Co.:** 1920 (52 pgs., B&W Sunday strip-r)			
nn-By Briggs	28.00	112.00	195.00
Special Railroad Edition (30¢)-r/strips from 1914-1920	24.00	96.00	170.00
JIMMY (James Swinnerton) **N. Y. American & Journal:** 1905 (10x15", 40 pgs., color)			
nn	114.00	456.00	800.00
JIMMY, STORY OF **McLoughlin Bros.:**1932 (9'1/2"X12", 16 pgs., soft cover	64.00	193.00	450.00
JOE PALOOKA **Cupples & Leon Co.:** 1933 (52 pgs., B&W daily strip-r)			
nn-(Scarce)-by Fisher	114.00	456.00	800.00
JUST KIDS **McLoughlin Bros.:** No. 283, 1932 (9-1/2x12", 16 pgs., paper-c)			
283-Three-color text, pictures on heavy paper	21.00	84.00	145.00
KATZENJAMMER KIDS, THE (Also see Hans Und Fritz) **New York American & Journal:** 1902,1903 (10x15-1/4", 50 pgs., color) (By Rudolph Dirks; strip 1st appeared in 1898)			
1902 (Rare)	314.00	1256.00	2200.00
1903 (Rare)-reprint	243.00	972.00	1700.00
1905	136.00	544.00	950.00
1905-A Series of Comic Pictures, 10x15", 40 pgs. in color	136.00	544.00	950.00
1905-Tricks of...(10x15)	136.00	544.00	950.00
1906-Stokes-10x16", 32 pgs. in color	114.00	456.00	800.00
1910-The Komical...(10x15)	79.00	316.00	550.00
1921-Embee Dist. Co., 10x16", 20 pgs. in color	64.00	256.00	450.00
KEEPING UP WITH THE JONESES **Cupples & Leon Co.:** 1920 - No. 2, 1921 (9-1/4x9-1/4", 52 pgs., B&W daily strip-r)			
1,2-By Pop Momand	37.00	148.00	260.00
LADY BOUNTIFUL **Saalfield Publ. Co./Press Publ. Co.:** 1917 (10-1/4x13-1/2", 24 pgs., B&W, cardboard-c)			
nn-By Gene Carr; 2 panels per page	36.00	144.00	250.00
LIFE'S LITTLE JOKES **M.S. Publ. Co.:** No date (1924) (52 pgs., B&W)			
nn-By Rube Goldberg	61.00	244.00	425.00
LILY OF THE ALLEY IN THE FUNNIES **Whitman Publishing Co.**(one of their first two books): No date (1927) (10-1/4x15-1/2"; 28 pgs., color)			
W936 - By T. Burke (Rare)	57.00	228.00	400.00
LITTLE ANNIE ROONEY **David McKay Co.:** 1935 (25¢, soft-c)			
Book 1	43.00	172.00	300.00
LITTLE JOHNNY & THE TEDDY BEARS **Reilly & Britton Co.:** 1907 (10x14", 32 pgs.; green, red, black interior color)			
nn-By J. R. Bray-a/Robert D. Towne-s	50.00	200.00	350.00
LITTLE NEMO (...in Slumberland) **Doffield & Co.(1906)/Cupples & Leon Co.(1909):** 1906, 1909 (Sunday strip-r in color, cardboard covers)			
1906-11x16-1/2" by Winsor McCay; 30 pgs. (Rare)	583.00	2335.00	3500.00
1909-10x14" by Winsor McCay (Rare)	500.00	2000.00	3000.00
LITTLE ORPHAN ANNIE (See Treasure Box of Famous Comics) **Cupples & Leon Co.:** 1926 - 1934 (7x8-3/4", 100 pgs., B&W daily strip-r, hard-c)			
1(1926)-Little Orphan Annie	50.00	200.00	350.00

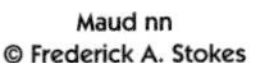

Maud nn
© Frederick A. Stokes

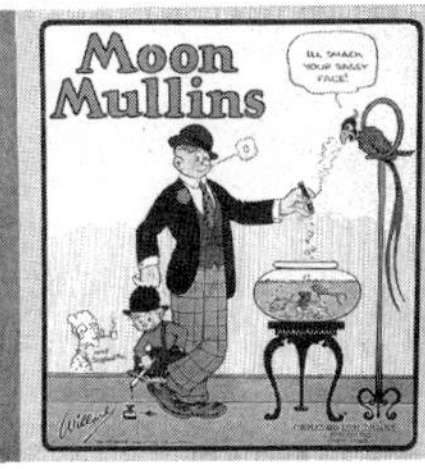

Moon Mullins #1
© C&L

Mutt & Jeff #1
© Ball Publ.

	GD25	FN65	VF82
1(1926)-softback (see Treasure Box...)			
2('27)-In the Circus	36.00	144.00	250.00
2('28)-softback (36 pgs.)	30.00	120.00	210.00
3('28)-The Haunted House	36.00	144.00	250.00
3('28)-softback (36 pgs.)	30.00	120.00	210.00
4('29)-Bucking the World	36.00	144.00	250.00
5('30)-Never Say Die	30.00	120.00	210.00
6('31)-Shipwrecked	30.00	120.00	210.00
7('32)-A Willing Helper	24.00	96.00	170.00
8('33)-In Cosmic City	24.00	96.00	170.00
9('34)-Uncle Dan (Rare)	43.00	172.00	300.00

NOTE: *Each book reprints dailies from the previous year.*

LITTLE SAMMY SNEEZE
New York Herald Co.: 1905 (11x16-1/2", 28 pgs., color)

	GD25	FN65	VF82
nn-By Winsor McCay (Rare)	665.00	2660.00	4000.00

NOTE: *Rarely found in fine to mint condition.*

MAUD
Frederick A. Stokes Co.: 1906 (10x15-1/2", 32 pgs., color, cardboard-c)

	GD25	FN65	VF82
nn-By Fred Opper (Scarce)	117.00	465.00	700.00

MICKEY MOUSE BOOK
Bibo & Lang: 1930-1931 (9"x12", stapled-c, 20 pgs., 4 printings)

nn-First Disney licensed publication (a magazine, not a book–see first book, Adventures of Mickey Mouse). Contains story of how Mickey met Walt and got his name; games, cartoons & song "Mickey Mouse (You Cute Little Feller)," written by Irving Bibo; Minnie, Clarabelle Cow, Horace Horsecollar & caricature of Walt shaking hands with Mickey. The changes made with the 2nd printing have been verified by billing affidavits in the Walt Disney Archives and include:Two Win Smith Mickey strips from 4/15/30 and 4/17/30 added to page 8 & back-c; "Printed in U.S.A." added to front cover; Bobette Bibo's age of 11 years added to title page; faulty type on the word "tail" corrected top of page 3; the word "start" added to bottom of page 7, removing the words "start 1 2 3 4" from the top of page 7; music and lyrics were rewritten on pages 12-14. A green ink border was added beginning with 2nd printing and some covers have inking variations. Art by Albert Barbelle, drawn in an Ub Iwerks style. Total circulation : 97,938 copies varying from 21,000 to 26,000 per printing.

	GD25	FN65	VF82
1st printing. Contains the song lyrics **censored** in later printings, "When little Minnie's pursued by a big bad villain we feel so bad then we're glad when you up and kill him." Attached to the Nov. 15, 1930 issue of the Official Bulletin of the Mickey Mouse Club notes: "Attached to this Bulletin is a new Mickey Mouse Book that has just been published." This is thought to be the reason why a slightly disproportionate larger number of copies of the first printing still exist	1200.00	5400.00	11,000.00
2nd printing with a theater/advertising. Christmas greeting added to inside front cover (1 copy known with Dec. 27, 1930 date)	----	12,000.00	----
2nd-4th printings	1100.00	5000.00	10,000.00

NOTE: Theater/advertising copies do not qualify as separate printings. Most copies are missing pages 9 & 10 which had a puzzle to be cut out. *Puzzle (pages 9 and 10) cut out or missing, subtract 60% to 75%.*

MICKEY MOUSE COMIC
David McKay Co.: 1931 - No. 4, 1934 (10"x9-3/4", 52 pgs., cardboard-c) (Later reprints exist)

	GD25	FN65	VF82
1(1931)-Reprints Floyd Gottfredson daily strips in black & white from 1930 & 1931, including the famous two week sequence in which Mickey tries to commit suicide	214.00	856.00	1500.00
2(1932)-1st app. of Pluto reprinted from 7/8/31 daily. All pgs. from 1931	164.00	656.00	1150.00
3(1933)-Reprints 1932 & 1933 Sunday pages in color, one strip per page, including the "Lair of Wolf Barker" continuity pencilled by Gottfredson and inked by Al Taliaferro & Ted Thwaites. First app. Mickey's nephews, Morty & Ferdie, one identified by name of Mortimer Fieldmouse, not to be confused with Uncle Mortimer Mouse who is introduced in the Wolf Barker story	214.00	856.00	1500.00
4(1934)-1931 dailies, include the only known reprint of the infamous strip of 2/4/31 where the villainous Kat Nipp snips off the end of Mickey's tail with a pair of scissors	121.00	484.00	850.00

MILITARY WILLY
J. I. Austen Co.: 1907 (7x9-1/2", 14 pgs., every other page in color, stapled)

	GD25	FN65	VF82
nn-By F. R. Morgan	50.00	200.00	350.00

MISCHIEVOUS MONKS OF CROCODILE ISLE, THE
J. I. Austen Co., Chicago: 1908 (8-1/2x11-1/2", 12 pgs., 4 pgs. in color)

	GD25	FN65	VF82
nn-By F. R. Morgan; reads longwise	71.00	284.00	500.00

MR. & MRS. (Also see Ain't It A Grand and Glorious Feeling?)
Whitman Publishing Co.: 1922 (9x9-1/2", 52 & 28 pgs., cardboard-c)

	GD25	FN65	VF82
nn-By Briggs (B&W, 52 pgs.)	36.00	144.00	250.00
nn-28 pgs.-(9x9-1/2")-Sunday strips-r in color	39.00	156.00	275.00

MONKEY SHINES OF MARSELEEN
Cupples & Leon Co.: 1909 (11-1/2x17", 28 pgs. in two colors)

	GD25	FN65	VF82
nn-By Norman E. Jennett	50.00	200.00	350.00

MOON MULLINS
Cupples & Leon Co.: 1927 - 1933 (52 pgs., B&W daily strip-r)

	GD25	FN65	VF82
Series 1('27)-By Willard	57.00	228.00	400.00
Series 2('28), Series 3('29), Series 4('30)	39.00	156.00	275.00
Series 5('31), 6('32), 7('33)	36.00	144.00	250.00
Big Book 1('30)-B&W	50.00	200.00	350.00

MUTT & JEFF (...Cartoon, The)
Ball Publications: 1910 - No. 5, 1916 (5-3/4x15-1/2", B&W, hard-c)

	GD25	FN65	VF82
1(1910)(68 pgs., 50¢)	186.00	744.00	1300.00
2,3: 2(1911, 68 pgs.)-Opium den panels; Jeff smokes opium (pipe dreams). 3(1912, 68 pgs.)	96.00	384.00	675.00
4(1915)(68 pgs., 50¢)(Rare)	96.00	384.00	675.00
5(1916)(68 pgs.)(Rare)-Photos of Fisher, 1st pg.	171.00	684.00	1200.00

NOTE: *Mutt & Jeff first appeared in newspapers in 1908. Cover variations exist showing Mutt & Jeff reading various newspapers; i.e., The Oregon Journal, The American, and The Detroit News. Reprinting of each issue began soon after publication. No. 5 may not have been reprinted. Values listed include the reprints.*

MUTT & JEFF
Cupples & Leon Co.: No. 6, 1919 - No. 22, 1933? (9-1/2x9-1/2", 52 pgs., B&W dailies, stiff-c)

	GD25	FN65	VF82
6-22-By Bud Fisher	57.00	228.00	400.00

NOTE: *Later issues are somewhat rarer.*

	GD25	FN65	VF82
nn(1920)-(Advs. of...) 16x11"; 20 pgs.; reprints 1919 Sunday strips	93.00	372.00	650.00
Big Book nn(1926, 144 pgs., hardcovers)	114.00	456.00	800.00
w/dust jacket	193.00	772.00	1350.00
Big Book 1(1928)-Thick book (hardcovers)	114.00	456.00	800.00
w/dust jacket (rare)	183.00	732.00	1275.00
Big Book 2(1929)-Thick book (hardcovers)	114.00	456.00	800.00
w/dust jacket (rare)	183.00	732.00	1275.00

NOTE: *The Big Books contain three previous issues rebound.*

MUTT & JEFF
Embee Publ. Co.: 1921 (9x15")

	GD25	FN65	VF82
nn-Sunday strips in color (Rare)	143.00	572.00	1000.00

NEBBS, THE
Cupples & Leon Co.: 1928 (52 pgs., B&W daily strip-r)

	GD25	FN65	VF82
nn-By Sol Hess; Carlson-a	40.00	160.00	280.00

NEWLYWEDS
Saalfield Publ. Co.: 1907; 1917 (cardboard-c)

	GD25	FN65	VF82
...& Their Baby' by McManus; Saalfield, (1907, 13x10", 52 pgs.); daily strips in full color	100.00	400.00	700.00

...& Their Baby's Comic Pictures, The, by McManus, Saalfield, (1917, 14x10",

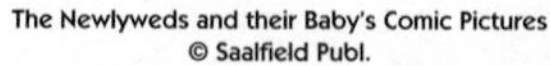
The Newlyweds and their Baby's Comic Pictures
© Saalfield Publ.

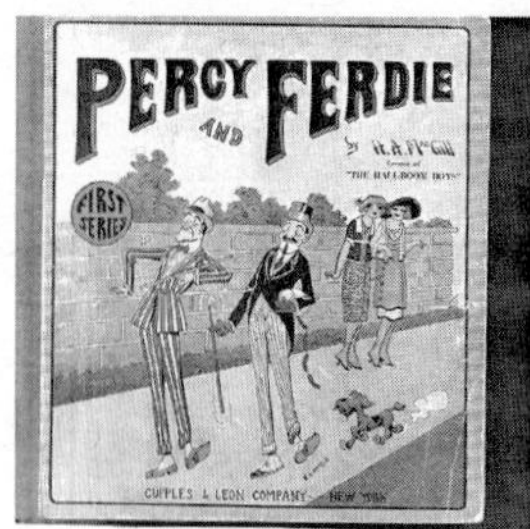

Percy and Ferdie
© C&L

Smitty in the North Woods
© C&L

	GD25	FN65	VF82
22 pgs, oblong, cardboard-c); reprints 'Newlyweds' (Baby Snookums stips) mainly from 1916; blue cover; says for painting & crayoning, but some pages in color. (Scarce)	70.00	280.00	490.00

NIPPY'S POP
The Saalfield Publishing Co.: 1917 (10-1/2x13-1/2", B&W, Sunday strip-r)

nn-32 pgs.	35.00	140.00	245.00

OH, MAN (A Bully Collection of Those Inimitable Humor Cartoons)
P.F. Volland & Co.: 1919 (8-1/2x13")

nn-By Briggs	35.00	140.00	245.00

OH SKIN-NAY!
P.F. Volland & Co.: 1913 (8-1/2x13")

nn-The Days Of Real Sport by Briggs	35.00	140.00	245.00

ON AND OFF MOUNT ARARAT (also see Tigers)
Heart's New York American & Journal: 1902

nn-Funny animal strip-r	86.00	344.00	600.00

ON THE LINKS
Associated Feature Service: Dec, 1926 (9x10", 48 pgs.)

nn-Daily strip-r	22.00	88.00	155.00

OUTBURSTS OF EVERETT TRUE
Saalfield Publ. Co.: 1921 (32 pgs., B&W)

1907 (2-panel strips reprint)	34.00	136.00	240.00

PECKS BAD BOY
Thompson of Chicago (by Walt McDougal): 1906 - 1908 (11-1/4x15-3/4", strip-r)

...& Cousin Cynthia(1907)-In color	68.00	272.00	475.00
...& His Chums (1908)-Hardcover; in full color; 16 pgs.	68.00	272.00	475.00
Advs. of...And His Country Cousins (1906)-In color, 18 pgs., oblong	68.00	272.00	475.00
Advs. of...in Pictures (1908)-In color; Stanton & Van V. Liet Co.	68.00	272.00	475.00

PERCY & FERDIE
Cupples & Leon Co.: 1921 (10x10", 52 pgs., B&W dailies, cardboard-c)

nn-By H. A. MacGill (Rare)	61.00	244.00	425.00

PETER RABBIT
John H. Eggers Co. The House of Little Books Publishers: 1922 - 1923 (9-1/4x6-1/4", paper-c)

B1-B4-(Rare)-(Set of 4 books which came in a cardboard box)-Each book reprints half of a Sunday page per page and contains 8 B&W and 2 color pages; by Harrison Cady each....	43.00	172.00	300.00
Box only	57.00	228.00	400.00

PINK LAFFIN
Whitman Publishing Co.: 1922 (9x12")(Strip-r)

...the Lighter Side of Life, ...He Tells 'Em, ...and His Family, ...Knockouts; Ray Gleason-a (All rare) each...	26.00	104.00	185.00

PORE LI'L MOSE
New York Herald Publ. by Grand Union Tea
Cupples & Leon Co.: 1902 (10-1/2x15", 30 pgs., color)

nn-By R. F. Outcault; 1 pg. strips about early Negroes (Very rare)	1000.00	2000.00	4000.00

REG'LAR FELLERS (See All-American Comics, Popular Comics & Treasure Box of Famous Comics)
Cupples & Leon Co./MS Publishng Co.: 1921 - 1929

	GD25	FN65	VF82
1(1921)-52 pgs. B&W dailies (Cupples & Leon, 10x10")	40.00	160.00	285.00
1925, 48 pgs. B&W dailies (MS Publ.)	36.00	144.00	250.00
Hardcover (1929, 96 pgs.)-B&W reprints	49.00	196.00	340.00

ROGER BEAN, R. G. (Regular Guy)
The Indiana News Co.: 1915 - No. 5, 1917 (4-3/4x16", 34 pgs., B&W, cardboard-c) (No. 1 & 4 bound on side, No. 3 bound at top)

1-By Chic Jackson (48 pgs.)(Scarce)	43.00	172.00	300.00
2-5 (Scarce)	29.00	116.00	200.00

SILK HAT HARRY'S DIVORCE SUIT
M. A. Donoghue & Co.: 1912 (5-3/4x15-1/2", B&W)

Newspaper-r by Tad (Thomas Dorgan)	26.00	104.00	180.00

SKEEZIX (Also see Gasoline Alley)
Reilly & Lee Co.: 1925 - 1928 (Strip-r, soft covers) (pictures & text)

...and Uncle Walt (1924)-Origin	26.00	104.00	180.00
...and Pal (1925)	21.00	84.00	150.00
...at the Circus (1926)	21.00	84.00	150.00
...& Uncle Walt (1927)	21.00	84.00	150.00
...Out West (1928)	21.00	84.00	150.00
Hardback Editions...	34.00	136.00	235.00

SKIPPY
No publisher listed: Circa 1920s (10x8", 16 pgs., color/B&W cartoons)

nn-By Percy Crosby	81.00	322.00	565.00

S'MATTER POP?
Saalfield Publ. Co.: 1917 (10x14", 44 pgs., B&W, cardboard-c)

nn-By Charlie Payne; in full color; pages printed on one side	39.00	156.00	275.00

SMITTY (See Treasure Box of Famous Comics)
Cupples & Leon Co.: 1928 - 1933 (9-1/2x9-1/2", 52 pgs., B&W strip-r, cardboard-c)

1928-(96 pgs. 7x8-3/4")	41.00	164.00	290.00
1929-At the Ball Game, 1930-The Flying Office Boy, 1931-The Jockey, 1932-In the North Woods each...	31.00	124.00	220.00
1933-At Military School	31.00	124.00	220.00
Hardback Editions-(7x8-1/4", 100 pgs.)(Rare)-With dust jacket each...	40.00	160.00	280.00

STRANGE AS IT SEEMS
Blue-Star Publishing Co.: 1932 (64 pgs., B&W, square binding)

1-Newspaper-r	32.00	128.00	225.00

NOTE: *Published with and without No. 1 and price on cover.*

Ex-Lax giveaway(1936, B&W, 24 pgs., 5x7")-McNaught Synd.	11.00	44.00	75.00

TAILSPIN TOMMY STORY & PICTURE BOOK
McLoughlin Bros.: No. 266, 1931? (nd) (10-1/2x10", color strip-r)

266-By Forrest	34.00	136.00	240.00

TAILSPIN TOMMY (Also see Famous Feature Stories & The Funnies)
Cupples & Leon Co.: 1932 (100 pgs., hard-c)

nn-(Rare)-B&W strip reprints from 1930 by Hal Forrest & Glenn Claffin	43.00	172.00	300.00

TARZAN BOOK (The Illustrated...)
Grosset & Dunlap: 1929 (7x9", 80 pgs.)

1(Rare)-Contains 1st B&W Tarzan newspaper comics from 1929. Cloth reinforced spine & dust jacket (50¢); Foster-c with dust jacket...	82.00	328.00	575.00
without dust jacket...	33.00	132.00	230.00
2nd Printing(1934, 25¢, 76 pgs.)-4 Foster pgs. dropped; paper spine, circle in lower right cover with 25¢ price. The 25¢ is barely visible on some copies	31.00	124.00	220.00

1967-House of Greystoke reprint-7x10", using the complete 300 illustrations/

The Three Funmakers nn
© Stokes & Company

Tigers nn
© Hearst's NY American & Journal

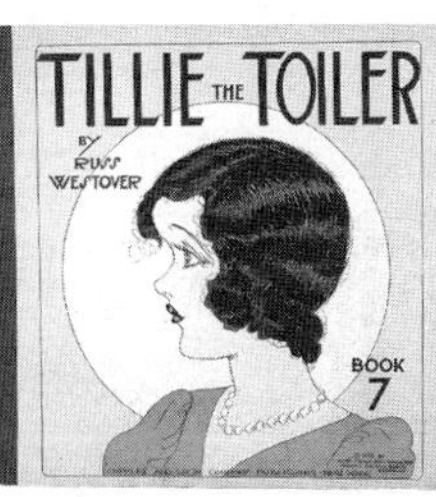

Tillie The Toiler #7
© C&L

	GD25	FN65	VF82

text from the 1929 edition minus the original indicia, foreword, etc. Initial version bound in gold paper & sold for $5.00. Officially titled **Burroughs Biblophile #2**. A very few additional copies were bound in heavier blue paper.

	GD25	FN65	VF82
Gold binding...	2.25	6.75	18.00
Blue binding...	2.50	7.50	24.00

TARZAN OF THE APES TO COLOR
Saalfield Publishing Co.: No. 988, 1933 (10-3/4x15-1/4", 24 pgs) (Coloring book)

	GD25	FN65	VF82
988-(Very Rare)-Contains 1929 daily reprints with some new art by Hal Foster. Two panels blown up large on each page with one at the top of opposing pages on every other double-page spread. Believed to be the only time these panels appeared in color. Most color panels are reproduced a second time in b&w to be colored	243.00	972.00	1700.00

THIMBLE THEATRE STARRING POPEYE
Sonnet Publishing Co.: 1931 - No. 2, 1932 (25¢, B&W, 52 pgs.)(Rare)

	GD25	FN65	VF82
1-Daily strip serial-r in both by Segar	157.00	628.00	1100.00
2	136.00	544.00	950.00

NOTE: *The very first Popeye reprint book. Popeye first entered Thimble Theatre in 1929.*

THREE FUNMAKERS, THE
Stokes and Company: 1908 (10x15", 64 pgs., color) (1904-06 Sunday strip-r)

	GD25	FN65	VF82
nn-Maude, Katzenjammer Kids, Happy Hooligan	250.00	500.00	1000.00

"TIGE" HIS STORY
Frederick A. Stokes Co.: 1905 (10x8", 63 pgs., B&W) (63 illos.)

	GD25	FN65	VF82
nn	86.00	344.00	600.00

TIGERS (Also see On and Off Mount Ararat)
Hearst's New York American & Journal: 1902

	GD25	FN65	VF82
nn-Funny animal strip reprints	86.00	344.00	600.00

TILLIE THE TOILER
Cupples & Leon Co.: 1925 - No. 8, 1933 (52 pgs., B&W, daily strip-r)

	GD25	FN65	VF82
nn (#1)	46.00	184.00	325.00
2-8	34.00	136.00	240.00

NOTE: *First strip appearance was January, 1921.*

TOM SAWYER & HUCK FINN
Stoll & Edwards Co.: 1925 (10-3/4x10", 52 pgs, stiff covers)(Sunday strips in color)

	GD25	FN65	VF82
nn-By Dwiggins; 1923, 1924-r	35.00	140.00	245.00

TOONERVILLE TROLLEY
Cupples & Leon Co.: 1921 (52 pgs., B&W, daily strip-r)

	GD25	FN65	VF82
1-By Fontaine Fox	50.00	200.00	350.00

TRAVELS OF HAPPY HOOLIGAN, THE
Frederick A. Stokes Co.: 1906 (10-1/4x15-3/4", 32 pgs., cardboard covers)

	GD25	FN65	VF82
nn-Contains reprints from 1905	71.00	284.00	500.00

TREASURE BOX OF FAMOUS COMICS
Cupples & Leon Co.: Mid 1930's (6-7/8x8-1/2", 36 pgs, soft covers) (Boxed set of 5 books)

	GD25	FN65	VF82
Little Orphan Annie (1926)	21.00	84.00	150.00
Reg'lar Fellers (1928)	19.00	76.00	130.00
Smitty (1928)	19.00	76.00	130.00
Harold Teen (1931)	19.00	76.00	130.00
How Dick Tracy & Dick Tracy Jr. Caught The Racketeers (1933)	26.00	104.00	185.00
Softcover set of five books in box	160.00	640.00	1125.00
Box only	57.00	228.00	400.00

NOTE: *Dates shown are copyright dates; all books actually came out in 1934 or later. The soft-covers are abbreviated versions of the hardcover editions listed under each character.*

Willie Westinghouse Edison Smith The Boy Inventor #1
© William A. Stokes

TRIALS OF LULU AND LEANDER, THE
William A. Stokes Co.: 1906 (10x16", 32 pgs. in color)

	GD25	FN65	VF82
nn-By F. M. Howarth	43.00	172.00	300.00

TROUBLE OF BRINGING UP FATHER, THE
Embee Publ. Co.: 1921 (9x15", Sunday-r in color)

	GD25	FN65	VF82
nn-(Rare)	75.00	300.00	525.00

VAUDEVILLE AND OTHER THINGS
Isaac H. Blandiard Co.: 1900 (10-1/2x13", 18+ pgs., color)

	GD25	FN65	VF82
nn-By Bunny (Scarce)	175.00	350.00	700.00

WILLIE WESTINGHOUSE EDISON SMITH THE BOY INVENTOR
William A. Stokes Co.: 1906 (10x16", 36 pgs. in color)

	GD25	FN65	VF82
nn-By Frank Crane (Scarce)	150.00	300.00	600.00

WINNIE WINKLE
Cupples & Leon Co.: 1930 - No. 4, 1933 (52 pgs., B&W daily strip-r)

	GD25	FN65	VF82
1	39.00	156.00	275.00
2-4	26.00	104.00	185.00

YELLOW KID, THE (Magazine)(becomes The Yellow Kid Book #10 on)
Howard Ainslee & Co., N.Y.: Mar. 20, 1897 - #9, July 17, 1897 (5¢, B&W w/color covers, 52p., stapled)

	GD25	FN65	VF82
1-R.F. Outcault Yellow kid on-c only #1-6. The same Yellow Kid color ad app. on back-c #1-6 (advertising the New York Sunday Journal)	650.00	2600.00	-
2 (4/3/97)	350.00	1400.00	-
3-6 (#6, 6/5/97)	243.00	975.00	-
7-9 (Yellow Kid not on-c)	106.00	425.00	-

NOTE: Richard Outcault's Yellow Kid from the Hearst New York American represents the very first successful comic strip in America. Eventually the first prototype comic books appeared reprinting these early strips. This magazine is listed here due to historical importance but is not a comic book.

YELLOW KID IN MCFADDEN'S FLATS, THE
G. W. Dillingham Company, New York: 1897 (50¢, 5 1/2x7 1/2", 196 pgs., B&W, squarebound)

	GD25	FN65	VF82
nn-The first "comic" book; E. W. Townsend narrative w/R. F. Outcault Sunday comic page art-r & some original drawings	4500.00	8000.00	-

The Yellow Kid in Mc Fadden's Flats

The American Comic Book: 1933-Present

THE GOLDEN AGE & BEYOND: THE ORIGIN OF THE MODERN COMIC BOOK

by Robert L. Beerbohm & Richard D. Olson, PhD © 1999

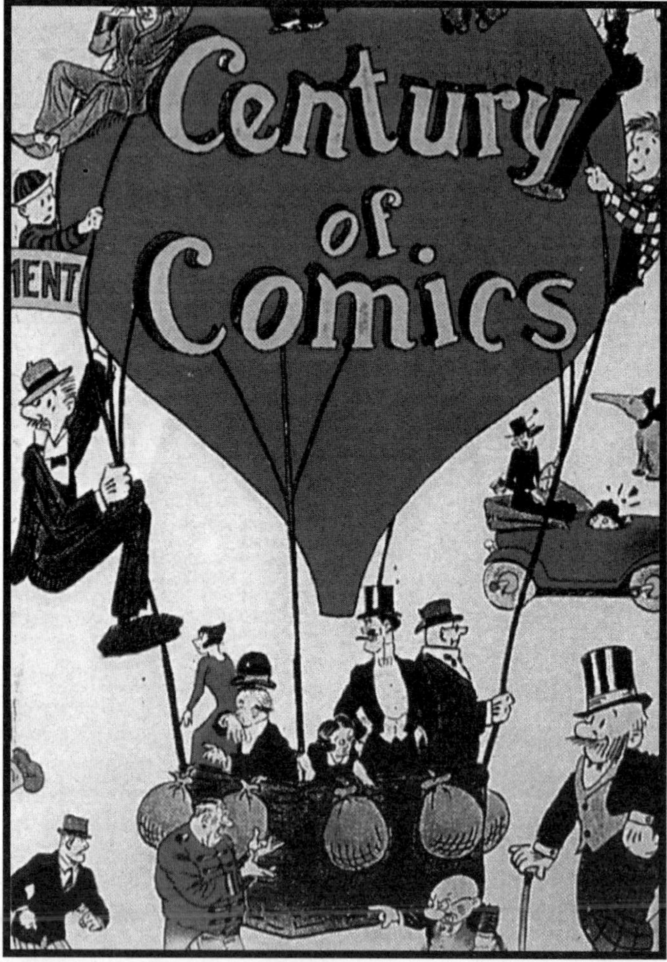

Century of Comics ©1933 Eastern Color Printing Co.

The formats that comic publishing pioneer Cupples & Leon popularized in 1919, although similar in appearance to comics of the Golden Age except for size, are quite different from today's comic format. Even so, the books and their styles were consistently successful until 1929 when they had to compete against The Great Depression—The Depression eventually won. The reason for the format change was that at a cost of 25¢ per book for the 10″ x 10″ cardboard style and 60¢ for the 7″ x 8

1/2" dustjacketed hardcovers, the price became increasingly prohibitive for most consumers already stifled by the crushed economy. As a result, all Cupples & Leon style books published between 1929-1935 are very rare and highly desireable as collectibles because most Americans had little money to spend after paying for necessities like food and shelter during the Depression.

By the early 1930s, the era of the Prestige Format black & white reprint comic book was over. In 1932-33 a lot of format variations arose, collecting such newspaper strips as **Bobby Thatcher**, **Bringing Up Father**, **Buck Rogers**, **Dick Tracy**, **Happy Hooligan**, **Joe Palooka**, **Just Kids**, **The Little King**, **Little Orphan Annie**, **Men of Daring**, **Mickey Mouse**, **Moon Mullins**, **Mutt & Jeff**, **Smitty**, **Tailspin Tommy**, **Tarzan**, **Thimble Theater starring Popeye**, **Tillie the Toiler**, **Winnie Winkle**, and the **Highlights of History** series. Until this point the previous formats had worked, but in light of the changing economic times, they no longer provided good value for the consumer.

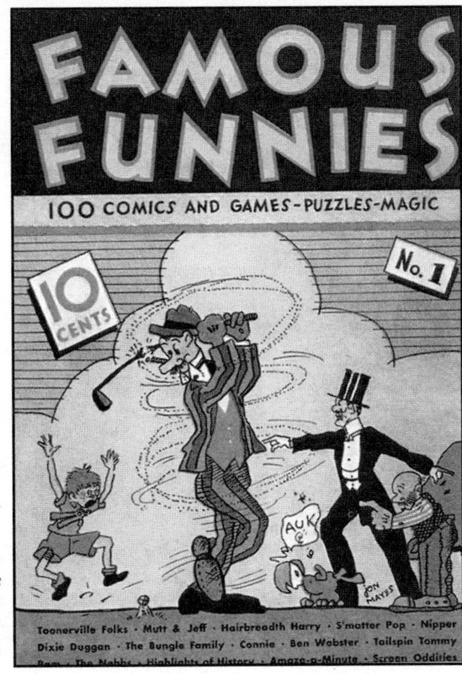

Famous Funnies #1, © 1934 Eastern Color

With the 1933 newsstand appearance of Humor's **Detective Dan**, **Adventures of Detective Ace King, Bob Scully**, **Two Fisted Hick Detective**, and others, these little understood original material comic books were the direct inspiration for Jerry Siegel and Joe Shuster to transform their fanzine character The Superman from **Science Fiction** #3, Jan, 1933 to a comic strip which evolved over the next couple years to what ended up in **Action Comics** #1. (For further information on how Superman's evolutionary process occurred, please refer to "The Big Bang Theory of Comic Book History," **Comic Book Marketplace** #50, June, 1997.) The stage was set for a new frontier to emerge.

Prior to Humor's very rare output, there was Embee's **Comic Monthly**'s dozen issues in 1922, and several dozen of Dell's **The Funnies** tabloid in 1929-30. All except **Comic Monthly** contained only original material and still failed. However, with another format change, including four colors, double page counts and a hefty price reduction (starting for free as promotional premiums due to the nationwide numbing effects of worldwide deflation), the birthing pangs of the modern American comic book occurred in late 1932. Created out of desperation to keep the printing presses rolling, the modern American comic book was born when a 45-year-old sales manager for Eastern Color Printing Company of New York reinvented the format.

Harry I. Wildenberg's job was to come up with ideas that would sell color printing for Eastern, a company which also printed the comic sections for a score of newspapers, including the **Boston Globe**, the **Brooklyn Times**, the **Providence Journal**, and the **Newark Ledger**. Down-time meant less take-home pay, so Wildenberg was

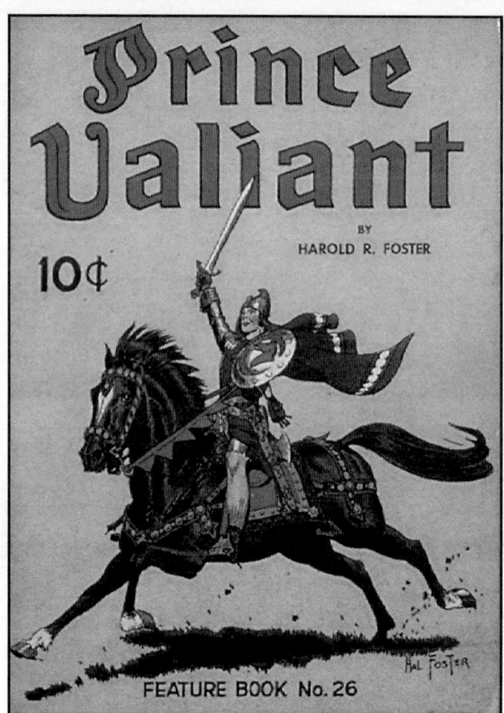

The only original comic book cover art by Hal Foster.
Feature Book #26, ©1941 David McKay Publications

always racking his brains for something to fit the color presses. He was fascinated by the miles of funny sheets which rolled off Eastern's presses each week, and he constantly sought new ways to exploit their commercial possibilities. If the funny papers were this popular, he reasoned, they should prove a good advertising medium. He decided to suggest a comics tabloid to one of his clients.

That client, Gulf Oil Company, liked the idea, hired a few artists and created its own original comics called **Gulf Comic Weekly** dated April, 1933 and was 10 1/2" x 15". It was the first comic to be advertised nationally on the radio beginning April 30. It's first artists were Stan Schendel doing "The Uncovered Wagon", Victor doing "Curly and the Kids" and Svess on a strip named "Smileage." All were full page, full color comic strips. Wildenberg promptly had Eastern print this 4 page comic, making it probably the first tabloid newsprint comic published for American distribution outside of a newspaper in the 20th Century. Wildenberg and Gulf were astonished when the tabloids were grabbed up as fast as Gulf service stations could offer them. Distribution shot up to 3,000,000 copies a week after Gulf changed the name to **Gulf Funny Weekly**. The series remained a tabloid until early 1939 and ran for 422 issues until May 23, 1941.

The idea for creating an actual comic book did not occur to Wildenberg, however, until a few weeks later in 1933, when he was idly folding a newspaper in halves then in quarters. As he looked at the twice-folded paper, it occurred to him that it was a convenient book size (actually it was late stage Dime Novel size which companies like Street & Smith were pumping out). The format had its hey-day from the 1880s through the 1910s, having been invented by the firm of Beadle and Adam in 1860 in more of a digest format. According to a 1942 article by Max Gaines, another contributing factor in the development of the format was an inspection of a promotional folder published by the Ledger Syndicate, in which four-color Sunday comic pages were printed in 7" x 9".

According to a 1949 interview with Wildenberg, he thought "why not a comic book? It would have 32 or 64 pages and make a fine item for concerns which distribute premiums."

Wildenberg obtained publishing rights to certain Associated, Bell, Fisher, McNaught and Public Ledger Syndicate comics, had an artist make up a few dummies by hand, and then had his sales staff walk them around to his biggest advertisers. Wildenberg received a telegram from Proctor & Gamble for an order of a million copies for a 32-page comic magazine in color called **Funnies on Parade**. The entire print run was given away in just a few weeks in the Spring of 1933.

Also working for Eastern Color at this time were quite a few future legends of the comics business, such as Max Gaines, Lev Gleason and a fellow named Harold Moore (all sales staff directly underneath the supervision of Wildenberg), Sol Harrison as a color separator, and George Dougherty Sr. as a printer. All of them worked on the **Funnies on Parade** project. Morris Margolis was brought in from Charlton Publications in Derby, Connecticut to solve binding problems centered on getting the pages in proper numerical sequence on that last fold to "modern" comic book size. All were infected with the comics bug for most of the rest of their lives.

The success of **Funnies on Parade** quickly led to Eastern publishing additional giveaway books in the same format by late 1933, including the 32 page **Famous Funnies A Carnival of Comics**, the 100 page **A Century of Comics** and **Skippy's Own Book of Comics**; the latter became the first "new" format comic book about a single character. These thicker issues had press runs up to half a million per title.

The idea that anyone would pay for them seemed fantastic to Wildenberg, so Max Gaines stickered ten cents on several dozen of the latest premium, **Famous Funnies A Carnival of Comics**, as a test, and talked a couple newsstands into participating in this experiment. The copies sold out over the weekend and newsies asked for more.

Eastern sales staffers first approached Woolworth's. The late Oscar Fitz-Alan Douglas, sales brains of Woolworth, showed some interest, but after several months of deliberation decided the book would not give enough value for ten cents. Kress, Kresge, McCrory, and several other dime stores turned them down even more abruptly. Wildenberg next went to George Hecht, editor of **Parents Magazine**, and tried to persuade him to run a comic supplement or publish a "higher level" comic magazine. Hecht also frowned on the idea.

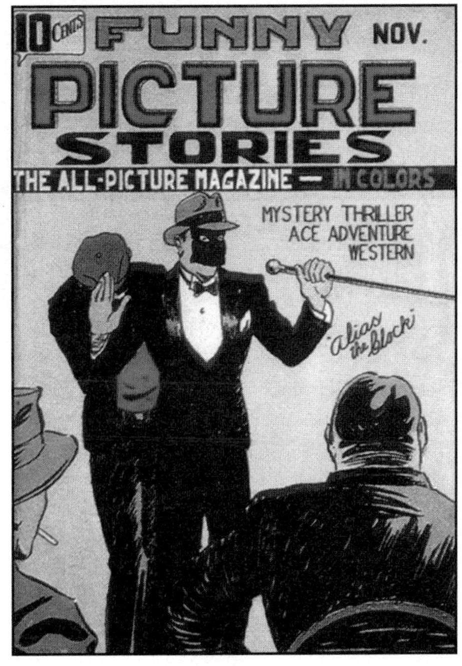

Funny Picture Stories #1 ©1936 Centaur Publications

In Wildenberg's 1949 interview, he noted that "even the comic syndicates couldn't see it. 'Who's going to read old comics?' they asked." With the failures of **Comic Monthly** and **The Funnies** still fresh in some minds, they couldn't see why children would pay ten cents for a comic magazine when they could get all they want for free in a Sunday newspaper.

But Wildenberg had become convinced that children—and grown-ups too—were not getting all the comics they wanted in the Sunday papers. Otherwise, the **Gulf Comic Weekly** and the premium comics would not have met with such success. Wildenberg said, "I decided that if boys and girls were willing to work for premium coupons to obtain comic

King Comics #1, featuring the first appearance of Flash Gordon, Popeye, and Mandrake the Magician.

books, they might be willing to pay ten cents on the newsstands." This conviction was also strengthened by Max Gaines' ten cent sticker experiment.

George Janosik, the president of Eastern Color, then called on George Delacorte to form a 50-50 joint venture to publish and market a comic book "magazine" for retail sales, but American News turned them down cold. The magazine monopoly also remembered Delacorte's abortive **The Funnies** from just a few years before. After much discussion on how to proceed, Delacorte finally agreed to publish it and a partnership was formed. They printed 40,000 copies for distribution to a few chain stores. Known today as **Famous Funnies Series One**, half of its pages came from reprints of the reprints in **Funnies on Parade** and **Famous Funnies A Carnival of Comics**.

With 68 full-color pages at only ten cents a piece, it sold out in thirty days with not a single returned copy. Delacorte refused to print a second edition. "Advertisers won't use it," he complained. "They say it's not dignified enough." The profit, however, was approximately $2,000. This particular edition is the rarest of all these early Eastern comic book experiments.

In early 1934, while riding the train, another Eastern Color employee named Harold A. Moore read an account from a prominent New York newspaper that indicated they owed much of their circulation success to their comics section. Mr. Moore went back to Harry Gold, President of American News, with the article in hand. He succeeded in acquiring a print order for 250,000 copies for a proposed monthly comics magazine.

In May 1934, **Famous Funnies** #1 (with a July cover date) hit the newsstands with Steven O. Douglass as its only editor (even though Harold Moore was listed as such in #1) until it ceased publication some twenty years later. It was a 64-page version of the 32-page giveaways, and more importantly, it still sold for a dime!

The first issue lost $4,150.60. Ninety percent of the copies sold out and a second issue dated September debuted in July. From then on, the comic book was published monthly. **Famous Funnies** also began carrying original material, apparently as early as the second issue. With #3, Buck Rogers took center stage and stayed there for the next twenty years, with covers by Frank Frazetta—some of his best comics work ever.

Delacorte got cold feet and sold back his interest to Eastern, even though the seventh issue cleared a profit of $2,664.25. Wildenberg emphasized that Eastern could make a manufacturer's profit by printing its own books as well as the publishing profits once it was distributed. Every issue showed greater sales than the preceding one, until within a year, close to a million 64-page books were being sold monthly at ten cents apiece; Eastern received the lion's share of the receipts. American News paid the publisher six cents a copy at first, then later six and a half cents. Of the remainder, the distributor received a cent to a cent and a half and the dealer received two to two and a half cents. Eastern soon found it was netting $30,000 per issue. The comic syndicates received $640 ($10 a page) for publishing rights. Original material could be obtained from budding professionals for just $5 a page. According to Will Eisner in R. C. Harvey's **The Art of the Comic Book**, the prices then paid for original material had the long range effect of keeping wages for creators very low for years.

Initially Eastern's experiment was eyed with skepticism by the publishing world, but within a year or so after **Famous Funnies** was nonchalantly placed on sale alongside slicker magazines like **Atlantic Monthly** or **Harper's** at least five other competitors entered the field.

In late 1934, pulp writer turned publisher Major Wheeler-Nicholson introduced **New Fun** #1 at almost tabloid-size and containing all original material. Around this same time, Whitman brought out the first original material movie adaptation—**Tim McCoy Police Car 17**—in the tabloid **New Fun** format with stiff card covers. A few years before, they had introduced the new comics formats known as the **Big Little Book** and the **Big Big Book**. The **BLB** and **BBB** formats would go toe-to-toe with Eastern's creation throughout the 1930s, but Eastern would win out.

The very last 10" x 10" comic books pioneered by Cupples & Leon were published in mid-1935 by the David McKay Company. In late 1935, Max Gaines (with his youthful assistant Sheldon Mayer) reached an agreement with George Delacorte (who was re-entering the comic book business a third time) and Chicago Tribune Syndicate (a powerhouse newspaper comic strip enterprise) to reprint newspaper comic strips in **Popular Comics**. Also by late 1935, Lev Gleason, another pioneer who participated **in Funnies on Parade**, had become the first editor of United Feature's own **Tip Top Comics**. In 1939 he would begin publishing his own titles, by 1942 creating the crime comic book as a popular genre with **Crime Does Not Pay**.

Industry giant King Features introduced **King Comics** #1, dated April 1936, through publisher David McKay, with Ruth Plumly Thompson as editor. McKay had

The birth of the Silver Age, Showcase #4, ©1956 DC Comics, introducing the Barry Allen Flash.

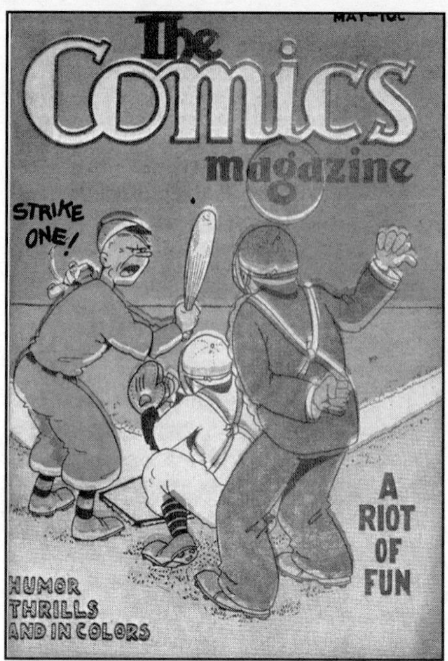

Top, The Comics Magazine #1 (1936) featured the first appearance of Dr. Mystic by Siegel & Shuster. Bottom, Ducks galore in Walt Disney's Uncle Scrooge, Four Color #386 1952 ©WDC.

already been issuing various format comic books with King Feature characters for a few years, including **Mickey Mouse**, **Henry**, **Popeye** and **Secret Agent X-9**, wherein Dashiell Hammett received cover billing and Alex Raymond was listed simply as "illustrator." McKay readily adapted to this format. Soon most young comic book illustrators were copying Raymond's style.

The following month, William Cook and John Mahon, former disgruntled employees of Wheeler-Nicholson, brought out **The Comics Magazine** #1 (May 1936). This was followed by Henle Publishing issuing **Wow** which contained the earliest comics work of Will Eisner, Bob Kane, Dick Briefer and others.

By the end of 1936 Cook and Mahon pioneered the first single theme comic books—**Funny Picture Stories** (adventure), **Detective Picture Stories** (crime), and **Western Picture Stories** (the Western). The company would eventually be known historically as Centaur Comics, and serve as the subject of endless debate amongst fandom historians regarding their earliest origins.

Almost forty years after the first newspaper strip comic book compilations were issued at the dawn of international popularity for American comic strips, the race was on to get out of the starting block.

Two years later, **Action Comics** #1 was published with a cover date of June 1938, and the Golden Age of superhero comics had begun. Early in 1938 at McClure Syndicate, Max Gaines and Shelly Mayer showed editor Vin Sullivan a many times rejected sample strip. Sullivan then talked Harry Donenfeld and Jack Liebowitz into publishing Jerry Siegel and Joe Shuster's creation—The Last Son of Krypton. This was followed by a lucrative partnership for Gaines with the **Detective Comics** people in the All-American Comics Group.

While there's a great deal of controversy surrounding such labeling, the Golden Age is often viewed these days as beginning with **Action Comics** #1 and continuing through the end of World War II. There was a time not that long ago, though, that the newspaper reprint comic book was collected with more fervor than the heroic ones of the '40s. **Feature Book** #26, **Four Color** #10 and **Single Series** #20 were the holy grails of collecting.

The Atomic Romance Age began in 1946, revamping the industry once again as circulations soon hit their all-time highs with over a billion issues sold a year. This continued until the advent of the self-censoring, industry-stifling Comics Code, created in response to a public outcry spearheaded by Dr. Frederic Wertham's tirade against the American comics industry, **Seduction of the Innocent**.

It took a year or two to recover from that moralistic assault, with many historians concluding that the Silver Age of Superheroes began with the publication of **Showcase** #4 in 1956, continuing through those turbulent times until Jack Kirby left Marvel for DC in 1969. Others point to the 1952 releases of Kurtzman's **MAD** #1 and Bark's **Uncle Scrooge Four Color** #386 (#1) as true Silver, since those titles soon broke the "million sold per issue" mark when the rest of the comic book industry was reeling from the effects of the public uproar fueled by Wertham.

The Bronze Age has been generally stated to begin when the Code approved newsstand comic book industry raised its standard cover price from 12 to 15 cents. As circulations plummeted after the Batman TV craze wore off by 1968 and the superhero glut died, out in San Francisco cartoonist Robert Crumb's creator-owned **Zap Comics** #1 appeared. As published by the Print Mint, **Zap**, which debuted in 1968, almost single-handedly spawned an industry with tremendous growth in alternative comix running through the 1970s. With the advent of the Direct Market by 1979, the last 20 years have generally been called The Modern Age, although there are hints of a new age emerging within these last 20 years.

In each of the above Ages, however, the secret for consumers and collectors has remained the same—buy what you enjoy. We did, and we're still collectors today!

(portions excerpted from Comic Book Store Wars. Those portions ©1999 by Robert Beerbohm. E-mail: beerbohm@teknetwork.com)

Underground "comix" were pioneered by creators like Robert Crumb and his Zap Comix #1 (1967)

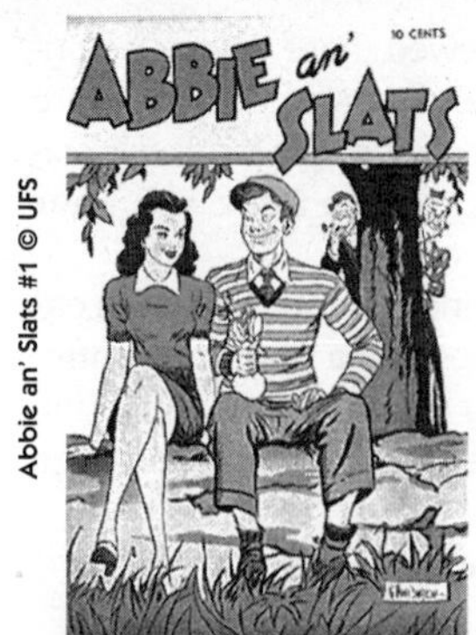

Abbie an' Slats #1 © UFS

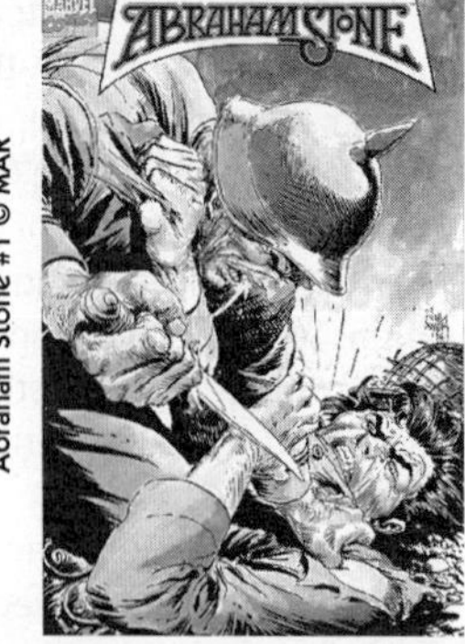

Abraham Stone #1 © MAR

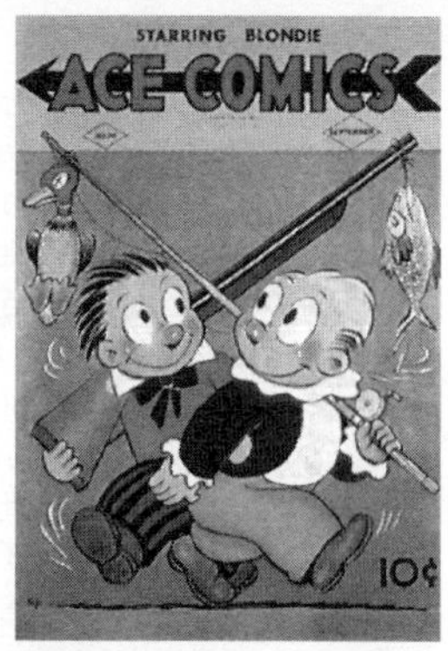

Ace Comics #30 © DMP

The correct title listing for each comic book can be determined by consulting the indicia (publication data) on the beginning interior pages of the comic. The official title is determined by those words of the title in capital letters only, and not by what is on the cover.

Titles are listed in this book as if they were one word, ignoring spaces, hyphens, and apostrophes, to make finding titles easier. Comic books listed should be assumed to be in color unless noted "B&W".

Comic publishers are invited to send us sample copies for possible inclusion in future guides.

Near Mint is the highest value listed in this price guide. True mint books from the 1970s and 1990s do exist, so the Near Mint value listed should be interpreted as a Mint value for those books.

A-1 (See A-One)

AARON STRIPS
Image Comics: Apr, 1997 - No. 4, Oct, 1997 ($2.95, B&W)

	GD25	FN65	NM94
1-4 -Reprints Adventures of Aaron newspaper strips			2.95

ABBIE AN' SLATS (...With Becky No. 1-4) (See Comics On Parade, Fight for Love, Giant Comics Edition 2, Giant Comics Editions #1, Sparkler Comics, Tip Topper, Treasury of Comics, & United Comics)
United Features Syndicate: 1940; March, 1948 - No. 4, Aug, 1948 (Reprints)

	GD25	FN65	NM94
Single Series 25 ('40)	35.00	105.00	260.00
Single Series 28	29.00	87.00	215.00
1 (1948)	15.00	45.00	110.00
2-4: 3-r/Sparkler #68-72	7.85	23.50	55.00

ABBOTT AND COSTELLO (...Comics)(See Giant Comics Editions #1 & Treasury of Comics)
St. John Publishing Co.: Feb, 1948 - No. 40, Sept, 1956 (Mort Drucker-a in most issues)

	GD25	FN65	NM94
1	46.00	138.00	390.00
2	25.00	75.00	185.00
3-9 (#8, 8/49; #9, 2/50)	15.00	45.00	115.00
10-Son of Sinbad story by Kubert (new)	19.00	57.00	140.00
11,13-20 (#11, 10/50; #13, 8/51; #15, 12/52)	11.00	33.00	80.00
12-Movie issue	13.00	39.00	95.00
21-30: 28-r/#8. 30-Painted-c	9.30	28.00	65.00
31-40: 33,38-Reprints	6.50	19.50	45.00
3-D #1 (11/53, 25¢)-Infinity-c	32.00	96.00	240.00

ABBOTT AND COSTELLO (TV)
Charlton Comics: Feb, 1968 - No. 22, Aug, 1971 (Hanna-Barbera)

	GD25	FN65	NM94
1	6.00	18.00	60.00
2	3.20	9.60	32.00
3-10	2.80	8.40	28.00
11-22	2.50	7.50	20.00

ABC (See America's Best TV Comics)

ABE SAPIEN: DRUMS OF THE DEAD
Dark Horse Comics: Mar, 1998 ($2.95, one-shot)

	GD25	FN65	NM94
1-McDonald-s/Thompson-a. Hellboy back-up; Mignola-s/a/c			3.00

ABOMINATIONS (See Hulk)
Marvel Comics: Dec, 1996 - No. 3, Feb, 1997 (1.50, limited series)

	GD25	FN65	NM94
1-3-Future Hulk stoyline			1.50

ABRAHAM LINCOLN LIFE STORY (See Dell Giants)

ABRAHAM STONE
Marvel Comics (Epic): July, 1995 - No. 2, Aug, 1995 ($6.95, limited series)

	GD25	FN65	NM94
1-Joe Kubert-s/a	.85	2.60	7.00

ABSENT-MINDED PROFESSOR, THE
Dell Publishing Co.: Apr, 1961 (Disney)

	GD25	FN65	NM94
Four Color #1199-Movie, photo-c	6.40	19.00	70.00

ABSOLUTE VERTIGO
DC Comics (Vertigo): Winter, 1995 (99¢, mature)

	GD25	FN65	NM94
nn-1st app. Preacher. Previews upcoming titles including Jonah Hex: Riders of the Worm, The Invisibles (King Mob), The Eaters, Ghostdancing & Preacher	1.50	4.50	15.00

ABYSS, THE (Movie)
Dark Horse Comics: June, 1989 - No. 2, July, 1989 ($2.25, limited series)

	GD25	FN65	NM94
1,2-Adaptation of film; Kaluta & Moebius-a			2.25

ACCLAIM ADVENTURE ZONE
Acclaim Books: 1997 ($4.50, digest size)

	GD25	FN65	NM94
1-Short stories of Turok, Troublemakers, Ninjak and others			4.50

ACE COMICS
David McKay Publications: Apr, 1937 - No. 151, Oct-Nov, 1949 (All contain some newspaper strip reprints)

	GD25	FN65	NM94
1-Jungle Jim by Alex Raymond, Blondie, Ripley's Believe It Or Not, Krazy Kat begin (1st app. of each)	260.00	780.00	2600.00
2	85.00	255.00	725.00
3-5	56.00	168.00	475.00
6-10	43.00	129.00	350.00
11-The Phantom begins (1st app., 2/38) (in brown costume)	65.00	195.00	550.00
12-20	36.00	108.00	270.00
21-25,27-30	31.00	93.00	235.00
26-Origin & 1st app. Prince Valiant (5/39); begins series?	82.00	246.00	700.00
31-40: 37-Krazy Kat ends	22.00	66.00	165.00
41-60	17.00	51.00	125.00
61-64,66-76-(7/43; last 68 pgs.)	15.00	44.00	110.00
65-(8/42)-Flag-c	15.00	46.00	115.00
77-84 (3/44; all 60 pgs.)	12.00	36.00	90.00
85-99 (52 pgs.)	10.00	30.00	75.00
100 (7/45; last 52 pgs.)	11.00	34.00	85.00
101-134: 128-(11/47)-Brick Bradford begins. 134-Last Prince Valiant (all 36 pgs.)	7.85	23.50	55.00
135-151: 135-(6/48)-Lone Ranger begins	7.15	21.50	50.00

ACE KELLY (See Tops Comics & Tops In Humor)

ACE KING (See Adventures of Detective...)

ACES
Acme Press (Eclipse): Apr, 1988 - No. 5, Dec, 1988 ($2.95, B&W, magazine)

	GD25	FN65	NM94
1-5			3.00

ACES HIGH
E.C. Comics: Mar-Apr, 1955 - No. 5, Nov-Dec, 1955

	GD25	FN65	NM94
1-Not approved by code	15.00	45.00	150.00
2	9.50	28.00	95.00
3-5	8.00	24.00	80.00

NOTE: *All have stories by* ***Davis, Evans, Krigstein,*** *and* ***Wood. Evans*** *c-1-5.*

ACTION ADVENTURE (War) (Formerly Real Adventure)
Gillmor Magazines: V1#2, June, 1955 - No. 4, Oct, 1955

	GD25	FN65	NM94
V1#2-4	4.00	12.00	24.00

ACTION COMICS (...Weekly #601-642) (Also see The Comics Magazine #1, More Fun #14-17 & Special Edition)
National Periodical Publ./Detective Comics/DC Comics: 6/38 - No. 583, 9/86; No. 584, 1/87 - Present

	GD25	FN65	VF82	VF/NM

1-Origin & 1st app. Superman by Siegel & Shuster, Marco Polo, Tex Thompson, Pep Morgan, Chuck Dawson & Scoop Scanlon; 1st app. Zatara & Lois Lane; Superman story missing 4 pgs. which were included when reprinted in Superman #1; Clark Kent works for Daily Star; story

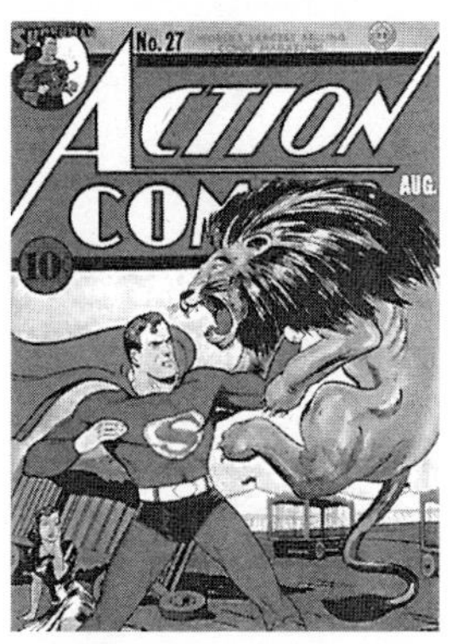

Action Comics #27 © DC

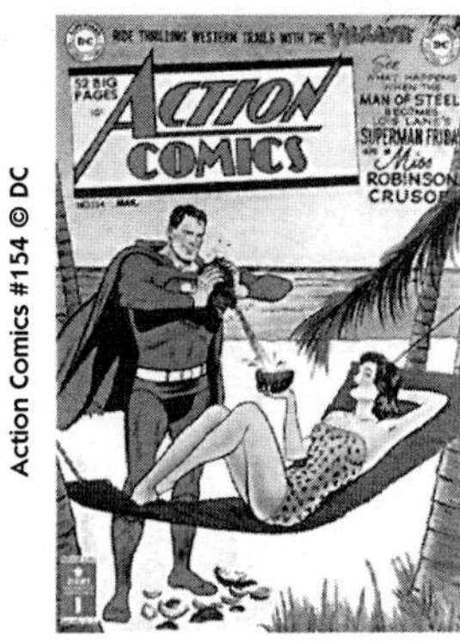

Action Comics #154 © DC

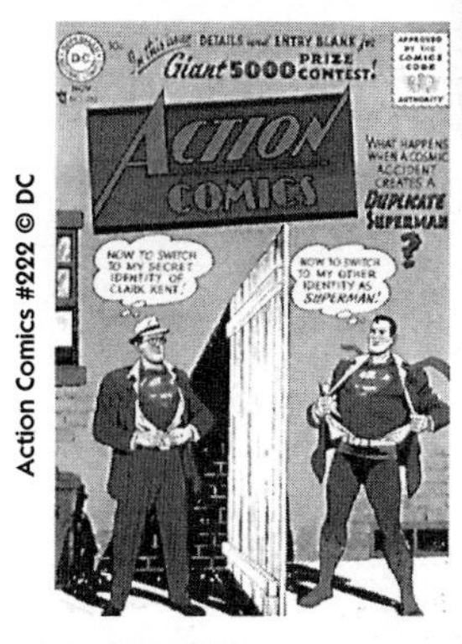

Action Comics #222 © DC

GD25 FN65 NM94

continued in #2 30,000.00 70,000.00 105,000.00 185,000.00
1-Reprint, Oversize 13-1/2x10". **WARNING:** This comic is an exact reprint of the original except for its size. DC published it in 1974 with a second cover titling it as a Famous First Edition. There have been many reported cases of the outer cover being removed and the interior sold as the original edition. The reprint with the new outer cover removed is practically worthless. See Famous First Edition for value.

GD25 FN65 NM94

1(1976,1983)-Giveaway; paper cover, 16pgs. in color; reprints complete Superman story from #1 ('38) 2.00 6.00 16.00
1(1987 Nestle Quik giveaway; 1988, 50¢) 2.00 6.00
1(1993)-Came w/Reign of Superman packs 1.50
2-O'Mealia non-Superman covers thru #6 2000.00 6000.00 20,000.00
3 (Scarce)-Superman apps. in costume in only one panel 1400.00 4200.00 14,000.00
4-6: 6-1st Jimmy Olsen (called office boy) 842.00 2525.00 8000.00
7-2nd Superman cover 1300.00 3900.00 13,000.00
8,9 631.00 1893.00 6000.00
10-3rd Superman cover by Siegel & Shuster 1000.00 3000.00 9500.00
11,14: 14-Clip Carson begins, ends #41; Zatara-c 316.00 950.00 3000.00
12-Has 1 pg. Batman ad for Det. #27 (5/39); Zatara sci-fi cover 326.00 978.00 3100.00
13-Shuster Superman-c; last Scoop Scanlon 526.00 1578.00 5000.00
15-Guardineer Superman-c; Detective Comics ad 463.00 1390.00 4400.00
16 258.00 775.00 2200.00
17-Superman cover; last Marco Polo 358.00 1075.00 3400.00
18-Origin 3 Aces; 1st X-Ray Vision? 258.00 775.00 2200.00
19-Superman covers begin; has full pg. ad for New York World's Fair 1939 333.00 1000.00 3000.00
20-The 'S' left off Superman's chest; Clark Kent works at 'Daily Star' 322.00 966.00 2900.00
21-Has 2 ads for More Fun #52 (1st Spectre) 224.00 672.00 1900.00
22,24,25: 24-Kent at Daily Planet. 25-Last app. Gargantua T. Potts, Tex Thompson's sidekick 212.00 636.00 1800.00
23-1st app. Luthor (w/red hair) & Black Pirate; Black Pirate by Moldoff; 1st mention of The Daily Planet (4/40)-Has 1 panel ad for Spectre in More Fun 547.00 1640.00 5200.00
26-28,30 167.00 500.00 1500.00
29-1st Lois Lane-c (10/40) 200.00 600.00 1800.00
31,32: 32-Intro/1st app. Krypto Ray Gun in Superman story by Burnley 105.00 315.00 950.00
33-Origin Mr. America; Superman by Burnley; has half page ad for All Star Comics #3 128.00 384.00 1150.00
34-36,38,39: 36-Robot cover 105.00 315.00 950.00
37,40: 37-Origin Congo Bill. 40-(9/41)-Intro/1st app. Star Spangled Kid & Stripesy 118.00 353.00 1000.00
41 97.00 291.00 875.00
42-1st app./origin Vigilante; Bob Daley becomes Fat Man; origin Mr. America's magic flying carpet; The Queen Bee & Luthor app; Black Pirate ends; not in #41 139.00 417.00 1250.00
43-46,48-50: 44-Fat Man's i.d. revealed to Mr. America. 45-1st app. Stuff (Vigilante's oriental sidekick) 97.00 291.00 875.00
47-1st Luthor cover in comics (4/42) 139.00 417.00 1250.00
51-1st app. The Prankster 97.00 291.00 875.00
52-Fat Man & Mr. America become the Ameri-commandos; origin Vigilante retold; classic Superman and back-ups-c 106.00 318.00 900.00
53-60: 56-Last Fat Man. 57-2nd Lois Lane-c in Action (3rd anywhere, 2/43). 59-Kubert Vigilante begins?, ends #70. 60-First app. Lois Lane as Superwoman 67.00 200.00 575.00
61-Historic Atomic Radiation-c (6/43) 63.00 189.00 540.00
62,63,65-70: 63-Last 3 Aces 61.00 183.00 520.00
64-Intro Toyman 70.00 210.00 600.00
71-79: 74-Last Mr. America 56.00 168.00 480.00
80-2nd app. & 1st Mr. Mxyztplk-c (1/45) 85.00 255.00 720.00
81-90: 83-Intro Hocus & Pocus 56.00 168.00 480.00

GD25 FN65 NM94

91-99: 93-X-Mas-c. 99-1st small logo (8/46) 54.00 162.00 460.00
100 122.00 366.00 975.00
101-Nuclear explosion-c (10/46) 122.00 366.00 975.00
102-120: 102-Mxyztplk-c. 105,117-X-Mas-c 51.00 153.00 440.00
121-126,128-140: 135,136,138-Zatara by Kubert 47.00 142.00 400.00
127-Vigilante by Kubert; Tommy Tomorrow begins (12/48, see Real Fact #6) 55.00 165.00 475.00
141-157,159-161: 151-Luthor/Mr. Mxyztplk/Prankster team-up. 156-Lois Lane as Super Woman. 160- Last 52 pgs. 42.00 126.00 375.00
158-Origin Superman retold 100.00 300.00 900.00
162-180: 168,176-Used in **POP**, pg. 90. 173-Robot-c 36.00 108.00 320.00
181-201: 191-Intro. Janu in Congo Bill. 198-Last Vigilante. 201-Last pre-code issue 36.00 108.00 300.00
202-220: 212-(1/56)-Includes 1956 Superman calendar that is part of story. 28.00 84.00 285.00
221-240: 221-1st S.A. issue. 224-1st Golden Gorilla story. 228-(5/57)-Kongorilla in Congo Bill story (Congorilla try-out) 22.00 66.00 220.00
241,243-251: 241-Batman x-over. 248-Origin/1st app. Congorilla; Congo Bill renamed Congorilla. 251-Last Tommy Tomorrow 17.50 52.00 175.00
242-Origin & 1st app. Brainiac (7/58); 1st mention of Shrunken City of Kandor 108.00 325.00 1400.00
252-Origin & 1st app. Supergirl (5/59); intro new Metallo 116.00 348.00 1400.00
253-2nd app. Supergirl 34.00 102.00 375.00
254-1st meeting of Bizarro & Superman-c/story 25.00 75.00 250.00
255-1st Bizarro Lois Lane-c/story & both Bizarros leave Earth to make Bizarro World 18.00 54.00 180.00
256-261: 259-Red Kryptonite used. 261-1st X-Kryptonite which gave Streaky his powers; last Congorilla in Action; origin & 1st app. Streaky The Super Cat 11.50 34.00 115.00
262,264-266,268-270 10.50 32.00 105.00
263-Origin Bizarro World 13.50 41.00 135.00
267(8/60)-3rd Legion app; 1st app. Chameleon Boy, Colossal Boy, & Invisible Kid, 1st app. of Supergirl as Superwoman. 34.00 102.00 375.00
271-275,277-282: 274-Lois Lane as Superwoman; 282-Last 10¢ issue 7.50 22.50 75.00
276(5/61)-6th Legion app; 1st app. Brainiac 5, Phantom Girl, Triplicate Girl, Bouncing Boy, Sun Boy, & Shrinking Violet; Supergirl joins Legion 17.00 51.00 170.00
283(12/61)-Legion of Super-Villains app. 1st 12¢ 9.00 27.00 90.00
284(1/62)-Mon-el app. 9.00 27.00 90.00
285(2/62)-12th Legion app; Brainiac 5 cameo; Supergirl's existence revealed to world; JFK & Jackie cameos 9.00 27.00 90.00
286(3/62)-Legion of Super Villains app. 6.00 18.00 60.00
287(4/62)-15th Legion app.(cameo) 6.00 18.00 60.00
288-Mon-el app.; r-origin Supergirl 6.00 18.00 60.00
289(6/62)-16th Legion app. (Adult); Lightning Man & Saturn Woman's marriage 1st revealed 6.00 18.00 60.00
290(7/62)-17th Legion app. (cameo); Phantom Girl app. 1st Supergirl emergency squad 6.00 18.00 60.00
291,292,294-299: 291-1st meeting Supergirl & Mr. Mxyzptlk. 292-2nd app. Superhorse (see Adv. #293). 297-Mon-el app. 298-Legion cameo 6.00 18.00 60.00
293-Origin Comet (Superhorse) 9.00 27.00 90.00
300-(5/63) 6.00 18.00 60.00
301-303,305-308,310-320: 306-Brainiac 5, Mon-el app. 307-Saturn Girl app. 314-retells origin Supergirl; J.L.A. x-over. 317-Death of Nor-Kan of Kandor. 319-Shrinking Violet app. 3.00 9.00 30.00
304-Origin & 1st app. Black Flame (9/63) 3.50 10.50 35.00
309-(2/64)-Legion app.; Batman & Robin-c & cameo; JFK app. (he died 11/22/63; on stands same time as death) 3.50 10.50 35.00
321-333,335-339: 336-Origin Akvar (Flamebird) 2.25 6.75 24.00
334-Giant G-20; origin Supergirl, Streaky, Superhorse & Legion (all-r) 5.00 15.00 55.00

Action Comics #586 © DC

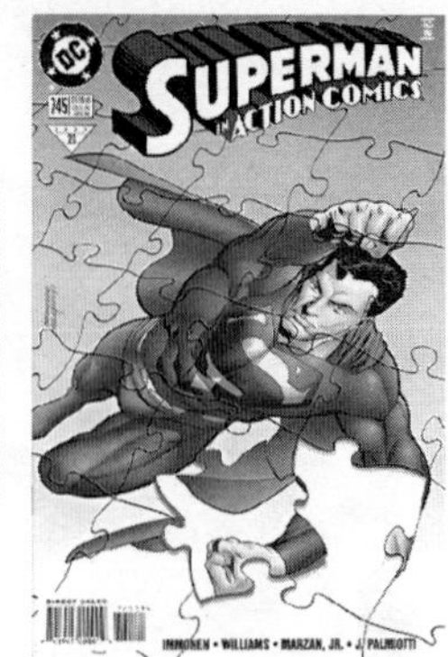

Action Comics #745 © DC

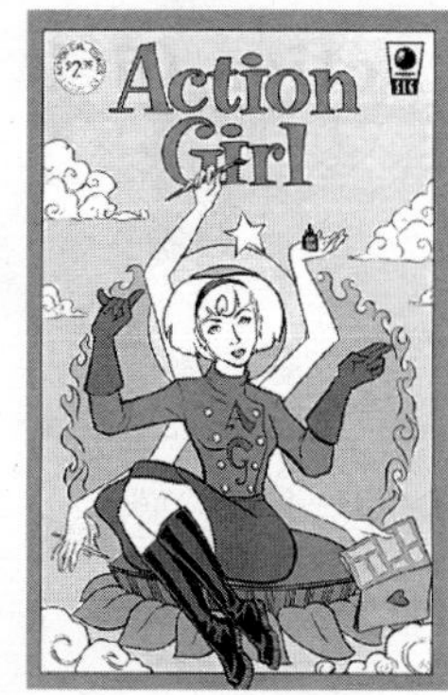

Action Girl #14 © Sarah Dyer

GD25 FN65 NM94

340-Origin, 1st app. of the Parasite 2.20 6.50 24.00
341-346,348-359: 344-Batman x-over. 350-Batman, Green Arrow & Green Lantern app. in Supergirl back-up story 1.80 5.40 18.00
347,360-Giant Supergirl G-33,G-45; 347-Origin Comet-r plus Bizarro story. 360-Legion-r; r/origin Supergirl 3.50 10.50 38.00
361-372,374-380: 361-2nd app. Parasite. 365-Legion app. 370-New facts about Superman's origin. 376-Last Supergirl in Action. 377-Legion begins. 1.40 4.20 14.00
373-Giant Supergirl G-57; Legion-r 3.00 9.00 33.00
381-399,401,402: 392-Last Legion in Action; Saturn Girl gets new costume. 393-402-All Superman issues 1.00 3.00 10.00
400 1.85 5.50 18.00
403-413: All 52 pg. issues. 411-Origin Eclipso-(r). 413-Metamorpho begins, ends #418 1.50 4.50 15.00
414-424: 419-Intro. Human Target. 421-Intro Capt. Strong; Green Arrow begins. 422,423-Origin Human Target .85 2.60 7.00
425-Neal Adams-a(p); The Atom begins 1.60 4.80 16.00
426-431,433-436,438,439 5.00
432-1st S.A. Toyman app (2/74). .90 2.70 9.00
437,443-(100 pg. giants) 2.00 6.00 20.00
440-1st Grell-a on Green Arrow .90 2.70 9.00
441,442,444-448: 441-Grell-a on Green Arrow continues 5.00
443,450-483,485-499: 454-Last Atom. 456-Grell Jaws-c. 458-Last Green Arrow. 485-Adams-c. 487,488-(44 pgs.). 487-Origin & 1st app. Microwave Man; origin Atom retold 4.00
449-(68 pgs.) .90 2.70 8.00
484-Earth II Superman & Lois Lane wed; 40th anniversary issue(6/78) 5.00
500-($1.00, 68 pgs.)-Infinity-c; Superman life story; shows Legion statues in museum 5.00
501-551,554-582: 511-514-Airwave II solo stories. 513-The Atom begins. 517-Aquaman begins; ends #541. 521-1st app. The Vixen. 532,536-New Teen Titans cameo. 535,536-Omega Men app. 544-(Mando paper, 68 pgs.)-Origins new Luthor & Brainiac; Omega Men cameo. 544-Shuster-a (pin-up); article by Siegel. 546-J.L.A., New Teen Titans app. 551-Starfire becomes Red-Star 2.25
552,553-Animal Man-c & app. (2/84 & 3/84) 4.00
583-Alan Moore scripts; last Earth 1 Superman story (cont'd from Superman #423) 5.00
584-Byrne-a begins; New Teen Titans app. 2.50
585-599: 586-Legends x-over. 596-Millennium x-over; Spectre app. 598-1st app. Checkmate 2.00
600-($2.50, 84 pgs., 5/88) 5.00
601-642-Weekly issues ($1.50, 52 pgs.): 601-Re-intro The Secret Six. 611-614-: Catwoman stories (new costume in #611). 613-618-Nightwing stories 2.00
643-Superman & monthly issues begin again; Perez-c/a/scripts begin; swipes cover to Superman #1 2.50
644-649,651-661,663-666,668-673,675-679: 645-1st app. Maxima. 654-Part 3 of Batman storyline. 655-Free extra 8 pgs. 660-Death of Lex Luthor. 661-Begin $1.00-c. 675-Deathstroke cameo. 679-Last $1.00 issue 2.00
650-($1.50, 52 pgs.)-Lobo cameo (last panel) 4.00
662-Clark Kent reveals i.d. to Lois Lane; story continued in Superman #53 5.00
667-($1.75, 52 pgs.) 2.00
674-Supergirl logo & c/story (reintro) 5.00
680-682 2.00
683-Doomsday cameo 1.50
683-2nd & 3rd printings 1.50
684-Doomsday battle issue 3.00
685,686-Funeral for a Friend issues; Supergirl app. 2.50
685-2nd & 3rd printings 1.25
687-($1.95)-Collector's Edition with die-cut-c 2.25
687-($1.50)-Newsstand Edition with mini-poster 2.00
688-694,696-699,701-703-($1.50): 688-Guy Gardner-c/story. 697-Bizarro-c/story. 703-(9/94)-Zero Hour 2.00
695-($2.50)-Collector's Edition w/embossed foil-c 2.50
700-($2.95, 68 pgs.)-Fall of Metropolis Pt 1; Pete Ross marries Lana Lang; Curt Swan & Murphy Anderson inks 3.00
700-Platinum 5.00
700-Gold 15.00
0,704-709: 0-(10/94). 704-(11/94) 1.50
710-719,721-731: 710-Begin $1.95-c. 714-Joker app. 719-Batman-c/app. 721-Mr. Mxyzptlk app. 723-Brainiac as Superman; Dave Johnson-c.727-Final Night x-over. 2.00
720-Lois breaks off engagement w/Clark 3.00
720-2nd print. 2.00
732-747: 732-New powers. 733-New costume, Ray app. 738-Immonen-s/a(p) begins. 741-Legion app. 744-Millennium Giants x-over. 745-747-70's-style Superman vs. Prankster 2.00
748,749,751: Begin $1.99-c 1.99
750-($2.95) 2.95
#1,000,000 (11/98) Gene Ha-c; 853rd Century x-over 1.99
Annual 1(1987)-Art Adams-c/a(p); Batman app. 3.00
Annual 2(1989, $1.75, 68 pgs.)-Perez-c/a(i) 2.00
Annual 3(1991, $2.00, 68 pgs.)-Armageddon 2001 2.00
Annual 4(1992, $2.50, 68 pgs.)-Eclipso vs. Shazam 2.50
Annual 5(1993, $2.50, 68 pgs.)-Bloodlines; 1st app. Loose Cannon 2.50
Annual 6(1994, $2.95)-Elseworlds story 3.00
Annual 7(1995, $3.95)-Year One story 4.00
Annual 8(1996, $2.95)-Legends of the Dead Earth story 3.00
Annual 9(1997, $3.95)-Pulp Heroes story 4.00
Theater Giveaway (1947, 32 pgs., 6-1/2 x 8-1/4", nn)-Vigilante story based on Columbia Vigilante serial; no Superman-c or story 66.00 198.00 525.00

NOTE: ***Supergirl's*** *origin in 262, 280, 285, 291, 305, 309.* ***N. Adams*** *c-356, 358, 359, 361-364, 366, 367, 370-374, 377-379i, 398-400, 402, 404,405, 419p, 466, 468, 469, 473i, 485.* ***Aparo*** *a-642.* ***Austin*** *c/a-682i.* ***Baily*** *a-24, 25.* ***Boring*** *a-164, 194, 211, 223, 233, 241, 250, 261, 266-268, 346, 348, 352, 356, 357.* ***Burnley*** *a-28-33; c-48?, 53-55, 58, 59?, 60-63, 65, 66p, 67p, 70p, 71p, 79p, 82p, 84-86p, 90-92p, 93p?, 94p, 107p, 108p.* ***Byrne*** *a-584-598p, 599i, 600p; c-584-591, 596-600.* ***Ditko*** *a-642.* ***Giffen*** *a-560, 563, 565, 577, 579; c-539, 560, 563, 565, 577, 579.* ***Grell*** *a-440-442, 444-446, 450-452, 456-458; c-456.* ***Guardineer*** *a-24, 25; c-8, 11, 12, 14-16, 18. 25.* ***Guice*** *a(p)-676-681, 683-698, 700; c-683, 685, 686, 687(direct), 688-693i, 694-696, 697i, 698-700.* ***Infantino*** *a-642.* ***Kaluta*** *c-613.* ***Bob Kane's*** *Clip Carson-14-41.* ***Gil Kane*** *a-443r, 493r, 539-541, 544-546, 551-554, 601-605, 642; c-535p, 540, 541, 544p, 545-549, 551-554, 580, 627.* ***Kirby*** *c-638.* ***Meskin*** *a-42-121(most).* ***Mignola*** *a-600, Annual 2; c-c-614.* ***Moldoff*** *a-23-25, 443r.* ***Mooney*** *a-667p.* ***Mortimer*** *c-153, 154, 159-172, 174, 178-181, 184, 186-189, 191-193, 196, 200, 206.* ***Orlando*** *a-617p; c-621.* ***Perez*** *a-600i, 643-652p, Annual 2p; c-529p, 602, 643-651, Annual 2p.* ***Quesada*** *c-Annual 4p.* ***Fred Ray*** *c-34, 36-46, 50-52.* ***Siegel & Shuster*** *a-1-27.* ***Paul Smith*** *c-608.* ***Starlin*** *a-509; c-631.* ***Leonard Starr*** *a-597i(part),* ***Staton*** *a-525p, 526p, 531p, 535p, 536p.* ***Swan/Moldoff*** *c-281, 286, 287, 293, 298, 334.* ***Thibert*** *c-676, 677p, 678-681, 684.* ***Toth*** *a-406, 407, 413, 431; c-616.* ***Tuska*** *a-486p, 550.* ***Williamson*** *a-568i.* ***Zeck*** *c-Annual 5*

ACTION FORCE (Also see G.I. Joe European Missions)
Marvel Comics Ltd. (British): Mar, 1987 - No. 40?, 1988 ($1.00, weekly, magazine)

1,3: British G.I. Joe series. 3-w/poster insert 3.00
2,4-40 1.50

ACTION GIRL
Slave Labor Graphics: Oct, 1994 - Present ($2.50/$2.75, B&W)

1-3 2.50
4-16: 4-Begin $2.75-c 2.75
1-6 ($2.75, 2nd printings): All read 2nd Print in indicia. 1-(2/96). 2-(10/95). 3-(2/96). 4-(7/96). 5-(2/97). 6-(9/97) 2.75
1-4 ($2.75, 3rd printings): All read 3rd Print in indicia. 2.75

ACTION PLANET COMICS
Action Planet: 1996 - No. 3, Sept, 1997 ($3.95, B&W, 44 pgs.)

1-3: 1-Intro Monster Man by Mike Manley & other stories 4.00
Giant Size Action Planet Halloween Special (1998, $5.96, oversized) 5.95

ACTUAL CONFESSIONS (Formerly Love Adventures)

Addam Omega #4 © Bill Hughes

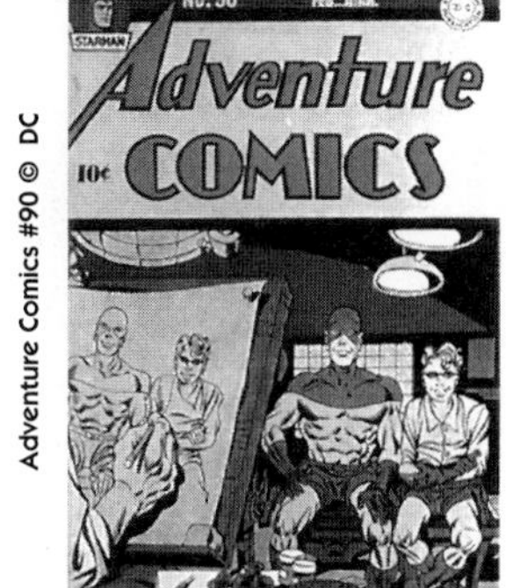

Adventure Comics #90 © DC

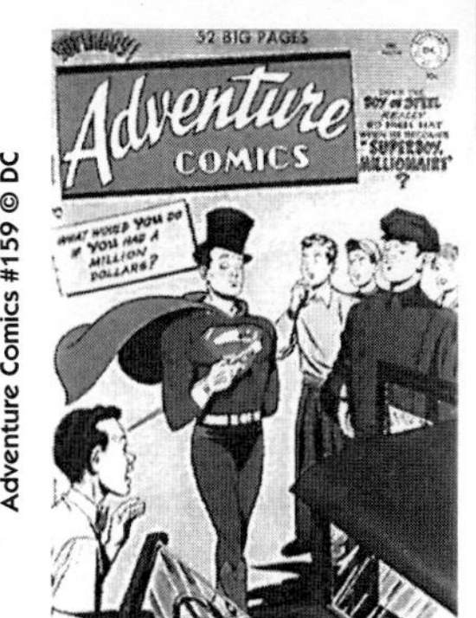

Adventure Comics #159 © DC

GD25 FN65 NM94

Atlas Comics (MPI): No. 13, Oct, 1952 - No. 14, Dec, 1952
13,14 5.00 15.00 30.00

ACTUAL ROMANCES (Becomes True Secrets #3 on?)
Marvel Comics (IPS): Oct, 1949 - No. 2, Jan, 1950 (52 pgs.)
1 8.75 26.25 62.00
2-Photo-c 5.70 17.00 38.00

ADAM AND EVE
Spire Christian Comics (Fleming H. Revell Co.): 1975,1978 (35¢/49¢)
nn-By Al Hartley 4.00

ADAM STRANGE (Also see Green Lantern #132, Mystery In Space #53 & Showcase #17)
DC Comics: 1990 - No. 3, 1990 ($3.95, 52 pgs, limited series, squarebound)
Book One - Three: Andy & Adam Kubert-c/a 4.00

ADAM-12 (TV)
Gold Key: Dec, 1973 - No. 10, Feb, 1976 (Photo-c)
1 5.50 16.50 60.00
2-10 1.80 5.50 20.00

ADDAM OMEGA
Antarctic Press: Feb, 1997 - No. 4, Aug, 1997 ($2.95. B&W)
1-4 2.95

ADDAMS FAMILY (TV cartoon)
Gold Key: Oct, 1974 - No. 3, Apr, 1975 (Hanna-Barbera)
1 8.25 25.00 90.00
2,3 4.50 13.50 50.00

ADLAI STEVENSON
Dell Publishing Co.: Dec, 1966
12-007-612-Life story; photo-c 2.25 7.00 25.00

ADOLESCENT RADIOACTIVE BLACK BELT HAMSTERS (See Clint)
Comic Castle/Eclipse Comics: 1986 - No. 9, Jan, 1988 ($1.50, B&W)
1-9: 1st & 2nd printings exist 1.00
1-Limited Edition 3.00
1-In 3-D (7/86) 1.80
2-4 ($2.50) 2.50
Massacre The Japanese Invasion #1 (8/89, $2.00) 2.00

ADULT TALES OF TERROR ILLUSTRATED (See Terror Illustrated)

ADVANCED DUNGEONS & DRAGONS (Also see TSR Worlds)
DC Comics: Dec, 1988 - No. 36, Dec, 1991 (Newsstand #1 is Holiday, 1988-89) ($1.25/$1.50/$1.75)
1-Based on TSR role playing game 2.00
2-24 1.50
25-36: 25-$1.75-c begins 1.75
Annual 1 (1990, $3.95, 68 pgs.) 4.00

ADVENTURE BOUND
Dell Publishing Co.: Aug, 1949
Four Color 239 4.25 13.00 48.00

ADVENTURE COMICS (Formerly New Adventure)(...Presents Dial H For Hero #479-490)
National Periodical Publications/DC Comics: No. 32, 11/38 - No. 490, 2/82; No. 491, 9/82 - No. 503, 9/83
32-Anchors Aweigh (ends #52), Barry O'Neil (ends #60, not in #33), Captain Desmo (ends #47), Dale Daring (ends #47), Federal Men (ends #70), The Golden Dragon (ends #36), Rusty & His Pals (ends #52) by Bob Kane, Todd Hunter (ends #38) and Tom Brent (ends #39) begin
466.00 1400.00 3100.00
33-38: 37-Cover used on Double Action #2 216.00 650.00 1450.00
39(6/39):-Jack Wood begins, ends #42; 1st mention of Marijuana in comics
216.00 650.00 1450.00

GD25 FN65 NM94

GD25 FN65 VF82 NM94
40-(Rare, 7/39, on stands 6/10/39)-The Sandman begins by Bert Christman (who died in WWII); believed to be 1st conceived story (see N.Y. World's Fair for 1st published app.); Socko Strong begins, ends #54
3000.00 9000.00 18,000.00 33,000.00

GD25 FN65 NM94
41-O'Mealia-c 430.00 1290.00 4000.00
42,44-Sandman-c by Flessel. 44-Opium story 550.00 1650.00 5200.00
43,45 265.00 795.00 2400.00
46,47-Sandman covers by Flessel. 47-Steve Conrad Adventurer begins, ends #76 380.00 1140.00 3600.00

GD25 FN65 VF82 NM94
48-Intro & 1st app. The Hourman by Bernard Baily; Baily-c (Hourman c-48,50,52-59) 1750.00 5250.00 10,500.00 20,000.00

GD25 FN65 NM94
49,50: 50-Cotton Carver by Jack Lehti begins, ends #64
210.00 630.00 1800.00
51,60-Sandman-c: 51-Sandman-c by Flessel. 270.00 810.00 2300.00
52-59: 53-1st app. Jimmy "Minuteman" Martin & the Minutemen of America in Hourman; ends #78. 58-Paul Kirk Manhunter begins (1st app.), ends #72
176.00 529.00 1500.00

GD25 FN65 VF82 NM94
61-1st app. Starman by Jack Burnley (4/41); Starman c-61-72; Starman by Burnley in #61-80 1000.00 3000.00 6000.00 11,000.00

GD25 FN65 NM94
62-65,67,68,70: 67-Origin & 1st app. The Mist; classic Burnley-c 70-Last Federal Men 153.00 459.00 1300.00
66-Origin/1st app. Shining Knight (9/41) 188.00 564.00 1600.00
69-1st app. Sandy the Golden Boy (Sandman's sidekick) by Paul Norris (in a Bob Kane style); Sandman dons new costume 165.00 495.00 1400.00
71-Jimmy Martin becomes costume aide to the Hourman; 1st app.Hourman's Miracle Ray machine 141.00 423.00 1200.00

GD25 FN65 VF82 NM94
72-1st Simon & Kirby Sandman (3/42, 1st DC work)
910.00 2730.00 5460.00 10,000.00
73-Origin Manhunter by Simon & Kirby; begin new series; Manhunter-c
1000.00 3000.00 6000.00 11,000.00

GD25 FN65 NM94
74-78,80: 74-Thorndyke replaces Jimmy, Hourman's assistant; new Sandman-c begin by S&K. 75-Thor app. by Kirby; 1st Kirby Thor (see Tales of the Unexpected #16). 77-Origin Genius Jones; Mist story. 80-Last S&K Manhunter & Burnley Starman 165.00 495.00 1400.00
79-Manhunter-c 176.00 529.00 1500.00
81-90: 83-Last Hourman. 84-Mike Gibbs begins, ends #102
112.00 336.00 900.00
91-Last Simon & Kirby Sandman 94.00 282.00 750.00
92-99,101,102: 92-Last Manhunter. 102-Last Starman, Sandman, & Genius Jones; most-S&K-c (Genius Jones cont'd in More Fun #108)
91.00 273.00 725.00
100-S&K-c 119.00 357.00 950.00
103-Aquaman, Green Arrow, Johnny Quick & Superboy all move over from More Fun Comics #107; 8th app. Superboy; Superboy-c begin; 1st small logo (4/46) 247.00 741.00 2100.00
104 94.00 282.00 750.00
105-110 66.00 198.00 525.00
111-120: 113-X-Mas-c 60.00 180.00 485.00
121-126,128-130: 128-1st meeting Superboy & Lois Lane
54.00 162.00 430.00
127-Brief origin Shining Knight retold 56.00 168.00 450.00
131-141,143-149: 132-Shining Knight 1st return to King Arthur time; origin aide Sir Butch 45.00 135.00 360.00
142-Origin Shining Knight & Johnny Quick retold 50.00 150.00 400.00
150,151,153,155,157,159,161,163-All have 6 pg. Shining Knight stories by Frank Frazetta. 159-Origin Johnny Quick 50.00 150.00 400.00

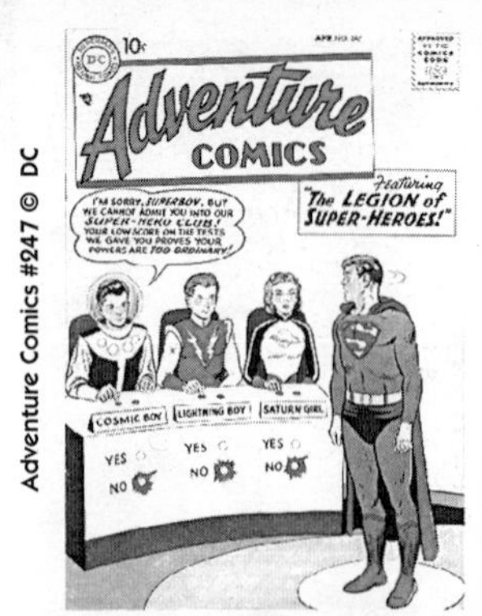

Adventure Comics #247 © DC

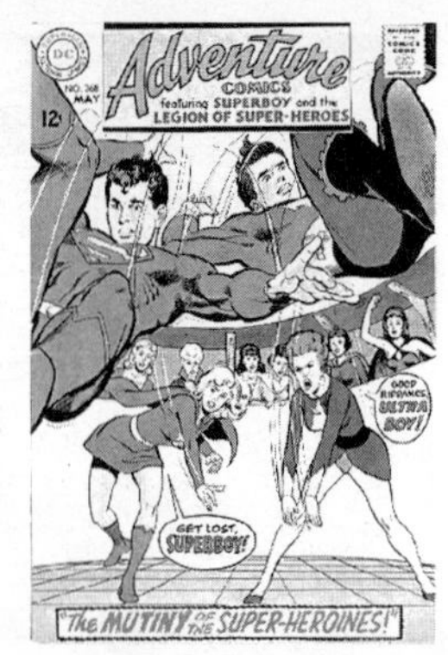

Adventure Comics #368 © DC

Adventure Comics #413 © DC

GD25 FN65 NM94 | GD25 FN65 NM94

152,154,156,158,160,162,164-169: 166-Last Shining Knight. 168-Last 52 pg. issue 41.00 123.00 310.00
170-180 40.00 120.00 290.00
181-199: 189-B&W and color illo in **POP** 40.00 120.00 280.00
200 (5/54) 38.00 114.00 420.00
201-208: 207-Last Johnny Quick (not in 205) 27.00 82.00 275.00
209-Last pre-code issue; origin Speedy 29.00 87.00 290.00

GD25 FN65 VF82 NM94

210-1st app. Krypto (Superdog)-c/story (3/55) 230.00 690.00 1500.00 3000.00

GD25 FN65 NM94

211-213,215-220: 220-Krypto app. 24.00 72.00 240.00
214-2nd app. Krypto 35.00 104.00 380.00
221-246: 229-1st S.A. issue. 237-1st Intergalactic Vigilante Squadron (6/57) 21.00 63.00 210.00

GD25 FN65 VF82 NM94

247(4/58)-1st Legion of Super Heroes app.; 1st app. Cosmic Boy, Lightning Boy (later Lightning Lad in #267), & Saturn Girl (origin) 307.00 920.00 2150.00 4600.00

GD25 FN65 NM94

248-252,254,255-Green Arrow in all: 255-Intro. Red Kryptonite in Superboy (used in #252 but with no effect) 16.50 50.00 165.00
253-1st meeting of Superboy & Robin; Green Arrow by Kirby in #250-255 (also see World's Finest #96-99) 22.00 66.00 220.00
256-Origin Green Arrow by Kirby 46.00 138.00 560.00
257-259: 258-Green Arrow x-over in Superboy 13.50 41.00 135.00
260-1st Silver-Age origin Aquaman (5/59) 51.00 153.00 610.00
261-265,268,270: 262-Origin Speedy in Green Arrow. 270-Congorilla begins, ends #281,283 11.00 33.00 110.00
266-(11/59)-Origin & 1st app. Aquagirl (tryout, not same as later character) 12.00 36.00 120.00
267(12/59)-2nd Legion of Super Heroes; Lightning Boy now called Lightning Lad; new costumes for Legion 64.00 192.00 770.00
269-Intro. Aqualad (2/60); last Green Arrow (not in #206) 21.00 63.00 210.00
271-Origin Luthor retold 23.00 69.00 230.00
272-274,277-280: 279-Intro White Kryptonite in Superboy. 280-1st meeting Superboy-Lori Lemaris 10.00 30.00 100.00
275-Origin Superman-Batman team retold (see World's Finest #94) 18.50 55.00 185.00
276-(9/60) Re-intro Metallo (3rd app?); story similar to Superboy #49 11.00 33.00 110.00
281,284,287-289: 281-Last Congorilla. 284-Last Aquaman in Adv. 287,288-Intro Dev-Em, the Knave from Krypton. 287-1st Bizarro Perry White & J. Olsen. 288-Bizarro-c. 289-Legion cameo (statues) 8.50 25.50 85.00
282(3/61)-5th Legion app; intro/origin Star Boy 16.00 48.00 160.00
283-Intro. The Phantom Zone 16.00 48.00 160.00
285-1st Tales of the Bizarro World-c/story (ends #299) in Adv. (see Action #255) 14.00 42.00 140.00
286-1st Bizarro Mxyzptlk; Bizarro-c 12.00 36.00 120.00
290(11/61)-9th Legion app; origin Sunboy in Legion (last 10¢ issue) 16.00 48.00 160.00
291,292,295-298: 291-1st 12¢ ish, (12/61). 292-1st Bizarro Lana Lang & Lucy Lane. 295-Bizarro-c; 1st Bizarro Titano 7.00 21.00 70.00
293(2/62)-13th Legion app; Mon-el & Legion Super Pets (1st app./origin) app. (1st Superhorse). 1st Bizarro Luthor & Kandor 10.50 32.00 105.00
294-1st Bizarro Marilyn Monroe, Pres. Kennedy. 10.00 30.00 100.00
299-1st Gold Kryptonite (8/62) 7.50 22.50 75.00
300-Tales of the Legion of Super-Heroes series begins (9/62); Mon-el leaves Phantom Zone (temporarily), joins Legion 31.00 93.00 350.00
301-Origin Bouncing Boy 12.00 36.00 120.00
302-305: 303-1st app. Matter-Eater Lad. 304-Death of Lightning Lad in Legion 8.00 24.00 80.00
306-310: 306-Intro. Legion of Substitute Heroes. 307-1st app. Element Lad in Legion. 308-1st app. Lightning Lass in Legion 7.00 21.00 70.00
311-320: 312-Lightning Lad back in Legion. 315-Last new Superboy story; Colossal Boy app. 316-Origins & powers of Legion given. 317-Intro. Dream Girl in Legion; Lightning Lass becomes Light Lass; Hall of Fame series begins. 320-Dev-Em 2nd app. 5.50 16.50 55.00
321-Intro Time Trapper 4.50 13.50 45.00
322-330: 327-Intro/1st app. Lone Wolf in Legion. 329-Intro The Bizarro Legionnaires 3.80 11.40 38.00
331-340: 337-Chlorophyll Kid & Night Girl app. 340-Intro Computo in Legion 2.70 8.00 30.00
341-Triplicate Girl becomes Duo Damsel 2.25 6.75 22.00
342-345,347,350,351: 345-Last Hall of Fame; returns in 356,371. 351-1st app. White Witch 1.60 4.80 16.00
346-1st app. Karate Kid, Princess Projectra, Ferro Lad, & Nemesis Kid. 2.00 6.00 20.00
348,349: 348-Origin Sunboy; intro Dr. Regulus in Legion. 349-Intro Universo & Rond Vidar 1.60 4.80 16.00
352,354-360: 355-Insect Queen joins Legion (4/67) 1.20 3.60 12.00
353-Death of Ferro Lad in Legion 2.00 6.00 20.00
361-364,366,368-370: 369-Intro Mordru in Legion 1.20 3.60 12.00
365,367: 365-Intro Shadow Lass; lists origins & powers of L.S.H. 367-New Legion headquarters. 1.20 3.60 12.00
371,372: 371-Intro. Chemical King. 372-Timber Wolf & Chemical King join. 1.60 4.80 16.00
373,374,376-380: 374-Article on comics fandom. 380-Last Legion in Adventure 1.20 3.60 12.00
375-Intro Quantum Queen & The Wanderers 1.60 4.80 16.00
381-Supergirl begins; 1st full length Supergirl story & her 1st solo book (6/69) 5.00 15.00 55.00
382-389,391-398 1.20 3.60 12.00
390-Giant Supergirl G-69 2.50 7.40 27.00
399-Unpubbed G.A. Black Canary story 1.80 5.40 18.00
400-New costume for Supergirl 2.20 6.25 22.00
401,402,404-408 1.00 3.00 10.00
403-68pg. Giant G-81; Legion-r/#304,305,308,312 2.50 7.60 28.00
409,410,411-(52 pgs.) 1.25 3.75 12.00
412-(52 pgs.) Reprints origin & 1st app. of Animal Man from Strange Adventures #180 1.75 5.25 16.00
413,418,419-(52 pgs.): 413-Hawkman by Kubert r/B&B #44; G.A. Robotman-r/Det. #178; Zatanna by Morrow. 418-Previously unpublished Dr. Mid-Nite story from 1948; No Zatanna. 1.30 3.90 13.00
414-(52 pgs.) Reprints 2nd Animal Man/Strange Advs. #184 1.30 3.90 13.00
415,420-(52 pgs.)Animal Man reprints from Strange Adventures #190 (origin recap) & #195 1.30 3.90 13.00
416-Also listed as DC 100 Pg. Super Spectacular #10; Golden Age-r; r/1st app. Black Canary from Flash #86; no Zatanna
(see DC 100 Pg. Super Spectacular #10 for price)
417-(52 pgs.) Morrow Vigilante; Frazetta Shining Knight-r/Adv. #161; origin The Enchantress; no Zatanna 1.40 4.20 14.00
421-424,427: Last Supergirl in Adventure. 427-Last Vigilante. 2.60 7.00
425-New look, content change to adventure; Kaluta-c; Toth-a, origin Capt. Fear 1.60 4.80 16.00
426-1st Adventurers Club. 1.00 3.00 10.00
428-Origin/1st app. Black Orchid (c/story, 6-7/73) 2.90 8.70 32.00
429,430-Black Orchid-c/stories 1.60 4.80 16.00
431-Spectre by Aparo begins, ends #440. 3.20 9.50 35.00
432-439-Spectre app. 433-437-Cover title is Weird Adv. Comics. 436-Last 20¢ issue. 1.60 4.80 16.00
440-New Spectre origin. 2.20 6.50 24.00
441,442,444,448-458: 441-452-Aquaman app. 450-Weather Wizard app. in Aquaman story. 449-451-Martian Manhunter app. 453-458-Superboy app. 453-Intro Mighty Girl. 457,458-Eclipso app. 3.00
443,445-447: 443-Fisherman app. 445-447-The Creeper app. 446-Flag-c 6.00

Adventures For Boys © Bailey Ent.

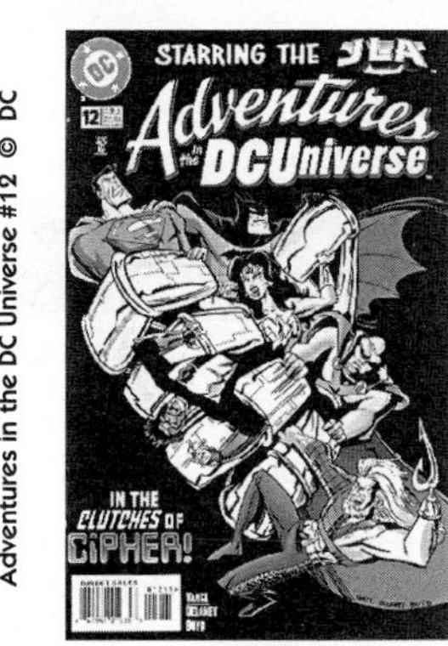

Adventures in the DC Universe #12 © DC

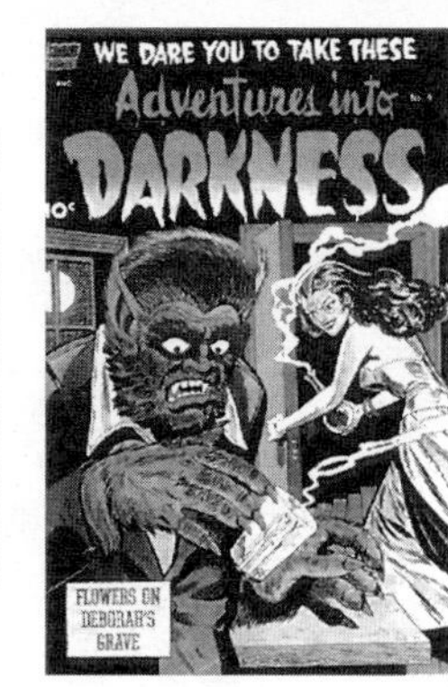

Adventures into Darkness #9 © STD

GD25 FN65 NM94

459,460: 459-New Gods/Darkseid storyline concludes from New Gods #19 (#459 is dated 9-10/78) without missing a month. 459-Flash (ends #466), Deadman (ends #466), Wonder Woman (ends #464), Green Lantern (ends #460). 460-Aquaman (ends #478) 1.10 3.30 11.00
461,462: 461-Justice Society begins; ends 466. 461,462-Death Earth II Batman (both $1.00, 68 pgs.) 1.10 3.30 11.00
463-466($1.00 size, 68 pgs.): .85 2.60 7.00
467-Starman by Ditko & Plastic Man begins; 1st app. Prince Gavyn (Starman). .90 2.70 9.00
468-470,479: 469,470-Origin Starman. 479-Dial 'H' For Hero begins, ends #490 3.50
471-478: 478-Last Starman & Plastic Man. 3.50
480-490: Dial 'H' For Hero 3.50
491-499: 491-100pg. Digest size begins; r/Legion of Super Heroes/Adv. #247, 267; Spectre, Aquaman, Superboy, S&K Sandman, Black Canary-r & new Shazam by Newton begin. 492,495,496,499-S&K Sandman-r/Adventure in all. 493-Challengers of the Unknown begins by Tuska w/brief origin. 493-495, 497-499-G.A. Captain Marvel-r. 494-499-Spectre-r/Spectre 1-3, 5-7. 496-Capt. Marvel Jr. new-s, Cockrum-a. 498-Mary Marvel new-s. Plastic Man-r begin; origin Bouncing Boy-r/ #301. 1.20 3.60 12.00
500-503: 500-Legion-r (Digest size, 148 pgs.). 501-503: G.A.-r 1.00 3.00 10.00
... 80 Page Giant (10/98, $4.95) Wonder Woman, Shazam, Superboy, Supergirl Green Arrow, Legion, Bizarro World stroies 5.00

NOTE: *Bizarro covers-285, 286, 288, 294, 295, 329. Vigilante app.-420, 426, 427.* **N. Adams** *a(r)-495i-498i; c-365-369, 371-373, 375-379, 381-383.* **Aparo** *a-431-433, 434i, 435, 436, 437i, 438i, 439-452, 503r; c-431-452.* **Austin** *a-449i 451i.* **Bernard Baily** *c-48, 50, 52-59.* **Bolland** *c-475.* **Burnley** *c-61-72, 116-120p.* **Chaykin** *a-438.* **Ditko** *a-467-478p; c-467p.* **Creig Flessel** *c-32, 33, 40, 42, 44, 46, 47, 51, 60.* **Giffen** *c-491p-494p, 500p.* **Grell** *a-435-437, 440.* **Guardineer** *c-34, 35, 45.* **Infantino** *a-416r.* **Kaluta** *c-425.* **Bob Kane** *a-38.* **G. Kane** *a-414r, 425; c-496-499, 537.* **Kirby** *a-250-256.* **Kubert** *a-413.* **Meskin** *a-81,127.* **Moldoff** *a-494i; c-49.* **Morrow** *a-413-415, 417, 422, 502r, 503r.* **Netzer/Nasser** *a-449-451.* **Newton** *a-459-461, 464-466, 491p, 492p.* **Paul Norris** *a-69.* **Orlando** *a-457p, 458p.* **Perez** *c-484-486, 490p.* **Simon/Kirby** *a-503r; c-73-97, 100-102.* **Starlin** *c-471.* **Staton** *a-445-447i, 456-458p, 459, 460, 461p-465p, 466,467p-478p, 502p(r); c-458, 461(back).* **Toth** *a-418, 419, 425, 431, 495p-497p.* **Tuska** *a-494p.*

ADVENTURE COMICS
IGA: No date (early 1940s) (Paper-c, 32 pgs.)

Two diff.issues; Super-Mystery-r from 1941 24.00 72.00 180.00

ADVENTURE IN DISNEYLAND
Walt Disney Productions (Dist. by Richfield Oil): May, 1955 (Giveaway, soft-c., 16 pgs)

nn 8.50 26.00 60.00

ADVENTURE INTO MYSTERY
Atlas Comics (BFP No. 1/OPI No. 2-8): May, 1956 - No. 8, July, 1957

1-Powell s/f-a; Forte-a; Everett-c 30.00 90.00 260.00
2-Flying Saucer story 17.00 51.00 145.00
3,6-Everett-c 14.00 42.00 120.00
4-Williamson-a, 4 pgs; Powell-a 15.00 45.00 130.00
5-Everett-c/a, Orlando-a 15.00 45.00 130.00
7-Torres-a; Everett-c 15.00 45.00 130.00
8-Moriera, Sale, Torres, Woodbridge-a, Severin-c 14.00 42.00 120.00

ADVENTURE IS MY CAREER
U.S. Coast Guard Academy/Street & Smith: 1945 (44 pgs.)

nn-Simon, Milt Gross-a 17.00 50.00 125.00

ADVENTURERS, THE
Aircel Comics/Adventure Publ.: Aug, 1986 - No. 10, 1987? ($1.50, B&W) V2#1, 1987 - V2#9, 1988; V3#1, Oct, 1989 - V3#6, 1990

1-Peter Hsu-a 3.00
1-Cover variant, limited ed. 5.00
1-2nd print (1986); 1st app. Elf Warrior 2.00
2,3 2.00
0 (#4, 12/86)-Origin 2.00
5-10 1.60
Book II, regular & limited ed. #1 1.60
Book II, #2,3,0,4-7 1.60
Book III, #1 (10/89, $2.25)-Regular & limited-c 2.25
Book III, #2-6 2.25

ADVENTURES (No. 2 Spectacular... on cover)
St. John Publishing Co.: Nov, 1949 - No. 2, Feb, 1950 (No. 1 ...in Romance on cover) (Slightly larger size)

1(Scarce); Bolle, Starr-a(2) 23.00 68.00 170.00
2(Scarce)-Slave Girl; China Bombshell app.; Bolle, L. Starr-a 37.00 112.00 280.00

ADVENTURES FOR BOYS
Bailey Enterprises: Dec, 1954

nn-Comics, text, & photos 5.00 15.00 30.00

ADVENTURES IN PARADISE (TV)
Dell Publishing Co.: Feb-Apr, 1962

Four Color#1301 3.60 11.00 40.00

ADVENTURES IN ROMANCE (See Adventures)

ADVENTURES IN SCIENCE (See Classics Illustrated Special Issue)

ADVENTURES IN THE DC UNIVERSE
DC Comics: Apr, 1997 - No. 19, Oct, 1998 ($1.75/$1.95/$1.99)

1-Animated style in all: JLA-c/app 3.00
2-8: 2-Flash app. 3-Wonder Woman. 4-Green Lantern. 6-Aquaman. 7-Shazam Family. 8-Blue Beetle & Booster Gold. 2.00
9-11,13-17,19: 9-Flash, begin $1.95-c. 10-Legion. 11-Green Lantern & Wonder Woman. 13-Impulse & Martian Manhunter. 14-Superboy/Flash race 19-$1.99-c 2.00
12,18-JLA-c/app 2.50
Annual 1(1997, $3.95)-Dr. Fate, Impulse, Rose & Thorn, Superboy, Mister Miracle app. 4.00

ADVENTURES IN 3-D
Harvey Publications: Nov, 1953 - No. 2, Jan, 1954 (25¢)

1-Nostrand, Powell-a, 2-Powell-a 16.00 48.00 120.00

ADVENTURES INTO DARKNESS (See Seduction of the Innocent 3-D)
Better-Standard Publications/Visual Editions: No. 5, Aug, 1952- No. 14, 1954

5-Katz-c/a; Toth-a(p) 28.00 84.00 210.00
6-Tuska, Katz-a 16.00 48.00 120.00
7-Katz-c/a 17.00 52.00 130.00
8,9-Toth-a(p) 18.00 54.00 135.00
10,11-Jack Katz-a 15.00 44.00 110.00
12-Toth-a?; lingerie panels 15.00 44.00 110.00
13-Toth-a(p); Cannibalism story cited by T. E. Murphy articles 17.00 52.00 130.00
14 12.00 36.00 90.00

NOTE: **Fawcette** *a-13.* **Moriera** *a-5.* **Sekowsky** *a-10, 11, 13(2).*

ADVENTURES INTO TERROR (Formerly Joker Comics)
Marvel/Atlas Comics (CDS): No. 43, Nov, 1950 - No. 31, May, 1954

43(#1) 54.00 162.00 460.00
44(#2, 2/51)-Sol Brodsky-c 39.00 118.00 315.00
3(4/51), 4 23.00 68.00 170.00
5-Wolverton-c panel/Mystic #6; Rico-c panel also; Atom Bomb story 27.00 82.00 205.00
6,8: 8-Wolverton text illo r-/Marvel Tales #104 21.00 64.00 160.00
7-Wolverton-a "Where Monsters Dwell", 6 pgs.; Tuska-c; Maneely-c panels 47.00 142.00 400.00
9,10,12-Krigstein-a. 9-Decapitation panels 19.00 58.00 145.00
11,13-20 16.00 48.00 120.00
21-24,26-31 14.00 42.00 105.00
25-Matt Fox-a 19.00 56.00 140.00

NOTE: **Ayers** *a-21.* **Colan** *a-3, 5, 14, 21, 24, 25, 28, 29; c-27.* **Colletta** *a-30.* **Everett** *c-13, 21,*

Adventures into Weird Worlds #16 © ACG

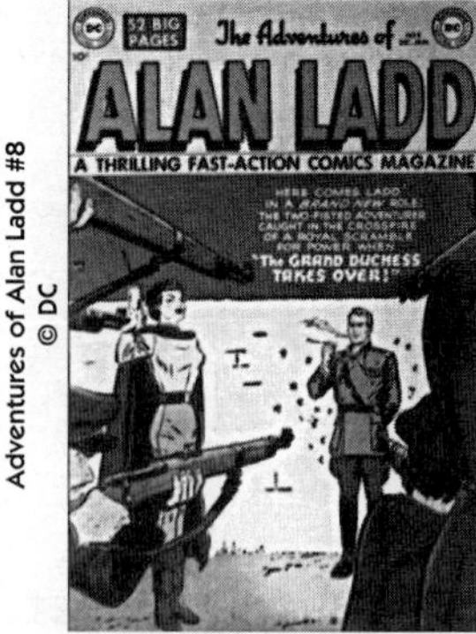

Adventures of Alan Ladd #8 © DC

Adventures of Bob Hope #5 © DC

	GD25	FN65	NM94

25. ***Fass*** *a-28, 29.* ***Forte*** *a-28.* ***Heath*** *a-43, 44, 4-6, 22, 24, 26; c-43, 9, 11.* ***Lazarus*** *a-7.* ***Maneely*** *a-7(3 pg.), 10, 11, 21., 22 c-15, 29.* ***Don Rico*** *a-4, 5(3 pg.).* ***Sekowsky*** *a-43, 3, 4.* ***Sinnott*** *a-8, 9, 11, 28.* ***Tuska*** *a-14; c-7.*

ADVENTURES INTO THE UNKNOWN
American Comics Group: Fall, 1948 - No. 174, Aug, 1967 (No. 1-33: 52 pgs.)
(1st continuous series horror comic; see Eerie #1)

	GD25	FN65	NM94
1-Guardineer-a; adapt. of 'Castle of Otranto' by Horace Walpole			
	165.00	494.00	1400.00
2	64.00	190.00	540.00
3-Feldstein-a (9 pgs)	64.00	190.00	540.00
4,5: 5-'Spirit Of Frankenstein' series begins, ends #12 (except #11)			
	33.00	100.00	250.00
6-10	27.00	80.00	200.00
11-16,18-20: 13-Starr-a	21.00	64.00	160.00
17-Story similar to movie 'The Thing'	25.00	76.00	190.00
21-26,28-30	17.00	52.00	130.00
27-Williamson/Krenkel-a (8 pgs.)	23.00	68.00	170.00
31-50: 38-Atom bomb panels	14.00	42.00	105.00
51-(1/54)-(3-D effect-c/story)-Only white cover	29.00	88.00	220.00
52-58: (3-D effect-c/stories with black covers). 52-E.C. swipe/Haunt Of Fear #14	28.00	84.00	210.00
59-3-D effect story only; new logo	23.00	68.00	170.00
60-Woodesque-a by Landau	9.35	28.00	70.00
61-Last pre-code issue (1-2/55)	9.35	28.00	70.00
62-70	5.00	15.00	50.00
71-90	3.50	10.50	35.00
91,96(#95 on inside),107,116-All have Williamson-a	5.00	15.00	50.00
92-95,97-99,101-106,108-115,117-127: 109-113,118-Whitney painted-c			
	3.20	9.60	32.00
100	3.50	10.50	35.00
128-Williamson/Krenkel/Torres-a(r)/Forbidden Worlds #63; last 10¢ issue			
	3.20	9.60	32.00
129-152	2.80	8.40	28.00
153, 157-Magic Agent app.	2.80	8.40	28.00
154-Nemesis series begins (origin), ends #170	3.20	9.60	32.00
155,156,158-167,170-174	2.50	7.50	24.00
168-Ditko-a(p)	3.20	9.60	32.00
169-Nemesis battles Hitler	2.60	7.80	26.00

NOTE: *"Spirit of Frankenstein" series in 5, 6, 8-10, 12, 16.* ***Buscema*** *a-100, 106, 108-110, 158r, 165r.* ***Cameron*** *a-34.* ***Craig*** *a-152, 160.* ***Goode*** *a-45, 47, 60.* ***Landau*** *a-51, 59-63.* ***Lazarus*** *a-34, 48, 51, 52, 56, 58, 79, 87; c-31-56, 58.* ***Reinman*** *a-102, 111, 112, 115-118, 124, 130, 137, 141, 145, 164.* ***Whitney*** *c-12-30, 57, 59-on (most.)* ***Torres/Williamson*** *a-116.*

ADVENTURES INTO WEIRD WORLDS
Marvel/Atlas Comics (ACI): Jan, 1952 - No. 30, June, 1954

	GD25	FN65	NM94
1-Atom bomb panels	45.00	136.00	385.00
2-Sci/fic stories (2); one by Maneely	31.00	94.00	235.00
3-10: 7-Tongue ripped out. 10-Krigstein, Everett-a	21.00	64.00	160.00
11-21: 21-Hitler in Hell story	17.00	52.00	130.00
22-26: 24-Man holds hypo & splits in two	15.00	44.00	110.00
27-Matt Fox end of world story-a; severed head-c	31.00	92.00	230.00
28-Atom bomb story; decapitation panels	17.00	52.00	130.00
29,30	12.00	36.00	90.00

NOTE: ***Ayers*** *a-8, 26.* ***Everett*** *a-4, 5; c-6, 8, 10-13, 18, 19, 22, 24, 25; a-4, 25.* ***Fass*** *a-7.* ***Forte*** *a-21, 24.* ***Al Hartley*** *a-2.* ***Heath*** *a-1, 4, 17, 22; c-7, 9, 20.* ***Maneely*** *a-2, 3, 11, 20, 22, 23, 25; c-1, 3, 22, 25-27, 29.* ***Reinman*** *a-24, 28.* ***Rico*** *a-13.* ***Robinson*** *a-13.* ***Sinnott*** *a-25, 30.* ***Tuska*** *a-1, 2, 12, 15.* ***Whitney*** *a-7.* ***Wildey*** *a-28. Bondage c-22.*

ADVENTURES IN WONDERLAND
Lev Gleason Publications: April, 1955 - No. 5, Feb, 1956 (Jr. Readers Guild)

	GD25	FN65	NM94
1-Maurer-a	7.85	23.50	55.00
2-4	5.35	16.00	32.00
5-Christmas issue	5.70	17.00	38.00

ADVENTURES OF AARON
Image Comics: Mar, 1997 - No. 3, Sept, 1997 (2.95, B&W)

	GD25	FN65	NM94
1,2,100(#3),3(#4)			2.95

ADVENTURES OF ALAN LADD, THE
National Periodical Publ.: Oct-Nov, 1949 - No. 9, Feb-Mar, 1951 (All 52 pgs.)

	GD25	FN65	NM94
1-Photo-c	85.00	255.00	725.00
2-Photo-c	46.00	138.00	390.00
3-6: Last photo-c	38.00	114.00	285.00
7-9	30.00	90.00	225.00

NOTE: ***Dan Barry*** *a-1.* ***Moreira*** *a-3-7.*

ADVENTURES OF ALICE (Also see Alice in Wonderland & ...at Monkey Island)
Civil Service Publ./Pentagon Publishing Co.: 1945

	GD25	FN65	NM94
1	9.30	27.90	70.00
2-Through the Magic Looking Glass	8.50	25.50	60.00

ADVENTURES OF BARON MUNCHAUSEN, THE
Now Comics: July, 1989 - No. 4, Oct, 1989 ($1.75, limited series)

	GD25	FN65	NM94
1-4: Movie adaptation			1.80

ADVENTURES OF BAYOU BILLY, THE
Archie Comics: Sept, 1989 - No. 5, June, 1990 ($1.00)

	GD25	FN65	NM94
1-5: Esposito-c/a(i). 5-Kelley Jones-c			2.00

ADVENTURES OF BOB HOPE, THE (Also see True Comics #59)
National Per. Publ.: Feb-Mar, 1950 - No. 109, Feb-Mar, 1968 (#1-10: 52pgs.)

	GD25	FN65	NM94
1-Photo-c	139.00	417.00	1250.00
2-Photo-c	69.00	207.00	590.00
3,4-Photo-c	43.00	129.00	350.00
5-10	39.00	117.00	290.00
11-20	21.00	63.00	160.00
21-31 (2-3/55; last precode)	14.00	42.00	105.00
32-40	8.50	25.50	85.00
41-50	7.00	21.00	70.00
51-70	5.00	15.00	50.00
71-93,96-105	2.80	8.40	28.00
94-Aquaman cameo	3.20	9.60	32.00
95-1st app. Super-Hip & 1st monster issue (11/65)	3.80	11.40	38.00
106-109-All monster-c/stories by N. Adams-c/a	4.20	12.60	42.00

NOTE: *Buzzy in #34. Kitty Karr of Hollywood in #15, 17-20, 23, 28. Liz in #26, 109. Miss Beverly Hills of Hollywood in #7, 8, 10, 13, 14. Miss Melody Lane of Broadway in #15. Rusty in #23, 25. Tommy in #24. No 2nd feature in #2-4, 6, 8, 11, 12, 28-108.*

ADVENTURES OF CAPTAIN AMERICA
Marvel Comics: Sept, 1991 - No. 4, Jan, 1992 ($4.95, 52 pgs., squarebound, limited series)

	GD25	FN65	NM94
1-4: 1-Embossed-c; Fabian Nicieza scripts; Kevin Maguire-c/a(p) begins, ends #3. 2-4-Austin-c/a(i)			5.00

ADVENTURES OF CYCLOPS AND PHOENIX (Also See Askani'son & The Further Adventures of Cyclops And Phoenix)
Marvel Comics: May, 1994 - No. 4, Aug, 1994 ($2.95, limited series)

	GD25	FN65	NM94
1-Characters from X-Men			3.00
2-4			3.00
Trade paperback ($14.95)-reprints #1-4			15.00

ADVENTURES OF DEAN MARTIN AND JERRY LEWIS, THE
(The Adventures of Jerry Lewis #41 on) (See Movie Love #12)
National Periodical Publications: July-Aug, 1952 - No. 40, Oct, 1957

	GD25	FN65	NM94
1	82.00	246.00	700.00
2-3 pg origin on how they became a team	43.00	129.00	350.00
3-10: 3- I Love Lucy text featurette	21.00	63.00	160.00
11-19: Last precode (2/55)	13.00	39.00	100.00
20-30	11.00	33.00	80.00
31-40	8.50	25.50	60.00

ADVENTURES OF DETECTIVE ACE KING, THE (Also see Bob Scully-- & Detective Dan)
Humor Publ. Corp.: No date (1933) (36 pgs., 9-1/2x12") (10¢, B&W, one-shot) (paper-c)

	GD25	FN65	VF82
Book 1-Along with Detective Dan, the first comic w/original art & the first of a single theme.; Not reprints; Ace King by Martin Nadle (The American			

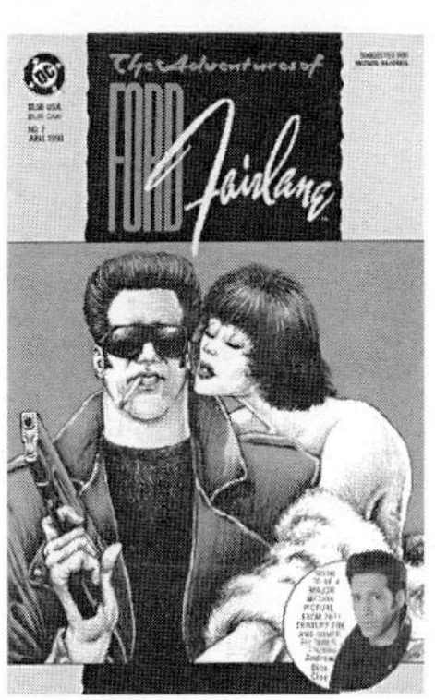

Adventures of Ford Fairlane #2 © DC

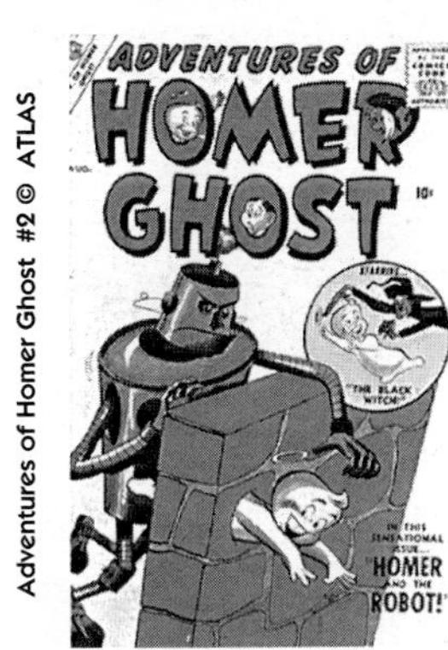

Adventures of Homer Ghost #2 © ATLAS

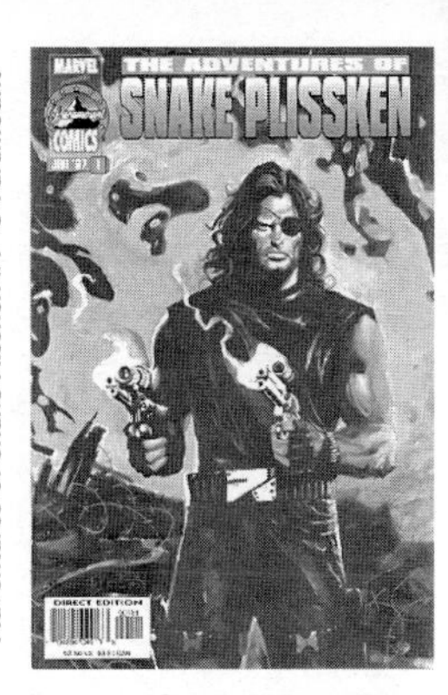

Adventures of Snake Plissken #1 © Paramount

	GD25	FN65	NM94
Sherlock Holmes). A Dick Tracy look-alike	250.00	750.00	1500.00

ADVENTURES OF FELIX THE CAT, THE
Harvey Comics: May, 1992 ($1.25)

	GD25	FN65	NM94
1-Messmer-r			1.50

ADVENTURES OF FORD FAIRLANE, THE
DC Comics: May, 1990 - No. 4, Aug, 1990 ($1.50, limited series, mature)

	GD25	FN65	NM94
1-4: Movie tie-in; Don Heck inks			1.50

ADVENTURES OF G. I. JOE
1969 (3-1/4x7") (20 & 16 pgs.)
Giveaways

First Series: 1-Danger of the Depths. 2-Perilous Rescue. 3-Secret Mission to Spy Island. 4-Mysterious Explosion. 5-Fantastic Free Fall. 6-Eight Ropes of Danger. 7-Mouth of Doom. 8-Hidden Missile Discovery. 9-Space Walk Mystery. 10-Fight for Survival. 11-The Shark's Surprise.
Second Series: 2-Flying Space Adventure. 4-White Tiger Hunt. 7-Capture of the Pygmy Gorilla. 12-Secret of the Mummy's Tomb.
Third Series: Reprinted surviving titles of First Series. Fourth Series: 13-Adventure Team Headquarters. 14-Search For the Stolen Idol.

	GD25	FN65	NM94
each....	1.00	3.00	10.00

ADVENTURES OF HOMER COBB, THE
Say/Bart Prod. : Sept, 1947 (Oversized)
(Published in the U.S., but printed in Canada)

	GD25	FN65	NM94
1-(Scarce)-Feldstein-c/a	26.00	78.00	195.00

ADVENTURES OF HOMER GHOST (See Homer The Happy Ghost)
Atlas Comics: June, 1957 - No. 2, Aug, 1957

	GD25	FN65	NM94
V1#1,2	5.70	17.00	38.00

ADVENTURES OF JERRY LEWIS, THE (Adventures of Dean Martin & Jerry Lewis No. 1-40)(See Super DC Giant)
National Periodical Publ.: No. 41, Nov, 1957 - No. 124, May-June, 1971

	GD25	FN65	NM94
41	6.00	18.00	60.00
42-60	5.00	15.00	50.00
61-67,69-73,75-80	3.80	11.40	38.00
68,74-Photo-c	4.20	12.60	42.00
81-91,93-96,98,99: 89-Bob Hope app.	2.50	7.50	24.00
92-Superman cameo	3.40	10.20	34.00
97-Batman/Robin/Joker-c/story; Riddler & Penguin app; Dick Sprang-c.	5.00	15.00	50.00
100	3.00	9.00	30.00
101,103,104-Neal Adams-c/a	4.20	12.60	42.00
102-Beatles app.; Neal Adams c/a	5.80	17.50	58.00
105-Superman x-over	3.20	9.50	35.00
106-111,113-116	1.80	5.40	18.00
112-Flash x-over	3.20	9.50	34.00
117-Wonder Woman x-over	3.20	9.50	34.00
118-124	1.40	4.20	14.00

ADVENTURES OF JO-JOY, THE (See Jo-Joy)

ADVENTURES OF LASSIE, THE (See Lassie)

ADVENTURES OF LUTHER ARKWRIGHT, THE
Valkyrie Press/Dark Horse Comics: Oct, 1987 - No. 9, Jan, 1989 ($2.00, B&W) V2, #1, Mar, 1990 - V2#9, 1990 ($1.95, B&W)

	GD25	FN65	NM94
1-9: 1-Alan Moore intro.			2.00
V2#1-9 (Dark Horse): Reprints 1st series; new-c			2.00
TPB (1997, $14.95) r/#1-9 w/Michael Moorcock intro.			15.00

ADVENTURES OF MARGARET O'BRIEN, THE
Bambury Fashions (Clothes): 1947 (20 pgs. in color, slick-c, regular size) (Premium)

	GD25	FN65	NM94
In "The Big City" movie adaptation (scarce)	19.00	56.00	140.00

ADVENTURES OF MIGHTY MOUSE (Mighty Mouse Adventures No. 1)
St. John Publishing Co.: No. 2, Jan, 1952 - No. 18, May, 1955

	GD25	FN65	NM94
2	23.00	68.00	170.00
3-5	11.00	34.00	85.00
6-18	8.50	26.00	60.00

ADVENTURES OF MIGHTY MOUSE (2nd Series)
(Two No. 144's; formerly Paul Terry's Comics; No. 129-137 have nn's)
(Becomes Mighty Mouse No. 161 on)
St. John/Pines/Dell/Gold Key: No. 126, Aug, 1955 - No. 160, Oct, 1963

	GD25	FN65	NM94
126(8/55), 127(10/55), 128(11/55)-St. John	6.85	21.00	48.00
nn(129, 4/56)-144(8/59)-Pines	4.00	12.00	40.00
144(10-12/59)-155(7-9/62) Dell	3.25	10.00	35.00
156(10/62)-160(10/63) Gold Key	3.50	10.50	38.00

NOTE: *Early issues titled "Paul Terry's Adventures of ...."*

ADVENTURES OF MIGHTY MOUSE (Formerly Mighty Mouse)
Gold Key: No. 166, Mar, 1979 - No. 172, Jan, 1980

	GD25	FN65	NM94
166-172			4.00

ADVS. OF MR. FROG & MISS MOUSE (See Dell Junior Treasury No. 4)

ADVENTURES OF OZZIE AND HARRIET, THE (Radio)
National Periodical Publications: Oct-Nov, 1949 - No. 5, June-July, 1950

	GD25	FN65	NM94
1-Photo-c	82.00	246.00	700.00
2	43.00	129.00	360.00
3-5	39.00	117.00	290.00

ADVENTURES OF PATORUZU
Green Publishing Co.: Aug, 1946 - Winter, 1946

	GD25	FN65	NM94
nn's-Contains Animal Crackers reprints	4.15	12.50	25.00

ADVENTURES OF PINKY LEE, THE (TV)
Atlas Comics: July, 1955 - No. 5, Dec, 1955

	GD25	FN65	NM94
1	24.00	72.00	180.00
2-5	15.00	44.00	110.00

ADVENTURES OF PIPSQUEAK, THE (Formerly Pat the Brat)
Archie Publications (Radio Comics): No. 34, Sept, 1959 - No. 39, July, 1960

	GD25	FN65	NM94
34	3.20	9.60	32.00
35-39	2.50	7.50	22.00

ADVENTURES OF QUAKE & QUISP, THE (See Quaker Oats "Plenty of Glutton")

ADVENTURES OF REX THE WONDER DOG, THE (Rex...No. 1)
National Periodical Publications: Jan-Feb, 1952 - No. 45, May-June, 1959; No. 46, Nov-Dec, 1959

	GD25	FN65	NM94
1-(Scarce)-Toth-c/a	92.00	276.00	850.00
2-(Scarce)-Toth-c/a	46.00	138.00	425.00
3-(Scarce)-Toth-a	36.00	108.00	325.00
4,5	29.00	86.00	240.00
6-10	21.00	64.00	175.00
11-Atom bomb-c/story	23.00	69.00	200.00
12-19: 19-Last precode (1-2/55)	12.00	36.00	100.00
20-46	7.00	21.00	75.00

NOTE: ***Infantino, Gil Kane** art in 5-19 (most)*

ADVENTURES OF ROBIN HOOD, THE (Formerly Robin Hood)
Magazine Enterprises (Sussex Publ. Co.): No. 7, 9/57 - No. 8, 11/57
(Based on Richard Greene TV Show)

	GD25	FN65	NM94
7,8-Richard Greene photo-c. 7-Powell-a	14.00	42.00	105.00

ADVENTURES OF ROBIN HOOD, THE
Gold Key: Mar, 1974 - No. 7, Jan, 1975 (Disney cartoon) (36 pgs.)

	GD25	FN65	NM94
1(90291-403)-Part-r of $1.50 editions	1.00	3.00	10.00
2-7: 1-7 are part-r		2.00	6.00

ADVENTURES OF SNAKE PLISSKEN
Marvel Comics: Jan, 1997 ($2.50, one-shot)

	GD25	FN65	NM94
1-Based on Escape From L.A. movie; Brereton-c			2.50

ADVENTURES OF SPIDER-MAN, THE (TV cartoon)
Marvel Comics: Apr, 1996 - No. 12, Mar, 1997 (99¢)

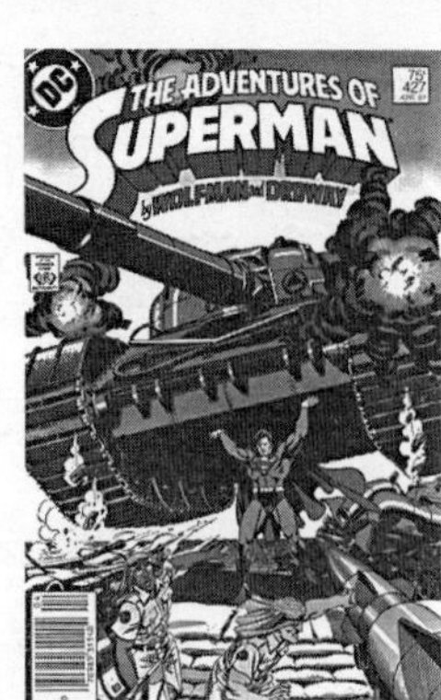

Adventures of Superman #427 © DC

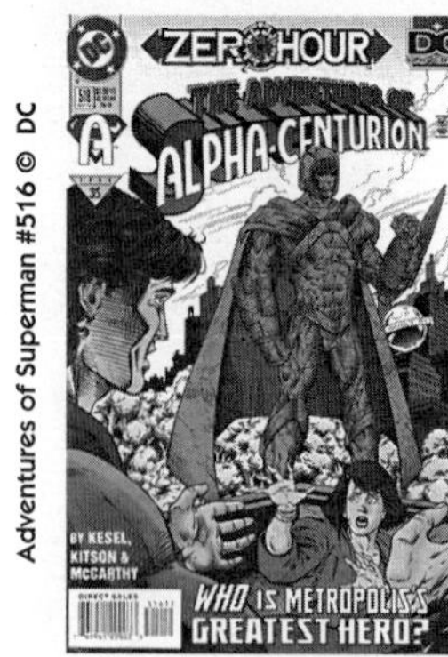

Adventures of Superman #516 © DC

Adventures of the Thing #3 © MAR

GD25 FN65 NM94

1-12: Based on animated television show. 1.00

ADVENTURES OF STUBBY, SANTA'S SMALLEST REINDEER, THE
W. T. Grant Co.: nd (early 1940s) (Giveaway, 12 pgs.)

nn 4.00 11.00 22.00

ADVENTURES OF SUPERBOY, THE (See Superboy, 2nd Series)

ADVENTURES OF SUPERMAN (Formerly Superman)
DC Comics: No. 424, Jan, 1987 - No. 499, Feb, 1993;
No. 500, Early June, 1993 - Present

424 2.25
425-449: 426-Legends x-over. 432-1st app. Jose Delgado who becomes Gangbuster in #434. 436-Byrne scripts begin. 436,437-Millennium x-over. 438-New Brainiac app. 440-Batman app. 449-Invasion 2.00
450-462: 457-Perez plots 2.00
463-Superman/Flash race; cover swipe/Superman #199 4.00
464-Lobo-c & app. (pre-dates Lobo #1) 3.00
465-479,481-491: 467-Part 2 of Batman story. 473-Hal Jordan, Guy Gardner x-over. 477-Legion app. 491-Last $1.00-c 2.00
480-($1.75, 52 pgs.) 2.00
492-495: 495-Forever People-c/story; Darkseid app. 2.00
496-Doomsday cameo 3.00
496,497-2nd printings 1.50
497-Doomsday battle issue 3.00
498,499-Funeral for a Friend; Supergirl app. 2.00
498-2nd & 3rd printings 1.50
500-($2.95, 68 pgs.)-Collector's edition w/card 3.25
500-($2.50, 68 pgs.)-Regular edition w/different-c 2.75
500-Platinum edition 2.25 6.80 25.00
501-($1.95)-Collector's edition with die-cut-c 2.00
501-($1.50)-Regular edition w/mini-poster & diff.-c 1.50
502-516: 502-Supergirl-c/story. 508-Challengers of the Unknown app. 510-Bizarro-c/story. 516-(9/94)-Zero Hour 2.50
505-($2.50)-Holo-grafx foil-c edition 2.50
0,517-523: 0-(10/94). 517-(11/94) 1.50
524-549,551-557: 524-Begin $1.95-c. 527-Return of Alpha Centurion (Zero Hour) 533-Impulse c/app. 535-Luthor-c/app. 536-Brainiac app. 537-Parasite app. 540-Final Night x-over. 541 Superboy-c/app.;Lois and Clark honeymoon 545-New powers. 546-New costume. 551-Cyborg app. 555-Red & blue Supermans battle. 557-Millennium Giants x-over 2.00
550-($3.50)-Double sized 3.50
558-560: Superman Silver Age-style story; Krypto app. 1.95
561-564: 561-Begin $1.99-c 1.99
#1,000,000 (11/98) Gene Ha-c; 853rd Century x-over 1.99
Annual 1 (1987, $1.25, 52 pgs.)-Starlin-c & scripts 1.50
Annual 2,3 (1990, 1991, $2.00, 68 pgs.): 2-Byrne-c/a(i); Legion '90 (Lobo) app. 3-Armageddon 2001 x-over .90 2.25
Annual 4,5 (1992, 1993, $2.50, 68 pgs.): 4-Guy Gardner/Lobo-c/story; Eclipso storyline; Quesada-c(p). 5-Bloodlines storyline 2.75
Annual 6 (1994, $2.95, 68 pgs.)-Elseworlds story 3.00
Annual 7 (1995, $3.95)-Year One story 4.00
Annual 8 (1996, $2.95)-Legends of the Dead Earth story 3.00
Annual 9 (1997, $3.95)-Pulp Heroes story 3.95
NOTE: *Erik Larsen a-431.*

ADVENTURES OF THE BIG BOY
Timely Comics/Webs Adv. Corp./Illus. Features: 1956 - No. 466, 1996? (Giveaway) (East & West editions of early issues)

1-Everett-a 54.00 162.00 650.00
2-Everett-a 22.50 68.00 225.00
3-5 8.00 24.00 80.00
6-10: 6-Sci/fic issue 5.00 15.00 50.00
11-20 2.50 7.50 25.00
21-30 1.75 5.25 14.00
31-50 1.00 3.00 8.00
51-100 5.00
101-150 4.00
151-240 3.00
241-265,267-269,271-300: 2.00
266-Superman x-over 1.00 3.00 10.00
270-TV's Buck Rogers-c/s 1.00 3.00 10.00
301-400 1.25
401-466 .50
1-50 ('76-'84,Paragon Prod.) (...Shoney's Big Boy) .20
Summer, 1959 issue, large size 3.50 10.50 35.00
NOTE: No. 467 was completed but never published.

ADVENTURES OF THE DOVER BOYS
Archie Comics (Close-up): September, 1950 - No. 2, 1950 (No month given)

1,2 7.15 21.50 50.00

ADVENTURES OF THE FLY (The Fly #1-6; Fly Man No. 32-39; See The Double Life of Private Strong, The Fly, Laugh Comics & Mighty Crusaders)
Archie Publications/Radio Comics: Aug, 1959 - No. 30, Oct, 1964; No. 31, May, 1965

1-Shield app.; origin The Fly; S&K-c/a 43.00 130.00 520.00
2-Williamson, S&K-a 28.00 84.00 280.00
3-Origin retold; Davis, Powell-a 22.00 66.00 220.00
4-Neal Adams-a(p)(1 panel); S&K-c; Powell-a; 2 pg. Shield story 11.50 34.00 115.00
5-10: 7-1st S.A. app. Black Hood (7/60). 8-1st S.A. app. Shield (9/60). 9-Shield app. 9-1st app. Cat Girl. 10-Black Hood app. 8.00 24.00 80.00
11-13,15-20: 13-1st app. Fly Girl w/o costume. 16-Last 10¢ issue. 20-Origin Fly Girl retold 5.00 15.00 50.00
14-Origin & 1st app. Fly Girl in costume 6.50 19.50 65.00
21-30: 23-Jaguar cameo. 27-29-Black Hood 1 pg. strips. 30-Comet x-over (1st S.A. app.) in Fly Girl 3.20 9.60 32.00
31-Black Hood, Shield, Comet app. 3.50 10.50 35.00
NOTE: ***Simon** c-2-4. **Tuska** a-1. Cover title to #31 is Flyman; Advs. of the Fly inside.*

ADVENTURES OF THE JAGUAR, THE (See Blue Ribbon Comics, Laugh Comics & Mighty Crusaders)
Archie Publications (Radio Comics): Sept, 1961 - No. 15, Nov, 1963

1-Origin Jaguar (1st app?) by J. Rosenberger 16.50 50.00 165.00
2,3: 3-Last 10¢ issue 8.50 25.50 85.00
4-6-Catgirl app. (#4's-c is same as splash pg.) 6.50 19.50 65.00
7-10 5.00 15.00 50.00
11-15: 13,14-Catgirl, Black Hood app. in both 4.00 12.00 40.00

ADVENTURES OF THE MASK (TV cartoon)
Dark Horse Comics: Jan, 1996 - No. 12, Dec, 1996 ($2.50)

1-12: Based on animated series 2.50

ADVENTURES OF THE NEW MEN (Formerly Newmen #1-21)
Maximum Press: No. 22, Nov, 1996; No. 23, March, 1997 ($2.50)

22,23-Sprouse-c/a 2.50

ADVENTURES OF THE OUTSIDERS, THE (Formerly Batman & The Outsiders; also see The Outsiders)
DC Comics: No. 33, May, 1986 - No. 46, June, 1987

33-46: 39-45-r/Outsiders #1-7 by Aparo 1.00

ADVENTURES OF THE SUPER MARIO BROTHERS (See Super Mario Bros.)
Valiant: 1990 - No. 9, Oct, 1991 ($1.50)

V2#1,6-9 2.00 6.00
2-5 4.00

ADVENTURES OF THE THING, THE (Also see The Thing)
Marvel Comics: Apr, 1992 - No. 4, July, 1992, ($1.25, limited series)

1-4: 1-r/Marvel Two-In-One #50 by Byrne; Kieth-c. 2-4-r/Marvel Two-In-One #80,51 & 77; 2-Ghost Rider-c/story. 3-Miller-r 1.25

ADVENTURES OF THE X-MEN, THE (TV cartoon)

Adventures on the Planet of the Apes #7 © MAR

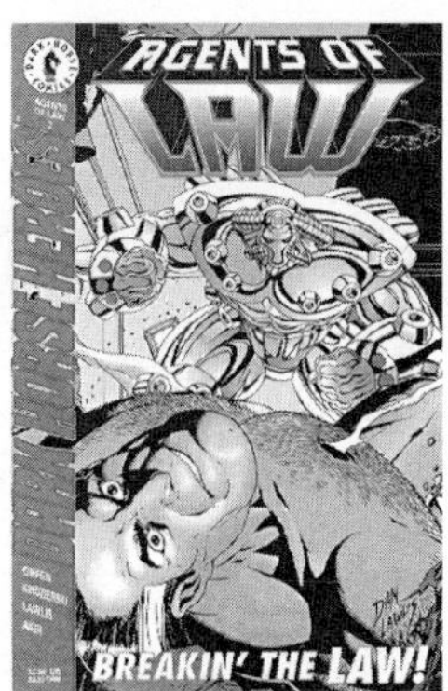

Agents of Law #2 © DH

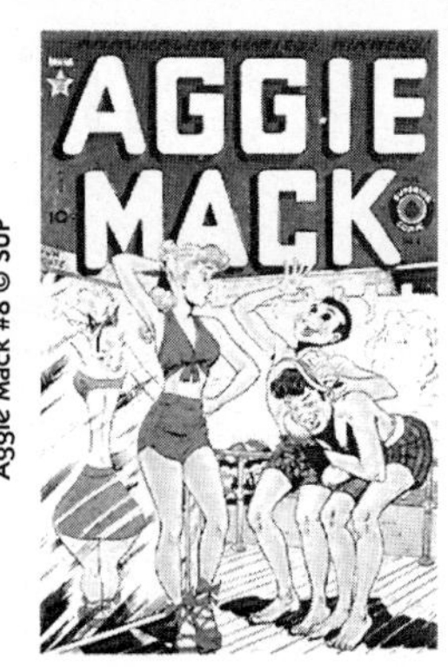

Aggie Mack #8 © SUP

	GD25	FN65	NM94
Marvel Comics: Apr, 1996 - No. 12, Mar, 1997 (99¢)			
1-12: Based on television show.			1.00
ADVENTURES OF TINKER BELL (See Tinker Bell, 4-Color No. 896 & 982)			
ADVENTURES OF TOM SAWYER (See Dell Junior Treasury No. 10)			
ADVENTURES OF YOUNG DR. MASTERS, THE			
Archie Comics (Radio Comics): Aug, 1964 - No. 2, Nov, 1964			
1	1.85	5.50	15.00
2	1.25	3.75	10.00
ADVENTURES ON OTHER WORLDS (See Showcase #17 & 18)			
ADVENTURES ON THE PLANET OF THE APES			
Marvel Comics Group: Oct, 1975 - No. 11, Dec, 1976			
1-Planet of the Apes-r in color; Starlin-c	1.00	3.00	10.00
2-5		2.00	6.00
6-11 (scarce)	.85	2.60	7.00
NOTE: ***Alcala*** a-6-11r. ***Buckler*** c-2p. ***Nasser*** c-7. ***Starlin*** c-6. ***Tuska*** a-1-5r.			
ADVENTURES WITH SANTA CLAUS			
Promotional Publ. Co. (Murphy's Store): No date (early 50's) (9-3/4x 6-3/4", 24 pgs., giveaway, paper-c)			
nn-Contains 8 pgs. ads	4.00	12.00	24.00
16 pg. version	4.00	12.00	24.00
AFRICA			
Magazine Enterprises: 1955			
1(A-1#137)-Cave Girl,Thun'da;Powell-c/a(4)	20.00	60.00	150.00
AFRICAN LION (Disney movie)			
Dell Publishing Co.: Nov, 1955			
Four Color #665	4.50	13.50	50.00
AFTER DARK			
Sterling Comics: No. 6, May, 1955 - No. 8, Sept, 1955			
6-8-Sekowsky-a in all	6.85	21.00	48.00
AGAINST BLACKSHARD 3-D (Also see SoulQuest)			
Sirius Comics: August, 1986 ($2.25)			
1			2.25
AGENT LIBERTY SPECIAL (See Superman, 2nd Series)			
DC Comics: 1992 ($2.00, 52 pgs, one-shot)			
1-1st solo adventure; Guice-c/a(i)			2.00
AGENT THREE-ZERO			
Galaxinovels, Inc.: Sept, 1993 ($3.95, 52 pgs.)			
1-Polybagged with card & mini-poster; Platt-c/a(1st work)			4.00
AGENT THREE–ZERO: THE BLUE SULTANS QUEST/ BLUE SULTAN–GALAXI FACT FILES			
Galaxi Novels: 1994 ($2.95, color w/text-no comics, limited series)			
1-($2.95)-Flip book w/Blue Sultan			3.00
1-($3.95)-Polybagged w/trading card; flip book w/Blue Sultan.			4.00
1-($5.95)-Platinum embossed edition; flip book w/ Blue Sultan			6.00
AGENTS OF LAW (Also see Comic's Greatest World)			
Dark Horse Comics: Mar, 1995 - No.6, Sept, 1995 ($2.50)			
1-6: 5-Predator app. 6-Predator app.; death of Law			2.50
AGE OF APOCALYPSE: THE CHOSEN			
Marvel Comics: Apr, 1995 ($2.50, one-shot)			
1-Wraparound-c			2.50
AGE OF BRONZE			
Image Comics: Nov, 1998 - Present ($2.95, B&W, limited series)			
1-Eric Shanower-c/s/a			2.95
AGE OF HEROES, THE			
Halloween Comics/Image Comics #3 on: 1996 - Present ($2.95, B&W)			
1-4: James Hudnall scripts; John Ridgway-c/a			3.00
...Special ($4.95) r/#1,2			4.95
...Wex 1 ('98, $2.95) Hudnall-s/Angel Fernandez-a			2.95
AGE OF INNOCENCE: THE REBIRTH OF IRON MAN			
Marvel Comics: Feb, 1996 ($2.50, one-shot)			
1-New origin of Tony Stark			2.50
AGE OF REPTILES			
Dark Horse Comics: Nov, 1993 - No. 4, Feb, 1994 ($2.50, limited series)			
1-4: Delgado-c/a/scripts in all			2.50
AGE OF REPTILES: THE HUNT			
Dark Horse Comics: May, 1996 - No. 5, Sept, 1996 ($2.95, limited series)			
1-5: Delgado-c/a/scripts in all; wraparound-c			3.00
AGGIE MACK			
Four Star Comics Corp./Superior Comics Ltd.: Jan, 1948 - No. 8, Aug, 1949			
1-Feldstein-a, "Johnny Prep"	25.00	76.00	190.00
2,3-Kamen-c	13.00	40.00	100.00
4-Feldstein "Johnny Prep"; Kamen-c	18.00	54.00	135.00
5-8-Kamen-c/a	15.00	44.00	110.00
AGGIE MACK			
Dell Publishing Co.: Apr - Jun, 1962			
Four Color #1335	2.75	8.00	30.00
AIR ACE (Formerly Bill Barnes No. 1-12)			
Street & Smith Publications: V2#1, Jan, 1944 - V3#8(No. 20), Feb-Mar, 1947			
V2#1	19.00	56.00	175.00
V2#2-Classic-c	11.00	34.00	85.00
V2#3-12: 7-Powell-a	10.00	30.00	75.00
V3#1-6	8.50	26.00	60.00
V3#7-Powell bondage-c/a; all atomic issue	17.00	51.00	130.00
V3#8 (V5#8 on-c)-Powell-c/a	9.30	28.00	70.00
AIRBOY (Also see Airmaidens, Skywolf, Target: Airboy & Valkyrie)			
Eclipse Comics: July, 1986 - No. 50, Oct, 1989 (#1-8, 50¢, 20 pgs., bi-weekly; #9-on, 36pgs.; #34-on monthly)			
1			1.00
2-4,6-8: 2-1st Marisa; Skywolf gets new costume. 3-The Heap begins			1.00
5-Valkyrie returns; Dave Stevens-c			1.00
9-32: 9-Begin $1.25-c; Skywolf begins. 11-Origin of G.A. Airboy & his plane Birdie. 28-Mr. Monster vs. The Heap.			1.25
33-41: 33-Begin $1.75-c. 38-40-The Heap by Infantino. 41-r/1st app. Valkyrie from Air Fighters			1.75
42-49: 42-Begin $1.95-c. 46,47-part-r/Air Fighters. 48-Black Angel-r/A.F			2.00
50 ($4.95, 52 pgs.)-Kubert-c			5.00
NOTE: ***Evans*** c-21. ***Gulacy*** c-7, 20. ***Spiegle*** a-34, 35, 37. ***Ken Steacy*** painted c-17, 33.			
AIRBOY COMICS (Air Fighters Comics No. 1-22)			
Hillman Periodicals: V2#11, Dec, 1945 - V10#4, May, 1953 (No V3#3)			
V2#11	62.00	186.00	525.00
12-Valkyrie app.	42.00	127.00	340.00
V3#1,2(no #3)	35.00	104.00	260.00
4-The Heap app. in Skywolf	31.00	92.00	230.00
5-8,10,11: 6-Valkyrie app.	25.00	76.00	190.00
9-Origin The Heap	31.00	92.00	230.00
12-Skywolf & Airboy x-over; Valkyrie app.	35.00	104.00	260.00
V4#1-Iron Lady app.	29.00	88.00	220.00
2,3,12: 2-Rackman begins	21.00	62.00	155.00
4-Simon & Kirby-c	23.00	70.00	175.00

Airboy V8 #7 © HILL

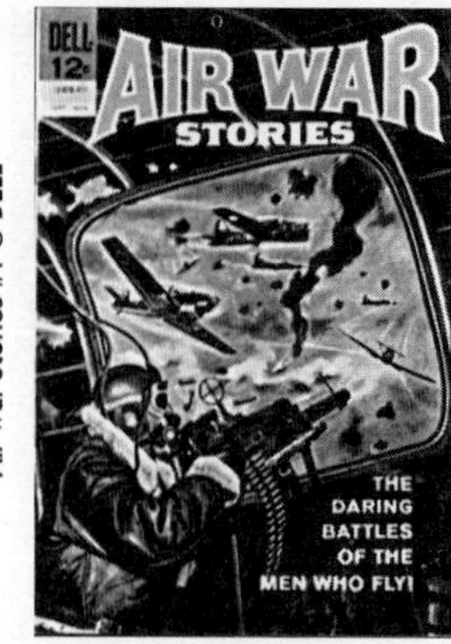

Air War Stories #1 © DELL

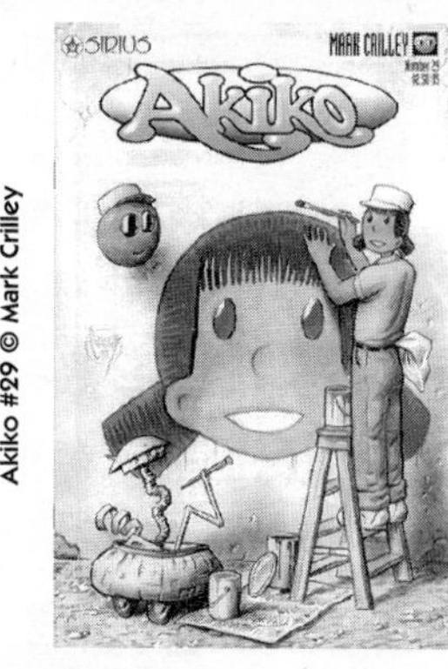

Akiko #29 © Mark Crilley

	GD25	FN65	NM94
5-11-All S&K-a	22.00	66.00	165.00
V5#1-4,6-11: 4-Infantino Heap. 10-Origin The Heap	13.00	40.00	110.00
5-Skull-c.	17.00	50.00	125.00
12-Krigstein-a(p)	17.00	52.00	130.00
V6#1-3,5-12: 6,8-Origin The Heap	15.00	44.00	110.00
4-Origin retold	19.00	56.00	140.00
V7#1-12: 7,8,10-Origin The Heap	15.00	44.00	110.00
V8#1-3,5-12	13.00	40.00	100.00
4-Krigstein-a	14.00	42.00	105.00
V9#1-4,6-12: 2-Valkyrie app. 7-One pg. Frazetta ad	11.00	32.00	80.00
5(#100)	12.00	36.00	90.00
V10#1-4	10.00	30.00	75.00

NOTE: ***Barry** a-V2#3, 7. **Bolle** a-V4#12. **McWilliams** a-V3#7, 9. **Powell** a-V7#2, 3, V8#1, 6. **Starr** a-V5#1, 12. **Dick Wood** a-V4#12. Bondage-c V5#8.*

AIRBOY MEETS THE PROWLER
Eclipse Comics: Aug, 1987 ($1.95, one-shot)

	GD25	FN65	NM94
1-John Snyder, III-c/a			1.95

AIRBOY-MR. MONSTER SPECIAL
Eclipse Comics: Aug, 1987 ($1.75, one-shot)

	GD25	FN65	NM94
1			1.80

AIRBOY VERSUS THE AIR MAIDENS
Eclipse Comics: July, 1988 ($1.95)

	GD25	FN65	NM94
1			1.95

AIR FIGHTERS CLASSICS
Eclipse Comics: Nov, 1987 - No. 6, May, 1989 ($3.95, 68 pgs., B&W)

	GD25	FN65	NM94
1-6: Reprints G.A. Air Fighters #2-7. 1-Origin Airboy			4.00

AIR FIGHTERS COMICS (Airboy Comics #23 (V2#11) on)
Hillman Periodicals: Nov, 1941; No. 2, Nov, 1942 - V2#10, Fall, 1945

	GD25	FN65	NM94
V1#1-(Produced by Funnies, Inc.); Black Commander only app.	182.00	546.00	1550.00
2(11/42)-(Produced by Quality artists & Biro for Hillman); Origin & 1st app. Airboy & Iron Ace; Black Angel (1st app.), Flying Dutchman & Skywolf (1st app.) begin; Fuje-a; Biro-c/a	278.00	834.00	2500.00
3-Origin/1st app. The Heap; origin Skywolf	141.00	423.00	1200.00
4	97.00	291.00	825.00
5,6	74.00	222.00	625.00
7-12	62.00	186.00	525.00
V2#1,3-9: 5-Flag-c; Fuje-a. 7-Valkyrie app.	56.00	168.00	475.00
2-Skywolf by Giunta; Flying Dutchman by Fuje; 1st meeting Valkyrie & Airboy (she worked for the Nazis in beginning); 1st app. Valkyrie (11/43)	82.00	246.00	700.00
10-Origin The Heap & Skywolf	62.00	186.00	525.00

NOTE: ***Fuje** a-V1#2, 5, 7, V2#2, 3, 5, 7-9. **Giunta** a-V2#2, 3, 7, 9.*

AIRFIGHTERS MEET SGT. STRIKE SPECIAL, THE
Eclipse Comics: Jan, 1988 ($1.95, one-shot, stiff-c)

	GD25	FN65	NM94
1-Airboy, Valkyrie, Skywolf app.			2.00

AIR FORCES (See American Air Forces)

AIRMAIDENS SPECIAL
Eclipse Comics: August, 1987 ($1.75, one-shot, Baxter paper)

	GD25	FN65	NM94
1-Marisa becomes La Lupina (origin)			1.80

AIR POWER (CBS TV & the U.S. Air Force Presents)
Prudential Insurance Co.: 1956 (5-1/4x7-1/4", 32 pgs., giveaway, soft-c)

	GD25	FN65	NM94
nn-Toth-a? Based on 'You Are There' TV program by Walter Cronkite	8.50	26.00	60.00

AIR RAIDERS
Marvel Comics (Star Comics)/Marvel #3 on: Nov, 1987- No. 5, Mar, 1988 ($1.00)

	GD25	FN65	NM94
1-5			2.00

AIRTIGHT GARAGE, THE
Marvel Comics (Epic Comics): July, 1993 - No. 4, Oct, 1993 ($2.50, limited series)

	GD25	FN65	NM94
1-4: Moebius-c/a/scripts			2.50

AIR WAR STORIES
Dell Publishing Co.: Sept-Nov, 1964 - No. 8, Aug, 1966

	GD25	FN65	NM94
1-Painted-c; Glanzman-c/a begins	2.80	8.40	28.00
2-8: 2-Painted-c (all painted?)	2.25	6.75	18.00

AKIKO
Sirius: Mar, 1996 - Present ($2.50, B&W)

	GD25	FN65	NM94
1-Crilley-c/a/scripts in all	.90	2.70	8.00
2		2.00	6.00
3-10			4.00
11-24			3.00
25-($2.95, 32 pgs.)-w/Asala back-up pages			2.95
26-29			2.50
TPB Volume 1 ('97, $14.95) r/#1-7	1.50	4.50	15.00
TPB Volume 2 ('98, $11.95) r/#8-13	1.20	3.60	12.00

AKIKO ON THE PLANET SMOO
Sirius: Dec, 1995 ($3.95, B&W)

	GD25	FN65	NM94
V1#1-($3.95)-Crilley-c/a/scripts; gatefold-c	.90	2.70	9.00
Ashcan ('95, mail offer)			2.00
Hardcover V1#1 (12/95, $19.95, B&W, 40 pgs.)	2.00	6.00	20.00

AKIRA
Marvel Comics (Epic Comics): Sept, 1988 - No. 38, Dec, 1995 ($3.50/$3.95/$6.95, deluxe, 68 pgs.)

	GD25	FN65	NM94
1	1.80	5.40	18.00
1,2-2nd printings (1989, $3.95)			4.00
2-5	.90	2.70	9.00
6-16			5.50
17-33: 17-$3.95-c begins			4.50
34-38: 34-(1994)-$6.95-c begins. 35-37: 35-(1995). 37-Texieira back-up, Gibbons, Williams pin-ups. 38-Moebius, Allred, Pratt, Toth, Romita, Van Fleet, O'Neill, Madureira pin-ups.	.85	2.60	7.00

ALADDIN & HIS WONDERFUL LAMP (See Dell Jr Treasury #2)

ALAN LADD (See The Adventures of...)

ALAN MOORE'S SONGBOOK
Caliber Comics: 1998 ($5.95, B&W)

	GD25	FN65	NM94
1-Alan Moore song lyrics w/illust. by various			5.95

ALARMING ADVENTURES
Harvey Publications: Oct, 1962 - No. 3, Feb, 1963

	GD25	FN65	NM94
1-Crandall/Williamson-a	6.50	19.50	65.00
2,3: 2-Williamson/Crandall-a	3.80	11.40	38.00

NOTE: ***Bailey** a-1, 3. **Crandall** a-1p, 2i. **Powell** a-2(2). **Severin** c-1-3. **Torres** a-2? **Tuska** a-1. **Williamson** a-1i, 2p.*

ALARMING TALES
Harvey Publications (Western Tales): Sept, 1957 - No. 6, Nov, 1958

	GD25	FN65	NM94
1-Kirby-c/a(4); Kamandi prototype story by Kirby	19.00	56.00	140.00
2-Kirby-a(4)	15.00	46.00	115.00
3,4-Kirby-a. 4-Powell, Wildey-a	10.00	30.00	75.00
5-Kirby/Williamson-a; Wildey-a; Severin-c	11.00	34.00	85.00
6-Williamson-a?; Severin-c	9.30	28.00	70.00

ALBEDO
Thoughts And Images: Apr, 1985 - No. 14, Spring, 1989 (B&W)

	GD25	FN65	NM94
0-Yellow cover; 50 copies	1.50	4.50	15.00
0-White cover, 450 copies	1.00	3.00	10.00
0-Blue, 1st printing, 500 copies			5.00
0-Blue, 2nd printing, 1000 copies			4.00
0-3rd printing			1.20
0-4th printing			1.20
1-Dark red; 1st app. Usagi Yojimbo			5.00

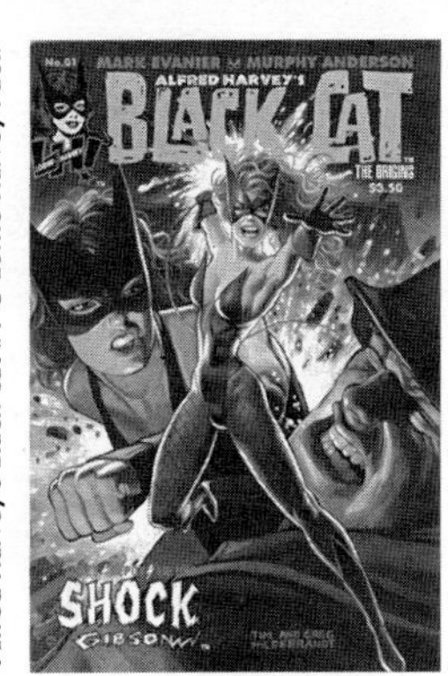

Alfred Harvey's Black Cat #1 © Lorne-Harvey Publ.

Alice #11 © Z-D

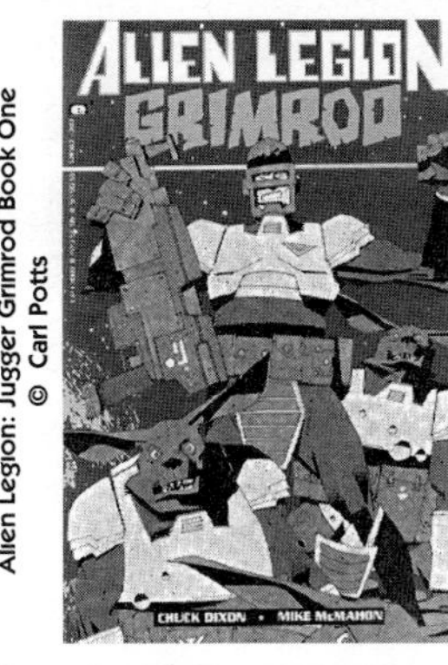

Alien Legion: Jugger Grimrod Book One © Carl Potts

	GD25	FN65	NM94
1-Bright red			4.00
2			3.00
3-14			1.20

ALBEDO ANTHROPOMORPHICS
Antartic Press: Spring, 1994

	GD25	FN65	NM94
V3#1-Steve Gallacci-c/a			2.00

ALBERTO (See The Crusaders)

ALBERT THE ALLIGATOR & POGO POSSUM (See Pogo Possum)

ALBINO SPIDER OF DAJETTE, THE
Verotik: Jan, 1997 - Present ($2.95, mature)

	GD25	FN65	NM94
1-3-Danzig-s			2.95

ALBUM OF CRIME (See Fox Giants)

ALBUM OF LOVE (See Fox Giants)

AL CAPP'S DOGPATCH (Also see Mammy Yokum)
Toby Press: No. 71, June, 1949 - No. 4, Dec, 1949

	GD25	FN65	NM94
71(#1)-Reprints from Tip Top #112-114	22.00	66.00	165.00
2-4: 4-Reprints from Li'l Abner #73	15.00	44.00	110.00

AL CAPP'S SHMOO (Also see Oxydol-Dreft & Washable Jones & Shmoo)
Toby Press: July, 1949 - No. 5, Apr, 1950 (None by Al Capp)

	GD25	FN65	NM94
1	33.00	100.00	250.00
2-5: 3-Sci-fi trip to moon. 4-X-Mas-c; origin/1st app. Super-Shmoo	23.00	70.00	175.00

AL CAPP'S WOLF GAL
Toby Press: 1951 - No. 2, 1952

	GD25	FN65	NM94
1,2-Edited-r from Li'l Abner #63,64	31.00	94.00	235.00

ALEXANDER THE GREAT (Movie)
Dell Publishing Co.: No. 688, May, 1956

	GD25	FN65	NM94
Four Color 688-Buscema-a; photo-c	6.00	19.00	68.00

ALF (TV) (See Star Comics Digest)
Marvel Comics: Mar, 1988 - No. 50, Feb, 1992 ($1.00)

	GD25	FN65	NM94
1-(Giant) Photo-c			3.00
2-49: 22-X-Men parody			2.00
50-($1.75, 52 pgs.)-Final issue; photo-c			2.50
Annual 1-3: 2-Sienkiewicz-c			2.50
...Comics Digest 1 (1988)-Reprints Alf #1,2		2.00	6.00
Holiday Special 1 (1988, $1.75, 68 pgs.)			2.50
Holiday Special 2 (Winter, 1989, $2.00, 68 pgs.)			2.50
Spring Special 1 (Spr/89, $1.75, 68 pgs.)			2.50

ALFRED HARVEY'S BLACK CAT
Lorne-Harvey Productions: 1995 ($3.50, B&W/color)

	GD25	FN65	NM94
1-Origin by Mark Evanier & Murphy Anderson; contains history of Alfred Harvey & Harvey Publications; 5 pg. B&W Sad Sack story; Hildebrandts-c			3.50

ALGIE
Timor Publ. Co.: Dec, 1953 - No. 3, 1954

	GD25	FN65	NM94
1-Teenage	4.15	12.50	25.00
1-Misprint exists w/Secret Mysteries #19 inside	5.00	15.00	30.00
2,3	3.60	9.00	18.00
Accepted Reprint #2(nd)	2.40	6.00	12.00
Super Reprint #15	2.00	5.00	10.00

ALIAS:
Now Comics: July, 1990 - No. 5, Nov, 1990 ($1.75)

	GD25	FN65	NM94
1-5: 1-Sienkiewicz-c			1.80

ALICE (New Adventures in Wonderland)
Ziff-Davis Publ. Co.: No. 10, 7-8/51 - No. 2, 11-12/51

	GD25	FN65	NM94
10-Painted-c; Berg-a	19.00	56.00	140.00
11-Dave Berg-a	10.00	30.00	75.00
2-Dave Berg-a	9.30	28.00	65.00

ALICE AT MONKEY ISLAND (See The Adventures of Alice)
Pentagon Publ. Co. (Civil Service): No. 3, 1946

	GD25	FN65	NM94
3	6.50	19.50	45.00

ALICE IN BLUNDERLAND
Industrial Services: 1952 (Paper cover, 16 pgs. in color)

	GD25	FN65	NM94
nn-Facts about big government waste and inefficiency	11.00	34.00	84.00

ALICE IN WONDERLAND (Disney; see Advs. of Alice, Dell Jr. Treasury #1, The Dreamery, Movie Comics, Walt Disney Showcase #22, and World's Greatest Stories)
Dell Publishing Co.: No. 24, 1940; No. 331, 1951; No. 341, July, 1951

	GD25	FN65	NM94
Single Series 24 (#1)(1940)	39.00	117.00	310.00
Four Color 331, 341-"Unbirthday Party w/...	14.00	41.00	150.00

ALICE IN WONDERLAND
Western Printing Company/Whitman Publ. Co.: 1965; 1982

	GD25	FN65	NM94
Meets Santa Claus(1950s), nd, 16 pgs.	4.00	11.00	22.00
Rexall Giveaway(1965, 16 pgs., 5x7-1/4) Western Printing (TV, Hanna-Barbera)	2.50	7.50	20.00
Wonder Bakery Giveaway(16 pgs, color, nn, nd) (Continental Baking Company, 1969)	2.50	7.50	20.00
1-(Whitman; 1982)-r/4-Color #331			1.20

ALICE IN WONDERLAND MEETS SANTA
No publisher: nd (6-5/8x9-11/16", 16 pgs., giveaway, paper-c)

	GD25	FN65	NM94
nn	9.30	28.00	65.00

ALIEN ENCOUNTERS (Replaces Alien Worlds)
Eclipse Comics: June, 1985 - No. 14, Aug, 1987 ($1.75, Baxter paper, mature)

	GD25	FN65	NM94
1-14: Nudity, strong language in all. 9-Snyder-a			3.00

ALIEN LEGION (See Epic & Marvel Graphic Novel #25)
Marvel Comics (Epic Comics): Apr, 1984 - No. 20, Sept, 1987 ($2.00/$1.50)

	GD25	FN65	NM94
1-High quality paper			2.00
2-20: 2-$1.50-c			1.50

ALIEN LEGION (2nd Series)
Marvel Comics (Epic Comics): Aug, 1987 (indicia) (10/87 on-c) - No. 18, Aug, 1990 ($1.25)

	GD25	FN65	NM94
V2#1-6			1.25
7-18: 7-Begin $1.50-c			1.50

ALIEN LEGION: BINARY DEEP
Marvel Comics (Epic Comics): 1993 ($3.50, one-shot, 52 pgs.)

	GD25	FN65	NM94
nn-With bound-in trading card			3.50

ALIEN LEGION: JUGGER GRIMROD
Marvel Comics (Epic Comics): Aug, 1992 ($5.95, one-shot, 52 pgs.)

	GD25	FN65	NM94
Book One		2.00	6.00

ALIEN LEGION: ONE PLANET AT A TIME
Marvel Comics (Epic Comics): May, 1993 - Book 3, July, 1993 ($4.95, squarebound, 52 pgs.)

	GD25	FN65	NM94
Book 1-3: Hoang Nguyen-a			5.00

ALIEN LEGION: ON THE EDGE (The... #2 & 3)
Marvel Comics (Epic Comics): Nov, 1990 - No. 3, Jan, 1991 ($4.50, limited series, 52 pgs.)

	GD25	FN65	NM94
1-3			4.50

ALIEN LEGION: TENANTS OF HELL
Marvel Comics (Epic): 1991 - No. 2, 1991 ($4.50, squarebound, 52 pgs.)

	GD25	FN65	NM94
Book 1,2-Stroman-c/a(p)			4.50

Aliens: Colonial Marines #1 © 20th Century Fox

Aliens: Hive #4 © 20th Century Fox

Aliens/Predator: The Deadliest of Species #3 © 20th Century Fox

GD25 FN65 NM94

ALIEN NATION (Movie)
DC Comics: Dec, 1988 ($2.50; 68 pgs.)
1-Adaptation of film; painted-c 2.50

ALIEN RESURRECTION (Movie)
Dark Horse Comics: Oct, 1997 - No. 2, Nov, 1997 ($2.50; limited series)
1,2-Adaptation of film; Dave McKean-c 2.50

ALIENS, THE (Captain Johner and...)(Also see Magnus Robot Fighter...)
Gold Key: Sept-Dec, 1967; No. 2, May, 1982
1-Reprints from Magnus #1,3,4,6-10; Russ Manning-a in all 1.85 5.50 20.00
2-Same contents as #1 5.00

ALIENS (Movie) (See Alien: The Illustrated..., Dark Horse Comics & Dark Horse Presents #24)
Dark Horse Comics: May, 1988 - No. 6, July, 1989 ($1.95, B&W, limited series)
1-Based on movie sequel;1st app. Aliens in comics 1.80 5.40 18.00
1-2nd printing 2.00
1-3rd - 6th printings; 4th w/new inside front-c 1.50
2 .90 2.70 8.00
2-2nd printing 1.50
2-3rd printing w/new inside front-c 1.50
3 5.00
4 3.50
5,6 3.00
3-6-2nd printings 1.50
Mini Comic #1 (2/89, 4x6")-Was included with Aliens Portfolio 4.00
Collection 1 ($10.95,)-r/#1-6 plus Dark Horse Presents #24 plus new-a 1.00 3.00 10.00
Collection 1-2nd printing (1991, $11.95)-Printed on higher quality paper than 1st print; Dorman painted-c 1.20 3.60 12.00
Hardcover ('90, $24.95, B&W)-r/1-6, DHP #24 2.25 6.80 25.00
Platinum Edition - (See Dark Horse Presents: Aliens Platinum Edition) -

ALIENS (Movie)
Dark Horse Comics: V2#1, Aug, 1989 - No. 4, 1990 ($2.25, limited series)
V2#1-Adapts sequel 4.50
1-2nd printing (1990, $2.25) 2.25
2-4 2.25

ALIENS: ALCHEMY
Dark Horse Comics: Oct, 1997 - No. 3, Nov, 1997 ($2.95, limited series)
1-3-Corben-c/a, Arcudi-s 2.95

ALIENS: BERSERKERS
Dark Horse Comics: Jan, 1995 - No. 4, Apr, 1995 ($2.50, limited series)
1-4 2.50

ALIENS: COLONIAL MARINES
Dark Horse Comics: Jan, 1993 - No. 10, July, 1994 ($2.50, limited series)
1-10 2.50

ALIENS: EARTH ANGEL
Dark Horse Comics: Aug, 1994 ($2.95, one-shot)
1-Byrne-a/story; wraparound-c 3.00

ALIENS: EARTH WAR
Dark Horse Comics: June, 1990 - No. 4, Oct, 1990 ($2.50, limited series)
1-All have Sam Kieth-a & Bolton painted-c 4.50
1-2nd printing 2.50
2 3.50
3,4 2.50

ALIENS: GENOCIDE
Dark Horse Comics: Nov, 1991 - No. 4, Feb, 1992 ($2.50, limited series)
1-4-Arthur Suydam painted-c. 4-Wraparound-c, poster 2.50

GD25 FN65 NM94

ALIENS: GLASS CORRIDOR
Dark Horse Comics: Jun, 1998 ($2.95, one-shot)
1-David Lloyd-s/a 3.00

ALIENS: HAVOC
Dark Horse Comics: June, 1997 - No. 2, July, 1997 ($2.95, limited series)
1,2: Schultz-s, Kent Williams-c, 40 artists including Art Adams, Kelley Jones, Duncan Fegredo, Kevin Nowlan 2.95

ALIENS: HIVE
Dark Horse Comics: Feb, 1992 - No. 4, May, 1992 ($2.50, limited series)
1-4: Kelley Jones-c/a in all 3.00
...Harvest TPB ('98, $16.95) r/series; Bolton-c 16.95

ALIENS: COLONIAL MARINES
Dark Horse Comics: Jan, 1993 - No. 10, July, 1994 ($2.50, limited series)
1-10 2.50

ALIENS KIDNAPPED
Dark Horse Comics: Dec, 1997 - No. 3, Feb, 1998 ($2.50, limited series)
1-3 2.50

ALIENS LABYRINTH
Dark Horse Comics: Sept, 1993 - No. 4, Jan, 1994 ($2.50, limited series)
1-4: 1-Painted-c 2.50

ALIENS: LOVESICK
Dark Horse Comics: Dec, 1996 ($2.95, one-shot)
1 2.95

ALIENS: MONDO HEAT
Dark Horse Comics: Feb, 1996 ($2.50, one-shot)
nn-Sequel to Mondo Pest 2.50

ALIENS: MONDO PEST
Dark Horse Comics: Apr, 1995 ($2.95, one-shot, 44 pgs.)
nn-Reprints Dark Horse Comics #22-24 2.95

ALIENS: MUSIC OF THE SPEARS
Dark Horse Comics: Jan, 1994 - No. 4, Apr, 1994 ($2.50, limited series)
1-4 2.50

ALIENS: PIG
Dark Horse Comics: Mar, 1997 ($2.95, one-shot)
1 2.95

ALIENS/PREDATOR: THE DEADLIEST OF SPECIES
Dark Horse Comics: July, 1993 - No. 12, Aug, 1995 ($2.50, limited series)
1-Bolton painted-c; Guice-a(p) 4.50
1-Embossed foil platinum edition 1.00 3.00 10.00
2-12: Bolton painted-c. 2,3-Guice-a(p) 3.00

ALIENS: PURGE
Dark Horse Comics: Aug, 1997 ($2.95, one-shot)
nn-Hester-a 2.95

ALIENS: ROGUE
Dark Horse Comics: Apr, 1993 - No. 4, July, 1993 ($2.50, limited series)
1-4: Painted-c 2.50

ALIENS: SACRIFICE
Dark Horse Comics: May, 1993 ($4.95, one-shot, 52 pgs.)
nn-Peter Milligan scripts; painted-c/a 5.00

ALIENS: SALVATION
Dark Horse Comics: Nov, 1993 ($4.95, one-shot, 52 pgs.)
nn-Mike Mignola-c/a(p); Dave Gibbons script 5.00

ALIENS: SPECIAL
Dark Horse Comics: June, 1997 ($2.50, one-shot)

Aliens: Survival #1 © 20th Century Fox

All-American Comics #21 © DC

All-American Comics #94 © DC

GD25 FN65 NM94

1 2.50

ALIENS: STALKER
Dark Horse Comics: June, 1998 ($2.50, one-shot)

1-David Wenzel-s/a 2.50

ALIENS: STRONGHOLD
Dark Horse Comics: May, 1994 - No. 4, Sept, 1994 ($2.50, limited series)

1-4 2.50

ALIENS: SURVIVAL
Dark Horse Comics: Feb, 1998 - No. 3, Apr, 1998 ($2.95, limited series)

1-3-Tony Harris-c 3.00

ALIENS VS. PREDATOR (See Dark Horse Presents #36)
Dark Horse Comics: June, 1990 - No. 4, Dec, 1990 ($2.50, limited series)

1-Painted-c 2.00 6.00
1-2nd printing 2.50
0-(7/90, $1.95, B&W)-r/Dark Horse Pres. #34-36 .90 2.70 8.00
2,3 5.00
4-Dave Dorman painted-c 2.50

ALIENS VS. PREDATOR: BOOTY
Dark Horse Comics: Jan, 1996 ($2.50, one-shot)

nn-painted-c 2.50

ALIENS VS. PREDATOR: DUEL
Dark Horse Comics: Mar, 1995 - No. 2, Apr, 1995 ($2.50, limited series)

1,2 2.50

ALIENS VS. PREDATOR: ETERNAL
Dark Horse Comics: June, 1998 - No. 4, Sept, 1998 ($2.50, limited series)

1-4: Edginton-s/Maleev-a; Fabry-c 2.50

ALIENS VS. PREDATOR: WAR
Dark Horse Comics: No. 0, May, 1995 - No. 4, Aug, 1995 ($2.50, limited series)

0-4: Corben painted-c 2.50

ALIENS: WRAITH
Dark Horse Comics: July, 1998 ($2.95, one-shot)

1-Jay Stephens-s 2.95

ALIEN TERROR (See 3-D Alien Terror)

ALIEN: THE ILLUSTRATED STORY (Also see Aliens)
Heavy Metal Books: 1980 ($3.95, soft-c, 8x11")

nn-Movie adaptation; Simonson-a 1.00 3.00 10.00

ALIEN^3 (Movie)
Dark Horse Comics: June, 1992 - No. 3, July, 1992 ($2.50, limited series)

1-3: Adapts 3rd movie; Suydam painted-c 2.50

ALIEN WORLDS (Also see Eclipse Graphic Album #22)
Pacific Comics/Eclipse: Dec, 1982 - No. 9, Jan, 1985

1,2,4: 2,4-Dave Stevens-c/a 4.00
3,5-9: 2.00
3-D No. 1-Art Adams 1st published art 4.00

ALISTER THE SLAYER
Midnight Press: Oct, 1995 ($2.50)

1-Boris-c 2.50

ALL-AMERICAN COMICS (...Western #103-126, ...Men of War #127 on; also see The Big All-American Comic Book)
All-American/National Periodical Publ.: April, 1939 - No. 102, Oct, 1948

1-Hop Harrigan (1st app.), Scribbly by Mayer (1st app.), Toonerville Folks, Ben Webster, Spot Savage, Mutt & Jeff, Red White & Blue (1st app.), Adv. in the Unknown, Tippie, Reg'lar Fellers, Skippy, Bobby Thatcher, Mystery Men of Mars, Daiseybelle, Wiley of West Point begin 830.00 2500.00 5500.00
2-Ripley's Believe It or Not begins, ends #24 230.00 700.00 1550.00

GD25 FN65 NM94

3-5: 5-The American Way begins, ends #10 165.00 500.00 1150.00
6,7: 6-Last Spot Savage; Popsicle Pete begins, ends #26, 28. 7-Last Bobby Thatcher 140.00 425.00 950.00
8-The Ultra Man begins & 1st-c app. 210.00 625.00 1350.00
9,10: 10-X-Mas-c 130.00 400.00 875.00
11-15: 11-Ultra Man-c. 12-Last Toonerville Folks. 15-Last Tippie & Reg'lar Fellars; Ultra Man-c 125.00 375.00 800.00

GD25 FN65 VF82 NM94

16-(Rare)-Origin/1st app. Green Lantern by Sheldon Moldoff (c/a)(7/40) & begin series; appears in costume on-c & only one panel inside; created by Martin Nodell. Inspired in 1940 by a switchman's green lantern that would give trains the go ahead to proceed.
6500.00 19,500.00 39,000.00 65,000.00

GD25 FN65 NM94

17-2nd Green Lantern 1090.00 3270.00 12,500.00
18-N.Y. World's Fair-c/story 800.00 2400.00 8,000.00

GD25 FN65 VF82 NM94

19-Origin/1st app. The Atom (10/40); last Ultra Man
1090.00 3270.00 6540.00 12,500.00

GD25 FN65 NM94

20-Atom dons costume; Ma Hunkle becomes Red Tornado (1st app.)(1st DC costumed heroine, before Wonder Woman, 11/40); Rescue on Mars begins, ends #25; 1 pg. origin Green Lantern 400.00 1200.00 3400.00
21-23: 21-Last Wiley of West Point & Skippy. 23-Last Daiseybelle; 3 Idiots begin, end #82 229.00 690.00 1950.00
24-Sisty & Dinky become the Cyclone Kids; Ben Webster ends; origin Dr. Mid-Nite & Sargon, The Sorcerer in text with app. 294.00 882.00 2500.00

GD25 FN65 VF82 NM94

25-Origin & 1st story app. Dr. Mid-Nite by Stan Asch; Hop Harrigan becomes Guardian Angel; last Adventure in the Unknown
800.00 2400.00 4800.00 8000.00

GD25 FN65 NM94

26-Origin/1st story app. Sargon, the Sorcerer 316.00 950.00 3000.00
27: #27-32 are misnumbered in indicia with correct No. appearing on-c. Intro. Doiby Dickles, Green Lantern's sidekick 337.00 1010.00 3200.00
28-Hop Harrigan gives up costumed i.d. 141.00 423.00 1200.00
29,30 141.00 423.00 1200.00
31-40: 35-Doiby learns Green Lantern's i.d. 106.00 318.00 900.00
41-50: 50-Sargon ends 88.00 264.00 750.00
51-60: 59-Scribbly & the Red Tornado ends 77.00 231.00 650.00
61-Origin/1st app. Solomon Grundy (11/44) 389.00 1170.00 3700.00
62-70: 70-Kubert Sargon; intro Sargon's helper, Maximillian O'Leary
71.00 213.00 600.00
71-88: 71-Last Red White & Blue. 72-Black Pirate begins (not in #74-82); last Atom. 73-Winky, Blinky & Noddy begins, ends #82. 79,83-Mutt & Jeff-c.
62.00 186.00 525.00
89-Origin & 1st app. Harlequin 88.00 264.00 750.00
90-99: 90-Origin/1st app. Icicle. 99-Last Hop Harrigan
76.00 228.00 650.00
100-1st app. Johnny Thunder by Alex Toth (8/48); western theme begins (Scarce) 165.00 495.00 1400.00
101-Last Mutt & Jeff (Scarce) 112.00 336.00 950.00
102-Last Green Lantern, Black Pirate & Dr. Mid-Nite (Scarce)
212.00 636.00 1800.00

NOTE: *No Atom in 47, 62-69.* ***Kinstler*** *Black Pirate-89.* ***Stan Aschmeier*** *a (Dr. Mid-Nite) 25-84; c-7.* ***Mayer*** *c-1, 2(part), 6, 10.* ***Moldoff*** *c-16-23.* ***Nodell*** *c-31.* ***Paul Reinman*** *a (Green Lantern)-53-55p, 56-84, 87; (Black Pirate)-83-88, 90; c-52, 55-76, 78, 80, 81, 87.* ***Toth*** *a-88, 92, 96, 98-102; c(p)-92, 96-102. Scribbly by* ***Mayer*** *in #1-59. Ultra Man by* ***Mayer*** *in #8-19.*

ALL-AMERICAN MEN OF WAR (Previously All-American Western)
National Periodical Publ.: No. 127, Aug-Sept, 1952 - No. 117, Sept-Oct, 1966

127 (#1, 1952) 71.00 213.00 850.00
128 (1952) 46.00 138.00 550.00
2(12-1/'52-53)-5 41.00 123.00 445.00
6-10 30.00 90.00 300.00

All-American Men of War #13 © DC

Alley Oop #17 © STD

All-Flash #8 © DC

	GD25	FN65	NM94
11-18: Last precode (2/55)	28.00	84.00	280.00
19-27	19.00	57.00	190.00
28 (12/55)-1st Sgt. Rock prototype; Kubert-a	22.50	68.00	225.00
29,30,32-Wood-a	20.00	60.00	200.00
31,33-38,40: 38-1st S.A. issue	16.00	48.00	160.00
.39 (11/56)-2nd Sgt. Rock prototype; 1st Easy Co.?	20.00	60.00	200.00
41-50	13.00	39.00	130.00
51-56,58-66	9.50	28.50	95.00
57 (5/58)-Pre-Sgt. Rock Easy Co. c/s	12.00	36.00	120.00
67-1st Gunner & Sarge by Andru & Esposito	27.00	81.00	270.00
68-70	10.00	30.00	100.00
71-80	6.50	19.50	65.00
81,83-88: 88-Last 10¢ issue	6.00	18.00	60.00
82-Johnny Cloud begins(1st app.), ends #111,114,115,117	11.00	33.00	110.00
89-100	4.00	12.00	40.00
101-117: 112-Balloon Buster series begins, ends #114,116. 117-Johnny Cloud-c & 3-part story	3.20	9.60	32.00

NOTE: *Colan a-112. **Drucker** a-47, 65, 71, 74, 77. **Grandenetti** c(p)-127, 128, 2-17(most). **Heath** a-27, 32, 47, 71, 95, 111, 112; c-85, 91, 94-96, 100, 101, 112, others? **Kirby** a-29. **Krigstein** a-128('52), 2, 3, 5. **Kubert** a-28, 29, 36, 38, 39, 41, 43, 47, 49, 50, 52, 53, 55, 56, 60, 63, 65, 69, 71-73, 102, 103, 105, 106, 108, 114; c-41, 77, 102, 103, 105, 106, 108, 114, others? Tank Killer in 69, 71, 76 by **Kubert. P. Reinman** c-55, 57, 61, 62, 71, 72, 74-76, 80.*

ALL-AMERICAN SPORTS
Charlton Comics: Oct, 1967

	GD25	FN65	NM94
1	2.25	6.75	18.00

ALL-AMERICAN WESTERN (Formerly All-American Comics; Becomes All-American Men of War)
National Periodical Publications: No. 103, Nov, 1948 - No. 126, June-July, 1952 (103-121: 52 pgs.)

	GD25	FN65	NM94
103-Johnny Thunder & his horse Black Lightning continues by Toth, ends #126; Foley of The Fighting 5th, Minstrel Maverick, & Overland Coach begin; Captain Tootsie by Beck; mentioned in Love and Death	44.00	132.00	375.00
104-Kubert-a	35.00	104.00	260.00
105,107-Kubert-a	29.00	86.00	215.00
106,108-110,112: 112-Kurtzman's "Pot-Shot Pete" (1 pg.)	21.00	64.00	160.00
111,114-116-Kubert-a	23.00	70.00	175.00
113-Intro. Swift Deer, J. Thunder's new sidekick (4-5/50); classic Toth-c; Kubert-a	25.00	76.00	190.00
117-126: 121-Kubert-a; bondage-c	17.00	52.00	130.00

NOTE: ***G. Kane** c(p)-119, 120, 123. **Kubert** a-103-105, 107, 111, 112(1 pg.), 113-116, 121. **Toth** a 103-126; c(p)-103-116, 121, 122, 124-126. Some copies of #125 have #12 on-c.*

ALL COMICS
Chicago Nite Life News: 1945

	GD25	FN65	NM94
1	11.00	32.00	80.00

ALLEGRA
Image Comics (WildStorm): Aug, 1996 - No. 4, Dec, 1996 ($2.50)

	GD25	FN65	NM94
1-4			2.50

ALLEY OOP (See The Comics, The Funnies, Red Ryder and Super Book #9)
Dell Publishing Co.: No. 3, 1942

	GD25	FN65	NM94
Four Color 3 (#1)	44.00	132.00	495.00

ALLEY OOP
Argo Publ.: Nov, 1955 - No. 3, Mar, 1956 (Newspaper reprints)

	GD25	FN65	NM94
1	15.00	44.00	110.00
2,3	10.00	30.00	75.00

ALLEY OOP
Dell Publishing Co.: 12-2/62-63 - No. 2, 9-11/63

	GD25	FN65	NM94
1,2	4.50	13.50	50.00

ALLEY OOP
Standard Comics: No. 10, 1947 - No. 18, Oct, 1949

	GD25	FN65	NM94
10	20.00	60.00	150.00
11-18: 17,18-Schomburg-c	15.00	46.00	115.00

ALLEY OOP ADVENTURES
Antarctic Press: Aug, 1998 - Present ($2.95)

	GD25	FN65	NM94
1,2-Jack Bender-s/a			3.00

ALL-FAMOUS CRIME (Formerly Law Against Crime #1-3; becomes All-Famous Police Cases #6 on)
Star Publications: No. 4, 2/50 - No. 5, 5/50; No. 8, 5/51 - No. 10, 11/51

	GD25	FN65	NM94
4 (#1-1st series)-Formerly Law-Crime	21.00	64.00	160.00
5 (#2)	14.00	42.00	105.00
8 (#3-2nd series)	13.00	40.00	100.00
9 (#4)-Used in **SOTI**, illo- "The wish to hurt or kill couples in lovers' lanes is a not uncommon perversion;" L.B. Cole-c/a(r)/Law-Crime #3	25.00	76.00	190.00
10 (#5)-Becomes All-Famous Police Cases #6	12.00	36.00	90.00

NOTE: *All have **L.B. Cole** covers.*

ALL FAMOUS CRIME STORIES (See Fox Giants)

ALL-FAMOUS POLICE CASES (Formerly All Famous Crime #10 [#5])
Star Publications: No. 6, Feb, 1952 - No. 16, Sept, 1954

	GD25	FN65	NM94
6	14.00	42.00	105.00
7,8: 7-Baker story; . 8-Marijuana story	13.00	38.00	95.00
9-16	11.00	32.00	80.00

NOTE: ***L. B. Cole** c-all; a-15, 1pg. **Hollingsworth** a-15.*

ALL-FLASH (...Quarterly No. 1-5)
National Per. Publ./All-American: Summer, 1941 - No. 32, Dec-Jan, 1947-48

	GD25	FN65	VF82	NM94
1-Origin The Flash retold by E. E. Hibbard; Hibbard c-1-10,12-14,16,31p.	1136.00	3400.00	6800.00	12,500.00

	GD25	FN65	NM94
2-Origin recap	265.00	800.00	2400.00
3,4	147.00	440.00	1250.00
5-Winky, Blinky & Noddy begins (1st app.), ends #32	106.00	318.00	900.00
6-10	88.00	264.00	750.00
11-13: 12-Origin/1st The Thinker. 13-The King app.	77.00	231.00	650.00
14-Green Lantern cameo	88.00	264.00	750.00
15-20: 18-Mutt & Jeff begins, ends #22	65.00	195.00	550.00
21-31	53.00	159.00	450.00
32-Origin/1st app. The Fiddler; 1st Star Sapphire	88.00	264.00	750.00

NOTE: *Book length stories in 2-13, 16. Bondage c-31, 32. **Martin Nodell** c-15, 17-28.*

ALL FOR LOVE (Young Love V3#5-on)
Prize Publications: Apr-May, 1957 - V3#4, Dec-Jan, 1959-60

	GD25	FN65	NM94
V1#1	5.50	16.50	55.00
2-6: 5-Orlando-c	3.20	9.60	32.00
V2#1-5(1/59), 5(3/59)	2.50	7.50	22.00
V3#1(5/59), 1(7/59)-4: 2-Powell-a	1.75	5.25	14.00

ALL FUNNY COMICS
Tilsam Publ./National Periodical Publications (Detective): Winter, 1943-44 - No. 23, May-June, 1948

	GD25	FN65	NM94
1-Genius Jones (1st app.), Buzzy (1st app., ends #4), Dover & Clover (see More Fun #93) begin; Bailey-a	44.00	132.00	375.00
2	21.00	64.00	160.00
3-10	13.00	38.00	95.00
11-13,15,18,19-Genius Jones app.	12.00	36.00	90.00
14,17,20-23	8.50	26.00	60.00
16-DC Super Heroes app.	29.00	88.00	220.00

ALL GOOD
St. John Publishing Co.: Oct, 1949 (50¢, 260 pgs.)

	GD25	FN65	NM94
nn-(8 St. John comics bound together)	55.00	166.00	470.00

All Humor Comics #9 © QUA

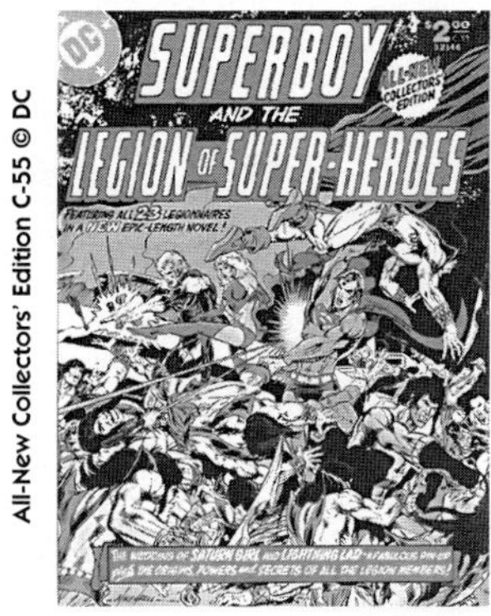

All-New Collectors' Edition C-55 © DC

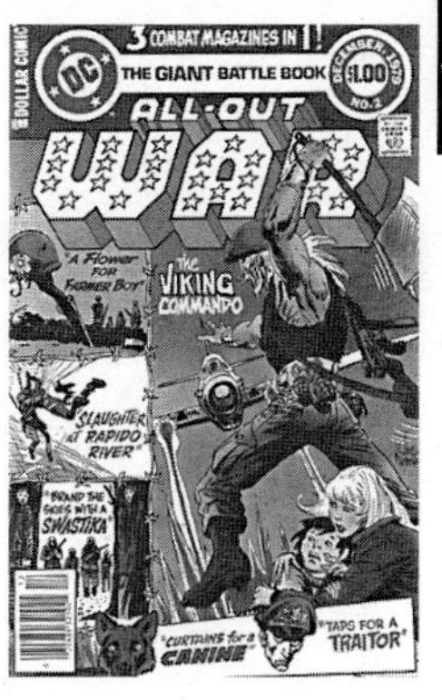

All-Out War #2 © DC

GD25 FN65 NM94

NOTE: *Also see Li'l Audrey Yearbook & Treasury of Comics.*

ALL GOOD COMICS (See Fox Giants)
Fox Features Syndicate: No.1, Spring, 1946 (36 pgs.)

1-Joy Family, Dick Transom, Rick Evans, One Round Hogan 19.00 56.00 140.00

ALL GREAT (See Fox Giants)
Fox Feature Syndicate: 1946 (36 pgs.)

1-Crazy House, Bertie Benson Boy Detective, Gussie the Gob 19.00 56.00 140.00

ALL GREAT
William H. Wise & Co.: nd (1945?) (132 pgs.)

nn-Capt. Jack Terry, Joan Mason, Girl Reporter, Baron Doomsday; Torture scenes 35.00 104.00 260.00

ALL GREAT COMICS (Formerly Phantom Lady #13? Dagar, Desert Hawk No. 14 on)
Fox Features Syndicate: No. 14, Oct, 1947 - No. 13, Dec, 1947 (Newspaper strip reprints)

14(#12)-Brenda Starr & Texas Slim-r (Scarce) 47.00 142.00 400.00
13-Origin Dagar, Desert Hawk; Brenda Starr (all-r); Kamen-c; Dagar covers begin 44.00 132.00 375.00

ALL-GREAT CONFESSIONS (See Fox Giants)

ALL GREAT CRIME STORIES (See Fox Giants)

ALL GREAT JUNGLE ADVENTURES (See Fox Giants)

ALL HALLOW'S EVE
Innovation Publishing: 1991 ($4.95, 52 pgs.)

1-Painted-c/a 5.00

ALL HERO COMICS
Fawcett Publications: Mar, 1943 (100 pgs., cardboard-c)

1-Capt. Marvel Jr., Capt. Midnight, Golden Arrow, Ibis the Invincible, Spy Smasher, Lance O'Casey; 1st Banshee O'Brien; Raboy-c 141.00 423.00 1200.00

ALL HUMOR COMICS
Quality Comics Group: Spring, 1946 - No. 17, December, 1949

1 17.00 50.00 125.00
2-Atomic Tot story; Gustavson-a 9.30 28.00 65.00
3-9: 3-Intro Kelly Poole who is cover feature #3 on. 5-1st app. Hickory? 8-Gustavson-a 5.35 16.00 32.00
10-17 4.00 12.00 24.00

ALLIANCE, THE
Image Comics (Shadowline Ink): Aug, 1995 - No. 3, Nov, 1995 ($2.50)

1-3: 2-(9/95) 2.50

ALL LOVE (...Romances No. 26)(Formerly Ernie Comics)
Ace Periodicals (Current Books): No. 26, May, 1949 - No. 32, May, 1950

26 (No. 1)-Ernie, Lily Belle app. 7.15 21.50 50.00
27-L. B. Cole-a 10.00 30.00 75.00
28-32 4.25 13.00 28.00

ALL-NEGRO COMICS
All-Negro Comics: June, 1947 (15¢)

1 (Rare) 300.00 900.00 2600.00

NOTE: *Seldom found in fine or mint condition; many copies have brown pages.*

ALL-NEW COLLECTORS' EDITION (Formerly Limited ...)
DC Comics, Inc.: Jan, 1978 - Vol. 8, No. C-62, 1979 (No. 54-58: 76 pgs.)

C-53-Rudolph the Red-Nosed Reindeer 3.00 9.00 35.00
C-54-Superman Vs. Wonder Woman 1.75 5.50 20.00
C-55-Superboy & the Legion of Super-Heroes; Wedding of Lightning Lad & Saturn Girl; Grell-c/a 1.75 5.50 22.00
C-56-Superman Vs. Muhammad Ali: story & wraparound N. Adams-c/a 2.25 7.00 28.00
C-58-Superman Vs. Shazam 1.50 4.50 18.00
C-60-Rudolph's Summer Fun(8/78) 2.50 7.50 30.00
C-61-(See Famous First Edition-Superman #1)
C-62-Superman the Movie (68 pgs.; 1979)-Photo-c from movie plus photos inside (also see DC Special Series #25) 1.00 3.00 12.00

NOTE: ***Buckler** a-C-58; c-C-58*

ALL-NEW COMICS (...Short Story Comics No. 1-3)
Family Comics (Harvey Publications): Jan, 1943 - No. 14, Nov, 1946; No. 15, Mar-Apr, 1947 (10 x 13-1/2")

1-Steve Case, Crime Rover, Johnny Rebel, Kayo Kane, The Echo, Night Hawk, Ray O'Light, Detective Shane begin (all 1st app.?); Red Blazer on cover only; Sultan-a 247.00 740.00 2100.00
2-Origin Scarlet Phantom by Kubert 88.00 264.00 750.00
3 67.00 200.00 565.00
4 54.00 162.00 460.00
5,6: 5-Schomburg-c thru #11. 6-The Boy Heroes & Red Blazer (text story) begin, end #12; Black Cat app.; intro. Sparky in Red Blazer 57.00 171.00 485.00
7-Kubert, Powell-a; Black Cat & Zebra app. 57.00 171.00 485.00
8,9: 8-Shock Gibson app.; Kubert, Powell-a; Schomburg bondage-c. 9-Black Cat app.; Kubert-a 57.00 171.00 485.00
10-12: 10-The Zebra app. (from Green Hornet Comics); Kubert-a(3). 11-Girl Commandos, Man In Black app. 12-Kubert-a 52.00 156.00 440.00
13-Stuntman by Simon & Kirby; Green Hornet, Joe Palooka, Flying Fool app.; Green Hornet-c 52.00 156.00 440.00
14-The Green Hornet & The Man in Black Called Fate by Powell, Joe Palooka app.; J. Palooka-c by Ham Fisher 49.00 147.00 415.00
15-(Rare)-Small size (5-1/2x8-1/2"; B&W; 32 pgs.). Distributed to mail subscribers only. Black Cat and Joe Palooka app. Estimated value....$250-350

NOTE: *Also see Boy Explorers No. 2, Flash Gordon No. 5, and Stuntman No. 3. **Powell** a-11. **Schomburg** c-5-11. Captain Red Blazer & Spark on c-5-11 (w/Boy Heroes #12).*

ALL NEW COMICS
Harvey Comics: Oct, 1993 (Giveaway, no cover price, 16 pgs.)(Hanna-Barbera)

1-Flintstones, Scooby Doo, Jetsons, Yogi Bear & Wacky Races previews for upcoming Harvey's new Hanna-Barbera line-up 1.00

NOTE: Material previewed in Harvey giveaway was eventually published by Archie.

ALL-OUT WAR
DC Comics: Sept-Oct, 1979 - No. 6, Aug, 1980 ($1.00, 68 pgs.)

1-6: 1-The Viking Commando(origin), Force Three(origin), & Black Eagle Squadron begin 4.50

NOTE: ***Ayers** a(p)-1-6. **Elias** r-2. **Evans** a-1-6. **Kubert** c-16.*

ALL PICTURE ADVENTURE MAGAZINE
St. John Publishing Co.: Oct, 1952 - No. 2, Nov, 1952 (100 pg. Giants, 25¢, squarebound)

1-War comics 23.00 68.00 170.00
2-Horror-crime comics 35.00 104.00 260.00

NOTE: *Above books contain three St. John comics rebound; variations possible. **Baker** art known in both.*

ALL PICTURE ALL TRUE LOVE STORY
St. John Publishing Co.: October, 1952 (100 pgs., 25¢)

1-Canteen Kate by Matt Baker 42.00 127.00 340.00

ALL-PICTURE COMEDY CARNIVAL
St. John Publishing Co.: October, 1952 (100 pgs., 25¢)(Contains 4 rebound comics)

1-Contents can vary; Baker-a 39.00 117.00 310.00

ALL REAL CONFESSION MAGAZINE (See Fox Giants)

ALL ROMANCES (Mr. Risk No. 7 on)
A. A. Wyn (Ace Periodicals): Aug, 1949 - No. 6, June, 1950

1 7.15 21.50 50.00
2 4.00 11.00 22.00
3-6 3.60 9.00 18.00

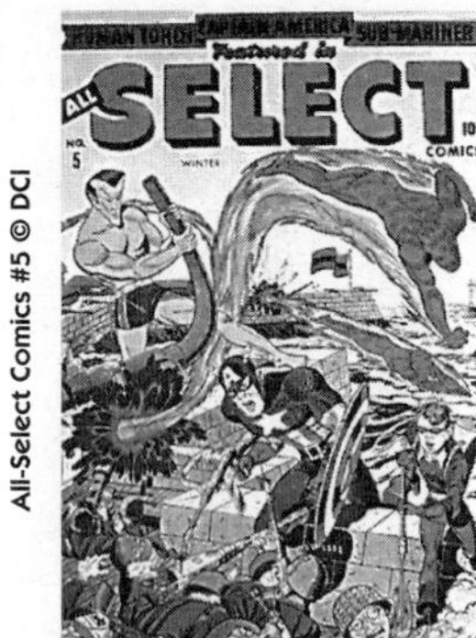

All-Select Comics #5 © DCI

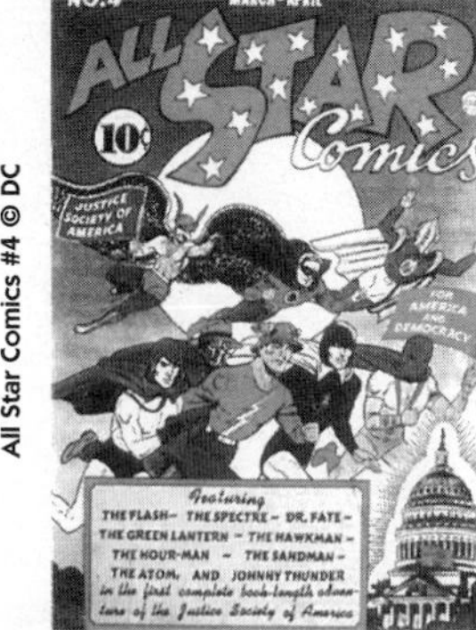

All Star Comics #4 © DC

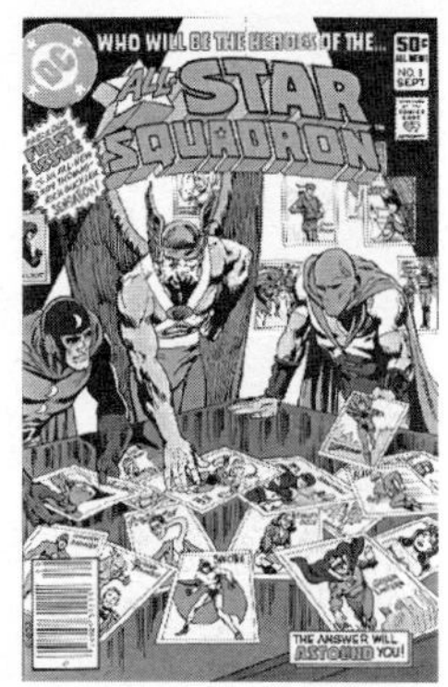

All-Star Squadron #1 © DC

GD25 FN65 NM94 | GD25 FN65 NM94

ALL-SELECT COMICS (Blonde Phantom No. 12 on)
Timely Comics (Daring Comics): Fall, 1943 - No. 11, Fall, 1946

1-Capt. America (by Rico #1), Human Torch, Sub-Mariner begin; Black Widow story (4 pgs.); Classic Schomburg-c 750.00 2250.00 7500.00
2-Red Skull app. 282.00 846.00 2400.00
3-The Whizzer begins 176.00 528.00 1500.00
4,5-Last Sub-Mariner 118.00 350.00 1000.00
6-9: 6-The Destroyer app. 8-No Whizzer 100.00 300.00 850.00
10-The Destroyer & Sub-Mariner app.; last Capt. America & Human Torch issue 100.00 300.00 850.00
11-1st app. Blonde Phantom; Miss America app.; all Blonde Phantom-c by Shores 200.00 600.00 1700.00

NOTE: ***Schomburg** c-1-10. **Sekowsky** a-7. #7 & 8 show 1944 in indicia, but should be 1945.*

ALL SPORTS COMICS (Formerly Real Sports Comics; becomes All Time Sports Comics No. 4 on)
Hillman Periodicals: No. 2, Dec-Jan, 1948-49; No. 3, Feb-Mar, 1949

2-Krigstein-a(p), Powell, Starr-a 31.00 92.00 230.00
3-Mort Lawrence-a 21.00 62.00 155.00

ALL STAR COMICS (All Star Western No. 58 on)
National Periodical Publ./All-American/DC Comics: Sum, '40 - No. 57, Feb-Mar, '51; No. 58, Jan-Feb, '76 -No. 74, Sept-Oct, '78

GD25 FN65 VF82 NM94

1-The Flash (#1 by E.E. Hibbard), Hawkman(by Shelly), Hourman(by Bernard Baily), The Sandman(by Creig Flessel), The Spectre(by Baily), Biff Bronson, Red White & Blue(ends #2) begin; Ultra Man's only app. (#1-3 are quarterly; #4 begins bi-monthly issues) 1100.00 3300.00 6600.00 12,000.00

GD25 FN65 NM94

2-Green Lantern (by Martin Nodell), Johnny Thunder begin; Green Lantern figure swipe from the cover of All-American Comics #16; Flash figure swipe from the cover of Flash Comics #8; Moldoff/Bailey-c (cut & paste-c.) 467.00 1400.00 4500.00

GD25 FN65 VF82 NM94

3-Origin & 1st app. The Justice Society of America (Win/40); Dr. Fate & The Atom begin, Red Tornado cameo 2700.00 8100.00 16,200.00 31,000.00
3-Reprint, Oversize 13-1/2x10". **WARNING:** This comic is an exact reprint of the original except for its size. DC published it in 1974 with a second cover titling it as a Famous First Edition. There have been many reported cases of the outer cover being removed and the interior sold as the original edition. The reprint with the new outer cover removed is practically worthless. See Famous First Edition for value.

GD25 FN65 NM94

4-1st adventure for J.S.A. 463.00 1389.00 4400.00
5-1st app. Shiera Sanders as Hawkgirl (1st costumed super-heroine, 6-7/41) 411.00 1233.00 3900.00
6-Johnny Thunder joins JSA 253.00 759.00 2400.00
7-Batman, Superman, Flash cameo; last Hourman; Doiby Dickles app. 295.00 885.00 2800.00

GD25 FN65 VF82 NM94

8-Origin & 1st app. Wonder Woman (12-1/41-42)(added as 9 pgs. making book 76 pgs.; origin cont'd in Sensation #1; see W.W. #1 for more detailed origin); Dr. Fate dons new helmet; Hop Harrigan text stories & Starman begin; Shiera app.; Hop Harrigan JSA guest; Starman & Dr. Mid-Nite become members 2182.00 6545.00 13,000.00 25,000.00

GD25 FN65 NM94

9,10: 9-JSA's girlfriends cameo; Shiera app.; J. Edgar Hoover of FBI made associate member of JSA. 10-Flash, Green Lantern cameo; Sandman new costume 265.00 800.00 2250.00
11-Wonder Woman begins; Spectre cameo; Shiera app. 271.00 810.00 2300.00
12-Wonder Woman becomes JSA Secretary 247.00 740.00 2100.00
13-15: Sandman w/Sandy in #14 & 15. 15-Origin & 1st app. Brain Wave; Shiera app. 224.00 672.00 1900.00
16-20: 19-Sandman w/Sandy. 20-Dr. Fate & Sandman cameo 165.00 495.00 1400.00
21-23: 21-Spectre & Atom cameo; Dr. Fate by Kubert; Dr. Fate, Sandman end. 22-Last Hop Harrigan; Flag-c. 23-Origin/1st app. Psycho Pirate; last Spectre & Starman 147.00 441.00 1250.00
24-Flash & Green Lantern cameo; Mr. Terrific only app.; Wildcat, JSA guest; Kubert Hawkman begins; Hitler-c 147.00 441.00 1250.00
25-27: 25-Flash & Green Lantern start again. 26-Robot-c. 27-Wildcat, JSA guest (#24-26: only All-American imprint) 123.00 370.00 1050.00
28-32 112.00 336.00 950.00
33-Solomon Grundy & Doiby Dickles app; classic Solomon Grundy cover. Last Solomon Grundy G.A. app. 271.00 813.00 2300.00
34,35-Johnny Thunder cameo in both 106.00 318.00 900.00
36-Batman & Superman JSA guests 259.00 775.00 2200.00
37-Johnny Thunder cameo; origin & 1st app. Injustice Society; last Kubert Hawkman 141.00 423.00 1200.00
38-Black Canary begins; JSA Death issue 165.00 500.00 1400.00
39,40: 39-Last Johnny Thunder 100.00 300.00 850.00
41-Black Canary joins JSA; Injustice Society app. (2nd app.?) 100.00 300.00 850.00
42-Atom & the Hawkman don new costumes 100.00 300.00 850.00
43-49,51-56: 43-New logo; Robot-c. 55-Sci/Fi story. 56-Robot-c 100.00 300.00 850.00
50-Frazetta art, 3 pgs. 112.00 336.00 950.00
57-Kubert-a, 6 pgs. (Scarce); last app. G.A. Green Lantern, Flash & Dr.Mid-Nite 141.00 423.00 1200.00
V12 #58-(1976) JSA (Flash, Hawkman, Dr. Mid-Nite, Wildcat, Dr. Fate, Green Lantern, Star Spangled Kid, & Robin) app.; intro Power Girl. 1.20 3.60 12.00
V12 #59-68,70-74(1976-78) .85 2.60 7.00
V12 #69-1st Earth-2 Huntress (Helena Wayne) 1.40 4.20 14.00

NOTE: *No Atom-27, 36; no Dr. Fate-13; no Flash-8, 9, 11-23; no Green Lantern-8, 9,11-23; Hawkman in 1-57 (only one to app. in all 57 issues); no Johnny Thunder-5, 36; no Wonder Woman-9, 10, 23. Book length stories in 4-9, 11-14, 18-22, 25, 26, 29, 30, 32-36, 42, 43. Johnny Peril in #42-46, 48, 49, 51, 52,54-57.* ***Baily** a-1-10, 12, 13, 14i, 15-20. **Burnley** Starman-8-13; c-12, 13. **Grell** c-58. **E.E. Hibbard** c-3, 4, 6-10. **Infantino** c-40. **Kubert** Hawkman-24-30, 33-37. **Lampert/Baily/Flessel** c-1, 2. **Moldoff** Hawkman-3-23; c-11. **Mart Nodell** c-25i, 26i, 27-32. **Purcell** c-5. **Simon & Kirby** Sandman 14-17, 19. **Staton** a-66-74p. c-74p. **Toth** a-37(2), 38(2), 40, 41; c-38, 41. **Wood** a-58i-63i, 64, 65; c-63i, 64, 65. Issues 1-7, 9-16 are 68 pgs.; #8 is 76 pgs.; #17-19 are 60 pgs.; #20-57 are 52 pgs.*

ALL STAR INDEX, THE
Independent Comics Group (Eclipse): Feb, 1987 ($2.00, Baxter paper)

1 2.00 6.00

ALL-STAR SQUADRON (See Justice League of America #193)
DC Comics: Sept, 1981 - No. 67, Mar, 1987

1-Original Atom, Hawkman, Dr. Mid-Nite, Robotman (origin), Plastic Man, Johnny Quick, Liberty Belle, Shining Knight begin 3.00
2-26: 4, 7-Spectre app. 5-Danette Reilly becomes new Firebrand. 8-Re-intro Steel, the Indestructable Man. 12-Origin G.A. Hawkman retold. 23-Origin/1st app. The Amazing Man. 24-Batman app. 25-1st app. Infinity, Inc. (9/83), 26-Origin Infinity, Inc. (2nd app.); Robin app. 2.00
27-46,48,49: 27-Dr. Fate vs. The Spectre. 30-35-Spectre app. 33-Origin Freedom Fighters of Earth-X. 36,37-Superman vs. Capt. Marvel; Ordway-c. 41-Origin Starman 2.00
47-Origin Dr. Fate; McFarlane-a (1st full story)/part-c (7/85) 5.00
50-Double size; Crisis x-over 3.00
51-67: 51-56-Crisis x-over. 61-Origin Liberty Belle. 62-Origin The Shining Knight. 63-Origin Robotman. 65-Origin Johnny Quick. 66-Origin Tarantula 2.00
Annual 1-3: 1(11/82)-Retells origin of G.A. Atom, Guardian & Wildcat; Jerry Ordway's 1st pencils for DC.(1st work was inking Carmine Infantino in House of Mystery #94) 2(11/83)-Infinity, Inc. app. 3(9/84) 2.00

NOTE: ***Buckler** a-1-5; c-1, 3-5, 51. **Kubert** c-2, 7-18. JLA app. in 14, 15. JSA app. in 4, 14, 15, 19, 27, 28.*

ALL-STAR STORY OF THE DODGERS, THE
Stadium Communications: Apr, 1979 ($1.00)

1 .90 2.70 8.00

All Star Western #106 © DC

All Top Comics #11 © FOX

All Western Winners #3 © MAR

GD25 FN65 NM94

ALL STAR WESTERN (Formerly All Star Comics No. 1-57)
National Periodical Publ.: No. 58, Apr-May, 1951 - No. 119, June-July, 1961

58-Trigger Twins (ends #116), Strong Bow, The Roving Ranger & Don Caballero begin 42.00 126.00 340.00
59,60: Last 52 pgs. 21.00 63.00 160.00
61-66: 61-64-Toth-a 18.00 54.00 135.00
67-Johnny Thunder begins; Gil Kane-a 21.00 63.00 160.00
68-81: Last precode (2-3/55) 9.30 28.00 70.00
82-98: 97-1st S.A. issue 9.30 28.00 65.00
99-Frazetta-r/Jimmy Wakely #4 9.30 28.00 70.00
100 9.30 28.00 70.00
101-107,109-116,118,119 6.85 20.50 48.00
108-Origin J. Thunder; J. Thunder logo begins 18.00 54.00 135.00
117-Origin Super Chie 11.00 32.00 80.00

NOTE: ***Gil Kane** c(p)-58, 59, 61, 63, 64, 68, 69, 70-95(most), 97-199(most). **Infantino** art in most issues. Madame .44 app.-#117-119.*

ALL-STAR WESTERN (Weird Western Tales No. 12 on)
National Periodical Publications: Aug-Sept, 1970 - No. 11, Apr-May, 1972

1-Pow-Wow Smith-r; Infantino-a 2.50 7.60 28.00
2-6: 2-Outlaw begins; El Diablo by Morrow begins; has cameos by Williamson, Torres, Kane, Giordano & Phil Seuling. 3-Origin El Diablo. 5-Last Outlaw issue. 6-Billy the Kid begins, ends #8 1.25 3.75 12.00
7-9-(52 pgs.) 9-Frazetta-a, 3pgs.(r) 1.65 4.80 16.00
10-(52 pgs.) Jonah Hex begins (1st app., 2-3/72) 18.50 55.00 195.00
11-(52 pgs.) 2nd app. Jonah Hex 9.00 27.00 95.00

NOTE: ***Neal Adams** c-2-5; **Aparo** a-5. **G. Kane** a-3, 4, 6, 8. **Kubert** a-4r, 7-9r. **Morrow** a-2-4, 10, 11. No. 7-11 have 52 pgs..*

ALL SURPRISE (Becomes Jeanie #13 on) (Funny animal)
Timely/Marvel (CPC): Fall, 1943 - No. 12, Winter, 1946-47

1-Super Rabbit, Gandy & Sourpuss begin 25.00 76.00 190.00
2 11.00 34.00 85.00
3-10,12 9.30 28.00 65.00
11-Kurtzman "Pigtales" art 11.00 32.00 80.00

ALL TEEN (Formerly All Winners; All Winners & Teen Comics No. 21 on)
Marvel Comics (WFP): No. 20, January, 1947

20-Georgie, Mitzi, Patsy Walker, Willie app.; Syd Shores-c 7.85 23.50 55.00

ALL-TIME SPORTS COMICS (Formerly All Sports Comics)
Hillman Per.: V2No. 4, Apr-May, 1949 - V2No. 7, Oct-Nov, 1949 (All 52 pgs.)

V2#4 20.00 60.00 150.00
5-7: 5-(V1#5 inside)-Powell-a; Ty Cobb sty. 7-Krigstein-p; Walter Johnson & Knute Rockne sty 15.00 44.00 110.00

ALL TOP
William H. Wise Co.: 1944 (132 pgs.)

Capt. V, Merciless the Sorceress, Red Robbins, One Round Hogan, Mike the M.P., Snooky, Pussy Katnip app. 26.00 78.00 195.00

ALL TOP COMICS (My Experience No. 19 on)
Fox Features Synd./Green Publ./Norlen Mag.: 1945; No. 2, Sum, 1946 - No. 18, Mar, 1949; 1957 - 1959

1-Cosmo Cat & Flash Rabbit begin (1st app.) 19.00 57.00 140.00
2 (#1-7 are funny animal) 9.30 28.00 65.00
3-7 7.15 21.50 50.00
8-Blue Beetle, Phantom Lady, & Rulah, Jungle Goddess begin (11/47); Kamen-c 194.00 582.00 1650.00
9-Kamen-c 102.00 305.00 865.00
10-Kamen bondage-c 109.00 326.00 925.00
11-13,15-17: 11-Rulah-c. 15-No Blue Beetle 88.00 265.00 750.00
14-No Blue Beetle; used in **SOTI**, illo- "Corpses of colored people strung up by their wrists" 109.00 326.00 925.00
18-Dagar, Jo-Jo app; no Phantom Lady or Blue Beetle 57.00 171.00 485.00
6(1957-Green Publ.)-Patoruzu the Indian; Cosmo Cat on cover only 3.60 9.00 18.00
6(1958-Literary Ent.)-Muggy Doo; Cosmo Cat on cover only 3.60 9.00 18.00
6(1959-Norlen)-Atomic Mouse; Cosmo Cat on cover only 3.60 9.00 18.00
6(1959)-Little Eva 3.60 9.00 18.00
6(Cornell)-Supermouse on-c 3.60 9.00 18.00

NOTE: *Jo-Jo by **Kamen**-12,18.*

ALL TRUE ALL PICTURE POLICE CASES
St. John Publishing Co.: Oct, 1952 - No. 2, Nov, 1952 (100 pgs.)

1-Three rebound St. John crime comics 40.00 120.00 285.00
2-Three comics rebound 29.00 86.00 200.00

NOTE: *Contents may vary.*

ALL-TRUE CRIME (...Cases No. 26-35; formerly Official True Crime Cases)
Marvel/Atlas Comics: No. 26, Feb, 1948 - No. 52, Sept, 1952
(OFI #26,27/CFI #28,29/LCC #30-46/LMC #47-52)

26(#1)-Syd Shores-c 25.00 76.00 190.00
27(4/48)-Electric chair-c 18.00 54.00 135.00
28-41,43-48,50-52: 35-37-Photo-c 7.85 23.50 55.00
42,49-Krigstein-a. 49-Used in **POP**, Pg 79 9.30 28.00 65.00

NOTE: ***Robinson** a-47, 50. **Shores** c-26. **Tuska** a-48(3).*

ALL-TRUE DETECTIVE CASES (Kit Carson No. 5 on)
Avon Periodicals: Feb-Mar, 1954 - No. 4, Aug-Sept, 1954

1 21.00 64.00 160.00
2-Wood-a 17.00 52.00 130.00
3-Kinstler-c 9.30 28.00 65.00
4-r/Gangsters And Gun Molls #2; Kamen-a 15.00 46.00 115.00
nn(100 pgs.)-7 pg. Kubert-a, Kinstler back-c 33.00 100.00 250.00

ALL TRUE ROMANCE (...Illustrated No. 3)
Artful Publ. #1-3/Harwell(Comic Media) #4-20?/Ajax-Farrell(Excellent Publ.) No. 22 on/Four Star Comic Corp.: 3/51 - No. 20, 12/54; No. 22, 3/55 - No. 30?, 7/57; No. 3(#31), 9/57;No. 4(#32), 11/57; No. 33, 2/58 - No. 34, 3/58

1 (3/51) 13.00 38.00 95.00
2 (10/51; 11/51 on-c) 6.00 18.00 42.00
3(12/51) - #5(5/52) 5.70 17.00 35.00
6-Wood-a, 9 pgs. (exceptional) 13.00 40.00 100.00
7-10 4.25 13.00 28.00
11-13,16-19 (9/54) 4.00 11.00 22.00
14-Marijuana story 4.15 12.50 25.00
20,22: Last precode issue (Ajax, 3/55) 3.60 9.00 18.00
23-27,29,30 3.00 7.50 15.00
28 (9/56)-L. B. Cole, Disbrow-a 7.15 21.50 50.00
3,4,33,34 (Farrell, '57- '58) 2.40 6.00 12.00

ALL WESTERN WINNERS (Formerly All Winners; becomes Western Winners with No. 5; see Two-Gun Kid No. 5)
Marvel Comics(CDS): No. 2, Winter, 1948-49 - No. 4, April, 1949

2-Black Rider (origin & 1st app.) & his horse Satan, Kid Colt & his horse Steel, & Two-Gun Kid & his horse Cyclone begin; Shores c-2-4 65.00 195.00 550.00
3-Anti-Wertham editorial 37.00 110.00 275.00
4-Black Rider i.d. revealed; Heath, Shores-a 37.00 110.00 275.00

ALL WINNERS COMICS (All Teen #20)
USA No. 1-7/WFP No. 10-19/YAI No. 21: Summer, 1941 - No. 19, Fall, 1946; No. 21, Winter, 1946-47; (No #20) (No. 21 continued from Young Allies No. 20)

GD25 FN65 VF82 NM94

1-The Angel & Black Marvel only app.; Capt. America by Simon & Kirby, Human Torch & Sub-Mariner begin (#1 was advertised as All Aces); 1st app. All-Winners Squad in text story by Stan Lee 1273.00 3820.00 7640.00 14,500.00

GD25 FN65 NM94

Alll Winners Comics #10 © WFP

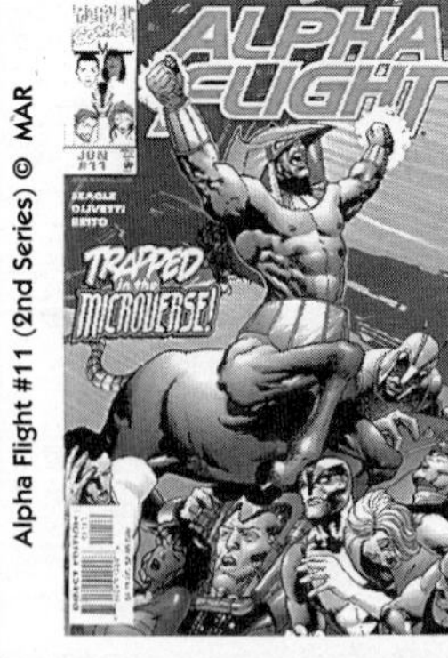

Alpha Flight #11 (2nd Series) © MAR

Altered Image #1 © Image

	GD25	FN65	NM94
2-The Destroyer & The Whizzer begin; Simon & Kirby Captain America	390.00	1170.00	3700.00
3	245.00	735.00	2200.00
4-Classic War-c by Al Avison	270.00	810.00	2400.00
5	165.00	495.00	1400.00
6-The Black Avenger only app.; no Whizzer story; Hitler, Hirohito & Mussolini-c	188.00	564.00	1600.00
7-10	141.00	423.00	1200.00
11,13-18: 11-1st Atlas globe on-c (Winter, 1943-44; also see Human Torch #14). 14-16-No Human Torch	112.00	336.00	950.00
12-Red Skull story; last Destroyer; no Whizzer story	129.00	387.00	1100.00
19-(Scarce)-1st story app. & origin All Winners Squad (Capt. America & Bucky, Human Torch & Toro, Sub-Mariner, Whizzer, & Miss America; r-in Fantasy Masterpieces #10	330.00	990.00	3000.00
21-(Scarce)-All Winners Squad; bondage-c	300.00	900.00	2700.00

NOTE: ***Everett*** *Sub-Mariner-1, 3, 4;* ***Burgos*** *Torch-1, 3, 4.* ***Schomburg*** *c-1, 7-18.* ***Shores*** *c-19p, 21.*

(2nd Series - August, 1948, Marvel Comics (CDS))
(Becomes All Western Winners with No. 2)

1-The Blonde Phantom, Capt. America, Human Torch, & Sub-Mariner app.	212.00	636.00	1800.00

ALL YOUR COMICS (See Fox Giants)
Fox Feature Syndicate (R. W. Voight): Spring, 1946 (36 pgs.)

1-Red Robbins, Merciless the Sorceress app.	15.00	44.00	110.00

ALMANAC OF CRIME (See Fox Giants)

AL OF FBI (See Little Al of the FBI)

ALPHA AND OMEGA
Spire Christian Comics (Fleming H. Revell): 1978 (49¢)

nn 4.00

ALPHA CENTURION (See Superman, 2nd Series & Zero Hour)
DC Comics: 1996 ($2.95, one-shot)

1 3.00

ALPHA FLIGHT (See X-Men #120,121 & X-Men/Alpha Flight)
Marvel Comics: Aug, 1983 - No. 130, Mar, 1994 (#52-on are direct sales only)

1-Byrne-a begins (52pgs.)-Wolverine & Nightcrawler cameo	2.00
2-12: 2-Vindicator becomes Guardian; origin Marrina & Alpha Flight. 3-Concludes origin Alpha Flight. 6-Origin Shaman. 7-Origin Snowbird. 10,11-Origin Sasquatch. 12-(52 pgs.)-Death of Guardian	1.50
13-Wolverine app.	2.50
14-16,18-28: 16-Wolverine cameo. 20-New headquarters. 25-Return of Guardian. 28-Last Byrne issue	1.25
17-X-Men x-over (70% reprinted from X-Men #109); Wolverine cameo	2.00
29-32,35-49: 39-47,49-Portacio-a(i)	1.00
33,34: 33-X-Men (Wolverine) app. 34-Origin Wolverine	2.50
50-Double size; Portacio-a(i)	1.25
51-Jim Lee's 1st work at Marvel (10/87); Wolverine cameo; 1st Jim Lee Wolverine; Portacio-a(i)	3.00
52,53-Wolverine app.; Lee-a on Wolverine; Portacio-a(i); 53-Lee/Portacio-a	2.00
54,63,64-No Jim Lee-a; 54-Portacio-a(i)	1.00
55-62-Jim Lee-a(p)	1.50
65-74,76-86: 65-Begin $1.50-c. 71-Intro The Sorcerer (villain). 74-Wolverine, Spider-Man & The Avengers app. 89-Original Guardian returns	1.50
75-Double size ($1.95, 52 pgs.)	2.00
87-90-Wolverine 4 part story w/Jim Lee covers	2.00
91-99,101-104: 91-Dr. Doom app. 94-F.F. x-over. 99-Galactus, Avengers app. 102-Intro Weapon Omega. 104-Last $1.50-c	1.50
100-($2.00, 52 pgs.)-Avengers & Galactus app.	2.00
105,107-119,121-129: 107-X-Factor x-over. 110-112-Infinity War x-overs. 110, 111-Wolverine app. (brief). 111-Thanos cameo	1.50
106-Northstar revelation issue	2.00
106-2nd printing (direct sale only)	1.25
120-($2.25)-Polybagged w/Paranormal Registration Act poster	2.25
130-($2.25, 52 pgs.)	2.25
Annual 1 (9/86, $1.25)	1.25
Annual 2(12/87, $1.25)	1.25
Special V2#1(6/92, $2.50, 52 pgs.)-Wolverine-c/story	2.50

NOTE: ***Austin*** *c-1i, 2i, 53i.* ***Byrne*** *c-81, 82.* ***Guice*** *c-85, 91-99.* ***Jim Lee*** *a(p)-51, 53, 55-62, 64; c-53, 87-90.* ***Mignola*** *a-29-31p.* ***Whilce Portacio*** *a(i)-39-47, 49-54.*

ALPHA FLIGHT (2nd Series)
Marvel Comics: Aug, 1997 - No. 20, Mar, 1999 ($2.99/$1.99)

1-($2.99)-Wraparound cover	4.00
2,3: 2-Variant-c	3.25
4-11,13-20: 8,9Wolverine-c/app.	2.00
12-($2.99) Death of Sasquatch; wraparound-c	3.00
.../Inhumans '98 Annual ($3.50) Raney-a	3.50

ALPHA FLIGHT: IN THE BEGINNING
Marvel Comics: July, 1997 ($1.95, one-shot)

(-1)-Flashback w/Wolverine 1.95

ALPHA FLIGHT SPECIAL
Marvel Comics: July, 1991 - No. 4, Oct, 1991 ($1.50, limited series)

1-3: Reprints Flight #97-99 w/covers	1.50
4 ($2.00, 52 pgs.)-Reprints Alpha Flight #100	2.00

ALPHA KORPS
Diversity Comics: Sept, 1996 ($2.50)

1-Origin/1st app. Alpha Korps 2.50

ALPHA WAVE
Darkline Comics: Mar, 1987 ($1.75, 36 pgs.)

1 1.50

ALTERED IMAGE
Image Comics: Apr, 1998 - No. 3, Sept, 1998 ($2.50, limited series)

1-3-Spawn, Witchblade, Savage Dragon; Valentino-s/a 2.50

ALTER EGO
First Comics: May, 1986 - No. 4, Nov, 1986 (Mini-series)

1-4 1.40

ALVIN (TV) (See Four Color Comics No. 1042)
Dell Publishing Co.: Oct-Dec, 1962 - No. 28, Oct, 1973

12-021-212 (#1)	8.00	25.00	90.00
2	4.50	13.50	50.00
3-10	3.60	11.00	40.00
11-28	2.75	8.00	30.00
Alvin For President (10/64)	2.75	8.00	30.00
...& His Pals in Merry Christmas with Clyde Crashcup & Leonardo 1 (02-120-402)-(12-2/64)	6.00	18.00	65.00
Reprinted in 1966 (12-023-604	4.50	13.50	50.00

ALVIN & THE CHIPMUNKS
Harvey Comics: July, 1992 - No. 5, May, 1994

1-5 1.50

AMALGAM AGE OF COMICS, THE: THE DC COMICS COLLECTION
DC Comics: 1996 ($12.95, trade paperback)

nn-r/Amazon, Assassins, Doctor Strangefate, JLX, Legends of the Dark Claw, & Super Soldier 12.95

AMANDA AND GUNN
Image Comics: Apr, 1997 - No. 4, Oct, 1997 ($2.95, B&W, limited series)

1-4 2.95

Amazing Adult Fantasy #7 © MAR

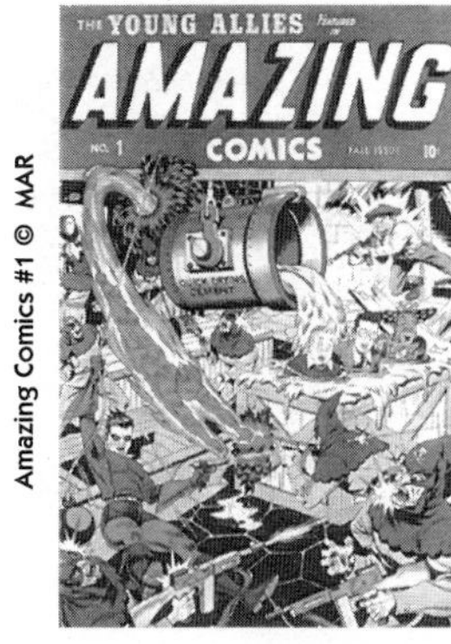

Amazing Comics #1 © MAR

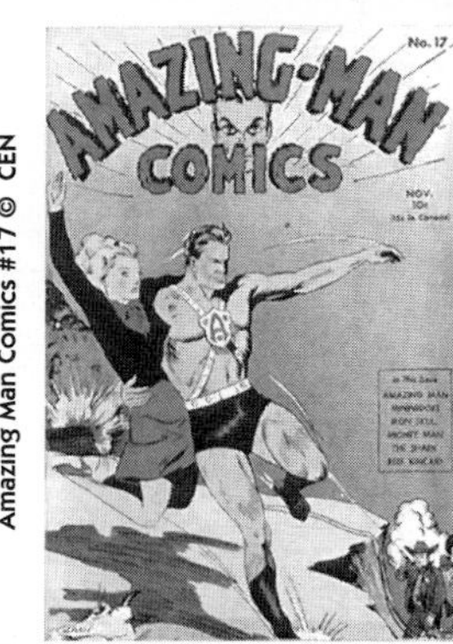

Amazing Man Comics #17 © CEN

GD25 FN65 NM94

AMAZING ADULT FANTASY (Formerly Amazing Adventures #1-6; becomes Amazing Fantasy #15)
Marvel Comics Group (AMI): No. 7, Dec, 1961 - No. 14, July, 1962

7-Ditko-c/a begins, ends #14 48.00 144.00 575.00
8-Last 10¢ issue 40.00 120.00 475.00
9-13: 12-1st app. Mailbag. 13-Anti-communist sty 38.00 114.00 420.00
14-Prototype issue (Professor X) 40.00 120.00 465.00

AMAZING ADVENTURE FUNNIES (Fantoman No. 2 on)
Centaur Publications: June, 1940 - No. 2, Sept. 1940

1-The Fantom of the Fair by Gustavson (r/Amaz. Mystery Funnies V2#7,V2#8), The Arrow, Skyrocket Steele From the Year X by Everett (r/AMF #2); Burgos-a 165.00 495.00 1400.00
2-Reprints; Published after Fantoman #2 106.00 318.00 900.00
NOTE: ***Burgos** a-1(2). **Everett** a-1(3). **Gustavson** a-1(5), 2(3). **Pinajian** a-2.*

AMAZING ADVENTURES (Also see Boy Cowboy & Science Comics)
Ziff-Davis Publ. Co.: 1950; No. 1, Nov, 1950 - No. 6, Fall, 1952 (Painted covers)

1950 (no month given) (8-1/2x11) (8 pgs.) Has the front & back cover plus Schomburg story used in Amazing Advs. #1 (Sent to subscribers of Z-D s/f magazines & ordered through mail for 10¢. Used to test market) Estimated value... 280.00
1-Wood, Schomburg, Anderson, Whitney-a 62.00 185.00 525.00
2-5: 2-Schomburg-a. 2,4,5-Anderson-a. 3,5-Starr-a 30.00 90.00 225.00
6-Krigstein-a 32.00 96.00 240.00

AMAZING ADVENTURES (Becomes Amazing Adult Fantasy #7 on)
Atlas Comics (AMI)/Marvel Comics No. 3 on: June, 1961 - No. 6, Nov, 1961

1-Origin Dr. Droom (1st Marvel-Age Superhero) by Kirby; Kirby/Ditko-a (5 pgs.) Ditko & Kirby-a in all; Kirby monster c-1-6 100.00 300.00 1200.00
2 41.00 123.00 500.00
3-6: 6-Last Dr. Droom 38.00 114.00 420.00

AMAZING ADVENTURES
Marvel Comics Group: Aug, 1970 - No. 39, Nov, 1976

1-Inhumans by Kirby(p) & Black Widow (1st app. in Tales of Suspense #52) double feature begins 3.50 10.50 38.00
2-4: 2-F.F. brief app. 4-Last Kirby Inhumans 1.50 4.50 14.00
5-8: Neal Adams-a(p); 8-Last Black Widow 2.20 6.25 22.00
9,10: Magneto app. 10-Last Inhumans (origin-r by Kirby) 1.10 3.30 11.00
11-New Beast begins(1st app. in mutated form; origin in flashback); X-Men cameo in flashback (#11-17 are X-Men tie-ins) 7.00 21.00 70.00
12-17: 13-Brotherhood of Evil Mutants x-over from X-Men. 15-X-Men app. 17-Last Beast (origin); X-Men app. 1.80 5.40 18.00
18-War of the Worlds begins (5/73); 1st app. Killraven; Neal Adams-a(p) 1.50 4.50 15.00
19-35,38,39: 35-Giffen's first published story (art), along with Deadly Hands of Kung-Fu #22 (3/76) 5.00
36,37-(Regular 25¢ edition)(7-8/76) 5.00
36,37-(30¢-c, limited distribution) 2.00 6.00 20.00
NOTE: ***N. Adams** c-6-8. **Buscema** a-1p, 2p. **Colan** a-3-5p, 26p. **Ditko** a-24r. **Everett** a(i)3-5, 7-9. **Giffen** a-35i, 38p. **G. Kane** c-11, 25p, 29p. **Ploog** a-12i. **Russell** a-27-32, 34-37, 39; c-28, 30-32, 33i, 34, 35, 37, 39i. **Starliing** a-17. **Starlin** c-15p, 16, 17, 27. **Sutton** a-11-15p.*

AMAZING ADVENTURES
Marvel Comics Group: Dec, 1979 - No. 14, Jan, 1981

V2#1-Reprints story/X-Men #1 & 38 (origins) 3.00
2-14: 2-6-Early X-Men-r. 7,8-Origin Iceman 2.00
NOTE: ***Byrne** c-6p, 9p. **Kirby** a-1-14r; c-7, 9. **Steranko** a-12r. **Tuska** a-7-9.*

AMAZING ADVENTURES
Marvel Comics: July, 1988 ($4.95, squarebound, one-shot, 80 pgs.)

1-Anthology; Austin, Golden-a 5.00

AMAZING ADVENTURES OF CAPTAIN CARVEL AND HIS CARVEL CRUSADERS, THE (See Carvel Comics)

GD25 FN65 NM94

AMAZING CHAN & THE CHAN CLAN, THE (TV)
Gold Key: May, 1973 - No. 4, Feb, 1974 (Hanna-Barbera)

1-Warren Tufts-a in all 2.00 6.00 20.00
2-4 1.40 4.20 14.00

AMAZING COMICS (Complete Comics No. 2)
Timely Comics (EPC): Fall, 1944

1-The Destroyer, The Whizzer, The Young Allies (by Sekowsky), Sergeant Dix; Schomburg-c 165.00 495.00 1400.00

AMAZING DETECTIVE CASES (Formerly Suspense No. 2?)
Marvel/Atlas Comics (CCC): No. 3, Nov, 1950 - No. 14, Sept, 1952

3 21.00 64.00 160.00
4-6 13.00 38.00 95.00
7-10 11.00 34.00 85.00
11,14: 11-(3/52)-Changes to horror 16.00 48.00 120.00
12-Krigstein-a 16.00 48.00 120.00
13-(Scarce)-Everett-a; electrocution-c/story 21.00 64.00 160.00
NOTE: ***Colan** a-9. **Maneely** c-13. **Sekowsky** a-12. **Sinnott** a-13. **Tuska** a-10.*

AMAZING FANTASY (Formerly Amazing Adult Fantasy #7-14)
Atlas Magazines/Marvel: #15, Aug, 1962 (Sept, 1962 shown in indicia); #16, Dec, 1995 - #18, Feb, 1996

GD25 FN65 VF82 NM94
15-Origin/1st app. of Spider-Man by Ditko (11 pgs.); 1st app. Aunt May & Uncle Ben; Kirby/Ditko-c 1100.00 3300.00 11,000.00 27,000.00
GD25 FN65 NM94
16-18 ('95-'96, $3.95): Kurt Busiek scripts; painted-c/a 1.60 4.00

AMAZING GHOST STORIES (Formerly Nightmare)
St. John Publishing Co.: No. 14, Oct, 1954 - No. 16, Feb, 1955

14-Pit & the Pendulum story by Kinstler; Baker-c 25.00 76.00 190.00
15-r/Weird Thrillers #5; Baker-c, Powell-a 17.00 52.00 130.00
16-Kubert reprints of Weird Thrillers #4; Baker-c; Roussos, Tuska-a; Kinstler-a (1 pg.) 18.00 54.00 135.00

AMAZING HIGH ADVENTURE
Marvel Comics: 8/84; No. 2, 10/85; No. 3, 10/86 - No. 5, 1987 ($2.00)

1-5: 3,4-Baxter paper 2.00
NOTE: ***Bissette** a-4. **Bolton** c/a-4. **Severin** a-1, 3. **Paul Smith** a-2. **Williamson** a-2i.*

AMAZING-MAN COMICS (Formerly Motion Picture Funnies Weekly?) (Also see Stars And Stripes Comics)
Centaur Publications: No. 5, Sept, 1939 - No. 26, Jan, 1942

GD25 FN65 VF82 NM94
5(#1)(Rare)-Origin/1st app. A-Man the Amazing Man by Bill Everett; The Cat-Man by Tarpe Mills (also #8), Mighty Man by Filchock, Minimidget & sidekick Ritty, & The Iron Skull by Burgos begins 1318.00 3955.00 7900.00 14,500.00
GD25 FN65 NM94
6-Origin The Amazing Man retold; The Shark begins; Ivy Menace by Tarpe Mills app. 274.00 822.00 2600.00
7-Magician From Mars begins; ends #11 182.00 546.00 1550.00
8-Cat-Man dresses as woman 129.00 387.00 1100.00
9-Magician From Mars battles the 'Elemental Monster,' swiped into The Spectre in More Fun #54 & 55. Ties w/Marvel Mystery #4 for 1st Nazi War-c on a comic (2/40) 129.00 387.00 1100.00
10,11: 11-Zardi, the Eternal Man begins; ends #16; Amazing Man dons costume; last Everett issue 112.00 336.00 950.00
12,13 97.00 291.00 825.00
14-Reef Kinkaid, Rocke Wayburn (ends #20), & Dr. Hypno (ends #21) begin; no Zardi or Chuck Hardy 82.00 246.00 700.00
15,17-20: 15-Zardi returns; no Rocke Wayburn. 17-Dr. Hypno returns; no Zardi 68.00 204.00 575.00
16-Mighty Man's powers of super strength & ability to shrink & grow explained; Rocke Wayburn returns; no Dr. Hypno; Al Avison (a character) begins, ends #18 (a tribute to the famed artist) 71.00 213.00 600.00

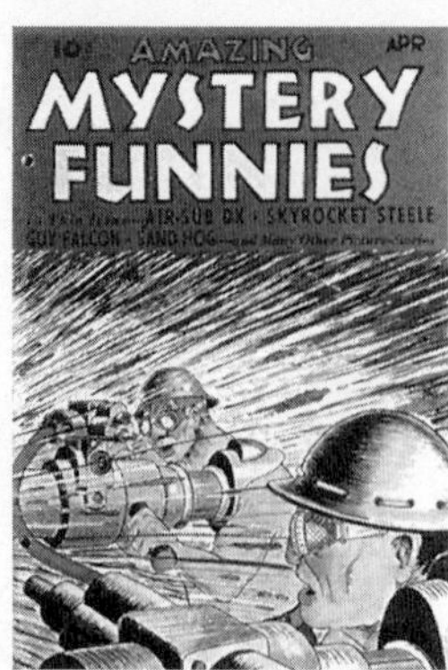

Amazing Mystery Funnies V2#4 © CEN

Amazing Spider-Man #9 © MAR

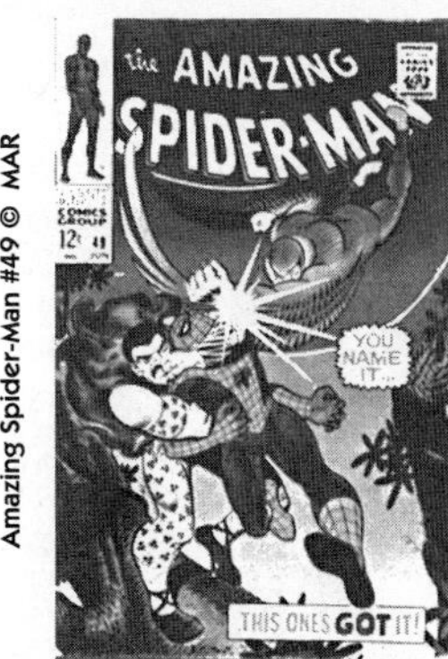

Amazing Spider-Man #49 © MAR

21-Origin Dash Dartwell (drug-use story); origin & only app. T.N.T.
68.00 204.00 575.00

22-Dash Dartwell, the Human Meteor & The Voice app; last Iron Skull & The Shark; Silver Streak app. (classic-c) 68.00 204.00 575.00

23-Two Amazing Man stories; intro/origin Tommy the Amazing Kid; The Marksman only app. 68.00 204.00 575.00

24-King of Darkness, Nightshade, & Blue Lady begin; end #26; 1st app. Super-Ann 65.00 195.00 550.00

25,26 (Scarce): Meteor Martin by Wolverton in both; 26-Electric Ray app.
100.00 300.00 850.00

NOTE: ***Everett*** *a-5-11; c-5-11.* ***Gilman*** *a-14-20.* ***Giunta/Mirando*** *a-7-10.* ***Sam Glanzman*** *a-14-16, 18-21, 23.* ***Louis Glanzman*** *a-6, 9-11, 14-21; c-13-19, 21.* ***Robert Golden*** *a-9.* ***Gustavson*** *a-6; c-22, 23.* ***Lubbers*** *a-14-21.* ***Simon*** *a-10.* ***Frank Thomas*** *a-6, 9-11, 14, 15, 17-21.*

AMAZING MYSTERIES (Formerly Sub-Mariner Comics No. 31)
Marvel Comics (CCC): No. 32, May, 1949 - No. 35, Jan, 1950 (1st Marvel Horror Comic)

32-The Witness app. 70.00 205.00 575.00
33-Horror format 28.00 84.00 210.00
34,35: Changes to Crime. 34,35-Photo-c 16.00 48.00 120.00

AMAZING MYSTERY FUNNIES
Centaur Publications: Aug, 1938 - No. 24, Sept, 1940 (All 52 pgs.)

V1#1-Everett-c(1st); Dick Kent Adv. story; Skyrocket Steele in the Year X on cover only 274.00 822.00 2600.00
2-Everett 1st-a (Skyrocket Steele) 153.00 459.00 1300.00
3 79.00 237.00 675.00
3(#4, 12/38)-nn on cover, #3 on inside; bondage-c
71.00 213.00 600.00

V2#1-4,6: 2-Drug use story. 3-Air-Sub DX begins by Burgos. 4-Dan Hastings, Hastings, Sand Hog begins (ends #5). 6-Last Skyrocket Steele
65.00 195.00 550.00
5-Classic Everett-c 82.00 246.00 700.00
7 (Scarce)-Intro. The Fantom of the Fair & begins; Everett, Gustavson, Burgos-a 280.00 840.00 2600.00
8-Origin & 1st app. Speed Centaur 115.00 345.00 975.00
9-11: 11-Self portrait and biog. of Everett; Jon Linton begins; early Robot cover (11/39) 67.00 200.00 565.00
12 (Scarce)-1st Space Patrol; Wolverton-a (12/39); new costume Phantom of the Fair 165.00 495.00 1400.00

V3#1(#17, 1/40)-Intro. Bullet; Tippy Taylor serial begins, ends #24 (continued in The Arrow #2) 67.00 200.00 565.00
18,20: 18-Fantom of the Fair by Gustavson 63.00 189.00 535.00
19,21-24: Space Patrol by Wolverton in all 87.00 261.00 735.00

NOTE: ***Burgos a****-V2#3-9.* ***Eisner*** *a-V1#2, 3(2).* ***Everett*** *a-V1#2-4, V2#1, 3-6; c-V1#1-4,V2#3, 5, 18.* ***Filchock*** *a-V2#9.* ***Flessel*** *a-V2#6.* ***Guardineer*** *a-V1#4, V2#4-6;* ***Gustavson*** *a-V2#4, 5, 9-12, V3#1, 18, 19; c-V2#7, 9, 12, V3#1, 21, 22;* ***McWilliams*** *a-V2#9, 10.* ***TarpeMills*** *a-V2#2, 4-6, 9-12, V3#1.* ***Leo Morey****(Pulp artist) c-V2#10; text illo-V2#11.* ***FrankThomas*** *a-6-V2#11.* ***Webster*** *a-V2#4.*

AMAZING SAINTS
Logos International: 1974 (39¢)

nn-True story of Phil Saint 4.00

AMAZING SCARLET SPIDER
Marvel Comics: Nov, 1995 - No. 2, Dec, 1995 ($1.95, limited series)

1,2: Replaces "Amazing Spider-Man" for two issues 2.00

AMAZING SPIDER-MAN, THE (See All Detergent Comics, Amazing Fantasy, America's Best TV Comics, Aurora, Deadly Foes of Spider-Man, Fireside Book Series, Giant-Size Spider-Man, Giant Size Super-Heroes Featuring..., Marvel Collectors Item Classics, Marvel Fanfare, Marvel Graphic Novel, Marvel Spec. Ed., Marvel Tales, Marvel Team-Up, Marvel Treasury Ed., Nothing Can Stop the Juggernaut, Official Marvel Index To..., Power Record Comics, Spectacular..., Spider-Man, Spider-Man Digest, Spider-Man Saga, Spider-Man 2099, Spider-Man Vs. Wolverine, Spidey Super Stories, Strange Tales Annual #2, Superman Vs. ..., Try-Out Winner Book, Web of Spider- Man & Within Our Reach)

AMAZING SPIDER-MAN, THE
Marvel Comics Group: March, 1963 - No. 441, Nov, 1998

GD25 FN65 VF82 NM94

1-Retells origin by Steve Ditko; 1st Fantastic Four x-over (ties w/F.F. #12 as first Marvel x-over); intro. John Jameson & The Chameleon; Spider-Man's 2nd app.; Kirby/Ditko-c; Ditko-c/a #1-38
700.00 2100.00 7000.00 18,000.00

GD25 FN65 NM94

1-Reprint from the Golden Record Comic set 10.00 30.00 100.00
with record (1966) 20.00 60.00 200.00
2-1st app. the Vulture & the Terrible Tinkerer 214.00 642.00 3000.00
3-1st full-length story; Human Torch cameo; intro. & 1st app. Doc Octopus; Spider-Man pin-up by Ditko 158.00 474.00 2050.00
4-Origin & 1st app. The Sandman (see Strange Tales #115 for 2nd app.); Intro. Betty Brant & Liz Allen 140.00 420.00 1675.00
5-Dr. Doom app. 121.00 363.00 1450.00
6-1st app. Lizard 100.00 300.00 1200.00
7,8,10: 7-Vs. The Vulture; 1st monthly issue. 8-Fantastic Four app. in back-up story by Kirby/Ditko. 10-1st app. Big Man & The Enforcers
67.00 200.00 800.00
9-Origin & 1st app. Electro (2/64) 73.00 219.00 875.00
11,12: 11-1st app. Bennett Brant. 12-Doc Octopus unmasks Spider-Man-c/story
41.00 123.00 475.00
13-1st app. Mysterio 53.00 159.00 640.00

GD25 FN65 VF82 NM94

14-(7/64)-1st app. The Green Goblin (c/story)(Norman Osborn); Hulk x-over
130.00 390.00 775.00 1550.00

GD25 FN65 NM94

15-1st app. Kraven the Hunter; 1st mention of Mary Jane Watson (not shown) 48.00 144.00 575.00
16-Spider-Man battles Daredevil (1st x-over 9/64); still in old yellow costume
34.00 102.00 375.00
17-2nd app. Green Goblin (c/story); Human Torch x-over (also in #18 & #21)
48.00 144.00 575.00
18-1st app. Ned Leeds who later becomes Hobgoblin; Fantastic Four back-up story; 3rd app. Sandman 33.00 100.00 370.00
19-Sandman app. 30.00 90.00 300.00
20-Origin & 1st app. The Scorpion 34.00 102.00 375.00
21-2nd app. The Beetle (see Strange Tales #123) 25.00 75.00 250.00
22-1st app. Princess Python 22.50 68.00 225.00
23-3rd app. The Green Goblin-c/story; Norman Osborn app.
31.00 93.00 340.00
24 19.50 58.00 195.00
25-(6/65)-1st app. Mary Jane Watson (cameo; face not shown); 1st app. Spencer Smythe; Norman Osborn app. 24.00 72.00 240.00
26-4th app. The Green Goblin-c/story; 1st app. Crime Master; dies in #27
27.00 81.00 270.00
27-5th app. The Green Goblin-c/story; Norman Osborn app.
25.00 75.00 250.00
28-Origin & 1st app. Molten Man (9/65, scarcer in high grade)
32.00 96.00 360.00
29,30 15.50 47.00 155.00
31-38: 31-1st app. Harry Osborn who later becomes 2nd Green Goblin, Gwen Stacy & Prof. Warren. 34-4th app. Kraven the Hunter. 36-1st app. Looter. 37-Intro. Norman Osborn. 38-(7/66)-2nd app. Mary Jane Watson (cameo; face not shown); last Ditko issue 15.50 47.00 155.00
39-The Green Goblin-c/story; Green Goblin's i.d. revealed as Norman Osborn; Romita-a begins (8/66; see Daredevil #16 for 1st Romita-a on Spider-Man)
21.00 63.00 210.00
40-1st told origin The Green Goblin-c/story 30.00 90.00 300.00
41-1st app. Rhino 16.00 48.00 160.00
42-(11/66)-3rd app. Mary Jane Watson (cameo in last 2 panels); 1st time face is shown 13.00 39.00 130.00
43-49: 44,45-2nd & 3rd app. The Lizard. 46-Intro. Shocker. 47-M. J. Watson & Peter Parker 1st date. 47-Green Goblin cameo; Harry & Norman Osborn app. 47,49-5th & 6th app. Kraven the Hunter 9.00 27.00 90.00

Amazing Spider-Man #90 © MAR

Amazing Spider-Man #187 © MAR

Amazing Spider-Man #243 © MAR

GD25 FN65 NM94

50-1st app. Kingpin (7/67) 35.00 105.00 390.00
51-2nd app. Kingpin 15.00 45.00 150.00
52-60: 52-1st app. Joe Robertson & 3rd app. Kingpin. 56-1st app. Capt. George Stacy. 57,58-Ka-Zar app. 59-1st app. Brainwasher (alias Kingpin); 1st-c app. M. J. Watson 6.80 20.50 68.00
61-74: 67-1st app. Randy Robertson. 69-Kingpin-c. 69,70-Kingpin app. 73-1st app. Silvermane. 74-Last 12¢ issue 4.40 13.20 48.00
75-89,91-93,95,99: 78,79-1st app. The Prowler. 83-1st app. Schemer & Vanessa (Kingpin's wife). 84,85-Kingpin-c/story. 86-Re-intro & origin Black Widow in new costume. 93-1st app. Arthur Stacy 3.60 10.80 39.00
90-Death of Capt. Stacey 4.50 13.50 50.00
94-Origin retold 6.00 18.00 65.00
96-98-Green Goblin app. (97,98-Green Goblin-c); drug books not approved by CCA 7.50 22.50 82.00
100-Anniversary issue (9/71); Green Goblin cameo (2 pgs.) 16.00 46.00 170.00
101-1st app. Morbius the Living Vampire; Wizard cameo; last 15¢ issue (10/71) 11.00 33.00 120.00
101-Silver ink 2nd printing (9/92, $1.75) 2.00
102-Origin & 2nd app. Morbius (25¢, 52 pgs.) 7.25 22.00 80.00
103-118: 104,111-Kraven the Hunter-c/stories. 108-1st app. Sha-Shan. 109-Dr. Strange-c/story (6/72). 110-1st app. Gibbon. 113-1st app. Hammerhead. 116-118-reprints story from Spectacular Spider-Man Mag. in color with some changes 2.50 7.50 27.00
119,120-Spider-Man vs. Hulk (4 & 5/73) 3.80 11.40 40.00
121-Death of Gwen Stacy (6/73) (killed by Green Goblin) (reprinted in Marvel Tales #98 & 192) 9.50 28.50 105.00
122-Death of The Green Goblin-c/story (7/73) (reprinted in Marvel Tales #99 & 192) 11.00 33.00 120.00
123,125-128: 123-Cage app. 125-Man-Wolf origin. 127-1st mention of Harry Osborn becoming Green Goblin 2.00 6.00 20.00
124-1st app. Man-Wolf (9/73) 3.00 9.00 33.00
129-1st app. Jackal & The Punisher (2/74) 13.00 38.00 140.00
130-133,138-141,152-158,160: 131-Last 20¢ issue. 139-1st app. Grizzly. 140-1st app. Glory Grant. 1.00 3.00 10.00
134-(7/74); 1st app. Tarantula; Harry Osborn discovers Spider-Man's ID; Punisher cameo 2.70 8.00 30.00
135-2nd full Punisher app. (8/74) 4.00 12.25 45.00
136-Reappearance of The Green Goblin (Harry Osborn; Norman Osborn's son) 3.80 11.50 40.00
137-Green Goblin-c/story (2nd Harry Osborn) 3.20 9.00 35.00
142,143-Gwen Stacy clone cameos: 143-1st app. Cyclone 2.20 6.25 22.00
144-Full app. of Gwen Stacy clone 1.60 4.80 16.00
145,146-Gwen Stacy clone storyline continues 1.60 4.80 16.00
147-Spider-Man learns Gwen Stacy is clone 1.60 4.80 16.00
148-Jackal revealed 2.20 6.50 24.00
149-Spider-Man clone story begins, clone dies (?); origin of Jackal 3.20 9.00 35.00
150-Spider-Man decides he is not the clone 1.00 3.00 10.00
151-Spider-Man disposes of clone body .90 2.70 9.00
159-(Regular 25¢ edition); last 25¢ issue(8/76) .90 2.70 8.00
159-(30¢-c, limited distribution) 2.90 8.70 32.00
161-Nightcrawler app. from X-Men; Punisher cameo; Wolverine & Colossus app. .90 2.70 9.00
162-Punisher, Nightcrawler app.; 1st Jigsaw .90 2.70 9.00
163-173,181-190: 167-1st app. Will O' The Wisp. 169-Clone story recapped. 171-Nova app. 181-Origin retold; gives life history of Spidey; Punisher cameo in flashback (1 panel). 182-(7/78)-Peter proposes to Mary Jane for 1st time, but she refuses 2.00 6.00
174,175-Punisher app. 1.20 3.60 12.00
176-180-Green Goblin app 1.30 3.90 13.00
191-193,195-199,203-208,210-219: 193-Peter & Mary Jane break up. 196-Faked death of Aunt May. 203-2nd app. Dazzler. 209-1st app. Calypso (Kraven's girlfriend). 210-1st app. Madame Web. 212-1st app. Hydro Man; origin Sandman 5.00
194-1st app. Black Cat 1.20 3.60 12.00
200-Giant origin issue (1/80) 1.80 5.40 18.00
201,202-Punisher app. 1.00 3.00 10.00
209-Origin & 1st app. Calypso (10/80) 2.00 6.00
220-237: 225-(2/82)-Foolkiller-c/story. 226,227-Black Cat returns. 236-Tarantula dies. 234-Free 16 pg. insert "Marvel Guide to Collecting Comics". 235-Origin Will-'O-The-Wisp 4.00
238-(3/83)-1st app. Hobgoblin (Ned Leeds); came with skin "Tattooz" decal. **Note:** The same decal appears in the more common Fantastic Four #252 which is being removed & placed in this issue as incentive to increase value (Value listed is with or without tattooz) 4.00 12.25 45.00
239-2nd app. Hobgoblin & 1st battle w/Spidey 2.70 8.00 30.00
240-243,246-248: 241-Origin The Vulture. 243-Reintro Mary Jane Watson after 4 year absence 4.00
244-3rd app. Hobgoblin (cameo) .90 2.70 8.00
245-(10/83)-4th app. Hobgoblin (cameo); Lefty Donovan gains powers of Hobgoblin & battles Spider-Man 1.00 3.00 10.00
249-251: 3 part Hobgoblin/Spider-Man battle. 249-Retells origin & death of 1st Green Goblin. 251-Last old costume .90 2.70 8.00
252-Spider-Man dons new black costume (5/84); ties with Marvel Team-Up #141 & Spectacular Spider-Man #90 for 1st new costume (See Marvel S-H Secret Wars #8) 2.00 6.00 20.00
253-1st app. The Rose 5.00
254 4.00
255,263,264,266-273,277-280,282,283: 277-Vess back-up art. 279-Jack O'Lantern-c/story. 282-X-Factor x-over 3.50
256-1st app. Puma 5.00
257-Hobgoblin cameo; 2nd app. Puma; M. J. Watson reveals she knows Spidey's i.d. 5.00
258-Hobgoblin app. (minor) 4.50
259-Full Hobgoblin app.; Spidey back to old costume; origin Mary Jane Watson .90 2.70 8.00
260-Hobgoblin app. 2.00 6.00
261-Hobgoblin-c/story; painted-c by Vess .85 2.60 7.00
262-Spider-Man unmasked; photo-c 5.00
265-1st app. Silver Sable (6/85) 2.00 6.00
265-Silver ink 2nd printing ($1.25) 1.50
274-Zarathos (The Spirit of Vengeance) app. (3/86) 3.00
275-($1.25, 52 pgs.)-Hobgoblin-c/story; origin-r by Ditko .90 2.70 7.50
276-Hobgoblin app. 2.00 6.00
281-Hobgoblin battles Jack O'Lantern .80 2.40 6.50
284-Punisher cameo; Gang War story begins; Hobgoblin-c/story .80 2.40 6.50
285-Punisher app.; minor Hobgoblin app. .85 2.60 7.00
286,287: 286-Hobgoblin-c & app. (minor). 287-Hobgoblin app. (minor) 4.50
288-Full Hobgoblin app.; last Gang War 5.00
289-(6/87, $1.25, 52 pgs.)-Hobgoblin's i.d. revealed as Ned Leeds; death of Ned Leeds; Macendale (Jack O'Lantern) becomes new Hobgoblin (1st app.) 1.80 5.40 18.00
290-292: 290-Peter proposes to Mary Jane. 292-She accepts; leads into Amazing Spider-Man Annual #21 3.00
293,294-Part 2 & 5 of Kraven story from Web of Spider-Man. 294-Death of Kraven 5.00
295-297 3.00
298-Todd McFarlane-c/a begins (3/88); 1st app. Eddie Brock who becomes Venom; (cameo on last pg.) 2.25 6.80 25.00
299-1st app. Venom with costume (cameo) 1.50 4.50 15.00
300 ($1.50, 52 pgs.; 25th Anniversary)-1st full Venom app.; last black costume (5/88) 5.00 15.00 55.00
301-305: 301 ($1.00 issues begin). 304-1st bi-weekly issue

Amazing Spider-Man #330 © MAR

Amazing Spider-Man #375 © MAR

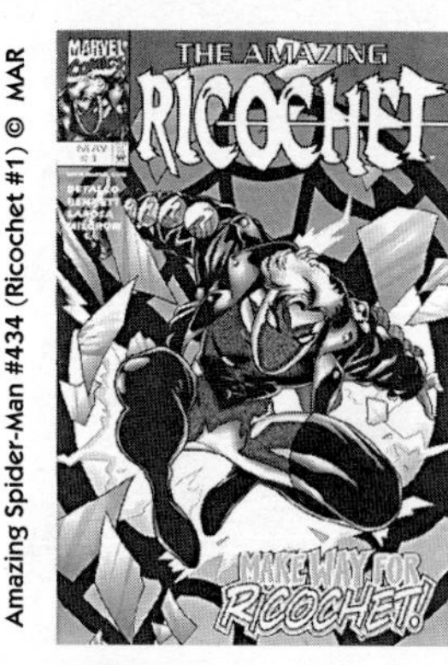

Amazing Spider-Man #434 (Ricochet #1) © MAR

	GD25	FN65	NM94
	.90	2.70	8.00
306-311,313,314: 306-Swipes-c from Action #1. 315-317-Venom app.		2.00	6.00
312-Hobgoblin battles Green Goblin	1.00	3.00	10.00
315-317-Venom app.	1.00	3.00	10.00
318-323,325: 319-Bi-weekly begins again			4.00
324-Sabretooth app.; McFarlane cover only		2.00	6.00
326,327,329: 327-Cosmic Spidey continues from Spectacular Spider-Man (no McFarlane-c/a)			2.50
328-Hulk x-over; last McFarlane issue	.85	2.60	7.00
330,331-Punisher app. 331-Minor Venom app.			3.00
332,333-Venom-c/story			5.00
334-336,338-343: 341-Tarantula app.			2.50
337-Hobgoblin app.			3.00
344-1st app. Cletus Kasady (Carnage)	.85	2.60	7.00
345-1st full app. Cletus Kasady; Venom cameo on last pg.	.90	2.70	8.00
346,347-Venom app.			4.50
348,349,351-359: 348-Avengers x-over. 351,352-Nova of New Warriors app. 353-Darkhawk app.; brief Punisher app. 354-Punisher cameo & Nova, Night Thrasher (New Warriors), Darkhawk & Moon Knight app. 357,358-Punisher, Darkhawk, Moon Knight, Night Thrasher, Nova x-over. 358-3 part gatefold-c; last $1.00-c. 360-Carnage cameo			2.00
350-($1.50, 52pgs.)-Origin retold; Spidey vs. Dr. Doom; pin-ups; Uncle Ben app.			2.50
360-Carnage cameo			3.00
361-Intro Carnage (the Spawn of Venom); begin 3 part story; recap of how Spidey's alien costume became Venom	.85	2.60	7.00
361-($1.25)-2nd printing; silver-c			2.00
362,363-Carnage & Venom-c/story			4.00
362-2nd printing			1.50
364,366-374,376-387: 364-The Shocker app. (old villain). 366-Peter's parents-c/story. 369-Harry Osborn back-up (Gr. Goblin II). 373-Venom back-up. 374-Venom-c/story. 376-Cardiac app. 378-Maximum Carnage part 3. 381,382-Hulk app. 383-The Jury app. 384-Venom/carnage app. 387-New costume Vulture			1.75
365-($3.95, 84 pgs.)-30th anniversary issue w/silver hologram on-c; Spidey/ Venom/Carnage pull-out poster; contains 5 pg. preview of Spider-Man 2099 (1st app.); Spidey's origin retold; Lizard app.; reintro Peter's parents in Stan Lee 3 pg. text w/illo (story continues thru #370).			3.00
365-Second printing; gold hologram on-c			2.00
375-($3.95, 68 pgs.)-Holo-grafx foil-c; vs. Venom story; ties into Venom: Lethal Protector #1; Pat Olliffe-a.			3.00
388-($2.25, 68 pgs.)-Newsstand edition; Venom back-up & Cardiac & chance back-up			2.25
388-($2.95, 68 pgs.)-Collector's edition w/foil-c			3.00
389-396,398,399,401-420: 389-$1.50-c begins; bound-in trading card sheet; Green Goblin app. 394-Power & Responsibility Pt. 2. 396-Daredevil-c & app. 403-Carnage app. 406-1st New Doc Octopus. 407-Human Torch, Silver Sable, Sandman app. 409-Kaine, Rhino app. 410-Carnage app. 414-The Rose app. 415-Onslaught story; Spidey vs. Sentinels. 416-Epilogue to Onslaught; Garney-a(p); Williamson-a(i)			1.50
390-($2.95)-Collector's edition polybagged w/16 pg. insert of new animated Spidey TV show plus animation cel			3.00
394-($2.95, 48 pgs.)-Deluxe edition; flip book w/Birth of a Spider-Man Pt. 2; silver foil both-c			3.00
397-($2.25)-Flip book w/Ultimate Spider-Man			2.25
400-($2.95)-Death of Aunt May			3.00
400-($3.95)-Death of Aunt May; embossed double-c			4.00
400-Collector's Edition; white-c	.85	2.60	7.00
408-Polybagged version with cassette			8.00
421-424, -1 (7/97)($1.95-c)			2.00
425-($2.99)-48 pgs., wraparound-c			3.00
426,428-433: 426-Begin $1.99-c. 432-Spiderhunt pt. 2			2.00

	GD25	FN65	NM94
427-($2.25) Return of Dr. Octopus; double gatefold-c			2.25
434-440: 434-Double cover with "Amazing Ricochet #1". 438-Daredevil app. 439-Avengers-c/app. 440-Byrne-s			2.00
441-Final issue; Byrne-s			2.00
Annual 1 (1964, 72 pgs.)-Origin Spider-Man; 1st app. Sinister Six (Dr. Octopus, Electro, Kraven the Hunter, Mysterio, Sandman, Vulture) (41 pg. story); plus gallery of Spidey foes	54.00	162.00	650.00
Annual 2 (1965, 25¢, 72 pgs.)-Reprints from #1,2,5 plus new Doctor Strange story	25.00	75.00	250.00
Special 3 (11/66, 25¢, 72 pgs.)-Avengers & Hulk x-over; Doctor Octopus-r from #11,12; Romita-a	9.00	27.00	90.00
Special 4 (11/67, 25¢, 68 pgs.)-Spidey battles Human Torch (new 41 pg. story)	8.50	25.50	85.00
Special 5 (11/68, 25¢, 68 pgs.)-New 40 pg. Red Skull story; 1st app. Peter Parker's parents; last annual with new-a	8.00	24 00	80.00
Special 6 (11/69, 25¢, 68 pgs.)-Reprints 41 pg. Sinister Six story from annual #1 plus 2 Kirby/Ditko stories (r)	3.00	9.00	33.00
Special 7 (12/70, 25¢, 68 pgs.)-All-r(#1,2)	3.00	9.00	33.00
Special 8 (12/71)-All-r	3.00	9.00	33.00
King Size 9 ('73)-Reprints Spectacular Spider-Man (mag.) #2; 40 pg. Green Goblin-c/story (re-edited from 58 pgs.)	2.80	8.40	31.00
Annual 10 (1976)-Origin Human Fly (vs. Spidey); new-a begins	1.50	4.50	15.00
Annual 11,12: 11 (1977). 12 (1978)-Spider-Man vs. Hulk-r/#119,120	1.00	3.00	10.00
Annual 13 (1979)-Byrne/Austin-a (new)	1.00	3.00	10.00
Annual 14 (1980)-Miller-c/a(p), 40pgs.	1.20	3.60	12.00
Annual 15 (1981)-Miller-c/a(p); Punisher app.	1.20	3.60	12.00
Annual 16-20: 16 (1982)-Origin/1st app. new Capt. Marvel (female heroine). 17 (1983). 18 (1984). 19 (1985). 20 (1986)-Origin Iron Man of 2020	.85	2.60	7.00
Annual 21 (1987)-Special wedding issue; newsstand & direct sale versions exist & are worth same	1.00	3.00	10.00
Annual 22 (1988, $1.75, 68 pgs.)-1st app. Speedball; Evolutionary War x-over; Daredevil app.		2.00	6.00
Annual 23 (1989, $2.00, 68 pgs.)-Atlantis Attacks; origin Spider-Man retold; She-Hulk app.; Byrne-c; Liefeld-a(p), 23 pgs.			4.00
Annual 24 (1990, $2.00, 68 pgs.)-Ant-Man app.			3.00
Annual 25 (1991, $2.00, 68 pgs.)-3 pg. origin recap; Iron Man app.; 1st Venom solo story; Ditko-a (6 pgs.)			5.00
Annual 26 (1992, $2.25, 68 pgs.)-New Warriors-c/story; Venom solo story cont'd in Spectacular Spider-Man Annual #12			4.00
Annual 27 (1993, $2.95, 68 pgs.)-Bagged w/card; 1st app. Annex			3.00
Annual 28 (1994, $2.95, 68 pgs.)-Carnage-c/story; Rhino & Cloak and Dagger back-ups			3.00
'96 Special-($2.95, 64 pgs.)-"Blast From The Past"-			3.00
'97 Special-($2.99)-Wraparound-c,Sundown app.			3.00
Super Special 1 (4/95, $3.95)-Flip Book			4.00
...: Skating on Thin Ice 1(1990, $1.25, Canadian)-McFarlane-c; anti-drug issue			5.00
...: Skating on Thin Ice 1 (2/93, $1.50, American)	.90	2.70	9.00
...: Double Trouble 2 (1990, $1.25, Canadian)		2.00	6.00
...: Double Trouble 2 (2/93, $1.50, American)			2.00
...: Hit and Run 3 (1990, $1.25, Canadian)-Ghost Rider-c/story	.90	2.70	8.00
...: Hit and Run 3 (2/93. $1.50, American)			2.00
... : Carnage (6/93, $6.95)-r/ASM #344,345,359-363	.85	2.60	7.00
...: Chaos in Calgary 4 (Canadian; part of 5 part series)	1.40	4.20	14.00
...: Chaos in Calgary 4 (2/93, $1.50, American)			2.00
...: Deadball 5 (1993, $1.60, Canadian)-Green Goblin-c/story; features Montreal Expos	1.80	5.40	18.00

Note: Prices listed above are for English Canadian editions. French editions

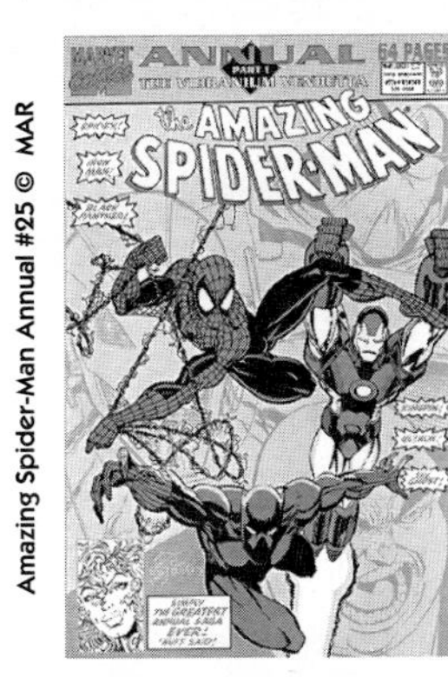

Amazing Spider-Man Annual #25 © MAR

Amazing Spider-Man V2 #1 © MAR

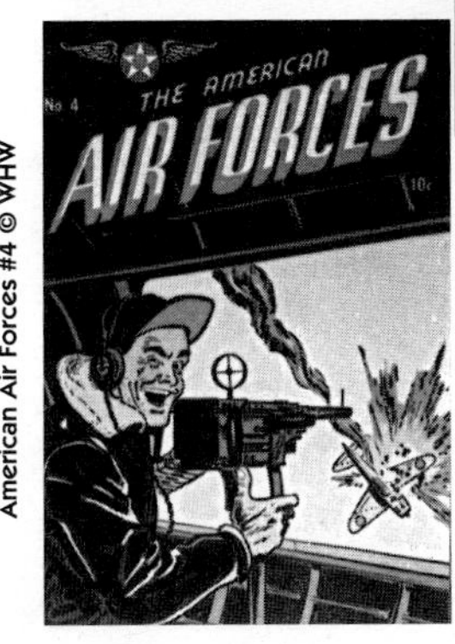

American Air Forces #4 © WHW

GD25 FN65 NM94

are worth double.
...: Soul of the Hunter nn (8/92, $5.95, 52 pgs.)-Zeck-c/a(p) 2.00 6.00
Parallel Lives (1990, $8.95, 68pgs.)-Graphic novel .90 2.70 9.00
Aim Toothpaste Giveaway (36 pgs., reg. size)-1 pg. origin recap; Green Goblin-c/story .90 2.70 9.00
Aim Toothpaste Giveaway (16 pgs., reg. size)-Dr. Octopus app. .90 2.70 9.00
All Detergent Giveaway (1979, 36 pgs.), nn-Origin-r 1.00 3.00 10.00
GiveawayY-Acme & Dingo Children's Boots (1980)-Spider-Woman app. 1.20 3.60 12.00
Amazing Spider-Man nn (1990, 6-1/8x9", 28 pgs.)-Shan-Lon giveaway; r/ Amazing Spider-Man #303 w/McFarlane-c/a 2.00 6.00
...& Power Pack (1984, nn)(Nat'l Committee for Prevention of Child Abuse (two versions, mail offer & store giveaway)-Mooney-a; Byrne-c
Mail offer 1.00 3.00 10.00
Store giveaway 3.00
...& The Hulk (Special Edition)(6/8/80; 20 pgs.)-Supplement to Chicago Tribune (giveaway) 1.20 3.60 12.00
...& The Incredible Hulk (1981, 1982; 36 pgs.)-Sanger Harris or May D&F supplement to Dallas Times, Dallas Herald, Denver Post, Kansas City Star, Tulsa World; Foley's supplement to Houston Chronicle (1982, 16 pgs.)-"Great Rodeo Robbery"; The Jones Store-giveaway (1983, 16 pgs.) 1.80 5.40 18.00
...and the New Mutants Featuring Skids nn (National Committee for Prevention of Child Abuse/K-Mart giveaway)-Williams-c(i) 3.00
...Captain America, The Incredible Hulk, & Spider-Woman (1981) (7-11 Stores giveaway; 36 pgs.) .90 2.70 8.00
...: Danger in Dallas (1983) (Supplement to Dallas Times Herald) giveaway .90 2.70 8.00
...: Danger in Denver (1983) (Supplement to Denver Post) giveaway for May D&F stores .90 2.70 8.00
..., Fire-Star, And Ice-Man at the Dallas Ballet Nutcracker (1983; supplement to Dallas Times Herald)-Mooney-p 1.00 3.00 10.00
Giveaway-Esquire Magazine (2/69)-Miniature-Still attached 9.00 27.00 100.00
Giveaway-Eye Magazine (2/69)-Miniature-Still attached 7.25 22.00 80.00
..., Storm & Powerman (1982; 20 pgs.)(American Cancer Society) giveaway 2.00 6.00
...Vs. The Hulk (Special Edition; 1979, 20 pgs.)(Supplement to Columbus Dispatch)-Giveaway 1.00 3.00 10.00
...Vs. The Prodigy (Giveaway, 16 pgs. in color (1976, 5x6-1/2")-Sex education; (1 million printed; 35-50¢) 1.50 4.50 15.00

NOTE: ***Austin** a(i)-248, 335, 337, Annual 13; c(i)-188, 241, 242, 248, 331, 334, 343, Annual 25. **J. Buscema** a(p)-72, 73, 76-81, 84, 85. **Byrne** a-189p, 190p, 206p, Annual 3r, 6r, 7r, 13p; c-189p, 268, 296, Annual 12. **Ditko** a-1-38, Annual 1, Special 3(r), 2, 24(2); c-1i, 2-38. **Guice** c/a-Annual 18i. **Gil Kane** a(p)-89-105, 120-124, 150, Annual 10, 12i, 24p; c-90p, 96, 98, 99, 101-105p, 129p, 131p, 132p, 137-140p, 143p, 148p, 149p, 151p, 153p, 160p, 161p, Annual 10p, 24. **Kirby** a-8. **Erik Larsen** a-324, 327, 329-350; c-327, 329-350, 354i, Annual 25. **McFarlane** a-298p, 299p, 300-303, 304-323p, 325p, 328; c-298-325, 328. **Miller** c-218, 219. **Mooney** a-65i, 67-82i, 84-88i, 173i, 178i, 189i, 190i, 192i, 193i, 196-202i, 207i, 211-219i, 221i, 222i, 226i, 227i, 229-233i, Annual 11i, 17i. **Nasser** c-228p. **Nebres** a-Annual 24i. **Russell** c-357i. **Simonson** c-222, 337i. **Starlin** a-113i, 114i, 187p. **Williamson** a-365i.*

AMAZING SPIDER-MAN (Volume 2)
Marvel Comics: Jan, 1998 - Present ($2.99/$1.99)
1-($2.99)-Byrne-a 3.00
1-($6.95) Dynamic Forces w/variant-c by the Romitas 7.00
2-($1.99) Two covers -by JohnByrne and Andy Kubert 2.00

AMAZING WILLIE MAYS, THE
Famous Funnies Publ.: No date (Sept, 1954)
nn 64.00 192.00 540.00

AMAZING WORLD OF SUPERMAN (See Superman)

GD25 FN65 NM94

AMAZING X-MEN
Marvel Comics: Mar, 1995 - No.4, July, 1995 ($1.95, limited series)
1-Age of Apocalypse 2.50
2-4 2.00

AMAZON
Comico: Mar, 1989 - No. 3, May, 1989 ($1.95, limited series)
1-3: Ecological theme 2.25

AMAZON (Also see Marvel Versus DC #3 & DC Versus Marvel #4)
DC Comics (Amalgam): Apr, 1996 ($1.95, one-shot)
1-John Byrne-c/a/scripts 2.00

AMAZON ATTACK 3-D
The 3-D Zone: Sept, 1990 ($3.95, 28 pgs.)
1-Chaykin-a 4.00

AMAZON WOMAN (1st Series)
FantaCo: Summer, 1994 - No. 2, Fall, 1994 ($2.95, B&W, limited series, mature)
1,2: Tom Simonton-c/a/scripts 3.00

AMAZON WOMAN (2nd Series)
FantaCo: Feb, 1996 - No. 4, May, 1996 ($2.95, B&W, limited series, mature)
1-4: Tom Simonton-a/scripts 3.00

AMAZON WOMAN: INVADERS OF TERROR
FantaCo: 1996 ($5.95, B&W, one-shot, mature)
nn-Tom Simonton-a/scripts 2.00 6.00

AMBUSH (See Zane Grey, Four Color 314)

AMBUSH BUG (Also see Son of...)
DC Comics: June, 1985 - No. 4, Sept, 1985 (75¢, limited series)
1-4: Giffen-c/a in all 1.00
Nothing Special 1 (9/92, $2.50, 68pg.)-Giffen-c/a 2.50
Stocking Stuffer (2/86, $1.25)-Giffen-c/a 1.25

AMERICA AT WAR - THE BEST OF DC WAR COMICS (See Fireside Book Series)

AMERICA IN ACTION
Dell(Imp. Publ. Co.)/Mayflower House Publ.: 1942; Winter, 1945 (36 pgs.)
1942-Dell-(68 pgs.) 15.00 44.00 110.00
1-(1945)-Has 3 adaptations from American history; Kiefer, Schrotter & Webb-a 10.00 30.00 75.00

AMERICA MENACED!
Vital Publications: 1950 (Paper-c)
nn-Anti-communism estimated value... 200.00

AMERICAN, THE
Dark Horse Comics: July, 1987 - No. 8, 1989 ($1.50/$1.75, B&W)
1-8: ($1.50) 1.50
Collection ($5.95, B&W)-Reprints 2.00 6.00
Special 1 (1990, $2.25, B&W) 2.25

AMERICAN AIR FORCES, THE (See A-1 Comics)
William H. Wise(Flying Cadet Publ. Co./Hasan(No.1)/Life's Romances/ Magazine Ent. No. 5 on): Sept-Oct, 1944-No. 4, 1945; No. 5, 1951-No. 12, 1954
1-Article by Zack Mosley, creator of Smilin' Jack 12.00 36.00 90.00
2-4 7.50 22.50 52.00

NOTE: *All part comic, part magazine. Art by **Whitney, Chas. Quinlan, H. C. Kiefer,** and **Tony Dipreta.***

5(A-1 45)(Formerly Jet Powers), 6(A-1 54), 7(A-1 58), 8(A-1 65), 9(A-1 67), 10(A-1 74), 11(A-1 79), 12(A-1 91) 5.70 17.00 34.00

NOTE: ***Powell** c/a-5-12.*

AMERICAN COMICS
Theatre Giveaways (Liberty Theatre, Grand Rapids, Mich. known): 1940's
Many possible combinations. "Golden Age" superhero comics with new cover added and given away at theaters. Following known: Superman #59, Capt. Marvel #20, Capt. Marvel Jr. #5, Action

American Flagg! #16 © FC

American Splendor: Transatlantic Comics #1 © Harvey Pekar

America's Best Comics #12 © Nedor

GD25 FN65 NM94

#33, Classics Comics #8, Whiz #39. Value would vary with book and should be 70-80 percent of the original.

AMERICAN FLAGG! (See First Comics Graphic Novel 3,9,12,21 & Howard Chaykin's..)
First Comics: Oct, 1983 - No. 50, Mar, 1988

1-Chaykin-c/a begins 2.00
2-50: 21-27-Alan Moore scripts. 31-Origin Bob Violence 1.00
Special 1 (11/86)-Introduces Chaykin's Time² 1.50

AMERICAN FREAK: A TALE OF THE UN-MEN
DC Comics (Vertigo): Feb, 1994 - No. 5, Jun, 1994 ($1.95, mini-series, mature)

1-5 2.00

AMERICAN GRAPHICS
Henry Stewart: No. 1, 1954; No. 2, 1957 (25¢)

1-The Maid of the Mist, The Last of the Eries (Indian Legends of Niagara) (sold at Niagara Falls) 8.50 26.00 60.00
2-Victory at Niagara & Laura Secord (Heroine of the War of 1812) 5.70 17.00 38.00

AMERICAN INDIAN, THE (See Picture Progress)

AMERICAN LIBRARY
David McKay Publ.: 1943 - No. 6, 1944 (15¢, 68 pgs., B&W, text & pictures)

nn (#1)-Thirty Seconds Over Tokyo (movie) 32.00 96.00 240.00
nn (#2)-Guadalcanal Diary; painted-c (only 10¢) 24.00 72.00 180.00
3-6: 3-Look to the Mountain. 4-Case of the Crooked Candle (Perry Mason). 5-Duel in the Sun. 6-Wingate's Raiders 11.00 32.00 80.00

AMERICAN: LOST IN AMERICA, THE
Dark Horse Comics: July, 1992 - No. 4, Oct, 1992 ($2.50, limited series)

1-4: 1-Dorman painted-c. 2-Joe Phillips painted-c. 3-Mignola-c. 4-Jim Lee-c. 2.50

AMERICAN SPLENDOR: COMIC-CON COMICS
Dark Horse Comics: Aug, 1996 ($2.95, B&W, one-shot)

1-H. Pekar script 3.00

AMERICAN SPLENDOR: MUSIC COMICS
Dark Horse Comics: Nov, 1997 ($2.95, B&W, one-shot)

nn-H. Pekar-s/Sacco-a; r/Village Voice jazz strips 3.00

AMERICAN SPLENDOR: ODDS AND ENDS
Dark Horse Comics: Dec, 1997 ($2.95, B&W, one-shot)

1-H. Pekar script 2.95

AMERICAN SPLENDOR: ON THE JOB
Dark Horse Comics: May, 1997 ($2.95, B&W, one-shot)

1-H. Pekar script 2.95

AMERICAN SPLENDOR SPECIAL: A STEP OUT OF THE NEST
Dark Horse Comics: Aug, 1994 ($2.95, B&W, one-shot)

1-H. Pekar script 3.00

AMERICAN SPLENDOR: TRANSATLANTIC COMICS
Dark Horse Comics: July, 1998 ($2.95, B&W, one-shot)

1-"American Splendour" on cover; Pekar script 3.00

AMERICAN SPLENDOR: WINDFALL
Dark Horse Comics: Sept, 1995 - No. 2, Oct,1995 ($3.95, B&W, limited series)

1,2-Pekar script 4.00

AMERICAN TAIL: FIEVEL GOES WEST, AN
Marvel Comics: Early Jan, 1992 - No. 3, Early Feb, 1992 ($1.00, limited series)

1-3-Adapts Universal animated movie; Wildman-a 1.50

AMERICAN WOMAN
Antarctic Press (Barrage Studios): Jun, 1998 - Present ($2.95)

1,2: 1-Denham-s/a. 2-Stockton-s 2.95

GD25 FN65 NM94

AMERICA'S BEST COMICS
Nedor/Better/Standard Publications: Feb, 1942; No. 2, Sept, 1942 - No. 31, July, 1949 (New logo with #9)

1-The Woman in Red, Black Terror, Captain Future, Doc Strange, The Liberator, & Don Davis, Secret Ace begin 200.00 600.00 1700.00
2-Origin The American Eagle; The Woman in Red ends 77.00 231.00 650.00
3-Pyroman begins (11/42, 1st app.; also see Startling Comics #18, 12/42) 59.00 177.00 500.00
4-6: 5-Last Capt. Future (not in #4); Lone Eagle app. 6-American Crusader app. 46.00 138.00 390.00
7-Hitler, Mussolini & Hirohito-c 59.00 177.00 500.00
8-Last Liberator 43.00 129.00 350.00
9-The Fighting Yank begins; The Ghost app. 50.00 150.00 425.00
10-21: 10-Flag-c. 11-Hirohito & Tojo-c. (10/44) 14-American Eagle ends. 21-Infinity-c. 41.00 123.00 325.00
22-Capt. Future app. 39.00 117.00 290.00
23-Miss Masque begins; last Doc Strange 43.00 129.00 360.00
24-Miss Masque bondage-c 42.00 126.00 340.00
25-Last Fighting Yank; Sea Eagle app. 36.00 108.00 270.00
26-31: 26-The Phantom Detective & The Silver Knight app.; Frazetta text illo & some panels in Miss Masque. 27,28-Commando Cubs. 27-Doc Strange. 28-Tuska Black Terror. 29-Last Pyroman 36.00 108.00 270.00

NOTE: *American Eagle not in 3, 8, 9, 13. Fighting Yank not in 10, 12. Liberator not in 2, 6, 7. Pyroman not in 9, 11, 14-16, 23, 25-27.* ***Schomburg (Xela)*** *c-5, 7-31. Bondage c-18, 24.*

AMERICA'S BEST TV COMICS (TV)
American Broadcasting Co. (Prod. by Marvel Comics): 1967 (25¢, 68 pgs.)

1-Spider-Man, Fantastic Four (by Kirby/Ayers), Casper, King Kong, George of the Jungle, Journey to the Center of the Earth stories (promotes new TV cartoon show) 9.00 27.00 90.00

AMERICA'S BIGGEST COMICS BOOK
William H. Wise: 1944 (196 pgs., one-shot)

1-The Grim Reaper, The Silver Knight, Zudo, the Jungle Boy, Commando Cubs, Thunderhoof app. 39.00 117.00 295.00

AMERICA'S FUNNIEST COMICS
William H. Wise: 1944 - No. 2, 1944 (15¢, 80 pgs.)

nn(#1), 2 25.00 74.00 185.00

AMERICA'S GREATEST COMICS
Fawcett Publications: May?, 1941 - No. 8, Summer, 1943 (15¢, 100 pgs., soft cardboard-c)

1-Bulletman, Spy Smasher, Capt. Marvel, Minute Man & Mr. Scarlet begin; Classic Mac Raboy-c. 1st time that Fawcett's major super-heroes appear together as a group on a cover. Fawcett's 1st squarebound comic. 259.00 777.00 2200.00
2 129.00 387.00 1100.00
3 91.00 273.00 775.00
4,5: 4-Commando Yank begins; Golden Arrow, Ibis the Invincible & Spy Smasher cameo in Captain Marvel 69.00 207.00 585.00
6,7: 7-Balbo the Boy Magician app.; Captain Marvel, Bulletman cameo in Mr. Scarlet 63.00 189.00 535.00
8-Capt. Marvel Jr. & Golden Arrow app.; Spy Smasher x-over in Capt. Midnight; no Minute Man or Commando Yank 63.00 189.00 535.00

AMERICA'S SWEETHEART SUNNY (See Sunny, ...)

AMERICA VS. THE JUSTICE SOCIETY
DC Comics: Jan, 1985 - No. 4, Apr, 1985 ($1.00, limited series)

1-Double size; Alcala-a(i) in all 4.00
2-4: 3,4-Spectre cameo 3.00

AMERICOMICS
Americomics: April, 1983 - No. 6, Mar, 1984 ($2.00, Baxter paper/slick paper)

1-Intro/origin The Shade; Intro. The Slayer, Captain Freedom and The Liberty

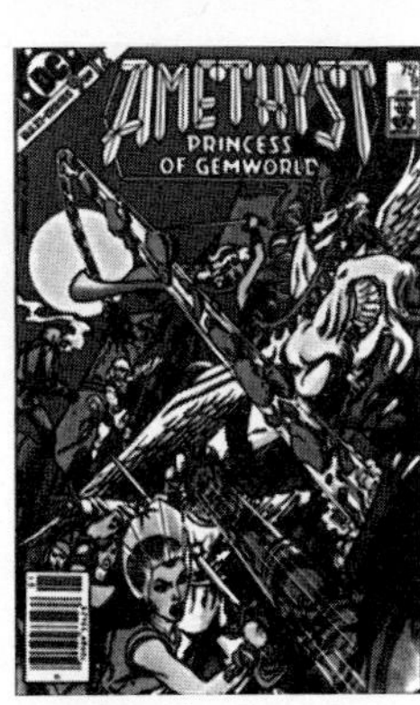

Amethyst, Princess of Gemworld #9 © DC

Anarky #2 © DC

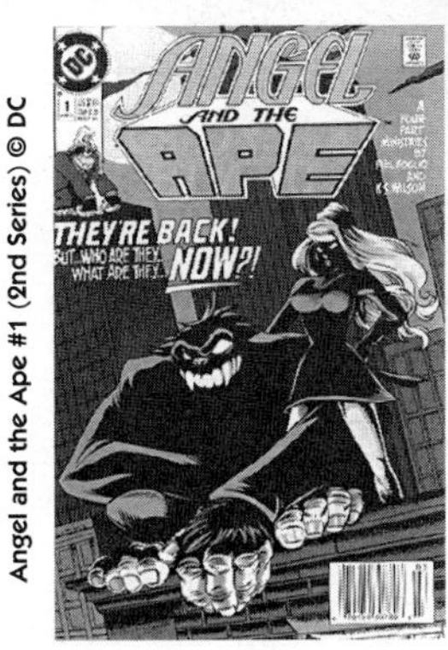

Angel and the Ape #1 (2nd Series) © DC

	GD25	FN65	NM94
Corps; Perez-c			3.00
1,2-2nd printings ($2.00)			2.00
2-6: 2-Messenger app. & 1st app. Tara on Jungle Island. 3-New & old Blue Beetle battle. 4-Origin Dragonfly & Shade. 5-Origin Commando D. 6-Origin the Scarlet Scorpion			2.00
Special 1 (8/83, $2.00)-Sentinels of Justice (Blue Beetle, Captain Atom, Nightshade & The Question)			3.00

AMETHYST
DC Comics: Jan, 1985 - No. 16, Aug, 1986 (75¢)

1-16: 8-Fire Jade's i.d. revealed			1.00
Special 1 (10/86, $1.25)			1.25

AMETHYST
DC Comics: Nov, 1987 - No. 4, Feb, 1988 ($1.25, limited series)

1-4			1.25

AMETHYST, PRINCESS OF GEMWORLD (See Legion of Super-Heroes #298)
DC Comics: May, 1983 - No. 12, Apr, 1984 (Maxi-series)

1-(60¢)			1.50
1,2-(35¢): Comic book tested in Austin & Kansas City	1.50	4.50	20.00
2-12: Perez-c(p) #6-11			1.00
Annual 1(9/84)			1.25

NOTE: *Perez c-4i, 5-11p.*

AMY RACECAR COLOR SPECIAL (See Stray Bullets)
El Capitán Books: July, 1997 ($2.95, one-shot)

1-David Laphan-a/scripts			3.00

ANARCHO DICTATOR OF DEATH (See Comics Novel)

ANARKY (See Batman)
DC Comics: May, 1997 - No. 4, Aug, 1997 ($2.50, limited series)

1-4			2.50

ANCHORS ANDREWS (The Saltwater Daffy)
St. John Publishing Co.: Jan, 1953 - No. 4, July, 1953
(Anchors the Saltwater... No. 4)

1-Canteen Kate by Matt Baker (9 pgs.)	17.00	52.00	130.00
2-4	5.70	17.00	35.00

ANDY & WOODY (See March of Comics No. 40, 55, 76)

ANDY BURNETT (TV, Disney)
Dell Publishing Co.: Dec, 1957

Four Color 865-Photo-c	9.00	27.00	100.00

ANDY COMICS (Formerly Scream Comics; becomes Ernie Comics)
Current Publications (Ace Magazines): No. 20, June, 1948-No. 21, Aug, 1948

20,21: Archie-type comic	5.70	17.00	35.00

ANDY DEVINE WESTERN
Fawcett Publications: Dec, 1950 - No. 2, 1951

1	50.00	150.00	425.00
2	39.00	117.00	310.00

ANDY GRIFFITH SHOW, THE (TV)(1st show aired 10/3/60)
Dell Publishing Co.: #1252, Jan-Mar, 1962 - #1341, Apr-Jun, 1962

Four Color 1252(#1), 1341-Photo-c	30.00	90.00	330.00

ANDY HARDY COMICS (See Movie Comics #3 by Fiction House)
Dell Publishing Co.: April, 1952 - No. 6, Sept-Nov, 1954

Four Color 389(#1)	2.70	8.00	30.00
Four Color 447,480,515,5,6	2.25	6.80	25.00
...& the New Automatic Gas Clothes Dryer (1952, 5x7-1/4", 16 pgs.) Bendix Giveaway (soft-c)	4.25	13.00	26.00

ANDY PANDA (Also see Crackajack Funnies #39, The Funnies, New Funnies & Walter Lantz...)
Dell Publishing Co.: 1943 - No. 56, Nov-Jan, 1961-62 (Walter Lantz)

	GD25	FN65	NM94
Four Color 25(#1, 1943)	45.00	135.00	495.00
Four Color 54(1944)	28.00	85.00	315.00
Four Color 85(1945)	15.00	44.00	160.00
Four Color 130(1946),154,198	9.00	27.00	100.00
Four Color 216,240,258,280,297	6.25	18.50	68.00
Four Color 326,345,358	3.80	11.50	40.00
Four Color 383,409	2.90	8.70	32.00
16(11-1/52-53) - 30	1.40	4.20	14.00
31-56	.90	2.70	9.00

(See March of Comics #5, 22, 79, & Super Book #4, 15, 27.)

A-NEXT (See Avengers)
Marvel Comics: Oct, 1998 - Present ($1.99)

1-Next generation of Avengers; Frenz-a			2.50
2-4: 2-Two covers. 3-Defenders app.			2.00

ANGEL
Dell Publishing Co.: Aug, 1954 - No. 16, Nov-Jan, 1958-59

Four Color 576(#1, 8/54)	2.25	6.75	25.00
2(5-7/55) - 16	1.50	4.50	12.00

ANGELA
Image Comics (Todd McFarlane Productions): Dec, 1994 - No. 3, Feb, 1995 ($2.95, limited series)

1-Gaiman scripts & Capullo-c/a in all; Spawn app.	1.40	4.20	14.00
2	1.20	3.60	12.00
3	1.20	3.60	12.00
Special Edition (1995)-Pirate Spawn-c	2.70	8.00	30.00
Special Edition (1995)-Angela-c	3.80	11.50	40.00
Trade paperback ($9.95, 1995) reprints #1-3 & Special Ed. w/additional pin-ups.			9.95

ANGELA/GLORY: RAGE OF ANGELS (See Glory/Angela: Rage of Angels)
Image Comics (Todd McFarlane Productions): Mar, 1996 ($2.50, one-shot)

1-Liefeld-c/Cruz-a(p); Darkchylde preview flip book		2.00	6.00
1-Variant-c		2.00	6.00

ANGEL AND THE APE (Meet Angel No. 7) (See Limited Collector's Edition C-34 & Showcase No. 77)
National Periodical Publications: Nov-Dec, 1968 - No. 6, Sept-Oct, 1969

1-(11-12/68)-Not Wood-a	3.50	10.50	35.00
2-6-Wood inks in all	2.50	7.50	22.00

ANGEL AND THE APE (2nd Series)
DC Comics: Mar, 1991 - No. 4, June, 1991 ($1.00, limited series)

1-4			1.00

ANGEL FIRE
Crusade Comics: June, 1997 - No. 3, Oct, 1997 ($2.95, limited series)

1-3: 1-(3 variant covers). 3-B&W			2.95

ANGEL LOVE
DC Comics: Aug, 1986 - No. 8, Mar, 1987 (75¢, limited series)

1-8			1.00
Special 1 (1987, $1.25, 52 pgs.)			1.25

ANGEL OF LIGHT, THE (See The Crusaders)

ANIMA
DC Comics: Mar, 1994 - No. 15, July, 1995 ($1.75/$1.95/$2.25)

1-6			1.75
7-(9/94)-Begin $1.95-c; Zero Hour x-over			2.00
0,8-14: 0-(10/94). 8-(11/94)			2.00
15-Begin $2.25-c			2.25

ANIMAL ADVENTURES
Timor Publications/Accepted Publ. (reprints): Dec, 1953 - No. 3, May?, 1954

Animal Antics #13 © DC

Animal Man #13 © DC

Animal Mystic Water Wars #5 © Greg Williams

GD25 FN65 NM94

1-Funny animal 5.00 15.00 30.00
2,3: 2-Featuring Soopermutt (2/54) 3.60 9.00 18.00
1-3 (reprints, nd) 1.60 4.00 8.00

ANIMAL ANTICS (Movie Town... No. 24 on)
National Periodical Publ: Mar-Apr, 1946 - No. 23, Nov-Dec, 1949 (All 52 pgs.?)

1-Raccoon Kids begins by Otto Feur; some-c by Grossman; Seaman Sy Wheeler by Kelly in some issues 43.00 129.00 350.00
2 23.00 70.00 175.00
3-10: 10-Post-c/a 14.00 42.00 105.00
11-23: 14,15,18,19-Post-a 9.30 28.00 70.00

ANIMAL COMICS
Dell Publishing Co.: Dec-Jan, 1941-42 - No. 30, Dec-Jan, 1947-48

1-1st Pogo app. by Walt Kelly (Dan Noonan art in most issues) 88.00 264.00 900.00
2-Uncle Wiggily begins 44.00 132.00 450.00
3,5 32.00 96.00 320.00
4,6,7-No Pogo 19.00 57.00 190.00
8-10 23.00 69.00 230.00
11-15 14.00 42.00 140.00
16-20 9.50 28.50 95.00
21-30: 25-30- "Jigger" by John Stanley 7.00 21.00 70.00
NOTE: ***Dan Noonan** a-18-30. **Gollub** art in most later issues; c-29, 30. **Kelly** c-7-26.*

ANIMAL CRACKERS (Also see Adventures of Patoruzu)
Green Publ. Co./Norlen/Fox Feat.(Hero Books): 1946; No. 31, July, 1950; No. 9, 1959

1-Super Cat begins (1st app.) 13.00 40.00 100.00
2 7.15 21.50 50.00
3-10 (Exist?) 4.00 11.00 22.00
31(Fox)-Formerly My Love Secret 5.35 16.00 32.00
9(1959-Norlen)-Infinity-c 3.00 7.50 15.00
nn, nd ('50s), no publ.; infinity-c 3.00 7.50 15.00

ANIMAL FABLES
E. C. Comics (Fables Publ. Co.): July-Aug, 1946 - No. 7, Nov-Dec, 1947

1-Freddy Firefly (clone of Human Torch), Korky Kangaroo, Petey Pig, Danny Demon begin 36.00 108.00 270.00
2-Aesop Fables begin 23.00 68.00 170.00
3-6 19.00 56.00 140.00
7-Origin Moon Girl 52.00 156.00 440.00

ANIMAL FAIR (Fawcett's...)
Fawcett Publications: Mar, 1946 - No. 11, Feb, 1947

1 21.00 64.00 160.00
2 10.00 30.00 75.00
3-6 7.50 22.50 52.00
7-11 5.70 17.00 38.00

ANIMAL FUN
Premier Magazines: 1953 (25¢, came w/glasses)

1-(3-D)-Ziggy Pig, Silly Seal, Billy & Buggy Bear 31.00 92.00 230.00

ANIMAL MAN (See Action Comics #552, 553, DC Comics Presents #77, 78, Secret Origins #39, Strange Adventures #180 & Wonder Woman #267, 268)
DC Comics (Vertigo imprint #57 on): Sept, 1988 - No. 89, Nov, 1995 ($1.25/$1.50/$1.75/$1.95/$2.25, mature)

1-Grant Morrison scripts begin, ends #26 5.00
2-Superman cameo 3.00
3,4 2.00
5-10: 6-Invasion tie-in. 9-Manhunter-c/story 1.50
11-26: 11-Begin $1.50-c; 24-Arkham Asylum story; Bizarro Superman app. 25-Inferior Five app. 26-Morrison apps. in story; part photo-c (of Morrison?) 1.50
27-49,51-55,57-59: 41-Begin $1.75-c, end #59 1.50
50-($2.95, 52 pgs.)-Last issue w/Veitch scripts 2.00
56-($3.50, 68 pgs.) 3.50
60-82: 60-Begin $1.95-c. 68-Photo-c. 71-Sutton-a(i) 2.00
83-89: 83-Begin $2.25-c 2.25
Annual 1 (1993, $3.95, 68 pgs.)-Bolland-c; Children's Crusade Pt. 3 4.00
NOTE: ***Bolland** c-1-63.*

ANIMAL MYSTIC (See Dark One...)
Cry For Dawn/Sirius: 1993 - No. 4, 1995 ($2.95?/$3.50, B&W)

1 2.25 6.80 25.00
1-Alternate 4.50 13.50 50.00
1-2nd printing 5.00
2 2.20 6.25 22.00
2,3-2nd prints (Sirius) 4.00
3 1.00 3.00 10.00
4-Color poster insert, Linsner-s 1.00 3.00 10.00
TPB ($14.95) r/ 14.95

ANIMAL MYSTIC WATER WARS
Sirius: 1996 - Present ($2.95, limited series)

1-6-Dark One-c/a/scripts 3.00

ANIMAL WORLD, THE (Movie)
Dell Publishing Co.: No. 713, Aug, 1956

Four Color 713 2.75 8.00 30.00

ANIMANIACS (TV)
DC Comics: May, 1995 - Present ($1.50/$1.75/$1.95/$1.99)

1-12 1.50
13-31: 13-Manga issue. 19-X-Files parody; Miran Kim-c; Adlard-a (4 pgs.) 26-E.C. parody-c 1.75
32-40: 32-Begin $1.95-c. 34-Xena parody 1.95
41-45: 41-Begin $1.99-c 1.99
A Christmas Special (12/94, $1.50, "1" on-c) 1.50

ANIMATED COMICS
E. C. Comics: No date given (Summer, 1947?)

1 (Rare) 62.00 186.00 525.00

ANIMATED FUNNY COMIC TUNES (See Funny Tunes)

ANIMATED MOVIE-TUNES (Movie Tunes No. 3)
Margood Publishing Corp. (Timely): Fall, 1945 - No. 2, Sum, 1946

1,2-Super Rabbit, Ziggy Pig & Silly Seal 17.00 51.00 130.00

ANIMAX
Marvel Comics (Star Comics): Dec, 1986 - No. 4, June, 1987

1-4: Based on toys 2.00

ANNE RICE'S THE MUMMY OR RAMSES THE DAMNED
Millennium Publications: Oct, 1990 - No. 12, 1991 ($2.50, limited series)

1-12: Adapts novel; Mooney-p in all 2.50

ANNETTE (Disney, TV)
Dell Publishing Co.: No. 905, May, 1958; No. 1100, May, 1960 (Mickey Mouse Club)

Four Color 905-Annette Funicello photo-c 26.00 78.00 285.00
Four Color 1100-...'s Life Story (Movie); A. Funicello photo-c 21.00 63.00 230.00

ANNEX
Marvel Comics: Aug, 1994 - No. 4, Nov, 1994 ($1.75)

1-4: 1-Spider-Man app. 1.75

ANNIE
Marvel Comics Group: Oct, 1982 - No. 2, Nov, 1982 (60¢)

1,2-Movie adaptation 1.50
Treasury Edition ($2.00, tabloid size) 1.20 3.60 12.00

ANNIE OAKLEY (See Tessie The Typist #19, Two-Gun Kid & Wild Western)
Marvel/Atlas Comics(MPI No. 1-4/CDS No. 5 on): Spring, 1948 - No. 4, 11/48;

A-1 Comics #49 © ME

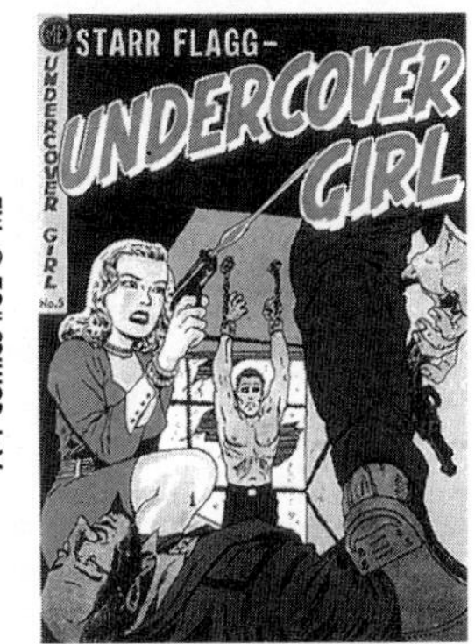

A-1 Comics #62 © ME

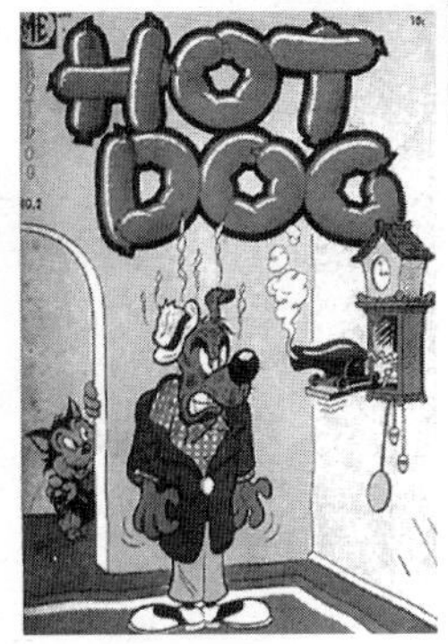

A-1 Comics #115 © ME

	GD25	FN65	NM94

No. 5, 6/55 - No. 11, 6/56

1 (1st Series, 1948)-Hedy Devine app.	39.00	117.00	310.00
2 (7/48, 52 pgs.)-Kurtzman-a, "Hey Look", 1 pg; Intro. Lana; Hedy Devine app; Captain Tootsie by Beck	24.00	72.00	180.00
3,4	20.00	60.00	150.00
5 (2nd Series, 1955)-Reinman-a ; Maneely-c	14.00	42.00	105.00
6-9: 6,8-Woodbridge-a. 9-Williamson-a (4 pgs.)	11.00	32.00	80.00
10,11: 11-Severin-c	9.30	28.00	70.00

ANNIE OAKLEY AND TAGG (TV)
Dell Publishing Co./Gold Key: 1953 - No. 18, Jan-Mar, 1959; July, 1965 (Gail Davis photo-c #3 on)

Four Color 438 (#1)	14.00	41.00	150.00
Four Color 481,575 (#2,3)	8.00	23.00	85.00
4(7-9/55)-10	6.40	19.00	70.00
11-18(1-3/59)	5.50	16.50	60.00
1(7/65-Gold Key)-Photo-c (c-r/#6)	4.50	13.50	50.00

NOTE: ***Manning** a-13. Photo back c-4, 9, 11.*

ANOTHER WORLD (See Strange Stories From...)

ANTARCTIC PRESS JAM 1996
Antarctic Press: Dec, 1996 ($2.95, one-shot)

1			2.95

ANTHRO (See Showcase #74)
National Periodical Publications: July-Aug, 1968 - No. 6, July-Aug, 1969

1-(7-8/68)-Howie Post-a in all	4.20	12.60	42.00
2-6: 6-Wood-c/a (inks)	2.50	7.50	25.00

ANTONY AND CLEOPATRA (See Ideal, a Classical Comic)

ANYTHING GOES
Fantagraphics Books: Oct, 1986 - No. 6, 1987 ($2.00, #1-5 color & B&W/#6 B&W, limited series)

1-Flaming Carrot app. (1st in color?); G. Kane-c			2.00
2-6: 2-Miller-c(p); Alan Moore scripts; early Sam Kieth-a (2 pgs.). 3-Capt. Jack, Cerebus app.; Cerebus-c by N. Adams. 4-Perez-c. 5-2nd color Teenage Mutant Ninja Turtles app.			2.00

A-1
Marvel Comics (Epic Comics): 1992 - No. 4, 1993 ($5.95, limited ser., mature)

1-4: 3-Bisley-c		2.00	6.00

A-1 COMICS (A-1 appears on covers No. 1-17 only)(See individual title listings.) (1st two issues not numbered.)
Life's Romances Publ.-No. 1/Compix/Magazine Ent.: 1944 - No. 139, Sept-Oct, 1955 (No #2)

(See Individual Alphabetical listings for prices)

nn-Kerry Drake, Johnny Devildog, Rocky, Streamer Kelly (slightly large size)
9-Texas Slim (all)
11-Teena; Ogden Whitney-c
12,15-Teena
13-Guns of Fact & Fiction (1948). Used in **SOTI**, pg. 19; Ingels & Johnny Craig-a
16-Vacation Comics; The Pixies, Tom Tom, Flying Fredd, & Koko & Kola
18,20-Jimmy Durante; photo covers
19-Tim Holt #3; photo-c
22-Dick Powell (1949)-Photo-c
23-Cowboys and Indians #6; Doc Holiday-c/story
25-Fibber McGee & Molly (1949) (Radio)
26-Trail Colt #2-Ingels-c
28-Christmas-(Koko & Kola #6) ("50)
1-Dotty Dripple (1 pg.), Mr. Ex, Bush Berry, Rocky, Lew Loyal (20 pgs.)
2-8,10-Texas Slim & Dirty Dalton, The Corsair, Teddy Rich, Dotty Dripple, Inca Dinca, Tommy Tinker, Little Mexico & Tugboat Tim, The Masquerader & others. 7-Corsair-c/s. 8-Intro. Rodeo Ryan
14-Tim Holt Western Adventures #1 (1948)
17-Tim Holt #2; photo-c; last issue to carry A-1 on cover (9-10/48)
21-Joan of Arc (1949)-Movie adaptation; Ingrid Bergman photo-covers & interior photos; Whitney-a
24-Trail Colt #1-Frazetta-r in-Manhunt #13; Ingels-c; L. B. Cole-a
27-Ghost Rider #1(1950)-Origin
29-Ghost Rider #2-Frazetta-c (1950)
30-Jet Powers #1-Powell-a
32-Jet Powers #2
33-Muggsy Mouse #1('51)
35-Jet Powers #3-Williamson/Evans-a
37-Ghost Rider #5-Frazetta-c (1951)
39-Muggsy Mouse #3
41-Cowboys 'N' Indians #7 (1951)
43-Dogface Dooley #2
45-American Air Forces #5-Powell-c/a
47-Thun'da, King of the Congo #1-Frazetta-c/a('52)
50-Danger Is Their Business #11 ('52)-Powell-a
53-Dogface Dooley #4
55-U.S. Marines #5-Powell-a
56-Thun'da #2-Powell-c/a
58-American Air Forces #7-Powell-a
60-The U.S. Marines #6-Powell-a
62-Starr Flagg, Undercover Girl #5 (#1) reprinted from A-1 #24
65-American Air Forces #8-Powell-a
67-American Air Forces #9-Powell-a
69-Ghost Rider #9(10/52)
71-Ghost Rider #10(12/52)-Vs. Frankenstein
74-American Air Forces #10-Powell-a
76-Best of the West #7
78-Thun'da #4-Powell-c/a
80-Ghost Rider #12(6/52)-One-eyed Devil-c
83-Thun'da #5-Powell-c/a
84-Ghost Rider #13(7-8/53)
86-Thun'da #6-Powell-c/a
88-Bobby Benson's B-Bar-B Riders #20
90-Red Hawk #11(1953)-Powell-c/a
91-American Air Forces #12-Powell-a
93-Great Western #8('54)-Origin The Ghost Rider; Powell-a
95-Muggsy Mouse #4
96-Cave Girl #12, with Thun'da; Powell-c/a
99-Muggsy Mouse #5
101-White Indian #12-Frazetta-a(r)
101-Dream Book of Romance #6 (4-6/54); Marlon Brando photo-c; Powell, Bolle, Guardineer-a
105-Great Western #9-Ghost Rider app.; Powell-a, 6 pgs.; Bolle-c
107-Hot Dog #1
108-Red Fox #15 (1954)-L.B. Cole c/a; Powell-a
110-Dream Book of Romance #8 (10/54)-Movie photo-c
112-Ghost Rider #14 ('54)
114-Dream Book of Love #2-Guardineer, Bolle-a; Piper Laurie, Victor Mature photo-c
118-Undercover Girl #7-Powell-c
120-Badmen of the West #2
121-Mysteries of Scotland Yard #1; reprinted from Manhunt (5 stories)
124-Dream Book of Romance #8 (10-11/54)
126-I'm a Cop #2-Powell-a
31-Ghost Rider #3-Frazetta-c & origin ('51)
34-Ghost Rider #4-Frazetta-c (1951)
36-Muggsy Mouse #2; Racist-c
38-Jet Powers #4-Williamson/Wood-a
40-Dogface Dooley #1('51)
42-Best of the West #1-Powell-a
44-Ghost Rider #6
46-Best of the West #2
48-Cowboys 'N' Indians #8
49-Dogface Dooley #3
51-Ghost Rider #7 ('52)
52-Best of the West #3
54-American Air Forces #6(8/52)-Powell-a
57-Ghost Rider #8
59-Best of the West #4
61-Space Ace #5(1953)-Guardineer-a
63-Manhunt #13-Frazetta
64-Dogface Dooley #5
66-Best of the West #5
68-U.S. Marines #7-Powell-a
70-Best of the West #6
72-U.S. Marines #8-Powell-a(3)
73-Thun'da #3-Powell-c/a
75-Ghost Rider #11(3/52)
77-Manhunt #14
79-American Air Forces #11-Powell-a
81-Best of the West #8
82-Cave Girl #11(1953)-Powell-c/a; origin (#1)
85-Best of the West #9
87-Best of the West #10(9-10/53)
89-Home Run #3-Powell-a; Stan Musial photo-c
92-Dream Book of Romance #5-Photo-c; Guardineer-a
94-White Indian #11-Frazetta-a(r); Powell-c
97-Best of the West #11
98-Undercover Girl #6-Powell-c
100-Badmen of the West #1-Meskin-a(?)
103-Best of the West #12-Powell-a
104-White Indian #13-Frazetta-a(r) ('54)
106-Dream Book of Love #1 (6-7/54) -Powell, Bolle-a; Montgomery Clift, Donna Reed photo-c
109-Dream Book of Romance #7 (7-8/54). Powell-a; movie photo-c
111-I'm a Cop #1 ('54); drug mention story; Powell-a
113-Great Western #10; Powell-a
115-Hot Dog #3
116-Cave Girl #13-Powell-c/a
117-White Indian #14
119-Straight Arrow's Fury #1 (origin); Fred Meagher-c/a
122-Black Phantom #1 (11/54)
123-Dream Book of Love #3 (10-11/54)-Movie photo-c
125-Cave Girl #14-Powell-c/a
127-Great Western #11('54)-Powell-a

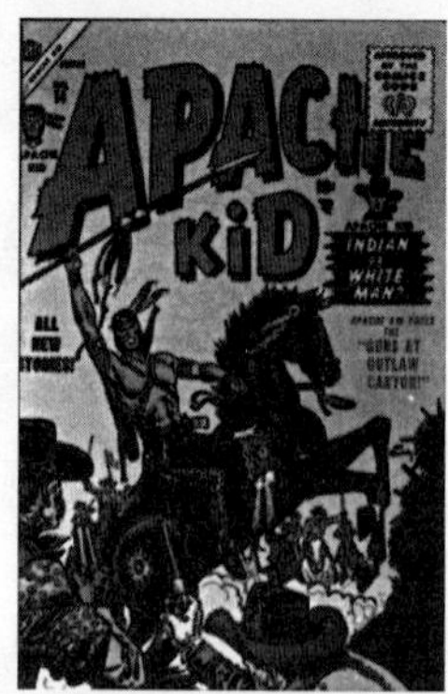

Apache Kid #14 © CPS

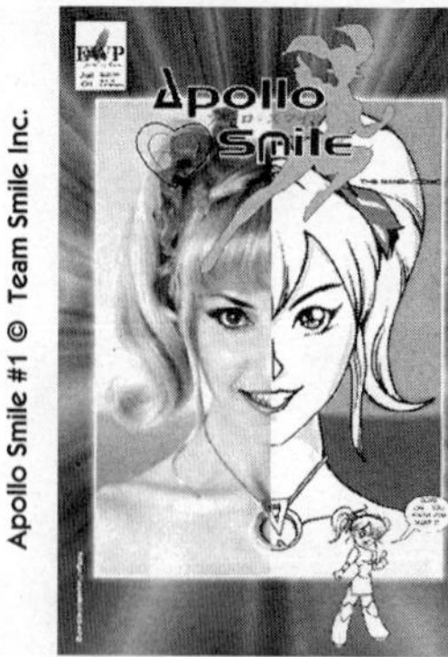

Apollo Smile #1 © Team Smile Inc.

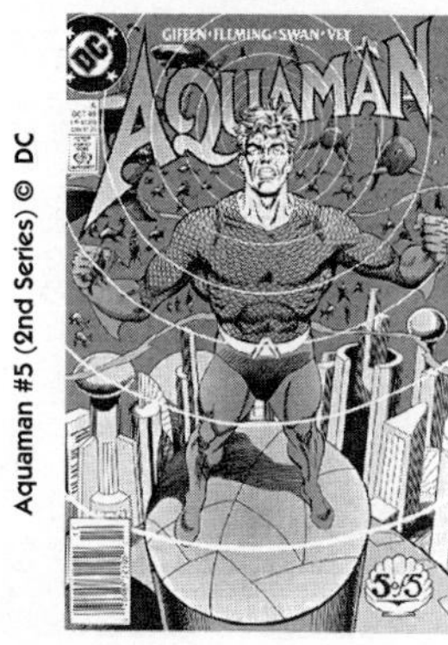

Aquaman #5 (2nd Series) © DC

GD25 FN65 NM94

128-I'm a Cop #3-Powell-a
129-The Avenger #1('55)-Powell-c
130-Strongman #1-Powell-a (2-3/55)
131-The Avenger #2('55)-Powell-c/a
132-Strongman #2
133-The Avenger #3-Powell-c/a
134-Strongman #3
135-White Indian #15
136-Hot Dog #4
137-Africa #1-Powell-c/a(4)
138-The Avenger #4-Powell-c/a
139-Strongman #4-Powell-a

NOTE: ***Bolle** a-110. Photo-c-17-22, 89, 92, 101, 106, 109, 110, 114, 123, 124.*

APACHE
Fiction House Magazines: 1951

1 18.00 54.00 135.00
I.W. Reprint No. 1-r/#1 above 2.50 7.50 20.00

APACHE HUNTER
Creative Pictorials: 1954 (18 pgs. in color) (promo copy) (saddle stitched)

nn-Severin, Heath stories 15.00 44.00 110.00

APACHE KID (Formerly Reno Browne; Western Gunfighters #20 on)
(Also see Two-Gun Western & Wild Western)
Marvel/Atlas Comics(MPC No. 53-10/CPS No. 11 on): No. 53, 12/50 - No. 10, 1/52; No. 11, 12/54 - No. 19, 4/56

53(#1)-Apache Kid & his horse Nightwind (origin), Red Hawkins by Syd Shores begins 29.00 88.00 220.00
2(2/51) 14.00 42.00 105.00
3-5 9.30 28.00 70.00
6-10 (1951-52): 7-Russ Heath-a 7.85 23.50 55.00
11-19 (1954-56) 6.50 19.50 45.00

NOTE: ***Heath** a-7. c-11, 13. **Maneely** a-53; c-53(#1), 12, 14-16. **Powell** a-14. **Severin** c-17.*

APACHE MASSACRE (See Chief Victorio's...)

APACHE TRAIL
Steinway/America's Best: Sept, 1957 - No. 4, June, 1958

1 9.30 28.00 65.00
2-4: 2-Tuska-a 5.70 17.00 38.00

APE (Magazine)
Dell Publishing Co.: 1961 (52 pgs., B&W)

1-Comics and humor 2.25 6.80 25.00

APOLLO SMILE
Eagle Wing Press: July, 1998 - Present ($2.95)

1,2-Manga 3.00

APPARITION
Caliber Comics: 1995 ($3.95, 52 pgs., B&W)

1 ($3.95) 4.00
V2#1-6 ($2.95) 3.00
Visitations 4.00

APPLESEED
Eclipse Comics: Sept, 1988 - Book 4, Vol. 4, Aug, 1991 ($2.50/$2.75/$3.50, 52/68 pgs, B&W)

Book One, Vol. 1 ($2.50) 3.00
Book One, Vol. 2-5: 5-(1/89, $2.75 cover) 3.00
Book Two, Vol. 1(2/89) -5(7/89): Art Adams-c 3.00
Book Three, Vol. 1(8/89) -4 ($2.75) 3.00
Book Three, Vol. 5 ($3.50) 3.00
Book Four, Vol. 1 (1/91) - 4 (8/91) ($3.50, 68 pgs.) 3.00

APPLESEED DATABOOK
Dark Horse Comics: Apr, 1994 - No. 2, May, 1994 ($3.50, B&W, limited series)

1,2: 1-Flip book format 3.50

APPROVED COMICS
St. John Publishing Co. (Most have no c-price): March, 1954 - No. 12, Aug, 1954 (All painted-c)

1-The Hawk #5-r 9.30 28.00 65.00
2-Invisible Boy (3/54)-Origin; Saunders-c 15.00 44.00 110.00

GD25 FN65 NM94

3-Wild Boy of the Congo #11-r (4/54) 9.30 28.00 65.00
4,5: 4-Kid Cowboy-r. 5-Fly Boy-r 9.30 28.00 65.00
6-Daring Adv.-r (5/54); Krigstein-a(2); Baker-c 11.00 32.00 80.00
7-The Hawk #6-r 9.30 28.00 65.00
8-Crime on the Run (6/54); Powell-a; Saunders-c 9.30 28.00 65.00
9-Western Bandit Trails #3-r, with new-c; Baker-c/a 11.00 32.00 80.00
11-Fightin' Marines #3-r (8/54); Canteen Kate app; Baker-c/a 11.00 34.00 85.00
12-North West Mounties #4-r(8/54); new Baker-c 11.00 34.00 85.00

AQUAMAN (See Adventure #260, Brave & the Bold, DC Comics Presents #5, DC Special #28, DC Special Series #1, DC Super Stars #7, Detective, Justice League of America, More Fun #73, Showcase #30-33, Super DC Giant, Super Friends, and World's Finest Comics)

AQUAMAN (1st Series)
National Periodical Publications/DC Comics: Jan-Feb, 1962 - #56, Mar-Apr, 1971; #57, Aug-Sept,1977 - #63, Aug-Sept, 1978

1-(1-2/62)-Intro. Quisp 54.00 162.00 650.00
2 27.00 81.00 270.00
3-5 15.00 45.00 150.00
6-10 9.00 27.00 95.00
11-20: 11-1st app. Mera. 18-Aquaman weds Mera; JLA cameo 8.00 24.00 80.00
21-32: 23-Birth of Aquababy. 26-Huntress app.(3-4/66). 29-1st app. Ocean Master, Aquaman's step-brother. 30-Batman & Superman-c & cameo 4.50 13.50 45.00
33-1st app. Aqua-Girl (see Adventure #266) 5.00 15.00 50.00
34-40: 40-Jim Aparo's 1st DC work (8/68) 2.50 7.60 28.00
41-47,49 1.80 5.40 18.00
48-Origin reprinted 2.00 6.00 20.00
50-52-Deadman by Neal Adams 4.00 12.00 45.00
53-56('71): 56-1st app. Crusader .85 2.60 7.00
57('77)-63: 58-Origin retold 5.00

NOTE: ***Aparo** a-40-45, 46p, 47-59; c-58-63. **Nick Cardy** c-1-39. **Newton** a-60-63.*

AQUAMAN (1st limited series)
DC Comics: Feb, 1986 - No. 4, May, 1986 (75¢, limited series)

1-New costume; 1st app. Nuada of Thierna Na Oge. 4.00
2-4: 3-Retelling of Aquaman & Ocean Master's origins. 3.00
Special 1 (1988, $1.50, 52 pgs.) 3.00

NOTE: ***Craig Hamilton** c/a-1-4p. **Russell** c-2-4i.*

AQUAMAN (2nd limited series)
DC Comics: June, 1989 - No. 5, Oct, 1989 ($1.00, limited series)

1-5: Giffen plots/breakdowns; Swan-a(p). 1.25
Special 1 (Legend of..., $2.00, 1989, 52 pgs.)-Giffen plots/breakdowns; Swan-a(p). 2.00

AQUAMAN (2nd Series)
DC Comics: Dec, 1991 - No. 13, Dec, 1992 ($1.00/$1.25)

1-5 2.00
6-13: 6-Begin $1.25-c. 9-Sea Devils app. 1.75

AQUAMAN (3rd Series)(Also see Atlantis Chronicles)
DC Comics: Aug, 1994 - Present ($1.50/$1.75/$1.95/$1.99)

1-(8/94)-Peter David scripts begin; reintro Dolphin .85 2.60 7.00
2-(9/94)-Aquaman loses hand .90 2.70 8.00
0-(10/94)-Aquaman replaces lost hand w/hook. .85 2.60 7.00
3-8: 3-(11/94)-Superboy-c/app. 4-Lobo app. 6-Deep Six app. 3.00
9-38: 9-Begin $1.75-c. 10-Green Lantern app. 11-Reintro Mera. 15-Reintro Kordax. 16-vs. JLA. 18-Reintro Ocean Master & Atlan (Aquaman's father). 19-Reintro Garth (Aqualad). 23-Ist app. Deep Blue (Neptune Perkins & Tsunami's daughter). 23,24-Neptune Perkins, Nuada, Tsunami, Arion, Power Girl, & The Sea Devils app. 26-Final Night. 28-Martian Manhunter-c/app. 29-Black Manta-c/app. 32-Swamp Thing-c/app. 37-Genesis x-over 2.00
39-42,44-46: 39-Begin $195-c. 41-Maxima-c/app. 44-G.A. Flash & Sentinel app.

Aquaman #47 (3rd Series) © DC

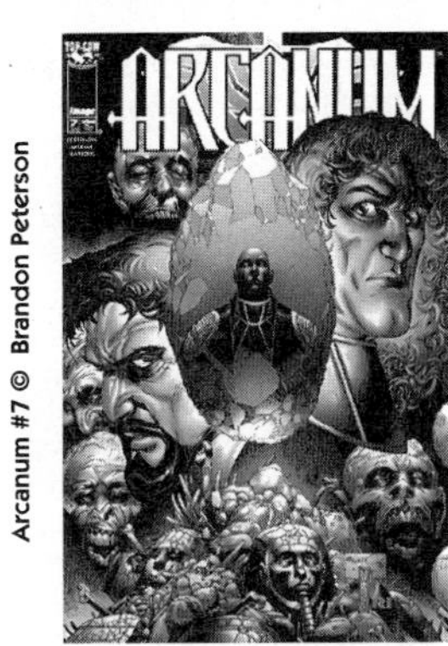

Arcanum #7 © Brandon Peterson

Archer & Armstrong #25 © VAL

GD25 FN65 NM94

1.95
43-Millennuim Giants x-over; Superman-c/app. 3.00
48-51: 48-Begin $1.99-c. 50-Larsen-s begins 1.99
#1,000,000 (11/98) 853rd Century x-over 2.00
Annual 1 (1995, $3.50)-Year One story 3.50
Annual 2 (1996, $2.95)-Legends of the Dead Earth story 3.00
Annual 3 (1997, $3.95)-Pulp Heroes story 4.00
Annual 4 (1998, $2.95)-Ghosts; Wrightson-c 2.95
...Secret Files 1 (12/98, $4.95) Origin-s and pin-ups 4.95
NOTE: ***Mignola** c-6.* ***Simonson** c-15.*

AQUAMAN: TIME & TIDE (3rd limited series) (Also see Atlantis Chronicles)
DC Comics: Dec, 1993 - No. 4, Mar, 1994 ($1.50, limited series)

1-4: Peter David scripts; origin retold. 3.00
Trade paperback ($9.95) 10.00

AQUANAUTS (TV)
Dell Publishing Co.: May - July, 1961

Four Color 1197-Photo-c 6.25 18.50 70.00

ARABIAN NIGHTS (See Cinema Comics Herald)

ARACHNOPHOBIA (Movie)
Hollywood Comics (Disney Comics): 1990 ($5.95, 68 pg. graphic novel)

nn-Adaptation of film; Spiegle-a 6.00
Comic edition ($2.95, 68 pgs.) 3.00

ARAKNIS
Mushroom Comics: 1995 - No. 4, 1996 ($2.50, limited series)

1,2 3.00
3,4: 3-w/pin-ups 2.50

ARAKNIS
Mushroom Comics: No. 0, Apr, 1996 - No. 2, 1996 ($2.95/$2.50)

0-(4/96, $2.95) 3.00
0-Special Edition 5.00
1,2: 1-Ongoing series (5/96) 2.50
1-Special Edition; polybagged w/certificate 10.00

ARAKNIS: RETRIBUTION
Morningstar Productions: May, 1997 ($2.50, unfinished limited series)

1-Ortiz Brothers-s/a 2.50

ARAK/SON OF THUNDER (See Warlord #48)
DC Comics: Sept, 1981 - No. 50, Nov, 1985

1-50: 1-Origin; 1st app. Angelica, Princess of White Cathay. 3-Intro Valda, The Iron Maiden. 12-Origin Valda. 20-Origin Angelica. 24,50-(52 pgs.) 1.00
Annual 1(10/84) 1.00

ARCANA (Also see Books of Magic limited & ongoing series and Mister E)
DC Comics (Vertigo): 1994 ($3.95, 68 pgs., annual)

1-Bolton painted-c; Children's Crusade/Tim Hunter story 4.00

ARCANUM
Image Comics (Top Cow Productions): Apr, 1997 - No. 8, Feb, 1998 ($2.50)

1/2 Gold Edition 10.00
1-Brandon Peterson-s/a(p); 4.00
1-Variant-c 4.00
2-8 2.50
3-Variant-c 3.50
4-American Ent. Ed. 3.00

ARCHANGEL (See Uncanny X-Men, X-Factor & X-Men)
Marvel Comics: Feb, 1996 ($2.50, B&W, one-shot)

1-Milligan story 2.50

ARCHER & ARMSTRONG

GD25 FN65 NM94

Valiant: July (June inside), 1992 - No. 26, Oct, 1994 ($2.50)

0-(7/92)-B. Smith-c/a; Reese-i assists 3.00
0-(Gold Logo) 6.00
1-(8/92)-Origin & 1st app. Archer; Miller-c; B. Smith/Layton-a 2.50
2-7: 2-2nd app. Turok(c/story); Smith/Layton-a; Simonson-c. 3,4-Smith-c&a(p) & scripts 2.50
8-($4.50, 52 pgs.)-Combined with Eternal Warrior #8; B. Smith-c/a & scripts; 1st app. Ivar the Time Walker 4.50
9-26: 10-2nd app. Ivar. 10,11-B. Smith-c. 21,22-Shadowman app. 22-w/bound-in trading card. 25-Eternal Warrior app. 26-Flip book w/Eternal Warrior #26 2.50

ARCHIE AMERICANA SERIES, BEST OF THE FORTIES
Archie Publications: 1991 ($10.95, trade paperback)

V1-r/early strips from 1940's; intro. by Steven King. 1.10 3.30 11.00

ARCHIE AMERICANA SERIES, BEST OF THE FIFTIES
Archie Publications: 1991 ($8.95, trade paperback)

V2-r/strips from 1950's; 1.20 3.60 12.00
2nd printing (1998, $9.95) 9.95

ARCHIE AMERICANA SERIES, BEST OF THE SIXTIES
Archie Publications: 1995 ($9.95, trade paperback)

V3-r/strips from 1960's; intro. by Frankie Avalon. 1.00 3.00 10.00

ARCHIE AND BIG ETHEL
Spire Christian Comics (Fleming H. Revell Co.): 1982 (69¢)

nn 5.00

ARCHIE & FRIENDS
Archie Comics: Dec, 1992 - Present ($1.25/$1.50/$1.75, quarterly/bi-monthly)

1-13 1.25
14-26: 14-Begin $1.50-c 1.50
27-33: 27-Begin $1.75-c 1.75

ARCHIE AND HIS GANG (Zeta Beta Tau Presents...)
Archie Publications: Dec. 1950 (St. Louis National Convention giveaway)

nn-Contains new cover stapled over Archie Comics #47 (11-12/50) on inside; produced for Zeta Beta Tau 13.00 40.00 100.00

ARCHIE AND ME (See Archie Giant Series Mag. #578, 591, 603, 616, 626)
Archie Publications: Oct, 1964 - No. 161, Feb, 1987

	GD25	FN65	NM94
1	14.00	42.00	140.00
2	7.00	21.00	70.00
3-5	3.80	11.40	38.00
6-10	2.50	7.50	20.00
11-20	1.60	4.85	13.00
21(6/68)-30: 26-X-Mas-c	1.00	3.00	10.00
31-42	.85	2.60	7.00
43-63-(All Giants): 43-(8/71). 63-(2/74)	1.20	3.60	12.00
64-99-(Regular size)			5.00
100-(4/78)	.85	2.60	7.00
101-120			3.00
121(8/80)-161			2.00

ARCHIE AND MR. WEATHERBEE
Spire Christian Comics (Fleming H. Revell Co.): 1980 (59¢)

nn 4.00

ARCHIE...ARCHIE ANDREWS, WHERE ARE YOU? (...Comics Digest #9, 10; ...Comics Digest Mag. No. 11 on)
Archie Publications: Feb, 1977 - Present (Digest size, 160-128 pgs., quarterly)

	GD25	FN65	NM94
1	1.40	4.20	14.00
2,3,5,7-9-N. Adams-a; 8-r-/origin The Fly by S&K. 9-Steel Sterling-r	1.00	3.00	10.00
4,6,10 ($1.00/$1.50): 17-Katy Keene story	.85	2.60	7.00
11-20		2.00	6.00

Archie Comics #26 © AP

Archie Comics #33 © AP

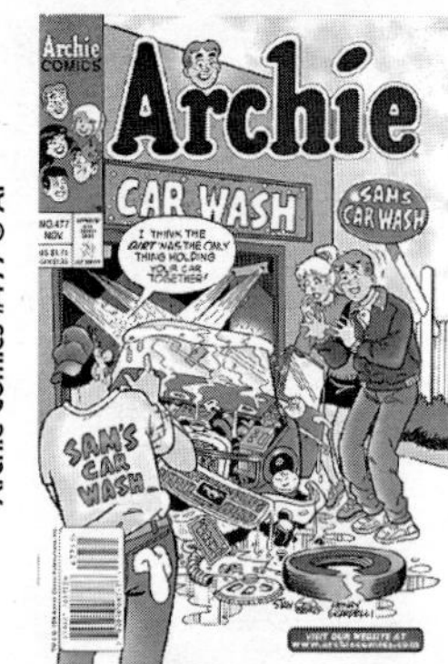

Archie Comics #477 © AP

	GD25	FN65	NM94
21-50,100			4.00
51-70			3.00
71-99			2.00
101-117: 113-Begin $1.95-c			1.95

ARCHIE AS PUREHEART THE POWERFUL (Also see Archie Giant Series #142, Jughead as Captain Hero, Life With Archie & Little Archie)
Archie Publications (Radio Comics): Sept, 1966 - No. 6, Nov, 1967

	GD25	FN65	NM94
1-Super hero parody	7.00	21.00	70.00
2	4.80	14.40	48.00
3-6	3.50	10.50	35.00

NOTE: *Evilheart cameos in all. Title: Archie As Pureheart the Powerful #1-3; ...As Capt. Pureheart-#4-6.*

ARCHIE AT RIVERDALE HIGH (See Archie Giant Series Magazine #573, 586, 604 & Riverdale High)
Archie Publications: Aug, 1972 - No. 113, Feb, 1987

	GD25	FN65	NM94
1	4.00	12.25	45.00
2	2.20	6.50	24.00
3-5	1.60	4.80	16.00
6-10	1.00	3.00	10.00
11-30		2.00	6.00
31(12/75)-50(12/77)			4.00
51-80,100 (12/84)			3.00
81(8/81)-99,101-114: 96-Anti-smoking issue			2.00

ARCHIE COMICS (Also see Christmas & Archie, Everything's..., Explorers of the Unknown, Jackpot, Little..., Oxydol-Dreft, Pep, Riverdale High, Teenage Mutant Ninja Turtles Adventures & To Riverdale and Back Again)

ARCHIE COMICS (Archie #114 on; 1st Teen-age comic; Radio show aired 6/2/45 by NBC)
MLJ Magazines No. 1-19/Archie Publ.No. 20 on: Winter, 1942-43 - No. 19, 3-4/46; No. 20, 5-6/46 - Present

	GD25	FN65	VF82	NM94
1 (Scarce)-Jughead, Veronica app.; 1st app. Mrs. Andrews	1045.00	3135.00	6270.00	11,500.00

	GD25	FN65	NM94
2	253.00	759.00	2400.00
3 (60 pgs.)(scarce)	212.00	636.00	1800.00
4,5: 4-Article about Archie radio series	112.00	336.00	950.00
6-10: 6-X-Mas-c. 7-1st definitive love triangle story	79.00	237.00	675.00
11-20: 15,17,18-Dotty & Ditto by Woggon. 16-Woggon-a	53.00	159.00	450.00
21-30: 23-Betty & Veronica by Woggon. 25-Woggon-a. 30-Coach Piffle app., a Coach Kleets prototype. 34-Pre-Dilton try-out (named Dilbert)	34.00	112.00	280.00
31-40	21.00	62.00	155.00
41-50	14.00	42.00	105.00
51-60: (1954) 51-Katy Keene app.	7.00	21.00	70.00
61-70 (1954): 65-70, Katy Keene app.	5.50	16.50	55.00
71-80: 72-74-Katy Keene app.	4.50	13.50	45.00
81-99: 94-1st Coach Kleets	3.50	10.50	35.00
100	4.80	14.40	48.00
101-130 (1962)	2.50	7.50	22.00
131-160	1.75	5.25	14.00
161(2/66)-199	1.10	3.30	9.00
200 (6/70)	1.20	3.60	12.00
201-230(11/73)	.85	2.60	7.00
231-260(3/77)			5.00
261-282			4.00
283(8/79)-Cover/story plugs "International Children's Appeal" which was a fraudulent charity, according to TV's 20/20 news program broadcast July 20, 1979			5.00
284-299,301-350			3.00
300(1/81)-Anniversary issue			5.00
351-399,401-466: 393-Infinity-c; 1st comic book printed on recycled paper. 423-Dan DeCarlo-c			2.00
400			4.00
467-480: 467-Begin $1.75-c; "A Storm Over Uniforms" x-over parts 3,4			1.75
Annual 1('50)-116 pgs. (Scarce)	152.00	456.00	1300.00
Annual 2('51)	76.00	228.00	650.00
Annual 3('52)	47.00	142.00	400.00
Annual 4,5(1953-54)	35.00	104.00	260.00
Annual 6-10(1955-59)	14.00	42.00	140.00
Annual 11-15(1960-65)	6.00	18.00	60.00
Annual 16-20(1966-70)	2.50	7.50	25.00
Annual 21-26(1971-75)	1.20	3.60	12.00
Annual Digest 27('75)	2.20	6.50	24.00
...28-30	1.60	4.80	16.00
...31-34	1.20	3.60	12.00
...35-40 (...Magazine #35 on)	.90	2.70	9.00
...41-65 ('94)			4.00
...66-69			2.00
...All-Star Specials(Winter '75, $1.25)-6 remaindered Archie comics rebound in each; titles: "The World of Giant Comics", "Giant Grab Bag of Comics", "Triple Giant Comics" & "Giant Spec. Comics	2.00	6.00	20.00
...And His Friends Help Raise Literacy Awareness In Mississippi nn (3/94)-Giveaway			3.00
...And the History of Electronics nn (5/90, 36 pgs.)-Radio Shack giveaway; Howard Bender-c/a			4.00
Mini-Comics (1970-Fairmont Potato Chips Giveaway-Miniature)(8 issues-nn's., 8 pgs. each)	1.40	4.20	14.00
Official Boy Scout Outfitter (1946, 9-1/2x6-1/2, 16 pgs.)-B. R. Baker Co. (Scarce)	43.00	129.00	350.00
Shoe Store giveaway (1948, Feb?)	14.00	42.00	105.00
Special Edition-Christmas With Archie 1(1/75)-Treasury (rare)	3.20	9.50	35.00

NOTE: ***Al Fagly** c-17-35. **Bob Montana** c-38, 41-50, 58, Annual 1-4. **Bill Woggon** c-53, 54.*

ARCHIE COMICS DIGEST (...Magazine No. 37-95)
Archie Publications: Aug, 1973 - Present (Small size, 160-128 pgs.)

	GD25	FN65	NM94
1	6.25	18.50	70.00
2	3.20	9.50	35.00
3-5	2.25	6.80	25.00
6-10	1.40	4.20	14.00
11-33: 32,33-The Fly-r by S&K	.90	2.70	8.00
34-60		2.00	6.00
61-80,100			4.00
81-99			3.00
101-140: 36-Katy Keene story			2.00
141-151			1.79
152-160-($1.95)			1.95

NOTE: ***Neal Adams** a-1, 2, 4, 5, 19-21, 24, 25, 27, 29, 31, 33. X-mas c-88, 94, 100, 106.*

ARCHIE COMICS PRESENTS: THE LOVE SHOWDOWN COLLECTION
Archie Publications: 1994 ($4.95, squarebound)

	GD25	FN65	NM94
nn-r/Archie #429, Betty #19, Betty & Veronica #82, & Veronica #39			5.00

ARCHIE GETS A JOB
Spire Christian Comics (Fleming H. Revell Co.): 1977

	GD25	FN65	NM94
nn			5.00

ARCHIE GIANT SERIES MAGAZINE
Archie Publications: 1954 - No. 632, July, 1992 (No #36-135, no #252-451) (#1 not code approved) (#1-233 are Giants)

	GD25	FN65	NM94
1-Archie's Christmas Stocking	106.00	318.00	900.00
2-Archie's Christmas Stocking('55)	64.00	192.00	550.00
3-6-Archie's Christmas Stocking('56- '59)	44.00	132.00	375.00

7-10: 7-Katy Keene Holiday Fun(9/60); Bill Woggon-c. 8-Betty & Veronica Summer Fun(10/60). 9-The World of Jughead (12/60). 10-Archie's

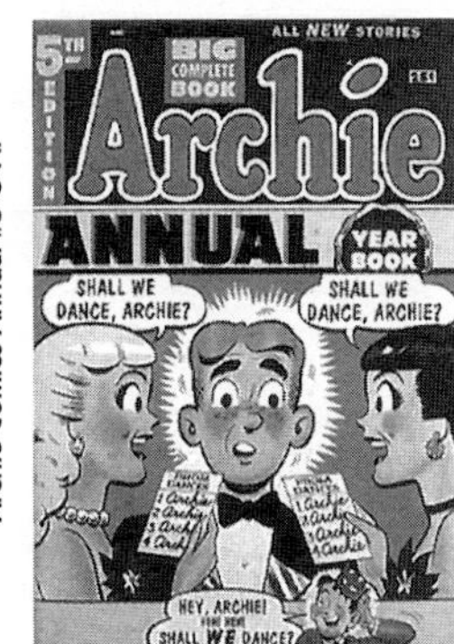

Archie Comics Annual #5 © AP

Archie Comics Digest #160 © AP

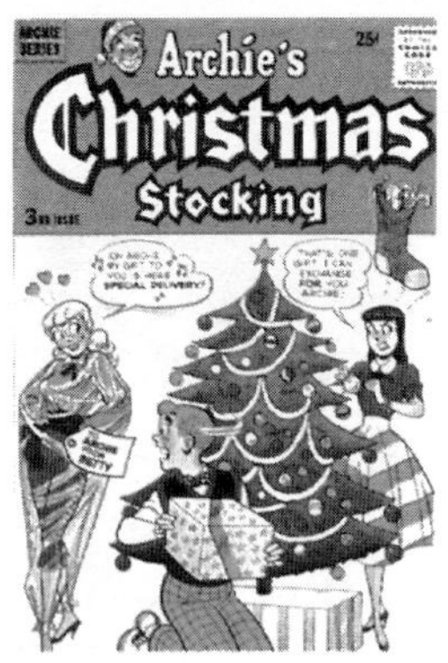

Archie Giant Series Magazine #3 © AP

GD25 FN65 NM94

Christmas Stocking(1/61) 31.00 94.00 250.00

11,13,16,18: 11-Betty & Veronica Spectacular (6/61). 13-Betty & Veronica Summer Fun (10/61). 16-Betty & Veronica Spectacular (6/62). 18-Betty & Veronica Summer Fun (10/62) 23.00 69.00 180.00

12,14,15,17,19,20: 12-Katy Keene Holiday Fun (9/61). 14-The World of Jughead (12/61). 15-Archie's Christmas Stocking (1/62). 17-Archie's Jokes (9/62); Katy Keene app. 19-The World of Jughead (12/62). 20-Archie's Christmas Stocking (1/63) 12.00 36.00 120.00

21,23,26,28: 21-Betty & Veronica Spectacular (6/63). 23-Betty & Veronica Summer Fun (10/63). 26-Betty & Veronica Spectacular (6/64). 28-Betty & Veronica Summer Fun (9/64) 9.00 27.00 90.00

22,24,25,27,29,30: 22-Archie's Jokes (9/63). 24-The World of Jughead (12/63). 25-Archie's Christmas Stocking (1/64). 27-Archie's Jokes (8/64). 29-Around the World with Archie (10/64). 30-The World of Jughead (12/64) 6.00 18.00 60.00

31-35,136-141: 31-Archie's Christmas Stocking (1/65). 32-Betty & Veronica Spectacular (6/65). 33-Archie's Jokes (8/65). 34-Betty & Veronica Summer Fun (9/65). 35-Around the World with Archie (10/65). 136-The World of Jughead (12/65). 137-Archie's Christmas Stocking (1/66). 138-Betty & Veronica Spectacular (6/66). 139-Archie's Jokes (6/66). 140-Betty & Veronica Summer Fun (8/66). 141-Around the World with Archie (9/66) 5.00 15.00 50.00

142-Archie's Super-Hero Special (10/66)-Origin Capt. Pureheart, Capt. Hero, and Evilheart 5.50 16.50 55.00

143-160: 143-The World of Jughead (12/66). 144-Archie's Christmas Stocking (1/67). 145-Betty & Veronica Spectacular (6/67). 146-Archie's Jokes (6/67). 147-Betty & Veronica Summer Fun (8/67) 148-World of Archie (9/67). 149-World of Jughead (10/67). 150-Archie's Christmas Stocking (1/68). 151-World of Archie (2/68). 152-World of Jughead (2/68). 153-Betty & Veronica Spectacular (6/68). 154-Archie Jokes (6/68). 155-Betty & VeronicaSummer Fun (8/68). 156-World of Archie (10/68). 157-World of Jughead (12/68). 158-Archie's Christmas Stocking (1/69). 159-Betty & Veronica Christmas Spectacular (1/69). 160-World of Archie (2/69)
each... 2.50 7.50 20.00

161-183: 161-World of Jughead (2/69). 162-Betty & Veronica Spectacular (6/69). 163-Archie's Jokes(8/69). 164-Betty & Veronica Summer Fun (9/69). 165-World of Archie (9/69). 166-World of Jughead (9/69). 167-Archie's Christmas Stocking (1/70). 168-Betty & Veronica Christmas Spect. (1/70). 169-Archie's Christmas Love-In (1/70). 170-Jughead's Eat-Out Comic Book Mag. (12/69). 171-World of Archie (2/70). 172-World of Jughead (2/70). 173-Betty & Veronica Spectacular (6/70). 174-Archie's Jokes (8/70). 175-Betty & Veronica Summer Fun (9/70). 176-Li'l Jinx Giant Laugh-Out (8/70). 177-World of Archie (9/70). 178-World of Jughead (9/70). 179-Archie's Christmas Stocking (1/71). 180-Betty & Veronica Christmas Spect. (1/71). 181-Archie's Christmas Love-In (1/71). 182-World of Archie (2/71). 183-World of Jughead (2/71)-Last squarebound each... 1.20 3.60 12.00

184-195,197-199 (52 pgs.): 184-Betty & Veronica Spectacular (6/71). 185-Li'l Jinx Giant Laugh-Out (6/71). 186-Archie's Jokes (8/71). 187-Betty & Veronica Summer Fun (9/71). 188-World of Archie (9/71). 189-World of Jughead (9/71). 190-Archie's Christmas Stocking (12/71). 191-Betty & Veronica Christmas Spect.(2/72). 192-Archie's Christmas Love-In (1/72). 193-World of Archie (3/72).194-World of Jughead (4/72). 195-Li'l Jinx Christmas Bag (1/72). 197-Betty & Veronica Spectacular (6/72). 198-Archie's Jokes (8/72). 199-Betty & Veronica Summer Fun (9/72
each... 1.50 4.50 15.00

196,200 952 pgs.): 196-Sabrina's Christmas Magic (1/72).200-World of Archie (10/72). 2.00 6.00 20.00

201-206,208-219,221-230,232,233 (All 52 pgs.): 201-Betty & Veronica Spectacular (10/72). 202-World of Jughead (11/72). 203-Archie's Christmas Stocking (12/72). 204-Betty & Veronica Christmas Spectacular (2/73). 205-Archie's Christmas Love-In (1/73). 206-Li'l Jinx Christmas Bag (12/72). 208-World of Archie (3/73). 209-World of Jughead (4/73). 210-Betty & Veronica Spectacular (6/73). 211-Archie's Jokes (8/73). 212-Betty & Veronica Summer Fun (9/73). 213-World of Archie (10/73). 214-Betty & Veronica Spectacular (10/73). 215-World of Jughead (11/73). 216-Archie's Christmas Stocking (12/73). 217-Betty & Veronica Christmas Spectacular (2/74). 218-Archie's Christmas Love-In (1/74). 219-Li'l Jinx Christmas Bag (12/73). 221-Betty & Veronica Spectacular (Advertised as World of Archie) (6/74). 222-Archie's Jokes (advertised as World of Jughead) (8/74). 223-Li'l Jinx (8/74). 224-Betty & Veronica Summer Fun (9/74). 225-World of Archie (9/74). 226-Betty & Veronica Spectacular (10/74). 227-World of Jughead (10/74). 228-Archie's Christmas Stocking (12/74). 229-Betty & Veronica Christmas Spectacular (12/74). 230-Archie's Christmas Love-In (1/75). 232-World of Archie (3/75). 233-World of Jughead (4/75)
each... .85 2.60 7.00

207,220,231,243: Sabrina's Christmas Magic. 207-(12/72). 220-(12/73). 231-(1/75). 243-(1/76)
each... 1.20 3.60 12.00

234-242,244-251 (36 pgs.): 234-Betty & Veronica Spectacular (6/75). 235-Archie's Jokes (8/75). 236-Betty & Veronica Summer Fun (9/75). 237-World of Archie (9/75) 238-Betty & Veronica Spectacular (10/75). 239-World of Jughead (10/75). 240-Archie's Christmas Stocking (12/75). 241-Betty & Veronica Christmas Spectacular (12/75). 242-Archie's Christmas Love-In (1/76). 244-World of Archie (3/76). 245-World of Jughead (4/76). 246-Betty & Veronica Spectacular (6/76). 247-Archie's Jokes (8/76). 248-Betty & Veronica Summer Fun (9/76). 249-World of Archie (9/76). 250-Betty & Veronica Spectacular (10/76). 251-World of Jughead
each.... .85 2.60 7.00

452-454,456-466,468-478, 480-490,492-499: 452-Archie's Christmas Stocking (12/76). 453-Betty & Veronica Christmas Spectacular (12/76). 454-Archie's Christmas Love-In (1/77). 456-World of Archie (3/77). 457-World of Jughead (4/77). 458-Betty & Veronica Spectacular (6/77). 459-Archie's Jokes (8/77)-Shows 8/76 in error. 460-Betty & Veronica Summer Fun (9/77). 461-World of Archie (9/77). 462-Betty & Veronica Spectacular (10/77). 463-World of Jughead (10/77). 464-Archie's Christmas Stocking (12/77). 465-Betty & Veronica Christmas Spectacular (12/77). 466-Archie's Christmas Love-In (1/78). 468-World of Archie (2/78). 469-World of Jughead (2/78). 470-Betty & Veronica Spectacular(6/78). 471-Archie's Jokes (8/78). 472-Betty & Veronica Summer Fun (9/78). 473-World of Archie (9/78). 474-Betty & Veronica Spectacular (10/78). 475-World of Jughead (10/78). 476-Archie's Christmas Stocking (12/78). 477-Betty & Veronica Christmas Spectacular (12/78). 478-Archie's Christmas Love-In (1/79). 480-The World of Archie (3/79). 481-World of Jughead (4/79). 482-Betty & Veronica Spectacular (6/79). 483-Archie's Jokes (8/79). 484-Betty & Veronica Summer Fun(9/79). 485-The World of Archie (9/79). 486-Betty & Veronica Spectacular(10/79). 487-The World of Jughead (10/79). 488-Archie's Christmas Stocking (12/79). 489-Betty & Veronica Christmas Spectacular (1/80). 490-Archie's Christmas Love-in (1/80). 492-The World of Archie (2/80). 493-The World of Jughead (4/80). 494-Betty & Veronica Spectacular (6/80). 495-Archie's Jokes (8/80). 496-Betty & Veronica Summer Fun (9/80). 497-The World of Archie (9/80). 498-Betty & Veronica Spectacular (10/80). 499-The World of Jughead (10/80).
each... 5.00

455,467,479,491-Sabrina's Christmas Magic: 455-(1/77). 467-(1/78). 479-(1/79). 491-(1/80) .90 2.70 9.00

500-Archie's Christmas Stocking (12/80) .90 2.70 8.00

501-514,516-527,529-532,534-539,541-543,545-550: 501-Betty & Veronica Christmas Spectacular (12/80). 502-Archie's Christmas Love-in (1/81). 503-Sabrina Christmas Magic (1/81). 504-The World of Archie (3/81). 505-The World of Jughead (4/81). 506-Betty & Veronica Spectacular (6/81). 507-Archie's Jokes (8/81). 508-Betty & Veronica Summer Fun (9/81). 509-The World of Archie (9/81). 510-Betty & Vernonica Spectacular (9/81). 511-The World of Jughead (10/81). 512-Archie's Christmas Stocking (12/81). 513-Betty & Veronica Christmas Spectacular (12/81). 514-Archie's Christmas Love-in (1/82). 516-The World of Archie (3/82). 517-The World of Jughead (4/82). 518-Betty & Veronica Spectacular (6/82). 519-Archie's Jokes (8/82). 520-Betty & Veronica Summer Fun (9/82). 521-The World of Archie (9/82). 522-Betty & Veronica Spectacular (10/82). 523-The World of Jughead (10/82). 524-Archie's Christmas Stocking (1/83). 525-Betty and Veronica Christmas

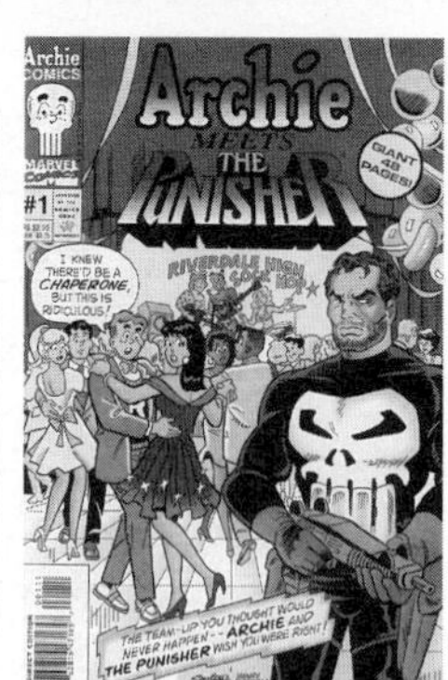

Archie Meets the Punisher #1 © AP/MAR

Archie's Double Digest #103 © AP

Archie's Girls, Betty and Veronica Annual #3 © AP

GD25 FN65 NM94

Spectacular (1/83). 526-Betty and Veronica Spectacular (5/83). 527-Little Archie (8/83). 529-Betty and Veronica Summer Fun (8/83). 530-Betty and Veronica Spectacular (9/83). 531-The World of Jughead (9/83). 532-The World of Archie (10/83). 534-Little Archie (1/84). 535-Archie's Christmas Stocking (1/84). 536-Betty and Veronica Christmas Spectacular (1/84). 537-Betty and Veronica Spectacular (6/84). 538-Little Archie (8/84). 539-Betty and Veronica Summer Fun (8/84). 541-Betty and Veronica Spectacular (9/84). 542-The World of Jughead (9/84). 543-The World of Archie (10/84). 545-Little Archie (12/84). 546-Archie's Christmas Stocking (12/84). 547-Betty and Veronica Christmas Spectacular (12/84). 548-? 549-Little Archie. 550-Betty and Veronica Summer Fun
each... 4.00

515,528,533,540,544: 515-Sabrina's Christmas Magic (1/82). 528-Josie and the Pussycats (8/83). 533-Space Pirates by Frank Bolling (10/83).540-Josie and the Pussycats (8/84). 544-Sabrina the Teen-Age Witch (10/84).
each... 2.00 6.00

551-600: 551-Josie and the Pussycats. 552-Betty and Veronica Spectacular. 553-The World of Jughead. 554-The World of Archie. 555-Betty's Diary. 556-Little Archie (1/86). 557-Archie's Christmas Stocking (1/86). 558-Betty & Veronica Christmas Spectacular (1/86). 559-Betty & Veronica Spectacular. 560-Little Archie. 561-Betty & Veronica Summer Fun. 562-Josie and the Pussycats. 563-Betty & Veronica Spectacular. 564-World of Jughead. 565-World of Archie. 566-Little Archie. 567-Archie's Christmas Stocking. 568-Betty & Veronica Christmas Spectacular. 569-Betty & Veronica Spring Spectacular. 570-Little Archie. 571-Josie & the Pussycats. 572-Betty & Veronica Summer Fun. 573-Archie At Riverdale High. 574-World of Archie. 575-Betty & Veronica Spectacular. 576-Pep. 577-World of Jughead. 578-Archie And Me. 579-Archie's Christmas Stocking. 580-Betty and Veronica Christmas Spectacular. 581-Little Archie Christmas Special. 582-Betty & Veronica Spring Spectacular. 583-Little Archie. 584-Josie and the Pussycats. 585-Betty & Veronica Summer Fun. 586-Archie At Riverdale High. 587-The World of Archie (10/88); 1st app. Explorers of the Unknown. 588-Betty & Veronica Spectacular. 589-Pep (10/88). 590-The World of Jughead. 591-Archie & Me. 592-Archie's Christmas Stocking. 593-Betty & Veronica Christmas Spectacular. 594-Little Archie. 595-Betty & Veronica Spring Spectacular. 596-Little Archie. 597-Josie and the Pussycats. 598-Betty & Veronica Summer Fun. 599-The World of Archie (10/89); 2nd app. Explorers of the Unknown. 600-Betty and Veronica Spectacular
each.... 3.00

601-609,611-629: 601-Pep. 602-The World of Jughead. 603-Archie and Me. 604-Archie at Riverdale High. 605-Archie's Christmas Stocking. 606-Betty and Veronica Christmas Spectacular. 607-Little Archie. 608-Betty and Veronica Spectacular. 609-Little Archie. 611-Betty and Veronica Summer Fun. 612-The World of Archie. 613-Betty and Veronica Spectacular. 614-Pep (10/90). 615-Veronica's Summer Special. 616-Archie and Me. 617-Archie's Christmas Stocking. 618-Betty & Veronica Christmas Spectacular. 619-Little Archie. 620-Betty and Veronica Spectacular. 621-Betty and Veronica Summer Fun. 622-Josie & the Pussycats; not published. 623-Betty and Veronica Spectacular. 624-Pep Comics. 625-Veronica's Summer Special. 626-Archie and Me. 627-World of Archie. 628-Archie's Pals 'n' Gals Holiday Special. 629-Betty & Veronica Christmas Spectacular.
each.... 2.00

610-Josie and the Pussycats 3.00

630-632: 630-Archie's Christmas Stocking. 631-Archie's Pals 'n' Gals. 632-Betty & Veronica Spectacular 2.25

ARCHIE MEETS THE PUNISHER (Same contents as The Punisher Meets Archie)
Marvel Comics & Archie Comics Publ.: Aug, 1994 ($2.95, 52 pgs., one-shot)

1-Batton Lash story, J. Buscema-a on Punisher, S. Goldberg-a on Archie 4.00

ARCHIE'S ACTIVITY COMICS DIGEST MAGAZINE
Archie Enterprises: 1985 - No. 4? (Annual, 128 pgs., digest size)

1 .85 2.60 7.00

GD25 FN65 NM94

2-4 5.00

ARCHIE'S CAR
Spire Christian Comics (Fleming H. Revell co.): 1979 (49¢)

nn 4.50

ARCHIE'S CHRISTMAS LOVE-IN (See Archie Giant Series Mag. No. 169, 181,192, 205, 218, 230, 242, 454, 466, 478, 490, 502, 514)

ARCHIE'S CHRISTMAS STOCKING (See Archie Giant Series Mag. No. 1-6,10, 15, 20, 25, 31, 137, 144, 150, 158, 167, 179, 190, 203, 216, 228, 240, 452, 464, 476, 488, 500, 512, 524, 535, 546, 557, 567, 579, 592, 605, 617, 630)

ARCHIE'S CHRISTMAS STOCKING
Archie Comics: 1993 -Present ($2.00, 52 pgs.)(Bound-in calendar poster in all)

1-5: 1-Dan DeCarlo-c/a 3.00
6-(1998, $2.25) 2.25

ARCHIE'S CLEAN SLATE
Spire Christian Comics (Fleming H. Revell Co.): 1973 (35/49¢)

1(Some issues have nn) 4.00

ARCHIE'S DATE BOOK
Spire Christian comics (Fleming H. Revell Co.): 1981

nn 4.50

ARCHIE'S DOUBLE DIGEST QUARTERLY MAGAZINE
Archie Comics: 1981 - Present ($1.95/$2.75/$2.95, 256pgs.) (A.D.D. Magazine No. 10 on)

	GD25	FN65	NM94
1	1.80	5.40	18.00
2-10; 6-Katy Keene story.	1.00	3.00	10.00
11-30: 29-Pureheart story	.90	2.70	8.00
31-50			5.00
51-70,100			4.00
71-99,101-105			3.00

ARCHIE'S FAMILY ALBUM
Spire Christian Comics (Fleming H. Revell Co.): 1978 (39¢, 36 pgs.)

nn 4.50

ARCHIE'S FESTIVAL
Spire Christian Comics (Fleming H. Revell Co.): 1980 (49¢)

nn 4.50

ARCHIE'S GIRLS, BETTY AND VERONICA (Becomes Betty & Veronica)(Also see Veronica)
Archie Publications (Close-Up): 1950 - No. 347, Apr, 1987

	GD25	FN65	NM94
1	133.00	400.00	1200.00
2	68.00	204.00	575.00
3-5	43.00	129.00	350.00
6-10: 6-Dan DeCarlo's 1st Archie work; Betty's 1st ponytail. 10-Katy Keene app. (2 pgs.)	37.00	111.00	275.00
11-20: 11,13,14,17-19-Katy Keene app. 17-Last pre-code issue (3/55). 20-Debbie's Diary (2 pgs.)	26.00	78.00	195.00
21-30: 27,30-Katy Keene app.	18.00	54.00	135.00
31-50: 44-Elvis Presley 1 pg. photo & bio. 45-Fabian 1 pg. photo & bio. 46-Bobby Darin 1 pg. photo & bio	11.00	33.00	85.00
51-74: 73-Sci-fi-c	6.50	19.50	65.00
75-Betty & Veronica sell souls to Devil	11.00	33.00	110.00
76-99: Bobby Rydell 1 pg. illustrated bio	3.20	9.60	32.00
100	4.20	12.60	42.00
101-117,120 (12/65)	2.50	7.50	20.00
118-Origin Superteen (see Betty & Me #3)	2.80	8.40	28.00
119-Last Superteen story	2.50	7.50	24.00
121-140 (8/67)	1.85	5.50	15.00
141-180 (12/70)	1.25	3.75	10.00
181-199	.90	2.70	8.00
200-(8/72)	1.00	3.00	10.00
201-240	.85	2.60	7.00

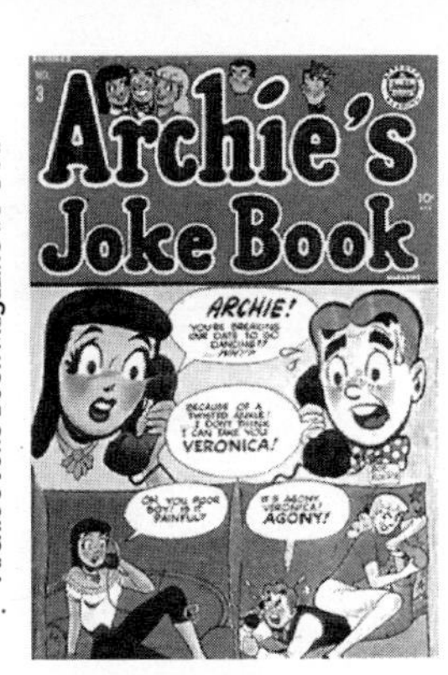

Archie's Joke Book Magazine #3 © AP

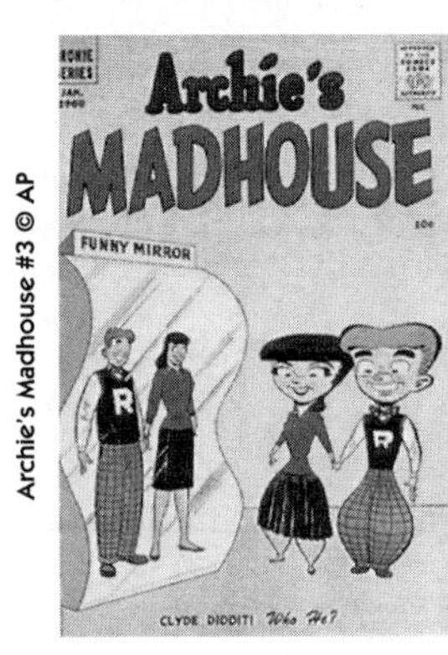

Archie's Madhouse #3 © AP

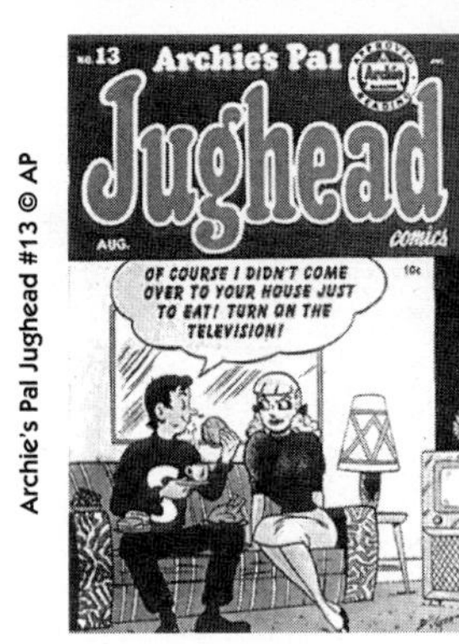

Archie's Pal Jughead #13 © AP

	GD25	FN65	NM94
241 (1/76)-270 (6/78)			5.00
271-299			4.00
300 (12/80)-Anniversary issue			6.00
301-319			3.00
320 (10/82)-1st Cheryl Blossom	1.00	3.00	10.00
321,322			6.00
323,326,327,329-347			2.00
324,325			4.00
Annual 1 (1953)	79.00	237.00	675.00
Annual 2(1954)	40.00	120.00	315.00
Annual 3-5 (1955-1957)	31.00	92.00	230.00
Annual 6-8 (1958-1960)	20.00	60.00	150.00

ARCHIE SHOE-STORE GIVEAWAY
Archie Publications: 1944-49 (12-15 pgs. of games, puzzles, stories like Superman-Tim books, No nos. - came out monthly)

	GD25	FN65	NM94
(1944-47)-issues	11.00	34.00	85.00
2/48-Peggy Lee photo-c	9.30	28.00	65.00
3/48-Marylee Robb photo-c	8.50	26.00	60.00
4/48-Gloria De Haven photo-c	8.50	26.00	60.00
5/48,6/48,7/48	8.50	26.00	60.00
8/48-Story on Shirley Temple	9.30	28.00	65.00
10/48-Archie as Wolf on cover	9.35	28.00	70.00
5/49-Kathleen Hughes photo-c	6.50	19.50	45.00
7/49	6.50	19.50	45.00
8/49-Archie photo-c from radio show	11.00	32.00	80.00
10/49-Gloria Mann photo-c from radio show	9.30	28.00	65.00
11/49,12/49	6.50	19.50	45.00

ARCHIE'S HOLIDAY FUN DIGEST
Archie Comics: 1997 - Present ($1.75/$1.95, annual)

	GD25	FN65	NM94
1-3-Christmas stories			1.95

ARCHIE'S JOKEBOOK COMICS DIGEST ANNUAL (See Jokebook...)

ARCHIE'S JOKE BOOK MAGAZINE (See Joke Book ...)
Archie Publ: 1953 - No. 3, Sum, 1954; No. 15, Fall, 1954 - No. 288, 11/82

	GD25	FN65	NM94
1953-One Shot (#1)	76.00	228.00	650.00
2	43.00	129.00	350.00
3 (no #4-14)	35.00	105.00	260.00
15-20: 15-Formerly Archie's Rival Reggie #14; last pre-code issue (Fall/54). 15-17-Katy Keene app.	20.00	60.00	150.00
21-30	12.00	36.00	90.00
31-40,42,43: 43-story about guitarist Duane Eddy	8.50	25.50	60.00
41-1st professional comic work by Neal Adams (9/59), 1 pg.	20.00	60.00	150.00
44-47-N. Adams-a in all, 1-3 pgs.	11.00	32.00	80.00
48-Four pgs. N. Adams-a	11.00	34.00	85.00
49-60 (1962)	2.50	7.50	24.00
61-80 (8/64)	1.75	5.25	14.00
81-99	1.25	3.75	10.00
100 (5/66)	1.75	5.25	14.00
101-140 (9/69)	1.00	3.00	8.00
141-199		2.00	6.00
200 (9/74)	.90	2.70	8.00
201-230 (3/77)			4.00
231-288: 270 (7/80)			3.00
Drug Store Giveaway (No. 39 w/new-c)	4.00	10.00	20.00

ARCHIE'S JOKES (See Archie Giant Series Mag. No. 17, 22, 27, 33, 139, 146, 154, 163, 174, 186, 198, 211, 222, 235, 247, 459, 471, 483, 495, 519)

ARCHIE'S LOVE SCENE
Spire Christian Comics (Fleming H. Revell Co.): 1973 (35¢/49¢)

	GD25	FN65	NM94
1(Some copies have nn)			4.50

ARCHIE'S MADHOUSE (Madhouse Ma-ad No. 67 on)
Archie Publications: Sept, 1959 - No. 66, Feb, 1969

	GD25	FN65	NM94
1-Archie begins	22.00	66.00	220.00
2	11.00	33.00	110.00
3-5	7.50	22.50	75.00
6-10	5.00	15.00	50.00
11-17 (Last w/regular characters)	3.40	10.20	34.00
18-21,29: 18-New format begins	2.50	7.50	22.00
22-1st app. Sabrina, the Teen-age Witch (10/62)	14.00	42.00	140.00
23,24-Sabrina app.	2.50	7.50	24.00
25,26,28-Sabrina app. 25-1st app. Captain Sprocket (4/63)	3.00	9.00	30.00
27-Sabrina-c; no story	3.00	9.00	30.00
30,34,38-40: No Sabrina. 34-Bordered-c begin.	1.85	5.50	15.00
31,32-Sabrina app.?	1.85	5.50	15.00
33,37-Sabrina app.	2.50	7.50	24.00
35-Beatles cameo. No Sabrina	2.50	7.50	20.00
36-1st Salem the Cat w/Sabrina sty	2.80	8.40	28.00
41-48,51-57,60-62,64-66; No Sabrina 43-Mighty Crusaders cameo. 44-Swipes Mad #4 (Super-Duperman) in "Bird Monsters From Outer Space"	1.25	3.75	10.00
49,50,58,59,63-Sabrina stories	1.85	5.50	15.00
Annual 1 (1962-63) no Sabrina	6.00	18.00	60.00
Annual 2 (1964) no Sabrina	3.60	10.80	36.00
Annual 3 (1965)-Origin Sabrina the Teen-Age Witch	4.50	13.50	45.00
Annual 4,5('66-68)(Becomes Madhouse Ma-ad Annual #7 on); no Sabrina	2.00	6.00	16.00
Annual 6 (1969)-Sabrina the Teen-Age Witch-sty	2.60	7.80	26.00

NOTE: *Cover title to 61-65 is "Madhouse" and to 66 is "Madhouse Ma-ad Jokes".*

ARCHIE'S MECHANICS
Archie Publications: Sept, 1954 - No. 3, 1955

	GD25	FN65	NM94
1-(15¢; 52 pgs.)	75.00	225.00	600.00
2-(10¢)-Last pre-code issue	46.00	138.00	365.00
3-(10¢)	40.00	120.00	300.00

ARCHIE'S ONE WAY
Spire Christian Comics (Fleming H. Revell Co.): 1972 (35/49¢, 36 pgs.)

	GD25	FN65	NM94
nn			4.00

ARCHIE'S PAL, JUGHEAD (Jughead No. 127 on)
Archie Publications: 1949 - No. 126, Nov, 1965

	GD25	FN65	NM94
1 (1949)-1st app. Moose (see Pep #33)	112.00	336.00	950.00
2 (1950)	56.00	168.00	475.00
3-5	39.00	117.00	290.00
6-10: 7-Suzie app.	26.00	78.00	195.00
11-20	16.00	48.00	120.00
21-30: 23-25,28-30-Katy Keene app. 28-Debbie's Diary app.	11.00	32.00	80.00
31-50	4.50	13.50	45.00
51-70	2.80	8.40	28.00
71-99	1.85	5.50	15.00
100	2.25	6.75	18.00
101-126	1.50	4.50	12.00
Annual 1 (1953, 25¢)	47.00	141.00	420.00
Annual 2 (1954, 25¢)-Last pre-code issue	35.00	104.00	260.00
Annual 3-5 (1955-57, 25¢)	24.00	72.00	180.00
Annual 6-8 (1958-60, 25¢)	15.00	44.00	110.00

ARCHIE'S PAL JUGHEAD COMICS (Formerly Jughead #1-45)
Archie Comic Publications: No. 46, June, 1993 - Present ($1.25/$1.50/$1.75)

	GD25	FN65	NM94
46-64			1.25
65-99			1.50
100-113- ($1.75): 100-"A Storm Over Uniforms" x-over part 1,2			1.75

ARCHIE'S PALS 'N' GALS (Also see Archie Giant Series Magazine #628)
Archie Publ: 1952-53 - No. 6, 1957-58; No. 7, 1958 - No. 224, Sept, 1991

	GD25	FN65	NM94
1-(116 pgs., 25¢)	61.00	183.00	550.00

No. 6
Archie's Rival
REGGIE
10¢
YOU MEAN TO SAY HE KISSED YOU WHEN YOU WEREN'T LOOKING! VERONICA, THAT ARCHIE OUGHTA BE TAUGHT A LESSON!
DON'T WORRY, REGGIE, ARCHIE DOESN'T NEED ANY LESSONS!

Archie's Rival Reggie #6 © AP

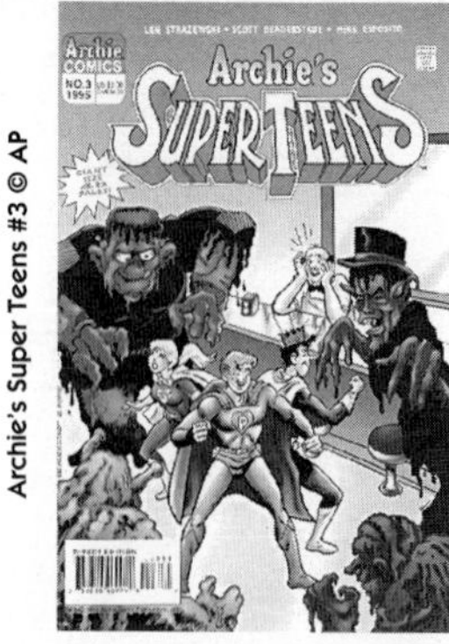

Archie's Super Teens #3 © AP

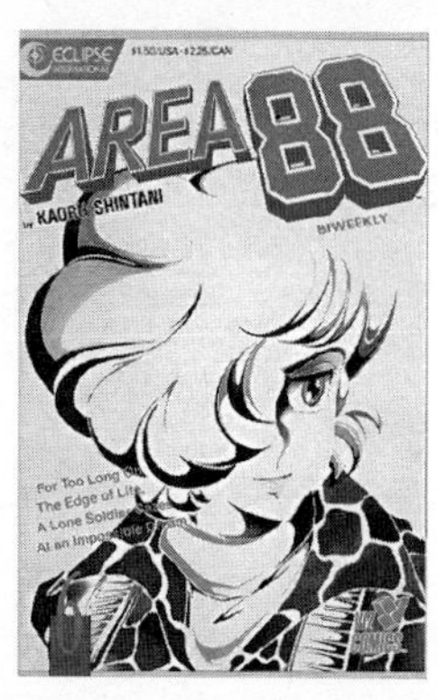

Area 88 #6 © ECL

	GD25	FN65	NM94
2(Annual)('54, 25¢)	36.00	108.00	290.00
3-5(Annual, '55-57, 25¢): 3-Last pre-code issue	26.00	78.00	200.00
6-10('58-'60)	15.00	46.00	115.00
11-20 (84 pgs.): 12-Harry Belafonte 2 pg. photos & bio	7.15	21.50	50.00
21-28,30 (68 pgs.)	3.00	9.00	30.00
29-Beatles satire (68 pgs.)	5.00	15.00	50.00
31(Wint. 64/65)-40 -(68 pgs.)	2.80	8.40	28.00
41(8/67)-50(2/69) (68 pgs.)	2.50	7.50	20.00
51(4/69)-64(6/71): 62-Last squarebound	2.00	6.00	16.00
65(8/70)-83(6/74) (52 pgs.)	1.50	4.50	12.00
84-99	.85	2.60	7.00
100	1.00	3.00	10.00
101-130(3/79)		2.00	6.00
131-170 (7/84)			4.00
171-199: 197-G. Colan-a			3.00
200(9/88)			4.00
201-224: Later issues $1.00 cover			2.00

ARCHIE'S PALS 'N' GALS DOUBLE DIGEST MAGAZINE
Archie Comic Publications: Nov, 1992 - Present ($2.50/$2.75/$2.95)

	GD25	FN65	NM94
1-3: 1-Capt. Hero story; Pureheart app. 2-Superduck story; Little Jinx in all			5.00
4-29: 4-Begin $2.75-c.			3.50
30-38-($2.95)			2.95

ARCHIE'S PARABLES
Spire Christian Comics (Fleming H. Revell Co.): 1973,1975 (39/49¢, 36 pgs.)

	GD25	FN65	NM94
nn-By Al Hartley			4.00

ARCHIE'S R/C RACERS
Archie Comics: Sept, 1989 - No. 10, Mar, 1991 (.95-$1)

	GD25	FN65	NM94
1			3.00
2-10: Radio control cars			2.00

ARCHIE'S RIVAL REGGIE (Reggie & Archie's Joke Book #15 on)
Archie Publications: 1950 - No. 14, Aug, 1954

	GD25	FN65	NM94
1-Reggie 1st app. in Jackpot Comics #5	64.00	192.00	575.00
2	36.00	108.00	285.00
3-5	24.00	71.00	195.00
6-10	17.50	53.00	140.00
11-14: Katy Keene in No. 10-14, 1-2 pgs.	12.00	38.00	100.00

ARCHIE'S RIVERDALE HIGH (See Riverdale High)

ARCHIE'S ROLLER COASTER
Spire Christian Comics (Fleming H. Revell Co.): 1981 (69¢)

	GD25	FN65	NM94
nn			4.50

ARCHIE'S SOMETHING ELSE
Spire Christian Comics (Fleming H. Revell Co.): 1975 (39/49¢, 36 pgs.)

	GD25	FN65	NM94
nn			4.50

ARCHIE'S SONSHINE
Spire Christian Comics (Fleming H. Revell Co.): 1973, 1974 (39/49¢, 36 pgs.)

	GD25	FN65	NM94
nn			4.50

ARCHIE'S SPORTS SCENE
Spire Christian Comics (Fleming H. Revell Co.): 1983

	GD25	FN65	NM94
nn			4.50

ARCHIE'S SPRING BREAK
Archie Comics: 1996 - Present ($2.00, 48 pgs., annual)

	GD25	FN65	NM94
1,2-Dan DeCarlo-c			2.00
3-($2.25)			2.25

ARCHIE'S STORY & GAME COMICS DIGEST MAGAZINE
Archie Enterprises: Nov, 1986 - Present ($1.25/$1.35/$1.50/$1.95, 128 pgs., digest-size)

	GD25	FN65	NM94
1	1.00	3.00	10.00
2-10	.85	2.60	7.00
11-20			5.00
21-38			2.50
39-42-($1.95)			1.95

ARCHIE'S SUPER HERO SPECIAL (See Archie Giant Series Mag. No. 142)

ARCHIE'S SUPER HERO SPECIAL (...Comics Digest Mag. 2)
Archie Publications (Red Circle): Jan, 1979 - No. 2, Aug, 1979(95¢, 148 pgs.)

	GD25	FN65	NM94
1-Simon & Kirby r-/Double Life of Pvt. Strong #1,2; Black Hood, The Fly, Jaguar, The Web app.	1.10	3.30	11.00
2-Contains contents to the never published Black Hood #1; origin Black Hood; N. Adams, Wood, McWilliams, Morrow, S&K-a(r); N. Adams-c. The Shield, The Fly, Jaguar, Hangman, Steel Sterling, The Web, The Fox-r	.90	2.70	8.00

ARCHIE'S SUPER TEENS
Archie Comic Publications, Inc.: 1994 - No. 4, 1996 ($2.00, 52 pgs.)

	GD25	FN65	NM94
1-4: 1-Staton/Esposito-c/a; pull-out poster. 2-Fred Hembeck script; Bret Blevins/Terry Austin-a			2.00

ARCHIE'S TV LAUGH-OUT
Archie Publications: Dec, 1969 - No. 106, Apr, 1986 (#1-7: 68 pgs.)

	GD25	FN65	NM94
1-Sabrina begins, thru #106	5.50	16.50	60.00
2 (68 pgs.)	2.70	8.00	30.00
3-6 (68 pgs.)	1.80	5.40	18.00
7-Josie begins, thru #105	2.70	8.00	30.00
8-23 (52 pgs.)	1.60	4.80	16.00
24-40	1.00	3.00	10.00
41-60,100	.85	2.60	7.00
61-80			5.00
81-99,101-106			3.00

ARCHIE'S VACATION SPECIAL
Archie Publications: Winter, 1994? - Present ($2.00, annually)

	GD25	FN65	NM94
1-5			2.00
6-($2.25)			2.25

ARCHIE'S WORLD
Spire Christian Comics (Fleming H. Revell Co.): 1973, 1976 (39/49¢)

	GD25	FN65	NM94
nn			5.00

ARCHIE 3000
Archie Comics: May, 1989 - No. 16, July, 1991 (75¢/95¢/$1.00)

	GD25	FN65	NM94
1-			3.00
2-16: 6-Begin $1.00-c; X-Mas-c			2.00

ARCOMICS PREMIERE
Arcomics: July, 1993 ($2.95)

	GD25	FN65	NM94
1-1st lenticular-c on a comic (flicker-c)			3.00

AREA 88
Eclipse Comics/VIZ Comics #37 on: May 26, 1987 - No. 42, 1989 ($1.50/$1.75, B&W)

	GD25	FN65	NM94
1-36: 1,2-2nd printings exist			1.50
37-42: 37-Begin $1.75-c			1.80

AREALA: ANGEL OF WAR (See Warrior Nun titles)
Antarctic Press: Sept, 1998 - Present ($2.95, color)

	GD25	FN65	NM94
1			2.95

ARENA
Alchemy Studios: Jan, 1990 ($1.50, 7x10-1/8", 20 pgs.)

	GD25	FN65	NM94
1-Science fiction			1.50
1-Signed & numbered ed. (500 copies)			2.95

ARGUS (See Flash, 2nd Series) (Also see Showcase '95 #1,2)
DC Comics: Apr, 1995 - No. 6, Oct, 1995 ($1.50, limited series)

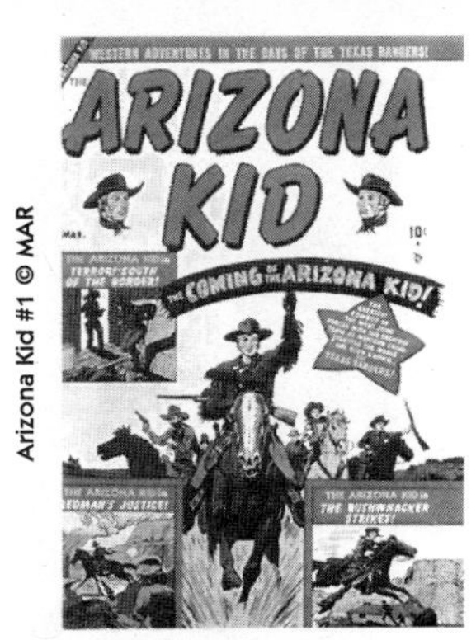

Arizona Kid #1 © MAR

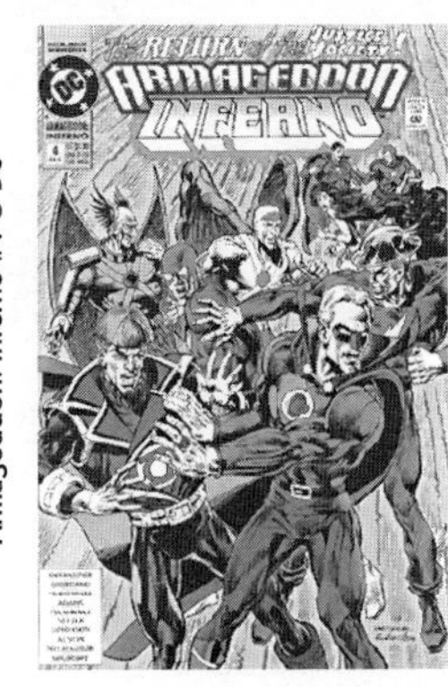

Armageddon: Inferno #4 © DC

Arrgh! #3 © MAR

	GD25	FN65	NM94
1-3			1.50
4-6: 4-Begin $1.75-c		.70	1.75

ARIANE AND BLUEBEARD (See Night Music #8)

ARIEL & SEBASTIAN (See Cartoon Tales & The Little Mermaid)

ARION, LORD OF ATLANTIS (Also see Warlord #55)
DC Comics: Nov, 1982 - No. 35, Sept, 1985

	GD25	FN65	NM94
1-35: 1-Story cont'd from Warlord #62			1.00
Special #1 (11/85)			1.00

ARION THE IMMORTAL (Also see Showcase '95 #7)
DC Comics: July, 1992 - No. 6, Dec, 1992 ($1.50, limited series)

	GD25	FN65	NM94
1-6: 4-Gustovich-a(i)			1.50

ARISTOCATS (See Movie Comics & Walt Disney Showcase No. 16)

ARISTOKITTENS, THE (...Meet Jiminy Cricket No. 1)(Disney)
Gold Key: Oct, 1971 - No. 9, Oct, 1975

	GD25	FN65	NM94
1	2.00	6.00	22.00
2-5,7-9	1.20	3.60	13.00
6-(52 pgs.)	1.50	4.50	16.00

ARIZONA KID, THE (Also see The Comics & Wild Western)
Marvel/Atlas Comics(CSI): Mar, 1951 - No. 6, Jan, 1952

	GD25	FN65	NM94
1	19.00	58.00	145.00
2-4: 2-Heath-a(3)	10.00	30.00	75.00
5,6	9.30	28.00	65.00

NOTE: ***Heath*** *a-1-3; c-1-3.* ***Maneely*** *c-4-6.* ***Morisi*** *a-4-6.* ***Sinnott*** *a-6.*

ARK, THE (See The Crusaders)

ARKAGA
Image Comics: Sept, 1997 ($2.95, one-shot)

	GD25	FN65	NM94
1-Jorgensen-s/a			3.00

ARMAGEDDON: ALIEN AGENDA
DC Comics: Nov, 1991 - No. 4, Feb, 1992 ($1.00, limited series)

	GD25	FN65	NM94
1-4			1.00

ARMAGEDDON FACTOR, THE
AC Comics: 1987 - No. 2, 1987; No. 3, 1990 ($1.95)

	GD25	FN65	NM94
1,2: Sentinels of Justice, Dragonfly, Femforce			2.00
3-($3.95, color)-Almost all AC characters app.			4.00

ARMAGEDDON: INFERNO
DC Comics: Apr, 1992 - No. 4, July, 1992 ($1.00, limited series)

	GD25	FN65	NM94
1-4: Many DC heroes app. 3-A. Adams/Austin-a			1.00

ARMAGEDDON 2001
DC Comics: May, 1991 - No. 2, Oct, 1991 ($2.00, squarebound, 68 pgs.)

	GD25	FN65	NM94
1-Features many DC heroes; intro Waverider			2.50
1-2nd & 3rd printings; 3rd has silver ink-c			1.75
2			2.50

ARMATURE
Olyoptics: Nov, 1996 - No. 2, ($2.95, limited series)

	GD25	FN65	NM94
1,2-Steve Oliff-c/s/a; Maxx app.			3.00

ARMED & DANGEROUS
Acclaim Comics (Armada): Apr, 1996 - No.4, July, 1996 ($2.95, B&W)

	GD25	FN65	NM94
1-4-Bob Hall-c/a & scripts			3.00
Special 1 (8/96, $2.95, B&W)-Hall-c/a & scripts.			3.00

ARMED & DANGEROUS HELL'S SLAUGHTERHOUSE
Acclaim Comics (Armada): Oct, 1996 - No. 4, Jan, 1997 ($2.95, B&W)

	GD25	FN65	NM94
1-4: Hall-c/a/scripts.			3.00

ARMOR (AND THE SILVER STREAK)
Continuity Comics: Sept, 1985 - No.13, Apr, 1992 ($2.00)

	GD25	FN65	NM94
1-13: 1-Intro/origin Armor & the Silver Streak; Neal Adams-c/a. 7-Origin Armor; Nebres-i			2.00

ARMOR (DEATHWATCH 2000)
Continuity Comics: Apr, 1993 - No.6, Nov, 1993 ($2.50)

	GD25	FN65	NM94
1-6: 1-3-Deathwatch 2000 x-over			2.50

ARMORED TROOPER VOTOMS (Manga)
CPM Comics: July, 1996 ($2.95)

	GD25	FN65	NM94
1			3.00

ARMORINES (See X-O Manowar #25)
Valiant: June, 1994 - No. 12, June, 1995 ($2.25)

	GD25	FN65	NM94
1-12: 7-Wraparound-c. 12-Byrne-c/swipe (X-Men, 1st Series #138)			2.25

ARMY AND NAVY COMICS (Supersnipe No. 6 on)
Street & Smith Publications: May, 1941 - No. 5, July, 1942

	GD25	FN65	NM94
1-Cap Fury & Nick Carter	44.00	132.00	375.00
2-Cap Fury & Nick Carter	27.00	81.00	200.00
3,4	19.00	57.00	140.00
5-Supersnipe app.; see Shadow V2#3 for 1st app.; Story of Douglas MacArthur; George Marcoux-c/a	44.00	132.00	375.00

ARMY ATTACK
Charlton Comics: July, 1964 - No. 4, Feb, 1965; V2#38, July, 1965 - No. 47, Feb, 1967

	GD25	FN65	NM94
V1#1	3.00	9.00	30.00
2-4(2/65)	2.25	6.75	18.00
V2#38(7/65)-47 (formerly U.S. Air Force #1-37)	1.85	5.50	15.00

NOTE: ***Glanzman*** *a-1-3.* ***Montes/Bache*** *a-44.*

ARMY AT WAR (Also see Our Army at War & Cancelled Comic Cavalcade)
DC Comics: Oct-Nov, 1978

	GD25	FN65	NM94
1-Kubert-c			4.00

ARMY OF DARKNESS (Movie)
Dark Horse Comics: Nov, 1992 - No. 2, Dec, 1992; No. 3, Oct, 1993 ($2.50, limited series)

	GD25	FN65	NM94
1-3-Bolton painted-c/a			2.50

ARMY SURPLUS KOMIKZ FEATURING CUTEY BUNNY
Army Surplus Komikz/Eclipse Comics: 1982 - No. 5, 1985 ($1.50, B&W)

	GD25	FN65	NM94
1-Cutey Bunny begins			5.00
2-5: 5-(Eclipse)-JLA/X-Men/Batman parody			3.00

ARMY WAR HEROES (Also see Iron Corporal)
Charlton Comics: Dec, 1963 - No. 38, June, 1970

	GD25	FN65	NM94
1	3.00	9.00	30.00
2-10	2.50	7.50	20.00
11-21,23-30: 24-Intro. Archer & Corp. Jack series	1.85	5.50	15.00
22-Origin/1st app. Iron Corporal series by Glanzman	2.25	6.75	18.00
31-38	1.25	3.75	10.00
Modern Comics Reprint 36 ('78)			4.00

NOTE: ***Montes/Bache*** *a-1, 16, 17, 21, 23-25, 27-30.*

AROUND THE BLOCK WITH DUNC & LOO (See Dunc and Loo)

AROUND THE WORLD IN 80 DAYS (Movie) (See A Golden Picture Classic)
Dell Publishing Co.: Feb, 1957

	GD25	FN65	NM94
Four Color 784-Photo-c	5.75	17.00	63.00

AROUND THE WORLD UNDER THE SEA (See Movie Classics)

AROUND THE WORLD WITH ARCHIE (See Archie Giant Series Mag. #29, 35, 141)

AROUND THE WORLD WITH HUCKLEBERRY & HIS FRIENDS (See Dell Giant No. 44)

ARRGH! (Satire)
Marvel Comics Group: Dec, 1974 - No. 5, Sept, 1975 (25¢)

	GD25	FN65	NM94
1	1.40	4.20	14.00

Arsenal #1 © DC

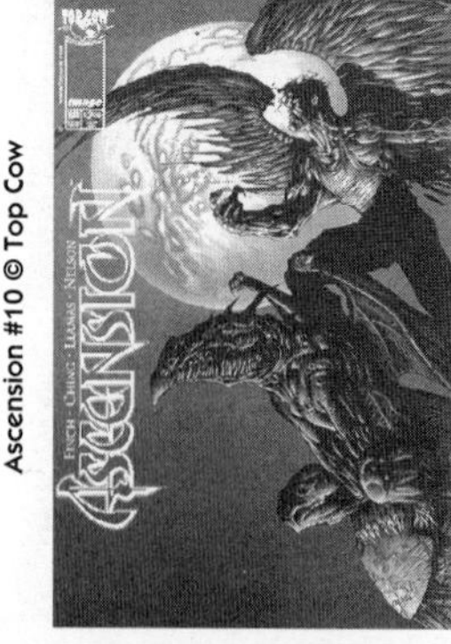
Ascension #10 © Top Cow

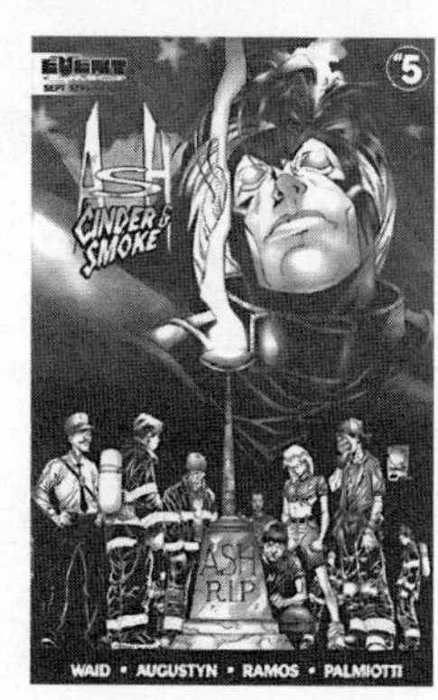

Ash: Cinder & Smoke #5 © Quesada & Palmiotti

GD25 FN65 NM94

2-5 1.00 3.00 10.00
NOTE *Alcala* a-2; c-3. *Everett* a-1r, 2r. *Maneely* a-4r. *Sekowsky* a-1p. *Sutton* a-1, 2.

ARROW (See Protectors)
Malibu Comics: Oct, 1992 ($1.95, one-shot)

1-Moder-a(p) 2.00

ARROW, THE (See Funny Pages)
Centaur Publications: Oct, 1940 - No. 2, Nov, 1940; No. 3, Oct, 1941

1-The Arrow begins(r/Funny Pages) 259.00 777.00 2200.00
2,3: 2-Tippy Taylor serial continues from Amazing Mystery Funnies #24. 3-Origin Dash Dartwell, the Human Meteor; origin The Rainbow-r; bondage-c 106.00 318.00 900.00
NOTE: *Gustavson* a-1, 2; c-3.

ARROWHEAD (See Black Rider and Wild Western)
Atlas Comics (CPS): April, 1954 - No. 4, Nov, 1954

1-Arrowhead & his horse Eagle begin 13.00 39.00 100.00
2-4: 4-Forte-a 9.30 28.00 65.00
NOTE: *Heath* c-3. *Jack Katz* a-3. *Maneely* c-2. *Pakula* a-2. *Sinnott* a-1-4; c-1.

ARSENAL (Teen Titans' Speedy)
DC Comics: Oct, 1998 - No. 4, Jan, 1999 ($2.50, limited series)

1-4: 1-Black Canary app. 2-Green Arrow app. 2.50

ARSENAL SPECIAL (See New Titans, Showcase '94 #7 & Showcase '95 #8)
DC Comics: 1996 ($2.95, one-shot)

1 3.00

ARTBABE
Fantagraphics Books: May, 1996 - Present ($2.50/$2.95, B&W)

V1 #5 2.50
V2 #1-3 2.95

ARTEMIS: REQUIEM (Also see Wonder Woman, 2nd Series #90)
DC Comics: June, 1996 - No. 6, Nov, 1996 ($1.75, limited series)

1-6: Messner-Loebs scripts & Ed Benes-c/a in all. 1,2-Wonder Woman app. 1.75

ART OF ZEN INTERGALACTIC NINJA, THE
Entity Comics: 1994 - No. 2, 1994 ($2.95)

1,2 3.00

ARZACH (See Moebius...)
Dark Horse Comics: 1996 ($6.95, one-shot)

nn-Moebius-c/a/scripts .85 2.60 7.00

ASCENSION
Image Comics (Top Cow Productions): Oct, 1997 - Present ($2.50)

Preview .85 2.60 7.00
Preview Gold Edition 10.00
Preview San Diego Edition 1.50 4.50 15.00
0 1.20 3.60 12.00
1/2 .90 2.70 8.00
1-David Finch-s/a(p)/Batt-s/a(i) 5.00
1-Variant-c w/Image logo at lower right .90 2.70 8.00
2-6 3.00
7-10 2.50
Fan Club Edition 1.00 3.00 10.00

ASCENSION COLLECTED EDITION
Image Comics (Top Cow Productions): 1998 - Present ($4.95, squarebound)

1,2: 1-r/#1,2. 2-r/#3,4 5.00

ASH
Event Comics: Nov, 1994 - No. 6, Dec, 1995; No. 0, May, 1996 ($2.50/$3.00)

0-(5/96, $3.00)-Present foil logo-c; w/pin-ups 3.00
0-(5/96, $3.00)-Future foil logo-c; w/pin-ups 3.00
0-Present Blue Foil logo-c (1000) 5.00

GD25 FN65 NM94

0-Future Blue Foil logo-c (1000) 5.00
0-Present Silver Prism logo-c (500) 12.00
0-Future Silver Prism logo-c (500) 12.00
0-Present Red Prism logo-c (250) 20.00
0-Future Red Prism logo-c (250) 20.00
0-Present Gold Hologram logo-c (1000) 10.00
0-Future Gold Hologram logo-c (1000) 10.00
1-Quesada-p/story; Palmiotti-i/story: Barry Windsor-Smith pin-up 1.10 3.30 11.00
2-Mignola Hellboy pin-up .85 2.60 7.00
3,4: 3-Big Guy pin-up by Geoff Darrow. 4-Jim Lee pin-up 5.00
4-Fahrenheit Gold 9.00
4-Fahrenheit Red 10.00
4-Fahrenheit White 15.00
5, 6-Double-c w/Hildebrandt Bros.-a, Quesada & Palmiotti. 6-Texiera-c 3.00
5-Fahrenheit Gold (2000) 5.00
5-Fahrenheit Red (1000) 9.00
5-Fahrenheit White (500) 15.00
6-Fahrenheit Gold (2000) 6.00
6-Fahrenheit Red (1000) 9.00
6-Fahrenheit White (500) 15.00
6-Fahrenheit White (500)-Texiera-c 15.00
Volume 1 (1996, $14.95, TPB)-r/#1-5, intro by James Robinson. 11.00

ASH: CINDER & SMOKE
Event Comics: May, 1997 - No. 6, Oct, 1997 ($2.95, limited series)

1-6:Ramos-a/Waid, Augustyn-s in all
2-6-variant covers by Ramos and Quesada 2.95

ASH: FILES
Event Comics: Mar, 1997 ($2.95, one-shot)

1-Comics w/text 2.95

ASH: FIRE WITHIN, THE
Event Comics: Sept, 1996 - No. 2, Jan, 1997 ($2.95, unfinished limited series)

1,2:Quesada & Palmiotti-c/s/a 2.95

ASH/ 22 BRIDES
Event Comics: Dec, 1996 - No. 2, Apr, 1997 ($2.95, limited series)

1,2:Nicieza-s/Ramos-c/a 2.95

ASKANI'SON (See Adventures of Cyclops & Phoenix limited series)
Marvel Comics: Jan, 1996 - No. 4, May, 1996 ($2.95, limited series)

1-4: Story cont'd from Advs. of Cyclops & Phoenix; Lobdell/Loeb story; Gene Ha-c/a(p) 3.00
TPB (1997, $12.99) r/#1-4; Gene Ha painted-c 1.30 3.90 13.00

ASSASSINETTE
Pocket Change Comics: 1994 - No.7, 1995? ($2.50, B&W)

1-7: 1-Silver foil-c 2.50

ASSASSINETTE HARDCORE
Pocket Change Comics: 1995 - No.2, 1995 ($2.50, B&W, limited series)

1,2 2.50

ASSASSINS
DC Comics (Amalgam): Apr, 1996 ($1.95)

1 2.00

ASSASSINS, INC.
Silverline Comics: 1987 - No. 2, 1987 ($1.95)

1,2 2.00

ASTER
Entity Comics: Oct, 1994 - No. 4, 1995 ($2.95)

0-4: 1,3,4-Foil Logo. 2-Foil-c. 3-Variant-c exists. 3.00

Astonishing #59 © ATLAS

Atari Force #13 © DC

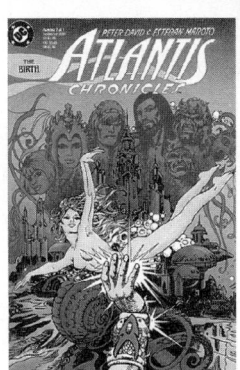

Atlantis Chronicles #7 © DC

GD25 FN65 NM94

ASTER: THE LAST CELESTIAL KNIGHT
Entity Comics: 1995 - No. 3, 1996 ($2.50)

1-3 2.50

ASTONISHING (Formerly Marvel Boy No. 1, 2)
Marvel/Atlas Comics(20CC): No. 3, Apr, 1951 - No. 63, Aug, 1957

3-Marvel Boy continues; 3-5-Marvel Boy-c 82.00 246.00 700.00
4-6-Last Marvel Boy; 4-Stan Lee app. 56.00 168.00 475.00
7-10: 7-Maneely s/f story. 10-Sinnott s/f story 25.00 75.00 190.00
11,12,15,17,20 22.00 66.00 165.00
13,14,16,18,19-Krigstein-a. 18-Jack The Ripper sty
23.00 70.00 175.00
21,22,24 20.00 60.00 150.00
23-E.C. swipe "The Hole In The Wall" from Vault Of Horror #16
20.00 60.00 150.00
25,29: 25-Crandall-a. 29-Decapitation-c 17.00 52.00 130.00
26-28 16.00 48.00 120.00
30-Tentacled eyeball story 20.00 60.00 150.00
31-37-Last pre-code issue 15.00 44.00 110.00
38-43,46,48-52,56,58,59,61 11.00 33.00 80.00
44,45,47,53-55,57,60: 44-Crandall swipe/Weird Fantasy #22. 45,47-Krigstein-a. 53-Ditko-a. 54-Torres-a, 55-Crandall, Torres-a. 57-Williamson/Krenkel-a (4 pgs.). 60-Williamson/Mayo-a (4 pgs.) 13.00 40.00 95.00
62,63: 62-Torres, Powell-a. 63-Woodbridge-a 11.00 34.00 85.00

NOTE: ***Ayers** a-16. **Berg** a-36, 53, 56. **Cameron** a-50. **Gene Colan** a-12, 20, 29, 56. **Ditko** a-53. **Drucker** a-41, 62. **Everett** a-3-6(3), 6, 10, 12, 37, 47, 48, 58; c-3-5, 13,15, 16, 18, 29, 47, 49, 51, 53-55, 57, 59-63. **Fass** a-11, 34. **Forte** a-53, 58, 60. **Fuje** a-11. **Heath** a-8, 29; c-8, 9, 19, 22, 25, 26. **Kirby** a-56. **Lawrence** a-28, 37, 38, 42. **Maneely** a-7(2); c-7, 31, 33, 34, 56. **Moldoff** a-33. **Morisi** a-10, 60. **Morrow** a-52, 61. **Orlando** a-47, 58, 61. **Pakula** a-10. **Powell** a-43, 44, 48. **Ravielli** a-28. **Reinman** a-32, 34, 38. **Robinson** a-20. **J. Romita** a-7, 18, 24, 43, 57,61. **Roussos** a-55. **Sale** a-28, 38, 59; c-32. **Sekowsky** a-13. **Severin** c-46. **Shores** a-16, 60. **Sinnott** a-11, 30. **Whitney** a-13. **Ed Win** a-20. Canadian reprints exist.*

ASTONISHING TALES (See Ka-Zar)
Marvel Comics Group: Aug, 1970 - No. 36, July, 1976 (#1-7: 15¢; #8: 25¢)

1-Ka-Zar (by Kirby(p) #1,2; by B. Smith #3-6) & Dr. Doom (by Wood #1-4; by Tuska #5,6; by Colan #7,8) double feature begins; Kraven the Hunter-c/story; Nixon cameo 3.25 10.00 36.00
2-Kraven the Hunter-c/story; Kirby, Wood-a 1.80 5.40 18.00
3-6: B. Smith-p; Wood-a-#3,4. 5,6-Red Skull 2-part story
2.25 6.80 25.00
7,9-11: 9-Lorna-r/Lorna #14. 10-B. Smith/Sal Buscema-a. 11-Origin Ka-Zar & Zabu 1.20 3.60 12.00
8-(25¢, 52 pgs.)-Last Dr. Doom 2.25 6.75 18.00
12-2nd app.Man-Thing; by Neal Adams (see Savage Tales #1 for 1st app.)
1.80 5.40 18.00
13-3rd app.Man-Thing 1.40 4.20 14.00
14-20: 14-Jann of the Jungle-r (1950s). 19-Starlin-a(p). 20-Last Ka-Zar
2.00 6.00
21-(12/73)-It! the Living Colossus begins, ends #24 (see Supernatural Thrillers #1) 1.40 4.20 14.00
22-24: 23,24-Fin Fang Foom app. 1.00 3.00 10.00
25-1st app. Deathlok the Demolisher; full length stories begin, end #36; Perez's 1st work, 2 pgs. (8/74) 2.20 6.50 24.00
26-28,30 .85 2.60 7.00
29-r/origin/1st app. Guardians of the Galaxy from Marvel Super-Heroes #18 plus-c w/4 pgs. omitted; no Deathlok story 1.00 3.00 10.00
31-34: 31-Watcher-r/Silver Surfer #3 2.00 6.00
35,36-(Regular 25¢ edition)(5,7/76) 5.00
35,36-(30¢-c, low distribution) 2.00 6.00 20.00

NOTE: ***Buckler** a-13i, 16p, 25, 26p, 27p, 28, 29p-36p; c-13, 25p, 26-30, 32-35p, 36. **John Buscema** a-9, 12p-14p, 16p; c-4-6p, 12p. **Colan** a-7p, 8p. **Ditko** a-21r. **Everett** a-6i. **G. Kane** a-11p, 15p; c-9, 10p, 11p, 14, 15p, 21p. **McWilliams** a-30i. **Starlin** a-19p; c-16p. **Sutton & Trimpe** a-8. **Tuska** a-5p, 6p, 8p. **Wood** a-1-4. **Wrightson** c-31i.*

ASTONISHING X-MEN
Marvel Comics: Mar, 1995 - No.4, July, 1995 ($1.95, limited series)

1-Age of Apocalypse 4.00
2-4 3.00

ASTRO BOY (TV) (See March of Comics #285 & The Original...)
Gold Key: August, 1965 (12¢)

1(10151-508)-Scarce;1st app. Astro Boy in comics 41.00 123.00 450.00

ASTRO CITY (See Kurt Busiek's Astro City)

ASTRO COMICS
American Airlines (Harvey): 1968 - 1979 (Giveaway)

Reprints of Harvey comics. 1968-Hot Stuff. 1969-Casper, Spooky, Hot Stuff, Stumbo the Giant, Little Audrey, Little Lotta, & Richie Rich reprints. 1970-r/Richie Rich #97. 1973-r/Richie Rich #122. 1975-Wendy. 1975-Richie Rich & Casper. 1977-r/Richie Rich & Casper #20. 1978-r/Richie Rich & Casper #25. 1979-r/Richie Rich & Casper #30 (scarce) 1.50 4.50 15.00

ASYLUM
Millennium Publications: 1993 ($2.50)

1-3: 1-Bolton-c/a; Russell 2-pg. illos 2.50

ASYLUM
Maximum Press: Dec, 1995 - No. 11, Jan, 1997 ($2.95/$2.99, anthology) (#1-6 are flip books)

1-10: 1-Warchild by Art Adams, Beanworld, Avengelyne, Battlestar Galactica. 2-Intro Mike Deodato's Deathkiss; Cybrid story begins, ends #5. 4-1st app.Christian; painted Battlestar Galactica story begins. 5-Intro Black Seed (formerly Black Flag) by Dan Fraga; B&W Christian story. 6-Intro Bionix (Six Million Dollar Man & the Bionic Woman). 7-Begin $2.99-c; Don Simpson's Megaton Man; Black Seed pinup. 8-B&W-a. 9- Foot Soldiers & Kid Supreme. 10-Lady Supreme by Terry Moore-c/app. 3.00

ATARI FORCE
DC Comics: 1982 - No. 5, 1983; Jan, 1984 - No. 20, Aug, 1985 (Mando paper)

1-3 (1982, 5X7", 52 pgs.)-Given away with Atari games 4.00
4,5 (1982-1983, 52 pgs.)-Given away with Atari games (scarcer)
.85 2.60 7.00
1-20: 1-(1/84)-Intro Tempest, Packrat, Babe, Morphea, & Dart 1.00
Special 1 (4/86) 1.00

NOTE: ***Byrne** c-Special 1i. **Giffen** a-12p, 13i. **Rogers** a-18p, Special 1p.*

A-TEAM, THE (TV)
Marvel Comics Group: Mar, 1984 - No. 3, May, 1984

1-3 2.00
1,2-(Whitman bagged set) w/75¢-c 4.00
3-(Whitman bagged set) w/75¢-c 2.00 6.00

ATLANTIS CHRONICLES, THE (Also see Aquaman, 3rd Series & Aquaman: Time & Tide)
DC Comics: Mar, 1990 - No. 7, Sept, 1990 ($2.95, limited series, 52 pgs.)

1-7: 1-Peter David scripts. 7-True origin of Aquaman; nudity panels
3.25

ATLANTIS, THE LOST CONTINENT
Dell Publishing Co.: May, 1961

Four Color #1188-Movie, photo-c 9.00 27.00 100.00

ATLAS (See 1st Issue Special)

ATLAS
Dark Horse Comics: Feb, 1994 - No. 4, 1994 ($2.50, limited series)

1-4 2.50

ATOM, THE (See Action #425, All-American #19, Brave & the Bold, D.C. Special Series #1, Detective, Flash Comics #80, Power Of The Atom, Showcase #34 -36 , Super Friends, Sword of The Atom, Teen Titans & World's Finest)

ATOM, THE (...& the Hawkman No. 39 on)
National Periodical Publ.: June-July, 1962 - No. 38, Aug-Sept, 1968

Atom #4 © DC

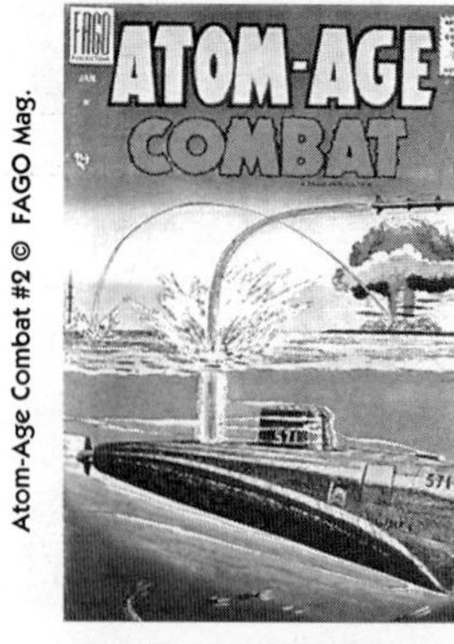

Atom-Age Combat #2 © FAGO Mag.

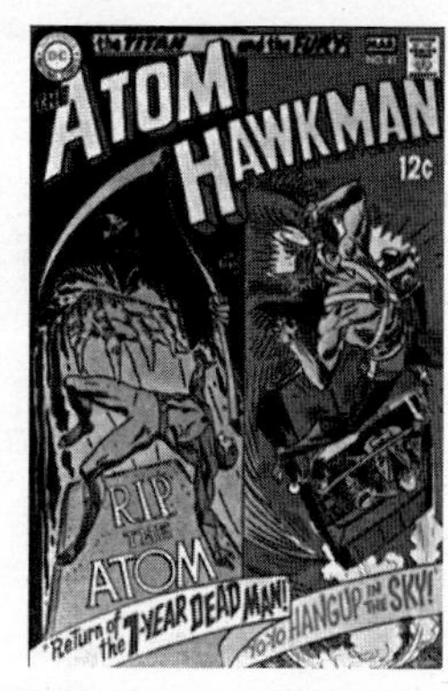

Atom & Hawkman #41 © DC

GD25 FN65 NM94

1-(6-7/62)-Intro Plant-Master; 1st app. Maya 63.00 188.00 750.00
2 30.00 90.00 300.00
3-1st Time Pool story; 1st app. Chronos (origin) 19.00 57.00 190.00
4,5: 4-Snapper Carr x-over 15.00 45.00 150.00
6,8-10: 8-Justice League, Dr. Light app. 10.00 30.00 100.00
7-Hawkman x-over (6-7/63; 1st Atom & Hawkman team-up); 1st app. Hawkman since Brave & the Bold tryouts 26.00 78.00 260.00
11-15: 13-Chronos-c/story 7.00 21.00 70.00
16-20: 19-Zatanna x-over 5.00 15.00 50.00
21-28,30: 28-Chronos-c/story 4.00 12.00 40.00
29-1st solo Golden Age Atom x-over in S.A. 14.00 42.00 140.00
31-35,37,38: 31-Hawkman x-over. 37-Intro. Major Mynah; Hawkman cameo 4.00 12.00 40.00
36-G.A. Atom x-over 5.00 15.00 50.00
NOTE: ***Anderson** a-1-11i, 13i; c-inks-1-25, 31-35, 37. **Sid Greene** a-8i-37i. **Gil Kane** a-1p-37p; c-1p-28p, 29, 33p, 34. **George Roussos** 38i **Mike Sekowsky** 38p Time Pool stories also in 6, 9,12, 17, 21, 27, 35.*

ATOM ,THE (See Tangent Comics/ The Atom)

ATOM AGE (See Classics Illustrated Special Issue)

ATOM-AGE COMBAT
St. John Publishing Co.: June, 1952 - No. 5, Apr, 1953; Feb, 1958
1-Buck Vinson in all 41.00 123.00 325.00
2-Flying saucer story 25.00 74.00 185.00
3,5: 3-Mayo-a (6 pgs.). 5-Flying saucer-c/story 20.00 60.00 150.00
4 (Scarce) 24.00 72.00 180.00
1(2/58-St. John) 16.00 48.00 120.00

ATOM-AGE COMBAT
Fago Magazines: Nov, 1958 - No. 3, Mar, 1959
1-All have Dick Ayers-c/a 23.00 70.00 175.00
2,3: 2-A-Bomb explosion-c 17.00 52.00 130.00

ATOMAN
Spark Publications: Feb, 1946 - No. 2, April, 1946
1-Origin & 1st app. Atoman; Robinson/Meskin-a; Kidcrusaders, Wild Bill Hickok, Marvin the Great app. 47.00 142.00 400.00
2-Robinson/Meskin-a; Robinson c-1,2 39.00 117.00 300.00

ATOM & HAWKMAN, THE (Formerly The Atom)
National Periodical Publ: No. 39, Oct-Nov, 1968 - No. 45, Oct-Nov, 1969
39-45: 40-41-Kubert/Anderson-a. 43-(7/69)-Last 12¢ issue; 1st app. Gentleman Ghost, origin in #44. 44-(9/69)-1st 15¢ issue 3.00 9.00 30.00
NOTE: ***M. Anderson** a-39, 40i, 41i, 43, 44. **Sid Greene** a-40i-45i. **Kubert** a-40p, 41p; c-39-45.*

ATOM ANT (TV) (See Golden Comics Digest #2)
Gold Key: January, 1966 (12¢)
1(10170-601)-Hanna-Barbera character 28.00 85.00 320.00

ATOM ANT & SECRET SQUIRREL
Archie Publications: Nov, 1995 - Present ($1.50, bi-monthly)
1-12-Hanna-Barbera characters 2.00

ATOMIC AGE
Marvel Comics (Epic Comics): Nov, 1990 - No. 4, Feb, 1991 ($4.50, limited series, squarebound, 52 pgs.)
1-4: Williamson-a(i) 4.50

ATOMIC ATTACK (True War Stories; formerly Attack, first series)
Youthful Magazines: No. 5, Jan, 1953 - No. 8, Oct, 1953 (1st story is sci/fi in all issues)
5-Atomic bomb-c; science fiction stories in all 35.00 104.00 260.00
6-8 21.00 64.00 160.00

ATOMIC BOMB
Jay Burtis Publications: 1945 (36 pgs.)
1-Airmale & Stampy 43.00 129.00 350.00

ATOMIC BUNNY (Formerly Atomic Rabbit)
Charlton Comics: No. 12, Aug, 1958 - No. 19, Dec, 1959
12 10.00 30.00 75.00
13-19 5.70 17.00 40.00

ATOMIC COMICS
Daniels Publications (Canadian): Jan, 1946 (Reprints, one-shot)
1-Rocketman, Yankee Boy, Master Key app. 29.00 86.00 215.00

ATOMIC COMICS
Green Publishing Co.: Jan, 1946 - No. 4, July-Aug, 1946 (#1-4 were printed w/o cover gloss)
1-Radio Squad by Siegel & Shuster; Barry O'Neal app.; Fang Gow cover-r/ Detective Comics (Classic-c) 118.00 353.00 1000.00
2-Inspector Dayton; Kid Kane by Matt Baker; Lucky Wings, Congo King, Prop Powers (only app.) begin 55.00 166.00 470.00
3,4: 3-Zero Ghost Detective app.; Baker-a(2) each; 4-Baker-c 39.00 118.00 315.00

ATOMIC KNIGHTS (See Strange Adventures #117)

ATOMIC MOUSE (TV, Movies) (See Blue Bird, Funny Animals, Giant Comics Edition & Wotalife Comics)
Capitol Stories/Charlton Comics: 3/53 - No. 54, 6/63; No. 1, 12/84; V2#10, 9/85 - No. 13, ?/86
1-Origin & 1st app.; Al Fago-c/a in all? 29.00 88.00 220.00
2 11.00 32.00 80.00
3-10: 5-Timmy The Timid Ghost app.; see Zoo Funnies 9.30 28.00 65.00
11-13,16-25 5.35 16.00 32.00
14,15-Hoppy The Marvel Bunny app. 6.50 19.50 45.00
26-(68 pgs.) 9.30 28.00 70.00
27-40: 36,37-Atom The Cat app. 4.25 13.00 28.00
41-54 3.00 7.50 15.00
1 (1984) 4.00
V2#10 (10/85) -13-Fago-r. #12(1/86) 3.00

ATOMIC RABBIT (Atomic Bunny #12 on; see Giant Comics #3 & Wotalife)
Charlton Comics: Aug, 1955 - No. 11, Mar, 1958
1-Origin & 1st app.; Al Fago-c/a in all? 25.00 76.00 190.00
2 10.00 30.00 75.00
3-10 7.15 21.50 45.00
11-(68 pgs.) 10.00 30.00 75.00

ATOMIC SPY CASES
Avon Periodicals: Mar-Apr, 1950 (Painted-c)
1-No Wood-a; A-bomb blast panels; Fass-a 27.00 80.00 200.00

ATOMIC THUNDERBOLT, THE
Regor Company: Feb, 1946 (one-shot)
1-Intro. Atomic Thunderbolt & Mr. Murdo 47.00 142.00 400.00

ATOMIC WAR!
Ace Periodicals (Junior Books): Nov, 1952 - No. 4, Apr, 1953
1-Atomic bomb-c 78.00 234.00 670.00
2,3: 3-Atomic bomb-c 52.00 156.00 440.00
4-Used in **POP**, pg. 96 & illo. 52.00 156.00 440.00

ATOMIK ANGELS
Crusade Comics: May, 1996 - Present ($2.50)
1-3: 1-Freefall from Gen 13 app 3.00
1-Variant-c 4.00
Intrep-Edition (2/96, B&W, giveaway at launch party)-Previews Atomik Angels #1; includes Billy Tucci interview. 4.00

ATOM SPECIAL (See Atom & Justice League of America)
DC Comics: 1993/1995 ($2.50/$2.95)
1-(1993, $2.50, 68 pgs.)-Dillon-c/a. 2.50
2-(1995, $2.95)-McDonnell-a/Bolland-c/Peyer-s. 3.00

Attack #4 © YM

Attack #54 © CC

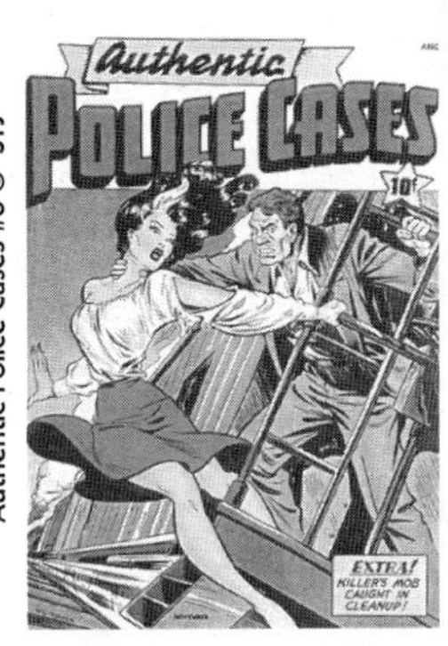

Authentic Police Cases #6 © STJ

GD25 FN65 NM94

ATOM THE CAT (Formerly Tom Cat; see Giant Comics #3)
Charlton Comics: No. 9, Oct, 1957 - No. 17, Aug, 1959

9 7.85 23.50 55.00
10,13-17 5.00 15.00 30.00
11,12: 11(64pgs)-Atomic Mouse app. 12(100 pgs.) 9.30 28.00 70.00

ATTACK
Youthful Mag./Trojan No. 5 on: May, 1952 - No. 4, Nov, 1952; No. 5, Jan, 1953 - No. 5, Sept, 1953

1-(1st series)-Extreme violence 23.00 70.00 175.00
2,3-Both Harrison-c/a; bondage, whipping 11.00 34.00 85.00
4-Krenkel-a (7 pgs.); Harrison-a (becomes Atomic Attack #5 on) 12.00 36.00 90.00
5-(#1, Trojan, 2nd series) 9.35 28.00 70.00
6-8 (#2-4), 5 6.50 19.50 45.00

ATTACK
Charlton Comics: No. 54, 1958 - No. 60, Nov, 1959

54 (25¢, 100 pgs.) 8.50 26.00 60.00
55-60 4.00 10.00 20.00

ATTACK!
Charlton Comics: 1962 - No. 15, 3/75; No. 16, 8/79 - No. 48, 10/84

nn(#1)-('62) Special Edition 2.80 8.40 28.00
2('63), 3(Fall, '64) 2.50 7.50 20.00
V4#3(10/66), 4(10/67)-(Formerly Special War Series #2; becomes Attack At Sea V4#5) 1.75 5.25 14.00
1(9/71) 1.40 4.20 14.00
2-5: 4-American Eagle app. 1.20 3.60 12.00
6-15(3/75): .90 2.70 8.00
16(8/79) - 48: 48(10/84)-Wood-r; S&K-c 3.00
Modern Comics 13('78)-r 3.00
NOTE: ***Sutton** a-9,10,13.*

ATTACK!
Spire Christian Comics (Fleming H. Revell Co.): 1975 (39¢/49¢, 36 pgs.)

nn 4.50

ATTACK AT SEA (Formerly Attack!, 1967)
Charlton Comics: V4#5, Oct, 1968

V4#5 1.75 5.25 14.00

ATTACK ON PLANET MARS (See Strange Worlds #18)
Avon Periodicals: 1951

nn-Infantino, Fawcette, Kubert & Wood-a; adaptation of Tarrano the Conqueror by Ray Cummings 65.00 194.00 550.00

ATTITUDE LAD
Slave Labor Graphics: Apr, 1994 - No. 3, Nov, 1994 ($2.95, B&W)

1-3 3.00

AUDREY & MELVIN (Formerly Little...)(See Little Audrey & Melvin)
Harvey Publications: No. 62, Sept, 1974

62 .85 2.60 7.00

AUGIE DOGGIE (TV) (See Hanna-Barbera Band Wagon, Quick-Draw McGraw, Spotlight #2, Top Cat & Whitman Comic Books)
Gold Key: October, 1963 (12¢)

1-Hanna-Barbera character 17.00 50.00 185.00

AURORA COMIC SCENES INSTRUCTION BOOKLET
Aurora Plastics Co.: 1974 (6-1/4x9-3/4," 8 pgs., slick paper)
(Included with superhero model kits)

181-140-Tarzan; Neal Adams-a 1.80 5.40 18.00
182-140-Spider-Man. 2.25 6.800 25.00
183-140-Tonto(Gil Kane art). 184-140-Hulk. 185-140-Superman. 186-140-Superboy. 187-140-Batman. 188-140-The Lone Ranger(1974-by Gil Kane). 192-140-Captain America(1975). 193-140-Robin 1.60 4.80 16.00

GD25 FN65 NM94

AUTHENTIC POLICE CASES
St. John Publishing Co.: 2/48 - No. 6, 11/48; No. 7, 5/50 - No. 38, 3/55

1-Hale the Magician by Tuska begins 35.00 104.00 260.00
2-Lady Satan, Johnny Rebel app. 22.00 66.00 165.00
3-Veiled Avenger app.; blood drainage story plus 2 Lucky Coyne stories; used in **SOTI**, illo. from Red Seal #16 40.00 120.00 320.00
4,5: 4-Masked Black Jack app. 5-Late 1930s Jack Cole-a(r); transvestism story 23.00 68.00 170.00
6-Matt Baker-c; used in **SOTI**, illo- "An invitation to learning", r-in Fugitives From Justice #3; Jack Cole-a; also used by the N.Y. Legis. Comm. 42.00 142.00 335.00
7,8,10-14: 7-Jack Cole-a; Matt Baker-a begins #8, ends #?; Vic Flint in #10-14. 10-12-Baker-a(2 each) 18.00 54.00 135.00
9-No Vic Flint 14.00 42.00 105.00
15-Drug-c/story; Vic Flint app.; Baker-c 18.00 54.00 135.00
16,18,20,21,23: Baker-a(i) 11.00 32.00 80.00
17,19,22-Baker-c 12.00 36.00 90.00
24-28 (All 100 pgs.): 26-Transvestism 20.00 60.00 150.00
29-32 6.00 18.00 42.00
33-38: 33-Transvestism; Baker-c. 34-Baker-c; r/#95. 35-Baker-c/a(2); r/#10 36-r/#11; Vic Flint strip-r; Baker-c/a(2) unsigned. 37-Baker-c; r/#17. 38-Baker-c/a; r/#18 9.35 28.00 70.00
NOTE: ***Matt Baker** c-6-16, 17, 19, 22, 27, 29, 31-38; a-13, 16. Bondage c-1, 3.*

AUTOMATON
Image Comics (Flypaper Press): Sept, 1998 - No. 3, 1998 ($2.95, lim. series)

1-3-R.A. Jones-s/Peter Vale-a 2.95

AUTUMN
Caliber Comics: 1995 - No. 3, 1995 ($2.95, B&W)

1-3 3.00

AUTUMN ADVENTURES (Walt Disney's...)
Disney Comics: Autumn, 1990; No. 2, Autumn, 1991 ($2.95, 68 pgs.)

1-Donald Duck-r(2) by Barks, Pluto-r, & new-a 3.50
2-D. Duck-r by Barks; new Super Goof story 3.50

AVATAR
DC Comics: Feb, 1991 - No. 3, Apr, 1991 ($5.95, limited series, 100 pgs.)

1-3: Based on TSR's Forgotten Realms 2.00 6.00

AVENGEBLADE
Maximum Press: July, 1996 - No. 2, Aug, 1996 ($2.99, limited series)

1,2: Bad Girls parody 3.00

AVENGELYNE
Maximum Press: May, 1995 - No. 3, July, 1995 ($2.50/$3.50, limited series)

1/2 1.00 3.00 10.00
1-Newstand ($2.50)-Photo-c; poster insert 4.00
1-Direct Market ($3.50)-Chromium-c; poster 8.00
1-Glossy edition 2.25 6.80 25.00
1-Gold 15.00
2-3: 2-Polybagged w/card 4.00
3-Variant-c; Deodato pin-up 5.00
...Swimsuit (8/95, $2.95)-Pin-ups/photos. 3-Variant-c exist (2 photo, 1 Liefeld-a) 3.00
...Swimsuit (1/96, $3.50, 2nd printing)-photo-c 3.50
Trade paperback (12/95, $9.95) 10.00

AVENGELYNE
Maximum Press: V2#1, Apr, 1996 - No. 14, Apr, 1997 ($2.95/$2.50)

V2#1-Four covers exist (2 photo-c). 5.00
V2#2-Three covers exist (1 photo-c); flip book w/Darkchylde 3.60 12.00
V2#0, 3-14: 0-(10/96).3-Flip book w/Priest preview. 4-Cybrid app; w/Darkchylde/Avengelyne poster. 5-Flip book w/Blindside. 6-Divinity-c/app. 3.00
...Bible (10/96, $3.50) 3.50

Avengelyne: Deadly Sins #1 © Rob Liefeld

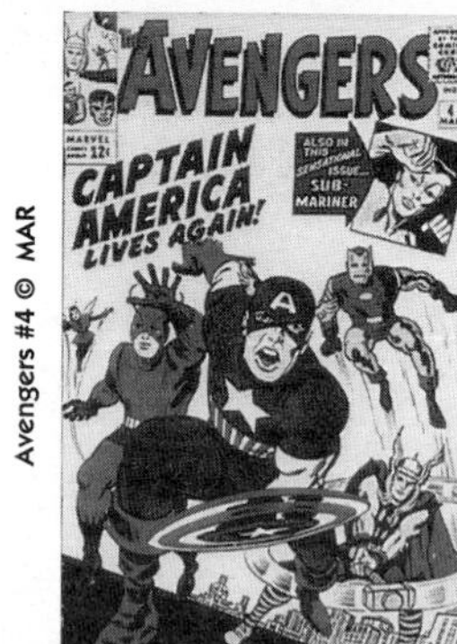

Avengers #4 © MAR

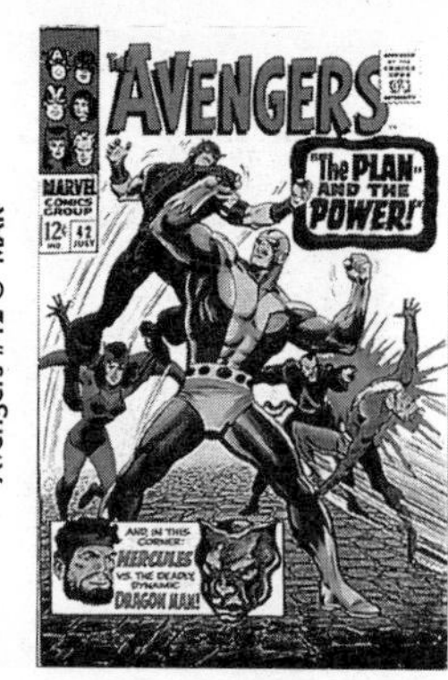

Avengers #42 © MAR

GD25 FN65 NM94

AVENGELYNE: ARMAGEDDON
Maximum Press: Dec, 1996 - No. 3, Feb, 1997 ($2.99, limited series)
1-3-Scott Clark-a(p) 3.00

AVENGELYNE: DEADLY SINS
Maximum Press: Feb, 1996 - No. 2, Mar, 1996 ($2.95, limited series)
1,2: 1-Two-c exist (1 photo, 1 Liefeld-a). 2-Liefeld-c; Pop Mhan-a(p). 3.00

AVENGELYNE/GLORY
Maximum Press: Sept, 1995 ($3.95, one-shot)
1-Chromium-c 4.00
1-Variant-c 4.00

AVENGELYNE/GLORY: GODYSSEY, THE (See Glory/...)
Maximum Press: Sept, 1996 ($2.99, one-shot)
1-Two covers (1 photo) 3.00

AVENGELYNE/GLORY SWIMSUIT SPECIAL
Maximum Press: June, 1996 ($2.95)
1-Pin-ups & photos of Avengelyne and Glory; photo-c (variant illos-c. also exists) 3.00

AVENGELYNE/POWER
Maximum Press: Nov, 1995 - No.3, Jan, 1996 ($2.95, limited series)
1-3: 1,2-Liefeld-c. 3-Three variant-c. exist (1 photo-c) 2.50
1-Variant-c 3.50

AVENGELYNE • PROPHET
Maximum Press: May, 1996; No. 2, Feb. 1997 ($2.95, unfinished lim. series)
1,2-Liefeld-c/a(p) 3.00

AVENGELYNE/ WARRIOR NUN AREALA (See Warrior Nun/...)
Maximum Press: Nov, 1996 ($2.99, one-shot)
1 3.00

AVENGER, THE (See A-1 Comics)
Magazine Enterprises: Feb-Mar, 1955 - No. 4, Aug-Sept, 1955
1(A-1 #129)-Origin 36.00 108.00 270.00
2(A-1 #131), 3(A-1 #133) Robot-c, 4(A-1 #138) 23.00 69.00 175.00
IW Reprint #9('64)-Reprints #1 (new cover) 2.50 7.50 24.00
NOTE: *Powell a-2-4; c-1-4.*

AVENGERS, THE (See Giant-Size..., Kree/Skrull War Starring..., Marvel Graphic Novel #27, Marvel Super Action, Marvel Super Heroes('66), Marvel Treasury Ed., Marvel Triple Action, Solo Avengers, Tales Of Suspense #49, West Coast Avengers & X-Men Vs....)

AVENGERS, THE (The Mighty Avengers on cover only #63-69)
Marvel Comics Group: Sept, 1963 - No. 402, Sept, 1996

GD25 FN65 VF82 NM94
1-Origin & 1st app. The Avengers (Thor, Iron Man, Hulk, Ant-Man, Wasp); Loki app. 167.00 500.00 1085.00 2350.00

GD25 FN65 NM94
2-Hulk leaves Avengers 52.00 156.00 620.00
3-1st Sub-Mariner x-over (outside the F.F.); Hulk & Sub-Mariner team-up & battle Avengers; Spider-Man cameo (1/64) 35.00 105.00 385.00
4-Revival of Captain America who joins the Avengers; 1st Silver Age app. of Captain America & Bucky (3/64) 125.00 375.00 1500.00
4-Reprint from the Golden Record Comic set 7.50 22.50 75.00
With Record (1966) 11.00 33.00 110.00
5-Hulk app. 22.50 68.00 225.00
6-8: 6-Intro/1st app. original Zemo & his Masters of Evil. 8-Intro Kang 18.00 54.00 180.00
9-Intro Wonder Man who dies in same story 18.50 55.00 185.00
10-Intro/1st app. Immortus; early Hercules app. (11/64) 15.50 47.00 155.00
11-Spider-Man-c & x-over (12/64) 18.50 55.00 185.00
12-15: 15-Death of original Zemo 11.50 34.00 115.00

GD25 FN65 NM94

16-New Avengers line-up (Hawkeye, Quicksilver, Scarlet Witch join; Thor, Iron Man, Giant-Man, Wasp leave) 12.50 38.00 125.00
17-19: 19-Intro/1st app. Swordsman; origin Hawkeye (8/65) 8.50 25.50 85.00
20-22: Wood inks 5.50 16.50 55.00
23-30: 25-Dr. Doom-c/story. 28-Giant-Man becomes Goliath (5/66) 4.00 12.00 40.00
31-40 2.50 7.50 25.00
41-52,54-56: 43,44-1st app. Red Guardian. 46-Ant-Man returns (re-intro, 11/67) 47-Magneto-c/story. 48-Origin/1st app. new Black Knight (1/68). 52-Black Panther joins; 1st app. The Grim Reaper. 54-1st app. new Masters of Evil. 56-Zemo app; story explains how Capt. America became imprisioned in ice dur ing WWII, only to be rescued in Avengers #4 2.25 6.75 22.00
53-X-Men app. 3.50 10.50 35.00
57-1st app. S.A. Vision (10/68) 6.50 19.50 65.00
58-Origin The Vision 4.50 13.50 45.00
59-67: 59-Intro. Yellowjacket. 60-Wasp & Yellowjacket wed. 63-Goliath becomes Yellowjacket; Hawkeye becomes the new Goliath. 65-Last 12¢ issue. 66,67-B. Smith-a 2.50 7.50 20.00
68-70: 70-Nighthawk on cover 1.25 3.75 10.00
71-1st app. The Invaders (12/69); 1st app. Nighthawk; Black Knight joins 3.00 9.00 30.00
72-79,81,82,84-86,88-91: 82-Daredevil app. 88-Written by Harlan Ellison 1.10 3.30 11.00
80-Intro. Red Wolf (9/70) 1.80 5.40 18.00
83-Intro. The Liberators (Wasp, Valkyrie, Scarlet Witch, Medusa & the Black Widow) 2.20 6.25 22.00
87-Origin The Black Panther 2.20 6.50 24.00
92-Last 15¢ issue; Neal Adams-c 1.60 4.80 16.00
93-(52 pgs.)-Neal Adams-c/a 5.00 15.00 55.00
94-96-Neal Adams-c/a 3.20 9.50 35.00
97-G.A. Capt. America, Sub-Mariner, Human Torch, Patriot, Vision, Blazing Skull, Fin, Angel, & new Capt. Marvel x-over 1.50 4.50 15.00
98,99: 98-Goliath becomes Hawkeye; Smith c/a(i). 99-Smith-c, Smith/Sutton-a 2.00 6.00 20.00
100-(6/72)-Smith-c/a; featuring everyone who was an Avenger 6.25 18.50 70.00
101 1.30 3.90 13.00
102-106,108,109: 101-Harlan Ellison scripts 1.00 3.00 10.00
107-Starlin-a(p) 1.30 3.90 13.00
110,111-X-Men app. 2.00 6.00 20.00
112-1st app. Mantis 1.20 3.60 12.00
113-115,119-124,126-130: 123-Origin Mantis .90 2.70 8.00
116-118-Defenders/Silver Surfer app. 1.40 4.20 14.00
125-Thanos-c & brief app. 1.50 4.50 15.00
131-133,136-140: 136-Ploog-r/Amazing Advs. #12 .80 2.40 6.50
134,135-True origin Vision .90 2.70 9.00
141-143,145,147,148,152-163 5.00
144,150,151:144-Origin & 1st app. Hellcat. 150-Kirby-a(r); new line-up: Capt. America, Scarlet Witch, Iron Man, Wasp, Yellowjacket, Vision & The Beast. 151-Wonder Man returns w/new costume .85 2.60 7.00
146,149-(Regular 25¢ edition)(4,7/76) 5.00
146,149-(30¢-c, limited distribution) 1.60 4.80 16.00
164-166: Byrne-a 2.00 6.00
167-191: 168-Guardians of the Galaxy app. 174-Thanos cameo. 176-Starhawk app. 181-191-Byrne-a. 181-New line-up: Capt. America, Scarlet Witch, Iron Man, Wasp, Vision, Beast & The Falcon. 183-Ms. Marvel joins. 185-Origin Quicksilver & Scarlet Witch 3.00
192-213,215-262: 195-1st Taskmaster. 200-(10/80, 52 pgs.)-Ms. Marvel leaves. 211-New line-up: Capt. America, Iron Man, Tigra, Thor, Wasp & Yellowjacket. 213-Yellowjacket leaves. 215,216-Silver Surfer app. 216-Tigra leaves. 217-Yellowjacket & Wasp return. 221-Hawkeye & She-Hulk join. 227-Capt. Marvel (female) joins; origins of Ant-Man, Wasp, Giant-Man, Goliath, Yellowjacket, & Avengers. 230-Yellowjacket quits. 231-Iron Man leaves. 232-Starfox (Eros)

Avengers #236 © MAR

Avengers #378 © MAR

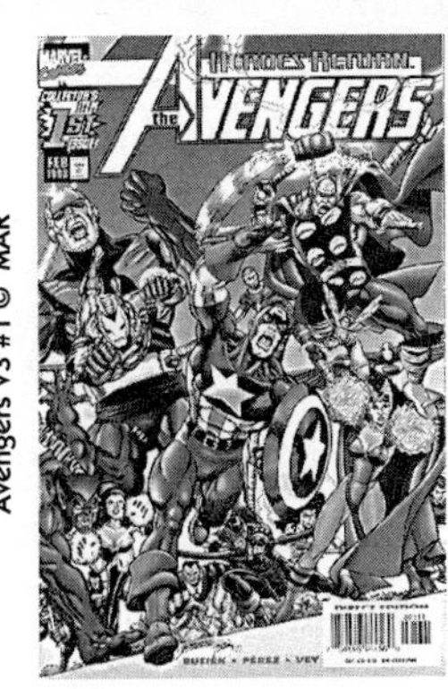

Avengers V3 #1 © MAR

GD25 FN65 NM94

joins. 234-Origin Quicksilver, Scarlet Witch. 236-New logo. 238-Origin Blackout. 239-Avengers app. on David Letterman show. 240-Spider-Woman revived. 250-($1.00, 52 pgs.) 2.25
214-Ghost Rider-c/story 5.00
263-1st app. X-Factor (1/86)(story continues in Fantastic Four #286) 4.00
264-299: 272-Alpha Flight app. 291-$1.00 issues begin. 297-Black Knight, She-Hulk & Thor resign. 298-Inferno tie-in 2.00
300 (2/89, $1.75, 68 pgs.)-Thor joins; Simonson-a 2.00
301-304,306-325,327,329-343: 302-Re-intro Quasar. 314-318-Spider-Man x-over. 320-324-Alpha Flight app. (320-cameo). 327-2nd app. Rage. 341, 342-New Warriors app. 343-Last $1.00-c 1.50
305-Byrne scripts begin 2.00
326-1st app. Rage (11/90) 4.00
328-Origin Rage 3.00
344-346,348,349,351-359,361,362,364,365,367: 365-Contains coupon for Hunt for Magneto contest 1.50
347-($1.75, 56 pgs.) 2.00
350-($2.50, 68 pgs.)-Double gatefold-c showing-c to #1; r/#53 w/cover in flip book format; vs. The Starjammers 2.50
360-($2.95, 52 pgs.)-Embossed all-foil-c; 30th ann. 3.50
363-($2.95, 52 pgs.)-All silver foil-c 2.50
366-($3.95, 68 pgs.)-Embossed all gold foil-c 4.00
368-Bloodties part 1; Avengers/X-Men x-over 1.50
369-($2.95)-Foil embossed-c; Bloodties part 5 3.00
370-373 1.50
374,376-399: 374-$1.50-c begins; bound-in trading card sheet. 380-Deodato-a. 390,391-"The Crossing." 395-Death of "old" Tony Stark; wraparound-c. 1.50
375-($2.00, 52 pgs.)-Regular ed.; Thunderstrike returns; leads into Malibu Comics' Black September. 2.00
375-($2.50, 52 pgs.)-Collector's ed. w/bound-in poster; leads into Malibu Comics' Black September. 2.50
400-Waid script 4.00
401,402: Waid-s; 402-Deodato breakdowns; cont'd in X-Men #56 & Onslaught: Marvel Universe. 2.50
Special 1(9/67, 25¢, 68 pgs.)-New-a; original & new Avengers team-up 6.00 18.00 60.00
Special 2(9/68, 25¢, 68 pgs.)-New-a; original vs. new Avengers 3.00 9.00 30.00
Special 3(9/69, 25¢, 68 pgs.)-r/Avengers #4 plus 3 Capt. America stories by Kirby (art); origin Red Skull 2.50 7.50 22.00
Special 4(1/71, 25¢, 68 pgs.)-Kirby-r/Avengers #5,6 1.20 3.60 12.00
Special 5(1/72)-Spider-Man x-over 1.20 3.60 12.00
Annual 6(11/76) .85 2.60 7.00
Annual 7(11/77)-Starlin-c/a; Warlock dies; Thanos app. 1.40 4.20 14.00
Annual 8(1978)-Dr. Strange, Ms. Marvel app. 5.00
Annual 9(1979)-Newton-a(p) 4.00
Annual 10(1981)-Golden-p; X-Men cameo; 1st app. Rogue & Madelyne Pryor 2.00 6.00 20.00
Annual 11-16: 11(1982)-Vs. The Defenders. 12(1983). 13(1984). 14(1985). 15(1986). 16(1987) 3.50
Annual 17(1988)-Evolutionary War x-over 4.00
Annual 18(1989, $2.00, 68 pgs.)-Atlantis Attacks 3.00
Annual 19,20(1990, 1991)(both $2.00, 68 pgs.) 2.50
Annual 21(1992, $2.25, 68 pgs.) 2.25
Annual 22(1993, $2.95, 68 pgs.)-Bagged w/card 3.00
Annual 23(1994, $2.95, 68 pgs.) 3.00
Marvel Double Feature...Avengers/Giant-Man #379 ($2.50, 52 pgs.)-Same as Avengers #379 w/Giant-Man flip book 2.50
The Yesterday Quest ($6.95)-r/#181,182,185-187 .85 2.60 7.00

NOTE: ***Austin** c(i)-157, 167, 168, 170-177, 181, 183-188, 198-201, Annual 8. **John Buscema** a-41-44p, 46p, 47p, 49, 50, 51-62p, 74-77, 79-85, 87-91, 97, 105p, 121p, 124p,125p, 152, 153p, 255-279p, 281-302p; c-41-66, 68-71, 73-91, 97-99, 178, 256-259p, 261-279p, 281-302p. **Byrne** a-164-166p, 181-191p, 233p, Annual 13i, 14p; c-186-190p, 233p, 260, 305p; scripts-305-312. **Colan** a(p)-63-65, 111, 206-208, 210, 211; c(p)-65, 206-208, 210, 211. **Ditko** a-Annual 13. **Guice** a-Annual 12p. **Don Heck** a-9-15, 17-40, 157. **Kane** c-37p, 159p. **Kane/Everett** c-97. **Kirby** a-1-8p, Special 3r, 4r(p); c-1-30, 148, 151-158; layouts-14-16. **Ron Lim** c(p)-335-341. **Miller** c-193p. **Mooney** a-86i, 179p, 180p. **Nebres** a-178i; c-179i. **Newton** a-204p, Annual 9p. **Perez** a(p)-141, 143, 144, 148, 150, 154, 155, 160, 161, 162, 167,168, 170, 171, 194-196, 198-202, Annual 6, 8; c(p)-160-162, 164-166, 170-174, 181,183-185, 191, 192, 194-201, 379-382, Annual 8. **Starlin** c-121, 135. **Staton** a-127-134i. **Tuska** a-47i,48i, 51i, 53i, 54i, 106p, 107p, 135p, 137-140p, 163p. Guardians of the Galaxy app. in #167, 168, 170, 173, 175, 181.*

AVENGERS, THE (Volume Two)
Marvel Comics: V2#1, Nov, 1996 - No. 13, Nov, 1997 ($2.95/$1.95/$1.99) (Produced by Extreme Studios)

1-($2.95)-Heroes Reborn begins; intro new team (Captain America, Swordsman, Scarlet Witch, Vision, Thor, Hellcat & Hawkeye); 1st app. Avengers Island; Loki & Enchantress app.; Rob Liefeld-p & plot; Chap Yaep-p; Jim Valentino scripts; variant-c exists 4.00
1-($1.95)-Variant-c 5.00
2,3: 2-Begin $1.95-c; Jeph Loeb scripts begin, Kang app. 2.00
4-9: 4-Hulk-c/app. 5-Thor/Hulk battle; 2 covers 2.00
10, 11: 10-Begin-$1.99-c 2.00
12-($2.99) "Heroes Reunited"-pt. 2 3.00
13-"World War 3"-pt. 2, x-over w/Image characters 2.00

AVENGERS, THE (Volume Three)
Marvel Comics: Feb, 1998 - Present ($2.99/$1.99)

1-($2.99, 48 pgs.) Busiek-s/Perez-a/wraparound-c; Avengers reassemble after Heroes Return 5.00
1-Variant Heroes Return cover 2.60 7.00
1-Rough Cut-Features original script and pencil pages 3.00
2-($1.99)Perez-c 3.00
2-Lago painted-c 3.00
3,4: 3-Wonder Man-c/app. 4-Final roster chosen; Perez poster 2.50
5-11: 5,6-Squadron Supreme-c/app. 8-Triathlon-c/app. 2.00
.../ Squadron Supreme '98 Annual ($2.99) 3.00

AVENGERS, THE (TV)(Also see Steed and Mrs. Peel)
Gold Key: Nov, 1968 ("John Steed & Emma Peel" cover title) (15¢)

1-Photo-c 22.00 66.00 240.00

AVENGERS COLLECTOR'S EDITION, THE
Marvel Comics: 1993 (Ordered through mail w/candy wrapper, 20 pgs.)

1-Contains 4 bound-in trading cards 2.00

AVENGERS FOREVER
Marvel Comics: Dec, 1998 - Present ($2.99)

1,2-Busiek-s/Pacheco-a 3.00

AVENGERS LOG, THE
Marvel Comics: Feb, 1994 ($1.95)

1-Gives history of all members; Perez-c 2.00

AVENGERS SPOTLIGHT (Formerly Solo Avengers #1-20)
Marvel Comics: No. 21, Aug, 1989 - No. 40, Jan, 1991 (75¢/$1.00)

21 (75¢)-Byrne-c/a 1.00
22-40 ($1.00): 26-Acts of Vengeance story. 31-34-U.S. Agent series. 36-Heck-i. 37-Mortimer-i. 40-The Black Knight app. 1.00

AVENGERS STRIKEFILE
Marvel Comics: Jan, 1994 ($1.75, one-shot)

1 1.75

AVENGERS: THE CROSSING
Marvel Comics: July, 1995 ($4.95, one-shot)

1-Deodato-c/a; 1st app. Thor's new costume 5.00

AVENGERS: THE LEGEND
Marvel Comics: Oct, 1996 ($3.95, one-shot)

1-Tribute issue 4.00

Avengers West Coast #69 © MAR

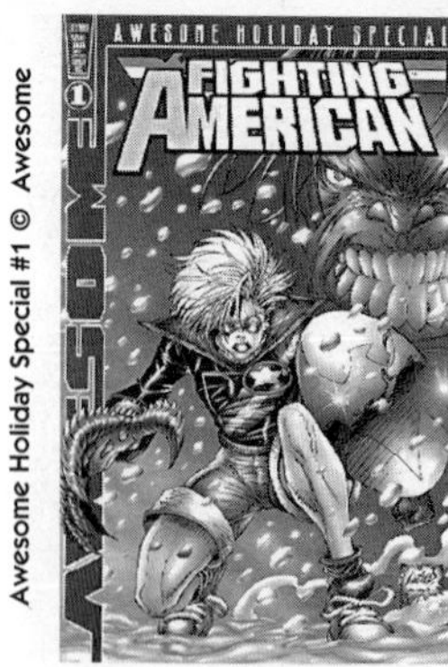

Awesome Holiday Special #1 © Awesome

Azrael #41 © DC

GD25 FN65 NM94 | GD25 FN65 NM94

AVENGERS: THE TERMINATRIX OBJECTIVE
Marvel Comics: Sept, 1993 - No. 4, Dec, 1993 ($1.25, limited series)
1 ($2.50)-Holo-grafx foil-c 2.50
2-4-Old vs. current Avengers 1.25

AVENGERS: TIMESLIDE
Marvel Comics: Feb, 1996 ($4.95, one-shot)
1-Foil-c 5.00

AVENGERS/ULTRAFORCE (See Ultraforce/Avengers)
Marvel Comics: Oct, 1995 ($3.95, one-shot)
1-Wraparound foil-c by Perez 4.00

AVENGERS UNPLUGGED
Marvel Comics: Oct, 1995 - No. 6, Aug, 1996 (99¢, bi-monthly)
1-6 1.00

AVENGERS WEST COAST (Formerly West Coast Avengers)
Marvel Comics: No. 48, Sept, 1989 - No. 102, Jan, 1994 ($1.00/$1.25)
48,49: 48-Byrne-c/a & scripts continue thru #57 1.10
50-Re-intro original Human Torch 1.50
51-74,76-99,101,102: 54-Cover swipe/F.F. #1. 70-Spider-Woman app. 78-Last $1.00-c. 79-Dr. Strange x-over. 84-Origin Spider-Woman retold; Spider-Man app. (also in #85,86). 87,88-Wolverine-c/story. 93-95-Darkhawk app. 101-X-Men x-over 1.25
75-($1.50, 52 pgs.)-Fantastic Four x-over 1.50
100-($3.95, 68 pgs.)-Embossed all red foil-c 4.00
Annual 5,6 ('90, '91, $2.00, 68 pgs.)-West Coast Avengers in indicia 2.00
Annual 7 (1992, $2.25, 68 pgs.)-Darkhawk app. 2.25
Annual 8 (1993, $2.95)-Polybagged w/card 3.00

AVIATION ADVENTURES AND MODEL BUILDING
Parents' Magazine Institute: No. 16, Dec, 1946 - No. 17, Feb, 1947 (True Aviation Advs. ...No. 15)
16,17-Half comics and half pictures 5.70 17.00 40.00

AVIATION CADETS
Street & Smith Publications: 1943
nn 14.00 42.00 105.00

A-V IN 3-D
Aardvark-Vanaheim: Dec, 1984 ($2.00, 28 pgs. w/glasses)
1-Cerebus, Flaming Carrot, Normalman & Ms. Tree 3.00

AWAKENING, THE
Image Comics: Oct, 1997 - No. 4, Apr, 1998 ($2.95, B&W, limited series)
1-4-Stephen Blue-s/c/a 3.00

AWFUL OSCAR (Formerly & becomes Oscar Comics with No. 13)
Marvel Comics: No. 11, June, 1949 - No. 12, Aug, 1949
11,12 6.85 21.00 48.00

AWKWARD UNIVERSE
Slave Labor Graphics: 12/95 ($9.95, graphic novel)
nn 10.00

AWESOME HOLIDAY SPECIAL
Awesome Entertainment: Dec, 1997 ($2.50, one-shot)
1-Flip book w/covers of Fighting American & Coven. Holiday stories also featuring Kaboom and Shaft by regular creators. 3.00
1-Gold Edition 5.00

AXA
Eclipse Comics: Apr, 1987 - No. 2, Aug, 1987 ($1.75)
1,2 1.80

AXEL PRESSBUTTON (Pressbutton No. 5; see Laser Eraser &...)
Eclipse Comics: Nov, 1984 - No. 6, July, 1985 ($1.50/$1.75, Baxter paper)
1-6: Reprints Warrior (British mag.). 1-Bolland-c; origin Laser Eraser & Pressbutton 1.80

AXIS ALPHA
Axis Comics: Feb, 1994 ($2.50, one-shot)
V1-Previews Axis titles including, Tribe, Dethgrip, B.E.A.S.T.I.E.S. & more; Pitt app. in Tribe story. 2.50

AZRAEL (...Agent of the Bat #47 on)(Also see Batman: Sword of Azrael)
DC Comics: Feb, 1995 - Present ($1.95/$2.25)
1-Dennis O'Neil scripts begin 5.00
2,3 4.00
4-44: 5,6-Ras Al Ghul app. 13-Nightwing-c/app. 15-Contagion Pt. 5 (Pt. 4 on-c). 16-Contagion Pt. 10. 22-Batman-c/app. 23, 27-Batman app. 27,28-Joker app. 35-Hitman app. 36-39-Batman, Bane app. 2.00
45,46,48,49: 45-Begin $2.25-c 2.25
47-($3.95) Flip book with Batman: Shadow of the Bat #80 3.95
#1,000,000 (11/98) Giarrano-a 2.25
Annual 1 (1995, $3.95)-Year One story 4.00
Annual 2 (1996, $2.95)-Legends of the Dead Earth story 3.00
Annual 3 (1997, $3.95)-Pulp Heroes story; Orbik-c 4.00
Plus (12/96, $2.95)-Question-c/app. 2.95

AZRAEL/ ASH
DC Comics: 1997 ($4.95, one-shot)
1-O'Neil-s/Quesada, Palmiotti-a 4.95

AZTEC ACE
Eclipse Comics: Mar, 1984 - No. 15, Sept, 1985 ($2.25/$1.50/$1.75, Baxter paper)
1-$2.25-c (52 pgs.) 2.30
2,3: 2-Begin $1.50-c & 36 pgs. 1.50
4-15: ($1.75/$1.50-c) 1.80
NOTE: ***N. Redondo*** *a-1i-8i, 10i. c-6-8i.*

AZTEK: THE ULTIMATE MAN
DC Comics: Aug, 1996 - No. 10, May 1997 ($1.75)
1-1st app. Aztek & Synth; Grant Morrison & Mark Millar scripts in all. 5.00
2-9: 2-Green Lantern app. 3-1st app. Death-Doll. 4-Intro The Lizard King. 5-Origin. 6-Joker app.; Batman cameo. 7-Batman app. 8-Luthor app. 9-vs. Parasite-c/app. 2.00
10-JLA-c/app. 1.00 3.00 10.00
NOTE: ***Breyfogle*** *c-5p.* ***N. Steven Harris*** *a-1-5p.* ***Porter*** *c-1p.* ***Wieringo*** *c-2p.*

BABE (...Darling of the Hills, later issues)(See Big Shot and Sparky Watts)
Prize/Headline/Feature: June-July, 1948 - No. 11, Apr-May, 1950
1-Boody Rogers-a 17.00 50.00 125.00
2-Boody Rogers-a 11.00 32.00 80.00
3-11-All by Boody Rogers 9.30 28.00 70.00

BABE
Dark Horse Comics (Legend): July, 1994 - No. 4, Jan, 1994 ($2.50, lim. series)
1-4: John Byrne-c/a/scripts; ProtoTykes back-up story 2.50

BABE RUTH SPORTS COMICS (Becomes Rags Rabbit #11 on?)
Harvey Publications: April, 1949 - No. 11, Feb, 1951
1-Powell-a 36.00 108.00 270.00
2-Powell-a 25.00 75.00 185.00
3-11: Powell-a in most 20.00 60.00 150.00
NOTE: *Baseball c-2-4, 9. Basketball c-1, 6. Football c-5. Yogi Berra c/story-8. Joe DiMaggio c/story-3. Bob Feller c/story-4. Stan Musial c-9.*

BABES IN TOYLAND (Disney, Movie) (See Golden Pix Story Book ST-3)
Dell Publishing Co.: No. 1282, Feb-Apr, 1962
Four Color 1282-Annette Funicello photo-c 11.00 34.00 125.00

BABES OF BROADWAY
Broadway Comics: May, 1996 ($2.95, one-shot)
1-Pin-ups of Broadway Comics' female characters; Alan Davis, Michael Kaluta,

Baby Huey Duckland #12 © HARV

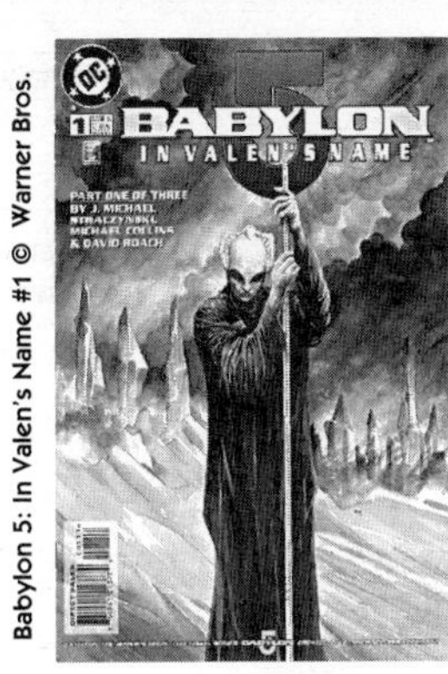

Babylon 5: In Valen's Name #1 © Warner Bros.

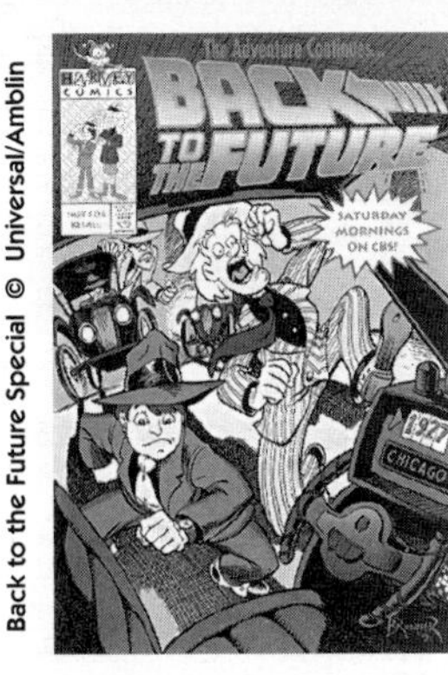

Back to the Future Special © Universal/Amblin

	GD25	FN65	NM94
J. G. Jones, Alan Weiss, Guy Davis & others-a; Giordano-c.			3.00

BABE 2
Dark Horse Comics (Legend): Mar, 1995 - No. 2, May, 1995 ($2.50, lim. series)

	GD25	FN65	NM94
1,2: John Byrne-c/a/scripts			2.50

BABY ANGEL X
Brainstorm Comics: 1995 ($2.95, B&W, mature)

	GD25	FN65	NM94
1-3			3.00
1-3-Gold ($5.00)			5.00

BABY HUEY
Harvey Comics: No. 100, Oct, 1990 - No. 101, Nov, 1990; No. 1, Oct, 1991 - No. 9, June, 1994 ($1.00/$1.25/$1.50, quarterly)

	GD25	FN65	NM94
100,101,1,2 ($1.00): 1-Cover says "Big Baby Huey"			3.00
3-9 ($1.25-$1.50)			2.00

BABY HUEY AND PAPA (See Paramount Animated...)
Harvey Publications: May, 1962 - No. 33, Jan, 1968 (Also see Casper The Friendly Ghost)

	GD25	FN65	NM94
1	15.00	45.00	150.00
2	7.00	21.00	70.00
3-5	4.80	14.40	48.00
6-10	2.40	7.20	24.00
11-20	2.00	6.00	16.00
21-33	1.60	4.85	13.00

BABY HUEY DIGEST
Harvey Publications: June, 1992 (Digest-size, one-shot)

	GD25	FN65	NM94
1-Reprints			4.00

BABY HUEY DUCKLAND
Harvey Publications: Nov, 1962 - No. 15, Nov, 1966 (25¢ Giants, 68 pgs.)

	GD25	FN65	NM94
1	11.50	34.00	115.00
2-5	4.80	14.40	48.00
6-15	2.40	7.20	24.00

BABY HUEY, THE BABY GIANT (Also see Big Baby Huey, Casper, Harvey Hits #22, Harvey Comics Hits #60, & Paramount Animated Comics)
Harvey Publ: 9/56 - #97, 10/71; #98, 10/72; #99, 10/80; #100, 10/90 - #102?

	GD25	FN65	NM94
1-Infinity-c	37.00	111.00	370.00
2	18.00	54.00	180.00
3-Baby Huey takes anti-pep pills	11.50	34.00	115.00
4,5	9.00	27.00	90.00
6-10	4.80	14.40	48.00
11-20	3.50	10.50	35.00
21-40	2.40	7.20	24.00
41-60	1.60	4.80	16.00
61-79 (12/67)	1.30	3.90	13.00
80(12/68) - 95-All 68 pg. Giants	1.80	5.40	18.00
96,97-Both 52 pg. Giants	1.30	3.90	13.00
98-99: Regular size		2.00	6.00
100-102 ($1.00)			3.00

BABYLON 5 (TV)
DC Comics: Jan, 1995 - No. 11, Dec, 1995 ($1.95/$2.50)

	GD25	FN65	NM94
1	1.50	4.50	15.00
2	1.20	3.60	12.00
3-6	1.00	3.00	10.00
7-11: 7-Begin $2.50-c	.90	2.70	8.00
... The Price of Peace (1998, $9.95, TPB) r/#1-4,11			9.95

BABYLON 5: IN VALEN'S NAME
DC Comics: Mar, 1998 - No. 3, May, 1998 ($2.50, limited series)

	GD25	FN65	NM94
1-3			3.00

BABY SNOOTS (Also see March of Comics #359, 371, 396, 401, 419, 431,443, 450, 462, 474, 485)
Gold Key: Aug, 1970 - No. 22, Nov, 1975

	GD25	FN65	NM94
1	1.80	5.40	18.00
2-11	.90	2.70	8.00
12-22: 22-Titled Snoots, the Forgetful Elefink			5.00

BACCHUS (Also see Eddie Campbell's ...)
Harrier Comics (New Wave): 1988 - No. 2, Aug, 1988 ($1.95, B&W)

	GD25	FN65	NM94
1,2: Eddie Campbell-c/a/scripts.			2.00

BACHELOR FATHER (TV)
Dell Publishing Co.: No. 1332, 4-6/62 - No. 2, 1962

	GD25	FN65	NM94
Four Color 1332 (#1), 2-Written by Stanley	7.25	22.00	80.00

BACHELOR'S DIARY
Avon Periodicals: 1949 (15¢)

	GD25	FN65	NM94
1(Scarce)-King Features panel cartoons & text-r; pin-up, girl wrestling photos; similar to Sideshow	37.00	110.00	275.00

BACK DOWN THE LINE
Eclipse Books: 1991 (Mature adults, 8-1/2 x 11", 52 pgs.)

	GD25	FN65	NM94
nn (Soft-c, $8.95)-Bolton-c/a	.90	2.70	9.00
nn (Limited Hard-c, $29.95)	2.70	8.00	30.00

BACKLASH (Also see The Kindred)
Image Comics (WildStorm Prod.): Nov,1994 - No. 32, May, 1997 ($1.95/$2.50)

	GD25	FN65	NM94
1-Double-c; variant-double-c			3.00
2-6:5-Intro Mindscape; 2 pinups			2.25
7,9-32: 7-Begin $2.50-c. 19-Fire From Heaven Pt 2. 20-Fire From Heaven Pt 10. 31-WildC.A.T.S app.			2.25
8-($1.95, newsstand)-Wildstorm Rising Pt. 8			2.00
8-($2.50, direct market)-Wildstorm Rising Pt. 8			2.50
25-($3.95)-Double-size			4.00

BACKLASH/SPIDER-MAN
Image Comics (WildStorm Productions): Aug, 1996 - No. 2, Sept, 1996 ($2.50, limited series)

	GD25	FN65	NM94
1,2: Pike (villain from WildC.A.T.S) & Venom app.			2.50

BACK TO THE FUTURE (Movie, TV cartoon)
Harvey Comics: Nov, 1991 - No. 4, June, 1992 ($1.25)

	GD25	FN65	NM94
1-4: 1,2-Gil Kane-c; based on animated cartoon			1.50
Special nn (1991, 20 pgs.)-Brunner-c; given away at Universal Studios in Florida			2.00

BACK TO THE FUTURE: FORWARD TO THE FUTURE
Harvey Comics: Oct, 1992 - No. 3, Feb, 1993 ($1.50, limited series)

	GD25	FN65	NM94
1-3			2.00

BAD APPLES
High Impact Entertainment: 1997- No. 2 ($2.95, B&W, limited series)

	GD25	FN65	NM94
1,2			2.95

BAD BOY
Oni Press: Dec, 1997 ($4.95, one-shot)

	GD25	FN65	NM94
1-Frank Miller-s/Simon Bisley-a/painted-c			5.00

BAD COMPANY
Quality Comics/Fleetway Quality #15 on: Aug, 1988 - No. 19?, 1990 ($1.50/$1.75, high quality paper)

	GD25	FN65	NM94
1-15: 5,6-Guice-c			1.50
16-19: ($1.75-c)			1.75

BAD EGGS, THE
Acclaim Comics (Armada): June, 1995 - No. 8, Jan, 1997 ($2.95)

	GD25	FN65	NM94
1-8: Layton scripts; Perlin-a. 5-8-"That Dirty Yellow Mustard." 5-William Shatner app.		1.20	3.00

BADGE OF JUSTICE
Charlton Comics: No. 22, 1/55 - No. 23, 3/55; 4/55 - No. 4, 10/55

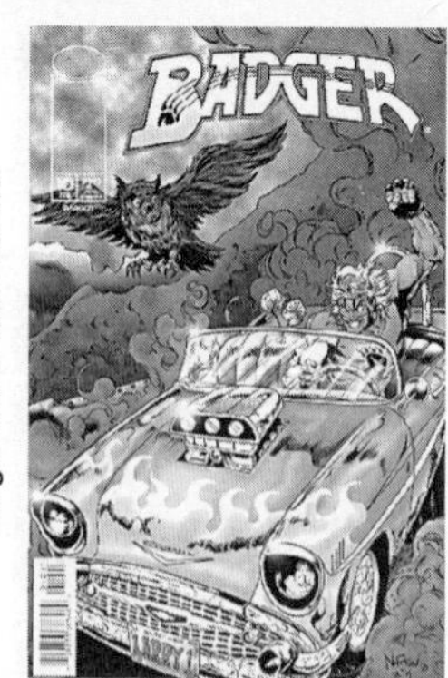

Badger #10 © First Pub. Inc.

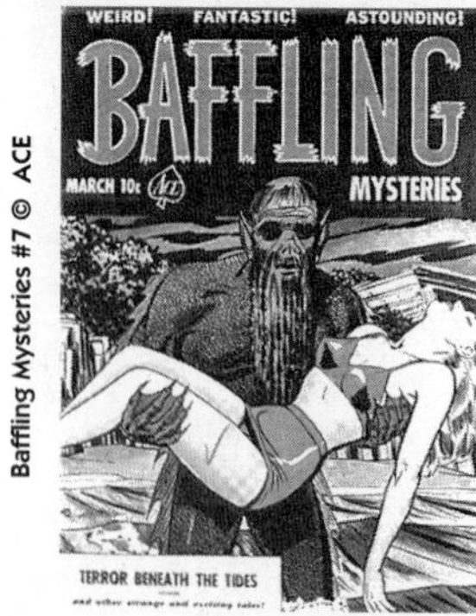

Baffling Mysteries #7 © ACE

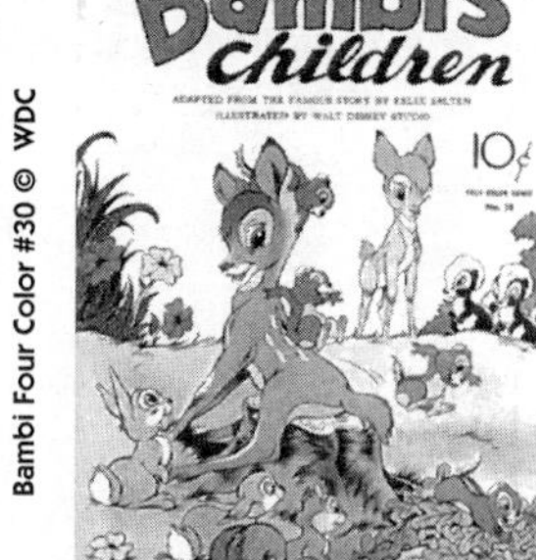

Bambi Four Color #30 © WDC

	GD25	FN65	NM94
22(1/55)	8.50	26.50	60.00
23(3/55), 1	5.70	17.00	38.00
2-4	4.25	13.00	28.00

BADGER, THE
Capital Comics(#1-4)/First Comics: Dec, 1983 - No. 70, Apr, 1991; V2#1, Spring, 1991

1-5 1.50
6-49 1.00
50-($3.95, 52 pgs.) 4.00
51-70: 52-54-Tim Vigil-c/a 2.00
V2#1 (Spring, 1991, $4.95) 5.00

BADGER, THE
Image Comics: V3#78, May, 1997 - Present ($2.95, B&W)

78-Cover lists #1, Baron-s 2.95
79/#2, 80/#3, 81(indicia lists #80)/#4,82-88/#5-11 2.95

BADGER GOES BERSERK
First Comics: Sept, 1989 - No. 4, Dec, 1989 ($1.95, lim. series, Baxter paper)

1-4: 2-Paul Chadwick-c/a(2pgs.) 2.00

BADGER: SHATTERED MIRROR
Dark Horse Comics: July, 1994 - No. Oct, 1994 ($2.50, limited series)

1-4 2.50

BADGER: ZEN POP FUNNY-ANIMAL VERSION
Dark Horse Comics: July, 1994 - No. 2, Aug, 1994 ($2.50, limited series)

1,2 2.50

BAD GIRLS OF BLACKOUT
Blackout Comics: July, 1995 ($3.50)

1 3.50
Annual 1 (1995, $3.50) 3.50
Annual 1 Commemorative (1995, $9.95) 1.00 3.00 10.00

BADLANDS
Vortex Comics: May, 1990 ($3.00, glossy stock, mature)

1-Chaykin-c 3.00

BADLANDS
Dark Horse Comics: July, 1991 - No. 6, Dec, 1991 ($2.25, B&W, limited series)

1-6: 1-John F. Kennedy-c; reprints Vortex Comics issue 2.30

BADMEN OF THE WEST
Avon Periodicals: 1951 (Giant) (132 pgs., painted-c)

1-Contains rebound copies of Jesse James, King of the Bad Men of Deadwood, Badmen of Tombstone; other combinations possible. Issues with Kubert-a... 32.00 96.00 240.00

BADMEN OF THE WEST! (See A-1 Comics)
Magazine Enterprises: 1953 - No. 3, 1954

1(A-1 100)-Meskin-a? 21.00 64.00 160.00
2(A-1 120), 3: 2-Larsen-a 13.00 40.00 100.00

BADMEN OF TOMBSTONE
Avon Periodicals: 1950

nn 13.00 38.00 95.00

BADROCK (Also see Youngblood)
Image Comics (Extreme Studios): Mar, 1995 - No. 2, Jan, 1996 ($1.75/$2.50)

1-Variant-c (3) .70 1.75
2-Liefeld-c/a & story; Savage Dragon app, flipbook w/Grifter/Badrock #2; variant-c exist 2.50
Annual 1(1995,$2.95)-Arthur Adams-c 3.00
Annual 1 Commemorative ($9.95)-3,000 printed 1.00 3.00 10.00
.../Wolverine (6/96, $4.95, squarebound)-Sauron app; pin-ups; variant-c exists 5.00
.../Wolverine (6/96)-Special Comicon Edition 5.00

BADROCK AND COMPANY (Also see Youngblood)
Image Comics (Extreme Studios): Sept, 1994 - No.6, Feb, 1995 ($2.50)

1-6 : 6-Indicia reads "October 1994"; story cont'd in Shadowhawk #17 2.50

BAFFLING MYSTERIES (Formerly Indian Braves No. 1-4; Heroes of the Wild Frontier No. 26-on)
Periodical House (Ace Magazines): No. 5, Nov, 1951 - No. 26, Oct, 1955

5 28.00 84.00 210.00
6-24: 8-Woodish-a by Cameron. 10-E.C. Crypt Keeper swipe on-c. 24-Last pre-code issue 17.00 51.00 125.00
25-Reprints; surrealistic-c 14.00 42.00 105.00
26-Reprints 12.00 36.00 90.00

NOTE: *Cameron a-8, 10, 16-18, 20-22.* ***Colan*** *a-5, 11, 25r/5.* ***Sekowsky*** *a-5, 6, 22. Bondage c-20, 23. Reprints in 18(1), 19(1), 24(3).*

BALBO (See Master Comics #33 & Mighty Midget Comics)

BALDER THE BRAVE
Marvel Comics Group: Nov, 1985 - No. 4, 1986 (Limited series)

1-4: Simonson-c/a; character from Thor 1.50

BALLAD OF HALO JONES, THE
Quality Comics: Sept, 1987 - No. 12, Aug, 1988 ($1.25/$1.50)

1-12: Alan Moore scripts in all 1.50

BALLISTIC (Also See Cyberforce)
Image Comics (Top Cow Productions): Sept, 1995 - No. 3, Dec, 1995 ($2.50, limited series)

1-3: Wetworks app, Turner-c/a 4.00

BALLISTIC ACTION
Image Comics (Top Cow Productions): May, 1996 ($2.95, one-shot)

1-Pin-ups of Top Cow characters participating in outdoor sports 3.00

BALLISTIC IMAGERY
Image Comics (Top Cow Productions): Jan, 1996 ($2.50, anthology, one-shot)

1-Cyberforce app. 2.50

BALLISTIC/ WOLVERINE
Image Comics (Top Cow Productions): Feb, 1997 ($2.95, one-shot)

1-Devil's Reign pt. 4; Witchblade cameo (1 page) 2.95

BALOO & LITTLE BRITCHES (Disney)
Gold Key: Apr, 1968

1-From the Jungle Book 2.40 7.00 26.00

BALTIMORE COLTS
American Visuals Corp.: 1950 (Giveaway)

nn-Eisner-c 44.00 132.00 375.00

BAMBI (Disney) (See Movie Classics, Movie Comics, and Walt Disney Showcase No. 31)
Dell Publishing Co.: No. 12, 1942; No. 30, 1943; No. 186, Apr, 1948

Four Color 12-Walt Disney's... 50.00 150.00 550.00
Four Color 30-Bambi's Children (1943) 50.00 150.00 550.00
Four Color 186-Walt Disney's...; reprinted as Movie Classic Bambi #3 (1956) 16.00 46.00 170.00

BAMBI (Disney)
K. K. Publications (Giveaways)/Whitman Publ. Co.: 1941, 1942, 1984

1941-Horlick's Malted Milk & various toy stores; text & pictures; most copies mailed out with store stickers on-c 23.00 69.00 190.00
1942-Same as 4-Color #12, but no price (Same as '41 issue?) (Scarce) 36.00 108.00 315.00
1-(Whitman, 1984; 60¢)-r/4-Color #186 5.00

BAMBI (Disney)

Bang-Up Comics #3 © Progressive Publ.

The Barker #1 © QUA

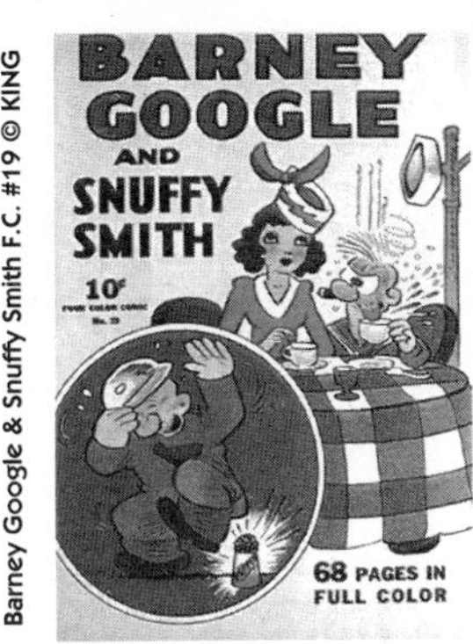

Barney Google & Snuffy Smith F.C. #19 © KING

GD25 FN65 NM94

Grosset & Dunlap: 1942 (50¢, 7"x8-1/2", 32pg, hard-c w/dust jacket)
nn-Given away w/a copy of Thumper for a $2.00, 2-yr. subscription to WDC&S in 1942 (Xmas offer). Book only 15.50 47.00 125.00
w/dust jacket 25.00 75.00 200.00

BAMM BAMM & PEBBLES FLINTSTONE (TV)
Gold Key: Oct, 1964 (Hanna-Barbera)
1 7.25 22.00 80.00

BANANA SPLITS, THE (TV) (See Golden Comics Digest & March of Comics No. 364)
Gold Key: June, 1969 - No. 8, Oct, 1971 (Hanna-Barbera)
1-Photo-c 8.50 26.00 95.00
2-8 5.00 15.00 55.00

BAND WAGON (See Hanna-Barbera Band Wagon)

BANDY MAN, THE
Caliber: 1996 - No. 3, ($2.95, B&W, limited series)
1-3-Stephan Petrucha scripts; 1-Jill Thompson-a; Miran Kim-c 3.00

BANG-UP COMICS
Progressive Publishers: Dec, 1941 - No. 3, June, 1942
1-Cosmo Mann & Lady Fairplay begin; Buzz Balmer by Rick Yager in all (origin #1) 82.00 246.00 700.00
2,3 44.00 132.00 375.00

BANNER COMICS (Becomes Captain Courageous No. 6)
Ace Magazines: No. 3, Sept, 1941 - No. 5, Jan, 1942
3-Captain Courageous (1st app.) & Lone Warrior & Sidekick Dicky begin; Jim Mooney-c 91.00 273.00 775.00
4,5: 4-Flag-c 57.00 171.00 485.00

BARABBAS
Slave Labor Graphics: Aug, 1986 - No. 2, Nov, 1986 ($1.50, B&W, lim. series)
1,2 1.50

BARBARIANS, THE
Atlas Comics/Seaboard Periodicals: June, 1975
1-Origin, only app. Andrax; Iron Jaw app. 3.00

BARBIE
Marvel Comics: Jan, 1991 - No. 66, Apr, 1996 ($1.00/$1.25/$1.50)
1-Polybagged w/Barbie Pink Card; Romita-c .90 2.70 8.00
2-49,51-66 4.00
50-(Giant) 2.00 6.00

BARBIE & KEN
Dell Publishing Co.: May-July, 1962 - No. 5, Nov-Jan, 1963-64
01-053-207(#1)-Based on Mattel toy dolls 35.00 105.00 380.00
2-4 25.00 75.00 275.00
5 (Rare) 30.00 90.00 330.00

BARBIE FASHION
Marvel Comics: Jan, 1991 - No. 63, Jan, 1996 ($1.00/$1.25/$1.50)
1-Polybagged w/doorknob hanger .90 2.70 8.00
2-49,51-63: 4-Contains preview to Sweet XVI. 14-Begin $1.25-c 4.00
50-(Giant) 2.00 6.00

BARBI TWINS, THE
Topps Comics: 1995 ($2.50/$5.00)
1-Razor app. 2.50
Swimsuit Art Calendar ($5.00)-art by Linsner, Bradstreet, Hughes; Julie Bell-c 5.00

BARB WIRE (See Comics' Greatest World)
Dark Horse Comics: Apr, 1994 - No. 9, Feb, 1995 ($2.00/$2.50)
1-4: 1-Foil logo 2.00
5-9-($2.50) 2.50

GD25 FN65 NM94

Trade paperback (1996, $8.95)-r/#2,3,5,6 w/Pamela Anderson bio 9.00

BARB WIRE: ACE OF SPADES
Dark Horse Comics: May, 1996 - No. 4, Sept, 1996 ($2.95, limited series)
1-4: Chris Warner-c/a(p)/scripts; Tim Bradstreet-c/a(i) in all 3.00

BARB WIRE COMICS MAGAZINE SPECIAL
Dark Horse Comics: May, 1996 ($3.50, B&W, magazine, one-shot)
nn-Adaptation of film; photo-c; poster insert. 3.50

BARB WIRE MOVIE SPECIAL
Dark Horse Comics: May, 1996 ($3.95, one-shot)
nn-Adaptation of film; photo-c; 1st app. new look 4.00

BARKER, THE (Also see National Comics #42)
Quality Comics Group/Comic Magazine: Autumn, 1946 - No. 15, Dec, 1949
1 17.00 50.00 125.00
2 9.30 28.00 65.00
3-10 6.00 18.00 42.00
11-14 4.25 13.00 28.00
15-Jack Cole-a(p) 5.70 17.00 35.00
NOTE: *Jack Cole* art in some issues.

BARNABY
Civil Service Publications Inc.: 1945 (25¢,102 pgs., digest size)
V1#1-r/Crocket Johnson strips from 1942 3.00 7.50 15.00

BARNEY AND BETTY RUBBLE (TV) (Flintstones' Neighbors)
Charlton Comics: Jan, 1973 - No. 23, Dec, 1976 (Hanna-Barbera)
1 2.70 8.00 30.00
2-10 1.50 4.50 15.00
11(2/75)-1st Mike Zeck-a (illos) 1.20 3.60 12.00
12-23 1.00 3.00 10.00

BARNEY BAXTER (Also see Magic Comics)
David McKay/Dell Publishing Co./Argo: 1938 - No. 2, 1956
Feature Books 15(McKay-1938) 26.00 76.00 280.00
Four Color 20(1942) 25.00 74.00 270.00
4,5 10.50 31.00 115.00
1,2 (1956-Argo) 7.00 21.00 50.00

BARNEY BEAR ...
Spire Christian Comics (Fleming H. Revell Co.): 1977-1981
...Home Plate nn-(1979, 49¢), ...Lost and Found nn-(1979, 49¢), Out of The Woods nn-(1980, 49¢), Sunday School Picnic nn-(1981, 69¢, The Swamp Gang!-(1977, 39¢) 4.00

BARNEY GOOGLE & SNUFFY SMITH
Dell Publishing Co./Gold Key: 1942 - 1943; April, 1964
Four Color 19(1942) 36.00 106.00 390.00
Four Color 40(1944) 21.00 63.00 230.00
Large Feature Comic 11(1943) 22.00 66.00 245.00
1(10113-404)-Gold Key (4/64) 3.20 9.50 35.00

BARNEY GOOGLE & SNUFFY SMITH
Toby Press: June, 1951 - No. 4, Feb, 1952 (Reprints)
1 11.00 32.00 80.00
2,3 6.50 19.50 45.00
4-Kurtzman-a "Pot Shot Pete", 5 pgs.; reprints John Wayne #5 11.00 32.00 80.00

BARNEY GOOGLE AND SNUFFY SMITH
Charlton Comics: Mar, 1970 - No. 6, Jan, 1971
1 1.80 5.40 18.00
2-6 1.20 3.60 12.00

BARNYARD COMICS (Dizzy Duck No. 32 on)
Nedor/Polo Mag./Standard(Animated Cartoons): June, 1944 - No. 31, Sept, 1950; No. 10, 1957

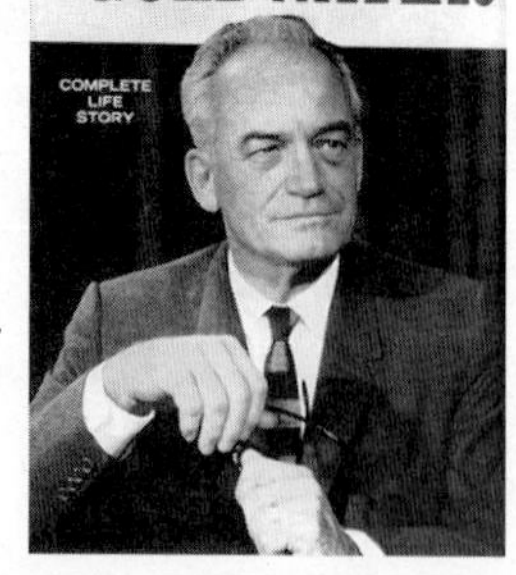

Barry M. Goldwater © DELL

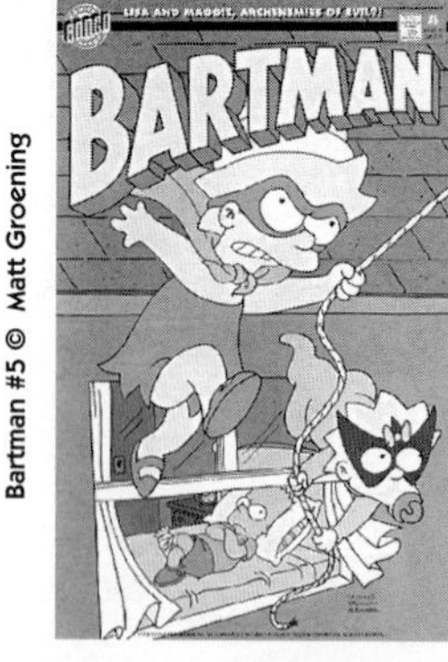

Bartman #5 © Matt Groening

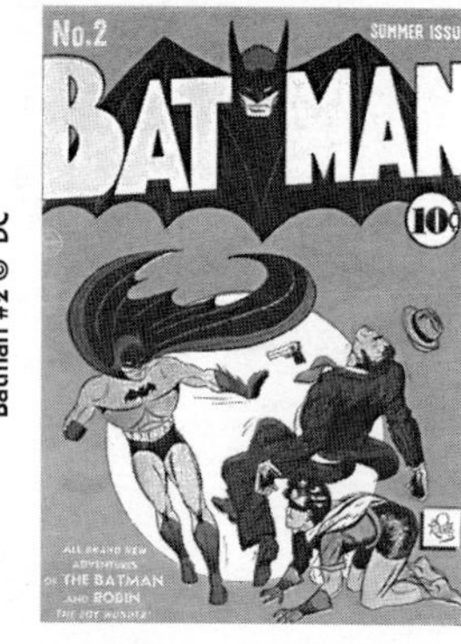

Batman #2 © DC

	GD25	FN65	NM94
1 (nn, 52 pgs.)-Funny animal	17.00	52.00	130.00
2 (52 pgs.)	9.30	28.00	65.00
3-5	5.70	17.00	40.00
6-12,16	5.35	16.00	32.00
13-15,17,21,23,26,27,29-All contain Frazetta text illos	5.70	17.00	40.00
18-20,22,24,25-All contain Frazetta-a & text illos	9.30	28.00	70.00
28,30,31	4.00	10.00	20.00
10 (1957)(Exist?)	2.00	5.00	10.00

BARRY M. GOLDWATER
Dell Publishing Co.: Mar, 1965 (Complete life story)

	GD25	FN65	NM94
12-055-503-Photo-c	2.50	7.50	28.00

BARRY WINDSOR-SMITH: STORYTELLER
Dark Horse Comics: Oct, 1996 - No. 9 ($4.95, oversize)

	GD25	FN65	NM94
1-9: 1-Intro Young Gods, Paradox Man & the Freebooters; Barry Smith-c/a/scripts			5.00

BAR SINISTER (Also see Shaman's Tears)
Acclaim Comics (Windjammer): Jun, 1995 - No. 4, Sept, 1995 ($2.50, lim. series)

	GD25	FN65	NM94
1-4: Mike Grell-c/a/scripts			2.50

BARTMAN (Also see Simpson's Comics & Radioactive Man)
Bongo Comics: 1993 - No. 6, 1994 ($1.95/$2.25)

	GD25	FN65	NM94
1-($2.95)-Foil-c; bound-in jumbo Bartman poster			3.25
2			2.00
3-6: 3-$2.25-c begins; w/trading card			2.25

BASEBALL COMICS
Will Eisner Productions: Spring, 1949 (Reprinted later as a Spirit section)

	GD25	FN65	NM94
1-Will Eisner-c/a	64.00	192.00	540.00

BASEBALL COMICS
Kitchen Sink Press: 1991 ($3.95, coated stock)

	GD25	FN65	NM94
1-r/1949 ish. by Eisner; contains trading cards			4.00

BASEBALL HEROES
Fawcett Publications: 1952 (one-shot)

	GD25	FN65	NM94
nn (Scarce)-Babe Ruth photo-c; baseball's Hall of Fame biographies	68.00	204.00	575.00

BASEBALL'S GREATEST HEROES
Magnum Comics: Dec, 1991 - No. 2, May, 1992 ($1.75)

	GD25	FN65	NM94
1-Mickey Mantle #1; photo-c; Sinnott-a(p)			1.75
2-Brooks Robinson #1; photo-c; Sinnott-a(i)			1.75

BASEBALL THRILLS
Ziff-Davis Publ. Co.: No. 10, Sum, 1951 - No. 3, Sum, 1952 (Saunders painted-c No.1,2)

	GD25	FN65	NM94
10(#1)-Bob Feller, Musial, Newcombe & Boudreau stories	39.00	116.00	290.00
2-Powell-a(2)(Late Sum, '51); Feller, Berra & Mathewson stories	26.00	78.00	195.00
3-Kinstler-c/a; Joe DiMaggio story	26.00	78.00	195.00

BASEBALL THRILLS 3-D
The 3-D Zone: May, 1990 ($2.95, w/glasses)

	GD25	FN65	NM94
1-New L.B. Cole-c; life stories of Ty Cobb & Ted Williams			4.00

BASICALLY STRANGE (Magazine)
John C. Comics (Archie Comics Group): Dec, 1982 ($1.95, B&W)

	GD25	FN65	NM94
1-(21,000 printed; all but 1,000 destroyed; pgs. out of sequence)	1.20	3.60	12.00
1-Wood, Toth-a; Corben-c; reprints & new art	.90	2.70	8.00

BASIC HISTORY OF AMERICA ILLUSTRATED
Pendulum Press: 1976 (B&W) (Soft-c $1.50; Hard-c $4.50)

07-1999-America Becomes a World Power 1890-1920. 07-2251-The Industrial Era 1865-1915. 07-226x-Before the Civil War 1830-1860. 07-2278-Americans Move Westward 1800-1850. 07-2286-The Civil War 1850-1876; Redondo-a. 07-2294-The Fight for Freedom 1750-1783. 07-2308-The New World 1500-1750. 07-2316-Problems of the New Nation 1800-1830. 07-2324-Roaring Twenties and the Great Depression 1920-1940. 07-2332-The United States Emerges 1783-1800. 07-2340-America Today 1945-1976. 07-2359-World War II 1940-1945

BASIL (...the Royal Cat)
St. John Publishing Co.: Jan, 1953 - No. 4, Sept, 1953

	GD25	FN65	NM94
1-Funny animal	4.25	13.00	28.00
2-4	3.20	8.00	16.00
I.W. Reprint 1	1.40	3.50	7.00

BASIL WOLVERTON'S FANTASTIC FABLES
Dark Horse Comics: Oct, 1993 - No. 2, Dec, 1993 ($2.50, B&W, limited series)

	GD25	FN65	NM94
1,2-Wolverton-c/a(r)			3.00

BASIL WOLVERTON'S GATEWAY TO HORROR
Dark Horse Comics: June, 1988 ($1.75, B&W, one-shot)

	GD25	FN65	NM94
1-Wolverton-r			3.00

BASIL WOLVERTON'S PLANET OF TERROR
Dark Horse Comics: Oct, 1987 ($1.75, B&W, one-shot)

	GD25	FN65	NM94
1-Wolverton-r; Alan Moore-c			3.00

BATGIRL ADVENTURES (See Batman Adventures, The)
DC Comics: Feb, 1998 ($2.95, one-shot) (Based on animated series)

	GD25	FN65	NM94
1-Harley Quinn and Poison Ivy app.; Timm-c			4.00

BATGIRL SPECIAL
DC Comics: 1988 ($1.50, one-shot, 52 pgs)

	GD25	FN65	NM94
1-Kitson-a/Mignola-c			4.50

BAT LASH (See DC Special Series #16, Showcase #76, Weird Western Tales)
National Periodical Publications: Oct-Nov, 1968 - No. 7, Oct-Nov, 1969 (All 12¢ issues)

	GD25	FN65	NM94
1-(10-11/68)-2nd app. Bat Lash	2.50	7.50	22.00
2-7	1.75	5.25	14.00

BATMAN (See Arkham Asylum, Aurora, The Best of DC #2, Blind Justice, The Brave & the Bold, Cosmic Odyssey, DC 100-Page Super Spec. #14,20, DC Special, DC Special Series, Detective, Dynamic Classics, 80-Page Giants, Gotham By Gaslight, Gotham Nights, Greatest Batman Stories Ever Told, Greatest Joker Stories Ever Told, Heroes Against Hunger, JLA,The Joker, Justice League of America, Justice League Int., Legends of the Dark Knight, Limited Coll. Ed., Man-Bat, Nightwing, Power Record Comics, Real Fact #5, Robin, Saga of Ra's Al Ghul, Shadow of the..., Star Spangled, Super Friends, 3-D Batman, Untold Legend of..., Wanted... & World's Finest Comics)

BATMAN
National Per. Publ./Detective Comics/DC Comics: Spring, 1940 - Present (#1-5 were quarterly)

	GD25	FN65	VF82	NM94
1-Origin The Batman reprinted (2 pgs.) from Det. #33 w/splash from #34 by Bob Kane; see Detective #33 for 1st origin; 1st app. Joker (2 stories intended for 2 separate issues of Det. Comics which would have been 1st & 2nd app.); splash pg. to 2nd Joker story is similar to cover of Det. #40 (story intended for #40); 1st app. The Cat (Catwoman)(1st villainess in comics); has Batman story (w/Hugo Strange) without Robin originally planned for Det. #38; mentions location (Manhattan) where Batman lives (see Det. #31). This book was created entirely from the inventory of Det. Comics; 1st Batman/Robin pin-up on back-c; has text piece & photo of Bob Kane	5,167.00	15,550.00	33,580.00	63,000.00

1-Reprint, oversize 13-1/2x10". **WARNING**: This comic is an exact duplicate reprint of the original except for its size. DC published it in 1974 with a second cover titling it as a Famous First Edition. There have been many reported cases of the outer cover being removed and the interior sold as the original edition. The reprint with the new outer cover removed is practically worthless. See Famous First Edition for value.

	GD25	FN65	NM94
2-2nd app. The Joker; 2nd app. Catwoman (out of costume) in Joker story; 1st time called Catwoman			

NOTE: A 15¢-c for Canadian distr. exists.

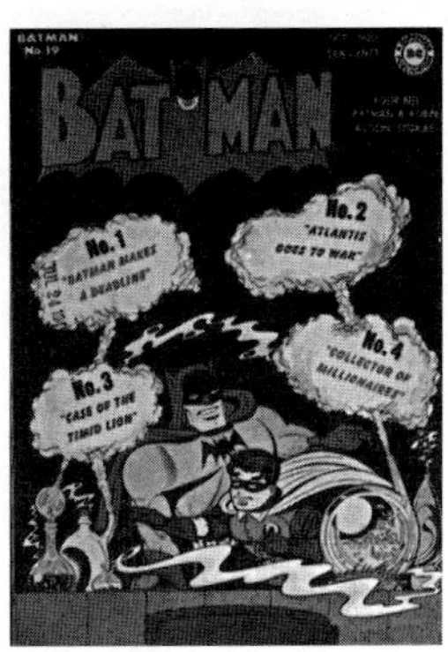

Batman #19 © DC

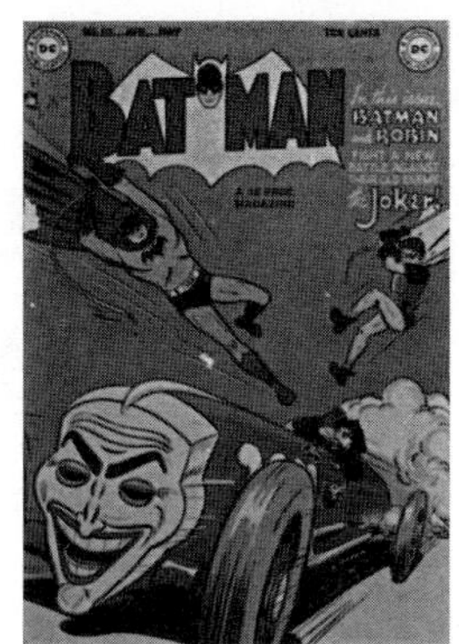

Batman #52 © DC

Batman #126 © DC

	GD25	FN65	NM94
	1018.00	3055.00	11,200.00
3-3rd app Catwoman (1st in costume & 1st costumed villainess); 1st Puppet Master app.; classic Kane & Moldoff-c	720.00	2160.00	7200.00
4-3rd app. The Joker (see Det. #45 for 4th); 1st mention of Gotham City in a Batman comic (on newspaper)(Win/40)	580.00	1740.00	5800.00
5-1st app. the Batmobile with its bat-head front	420.00	1260.00	4200.00
6,7: 7-Bullseye-c	360.00	1080.00	3600.00
8-Infinity-c.	300.00	900.00	3000.00
9-10:9-1st Batman x-mas story; Burnley-c. 10-Catwoman story (gets new costume)	275.00	825.00	2750.00
11-Classic Joker-c by Ray/Robinson (3rd Joker-c, 6-7/42); Joker & Penguin app.	530.00	1590.00	5300.00
12,15: 15-New costume Catwoman	247.00	741.00	2100.00
13-Jerry Siegel (Superman's co-creator) appears in a Batman story.	282.00	746.00	2400.00
14-2nd Penguin-c; Penguin app. (12-1/42-43)	276.00	825.00	2350.00
16-Intro/origin Alfred (4-5/43); cover is a reverse of #9 cover by Burnley; 1st small logo	463.00	1390.00	4400.00
17,19,20: 17-Penguin app. 20-1st Batmobile-c (12-1/43-44)	171.00	513.00	1450.00
18-Hitler, Hirohito, Mussolini-c.	212.00	636.00	1800.00
21,22,24,26,28-30: 21-1st skinny Alfred in Batman (2-3/44). 21,30-Penguin app. 22-1st Alfred solo-c/story (Alfred solo stories in 22-32,36); Catwoman & The Cavalier app. 28-Joker story	124.00	372.00	1050.00
23-Joker-c/story	182.00	546.00	1550.00
25-Only Joker/Penguin team-up; 1st team-up between two major villains	188.00	564.00	1600.00
27-Burnley Christmas-c; Penguin app.	165.00	495.00	1400.00
31,32,34-36,39: 32-Origin Robin retold. 35-Catwoman story (in new costume w/o cat head mask). 36-Penguin app.	94.00	282.00	800.00
33-Christmas-c	103.00	318.00	900.00
37,40,44-Joker-c/stories	124.00	372.00	1050.00
38-Penguin-c/story	103.00	309.00	875.00
41,45,46: 41-1st Sci-fi cover/story in Batman; Penguin app.(6-7/47). 45-Christmas-c/story; Catwoman story; Vicki Vale app. (1st app?)	71.00	213.00	600.00
42,43: 42-2nd Catwoman-c (1st in Batman)(8-9/47); Catwoman story also. 43-Penguin-c/story	88.00	264.00	750.00
47-1st detailed origin The Batman (6-7/48); 1st Bat-signal-c this title (see Detective #108); Batman tracks down his parent's killer and reveals i.d. to him	289.00	867.00	2600.00
48-1000 Secrets of the Batcave; r-in #203; Penguin story	94.00	282.00	800.00
49-Joker-c/story; 1st app. Mad Hatter; Vicki Vale app.	147.00	441.00	1250.00
50-Two-Face impostor app.	79.00	237.00	675.00
51,54,56,57,59: 57-Centerfold is a 1950 calendar. 59-1st app. Deadshot; Batman in the future-c/story	68.00	204.00	575.00
52,55-Joker-c/stories	85.00	255.00	725.00
53,58,60,61: 58-Penguin-c. 61-Origin Batman Plane II	75.00	225.00	640.00
62-Origin Catwoman; Catwoman-c	100.00	300.00	850.00
63,80-Joker stories. 63-Flying saucer story(2-3/51)	61.00	183.00	520.00
64,67,70-72,74-77,79: 70-Robot-c. 72-Last 52 pg. issue. 74-Used in **POP**, Pg. 90. 79-Vicki Vale in "The Bride of Batman"	53.00	159.00	450.00
65,69,84-Catwoman-c/stories. 84-Two-Face app.	61.00	183.00	520.00
66,73-Joker-c/stories. 66-Pre-2nd Batman & Robin team try-out. 73-Vicki Vale story	71.00	213.00	600.00
68,81-Two-Face-c/stories	56.00	168.00	480.00
78-(8-9/53)-Roh Kar, The Man Hunter from Mars story-the 1st lawman of Mars to come to Earth (green skinned)	68.00	204.00	575.00
82,83,85-89: 86-Intro Batmarine (Batman's submarine). 89-Last pre-code issue	52.00	156.00	440.00
90,91,93-99: 97-2nd app. Bat-Hound-c/story; Joker app. 99-(4/56)-Last S.A. Penguin app.	40.00	120.00	360.00
92-1st app. Bat-Hound-c/story	50.00	150.00	475.00
100-(6/56)	211.00	633.00	1950.00
101-(8/56)-Clark Kent x-over who protects Batman's i.d. (3rd story)	43.00	130.00	390.00
102-104,106-109: 103-1st S.A. issue; 3rd Bat-Hound-c/story	31.00	93.00	350.00
105-1st Batwoman in Batman (2nd anywhere)	39.00	117.00	440.00
110-Joker story	33.00	99.00	360.00
111-120: 112-1st app. Signalman (super villain). 113-1st app. Fatman; Batman meets his counterpart on Planet X w/a chest plate similar to S.A. Batman's design (yellow oval w/black design inside).	29.00	87.00	290.00
121- Origin/1st app. of Mr. Zero (Mr. Freeze).	31.00	93.00	350.00
122,124-126,128,130: 124-2nd app. Signal Man. 126-Batwoman-c/story. 128-Batwoman cameo. 130-Lex Luthor app.	19.50	58.00	195.00
123,127: 123-Joker story; Bat-Hound app. 127-(10/59)-Batman vs. Thor the Thunder God-c/story; Joker story; Superman cameo	22.50	68.00	225.00
129-Origin Robin retold; bondage-c; Batwoman-c/story (reprinted in Batman Family #8)	24.00	72.00	240.00
131-135,137-139,141-143: 131-Intro 2nd Batman & Robin series (see #66; also in #135,145,154,159,163). 133-1st Bat-Mite in Batman (3rd app. anywhere). 134-Origin The Dummy (not Vigilante's villain). 139-Intro 1st original Bat-Girl; only app. Signalman as the Blue Bowman. 141-2nd app. original Bat-Girl. 143-(10/61)-Last 10¢ issue	15.50	47.00	155.00
136-Joker-c/story	18.00	54.00	180.00
140,144-Joker stories. 140-Batwoman-c/story; Superman cameo. 144-(12/61)-3rd app. original Bat-Girl; 1st 12¢ issue	15.00	45.00	150.00
145,148-Joker-c/stories	16.00	48.00	160.00
146,147,149,150	11.50	34.00	115.00
151,152,153,154,156-158,160-162,164-168,170: 152-Joker story. 153-4th app. original Bat-Girl. 156-Ant-Man/Robin team-up(6/63). 164-New Batmobile(6/64) new look & Mystery Analysts series begins	9.00	27.00	90.00
155-1st S.A. app. The Penguin (5/63)	27.00	81.00	300.00
159,163-Joker-c/stories. 159-Bat-Girl app. 163-Bat-Girl appears as Batwoman II (last Silver Age app.)	11.00	33.00	110.00
169-2nd SA Penguin app.	12.00	36.00	120.00
171-1st Riddler app.(5/65) since Dec. 1948	36.00	108.00	390.00
172-175,177,178,180,184	5.50	16.50	55.00
176-(80-Pg. Giant G-17); Joker-c/story; Penguin app. in strip-r; Catwoman reprint	7.00	21.00	70.00
179-2nd app. Silver Age Riddler	11.50	34.00	115.00
181-Batman & Robin poster insert; intro. Poison Ivy.	13.00	39.00	130.00
182,187-(80 Pg. Giants G-24, G-30); Joker-c/stories	6.00	18.00	60.00
183-2nd app. Poison Ivy	9.00	27.00	90.00
185-(80 Pg. Giant G-27)	8.00	24.00	60.00
186-Joker-c/story	4.50	13.50	45.00
188,191,192,194-196,199	2.80	7.60	28.00
189-1st S.A. app. Scarecrow; retells origin of G.A. Scarecrow from World's Finest #3(1st app.)	6.00	18.00	60.00
190-Penguin app.	3.00	9.00	30.00
193-(80-Pg. Giant G-37)	4.80	13.50	48.00
197-4th S.A. Catwoman app. cont'd from Det. #369; 1st new Batgirl app. in Batman (5th anywhere)	5.00	15.00	50.00
198-(80-Pg. Giant G-43); Joker-c/story-r/World's Finest #61; Catwoman-r/ Det. #211; Penguin-r; origin-r/#47	6.50	19.50	65.00
200-(3/68)-Joker cameo; retells origin of Batman & Robin; 1st Neal Adams work this title (cover only)	11.00	33.00	110.00
201-Joker story	3.20	9.40	32.00
202,204-207,209,210	2.50	7.50	20.00
203-(80 Pg. Giant G-49); r/#48, 61, & Det. 185; Batcave Blueprints	4.20	12.60	42.00
208-(80 Pg. Giant G-55); New origin Batman by Gil Kane plus 3 G.A. Batman reprints w/Catwoman, Vicki Vale & Batwoman	4.20	12.60	42.00

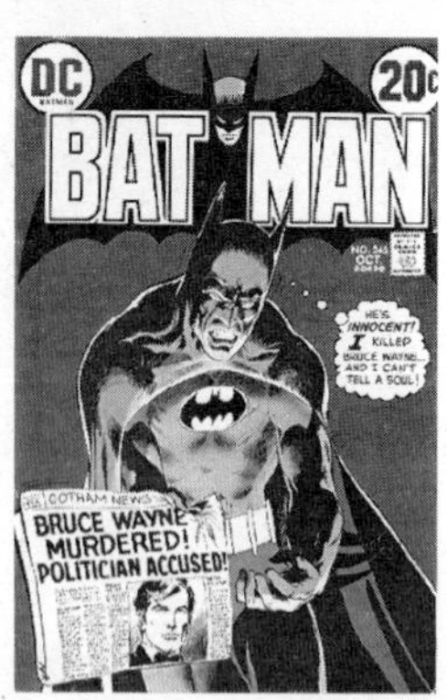

Batman #245 © DC

Batman #408 © DC

Batman #477 © DC

GD25 FN65 NM94

211,212,214-217: 212-Last 12¢ issue. 214-Alfred given a new last name- "Pennyworth" (see Detective #96). 2.00 6.00 20.00
213-(80-Pg. Giant G-61); 30th anniversary issue (7-8/69); origin Alfred (r/Batman #16), Joker(r/Det. #168), Clayface; new origin Robin with new facts 5.50 16.50 60.00
218-(80-Pg. Giant G-67) 3.80 11.40 40.00
219-Neal Adams-a 3.80 11.40 40.00
220,221,224-227,229-231 1.70 5.10 17.00
222-Beatles take-off; art lesson by Joe Kubert 2.80 8.40 31.00
223,228,233-(80-Pg. Giants G-73,G-79,G-85) 2.80 8.40 31.00
232-N. Adams-a. Intro/1st app. Ras Al Ghul; origin Batman & Robin retold. 8.00 23.00 85.00
234-(9/71)-Two-Face app.; (see World's Finest #173); N. Adams-a; 52 pg. issues begin, end #242 10.00 30.00 110.00
235,236,239-242: 239-XMas-c. 241-Reprint/#5 2.00 6.00 20.00
237-N. Adams-a. G.A. Batman-r/Det. #37; 1st app. The Reaper; Wrightson/Ellison plots 4.20 12.60 46.00
238-Also listed as DC 100 Page Super Spectacular #8; Batman, Legion, Aquaman-r; G.A. Atom, Sargon (r/Sensation #57), Plastic Man (r/Police #14) stories; Doom Patrol origin-r; N. Adams wraparound-c (see DC 100 Pg. Super Spectacular #8 for price)
243-245-Neal Adams-a 3.00 9.00 33.00
246-250,252,253: 246-Scarecrow app. 253-Shadow-c & app. 2.00 6.00 20.00
251-(9/73)-N. Adams-c/a; Joker-c/story 4.80 14.40 53.00
254,256-259,261-All 100 pg. editions; part-r: 254-(2/74)-Man-Bat-c & app. 256-Catwoman app. 257-Joker & Penguin app. 258-The Cavalier-r. 259-Shadow-c/app. 2.20 6.25 22.00
255-(100 pgs.)-N. Adams-c/a; tells of Bruce Wayne's father who wore bat costume & fought crime (r/Det. #235); r/story Batman #22 3.50 10.50 38.00
260-Joker-c/story (100 pgs.) 3.50 10.50 38.00
262 (68pgs.) 2.00 6.00 20.00
263,264,266-285,287-290,292,293,295-299: 266-Catwoman back to old costume 1.00 3.00 10.00
265-Wrightson-a(i) 1.20 3.60 12.00
286,291,294: 294-Joker-c/stories 1.30 3.90 13.00
300-Double-size 1.80 5.40 18.00
301-(7/78)-320,322-331,333-352: 304-(44 pgs.). 306-3rd app. Black Spider. 308-Mr. Freeze app. 310-1st modern app. The Gentleman Ghost in Batman; Kubert-c. 311-Batgirl-c/story; Batgirl reteams w/Batman. 312,314,346-Two-Face-c/stories. 313-2nd app. Calendar Man. 316-Robin returns. 318-Intro Firebug. 319-2nd modern age app. The Gentleman Ghost; Kubert-c. 322-324-Catwoman (Selina Kyle) app. 322,323-Cat-Man cameos (1st in Batman, 1 panel each). 323-1st meeting Catwoman & Cat-Man. 324-1st full app. Cat-Man this title. 344-Poison Ivy app. 345-1st app. new Dr. Death. 345,346,351-7 pg. Catwoman back-ups .90 2.70 9.00
321,353,359-Joker-c/stories. 1.00 3.00 10.00
332-Catwoman's 1st solo. 1.00 3.00 10.00
354-356,358,360-365,369,370: 358-1st app. Killer Croc. 361-1st app Harvey Bullock 2.00 6.00
357-1st app. Jason Todd (3/83); see Det. #524 1.00 3.00 10.00
366-Jason Todd 1st in Robin costume; Joker-c/story 1.00 3.00 10.00
367-Jason in red & green costume (not as Robin) 2.00 6.00
368-1st new Robin in costume (Jason Todd) .85 2.60 7.00
371-399,401-403: 371-Cat-Man-c/story; brief origin Cat-Man (cont'd in Det. #538). 386,387-Intro Black Mask (villain). 380-391-Catwoman app. 398-Catwoman & Two-Face app. 401-2nd app. Magpie (see Man of Steel #3 for 1st). 403-Joker cameo 1.20 3.00

NOTE: *Most issues between 397 & 432 were reprinted in 1989 and sold in multi-packs. Some are not identified as reprints but have newer ads copyrighted after cover dates. 2nd and 3rd printings exist.*

400 ($1.50, 68pgs.)-Dark Knight special; intro by Stephen King; Art Adams/ Austin-a 1.50 4.50 15.00

GD25 FN65 NM94

404-Miller scripts begin (end 407); Year 1; 1st modern app. Catwoman (2/87) .85 2.60 7.00
405-407: 407-Year 1 ends (See Det. Comics for Year 2) 4.00
408-410: New Origin Jason Todd (Robin) 4.00
411-416,421-425: 411-Two-face app. 412-Origin/1st app. Mime. 414-Starlin scripts begin, end #429. 416-Nightwing-c/story. 423-McFarlane-c 3.00
417-420: "Ten Nights of the Beast" storyline 5.00
426-($1.50, 52 pgs.)- "A Death In The Family" storyline begins, ends #429 .85 2.60 7.00
427- "A Death In The Family" part 2. .85 2.60 7.00
428-Death of Robin (Jason Todd) 4.00
429-Joker-c/story; Superman app. 4.00
430-432 2.00
433-435-Many Deaths of the Batman story by John Byrne-c/scripts 2.00
436-Year 3 begins (ends #439); origin original Robin retold by Nightwing (Dick Grayson); 1st app. Timothy Drake (8/89) 3.00
436-2nd printing 1.00
437-439: 437-Origin Robin continued 2.00
440,441: "A Lonely Place of Dying" Parts 1 & 3 1.25
442-1st app. Timothy Drake in Robin costume 2.50
443-456,458,459,462-464: 445-447-Batman goes to Russia. 448,449-The Penguin Affair Pts 1 & 3. 450-Origin Joker. 450,451-Joker-c/stories. 452-454-Dark Knight Dark City storyline; Riddler app. 455-Alan Grant scripts begin, ends #466, 470. 464-Last solo Batman story; free 16 pg. preview of Impact Comics line 1.50
457-Timothy Drake officially becomes Robin & dons new costume 3.00
457-Direct sale edition (has #000 in indicia) 2.50
460,461-Two part Catwoman story 2.00
465-487: 465-Robin returns to action with Batman. 470-War of the Gods x-over. 475,476-Return of Scarface-c/story. 476-Last $1.00-c. 477,478-Photo-c 1.50
488-Cont'd from Batman: Sword of Azrael #4; Azrael-c & app. 2.00 6.00
489-Bane-c/story; 1st app. Azrael in Bat-costume 4.00
490-Riddler-c/story; Azrael & Bane app. 3.00
491,492: 491-Knightfall lead-in; Joker-c/story; Azrael & Bane app.; Kelley Jones-c begin. 492-Knightfall part 1; Bane app. 3.00
492-Platinum edition (promo copy) 7.00
493-Knightfall Pt. 3 2.50
494-Knightfall Pt. 5; Joker-c & app. 2.00
495,496: 495-Knightfall Pt. 7; brief Bane & Joker apps. 496-Knightfall Pt. 9; Joker-c/story; Bane cameo 2.00
497-(Late 7/93)-Knightfall Pt. 11; Bane breaks Batman's back; B&W outer-c; Aparo-a(p); Giordano-a(i) 3.00
497-499: 497-2nd printing. 497-Newsstand edition w/o outer cover. 498-Knightfall part 15; Bane & Catwoman-c & app. (see Showcase 93 #7 & 8) 499-Knightfall Pt. 17; Bane app. 2.00
500-($2.50, 68 pgs.)-Knightfall Pt. 19; Azrael in new Bat-costume; Bane-c/ story 2.50
500-($3.95, 68 pgs.)-Collector's Edition w/die-cut double-c w/foil by Joe Quesada & 2 bound-in post cards 4.50
501-508,510,511: 501-Begin $1.50-c. 501-508-Knightquest. 503,504-Catwoman app. 507-Ballistic app.; Jim Balent-a(p). 510-KnightsEnd Pt. 7. 511-(9/94)-Zero Hour; Batgirl-c/story 1.75
509-($2.50, 52 pgs.)-KnightsEnd Pt. 1 2.50
0,512-514,516-518: 0-(10/94)-Origin retold. 512-(11/94)-Dick Grayson assumes Batman role 1.75
515-Special Ed.($2.50)-Kelley Jones-a begins; all black embossed-c; Troika Pt. 1 3.00
515-Regular Edition 2.00
519-534,536-549: 519-Begin $1.95-c. 521-Return of Alfred, 522-Swamp Thing app. 525-Mr. Freeze app. 527,528-Two Face app. 529-Contagion Pt. 6. 530-532-Deadman app. 533-Legacy prelude. 534-Legacy Pt. 5. 536-Final

Batman #558 © DC

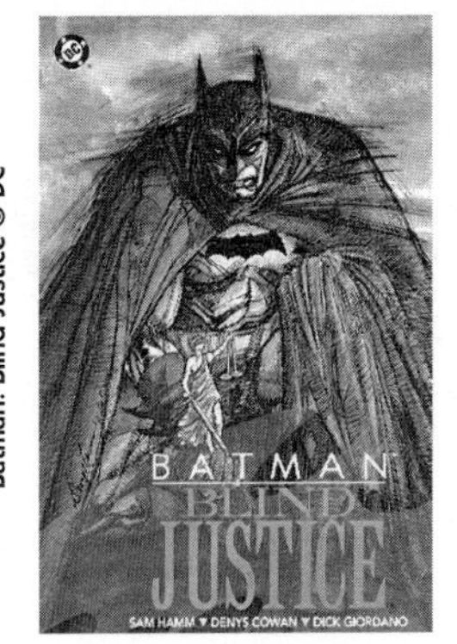

Batman: Blind Justice © DC

Batman: Prey © DC

GD25 FN65 NM94

Night x-over; Man-Bat-c/app. 540,541-Spectre-c-app. 544-546-Joker & The Demon. 548,549-Penguin-c/app. 2.00
530-532 ($2.50)-Enhanced edition; glow-in-the-dark-c. 2.75
535-(10/96, $2.95)-1st app. The Ogre 3.00
535-(10/96, $3.95)-1st app. The Ogre; variant, cardboard, foldout-c 4.00
550-($3.50)-Collector's Ed., includes 4 collector cards; intro. Chase, return of Clayface; Kelley Jones-c 3.50
550-($2.95)-Standard Ed.; Williams & Gray-c 2.95
551-557: 551,552-Ragman c/app. 553,554-Cataclysm pts.3,12 2.00
558-562: 558-Begin $1.99-c 1.99
#1,000,000 (11/98) 853rd Century x-over 1.99
Annual 1 (8-10/61)-Swan-c 54.00 162.00 650.00
Annual 2 28.00 85.00 285.00
Annual 3 (Summer, '62)-Joker-c/story 29.00 88.00 295.00
Annual 4,5 13.00 39.00 130.00
Annual 6,7 (7/64, 25¢, 80 pgs.) 10.00 30.00 100.00
Annual V5#8 (1982)-Painted-c 4.50
Annual 9,10,12: 9(7/85). 10(1986). 12(1988, $1.50) 3.00
Annual 11 (1987, $1.25)-Penguin-c/story; Alan Moore scripts 4.00
Annual 13 (1989, $1.75, 68 pgs.)-Gives history of Bruce Wayne, Dick Grayson, Jason Todd, Alfred, Comm. Gordon, Barbara Gordon (Batgirl) & Vicki Vale; Morrow-i 2.25
Annual 14 (1990, $2.00, 68 pgs.)-Origin Two-Face 2.25
Annual 15 (1991, $2.00, 68 pgs.)-Armageddon 2001 x-over; Joker app. 2.25
Annual 15 (2nd printing) 2.00
Annual 16 (1992, $2.50, 68 pgs.)-Joker-c/s; Kieth-c 2.50
Annual 17 (1993, $2.50, 68 pgs.)-Azrael in Bat-costume; intro Ballistic 2.50
Annual 18 (1994, $2.95) 3.00
Annual 19 (1995, $3.95)-Year One story; retells Scarecrow's origin 4.00
Annual 20 (1996, $2.95)-Legends of the Dead Earth story; Giarrano-a 3.00
Annual 21 (1997, $3.95)-Pulp Heroes story 3.95
Annual 22 (1998, $2.95)-Ghosts; Wrightson-c 2.95
Special 1 (4/84)-Mike W. Barr story; Golden-c/a 5.00
Pizza Hut giveaway(12/77)-exact-r of #122,123; Joker-c/story 2.00 6.00
Prell Shampoo giveaway(1966, 16 pgs.)- "The Joker's Practical Jokes" (6-7/8x3-3/8") 3.20 9.60 32.00

NOTE: **Art Adams** *a-400p.* **Neal Adams** *c-200, 203, 210, 217, 219-222, 224-227, 229, 230, 232, 234, 236-241, 243-246, 251, 255, Annual 14.* **Aparo** *a-414-420, 426-435, 440-448, 450, 451, 480-483, 486-491, 494-500; c-414-416, 481, 482, 463i, 486, 487i.* **Bolland** *a-400; c-445-447.* **Burnley** *a-10, 12-18, 20, 22, 25, 27; c-9, 15, 16, 27, 28p, 40p, 42p.* **Byrne** *c-401, 433-435, 533-535, Annual 11.* **Travis Charest** *c-488-490p.* **Colan** *a-340p, 343-345p, 348-351p, 373p, 383p; c-343p, 345p, 350p.* **J. Cole** *a-238r.* **Cowan** *a-Annual 10p.* **Golden** *a-295p, 303p, 484, 485.* **Alan Grant** *scripts-455-466, 470, 474-476, 479, 480, Annual 16(part).* **Grell** *a-287, 288p, 289p, 290; c-287-290.* **Infantino/Anderson** *c-167, 173, 175, 181, 186, 191, 192, 194, 195, 198, 199.* **Kelley Jones** *a-513-519, 521-525, 527; c-491-499, 500(newsstand), 501-510, 513.* **Kaluta** *c-242, 248, 253, Annual 12.* **G. Kane/Anderson** *c-178-180.* **Bob Kane** *a-1, 2, 5; c-1-5, 7, 17.* **G. Kane** *a-(r)-254, 255, 259, 261, 353i.* **Kubert** *a-238r, 400; c-310, 319p, 327, 328, 344.* **McFarlane** *c-423.* **Mignola** *c-426-429, 452-454, Annual 18.* **Moldoff** *c-101-140.* **Moldoff/Giella** *a-164-175, 177-181, 183, 184, 186.* **Moldoff/Greene** *a-169, 172-174, 177-179, 181, 184.* **Mooney** *a-255r.* **Morrow** *a-Annual 13i.* **Newton** *a-305, 306, 328p, 331p, 332p, 337p, 338p, 346p, 352-357p, 360-372p, 374-378p; c-374p, 378p.* **Nino** *a-Annual 9.* **Irv Novick** *c-201, 202.* **Perez** *a-400; c-436-442.* **Fred Ray** *c-8, 10; w/***Robinson***-11.* **Robinson/Roussos** *a-12-17, 20, 22, 24, 25, 27, 28, 31, 33, 37.* **Robinson** *a-12, 14, 18, 22-32,34, 36, 37, 255r, 260r, 261r; c-6, 8, 10, 12-15, 18, 21, 24, 26, 30, 37, 39.* **Simonson** *a-300p, 312p, 321p; c-300p, 312p, 366, 413i.* **P. Smith** *a-Annual 9.* **Dick Sprang** *c-19, 20, 22, 23, 25, 29, 31-36, 38, 51, 55, 66, 73, 76.* **Starlin** *c/a-402.* **Staton** *a-334.* **Sutton** *a-400.* **Wrightson** *a-265i, 400; c-320r. Bat-Hound app. in 92, 97, 103, 123, 125, 133, 156, 158. Bat-Mite app. in 133, 136, 144, 146, 158, 161. Batwoman app. in 105, 116, 122, 125, 128, 129, 131, 133, 139, 140, 141, 144, 145, 150, 151, 153, 154, 157, 159, 162, 163.* **Zeck** *c-417-420. Catwoman back-ups in 332, 345, 346, 348-351. Joker app. in 1, 2, 4, 5, 7-9, 11-13, 19, 20, 23, 25, 28, 32 & many more. Robin solo back-up stories in 337-339, 341-343.*

BATMAN (Books and trade paperbacks)
...: A LONELY PLACE OF DYING (1990, $3.95, 132 pgs.)-r/Batman #440-442 & New Titans #60,61; Perez-c 4.00
...AND DRACULA: RED RAIN nn (1991, $24.95)-Hard-c.; Elseworlds storyline 2.70 8.00 30.00
...AND DRACULA: Red Rain nn (1992, $9.95)-SC 1.00 3.00 10.00
ARKHAM ASYLUM Hard-c (1989, $24.95) 2.25 6.75 25.00
ARKHAM ASYLUM Soft-c ($14.95) 1.50 4.50 15.00

GD25 FN65 NM94

BIRTH OF THE DEMON Hard-c (1992, $24.95)-Origin of Ras al Ghul 2.25 6.75 25.00
BIRTH OF THE DEMON Soft-c (1993, $12.95) 1.30 3.90 13.00
BLIND JUSTICE nn (1992, $7.50)-r/Det. #598-600 .90 2.70 7.50
BRIDE OF THE DEMON Hard-c (1990, $19.95) 2.00 6.00 20.00
BRIDE OF THE DEMON Soft-c ($12.95) 1.30 3.90 13.00
...: CASTLE OF THE BAT ($5.95)-Elseworlds story 2.00 6.00
...: COLLECTED LEGENDS OF THE DARK KNIGHT nn (1994, $12.95)-r/Legends of the Dark Knight #32-34,38,42,43 1.30 3.90 13.00
...: CRIMSON MIST (1999, $24.95,HC)-Elseworlds story Doug Moench-s/Kelley Jones-c/a 24.95
...: DARK JOKER-THE WILD (1993, $24.95,HC)-Elseworlds story Doug Moench-s/Kelley Jones-c/a 2.25 6.80 25.00
...: DARK JOKER-THE WILD (1993, $9.95,SC) 1.00 3.00 10.00
...DARK KNIGHT DYNASTY nn (1997, $24.95)-Hard-c.; 3 Elseworlds stories; Barr-s/ S. Hampton painted-a, Gary Frank, McDaniel-a(p) 24.95
...DEADMAN: DEATH AND GLORY nn (1996, $24.95)-Hard-c.; Robinson-s/ Estes-c/a 2.25 6.75 25.00
...DEADMAN: DEATH AND GLORY ($12.95)-SC 1.30 3.90 13.00
DEATH IN THE FAMILY (1988, $3.95, trade paperback)-r/Batman #426-429 by Aparo 5.00
DEATH IN THE FAMILY: (2nd - 5th printings) 4.00
DIGITAL JUSTICE nn (1990, $24.95, Hard-c.)-Computer generated art 2.25 6.75 25.00
... FACES (1995, $9.95, TPB) 1.00 3.00 10.00
FOUR OF A KIND TPB (1998, $14.95)-r/1995 Year One Annuals featuring Poison Ivy, Riddler, Scarecrow, & Man-Bat 1.50 4.50 15.00
...GOTHIC (1992, $12.95, TPB)-r/Legends of the Dark Knight #6-10 1.30 3.90 13.00
GREATEST BATMAN STORIES Hard-c ($24.95) 3.20 9.50 35.00
GREATEST BATMAN STORIES Soft-c ($15.95) 1.60 4.80 16.00
GREATEST BATMAN STORIES Vol. 2 (1992, $16.95)1.70 5.10 17.00
GREATEST JOKER STORIES Hard-c ($19.95) 2.20 6.50 24.00
GREATEST JOKER STORIES Soft-c ($14.95) 1.85 5.50 15.00
GREATEST JOKER STORIES (Stacked Deck...Expanded Edition) (1992, $29.95)-Longmeadow Press Publ. 2.70 8.00 30.00
...: HAUNTED KNIGHT-(1997,12.95) r/ Halloween sp..1.30 3.90 13.00
... LEGACY-(1996,17.95) reprints Legacy 17.95
...: THE MANY DEATHS OF THE BATMAN (1992, $3.95, 84 pgs.)-r/Batman #433-435 w/new Byrne-c 4.00
...: THE MOVIES (1997, $19.95)-r/movie adaptions of Batman, Batman Returns, Batman Forever, Batman and Robin 2.00 6.00 20.00
...: PREY (1992, $12.95)-Gulacy/Austin-a 1.30 3.90 13.00
...: PRODIGAL (1997, $14.95)-Gulacy/Austin-a 1.50 4.50 15.00
SHAMAN (1993, $12.95)-r/Legends/D.K. #1-5 1.30 3.90 13.00
...: SON OF THE DEMON Hard-c (9/87, $14.95) 2.70 8.00 30.00
...: SON OF THE DEMON limited signed & numbered Hard-c (1,700) 4.00 12.00 45.00
...: SON OF THE DEMON Soft-c w/new-c ($8.95) .90 2.70 9.00
...: SON OF THE DEMON Soft-c (1989, $9.95, 2nd printing - 4th printing) 1.00 3.00 10.00
...: TALES OF THE DEMON (1991, $17.95, 212 pgs.)-Intro by Sam Hamm; reprints by N. Adams(3) & Golden; contains Saga of Ra's Al Ghul #1 1.80 5.40 18.00
...: TEN NIGHTS OF THE BEAST (1994, $5.95)-r/Batman #417-420 2.00 6.00
...:THE LAST ANGEL (1994, $12.95, TPB) 1.30 3.90 13.00
...: THRILLKILLER (1998, $12.95, TPB)-r/series & ...'62 12.95
...: VENOM (1993, $9.95, TPB)-r/Legends of the Dark Knight #16-20; embossed-c 1.00 3.00 10.00
YEAR ONE Hard-c (1988, $12.95) 1.80 5.40 18.00
YEAR ONE (1988, $9.95, TPB)-r/Batman #404-407 by Miller; intro by Miller 1.00 3.00 10.00

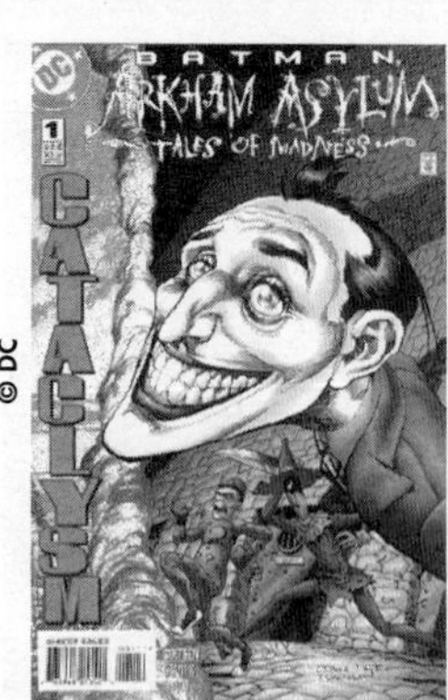

Batman: Arkham Asylum - Tales of Madness #1 © DC

Batman: Batgirl © DC

Batman: Scottish Connection © DC

GD25 FN65 NM94

YEAR ONE (TPB, 2nd & 3rd printings) 1.00 3.00 10.00
YEAR TWO (1990, $9.95, TPB)-r/Det. 575-578 by McFarlane; wraparound-c 1.00 3.00 10.00

BATMAN (one-shots)
BATMAN AND OTHER DC CLASSICS 1 (1989, giveaway)-DC Comics/Diamond Comic Distributors; Batman origin-r/Batman #47, Camelot 3000-r by Bolland, Justice League-r('87), New Teen Titans-r by Perez. 1.00
... & ROBIN (1997, $5.95)-Movie adaption 5.95
...: ARKHAM ASYLUM - TALES OF MADNESS (5/98, $2.95) Cataclysm x-over pt. 16; Grant-s/Taylor-a 3.00
... : BANE (1997, $4.95)-Dixon-s/Burchett-a; Stelfreeze-c; cover interlocks w/Batman:(Batgirl, Mr. Freeze, Poison Ivy) 4.95
... : BATGIRL (1997, $4.95)-Puckett-s/Haley,Kesel-a; Stelfreeze-c; cover interlocks w/Batman:(Bane, Mr. Freeze, Poison Ivy) 4.95
... : BATGIRL (6/98, $1.95)-Girlfrenzy; Balent-a 2.00
... : BLACKGATE (1/97, $3.95) Dixon-s 3.95
... : BLACKGATE - ISLE OF MEN (4/98, $2.95) Cataclysm x-over pt. 8; Moench-s/Aparo-a 3.00
BROTHERHOOD OF THE BAT (1995, $5.95)-Elseworlds-s 2.00 6.00
.../CAPTAIN AMERICA (1996, $5.95, DC/Marvel) Elseworlds story; Byrne-c/s/a 5.95
... : CATWOMAN DEFIANT nn (1992, $4.95, prestige format)-Milligan scripts; cover interlocks w/Batman: Penguin Triumphant; special foil logo. 5.00
... : DARK ALLEGIANCES (1996, $5.95)-Elseworlds story, Chaykin-c/a. 2.00 6.00
... : DARK KNIGHT GALLERY (1995, $3.50)-Pin-ups by Pratt, Balent, & others. 3.50
...:DEATH OF INNOCENTS (12/96, $3.95)-O'Neil-s/ Staton-a(p) 4.00
.../DEMON (1996, $4.95)-Alan Grant scripts 5.00
... 80-PAGE GIANT (8/98, $4.95) Stelfreeze-c 5.00
... FOREVER (1995, $5.95, direct market) 2.00 6.00
... FOREVER (1995, $3.95, newsstand) 4.00
FULL CIRCLE nn (1991, $5.95, stiff-c, 68 pgs.)-Sequel to Batman: Year Two 2.00 6.00
...GALLERY, The 1 (1992, $2.95)-Pin-ups by Miller, N. Adams & others 3.00
...GOTHAM BY GASLIGHT (1989, $3.95) 4.00
.../GREEN ARROW: THE POISON TOMORROW nn (1992, $5.95, square-bound, 68 pgs.)-Netzer-c/a 2.00 6.00
HOLY TERROR nn (1991, $4.95, 52 pgs.)-Elseworlds story 5.00
.../HOUDINI: THE DEVIL'S WORKSHOP (1993, $5.95) 2.00 6.00
... :HUNTRESS/SPOILER - BLUNT TRAUMA (5/98, $2.95) Cataclysm pt. 13 Dixon-s/Barreto & Sienkiewicz-a 3.00
...: IN DARKEST KNIGHT nn (1994, $4.95, 52 pgs.)-Elseworlds story; Batman w/Green Lantern's ring. 5.00
...:JUDGE DREDD: JUDGEMENT ON GOTHAM nn (1991, $5.95, 68 pgs.) Grant/Wagner scripts; Simon Bisley-c/a 2.00 6.00
...:JUDGE DREDD: JUDGEMENT ON GOTHAM nn (2nd printing) 2.00 6.00
...:JUDGE DREDD: THE ULTIMATE RIDDLE (1995, $4.95) 5.00
...:JUDGE DREDD: VENDETTA IN GOTHAM (1993, $5.95) 2.00 6.00
...: KNIGHTGALLERY (1995, $3.50)-Elseworlds sketchbook. 3.50
...: MASK OF THE PHANTASM (1994, $2.95)-Movie adapt. 3.00
...: MASK OF THE PHANTASM (1994, $4.95)-Movie adapt. 5.00
...: MASQUE (1997, $6.95)-Elseworlds; Grell-c/s/a 6.95
...: MASTER OF THE FUTURE nn (1991, $5.95, 68 pgs.)-Elseworlds storyline; sequel to Gotham By Gaslight; embossed-c 2.00 6.00
...: MITEFALL (1995, $4.95)-Alan Grant script, Kevin O'Neill-a 5.00
... : MR. FREEZE (1997, $4.95)-Dini-s/Buckingham-a; Stelfreeze-c; cover interlocks w/Batman:(Bane, Batgirl, Poison Ivy) 4.95
...: PENGUIN TRIUMPHANT nn (1992, $4.95)-Staton-a(p); special foil logo 5.00
...•PHANTOM STRANGER nn (1997, $4.95) nn-Grant-s/Ransom-a 4.95

GD25 FN65 NM94

... : PLUS (2/97, $2.95) Arsenal-c/app. 3.00
... : POISON IVY (1997, $4.95)-J.F. Moore-s/Apthorp-a; Stelfreeze-c; cover interlocks w/Batman:(Bane, Batgirl, Mr. Freeze) 4.95
.../PUNISHER: LAKE OF FIRE (1994, $4.95, DC/Marvel) 5.00
... :REIGN OF TERROR ('99, $4.95) Elseworlds 4.95
...RETURNS MOVIE SPECIAL (1992, $3.95) 4.00
...RETURNS MOVIE PRESTIGE (1992, $5.95, squarebound)-Dorman painted-c 2.00 6.00
...:RIDDLER-THE RIDDLE FACTORY (1995, $4.95)-Wagner script 5.00
...: SCARECROW 3-D (12/98, $3.95) w/glasses 3.95
...: SCAR OF THE BAT nn (1996, $4.95)-Elseworlds story; Max Allan Collins script; Barreto-a. 5.00
... :SCOTTISH CONNECTION (1998, $5.95) Quitely-a 5.95
... :SEDUCTION OF THE GUN nn (1992, $2.50, 68 pgs.) 2.50
.../SPAWN: WAR DEVIL nn (1994, $4.95, 52 pgs.) 5.00
.../SPIDER-MAN (1997, $4.95) Dematteis-s/Nolan & Kesel-a 4.95
... : THE ABDUCTION ('98, $5.95) 5.95
... :THE BLUE, THE GREY, & THE BAT nn (1992, $5.95, 68 pgs.)-Weiss/Lopez-a 2.00 6.00
... :THE KILLING JOKE (1988, deluxe 52 pgs., mature readers)-Bolland-c/a; Alan Moore scripts. 1.20 3.60 12.00
...: THE KILLING JOKE (2nd thru 8th printings) 3.50
...: THE OFFICIAL COMIC ADAPTATION OF THE WARNER BROS. MOTION PICTURE (1989, $2.50, regular format, 68 pgs.)-Ordway-c. 3.00
...: THE OFFICIAL COMIC ADAPTATION OF THE WARNER BROS. MOTION PICTURE (1989, $4.95, prestige format, 68 pgs.)-same interiors but different-c than regular format. 5.00
...: TWO-FACE-CRIME AND PUNISHMENT-(1995, $4.95)-Scott McDaniel-a 5.00
... : TWO FACES (11/98, $4.95) Elseworlds 4.95
...: VENGEANCE OF BANE SPECIAL 1 (1992, $2.50, 68 pgs.)-Origin & 1st app. Bane (see Batman #491) 1.00 3.00 10.00
...: VENGEANCE OF BANE SPECIAL 1 (2nd printing) 2.50
....:VENGEANCE OF BANE II nn (1995, $3.95)-sequel 4.00
...Vs. THE INCREDIBLE HULK (1995, $3.95)-r/DC Special Series #27 4.00
...: VILLAINS SECRET FILES (10/98, $4.95) Origin-s 4.95

BATMAN (Kellogg's Poptarts comics)
National Periodical Publications: 1966 (Set of 6) (16 pgs.)

"The Man in the Iron Mask", "The Penguin's Fowl Play", "The Joker's Happy Victims", "The Catwoman's Catnapping Caper", "The Mad Hatter's Hat Crimes", "The Case of the Batman II" each.... 2.80 8.40 28.00
NOTE: *All above were folded and placed in Poptarts boxes.* ***Infantino*** *art on Catwoman and Joker issues.*

BATMAN ADVENTURES, THE (Based on animated series)
DC Comics: Oct, 1992 - No. 36, Oct, 1995 ($1.25/$1.50)

1-Penguin-c/story 4.00
1 ($1.95, Silver Edition)-2nd printing 2.25
2-6,8-19: 2,12-Catwoman-c/story. 3-Joker-c/story. 5-Scarecrow-c/story. 10-Riddler-c/story. 11-Man-Bat-c/story. 12-Batgirl & Catwoman-c/story. 16-Joker-c/story; begin $1.50-c. 18-Batgirl-c/story. 19-Scarecrow-c/story. 2.50
7-Special edition polybagged with Man-Bat trading card 2.00 6.00
20-24,26-32: 26-Batgirl app. 1.75
25-($2.50, 52 pgs.)-Superman app. 2.50
33-36: 33-Begin $1.75-c 1.75
Annual 1 (1994, $2.95) 3.00
Annual 2 (1995, $3.50)-Demon-c/story; Ras al Ghul app. 3.50
Holiday Special 1 (1995, $2.95) 3.00
Mad Love nn (2/94, $3.95, 68 pgs.)-Joker-c/story 4.00
The Collected Adventures Vol. 1 (1993, $5.95) 2.00 6.00
The Collected Adventures Vol. 2 (1994, $5.95) 2.00 6.00

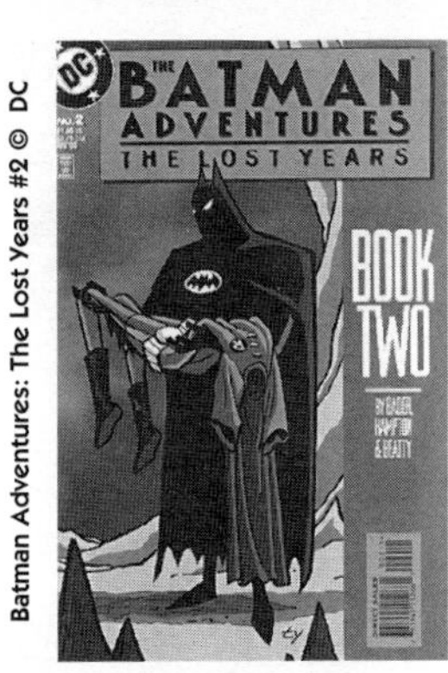

Batman Adventures: The Lost Years #2 © DC

Batman Family #10 © DC

Batman: Gotham Adventures #1 © DC

GD25 FN65 NM94

TPB ('98, $7.95) r/#1-6; painted wraparound-c 7.95

BATMAN ADVENTURES, THE: THE LOST YEARS (TV)
DC Comics: Jan, 1998 - No. 5, May, 1998 ($1.95) (Based on animated series)

1-5-Leads into Fall '97's new animated episodes. 4-Tim Drake becomes Robin. 5-Dick becomes Nightwing 2.00

BATMAN/ALIENS
DC Comics/Dark Horse: Mar, 1997 - No. 2, Apr, 1997 ($4.95, lim. series)

1,2: Wrightson-c/a. 5.00
TPB-(1997, $14.95) w/prequel from DHP #101,102 1.50 4.50 15.00

BATMAN AND ROBIN ADVENTURES (TV)
DC Comics: Nov, 1995 - No. 25, Dec, 1997 ($1.75) (Based on animated series)

1-Dini-s. 4.00
2-24: 2-4-Dini script. 4-Penguin-c/story. 5-Joker-c/story; Poison Ivy, Harley Quinn-c/app. 9-Batgirl & Talia-c/story. 10-Ra's Al Ghul-c/story 11-Man-Bat app. 12-Bane-c/app. 13-Scarecrow-c/app. 15 Deadman-c/app. 16-Catwoman-c/app. 18-Joker-c/app. 24-Poison Ivy app. 2.00
25-($2.95, 48 pgs.) 3.00
Annual 1(11/96, $2.95) Phantasm-c/app. 4.00
Annual 2(11/97, $3.95) Zatara and Zatanna-c/app. 3.95
...: Sub-Zero(1998, $3.95) Adaption of animated video 3.95

BATMAN AND SUPERMAN ADVENTURES: WORLD'S FINEST
DC Comics: 1997 ($6.95, square-bound, one-shot) (Based on animated series)

1-Adaption of animated crossover episode; Dini-s/Timm-c. 6.95

BATMAN AND THE OUTSIDERS (The Adventures of the Outsiders#33 on) (Also see Brave & The Bold #200 & The Outsiders) (Replaces The Brave and the Bold)
DC Comics: Aug, 1983 - No. 32, Apr, 1986 (Mando paper #5 on)

1-Batman, Halo, Geo-Force, Katana, Metamorpho & Black Lightning begin. 2.50
2-32: 5-New Teen Titans x-over. 9-Halo begins. 11,12-Origin Katana. 18-More facts about Metamorpho's origin. 28-31-Lookers origin. 32-Team disbands 1.00
Annual 1 (9/84)-Miller/Aparo-c; Aparo-i 1.00
Annual 2 (9/85)-Metamorpho & Sapphire Stagg wed; Aparo-c 1.00

NOTE: ***Aparo*** *a-1-9, 11-13p, 16-20; c-1-4, 5i, 6-21.* ***B. Kane*** *a-3r.* ***Layton*** *a-19i, 20i.* ***Lopez*** *a-3p.* ***Perez*** *c-5p.* ***B. Willingham*** *a-14p.*

BATMAN: BANE OF THE DEMON
DC Comics: Mar, 1998 - No. 4, June, 1998 ($1.95, limited series)

1-4-Dixon-s/Nolan-a; prelude to Legacy x-over 2.00

BATMAN: BLACK & WHITE
DC Comics: June, 1996 - No. 4, Sept, 1996 ($2.95, B&W, limited series)

1-Stories by McKeever, Timm, Kubert, Chaykin, Goodwin; Jim Lee-c; Allred inside front-c; Moebius inside back-c 5.00
2-4: 2-Stories by Simonson, Corben, Bisley & Gaiman; Miller-c. 3-Stories by M. Wagner, Janson, Sienkiewicz, O'Neil & Kristiansen; B. Smith-c; Russell inside front-c; Silvestri inside back-c. 4-Stories by Bolland, Goodwin & Gianni, Strnad & Nowlan, O'Neil & Stelfreeze; Toth-c; Neal Adams & Alex Ross pin-ups 4.50
Hardcover ('97, $39.95) r/series w/new art & cover plate 40.00

BATMAN: CATWOMAN DEFIANT (See Batman one-shots)

BATMAN CHRONICLES, THE
DC Comics: Summer, 1995 - Present ($2.95, quarterly)

1-3,5-15: 1-Dixon/Grant/Moench script. 3-Bolland-c. 5-Oracle Year One story, Richard Dragon app.,Chaykin-c. 6-Kaluta-c; Ra's Al Ghul story. 7-Superman-c/app.11-Paul Pope-s/a. 12-Cataclysm pt. 10 3.00
4-Hitman story by Garth Ennis, Contagion tie-in; Balent-c 1.00 3.00 10.00

GD25 FN65 NM94

...Gallery (3/97, $3.50) Pin-ups 3.50
Gauntlet, The (1997, $4.95, one-shot) 5.00

BATMAN: DARK KNIGHT OF THE ROUND TABLE
DC Comics: 1999 - No. 2, 1999 ($4.95, limited series, prestige format)

1,2-Elseworlds: Giordano-a 4.95

BATMAN FAMILY, THE
National Periodical Pub./DC Comics: Sept-Oct, 1975 - No. 20, Oct-Nov, 1978 (#1-4, 17-on: 68 pgs.) (Combined with Detective Comics with No. 481)

1-Origin/2nd app. Batgirl-Robin team-up (The Dynamite Duo); reprints plus one new story begins; N. Adams-a(r); r/1st app. Man-Bat from Det. #400 1.60 4.80 16.00
2-5: 2-r/Det. #369. 3-Batgirl & Robin learn each's i.d.; r/Batwoman app. from Batman #105. 4-r/1st Fatman app. from Batman #113. 5-r/1st Bat-Hound app. from Batman #92 1.00 3.00 10.00
6,9-Joker's daughter on cover (1st app?) 1.40 4.20 14.00
7,8,14-16: 8-r/Batwoman app.14-Batwoman app. 15-3rd app. Killer Moth. 16-Bat-Girl cameo (last app. in costume until New Teen Titans #47) .90 2.70 8.00
10-1st revival Batwoman; Cavalier app.; Killer Moth app. 1.50 4.50 15.00
11-13-Rogers-a(p): 11-New stories begin; Man-Bat begins. 13-Batwoman cameo 1.20 3.60 12.00
17-20: 17-($1.00 size)-Batman, Huntress begin; Batwoman & Catwoman 1st meet. 18-20: Huntress by Staton in all. 20-Origin Ragman retold 1.20 3.60 12.00

NOTE: ***Aparo*** *a-17; c-11-16.* ***Austin*** *a-12i.* ***Chaykin*** *a-14p.* ***Michael Golden*** *a-15-17,18-20p.* ***Grell*** *a-1; c-1.* ***Gil Kane*** *a-2r.* ***Kaluta*** *c-17, 19.* ***Newton*** *a-13.* ***Robinson*** *a-1r, 3i(r), 9r.* ***Russell*** *a-18i, 19i.* ***Starlin*** *a-17; c-18, 20.*

BATMAN: GCPD
DC Comics: Aug, 1996 - No. 4, Nov, 1996 ($2.25, limited series)

1-4: Features Jim Gordon; Aparo/Sienkiewicz-a 2.25

BATMAN: GORDON OF GOTHAM
DC Comics: June, 1998 - No. 4, Sept, 1998 ($1.95, limited series)

1-4: Gordon's early days in Chicago 2.00

BATMAN: GORDON'S LAW
DC Comics: Dec, 1996 - No. 3, Feb, 1997 ($1.95, limited series)

1-3: Dixon-s/Janson-c/a 1.95

BATMAN: GOTHAM ADVENTURES (TV)
DC Comics: June, 1998 - Present ($2.95/$1.95)

1-($2.95) Based on Kids WB Batman animated series 3.00
2-3-($1.95): 2-Two-Face-c/app. 2.00
4-9: 4-Begin $1.99-c. 5-Deadman-c 1.99

BATMAN: GOTHAM NIGHTS II (First series listed under Gotham Nights)
DC Comics: Mar, 1995 - No. 4, June, 1995 ($1.95, limited series)

1-4 2.00

BATMAN/GRENDEL (1st limited series)
DC Comics: 1993 - No. 2, 1993 ($4.95, limited series, squarebound; 52 pgs.)

1,2: Batman vs. Hunter Rose. 1-Devil's Riddle; Matt Wagner-c/a/scripts. 2-Devil's Masque; Matt Wagner-c/a/scripts 2.00 6.00

BATMAN/GRENDEL (2nd limited series)
DC Comics: June, 1996 - No. 2, July, 1996 ($4.95, limited series, squarebound)

1,2: Batman vs. Grendel Prime. 1-Devil's Bones; Matt Wagner-c/a/s 5.00

BATMAN/ JUDGE DREDD "DIE LAUGHING"
DC Comics: 1998 - No. 2, 1999 ($4.95, limited series, squarebound)

1,2: 1-Fabry-c/a. 2-Jim Murray-c/a 4.95

BATMAN: KNIGHTGALLERY (See Batman one-shots)

BATMAN: LEGENDS OF THE DARK KNIGHT (Legends of the Dark...#1-36)
DC Comics: Nov, 1989 - Present ($1.50/$1.75/$1.95/$1.99)

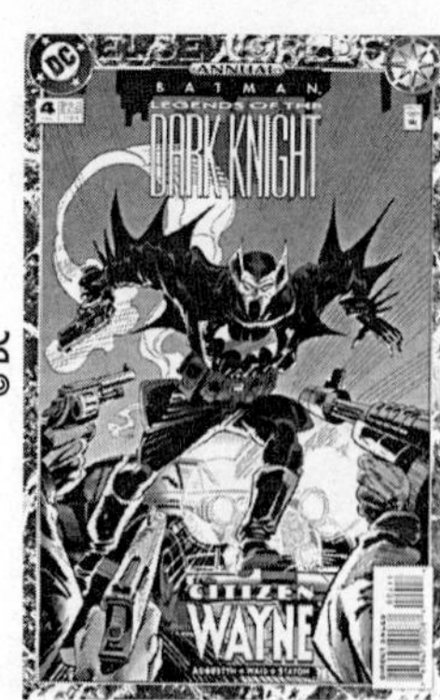

Batman: Legends of the Dark Knight Annual #4 © DC

Batman/Predator III #4 © DC

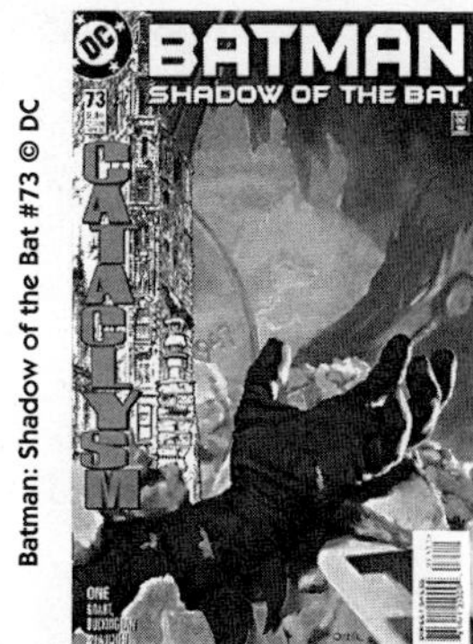

Batman: Shadow of the Bat #73 © DC

GD25 FN65 NM94

1- "Shaman" begins, ends #5; outer cover has four different color variations, all worth same 3.00
2 2.00
3-5 2.00
6-10- "Gothic" by Grant Morrison (scripts) 2.00
11-15,17,18: 11-15-Gulacy/Austin-a. 13-Catwoman app. 18-Last $1.50-c 2.00
16-Intro drug Bane uses; begin Venom story 4.00
19-49,51-63: 38-Bat-Mite-c/story. 46-49-Catwoman app. w/Heath-c/a. 51-Ragman app.; Joe Kubert-c. 59,60,61-Knightquest x-over. 62,63-KnightsEnd Pt. 4 & 10 2.00
50-($3.95, 68 pgs.)-Bolland embossed gold foil-c; Joker-c/story; pin-ups by Chaykin, Simonson, Williamson, Kaluta, Russell, others 4.00
64,0,65-99: 64-(9/94)-Begin $1.95-c. 0-(10/94)-Quesada/Palmiotti-c; various artists on story. 71-73-James Robinson-s, J. Watkiss-c/a. 74,75-Ted McKeever-c/a/s. 76-78-Scott Hampton-c/a/s. 81-Card insert. 83,84-Ellis-s. 85-Robinson-s. 91-93-Ennis-s. 94-Michael T. Gilbert-s/a. 2.00
100-($3.95) Alex Ross painted-c; gallery by various 5.00
101-109: 101-Ezquerra-a. 102-104-Robinson-s 2.00
110-114: 110-Begin $1.99-c. 114-Brereton-c/a 1.99
Annual 1 (1991, $3.95, 68 pgs.)-Joker app. 4.00
Annual 2 (1992, $3.50, 68 pgs.)-Netzer-c/a 3.50
Annual 3 (1993, $3.50, 68 pgs.)-New Batman (Azrael) app. 3.50
Annual 4 (1994, $3.50, 68 pgs.)-Elseworlds story 3.50
Annual 5 (1995, $3.95, 68 pgs.)-Year One; Man-Bat app. 4.00
Annual 6 (1996, $2.95)-Legend of the Dead Earth story 3.00
Annual 7 (1997, $3.95)-Pulp Heroes story 4.00
Halloween Special 1 (12/93, $6.95, 84 pgs.)-Embossed & foil stamped-c .85 2.60 7.00
Batman Madness-...Halloween Special (1994, $4.95) 2.00 5.00
Batman Ghosts-...Halloween Special (1995, $4.95) 2.00 5.00

NOTE: *Aparo a-Annual 1.* ***Chaykin*** *scripts-24-26.* ***Giffen*** *a-Annual 1.* ***Golden*** *a-Annual 1.* ***Alan Grant*** *scripts-38, 52, 53.* ***Gil Kane*** *c/a-24-26.* ***Mignola*** *a-54; c-54, 62.* ***Morrow*** *a-Annual 3i.* ***Quesada*** *a-Annual 1.* ***James Robinson*** *scripts- 71-73.* ***Russell*** *c/a-42, 43.* ***Sears*** *a-21, 23; c-21, 23.* ***Zeck*** *a-69, 70; c-69, 70.*

BATMAN-LEGENDS OF THE DARK KNIGHT: JAZZ
DC Comics: Apr, 1995 - No. 3, June, 1995 ($2.50, limited series)
1-3 2.50

BATMAN: MANBAT
DC Comics: Oct, 1995 - No. 3, Dec, 1995 ($4.95, limited series)
1-3-Elseworlds-Delano-script; Bolton-a. 5.00
TPB-(1997, $14.95) r/#1-3 14.95

BATMAN: MITEFALL (See Batman one-shots)

BATMAN MINIATURE (See Batman Kellogg's)

BATMAN: PENGUIN TRIUMPHANT (See Batman one-shots)

BATMAN/PREDATOR III: BLOOD TIES
DC Comics/Dark Horse Comics: Nov, 1997 - No. 4, Feb, 1998 ($1.95, lim. series)
1-4: Dixon-s/Damaggio-c/a 2.00
TPB-(1998, $7.95) r/#1-4 .90 2.70 8.00

BATMAN RECORD COMIC
National Periodical Publications: 1966 (one-shot)
1-With record (still sealed) 12.50 38.00 125.00
Comic only 7.00 21.00 70.00

BATMAN RETURNS MOVIE SPECIAL (See Batman one-shots)

BATMAN: RIDDLER-THE RIDDLE FACTORY (See Batman one-shots)

BATMAN: RUN, RIDDLER, RUN
DC Comics: 1992 - Book 3, 1992 ($4.95, limited series)
Book 1-3: Mark Badger-a & plot 5.00

BATMAN: SCAR OF THE BAT (See Batman one-shots)

GD25 FN65 NM94

BATMAN: SECRET FILES
DC Comics: Oct, 1997 ($4.95)
1-New origin-s and profiles 5.00

BATMAN: SHADOW OF THE BAT
DC Comics: June, 1992 - Present ($1.50/$1.75/$1.95/$1.99)
1-The Last Arkham-c/story begins; Alan Grant scripts in all 3.00
1-($2.50)-Deluxe edition polybagged w/poster, pop-up & book mark 4.00
2-7: 4-The Last Arkham ends. 7-Last $1.50-c 1.50
8-28: 14,15-Staton-a(p). 16-18-Knightfall tie-ins. 19-28-Knightquest tie-ins w/Azrael as Batman. 19,20-Painted-c. 25-Silver ink-c; anniversary issue 1.75
29-($2.95, 52 pgs.)-KnightsEnd Pt. 2 3.00
30,31,0,32-72: 30-KnightsEnd Pt. 8. 31-(9.94)-Begin $1.95-c; Zero Hour. 0-(10/94). 32-(11/94). 33-Robin-c. 35-Troika-Pt.2. 43,44-Cat-Man & Catwoman-c. 48-Contagion Pt. 1; card insert. 49-Contagion Pt.7. 56,57,58-Poison Ivy-c/app. 62-Two-Face app. 69,70-Fate app. 2.00
35-($2.95)-Variant embossed-c 3.00
73,74,76-78: Cataclysm x-over pts. 1,9. 76-78-Orbik-c 2.00
75-($2.95) Mr. Freeze & Clayface app.; Orbik-c 3.00
79,81,82: 79-Begin $1.99-c; Orbik-c 1.99
80-($3.95) Flip book with Azrael #47 3.95
#1,000,000 (11/98) 853rd Century x-over; Orbik-c 1.99
Annual 1 (1993, $3.50, 68 pgs.) 3.50
Annual 2 (1994, $3.95, 68 pgs.) 4.00
Annual 3 (1995, $3.95)-Year One story; Poison Ivy app. 4.00
Annual 4 (1996, $2.95)-Legends of the Dead Earth story; Starman cameo 3.00
Annual 5 (1997, $3.95)-Pulp Heroes story; Poison Ivy app. 3.95

BATMAN-SPAWN: WAR DEVIL (See Batman one-shots)

BATMAN SPECTACULAR (See DC Special Series No. 15)

BATMAN: SWORD OF AZRAEL (Also see Azrael & Batman #488,489)
DC Comics: Oct, 1992 - No. 4, Jan, 1993 ($1.75, limited series)
1-Wraparound gatefold-c; Quesada-c/a(p) in all; 1st app. Azrael 1.00 3.00 10.00
2-4: 4-Cont'd in Batman #488 .85 2.60 7.00
Silver Edition 1-4 (1993, $1.95)-Reprints #1-4 2.00
Trade Paperback (1993, $9.95)-Reprints #1-4 1.00 3.00 10.00
Trade Paperback Gold Edition 1.50 4.50 15.00

BATMAN: THE CULT
DC Comics: 1988 - No. 4, Nov, 1988 ($3.50, deluxe limited series)
1-Wrightson-a/painted-c in all 4.00
2-4 3.50
Trade Paperback ('91, $14.95)-New Wrightson-c 1.50 4.50 15.00

BATMAN: THE DARK KNIGHT RETURNS
DC Comics: Mar, 1986 - No. 4, 1986 ($2.95, squarebound, limited series)
1-Miller story & c/a(p); set in the future 2.20 6.25 22.00
1-2nd & 3rd printings 1.20 3.00
2-Carrie Kelly becomes 1st female Robin 1.20 3.60 12.00
2-2nd & 3rd printings 1.20 3.00
3-Death of Joker; Superman app. .90 2.70 9.00
3-2nd printing 1.20 3.00
4-Death of Alfred; Superman app. .85 2.60 7.00
Hard-c, signed & numbered edition ($40.00)(4000 copies) 250.00
Hard-c, trade edition 3.80 11.50 40.00
Soft-c, trade edition (1st printing only) 1.25 3.75 10.00
Soft-c, trade edition (2nd thru 8th printings) .90 2.70 7.50
10th Anniv. Slipcase set ('96, $100.00): Signed & numbered hard-c edition (10,000 copies), sketchbook, copy of script for #1, 2 colorprints 90.00
10th Anniv. Hard-c ('96, $45.00) 45.00
10th Anniv. Soft-c ('97, $14.95) 14.95

NOTE: *The #2 second printings can be identified by matching the grey background colors on the inside front cover and facing page. The inside front cover of the second printing has a dark grey*

Batman: The Long Halloween #6 © DC

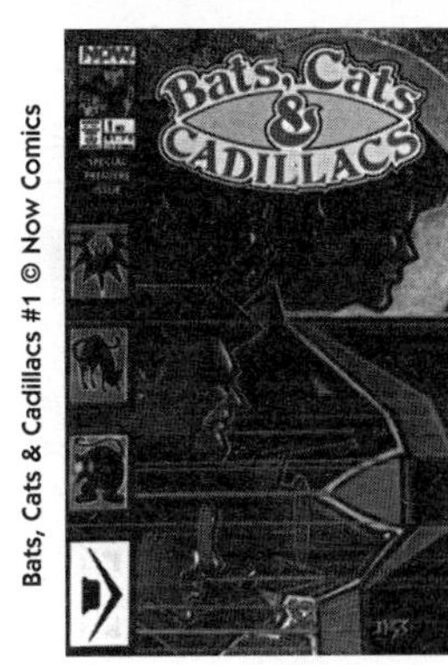

Bats, Cats & Cadillacs #1 © Now Comics

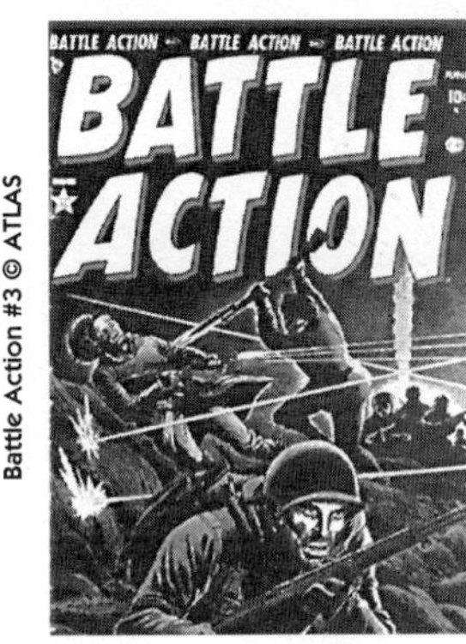

Battle Action #3 © ATLAS

GD25 FN65 NM94

background which does not match the lighter grey of the facing page. On the true 1st printings, the backgrounds are both light grey. All other issues are clearly marked.

BATMAN: THE KILLING JOKE (See Batman one-shots)

BATMAN: THE LONG HALLOWEEN
DC Comics: Oct, 1996 - No. 13, Oct, 1997 ($2.95/$4.95, limited series)

1-($4.95)-Loeb-s/Sale-c/a in all 1.00 3.00 10.00
2-5($2.95): 2-Solomon Grundy-c/app. 3-Joker-c/app., Catwoman, Poison Ivy app. 2.00 6.00
6-10: 6-Poison Ivy-c. 7-Riddler-c/app. 5.00
11,12 4.00
13-($4.95, 48 pgs.)-Killer revelations 5.00

BATMAN: THE OFFICIAL COMIC ADAPTATION OF THE WARNER BROS. MOTION PICTURE (See Batman one-shots)

BATMAN: THE ULTIMATE EVIL
DC Comics: 1995 ($5.95, limited series, prestige format)

1,2-Barrett, Jr. adaptation of Vachss novel. 2.00 6.00

BATMAN 3-D (Also see 3-D Batman)
DC Comics: 1990 ($9.95, w/glasses, 8-1/8x10-3/4")

nn-Byrne-a/scripts; Riddler, Joker, Penguin & Two-Face app. plus r/1953 3-D Batman; pin-ups by many artists 1.20 3.60 12.00

BATMAN: TOYMAN
DC Comics: Nov, 1998 - No. 4, Feb, 1999 ($2.25, limited series)

1-4-Hama-s 2.25

BATMAN: TWO-FACE-CRIME AND PUNISHMENT (See Batman one-shots)

BATMAN: TWO-FACE STRIKES TWICE
DC Comics: 1993 - No. 2, 1993 ($4.95, 52 pgs.)

1,2-Flip book format w/Staton-a (G.A. side) 5.00

BATMAN VERSUS PREDATOR
DC Comics/Dark Horse Comics: 1991 - No. 3, 1992 ($4.95/$1.95, limited series) (1st DC/Dark Horse x-over)

1 (Prestige format, $4.95)-1 & 3 contain 8 Batman/Predator trading cards; Andy & Adam Kubert-a; Suydam painted-c 5.50
1 (Regular format, $1.95)-No trading cards 2.50
2-(Prestige)-Extra pin-ups inside; Suydam-c 5.00
2-(Regular)-w/o cards 2.50
3-(Prestige)-Suydam-c 5.00
3-(Regular)-w/o cards 2.50
TPB (1993, $5.95, 132 pgs.)-r/#1-3 w/new introductions & forward plus new wraparound-c by Gibbons 2.00 6.00

BATMAN VERSUS PREDATOR II: BLOODMATCH
DC Comics: Late 1994 - No. 4, 1995 ($2.50, limited series)

1-4-Huntress app.; Moench scripts; Gulacy-a 2.50
TPB (1995, $6.95)-r/#1-4 .85 2.60 7.00

BATMAN VS. THE INCREDIBLE HULK (See DC Special Series No. 27)

BATMAN/ WILDCAT
DC Comics: Apr, 1997 - No.3, June, 1997 ($2.25, mini-series)

1-3: Dixon/Smith-s: 1-Killer Croc app. 2.25

BAT MASTERSON (TV) (Also see Tim Holt #28)
Dell Publishing Co.: Aug-Oct, 1959; Feb-Apr, 1960 - No. 9, Nov-Jan, 1961-62

Four Color 1013 (#1) (8-10/59) 11.00 34.00 125.00
2-9: Gene Barry photo-c on all. 2-Two different back-c exist 5.50 16.50 60.00

BATS (See Tales Calculated to Drive You Bats)

BATS, CATS & CADILLACS
Now Comics: Oct, 1990 - No. 2, Nov, 1990 ($1.75)

1,2: 1-Gustovich-a(i); Snyder-c 1.80

GD25 FN65 NM94

BAT-THING
DC Comics (Amalgam): June, 1997 ($1.95, one-shot)

1-Hama-s/Damaggio & Sienkiewicz-a 1.95

BATTLE
Marvel/Atlas Comics(FPI #1-62/ Male #63 on): Mar, 1951 - No. 70, Jun, 1960

1 25.00 74.00 185.00
2 11.00 34.00 85.00
3-10: 4-1st Buck Pvt. O'Toole. 10-Pakula-a 8.50 26.00 60.00
11-20: 11-Check-a 6.50 19.50 45.00
21,23-Krigstein-a 8.00 24.00 55.00
22,24-36: 32-Tuska-a. 36-Everett-a 5.70 17.00 35.00
37-Kubert-a (Last precode, 2/55) 5.70 17.00 40.00
38-40,42-48 4.25 13.00 28.00
41-Kubert/Moskowitz-a 5.70 17.00 40.00
49-Davis-a 5.70 17.00 40.00
50-54,56-58 4.25 13.00 28.00
55-Williamson-a (5 pgs.) 6.00 18.00 42.00
59-Torres-a 5.70 17.00 35.00
60-62: 60,62-Combat Kelly app. 61-Combat Casey app. 4.25 13.00 28.00
63-Ditko-a 7.85 23.50 55.00
64-66-Kirby-a. 66-Davis-a; has story of Fidel Castro in pre-Communism days (an admiring profile) 9.30 28.00 65.00
67,68: 67-Williamson/Crandall-a (4 pgs.); Kirby, Davis-a. 68-Kirby/ Williamson-a (4 pgs.); Kirby/Ditko-a 9.35 28.00 70.00
69,70: 69-Kirby-a. 70-Kirby/Ditko-a 8.50 26.00 60.00

NOTE: *Andru a-37. **Berg** a-38, 14, 60-62. **Colan** a-33, 55. **Everett** a-36, 50, 70; c-56, 57. **Heath** a-6, 9, 13, 31, 69; c-6, 9, 12, 26, 35, 37. **Kirby** c-64-69. **Maneely** a-4, 6, 31, 61; c-4, 33, 59, 61. **Orlando** a-47. **Powell** a-53, 55. **Reinman** a-8, 9, 26, 32. **Robinson** a-9, 39. **Romita** a-26. **Severin** a-28, 32-34, 66-69; c-36, 55. **Sinnott** a-33, 37. **Woodbridge** a-52, 55.*

BATTLE ACTION
Atlas Comics (NPI): Feb, 1952 - No. 12, 5/53; No. 13, 11/54 - No. 30, 8/57

1-Pakula-a 20.00 60.00 150.00
2 10.00 30.00 75.00
3,4,6,7,9,10: 6-Robinson-c/a. 7-Partial nudity 5.70 17.00 40.00
5-Used in **POP**, pg. 93,94 6.50 19.50 45.00
8-Krigstein-a 6.85 21.00 48.00
11-15 (Last precode, 2/55) 5.70 17.00 40.00
16-26,28,29 5.70 17.00 35.00
27,30-Torres-a 5.70 17.00 35.00

NOTE: *Battle Brady app. 5-7, 10-12. **Berg** a-3. **Check** a-11. **Everett** a-7; c-13, 25. **Heath** a-3, 8, 18; c-3,15, 18, 21. **Maneely** a-1; c-5. **Reinman** a-1. **Robinson** a-6, 7; c-6. **Shores** a-7(2). **Sinnott** a-3. **Woodbridge** a-28, 30.*

BATTLE ATTACK
Stanmor Publications: Oct, 1952 - No. 8, Dec, 1955

1 8.50 26.00 60.00
2 5.35 16.00 32.00
3-8: 3-Hollingsworth-a 4.00 11.00 22.00

BATTLE BEASTS
Blackthorne Publishing: Feb, 1988 - No. 4, 1988 ($1.50/$1.75, B&W/color)

1-3 (B&W)-Based on Hasbro toys 1.50
4 ($1.75, color) 1.80

BATTLE BRADY (Formerly Men in Action No. 1-9; see 3-D Action)
Atlas Comics (IPC): No. 10, Jan, 1953 - No. 14, June, 1953

10: 10-12-Syd Shores-c 12.00 36.00 90.00
11-Used in **POP**, pg. 95 plus B&W & color illos 7.85 23.50 55.00
12-14 6.50 19.50 45.00

BATTLE CHASERS
Image Comics (Cliffhanger): Apr, 1998 - Present ($2.50)

Prelude (2/98) 1.00 3.00 10.00
Prelude Gold Ed. 10.00

Battle Chasers #2 © Joe Madureira

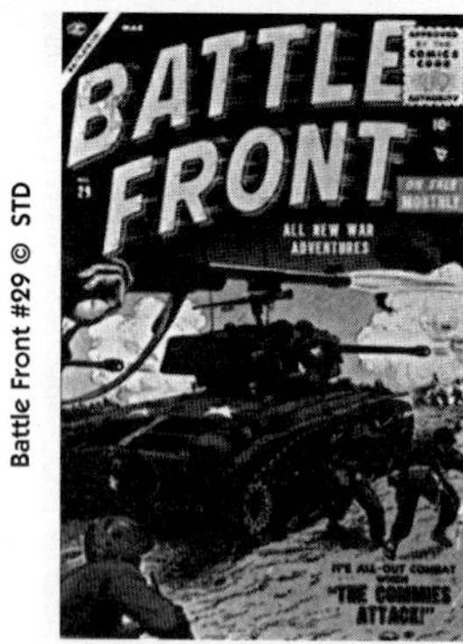

Battle Front #29 © STD

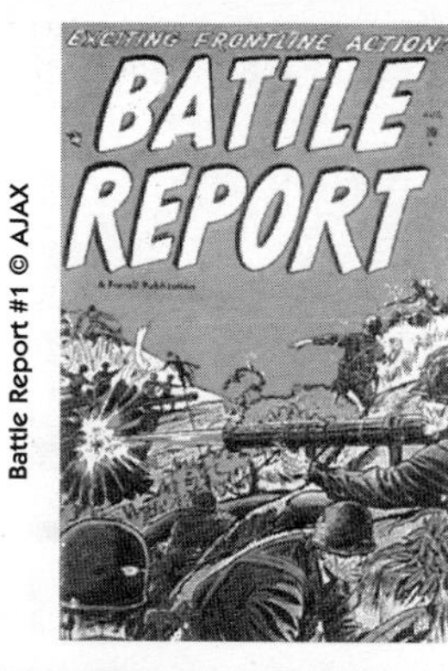

Battle Report #1 © AJAX

	GD25	FN65	NM94
1-Madureira & Sharrieff-s/Madureira-a(p)/Charest-c	1.50	4.50	15.00
1-American Ent. Ed. w/"racy" cover	2.00	6.00	20.00
1-Gold Edition			18.00
1-Chromium cover			100.00
1-2nd printing			3.00
2	1.00	3.00	10.00
2-Dynamic Forces BattleChrome cover	1.50	4.50	15.00
3-Red Monika cover by Madureira			5.00
4-Four covers			2.50
...Collected Edition 1 (11/98, $5.95) r/#1,2			5.95

BATTLE CLASSICS (See Cancelled Comic Cavalcade)
DC Comics: Sept-Oct, 1978 (44 pgs.)

	GD25	FN65	NM94
1-Kubert-r; new Kubert-c			4.00

BATTLE CRY
Stanmor Publications: 1952 (May) - No. 20, Sept, 1955

	GD25	FN65	NM94
1	10.00	30.00	75.00
2	5.70	17.00	38.00
3,5-10: 8-Pvt. Ike begins, ends #13,17	4.00	12.00	24.00
4-Classic E.C. swipe	5.70	17.00	35.00
11-20	4.00	10.00	20.00

NOTE: ***Hollingsworth*** *a-9; c-20.*

BATTLEFIELD (War Adventures on the...)
Atlas Comics (ACI): April, 1952 - No. 11, May, 1953

	GD25	FN65	NM94
1-Pakula, Reinman-a	17.00	50.00	125.00
2-5: 2-Heath, Maneely, Pakula, Reinman-a	8.50	26.00	60.00
6-11	5.70	17.00	38.00

NOTE: ***Colan*** *a-11.* ***Everett*** *a-8.* ***Heath*** *a-1, 2, 5p; c-2, 8, 9, 11.* ***Ravielli*** *a-11.*

BATTLEFIELD ACTION (Formerly Foreign Intrigues)
Charlton Comics: No. 16, Nov, 1957 - No. 62, 2-3/66; No. 63, 7/80 - No. 89, 11/84

	GD25	FN65	NM94
V2#16	4.25	13.00	28.00
17,20-30	3.00	7.50	15.00
18,19-Check-a (2 stories in #18)	3.60	9.00	18.00
31-62(1966)	1.50	4.50	12.00
63-89(1983-84)		1.20	3.00

NOTE: ***Montes/Bache*** *a-43, 55, 62.* ***Glanzman*** *a-87r.*

BATTLE FIRE
Aragon Magazine/Stanmor Publications: Apr, 1955 - No. 7, 1955

	GD25	FN65	NM94
1	6.70	20.00	46.00
2	4.00	11.00	22.00
3-7	2.80	7.00	14.00

BATTLE FOR A THREE DIMENSIONAL WORLD
3D Cosmic Publications: May, 1983 (20 pgs., slick paper w/stiff-c, $3.00)

	GD25	FN65	NM94
nn-Kirby c/a in 3-D; shows history of 3-D			5.00

BATTLEFORCE
Blackthorne Publishing: Nov, 1987 - No. 2, 1988 ($1.75, color/B&W)

	GD25	FN65	NM94
1,2: Based on game. 1-In color. 2-B&W			1.75

BATTLE FOR INDEPENDENTS, THE (Also See Cyblade/Shi & Shi/Cyblade: The Battle For Independents)
Image Comics (Top Cow Productions)/Crusade Comics: 1995 ($29.95)

	GD25	FN65	NM94
nn-boxed set of all editions of Shi/Cyblade & Cyblade/Shi plus new variant.	3.80	11.50	40.00

BATTLE FOR THE PLANET OF THE APES (See Power Record Comics)

BATTLEFRONT
Atlas Comics (PPI): June, 1952 - No. 48, Aug, 1957

	GD25	FN65	NM94
1-Heath-c	23.00	68.00	170.00
2-Robinson-a(4)	11.00	32.00	80.00
3-5-Robinson-a(4) in each	9.30	28.00	65.00
6-10: Combat Kelly in No. 6-10	7.85	23.50	55.00
11-22,24-28: 14,16-Battle Brady app. 22-Teddy Roosevelt & His Rough Riders story. 28-Last pre-code (2/55)	5.70	17.00	38.00
23,43-Check-a	6.00	18.00	42.00
29-39,41,44-47	5.00	15.00	30.00
40,42-Williamson-a	7.15	21.50	50.00
48-Crandall-a	5.70	17.00	38.00

NOTE: ***Ayers*** *a-19, 32.* ***Berg*** *a-44.* ***Colan*** *a-21, 22, 32, 33, 40.* ***Drucker*** *a-28, 29.* ***Everett*** *a-44.* ***Heath*** *c-23, 26, 27, 29, 32.* ***Maneely*** *a-22, 23; c-2, 13, 22, 35.* ***Morisi*** *a-42.* ***Morrow*** *a-41.* ***Orlando*** *a-47.* ***Powell*** *a-19, 21, 25, 29, 32, 40, 47.* ***Robinson*** *a-1-4, 5(4); c-4, 5.* ***Robert Sale*** *a-19.* ***Severin*** *a-32; c-40.* ***Woodbridge*** *a-45, 46.*

BATTLEFRONT
Standard Comics: No. 5, June, 1952

	GD25	FN65	NM94
5-Toth-a	13.00	38.00	95.00

BATTLE GROUND
Atlas Comics (OMC): Sept, 1954 - No. 20, Aug, 1957

	GD25	FN65	NM94
1	17.00	50.00	125.00
2-Jack Katz-a	9.30	28.00	65.00
3,4-Last precode (3/55)	6.00	18.00	42.00
5-8,10	5.70	17.00	38.00
9,11,13,18: 9-Krigstein-a. 11,13,18-Williamson-a in each	7.85	23.50	55.00
12,15-17,19,20	5.70	17.00	35.00
14-Kirby-a	7.85	23.50	55.00

NOTE: ***Ayers*** *a-13.* ***Colan*** *a-11, 13.* ***Drucker*** *a-7, 12, 13, 20.* ***Heath*** *c-2, 5, 13.* ***Maneely*** *a-19; c-1, 19.* ***Orlando*** *a-17.* ***Pakula*** *a-11.* ***Severin*** *a-5, 12, 19. c-20.* ***Tuska*** *a-11.*

BATTLE HEROES
Stanley Publications: Sept, 1966 - No. 2, Nov, 1966 (25¢)

	GD25	FN65	NM94
1,2	1.00	3.00	8.00

BATTLE OF THE BULGE (See Movie Classics)

BATTLE OF THE PLANETS (TV)
Gold Key/Whitman No. 6 on: 6/79 - No. 10, 12/80
(Based on syndicated cartoon by Sandy Frank)

	GD25	FN65	NM94
1: Mortimer a-1-4,7-10	.90	2.70	8.00
2-6,10			5.00
7,8(11/80),9 (3-pack only?)	1.00	3.00	10.00

BATTLE REPORT
Ajax/Farrell Publications: Aug, 1952 - No. 6, June, 1953

	GD25	FN65	NM94
1	7.15	21.50	50.00
2-6	5.00	15.00	30.00

BATTLE SQUADRON
Stanmor Publications: April, 1955 - No. 5, Dec, 1955

	GD25	FN65	NM94
1	5.70	17.00	38.00
2-5: 3-Iwo Jima & flag-c	4.00	11.00	22.00

BATTLESTAR GALACTICA (TV) (Also see Marvel Comics Super Special #8)
Marvel Comics Group: Mar, 1979 - No. 23, Jan, 1981

	GD25	FN65	NM94
1: 1-5 adapt TV episodes			4.50
2-23: 1-3-Partial-r			3.00

NOTE: ***Austin*** *c-9i, 10i.* ***Golden*** *c-18.* ***Simonson*** *a(p)-4, 5, 11-13, 15-20, 22, 23; c(p)-4, 5,11-17, 19, 20, 22, 23.*

BATTLESTAR GALACTICA (TV) (Also see Asylum)
Maximum Press: July, 1995 - No.4, Nov, 1995 ($2.50, limited series)

	GD25	FN65	NM94
1-4: Continuation of TV series			3.25
Trade paperback (12/95, $12.95)-reprints series			13.00

BATTLESTAR GALACTICA: APOLLO'S JOURNEY (TV)
Maximum Press: Apr, 1996 - No. 3, June, 1996 ($2.95, limited series)

	GD25	FN65	NM94
1-3: Richard Hatch scripts			3.00

BATTLESTAR GALACTICA: JOURNEY'S END (TV)
Maximum Press: Aug, 1996 - No. 4, Nov, 1996 ($2.99, limited series)

	GD25	FN65	NM94
1-4-Continuation of the T.V. series			3.00

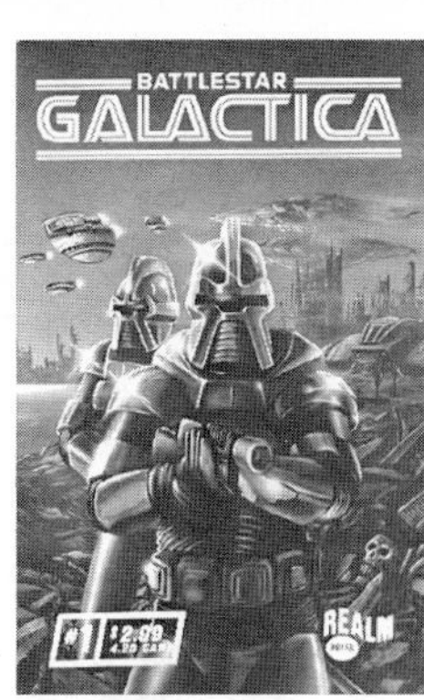

Battlestar Galactica #1 © Universal Studios

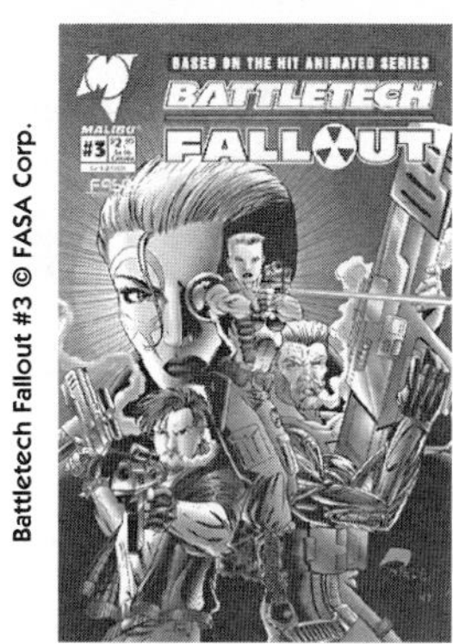

Battletech Fallout #3 © FASA Corp.

Battletide #3 © MAR

GD25 FN65 NM94

BATTLESTAR GALACTICA: SPECIAL EDITION (TV)
Maximum Press: Jan, 1997 ($2.99, one-shot)
1-Fully painted; Scalf-c/s/a; r/Asylum 2.99

BATTLESTAR GALACTICA: STARBUCK (TV)
Maximum Press: Dec, 1995 - No. 3, Mar, 1996 ($2.50, limited series)
1-3 2.50

BATTLESTAR GALACTICA: THE COMPENDIUM (TV)
Maximum Press: Feb, 1997 ($2.99, one-shot)
1 2.99

BATTLESTAR GALACTICA: THE ENEMY WITHIN (TV)
Maximum Press: Nov, 1995 - No. 3, Feb, 1996 ($2.50, limited series)
1-3: 3-Indicia reads Feb, 1995 in error. 2.50

BATTLESTAR GALACTICA (TV)
Realm Press: Dec, 1997 - Present ($2.99)
1-5-Chris Scalf-s/painted-a/c 3.00

BATTLESTAR GALACTICA: SEARCH FOR SANCTUARY (TV)
Realm Press: Sept, 1998 - Present ($2.99)
1-Scalf & Kuhoric-s 3.00

BATTLESTONE (Also see Brigade & Youngblood)
Image Comics (Extreme): Nov, 1994 - No. 2, Dec, 1994 ($2.50, limited series)
1,2-Liefeld plots 2.50

BATTLE STORIES (See XMas Comics)
Fawcett Publications: Jan, 1952 - No. 11, Sept, 1953
1-Evans-a 11.00 34.00 85.00
2 6.00 18.00 42.00
3-11 5.35 16.00 32.00

BATTLE STORIES
Super Comics: 1963 - 1964
Reprints #10-12,15-18: 10-r/U.S Tank Commandos #? 11-r/? 11, 12,17-r/Monty Hall #?; 13-Kintsler-a (1pg).15-r/American Air Forces #7 by Powell; Bolle-r. 18-U.S. Fighting Air Force #? 1.00 2.80 7.00

BATTLETECH (See Blackthorne 3-D Series #41 for 3-D issue)
Blackthorne Publishing: Oct, 1987 - No. 6, 1988 ($1.75/$2.00)
1-6: Based on game. 1-Color. 2-Begin B&W 1.75
Annual 1 ($4.50, B&W) 4.50

BATTLETECH
Malibu Comics: Feb, 1995 ($2.95)
0 1.20 3.00

BATTLETECH FALLOUT
Malibu Comics: Dec, 1994 - No. 4, Mar, 1995 ($2.95)
1-Two editions exist; normal logo and gold version w/foil logo stamped "Gold Limited Edition 3.00
1-Full-c holographic limited edition 2.00 6.00
2-4 3.00

BATTLETIDE (Death's Head II & Killpower...)
Marvel Comics UK, Ltd.: Dec, 1992 - No. 4, Mar, 1993 ($1.75, mini-series)
1-4: Wolverine, Psylocke, Dark Angel app. 2.00

BATTLETIDE II (Death's Head II & Killpower...)
Marvel Comics UK, Ltd.: Aug, 1993 - No. 4, Nov, 1993 ($1.75, mini-series)
1-($2.95)-Foil embossed logo 3.00
2-4: 2-Hulk-c/story 1.75

BATTLEZONES: DREAM TEAM 2 (See Dream Team)
Malibu Comics (Ultraverse): Mar, 1996 ($3.95)
1-pin-ups between Marvel & Malibu characters by Mike Wieringo, Phil Jimenez, Mike McKone, Cully Hamner, Gary Frank & others 4.00

BAYWATCH COMIC STORIES (TV) (Magazine)
Acclaim Comics (Armada): May, 1996 - No. 4, 1997 ($4.95) (Photo-c on all)
1-4: Photo comics based on TV show 5.00

BEACH BLANKET BINGO (See Movie Classics)

BEAGLE BOYS, THE (Walt Disney)(See The Phantom Blot)
Gold Key: 11/64; No. 2, 11/65; No. 3, 8/66 - No. 47, 2/79 (See WDC&S #134)
1 2.70 8.00 30.00
2-5 1.40 4.10 15.00
6-10 .90 2.70 10.00
11-20: 11,14,19-r 2.20 8.00
21-30: 27-r 5.00
31-47 3.00

BEAGLE BOYS VERSUS UNCLE SCROOGE
Gold Key: Mar, 1979 - No. 12, Feb, 1980
1 .90 2.70 9.00
2-12: 9-r 4.50

BEANBAGS
Ziff-Davis Publ. Co. (Approved Comics): Winter, 1951 - No. 2, Spring, 1952
1,2 8.50 26.00 60.00

BEANIE THE MEANIE
Fago Publications: 1958 - No. 3, May, 1959
1-3 4.00 12.00 24.00

BEANY AND CECIL (TV) (Bob Clampett's...)
Dell Publishing Co.: Jan, 1952 - 1955; July-Sept, 1962 - No. 5, July-Sept, 1963
Four Color 368 25.00 75.00 275.00
Four Color 414,448,477,530,570,635(1/55) 16.00 47.00 170.00
01-057-209 (#1) 15.00 45.00 165.00
2-5 10.00 30.00 110.00

BEAR COUNTRY (Disney)
Dell Publishing Co.: No. 758, Dec, 1956
Four Color 758-Movie 4.50 13.50 50.00

BEAST (See X-Men)
Marvel Comics: May, 1997 - No. 3, 1997 ($2.50, mini-series)
1-3-Giffen-s/Nocon-a 2.50

B.E.A.S.T.I.E.S. (Also see Axis Alpha)
Axis Comics: Apr, 1994 ($1.95)
1-Javier Saltares-c/a/scripts 2.00

BEATLES, THE (See Girls' Romances #109, Go-Go, Heart Throbs #101, Herbie #5, Howard the Duck Mag. #4, Laugh #166, Marvel Comics Super Special #4, My LittleMargie #54, Not Brand Echh, Strange Tales #130, Summer Love, Superman's Pal Jimmy Olsen #79, Teen Confessions #37, Tippy's Friends & Tippy Teen)

BEATLES, THE (Life Story)
Dell Publishing Co.: Sept-Nov, 1964 (35¢)
1-(Scarce)-Stories with color photo pin-ups 41.00 123.00 500.00

BEATLES EXPERIENCE, THE
Revolutionary Comics: Mar, 1991 - No. 8, 1991 ($2.50, B&W, limited series)
1-8: 1-Gold logo 2.50

BEATLES YELLOW SUBMARINE (See Movie Comics under Yellow...)

BEAUTIFUL PEOPLE
Slave Labor Graphics: Apr, 1994 ($4.95, 8-1/2x11", one-shot)
nn 5.00

BEAUTIFUL STORIES FOR UGLY CHILDREN
DC Comics (Piranha Press): 1989 - No. 30, 1991 ($2.00/$2.50, B&W, mature)
V1-11 2.00
12-30: 12-$2.50-c begins 2.50
A Cotton Candy Autopsy ($12.95, B&W)-Reprints 1st two volumes 13.00

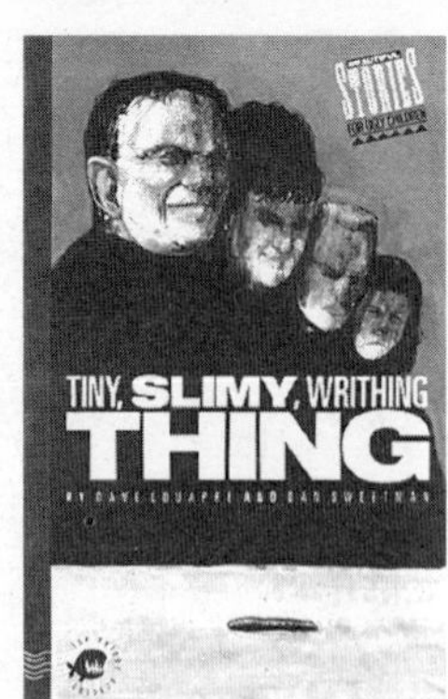

Beautiful Stories For Ugly Children Vol. 23
© Dave Louapre and Dan Sweetman

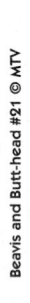

Beavis and Butt-head #21 © MTV

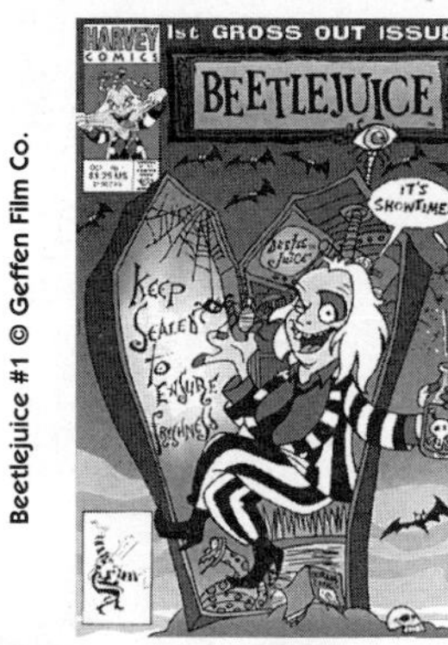

Beetlejuice #1 © Geffen Film Co.

GD25 FN65 NM94

BEAUTY AND THE BEAST, THE
Marvel Comics Group: Jan, 1985 - No. 4, Apr, 1985 (limited series)

1-4: Dazzler & the Beast from X-Men 1.50

BEAUTY AND THE BEAST (Graphic novel)(Also see Cartoon Tales & Disney's New Adventures of...)
Disney Comics: 1992

nn-($4.95, prestige edition)-Adapts animated film 5.00
nn-($2.50, newsstand edition) 2.50

BEAUTY AND THE BEAST
Disney Comics: Sept., 1992 - No. 2, 1992 ($1.50, limited series)

1 2.00
2 1.50

BEAUTY AND THE BEAST: PORTRAIT OF LOVE (TV)
First Comics: May, 1989 - No. 2, Mar, 1990 ($5.95, 60 pgs., squarebound)

1,2: 1-Based on TV show, Wendy Pini-a/scripts. 2-...: Night of Beauty; by Wendy Pini 2.00 6.00

BEAVER VALLEY (Movie)(Disney)
Dell Publishing Co.: No. 625, Apr, 1955

Four Color 625 5.50 16.50 60.00

BEAVIS AND BUTTHEAD (MTV's...)(TV cartoon)
Marvel Comics: Mar, 1994 - No. 28, June, 1996 ($1.95)

1-Silver ink-c. 1, 2-Punisher & Devil Dinosaur app. 5.00
1-2nd printing 2.00
2,3: 2-Wolverine app. 3-Man-Thing, Spider-Man, Venom, Carnage, Mary Jane & Stan Lee cameos; John Romita, Sr. art (2 pgs.) 1.00 3.00
4-28: 5-War Machine, Thor, Loki, Hulk, Captain America & Rhino cameos. 6-Psylocke, Polaris, Daredevil & Bullseye app. 7-Ghost Rider & Sub-Mariner app. 8-Quasar & Eon app.9-Prowler & Nightwatch app. 11-Black Widow app. 12-Thunderstrike & Bloodaxe app. 13-Night Thrasher app. 14-Spider-Man 2099 app. 15-Warlock app. 16-X-Factor app. 25-Juggernaut app. .80 2.00

BECK & CAUL INVESTIGATIONS
Gauntlet Comics (Caliber): Jan, 1994 - No. 5, 1995? ($2.95, B&W)

1-5 3.00
Special 1 ($4.95) 5.00

BEDKNOBS AND BROOMSTICKS (See Walt Disney Showcase No. 6 & 50)

BEDLAM!
Eclipse Comics: Sept, 1985 - No. 2, Sept, 1985 (B&W-r in color)

1,2: Bissette-a 1.80

BEDTIME STORY (See Cinema Comics Herald)

BEELZELVIS
Slave Labor Graphics: Feb, 1994 ($2.95, B&W, one-shot)

1 3.00

BEEP BEEP, THE ROAD RUNNER (TV)(See Daffy & Kite Fun Book)
Dell Publishing Co./Gold Key No. 1-88/Whitman No. 89 on: July, 1958 - No. 14, Aug-Oct, 1962; Oct, 1966 - No. 105, 1983

Four Color 918 (#1, 7/58) 8.50 26.00 95.00
Four Color 1008,1046 (11-1/59-60) 4.40 13.00 48.00
4(2-4/60)-14(Dell) 3.25 10.00 36.00
1(10/66, Gold Key) 3.80 11.50 40.00
2-5 2.50 7.60 28.00
6-14 1.60 4.80 18.00
15-18,20-40 1.30 4.00 14.00
19-With pull-out poster 2.40 7.00 26.00
41-50 .90 2.70 9.00
51-70 2.00 6.00
71-88 3.00
89,90,94-101 5.00

GD25 FN65 NM94

91(8/80), 92(9/80), 93 (3-pack?) .90 2.70 8.00
102-105 (All #90189 on-c; no date or date code; pre-pack?) 2.00 6.00
NOTE: *See March of Comics #351, 353, 375, 387, 397, 416, 430, 442, 455. #5, 8-10, 35, 53, 59-62, 68-r; 96-102, 104 are 1/3-r.*

BEETLE BAILEY (See Comics Reading Library, Giant Comic Album & Sarge Snorkel)
Dell Publishing Co./Gold Key #39-53/King #54-66/Charlton #67-119/ Gold Key #120-131/Whitman #132: #459, 5/53 - #38, 5-7/62; #39, 11/62 - #53, 5/66; #54, 8/66 - #65, 12/67;#67, 2/69 - #119, 11/76; #120, 4/78 - #132, 4/80

Four Color 469 (#1)-By Mort Walker 9.00 27.00 100.00
Four Color 521,552,622 4.50 13.50 50.00
5(2-4/56)-10(5-7/57) 3.60 11.00 40.00
11-20(4-5/59) 2.75 8.00 30.00
21-38(5-7/62) 1.65 5.00 18.00
39-53(5/66) 1.50 4.50 15.00
54-65 1.20 3.60 12.00
67-99 (No. 66 publ. overseas only?) .90 2.70 9.00
100 1.20 3.60 12.00
101-119 .85 2.60 7.00
120-132 4.00
Bold Detergent Giveaway('69)-same as regular issue (#67) minus price 5.00
Cerebral Palsy Assn. Giveaway V2#71('69) - V2#73(#1,1/70) (Charlton) 5.00
Red Cross Giveaway-(1969, 5x7", 16 pgs., paper-c 5.00

BEETLE BAILEY
Harvey Comics: V2#1, Sept, 1992 - V2#9, Aug, 1994 ($1.25/$1.50)

V2#1-4 2.00
5-9-($1.50) 1.50
Big Book 1(11/92),2(5/93)(Both $1.95, 52 pgs.) 2.50
Giant Size V2#1(10/92),2(3/93)(Both $2.25,68 pgs.) 2.50

BEETLEJUICE (TV)
Harvey Comics: Oct, 1991 ($1.25)

1 1.50

BEETLEJUICE CRIMEBUSTERS ON THE HAUNT
Harvey Comics: Sept, 1992 - No. 3, Jan, 1993 ($1.50, limited series)

1-3 1.50

BEE 29, THE BOMBARDIER
Neal Publications: Feb, 1945

1-(Funny animal) 19.00 56.00 140.00

BEHIND PRISON BARS
Realistic Comics (Avon): 1952

1-Kinstler-c 25.00 76.00 190.00

BEHOLD THE HANDMAID
George Pflaum: 1954 (Religious) (25¢ with a 20¢ sticker price)

nn 3.60 9.00 18.00

BELIEVE IT OR NOT (See Ripley's...)

BEN AND ME (Disney)
Dell Publishing Co.: No. 539, Mar, 1954

Four Color 539 3.00 9.00 32.00

BEN BOWIE AND HIS MOUNTAIN MEN
Dell Publishing Co.: 1952 - No. 17, Nov-Jan, 1958-59

Four Color 443 (#1) 5.50 16.50 60.00
Four Color 513,557,599,626,657 2.75 8.00 30.00
7(5-7/56)-11: 11-Intro/origin Yellow Hair 2.75 8.00 30.00
12-17 2.25 6.75 24.00

BEN CASEY (TV)
Dell Publishing Co.: June-July, 1962 - No. 10, June-Aug, 1965 (Photo-c)

Beowulf #1 © DC

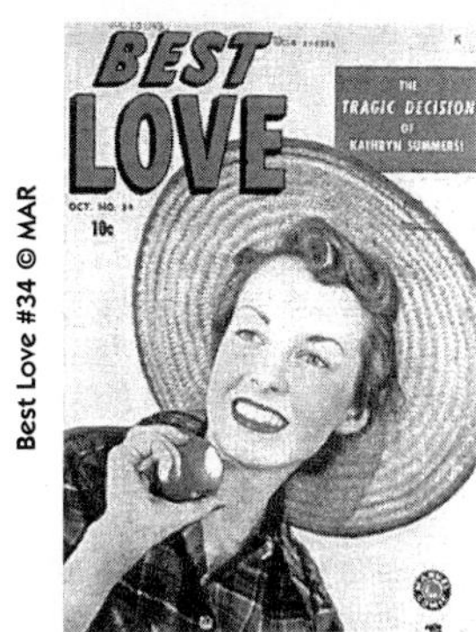

Best Love #34 © MAR

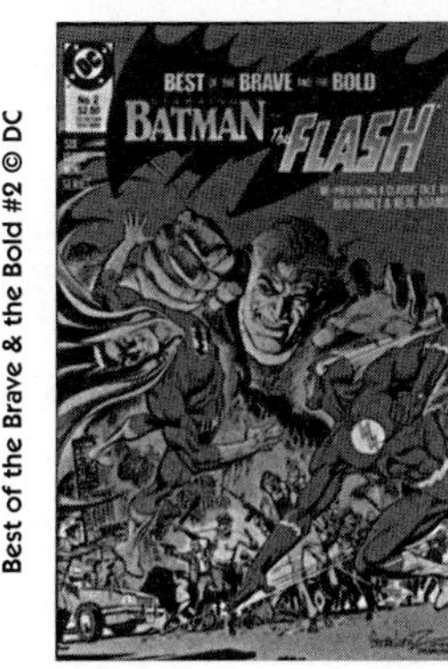

Best of the Brave & the Bold #2 © DC

GD25 FN65 NM94

12-063-207 (#1) 4.00 12.00 45.00
2(10/62)-10: 4-Marijuana & heroin use story 3.00 9.00 32.00

BEN CASEY FILM STORY (TV)
Gold Key: Nov, 1962 (25¢) (Photo-c)
30009-211-All photos 7.00 21.00 75.00

BENEATH THE PLANET OF THE APES (See Movie Comics & Power Record Comics)

BEN FRANKLIN (See Kite Fun Book)

BEN HUR
Dell Publishing Co.: No. 1052, Nov, 1959
Four Color 1052-Movie, Manning-a 9.00 27.00 100.00

BEN ISRAEL
Logos International: 1974 (39¢)
nn 3.00

BEOWULF (Also see First Comics Graphic Novel #1)
National Periodical Publications: Apr-May, 1975 - No. 6, Feb-Mar, 1976
1-6: 4-Dracula-c/s. 5-Flying saucer-c/story 3.00

BERLIN
Black Eye Productions: Apr, 1996 - Present ($2.50, B&W)
1-4: Jason Lutes-c/a/scripts. 2.50

BERNI WRIGHTSON, MASTER OF THE MACABRE
Pacific Comics/Eclipse Comics No. 5: July, 1983 - No. 5, Nov, 1984 ($1.50, Baxter paper)
1-5: Wrightson-c/a(r). 4-Jeff Jones-r (11 pgs.) 3.00

BERRYS, THE (Also see Funny World)
Argo Publ.: May, 1956
1-Reprints daily & Sunday strips & daily Animal Antics by Ed Nofziger 5.00 15.00 30.00

BERZERKERS (See Youngblood V1#2)
Image Comics (Extreme Studios): Aug, 1995 - No. 3, Oct, 1995 ($2.50, limited series)
1-3: Beau Smith scripts, Fraga-a 2.50

BEST COMICS
Better Publications: Nov, 1939 - No. 4, Feb, 1940(Large size, reads sideways)
1-(Scarce)-Red Mask begins(1st app.) & c/s-all. Contains 6 pg. Boston Celtics photo story 68.00 204.00 575.00
2-4: 4-Cannibalism story 43.00 129.00 360.00

BEST FROM BOY'S LIFE, THE
Gilberton Company: Oct, 1957 - No. 5, Oct, 1958 (35¢)
1-Space Conquerors & Kam of the Ancient Ones begin, end #5 9.30 28.00 65.00
2,3,5 5.70 17.00 35.00
4-L.B. Cole-a 6.00 18.00 42.00

BEST LOVE (Formerly Sub-Mariner Comics No. 32)
Marvel Comics (MPI): No. 33, Aug, 1949 - No. 36, April, 1950 (Photo-c 33-36)
33-Kubert-a 9.35 28.00 70.00
34 5.70 17.00 35.00
35,36-Everett-a 6.50 19.50 45.00

BEST OF BUGS BUNNY, THE
Gold Key: Oct, 1966 - No. 2, Oct, 1968
1,2-Giants 3.75 11.25 45.00

BEST OF DC, THE (Blue Ribbon Digest) (See Limited Coll. Ed. C-52)
DC Comics: Sept-Oct, 1979 - No. 71, Apr, 1986 (100-148 pgs; mostly reprints)
1-3,5-10: 1-Superman, w/"Death of Superman"-r. 2-Batman 40th Ann. Special. 3-Superfriends. 5-Best of 1979. 6,8-Superman. 7-Superboy. 9-Batman, Creeper app. 10-Secret Origins of Super Villains 5.00
4-Rudolph the Red Nosed Reindeer .90 2.70 8.00
11-20: 11-The Year's Best Stories. 12-Superman Time and Space Stories. 13-Best of DC Comics Presents. 14-Origins of Batman Villains. 15-Superboy 16-Superman Anniv. 17-Supergirl. 18-Teen Titans new-s., Adams, Kane-a; Perez-c. 19-Superman. 20-World's Finest 4.00
21-27: 21-Justice Society. 22-Christmas. 23-(148 pgs.)-Best of 1981. 24 Legion, new story and 16 pgs. new costumes. 25-Superman. 26-Brave & Bold. 27-Superman vs. Luthor 2.00 6.00
28,29: 28-Binky, Sugar & Spike app. 29-Sugar & Spike, 3 new stories; new Stanley & his Monster story .90 2.70 8.00
30-36,38,40: 30-Detective Comics. 31-JLA. 32-Superman. 33-Secret origins of Legion Heroes and Villains. 34-Metal Men; has #497 on-c from Adv. Comics. 35-The Year's Best Comics Stories(148 pgs.). 36-Superman vs. Kryptonite. 38-Superman. 40-World of Krypton 2.00 6.00
37,39: 37-"Funny Stuff", Mayer-a. 39-Binky .90 2.70 8.00
41,43,45,47,49,53,55,58,60,63,65,68,70: 41-Sugar & Spike new stories with Mayer-a. 43,49,55-Funny Stuff. 45,53,70-Binky. 47,58,65,68-Sugar & Spike. 60-Plop!; Wood-c(r) & Aragonés-r (5/85). 63-Plop!; Wrightson-a(r) 1.20 3.60 12.00
42,44,46,48,50-52,54,56,57,59,61,62,64,66,67,69,71: 42,56-Superman vs. Aliens. 44,57,67-Superboy & LSH. 46-Jimmy Olsen. 48-Superman Team-ups 50-Year's best Superman. 51-Batman Family. 52 Best of 1984. 54,56,59-Superman. 61-(148 pgs.)Year's best. 62-Best of Batman 1985. 69-Year's best Team stories. 71-Year's best .90 2.70 9.00

NOTE: ***N. Adams*** *a-2r, 14r, 18r, 26, 51.* ***Aparo*** *a-9, 14, 26, 30; c-9, 14, 26.* ***Austin*** *a-51i.* ***Buckler*** *a-40p; c-16, 22.* ***Giffen*** *a-50, 52; c-33p.* ***Grell*** *a-33p.* ***Grossman*** *a-37.* ***Heath*** *a-26.* ***Infantino*** *a-10r, 18.* ***Kaluta*** *a-40.* ***G. Kane*** *a-10r, 18r; c-40, 44.* ***Kubert*** *a-10r, 21, 26.* ***Layton*** *a-21.* ***S. Mayer*** *c-29, 37, 41, 43, 47; a-28, 29, 37, 41, 43, 47, 58, 65, 68.* ***Moldoff*** *c-64p.* ***Morrow*** *a-40; c-40.* ***W. Mortimer*** *a-39p.* ***Newton*** *a-5, 51.* ***Perez*** *a-24, 50p; c-18, 21, 23.* ***Rogers*** *a-14, 51p.* ***Simonson*** *a-11r.* ***Spiegle*** *a-52.* ***Starlin*** *a-51.* ***Staton*** *a-5, 21.* ***Tuska*** *a-24.* ***Wolverton*** *a-60.* ***Wood*** *a-60, 63; c-60, 63.* ***Wrightson*** *a-60. New art in #14, 18, 24.*

BEST OF DENNIS THE MENACE, THE
Hallden/Fawcett Publications: Summer, 1959 - No. 5, Spring, 1961 (100 pgs.)
1-All reprints; Wiseman-a 6.00 18.00 60.00
2-5 4.00 12.00 40.00

BEST OF DONALD DUCK, THE
Gold Key: Nov, 1965 (12¢, 36 pgs.)(Lists 2nd printing in indicia)
1-Reprints Four Color #223 by Barks 6.40 19.00 70.00

BEST OF DONALD DUCK & UNCLE SCROOGE, THE
Gold Key: Nov, 1964 - No. 2, Sept, 1967 (25¢ Giants)
1(30022-411)('64)-Reprints 4-Color #189 & 408 by Carl Barks; cover of F.C. #189 redrawn by Barks 6.40 19.00 70.00
2(30022-709)('67)-Reprints 4-Color #256 & "Seven Cities of Cibola" & U.S. #8 by Barks 6.40 19.00 70.00

BEST OF HORROR AND SCIENCE FICTION COMICS
Bruce Webster: 1987 ($2.00)
1-Wolverton, Frazetta, Powell, Ditko-r 3.00

BEST OF MARMADUKE, THE
Charlton Comics: 1960
1-Brad Anderson's strip reprints 2.50 7.50 24.00

BEST OF MS. TREE, THE
Pyramid Comics: 1987 - No. 4, 1988 ($2.00, B&W, limited series)
1-4 2.00

BEST OF THE BRAVE AND THE BOLD, THE (See Super DC Giant)
DC Comics: Oct, 1988 - No. 6, Jan, 1989 ($2.50, limited series)
1-6: Neal Adams-r, Kubert-r & Heath-r in all 2.50

BEST OF THE WEST (See A-1 Comics)
Magazine Enterprises: 1951 - No. 12, April-June, 1954
1(A-1 42)-Ghost Rider, Durango Kid, Straight Arrow, Bobby Benson begin 39.00 117.00 310.00

Best Western #58 © MAR

Betty #66 © AP

Betty and Veronica (Double) Digest Magazine #76 © AP

	GD25	FN65	NM94
2(A-1 46)	19.00	58.00	145.00
3(A-1 52), 4(A-1 59), 5(A-1 66)	17.00	50.00	125.00
6(A-1 70), 7(A-1 76), 8(A-1 81), 9(A-1 85), 10(A-1 87), 11(A-1 97), 12(A-1 103)	12.00	36.00	90.00

NOTE: ***Bolle** a-9. **Borth** a-12. **Guardineer** a-5, 12. **Powell** a-1, 12.*

BEST OF UNCLE SCROOGE & DONALD DUCK, THE
Gold Key: Nov, 1966 (25¢)

	GD25	FN65	NM94
1(30030-611)-Reprints part 4-Color #159 & 456 & Uncle Scrooge #6,7 by Carl Barks	6.40	19.00	70.00

BEST OF WALT DISNEY COMICS, THE
Western Publishing Co.: 1974 ($1.50, 52 pgs.) (Walt Disney)
(8-1/2x11" cardboard covers; 32,000 printed of each)

	GD25	FN65	NM94
96170-Reprints 1st two stories less 1 pg. each from 4-Color #62	2.50	7.60	28.00
96171-Reprints Mickey Mouse and the Bat Bandit of Inferno Gulch from 1934 (strips) by Gottfredson	2.50	7.60	28.00
96172-r/Uncle Scrooge #386 & two other stories	2.50	7.60	28.00
96173-Reprints "Ghost of the Grotto" (from 4-Color #159) & "Christmas on Bear Mountain" (from 4-Color #178)	2.50	7.60	28.00

BEST ROMANCE
Standard Comics (Visual Editions): No. 5, Feb-Mar, 1952 - No. 7, Aug, 1952

	GD25	FN65	NM94
5-Toth-a; photo-c	10.00	30.00	75.00
6,7-Photo-c	4.25	13.00	28.00

BEST SELLER COMICS (See Tailspin Tommy)

BEST WESTERN (Formerly Terry Toons? or Miss America Magazine
Marvel Comics (IPC): V7#24(#57)?; Western Outlaws & Sheriffs No. 60 on)
No. 58, June, 1949 - No. 59, Aug, 1949

	GD25	FN65	NM94
58,59-Black Rider, Kid Colt, Two-Gun Kid app.; both have Syd Shores-c	18.00	54.00	135.00

BETTIE PAGE COMICS
Dark Horse Comics: Mar, 1996 ($3.95)

	GD25	FN65	NM94
1-Dave Stevens-c; Blevins & Heath-a; Jaime Hernandez pin-up			4.50

BETTIE PAGE COMICS: SPICY ADVENTURE
Dark Horse Comics: Jan, 1997 ($2.95, one-shot, mature)

	GD25	FN65	NM94
nn-Silke-c/s/a			4.00

BETTY (See Pep Comics #22 for 1st app.)
Archie Comics: Sept, 1992 - Present ($1.25/$1.50/$1.75)

	GD25	FN65	NM94
1			3.00
2-24			2.00
25-56			1.50
57-70: 57-Begin $1.75-c; "A Storm Over Uniforms" x-over part 5,6			1.75

BETTY AND HER STEADY (Going Steady with Betty No. 1)
Avon Periodicals: No. 2, Mar-Apr, 1950

	GD25	FN65	NM94
2	7.85	23.50	55.00

BETTY AND ME
Archie Publications: Aug, 1965 - No. 200, Aug, 1992

	GD25	FN65	NM94
1	9.00	27.00	90.00
2,3: 3-Origin Superteen	4.50	13.50	45.00
4-8: Superteen in new costume #4-7; dons new helmet in #5, ends #8 (see Archie's Girls #118)	2.50	7.50	30.00
9-20(4/69)	1.80	5.40	18.00
21-35	.90	2.70	8.00
36(8/71)-55 (52 pgs.)	1.20	3.60	12.00
56(4/71)-80(12/76)		2.00	6.00
81-99			4.00
100(3/79)		2.00	6.00
101-130(9/82)			3.00
131-160(8/87)			2.50
156-199			2.00
200			4.00

BETTY AND VERONICA (Also see Archie's Girls...)
Archie Enterprises: June, 1987 - Present (75¢ /$1.25/$1.50/$1.75)

	GD25	FN65	NM94
1			4.00
2-10			3.00
11-120			2.00
121-132			1.75
Summer Fun 1 (1994, $2.00, 52 pgs. plus poster)			2.00

BETTY & VERONICA ANNUAL DIGEST (...Digest Magazine #1-4, 44 on; ...Comics Digest Mag. #5-43)
Archie Publications: Nov, 1980 - Present ($1.00/$1.50/$1.75/$1.95, digest size)

	GD25	FN65	NM94
1	1.60	4.80	16.00
2-10: 2(11/81-Katy Keene story), 3(8/82)	.90	2.70	8.00
11-30			5.00
31-50			4.00
51-101			2.00

BETTY & VERONICA ANNUAL DIGEST MAGAZINE
Archie Comics: Sept, 1989 - Present ($1.50/$1.75/$1.79, 128 pgs.)

	GD25	FN65	NM94
1			4.50
2-17: 9-Neon ink logo. 16-Begin $1.79-c			3.00

BETTY & VERONICA CHRISTMAS SPECTACULAR (See Archie Giant Series Magazine #159, 168, 180, 191, 204, 217, 229, 241, 453, 465, 477, 489, 501, 513, 525, 536, 547, 558, 568, 580, 593, 606, 618)

BETTY & VERONICA DOUBLE DIGEST MAGAZINE
Archie Enterprises: 1987 - Present ($2.25/$2.75/$1.50/$2.79/$2.95, digest size, 256 pgs.)(...Digest #12 on)

	GD25	FN65	NM94
1	.90	2.70	9.00
2-10			5.00
11-25: 5,17-Xmas-c. 16-Capt. Hero story			3.50
26-77			3.00

BETTY & VERONICA SPECTACULAR (See Archie Giant Series Mag. #11, 16, 21, 26, 32, 138, 145, 153, 162, 173, 184, 197, 201, 210, 214, 221, 226, 234, 238, 246, 250, 458, 462, 470, 482, 486, 494, 498, 506, 510, 518, 522, 526, 530, 537, 552, 559, 563, 569, 575, 582, 588, 600, 608, 613, 620, 623, and Betty & Veronica)

BETTY AND VERONICA SPECTACULAR
Archie Comics: Oct, 1992 - Present ($1.25/$1.50/$1.75)

	GD25	FN65	NM94
1			3.00
2-10: 1-Dan DeCarlo-c/a			2.00
11-33			1.75

BETTY & VERONICA SPRING SPECTACULAR (See Archie Giant Series Magazine #569, 582, 595)

BETTY & VERONICA SUMMER FUN (See Archie Giant Series Mag. #8, 13, 18, 23, 28, 34, 140, 147, 155, 164, 175, 187, 199, 212, 224, 236, 248, 460, 484, 496, 508, 520, 529, 539, 550, 561, 572, 585, 598, 611, 621)
Archie Comics: 1994 - Present ($2.00)

	GD25	FN65	NM94
1-5			2.00

BETTY BOOP'S BIG BREAK
First Publishing: 1990 ($5.95, 52 pgs.)

	GD25	FN65	NM94
nn-By Joshua Quagmire; 60th anniversary ish.		2.00	6.00

BETTY PAGE 3-D COMICS
The 3-D Zone: 1991 ($3.95, "7-1/2x10-1/4," 28 pgs., no glasses)

	GD25	FN65	NM94
1-Photo inside covers; back-c nudity			5.00

BETTY'S DIARY (See Archie Giant Series Magazine No. 555)
Archie Enterprises: April, 1986 - No. 40, Apr, 1991 (#1:65¢; 75¢/95¢)

	GD25	FN65	NM94
1			4.00
2-10			3.00
11-40			2.00

Beware the Creeper #1 © DC

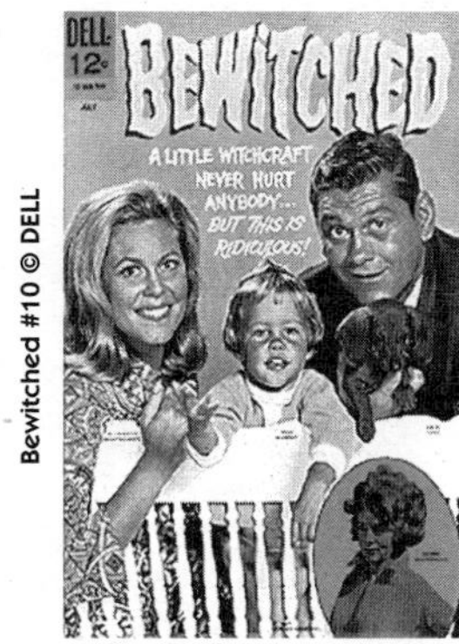

Bewitched #10 © DELL

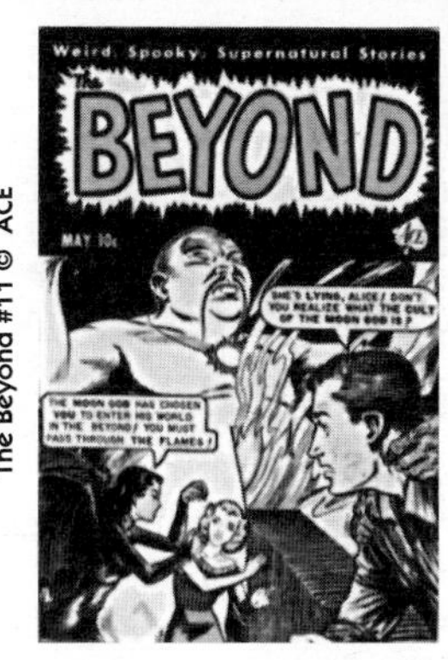

The Beyond #11 © ACE

BETTY'S DIGEST
Archie Enterprises: Nov, 1996 - Present ($1.75/$1.79)

	GD25	FN65	NM94
1,2			1.79

BEVERLY HILLBILLIES (TV)
Dell Publishing Co.: 4-6/63 - No. 18, 8/67; No. 19, 10/69; No. 20, 10/70; No. 21, Oct, 1971

	GD25	FN65	NM94
1-Photo-c	15.00	45.00	165.00
2-Photo-c	8.00	24.00	90.00
3-9: All have photo covers	5.50	16.50	60.00
10: No photo cover	3.80	11.50	40.00
11-21: All have photo covers. 18-Last 12¢ issue	4.50	13.50	50.00

NOTE: *#1-9, 11-21 are photo covers. #19 reprints cover to #1, but not insides.*

BEWARE (Formerly Fantastic; Chilling Tales No. 13 on)
Youthful Magazines: No. 10, June, 1952 - No. 12, Oct, 1952

	GD25	FN65	NM94
10-E.A. Poe's Pit & the Pendulum adaptation by Wildey; Harrison/Bache-a; atom bomb and shrunken head-c	39.00	117.00	300.00
11-Harrison-a; Ambrose Bierce adapt.	27.00	80.00	200.00
12-Used in **SOTI**, pg. 388; Harrison-a	27.00	80.00	200.00

BEWARE
Trojan Magazines/Merit Publ. No. ?: No. 13, 1/53 - No. 16, 7/53; No. 5, 9/53 - No. 15, 5/55

	GD25	FN65	NM94
13(#1)-Harrison-a	42.00	127.00	340.00
14(#2, 3/53)-Krenkel/Harrison-c; dismemberment, severed head panels	28.00	84.00	210.00
15,16(#3, 5/53; #4, 7/53)-Harrison-a	21.00	64.00	160.00
5,9,12,13	21.00	64.00	160.00
6-Ill. in **SOTI**- "Children are first shocked and then desensitized by all this brutality." Corpse on cover swipe/V.O.H. #26; girl on cover swipe/Advs. Into Darkness #10	43.00	129.00	360.00
7,8-Check-a	21.00	64.00	160.00
10-Frazetta/Check-c; Disbrow, Check-a	49.00	147.00	415.00
11-Disbrow-a; heart torn out, blood drainage	24.00	72.00	180.00
14,15: 14-Myron Fass-c. 15-Harrison-a	19.00	56.00	140.00

NOTE: ***Fass** a-5, 6, 8; c-6, 11, 14. **Forte** a-8. **Hollingsworth** a-15(#3), 16(#4), 9; c-16(#4), 8, 9. **Kiefer** a-16(#4), 5, 6, 10.*

BEWARE (Becomes Tomb of Darkness No. 9 on)
Marvel Comics Group: Mar, 1973 - No. 8, May, 1974 (All reprints)

	GD25	FN65	NM94
1-Everett-c; Sinnott-r ('54)	1.50	4.50	15.00
2-8: 2-Forte, Colan-r. 6-Tuska-a. 7-Torres-r/Mystical Tales #7	1.00	3.00	10.00

NOTE: ***Infantino** a-4r. **Gil Kane** c-4. **Wildey** a-7r.*

BEWARE TERROR TALES
Fawcett Publications: May, 1952 - No. 8, July, 1953

	GD25	FN65	NM94
1-E.C. art swipe/Haunt of Fear #5 & Vault of Horror #26	39.00	117.00	300.00
2	24.00	72.00	180.00
3-7	19.00	56.00	140.00
8-Tothish-a; people being cooked-c	21.00	64.00	160.00

NOTE: ***Andru** a-2. **Bernard Bailey** a-1; c-1-5. **Powell** a-1, 2, 8. **Sekowsky** a-2.*

BEWARE THE CREEPER (See Adventure, Best of the Brave & the Bold, Brave & the Bold, 1st Issue Special, Flash #318-323, Showcase #73, World's Finest #249)
National Periodical Publications: May-June, 1968 - No. 6, Mar-Apr, 1969 (All 12¢ issues)

	GD25	FN65	NM94
1-(5-6/68)-Classic Ditko-c; Ditko-a in all	6.50	19.50	65.00
2-6: 2-5-Ditko-c. 6-Gil Kane-c	4.20	12.60	42.00

BEWITCHED (TV)
Dell Publishing Co.: 4-6/65 - No. 11, 10/67; No. 12, 10/68 - No. 13, 1/69; No. 14, 10/69

	GD25	FN65	NM94
1-Photo-c	14.00	41.00	150.00
2-No photo-c	7.00	21.00	75.00
3-13-All have photo-c	5.00	15.00	55.00
14-No photo-c	3.20	9.50	35.00

BEYOND, THE
Ace Magazines: Nov, 1950 - No. 30, Jan, 1955

	GD25	FN65	NM94
1-Bakerish-a(p)	35.00	104.00	260.00
2-Bakerish-a(p)	21.00	64.00	160.00
3-10: 10-Woodish-a by Cameron	13.00	40.00	100.00
11-20: 18-Used in **POP**, pgs. 81,82	11.00	32.00	80.00
21-26,28-30	10.00	30.00	75.00
27-Used in **SOTI,** pg. 111	11.00	32.00	80.00

NOTE: ***Cameron** a-10, 11p, 12p, 15, 16, 21-27, 30; c-20. **Colan** a-6, 13, 17. **Sekowsky** a-2, 3, 5, 7, 11, 14, 27r. No. 1 was to appear as Challenge of the Unknown No. 7.*

BEYOND THE GRAVE
Charlton Comics: July, 1975 - No. 6, June, 1976; No. 7, Jan, 1983 - No. 17, Oct, 1984

	GD25	FN65	NM94
1-Ditko-a (6 pgs.); Sutton painted-c	1.20	3.60	12.00
2-6: 2-5-Ditko-a; Ditko c-2,3,6	.90	2.70	8.00
7-17: ('83-'84) Reprints. 13-Aparo-c(r). 15-Sutton-c			5.00
Modern Comics Reprint 2('78)			3.00

NOTE: ***Howard** a-4. **Kim** a-1. **Larson** a-4, 6.*

BIBLE TALES FOR YOUNG FOLK (...Young People No. 3-5)
Atlas Comics (OMC): Aug, 1953 - No. 5, Mar, 1954

	GD25	FN65	NM94
1	21.00	64.00	160.00
2-Everett, Krigstein-a	15.00	46.00	115.00
3-5: 4-Robinson-c	11.00	34.00	85.00

BIG (Movie)
Hit Comics (Dark Horse Comics): Mar, 1989 ($2.00)

	GD25	FN65	NM94
1-Adaptaiton of film; Paul Chadwick-c			2.00

BIG ALL-AMERICAN COMIC BOOK, THE (See All-American Comics)
All-American/National Per. Publ.: 1944 (132 pgs., one-shot) (Early DC Annual)

	GD25	FN65	VF82	NM94
1-Wonder Woman, Green Lantern, Flash, The Atom, Wildcat, Scribbly, The Whip, Ghost Patrol, Hawkman by Kubert (1st on Hawkman), Hop Harrigan, Johnny Thunder, Little Boy Blue, Mr. Terrific, Mutt & Jeff app.; Sargon on cover only; cover by Kubert/Hibbard/Mayer/others	900.00	2700.00	6600.00	10,800.00

BIG BABY HUEY (Also see Baby Huey)
Harvey Comics: Oct, 1991 - No. 4, Mar, 1992 ($1.00, quarterly)

	GD25	FN65	NM94
1-4			2.00

BIG BANG COMICS (Becomes Big Bang #4)
Caliber Press: Spring, 1994 - No. 4, Feb, 1995 ($1.95, limited series)

	GD25	FN65	NM94
0-4: 0-Alex Ross-c.			2.00
Your Big Book of Big Bang Comics TPB ('98, $11.00) r/#0-2			11.00

BIG BANG COMICS (Volume 2)
Image Comics (Highbrow Entertainment): V2#1, May, 1996 - Present ($1.95/$2.50/$2.95)

	GD25	FN65	NM94
1-Mighty Man app.			2.00
2-4: 2-Begin $2.50-c., S.A. Shadowhawk app.			2.50
5-22: 5-Begin $2.95-c. 6-Curt Swan/Murphy Anderson-c. 7-Begin B&W. 12-Savage Dragon-c/app. 15-Bissette-c. 16,17,21-Shadow Lady			3.00

BIG BLACK KISS
Vortex Comics: Sep, 1989 - No, 3, Nov, 1989 ($3.75, B&W, lim. series, mature)

	GD25	FN65	NM94
1-3-Chaykin-s/a			4.00

BIG BLOWN BABY (Also see Dark Horse Presents)
Dark Horse Comics: Aug, 1996 - No. 4, Nov, 1996 ($2.95, lim. series, mature)

	GD25	FN65	NM94
1-4: Bill Wray-c/a/scripts			3.00

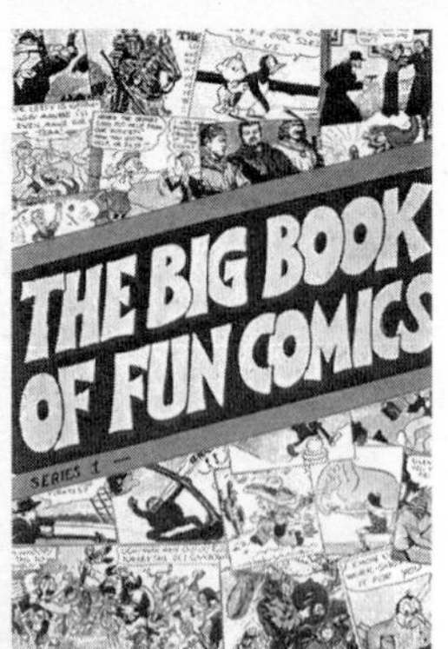

Big Book of Fun Comics #1 © DC

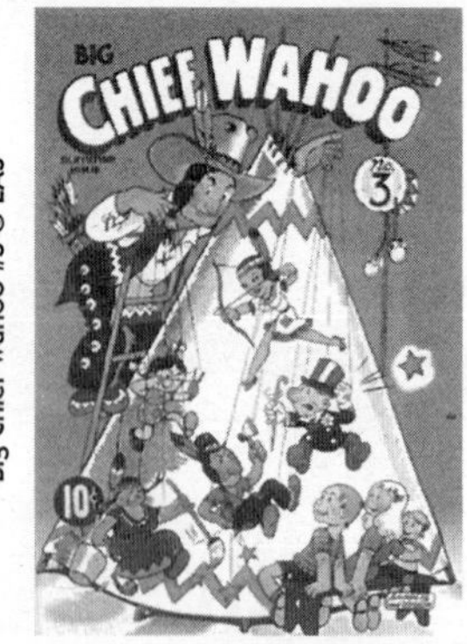

Big Chief Wahoo #3 © EAS

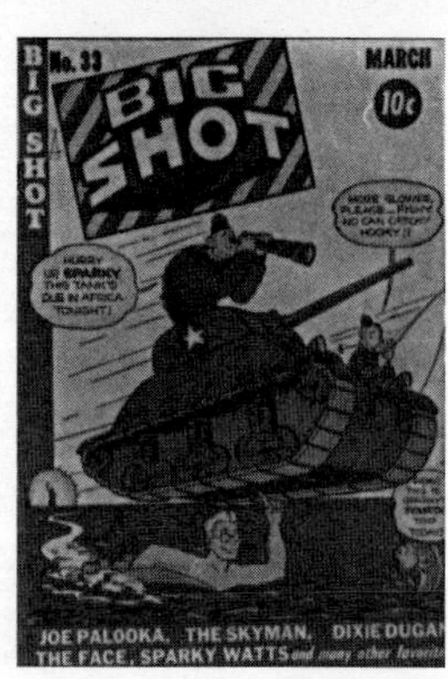

Big Shot Comics #33 © CCG

GD25 FN65 NM94

BIG BOOK OF ..., THE
DC Comics (Paradox Press): 1994 - Present

BIG BOOK OF BAD, THE
1998 ($14.95, B&W,TPB) Jonathan Vankin-s/art by various 14.95

BIG BOOK OF CONSPIRACIES, THE
1995 ($12.95, B&W,TPB) Doug Moench-s/art by various 13.00

BIG BOOK OF DEATH, THE
1994 ($12.95, B&W, TPB) 13.00

BIG BOOK OF FREAKS, THE
1996 ($14.95, B&W, TPB) 15.00

BIG BOOK OF HOAXES, THE
1996 ($14.95, B&W,TPB) 15.00

BIG BOOK OF LITTLE CRIMINALS, THE
1996 ($14.95, B&W,TPB) 15.00

BIG BOOK OF LOSERS, THE
1997 ($14.95, B&W, TPB) 15.00

BIG BOOK OF MARTYRS, THE
1997 ($14.95, B&W, TPB) 15.00

BIG BOOK OF SCANDAL, THE
1997 ($14.95, B&W, TPB) Jonathan Vankin-s/art by various 15.00

BIG BOOK OF THE WEIRD WILD WEST, THE
1998 ($14.95, B&W, TPB) John Whalen-s/ art by various 15.00

BIG BOOK OF THUGS, THE
1997 ($14.95, B&W, TPB) Joel Rose-s/art by various 15.00

BIG BOOK OF UNEXPLAINED, THE
1997 ($14.95, B&W, TPB) Doug Moench-s/art by various 15.00

BIG BOOK OF URBAN LEGENDS, THE
1994 ($12.95, B&W, TPB) 13.00

BIG BOOK OF WEIRDOS, THE
1995 ($12.95, B&W, TPB) 13.00

BIG BOOK OF FUN COMICS (See New Book of Comics)
National Periodical Publications: Spring, 1936 (Large size, 52 pgs.)
(1st comic book annual & DC annual)

	GD25	FN63	VF82
1 (Very rare)-r/New Fun #1-5	2000.00	6000.00	12,000.00

BIG BOOK ROMANCES
Fawcett Publications: Feb, 1950 (no date given) (148 pgs.)

	GD25	FN63	NM92
1-Contains remaindered Fawcett romance comics - several combinations possible	32.00	96.00	240.00

BIG BOY (See Adventures of the Big Boy)

BIG BRUISERS
Image Comics (WildStorm Productions): July, 1996 ($3.50, one-shot)
1-Features Maul from WildC.A.T.S, Impact from Cyberforce & Badrock from Youngblood; wraparound-c 3.50

BIG CHIEF WAHOO
Eastern Color Printing/George Dougherty (distr. by Fawcett): July, 1942 - No. 7, Wint., 1943/44?(no year given)(Quarterly)

	GD25	FN65	NM94
1-Newspaper-r (on sale 6/15/42)	39.00	117.00	300.00
2-Steve Roper app.	20.00	60.00	150.00
3-5: 4-Chief is holding a Katy Keene comic	15.00	44.00	110.00
6-7	10.00	30.00	75.00

NOTE: *Kerry Drake in some issues.*

BIG CIRCUS, THE (Movie)
Dell Publishing Co.: No. 1036, Sept-Nov, 1959
Four Color 1036-Photo-c 5.50 16.50 60.00

BIG COUNTRY, THE (Movie)
Dell Publishing Co.: No. 946, Oct, 1958
Four Color 946-Photo-c 6.40 19.00 70.00

GD25 FN65 NM94

BIG DADDY ROTH (Magazine)
Millar Publications: Oct-Nov, 1964 - No. 4, Apr-May, 1965 (35¢)

	GD25	FN65	NM94
1-Toth-a	14.00	42.00	140.00
2-4-Toth-a	10.50	32.00	105.00

BIG GUY AND RUSTY THE BOY ROBOT, THE (Also See Madman Comics #6,7 & Martha Washington Stranded In Space)
Dark Horse (Legend): July, 1995 - No. 2, Aug, 1995 ($4.95, oversize, lim. series)
1,2-Frank Miller scripts & Geoff Darrow-c/a .85 2.60 7.00
Trade paperback (10/96, $14.95)-r/1,2 w/cover gallery 15.00

BIG HERO ADVENTURES (See Jigsaw)

BIG JIM'S P.A.C.K.
Mattel, Inc. (Marvel Comics): No date (1975) (16 pgs.)
nn-Giveaway with Big Jim doll; Buscema/Sinnott-c/a 2.00 6.00 20.00

BIG JON & SPARKIE (Radio)(Formerly Sparkie, Radio Pixie)
Ziff-Davis Publ. Co.: No. 4, Sept-Oct, 1952 (Painted-c)
4-Based on children's radio program 16.00 48.00 120.00

BIG LAND, THE (Movie)
Dell Publishing Co.: No. 812, July, 1957
Four Color 812-Alan Ladd photo-c 9.00 27.00 100.00

BIG RED (See Movie Comics)

BIG SHOT COMICS
Columbia Comics Group: May, 1940 - No. 104, Aug, 1949

	GD25	FN65	NM94
1-Intro. Skyman; The Face (1st app.; Tony Trent), The Cloak (Spy Master), Marvelo, Monarch of Magicians, Joe Palooka, Charlie Chan, Tom Kerry, Dixie Dugan, Rocky Ryan begin; Charlie Chan moves over from Feature Comics #31 (4/40).	176.00	528.00	1500.00
2	68.00	204.00	575.00
3-The Cloak called Spy Chief; Skyman-c	56.00	168.00	475.00
4,5	44.00	132.00	375.00
6-10: 8-Christmas-c	39.00	117.00	310.00
11-14: 14-Origin & 1st app. Sparky Watts (6/41)	37.00	111.00	280.00
15-Origin The Cloak	39.00	117.00	310.00
16-20	28.00	84.00	210.00
21-27,29,30: 24-Tojo-c. 25-Hitler-c. 29-Intro. Capt. Yank; Bo (a dog) newspaper strip-r by Frank Beck begin, ends #104. 30-X-Mas-c	23.00	69.00	170.00
28-Hitler, Tojo & Mussolini-c	32.00	96.00	240.00
31,33-40	17.00	51.00	125.00
32-Vic Jordan newspaper strip reprints begin, ends #52; Hitler, Tojo & Mussolini-c	21.00	63.00	160.00
41-50: 42-No Skyman. 43,46-Hitler-c. 50-Origin The Face retold	13.00	39.00	100.00
51-60	11.00	32.00	80.00
61-70: 63 on-Tony Trent, the Face	9.30	28.00	65.00
71-80: 73-The Face cameo. 74-(2/47)-Mickey Finn begins. 74,80-The Face app. in Tony Trent. 78-Last Charlie Chan strip-r	8.50	26.00	60.00
81-90: 85-Tony Trent marries Babs Walsh. 86-Valentines-c	7.15	21.50	50.00
91-99,101-104: 69-94-Skyman in Outer Space. 96-Xmas-c	5.70	17.00	40.00
100	7.85	23.50	55.00

NOTE: ***Mart Bailey** art on "The Face" No. 1-104. **Guardineer** a-5. Sparky Watts by **Boody Rogers**-No. 14-42, 77-104, (by others No. 43-76). Others than Tony Trent wear "The Face" mask in No. 46-63, 93. Skyman by **Ogden Whitney**-No. 1, 2, 4, 12-37, 49, 70-101. Skyman covers-No. 1, 3, 7-12, 14, 16, 20, 27, 89, 95, 100.*

BIG TEX
Toby Press: June, 1953
1-Contains (3) John Wayne stories-r with name changed to Big Tex 8.50 26.00 60.00

Biker Mice From Mars #1 © MAR

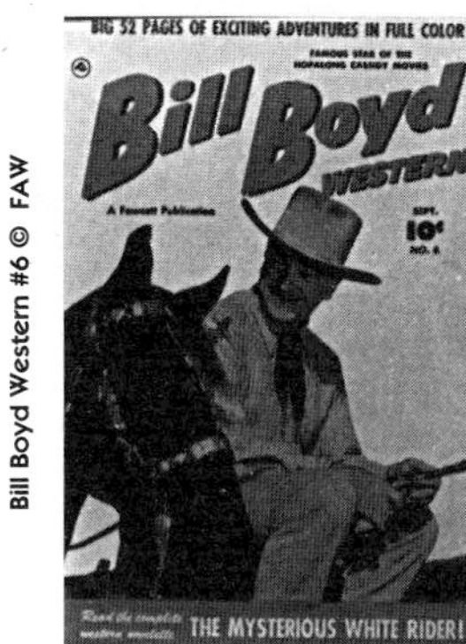

Bill Boyd Western #6 © FAW

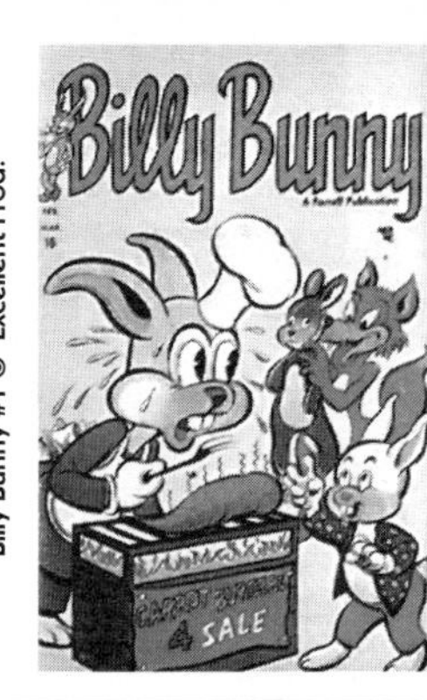

Billy Bunny #1 © Excellent Prod.

BIG-3
Fox Features Syndicate: Fall, 1940 - No. 7, Jan, 1942

	GD25	FN65	NM94
1-Blue Beetle, The Flame, & Samson begin	188.00	564.00	1600.00
2	80.00	240.00	680.00
3-5	56.00	168.00	480.00
6,7: 6-Last Samson. 7-V-Man app.	46.00	138.00	390.00

BIG TOP COMICS, THE (TV's Great Circus Show)
Toby Press: 1951 - No. 2, 1951 (No month)

	GD25	FN65	NM94
1,2	6.85	21.00	48.00

BIG TOWN (Radio/TV) (Also see Movie Comics, 1946)
National Periodical Publ: Jan, 1951 - No. 50, Mar-Apr, 1958 (No. 1-9: 52pgs.)

	GD25	FN65	NM94
1-Dan Barry-a begins	56.00	168.00	475.00
2	31.00	93.00	235.00
3-10	17.00	51.00	130.00
11-20	12.00	36.00	90.00
21-31: Last pre-code (1-2/55)	9.30	28.00	70.00
32-50	7.15	21.50	50.00

BIG VALLEY, THE (TV)
Dell Publishing Co.: June, 1966 - No. 5, Oct, 1967; No. 6, Oct, 1969

	GD25	FN65	NM94
1: Photo-c #1-5	3.80	11.50	42.00
2-6: 6-Reprints #1	2.20	6.50	24.00

BIKER MICE FROM MARS (TV)
Marvel Comics: Nov, 1993 - No. 3, Jan, 1994 ($1.50, limited series)

	GD25	FN65	NM94
1-3: 1-Intro Vinnie, Modo & Throttle. 2-Origin			2.00

BILL & TED'S BOGUS JOURNEY
Marvel Comics: Sept, 1991 ($2.95, squarebound, 84 pgs.)

	GD25	FN65	NM94
1-Adapts movie sequel			3.00

"BILL AND TED'S EXCELLENT ADVENTURE" MOVIE ADAPTATION
DC Comics: 1989 (No cover price)

	GD25	FN65	NM94
nn-Torres-a.			1.00

BILL & TED'S EXCELLENT COMIC BOOK (Movie)
Marvel Comics: Dec, 1991 - No. 12, 1992 ($1.00/$1.25)

	GD25	FN65	NM94
1,2: 2-Last $1.00-c			1.00
3-12			1.25

BILL BARNES COMICS (...America's Air Ace Comics No. 2 on)
(Becomes Air Ace V2#1 on; also see Shadow Comics)
Street & Smith Publications: Oct, 1940(No. month given) - No. 12, Oct, 1943

	GD25	FN65	NM94
1-23 pgs.-comics; Rocket Rooney begins	68.00	204.00	575.00
2-Barnes as The Phantom Flyer app.; Tuska-a	39.00	117.00	310.00
3-5	31.00	93.00	235.00
6-12	27.00	81.00	200.00

BILL BATTLE, THE ONE MAN ARMY (Also see Master Comics No. 133)
Fawcett Publications: Oct, 1952 - No. 4, Apr, 1953 (All photo-c)

	GD25	FN65	NM94
1	9.35	28.00	70.00
2	5.70	17.00	40.00
3,4	5.35	16.00	32.00

BILL BLACK'S FUN COMICS
Paragon #1-3/Americomics #4: Dec, 1982 - No. 4, Mar, 1983 ($1.75, Baxter paper)(1st AC comic)

	GD25	FN65	NM94
1-Intro. Capt. Paragon, Phantom Lady & Commando D (#1-3 are B&W fanzines; 8-1/2x11")			2.00
2-4: 4-($2.00, color)-Origin Nightfall (formerly Phantom Lady); Nightveil app.			2.00

BILL BOYD WESTERN (Movie star; see Hopalong Cassidy & Western Hero)
Fawcett Publ: Feb, 1950 - No. 23, June, 1952 (1-3,7,11,14-on: 36 pgs.)

	GD25	FN65	NM94
1-Bill Boyd & his horse Midnite begin; photo front/back-c	45.00	135.00	380.00
2-Painted-c	25.00	75.00	190.00
3-Photo-c begin, end #23; last photo back-c	19.00	57.00	145.00
4-6(52 pgs.)	15.00	45.00	115.00
7,11(36 pgs.)	12.00	36.00	90.00
8-10,12,13(52 pgs.)	13.00	39.00	95.00
14-22	11.00	33.00	85.00
23-Last issue	13.00	39.00	95.00

BILL BUMLIN (See Treasury of Comics No. 3)

BILL ELLIOTT (See Wild Bill Elliott)

BILLI 99
Dark Horse Comics: Sept, 1991 - No. 4, 1991 ($3.50, B&W, lim. series, 52 pgs.)

	GD25	FN65	NM94
1-4: Tim Sale-c/a			3.50

BILL STERN'S SPORTS BOOK
Ziff-Davis Publ. Co.(Approved Comics): Spring-Sum, 1951 - V2#2, Win, 1952

	GD25	FN65	NM94
V1#10-(1951)	17.00	51.00	130.00
2-(Sum/52; reg. size)	13.00	39.00	95.00
V2#2-(1952, 96 pgs.)-Krigstein, Kinstler-a	17.00	51.00	130.00

BILL THE BULL: ONE SHOT, ONE BOURBON, ONE BEER
Boneyard Press: Dec, 1994 ($2.95, B&W, mature)

	GD25	FN65	NM94
1			3.00

BILL THE CLOWN
Slave Labor Graphics: Feb, 1992 ($2.50, one-shot)

	GD25	FN65	NM94
1			2.50
1-(2nd printing, 4/93, $2.95)			3.00
Comedy Isn't Pretty 1 (11/92, $2.50)			2.50
Death & Clown White 1 (9/93, $2.95)			3.00

BILLY AND BUGGY BEAR (See Animal Fun)
I.W. Enterprises/Super: 1958; 1964

	GD25	FN65	NM94
I.W. Reprint #1, #7('58)-All Surprise Comics #?(Same issue-r for both)	1.00	2.80	7.00
Super Reprint #10(1964)	1.00	2.80	7.00

BILLY BUCKSKIN WESTERN (2-Gun Western No. 4)
Atlas Comics (IMC No. 1/MgPC No. 2,3): Nov, 1955 - No. 3, Mar, 1956

	GD25	FN65	NM94
1-Mort Drucker-a; Maneely-c/a	12.00	36.00	90.00
2-Mort Drucker-a	9.30	28.00	65.00
3-Williamson, Drucker-a	9.30	28.00	70.00

BILLY BUNNY (Black Cobra No. 6 on)
Excellent Publications: Feb-Mar, 1954 - No. 5, Oct-Nov, 1954

	GD25	FN65	NM94
1	5.70	17.00	35.00
2	4.00	10.00	20.00
3-5	3.20	8.00	16.00

BILLY BUNNY'S CHRISTMAS FROLICS
Farrell Publications: 1952 (25¢ Giant, 100 pgs.)

	GD25	FN65	NM94
1	12.00	36.00	120.00

BILLY COLE
Cult Press: May, 1994 - No. 4, Aug, 1994 ($2.75, B&W, limited series)

	GD25	FN65	NM94
1-4			2.75

BILLY MAKE BELIEVE
United Features Syndicate: No. 14, 1939

	GD25	FN65	NM94
Single Series 14	25.00	76.00	190.00

BILLY NGUYEN, PRIVATE EYE
Caliber Press: V2#1, 1990 ($2.50)

	GD25	FN65	NM94
V2#1			2.50

BILLY THE KID (Formerly The Masked Raider; also see Doc Savage Comics & Return of the Outlaw)
No. 9, Nov, 1957 - No. 121, Dec, 1976; No. 122, Sept, 1977 - No. 123,

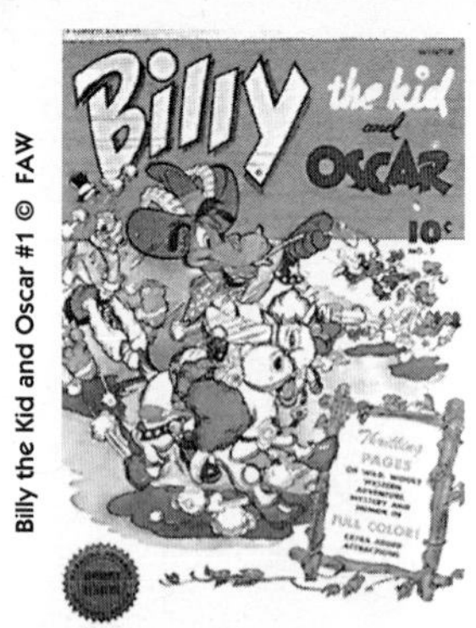

Billy the Kid and Oscar #1 © FAW

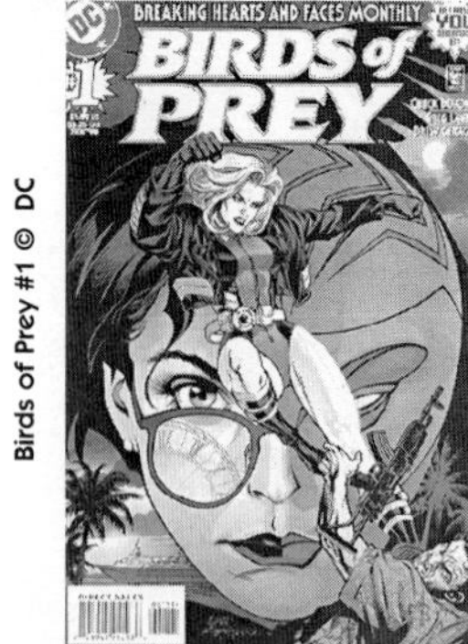

Birds of Prey #1 © DC

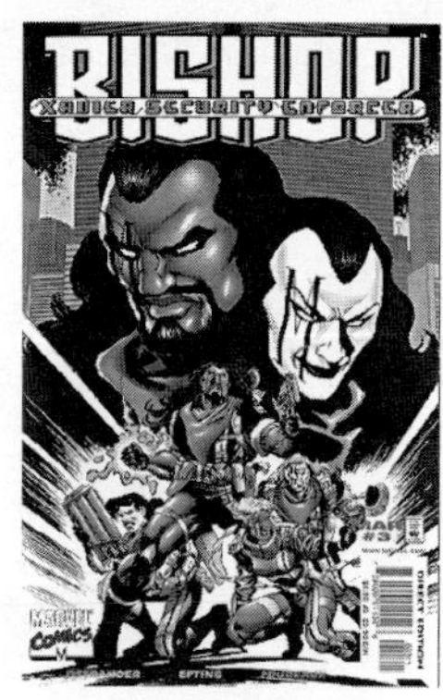

Bishop XSE #3 © MAR

GD25 FN65 NM94

Charlton Publ. Co.: Oct, 1977; No. 124, Feb, 1978 - No. 153, Mar, 1983

9 8.50 26.00 60.00
10,12,14,17-19: 12-2 pg Check-sty 5.35 16.00 32.00
11-(68 pgs.)-Origin & 1st app. The Ghost Train 5.70 17.00 38.00
13-Williamson/Torres-a 5.70 17.00 40.00
15-Origin; 2 pgs. Williamson-a 5.70 17.00 40.00
16-Williamson-a, 2 pgs. 5.70 17.00 38.00
20-26-Severin-a(3-4 each) 5.70 17.00 40.00
27-30: 30-Masked Rider app. 2.50 7.50 22.00
31-40 2.00 6.00 16.00
41-60 1.60 4.85 13.00
61-65 .90 2.70 9.00
66-Bounty Hunter series begins. 1.20 3.60 12.00
67-80: Bounty Hunter series; not in #79,82,84-86 .90 2.70 9.00
81-90: 87-Last Bounty Hunter 2.00 6.00
91-123: 110-Dr. Young of Boothill app. 111-Origin The Ghost Train. 117-Gunsmith & Co., The Cheyenne Kid app. 5.00
124(2/78)-153 3.00
Modern Comics 109 (1977 reprint) 3.00
NOTE: ***Boyette*** *a-91-110.* ***Kim*** *a-73.* ***Morsi*** *a-12,14.* ***Sattler*** *a-118-123.* ***Severin*** *a(r)-121-129, 134; c-23, 25.* ***Sutton*** *a-111.*

BILLY THE KID ADVENTURE MAGAZINE
Toby Press: Oct, 1950 - No. 30, 1955

1-Williamson/Frazetta-a (2 pgs) r/from John Wayne Adventure Comics #2; photo-c 28.00 84.00 210.00
2-Photo-c 8.50 26.00 60.00
3-Williamson/Frazetta "The Claws of Death", 4 pgs. plus Williamson art 31.00 92.00 230.00
4,5,7,8,10: 4,7-Photo-c 5.70 17.00 40.00
6-Frazetta assist on "Nightmare"; photo-c 13.00 38.00 95.00
9-Kurtzman Pot-Shot Pete; photo-c 10.00 30.00 75.00
11,12: 11-Photo-c 5.70 17.00 35.00
13-Kurtzman-r/John Wayne #12 (Genius) 5.70 17.00 40.00
14-Williamson/Frazetta; r-of #1 (2 pgs.) 8.50 26.00 60.00
15-20 5.70 17.00 35.00
21 4.25 13.00 28.00
22-Williamson/Frazetta-r(1pg.)/#1; photo-c 5.70 17.00 35.00
23-30 4.25 13.00 28.00

BILLY THE KID AND OSCAR (Also see Fawcett's Funny Animals)
Fawcett Publications: Winter, 1945 - No. 3, Summer, 1946 (Funny animal)

1 12.00 36.00 90.00
2,3 8.50 26.00 60.00

BILLY WEST (Bill West No. 9,10)
Standard Comics (Visual Editions): 1949-No. 9, Feb, 1951; No. 10, Feb, 1952

1 9.30 28.00 70.00
2 5.70 17.00 35.00
3-10: 7,8-Schomburg-c 4.15 12.50 25.00
NOTE: ***Celardo*** *a-1-6, 9; c-1-3.* ***Moreira*** *a-3.* ***Roussos*** *a-2.*

BING CROSBY (See Feature Films)

BINGO (...Comics) (H. C. Blackerby)
Howard Publ.: 1945 (Reprints National material)

1-L. B. Cole opium-c 25.00 74.00 185.00

BINGO, THE MONKEY DOODLE BOY
St. John Publishing Co.: Aug, 1951; Oct, 1953

1(8/51)-By Eric Peters 5.00 15.00 30.00
1(10/53) 4.00 12.00 24.00

BINKY (Formerly Leave It to...)
National Periodical Publ./DC Comics: No. 72, 4-5/70 - No. 81, 10-11/71; No. 82, Summer/77

72-76 1.40 4.20 14.00

GD25 FN65 NM94

77-79: (68pgs.). 77-Bobby Sherman 1pg. story w/photo. 78-1 pg. sty on Barry Williams of Brady Bunch. 79-Osmonds 1pg. story 2.40 7.00 26.00
80,81 (52pgs.)-Sweat Pain story 2.00 6.00 20.00
82 (1977, one-shot) 1.00 3.00 10.00

BINKY'S BUDDIES
National Periodical Publications: Jan-Feb, 1969 - No. 12, Nov-Dec, 1970

1 2.70 8.00 30.00
2-12 1.40 4.20 14.00

BIONEERS
Mirage Publishing: Aug, 1994 ($2.75)

1-w/bound-in trading card 2.75

BIONIC WOMAN, THE (TV)
Charlton Publications: Oct, 1977 - No. 5, June, 1978

1 .85 2.60 7.00
2-5 4.50

BIRDS OF PREY (Also see Black Canary/Oracle: Birds of Prey)
DC Comics: Jan,1999 - Present ($1.99)

1-Dixon-s/Land-c/a 2.00
2-4 2.00
TPB (1999, $17.95) reprints previous series 17.95

BIRDS OF PREY: BATGIRL
DC Comics: Feb,1998 ($2.95, one-shot)

1-Dixon-s/Frank-c 3.00

BIRDS OF PREY: MANHUNT
DC Comics: Sept, 1996 - No. 4, Dec, 1996 ($1.95, limited series)

1-4: Features Black Canary, Oracle, Huntress, & Catwoman; Chuck Dixon scripts; Gary Frank-c on all. 1-Catwoman cameo only 3.00
NOTE: ***Gary Frank*** *c-1-4.* ***Matt Haley*** *a-1-4p.* ***Wade Von Grawbadger*** *a-1i.*

BIRDS OF PREY: REVOLUTION
DC Comics: 1997 ($2.95, one-shot)

1-Frank-c/Dixon-s 3.00

BIRDS OF PREY: THE RAVENS
DC Comics: June,1998 ($1.95, one-shot)

1-Dixon-s; Girlfrenzy issue 2.00

BIRDS OF PREY: WOLVES
DC Comics: Oct, 1997 ($2.95, one-shot)

1-Dixon-s/Giordano & Faucher-a 3.00

BIRTH OF THE DEFIANT UNIVERSE, THE
Defiant Comics: May, 1993 (Giveaway)

nn-contains promotional artwork & text; limited print run of 1000 copies. 1.00 3.00 10.00

BISHOP (See Uncanny X-Men & X-Men)
Marvel Comics: Dec, 1994 - No.4, Mar, 1995 ($2.95, limited series)

1-4: Foil-c 3.00

BISHOP: XAVIER SECURITY ENFORCER
Marvel Comics: Jan, 1998 - No.3, Mar, 1998 ($2.50, limited series)

1-3: Ostrander-s 2.50

BIZARRE ADVENTURES (Formerly Marvel Preview)
Marvel Comics Group: No. 25, 3/81 - No. 34, 2/83 (#25-33: Magazine-$1.50)

25-Lethal Ladies. 26-King Kull; Bolton-c/a 5.00
27-Phoenix, Iceman & Nightcrawler app. 28-The Unlikely Heroes; Elektra by Miller; Neal Adams-a .85 2.60 7.00
29-Stephen King's Lawnmower Man. 30-Tomorrow; 1st app. Silhouette. 31-After The Violence Stops; new Hangman story; Miller-a. 32-Gods; Thor-c/s. 33-Horror; Dracula app.; photo-c 4.50
34 ($2.00, Baxter paper, comic size)-Son of Santa; Christmas special; Howard

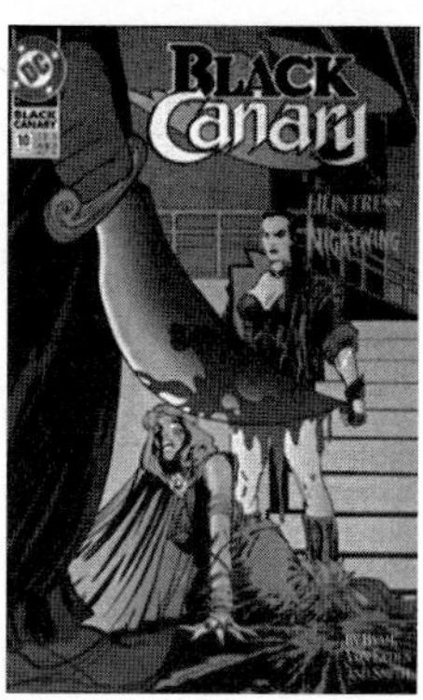

Black Canary #10 © DC

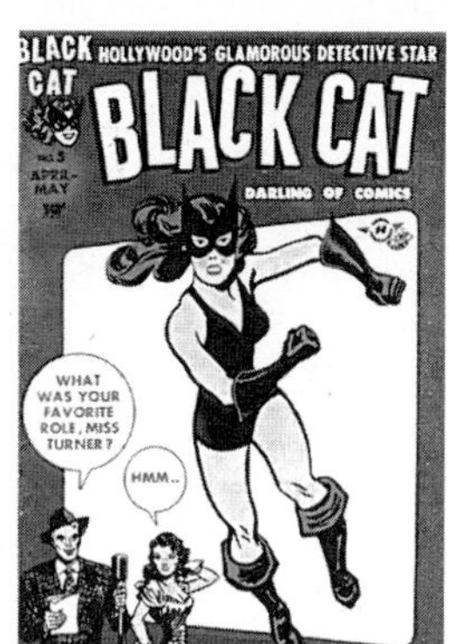

Black Cat Comics #5 © HARV

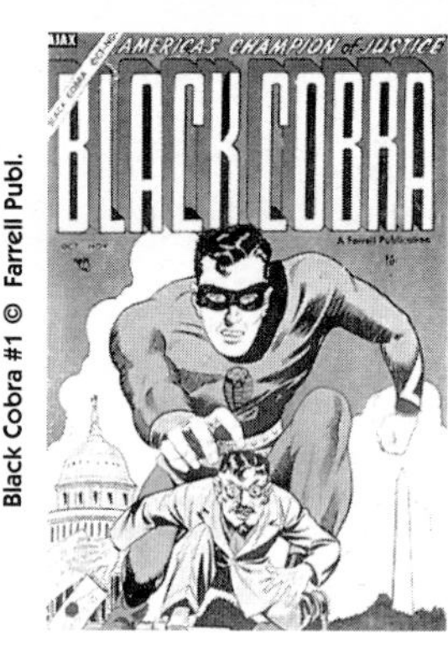

Black Cobra #1 © Farrell Publ.

	GD25	FN65	NM94

the Duck by Paul Smith 4.50
NOTE: ***Alcala*** *a-27i.* ***Austin*** *a-25i, 28i.* ***Bolton*** *a-26, 32.* ***J. Buscema*** *a-27p, 29, 30p; c-26.* ***Byrne*** *a-31 (2 pg.).* ***Golden*** *a-25p, 28p.* ***Perez*** *a-27p.* ***Rogers*** *a-25p.* ***Simonson*** *a-29; c-29.* ***Paul Smith*** *a-34.*

BLACK AND WHITE (See Large Feature Comic, Series I)

BLACK & WHITE (Also see Codename: Black & White)
Image Comics (Extreme): Oct,1994 - No. 3, Jan,1995 ($1.95, limited series)

1-3: Thibert-c/story 2.00

BLACK & WHITE MAGIC
Innovation Publishing: 1991 ($2.95, 98 pgs., B&W w/30 pgs. color, square-bound)

1-Contains rebound comics w/covers removed; contents may vary 2.95

BLACKBALL COMICS
Blackball Comics: Mar, 1994 ($3.00)

1-Trencher-c/story by Giffen; John Pain by O'Neill 3.00

BLACKBEARD'S GHOST (See Movie Comics)

BLACK BEAUTY (See Son of Black Beauty)
Dell Publishing Co.: No. 440, Dec, 1952

	GD25	FN65	NM94
Four Color 440	2.78	8.00	30.00

BLACK CANARY (See All Star Comics #38, Flash Comics #86, Justice League of America #75 & World's Finest #244)
DC Comics: Nov, 1991 - No. 4, Feb, 1992 ($1.75, limited series)

1-4 1.75

BLACK CANARY
DC Comics: Jan, 1993 - No. 12, Dec, 1993 ($1.75)

1-12: 8-The Ray-c/story. 9,10-Huntress-c/story 1.75

BLACK CANARY/ORACLE: BIRDS OF PREY (Also see Showcase '96 #3)
DC Comics: 1996 ($3.95, one-shot)

1-Chuck Dixon scripts & Gary Frank-c/a. 4.50

BLACK CAT COMICS (...Western #16-19; ...Mystery #30 on)
(See All-New #7,9, The Original Black Cat, Pocket & Speed Comics)
Harvey Publications (Home Comics): June-July, 1946 - No. 29, June, 1951

	GD25	FN65	NM94
1-Kubert-a; Joe Simon c-1-3	54.00	162.00	475.00
2-Kubert-a	32.00	96.00	240.00
3,4: 4-The Red Demons begin (The Demon #4 & 5)	25.00	75.00	190.00
5,6,7: 5,6-The Scarlet Arrow app. in ea. by Powell; S&K-a in both. 6-Origin Red Demon. 7-Vagabond Prince by S&K plus 1 more story	32.00	96.00	240.00
8-S&K-a; Kerry Drake begins, ends #13	28.00	84.00	210.00
9-Origin Stuntman (r/Stuntman #1)	35.00	105.00	260.00
10-20: 14,15,17-Mary Worth app. plus Invisible Scarlet O'Neil-#15,20,24	21.00	63.00	160.00
21-26	17.00	51.00	130.00
27,28: 27-Used in **SOTI**, pg. 193; X-Mas-c; 2 pg. John Wayne story. 28-Intro. Kit, Black Cat's new sidekick	19.00	56.00	140.00
29-Black Cat bondage-c; Black Cat stories	18.00	54.00	135.00

BLACK CAT MYSTERY (Formerly Black Cat; ...Western Mystery #54; ...Western #55,56;...Mystery #57; ...Mystic #58-62; Black Cat #63-65)
Harvey Publications: No. 30, Aug, 1951 - No. 65, Apr, 1963

	GD25	FN65	NM94
30-Black Cat on cover only	22.00	66.00	165.00
31,32,34,37,38,40	16.00	48.00	120.00
33-Used in **POP**, pg. 89; electrocution-c	17.00	52.00	130.00
35-Atomic disaster cover/story	19.00	56.00	140.00
36,39-Used in **SOTI**: #36-Pgs. 270,271; #39-Pgs. 386-388	20.00	60.00	150.00
41-43	16.00	48.00	120.00
44-Eyes, ears, tongue cut out; Nostrand-a	17.00	50.00	125.00
45-Classic "Colorama" by Powell; Nostrand-a	27.00	80.00	200.00
46-49,51-Nostrand-a in all	17.00	50.00	125.00
50-Check-a; classic Warren Kremer?-c showing a man's face burning away	39.00	116.00	290.00
52,53 (r/#34 & 35)	11.00	32.00	80.00
54-Two Black Cat stories (2/55, last pre-code)	14.00	42.00	105.00
55,56-Black Cat app.	11.00	32.00	80.00
57(7/56)-Kirby-c	9.35	28.00	70.00
58-60-Kirby-a(4). 58,59-Kirby-c. 60,61-Simon-c	13.00	40.00	100.00
61-Nostrand-a; "Colorama" r/#45	13.00	40.00	100.00
62 (3/58)-E.C. story swipe	9.30	28.00	65.00
63-Giant(10/62); Reprints; Black Cat app.; origin Black Kitten	12.00	36.00	90.00
64-Giant(1/63); Reprints; Black Cat app.	12.00	36.00	90.00
65-Giant(4/63); Reprints; Black Cat app.; 1 pg. Powell-a	12.00	36.00	90.00

NOTE: ***Kremer*** *a-37, 39, 43; c-36, 37, 47.* ***Meskin*** *a-51.* ***Palais*** *a-30, 31(2), 32(2), 33-35, 37-40.* ***Powell*** *a-32-35, 36(2), 40, 41, 43-53, 57.* ***Simon*** *c-63-65.* ***Sparling*** *a-44. Bondage c-32, 34, 43.*

BLACK COBRA (Bride's Diary No. 4 on) (See Captain Flight #8)
Ajax/Farrell Publications(Excellent Publ.): No. 1, 10-11/54; No. 6(No. 2), 12-1/54-55; No. 3, 2-3/55

	GD25	FN65	NM94
1-Re-intro Black Cobra & The Cobra Kid (costumed heroes)	25.00	76.00	190.00
6(#2)-Formerly Billy Bunny	15.00	46.00	115.00
3-(Pre-code)-Torpedoman app.	14.00	42.00	105.00

BLACK CONDOR (Also see Crack Comics, Freedom Fighters & Showcase '94 #10,11)
DC Comics: June, 1992 - No. 12, May, 1993 ($1.25)

1-12: 1-10,12-Heath-c. 9,10-The Ray app. 12-Batman-c/scripts 1.25

BLACK CROSS SPECIAL (See Dark Horse Presents)
Dark Horse Comics: Jan, 1988 ($1.75, B&W, one-shot)(Reprints & new-a)

1-1st & 2nd print; 2nd has 2pgs new-a 1.75

BLACK CROSS: DIRTY WORK (See Dark Horse Presents)
Dark Horse Comics: Apr, 1997 ($2.95, one-shot)

1-Chris Warner-c/s/a 2.95

BLACK DIAMOND
Americomics: May, 1983 - No. 5, 1984 (no month)($2.00-$1.75, Baxter paper)

1-3-Movie adapt.; 1-Colt back-up begins 2.50
4,5 1.50

NOTE: ***Bill Black*** *a-1i; c-1.* ***Gulacy*** *c-2-5. Sybil Danning photo back-c-1.*

BLACK DIAMOND WESTERN (Formerly Desperado No. 1-8)
Lev Gleason Publ: No. 9, Mar, 1949 - No. 60, Feb, 1956 (No. 9-28: 52 pgs.)

	GD25	FN65	NM94
9-Black Diamond & his horse Reliapon begin; origin & 1st app. Black Diamond	17.00	52.00	130.00
10	8.50	26.00	60.00
11-15	6.50	19.50	45.00
16-28(11/49-11/51)-Wolverton's Bing Bang Buster	8.50	26.00	60.00
29-40: 31-One pg. Frazetta anti-drug ad	5.00	15.00	30.00
41-50,53-59	4.15	12.50	25.00
51-3-D effect-c/story	11.00	34.00	85.00
52-3-D effect story	11.00	32.00	80.00
60-Last issue	5.35	16.00	32.00

NOTE: ***Biro*** *c-9-35?.* ***Fass*** *a-58, c-54-56, 58.* ***Guardineer*** *a-9, 15, 18.* ***Kida*** *a-9.* ***Maurer*** *a-10.* ***Ed Moore*** *a-16.* ***Morisi*** *a-55.* ***Tuska*** *a-10, 48.*

BLACK DRAGON, THE
Marvel Comics (Epic Comics): May, 1985 - No. 6, Oct, 1985 (Limited series, Baxter paper, mature)

1-Chris Claremont story & John Bolton-c/a in all. 2.00
2-6 1.00

BLACK DRAGON, THE

Black Fury #1 © CC

Blackhawk #12 © QUA

Blackhawk #253 © DC

GD25 FN65 NM94

Dark Horse Comics: Apr, 1996 ($17.95, B&W, trade paperback)
nn-Reprints Epic Comics limited series; intro by Anne McCaffrey 18.00

BLACK FLAG (See Asylum #5)
Maximum Press: Jan, 1995 - No.4, 1995; No. 0, July, 1995 ($2.50, B&W) (No. 0 in color)

Preview Edition (6/94, $1.95, B&W)-Fraga/McFarlane-c. 2.00
0-4: 0-(7/95)-Liefeld/Fraga-c. 1-(1/95). 3.00
1-Variant cover 5.00
2,4-Variant covers 3.00

NOTE: ***Fraga*** *a-0-4, Preview Edition; c-1-4.* ***Liefeld/Fraga*** *c-0.* ***McFarlane/Fraga*** *c-Preview Edition.*

BLACK FURY (Becomes Wild West No. 58) (See Blue Bird)
Charlton Comics Group: May, 1955 - No. 57, Mar-Apr, 1966 (Horse stories)

1 5.70 17.00 35.00
2 3.20 8.00 16.00
3-10 2.40 6.00 12.00
11-15,19,20 1.60 4.00 8.00
16-18-Ditko-a 5.70 17.00 35.00
21-30 2.40 6.00
31-57 4.00

BLACK GOLD
Esso Service Station (Giveaway): 1945? (8 pgs. in color)
nn-Reprints from True Comics 5.00 15.00 30.00

BLACK GOLIATH
Marvel Comics Group: Feb, 1976 - No. 5, Nov, 1976

1: 1-3-Tuska-a(p) 2.00 6.00
2-5: 4-Kirby-c 4.00

BLACKHAWK (Formerly Uncle Sam #1-8; see Military & Modern Comics)
Comic Magazines(Quality)No. 9-107(12/56); National Periodical PublicationsNo. 108(1/57)-250; DC Comics No. 251 on: No. 9, Winter, 1944 - No. 243, 10-11/68; No. 244, 1-2/76 - No. 250, 1-2/77; No. 251, 10/82 - No. 273, 11/84

9 (1944) 289.00 867.00 2600.00
10 (1946) 97.00 291.00 825.00
11-15: 14-Ward-a; 13,14-Fear app. 64.00 192.00 540.00
16-20: 20-Ward Blackhawk 52.00 156.00 440.00
21-30 42.00 126.00 340.00
31-40: 31-Chop Chop by Jack Cole 32.00 96.00 240.00
41-49,51-60: 42-Robot-c 25.00 75.00 190.00
50-1st Killer Shark; origin in text 28.00 84.00 210.00
61,62: 61-Used in **POP**, pg. 91. 62-Used in **POP**, pg. 92 & color illo 22.00 66.00 165.00
63-70,72-80: 65-H-Bomb explosion panel. 66-B&W & color illos **POP**. 70-Return of Killer Shark; atomic explosion panel. 75-Intro. Blackie the Hawk 21.00 63.00 155.00
71-Origin retold; flying saucer-c; A-Bomb panels 24.00 72.00 180.00
81-86: Last precode (3/55) 19.00 58.00 145.00
87-92,94-99,101-107: 91-Robot-c. 105-1st S.A. ish 15.00 45.00 115.00
93-Origin in text 16.00 48.00 120.00
100 19.00 58.00 145.00
108-1st DC issue (1/57); re-intro. Blackie, the Hawk, their mascot; not in #115 39.00 117.00 440.00
109-117: 117-(10/57)-Mr. Freeze app. 14.50 44.00 145.00
118-(11/57)-Frazetta-r/Jimmy Wakely #4 (3 pgs.) 15.50 47.00 155.00
119-130 (11/58): 120-Robot-c 9.50 28.50 95.00
131-140 (2/59): 133-Intro. Lady Blackhawk 7.00 21.00 70.00
141-150,152-163,165,166: 143-Kurtzman-r/Jimmy Wakely #4. 150-(7/60)-King Condor returns. 166-Last 10¢ issue 5.00 15.00 50.00
151-Lady Blackhawk receives & loses super powers 5.50 16.50 55.00
164-Origin retold 6.00 18.00 60.00

GD25 FN65 NM94

167-180 2.60 7.80 26.00
181-190 2.50 7.50 20.00
191-196,199,201,204-210: 196-Combat Diary series begins. 2.00 6.00 16.00
197-New look for Blackhawks 2.50 7.50 20.00
198,200: 198-Origin retold 2.50 7.50 20.00
203-Origin Chop Chop (12/64) 2.50 7.50 20.00
211-227,229,231-243(1968): 242-Return to old costumes 1.20 3.60 12.00
228-Batman, Green Lantern, Superman, The Flash cameos. 230-Blackhawks become superheroes. 1.40 4.20 14.00
244 ('76) -250: 250-Chuck dies 4.00
251-273: 251-Origin retold; Black Knights return. 252-Intro Domino. 253-Part origin Hendrickson. 258-Blackhawk's Island destroyed. 259-Part origin Chop-Chop. 265-273 (75¢ cover price) 1.50

NOTE: ***Chaykin*** *a-260; c-257-260, 262.* ***Crandall*** *a-10, 11, 13, 16?, 18-20, 22-26, 30-33, 35p, 36(2), 37, 38?, 39-44, 46-50, 52-58, 60, 63, 64, 66, 67; c-14-20, 22-63(most except #28-33, 36, 37, 39).* ***Evans*** *a-244, 245,246i, 248-250i.* ***G. Kane*** *c-263, 264.* ***Kubert c****-244, 245.* ***Newton*** *a-266p.* ***Severin*** *a-257.****Spiegle*** *a-261-267, 269-273; c-265-272.* ***Toth*** *a-260p.* ***Ward*** *a-16-27(Chop Chop, 8pgs. ea.); pencilled stories-No. 17-63(approx.).* ***Wildey*** *a-268. Chop Chop solo stories in #10-95?*

BLACKHAWK
DC Comics: Mar, 1988 - No. 3, May, 1988 ($2.95, limited series, mature)

1-3: Chaykin painted-c/a/scripts 3.00

BLACKHAWK (Also see Action Comics #601)
DC Comics: Mar, 1989 - No. 16, Aug, 1990 ($1.50, mature)

1-6,8-16: 16-Crandall-c swipe 1.50
7-($2.50, 52 pgs.)-Story-r/Military #1 2.50
Annual 1 (1989, $2.95, 68 pgs.)-Recaps origin of Blackhawk, Lady Blackhawk, and others 3.00
Special 1 (1992, $3.50, 68 pgs.)-Mature readers 3.50

BLACKHAWK INDIAN TOMAHAWK WAR, THE
Avon Periodicals: 1951 (Also see Fighting Indians of the Wild West)
nn-Kinstler-c; Kit West story 16.00 48.00 120.00

BLACK HEART ASSASSIN
Iguana Comics: Jan, 1994 ($2.95)
1 3.00

BLACK HOLE (See Walt Disney Showcase #54) (Disney, movie)
Whitman Publishing Co.: Mar, 1980 - No. 4, Sept, 1980

11295(#1) (1979, Golden, $1.50-c, 52 pgs., graphic novel; 8 1/2x11") Photo-c; Spiegle-a. 1,2-Movie adaptation. 1.50 4.50 15.00
2-4: 2-4-Spiegle-a. 3-McWilliams-a; photo-c. 3,4-New stories 5.00

BLACK HOOD, THE (See Blue Ribbon, Flyman & Mighty Comics)
Red Circle Comics (Archie): June, 1983 - No. 3, Oct, 1983 (Mandell paper)

1-Morrow, McWilliams, Wildey-a; Toth-c 3.00
2,3: MLJ's The Fox by Toth-c/a. 3-Morrow-a 2.00
(Also see Archie's Super-Hero Special Digest #2)

BLACK HOOD
DC Comics (Impact Comics): Dec, 1991 - No. 12, Dec, 1992 ($1.00)

1-12: 11-Intro The Fox. 12-Origin Black Hood 1.00
Annual 1 (1992, $2.50, 68 pgs.)-w/Trading card 2.50

BLACK HOOD COMICS (Formerly Hangman #2-8; Laugh Comics #20 on; also see Black Swan, Jackpot, Roly Poly & Top-Notch #9)
MLJ Magazines: No. 9, Wint., 1943-44 - No. 19, Sum., 1946 (on radio in 1943)

9-The Hangman & The Boy Buddies cont'd 88.00 264.00 750.00
10-Hangman & Dusty, the Boy Detective app. 50.00 150.00 425.00
11-Dusty app.; no Hangman 40.00 120.00 315.00
12-18: 14-Kinstler blood-c. 17-Hal Foster swipe from Prince Valiant; 1st issue with "An Archie Magazine" on-c 38.00 114.00 285.00
19-I.D. exposed 44.00 132.00 375.00

NOTE: *Hangman by* ***Fuje*** *in 9, 10.* ***Kinstler*** *a-15, c-14-16.*

Black Lightning #8 (1st Series) © DC

Black Magic #1 © HEAD

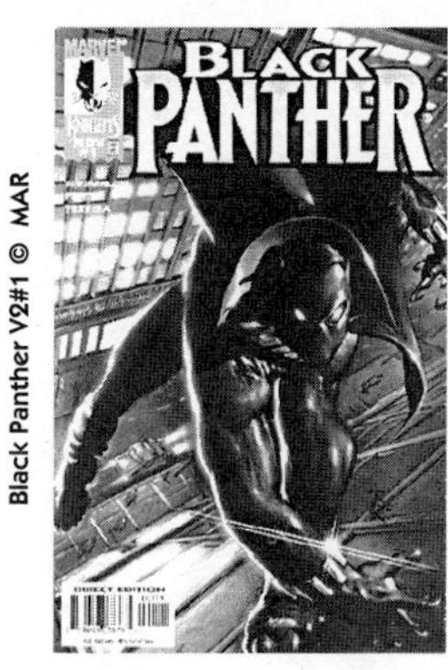

Black Panther V2#1 © MAR

BLACK JACK (Rocky Lane's...; formerly Jim Bowie)
Charlton Comics: No. 20, Nov, 1957 - No. 30, Nov, 1959

	GD25	FN65	NM94
20	7.15	21.50	50.00
21,27,29,30	4.25	13.00	28.00
22-(68 pgs.)	5.70	17.00	38.00
23-Williamson/Torres-a	5.70	17.00	40.00
24-26,28-Ditko-a	7.85	23.50	55.00

BLACK KNIGHT, THE
Toby Press: May, 1953; 1963

	GD25	FN65	NM94
1-Bondage-c	20.00	60.00	150.00
Super Reprint No. 11 (1963)-Reprints 1953 issue	2.25	6.75	18.00

BLACK KNIGHT, THE (Also see The Avengers #48, Marvel Super Heroes & Tales To Astonish #52)
Atlas Comics (MgPC): May, 1955 - No. 5, April, 1956

	GD25	FN65	NM94
1-Origin Crusader; Maneely-c/a	75.00	225.00	600.00
2-Maneely-c/a(4)	56.00	170.00	450.00
3-5: 4-Maneely-c/a. 5-Maneely-c, Shores-a	44.00	132.00	350.00

BLACK KNIGHT (Also see Avengers & Ultraforce)
Marvel Comics: June, 1990 - No. 4, Sept, 1990 ($1.50, limited series)

	GD25	FN65	NM94
1-4: 1-Original Black Knight returns			1.50

NOTE: ***Buckler** c-1-4p*

BLACK KNIGHT: EXODUS
Marvel Comics: Dec, 1996 ($2.50, one-shot)

	GD25	FN65	NM94
1-Raab-s; Apocalypse-c/app.			2.50

BLACK LAMB, THE
DC Comics (Helix): Nov, 1996 - No, 6, Apr, 1997 ($2.50, limited series)

	GD25	FN65	NM94
1-6: Tim Truman-c/a/scripts			2.50

BLACK LIGHTNING (See The Brave & The Bold, Cancelled Comic Cavalcade, DC Comics Presents #16, Detective #490 and World's Finest #257)
National Periodical Publ./DC Comics: Apr, 1977 - No. 11, Sept-Oct, 1978

	GD25	FN65	NM94
1,11: 1-Origin Black Lightning. 11-The Ray app.			5.00
2-10: 4-Intro Cyclotronic Man.			3.50

NOTE: ***Buckler** c-1-3p, 6-11p. #11 is 44 pgs.*

BLACK LIGHTNING (2nd Series)
DC Comics: Feb, 1995 - No. 13, Feb, 1996 ($1.95/$2.25)

	GD25	FN65	NM94
1-5-Tony Isabella scripts begin, ends #8			2.00
6-13; 6-Begin $2.25-c. 13-Batman-c/app.			2.25

BLACK MAGIC (...Magazine) (Becomes Cool Cat V8#6 on)
Crestwood Publ. V1#1-4,V6#1-V7#5/Headline V1#5-V5#3,V7#6-V8#5: 10-11/50 - V4#1, 6-7/53: V4#2, 9-10/53 - V5#3, 11-12/54; V6#1, 9-10/57 - V7#2, 11-12/58: V7#3, 7-8/60 - V8#5, 11-12/61
(V1#1-5, 52pgs.; V1#6-V3#3, 44pgs.)

	GD25	FN65	NM94
V1#1-S&K-a, 10 pgs.; Meskin-a(2)	78.00	234.00	750.00
2-S&K-a, 17 pgs.; Meskin-a	40.00	120.00	350.00
3-6(8-9/51)-S&K, Roussos, Meskin-a	36.00	107.00	300.00
V2#1(10-11/51),4,5,7(#13),9(#15),12(#18)-S&K-a	26.00	77.00	200.00
2,3,6,8,10,11(#17)	17.00	49.00	130.00
V3#1(#19, 12/52) - 6(#24, 5/53)-S&K-a	19.00	58.00	150.00
V4#1(#25, 6-7/53), 2(#26, 9-10/53)-S&K-a(3-4)	21.00	62.00	160.00
3(#27, 11-12/53)-S&K-a; Ditko-a (2nd published-a); also see Captain 3-D, Daring Love #1, Strange Fantasy #9, & Fantastic Fears #5 (Fant. Fears was 1st drawn, but not 1st publ.)	40.00	120.00	325.00
4(#28)-Eyes ripped out/story-S&K, Ditko-a	29.00	86.00	225.00
5(#29, 3-4/54)-S&K, Ditko-a	22.00	66.00	170.00
6(#30, 5-6/54)-S&K, Powell?-a	17.00	49.00	130.00
V5#1(#31, 7-8/54 - 3(#33, 11-12/54)-S&K-a	13.50	41.00	110.00
V6#1(#34, 9-10/57), 2(#35, 11-12/57)	7.50	22.50	55.00
3(1-2/58) - 6(7-8/58)	7.50	22.50	55.00
V7#1(9-10/58) - 3(7-8/60)	5.70	17.00	45.00
4(9-10/60), 5(11-12/60)-Torres-a	7.50	22.50	55.00
6(1-2/61)-Powell-a(2)	5.70	17.00	45.00
V8#1(3-4/61)-Powell-c/a	5.70	17.00	45.00
2(5-6/61)-E.C. story swipe/W.F. #22; Ditko, Powell-a	7.50	22.50	55.00
3(7-8/61)-E.C. story swipe/W.F. #22; Powell-a(2)	7.50	22.50	55.00
4(9-10/61)-Powell-a(5)	5.70	17.00	45.00
5-E.C. story swipe/W.S.F. #28; Powell-a(3)	7.50	22.50	55.00

NOTE: ***Bernard Baily** a-V4#6?, V5#3(2). **Grandenetti** a-V2#3, 11. **Kirby** c-V1#1-6, V2#1-12, V3#1-6, V4#1, 2, 4-6, V5#1-3. **McWilliams** a-V3#2i. **Meskin** a-V1#1(2), 2, 3, 4(2), 5(2), 6, V2/1, 2, 3(2), 4(3), 5, 6(2), 7-9, 11, 12i, V3#1(2), 5, 6, V5#1(2), 2. **Orlando** a-V6#1, 4, V7#2; c-V6/1-6. **Powell** a-V5#1?. **Roussos** a-V1#3-5, 6(2), V2#3(2), 4, 5(2), 6, 8, 9, 10(2), 11, 12p, V3#1(2), 2i, 5, V5#2. **Simon** a-V2#12, V3#2, V7#5? c-V4#3?, V7#3?, 4, 5?, 6?, V8#1-5. **Simon & Kirby** a-V1#1, 2(2), 3-6, V2#1, 4, 5, 7, 9, 12, V3#1-6, V4#1(3), 2(4), 3(2), 4(2), 5, 6, V5#1-3; c-V2#1. **Leonard Starr** a-V1#1. **Tuska** a-V6#3, 4. **Woodbridge** a-V7#4.*

BLACK MAGIC
National Periodical Publications: Oct-Nov, 1973 - No. 9, Apr-May, 1975

	GD25	FN65	NM94
1-S&K reprints	2.00	6.00	20.00
2-9-S&K reprints	.90	2.70	9.00

BLACK MAGIC
Eclipse International: Apr, 1990 - No. 4, Oct, 1990 ($2.75, B&W, mini-series)

	GD25	FN65	NM94
1-($3.50, 68pgs.)-Japanese manga			3.50
2-4 ($2.75, 52 pgs.)			2.80

BLACKMAIL TERROR (See Harvey Comics Library)

BLACK MASK
DC Comics: 1993 - No. 3, 1994 ($4.95, limited series, 52 pgs.)

	GD25	FN65	NM94
1-3			5.00

BLACK OPS
Image Comics (WildStorm): Jan, 1996 - No. 5, May, 1996 ($2.50, lim. series)

	GD25	FN65	NM94
1-5			2.50

BLACK ORCHID (See Adventure Comics #428 & Phantom Stranger)
DC Comics: Holiday, 1988-89 - No. 3, 1989 ($3.50, lim. series, prestige format)

	GD25	FN65	NM94
Book 1,3: Gaiman scripts & McKean painted-a in all			5.00
Book 2-Arkham Asylum story; Batman app.		2.00	6.00

BLACK ORCHID
DC Comics: Sept, 1993 - No. 22, June, 1995 ($1.95/$2.25)

	GD25	FN65	NM94
1-20: Dave McKean-c all issues			2.00
1-Platinum Edition	1.20	3.60	12.00
21,22			2.25
Annual 1 (1993, $3.95, 68 pgs.)-Children's Crusade			4.00

BLACKOUTS (See Broadway Hollywood...)

BLACK PANTHER, THE (Also see Avengers #52, Fantastic Four #52, Jungle Action & Marvel Premiere #51-53)
Marvel Comics Group: Jan, 1977 - No. 15, May, 1979

	GD25	FN65	NM94
1	1.40	4.20	14.00
2-12	.85	2.60	7.00
13-15: 14,15-Avengers x-over			4.50

NOTE: ***J. Buscema** c-15p. **Kirby** c/a & scripts-1-12. **Layton** c-13i.*

BLACK PANTHER
Marvel Comics Group: July, 1988 - No. 4, Oct, 1988 ($1.25)

	GD25	FN65	NM94
1-4			1.25

BLACK PANTHER (Marvel Knights)
Marvel Comics: Nov, 1998 - Present ($2.50)

	GD25	FN65	NM94
1-Texeira-a/c; Priest-s			2.50
1-($6.95) DF edition w/Quesada& Palmiotti-c			6.95
2,3: 2-Two covers by Texeira and Timm. 3-Fantastic Four app.			2.50

BLACK PANTHER: PANTHER'S PREY
Marvel Comics: 1991 - No. 4, 1991 ($4.95, squarebound, lim. series, 52 pgs.)

Blackstone, Master Magician Comics #1 © Vital

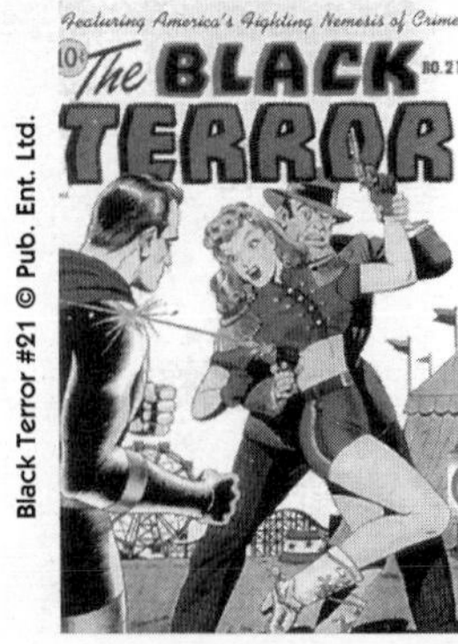

Black Terror #21 © Pub. Ent. Ltd.

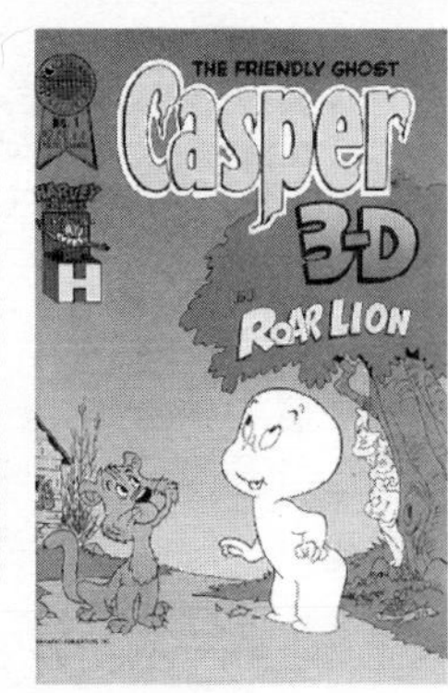

Blackthorne 3-D Series #57 © HARV

GD25 FN65 NM94

1-4 5.00

BLACK PEARL, THE
Dark Horse Comics: Sept, 1996 - No. 5, Jan, 1997 ($2.95, limited series)

1-5: Mark Hamill scripts 3.00

BLACK PHANTOM (See Tim Holt #25, 38)
Magazine Enterprises: Nov, 1954 (one-shot) (Female outlaw)

1 (A-1 #122)-The Ghost Rider story plus 3 Black Phantom stories; Headlight-c/a 35.00 104.00 260.00

BLACK PHANTOM
AC Comics: 1989 - No. 3, 1990 ($2.50, B&W; #2 color)(Reprints & new-a)

1,2: 1-Ayers-r, Bolle-r/B.P. #1. 2-Redmask-r 2.50
3 ($2.75, B&W)-B.P., Redmask-r & new-a 2.75

BLACK PHANTOM, RETURN OF THE (See Wisco)

BLACK RIDER (Western Winners #1-7; Western Tales of Black Rider #28-31; Gunsmoke Western #32 on)(See All Western Winners, Best Western, Kid Colt, Outlaw Kid, Rex Hart, Two-Gun Kid, Two-Gun Western, Western Gunfighters, Western Winners, & Wild Western)
Marvel/Atlas Comics(CDS No. 8-17/CPS No. 19 on): No. 8, 3/50 - No. 18, 1/52; No. 19, 11/53 - No. 27, 3/55

8 (#1)-Black Rider & his horse Satan begin; 36 pgs; Stan Lee photo-c as Black Rider) 40.00 120.00 320.00
9-52 pgs. begin, end #14 20.00 60.00 150.00
10-Origin Black Rider 24.00 72.00 180.00
11-14: 14-Last 52pgs. 14.00 42.00 105.00
15-19: 19-Two-Gun Kid app. 12.00 36.00 90.00
20-Classic-c; Two-Gun Kid app. 13.00 40.00 100.00
21-27: 21-23-Two-Gun Kid app. 24,25-Arrowhead app. 26-Kid Colt app. 27-Last issue; last precode. Kid Colt app. The Spider (a villain) burns to death 11.00 32.00 80.00

NOTE: ***Ayers** c-22. **Jack Keller** a-15, 26, 27. **Maneely** a-14; c-16, 17, 25, 27. **Syd Shores** a-19, 21, 22, 23(3), 24(3), 25-27; c-19, 21, 23. **Sinnott** a-24, 25. **Tuska** a-12, 19-21.*

BLACK RIDER RIDES AGAIN!, THE
Atlas Comics (CPS): Sept, 1957

1-Kirby-a(3); Powell-a; Severin-c 21.00 64.00 160.00

BLACK SEPTEMBER (Also see Avengers/Ultraforce, Ultraforce (1st series) #10 & Ultraforce/Avengers)
Malibu Comics (Ultraverse): 1995 ($1.50, one-shot)

Infinity-Intro to the newUltraverse; variant-c exists. 1.50

BLACKSTONE (See Super Magician Comics & Wisco Giveaways)

BLACKSTONE, MASTER MAGICIAN COMICS
Vital Publ./Street & Smith Publ.: Mar-Apr, 1946 - No. 3, July-Aug, 1946

1 25.00 74.00 185.00
2,3 18.00 54.00 130.00

BLACKSTONE, THE MAGICIAN (...Detective on cover only #3 & 4)
Marvel Comics (CnPC): No. 2, May, 1948 - No. 4, Sept, 1948 (No #1) (Cont'd from E.C. #1?)

2-The Blonde Phantom begins, ends #4 52.00 156.00 440.00
3,4: 3-Blonde Phantom by Sekowsky 39.00 117.00 300.00

BLACKSTONE, THE MAGICIAN DETECTIVE FIGHTS CRIME
E. C. Comics: Fall, 1947

1-1st app. Happy Houlihans 43.00 129.00 350.00

BLACK SWAN COMICS
MLJ Magazines (Pershing Square Publ. Co.): 1945

1-The Black Hood reprints from Black Hood No. 14; Bill Woggon-a; Suzie app. 20.00 60.00 150.00

BLACK TARANTULA (See Feature Presentations No. 5)

BLACK TERROR (See America's Best Comics & Exciting Comics)

GD25 FN65 NM94

Better Publications/Standard: Winter, 1942-43 - No. 27, June, 1949

1-Black Terror, Crime Crusader begin 235.00 705.00 2000.00
2 85.00 255.00 725.00
3 62.00 186.00 525.00
4,5 52.00 156.00 440.00
6-10: 7-The Ghost app. 46.00 138.00 390.00
11-20: 20-The Scarab app. 39.00 117.00 310.00
21-Miss Masque app. 42.00 126.00 340.00
22-Part Frazetta-a on one Black Terror story 39.00 117.00 310.00
23,25-27 39.00 117.00 290.00
24-Frazetta-a (1/4 pg.) 39.00 117.00 300.00

NOTE: ***Schomburg (Xela)** c-2-27; bondage c-2, 17, 24. **Meskin** a-27. **Moreira** a-27. **Robinson/Meskin** a-23, 24(3), 25, 26. **Roussos/Mayo** a-24. **Tuska** a-26, 27.*

BLACK TERROR, THE (Also see Total Eclipse)
Eclipse Comics: Oct, 1989 - No. 3, June, 1990 ($4.95, 52 pgs., squarebound, limited series)

1-3: Beau Smith & Chuck Dixon scripts; Dan Brereton painted-c/a 5.00

BLACKTHORNE 3-D SERIES
Blackthorne Publishing Co.: May, 1985 - No. 80, 1989 ($2.25/$2.50)

1-Sheena in 3-D #1. D. Stevens-c/retouched-a 4.00
2-10: 2-MerlinRealm in 3-D #1. 3-3-D Heroes #1. Goldyn in 3-D #1. 5-Bizarre 3-D Zone #1. 6-Salimba in 3-D #1. 7-Twisted Tales in 3-D #1. 8-Dick Tracy in 3-D #1. 9-Salimba in 3-D #2. 10-Gumby in 3-D #1 4.00
11-20: 11-Betty Boop in 3-D #1. 12-Hamster Vice in 3-D #1. 13-Little Nemo in 3-D #1. 14-Gumby in 3-D #2. 15-Hamster Vice #6 in 3-D. 16-Laffin' Gas #6 in 3-D. 17-Gumby in 3-D #3. 18-Bullwinkle and Rocky in 3-D #1. 19-The Flintstones in 3-D #1. 20-G.I. Joe in 3-D #1 4.00
21-29: 21-Gumby in 3-D #4. 22-The Flintstones in 3-D #2. 23-Laurel & Hardy in 3-D #1. 24-Bozo the Clown in 3-D #1. 25-The Transformers in 3-D #1. 26-G.I. Joe in 3-D #2. 27-Bravestarr in 3-D #1. 28- Gumby in 3-D #5. 29-The Transformers in 3-D #2 4.00
30-Star Wars in 3-D #1 2.00 6.00
31-40: 31-The California Raisins in 3-D #1. 32-Richie Rich & Casper in 3-D #1. 33-Gumby in 3-D #6. 34-Laurel & Hardy in 3-D #2. 35-G.I. Joe in 3-D #3. 36-The Flintstones in 3-D #3. 37-The Transformers in 3-D #3. 38-Gumby in 3-D #7. 39-G.I. Joe in 3-D #4. 40-Bravestarr in 3-D #2 4.00
41-46,49,50: 41-Battletech in 3-D #1. 42-The Flintstones in 3-D #4. 43-Underdog in 3-D #1 44-The California Raisins in 3-D #2. 45-Red Heat in 3-D #1 (movie adapt.). 46-The California Raisins in 3-D #3. 49-Rambo in 3-D #1. 49-Sad Sack in 3-D #1. 50-Bullwinkle For President in 3-D #1 4.00
47, 48-Star Wars in 3-D #2,3. 5.00
51-60: 51-Kull in 3-D #1. 52-G.I. Joe in 3-D #5. 53-Red Sonja in 3-D #1. 54-Bozo in 3-D #2. 55-Waxwork in 3-D #1 (movie adapt.). 56. 57-Casper in 3-D #1. 58- Baby Huey in 3-D #1. 59-Little Dot in 3-D #1. 60-Solomon Kane in 3-D #1 0 4.00
61-70: 61-Werewolf in 3-D #1. 62-G.I. Joe in 3-D Annual #1. 63-The California Raisins in 3-D #4. 64-To Die For in 3-D #1. 65-Capt. Holo in 3-D #1. 66-Playful Little Audrey in 3-D #1. 67-Kull in 3-D #2. 68. 69-The California Raisins in 3-D#5. 70-Wendy in 3-D #1 4.00
71-80: 71. 72-Sports Hall of Shame #1. 73. 74-The Noid in 3-D #1. 75-Moonwalker in 3-D #1 (Michael Jackson movie adapt.). 76-79. 80-The Noid in 3-D #2 3.00

BLACKWULF
Marvel Comics: June, 1994 - No. 10, Mar, 1995 ($1.50)

1-($2.50)-Embossed-c; Angel Medina-a 2.50
2-10 1.50

BLADE (The Vampire Hunter)
Marvel Comics: Mar, 1998 ($3.50, one-shot)

1-Colan-a(p)/Christopher Golden-s 3.50

Blade #2 © MAR

Blaze: Legacy of Blood #4 © MAR

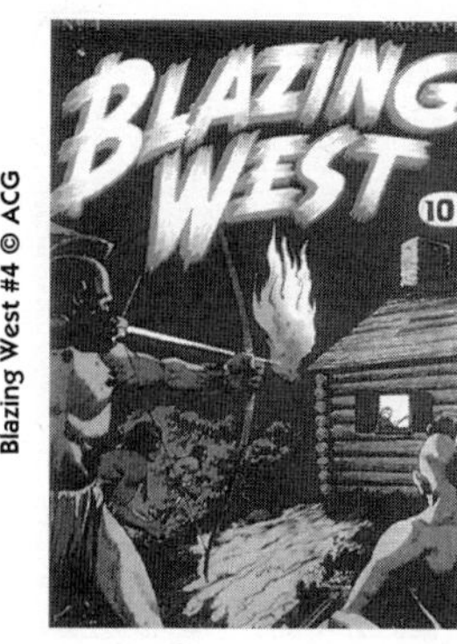

Blazing West #4 © ACG

GD25 FN65 NM94

BLADE (The Vampire Hunter)
Marvel Comics: Nov, 1998 - Present ($3.50/$2.99)
1-($3.50) Contains Movie insider pages; McKean-a 3.50
2,3-($2.99): 2-Two covers 2.99

BLADE OF THE IMMORTAL (Manga)
Dark Horse Comics: June, 1996 - Present ($2.95, B&W)
1-10: 2-#1 on cover in error 3.00
11,19,20-($3.95, 48 pgs.) 4.00
12-18:12-Begin Dreamsong 3.00
21-25: 21-Begin On Silent Wings 2.95

BLADE RUNNER (Movie)
Marvel Comics Group: Oct, 1982 - No. 2, Nov, 1982
1,2-r/Marvel Super Special #22; 1-Williamson-c/a. 2-Williamson-a .75

BLADESMEN UNDERSEA
Blue Comet Press: 1994 ($3.50, B&W)
1-Polybagged w/trading card 3.50

BLADE: THE VAMPIRE-HUNTER
Marvel Comics: July, 1994 - No. 10, Apr, 1995 ($1.95)
1-($2.95)-Foil-c 3.00
2-10 2.00

BLAST (Satire Magazine)
G & D Publications: Feb, 1971 - No. 2, May, 1971
1-Wrightson & Kaluta-a/Everette-c 4.50 13.50 50.00
2-Kaluta-c/a 3.20 9.50 35.00

BLAST CORPS
Dark Horse Comics: Oct, 1998 ($2.50, one-shot, based on Nintendo game)
1-Reprints from Nintendo Power magazine; Mahn-a 2.50

BLASTERS SPECIAL
DC Comics: 1989 ($2.00, one-shot)
1-Peter David scripts; Invasion spin-off 2.00

BLAST-OFF (Three Rocketeers)
Harvey Publications (Fun Day Funnies): Oct, 1965 (12¢)
1-Kirby/Williamson-a(2); Williamson/Crandall-a; Williamson/Torres/Krenkel-a; Kirby/Simon-c 3.80 11.40 38.00

BLAZE
Marvel Comics: Aug, 1994 - No. 12, July, 1995 ($1.95)
1-($2.95)-Foil embossed-c 3.00
2-12: 2-Man-Thing-c/story 2.00

BLAZE CARSON (Rex Hart #6 on)(See Kid Colt, Tex Taylor, Wild Western, Wisco)
Marvel Comics (USA): Sept, 1948 - No. 5, June, 1949
1: 1,2-Shores-c 23.00 68.00 170.00
2,4,5: 4-Two-Gun Kid app. 5-Tex Taylor app. 17.00 50.00 125.00
3-Used by N.Y. State Legis. Comm. (injury to eye splash); Tex Morgan app. 18.00 54.00 135.00

BLAZE: LEGACY OF BLOOD (See Ghost Rider & Ghost Rider/Blaze)
Marvel Comics (Midnight Sons imprint): Dec, 1993 - No. 4, Mar, 1994 ($1.75, limited series)
1-4 1.75

BLAZE THE WONDER COLLIE (Formerly Molly Manton's Romances #1?)
Marvel Comics(SePI): No. 2, Oct, 1949 - No. 3, Feb, 1950 (Both have photo-c)
2(#1), 3-(Scarce) 20.00 60.00 150.00

BLAZING BATTLE TALES
Seaboard Periodicals (Atlas): July, 1975
1-Intro. Sgt. Hawk & the Sky Demon; Severin, McWilliams, Sparling-a; Thorne-c 4.00

BLAZING COMBAT (Magazine)
Warren Publishing Co.: Oct, 1965 - No. 4, July, 1966 (35¢, B&W)
1-Frazetta painted-c on all 15.00 45.00 150.00
2 3.20 9.60 32.00
3,4: 4-Frazetta half pg. ad 2.50 7.50 24.00
...Anthology (reprints from No. 1-4) 4.20 12.60 42.00
NOTE: *Above has art by* ***Colan, Crandall, Evans, Morrow, Orlando, Severin, Torres, Toth, Williamson,*** *and* ***Wood.***

BLAZING COMBAT: WORLD WAR I AND WORLD WAR II
Apple Press: Mar, 1994 ($3.75, B&W)
1,2: 1-r/Colan, Toth, Goodwin, Severin, Wood-a. 2-r/Crandall, Evans, Severin, Torres, Williamson-a 3.75

BLAZING COMICS
Enwil Associates/Rural Home: 6/44 - #3, 9/44; #4, 2/45; #5, 3/45; #5(V2#2), 3/55 - #6(V2#3), 1955?
1-The Green Turtle, Red Hawk, Black Buccaneer begin; origin Jun-Gal 43.00 129.00 360.00
2-5: 3-Briefer-a. 5-(V2#2 inside) 29.00 88.00 220.00
5(3/55, V2#2-inside)-Black Buccaneer-c, 6(V2#3-inside, 1955)-Indian/Japanese-c 11.00 32.00 80.00
NOTE: *No. 5 & 6 contain remaindered comics rebound and the contents can vary. Cloak & Daggar, Will Rogers, Superman 64, Star Spangled 130, Kaanga known. Value would be half of contents.*

BLAZING SIXGUNS
Avon Periodicals: Dec, 1952
1-Kinstler-c/a; Larsen/Alascia-a(2), Tuska?-a; Jesse James, Kit Carson, Wild Bill Hickok app. 13.00 38.00 95.00

BLAZING SIXGUNS
I.W./Super Comics: 1964
I.W. Reprint #1,8,9: 1-r/Wild Bill Hickok #26, Western True Crime #? & Blazing Sixguns #1 by Avon; Kinstler-c. 8-r/Blazing Western #?; Kinstler-c. 9-r/Blazing Western #1; Ditko-r; Kintsler-c reprinted from Dalton Boys #1. 1.25 3.75 10.00
Super Reprint #10,11,15,16: 10,11-r/The Rider #2,1. 15-r/Silver Kid Western #?. 16-r/Buffalo Bill #?; Wildey-r; Severin-c. 17(1964)-r/Western True Crime #? 1.25 3.75 10.00
12-Reprints Bullseye #3; S&K-a 2.50 7.50 25.00
18-r/Straight Arrow #? by Powell; Severin-c 1.50 4.50 12.00

BLAZING SIX-GUNS (Also see Sundance Kid)
Skywald Comics: Feb, 1971 - No. 2, Apr, 1971 (52 pgs.)
1-The Red Mask, Sundance Kid begin, Avon's Geronimo reprint by Kinstler; Wyatt Earp app. 1.00 3.00 10.00
2-Wild Bill Hickok, Jesse James, Kit Carson-r plus M.E. Red Mask-r .85 2.60 7.00

BLAZING WEST (Also see The Hooded Horseman)
American Comics Group (B&I Publ./Michel Publ.): Fall, 1948 - No. 22, Mar-Apr, 1952
1-Origin & 1st app. Injun Jones, Tenderfoot & Buffalo Belle; Texas Tim & Ranger begins, ends #13 17.00 52.00 130.00
2,3 9.30 28.00 65.00
4-Origin & 1st app. Little Lobo; Starr-a 6.50 19.50 45.00
5-10: 5-Starr-a 5.70 17.00 40.00
11-13 5.00 15.00 30.00
14-Origin & 1st app. The Hooded Horseman 9.30 28.00 70.00
15-22: 15,16,18,19-Starr-a 6.50 19.50 45.00

BLAZING WESTERN
Timor Publications: Jan, 1954 - No. 5, Sept, 1954
1-Ditko-a (1st Western-a?); text story by Bruce Hamilton 13.00 38.00 95.00

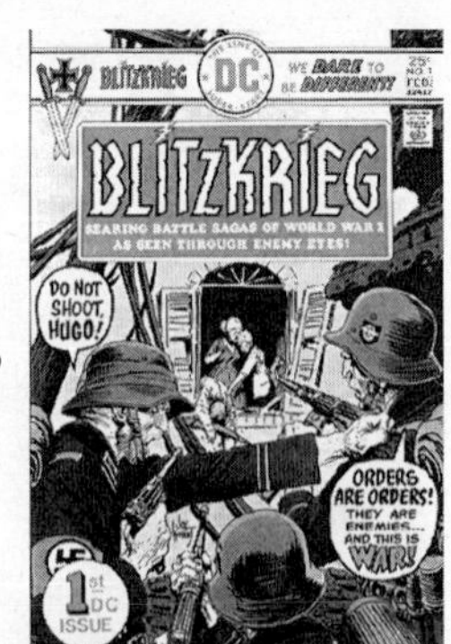

Blitzkrieg #1 © DC

Blood and Shadows Book Three
© Joe R. Lansdale & Mark A. Nelson

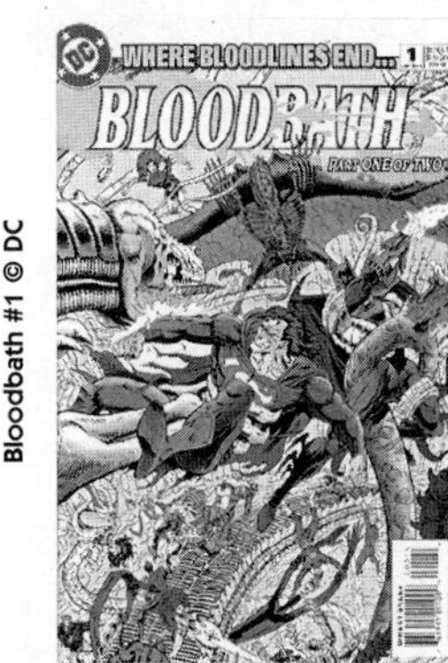

Bloodbath #1 © DC

	GD25	FN65	NM94
2-4	5.70	17.00	35.00
5-Disbrow-a	5.70	17.00	40.00

BLEAT
Slave Labor Graphics: Aug, 1995 ($2.95)

	GD25	FN65	NM94
1			3.00

BLESSED PIUS X
Catechetical Guild (Giveaway): No date (Text/comics, 32 pgs., paper-c)

	GD25	FN65	NM94
nn	3.60	9.00	18.00

BLIND JUSTICE (Also see Batman: Blind Justice)
DC Comics/Diamond Comic Distributors: 1989 (Giveaway, squarebound)

	GD25	FN65	NM94
nn-Contains Detective #598-600 by Batman movie writer Sam Hamm, w/covers; published same time as originals?			2.00

BLINDSIDE
Image Comics (Extreme Studios): Aug, 1996 ($2.50)

	GD25	FN65	NM94
1-Variant-c exists			2.50

BLIP
Marvel Comics Group: 2/1983 - 1983 (Video game mag. in comic format)

	GD25	FN65	NM94
1-1st app. Donkey Kong & Mario Bros. in comics, 6pgs. comics; photo-c		2.00	6.00
2-Spider-Man photo-c; 6pgs. Spider-Man comics w/Green Goblin	.85	2.60	7.00
3,4,6			3.50
5-E.T., Indiana Jones; Rocky-c			4.00
7-6pgs. Hulk comics; Pac-Man & Donkey Kong Jr. Hints			5.00

BLISS ALLEY
Image Comics: July, 1997 - No. 2($2.95, B&W)

	GD25	FN65	NM94
1,2-Messner-Loebs-s/a			2.95

BLITZKRIEG
National Periodical Publications: Jan-Feb, 1976 - No. 5, Sept-Oct, 1976

	GD25	FN65	NM94
1-Kubert-c on all	2.70	8.00	30.00
2-5	1.80	5.40	18.00

BLONDE PHANTOM (Formerly All-Select #1-11; Lovers #23 on)(Also see Blackstone, Marvel Mystery, Millie The Model #2, Sub-Mariner Comics #25 & Sun Girl)
Marvel Comics (MPC): No. 12, Winter, 1946-47 - No. 22, Mar, 1949

	GD25	FN65	NM94
12-Miss America begins, ends #14	124.00	372.00	1050.00
13-Sub-Mariner begins (not in #16)	77.00	231.00	650.00
14,15: 15-Kurtzman's "Hey Look"	71.00	213.00	600.00
16-Captain America with Bucky story by Rico(p), 6 pgs.; Kurtzman's "Hey Look" (1 pg.)	97.00	291.00	825.00
17-22: 22-Anti Wertham editorial	65.00	195.00	550.00

NOTE: ***Shores** c-12-18.*

BLONDIE (See Ace Comics, Comics Reading Libraries, Dagwood, Daisy & Her Pups, Eat Right to Work..., King & Magic Comics)
David McKay Publications: 1942 - 1946

	GD25	FN65	NM94
Feature Books 12 (Rare)	62.00	186.00	620.00
Feature Books 27-29,31,34(1940)	17.00	50.00	125.00
Feature Books 36,38,40,42,43,45,47	15.00	46.00	115.00
...1944 (Hard-c, 1938, B&W, 128 pgs.)-1944 daily strip-r	12.00	36.00	90.00

BLONDIE & DAGWOOD FAMILY
Harvey Publ. (King Features Synd.): Oct, 1963 - No. 4, Dec, 1965 (68 pgs.)

	GD25	FN65	NM94
1	2.00	6.00	20.00
2-4	1.20	3.60	12.00

BLONDIE COMICS (...Monthly No. 16-141)
David McKay #1-15/Harvey #16-163/King #164-175/Charlton #177 on: Spring, 1947 - No. 163, Nov, 1965; No. 164, Aug, 1966 - No. 175, Dec, 1967; No. 177, Feb, 1969 - No. 222, Nov, 1976

	GD25	FN65	NM94
1	21.00	64.00	160.00
2	10.00	30.00	75.00
3-5	7.85	23.50	55.00
6-10	5.70	17.00	40.00
11-15	5.00	15.00	30.00
16-(3/50; 1st Harvey issue)	5.70	17.00	38.00
17-20: 20-(3/51)-Becomes Daisy & Her Pups #21 & Chamber of Chills #21	2.80	8.40	28.00
21-30	2.00	6.00	20.00
31-50	1.60	4.80	16.00
51-80	1.40	4.20	14.00
81-99	1.20	3.60	12.00
100	1.60	4.80	16.00
101-124,126-130	1.10	3.30	11.00
125 (80 pgs.)	2.20	6.60	22.00
131-136,138,139	.80	2.40	8.00
137,140-(80 pgs.)	2.00	6.00	20.00
141-147,149-154,156,160,164-167	1.10	3.30	11.00
148,155,157-159,161-163 are 68 pgs.	1.80	5.40	18.00
168-175		2.00	7.00
177-199 (no #176)		2.00	6.00
200	.80	2.40	8.00
201-222: 211,212-1st & 2nd app. Super Dagwood			5.00
Blondie, Dagwood & Daisy 1(100 pgs., 1953)	16.00	48.00	120.00
1950 Giveaway	5.00	15.00	30.00
1962,1964 Giveaway	1.20	3.60	12.00
N. Y. State Dept. of Mental Hygiene Giveaway-('50, '56, '61) Regular size (Diff. issues) 16 pgs.; no #	1.20	3.60	12.00

BLOOD
Marvel Comics (Epic Comics): Feb, 1988 - No. 4, Apr, 1988 ($3.25, mature)

	GD25	FN65	NM94
1-4: DeMatteis scripts & Kent Williams-c/a			3.50

BLOOD AND GLORY (Punisher & Captain America)
Marvel Comics: Oct, 1992 - No. 3, Dec, 1992 ($5.95, limited series)

	GD25	FN65	NM94
1-3: 1-Embossed wraparound-c		2.00	6.00

BLOOD & ROSES: FUTURE PAST TENSE (Bob Hickey's...)
Sky Comics: Dec, 1993 ($2.25)

	GD25	FN65	NM94
1-Silver ink logo			2.25

BLOOD & ROSES: SEARCH FOR THE TIME-STONE (Bob Hickey's...)
Sky Comics: Apr, 1994 ($2.50)

	GD25	FN65	NM94
1			2.50

BLOOD AND SHADOWS
DC Comics (Vertigo): 1996 - Book 4, 1996 ($5.95, squarebound, mature)

	GD25	FN65	NM94
Books 1-4: Joe R. Lansdale scripts; Mark A. Nelson-c/a.		2.00	6.00

BLOOD: A TALE
DC Comics (Vertigo): Nov, 1996 - No. 4, Feb, 1997 ($2.95, limited series)

	GD25	FN65	NM94
1-4: Reprints Epic series w/new-c; DeMatteis scripts; Kent Williams-c/a			3.00

BLOODBATH
DC Comics: Early Dec, 1993 - No. 2, Late Dec, 1993 ($3.50, 68 pgs.)

	GD25	FN65	NM94
1-Neon ink-c; Superman app.: 1-New Batman-c & app.			3.50
2-Hitman 2nd app.	1.00	3.00	10.00

BLOODFIRE
Lightning Comics: June, 1993 - No. 12, May, 1994 ($2.95)

	GD25	FN65	NM94
1-($3.50)-Foil-c; 1st app. Bloodfire			3.50
2-12: 2-Origin; contracts HIV virus via transfusion. 5-Polybagged w/card & collectors warning on bag. 12-(5/94)			3.00
0-(Indicia reads June 1994, MAY on-c, $3.50)			3.50
.../Hellina 1 (7/95, $3.00)			3.00
.../Hellina 1 (7/95, $9.95)-Nude edition; Deodato-c			

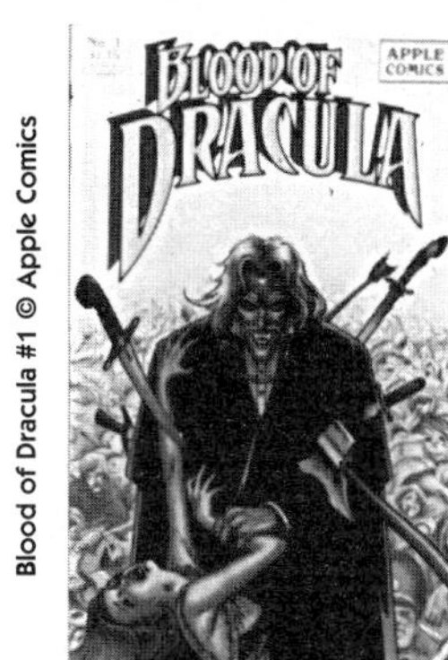

Blood of Dracula #1 © Apple Comics

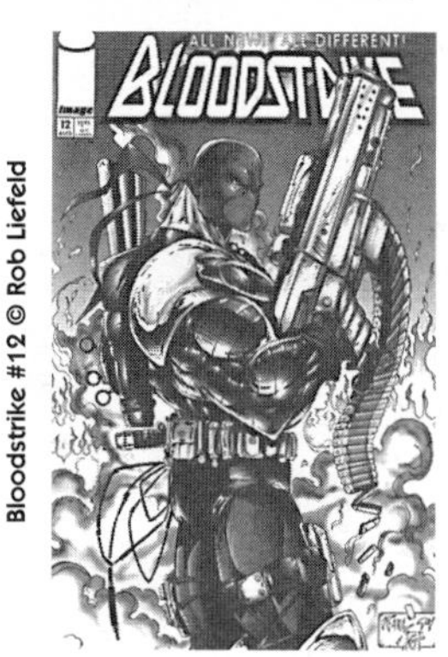

Bloodstrike #12 © Rob Liefeld

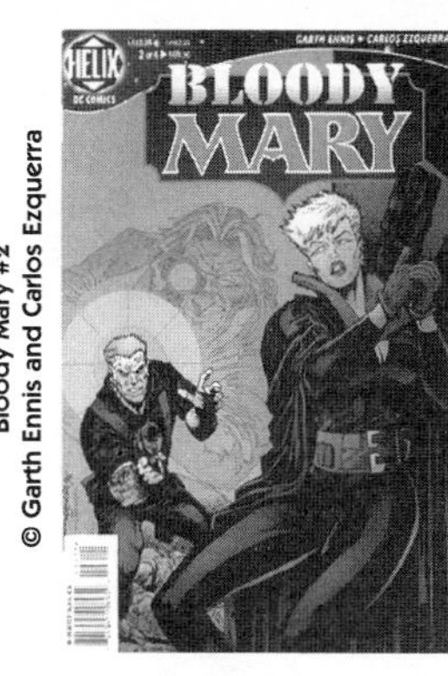

Bloody Mary #2 © Garth Ennis and Carlos Ezquerra

	GD25	FN65	NM94
	1.00	3.00	10.00
.../Hellina (8/95, $9.95)-Commemorative edition	1.00	3.00	10.00

BLOOD IS THE HARVEST
Catechetical Guild: 1950 (32 pgs., paper-c)

(Scarce)-Anti-communism (13 known copies) 94.00 282.00 800.00
Black & white version (5 known copies), saddle stitched 39.00 118.00 275.00
Untrimmed version (only one known copy); estimated value-$600
NOTE: *In 1979 nine copies of the color version surfaced from the old Guild's files plus the five black & white copies.*

BLOODLINES: A TALE FROM THE HEART OF AFRICA (See Tales From the Heart of Africa)
Marvel Comics (Epic Comics): 1992 ($5.95, 52 pgs.)

1-Story cont'd from Tales From... 2.00 6.00

BLOOD OF DRACULA
Apple Comics: Nov, 1987 - No. 20?, 1990 ($1.75/$1.95, B&W)($2.25 #14,16 on)

1-13: 6-Begin $1.95-c. 10-Chadwick-c 2.00
14,16-20 ($2.25): 14,16-19-Lost Frankenstein pgs. by Wrightson 2.25
15-Contains stereo flexidisc ($3.75) 3.75

BLOOD OF THE INNOCENT (See Warp Graphics Annual)
WaRP Graphics: 1/7/86 - No. 4, 1/28/86 (Weekly mini-series, mature)

1-4 2.00

BLOODPACK
DC Comics: Mar, 1995 - No. 4, June,1995 ($1.50, limited series)

1-4 1.50

BLOODPOOL
Image Comics (Extreme): Aug, 1995 - No. 4, Nov, 1995 ($2.50, limited series)

1-4: Jo Duffy scripts in all 2.50
Special (3/96, $2.50)-Jo Duffy scripts 2.50
Trade Paperback (1996, $12.95)-r/#1-4 13.00

BLOOD REIGN SAGA
London Night Studios: 1996 ($3.00, B&W, mature)

1-"Encore Edition" 3.00

BLOODSCENT
Comico: Oct, 1988 ($2.00, one-shot, Baxter paper)

1-Colan-p 2.00

BLOODSEED
Marvel Comics (Frontier Comics): Oct, 1993 - No. 2, Nov, 1993 ($1.95)

1,2: Sharp/Cam Smith-a 2.00

BLOODSHOT (See Eternal Warrior #4 & Rai #0)
Valiant/Acclaim Comics (Valiant): Nov, 1992 - No. 51, Aug, 1996 ($2.25/$2.50)

1-($3.50)-Chromium embossed-c by B. Smith w/poster 3.50
2-($2.50) 2.50
3-5,8-14: 3-$2.25-c begins; cont'd in Hard Corps #5. 4-Eternal Warrior-c/story. 5-Rai & Eternal Warrior app. 14-(3/94)-Reese-c(i) 2.25
6-1st app. Ninjak (out of costume) 3.00
7-1st app. Ninjak in costume 3.50
0-(3/94, $3.50)-Wraparound chromium-c by Quesada(p); origin 3.50
0-Gold variant 2.00 6.00
15-49: 15-(4/94). 16-w/bound-in trading card 2.25
50,51: 50-$2.50-c begins. 51-Bloodshot dies? 2.50
Yearbook 1 (1994, $3.95) 4.00
Special 1 (3/94, $5.95)-Zeck-c/a(p) 2.00 6.00

BLOODSHOT (Volume Two)
Acclaim Comics (Valiant): July, 1997 - No. 16, Oct, 1998 ($2.50)

1-16: 1-Two covers. 5-Copycat-c. X-O Manowar-c/app 2.50

BLOODSTRIKE (See Supreme V2#3)
Image Comics (Extreme Studios): 1993 - No. 22, May, 1995; No. 25, May, 1994 ($1.95/$2.50)

1-12, 25: Liefeld layouts in early issues. 1-Blood Brothers prelude. 2-1st app. Lethal. 5-1st app. Noble. 9-Black and White part 6 by Art Thibert; Liefeld pin-up. 9,10-Have coupon #3 & 7 for Extreme Prejudice #0. 10-(4/94). 11-(7/94). 25-(5/94) -Liefeld/Fraga-c 2.00
13-22: 13-$2.50-c begins. 16:Platt-c; Prophet app. 17-19-polybagged w/card 2.50
NOTE: ***Giffen** story/layouts-4-6. **Jae Lee** c-7, 8. **Rob Liefeld** layouts-1-3. **Art Thibert** c-6i.*

BLOODSTRIKE ASSASSIN
Image Comics (Extreme Studios): June, 1995 - No. 3, Aug, 1995; No. 0, Oct, 1995 ($2.50, limited series)

0-3: 3-(8/95)-Quesada-c. 0-(10/95)-Battlestone app. 2.50

BLOOD SWORD, THE
Jademan Comics: Aug, 1988 - No. 53, Dec, 1992 ($1.50/$1.95, 68 pgs.)

1-8 ($1.50)-Kung Fu stories 1.50
9-53: ($1.95) 2.00

BLOOD SWORD DYNASTY
Jademan Comics: 1989 -No. 41, Jan, 1993 ($1.25, 36 pgs.)

1-41: Ties into Blood Sword 1.30

BLOOD SYNDICATE
DC Comics (Milestone): Apr, 1993 - No. 35, Feb, 1996 ($1.50/$1.75/$2.50/$3.50)

1-($2.95)-Collector's Edition; polybagged with poster, trading card, & acid-free backing board (direct sale only) 3.00
1-9,11-17: 8-Intro Kwai. 15-Byrne-c. 16-Worlds Collide Pt. 6; Superman-c/app. 17-Worlds Collide Pt. 13 1.50
10-($2.50, 52 pgs.)-Simonson-c 2.50
18-27: 18-Begin $1.75-c 1.75
25-($2.95, 52 pgs.) 3.00
28, 30-32: 28-Begin $2.50-c. 30-Long Hot Summer x-over 2.50
29, 33-34: 29-(99¢); Long Hot Summer x-over 1.00
35-Kwai disappears 3.50

BLOODWULF
Image Comics (Extreme): Feb, 1995 - No. 4, May, 1995 ($2.50, limited series)

1-4: 1-Liefeld-c w/4 diferent captions & alternate-c. 2.50
Summer Special (8/95, $2.50)-Jeff Johnson-c/a; Supreme app; story takes place between Legend of Supreme #3 & Supreme #23. 2.50

BLOODY MARY
DC Comics (Helix): Oct, 1996 - No. 4, Jan, 1997 ($2.25, limited series)

1-4: Garth Ennis scripts; Ezquerra-c/a in all 2.25

BLOODY MARY: LADY LIBERTY
DC Comics (Helix): Sept, 1997 - No. 4, Dec, 1997 ($2.50, limited series)

1-4: Garth Ennis scripts; Ezquerra-c/a in all 2.50

BLUEBEARD
Slave Labor Graphics: Nov, 1993 - No. 3, Mar, 1994 ($2.95, B&W, lim. series)

1-3: James Robinson scripts. 2-(12/93) 3.00
Trade paperback (6/94, $9.95) 9.95
Trade paperback (2nd printing, 7/96, $12.95)-New-c 12.95

BLUE BEETLE, THE (Also see All Top, Big-3, Mystery Men & Weekly Comic Magazine)
Fox Publ. No. 1-11, 31-60; Holyoke No. 12-30: Winter, 1939-40 - No. 57, 7/48; No. 58, 4/50 - No. 60, 8/50

1-Reprints from Mystery Men 1-5; Blue Beetle origin; Yarko the Great-r/from Wonder/Wonderworld 2-5 all by Eisner; Master Magician app.; (Blue Beetle in 4 different costumes) 368.00 1100.00 3500.00

Blue Beetle #48 © FOX

Blue Beetle #14 © DC

Blue Bolt #6 © Premium Service Co.

	GD25	FN65	NM94
2-K-51-r by Powell/Wonderworld 8,9	129.00	387.00	1100.00
3-Simon-c	91.00	273.00	775.00
4-Marijuana drug mention story	62.00	186.00	525.00
5-Zanzibar The Magician by Tuska	56.00	168.00	475.00
6-Dynamite Thor begins (1st); origin Blue Beetle	53.00	159.00	450.00
7,8-Dynamo app. in both. 8-Last Thor	50.00	150.00	425.00
9-12: 9,10-The Blackbird & The Gorilla app. in both. 10-Bondage/hypo-c 11(2/42)-The Gladiator app. 12(6/42)-The Black Fury app.	44.00	132.00	375.00
13-V-Man begins (1st app.), ends #18; Kubert-a	53.00	159.00	450.00
14,15-Kubert-a in both. 14-Intro. side-kick (c/text only), Sparky (called Spunky #17-19)	46.00	138.00	390.00
16-18: 17-Brodsky-c	39.00	117.00	300.00
19-Kubert-a	39.00	117.00	310.00
20-Origin/1st app. Tiger Squadron; Arabian Nights begin	42.00	126.00	340.00
21-26: 24-Intro. & only app. The Halo. 26-General Patton story & photo	29.00	87.00	220.00
27-Tamaa, Jungle Prince app.	27.00	81.00	200.00
28-30(2/44)	25.00	75.00	185.00
31(6/44), 33,34,36-40: 34-38-"The Threat from Saturn" serial.	23.00	69.00	170.00
32-Hitler-c	31.00	93.00	230.00
35-Extreme violence	27.00	81.00	200.00
41-45	20.00	60.00	150.00
46-The Puppeteer app.	23.00	69.00	170.00
47-Kamen & Baker-a begin	100.00	300.00	850.00
48-50	81.00	242.00	685.00
51,53	68.00	204.00	575.00
52-Kamen bondage-c; true crime stories begin	102.00	305.00	865.00
54-Used in **SOTI**. Illo, "Children call these 'headlights' comics"	109.00	330.00	925.00
55-57: 56-Used in **SOTI**, pg. 145. 57(7/48)-Last Kamen issue; becomes Western Killers?	67.00	201.00	570.00
58(4/50)-60-No Kamen-a	13.50	41.00	100.00

NOTE: ***Kamen** a-47-51, 53, 55-57; c-47, 49-52. **Powell** a-4(2). Bondage-c 9-12, 46, 52.*

BLUE BEETLE (Formerly The Thing; becomes Mr. Muscles No. 22 on) (See Charlton Bullseye & Space Adventures)
Charlton Comics: No. 18, Feb, 1955 - No. 21, Aug, 1955

	GD25	FN65	NM94
18,19-(Pre-1944-r). 18-Last pre-code issue. 19-Bouncer, Rocket Kelly-r	17.00	50.00	125.00
20-Joan Mason by Kamen	21.00	64.00	160.00
21-New material	15.00	44.00	110.00

BLUE BEETLE (Unusual Tales #1-49; Ghostly Tales #55 on)(See Captain Atom #83 & Charlton Bullseye)
Charlton Comics: V2#1, June, 1964 - V2#5, Mar-Apr, 1965; V3#50, July, 1965 - V3#54, Feb-Mar, 1966; #1, June, 1967 - #5, Nov, 1968

	GD25	FN65	NM94
V2#1-Origin/1st S.A. app. Dan Garrett-Blue Beetle	6.00	18.00	60.00
2-5: 5-Weiss illo; 1st published-a?	4.20	12.60	42.00
V3#50-54-Formerly Unusual Tales	4.20	12.60	42.00
1(1967)-Question series begins by Ditko	9.00	27.00	90.00
2-Origin Ted Kord-Blue Beetle (see Capt. Atom #83 for 1st Ted Kord Blue Beetle); Dan Garrett x-over	3.80	11.40	38.00
3-5 (All Ditko-c/a in #1-5)	3.00	9.00	30.00
1,3(Modern Comics-1977)-Reprints			3.00

NOTE: *#6 only appeared in the fanzine 'The Charlton Portfolio.'*

BLUE BEETLE (Also see Americomics, Crisis On Infinite Earths, Justice League & Showcase '94 #2-4)
DC Comics: June, 1986 - No. 24, May, 1988

	GD25	FN65	NM94
1-Origin retold; intro. Firefist			1.00
2-24: 2-Origin Firefist. 5-7-The Question app. 11-14-New Teen Titans x-over. 20-Justice League app. 20,21-Millennium tie-ins			1.00

BLUEBERRY (See Lt. Blueberry & Marshal Blueberry)
Marvel Comics (Epic Comics): 1989 - No. 5, 1990 ($12.95/$14.95, graphic novel)

	GD25	FN65	NM94
1,3,4,5-($12.95)-Moebius-a in all			13.00
2-($14.95)			15.00

BLUE BIRD COMICS
Various Shoe Stores/Charlton Comics: Late 1940's - 1964 (Giveaway)

	GD25	FN65	NM94
nn(1947-50)(36 pgs.)-Several issues; Human Torch, Sub-Mariner app. in some	11.00	32.00	80.00
1959-Li'l Genius, Timmy the Timid Ghost, Wild Bill Hickok (All #1)	1.25	3.75	10.00
1959-(6 titles; all #2) Black Fury #1,4,5, Freddy #4, Li'l Genius, Timmy the Timid Ghost #4, Masked Raider #4, Wild Bill Hickok (Charlton)	1.25	3.75	10.00
1959-(#5) Masked Raider #21	1.25	3.75	10.00
1960-(6 titles)(All #4) Black Fury #8,9, Masked Raider, Freddy #8,9, Timmy the Timid Ghost #9, Li'l Genius #7,9 (Charlt.)	1.25	3.75	10.00
1961,1962-(All #10's) Atomic Mouse #12,13,16, Black Fury #11,12, Freddy, Li'l Genius, Masked Raider, Six Gun Heroes, Texas Rangers in Action, Timmy the Ghost, Wild Bill Hickok, Wyatt Earp #3,11-13,16-18 (Charlton)	1.00	3.00	8.00
1963-Texas Rangers #17 (Charlton)		2.00	5.00
1964-Mysteries of Unexplored Worlds #18, Teenage Hotrodders #18, War Heroes #18 (Charlton)	1.00	2.80	7.00
1965-War Heroes #18			3.00

NOTE: *More than one issue of each character could have been published each year. Numbering is sporadic.*

BLUE BIRD CHILDREN'S MAGAZINE, THE
Graphic Information Service: V1#2, 1957 - No. 10 1958 (16 pgs., soft-c, regular size)

	GD25	FN65	NM94
V1#2-10: Pat, Pete & Blue Bird app.			4.00

BLUE BOLT
Funnies, Inc. No. 1/Novelty Press/Premium Group of Comics: June, 1940 - No. 101 (V10#2), Sept-Oct, 1949

	GD25	FN65	NM94
V1#1-Origin Blue Bolt by Joe Simon, Sub-Zero Man, White Rider & Super Horse, Dick Cole, Wonder Boy & Sgt. Spook (1st app. of each)	271.00	813.00	2300.00
2-Simon & Kirby's 1st art & 1st super-hero (Blue Bolt)	124.00	372.00	1050.00
3-1 pg. Space Hawk by Wolverton; 2nd S&K-a on Blue Bolt (same cover date as Red Raven #1); 1st time S&K names app. in a comic; Simon-c	106.00	318.00	900.00
4,5-S&K-a in each; 5-Everett-a begins on Sub-Zero	100.00	300.00	850.00
6,8-10-S&K-a	88.00	264.00	750.00
7-S&K-c/a	100.00	300.00	850.00
11,12: 11-Robot-c	94.00	282.00	800.00
V2#1-Origin Dick Cole & The Twister; Twister x-over in Dick Cole, Sub-Zero, & Blue Bolt; origin Simba Karno who battles Dick Cole thru V2#5 & becomes main supporting character V2#6 on; battle-c	30.00	90.00	225.00
2-Origin The Twister retold in text	24.00	72.00	180.00
3-5: 5-Intro. Freezum	21.00	63.00	160.00
6-Origin Sgt. Spook retold	17.00	51.00	130.00
7-12: 7-Lois Blake becomes Blue Bolt's costume aide; last Twister. 12-Text-sty by Mickey Spillaine	15.00	45.00	110.00
V3#1-3	12.00	36.00	90.00
4-12: 4-Blue Bolt abandons costume	9.30	28.00	65.00
V4#1-Hitler, Tojo, Mussolini-c	15.00	45.00	115.00
V4#2-12: 3-Shows V4#3 on-c, V4#4 inside (9-10/43). 5-Infinity-c. 8-Last Sub-Zero	7.85	23.50	55.00
V5#1-8, V6#1-3,5-10, V7#1-12	7.15	21.50	50.00
V6#4-Racist cover	8.50	26.00	60.00
V8#1-6,8-12, V9#1-5,7,8	6.50	19.50	45.00

Blue Devil #15 © DC

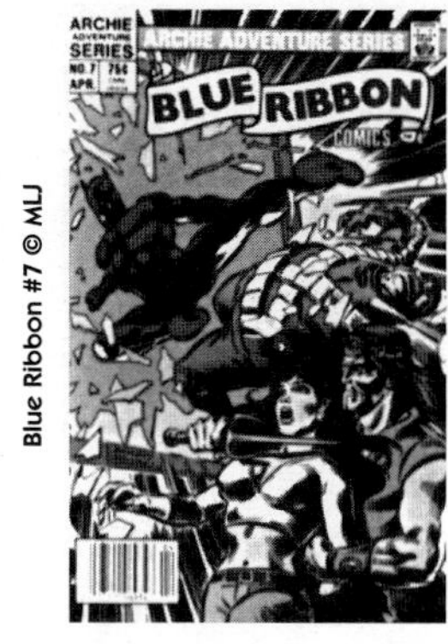

Blue Ribbon #7 © MLJ

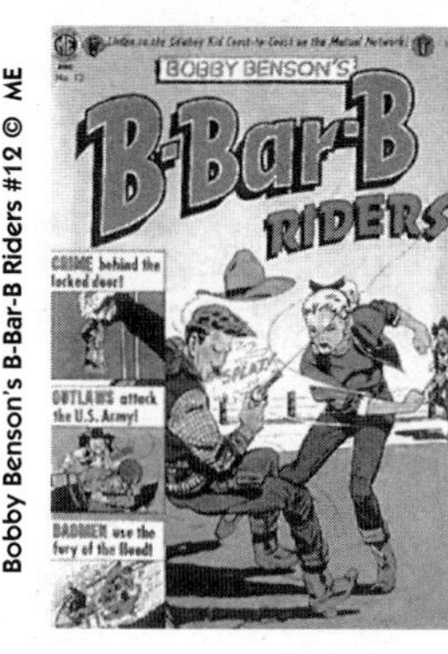

Bobby Benson's B-Bar-B Riders #12 © ME

	GD25	FN65	NM94
V8#7,V9#6,9-L. B. Cole-c	15.00	45.00	110.00
V10#1(#100)	6.50	19.50	45.00
V10#2(#101)-Last Dick Cole, Blue Bolt	6.50	19.50	45.00

NOTE: ***Everett*** *c-V1#4, 11, V2#1, 2.* ***Gustavson*** *a-V1#1-12, V2#1-7.* ***Kiefer*** *c-V3#1.* ***Rico*** *a-V6#10, V7#4. Blue Bolt not in V9#8.*

BLUE BOLT (Becomes Ghostly Weird Stories #120 on; continuation of Novelty Blue Bolt) (...Weird Tales of Terror #111,...Weird Tales #112-119)
Star Publications: No. 102, Nov-Dec, 1949 - No. 119, May-June, 1953

	GD25	FN65	NM94
102-The Chameleon, & Target app.	27.00	80.00	200.00
103,104-The Chameleon app. 104-Last Target	25.00	76.00	190.00
105-Origin Blue Bolt (from #1) retold by Simon; Chameleon & Target app.; opium den story	42.00	127.00	340.00
106-Blue Bolt by S&K begins; Spacehawk reprints from Target by Wolverton begin, ends #110; Sub-Zero begins; ends #109	41.00	122.00	325.00
107-110: 108-Last S&K Blue Bolt reprint. 109-Wolverton-c(r)/inside Spacehawk splash. 110-Target app.	39.00	117.00	310.00
111,112: 111-Red Rocket & The Mask-r; last Blue Bolt; 1pg. L. B. Cole-a 112-Last Torpedo Man app.	37.00	112.00	280.00
113-Wolverton's Spacehawk-r/Target V3#7	39.00	117.00	300.00
114,116: 116-Jungle Jo-r	37.00	112.00	280.00
115-Sgt. Spook app.	39.00	117.00	300.00
117-Jo-Jo & Blue Bolt-r	39.00	116.00	290.00
118-"White Spirit" by Wood	39.00	117.00	300.00
119-Disbrow/Cole-c; Jungle Jo-r	39.00	116.00	290.00
Accepted Reprint #103(1957?, nd)	8.50	26.00	60.00

NOTE: ***L. B. Cole*** *c-102-108, 110 on.* ***Disbrow*** *a-112(2), 113(3), 114(2), 115(2), 116-118.* ***Hollingsworth*** *a-117.* ***Palais*** *a-112r. Sci/Fi c-105-110. Horror c-111.*

BLUE BULLETEER, THE (Also see Femforce Special)
AC Comics: 1989 ($2.25, B&W, one-shot)

	GD25	FN65	NM94
1-Origin by Bill Black; Bill Ward-a			3.00

BLUE BULLETEER (Also see Femforce Special)
AC Comics: 1996 ($5.95, B&W, one-shot)

	GD25	FN65	NM94
1-Photo-c		2.00	6.00

BLUE CIRCLE COMICS (Also see Roly Poly Comic Book)
Enwil Associates/Rural Home: June, 1944 - No. 5, Mar, 1945; No. 6, 1950s

	GD25	FN65	NM94
1-The Blue Circle begins (1st app.); origin & 1st app. Steel Fist	23.00	68.00	170.00
2	16.00	48.00	120.00
3-Hitler parody-c	17.00	52.00	130.00
4-6: 5-Last Steel Fist. 6-(1950s)-Colossal Features-r	9.30	28.00	65.00

BLUE DEVIL (See Fury of Firestorm #24, Underworld Unleashed, Starman #38)
DC Comics: June, 1984 - No. 31, Dec, 1986 (75¢/$1.25)

	GD25	FN65	NM94
1-30: 4-Origin Nebiros. 7-Gil Kane-a. 8-Giffen-a. 17,18-Crisis x-over			1.00
31-($1.25, 52 pgs.)			1.25
Annual 1 (11/85)-Team-ups w/Black Orchid, Creeper, Demon, Madame Xanadu, Man-Bat & Phantom Stranger			1.25

BLUE PHANTOM, THE
Dell Publishing Co.: June-Aug, 1962

	GD25	FN65	NM94
1(01-066-208)-by Fred Fredericks	2.25	6.75	24.00

BLUE RIBBON COMICS (...Mystery Comics No. 9-18)
MLJ Magazines: Nov, 1939 - No. 22, Mar, 1942 (1st MLJ series)

	GD25	FN65	NM94
1-Dan Hastings, Richy the Amazing Boy, Rang-A-Tang the Wonder Dog begin (1st app. of each); Little Nemo app. (not by W. McCay); Jack Cole-a(3)	288.00	864.00	2600.00
2-Bob Phantom, Silver Fox (both in #3), Rang-A-Tang Club & Cpl. Collins begin (1st app. of each); Jack Cole-a	112.00	336.00	950.00
3-J. Cole-a	77.00	231.00	650.00
4-Doc Strong, The Green Falcon, & Hercules begin (1st app. each); origin & 1st app. The Fox & Ty-Gor, Son of the Tiger	82.00	246.00	700.00
5-8: 8-Last Hercules; 6,7-Biro, Meskin-a. 7-Fox app. on-c	58.00	174.00	490.00
9-(Scarce)-Origin & 1st app. Mr. Justice (2/41)	233.00	700.00	2100.00
10-13: 12-Last Doc Strong. 13-Inferno, the Flame Breather begins, ends #19; Devil-c	88.00	264.00	750.00
14,15,17,18: 15-Last Green Falcon	76.00	228.00	650.00
16-Origin & 1st app. Captain Flag (9/41)	150.00	450.00	1275.00
19-22: 20-Last Ty-Gor. 22-Origin Mr. Justice retold	76.00	228.00	650.00

NOTE: ***Biro*** *c-3-5; a-2 (Cpl. Collins & Scoop Cody).* ***S. Cooper*** *c-9-17. 20-22 contain "Tales From the Witch's Cauldron" (same strip as "Stories of the Black Witch" in Zip Comics). Mr. Justice c-9-18. Captain Flag c-16(w/Mr. Justice), 19-22.*

BLUE RIBBON COMICS (Becomes Teen-Age Diary Secrets #4)(See Heckle & Jeckle)
Blue Ribbon (St. John): Feb, 1949 - No. 6, Aug, 1949

	GD25	FN65	NM94
1,3-Heckle & Jeckle	7.85	23.50	55.00
2(4/49)-Diary Secrets; Baker-c	17.00	50.00	125.00
4(6/49)-Teen-Age Diary Secrets; Baker c/a(2)	17.00	52.00	130.00
5(8/49)-Teen-Age Diary Secrets; Oversize; photo-c; Baker-a(2)- Continues as Teen-Age Diary Secrets	22.00	66.00	165.00
6-Dinky Duck(8/49)	4.00	11.00	22.00

BLUE-RIBBON COMICS
Red Circle Prod./Archie Ent. No. 5 on: Nov, 1983 - No. 14, Dec, 1984

	GD25	FN65	NM94
1-S&K-r/Advs. of the Fly #1,2; Williamson/Torres-r/Fly #2; Ditko-c			3.00
2-14: 3-Origin Steel Sterling. 5-S&K Shield-r. 6,7-The Fox app. 8-Toth centerspread. 8,11-Black Hood. 12-Thunder Agents. 13-Thunder Bunny. 14-Web & Jaguar			2.00

NOTE: ***N. Adams*** *a(r)-8.* ***Buckler*** *a-4i.* ***Nino*** *a-2i.* ***McWilliams*** *a-8.* ***Morrow*** *a-8.*

BLUE STREAK (See Holyoke One-Shot No. 8)

BLYTHE (Marge's)
Dell Publishing Co.: No. 1072, Jan-Mar, 1960

	GD25	FN65	NM94
Four Color 1072	4.50	13.50	50.00

B-MAN (See Double-Dare Adventures)

BO (Tom Cat #4 on) (Also see Big Shot #29 & Dixie Dugan)
Charlton Comics Group: June, 1955 - No. 3, Oct, 1955 (A dog)

	GD25	FN65	NM94
1-3: Newspaper reprints by Frank Beck	6.00	18.00	42.00

BOATNIKS, THE (See Walt Disney Showcase No. 1)

BOB & BETTY & SANTA'S WISHING WHISTLE
Sears Roebuck & Co.: 1941 (Christmas giveaway, 12 pgs.)

	GD25	FN65	NM94
nn	8.50	26.00	60.00

BOBBY BENSON'S B-BAR-B RIDERS (Radio) (See Best of The West, The Lemonade Kid & Model Fun)
Magazine Enterprises/AC Comics: May-June, 1950 - No. 20, May-June, 1953

	GD25	FN65	NM94
1-The Lemonade Kid begins; Powell-a (Scarce)	42.00	126.00	335.00
2	15.00	44.00	110.00
3-5: 4,5-Lemonade Kid-c (#4-Spider-c)	11.00	34.00	85.00
6-8,10	10.00	30.00	75.00
9,11,13-Frazetta-c; Ghost Rider in #13-15 by Ayers-a. 13-Ghost Rider-c	29.00	86.00	215.00
12,17-20: 20-(A-1 #88)	9.30	28.00	70.00
14-Decapitation/Bondage-c & story; classic horror-c	17.00	52.00	130.00
15-Ghost Rider-c	13.00	40.00	100.00
16-Photo-c	11.00	34.00	85.00
...in the Tunnel of Gold-(1936, 5-1/4x8"; 100 pgs.) Radio giveaway by Hecker-H.O. Company(H.O. Oats); contains 22 color pgs. of comics, rest in novel form	9.15	27.50	55.00
...And The Lost Herd-same as above	9.15	27.50	55.00
1 (1990, $2.75, B&W)-Reprints; photo-c & inside covers			2.75

NOTE: ***Ayers*** *a-13-15, 20.* ***Powell*** *a-1-12(4 ea.), 13(3), 14-16(Red Hawk only); c-1-8,1 0, 12. Lemonade Kid in most 1-13.*

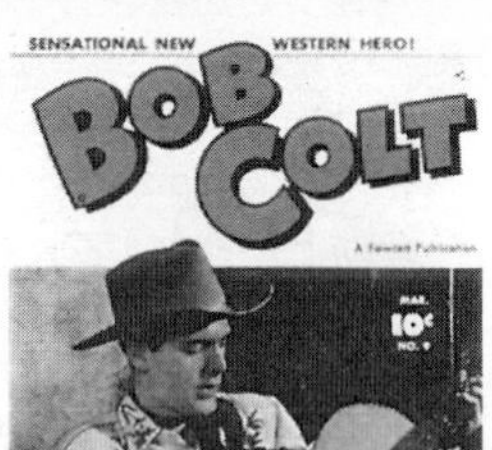

Bob Colt #9 © FAW

Body Doubles #1 © DC

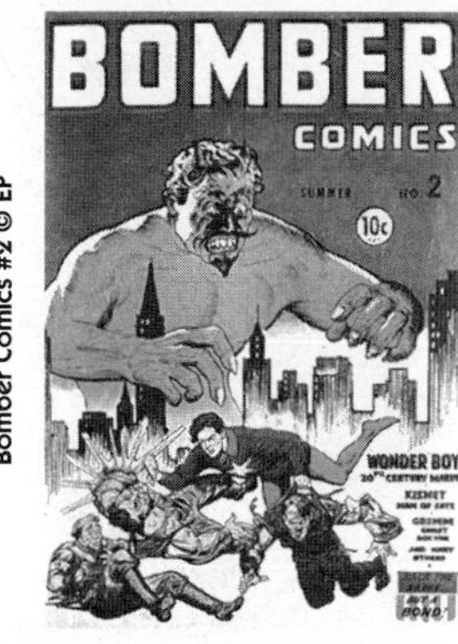

Bomber Comics #2 © EP

	GD25	FN65	NM94

BOBBY COMICS
Universal Phoenix Features: May, 1946

1-By S. M. Iger	6.50	19.50	45.00

BOBBY SHELBY COMICS
Shelby Cycle Co./Harvey Publications: 1949

nn	3.20	8.00	16.00

BOBBY SHERMAN (TV)
Charlton Comics: Feb, 1972 - No. 7, Oct, 1972

1-Based on TV show "Getting Together"	2.90	8.70	32.00
2-7: 4-Photo-c	2.20	6.25	22.00

BOB COLT (Movie star)(See XMas Comics)
Fawcett Publications: Nov, 1950 - No. 10, May, 1952

1-Bob Colt, his horse Buckskin & sidekick Pablo begin; photo front/back-c begin	42.00	127.00	340.00
2	27.00	80.00	200.00
3-5	21.00	64.00	160.00
6-Flying Saucer story	19.00	56.00	140.00
7-10: 9-Last photo back-c	17.00	52.00	130.00

BOB HOPE (See Adventures of... & Calling All Boys #12)

BOB MARLEY, TALE OF THE TUFF GONG (Music star)
Marvel Comics: Aug, 1994 - No, 3, Nov, 1994 ($5.95, limited series)

1-3		2.00	6.00

BOB POWELL'S TIMELESS TALES
Eclipse Comics: March, 1989 ($2.00, B&W)

1-Powell-r/Black Cat #5 (Scarlet Arrow), 9 & Race for the Moon #1			2.00

BOB SCULLY, THE TWO-FISTED HICK DETECTIVE (Also see Advs. of Detective Ace King and Detective Dan)
Humor Publ. Co.: No date (1933) (36 pgs., 9-1/2x11", B&W, paper-c; 10¢-c)

nn-By Howard Dell; not reprints	75.00	225.00	600.00

BOB SON OF BATTLE
Dell Publishing Co.: No. 729, Nov, 1956

Four Color 729	2.75	8.00	30.00

BOB STEELE WESTERN (Movie star)
Fawcett Publications/AC Comics: Dec, 1950 - No. 10, June, 1952; 1990

1-Bob Steele & his horse Bullet begin; photo front/back-c begin	52.00	156.00	440.00
2	29.00	87.00	220.00
3-5: 4-Last photo back-c	23.00	69.00	170.00
6-10: 10-Last photo-c	17.00	51.00	130.00
1 (1990, $2.75, B&W)-Bob Steele & Rocky Lane reprints; photo-c & inside covers			2.75

BOB SWIFT (Boy Sportsman)
Fawcett Publications: May, 1951 - No. 5, Jan, 1952

1	7.85	23.50	55.00
2-5: Saunders painted-c #1-5	5.00	15.00	30.00

BOB, THE GALACTIC BUM
DC Comics: Feb, 1995 - No. 4, June, 1995 ($1.95, limited series)

1-4: 1-Lobo app.			2.00

BODY BAGS
Dark Horse Comics (Blanc Noir): Sept, 1996 - No. 4, Jan, 1997 ($2.95, mini-series, mature)(1st Blanc Noir series)

1-Jason Pearson-c/a/scripts in all. 1-Intro Clownface & Panda.	.90	2.70	8.00
2	1.00	3.00	10.00
3,4		2.00	6.00

BODYCOUNT (Also see Casey Jones & Raphael)
Image Comics (Highbrow Entertainment): Mar, 1996 - No. 4, July, 1996 ($2.50, limited series)

1-4: Kevin Eastman-a(p)/scripts; Simon Bisley-c/a(i); Turtles app.			2.50

BODY DOUBLES (VILLAINS) (See Resurrection Man)
DC Comics: Feb, 1998 ($1.95, one-shot)

1-Pearson-c; Deadshot app.			2.00

BOHOS
Image Comics (Flypaper Press): June, 1998 - Present ($2.95)

1-3-Whorf-s/Penaranda-a			3.00

BOLD ADVENTURES
Pacific Comics: Oct, 1983 - No. 3, June, 1984 ($1.50)

1-Time Force, Anaconda, & The Weirdling begin			1.50
2,3: 2-Soldiers of Fortune begins. 3-Spitfire			1.50

NOTE: ***Kaluta** c-3. **Nebres** a-1-3. **Nino** a-2, 3. **Severin** a-3.*

BOLD STORIES (Also see Candid Tales & It Rhymes With Lust)
Kirby Publishing Co.: Mar, 1950 - July, 1950 (Digest size, 144 pgs.)

Mar issue (Very Rare) - Contains "The Ogre of Paris" by Wood	111.00	332.00	940.00
May issue (Very Rare) - Contains "The Cobra's Kiss" by Graham Ingels (21 pgs.)	94.00	282.00	800.00
July issue (Very Rare) - Contains "The Ogre of Paris" by Wood	82.00	246.00	700.00

BOLT AND STAR FORCE SIX
Americomics: 1984 ($1.75)

1-Origin Bolt & Star Force Six			2.00
Special 1 (1984, $2.00, 52pgs., B&W)			2.00

BOMBARDIER (See Bee 29, the Bombardier & Cinema Comics Herald)

BOMBAST
Topps Comics: 1993 ($2.95, one-shot) (Created by Jack Kirby)

1-Polybagged w/Kirbychrome trading card; Savage Dragon app.; Kirby-c; has coupon for Amberchrome Secret City Saga #0			3.00

BOMBA THE JUNGLE BOY (TV)
National Periodical Publ.: Sept-Oct, 1967 - No. 7, Sept-Oct, 1968 (12¢)

1-Intro. Bomba; Infantino/Anderson-c	2.50	7.50	20.00
2-7	1.60	5.25	14.00

BOMBER COMICS
Elliot Publ. Co./Melverne Herald/Farrell/Sunrise Times: Mar, 1944 - No. 4, Winter, 1944-45

1-Wonder Boy, & Kismet, Man of Fate begin	53.00	159.00	450.00
2,3: 2-Hitler-c. 2-4-Have Classics Comics ad to HRN 20.	33.00	100.00	250.00
4-Hitler, Tojo & Mussolini-c; Sensation Comics #13-c/swipe; has Classics Comics ad to HRN 20.	40.00	120.00	320.00

BONANZA (TV)
Dell/Gold Key: June-Aug, 1960 - No. 37, Aug, 1970 (All Photo-c)

Four Color 1110 (6-8/60)	34.00	102.00	375.00
Four Color 1221,1283, & #01070-207, 01070-210	16.00	49.00	180.00
1(12/62-Gold Key)	17.00	52.00	190.00
2	8.75	26.50	95.00
3-10	7.00	20.00	75.00
11-20	5.50	16.50	60.00
21-37: 29-Reprints	4.50	13.50	50.00

BONE
Cartoon Books/Image Comics #21 on: July, 1991 - Present ($2.95, B&W)

1-Jeff Smith-c/a in all	7.00	21.00	75.00
1-2nd printing	1.20	3.60	12.00
1-3rd thru 5th printings			4.00

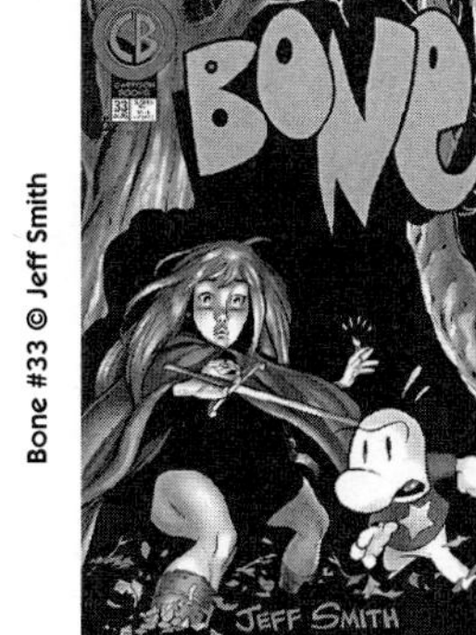

Bone #33 © Jeff Smith

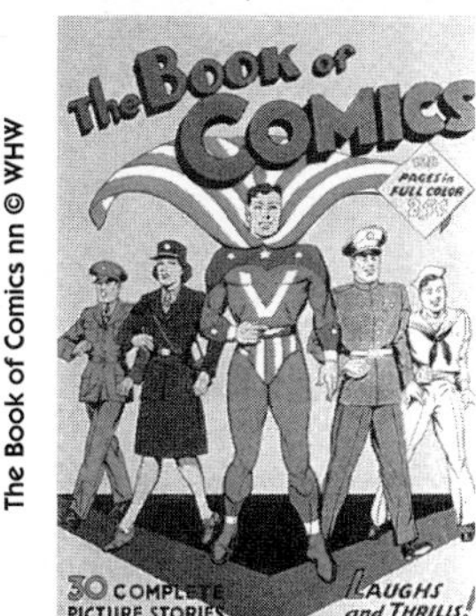

The Book of Comics nn © WHW

Books of Magic #50 © DC

	GD25	FN65	NM94
2-1st printing	4.00	12.25	45.00
2-2nd & 3rd printings			5.00
3-1st printing	3.20	9.50	35.00
3-2nd thru 4th printings			4.00
4,5	1.50	4.50	15.00
6-8	1.00	3.00	10.00
9,10	.85	2.60	7.00
11,12			3.00
13-20			2.50
13 1/2	.90	2.70	8.00
13 1/2 (Gold)	1.00	3.00	10.00
21,22: 21-1st Image issue ($2.95)			2.50
23-34			3.00
1-24-($2.95): 1-Image reprints begin w/new-c. 2-Allred pin-up.			3.00
Holiday Special (1993, giveaway)			3.00
Sourcebook-San Diego Edition	.85	2.60	7.00
Complete Bone Adventures Vol 1 (1993, $12.95, r/#1-6)	1.30	3.90	13.00
Complete Bone Adventures Vol 2 (1994, $12.95, r/#7-12)	1.30	3.90	13.00
Volume 1-($19.95, hard-c)-"Out From Boneville"			20.00
Volume 1-($12.95, soft-c)			13.00
Volume 2-($22.95, hard-c)-"The Great Cow Race"			23.00
Volume 2-($14.95, soft-c)			15.00
Volume 3-($24.95, hard-c)-"Eyes of the Storm"			25.00
Volume 3-($16.95, soft-c)			17.00
Volume 4-($24.95, hard-c)-"The Dragonslayer"			25.00
Volume 4-($16.95, soft-c)			17.00
Volume 5-($22.95, hard-c)-"Rock Jaw"			23.00
Volume 5-($14.95, soft-c)			15.00

NOTE: *Printings not listed sell for cover price.*

BONGO (See Story Hour Series)

BONGO & LUMPJAW (Disney, see Walt Disney Showcase #3)
Dell Publishing Co.: No. 706, June, 1956; No. 886, Mar, 1958

	GD25	FN65	NM94
Four Color 706 (#1)	4.50	13.50	50.00
Four Color 886	3.80	11.50	40.00

BON VOYAGE (See Movie Classics)

BOOF
Image Comics (Todd McFarlane Prod.): July, 1994 - No. 6, Dec, 1994 ($1.95)

	GD25	FN65	NM94
1-6			2.00

BOOF AND THE BRUISE CREW
Image Comics (Todd McFarlane Prod.): July, 1994 - No. 6, Dec, 1994 ($1.95)

	GD25	FN65	NM94
1-6			2.00

BOOK AND RECORD SET (See Power Record Comics)

BOOK OF ALL COMICS
William H. Wise: 1945 (196 pgs.)(Inside f/c has Green Publ. blacked out)

	GD25	FN65	NM94
nn-Green Mask, Puppeteer & The Bouncer	35.00	104.00	260.00

BOOK OF ANTS, THE
Artisan Entertainment: 1998 ($2.95, B&W)

	GD25	FN65	NM94
1-Based on the movie Pi; Aronofsky-s			2.95

BOOK OF BALLADS AND SAGAS, THE
Green Man Press: Oct, 1995 - Present ($2.95/$3.50/$3.25, B&W)

	GD25	FN65	NM94
1,2: 1-Vess-c/a; Gaiman story.			3.00
3-($3.50)			3.50
4-($3.25)			3.25

BOOK OF COMICS, THE
William H. Wise: No date (1944) (25¢, 132 pgs.)

	GD25	FN65	NM94
nn-Captain V app.	35.00	104.00	260.00

BOOK OF FATE, THE (See Fate)
DC Comics: Feb, 1997 - Present ($2.25/$2.50)

	GD25	FN65	NM94
1-7: 4-Two-Face-c/app. 6-Convergence			2.25
8-11: 8-Begin 2.50-c. 11-Sentinel app.			2.50

BOOK OF LOVE (See Fox Giants)

BOOK OF NIGHT, THE
Dark Horse Comics: July, 1987 - No. 3, 1987 ($1.75, B&W)

	GD25	FN65	NM94
1-3: Reprints from Epic Illustrated; Vess-a			1.80

BOOK OF THE DEAD
Marvel Comics: Dec, 1993 - No. 4, Mar, 1994 ($1.75, limited series, 52 pgs.)

	GD25	FN65	NM94
1-4: 1-Ploog Frankenstein & Morrow Man-Thing-r begin; Wrightson-r/Chamber of Darkness #7. 2-Morrow new painted-c; Chaykin/Morrow Man-Thing; Krigstein-r/Uncanny Tales #54; r/Fear #10. 3-r/Astonishing Tales #10 & Starlin Man-Thing. 3,4-Painted-c			3.00

BOOKS OF FAERIE, THE
DC Comics (Vertigo): Mar, 1997 - No. 3, May,1997 ($2.50, limited series)

	GD25	FN65	NM94
1-3-Gross-a			2.50
TPB (1998, $14.95) r/#1-3 & Arcana Annual #1			14.95

BOOKS OF FAERIE, THE :AUBERON'S TALE
DC Comics (Vertigo): Aug, 1998 - No. 3, Oct,1998 ($2.50, limited series)

	GD25	FN65	NM94
1-3-Gross-a			2.50

BOOKS OF MAGIC
DC Comics: 1990 - No. 4, 1991 ($3.95, 52 pgs., limited series, mature)

	GD25	FN65	NM94
1-Bolton painted-c/a; Phantom Stranger app.; Gaiman scripts in all	.90	2.70	8.50
2,3: 2-John Constantine, Dr. Fate, Spectre, Deadman app. 3-Dr. Occult app.; minor Sandman app.			5.25
4-Early Death-c/app. (early 1991)		2.10	6.25
Trade paperback-($19.95)-Reprints limited series			20.00

BOOKS OF MAGIC
DC Comics (Vertigo): May, 1994 - Present ($1.95/$2.50, mature)

	GD25	FN65	NM94
1-Charles Vess-c			4.00
1-Platinum	.90	2.70	8.00
2,3			4.00
4-Death app.			5.00
5-14; Charles Vess-c			2.50
15-50: 15-$2.50-c begins. 22-Kaluta-c. 25-Death-c/app; Bachalo-c			2.50
51-57: 51-Peter Gross-s/a begins. 55-Medley-a			2.50
Annual 1 (2/97, $3.95)			4.00
Annual 2 (2/98, $3.95)			4.00
Bindings (1995, $12.95, TPB)-r/#1-4			13.00
Reckonings (1997, $12.95, TPB)-r/#14-20			13.00
Summonings (1996, $17.50, TPB)-r/#5-13, Vertigo Rave #1			17.50
Transformations (1998, $12.95, TPB)-r/#21-25			12.95

BOONDOGGLE
Knight Press: Mar, 1995 - No. 4 ($2.95, B&W)

	GD25	FN65	NM94
1-4: Stegelin-c/a/scripts			3.00

BOONDOGGLE
Caliber Press: Jan, 1997 - Present ($2.95, B&W)

	GD25	FN65	NM94
1,2: Stegelin-c/a/scripts			3.00

BOOSTER GOLD (See Justice League #4)
DC Comics: Feb, 1986 - No. 25, Feb, 1988 (75¢)

	GD25	FN65	NM94
1-25: 4-Rose & Thorn app. 6-Origin. 6,7,23-Superman app. 8,9-LSH app. 22-JLI app. 24,25-Millennium tie-ins			1.00

NOTE: ***Austin*** *c-22i.* ***Byrne*** *c-23i.*

BOOTS AND HER BUDDIES

Boots and Her Buddies #7 © STD

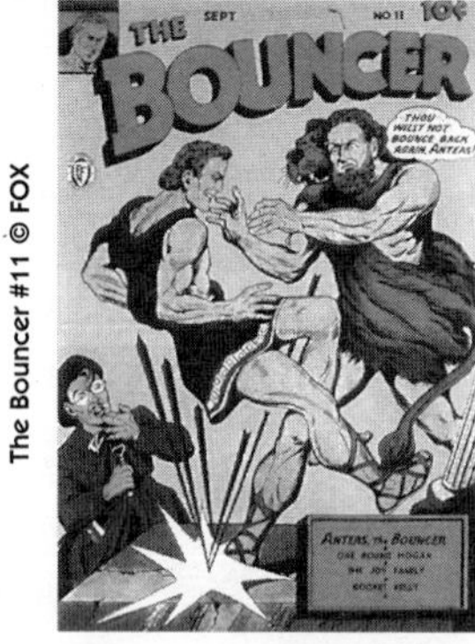

The Bouncer #11 © FOX

Boy Comics #11 © LEV

	GD25	FN65	NM94

Standard Comics/Visual Editions/Argo (NEA Service): No. 5, 9/48 - No. 9, 9/49; 12/55 - No. 3, 1956

	GD25	FN65	NM94
5-Strip-r	14.00	42.00	105.00
6,8	9.30	28.00	70.00
7-(Scarce)-Spanking panels(3)	11.00	32.00	80.00
9-(Scarce)-Frazetta-a (2 pgs.)	23.00	70.00	175.00
1-3(Argo-1955-56)-Reprints	5.00	15.00	30.00

BOOTS & SADDLES (TV)
Dell Publ. Co.: No. 919, July, 1958; No. 1029, Sept, 1959; No. 1116, Aug, 1960

	GD25	FN65	NM94
Four Color 919 (#1)-Photo-c	7.00	22.00	80.00
Four Color 1029, 1116-Photo-c	4.50	13.50	50.00

BORDERLINE
Friction Press: June, 1992 ($2.25, B&W)

	GD25	FN65	NM94
0-Ashcan edition; 1st app. of Cliff Broadway			2.00
1-Painted-c			3.00
1-Special Edition (bagged w/ photo, S&N)			4.00

BORDER PATROL
P. L. Publishing Co.: May-June, 1951 - No. 3, Sept-Oct, 1951

	GD25	FN65	NM94
1	10.00	30.00	75.00
2,3	7.15	21.50	50.00

BORDER WORLDS (Also see Megaton Man)
Kitchen Sink Press: 7/86 - No. 7, 1987; V2#1, 1990 - No. 4, 1990 ($1.95-$2.00, B&W, mature)

	GD25	FN65	NM94
1-7: ($1.95)-Donald Simpson-c/a/scripts			2.00
V2#1-4 ($2.00)-Donald Simpson-c/a/scripts			2.00

BORIS KARLOFF TALES OF MYSTERY (TV) (...Thriller No. 1,2)
Gold Key: No. 3, April, 1963 - No. 97, Feb, 1980

	GD25	FN65	NM94
3-8,10-(Two #5's, 10/63,11/63): 5-(10/63)-11 pgs. Toth-a. 10-Orlando-a	2.50	7.50	22.00
9-Wood-a	2.50	7.50	26.00
11-Williamson-a, 8 pgs.; Orlando-a, 5 pgs.	2.50	7.50	26.00
12-Torres, McWilliams-a; Orlando-a(2)	2.25	6.75	20.00
13,14,16-20	1.75	5.75	16.00
15-Crandall	2.00	6.00	18.00
21-Jeff Jones-a(3 pgs.) "The Screaming Skull"	2.00	6.00	18.00
22-30: 23-Reprint; photo-c	1.25	3.75	12.00
31-50: 36-Weiss-a	.90	2.70	8.00
51-74: 74-Origin & 1st app. Taurus		2.00	6.00
75-79,87-97: 90-r/Torres, McWilliams-a/#12; Morrow-c			4.00
80-86-(52 pgs.)	.85	2.60	7.00
Story Digest 1(7/70-Gold Key)-All text	2.40	7.00	26.00

(See Mystery Comics Digest No. 2, 5, 8, 11, 14, 17, 20, 23, 26)
NOTE: ***Bolle** a-51-54, 56, 58, 59. **McWilliams** a-12, 14, 18, 19, 72, 80, 81, 93. **Orlando** a-11-15, 21. Reprints: 78, 81-86, 88, 90, 92, 95, 97.*

BORIS KARLOFF THRILLER (TV) (Becomes Boris Karloff Tales...)
Gold Key: Oct, 1962 - No. 2, Jan, 1963 (80 pgs.)

	GD25	FN65	NM94
1-Photo-c	5.50	16.50	60.00
2	4.00	12.00	45.00

BORIS THE BEAR
Dark Horse Comics/Nicotat Comics #13 on: Aug, 1986 - No. 34, 1990 ($1.50/$1.75/$1.95, B&W)

	GD25	FN65	NM94
1			3.00
1-2nd printing			1.50
2,3,4A,4B,5-12: 8-(44 pgs.)			2.00
13-1st Nicotat Comics issue			4.00
14-24			2.00
25-29			4.00
30-34			5.00
Annual 1 (1988, $2.50)			3.00

BORIS THE BEAR INSTANT COLOR CLASSICS
Dark Horse Comics: July, 1987 - No. 3, 1987 ($1.75/$1.95)

	GD25	FN65	NM94
1-3			2.00

BORN AGAIN
Spire Christian Comics (Fleming H. Revell Co.): 1978 (39¢)

	GD25	FN65	NM94
nn-Watergate, Nixon, etc.			3.00

BOUNCER, THE (Formerly Green Mask #9)
Fox Features Syndicate: 1944 - No. 14, Jan, 1945

	GD25	FN65	NM94
nn(1944, #10?)	23.00	68.00	170.00
11(#1)(9/44)-Origin; Rocket Kelly, One Round Hogan app.	19.00	56.00	140.00
12-14: 14-Reprints no # issue	15.00	44.00	110.00

BOUNTY GUNS (See Luke Short's..., Four Color 739)

BOX OFFICE POISON
Antarctic Press: 1996 - Present ($2.95, B&W)

	GD25	FN65	NM94
1-Alex Robinson-s/a in all			4.00
2-11			3.00
...Super Special 0 (5/97, $4.95)			4.95
Sherman's March: Collected BOP Vol. 1 (9/98, $14.95) r/#0-4			14.95

BOY AND HIS 'BOT, A
Now Comics: Jan, 1987 ($1.95)

	GD25	FN65	NM94
1-A Holiday Special			2.00

BOY AND THE PIRATES, THE (Movie)
Dell Publishing Co.: No. 1117, Aug, 1960

	GD25	FN65	NM94
Four Color 1117-Photo-c	5.50	16.50	60.00

BOY COMICS (Captain Battle No. 1 & 2; Boy Illustories No. 43-108) (Stories by Charles Biro)(Also see Squeeks)
Lev Gleason Publ. (Comic House): No. 3, Apr, 1942 - No. 119, Mar, 1956

	GD25	FN65	NM94
3(No.1)-Origin Crimebuster, Bombshell & Young Robin Hood; Yankee Longago, Case 1001-1008, Swoop Storm, & Boy Movies begin; 1st app. Iron Jaw; Crimebuster's pet monkey Squeeks begins	271.00	810.00	2300.00
4-Hitler, Tojo, Mussolini-c	106.00	318.00	900.00
5	79.00	237.00	675.00
6-Origin Iron Jaw; origin & death of Iron Jaw's son; Little Dynamite begins, ends #39; 1st Iron Jaw-c	212.00	636.00	1800.00
7-Flag & Hitler, Tojo, Mussolini-c	74.00	222.00	625.00
8-Death of Iron Jaw; Iron Jaw-c	79.00	237.00	675.00
9-Iron Jaw-c	71.00	213.00	600.00
10-Return of Iron Jaw; classic Biro-c; Iron Jaw-c	106.00	318.00	900.00
11-Classic Iron Jaw-c	68.00	204.00	575.00
12,13	49.00	147.00	420.00
14-Iron Jaw-c	52.00	156.00	440.00
15-Death of Iron Jaw	64.00	192.00	540.00
16,18-20	33.00	100.00	250.00
17-Flag-c	37.00	111.00	275.00
21-29,31,32-(All 68 pgs.). 28-Yankee Longago ends. 32-Swoop Storm & Young Robin Hood end	22.00	66.00	165.00
30-(68 pgs.)-Origin Crimebuster retold	32.00	96.00	240.00
33-40: 34-Crimebuster story(2); suicide-c/story	16.00	48.00	120.00
41-50	14.00	42.00	105.00
51-59: 57-Dilly Duncan begins, ends #71	13.00	38.00	95.00
60-Iron Jaw returns	14.00	42.00	105.00
61-Origin Crimebuster & Iron Jaw retold	16.00	48.00	120.00
62-Death of Iron Jaw explained	15.00	44.00	110.00
63-73: 63-McWilliams-a. 73-Frazetta 1-pg. ad	11.00	32.00	80.00
74-88: 80-1st app. Rocky X of the Rocketeers; becomes "Rocky X" #101; Iron Jaw, Sniffer & the Deadly Dozen in 80-118	9.30	28.00	65.00
89-92-The Claw serial app. in all	9.30	28.00	70.00
93-Claw cameo; Rocky X by Sid Check	9.30	28.00	65.00

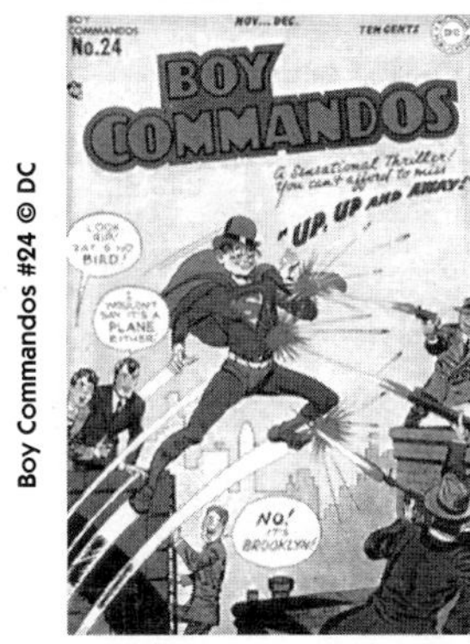

Boy Commandos #24 © DC

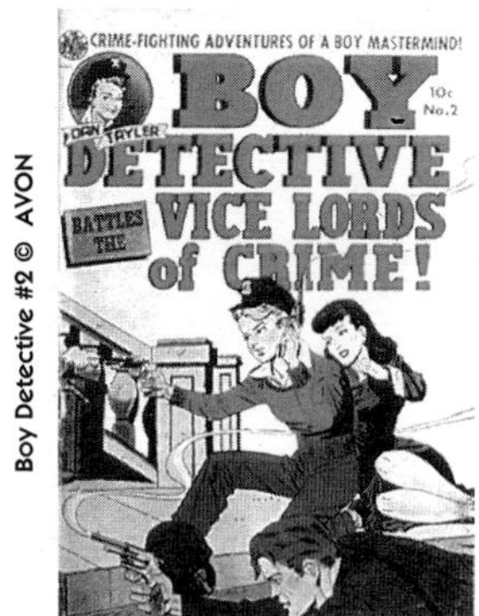

Boy Detective #2 © AVON

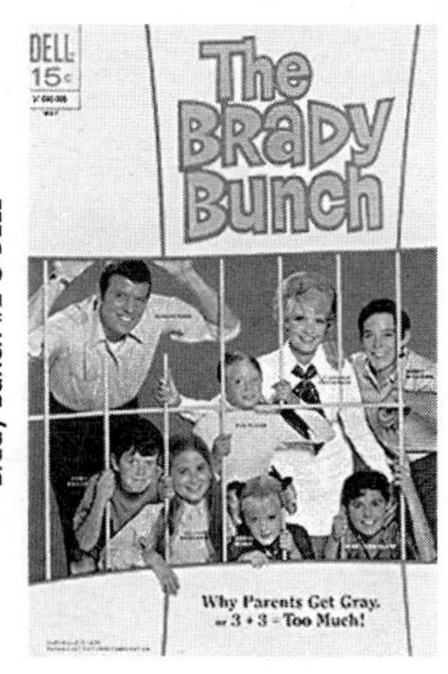

Brady Bunch #2 © DELL

	GD25	FN65	NM94
94-97,99	8.50	26.00	60.00
98-Rocky X by Sid Check	9.30	28.00	65.00
100	9.30	28.00	65.00
101-107,109,111,119: 111-Crimebuster becomes Chuck Chandler. 119-Last Crimebuster	7.15	21.50	50.00
108,110,112-118-Kubert-a	8.50	26.00	60.00

(See Giant Boy Book of Comics)

NOTE: *Boy Movies in 3-5,40,41. Iron Jaw app.-3, 4, 6, 8, 10, 11, 13-15; returns-60-62, 68, 69, 72-79, 81-118.* ***Biro*** *c-all.* ***Briefer*** *a-5, 13, 14, 16-20 among others.* ***Fuje*** *a-55, 18 pgs.* ***Palais*** *a-14, 16, 17, 19, 20 among others.*

BOY COMMANDOS (See Detective #64 & World's Finest Comics #8)
National Periodical Publications: Winter, 1942-43 - No. 36, Nov-Dec, 1949

	GD25	FN65	NM94
1-Origin Liberty Belle; The Sandman & The Newsboy Legion x-over in Boy Commandos; S&K-a, 48 pgs.; S&K cameo? (classic-c)	450.00	1350.00	4500.00
2-Last Liberty Belle; Hitler-c; S&K-a, 46 pgs.	141.00	423.00	1200.00
3-S&K-a, 45 pgs.	94.00	282.00	800.00
4-6: 6-S&K-a	65.00	195.00	550.00
7-10	44.00	132.00	375.00
11-Infinity-c	33.00	100.00	250.00
12-14,16,18-19-More S&K	25.00	76.00	190.00
15-1st app. Crazy Quilt, their arch nemesis	27.00	80.00	200.00
17,20-Sci/fi-c/stories	28.00	84.00	210.00
21,22,25: 22-Judy Canova x-over	19.00	58.00	145.00
23-S&K-c/a(all)	23.00	70.00	175.00
24-1st costumed superhero satire-c (11-12/47).	23.00	68.00	170.00
26-Flying Saucer story (3-4/48)-4th of this theme	21.00	64.00	160.00
27,28,30: 30-Cleveland Indians story	19.00	56.00	140.00
29-S&K story (1)	21.00	62.00	155.00
31-35: 32-Dale Evans app. on-c & in story. 34-Intro. Wolf, their mascot	18.00	54.00	135.00
36-Intro The Atomobile c/sci-fi story (Scarce)	29.00	88.00	220.00

NOTE: *Most issues signed by* ***Simon & Kirby*** *are not by them.* ***S&K*** *c-1-9, 13, 14, 17, 21, 23, 24, 30-32.* ***Feller*** *c-30.*

BOY COMMANDOS
National Per. Publ.: Sept-Oct, 1973 - No. 2, Nov-Dec, 1973 (G.A. S&K reprints)

	GD25	FN65	NM94
1,2: 1-Reprints story from Boy Commandos #1 plus-c & Detective #66 by S&K. 2-Infantino/Orlando-c	.90	2.70	8.00

BOY COWBOY (Also see Amazing Adventures & Science Comics)
Ziff-Davis Publ. Co.: 1950 (8 pgs. in color)

nn-Sent to subscribers of Ziff-Davis mags. & ordered through mail for 10¢; used to test market for Kid Cowboy Estimated value 150.00

BOY DETECTIVE
Avon Periodicals: May-June, 1951 - No. 4, May, 1952

	GD25	FN65	NM94
1	16.00	48.00	120.00
2,3: 3-Kinstler-c	9.30	28.00	70.00
4-Kinstler-c	13.00	38.00	95.00

BOY EXPLORERS COMICS (Terry and The Pirates No. 3 on)
Family Comics (Harvey Publ.): May-June, 1946 - No. 2, Sept-Oct, 1946

	GD25	FN65	NM94
1-Intro The Explorers, Duke of Broadway, Calamity Jane & Danny Dixon... Cadet; S&K-c/a, 24 pgs.	53.00	159.00	450.00

2-(Scarce)-Small size (5-1/2x8-1/2"; B&W; 32 pgs.) Distributed to mail subscribers only; S&K-a Estimated value $250.00-$400.00

(Also see All New No. 15, Flash Gordon No. 5, and Stuntman No. 3)

BOY ILLUSTORIES (See Boy Comics)

BOY LOVES GIRL (Boy Meets Girl No. 1-24)
Lev Gleason Publications: No. 25, July, 1952 - No. 57, June, 1956

	GD25	FN65	NM94
25(#1)	5.70	17.00	35.00
26,27,29-33: 30-33-Serial, 'Loves of My Life	4.00	10.00	20.00
34-42: 39-Lingerie panels	3.60	9.00	18.00
28-Drug propaganda story	4.15	12.50	25.00
43-Toth-a	5.70	17.00	35.00
44-50: 50-Last pre-code (2/55)	2.80	7.00	14.00
51-57: 57-Ann Brewster-a	2.00	5.00	10.00

BOY MEETS GIRL (Boy Loves Girl No. 25 on)
Lev Gleason Publications: Feb, 1950 - No. 24, June, 1952 (No. 1-17: 52 pgs.)

	GD25	FN65	NM94
1-Guardineer-a	6.50	19.50	45.00
2	4.15	12.50	25.00
3-10	4.00	11.00	22.00
11-24	3.60	9.00	18.00

NOTE: ***Briefer*** *a-24.* ***Fuje*** *c-3,7. Painted-c 1-17. Photo-c 19-21, 23.*

BOYS' AND GIRLS' MARCH OF COMICS (See March of Comics)

BOYS' RANCH (Also see Western Tales & Witches' Western Tales)
Harvey Publ.: Oct, 1950 - No. 6, Aug, 1951 (No.1-3, 52 pgs.; No. 4-6, 36 pgs.)

	GD25	FN65	NM94
1-S&K-c/a(3)	56.00	168.00	475.00
2-S&K-c/a(3)	41.00	123.00	325.00
3-S&K-c/a(2); Meskin-a	39.00	117.00	290.00
4-S&K-c/a, 5 pgs.	33.00	100.00	250.00
5,6-S&K-c, splashes & centerspread only; Meskin-a	19.00	56.00	140.00
Shoe Store Giveaway #5,6 (Identical to regular issues except S&K centerfold replaced with ad)	17.00	52.00	130.00

BOZO (Larry Harmon's Bozo, the World's Most Famous Clown)
Innovation Publishing: 1992 ($6.95, 68 pgs.)

	GD25	FN65	NM94
1-Reprints Four Color #285(#1)	.85	2.60	7.00

BOZO THE CLOWN (TV) (Bozo No. 7 on)
Dell Publishing Co.: July, 1950 - No. 4, Oct-Dec, 1963

	GD25	FN65	NM94
Four Color 285(#1)	17.00	52.00	190.00
2(7-9/51)-7(10-12/52)	10.00	30.00	110.00
Four Color 464,508,551,594(10/54)	8.00	25.00	90.00
1(nn, 5-7/62)	5.50	16.50	60.00
2 - 4(1963)	4.50	13.50	50.00
Giveaway-1961, 16 pgs., 3-1/2x7-1/4", Apsco Products	2.75	8.00	30.00

BOZZ CHRONICLES, THE
Marvel Comics (Epic Comics): Dec, 1985 - No. 6, 1986 (Lim. series, mature)

	GD25	FN65	NM94
1-6-Logan/Wolverine look alike in 19th century			2.50

BRADY BUNCH, THE (TV)(See Kite Fun Book and Binky #78)
Dell Publishing Co.: Feb, 1970 - No. 2, May, 1970

	GD25	FN65	NM94
1	8.25	25.00	90.00
2	6.00	18.00	65.00

BRAIN, THE
Sussex Publ. Co./Magazine Enterprises: Sept, 1956 - No. 7, 1958

	GD25	FN65	NM94
1-Dan DeCarlo-a in all including reprints	6.50	19.50	45.00
2,3	4.15	12.50	25.00
4-7	3.60	9.00	18.00
I.W. Reprints #1-4,8-10('63),14: 2-Reprints Sussex #2 with new cover added	1.10	3.30	9.00
Super Reprint #17,18(nd)	1.10	3.30	9.00

BRAINBANX
DC Comics (Helix): Mar, 1997 - No. 6, Aug, 1997 ($2.50, limited series)

	GD25	FN65	NM94
1-6: Elaine Lee-s/Temujin-a			2.50

BRAIN BOY
Dell Publishing Co.: Apr-June, 1962 - No. 6, Sept-Nov, 1963 (Painted c-#1-6)

	GD25	FN65	NM94
Four Color 1330(#1)-Gil Kane-a; origin	12.00	37.00	135.00
2(7-9/62),3-6: 4-Origin retold	7.00	20.00	75.00

BRAM STOKER'S BURIAL OF THE RATS (Movie)
Roger Corman's Cosmic Comics: Apr, 1995 - No.3, June, 1995 ($2.50)

	GD25	FN65	NM94
1-3: Adaptation of film; Jerry Prosser scripts			2.50

BRAM STOKER'S DRACULA (Movie)(Also see Dracula: Vlad the Impaler)

Brand New York: What Justice #1 © Z-A-C

Brave And The Bold #14 © DC

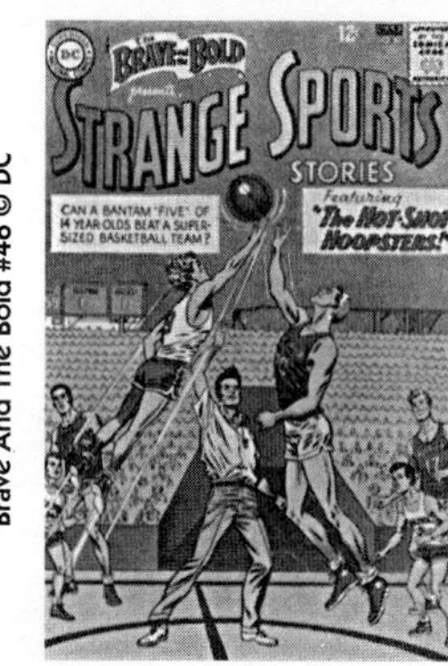

Brave And The Bold #46 © DC

Topps Comics: Oct, 1992 - No. 4, Jan, 1993 ($2.95, limited series, polybagged)

1-Adaptation of film begins; Mignola-c/a in all; 4 trading cards & poster; photo scenes of movie 3.00
1-2nd printing 3.00
1-Crimson foil edition (limited to 500) 1.00 3.00 10.00
2-Bound-in poster & cards 3.00
3,4: 4 trading cards in both. 3-Contains coupon to win 1 of 500 crimson foil-c edition of #1. 4-Contains coupon to win 1 of 500 uncut sheets of all 16 trading cards 3.00
3,4-Without coupon 3.00

BRAND ECHH (See Not Brand Echh)

BRAND NEW YORK: WHAT JUSTICE
Comic Box Inc.: July, 1997 ($3.95, B&W&Red)

1-Zoltan-s/a, Peter Avanti-s 3.95

BRAND OF EMPIRE (See Luke Short's...Four Color 771)

BRASS
Image Comics (WildStorm Productions): Aug, 1996 - No. 3, May, 1997 ($2.50, limited series)

1-($4.50) Folio Ed.; oversized 4.50
1-3: Wiesenfeld-s/Bennett-a. 3-Grunge & Roxy(Gen 13) cameo 2.50

BRATPACK/MAXIMORTAL SUPER SPECIAL
King Hell Press: 1996 ($2.95, B&W, limited series)

1,2: Veitch-s/a 2.95

BRATS BIZARRE
Marvel Comics (Epic/Heavy Hitters): 1994 - No. 4, 1994 ($2.50, limited series)

1-4: All w/bound-in trading cards 2.50

BRAVADOS, THE (See Wild Western Action)
Skywald Publ. Corp.: Aug, 1971 (52 pgs., one-shot)

1-Red Mask, The Durango Kid, Billy Nevada-r; Bolle-a; 3-D effect story 1.00 3.00 10.00

BRAVE AND THE BOLD, THE (See Best Of... & Super DC Giant) (Replaced by Batman & The Outsiders)
National Periodical Publ./DC Comics: Aug-Sept, 1955 - No. 200, July, 1983

1-Viking Prince by Kubert, Silent Knight, Golden Gladiator begin; part Kubert-c 208.00 624.00 2700.00
2 100.00 300.00 1200.00
3,4 52.00 156.00 625.00
5-Robin Hood begins (4-5/56, 1st DC app.), ends #15; see Robin Hood Tales #7 56.00 168.00 675.00
6-10: 6-Robin Hood by Kubert; last Golden Gladiator app.; Silent Knight; no Viking Prince. 8-1st S.A. issue 40.00 120.00 450.00
11-22,24: 12,14-Robin Hood-c. 18,21-23-Grey tone-c. 22-Last Silent Knight. 24-Last Viking Prince by Kubert (2nd solo book) 31.00 93.00 340.00
23-Viking Prince origin by Kubert; 1st B&B single theme issue & 1st Viking Prince solo book 40.00 120.00 450.00
25-1st app. Suicide Squad (8-9/59) 32.00 96.00 360.00
26,27-Suicide Squad 30.00 90.00 300.00

GD25 FN65 VF82 NM94

28-(2-3/60)-Justice League intro./1st app.; origin/1st app. Snapper Carr 300.00 900.00 2250.00 5100.00
29-Justice League (4-5/60)-2nd app. battle the Weapons Master; robot-c 150.00 450.00 1050.00 2250.00
30-Justice League (6-7/60)-3rd app.; vs. Amazo 128.00 384.00 832.00 1800.00

GD25 FN65 NM94

31-1st app. Cave Carson (8-9/60); scarce in high grade; 1st try-out series 31.00 93.00 320.00
32,33-Cave Carson 21.00 63.00 210.00

GD25 FN65 VF82 NM94

34-Origin/1st app. Silver-Age Hawkman, Hawkgirl & Byth by Kubert (2-3/61); 1st S.A. Hawkman tryout series; all predate Hawkman #1 133.00 400.00 865.00 1850.00

GD25 FN65 NM94

35-Hawkman by Kubert (4-5/61)-2nd app. 40.00 120.00 485.00
36-Hawkman by Kubert; origin & 1st app. Shadow Thief (6-7/61)-3rd app. 37.00 111.00 410.00
37-Suicide Squad (2nd tryout series) 22.00 66.00 220.00
38,39-Suicide Squad. 38-Last 10¢ issue 19.00 57.00 190.00
40,41-Cave Carson Inside Earth (2nd try-out series). 40-Kubert-a. 41-Meskin-a 13.50 41.00 135.00
42-Hawkman by Kubert (2nd tryout series) 28.00 84.00 285.00
43-Hawkman by Kubert; more detailed origin 33.00 100.00 330.00
44-Hawkman by Kubert; grey-tone-c 24.00 72.00 240.00
45-49-Strange Sports Stories by Infantino 6.00 18.00 60.00
50-The Green Arrow & Manhunter From Mars (10-11/63); 1st Manhunter x-over outside of Detective (pre-dates House of Mystery #143); team-ups begin 16.00 48.00 160.00
51-Aquaman & Hawkman (12-1/63-64); pre-dates Hawkman #1 22.00 66.00 220.00
52-(2-3/64)-3 Battle Stars; Sgt. Rock, Haunted Tank, Johnny Cloud, & Mlle. Marie team-up for 1st time by Kubert (c/a) 14.00 42.00 140.00
53-Atom & The Flash by Toth 6.00 18.00 60.00
54-Kid Flash, Robin & Aqualad; 1st app./origin Teen Titans (6-7/64) 26.00 78.00 260.00
55-Metal Men & The Atom 4.50 13.50 45.00
56-The Flash & Manhunter From Mars 4.50 13.50 45.00
57-Origin & 1st app. Metamorpho (12-1/64-65) 14.00 42.00 140.00
58-2nd app. Metamorpho by Fradon 7.00 21.00 70.00
59-Batman & Green Lantern; 1st Batman team-up in Brave and the Bold 9.00 27.00 90.00
60-Teen Titans (2nd app.)-1st app. new Wonder Girl (Donna Troy), who joins Titans (6-7/65) 8.00 24.00 80.00
61-Origin Starman & Black Canary by Anderson 11.00 33.00 110.00
62-Origin Starman & Black Canary cont'd. 62-1st S.A. app. Wildcat (10-11/65); 1st S.A. app. of G.A. Huntress 9.00 27.00 90.00
63-Supergirl & Wonder Woman 4.00 12.00 40.00
64-Batman Versus Eclipso (see H.O.S. #61) 6.00 18.00 60.00
65-Flash & Doom Patrol (4-5/66) 2.50 7.50 22.00
66-Metamorpho & Metal Men (6-7/66) 2.50 7.50 22.00
67-Batman & The Flash by Infantino; Batman team-ups begin, end #200 (8-9/66) 4.20 12.60 42.00
68-Batman/Metamorpho/Joker/Riddler/Penguin-c/story; Batman as Bat-Hulk (Hulk parody) 6.00 18.00 60.00
69-Batman & Green Lantern 3.00 9.00 30.00
70-Batman & Hawkman; Craig-a(p) 3.00 9.00 30.00
71-Batman & Green Arrow 3.00 9.00 30.00
72-Spectre & Flash (6-7/67); 4th app. The Spectre; predates Spectre #1 3.50 10.50 35.00
73-Aquaman & The Atom 2.70 8.10 27.00
74-Batman & Metal Men 2.70 8.10 27.00
75-Batman & The Spectre (12-1/67-68); 6th app. Spectre; came out between Spectre #1 & #2 3.00 9.00 30.00
76-Batman & Plastic Man (2-3/68); came out between Plastic Man #8 & #9 2.70 8.10 27.00
77-Batman & The Atom 2.70 8.10 27.00
78-Batman, Wonder Woman & Batgirl 2.70 8.10 27.00
79-Batman & Deadman by Neal Adams (8-9/68); early Deadman app. 5.00 15.00 50.00
80-Batman & Creeper (10-11/68); N. Adams-a; early app. The Creeper; came out between Creeper #3 & #4 4.00 12.00 40.00
81-Batman & Flash; N. Adams-a 4.00 12.00 40.00
82-Batman & Aquaman; N. Adams-a; origin Ocean Master retold (2-3/69) 4.00 12.00 40.00

Brave And The Bold #133 © DC

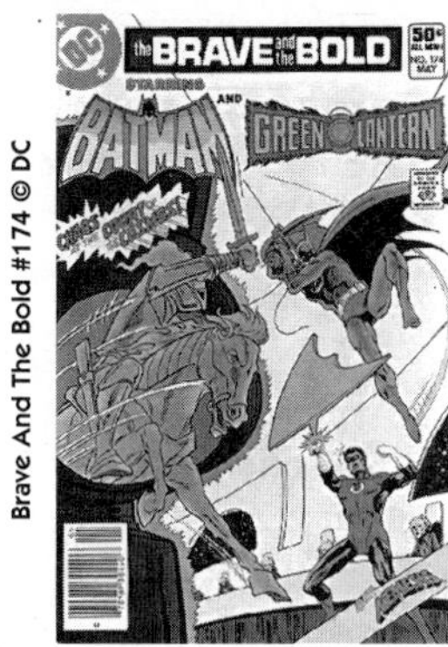

Brave And The Bold #174 © DC

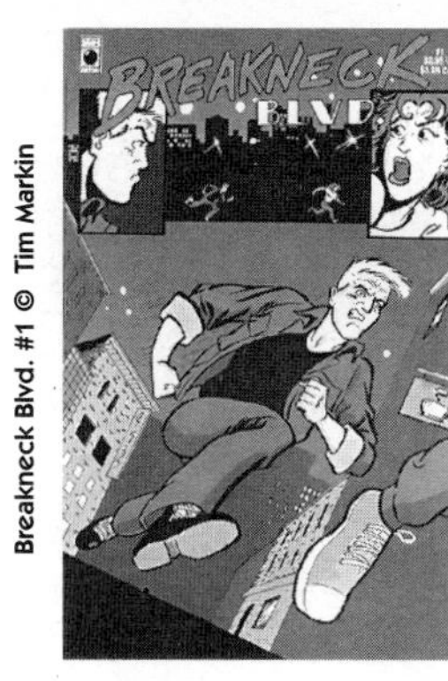

Breakneck Blvd. #1 © Tim Markin

	GD25	FN65	NM94
83-Batman & Teen Titans; N. Adams-a (4-5/69); last 12¢ issue	4.00	12.00	40.00
84-Batman (G.A., 1st S.A. app.) & Sgt. Rock; N. Adams-a	4.00	12.00	40.00
85-Batman & Green Arrow; 1st new costume for Green Arrow by Neal Adams (8-9/69)	4.00	12.00	40.00
86-Batman & Deadman (10-11/69); N. Adams-a; story concludes from Strange Adventures #216 (1-2/69)	4.00	12.00	40.00
87-Batman & Wonder Woman	2.20	6.50	24.00
88-Batman & Wildcat	2.20	6.50	24.00
89-Batman & Phantom Stranger (4-5/70); early Phantom Stranger app. (came out between Phantom Stranger #6 & 7	2.20	6.50	24.00
90-Batman & Adam Strange	2.20	6.50	24.00
91-Batman & Black Canary (8-9/70)	2.20	6.50	24.00
92-Batman; intro the Bat Squad	2.20	6.50	24.00
93-Batman-House of Mystery; N. Adams-a	3.20	9.50	35.00
94-Batman-Teen Titans	1.60	4.80	16.00
95-Batman & Plastic Man	2.00	6.00	20.00
96-Batman & Sgt. Rock	2.20	6.25	22.00
97-Batman & Wildcat; 52 pg. issues begin, end #102; reprints origin & 1st app. Deadman from Strange Advs. #205	1.80	5.40	18.00
98-Batman & Phantom Stranger; 1st Jim Aparo Batman-a?	1.80	5.40	18.00
99-Batman & Flash	1.80	5.40	18.00
100-(2-3/72, 25¢, 52 pgs.)-Batman-Gr. Lantern-Gr. Arrow-Black Canary-Robin; Deadman-r by Adams/Str. Advs. #210	3.80	11.50	42.00
101-Batman & Metamorpho; Kubert Viking Prince	1.00	3.00	10.00
102-Batman-Teen Titans; N. Adams-a(p)	1.60	4.80	16.00
103-107,109,110: Batman team-ups: 103-Metal Men. 104-Deadman. 105-Wonder Woman. 106-Green Arrow. 107-Black Canary. 109-Demon. 110-Wildcat	.85	2.60	7.00
108-Sgt. Rock	1.00	3.00	10.00
111-Batman/Joker-c/story	1.20	3.60	12.00
112-117: All 100 pgs.; Batman team-ups: 112-Mr. Miracle. 113-Metal Men; reprints origin/1st Hawkman from Brave and the Bold #34; r/origin Multi-Man/ Challengers #14. 114-Aquaman. 115-Atom; r/origin Viking Prince from #23; r/Dr. Fate/Hourman/Solomon Grundy/Green Lantern from Showcase #55. 116-Spectre. 117-Sgt. Rock; last 100 pg. issue	1.60	4.80	16.00
118-Batman/Wildcat/Joker-c/story	1.30	3.90	13.00
119,121-123,125-128,132-140: Batman team-ups: 119-Man-Bat. 121-Metal Men. 122-Swamp Thing. 123-Plastic Man/Metamorpho. 125-Flash. 126-Aquaman. 127-Wildcat. 128-Mr. Miracle. 132-Kung-Fu Fighter. 133-Deadman. 134-Green Lantern. 135-Metal Men. 136-Metal Men/Green Arrow. 137-Demon. 138-Mr. Miracle. 139-Hawkman. 140-Wonder Woman		2.00	6.00
120-Kamandi(68 pgs.)	.90	2.70	8.00
124-Sgt. Rock`	1.00	3.00	10.00
129,130-Batman/Green Arrow/Atom parts 1 & 2; Joker & Two Face-c/stories	1.20	3.60	12.00
131-Batman & Wonder Woman vs. Catwoman-c/sty	.85	2.60	7.00
141-Batman/Black Canary vs. Joker-c/story	1.20	3.60	12.00
142-190,192-195,198,199: Batman team-ups: 142-Aquaman. 143-Creeper; origin Human Target (44 pgs.). 144-Green Arrow; origin Human Target part 2 (44 pgs.).145-Phantom Stranger. 146-G.A. Batman/Unknown Soldier. 147-Supergirl.148-Plastic Man; X-Mas-c. 149-Teen Titans. 150-Anniversary issue; Superman. 151-Flash. 152-Atom. 153-Red Tornado. 154-Metamorpho. 155-Green Lantern. 156-Dr. Fate. 157-Batman vs. Kamandi (ties into Kamandi #59). 158-Wonder Woman. 159-Ra's Al Ghul. 160-Supergirl. 161-Adam Strange. 162-G.A. Batman/Sgt. Rock. 163-Black Lightning. 164-Hawkman. 165-Man-Bat. 166-Black Canary; Nemesis (intro) back-up story begins, ends #192; Penguin-c/story. 167-G.A. Batman/Blackhawk; origin Nemesis. 168-Green Arrow. 169-Zatanna. 170-Nemesis. 171-Scalphunter. 172-Firestorm. 173-Guardians of the Universe. 174-Green Lantern. 175-Lois Lane. 176-Swamp Thing. 177-Elongated Man. 178-Creeper. 179-Legion. 180-Spectre. 181-Hawk & Dove. 182-G.A. Robin; G.A. Starman app.; 1st modern app. G.A. Batwoman. 183-Riddler. 184-Huntress. 185-Green Arrow. 186-Hawkman. 187-Metal Men. 188,189-Rose & the Thorn. 190-Adam Strange. 192-Superboy vs. Mr. I.Q. 193-Nemesis. 194-Flash. 195-I... Vampire. 198-Karate Kid. 199-Batman vs. The Spectre			3.50
191-Batman/Joker-c/story; Nemesis app.	.90	2.70	8.00
196-Ragman; origin Ragman retold.		2.00	6.00
197-Catwoman; Earth II Batman & Catwoman marry; 2nd modern app. of G.A. Batwoman	.90	2.70	8.00
200-Double-sized (64 pgs.); printed on Mando paper; Earth One & Earth Two Batman app. in separate stories; intro/1st app. Batman & The Outsiders	.90	2.70	9.00

NOTE: ***Neal Adams** a-79-86, 93, 100r, 102; c-75, 76, 79-86, 88-90, 93, 95, 99, 100r. **M. Anderson** a-115r; c-72i, 96i. **Andru/Esposito** c-25-27. **Aparo** a-98, 100-102, 104-125, 126i, 127-136, 138-145, 147, 148i, 149-152, 154, 155, 157-162, 168-170, 173-178, 180-182, 184, 186i-189i, 191i-193i, 195, 196, 200; c-105-109, 111-136, 137i, 138-175, 177, 180-184, 186-200. **Austin** a-166i. **Bernard Baily** c-32, 33, 58. **Buckler** a-185, 186p; c-137, 178p, 185p, 186p. **Giordano** a-143, 144. **Infantino** a-67p, 72p, 97r, 98r, 115r, 172p, 183p, 190p, 194p; c-45-49, 67p, 69p, 70p, 72p, 96p, 98r. **Kaluta** c-176. **Kane** a-115r; c-59, 64. **Kubert** &/or **Heath** a-1-24; reprints-101, 113, 115, 117. **Kubert** a-99r; c-22-24, 34-36, 40, 42-44, 52. **Mooney** a-114r. **Mortimer** a-64, 69. **Newton** a-153p, 156p, 165p. **Irv Novick** c-1(part), 2-21. **Fred Ray** a-78r. **Roussos** a-50, 76i, 114r. **Staton** 148p. 52 pgs.-97, 100; 68 pgs.-120; 100 pgs.-112-117.*

BRAVE AND THE BOLD, THE
DC Comics: Dec, 1991 - No. 6, June, 1992 ($1.75, limited series)

	GD25	FN65	NM94
1-6: Green Arrow, The Butcher, The Question in all; Grell scripts in all.			1.75

NOTE: ***Grell** c-3, 4-6.*

BRAVE AND THE BOLD SPECIAL, THE (See DC Special Series No. 8)

BRAVE EAGLE (TV)
Dell Publishing Co.: No. 705, June, 1956 - No. 929, July, 1958

	GD25	FN65	NM94
Four Color 705 (#1)-Photo-c	5.50	16.50	60.00
Four Color 770, 816, 879 (2/58), 929-All photo-c	2.75	8.00	30.00

BRAVE ONE, THE (Movie)
Dell Publishing Co.: No. 773, Mar, 1957

	GD25	FN65	NM94
Four Color 773-Photo-c	4.50	13.50	50.00

BRAVURA
Malibu Comics (Bravura): 1995 (mail-in offer)

	GD25	FN65	NM94
0-wraparound holographic-c; short stories and promo pin-ups of Chaykin's Power &Glory, Gil Kane's & Steven Grant's Edge, Starlin's Breed, & Simonson's Star Slammers.			5.00

BREAKNECK BLVD.
MotioN Comics/Slave Labor Graphics Vol. 2: No. 0, Feb, 1994 - No. 2, Nov, 1994; Vol. 2#1, Jul, 1995 - Present ($2.50/$2.95, B&W)

	GD25	FN65	NM94
0-2: 0-Perez/Giordano-c			2.50
V2#1-6: 6-(12/96)			3.00

BREAK-THRU (Also see Exiles V1#4)
Malibu Comics (Ultraverse): Dec, 1993 - No. 2, Jan, 1994 ($2.50, 44 pgs.)

	GD25	FN65	NM94
1,2-Perez-c/a(p); has x-overs in Ultraverse titles			2.50

BREATHTAKER
DC Comics: 1990 - No. 4, 1990 ($4.95, 52 pgs., prestige format, mature)

	GD25	FN65	NM94
Book 1-4: Mark Wheatley-painted-c/a & scripts; Marc Hempel-a			5.00
TPB (1994, $14.95) r/#1-4; intro by Neil Gaiman	1.50	4.50	15.00

'BREED
Malibu Comics (Bravura): Jan, 1994 - No. 6, 1994 ($2.50, limited series)

	GD25	FN65	NM94
1-(48 pgs.)-Origin & 1st app. of 'Breed by Starlin; contains Bravura stamps; spot varnish-c			2.50
2-6: 2-5-contains Bravura stamps. 6-Death of Rachel			2.50
...:Book of Genesis (1994, $12.95)-reprints #1-6			12.95

'BREED II
Malibu Comics (Bravura): Nov, 1994 - No. 6, Apr, 1995 ($2.95, limited series)

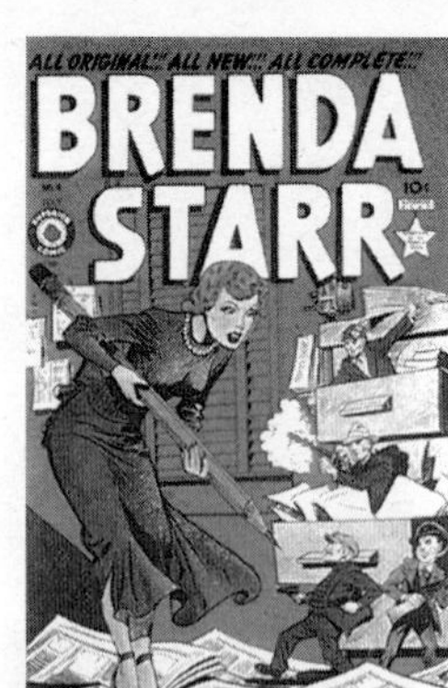

Brenda Starr #9 © SUPR

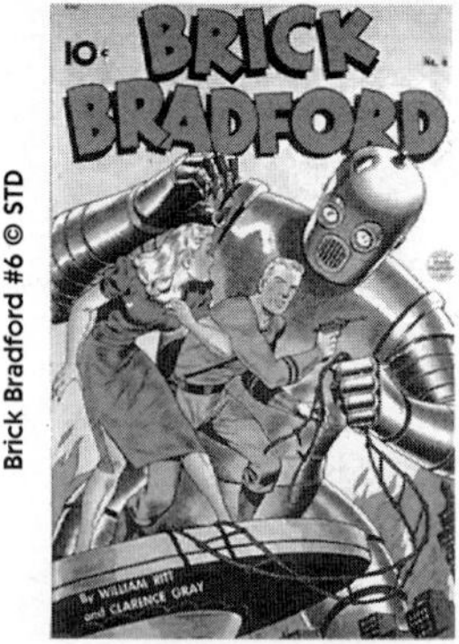

Brick Bradford #6 © STD

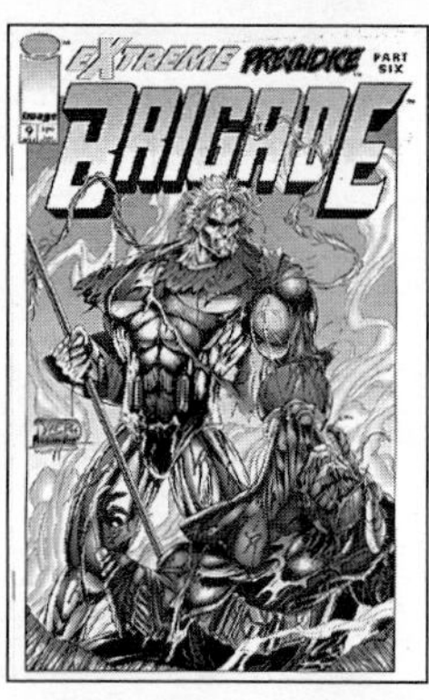

Brigade #9 © Rob Liefeld

	GD25	FN65	NM94
1-6: Starlin-c/a/scripts in all. 1-Gold edition			3.00

BREEZE LAWSON, SKY SHERIFF (See Sky Sheriff)

BRENDA LEE STORY, THE
Dell Publishing Co.: Sept, 1962

	GD25	FN65	NM94
01-078-209	8.00	23.00	85.00

BRENDA STARR (Also see All Great)
Four Star Comics Corp./Superior Comics Ltd.: No. 13, 9/47; No. 14, 3/48; V2#3, 6/48 - V2#12, 12/49

	GD25	FN65	NM94
V1#13-By Dale Messick	71.00	212.00	600.00
14-Kamen bondage-c	74.00	221.00	625.00
V2#3-Baker-a?	60.00	180.00	510.00
4-Used in **SOTI**, pg. 21; Kamen bondage-c	71.00	212.00	600.00
5-10	58.00	173.00	490.00
11,12 (Scarce)	59.00	178.00	500.00

NOTE: *Newspaper reprints plus original material through #6. All original #7 on.*

BRENDA STARR (...Reporter)(Young Lovers No. 16 on?)
Charlton Comics: No. 13, June, 1955 - No. 15, Oct, 1955

	GD25	FN65	NM94
13-15-Newspaper-r	32.00	96.00	240.00

BRENDA STARR REPORTER
Dell Publishing Co.: Oct, 1963

	GD25	FN65	NM94
1	14.00	44.00	160.00

BRER RABBIT (See Kite Fun Book, Walt Disney Showcase #28 and Wheaties)
Dell Publishing Co.: No. 129, 1946; No. 208, Jan, 1949; No. 693, 1956 (Disney)

	GD25	FN65	NM94
Four Color 129 (#1)-Adapted from Disney movie "Song of the South"	26.00	79.00	290.00
Four Color 208 (1/49)	11.00	32.00	115.00
Four Color 693-Part-r 129	8.00	25.00	90.00

BRER RABBIT IN "ICE CREAM FOR THE PARTY"
American Dairy Association: 1955 (5x7-1/4", 16 pgs., soft-c) (Walt Disney) (Premium)

	GD25	FN65	NM94
nn-(Scarce)	39.00	116.00	290.00

BRIAN BOLLAND'S BLACK BOOK
Eclipse Comics: July, 1985 (one-shot)

	GD25	FN65	NM94
1-British B&W-r in color			1.50

BRICK BRADFORD (Also see Ace Comics & King Comics)
King Features Syndicate/Standard: No. 5, July, 1948 - No. 8, July, 1949 (Ritt & Grey reprints)

	GD25	FN65	NM94
5	17.00	50.00	125.00
6-Robot-c (by Schomburg?).	23.00	68.00	170.00
7-Schomburg-c. 8-Says #7 inside, #8 on-c	13.00	38.00	95.00

BRIDE'S DIARY (Formerly Black Cobra No. 3)
Ajax/Farrell Publ.: No. 4, May, 1955 - No. 10, Aug, 1956

	GD25	FN65	NM94
4 (#1)	5.70	17.00	35.00
5-8	4.00	11.00	22.00
9,10-Disbrow-a	5.70	17.00	35.00

BRIDES IN LOVE (Hollywood Romances & Summer Love No. 46 on)
Charlton Comics: Aug, 1956 - No. 45, Feb, 1965

	GD25	FN65	NM94
1	7.15	21.50	50.00
2	4.25	13.00	28.00
3-6,8-10	2.50	7.50	22.00
7-(68 pgs.)	3.00	9.00	30.00
11-20	1.75	5.25	14.00
21-45	1.00	3.00	8.00

BRIDES ROMANCES
Quality Comics Group: Nov, 1953 - No. 23, Dec, 1956

	GD25	FN65	NM94
1	9.30	28.00	70.00
2	5.35	16.00	32.00
3-10: Last precode (3/55)	4.15	12.50	25.00
11-14,16,17,19-22	3.60	9.00	18.00
15-Baker-a(p)?; Colan-a	4.00	10.00	20.00
18-Baker-a	5.00	15.00	30.00
23-Baker-c/a	6.50	19.50	45.00

BRIDE'S SECRETS
Ajax/Farrell(Excellent Publ.)/Four-Star: Apr-May, 1954 - No. 19, May, 1958

	GD25	FN65	NM94
1	8.50	26.00	60.00
2	5.00	15.00	30.00
3-6: Last precode (3/55)	4.00	11.00	22.00
7-11,13-19: 18-Hollingsworth-a	4.00	10.00	20.00
12-Disbrow-a	4.00	12.00	24.00

BRIDE-TO-BE ROMANCES (See True...)

BRIGADE
Image Comics (Extreme Studios): Aug, 1992 - No. 4, 1993 ($1.95, lim. series)

	GD25	FN65	NM94
1-Liefeld part plots/scripts in all, Liefeld-c(p); contains 2 Brigade trading cards; 1st app. Genocide			3.00
1-Gold foil stamped logo edition			8.00
2-Contains coupon for Image Comics #0 & 2 trading cards			3.00
2-With coupon missing			2.00
3-Contains 2 bound-in trading cards; 1st Birds of Prey			2.00
4-Flip book format featuring Youngblood #5			2.00

BRIGADE
Image Comics (Extreme): V2#1, May, 1993 - V2#22, July, 1995 ($1.95/$2.50)

	GD25	FN65	NM94
V2#1-Gatefold-c; Liefeld co-plots; Blood Brothers part 1; Bloodstrike app.; 1st app. Boone & Hacker			2.00
2-10, 13, 14: 2-(6/93, V2#1 on inside)-Foil merricote-c (newsstand ed. w/out foil-c exists). 3-1st app. Roman; Perez-c(i); Liefeld scripts. 6-1st app. Coral & Worlok. 6-8-Thibert-c(i). 8-Liefeld scripts; Black and White part 5 by Art Thibert. 8,9-Coupons #2 & 6 for Extreme Prejudice #0 bound-in. 9-(4/94). 10-(6/94).			2.00
0-(9/93)-Liefeld scripts; 1st app. Warcry; Youngblood & Wildcats app.; Thibert-c(i)			3.00
11,12,15-22: 11-(8/94, $2.50) WildC.A.T.S app. 16-Polybagged w/ trading card. 19-Glory app. 20 (Regular-c.)-Troll, Supreme, Shadowhawk, Glory, Vanguard, & Roman form new team. 22-"Supreme Apocalypse" Pt. 4; Marv Wolfman scripts; polybagged w/ trading card			2.50
20-(Variant-c. by Quesada & Palmiotti)-Troll, Supreme, Shadowhawk, Glory, Vanguard, & Roman form new team.			3.00
Sourcebook 1 (8/94, $2.95)			3.00

BRIGAND, THE (See Fawcett Movie Comics No. 18)

BRINGING UP FATHER
Dell Publishing Co.: No. 9, 1942 - No. 37, 1944

	GD25	FN65	NM94
Large Feature Comic 9	18.00	55.00	200.00
Four Color 37	18.00	55.00	200.00

BRING BACK THE BAD GUYS
Marvel Comics: 1998($24.95, TPB)

	GD25	FN65	NM94
1-Reprints stories of Marvel villains' secrets			25.00

BRING ON THE BAD GUYS (See Fireside Book Series)

BRINKE OF DESTRUCTION
High-Top and Brinke Stevens: Dec, 1995 - Jan, 1997($2.95)

	GD25	FN65	NM94
1-3: 1-Boris-c. 2-Julie Bell-c. 3-Garris-c			3.00
Holiday Special ($6.99)-Comic w/audio tape	.85	2.60	7.00

BRINKE OF DISASTER
Revenge Entertainment Group: 1996 ($2.25, B&W, one-shot)

	GD25	FN65	NM94
nn-Photo-c			2.25

BRINKE OF ETERNITY
Chaos! Comics: Apr, 1994 ($2.75, one-shot)

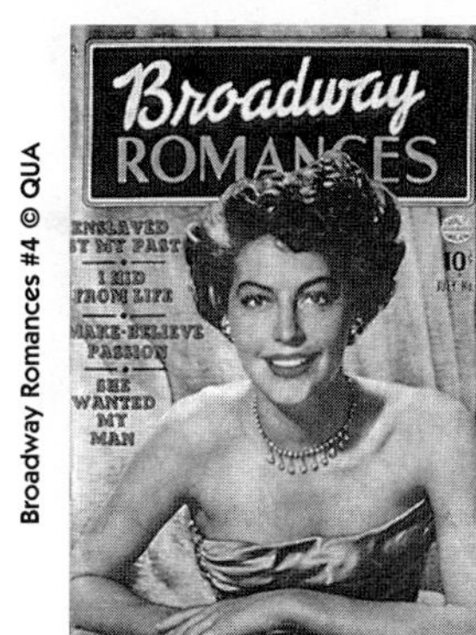

Broadway Romances #4 © QUA

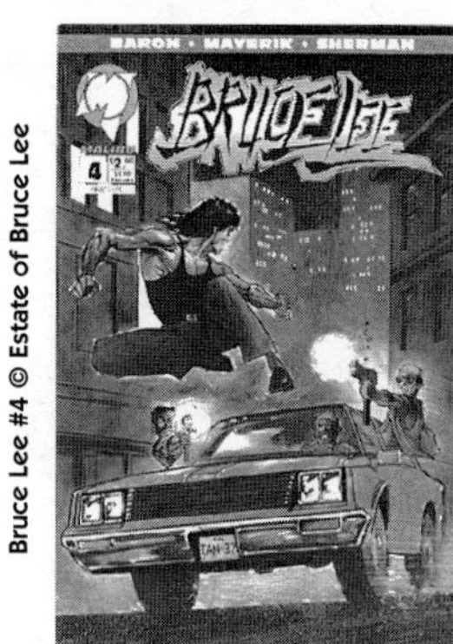

Bruce Lee #4 © Estate of Bruce Lee

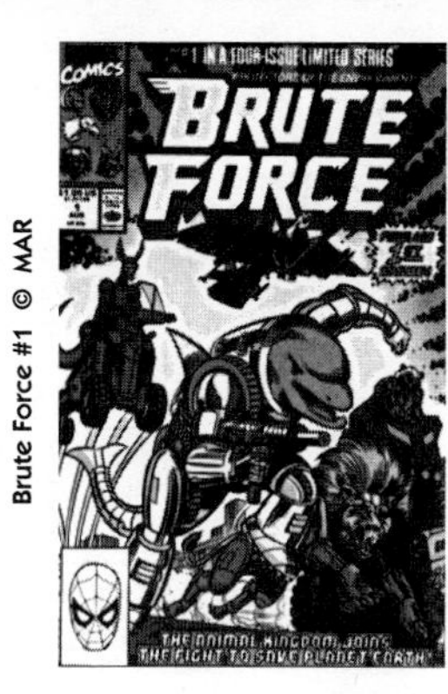

Brute Force #1 © MAR

GD25 FN65 NM94

1 — 2.00
1-Signed Edition — 3.00

BROADWAY HOLLYWOOD BLACKOUTS
Stanhall: Mar-Apr, 1954 - No. 3, July-Aug, 1954

1 — 9.30 28.00 65.00
2,3 — 6.00 18.00 42.00

BROADWAY ROMANCES
Quality Comics Group: January, 1950 - No. 5, Sept, 1950

1-Ward-c/a (9 pgs.); Gustavson-a — 29.00 88.00 220.00
2-Ward-a (9 pgs.); photo-c — 22.00 66.00 165.00
3-5: All-Photo-c — 9.30 28.00 70.00

BROKEN ARROW (TV)
Dell Publishing Co.: No. 855, Oct, 1957 - No. 947, Nov, 1958

Four Color 855 (#1)-Photo-c — 5.00 15.00 54.00
Four Color 947-Photo-c — 4.00 12.00 45.00

BROKEN CROSS, THE (See The Crusaders)

BRONCHO BILL (See Comics On Parade, Sparkler & Tip Top Comics)
United Features Syndicate/Standard(Visual Editions) No. 5-on: 1939 - 1940; No. 5, 1?/48 - No. 16, 8?/50

Single Series 2 ('39) — 44.00 132.00 370.00
Single Series 19 ('40)(#2 on cvr) — 39.00 118.00 315.00
5 — 11.00 32.00 80.00
6(4/48)-10(4/49) — 6.00 18.00 42.00
11(6/49)-16 — 5.35 16.00 32.00

NOTE: ***Schomburg** c-6, 7, 9-13, 16.*

BROOKLYN DREAMS
DC Comics (Paradox Press): 1994, ($4.95, B&W, limited series, mature)

1-4 — 5.00

BROOKS ROBINSON (See Baseball's Greatest Heroes #2)

BROTHER BILLY THE PAIN FROM PLAINS
Marvel Comics Group: 1979 (68pgs.)

1-B&W comics, satire, Jimmy Carter-c & x-over w/Brother Billy peanut jokes. Joey Adams-a (scarce) — 1.80 5.40 18.00

BROTHER POWER, THE GEEK (See Saga of Swamp Thing Annual & Vertigo Visions)
National Periodical Publications: Sept-Oct, 1968 - No. 2, Nov-Dec, 1968

1-Origin; Simon-c(i?) — 4.00 12.00 40.00
2 — 2.50 7.50 20.00

BROTHERS, HANG IN THERE, THE
Spire Christian Comics (Fleming H. Revell Co.): 1979 (49¢)

nn — 3.00

BROTHERS OF THE SPEAR (Also see Tarzan)
Gold Key/Whitman No. 18: June, 1972 - No. 17, Feb, 1976; No. 18, May, 1982

1 — 2.20 6.50 24.00
2-Painted-c begin, end #17 — 1.20 3.60 12.00
3-10 — .85 2.60 7.00
11-17: 12-Line drawn-c. 13-17-Spiegle-a — 1.60 4.00
18-r/#2; Leopard Girl-r — 1.60 4.00

BROTHERS, THE CULT ESCAPE, THE
Spire Christian Comics (Fleming H. Revell Co.): 1980 (49¢)

nn — 3.00

BROWNIES (See New Funnies)
Dell Publishing Co.: No. 192, July, 1948 - No. 605, Dec, 1954

Four Color 192(#1)-Kelly-a — 11.00 33.00 120.00
Four Color 244(9/49), 293 (9/50)-Last Kelly c/a — 10.00 30.00 110.00
Four Color 337(7-8/51), 365(12-1/51-52), 398(5/52) — 3.00 10.00 36.00
Four Color 436(11/52), 482(7/53), 522(12/53), 605 — 3.00 9.00 32.00

GD25 FN65 NM94

BRUCE GENTRY
Better/Standard/Four Star Publ./Superior No. 3: Jan, 1948 - No. 8, Jul, 1949

1-Ray Bailey strip reprints begin, end #3; E. C. emblem appears as a monogram on stationery in story; negligee panels — 42.00 127.00 340.00
2,3 — 32.00 96.00 240.00
4-8 — 22.00 66.00 165.00

NOTE: ***Kamenish** a-2-7; c-1-8.*

BRUCE LEE
Malibu Comics: July, 1994 - No. 6, Dec, 1994 ($2.95, 36 pgs.)

1-6: 1-(44 pgs.)-Mortal Kombat preview, 1st app. in comics. 2,6-(36 pgs.) — 1.00

BRUCE JONES' OUTER EDGE
Innovation: 1993 ($2.50, B&W, one-shot)

1-Bruce Jones-c/a/script — 2.50

BRUCE WAYNE: AGENT OF S.H.I.E.L.D. (Also see Marvel Versus DC #3 & DC Versus Marvel #4)
Marvel Comics (Amalgam): Apr, 1996 ($1.95, one-shot)

1-Chuck Dixon scripts & Cary Nord-c/a. — 2.00

BRU-HEAD: AMERICA'S FAVORITE BLOCKHEAD
Schism Comics: Mar, 1994 - No. 4, 1994 ($2.50, B&W, limited series)

1 — 2.50

BRUISER
Anthem Publications: Feb, 1994 ($2.45)

1 — 2.45

BRUTE, THE
Seaboard Publ. (Atlas): Feb, 1975 - No. 3, July, 1975

1,2: 1-Origin & 1st app; Sekowsky-a(p). 2-Sekowsky-a(p) — 3.00
3-Brunner/Starlin/Weiss-a(p) — 5.00

BRUTE & BABE
Ominous Press: July, 1994 - No. 2, Aug, 1994

1-($3.95, 8 tablets plus-c)-"...It Begins..."; tablet format — 4.00
2-($2.50, 36 pgs.)-"Mael's Rage" — 2.50
2-(40 pgs.)-Stiff additional variant-c — 2.50

BRUTE FORCE
Marvel Comics: Aug, 1990 - No. 4, Nov, 1990 ($1.00, limited series)

1-4: Animal super-heroes — 1.00

BUBBLEGUM CRISIS: GRAND MAL
Dark Horse Comics: Mar, 1994 - No. 4, June, 1994 ($2.50, limited series)

1-4-Japanese manga — 2.50

BUCCANEER
I. W. Enterprises: No date (1963)

I.W. Reprint #1(r-/Quality #20), #8(r-/#23): Crandall-a in each — 2.50 7.50 22.00

BUCCANEERS (Formerly Kid Eternity)
Quality Comics: No. 19, Jan, 1950 - No. 27, May, 1951 (No. 24-27: 52 pgs.)

19-Captain Daring, Black Roger, Eric Falcon & Spanish Main begin; Crandall-a — 44.00 132.00 375.00
20,23-Crandall-a — 32.00 96.00 240.00
21-Crandall-c/a — 40.00 120.00 300.00
22-Bondage-c — 26.00 78.00 195.00
24-26: 24-Adam Peril, U.S.N. begins. 25-Origin & 1st app. Corsair Queen. 26-last Spanish Main — 22.00 66.00 165.00
27-Crandall-c/a — 34.00 101.00 250.00
Super Reprint #12 (1964)-Crandall-r/#21 — 2.50 7.50 25.00

BUCCANEERS, THE (TV)
Dell Publishing Co.: No. 800, 1957

Buck Duck #2 © MAR

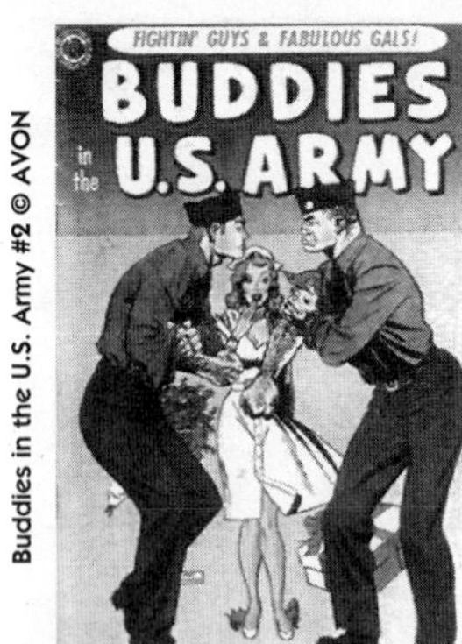

Buddies in the U.S. Army #2 © AVON

Buffy The Vampire Slayer #1 © 20th Century Fox

	GD25	FN65	NM94
Four Color 800-Photo-c	6.40	19.00	70.00

BUCKAROO BANZAI (Movie)
Marvel Comics Group: Dec, 1984 - No. 2, Feb, 1985

1,2-Movie adaptation; r/Marvel Super Special #33 — 1.00

BUCK DUCK
Atlas Comics (ANC): June, 1953 - No. 4, Dec, 1953

1-Funny animal stories in all 11.00 34.00 85.00
2-4: 2-Ed Win-a(5) 5.70 17.00 35.00

BUCK JONES (Also see Crackajack Funnies, Famous Feature Stories, Master Comics #7 & Wow Comics #1, 1936)
Dell Publishing Co.: No. 299, Oct, 1950 - No. 850, Oct, 1957 (All Painted-c)

Four Color 299(#1)-Buck Jones & his horse Silver-B begin; painted back-c begins, ends #5 11.00 34.00 125.00
2(4-6/51) 6.00 18.00 65.00
3-8(10-12/52) 5.00 15.00 55.00
Four Color 460,500,546,589 4.50 13.50 50.00
Four Color 652,733,850 2.75 8.00 30.00

BUCK ROGERS (In the 25th Century)
Kelloggs Corn Flakes Giveaway: 1933 (6x8", 36 pgs)

370A-By Phil Nowlan & Dick Calkins; 1st Buck Rogers radio premium & 1st app. in comics (tells origin) (Reissued in 1995) 60.00 250.00 425.00
with envelope 68.00 272.00 475.00

BUCK ROGERS (Also see Famous Funnies, Pure Oil Comics, Salerno Carnival of Comics, 24 Pages of Comics, & Vicks Comics)
Famous Funnies: Winter, 1940-41 - No. 6, Sept, 1943

1-Sunday strip reprints by Rick Yager; begins with strip #190; Calkins-c 300.00 900.00 2700.00
2 (7/41)-Calkins-c 118.00 354.00 1000.00
3 (12/41), 4 (7/42) 100.00 300.00 850.00
5-Story continues with Famous Funnies No. 80; Buck Rogers, Sky Roads 88.00 264.00 750.00
6-Reprints of 1939 dailies; contains B.R. story "Crater of Doom" (2 pgs.) by Calkins not-r from Famous Funnies 88.00 264.00 750.00

BUCK ROGERS
Toby Press: No. 100, Jan, 1951 - No. 9, May-June, 1951

100(#7)-All strip-r begin 25.00 76.00 190.00
101(#8), 9-All Anderson-a(1947-49-r/dailies) 20.00 60.00 150.00

BUCK ROGERS (...in the 25th Century No. 5 on) (TV)
Gold Key/Whitman No. 7 on: Oct, 1964; No. 2, July, 1979 - No. 16, May, 1982 (No #10)

1(10128-410, 12¢)-1st S.A. app. Buck Rogers & 1st new B. R. in comics since 1933 giveaway; painted-c; back-c pin-up 4.50 13.50 50.00
2(7/79)-6: 3,4,6-Movie adaptation; painted-c — 4.50
7,11 (Whitman) — 5.00
8-10 (prepack)(scarce) .90 2.70 8.00
12-16 — 3.00
Giant Movie Edition 11296(64pp, Whitman, $1.50), reprints GK #2-4 minus cover; tabloid size; photo-c (See Marvel Treasury) 1.50 4.50 15.00
Giant Movie Edition 02489(Western/Marvel, $1.50), reprints GK #2-4 minus cover 1.40 4.20 14.00
NOTE: *Bolle a-2p,3p, Movie Ed.(p).* ***McWilliams*** *a-2i,3i, 5-11, Movie Ed.(i). Painted c-1-9,11-13.*

BUCK ROGERS (Comics Module)
TSR, Inc.: 1990 - No. 10, 1991 ($2.95, 44 pgs.)

1-5 (1990): 1-Begin origin in 3 parts. 2-Indicia says #1. 2,3-Black Barney back-up story. 4-All Black Barney issue; B. B.-c. 5-Indicia says #6; Black Barney-c & lead story; Buck Rogers back-up story. — 3.00
6-10 (1991): 10-Flip book (72 pgs.) — 3.00

BUCKSKIN (TV)
Dell Publishing Co.: No. 1011, July, 1959 - No. 1107, June-Aug, 1960

	GD25	FN65	NM94
Four Color 1011 (#1)-Photo-c	6.40	19.00	70.00
Four Color 1107-Photo-c	5.50	16.50	60.00

BUCKY O'HARE (Funny Animal)
Continuity Comics: 1988 ($5.95, graphic novel)

1-Michael Golden-c/a(r); r/serial-Echo of Futurepast #1-6. 2.00 6.00
Deluxe Hardcover ($40, 52pg, 8x11") — 40.00

BUCKY O'HARE
Continuity Comics: Jan, 1991 - No. 5, 1991 ($2.00)

1-6: 1-Michael Golden-c/a — 2.00

BUDDIES IN THE U.S. ARMY
Avon Periodicals: Nov, 1952 - No. 2, 1953

1-Lawrence-c 11.00 32.00 80.00
2-Mort Lawrence-c/a 7.15 21.50 50.00

BUFFALO BEE (TV)
Dell Publishing Co.: No. 957, Nov, 1958 - No. 1061, Dec-Feb, 1959-60

Four Color 957 (#1) 9.00 27.00 100.00
Four Color 1002 (8-10/59), 1061 6.00 18.00 65.00

BUFFALO BILL (See Frontier Fighters, Super Western Comics &Western Action Thrillers)
Youthful Magazines: No. 2, Oct, 1950 - No. 9, Dec, 1951

2-Annie Oakley story 10.00 30.00 75.00
3-9: 2-4-Walter Johnson-c/a. 9-Wildey-a 6.70 20.00 45.00

BUFFALO BILL CODY (See Cody of the Pony Express)

BUFFALO BILL, JR. (TV) (See Western Roundup)
Dell/Gold Key: Jan, 1956 - No. 13, Aug-Oct, 1959; 1965 (All photo-c)

Four Color 673 (#1) 5.75 17.00 63.00
Four Color 742,766,798,828,856(11/57) 4.00 12.00 45.00
7(2-4/58)-13 3.00 10.00 36.00
1(6/65, Gold Key)-Photo-c(r/F.C. #798); photo-b/c 3.00 10.00 36.00

BUFFALO BILL PICTURE STORIES
Street & Smith Publications: June-July, 1949 - No. 2, Aug-Sept, 1949

1,2-Wildey, Powell-a in each 11.00 32.00 80.00

BUFFY THE VAMPIRE SLAYER (Based on the TV series)
Dark Horse Comics: 1998 - Present ($2.95)

1-Bennett-a/Watson-s; Art Adams-c — 4.00
1-Variant photo-c — 4.00
1-Gold foil logo Art Adams-c — 12.00
1-Gold foil logo photo-c — 15.00
2-Bachalo-c and photo-c — 3.00

BUG
Marvel Comics: Mar, 1997 ($2.99, one-shot)

1-Micronauts character — 3.00

BUGALOOS (TV)
Charlton Comics: Sept, 1971 - No. 4, Feb, 1972

1 2.20 6.25 22.00
2-4 1.60 4.80 16.00
NOTE: *No. 3(1/72) went on sale late in 1972 (after No. 4) with the 1/73 issues.*

BUGBOY
Image Comics: June, 1998 ($3.95, B&W, one-shot)

1-Mark Lewis-s/a — 3.95

BUGHOUSE (Satire)
Ajax/Farrell (Excellent Publ.): Mar-Apr, 1954 - No. 4, Sept-Oct, 1954

V1#1 16.00 48.00 120.00
2-4 9.30 28.00 70.00

BUGS BUNNY (See The Best of..., Camp Comics, Comic Album #2, 6, 10, 14, Dell Giant #28, 32, 46, Dynabrite, Golden Comics Digest #1, 3, 5, 6, 8, 10, 14, 15, 17, 21, 26, 30, 34, 39,

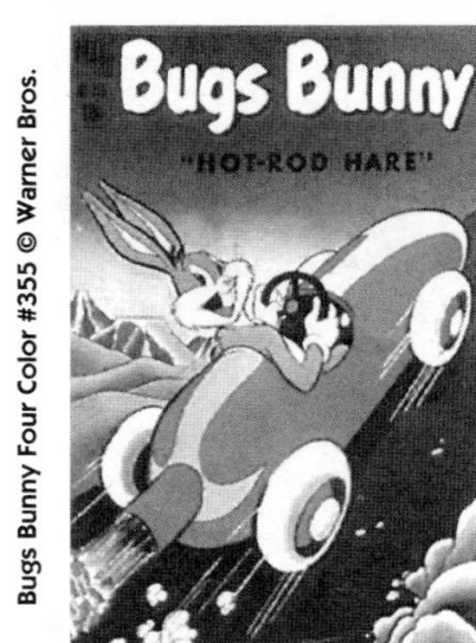

Bugs Bunny Four Color #355 © Warner Bros.

Bugs Bunny #1 © Warner Bros.

Bulletman #6 © FAW

	GD25	FN65	NM94

42, 47, Kite Fun Book, Large Feature Comic #8, Looney Tunes and Merry Melodies, March of Comics #44, 59, 75, 83, 97, 115, 132, 149, 160, 179, 188, 201, 220, 231, 245, 259, 273, 287, 301, 315, 329, 343, 363, 367, 380, 392, 403, 415, 428, 440, 452, 464, 476, 487, Porky Pig, Puffed Wheat, Story Hour Series #802, Super Book #14, 26 and Whitman Comic Books)

BUGS BUNNY (See Dell Giants for annuals)
Dell Publishing Co./Gold Key No. 86-218/Whitman No. 219 on: 1942 - No. 245, 1983

	GD25	FN65	NM94
Large Feature Comic 8(1942)-(Rarely found in fine-mint condition)	105.00	315.00	1150.00
Four Color 33 ('43)	105.00	315.00	1150.00
Four Color 51	34.00	102.00	370.00
Four Color 88	19.00	57.00	210.00
Four Color 123('46),142,164	14.00	42.00	155.00
Four Color 187,200,217,233	9.50	28.50	105.00
Four Color 250-Used in **SOTI**, pg. 309	11.00	33.00	120.00
Four Color 266,274,281,289,298('50)	8.00	25.00	90.00
Four Color 307,317(#1),327(#2),338,347,355,366,376,393	7.00	20.00	75.00
Four Color 407,420,432(10/52)	5.50	16.50	60.00
Four Color 498(9/53),585(9/54), 647(9/55)	4.50	13.50	50.00
Four Color 724(9/56),838(9/57),1064(12/59)	3.60	11.00	40.00
28(12-1/52-53)-30	3.50	10.50	38.00
31-50	2.50	7.50	28.00
51-85(7-9/62)	2.25	6.75	18.00
86(10/62)-88-Bugs Bunny's Showtime-(25¢, 80pgs.)	5.00	15.00	55.00
89-99	1.75	5.25	14.00
100	2.00	6.00	16.00
101-120	1.00	3.00	10.00
121-140	.90	2.70	8.00
141-170		2.00	6.00
171-218			3.50
219,220,225-237: 229-Swipe of Barks story/WDC&S #223			4.00
221(9/80),222(11/80)-Pre-pack?	.90	2.70	8.00
223 (1/81),224 (3/81)-Low distr.			5.00
238-245 (#90070 on-c, nd, nd code; pre-pack?		2.00	6.00

NOTE: *Reprints-100, 102, 104, 123, 143, 144, 147, 167, 173, 175-177, 179-185, 187, 190.*

	GD25	FN65	NM94
...Comic-Go-Round 11196-(224 pgs.)($1.95)(Golden Press, 1979)	1.50	4.50	15.00
...Winter Fun 1(12/67-Gold Key)-Giant	2.70	8.00	30.00

BUGS BUNNY (Puffed Rice Giveaway)
Quaker Cereals: 1949 (32 pgs. each, 3-1/8x6-7/8")

A1-Traps the Counterfeiters, A2-Aboard Mystery Submarine, A3- Rocket to the Moon, A4-Lion Tamer, A5-Rescues the Beautiful Princess, B1-Buried Treasure, B2-Outwits the Smugglers, B3-Joins the Marines, B4-Meets the Dwarf Ghost, B5-Finds Aladdin's Lamp, C1-Lost in the Frozen North, C2-Secret Agent, C3-Captured by Cannibals, C4-Fights the Man from Mars, C5-And the Haunted Cave

	GD25	FN65	NM94
each....	5.70	17.00	40.00

BUGS BUNNY (3-D)
Cheerios Giveaway: 1953 (Pocket size) (15 titles)

	GD25	FN65	NM94
each....	6.85	21.00	48.00

BUGS BUNNY
DC Comics: June, 1990 - No. 3, Aug, 1990 ($1.00, limited series)

	GD25	FN65	NM94
1-3: Daffy Duck, Elmer Fudd, others app.			1.00

BUGS BUNNY (...Monthly on-c)
DC Comics: 1993 - No. 3, 1994? ($1.95)

	GD25	FN65	NM94
1-3-Bugs, Porky Pig, Daffy, Road Runner			2.00

BUGS BUNNY & PORKY PIG
Gold Key: Sept, 1965 (Paper-c, giant, 100 pgs.)

	GD25	FN65	NM94
1(30025-509)	7.00	20.00	80.00

BUGS BUNNY'S ALBUM (See Bugs Bunny, Four Color No. 498,585,647,724)

BUGS BUNNY LIFE STORY ALBUM (See Bugs Bunny, Four Color No. 838)

BUGS BUNNY MERRY CHRISTMAS (See Bugs Bunny, Four Color No. 1064)

BULLET CROW, FOWL OF FORTUNE
Eclipse Comics: Mar, 1987 - No. 2, Apr, 1987 ($2.00, B&W, limited series)

	GD25	FN65	NM94
1,2-The Comic Reader-r & new-a			2.00

BULLETMAN (See Fawcett Miniatures, Master Comics, Mighty Midget Comics, Nickel Comics & XMas Comics)
Fawcett Publications: Sum, 1941 - #12, 2/12/43; #14, Spr, 1946 - #16, Fall, 1946 (No #13)

	GD25	FN65	NM94
1-Silver metallic-c	295.00	885.00	2800.00
2-Raboy-c	135.00	405.00	1150.00
3,5-Raboy-c each	98.00	294.00	835.00
4	86.00	258.00	730.00
6-10: 7-Ghost Stories told by night watchman of cemetery begins; Eisnerish-a; hidden message "Chic Stone is a jerk"	71.00	213.00	600.00
11,12,14-16 (nn 13): 12-Robot-c	53.00	159.00	450.00
Well Known Comics (1942)-Paper-c, glued binding; printed in red (Bestmaid/Samuel Lowe giveaway)	13.50	41.00	95.00

NOTE: ***Mac Raboy** c-1-3, 5, 6, 10. "Bulletman the Flying Detective" on cover #8 on.*

BULLETS AND BRACELETS (Also see Marvel Versus DC #3 & DC Versus Marvel #4)
Marvel Comics (Amalgam): Apr, 1996 ($1.95)

	GD25	FN65	NM94
1-John Ostrander script & Gary Frank-c/a			2.00

BULLS-EYE (Cody of The Pony Express No. 8 on)
Mainline No. 1-5/Charlton No. 6,7: 7-8/54-No. 5, 3-4/55; No. 6, 6/55; No. 7, 8/55

	GD25	FN65	NM94
1-S&K-c, 2 pgs.-a	46.00	138.00	390.00
2-S&K-c/a	41.00	122.00	325.00
3-5-S&K-c/a(2 each). 4-Last pre-code issue (1-2/55). 5-Censored issue with tomahawks removed in battle scene	33.00	100.00	250.00
6-S&K-c/a	26.00	78.00	195.00
7-S&K-c/a(3)	33.00	100.00	250.00
Great Scott Shoe Store giveaway-Reprints #2 with new cover	17.00	52.00	130.00

BULLS-EYE COMICS (Formerly Komik Pages #10; becomes Kayo #12)
Harry 'A' Chesler: No. 11, 1944

	GD25	FN65	NM94
11-Origin K-9, Green Knight's sidekick, Lance; The Green Knight, Lady Satan, Yankee Doodle Jones app.	37.00	110.00	275.00

BULLWHIP GRIFFIN (See Movie Comics)

BULLWINKLE (...and Rocky No. 20 on; See March of Comics #233 and Rocky & Bullwinkle)(TV) (Jay Ward)
Dell/Gold Key: 3-5/62 - #11, 4/74; #12, 6/76 - #19, 3/78; #20, 4/79 - #25, 2/80

	GD25	FN65	NM94
Four Color 1270 (3-5/62)	18.00	55.00	200.00
01-090-209 (Dell, 7-9/62)	14.00	44.00	160.00
1(11/62, Gold Key)	13.00	39.00	145.00
2(2/63)	7.50	22.50	85.00
3(4/72)-11(4/74-Gold Key)	4.00	12.00	45.00
12(6/76)-Reprints	2.25	6.75	18.00
13(9/76), 14-New stories	2.25	6.75	18.00
15-25	1.25	3.75	10.00
Mother Moose Nursery Pomes 01-530-207 (5-7/62, Dell)	18.00	55.00	200.00

NOTE: *Reprints: 6, 7, 20-24.*

BULLWINKLE (...& Rocky No. 2 on)(TV)
Charlton Comics: July, 1970 - No. 7, July, 1971

	GD25	FN65	NM94
1	4.00	12.25	45.00
2-7	3.20	9.50	34.00

BULLWINKLE AND ROCKY
Star Comics/Marvel Comics No. 3 on: Nov, 1987 - No. 9, Mar, 1989

	GD25	FN65	NM94
1-9: 3,5,8-Dudley Do-Right app. 4-Reagan-c			4.00

BUMMER

Buster Bear #1 © QUA

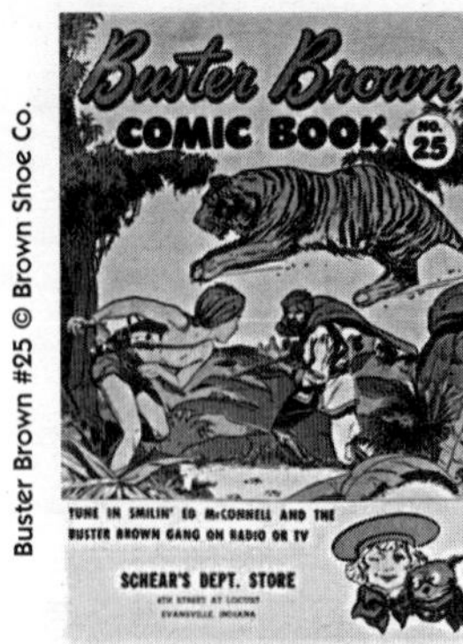

Buster Brown #25 © Brown Shoe Co.

Cable #14 © MAR

GD25 FN65 NM94

Fantagraphics Books: June, 1995 ($3.50, B&W, mature)
1 — 3.50

BUNNY (Also see Rock Happening)
Harvey Publications: Dec, 1966 - No. 20, Dec, 1971; No. 21, Nov, 1976
1-68 pg. Giants begin 4.50 13.50 50.00
2-10 2.70 8.00 30.00
11-18: 18-Last 68 pg. Giant 2.20 6.50 24.00
19-21-52 pg. Giants: 21-Fruitman app. 2.00 6.00 20.00

BURKE'S LAW (TV)
Dell Publ.: 1-3/64; No. 2, 5-7/64; No. 3, 3-5/65 (All have Gene Barry photo-c)
1-Photo-c 4.00 12.00 45.00
2,3-Photo-c 3.00 9.00 35.00

BURNING ROMANCES (See Fox Giants)

BUSTER BEAR
Quality Comics Group (Arnold Publ.): Dec, 1953 - No. 10, June, 1955
1-Funny animal 7.15 21.50 50.00
2 4.15 12.50 25.00
3-10 4.00 10.00 20.00
I.W. Reprint #9,10 (Super on inside) 1.00 3.00 8.00

BUSTER BROWN COMICS (Radio)(Also see My Dog Tige)
Brown Shoe Co: 1945 - No. 43, 1959 (No. 5: paper-c)
nn, nd (#1,scarce)-Featuring Smilin' Ed McConnell & the Buster Brown gang "Midnight" the cat, "Squeaky" the mouse & "Froggy" the Gremlin; covers mention diff. shoe stores. Contains adventure stories 59.00 177.00 500.00
2 18.00 54.00 135.00
3,5-10 9.30 28.00 70.00
4 (Rare)-Low print run due to paper shortage 15.00 44.00 110.00
11-20 6.50 19.50 45.00
21-24,26-28 5.35 16.00 32.00
25,33-37,40,41-Crandall-a in all 9.30 28.00 65.00
29-32-"Interplanetary Police Vs. the Space Siren" by Crandall (pencils only #29) 9.30 28.00 65.00
38,39,42,43 5.35 16.00 32.00
...Goes to Mars (2/58-Western Printing), slick-c, 20 pgs., reg. size 9.30 28.00 70.00
...In "Buster Makes the Team!" (1959-Custom Comics) 5.70 17.00 40.00
...In The Jet Age ('50s), slick-c, 20 pgs., 5x7-1/4" 9.30 28.00 65.00
...Of the Safety Patrol ('60-Custom Comics) 4.00 12.00 24.00
...Out of This World ('59-Custom Comics) 5.70 17.00 40.00
...Safety Coloring Book ('58, 16 pgs.)-Slick paper 5.70 17.00 35.00

BUSTER BUNNY
Standard Comics(Animated Cartoons)/Pines: Nov, 1949 - No. 16, Oct, 1953
1-Frazetta 1 pg. text illo. 7.15 21.50 50.00
2 4.15 12.50 25.00
3-16: 15-Racist-c 3.60 9.00 18.00

BUSTER CRABBE (TV)
Famous Funnies Publ.: Nov, 1951 - No. 12, 1953
1-1st app.(?) Frazetta anti-drug ad; text story about Buster Crabbe & Billy the Kid 31.00 92.00 230.00
2-Williamson/Evans-c; text story about Wild Bill Hickok & Pecos Bill 32.00 96.00 240.00
3-Williamson/Evans-c/a 36.00 108.00 270.00
4-Frazetta-c/a, 1pg.; bondage-c 42.00 127.00 340.00
5-Frazetta-c; Williamson/Krenkel/Orlando-a, 11pgs. (per Mr. Williamson) 97.00 291.00 825.00
6,8 15.00 44.00 110.00
7-Frazetta one pg. ad 16.00 48.00 120.00
9-One pg. Frazetta Boy Scouts ad (1st?) 13.00 40.00 100.00

GD25 FN65 NM94

10-12 9.30 28.00 65.00
NOTE: Eastern Color sold 3 dozen each NM file copies of #s 9-12 a few years ago.

BUSTER CRABBE (The Amazing Adventures of...)(Movie star)
Lev Gleason Publications: Dec, 1953 - No. 4, June, 1954
1,4: 1-Photo-c. 4-Flash Gordon-c 19.00 56.00 140.00
2,3-Toth-a 17.00 52.00 130.00

BUTCH CASSIDY
Skywald Comics: June, 1971 - No. 3, Oct, 1971 (52 pgs.)
1-Red Mask reprint, retitled Maverick; Bolle-a; Sutton-a 1.00 3.00 10.00
2,3: 2-Whip Wilson-r. 3-Dead Canyon Days reprint/Crack Western No. 63; Sundance Kid app.; Crandall-a .90 2.70 8.00

BUTCH CASSIDY (...& the Wild Bunch)
Avon Periodicals: 1951
1-Kinstler-c/a 15.00 46.00 115.00
NOTE: ***Reinman*** *story; Issue number on inside spine.*

BUTCH CASSIDY (See Fun-In No. 11 & Western Adventure Comics)

BUTCHER, THE (Also see Brave and the Bold, 2nd Series))
DC Comics: May, 1990 - No. 5, Sept, 1990 ($1.50, mature)
1-5: 1-No indicia inside — 1.50

BUZ SAWYER (Sweeney No. 4 on)
Standard Comics: June, 1948 - No. 3, 1949
1-Roy Crane-a 20.00 60.00 150.00
2-Intro his pal Sweeney 11.00 34.00 85.00
3 9.30 28.00 70.00

BUZ SAWYER'S PAL, ROSCOE SWEENEY (See Sweeney)

BUZZ BUZZ COMICS MAGAZINE
Horse Press: May, 1996 ($4.95, B&W, over-sized magazine)
1-Paul Pope-c/a/scripts; Moebius-a — 5.00

BUZZY (See All Funny Comics)
National Periodical Publications/Detective Comics: Winter, 1944-45 - No. 75, 1-2/57; No. 76, 10/57; No. 77, 10/58
1 (52 pgs. begin); "America's favorite teenster" 25.00 76.00 190.00
2 (Spr, 1945) 12.00 36.00 90.00
3-5 8.50 26.00 60.00
6-10 5.70 17.00 38.00
11-20 5.35 16.00 32.00
21-30 4.00 12.00 24.00
31,35-38 4.00 10.00 20.00
32-34,39-Last 52 pgs. Scribbly story by Mayer in each (these four stories were done for Scribbly #14 which was delayed for a year) 4.00 12.00 24.00
40-77: 62-Last precode (2/55) 3.60 9.00 18.00

BUZZY THE CROW (See Harvey Comics Hits #60 & 62, Harvey Hits #18 & Paramount Animated Comics #1)

BY BIZARRE HANDS
Dark Horse Comics: Apr, 1994 - No. 3, June, 1994 ($2.50, B&W, mature)
1-3: Lansdale stories — 2.50

CABBOT: BLOODHUNTER (Also see Bloodstrike & Bloodstrike: Assassin)
Maximum Press: Jan, 1997 ($2.50, one-shot)
1-Rick Veitch-a/script; Platt-c; Thor, Chapel & Prophet cameos — 2.50

CABLE (See Ghost Rider &..., & New Mutants #87)
Marvel Comics: May, 1993 - Present ($3.50/$1.95/$1.50)
1-($3.50, 52 pgs.)-Gold foil & embossed-c; Thibert a-1-4p; c-1-3; Liefeld-a assist #4 — 3.50
2-15: 3-Extra 16 pg. X-Men/Avengers ann. preview. 4-Liefeld-a assist; last

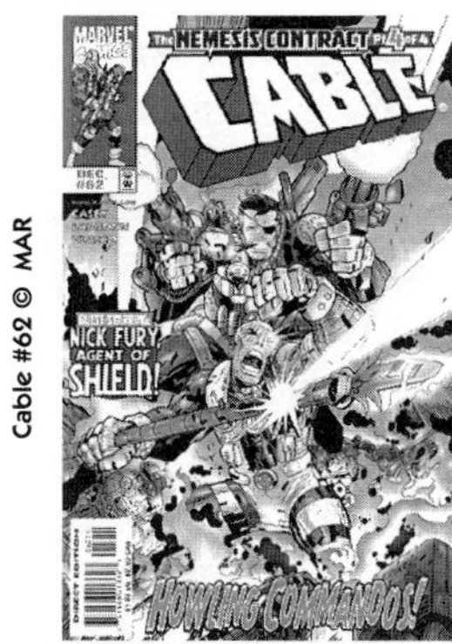

Cable #62 © MAR

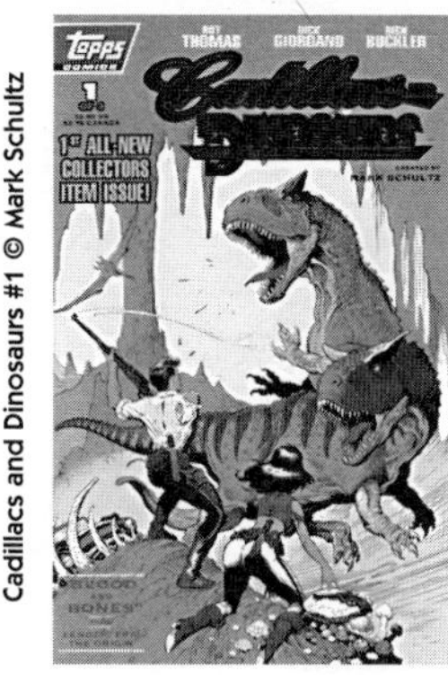

Cadillacs and Dinosaurs #1 © Mark Schultz

Calling All Boys #9 © PMI

GD25 FN65 NM94

Thibert-a(p). 6-8-Reveals that Baby Nathan is Cable; gives background on Stryfe. 9-Omega Red-c/story. 11-Bound-in trading card sheet 2.00
16-Newsstand edition 2.00
16-Enhanced edition 2.00 6.00
17-20-($1.95)-Deluxe edition, 20-w/bound in '95 Fleer Ultra cards 2.00
17-20-($1.50)-Standard edition 1.50
21-24, 26-44, -1(7/97): 21-Begin $1.95-c; return from Age of Apocalyse. 24-Grizzly dies. 28-vs. Sugarman; Mr. Sinister app. 30-X-Man-c/app.; Exodus app. 31-vs. X-Man. 32-Post app. 33-Post-c/app; Mandarin app (flashback); includes "Onslaught Update". 34-Onslaught x-over; Hulk-c/app.; Apocalypse app (cont'd in Hulk #444). 35-Onslaught x-over; Apocalypse vs. Cable. 36-w/card insert. 38-Weapon X-c/app; Psycho Man & Micronauts app. 40-Scott Clark-a(p). 41-Bishop-c/app. 2.00
25 ($3.95)-Foil gatefold-c 4.00
45-49: 45-Begin $1.99-c; Operation Zero Tolerance. 2.00
50-($2.99) Double sized w/wraparound-c 3.00
51-58: 51-1st Casey-s. 54-Black Panther. 55-Domino-c/app. 62-Nick Fury-c/app. 63-Stryfe-c/app. 2.00
.../Machine Man '98 Annual ($2.99) Wraparound-c 3.00
.../X-Force '96 Annual ($2.95) Wraparound-c 3.00

CABLE - BLOOD AND METAL (Also see New Mutants #87 & X-Force #8)
Marvel Comics: Oct, 1992 - No. 2, Nov, 1992 ($2.50, limited series, 52 pgs.)

1-Fabian Nicieza scripts; John Romita, Jr.-c/a in both; Cable vs. Stryfe; 2nd app. of The Wild Pack (becomes The Six Pack); wraparound-c. 3.50
2-Prelude to X-Cutioner's Song 2.50

CADET GRAY OF WEST POINT (See Dell Giants)

CADILLACS & DINOSAURS (TV)
Marvel Comics (Epic Comics): Nov, 1990 - No. 6, Apr, 1991 ($2.50, limited series, coated paper)

1-6: r/Xenozoic Tales in color w/new-c 2.50
...In 3-D #1 (7/92, $3.95, Kitchen Sink)-With glasses 5.00

CADILLACS AND DINOSAURS (TV)
Topps Comics: V2#1, Feb, 1994 - V2#9, 1995 ($2.50, limited series)

V2#1-($2.95)-Collector's edition w/Stout-c & bound-in poster; Buckler-a; foil stamped logo; Giordano-a in all 3.00
V2#1-Newsstand edition w/Giordano-c 2.50
2,3-Collector's editions w/Stout-c & posters 2.50
2,3-Newsstand ed. w/Giordano-c; w/o posters 2.50
4-6-Collectors edition; Kieth-c 2.50
4-6-Newsstand edition 2.50
7-9-Linsner-c 2.75

CAFFEINE
Slave Labor Graphics: Jan, 1996 - Present ($2.95, B&W)

1-9 3.00

CAGE (Also see Hero for Hire, Power Man & Punisher)
Marvel Comics: Apr, 1992 - No. 20, Nov, 1993 ($1.25)

1-($1.50)-Has extra color on-c 1.50
2-11,13-20: 3-Punisher-c & minor app. 9-Rhino-c/story; Hulk cameo. 10-Rhino & Hulk-c/story 1.25
12-($1.75, 52 pgs.)-Iron Fist app. 1.75

CAGED HEAT 3000 (Movie)
Roger Corman's Cosmic Comics: Nov, 1995 - No. 3, Jan, 1996 ($2.50)

1-3: Adaptation of film 2.50

CAGES
Tundra Publ.: 1991 - No. 10, May, 1996 ($3.50/$3.95/$4.95, limited series)

1-Dave McKean-c/a in all 1.20 3.60 12.00
2-Misprint exists .90 2.70 8.00
3-9: 5-$3.95-c begins 4.00

GD25 FN65 NM94

10-($4.95) 5.00

CAIN'S HUNDRED (TV)
Dell Publishing Co.: May-July, 1962 - No. 2, Sept-Nov, 1962

nn(01-094-207) 1.80 5.40 20.00
2 1.40 4.20 14.00

CAIN/VAMPIRELLA FLIP BOOK
Harris Comics: Oct, 1994 ($6.95, one-shot, squarebound)

nn-contains Cain #3 & #4; flip book is r/Vampirella story from 1993 Creepy Fearbook. .90 2.70 7.50

CALIBER PRESENTS
Caliber Press: Jan, 1989 - No. 24, 1991 ($1.95/$2.50, B&W, 52 pgs.)

1-Anthology; 1st app. The Crow; Tim Vigil-c/a 5.50 16.50 60.00
2-Deadworld story; Tim Vigil-a 5.00
3-14: 9-Begin $2.50-c 3.00
15-24 ($3.50, 68 pgs.) 3.50

CALIBER PRESENTS: CINDERELLA ON FIRE
Caliber Press: 1994 ($2.95, B&W, mature)

1 3.00

CALIBER SPOTLIGHT
Caliber Press: May, 1995 ($2.95, B&W)

1-Kabuki app 3.50

CALIBRATIONS
Caliber: 1996 - No. 5 (99¢, anthology)

1-5: 1-Jill Thompson-c/a. 1,2-Atmospherics by Warren Ellis 1.00

CALIFORNIA GIRLS
Eclipse Comics: June, 1987 - No. 8, May, 1988 ($2.00, 40 pgs, B&W)

1-8: All contain color paper dolls 2.00

CALL FROM CHRIST
Catechetical Educational Society: 1952 (Giveaway, 36 pgs.)

nn 2.40 6.00 12.00

CALLING ALL BOYS (Tex Granger No. 18 on)
Parents' Magazine Institute: Jan, 1946 - No. 17, May, 1948 (Photo c-1-5,7,8)

1 9.30 28.00 70.00
2-Contains Roy Rogers article 5.00 15.00 30.00
3-7,9,11,14-17: 6-Painted-c. 11-Rin Tin Tin photo on-c; Tex Granger begins. 14-J. Edgar Hoover photo on-c. 15-Tex Granger-c begin 4.00 11.00 22.00
8-Milton Caniff story 5.70 17.00 38.00
10-Gary Cooper photo on-c 5.70 17.00 35.00
12-Bob Hope photo on-c 7.85 23.50 55.00
13-Bing Crosby photo on-c 6.50 19.50 45.00

CALLING ALL GIRLS
Parents' Magazine Institute: Sept, 1941 - No. 89, Sept, 1949 (Part magazine, part comic)

1 11.00 34.00 85.00
2-Photo-c 6.00 18.00 42.00
3-Shirley Temple photo-c 7.15 21.50 50.00
4-10: 4,5,7,9-Photo-c. 9-Flag-c 4.25 13.00 28.00
11-Tina Thayer photo-c; Mickey Rooney photo-b/c; B&W photo inside of Gary Cooper as Lou Gehrig in "Pride of Yankees" 4.15 12.50 25.00
12-20 4.00 11.00 22.00
21-39,41-43(10-11/45)-Last issue with comics 3.20 8.00 16.00
40-Liz Taylor photo-c 8.50 26.00 60.00
44-51(7/46)-Last comic book size issue 3.00 7.50 15.00
52-89 2.40 6.00 12.00

NOTE: ***Jack Sparling*** *art in many issues; becomes a girls' magazine "Senior Prom" with #90.*

CALLING ALL KIDS (Also see True Comics)
Parents' Magazine Institute: Dec-Jan, 1945-46 - No. 26, Aug, 1949

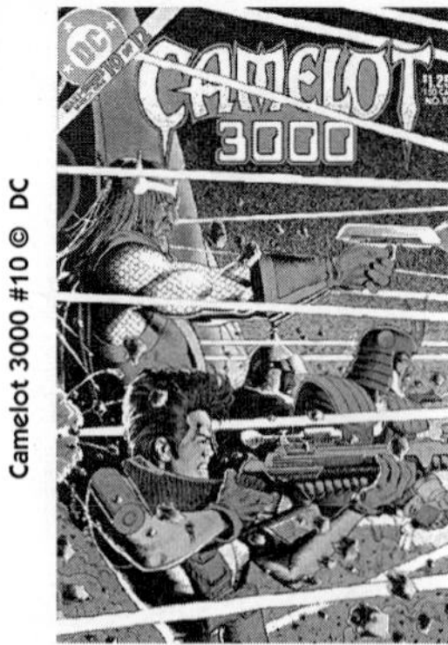

Camelot 3000 #10 © DC

Camp Comics #2 © WHIT

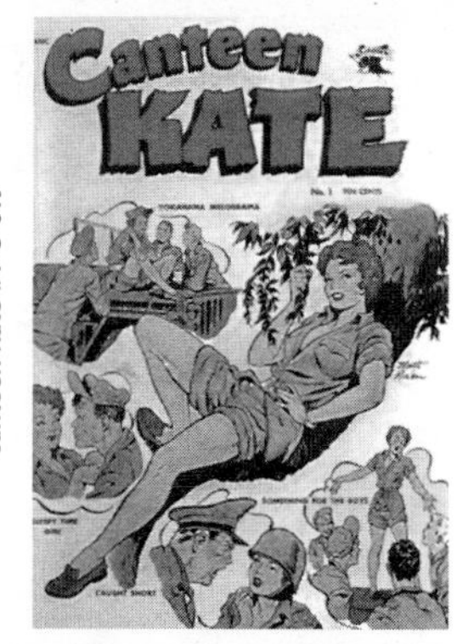

Canteen Kate #1 © STJ

	GD25	FN65	NM94
1-Funny animal	9.30	28.00	65.00
2	5.00	15.00	30.00
3-10	3.00	7.50	15.00
11-26	2.40	6.00	12.00

CALVIN (See Li'l Kids)

CALVIN & THE COLONEL (TV)
Dell Publishing Co.: No. 1354, Apr-June, 1962 - No. 2, July-Sept, 1962

	GD25	FN65	NM94
Four Color 1354(#1)	7.00	22.00	80.00
2	4.50	13.50	50.00

CAMBION
Slave Labor Graphics: Dec, 1995 - No. 2, Feb, 1996 ($2.95, B&W)

	GD25	FN65	NM94
1,2			3.00

CAMELOT 3000
DC Comics: Dec, 1982 - No. 11, July, 1984; No. 12, Apr, 1985 (Direct sales, maxi series, Mando paper)

	GD25	FN65	NM94
1-12: 1-Mike Barr scripts & Brian Bolland-c/a begin. 5-Intro Knights of New Camelot			2.50

NOTE: ***Austin** a-7i-12i. **Bolland** a-1-12p; c-1-12.*

CAMERA COMICS
U.S. Camera Publishing Corp./ME: July, 1944 - No. 9, Summer, 1946

	GD25	FN65	NM94
nn (7/44)	21.00	64.00	160.00
nn (9/44)	17.00	52.00	130.00
1(10/44)-The Grey Comet	17.00	52.00	130.00
2	11.00	34.00	85.00
3-Nazi WW II-c; photos	10.00	30.00	75.00
4-9: All half photos	9.30	28.00	70.00

CAMP CANDY (TV)
Marvel Comics: May, 1990 - No. 6, Oct, 1990 ($1.00, limited series)

	GD25	FN65	NM94
1-6: Post-c/a(p); featuring John Candy			2.00

CAMP COMICS
Dell Publishing Co.: Feb, 1942 - No. 3, April, 1942 (All have photo-c)

	GD25	FN65	NM94
1- "Seaman Sy Wheeler" by Kelly, 7 pgs.; Bugs Bunny app.; Mark Twain adaptation	46.00	138.00	390.00
2-Kelly-a, 12 pgs.; Bugs Bunny app.	38.00	114.00	285.00
3-(Scarce)-Dave Berg & Walt Kelly-a	46.00	138.00	390.00

CAMP RUNAMUCK (TV)
Dell Publishing Co.: Apr, 1966

	GD25	FN65	NM94
1-Photo-c	2.25	6.75	25.00

CAMPUS LOVES
Quality Comics Group (Comic Magazines): Dec, 1949 - No. 5, Aug, 1950

	GD25	FN65	NM94
1-Ward-c/a (9 pgs.)	27.00	80.00	200.00
2-Ward-c/a	20.00	60.00	150.00
3-5: 5-Spanking panels (2)	10.00	30.00	75.00

NOTE: ***Gustavson** a-1-5. Photo c-3-5.*

CAMPUS ROMANCE (...Romances on cover)
Avon Periodicals/Realistic: Sept-Oct, 1949 - No. 3, Feb-Mar, 1950

	GD25	FN65	NM94
1-Walter Johnson-a; c-/Avon paperback #348	20.00	60.00	150.00
2-Grandenetti-a; c-/Avon paperback #151; spanking panel	15.00	44.00	110.00
3-c-/Avon paperback #201	15.00	44.00	110.00
Realistic reprint	5.70	17.00	40.00

CANADA DRY PREMIUMS (See Swamp Fox, The & Terry & The Pirates)

CANCELLED COMIC CAVALCADE
DC Comics, Inc.: Summer, 1978 - No. 2, Fall, 1978 (8-1/2x11", B&W)
(Xeroxed pgs. on one side only w/blue cover and taped spine)

1-(412 pgs.) Contains xeroxed copies of art for: Black Lightning #12, cover to #13; Claw #13, 14; The Deserter #1; Doorway to Nightmare #6; Firestorm #6; The Green Team #2,3.
2-(532 pgs.) Contains xeroxed copies of art for: Kamandi #60 (including Omac), #61; Prez #5; Shade #9 (including The Odd Man); Showcase #105 (Deadman), 106 (The Creeper); The Vixen #1; and covers to Army at War #2, Battle Classics #3, Demand Classics #1 & 2, Dynamic Classics #3, Mr. Miracle #26, Ragman #6, Weird Mystery #25 & 26, & Western Classics #1 & 2. (Rare) (One set sold in 1989 for $1,200.00)

NOTE: *In June, 1978, DC cancelled several of their titles. For copyright purposes, the unpublished original art for these titles was xeroxed, bound in the above books, published and distributed. Only 35 copies were made.*

CANDID TALES (Also see Bold Stories & It Rhymes With Lust)
Kirby Publ. Co.: April, 1950; June, 1950 (Digest size) (144 pgs.) (Full color)

	GD25	FN65	NM94
nn-(Scarce) Contains Wood female pirate story, 15 pgs., and 14 pgs. in June issue; Powell-a	79.00	238.00	675.00

NOTE: *Another version exists with Dr. Kilmore by Wood; no female pirate story.*

CANDY
William H. Wise & Co.: Fall, 1944 - No. 3, Spring, 1945

	GD25	FN65	NM94
1-Two Scoop Scuttle stories by Wolverton	33.00	100.00	250.00
2,3-Scoop Scuttle by Wolverton, 2-4 pgs.	26.00	78.00	195.00

CANDY (Teen-age)(Also see Police Comics #37)
Quality Comics Group (Comic Magazines): Autumn, 1947 - No. 64, Jul, 1956

	GD25	FN65	NM94
1-Gustavson-a	19.00	56.00	140.00
2-Gustavson-a	9.30	28.00	70.00
3-10	6.00	18.00	42.00
11-30	4.25	13.00	28.00
31-63	4.15	12.50	25.00
64-Ward-c(p)?	4.15	12.50	25.00
Super Reprint No. 2,10,12,16,17,18('63- '64):17-Candy #12	1.50	4.50	12.00

NOTE: ***Jack Cole** 1-2 pg. art in many issues.*

CANNON (See Heroes, Inc. Presents Cannon)

CANNONBALL COMICS
Rural Home Publishing Co.: Feb, 1945 - No. 2, Mar, 1945

	GD25	FN65	NM94
1-The Crash Kid, Thunderbrand, The Captive Prince & Crime Crusader begin; skull-c	65.00	194.00	550.00
2-Devil-c	53.00	159.00	450.00

CANTEEN KATE (See All Picture All True Love Story & Fightin' Marines)
St. John Publishing Co.: June, 1952 - No. 3, Nov, 1952

	GD25	FN65	NM94
1-Matt Baker-c/a	43.00	129.00	360.00
2-Matt Baker-c/a	39.00	118.00	290.00
3-(Rare)-Used in **POP**, pg. 75; Baker-c/a	43.00	129.00	360.00

CAP'N CRUNCH COMICS (See Quaker Oats)
Quaker Oats Co.: 1963; 1965 (16 pgs.; miniature giveaways; 2-1/2x6-1/2")

	GD25	FN65	NM94
(1963 titles)- "The Picture Pirates", "The Fountain of Youth", "I'm Dreaming of a Wide Isthmus". (1965 titles)- "Bewitched, Betwitched, & Betweaked", "Seadog Meets the Witch Doctor", "A Witch in Time"	4.00	12.00	40.00

CAP'N QUICK & A FOOZLE (Also see Eclipse Mag. & Monthly)
Eclipse Comics: July, 1984 - No. 3, Nov, 1985 ($1.50, color, Baxter paper)

	GD25	FN65	NM94
1-3-Rogers-c/a			1.50

CAPTAIN ACTION (Toy)
National Periodical Publications: Oct-Nov, 1968 - No. 5, June-July, 1969 (Based on Ideal toy)

	GD25	FN65	NM94
1-Origin; Wood-a; Superman-c app.	9.00	27.00	90.00
2,3,5-Kane/Wood-a	5.50	16.50	55.00
4	4.00	12.00	40.00
...& Action Boy('67)-Ideal Toy Co. giveaway (1st app. Captain Action)	9.00	27.00	90.00

CAPTAIN AERO COMICS (Samson No. 1-6; also see Veri Best Sure Fire &Veri Best Sure Shot Comics)
Holyoke Publishing Co.: V1#7(#1), Dec, 1941 - V2#4(#10), Jan, 1943; V3#9(#11), Sept, 1943 -V4#3(#17), Oct, 1944; #21, Dec, 1944 - #26, Aug, 1946

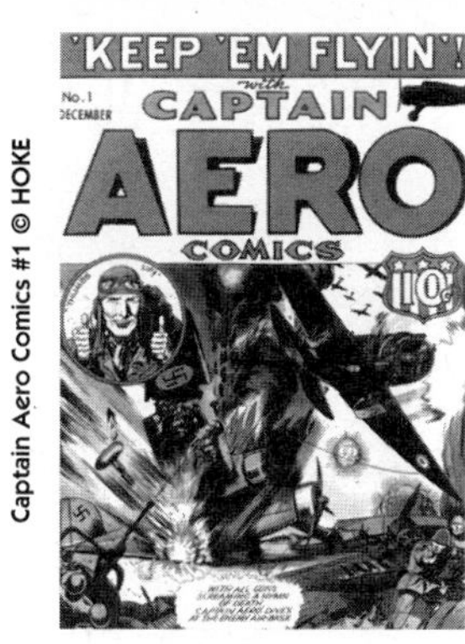

Captain Aero Comics #1 © HOKE

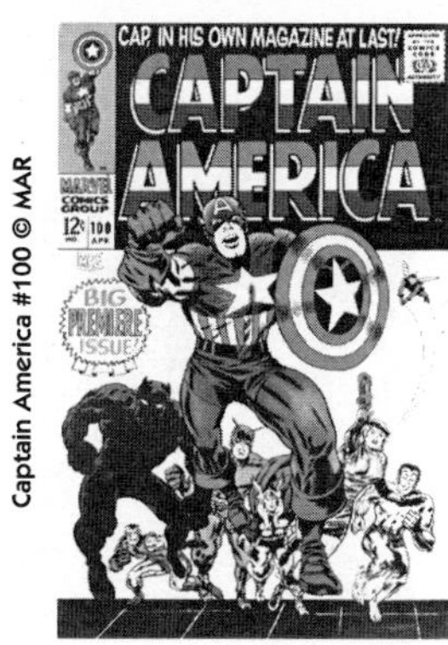

Captain America #100 © MAR

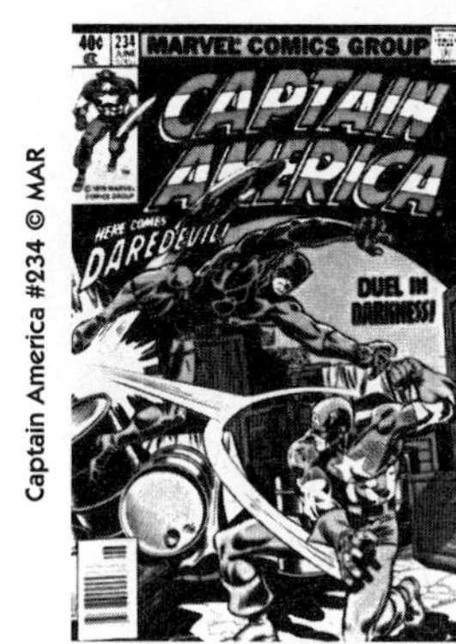

Captain America #234 © MAR

GD25 FN65 NM94

(No #18-20)
V1#7(#1)-Flag-Man & Solar, Master of Magic, Captain Aero, Cap Stone, Adventurer begin 135.00 405.00 1150.00
8(#2)-Pals of Freedom app. 68.00 204.00 575.00
9(#3)-Alias X begins; Pals of Freedom app. 68.00 204.00 575.00
10(#4)-Origin The Gargoyle; Kubert-a 68.00 204.00 575.00
11,12(#5,6)-Kubert-a; Miss Victory in #6 56.00 168.00 475.00
V2#1,2(#7,8): 8-Origin The Red Cross; Miss Victory app.; Brodsky-c(i) 37.00 110.00 275.00
3(#9)-Miss Victory app. 30.00 90.00 225.00
4(#10)-Miss Victory app. 23.00 70.00 175.00
V3#9 - V3#13(#11-15): 11,15-Miss Victory app. 19.00 56.00 140.00
V4#2(#16) 17.00 52.00 130.00
V4#3(#17), 21-24-L. B. Cole covers. 22-Intro/origin Mighty Mite. 25 30.00 90.00 225.00
26--L. B. Cole S/F-c; Palais-a(2) (scarce) 59.00 177.00 500.00
NOTE: ***L.B. Cole*** *c-17.* ***Hollingsworth*** *a-23.* ***Infantino*** *a-23, 26.* ***Schomburg*** *c-15, 16.*

CAPTAIN AMERICA (See Adventures of..., All-Select, All Winners, Aurora, Avengers #4, Blood and Glory, Captain Britain 16-20, Giant-Size..., The Invaders, Marvel Double Feature, Marvel Fanfare, Marvel Mystery, Marvel Super-Action, Marvel Super Heroes V2#3, Marvel Team-Up, Marvel Treasury Special, Power Record Comics, USA Comics, Young Allies & Young Men)

CAPTAIN AMERICA (Formerly Tales of Suspense #1-99) (Captain America and the Falcon #134-223 & Steve Rogers: Captain America #444-454 appears on cover only)
Marvel Comics Group: No. 100, Apr, 1968 - No. 454, Aug, 1996

100-Flashback on Cap's revival with Avengers & Sub-Mariner; story continued from Tales of Suspense #99; Kirby-c/a begins 20.00 60.00 275.00
101-The Sleeper-c/story; Red Skull app. 5.00 15.00 50.00
102-108: 102-Sleeper-c/s. 103,104-Red Skull-c/sty 3.00 9.00 30.00
109-Origin Capt. America retold 4.50 13.50 45.00
110,111,113-Classic Steranko-c/a: 110-Rick becomes Cap's partner; Hulk x-over; 1st app. Viper. 111-Death of Steve Rogers. 113-Cap's funeral 4.50 13.50 45.00
112-Origin retold; last Kirby-c/a 2.80 8.40 28.00
114-116,118-120: 115-Last 12¢ issue 2.25 6.75 18.00
117-1st app. The Falcon (9/69) 4.50 13.50 45.00
121-140: 121-Retells origin. 133-The Falcon becomes Cap's partner; origin Modok. 137,138-Spider-Man x-over. 140-Origin Grey Gargoyle retold .90 2.70 9.00
141,142,144-153,155-171,176-179: 142-Last 15¢ issue. 144-New costume Falcon. 153-1st app. (cameo) Jack Monroe. 155-Origin; redrawn w/Falcon added; origin J. Monroe. 158-Cap's strength increased. 160-1st app. Solarr. 164-1st app. Nightshade. 176-End of Capt. America 2.00 6.00
143-(52 pgs). 1.00 3.00 10.00
154-1st full app. Jack Monroe (Nomad)(10/72) 2.00 6.00
172-175: X-Men x-over 1.20 3.60 12.00
180-Intro/origin of Nomad (Steve Rogers) .85 2.60 7.00
181-Intro/origin new Cap. 2.00 6.00
182,184-192,194-197,199(7/76): 186-True origin The Falcon 4.00
183-Death of new Cap; Nomad becomes Cap 2.00 6.00
193,200: 193-Kirby-a returns 2.00 6.00
198-(Regular 25¢ edition)(6/76) 4.00
198-(30¢-c, limited distribution) 1.60 4.80 16.00
201-240,242-246: 215-Retells Cap's origin. 216-r/story from Strange Tales #114. 217-1st app. Marvel Man (later Quasar). 229-Marvel Man app. 230-Battles Hulk-c/story cont'd in Hulk #232. 233-Death of Sharon Carter. 234,235-Daredevil x-over; 235(7/79)-Miller-a(p). 244,245-Miller-c. 3.00
241-Punisher app.; Miller-c. .90 2.70 8.00
241-2nd print 2.00
247-255-Byrne-a. 255-Origin; Miller-c. 3.50
256-281,284,285,289-322,324-326,329-331: 264-Old X-Men cameo in flash-back. 265,266-Nick Fury & Spider-Man app. 267-1st app. Everyman. 269-1st Team America. 279-(3/83)-Contains Tattooz skin decals. 281-1950s Bucky returns. 284-Patriot (Jack Mace) app. 285-Death of Patriot. 298-Origin Red Skull 2.00
282-Bucky becomes new Nomad (Jack Monroe) 4.00
282-Silver ink 2nd print ($1.75) w/original date (6/83) 1.75
283-2nd app. Nomad 3.00
286-288-Deathlok app. 2.50
323-1st app. new Super Patriot (see Nick Fury) 4.00
327-Captain America battles Super Patriot 3.00
328-Origin & 1st app. D-Man 2.50
332-Old Cap resigns 5.00
333-Intro & origin new Captain (Super Patriot) 3.00
334-340: 339-Fall of the Mutants tie-in 3.00
341-343,345-349 1.50
344-($1.50, 52 pgs.)-Ronald Reagan cameo 2.00
350-($1.75, 68 pgs.)-Return of Steve Rogers (original Cap) to original costume 3.00
351-354: 351-Nick Fury app. 354-1st app. U.S. Agent (6/89, see Avengers West Coast) 1.50
355-382,384-396: 373-Bullseye app. 375-Daredevil app. 386-U.S. Agent app. 387-389-Red Skull back-up stories. 396-Last $1.00-c. 396,397-1st app. all new Jack O'Lantern 1.50
383-($2.00, 68 pgs.)-50th anniversary issue; Red Skull story; Jim Lee-c(i) 3.00
397-399,401-424,426: 402-Begin 6 part Man-Wolf story w/Wolverine in #403-407. 405-410-New Jack O'Lantern app. in back-up story. 406-Cable & Shatterstar cameo. 407-Capwolf vs. Cable-c/story. 408-Infinity War x-over; Falcon solo back-up. 423-Vs. Namor-c/story 1.25
400-($2.25, 84 pgs.)-Flip book format w/double gatefold-c; r/Avengers #4 plus-c; contains cover pin-ups. 2.50
425-($2.95, 52 pgs.)-Embossed Foil-c edition; Fighting Chance Pt. 1 3.00
425-($1.75, 52 pgs.)-Regular edition 1.80
427-443,446,447,449-454: 427-Begin $1.50-c; bound-in trading card sheet. 449-Thor app. 450-"Man Without A Country" storyline begins, ends #453; Bill Clinton app; variant-c exists. 451-1st app.Cap's new costume. 452-Machinesmith app. 453-Cap gets old costume back; Bill Clinton app. 1.50
444-Mark Waid scripts & Ron Garney-c/a(p) begins, ends #454; Avengers app. 5.00
445-Sharon Carter & Red Skull return. 2.50
448-($2.95, double-sized issue)-Waid script & Garney-c/a; Red Skull dies? 3.50
Special 1(1/71)-Origin retold 2.20 6.50 24.00
Special 2(1/72)-Colan-r/Not Brand Echh; all-r 1.20 3.60 12.00
Annual 3,4('76,'77, 52 pgs.)-Kirby-c/a(new); 4-Magneto-c/story (34 pgs.) .85 2.60 7.00
Annual 5-7: (52 pgs.)('81-'83) 2.50
Annual 8(9/86)-Wolverine-c/story 1.50 4.50 15.00
Annual 9(1990, $2.00, 68 pgs.)-Nomad back-up 3.00
Annual 10(1991, $2.00, 68 pgs.)-Origin retold (2 pgs.) 2.00
Annual 11(1992, $2.25, 68 pgs.)-Falcon solo story 2.25
Annual 12(1993, $2.95, 68 pgs.)-Bagged w/card 3.00
Annual 13(1994, $2.95, 68 pgs.)-Red Skull-c/story 3.00
...ASHCAN EDITION ('95, 75¢) .75
...: DEATHLOK LIVES! nn(10/93, $4.95)-r/#286-288 5.00
...DRUG WAR 1-(1994, $2.00, 52 pgs.)-New Warriors app. 2.00
...MAN WITHOUT A COUNTRY (1998, $12.99, TPB)-r/#450-453 13.00
...MEDUSA EFFECT 1 (1994, $2.95, 68 pgs.)-Origin Baron Zemo 3.00
...OPERATION REBIRTH (1996, $9.95)-r/#445-448 1.00 3.00 10.00
...STREETS OF POISON ($15.95)-r/#372-378 1.60 4.80 16.00
...: THE MOVIE SPECIAL nn (5/92, $3.50, 52 pgs.)-Adapts movie; printed on coated stock; The Red Skull app. 3.00
...& THE CAMPBELL KIDS (1980, 36pg. giveaway, Campbell's Soup/U.S. Dept. of Energy) .90 2.70 8.00
...GOES TO WAR AGAINST DRUGS (1990, no #, giveaway)-Distributed to

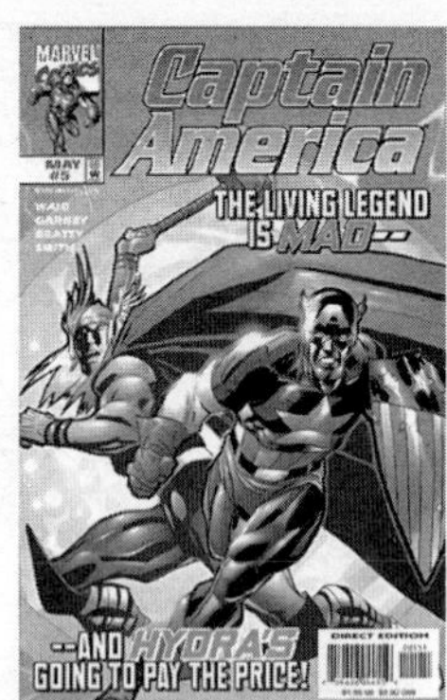

Captain America V3 #5 © MAR

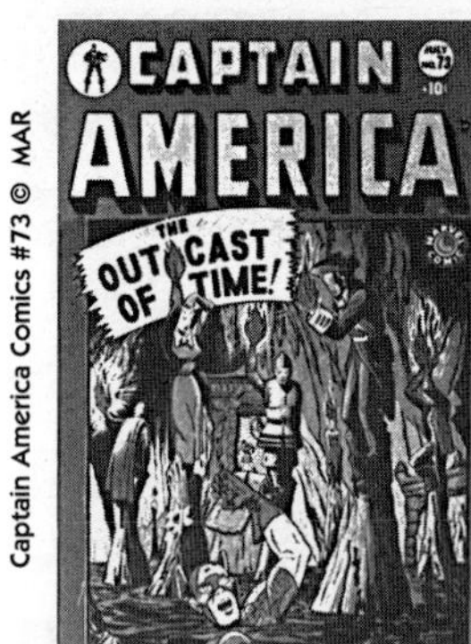

Captain America Comics #73 © MAR

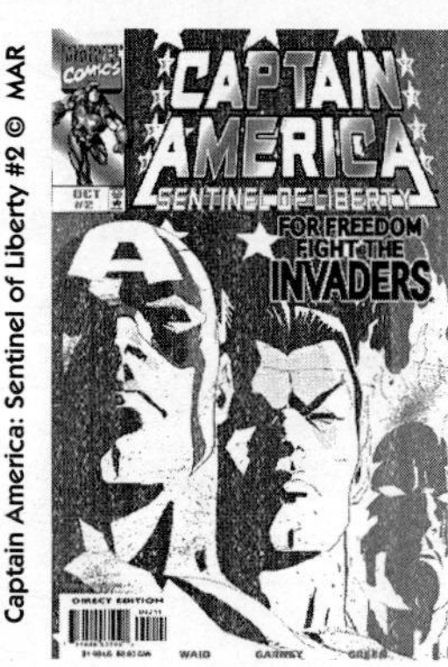

Captain America: Sentinel of Liberty #2 © MAR

GD25 FN65 NM94 GD25 FN65 NM94

direct sales shops; 2nd printing exists 4.00
...MEETS THE ASTHMA MONSTER (1987, no #, giveaway, Your Physician and Glaxo, Inc.) 2.00 6.00
...VS. ASTHMA MONSTER (1990, no #, giveaway, Your Physician & Allen & Hanbury's) 4.00

NOTE: ***Austin*** *c-225i, 239i, 246i.* ***Buscema*** *a-115p, 217p; c-136p, 217, 297.* ***Byrne*** *c-223(part), 238, 239, 247p-254p, 290, 291, 313p; a-247-254p, 255, 313p, 350.* ***Colan*** *a(p)-116-137, 256, Annual 5; c(p)-116-123, 126, 129.* ***Everett*** *a-136i, 137i; c-126i.* ***Garney*** *a(p)-444-454.* ***Gil Kane*** *a-145p; c-147p, 149p, 150p, 170p, 172-174, 180, 181p, 183-190p, 215, 216, 220, 221.* ***Kirby*** *a(p)-100-109, 112, 193-214, 216, Special 1, 2(layouts), Annual 3, 4; c-100-109, 112, 126p, 193-214.* ***Ron Lim*** *a(p)-366, 368-378, 380-386; c-366p, 368-378p, 379, 380-393p.* ***Miller*** *c-241p, 244p, 245p, 255p, Annual 5.* ***Mooney*** *a-149i.* ***Morrow*** *a-144.* ***Perez*** *c-243p, 246p.* ***Robbins*** *c(p)-183-187, 189-192, 225.* ***Roussos*** *a-140i, 168i.* ***Starlin/Sinnott*** *c-162.* ***Sutton*** *a-244i.* ***Tuska*** *a-112i, 215p, Special 2.* ***Waid*** *scripts-444-454.* ***Williamson*** *a-313i.* ***Wood*** *a-127i.* ***Zeck*** *a-263-289; c-300.*

CAPTAIN AMERICA (Volume Two)
Marvel Comics: V2#1, Nov, 1996 - No. 13, Nov, 1997($2.95/$1.95/$1.99) (Produced by Extreme Studios)

1-($2.95)-Heroes Reborn begins; Rob Liefeld-c/a; Jeph Loeb scripts; reintro Nick Fury 5.00
1-($2.95)-(Variant-c)-Liefeld-c/a 5.00
1-(7/96, $2.95)-(Exclusive Comicon Edition)-Liefeld-c/a 2.60 7.00
2-9-($1.95): 5-Two covers. 6-Cable-c/app. 2.00
10, 11: 10-Begin-$1.99-c 2.00
12-($2.99) "Heroes Reunited"-pt. 4 3.00
13-"World War 3"-pt. 4, x-over w/Image 2.00

CAPTAIN AMERICA (Vol. Three) (Also see Capt. America: Sentinel of Liberty)
Marvel Comics: Jan, 1998 - Present ($2.99/$1.99)

1-($2.99) Mark Waid-s/Ron Garney-a 3.00
1-Variant cover 5.00
2-($1.99): 2-Two covers 3.00
3-11: 3-Returns to old shield. 4-Hawkeye app. 5-Thor-c/app. 7-Andy Kubert-c/a begin. 9-New shield 2.00
12-($2.99) Battles Nightmare; Red Skull back-up story 3.00
.../Citizen V '98 Annual ($3.50) Busiek & Kesel-s 3.50

CAPTAIN AMERICA COMICS
Timely/Marvel Comics (TCI 1-20/CmPS 21-68/MjMC 69-75/Atlas Comics (PrPI 76-78): Mar, 1941 - No. 75, Jan, 1950; No. 76, 5/54 - No. 78, 9/54 (No. 74 & 75 titled Capt. America's Weird Tales)

GD25 FN65 VF82 NM94
1-Origin & 1st app. Captain America & Bucky by S&K; Hurricane, Tuk the Caveboy begin by S&K; 1st app. Red Skull; Hitler-c (by Simon?); intro of the "Capt. America Sentinels of Liberty Club" (advertised on inside front-c.); indicia reads Vol. 2, Number 1 4,667.00 14,000.00 30,335.00 56,000.00

GD25 FN65 NM94
2-S&K Hurricane; Tuk by Avison (Kirby splash); classic Hitler-c 950.00 2850.00 10,000.00
3-Classic Red Skull-c & app; Stan Lee's 1st text (1st work for Marvel) 820.00 2460.00 8200.00
4-1st full pg. panel in comics 490.00 1470.00 4900.00
5 460.00 1380.00 4600.00
6-Origin Father Time; Tuk the Caveboy ends 410.00 1230.00 4100.00
7-Red Skull app.; classic-c 460.00 1380.00 4600.00
8-10-Last S&K issue, (S&K centerfold #6-10) 347.00 1040.00 3300.00
11-Last Hurricane, Headline Hunter; Al Avison Captain America begins, ends #20; Avison-c(p) 305.00 915.00 2900.00
12-The Imp begins, ends #16; last Father Time 284.00 850.00 2700.00
13-Origin The Secret Stamp; classic-c 305.00 915.00 2900.00
14,15 284.00 850.00 2700.00
16-Red Skull unmasks Cap; Red Skull-c 337.00 1010.00 3200.00
17-The Fighting Fool only app. 259.00 775.00 2200.00
18-classic-c 259.00 775.00 2200.00
19-Human Torch begins #19 200.00 600.00 1700.00
20-Sub-Mariner app.; no H. Torch 200.00 600.00 1700.00
21-25: 25-Cap drinks liquid opium 188.00 564.00 1600.00
26-30: 27-Last Secret Stamp; last 68 pg. issue. 28-60 pg. issues begin. 176.00 529.00 1500.00
31-35,38-40: 34-Centerfold poster of Cap 153.00 460.00 1300.00
36-Classic Hitler-c 235.00 700.00 2000.00
37-Red Skull app. 188.00 564.00 1600.00
41-47: 41-Last Jap War-c. 46-German Holocaust-c. 47-Last German War-c 135.00 400.00 1150.00
48-58,60 112.00 336.00 950.00
59-Origin retold 271.00 813.00 2300.00
61-Red Skull-c/story 212.00 636.00 1800.00
62,64,65: 65-Kurtzman's "Hey Look" 141.00 423.00 1200.00
63-Intro/origin Asbestos Lady 147.00 441.00 1250.00
66-Bucky is shot; Golden Girl teams up with Captain America & learns his i.d; origin Golden Girl 153.00 460.00 1300.00
67-Captain America/Golden Girl team-up; Mxyztplk swipe; last Toro in Human Torch 147.00 441.00 1250.00
68,70-Sub-Mariner/Namora, and Captain America/Golden Girl team-up in each. 70-Science fiction-c/story 147.00 441.00 1250.00
69,71-73: 69-Human Torch/Sun Girl team-up. 71-Anti Wertham editorial; The Witness, Bucky app. 147.00 441.00 1250.00
74-(Scarce)(1949)-Titled "Captain America's Weird Tales"; Red Skull-c & app.; classic-c 379.00 1140.00 3600.00
75(2/50)-Titled "C.A.'s Weird Tales"; no C.A. app.; horror cover/stories 147.00 441.00 1250.00
76-78(1954): Human Torch/Toro stories; all have communist-c/stories 91.00 273.00 775.00
132-Pg. Issue (B&W-1942)(Canadian)-Has blank inside-c and back-c; contains Marvel Mystery #33 & Capt. America #18 w/cover from Capt. America #22; same contents as Marvel Mystery annual 2000.00 6000.00 12000.00
Shoestore Giveaway #77 53.00 160.00 425.00

NOTE: ***Crandall*** *a-2i, 3i, 9i, 10i.* ***Kirby*** *c-8p.* ***Rico*** *c-69-71.* ***Romita*** *c-77, 78.* ***Schomburg*** *c-3, 4, 26-29, 31, 33, 37-39, 41, 42, 45-54, 58.* ***Sekowsky*** *c-55, 56.* ***Shores*** *c-1, 2, 5-7, 11i, 20-25, 30, 32, 34, 35, 40, 57, 59-67.* ***S&K*** *c-1, 2, 5-7, 9, 10. Bondage c-3, 7, 15, 16, 34, 38.*

CAPTAIN AMERICA/NICK FURY: BLOOD TRUCE
Marvel Comics: Feb, 1995 ($5.95, one-shot, squarebound)

nn-Chaykin story 2.00 6.00

CAPTAIN AMERICA, SENTINEL OF LIBERTY (See Fireside Book Series)

CAPTAIN AMERICA: SENTINEL OF LIBERTY
Marvel Comics: Sept, 1998 - Present ($1.99)

1-Waid-s/Garney-a 2.00
1-Rough Cut ($2.99) Features original script and pencil pages 3.00
2-5: 2-Two covers; Invaders WW2 story 2.00
6-($2.99) Iron Man-c/app. 2.99

CAPTAIN AMERICA SPECIAL EDITION
Marvel Comics Group: Feb, 1984 - No. 2, Mar, 1984 ($2.00, Baxter paper)

1-Steranko-c/a(r) in both 3.00
2-Reprints the scarce Our Love Story #5 4.00

CAPTAIN AMERICA: THE LEGEND
Marvel Comics: Sept, 1996 ($3.95, one-shot)

1-Tribute issue; wraparound-c 4.00

CAPTAIN AND THE KIDS, THE (See Famous Comics Cartoon Books)

CAPTAIN AND THE KIDS, THE (See Comics on Parade, Katzenjammer Kids, Okay Comics & Sparkler Comics)
United Features Syndicate/Dell Publ. Co.: 1938 -12/39; Sum, 1947 - No. 32, 1955; Four Color No. 881, Feb, 1958

Single Series 1(1938) 79.00 237.00 675.00
Single Series 1(Reprint)(12/39- "Reprint" on-c) 43.00 129.00 360.00
1(Summer, 1947-UFS)-Katzenjammer Kids 12.00 36.00 90.00
2 7.15 21.50 50.00
3-10 5.70 17.00 38.00

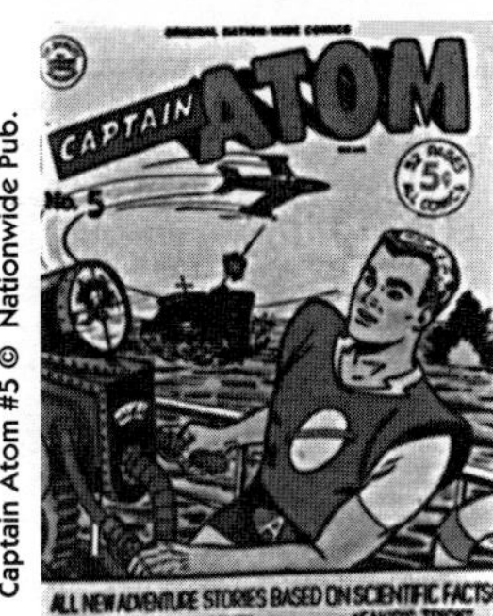

Captain Atom #5 © Nationwide Pub.

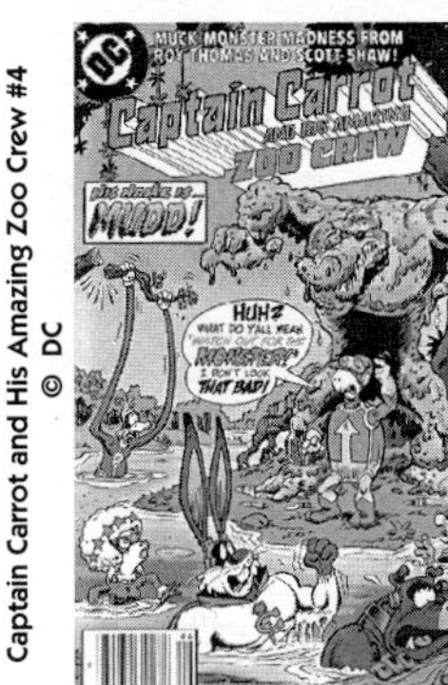

Captain Carrot and His Amazing Zoo Crew #4 © DC

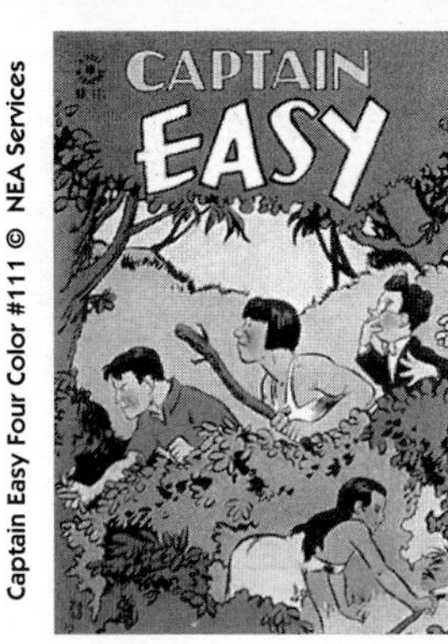

Captain Easy Four Color #111 © NEA Services

GD25 FN65 NM94

11-20 4.15 12.50 25.00
21-32(1955) 4.00 11.00 22.00
50th Anniversary issue-(1948)-Contains a 2 pg. history of the strip, including an account of the famous Supreme Court decision allowing both Pulitzer & Hearst to run the same strip under different names 7.85 23.50 55.00
Special Summer issue, Fall issue (1948) 5.70 17.00 35.00
Four Color 881 (Dell) 2.75 8.00 30.00

CAPTAIN ATOM
Nationwide Publishers: 1950 - No. 7, 1951 (5¢, 5x7-1/4", 52 pgs.)

1-Science fiction 32.00 96.00 240.00
2-7 17.00 52.00 130.00
...- Secret of the Columbian Jungle (16 pgs. in color, paper-c, 3-3/4x5-1/8")-Fireside Marshmallow giveaway 4.15 12.50 25.00

CAPTAIN ATOM (Formerly Strange Sus. Stories #77)(Also see Space Adv.)
Charlton Comics: V2#78, Dec, 1965 - V2#89, Dec, 1967

V2#78-Origin retold; Bache-a (3 pgs.) 7.00 21.00 70.00
79-82: 79-1st app. Dr. Spectro; 3 pg. Ditko cut & paste /Space Adventures #24. 82-Intro. Nightshade (9/66) 4.50 13.50 45.00
83-86: Ted Kord Blue Beetle in all. 83-(11/66)-1st app. Ted Kord. 84-1st app. new Captain Atom 3.80 11.40 38.00
87-89: Nightshade by Aparo in all 3.80 11.40 38.00
83-85(Modern Comics-1977)-reprints 3.00
NOTE: *Aparo a-87-89.* ***Ditko*** *c/a(p) 78-89. #90 only published in fanzine 'The Charlton Bullseye' #1, 2.*

CAPTAIN ATOM (Also see Americomics & Crisis On Infinite Earths)
DC Comics: Mar, 1987 - No. 57, Sept, 1991 (Direct sales only #35 on)

1-(44 pgs.)-Origin/1st app. with new costume 2.00
2-41,43-49: 5-Firestorm x-over. 6-Intro. new Dr. Spectro. 11-Millennium tie-in 14-Nightshade app. 16-Justice League app. 17-$1.00-c begins; Swamp Thing app. 20-Blue Beetle x-over. 24,25-Invasion tie-in 1.00
42 3.00
50-($2.00, 52 pgs.) 2.00
51-57: 57-War of the Gods x-over 1.00
Annual 1 (1988, $1.25)-Intro Major Force 1.50
Annual 2 (1988, $1.50) 1.50

CAPTAIN BATTLE (Boy Comics #3 on) (See Silver Streak Comics)
New Friday Publ./Comic House: Summer, 1941 - No. 2, Fall, 1941

1-Origin Blackout by Rico; Captain Battle begins (1st appeared in Silver Streak #10, 5/41) 106.00 318.00 900.00
2 74.00 222.00 625.00

CAPTAIN BATTLE (2nd Series)
Magazine Press/Picture Scoop No. 5: No. 3, Wint, 1942-43 - No. 5, Sum, 1943 (#3: 52pgs., nd)(#5: 68pgs.)

3-Origin Silver Streak-r/SS#3; origin Lance Hale-r/Silver Streak; Simon-a(r) 62.00 186.00 525.00
4,5: 5-Origin Blackout retold 44.00 132.00 370.00

CAPTAIN BATTLE, JR.
Comic House (Lev Gleason): Fall, 1943 - No. 2, Winter, 1943-44

1-The Claw vs. The Ghost 91.00 273.00 775.00
2-Wolverton's Scoop Scuttle; Don Rico-c/a; The Green Claw story is reprinted from Silver Streak #6 74.00 222.00 625.00

CAPTAIN BEN DIX
Bendix Aviation Corporation: 1943 (Small size)

nn 6.70 20.00 40.00

CAPTAIN BRITAIN (Also see Marvel Team-Up No. 65, 66)
Marvel Comics International: Oct. 13, 1976 - No. 39, July 6, 1977 (Weekly)

1-Origin; with Capt. Britain's face mask inside 1.00 3.00 10.00
2-Origin, part II; Capt. Britain's Boomerang inside 2.00 6.00

GD25 FN65 NM94

3-8: 3,8-Vs. Bank Robbers. 4-7-Vs. Hurricane 4.00
9-11: Vs. Dr. Synne 3.00
12-27: (scarce)-12,13-Vs. Dr. Synne. 14,15-Vs. Mastermind. 16-20-With Capt. America; 17 misprinted & color section reprinted in #18. 21-23,25,26-With Capt. America. 24-With C.B.'s Jet Plane inside. 27-Origin retold 1.20 3.60 12.00
28-32,36-39: 28-32-Vs. Lord Hawk. 36-Star Sceptre. 37-39-Vs. Highwayman & Munipulator 2.00
33-35-More on origin 2.50
Annual (1978, Hardback, 64 pgs.)-Reprints #1-7 with pin-ups of Marvel characters .90 2.70 8.00
Summer Special (1980, 52 pgs.)-Reprints 2.00
NOTE: *No. 1, 2, & 24 are rarer in mint due to inserts. Distributed in Great Britain only. Nick Fury-r by* ***Steranko*** *in 1-20, 24-31, 35-37. Fantastic Four-r by* ***J. Buscema*** *in all. New* ***Buscema****-a in 24-30. Story from No. 39 continues in Super Spider-Man (British weekly) No. 231-247. Following cancellation of his series, new Captain Britain stories appeared in "Super Spider-Man" (British weekly) No. 231-247. Captain Britain stories which appear in Super-Spider-Man No 248-253 are reprints of Marvel Team-Up No. 65&66. Capt. Britain strips also appeared in Hulk Comic (weekly) 1, 3-30, 42-55, 57-60, in Marvel Superheroes (monthly) 377-388, in Daredevils (monthly) 1-11, Mighty World of Marvel (monthly) 7-16 & Captain Britain (monthly) 1-14. Issues 1-23 have B&W & color, paper-c, & are 32 pgs. Issues 24 on are all B&W w/glossy-c & are 36 pgs.*

CAPTAIN CANUCK
Comely Comix (Canada) (All distr. in U. S.): 7/75 - No. 4, 7/77; No. 4, 7-8/79 - No. 14, 3-4/81

1-1st app. Bluefox 4.00
2-1st app. Dr. Walker, Redcoat & Kebec 3.00
3(5-7/76)-1st app. Heather 3.00
4(1st printing-2/77)-10x14-1/2"; (5.00); B&W; 300 copies serially numbered and signed with one certificate of authenticity 8.00 23.00 85.00
4(2nd printing-7/77)-11x17", B&W; only 15 copies printed; signed by creator Richard Comely, serially #'d and two certificates of authenticity inserted; orange cardboard covers (Very Rare) 11.00 33.00 120.00
4-14: 4(7-8/79)-1st app. Tom Evans & Mr. Gold; origin The Catman. 5-Origin Capt. Canuck's powers; 1st app. Earth Patrol & Chaos Corps. 8-Jonn 'The Final Chapter'. 9-1st World Beyond. 11-1st 'Chariots of Fire' story 2.00
Special Collectors Pack (polybagged) .90 2.70 8.00
Summer Special 1(7-9/80, 95¢, 64 pgs.) 2.00
NOTE: *30,000 copies of No. 2 were destroyed in Winnipeg.*

CAPTAIN CARROT AND HIS AMAZING ZOO CREW (Also see New Teen Titans & Oz-Wonderland War)
DC Comics: Mar, 1982 - No. 20, Nov, 1983

1-20: 1-Superman app. 3-Re-intro Dodo & The Frog. 9-Re-intro Three Mouseketeers, the Terrific Whatzit. 10,11- Pig Iron reverts back to Peter Porkchops. 20-The Changeling app. 1.00

CAPTAIN CARVEL AND HIS CARVEL CRUSADERS (See Carvel Comics)

CAPTAIN CONFEDERACY
Marvel Comics (Epic Comics): Nov, 1991 - No. 4, Feb, 1992 ($1.95)

1-4: All new stories 2.00

CAPTAIN COURAGEOUS COMICS (Banner #3-5; see Four Favorites #5)
Periodical House (Ace Magazines): No. 6, March, 1942

6-Origin & 1st app. The Sword; Lone Warrior, Capt. Courageous app.; Capt. moves to Four Favorites #5 in May 68.00 204.00 575.00

CAPT'N CRUNCH COMICS (See Cap'n...)

CAPTAIN DAVY JONES
Dell Publishing Co.: No. 598, Nov, 1954

Four Color 598 3.60 11.00 40.00

CAPTAIN EASY (See The Funnies & Red Ryder #3-32)
Hawley/Dell Publ./Standard(Visual Editions)/Argo: 1939 - No. 17, Sept, 1949; April, 1956

nn-Hawley(1939)-Contains reprints from The Funnies & 1938 Sunday strips by

Captain Flash #1 © Sterling Comics

Captain Hobby #1 © Export Publ.

Captain Marvel #1 © M.F. Enterprises

	GD25	FN65	NM94
Roy Crane	79.00	237.00	670.00
Four Color 24 (1943)	40.00	120.00	435.00
Four Color 111(6/46)	13.00	40.00	145.00
10(Standard-10/47)	9.50	28.00	75.00
11-17: All contain 1930s & '40s strip-r	7.85	23.50	55.00
Argo 1(4/56)-Reprints	5.70	17.00	40.00

NOTE: ***Schomburg*** *c-13, 16.*

CAPTAIN EASY & WASH TUBBS (See Famous Comics Cartoon Books)

CAPTAIN ELECTRON
Brick Computer Science Institute: Aug, 1986 ($2.25)

1-Disbrow-a 2.25

CAPTAIN EO 3-D (Disney)
Eclipse Comics: July, 1987 (Eclipse 3-D Special #18, $3.50, Baxter)

1-Adapts 3-D movie 3.50
1-2-D limited edition 5.00
1-Large size (11x17", 8/87)-Sold only at Disney Theme parks ($6.95) 1.20 3.60 12.00

CAPTAIN FEARLESS COMICS (Also see Holyoke One-Shot #6, Old Glory Comics & Silver Streak #1)
Helnit Publishing Co. (Holyoke Publ. Co.): Aug, 1941 - No. 2, Sept, 1941

1-Origin Mr. Miracle, Alias X, Captain Fearless, Citizen Smith Son of the Unknown Soldier; Miss Victory (1st app.) begins (1st patriotic heroine? before Wonder Woman) 71.00 213.00 600.00
2-Grit Grady, Captain Stone app. 44.00 132.00 375.00

CAPTAIN FLAG (See Blue Ribbon Comics #16)

CAPTAIN FLASH
Sterling Comics: Nov, 1954 - No. 4, July, 1955

1-Origin; Sekowsky-a; Tomboy (female super hero) begins; only pre-code issue; atomic rocket-c 36.00 108.00 270.00
2-4: 4-Flying saucer invasion-c 20.00 60.00 150.00

CAPTAIN FLEET (Action Packed Tales of the Sea)
Ziff-Davis Publishing Co.: Fall, 1952

1-Painted-c 13.00 39.00 95.00

CAPTAIN FLIGHT COMICS
Four Star Publications: Mar, 1944 - No. 10, Dec, 1945; No. 11, Feb-Mar, 1947

nn 37.00 112.00 280.00
2-4: 4-Rock Raymond begins, ends #7 19.00 58.00 145.00
5-Bondage, classic torture-c; Red Rocket begins; the Grenade app. (scarce) 56.00 168.00 475.00
6 19.00 56.00 140.00
7-10: 7-L. B. Cole covers begin, end #11. 8-Yankee Girl begins; intro. Black Cobra & Cobra Kid & begins. 9-Torpedoman app.; last Yankee Girl; Kinstler-a. 10-Deep Sea Dawson, Zoom of the Jungle, Rock Raymond, Red Rocket, & Black Cobra app; bondage-c 39.00 117.00 300.00
11-Torpedoman, Blue Flame (Human Torch clone) app.; last Black Cobra, Red Rocket; classic L. B. Cole robot-c (scarce) 53.00 159.00 450.00

CAPTAIN FORTUNE PRESENTS
Vital Publications: 1955 - 1959 (Giveaway, 3-1/4x6-7/8", 16 pgs.)

"Davy Crockett in Episodes of the Creek War", "Davy Crockett at the Alamo", "In Sherwood Forest Tells Strange Tales of Robin Hood" ('57), "Meets Bolivar the Liberator" ('59), "Tells How Buffalo Bill Fights the Dog Soldiers" ('57), "Young Davy Crockett" 1.80 4.50 9.00

CAPTAIN GALLANT (...of the Foreign Legion) (TV) (Texas Rangers in Action No. 5 on?)
Charlton Comics: 1955; No. 2, Jan, 1956 - No. 4, Sept, 1956

Heinz Foods Premium (#1?)(1955; regular size)-U.S. Pictorial; contains Buster Crabbe photos; Don Heck-a 1.80 4.50 9.00
Non-Heinz version (same as above except pictures of show replaces ads) (#1)-Buster Crabbe photo on-c; full page Buster Crabbe photo inside front-c 8.50 26.00 60.00
2-4: Buster Crabbe in all 7.15 21.50 50.00

CAPTAIN GLORY
Topps Comics: Apr, 1993 ($2.95) (Created by Jack Kirby)

1-Polybagged w/Kirbychrome trading card; Ditko-a & Kirby-c; has coupon for Amberchrome Secret City Saga #0 3.00

CAPTAIN HERO (See Jughead as...)

CAPTAIN HERO COMICS DIGEST MAGAZINE
Archie Publications: Sept, 1981

1-Reprints of Jughead as Super-Guy .90 2.70 8.00

CAPTAIN HOBBY COMICS
Export Publication Ent. Ltd. (Dist. in U.S. by Kable News Co.): Feb, 1948 (Canadian)

1 5.70 17.00 35.00

CAPT. HOLO IN 3-D (See Blackthorne 3-D Series #65)

CAPTAIN HOOK & PETER PAN (Movie)(Disney)
Dell Publishing Co.: No. 446, Jan, 1953

Four Color 446 8.00 25.00 90.00

CAPTAIN JET (Fantastic Fears No. 7 on)
Four Star Publ./Farrell/Comic Media: May, 1952 - No. 5, Jan, 1953

1-Bakerish-a 16.00 48.00 120.00
2 9.30 28.00 70.00
3-5,6(?) 7.85 23.50 55.00

CAPTAIN JOHNER & THE ALIENS
Valiant: May, 1995 - No. 2, May, 1995 ($2.95, shipped in same month)

1,2: Reprints Magnus Robot Fighter 4000 A.D. back-up stories; new Paul Smith-c 3.00

CAPTAIN JUSTICE (TV)
Marvel Comics: Mar, 1988 - No. 2, Apr, 1988 (limited series)

1,2-Based on True Colors television series. 1.25

CAPTAIN KANGAROO (TV)
Dell Publishing Co.: No. 721, Aug, 1956 - No. 872, Jan, 1958

Four Color 721 (#1)-Photo-c 13.00 40.00 145.00
Four Color 780, 872-Photo-c 11.00 34.00 125.00

CAPTAIN KIDD (Formerly Dagar; My Secret Story #26 on)(Also see Comic Comics & Fantastic Comics)
Fox Feature Syndicate: No. 24, June, 1949 - No. 25, Aug, 1949

24,25: 24-Features Blackbeard the Pirate 13.00 38.00 95.00

CAPTAIN MARVEL (See All Hero, All-New Collectors' Ed., America's Greatest, Fawcett Miniature, Gift, Legends, Limited Collectors' Ed., Marvel Family, Master No. 21, Mighty Midget Comics, Shazam, Special Edition Comics, Whiz, Wisco, World's Finest #253 and XMas Comics)

CAPTAIN MARVEL (Becomes ...Presents the Terrible 5 No. 5)
M. F. Enterprises: April, 1966 - No. 4, Nov, 1966 (25¢ Giants)

nn-(#1 on pg. 5)-Origin; created by Carl Burgos 2.50 7.50 22.00
2-4: 3-(#3 on pg. 4)-Fights the Bat 1.75 5.25 14.00

CAPTAIN MARVEL (Marvel's Space-Born Super-Hero! Captain Marvel #1-6; see Giant-Size..., Life Of..., Marvel Graphic Novel #1, Marvel Spotlight V2#1 & Marvel Super-Heroes #12)
Marvel Comics Group: May, 1968 - No. 19, Dec, 1969; No. 20, June, 1970 - No. 21, Aug, 1970; No. 22, Sept, 1972 - No. 62, May, 1979

1 6.00 18.00 60.00
2-Super Skrull-c/story 1.85 5.50 15.00
3-5: 4-Captain Marvel battles Sub-Mariner 1.25 3.75 10.00
6-11: 11-Capt. Marvel given great power by Zo the Ruler; Smith/Trimpe-c; Death of Una 1.10 3.30 9.00
12-24: 14-Capt. Marvel vs. Iron Man; last 12¢ issue. 16,17-New costume.

Captain Marvel #1 © MAR

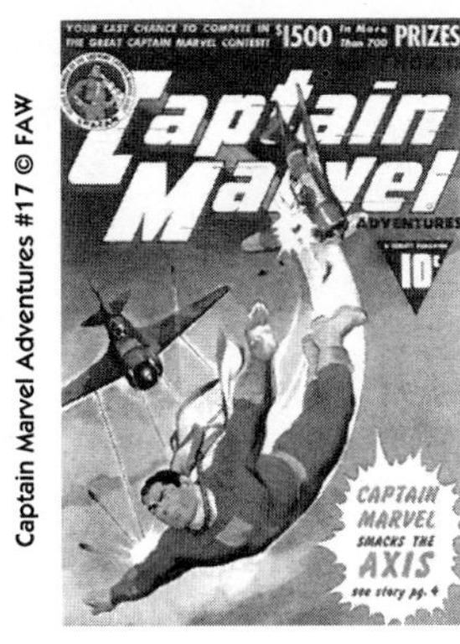

Captain Marvel Adventures #17 © FAW

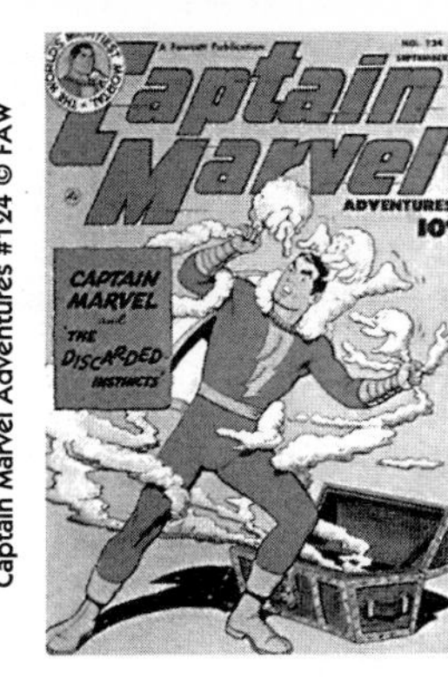

Captain Marvel Adventures #124 © FAW

GD25 FN65 NM94

21-Capt. Marvel battles Hulk; last 15¢ issue 2.00 6.00
25-Starlin-c/a begins; Starlin's 1st Thanos saga begins (3/73), ends #34; Thanos cameo (5 panels) 1.20 3.60 12.00
26-Minor Thanos app. (see Iron Man #55); 1st Thanos-c 1.40 4.20 14.00
27,28-1st & 2nd full app. Thanos. 28-Thanos-c/s 1.00 3.00 10.00
29,30-Thanos cameos. 29-C.M. gains more powers .90 2.70 8.00
31,32: Thanos app. 31-Last 20¢ issue. 32-Thanos-c 1.00 3.00 10.00
33-Thanos-c & app.; Capt. Marvel battles Thanos; 1st origin Thanos 1.20 3.60 12.00
34-1st app. Nitro; C.M. contracts cancer which eventually kills him; last Starlin-c/a .85 2.60 7.00
35,37-40,42,44,46-56,58-62: 39-Origin Watcher. 49-Starlin & Weiss-p assists. 58-Thanos cameo 1.50
36-Reprints origin/1st app. Capt. Marvel from Marvel Super-Heroes #12; Starlin-a (3 pgs.) 2.00 6.00
41,43-Wrightson part inks; #43-c(i). 2.00 6.00
45-(Regular 25¢ edition)(7/76) 1.50
45-(30¢-c, limited distribution) 2.00 6.00
57-Thanos appears in flashback 2.00 6.00

NOTE: *Alcala a-35. Austin a-46i, 49-53i; c-52i. Buscema a-18p-21p. Colan a(p)-1-4; c(p)-1-4, 8, 9. Heck a-5-10p, 16p. Gil Kane a-17-21p; c-17-24p, 37p, 53. McWilliams a-40i. #25-34 were reprinted in The Life of Captain Marvel.*

CAPTAIN MARVEL
Marvel Comics: Nov, 1989 ($1.50, one-shot, 52 pgs.)

1-Super-hero from Avengers; new powers 1.50

CAPTAIN MARVEL
Marvel Comics: Feb, 1994 ($1.75, 52 pgs.)

1-(Indicia reads Vol 2 #2)-Minor Captain America app. 1.75

CAPTAIN MARVEL
Marvel Comics: Dec, 1995 - No. 6, May, 1996 ($2.95/$1.95)

1 ($2.95)-Advs. of Mar-Vell's son begins; Fabian Nicieza scripts; foil-c 3.00
2-6: 2-Begin $1.95-c 2.00

CAPTAIN MARVEL ADVENTURES (See Special Edition Comics for pre #1)
Fawcett Publications: 1941 (March) - No. 150, Nov, 1953
(#1 on stands 1/16/41)

GD25 FN65 VF82 NM94

nn(#1)-Captain Marvel & Sivana by Jack Kirby. The cover was printed on unstable paper stock and is rarely found in Fine or Mint condition; blank back inside-c 2333.00 7000.00 14,000.00 28,000.00

GD25 FN65 NM94

2-(Advertised as #3, which was counting Special Edition Comics as the real #1); Tuska-a 347.00 1040.00 3300.00
3-Metallic silver-c 235.00 700.00 2000.00
4-Three Lt. Marvels app. 159.00 480.00 1350.00
5 118.00 350.00 1000.00
6-10: 9-1st Otto Binder scripts on Capt. Marvel 94.00 280.00 800.00
11-15: 12-Capt. Marvel joins the Army. 13-Two pg. Capt. Marvel pin-up. 15-Comic cards on back-c begin, end #26 76.00 228.00 650.00
16,17: 17-Painted-c 71.00 213.00 600.00
18-Origin & 1st app. Mary Marvel & Marvel Family (12/11/42); painted-c; Mary Marvel by Marcus Swayze 171.00 513.00 1450.00
19-Mary Marvel x-over; Christmas-c 59.00 177.00 500.00
20,21-Attached to the cover, each has a miniature comic just like the Mighty Midget Comics #11, except that each has a full color promo ad on the back cover. Most copies were circulated without the miniature comic. These issues with miniatures attached are very rare, and should not be mistaken for copies with the similar Mighty Midget glued in its place. The Mighty Midgets had blank back covers except for a small victory stamp seal. Only the Capt. Marvel and Captain Marvel Jr. No. 11 miniatures have been positively documented as having been affixed to these covers. Each miniature was only partially glued by its back cover to the Captain Marvel comic making it easy to see if it's the genuine miniature rather than a Mighty Midget.
with comic attached.... 320.00 960.00 3200.00
20-Without miniature 56.00 168.00 475.00
21-Without miniature; Hitler-c 71.00 213.00 600.00
22-Mr. Mind serial begins; 1st app. Mr. Mind 79.00 237.00 670.00
23-25 53.00 159.00 450.00
26-30: 26-Flag-c. 29-1st Mr. Mind-c & 1st app. (his voice was heard over the radio before now)(11/43) 45.00 135.00 385.00
31-35: 35-Origin Radar (5/44, see Master #50) 43.00 129.00 350.00
36-40: 37-Mary Marvel x-over 39.00 117.00 295.00
41-46: 42-Christmas-c. 43-Capt. Marvel 1st meets Uncle Marvel (1st app.); Mary Batson cameo. 46-Mr. Mind serial ends 31.00 93.00 235.00
47-50 29.00 87.00 215.00
51-53,55-60: 51-63-Bi-weekly issues. 52-Origin & 1st app. Sivana Jr.; Capt. Marvel Jr. x-over 24.00 72.00 180.00
54-Special oversize 68 pg. issue 25.00 75.00 185.00
61-The Cult of the Curse serial begins 29.00 87.00 215.00
62-65-Serial cont.; Mary Marvel x-over in #65 24.00 72.00 180.00
66-Serial ends; Atomic War-c 27.00 81.00 200.00
67-77,79: 69-Billy Batson's Christmas; Uncle Marvel, Mary Marvel, Capt. Marvel Jr. x-over. 71-Three Lt. Marvels app. 79-Origin Mr. Tawny 22.00 66.00 165.00
78-Origin Mr. Atom 25.00 75.00 185.00
80-Origin Capt. Marvel retold 43.00 129.00 360.00
81-84,86-90: 81,90-Mr. Atom app. 82-Infinity-c. 86-Mr. Tawny app. 21.00 63.00 155.00
85-Freedom Train issue 25.00 75.00 190.00
91-99: 96-Mr. Tawny app. 20.00 60.00 150.00
100-Origin retold; silver metallic-c 39.00 117.00 295.00
101-115,117-120 19.00 58.00 145.00
116-Flying Saucer issue (1/51) 21.00 64.00 160.00
121-Origin retold 26.00 78.00 195.00
122-137,139-149: 141-Pre-code horror story "The Hideous Head-Hunter". 142-used in **POP**, pgs. 92,96 19.00 56.00 140.00
138-Flying Saucer issue (11/52) 22.00 66.00 165.00
150-(Low distribution) 35.00 105.00 260.00
Bond Bread Giveaways-(24 pgs.; pocket size-7-1/4x3-1/2"; paper cover): "...& the Stolen City" ('48), "The Boy Who Never Heard of Capt. Marvel", "Meets the Weatherman" -(1950)(reprint) each.... 26.00 77.00 185.00
...Well Known Comics (1944; 12 pgs.; 8-1/2x10-1/2")-printed in red & in blue; soft-c; glued binding)-Bestmaid/Samuel Lowe Co. giveaway 17.00 51.00 120.00

NOTE: *Swayze a-12, 14, 15, 18, 19, 40; c-12, 15, 19.*

CAPTAIN MARVEL ADVENTURES
Fawcett Publications (Wheaties Giveaway): 1945 (6x8", full color, paper-c)

nn- "Captain Marvel & the Threads of Life" plus 2 other stories (32 pgs.) 50.00 150.00 425.00

NOTE: *All copies were taped at each corner to a box of Wheaties and are never found in Fine or Mint condition. Prices listed for each grade include tape.*

CAPTAIN MARVEL AND THE GOOD HUMOR MAN (Movie)
Fawcett Publications : 1950

nn-Partial photo-c w/Jack Carson & the Captain Marvel Club Boys 42.00 127.00 340.00

CAPTAIN MARVEL AND THE LTS. OF SAFETY
Ebasco Services/Fawcett Publications: 1950 - 1951 (3 issues - no No.'s)

GD25 FN65 VF82

"Danger Flies a Kite" ('50, scarce), "Danger Takes to Climbing" ('50), "Danger Smashes Street Lights" ('51) 106.00 318.00 850.00

CAPTAIN MARVEL COMIC STORY PAINT BOOK (See Comic Story...)

CAPTAIN MARVEL, JR. (See Fawcett Miniatures, Marvel Family, Master Comics, Mighty Midget Comics, Shazam & Whiz Comics)

CAPTAIN MARVEL, JR.
Fawcett Publications: Nov, 1942 - No. 119, June, 1953 (No #34)

1-Origin Capt. Marvel Jr. retold (Whiz #25); Capt. Nazi app. Classic Raboy-c

Captain Marvel, Jr. #4 © FAW

Captain Midnight #8 © FAW

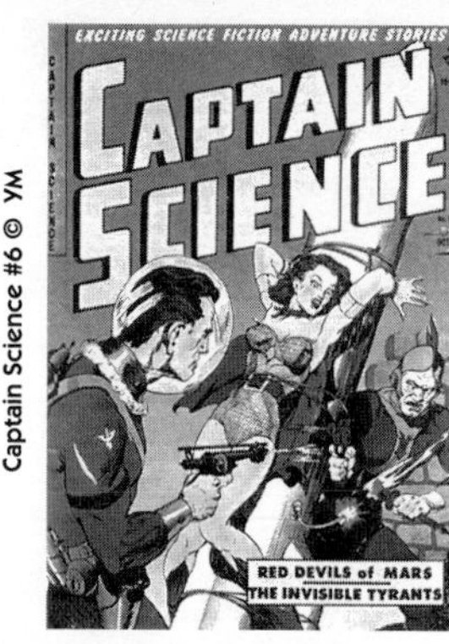

Captain Science #6 © YM

	GD25	FN65	NM94
	440.00	1320.00	4400.00
2-Vs. Capt. Nazi; origin Capt. Nippon	171.00	513.00	1450.00
3	91.00	273.00	775.00
4-Classic Raboy-c	100.00	300.00	850.00
5-Vs. Capt. Nazi	86.00	258.00	735.00
6-8: 8-Vs. Capt. Nazi	66.00	198.00	560.00
9,10: 9-Classic flag-c. 10-Hitler-c	68.00	204.00	580.00
11,12,15-Capt. Nazi app.	56.00	168.00	480.00
13,14,16-20: 13-Hitler-c. 14-X-Mas-c. 16-Capt. Marvel & Sivana x-over. 19-Capt. Nazi & Capt. Nippon app.	50.00	150.00	425.00
21-30: 25-Flag-c	40.00	120.00	320.00
31-33,36-40: 37-Infinity-c	27.00	80.00	200.00
35-#34 on inside; cover shows origin of Sivana Jr. which is not on inside. Evidently the cover to #35 was printed out of sequence and bound with contents to #34	27.00	80.00	200.00
41-70: 42-Robot-c. 53-Atomic Bomb-c/story	19.00	58.00	145.00
71-99,101-104: 104-Used in **POP**, pg. 89	14.00	42.00	105.00
100	17.00	50.00	125.00
105-114,116-118: 116-Vampira, Queen of Terror app. 119-Electric chair-c	13.00	38.00	95.00
115-Injury to eye-c; Eyeball story w/injury-to-eye panels	21.00	64.00	160.00
119-Electric chair-c (scarce)	28.00	84.00	210.00
...Well Known Comics (1944; 12 pgs.; 8-1/2x10-1/2")(Printed in blue; paper-c, glued binding)-Bestmaid/Samuel Lowe Co. giveaway	11.00	32.00	80.00

NOTE: ***Mac Raboy** c-1-28, 30-32, 57, 59 among others.*

CAPTAIN MARVEL PRESENTS THE TERRIBLE FIVE
M. F. Enterprises: Aug, 1966; V2#5, Sept, 1967 (No #2-4) (25¢)

	GD25	FN65	NM94
1	2.25	6.75	18.00
V2#5-(Formerly Captain Marvel)	1.25	3.75	10.00

CAPTAIN MARVEL'S FUN BOOK
Samuel Lowe Co.: 1944 (1/2" thick) (cardboard covers)

	GD25	FN65	NM94
nn-Puzzles, games, magic, etc.; infinity-c	30.00	90.00	225.00

CAPTAIN MARVEL SPECIAL EDITION (See Special Edition)

CAPTAIN MARVEL STORY BOOK
Fawcett Publications: Summer, 1946 - No. 4, Summer?, 1948

	GD25	FN65	NM94
1-Half text	49.00	148.00	420.00
2-4	37.00	112.00	280.00

CAPTAIN MARVEL THRILL BOOK (Large-Size)
Fawcett Publications: 1941 (B&W w/color-c)

	GD25	FN65	VF82
1-Reprints from Whiz #8,10, & Special Edition #1 (Rare)	250.00	750.00	2500.00

NOTE: *Rarely found in Fine or Mint condition.*

CAPTAIN MIDNIGHT (TV, radio, films) (See The Funnies & Popular Comics) (Becomes Sweethearts No. 68 on)
Fawcett Publications: Sept, 1942 - No. 67, Fall, 1948 (#1-14: 68 pgs.)

	GD25	FN65	NM94
1-Origin Captain Midnight; Captain Marvel cameo on cover	259.00	777.00	2200.00
2	118.00	354.00	1000.00
3-5	87.00	261.00	740.00
6-10: 9-Raboy-c. 10-Raboy Flag-c	62.00	186.00	530.00
11-20: 11,17,18-Raboy-c	45.00	135.00	380.00
21-30	38.00	114.00	285.00
31-40	27.00	80.00	200.00
41-59,61-67: 50-Sci/fi theme begins?	21.00	62.00	155.00
60-Flying Saucer issue (2/48)-3rd of this theme; see Shadow Comics V7#10 & Boy Commandos #26	28.00	84.00	210.00

CAPTAIN NICE (TV)
Gold Key: Nov, 1967 (one-shot)

	GD25	FN65	NM94
1(10211-711)-Photo-c	6.00	18.00	65.00

CAPTAIN N: THE GAME MASTER (TV)
Valiant Comics: 1990 - No. 6? ($1.95, thick stock, coated-c)

	GD25	FN65	NM94
1-6: 4-6-Layton-c			2.00

CAPTAIN PARAGON (See Bill Black's Fun Comics)
Americomics: Dec, 1983 - No. 4, 1985

	GD25	FN65	NM94
1-4: 1-Intro/1st app. Ms. Victory			1.50

CAPTAIN PARAGON AND THE SENTINELS OF JUSTICE
AC Comics: April, 1985 - No. 6, 1986 ($1.75)

	GD25	FN65	NM94
1-6: 1-Capt. Paragon, Commando D., Nightveil, Scarlet Scorpion, Stardust & Atoman begin			1.80

CAPTAIN PLANET AND THE PLANETEERS (TV cartoon)
Marvel Comics: Oct, 1991 - No. 12, Oct, 1992 ($1.00/$1.25)

	GD25	FN65	NM94
1-N. Adams painted-c			3.00
2-12: 3-Romita-c			2.00

CAPTAIN POWER AND THE SOLDIERS OF THE FUTURE (TV)
Continuity Comics: Aug, 1988 - No. 2, 1988 ($2.00)

	GD25	FN65	NM94
1,2: 1-Neal Adams-c/layouts/inks; variant-c exists.			2.00

CAPTAIN PUREHEART (See Archie as...)

CAPTAIN ROCKET
P. L. Publ. (Canada): Nov, 1951

	GD25	FN65	NM94
1	37.00	112.00	280.00

CAPT. SAVAGE AND HIS LEATHERNECK RAIDERS (...And His Battlefield Raiders #9 on)
Marvel Comics Group (Animated Timely Features): Jan, 1968 - No. 19, Mar, 1970 (See Sgt. Fury No. 10)

	GD25	FN65	NM94
1-Sgt. Fury & Howlers cameo	2.20	6.25	22.00
2,7,11: 2-Origin Hydra. 1-5,7-Ayers/Shores-a. 7-Pre-"Thing" Ben Grimm story. 11-Sgt. Fury app.	1.40	4.20	14.00
3-6,8-10,12-19	1.00	3.00	10.00

CAPTAIN SCIENCE (Fantastic No. 8 on)
Youthful Magazines: Nov, 1950 - No. 7, Dec, 1951

	GD25	FN65	NM94
1-Wood-a; origin; 2 pg. text w/ photos of George Pal's "Destination Moon."	71.00	213.00	600.00
2	39.00	118.00	300.00
3,6,7; 3,6-Bondage c-swipes/Wings #94,91	36.00	108.00	270.00
4,5-Wood/Orlando-c/a(2) each	68.00	206.00	575.00

NOTE: ***Fass** a-4. Bondage c-3, 6, 7.*

CAPTAIN SILVER'S LOG OF SEA HOUND (See Sea Hound)

CAPTAIN SINBAD (Movie Adaptation) (See Fantastic Voyages of... & Movie Comics)

CAPTAIN STERNN: RUNNING OUT OF TIME
Kitchen Sink Press: Sept, 1993 - No. 5, 1994 ($4.95, limited series, coated stock, 52 pgs.)

	GD25	FN65	NM94
1-5: Berni Wrightson-c/a/scripts			5.00
1-Gold ink variant			10.00

CAPTAIN STEVE SAVAGE (...& His Jet Fighters, No. 2-13)
Avon Periodicals: 1950 - No. 8, 1/53; No. 5, 9-10/54 - No. 13, 5-6/56

	GD25	FN65	NM94
nn(1st series)-Wood art, 22 pgs. (titled "...Over Korea")	36.00	107.00	250.00
1(4/51)-Reprints nn issue (Canadian)	15.00	45.00	105.00
2-Kamen-a	10.00	30.00	60.00
3-11 (#6, 9-10/54, last precode)	5.70	17.00	35.00
12-Wood-a (6 pgs.)	10.00	30.00	70.00
13-Check, Lawrence-a	7.50	26.25	45.00

NOTE: ***Kinstler** c-2-5, 7-9, 11. **Lawrence** a-8. **Ravielli** a-5, 9.*

5(9-10/54-2nd series)(Formerly Sensational Police Cases)

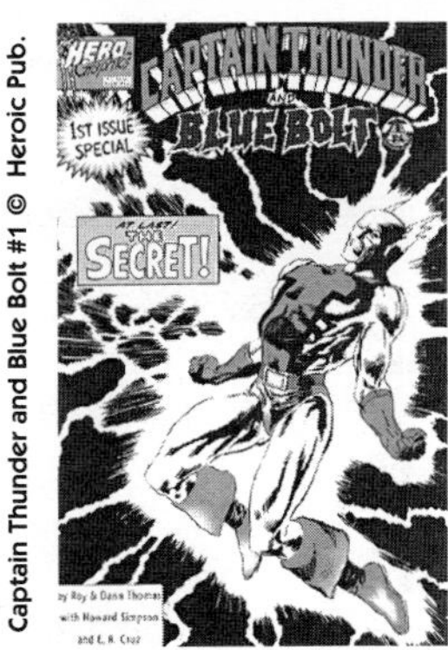

Captain Thunder and Blue Bolt #1 © Heroic Pub.

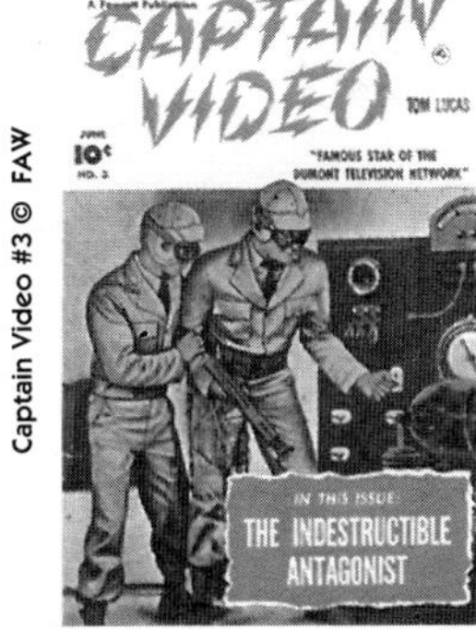

Captain Video #3 © FAW

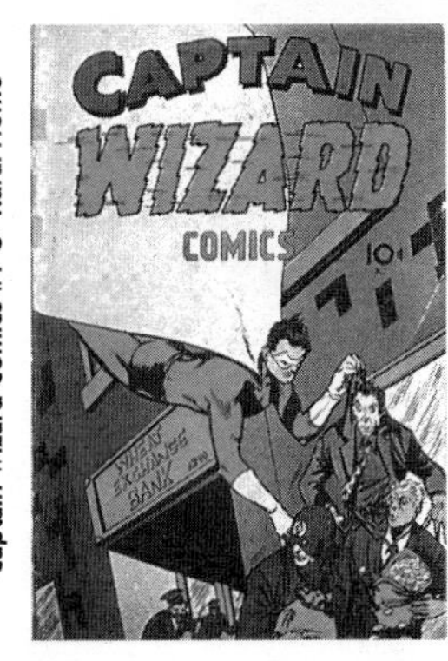

Captain Wizard Comics #1 © Rural Home

GD25 FN65 NM94

5.70 17.00 38.00
6-Reprints nn issue; Wood-a 8.50 26.00 60.00
7-13: 9,10-Kinstler-c. 10-r/cover #2 (1st series). 13-r/cover #8 (1st series) 4.00 12.00 24.00

CAPTAIN STONE (See Holyoke One-Shot No. 10)

CAPT. STORM (Also see G. I. Combat #138)
National Periodical Publications: May-June, 1964 - No. 18, Mar-Apr, 1967 (Grey tone c-8)

1-Origin 3.20 9.60 32.00
2-18: 3,6,13-Kubert-a. 4-Colan-a. 12-Kubert-c 2.50 7.50 22.00

CAPTAIN 3-D (Super hero)
Harvey Publications: December, 1953 (25¢, came with 2 pairs of glasses)

1-Kirby/Ditko-a (Ditko's 3rd published work tied with Strange Fantasy #9, see also Daring Love #1 & Black Magic V4 #3); shows cover in 3-D on inside; Kirby/Meskin-c 9.30 28.00 65.00

CAPTAIN THUNDER AND BLUE BOLT
Hero Comics: Sept, 1987 - No. 10, 1988 ($1.95)

1-10: 1-Origin Blue Bolt. 3-Origin Capt. Thunder. 6-1st app. Wicket. 8-Champions x-over 2.00

CAPTAIN TOOTSIE & THE SECRET LEGION (Advs. of...)(Also see Monte Hale #30,39 & Real Western Hero)
Toby Press: Oct, 1950 - No. 2, Dec, 1950

1-Not Beck-a; both have sci/fi covers 25.00 76.00 190.00
2-The Rocketeer Patrol app.; not Beck-a 16.00 48.00 120.00

CAPTAIN TRIUMPH (See Crack Comics #27)

CAPTAIN VENTURE & THE LAND BENEATH THE SEA (See Space Family Robinson)
Gold Key: Oct, 1968 - No. 2, Oct, 1969)

1,2: 1-r/Space Family Robinson serial; Spiegle-a in both 3.00 9.00 35.00

CAPTAIN VICTORY AND THE GALACTIC RANGERS
Pacific Comics: 11/81 - #13, 1/84 ($1.00, direct sales, 36-48 pgs.) (Created by Jack Kirby)

1-13: 1-1st app. Mr. Mind. 3-N. Adams-a 1.00
Special 1-(10/83)-Kirby c/a(p) 1.00
*NOTE: **Conrad** a-10, 11. **Ditko** a-6. **Kirby** a-1-3p; c-1-13.*

CAPTAIN VIDEO (TV) (See XMas Comics)
Fawcett Publications: Feb, 1951 - No. 6, Dec, 1951 (No. 1,5,6-36pgs.; 2-4, 52pgs.) (All photo-c)

1-George Evans-a(2) 94.00 282.00 800.00
2-Used in **SOTI**, pg. 382 62.00 187.00 525.00
3-6-All Evans-a except #5 mostly Evans 52.00 157.00 440.00
*NOTE: Minor **Williamson** assists on most issues. Photo c-1, 5, 6; painted c-2-4.*

CAPTAIN WILLIE SCHULTZ (Also see Fightin' Army)
Charlton Comics: No. 76, Oct, 1985 - No. 77, Jan, 1986

76,77 1.00

CAPTAIN WIZARD COMICS (See Meteor, Red Band & Three Ring Comics)
Rural Home: 1946

1-Capt. Wizard dons new costume; Impossible Man, Race Wilkins app. 23.00 70.00 175.00

CARDINAL MINDSZENTY (The Truth Behind the Trial of...)
Catechetical Guild Education Society: 1949 (24 pgs., paper cover)

nn-Anti-communism 5.70 17.00 35.00
Press Proof-(Very Rare)-(Full color, 7-1/2x11-3/4", untrimmed)
Only two known copies 150.00
Preview Copy (B&W, stapled), 18 pgs.; contains first 13 pgs. of Cardinal Mindszenty and was sent out as an advance promotion.
Only one known copy 150.00 - 200.00
NOTE: Regular edition also printed in French. There was also a movie released in 1949 called "Guilty of Treason" which is a fact-based account of the trial and imprisonment of Cardinal Mindszenty by the Communist regime in Hungary.

CARE BEARS (TV, Movie)(See Star Comics Magazine)
Star Comics/Marvel Comics No. 15 on: Nov, 1985 - No. 20, Jan, 1989 ($1.00 #11 on)

1-20: Post-a begins. 13-Madballs app. 2.50

CAREER GIRL ROMANCES (Formerly Three Nurses)
Charlton Comics: June, 1964 - No. 78, Dec, 1973

V4#24-31 1.25 3.75 10.00
32-Elvis Presley, Hermans Hermits, Johnny Rivers line drawn-c 9.00 27.00 90.00
33-50 1.00 3.00 8.00
51-78 5.00

CAR 54, WHERE ARE YOU? (TV)
Dell Publishing Co.: Mar-May, 1962 - No. 7, Sept-Nov, 1963; 1964 - 1965 (All photo-c)

Four Color 1257(#1, 3-5/62) 6.40 19.00 70.00
2(6-8/62)-7 3.00 9.00 35.00
2,3(10-12/64), 4(1-3/65)-Reprints #2,3,&4 of 1st series 2.25 6.75 25.00

CARL BARKS LIBRARY OF WALT DISNEY'S GYRO GEARLOOSE COMICS AND FILLERS IN COLOR, THE
Gladstone: 1993 ($7.95, 8-1/2x11", limited series, 52 pgs.)

1-6: Carl Barks reprints 1.00 3.00 10.00

CARL BARKS LIBRARY OF WALT DISNEY'S COMICS AND STORIES IN COLOR, THE
Gladstone: Jan, 1992 - No. 51, Mar, 1996 ($8.95, 8-1/2x11", 60 pgs.)

1,2,6,8-51: 1-Barks Donald Duck-r/WDC&S #31-35; 2-r/#36,38-41; 6-r/#57-61; 8-r/#67-71; 9-r/#72-76; 10-r/#77-81; 11-r/#82-86; 12-r/#87-91; 13-r/#92-96; 14-r/#97-101; 15-r/#102-106; 16-r/#107-111; 17-r/#112,114,117,124,125; 18-r/#126-130; 19-r/#131,132(2),133,134; 20-r/#135-139; 21-r/#140-144; 22-r/#145-149; 23-r/#150-154; 24-r/#155-159; 25-r/#160-164; 26-r/#165-169; 27-r/#170-174;28-r/#175-179; 29-r/#180-184; 30-r/#185-189; 31-r/#190-194; 32-r/#195-199;33-r/#200-204; 34-r/#205-209; 35-r/#210-214; 36-r/#215-219; 37-r/#220-224; 38-r/#225-229; 39-r/#230-234; 40-r/#235-239; 41-r/#240-244; 42r/#245-249; 43-r/#250-254; 44-50; All contain one Heroes & Villains trading card each 1.00 3.00 10.00
3,4,7: 3-r/#42-46. 4-r/#47-51. 7-r/#62-66. 1.50 4.50 15.00
5-r/#52-56 2.00 6.00 20.00

CARL BARKS LIBRARY OF WALT DISNEY'S DONALD DUCK ADVENTURES IN COLOR, THE
Gladstone: 1994 - Present ($7.95/$9.95, 44-68 pgs., 8-1/2"x11") (all contain one Donald Duck trading card each)

1-16-Carl Barks-r: 1-r/FC #9; 2-r/FC #29; 3-r/FC #62; 4-r/FC #108; 5-r/FC #147 & #79(Mickey Mouse); 6-r/MOC #4, Cheerios "Atom Bomb," D.D. Tells About Kites; 7-r/FC #159. 8-r/FC #178 & 189. 9-r/FC #199 & 203; 10-r/FC 223 & 238; 11-r/Christmas Parade #1 & 2; 12-r/FC #296; 13-r/FC #263; 14-r/MOC #20 & 41; 15-r/FC 275 & 282; 16-r/FC #291&300; 17-r/FC #308 & 318; 18-r/Vac. Parade #1 & Summer Fun #2; 19-r/FC #328 & 367 1.20 3.60 12.00

CARL BARKS LIBRARY OF WALT DISNEY'S DONALD DUCK CHRISTMAS STORIES IN COLOR, THE
Gladstone: 1992 ($7.95, 44pgs., one-shot)

nn-Reprints Firestone giveaways 1945-1949 1.50 4.50 15.00

CARL BARKS LIBRARY OF WALT DISNEY'S UNCLE SCROOGE COMICS ONE PAGERS IN COLOR, THE
Gladstone: 1992 - No. 2, 1993 ($8.95, limited series, 60 pgs., 8-1/2x11")

1-Carl Barks one pg. reprints 2.25 6.80 25.00

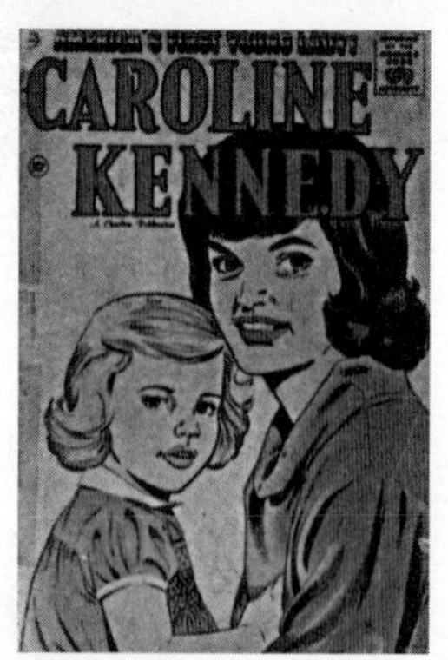

Caroline Kennedy nn © CC

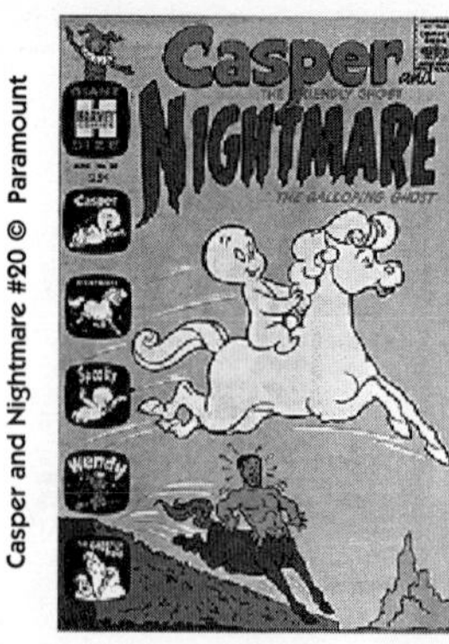

Casper and Nightmare #20 © Paramount

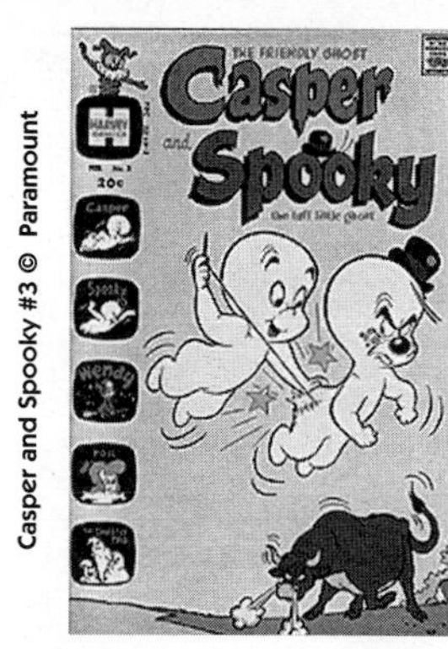

Casper and Spooky #3 © Paramount

	GD25	FN65	NM94
2-Carl Barks one pg. reprints	1.50	4.50	15.00

CARNAGE: IT'S A WONDERFUL LIFE
Marvel Comics: Oct, 1996 ($1.95, one-shot)

	GD25	FN65	NM94
1-David Quinn scripts			2.00

CARNAGE: MIND BOMB
Marvel Comics: Feb, 1996 ($2.95, one-shot)

	GD25	FN65	NM94
1-Warren Ellis script; Kyle Hotz-a			3.00

CARNATION MALTED MILK GIVEAWAYS (See Wisco)

CARNEYS, THE
Archie Comics: Summer, 1994 ($2.00, 52 pgs)

	GD25	FN65	NM94
1-Bound-in pull-out poster			2.00

CARNIVAL COMICS (Formerly Kayo #12; becomes Red Seal Comics #14)
Harry 'A' Chesler/Pershing Square Publ. Co.: 1945

	GD25	FN65	NM94
nn (#13)-Guardineer-a	14.00	42.00	105.00

CARNIVAL OF COMICS
Fleet-Air Shoes: 1954 (Giveaway)

	GD25	FN65	NM94
nn-Contains a comic bound with new cover; several combinations possible; Charlton's Eh! known	2.40	6.00	12.00

CAROLINE KENNEDY
Charlton Comics: 1961 (one-shot)

	GD25	FN65	NM94
nn-Interior photo covers of Kennedy family	8.50	25.50	85.00

CAROUSEL COMICS
F. E. Howard, Toronto: V1#8, April, 1948

	GD25	FN65	NM94
V1#8	5.35	16.00	32.00

CARTOON KIDS
Atlas Comics (CPS): 1957 (no month)

	GD25	FN65	NM94
1-Maneely-c/a; Dexter The Demon, Willie The Wise-Guy, Little Zelda app.	8.50	26.00	60.00

CARTOON NETWORK PRESENTS
DC Comics: Aug, 1997 - Present ($1.75/$1.95/$1.99)

	GD25	FN65	NM94
1-4: 1-Dexter's Lab. 2-Space Ghost			1.75
1-Platinum Edition			1.75
5-12: 5-Begin $1.95-c. 12-Bizarro World			1.95
13-17: 13-Begin $1.99-c			1.99

CARTOON TALES (Disney's...)
W.D. Publications (Disney): No date (1992) ($2.95, 6-5/8x9-1/2", 52 pgs.)

	GD25	FN65	NM94
nn-Ariel & Sebastian - Serpent Teen			4.00
nn-Beauty and the Beast - A Tale of Enchantment			4.00
nn-Darkwing Duck - Just Us Justice Ducks			4.00
nn-101 Dalmations - Canine Classics			4.00
nn-Tale Spin - Surprise in the Skies			4.00
nn-Uncle Scrooge - Blast to the Past			4.00

CARVEL COMICS (Amazing Advs. of Capt. Carvel)
Carvel Corp. (Ice Cream): 1975 - No. 5, 1976 (25¢; #3-5: 35¢) (#4,5: 3-1/4x5")

	GD25	FN65	NM94
1-3			1.00
4,5(1976)-Baseball theme		2.00	6.00

CARVERS
Image Comics (Flypaper Press): 1998 - Present ($2.95)

	GD25	FN65	NM94
1			2.95

CAR WARRIORS
Marvel Comics (Epic): June, 1991 - No. 4, Sept, 1991 ($2.25, lim. series)

	GD25	FN65	NM94
1-4: 1-Says April in indicia			2.25

CASE OF THE SHOPLIFTER'S SHOE (See Perry Mason, Feature Book No.50)

CASE OF THE WASTED WATER, THE
Rheem Water Heating: 1972? (Giveaway)

	GD25	FN65	NM94
nn-Neal Adams-a	3.20	9.50	35.00

CASE OF THE WINKING BUDDHA, THE
St. John Publ. Co.: 1950 (132 pgs.; 25¢; B&W; 5-1/2x7-5-1/2x8")

	GD25	FN65	NM94
nn-Charles Raab-a; reprinted in Authentic Police Cases No. 25	23.00	70.00	175.00

CASEY-CRIME PHOTOGRAPHER (Two-Gun Western No. 5 on)(Radio)
Marvel Comics (BFP): Aug, 1949 - No. 4, Feb, 1950

	GD25	FN65	NM94
1-Photo-c; 52 pgs.	19.00	56.00	140.00
2-4: Photo-c	12.00	36.00	90.00

CASEY JONES (TV)
Dell Publishing Co.: No. 915, July, 1958

	GD25	FN65	NM94
Four Color 915-Alan Hale photo-c	4.50	13.50	50.00

CASEY JONES & RAPHAEL (See Bodycount)
Mirage Studios: Oct, 1994 ($2.75, unfinished limited series)

	GD25	FN65	NM94
1-Bisley-c; Eastman story & pencils			2.75

CASEY JONES: NORTH BY DOWNEAST
Mirage Studios: June, 1994? - No. 2, July, 1994 ($2.75, limited series)

	GD25	FN65	NM94
1,2-Rick Veitch script & pencils; Kevin Eastman story & inks			2.75

CASPER ADVENTURE DIGEST
Harvey Comics: V2#1, Oct, 1992 - V2#8, Apr, 1994 ($1.75/$1.95, digest-size)

	GD25	FN65	NM94
V2#1: Casper, Richie Rich, Spooky, Wendy			4.00
2-8			2.50

CASPER AND...
Harvey Comics: Nov, 1987 - No. 12, June, 1990 (.75/$1.00, all reprints)

	GD25	FN65	NM94
1-Ghostly Trio			3.50
2-12: 2-Spooky; begin $1.00-c. 3-Wendy. 4-Nightmare. 5-Ghostly Trio. 6-Spooky. 7-Wendy. 8-Hot Stuff. 9-Baby Huey. 10-Wendy.11-Ghostly Trio. 12-Spooky			2.50

CASPER AND FRIENDS
Harvey Comics: Oct, 1991 - No. 5, July, 1992 ($1.00/$1.25)

	GD25	FN65	NM94
1-Nightmare, Ghostly Trio, Wendy, Spooky			3.50
2-5			2.50

CASPER AND FRIENDS MAGAZINE: Mar, 1997 - No. 3, July, 1997 ($3.99)

	GD25	FN65	NM94
1-3			4.00

CASPER AND NIGHTMARE (See Harvey Hits# 37, 45, 52, 56, 59, 62, 65, 68,71, 75)

CASPER AND NIGHTMARE (Nightmare & Casper No. 1-5)
Harvey Publications: No. 6, 11/64 - No. 44, 10/73; No. 45, 6/74 - No. 46, 8/74 (25¢)

	GD25	FN65	NM94
6: 68 pg. Giants begin, ends #32	3.50	10.50	35.00
7-10	2.40	7.20	24.00
11-20	1.60	4.80	16.00
21-37: 33-37-(52 pg. Giants)	1.20	3.60	12.00
38-46	.85	2.60	7.00

NOTE: *Many issues contain reprints.*

CASPER AND SPOOKY (See Harvey Hits No. 20)
Harvey Publications: Oct, 1972 - No. 7, Oct, 1973

	GD25	FN65	NM94
1	2.00	6.00	20.00
2-7	1.00	3.00	10.00

CASPER AND THE GHOSTLY TRIO
Harvey Pub.: Nov, 1972 - No. 7, Nov, 1973; No. 8, Aug, 1990 - No. 10, Dec, 1990

	GD25	FN65	NM94
1	2.00	6.00	20.00
2-7	1.00	3.00	10.00
8-10			4.00

CASPER AND WENDY
Harvey Publications: Sept, 1972 - No. 8, Nov, 1973

	GD25	FN65	NM94
1: 52 pg. Giant	2.20	6.25	22.00

Casper's Ghostland #17 © Paramount

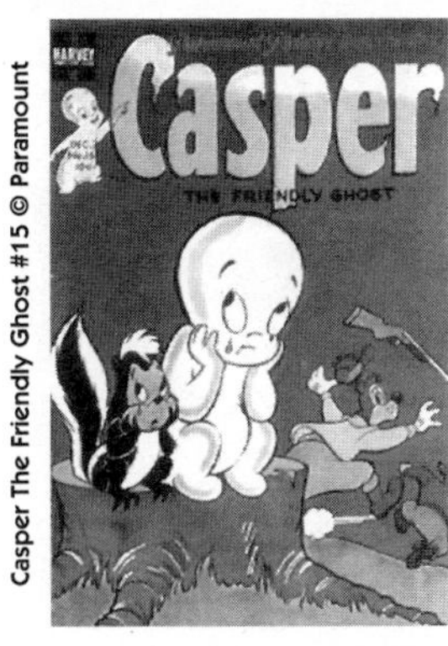

Casper The Friendly Ghost #15 © Paramount

Casper The Friendly Ghost #20 © Paramount

	GD25	FN65	NM94
2-8	1.00	3.00	10.00

CASPER BIG BOOK
Harvey Comics: V2#1, Aug, 1992 - No. 3, May, 1993 ($1.95, 52 pgs.)

	GD25	FN65	NM94
V2#1-Spooky app.			3.50
2,3			2.00

CASPER CAT (See Dopey Duck)
I. W. Enterprises/Super: 1958; 1963

	GD25	FN65	NM94
1,7:1-Wacky Duck #?.7-Reprint, Super No. 14('63)	1.00	2.80	7.00

CASPER DIGEST (...Magazine #?; ...Halloween Digest #8, 10)
Harvey Publications: Oct, 1986 - No. 18, Jan, 1991 ($1.25/$1.75, digest-size)

	GD25	FN65	NM94
1	.85	2.60	7.00
2-18: 11-Valentine-c. 18-Halloween-c			4.00

CASPER DIGEST (...Magazine #? on)
Harvey Comics: V2#1, Sept, 1991 - V2#14, Nov, 1994 ($1.75/$1.95, digest-size)

	GD25	FN65	NM94
V2#1			3.50
2-14			2.50

CASPER DIGEST STORIES
Harvey Publications: Feb, 1980 - No. 4, Nov, 1980 (95¢, 132 pgs., digest size)

	GD25	FN65	NM94
1	1.00	3.00	10.00
2-4		2.00	6.00

CASPER DIGEST WINNERS
Harvey Publications: Apr, 1980 - No. 3, Sept, 1980 (95¢, 132 pgs., digest size)

	GD25	FN65	NM94
1	1.00	3.00	10.00
2,3		2.00	6.00

CASPER ENCHANTED TALES DIGEST
Harvey Comics: May, 1992 - No. 10, Oct, 1994 ($1.75, digest-size, 98 pgs.)

	GD25	FN65	NM94
1-Casper, Spooky, Wendy stories			3.50
2-10			2.50

CASPER GHOSTLAND
Harvey Comics: May, 1992 ($1.25)

	GD25	FN65	NM94
1			2.50

CASPER GIANT SIZE
Harvey Comics: Oct, 1992 - No. 4, Nov, 1993 ($2.25, 68 pgs.)

	GD25	FN65	NM94
V2#1-4-Casper, Wendy, Spooky stories			3.00

CASPER HALLOWEEN TRICK OR TREAT
Harvey Publications: Jan, 1976 (52 pgs.)

	GD25	FN65	NM94
1	1.80	5.40	18.00

CASPER IN SPACE (Formerly Casper Spaceship)
Harvey Publications: No. 6, June, 1973 - No. 8, Oct, 1973

	GD25	FN65	NM94
6-8	.90	2.70	8.00

CASPER'S GHOSTLAND
Harvey Publications: Winter, 1958-59 - No. 97, 12/77; No. 98, 12/79 (25¢)

	GD25	FN65	NM94
1-84 pgs. begin, ends #10	16.00	48.00	160.00
2	8.50	25.50	85.00
3-10	5.80	17.40	58.00
11-20: 11-68 pgs. begin, ends #61. 13-X-Mas-c	4.20	12.60	42.00
21-40	3.20	9.60	32.00
41-61	1.60	4.80	16.00
62-77: 62-52 pgs. begin	.90	2.70	9.00
78-98: 94-X-Mas-c			4.50

NOTE: *Most issues contain reprints w/new stories.*

CASPER SPACESHIP (Casper in Space No. 6 on)
Harvey Publications: Aug, 1972 - No. 5, April, 1973

	GD25	FN65	NM94
1: 52 pg. Giant	2.00	6.00	20.00
2-5	1.00	3.00	10.00

CASPER SPECIAL
Target Stores (Harvey): nd (Dec, 1990) (Giveaway with $1.00 cover)

	GD25	FN65	NM94
Three issues-Given away with Casper video			4.00

CASPER STRANGE GHOST STORIES
Harvey Publications: October, 1974 - No. 14, Jan, 1977 (All 52 pgs.)

	GD25	FN65	NM94
1	1.50	4.50	15.00
2-14	1.00	3.00	10.00

CASPER, THE FRIENDLY GHOST (See America's Best TV Comics, Famous TV Funday Funnies, The Friendly Ghost..., Nightmare &..., Richie Rich and..., Tastee-Freez, Treasury of Comics, Wendy the Good Little Witch & Wendy Witch World)

CASPER, THE FRIENDLY GHOST (Becomes Harvey Comics Hits No. 61 (No. 6), and then continued with Harvey issue No. 7)(1st Series)
St. John Publishing Co.: Sept, 1949 - No. 5, Aug, 1951

	GD25	FN65	NM94
1(1949)-Origin & 1st app. Baby Huey & Herman the Mouse (1st time the name Casper app. in any media, even films)	141.00	423.00	1200.00
2,3 (2/50 & 8/50)	62.00	186.00	525.00
4,5 (3/51 & 8/51)	47.00	141.00	400.00

CASPER, THE FRIENDLY GHOST (Paramount Picture Star...)(2nd Series)
Harvey Publications (Family Comics): No. 7, Dec, 1952 - No. 70, July, 1958
Note: No. 6 is Harvey Comics Hits No. 61 (10/52)

	GD25	FN65	NM94
7-Baby Huey begins, ends #9	30.00	90.00	295.00
8,9	16.50	50.00	165.00
10-Spooky begins (1st app., 6/53), ends #70?	18.00	54.00	180.00
11-18: Alfred Harvey app. in story	9.50	28.50	95.00
19-1st app. Nightmare (4/54)	12.50	38.00	125.00
20-Wendy the Witch begins (1st app., 5/54)	16.00	48.00	160.00
21-30: 24-Infinity-c	7.50	22.50	75.00
31-40	5.00	15.00	50.00
41-50	4.00	12.00	40.00
51-70 (Continues as Friendly Ghost... 8/58)	3.80	11.40	38.00
American Dental Association (Giveaways):			
...'s Dental Health Activity Book-1977		2.00	6.00
...Presents Space Age Dentistry-1972	.90	2.70	8.00
..., His Den, & Their Dentist Fight the Tooth Demons-1974	.90	2.70	8.00

CASPER THE FRIENDLY GHOST (Formerly The Friendly Ghost...)(3rd Series)
Harvey Comics: No. 254, July, 1990 - No. 260, Jan, 1991 ($1.00)

	GD25	FN65	NM94
254-260			2.00

CASPER THE FRIENDLY GHOST (4th Series)
Harvey Comics: Mar, 1991 - No. 28, Nov, 1994 ($1.00/$1.25/$1.50)

	GD25	FN65	NM94
1-Casper becomes Mighty Ghost; Spooky & Wendy app.			3.50
2-10: 7,8-Post-a			2.00
11-28-($1.50)			1.50

CASPER T.V. SHOWTIME
Harvey Comics: Jan, 1980 - No. 5, Oct, 1980

	GD25	FN65	NM94
1	.85	2.60	7.00
2-5			4.50

CASSETTE BOOKS (Classics Illustrated)
Cassette Book Co./I.P.S. Publ.: 1984 (48 pgs, b&w comic with cassette tape)

NOTE: *This series was illegal. The artwork was illegally obtained, and the Classics Illustrated copyright owner, Twin Circle Publ. sued to get an injunction to prevent the continued sale of this series. Many C.I. collectors obtained copies before the 1987 injunction, but now they are already scarce. Here again the market is just developing, but sealed mint copies of com ic and tape should be worth at least $25.*

1001 (CI#1-A2)New-PC 1002(CI#3-A2)CI-PC 1003(CI#13-A2)CI-PC
1004(CI#25)CI-LDC 1005(CI#10-A2)New-PC 1006(CI#64)CI-LDC

CASTILIAN (See Movie Classics)

CASUAL HEROES
Image Comics (Motown Machineworks): Apr, 1996 ($2.25, unfinished lim. series

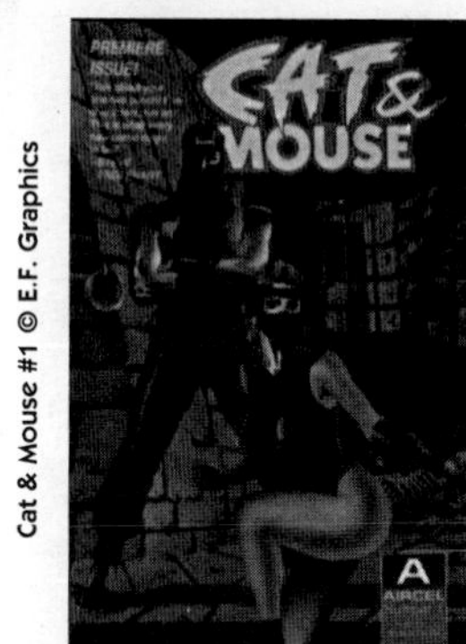

Cat & Mouse #1 © E.F. Graphics

Catwoman #13 © DC

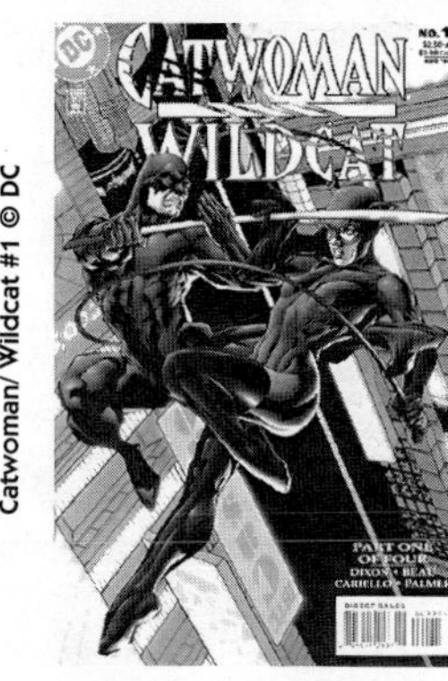

Catwoman/ Wildcat #1 © DC

1-Steve Rude-c 2.25

CAT, T.H.E. (TV) (See T.H.E. Cat)

CAT, THE (See Movie Classics)

CAT, THE (Female hero)
Marvel Comics Group: Nov, 1972 - No. 4, June, 1973

1-Origin & 1st app. The Cat (who later becomes Tigra); Mooney-a(i); Wood-c(i)/a(i) 2.00 6.00 20.00
2,3: 2-Marie Severin/Mooney-a. 3-Everett inks 1.20 3.60 12.00
4-Starlin/Weiss-a(p) 1.40 4.20 14.00

CATALYST: AGENTS OF CHANGE (Also see Comics' Greatest World)
Dark Horse Comics: Feb, 1994 - No.7, Nov, 1994 ($2.00, limited series)

1-7: 1-Foil stamped logo 2.00

CAT & MOUSE
EF Graphics (Silverline): Dec, 1988 ($1.75, color w/part B&W)

1-1st printing (12/88, 32 pgs.) 1.75
1-2nd printing (5/89, 36 pgs.) 1.75

CAT FROM OUTER SPACE (See Walt Disney Showcase #46)

CATHOLIC COMICS (See Heroes All Catholic...)
Catholic Publications: June, 1946 - V3#10, July, 1949

1 25.00 76.00 190.00
2 13.00 40.00 100.00
3-13(7/47) 11.00 34.00 85.00
V2#1-10 7.85 23.50 55.00
V3#1-10: Reprints 10-part Treasure Island serial from Target V2#2-11 (see Key Comics #5) 8.50 26.00 60.00

CATHOLIC PICTORIAL
Catholic Guild: 1947

1-Toth-a(2) (Rare) 35.00 104.00 260.00

CATMAN COMICS (Formerly Crash Comics No. 1-5)
Holyoke Publishing Co./Continental Magazines V2#12, 7/44 on:
5/41 - No. 17, 1/43; No. 18, 7/43 - No. 22, 12/43; No. 23, 3/44 - No. 26, 11/44; No. 27, 4/45 - No. 30, 12/45; No. 31, 6/46 - No. 32, 8/46

1(V1#6)-Origin The Deacon & Sidekick Mickey, Dr. Diamond & Rag-Man; The Black Widow app.; The Catman by Chas. Quinlan & Blaze Baylor begin 306.00 918.00 2600.00
2(V1#7) 100.00 300.00 850.00
3(V1#8)-The Pied Piper begins; classic Hitler, Stalin & Mussolini-c 82.00 246.00 700.00
4(V1#9) 77.00 231.00 650.00
5(V2#10)-Origin Kitten; The Hood begins (c-redated), 6,7(V2#11,12) 62.00 186.00 525.00
8(V2#13,3/42)-Origin Little Leaders; Volton by Kubert begins (his 1st comic book work) 77.00 231.00 650.00
9,10(V2#14,15): 10-Origin Blackout retold; Phantom Falcon begins 49.00 147.00 420.00
11 (V3#1)-Kubert-a 49.00 147.00 420.00
12 (V3#2), 14, 15, 17, 18(V3#8, 7/43) 44.00 132.00 375.00
13-(scarce) 59.00 177.00 500.00
16 (V3#5)-Hitler, Tojo, Mussolini, Stalin-c 56.00 168.00 475.00
19 (V2#6)-Hitler, Tojo, Mussolini-c 56.00 168.00 475.00
20 (V2#7): Classic Hitler-c 56.00 168.00 475.00
21- 23 (V2#10, 3/44) 41.00 122.00 325.00
nn(V3#13, 5/44)-Rico-a; Schomburg bondage-c 39.00 116.00 290.00
nn(V2#12, 7/44) 39.00 116.00 290.00
nn(V3#1, 9/44)-Origin The Golden Archer; Leatherface app. 39.00 116.00 290.00
nn(V3#2, 11/44)-L. B. Cole-c 62.00 186.00 525.00
27-Origin Kitten retold; L. B. Cole Flag-c 68.00 204.00 575.00
28-Catman learns Kitten's I.D.; Dr. Macabre, Deacon app.; L. B. Cole c/a 71.00 213.00 600.00
29-32-L. B. Cole-c; bondage-#30 62.00 186.00 525.00
NOTE: *Fuje a-11, 29(3), 30.* ***Palais*** *a-11, 29(2), 30(2), 32; c-25(7/44).* ***Rico*** *a-11(2).*

CAT TALES (3-D)
Eternity Comics: Apr, 1989 ($2.95)

1-Felix the Cat-r in 3-D 4.00

CATWOMAN (Also see Action Comics Weekly #611, Batman #404-407, Detective Comics, & Superman's Girlfriend Lois Lane #70, 71)
DC Comics: Feb, 1989 - No. 4, May, 1989 ($1.50, limited series, mature)

1 3.00
2 2.00
3,4: 3-Batman cameo. 4-Batman app. 2.00
Her Sister's Keeper (1991, $9.95, trade paperback)-r/#1-4 1.00 3.00 10.00

CATWOMAN (Also see Showcase '93, Showcase '95 #4, & Batman #404-407)
DC Comics: Aug, 1993 - Present ($1.50/$1.95/$1.99)

1-($1.95)-Embossed-c; Bane app.; Balent c-1-10; a-1-10p 4.00
2,3: 3-Bane flashback cameo 3.00
0,4-11, 13-20: 4-Brief Bane app. 6,7-Knightquest tie-ins; new Batman (Azrael) app. 8-1st app. Zephyr. 13-KnightsEnd Aftermath. 14-(9/94)-Zero Hour. 0-(10/94)-Origin retold 3.00
12-KnightsEnd pt. 6. 4.00
21-24, 26-30, 33-49: 21-$1.95-c begins. 28,29-Penguin cameo app. 36-Legacy pt. 2. 38-40-Year Two; Batman, Joker, Penguin & Two-Face app. 46-Two-Face app. 2.00
25-($2.95)-Robin app. 3.00
31, 32: 31-Contagion pt. 4 (Reads pt. 5 on-c). 32-Contagion pt. 9. 3.00
50-($2.95, 48 pgs.)-New armored costume 3.00
50-($2.95, 48 pgs.)-Collector's Ed.w/metallic ink-c 3.00
51-60: 51-Huntress-c/app. 54-Grayson-s begins. 56-Cataclysm pt.6. 57-Poison Ivy-c/app. 2.00
61-65: 61-Begin $1.99-c. 63-65-Joker-c/app. 1.99
#1,000,000 (11/98) 853rd Century x-over 2.00
Annual 1 (1994, $2.95, 68 pgs.)-Elseworlds story; Batman app.; no Balent-a 3.00
Annual 2 (1995, $3.95)-Year One story 4.00
Annual 3 (1996, $2.95)-Legends of the Dead Earth story 3.00
Annual 4 (1997, $3.95)-Pulp Heroes story 3.95
...Plus 1 (11/97, $2.95) Screamqueen (Scare Tactics) app. 2.95
TPB ($9.95) r/#15-19, Balent-c 1.00 3.00 10.00

CATWOMAN/VAMPIRELLA: THE FURIES
DC Comics/Harris Publ.: Feb, 1997 ($4.95, squarebound, one-shot, 46 pgs.) (1st DC/Harris x-over)

nn-Reintro Pantha; Chuck Dixon scripts; Jim Balent-c/a 5.00

CATWOMAN/WILDCAT
DC Comics: Aug, 1998 - No. 4, Nov, 1998 ($2.50, limited series)

1-Chuck Dixon & Beau Smith-s; Stelfreeze-c 2.50

CAUGHT
Atlas Comics (VPI): Aug, 1956 - No. 5, Apr, 1957

1 17.00 52.00 130.00
2,4: 4-Maneely-a (4 pgs.) 9.30 28.00 65.00
3-Maneely, Pakula, Torres-a 9.30 28.00 65.00
5-Crandall, Krigstein-a 10.00 30.00 75.00
NOTE: ***Drucker*** *a-2.* ***Heck*** *a-4.* ***Severin*** *c-1, 2, 4, 5.* ***Shores*** *a-4.*

CAVALIER COMICS
A. W. Nugent Publ. Co.: 1945; 1952 (Early DC reprints)

2(1945)-Speed Saunders, Fang Gow 17.00 52.00 130.00
2(1952) 9.30 28.00 65.00

CAVE GIRL (Also see Africa)

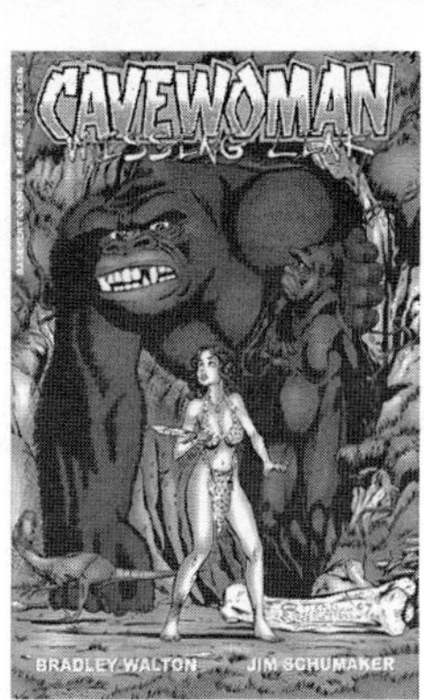

Cavewoman: Missing Link #4 © Budd Root

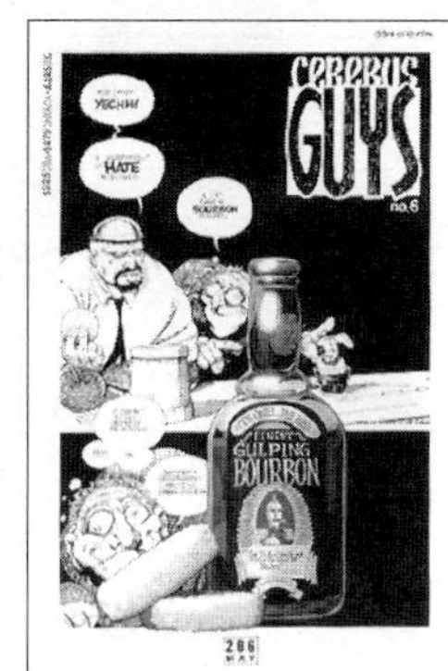

Cerebus #206 © Dave Sim

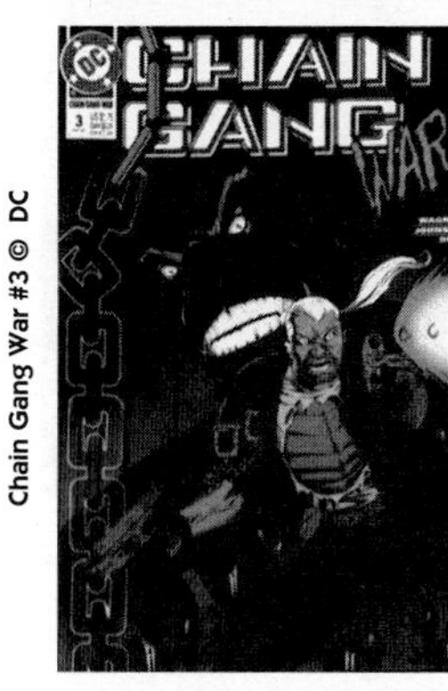

Chain Gang War #3 © DC

	GD25	FN65	NM94
Magazine Enterprises: No. 11, 1953 - No. 14, 1954			
11(A-1 82)-Origin; all Cave Girl stories	40.00	120.00	320.00
12(A-1 96), 13(A-1 116), 14(A-1 125)-Thunda by Powell in each	29.00	86.00	215.00

NOTE: ***Powell** c/a in all.*

CAVE GIRL
AC Comics: 1988 ($2.95, 44 pgs.) (16 pgs. of color, rest B&W)

1-Powell-r/Cave Girl #11; Nyoka photo back-c from movie; Powell/Bill Black-c; Special Limited Edition on-c			3.00

CAVE KIDS (TV) (See Comic Album)
Gold Key: Feb, 1963 - No. 16, Mar, 1967 (Hanna-Barbera)

1	6.00	18.00	65.00
2-5	3.00	9.00	32.00
6-16: 7,12-Pebbles & Bamm Bamm app.	2.00	6.00	22.00

CAVEWOMAN
Basement Comics: Jan, 1994 - No. 6, 1995 ($2.95)

1	4.00	12.25	45.00
2	2.40	7.00	26.00
3-6	1.80	5.40	18.00

CAVEWOMAN MEETS EXPLORERS
Basement Comics: 1997 ($2.95, B&W, one-shot)

1			3.00

CAVEWOMAN: MISSING LINK
Basement Comics: 1997 - No. 4, 1998 ($2.95, B&W, limited series)

1-4			3.00

CAVEWOMAN: RAIN
Caliber: 1996 - No. 8, 1998 ($2.95, limited series)

1			3.00
2			5.00
3,4			3.50
5-8			2.95
8-Alternate cover			5.00
8-Green foil cover			9.00

CELESTINE (See Violator Vs. Badrock #1)
Image Comics (Extreme): May, 1996 - No. 2, June, 1996 ($2.50, limited series)

1,2: Warren Ellis scripts			2.50

CENTURION OF ANCIENT ROME, THE
Zondervan Publishing House: 1958 (no month listed) (B&W, 36 pgs.)

(Rare) All by Jay Disbrow	30.00	90.00	225.00

CENTURIONS (TV)
DC Comics: June, 1987 - No. 4, Sept, 1987 (75¢, limited series)

1-4			1.00

CENTURY: DISTANT SONS
Marvel Comics: Feb, 1996 ($2.95, one-shot)

1-Wraparound-c			3.00

CENTURY OF COMICS
Eastern Color Printing Co.: 1933 (100 pgs.) (Probably the 3rd comic book)

Bought by Wheatena, Milk-O-Malt, John Wanamaker, Kinney Shoe Stores, & others to be used as premiums and radio giveaways. No publisher listed.

	GD25	FN65	VF82
nn-Mutt & Jeff, Joe Palooka, etc. reprints	3000.00	9000.00	17,000.00

CEREBUS BI-WEEKLY
Aardvark-Vanaheim: Dec. 2, 1988 - No. 26, Nov. 11, 1989 ($1.25, B&W)

	GD25	FN65	NM94
Reprints Cerebus The Aardvark#1-26			
1-16, 18, 19, 21-26:			2.00
17-Hepcats app.	1.50	4.50	15.00
20-Milk & Cheese app.	2.00	6.00	20.00

CEREBUS: CHURCH & STATE
Aardvark-Vanaheim: Feb, 1991 - No. 30, Apr, 1992 ($2.00, B&W, bi-weekly)

1-30: r/Cerebus #51-80			2.50

CEREBUS: HIGH SOCIETY
Aardvark-Vanaheim: Feb, 1990 - No. 25, 1991 ($1.70, B&W)

1-25: r/Cerebus #26-50			2.25

CEREBUS JAM
Aardvark-Vanaheim: Apr, 1985

1-Eisner, Austin, Dave Sim-a (Cerebus vs. Spirit)			5.00

CEREBUS THE AARDVARK (See A-V in 3-D, Nucleus, Power Comics)
Aardvark-Vanaheim: Dec, 1977 - Present ($1.70/$2.00/$2.25, B&W)

0			3.00
0-Gold			25.00
1-1st app. Cerebus; 2000 print run; most copies poorly printed	23.00	68.00	250.00

Note: *There is a counterfeit version known to exist. It can be distinguished from the original in the following ways: inside cover is glossy instead of flat, black background on the front cover is blotted or spotty. Reports show that a counterfeit #2 also exists.*

2-Dave Sim art in all	7.00	21.00	75.00
3-Origin Red Sophia	6.00	18.00	65.00
4-Origin Elrod the Albino	4.00	12.00	45.00
5,6	3.50	10.50	38.00
7-10	2.25	6.80	25.00
11,12: 11-Origin The Cockroach	2.00	6.00	20.00
13-15: 14-Origin Lord Julius	1.00	3.00	10.00
16-20		2.00	6.00
21-B. Smith letter in letter column	3.20	9.50	35.00
22-Low distribution; no cover price	1.30	3.90	13.00
23-30: 23-Preview of Wandering Star by Teri S. Wood. 26-High Society begins, ends #50		2.00	6.00
31-Origin Moonroach	.90	2.70	8.00
32-40			5.00
41-50,52: 52-Church & State begins, ends #111; Cutey Bunny app.			4.00
51-Cutey Bunny app.	1.00	3.00	10.00
53-Intro. Wolveroach (cameo)			5.00
54-1st full Wolveroach story		2.00	6.00
55,56-Wolveroach app.; Normalman back-ups by Valentino			5.00
57-79: 61,62: Flaming Carrot app. 65-Gerhard begins			2.50
80-237: 104-Flaming Carrot app. 112/113-Double issue. 114-Jaka's Story begins, ends #136. 137-$2.25-c begins. 139-Melmoth begins, ends #150. 175-($2.25, 44 pgs). 151-Mothers & Daughters begins, ends #200 201-Guys storyline begins; Eddie Campbell's Bacchus app. 220-231-Rick's Story. 232-Going Home begins			2.25
151-153-2nd printings			2.25
Free Cerebus (Giveaway, 1991-92?, 36 pgs.)-All-r			1.00

CHAIN GANG WAR
DC Comics: July, 1993 - No. 12, June, 1994 ($1.75)

1-($2.50)-Embossed silver foil-c, Dave Johnson-c/a			2.50
2-4,6-12: 3-Deathstroke app. 4-Brief Deathstroke app. 6-New Batman (Azrael) cameo. 11-New Batman-c/story. 12-New Batman app.			1.75
5-($2.50)-Foil embossed-c; Deathstroke app; new Batman cameo (1 panel).			2.50

CHAINS OF CHAOS
Harris Comics: Nov, 1994 - No. 3, Jan, 1995 ($2.95, limited series)

1-3-Re-Intro of The Rook w/ Vampirella			3.00

CHALLENGE OF THE UNKNOWN (Formerly Love Experiences)
Ace Magazines: No. 6, Sept, 1950 (See Web Of Mystery No. 19)

The Challenger #2 © Interfaith Publ.

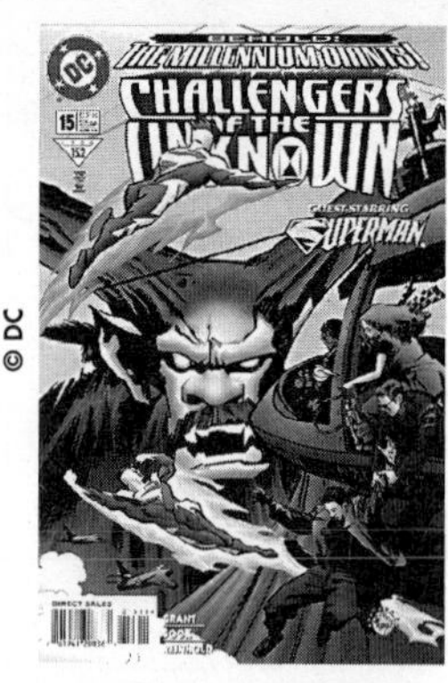

Challengers of the Unknown #15 (3rd Series) © DC

The Champions #10 © MAR

GD25 FN65 NM94

6- "Villa of the Vampire" used in N.Y. Joint Legislative Comm. Publ; Sekowsky-a 24.00 72.00 180.00

CHALLENGER, THE
Interfaith Publications/T.C. Comics: 1945 - No. 4, Oct-Dec, 1946

nn; nd; 32 pgs.; Origin the Challenger Club; Anti-Fascist with funny animal filler 32.00 96.00 240.00
2-4: Kubert-a; 4-Fuje-a 25.00 76.00 190.00

CHALLENGERS OF THE FANTASTIC
Marvel Comics (Amalgam): June 1997 ($1.95, one-shot)

1-Karl Kesel-s/Tom Grummett-a 1.95

CHALLENGERS OF THE UNKNOWN (See Showcase #6, 7, 11, 12, Super DC Giant, and Super Team Family)
National Per. Publ./DC Comics: 4-5/58 - No. 77, 12-1/70-71; No. 78, 2/73 - No. 80, 6-7/73; No. 81, 6-7/77 - No. 87, 6-7/78

1-(4-5/58)-Kirby/Stein-a(2); Kirby-c 162.00 485.00 2100.00
2-Kirby/Stein-a(2) 64.00 193.00 770.00
3-Kirby/Stein-a(2) 55.00 165.00 660.00
4-8-Kirby/Wood-a plus cover to #8 44.00 133.00 530.00
9,10 26.00 78.00 260.00
11-15: 11-Grey tone-c. 14-Origin/1st app. Multi-Man (villain) 17.50 53.00 175.00
16-22: 18-Intro. Cosmo, the Challengers Spacepet. 22-Last 10¢ issue 12.00 36.00 120.00
23-30 6.00 18.00 60.00
31-Retells origin of the Challengers 6.50 19.50 65.00
32-40 3.00 9.00 30.00
41-60: 43-New look begins. 48-Doom Patrol app. 49-Intro. Challenger Corps. 51-Sea Devils app. 55-Death of Red Ryan. 60-Red Ryan returns 2.25 6.75 18.00
61-68: 64,65-Kirby origin-r, parts 1 & 2. 66-New logo. 68-Last 12¢ issue. 1.10 3.30 9.00
69-73,75-80: 69-1st app. Corinna 5.00
74-Deadman by Tuska/Adams; 1 pg. Wrightson-a 1.50 4.50 15.00
81,83-87: 83-87-Swamp Thing app. 2.00 6.00
82-Swamp Thing begins, c/s .90 2.70 9.00

NOTE: ***N. Adams*** *c-67, 68, 70, 72, 74i, 81i.* ***Buckler*** *c-83-86p.* ***Giffen*** *a-83-87p.* ***Kirby*** *a-75-80r; c-75, 77, 78.* ***Kubert*** *c-64, 66, 69, 76, 79.* ***Nasser*** *c/a-81p, 82p.* ***Tuska*** *a-73.* ***Wood*** *r-76.*

CHALLENGERS OF THE UNKNOWN
DC Comics: Mar, 1991 - No. 8, Oct, 1991 ($1.75, limited series)

1-Jeph Loeb scripts & Tim Sale-a in all (1st work together); Bolland-c 2.00
2-8: 2-Superman app. 3-Dr. Fate app. 6-G. Kane-c(p). 7-Steranko-c/swipe by Art Adams 1.75

NOTE: ***Art Adams*** *c-7.* ***Hempel*** *c-5.* ***Gil Kane*** *c-6p.* ***Sale*** *a-1-8; c-3, 8.* ***Wagner*** *c-4.*

CHALLENGERS OF THE UNKNOWN
DC Comics: Feb, 1997 - No. 18, July, 1998 ($2.25)

1-15: 1-Intro new team; Leon-c/a(p) begins. 4-Origin of new team. 11,12-Batman app. 15-Millennium Giants x-over; Superman-c/app. 2.25
16-18-($2.50) 2.50

CHALLENGE TO THE WORLD
Catechetical Guild: 1951 (10¢, 36 pgs.)

nn 4.00 10.00 20.00

CHAMBER OF CHILLS (Formerly Blondie Comics #20; ...of Clues No. 27 on)
Harvey Publications/Witches Tales: No. 21, June, 1951 - No. 26, Dec, 1954

21 (#1) 37.00 112.00 280.00
22,24 (#2,4) 23.00 68.00 170.00
23 (#3)-Excessive violence; eyes torn out 25.00 76.00 190.00
5(2/52)-Decapitation, acid in face scene 25.00 76.00 190.00
6-Woman melted alive 24.00 72.00 180.00
7-Used in **SOTI**, pg. 389; decapitation/severed head panels 23.00 68.00 170.00
8-10: 8-Decapitation panels 18.00 54.00 135.00
11,12,14 13.00 40.00 100.00
13,15-24-Nostrand-a in all. 13,21-Decapitation panels. 18-Atom bomb panels. 20-Nostrand-c 20.00 60.00 150.00
25,26 11.00 34.00 85.00

NOTE: *About half the issues contain bondage, torture, sadism, perversion, gore, cannabalism, eyes ripped out, acid in face, etc.* ***Elias*** *c-4-11, 14-19, 21-26.* ***Kremer*** *a-12, 17.* ***Palais*** *a-21(1), 23.* ***Nostrand/Powell*** *a-13, 15, 16.* ***Powell*** *a-21, 23, 24('51), 5-8, 11, 13, 18-21, 23-25. Bondage-c-21, 24('51), 7. 25-r/#5; 26-r/#9.*

CHAMBER OF CHILLS
Marvel Comics Group: Nov, 1972 - No. 25, Nov, 1976

1-Harlan Ellison adaptation 1.60 4.80 16.00
2-5: 2-1st app. John Jakes (Brak the Barbarian) 1.00 3.00 10.00
6-25 .90 2.70 8.00

NOTE: ***Adkins*** *a-1i, 2i.* ***Brunner*** *a-2-4; c-4.* ***Chaykin*** *a-4.* ***Ditko*** *r-14, 16, 19, 23, 24.* ***Everett*** *a-3i, 11r,21r.* ***Heath*** *a-1r.* ***Gil Kane*** *c-2p.* ***Powell*** *a-13r.* ***Russell*** *a-1p, 2p.* ***Williamson/Mayo*** *a-13r.* ***Robert E. Howard*** *horror story adaptation-2, 3.*

CHAMBER OF CLUES (Formerly Chamber of Chills)
Harvey Publications: No. 27, Feb, 1955 - No. 28, April, 1955

27-Kerry Drake-r/#19; Powell-a; last pre-code 9.30 28.00 65.00
28-Kerry Drake 5.70 17.00 40.00

CHAMBER OF DARKNESS (Monsters on the Prowl #9 on)
Marvel Comics Group: Oct, 1969 - No. 8, Dec, 1970

1-Buscema-a(p) 4.20 12.60 42.00
2,3: 2-Neal Adams scripts. 3-Smith, Buscema-a 2.20 6.25 22.00
4-A Conanesque tryout by Smith (4/70); reprinted in Conan #16; Marie Severin/Everett-c 3.80 11.50 40.00
5,8: 5-H.P. Lovecraft adaptation. 8-Wrightson-c 1.60 4.80 16.00
6 1.20 3.60 12.00
7-Wrightson-c/a, 7pgs. (his 1st work at Marvel); Wrightson draws himself in 1st & last panels; Kirby/Ditko-r 1.60 4.80 16.00
1-(1/72; 25¢ Special) 2.00 6.00 20.00

NOTE: ***Adkins/Everett*** *a-8.* ***Buscema*** *a-Special 1r.* ***Craig*** *a-5.* ***Ditko*** *a-6-8r.* ***Heck*** *a-1, 2, 8, Special 1r.* ***Kirby*** *a(p)-4, 5, 7r.* ***Kirby/Everett*** *c-5.* ***Severin/Everett*** *c-6.* ***Shores*** *a-2, 3i, Special 1r.* ***Sutton*** *a-1, 2i, 4, 7, Special 1r.* ***Wrightson*** *c-7, 8.*

CHAMP COMICS (Formerly Champion No. 1-10)
Worth Publ. Co./Champ Publ./Family Comics(Harvey Publ.): No. 11, Oct, 1940 - No. 29, March, 1944

11-Human Meteor cont'd. from Champion 77.00 231.00 650.00
12-17,20: 14,15-Crandall-c. 20-The Green Ghost app. 56.00 168.00 475.00
18,19-Simon-c. 19-The Wasp app. 71.00 213.00 600.00
21-29: 22-The White Mask app. 23-Flag-c. 24-Hitler, Tojo & Mussolini-c 44.00 132.00 375.00

CHAMPION (See Gene Autry's...)

CHAMPION COMICS (Formerly Speed Comics #1?; Champ Comics No. 11 on)
Worth Publ. Co.(Harvey Publications): No. 2, Dec, 1939 - No. 10, Aug, 1940 (no No.1)

2-The Champ, The Blazing Scarab, Neptina, Liberty Lads, Jungleman, Bill Handy, Swingtime Sweetie begin 124.00 372.00 1050.00
3-7: 7-The Human Meteor begins? 65.00 195.00 550.00
8-10: 8-Simon-c. 9-1st S&K-c (1st collaboration together). 10-Bondage-c by Kirby 115.00 345.00 975.00

CHAMPIONS, THE
Marvel Comics Group: Oct, 1975 - No. 17, Jan, 1978

1-Origin & 1st app. The Champions (The Angel, Black Widow, Ghost Rider, Hercules, Iceman); Venus x-over 1.20 3.60 12.00
2-4,8-14,16,17: 2,3-Venus x-over. 11-14,17-Byrne-a. .90 2.70 8.00
5-7-(Regular 25¢ edition)(4-8/76) .90 2.70 8.00
5-7-(30¢-c, limited distribution) 2.20 6.50 24.00
15-(Regular 30¢ edition)(9/77)-Byrne-a .90 2.70 8.00
15-(35¢-c, limited distribution) 2.20 6.50 24.00

CH

Chapel V2 #5 © Rob Liefeld

Charlie Chan #1 © PRIZE

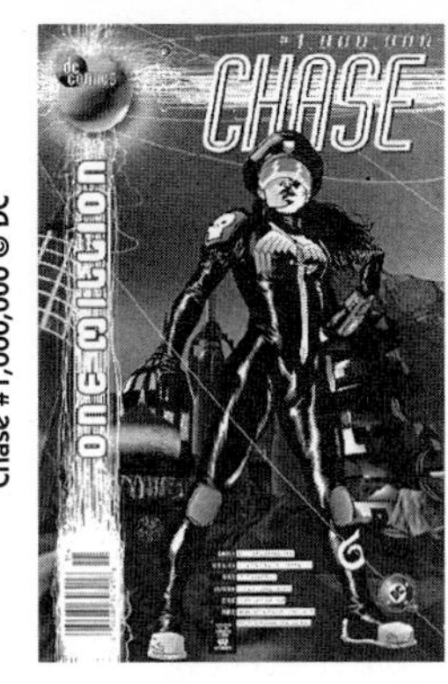

Chase #1,000,000 © DC

GD25 FN65 NM94 | GD25 FN65 NM94

NOTE: ***Buckler/Adkins** c-3. **Byrne** a-11-15, 17. **Kane/Adkins** c-1. **Kane/Layton** c-11. **Tuska** a-3p, 4p, 6p, 7p. Ghost Rider c-1-4, 7, 8, 10, 14, 16, 17 (4, 10, 14 are more prominent).*

CHAMPIONS (Game)
Eclipse Comics: June, 1986 - No. 6, Feb, 1987 (limited series)

1-6: 1-Intro Flare; based on game. 5-Origin Flare 1.50

CHAMPIONS (Also see The League of Champions)
Hero Comics: Sept, 1987 - No. 12, 1989 ($1.95)

1-12: 1-Intro The Marksman & The Rose. 14-Origin Malice 2.00
Annual 1(1988, $2.75, 52pgs.)-Origin of Giant 2.75

CHAMPION SPORTS
National Periodical Publications: Oct-Nov, 1973 - No. 3, Feb-Mar, 1974

	GD25	FN65	NM94
1	2.00	6.00	20.00
2,3	1.00	3.00	10.00

CHANNEL ZERO
Image Comics: Feb, 1998 - No. 4, Aug, 1998 ($2.95, B&W, limited series)

1-4-Brian Wood-s/a 2.95

CHAOS (See The Crusaders)

CHAOS! BIBLE
Chaos! Comics: Nov, 1995 ($3.30, one-shot)

1-Profiles of characters & creators 3.50

CHAOS EFFECT, THE
Valiant: 1994

Alpha (Giveaway w/trading card checklist) 1.00
Alpha-Gold variant 5.00
Omega (11/94, $2.25) 2.25
Omega-Gold variant 5.00
Epilogue Pt. 1, 2 (12/94, 1/95; $2.95) 3.00

CHAOS! GALLERY
Chaos! Comics: Aug, 1997 ($2.95, one-shot)

1-Pin-ups of characters 2.95

CHAOS! QUARTERLY
Chaos! Comics: Oct, 1995 -No. 3, May, 1996 ($4.95, quarterly)

1-3: 1-anthology; Lady Death-c by Julie Bell. 2-Boris "Lady Demon"-c. 5.00
1-Premium Edition (7,500) 35.00

CHAPEL (Also see Youngblood & Youngblood Strikefile #1-3)
Image Comics (Extreme Studios): No. 1 Feb, 1995 - No. 2, Mar, 1995 ($2.50, limited series)

1,2 2.50

CHAPEL (Also see Youngblood & Youngblood Strikefile #1-3)
Image Comics (Extreme Studios): V2 #1, Aug, 1995 - No. 7, Apr, 1996 ($2.50)

V2#1-7: 4-Babewatch x-over. 5-vs. Spawn. 7-Shadowhawk-c/app; Shadowhunt x-over 2.50
#1-Quesada & Palmiotti variant-c 3.00

CHAPEL (Also see Youngblood & Youngblood Strikefile #1-3)
Awesome Entertainment: Sept, 1997 ($2.99, one-shot)

	FN65	NM94
1		3.00
1-Alternate cover	2.00	6.00

CHARLEMAGNE (Also see War Dancer)
Defiant Comics: Mar, 1994 - No. 5, July, 1994 ($2.50)

1/2 (Hero Illustrated giveaway)-Adam Pollina-c/a.
1-(3/94, $3.50, 52 pgs.)-Adam Pollina-c/a. 3.50
2,3,5: Adam Pollina-c/a. 2-War Dancer app. 5-Pre-Schism issue. 2.50
4-($3.25, 52 pgs.) 3.25

CHARLIE CHAN (See Big Shot Comics, Columbia Comics, Feature Comics & The New Advs. of...)

CHARLIE CHAN (The Adventures of...) (Zaza The Mystic No. 10 on) (TV)
Crestwood(Prize) No. 1-5; Charlton No. 6(6/55) on: 6-7/48 - No. 5, 2-3/49; No.6, 6/55 - No. 9, 3/56

	GD25	FN65	NM94
1-S&K-c, 2 pgs.; Infantino-a	65.00	195.00	550.00
2-5-S&K-c: 3-S&K-c/a	43.00	129.00	360.00
6 (6/55-Charlton)-S&K-c	29.00	87.00	220.00
7-9	15.00	45.00	110.00

CHARLIE CHAN
Dell Publishing Co.: Oct-Dec, 1965 - No. 2, Mar, 1966

	GD25	FN65	NM94
1-Springer-a	3.50	10.50	38.00
2	2.20	6.50	24.00

CHARLIE McCARTHY (See Edgar Bergen Presents...)
Dell Publishing Co.: No. 171, Nov, 1947 - No. 571, July, 1954 (See True Comics #14)

	GD25	FN65	NM94
Four Color 171	23.00	68.00	250.00
Four Color 196-Part photo-c; photo back-c	16.00	47.00	170.00
1(3-5/49)-Part photo-c; photo back-c	14.00	44.00	160.00
2-9(7/52; #5,6-52 pgs.)	6.40	19.00	70.00
Four Color 445,478,527,571	4.50	13.50	50.00

CHARLTON BULLSEYE
CPL/Gang Publications: 1975 - No. 5, 1976 ($1.50, B&W, bi-monthly, magazine format)

	GD25	FN65	NM94
1: 1 & 2 are last Capt. Atom by Ditko/Byrne intended for the never published Capt. Atom #90; Nightshade app.; Jeff Jones-a	2.50	7.60	28.00
2-Part 2 Capt. Atom story by Ditko/Byrne	1.80	5.40	18.00
3-Wrong Country by Sanho Kim	1.40	4.20	14.00
4-Doomsday + 1 by John Byrne	1.40	4.20	14.00
5-Doomsday + 1 by Byrne, The Question by Toth; Neal Adams back-c; Toth-c	2.20	6.50	24.00

CHARLTON BULLSEYE
Charlton Publications: June, 1981 - No. 10, Dec, 1982; Nov, 1986

1-Blue Beetle, The Question app.; 1st app. Rocket Rabbit 4.00
2-10: 2-1st app. Neil The Horse; Rocket Rabbit app. 4-Vanguards. 6-Origin & 1st app. Thunderbunny 2.50
Special 1(11/86) (Half in B&W) 3.50
Special 2-Atomic Mouse app. (1987) 2.50

CHARLTON CLASSICS
Charlton Comics: Apr, 1980 - No. 9, Aug, 1981

1 4.00
2-9 2.50

CHARLTON CLASSICS LIBRARY (1776)
Charlton Comics: V10 No.1, Mar, 1973 (one-shot)

	GD25	FN65	NM94
1776 (title) - Adaptation of the film musical "1776"; given away at movie theatres	1.00	3.00	10.00

CHARLTON PREMIERE (Formerly Marine War Heroes)
Charlton Comics: V1#19, July, 1967; V2#1, Sept, 1967 - No. 4, May, 1968

	GD25	FN65	NM94
V1#19-Marine War Heroes. V2#1-Trio; intro. Shape. Tyro Team. & Spookman. 2-Children of Doom. 3-Sinistro Boy Fiend; Blue Beetle & Peacemaker x-over. 4-Unlikely Tales; Aparo, Ditko-a	1.50	4.50	15.00

CHARLTON SPORT LIBRARY - PROFESSIONAL FOOTBALL
Charlton Comics: Winter, 1969-70 (Jan. on cover) (68 pgs.)

	GD25	FN65	NM94
1	2.40	7.00	26.00

CHASE (See Batman #550 for 1st app.)
DC Comics: Feb, 1998 - No. 8, Oct, 1998; #1,000,000 Nov, 1998 ($2.50)

1-9: Williams III & Gray-a. 1-Includes 4 Chase cards. 4-Teen Titans app. 7,8-Batman app. 9-GL Hal Jordan-c/app. 2.50
#1,000,000 (11/98) Final issue; 853rd Century x-over 2.50

CHASSIS

Chastity: Rocked #1 © Chaos! Comics

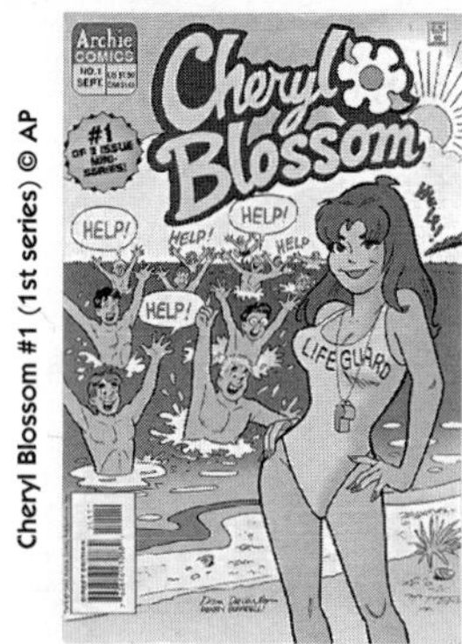

Cheryl Blossom #1 (1st series) © AP

Chesty Sanchez #2 © Antarctic Press

GD25 FN65 NM94

Millenium Publications: 1996 - No. 2 ($2.95)

1,2: 1-Adam Hughes-c — 2.95

CHASTITY: ROCKED
Chaos! Comics: Nov, 1998 - No. 4 ($2.95, limited series)

1,2-Nutman-s/Justiniano-c/a — 2.95

CHASTITY: THEATER OF PAIN
Chaos! Comics: Feb, 1997 - No. 3, June, 1997 ($2.95, limited series)

1-3-Pulido-s/Justiniano-c/a — 2.95
TPB (1997, $9.95) r/#1-3 — 9.95

CHECKMATE (TV)
Gold Key: Oct, 1962 - No. 2, Dec, 1962

	GD25	FN65	NM94
1,2-Photo-c	4.00	12.00	45.00

CHECKMATE! (See Action Comics #598)
DC Comics: Apr, 1988 - No. 33, Jan, 1991 ($1.25)

1-12 — 1.25
13-33: $1.50/$2.00, new format — 1.50
NOTE: ***Gil Kane*** *c-2, 4, 7, 8, 10, 11, 15-19.*

CHEERIOS PREMIUMS (Disney)
Walt Disney Productions: 1947 (16 titles, pocket size, 32 pgs.)

	GD25	FN65	NM94
Set "W"			
W1-Donald Duck & the Pirates	7.15	21.50	50.00
W2-Bucky Bug & the Cannibal King	4.00	12.00	24.00
W3-Pluto Joins the F.B.I.	4.00	12.00	24.00
W4-Mickey Mouse & the Haunted House	5.35	16.00	32.00
Set "X"			
X1-Donald Duck, Counter Spy	7.15	21.50	50.00
X2-Goofy Lost in the Desert	4.00	11.00	22.00
X3-Br'er Rabbit Outwits Br'er Fox	4.00	11.00	22.00
X4-Mickey Mouse at the Rodeo	5.35	16.00	32.00
Set "Y"			
Y1-Donald Duck's Atom Bomb by Carl Barks. Disney has banned reprinting this book	78.00	234.00	700.00
Y2-Br'er Rabbit's Secret	4.00	11.00	22.00
Y3-Dumbo & the Circus Mystery	5.00	15.00	30.00
Y4-Mickey Mouse Meets the Wizard	5.35	16.00	32.00
Set "Z"			
Z1-Donald Duck Pilots a Jet Plane (not by Barks)	7.15	21.50	50.00
Z2-Pluto Turns Sleuth Hound	4.00	11.00	22.00
Z3-The Seven Dwarfs & the Enchanted Mtn.	5.35	16.00	32.00
Z4-Mickey Mouse's Secret Room	5.35	16.00	32.00

CHEERIOS 3-D GIVEAWAYS (Disney)
Walt Disney Productions: 1954 (24 titles, pocket size) (Glasses were cut-outs on boxes)

	GD25	FN65	NM94
Glasses only...	5.70	17.00	40.00

(Set 1) 1-Donald Duck & Uncle Scrooge, the Firefighters
2-Mickey Mouse & Goofy, Pirate Plunder
3-Donald Duck's Nephews, the Fabulous Inventors
4-Mickey Mouse, Secret of the Ming Vase
5-Donald Duck with Huey, Dewey, & Louie; ...the Seafarers (title on 2nd page)
6-Mickey Mouse, Moaning Mountain
7-Donald Duck, Apache Gold
8-Mickey Mouse, Flight to Nowhere (per book) — 7.85 — 23.50 — 55.00

(Set 2) 1-Donald Duck, Treasure of Timbuktu
2-Mickey Mouse & Pluto, Operation China
3-Donald Duck in the Magic Cows
4-Mickey Mouse & Goofy, Kid Kokonut
5-Donald Duck, Mystery Ship
6-Mickey Mouse, Phantom Sheriff
7-Donald Duck, Circus Adventures
8-Mickey Mouse, Arctic Explorers (per book) — 7.85 — 23.50 — 55.00

(Set 3) 1-Donald Duck & Witch Hazel
2-Mickey Mouse in Darkest Africa
3-Donald Duck & Uncle Scrooge, Timber Trouble
4-Mickey Mouse, Rajah's Rescue
5-Donald Duck in Robot Reporter
6-Mickey Mouse, Slumbering Sleuth
7-Donald Duck in the Foreign Legion
8-Mickey Mouse, Airwalking Wonder (per book).... — 7.85 — 23.50 — 55.00

CHERYL BLOSSOM (See Archie's Girls, Betty and Veronica #320 for 1st app.)
Archie Publications: Sept, 1995 - No. 3, Nov, 1995 ($1.50, limited series)

1-3 — 1.50
Special 1,2 (1995, $2.00) — 2.00
Special 3,4 (1996, $2.00) — 2.00

CHERYL BLOSSOM (Cheryl's Summer Job)
Archie Publications: July, 1996 - No. 3, Sept, 1996 ($1.50, limited series)

1-3 — 1.50

CHERYL BLOSSOM (...Goes Hollywood)
Archie Publications: Dec, 1996 - No. 3, Feb, 1997 ($1.50, limited series)

1-3 — 1.50

CHERYL BLOSSOM
Archie Publications: Apr, 1997 - Present ($1.50/$1.75)

1-7: Dan DeCarlo-c/a — 1.50
8-19: 8-Begin $1.75-c — 1.75

CHESTY AND COPTIE (Disney)
Los Angeles Community Chest: 1946 (Giveaway, 4pgs.)

	GD25	FN65	NM94
nn-(One known copy) by Floyd Gottfredson	91.00	274.00	775.00

CHESTY AND HIS HELPERS (Disney)
Los Angeles War Chest: 1943 (Giveaway, 12 pgs., 5-1/2x7-1/4")

	GD25	FN65	NM94
nn-Chesty & Coptie	62.00	185.00	525.00

CHESTY SANCHEZ
Antarctic Press: Nov, 1995 - No. 2, Mar, 1996 ($2.95, B&W)

1,2 — 3.00

CHEVAL NOIR
Dark Horse Comics: 1989 - No. 48, Nov, 1993 ($3.50, B&W, 68 pgs.)

1-8,10 ($3.50): 6-Moebius poster insert — 3.50
9,11,13,15,17,20,22 ($4.50, 84 pgs.) — 4.50
12,18,19,21,23,25,26 ($3.95): 12-Geary-a; Mignola-c. 26-Moebius-a begins — 4.00
14 ($4.95, 76 pgs.)(7 pgs. color) — 5.00
16,24 ($3.75): 16-19-Contain trading cards — 3.75
27-48 ($2.95): 33-Snyder III-c — 3.00
NOTE: ***Bolland*** *a-2, 6, 7, 13, 14.* ***Bolton*** *a-2, 4, 45; c-4, 20.* ***Chadwick*** *c-13.* ***Dorman*** *painted c-16.* ***Geary*** *a-13, 14.* ***Kelley Jones*** *c-27.* ***Kaluta*** *a-6; c-6, 18.* ***Moebius*** *c-5, 9, 26.* ***Dave Stevens*** *c-1, 7.* ***Sutton*** *painted c-36.*

CHEYENNE (TV)
Dell Publishing Co.: No. 734, Oct, 1956 - No. 25, Dec-Jan, 1961-62

	GD25	FN65	NM94
Four Color 734(#1)-Clint Walker photo-c	16.00	47.00	170.00
Four Color 772,803: Clint Walker photo-c	7.00	20.00	75.00
4(8-10/57) - 12: 4-9-Clint Walker photo-c. 10-12-Ty Hardin photo-c	4.50	13.50	50.00
13-20 (All Clint Walker photo-c)	4.50	13.50	50.00
21-25 (All Clint Walker photo-c)	5.00	15.00	55.00

CHEYENNE AUTUMN (See Movie Classics)

CHEYENNE KID (Formerly Wild Frontier No. 1-7)

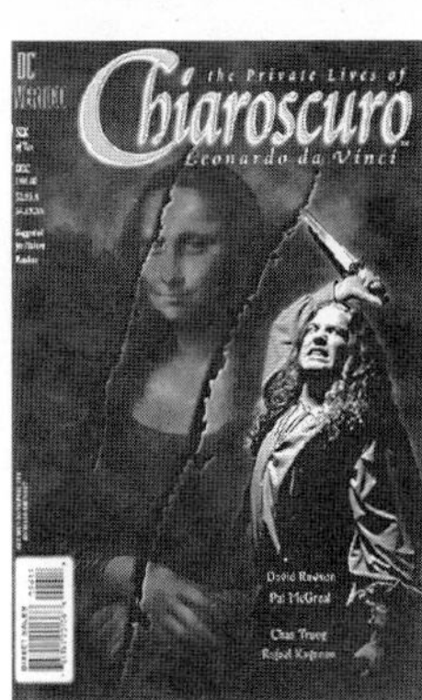

Chiaroscuro (The Private Lives of Leonardo da Vinci) #6 © DC

Child's Play 2 #1 © Universal

Chip 'n' Dale Four Color #517 © WDC

	GD25	FN65	NM94
Charlton Comics: No. 8, July, 1957 - No. 99, Nov, 1973			
8 (#1)	5.70	17.00	35.00
9,15-19	4.00	10.00	20.00
10-Williamson/Torres-a(3); Ditko-c	7.85	23.50	55.00
11,12-Williamson/Torres-a(2) ea.; 11-(68 pgs.)-Cheyenne Kid meets Geronimo	8.50	26.00	60.00
13-Williamson/Torres-a (5 pgs.)	5.70	17.00	35.00
14-Williamson-a (5 pgs.?)	5.70	17.00	35.00
20-22,24,25-Severin c/a(3) each	2.50	7.50	22.00
23,27-29	1.25	3.75	10.00
26,30-Severin-a	2.00	6.00	16.00
31-59	1.25	3.75	10.00
60-80: 66-Wander by Aparo begins, ends #87	.85	2.60	7.00
81-99: . Apache Red begins #88, origin in #89			5.00
Modern Comics Reprint 87,89(1978)			3.00

CHIAROSCURO (THE PRIVATE LIVES OF LEONARDO DA VINCI)
DC Comics (Vertigo): July, 1995 - No. 10, Apr, 1996 ($2.50/$2.95, limited series, mature)

	GD25	FN65	NM94
1-9			2.50
10-($2.95)			2.95

CHICAGO MAIL ORDER (See C-M-O Comics)

CHI-CHIAN
Sirius Entertainment: 1997 - No. 6, 1998 ($2.95, limited series)

	GD25	FN65	NM94
1-6-Voltaire-s/a			3.00

CHIEF, THE (Indian Chief No. 3 on)
Dell Publishing Co.: No. 290, Aug, 1950 - No. 2, Apr-June, 1951

	GD25	FN65	NM94
Four Color 290(#1), 2	4.50	13.50	50.00

CHIEF CRAZY HORSE (See Wild Bill Hickok #21)
Avon Periodicals: 1950 (Also see Fighting Indians of the Wild West!)

	GD25	FN65	NM94
nn-Fawcette-c	18.00	54.00	135.00

CHIEF VICTORIO'S APACHE MASSACRE (See Fight Indians of/Wild West!)
Avon Periodicals: 1951

	GD25	FN65	NM94
nn-Williamson/Frazetta-a (7 pgs.); Larsen-a; Kinstler-c	39.00	118.00	300.00

CHILDHOOD'S END
Image Comics: Oct, 1997 ($2.95, B&W)

	GD25	FN65	NM94
1-Bourne-s/Calafiore-a			2.95

CHILDREN OF FIRE
Fantagor Press: Nov, 1987 - No. 3, 1988 ($2.00, limited series)

	GD25	FN65	NM94
1-3: by Richard Corben			2.00

CHILDREN OF THE VOYAGER (See Marvel Frontier Comics Unlimited)
Marvel Frontier Comics: Sept, 1993 - No. 4, Dec, 1993 ($1.95, limited series)

	GD25	FN65	NM94
1-($2.95)-Embossed glow-in-the-dark-c			3.00
2-4			1.50

CHILDREN'S BIG BOOK
Dorene Publ. Co.: 1945 (25¢, stiff-c, 68 pgs.)

	GD25	FN65	NM94
nn-Comics & fairy tales; David Icove-a	9.30	28.00	65.00

CHILDREN'S CRUSADE, THE
DC Comics (Vertigo): Dec, 1993 - No. 2, Jan, 1994 ($3.95, limited series)

	GD25	FN65	NM94
1,2-Neil Gaiman scripts & Chris Bachalo-a; framing issues for Children's Crusade x-over			4.00

CHILD'S PLAY: THE SERIES (Movie)
Innovation Publishing: May, 1991 - #3, 1991 ($2.50, 28pgs.)

	GD25	FN65	NM94
1-3			2.50

CHILD'S PLAY 2 THE OFFICIAL MOVIE ADAPTATION (Movie)
Innovation Publishing: 1990 - No. 3, 1990 ($2.50, bi-weekly limited series)

	GD25	FN65	NM94
1-3: Adapts movie sequel			2.50

CHILI (Millie's Rival)
Marvel Comics Group: 5/69 - No. 17, 9/70; No. 18, 8/72 - No. 26, 12/73

	GD25	FN65	NM94
1	4.00	12.25	45.00
2-5	2.20	6.25	22.00
6-17	1.40	4.20	14.00
18-26	.90	2.70	9.00
Special 1(12/71)	2.40	7.00	26.00

CHILLER
Marvel Comics (Epic): Nov, 1993 - No. 2, Dec, 1993 ($7.95, lim. series)

	GD25	FN65	NM94
1,2-(68 pgs.)	.90	2.70	8.00

CHILLING ADVENTURES IN SORCERY (...as Told by Sabrina #1, 2) (Red Circle Sorcery No. 6 on)
Archie Publications (Red Circle Productions): 9/72 - No. 2, 10/72; No. 3, 10/73 - No. 5, 2/74

	GD25	FN65	NM94
1-Sabrina cameo	2.40	7.00	26.00
2-Sabrina cameo	1.20	3.60	12.00
3-5: Morrow-c/a, all	.90	2.70	8.00

CHILLING TALES (Formerly Beware)
Youthful Magazines: No. 13, Dec, 1952 - No. 17, Oct, 1953

	GD25	FN65	NM94
13(No.1)-Harrison-a; Matt Fox-c/a	43.00	129.00	360.00
14-Harrison-a	29.00	88.00	220.00
15-Has #14 on-c; Matt Fox-c; Harrison-a	36.00	108.00	270.00
16-Poe adapt.-`Metzengerstein'; Rudyard Kipling adapt.- 'Mark of the Beast,' by Kiefer; bondage-c	25.00	74.00	185.00
17-Matt Fox-c; Sir Walter Scott & Poe adapt.	32.00	96.00	240.00

CHILLING TALES OF HORROR (Magazine)
Stanley Publications: V1#1, 6/69 - V1#7, 12/70; V2#2, 2/71 - V2#5, 10/71 (50¢, B&W, 52 pgs.)

	GD25	FN65	NM94
V1#1	4.00	12.25	45.00
2-7: 7-Cameron-a	2.70	8.00	30.00
V2#2,3,5: 2-Spirit of Frankenstein-r/Adventures into the Unknown #16	2.40	7.00	26.00
V2#4-r/9 pg. Feldstein-a from Adventures into the Unknown #3	2.70	8.00	30.00

NOTE: *Two issues of V2#2 exist, Feb, 1971 and April, 1971.*

CHILLY WILLY
Dell Publ. Co.: No. 740, Oct, 1956 - No. 1281, Apr-June, 1962 (Walter Lantz)

	GD25	FN65	NM94
Four Color 740 (#1)	3.60	11.00	40.00
Four Color 852 (2/58),967 (2/59),1017 (9/59), 1074 (2-4/60),1122 (8/60), 1177 (4-6/61), 1212 (7-9/61), 1281	2.75	8.00	30.00

CHINA BOY (See Wisco)

CHIP 'N' DALE (Walt Disney)(See Walt Disney's C&S #204)
Dell Publishing Co./Gold Key/Whitman No. 65 on: Nov, 1953 - No. 30, June-Aug, 1962; Sept, 1967 - No. 83, 1982

	GD25	FN65	NM94
Four Color 517(#1)	7.00	22.00	80.00
Four Color 581,636	4.50	13.50	50.00
4(12/55-2/56)-10	3.60	11.00	40.00
11-30	2.75	8.00	30.00
1(Gold Key, 1967)-Reprints	1.80	5.40	20.00
2-10	1.00	3.00	10.00
11-20		2.00	6.00
21-64			2.00
65,66 (Whitman)			3.00
67-69 (3-pack? 1980)	.90	2.70	8.00
70-77			4.00
78-83 (All #90214; 3-pack?, nd, dn code		2.00	6.00

NOTE: *All Gold Key/Whitman issues have reprints except No. 32-35, 38-41, 45-47. No. 23-28, 30-42, 45-47, 49 have new covers.*

CHIP 'N DALE RESCUE RANGERS

C.H.I.X. #1 © Image

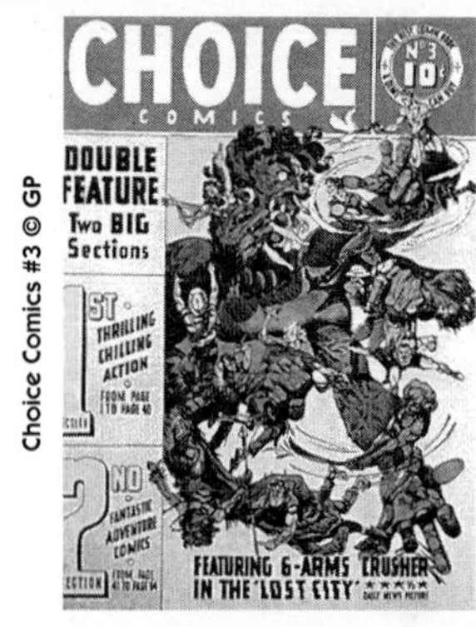

Choice Comics #3 © GP

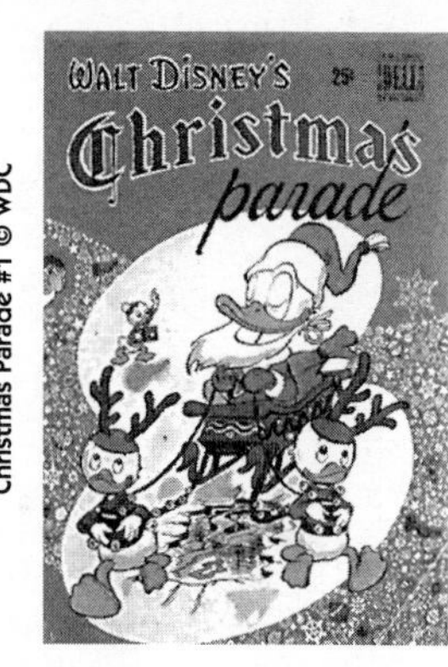

Christmas Parade #1 © WDC

GD25 FN65 NM94

Disney Comics: June, 1990 - No. 19, Dec, 1991 ($1.50)

1-19: New stories; 1,2-Origin 1.50

CHITTY CHITTY BANG BANG (See Movie Comics)

C.H.I.X.
Image Comics (Studiosaurus): Jan, 1998 ($2.50)

1-Dodson, Haley, Lopresti, Randall, and Warren-s/c/a 3.00
1-($5.00) "X-Ray Variant" cover 5.00
C.H.I.X. That Time Forgot 1 (8/98, $2.95) 2.95

CHOICE COMICS
Great Publications: Dec, 1941 - No. 3, Feb, 1942

1-Origin Secret Circle; Atlas the Mighty app.; Zomba, Jungle Fight, Kangaroo Man, & Fire Eater begin 129.00 387.00 1100.00
2 71.00 213.00 600.00
3-Double feature; Features movie "The Lost City" (classic cover); continued from Great Comics #3 100.00 300.00 850.00

CHOO CHOO CHARLIE
Gold Key: Dec, 1969

1-John Stanley-a (scarce) 9.00 26.00 95.00

CHRISTIAN (See Asylum)
Maximum Press: Jan, 1996 ($2.99, one-shot)

1-Pop Mhan-a 3.00

CHRISTIAN HEROES OF TODAY
David C. Cook: 1964 (36 pgs.)

nn 1.00 3.00 8.00

CHRISTMAS (Also see A-1 Comics)
Magazine Enterprises: No. 28, 1950

A-1 28 4.25 13.00 28.00

CHRISTMAS ADVENTURE, A (See Classics Comics Giveaways, 12/69)

CHRISTMAS ADVENTURE, THE
S. Rose (H. L. Green Giveaway): 1963 (16 pgs.)

nn 1.00 3.00 8.00

CHRISTMAS ALBUM (See March of Comics No. 312)

CHRISTMAS & ARCHIE
Archie Comics: Jan, 1975 ($1.00, 68 pgs., 10-1/4x13-1/4")

1 3.20 9.50 35.00

CHRISTMAS AT THE ROTUNDA (Titled Ford Rotunda Christmas Book 1957 on) (Regular size)
Ford Motor Co. (Western Printing): 1954 - 1961 (Given away every Christmas at one location)

1954-56 issues (nn's) 5.00 15.00 30.00
1957-61 issues (nn's) 4.00 12.00 24.00

CHRISTMAS BELLS (See March of Comics No. 297)

CHRISTMAS CARNIVAL
Ziff-Davis Publ. Co./St. John Publ. Co. No. 2: 1952 (25¢, one-shot, 100 pgs.)

nn 25.00 76.00 190.00
2-Reprints Ziff-Davis issue plus-c 15.00 44.00 110.00

CHRISTMAS CAROL, A (See March of Comics No. 33)

CHRISTMAS CAROL, A
Sears Roebuck & Co.: No date (1942-43) (Giveaway, 32 pgs., 8-1/4x10-3/4", paper cover)

nn-Comics & coloring book 16.00 48.00 120.00

CHRISTMAS CAROL, A
Sears Roebuck & Co.: 1940s ? (Christmas giveaway, 20 pgs.)

nn-Comic book & animated coloring book 14.00 42.00 105.00

GD25 FN65 NM94

CHRISTMAS CAROLS
Hot Shoppes Giveaway: 1959? (16 pgs.)

nn 3.60 9.00 18.00

CHRISTMAS COLORING FUN
H. Burnside: 1964 (20 pgs., slick-c, B&W)

nn 1.10 3.30 9.00

CHRISTMAS DREAM, A
Promotional Publishing Co.: 1950 (Kinney Shoe Store Giveaway, 16 pgs.)

nn 4.00 10.00 20.00

CHRISTMAS DREAM, A
J. J. Newberry Co.: 1952? (Giveaway, paper cover, 16 pgs.)

nn 4.00 10.00 18.00

CHRISTMAS DREAM, A
Promotional Publ. Co.: 1952 (Giveaway, 16 pgs., paper cover)

nn 4.00 10.00 20.00

CHRISTMAS EVE, A (See March of Comics No. 212)

CHRISTMAS FUN AROUND THE WORLD
No publisher: No date (early 50's) (16 pgs., paper cover)

nn 4.00 10.00 20.00

CHRISTMAS IN DISNEYLAND (See Dell Giants)

CHRISTMAS JOURNEY THROUGH SPACE
Promotional Publishing Co.: 1960

nn-Reprints 1954 issue Jolly Christmas Book with new slick cover 2.50 7.50 25.00

CHRISTMAS ON THE MOON
W. T. Grant Co.: 1958 (Giveaway, 20 pgs., slick cover)

nn 7.15 21.50 50.00

CHRISTMAS PARADE (See Dell Giant No. 26, Dell Giants, March of Comics No. 284, Walt Disney Christmas Parade & Walt Disney's...)

CHRISTMAS PARADE (Walt Disney's)
Gold Key: Jan, 1963 (no month listed) - No. 9, Jan, 1972 (#1,5: 80 pgs.; #2-4,7-9: 36 pgs.)

1 (30018-301)-Giant 7.70 22.00 85.00
2-6: 2-r/F.C. #367 by Barks. 3-r/F.C. #178 by Barks. 4-r/F.C. #203 by Barks. 5-r/Christ. Parade #1 (Dell) by Barks; giant. 6-r/Christmas Parade #2 (Dell) by Barks (64 pgs.); giant 5.50 16.50 60.00
7-Pull-out poster 3.00 9.00 35.00
8-r/F.C. #367 by Barks; pull-out poster 5.50 16.50 60.00
9 2.75 8.00 30.00

CHRISTMAS PARTY (See March of Comics No. 256)

CHRISTMAS PLAY BOOK
Gould-Stoner Co.: 1946 (Giveaway, 16 pgs., paper cover)

nn 5.00 15.00 30.00

CHRISTMAS ROUNDUP
Promotional Publishing Co.: 1960

nn-Marv Levy-c/a 1.10 3.30 9.00

CHRISTMAS STORIES (See Little People No. 959, 1062)

CHRISTMAS STORY (See March of Comics No. 326)

CHRISTMAS STORY BOOK (See Woolworth's Christmas Story Book)

CHRISTMAS STORY CUT-OUT BOOK, THE
Catechetical Guild: No. 393, 1951 (15¢, 36 pgs.)

393-Half text & half comics 4.25 13.00 28.00

CHRISTMAS TREASURY, A (See Dell Giants & March of Comics No. 227)

CHRISTMAS USA (Through 300 Years) (Also see Uncle Sam's...)

Chronos #4 © DC

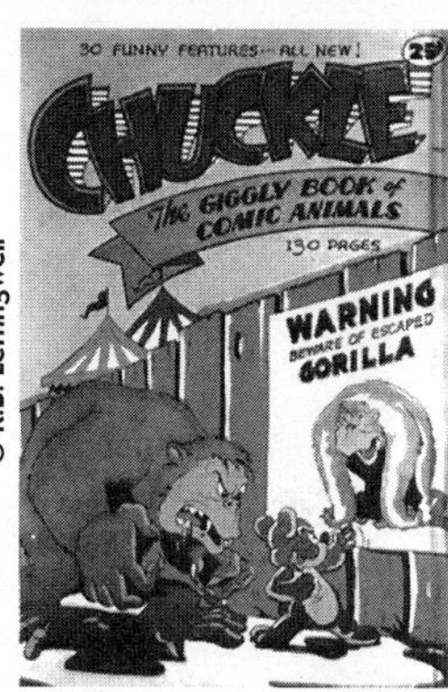

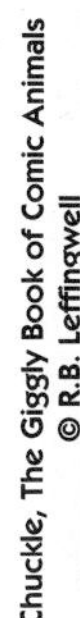
Chuckle, The Giggly Book of Comic Animals © R.B. Leffingwell

Cinderella Love #29 © STJ

GD25 FN65 NM94

Promotional Publ. Co.: 1956 (Giveaway)

nn-Marv Levy-c/a 1.80 4.50 9.00

CHRISTMAS WITH ARCHIE
Spire Christian Comics (Fleming H. Revell Co.): 1973, 1974 (49¢, 52 pgs.)

nn 5.00

CHRISTMAS WITH MOTHER GOOSE
Dell Publishing Co.: No. 90, Nov, 1945 - No. 253, Nov, 1949

Four Color 90 (#1)-Kelly-a 16.00 49.00 180.00
Four Color 126 ('46), 172 (11/47)-By Walt Kelly 13.00 38.00 140.00
Four Color 201 (10/48), 253-By Walt Kelly 11.00 33.00 120.00

CHRISTMAS WITH SANTA (See March of Comics No. 92)

CHRISTMAS WITH SNOW WHITE AND THE SEVEN DWARFS
Kobackers Giftstore of Buffalo, N.Y.: 1953 (16 pgs., paper-c)

nn 4.25 13.00 28.00

CHRISTMAS WITH THE SUPER-HEROES (See Limited Collectors' Edition)
DC Comics: 1988; No. 2, 1989 ($2.95)

1,2: 1-(100 pgs.)-All reprints; N. Adams-r, Byrne-c; Batman, Superman, JLA, LSH Christmas stories; r-Miller's 1st Batman/DC Special Series #21. 2-(68 pgs.)-Superman by Chadwick; Batman, Wonder Woman, Deadman, Gr. Lantern, Flash app.; Morrow-a; Enemy Ace by Byrne; all new-a 3.50

CHRISTOPHERS, THE
Catechetical Guild: 1951 (Giveaway, 36 pgs.) (Some copies have 15¢ sticker)

nn-Stalin as Satan in Hell 23.00 68.00 170.00

CHROMA-TICK, THE (...Special Edition, #1,2) (Also see The Tick)
New England Comics Press: Feb, 1992 - No. 8, Nov, 1993 ($3.95/$3.50, 44 pgs.)

1,2-Includes serially numbered trading card set 4.00
3-8 ($3.50, 36 pgs.): 6-Bound-in card 3.50

CHROME
Hot Comics: 1986 - No. 3, 1986 ($1.50, limited series)

1-3 1.50

CHROMIUM MAN, THE
Triumphant Comics: Aug, 1993 - No.10, May, 1994 ($2.50)

1-1st app. Mr. Death; all serially numbered 2.50
2-10: 2-1st app. Prince Vandal. 3-1st app. Candi, Breaker & Coil. 4,5-Triumphant Unleashed x-over. 8,9-(3/94). 10-(5/94) 2.50
0-(4/94)-Four color-c 2.50
0-All pink-c & all blue-c; no cover price 2.50

CHROMIUM MAN: VIOLENT PAST, THE
Triumphant Comics: Jan, 1994 - No. 2, Jan, 1994 ($2.50, limited series)

1,2-Serially numbered to 22,000 each 2.50

CHRONICLES OF CORUM, THE (Also see Corum...)
First Comics: Jan, 1987 - No. 12, Nov, 1988 ($1.75/$1.95, deluxe series)

1-12: Adapts Michael Moorcock's novel 2.00

CHRONOS
DC Comics: Mar, 1998 - No. 11, Feb. 1999 ($2.50)

1-11-J.F. Moore-s/Guinan-a 2.50
#1,000,000 (11/98) 853rd Century x-over 2.50

CHRONOWAR (Manga)
Dark Horse Comics: Aug, 1996 - No. 9, Apr, 1997 ($2.95, limited series)

1-9 3.00

CHUCKLE, THE GIGGLY BOOK OF COMIC ANIMALS
R. B. Leffingwell Co.: 1945 (132 pgs., one-shot)

1-Funny animal 17.00 52.00 130.00

CHUCK NORRIS (TV)
Marvel Comics (Star Comics): Jan, 1987 - No. 4, July, 1987

1-3: Ditko-a 3.00
4-No Ditko-a (scarce) 5.00

CHUCK WAGON (See Sheriff Bob Dixon's...)

CICERO'S CAT
Dell Publishing Co.: July-Aug, 1959 - No. 2, Sept-Oct, 1959

1,2-Cat from Mutt & Jeff 3.00 9.00 35.00

CIMARRON STRIP (TV)
Dell Publishing Co.: Jan, 1968

1-Stuart Whitman photo-c 2.90 8.70 32.00

CINDER AND ASHE
DC Comics: May, 1988 - No. 4, Aug, 1988 ($1.75, limited series)

1-4: Mature readers 1.75

CINDERELLA (Disney) (See Movie Comics)
Dell Publishing Co.: No. 272, Apr, 1950 - No. 786, Apr, 1957

Four Color 272 9.00 27.00 100.00
Four Color 786-Partial-r 272 5.50 16.50 60.00

CINDERELLA
Whitman Publishing Co.: Apr, 1982

nn-Reprints 4-Color #272 3.00

CINDERELLA IN "FAIREST OF THE FAIR"
American Dairy Association (Premium): 1955 (5x7-1/4", 16 pgs., soft-c) (Walt Disney)

nn 9.30 28.00 65.00

CINDERELLA LOVE
Ziff-Davis/St. John Publ. Co. No. 12 on: No. 10, 1950; No. 11, 4-5/51; No. 12, 9/51; No. 4, 10-11/51 - No. 11, Fall, 1952; No. 12, 10/53 - No. 15, 8/54; No. 25, 12/54 - No. 29, 10/55 (No #16-24)

10(#1)(1st Series, 1950)-Painted-c 11.00 32.00 80.00
11(#2, 4-5/51)-Crandall-a; Saunders painted-c 7.85 23.50 55.00
12(#3, 9/51)-Photo-c 5.70 17.00 38.00
4-8: 4,6,7-Photo-c 5.00 15.00 30.00
9-Kinstler-a; photo-c 6.00 18.00 42.00
10,11(Fall/'52), 14: 10,11-Photo-c. 14-Baker-a 5.70 17.00 38.00
12(St. John-10/53)-#13:13-Painted-c. 4.25 13.00 28.00
15 (8/54)-Matt Baker-c 6.50 19.50 45.00
25(2nd Series)(Formerly Romantic Marriage) 4.25 13.00 28.00
26-Baker-c; last precode (2/55) 6.50 19.50 45.00
27,29-Matt Baker-c 6.50 19.50 45.00
28 4.00 11.00 22.00

CINDY COMICS (...Smith No. 39, 40; Crime Can't Win No. 41 on)(Formerly Krazy Komics) (See Junior Miss & Teen Comics)
Timely Comics: No. 27, Fall, 1947 - No. 40, July, 1950

27-Kurtzman-a, 3 pgs: Margie, Oscar begin 17.00 50.00 125.00
28-31-Kurtzman-a 10.00 30.00 75.00
32-40: 33-Georgie story; anti-Wertham editorial 6.50 19.50 45.00

NOTE: *Kurtzman's "Hey Look"-#27(3), 29(2), 30(2), 31; "Giggles 'n' Grins"-28.*

CINEMA COMICS HERALD
Paramount Pictures/Universal/RKO/20th Century Fox/Republic: 1941 - 1943 (4-pg. movie "trailers", paper-c, 7-1/2x10-1/2")(Giveaway)

"Mr. Bug Goes to Town" (1941) 6.50 19.50 45.00
"Bedtime Story" 5.00 15.00 30.00
"Lady For A Night", John Wayne, Joan Blondell (1942) 11.00 32.00 80.00
"Reap The Wild Wind" (1942) 7.15 21.50 50.00
"Thunder Birds" (1942) 6.50 19.50 45.00
"They All Kissed the Bride" 6.50 19.50 45.00
"Arabian Nights" (nd) 6.50 19.50 45.00

Cisco Kid #2 © DELL

Claire Voyant #2 © STD

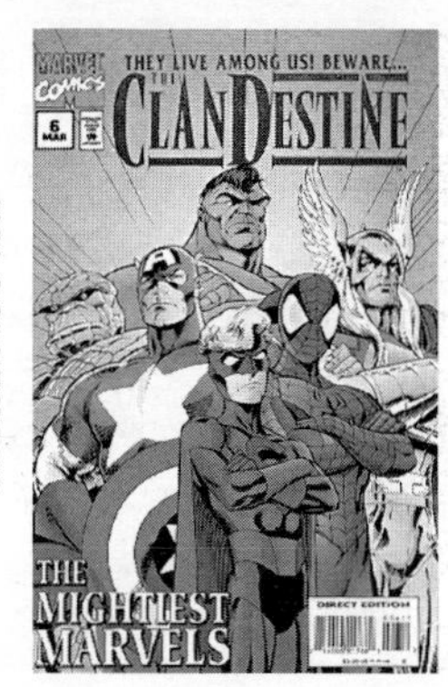

ClanDestine #6 © MAR

"Bombardie" (1943) 6.50 19.50 45.00
"Crash Dive" (1943)-Tyrone Power 6.50 19.50 45.00
NOTE: *The 1941-42 issues contain line art with color photos. 1943 issues are line art.*

CIRCUS (...the Comic Riot)
Globe Syndicate: June, 1938 - No. 3, Aug, 1938

1-(Scarce)-Spacehawks (2 pgs.), & Disk Eyes by Wolverton (2 pgs.), Pewee Throttle by Cole (2nd comic book work; see Star Comics V1#11), Beau Gus, Ken Craig & The Lords of Crillon, Jack Hinton by Eisner, Van Bragger by Kane 750.00 2250.00 4900.00
2,3-(Scarce)-Eisner, Cole, Wolverton, Bob Kane-a in each 383.00 1150.00 2500.00

CIRCUS BOY (TV) (See Movie Classics)
Dell Publishing Co.: No. 759, Dec, 1956 - No. 813, July, 1957

Four Color 759 (#1)-The Monkees' Mickey Dolenz photo-c 10.50 31.50 115.00
Four Color 785 (4/57),813-Mickey Dolenz photo-c 10.00 30.00 110.00

CIRCUS COMICS
Farm Women's Pub. Co./D. S. Publ.: 1945 - No. 2, Jun, 1945; Wint., 1948-49

1-Funny animal 10.00 30.00 75.00
2 6.50 19.50 45.00
1(1948)-D.S. Publ.; 2 pgs. Frazetta 21.00 64.00 160.00

CIRCUS OF FUN COMICS
A. W. Nugent Publ. Co.: 1945 - No. 3, Dec, 1947 (A book of games & puzzles)

1 11.00 34.00 85.00
2,3 7.15 21.50 50.00

CISCO KID, THE (TV)
Dell Publishing Co.: July, 1950 - No. 41, Oct-Dec, 1958

Four Color 292(#1)-Cisco Kid, his horse Diablo, & sidekick Pancho & his horse Loco begin; painted-c begin 22.00 66.00 240.00
2(1/51)-5 9.50 28.50 105.00
6-10 7.00 22.00 80.00
11-20 6.40 19.00 70.00
21-36-Last painted-c 4.50 13.50 50.00
37-41: All photo-c 9.00 27.00 100.00
NOTE: ***Buscema** a-40. **Ernest Nordli** painted c-5-16, 20, 35.*

CISCO KID COMICS
Bernard Bailey/Swappers Quarterly: Winter, 1944 (one-shot)

1-Illustrated Stories of the Operas: Faust; Funnyman by Giunta; Cisco Kid (1st app.) & Superbaby begin; Giunta-c 39.00 117.00 300.00

CITIZEN SMITH (See Holyoke One-Shot No. 9)

CITY OF THE LIVING DEAD (See Fantastic Tales No. 1)
Avon Periodicals: 1952

nn-Hollingsworth-c/a 39.00 116.00 290.00

CITY SURGEON (Blake Harper...)
Gold Key: August, 1963

1(10075-308)-Painted-c 3.20 9.60 32.00

CIVIL WAR MUSKET, THE (Kadets of America Handbook)
Custom Comics, Inc.: 1960 (25¢, half-size, 36 pgs.)

nn 2.50 7.50 22.00

CLAIRE VOYANT (Also see Keen Teens)
Leader Publ./Standard/Pentagon Publ.: 1946 - No. 4, 1947 (Sparling strip reprints)

nn 51.00 152.00 430.00
2,4: 2-Kamen-c. 4-Kamen bondage-c 42.00 127.00 340.00
3-Kamen bridal-c; contents mentioned in Love and Death, a book by Gershom Legman(1949) referenced by Dr. Wertham in **SOTI** 48.00 143.00 405.00

CLAIRE VOYANTE
Lightning Comics: June, 1996 ($3.50, B&W)

1-Cleary-c 3.50
1-($9.95)-Platinum Edition, Nude A ,Nude B 10.00

CLANDESTINE (Also see Marvel Comics Presents & X-Men: ClanDestine)
Marvel Comics: Oct, 1994 - No.12, Sept, 1995 ($2.95/$2.50)

1-($2.95)-Alan Davis-c/a(p)/scripts & Mark Farmer-c/a(i) begin, ends #8; Modok app.; Silver Surfer cameo; gold foil-c 3.00
2-12: 2-Wraparound-c. 2,3-Silver Surfer app. 5-Origin of ClanDestine. 6-Capt. America, Hulk, Spider-Man, Thing & Thor-c; Spider-Man cameo. 7-Spider-Man-c/app; Punisher cameo. 8-Invaders & Dr. Strange app. 9-12-Modok app. 10-Captain Britain-c/app. 11-Sub-Mariner app 2.50
Preview (10/94, $1.50) 1.50

CLASH
DC Comics: 1991 - No. 3, 1991 ($4.95, limited series, 52 pgs.)

Book One - Three: Adam Kubert-c/a 5.00

CLASSIC COMICS/ILLUSTRATED - INTRODUCTION
by Dan Malan

Further revisions have been made to help in understanding the **Classics** section. **Classics** reprint editions prior to 1963 had either incorrect dates or no dates listed. Those reprint editions should be identified only by the highest number on the reorder list (HRN). Past price guides listed what were calculated to be approximately correct dates, but many people found it confusing for the price guide to list a date not listed in the comic itself.

We have also attempted to clear up confusion about edition variations, such as color, printer, etc. Such variations will be identified by letters. Editions will now be determined by three categories. Original edition variations will be Edition 1A, 1B, etc. All reprint editions prior to 1963 will be identified by HRN only. All reprint editions from 9/63 on will be identified by the correct date listed in the comic.

We have also included new information on four recent reprintings of **Classics** not previously listed. From 1968-1976 Twin Circle, the Catholic newspaper, serialized over 100 **Classics** titles. That list can be found under non-series items at the end of this section. In 1972 twelve **Classics** were reissued as **Now Age Books Illustrated**. They are listed under **Pendulum Illustrated Classics**. In 1982, 20 **Classics** were reissued, adapted for teaching English as a second language. They are listed under **Regents Illustrated Classics**. Then in 1984, six **Classics** were reissued with cassette tapes. See the listing under **Cassette Books**.

UNDERSTANDING CLASSICS ILLUSTRATED
by Dan Malan

Since **Classics Illustrated** is the most complicated comic book series, with all its reprint editions and variations, with changes in covers and artwork, with a variety of means of identifying editions, and with the most extensive worldwide distribution of any comic-book series; therefore this introductory section is provided to assist you in gaining expertise about this series.

THE HISTORY OF CLASSICS

The **Classics** series was the brain child of Albert L. Kanter, who saw in the new comic-book medium a means of introducing children to the great classics of literature. In October of 1941 his Gilberton Co. began the **Classic Comics** series with **The Three Musketeers**, with 64 pages of storyline. In those early years, the struggling series saw irregular schedules and numerous printers, not to mention variable art quality and liberal story adaptations. With No.13 the page total was reduced to 56 (except for No. 33, originally scheduled to be No. 9), and with No. 15 the coming-next ad on the outside back cover moved inside. In 1945 the Jerry Iger Shop began producing all new CC titles, beginning with No. 23. In 1947 the search for a classier logo resulted in **Classics Illustrated**, beginning with No. 35, **Last Days of Pompeii**. With No. 45 the page total dropped again to 48, which was to become the standard.

Two new developments in 1951 had a profound effect upon the success of the series. One was the introduction of painted covers, instead of the old line drawn covers, beginning with No. 81, **The Odyssey**. The second was the switch to the

Classic Comics #1 © GIL

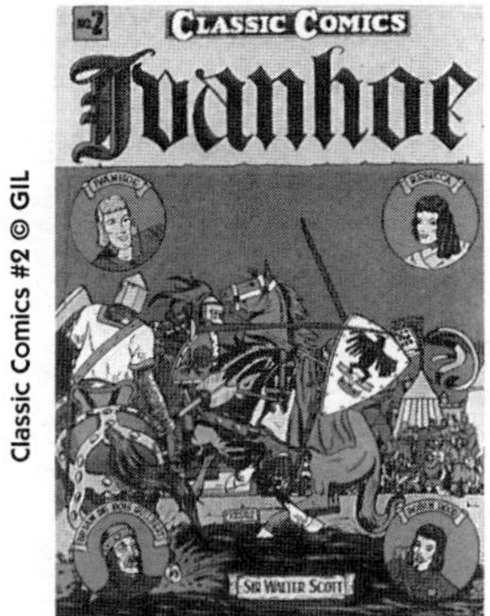

Classic Comics #2 © GIL

Classic Comics #3 © GIL

major national distributor Curtis. They raised the cover price from 10 to 15 cents, making it the highest priced comic-book, but it did not slow the growth of the series, because they were marketed as books, not comics. Because of this higher quality image, **Classics** flourished during the fifties while other comic series were reeling from outside attacks. They diversified with their new **Juniors**, **Specials**, and **World Around Us** series.

Classics artwork can be divided into three distinct periods. The pre-Iger era (1941-44) was mentioned above for its variable art quality. The Iger era (1945-53) was a major improvement in art quality and adaptations. It came to be dominated by artists Henry Kiefer and Alex Blum, together accounting for some 50 titles. Their styles gave the first real personality to the series. The EC era (1954-62) resulted from the demise of the EC horror series, when many of their artists made the major switch to classical art.

But several factors brought the production of new CI titles to a complete halt in 1962. Gilberton lost its 2nd class mailing permit. External factors like television, cheap paperback books, and Cliff Notes were all eating away at their market. Production halted with No.167, **Faust**, even though many more titles were already in the works. Many of those found their way into foreign series, and are very desirable to collectors. In 1967, **Classics Illustrated** was sold to Patrick Frawley and his Catholic publication, Twin Circle. They issued two new titles in 1969 as part of an attempted revival, but succumbed to major distribution problems in 1971. In 1988, the trio: First Publishing, Berkley Press, and Classics Media Group acquired the use rights for the old CI series art, logo, and name from the Frawley Group. So far they have used only the name in the new series, but do have plans to reprint the old CI.

One of the unique aspects of the **Classics Illustrated** (CI) series was the proliferation of reprint variations. Some titles had as many as 25 editions. Reprinting began in 1943. Some **Classic Comics** (CC) reprints (r) had the logo format revised to a banner logo, and added a motto under the banner. In 1947 CC titles changed to the CI logo, but kept their line drawn covers (LDC). In 1948, Nos. 13, 18, 29 and 41 received second covers (LDC2), replacing covers considered too violent, and reprints of Nos. 13-44 had pages reduced to 48, except for No. 26, which had 48 pages to begin with.

Starting in the mid-1950s, 70 of the 80 LDC titles were reissued with new painted covers (PC). Thirty of them also received new interior artwork (A2). The new artwork was generally higher quality with larger art panels and more faithful but abbreviated storylines. Later on, there were 29 second painted covers (PC2), mostly by Twin Circle. Altogether there were 199 interior art variations (169 (O)s and 30 A2 editions) and 272 different covers (169 (O)s, four LDC2s, 70 new PCs of LDC (O)s, and 29 PC2s). It is mildly astounding to realize that there are nearly 1400 different editions in the U.S. CI series.

FOREIGN CLASSICS ILLUSTRATED

If U.S. Classics variations are mildly astounding, the veritable plethora of foreign CI variations will boggle your imagination. While we still anticipate additional discoveries, we presently know about series in 25 languages and 27 countries. There were 250 new CI titles in foreign series, and nearly 400 new foreign covers of U.S. titles. The 1400 U.S. CI editions pale in comparison to the 4000 plus foreign editions. The very nature of CI lent itself to flourishing as an international series. Worldwide, they published over one billion copies! The first foreign CI series consisted of six Canadian Classic Comic reprints in 1946.

The following chart shows when CI series first began in each country:
1946: Canada. 1947: Australia. 1948: Brazil/The Netherlands. 1950: Italy. 1951: Greece/Japan/Hong Kong(?)/England/Argentina/Mexico. 1952: West Germany. 1954: Norway. 1955: New Zealand/South Africa. 1956: Denmark/Sweden/Iceland. 1957: Finland/France. 1962: Singapore(?). 1964: India (8 languages). 1971: Ireland (Gaelic). 1973: Belgium(?) /Philippines(?) & Malaysia(?).

Significant among the early series were Brazil and Greece. In 1950, Brazil was the first country to begin doing its own new titles. They issued nearly 80 new CI titles by Brazilian authors. In Greece in 1951 they actually had debates in parliament about the effects of Classics Illustrated on Greek culture, leading to the inclusion of 88 new Greek History & Mythology titles in the CI series.

But by far the most important foreign CI development was the joint European series which began in 1956 in 10 countries simultaneously. By 1960, CI had the largest European distribution of any American publication, not just comics! So when all the problems came up with U.S. distribution, they literally moved the CI operation to Europe in 1962, and continued producing new titles in all four CI series. Many of them were adapted and drawn in the U.S., the most famous of which was the British CI #158A. Dr. No, drawn by Norman Nodel. Unfortunately, the British CI series ended in late 1963, which limited the European CI titles available in English to 15. Altogether there were 82 new CI art titles in the joint European series, which ran until 1976.

IDENTIFYING CLASSICS EDITIONS

HRN: This is the highest number on the reorder list. It should be listed in ( ) after the title number. It is crucial to understanding various CI editions.

ORIGINALS (O): This is the all-important First Edition. To determine (O)s,there is one primary rule and two secondary rules (with exceptions):

Rule No. 1: All (O)s and only (O)s have coming-next ads for the next number. **Exceptions**: No. 14(15) (reprint) has an ad on the last inside text page only. No. 14(0) also has a full-page outside back cover ad (also rule 2). Nos.55(75) and 57(75) have coming-next ads. (Rules 2 and 3 apply here). Nos. 168(0) and 169(0) do not have coming-next ads. No.168 was never reprinted; No. 169(0) has HRN (166). No. 169(169) is the only reprint.

Rule No. 2: On nos.1-80, all (O)s and only (O)s list 10c on the front cover. **Exceptions**: Reprint variations of Nos. 37(62), 39(71), and 46(62) list 10c on the front cover. (Rules 1 and 3 apply here.)

Rule No. 3: All (O)s have HRN close to that title No. **Exceptions**: Some reprints also have HRNs close to that title number: a few CC(r)s, 58(62), 60(62), 149(149), 152(149) 153(149), and title nos. in the 160's. (Rules 1 and 2 apply here.)

DATES: Many reprint editions list either an incorrect date or no date. Since Gilberton apparently kept track of CI editions by HRN, they often left the (O) date on reprints. Often, someone with a CI collection for sale will swear that all their copies are originals. That is why we are so detailed in pointing out how to identify original editions. Except for original editions, which should have a coming-next ad, etc., all CI dates prior to 1963 are incorrect! So you want to go by HRN only if it is (165) or below, and go by listed date if it is 1963 or later. There are a few (167) editions with incorrect dates. They could be listed either as (167) or (62/3), which is meant to indicate that they were issued sometime between late 1962 and early 1963.

COVERS: A change from CC to LDC indicates a logo change, not a cover change; while a change from LDC to LDC2, LDC to PC, or from PC to PC2 does indicate a new cover. New PCs can be identified by HRN, and PC2s can be identified by HRN and date. Several covers had color changes, particularly from purple to blue.

Notes: If you see 15 cents in Canada on a front cover, it does not necessarily indicate a Canadian edition. Editions with an HRN between 44 and 75, with 15 cents on the cover are Canadian. Check the publisher's address. An HRN listing two numbers with a / between them indicates that there are two different reorder lists in the front and back covers. Official Twin Circle editions have a full-page back cover ad for their TC magazine, with no CI reorder list. Any CI with just a Twin Circle sticker on the front is not an official TC edition.

TIPS ON LISTING CLASSICS FOR SALE

It may be easy to just list Edition 17, but Classics collectors keep track of CI editions in terms of HRN and/or date, (O) or (r), CC or LDC, PC or PC2, A1 or A2, soft or stiff cover, etc. Try to help them out. For originals, just list (0), unless there are variations such as color (Nos. 10 and 61), printer (Nos. 18-22), HRN (Nos. 95, 108, 160), etc. For reprints, just list HRN if it's (165) or below. Above that, list HRN and date. Also, please list type of logo/cover/art for the convenience of buyers. They will appreciate it.

CLASSIC COMICS (Also see Best from Boys Life, Cassette Books, Famous Stories, Fast Fiction, Golden Picture Classics, King Classics, Marvel Classics Comics, Pendulum Illustrated Classics, Picture Parade, Picture Progress, Regents Ill. Classics, Spitfire, Stories by Famous Authors, Superior Stories, and World Around Us.)

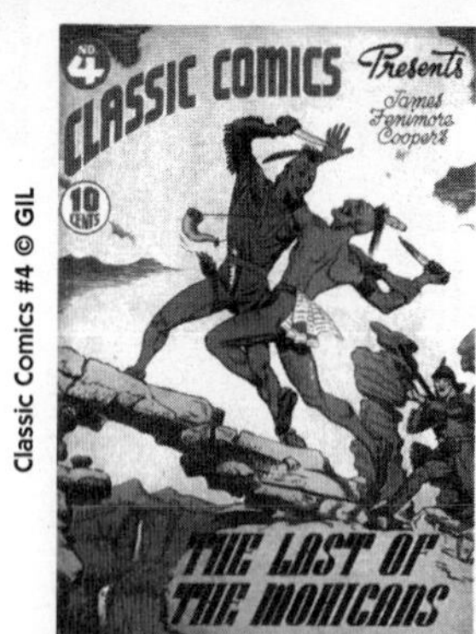

Classic Comics #4 © GIL

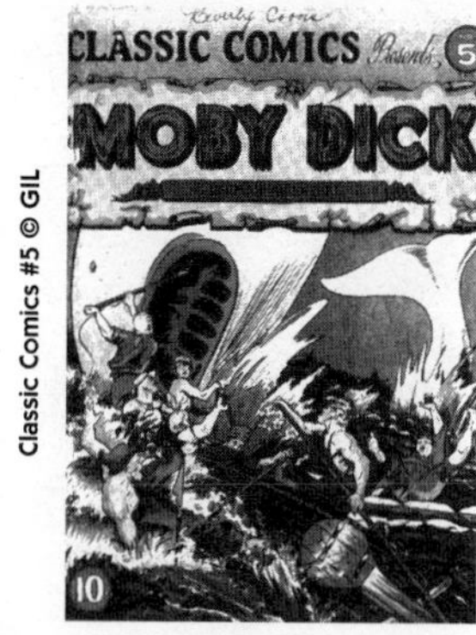

Classic Comics #5 © GIL

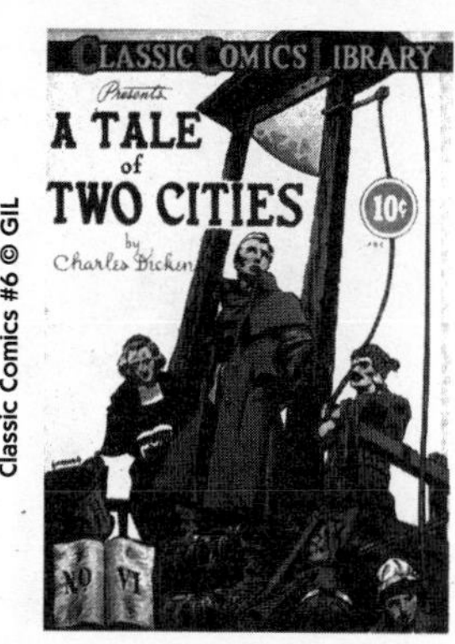

Classic Comics #6 © GIL

CLASSIC COMICS (Classics Illustrated No. 35 on)
Elliot Publishing #1-3 (1941-1942)/Gilberton Publications #4-167 (1942-1967) /Twin Circle Pub. (Frawley) #168-169 (1968-1971):
10/41 - No. 34, 2/47; No. 35, 3/47 - No. 169, Spring 1969
(Reprint Editions of almost all titles 5/43 - Spring 1971)
(Painted Covers (0)s No. 81 on, and (r)s of most Nos. 1-80)

Abbreviations:
A–Art; C or c–Cover; CC–Classic Comics; CI–Classics Ill.; Ed–Edition; LDC–Line Drawn Cover; PC–Painted Cover; r–Reprint

1. The Three Musketeers

Ed	HRN	Date	Details	A	C	GD25	FN65	NM94
1	–	10/41	Date listed-1941; Elliot Pub; 68 pgs.	1	1	430.00	1290.00	4300.00
2	10	–	10¢ price removed on all (r)s; Elliot Pub; CC-r	1	1	33.00	100.00	250.00
3	15	–	Long Isl. Ind. Ed.; CC-r	1	1	24.00	72.00	180.00
4	18/20		Sunrise Times Ed.; CC-r	1	1	16.00	48.00	120.00
5	21	–	Richmond Courier Ed.; CC-r	1	1	15.00	44.00	110.00
6	28	1946	CC-r	1	1	11.00	34.00	85.00
7	36	–	LDC-r	1	1	5.70	17.00	40.00
8	60	–	LDC-r	1	1	4.25	13.00	28.00
9	64	–	LDC-r	1	1	4.00	10.00	20.00
10	78	–	C-price 15¢;LDC-r	1	1	3.60	9.00	18.00
11	93	–	LDC-r	1	1	3.60	9.00	18.00
12	114	–	Last LDC-r	1	1	2.80	7.00	14.00
13	134	–	New-c; old-a; 64 pg. PC-r	1	2	3.20	8.00	16.00
14	143	–	Old-a; PC-r; 64 pg.	1	2	2.40	6.00	12.00
15	150	–	New-a; PC-r; Evans/Crandall-a	2	2	2.80	7.00	14.00
16	149	–	PC-r	2	2	1.00	2.40	6.00
17	167	–	PC-r	2	2	1.00	2.40	6.00
18	167	4/64	PC-r	2	2	1.00	2.40	6.00
19	167	1/65	PC-r	2	2	1.00	2.40	6.00
20	167	3/66	PC-r	2	2	1.00	2.40	6.00
21	166	11/67	PC-r	2	2	1.00	2.40	6.00
22	166	Spr/69	C-price 25¢ ; stiff-c; PC-r	2	2	1.00	2.40	6.00
23	169	Spr/71	PC-r; stiff-c	2	2	1.00	2.40	6.00

2. Ivanhoe

Ed	HRN	Date	Details	A	C	GD25	FN65	NM94
1	(O)	12/41?	Date listed-1941; Elliot Pub; 68 pgs.	1	1	212.00	635.00	1800.00
2	10	–	Price & 'Presents' removed; Elliot Pub; CC-r	1	1	29.00	88.00	220.00
3	15	–	Long Isl. Ind. ed.; CC-r	1	1	19.00	56.00	140.00
4	18/20		Sunrise Times ed.; CC-r	1	1	16.00	48.00	120.00
5	21	–	Richmond Courier ed.; CC-r	1	1	15.00	44.00	110.00
6	28	1946	Last 'Comics'-r	1	1	11.00	34.00	85.00
7	36	–	1st LDC-r	1	1	6.50	19.50	45.00
8	60	–	LDC-r	1	1	4.25	13.00	28.00
9	64	–	LDC-r	1	1	4.00	11.00	22.00
10	78	–	C-price 15¢; LDC-r	1	1	3.60	9.00	18.00
11	89	–	LDC-r	1	1	3.20	8.00	16.00
12	106	–	LDC-r	1	1	2.80	7.00	14.00
13	121	–	Last LDC-r	1	1	2.80	7.00	14.00
14	136	–	New-c&a; PC-r	2	2	3.60	9.00	18.00
15	142	–	PC-r	2	2	1.00	2.80	7.00
16	153	–	PC-r	2	2	1.00	2.80	7.00
17	149	–	PC-r	2	2	1.00	2.80	7.00
18	167	–	PC-r	2	2	1.00	2.40	6.00
19	167	5/64	PC-r	2	2	1.00	2.40	6.00
20	167	1/65	PC-r	2	2	1.00	2.40	6.00
21	167	3/66	PC-r	2	2	1.00	2.40	6.00
22A	166	9/67	PC-r	2	2	1.00	2.40	6.00
22B	166	–	Center ad for Children's Digest & Young Miss; rare; PC-r	2	2	7.00	21.00	70.00
23	166	R/68	C-Price 25¢; PC-r	2	2	1.00	2.00	5.00
24	169	Win/69	Stiff-c	2	2	1.00	2.00	5.00
25	169	Win/71	PC-r; stiff-c	2	2	1.00	2.00	5.00

3. The Count of Monte Cristo

Ed	HRN	Date	Details	A	C	GD25	FN65	NM94
1	(O)	3/42	Elliot Pub; 68 pgs.	1	1	135.00	406.00	1150.00
2	10	–	Conray Prods; CC-r	1	1	25.00	76.00	190.00
3	15	–	Long Isl. Ind. ed.; CC-r	1	1	20.00	60.00	150.00
4	18/20		Sunrise Times ed.; CC-r	1	1	17.00	52.00	130.00
5	20	–	Sunrise Times ed.; CC-r	1	1	15.00	46.00	115.00
6	21	–	Richmond Courier ed.; CC-r	1	1	15.00	44.00	110.00
7	28	1946	CC-r; new Banner logo	1	1	11.00	34.00	85.00
8	36	–	1st LDC-r	1	1	6.50	19.50	45.00
9	60	–	LDC-r	1	1	4.25	13.00	28.00
10	62	–	LDC-r	1	1	5.35	16.00	32.00
11	71	–	LDC-r	1	1	4.00	10.00	20.00
12	87	–	C-price 15¢; LDC-r	1	1	3.60	9.00	18.00
13	113	–	LDC-r	1	1	2.80	7.00	14.00
14	135	–	New-c&a; PC-r; Cameron-a	2	2	3.20	8.00	16.00
15	143	–	PC-r	2	2	1.00	2.80	7.00
16	153	–	PC-r	2	2	1.00	2.80	7.00
17	161	–	PC-r	2	2	1.00	2.80	7.00
18	167	–	PC-r	2	2	1.00	2.40	6.00
19	167	7/64	PC-r	2	2	1.00	2.40	6.00
20	167	7/65	PC-r	2	2	1.00	2.40	6.00
21	167	7/66	PC-r	2	2	1.00	2.40	6.00
22	166	R/68	C-price 25¢; PC-r	2	2	1.00	2.40	6.00
23	169	–	Win/69 Stiff-c; PC-r	2	2	1.00	2.40	6.00

4. The Last of the Mohicans

Ed	HRN	Date	Details	A	C	GD25	FN65	NM94
1	(O)	8/42	Date listed-1942; Gilberton #4(0) on; 68 pgs.	1	1	112.00	335.00	950.00
2	12	–	Elliot Pub; CC-r	1	1	25.00	76.00	190.00
3	15	–	Long Isl. Ind. ed.; CC-r	1	1	20.00	60.00	150.00
4	20	–	Long Isl. Ind. ed.; CC-r; banner logo	1	1	17.00	50.00	125.00
5	21	–	Queens Home News ed.; CC-r	1	1	15.00	46.00	115.00
6	28	1946	Last CC-r; new	1	1	11.00	34.00	85.00
7	36	–	1st LDC-r	1	1	6.50	19.50	45.00
8	60	–	LDC-r	1	1	4.25	13.00	28.00

Classic Comics #7 © GIL

Classic Comics #8 © GIL

Classic Comics #9 © GIL

						GD25	FN65	NM94
9	64	–	LDC-r	1	1	4.00	10.00	20.00
10	78	–	C-price 15¢; LDC-r	1	1	3.60	9.00	18.00
11	89	–	LDC-r	1	1	3.20	8.00	16.00
12	117	–	Last LDC-r	1	1	2.80	7.00	14.00
13	135	–	New-c; PC-r	1	2	3.20	8.00	16.00
14	141	–	PC-r	1	2	2.00	5.00	10.00
15	150	–	New-a; PC-r; Severin, L.B. Cole-a	2	2	3.60	9.00	18.00
16	161	–	PC-r	2	2	1.00	2.40	6.00
17	167	–	PC-r	2	2	1.00	2.40	6.00
18	167	6/64	PC-r	2	2	1.00	2.40	6.00
19	167	8/65	PC-r	2	2	1.00	2.40	6.00
20	167	8/66	PC-r	2	2	1.00	2.40	6.00
21	166	R/67	C-price 25¢; PC-r	2	2	1.00	2.40	6.00
22	169	Spr/69	Stiff-c; PC-r	2	2	1.00	2.40	6.00

5. Moby Dick

Ed	HRN	Date	Details	A	C	GD25	FN65	NM94
1A	(O)	9/42	Date listed-1942; Gilberton; 68 pgs.	1	1	141.00	424.00	1200.00
1B			inside-c, rare free promo			212.00	635.00	1800.00
2	10	–	Conray Prods; Pg. 64 changed from 105 title list to letter from Editor; CC-r	1	1	27.00	80.00	200.00
3	15	–	Long Isl. Ind. ed.; Pg. 64 changed from Letter to the Editor to Ill. poem-Concord Hymn; CC-r	1	1	23.00	68.00	170.00
4	18/20	–	Sunrise Times ed.; CC-r	1	1	17.00	52.00	130.00
5	20	–	Sunrise Times ed.; CC-r	1	1	17.00	50.00	125.00
6	21	–	Sunrise Times ed.; CC-r	1	1	15.00	46.00	115.00
7	28	1946	CC-r; new banner logo	1	1	13.00	38.00	95.00
8	36	–	1st LDC-r	1	1	6.50	19.50	45.00
9	60	–	LDC-r	1	1	4.25	13.00	28.00
10	62	–	LDC-r	1	1	5.35	16.00	32.00
11	71	–	LDC-r	1	1	4.00	11.00	22.00
12	87	–	C-price 15¢; LDC-r	1	1	4.00	10.00	20.00
13	118	–	LDC-r	1	1	3.20	8.00	16.00
14	131	–	New c&a; PC-r	2	2	3.60	9.00	18.00
15	138	–	PC-r	2	2	1.00	2.80	7.00
16	148	–	PC-r	2	2	1.00	2.80	7.00
17	158	–	PC-r	2	2	1.00	2.80	7.00
18	167	–	PC-r	2	2	1.00	2.40	6.00
19	167	6/64	PC-r	2	2	1.00	2.40	6.00
20	167	7/65	PC-r	2	2	1.00	2.40	6.00
21	167	3/66	PC-r	2	2	1.00	2.40	6.00
22	166	9/67	PC-r	2	2	1.00	2.40	6.00
23	166	Win/69	New-c & c-price 25¢; Stiff-c; PC-r	2	3	1.75	5.25	14.00
24	169	Win/71	PC-r	2	3	1.50	4.50	12.00

6. A Tale of Two Cities

Ed	HRN	Date	Details	A	C	GD25	FN65	NM94
1	(O)	10/42	Date listed-1942; 68 pgs. Zeckerberg c/a	1	1	112.00	335.00	950.00
2	14	–	Elliot Pub; CC-r	1	1	24.00	72.00	180.00
3	18	–	Long Isl. Ind. ed.; CC-r	1	1	19.00	56.00	140.00
4	20	–	Sunrise Times ed.; CC-r	1	1	17.00	50.00	125.00
5	28	1946	Last CC-r; new banner logo	1	1	11.00	34.00	85.00
6	51	–	1st LDC-r	1	1	5.70	17.00	40.00
7	64	–	LDC-r	1	1	4.00	12.00	24.00
8	78	–	C-price 15¢; LDC-r	1	1	4.00	10.00	20.00
9	89	–	LDC-r	1	1	2.80	7.00	14.00
10	117	–	LDC-r	1	1	2.80	7.00	14.00
11	132	–	New-c&a; PC-r; Joe Orlando-a	2	2	3.60	9.00	18.00
12	140	–	PC-r	2	2	1.00	2.00	7.00
13	147	–	PC-r	2	2	1.00	2.00	7.00
14	152	–	PC-r; very rare	2	2	14.50	43.00	120.00
15	153	–	PC-r	2	2	1.00	2.80	7.00
16	149	–	PC-r	2	2	1.00	2.80	7.00
17	167	–	PC-r	2	2	1.00	2.40	6.00
18	167	6/64	PC-r	2	2	1.00	2.40	6.00
19	167	8/65	PC-r	2	2	1.00	2.40	6.00
20	166	5/67	PC-r	2	2	1.00	2.40	6.00
21	166	Fall/68	New-c & 25¢; PC-r	2	3	2.00	6.00	16.00
22	169	Sum/70	Stiff-c; PC-r	2	3	1.50	4.50	12.00

7. Robin Hood

Ed	HRN	Date	Details	A	C	GD25	FN65	NM94
1	(O)	12/42	Date listed-1942; first Gift Box ad-bc; 68 pgs.	1	1	82.00	247.00	700.00
2	12	–	Elliot Pub; CC-r	1	1	23.00	70.00	175.00
3	18	–	Long Isl. Ind. ed.; CC-r	1	1	17.00	52.00	130.00
4	20	–	Nassau Bulletin ed.; CC-r	1	1	16.00	48.00	120.00
5	22	–	Queens Cty. Times ed.; CC-r	1	1	15.00	44.00	110.00
6	28	–	CC-r	1	1	11.00	34.00	85.00
7	51	–	LDC-r	1	1	5.70	17.00	40.00
8	64	–	LDC-r	1	1	4.00	12.00	24.00
9	78	–	LDC-r	1	1	3.60	9.00	18.00
10	97	–	LDC-r	1	1	3.20	8.00	16.00
11	106	–	LDC-r	1	1	2.80	7.00	14.00
12	121	–	LDC-r	1	1	2.80	7.00	14.00
13	129	–	New-c; PC-r	1	2	2.25	6.75	18.00
14	136	–	New-a; PC-r	2	2	2.25	6.75	18.00
15	143	–	PC-r	2	2	1.00	2.80	7.00
16	153	–	PC-r	2	2	1.00	2.80	7.00
17	164	–	PC-r	2	2	1.00	2.40	6.00
18	167	–	PC-r	2	2	1.00	2.40	6.00
19	167	6/64	PC-r	2	2	1.20	2.40	6.00
20	167	5/65	PC-r	2	2	1.00	2.40	6.00
21	167	7/66	PC-r	2	2	1.00	2.40	6.00
22	166	12/67	PC-r	2	2	1.20	2.40	6.00
23	169	Sum/69	Stiff-c; c-price 25¢; PC-r	2	2	1.00	2.40	6.00

8. Arabian Nights

Ed	HRN	Date	Details	A	C	GD25	FN65	NM94
1	(O)	2/43	Original; 68 pgs. Lilian Chestney-c/a	1	1	141.00	424.00	1200.00
2	17	–	Long Isl. ed.; pg. 64 changed from Gift Box ad to Letter from British Medical Worker; CC-r	1	1	52.00	155.00	440.00
3	20	–	Nassau Bulletin;	1	1	43.00	129.00	350.00

Classic Comics #10 © GIL

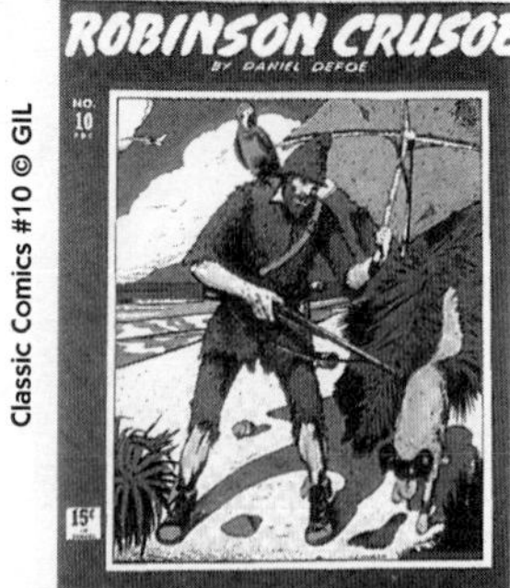

Classic Comics #11 © GIL

Classic Comics #12 © GIL

Ed	HRN	Date	Details	A	C	GD25	FN65	NM94
			Pg. 64 changed from letter to article-Three Men Named Smith; CC-r					
4A	28	1946	CC-r; new banner logo, slick-c	1	1	31.00	92.00	230.00
4B	28	1946	Same, but w/stiff-c	1	1	31.00	92.00	230.00
5	51	–	LDC-r	1	1	21.00	64.00	160.00
6	64	–	LDC-r	1	1	17.00	52.00	130.00
7	78	–	LDC-r	1	1	16.00	48.00	120.00
8	164	–	New-c&a; PC-r	2	2	15.00	44.00	110.00

9. Les Miserables

Ed	HRN	Date	Details	A	C	GD25	FN65	NM94
1A	(O)	3/43	Original; slick paper cover; 68 pgs.	1	1	82.00	247.00	700.00
1B	(O)	3/43	Original; rough, pulp type-c; 68 pgs.	1	1	103.00	309.00	875.00
2	14	–	Elliot Pub; CC-r	1	1	25.00	76.00	190.00
3	18	3/44	Nassau Bul. Pg. 64 changed from Gift Box ad to Bill of Rights article; CC-r	1	1	21.00	62.00	155.00
4	20	–	Richmond Courier ed.; CC-r	1	1	17.00	50.00	125.00
5	28	1946	Gilberton; pgs. 60-64 rearranged/ illos added; CC-r	1	1	12.00	36.00	90.00
6	51	–	LDC-r	1	1	6.50	19.50	45.00
7	71	–	LDC-r	1	1	5.35	16.00	32.00
8	87	–	C-price 15¢; LDC-r	1	1	4.25	13.00	28.00
9	161	–	New-c&a; PC-r	2	2	4.25	13.00	28.00
10	167	9/63	PC-r	2	2	1.50	4.50	12.00
11	167	12/65	PC-r	2	2	1.50	4.50	12.00
12	166	R/1968	New-c & price 25¢; PC-r	2	3	2.25	6.75	18.00

10. Robinson Crusoe (Used in **SOTI**, pg. 142)

Ed	HRN	Date	Details	A	C	GD25	FN65	NM94
1A	(O)	4/43	Original; Violet-c; 68 pgs; Zuckerberg c/a	1	1	71.00	212.00	600.00
1B	(O)	4/43	Original; blue-grey-c, 68 pgs.	1	1	79.00	238.00	675.00
2A	14	–	Elliot Pub; violet-c; 68 pgs; CC-r	1	1	27.00	80.00	200.00
2B	14	–	Elliot Pub; blue-grey-c; CC-r	1	1	24.00	72.00	180.00
3	18	–	Nassau Bul. Pg. 64 changed from Gift Box ad to Bill of Rights article; CC-r	1	1	17.00	52.00	130.00
4	20	–	Queens Home News ed.; CC-r	1	1	15.00	46.00	115.00
5	28	1946	Gilberton; pg. 64 changes from Bill of Rights to WWII article-One Leg Shot Away; last CC-r	1	1	11.00	34.00	85.00
6	51	–	LDC-r	1	1	5.70	17.00	40.00
7	64	–	LDC-r	1	1	4.25	13.00	28.00
8	78	–	C-price 15¢; LDC-r	1	1	4.00	10.00	20.00
9	97	–	LDC-r	1	1	3.60	9.00	18.00
10	114	–	LDC-r	1	1	2.80	7.00	14.00
11	130	–	New-c; PC-r	1	2	3.60	9.00	18.00
12	140	–	New-a; PC-r	2	2	3.60	9.00	18.00
13	153	–	PC-r	2	2	1.00	2.80	7.00
14	164	–	PC-r	2	2	1.00	2.40	6.00
15	167	–	PC-r	2	2	1.00	2.40	6.00
16	167	7/64	PC-r	2	2	1.25	3.75	10.00
17	167	5/65	PC-r	2	2	1.25	3.75	10.00
18	167	6/66	PC-r	2	2	1.00	2.40	6.00
19	166	Fall/68	C-price 25¢; PC-r	2	2	1.00	2.40	6.00
20	166	R/68	(No Twin Circle ad)	2	2	1.00	2.80	7.00
21	169	Sm/70	Stiff-c; PC-r	2	2	1.00	2.80	7.00

11. Don Quixote

Ed	HRN	Date	Details	A	C	GD25	FN65	NM94
1	10	5/43	First (O) with HRN list; 68 pgs.	1	1	77.00	229.00	650.00
2	18	–	Nassau Bulletin ed.; CC-r	1	1	23.00	68.00	170.00
3	21	–	Queens Home News ed.; CC-r	1	1	17.00	52.00	130.00
4	28	–	CC-r	1	1	12.00	36.00	90.00
5	110	–	New-PC; PC-r	1	2	4.15	12.50	25.00
6	156	–	Pgs. reduced 68 to 52; PC-r	1	2	2.80	7.00	14.00
7	165	–	PC-r	1	2	1.10	3.30	9.00
8	167	1/64	PC-r	1	2	1.10	3.30	9.00
9	167	11/65	PC-r	1	2	1.10	3.30	9.00
10	166	R/1968	New-c & price 25¢; PC-r	1	3	2.50	7.50	20.00

12. Rip Van Winkle and the Headless Horseman

Ed	HRN	Date	Details	A	C	GD25	FN65	NM94
1	11	6/43	Original; 68 pgs.	1	1	77.00	229.00	650.00
2	15	–	Long Isl. Ind. ed.; CC-r	1	1	22.00	66.00	165.00
3	20	–	Long Isl. Ind. ed.;	1	1	17.00	52.00	130.00
4	22	–	Queens Cty. Times ed.; CC-r	1	1	15.00	44.00	110.00
5	28	–	CC-r	1	1	11.00	34.00	85.00
6	60	–	1st LDC-r	1	1	5.70	17.00	35.00
7	62	–	LDC-r	1	1	4.00	12.00	24.00
8	71	–	LDC-r	1	1	3.60	9.00	18.00
9	89	–	C-price 15¢; LDC-r	1	1	3.20	8.00	16.00
10	118	–	LDC-r	1	1	2.80	7.00	14.00
11	132	–	New-c; PC-r	1	2	3.60	9.00	18.00
12	150	–	New-a; PC-r	2	2	3.60	9.00	18.00
13	158	–	PC-r	2	2	1.00	2.80	7.00
14	167	–	PC-r	2	2	1.00	2.80	7.00
15	167	12/63	PC-r	2	2	1.00	2.40	6.00
16	167	4/65	PC-r	2	2	1.20	2.40	6.00
17	167	4/66	PC-r	2	2	1.00	2.40	6.00
18	166	R/1968	New-c&price 25¢; PC-r; stiff-c	2	3	1.50	4.50	12.00
19	169	Sm/70	PC-r; stiff-c	2	3	1.25	3.75	10.00

13. Dr. Jekyll and Mr. Hyde (Used in **SOTI**, pg. 143)(1st horror comic?)

Ed	HRN	Date	Details	A	C	GD25	FN65	NM94
1	12	8/43	Original 60 pgs.	1	1	109.00	327.00	925.00
2	15	–	Long Isl. Ind. ed.; CC-r	1	1	31.00	92.00	230.00
3	20	–	Long Isl. Ind. ed.; CC-r	1	1	21.00	64.00	160.00
4	28	–	No c-price; CC-r	1	1	16.00	48.00	120.00
5	60	–	New-c; Pgs. reduced from 60 to 52; H.C. Kiefer-c; LDC-r	1	2	5.70	17.00	38.00
6	62	–	LDC-r	1	2	4.25	13.00	28.00
7	71	–	LDC-r	1	2	4.00	11.00	22.00

Classic Comics #13 © GIL

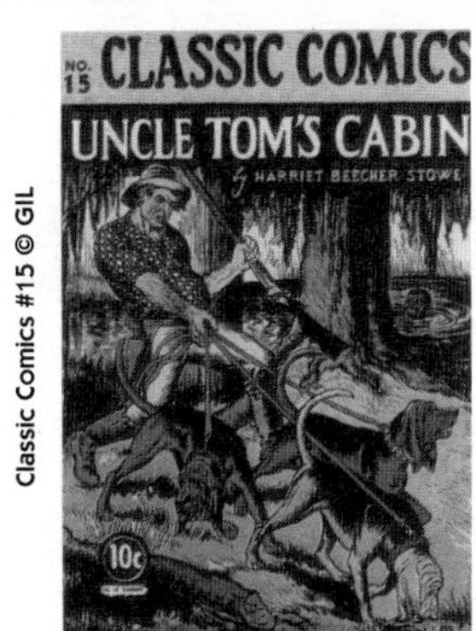

Classic Comics #15 © GIL

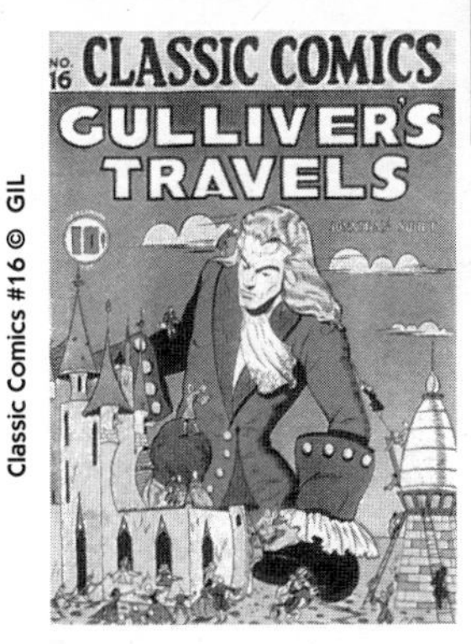

Classic Comics #16 © GIL

Ed	HRN	Date	Details	A	C	GD25	FN65	NM94
8	87	–	Date returns (erroneous); LDC-r	1	2	4.00	10.00	20.00
9	112	–	New-c&a; PC-r; Cameron-a	2	3	4.25	13.00	26.00
10	153	–	PC-r	2	3	1.00	2.80	7.00
11	161	–	PC-r	2	3	1.00	2.80	7.00
12	167	–	PC-r	2	3	1.00	2.40	6.00
13	167	8/64	PC-r	2	3	1.00	2.40	6.00
14	167	11/65	PC-r	2	3	1.00	2.40	6.00
15	166	R/68	C-price 25¢; PC-r	2	3	1.20	2.40	6.00
16	169	Wn/69	PC-r; stiff-c	2	3	1.00	2.40	6.00

14. Westward Ho!

Ed	HRN	Date	Details	A	C	GD25	FN65	NM94
1	13	9/43	Original; last outside bc coming-next ad; 60 pgs.	1	1	182.00	547.00	1550.00
2	15	–	Long Isl. Ind. ed.; CC-r	1	1	55.00	166.00	470.00
3	21	–	Queens Home News; Pg. 56 changed from coming-next ad to Three Men Named Smith; CC-r	1	1	42.00	126.00	335.00
4	28	1946	Gilberton; Pg. 56 changed again to WWII article-Speaking for America; last CC-r	1	1	35.00	104.00	260.00
5	53	–	Pgs. reduced from 60 to 52; LDC-r	1	1	32.00	96.00	240.00

15. Uncle Tom's Cabin (Used in **SOTI**, pgs. 102, 103)

Ed	HRN	Date	Details	A	C	GD25	FN65	NM94
1	14	11/43	Original; Outside-bc ad: 2 Gift Boxes; 60 pgs.; color var. on-c; green trunk,root on left & brown trunk, root on left	1	1	65.00	194.00	550.00
2	15	–	Long Isl. Ind. listed- bottom inside-fc; also Gilberton listed bottom-pg. 1; CC-r; green root vs. brown root var. occurs again	1	1	24.00	72.00	180.00
3	21	–	Nassau Bulletin ed.; CC-r	1	1	19.00	56.00	140.00
4	28	–	No c-price; CC-r	1	1	12.00	36.00	90.00
5	53	–	Pgs. reduced 60 to 52; LDC-r	1	1	5.70	17.00	40.00
6	71	–	LDC-r	1	1	4.25	13.00	28.00
7	89	–	C-price 15¢; LDC-r	1	1	4.25	13.00	26.00
8	117	–	New-c/lettering changes; PC-r	1	2	3.60	9.00	18.00
9	128	–	'Picture Progress' promo; PC-r	1	2	2.00	5.00	10.00
10	137	–	PC-r	1	2	1.00	2.80	7.00
11	146	–	PC-r	1	2	1.00	2.80	7.00
12	154	–	PC-r	1	2	1.00	2.80	7.00
13	161	–	PC-r	1	2	1.00	2.40	6.00
14	167	–	PC-r	1	2	1.00	2.40	6.00
15	167	6/64	PC-r	1	2	1.00	2.40	6.00
16	167	5/65	PC-r	1	2	1.00	2.40	6.00
17	166	5/67	PC-r	1	2	1.00	2.40	6.00
18	166	Wn/69	New-stiff-c; PC-r	1	3	1.50	4.50	12.00
19	169	Sm/70	PC-r; stiff-c	1	3	1.25	5.00	10.00

16. Gullivers Travels

Ed	HRN	Date	Details	A	C	GD25	FN65	NM94
1	15	12/43	Original-Lilian Chestney c/a; 60 pgs.	1	1	66.00	198.00	560.00
2	18/20	–	Price deleted; Queens Home News ed; CC-r	1	1	21.00	64.00	160.00
3	22	–	Queens Cty. Times ed.; CC-r	1	1	17.00	50.00	125.00
4	28	–	CC-r	1	1	11.00	34.00	85.00
5	60	–	Pgs. reduced to 48; LDC-r	1	1	5.35	16.00	32.00
6	62	–	LDC-r	1	1	4.00	12.00	24.00
7	78	–	C-price 15¢; LDC-r	1	1	4.00	10.00	20.00
8	89	–	LDC-r	1	1	3.20	8.00	16.00
9	155	–	New-c; PC-r	1	2	3.60	9.00	18.00
10	165	–	PC-r	1	2	1.00	2.40	6.00
11	167	5/64	PC-r	1	2	1.00	2.40	6.00
12	167	11/65	PC-r	1	2	1.00	2.40	6.00
13	166	R/1968	C-price 25¢; PC-r	1	2	1.00	2.40	6.00
14	169	Wn/69	PC-r; stiff-c	1	2	1.00	2.40	6.00

17. The Deerslayer

Ed	HRN	Date	Details	A	C	GD25	FN65	NM94
1	16	1/44	Original; Outside-bc ad: 3 Gift Boxes; 60 pgs.	1	1	57.00	171.00	485.00
2A	18	–	Queens Cty Times (inside-fc); CC-r	1	1	22.00	66.00	165.00
2B	18	–	Gilberton (bottom-pg. 1); CC-r; Scarce	1	1	32.00	96.00	240.00
3	22	–	Queens Cty. Times ed.; CC-r	1	1	17.00	52.00	130.00
4	28	–	CC-r	1	1	12.00	36.00	90.00
5	60	–	Pgs.reduced to 52; LDC-r	1	1	5.70	17.00	38.00
6	64	–	LDC-r	1	1	4.00	11.00	22.00
7	85	–	C-price 15¢; LDC-r	1	1	3.20	8.00	16.00
8	118	–	LDC-r	1	1	1.75	5.25	14.00
9	132	–	LDC-r	1	1	1.75	5.25	14.00
10	167	11/66	Last LDC-r	1	1	1.50	4.50	12.00
11	166	R/1968	New-c & price 25¢; PC-r	1	2	2.25	6.75	18.00
12	169	Spr/71	Stiff-c; letters from parents & educators; PC-r	1	2	1.50	4.50	12.00

18. The Hunchback of Notre Dame

Ed	HRN	Date	Details	A	C	GD25	FN65	NM94
1A	17	3/44	Orig.; Gilberton ed; 60 pgs.	1	1	76.00	229.00	650.00
1B	17	3/44	Orig.; Island Pub. Ed.; 60 pgs.	1	1	68.00	203.00	575.00
2	18/20	–	Queens Home News ed.; CC-r	1	1	24.00	72.00	180.00
3	22	–	Queens Cty. Times ed.; CC-r	1	1	18.00	54.00	135.00
4	28	–	CC-r	1	1	15.00	46.00	115.00
5	60	–	New-c; 8pgs. deleted; Kiefer-c; LDC-r	1	2	5.70	17.00	36.00
6	62	–	LDC-r	1	2	4.00	11.00	22.00
7	78	–	C-price 15¢; LDC-r	1	2	4.00	10.00	20.00
8A	89	–	H.C.Kiefer on bottom right-fc; LDC-r	1	2	3.60	9.00	18.00
8B	89	–	Name omitted; LDC-r	1	2	4.25	13.00	26.00

Classic Comics #17 © GIL

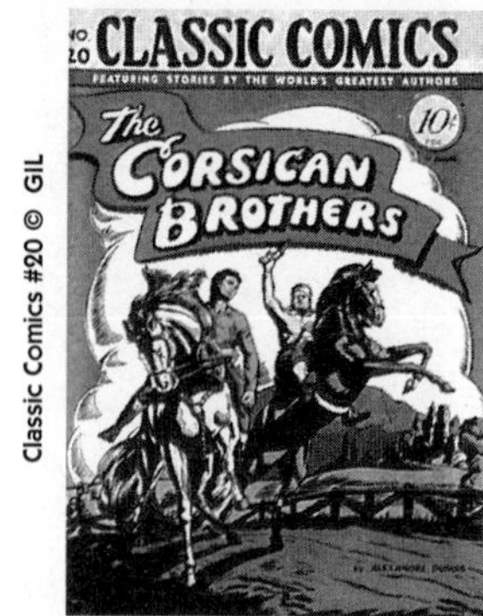

Classic Comics #20 © GIL

Classic Comics #22 © GIL

Ed	HRN	Date	Details	A	C	GD25	FN65	NM94
9	118	–	LDC-r	1	2	3.20	8.00	16.00
10	140	–	New-c; PC-r	1	3	4.25	13.00	26.00
11	146	–	PC-r	1	3	3.60	9.00	18.00
12	158	–	New-c&a; PC-r; Evans/Crandall-a	2	4	4.00	10.00	20.00
13	165	–	PC-r	2	4	1.00	2.80	7.00
14	167	9/63	PC-r	2	4	1.00	2.80	7.00
15	167	10/64	PC-r	2	4	1.00	2.80	7.00
16	167	4/66	PC-r	2	4	1.00	2.00	6.00
17	166	R/1968	New price 25¢; PC-r	2	4	1.00	2.40	6.00
18	169	Sp/70	Stiff-c; PC-r	2	4	1.00	2.40	6.00

19. Huckleberry Finn

Ed	HRN	Date	Details	A	C	GD25	FN65	NM94
1A	18	4/44	Orig.; Gilberton ed.; 60 pgs.	1	1	47.00	142.00	400.00
1B	18	4/44	Orig.; Island Pub.; 60 pgs.	1	1	51.00	154.00	435.00
2	18	–	Nassau Bulletin ed.; fc-price 15¢-Canada; no coming-next ad; CC-r	1	1	23.00	68.00	170.00
3	22	–	Queens City Times ed.; CC-r	1	1	17.00	50.00	125.00
4	28	–	CC-r	1	1	11.00	34.00	85.00
5	60	–	Pgs. reduced to 48; LDC-r	1	1	5.35	16.00	32.00
6	62	–	LDC-r	1	1	4.00	12.00	24.00
7	78	–	LDC-r	1	1	3.60	9.00	18.00
8	89	–	LDC-r	1	1	3.20	8.00	16.00
9	117	–	LDC-r	1	1	2.80	7.00	14.00
10	131	–	New-c&a; PC-r	2	2	3.20	8.00	16.00
11	140	–	PC-r	2	2	1.00	2.80	7.00
12	150	–	PC-r	2	2	1.00	2.80	7.00
13	158	–	PC-r	2	2	1.00	2.80	7.00
14	165	–	PC-r (scarce)	2	2	3.20	8.00	16.00
15	167	–	PC-r	2	2	1.00	2.40	6.00
16	167	6/64	PC-r	2	2	1.00	2.40	6.00
17	167	6/65	PC-r	2	2	1.00	2.40	6.00
18	167	10/65	PC-r	2	2	1.00	2.40	6.00
19	166	9/67	PC-r	2	2	1.00	2.40	6.00
20	166	Win/69	C-price 25¢; PC-r; stiff-c	2	2	1.00	2.40	6.00
21	169	Sm/70	PC-r; stiff-c	2	2	1.00	2.40	6.00

20. The Corsican Brothers

Ed	HRN	Date	Details	A	C	GD25	FN65	NM94
1A	20	6/44	Orig.; Gilberton ed.; bc-ad: 4 Gift Boxes; 60 pgs.	1	1	41.00	124.00	330.00
1B	20	6/44	Orig.; Courier ed.; 60 pgs.	1	1	39.00	117.00	300.00
1C	20	6/44	Orig.; Long Island Ind. ed.; 60 pgs.	1	1	39.00	117.00	300.00
2	22	–	Queens Cty. Times ed.; white logo banner; CC-r	1	1	19.00	56.00	140.00
3	28	–	CC-r	1	1	17.00	50.00	125.00
4	60	–	Cl logo; no price; 48 pgs.; LDC-r	1	1	15.00	44.00	110.00
5A	62	–	LDC-r; Classics Ill. logo at top of pgs.	1	1	12.00	36.00	90.00
5B	62	–	w/o logo at top of pg. (scarcer)	1	1	13.00	40.00	100.00
6	78	–	C-price 15¢; LDC-r	1	1	11.00	34.00	85.00
7	97	–	LDC-r	1	1	10.00	30.00	75.00

21. 3 Famous Mysteries ("The Sign of the 4", "The Murders in the Rue Morgue", "The Flayed Hand")

Ed	HRN	Date	Details	A	C	GD25	FN65	NM94
1A	21	7/44	Orig.; Gilberton ed.; 60 pgs.	1	1	87.00	261.00	740.00
1B	21	7/44	Orig. Island Pub. Co.; 60 pgs.	1	1	89.00	268.00	760.00
1C	21	7/44	Original; Courier Ed.; 60 pgs.	1	1	76.00	229.00	650.00
2	22	–	Nassau Bulletin ed.; CC-r	1	1	35.00	104.00	260.00
3	30	–	CC-r	1	1	27.00	82.00	205.00
4	62	–	LDC-r; 8 pgs. deleted; LDC-r	1	1	21.00	64.00	160.00
5	70	–	LDC-r	1	1	19.00	58.00	145.00
6	85	–	C-price 15¢; LDC-r	1	1	17.00	50.00	125.00
7	114	–	New-c; PC-r	1	2	17.00	50.00	125.00

22. The Pathfinder

Ed	HRN	Date	Details	A	C	GD25	FN65	NM94
1A	22	10/44	Orig.; No printer listed; ownership statement inside fc lists Gilberton & date; 60 pgs.	1	1	42.00	127.00	340.00
1B	22	10/44	Orig.; Island Pub. ed.; 60 pgs.	1	1	39.00	116.00	290.00
1C	22	10/44	Orig.; Queens Cty Times ed. 60 pgs.	1	1	39.00	116.00	290.00
2	30	–	C-price removed; CC-r	1	1	12.00	36.00	90.00
3	60	–	Pgs. reduced to 52; LDC-r	1	1	4.25	13.00	28.00
4	70	–	LDC-r	1	1	4.00	11.00	22.00
5	85	–	C-price 15¢; LDC-r	1	1	3.60	9.00	18.00
6	118	–	LDC-r	1	1	3.20	8.00	16.00
7	132	–	LDC-r	1	1	2.80	7.00	14.00
8	146	–	LDC-r	1	1	2.80	7.00	14.00
9	167	11/63	New-c; PC-r	1	2	2.60	7.80	26.00
10	167	12/65	PC-r	1	2	1.75	5.25	14.00
11	166	8/67	PC-r	1	2	1.75	5.25	14.00

23. Oliver Twist (1st Classic produced by the Iger Shop)

Ed	HRN	Date	Details	A	C	GD25	FN65	NM94
1	23	7/45	Original; 60 pgs.	1	1	40.00	120.00	315.00
2A	30	–	Printers Union logo on bottom left-fc same as 23(Orig.) (very rare); CC-r	1	1	29.00	88.00	220.00
2B	30	–	Union logo omitted; CC-r	1	1	11.00	34.00	85.00
3	60	–	Pgs. reduced to 48; LDC-r	1	1	5.00	15.00	30.00
4	62	–	LDC-r	1	1	4.00	12.00	24.00
5	71	–	LDC-r	1	1	4.00	10.00	20.00
6	85	–	C-price 15¢; LDC-r	1	1	3.60	9.00	18.00
7	94	–	LDC-r	1	1	2.80	7.00	14.00
8	118	–	LDC-r	1	1	2.80	7.00	14.00
9	136	–	New-PC, old-a; PC-r	1	2	3.20	8.00	16.00
10	150	–	Old-a; PC-r	1	2	2.40	6.00	12.00
11	164	–	Old-a; PC-r	1	2	3.00	7.50	15.00
12	164	–	New-a; PC-r; Evans/Crandall-a	2	2	4.25	13.00	26.00

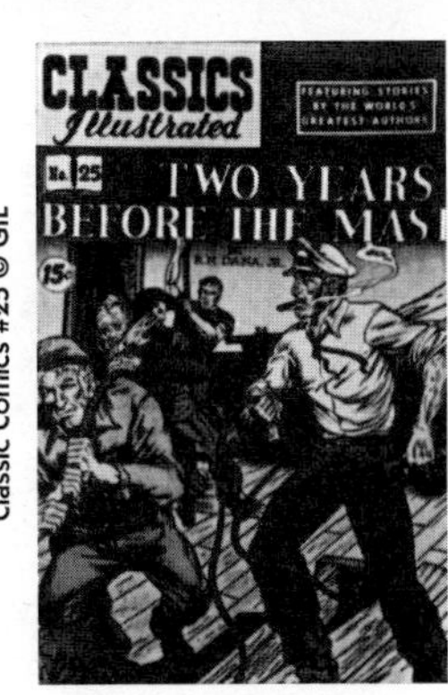

Classic Comics #25 © GIL

Classic Comics #28 © GIL

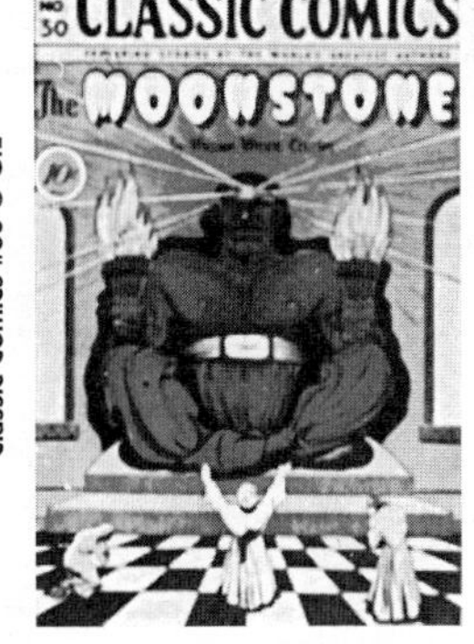

Classic Comics #30 © GIL

Ed	HRN	Date	Details	A	C	GD25	FN65	NM94
13	167	–	PC-r	2	2	2.80	7.00	14.00
14	167	8/64	PC-r	2	2	1.00	2.40	6.00
15	167	12/65	PC-r	2	2	1.00	2.40	6.00
16	166	R/1968	New 25¢; PC-r	2	2	1.00	2.40	6.00
17	169	Win/69	Stiff-c; PC-r	2	2	1.00	2.40	6.00

24. A Connecticut Yankee in King Arthur's Court

Ed	HRN	Date	Details	A	C	GD25	FN65	NM94
1	9/45	–	Original	1	1	37.00	110.00	275.00
2	30	–	No price circle; CC-r	1	1	11.00	32.00	80.00
3	60	–	8 pgs. deleted; LDC-r	1	1	4.25	13.00	28.00
4	62	–	LDC-r	1	1	4.00	12.00	24.00
5	71	–	LDC-r	1	1	4.00	10.00	20.00
6	87	–	C-price 15¢; LDC-r	1	1	3.60	9.00	18.00
7	121	–	LDC-r	1	1	3.20	8.00	16.00
8	140	–	New-c&a; PC-r	2	2	3.60	9.00	18.00
9	153	–	PC-r	2	2	1.00	2.80	7.00
10	164	–	PC-r	2	2	1.00	2.40	6.00
11	167	–	PC-r	2	2	1.00	2.40	6.00
12	167	7/64	PC-r	2	2	1.00	2.40	6.00
13	167	6/66	PC-r	2	2	1.00	2.40	6.00
14	166	R/1968	C-price 25¢; PC-r	2	2	1.00	2.40	6.00
15	169	Spr/71	PC-r; stiff-c	2	2	1.00	2.40	6.00

25. Two Years Before the Mast

Ed	HRN	Date	Details	A	C	GD25	FN65	NM94
1	10/45	–	Original; Webb/Heames-a&c	1	1	35.00	104.00	275.00
2	30	–	Price circle blank; CC-r	1	1	11.00	34.00	85.00
3	60	–	8 pgs. deleted; LDC-r	1	1	4.25	13.00	28.00
4	62	–	LDC-r	1	1	4.00	12.00	24.00
5	71	–	LDC-r	1	1	3.60	9.00	18.00
6	85	–	C-price 15¢; LDC-r	1	1	3.20	8.00	16.00
7	114	–	LDC-r	1	1	2.80	7.00	14.00
8	156	–	3 pgs. replaced by fillers; new-c; PC-r	1	2	3.60	9.00	18.00
9	167	12/63	PC-r	1	2	1.00	2.40	6.00
10	167	12/65	PC-r	1	2	1.00	2.40	6.00
11	166	9/67	PC-r	1	2	1.00	2.40	6.00
12	169	Win/69	C-price 25¢; stiff-c PC-r	1	2	1.00	2.40	6.00

26. Frankenstein (2nd horror comic?)

Ed	HRN	Date	Details	A	C	GD25	FN65	NM94
1	26	12/45	Orig.; Webb/Brewster a&c; 52 pgs.	1	1	88.00	265.00	750.00
2A	30	–	Price circle blank; no indicia; CC-r	1	1	27.00	80.00	200.00
2B	30	–	With indicia; scarce; CC-r	1	1	31.00	94.00	235.00
3	60	–	LDC-r	1	1	7.50	22.50	52.00
4	62	–	LDC-r	1	1	11.00	34.00	85.00
5	71	–	LDC-r	1	1	5.35	16.00	32.00
6A	82	–	C-price 15¢; soft-c LDC-r	1	1	4.25	13.00	28.00
6B	82	–	Stiff-c; LDC-r	1	1	5.75	17.00	35.00
7	117	–	LDC-r	1	1	3.20	8.00	16.00
8	146	–	New Saunders-c; PC-r	1	2	4.00	10.00	20.00
9	152	–	Scarce; PC-r	1	2	5.70	17.00	36.00
10	153	–	PC-r	1	2	1.00	2.80	7.00
11	160	–	PC-r	1	2	1.00	2.80	7.00
12	165	–	PC-r	1	2	1.00	2.40	6.00
13	167	–	PC-r	1	2	1.00	2.40	6.00
14	167	6/64	PC-r	1	2	1.00	2.40	6.00
15	167	6/65	PC-r	1	2	1.00	2.40	6.00
16	167	10/65	PC-r	1	2	1.00	2.40	6.00
17	166	9/67	PC-r	1	2	1.00	2.40	6.00
18	169	Fall/69	C-price 25¢; stiff-c PC-r	1	2	1.00	2.40	6.00
19	169	Spr/71	PC-r; stiff-c	1	2	1.00	2.40	6.00

27. The Adventures of Marco Polo

Ed	HRN	Date	Details	A	C	GD25	FN65	NM94
1	4/46	–	Original	1	1	39.00	117.00	300.00
2	30	–	Last 'Comics' reprint; CC-r	1	1	11.00	34.00	85.00
3	70	–	8 pgs. deleted; no c-price; LDC-r	1	1	4.25	13.00	26.00
4	87	–	C-price 15¢; LDC-r	1	1	3.60	9.00	18.00
5	117	–	LDC-r	1	1	2.40	6.00	12.00
6	154	–	New-c; PC-r	1	2	3.20	8.00	16.00
7	165	–	PC-r	1	2	1.00	2.40	6.00
8	167	4/64	PC-r	1	2	1.00	2.40	6.00
9	167	6/66	PC-r	1	2	1.00	2.40	6.00
10	169	Spr/69	New price 25¢; stiff-c; PC-r	1	2	1.00	2.40	6.00

28. Michael Strogoff

Ed	HRN	Date	Details	A	C	GD25	FN65	NM94
1	6/46	–	Original	1	1	39.00	117.00	310.00
2	51	–	8 pgs. cut; LDC-r	1	1	11.00	34.00	85.00
3	115	–	New-c; PC-r	1	2	4.00	12.00	24.00
4	155	–	PC-r	1	2	1.50	4.50	12.00
5	167	11/63	PC-r	1	2	1.25	3.75	10.00
6	167	7/66	PC-r	1	2	1.25	3.75	10.00
7	169	Sm/69	C-price 25¢; stiff-c PC-r	1	3	1.50	4.50	12.00

29. The Prince and the Pauper

Ed	HRN	Date	Details	A	C	GD25	FN65	NM94
1	7/46	–	Orig.; "Horror"-c	1	1	53.00	159.00	450.00
2	60	–	8 pgs. cut; new-c by Kiefer; LDC-r	1	2	5.35	16.00	32.00
3	62	–	LDC-r	1	2	4.25	13.00	26.00
4	71	–	LDC-r	1	2	3.60	9.00	18.00
5	93	–	LDC-r	1	2	3.20	8.00	16.00
6	114	–	LDC-r	1	2	2.80	7.00	14.00
7	128	–	New-c; PC-r	1	3	3.20	8.00	16.00
8	138	–	PC-r	1	3	1.00	2.80	7.00
9	150	–	PC-r	1	3	1.00	2.80	7.00
10	164	–	PC-r	1	3	1.00	2.40	6.00
11	167	–	PC-r	1	3	1.00	2.40	6.00
12	167	7/64	PC-r	1	3	1.00	2.40	6.00
13	167	11/65	PC-r	1	3	1.00	2.40	6.00
14	166	R/68	C-price 25¢; PC-r	1	3	1.00	2.40	6.00
15	169	Sm/70	PC-r; stiff-c	1	3	1.00	2.40	6.00

30. The Moonstone

Ed	HRN	Date	Details	A	C	GD25	FN65	NM94
1	9/46	–	Original; Rico-c/a	1	1	39.00	117.00	300.00
2	60	–	LDC-r; 8pgs. cut	1	1	5.70	17.00	38.00
3	70	–	LDC-r	1	1	5.35	16.00	32.00
4	155	–	New L.B. Cole-c; PC-r	1	2	5.70	17.00	34.00
5	165	–	PC-r; L.B. Cole-c	1	2	3.60	9.00	18.00
6	167	1/64	PC-r; L.B. Cole-c	1	2	1.10	3.30	9.00
7	167	9/65	PC-r; L.B. Cole-c	1	2	1.00	2.80	7.00
8	166	R/1968	C-price 25¢; PC-r	1	2	1.00	2.40	6.00

Classic Comics #32 © GIL

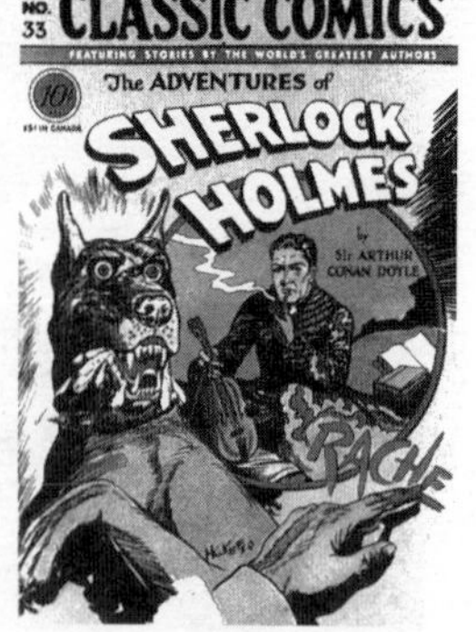

Classic Comics #33 © GIL

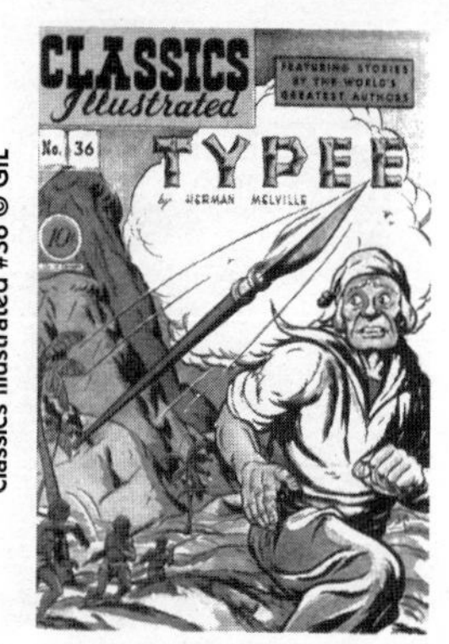

Classics Illustrated #36 © GIL

31. The Black Arrow

Ed	HRN	Date	Details	A	C	GD25	FN65	NM94
1	10/46	–	Original	1	1	29.00	88.00	220.00
2	51	–	CI logo; LDC-r 8pgs. deleted	1	1	5.00	15.00	30.00
3	64	–	LDC-r	1	1	3.60	9.00	18.00
4	87	–	C-price 15¢; LDC-r	1	1	3.20	8.00	16.00
5	108	–	LDC-r	1	1	2.80	7.00	14.00
6	125	–	LDC-r	1	1	2.40	6.00	12.00
7	131	–	New-c; PC-r	1	2	2.80	7.00	16.00
8	140	–	PC-r	1	2	1.00	2.80	7.00
9	148	–	PC-r	1	2	1.00	2.80	7.00
10	161	–	PC-r	1	2	1.00	2.40	6.00
11	167	–	PC-r	1	2	1.00	2.40	6.00
12	167	7/64	PC-r	1	2	1.20	2.40	6.00
13	167	11/65	PC-r	1	2	1.00	2.40	6.00
14	166	R/1968	C-price 25¢; PC-r	1	2	1.00	2.40	6.00

32. Lorna Doone

Ed	HRN	Date	Details	A	C	GD25	FN65	NM94
1	12/46	–	Original; Matt Baker c&a	1	1	37.00	110.00	275.00
2	53/64	–	8 pgs. deleted; LDC-r	1	1	5.70	17.00	40.00
3	85	–	C-price 15¢; LDC-r; Baker c&a	1	1	5.35	16.00	32.00
4	118	–	LDC-r	1	1	3.60	9.00	18.00
5	138	–	New-c; old-c becomes new title pg.; PC-r	1	2	3.60	9.00	18.00
6	150	–	PC-r	1	2	1.00	2.40	6.00
7	165	–	PC-r	1	2	1.00	2.40	6.00
8	167	1/64	PC-r	1	2	1.00	3.00	8.00
9	167	11/65	PC-r	1	2	1.00	3.00	8.00
10	166	R/1968	New-c; PC-r	1	3	2.25	6.75	18.00

33. The Adventures of Sherlock Holmes

Ed	HRN	Date	Details	A	C	GD25	FN65	NM94
1	33	1/47	Original; Kiefer-c; contains Study in Scarlet & Hound of the Baskervilles; 68 pgs.	1	1	112.00	335.00	950.00
2	53	–	"A Study in Scarlet" (17 pgs.) deleted; LDC-r	1	1	42.00	127.00	340.00
3	71	–	LDC-r	1	1	33.00	100.00	250.00
4A	89	–	C-price 15¢; LDC-r	1	1	27.00	80.00	200.00
4B	89	–	Kiefer's name omitted from-c	1	1	28.00	84.00	210.00

34. Mysterious Island (Last "Classic Comic")

Ed	HRN	Date	Details	A	C	GD25	FN65	NM94
1	2/47	–	Original; Webb/Heames-c/a	1	1	39.00	117.00	300.00
2	60	–	8 pgs. deleted; LDC-r	1	1	5.35	16.00	32.00
3	62	–	LDC-r	1	1	4.00	12.00	24.00
4	71	–	LDC-r	1	1	5.35	16.00	32.00
5	78	–	C-price 15¢ in circle; LDC-r	1	1	4.00	10.00	20.00
6	92	–	LDC-r	1	1	3.60	9.00	18.00
7	117	–	LDC-r	1	1	2.80	7.00	14.00
8	140	–	New-c; PC-r	1	2	3.20	8.00	16.00
9	156	–	PC-r	1	2	1.00	2.80	7.00
10	167	10/63	PC-r	1	2	1.00	2.40	6.00
11	167	5/64	PC-r	1	2	1.00	2.40	6.00
12	167	6/66	PC-r	1	2	1.00	2.40	6.00
13	166	R/1968	C-price 25¢; PC-r	1	2	1.00	2.40	6.00

35. Last Days of Pompeii (First "Classics Illustrated")

Ed	HRN	Date	Details	A	C	GD25	FN65	NM94
1	–	3/47	Original; LDC; Kiefer-c/a	1	1	39.00	117.00	300.00
2	161	–	New c&a; 15¢; PC-r; Kirby/Ayers-a	2	2	4.25	13.00	26.00
3	167	1/64	PC-r	2	2	1.75	5.25	14.00
4	167	7/66	PC-r	2	2	1.75	5.25	14.00
5	169	Spr/70	New price 25¢; stiff-c; PC-r	2	2	1.75	5.25	14.00

36. Typee

Ed	HRN	Date	Details	A	C	GD25	FN65	NM94
1	4/47	–	Original	1	1	21.00	62.00	155.00
2	64	–	No c-price; 8 pg. ed.; LDC-r	1	1	5.70	17.00	35.00
3	155	–	New-c; PC-r	1	2	3.20	8.00	16.00
4	167	9/63	PC-r	1	2	1.00	3.00	8.00
5	167	7/65	PC-r	1	2	1.00	3.00	8.00
6	169	Sm/69	C-price 25¢; stiff-c PC-r	1	2	1.00	3.00	8.00

37. The Pioneers

Ed	HRN	Date	Details	A	C	GD25	FN65	NM94
1	37	5/47	Original; Palais-c/a	1	1	15.00	44.00	110.00
2A	62	–	8 pgs. cut; LDC-r; price circle blank	1	1	4.00	12.00	24.00
2B	62	–	10¢; LDC-r;	1	1	23.00	70.00	175.00
3	70	–	LDC-r	1	1	3.20	8.00	16.00
4	92	–	15¢; LDC-r	1	1	2.80	7.00	14.00
5	118	–	LDC-r	1	1	2.40	6.00	12.00
6	131	–	LDC-r	1	1	2.40	6.00	12.00
7	132	–	LDC-r	1	1	2.40	6.00	12.00
8	153	–	LDC-r	1	1	2.40	6.00	12.00
9	167	5/64	LDC-r	1	1	1.00	3.00	8.00
10	167	6/66	LDC-r	1	1	1.00	3.00	8.00
11	166	R/1968	New-c; 25¢; PC-r	1	2	2.25	6.75	18.00

38. Adventures of Cellini

Ed	HRN	Date	Details	A	C	GD25	FN65	NM94
1	6/47	–	Original; Froehlich c/a	1	1	27.00	80.00	200.00
2	164	–	New-c&a; PC-r	2	2	3.20	8.00	16.00
3	167	12/63	PC-r	2	2	1.10	3.30	9.00
4	167	7/66	PC-r	2	2	1.10	3.30	9.00
5	169	Spr/70	Stiff-c; new price 25¢; PC-r	2	2	1.25	3.75	10.00

39. Jane Eyre

Ed	HRN	Date	Details	A	C	GD25	FN65	NM94
1	7/47	–	Original	1	1	26.00	78.00	195.00
2	60	–	No c-price; 8 pgs. cut; LDC-r	1	1	5.00	15.00	30.00
3	62	–	LDC-r	1	1	4.15	12.50	25.00
4	71	–	LDC-r; c-price 10¢	1	1	4.00	11.00	22.00
5	92	–	C-price 15¢; LDC-r	1	1	3.60	9.00	18.00
6	118	–	LDC-r	1	1	3.20	8.00	16.00
7	142	–	New-c; old-a; PC-r	1	2	4.00	10.00	20.00
8	154	–	Old-a; PC-r	1	2	3.20	8.00	16.00
9	165	–	New-a; PC-r	2	2	4.00	10.00	20.00
10	167	12/63	PC-r	2	2	2.00	6.00	16.00
11	167	4/65	PC-r	2	2	1.85	5.50	15.00
12	167	8/66	PC-r	2	2	1.85	5.50	15.00
13	166	R/1968	New-c; PC-r	2	3	4.20	12.60	42.00

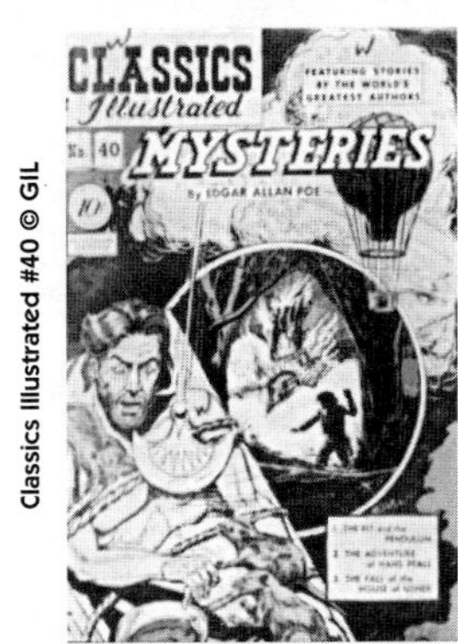

Classics Illustrated #40 © GIL

Classics Illustrated #42 © GIL

Classics Illustrated #46 © GIL

40. Mysteries ("The Pit and the Pendulum", "The Advs. of Hans Pfall" & "The Fall of the House of Usher")

Ed	HRN	Date	Details	A	C	GD25	FN65	NM94
1	8/47	–	Original; Kiefer-c/a, Froehlich, Griffiths-a	1	1	57.00	169.00	480.00
2	62	–	LDC-r; 8pgs. cut	1	1	23.00	70.00	175.00
3	75	–	LDC-r	1	1	20.00	60.00	150.00
4	92	–	C-price 15¢; LDC-r	1	1	16.00	48.00	120.00

41. Twenty Years After

Ed	HRN	Date	Details	A	C	GD25	FN65	NM94
1	9/47	–	Original; 'horror'-c	1	1	39.00	117.00	300.00
2	62	–	New-c; no c-price 8 pgs. cut; LDC-r; Kiefer-c	1	2	5.35	16.00	32.00
3	78	–	C-price 15¢; LDC-r	1	2	4.00	11.50	23.00
4	156	–	New-c; PC-r	1	3	3.20	8.00	16.00
5	167	12/63	PC-r	1	3	1.00	2.80	7.00
6	167	11/66	PC-r	1	3	1.00	2.80	7.00
7	169	Spr/70	New price 25¢; stiff-c; PC-r	1	3	1.00	2.80	7.00

42. Swiss Family Robinson

Ed	HRN	Date	Details	A	C	GD25	FN65	NM94
1	42	10/47	Orig.; Kiefer-c&a;	1	1	19.00	58.00	145.00
2A	62	–	8 pgs. cut; outside bc: Gift Box ad; LDC-r	1	1	5.00	15.00	30.00
2B	62	–	8 pgs. cut; outside-bc: Reorder list; scarce; LDC-r	1	1	7.85	23.50	55.00
3	75	–	LDC-r	1	1	4.00	10.00	20.00
4	93	–	LDC-r	1	1	3.60	9.00	18.00
5	117	–	LDC-r	1	1	3.20	8.00	16.00
6	131	–	New-c; old-a; PC-r	1	2	3.20	8.00	16.00
7	137	–	Old-a; PC-r	1	2	2.40	6.00	12.00
8	141	–	Old-a; PC-r	1	2	2.40	6.00	12.00
9	152	–	New-a; PC-r	2	2	3.20	8.00	16.00
10	158	–	PC-r	2	2	1.00	2.80	7.00
11	165	–	PC-r	2	2	2.40	6.00	12.00
12	167	12/63	PC-r	2	2	1.10	3.30	9.00
13	167	4/65	PC-r	2	2	1.00	2.40	6.00
14	167	5/66	PC-r	2	2	1.00	2.40	6.00
15	166	11/67	PC-r	2	2	1.00	2.40	6.00
16	169	Spr/69	PC-r; stiff-c	2	2	1.00	2.40	6.00

43. Great Expectations (Used in **SOTI**, pg. 311)

Ed	HRN	Date	Details	A	C	GD25	FN65	NM94
1	11/47	–	Original; Kiefer-a/c	1	1	81.00	244.00	690.00
2	62	–	No c-price; 8 pgs. cut; LDC-r	1	1	47.00	141.00	400.00

44. Mysteries of Paris (Used in **SOTI**, pg. 323)

Ed	HRN	Date	Details	A	C	GD25	FN65	NM94
1A	44	12/47	Original; 56 pgs.; Kiefer-c/a	1	1	62.00	185.00	525.00
1B	44	12/47	Orig.; printed on white/heavier paper; (rare)	1	1	68.00	203.00	575.00
2A	62	–	8 pgs. cut; outside-bc: Gift Box ad; LDC-r	1	1	27.00	80.00	200.00
2B	62	–	8 pgs. cut; outside-bc: reorder list; LDC-r	1	1	27.00	80.00	200.00
3	78	–	C-price 15¢; LDC-r	1	1	23.00	68.00	170.00

45. Tom Brown's School Days

Ed	HRN	Date	Details	A	C	GD25	FN65	NM94
1	44	1/48	Original; 1st 48pg. issue	1	1	12.00	36.00	90.00
2	64	–	No c-price; LDC-r	1	1	5.35	16.00	32.00
3	161	–	New-c&a; PC-r	2	2	3.20	8.00	14.00
4	167	2/64	PC-r	2	2	1.10	3.30	9.00
5	167	8/66	PC-r	2	2	1.10	3.30	9.00
6	166	R/1968	C-price 25¢; PC-r	2	2	1.10	3.30	9.00

46. Kidnapped

Ed	HRN	Date	Details	A	C	GD25	FN65	NM94
1	47	4/48	Original; Webb-c/a	1	1	11.00	34.00	85.00
2A	62	–	Price circle blank; LDC-r	1	1	4.25	13.00	26.00
2B	62	–	C-price 10¢; rare; LDC-r	1	1	26.00	78.00	195.00
3	78	–	C-price 15¢; LDC-r	1	1	4.00	10.00	20.00
4	87	–	LDC-r	1	1	3.20	8.00	16.00
5	118	–	LDC-r	1	1	2.80	7.00	14.00
6	131	–	New-c; PC-r	1	2	3.20	8.00	16.00
7	140	–	PC-r	1	2	1.00	2.80	7.00
8	150	–	PC-r	1	2	1.00	2.80	7.00
9	164	–	Reduced pg.width; PC-r	1	2	1.00	2.40	6.00
10	167	–	PC-r	1	2	1.00	2.40	6.00
11	167	3/64	PC-r	1	2	1.00	2.40	6.00
12	167	6/65	PC-r	1	2	1.00	2.40	6.00
13	167	12/65	PC-r	1	2	1.00	2.40	6.00
14	166	9/67	PC-r	1	2	1.00	2.40	6.00
15	166	Win/69	New price 25¢; PC-r; stiff-c	1	2	1.00	2.40	6.00
16	169	Sm/70	PC-r; stiff-c	1	2	1.00	2.40	6.00

47. Twenty Thousand Leagues Under the Sea

Ed	HRN	Date	Details	A	C	GD25	FN65	NM94
1	47	5/48	Orig.; Kiefer-a&c;	1	1	11.00	34.00	85.00
2	64	–	No c-price; LDC-r	1	1	4.25	13.00	26.00
3	78	–	C-price 15¢; LDC-r	1	1	3.60	9.00	18.00
4	94	–	LDC-r	1	1	3.20	8.00	16.00
5	118	–	LDC-r	1	1	2.80	7.00	14.00
6	128	–	New-c; PC-r	1	2	3.00	7.50	15.00
7	133	–	PC-r	1	2	2.00	5.00	10.00
8	140	–	PC-r	1	2	1.00	2.80	7.00
9	148	–	PC-r	1	2	1.00	2.80	7.00
10	156	–	PC-r	1	2	1.00	2.80	7.00
11	165	–	PC-r	1	2	1.00	2.40	6.00
12	167	–	PC-r	1	2	1.00	2.40	6.00
13	167	3/64	PC-r	1	2	1.00	2.40	6.00
14	167	8/65	PC-r	1	2	1.00	2.40	6.00
15	167	10/66	PC-r	1	2	1.00	2.40	6.00
16	166	R/1968	C-price 25¢; new-c PC-r	1	3	1.25	3.75	10.00
17	169	Spr/70	Stiff-c; PC-r	1	3	1.50	4.50	12.00

48. David Copperfield

Ed	HRN	Date	Details	A	C	GD25	FN65	NM94
1	47	6/48	Original; Kiefer-c/a	1	1	11.00	34.00	85.00
2	64	–	Price circle replaced by motif of boy reading; LDC-r	1	1	4.25	13.00	26.00
3	87	–	C-price 15¢; LDC-r	1	1	3.20	8.00	16.00
4	121	–	New-c; PC-r	1	2	2.80	7.00	14.00
5	130	–	PC-r	1	2	1.50	3.50	7.00
6	140	–	PC-r	1	2	1.50	3.50	7.00
7	148	–	PC-r	1	2	1.50	3.50	7.00

Classics Illustrated #51 © GIL

Classics Illustrated #53 © GIL

Classics Illustrated #56 © GIL

Ed	HRN	Date	Details	A	C	GD25	FN65	NM94
8	156	–	PC-r	1	2	1.50	3.50	7.00
9	167	–	PC-r	1	2	1.00	2.40	6.00
10	167	4/64	PC-r	1	2	1.00	2.40	6.00
11	167	6/65	PC-r	1	2	1.00	2.40	6.00
12	166	5/67	PC-r	1	2	1.00	2.40	6.00
13	166	R/67	PC-r; C-price 25¢	1	2	1.25	3.75	10.00
14	166	Spr/69	C-price 25¢; stiff-c PC-r	1	2	1.00	2.00	4.00
15	169	Win/69	Stiff-c; PC-r	1	2	1.00	2.40	6.00

49. Alice in Wonderland

Ed	HRN	Date	Details	A	C	GD25	FN65	NM94
1	47	7/48	Original; 1st Blum a & c	1	1	17.00	50.00	125.00
2	64	–	No c-price; LDC-r	1	1	5.70	17.00	35.00
3A	85	–	C-price 15¢; soft-c LDC-r	1	1	4.25	13.00	28.00
3B	85	–	Stiff-c; LDC-r	1	1	5.35	16.00	32.00
4	155	–	New PC, similar to orig.; PC-r	1	2	4.25	13.00	28.00
5	165	–	PC-r	1	2	4.00	10.00	20.00
6	167	3/64	PC-r	1	2	2.00	6.00	16.00
7	167	6/66	PC-r	1	2	2.00	6.00	16.00
8A	166	Fall/68	New-c; soft-c; 25¢ c-price; PC-r	1	3	2.85	8.40	28.00
8B	166	Fall/68	New-c; stiff-c; 25¢ c-price; PC-r	1	3	5.00	15.00	50.00

50. Adventures of Tom Sawyer (Used in **SOTI**, pg. 37)

Ed	HRN	Date	Details	A	C	GD25	FN65	NM94
1A	51	8/48	Orig.; Aldo Rubano a&c	1	1	13.00	38.00	95.00
1B	51	9/48	Orig.; Rubano c&a	1	1	13.00	38.00	95.00
1C	51	9/48	Orig.; outside-bc: blue & yellow only; rare	1	1	19.00	58.00	145.00
2	64	–	No c-price; LDC-r	1	1	4.00	11.00	22.00
3	78	–	C-price 15¢; LDC-r	1	1	3.20	8.00	16.00
4	94	–	LDC-r	1	1	2.80	7.00	14.00
5	117	–	LDC-r	1	1	2.40	6.00	12.00
6	132	–	LDC-r	1	1	2.40	6.00	12.00
7	140	–	New-c; PC-r	1	2	3.20	8.00	16.00
8	150	–	PC-r	1	2	1.80	4.50	9.00
9	164	–	New-a; PC-r	2	2	3.20	8.00	16.00
10	167	–	PC-r	2	2	1.80	4.50	9.00
11	167	1/65	PC-r	2	2	1.00	2.40	6.00
12	167	5/66	PC-r	2	2	1.00	2.40	6.00
13	166	12/67	PC-r	2	2	1.00	2.40	6.00
14	169	Fall/69	C-price 25¢; stiff-c; PC-r	2	2	1.00	2.40	6.00
15	169	Win/71	PC-r	2	2	1.00	2.40	6.00

51. The Spy

Ed	HRN	Date	Details	A	C	GD25	FN65	NM94
1A	51	9/48	Original; inside-bc illo: Christmas Carol	1	1	11.00	32.00	80.00
1B	51	9/48	Original; inside-bc illo: Man in Iron Mask	1	1	11.00	32.00	80.00
1C	51	8/48	Original; outside-bc: full color	1	1	11.00	32.00	80.00
1D	51	8/48	Original; outside-bc: blue & yellow only; scarce	1	1	15.00	46.00	115.00
2	89	–	C-price 15¢; LDC-r	1	1	4.00	10.00	20.00
3	121	–	LDC-r	1	1	3.20	8.00	16.00
4	139	–	New-c; PC-r	1	2	3.20	8.00	16.00
5	156	–	PC-r	1	2	1.00	2.80	7.00
6	167	11/63	PC-r	1	2	1.00	2.40	6.00
7	167	7/66	PC-r	1	2	1.00	2.40	6.00
8A	166	Win/69	C-price 25¢; soft-c; scarce; PC-r	1	2	2.25	6.75	18.00
8B	166	Win/69	C-price 25¢; stiff-c; PC-r	1	2	1.00	2.40	6.00

52. The House of the Seven Gables

Ed	HRN	Date	Details	A	C	GD25	FN65	NM94
1	53	10/48	Orig.; Griffiths a&c	1	1	11.00	32.00	80.00
2	89	–	C-price 15¢; LDC-r	1	1	4.00	10.00	20.00
3	121	–	LDC-r	1	1	3.20	8.00	16.00
4	142	–	New-c&a; PC-r; Woodbridge-a	2	2	3.60	9.00	18.00
5	156	–	PC-r	2	2	1.00	2.80	7.00
6	165	–	PC-r	2	2	1.00	2.40	6.00
7	167	5/64	PC-r	2	2	1.10	3.30	9.00
8	167	3/66	PC-r	2	2	1.00	2.40	6.00
9	166	R/1968	C-price 25¢; PC-r	2	2	1.00	2.40	6.00
10	169	Spr/70	Stiff-c; PC-r	2	2	1.00	2.40	6.00

53. A Christmas Carol

Ed	HRN	Date	Details	A	C	GD25	FN65	NM94
1	53	11/48	Original & only ed; Kiefer-c/a	1	1	15.00	46.00	115.00

54. Man in the Iron Mask

Ed	HRN	Date	Details	A	C	GD25	FN65	NM94
1	55	12/48	Original; Froehlich-a, Kiefer-c	1	1	10.00	30.00	75.00
2	93	–	C-price 15¢; LDC-r	1	1	4.00	12.00	24.00
3A	111	–	(O) logo lettering; scarce; LDC-r	1	1	5.35	16.00	32.00
3B	111	–	New logo as PC; LDC-r	1	1	4.00	11.00	22.00
4	142	–	New-c&a; PC-r	2	2	3.60	9.00	18.00
5	154	–	PC-r	2	2	1.00	2.80	7.00
6	165	–	PC-r	2	2	1.00	2.40	6.00
7	167	5/64	PC-r	2	2	1.00	2.40	6.00
8	167	4/66	PC-r	2	2	1.00	2.40	6.00
9A	166	Win/69	C-price 25¢; soft-c PC-r	2	2	2.25	6.75	18.00
9B	166	Win/69	Stiff-c	2	2	1.00	2.40	6.00

55. Silas Marner (Used in **SOTI**, pgs. 311, 312)

Ed	HRN	Date	Details	A	C	GD25	FN65	NM94
1	55	1/49	Original-Kiefer-c	1	1	11.00	32.00	80.00
2	75	–	Price circle blank; 'Coming Next' ad; LDC-r	1	1	4.25	13.00	26.00
3	97	–	LDC-r	1	1	3.20	8.00	16.00
4	121	–	New-c; PC-r	1	2	3.20	8.00	16.00
5	130	–	PC-r	1	2	1.00	2.80	7.00
6	140	–	PC-r	1	2	1.00	2.80	7.00
7	154	–	PC-r	1	2	1.00	2.80	7.00
8	165	–	PC-r	1	2	1.00	2.40	6.00
9	167	2/64	PC-r	1	2	1.00	2.40	6.00
10	167	6/65	PC-r	1	2	1.00	2.40	6.00
11	166	5/67	PC-r	1	2	1.00	2.40	6.00
12A	166	Win/69	C-price 25¢; soft-c PC-r	1	2	2.25	6.75	18.00
12B	166	Win/69	C-price 25¢; stiff-c PC-r	1	2	1.00	2.40	6.00

56. The Toilers of the Sea

Ed	HRN	Date	Details	A	C

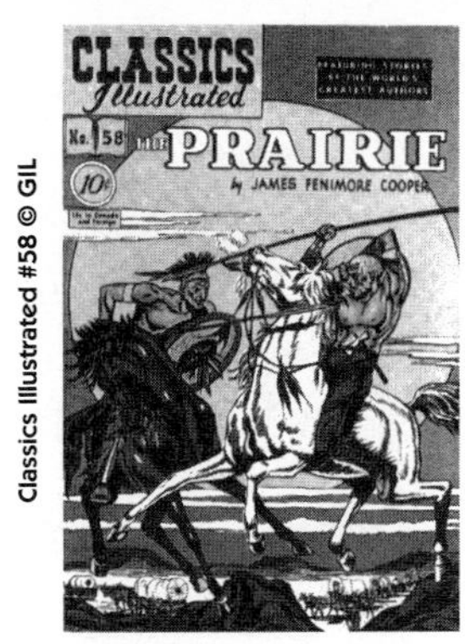

Classics Illustrated #58 © GIL

Classics Illustrated #61 © GIL

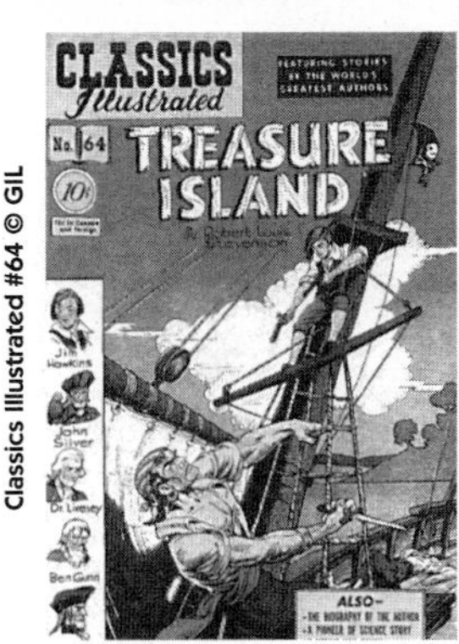

Classics Illustrated #64 © GIL

Ed	HRN	Date	Details	A	C	GD25	FN65	NM94
1	55	2/49	Original; A.M. Froehlich-c/a	1	1	20.00	60.00	150.00
2	165	–	New-c&a; PC-r; Angelo Torres-a	2	2	5.35	16.00	32.00
3	167	3/64	PC-r	2	2	2.25	6.75	18.00
4	167	10/66	PC-r	2	2	2.25	6.75	18.00

57. The Song of Hiawatha

Ed	HRN	Date	Details	A	C	GD25	FN65	NM94
1	55	3/49	Original; Alex Blum-c/a	1	1	11.00	32.00	80.00
2	75	–	No c-price w/15¢ sticker; 'Coming Next' ad; LDC-r	1	1	4.25	13.00	26.00
3	94	–	C-price 15¢; LDC-r	1	1	4.00	10.00	20.00
4	118	–	LDC-r	1	1	3.20	8.00	16.00
5	134	–	New-c; PC-r	1	2	3.20	8.00	16.00
6	139	–	PC-r	1	2	1.00	2.80	7.00
7	154	–	PC-r	1	2	1.00	2.80	7.00
8	167	–	Has orig.date; PC-r	1	2	1.00	2.40	6.00
9	167	9/64	PC-r	1	2	1.00	2.40	6.00
10	167	10/65	PC-r	1	2	1.00	2.40	6.00
11	166	F/1968	C-price 25¢; PC-r	1	2	1.00	2.40	6.00

58. The Prairie

Ed	HRN	Date	Details	A	C	GD25	FN65	NM94
1	60	4/49	Original; Palais c/a	1	1	11.00	32.00	80.00
2A	62	–	No c-price; no coming-next ad; LDC-r	1	1	5.70	17.00	40.00
2B	62		10¢ (rare)	1	1	15.00	46.00	115.00
3	78	–	C-price 15¢ in dbl. circle; LDC-r	1	1	4.00	10.00	20.00
4	114	–	LDC-r	1	1	3.20	8.00	16.00
5	131	–	LDC-r	1	1	2.80	7.00	14.00
6	132	–	LDC-r	1	1	2.80	7.00	14.00
7	146	–	New-c; PC-r	1	2	3.20	8.00	16.00
8	155	–	PC-r	1	2	1.00	2.80	7.00
9	167	5/64	PC-r	1	2	1.00	2.40	6.00
10	167	4/66	PC-r	1	2	1.00	2.40	6.00
11	169	Sm/69	New price 25¢; stiff-c; PC-r	1	2	1.00	2.40	6.00

59. Wuthering Heights

Ed	HRN	Date	Details	A	C	GD25	FN65	NM94
1	60	5/49	Original; Kiefer-c/a	1	1	12.00	36.00	90.00
2	85	–	C-price 15¢; LDC-r	1	1	5.00	15.00	30.00
3	156	–	New-c; PC-r	1	2	3.60	9.00	18.00
4	167	1/64	PC-r	1	2	1.00	3.00	8.00
5	167	10/66	PC-r	1	2	1.00	3.00	8.00
6	169	Sm/69	C-price 25¢; stiff-c; PC-r	1	2	1.00	3.00	8.00

60. Black Beauty

Ed	HRN	Date	Details	A	C	GD25	FN65	NM94
1	62	6/49	Original; Froehlich-c/a	1	1	11.00	34.00	85.00
2	62	–	No c-price; no coming-next ad; LDC-r (rare)	1	1	14.00	42.00	105.00
3	85	–	C-price 15¢; LDC-r	1	1	4.00	12.00	24.00
4	158	–	New L.B. Cole-c/a; PC-r	2	2	4.25	13.00	28.00
5	167	2/64	PC-r	2	2	1.50	4.50	12.00
6	167	3/66	PC-r	2	2	1.50	4.50	12.00
7	166	R/1968	New-c&price, 25¢; PC-r	2	3	4.50	13.50	45.00

61. The Woman in White

Ed	HRN	Date	Details	A	C	GD25	FN65	NM94
1A	62	7/49	Original; Blum-c/a fc-purple; bc: top illos light blue	1	1	12.00	36.00	90.00
1B	62	7/49	Original; Blum-c/a fc-pink; bc: top illos light violet	1	1	12.00	36.00	90.00
2	156	–	New-c; PC-r	1	2	4.00	11.00	22.00
3	167	1/64	PC-r	1	2	1.75	5.25	14.00
4	166	R/1968	C-price 25¢; PC-r	1	2	1.75	5.25	14.00

62. Western Stories ("The Luck of Roaring Camp" and "The Outcasts of Poker Flat")

Ed	HRN	Date	Details	A	C	GD25	FN65	NM94
1	62	8/49	Original; Kiefer-c/a	1	1	10.00	30.00	75.00
2	89	–	C-price 15¢; LDC-r	1	1	4.00	12.00	24.00
3	121	–	LDC-r	1	1	3.60	9.00	18.00
4	137	–	New-c; PC-r	1	2	3.20	8.00	16.00
5	152	–	PC-r	1	2	1.00	2.80	7.00
6	167	10/63	PC-r	1	2	1.00	2.40	6.00
7	167	6/64	PC-r	1	2	1.00	2.40	6.00
8	167	11/66	PC-r	1	2	1.00	2.40	6.00
9	166	R/1968	New-c&price 25¢; PC-r	1	3	2.50	7.50	16.00

63. The Man Without a Country

Ed	HRN	Date	Details	A	C	GD25	FN65	NM94
1	62	9/49	Original; Kiefer-c/a	1	1	11.00	32.00	80.00
2	78	–	C-price 15¢ in double circle; LDC-r	1	1	4.00	12.00	24.00
3	156	–	New-c, old-a; PC-r	1	2	4.00	10.00	20.00
4	165	–	New-a & text pgs.; PC-r; A. Torres-a	2	2	3.60	9.00	18.00
5	167	3/64	PC-r	2	2	1.00	2.40	6.00
6	167	8/66	PC-r	2	2	1.00	2.40	6.00
7	169	Sm/69	New price 25¢; stiff-c; PC-r	2	2	1.00	2.40	6.00

64. Treasure Island

Ed	HRN	Date	Details	A	C	GD25	FN65	NM94
1	62	10/49	Original; Blum-c/a	1	1	11.00	32.00	80.00
2A	82	–	C-price 15¢; soft-c LDC-r	1	1	4.00	11.00	22.00
2B	82	–	Stiff-c; LDC-r	1	1	4.00	12.00	24.00
3	117	–	LDC-r	1	1	3.60	9.00	18.00
4	131	–	New-c; PC-r	1	2	3.20	8.00	16.00
5	138	–	PC-r	1	2	1.00	2.80	7.00
6	146	–	PC-r	1	2	1.00	2.80	7.00
7	158	–	PC-r	1	2	1.00	2.80	7.00
8	165	–	PC-r	1	2	1.00	2.40	6.00
9	167	–	PC-r	1	2	1.00	2.40	6.00
10	167	6/64	PC-r	1	2	1.00	2.40	6.00
11	167	12/65	PC-r	1	2	1.00	2.40	6.00
12A	166	10/67	PC-r	1	2	1.10	3.30	9.00
12B	166	10/67	w/Grit ad stapled in book	1	2	8.00	24.00	80.00
13	169	Spr/69	New price 25¢; stiff-c; PC-r	1	2	1.00	2.80	7.00
14	–	1989	Long John Silver's Seafood Shoppes; $1.95, First/Berkley Publ.; Blum-r	1	2		.80	2.00

65. Benjamin Franklin

Ed	HRN	Date	Details	A	C

Classics Illustrated #71 © GIL

Classics Illustrated #72 © GIL

Classics Illustrated #76 © GIL

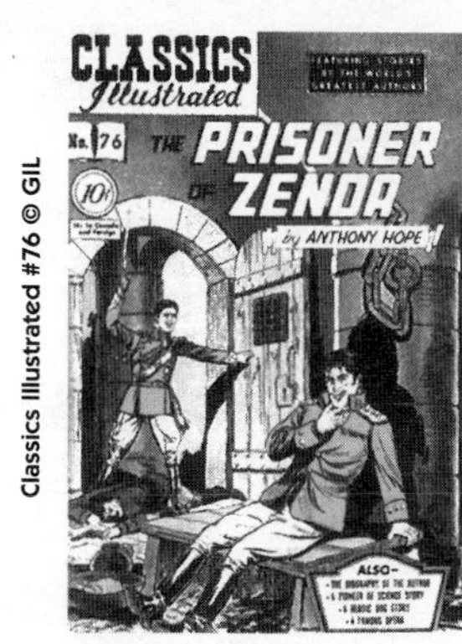

Ed	HRN	Date	Details	A	C	GD25	FN65	NM94
1	64	11/49	Original; Kiefer-c; Iger Shop-a	1	1	11.00	32.00	80.00
2	131	–	New-c; PC-r	1	2	3.60	9.00	18.00
3	154	–	PC-r	1	2	1.00	3.00	8.00
4	167	2/64	PC-r	1	2	1.00	2.80	7.00
5	167	4/66	PC-r	1	2	1.00	2.80	7.00
6	169	Fall/69	New price 25¢; stiff-c; PC-r	1	2	1.00	2.80	7.00

66. The Cloister and the Hearth

Ed	HRN	Date	Details	A	C	GD25	FN65	NM94
1	67	12/49	Original & only ed; Kiefer-a & c	1	1	23.00	70.00	175.00

67. The Scottish Chiefs

Ed	HRN	Date	Details	A	C	GD25	FN65	NM94
1	67	1/50	Original; Blum-a&c	1	1	9.30	28.00	70.00
2	85	–	C-price 15¢; LDC-r	1	1	4.00	12.00	24.00
3	118	–	LDC-r	1	1	3.60	9.00	18.00
4	136	–	New-c; PC-r	1	2	3.60	9.00	18.00
5	154	–	PC-r	1	2	1.10	3.30	9.00
6	167	11/63	PC-r	1	2	1.40	4.50	11.00
7	167	8/65	PC-r	1	2	1.10	3.30	9.00

68. Julius Caesar (Used in **SOTI**, pgs. 36, 37)

Ed	HRN	Date	Details	A	C	GD25	FN65	NM94
1	70	2/50	Original; Kiefer-c/a	1	1	9.30	28.00	65.00
2	85	–	C-price 15¢; LDC-r	1	1	4.00	11.00	22.00
3	108	–	LDC-r	1	1	3.60	9.00	18.00
4	156	–	New L.B. Cole-c; PC-r	1	2	4.00	10.00	20.00
5	165	–	New-a by Evans, Crandall; PC-r	2	2	4.00	10.00	20.00
6	167	2/64	PC-r	2	2	1.00	2.40	6.00
7	167	10/65	Tarzan books inside cover; PC-r	2	2	1.00	2.40	6.00
8	166	R/1967	PC-r	2	2	1.00	2.40	6.00
9	169	Win/69	PC-r; stiff-c	2	2	1.00	2.00	6.00

69. Around the World in 80 Days

Ed	HRN	Date	Details	A	C	GD25	FN65	NM94
1	70	3/50	Original; Kiefer-c/a	1	1	9.30	28.00	65.00
2	87	–	C-price 15¢; LDC-r	1	1	4.00	11.00	22.00
3	125	–	LDC-r	1	1	3.60	9.00	18.00
4	136	–	New-c; PC-r	1	2	3.60	9.00	18.00
5	146	–	PC-r	1	2	1.00	2.80	7.00
6	152	–	PC-r	1	2	1.00	2.80	7.00
7	164	–	PC-r	1	2	1.00	2.40	6.00
8	167	–	PC-r	1	2	1.00	2.40	6.00
9	167	7/64	PC-r	1	2	1.00	2.40	6.00
10	167	11/65	PC-r	1	2	1.00	2.40	6.00
11	166	7/67	PC-r	1	2	1.00	2.40	6.00
12	169	Spr/69	C-price 25¢; stiff-c; PC-r	1	2	1.00	2.40	6.00

70. The Pilot

Ed	HRN	Date	Details	A	C	GD25	FN65	NM94
1	71	4/50	Original; Blum-c/a	1	1	8.50	26.00	60.00
2	92	–	C-price 15¢; LDC-r	1	1	4.00	12.00	24.00
3	125	–	LDC-r	1	1	3.60	9.00	18.00
4	156	–	New-c; PC-r	1	2	4.00	10.00	20.00
5	167	2/64	PC-r	1	2	1.60	4.85	13.00
6	167	5/66	PC-r	1	2	1.25	3.75	10.00

71. The Man Who Laughs

Ed	HRN	Date	Details	A	C	GD25	FN65	NM94
1	71	5/50	Original; Blum-c/a	1	1	15.00	44.00	110.00
2	165	–	New-c&a; PC-r	2	2	8.50	26.00	60.00
3	167	4/64	PC-r	2	2	7.50	22.50	52.00

72. The Oregon Trail

Ed	HRN	Date	Details	A	C	GD25	FN65	NM94
1	73	6/50	Original; Kiefer-c/a	1	1	8.50	26.00	60.00
2	89	–	C-price 15¢; LDC-r	1	1	4.00	12.00	24.00
3	121	–	LDC-r	1	1	3.60	9.00	18.00
4	131	–	New-c; PC-r	1	2	3.60	9.00	18.00
5	140	–	PC-r	1	2	1.00	2.80	7.00
6	150	–	PC-r	1	2	1.00	2.80	7.00
7	164	–	PC-r	1	2	1.00	2.40	6.00
8	167	–	PC-r	1	2	1.00	2.40	6.00
9	167	8/64	PC-r	1	2	1.00	2.40	6.00
10	167	10/65	PC-r	1	2	1.00	2.40	6.00
11	166	R/1968	C-price 25¢; PC-r	1	2	1.00	2.40	6.00

73. The Black Tulip

Ed	HRN	Date	Details	A	C	GD25	FN65	NM94
1	75	7/50	1st & only ed.; Alex Blum-c/a	1	1	30.00	90.00	225.00

74. Mr. Midshipman Easy

Ed	HRN	Date	Details	A	C	GD25	FN65	NM94
1	75	8/50	1st & only edition	1	1	30.00	90.00	225.00

75. The Lady of the Lake

Ed	HRN	Date	Details	A	C	GD25	FN65	NM94
1	75	9/50	Original; Kiefer-c/a	1	1	8.50	26.00	60.00
2	85	–	C-price 15¢; LDC-r	1	1	4.25	13.00	26.00
3	118	–	LDC-r	1	1	4.00	10.00	20.00
4	139	–	New-c; PC-r	1	2	3.60	9.00	18.00
5	154	–	PC-r	1	2	1.00	2.80	7.00
6	165	–	PC-r	1	2	1.00	2.40	6.00
7	167	4/64	PC-r	1	2	1.00	2.40	6.00
8	167	5/66	PC-r	1	2	1.00	2.40	6.00
9	169	Spr/69	New price 25¢; stiff-c; PC-r	1	2	1.00	2.40	6.00

76. The Prisoner of Zenda

Ed	HRN	Date	Details	A	C	GD25	FN65	NM94
1	75	10/50	Original; Kiefer-c/a	1	1	7.85	23.50	55.00
2	85	–	C-price 15¢; LDC-r	1	1	4.00	12.00	24.00
3	111	–	LDC-r	1	1	3.60	9.00	18.00
4	128	–	New-c; PC-r	1	2	3.60	9.00	18.00
5	152	–	PC-r	1	2	1.00	2.80	7.00
6	165	–	PC-r	1	2	1.00	2.40	6.00
7	167	4/64	PC-r	1	2	1.00	2.40	6.00
8	167	9/66	PC-r	1	2	1.00	2.40	6.00
9	169	Fall/69	New price 25¢; stiff-c; PC-r	1	2	1.00	2.40	6.00

77. The Iliad

Ed	HRN	Date	Details	A	C	GD25	FN65	NM94
1	78	11/50	Original; Blum-c/a	1	1	8.50	26.00	60.00
2	87	–	C-price 15¢; LDC-r	1	1	4.25	13.00	26.00
3	121	–	LDC-r	1	1	3.60	9.00	18.00
4	139	–	New-c; PC-r	1	2	3.20	8.00	16.00
5	150	–	PC-r	1	2	1.00	2.80	7.00
6	165	–	PC-r	1	2	1.00	2.40	6.00
7	167	10/63	PC-r	1	2	1.00	2.40	6.00
8	167	7/64	PC-r	1	2	1.00	2.40	6.00
9	167	5/66	PC-r	1	2	1.00	2.40	6.00
10	166	R/1968	C-price 25¢; PC-r	1	2	1.00	2.40	6.00

78. Joan of Arc

Ed	HRN	Date	Details	A	C	GD25	FN65	NM94
1	78	12/50	Original; Kiefer-c/a	1	1	7.85	23.50	55.00
2	87	–	C-price 15¢; LDC-r	1	1	4.00	12.00	24.00
3	113	–	LDC-r	1	1	3.60	9.00	18.00

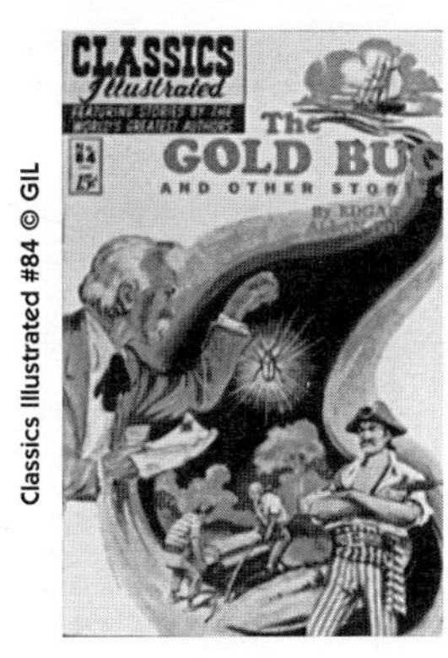
Classics Illustrated #84 © GIL

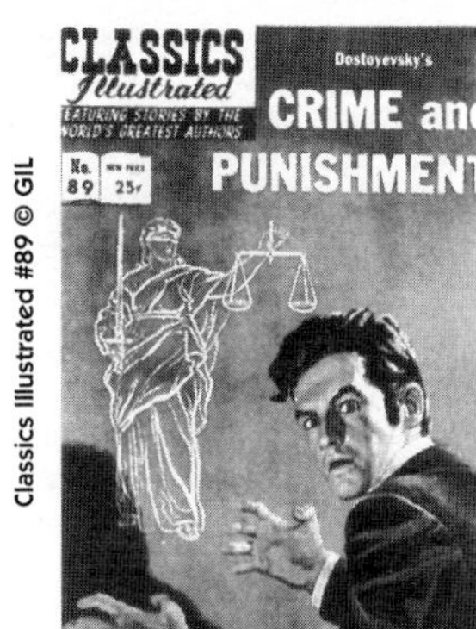
Classics Illustrated #89 © GIL

Classics Illustrated #90 © GIL

Ed	HRN	Date	Details	A	C	GD25	FN65	NM94
4	128	–	New-c; PC-r	1	2	3.60	9.00	18.00
5	140	–	PC-r	1	2	1.00	2.80	7.00
6	150	–	PC-r	1	2	1.00	2.80	7.00
7	159	–	PC-r	1	2	1.00	2.80	7.00
8	167	–	PC-r	1	2	1.00	2.40	6.00
9	167	12/63	PC-r	1	2	1.00	2.40	6.00
10	167	6/65	PC-r	1	2	1.00	2.40	6.00
11	166	6/67	PC-r	1	2	1.00	2.40	6.00
12	166	Win/69	New-c&price, 25¢; PC-r; stiff-c	1	3	2.50	7.50	20.00

79. Cyrano de Bergerac

Ed	HRN	Date	Details	A	C	GD25	FN65	NM94
1	78	1/51	Orig.; movie promo inside front-c; Blum-c/a	1	1	7.85	23.50	55.00
2	85	–	C-price 15¢; LDC-r	1	1	4.00	12.00	24.00
3	118	–	LDC-r	1	1	3.60	9.00	18.00
4	133	–	New-c; PC-r	1	2	3.60	9.00	18.00
5	156	–	PC-r	1	2	1.50	4.50	12.00
6	167	8/64	PC-r	1	2	1.50	4.50	12.00

80. White Fang (Last line drawn cover)

Ed	HRN	Date	Details	A	C	GD25	FN65	NM94
1	79	2/51	Orig.; Blum-c/a	1	1	7.85	23.50	55.00
2	87	–	C-price 15¢; LDC-r	1	1	4.25	13.00	26.00
3	125	–	LDC-r	1	1	3.60	9.00	18.00
4	132	–	New-c; PC-r	1	2	3.20	8.00	16.00
5	140	–	PC-r	1	2	1.00	2.80	7.00
6	153	–	PC-r	1	2	1.00	2.80	7.00
7	167	–	PC-r	1	2	1.00	2.40	6.00
8	167	9/64	PC-r	1	2	1.00	2.40	6.00
9	167	7/65	PC-r	1	2	1.00	2.40	6.00
10	166	6/67	PC-r	1	2	1.00	2.40	6.00
11	169	Fall/69	New price 25¢; PC-r; stiff-c	1	2	1.00	2.40	6.00

81. The Odyssey (1st painted cover)

Ed	HRN	Date	Details	A	C	GD25	FN65	NM94
1	82	3/51	First 15¢ Original; Blum-c	1	1	7.15	21.50	50.00
2	167	8/64	PC-r	1	1	1.50	4.50	12.00
3	167	10/66	PC-r	1	1	1.50	4.50	12.00
4	169	Spr/69	New, stiff-c; PC-r	1	2	2.25	6.75	18.00

82. The Master of Ballantrae

Ed	HRN	Date	Details	A	C	GD25	FN65	NM94
1	82	4/51	Original; Blum-c	1	1	5.70	17.00	35.00
2	167	8/64	PC-r	1	1	2.00	6.00	16.00
3	166	Fall/68	New, stiff-c; PC-r	1	2	2.25	6.75	18.00

83. The Jungle Book

Ed	HRN	Date	Details	A	C	GD25	FN65	NM94
1	85	5/51	Original; Blum-c Bossert/Blum-a	1	1	5.70	17.00	34.00
2	110	–	PC-r	1	1	2.00	5.00	10.00
3	125	–	PC-r	1	1	1.00	2.80	7.00
4	134	–	PC-r	1	1	1.00	2.80	7.00
5	142	–	PC-r	1	1	1.00	2.80	7.00
6	150	–	PC-r	1	1	1.00	2.80	7.00
7	159	–	PC-r	1	1	1.00	2.80	7.00
8	167	–	PC-r	1	1	1.00	2.40	6.00
9	167	3/65	PC-r	1	1	1.00	2.40	6.00
10	167	11/65	PC-r	1	1	1.00	2.40	6.00
11	167	5/66	PC-r	1	1	1.00	2.40	6.00
12	166	R/1968	New c&a; stiff-c; PC-r	2	2	2.25	6.75	18.00

84. The Gold Bug and Other Stories ("The Gold Bug", "The Tell-Tale Heart", "The Cask of Amontillado")

Ed	HRN	Date	Details	A	C	GD25	FN65	NM94
1	85	6/51	Original; Blum-c/a; Palais, Laverly-a	1	1	10.00	30.00	75.00
2	167	7/64	PC-r	1	1	9.30	28.00	65.00

85. The Sea Wolf

Ed	HRN	Date	Details	A	C	GD25	FN65	NM94
1	85	7/51	Original; Blum-c/a	1	1	4.15	12.50	25.00
2	121	–	PC-r	1	1		2.80	7.00
3	132	–	PC-r	1	1		2.80	7.00
4	141	–	PC-r	1	1		2.80	7.00
5	161	–	PC-r	1	1		2.40	6.00
6	167	2/64	PC-r	1	1		2.40	6.00
7	167	11/65	PC-r	1	1		2.40	6.00
8	169	Fall/69	New price 25¢; stiff-c; PC-r	1	1		2.40	6.00

86. Under Two Flags

Ed	HRN	Date	Details	A	C	GD25	FN65	NM94
1	87	8/51	Original; first delBourgo-a	1	1	4.00	12.00	24.00
2	117	–	PC-r	1	1	2.00	5.00	10.00
3	139	–	PC-r	1	1	1.60	4.00	8.00
4	158	–	PC-r	1	1	1.60	4.00	8.00
5	167	2/64	PC-r	1	1	1.00	2.40	6.00
6	167	8/66	PC-r	1	1	1.00	2.40	6.00
7	169	Sm/69	New price 25¢; stiff-c; PC-r	1	1	1.00	2.40	6.00

87. A Midsummer Nights Dream

Ed	HRN	Date	Details	A	C	GD25	FN65	NM94
1	87	9/51	Original; Blum c/a	1	1	4.25	13.00	26.00
2	161	–	PC-r	1	1	1.00	2.80	7.00
3	167	4/64	PC-r	1	1	1.00	2.40	6.00
4	167	5/66	PC-r	1	1	1.00	2.40	6.00
5	169	Sm/69	New price 25¢; stiff-c; PC-r	1	1	1.00	2.40	6.00

88. Men of Iron

Ed	HRN	Date	Details	A	C	GD25	FN65	NM94
1	89	10/51	Original	1	1	4.25	13.00	28.00
2	154	–	PC-r	1	1	1.60	4.00	8.00
3	167	1/64	PC-r	1	1	1.00	2.40	6.00
4	166	R/1968	C-price 25¢; PC-r	1	1	1.00	2.40	6.00

89. Crime and Punishment (Cover illo. in **POP**)

Ed	HRN	Date	Details	A	C	GD25	FN65	NM94
1	89	11/51	Original; Palais-a	1	1	5.00	15.00	30.00
2	152	–	PC-r	1	1	1.60	4.00	8.00
3	167	4/64	PC-r	1	1	1.00	2.40	6.00
4	167	5/66	PC-r	1	1	1.00	2.40	6.00
5	169	Fall/69	New price 25¢ stiff-c; PC-r	1	1	1.00	2.40	6.00

90. Green Mansions

Ed	HRN	Date	Details	A	C	GD25	FN65	NM94
1	89	12/51	Original; Blum-c/a	1	1	4.25	13.00	28.00
2	148	–	New L.B. Cole-c; PC-r	1	2	2.80	7.00	14.00
3	165	–	PC-r	1	2	1.00	2.40	6.00
4	167	4/64	PC-r	1	2	1.00	2.40	6.00
5	167	9/66	PC-r	1	2	1.00	2.40	6.00
6	169	Sm/69	New price 25¢; stiff-c; PC-r	1	2	1.00	2.40	6.00

91. The Call of the Wild

Ed	HRN	Date	Details	A	C

Classics Illustrated #91 © GIL

Classics Illustrated #95 © GIL

Classics Illustrated #101 © GIL

Ed	HRN	Date	Details	A	C	GD25	FN65	NM94
1	92	1/52	Orig.; delBourgo-a	1	1	4.25	13.00	26.00
2	112	–	PC-r	1	1	1.60	4.00	8.00
3	125	–	'Picture Progress' on back-c; PC-r	1	1	1.60	4.00	8.00
4	134	–	PC-r	1	1	1.60	4.00	8.00
5	143	–	PC-r	1	1	1.60	4.00	8.00
6	165	–	PC-r	1	1	1.60	4.00	8.00
7	167	–	PC-r	1	1	1.00	2.40	6.00
8	167	4/65	PC-r	1	1	1.00	2.40	6.00
9	167	3/66	PC-r	1	1	1.00	2.40	6.00
10	166	11/67	PC-r	1	1	1.00	2.40	6.00
11	169	Spr/70	New price 25¢; stiff-c; PC-r	1	1	1.00	2.40	6.00

92. The Courtship of Miles Standish

Ed	HRN	Date	Details	A	C	GD25	FN65	NM94
1	92	2/52	Original; Blum-c/a	1	1	4.25	13.00	26.00
2	165	–	PC-r	1	1	1.00	2.80	7.00
3	167	3/64	PC-r	1	1	1.00	2.80	7.00
4	166	5/67	PC-r	1	1	1.00	2.80	7.00
5	169	Win/69	New price 25¢ stiff-c; PC-r	1	1	1.00	2.80	7.00

93. Pudd'nhead Wilson

Ed	HRN	Date	Details	A	C	GD25	FN65	NM94
1	94	3/52	Orig.; Kiefer-c/a;	1	1	4.25	13.00	28.00
2	165	–	New-c; PC-r	1	2	2.40	6.00	12.00
3	167	3/64	PC-r	1	2	1.00	3.00	8.00
4	166	R/1968	New price 25¢; soft-c; PC-r	1	2	1.00	3.00	8.00

94. David Balfour

Ed	HRN	Date	Details	A	C	GD25	FN65	NM94
1	94	4/52	Original; Palais-a	1	1	4.25	13.00	28.00
2	167	5/64	PC-r	1	1	1.50	4.50	12.00
3	166	R/1968	C-price 25¢; PC-r	1	1	1.50	4.50	12.00

95. All Quiet on the Western Front

Ed	HRN	Date	Details	A	C	GD25	FN65	NM94
1A	96	5/52	Orig.; del Bourgo-a	1	1	9.30	28.00	70.00
1B	99	5/52	Orig.; del Bourgo-a	1	1	7.50	22.50	52.00
2	167	10/64	PC-r	1	1	2.25	6.75	18.00
3	167	11/66	PC-r	1	1	2.25	6.75	18.00

96. Daniel Boone

Ed	HRN	Date	Details	A	C	GD25	FN65	NM94
1	97	6/52	Original; Blum-a	1	1	4.00	12.00	24.00
2	117	–	PC-r	1	1	1.00	2.80	7.00
3	128	–	PC-r	1	1	1.00	2.80	7.00
4	132	–	PC-r	1	1	1.00	2.80	7.00
5	134	–	"Story of Jesus" on back-c; PC-r	1	1	1.00	2.80	7.00
6	158	–	PC-r	1	1	1.00	2.80	7.00
7	167	1/64	PC-r	1	1	1.00	2.40	6.00
8	167	5/65	PC-r	1	1	1.00	2.40	6.00
9	167	11/66	PC-r	1	1	1.00	2.40	6.00
10	166	Win/69	New-c; price 25¢; PC-r; stiff-c	1	2	1.50	4.50	12.00

97. King Solomon's Mines

Ed	HRN	Date	Details	A	C	GD25	FN65	NM94
1	96	7/52	Orig.; Kiefer-a	1	1	4.00	12.00	24.00
2	118	–	PC-r	1	1	1.60	4.00	8.00
3	131	–	PC-r	1	1	1.60	4.00	8.00
4	141	–	PC-r	1	1	1.60	4.00	8.00
5	158	–	PC-r	1	1	1.60	4.00	8.00
6	167	2/64	PC-r	1	1	1.00	2.40	6.00
7	167	9/65	PC-r	1	1	1.00	2.40	6.00
8	169	Sm/69	New price 25¢; stiff-c; PC-r	1	1	1.00	2.40	6.00

98. The Red Badge of Courage

Ed	HRN	Date	Details	A	C	GD25	FN65	NM94
1	98	8/52	Original	1	1	4.25	13.00	26.00
2	118	–	PC-r	1	1	1.60	4.00	8.00
3	132	–	PC-r	1	1	1.60	4.00	8.00
4	142	–	PC-r	1	1	1.60	4.00	8.00
5	152	–	PC-r	1	1	1.60	4.00	8.00
6	161	–	PC-r	1	1	1.00	2.40	6.00
7	167	–	Has orig.date; PC-r	1	1	1.00	2.40	6.00
8	167	9/64	PC-r	1	1	1.00	2.40	6.00
9	167	10/65	PC-r	1	1	1.00	2.40	6.00
10	166	R/1968	New-c&price 25¢; PC-r; stiff-c	1	2	2.00	6.00	16.00

99. Hamlet (Used in **POP**, pg. 102)

Ed	HRN	Date	Details	A	C	GD25	FN65	NM94
1	98	9/52	Original; Blum-a	1	1	4.25	13.00	28.00
2	121	–	PC-r	1	1	1.60	4.00	8.00
3	141	–	PC-r	1	1	1.60	4.00	8.00
4	158	–	PC-r	1	1	1.60	4.00	8.00
5	167	–	Has orig.date; PC-r	1	1	1.00	2.40	6.00
6	167	7/65	PC-r	1	1	1.00	2.40	6.00
7	166	4/67	PC-r	1	1	1.00	2.40	6.00
8	169	Spr/69	New-c&price 25¢; PC-r; stiff-c	1	2	2.00	6.00	16.00

100. Mutiny on the Bounty

Ed	HRN	Date	Details	A	C	GD25	FN65	NM94
1	100	10/52	Original	1	1	4.00	12.00	24.00
2	117	–	PC-r	1	1	1.60	4.00	8.00
3	132	–	PC-r	1	1	1.60	4.00	8.00
4	142	–	PC-r	1	1	1.60	4.00	8.00
5	155	–	PC-r	1	1	1.60	4.00	8.00
6	167	–	Has orig. date;PC-r	1	1	1.00	2.40	6.00
7	167	5/64	PC-r	1	1	1.00	2.40	6.00
8	167	3/66	PC-r	1	1	1.00	2.40	6.00
9	169	Spr/70	PC-r; stiff-c	1	1	1.00	2.40	6.00

101. William Tell

Ed	HRN	Date	Details	A	C	GD25	FN65	NM94
1	101	11/52	Original; Kiefer-c delBourgo-a	1	1	4.00	12.00	24.00
2	118	–	PC-r	1	1	1.60	4.00	8.00
3	141	–	PC-r	1	1	1.60	4.00	8.00
4	158	–	PC-r	1	1	1.60	4.00	8.00
5	167	–	Has orig.date; PC-r	1	1	1.00	2.40	6.00
6	167	11/64	PC-r	1	1	1.00	2.40	6.00
7	166	4/67	PC-r	1	1	1.00	2.40	6.00
8	169	Win/69	New price 25¢; stiff-c; PC-r	1	1	1.00	2.40	6.00

102. The White Company

Ed	HRN	Date	Details	A	C	GD25	FN65	NM94
1	101	12/52	Original; Blum-a	1	1	7.50	22.50	52.00
2	165	–	PC-r	1	1	2.50	7.50	20.00
3	167	4/64	PC-r	1	1	2.50	7.50	20.00

103. Men Against the Sea

Ed	HRN	Date	Details	A	C	GD25	FN65	NM94
1	104	1/53	Original; Kiefer-c; Palais-a	1	1	4.25	13.00	28.00
2	114	–	PC-r	1	1	3.20	8.00	16.00
3	131	–	New-c; PC-r	1	2	3.60	9.00	18.00
4	158	–	PC-r	1	2	2.40	6.00	12.00
5	149	–	White reorder list;	1	2	4.00	11.00	22.00

Classics Illustrated #104 © GIL

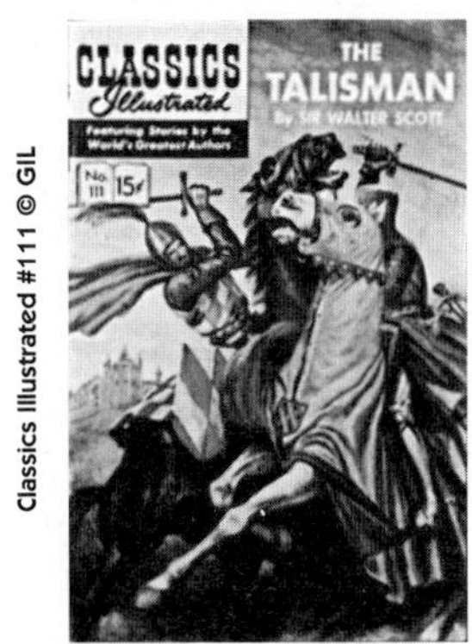

Classics Illustrated #111 © GIL

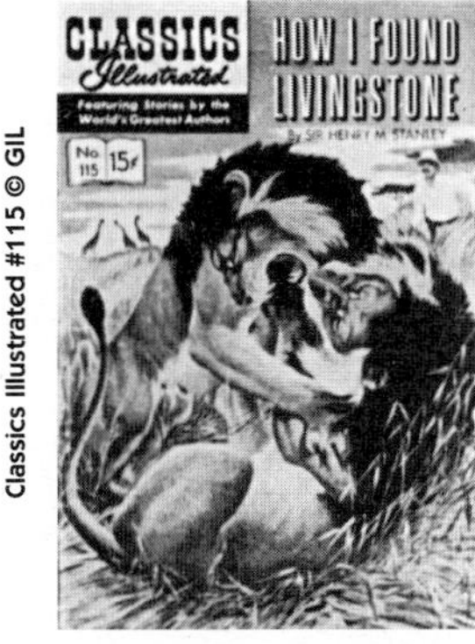

Classics Illustrated #115 © GIL

Ed	HRN	Date	Details	A	C	GD25	FN65	NM94
			came after HRN-158; PC-r					
6	167	3/64	PC-r	1	2	1.10	3.30	9.00

104. Bring 'Em Back Alive

Ed	HRN	Date	Details	A	C	GD25	FN65	NM94
1	105	2/53	Original; Kiefer-c/a	1	1	4.00	11.00	22.00
2	118	–	PC-r	1	1	1.00	2.80	7.00
3	133	–	PC-r	1	1	1.00	2.80	7.00
4	150	–	PC-r	1	1	1.00	2.80	7.00
5	158	–	PC-r	1	1	1.00	2.80	7.00
6	167	10/63	PC-r	1	1	1.00	2.40	6.00
7	167	9/65	PC-r	1	1	1.00	2.40	6.00
8	169	Win/69	New price 25¢; stiff-c; PC-r	1	1	1.00	2.40	6.00

105. From the Earth to the Moon

Ed	HRN	Date	Details	A	C	GD25	FN65	NM94
1	106	3/53	Original; Blum-a	1	1	4.00	11.00	22.00
2	118	–	PC-r	1	1	1.00	2.80	7.00
3	132	–	PC-r	1	1	1.00	2.80	7.00
4	141	–	PC-r	1	1	1.00	2.80	7.00
5	146	–	PC-r	1	1	1.00	2.80	7.00
6	156	–	PC-r	1	1	1.00	2.80	7.00
7	167	–	Has orig. date; PC-r	1	1	1.00	2.40	6.00
8	167	5/64	PC-r	1	1	1.00	2.40	6.00
9	167	5/65	PC-r	1	1	1.00	2.40	6.00
10A	166	10/67	PC-r	1	1	1.00	2.40	6.00
10B	166	10/67	w/Grit ad stapled in book	1	1	7.50	22.50	75.00
11	169	Sm/69	New price 25¢; stiff-c; PC-r	1	1	1.00	2.40	6.00
12	169	Spr/71	PC-r	1	1	1.00	2.40	6.00

106. Buffalo Bill

Ed	HRN	Date	Details	A	C	GD25	FN65	NM94
1	107	4/53	Orig.; delBourgo-a	1	1	4.00	11.00	22.00
2	118	–	PC-r	1	1	1.00	2.80	7.00
3	132	–	PC-r	1	1	1.00	2.80	7.00
4	142	–	PC-r	1	1	1.00	2.80	7.00
5	161	–	PC-r	1	1	1.00	2.40	6.00
6	167	3/64	PC-r	1	1	1.00	2.40	6.00
7	166	7/67	PC-r	1	1	1.00	2.40	6.00
8	169	Fall/69	PC-r; stiff-c	1	1	1.00	2.40	6.00

107. King of the Khyber Rifles

Ed	HRN	Date	Details	A	C	GD25	FN65	NM94
1	108	5/53	Original	1	1	4.00	12.00	24.00
2	118	–	PC-r	1	1	1.00	2.80	7.00
3	146	–	PC-r	1	1	1.00	2.80	7.00
4	158	–	PC-r	1	1	1.00	2.80	7.00
5	167	–	Has orig.date; PC-r	1	1	1.00	2.40	6.00
6	167	–	PC-r	1	1	1.00	2.40	6.00
7	167	10/66	PC-r	1	1	1.00	2.40	6.00

108. Knights of the Round Table

Ed	HRN	Date	Details	A	C	GD25	FN65	NM94
1A	108	6/53	Original; Blum-a	1	1	4.25	13.00	28.00
1B	109	6/53	Original; scarce	1	1	5.70	17.00	36.00
2	117	–	PC-r	1	1	1.00	2.80	7.00
3	165	–	PC-r	1	1	1.00	2.40	6.00
4	167	4/64	PC-r	1	1	1.00	2.40	6.00
5	166	4/67	PC-r	1	1	1.00	2.40	6.00
6	169	Sm/69	New price 25¢; stiff-c; PC-r	1	1	1.00	2.40	6.00

109. Pitcairn's Island

Ed	HRN	Date	Details	A	C	GD25	FN65	NM94
1	110	7/53	Original; Palais-a	1	1	4.25	13.00	28.00
2	165	–	PC-r	1	1	1.00	3.00	8.00
3	167	3/64	PC-r	1	1	1.00	3.00	8.00
4	166	6/67	PC-r	1	1	1.00	3.00	8.00

110. A Study in Scarlet

Ed	HRN	Date	Details	A	C	GD25	FN65	NM94
1	111	8/53	Original	1	1	10.00	30.00	75.00
2	165	–	PC-r	1	1	8.50	26.00	60.00

111. The Talisman

Ed	HRN	Date	Details	A	C	GD25	FN65	NM94
1	112	9/53	Original; last H.C. Kiefer-a	1	1	4.00	12.00	28.00
2	165	–	PC-r	1	1	1.00	2.80	7.00
3	167	5/64	PC-r	1	1	1.00	2.80	7.00
4	166	Fall/68	C-price 25¢; PC-r	1	1	1.00	2.80	7.00

112. Adventures of Kit Carson

Ed	HRN	Date	Details	A	C	GD25	FN65	NM94
1	113	10/53	Original; Palais-a	1	1	4.25	13.00	26.00
2	129	–	PC-r	1	1	1.00	2.80	7.00
3	141	–	PC-r	1	1	1.00	2.80	7.00
4	152	–	PC-r	1	1	1.00	2.80	7.00
5	161	–	PC-r	1	1	1.00	2.40	6.00
6	167	–	PC-r	1	1	1.00	2.40	6.00
7	167	2/65	PC-r	1	1	1.00	2.40	6.00
8	167	5/66	PC-r	1	1	1.00	2.40	6.00
9	166	Win/69	New-c&price 25¢; PC-r; stiff-c	1	2	1.50	4.50	12.00

113. The Forty-Five Guardsmen

Ed	HRN	Date	Details	A	C	GD25	FN65	NM94
1	114	11/53	Orig.; delBourgo-a	1	1	6.50	19.50	45.00
2	166	7/67	PC-r	1	1	2.50	7.50	25.00

114. The Red Rover

Ed	HRN	Date	Details	A	C	GD25	FN65	NM94
1	115	12/53	Original	1	1	6.50	19.50	45.00
2	166	7/67	PC-r	1	1	2.50	7.50	25.00

115. How I Found Livingstone

Ed	HRN	Date	Details	A	C	GD25	FN65	NM94
1	116	1/54	Original	1	1	8.30	25.00	58.00
2	167	1/67	PC-r	1	1	3.60	10.80	36.00

116. The Bottle Imp

Ed	HRN	Date	Details	A	C	GD25	FN65	NM94
1	117	2/54	Orig.; Cameron-a	1	1	8.30	25.00	58.00
2	167	1/67	PC-r	1	1	3.60	10.80	36.00

117. Captains Courageous

Ed	HRN	Date	Details	A	C	GD25	FN65	NM94
1	118	3/54	Orig.; Costanza-a	1	1	6.85	21.50	48.00
2	167	2/67	PC-r	1	1	2.25	6.75	18.00
3	169	Fall/69	New price 25¢; stiff-c; PC-r	1	1	2.25	6.75	18.00

118. Rob Roy

Ed	HRN	Date	Details	A	C	GD25	FN65	NM94
1	119	4/54	Original; Rudy & Walter Palais-a	1	1	8.30	25.00	58.00
2	167	2/67	PC-r	1	1	3.60	10.80	36.00

119. Soldiers of Fortune

Ed	HRN	Date	Details	A	C	GD25	FN65	NM94
1	120	5/54	Schaffenberger-a	1	1	6.00	18.00	42.00
2	166	3/67	PC-r	1	1	2.25	6.75	18.00
3	169	Spr/70	New price 25¢;	1	1	2.25	6.75	18.00

Classics Illustrated #125 © GIL

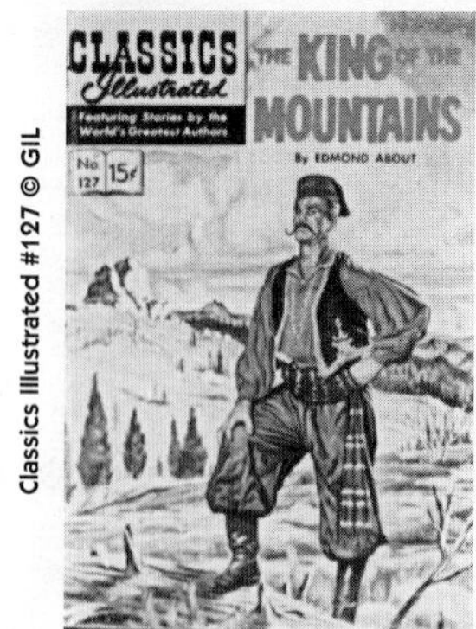

Classics Illustrated #127 © GIL

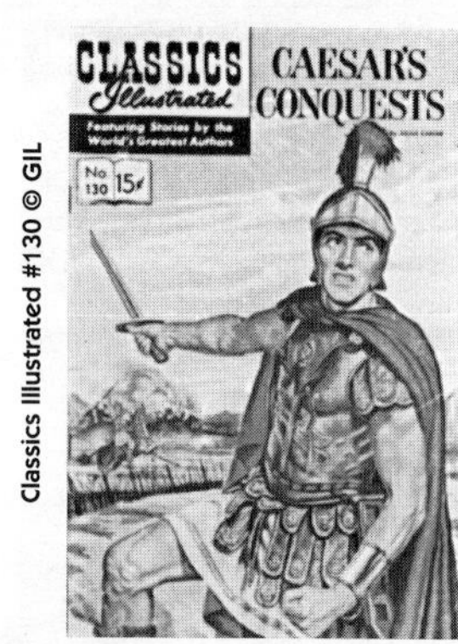

Classics Illustrated #130 © GIL

						GD25	FN65	NM94
			stiff-c; PC-r					

120. The Hurricane

Ed	HRN	Date	Details	A	C	GD25	FN65	NM94
1	121	6/54	Orig.; Cameron-a	1	1	6.00	18.00	42.00
2	166	3/67	PC-r	1	1	2.60	7.80	26.00

121. Wild Bill Hickok

Ed	HRN	Date	Details	A	C	GD25	FN65	NM94
1	122	7/54	Original	1	1	4.00	10.00	20.00
2	132	–	PC-r	1	1	1.00	2.80	7.00
3	141	–	PC-r	1	1	1.00	2.80	7.00
4	154	–	PC-r	1	1	1.00	2.80	7.00
5	167	–	PC-r	1	1	1.00	2.40	6.00
6	167	8/64	PC-r	1	1	1.00	2.40	6.00
7	166	4/67	PC-r	1	1	1.00	2.40	6.00
8	169	Win/69	PC-r; stiff-c	1	1	1.00	2.40	6.00

122. The Mutineers

Ed	HRN	Date	Details	A	C	GD25	FN65	NM94
1	123	9/54	Original	1	1	4.00	12.00	28.00
2	136	–	PC-r	1	1	1.00	2.80	7.00
3	146	–	PC-r	1	1	1.00	2.80	7.00
4	158	–	PC-r	1	1	1.00	2.80	7.00
5	167	11/63	PC-r	1	1	1.00	2.40	6.00
6	167	3/65	PC-r	1	1	1.00	2.40	6.00
7	166	8/67	PC-r	1	1	1.00	2.40	6.00

123. Fang and Claw

Ed	HRN	Date	Details	A	C	GD25	FN65	NM94
1	124	11/54	Original	1	1	4.00	12.00	28.00
2	133	–	PC-r	1	1	1.00	2.80	7.00
3	143	–	PC-r	1	1	1.00	2.80	7.00
4	154	–	PC-r	1	1	1.00	2.80	7.00
5	167	–	Has orig.date; PC-r	1	1	1.00	2.40	6.00
6	167	9/65	PC-r	1	1	1.00	2.40	6.00

124. The War of the Worlds

Ed	HRN	Date	Details	A	C	GD25	FN65	NM94
1	125	1/55	Original; Cameron-c/a	1	1	5.70	17.00	36.00
2	131	–	PC-r	1	1	1.60	4.00	8.00
3	141	–	PC-r	1	1	1.60	4.00	8.00
4	148	–	PC-r	1	1	1.60	4.00	8.00
5	156	–	PC-r	1	1	1.60	4.00	8.00
6	165	–	PC-r	1	1	2.00	5.00	10.00
7	167	–	PC-r	1	1	1.40	3.50	7.00
8	167	11/64	PC-r	1	1	1.00	3.00	8.00
9	167	11/65	PC-r	1	1	1.00	2.80	7.00
10	166	R/1968	C-price 25¢; PC-r	1	1	1.00	2.80	7.00
11	169	Sm/70	PC-r; stiff-c	1	1	1.00	2.80	7.00

125. The Ox Bow Incident

Ed	HRN	Date	Details	A	C	GD25	FN65	NM94
1	3/55	–	Original; Picture Progress replaces reorder list	1	1	4.00	10.00	20.00
2	143	–	PC-r	1	1	1.40	3.50	7.00
3	152	–	PC-r	1	1	1.40	3.50	7.00
4	149	–	PC-r	1	1	1.40	3.50	7.00
5	167	–	PC-r	1	1	1.00	2.40	6.00
6	167	11/64	PC-r	1	1	1.00	2.40	6.00
7	166	4/67	PC-r	1	1	1.00	2.40	6.00
8	169	Win/69	New price 25¢; stiff-c; PC-r	1	1	1.00	2.40	6.00

126. The Downfall

Ed	HRN	Date	Details	A	C	GD25	FN65	NM94
1	5/55	–	Orig.; 'Picture Progress' replaces reorder list; Cameron-c/a	1	1	4.00	12.00	28.00
2	167	8/64	PC-r	1	1	1.25	3.75	10.00
3	166	R/1968	C-price 25¢; PC-r	1	1	1.25	3.75	10.00

127. The King of the Mountains

Ed	HRN	Date	Details	A	C	GD25	FN65	NM94
1	128	7/55	Original	1	1	4.00	12.00	28.00
2	167	6/64	PC-r	1	1	1.10	3.30	9.00
3	166	F/1968	C-price 25¢; PC-r	1	1	1.10	3.30	9.00

128. Macbeth (Used in **POP**, pg. 102)

Ed	HRN	Date	Details	A	C	GD25	FN65	NM94
1	128	9/55	Orig.; last Blum-a	1	1	4.00	12.00	28.00
2	143	–	PC-r	1	1	1.40	3.50	7.00
3	158	–	PC-r	1	1	1.40	3.50	7.00
4	167	–	PC-r	1	1	1.00	2.40	6.00
5	167	6/64	PC-r	1	1	1.00	2.40	6.00
6	166	4/67	PC-r	1	1	1.00	2.40	6.00
7	166	R/1968	C-Price 25¢; PC-r	1	1	1.00	2.40	6.00
8	169	Spr/70	Stiff-c; PC-r	1	1	1.00	2.40	6.00

129. Davy Crockett

Ed	HRN	Date	Details	A	C	GD25	FN65	NM94
1	129	11/55	Orig.; Cameron-a	1	1	10.00	30.00	75.00
2	167	9/66	PC-r	1	1	8.50	26.00	60.00

130. Caesar's Conquests

Ed	HRN	Date	Details	A	C	GD25	FN65	NM94
1	130	1/56	Original; Orlando-a	1	1	5.35	16.00	32.00
2	142	–	PC-r	1	1	1.40	3.50	7.00
3	152	–	PC-r	1	1	1.40	3.50	7.00
4	149	–	PC-r	1	1	1.40	3.50	7.00
5	167	–	PC-r	1	1	1.00	2.40	6.00
6	167	10/64	PC-r	1	1	1.00	2.40	6.00
7	167	4/66	PC-r	1	1	1.00	2.40	6.00

131. The Covered Wagon

Ed	HRN	Date	Details	A	C	GD25	FN65	NM94
1	131	3/56	Original	1	1	4.00	10.00	20.00
2	143	–	PC-r	1	1	1.40	3.50	7.00
3	152	–	PC-r	1	1	1.40	3.50	7.00
4	158	–	PC-r	1	1	1.40	3.50	7.00
5	167	–	PC-r	1	1	1.00	2.40	6.00
6	167	11/64	PC-r	1	1	1.00	2.40	6.00
7	167	4/66	PC-r	1	1	1.00	2.40	6.00
8	169	Win/69	New price 25¢; stiff-c; PC-r	1	1	1.00	2.40	6.00

132. The Dark Frigate

Ed	HRN	Date	Details	A	C	GD25	FN65	NM94
1	132	5/56	Original	1	1	4.00	12.00	28.00
2	150	–	PC-r	1	1	1.80	4.50	9.00
3	167	1/64	PC-r	1	1	1.00	3.00	8.00
4	166	5/67	PC-r	1	1	1.00	3.00	8.00

133. The Time Machine

Ed	HRN	Date	Details	A	C	GD25	FN65	NM94
1	132	7/56	Orig.; Cameron-a	1	1	5.35	16.00	32.00
2	142	–	PC-r	1	1	1.80	4.50	9.00
3	152	–	PC-r	1	1	1.80	4.50	9.00
4	158	–	PC-r	1	1	1.80	4.50	9.00
5	167	–	PC-r	1	1	1.60	4.00	8.00
6	167	6/64	PC-r	1	1	1.25	3.75	10.00
7	167	3/66	PC-r	1	1	1.00	3.00	8.00
8	166	12/67	PC-r	1	1	1.00	3.00	8.00
9	169	Win/71	New price 25¢; stiff-c; PC-r	1	1	1.00	3.00	8.00

Classics Illustrated #132 © GIL

Classics Illustrated #140 © GIL

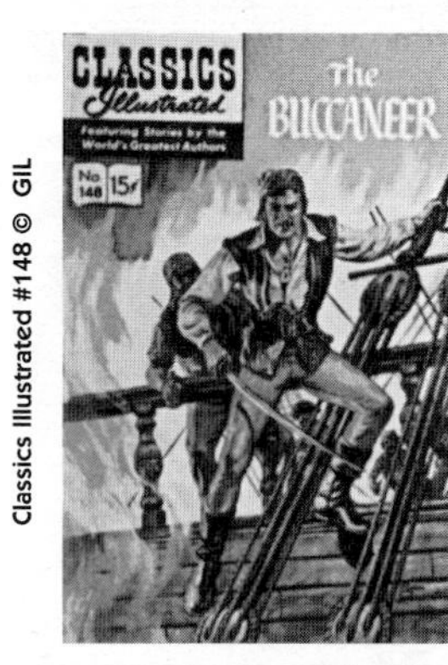

Classics Illustrated #148 © GIL

134. Romeo and Juliet

Ed	HRN	Date	Details	A	C	GD25	FN65	NM94
1	134	9/56	Original; Evans-a	1	1	4.00	12.00	28.00
2	161	–	PC-r	1	1	1.40	3.50	7.00
3	167	9/63	PC-r	1	1	1.00	2.40	6.00
4	167	5/65	PC-r	1	1	1.00	2.40	6.00
5	166	6/67	PC-r	1	1	1.00	2.40	6.00
6	166	Win/69	New c&price 25¢; stiff-c; PC-r	1	2	2.50	7.50	20.00

135. Waterloo

Ed	HRN	Date	Details	A	C	GD25	FN65	NM94
1	135	11/56	Orig.; G. Ingels-a	1	1	4.00	12.00	28.00
2	153	–	PC-r	1	1	1.40	3.50	7.00
3	167	–	PC-r	1	1	1.00	2.40	6.00
4	167	9/64	PC-r	1	1	1.00	2.40	6.00
5	166	R/1968	C-price 25¢; PC-r	1	1	1.00	2.40	6.00

136. Lord Jim

Ed	HRN	Date	Details	A	C	GD25	FN65	NM94
1	136	1/57	Original; Evans-a	1	1	4.00	12.00	28.00
2	165	–	PC-r	1	1	1.00	2.40	6.00
3	167	3/64	PC-r	1	1	1.00	2.40	6.00
4	167	9/66	PC-r	1	1	1.00	2.40	6.00
5	169	Sm/69	New price 25 ¢; stiff-c; PC-r	1	1	1.00	2.40	6.00

137. The Little Savage

Ed	HRN	Date	Details	A	C	GD25	FN65	NM94
1	136	3/57	Original; Evans-a	1	1	4.00	12.00	28.00
2	148	–	PC-r	1	1	1.40	3.50	7.00
3	156	–	PC-r	1	1	1.40	3.50	7.00
4	167	–	PC-r	1	1	1.00	2.40	6.00
5	167	10/64	PC-r	1	1	1.00	2.40	6.00
6	166	8/67	PC-r	1	1	1.00	2.40	6.00
7	169	Spr/70	New price 25¢; stiff-c; PC-r	1	1	1.00	2.40	6.00

138. A Journey to the Center of the Earth

Ed	HRN	Date	Details	A	C	GD25	FN65	NM94
1	136	5/57	Original	1	1	5.70	17.00	38.00
2	146	–	PC-r	1	1	1.40	3.50	7.00
3	156	–	PC-r	1	1	1.40	3.50	7.00
4	158	–	PC-r	1	1	1.40	3.50	7.00
5	167	–	PC-r	1	1	1.20	3.00	6.00
6	167	6/64	PC-r	1	1	1.00	3.00	8.00
7	167	4/66	PC-r	1	1	1.00	3.00	8.00
8	166	R/68	C-price 25¢; PC-r	1	1	1.00	2.40	6.00

139. In the Reign of Terror

Ed	HRN	Date	Details	A	C	GD25	FN65	NM94
1	139	7/57	Original; Evans-a	1	1	3.60	9.00	18.00
2	154	–	PC-r	1	1	1.60	4.00	8.00
3	167	–	Has orig.date; PC-r	1	1	1.20	3.00	6.00
4	167	7/64	PC-r	1	1	1.00	2.40	6.00
5	166	R/1968	C-price 25¢; PC-r	1	1	1.00	2.40	6.00

140. On Jungle Trails

Ed	HRN	Date	Details	A	C	GD25	FN65	NM94
1	140	9/57	Original	1	1	3.60	9.00	18.00
2	150	–	PC-r	1	1	1.40	3.50	7.00
3	160	–	PC-r	1	1	1.40	3.50	7.00
4	167	9/63	PC-r	1	1	1.00	2.40	6.00
5	167	9/65	PC-r	1	1	1.00	2.40	6.00

141. Castle Dangerous

Ed	HRN	Date	Details	A	C	GD25	FN65	NM94
1	141	11/57	Original	1	1	5.70	17.00	35.00
2	152	–	PC-r	1	1	1.40	3.50	7.00
3	167	–	PC-r	1	1	1.40	3.50	7.00
4	166	7/67	PC-r	1	1	1.00	2.80	7.00

142. Abraham Lincoln

Ed	HRN	Date	Details	A	C	GD25	FN65	NM94
1	142	1/58	Original	1	1	5.35	16.00	32.00
2	154	–	PC-r	1	1	1.40	3.50	7.00
3	158	–	PC-r	1	1	1.40	3.50	7.00
4	167	10/63	PC-r	1	1	1.00	2.40	6.00
5	167	7/65	PC-r	1	1	1.00	2.40	6.00
6	166	11/67	PC-r	1	1	1.00	2.40	6.00
7	169	Fall/69	New price 25¢; stiff-c; PC-r	1	1	1.00	2.40	6.00

143. Kim

Ed	HRN	Date	Details	A	C	GD25	FN65	NM94
1	143	3/58	Original; Orlando-a	1	1	4.15	12.50	25.00
2	165	–	PC-r	1	1	1.20	3.00	6.00
3	167	11/63	PC-r	1	1	1.00	2.40	6.00
4	167	8/65	PC-r	1	1	1.00	2.40	6.00
5	169	Win/69	New price 25¢; stiff-c; PC-r	1	1	1.00	2.40	6.00

144. The First Men in the Moon

Ed	HRN	Date	Details	A	C	GD25	FN65	NM94
1	143	5/58	Original; Woodbridge/Williamson/Torres-a	1	1	4.00	12.00	28.00
2	152	–	(Rare)-PC-r	1	1	6.00	18.00	42.00
3	153	–	PC-r	1	1	1.40	3.50	7.00
4	161	–	PC-r	1	1	1.20	3.00	6.00
5	167	–	PC-r	1	1	1.20	3.00	6.00
6	167	12/65	PC-r	1	1	1.00	2.40	6.00
7	166	Fall/68	New-c&price 25¢; PC-r; stiff-c	1	2	1.75	5.25	14.00
8	169	Win/69	Stiff-c; PC-r	1	2	1.25	3.75	10.00

145. The Crisis

Ed	HRN	Date	Details	A	C	GD25	FN65	NM94
1	143	7/58	Original; Evans-a	1	1	4.00	12.00	28.00
2	156	–	PC-r	1	1	1.40	3.50	7.00
3	167	10/63	PC-r	1	1	1.00	2.40	6.00
4	167	3/65	PC-r	1	1	1.00	2.40	6.00
5	166	R/68	C-price 25¢; PC-r	1	1	1.00	2.40	6.00

146. With Fire and Sword

Ed	HRN	Date	Details	A	C	GD25	FN65	NM94
1	143	9/58	Original; Woodbridge-a	1	1	5.35	16.00	32.00
2	156	–	PC-r	1	1	2.00	5.00	10.00
3	167	11/63	PC-r	1	1	1.10	3.30	9.00
4	167	3/65	PC-r	1	1	1.10	3.30	9.00

147. Ben-Hur

Ed	HRN	Date	Details	A	C	GD25	FN65	NM94
1	147	11/58	Original; Orlando-a	1	1	4.15	12.50	25.00
2	152	–	Scarce; PC-r	1	1	5.00	15.00	30.00
3	153	–	PC-r	1	1	1.40	3.50	7.00
4	158	–	PC-r	1	1	1.40	3.50	7.00
5	167	–	Orig.date; but PC-r	1	1	1.20	3.00	6.00
6	167	2/65	PC-r	1	1	1.00	2.40	6.00
7	167	9/66	PC-r	1	1	1.00	2.40	6.00
8A	166	Fall/68	New-c&price 25¢; PC-r; soft-c	1	2	2.25	6.75	18.00
8B	166	Fall/68	New-c&price 25¢; PC-r; stiff-c; scarce	1	2	3.00	9.00	30.00

148. The Buccaneer

Ed	HRN	Date	Details	A	C	GD25	FN65	NM94

Classics Illustrated #149 © GIL

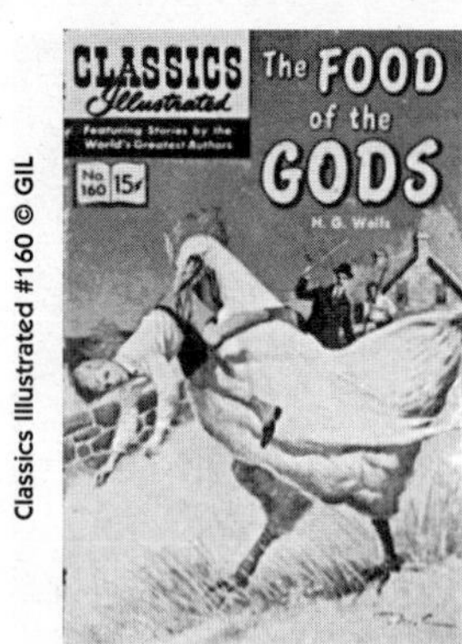

Classics Illustrated #160 © GIL

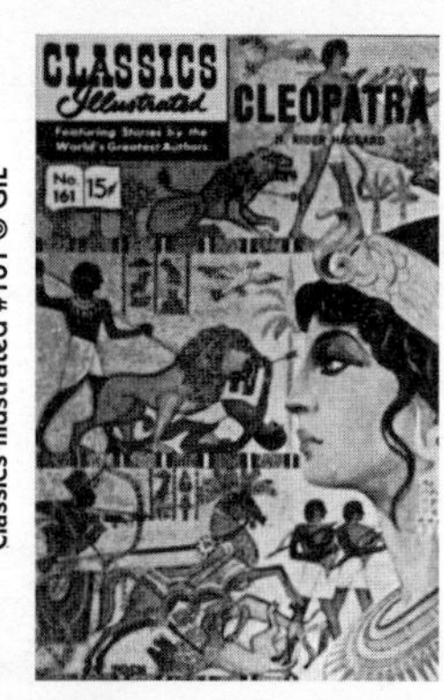

Classics Illustrated #161 © GIL

Ed	HRN	Date	Details	A	C	GD25	FN65	NM94
1	148	1/59	Orig.; Evans/Jenny-a; Saunders-c	1	1	4.15	12.50	25.00
2	568	–	Juniors list only PC-r	1	1	1.80	4.50	9.00
3	167	–	PC-r	1	1	1.20	3.00	6.00
4	167	9/65	PC-r	1	1	1.00	2.40	6.00
5	169	Sm/69	New price 25¢; PC-r; stiff-c	1	1	1.00	2.40	6.00

149. Off on a Comet

Ed	HRN	Date	Details	A	C	GD25	FN65	NM94
1	149	3/59	Orig.;G.McCann-a; blue reorder list	1	1	4.00	12.00	28.00
2	155	–	PC-r	1	1	1.40	3.50	7.00
3	149	–	PC-r; white reorder list; no coming-next ad	1	1	1.40	3.50	7.00
4	167	12/63	PC-r	1	1	1.00	2.40	6.00
5	167	2/65	PC-r	1	1	1.00	2.40	6.00
6	167	10/66	PC-r	1	1	1.00	2.40	6.00
7	166	Fall/68	New-c & price 25¢; PC-r	1	2	2.00	6.00	16.00

150. The Virginian

Ed	HRN	Date	Details	A	C	GD25	FN65	NM94
1	150	5/59	Original	1	1	5.70	17.00	36.00
2	164	–	PC-r	1	1	3.00	7.50	15.00
3	167	10/63	PC-r	1	1	2.50	7.50	20.00
4	167	12/65	PC-r	1	1	1.85	5.50	15.00

151. Won By the Sword

Ed	HRN	Date	Details	A	C	GD25	FN65	NM94
1	150	7/59	Original	1	1	5.35	16.00	32.00
2	164	–	PC-r	1	1	2.40	6.00	12.00
3	167	10/63	PC-r	1	1	1.50	4.50	12.00
4	166	7/67	PC-r	1	1	1.50	4.50	12.00

152. Wild Animals I Have Known

Ed	HRN	Date	Details	A	C	GD25	FN65	NM94
1	152	9/59	Orig.; L.B. Cole c/a	1	1	5.70	17.00	38.00
2A	149	–	PC-r; white reorder list; no coming-next ad; IBC: Jr. list #572	1	1	1.40	3.50	7.00
2B	149	–	PC-r; inside-bc: Jr. list to #555	1	1	1.60	4.00	8.00
2C	149	–	PC-r; inside-bc: has World Around Us ad; scarce	1	1	3.60	9.00	18.00
3	167	9/63	PC-r	1	1	1.00	2.40	6.00
4	167	8/65	PC-r	1	1	1.00	2.40	6.00
5	169	Fall/69	New price 25¢; stiff-c; PC-r	1	1	1.00	2.40	6.00

153. The Invisible Man

Ed	HRN	Date	Details	A	C	GD25	FN65	NM94
1	153	11/59	Original	1	1	5.70	17.00	38.00
2A	149	–	PC-r; white reorder list; no coming-next ad; inside-bc: Jr. list to #572	1	1	1.00	2.00	7.00
2B	149	–	PC-r; inside-bc: Jr. list to #555	1	1	1.40	3.50	8.00
3	167	–	PC-r	1	1	1.20	3.00	6.00
4	167	2/65	PC-r	1	1	1.00	2.40	6.00
5	167	9/66	PC-r	1	1	1.00	2.40	6.00
6	166	Win/69	New price 25¢; PC-r; stiff-c	1	1	1.00	2.40	6.00
7	169	Spr/71	Stiff-c; letters spelling 'Invisible Man' are 'solid' not 'invisible;' PC-r	1	1	1.00	2.40	6.00

154. The Conspiracy of Pontiac

Ed	HRN	Date	Details	A	C	GD25	FN65	NM94
1	154	1/60	Original	1	1	3.80	11.40	38.00
2	167	11/63	PC-r	1	1	1.75	5.25	14.00
3	167	7/64	PC-r	1	1	1.75	5.25	14.00
4	166	12/67	PC-r	1	1	1.75	5.25	14.00

155. The Lion of the North

Ed	HRN	Date	Details	A	C	GD25	FN65	NM94
1	154	3/60	Original	1	1	3.20	9.60	32.00
2	167	1/64	PC-r	1	1	1.50	4.50	12.00
3	166	R/1967	C-price 25¢; PC-r	1	1	1.25	3.75	10.00

156. The Conquest of Mexico

Ed	HRN	Date	Details	A	C	GD25	FN65	NM94
1	156	5/60	Orig.; Bruno Premiani-c/a	1	1	3.20	9.60	32.00
2	167	1/64	PC-r	1	1	1.10	3.30	9.00
3	166	8/67	PC-r	1	1	1.10	3.30	9.00
4	169	Spr/70	New price 25¢; stiff-c; PC-r	1	1	1.00	2.40	6.00

157. Lives of the Hunted

Ed	HRN	Date	Details	A	C	GD25	FN65	NM94
1	156	7/60	Orig.; L.B. Cole-c	1	1	3.80	11.40	38.00
2	167	2/64	PC-r	1	1	1.75	5.25	14.00
3	166	10/67	PC-r	1	1	1.75	5.25	14.00

158. The Conspirators

Ed	HRN	Date	Details	A	C	GD25	FN65	NM94
1	156	9/60	Original	1	1	3.60	10.80	36.00
2	167	7/64	PC-r	1	1	1.75	5.25	14.00
3	166	10/67	PC-r	1	1	1.75	5.25	14.00

159. The Octopus

Ed	HRN	Date	Details	A	C	GD25	FN65	NM94
1	159	11/60	Orig.; Gray Morrow-a; L.B. Cole-c	1	1	3.60	10.80	36.00
2	167	2/64	PC-r	1	1	1.50	4.50	12.00
3	166	R/1967	C-price 25¢; PC-r	1	1	1.50	4.50	12.00

160. The Food of the Gods

Ed	HRN	Date	Details	A	C	GD25	FN65	NM94
1A	159	1/61	Original	1	1	3.80	11.40	38.00
1B	160	1/61	Original; same, except for HRN	1	1	3.50	10.50	35.00
2	167	1/64	PC-r	1	1	1.50	4.50	12.00
3	166	6/67	PC-r	1	1	1.50	4.50	12.00

161. Cleopatra

Ed	HRN	Date	Details	A	C	GD25	FN65	NM94
1	161	3/61	Original	1	1	3.80	11.40	38.00
2	167	1/64	PC-r	1	1	2.00	6.00	16.00
3	166	8/67	PC-r	1	1	2.00	6.00	16.00

162. Robur the Conqueror

Ed	HRN	Date	Details	A	C	GD25	FN65	NM94
1	162	5/61	Original	1	1	3.80	11.40	38.00
2	167	7/64	PC-r	1	1	1.75	5.25	14.00
3	166	8/67	PC-r	1	1	1.75	5.25	14.00

163. Master of the World

Ed	HRN	Date	Details	A	C	GD25	FN65	NM94
1	163	7/61	Original; Gray Morrow-a	1	1	3.60	9.60	36.00
2	167	1/65	PC-r	1	1	1.75	5.25	14.00

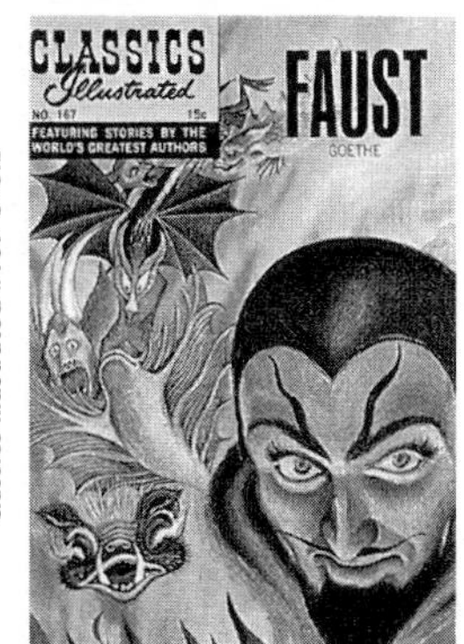

Classics Illustrated #167 © GIL

Classics Illustrated #168 © GIL

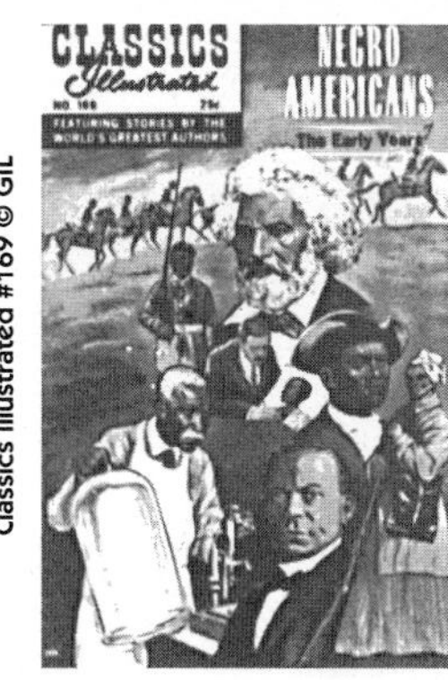

Classics Illustrated #169 © GIL

						GD25	FN65	NM94
3	166	R/1968	C-price 25¢; PC-r	1	1	1.75	5.25	14.00

164. The Cossack Chief

Ed	HRN	Date	Details	A	C			
1	164	(1961)	Orig.; nd(10/61?)	1	1	3.60	10.50	36.00
2	167	4/65	PC-r	1	1	1.75	5.25	14.00
3	166	Fall/68	C-price 25¢; PC-r	1	1	1.75	5.25	14.00

165. The Queen's Necklace

Ed	HRN	Date	Details	A	C			
1	164	1/62	Original; Morrow-a	1	1	3.60	10.50	36.00
2	167	4/65	PC-r	1	1	1.75	5.25	14.00
3	166	Fall/68	C-price 25¢; PC-r	1	1	1.75	5.25	14.00

166. Tigers and Traitors

Ed	HRN	Date	Details	A	C			
1	165	5/62	Original	1	1	6.50	19.50	65.00
2	167	2/64	PC-r	1	1	2.50	7.50	22.00
3	167	11/66	PC-r	1	1	2.50	7.50	22.00

167. Faust

Ed	HRN	Date	Details	A	C			
1	165	8/62	Original	1	1	9.00	27.00	90.00
2	167	2/64	PC-r	1	1	3.80	11.40	38.00
3	166	6/67	PC-r	1	1	3.80	11.40	38.00

168. In Freedom's Cause

Ed	HRN	Date	Details	A	C			
1	169	Win/69	Original; Evans/ Crandall-a; stiff-c; 25¢; no coming-next ad;	1	1	11.50	34.00	115.00

169. Negro Americans The Early Years

Ed	HRN	Date	Details	A	C			
1	166	Spr/69	Orig. & last issue; 25¢; Stiff-c; no coming-next ad; other sources indicate publication date of 5/69	1	1	8.00	24.00	80.00
2	169	Spr/69	Stiff-c	1	1	4.20	12.60	42.00

NOTE: *Many other titles were prepared or planned but were only issued in British/European series.*

CLASSIC PUNISHER (Also see Punisher)
Marvel Comics: Dec, 1989 ($4.95, B&W, deluxe format, 68 pgs.)

1-Reprints Marvel Super Action #1 & Marvel Preview #2 plus new story 5.00

CLASSICS GIVEAWAYS (Arranged in chronological order)

12/41–Walter Theatre Enterprises (Huntington, WV) giveaway containing #2 (orig.) w/new generic-c (only 1 known copy) 113.00 339.00 900.00

1942–Double Comics containing CC#1 (orig.) (diff. cover) (not actually a giveaway) (very rare) (also see Double Comics) (only one known copy) 218.00 654.00 1850.00

12/42–Saks 34th St. Giveaway containing CC#7 (orig.) (diff. cover) (very rare; only 6 known copies) 714.00 2142.00 5000.00

2/43–American Comics containing CC#8 (orig.) (Liberty Theatre giveaway) (different cover) (only one known copy) (see American Comics) 163.00 490.00 1300.00

12/44–Robin Hood Flour Co. Giveaway - #7-CC(R) (diff. cover) (rare) (edition probably 5 [22]) 300.00 900.00 2400.00

NOTE: How are above editions determined without CC covers? 1942 is dated 1942, and CC#1-first reprint did not come out until 5/43. 12/42 and 2/43 are determined by blue note at bottom of first text page only in original edition. 12/44 is estimated from page width each reprint edition had progressively slightly smaller page width.

1951–Shelter Thru the Ages (C.I. Educational Series) (actually Giveaway by the Ruberoid Co.) (16 pgs.) (contains original artwork by H. C. Kiefer) (there are 5 diff. back cover ad variations: "Ranch" house ad, "Igloo" ad, "Doll House" ad, "Tree House" ad & blank)(scarce) 88.00 264.00 700.00

1952–George Daynor Biography Giveaway (CC logo) (partly comic book/ pictures/newspaper articles) (story of man who built Palace Depression out of junkyard swamp in NJ) (64 pgs.)(very rare; only 3 known copies, one missing-bc) 857.00 2571.00 6300.00

1953–Westinghouse/Dreams of a Man (C.I. Educational Series) (Westinghouse bio./Westinghouse Co. giveaway) (contains original artwork by H. C. Kiefer) (16 pgs.) (also French/Spanish/Italian versions) (scarce) 84.00 252.00 675.00

NOTE: Reproductions of 1951, 1952, and 1953 exist with color photocopy covers and black & white photocopy interior ("W.C.N. Reprint") 2.00 5.00 10.00

1951-53–Coward Shoe Giveaways (all editions very rare); 2 variations of back-c ad exist:

With back-c photo ad: 5 (87), 12 (89), 22 (85), 32 (85),49 (85), 69 (87), 72 (no HRN), 80 (0), 91 (0), 92 (0), 96 (0), 98 (0), 100 (0), 101 (0), 103-105 (all Os) 42.00 126.00 340.00

With back-c cartoon ad: 106-109 (all 0s), 110 (111), 112 (0) 47.00 141.00 400.00

1956–Ben Franklin 5-10 Store Giveaway (#65-PC with back cover ad) (scarce) 39.00 117.00 290.00

1956–Ben Franklin Insurance Co. Giveaway (#65-PC with diff. back cover ad) (very rare) 71.00 213.00 600.00

11/56–Sealtest Co. Edition - #4 (135) (identical to regular edition except for Sealtest logo printed, not stamped, on front cover) (only two copies known to exist) 43.00 129.00 350.00

1958–Get-Well Giveaway containing #15-CI (new cartoon-type cover) (Pressman Pharmacy) (only one copy known to exist) 39.00 117.00 300.00

1967-68–Twin Circle Giveaway Editions - all HRN 166, with back cover ad for National Catholic Press.

	GD25	FN65	NM94
2(R68), 4(R67), 10(R68), 13(R68)	3.00	9.00	30.00
48(R67), 128(R68), 535(576-R68)	3.50	10.50	35.00
16(R68), 68(R67)	5.00	15.00	50.00

12/69–Christmas Giveaway ("A Christmas Adventure") (reprints Picture Parade #4-1953, new cover) (4 ad variations)

	GD25	FN65	NM94
Stacy's Dept. Store	2.50	7.50	25.00
Anne & Hope Store	5.50	16.50	55.00
Gibson's Dept. Store (rare)	5.50	16.50	55.00
"Merry Christmas" & blank ad space	2.50	7.50	25.00

CLASSICS ILLUSTRATED
First Publishing/Berkley Publishing: Feb, 1990 - No. 27, July, 1991 ($3.75/$3.95, 52 pgs.)

1-17: 1-Gahan Wilson-c/a. 4-Sienkiewicz painted-c/a. 6-Russell scripts/ layouts. 7-Spiegle-a. 9-Ploog-c/a. 16-Staton-a 3.75

18-27: 18-Gahan Wilson-c/a; begin $3.95-c. 20-Geary-a. 26-Aesop's Fables (6/91). 26,27-Direct sale only 4.00

CLASSICS ILLUSTRATED
Acclaim Books/Twin Circle PublishingCo.: Feb, 1997 - Present ($4.99, digest-size) (Each book contains study notes)

A Christmas Carol-(12/97), A Connecticut Yankee in King Arthur's Court-(5/97), All Quiet on the Western Front-(1/98), A Midsummer's Night Dream-(4/97) Around the World in 80 Days-(1/98), A Tale of Two Cities-(2/97)Joe Orlando-r, Captains Courageous-(11/97), Crime and Punishment-(3/97), Dr. Jekyll and Mr. Hyde-(10/97), Don Quixote-(12/97), Frankenstein-(10/97), Great Expectations-(4/97), Hamlet-(3/97), Huckleberry Finn-(3/97), Jane Eyre-(2/97), Kidnapped-(1/98), Les Miserables-(5/97), Lord Jim-(9/97), Macbeth-(5/97), Moby Dick-(4/97), Oliver Twist-(5/97), Robinson Crusoe-(9/97), Romeo & Juliet-(2/97), Silas Marner-(11/97), The Call of the Wild-(9/97), The Count of Monte Cristo-(1/98), The House of the Seven Gables-(9/97), The Iliad-(12/97), The Invisible Man-(10/97), The Last of the Mohicans-(12/97), The Master of Ballantrae-(11/97), The Odyssey-(3/97), The Prince and the Pauper-(4/97), The Red Badge Of Courage-(9/97), Tom Sawyer-(2/97) Wuthering Heights-(11/97) 5.00

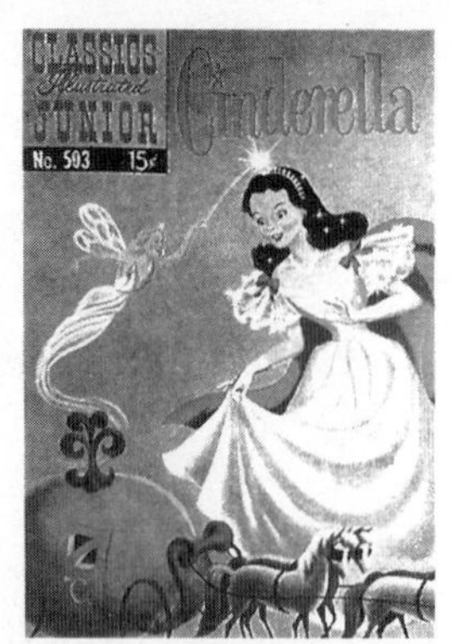

Classics Illustrated Junior #503 © GIL

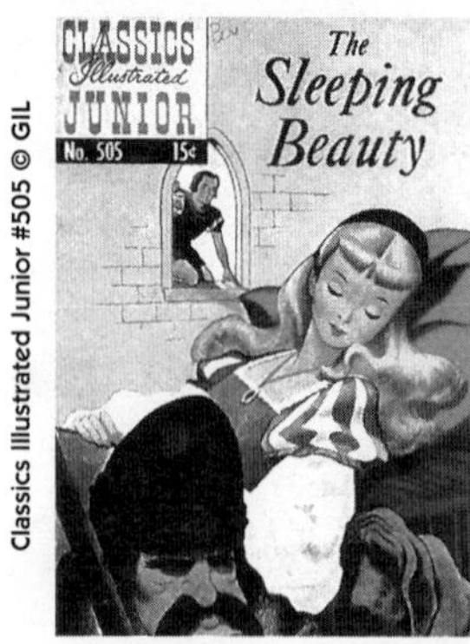

Classics Illustrated Junior #505 © GIL

Classics Illustrated Special Issue #141A © GIL

GD25 FN65 NM94

NOTE: *Stories reprinted from the original Gilberton Classic Comics and Classics Illustrated.*

CLASSICS ILLUSTRATED GIANTS
Gilberton Publications: Oct, 1949 (One-Shots - "OS")
These Giant Editions, all with new Kiefer front and back covers, were advertised from 10/49 to 2/52. They were 50¢ on the newsstand and 60¢ by mail. They are actually four Classics in one volume. All the stories are reprints of the Classics Illustrated Series. NOTE: There were also British hardback Adventure & Indian Giants in 1952, with the same covers but different contents: Adventure - 2, 7, 10; Indian - 17, 22, 37, 58. They are also rare.
"An Illustrated Library of Great Adventure Stories" - reprints of No. 6,7,8,10 (Rare); Kiefer-c 129.00 387.00 1100.00
"An Illustrated Library of Exciting Mystery Stories" - reprints of No. 30,21,40, 13 (Rare) 141.00 423.00 1200.00
"An Illustrated Library of Great Indian Stories" - reprints of No. 4,17,22,37 (Rare) 129.00 387.00 1100.00

INTRODUCTION TO CLASSICS ILLUSTRATED JUNIOR

Collectors of Juniors can be put into one of two categories: those who want any copy of each title, and those who want all the originals. Those seeking every original and reprint edition are a limited group, primarily because Juniors have no changes in art or covers to spark interest, and because reprints are so low in value it is difficult to get dealers to look for specific reprint editions.

In recent years it has become apparent that most serious Classics collectors seek Junior originals. Those seeking reprints seek them for low cost. This has made the previous note about the comparative market value of reprints inadequate. Most dealers report difficulty in moving reprints for more than $2-$4 for mint copies. Some may be worth $5-$7, just because of the popularity of the title, such as Snow White, Sleeping Beauty, and Wizard of Oz. Others may be worth $5-$7, because of the scarcity of particular title nos., such as 514, 560, 562, 575 & 576. Three particular reprint editions are worth even more. For the 535-Twin Circle edition, see Giveaways. There are also reprint editions of 501 and 503 which have a full-page bc ad for the very rare Junior record. Those may sell as high as $10-$15 in mint. Original editions of 557 and 558 also have that ad.

There are no reprint editions of 577. The only edition, from 1969, is a 25 cent stiff-cover edition with no ad for the next issue. All other original editions have coming-next ad. But 577, like C.I. #168, was prepared in 1962 but not issued. Copies of 577 can be found in 1963 British/European series, which then continued with dozens of additional new Junior titles.

PRICES LISTED BELOW ARE FOR ORIGINAL EDITIONS, WHICH HAVE AN AD FOR THE NEXT ISSUE.

NOTE: *Non HRN 576 copies- many are written on or colored . Reprints with 576 HRN are worth about 1/3 original prices. All other HRN #'s are 1/2 original price*

CLASSICS ILLUSTRATED JUNIOR
Famous Authors Ltd. (Gilberton Publications): Oct, 1953 - Spring, 1971
501-Snow White & the Seven Dwarfs; Alex Blum-a 9.30 28.00 65.00
502-The Ugly Duckling 5.70 17.00 40.00
503-Cinderella 4.00 12.00 24.00
504-512: 504-The Pied Piper. 505-The Sleeping Beauty. 506-The Three Little Pigs. 507-Jack & the Beanstalk. 508-Goldilocks & the Three Bears. 509-Beauty and the Beast. 510-Little Red Riding Hood. 511-Puss-N Boots. 512-Rumpelstiltskin 3.60 9.00 18.00
513-Pinocchio 4.00 12.00 24.00
514-The Steadfast Tin Soldier 5.70 17.00 36.00
515-Johnny Appleseed 3.60 9.00 18.00
516-Aladdin and His Lamp 4.00 12.00 24.00
517-519: 517-The Emperor's New Clothes. 518-The Golden Goose. 519-Paul Bunyan 3.60 9.00 18.00
520-Thumbelina 4.00 12.00 24.00
521-King of the Golden River 3.60 9.00 18.00
522,523,528,530: 522-The Nightingale. 523-The Gallant Tailor. 528-The Penny Prince. 530-The Golden Bird 3.00 7.50 15.00
524,527: 524-The Wild Swans. 527-The Golden-Haired Giant 4.00 10.00 20.00

GD25 FN65 NM94

525,526: 525-The Little Mermaid. 526-The Frog Prince 3.60 9.00 18.00
529-The Magic Servants 2.60 6.50 13.00
531-Rapunzel 3.60 9.00 18.00
532-534: 532-The Dancing Princesses. 533-The Magic Fountain. 534-The Golden Touch 2.80 7.00 14.00
535-The Wizard of Oz 5.35 16.00 32.00
536,537: 536-The Chimney Sweep. 537-The Three Fairies. 3.60 9.00 18.00
538-Silly Hans 2.80 7.00 14.00
539-The Enchanted Fish 4.25 13.00 26.00
540-The Tinder-Box 4.00 12.00 24.00
541-Snow White & Rose Red 3.20 8.00 16.00
542-The Donkey's Tale 3.20 8.00 16.00
543-The House in the Woods 3.60 9.00 18.00
544-The Golden Fleece 5.00 15.00 30.00
545-The Glass Mountain 3.20 8.00 16.00
546-The Elves & the Shoemaker 3.20 8.00 16.00
547-The Wishing Table 3.60 9.00 18.00
548-551: 548-The Magic Pitcher. 549-Simple Kate. 550-The Singing Donkey. 551-The Queen Bee 2.80 7.00 14.00
552-The Three Little Dwarfs 3.60 9.00 18.00
553,556: 553-King Thrushbeard. 556-The Elf Mound 2.80 7.00 14.00
554,555: 554-The Enchanted Deer. 555-The Three Golden Apples 3.20 8.00 16.00
557-Silly Willy 4.00 11.00 22.00
558-The Magic Dish; L.B. Cole-c; soft and stiff-c exist on original 5.00 15.00 30.00
559-The Japanese Lantern; 1 pg. Ingels-a; L.B. Cole-c 5.00 15.00 30.00
560-The Doll Princess; L.B. Cole-c 5.00 15.00 30.00
561-Hans Humdrum; L.B. Cole-c 3.20 8.00 16.00
562-The Enchanted Pony; L.B. Cole-c 5.00 15.00 30.00
563-570: 563-The Wishing Well; L.B. Cole-c. 564-The Salt Mountain; L.B.Cole-c. 565-The Silly Princess; L.B. Cole-c. 566-Clumsy Hans; L.B. Cole-c. 567-The Bearskin Soldier; L.B. Cole-c. 568-The Happy Hedgehog; L.B. Cole-c. 569-The Three Giants. 570-The Pearl Princess 2.80 7.00 14.00
571-573: 571-How Fire Came to the Indians. 572-The Drummer Boy. 573-The Crystal Ball. 4.00 12.00 20.00
574-Brightboots 3.00 7.50 15.00
575-The Fearless Prince 3.60 9.00 18.00
576-The Princess Who Saw Everything 4.25 13.00 28.00
577-The Runaway Dumpling 5.70 17.00 34.00
NOTE: *Prices are for original editions. Last reprint - Spring, 1971.* **Costanza** & **Schaffenberger** *art in many issues.*

CLASSICS ILLUSTRATED SPECIAL ISSUE
Gilberton Co.: (Came out semi-annually) Dec, 1955 - Jul, 1962 (35¢, 100 pgs.)
129-The Story of Jesus (titled ...Special Edition) "Jesus on Mountain" cover 7.85 23.50 55.00
"Three Camels" cover (12/58) 10.00 30.00 75.00
"Mountain" cover (no date)-Has checklist on inside b/c to HRN #161 & different testimonial on back-c 5.70 17.00 40.00
"Mountain" cover (1968 re-issue; has white 50¢ circle) 5.70 17.00 38.00
132A-The Story of America (6/56); Cameron-a 5.70 17.00 40.00
135A-The Ten Commandments(12/56) 5.70 17.00 38.00
138A-Adventures in Science(6/57); HRN to 137 5.35 16.00 32.00
138A-(6/57)-2nd version w/HRN to 149 4.25 13.00 26.00
138A-(12/61)-3rd version w/HRN to 149 5.35 16.00 32.00
141A-The Rough Rider (Teddy Roosevelt)(12/57); Evans-a 5.70 17.00 38.00
144A-Blazing the Trails West(6/58)- 73 pgs. of Crandall/Evans plus Severin-a 5.70 17.00 36.00
147A-Crossing the Rockies(12/58)-Crandall/Evans-a 5.70 17.00 38.00
150A-Royal Canadian Police(6/59)-Ingels, Sid Check-a

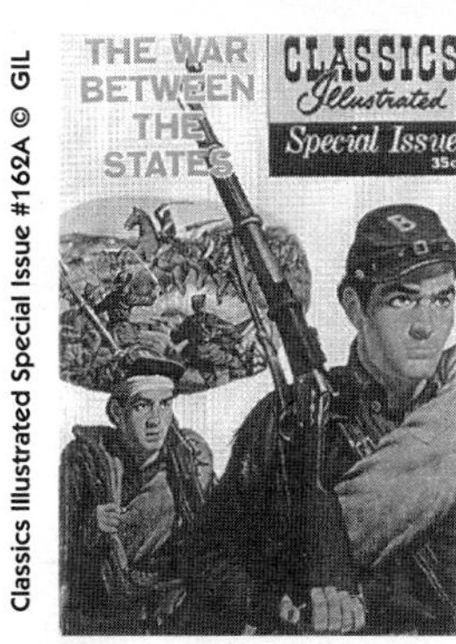

Classics Illustrated Special Issue #162A © GIL

Classic Star Wars: A New Hope #2 © Lucasfilm

Clerks #1 © Miramax, Inc.

GD25 FN65 NM94

5.70 17.00 38.00
153A-Men, Guns & Cattle(12/59)-Evans-a (26 pgs.); Kinstler-a 5.70 17.00 38.00
156A-The Atomic Age(6/60)-Crandall/Evans, Torres-a 5.70 17.00 38.00
159A-Rockets, Jets and Missiles(12/60)-Evans, Morrow-a 5.70 17.00 38.00
162A-War Between the States(6/61)-Kirby & Crandall/Evans-a; Ingels-a 12.00 36.00 90.00
165A-To the Stars(12/61)-Torres, Crandall/Evans, Kirby-a 5.70 17.00 38.00
166A-World War II('62)-Torres, Crandall/Evans, Kirby-a 9.30 28.00 65.00
167A-Prehistoric World(7/62)-Torres & Crandall/Evans-a; two versions exist (HRN to 165 & HRN to 167) 9.30 28.00 65.00
nn Special Issue-The United Nations (1964; 50¢; scarce); this is actually part of the European Special Series, which cont'd on after the U.S. series stopped issuing new titles in 1962. This English edition was prepared specifically for sale at the U.N. It was printed in Norway 28.00 83.00 220.00

NOTE: *There was another U.S. Special Issue prepared in 1962 with artwork by **Torres** entitled World War I. Unfortunately, it was never issued in any English-language edition. It was issued in 1964 in West Germany, The Netherlands, and some Scandanavian countries, with another edition in 1974 with a new cover.*

CLASSICS LIBRARY (See King Classics)

CLASSIC STAR WARS (Also see Star Wars)
Dark Horse Comics: Aug, 1992 - No. 20, June, 1994 ($2.50)

1-19: Star Wars strip-r by Williamson; Williamson redrew portions of the panels to fit comic book format; Williamson c-1-5,7,9,10,14,15,20: 8-Polybagged w/ Star Wars Galaxy trading card. 8,17-M. Schultz-c. 13-Yeates-c. 19-Evans-c 3.00
20-($3.50, 52 pgs.)-Polybagged w/trading card 3.50
Escape To Hoth TPB ($16.95) r/#15-20 1.70 5.10 17.00
Trade paperback ($29.95, slip-cased)-Reprints all movie adaptations 30.00

CLASSIC STAR WARS: A NEW HOPE
Dark Horse Comics: June, 1994 - No. 2, July, 1994 ($3.95, limited series)

1-r/Star Wars #1-3, 7-9 publ. by Marvel Comics 4.00
2-r/Star Wars #4-6, 10-12 publ. by Marvel Comics 4.00

CLASSIC STAR WARS: DEVIL WORLDS
Dark Horse Comics: Aug, 1996 - No.2, Sept, 1996 ($2.50, limited series)

1,2: r/Alan Moore-s 2.50

CLASSIC STAR WARS: HAN SOLO AT STARS' END
Dark Horse Comics: Mar, 1997 - No.3, May, 1997 ($2.95, limited series)

1-3: r/strips by Alfredo Alcala 2.95

CLASSIC STAR WARS: RETURN OF THE JEDI
Dark Horse Comics: Oct, 1994 - No.2, Nov, 1994 ($3.50, limited series)

1,2: 1-r/1983-84 Marvel series; polybagged with w/trading card 3.50

CLASSIC STAR WARS: THE EARLY ADVENTURES
Dark Horse Comics: Aug, 1994 - No. 9, Apr, 1995 ($2.50, limited series)

1-9 2.50

CLASSIC STAR WARS: THE EMPIRE STRIKES BACK
Dark Horse Comics: Aug, 1994 - No. 2, Sept, 1994 ($3.95, limited series)

1-r/Star Wars #39-44 published by Marvel Comics 4.00

CLASSIC X-MEN (Becomes X-Men Classic #46 on)
Marvel Comics Group: Sept, 1986 - No. 45, Mar, 1990

1-Begins-r of New X-Men 3.00
2-4 2.25
5-9 2.00
10-Sabretooth app. 2.25
11-15: 11-1st origin of Magneto in back-up story 1.75

GD25 FN65 NM94

16,18-20 1.50
17-Wolverine-c 2.00
21-25,27-30: 27-r/X-Men #121; $1.25-c begins 1.50
26-r/X-Men #120; Wolverine-c/app. 2.00
31-38,40-42,44,45: 35-r/X-Men #129 1.50
39-New Jim Lee back-up story (2nd-a on X-Men) 2.00
43-Byrne-c/a(r); $1.75, double-size 1.75

NOTE: ***Art Adams** c(p)-1-10, 12-16, 18-23. **Austin** c-10,15-21,24-28i. **Bolton** back up stories in 1-28,30-35. **Williamson** c-12-14i.*

CLAW (See Capt. Battle, Jr. Daredevil Comics & Silver Streak Comics)

CLAW THE UNCONQUERED (See Cancelled Comic Cavalcade)
National Periodical Publications/DC Comics: 5-6/75 - No. 9, 9-10/76; No. 10, 4-5/78 - No. 12, 8-9/78

1,3,9:-1st app. Claw. 3-Nudity panel. 9-Origin 4.00
2,4-8,10-12 3.00

NOTE: ***Giffen** a-8-12p. **Kubert** c-10-12. **Layton** a-9i, 12i.*

CLAY CODY, GUNSLINGER
Pines Comics: Fall, 1957

1-Painted-c 5.00 15.00 30.00

CLEAN FUN, STARRING "SHOOGAFOOTS JONES"
Specialty Book Co.: 1944 (10¢, B&W, oversized covers, 24 pgs.)

nn-Humorous situations involving Negroes in the Deep South
White cover issue... 7.15 21.50 50.00
Dark grey cover issue... 8.50 26.00 60.00

CLEMENTINA THE FLYING PIG (See Dell Jr. Treasury)

CLEOPATRA (See Ideal, a Classical Comic No. 1)

CLERKS: THE COMIC BOOK (Also see Oni Double Feature #1)
Oni Press: Feb, 1998 ($2.95, B&W, one-shot)

1-Kevin Smith-s 1.20 3.60 12.00
1-Second printing 4.00

CLIFFHANGER (See Battle Chasers, Crimson, and Danger Girl)
WildStorm Prod./Wizard Press: 1997 (Wizard supplement)

0-Sketchbook preview of Cliffhanger titles 1.00 3.00 10.00

CLIFF MERRITT SETS THE RECORD STRAIGHT
Brotherhood of Railroad Trainsmen: Giveaway (2 different issues)

...and the Very Candid Candidate by Al Williamson 3.00
...Sets the Record Straight by Al Williamson (2 different-c: one by Williamson, the other by McWilliams) 3.00

CLIMAX! (Mystery)
Gillmor Magazines: July, 1955 - No. 2, Sept, 1955

1,2 11.50 34.00 80.00

CLINT (Also see Adolescent Radioactive Black Belt Hamsters)
Eclipse Comics: Sept, 1986 - No. 2, Jan, 1987 ($1.50, B&W)

1,2 1.50

CLINT & MAC (TV, Disney)
Dell Publishing Co.: No. 889, Mar, 1958

Four Color 889-Alex Toth-a, photo-c 12.00 35.00 135.00

CLIVE BARKER'S BOOK OF THE DAMNED: A HELLRAISER COMPANION
Marvel Comics (Epic): Oct, 1991 - No. 3, Nov, 1992 ($4.95, semi-annual)

Volume 1-3-(52 pgs.): 1-Simon Bisley-c. 2-(4/92). 3-(11/92)-McKean-a (1 pg.) 5.00

CLIVE BARKER'S HELLRAISER (Also see Epic, Hellraiser Nightbreed –Jihad, Revelations, Son of Celluloid, Tapping the Vein & Weaveworld)
Marvel Comics (Epic Comics): 1989 - No. 20, 1993 ($4.95, mature readers, quarterly, 68 pgs.)

Book 1-Based on Hellraiser & Hellbound movies; Bolton-c/a; Spiegle &

Cloak and Dagger #1 © Z-D

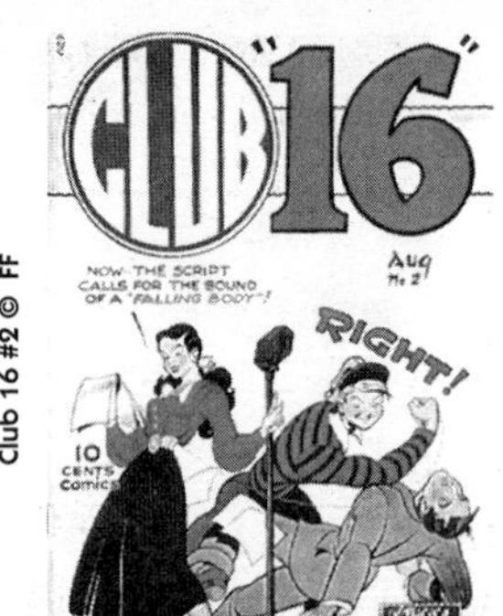

Club 16 #2 © FF

Clue Comics V2 #1 © HP

GD25 FN65 NM94

Wrightson-a (graphic album) 5.00
Book 2-4,14-16,18,19 5.00
Book 5-9 ($5.95): 7-Bolton-a. 8-Morrow-a 2.00 6.00
Book 10,11,13($4.50, 52 pgs.): 10-Foil-c. 11-Guice-p 4.50
Book 12-Sam Kieth-a 4.50
Book 17-Alex Ross-a, 34 pgs. 1.00 3.00 10.00
Book 20-By Gaiman/McKean .90 2.70 9.00
...Dark Holiday Special ('92, $4.95)-Conrad-a 5.00
...Spring Slaughter 1 ('94, $6.95, 52 pgs.)-Painted-c .85 2.60 7.00
...Summer Special 1 ('92, $5.95, 68 pgs.) 2.00 6.00

CLIVE BARKER'S NIGHTBREED (Also see Epic)
Marvel Comics (Epic Comics): Apr, 1990 - No. 25, Mar, 1993 ($1.95/$2.25/$2.50, mature readers)

1: 1-4-Adapt horror movie 2.00
2-19: 5-New stories & $2.25-c begin; Guice-a(p) 2.25
20-25: 20-Begin $2.50-c 2.50

CLIVE BARKER'S THE HARROWERS
Marvel Comics (Epic Comics): Dec, 1993 - No. 6, May, 1994 ($2.50)

1-($2.95)-Glow-in-the-dark-c; Colan-c/a in all 3.00
2-6 2.50
NOTE: ***Colan*** *a(p)-1-6; c-1-3, 4p, 5p.* ***Williamson*** *a(i)-2, 4, 5(part).*

CLOAK AND DAGGER
Ziff-Davis Publishing Co.: Fall, 1952

1-Saunders painted-c 22.00 66.00 165.00

CLOAK AND DAGGER (Also see Marvel Fanfare)
Marvel Comics Group: Oct, 1983 - No. 4, Jan, 1984 (Mini-series) (See Spectacular Spider-Man #64)

1-4-Austin-c/a(i) in all. 4-Origin 1.50

CLOAK AND DAGGER (Also see Marvel Graphic Novel #34, Mutant Misadventures Of... & Strange Tales, 2nd Series)
Marvel Comics Group: July, 1985 - No. 11, Jan, 1987

1 1.50
2-8,10,11 1.00
9-Art Adams-p 2.00
...And Power Pack (1990, $7.95, 68 pgs.) .90 2.70 8.00
NOTE: ***Mignola*** *c-7, 8.*

CLOBBERIN' TIME
Marvel Comics: Sept, 1995 ($1.95) (Based on card game)

nn-Overpower game guide; Ben Grimm story 2.00

CLONEZONE SPECIAL
Dark Horse Comics/First Comics: 1989 ($2.00, B&W)

1-Back-up series from Badger & Nexus 2.00

CLOSE ENCOUNTERS (See Marvel Comics Super Special & Marvel Special Edition)

CLOSE SHAVES OF PAULINE PERIL, THE (TV?)
Gold Key: June, 1970 - No. 4, March, 1971

1 2.20 6.25 22.00
2-4 1.40 4.20 14.00

CLOWN COMICS (No. 1 titled Clown Comic Book)
Clown Comics/Home Comics/Harvey Publ.: 1945 - No. 3, Win, 1946

nn (#1) 9.30 28.00 65.00
2,3 5.70 17.00 40.00

CLOWNS, THE (I Pagliacci)
Dark Horse Comics: 1998 ($2.95, B&W, one-shot)

1-Adaption of the opera; P. Craig Russell-script 2.95

CLUBHOUSE RASCALS (#1 titled ...Presents?) (Also see Three Rascals)
Sussex Publ. Co. (Magazine Enterprises): June, 1956 - No. 2, Oct, 1956

1,2: The Brain app. 5.00 15.00 30.00

CLUB "16"
Famous Funnies: June, 1948 - No. 4, Dec, 1948

1-Teen-age humor 9.30 28.00 70.00
2-4 5.70 17.00 38.00

CLUE COMICS (Real Clue Crime V2#4 on)
Hillman Periodicals: Jan, 1943 - No. 15(V2#3), May, 1947

1-Origin The Boy King, Nightmare, Micro-Face, Twilight, & Zippo 94.00 282.00 800.00
2 44.00 132.00 375.00
3-5 33.00 100.00 250.00
6,8,9: 8-Palais-c/a(2) 25.00 75.00 185.00
7-Classic torture-c 39.00 117.00 290.00
10-Origin/1st app. The Gun Master & begin series; content changes to crime 25.00 75.00 185.00
11 17.00 51.00 130.00
12-Origin Rackman; McWilliams-a, Guardineer-a(2) 23.00 70.00 170.00
V2#1-Nightmare new origin; Iron Lady app.; Simon & Kirby-a 42.00 126.00 340.00
V2#2-S&K-a(2)-Bondage/torture-c; man attacks & kills people with electric iron. Infantino-a 42.00 126.00 340.00
V2#3-S&K-a(3) 42.00 126.00 340.00

CLUELESS SPRING SPECIAL (TV)
Marvel Comics: May, 1997 ($3.99, magazine sized, one-shot)

1-Photo-c from TV show 4.00

CLUTCHING HAND, THE
American Comics Group: July-Aug, 1954

1 30.00 90.00 225.00

CLYDE BEATTY COMICS (Also see Crackajack Funnies)
Commodore Productions & Artists, Inc.: October, 1953 (84 pgs.)

1-Photo front/back-c; movie scenes and comics 25.00 75.00 185.00
...African Jungle Book('56)-Richfield Oil Co. 16 pg. giveaway, soft-c 9.30 28.00 70.00

CLYDE CRASHCUP (TV)
Dell Publishing Co.: Aug-Oct, 1963 - No. 5, Sept-Nov, 1964

1-All written by John Stanley 12.00 36.00 130.00
2-5 11.00 33.00 120.00

C-M-O COMICS
Chicago Mail Order Co.(Centaur): 1942 - No. 2, 1942 (68 pgs., full color)

1-Invisible Terror, Super Ann, & Plymo the Rubber Man app. (all Centaur costume heroes) 74.00 222.00 625.00
2-Invisible Terror, Super Ann app. 47.00 141.00 400.00

COBALT BLUE (Also see Power Comics)
Innovation Publishing: Sept, 1989 - No. 2, Oct, 1989 ($1.95, 28 pgs.)

1,2-Gustovich-c/a/scripts 2.00
The Graphic Novel ($6.95, color, 52 pgs.)-r/1,2 .85 2.60 7.00

COCOMALT BIG BOOK OF COMICS
Harry 'A' Chesler (Cocomalt Premium): 1938 (Reg. size, full color, 52 pgs.)

1-(Scarce)-Biro-c/a; Little Nemo by Winsor McCay Jr., Dan Hastings; Jack Cole, Guardineer, Gustavson, Bob Wood-a 200.00 600.00 1800.00

CODE BLUE
Image Comics (Jet-Black): Apr, 1998 ($2.95, B&W)

1-Jimmie Robinson-s/a 2.95

CODE NAME: ASSASSIN (See 1st Issue Special)

CODENAME: DANGER
Lodestone Publishing: Aug, 1985 - No. 4, May, 1986 ($1.50)

1-4 1.50

CODENAME DOUBLE IMPACT

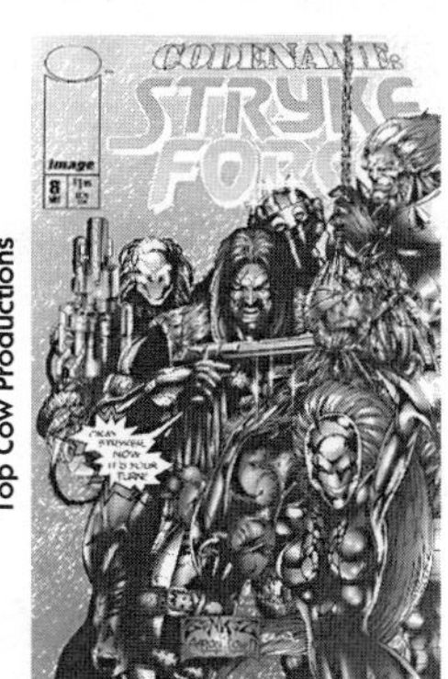

Codename: Stryke Force #8 © Top Cow Productions

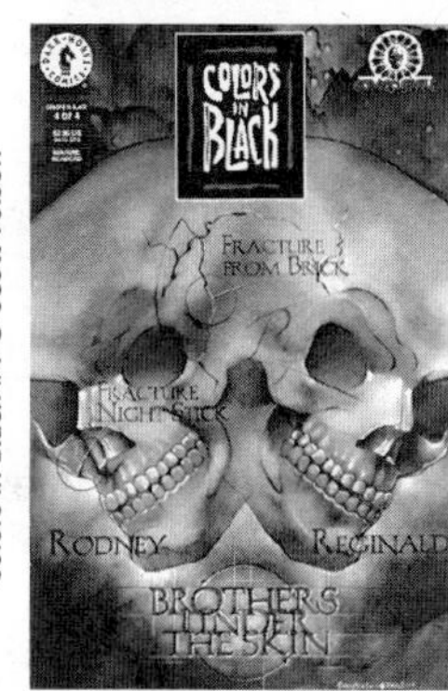

Colors in Black #4 © Scott Tolson

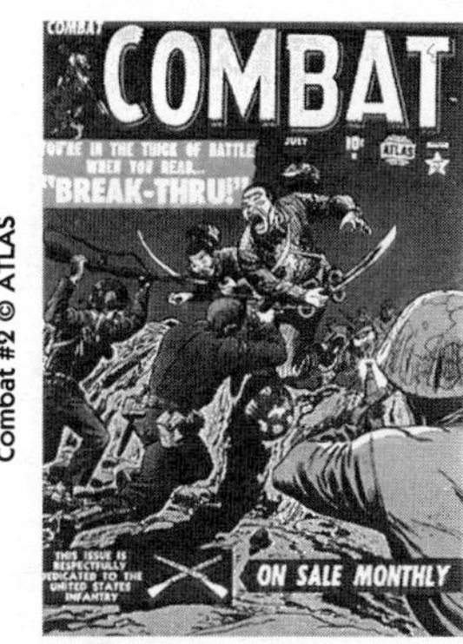

Combat #2 © ATLAS

	GD25	FN65	NM94

High Impact Entertainment: 1997 ($2.95, B&W)

1,2			2.95

CODENAME: FIREARM (Also see Firearm)
Malibu Comics (Ultraverse): June, 1995 - No. 5, Sept, 1995 ($2.95, bimonthly limited series)

0-5: 0-2-Alec Swan back-up story by James Robinson			3.00

NOTE: *Perez c-0.*

CODENAME: GENETIX
Marvel Comics UK: Jan, 1993 - No. 4, May, 1993 ($1.75, limited series)

1-4: Wolverine in all			1.75

CODENAME SPITFIRE (Formerly Spitfire And The Troubleshooters)
Marvel Comics Group: No. 10, July, 1987 - No. 13, Oct, 1987

10-13: 10-Rogers-c/a			1.00

CODENAME: STRYKE FORCE (Also See Cyberforce V1#4 & Cyberforce/Stryke Force: Opposing Forces)
Image Comics (Top Cow Productions): Jan, 1994 - No. 14, Sept, 1995 ($1.95/$2.25)

0			2.50
1-12-Silvestri stories, Peterson-a. 1-wraparound-c. 4-Stormwatch app.			2.00
1-Gold			5.00
1-Blue			5.00
13-14: 13-$2.25-c begins. 14-Story continues in Cyberforce/Stryke Force: Opposing Forces; Turner-a			2.25

CODE NAME: TOMAHAWK
Fantasy General Comics: Sept, 1986 ($1.75, high quality paper)

1-Sci/fi			1.75

CODE OF HONOR
Marvel Comics: Feb, 1997 - No. 4, May, 1997 ($5.95, limited series)

1-4-Fully painted by various; Dixon-s			5.95

CODY OF THE PONY EXPRESS (See Colossal Features Magazine)
Fox Features Syndicate: Sept, 1950 - No. 3, Jan, 1951 (See Women Outlaws)

1-3 (Actually #3-5). 1-Painted-c	11.00	34.00	85.00

CODY OF THE PONY EXPRESS (Buffalo Bill...) (Outlaws of the West #11 on; Formerly Bullseye)
Charlton Comics: No. 8, Oct, 1955; No. 9, Jan, 1956; No. 10, June, 1956

8-Bullseye on splash pg; not S&K-a	5.70	17.00	40.00
9,10: Buffalo Bill app. in all	4.25	13.00	26.00

CODY STARBUCK (1st app. in Star Reach #1)
Star Reach Productions: July, 1978 (2nd printing exists)

nn-Howard Chaykin-c/a			5.00

NOTE: *Both printings say First Printing. True first printing is on lower-grade paper, somewhat off-register, and snow in snow sequence has green tint.*

CO-ED ROMANCES
P. L. Publishing Co.: November, 1951

1	5.70	17.00	35.00

COFFEE WORLD
World Comics: Oct, 1995 ($1.50, B&W, anthology)

1-Shannon Wheeler's Too Much Coffee Man story			2.00

COLLECTORS DRACULA, THE
Millennium Publications: 1994 - No. 2, 1994 ($3.95, color/B&W, 52 pgs., limited series)

1,2-Bolton-a (7 pgs.)			4.00

COLLECTORS ITEM CLASSICS (See Marvel Collectors Item Classics)

COLONIA
Colonia Press: 1998 ($2.95, B&W)

1-Jeff Nicholson-s/a			3.00

COLORS IN BLACK
Dark Horse Comics: Mar, 1995 - No. 4, June, 1995 ($2.95, limited series)

1-4			3.00

COLOSSAL FEATURES MAGAZINE (Formerly I Loved) (See Cody of the Pony Express)
Fox Features Syndicate: No. 33, 5/50 - No. 34, 7/50; No. 3, 9/50 (Based on Columbia serial)

33,34: Cody of the Pony Express begins. 33-Painted-c. 34-Photo-c	11.00	32.00	80.00
3-Authentic criminal cases	11.00	32.00	80.00

COLOSSAL SHOW, THE (TV)
Gold Key: Oct, 1969

1	4.00	12.00	40.00

COLOSSUS (See X-Men)
Marvel Comics: Oct, 1997 ($2.99, 48 pgs., one-shot)

1-Raab-s/Hitch & Nealy-a, wraparound-c			3.00

COLOSSUS COMICS (See Green Giant & Motion Picture Funnies Weekly)
Sun Publications (Funnies, Inc.?): March, 1940

1-(Scarce)-Tulpa of Tsang(hero); Colossus app.	289.00	867.00	2800.00

NOTE: *Cover by artist that drew Colossus in Green Giant Comics.*

COLOUR OF MAGIC, THE (Terry Pratchett's...)
Innovation Publishing: 1991 - No. 4, 1991 ($2.50, limited series)

1-4: Adapts 1st novel of the Discworld series			2.50

COLT .45 (TV)
Dell Publishing Co.: No. 924, 8/58 - No. 1058, 11-1/59-60; No. 4, 2-4/60 - No. 9, 5-7/61

Four Color 924(#1)-Wayde Preston photo-c on all	9.00	27.00	100.00
Four Color 1004,1058, #4,5,7-9: 1004-Photo-b/c	7.00	20.00	75.00
6-Toth-a	8.00	23.00	85.00

COLUMBIA COMICS
William H. Wise Co.: 1943

1-Joe Palooka, Charlie Chan, Capt. Yank, Sparky Watts, Dixie Dugan app.	25.00	74.00	185.00

COLUMBUS
Dark Horse Comics: Sept, 1992 ($2.50, B&W, one-shot)

1-Yeates painted-c			2.50

COMANCHE (See Four Color No. 1350)

COMANCHEROS, THE
Dell Publishing Co.: No. 1300, Mar-May, 1962

Four Color 1300-Movie, John Wayne photo-c	14.00	44.00	160.00

COMBAT
Atlas Comics (ANC): June, 1952 - No. 11, April, 1953

1	19.00	56.00	140.00
2-Heath-c/a	9.30	28.00	70.00
3,5-9,11: 9-Robert Q. Sale-a	6.50	19.50	45.00
4-Krigstein-a	7.15	21.50	50.00
10-B&W and color illos. in **POP**	6.50	19.50	45.00

NOTE: *Combat Casey in 7-11.* **Heath** *c-1, 2, 9.* **Maneely** *a-1; c-3.* **Pakula** *a-1.* **Reinman** *a-1.*

COMBAT
Dell Publishing Co.: Oct-Nov, 1961 - No. 40, Oct, 1973 (No #9)

1	3.60	10.80	40.00
2,3,5:	2.20	6.60	24.00
4-John F. Kennedy c/story (P.T. 109)	2.75	8.00	30.00
6,7,8(4-6/63), 8(7-9/63)	1.80	5.50	20.00
10-26	1.50	4.50	15.00

Combat Kelly #2 © ATLAS

The Comet #15 © AP

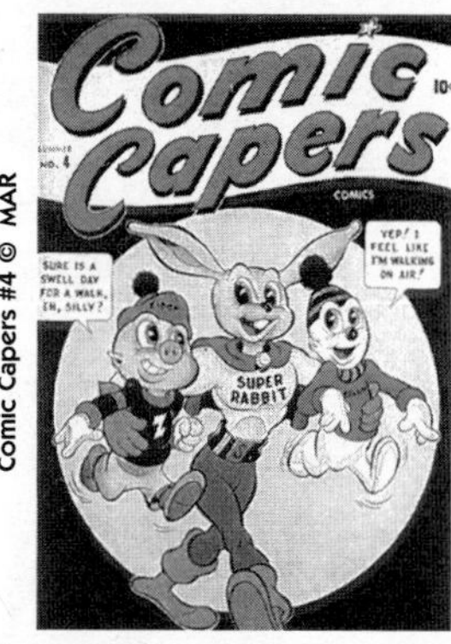

Comic Capers #4 © MAR

GD25 FN65 NM94

27-40(reprints #1-14). 30-r/#4 1.30 4.00 12.00
NOTE: ***Glanzman** c/a-1-27, 28-40r.*

COMBAT CASEY (Formerly War Combat)
Atlas Comics (SAI): No. 6, Jan, 1953 - No. 34, July, 1957

6 (Indicia shows 1/52 in error) 11.00 34.00 85.00
7-Spanking panel 7.15 21.50 50.00
8-Used in **POP**, pg. 94 5.70 17.00 40.00
9 5.70 17.00 35.00
10,13-19-Violent art by R. Q. Sale; Battle Brady x-over #10 9.30 28.00 65.00
11,12,20-Last Precode (2/55) 5.70 17.00 35.00
21-34 5.00 15.00 30.00
NOTE: ***Everett** a-6. **Heath** c-10, 17, 19, 30. **Maneely** c-6, 8. **Powell** a-29(5), 30(5), 34. **Severin** c-26, 33.*

COMBAT KELLY
Atlas Comics (SPI): Nov, 1951 - No. 44, Aug, 1957

1-1st app. Combat Kelly; Heath-a 23.00 68.00 170.00
2 11.00 32.00 80.00
3-10 7.85 23.50 55.00
11-Used in **POP**, pgs. 94,95 plus color illo. 6.50 19.50 45.00
12-Color illo. in **POP** 6.50 19.50 45.00
13-16 5.70 17.00 35.00
17-Violent art by R. Q. Sale; Combat Casey app. 9.30 28.00 65.00
18-20,22-44: 18-Battle Brady app. 28-Last precode (1/55). 38-Green Berets story (8/56) 5.70 17.00 35.00
21-Transvestism-c 5.70 17.00 40.00
NOTE: ***Berg** a-8, 12-14, 16, 17, 19-23, 25, 26, 28, 31-36, 42-44; c-2. **Colan** a-42. **Heath** a-4; c-31. **Lawrence** a-23. **Maneely** a-4(2), 6, 7(3), 8; c-4, 5, 7, 8, 10, 25. **R.Q. Sale** a-17, 25. **Severin** c-41, 42. **Whitney** a-5.*

COMBAT KELLY (...and the Deadly Dozen)
Marvel Comics Group: June, 1972 - No. 9, Oct, 1973

1-Intro & origin new Combat Kelly; Ayers/Mooney-a; Severin-c (20¢) 1.50 4.50 15.00
2,5-8 .90 2.70 9.00
3,4: 3-Origin. 4-Sgt. Fury-c/s 1.20 3.60 12.00
9-Death of the Deadly Dozen 1.20 3.60 12.00

COMBINED OPERATIONS (See The Story of the Commandos)

COMEBACK (See Zane Grey 4-Color 357)

COMEDY CARNIVAL
St. John Publishing Co.: no date (1950's) (100 pgs.)

nn-Contains rebound St. John comics 31.00 92.00 230.00

COMEDY COMICS (1st Series) (Daring Mystery #1-8) (Becomes Margie Comics #35 on)
Timely Comics (TCI 9,10): No. 9, April, 1942 - No. 34, Fall, 1946

9-(Scarce)-The Fin by Everett, Capt. Dash, Citizen V, & The Silver Scorn app.; Wolverton-a; 1st app. Comedy Kid; satire on Hitler & Stalin; The Fin, Citizen V & Silver Scorn cont. from Daring Mystery 247.00 741.00 2100.00
10-(Scarce)-Origin The Fourth Musketeer, Victory Boys; Monstro, the Mighty app. 176.00 529.00 1500.00
11-Vagabond, Stuporman app. 44.00 132.00 375.00
12,13 13.00 38.00 95.00
14-Origin/1st app. Super Rabbit (3/43) plus-c 44.00 132.00 375.00
15-20 11.00 34.00 85.00
21-32 9.30 28.00 65.00
33-Kurtzman-a (5 pgs.) 11.00 32.00 80.00
34-Intro Margie; Wolverton-a (5 pgs.) 17.00 50.00 125.00

COMEDY COMICS (2nd Series)
Marvel Comics (ACI): May, 1948 - No. 10, Jan, 1950

1-Hedy, Tessie, Millie begin; Kurtzman's "Hey Look" (he draws himself) 29.00 88.00 220.00
2 11.00 32.00 80.00

GD25 FN65 NM94

3,4-Kurtzman's "Hey Look" (?&3) 13.00 38.00 95.00
5-10 6.00 18.00 42.00

COMET, THE (See The Mighty Crusaders & Pep Comics #1)
Red Circle Comics (Archie): Oct, 1983 - No. 2, Dec, 1983

1,2: 1-Re-intro & origin The Comet; The American Shield begins. 2-Origin continues. Nino & Infantino art in both 1.00

COMET, THE
DC Comics (Impact Comics): July, 1991 - No. 18, Dec, 1992 ($1.00/$1.25)

1-13: 4-Black Hood app. 6-Re-intro Hangman. 8-Web x-over. 10-Contains Crusaders trading card. 13-Last $1.00-c 1.00
14-18: 14-Origin. Netzer(Nasser) c(p)-11,14-17 1.25
Annual 1 (1992, $2.50, 68 pgs.)-Contains Impact trading card; Shield back-up story 2.50

COMET MAN, THE (Movie)
Marvel Comics Group: Feb, 1987 - No. 6, July, 1987 (limited series)

1-3,5,6: 3-Hulk app. 5-Fantastic 4 app. 1.50
4-She Hulk shower scene c/s. Fantastic 4 app. 3.00
NOTE: ***Kelley Jones** a-1-6p.*

COMIC ALBUM (Also see Disney Comic Album)
Dell Publishing Co.: Mar-May, 1958 - No. 18, June-Aug, 1962

1-Donald Duck 7.00 22.00 80.00
2-Bugs Bunny 3.60 11.00 40.00
3-Donald Duck 5.50 16.50 60.00
4-6,8-10: 4-Tom & Jerry. 5-Woody Woodpecker. 6,10-Bugs Bunny. 8-Tom & Jerry. 9-Woody Woodpecker 2.75 8.00 30.00
7,11: 7-Popeye (9-11/59). 11-Popeye (9-11/60) 3.60 11.00 40.00
12-14: 12-Tom & Jerry. 13-Woody Woodpecker. 14-Bugs Bunny 2.75 8.00 30.00
15-Popeye 3.60 11.00 40.00
16-Flintstones (12-2/61-62)-3rd app. Early Cave Kids app. 6.40 19.00 70.00
17-Space Mouse (3rd app.) 3.60 11.00 40.00
18-Three Stooges; photo-c 6.40 19.00 70.00

COMIC BOOK (Also see Comics From Weatherbird)
American Juniors Shoe: 1954 (Giveaway)

Contains a comic rebound with new cover. Several combinations possible. Contents determines price.

COMIC BOOK
Marvel Comics-#1/Dark Horse Comics-#2: 1995 ($5.95, oversize)

1-Spumco characters by John K. .85 2.60 7.00
2-(Dark Horse) 2.00 6.00

COMIC BOOK MAGAZINE
Chicago Tribune & other newspapers: 1940 - 1943 (Similar to Spirit Sections) (7-3/4x10-3/4"; full color; 16-24 pgs. ea.)

1940 issues 5.70 17.50 35.00
1941, 1942 issues 4.25 13.00 28.00
1943 issues 4.00 12.00 24.00
NOTE: *Published weekly. Texas Slim, Kit Carson, Spooky, Josie, Nuts & Jolts, Lew Loyal, Brenda Starr, Daniel Boone, Captain Storm, Rocky, Smokey Stover, Tiny Tim, Little Joe, Fu Manchu appear among others. Early issues had photo stories with pictures from the movies; later issues had comic art.*

COMIC BOOKS (Series 1)
Metropolitan Printing Co. (Giveaway): 1950 (16 pgs.; 5-1/4x8-1/2"; full color; bound at top; paper cover)

1-Boots and Saddles; intro The Masked Marshal 5.00 15.00 30.00
1-The Green Jet; Green Lama by Raboy 27.00 80.00 200.00
1-My Pal Dizzy (Teen-age) 2.80 7.00 14.00
1-New World; origin Atomaster (costumed hero) 7.85 23.50 55.00
1-Talullah (Teen-age) 2.80 7.00 14.00

COMIC CAPERS

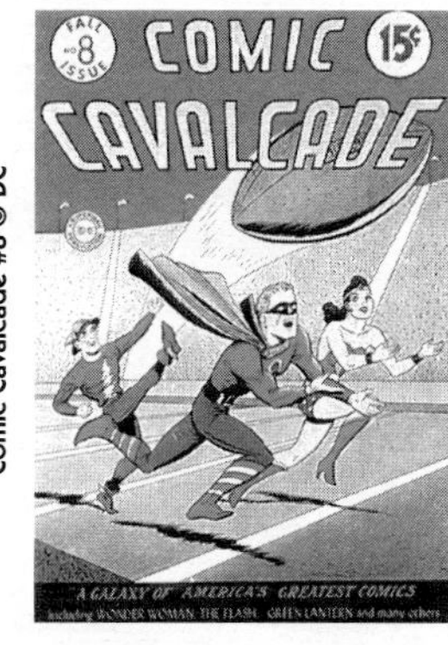

Comic Cavalcade #8 © DC

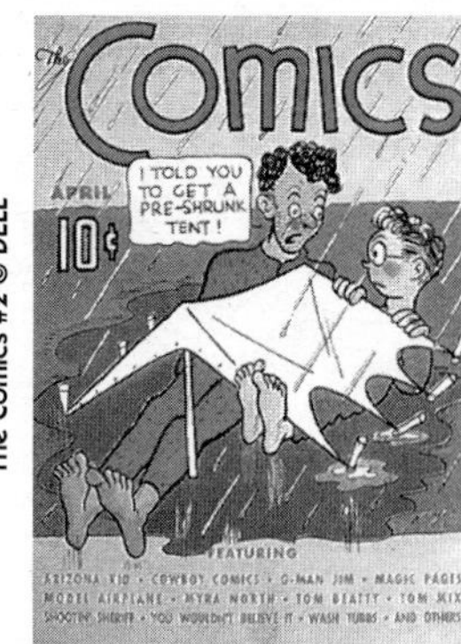

The Comics #2 © DELL

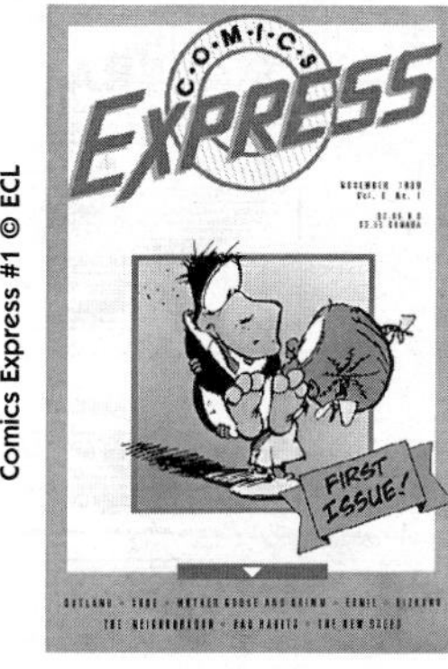

Comics Express #1 © ECL

GD25 FN65 NM94

Red Circle Mag./Marvel Comics: Fall, 1944 - No. 6, Summer, 1946

1-Super Rabbit, The Creeper, Silly Seal, Ziggy Pig, Sharpy Fox begin 21.00 64.00 160.00
2 11.00 32.00 80.00
3-6 9.30 28.00 65.00

COMIC CAVALCADE
All-American/National Periodical Publications: Winter, 1942-43 - No. 63, June-July, 1954 (Contents change with No. 30, Dec-Jan, 1948-49 on)

GD25 FN65 VF82 NM94
1-The Flash, Green Lantern, Wonder Woman, Wildcat, The Black Pirate by Moldoff (also #2), Ghost Patrol, and Red White & Blue begin; Scribbly app.; Minute Movie 800.00 2400.00 4800.00 8000.00
(Estimated up to 175 total copies exist, 6 in NM/Mint)

GD25 FN65 NM94
2-Mutt & Jeff begin; last Ghost Patrol & Black Pirate; Minute Movies 206.00 618.00 1750.00
3-Hop Harrigan & Sargon, the Sorcerer begin; The King app. 150.00 450.00 1275.00
4,5: 4-The Gay Ghost, The King, Scribbly, & Red Tornado app. 5-Christmas-c. 5-Prints ad for Jr. JSA membership kit that includes "The Minute Man Answers The Call" 127.00 379.00 1075.00
6-10: 7-Red Tornado & Black Pirate app.; last Scribbly. 9-Fat & Slat app.; X-Mas-c 97.00 291.00 825.00
11,12,14,16-20: 12-Last Red White & Blue. 19-Christmas-c 82.00 247.00 700.00
13-Solomon Grundy app.; X-Mas-c 129.00 388.00 1100.00
15-Johnny Peril begins (1st app.,6-7/46), ends #29 (See Danger Trail & Sensation Mystery) 88.00 265.00 750.00
21-23: 23-Harry Lampert-c (Toth swipes) 79.00 238.00 675.00
24-Solomon Grundy x-over in Green Lantern 94.00 282.00 800.00
25-28: 25-Black Canary app.; X-Mas-c. 26-28-Johnny Peril app. 28-Last Mutt & Jeff 68.00 203.00 575.00
29-(10-11/48)-Last Flash, Wonder Woman, Green Lantern & Johnny Peril; Wonder Woman invents "Thinking Machine"; 2nd computer in comics (after Flash Comics #52); Leave It to Binky story (early app.) 77.00 229.00 650.00
30-(12-1/48-49)-The Fox & the Crow, Dodo & the Frog & Nutsy Squirrel begin 40.00 120.00 320.00
31-35 21.00 64.00 160.00
36-49 15.00 44.00 110.00
50-62(Scarce) 19.00 56.00 140.00
63(Rare) 31.00 92.00 230.00
Giveaway (1944, 8 pgs., paper-c, in color)-One Hundred Years of Co-operation-r/Comic Cavalcade #9 68.00 206.00 550.00
Giveaway (1945, 16 pgs., paper-c, in color)-Movie "Tomorrow The World" (Nazi theme); r/Comic Cavalcade #10 93.00 281.00 750.00
Giveaway (c. 1944-45; 8 pgs, paper-c, in color)-The Twain Shall Meet-r/Comic Cavalcade #8 81.00 243.00 650.00

NOTE: ***Grossman** a-30-63. **E.E. Hibbard** c-(Flash only)-1-4, 7-14, 16-19, 21. **Sheldon Mayer** a(2-3)-40-63. **Moulson** c(G.L.)-7, 15. **Nodell** c(G.L.)-9. **H.G. Peter** c(W. Woman only)-1, 3-21, 24. **Post** a-31, 36. **Purcell** c(G.L.)-2-5, 10. **Reinman** a(Green Lantern)-4-6, 8, 9, 13, 15-21; c(Gr. Lantern)-6, 8, 19. **Toth** a(Green Lantern)-26-28; c-27. Atom app.-22, 23.*

COMIC COMICS
Fawcett Publications: Apr, 1946 - No. 10, Feb, 1947

1-Captain Kidd; Nutty Comics #1 in indicia 11.00 32.00 80.00
2-10-Wolverton-a, 4 pgs. each. 5-Captain Kidd app. Mystic Moot by Wolverton in #2-10? 12.00 36.00 90.00

COMIC CUTS (Also see The Funnies)
H. L. Baker Co., Inc.: 5/19/34 - 7/28/34 (5¢, 24 pgs.) (Tabloid size in full color) (Not reprints; published weekly; created for newsstand sale)

V1#1 - V1#7(6/30/34), V1#8(7/14/34), V1#9(7/28/34)-Idle Jack strips 8.50 26.00 60.00

COMIC LAND

GD25 FN65 NM94

Fact and Fiction Publ.: March, 1946

1-Sandusky & the Senator, Sam Stupor, Sleuth, Marvin the Great, Sir Passer, Phineas Gruff app.; Irv Tirman & Perry Williams art 11.00 34.00 85.00

COMICO CHRISTMAS SPECIAL
Comico: Dec, 1988 ($2.50, 44pgs.)

1-Rude/Williamson-a; Dave Stevens-c 3.00

COMICO PRIMER (See Primer)

COMIC PAGES (Formerly Funny Picture Stories)
Centaur Publications: V3#4, July, 1939 - V3#6, Dec, 1939

V3#4-Bob Wood-a 65.00 194.00 550.00
5,6: 6-Schwab-c 49.00 148.00 420.00

COMICS (See All Good)

COMICS, THE
Dell Publ. Co.: Mar, 1937 - No. 11, Nov, 1938 (Newspaper strip-r; bi-monthly)

1-1st app. Tom Mix in comics; Wash Tubbs, Tom Beatty, Myra North, Arizona Kid, Erik Noble & International Spy w/Doctor Doom begin 153.00 460.00 1300.00
2 74.00 222.00 625.00
3-11: 3-Alley Oop begins 59.00 171.00 500.00

COMICS AND STORIES (See Walt Disney's Comics and Stories)

COMICS & STORIES (Also see Wolf & Red)
Dark Horse Comics: Apr, 1996 - No. 3, June, 1996 ($2.95, limited series) (Created by Tex Avery)

1-3: Wolf & Red app; reads Comics and Stories on-c. 1-Terry Moore-a. 2-Reed Waller-a. 3.00

COMICS CALENDAR, THE (The 1946...)
True Comics Press (ordered through the mail): 1946 (25¢, 116 pgs.) (Stapled at top)

nn-(Rare) Has a "strip" story for every day of the year in color 37.00 112.00 280.00

COMICS DIGEST (Pocket size)
Parents' Magazine Institute: Winter, 1942-43 (B&W, 100 pgs)

1-Reprints from True Comics (non-fiction World War II stories) 7.85 23.50 55.00

COMIC SELECTIONS (Shoe store giveaway)
Parents' Magazine Press: 1944-46 (Reprints from Calling All Girls, True Comics, True Aviation, & Real Heroes)

1 4.00 10.00 20.00
2-5 3.20 8.00 16.00

COMICS EXPRESS
Eclipse Comics: Nov, 1989 - No. 2, Jan, 1990 ($2.95, B&W, 68pgs.)

1,2: Collection of strip-r; 2(12/89-c, 1/90 inside) 3.00

COMICS FOR KIDS
London Publ. Co./Timely: 1945 (no month); No. 2, Sum, 1945 (Funny animal)

1,2-Puffy Pig, Sharpy Fox 11.00 34.00 85.00

COMICS FROM WEATHER BIRD (Also see Comic Book, Edward's Shoes, Free Comics to You & Weather Bird)
Weather Bird Shoes: 1954 - 1957 (Giveaway)
Contains a comic bound with new cover. Many combinations possible. Contents would determine price. Some issues do not contain complete comics, but only parts of comics.Value equals 40 to 60 percent of contents.

COMICS' GREATEST WORLD
Dark Horse Comics: Jun, 1993 - V4#4, Sept, 1993 ($1.00, weekly, lim. series)

Arcadia (Week 1)
V1#1,2,4: 1-X: Frank Miller-c. 2-Pit Bulls. 4-Monster. 1.00
1-B&W Press Proof Edition (1500 copies) 1.00 3.00 10.00

Comics' Greatest World V1#4 © DH

Comics On Parade #13 © UFS

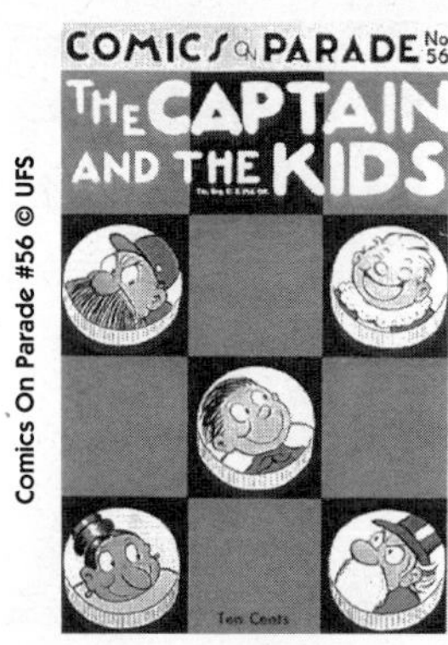

Comics On Parade #56 © UFS

	GD25	FN65	NM94
1-Silver-c; distr. retailer bonus w/print & cards	.90	2.70	8.00
3-Ghost, Dorman-c; Hughes-a			4.00
Retailer's Premium Embossed Silver Foil Logo-r/V1#1-4.	1.00	3.00	10.00
Golden City (Week 2)			
V2#1-4: 1-Rebel; Ordway-c. 2-Mecha; Dave Johnson-c. 3-Titan; Walt Simonson-c. 4-Catalyst; Perez-c.			1.00
1-Gold-c; distr. retailer bonus w/print & cards.		2.00	6.00
Retailer's Premium Embossed Gold Foil Logo-r/V2#1-4.	.90	2.70	8.00
Steel Harbor (Week 3)			
V3#1-Barb Wire; Dorman-c; Gulacy-a(p)			4.00
2-4: 2-The Machine; Mignola-c. 3-Wolfgang; Warner-c. 4-Motorhead			1.00
1-Silver-c; distr. retailer bonus w/print & cards	.90	2.70	8.00
Retailer's Premium Embossed Red Foil Logo-r/V3#1-4.	1.00	3.00	10.00
Vortex (Week 4)			
V4#1-4: 1-Division 13; Dorman-c. 2-Hero Zero; Art Adams-c. 3-King Tiger; Chadwick-a(p); Darrow-c. 4-Vortex; Miller-c.			1.00
1-Gold-c; distr. retailer bonus w/print & cards.		2.00	6.00
Retailer's Premium Embossed Blue Foil Logo-r/V4#1-4.	.90	2.70	8.00

COMICS' GREATEST WORLD: OUT OF THE VORTEX (See Out of The Vortex)

COMICS HITS (See Harvey Comics Hits)

COMICS MAGAZINE, THE (...Funny Pages #3)(Funny Pages #6 on)
Comics Magazine Co. (1st Comics Mag./Centaur Publ.): May, 1936 - No. 5, Sept, 1936 (Paper covers)

	GD25	FN65	VF82
1-1st app. Dr. Mystic (a.k.a. Dr. Occult) by Siegel & Shuster (the 1st app. of a Superman prototype in comics). Dr. Mystic is not in costume but later appears in costume as a more pronounced prototype in More Fun #14-17. (1st episode of "The Koth and the Seven"; continues in More Fun #14; originally scheduled for publication at DC). 1 pg. Kelly-a; Sheldon Mayer-a	1000.00	3000.00	9500.00
	GD25	**FN65**	**NM94**
2-Federal Agent (a.k.a. Federal Men) by Siegel & Shuster; 1 pg. Kelly-a	218.00	654.00	1850.00
3-5	176.00	528.00	1500.00

COMICS NOVEL (Anarcho, Dictator of Death)
Fawcett Publications: 1947

	GD25	FN65	NM94
1-All Radar; 51 pg anti-fascism story	26.00	78.00	195.00

COMICS ON PARADE (No. 30 on are a continuation of Single Series)
United Features Syndicate: Apr, 1938 - No. 104, Feb, 1955

	GD25	FN65	NM94
1-Tarzan by Foster; Captain & the Kids, Little Mary Mixup, Abbie & Slats, Ella Cinders, Broncho Bill, Li'l Abner begin	300.00	900.00	3000.00
2 (Tarzan & others app. on-c of #1-3,17)	118.00	354.00	1000.00
3	94.00	282.00	800.00
4,5	71.00	213.00	600.00
6-10	47.00	141.00	400.00
11-16,18-20	41.00	123.00	325.00
17-Tarzan-c	45.00	135.00	385.00
21-29: 22-Son of Tarzan begins. 22,24,28-Tailspin Tommy-c. 29-Last Tarzan issue	33.00	100.00	250.00
30-Li'l Abner	21.00	64.00	160.00
31-The Captain & the Kids	15.00	44.00	110.00
32-Nancy & Fritzi Ritz	12.00	36.00	90.00
33-Li'l Abner	17.00	52.00	130.00
34-The Captain & the Kids (10/41)	15.00	44.00	110.00
35-Nancy & Fritzi Ritz	12.00	36.00	90.00
36-Li'l Abner	17.00	52.00	130.00
37-The Captain & the Kids (6/42)	15.00	44.00	110.00
38-Nancy & Fritzi Ritz; infinity-c	12.00	36.00	90.00
39-Li'l Abner	17.00	52.00	130.00
40-The Captain & the Kids (3/43)	15.00	44.00	110.00
41-Nancy & Fritzi Ritz	9.30	28.00	70.00
42-Li'l Abner	17.00	52.00	130.00
43-The Captain & the Kids	15.00	44.00	110.00
44-Nancy & Fritzi Ritz (3/44)	9.30	28.00	70.00
45-Li'l Abner	15.00	44.00	110.00
46-The Captain & the Kids	12.00	36.00	90.00
47-Nancy & Fritzi Ritz	9.30	28.00	70.00
48-Li'l Abner (3/45)	15.00	44.00	110.00
49-The Captain & the Kids	12.00	36.00	90.00
50-Nancy & Fritzi Ritz	9.30	28.00	70.00
51-Li'l Abner	12.00	36.00	90.00
52-The Captain & the Kids (3/46)	8.50	26.00	60.00
53-Nancy & Fritzi Ritz	8.50	26.00	60.00
54-Li'l Abner	12.00	36.00	90.00
55-Nancy & Fritzi Ritz	8.50	26.00	60.00
56-The Captain & the Kids (r/Sparkler)	8.50	26.00	60.00
57-Nancy & Fritzi Ritz	8.50	26.00	60.00
58-Li'l Abner; continues as Li'l Abner #61?	12.00	36.00	90.00
59-The Captain & the Kids	6.85	21.00	48.00
60-70-Nancy & Fritzi Ritz	6.85	21.00	48.00
71-76-Nancy only	5.70	17.00	35.00
77-99,101-104-Nancy & Sluggo	5.70	17.00	35.00
100-Nancy & Sluggo	6.50	19.50	45.00
Special Issue, 7/46; Summer, 1948 - The Captain & the Kids app.	5.70	17.00	35.00
NOTE: Bound Volume (Very Rare) includes No. 1-12; bound by publisher in pictorial comic boards & distributed at the 1939 World's Fair and through mail order from ads in comic books (also see Tip Top)	235.00	706.00	2000.00

NOTE: *Li'l Abner reprinted from Tip Top.*

COMICS READING LIBRARIES (Educational Series)
King Features (Charlton Publ.): 1973, 1977, 1979 (36 pgs. in color) (Giveaways)

	GD25	FN65	NM94
R-01-Tiger, Quincy		2.00	6.00
R-02-Beetle Bailey, Blondie & Popeye	.90	2.70	9.00
R-03-Blondie, Beetle Bailey		2.00	6.00
R-04-Tim Tyler's Luck, Felix the Cat	1.60	4.80	16.00
R-05-Quincy, Henry		2.00	6.00
R-06-The Phantom, Mandrake	1.60	4.80	16.00
1977 reprint(R-04)	.90	2.70	9.00
R-07-Popeye, Little King	1.10	3.30	11.00
R-08-Prince Valiant(Foster), Flash Gordon	2.00	6.00	20.00
1977 reprint	1.30	3.90	13.00
R-09-Hagar the Horrible, Boner's Ark	.90	2.70	9.00
R-10-Redeye, Tiger		2.00	6.00
R-11-Blondie, Hi & Lois		2.00	6.00
R-12-Popeye-Swee'pea, Brutus	1.10	3.30	11.00
R-13-Beetle Bailey, Little King		2.00	6.00
R-14-Quincy-Hamlet		2.00	6.00
R-15-The Phantom, The Genius	1.10	3.30	11.00
R-16-Flash Gordon, Mandrake	2.00	6.00	20.00
1977 reprint	1.10	3.30	11.00
Other 1977 editions....			5.00
1979 editions(68pgs.)			5.00

NOTE: *Above giveaways available with purchase of $45.00 in merchandise. Used as a reading skills aid for small children.*

COMICS REVUE
St. John Publ. Co. (United Features Synd.): June, 1947 - No. 5, Jan, 1948

	GD25	FN65	NM94
1-Ella Cinders & Blackie	9.30	28.00	65.00
2-Hap Hopper (7/47)	6.50	19.50	45.00
3-Iron Vic (8/47)	5.70	17.00	40.00
4-Ella Cinders (9/47)	6.50	19.50	45.00

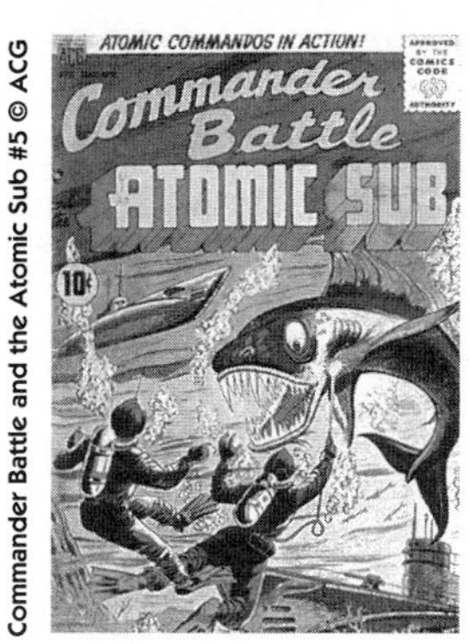

Commander Battle and the Atomic Sub #5 © ACG

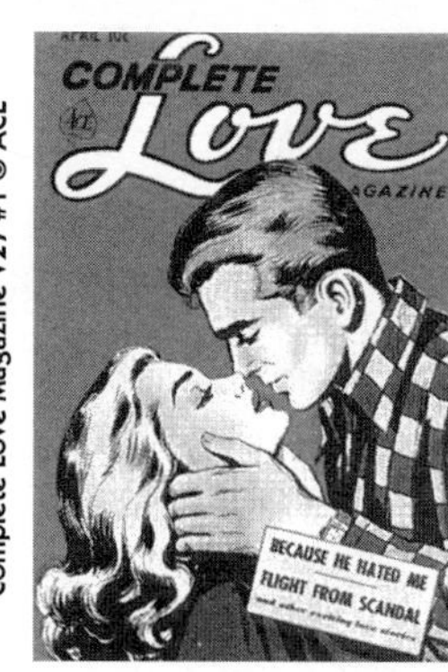

Complete Love Magazine V27 #1 © ACE

The Conan Saga #32 © MAR

GD25 FN65 NM94

5-Gordo No. 1 (1/48) 5.70 17.00 40.00

COMIC STORY PAINT BOOK
Samuel Lowe Co.: 1943 (Large size, 68 pgs.)

1055-Captain Marvel & a Captain Marvel Jr. story to read & color; 3 panels in color per pg. (reprints) 60.00 180.00 600.00

COMIX BOOK
Marvel Comics Group/Krupp Comics Works No. 4,5: 1974 - No. 5, 1976 ($1.00, B&W, magazine)

1-Underground comic artists; 2 pgs. Wolverton-a 2.20 6.50 24.00
2-Wolverton-a (1 pg.) 1.80 5.40 18.00
3-Low distribution (3/75) 2.20 6.50 24.00
4(2/76), 4(5/76), 5 1.40 4.20 14.00
NOTE: *Print run No. 1-3: 200-250M; No. 4&5: 10M each.*

COMIX INTERNATIONAL
Warren Magazines: July, 1974 - No. 5, Spring, 1977 (Full color)

1-Low distribution; all Corben story remainders from Warren 7.00 21.00 75.00
2-Wood, Wrightson-r 2.25 6.80 25.00
3-5: 4-(printing without Corben story). 4-Crandall-a. 5-Spirit story 2.00 6.00 20.00
4-printing w/Corben story 2.25 6.80 25.00
NOTE: *No. 4 had two printings with extra* ***Corben*** *story in one. No. 3 may also have a variation. No. 3 has two Jeff Jones reprints from Vampirella.*

COMMANDER BATTLE AND THE ATOMIC SUB
Amer. Comics Group (Titan Publ. Co.): Jul-Aug, 1954 - No. 7, Aug-Sep, 1955

1 (3-D effect)-Moldoff flying saucer-c 42.00 127.00 340.00
2,4-7: 2-Moldoff-c. 4-(1-2/55)-Last pre-code; Landau-a. 5-3-D effect story (2 pgs.). 6,7-Landau-a. 7-Flying saucer-c 27.00 80.00 200.00
3-H-Bomb-c; Atomic Sub becomes Atomic Spaceship 28.00 84.00 210.00

COMMANDMENTS OF GOD
Catechetical Guild: 1954, 1958

300-Same contents in both editions; diff-c 2.40 6.00 12.00

COMMANDO ADVENTURES
Atlas Comics (MMC): June, 1957 - No. 2, Aug, 1957

1,2-Severin-c. 2-Drucker-a? 7.15 21.50 50.00

COMMANDO YANK (See The Mighty Midget Comics & Wow Comics)

COMPLETE BOOK OF COMICS AND FUNNIES
William H. Wise & Co.: 1944 (25¢, one-shot, 196 pgs.)

1-Origin Brad Spencer, Wonderman; The Magnet, The Silver Knight by Kinstler, & Zudo the Jungle Boy app. 38.00 114.00 285.00

COMPLETE BOOK OF TRUE CRIME COMICS
William H. Wise & Co.: No date (Mid 1940's) (25¢, 132 pgs.)

nn-Contains Crime Does Not Pay rebound (includes #22) 88.00 265.00 750.00

COMPLETE COMICS (Formerly Amazing Comics No. 1)
Timely Comics (EPC): No. 2, Winter, 1944-45

2-The Destroyer, The Whizzer, The Young Allies & Sergeant Dix; Schomburg-c 129.00 388.00 1100.00

COMPLETE LOVE MAGAZINE (Formerly a pulp with same title)
Ace Periodicals (Periodical House): V26#2, May-June, 1951 - V32#4(#191), Sept, 1956

V26#2-Painted-c (52 pgs.) 5.00 15.00 30.00
V26#3-6(2/52), V27#1(4/52)-6(1/53) 4.00 11.00 22.00
V28#1(3/53), V28#2(5/53), V29#3(7/53)-6(12/53) 3.60 9.00 18.00
V30#1(2/54), V30#1(#176, 4/54),2,4-6(#181, 1/55) 3.60 9.00 18.00
V30#3(#178)-Rock Hudson photo-c 4.25 13.00 26.00
V31#1(#182, 3/55)-Last precode 3.60 9.00 18.00
V31#2(5/55)-6(#187, 1/56) 2.40 6.00 12.00
V32#1(#188, 3/56)-4(#191, 9/56) 2.40 6.00 12.00
NOTE: *(34 total issues). Photo-c V27#5-on. Painted-c V26#3.*

COMPLETE MYSTERY (True Complete Mystery No. 5 on)
Marvel Comics (PrPl): Aug, 1948 - No. 4, Feb, 1949 (Full length stories)

1-Seven Dead Men 41.00 122.00 325.00
2-Jigsaw of Doom! 39.00 118.00 295.00
3-Fear in the Night; Burgos-c/a (28 pgs.) 39.00 118.00 295.00
4-A Squealer Dies Fast 39.00 118.00 295.00

COMPLETE ROMANCE
Avon Periodicals: 1949

1-(Scarce)-Reprinted as Women to Love 35.00 104.00 260.00

COMPLIMENTARY COMICS
Sales Promotion Publ.: No date (1950's) (Giveaway)

1-Strongman by Powell, 3 stories 5.70 17.00 38.00

CONAN (See Chamber of Darkness #4, Giant-Size..., Handbook of..., King Conan, Marvel Graphic Novel #19, 28, Marvel Treasury Ed., Power Record Comics, Robert E. Howard's.., Savage Sword of Conan, and Savage Tales)

CONAN
Marvel Comics: Aug, 1995 - No. 11, June, 1996 ($2.95)

1-11: 4-Malibu Comic's Rune app. 3.00

CONAN CLASSIC
Marvel Comics: June, 1994 - No. 11, Apr, 1995 ($1.50)

1-11: 1-r/Conan #1 by B. Smith, r/covers w/changes. 2-11-r/Conan #2-11 by Smith 1.50
2-Bound w/cover to Conan The Adventurer #2 by mistake 1.50

CONAN: RRETURN OF STRYM
Marvel Comics: Sept, 1998 - No. 3, Nov, 1998 ($2.99, limited series)

1-3-Parente & Soresina-a; painted-c 3.00

CONAN: RIVER OF BLOOD
Marvel Comics: June, 1998 - No. 3, Aug, 1998 ($2.50, limited series)

1-3 2.50

CONAN: SCARLET SWORD
Marvel Comics: Dec, 1998 - No. 3, Feb, 1999 ($2.99, limited series)

1-3-Thomas-s/Raffaele-a 3.00

CONAN SAGA, THE
Marvel Comics: June, 1987 - No. 97, Apr, 1995 ($2.00/$2.25, B&W, magazine)

1-Barry Smith-r 1-9,11; new Barry Smith-c 1-9 2.00
2-27: 13,15-Boris-c. 17-Adams-r. 18,25-Chaykin-r. 22-r/Giant-Size Conan 1,2 2.00
28-97 ($2.25): 31-Red Sonja-r by N. Adams/SSOC #1; 1 pg. Jeff Jones-r. 32-Newspaper strip-r begin by Buscema. 33-Smith/Conrad-a. 39-r/Kull #1('71) by Andru/Wood. 44-Swipes-c/Savage Tales #1. 57-Brunner-r/SSOC #30. 66-r/Conan Annual #2 by Buscema. 79-r/Conan #43-45 w/Red Sonja. 85-Based on Conan #57-63 2.25
NOTE: ***J. Buscema*** *r-32-on; c-86.* ***Chaykin*** *r-34.* ***Chiodo*** *painted c-63, 65, 66, 82.* ***G. Colan*** *a-47p.* ***Jusko*** *painted c-64, 83.* ***Kaluta*** *c-84.* ***Nino*** *a-37.* ***Ploog*** *a-50.* ***N. Redondo*** *painted c-48, 50, 51, 53, 57, 62.* ***Simonson*** *r-50-54, 56.* ***B. Smith*** *r-51.* ***Starlin*** *c-34.* ***Williamson*** *r-50i.*

CONAN THE ADVENTURER
Marvel Comics: June, 1994 - No. 14, July, 1995 ($1.50)

1-($2.50)-Embossed foil-c; Kayaran-a 2.50
2-14 1.50
2-Contents are Conan Classics #2 by mistake 1.50

CONAN THE BARBARIAN
Marvel Comics: Oct, 1970 - No. 275, Dec, 1993

1-Origin/1st app. Conan (in comics) by Barry Smith; 1st app. Kull (cameo); #1-9 are 15¢ issues 17.00 52.00 190.00
2 6.50 19.00 70.00

Conan The Barbarian #9 © MAR

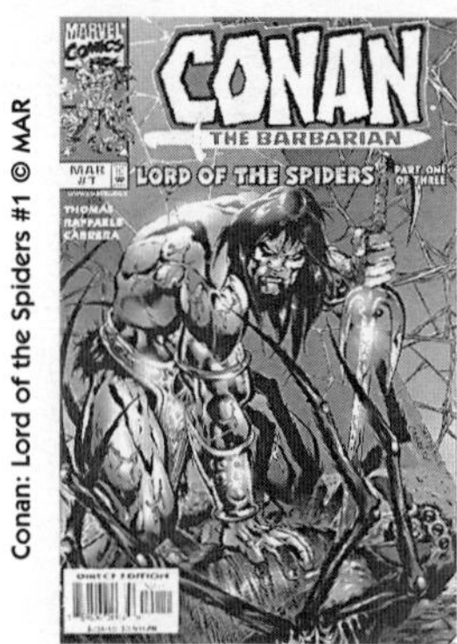

Conan: Lord of the Spiders #1 © MAR

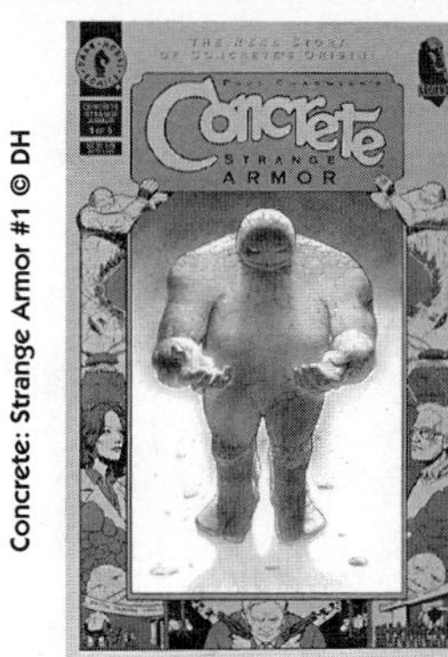

Concrete: Strange Armor #1 © DH

GD25 FN65 NM94

3-(Low distribution in some areas) 11.00 33.00 120.00
4,5 4.50 13.50 50.00
6-9: 8-Hidden panel message, pg. 14 2.90 8.70 32.00
10,11 (25¢ giants): 10-Black Knight-r; Kull story by Severin 3.80 11.50 42.00
12,13: 12-Wrightson-c(i) 2.00 6.00 20.00
14,15-Elric app. 2.90 8.70 32.00
16,19,20: 16-Conan-r/Savage Tales #1 1.80 5.40 18.00
17,18-No Barry Smith-a .90 2.70 9.00
21,22: 22-Has reprint from #1 1.50 4.50 15.00
23-1st app. Red Sonja (2/73) 2.20 6.50 24.00
24-1st full Red Sonja story; last Smith-a 2.00 6.00 20.00
25-John Buscema-c/a begins 5.00
26-30 4.00
31-36,38-40 3.00
37-Neal Adams-c/a; last 20¢ issue; contains pull-out subscription form .90 2.70 8.00
41-57,59,60: 44,45-N. Adams-i(Crusty Bunkers). 45-Adams-c. 48-Origin retold. 59-Origin Belit 4.00
58-2nd Belit app. (see Giant-Size Conan #1) 5.00
61-99: 68-Red Sonja story cont'd from Marvel Feature #7. 84-Intro. Zula. 85-Origin Zula. 87-r/Savage Sword of Conan #3 in color 3.00
100-(52 pg. Giant)-Death of Belit 3.00
101-114,116-199: 116-r/Power Record Comic PR31 1.25
115-Double size 1.50
200,250 ($1.50): 200-(52 pgs.). 250-(60 pgs.) 1.50
201-249,251,252: 232-Young Conan storyline begins; Conan is born. 244-Return of Zula. 252-Last $1.00-c 1.25
253-274: 262-Adapted from R.E. Howard story 1.25
275-($2.50, 68 pgs.)-Final issue; painted-c 2.50
King Size 1(1973, 35¢)-Smith-r/#2,4; Smith-c 1.00 3.00 10.00
Annual 2(1976, 50¢)-New full length story 3.50
Annual 3(1978)-Chaykin/N. Adams-r/SSOC #2 2.00
Annual 4-6: 4(1978)-New full length story. 5(1979)-New full length Buscema story & part-c, 6(1981)-Kane-c/a 1.50
Annual 7-12: 7(1982)-Based on novel "Conan of the Isles" (new-a). 8(1984). 9(1984), 10(1986). 11(1986). 12(1987) 1.25
Special Edition 1 (Red Nails) 3.50

NOTE: ***Arthur Adams*** *c-248, 249.* ***Neal Adams*** *a-116r(i); c-49i.* ***Austin*** *a-125, 126; c-125i, 126i.* ***Brunner*** *c-17i. c-40.* ***Buscema*** *a-25-36p, 38, 39, 41-56p, 58-63p, 65-67p, 68, 70-78p, 84-86p, 88-91p, 93-126p, 136p, 140, 141-144p, 146-158p, 159, 161, 162, 163p, 165-185p, 187-190p, Annual 2(3pgs.). 3-5p, 7p; c(p)-26, 36, 44, 46, 52, 56, 58, 59, 64, 65, 72, 78-80, 83-91, 93-103, 105-126, 136-151, 155-159, 161, 162, 168, 169, 171, 172, 174, 175, 178-185, 188, 189, Annual 4, 5, 7.* ***Chaykin*** *a-79-83.* ***Golden*** *c-152.* ***Kaluta*** *c-167.* ***Gil Kane*** *a-12p, 17p, 18p, 127-130, 131-134p; c-12p, 17p, 18p, 23, 25, 27-32, 34, 35, 38, 39, 41-43, 45-51, 53-55, 57, 60-63, 65-71, 73p, 76p, 127-134.* ***Jim Lee*** *c-242.* ***McFarlane*** *c-241p.* ***Ploog*** *a-57.* ***Russell*** *a-21; c-251i.* ***Simonson*** *c-135.* ***B. Smith*** *a-1-11p, 12, 13-15p, 16, 19-21, 23, 24; c-1-11, 13-16, 19-24p.* ***Starlin*** *a-64.* ***Wood*** *a-47r. Issue Nos. 3-5, 7-9, 11, 16-18, 21, 23, 25, 27-30, 35, 37, 38, 42, 45, 52, 57, 58, 65, 69-71, 73, 79-83, 99, 100, 104, 114, Annual 2 have original Robert E. Howard stories adapted. Issues #32-34 adapted from Norvell Page's novel* ***Flame Winds****.*

CONAN THE BARBARIAN (Volume 2)
Marvel Comics: July, 1997 - No. 3, Oct, 1997 ($2.50, limited series)

1-3-Castellini-a 2.50

CONAN THE BARBARIAN MOVIE SPECIAL (Movie)
Marvel Comics Group: Oct, 1982 - No. 2, Nov, 1982

1,2-Movie adaptation; Buscema-a 1.00

CONAN THE BARBARIAN: THE USURPER
Marvel Comics: Dec, 1997 - No. 3, Feb, 1998 ($2.50, limited series)

1-3-Dixon-s 2.50

CONAN THE DESTROYER (Movie)
Marvel Comics Group: Jan, 1985 - No. 2, Mar, 1985

1,2-r/Marvel Super Special 1.00

CONAN THE KING (Formerly King Conan)

GD25 FN65 NM94

Marvel Comics Group: No. 20, Jan, 1984 - No. 55, Nov, 1989

20-55: 48-55 ($1.50) 1.50

NOTE: ***Kaluta*** *c-20-23, 24i, 26, 27, 30, 50, 52.* ***Williamson*** *a-37i; c-37i, 38i.*

CONAN: THE LORD OF THE SPIDERS
Marvel Comics: Mar, 1998 - No. 3, May, 1998 ($2.50, limited series)

1-3-Roy Thomas-s/Raffaele-a 2.50

CONAN THE SAVAGE
Marvel Comics: Aug, 1995 - No. 10, May, 1996 ($2.95, B&W, Magazine)

1-10: 1-Bisley-c. 4-vs. Malibu Comic's Rune. 5,10-Brereton-c 3.00

CONAN VS. RUNE (Also See Conan #4)
Marvel Comics: Nov, 1995 ($2.95, one-shot)

1-Barry Smith-c/a/scripts 3.00

CONCRETE (Also see Dark Horse Presents & Within Our Reach)
Dark Horse Comics: March, 1987 - No. 10, Nov, 1988 ($1.50, B&W)

1-Paul Chadwick-c/a in all 5.00
1-2nd print 1.50
2 3.00
3-Origin 2.00
4-10 1.50
A New Life 1 (1989, $2.95, B&W)-r/#3,4 plus new-a (11 pgs.) 3.00
Celebrates Earth Day 1990 ($3.50, 52 pgs.) 3.50
Color Special 1 (2/89, $2.95, 44 pgs.)-r/1st two Concrete apps. from Dark Horse Presents #1,2 plus new-a 3.00
Land And Sea 1 (2/89, $2.95, B&W)-r/#1,2 3.00
Odd Jobs 1 (7/90, $3.50)-r/5,6 plus new-a 3.50

CONCRETE: ECLECTICA
Dark Horse Comics: Apr, 1993 - No. 2, May, 1993 ($2.95, limited series)

1,2 3.00

CONCRETE: FRAGILE CREATURE
Dark Horse Comics: June, 1991 - No. 4, Feb, 1992 ($2.50, limited series)

1-4 2.50

CONCRETE: KILLER SMILE
Dark Horse Comics (Legend): July, 1994 - No. 4, Oct, 1994 ($2.95, lim. series)

1-4: 1st Concrete limited series under Legend Imprint 3.00

CONCRETE: STRANGE ARMOR
Dark Horse Comics: Dec, 1997 - No. 5, May, 1998 ($2.95, color, limited series)

1-5-Chadwick-s/c/a; retells origin 3.00

CONCRETE: THINK LIKE A MOUNTAIN
Dark Horse Comics (Legend): Mar, 1996 - No. 6, Aug, 1996 ($2.95, lim. series)

1-6: Chadwick-a/scripts & Darrow-c in all 3.00

CONDORMAN (Walt Disney)
Whitman Publishing: Oct, 1981 - No. 3, Jan, 1982

1-3: 1,2-Movie adaptation; photo-c 1.00

CONEHEADS
Marvel Comics: June, 1994 - No. 4, 1994 ($1.75, limited series)

1-4 1.75

CONFESSIONS ILLUSTRATED (Magazine)
E. C. Comics: Jan-Feb, 1956 - No. 2, Spring, 1956

1-Craig, Kamen, Wood, Orlando-a 14.00 42.00 105.00
2-Craig, Crandall, Kamen, Orlando-a 12.00 36.00 90.00

CONFESSIONS OF LOVE
Artful Publ.: Apr, 1950 - No. 2, July, 1950 (25¢, 7-1/4x5-1/4", 132 pgs.)

1-Bakerish-a 24.00 72.00 180.00
2-Art & text; Bakerish-a 13.00 40.00 100.00

CONFESSIONS OF LOVE (Formerly Startling Terror Tales #10; becomes

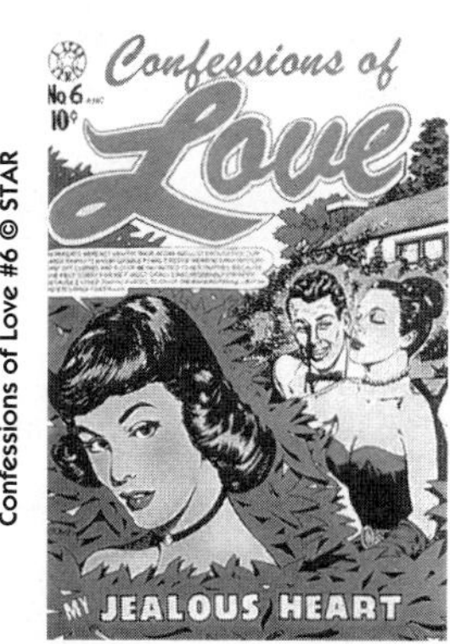

Confessions of Love #6 © STAR

Conspiracy #1 © MAR

Coo Coo Comics #34 © STD

Confessions of Romance No. 7 on)
Star Publications: No. 11, 7/52 - No. 14, 1/53; No. 4, 3/53- No. 6, 8/53

	GD25	FN65	NM94
11-13: 12,13-Disbrow-a	12.00	36.00	90.00
14,5,6	9.30	28.00	65.00
4-Disbrow-a	10.00	30.00	75.00

NOTE: *All have **L. B. Cole** covers.*

CONFESSIONS OF ROMANCE (Formerly Confessions of Love)
Star Publications: No. 7, Nov, 1953 - No. 11, Nov, 1954

	GD25	FN65	NM94
7	12.00	36.00	90.00
8	9.30	28.00	65.00
9-Wood-a	11.00	34.00	85.00
10,11-Disbrow-a	10.00	30.00	75.00

NOTE: *All have **L. B. Cole** covers.*

CONFESSIONS OF THE LOVELORN (Formerly Lovelorn)
American Comics Group (Regis Publ./Best Synd. Features): No. 52, Aug, 1954 - No. 114, June-July, 1960

	GD25	FN65	NM94
52 (3-D effect)	25.00	76.00	190.00
53,55	6.50	19.50	45.00
54 (3-D effect)	25.00	76.00	190.00
56-Anti-communist propaganda story, 10 pgs; last pre-code (2/55)	8.50	26.00	60.00
57-90	4.15	12.50	25.00
91-Williamson-a	6.50	19.50	45.00
92-99,101-114	4.00	12.00	20.00
100	4.15	12.50	25.00

NOTE: ***Whitney** a-most issues; c-52, 53. Painted c-106, 107.*

CONFIDENTIAL DIARY (Formerly High School Confidential Diary; Three Nurses #18 on)
Charlton Comics: No. 12, May, 1962 - No. 17, Mar, 1963

	GD25	FN65	NM94
12-17	1.85	5.50	15.00

CONGO BILL (See Action Comics & More Fun Comics #56)
National Periodical Publication: Aug-Sept, 1954 - No. 7, Aug-Sept, 1955

	GD25	FN65	VF82
1 (Scarce)	83.00	249.00	700.00
2,7 (Scarce)	65.00	195.00	550.00
3-6 (Scarce). 4-Last pre-code issue	59.00	177.00	475.00

NOTE: *(Rarely found in fine to mint condition.)* ***Nick Cardy** c-1-7.*

CONGORILLA (Also see Actions Comics #224)
DC Comics: Nov, 1992 - No. 4, Feb, 1993 ($1.75, limited series)

	GD25	FN65	NM94
1-4: 1,2-Brian Bolland-c			1.75

CONNECTICUT YANKEE, A (See King Classics)

CONQUEROR, THE
Dell Publishing Co.: No., 690, Mar, 1956

	GD25	FN65	NM94
Four Color 690-Movie, John Wayne photo-c	14.00	44.00	160.00

CONQUEROR COMICS
Albrecht Publishing Co.: Winter, 1945

	GD25	FN65	NM94
nn	16.00	48.00	120.00

CONQUEROR OF THE BARREN EARTH (See The Warlord #63)
DC Comics: Feb, 1985 - No. 4, May, 1985 (Limited series)

	GD25	FN65	NM94
1-4: Back-up series from Warlord			1.00

CONQUEST
Store Comics: 1953 (6¢)

	GD25	FN65	NM94
1-Richard the Lion Hearted, Beowulf, Swamp Fox	4.15	12.50	25.00

CONQUEST
Famous Funnies: Spring, 1955

	GD25	FN65	NM94
1-Crandall-a, 1 pg.; contains contents of 1953 ish.	4.00	11.00	22.00

CONSPIRACY
Marvel Comics: Feb, 1998 - No. 2, Mar, 1998 ($2.99, limited series)

	GD25	FN65	NM94
1,2-Painted art by Korday/Abnett-s			3.00

CONSTRUCT
Caliber (New Worlds): 1996 - No. 6, 1997 ($2.95, B&W, limited series)

	GD25	FN65	NM94
1-6: Paul Jenkins scripts			3.00

CONTACT COMICS
Aviation Press: July, 1944 - No. 12, May, 1946

	GD25	FN65	NM94
nn-Black Venus, Flamingo, Golden Eagle, Tommy Tomahawk begin	43.00	129.00	360.00
2-5: 3-Last Flamingo. 3,4-Black Venus by L. B. Cole. 5-The Phantom Flyer app.	37.00	110.00	275.00
6,11-Kurtzman's Black Venus; 11-Last Golden Eagle, last Tommy Tomahawk; Feldstein-a	39.00	117.00	300.00
7-10	32.00	96.00	240.00
12-Sky Rangers, Air Kids, Ace Diamond app.; L.B. Cole sci-fi cover	43.00	129.00	350.00

NOTE: ***L. B. Cole** a-3, 9; c-1-12. **Giunta** a-3. **Hollingsworth** a-5, 7, 10. **Palais** a-11, 12.*

CONTEMPORARY MOTIVATORS
Pendelum Press: 1977 - 1978 ($1.45, 5-3/8x8", 31 pgs., B&W)

	GD25	FN65	NM94
14-3002 The Caine Mutiny; 14-3010 Banner in the Sky; 14-3029 God Is My Co-Pilot; 14-3037 Guadalcanal Diary; 14-3045 Hiroshima; 14-3053 Hot Rod; 14-3061 Just Dial a Number; 14-307x Star Wars; 14-3088 The Diary of Anne Frank; 14-3096 Lost Horizon			3.00

NOTE: *Also see Pendulum Illustrated Classics. Above may have been distributed the same.*

CONTEST OF CHAMPIONS (See Marvel Super-Hero...)

CONTRACTORS
Eclipse Comics: June, 1987 ($2.00, B&W, one-shot)

	GD25	FN65	NM94
1-Funny animal			2.00

CONVOCATIONS: A MAGIC THE GATHERING GALLERY
Acclaim Comics (Armada): Jan, 1996 ($2.50, one-shot)

	GD25	FN65	NM94
1-pin-ups by various artists including Kaluta, Vess, and Dringenberg			2.50

COO COO COMICS (...the Bird Brain No. 57 on)
Nedor Publ. Co./Standard (Animated Cartoons): Oct, 1942 - No. 62, Apr, 1952

	GD25	FN65	NM94
1-Origin/1st app. Super Mouse & begin series (cloned from Superman); the first funny animal super hero series (see Looney Tunes #5 for 1st funny animal super hero)	25.00	76.00	190.00
2	11.00	34.00	85.00
3-10: 10-(3/44)	6.50	19.50	45.00
11-33: 33-1 pg. Ingels-a	5.35	16.00	32.00
34-40,43-46,48-Text illos by Frazetta in all. 36-Super Mouse covers begin	7.85	23.50	55.00
41-Frazetta-a (6-pg. story & 3 text illos)	15.00	44.00	110.00
42,47-Frazetta-a & text illos.	10.00	30.00	75.00
49-(1/50)-3-D effect story; Frazetta text illo	9.30	28.00	65.00
50,51-3-D effect-c only. 50-Frazetta text illo	8.30	25.00	58.00
52-62: 56-Last Supermouse?	4.15	12.50	25.00

"COOKIE" (Also see Topsy-Turvy)
Michel Publ./American Comics Group(Regis Publ.): Apr, 1946 - No. 55, Aug-Sept, 1955

	GD25	FN65	NM94
1-Teen-age humor	19.00	56.00	140.00
2	9.30	28.00	70.00
3-10	6.50	19.50	45.00
11-20	5.70	17.00	35.00
21-23,26,28-30	4.25	13.00	26.00
24,25,27-Starlett O'Hara stories	5.00	15.00	30.00
31-34,37-50,52-55	4.00	12.00	24.00
35,36-Starlett O'Hara stories	4.25	13.00	26.00
51-(10-11/54) 8pg. TrueVision 3-D effect story	6.85	21.00	48.00

COOL CAT (Formerly Black Magic)

Corum #4 © FC

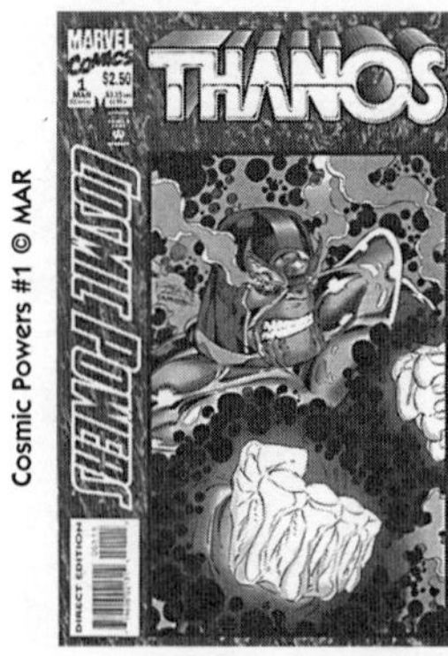

Cosmic Powers #1 © MAR

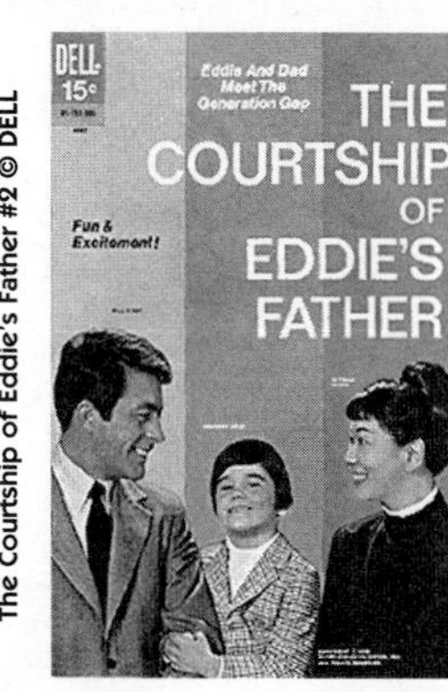

The Courtship of Eddie's Father #2 © DELL

GD25 FN65 NM94

Prize Publications: V8#6, Mar-Apr, 1962 - V9#2, July-Aug, 1962
V8#6, nn(V9#1, 5-6/62), V9#2 2.50 7.50 24.00

COOL WORLD (Movie)
DC Comics: Apr, 1992 - No. 4, Sept, 1992 ($1.75, limited series)
1-4: Prequel to animated/live action movie by Ralph Bakshi. 1-Bakshi-c. Bill Wray inks in all 1.75
Movie Adaptation nn ('92, $3.50, 68pg.)-Bakshi-c 3.50

COPPER CANYON (See Fawcett Movie Comics)

COPS (TV)
DC Comics: Aug, 1988 - No. 15, Aug, 1989 ($1.00)
1 ($1.50, 52 pgs.)-Based on Hasbro Toys 1.50
2-15: 14-Orlando-c(p) 1.00

COPS: THE JOB
Marvel Comics: June, 1992 - No. 4, Sept, 1992 ($1.25, limited series)
1-4: All have Jusko scripts & Golden-c 1.25

CORBEN SPECIAL, A
Pacific Comics: May, 1984 (one-shot)
1-Corben-c/a; E.A. Poe adaptation 3.00

CORKY & WHITE SHADOW (Disney, TV)
Dell Publishing Co.: No. 707, May, 1956 (Mickey Mouse Club)
Four Color 707-Photo-c 6.40 19.00 70.00

CORLISS ARCHER (See Meet Corliss Archer)

CORMAC MAC ART (Robert E. Howard's...)
Dark Horse Comics: 1990 - No. 4, 1990 ($1.95, B&W, mini-series)
1-4: All have Bolton painted-c; Howard adapts. 2.00

CORNY'S FETISH
Dark Horse Comics: Apr, 1998 ($4.95, B&W, one-shot)
1-Renée French-s/a; Bolland-c 4.95

CORPORAL RUSTY DUGAN (See Holyoke One-Shot #2)

CORPSES OF DR. SACOTTI, THE (See Ideal a Classical Comic)

CORSAIR, THE (See A-1 Comics No. 5, 7, 10)

CORTEZ AND THE FALL OF THE AZTECS
Tome Press: 1993 ($2.95, B&W, limited series)
1,2 3.00

CORUM: THE BULL AND THE SPEAR (See Chronicles Of Corum)
First Comics: Jan, 1989 - No. 4, July, 1989 ($1.95)
1-4: Adapts Michael Moorcock's novel 2.00

COSMIC BOOK, THE
Ace Comics: Dec, 1986 - No. 1, 1987 ($1.95)
1-(44pgs.)-Wood, Toth-a 2.00
2-(B&W) 1.60

COSMIC BOY (Also see The Legion of Super-Heroes)
DC Comics: Dec, 1986 - No. 4, Mar, 1987 (limited series)
1-4: Legends tie-ins all issues 1.00

COSMIC ODYSSEY
DC Comics: 1988 - No. 4, 1988 ($3.50, limited series, squarebound)
1-4: Reintro. New Gods into DC continuity; Superman, Batman, Green Lantern (John Stewart) app; Starlin scripts, Mignola-c/a in all. 2-Darkseid merges Demon & Jason Blood (seperated in Demon limited series #4); John Stewart responsible for the death of a star system. 3.50
Trade paperback-r/#1-4. 19.95

COSMIC POWERS
Marvel Comics: Mar, 1994 - No. 6, Aug, 1994 ($2.50, limited series)
1-6: 1-Ron Lim-c/a(p). 1,2-Thanos app. 2-Terrax. 3-Ganymede & Jack of Hearts app. 2.50

COSMIC POWERS UNLIMITED
Marvel Comics: May, 1995 - No. 5, May, 1996 ($3.95, quarterly)
1-5 4.00

COSMO CAT (Becomes Sunny #11 on; also see All Top & Wotalife Comics)
Fox Publications/Green Publ. Co./Norlen Mag.: July-Aug, 1946 - No. 10, Oct, 1947; 1957; 1959
1 25.00 76.00 190.00
2 13.00 38.00 95.00
3-Origin (11-12/46) 17.00 50.00 125.00
4-10: 4-Robot-c 7.85 23.50 55.00
2-4(1957-Green Publ. Co.) 4.25 13.00 28.00
2-4(1959-Norlen Mag.) 4.00 10.00 20.00
I.W. Reprint #1 1.50 4.50 12.00

COSMO THE MERRY MARTIAN
Archie Publications (Radio Comics): Sept, 1958 - No. 6, Oct, 1959
1-Bob White-a in all 13.00 38.00 95.00
2-6 9.30 28.00 65.00

COTTON WOODS
Dell Publishing Co.: No. 837, Sept, 1957
Four Color 837 2.75 8.00 30.00

COUGAR, THE (Cougar No. 2)
Seaboard Periodicals (Atlas): April, 1975 - No. 2, July, 1975
1,2: 1-Adkins-a(p). 2-Origin; Buckler-c(p) 3.00

COUNTDOWN (See Movie Classics)

COUNT DUCKULA (TV)
Marvel Comics: Nov, 1988 - No. 15, Jan, 1991 ($1.00)
1-7,9-15: Dangermouse back-ups. 3.00
8-Geraldo Rivera photo-c/& app.; Sienkiewicz-a(i) 5.00

COUNT OF MONTE CRISTO, THE
Dell Publishing Co.: No. 794, May, 1957
Four Color 794-Movie, Buscema-a 8.00 25.00 90.00

COURAGE COMICS
J. Edward Slavin: 1945
1,2,77 7.85 23.50 55.00

COURTSHIP OF EDDIE'S FATHER (TV)
Dell Publishing Co.: Jan, 1970 - No. 2, May, 1970
1,2-Bill Bixby photo-c 2.70 8.10 30.00

COVEN
Awesome Entertainment: Aug, 1997 - Present ($2.50)
Preview .90 2.70 8.00
1-Loeb-s/Churchill-a; Churchill-c .90 2.70 8.00
1-Liefeld variant-c .85 2.60 7.00
1-Pollina variant-c .90 2.70 8.00
1-American Entertainment Ed. .90 2.70 8.00
1-American Entertainment Gold Ed. 10.00
1-Fan Appreciation Ed.(3/98); new Churchill-c 3.00
1-Fan Appreciation Gold Ed. 10.00
1+ :Includes B&W art from Kaboom 1.00 3.00 10.00
1+ :Gold Ed. 7.50
1+ :Red Foil cover 12.00
2-Regular-c w/leaping Fantom 2.00 6.00
2-Variant-c w/circle of candles .90 2.70 8.00
2-American Entertainment Gold Ed. 8.00
2-Dynamic Forces Gold Ed. 10.00
3-6-Contains flip book preview of ReGex 3.00
3-White variant-c .85 2.60 7.00

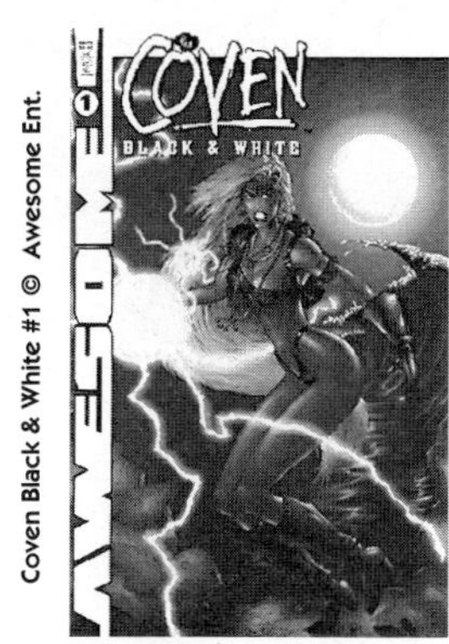

Coven Black & White #1 © Awesome Ent.

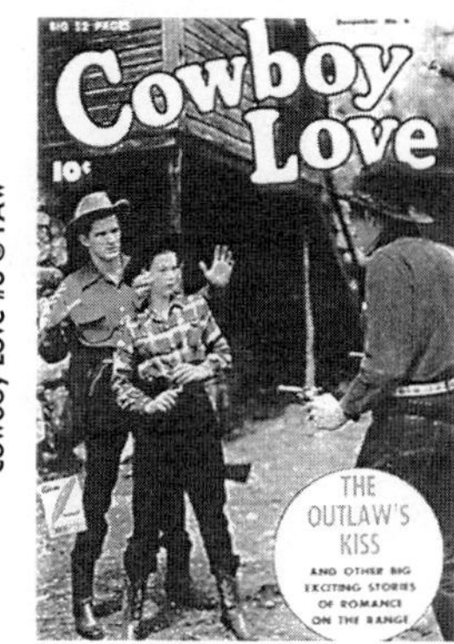

Cowboy Love #6 © FAW

Cowgirl Romances #8 © FH

GD25 FN65 NM94

3-Halloween wraparound-c 3.00
4-Purple variant-c 3.00
4-Dynamic Forces Ed. 5.00
4,5-Dynamic Forces Gold Ed. .90 2.70 8.00
5-Dynamic Forces Ed. 4.00
...Black & White (9/98) Short stories 3.00
...Fantom Special (2/98) w/sketch pages 5.00
...Fantom Special Gold Ed. 10.00

COVERED WAGONS, HO (Disney, TV)
Dell Publishing Co.: No. 814, June, 1957 (Donald Duck)

Four Color 814-Mickey Mouse app. 4.50 13.50 50.00

COWBOY ACTION (Formerly Western Thrillers No. 1-4; Becomes Quick-Trigger Western No. 12 on)
Atlas Comics (ACI): No. 5, March, 1955 - No. 11, March, 1956

5 11.00 32.00 80.00
6-10: 6-8-Heath-c 7.85 23.50 55.00
11-Williamson-a (4 pgs.); Baker-a 9.30 28.00 65.00
NOTE: *Ayers a-8. Drucker a-6. Maneely c/a-5, 6. Severin c-10. Shores a-7.*

COWBOY COMICS (Star Ranger #12, Stories #14)(Star Ranger Funnies #15)
Centaur Publishing Co.: No. 13, July, 1938 - No. 14, Aug, 1938

13-(Rare)-Ace and Deuce, Lyin Lou, Air Patrol, Aces High, Lee Trent, Trouble Hunters begin 112.00 336.00 950.00
14-Filchock-c 79.00 237.00 675.00
NOTE: *Guardineer a-13, 14. Gustavson a-13, 14.*

COWBOY IN AFRICA (TV)
Gold Key: Mar, 1968

1(10219-803)-Chuck Connors photo-c 3.50 10.50 38.00

COWBOY LOVE (Becomes Range Busters?)
Fawcett Publications/Charlton Comics No. 28 on: 7/49 - V2#10, 6/50; No. 11, 1951; No. 28, 2/55 - No. 31, 8/55

V1#1-Rocky Lane photo back-c 16.00 48.00 120.00
2 5.70 17.00 35.00
V1#3,4,6 (12/49) 5.00 15.00 30.00
5-Bill Boyd photo back-c (11/49) 5.70 17.00 40.00
V2#7-Williamson/Evans-a 7.85 23.50 55.00
V2#8-11 4.15 12.50 25.00
V1#28 (Charlton)-Last precode (2/55) (Formerly Romantic Story?) 4.15 12.50 25.00
V1#29-31 (Charlton; becomes Sweetheart Diary #32 on) 4.00 11.00 22.00
NOTE: *Powell a-10. Marcus Swayze a-2, 3. Photo c-1-11. No. 1-3, 5-7, 9, 10 are 52 pgs.*

COWBOY ROMANCES (Young Men No. 4 on)
Marvel Comics (IPC): Oct, 1949 - No. 3, Mar, 1950 (All photo-c & 52 pgs.)

1-Photo-c 20.00 60.00 150.00
2-William Holden, Mona Freeman "Streets of Laredo" photo-c 13.00 38.00 95.00
3-Photo-c 11.00 32.00 80.00

COWBOYS 'N' INJUNS (...and Indians No. 6 on)
Com No. 1-5/Magazine Enterprises No. 6 on: 1946 - No. 5, 1947; No. 6, 1949 - No. 8, 1952

1 9.30 28.00 70.00
2-5-All funny animal western 6.50 19.50 45.00
6(A-1 23)-Half violent, half funny; Ayers-a 8.50 26.00 60.00
7(A-1 41, 1950), 8(A-1 48)-All funny 6.50 19.50 45.00
I.W. Reprint No. 1,7 (Reprinted in Canada by Superior, No. 7) 1.50 4.50 12.00
Super Reprint #10 (1963) 1.50 4.50 12.00

COWBOY WESTERN COMICS (TV)(Formerly Jack In The Box; Becomes Space Western No. 40-45 & Wild Bill Hickok & Jingles No. 68 on; title:Cowboy Western Heroes No. 47 & 48; Cowboy Western No. 49 on)
Charlton (Capitol Stories): No. 17, 7/48 - No. 39, 8/52; No. 46, 10/53; No. 47, 12/53; No. 48, Spr, '54;
No. 49, 5-6/54 - No. 67, 3/58 (nn 40-45)

17-Jesse James, Annie Oakley, Wild Bill Hickok begin; Texas Rangers app. 16.00 48.00 120.00
18,19-Orlando-c/a. 18-Paul Bunyan begins. 19-Wyatt Earp story 9.30 28.00 70.00
20-25: 21-Buffalo Bill story. 22-Texas Rangers-c/story. 24-Joel McCrea photo-c & adaptation from movie "Three Faces West". 25-James Craig photo-c & adaptation from movie "Northwest Stampede" 8.50 26.00 60.00
26-George Montgomery photo-c and adaptation from movie "Indian Scout"; 1 pg. bio on Will Rogers 10.00 30.00 75.00
27-Sunset Carson photo-c & adapts movie "Sunset Carson Rides Again" plus 1 other Sunset Carson story 53.00 159.00 450.00
28-Sunset Carson line drawn-c; adapts movies "Battling Marshal" & "Fighting Mustangs" starring Sunset Carson 30.00 90.00 225.00
29-Sunset Carson line drawn-c; adapts movies "Rio Grande" with Sunset Carson & "Winchester '73" w/James Stewart plus 5 pg. life history of Sunset Carson featuring Tom Mix 30.00 90.00 225.00
30-Sunset Carson photo-c; adapts movie "Deadline" starring Sunset Carson plus 1 other Sunset Carson story 53.00 159.00 450.00
31-34,38,39,47-50 (no #40-45): 50-Golden Arrow, Rocky Lane & Blackjack (r?) stories 6.50 19.50 45.00
35,36-Sunset Carson-c/stories (2 in each). 35-Inside front-c photo of Sunset Carson plus photo on-c 30.00 90.00 225.00
37-Sunset Carson stories (2) 19.00 56.00 140.00
46-(Formerly Space Western)-Space western story 17.00 52.00 130.00
51-57,59-66: 51-Golden Arrow(r?) & Monte Hale-r renamed Rusty Hall. 53,54-Tom Mix-r. 55-Monte Hale story(r?). 66-Young Eagle story. 67-Wild Bill Hickok and Jingles-c/story 5.00 15.00 30.00
58-(1/56, 15¢, 68 pgs.)-Wild Bill Hickok, Annie Oakley & Jesse James stories; Forgione-a 5.70 17.00 35.00
67-(15¢, 68 pgs.)-Williamson/Torres-a, 5 pgs. 8.50 26.00 60.00
NOTE: *Many issues trimmed 1" shorter. Maneely a-67(5). Inside front/back photo c-29.*

COWGIRL ROMANCES (Young Men No. 4 on)
Marvel Comics (CCC): No. 28, Jan, 1950 (52 pgs.)

28(#1)-Photo-c 18.00 54.00 135.00

COWGIRL ROMANCES
Fiction House Magazines: 1950 - No. 12, Winter, 1952-53 (No. 1-3: 52 pgs.)

1-Kamen-a 29.00 88.00 220.00
2 15.00 44.00 110.00
3-5: 5-12-Whitman-c (most) 13.00 40.00 100.00
6-9,11,12 12.00 36.00 90.00
10-Frazetta?/Williamson?-a; Kamen?/Baker-a; r/Mitzi story from Movie Comics #4 w/all new dialogue 29.00 88.00 220.00

COW PUNCHER (...Comics)
Avon Periodicals: Jan, 1947; No. 2, Sept, 1947 - No. 7, 1949

1-Clint Cortland, Texas Ranger, Kit West, Pioneer Queen begin; Kubert-a; Alabam stories begin 39.00 117.00 290.00
2-Kubert, Kamen/Feldstein-a; Kamen-c 31.00 93.00 230.00
3-5,7: 3-Kiefer story 21.00 63.00 160.00
6-Opium drug mention story; bondage, headlight-c; Reinman-a 27.00 81.00 200.00

COWPUNCHER
Realistic Publications: 1953 (nn) (Reprints Avon's No. 2)

nn-Kubert-a 10.00 30.00 70.00

COWSILLS, THE (See Harvey Pop Comics)

COYOTE
Marvel Comics (Epic Comics): June, 1983 - No. 16, Mar, 1986

1-10,15: 7-10-Ditko-a 2.00
11-1st McFarlane-a. 2.00 6.00

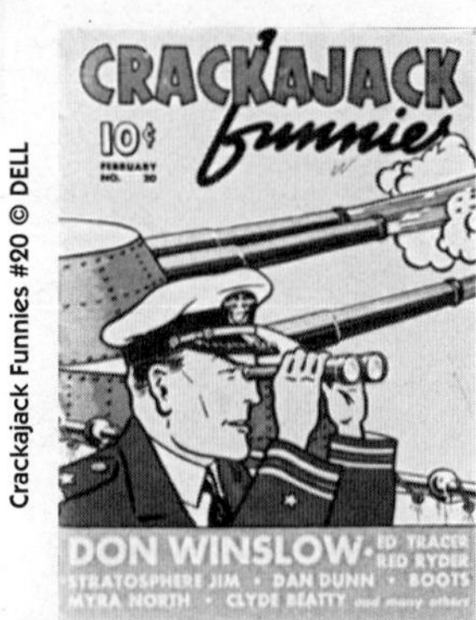

Crackajack Funnies #20 © DELL

Crack Comics #42 © QUA

Cracked #266 © Globe Comm. Corp.

	GD25	FN65	NM94
12-14,16: 12-14-McFarlane-a. 14-Badger x-over. 16-Reagan c/app.			4.00

CRACKAJACK FUNNIES (Giveaway)
Malto-Meal: 1937 (Full size, soft-c, full color, 32 pgs.)(Before No. 1?)

	GD25	FN65	NM94
nn-Features Dan Dunn, G-Man, Speed Bolton, Freckles, Buck Jones, Clyde Beatty, The Nebbs, Major Hoople, Wash Tubbs	88.00	265.00	750.00

CRACKAJACK FUNNIES (Also see The Owl)
Dell Publishing Co.: June, 1938 - No. 43, Jan, 1942

	GD25	FN65	NM94
1-Dan Dunn, Freckles, Myra North, Wash Tubbs, Apple Mary, The Nebbs, Don Winslow, Tom Mix, Buck Jones, Major Hoople, Clyde Beatty, Boots begin	224.00	672.00	1900.00
2	91.00	273.00	775.00
3	65.00	195.00	550.00
4	49.00	147.00	420.00
5-Nude woman on cover	52.00	156.00	440.00
6-8,10: 8-Speed Bolton begins (1st app.)	41.00	123.00	325.00
9-(3/39)-Red Ryder strip-r begin by Harman; 1st app. in comics & 1st cover app.	115.00	345.00	975.00
11-14	39.00	117.00	310.00
15-Tarzan text feature begins by Burroughs (9/39); not in #26,35	42.00	127.00	340.00
16-24: 18-Stratosphere Jim begins (1st app., 12/39). 23-Ellery Queen begins plus-c (1st comic book app., 5/40)	31.00	92.00	230.00
25-The Owl begins (1st app., 7/40); in new costume #26 by Frank Thomas (also see Popular Comics #72)	65.00	194.00	550.00
26-30: 28-Part Owl-c	46.00	138.00	390.00
31-Owl covers begin, end #42	44.00	132.00	375.00
32-Origin Owl Girl	52.00	156.00	440.00
33-38: 36-Last Tarzan issue. 37-Cyclone & Midge begin (1st app.)	39.00	117.00	300.00
39-Andy Panda begins (intro/1st app., 9/41)	44.00	132.00	375.00
40-42: 42-Last Owl-c.	39.00	116.00	290.00
43-Terry & the Pirates-r	33.00	100.00	250.00

NOTE: ***McWilliams** art in most issues.*

CRACK COMICS (Crack Western No. 63 on)
Quality Comics Group: May, 1940 - No. 62, Sept, 1949

	GD25	FN65	NM94
1-Origin & 1st app. The Black Condor by Lou Fine, Madame Fatal, Red Torpedo, Rock Bradden & The Space Legion; The Clock, Alias the Spider (by Gustavson), Wizard Wells, & Ned Brant begin; Powell-a; Note: Madame Fatal is a man dressed as a woman	421.00	1263.00	4000.00
2	188.00	564.00	1600.00
3	129.00	387.00	1100.00
4	115.00	345.00	975.00
5-10: 5-Molly The Model begins. 10-Tor, the Magic Master begins	88.00	264.00	750.00
11-20: 13-1 pg. J. Cole-a. 18-1st app. Spitfire?	77.00	231.00	650.00
21-24: 23-Pen Miller begins; continued from National Comics #22. 24-Last Fine Black Condor	59.00	177.00	500.00
25,26: 26-Flag-c	50.00	150.00	425.00
27-(1/43)-Intro & origin Captain Triumph by Alfred Andriola (Kerry Drake artist) & begin series	88.00	264.00	750.00
28-30	41.00	123.00	325.00
31-39: 31-Last Black Condor	25.00	74.00	185.00
40-46	17.00	52.00	130.00
47-57,59,60-Capt. Triumph by Crandall	19.00	58.00	145.00
58,61,62-Last Captain Triumph	13.00	38.00	95.00

NOTE: *Black Condor by **Fine**: No. 1, 2, 4-6, 8, 10-24; by **Sultan**: No. 3, 7; by **Fugitani**: No. 9. **Cole** a-34. **Crandall** a-61(unsigned); c-48, 49, 51-61. **Guardineer** a-17. **Gustavson** a-1, 13, 17. **McWilliams** a-15-27. Black Condor c-2, 4, 6, 8, 10, 12, 14, 16, 18, 20-26. Capt. Triumph c-27-62. The Clock c-1, 3, 5, 7, 9, 11, 13, 15, 17, 19.*

CRACKED (Magazine) (Satire) (Also see The 3-D Zone #19)
Major Magazines(#1-212)/Globe Communications(#213 on): Feb-Mar, 1958 - Present

	GD25	FN65	NM94
1-One pg. Williamson-a	12.00	36.00	120.00
2-1st Shut-Ups & Bonus Cut-Outs	5.00	15.00	50.00
3-6	3.00	9.00	30.00
7-10: 7-Reprints 1st 6 covers on-c	2.50	7.50	24.00
11-12, 13(nn,3/60), 14-17, 18(nn,2/61), 19,20	2.50	7.50	22.00
21-27(11/62), 27(No.28, 2/63; mis-#d), 29(5/63)	2.25	6.75	18.00
31-60	2.00	6.00	16.00
61-98,100	1.50	4.50	12.00
99-Alfred E. Neuman on-c	2.80	8.40	32.00
101-150: 131-Bill Ward-a	1.10	3.30	9.00
151-200: 234-Don Martin-a begins ($1.75 #? on)		2.00	6.00
201-300			4.00
301-341			2.50
Biggest... (Winter, 1977)	1.70	5.25	14.00
Biggest, Greatest... nn('65)	3.20	9.60	32.00
Biggest, Greatest... 2('66) - #5('69)	2.50	7.50	20.00
Biggest, Greatest... 6('70) - #12('76)	2.00	6.00	16.00
...Blockbuster 1,2 ('88)		2.40	6.00
...Digest 1(Fall, '86, 148 pgs.) - #5		2.40	6.00
...Collectors' Edition 4 ('73; formerly ...Special)	1.50	4.50	12.00
5-10	1.50	4.50	12.00
11-30: 23-Ward-a	1.10	3.30	9.00
31-50	1.00	2.80	7.00
51-70			5.00
71-84: 83-Elvis, Batman parodies			4.00
...Party Pack 1,2('88)			4.00
...Shut-Ups (2/72-'72; Cracked Spec. #3) 1	2.50	7.50	20.00
2	1.50	4.50	12.00
...Special 3('73; formerly Cracked Shut-Ups; ...Collectors' Edition#4 on)	1.00	3.00	8.00
Extra Special... 1('76)	1.50	4.50	12.00
Extra Special... 2('76)	1.00	3.00	8.00
Giant... nn('65)	4.00	12.00	40.00
Giant... 2('66)-5('69)	2.80	8.40	28.00
Giant...6('70)-12('76)	2.50	7.50	22.00
Giant...nn(9/77)-24	1.85	5.50	15.00
Giant...25-35	1.50	4.50	12.00
Giant...36-48('87)	1.00	3.00	8.00
King Sized... 1('67)	3.80	11.40	38.00
King Sized... 2('68)-5('71)	2.60	7.80	26.00
King Sized... 6('72)-11('77)	2.50	7.50	22.00
King Sized... 12-17	1.50	4.50	12.00
King Sized... 18-22 (Sum/'86)	1.00	3.00	8.00
Super... 1('68)	3.00	9.00	30.00
Super... 2('69)-5	2.60	7.80	26.00
Super... 6-10	2.50	7.50	20.00
Super... 11-16	2.00	6.00	16.00
Super... 17-24('88)	1.50	4.50	12.00
Super... 1('87, 100 pgs.)-Severin & Elder-a	1.00	3.00	8.00

NOTE: ***Burgos** a-1-10. **Colan** a-257. **Davis** a-5, 11-17, 24, 40, 80; c-12-14, 16. **Elder** a-5, 6, 10-13; c-10. **Everett** a-1-10, 23-25, 61; c-1. **Heath** a-1-3, 6, 13, 14, 17, 110; c-6. **Jaffee** a-5, 6. **Don Martin** c-235, 244, 247, 259, 261, 264. **Morrow** a-8-10. **Reinman** a-1-4. **Severin** c/a-in most all issues. **Shores** a-3-7. **Torres** a-7-10. **Ward** a-22-24, 27, 35, 40, 143, 144, 149, 150, 152, 153, 156. **Williamson** a-1 (1 pg.). **Wolverton** a-10 (2 pgs.), Giant nn('65). **Wood** a-27, 35, 40. Alfred E. Neuman c-177, 200, 202. Batman c-234, 248, 249, 256. Captain America c-256. Christmas c-234, 243. Spider-Man c-260. Star Trek c-127, 169, 207, 228. Star Wars c-145, 146, 148, 149, 152, 155, 173, 174, 199. Superman c-183, 233. #144, 146 have free full-color pre-glued stickers. #145, 147, 155, 163 have free full-color postcards. #123, 137, 154, 157 have free iron-ons.*

CRACKED MONSTER PARTY
Globe Communications: July, 1988 - No. 26, 1990?

	GD25	FN65	NM94
1	1.20	3.60	12.00
2-10	.90	2.70	8.00
11-26			5.00

CRACKED'S FOR MONSTERS ONLY
Major Magazines: Sept, 1969 - No. 9, Sept, 1969

	GD25	FN65	NM94
1	2.80	8.40	28.00

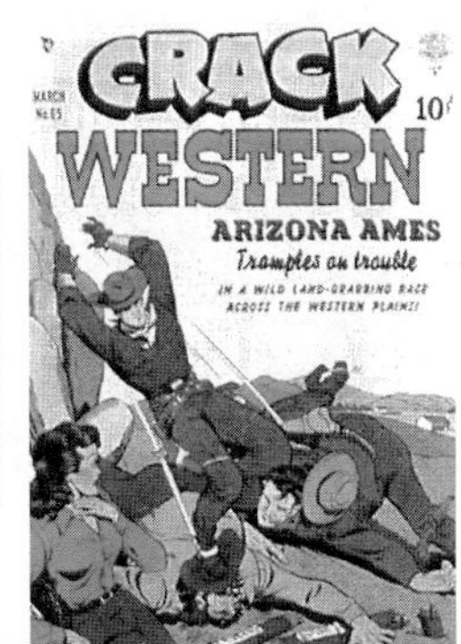

Crack Western #65 © QUA

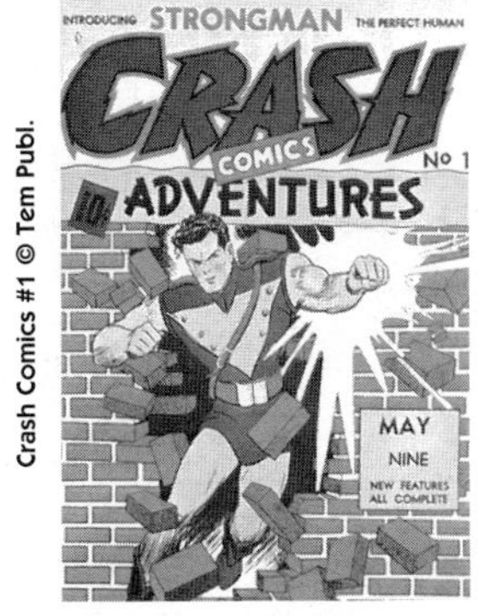

Crash Comics #1 © Tem Publ.

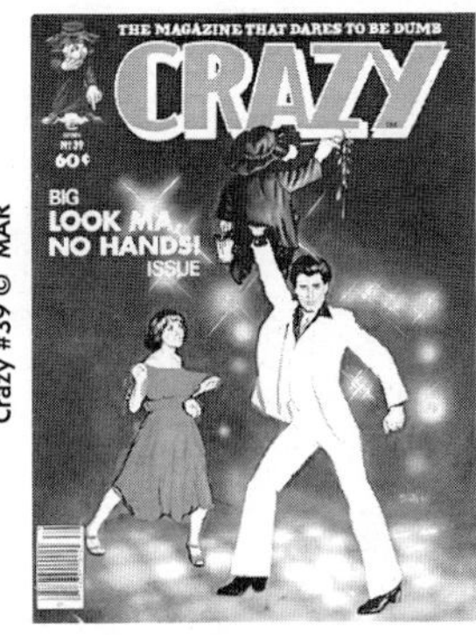

Crazy #39 © MAR

	GD25	FN65	NM94
2-9	1.75	5.25	14.00

CRACKED SPACED OUT
Globe Communications: Fall, 1993 - No. 4, 1994?

1-4			3.00

CRACK WESTERN (Formerly Crack Comics; Jonesy No. 85 on)
Quality Comics Group: No. 63, Nov, 1949 - No. 84, May, 1953 (36 pgs., 63-68,74-on)

63(#1)-Ward-c; Two-Gun Lil (origin & 1st app.)(ends #84), Arizona Ames, his horse Thunder (with sidekick Spurs & his horse Calico), Frontier Marshal (ends #70), & Dead Canyon Days (ends #69) begin; Crandall-a	20.00	60.00	150.00
64,65: 64-Ward-c. Crandall-a in both.	15.00	44.00	110.00
66,68-Photo-c. 66-Arizona Ames becomes A. Raines (ends #84)	13.00	38.00	95.00
67-Randolph Scott photo-c; Crandall-a	15.00	44.00	110.00
69(52pgs.)-Crandall-a	13.00	38.00	95.00
70(52pgs.)-The Whip (origin & 1st app.) & his horse Diablo begin (ends #84); Crandall-a	13.00	38.00	95.00
71(52pgs.)-Frontier Marshal becomes Bob Allen F. Marshal (ends #84); Crandall-c/a	15.00	44.00	110.00
72(52pgs.)-Tim Holt photo-c	12.00	36.00	90.00
73(52pgs.)-Photo-c	8.50	26.00	60.00
74-76,78,79,81,83-Crandall-c. 83-Crandall-a(p)	11.00	32.00	80.00
77,80,82	7.15	21.50	50.00
84-Crandall-c/a	12.00	36.00	90.00

NOTE: *Crandall c-71p, 74-81, 83p(w/**Cuidera**-i).*

CRASH COMICS (Catman Comics No. 6 on)
Tem Publishing Co.: May, 1940 - No. 5, Nov, 1940

1-The Blue Streak, Strongman (origin), The Perfect Human, Shangra begin (1st app. of each); Kirby-a	271.00	813.00	2300.00
2-Simon & Kirby-a	129.00	387.00	1100.00
3,5-Simon & Kirby-a	112.00	336.00	950.00
4-Origin & 1st app. The Catman; S&K-a	259.00	777.00	2200.00

NOTE: *Solar Legion by **Kirby** No. 1-5 (5 pgs. each). Strongman c-1-4. Catman c-5.*

CRASH DIVE (See Cinema Comics Herald)

CRASH RYAN (Also see Dark Horse Presents #44)
Marvel Comics (Epic): Oct, 1984 - No. 4, Jan, 1985 (Baxter paper, lim. series)

1-4			1.50

CRAZY (Also see This Magazine is Crazy)
Atlas Comics (CSI): Dec, 1953 - No. 7, July, 1954

1-Everett-c/a	23.00	68.00	170.00
2	17.00	50.00	125.00
3-7: 4-I Love Lucy satire. 5-Satire on censorship	14.00	42.00	105.00

NOTE: ***Ayers** a-5. **Berg** a-1, 2. **Burgos** c-5, 6. **Drucker** a-6. **Everett** a-1-4. **Al Hartley** a-4. **Heath** a-3, 7; c-7. **Maneely** a-1-7, c-3, 4. **Post** a-3-6. Funny monster c-1-4.*

CRAZY (Satire)
Marvel Comics Group: Feb, 1973 - No. 3, June, 1973

1-Not Brand Echh-r; Beatles cameo (r)	1.60	4.80	16.00
2,3-Not Brand Echh-r	1.10	3.30	11.00

CRAZY MAGAZINE (Satire)
Oct, 1973 - No. 94, Apr, 1983 (40-90¢, B&W magazine)
Marvel Comics: (#1, 44 pgs; #2-90, reg. issues, 52 pgs; #92-95, 68 pgs)'

1-Wolverton(1 pg.), Bode-a; 3 pg. photo story of Neal Adams & Dick Giordano; Harlan Ellison story; TV Kung Fu sty.	2.25	6.80	25.00
2-"Live & Let Die" c/s; 8pgs; Adams/Buscema-a; McCloud w5 pgs. Adams-a; Kurtzman's "Hey Look" 2 pg.-r	2.00	6.00	20.00
3-5: 3-"High Plains Drifter" w/Clint Eastwood c/s; Waltons app; Drucker, Reese-a. 4-Shaft-c/s; Ploog-a; Nixon 3 pg. app; Freas-a. 5-Michael Crichton's "Westworld" c/s; Nixon app.	1.50	4.50	15.00
6,7,18: 6-Exorcist c/s; Nixon app. 7-TV's Kung Fu c/s; Nixon app.; Ploog & Freas-a. 18-Six Million Dollar Man/Bionic Woman c/s; Welcome Back Kotter story	1.20	3.60	12.00
8-10: 8-Serpico c/s; Casper parody; TV's Police Story. 9-Joker cameo; China-town story; Eisner s/a begins; Has 1st 8 covers on-c. 10-Playboy Bunny-c; M. Severin-a; Lee Marrs-a begins; "Deathwish" story	1.00	3.00	10.00
11-17,19: 11-Towering Inferno. 12-Rhoda. 13-"Tommy" the Who Rock Opera. 14-Mandingo. 15-Jaws story. 16-Santa/Xmas-c; "Good Times" TV story; Jaws. 17-Bi-Centennial ish; Baretta; Woody Allen. 19-King Kong c/s; Reagan, J. Carter, Howard the Duck cameos, "Laverne & Shirley"	.90	2.70	8.00
20,27: 20-Bi-Centennial-c; Space 1999 sty; Superheroes song sheet, 4pgs. 27-Charlies Angels/Travolta/Fonz-c; Bionic Woman sty	1.00	3.00	10.00
21-23,25,26,28-30: 21-Starskey & Hutch. 22-Mount Rushmore/J. Carter-c; TV's Barney Miller; Superheroes spoof. 23-Santa/Xmas-c; "Happy Days" sty; "Omen" sty. 25-J. Carter-c/s; Grandenetti-a begins; TV's Alice; Logans Run. 26-TV Stars-c; Mary Hartman, King Kong. 28-Donny & Marie Osmond-c/s; Marathon Man. 29-Travolta/Kotter-c; "One Day at a Time", Gong Show. 30-1977, 84 pgs. w/bonus; Jaws, Baretta, King Kong, Happy Days	.90	2.70	8.00
24-Charlies Angels	1.20	3.60	12.00
31,33-35,38,40: 31-"Rocky"-c/s; TV game shows. 33-Peter Benchley's "Deep". 34-J. Carter-c; TV's "Fish". 35-Xmas-c with Fonz/Six Million Dollar Man/ Wonder Woman/Darth Vader/Travolta, TV's "Mash" & "Family Matters". 38-Close Encounters of the Third Kind-c/s. 40-"Three's Company-c/s		2.00	6.00
32-Star Wars/Darth Vader-c/s; "Black Sunday"	1.50	4.50	15.00
36,42,47,49: 36-Farrah Fawcett/Six Million Dollar Man-c; TV's Nancy Drew & Hardy Boys; 1st app. Howard The Duck in Crazy, 2 pgs. 42-84 pgs. w/bonus; TV Hulk/Spider-Man-c; Mash, Gong Show, One Day at a Time, Disco, Alice. 47-Battlestar Galactica xmas-c; movie "Foul Play". 49-1979, 84 pgs. w/bonus; Mork & Mindy-c; Jaws, Saturday Night Fever, Three's Company	.90	2.70	8.00
37-1978, 84 pgs. w/bonus. Darth Vader-c; Barney Miller, Laverne & Shirley, Good Times, Rocky, Donny & Marie Osmond, Bionic Woman	1.20	3.60	12.00
39,44: 39-Saturday Night Fever-c/s. 44-"Grease"-c w/Travolta/O. Newton-John	1.00	3.00	10.00
41-Kiss-c & 1pg. photos; Disaster movies, TV's "Family", Annie Hall	2.25	6.80	25.00
43,45,46,48,51: 43-Jaws-c; Saturday Night Fever; Stallone's "Fist".43-E.C. swipe from Mad #131 45-Travolta/O. Newton-John/J. Carter-c; Eight is Enough. 46-TV Hulk-c/s; Punk Rock. 48-"Wiz"-c, Battlestar Galactica-s. 51-Grease/Mork & Mindy/D&M Osmond-c, Mork & Mindy-sty. "Boys from Brazil"		2.00	6.00
50,58: 50-Superman movie-c/sty, Playboy Mag., TV Hulk, Fonz; Howard the Duck, 1 pg. 58-1980, 84 pgs. w/32 pg. color comic bonus insert-Full reprint of Crazy Comic #1, Battlestar Galactica, Charlie's Angels, Starsky & Hutch	1.20	3.60	12.00
52,59,60,64: 52-1979, 84 pgs. w/bonus. Marlon Brando-c; TV Hulk, Grease. Kiss, 1 pg. photos. 59-Santa Ptd-c by Larkin; "Alien", "Moonraker", Rocky-2, Howard the Duck, 1 pg. 60-Star Trek w/Muppets-c; Star Trek sty; 1st app/origin Teen Hulk; Severin-a. 64-84 pgs. w/bonus Monopoly game satire. "Empire Strikes Back", 8 pgs,.One Day at a Time.	1.00	3.00	10.00
53,54,65,67-70: 53-"Animal House"-c/sty; TV's "Vegas", Howard the Duck, 1 pg. 54-Love at First Bite-c/sty, Fantasy Island sty, Howard the Duck 1 pg. 65-(Has #66 on-c, Aug/'80). "Black Hole" w/Janson-a; Kirby,Wood/Severin-a(r), 5 pgs. Howard the Duck, 3 pgs.; Broderick-a; Buck Rogers, Mr. Rogers. 67-84 pgs. w/bonus; TV's Kung Fu, Excorcist; Ploog-a(r). 68-American Gigalo, Dukes of Hazard, Teen Hulk; Howard the Duck, 3 pgs. Broderick-a; Monster sty/5 pg. Ditko-a(r). 69-Obnoxio the Clown-c/sty; Stephen King's "Shining", Teen Hulk, Richie Rich, Howard the Duck, 3pgs; Broderick-a. 70-84 pgs. Towering Inferno, Daytime TV; Trina Robbins-a		2.00	6.00

55-57,61,63: 55-84 pgs. w/bonus; Love Boat, Mork & Mindy, Fonz, TV Hulk. 56-

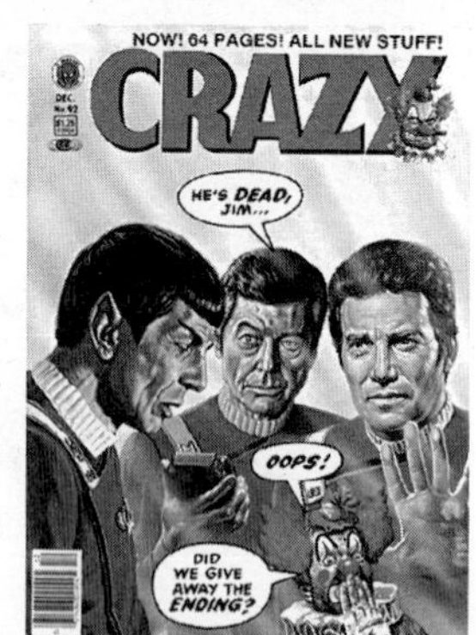

Crazy #92 © MAR

Crazyman #2 © Continuity Assoc.

Creed: Use Your Delusion #1 © Trent Kaniuga

Mork/Rocky/J. Carter-c; China Syndrome. 57-TV Hulk with Miss Piggy-c, Dracula, Taxi, Muppets. 61-1980, 84 pgs. Adams-a(r), McCloud, Pro wrestling, Casper, TV's Police Story. 63-Apocalypse Now-Coppola's cult movie; 3rd app. Teen Hulk, Howard the Duck, 3 pgs. .90 2.70 8.00

62-Kiss Ptd-c & 2 pg. app; Quincy, 2nd app. Teen Hulk 2.25 6.80 25.00

66-Sept/'80, Empire Strikes Back-c/sty; Teen Hulk by Severin, Howard the Duck, 3pgs. by Broderick 1.00 3.00 10.00

71,72,75-77,79: 71-Blues Brothers parody, Teen Hulk, Superheroes parody, WKRP in Cincinnati, Howard the Duck, 3pgs. by Broderick. 72-Jackie Gleason/Smokey & the Bandit II-c/sty, Shogun, Teen Hulk. Howard the Duck, 3pgs. by Broderick. 75-Flash Gordon movie c/sty; Teen Hulk, Cat in the Hat, Howard the Duck 3pgs. by Broderick. 76-84 pgs. w/bonus; Monster-sty w/ Crandall-a(r), Monster-stys(2) w/Kirby-a(r), 5pgs. ea; Mash, TV Hulk, Chinatown. 77-Popeye movie/R. Williams-c/sty; Teen Hulk, Love Boat, Howard the Duck 3 pgs. 79-84 pgs. w/bonus color stickers; has new materi al; "9 to 5" w/Dolly Parton, Teen Hulk, Magnum P.I., Monster-sty w/5pgs, Ditko-a(r), "Rat" w/Sutton-a(r), Everett-a, 4 pgs.(r) 2.00 6.00

73,74,78,80: 73-84 pgs. w/bonus Hulk/Spiderman Finger Puppets-c & bonus; "Live & Let Die, Jaws, Fantasy Island. 74-Dallas/"Who Shot JR"-c/sty; Elephant Man, Howard the Duck 3pgs. by Broderick. 78-Clint Eastwood-c/sty; Teen Hulk, Superheroes parody, Lou Grant. 80-Star Wars, 2 pg. app; "Howling", TV's "Greatest American Hero" .90 2.70 8.00

81,84,86,87,89: 81-.Superman Movie II-c/sty; Wolverine cameo, Mash, Teen Hulk. 84-American Werewolf in London, Johnny Carson app; Teen Hulk. 86-Time Bandits-c/sty; Private Benjamin. 87-Rubix Cube-c; Hill Street Blues, "Ragtime", Origin Obnoxio the Clown; Teen Hulk. 89-Burt Reynolds "Sharkeys Machine", Teen Hulk 2.00 6.00

82-X-Men-c w/new Byrne-a, 84 pgs. w/new material; Fantasy Island, Teen Hulk, "For Your Eyes Only", Spiderman/Human Torch-r by Kirby/Ditko; Sutton-a(r); Rogers-a; Hunchback of Notre Dame, 5 pgs. 1.50 4.50 15.00

83-Raiders of the Lost Ark-c/sty; Hart to Hart; Reese-a; Teen Hulk 1.00 3.00 10.00

85,88: 85-84 pgs; Escape from New York, Teen Hulk; Kirby-a(r), 5 pgs, Posiedon Adventure, Flintstones, Sesame Street. 88-84 pgs. w/bonus Dr. Strange Game; some new material; Jeffersons, X-Men/Wolverine, 10 pgs.; Byrne-a; Apocalypse Now, Teen Hulk .90 2.70 8.00

90-94: 90-Conan-c/sty; M. Severin-a; Teen Hulk. 91-84 pgs, some new materi al; Bladerunner-c/sty, "Deathwish-II, Teen Hulk, Black Knight, 10 pgs.-'50s-r w/Maneely-a. 92-Wrath of Khan Star Trek-c/sty; Joanie & Chachi, Teen Hulk. 93-"E.T."-c/sty, Teen Hulk, Archie Bunkers Place, Dr. Doom Game. 94-Poltergeist, Smurfs, Teen Hulk, Casper, Avengers parody-8pgs. Adams-a. 1.20 3.60 12.00

Crazy Summer Special #1 (Sum, '75, 100 pgs.)-Nixon, TV Kung Fu, Babe Ruth, Joe Namath, Waltons, McCloud, Chariots of the Gods 1.20 3.60 12.00

NOTE: ***N. Adams** a-2, 61r, 94p. **Austin** a-82i. **Buscema** a-2, 82. **Byrne** c-82p. **Nick Cardy** c-7, 8, 10, 12-16, Super Special 1. **Crandall** a-76r. **Ditko** a-68r, 79r, 82r. **Drucker** a-3. **Eisner** a-9-16. **Kelly Freas** c-1-6, 9, 11; a-7. **Kirby/Wood** a-66r. **Ploog** a-1, 4, 7, 67r, 73r. **Rogers** a-82. **Sparling** a-92. **Wood** a-65r. Howard the Duck in 36, 50, 51, 53, 54, 59, 63, 65, 66, 68, 69, 71, 72, 74, 75, 77. Hulk in 46, c-42, 46, 57, 73. Star Wars in 32, 66; c-37.*

CRAZYMAN
Continuity Comics: Apr, 1992 - No. 3, 1992 ($2.50, high quality paper)

1-($3.95, 52 pgs.)-Embossed-c; N. Adams part-i 4.00
2,3 ($2.50): 2-N. Adams/Bolland-c 2.50

CRAZYMAN
Continuity Comics: V2#1, May, 1993 - No. 4, Jan, 1994 ($2.50, high quality paper)

V2#1-($2.50)-Entire book is die-cut 2.50
2-4: 2-(12/93)-Adams-c(p) & part scripts. 3-(12/93). 4-Indicia says #3, Jan. 1993 2.50

CRAZY, MAN, CRAZY (Magazine) (Becomes This Magazine is...?) (Formerly From Here to Insanity)
Humor Magazines (Charlton): V2#1, Dec, 1955 - V2#2, June, 1956

V2#1,V2#2-Satire; Wolverton-a, 3 pgs. 11.00 32.00 80.00

CREATURE, THE (See Movie Classics)

CREATURE
Antarctic Press: Oct, 1997 - Present ($2.95, B&W)

1,2-Don Walker-s/a 2.95

CREATURES OF THE ID
Caliber Press: 1990 ($2.95, B&W)

1-Frank Einstein (Madman) app.; Allred-a 4.50 13.50 50.00

CREATURES ON THE LOOSE (Formerly Tower of Shadows No. 1-9)(See Kull)
Marvel Comics: No. 10, March, 1971 - No. 37, Sept, 1975 (New-a & reprints)

10-(15¢)-1st full app. King Kull; see Kull the Conqueror; Wrightson-a 3.25 10.00 36.00
11-15 1.20 3.60 12.00
16-Origin Warrior of Mars (begins, ends #21) 1.00 3.00 10.00
17-20 2.00 6.00
21-Steranko-c .90 2.70 8.00
22-Steranko-c; Thongor stories begin 1.00 3.00 10.00
23-29-Thongor-c/stories 4.00
30-Manwolf begins 1.20 3.60 12.00
31-33 .90 2.70 9.00
34-37 .85 2.60 7.00

NOTE: ***Crandall** a-13. **Ditko** r-15, 17, 18, 20, 22, 24, 27, 28. **Everett** a-16i(new). **Matt Fox** r-21i. **Howard** a-26i. **Gil Kane** a-16p, 17p, 19i; c-16, 17, 19, 20, 25, 29, 33p, 35p, 36p. **Kirby** a-10-15r, 16(2)r, 17r, 19r. **Morrow** a-20, 21. **Perez** a-33-37; c-34p. **Shores a-11. innott** r-21. **Sutton** c-10. **Tuska** a-31p, 32p.*

CREECH, THE
Image Comics: Oct, 1997 - No. 3, Dec, 1997 ($1.95/$2.50, limited series)

1-Capullo-s/c/a(p) 2.00
2,3-($2.50) 2.50

CREED
Hall of Heroes Comics: Dec, 1994 - No. 2, Jan, 1995 ($2.50, B&W)

1 1.50 4.50 15.00
2 1.20 3.60 12.00

CREED
Lightning Comics: June, 1995 - Present ($2.75/$3.00, B&W/color)

1-($2.75) 4.00
1-($3.00, color) 4.50
1-($9.95)-Commemorative Edition 1.00 3.00 10.00
1-Twin Variant Edition (1250? print run) 1.00 3.00 10.00
1-Special Edition; polybagged w/certificate 4.00
1 Gold Collectors Edition; polybagged w/certificate 3.00
2,3-($3.00, color)-Butt Naked Edition & regular-c 3.00
3-($9.95)-Commemorative Edition; polybagged w/certificate & card 1.00 3.00 10.00

CREED: CRANIAL DISORDER
Lightning Comics: Oct, 1996 ($3.00, one-shot)

1-3-Two covers 3.00
1-($5.95)-Platinum Edition 2.00 6.00
2,3-($9.95)Ltd.l Edition 1.00 3.00 10.00

CREED/TEENAGE MUTANT NINJA TURTLES
Lightning Comics: May, 1996 ($3.00, one-shot)

1-Kaniuga-a(p)/scripts; Laird-c; variant-c exists 3.00
1-($9.95)-Platinum Edition 1.00 3.00 10.00
1-Special Edition; polybagged w/certificate 5.00

CREED: USE YOUR DELUSION
Avatar Press: Jan, 1998 - No. 2, Feb, 1998 ($3.00, B&W)

1,2-Kaniuga-s/c/a 3.00

The Creeper #7 © DC

Cremator #1 © Chaos! Comics

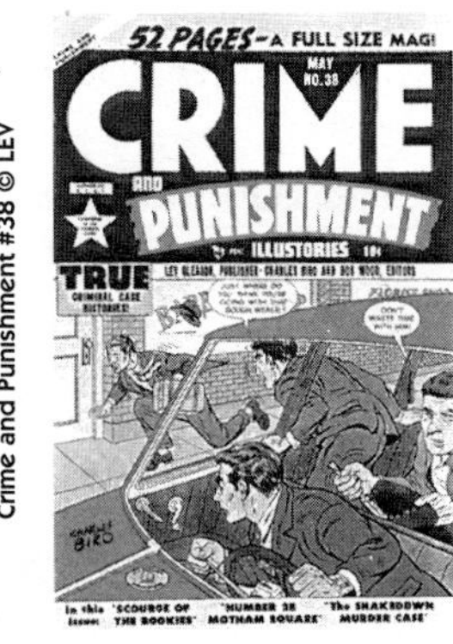

Crime and Punishment #38 © LEV

GD25 FN65 NM94

1,2-($4.95) Foil cover 5.00

CREEPER, THE (See Beware… , Showcase #73 & 1st Issue Special #7)
DC Comics: Dec, 1997 - No. 11; #1,000,000 Nov, 1998 ($2.50)

1-11-Kaminski-s/Martinbrough-a(p). 7,8-Joker-c/app. 2.50
#1,000,000 (11/98) 853rd Century x-over 2.50

CREEPSVILLE
Laughing Reindeer Press: V2#1, Winter, 1995 ($4.95)

V2#1-Comics w/text 5.00

CREEPY (See Warren Presents)
Warren Publishing Co./Harris Publ. #146: 1964 - No. 145, Feb, 1983; No. 146, 1985 (B&W, magazine)

1-Frazetta-a (his last story in comics?); Jack Davis-c; 1st Warren all comics magazine 8.00 24.00 90.00
2: 2-Frazetta-c & 1 pg. strip 4.00 12.00 45.00
3-13: 3-7,9-11-Frazetta-c. 7-Frazetta 1 pg. strip. 9-Creepy fan club sketch by Wrightson (1st published-a); has 1/2 pg. anti-smoking strip by Frazetta. 10-Brunner fan club sketch (1st published work) 2.25 6.75 20.00
14-Neal Adams 1st Warren work 2.50 7.50 24.00
15-20: 15-17-Frazetta-c 1.75 5.25 16.00
21-30: 27-Frazetta-c 2.25 6.75 18.00
31,33-37,39-47,49 1.50 4.50 22.00
32-Frazetta-c; Harlan Ellison sty 3.60 10.80 36.00
38 (scarce) 3.00 9.00 30.00
48,55,65-(1973, 1974, 1975 Annuals) #55 & 65 contain an 8 pg. slick comic insert. 1.50 4.50 22.00
50-Vampirella-c 1.50 4.50 22.00
51,54,56-64: All contain an 8 pg. slick comic insert in middle 2.25 6.75 18.00
52,53,66-112,114-140: 93-Sports issue. 96-Aliens issue. 102-All monster issue. 121-All Severin-r issue. 125-All N. Adams-r issue. 137-All Williamson-r issue. 139-All Toth-r issue 1.00 3.00 8.00
113-All Wrightson-r issue 1.25 3.75 10.00
141-145 (low dist.) 144-Giant, $2.25; Frazetta-c 1.85 5.50 15.00
146 ($2.95)-1st from Harris; resurrection issue 5.00 15.00 50.00
Year Book 1968, 1969 3.00 9.00 30.00
Year Book 1970-Neal Adams, Ditko-a(r) 3.00 9.00 30.00
Annual 1971,1972 3.00 9.00 30.00
1993 Fearbook ($3.95)-Harris Publ. Vampirella app. 3.00 9.00 30.00

NOTE: *All issues contain many good artists works:* ***Neal Adams, Brunner, Corben, Craig (Taycee), Crandall, Ditko, Evans, Frazetta, Heath, Jeff Jones, Krenkel, McWilliams, Morrow, Nino, Orlando, Ploog, Severin, Torres, Toth, Williamson, Wood, & Wrightson****; covers by* ***Crandall, Davis, Frazetta, Morrow, San Julian, Todd/Bode****; Otto Binder's "Adam Link" stories in No. 2, 4, 6, 8, 9, 12, 13, 15 with* ***Orlando*** *art.* ***Frazetta*** *c-2-7, 9-11, 15-17, 27, 32, 83r, 89r, 91r.* ***E.A. Poe*** *adaptations in 66, 69, 70.*

CREEPY THINGS
Charlton Comics: July, 1975 - No. 6, June, 1976

1 1.10 3.30 11.00
2-6: Ditko-a in 3,5. Sutton c-3,4 5.00
Modern Comics Reprint 2-6(1977) 4.00

NOTE: ***Larson*** *a-2,6.* ***Sutton*** *a-1,2,4,6.* ***Zeck*** *a-2.*

CREMATOR
Chaos! Comics: Dec, 1998 - No. 5, Apr, 1999 ($2.95, limited series)

1,2-Leonardo Jimenez-s/a 3.00

CRIME AND JUSTICE (Rookie Cop? No. 27 on)
Capitol Stories/Charlton Comics: March, 1951 - No. 26, Sept, 1955

1 27.00 80.00 200.00
2 8.50 26.00 60.00
3-8,10-13: 6-Negligee panels 7.50 22.50 52.00
9-Classic story "Comics Vs. Crime" 19.00 58.00 145.00
14-Color illos in **POP**; gory story of man who beheads women 13.00 40.00 100.00
15-17,19-26; 15-Negligee panels 5.35 16.00 32.00
18-Ditko-a 20.00 60.00 150.00

NOTE: ***Alascia*** *c-20.* ***Ayers*** *a-17.* ***Shuster*** *a-19-21; c-19. Bondage c-11, 12.*

CRIME AND PUNISHMENT (Title inspired by 1935 film)
Lev Gleason Publications: April, 1948 - No. 74, Aug, 1955

1-Mr. Crime app. on-c 27.00 80.00 200.00
2 14.00 42.00 105.00
3-Used in **SOTI**, pg. 112; injury-to-eye panel; Fuje-a 17.00 50.00 125.00
4,5 10.00 30.00 75.00
6-10 8.75 26.00 62.00
11-20 7.50 22.50 52.00
21-30 5.70 17.00 40.00
31-38,40-44,46: 46-One pg. Frazetta-a 5.35 16.00 32.00
39-Drug mention story "The 5 Dopes" 8.35 25.00 58.00
45- "Hophead Killer" drug story 8.35 25.00 58.00
47-57,60-65,70-74: 5.35 16.00 32.00
58-Used in **POP**, pg. 79 5.70 17.00 35.00
59-Used in **SOTI**, illo "What comic-book America stands for" 23.00 69.00 170.00
66-Toth-c/a(4); 3-D effect issue (3/54); 1st "Deep Dimension" process 31.00 94.00 235.00
67- "Monkey on His Back" heroin story; 3-D effect issue 25.00 76.00 190.00
68-3-D effect issue; Toth-c (7/54) 23.00 69.00 170.00
69- "The Hot Rod Gang" dope crazy kids 9.30 28.00 65.00

NOTE: ***Biro*** *c-most.* ***Everett*** *a-31.* ***Fuje*** *a-3, 4, 12, 13, 17, 18, 20, 26, 27.* ***Guardineer*** *a-2-4, 10, 14, 17, 18, 20, 26-28, 32, 38-44.* ***Kinstler*** *c-69.* ***McWilliams*** *a-41, 48, 49.* ***Tuska*** *a-28, 30, 51, 64, 70.*

CRIME AND PUNISHMENT: MARSHALL LAW TAKES MANHATTAN
Marvel Comics (Epic Comics): 1989 ($4.95, 52 pgs., direct sales only, mature)

nn-Graphic album featuring Marshall Law 5.00

CRIME CAN'T WIN (Formerly Cindy Smith)
Marvel/Atlas Comics (TCI 41/CCC 42,43,4-12): No. 41, 9/50 - No. 43, 2/51; No. 4, 4/51 - No. 12, 9/53

41(#1) 22.00 66.00 165.00
42(#2) 13.00 38.00 95.00
43(#3)-Horror story 14.00 42.00 105.00
4(4/51),5-12: 10-Possible use in **SOTI**, pg. 161 9.30 28.00 65.00

NOTE: ***Robinson*** *a-9-11.* ***Tuska*** *a-43.*

CRIME CASES COMICS (Formerly Willie Comics)
Marvel/Atlas Comics(CnPC No.24-8/MJMC No.9-12): No. 24, 8/50 - No. 27, 3/51; No. 5, 5/51 - No. 12, 7/52

24 (#1, 52 pgs.)-True police cases 13.00 40.00 100.00
25-27(#2-4): 27-Morisi-a 9.30 28.00 65.00
5-12: 11-Robinson-a. 12-Tuska-a 7.85 23.50 55.00

CRIME CLINIC
Ziff-Davis Publishing Co.: No. 10, July-Aug, 1951 - No. 5, Summer, 1952

10(#1)-Painted-c; origin Dr. Tom Rogers 22.00 66.00 165.00
11(#2),4,5: 4,5-Painted-c 15.00 46.00 115.00
3-Used in **SOTI**, pg. 18 17.00 50.00 125.00

NOTE: *All have painted covers by* ***Saunders. Starr*** *a-10.*

CRIME CLINIC
Slave Labor Graphics: May, 1995 - No. 2, Oct, 1995 ($2.95, B&W, limited series)

1,2 3.00

CRIME DETECTIVE COMICS
Hillman Periodicals: Mar-Apr, 1948 - V3#8, May-June, 1953

V1#1-The Invisible 6, costumed villains app; Fuje-c/a, 15 pgs. 22.00 66.00 165.00
2,5: 5-Krigstein-a 9.30 28.00 65.00
3,4,6,7,10-12: 6-McWilliams-a 7.85 23.50 55.00

Crime Does Not Pay #40 © LEV

Crimefighters #6 © MAR

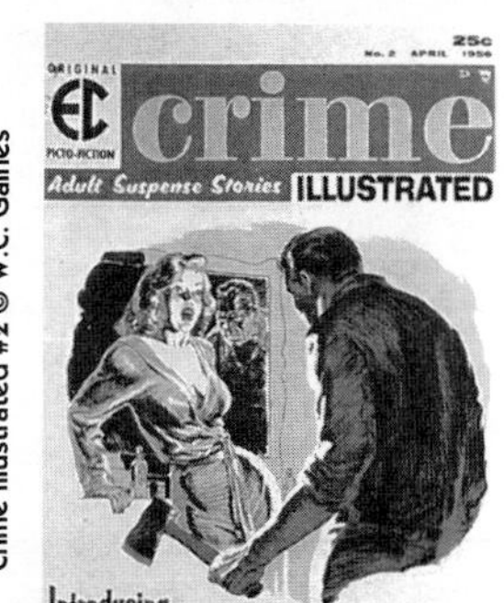

Crime Illustrated #2 © W.C. Gaines

	GD25	FN65	NM94
8-Kirbyish-a by McCann	7.85	23.50	55.00
9-Used in **SOTI**, pg. 16 & "Caricature of the author in a position comic book publishers wish he were in permanently" illo.	29.00	88.00	220.00
V2#1,4,7-Krigstein-a: 1-Tuska-a	8.50	26.00	60.00
2,3,5,6,8-12 (1-2/52)	5.70	17.00	35.00
V3#1-Drug use-c	5.70	17.00	38.00
2-8	5.00	15.00	30.00

NOTE: ***Briefer** a-11, V3#1. **Kinstlerish**-a by **McCann**-V2#7, V3#2. **Powell** a-10, 11. **Starr** a-10.*

CRIME DETECTOR
Timor Publications: Jan, 1954 - No. 5, Sept, 1954

	GD25	FN65	NM94
1	15.00	44.00	110.00
2	7.85	23.50	55.00
3,4	7.15	21.50	50.00
5-Disbrow-a (classic)	15.00	46.00	115.00

CRIME DOES NOT PAY (Formerly Silver Streak Comics No. 1-21)
Comic House/Lev Gleason/Golfing (Title inspired by film):
No. 22, June, 1942 - No. 147, July, 1955 (1st crime comic)

	GD25	FN65	NM94
22(23 on cover, 22 on indicia)-Origin The War Eagle & only app.; Chip Gardner begins; #22 was rebound in Complete Book of True Crime (Scarce)	194.00	582.00	1650.00
23 (Scarce)	112.00	335.00	950.00
24-Intro. & 1st app. Mr. Crime (Scarce)	88.00	265.00	750.00
25-30: 27-Classic Bird-c. 30-Wood and Biro app.	50.00	150.00	425.00
31-40	32.00	96.00	240.00
41-Origin & 1st app. Officer Common Sense	23.00	68.00	170.00
42-Electrocution-c	27.00	80.00	200.00
43-46,48-50: 44,45,50 are 68 pg. issues	15.00	44.00	110.00
47-Electric chair-c	25.00	76.00	190.00
51-70: 63,64-Possible use in **SOTI**, pg. 306. 63-Contains Biro & Gleason's self censorship code of 12 listed restrictions (5/48)	13.00	40.00	100.00
71-99: 87-Chip Gardner begins, ends #100	10.00	30.00	75.00
100	11.00	32.00	80.00
101-104,107-110: 102-Chip Gardner app	7.85	23.50	55.00
105-Used in **POP**, pg. 84	9.30	28.00	65.00
106,114-Frazetta-a, 1 pg.	7.85	23.50	55.00
111-Used in **POP**, pgs. 80 & 81; injury-to-eye sty illo	7.85	23.50	55.00
112,113,115-130	5.70	17.00	40.00
131-140	5.00	15.00	30.00
141,142-Last pre-code issue; Kubert-a(1)	7.85	23.50	55.00
143-Kubert-a in one story	7.85	23.50	55.00
144-146	5.00	15.00	30.00
147-Last issue (scarce); Kubert-a	10.00	30.00	75.00
1(Golfing-1945)	5.70	17.00	35.00
The Best of...(1944, 128 pgs.)-Series contains 4 rebound issues	75.00	225.00	600.00
...1945 issue	56.00	168.00	450.00
...1946-48 issues	41.00	124.00	330.00
...1949-50 issues	40.00	120.00	285.00
...1951-53 issues	32.00	96.00	225.00

NOTE: *Many issues contain violent covers and stories. Who Dunnit by **Guardineer**-39-42, 44-105, 108-110; Chip Gardner by **Bob Fujitani (Fuje)**-88-103. **Alderman** a-29, 41-44, 49. **Dan Barry** a-75. **Biro** c-1-76, 122, 142. **Briefer** a-29(2), 30, 31, 33, 37, 39. **G. Colan** a-105. **Fuje** c-88, 89, 91-94, 96, 98, 99, 102, 103. **Guardineer** a-57, 71. **Kubert** c-143. **Landau** a-118. **Maurer** a-29, 39, 41, 42. **McWilliams** a-91, 93, 95, 100-103. **Palais** a-30, 33, 37, 39, 41-43, 44(2), 46, 49. **Powell** a-146, 147. **Tuska** a-48, 50(2), 51, 52, 56, 57(2), 60-64, 66, 67, 71. Painted c-87-102. Bondage c-43, 62, 98.*

CRIME EXPOSED
Marvel Comics (PPI)/Marvel Atlas Comics (PrPI): June, 1948; Dec, 1950 - No. 14, June, 1952

	GD25	FN65	NM94
1(6/48)	25.00	76.00	190.00
1(12/50)	16.00	48.00	120.00
2	11.00	32.00	80.00
3-9,11,14	8.50	26.00	60.00
10-Used in **POP**, pg. 81	8.75	26.25	65.00
12-Krigstein & Robinson-a	8.75	26.25	65.00
13-Used in **POP**, pg. 81; Krigstein-a	8.75	26.25	70.00

NOTE: ***Maneely** c-8. **Robinson** a-11, 12. **Tuska** a-3, 4.*

CRIMEFIGHTERS
Marvel Comics (CmPS 1-3/CCC 4-10): Apr, 1948 - No. 10, Nov, 1949

	GD25	FN65	NM94
1-Some copies are undated & could be reprints	21.00	64.00	150.00
2,3: 3-Morphine addict story	11.00	32.00	80.00
4-10: 6-Anti-Wertham editorial. 9,10-Photo-c	9.30	28.00	65.00

CRIME FIGHTERS (...Always Win)
Atlas Comics (CnPC): No. 11, Sept, 1954 - No. 13, Jan, 1955

	GD25	FN65	NM94
11-13: 11-Maneely-a,13-Pakula, Reinman, Severin-a	9.30	28.00	70.00

CRIME-FIGHTING DETECTIVE (Shock Detective Cases No. 20 on; formerly Criminals on the Run)
Star Publications: No. 11, Apr-May, 1950 - No. 19, June, 1952
(Based on true crime cases)

	GD25	FN65	NM94
11-L. B. Cole-c/a (2 pgs.); L. B. Cole-c on all	15.00	44.00	110.00
12,13,15-19: 17-Young King Cole & Dr. Doom app.	11.00	32.00	80.00
14-L. B. Cole-c/a, r/Law-Crime #2	13.00	38.00	95.00

CRIME FILES
Standard Comics: No. 5, Sept, 1952 - No. 6, Nov, 1952

	GD25	FN65	NM94
5-1pg. Alex Toth-a; used in **SOTI**, pg. 4 (text)	21.00	64.00	160.00
6-Sekowsky-a	11.00	32.00	80.00

CRIME ILLUSTRATED (Magazine)
E. C. Comics: Nov-Dec, 1955 - No. 2, Spring, 1956 (25¢, Adult Suspense Stories on-c)

	GD25	FN65	NM94
1-Ingels & Crandall-a	11.30	34.00	95.00
2-Ingels & Crandall-a	9.50	28.00	80.00

NOTE: ***Craig** a-2. **Crandall** a-1, 2; c-2. **Evans** a-1. **Davis** a-2. **Ingels** a-1, 2. **Krigstein/Crandall** a-1. **Orlando** a-1, 2; c-1.*

CRIME INCORPORATED (Formerly Crimes Incorporated)
Fox Features Syndicate: No. 2, Aug, 1950; No. 3, Aug, 1951

	GD25	FN65	NM94
2	22.00	66.00	165.00
3(1951)-Hollingsworth-a	16.00	48.00	120.00

CRIME MACHINE (Magazine)
Skywald Publications: Feb, 1971 - No. 2, May, 1971 (B&W)

	GD25	FN65	NM94
1-Kubert-a(2)(r)(Avon)	4.00	12.25	45.00
2-Torres, Wildey-a; violent-c/a	2.70	8.00	30.00

CRIME MUST LOSE! (Formerly Sports Action?)
Sports Action (Atlas Comics): No. 4, Oct, 1950 - No. 12, April, 1952

	GD25	FN65	NM94
4-Ann Brewster-a in all; c-used in N.Y. Legis. Comm. documents	15.00	46.00	115.00
5-10,12: 9-Robinson-a	11.00	32.00	80.00
11-Used in **POP**, pg. 89	10.00	30.00	75.00

CRIME MUST PAY THE PENALTY (Formerly Four Favorites; Penalty #47, 48)
Ace Magazines (Current Books): No. 33, Feb, 1948; No. 2, Jun, 1948 - No. 48, Jan, 1956

	GD25	FN65	NM94
33(#1, 2/48)-Becomes Four Teeners #34?	27.00	80.00	200.00
2(6/48)-Extreme violence; Palais-a?	17.00	52.00	130.00
3- "Frisco Mary" story used in Senate Investigation report, pg. 7	12.00	36.00	90.00
4,8-Transvestism stories	13.00	38.00	95.00
5-7,9,10	7.85	23.50	55.00
11-20-Drug story "Dealers in White Death"	7.15	21.50	50.00
21-32,34-40,42-48	5.70	17.00	35.00
33(7/53)- "Dell Fabry-Junk King" drug story; mentioned in Love and Death	7.85	23.50	55.00
41-reprints "Dealers in White Death"	7.85	23.50	55.00

NOTE: ***Cameron** a-29-31, 34, 35, 39-41. **Colan** a-20, 31. **Kremer** a-3, 37r. **Larsen** a-32. **Palais***

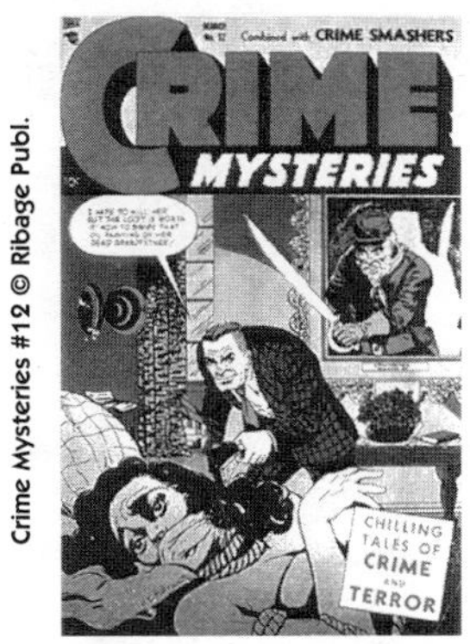

Crime Mysteries #12 © Ribage Publ.

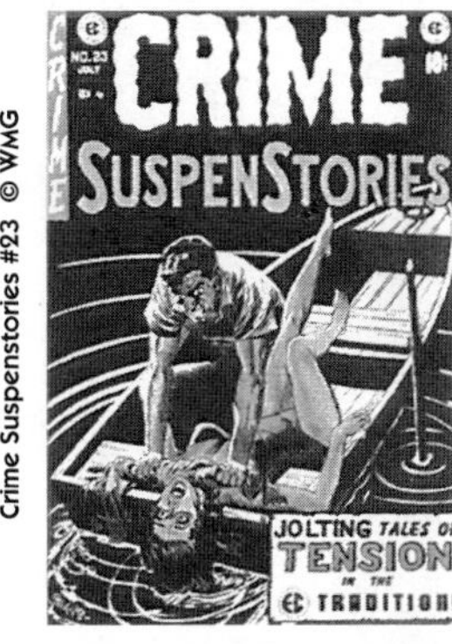

Crime Suspenstories #23 © WMG

Crimson #2 © Wildstorm Prod.

GD25 FN65 NM94

a-5?,37.

CRIME MUST STOP
Hillman Periodicals: October, 1952 (52 pgs.)

V1#1(Scarce)-Similar to Monster Crime; Mort Lawrence, Krigstein-a 54.00 162.00 460.00

CRIME MYSTERIES (Secret Mysteries #16 on; combined with Crime Smashers #7 on)
Ribage Publ. Corp. (Trojan Magazines): May, 1952 - No. 15, Sept, 1954

1-Transvestism story; crime & terror stories begin 43.00 129.00 365.00
2-Marijuana story (7/52) 32.00 96.00 240.00
3-One pg. Frazetta-a 27.00 80.00 200.00
4-Cover shows girl in bondage having her blood drained; 1 pg. Frazetta-a 43.00 129.00 360.00
5-10 22.00 66.00 165.00
11,12,14 21.00 62.00 155.00
13-(5/54)-Angelo Torres 1st comic work (inks over Check's pencils); Check-a 27.00 80.00 200.00
15-Acid in face-c 31.00 94.00 235.00

NOTE: ***Fass** a-13; c-4, 10. **Hollingsworth** a-10-13, 15; c-2, 12, 13, 15. **Kiefer** a-4. **Woodbridge** a-13? Bondage-c-1, 8, 12.*

CRIME ON THE RUN (See Approved Comics #8)

CRIME ON THE WATERFRONT (Formerly Famous Gangsters)
Realistic Publications: No. 4, May, 1952 (Painted cover)

4 25.00 76.00 190.00

CRIME PATROL (Formerly International #1-5; International Crime Patrol #6; becomes Crypt of Terror #17 on)
E. C. Comics: No. 7, Summer, 1948 - No. 16, Feb-Mar, 1950

7-Intro. Captain Crime 50.00 150.00 440.00
8-14: 12-Ingels-a 44.00 132.00 380.00
15-Intro. of Crypt Keeper (inspired by Witches Tales radio show) & Crypt of Terror (see Tales From the Crypt #33 for origin); used by N.Y. Legis. Comm.; last pg. Feldstein-a 212.00 638.00 1900.00
16-2nd Crypt Keeper app.; Roussos-a 138.00 412.00 1200.00

NOTE: ***Craig** c/a in most issues. **Feldstein** a-9-16. **Kiefer** a-8, 10, 11. **Moldoff** a-7.*

CRIME PHOTOGRAPHER (See Casey...)

CRIME REPORTER
St. John Publ. Co.: Aug, 1948 - No. 3, Dec, 1948 (Indicia shows Oct.)

1-Drug club story 42.00 132.00 335.00
2-Used in **SOTI**: illo- "Children told me what the man was going to do with the red-hot poker;" r/Dynamic #17 with editing; Baker-c; Tuska-a 60.00 180.00 510.00
3-Baker-c; Tuska-a 33.00 100.00 245.00

CRIMES BY WOMEN
Fox Features Syndicate: June, 1948 - No. 15, Aug, 1951; 1954 (True crime cases)

1-True story of Bonnie Parker 108.00 324.00 920.00
2,3: 3-Used in **SOTI**, pg. 234 57.00 171.00 485.00
4,5,7-9,11-15: 8-Used in **POP**.14-Spanking panel r/from All Famous Crime Stories (1949) (Fox Giant) 50.00 150.00 425.00
6-Classic girl fight-c; acid-in-face panel 55.00 164.00 465.00
10-Used in **SOTI**, pg. 72; girl fight-c 47.00 142.00 400.00
54(M.S. Publ.-'54)-Reprint; (formerly My Love Secret) 23.00 68.00 170.00

CRIMES INCORPORATED (Formerly My Past)
Fox Features Syndicate: No. 12, June, 1950 (Crime Incorporated No. 2 on)

12 12.00 36.00 90.00

CRIMES INCORPORATED (See Fox Giants)

CRIME SMASHER (See Whiz #76)
Fawcett Publications: Summer, 1948 (one-shot)

1-Formerly Spy Smasher 39.00 118.00 300.00

CRIME SMASHERS (Becomes Secret Mysteries No. 16 on)
Ribage Publishing Corp.(Trojan Magazines): Oct, 1950 - No. 15, Mar, 1953

1-Used in **SOTI**, pg. 19,20, & illo "A girl raped and murdered;" Sally the Sleuth begins 68.00 203.00 575.00
2-Kubert-c 37.00 112.00 280.00
3,4 28.00 84.00 210.00
5-Wood-a 35.00 104.00 260.00
6,8-11: 8-Lingerie panel 21.00 62.00 155.00
7-Female heroin junkie story 22.00 66.00 165.00
12-Injury to eye panel; 1 pg. Frazetta-a 23.00 68.00 170.00
13-Used in **POP**, pgs. 79,80; 1 pg. Frazetta-a 23.00 68.00 170.00
14,15 19.00 56.00 140.00

NOTE: ***Hollingsworth** a-14. **Kiefer** a-15. Bondage c-7, 9.*

CRIME SUSPENSTORIES (Formerly Vault of Horror No. 12-14)
E. C. Comics: No. 15, Oct-Nov, 1950 - No. 27, Feb-Mar, 1955

15-Identical to #1 in content; #1 printed on outside front cover. #15 (formerly "The Vault of Horror") printed and blackened out on inside front cover with Vol. 1, No. 1 printed over it. Evidently, several of No. 15 were printed before a decision was made not to drop the Vault of Horror and Haunt of Fear series. The print run was stopped on No. 15 and continued on No. 1. All of No. 15 were changed as described above. 115.00 345.00 1100.00
1 90.00 270.00 850.00
2 47.00 141.00 440.00
3-5: 3-Poe adaptation. 3-Old Witch stories begin 33.00 100.00 300.00
6-10 27.00 80.00 240.00
11,12,14,15: 15-The Old Witch guest stars 20.00 60.00 180.00
13,16-Williamson-a 22.00 66.00 200.00
17-Williamson/Frazetta-a (6 pgs.) 24.00 73.00 220.00
18,19: 19-Used in **SOTI**, pg. 235 17.00 50.00 150.00
20-Cover used in **SOTI**, illo "Cover of a children's comic book" 22.00 66.00 200.00
21,24-27: 24- "Food For Thought" similar to "Cave In" in Amazing Detective Cases #13 (1952) 11.00 33.00 100.00
22,23-Used in Senate investigation on juvenile delinquency. 22-Ax decapitation-c 17.00 50.00 150.00

NOTE: ***Craig** a-1-21; c-1-18, 20-22. **Crandall** a-18-26. **Davis** a-4, 5, 7, 9-12, 20. **Elder** a-17,18. **Evans** a-15, 19, 21, 23, 25, 27; c-23, 24. **Feldstein** c-19. **Ingels** a-1-12, 14, 15, 27. **Kamen** a-2, 4-18, 20-27; c-25-27. **Krigstein** a-22, 24, 25, 27. **Kurtzman** a-1, 3. **Orlando** a-16, 22, 24, 26. **Wood** a-1, 3. Issues No. 11-15 have E. C. "quickie" stories. No. 25 contains the famous "Are You a Red Dupe?" editorial. Ray Bradbury adaptations-15, 17.*

CRIME SUSPENSTORIES
Russ Cochran/Gemstone Publ.: Nov, 1992 - Present ($1.50/$2.00/$2.50)

1-3:Reprints Crime SuspenStories series 1.50
4-15-($2.00) 2.00
16-24-($2.50) 2.50

CRIMINALS ON THE RUN (Formerly Young King Cole) (Crime Fighting Detective No. 11 on)
Premium Group (Novelty Press): V4#1, Aug-Sep, 1948-#10, Dec-Jan, 1949-50

V4#1-Young King Cole continues 25.00 74.00 185.00
2-6: 6-Dr. Doom app. 21.00 62.00 155.00
7-Classic "Fish in the Face" c by L. B. Cole 43.00 129.00 350.00
V5#1,2 (#8,9): 9-L. B. Cole-c 18.00 54.00 135.00
10-L. B. Cole-c 18.00 54.00 135.00

NOTE: *Most issues have **L. B. Cole** covers. **McWilliams** a-V4#6, 7, V5#2; c-V4#5.*

CRIMSON (Also see Cliffhanger #0)
Image Comics (Cliffhanger Prod.): May, 1998 - Present ($2.50)

1-Humberto Ramos-a/Augustyn-s 5.00
1-Variant-c by Warren .85 2.60 7.00
1-Chromium-c 25.00
2-Ramos-c with street crowd 3.00
2-Variant-c by Art Adams 3.00
2-Dynamic Forces CrimsonChrome cover 15.00
3-6: 3-Ramos Moon background-c 2.50

Crisis On Infinite Earths #9 © DC

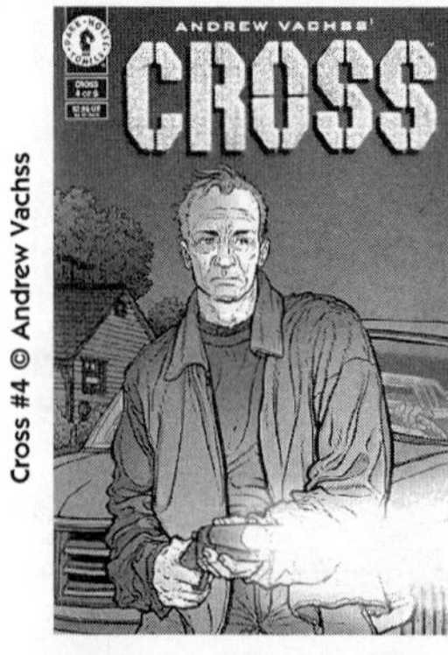

Cross #4 © Andrew Vachss

The Crow: Razor - Kill The Pain #10 © James O'Barr & Everette Hartsoe

GD25 FN65 NM94

DF Premiere Ed. 1998 ($6.95) covers by Ramos and Jae Lee 6.95

CRIMSON AVENGER, THE (See Detective Comics #20 for 1st app.)(Also see Leading Comics #1 & World's Best/Finest Comics)
DC Comics: June, 1988 - No. 4, Sept, 1988 ($1.00, limited series)

1-4 1.00

CRIMSON NUN
Antarctic Press: May, 1997 - No. 4, Nov, 1997 ($2.95, limited series)

1-4 2.95

CRIMSON PLAGUE
Event Comics: June, 1997 ($2.95)

1-George Perez-a 4.00

CRISIS ON INFINITE EARTHS (Also see Official... Index)
DC Comics: Apr, 1985 - No. 12, Mar, 1986 (maxi-series)

1-1st DC app. Blue Beetle & Detective Karp from Charlton; Perez-c on all .90 2.70 8.00
2-6: 6-Intro Charlton's Capt. Atom, Nightshade, Question, Judomaster, Peacemaker & Thunderbolt into DC Universe .85 2.60 7.00
7-Double size; death of Supergirl .90 2.70 8.00
8-Death of the Flash (Barry Allen) 1.00 3.00 10.00
9-11: 9-Intro. Charlton's Ghost into DC Universe. 10-Intro. Charlton's Banshee, Dr. Spectro, Image, Punch & Jewellee into DC Universe; Starman (Prince Gavyn) dies. .85 2.60 7.00
12-(52 pgs.)-Deaths of Dove, Kole, Lori Lemaris, Sunburst, G.A. Robin & Huntress; Kid Flash becomes new Flash; 3rd & final DC app. of the 3 Lt. Marvels; Green Fury gets new look (becomes Green Flame in Infinity, Inc. #32) .85 2.60 7.00

CRITICAL MASS (See A Shadowline Saga: Critical Mass)

CRITTERS (Also see Usagi Yojimbo Summer Special)
Fantagraphics Books: 1986 - No. 50, 1990 ($1.70/$2.00, B&W)

1-Cutey Bunny, Usagi Yojimbo app. 5.00
2-11: 3,6,7,10,11-Usagi Yojimbo app. 11-Christmas Special (68 pgs.); Usagi Yojimbo 2.00
12-22,24-49: 14,38-Usagi Yojimbo app. 22-Watchmen parody; two diff. covers exist 1.75
23-With Alan Moore Flexi-disc ($3.95) 5.00
50 ($4.95, 84 pgs.)-Neil the Horse, Capt. Jack, Sam & Max & Usagi Yojimbo app.; Quagmire, Shaw-a 5.00
Special 1 (1/88, $2.00) 2.00

CROSLEY'S HOUSE OF FUN (Also see Tee and Vee Crosley...)
Crosley Div. AVCO Mfg. Corp.: 1950 (Giveaway, paper cover, 32 pgs.)

nn-Strips revolve around Crosley appliances 4.25 13.00 26.00

CROSS
Dark Horse Comics: No. 0, Oct, 1995 - No. 6, Apr, 1995 ($2.95, limited series, mature)

0-6: Darrow-c & Vachss scripts in all 3.00

CROSS AND THE SWITCHBLADE, THE
Spire Christian Comics (Fleming H. Revell Co.): 1972 (35-49¢)

1-Some issues have nn 4.00

CROSSFIRE
Spire Christian Comics (Fleming H. Revell Co.): 1973 (39/49¢)

nn 4.00

CROSSFIRE (Also see DNAgents)
Eclipse Comics: 5/84 - No. 17, 3/86; No. 18, 1/87 - No. 26, 2/88 ($1.50, Baxter paper)

1-11,14-17: 1-DNAgents x-over; Spiegle-c/a begins 1.50
12,13-Death of Marilyn Monroe. 12-Dave Stevens-c 3.00
18-26-(B&W) 1.80

GD25 FN65 NM94

CROSSFIRE AND RAINBOW (Also see DNAgents)
Eclipse Comics: June, 1986 - No. 4, Sept, 1986 ($1.25, deluxe format)

1-3: Spiegle-a 1.30
4-Dave Stevens-c 2.00

CROSSING THE ROCKIES (See Classics Illustrated Special Issue)

CROSSROADS
First Comics: July, 1988 - No. 5, Nov, 1988 ($3.25, lim. series, deluxe format)

1-5 3.25

CROW, THE (Also see Caliber Presents)
Caliber Press: Feb, 1989 - No. 4, 1989 ($1.95, B&W, limited series)

1-James O'Barr-c/a/scripts 7.00 21.00 75.00
1-3-2nd printing 1.20 3.60 12.00
2,4 3.80 11.50 40.00
2-3rd printing 1.00 3.00 10.00
3 4.20 12.60 42.00

CROW, THE
Tundra Publishing, Ltd.: Jan, 1992 - No. 3, 1992 ($4.95, B&W, 68 pgs.)

1-3: 1-r/#1,2 of Caliber series. 2-r/#3 of Caliber series w/new material. 3-All new material 1.00 3.00 10.00

CROW, THE
Kitchen Sink Press: Jan, 1996 - No. 3, Mar, 1996 ($2.95, B&W, limited series)

1-3: James O'Barr-c/scripts 3.00

CROW, THE: CITY OF ANGELS (Movie)
Kitchen Sink Press: July, 1996 - No. 3, Sept, 1996 ($2.95, limited series)

1-3: Adaptation of film; two-c (photo & illos.). 1-Vincent Perez interview 3.00

CROW, THE: FLESH AND BLOOD
Kitchen Sink Press: May, 1996 - No. 3, July, 1996 ($2.95, limited series)

1-3: O'Barr-c 3.00

CROW, THE: RAZOR - KILL THE PAIN
London Night Studios: Apr, 1998 - No.3, July, 1998 ($2.95, B&W, lim. series)

1-3-Hartsoe-s/O'Barr-painted-c 3.00
Tour Book-(12/97) pin-ups; 4 diferent covers 5.00
0(10/98) Dorien painted-c 3.00

CROW, THE: WAKING NIGHTMARES
Kitchen Sink Press: Jan, 1997 - No.4, 1998 ($2.95, B&W, limited series)

1-4-Miran Kim-c 3.00

CROW, THE: WILD JUSTICE
Kitchen Sink Press: Oct, 1996 ($2.95, B&W, unfinished limited series)

1-Prosser-s/Adlard-a 3.00

CROWN COMICS
Golfing/McCombs Publ.: Wint, 1944-45; No. 2, Sum, 1945 - No. 19, July, 1949

1- "The Oblong Box" E.A. Poe adaptation 31.00 92.00 230.00
2,3-Baker-a; 3-Voodah by Baker 20.00 60.00 150.00
4-6-Baker-c/a; Voodah app. #4,5 21.00 64.00 160.00
7-Feldstein, Baker, Kamen-a; Baker-c 20.00 60.00 150.00
8-Baker-a; Voodah app. 18.00 54.00 135.00
9-11,13-19: Voodah in #10-19. 13-New logo 11.00 33.00 80.00
12-Master Marvin by Feldstein, Starr-a; Voodah-c 11.00 34.00 85.00
NOTE: ***Bolle** a-11, 13-16, 18, 19; c-11p, 15. **Powell** a-19. **Starr** a-11-13; c-11i.*

CRUCIBLE
DC Comics (Impact): Feb, 1993 - No. 6, July, 1993 ($1.25, limited series)

1-(99¢)-Quesada-c(p) & layouts begin; neon ink-c 1.00
2-6: 2-Last Quesada-c. 4-Last Quesada layouts 1.25

CRUSADER FROM MARS (See Tops in Adventure)
Ziff-Davis Publ. Co.: Jan-Mar, 1952 - No. 2, Fall, 1952 (Painted-c)

Crusaders #1 © AP

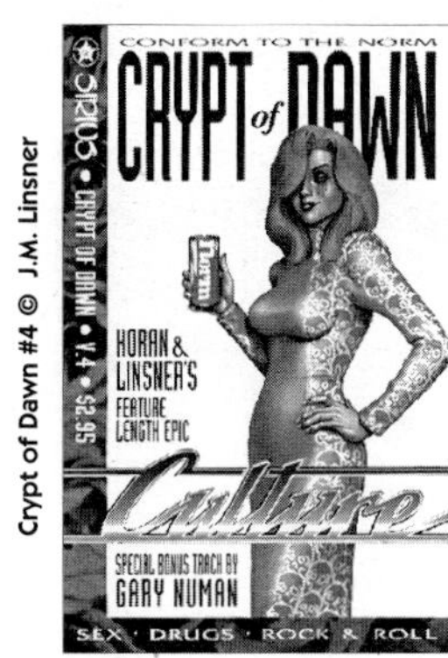

Crypt of Dawn #4 © J.M. Linsner

C•23 #1 © Wizards of the Coast

	GD25	FN65	NM94
1-Cover is dated Spring	62.00	186.00	525.00
2-Bondage-c	49.00	147.00	415.00

CRUSADER RABBIT (TV)
Dell Publishing Co.: No. 735, Oct, 1956 - No. 805, May, 1957

	GD25	FN65	NM94
Four Color 735 (#1)	31.00	93.00	340.00
Four Color 805	24.00	70.00	260.00

CRUSADERS, THE (Religious)
Chick Publications: 1974 - Vol. 16, 1985 (39/69¢, 36 pgs.)

Vol.1-Operation Bucharest ('74). Vol.2-The Broken Cross ('74). Vol.3-Scarface ('74). Vol.4-Exorcists ('75). Vol.5-Chaos ('75) 3.00

Vol.6-Primal Man? ('76)-(Disputes evolution theory). Vol.7-The Ark-(claims proof of existence, destroyed by Bolsheviks). Vol.8-The Gift-(Life story of Christ). Vol.9-Angel of Light-(Story of the Devil). Vol.10-Spellbound?-(Tells how rock music is Satanical & produced by witches). 11-Sabotage?. 12-Alberto. 13-Double Cross. 14-The Godfathers. (No. 6-14 low in distribution; loaded in religious propaganda.). 15-The Force. 16-The Four Horsemen 3.00

CRUSADERS (Southern Knights No. 2 on)
Guild Publications: 1982 (B&W, magazine size)

1-1st app. Southern Knights 3.00

CRUSADERS, THE (Also see Black Hood, The Jaguar, The Comet, The Fly, Legend of the Shield, The Mighty... & The Web)
DC Comics (Impact): May, 1992 - No. 8, Dec, 1992 ($1.00/$1.25)

1-Contains 3 Impact trading cards 1.25
2-8 1.00

CRUSH, THE
Image Comics (Motown Machineworks): Jan, 1996 - No. 5, July, 1996 ($2.25, limited series)

1-5: Baron scripts 2.25

CRY FOR DAWN
Cry For Dawn Pub.: 1989 - No. 9 ($2.25, B&W, mature)

	GD25	FN65	NM94
1	14.00	41.00	150.00
1-2nd printing	4.50	13.50	50.00
1-3rd printing	3.80	11.50	40.00
2	7.00	21.00	70.00
2-2nd printing	1.80	5.40	18.00
3	4.00	12.25	45.00
4-6	2.25	6.80	25.00
5-2nd printing	.90	2.70	8.00
7-9	2.00	6.00	20.00
4-9-Signed & numbered editions	3.80	11.50	40.00
...Calendar (1993)			47.00

CRYIN' LION COMICS
William H. Wise Co.: Fall, 1944 - No. 3, Spring, 1945

	GD25	FN65	NM94
1-Funny animal	13.00	38.00	95.00
2-Hitler app.	10.00	30.00	75.00
3	8.50	26.00	60.00

CRYPT
Image Comics (Extreme): Aug, 1995 - No.2, Oct. 1995 ($2.50, limited series)

1,2-Prophet app. 2.50

CRYPTIC WRITINGS OF MEGADETH
Chaos! Comics: Sept, 1997 - Present ($2.95, quarterly)

1-4-Stories based on song lyrics by Dave Mustaine 2.95

CRYPT OF DAWN (see Dawn)
Sirius: 1996 ($2.95, B&W, limited series)

	GD25	FN65	NM94
1-Linsner-c/s; anthology.	.85	2.60	7.00
2			5.00
3 (2/98)			5.00
4 (6/98)			2.95
Ltd. Edition	2.00	6.00	20.00

CRYPT OF SHADOWS
Marvel Comics Group: Jan, 1973 - No. 21, Nov, 1975 (#1-9 are 20¢)

	GD25	FN65	NM94
1-Wolverton-r/Advs. Into Terror #7	1.40	4.20	14.00
2-10: 2-Starlin/Everett-c	1.00	3.00	10.00
11-21	.85	2.60	7.00

NOTE: ***Briefer*** *a-2r.* ***Ditko*** *a-13r, 18-20r.* ***Everett*** *a-6, 14r; c-2i.* ***Heath*** *a-1r.* ***Gil Kane*** *c-1, 6.* ***Mort Lawrence*** *a-1r, 8r.* ***Maneely*** *a-2r.* ***Moldoff*** *a-8.* ***Powell*** *a-12r, 14r.* ***Tuska*** *a-2r.*

CRYPT OF TERROR (Formerly Crime Patrol; Tales From the Crypt No. 20 on)
E. C. Comics: No. 17, Apr-May, 1950 - No. 19, Aug-Sept, 1950

	GD25	FN65	NM94
17-1st New Trend to hit stands	230.00	690.00	2200.00
18,19	130.00	390.00	1200.00

NOTE: ***Craig*** *c/a-17-19.* ***Feldstein*** *a-17-19.* ***Ingels*** *a-19.* ***Kurtzman*** *a-18.* ***Wood*** *a-18. Canadian reprints known; see Table of Contents.*

C•23 (Jim Lee's...) (Based on Wizards of the Coast card game)
Image Comics: Apr, 1998 - Present ($2.50)

1,2-Choi & Mariotte-s/ Charest-c 2.50
2-Variant-c by Jim Lee 2.50
3-5,7,8: 4-Ryan Benjamin-c. 5,8-Corben var-c 2.50
6-Flip book with Planetary preview; Corben-c 2.50

CUD
Fantagraphics Books: Aug, 1992 - No. 8, Dec, 1994 ($2.25/$2.50/$2.75, B&W, mature)

1($2.25)-Terry LaBan scripts & art in all 2.50
2-7 ($2.50): 6-1st Eno & Plum 2.75
8 ($2.75) 3.00

CUD COMICS
Dark Horse Comics: Jan, 1995 - Present ($2.95, B&W)

1-8: Terry LaBan-c/a/scripts. 5-Nudity; marijuana story 3.00
Eno and Plum TPB (1997, $12.95) r/#1-4, DHP #93-95 12.95

CUPID
Marvel Comics (U.S.A.): Dec, 1949 - No. 2, Mar, 1950

	GD25	FN65	NM94
1-Photo-c	11.00	34.00	85.00
2-Betty Page ('50s pin-up queen) photo-c; Powell-a (see My Love #4)	25.00	76.00	190.00

CURIO
Harry 'A' Chesler: 1930's(?) (Tabloid size, 16-20 pgs.)

	GD25	FN65	NM94
nn	17.00	52.00	130.00

CURLY KAYOE COMICS (Boxing)
United Features Syndicate/Dell Publ. Co.: 1946 - No. 8, 1950; Jan, 1958

	GD25	FN65	NM94
1 (1946)-Strip-r (Fritzi Ritz); biography of Sam Leff, Kayoe's artist	15.00	44.00	110.00
2	7.85	23.50	55.00
3-8	5.70	17.00	40.00
United Presents...(Fall, 1948)	5.00	15.00	30.00
Four Color 871 (Dell, 1/58)	1.80	5.50	20.00

CURSE OF DRACULA, THE
Dark Horse Comics: July, 1998 - No. 3, Sept, 1998 ($2.95, limited series)

1-3-Wolfman-s/Colan-a 2.95

CURSE OF DREADWOLF
Lightning Comics: Sept, 1994 ($2.75, B&W)

1 2.75

CURSE OF RUNE (Becomes Rune, 2nd Series)
Malibu Comics (Ultraverse): May, 1995 - No. 4, Aug, 1995 ($2.50, lim. series)

1-4: 1-Two covers form one image 2.50

CURSE OF THE SPAWN

Curse of the Spawn #12 © Todd McFarlane Prod.

Cyberella #8 © Howard Chaykin & Don Cameron

Cyberforce #24 © Top Cow

GD25 FN65 NM94

Image Comics (Todd McFarlane Productions): Sept, 1996 - Present ($1.95)

	GD25	FN65	NM94
1-Dwayne Turner-a(p)	1.00	3.00	10.00
1-B&W Edition	2.70	8.00	30.00
2-3	.90	2.70	8.00
4-10		2.00	6.00
11-13: 12-Movie photo-c of Melinda Clarke (Priest)			4.00
14-26			2.00

CURSE OF THE WEIRD
Marvel Comics: Dec, 1993 - No. 4, Mar, 1994 ($1.25, limited series) (Pre-code horror-r)

1-4: 1,3,4-Wolverton-r(1-Eye of Doom; 3-Where Monsters Dwell; 4-The End of the World). 2-Orlando-r. 4-Zombie-r by Everett; painted-c — 2.00

NOTE: *Briefer r-2. Jack Davis a-4r. Ditko a-1r, 2r, 4r; c-1r. Everett r-1. Heath r-1-3. Kubert r-3. Wolverton a-1r, 3r, 4r.*

CUSTER'S LAST FIGHT
Avon Periodicals: 1950

nn-Partial reprint of Cowpuncher #1 — 15.00 44.00 110.00

CUTEY BUNNY (See Army Surplus Komikz Featuring...)

CUTIE PIE
Junior Reader's Guild (Lev Gleason): May, 1955 - No. 3, Dec, 1955; No. 4, Feb, 1956; No. 5, Aug, 1956

	GD25	FN65	NM94
1	5.35	16.00	32.00
2-5: 4-Misdated 2/55	3.60	9.00	18.00

CUTTING EDGE
Marvel Comics: Dec, 1995 ($2.95)

1-Hulk-c/story; Messner-Loebs scripts — 3.00

CYBERCITY
CPM Comics: Sept, 1995- Present ($2.95, bi-monthly)

Part One #1,2; Part Two #1,2; Part Three #1,2 — 3.00

CYBERELLA
DC Comics (Helix): Sept, 1996 - No. 12, Aug, 1997 ($2.25/$2.50) (1st Helix series)

1-5: Chaykin-s & Cameron-a in all. 1,2-Chaykin-c. 3-5-Cameron-c — 2.25
6-12: 6-Begin $2.50-c — 2.50

CYBERFORCE
Image Comics (Top Cow Productions): Oct, 1992 - No. 4, 1993; No. 0, Sept, 1993 ($1.95, limited series)

	GD25	FN65	NM94
1-Silvestri-c/a in all; coupon for Image Comics #0; 1st Top Cow Productions title.	.85	2.60	7.00
1-With coupon missing			2.00
2-4: 2-(3/93). 3-Pitt-c/story. 4-Codename: Stryke Force back-up (1st app.); foil-c			2.00
0-(9/93)-Walt Simonson-c/a/scripts			2.50

CYBERFORCE
Image Comics (Top Cow Productions)/Top Cow Comics No. 28 on: V2#1, Nov, 1993 - No. 35, Sept. 1997 ($1.95)

V2#1-24: 1-7-Marc Silvestri/Keith Williams-c/a. 8-McFarlane-c/a. 10-Painted variant-c exists. 18-Variant-c exists. 23-Velocity-c. — 2.00
1-3: 1-Gold Logo-c. 2-Silver embossed-c. 3-Gold embossed-c — 10.00
1-(99¢, 3/96, 2nd printing) — 1.00
25-($3.95)-Wraparound, foil-c — 4.00
26-35: 26-Begin $2.50-c. 28-(11/96)-1st Top Cow Comics issue; Quesada & Palmiotti's Gabriel app. — 2.50
27-Quesada & Palmiotti's Ash app. — 3.00
Annual 1 (3/95, $2.50) — 2.50
Annual 2 (8/96, $2.95) — 3.00

NOTE: *Annuals read Volume One in the indica.*

CYBERFORCE ORIGINS
Image Comics (Top Cow Productions): Jan, 1995 - No. 3, Nov, 1995 ($2.50)

GD25 FN65 NM94

	GD25	FN65	NM94
1-Cyblade (1/95)	.85	2.60	7.00
1-Cyblade (3/96, 99¢, 2nd printing)			1.00
1A-Exclusive Ed.; Tucci-c			5.00
2-Stryker (2/95)-1st Mike Turner-a			2.50
3-Impact			2.50

CYBERFORCE/STRYKEFORCE: OPPOSING FORCES (See Codename: Stryke Force #15)
Image Comics (Top Cow Productions): Sept, 1995 - No.2, Oct, 1995 ($2.50, limited series)

1,2: 2-Stryker disbands Strykeforce. — 2.50

CYBERFORCE UNIVERSE SOURCEBOOK
Image Comics (Top Cow Productions): Aug, 1994/Feb, 1995 ($2.50)

1-Silvestri-c (8/94) — 2.50
2-Silvestri-c (2/95) — 2.50

CYBERFROG
Hall of Heroes: June, 1994 - No. 2, Dec, 1994 ($2.50, B&W, limited series)

1,2 — 2.50

CYBERFROG
Harris Comics: Feb, 1996 - No. 3, Apr, 1996 ($2.95)

0-3: Van Sciver-c/a/scripts. 2-Variant-c exists — 1.00 3.00 10.00

CYBERFROG: RESERVOIR FROG
Harris Comics: Sept, 1996 - No. 2, Oct, 1996 ($2.95, limited series)

1,2: Van Sciver-c/a/scripts; wraparound-c — 3.00

CYBERFROG: 3RD ANNIVERSARY SPECIAL
Harris Comics: Jan, 1997 - Present ($2.50, B&W, limited series)

1,2 — 2.50

CYBERFROG VS. CREED
Harris Comics: July, 1997 - Present ($2.95, B&W, limited series)

1 — 2.95

CYBERNARY (See Deathblow #1)
Image Comics (WildStorm Productions): Nov, 1995 - No.5, Mar, 1996 ($2.50, limited series)

1-5 — 2.50

CYBERPUNK
Innovation Publishing: Sept, 1989 - No. 2, Oct, 1989 ($1.95, limited series, 28 pgs.) Book 2, #1, May, 1990 - No. 2, 1990 ($2.25, 28 pgs.)

1,2-Both have Ken Steacy painted-c (Adults) — 2.00
Book 2, #1,2 — 2.30

CYBERPUNK: THE SERAPHIM FILES
Innovation Publishing: Nov, 1990 - No. 2, Dec, 1990 ($2.50, 28 pgs., mature)

1,2: 1-Painted-c; story cont'd from Seraphim — 2.50

CYBERPUNX
Image Comics (Extreme Studios): Mar, 1996 ($2.50)

1 — 2.50

CYBERRAD
Continuity Comics: 1991 - No. 7, 1992 ($2.00)(Direct sale & newsstand-c variations)
V2#1, 1993 ($2.50)

1-7: 5-Glow-in-the-dark-c by N. Adams (direct sale only). 6-Contains 4 pg. fold-out poster; N. Adams layouts — 2.00
V2#1-($2.95, direct sale ed.)-Die-cut-c w/B&W hologram on-c; Neal Adams sketches — 3.00
V2#1-($2.50, newsstand ed.)-Without sketches — 2.50

CYBERRAD DEATHWATCH 2000 (Becomes CyberRad w/#2, 7/93)
Continuity Comics: Apr, 1993 - No. 2, 1993 ($2.50)

1,2: 1-Bagged w/2 cards; Adams-c & layouts & plots. 2-Bagged w/card; Adams

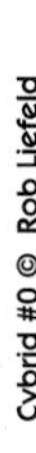
Cybrid #0 © Rob Liefeld

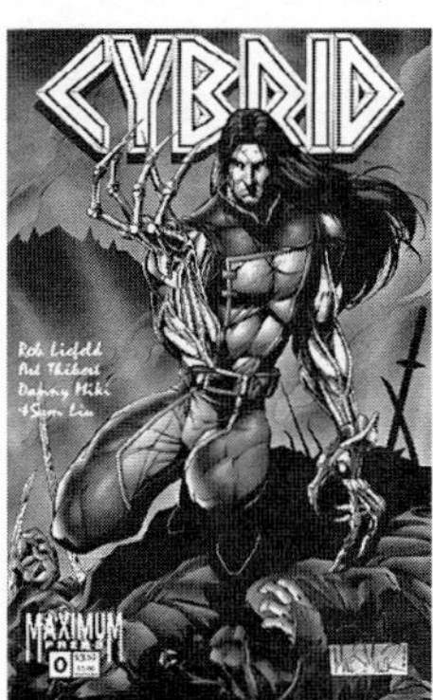

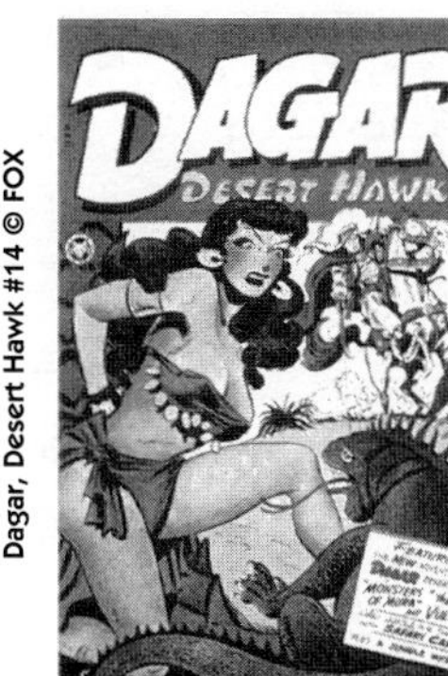

Dagar, Desert Hawk #14 © FOX

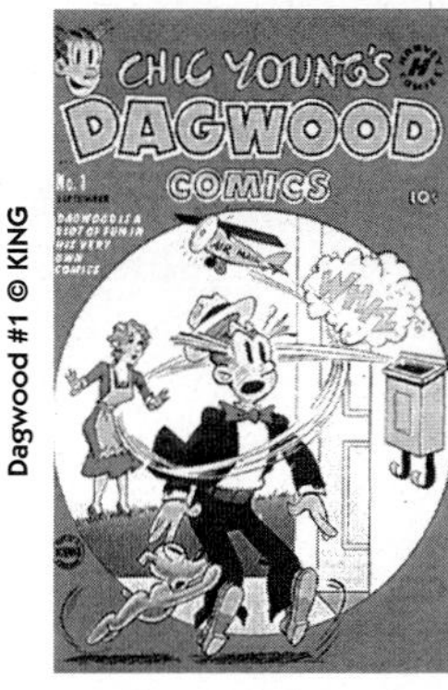

Dagwood #1 © KING

GD25 FN65 NM94

scripts 2.50

CYBER 7
Eclipse Comics: Mar, 1989 - #7, Sept, 1989; V2#1, Oct, 1989 - #10, 1990 ($2.00, B&W)

1-7: Stories translated from Japanese 2.00
Book Two, #1-10 2.00

CYBLADE/ GHOST RIDER
Marvel Comics /Top Cow Productions: Jan 1997 ($2.95, one-shot)

1-Devil's Reign pt. 2 3.00

CYBLADE/SHI (Also see Battle For The Independents & Shi/Cyblade: The Battle For The Independents)
Image Comics (Top Cow Productions): 1995 ($2.95, one-shot)

San Diego Preview 2.00 6.00 20.00
1-($2.95)-1st app. Witchblade 1.20 3.60 12.00
1-($2.95)-variant-c; Tucci-a .90 2.70 8.00

CYBRID
Maximum Press: July, 1995; No. 0, Jan, 1997 ($2.95/$3.50)

1-(7/95) 3.00
0-(1/97)-Liefeld-a/script; story cont'd in Avengelyne #4 3.50

CYCLONE COMICS (Also see Whirlwind Comics)
Bilbara Publishing Co.: June, 1940 - No. 5, Nov, 1940

1-Origin Tornado Tom; Volton (the human generator), Tornado Tom, Kingdom of the Moon, Mister Q begin (1st app. of each) 124.00 371.00 1050.00
2,3 62.00 185.00 525.00
4,5 50.00 150.00 425.00

CYCLOPS: RETRIBUTION
Marvel Comics: 1994 ($5.95, trade paperback)

nn-r/Marvel Comics Presents #17-24 2.00 6.00

CYNDER
Immortelle Studios: 1995 - No. 3, 1996 ($2.50, B&W)

1-3: 2-Tucci centerfold 2.50
Annual 1-(5/96, $2.95, color) 3.00

CYNDER (Series 2)
Immortelle Studios: 1996 - No.2, 1996 ($2.95, color)

1,2 2.50

CYNDER/NIRA X
Immortelle Studios: 1996 ($2.95, one-shot)

1-w/centerfold 3.00
1-Hughes variant-c. 3.00
1 (Gold)-Hughes-c. 10.00

CYNTHIA DOYLE, NURSE IN LOVE (Formerly Sweetheart Diary)
Charlton Publications: No. 66, Oct, 1962 - No. 74, Feb, 1964

66-74 1.20 3.60 12.00

DAEMONSTORM
Caliber Comics: 1997 ($3.95, one-shot)

1-McFarlane-c 3.95

DAEMONSTORM: STORMWALKER
Caliber Comics: 1997 ($3.95, B&W, one-shot)
nn 3.95

DAFFY (Daffy Duck No. 18 on)(See Looney Tunes)
Dell Publishing Co./Gold Key No. 31-127/Whitman No. 128 on: #457, 3/53 - #30, 7-9/62; #31, 10-12/62 - #145, 1983 (No #132,133)

Four Color 457(#1)-Elmer Fudd x-overs begin 8.00 25.00 90.00
Four Color 536,615('55) 4.00 12.00 45.00
4(1-3/56)-11('57) 2.50 7.50 27.00
12-19(1958-59) 1.65 5.00 18.00
20-40(1960-64) 1.50 4.50 12.00
41-60(1964-68) 1.25 3.75 10.00
61-90(1969-74)-Road Runner in most .85 2.60 7.00
91-110 5.00
111-127 3.00
128,134-141 4.00
129(8/80), 130,131 (pe-pack?) .90 2.70 8.00
142-145(#90029 on-c; nd, nd code, pre-pack?) 2.00 6.00
Mini-Comic 1 (1976; 3-1/4x6-1/2") 4.00

NOTE: *Reprint issues-No.41-46, 48, 50, 53-55, 58, 59, 65, 67, 69, 73, 81, 96, 103-108; 136-142, 144, 145(1/3-2/3-r). (See March of Comics No. 277, 288, 303, 313, 331, 347, 357,375, 387, 397, 402, 413, 425, 437, 460).*

DAFFY TUNES COMICS
Four-Star Publications: June, 1947; No. 12, Aug, 1947

nn 6.50 19.50 45.00
12-Al Fago-c/a; funny animal 5.70 17.00 38.00

DAGAR, DESERT HAWK (Captain Kidd No. 24 on; formerly All Great)
Fox Features Syndicate: No. 14, Feb, 1948 - No. 23, Apr, 1949 (No #17,18)

14-Tangi & Safari Cary begin; Good bondage-c/a 65.00 194.00 550.00
15,16-E. Good-a; 15-Bondage-c 42.00 132.00 340.00
19,20,22: 19-Used in **SOTI**, pg. 180 (Tangi) 38.00 114.00 285.00
21- "Bombs & Bums Away" panel in "Flood of Death" story used in **SOTI** 41.00 123.00 325.00
23-Bondage-c 41.00 123.00 325.00

NOTE: *Tangi by* ***Kamen****-14-16, 19, 20; c-20, 21.*

DAGAR THE INVINCIBLE (Tales of Sword & Sorcery...) (Also see Dan Curtis Giveaways & Gold Key Spotlight)
Gold Key: Oct, 1972 - No. 18, Dec, 1976; No. 19, Apr, 1982

1-Origin; intro. Villains Olstellon & Scor 1.80 5.40 18.00
2-5: 3-Intro. Graylin, Dagar's woman; Jarn x-over 2.00 6.00
6-1st Dark Gods story 5.00
7-10: 9-Intro. Torgus. 10-1st Three Witches story 5.00
11-18: 13-Durak & Torgus x-over; story continues in Dr. Spektor #15. 14-Dagar's origin retold. 18-Origin retold 4.00
19-Origin-r/#18 4.00

NOTE: *Durak app. in 7, 12, 13. Tragg app. in 5, 11.*

DAGWOOD (Chic Young's) (Also see Blondie Comics)
Harvey Publications: Sept, 1950 - No. 140, Nov, 1965

1 10.00 30.00 100.00
2 5.00 15.00 50.00
3-10 4.00 12.00 40.00
11-20 3.00 9.00 30.00
21-30 2.50 7.50 25.00
31-50 2.00 6.00 20.00
51-70 1.80 5.40 18.00
71-100 1.20 3.60 12.00
101-128,130,135 1.00 3.00 8.00
129,131-134,136-140-All are 68-pg. issues 1.40 4.20 14.00

NOTE: *Popeye and other one page strips appeared in early issues.*

DAGWOOD SPLITS THE ATOM (Also see Topix V8#4)
King Features Syndicate: 1949 (Science comic with King Features characters) (Giveaway)

nn-Half comic, half text; Popeye, Olive Oyl, Henry, Mandrake, Little King, Katzenjammer Kids app. 4.00 12.00 40.00

DAI KAMIKAZE!
Now Comics: June, 1987 - No. 12, Aug, 1988 ($1.75)

1-12: 1-1st app. Speed Racer; 2nd print exists 1.80

DAILY BUGLE (See Spider-Man)
Marvel Comics: Dec, 1996 - No. 3, Feb, 1997 ($2.50, B&W, limited series)

1-3-Paul Grist-s 2.50

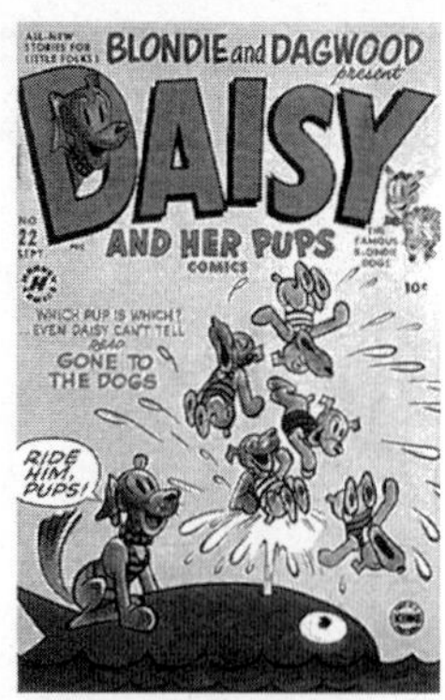

Daisy and Her Pups #22 © KING

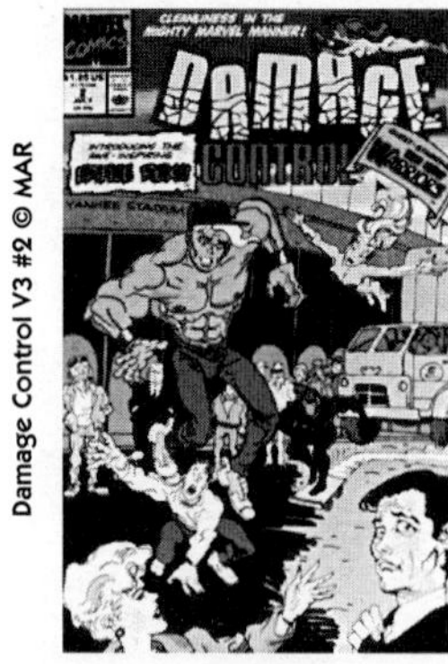

Damage Control V3 #2 © MAR

Dale Evans Comics #12 © DC

DAISY AND DONALD (See Walt Disney Showcase No. 8)
Gold Key/Whitman No. 42 on: May, 1973 - No. 59, 1984 (no No. 48)

	GD25	FN65	NM94
1-Barks-r/WDC&S #280,308	2.00	6.00	20.00
2-5: 4-Barks-r/WDC&S #224	1.00	3.00	10.00
6-10		2.00	6.00
11-20			5.00
21-41: 32-r/WDC&S #308			4.00
42-44 (Whitman)			5.00
45 (8/80),46-(pre-pack?)	1.60	4.80	16.00
47-(12/80)-Only distr. in Whitman 3-pack	3.20	9.60	35.00
48(3/81)-50(8/81): 50-r/#3	.90	2.70	8.00
51-54: 51-Barks-r/4-Color #1150. 52-r/#2		2.00	6.00
55-59-(all #90284 on-c, nd, nd code, pre-pack?)	1.00	3.00	10.00

DAISY & HER PUPS (Blondie's Dogs)(Formerly Blondie Comics #20)
Harvey Publications: No. 21, 7/51 - No. 27, 7/52; No. 8, 9/52 - No. 18, 5/54

	GD25	FN65	NM94
21 (#1)-Blondie's dog Daisy and her 5 pups led by Elmer begin. Rags Rabbit app	3.00	9.00	30.00
22-27 (#2-7): 26,27 have No. 6 & 7 on cover but No. 26 & 27 on inside. 23,25-The Little King app. 24-Bringing Up Father by McManus app. 25-27-Rags Rabbit app.	2.00	6.00	20.00
8-18: 8,9-Rags Rabbit app. 8,17-The Little King app. 11-The Flop Family Swan begins. 22-Cookie app. 11-Felix The Cat app. by 17,18-Popeye app.	1.50	4.50	15.00

DAISY COMICS
Eastern Color Printing Co.: Dec, 1936 (5-1/4x7-1/2")

	GD25	FN65	NM94
nn-Joe Palooka, Buck Rogers (2 pgs. from Famous Funnies No. 18), Napoleon Flying to Fame, Butty & Fally	29.00	88.00	220.00

DAISY DUCK & UNCLE SCROOGE PICNIC TIME (See Dell Giant #33)

DAISY DUCK & UNCLE SCROOGE SHOW BOAT (See Dell Giant #55)

DAISY DUCK'S DIARY (See Dynabrite Comics, & Walt Disney's C&S #298)
Dell Publishing Co.: No. 600, Nov, 1954 - No. 1247, Dec-Fef, 1961-62 (Disney)

	GD25	FN65	NM94
Four Color 600 (#1)	6.00	18.00	65.00
Four Color 659, 743 (11/56)	5.00	15.00	55.00
Four Color 858 (11/57), 948 (11/58), 1247 (12-2/61-62)	4.00	12.00	45.00
Four Color 1055 (11-1/59-60), 1150 (12-1/60-61)-By Carl Barks)	9.00	27.00	100.00

DAISY HANDBOOK
Daisy Manufacturing Co.: 1946; No. 2, 1948 (10¢, pocket-size, 132 pgs.)

	GD25	FN65	NM94
1-Buck Rogers, Red Ryder; Wolverton-a(2 pgs.)	37.00	110.00	275.00
2-Captain Marvel & Ibis the Invincible, Red Ryder, Boy Commandos & Robotman; Wolverton-a (2 pgs.); contains 8 pg. color catalog	37.00	110.00	275.00

DAISY LOW OF THE GIRL SCOUTS
Girl Scouts of America: 1954, 1965 (16 pgs., paper-c)

	GD25	FN65	NM94
1954-Story of Juliette Gordon Low	4.00	10.00	20.00
1965	1.00	3.00	8.00

DAISY MAE (See Oxydol-Dreft)

DAISY'S RED RYDER GUN BOOK
Daisy Manufacturing Co.: 1955 (25¢, pocket-size, 132 pgs.)

	GD25	FN65	NM94
nn-Boy Commandos, Red Ryder; 1pg. Wolverton-a	23.00	70.00	175.00

DAKKON BLACKBLADE ON THE WORLD OF MAGIC: THE GATHERING
Acclaim Comics (Armada): June, 1996 ($5.95, one-shot)

	GD25	FN65	NM94
1-Jerry Prosser scripts; Rags Morales-c/a.		2.00	6.00

DAKOTA LIL (See Fawcett Movie Comics)

DAKOTA NORTH
Marvel Comics Group: June, 1986 - No. 5, Feb, 1987

	GD25	FN65	NM94
1-5			1.00

DAKTARI (Ivan Tors) (TV)
Dell Publishing Co.: July, 1967 - No. 3, Oct, 1968; No. 4, Sept, 1969 (All have photo-c)

	GD25	FN65	NM94
1	2.25	6.80	25.00
2-4	1.80	5.40	18.00

DALE EVANS COMICS (Also see Queen of the West...)
National Periodical Publications: Sept-Oct, 1948 - No. 24, July-Aug, 1952 (No. 1-19: 52 pgs.)

	GD25	FN65	NM94
1-Dale Evans & her horse Buttermilk begin; Sierra Smith begins by Alex Toth	90.00	270.00	765.00
2-Alex Toth-a	44.00	132.00	370.00
3-11-Alex Toth-a	29.00	86.00	215.00
12-24: 12-Target-c	13.00	40.00	100.00

NOTE: *Photo-c-1, 2, 4-14.*

DALGODA
Fantagraphics Books: Aug, 1984 - No. 8, Feb, 1986 (High quality paper)

	GD25	FN65	NM94
1-($2.25); Fujitake-c/a in all			2.25
2-7-($1.50). 2,3-Debut Grimwood's Daughter			1.50
8-Alan Moore story			3.00

DALTON BOYS, THE
Avon Periodicals: 1951

	GD25	FN65	NM94
1-(Number on spine)-Kinstler-c	14.00	43.00	105.00

DAMAGE
DC Comics: Apr, 1994 - No. 20, Jan, 1996 ($1.75/$1.95)

	GD25	FN65	NM94
1-4			1.75
5,6,0,7-12: 5-Begin $1.95-c. 6-(9/94)-Zero Hour. 0-(10/94). 7-(11/94)			2.00
13-20: 13-Begin $2.25-c. 14-Ray app.			2.25

DAMAGE CONTROL (See Marvel Comics Presents #19)
Marvel Comics: 5/89 - No. 4, 8/89; V2#1, 12/89 - No. 4, 2/90 ($1.00) V3#1, 6/91 - No. 4, 9/91 ($1.25, all are limited series)

	GD25	FN65	NM94
V1#1-4,V2#1,3: V1#4-Wolverine app.			1.00
V2#2,4-Punisher app.			1.00
V3#1-4: 1-Spider-Man app. 2-New Warriors app. 3,4-Silver Surfer app. 4-Infinity Guantlet parody			1.25

DAMNED
Image Comics (Homage Comics): June, 1997 - No. 4, Sept, 1997 ($2.50, limited series)

	GD25	FN65	NM94
1-4-Steven Grant-s/Mike Zeck-c/a in all			4.00

DANCES WITH DEMONS (See Marvel Frontier Comics Unlimited)
Marvel Frontier Comics: Sept, 1993 - No. 4, Dec, 1993 ($1.95, limited series)

	GD25	FN65	NM94
1-($2.95)-Foil embossed-c			3.00
2-4			2.00

DAN CURTIS GIVEAWAYS
Western Publishing Co.:1974 (3x6", 24 pgs., reprints)

	GD25	FN65	NM94
1-Dark Shadows, 2-Star Trek, 3-The Twilight Zone, 4-Ripley's Believe It or Not!, 5-Turok, Son of Stone (partial-r/Turok #78), 6-Star Trek, 7-The Occult Files of Dr. Spektor, 8-Dagar the Invincible, 9-Grimm's Ghost Stories Set...	2.70	8.00	30.00

DANDEE
Four Star Publications: 1947

	GD25	FN65	NM94
nn	5.70	17.00	35.00

DAN DUNN (See Crackajack Funnies, Detective Dan, Famous Feature Stories & Red Ryder)

DANDY COMICS (Also see Happy Jack Howard)
E. C. Comics: Spring, 1947 - No. 7, Spring, 1948

	GD25	FN65	NM94
1-Funny animal; Vince Fago-a in all; Dandy in all	31.00	92.00	230.00
2	23.00	68.00	170.00

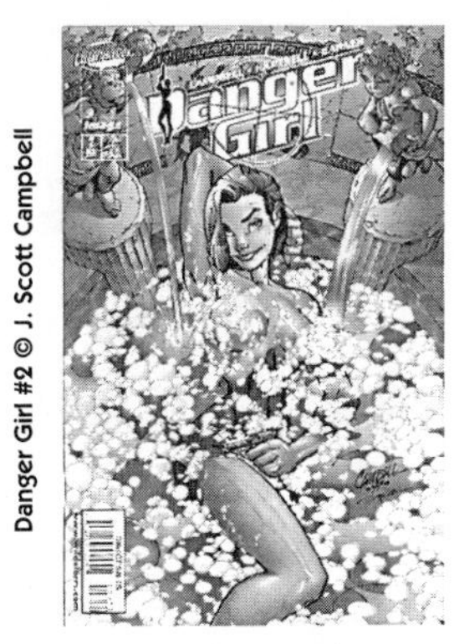

Danger Girl #2 © J. Scott Campbell

Danger Unlimited #1 © Comic Media

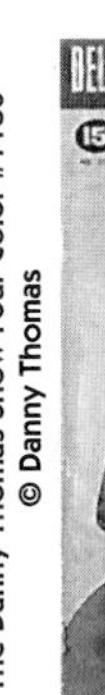
The Danny Thomas Show Four Color #1180 © Danny Thomas

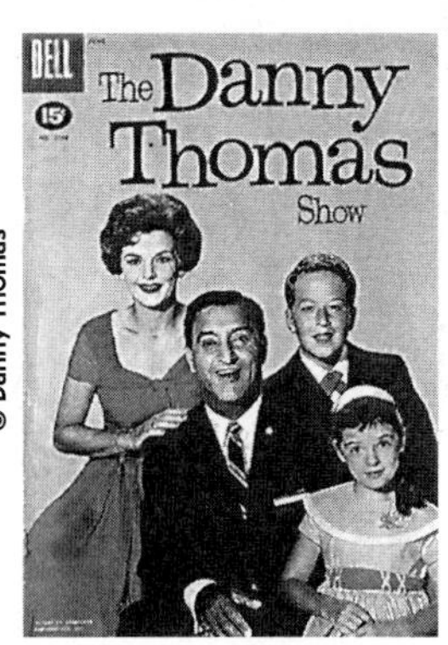

	GD25	FN65	NM94
3-7: 3-Intro Handy Andy who is c-feature #3 on	17.00	50.00	125.00

DANGER
Comic Media/Allen Hardy Assoc.: Jan, 1953 - No. 11, Aug, 1954

	GD25	FN65	NM94
1-Heck-c/a	14.00	42.00	105.00
2,3,5,7,9-11:	7.85	23.50	55.00
6- "Narcotics" story; begin spy theme	8.50	26.00	60.00
4-Marijuana cover/story	9.35	28.00	70.00
8-Bondage/torture/headlights panels	11.00	32.00	80.00

NOTE: ***Morisi** a-2, 5, 6(3), 10; c-2. Contains some reprints from Danger & Dynamite.*

DANGER (Jim Bowie No. 15 on) (Formerly Comic Media title)
Charlton Comics Group: No. 12, June, 1955 - No. 14, Oct, 1955

	GD25	FN65	NM94
12(#1)	7.15	21.50	50.00
13,14: 14-r/#12	5.70	17.00	38.00

DANGER
Super Comics: 1964

	GD25	FN65	NM94
Super Reprint #10-12 (Black Dwarf; #10-r/Great Comics #1 by Novack. #11-r/Johnny Danger #1. #12-r/Red Seal #14), #15-r/Spy Cases #26. #16-Unpublished Chesler material (Yankee Girl), #17-r/Scoop #8 (Capt. Courage & Enchanted Dagger), #18(nd)-r/Guns Against Gangsters #5 (Gun-Master, Annie Oakley, The Chameleon; L.B. Cole-r)	1.50	4.50	12.00

DANGER AND ADVENTURE (Formerly This Magazine Is Haunted; Robin Hood and His Merry Men No. 28 on)
Charlton Comics: No. 22, Feb, 1955 - No. 27, Feb, 1956

	GD25	FN65	NM94
22-Ibis the Invincible-c/story; Nyoka app.; last pre-code issue	8.50	26.00	60.00
23-Lance O'Casey-c/story; Nyoka app.; Ditko-a thru #27	10.00	30.00	75.00
24-27: 24-Mike Danger & Johnny Adventure begin	6.50	19.50	45.00

DANGER GIRL (Also see Cliffhanger #0)
Image Comics (Cliffhanger Productions): Mar, 1998 - Present ($2.95/$2.50)

	GD25	FN65	NM94
Preview-Bagged in DV8 #14 Voyager Pack			5.00
Preview Gold Edition			10.00
1-($2.95) Hartnell & Campbell-s/Campbell & Garner-a		3.00	10.00
1-($4.95) Chromium cover			100.00
1-American Entertainment Ed.	1.20	3.60	12.00
1-American Entertainment Gold Ed.			16.00
1-"Danger-sized" ed.; over-sized format	3.80	11.50	40.00
1-Tourbook edition	1.20	3.60	12.00
2-($2.50)			5.00
2-Smoking Gun variant cover	1.00	3.00	10.00
2-Platinum Ed.	2.00	6.00	20.00
2-Dynamic Forces Omnichrome variant-c	2.70	8.00	30.00
2-Gold foil cover			15.00
2-Ruby red foil cover			60.00
3-Campbell cover			3.00
3-Charest-c			3.00
3-Adam Hughes-c			3.00
San Diego Preview (8/98, B&W) flip book w/Wildcats preview			5.00

DANGER IS OUR BUSINESS!
Toby Press: 1953(Dec.) - No. 10, June, 1955

	GD25	FN65	NM94
1-Captain Comet by Williamson/Frazetta-a, 6 pgs. (science fiction)	41.00	123.00	325.00
2	10.00	30.00	75.00
3-10	9.30	28.00	65.00
I.W. Reprint #9('64)-Williamson/Frazetta-r/#1; Kinstler-c	9.30	28.00	70.00

DANGER IS THEIR BUSINESS (Also see A-1 Comic)
Magazine Enterprises: No. 50, 1952

	GD25	FN65	NM94
A-1 50-Powell-a	10.50	32.00	85.00

DANGER MAN (TV)
Dell Publishing Co.: No. 1231, Sept-Nov, 1961

	GD25	FN65	NM94
Four Color 1231-Patrick McGoohan photo-c	10.00	30.00	110.00

DANGER TRAIL (Also see Showcase #50, 51)
National Periodical Publ.: July-Aug, 1950 - No. 5, Mar-Apr, 1951 (52 pgs.)

	GD25	FN65	NM94
1-King Faraday begins, ends #4; Toth-a in all	103.00	310.00	875.00
2	74.00	222.00	625.00
3-(Rare) one of the rarest early '50s DCs	103.00	310.00	875.00
4,5: 5-Johnny Peril-c/story (moves to Sensation Comics #107); new logo	62.00	186.00	530.00

DANGER TRAIL
DC Comics: Apr, 1993 - No. 4, July, 1993 ($1.50, limited series)

	GD25	FN65	NM94
1-4: Gulacy-c on all			1.50

DANGER UNLIMITED (See San Diego Comic Con Comics #2 & Torch of Liberty Special)
Dark Horse (Legend): Feb, 1994 - No. 4, May, 1994 ($2.00, limited series)

	GD25	FN65	NM94
1-4: Byrne-c/a/scripts in all; origin stories of both original team (Doc Danger, Thermal, Miss Mirage, & Hunk) & future team (Thermal, Belebet, & Caucus). 1-Intro Torch of Liberty & Golgotha (cameo) in back-up story. 4-Hellboy & Torch of Liberty cameo in lead story			2.00
Trade paperback (1995, $14.95)-r/#1-4; includes last pg. originally cut from #4			15.00

DAN HASTINGS (See Syndicate Features)

DANIEL BOONE (See The Exploits of..., Fighting... Frontier Scout...,The Legends of... & March of Comics No. 306)
Dell Publishing Co.: No. 1163, Mar-May, 1961

	GD25	FN65	NM94
Four Color 1163-Marsh-a	4.50	13.50	50.00

DANIEL BOONE (TV) (See March of Comics No. 306)
Gold Key: Jan, 1965 - No. 15, Apr, 1969 (All have Fess Parker photo-c)

	GD25	FN65	NM94
1	8.00	23.00	85.00
2	4.00	12.00	42.00
3-5	2.90	8.70	32.00
6-15	1.80	5.50	20.00

DAN'L BOONE
Sussex Publ. Co.: Sept, 1955 - No. 8, Sept, 1957

	GD25	FN65	NM94
1	13.00	40.00	100.00
2	7.85	23.50	55.00
3-8	5.70	17.00	40.00

DANNY BLAZE (...Firefighter) (Nature Boy No. 3 on)
Charlton Comics: Aug, 1955 - No. 2, Oct, 1955

	GD25	FN65	NM94
1,2	6.50	19.50	45.00

DANNY DINGLE (See Sparkler Comics)
United Features Syndicate: No. 17, 1940

	GD25	FN65	NM94
Single Series 17	21.00	64.00	160.00

DANNY KAYE'S BAND FUN BOOK
H & A Selmer: 1959 (Giveaway)

	GD25	FN65	NM94
nn	5.70	17.00	35.00

DANNY THOMAS SHOW, THE (TV)
Dell Publishing Co.: No. 1180, Apr-June, 1961 - No. 1249, Dec-Feb, 1961-62

	GD25	FN65	NM94
Four Color 1180-Toth-a, photo-c	15.00	44.00	160.00
Four Color 1249-Manning-a, photo-c	15.00	44.00	160.00

DARBY O'GILL & THE LITTLE PEOPLE (Movie)(See Movie Comics)
Dell Publishing Co.: 1959 (Disney)

	GD25	FN65	NM94
Four Color 1024-Toth-a; photo-c.	9.00	27.00	100.00

DAREDEVIL (...& the Black Widow #92-107 on-c only; see Giant-Size...,Marvel Advs., Marvel Graphic Novel #24, Marvel Super Heroes, '66 & Spider-Man &...)
Marvel Comics Group: Apr, 1964 - No. 380, Oct, 1998

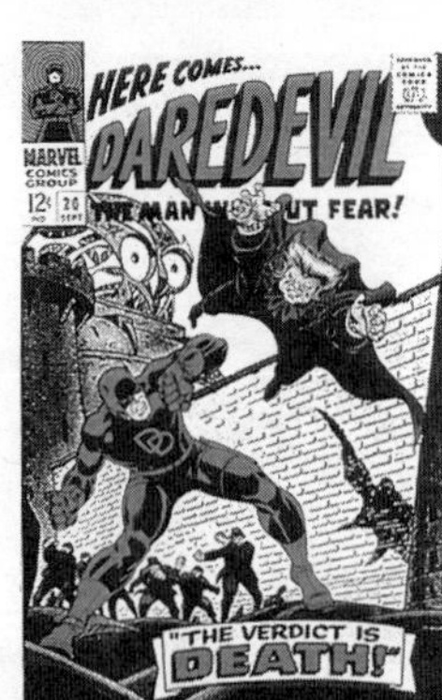

Daredevil #20 © MAR

Daredevil #212 © MAR

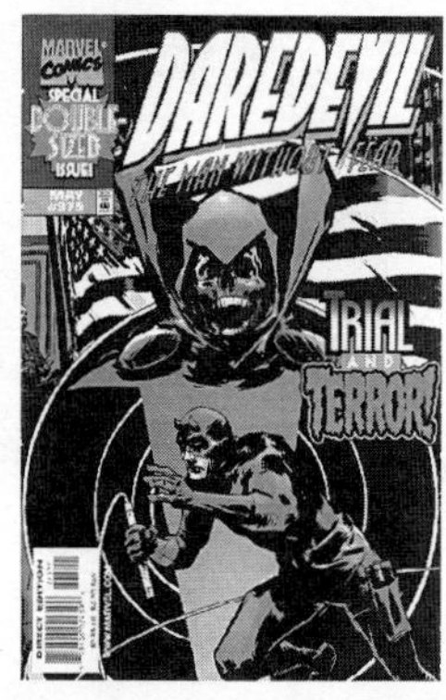

Daredevil #375 © MAR

GD25 FN65 VF82 NM94
1-Origin/1st app. Daredevil; reprinted in Marvel Super Heroes #1 (1966); death of Battling Murdock; intro Foggy Nelson & Karen Page; Everett-c/a 135.00 405.00 875.00 1900.00

GD25 FN65 NM94
2-Fantastic Four cameo; 2nd app. Electro (Spidey villain); Thing guest star 40.00 120.00 475.00
3-Origin & 1st app. The Owl (villain) 31.00 93.00 310.00
4 27.00 82.00 275.00
5-Minor costume change; Wood-a begins 19.00 57.00 190.00
6,8-10: 8-Origin/1st app. Stilt-Man 13.00 39.00 130.00
7-Daredevil battles Sub-Mariner & dons new red costume (4/65) 25.00 75.00 250.00
11-15: 12-Romita's 1st work at Marvel; 1st app. Plunderer; Ka-Zar app. 13-Facts about Ka-Zar's origin; Kirby-a 6.00 18.00 60.00
16,17-Spider-Man x-over. 16-1st Romita-a on Spider-Man (5/66) 9.00 27.00 90.00
18-20: 18-Origin & 1st app. Gladiator 4.50 13.50 45.00
21-26,28-30: 24-Ka-Zar app. 3.00 9.00 30.00
27-Spider-Man x-over 3.20 9.40 32.00
31-40: 38-Fantastic Four x-over; cont'd in F.F. #73. 39-1st Exterminator (later becomes Death-Stalker) 2.50 7.50 22.00
41-49: 41-Death Mike Murdock. 42-1st app. Jester. 43-Daredevil battles Captain America; origin partially retold. 45-Statue of Liberty photo-c 2.00 6.00 16.00
50-52-B. Smith-a 2.50 7.50 20.00
53-Origin retold; last 12¢ issue 2.50 7.50 20.00
54-56,58-60: 54-Spider-Man cameo. 56-1st app. Death's Head (9/69); story cont'd in #57 (not same as new Death's Head) 1.40 4.20 14.00
57-Reveals i.d. to Karen Page; Death's Head app. 1.50 4.50 15.00
61-76,78-80,82-99: 79-Stan Lee cameo. 83-B. Smith layouts/Weiss-p. 87-Electro-c/story 1.20 3.60 12.00
77-Spider-Man x-over 1.50 4.50 15.00
81-Oversize issue; Black Widow begins (11/71). 2.00 6.00 20.00
100-Origin retold 1.80 5.40 18.00
101-104,106,108-113,115-120: 113-1st app. Deathstalker (cameo) 5.00
105-Origin Moondragon by Starlin (12/73); Thanos cameo in flashback (early app.) 1.20 3.60 12.00
107-Starlin-c; Thanos cameo 5.00
114-1st full app. Deathstalker 5.00
121-130,133-137: 124-1st app. Copperhead; Black Widow leaves. 126-1st new Torpedo 3.50
131-Origin/1st app. new Bullseye (see Nick Fury #15) 1.80 5.40 18.00
132-Bullseye app. 3.50
138-Ghost Rider-c/story; Death's Head is reincarnated; Byrne-a .85 2.60 7.00
139-147-149-157: 142-Nova cameo. 146-Bullseye app. 150-1st app. Paladin. 151-Reveals i.d. to Heather Glenn. 155-Black Widow returns. 156-The 1960s Daredevil app. 2.50
148-(Regular 30¢ edition)(9/77) 2.50
148-(35¢-c, limited distribution) 1.00 3.00 10.00
158-Frank Miller art begins (5/79); origin/death of Deathstalker (see Captain America #235 & Spectacular Spider-Man #27 2.70 8.00 30.00
159 1.80 5.40 18.00
160,161 .90 2.70 8.00
162-Ditko-a; no Miller-a 3.00
163,164: 163-Hulk cameo. 164-Origin retold .90 2.70 8.00
165-167,170 .90 2.70 8.00
168-Origin/1st app. Elektra 3.50 10.50 38.00
169-Elektra app. .90 2.70 8.00
171-175: 174,175-Elektra app. 2.00 6.00
176-180-Elektra app. 178-Cage app. 179-Anti-smoking issue mentioned in the Congressional Record 5.00
181-(52 pgs.)-Death of Elektra; Punisher cameo out of costume 1.00 3.00 10.00
182-184-Punisher app. by Miller (drug issues) 4.00
185-191: 187-New Black Widow. 189-Death of Stick. 190-($1.00, 52 pgs.)-Elektra returns, part origin. 191-Last Miller Daredevil 2.50
192-195,197-210: 197,200-Bullseye app. 208-Harlan Ellison scripts borrowed from Avengers TV episode "House that Jack Built" 1.50
196-Wolverine app. .90 2.70 7.50
211-225: 219-Miller-c/script 1.25
226-Frank Miller plots begin 2.00
227-Miller scripts begin 3.00
228-233-Last Miller scripts 2.00
234-237,239,240,242-247 1.25
238-Mutant Massacre; Sabretooth app. 4.00
241-Todd McFarlane-a(p) 2.00
248,249-Wolverine app. 4.00
250,251,253,258: 250-1st app. Bullet. 258-Intro The Bengal (a villain) 1.25
252-(52 pgs.); Fall of the Mutants 3.00
254-Origin & 1st app. Typhoid Mary (5/88) .90 2.70 7.50
255-2nd app. Typhoid Mary 4.00
256-3rd app. Typhoid Mary 3.00
257-Punisher app. (x-over w/Punisher #10) 5.00
259,260-Typhoid Mary app. 260-(52 pgs.) 3.00
261-291,294,296-299: 270-1st app. Black Heart. 272-Intro Shotgun (villain). 282-Silver Surfer app. (cameo in #281). 283-Capt. America app. 297-Typhoid Mary app.; Kingpin storyline begins. 299-Last $1.00-c 1.25
292,293,295: 293-Punisher app. 292-D. G. Chichester scripts begin. 295-Ghost Rider app. 2.00
300-($2.00, 52 pgs.)-Kingpin story ends 2.50
301-318: 301-303-Re-intro the Owl. 304-Garney-c/a. 305,306-Spider-Man-c. 309-Punisher-c.; Terror app. 310-Calypso-c. 1.25
319-Prologue to Fall From Grace; Elektra returns 4.00
319-2nd printing w/black-c 1.25
320-Fall From Grace Pt 1 4.00
321-Fall From Grace regular ed.; Pt 2; new costume; Venom app. 2.00
321-($2.00)-Wraparound Glow-in-the-dark-c ed. 3.00
322-Fall From Grace Pt 3; Eddie Brock app. 3.00
323,324-Fall From Grace Pt. 4 & 5: 323-Vs. Venom-c/story. 324-Morbius-c/story 1.75
325-($2.50, 52 pgs.)-Fall From Grace ends; contains bound-in poster 2.50
326,327: 326-New logo 1.25
328-343: 328-$1.50-c begins; bound-in trading card sheet. 330-Gambit app. 1.50
344-349, 351-353: 344-Begin $1.95-c. 348-1st Cary Nord art in DD (1/96); "Dec" on-c. 353-Karl Kesel scripts; Nord-c/a begins; Mr. Hyde-c/app. 2.00
350-($2.95)-Double-sized 3.00
350-($3.50)-Double-sized; gold ink-c 3.50
354-368: Kesel scripts, Nord-c/a in all. 354-$1.50-c begins. 355-Larry Hama layouts; Pyro app. 358-Mysterio-c/app. 359-Absorbing Man cameo 360-Absorbing Man-c/app. 361-Black Widow-c/app. 363-Gene Colan-a(p) begins 1.50
364, 365, -1(7/97): 364-Begin $1.95-c 2.00
366-374: 366-Begin $1.99-c. 368-Omega Red-c/app. 372-Ghost Rider-c/app. 1.99
375-($2.99) Wraparound-c; Mr. Fear-c/app. 3.00
376-379-"Flying Blind", DD goes undercover for S.H.I.E.L.D. 2.00
380-($2.99) Final issue; flashback story 3.00
Special 1(9/67, 25¢, 68 pgs.)-New art/story 2.50 7.50 24.00
Special 2,3: 2(2/71, 25¢, 52 pgs.)-Entire book has Powell/Wood-r; Wood-c. 3(1/72)-Reprints .85 2.60 7.00
Annual 4(10/76) 2.00 6.00
Annual 4(#5)(1989, $2.00, 68 pgs.)-Atlantis Attacks 3.00
Annual 6(1990, $2.00, 68 pgs.)-Sutton-a 2.00

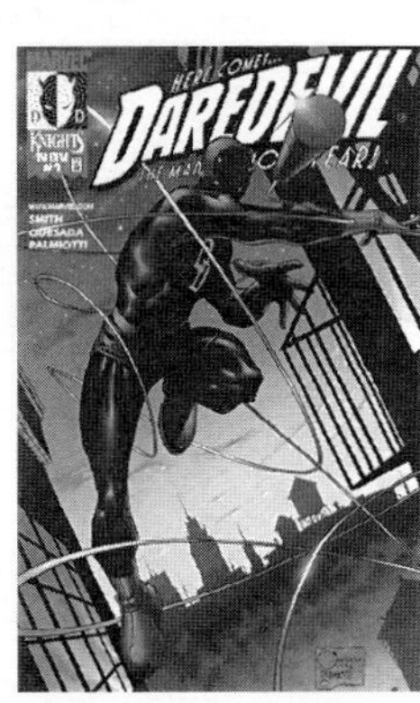

Daredevil V2 #1 (DF Edition) © MAR

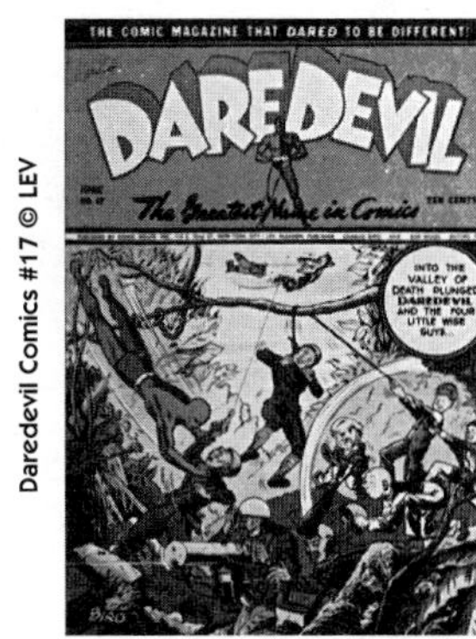

Daredevil Comics #17 © LEV

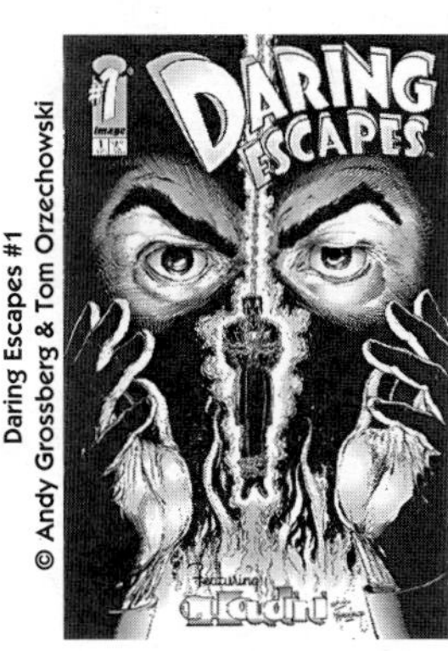

Daring Escapes #1
© Andy Grossberg & Tom Orzechowski

GD25 FN65 NM94

Annual 7(1991, $2.00, 68 pgs.)-Guice-a (7 pgs.) 2.00
Annual 8(1992, $2.25, 68 pgs.)-Deathlok-c/story 2.25
Annual 9(1993, $2.95, 68 pgs.)-Polybagged w/card 3.00
Annual 10(1994, $2.95, 68 pgs.) 3.00
.../DEADPOOL- (Annual '97, $2.99)-Wraparound-c 3.00
...:FALL FROM GRACE TPB ($19.95)-r #319-325 20.00
.../PUNISHER TPB (1988, $4.95)-r/D.D. #182-184 5.00
.../PUNISHER TPB, 2nd & 3rd printings 5.00
...VS. VAPORA 1(Engineering Show Giveaway, 1993, 16 pg.)–Intro Vapora 3.00

NOTE: ***Art Adams*** *c-238p, 239.* ***Austin*** *a-191i; c-151i, 200i.* ***John Buscema*** *a-136, 137p, 234p, 235p; c-86p, 136i, 137p, 142, 219.* ***Byrne*** *c-200p, 201, 203, 223.* ***Capullo*** *a-286p.* ***Colan*** *a(p)-20-49, 53-82, 84-98, 100, 110, 112, 124, 153, 154, 156, 157, Spec. 1p; c(p)-20-42, 44-49, 53-60, 71, 92, 98, 138, 153, 154, 156, 157, Annual 1.* ***Craig*** *a-50i, 52i.* ***Ditko*** *a-162, 234p, 235p, 264p; c-162.* ***Everett*** *c/a-1; inks-21, 83.* ***Garney*** *c/a-304.* ***Gil Kane*** *a-141p, 146-148p, 151p; c(p)-85, 90, 91, 93, 94, 115, 116, 119, 120, 125-128, 133, 139, 147, 152.* ***Kirby*** *c-2-4, 5p, 12p, 13p, 43, 136p.* ***Layton*** *c-202.* ***Miller*** *scripts-168-182, 183(part), 184-191, 219, 227-233; a-158-161p, 163-184p, 191p; c-158-161p, 163-184p, 185-189, 190p, 191.* ***Orlando*** *a-2-4p.* ***Powell*** *a-9p, 11p, Special 1r, 2r.* ***Simonson*** *c-199, 236p.* ***B. Smith*** *a-236p; c-51p, 52p.* ***Starlin*** *a-105p.* ***Steranko*** *c-44i.* ***Tuska*** *a-39i, 145p.* ***Williamson*** *a(i)-237, 239, 240, 243, 248-257, 259-282, 283(part), 284, 285, 287, 288(part), 289(part), 293-300; c(i)-237, 243, 244, 248-257, 259-263, 265-278, 280-289, Annual 8.* ***Wood*** *a-5-8, 9i, 10, 11i, Spec. 2i; c-5i, 6-11, 164i.*

DAREDEVIL (Volume 2) (Marvel Knights)
Marvel Comics: Nov, 1998 - Present ($2.50)

1-Kevin Smith-s/Quesada & Palmiotti-a 3.00
1-($6.95) DF Edition w/Quesada & Palmiotti var.-c 7.00
1-($6.00) DF Sketch Ed. w/B&W-c 6.00
2-4: 2-Two covers by Campbell and Quesada/Palmiotti 2.50

DAREDEVIL/ BATMAN
Marvel Comics/ DC Comics: 1997 ($5.99, one-shot)

nn-McDaniel-c/a 2.00 6.00

DAREDEVIL/ SHI (See Shi/ Daredevil)
Marvel Comics/ Crusade Comics: Feb,1997 ($2.95, limited series)

1- 3.00

DAREDEVIL THE MAN WITHOUT FEAR
Marvel Comics: Oct, 1993 - No. 5, Feb, 1994 ($2.95, limited series) (foil embossed covers)

1-5: Miller scripts; Romita, Jr./Williamson-c/a 4.00
Hardcover 100.00
Trade paperback 20.00

DAREDEVIL COMICS (See Silver Streak Comics)
Lev Gleason Publications (Funnies, Inc. No. 1): July, 1941 - No. 134, Sept, 1956 (Charles Biro stories)

GD25 FN65 VF82 NM94
1-No. 1 titled "Daredevil Battles Hitler"; The Silver Streak, Lance Hale, Cloud Curtis, Dickey Dean, Pirate Prince team up w/Daredevil and battle Hitler; Daredevil battles the Claw; Origin of Hitler feature story. Hitler photo app. on-c 900.00 2700.00 5400.00 9500.00

GD25 FN65 NM94
2-London, Pat Patriot (by Reed Crandall), Nightro, Real American No. 1 (by Briefer #2-11), Dickie Dean, Pirate Prince, & Times Square begin; intro. & only app. The Pioneer, Champion of America 263.00 790.00 2500.00
3-Origin of 13 165.00 495.00 1400.00
4 141.00 423.00 1200.00
5-Intro. Sniffer & Jinx; Ghost vs. Claw begins by Bob Wood, ends #20 112.00 336.00 950.00
6-(#7 in indicia) 94.00 282.00 800.00
7-10: 8-Nightro ends 79.00 237.00 675.00
11-London, Pat Patriot end; classic bondage/torture-c 88.00 264.00 750.00
12-Origin of The Claw; Scoop Scuttle by Wolverton begins (2-4 pgs.), ends #22, not in #21 124.00 372.00 1050.00
13-Intro. of Little Wise Guys (10/42) 106.00 318.00 900.00
14 56.00 168.00 475.00
15-Death of Meatball 82.00 246.00 700.00
16,17 52.00 156.00 440.00
18-New origin of Daredevil (not same as Silver Streak #6) 112.00 336.00 950.00
19,20 44.00 132.00 375.00
21-Reprints cover of Silver Streak #6 (on inside) plus intro. of The Claw from Silver Streak #1 77.00 231.00 650.00
22-30: 27-Bondage/torture-c 37.00 112.00 280.00
31-Death of The Claw 71.00 213.00 600.00
32-37,39,41: 35-Two Daredevil stories begin, end #68 (35-41 are 64 pgs.) 25.00 75.00 190.00
38-Origin Daredevil retold from #18 40.00 120.00 320.00
42-50: 42-Intro. Kilroy in Daredevil; 1 panel Steranko-a 20.00 60.00 150.00
51-69-Last Daredevil issue (12/50) 14.00 42.00 105.00
70-Little Wise Guys take over book; McWilliams-a; Hot Rock Flanagan begins, ends #80 11.00 34.00 85.00
71-79,81: 79-Daredevil returns 9.30 28.00 70.00
80-Daredevil x-over 10.00 30.00 75.00
82,90-One pg. Frazetta ad in both 9.30 28.00 70.00
83-89,91-99,101-134 8.50 26.00 60.00
100 9.30 28.00 70.00

NOTE: ***Biro*** *c/a-all?* ***Bolle*** *a-125.* ***Maurer*** *a-75.* ***McWilliams*** *a-73, 75, 79, 80.*

DARING ADVENTURES (Also see Approved Comics)
St. John Publishing Co.: Nov, 1953 (25¢, 3-D, came w/glasses)

1 (3-D)-Reprints lead story from Son of Sinbad #1 by Kubert 35.00 105.00 245.00

DARING ADVENTURES
I.W. Enterprises/Super Comics: 1963 - 1964

I. W. Reprint #8-r/Fight Comics #53; Matt Baker-a 4.50 13.50 45.00
I.W. Reprint #9-r/Blue Bolt #115; Disbrow-a(3) 4.50 13.50 45.00
Super Reprint #10,11('63)-r/Dynamic #24,16; 11-Marijuana story; Yankee Boy app.; Mac Raboy-a 2.50 7.50 22.00
Super Reprint #12('64)-Phantom Lady from Fox (r/#14 only? w/splash pg. omitted); Matt Baker-a 10.50 32.00 105.00
Super Reprint #15('64)-r/Hooded Menace #1 7.00 21.00 70.00
Super Reprint #16('64)-r/Dynamic #12 2.25 6.75 18.00
Super Reprint #17('64)-r/Green Lama #3 by Raboy 3.50 10.50 35.00
Super Reprint #18-Origin Atlas from unpublished Atlas Comics #1 2.50 7.50 24.00

DARING COMICS (Formerly Daring Mystery) (Jeanie Comics No. 13 on)
Timely Comics (HPC): No. 9, Fall, 1944 - No. 12, Fall, 1945

9-Human Torch, Toro & Sub-Mariner begin 102.00 306.00 865.00
10-The Angel only app. 87.00 261.00 740.00
11,12-The Destroyer app. 87.00 261.00 740.00

NOTE: ***Schomburg*** *c-9-11.* ***Sekowsky*** *c-12? Human Torch, Toro & Sub-Mariner c-9-12.*

DARING CONFESSIONS (Formerly Youthful Hearts)
Youthful Magazines: No. 4, 11/52 - No. 7, 5/53; No. 8, 10/53

4-Doug Wildey-a; Tony Curtis story 11.00 32.00 80.00
5-8: 5-Ray Anthony photo on-c. 6,8-Wildey-a 8.50 26.00 60.00

DARING ESCAPES
Image Comics: Sept, 1998 - No. 4 ($2.95/$2.50, mini-series)

1-Houdini; following app. in Spawn #19,20 3.00
2-($2.50) 2.50

DARING LOVE (Radiant Love No. 2 on)
Gilmor Magazines: Sept-Oct, 1953

1–Steve Ditko's 1st published work (1st drawn was Fantastic Fears #5)(Also See Black Magic #27)(scarce) 32.00 96.00 240.00

DARING LOVE (Formerly Youthful Romances)
Ribage/Pix: No. 15, 12/52; No. 16, 2/53-c, 4/53-Indicia; No. 17-4/53-c & indicia

Daring Mystery Comics #6 © MAR

Dark Angel #8 © MAR

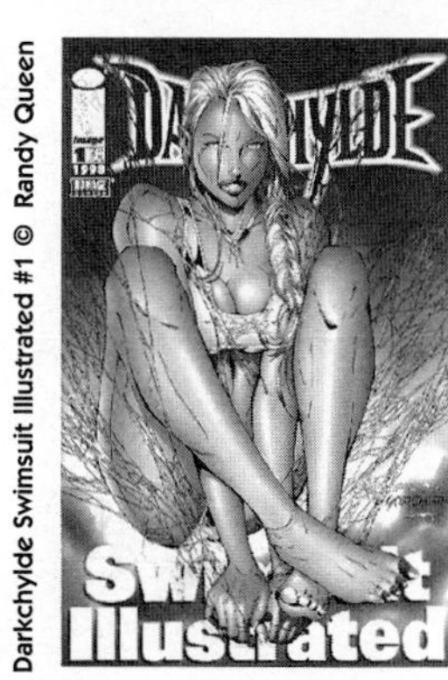
Darkchylde Swimsuit Illustrated #1 © Randy Queen

GD25 FN65 NM94

15 — 8.50 26.00 60.00
16,17: 17-Photo-c — 7.15 21.50 50.00
NOTE: ***Colletta** a-15. **Wildey** a-17.*

DARING LOVE STORIES (See Fox Giants)

DARING MYSTERY COMICS (Comedy Comics No. 9 on; title changed to Daring Comics with No. 9)
Timely Comics (TPI 1-6/TCI 7,8): 1/40 - No. 5, 6/40; No. 6, 9/40; No. 7, 4/41 - No. 8, 1/42

GD25 FN65 VF82 NM94

1-Origin The Fiery Mask (1st app.) by Joe Simon; Monako, Prince of Magic (1st app.), John Steele, Soldier of Fortune (1st app.), Doc Doyle (1st app.) begin; Flash Foster & Barney Mullen, Sea Rover only app; bondage-c — 1375.00 4125.00 8250.00 16,500.00

GD25 FN65 NM94

2-(Rare)-Origin The Phantom Bullet (1st & only app.); The Laughing Mask & Mr. E only app.; Trojak the Tiger Man begins, ends #6; Zephyr Jones & K-4 & His Sky Devils app., also #4 — 600.00 1800.00 6000.00
3-The Phantom Reporter, Dale of FBI, Breeze Barton, Captain Strong & Marvex the Super-Robot only app.; The Purple Mask begins — 360.00 1080.00 3600.00
4-Last Purple Mask; Whirlwind Carter begins; Dan Gorman, G-Man app. — 260.00 780.00 2200.00
5-The Falcon begins (1st app.); The Fiery Mask, Little Hercules app. by Sagendorf in the Segar style; bondage-c — 260.00 780.00 2200.00
6-Origin & only app. Marvel Boy by S&K; Flying Flame, Dynaman, & Stupor-man only app.; The Fiery Mask by S&K; S&K-c — 315.00 945.00 3000.00
7-Origin The Blue Diamond, Captain Daring by S&K, The Fin by Everett, The Challenger, The Silver Scorn & The Thunderer by Burgos; Mr. Millions app — 263.00 790.00 2500.00
8-Origin Citizen V; Last Fin, Silver Scorn, Capt. Daring by Borth, Blue Diamond & The Thunderer; Kirby & part solo Simon-c; Rudy the Robot only app.; Citizen V, Fin & Silver Scorn continue in Comedy #9 — 229.00 688.00 1950.00
NOTE: ***Schomburg** c-1-4, 7. **Simon** a-2, 3, 5. Cover features: 1-Fiery Mask; 2-Phantom Bullet; 3-Purple Mask; 4-G-Man; 5-The Falcon; 6-Marvel Boy; 7, 8-Multiple characters.*

DARING NEW ADVENTURES OF SUPERGIRL, THE
DC Comics: Nov, 1982 - No. 13, Nov, 1983 (Supergirl No. 14 on)

1-Origin retold; Lois Lane back-ups in #2-12 — 2.00
2-13: 8,9-Doom Patrol app. 13-New costume; flag-c — 1.50
NOTE: ***Buckler** c-1p, 2p. **Giffen** c-3p, 4p. **Gil Kane** c-6, ,8, 9, 11-13.*

DARK, THE
Continum Comics: Nov, 1990 - No. 4, Feb, 1993; V2#1, May, 1993 - V2#7, Apr?, 1994 ($1.95)

1-($2.00)-Bright-p; Panosian, Hanna-i; Stroman-c — 2.00
2-(1/92, $2.25)-Stroman-c/a(p) — 2.25
3,4-($2.50): 4-Perez-c & part-i — 2.50
V2#1-Red foil Bart Sears-c — 2.00
V2#1-Red non-foil variant-c — 2.00
V2#1-2nd printing w/blue foil Bart Sears-c — 2.00
V2#2-6: 2-Stroman/Bryant-a. 3-Perez-c(i). 3-6-Foil-c. 4-Perez-c & part-i; bound-in trading cards. 5,6-(2,3/94)-Perez-c(i) — 2.00
V2#7-(B&W)-Perez-c(i) — 2.00
Convention Book 1 (Fall/94, $2.00)-Perez-c — 2.00
Convention Book 2 (10/94, $2.00)-Perez-c(i) — 2.00

DARK ANGEL (Formerly Hell's Angel)
Marvel Comics UK, Ltd.: No. 6, Dec, 1992 - No. 16, Dec, 1993 ($1.75)

6-8,13-16: 6-Excalibur-c/story. 8-Psylocke app. — 1.75
9-12-Wolverine/X-Men app. — 3.00

DARKCHYLDE
Maximum Press #1-3/ Image Comics #4 on: June, 1996 - No. 5, Sept, 1997 ($2.95/ $2.50)

GD25 FN65 NM94

1-Randy Queen-c/a/scripts; "Roses" cover — .90 2.70 8.00
1-American Entertainment Edition-wraparound-c — .90 2.70 8.00
1-"Fashion magazine-style" variant-c — .90 2.70 9.00
1-Special Comicon Edition (contents of #1) Winged devil variant-c — 2.00 6.00
1-($2.50)-Remastered Ed.-wraparound-c — 5.00
2 — .90 2.70 9.00
2-Spiderweb and Moon variant-c — .90 2.70 9.00
3 — 5.00
3-"Kalvin Clein" variant-c by Drew — 5.00
4-($2.50) — 5.00
4-Variant-c — .90 2.70 8.00
5 — 5.00
5-B&W Edition — 1.00 3.00 10.00
5-Dynamic Forces Gold Ed. — 1.00 3.00 10.00
0-(3/98, $2.50) — 2.50
0-American Entertainment Ed. — 5.00
0-Dynamic Forces Ed. — 6.00
0-Dynamic Forces Gold Ed. — .90 2.70 9.00
1/2-WIzard offer — 5.00
1/2 Variant-c — .90 2.70 8.00
1/2 Gold Ed. — 1.20 3.60 12.00
... The Descent TPB ('98, $19.95) r/#1-5; bagged with Darkchylde The Legacy Preview Special 1998; listed price is for TPB only — 25.00

DARKCHYLDE SKETCH BOOK
Image Comics (Dynamic Forces): 1998

1-Regular-c — 7.95
1-DarkChrome cover — 1.60 4.80 16.00

DARKCHYLDE SWIMSUIT ILLUSTRATED
Image Comics: 1998

1-Pin-up art by various — 2.50
1-(6.95) Variant cover — 6.95
1-American Entertainment Ed. — 3.50
1-Dynamic Forces Ed. — 4.50
1-Dynamic Forces Gold Ed. — 8.00
1-Chromium cover — 20.00

DARKCHYLDE THE DIARY
Image Comics: June, 1997 ($2.50, one-shot)

1-Queen-c/s/ art by various — 2.50
1-Variant-c — 5.00
1-Holochrome variant-c — 10.00

DARK CLAW ADVENTURES
DC Comics (Amalgam): June, 1997 ($1.95, one-shot)

1-Templeton-c/s/a & Burchett-a — 2.00

DARK CRYSTAL, THE (Movie)
Marvel Comics Group: April, 1983 - No. 2, May, 1983

1,2-Adaptation of film — 1.50

DARK DOMINION
Defiant: Oct, 1993 - No. 10, July, 1994 ($2.50)

1-9-Len Wein scripts begin. 4-Free extra 16 pgs. 7-9-J.G. Jones-c/a — 2.50
10-Pre-Schism issue; Shooter/Wein script; John Ridgway-a — 2.50

DARKER IMAGE (Also see Deathblow, The Maxx, & Bloodwulf)
Image Comics: Mar, 1993 ($1.95, one-shot)

1-The Maxx by Sam Kieth begins; Bloodwulf by Rob Liefeld & Deathblow by Jim Lee begin (both 1st app.); polybagged w/1 of 3 cards by Kieth, Lee or Liefeld — 2.50
1-B&W interior pgs. w/silver foil logo — 2.00 6.00

DARKEWOOD
Aircel Publishing: 1987 - No. 5, 1988 ($2.00, 28pgs, limited series)

Darkhawk #6 © MAR

Dark Horse Presents #50 © DH

Dark Horse Presents Annual 1998 © DH

GD25 FN65 NM94

1-5 2.00

DARK FANTASIES
Dark Fantasy: 1994 - No. 8, 1995 ($2.95)

1-Test print Run (3,000)-Linsner-c .90 2.70 8.00
1-Linsner-c 5.00
2-4 (Deluxe): 4-($3.95) 4.00
2-4 (Regular) 3.00
5-8 (Deluxe; $3.95) 4.00
5-8 (Regular; $3.50) 3.50

DARK GUARD
Marvel Comics UK: Oct, 1993 - No. 4, Jan, 1994 ($1.75)

1-($2.95)-Foil stamped-c 3.00
2-4 1.75

DARKHAWK
Marvel Comics: Mar, 1991 - No. 50, Apr, 1995 ($1.00/$1.25/$1.50)

1-Origin/1st app. Darkhawk; Hobgoblin cameo 1.50
2-14: 2-Spider-Man & Hobgoblin app. 3-Spider-Man & Hobgoblin app. 6-Capt. America & Daredevil x-over. 9-Punisher app. 11-Last $1.00-c. 11,12-Tombstone app. 13,14-Venom-c/story 1.50
15-24,26-38: 19-Spider-Man & Brotherhood of Evil Mutants-c/story. 20-Spider-Man app. 22-Ghost Rider-c/story. 23-Origin begins, ends #25. 27-New Warriors-c/story. 35-Begin 3 part Venom story 1.25
25-($2.95, 52 pgs.)-Red holo-grafx foil-c w/double gatefold poster; origin of Darkhawk armor revealed 3.00
39-49: 39-Begin $1.50-c; bound-in trading card sheet 1.50
50-($2.50, 52 pgs) 2.50
Annual 1 (1992, $2.25, 68 pgs.)-Vs. Iron Man 2.25
Annual 2 (1993, $2.95, 68 pgs.)-Polybagged w/card 3.00
Annual 3 (1994, $2.95) 3.00

DARKHOLD: PAGES FROM THE BOOK OF SINS (See Midnight Sons Unlimited)
Marvel Comics (Midnight Sons imprint #15 on): Oct, 1992 - No. 16, Jan, 1994 ($1.75)

1-($2.75, 52 pgs.)-Polybagged w/poster by Andy & Adam Kubert; part 4 of Rise of the Midnight Sons storyline 2.75
2-10,12-16: 3-Reintro Modred the Mystic (see Marvel Chillers #1). 4-Sabertooth-c/sty. 5-Punisher & Ghost Rider app. 15-Spot varnish-c. 15,16-Siege of Darkness part 4&12 1.75
11-($2.25)-Outer-c is a Darkhold envelope made of black parchment w/gold ink 2.25

DARK HORSE CLASSICS
Dark Horse Comics: 1992 ($3.95, B&W, 52 pgs.)

nn's: The Last of the Mohicans. 20,000 Leagues Under the Sea 4.00

DARK HORSE CLASSICS
Dark Horse Comics: May, 1996 ($2.95, one-shot)

1-r/Predator: Jungle Tales 3.00

DARK HORSE CLASSICS- ALIENS VERSUS PREDATOR
Dark Horse Comics: Feb, 1997 - No. 6, July, 1997 ($2.95, mini-series)

1-6: r/Aliens Versus Predator 3.00

DARK HORSE CLASSICS- GODZILLA: KING OF THE MONSTERS
Dark Horse Comics: Apr, 1998 ($2.95)

1-4: 1-r/Godzilla: Color Special; Art Adams-a 3.00

DARK HORSE CLASSICS- STAR WARS: DARK EMPIRE
Dark Horse Comics: Mar, 1997 - No. 5 ($2.95, mini-series)

1-5: r/Star Wars: Dark Empire 3.00

DARK HORSE CLASSICS- TERROR OF GODZILLA
Dark Horse Comics: Aug, 1998 - Present ($2.95, limited series)

1-3-r/manga Godzilla in color; Art Adams-c 2.95

GD25 FN65 NM94

DARK HORSE COMICS
Dark Horse Comics: Aug, 1992 - No. 25, Sept, 1994 ($2.50)

1-Dorman double gategold painted-c; Predator, Robocop, Timecop (3-part) & Renegade stories begin 3.00
2-6,11-25: 2-Mignola-c. 3-Begin 3-part Aliens story; Aliens-c. 4-Predator-c. 6-Begin 4 part Robocop story. 12-Begin 2-part Aliens & 3-part Predator stories. 13-Thing From Another World begins w/Nino-a(i). 15-Begin 2-part Aliens: Cargo story. 16-Begin 3-part Predator story. 17-Begin 3-part Star Wars: Droids story & 3-part Aliens: Alien story; Droids-c. 19-Begin 2-part X story; X cover 2.50
7-Begin Star Wars: Tales of the Jedi 3-part story 4.00
8-1st app. X and begins; begin 4-part James Bond 3.00
9,10: 9-Star Wars ends. 10-X ends; Begin 3-part Predator & Godzilla stories 3.00

NOTE: *Art Adams c-11.*

DARK HORSE DOWN UNDER
Dark Horse Comics: June, 1994 - No. 3, Oct, 1994 ($2.50, B&W, limited series)

1-3 2.50

DARK HORSE MONSTERS
Dark Horse Comics: Feb, 1997 ($2.95, one-shot)

1-reprints 3.00

DARK HORSE PRESENTS
Dark Horse Comics: July, 1986 - Present ($1.50/$1.75/$1.95/$2.25/$2.50/$2.95, B&W)

1-1st app. Concrete by Paul Chadwick 1.00 3.00 10.00
1-2nd printing (1988, $1.50) 2.50
1-Silver ink 3rd printing (1992, $2.25)-Says 2nd printing inside 2.25
2-Concrete app. 4.00
3-Concrete app. 3.00
4,5-Concrete app. 2.50
6-10: 6,8,10-Concrete app. 10-1st app. The Mask 2.50
11-19,21-23: 11-19,21-Mask stories. 12,14,16,18,22-Concrete app. 15(2/88) 17-All Roachmill issue 2.00
20-($2.95, 68 pgs.)-Concrete, Flaming Carrot, Mask 2.50
24-Origin Aliens-c/story (11/88); Mr. Monster app. 1.80 5.40 18.00
25-31,33: 28-($2.95, 52 pgs.)-Concrete app.; Mr. Monster story (homage to Graham Ingels). 33-($2.25, 44 pgs.) 2.50
32-($3.50, 68 pgs.)-Annual; Concrete, American 4.00
34-Aliens-c/story 3.00
35-Predator-c/story; begin $1.95-c 3.00
36-1st Aliens Vs. Predator story; painted-c 2.00 6.00
36-Same as above, but line drawn-c 5.00
37-39,41,44,45,47-50: 38-Concrete. 44-Crash Ryan. 48-50-Contain 2 trading cards. 50-S/F story by Perez 2.00
40-($2.95, 52 pgs.)-1st Argosy story 3.00
42,43-Aliens-c/stories 5.00
46-Prequel to new Predator II mini-series 3.00
51-53-Sin City by Frank Miller, parts 2-4; 51,53-Miller-c (see D.H.P. Fifth Anniv. Special for pt. 1) 4.00
54-The Next Men begins(1st app.) by Byrne(9/91); Miller-a 4.00
55-2nd app. The Next Men; parts 5 & 6 of Sin City by Miller; Homocide by Morrow in both. 54-Morrow-c; begin $2.25-c. 55-Miller-c 3.00
56-($3.95, 68 pg. annual)-2-part prologue to Aliens: Genocide; part 7 of Sin City by Miller; Next Men by Byrne 3.00
57-($3.50, 52 pgs.)-Part 8 of Sin City by Miller; Next Men by Byrne; Byrne & Miller-c; Alien Fire story; swipes cover to Daredevil #1 3.00
58-66,68-79,81-84-($2.25): 58,59-Part 9,10 Sin City by Miller; Alien Fire stories. 60,61-Part 11,12 Sin City by Miller. 62-Last Sin City (entire book by Miller, c/a;52 pgs.). 64-Dr. Giggles begins (1st app.), ends #66; Boris the Bear story. 66-New Concrete-c/story by Chadwick. 71-Begin 3 part Dominque story by Jim Balent; Balent-c. 72-(3/93)-Begin 3-part Eudaemon (1st app.) story by Nelson. 2.25

Darkminds #1 © Dreamwave Prod.

The Darkness #10 © Top Cow

Darkseid (Villains) #1 © DC

GD25 FN65 NM94

67-($3.95, 68 pgs.)-Begin 3-part prelude to Predator: Race War mini-series; Oscar Wilde adapt. by Russell 4.00
80-Art Adams-c/a (Monkeyman & O'Brien) 5.00
85-87,92-99,101-108: 85-Begin $2.50-c. 92, 93, 95-Too Much Coffee Man. 101-Aliens c/a by Wrightson, story by Paul Pope. 103-Kirby gatefold-c. 106-Big Blown Baby by Bill Wray. 107-Mignola-c/a 2.50
88-91-Hellboy by Mignola. 5.00
100-1-Intro Lance Blastoff by Miller; Milk & Cheese by Evan Dorkin 5.00
100-2-Hellboy-c by Wrightson; Hellboy story by Mignola; includes Roberta Gregory & Paul Pope stories 3.50
100-3-Darrow-c, Concrete by Chadwick; Pekar story 2.50
100-4-Gibbons-c: Miller story, Geary story/a 2.50
100-5-Allred-c, Adams, Dorkin, Pope 2.50
109-125: 109-Begin $2.95-c; Paul Pope-c. 110-Ed Brubaker-a/scripts. 114-Flip books begin; Lance Blastoff by Miller; Star Slammers by Simonson. 115-Miller-c. 117-Aliens-c/app. 118-Evan Dorkin-c/a. 119-Monkeyman & O'Brien. 121-Jack Zero. 122-Lords of Misrue 123-Imago. 124-Predator. 125-Nocturnals 3.00
126-($3.95, 48 pgs.)-Flip book: Nocturnals, Starship Troopers 3.95
127-134,136: 127-Nocturnals. 129-The Hammer. 132-134-Warren-a 2.95
135-($3.50) The Mark 3.50
Annual 1997 ($4.95, 64 pgs.)-Flip book; Body Bags, Aliens. Pearson-c; stories by Allred & Stephens, Pope, Smith & Morrow, Pearson 5.00
Annual 1998 ($4.95, 64 pgs.) 1st Buffy the Vampire Slayer app. Hellboy story and cover by Mignola 6.00
...Aliens Platinum Edition (1992)-r/DHP #24,43,43,56 & Special 11.00
...Fifth Anniversary Special nn (4/91, $9.95)-Part 1 of Sin City by Frank Miller (c/a); Aliens, Aliens vs. Predator, Concrete, Roachmill, Give Me Liberty & The American stories 1.00 3.00 10.00
The One Trick Rip-off (1997, $12.95, TPB)-r/stories from #101-112 13.00

NOTE: ***Geary*** *a-59, 60.* ***Miller*** *a-Special, 51-53, 55-62; c-59-62, 100-1; c-51, 53, 55, 59-62, 100-1.* ***Moebius*** *a-63; c-63, 70.* ***Vess*** *a-78; c-75, 78.*

DARK KNIGHT (See Batman: The Dark Knight Returns & Legends of the...)

DARKLON THE MYSTIC (Also see Eerie Magazine #79,80)
Pacific Comics: Oct, 1983 (one-shot)

1-Starlin-c/a(r) 1.50

DARKMAN (Movie)
Marvel Comics: Sept, 1990; Oct, 1990 - No. 3, Dec, 1990 ($1.50)

1 (9/90, $2.25, B&W mag., 68 pgs.)-Adaptation of film 2.25
1-3: Reprints B&W magazine 1.50

DARKMAN
Marvel Comics: V2#1, Apr, 1993 -No. 6, Sept, 1993 ($2.95, limited series)

V2#1 ($3.95, 52 pgs.) 4.00
2-6 3.00

DARK MANSION OF FORBIDDEN LOVE, THE (Becomes Forbidden Tales of Dark Mansion No. 5 on)
National Periodical Publ.: Sept-Oct, 1971 - No. 4, Mar-Apr, 1972 (52 pgs.)

1 11.00 33.00 120.00
2-4: 2-Adams-c. 3-Jeff Jones-c 3.80 11.50 40.00

DARKMINDS
Image Comics (Dreamwave Prod.): July, 1998 - Present ($2.50)

1-Manga; Pat Lee-s/a; 2 covers 1.00 3.00 10.00
1-2nd printing 2.50
2 5.00
3-5 2.50

DARK MYSTERIES (Thrilling Tales of Horror & Suspense)
"Master" - "Merit" Publications: June-July, 1951 - No. 25?, 1955

1-Wood-c/a (8 pgs.) 82.00 247.00 700.00
2-Wood/Harrison-c/a (8 pgs.) 56.00 168.00 475.00
3-9: 7-Dismemberment, hypo blood drainage stys 31.00 92.00 230.00
10-Cannibalism story; witch burning-c 32.00 96.00 240.00
11-13,15-18: 11-Severed head panels. 13-Dismemberment-c/story. 17-The Old Gravedigger host 23.00 68.00 170.00
14-Several E.C. Craig swipes 23.00 70.00 175.00
19-Injury-to-eye panel; E.C. swipe; torture-c 30.00 90.00 225.00
20-Female bondage, blood drainage story 27.00 80.00 200.00
21,22-Last pre-code issue, misdated 3/54 instead of 3/55 16.00 48.00 120.00
23-25 (#25-Exist?) 13.00 40.00 100.00

NOTE: ***Cameron*** *a-1, 2.* ***Myron Fass*** *c/a-21.* ***Harrison*** *a-3, 7; c-3.* ***Hollingsworth*** *a-7-17, 20, 21, 23.* ***Wildey*** *a-5. Woodish art by* ***Fleishman****-9; c-10, 14-17. Bondage c-10, 18, 19.*

DARK NEMESIS (VILLAINS) (See Teen Titans)
DC Comics: Feb, 1998 ($1.95, one-shot)

1-Jurgens-s/Pearson-c 2.00

DARKNESS, THE (See Witchblade #10)
Image Comics (Top Cow Productions): Dec, 1996 - Present ($2.50)

Special Preview Edition-(7/96, B&W)-Ennis script; Silvestri-a(p) 1.80 5.40 18.00
0 2.00 6.00 20.00
0-Gold Edition 22.00
1/2 1.60 4.80 16.00
1/2-Christmas-c 2.70 8.00 30.00
1-Ennis-s/Silvestri-a 1.50 4.50 15.00
1-Black variant-c 1.50 4.50 15.00
1-Platinum variant-c 30.00
1-Fan Club Ed. 1.00 3.00 10.00
2 1.50 4.50 15.00
3 1.20 3.60 12.00
4, 5 1.00 3.00 10.00
6-10: 9,10-Witchblade "Family Ties" x-over pt. 2,3 5.00
7-Variant-c w/concubine 1.40 4.20 14.00
8-American Entertainment 1.50 4.50 15.00
8-American Entertainment Gold Ed. 20.00
9-American Entertainment Gold Ed. 10.00
10-American Entertainment Gold Ed. 15.00
11-Regular Ed.; Ennis-s/Silverstri & D-Tron-c 1.20 3.00
11-Nine (non-chromium) variant-c (Benitez, Cabrera, the Hildebrandts, Finch, Keown, Peterson, Portacio, Tan, Turner .90 2.70 8.00
11-Chromium-c by Silvestri & Batt 40.00
12-18: 13-Begin Benitez-a(p) 3.00
Holiday Pin-up-American Entertainment .90 2.70 8.00
Holiday Pin-up Gold Ed.-American Entertainment 14.00
Prelude-American Entertainment .85 2.60 7.00
Prelude Gold Ed.-American Entertainment 14.00
Wizard ACE Ed.- Reprints #1 1.80 5.40 18.00
...Collected Editions #1 ($4.95, trade paperback) r/#1,2 4.95
...Collected Editions #2 ($4.95, trade paperback) r/#3,4 4.95
...Collected Editions #3 ($4.95, trade paperback) r/#5,6 4.95
...Collected Editions #4 ($4.95, trade paperback) r/#7,8 4.95
Deluxe Collected Editions #1 (12/98, $14.95, TPB) r/#1-6 & Preview 14.95

DARK ONE'S THIRD EYE
Sirius Entertainment: 1996 ($4.95, squarebound, one-shot)

nn-Dark One-a; pinups 5.00

DARK OZ
Arrow Comics: 1997 - No. 5 ($2.75, B&W, limited series)

1-Bill Bryan-a 2.75

DARKSEID (VILLAINS) (See Jack Kirby's New Gods and New Gods)
DC Comics: Feb, 1998 ($1.95, one-shot)

1-Byrne-s/Pearson-c 2.00

DARKSEID VS. GALACTUS: THE HUNGER
DC Comics: 1995 ($4.95, one-shot) (1st DC/Marvel x-over by John Byrne)

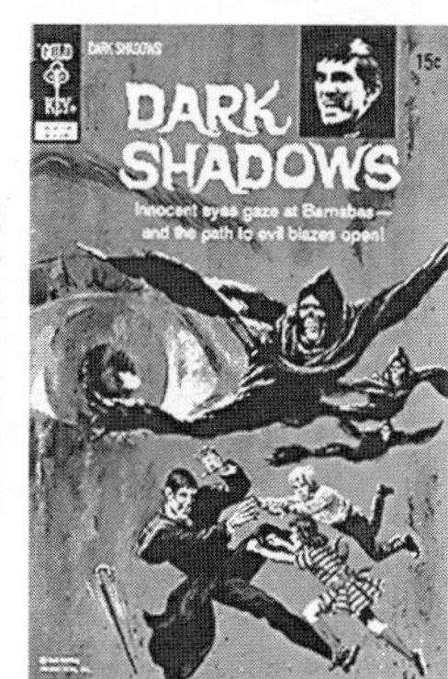

Dark Shadows #15 © GK

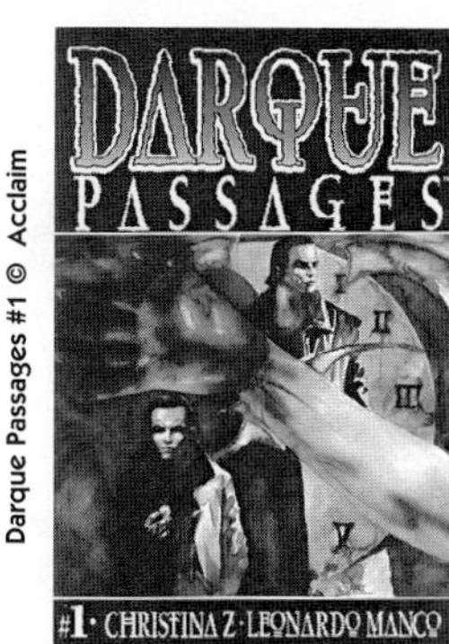

Darque Passages #1 © Acclaim

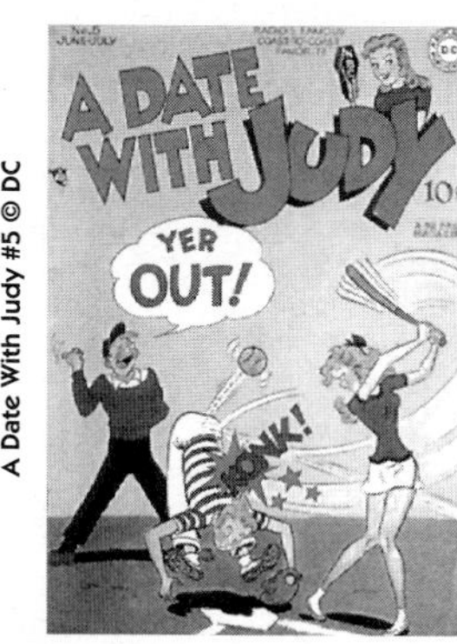

A Date With Judy #5 © DC

	GD25	FN65	NM94
nn-John Byrne-c/a/script			5.00

DARK SHADOWS
Steinway Comic Publ. (Ajax)(America's Best): Oct, 1957 - No. 3, May, 1958

	GD25	FN65	NM94
1	14.00	42.00	105.00
2,3	11.00	32.00	80.00

DARK SHADOWS (TV) (See Dan Curtis Giveaways)
Gold Key: Mar, 1969 - No. 35, Feb, 1976 (Photo-c: 1-7)

	GD25	FN65	NM94
1(30039-903)-With pull-out poster (25¢)	22.00	66.00	245.00
1-With poster missing	8.00	24.00	90.00
2	7.00	22.00	80.00
3-With pull-out poster	10.00	30.00	115.00
3-With poster missing	5.50	16.50	60.00
4-7: 7-Last photo-c	6.40	19.00	70.00
8-10	5.00	15.00	55.00
11-20	4.00	12.00	45.00
21-35: 30-Last painted-c	3.00	9.00	35.00
Story Digest 1 (6/70)-Photo-c	8.00	25.00	90.00

DARK SHADOWS (TV) (See Nightmare on Elm Street)
Innovation Publishing: June, 1992 - No. 4, Spring, 1993 ($2.50, limited series, coated stock)

	GD25	FN65	NM94
1-Based on 1991 NBC TV mini-series; painted-c			4.00
2-4			3.00

DARK SHADOWS: BOOK TWO
Innovation Publishing: 1993 - No. 4, July, 1993 ($2.50, limited series)

	GD25	FN65	NM94
1-4-Painted-c. 4-Maggie Thompson scripts			3.00

DARK SHADOWS: BOOK THREE
Innovation Publishing: Nov, 1993 ($2.50)

	GD25	FN65	NM94
1-(Whole #9)			3.00

DARKSIDE
Maximum Press: Oct, 1996 ($2.99, one-shot)

	GD25	FN65	NM94
1-Avengelyne-c/app.			3.00

DARKSTARS, THE
DC Comics: Oct, 1992 - No. 38, Jan, 1996 ($1.75/$1.95)

	GD25	FN65	NM94
1-1st app. The Darkstars			2.00
2-21: 5-Hawkman & Hawkwoman app. 18-20-Flash app.			1.75
22-24: 22-Begin $1.95-c. 24-(9/94)-Zero Hour			2.00
0,25-30: 0-(10/94). 25-(11/94). 30-Green Lantern app.			2.00
31-38: 31-...vs, Darkseid. 32-Green Lantern app.			2.25

NOTE: ***Travis Charest*** *a(p)-4-7; c(p)-2-5; c-6-11.* ***Stroman*** *a-1-3; c-1.*

DARK TOWN
Mad Monkey Press: 1995 ($3.95, magazine-size, quarterly)

	GD25	FN65	NM94
1-Kaja Blackley scripts; Vanessa Chong-a			4.00

DARKWING DUCK (TV cartoon) (Also see Cartoon Tales)
Disney Comics: Nov, 1991 - No. 4, Feb, 1992 ($1.50, limited series)

	GD25	FN65	NM94
1-4: Adapts hour-long premiere TV episode			1.50

DARLING LOVE
Close Up/Archie Publ. (A Darling Magazine): Oct-Nov, 1949 - No. 11, 1952 (no month) (52 pgs.)(All photo-c?)

	GD25	FN65	NM94
1-Photo-c	12.00	36.00	90.00
2-Photo-c	8.50	26.00	60.00
3-8,10,11: 3-6-photo-c	6.50	19.50	45.00
9-Krigstein-a	7.85	23.50	55.00

DARLING ROMANCE
Close Up (MLJ Publications): Sept-Oct, 1949 - No. 7, 1951 (All photo-c)

	GD25	FN65	NM94
1-(52 pgs.)-Photo-c	19.00	58.00	145.00
2	8.50	26.00	60.00
3-7	7.15	21.50	50.00

DARQUE PASSAGES (See Master Darque)
Acclaim (Valiant): April, 1998 ($2.50)

	GD25	FN65	NM94
1-Christina Z.-s/Manco-c/a			2.50

DARQUE RAZOR
London Night Studios: Aug, 1997 ($2.25/$3.00)

	GD25	FN65	NM94
1/2			2.25
1-($3.00)			3.00
1-($10.00) Nude Edition	1.00	3.00	10.00

DART (Also see Freak Force & Savage Dragon)
Image Comics (Highbrow Entertainment): Feb, 1996 - No. 3, May, 1996 ($2.50, limited series)

	GD25	FN65	NM94
1-3			2.50

DASTARDLY & MUTTLEY (See Fun-In No. 1-4, 6 and Kite Fun Book)

DATE WITH DANGER
Standard Comics: No. 5, Dec, 1952 - No. 6, Feb, 1953

	GD25	FN65	NM94
5,6-Secret agent stories: 6-Atom bomb story	6.50	19.50	45.00

DATE WITH DEBBI (Also see Debbi's Dates)
National Periodical Publ.: Jan-Feb, 1969 - No. 17, Sept-Oct, 1971; No. 18, Oct-Nov, 1972

	GD25	FN65	NM94
1-Teenage	3.20	9.50	35.00
2-5	1.60	4.80	16.00
6-13	1.40	4.20	14.00
14,15-(68 pgs.): 14-1 pg. story on Jack Wild. 15-Marlo Thomas/"That Girl" sty	1.80	5.40	18.00
16,17: 17-52 pgs; James Taylor sty.	1.60	4.80	16.00
18-Last issue	1.40	4.20	14.00

DATE WITH JUDY, A (Radio/TV, and 1948 movie)
National Periodical Publications: Oct-Nov, 1947 - No. 79, Oct-Nov, 1960 (No. 1-25: 52 pgs.)

	GD25	FN65	NM94
1-Teenage	25.00	76.00	190.00
2	12.00	36.00	90.00
3-10	9.30	28.00	70.00
11-20	5.70	17.00	40.00
21-40	5.35	16.00	32.00
41-45: 45-Last pre-code (2-3/55)	4.25	13.00	28.00
46-79: 79-Drucker-c/a	4.00	11.00	22.00

DATE WITH MILLIE, A (Life With Millie No. 8 on)(Teenage)
Atlas/Marvel Comics (MPC): Oct, 1956 - No. 7, Aug, 1957; Oct, 1959 - No. 7, Oct, 1960

	GD25	FN65	NM94
1(10/56)-(1st Series)-Dan DeCarlo-a in #1-7	21.00	63.00	160.00
2	11.00	32.00	80.00
3-7	7.85	23.50	55.00
1(10/59)-(2nd Series)	11.00	32.00	80.00
2-7	7.85	23.50	55.00

DATE WITH PATSY, A (Also see Patsy Walker)
Atlas Comics: Sept, 1957 (One-shot)

	GD25	FN65	NM94
1-Starring Patsy Walker	9.30	28.00	65.00

DAVID AND GOLIATH (Movie)
Dell Publishing Co.: No. 1205, July, 1961

	GD25	FN65	NM94
Four Color 1205-Photo-c	5.50	16.50	60.00

DAVID CASSIDY (TV)(See Partridge Family, Swing With Scooter #33 & Time For Love #30)
Charlton Comics: Feb, 1972 - No. 14, Sept, 1973

	GD25	FN65	NM94
1	3.50	10.50	38.00
2-4,6,8,10-13	1.80	5.40	18.00
5,7,9,14-Photo-c	2.40	7.00	26.00

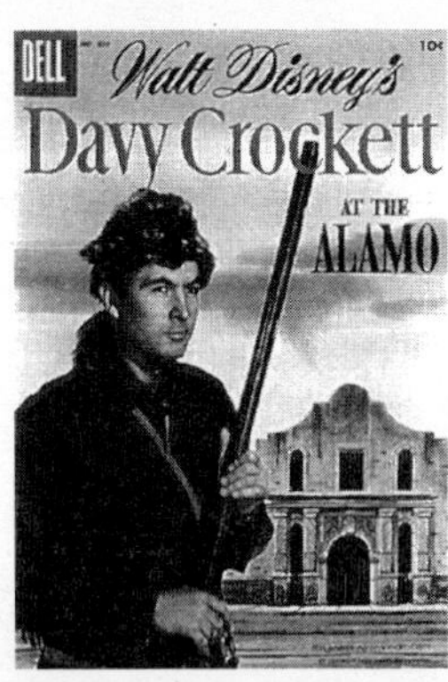

Davy Crockett Four Color #639 © WDC

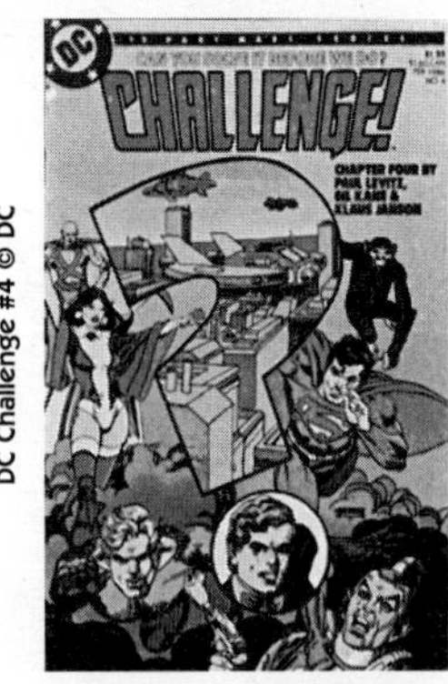

DC Challenge #4 © DC

DC 100 Page Super Spectacular #5 © DC

GD25 FN65 NM94

DAVID LADD'S LIFE STORY (See Movie Classics)

DAVY CROCKETT (See Dell Giants, Fightin..., Frontier Fighters, It's Game Time, Power Record Comics, Western Tales & Wild Frontier)

DAVY CROCKETT (Frontier Fighter...)
Avon Periodicals: 1951

nn-Tuska?, Reinman-a; Fawcette-c 15.00 46.00 115.00

DAVY CROCKETT (...King of the Wild Frontier No. 1,2)(TV)
Dell Publishing Co./Gold Key: 5/55 - No. 671, 12/55; No. 1, 12/63; No. 2, 11/69 (Walt Disney)

Four Color 631(#1)-Fess Parker photo-c 16.75 50.00 185.00
Four Color 639-Photo-c 13.25 40.00 145.00
Four Color 664,671(Marsh-a)-Photo-c 12.00 37.00 135.00
1(12/63-Gold Key)-Fess Parker photo-c; reprints 12.00 37.00 135.00
2(11/69)-Fess Parker photo-c; reprints 3.60 11.00 40.00
...Christmas Book (no date, 16 pgs., paper-c)-Sears giveaway 5.70 17.00 35.00
...In the Raid at Piney Creek (1955, 16 pgs., 5x7-1/4")-American Motors giveaway; slick, photo-c 6.50 19.50 45.00
...Safety Trails (1955, 16pgs, 3-1/4x7")-Cities Service giveaway 6.50 19.50 45.00

DAVY CROCKETT (...Frontier Fighter #1,2; Kid Montana #9 on)
Charlton Comics: Aug, 1955 - No. 8, Jan, 1957

1 7.85 23.50 55.00
2 5.35 16.00 32.00
3-8 4.00 12.00 24.00
Hunting With... nn ('55, 16 pgs.)-Ben Franklin Store giveaway (Publ.-S. Rose) 5.00 15.00 30.00

DAWN
Sirius Entertainment: June, 1995 - No. 6, 1996 ($2.95)

1/2-w/certificate .90 2.70 8.00
1/2-Variant-c 2.00 6.00 20.00
1-Linsner-c/a 1.00 3.00 10.00
1-Black Light Edition 1.50 4.50 15.00
1-White Trash Edition 2.25 6.80 25.00
1-Look Sharp Edition 4.00 12.25 45.00
2-4: Linsner-c/a 5.00
2-Variant-c 2.25 6.80 25.00
3-Limited Edition 2.25 6.80 25.00
4-6-Vibrato-c 4.00
4, 5-Limited Edition 1.50 4.50 15.00
6-Limited Edition 1.80 5.40 18.00
Lucifer's Halo TPB (11/97, $19.95) r/Drama, Dawn #1-6 plus 12 pages of new artwork 19.95

DAYDREAMERS (See Generation X)
Marvel Comics: Aug, 1997 - No. 3, Oct, 1997 ($2.50, limited series)

1-3-Franklin Richards, Howard the Duck, Man-Thing app. 2.50

DAYS OF THE MOB (See In the Days of the Mob)

DAZEY'S DIARY
Dell Publishing Co.: June-Aug, 1962

01-174-208: Bill Woggon-c/a 2.75 8.00 30.00

DAZZLER, THE (Also see Marvel Graphic Novel & X-Men #130)
Marvel Comics Group: Mar, 1981 - No. 42, Mar, 1986

1,2-X-Men app. 2.50
3-21: 10,11-Galactus app. 21-Double size; photo-c. 1.00
22 (12/82)-vs. Rogue Battle-c/sty 3.00
23,26: 23-Rogue/Mystique 1 pg. app. 26-Jusko-c 2.00
24,28: 24-Full app. Rogue w/Powerman (Iron Fist). 28-Full app. Rogue; Mystique app. 3.00
25,29-32,34-37,39 1.00
27,33,38,40-42: 27-Rogue app. 33-Michael Jackson thriller swipe-c/sty. 38-Wolverine-c/app.; X-Men app. 40-Secret Wars II. 42-Beast-c/sty 3.00
NOTE: *No. 1 distributed only through comic shops.* ***Alcala*** *a-1i, 2i.* ***Chadwick*** *a-38-42p; c(p)-39, 41, 42.* ***Guice*** *a-38i, 42i; c-38, 40.*

GD25 FN65 NM94

DC CHALLENGE
DC Comics: Nov, 1985 - No. 12, Oct, 1986 ($1.25, maxi-series)

1-11: 1-Colan-a. 2,8-Batman-c/app. 4-Gil Kane-c/a 1.25
12-($2.00)-Ordway-c 2.00
NOTE: *Batman app. in 1-4, 6-12. Joker app. in 7.* ***Giffen*** *c/a-11.* ***Infantino*** *a-3.* ***Ordway*** *c-12.* ***Swan/Austin*** *c-10.*

DC COMICS PRESENTS
DC Comics: July-Aug, 1978 - No. 97, Sept, 1986 (Superman team-ups in all)

1-4th & final Superman/Flash race .85 2.60 7.00
2-10: 2-4th & final Superman/Flash race. 4-Metal Men. 9-Wonder Woman 4.00
11,12,14-26,30-32,38-40,43-46,48,50,51,53-71,73-76,79-84: 19-Batgirl. 31,58-Robin.. 43,80-Legion of Super Heroes. .82-Adam Strange. 83-Batman & Outsiders. 3.00
13,27-29,33-37,42,47,49,52,86-96: 13-Legion of Super Heroes. 35-Man-Bat. 42,47-Sandman. 52-Doom Patrol. 86-88-Crisis x-over. 88-Creeper 4.00
26-(10/80)-Green Lantern; intro Cyborg, Starfire, Raven (1st app. New Teen Titans in 16 pg. preview); Starlin-c/a; Sargon the Sorcerer back-up 1.40 4.20 14.00
41,72,77,78,97: 41-Superman/Joker-c/story. 72-Joker/Phantom Stranger-c/story.77,78-Animal Man app. (77-cover app. also) 2.00 6.00
85-Swamp Thing; Alan Moore scripts .90 2.70 8.00
Annual 1,4: 1(9/82)-G.A. Superman. 4(10/85)-Superwoman 3.00
Annual 2,3: 2(7/83)-Intro/origin Superwoman. 3(9/84)-Shazam. 4.00
NOTE: ***Adkins*** *a-2, 54; c-2.* ***Buckler*** *a-33, 34; c-30, 33, 34.* ***Giffen*** *a-39; c-59.* ***Gil Kane*** *a-28, 35, Annual 3; c-48p, 56, 58, 60, 62, 64, 68, Annual 2, 3.* ***Kirby*** *c/a-84.* ***Kubert*** *c/a-66.* ***Morrow*** *c/a-65.* ***Newton*** *c/a-54p.* ***Orlando*** *c-53i.* ***Perez*** *a-26p, 61p; c-38, 61, 94.* ***Starlin*** *a-26-29p, 36p, 37p; c-26-29, 36, 37, 93.* ***Toth*** *a-84.* ***Williamson*** *i-79, 85, 87.*

DC GRAPHIC NOVEL (Also see DC Science Fiction...)
DC Comics: Nov, 1983 - No. 7, 1986 ($5.95, 68 pgs.)

1-3,5,7: 1-Star Raiders. 2-Warlords; not from regular Warlord series. 3-The Medusa Chain; Ernie Colon story/a. 5-Me and Joe Priest; Chaykin-c. 7-Space Clusters; Nino-c/a. 1.00 3.00 10.00
4-The Hunger Dogs by Kirby; Darkseid kills Himon from Mister Miracle & destroys New Genesis 2.20 6.25 22.00
6-Metalzoic; Sienkiewicz-c ($6.95) .90 2.70 9.00

DC/MARVEL: ALL ACCESS (Also see DC Versus Marvel & Marvel Versus DC)
DC Comics: 1996 - No. 4, 1997 ($2.95, limited series)

1-4: 1-Superman & Spider-Man app. 2-Robin & Jubilee app. 3-Dr. Strange & Batman-c/app., X-Men , JLA app. 4-X-Men vs. JLA-c/app. rebirth of Amalgam 3.00

DC/MARVEL: CROSSOVER CLASSICS II
DC Comics: 1998 ($14.95, TPB)

1-Reprints Batman/Punisher: Lake of Fire, Punisher/Batman: Deadly Knights, Silver Surfer/Superman, Batman & Capt. America 14.95

DC 100 PAGE SUPER SPECTACULAR
(Title is 100 Page... No. 14 on)(Square bound) (Reprints, 50¢)
National Periodical Publications: No. 4, Summer, 1971 - No. 13, 6/72; No. 14, 2/73 - No. 22, 11/73 (No #1-3)

4-Weird Mystery Tales; Johnny Peril & Phantom Stranger; cover & splashes by Wrightson; origin Jungle Boy of Jupiter 10.00 30.00 110.00
5-Love Stories; Wood inks (7 pgs.)(scarcer) 33.00 100.00 400.00
6- "World's Greatest Super-Heroes"; JLA, JSA, Spectre, Johnny Quick, Vigilante & Hawkman; contains unpublished Wildcat story; N. Adams wrap-around-c; r/JLA #21,22 10.00 30.00 110.00
7-(Also listed as Superman #245) Air Wave, Kid Eternity, Hawkman-r; Atom-r/Atom #3 3.00 9.00 32.00

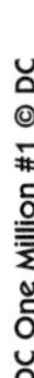
DC One Million #1 © DC

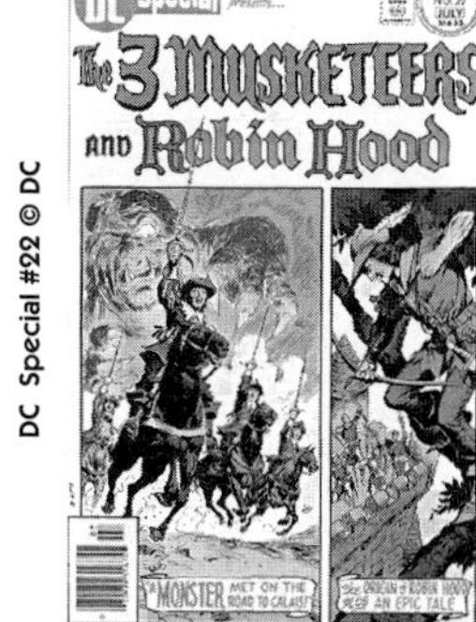

DC Special #22 © DC

DC Special Series #22 © DC

GD25 FN65 NM94

8-(Also listed as Batman #238) Batman, Legion, Aquaman-r; G.A. Atom, Sargon (r/Sensation #57), Plastic Man (r/Police #14) stories; Doom Patrol origin-r; N. Adams wraparound-c 4.00 12.00 45.00
9-(Also listed as Our Army at War #242) Kubert-c 5.00 15.00 55.00
10-(Also listed as Adventure Comics #416) Golden Age-reprints; r/1st app. Black Canary from Flash #86; no Zatanna 3.25 10.00 35.00
11-(Also listed as Flash #214) origin Metal Men-r/Showcase #37; never before pubbed G.A. Flash story. 3.75 11.50 40.00
12-(Also listed as Superboy #185) Legion-c/story; Teen Titans, Kid Eternity (r/Hit #46), Star Spangled Kid-r(S.S. #55) 2.75 8.50 30.00
13-(Also listed as Superman #252) Ray(r/Smash #17), Black Condor, (r/Crack #18), Hawkman(r/Flash #24); Starman-r/Adv. #67; Dr. Fate & Spectre-r/More Fun #57; N. Adams-c 2.75 8.50 30.00
14-Batman-r/Detective #31,32,156; Atom-r/Showcase#34
2.75 8.50 30.00
15-22: 15-r/2nd Boy Commandos/Det. #64. 17-JSA-r/All Star #37 (10-11/47, 38 pgs.), Sandman-r/Adv. #65 (8/41), JLA #23 (11/63) & JLA #43 (3/66). 20-Batman-r/Det. #66,68, Spectre; origin Two-Face. 21-Superboy; r/Brave & the Bold #54. 22-r/All-Flash #13. 1.60 4.80 18.00
NOTE: ***Anderson*** *r-11, 14, 18i, 22.* ***B. Baily*** *r-18, 20.* ***Burnley*** *r-18, 20.* ***Crandall*** *r-14p, 20.* ***Drucker*** *r-4.* ***Grandenetti*** *a-22(2)r.* ***Heath*** *a-22r.* ***Infantino*** *r-17, 20, 22.* ***G. Kane*** *r-18.* ***Kubert*** *r-6, 7, 16, 17; c-16, 19.* ***Manning*** *a-19r.* ***Meskin*** *r-4, 22.* ***Mooney*** *r-15, 21.* ***Toth*** *r-17, 20.*

DC ONE MILLION (Also see crossover #1,000,000 issues)
DC Comics: Nov, 1998 - No. 4, Nov, 1998 ($2.95/$1.99, weekly lim. series)

1-($2.95) JLA travels to the 853rd century; Morrison-s 3.00
2-4-($1.99) 2.00

DC SCIENCE FICTION GRAPHIC NOVEL
DC Comics: 1985 - No. 7, 1987 ($5.95)

SF1-SF7: SF1-Hell on Earth by Robert Bloch; Giffen-p. SF2-Nightwings by Robert Silverberg; G. Colan-p. SF3-Frost & Fire by Bradbury. SF4-Merchants of Venus. SF5-Demon With A Glass Hand by Ellison; M. Rogers-a. SF6-The Magic Goes Away by Niven. SF7-Sandkings by George R.R. Martin .90 2.70 9.00

DC SILVER AGE CLASSICS
DC Comics: 1992 ($1.00, all reprints)

...Action Comics #252; r/1st Supergirl; Adventure Comics #247; r/1st Legion of S.H....The Brave and the Bold #28; r/1st JLA; Detective Comics #225; r/1st Martian Manhunter; Detective Comics #327; r/1st new look Batman; Green Lantern #76; r/Green Lantern/Gr. Arrow; House of Secrets #92; r/1st Swamp Thing; Showcase #4; r/1st S.A. Flash; Showcase #22; r/1st S.A. Green Lantern; Sugar and Spike #99; 2 unpublished stories 1.00

DC SPECIAL (Also see Super DC...)
National Per. Publ.: 10-12/68 - No. 15, 11-12/71; No. 16, Spr/75 - No. 29, 8-9/77

1-All Infantino issue; Flash, Batman, Adam Strange-r; begin 68 pg. issues, end #21 3.20 9.50 35.00
2-Teen humor; Binky, Buzzy, Harvey app. 5.50 16.50 60.00
3-All-Girl issue; unpubl. GA Wonder Woman story 3.20 9.60 35.00
4-13: 4-Horror. 5-All Kubert issue; Viking Prince, Sgt. Rock-r. 6-Western. 7,9,13-Strangest Sports. 11-Monsters. 12-Viking Prince; Kubert-c/a (r/B&B almost entirely) 2.20 6.25 22.00
14,15: 15-G.A. Plastic Man origin-r/Police #1; origin Woozy by Cole; 14,15-(52 pgs.) 2.20 6.25 22.00
16-29: 16-Super Heroes Battle Super Gorillas; r/Capt. Storm #1, 1st Johnny Cloud/All-Amer. Men of War #82. 17-Early S.A. Green Lantern-r. 22-Origin Robin Hood. 26-Enemy Ace on-c only. 27-Captain Comet story. 28-Earth Shattering Disaster Stories; Legion of Super-Heroes story. 29-New "The Untold Origin of the Justice Society"; Staton-a .90 2.70 9.00
NOTE: ***N. Adams*** *c-3, 4, 6, 11, 29.* ***Grell*** *a-20; c-17, 20.* ***Heath*** *a-12r.* ***G. Kane*** *a-6p, 13r, 17r, 19-21r.* ***Kubert*** *a-6r, 12r, 22.* ***Meskin*** *a-10.* ***Moreira*** *a-10.* ***Staton*** *a-29p.* ***Toth*** *a-13, 20r. #1-15: 25¢; 16-27: 50¢; 28, 29: 60¢. #1-13, 16-21: 68 pgs.; 14, 15: 52 pgs.; 25-27: oversized.*

DC SPECIAL BLUE RIBBON DIGEST
DC Comics: Mar-Apr, 1980 - No. 24, Aug, 1982

GD25 FN65 NM94

1-5: 1-Legion reprints. 2-Flash. 3-Justice Society. 4-Green Lantern 5-Secret Origins; new Zatara and Zatanna 2.00 6.00
6-10: 6-Ghosts. 7-Sgt. Rock's Prize Battle Tales. 8-Legion. 9-Secret Origins. 10-Warlord-"The Deimos Saga"-Grell-s/c/a 5.00
11-15: 11-Justice League. 12-Haunted Tank; reprints 1st app. 13-Strange Sports Stories. 14-UFO Invaders; Adam Strange app. 15-Secret Origins of Super Villains; JLA app. .85 2.60 7.00
16-19: 16-Green Lantern/Green Arrow-r; all Adams-a. 17-Ghosts. 18-Sgt. Rock; Kubert front & back-c. 19-Doom Patrol; new Perez-c .85 2.60 7.00
20-Dark Mansion of Forbidden Love (scarce) 2.20 6.50 24.00
21-24: 21-Our Army at War. 22-Secret Origins. 23-Green Arrow, w/new 7 pg. story. 24-House of Mystery; new Kubert wraparound-c .90 2.70 8.00
NOTE: ***N. Adams*** *a-16(6)r, 17r, 23r; c-16.* ***Aparo*** *a-6r, 24r; c-23.* ***Grell*** *a-8, 10; c-10.* ***Heath*** *a-14.* ***Infantino*** *a-15r.* ***Kaluta*** *a-17r.* ***Gil Kane*** *a-15r, 22r.* ***Kirby*** *a-23r.* ***Kubert*** *a-3, 18r, 21r; c-7, 12, 14, 17, 18, 21, 24.* ***Morrow*** *a-24r.* ***Orlando*** *a-17r, 22r; c-1, 20.* ***Toth*** *a-21r, 24r.* ***Wood*** *a-3, 17r, 24r.* ***Wrightson*** *a-16r, 17r, 24r.*

DC SPECIAL SERIES
National Periodical Publications/DC Comics: 9/77 - No. 16, Fall, 1978; No. 17, 8/79 - No. 27, Fall, 1981 (No. 18, 19, 23, 24 - digest size, 100 pgs.; No. 25-27 - Treasury sized)

1-"5-Star Super-Hero Spectacular 1977"; Batman, Atom, Flash, Green Lantern, Aquaman, in solo stories, Kobra app.; N. Adams-c
1.00 3.00 10.00
2(#1)-"The Original Swamp Thing Saga 1977"-r/Swamp Thing #1&2 by Wrightson; new Wrightson wraparound-c. 2.00 6.00
3,4,6-9: 3-Sgt Rock. 4-Unexpected. 6-Secret Society of Super Villains, Jones-a. 7-Ghosts Special. 8-Brave and Bold w/ new Batman, Deadman & Sgt Rock team-up. 9-Wonder Woman; Ditko-a (11 pgs.)
.85 2.60 7.00
5-"Superman Spectacular 1977"-(84 pg, $1.00)-Superman vs. Brainiac & Lex Luthor, new 63 pg. story .85 2.60 7.00
10-"Secret Origins of Superheroes Special 1978"-(52. pgs)-Dr. Fate, Lightray & Black Canary-c/new origin stories; Staton, Newton-a .85 2.60 7.00
11-"Flash Spectacular 1978"-(84 pgs.) Flash, Kid Flash, GA Flash & Johnny Quick vs. Grodd; Wood-i on Kid Flash chapter .85 2.60 7.00
12-"Secrets of Haunted House Special Spring 1978" .85 2.60 7.00
13-"Sgt. Rock Special Spring 1978", 50 pg new story .85 2.60 7.00
14,17,20-"Original Swamp Thing Saga", Wrightson-a: 14-Sum '78, r/#3,4. 17-Sum '79 r/#5-7. 20-Jan/Feb '80, r/#8-10 .85 2.60 7.00
15-"Batman Spectacular Summer 1978", Ra's Al Ghul-app.; Golden-a. Rogers-a/front & back-c .90 2.70 8.00
16-"Jonah Hex Spectacular Fall 1978"; death of Jonah Hex, Heath-a; Bat Lash and Scalphunter stories 2.70 8.00 30.00
18,19-Digest size: 18-"Sgt. Rock's Prize Battle Tales Fall 1979". 19-"Secret Origins of Super-Heroes Fall 1979"; origins Wonder Woman (new-a),r/Robin, Batman-Superman team, Aquaman, Hawkman and others
.90 2.70 8.00
21-"Super-Star Holiday Special Spring 1980", Frank Miller-a in "Batman--Wanted Dead or Alive" (1st Batman story); Jonah Hex, Sgt. Rock, Superboy &LSH and House of Mystery/Witching Hour-c/stories 1.50 4.50 15.00
22-"G.I. Combat Sept. 1980", Kubert-c. Haunted Tank-s .90 2.70 8.00
23,24-Digest size: 23-World's Finest-r. 24-Flash .90 2.70 9.00
V5#25-($2.95)-"Superman II, the Adventure Continues Summer 1981"; photos from movie & photo-c (see All-New Coll. Ed. C-62) 1.00 3.00 10.00
26-($2.50)-"Superman and His Incredible Fortress of Solitude Summer 1981"
1.00 3.00 10.00
27-($2.50)-"Batman vs. The Incredible Hulk Fall 1981" 1.80 5.40 18.00
NOTE: ***Aparo*** *c-8.* ***Heath*** *a-12i, 16.* ***Infantino*** *a-19r.* ***Kubert*** *c-13, 19r.* ***Nasser/Netzer*** *a-1, 10i, 15.* ***Newton*** *a-10.* ***Nino*** *a-4, 7.* ***Starlin*** *c-12.* ***Staton*** *a-1.* ***Tuska*** *a-19r. #25 & 26. were advertised as All-New Collectors' Edition C-63, C-64. #26 was originally planned as All-New Collectors' Ed. C-30?; has C-630 & A.N.C.E. on cover.*

DC SPOTLIGHT
DC Comics : 1985 (50th anniversary special) (giveaway)

1-Includes profiles on Batman:The Dark Knight & Watchmen 3.00

DC Super-Stars #7 © DC

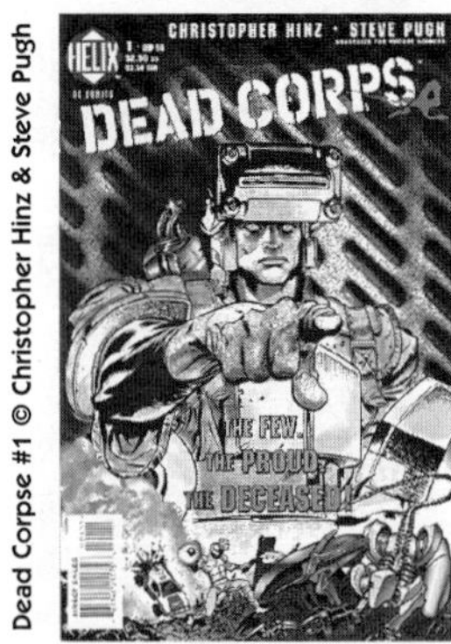

Dead Corpse #1 © Christopher Hinz & Steve Pugh

Dead King #1 © Chaos!

GD25 FN65 NM94

DC SUPER-STARS
National Periodical Publications/DC Comics: March, 1976 - No. 18, Winter, 1978 (No.3-18: 52 pgs.)

1-(68 pgs.)-Re-intro Teen Titans (predates T. T. #44 (11/76); tryout iss.) plus r/Teen Titans; W.W. as girl was original Wonder Girl 1.20 3.60 12.00
2-7,9,11,12,16,18: 2,4,6,8-Adam Strange; 2-(68 pgs.)-r/1st Adam Strange/Hawkman team-up from Mystery in Space #90 plus Atomic Knights origin-r. 3-Legion issue. 4-r/Tales/Unexpected #45 .90 2.70 8.00
8-r/1st Space Ranger from Showcase #15, Adam Strange-r/Mystery in Space #89 & Star Rovers-r/M.I.S. #80 1.00 3.00 10.00
10-Strange Sports Stories; Batman/Joker-c/story 1.10 3.30 9.00
13-Sergio Aragones Special 1.20 3.60 12.00
14,15: 15-Sgt. Rock .90 2.70 9.00
17-Secret Origins of Super-Heroes (origin of The Huntress); origin Green Arrow by Grell; Legion app.; Earth II Batman & Catwoman marry (1st revealed; also see B&B #197 & Superman Family #211) 1.20 3.60 12.00

NOTE: ***M. Anderson** r-2, 4, 6. **Aparo** c-7, 14, 18. **Austin** a-11i. **Buckler** a-14p; c-10. **Grell** a-17. **G. Kane** a-1r, 10r. **Kubert** c-15. **Layton** c/a-16i, 17i. **Mooney** a-4r, 6r. **Morrow** c/a-11r. **Nasser** a-11. **Newton** c/a-16p. **Staton** a-17; c-17. No. 10, 12-18 contain all new material; the rest are reprints. #1 contains new and reprint material.*

DC UNIVERSE HOLIDAY BASH
DC Comics: 1997, 1998 ($3.95)

1-(X-mas '96) Christmas stories by various 4.00
II (1998, for Christmas '97, $3.95) 4.00
III (1999, for Christmas '98, $4.95) 4.95

DC UNIVERSE: TRINITY
DC Comics: Aug, 1993 - No. 2, Sept, 1993 ($2.95, 52 pgs, limited series)

1,2-Foil-c; Green Lantern, Darkstars, Legion app. 3.00

DC VERSUS MARVEL (See Marvel Versus DC) (Also see Amazon, Assassins, Bruce Wayne: Agent of S.H.I. E. L.D., Bullets & Bracelets, Doctor Strangefate, JLX, Legend of the Dark Claw, Magneto & The Magnetic Men, Speed Demon, Spider-Boy, Super Soldier, X-Patrol)
DC Comics: No. 1, 1996, No. 4, 1996 ($3.95, limited series)

1,4: 1-Marz script, Jurgens-a(p); 1st app. of Access. 4.00
.../Marvel Versus DC ($12.95, trade paperback) r/1-4 12.95

D-DAY (Also see Special War Series)
Charlton Comics (no No. 3): Sum/63; No. 2, Fall/64; No. 4, 9/66; No. 5, 10/67; No. 6, 11/68

1(1963)-Montes/Bache-c 2.50 7.50 24.00
2(Fall,'64)-Wood-a(4) 2.50 7.50 24.00
4-6('66-'68)-Montes/Bache-a #5 1.75 5.25 14.00

DEAD AIR
Slave Labor Graphics: July, 1989 ($5.95, graphic novel)

nn-Mike Allred's 1st published work 2.00 6.00

DEAD CORPSe
DC Comics (Helix): Sept, 1998 - No. 4, Dec, 1998 ($2.50, limited series)

1-4-Pugh-a/Hinz-s 2.50

DEAD END CRIME STORIES
Kirby Publishing Co.: April, 1949 (52 pgs.)

nn-(Scarce)-Powell, Roussos-a; painted-c 44.00 132.00 375.00

DEAD-EYE WESTERN COMICS
Hillman Periodicals: Nov-Dec, 1948 - V3#1, Apr-May, 1953

V1#1-(52 pgs.)-Krigstein, Roussos-a 16.00 48.00 120.00
V1#2,3-(52 pgs.) 8.50 26.00 60.00
V1#4-12-(52 pgs.) 5.70 17.00 35.00
V2#1,2,5-8,10-12: 1-7-(52 pgs.) 4.25 13.00 28.00
3,4-Krigstein-a 5.70 17.00 40.00

GD25 FN65 NM94

9-One pg. Frazetta ad 4.25 13.00 28.00
V3#1 4.15 12.50 25.00

NOTE: ***Briefer** a-V1#8. Kinstleresque stories by **McCann**-12, V2#1, 2, V3#1. **McWilliams** a-V1#5. **Ed Moore** a-V1#4.*

DEADFACE: DOING THE ISLANDS WITH BACCHUS
Dark Horse Comics: July, 1991 - No. 3, Sept, 1991 ($2.95, B&W, lim. series)

1-3: By Eddie Campbell 3.00

DEADFACE: EARTH, WATER, AIR, AND FIRE
Dark Horse Comics: July, 1992 - No. 4, Oct, 1992 ($2.50, B&W, limited series; British-r)

1-4: By Eddie Campbell 2.50

DEAD IN THE WEST
Dark Horse Comics: Oct, 1993 - No. 2, Mar, 1994 ($3.95, B&W, 52 pgs.)

1,2-Timothy Truman-c 4.00

DEAD KING (See Evil Ernie)
Chaos! Comics: May, 1998 - No. 4, Aug, 1998, ($2.95, limited series)

1-4-Fisher-s 3.00

DEADLIEST HEROES OF KUNG FU (Magazine)
Marvel Comics Group: Summer, 1975 (B&W)(76 pgs.)

1 -Bruce Lee vs. Carradine painted-c; TV Kung Fu, 4pgs. photos/article; Enter the Dragon, 24 pgs. photos/article w/ Bruce Lee; Bruce Lee photo pinup 1.60 4.80 16.00

DEADLINE USA
Dark Horse Comics: Apr, 1992 - No. 8, Nov, 1992 ($3.95, B&W, 52 pgs.)

1-8: Johnny Nemo w/Milligan scripts in all 4.00

DEADLY DUO, THE
Image Comics (Highbrow Entertainment): Nov, 1994 - No. 3, Jan, 1995 ($2.50, limited series)

1-3: 1-Ist app. of Kill Cat 2.50

DEADLY DUO, THE
Image Comics (Highbrow Entertainment): June, 1995 - No. 4, Oct, 1995 ($2.50, limited series)

1-4: 1-Spawn app. 2-Savage Dragon app. 3-Gen 13 app. 2.50

DEADLY FOES OF SPIDER-MAN (See Lethal Foes of...)
Marvel Comics: May, 1991 - No. 4, Aug, 1991 ($1.00, limited series)

1-4: 1-Punisher, Kingpin, Rhino app. 1.00

DEADLY HANDS OF KUNG FU, THE (See Master of Kung Fu)
Marvel Comics Group: April, 1974 - No. 33, Feb, 1977 (75¢) (B&W, magazine)

1(V1#4 listed in error)-Origin Sons of the Tiger; Shang-Chi, Master of Kung Fu begins (ties w/Master of Kung Fu #17 as 3rd app. Shang-Chi); Bruce Lee painted-c by Neal Adams; 2pg. memorial photo pinup w/8 pgs. photos/articles; TV Kung Fu, 9 pgs. photos/articles; 15 pgs. Starlin-a. 2.20 6.50 24.00
2-Adams painted-c; 1st time origin of Shang-Chi, 34 pgs. by Starlin. TV Kung Fu, 6 pgs. ph/a w/2 pg. pinup. Bruce Lee, 11 pgs. ph/a 2.00 6.00 20.00
3,4,7,10: 3-Adams painted-c; Gulacy-a. Enter the Dragon, photos/articles, 8 pgs. 4-TV Kung Fu painted-c by Neal Adams; TV Kung Fu 7 pg. article/art; Fu Manchu; Enter the Dragon, 10 pg. photos/article w/Bruce Lee. 7-Bruce Lee painted-c & 9 pgs. photos/articles-Return of Dragon plus 1 pg. photo pinup. 10-(3/75)-Iron Fist painted-c & 34 pg. sty-Early app. 1.50 4.50 15.00
5,6: 5-1st app. Manchurian, 6 pgs. Gulacy-a. TV Kung Fu, 4 pg. article; re books w/Barry Smith-a. Capt. America-sty, 10 pgs. Kirby-a(r). 6-Bruce Lee photos/article, 6 pgs.; 15 pgs. early Perez-a 1.20 3.60 12.00
8,9,11: 9-Iron Fist, 2 pg. Preview pinup; Nebres-a. 11-Billy Jack painted-c by Adams; 17 pgs. photos/article 1.00 3.00 10.00

Deadman: Love After Death #2 © DC

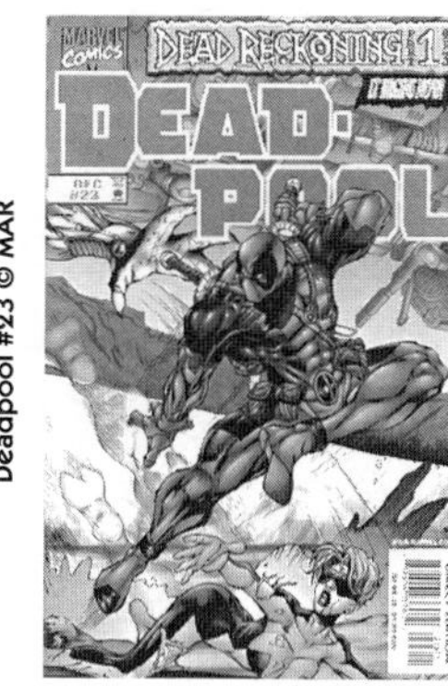

Deadpool #23 © MAR

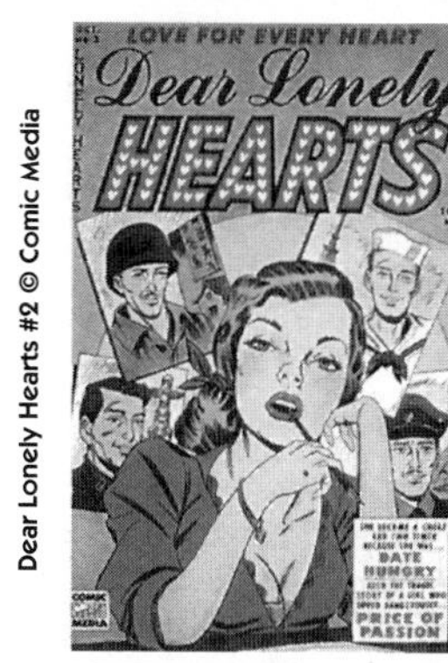

Dear Lonely Hearts #2 © Comic Media

GD25 FN65 NM94

12,13: 12-James Bond painted-c by Adams; 14 pg. photos/article. 13-16 pgs. early Perez-a; Piers Anthony, 7 pgs. photos/article .90 2.70 8.00
14-Classic Bruce Lee painted-c by Adams. Lee pinup by Chaykin. Lee 16 pg. photos/article w/2 pgs. Green Hornet TV 2.90 8.70 32.00
15,19: 15-Sum, '75 Giant Annual #1. 20pgs. Starlin-a. Bruce Lee photo pinup & 3 pg photos/article re book; Man-Thing app. Iron Fist-c/sty; Gulacy-a 18pgs. 19-Iron Fist painted-c & series begins; 1st White Tiger1.20 3.60 12.00
16,18,20: 16-1st app. Corpse Rider, a Samurai w/Sanho Kim-a. 20-Chuck Norris painted-c & 16 pgs. interview w/photos/article; Bruce Lee vs. C. Norris pinup by Ken Barr. Origin The White Tiger, Perez-a .90 2.70 9.00
17-Bruce Lee painted-c by Adams; interview w/R. Clouse, director Enter Dragon 7 pgs. w/B. Lee app. 1st Giffen-a (1pg. 11/75) 2.00 6.00 20.00
21-Bruce Lee 1pg. photos/article .85 2.60 7.00
22,30-32: 22-1st app. Jack of Hearts (cameo). 1st Giffen sty-a (along w/Amazing Adv. #35, 3/76). 30-Swordquest-c/sty & conclusion; Jack of Hearts app. 31-Jack of Hearts app; Staton-a. 32-1st Daughters of the Dragon -c/sty, 21 pgs. M. Rogers-a/Claremont-sty; Iron Fist pinup 1.00 3.00 10.00
23-26,29: 23-1st full app. Jack of Hearts. 24-Iron Fist-c & centerfold pinup. early Zeck-a; Shang Chi pinup; 6 pgs. Piers Anthony text sty w/Perez/Austin-a; Jack of Hearts app. early Giffen-a. 25-1st app. Shimuru, "Samurai", 20 pgs. Mantlo-sty/Broderick-a; "Swordquest"-c & begins 17 pg. sty by Sanho Kim; 11 pg. photos/article; partly Bruce Lee. 26-Bruce Lee painted-c & pinup; 16 pgs. interviews w/Kwon & Clouse; talk about B. Lee re filming of B. Lee legend. 29-Ironfist vs. Shang Chi battle-c/sty; Jack of Hearts app. 1.20 3.60 12.00
27 .90 2.70 8.00
28-All Bruce Lee Special Issue; (1st time in comics). Bruce Lee painted-c by Ken Barr & pinup. 36 pgs. comics chronicaling Bruce Lee's life; 15 pgs. B. Lee photos/article (Rare in high grade) 3.80 11.50 40.00
33-Shang Chi-c/sty; Classic Daughters of the Dragon, 21 pgs. M. Rogers-a/ Claremont-sty with Nudity; Bob Wall interview, photos/article, 14 pgs. 1.20 3.60 12.00
...Special Album Edition 1(Summer, '74)-Iron Fist-c/story (early app., 3rd?); 10 pgs. Adams-i; Shang Chi/Fu Manchu, 10 pgs.; Sons of Tiger, 11 pgs.; TV Kung Fu, 6 pgs. photos/article 1.60 4.80 16.00

NOTE: ***Bruce Lee:*** *1-7, 14, 15, 17, 25, 26, 28.* ***Kung Fu (TV):*** *1, 2, 4.* ***Jack of Hearts:*** *22, 23, 29-33.* ***Shang Chi Master of Kung Fu:*** *1-9, 11-18, 29, 31, 33.* ***Sons of Tiger:*** *1, 3, 4, 6-14, 16-19.* ***Swordquest:*** *25-27, 29-33.* ***White Tiger:*** *19-24, 26, 27, 29-33.* ***N. Adams*** *a-1i(part), 27i; c-1, 2-4, 11, 12, 14, 17.* ***Giffen*** *a-22p, 24p.* ***G. Kane*** *a-23p.* ***Kirby*** *a-5r.* ***Nasser*** *a-27p, 28.* ***Perez*** *a(p)-6-14, 16, 17, 19, 21.* ***Rogers*** *a-26, 32, 33.* ***Starlin*** *a-1, 2r, 15r.* ***Staton*** *a-28p, 31, 32.*

DEADMAN (See The Brave and the Bold & Phantom Stranger #39)
DC Comics: May, 1985 - No. 7, Nov, 1985 ($1.75, Baxter paper)

1-Deadman-r by Infantino, N. Adams in all 1.75
2-7: 5-Batman-c/story-r/Str. Advs. 7-Batman-r 1.75

DEADMAN
DC Comics: Mar, 1986 - No. 4, June, 1986 (75¢, limited series)

1-4: Lopez-c/a. 4-Byrne-c(p) 1.00

DEADMAN: EXORCISM
DC Comics: 1992 - No. 2, 1992 ($4.95, limited series, 52 pgs.)

1,2: Kelley Jones-c/a in both. 5.00

DEADMAN: LOVE AFTER DEATH
DC Comics: 1989 - No. 2, 1990 ($3.95, 52 pgs., limited series, mature)

Book One, Two: Kelley Jones-c/a in both. 1-contains nudity. 4.00

DEAD OF NIGHT
Marvel Comics Group: Dec, 1973 - No. 11, Aug, 1975

	GD25	FN65	NM94
1-Horror reprints	1.20	3.60	12.00
2-10	.85	2.60	8.00
11-Intro Scarecrow; Kane/Wrightson-c	1.40	4.20	14.00

NOTE: ***Ditko*** *r-7, 10.* ***Everett*** *c-2.* ***Sinnott*** *r-1.*

GD25 FN65 NM94

DEAD OR ALIVE - A CYBERPUNK WESTERN
Image Comics (Shok Studio): Apr, 1998 - No. 4, July, 1998 ($2.50, lim. series)

1-4 2.50

DEADPOOL (See New Mutants #98)
Marvel Comics: Aug, 1994 - No. 4, Nov, 1994 ($2.50, limited series)

1: Mark Waid's 1st Marvel work; Ian Churchill-c/a 4.00
2--4 3.00

DEADPOOL
Marvel Comics: Jan, 1997 - Present ($2.95/$1.95/$1.99)

1-($2.95)-Wraparound-c 4.00
2-Begin-$1.95-c. 3.00
3 2.50
4-6, -1(7/97): 4-Hulk-c/app. 2.00
7-10,12,13: 7-Begin $1.99-c. 12-Variant-c 2.00
11-($3.99)-Deadpool replaces Spider-Man from Amazing Spider-Man #47; Kraven, Gwen Stacy app. 5.00
14-22,24: 14-Begin McDaniel-a. 22-Cable app. 2.00
23-($2.99) Dead Reckoning pt. 1; wraparound-c 3.00
.../Death '98 Annual ($2.99) Kelly-s 3.00
... Team-Up (12/98, $2.99) Widdle Wade-c/app. 3.00
Baby's First Deadpool Book (12/98, $2.99) 3.00
Encyclopædia Deadpoolica (12/98, $2.99) Synopses 3.00
Mission Improbable TPB (9/98, $14.95) r/#1-5 14.95
#0 ('98, bagged with Wizard #87) 1.00

DEADPOOL: THE CIRCLE CHASE (See New Mutants #98)
Marvel Comics: Aug, 1993 - No. 4, Nov, 1993 ($2.00, limited series)

1-($2.50)-Embossed-c 2.50
2-4 2.00

DEADSHOT (See Batman #59, Detective Comics #474, & Showcase '93 #8)
DC Comics: Nov, 1988 - No. 4, Feb, 1989 ($1.00, limited series)

1-4 1.00

DEAD WHO WALK, THE (See Strange Mysteries, Super Reprint #15, 16)
Realistic Comics: 1952 (one-shot)

nn 42.00 132.00 360.00

DEADWORLD (Also see The Realm)
Arrow Comics/Caliber Comics: Dec, 1986 - No. 26 ($1.50/$1.95/#15-28: $2.50, B&W, mature)

1 1.50
2 2.00
3-11: 5-11-Graphic covers 1.50
5-11: Tame covers 1.75
12-26: Graphic covers, 12-26: Tame covers 1.75
...Archives 1-3 (1992, $2.50) 2.50

DEAN MARTIN & JERRY LEWIS (See Adventures of...)

DEAR BEATRICE FAIRFAX
Best/Standard Comics (King Features): No. 5, Nov, 1950 - No. 9, Sept, 1951 (Vern Greene art)

	GD25	FN65	NM94
5-All have Schomburg air brush-c	7.15	21.50	50.00
6-9	5.35	16.00	32.00

DEAR HEART (Formerly Lonely Heart)
Ajax: No. 15, July, 1956 - No. 16, Sept, 1956

15,16 5.00 15.00 30.00

DEAR LONELY HEART (...Illustrated No. 1-6)
Artful Publications: Mar, 1951; No. 2, Oct, 1951 - No. 8, Oct, 1952

	GD25	FN65	NM94
1	13.00	40.00	100.00
2	6.00	18.00	42.00
3-Matt Baker Jungle Girl story	14.00	42.00	105.00
4-8	5.70	17.00	38.00

Deathblow #7 © Aegis Entertainment

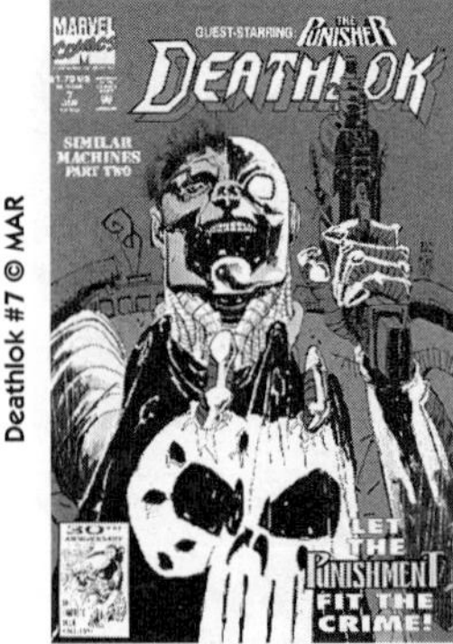

Deathlok #7 © MAR

Deathmate Blue © VAL

GD25 FN65 NM94

DEAR LONELY HEARTS (Lonely Heart #9 on)
Harwell Publ./Mystery Publ. Co. (Comic Media): Aug, 1953 -No. 8, Oct, 1954

1 6.00 18.00 42.00
2-8 4.00 12.00 24.00

DEARLY BELOVED
Ziff-Davis Publishing Co.: Fall, 1952

1-Photo-c 13.00 38.00 95.00

DEAR NANCY PARKER
Gold Key: June, 1963 - No. 2, Sept, 1963

1,2-Painted-c 1.80 5.40 20.00

DEATHBLOW (Also see Darker Image)
Image Comics (WildStorm Productions): May (Apr. inside), 1993 - No. 29, Aug, 1996 ($1.75/$1.95/$2.50)

0-(8/96, $2.95, 32 pgs.)-r/Darker Image w/new story & art; Jim Lee & Trevor Scott-a; new Jim Lee-c 3.00
1-($2.50)-Red foil stamped logo on black varnish-c; Jim Lee-c/a; flip-book side has Cybernary -c/story (#2 also) 2.50
1-($1.95)-Newsstand version w/o foil-c & varnish 2.00
2,4: 2-(8/93)-Lee-a; with bound-in poster. 4-Jim Lee-c 1.75
2-($1.75)-Newsstand version w/o poster 1.75
3 2.00
5-9: Jim Lee-c in all. 5-Begin $1.95-c 2.00
5-Alternate Portacio-c (Forms larger picture when combined with alternate-c for Gen 13 #5, Kindred #3, Stormwatch #10, Team 7 #1, Union #0, Wetworks #2 & WildC.A.T.S # 11) 2.00 6.00
10-14,15,19-29: 10-Begin $2.50-c. 13-W/pinup poster by Tim Sale & Jim Lee. 17-Variant "Chicago Comicon" edition exists. 20,21-Gen 13 app. 23-Backlash-c/app. 24,25-Grifter-c/app; Gen 13 & Dane from Wetworks app. 28-Deathblow dies. 29-Memorial issue 2.50
16 ($1.95, Newsstand)-Wildstorm Rising Pt. 6 2.00
16 ($2.50, Direct Market)-Wildstorm Rising Pt. 6 2.50

DEATHBLOW/WOLVERINE
Image Comics (WildStorm Productions)/ Marvel Comics: Sept, 1996 - No. 2, Feb, 1997 ($2.50, limited series)

1,2: Wiesenfeld-s/Bennett-a 2.50
TPB (1997, $8.95) r/#1,2 8.95

DEATHDEALER
Verotik: July, 1995 - Present ($5.95)

1-Frazetta-c; Bisley-a .90 2.70 8.00
1-2nd print .85 2.60 7.00
2,3-($6.95)-Frazetta-c; embossed logo .85 2.60 7.00
4-($6.95)-Frazetta-c; Suydam-a 6.95

DEATHLOK (Also see Astonishing Tales #25)
Marvel Comics: July, 1990 - No. 4, Oct, 1990 ($3.95, limited series, 52 pgs.)

1-4: 1,2-Guice-a(p). 3,4-Denys Cowan-a, c-4 4.00

DEATHLOK
Marvel Comics: July, 1991 - No. 34, Apr, 1994 ($1.75)

1-Silver ink cover; Denys Cowan-c/a(p) begins 2.00
2-5: 2-Forge (X-Men) app. 3-Vs. Dr. Doom. 5-X-Men & F.F. x-over 1.75
6-10: 6,7-Punisher x-over. 9,10-Ghost Rider-c/story 1.75
11-18,20-24,26-34: 16-Infinity War x-over. 17-Jae Lee-c. 22-Black Panther app. 27-Siege app. 1.75
19-($2.25)-Foil-c 2.25
25-($2.95, 52 pgs.)-Holo-grafx foil-c 3.00
Annual 1 (1992, $2.25, 68 pgs.)-Guice-p; Quesada-c(p) 2.50
Annual 2 (1993, $2.95, 68 pgs.)-Bagged w/card; intro Tracer 3.00
NOTE: *Denys Cowan a(p)-9-13, 15, Annual 1; c-9-12, 13p, 14.* ***Guice/Cowan*** *c-8.*

DEATHLOK SPECIAL
Marvel Comics: May, 1991 - No. 4, June, 1991 ($2.00, bi-weekly lim. series)

GD25 FN65 NM94

1-4: r/1-4(1990) w/new Guice-c #1,2; Cowan c-3,4 2.00
1-2nd printing w/white-c 2.00

DEATHMARK
Lightning Comics: Dec, 1994 ($2.95, B&W)

1 3.00

DEATHMATE
Valiant (Prologue/Yellow/Blue)/Image Comics (Black/Red/Epilogue): Sept, 1993 - Epilogue (#6), Feb, 1994 ($2.95/$4.95, limited series)

Preview-(7/93, 8 pgs.) 1.00
Prologue (#1)–Silver foil; Jim Lee/Layton-c; B. Smith/Lee-a; Liefeld-a(p) 2.50
Prologue–Special gold foil ed. of silver ed. 4.00
Black (#2)-(9/93, $4.95, 52 pgs.)-Silvestri/Jim Lee-c; pencils by Peterson/Silvestri/Capullo/Jim Lee/Portacio; 1st story app. Gen 13 telling their rebellion against the Troika (see WildC.A.T.S. Trilogy) 5.50
Black-Special gold foil edition 2.00 6.00
Yellow (#3)-(10/93, $4.95, 52 pgs)-Yellow foil-c; Indicia says Prologue Sept 1993 by mistake; 3rd app. Ninjak; Thibert-c(i) 3.50
Yellow-Special gold foil edition 4.00
Blue (#4)-(10/93, $4.95, 52 pgs.)-Thibert blue foil-c(i); Reese-a(i) 4.50
Blue-Special gold foil edition 4.00
Red (#5) 3.00
Epilogue (#6)-(2/94, $2.95)-Silver foil Quesada/Silvestri-c; Silvestri-a(p) 3.00

DEATH METAL
Marvel Comics UK: Jan, 1994 - No. 4, Apr, 1994 ($1.95, limited series)

1-4: 1-Silver ink-c. Alpha Flight app. 2.00

DEATH METAL VS. GENETIX
Marvel Comics UK: Dec, 1993 - No. 2, Jan, 1994 (Limited series)

1-($2.95)-Polybagged w/2 trading cards 3.00
2-($2.50)-Polybagged w/2 trading cards 2.50

DEATH OF CAPTAIN MARVEL (See Marvel Graphic Novel #1)

DEATH OF HARI KARI
Blackout Comics: 1997 ($2.95, limited series)

0-Regular Edition 2.95
0-($9.95)-"Super Sexy Parody Cover" 9.95
0-($14.95)-"3-D Parody Cover" 14.95

DEATH OF LADY VAMPRE
Blackout Comics: 1995 ($2.95, bi-monthly)

1-Mignola, Colan flip-c 3.00

DEATH OF MR. MONSTER, THE (See Mr. Monster #8)

DEATH OF SUPERMAN (See Superman, 2nd Series)

DEATH RACE 2020
Roger Corman's Cosmic Comics: Apr, 1995 - No. 8, Nov, 1995 ($2.50)

1-8: Sequel to the Movie 2.50

DEATH RATTLE (Formerly an Underground)
Kitchen Sink Press: V2#1, 10/85 - No. 18, 1988, 1994 ($1.95, Baxter paper, mature)

V2#1-7,9-18: 1-Corben-c. 2-Unpubbed Spirit story by Eisner. 5-Robot Woman-r by Wolverton. 6-B&W issues begin. 10-Savage World-r by by Williamson/ Torres/ Krenkel/Frazetta from Witzend #1. 16-Wolverton Spacehawk-r 2.00
8-(12/86)-1st app. Mark Schultz's Xenozoic Tales/Cadillacs & Dinosaurs 3.00
8-(1994)-r plus interview w/Mark Schultz 2.00

DEATH'S HEAD (See Daredevil #56, Dragon's Claws #5 & Incomplete...)
Marvel Comics: Dec, 1988 - No. 10, Sept, 1989 ($1.75)

1-Dragon's Claws spin-off 3.00
2-Fantastic Four app.; Dragon's Claws x-over 2.00

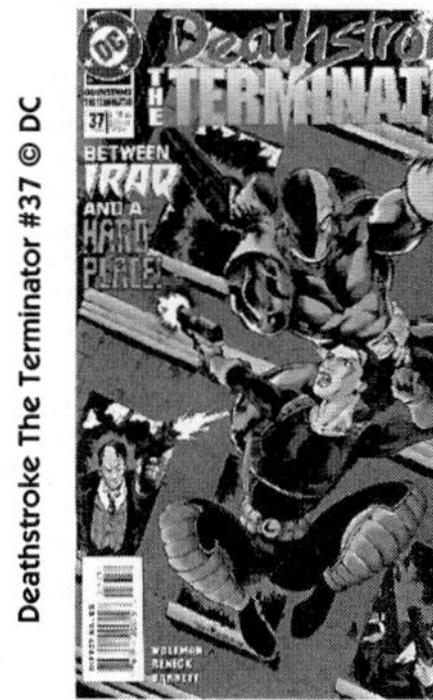

Deathstroke The Terminator #37 © DC

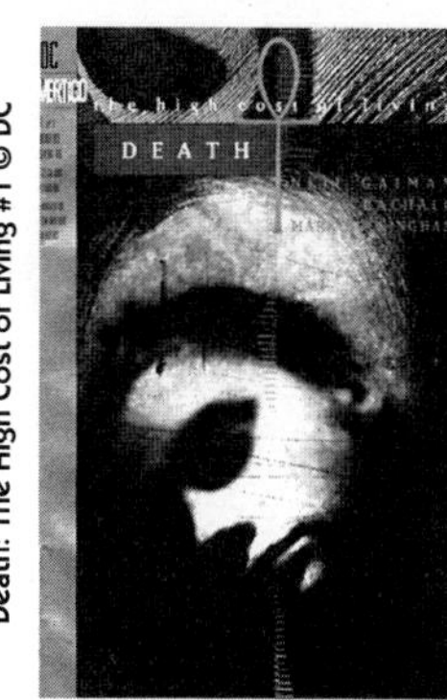

Death: The High Cost of Living #1 © DC

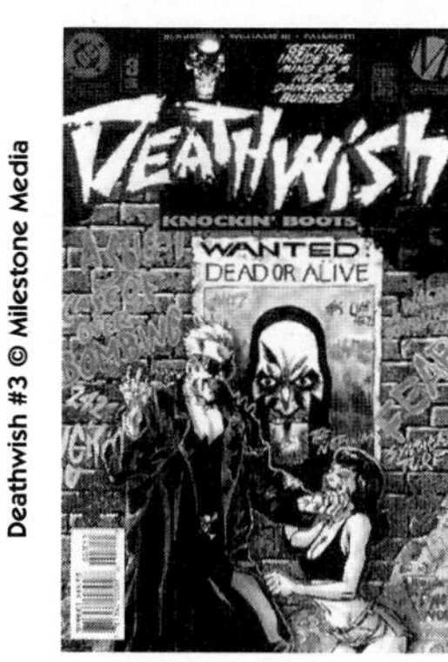

Deathwish #3 © Milestone Media

GD25 FN65 NM94

3,4 2.00
5-10: 8-Dr. Who app. 9-F. F. x-over; Simonson-c(p) 2.00
...Gold 1 (1/94, $3.95, 68 pgs.)-Gold foil-c 4.00

DEATH'S HEAD II (Also see Battletide)
Marvel Comics UK, Ltd.: Mar, 1992 - No. 4, June (May inside), 1992 ($1.75, color, limited series)

1 2.00
1,2-Silver ink 2nd printiings 1.75
2-4: 2-Fantastic Four app. 4-Punisher, Spider-Man , Daredevil, Dr. Strange, Capt. America & Wolverine in the year 2020 2.00

DEATH'S HEAD II (Also see Battletide)
Marvel Comics UK, Ltd.: Dec, 1992 - Present ($1.75/$1.95)

V2#1-5: 1-Gatefold-c. 1-4-X-Men app. 1.75
6-13,15,16 ($1.95): 15-Capt. America & Wolverine app. 2.00
14-($2.95)-Foil flip-c w/Death's Head II Gold #0 3.00

DEATH'S HEAD II & THE ORIGIN OF DIE CUT
Marvel Comics UK, Ltd.: Aug, 1993 - No. 2, Sept, 1993 (limited series)

1-($2.95)-Embossed-c 3.00
2 ($1.75) 1.75

DEATHSTROKE: THE TERMINATOR (Deathstroke: The Hunted #0-47; Deathstroke #48-60) (Also see Marvel & DC Present, New Teen Titans #2, New Titans, Showcase '93 #7,9 & Tales of the Teen Titans #42-44)
DC Comics: Aug, 1991 - No. 60, June, 1996 ($1.75/$1.95/$2.25)

1-New Titans spin-off; Mike Zeck c-1-28 3.00
1-Gold ink 2nd printing ($1.75) 2.00
2 3.00
3-5 2.00
6-37: 6,8-Batman cameo. 7,9-Batman-c/story. 9-1st new Vigilante (female) in cameo. 10-1st full app. new Vigilante; Perez-i. 13-Vs. Justice League; Team Titans cameo on last pg. 14-Total Chaos, part 1; Team Titans-c/story cont'd in New Titans #90. 15-Total Chaos, part 4 1.75
38-40: 38-Begin $1.95-c. 40-(9/94) 2.00
0 (10/94)-Begin Deathstroke, The Hunted, ends #47. 2.00
41 (11/94) - 47 2.00
48,49,51-60: 48-Begin 2.25-c. 2.25
50 ($3.50) 3.50
Annual 1,2 (1992, 1993, $3.50, 68 pgs.): 1-Nightwing & Vigilante app.; minor Eclipso app. 2-Bloodlines Deathstorm; 1st app. Gunfire. 3.50
Annual 3 (1994, $3.95, 68 pgs.)-Elseworlds story 4.00
Annual 4 (1995, $3.95)-Year One story 4.00
NOTE: ***Golden*** *a-12.* ***Perez*** *a-11i.* ***Zeck*** *c-Annual 1, 2.*

DEATH: THE HIGH COST OF LIVING (See Sandman #8) (Also see the Books of Magic limited & ongoing series)
DC Comics (Vertigo): Mar, 1993 - No. 3, May, 1993 ($1.95, limited series)

1-Bachalo/Buckingham-a; Dave McKean-c; Neil Gaiman scripts in all 2.00 6.00
1-Platinum edition 25.00
2 5.00
3-Pgs. 19 & 20 had wrong placement 3.00
3-Corrected version w/pgs. 19 & 20 facing each other; has no-c price plus has ads for Sebastion O & The Geek added 4.00
Death Talks About Life-giveaway about AIDS prevention 4.00
Hardcover (1994, $19.95)-r/#1-3 & Death Talks About Life; intro. by Tori Amos. 20.00
Trade paperback (6/94, $12.95, Titan Books)-r/#1-3 & Death Talks About Life; prism-c 13.00

DEATH: THE TIME OF YOUR LIFE (See Sandman #8)
DC Comics (Vertigo): Apr, 1996 - No. 3, July, 1996 ($2.95, limited series)

1-3: Neil Gaiman story & Bachalo/Buckingham-a; Dave McKean-c. 2-(5/96). 3.00
Hardcover (1997, $19.95)-r/#1-3 w/3 new pages & gallery art by various 20.00
Trade paperback (1997, $12.95)-r/#1-3 & Visions of Death gallery; Intro. by Claire Danes 12.95

DEATH 3
Marvel Comics UK: Sept, 1993 - No. 4, Dec, 1993 ($1.75, limited series)

1-($2.95)-Embossed-c 3.00
2-4 1.75

DEATH VALLEY (Cowboys and Indians)
Comic Media: Oct, 1953 - No. 6, Aug, 1954

1-Billy the Kid; Morisi-a; Andru/Esposito-c/a 7.85 23.50 55.00
2-Don Heck-c 5.35 16.00 32.00
3-6: 3,5-Morisi-a. 5-Discount-a 4.25 13.00 28.00

DEATH VALLEY (Becomes Frontier Scout, Daniel Boone No.10-13)
Charlton Comics: No. 7, 6/55 - No. 9, 10/55 (Cont'd from Comic Media series)

7-9: 8-Wolverton-a (half pg.) 4.25 13.00 28.00

DEATHWISH
DC Comics (Milestone Media): Dec, 1994 - No. 4, Mar, 1995 (2.50, lim. series)

1-4 2.50

DEATH WRECK
Marvel Comics UK: Jan, 1994 - No. 4, Apr, 1994 ($1.95, limited series)

1-4: 1-Metallic ink logo; Death's Head II app. 2.00

DEBBIE DEAN, CAREER GIRL
Civil Service Publ.: April, 1945 - No. 2, July, 1945

1,2-Newspaper reprints by Bert Whitman 11.00 34.00 85.00

DEBBI'S DATES (Also see Date With Debbi)
National Periodical Publications: Apr-May, 1969 - No. 11, Dec-Jan, 1970-71

1 3.50 10.50 35.00
2,3,5,7-11 1.75 5.25 14.00
4-Neal Adams text illo 2.60 7.80 26.00
6-Superman cameo 3.80 11.40 38.00

DECADE OF DARK HORSE, A
Dark Horse Comics: Jul, 1996 - No. 4, Oct, 1996 ($2.95, B&W/color, lim. series)

1-4: 1-Sin City-c/story by Miller; Grendel by Wagner; Predator. 2-Star Wars wraparound-c. 3-Aliens-c/story; Nexus, Mask stories 3.00

DECAPITATOR (Randy Bowen's...)
Dark Horse Comics: Jun, 1998 - No. 4, ($2.95)

1-3-Bowen-s/art by various. 1-Mahnke-c. 3-Jones-c 3.00

DEEP, THE (Movie)
Marvel Comics Group: Nov, 1977

1-Infantino-c/a 1.50

DEEP DARK FANTASIES
Dark Fantasy Productions: Oct, 1995 ($4.50/$4.95, B&W)

1-($4.50)-Clive Barker-c, anthology 4.50
1-($4.95)-Red foil logo-c 5.00

DEFCON 4
Image Comics (WildStorm Productions): Feb, 1996 - No. 4, Sept, 1996 ($2.50, limited series)

1/2 .90 2.70 9.00
1/2 Gold-(1000 printed) 14.00
1-Main Cover by Mat Broome & Edwin Rosell 3.00
1-Hordes of Cymulants variant-c by Michael Golden 5.00
1-Backs to the Wall variant-c by Humberto Ramos & Alex Garner 5.00
1-Defcon 4-Way variant-c by Jim Lee .85 2.60 7.00
2-4 2.50

DEFENDERS, THE (TV)
Dell Publishing Co.: Sept-Nov, 1962 - No. 2, Feb-Apr, 1963

The Defenders #25 © MAR

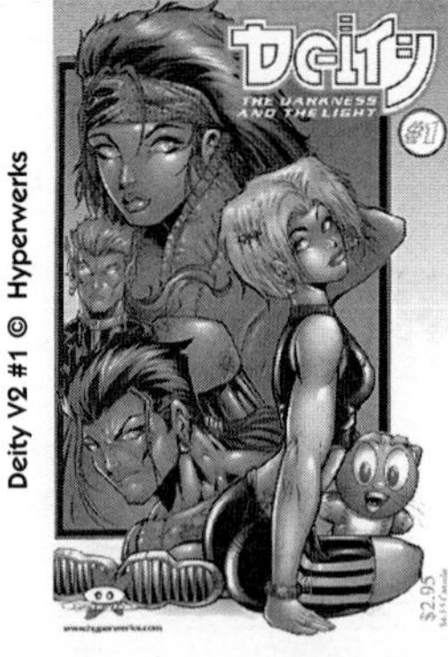

Deity V2 #1 © Hyperwerks

Della Vision #1 © ATL

	GD25	FN65	NM94
12-176-211(#1), 12-176-304(#2)	2.25	6.75	26.00

DEFENDERS, THE (Also see Giant-Size..., Marvel Feature, Marvel Treasury Edition, Secret Defenders & Sub-Mariner #34, 35; The New...#140-on)
Marvel Comics Group: Aug, 1972 - No. 152, Feb, 1986

	GD25	FN65	NM94
1-The Hulk, Doctor Strange, Sub-Mariner begin	5.00	15.00	55.00
2-Silver Surfer x-over	2.25	6.80	25.00
3-5: 3-Silver Surfer x-over. 4-Valkyrie joins	1.80	5.40	18.00
6,7: 6-Silver Surfer x-over	1.30	3.90	13.00
8-11: Defenders vs. the Avengers (Crossover with Avengers #115-118) 8,11-Silver Surfer x-over. 10-Hulk vs. Thor battle	1.80	5.40	18.00
12-14: 12-Last 20¢ issue		2.00	6.00
15,16-Magneto & Brotherhood of Evil Mutants app. from X-Men	.90	2.70	9.00
17-20: 17-Power Man x-over (11/74)			5.00
21-25: 24,25-Son of Satan app.			4.00
26-29-Guardians of the Galaxy app. (#26 is 8/75; pre-dates Marvel Presents #3): 28-1st full app. Starhawk (cameo #27). 29-Starhawk joins Guardians		2.00	6.00
30-35,37,39-50: 31,32-Origin Nighthawk. 35-Intro New Red Guardian. 44-Hellcat joins. 45-Dr. Strange leaves. 47-49-Early Moon Knight app. (5/77)			3.00
36,38-(Regular 25¢ edition)			3.00
36,38-(30¢-c, limited distribution)	1.20	3.60	12.00
51-60: 53-1st app. Lunatik (cameo, Lobo lookalike). 55-Origin Red Guardian; Lunatik cameo. 56-1st full Lunatik story			2.50
61-75: 61-Lunatik & Spider-Man app. 70-73-Lunatik (origin #71). 73-75-Foolkiller II app. (Greg Salinger). 74-Nighthawk resigns			2.00
76-95,97-124,126-149,151: 77-Origin Omega. 78-Original Defenders return thru #101. 94-1st Gargoyle. 100-(52 pgs.)-Hellcat (Patsy Walker) revealed as Satan's daughter. 101-Silver Surfer-c & app. 104-The Beast joins. 105-Son of Satan joins. 106-Death of Nighthawk. 120,121-Son of Satan-c/ stories. 122-Final app. Son of Satan (2 pgs.). 129-New Mutants cameo (3/84, early x-over)			1.75
96-Ghost Rider app.			3.00
125,150,152: 125-(52 pgs.)-Intro new Defenders. 150-(52 pgs.)-Origin Cloud. 152-(52 pgs.)-Ties in with X-Factor & Secret Wars II			2.50
Annual 1 (1976, 52 pgs.)-New book-length story			3.00

NOTE: ***Art Adams*** *c-142p.* ***Austin*** *a-53i; c-65i, 119i, 145i.* ***Frank Bolle*** *a-7i, 10i, 11i.* ***Buckler*** *c(p)-34, 38, 76, 77, 79-86, 90, 91.* ***J. Buscema*** *c-66.* ***Giffen*** *a-42-49p, 50, 51-54p.* ***Golden*** *a-53p, 54p; c-94, 96.* ***Guice*** *c-129.* ***G. Kane*** *c(p)-13, 16, 18, 19, 21-26, 31-33, 35-37, 40, 41, 52, 55.* ***Kirby*** *c-42-45.* ***Mooney*** *a-3i, 31-34i, 62i, 63i, 85i.* ***Nasser*** *c-88p.* ***Perez*** *c(p)-51, 53, 54.* ***Rogers*** *c-98.* ***Starlin*** *c-110.* ***Tuska*** *a-57p. Silver Surfer in No. 2, 3, 6, 8-11, 92, 98-101, 107, 112-115, 122-125.*

DEFENDERS OF DYNATRON CITY
Marvel Comics: Feb, 1992 - No. 6, July, 1992 ($1.25, limited series)

1-6-Lucasarts characters. 2-Origin	1.25

DEFENDERS OF THE EARTH (TV)
Marvel Comics (Star Comics): Jan, 1987 - No. 5, Sept, 1987

1-5: The Phantom, Mandrake The Magician, Flash Gordon begin. 3-Origin Phantom. 4-Origin Mandrake	2.00

DEFINITIVE DIRECTORY OF THE DC UNIVERSE, THE (See Who's Who...)

DEITY
Hyperwerks Comics: Sept, 1997 - No. 6, Apr, 1998, ($2.95, limited series)

1-6	3.00
1-Variant-c	8.00
2-6-Variant covers	4.00
0(5/98)	3.00
0-Variant-c	4.00
0-NDC Edition	6.00
0-NDC Silver Ed.	10.00
0-NDC Gold Ed.	15.00

DEITY (Volume 2)
Hyperwerks Comics: Sept, 1998 - Present ($2.95)

	GD25	FN65	NM94
Preview (6/98) Flip book with Lady Pendragon preview			3.00
1,2: 1-Flip book w/Catseye preview			2.95

DELECTA OF THE PLANETS (See Don Fortune & Fawcett Miniatures)

DELLA VISION (...The Television Queen) (Patty Powers #4 on)
Atlas Comics: April, 1955 - No. 3, Aug, 1955

	GD25	FN65	NM94
1-Al Hartley-c	13.00	38.00	95.00
2,3	9.30	28.00	70.00

DELL GIANT COMICS

Dell Publishing began to release square bound comics in 1949 with a 132-page issue called Christmas Parade #1. The covers were of a heavier stock to accommodate the increased number of pages. The books proved profitable at 25 cents, but the average number of pages was quickly reduced to 100. Ten years later they were converted to a numbering system similar to the Four Color Comics, for greater ease in distribution and the page counts cut back to mostly 84 pages. The label "Dell Giant" began to appear on the covers in 1954. Because of the size of the books and the heavier, less pliant cover stock, they are rarely found in high grade condition, and with the exception of a small quantity of copies released from Western Publishing's warehouse–are almost never found in near mint.

	GD25	FN65	VF82	NM94
Abraham Lincoln Life Story 1(3/58)	5.00	15.00	30.00	90.00
Bugs Bunny Christmas Funnies 1(11/50, 116pp)	13.50	40.50	91.00	240.00
...Christmas Funnies 2(11/51, 116pp)	9.00	27.00	54.00	160.00
...Christmas Funnies 3-5(11/52-11/54,)-Becomes Christmas Party #6	8.00	24.00	48.00	145.00
...Christmas Funnies 7-9(12/56-12/58)	7.00	21.00	42.00	130.00
...Christmas Party 6(11/55)-Formerly Bugs Bunny Christmas Funnies	6.00	18.00	36.00	105.00
...County Fair 1(9/57)	9.00	27.00	54.00	160.00
...Halloween Parade 1(10/53)	8.50	25.50	51.00	150.00
...Halloween Parade 2(10/54)-Trick 'N' Treat Halloween Fun #3 on	7.00	21.00	42.00	130.00
...Trick 'N' Treat Halloween Fun 3,4(10/55-10/56)-Formerly Halloween Parade #2	8.00	24.00	48.00	140.00
...Vacation Funnies 1(7/51, 112pp)	13.50	40.50	81.00	240.00
...Vacation Funnies 2('52)	10.50	31.50	63.00	190.00
...Vacation Funnies 3-5('53-'55)	8.00	24.00	48.00	145.00
...Vacation Funnies 6-9('54-6/59)	7.00	21.00	42.00	130.00
Cadet Gray of West Point 1(4/58)-Williamson-a, 10pgs.; Buscema-a; photo-c	5.00	15.00	30.00	90.00
Christmas In Disneyland 1(12/57)-Barks-a, 18 pgs.	21.00	63.00	126.00	380.00
Christmas Parade 1(11/49)(132 pgs.)(1st Dell Giant)-Donald Duck (25pgs. by Barks, r-in G.K. Christmas Parade #5); Mickey Mouse & other film oriented stories; Cinderella (prior to movie), 7 Dwarfs, Bambi & Thumper, So Dear To My Heart, Flying Mouse, Dumbo, Cookieland & others	47.00	141.00	282.00	850.00
Christmas Parade 2('50)-Donald Duck (132 pgs.)(25 pgs. by Barks, r-in G.K. Christmas Parade #6). Mickey, Pluto, Chip & Dale, etc. Contents shift to a holiday expansion of W.D. C&S type format	36.00	108.00	216.00	650.00
Christmas Parade 3-7('51-'55, #3-116pgs; #4-7, 100 pgs.)	10.00	30.00	60.00	180.00
Christmas Parade 8(12/56)-Barks-a, 8 pgs.	18.00	54.00	108.00	320.00
Christmas Parade 9(12/58)-Barks-a, 20 pgs.	21.00	63.00	126.00	380.00
Christmas Treasury, A 1(11/54)	6.50	19.50	40.00	115.00
Davy Crockett, King Of The Wild Frontier 1(9/55)-Fess Parker photo-c; Marsh-a	14.50	43.50	87.00	260.00
Disneyland Birthday Party 1(10/58)-Barks-a, 16 pgs. r-by Gladstone				

Dell Giant - Lone Ranger Western Treasury #1 © Lone Ranger, Inc.

Dell Giant - Nancy and Sluggo Travel Time © UFS

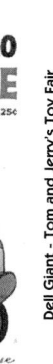

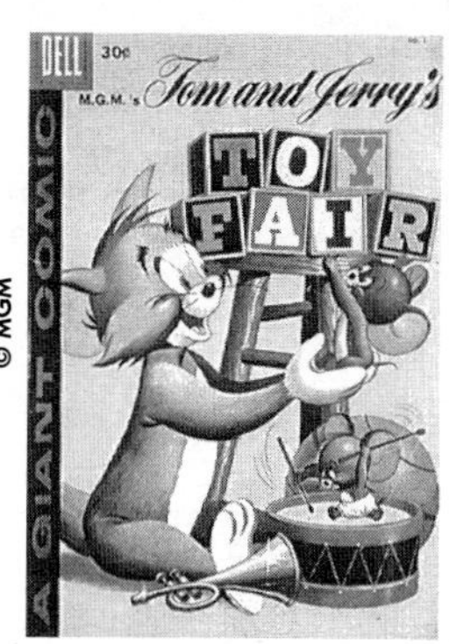
Dell Giant - Tom and Jerry's Toy Fair © MGM

	GD25	FN65		NM94
	21.00	63.00	126.00	380.00
Donald and Mickey In Disneyland 1(5/58)	9.00	27.00	54.00	160.00
Donald Duck Beach Party 1(7/54)-Has an Uncle Scrooge story (not by Barks) that prefigures the later rivalry with Flintheart Glomgold and tells of Scrooge's wild rivalry with another millionaire	11.00	33.00	66.00	200.00
...Beach Party 2(1955)-Lady & Tramp	8.50	25.50	50.00	150.00
...Beach Party 3-5(1956-58)	8.50	25.50	50.00	150.00
...Beach Party 6(8/59, 84pp)-Stapled	5.50	16.50	33.00	100.00
Donald Duck Fun Book 1,2(1953 & 10/54)-Games, puzzles, comics & cut-outs (very rare in unused condition)(most copies commonly have defaced interior pgs.)	30.50	91.50	183.00	550.00
Donald Duck In Disneyland 1(9/55)-1st Disneyland Dell Giant	11.00	33.00	66.00	200.00
Golden West Rodeo Treasury 1(10/57)	7.00	21.00	42.00	125.00
Huey, Dewey and Louie Back To School 1(9/58)	7.00	21.00	42.00	120.00
Lady and The Tramp 1(6/55)	14.00	42.00	84.00	250.00
Life Stories of American Presidents 1(11/57)-Buscema-a	4.00	12.00	24.00	75.00
Lone Ranger Golden West 3(8/55)-Formerly Lone Ranger Western Treasury	14.50	43.50	87.00	260.00
Lone Ranger Movie Story nn(3/56)-Origin Lone Ranger in text; Clayton Moore photo-c	27.00	81.00	162.00	490.00
...Western Treasury 1(9/53)-Origin Lone Ranger, Silver, & Tonto; painted cover	16.00	48.00	96.00	290.00
...Western Treasury 2(8/54)-Becomes Lone Ranger Golden West #3	10.50	31.50	63.00	185.00
Marge's Little Lulu & Alvin Story Telling Time 1(3/59)-r/#2,5,3,11,30,10,21,17,8, 14,16; Stanley-a	11.00	33.00	66.00	195.00
...& Her Friends 4(3/56)-Tripp-a	9.00	27.00	54.00	165.00
...& Her Special Friends 3(3/55)-Tripp-a	11.00	33.00	66.00	200.00
...& Tubby At Summer Camp 5(10/57)-Tripp-a	9.00	27.00	54.00	165.00
...& Tubby At Summer Camp 2(10/58)-Tripp-a	9.00	27.00	54.00	165.00
...& Tubby Halloween Fun 6(10/57)-Tripp-a	9.00	27.00	54.00	165.00
...& Tubby Halloween Fun 2(10/58)-Tripp-a	9.00	27.00	54.00	165.00
...& Tubby In Alaska 1(7/59)-Tripp-a	9.00	27.00	54.00	165.00
...On Vacation 1(7/54)-r/4C-110,14,4C-146,5,4C-97,4,4C-158,3,1;Stanley-a	20.00	60.00	120.00	360.00
...& Tubby Annual 1(3/53)-r/4C-165,4C-74,4C-146,4C-97,4C-158, 4C-139, 4C -131; Stanley-a (1st Lulu Dell Gnt)	24.50	73.50	147.00	435.00
...& Tubby Annual 2('54)-r/4C-139,6,4C-115,4C-74,5,4C-97,3,4C-146,18; Stanley-a	21.50	64.50	130.00	390.00
Marge's Tubby & His Clubhouse Pals 1(10/56)-1st app. Gran'pa Feeb;1st app. Janie; written by Stanley; Tripp-a	10.50	31.50	63.00	190.00
Mickey Mouse Almanac 1(12/57)-Barks-a, 8pgs.	21.50	64.50	130.00	390.00
...Birthday Party 1(9/53)-r/entire 48pgs. of Gottfredson's "Mickey Mouse in Love Trouble" from WDC&S 36-39. Quality equal to original. Also reprints one story each from 4-Color 27, 29, & 181 plus 6 panels of highlights in the career of Mickey Mouse	26.00	78.00	156.00	470.00
...Club Parade 1(12/55)-r/4-Color 16 with some death trap scenes redrawn by Paul Murry & recolored with night turned into day; quality less than original	20.00	60.00	120.00	360.00
...In Fantasy Land 1(5/57)	10.00	30.00	60.00	180.00
...In Frontier Land 1(5/56)-Mickey Mouse Club issue	10.00	30.00	60.00	180.00
...Summer Fun 1(8/58)-Mobile cut-outs on back-c; becomes Summer Fun with #2	10.00	30.00	60.00	180.00
Moses & The Ten Commandments 1(8/57)-Not based on movie; Dell's adaptation; Sekowsky-a	4.00	12.00	24.00	70.00

	GD25	FN65	VF82	NM94
Nancy & Sluggo Travel Time 1(9/58)	5.50	16.50	33.00	95.00
Peter Pan Treasure Chest 1(1/53, 212pp)-Disney; contains 54-page movie adaptation & other P. Pan stories; plus Donald & Mickey stories w/P. Pan; a 32-page retelling of "D. Duck Finds Pirate Gold" with yellow beak, called "Capt. Hook & the Buried Treasure"	83.50	250.00	500.00	1500.00
Picnic Party 6,7(7/55-6/56)(Formerly Vacation Parade)-Uncle Scrooge, Mickey & Donald	8.50	25.50	50.00	150.00
Picnic Party 8(7/57)-Barks-a, 6pgs	18.00	54.00	108.00	320.00
Pogo Parade 1(9/53)-Kelly-a(r-/Pogo from Animal Comics in this order: #11,13,21,14,27,16,23,9,18,15,17)	23.50	70.50	141.00	425.00
Raggedy Ann & Andy 1(2/55)	12.00	36.00	72.00	220.00
Santa Claus Funnies 1(11/52)-Dan Noonan -A Christmas Carol adaptation	6.50	19.50	39.00	115.00
Silly Symphonies 1(9/52)-Redrawing of Gotfredson's Mickey Mouse strip of "The Brave Little Tailor;" 2 Good Housekeeping pages (from 1943); Lady and the Two Siamese Cats, three years before "Lady & the Tramp;" a retelling of Donald Duck's first app. in "The Wise Little Hen" & other stories based on 1930's Silly Symphony cartoons	23.50	70.50	141.00	425.00
Silly Symphonies 2(9/53)-M. Mouse in "The Sorcerer's Apprentice", 2 Good Housekeeping pages (from 1944); The Pelican & the Snipe, Elmer Elephant, Peculiar Penguins, Little Hiawatha, & others	21.00	63.00	126.00	380.00
Silly Symphonies 3(2/54)-r/Mickey & The Beanstalk (4-Color #157, 39pgs.), Little Minnehaha, Pablo, The Flying Gauchito, Pluto, & Bongo, & 2 Good Housekeeping pages (1944)	18.00	54.00	108.00	320.00
Silly Symphonies 4(8/54)-r/Dumbo (4-Color 234), Morris The Midget Moose, The Country Cousin, Bongo, & Clara Cluck	18.00	54.00	108.00	320.00
Silly Symphonies 5(2/55)-r/Cinderella (4-Color 272), Bucky Bug, Pluto, Little Hiawatha, The 7 Dwarfs & Dumbo, Pinocchio	15.00	45.00	90.00	270.00
Silly Symphonies 6(8/55)-r/Pinocchio(WDC&S 63), The 7 Dwarfs & Thumper (WDC&S 45), M. Mouse "Adventures With Robin Hood" (40 pgs.), Johnny Appleseed, Pluto & Peter Pan, & Bucky Bug; Cut-out on back-c	15.00	45.00	90.00	270.00
Silly Symphonies 7(2/57)-r/Reluctant Dragon, Ugly Duckling, M. Mouse & Peter Pan, Jiminy Cricket, Peter & The Wolf, Brer Rabbit, Bucky Bug; Cut-out on back-c	15.00	45.00	90.00	270.00
Silly Symphonies 8(2/58)-r/Thumper Meets The 7 Dwarfs (4-Color #19), Jiminy Cricket, Niok, Brer Rabbit; Cut-out on back-c	15.00	45.00	90.00	270.00
Silly Symphonies 9(2/59)-r/Paul Bunyan, Humphrey Bear, Jiminy Cricket, The Social Lion, Goliath II; cut-out on back-c	14.00	42.00	84.00	250.00
Sleeping Beauty 1(4/59)	23.50	70.50	141.00	425.00
Summer Fun 2(8/59, 84pp, stapled binding)(Formerly Mickey Mouse...)-Barks-a(2), 24 pgs.	21.00	63.00	126.00	380.00
Tarzan's Jungle Annual 1(8/52)-Lex Barker photo on-c of #1,2	11.00	33.00	66.00	200.00
...Annual 2(8/53)	8.50	25.50	50.00	150.00
...Annual 3-7('54-9/58)(two No. 5s)-Manning-a-No. 3,5-7; Marsh-a in No. 1-7 plus painted-c 1-7	7.00	21.00	42.00	125.00
Tom And Jerry Back To School 1(9/56)	10.50	31.50	63.00	190.00
...Picnic Time 1(7/58)	8.00	24.00	48.00	145.00
...Summer Fun 1(7/54)-Droopy written by Barks	13.00	39.00	78.00	230.00
...Summer Fun 2-4(7/55-7/57)	5.50	16.50	32.00	95.00
...Toy Fair 1(6/58)	8.00	24.00	48.00	145.00
...Winter Carnival 1(12/52)-Droopy written by Barks	18.00	54.00	108.00	320.00
...Winter Carnival 2(12/53)-Droopy written by Barks	15.00	45.00	90.00	265.00
...Winter Fun 3(12/54)	5.50	16.50	31.00	95.00
...Winter Fun 4-7(12/55-11/58)	4.50	13.50	27.00	80.00

Dell Giant #31 © H-B

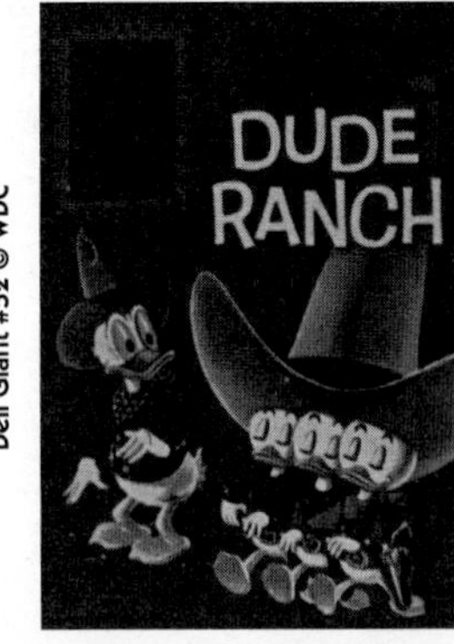

Dell Giant #52 © WDC

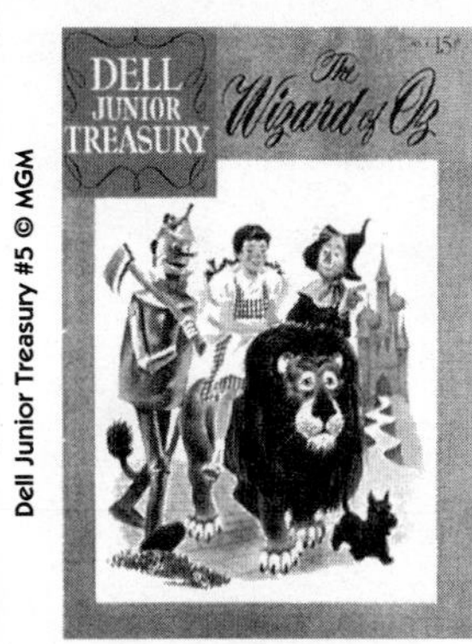

Dell Junior Treasury #5 © MGM

GD25 FN65 VF82 NM94

Treasury of Dogs, A 1(10/56) 4.50 13.50 28.00 85.00
Treasury of Horses, A (9/55) 4.50 13.50 28.00 85.00
Uncle Scrooge Goes To Disneyland 1(8/57p)-Barks-a, 20pgs.r-by Gladstone 21.00 63.00 126.00 380.00
Vacation In Disneyland 1(8/58) 9.00 27.00 54.00 160.00
Vacation Parade 1(7/50, 132pp)-Donald Duck & Mickey Mouse; Barks-a, 55 pgs. 66.50 200.00 400.00 1200.00
Vacation Parade 2(7/51,116pp) 22.00 66.00 133.00 400.00
Vacation Parade 3-5(7/52-7/54)-Becomes Picnic Party No. 6 on. #4-Robin Hood Advs. 10.50 31.50 63.00 190.00
Western Roundup 1(6/52)-Photo-c; Gene Autry, Roy Rogers, Johnny Mack Brown, Rex Allen, & Bill Elliott begin; photo back-c begin, end No. 14,16,18 19.50 58.50 117.00 350.00
Western Roundup 2(2/53)-Photo-c 10.50 31.00 62.00 190.00
Western Roundup 3-5(7-9/53 - 1-3/54)-Photo-c 8.50 25.50 50.00 150.00
Western Roundup 6-10(4-6/54 - 4-6/55)-Photo-c 8.00 24.00 48.00 140.00
Western Roundup 11-13,16,17-Photo-c; Manning-a. 11-Flying A's Range Rider, Dale Evans begin 7.00 21.00 42.00 130.00
Western Roundup 14,15,25(1-3/59)-Photo-c 7.00 21.00 42.00 130.00
Western Roundup 18-Toth-a; last photo-c; Gene Autry ends 7.50 22.50 45.00 135.00
Western Roundup 19-24-Manning-a. 19-Buffalo Bill Jr. begins (7-9/57; early app.). 19,20,22-Toth-a. 21-Rex Allen, Johnny Mack Brown end. 22-Jace Pearson's Texas Rangers, Rin Tin Tin, Tales of Wells Fargo (2nd app., 4-6/58) & Wagon Train (2nd app.) begin 6.50 19.00 38.00 115.00
Woody Woodpecker Back To School 1(10/52) 8.00 24.00 48.00 140.00
...Back To School 2-4,6('53-10/57)-County Fair No. 5 5.50 16.50 32.00 95.00
...County Fair 5(9/56)-Formerly Back To School 5.50 16.50 32.00 95.00
...County Fair 2(11/58) 4.50 13.50 27.00 80.00

DELL GIANTS (Consecutive numbering)
Dell Publishing Co.: No. 21, Sept, 1959 - No. 55, Sept, 1961 (Most 84 pgs., 25¢)

21-(#1)-M.G.M.'s Tom & Jerry Picnic Time (84pp, stapled binding)-Painted-c 9.00 27.00 54.00 160.00
22-Huey, Dewey & Louie Back to School (Disney; 10/59, 84pp, square binding begins) 6.50 19.50 40.00 120.00
23-Marge's Little Lulu & Tubby Halloween Fun (10/59)-Tripp-a 9.00 27.00 54.00 160.00
24-Woody Woodpecker's Family Fun (11/59)(Walter Lantz) 6.50 19.50 39.00 115.00
25-Tarzan's Jungle World(11/59)-Marsh-a; painted-c 8.50 25.50 50.00 150.00
26-Christmas Parade(Disney; 12/59)-Barks-a, 16pgs.; Barks draws himself on wanted poster pg. 13 18.00 54.00 108.00 320.00
27-Man in Space r-/4-Color 716,866, & 954 (100 pgs., 35¢)(Disney)(TV) 8.00 24.00 48.00 145.00
28-Bugs Bunny's Winter Fun (2/60) 8.00 24.00 48.00 145.00
29-Marge's Little Lulu & Tubby in Hawaii (4/60)-Tripp-a 8.50 25.50 50.00 150.00
30-Disneyland USA(Disney; 6/60) 7.00 21.00 42.00 130.00
31-Huckleberry Hound Summer Fun (7/60)(TV)(HannaBarbera)-Yogi Bear & Pixie & Dixie app. 10.50 31.50 63.00 190.00
32-Bugs Bunny Beach Party 4.50 13.50 27.00 85.00
33-Daisy Duck & Uncle Scrooge Picnic Time (Disney; 9/60) 7.00 21.00 42.00 130.00
34-Nancy & Sluggo Summer Camp (8/60) 5.50 16.50 33.00 100.00
35-Huey, Dewey & Louie Back to School (Disney; 10/60)-1st app. Daisy Duck's Nieces, April, May & June 8.50 25.50 50.00 150.00
36-Marge's Little Lulu & Witch Hazel Halloween Fun (10/60)-Tripp-a 8.50 25.50 50.00 150.00
37-Tarzan, King of the Jungle (11/60)-Marsh-a; painted-c 8.00 24.00 48.00 140.00
38-Uncle Donald & His Nephews Family Fun (Disney; 11/60)-Cover painting based on a pencil sketch by Barks 10.50 31.50 63.00 190.00
39-Walt Disney's Merry Christmas (Disney; 12/60)-Cover painting based on a pencil sketch by Barks 10.50 31.50 63.00 190.00
40-Woody Woodpecker Christmas Parade (12/60)(Walter Lantz) 4.50 13.50 27.00 85.00
41-Yogi Bear's Winter Sports (12/60)(TV)(Hanna-Barbera)-Huckleberry Hound & Top Cat app. 10.50 31.50 63.00 190.00
42-Marge's Little Lulu & Tubby in Australia (4/61) 9.00 27.00 54.00 160.00
43-Mighty Mouse in Outer Space (5/61) 17.00 51.00 102.00 305.00
44-Around the World with Huckleberry and His Friends (7/61)(TV)(Hanna-Barbera)-Yogi Bear app. 10.50 31.50 63.00 190.00
45-Nancy & Sluggo Summer Camp (8/61) 4.50 13.50 27.00 85.00
46-Bugs Bunny Beach Party (8/61) 4.50 13.50 27.00 85.00
47-Mickey & Donald in Vacationland (Disney; 8/61) 6.50 19.50 40.00 120.00
48-The Flintstones (No. 1)(Bedrock Bedlam)(7/61)(TV)(Hanna-Barbera) 16.00 48.00 95.00 285.00
49-Huey, Dewey & Louie Back to School (Disney; 9/61) 6.50 19.50 40.00 120.00
50-Marge's Little Lulu & Witch Hazel Trick 'N' Treat (10/61) 8.50 25.50 50.00 150.00
51-Tarzan, King of the Jungle by Jesse Marsh (11/61)-Painted-c 6.00 18.00 35.00 105.00
52-Uncle Donald & His Nephews Dude Ranch (Disney; 11/61) 5.50 16.50 33.00 100.00
53-Donald Duck Merry Christmas (Disney; 12/61) 5.50 16.50 33.00 100.00
54-Woody Woodpecker's Christmas Party (12/61)-Issued after No. 55 5.50 16.50 33.00 100.00
55-Daisy Duck & Uncle Scrooge Showboat (Disney; 9/61) 6.50 19.50 40.00 120.00
NOTE: All issues printed with & without ad on back cover.

DELL JUNIOR TREASURY
Dell Publishing Co.: June, 1955 - No. 10, Oct, 1957 (15¢) (All painted-c)

	GD25	FN65	NM94
1-Alice in Wonderland; r/4-Color #331 (52 pgs.)	9.00	27.00	100.00
2-Aladdin & the Wonderful Lamp	6.00	18.00	65.00
3-Gulliver's Travels (1/56)	5.00	15.00	55.00
4-Adventures of Mr. Frog & Miss Mouse	5.50	16.50	60.00
5-The Wizard of Oz (7/56)	6.00	18.00	65.00
6-Heidi (10/56)	5.00	15.00	55.00
7-Santa and the Angel	5.00	15.00	55.00
8-Raggedy Ann and the Camel with the Wrinkled Knees	5.00	15.00	55.00
9-Clementina the Flying Pig	5.00	15.00	55.00
10-Adventures of Tom Sawyer	5.00	15.00	55.00

DEMOLITION MAN
DC Comics: Nov, 1993 - No. 4, Feb, 1994 ($1.75, color, limited series)

1-4-Movie adaptation 1.75

DEMON, THE (See Detective Comics No. 482-485)
National Periodical Publications: Aug-Sept, 1972 - V3#16, Jan, 1974

1-Origin; Kirby-c/a in all 1.40 4.20 14.00
2-5 .85 2.60 7.00
6-16 4.00

Demon #51 (2nd series) © DC

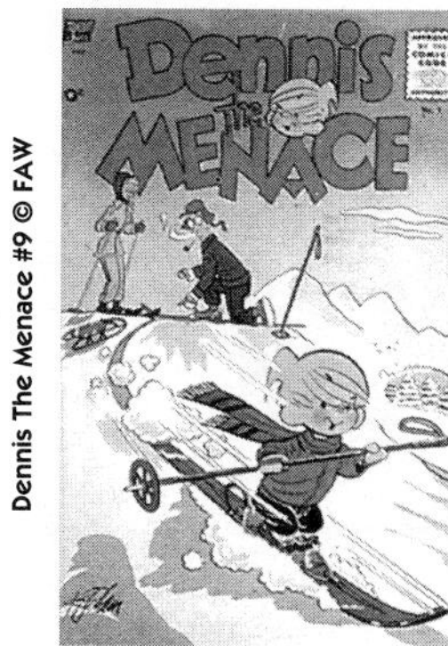

Dennis The Menace #9 © FAW

Dennis The Menace #9 © Field Ent.

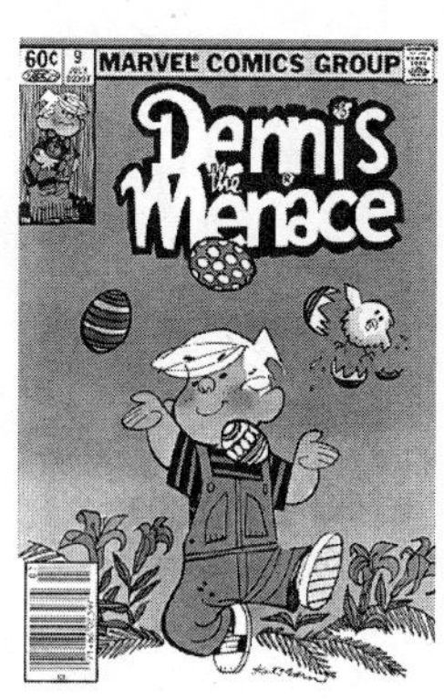

GD25 FN65 VF82 NM94

DEMON, THE (1st limited series)(Also see Cosmic Odyssey #2)
DC Comics: Nov, 1986 - No. 4, Feb, 1987 (75¢, limited series)
(#2 has #4 of 4 on-c)

1-4: Matt Wagner-a(p) & scripts in all. 4-Demon & Jason Blood become separate entities. 1.00

DEMON, THE (2nd Series)
DC Comics: July, 1990 - No. 57, May, 1995 ($1.50/$1.75/$1.95)

1-Grant scripts begin, ends #39: 1-4-Painted-c 1.80
2-18,20-27: 3,8-Batman app. (cameo #4). 12-Bisley painted-c. 12-15,21-Lobo app. (1 pg. cameo #11). 23-Robin app. 1.60
19-($2.50, 44 pgs.)-Lobo poster stapled inside 2.50
28-42,46,47: 28-Superman-c/story; begin $1.75-c. 29-Superman app. 31,33-39-Lobo app. 40-Garth Ennis scripts begin. 46-48 Return of The Haunted Tank-c/s. 1.75
43-45-Hitman app. 1.40 4.20 14.00
48,49,51: 48-Begin $1.95-c. 51-(9/94) 2.00
50 ($2.95, 52 pgs.) 3.00
0,52-57: 0-(10/94). 52-54-Hitman-s 2.00
Annual 1 (1992, $3.00, 68 pgs.)-Eclipso-c/story 3.00
Annual 2 (1993, $3.50, 68 pgs.)-1st app. of Hitman 1.50 4.50 15.00

NOTE: *Alan Grant scripts in #1-16, 20, 21, 23-25, 30-39, Annual 1.* ***Wagner*** *a/scripts-22.*

DEMON DREAMS
Pacific Comics: Feb, 1984 - No. 2, May, 1984

1,2-Mostly r-/Heavy Metal 1.50

DEMONGATE
Sirius Entertainment: May, 1996 - Present ($2.50, B&W)

1-10-Bao Lin Hum/Steve Blevins-s/a 2.50

DEMON GUN
Crusade Ent.: June, 1996 - No. 3, Jan, 1997 ($2.95, B&W, limited series)

1-3: Gary Cohn scripts in all. 2-(10/96) 3.00

DEMON-HUNTER
Seaboard Periodicals (Atlas): Sept, 1975

1-Origin; Buckler-c/a 3.00

DEMONIQUE
London Night Studios: 1994 - No. 4, 1995 ($3.00, B&W, limited series)

1-4 3.00

DEMONIQUE
London Night Studios: No. 0, Aug, 1996 - Present ($3.00, mature)

0,1, 1/2 (8/97) 3.00
1,1/2 (8/97)-($6.00)-Nude Edition 2.00 6.00

DEMON KNIGHT: A GRIMJACK GRAPHIC NOVEL
First Publishing: 1990 ($8.95, 52 pgs.)

nn-Flint Henry-a .90 2.70 9.00

DENNIS THE MENACE (TV with 1959 issues) (Becomes ...Fun Fest Series; See The Best of... & The Very Best of...)(...Fun Fest on-c only to #156-166)
Standard Comics/Pines No.15-31/Hallden (Fawcett) No.32 on: 8/53 - #14, 1/56; #15, 3/56 - #31, 11/58; #32, 1/59 - #166, 11/79

1-1st app. Dennis, Mr. & Mrs. Wilson, Ruff & Dennis' mom & dad; Wiseman-a, written by Fred Toole-most issues 48.00 144.00 410.00
2 25.00 75.00 185.00
3-10: 8-Last pre-code issue 14.00 42.00 105.00
11-20 11.00 32.00 80.00
21-30: 22-1st app. Margaret w/blonde hair 7.85 23.50 55.00
31-1st app. Joey 5.70 17.00 40.00
32-40: 37-A-Bomb blast panel. 39-1st app. Gina (11/59) 5.35 16.00 32.00
41-60 2.50 7.50 20.00
61-80,100 1.75 5.25 14.00

GD25 FN65 NM94

81-99 1.50 4.50 12.00
101-166 2.40 6.00
...& Dirt('59,'68)-Soil Conservation giveaway; r-# 36; Wiseman-c/a 2.40 6.00
...Away We Go('70)-Caladayl giveaway 2.40 6.00
...Coping with Family Stress-giveaway 4.00
...Takes a Poke at Poison('61)-Food & Drug Assn. giveaway; Wiseman-c/a 2.40 6.00
...Takes a Poke at Poison-Revised 1/66, 11/70, 1972, 1974, 1977, 1981 4.00

NOTE: ***Wiseman*** *c/a-1-46, 53, 68, 69.*

DENNIS THE MENACE (Giants) (No. 1 titled Giant Vacation Special; becomes Dennis the Menace Bonus Magazine No. 76 on)
(#1-8,18,23,25,30,38: 100 pgs.; rest to #41: 84 pgs.; #42-75: 68 pgs.)
Standard/Pines/Hallden(Fawcett): Summer, 1955 - No. 75, Dec, 1969

nn-Giant Vacation Special(Summ/55-Standard) 17.00 52.00 130.00
nn-Christmas issue (Winter '55) 15.00 44.00 110.00
2-Giant Vacation Special (Summer '56-Pines) 13.00 40.00 100.00
3-Giant Christmas issue (Winter '56-Pines) 12.00 36.00 90.00
4-Giant Vacation Special (Summer '57-Pines) 11.00 34.00 85.00
5-Giant Christmas issue (Winter '57-Pines) 11.00 34.00 85.00
6-In Hawaii (Giant Vacation Special)(Summer '58-Pines) 11.00 32.00 80.00
6-In Hawaii (Summer '59-Hallden)-2nd printing; says 3rd large printing on-c
6-In Hawaii (Summer '60)-3rd printing; says 4th large printing on-c
6-In Hawaii (Summer '62)-4th printing; says 5th large printing on-c
each.... 7.15 21.50 50.00
6-Giant Christmas issue (Winter '58) 10.00 30.00 75.00
7-In Hollywood (Winter '59-Hallden) 5.00 15.00 50.00
7-In Hollywood (Summer '61)-2nd printing 3.50 10.50 35.00
8-In Mexico (Winter '60, 100 pgs.-Hallden/Fawcett) 5.00 15.00 50.00
8-In Mexico (Summer '62, 2nd printing) 3.50 10.50 35.00
9-Goes to Camp (Summer '61, 84 pgs.)-1st CCA approved issue 5.00 15.00 50.00
9-Goes to Camp (Summer '62)-2nd printing 3.50 10.50 35.00
10-X-Mas issue (Winter '61) 5.50 16.50 55.00
11-Giant Christmas issue (Winter '62) 5.50 16.50 55.00
12-Triple Feature (Winter '62) 5.50 16.50 55.00
13-Best of Dennis the Menace (Spring '63)-Reprints 3.00 9.00 30.00
14-And His Dog Ruff (Summer '63) 3.00 9.00 30.00
15-In Washington, D.C. (Summer '63) 3.00 9.00 30.00
16-Goes to Camp (Summer '63)-Reprints No. 9 3.00 9.00 30.00
17-& His Pal Joey (Winter '63) 3.00 9.00 30.00
18-In Hawaii (Reprints No. 6) 2.50 7.50 25.00
19-Giant Christmas issue (Winter '63) 3.50 10.50 35.00
20-Spring Special (Spring '64) 3.50 10.50 35.00
21-40: 30-r/#6 2.50 7.50 20.00
41-60 1.75 5.25 14.00
61-75: 68-Partial-r/#6 1.50 4.50 12.00

NOTE: ***Wiseman*** *c/a-1-8, 12, 14, 15, 17, 20, 22, 27, 28, 31, 35, 36, 41, 49.*

DENNIS THE MENACE
Marvel Comics Group: Nov, 1981 - No. 13, Nov, 1982

1-New-a 2.00 6.00
2-13: 2-New art. 3-Part-r. 4,5-r. 5-X-Mas-c & issue. 7-Spider Kid-c/sty 4.00

NOTE: ***Hank Ketcham*** *c-most; a-3, 12.* ***Wiseman*** *a-4, 5.*

DENNIS THE MENACE AND HIS DOG RUFF
Hallden/Fawcett: Summer, 1961

1-Wiseman-c/a 4.20 12.60 42.00

DENNIS THE MENACE AND HIS FRIENDS
Fawcett Publ.: 1969; No. 5, Jan, 1970 - No. 46, April, 1980 (All reprints)

Dennis the Menace & Joey No. 2 (7/69) 1.75 5.25 14.00

Desperado #4 © LEV

Desperadoes #4 © Aegis Ent.

Destroyer #1 © Warren Murphy

Dennis the Menace & Ruff No. 2 (9/69) 1.75 5.25 14.00
Dennis the Menace & Mr. Wilson No. 1 (10/69) 2.50 7.50 20.00
Dennis & Margaret No. 1 (Winter '69) 2.50 7.50 20.00
5-20: 5-Dennis the Menace & Margaret. 6-...& Joey. 7-...& Ruff. 8-...& Mr. Wilson .90 2.70 8.00
21-37 2.00 6.00
38-46 (Digest size, 148 pgs., 4/78, 95¢) 1.00 2.80 7.00
NOTE: *Titles rotate every four issues, beginning with No. 5.*

DENNIS THE MENACE AND HIS PAL JOEY
Fawcett Publ.: Summer, 1961 (10¢) (See Dennis the Menace Giants No. 45)
1-Wiseman-c/a 4.50 13.50 45.00

DENNIS THE MENACE AND THE BIBLE KIDS
Word Books: 1977 (36 pgs.)
1-10: 1-Jesus. 2-Joseph. 3-David. 4-The Bible Girls. 5-Moses. 6-More About Jesus. 7-The Lord's Prayer. 8-Stories Jesus told. 9-Paul, God's Traveller. 10-In the Beginning 5.00
NOTE: ***Ketcham** c/a in all.*

DENNIS THE MENACE BIG BONUS SERIES
Fawcett Publications: No. 10, Feb, 1980 - No. 11, Apr, 1980
10,11 4.00

DENNIS THE MENACE BONUS MAGAZINE (Formerly Dennis the Menace Giants Nos. 1-75)
Fawcett Publications: No. 76, 1/70 - No. 194, 10/79; (No. 76-124: 68 pgs.; No. 125-163: 52 pgs.; No. 164 on: 36 pgs.)
76-90 .90 2.70 8.00
91-110 .85 2.60 7.00
111-150 5.00
151-194: 166-Indicia printed backwards 4.00

DENNIS THE MENACE COMICS DIGEST
Marvel Comics Group: April, 1982 - No. 3, Aug, 1982 ($1.25, digest-size)
1-3-Reprints .90 2.70 8.00
NOTE: ***Ketcham** c-all. **Wiseman** a-all. A few thousand #1's were published with a DC emblem on cover.*

DENNIS THE MENACE FUN BOOK
Fawcett Publications/Standard Comics: 1960 (100 pgs.)
1-Part Wiseman-a 6.00 18.00 60.00

DENNIS THE MENACE FUN FEST SERIES (Formerly Dennis the Menace #166)
Hallden (Fawcett): No. 16, Jan, 1980 - No. 17, Mar, 1980 (40¢)
16,17-By Hank Ketcham 3.00

DENNIS THE MENACE POCKET FULL OF FUN!
Fawcett Publications (Hallden): Spring, 1969 - No. 50, March, 1980 (196 pgs.) (Digest size)
1-Reprints in all issues 3.50 10.50 35.00
2-10 2.50 7.50 22.00
11-20 1.75 5.25 14.00
21-28 .90 2.70 9.00
29-50: 35,40,46-Sunday strip-r 2.00 6.00
NOTE: *No. 1-28 are 196 pgs.; No. 29-36: 164 pgs.; No. 37: 148 pgs.; No. 38 on: 132 pgs. No. 8, 11, 15, 21, 25, 29 all contain strip reprints.*

DENNIS THE MENACE TELEVISION SPECIAL
Fawcett Publ. (Hallden Div.): Summer, 1961 - No. 2, Spring, 1962 (Giant)
1 5.50 16.50 55.00
2 3.00 9.00 30.00

DENNIS THE MENACE TRIPLE FEATURE
Fawcett Publications: Winter, 1961 (Giant)
1-Wiseman-c/a 5.50 16.50 55.00

DEPUTY, THE (TV)
Dell Publishing Co.: No. 1077, Feb-Apr, 1960 - No. 1225, Oct-Dec, 1961 (all-Henry Fonda photo-c)
Four Color 1077 (#1)-Buscema-a 12.00 35.00 130.00
Four Color 1130 (9-11/60)-Buscema-a,1225 9.00 27.00 100.00

DEPUTY DAWG (TV) (Also see New Terrytoons)
Dell Publishing Co./Gold Key: Oct-Dec, 1961 - No. 1299, 1962; No. 1, Aug, 1965
Four Color 1238,1299 10.00 30.00 110.00
1(10164-508)(8/65)-Gold Key 10.00 30.00 110.00

DEPUTY DAWG PRESENTS DINKY DUCK AND HASHIMOTO-SAN (TV)
Gold Key: August, 1965
1(10159-508) 9.00 275.00 100.00

DESERT GOLD (See Zane Grey 4-Color 467)

DESIGN FOR SURVIVAL (Gen. Thomas S. Power's...)
American Security Council Press: 1968 (36 pgs. in color) (25¢)
nn-Propaganda against the Threat of Communism-Aircraft cover; H-Bomb panel 2.50 7.50 20.00
Twin Circle Edition-Cover shows panels from inside 1.50 4.50 12.00

DESPERADO (Becomes Black Diamond Western No. 9 on)
Lev Gleason Publications: June, 1948 - No. 8, Feb, 1949 (All 52 pgs.)
1-Biro-c on all; contains inside photo-c of Charles Biro, Lev Gleason & Bob Wood 11.00 34.00 85.00
2 6.00 18.00 42.00
3-Story with over 20 killings 6.50 19.50 45.00
4-8 5.35 16.00 32.00
NOTE: ***Barry** a-2. **Fuje** a-4, 8. **Guardineer** a-5-7. **Kida** a-3-7. **Ed Moore** a-4, 6.*

DESPERADOES
Image Comics (Homage): Sept, 1997 - No. 5, June, 1998 ($2.50/$2.95)
1-Mariotte-s/Cassaday-c/a 5.00
2-5-($2.95) 2.95
...: A Moment's Sunlight TPB ('98, $16.95) r/#1-5 16.95

DESPERATE TIMES (See Savage Dragon)
Image Comics: Jun, 1998 - Present ($2.95, B&W)
1-3-Chris Eliopoulos-s/a 3.00

DESTINATION MOON (See Fawcett Movie Comics, Space Adventures #20, 23, & Strange Adventures #1)

DESTINY: A CHRONICLE OF DEATHS FORETOLD (See Sandman)
DC Comics (Vertigo): 1997 - No.3, 1998 ($5.95, limited series)
1-3-Kwitney-s in all: 1-Williams & Zulli-a, Williams painted-c. 2-Williams & Scott Hampton-painted-c/a. 3-Williams & Guay-a 2.00 6.00

DESTROY!!
Eclipse Comics: 1986 ($4.95, B&W, magazine-size, one-shot)
1 5.00
3-D Special 1-r-/#1 ($2.50) 4.00

DESTROYER, THE
Marvel Comics: Nov, 1989 - No. 9, Jun, 1990 ($2.25, B&W, magazine, 52 pgs.)
1-Based on Remo Williams movie, paperbacks 2.25
2-9: 2-Williamson part inks. 4-Ditko-a 2.25

DESTROYER, THE
Marvel Comics: V2#1, March, 1991 ($1.95, 52 pgs.)
V3#1, Dec, 1991 - No. 4, Mar, 1992 ($1.95, mini-series)
V2#1,V3#1-4: Based on Remo Williams paperbacks. V3#1-4-Simonson-c. 3-Morrow-a 2.00

DESTROYER, THE (Also see Solar, Man of the Atom)
Valiant: Apr, 1995 ($2.95, color, one-shot)
0-Indicia indicates #1 3.00

Detective Comics #1 © DC

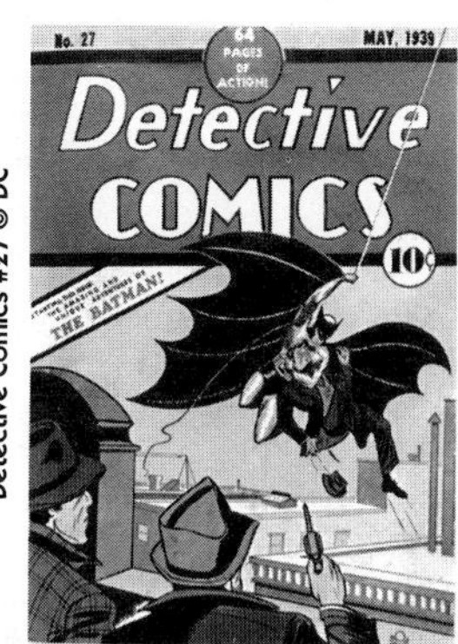

Detective Comics #27 © DC

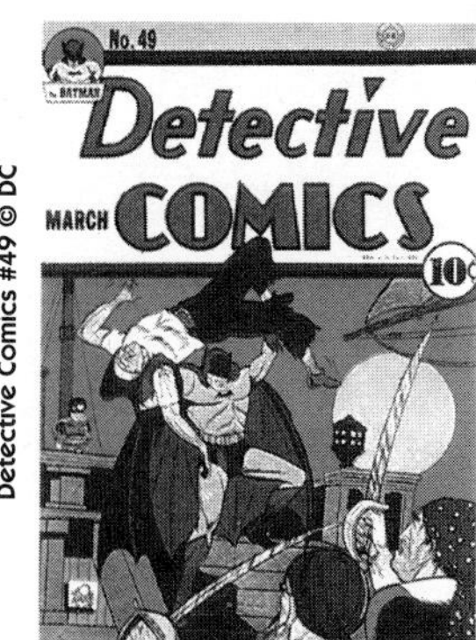

Detective Comics #49 © DC

DESTROYER DUCK
Eclipse Comics: Feb, 1982 - No. 7, May, 1984 (#2-7: Baxter paper) ($1.50)

	GD25	FN65	NM94
1-Origin Destroyer Duck; 1st app. Groo		2.00	6.00
2-7: 2-Starling back-up begins			1.25

NOTE: ***Neal Adams*** *c-1i.* ***Kirby*** *c/a-1-5p.* ***Miller*** *c-7.*

DESTRUCTOR, THE
Atlas/Seaboard: February, 1975 - No. 4, Aug, 1975

1-Origin; Ditko/Wood-a; Wood-c(i)		4.00
2-4: 2-Ditko/Wood-a. 3,4-Ditko-a(p)		3.00

DETECTIVE COMICS (Also see other Batman titles)
National Periodical Publications/DC Comics: Mar, 1937 - Present

	GD25	FN65	VF82
1-(Scarce)-Slam Bradley & Spy by Siegel & Shuster, Speed Saunders by Guardineer, Flat Foot Flannigan by Gustavson, Cosmo, the Phantom of Disguise, Buck Marshall, Bruce Nelson begin; Chin Lung in 'Claws of the Red Dragon' serial begins; Vincent Sullivan-c.	8,333.00	25,000.00	50,000.00
2 (Rare)-Creig Flessel-c begin; new logo	2333.00	6999.00	14,300.00
3 (Rare)	1666.00	5000.00	10,200.00

	GD25	FN65	NM94
4,5: 5-Larry Steele begins	1033.00	3099.00	6500.00
6,7,9,10	750.00	2250.00	4700.00
8-Mister Chang-c; classic-c	1133.00	3399.00	7200.00
11-17,19: 17-1st app. Fu Manchu in Det.	566.00	1700.00	3600.00
18-Fu Manchu-c; last Flessel-c	950.00	2850.00	6000.00
20-The Crimson Avenger begins (1st app.)	866.00	2600.00	5500.00
21,23-25	450.00	1350.00	2800.00
22-1st Crimson Avenger-c by Chambers (12/38)	583.00	1749.00	3700.00
26	400.00	1200.00	2500.00

	GD25	FN65	VF82	NM94
27-The Bat-Man & Commissioner Gordon begin (1st app.), created by Bill Finger & Bob Kane (5/39); Batman-c (1st)(by Kane). Bat-Man's secret identity revealed as Bruce Wayne in 6pg. sty. Signed Rob't Kane (also see Det. Picture Stories #5)	25,000.00	65,000.00	100,000.00	165,000.00

27-Reprint, Oversize 13-1/2x10". WARNING: This comic is an exact duplicate reprint of the original except for its size. DC published it in 1974 with a second cover titling it as Famous First Edition. There have been many reported cases of the outer cover being removed and the interior sold as the original edition. The reprint with the new outer cover removed is practically worthless; see Famous First Edition for value.

	GD25	FN65	NM94
27(1984)-Oreo Cookies giveaway (32 pgs., paper-c, r-/Det. 27, 38 & Batman No. 1 (1st Joker)	2.50	7.60	28.00
28-2nd app. The Batman (6 pg. story); non-Bat-Man-c; signed Rob't Kane	1300.00	3900.00	15,000.00

	GD25	FN65	VF82	NM94
29-1st app. Doctor Death-c/story, Batman's 1st name villain. 1st 2 part story (10 pgs.). 2nd Batman-c by Kane	2154.00	6460.00	14,000.00	25,000.00

	GD25	FN65	NM94
30-Dr. Death app. Story concludes from issue #29. Classic Batman splash panel by Kane.	520.00	1560.00	5600.00

	GD25	FN65	VF82	NM94
31-Classic Batman over castle-c; 1st app. The Monk & 1st Julie Madison (Bruce Wayne's 1st love interest); 1st Batplane (Bat-Gyro) and Batarang; 2nd 2-part Batman adventure. Gardner Fox takes over script from Bill Finger. 1st men tion of Locale (New York City) where Batman lives	2154.00	6460.00	14,000.00	25,000.00

	GD25	FN65	NM94
32-Batman story concludes from issue #31. 1st app. Dala (Monk's assistant). Batman uses gun for 1st time to slay The Monk and Dala. This was the 1st time a costumed hero used a gun in comic books. 1st Batman head logo on cover	500.00	1500.00	5200.00

	GD25	FN65	VF82	NM94
33-Origin The Batman (2 pgs.)(1st told origin); Batman gun holster-c; Batman w/smoking gun panel at end of story. Batman story now 12 pgs. Classic Batman-c	2900.00	8700.00	18,850.00	35,000.00

	GD25	FN65	NM94
34-2nd Crimson Avenger-c by Creig Flessel and last non Batman-c. Story from issue #32 x-over as Bruce Wayne sees Julie Madison off to America from Paris. Classic Batman splash panel used later in Batman #1 for origin story. Steve Malone begins	400.00	1200.00	4200.00
35-Classic Batman hypodermic needle-c that reflects story in issue #34. Classic Batman with smoking .45 automatic splash panel. Last time a costumed hero used a gun in comic books. Batman-c begin	720.00	2160.00	7500.00
36-Batman-c that reflects adventure in issue #35. Origin/1st app. of Dr. Hugo Strange (1st major villain, 2/40). 1st finned-gloves worn by Batman	520.00	1560.00	5500.00
37-Last solo Golden-Age Batman adventure in Detective Comics. Panel at end of story reflects solo Batman adventure in Batman #1 that was originally planned for Detective #38. Cliff Crosby begins	520.00	1560.00	5500.00

	GD25	FN65	VF82	NM94
38-Origin/1st app. Robin the Boy Wonder (4/40); Batman and Robin-c begin; cover by Kane & Robinson taken from splash pg.	2545.00	7635.00	16,542.00	30,000.00

	GD25	FN65	NM94
39-Opium story	460.00	1380.00	4800.00
40-Origin & 1st app. Clay Face (Basil Karlo); 1st Joker cover app. (6/40); Joker story intended for this issue was used in Batman #1 instead; cover is similar to splash pg. in 2nd Joker story in Batman #1	580.00	1740.00	5800.00
41-Robin's 1st solo	284.00	852.00	2700.00
42-44: 44-Crimson Avenger-new costume	206.00	618.00	1750.00
45-1st Joker story in Det. (3rd book app. & 4th story app. over all, 11/40)	284.00	852.00	2700.00
46-50: 46-Death of Hugo Strange. 48-1st time car called Batmobile (2/41); Gotham City 1st mention in Det. (1st mentioned in Wow #1; also see Batman #4). 49-Last Clay Face	182.00	546.00	1550.00
51-57	126.00	378.00	1075.00
58-1st Penguin app. (12/41); last Speed Saunders; Fred Ray-c	337.00	1010.00	3200.00
59-Last Steve Malone; 2nd Penguin; Wing becomes Crimson Avenger's aide	147.00	441.00	1250.00
60-Intro. Air Wave; Joker app. (2nd in Det.)	147.00	441.00	1250.00
61,63: 63-Last Cliff Crosby; 1st app. Mr. Baffle	129.00	387.00	1100.00
62-Joker-c/story (2nd Joker-c, 4/42)	200.00	600.00	1700.00
64-Origin & 1st app. Boy Commandos by Simon & Kirby (6/42); Joker app.	337.00	1010.00	3200.00
65-1st Boy Commandos-c (S&K-a on Boy Commandos & Ray/Robinson-a on Batman & Robin on-c; 4 artists on one-c)	276.00	828.00	2350.00
66-Origin & 1st app. Two-Face	295.00	885.00	2800.00
67-1st Penguin-c (9/42)	188.00	564.00	1600.00
68-Two-Face-c/story; 1st Two-Face-c	147.00	441.00	1250.00
69-Joker-c/story	147.00	441.00	1250.00
70	100.00	300.00	850.00
71-Joker-c/story	114.00	342.00	965.00
72,74,75: 74-1st Tweedledum & Tweedledee plus-c; S&K-a	91.00	273.00	775.00
73-Scarecrow-c/story (1st Scarecrow-c)	106.00	318.00	900.00
76-Newsboy Legion & The Sandman x-over in Boy Commandos; S&K-a; Joker-c/story	147.00	441.00	1250.00
77-79: All S&K-a	100.00	300.00	850.00
80-Two-Face app.; S&K-a	108.00	324.00	915.00
81,82,84,86-90: 81-1st Cavalier-c & app. 89-Last Crimson Avenger; 2nd Cavalier-c & app.	79.00	237.00	675.00
83-1st "skinny" Alfred (2/44)(see Batman #21; last S&K Boy Commandos. (also #92,128); most issues #84 on signed S&K are not by them	88.00	264.00	750.00
85-Joker-c/story; last Spy; Kirby/Klech Boy Commandos			

Detective Comics #118 © DC

Detective Comics #259 © DC

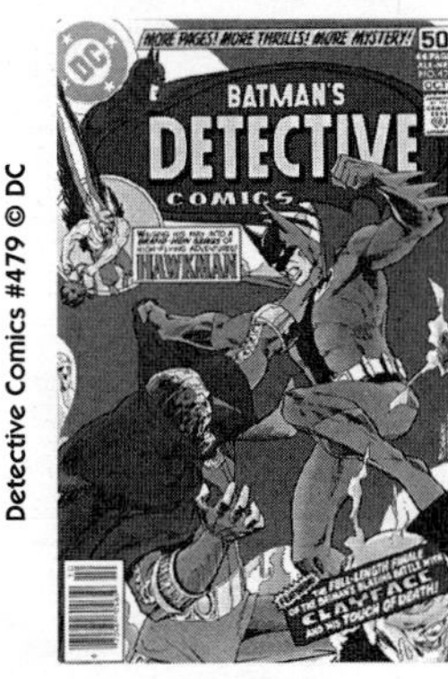

Detective Comics #479 © DC

	GD25	FN65	NM94
	103.00	309.00	875.00
91,102-Joker-c/story	97.00	291.00	825.00
92-98: 96-Alfred's last name 'Beagle' revealed, later changed to 'Pennyworth' in #214	68.00	204.00	575.00
99-Penguin-c	103.00	309.00	875.00
100 (6/45)	106.00	318.00	900.00
101,103-108,110-113,115-117,119: 108-1st Bat-signal-c (2/46). 114-1st small logo (8/46)	65.00	195.00	550.00
109,114,118-Joker-c/stories	88.00	264.00	750.00
120-Penquin-c (white-c, rare above fine)	133.00	400.00	1400.00
121,123,125,127,129,130	62.00	186.00	525.00
122-1st Catwoman-c (4/47)	112.00	336.00	950.00
124,128-Joker-c/stories	82.00	246.00	700.00
126-Penguin-c	85.00	255.00	725.00
131-136,139: 135-Frankenstein-c/story	53.00	159.00	450.00
137-Joker-c/story; last Air Wave	68.00	204.00	575.00
138-Origin Robotman (see Star Spangled #7 for 1st app.); series ends #202	100.00	300.00	850.00
140-The Riddler-c/story (1st app., 10/48)	380.00	1140.00	3800.00
141,143-148,150: 150-Last Boy Commandos	53.00	159.00	450.00
142-2nd Riddler-c/story	100.00	300.00	850.00
149-Joker-c/story	74.00	222.00	625.00
151-Origin & 1st app. Pow Wow Smith, Indian lawman (9/49) & begins series	65.00	195.00	550.00
152,154,155,157-160: 152-Last Slam Bradley	53.00	159.00	450.00
153-1st app. Roy Raymond TV Detective (11/49); origin The Human Fly	60.00	180.00	510.00
156(2/50)-The new classic Batmobile	74.00	222.00	625.00
161-167,169,170,172-176: Last 52 pg. issue	51.00	153.00	430.00
168-Origin the Joker	300.00	900.00	3000.00
171-Penguin-c	79.00	237.00	675.00
177-179,181-186,188,189,191,192,194-199,201,202,204,206-210,212,214-216: 184-1st app. Fire Fly. 185-Secret of Batman's utility belt. 187-Two-Face app. 202-Last Robotman & Pow Wow Smith. 215-1st app. of Batmen of all Nations. 216-Last precode (2/55)	44.00	132.00	380.00
180,193-Joker-c/story	48.00	144.00	410.00
187-Two-Face-c/story	48.00	144.00	410.00
190-Origin Batman retold	65.00	195.00	550.00
200 (10/53)	61.00	183.00	520.00
203,211-Catwoman-c/stories	48.00	144.00	410.00
205-Origin Batcave	61.00	183.00	520.00
213-Origin & 1st app. Mirror Man	53.00	159.00	450.00
217-224: 218-Batman Jr. & Robin Sr. app.	41.00	123.00	325.00

	GD25	FN65	VF82	NM94
225-(11/55)-1st app. Martian Manhunter, John Jones; later changed to J'onn J'onzz; origin begins; also see Batman #78	329.00	988.00	2470.00	5600.00

	GD25	FN65	NM94
226-Origin Martian Manhunter cont'd (2nd app.)	105.00	315.00	1260.00
227-229: Martian Manhunter stories in all	40.00	120.00	470.00
230-1st app. Mad Hatter; brief recap origin of Martian Manhunter	41.00	123.00	495.00
231-Brief origin recap Martian Manhunter	31.00	93.00	320.00
232,234,237-240: 232-Batwoman app. 239-Early DC grey tone-c	30.00	90.00	300.00
233-Origin & 1st app. Batwoman (7/56)	96.00	288.00	1150.00
235-Origin Batman & his costume; tells how Bruce Wayne's father (Thomas Wayne) wore Bat costume & fought crime (reprinted in Batman #255)	46.00	138.00	560.00
236-1st S.A. issue; J'onn J'onzz talks to parents and Mars-1st since being stranded on Earth; 1st app. Bat-Tank?	31.00	93.00	350.00
241-260: 246-Intro. Diane Meade, John Jones' girl. 249-Batwoman-c/app. 253-1st app. The Terrible Trio. 254-Bat-Hound-c/story. 257-Intro. & 1st app. Whirly Bats. 259-1st app. The Calendar Man	25.00	75.00	250.00
261-J. Jones tie-in to sci/fi movie "Incredible Shrinking Man"	18.50	55.00	185.00
262-264,266,269,270: 261-1st app. Dr. Double X. 262-Origin Jackal	18.50	55.00	185.00
265-Batman's origin retold with new facts	29.00	88.00	295.00
267-Origin & 1st app. Bat-Mite (5/59)	25.00	76.00	255.00
268,271-Manhunter origin recap	18.00	54.00	180.00
272,274-280: 276-2nd app. Bat-Mite	14.50	44.00	145.00
273-J'onn J'onzz i.d. revealed for 1st time	15.50	47.00	155.00
281-292, 294-297: 285,286,292-Batwoman-c/app. 287-Origin J'onn J'onzz retold. 289-Bat-Mite-c/story. 292-Last Roy Raymond. 297-Last 10¢ issue (11/61)	11.50	34.00	115.00
293-(7/61)-Aquaman begins (pre #1); ends #300	12.00	36.00	120.00
298-(12/61)-1st modern Clayface (Matt Hagen)	22.00	66.00	220.00
299,300: 300-(2/62)-Aquaman ends	8.50	25.50	85.00
301-(3/62)-J'onn J'onzz returns to Mars (1st since stranded on Earth 6 years before)	8.50	25.50	85.00
302-326,329,330: 302,307,311,318,321,325-Batwoman-c/app. 311-Intro. Zook in John Jones; 1st app. Cat-Man. 318,325-Cat-Man-c/story (2nd & 3rd app.); also 1st & 2nd app. Batwoman as the Cat-Woman. 321-2nd Terrible Trio. 322-Bat-Girl's 1st/only app. in Det. (6th in all); Batman cameo in J'onn J'onzz (only hero to app. in series). 326-Last J'onn J'onzz, story cont'd in H.O.M. #143; intro. Idol-Head of Diabolu	6.50	19.50	65.00
327-(5/64)-Elongated Man begins, ends #383; 1st new look Batman with new costume; Infantino/Giella new look-a begins; Batman with gun	10.50	32.00	105.00
328-Death of Alfred; Bob Kane biog, 2 pgs.	9.00	27.00	90.00
331,333-340,342-358,360-364,366-368,370: 334-1st app. The Outsider. 345-Intro Block Buster. 347-"What If" theme story (1/66). 351-Elongated Man new costume. 355-Zatanna x-over in Elongated Man. 356-Alfred brought back in Batman, 1st SA app.? 362,364-S.A. Riddler app. (early). 363-2nd app. new Batgirl. 370-1st Neal Adams-a on Batman (cover only, 12/67)	4.00	12.00	40.00
332,341,365-Joker-c/stories	4.80	14.40	48.00
359-Intro/origin new Batgirl-c/story (1/67); 1st app. Killer Moth.	9.50	28.50	95.00
369(11/67)-N. Adams-a (Elongated Man); 3rd app. S.A. Catwoman (cameo; leads into Batman #197); 4th app. new Batgirl	5.00	15.00	50.00
371-1st new Batmobile from TV show (1/68)	4.50	13.50	45.00
372-386,389,390: 375-New Batmobile-c. 377-S.A. Riddler app.	3.20	9.50	35.00
387-r/1st Batman story from #27 (30th anniversary, 5/69); Joker-c	3.80	11.50	40.00
388-Joker-c/story; last 12¢ issue	2.90	8.70	32.00
391-394,396,398,399,401,403,405,406,409: 392-1st app. Jason Bard. 401-2nd Batgirl/Robin team-up	2.20	6.50	24.00
395,397,402,404,407,408,410-Neal Adams-a. 404-Tribute to Enemy Ace	2.50	7.50	27.00
400-(6/70)-Origin & 1st app. Man-Bat; 1st Batgirl/Robin team-up (cont'd in #401); Neal Adams-a	4.50	13.50	50.00
411-413: 413-Last 15¢ issue	1.80	5.40	18.00
414-424: All-25¢, 52 pgs. 418-Creeper x-over. 424-Last Batgirl.	2.20	6.25	22.00
425-436: 426,430,436-Elongated Man app. 428,434-Hawkman begins, ends #467	1.25	3.75	12.00
437-New Manhunter begins (10-11/73, 1st app.) by Simonson, ends #443	1.80	5.40	18.00
438-445 (All 100 Page Super Spectaculars): 438-Kubert Hawkman-r. 439-Origin Manhunter. 440-G.A. Manhunter(Adv. #79) by S&K, Hawkman, Dollman, Gr. Lantern; Toth-a. 441-G.A. Plastic Man, Batman, Ibis-r. 442-G.A. Newsboy Legion, Bl. Canary, Elongated Man, Dr. Fate-r. 443-Origin The Creeper-r; death of Manhunter; G.A. Green Lantern, Spectre-r; Batman-r/Batman #18. 444-G.A. Kid Eternity-r. 445-G.A. Dr. Midnite-r	2.90	8.70	32.00
446-460: 457-Origin retold & updated	1.00	3.00	10.00

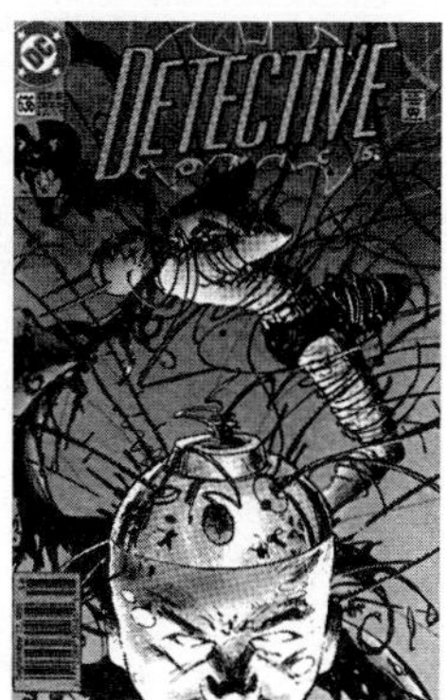

Detective Comics #636 © DC

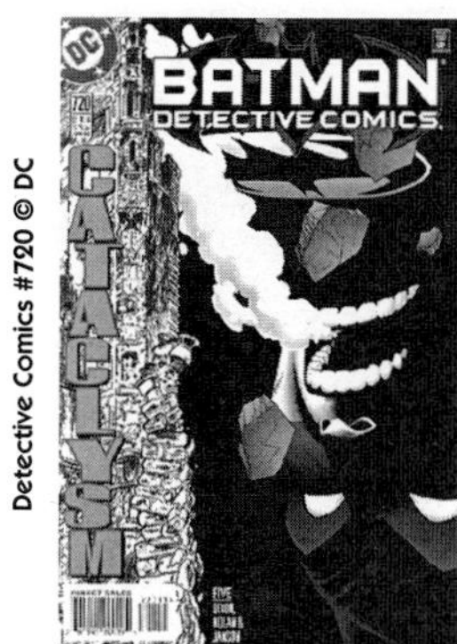

Detective Comics #720 © DC

Detective Dan #1 © Humor Publ.

GD25 FN65 NM94

461-465,469,470,480: 480-(44 pgs.). 463-1st app. Black Spider. 464-2nd app. Black Spider .90 2.70 8.00
466-468,471-474,478,479-Rogers-a in all: 466-1st app. Signalman since Batman #139. 469-Intro/origin Dr. Phosphorous. 470,471-1st modern app. Hugo Strange. 474-1st app. new Deadshot. 478-1st app. 3rd Clayface (Preston Payne). 479-(44 pgs.)-Clayface app. 1.50 4.50 15.00
475,476-Joker-c/stories; Rogers-a 2.25 6.80 25.00
477-Neal Adams-a(r); Rogers-a (3 pgs.) 1.80 5.40 18.00
481-(Combined with Batman Family, 12-1/78-79, begin $1.00, 68 pg. issues, ends #495); 481-495-Batgirl, Robin solo stories 1.20 3.60 12.00
482-Starlin/Russell, Golden-a; The Demon begins (origin-r), ends #485 (by Ditko #483-485) .90 2.70 7.50
483-40th Anniversary issue; origin retold; Newton Batman begins 1.00 3.00 10.00
484-499: 484-Origin Robin. 485-Death of Batwoman. 487-The Odd Man by Ditko. 489-Robin/Batgirl team-up. 490-Black Lightning begins. 491-(#492 on inside) 5.00
500-($1.50, 52 pgs.)-Batman/Deadman team-up; new Hawkman story by Joe Kubert; incorrectly says 500th anniv. of Det. 1.10 3.30 11.00
501-503,505-523: 512-2nd app. new Dr. Death. 519-Last Batgirl. 521-Green Arrow series begins. 523-Solomon Grundy app. 5.00
504-Joker-c/story .85 2.60 7.00
524-2nd app. Jason Todd (cameo)(3/83) 3.50
525-3rd app. Jason Todd (See Batman #357) 4.00
526-Batman's 500th app. in Detective Comics ($1.50, 68 pgs.); Death of Jason Todd's parents, Joker-c/story (55 pgs.); Bob Kane pin-up 1.20 3.60 12.00
527-531,533,534,536-568,571,573: 538-Cat-Man-c/story cont'd from Batman #371. 542-Jason Todd quits as Robin (becomes Robin again #547). 549, 550-Alan Moore scripts (Green Arrow). 554-1st new Black Canary (9/85). 566-Batman villains profiled. 567-Harlan Ellison scripts 3.00
532,569,570-Joker-c/stories 5.00
535-Intro new Robin (Jason Todd)-1st appeared in Batman 3.00
572-(3/87, $1.25, 60 pgs.)-50th Anniv. of Det. Comics 3.00
574-Origin Batman & Jason Todd retold 3.00
575-Year 2 begins, ends #578 .90 2.70 8.00
576-578: McFarlane-c/a. 578-Clay Face app. 2.00 6.00
579-597,601-610: 579-New bat wing logo. 583-1st app. villains Scarface & Ventriloquist. 589-595-(52 pgs.)-Each contain free 16 pg. Batman stories. 604-607-Mudpack storyline; 604,607-Contain Batman mini-posters. 610-Faked death of Penguin; artists names app. on tombstone on-c 1.50
598-($2.95, 84 pgs.)- "Blind Justice" storyline begins by Batman movie writer Sam Hamm, ends #600 3.00
599 2.50
600-(5/89, $2.95, 84 pgs.)-50th Anniv. of Batman in Det.; 1 pg. Neal Adams pin-up, among other artists 4.00
611-626,628-658: 612-1st new look Cat-Man; Catwoman app. 615- "The Penguin Affair" part 2 (See Batman #448,449). 617-Joker-c/story. 624-1st new Catwoman (w/death) & 1st new Batwoman. 626-Batman's 600th app. in Det. 642-Return of Scarface, part 2. 644-Last $1.00-c. 652,653-Huntress-c/story w/new costume plus Travis Charest-c on both 1.50
627-($2.95, 84 pgs.)-Batman's 601st app. in Det.; reprints 1st story/#27 plus 3 versions (2 new) of same story 3.00
659,660: 659-Knightfall part 2; Kelley Jones-c. 660-Knightfall part 4; Bane-c by Sam Kieth 3.00
661-664: 661-Knightfall part 6; brief Joker & Riddler app. 662-Knightfall part 8; Riddler app.; Sam Kieth-c. 663-Knightfall part 10; Kelley Jones-c. 664-Knightfall part 12; Bane-c/story; Joker app.; continued in Showcase 93 #7 & 8; Jones-c 3.00
665,666-Knightfall parts 16 & 18; 666-Bane-c/story 2.00
667,668: 667-Knightquest: The Crusade & new Batman begins (1st app. in Batman #500) 1.75
669-675: 669-Begin $1.50-c; Knightquest, cont'd in Robin #1. 671,673-Joker app. 1.75
675-($2.95)-Collectors edition w/foil-c 3.00
676-($2.50, 52 pgs.)-KnightsEnd Pt. 3 2.50
677,678: 677-KnightsEnd Pt. 9. 678-(9/94)-Zero Hour tie-in. 1.50
0,679-684: 0-(10/94). 679-(11/94). 682-Troika Pt. 3 1.50
682-($2.50) Embossed-c Troika Pt. 3 2.50
686-699,701-719: 686-Begin $1.95-c. 693,694-Poison Ivy-c/app. 695-Contagion Pt. 2; Catwoman, Penguin app. 696-Contagion Pt. 8. 698-Two-Face-c/app. 701-Legacy Pt. 6; Batman vs. Bane-c/app. 702-Legacy Epilogue. 703-Final Night x-over. 705-707-Riddler-app. 714,715-Martian Manhunter-app. 2.00
700-($4.95, Collectors Edition)-Legacy Pt. 1; Ra's Al Ghul-c/app; Talia & Bane app; book displayed at shops in envelope 5.00
700-($2.95, Regular Edition)-Different-c 3.00
720-724: 720,721-Cataclysm pts. 5,14. 723-Green Arrow app. 2.00
725-728: 725-Begin $1.99-c 1.99
#1,000,000 (11/98) 853rd Century x-over 2.00
Annual 1 (1988, $1.50) 5.00
Annual 2 (1989, $2.00, 68 pgs.) 3.00
Annual 3 (1990, $2.00, 68 pgs.) 2.00
Annual 4 (1991, $2.00, 68 pgs.)-Painted-c 2.00
Annual 5 (1992, $2.50, 68 pgs.)-Joker-c/story (54 pgs.) continued in Robin Annual #1; Sam Kieth-c; Eclipso app. 2.50
Annual 6 (1993, $2.50, 68 pgs.)-Azrael as Batman in new costume; intro Geist the Twilight Man; Bloodlines storyline 2.50
Annual 7 (1994, $2.95, 68 pgs.)-Elseworlds story 3.00
Annual 8 (1995, $3.95, 68 pgs.)-Year One story 4.00
Annual 9 (1996, $2.95)-Legends of the Dead Earth story 3.00
Annual 10 (1997, $3.95)-Pulp Heroes story 4.00

NOTE: ***Neal Adams*** *c-370, 372, 383, 385, 389, 391, 392, 394-422, 439.* ***Aparo*** *a-437, 438, 444-446, 500, 625-632p, 638-643p; c-430, 437, 440-446, 448, 468-470, 480, 484(back), 492-502,508, 509, 515, 518-522, 641, 716, 719, 722, 724.* ***Austin*** *a(i)-450, 451, 463-468, 471-476; c(i)-474-476, 478.* ***Baily*** *a-443r.* ***Buckler*** *a-434, 446p, 479p; c(p)-467, 482, 505-507, 511, 513-516, 518.* ***Burnley*** *a(Batman)-65, 75, 78, 83, 100, 103, 125; c-62i, 63i, 64, 73i, 78, 83p, 96p, 103p, 105p, 106, 108, 121p, 123p, 125p.* ***Chaykin*** *a-441.* ***Colan*** *a(p)-510, 512, 517, 523, 528-538, 540-546, 555-567; c(p)-510, 512, 528, 530-535, 537, 538, 540, 541, 543-545, 556-558, 560-564.* ***J. Craig*** *a-488.* ***Ditko*** *a-443r, 483-485, 487.* ***Golden*** *a-482p; c-625, 626, 628-631, 633, 644-646.* ***Alan Grant*** *scripts-584-597, 601-621, 641, 642, Annual 5.* ***Grell*** *a-445, 455, 463p, 464p; c-455.* ***Guardineer*** *c-23, 24, 26, 28, 30, 32.* ***Gustavson*** *a-441r.* ***Infantino*** *a-442(2)r, 500, 572.* ***Infantino/Anderson*** *c-333, 337-340, 343, 344, 347, 351, 352, 359, 361-368, 371.* ***Kelley Jones*** *c-651, 657i, 658i, 659, 661, 663-675.* ***Kaluta*** *c-423, 424, 426-428, 431, 434, 438, 484, 486, 572.* ***Bob Kane*** *a-Most early issues #27 on, 297r, 356r, 438-440r, 442r, 443r.* ***Kane/Robinson*** *c-33.* ***Gil Kane*** *a(p)-368, 370-374, 384, 385, 388-407, 438r, 439r, 520.* ***Kane/Anderson*** *c-369.* ***Sam Kieth*** *c-654-656 (657, 658 w/**Kelley Jones**), 660, 662, Annual #5.* ***Kubert*** *a-438r, 439r, 500; c-348, 350.* ***McFarlane*** *c/a(p)-576-578.* ***Meskin*** *a-420r.* ***Mignola*** *c-583.* ***Moldoff*** *c-233-354, 259, 266, 267, 275, 287, 289, 290, 297, 300.* ***Moldoff/Giella*** *a-328, 330, 332, 334, 336, 338, 340, 342, 344, 346, 348, 350, 352, 354, 356.* ***Mooney*** *a-444r.* ***Moreira*** *a-153-300, 419r, 444r, 445r.* ***Nasser/Netzer*** *a-654, 655, 657, 658.* ***Newton*** *a(p)-480, 481, 483-499, 501-509, 511, 513-516, 518-520, 524, 526, 539; c-526p.* ***Irv Novick*** *c-375-377.* ***Robbins*** *a-426p, 429p.* ***Robinson*** *a-part: 66, 68, 71-73; all: 74-76, 79, 80; c-62, 64, 66, 68-74, 76, 79, 82, 86, 88, 442r, 443r.* ***Rogers*** *a-466-468, 471-479p, 481p; c-471p, 472p, 473, 474-479p.* ***Roussos*** *Airwave-76-105(most); c(i)-71, 72, 74-76, 79, 107.* ***Russell*** *a-481i, 482i.* ***Simon/Kirby*** *a-440r, 442r.* ***Simonson*** *a-437-443, 450, 469, 470, 500.* ***Dick Sprang*** *c-77, 82, 84, 85, 87, 89-93, 95-100, 102, 103i, 104i, 106, 108, 114, 117, 118, 122, 123, 128, 129, 131, 133, 135, 141, 148, 149, 168, 622-624.* ***Starlin*** *a-481p, 482p; c-503, 504, 567p.* ***Starr*** *a-444r.* ***Toth*** *a-442; r-414, 416, 418, 424, 440-441, 443, 444.* ***Tuska*** *a-486p, 490p.* ***Matt Wagner*** *c-647-649.* ***Wrightson*** *c-425.*

DETECTIVE DAN, SECRET OP. 48 (Also see Adventures of Detective Ace King and Bob Scully, The Two-Fisted Hick Detective)
Humor Publ. Co. (Norman Marsh): 1933 (10¢, 10x13", 36 pgs., B&W, one-shot) (3 color, cardboard-c)

	GD	FN	VF
nn-By Norman Marsh, 1st comic w/ original-a; 1st newsstand-c; Dick Tracy look-alike; forerunner of Dan Dunn. (Title and Wu Fang character inspired Detective #1 four years later.) (1st comic of a single theme)	1400.00	4200.00	5500.00

DETECTIVE EYE (See Keen Detective Funnies)
Centaur Publications: Nov, 1940 - No. 2, Dec, 1940

GD FN NM

1-Air Man (see Keen Detective) & The Eye Sees begins; The Masked Marvel

Detectives, Inc. #2 © Don McGregor

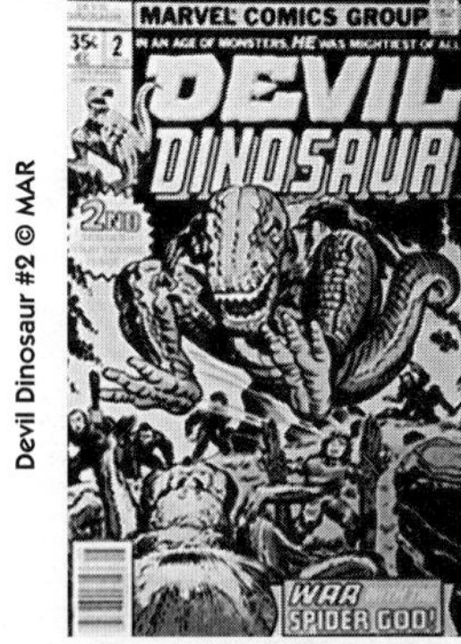

Devil Dinosaur #2 © MAR

Diary Loves #5 © QUA

	GD25	FN65	NM94

& Dean Denton app. 188.00 564.00 1600.00
2-Origin Don Rance and the Mysticape; Binder-a; Frank Thomas-c 118.00 354.00 1000.00

DETECTIVE PICTURE STORIES (Keen Detective Funnies No. 8 on?)
Comics Magazine Company: Dec, 1936 - No. 5, Apr, 1937
(1st comic of a single theme)

1 (all issues are very scarce) 550.00 1650.00 3500.00
2-The Clock app. (1/37, early app.) 233.00 699.00 1500.00
3,4: 4-Eisner-a 150.00 450.00 950.00
5-The Clock-c/story (4/37); 1st detective/adventure art by Bob Kane; Bruce Wayne prototype app. 166.00 500.00 1050.00

DETECTIVES, THE (TV)
Dell Publishing Co.: No. 1168, Mar-May, 1961 - No. 1240, Oct-Dec, 1961

Four Color 1168 (#1)-Robert Taylor photo-c 9.00 27.00 100.00
Four Color 1219-Robert Taylor, Adam West photo-c 7.00 22.00 80.00
Four Color 1240-Tufts-a; Robert Taylor photo-c 7.00 22.00 80.00

DETECTIVES, INC. (See Eclipse Graphic Album Series)
Eclipse Comics: Apr, 1985 - No. 2, Apr, 1985 ($1.75, both w/April dates)

1,2: 2-Nudity 1.80

DETECTIVES, INC.: A TERROR OF DYING DREAMS
Eclipse Comics: Jun, 1987 - No. 3, Dec, 1987 ($1.75, B&W& sepia)

1-3: Colan-a 1.80

DETENTION COMICS
DC Comics: Oct, 1996 ($3.50, 56 pgs., one-shot)

1-Robin story by Dennis O'Neil & Norm Breyfogle; Superboy story by Ron Marz & Ron Lim; Warrior story by Ruben Diaz & Joe Phillips; Phillips-c 3.50

DETONATOR
Chaos! Comics: Dec, 1994 - No. 2, 1995 ($2.95, limited series)

1,2-Brian Pulido scripts; Steven Hughes-a 3.00

DEVASTATOR
Image Comics/Halloween: 1998 - No. 3 ($2.95, B&W, limited series)

1,2-Hudnall-s/Horn-c/a 3.00

DEVIL CHEF
Dark Horse Comics: July, 1994 ($2.50, B&W, one-shot)

nn 2.50

DEVIL DINOSAUR
Marvel Comics Group: Apr, 1978 - No. 9, Dec, 1978

1-Kirby/Royer-a in all; all have Kirby-c .90 2.70 8.00
2,3,8,9: 8-Dinoriders-c/sty 4.00
4-7-UFO/sci. fic 5.00

DEVIL DINOSAUR SPRING FLING
Marvel Comics: June, 1997 ($2.99. one-shot)

1-(48pgs.) Moon-Boy-c/app. 2.99

DEVIL-DOG DUGAN (Tales of the Marines No. 4 on)
Atlas Comics (OPI): July, 1956 - No. 3, Nov, 1956

1-Severin-c 9.30 28.00 70.00
2-Iron Mike McGraw x-over; Severin-c 6.00 18.00 42.00
3 5.35 16.00 32.00

DEVIL DOGS
Street & Smith Publishers: 1942

1-Boy Rangers, U.S. Marines 24.00 72.00 180.00

DEVLIN (See Avengelyne/Glory)
Maximum Press: Apr, 1996 ($2.50, one-shot)

1-Avengelyne app. 2.50

	GD25	FN65	NM94

DEVILINA (Magazine)
Atlas/Seaboard: Feb, 1975 - No. 2, May, 1975 (B&W)

1-Reese-a 1.20 3.60 12.00
2 1.80 5.40 18.00

DEVIL KIDS STARRING HOT STUFF
Harvey Publications (Illustrated Humor): July, 1962 - No. 107, Oct, 1981
(Giant-Size #41-55)

1 (12¢ cover price #1-#41-9/69) 13.00 39.00 130.00
2 6.50 19.50 65.00
3-10 (1/64) 4.80 14.40 48.00
11-20 2.50 7.50 24.00
21-30 2.25 6.75 18.00
31-40: 40-(6/69) 1.85 5.50 15.00
41-50: All 68 pg. Giants 2.25 6.75 18.00
51-55: All 52 pg. Giants 2.00 6.00 16.00
56-70 .90 2.70 8.00
71-90 5.00
91-107 3.00

DEVILMAN
Verotik: June, 1995 - Present ($2.95, mature)

1-3: Go Nagai story and art. 3-Bisley-c 3.00

DEXTER COMICS
Dearfield Publ.: Summer, 1948 - No. 5, July, 1949

1-Teen-age humor 7.15 21.50 50.00
2-Junie Prom app. 5.70 17.00 35.00
3-5 4.15 12.50 25.00

DEXTER THE DEMON (Formerly Melvin The Monster)(See Cartoon Kids & Peter the Little Pest)
Atlas Comics (HPC): No. 7, Sept, 1957

7 5.00 15.00 30.00

DHAMPIRE: STILLBORN
DC Comics (Vertigo): 1996 ($5.95, one-shot, mature)

1-Nancy Collins script; Paul Lee-c/a 2.00 6.00

DIARY CONFESSIONS (Formerly Ideal Romance)
Stanmor/Key Publ.(Medal Comics): No. 9, May, 1955 - No. 14, Apr, 1955

9 5.70 17.00 35.00
10-14 4.00 12.00 24.00

DIARY LOVES (Formerly Love Diary #1; G. I. Sweethearts #32 on)
Quality Comics Group: No. 2, Nov, 1949 - No. 31, April, 1953

2-Ward-c/a, 9 pgs. 13.00 40.00 100.00
3 (1/50)-Photo-c begin, end #27? 5.00 15.00 30.00
4-Crandall-a 6.50 19.50 45.00
5-7,10 4.00 11.00 22.00
8,9-Ward-a 6,8 pgs. 8-Gustavson-a 9.30 28.00 65.00
11,13,14,17-20 4.00 11.00 22.00
12,15,16-Ward-a 9,7,8 pgs. 8.50 26.00 60.00
21-Ward-a, 7 pgs. 6.50 19.50 45.00
22-31: 31-Whitney-a 2.80 7.00 14.00
NOTE: *Photo c-3-10, 12-27.*

DIARY OF HORROR
Avon Periodicals: December, 1952

1-Hollingsworth-c/a; bondage-c 33.00 98.00 245.00

DIARY SECRETS (Formerly Teen-Age Diary Secrets)
St. John Publishing Co.: No. 10, Feb, 1952 - No. 30, Sept, 1955

10-Baker-c/a most issues 13.00 40.00 100.00
11-16,18,19 10.00 30.00 75.00
17,20: Kubert-r/Hollywood Confessions #1. 17-r/Teen Age Romances #9 10.00 30.00 75.00

Dick Cole #2 © STAR

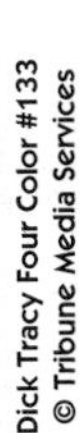
Dick Tracy Four Color #133 © Tribune Media Services

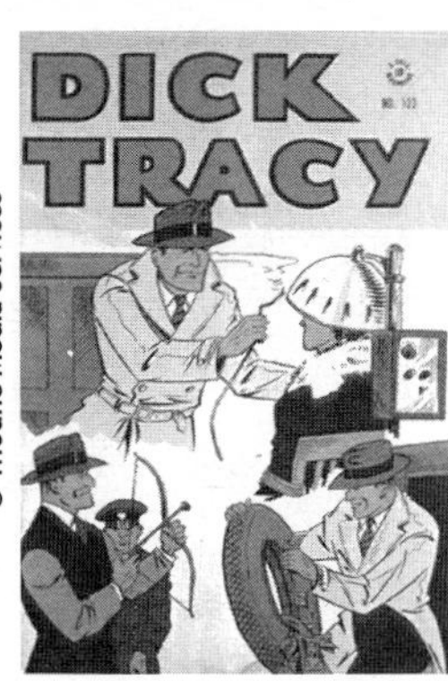

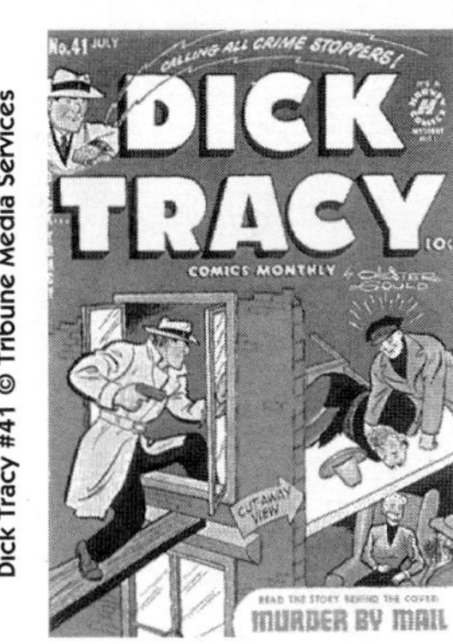

Dick Tracy #41 © Tribune Media Services

GD25 FN65 NM94

21-30: 22,27-Signed stories by Estrada. 28-Last precode (3/55) 6.50 19.50 45.00
(See Giant Comics Edition for Annual)

DIATOM
Photographics: Apr, 1995 ($4.95, unfinished limited series)
1-Photo/computer-a 5.00

DICK COLE (Sport Thrills No. 11 on)(See Blue Bolt & Four Most #1)
Curtis Publ./Star Publications: Dec-Jan, 1948-49 - No. 10, June-July, 1950
1-Sgt. Spook; L. B. Cole-c; McWilliams-a; Curt Swan's 1st work 24.00 72.00 180.00
2,5 12.00 36.00 90.00
3,4,6-10: All-L.B. Cole-c. 10-Joe Louis story 15.00 46.00 115.00
Accepted Reprint #7(V1#6 on-c)(1950's)-Reprints #7; L.B. Cole-c 5.70 17.00 40.00
Accepted Reprint #9(nd)-(Reprints #9 & #8-c) 5.70 17.00 40.00
NOTE: *L. B. Cole c-1, 3, 4, 6-10. Al McWilliams a-6. Dick Cole in 1-9. Baseball c-10. Basketball c-9. Football c-8.*

DICKIE DARE
Eastern Color Printing Co.: 1941 - No. 4, 1942 (#3 on sale 6/15/42)
1-Caniff-a, Everett-c 37.00 112.00 280.00
2 23.00 70.00 175.00
3,4-Half Scorchy Smith by Noel Sickles who was very influential in Milton Caniff's development 26.00 78.00 195.00

DICK POWELL (Also see A-1 Comics)
Magazine Enterprises: No. 22, 1949 (one shot)
A-1 22-Photo-c 24.00 71.00 175.00

DICK QUICK, ACE REPORTER (See Picture News #10)

DICKS
Caliber Comics: 1997 - No. 4, 1998 ($2.95, B&W)
1-4-Ennis-s/McCrea-c/a; r/Fleetway 4.50

DICK'S ADVENTURES
Dell Publishing Co.: No. 245, Sept, 1949
Four Color 245 4.50 13.50 50.00

DICK TRACY (See Famous Feature Stories, Harvey Comics Library, Limited Collectors' Ed., Mammoth Comics, Merry Christmas, The Original..., Popular Comics, Super Book No. 1, 7, 13, 25, Super Comics & Tastee-Freez)

DICK TRACY
David McKay Publications: May, 1937 - Jan, 1938
Feature Books nn - 100 pgs., partially reprinted as 4-Color No. 1 (appeared before Large Feature Comics, 1st Dick Tracy comic book) (Very Rare-three known copies) Estimated Value.... 600.00 1800.00 6000.00
Feature Books 4 - Reprints nn ish. w/new-c 110.00 330.00 1100.00
Feature Books 6,9 80.00 240.00 800.00

DICK TRACY (...Monthly #1-24)
Dell Publishing Co.: 1939 - No. 24, Dec, 1949
Large Feature Comic 1 (1939) -Dick Tracy Meets The Blank 118.00 355.00 1300.00
Large Feature Comic 4,8 59.00 177.00 650.00
Large Feature Comic 11,13,15 68.00 205.00 750.00

	GD25	FN65	VF82	NM94
Four Color 1(1939)('35-r)	590.00	1775.00	3540.00	6500.00

(Estimated up to 75+ total copies exist, 5 in NM/Mint)

	GD25	FN65	NM94
Four Color 6(1940)('37-r)-(Scarce)	134.00	400.00	1470.00
Four Color 8(1940)('38-'39-r)	67.00	200.00	735.00
Large Feature Comic 3(1941, Series II)	58.00	175.00	640.00
Four Color 21('41)('38-r)	57.00	170.00	625.00
Four Color 34('43)('39-'40-r)	39.00	116.00	425.00
Four Color 56('44)('40-r)	31.00	83.00	340.00
Four Color 96('46)('40-r)	22.00	67.00	245.00
Four Color 133('47)('40-'41-r)	19.00	57.00	210.00
Four Color 163('47)('41-r)	15.00	45.00	165.00
Four Color 215('48)-Titled "Sparkle Plenty", Tracy-r	9.00	27.00	100.00
1(1/48)('34-r)	36.00	107.00	390.00
2,3	19.00	57.00	210.00
4-10	18.00	55.00	200.00
11-18: 13-Bondage-c	12.00	37.00	135.00
19-1st app. Sparkle Plenty, B.O. Plenty & Gravel Gertie in a 3-pg. strip not by Gould	13.00	40.00	145.00
20-1st app. Sam Catchem; c/a not by Gould	10.00	30.00	110.00
21-24-Only 2 pg. Gould-a in each	10.00	30.00	110.00

NOTE: *No. 19-24 have a 2 pg. biography of a famous villain illustrated by **Gould**: 19-Little Face; 20-Flattop; 21-Breathless Mahoney; 22-Measles; 23-Itchy; 24-The Brow.*

DICK TRACY (Continued from Dell series)(...Comics Monthly #25-140)
Harvey Publications: No. 25, Mar, 1950 - No. 145, April, 1961
25-Flat Top-c/story (also #26,27) 16.50 49.50 165.00
26-28,30: 28-Bondage-c. 28,29-The Brow-c/stories 11.50 34.50 115.00
29-1st app. Gravel Gertie in a Gould-r 15.50 46.50 155.00
31,32,34,35,37-40: 40-Intro/origin 2-way wrist radio (6/51) 10.50 31.50 105.00
33- "Measles the Teen-Age Dope Pusher" 11.50 34.50 115.00
36-1st app. B.O. Plenty in a Gould-r 11.50 34.50 115.00
41-50 8.50 25.50 85.00
51-56,58-80: 51-2pgs Powell-a 7.50 22.50 75.00
57-1st app. Sam Catchem in a Gould-r 9.50 28.50 95.00
81-99,101-140 5.80 17.40 58.00
100 6.50 19.50 65.00
141-145 (25¢)(titled "Dick Tracy") 6.50 19.50 65.00
NOTE: ***Powell** a(1-2pgs.)-43, 44, 104, 108, 109, 145. No. 110-120, 141-145 are all reprints from earlier issues.*

DICK TRACY
Blackthorne Publishing: 12/84 - No. 24, 6/89 (1-12: $5.95; 13-24: $6.95, B&W, 76 pgs.)
1-3-1st printings; hard-c ed. ($14.95) 1.50 4.50 15.00
1-3-1st printings; squarebound. thick-c 2.00 6.00
1-3-2nd printings, 1986; hard-c ed. 1.50 4.50 15.00
1-3-2nd printings, 1986; squarebound, thick-c 2.00 6.00
4-8-Hardcover ed. ($14.95) 1.50 4.50 15.00
4-12: Squarebound, thick-c 2.00 6.00
13-24 ($6.95): 21,22-Regular-c & stapled .85 2.60 7.00
NOTE: **Gould** daily & Sunday strip-r in all. 1-12 r-12/31/45-4/5/49; 13-24 r-7/13/41-2/20/44.

DICK TRACY (Disney)
WD Publications: 1990 - No. 3, 1990 (color) (Book 3 adapts 1990 movie)
Book One ($3.95, 52pgs.)-Kyle Baker-c/a 4.00
Book Two, Three ($5.95, 68pgs.)-Direct sale 2.00 6.00
Book Two, Three ($2.95, 68pgs.)-Newsstand 3.00

DICK TRACY ADVENTURES
Gladstone Publishing: May, 1991 ($4.95, 76 pgs.)
1-Reprints strips 2/1/42-4/18/42 5.00

DICK TRACY, EXPLOITS OF
Rosdon Books, Inc.: 1946 ($1.00, hard-c strip reprints)
1-Reprints the near complete case of "The Brow" from 6/12/44 to 9/24/44 (story starts a few weeks late) 22.00 66.00 175.00
with dust jacket... 36.00 108.00 300.00

DICK TRACY GIVEAWAYS
1939 - 1958; 1990
Buster Brown Shoes Giveaway (1940s?, 36 pgs. in color); 1938-39-r by Gould 29.00 88.00 235.00
Gillmore Giveaway (See Superbook)
...Hatful of Fun (No date, 1950-52, 32pgs.; 8-1/2x10")-Dick Tracy hat promotion; Dick Tracy games, magic tricks. Miller Bros. premium

Die Cut #4 © MEG

Dilton's Strange Science #5 © AP

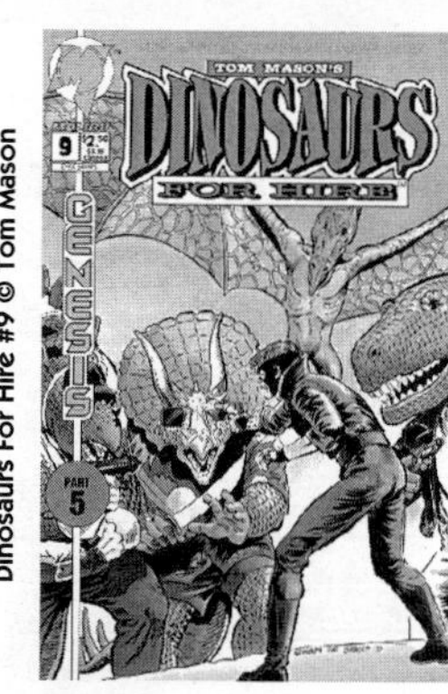

Dinosaurs For Hire #9 © Tom Mason

GD25 FN65 NM94

14.00 41.00 110.00
Motorola Giveaway (1953)-Reprints Harvey Comics Library #2; "The Case of the Sparkle Plenty TV Mystery" 5.00 15.00 30.00
Original Dick Tracy by Chester Gould, The (Aug, 1990, 16 pgs., 5-1/2x8-1/2")-Gladstone Publ.; Bread Giveaway 2.50 7.50 20.00
Popped Wheat Giveaway (1947, 16 pgs. in color)-1940-r; Sig Feuchtwanger Publ.; Gould-a 2.40 6.00 12.00
...Presents the Family Fun Book; Tip Top Bread Giveaway, no date or number (1940, Fawcett Publ., 16 pgs. in color)-Spy Smasher, Ibis, Lance O'Casey app. 50.00 50.00 450.00
Same as above but without app. of heroes & Dick Tracy on cover only 9.50 28.00 75.00
Service Station Giveaway (1958, 16 pgs. in color)(regular size, slick cover)-Harvey Info. Press 3.60 9.00 18.00
Shoe Store Giveaway (Weatherbird)(1939, 16 pgs.)-Gould-a 12.00 36.00 95.00

DICK TRACY MONTHLY/WEEKLY
Blackthorne Publishing: May, 1986 - No. 99, 1989 ($2.00, B&W) (Becomes Weekly #26 on)
1-99: Gould-r. 30,31-Mr. Crime app. 2.00
NOTE: *#1-10 reprint strips 3/10/40-7/13/41; #10(pg.8)-51 reprint strips 4/6/49-12/31/55; #52-99 reprint strips 12/26/56-4/26/64.*

DICK TRACY SHEDS LIGHT ON THE MOLE
Western Printing Co.: 1949 (16 pgs.) (Ray-O-Vac Flashlights giveaway)
nn-Not by Gould 5.70 17.00 40.00

DICK TRACY SPECIAL
Blackthorne Publ.: Jan, 1988 - No. 3, Aug. (no month), 1989 ($2.95, B&W)
1-3: 1-Origin D. Tracy; 4/strips 10/12/31-3/30/32 3.00

DICK TRACY: THE EARLY YEARS
Blackthorne Publishing: Aug, 1987 - No. 4, Aug (no month) 1989 ($6.95, B&W, 76 pgs.)
1-3: 1-4-r/strips 10/12/31(1st daily)-8/31/32 & Sunday strips 6/12/32-8/28/32; Big Boy apps. in #1-3 .85 2.60 7.00
4 ($2.95, 52pgs.) 3.00

DICK TRACY UNPRINTED STORIES
Blackthorne Publishing: Sept, 1987 - No. 4, June, 1988 ($2.95, B&W)
1-4: Reprints strips 1/1/56-12/25/56 3.00

DICK TURPIN (See Legend of Young...)

DICK WINGATE OF THE U.S. NAVY
Superior Publ./Toby Press: 1951; 1953 (no month)
nn-U.S. Navy giveaway 2.40 6.00 12.00
1(1953, Toby)-Reprints nn issue? (same-c) 4.00 10.00 20.00

DIE-CUT
Marvel Comics UK, Ltd: Nov, 1993 - No. 4, Feb, 1994 ($1.75, limited series)
1-($2.50)-Die-cut-c; The Beast app. 2.50
2-4 1.75

DIE-CUT VS. G-FORCE
Marvel Comics UK, Ltd: Nov, 1993 - No. 2, Dec, 1993 ($2.75, limited series)
1,2-($2.75)-Gold foil-c on both 2.75

DIE, MONSTER, DIE (See Movie Classics)

DIESEL
Antarctic Press: Apr, 1997 - Present ($2.95)
1 2.95

DIG 'EM
Kellogg's Sugar Smacks Giveaway: 1973 (2-3/8x6", 16 pgs.)
nn-4 different issues 5.00

DIGITEK
Marvel UK, Ltd: Dec, 1992 - No. 4, Mar, 1993 ($1.95/$2.25, mini-series)
1,2 ($1.95) 2.00
3,4 ($2.25): 3-Deathlock-c/story 2.25

DILLY (Dilly Duncan from Daredevil Comics; see Boy Comics #57)
Lev Gleason Publications: May, 1953 - No. 3, Sept, 1953
1-Teenage; Biro-c 5.00 15.00 30.00
2,3-Biro-c 4.00 10.00 20.00

DILTON'S STRANGE SCIENCE (See Pep Comics #78)
Archie Comics: May, 1989 - No. 5, May, 1990 (75¢/$1.00)
1-5 2.00

DIME COMICS
Newsbook Publ. Corp.: 1945; 1951
1-Silver Streak-c/story; L. B. Cole-c 47.00 142.00 400.00
1(1951), 5 4.00 10.00 20.00

DINGBATS (See 1st Issue Special)

DING DONG
Compix/Magazine Enterprises: Summer?, 1946 - No. 5, 1947 (52 pgs.)
1-Funny animal 19.00 56.00 140.00
2 (9/46) 9.30 28.00 70.00
3 (Wint '46-'47) - 5 7.85 23.50 55.00

DINKY DUCK (Paul Terry's...) (See Blue Ribbon, Giant Comics Edition #5A & New Terrytoons)
St. John Publishing Co./Pines No. 16 on: Nov, 1951 - No. 16, Sept, 1955; No. 16, Fall, 1956; No. 17, May, 1957 - No. 19, Summer, 1958
1-Funny animal 9.30 28.00 70.00
2 5.70 17.00 35.00
3-10 4.00 11.00 22.00
11-16(9/55) 3.20 8.00 16.00
16(Fall,'56) - 19 2.40 6.00 12.00

DINKY DUCK & HASHIMOTO-SAN (See Deputy Dawg Presents...)

DINO (TV)(The Flintstones)
Charlton Publications: Aug, 1973 - No. 20, Jan, 1977 (Hanna-Barbera)
1 2.20 6.25 22.00
2-10 1.40 4.20 14.00
11-20 1.00 3.00 10.00

DINO ISLAND
Mirage Studios: Feb, 1994 - No. 2, Mar, 1994 ($2.75, limited series)
1,2-By Jim Lawson 2.75

DINO RIDERS
Marvel Comics: Feb, 1989 - No. 3, 1989 ($1.00)
1-3: Based on toys 1.50

DINOSAUR REX
Upshot Graphics (Fantagraphics): 1986 - No. 3, 1986 ($2.00, limited series)
1-3 2.00

DINOSAURS, A CELEBRATION
Marvel Comics (Epic): Oct, 1992 - No. 4, Oct, 1992 ($4.95, lim. series, 52 pgs.)
1-4: 2-Bolton painted-c 5.00

DINOSAURS ATTACK! THE GRAPHIC NOVEL
Eclipse Comics: 1991 ($3.95, coated stock, stiff-c)
Book One- Based on Topps trading cards 4.00

DINOSAURS FOR HIRE
Malibu Comics: Feb, 1993 - No. 12, Feb, 1994 ($1.95/$2.50)
1-Flip book 2.00
2-12: 8-($2.50)-Bagged w/Skycap; Staton-c. 10-Flip book 2.50

DINOSAURS GRAPHIC NOVEL (TV)

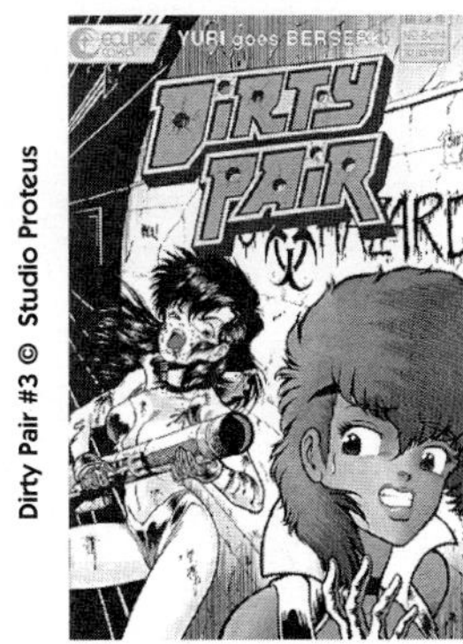

Dirty Pair #3 © Studio Proteus

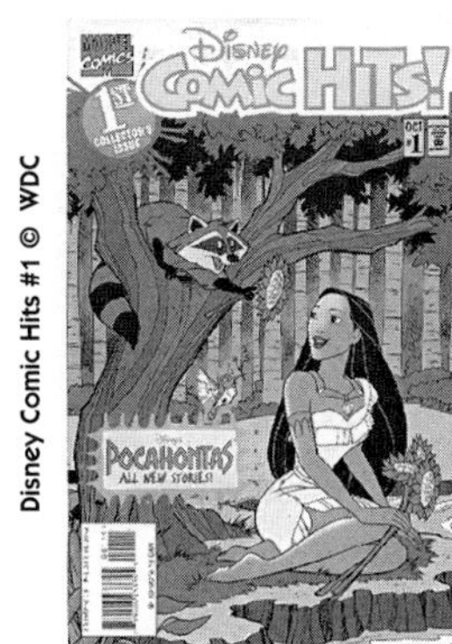

Disney Comic Hits #1 © WDC

Disney's The Lion King #1 © WDC

GD25 FN65 NM94

Disney Comics: 1992 - No. 2, 1993 ($2.95, 52 pgs.)
1,2-Staton-a; based on Dinosaurs TV show 3.00

DINOSAURUS
Dell Publishing Co.: No. 1120, Aug, 1960
Four Color 1120-Movie, painted-c 6.40 19.00 70.00

DIPPY DUCK
Atlas Comics (OPI): October, 1957
1-Maneely-a; code approved 7.15 21.50 50.00

DIRECTORY TO A NONEXISTENT UNIVERSE
Eclipse Comics: Dec, 1987 ($2.00, B&W)
1 2.00

DIRTY DOZEN (See Movie Classics)

DIRTY PAIR (Manga)
Eclipse Comics: Dec, 1988 - No. 4, Apr, 1989 ($2.00, B&W, limited series)
1-4: Japanese manga with original stories 2.00

DIRTY PAIR: FATAL BUT NOT SERIOUS (Manga)
Dark Horse Comics: July, 1995 - No. 5, Nov, 1995 ($2.95, limited series)
1-5 3.00

DIRTY PAIR: SIM HELL (Manga)
Dark Horse Comics: May, 1993 - No. 4, Aug, 1993 ($2.50, B&W, limited series)
1-4 2.50

DIRTY PAIR II (Manga)
Eclipse Comics: June, 1989 - No. 5, Mar, 1990 ($2.00, B&W, limited series)
1-5: 3-Cover is misnumbered as #1 2.00

DIRTY PAIR III, THE (A Plague of Angels) (Manga)
Eclipse Comics: Aug, 1990 - No. 5, Aug, 1991 ($2.00, B&W, limited series)
1,2 2.00
3-5: ($2.25) 2.25

DISHMAN
Eclipse Comics: Sept, 1988 ($2.50, B&W, 52 pgs.)
1 2.50

DISNEY AFTERNOON, THE (TV)
Marvel Comics: Nov, 1994 - No. 10?, Aug, 1995 ($1.50)
1-10: 3-w/bound-in Power Ranger Barcode Card 2.50

DISNEY COMIC ALBUM
Disney Comics: 1990(no month, year) - No. 8, 1991 ($6.95/$7.95)
1,2 ($6.95): 1-Donald Duck and Gyro Gearloose by Barks(r). 2-Uncle Scrooge by Barks(r); Jr. Woodchucks app. .85 2.60 7.00
3-8: 3-Donald Duck-r/F.C. 308 by Barks; begin $7.95-c. 4-Mickey Mouse Meets the Phantom Blot; r/M.M Club Parade(censored 1956 version of story). 5-Chip 'n' Dale Rescue Rangers; new-a. 6-Uncle Scrooge. 7-Donald Duck in Too Many Pets; Barks-r(4) including F.C. #29. 8-Super Goof; r/S.G. #1, D.D. #102 .90 2.70 8.00

DISNEY COMIC HITS
Marvel Comics: Oct, 1995 - Present ($1.50/$2.50)
1-9,11-15: 4-Toy Story. 6-Aladdin. 7-Pocahontas. 13-Aladdin and the Forty Thieves 3.00
10-(7/96, $2.50)-The Hunchback of Notre Dame (Same story in Disney's The Hunchback of Notre Dame) 4.00

DISNEY COMICS
Disney Comics: June, 1990
Boxed set of #1 issues includes Donald Duck Advs., Ducktales, Chip 'n Dale Rescue Rangers, Roger Rabbit, Mickey Mouse Advs. & Goofy Advs.; limited to 10,000 sets 1.20 3.60 12.00

DISNEYLAND BIRTHDAY PARTY (Also see Dell Giants)
Gladstone Publishing Co.: Aug, 1985 ($2.50)
1-Reprints Dell Giant with new-photo-c 1.20 3.60 12.00
...Comics Digest #1-(Digest) 1.40 4.20 14.00

DISNEYLAND MAGAZINE
Fawcett Publications: Feb. 15, 1972 - ? (10-1/4"x12-5/8", 20 pgs, weekly)
1-One or two page painted art features on Dumbo, Snow White, Lady & the Tramp, the Aristocats, Brer Rabbit, Peter Pan, Cinderella, Jungle Book, Alice & Pinocchio. Most standard characters app. 2.00 6.00 20.00

DISNEYLAND, USA (See Dell Giant No. 30)

DISNEY MOVIE BOOK
Walt Disney Productions (Gladstone): 1990 ($7.95, 8-1/2"x11", 52 pgs.) (w/pull-out poster)
1-Roger Rabbit in Tummy Trouble; from the cartoon film strips adapted to the comic format. Ron Dias-c 1.20 3.60 12.00

DISNEY'S ACTION CLUB
Acclaim Books: 1997 - Present ($4.50, digest size)
1-4: 1-Hercules. 4-Mighty Ducks 4.50

DISNEY'S ALADDIN (Movie)
Marvel Comics: Oct, 1994 - No. 11, 1995 ($1.50)
1-11 3.00

DISNEY'S BEAUTY AND THE BEAST (Movie)
Marvel Comics: Sept, 1994 - No. 13, 1995 ($1.50)
1-13 3.00

DISNEY'S BEAUTY AND THE BEAST HOLIDAY SPECIAL
Acclaim Books: 1997 ($4.50, digest size, one-shot)
1-Based on The Enchanted Christmas video 4.50

DISNEY'S COLOSSAL COMICS COLLECTION
Disney Comics: 1991 - No. 10, 1993 ($1.95, digest-size, 96/132 pgs.)
1-10: Ducktales, Talespin, Chip 'n Dale's Rescue Rangers. 4-r/Darkwing Duck #1-4. 6-Goofy begins. 8-Little Mermaid 4.00

DISNEY'S COMICS IN 3-D
Disney Comics: 1992 ($2.95, w/glasses, polybagged)
1-Infinity-c; Barks, Rosa, Gottfredson-r 5.00

DISNEY'S ENCHANTING STORIES
Acclaim Books: 1997 - Present ($4.50, digest size)
1-5: 1-Hercules. 2-Pocahontas 1.50

DISNEY'S NEW ADVENTURES OF BEAUTY AND THE BEAST (Also see Beauty and the Beast & Disney's Beauty and the Beast)
Disney Comics: 1992 - No. 2, 1992 ($1.50, limited series)
1,2-New stories based on movie 3.00

DISNEY'S POCAHONTAS (Movie)
Marvel Comics: 1995 ($4.95, one-shot)
1-Movie adaptation .85 2.60 7.00

DISNEY'S TALESPIN LIMITED SERIES: "TAKE OFF" (TV) (See Talespin)
W. D. Publications (Disney Comics): Jan, 1991 - No. 4, Apr, 1991 ($1.50, limited series, 52 pgs.)
1-4: Based on animated series; 4 part origin 2.50

DISNEY'S THE LION KING (Movie)
Marvel Comics: July, 1994 - No. 2, July, 1994 ($1.50, limited series)
1,2: 2-part movie adaptation 3.00
1-($2.50, 52 pgs.)-Complete story 4.00

DISNEY'S THE LITTLE MERMAID (Movie)
Marvel Comics: Sept, 1994 - No. 12, 1995 ($1.50)
1-12 3.00

A Distant Soil #13 © Colleen Doran

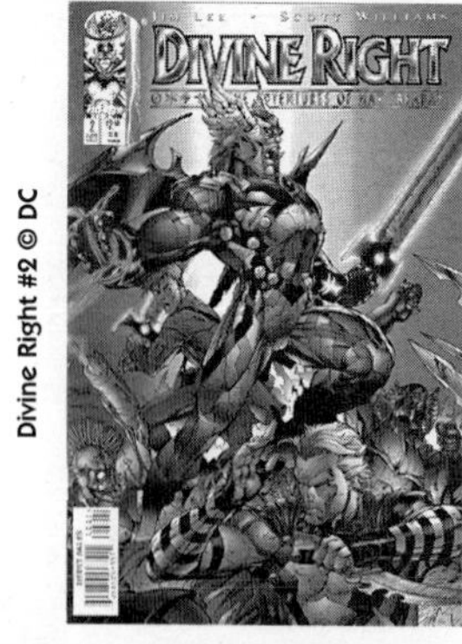

Divine Right #2 © DC

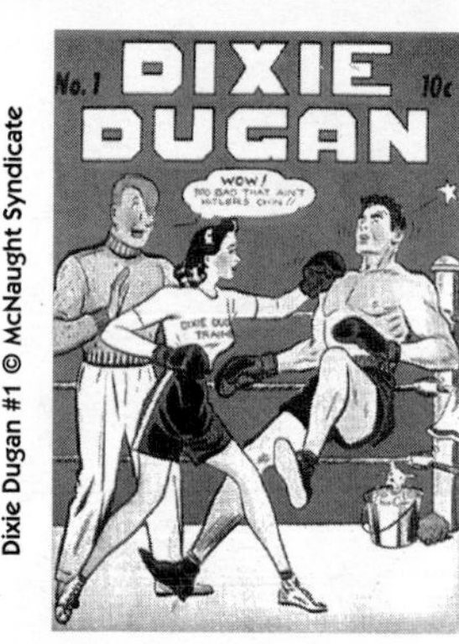

Dixie Dugan #1 © McNaught Syndicate

GD25 FN65 NM94

DISNEY'S THE LITTLE MERMAID LIMITED SERIES (Movie)
Disney Comics: Feb, 1992 - No. 4, May, 1992 ($1.50, limited series)
1-4: Peter David scripts 3.00

DISNEY'S THE LITTLE MERMAID: UNDERWATER ENGAGEMENTS
Acclaim Books: 1997 ($4.50, digest size)
1-Flip book 4.50

DISNEY'S THE HUNCHBACK OF NOTRE DAME (Movie)(See Disney's Comic Hits #10)
Marvel Comics: July, 1996 ($4.95, squarebound, one-shot)
1-Movie adaptation. .85 2.60 7.00
NOTE: A different edition of this series was sold at Wal-Mart stores with new covers depicting scenes from the 1989 feature film. Inside contents and price were identical.

DISNEY'S THE THREE MUSKETEERS (Movie)
Marvel Comics: Jan, 1994 - No. 2, Feb, 1994 ($1.50, limited series)
1,2-Morrow-c; Spiegle-a; Movie adaptation 2.00

DISNEY'S TOY STORY (Movie)
Marvel Comics: Dec, 1995 ($4.95, one-shot)
nn-Adaptation of film .85 2.60 7.00

DISTANT SOIL, A (1st Series)
WaRP Graphics: Dec, 1983 - No. 9, Mar 1986 ($1.50, B&W)
1-9 3.00
NOTE: Second printings exist of #1, 2, 3 & 6.

DISTANT SOIL, A
Donning (Star Blaze): Mar, 1989 ($12.95, trade paperback)
nn-new material 13.00

DISTANT SOIL, A (2nd Series)
Aria Press/Image Comics (Highbrow Entertainment) #15 on: June, 1991 - Present ($1.75/$2.50/$2.95, B&W)
1-8 2.50
9-12: 9-$2.50-c begins 2.50
13-24: 13-$2.95-c begins. 14-Sketchbook. 15-(8/96)-1st Image issue. 3.00
The Ascendant ('98, $18.95,TPB) r/#13-25 18.95
The Gathering ('97, $18.95,TPB) r/#1-13; intro. Neil Gaiman 18.95
NOTE: Four separate printings exist for #1 and are clearly marked. Second printings exist of #2-4 and are also clearly marked.

DISTANT SOIL, A: IMMIGRANT SONG
Donning (Star Blaze): Aug, 1987 ($6.95, trade paperback)
nn-new material 7.00

DIVER DAN (TV)
Dell Publishing Co.: Feb-Apr, 1962 - No. 2, June-Aug, 1962
Four Color 1254(#1), 2 4.50 13.50 50.00

DIVINE RIGHT
Image Comics (WildStorm Productions): Sept, 1997 - Present ($2.50)
Preview 4.50
1-Jim Lee-s/a(p); cover by Lee 3.00
1-Variant-c by Charest 2.50
1-($3.50)-Voyager Pack w/Stormwatch preview 3.50
1-American Entertainment Ed. 5.50
2 3.00
2-Variant-c of Exotica & Blaze 4.00
3-5-Fairchild & Lynch app. 2.50
3-Chromium-c by Jim Lee 5.00
4-American Entertainment Ed. 3.00
5-Pacific Comicon Ed. 6.00
6 2.50
European Tour Edition 15.00
...Collected Edition #1 ($5.95, trade paperback) r/#1,2 5.95
...Collected Edition #2 ($5.95, trade paperback) r/#3,4 5.95

DIVISION 13 (See Comic's Greatest World)
Dark Horse Comics: Sept, 1994 - Jan, 1995 ($2.50, color)
1-4: Giffen story in all. 1-Art Adams-c 2.50

DIXIE DUGAN (See Big Shot, Columbia Comics & Feature Funnies)
McNaught Syndicate/Columbia/Publication Ent.: July, 1942 - No. 13, 1949 (Strip reprints in all)
1-Joe Palooka x-over by Ham Fisher 25.00 75.00 190.00
2 14.00 42.00 105.00
3 10.00 30.00 75.00
4,5(1945-46)-Bo strip-r 7.15 21.50 50.00
6-13(1/47-49): 6-Paperdoll cut-outs 5.70 17.00 38.00

DIXIE DUGAN
Prize Publications (Headline): V3#1, Nov, 1951 - V4#4, Feb, 1954
V3#1 6.50 19.50 45.00
2-4 5.00 15.00 30.00
V4#1-4(#5-8) 4.00 12.00 24.00

DIZZY DAMES
American Comics Group (B&M Distr. Co.): Sept-Oct, 1952 - No. 6, Jul-Aug, 1953
1-Whitney-c 11.00 32.00 80.00
2 6.50 19.50 45.00
3-6 5.70 17.00 35.00

DIZZY DON COMICS
F. E. Howard Publications/Dizzy Don Ent. Ltd (Canada): 1942 - No. 22, Oct, 1946; No. 3, Apr, 1947 (Most B&W)
1 (B&W) 9.30 28.00 70.00
2 (B&W) 5.70 17.00 35.00
4-21 (B&W) 5.35 16.00 32.00
22-Full color, 52 pgs. 9.30 28.00 70.00
3 (4/47)-Full color, 52 pgs. 8.50 26.00 60.00

DIZZY DUCK (Formerly Barnyard Comics)
Standard Comics: No. 32, Nov, 1950 - No. 39, Mar, 1952
32-Funny animal 7.85 23.50 55.00
33-39 4.25 13.00 28.00

DNAGENTS (The New DNAgents V2/1 on)(Also see Surge)
Eclipse Comics: March, 1983 - No. 24, July, 1985 ($1.50, Baxter paper)
1-10: 1-Origin. 4-Amber app. 9-Spiegle-a 1.50
11-24: 18-Infinity-c. 24-Dave Stevens-c 1.50

DOBERMAN (See Sgt. Bilko's Private...)

DOBIE GILLIS (See The Many Loves of...)

DOC CARTER VD COMICS
Health Publications Institute, Raleigh, N. C. (Giveaway): 1949 (16 pgs. in color) (Paper-c)
nn 18.00 54.00 135.00

DOC CHAOS: THE STRANGE ATTRACTOR
Vortex Comics: Apr, 1990 - #3, 1990 ($3.00, 32 pgs.)
1-3: The Lust For Order 3.00

DOC SAMSON (Also see Incredible Hulk)
Marvel Comics: Jan, 1996 - No. 4, Apr, 1996 ($1.95, limited series)
1-4: 1-Hulk c/app. 2-She-Hulk-c/app. 3-Punisher-c/app. 4-Polaris-c/app. 2.00

DOC SAVAGE
Gold Key: Nov, 1966
1-Adaptation of the Thousand-Headed Man; James Bama c-r/1964 Doc Savage paperback 9.00 27.00 100.00

Doc Savage #19 © Condé Nast

Dr. Fate #8 © DC

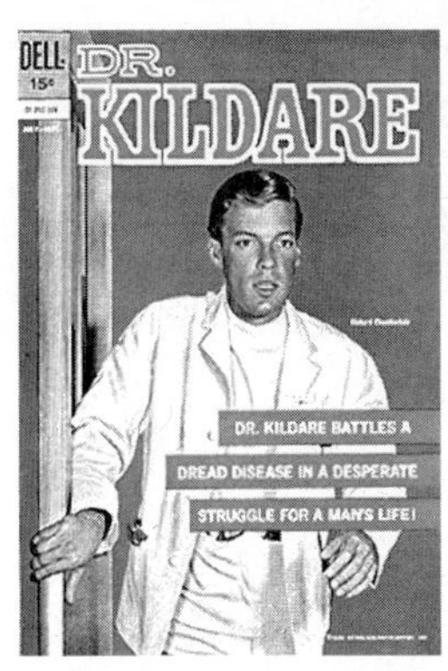

Dr. Kildare #2 © DELL

GD25 FN65 NM94

DOC SAVAGE (Also see Giant-Size...)
Marvel Comics Group: Oct, 1972 - No. 8, Jan, 1974

1 1.20 3.60 12.00
2,3-Steranko-c .90 2.70 8.00
4-8 2.00 6.00

NOTE: ***Gil Kane** c-5, 6. **Mooney** a-1i. No. 1, 2 adapts pulp story "The Man of Bronze"; No. 3, 4 adapts "Death in Silver"; No. 5, 6 adapts "The Monsters"; No. 7, 8 adapts "The Brand of The Werewolf".*

DOC SAVAGE (Magazine)
Marvel Comics Group: Aug, 1975 - No. 8, Spring, 1977 ($1.00, B&W)

1-Cover from movie poster; Ron Ely photo-c .90 2.70 8.00
2-5: 3-Buscema-a. 5-Adams-a(1 pg.), Rogers-a(1 pg) 5.00
6-8 2.00 6.00

DOC SAVAGE
DC Comics: Nov, 1987 - No. 4, Feb, 1988 ($1.75, limited series)

1-4 1.75

DOC SAVAGE
DC Comics: Nov, 1988 - No. 24, Oct, 1990 ($1.75/$2.00: #13-24)

1-24 2.00
Annual 1 (1989, $3.50, 68 pgs.) 3.50

DOC SAVAGE COMICS (Also see Shadow Comics)
Street & Smith Publications: May, 1940 - No. 20, Oct, 1943 (1st app. in Doc Savage pulp, 3/33)

1-Doc Savage, Cap Fury, Danny Garrett, Mark Mallory, The Whisperer, Captain Death, Billy the Kid, Sheriff Pete & Treasure Island begin; Norgil, the Magician app. 400.00 1200.00 4000.00
2-Origin & 1st app. Ajax, the Sun Man; Danny Garrett, The Whisperer end 135.00 405.00 1150.00
3 106.00 318.00 900.00
4-Treasure Island ends; Tuska-a 88.00 264.00 750.00
5-Origin & 1st app. Astron, the Crocodile Queen, not in #9 & 11; Norgi the Magician app. 68.00 204.00 575.00
6-10: 6-Cap Fury ends; origin & only app. Red Falcon in Astron story. 8-Mark Mallory ends; Charlie McCarthy app. on-c plus true life story. 9-Supersnipe app. 10-Origin & only app. The Thunderbolt 56.00 168.00 475.00
11,12 46.00 138.00 395.00
V2#1-8(#13-20): 16-The Pulp Hero, The Avenger app.; Fanny Brice story. 17-Sun Man ends; Nick Carter begins; Duffy's Tavern part photo-c & story. 18-Huckleberry Finn part-c/story. 19-Henny Youngman part photo-c & life story. 20-Only all funny-c w/Huckleberry Finn 46.00 138.00 395.00

DOC SAVAGE: CURSE OF THE FIRE GOD
Dark Horse Comics: Sept, 1995 - No, 4, Dec, 1995 ($2.95, limited series)

1-4 3.00

DOC SAVAGE: THE MAN OF BRONZE
Millennium Publications: 1991 - No. 4, 1991 ($2.50, limited series)

1-4: 1-Bronze logo 2.50
...: The Manual of Bronze 1 ($2.50, B&W, color, one-shot)-Unpublished proposed Doc Savage strip in color, B&W strip-r 2.50

DOC SAVAGE: THE MAN OF BRONZE, DOOM DYNASTY
Millennium Publ.: 1992 (Says 1991) - No. 2, 1992 ($2.50, limited series)

1,2 2.50

DOC SAVAGE: THE MAN OF BRONZE - REPEL
Innovation Publishing: 1992 ($2.50)

1-Dave Dorman painted-c 2.50

DOC SAVAGE: THE MAN OF BRONZE THE DEVIL'S THOUGHTS
Millennium Publ.: 1992 (Says 1991) - No. 3, 1992 ($2.50, limited series)

1-3 2.50

DOC STEARN...MR. MONSTER (See Mr. Monster)

GD25 FN65 NM94

DR. ANTHONY KING, HOLLYWOOD LOVE DOCTOR
Minoan Publishing Corp./Harvey Publications No. 4: 1952(Jan) - No. 3, May, 1953; No. 4, May, 1954

1 11.00 32.00 80.00
2-4: 4-Powell-a 6.70 20.00 45.00

DR. ANTHONY'S LOVE CLINIC (See Mr. Anthony's...)

DR. BOBBS
Dell Publishing Co.: No. 212, Jan, 1949

Four Color 212 3.80 11.50 40.00

DOCTOR BOOGIE
Media Arts Publishing: 1987 ($1.75)

1-Airbrush waparound-c; Nick Cuti-i 1.80

DOCTOR CHAOS
Triumphant Comics: Nov, 1993 - No. 6, Mar, 1994 ($2.50)

1-6: 1,2-Triumphant Unleashed x-over. 2-1st app. War Dancer in pin-up. 3-Intro The Cry 2.50

DOCTOR CYBORG
Attention! Publishing: 1996 - No. 5 ($2.95, B&W)

1-5 3.00
The Clone Conspiracy TPB (1998, $14.95) r/#1-5 14.95

DR. DOOM'S REVENGE
Marvel Comics: 1989 (Came w/computer game from Paragon Software)

V1#1-Spider-Man & Captain America fight Dr. Doom 3.00

DR. FATE (See 1st Issue Special, The Immortal..., Justice League, More Fun #55, & Showcase)

DOCTOR FATE
DC Comics: July, 1987 - No. 4, Oct, 1987 ($1.50, limited series, Baxter paper)

1-4: Giffen-c/a in all 2.00

DOCTOR FATE
DC Comics: Winter, 1988-`89 - No. 41, June, 1992 ($1.25/$1.50 #5 on)

1-31: 15-Justice League app. 25-1st new Dr. Fate 1.50
32-41: 32-Begin $1.75-c. 36-Original Dr. returns 1.75
Annual 1(1989, $2.95, 68 pgs.)-Sutton-a 3.00

DR. FU MANCHU (See The Mask of...)
I.W. Enterprises: 1964

1-r/Avon's "Mask of Dr. Fu Manchu"; Wood-a 7.00 21.00 70.00

DR. GIGGLES (See Dark Horse Presents #64-66)
Dark Horse Comics: Oct, 1992 - No. 2, Oct, 1992 ($2.50, limited series)

1,2-Based on movie 2.50

DOCTOR GRAVES (Formerly The Many Ghosts of...)
Charlton Comics: No. 73, Sept, 1985 - No. 75, Jan, 1986

73-75 2.00

DR. JEKYLL AND MR. HYDE (See A Star Presentation & Supernatural Thrillers #4)

DR. KILDARE (TV)
Dell Publishing Co.: No. 1337, 4-6/62 - No. 9, 4-6/65 (All Richard Chamberlain photo-c)

Four Color 1337(#1, 1962) 8.00 25.00 90.00
2-9 5.50 16.50 60.00

DR. MASTERS (See The Adventures of Young...)

DOCTOR SOLAR, MAN OF THE ATOM (Also see The Occult Files of Dr. Spektor #14 & Solar)
Gold Key/Whitman No. 28 on: 10/62 - No. 27, 4/69; No. 28, 4/81 - No. 31, 3/82 (1-27 have painted-c)

1-(#10000-210)-Origin/1st app. Dr. Solar (1st original Gold Key character) 18.00 55.00 200.00

Doctor Solar, Man of the Atom #1 © GK

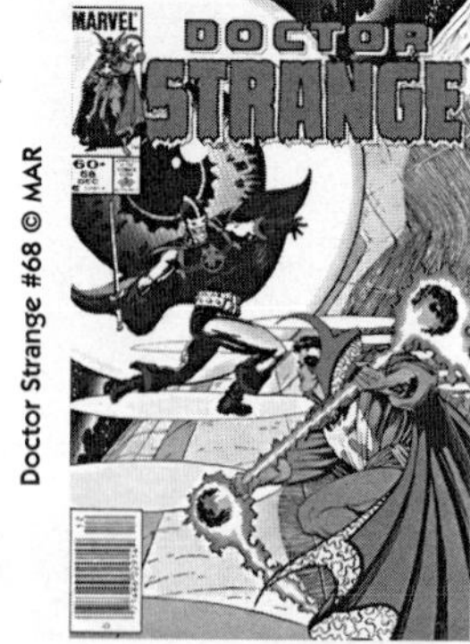

Doctor Strange #68 © MAR

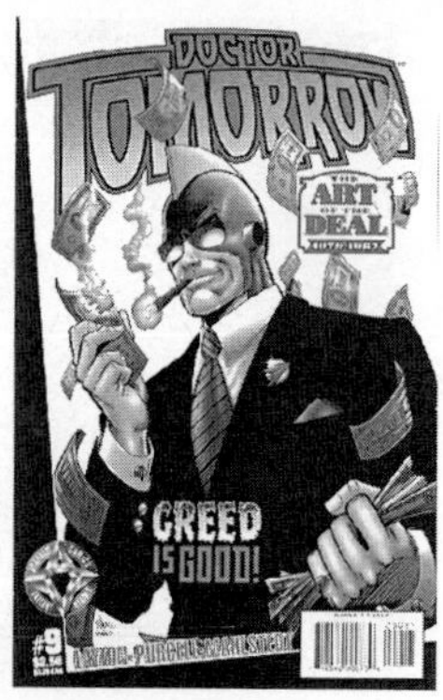

Doctor Tomorrow #9 © Acclaim

	GD25	FN65	NM94
2-Prof. Harbinger begins	7.00	20.00	75.00
3,4	4.50	13.50	50.00
5-Intro. Man of the Atom in costume	5.00	15.00	55.00
6-10	2.75	8.00	30.00
11-14,16-20	2.20	6.50	24.00
15-Origin retold	2.50	7.60	28.00
21-27	1.80	5.40	18.00
28-31: 29-Magnus Robot Fighter begins. 31-The Sentinel app.	.90	2.70	8.00

NOTE: ***Frank Bolle*** *a-6-19, 29-31; c-29i, 30i.* ***Bob Fugitani*** *a-1-5.* ***Spiegle*** *a-29-31.* ***Al McWilliams*** *a-20-23.*

DOCTOR SOLAR, MAN OF THE ATOM
Valiant Comics: 1990 - No. 2, 1991 ($7.95, card stock-c, high quality, 96 pgs.)

1,2: Reprints Gold Key series	.90	2.70	8.00

DOCTOR SPEKTOR (See The Occult Files of..., & Spine-Tingling Tales)

DOCTOR STRANGE (Formerly Strange Tales #1-168) (Also see The Defenders, Giant-Size..., Marvel Fanfare, Marvel Graphic Novel, Marvel Premiere, Marvel Treasury Edition & Strange Tales, 2nd Series)
Marvel Comics Group: No. 169, 6/68 - No. 183, 11/69; 6/74 - No. 81, 2/87

169(#1)-Origin retold; panel swipe/M.D. #1-c	11.00	33.00	110.00
170-176	3.00	9.00	30.00
177-New costume	3.00	9.00	30.00
178-183: 178-Black Knight app. 179-Spider-Man story-r. 180-Photo montage-c. 181-Brunner-c(part-i)	2.50	7.50	25.00
1(6/74, 2nd series)-Brunner-c/a	2.90	8.70	32.00
2	1.50	4.50	15.00
3-5	.85	2.60	7.00
6-10			4.00
11-20: 14-Dracula app.			3.00
21-26: 21-Origin-r/Doctor Strange #169			2.50
27-77,79-81: 31-Sub-Mariner-c/story. 56-Origin retold. 58-Re-intro Hannibal King (cameo). 59-Hannibal King full app. 59-62-Dracula app. (Darkhold storyline). 61,62-Doctor Strange, Blade, Hannibal King & Frank Drake team-up to battle Dracula. 62-Death of Dracula & Lilith			2.00
78-New costume			2.50
Annual 1(1976, 52 pgs.)-New Russell-a (35 pgs.)			4.00
.../Silver Dagger Special Edition 1 (3/83, $2.50)-r/#1,2,4,5; Wrightson-c			2.50
...What Is It That Disturbs You, Stephen? #1 (10/97, $5.99, 48 pgs.) Russell-a/Andreyko & Russell-s, retelling of Annual #1 story		2.00	6.00

NOTE: ***Adkins*** *a-169, 170, 171i; c-169-171, 172i, 173.* ***Adams*** *a-4i.* ***Austin*** *a(i)-48-60, 66, 68, 70, 73; c(i)-38, 47-53, 55, 58-60, 70.* ***Brunner*** *a-1-5p; c-1-6, 22, 28-30, 33.* ***Colan*** *a(p)-172-178, 180-183, 6-18, 36-45, 47; c(p)-172, 174-183, 11-21, 23, 27, 35, 36, 47.* ***Ditko*** *a-179r, 3r.* ***Everett*** *c-183i.* ***Golden*** *a-46p, 55p; c-42-44, 46, 55p.* ***G. Kane*** *c(p)-8-10.* ***Miller*** *c-46p.* ***Nebres*** *a-20, 22, 23, 24i, 26i, 32i; c-32i, 34.* ***Rogers*** *a-48-53p; c-47p-53p.* ***Russell*** *a-34i, 46i, Annual 1.* ***B. Smith*** *c-179.* ***Paul Smith*** *a-54p, 56p, 65, 66p, 68p, 69, 71-73; c-56, 65, 66, 68, 71.* ***Starlin*** *a-23p, 26; c-25, 26.* ***Sutton*** *a-27-29p, 31i, 33, 34p. Painted c-62, 63.*

DOCTOR STRANGE CLASSICS
Marvel Comics Group: Mar, 1984 - No. 4, June, 1984 ($1.50, Baxter paper)

1-4: Ditko-r; Byrne-c. 4-New Golden pin-up 2.00

NOTE: ***Byrne*** *c-1i, 2-4.*

DOCTOR STRANGEFATE (See Marvel Versus DC #3 & DC Versus Marvel #4)
DC Comics (Amalgam): Apr, 1996 ($1.95)

1-Ron Marz script w/Jose Garcia-Lopez-(p) & Kevin Nowlan-(i). Access & Charles Xavier app. .80 2.00

DOCTOR STRANGE MASTER OF THE MYSTIC ARTS (See Fireside Book Series)

DOCTOR STRANGE, SORCERER SUPREME
Marvel Comics (Midnight Sons imprint #60 on): Nov, 1988 - No. 90, June, 1996 ($1.25/$1.50/$1.75/$1.95, direct sales only, Mando paper)

1 ($1.25)	2.00
2-9,12-14,16-27,29,30 ($1.50): 3-New Defenders app. 5-Guice-96c/a begins. 14-18-Morbius story line. 26-Werewolf by Night app.	1.50
10-Re-intro Morbius w/new costume (11/89)	2.00
11-Hobgoblin app.	2.50
15-Unauthorized Amy Grant photo-c	2.00
28-Ghost Rider story cont'd from G.R. #12; same book published at same time as Doctor Strange/Ghost Rider Special #1 (4/91)	2.00
31-36-Infinity Gauntlet x-overs: 31-Silver Surfer app. 33-Thanos-c & cameo. 36-Warlock app.	2.00
37-49,51-64: 37-Silver Surfer app. 38-Begin $1.75-c. 40-Daredevil x-over. 41-Wolverine-c/story. 42-47-Infinity War x-overs. 47-Gamora app. 52,53-Morbius-c/stories. 60,61-Siege of Darkness pt. 7 & 15. 60-Spot varnish-c. 61-New Doctor Strange begins (cameo, 1st app.). 62-Dr. Doom & Morbius app.	1.75
50-($2.95, 52 pgs.)-Holo-grafx foil-c; Hulk, Ghost Rider & Silver Surfer app.; leads into new Secret Defenders series	3.00
65-74, 76-90: 65-Begin $1.95-c; bound-in card sheet. 72-Silver ink-c. 80-82-Ellis story. 84-DeMatteis story begins. 87-Death of Baron Mordo.	2.00
75 ($2.50)	2.50
75 ($3.50)-Foil-c	3.50
Annual 2 ('92, $2.25, 68 pgs.)-Return of Defenders	2.25
Annual 3 ('93, $2.95, 68 pgs.)-Polybagged w/card	3.00
Annual 4 ('94, $2.95)	3.00
Ashcan (1995, 75¢)	0.75
.../Ghost Rider Special 1 (4/91, $1.50)-Same book as D.S.S.S. #28	2.00
...Vs. Dracula 1 (3/94, $1.75, 52 pgs.)-r/Tomb of Dracula #44 & Dr. Strange #14	1.75

NOTE: ***Colan*** *c/a-19.* ***Golden*** *c-28.* ***Guice*** *a-5-16, 18, 20-24; c-5-12, 20-24. See 1st series for Annual #1.*

DR. TOM BRENT, YOUNG INTERN
Charlton Publications: Feb, 1963 - No. 5, Oct, 1963

1	1.50	4.50	12.00
2-5	.90	2.70	8.00

DR. TOMORROW
Acclaim Comics (Valiant): Sept, 1997 - No. 12 ($2.50)

1-12: 1-Mignola-c 2.50

DR. VOLTZ (See Mighty Midget Comics)

DR. WEIRD
Big Bang Comics: 1994 ($2.95, B&W)

1,2: 1-Frank Brunner-c 4.00

DR. WEIRD SPECIAL
Big Bang Comics: Feb, 1994 ($3.95, B&W, 68 pgs.)

1-Origin-r by Starlin; Starlin-c. 4.00

DOCTOR WHO (Also see Marvel Premiere #57-60)
Marvel Comics Group: Oct, 1984 - No. 23, Aug, 1986 ($1.50, color, direct sales, Baxter paper)

1-23-British-r. 3.00

DR. WHO & THE DALEKS (See Movie Classics)

DR. WONDER
Old Town Publishing: June, 1996 - Present ($2.95, B&W)

1-5: 1-Intro & origin of Dr. Wonder; Dick Ayers-c/a; Irwin Hasen-a; contains profiles of the artists 3.00

DOCTOR ZERO
Marvel Comics (Epic Comics): Apr, 1988 - No. 8, Aug, 1989 ($1.25/$1.50)

1-8: 1-Sienkiewicz-c. 6,7-Spiegle-a 1.50

NOTE: ***Sienkiewicz*** *a-3i, 4i; c-1.* ***Spiegle*** *a-6, 7.*

DO-DO (Funny Animal Circus Stories)
Nation-Wide Publishers: 1950 - No. 7, 1951 (5¢, 5x7-1/4" Miniature)

1 (52 pgs.)	19.00	56.00	140.00
2-7	9.30	28.00	70.00

DODO & THE FROG, THE (Formerly Funny Stuff; also see It's Game Time #2)

Do-Do #1 © Nation-Wide Publ.

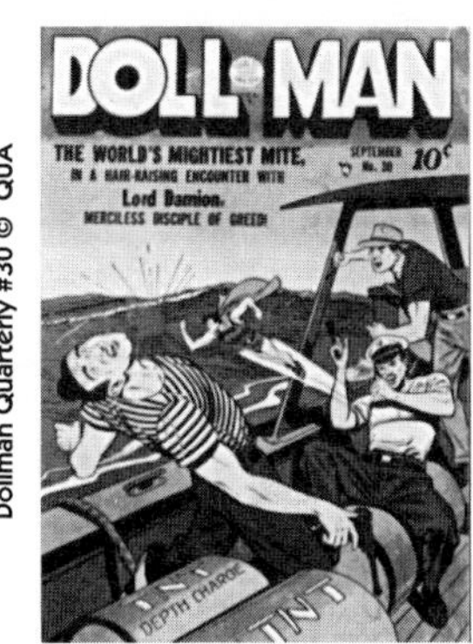

Dollman Quarterly #30 © QUA

Dominion #6 © ECL

National Periodical Publications: No. 80, 9-10/54 - No. 88, 1-2/56; No. 89, 8-9/56; No. 90, 10-11/56; No. 91, 9/57; No. 92, 11/57 (See Comic Cavalcade)

80-1st app. Doodles Duck by Sheldon Mayer 19.00 56.00 140.00
81-91: Doodles Duck by Mayer in #81,83-90 12.00 36.00 90.00
92-(Scarce)-Doodles Duck by S. Mayer 16.00 48.00 120.00

DOGFACE DOOLEY
Magazine Enterprises: 1951 - No. 5, 1953

1(A-1 40) 5.70 17.00 35.00
2(A-1 43), 3(A-1 49), 4(A-1 53), 5(A-1 64) 4.25 13.00 26.00
I.W. Reprint #1('64), Super Reprint #17 2.40 6.00 12.00

DOG MOON
DC Comics (Vertigo): 1996 ($6.95, one-shot)

1-Robert Hunter-scripts; Tim Truman-c/a. .85 2.60 7.00

DOG OF FLANDERS, A
Dell Publishing Co.: No. 1088, Mar, 1960

Four Color 1088-Movie, photo-c 3.60 11.00 40.00

DOGPATCH (See Al Capp's... & Mammy Yokum)

DOGS OF WAR (Also see Warriors of Plasm)
Defiant: Apr, 1994 - No. 5, Aug, 1994 ($2.50)

1-5 2.50

DOGS-O-WAR
Crusade Comics: June, 1996 - No. 3, Jan, 1997 ($2.95, B&W, limited series)

1-3: 1,2-Photo-c 3.00

DOLLFACE & HER GANG (Betty Betz'...)
Dell Publishing Co.: No. 309, Jan, 1951

Four Color 309 4.50 13.50 50.00

DOLLMAN (Movie)
Eternity Comics: Sept, 1991 - No. 4, Dec, 1991 ($2.50, limited series)

1-4: Adaptation of film 2.50

DOLL MAN QUARTERLY, THE (Doll Man #17 on; also see Feature Comics #27 & Freedom Fighters)
Quality Comics: Fall, 1941 - No. 7, Fall, '43; No. 8, Spr, '46 - No. 47, Oct, 1953

1-Dollman (by Cassone), Justin Wright begin 263.00 790.00 2500.00
2-The Dragon begins; Crandall-a(5) 112.00 336.00 950.00
3,4 79.00 238.00 675.00
5-Crandall-a 62.00 185.00 525.00
6,7(1943) 46.00 138.00 390.00
8(1946)-1st app. Torchy by Bill Ward 124.00 371.00 1050.00
9 46.00 138.00 390.00
10-20 37.00 110.00 275.00
21-30: 28-Vs. The Flame 31.00 92.00 230.00
31-36,38,40: 31-(12/50)-Intro Elmo, the wonder dog (Dollman's faithful dog). 32-34-Jeb Rivers app.; 34 by Crandall(p) 25.00 74.00 185.00
37-Origin & 1st app. Dollgirl; Dollgirl bondage-c 36.00 108.00 270.00
39- "Narcotics...the Death Drug" c-/story 25.00 76.00 190.00
41-47 19.00 56.00 140.00
Super Reprint #11('64, r/#20),15(r/#23),17(r/#28): 15,17-Torchy app.; Andru/Esposito-c 2.80 8.40 28.00

NOTE: ***Ward** Torchy in 8, 9, 11, 12, 14-24, 26, 27; by Fox-#30, 35-47. **Crandall** a-2, 5, 10, 13 & Super #11, 17, 18. **Crandall/Cuidera** c-40-42. **Guardineer** a-3. Bondage c-27, 37, 38, 39.*

DOLLS
Sirius: June, 1996 ($2.95, B&W, one-shot)

1 3.00

DOLLY
Ziff-Davis Publ. Co.: No. 10, July-Aug, 1951 (Funny animal)

10-Painted-c 5.35 16.00 32.00

DOLLY DILL
Marvel Comics/Newsstand Publ.: 1945

1 13.00 38.00 95.00

DOMINION (Manga)
Eclipse Comics: Dec, 1990 - No. 6., July, 1990 ($2.00, B&W, limited series)

1-6 2.00

DOMINION: CONFLICT 1 (Manga)
Dark Horse Comics: Mar, 1996 - Present ($2.95, B&W, limited series)

1-5: Shirow-c/a/scripts 3.00

DOMINIQUE: KILLZONE
Caliber Comics: May, 1995 ($2.95, B&W)

1 3.00

DOMINO (See X-Force)
Marvel Comics: Jan, 1997 - No. 3, Mar, 1997 ($1.95, limited series)

1-3: 2-Deathstrike-c/app. 2.00

DOMINO CHANCE
Chance Enterprises: May-June, 1982 - No. 9, May, 1985 (B&W)

1 3.00
1-Reprint, May, 1985 2.50
2-6,9 1.00
7-1st app. Gizmo, 2 pgs. 2.00
8-1st full Gizmo story 3.00

DONALD AND MICKEY IN DISNEYLAND (See Dell Giants)

DONALD AND MICKEY MERRY CHRISTMAS (Formerly Famous Gang Book Of Comics)
K. K. Publ./Firestone Tire & Rubber Co.: 1943 - 1949 (Giveaway, 20 pgs.)
Put out each Christmas; 1943 issue titled "Firestone Presents Comics" (Disney)

1943-Donald Duck-r/WDC&S #32 by Carl Barks 59.00 177.00 650.00
1944-Donald Duck-r/WDC&S #35 by Barks 59.00 177.00 650.00
1945- "Donald Duck's Best Christmas", 8 pgs. Carl Barks; intro. & 1st app. Grandma Duck in comic books 80.00 240.00 875.00
1946-Donald Duck in "Santa's Stormy Visit", 8 pgs. Carl Barks 64.00 192.00 700.00
1947-Donald Duck in "Three Good Little Ducks", 8 pgs. Carl Barks 55.00 165.00 600.00
1948-Donald Duck in "Toyland", 8 pgs. Carl Barks 55.00 165.00 600.00
1949-Donald Duck in "New Toys", 8 pgs. Barks 55.00 165.00 600.00

DONALD AND SCROOGE
Disney Comics: 1992 ($8.95, squarebound, 100 pgs.)

nn-Don Rosa reprint special; r/U.S., D.D. Advs. 1.00 3.00 10.00
1-3 (1992, $1.50)-r/D.D. Advs. (Disney) #1,22,24 & U.S. #261-263,269 2.00

DONALD AND THE WHEEL (Disney)
Dell Publishing Co.: No. 1190, Nov, 1961

Four Color 1190-Movie, Barks-c 6.40 19.00 70.00

DONALD DUCK (See Adventures of Mickey Mouse, Cheerios, Donald & Mickey, Ducktales, Dynabrite Comics, Gladstone Comic Album, Mickey & Donald, Mickey Mouse Mag., Story Hour Series, Uncle Scrooge, Walt Disney's Comics & Stories, W. D.'s Donald Duck, Wheaties & Whitman Comic Books, Wise Little Hen, The)

DONALD DUCK
Whitman Publishing Co./Grosset & Dunlap/K.K.: 1935, 1936 (All pages on heavy linen-like finish cover stock in color;1st book ever devoted to Donald Duck; see Advs. of Mickey Mouse for 1st app.) (9-1/2x13")

978(1935)-16 pgs.; Illustrated text story book 265.00 800.00 2000.00
nn(1936)-36 pgs.plus hard cover & dust jacket. Story completely rewritten with B&W illos added. Mickey appears and his nephews are named Morty & Monty
Book only 265.00 800.00 2000.00
Dust jacket only.... 71.00 214.00 500.00

DONALD DUCK (Walt Disney's) (10¢)

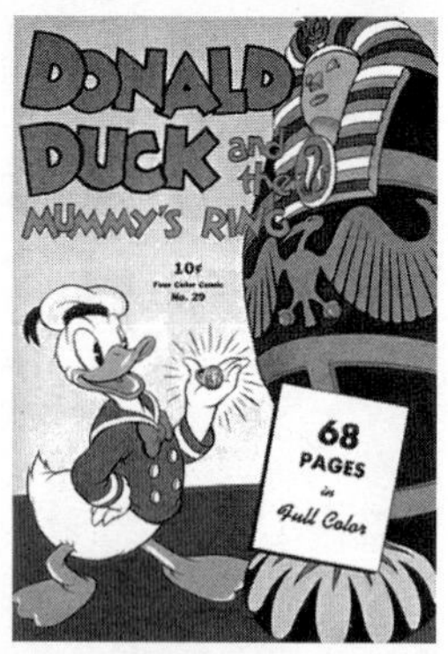

Donald Duck Four Color #29 © WDC

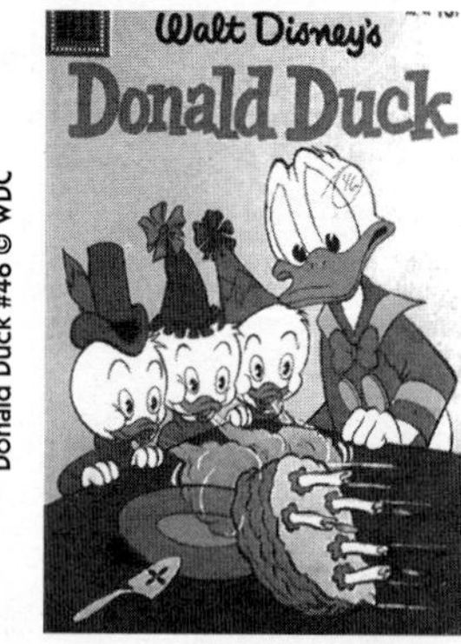

Donald Duck #46 © WDC

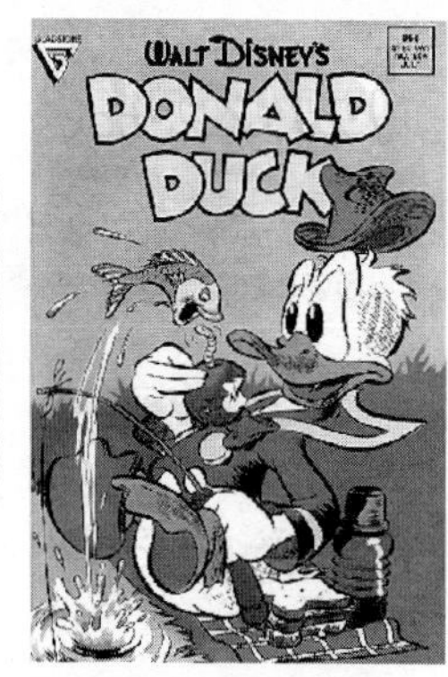

Donald Duck #264 © WDC

Whitman/K.K. Publications: 1938 (8-1/2x11-1/2", B&W, cardboard-c)
(Has D. Duck with bubble pipe on-c)

GD25 FN65 VF82 NM94

nn-The first Donald Duck & Walt Disney comic book; 1936 & 1937 Sunday strip-r(in B&W); same format as the Feature Books; 1st strips with Huey, Dewey & Louie from 10/17/37 250.00 750.00 1500.00 2250.00

DONALD DUCK (Walt Disney's...#262 on; see 4-Color listings for titles & Four Color No. 1109 for origin story)
Dell Publ. Co./Gold Key #85-216/Whitman #217-245/Gladstone #246 on:
1940 - No. 84, Sept-Nov, 1962; No. 85, Dec, 1962 - No. 245, 1984; No. 246, Oct, 1986 - No. 279, May, 1990; No. 280, Sept, 1993 - Present

GD25 FN65 VF82 NM94

Four Color 4(1940)-Daily 1939 strip-r by Al Taliaferro
808.00 2423.00 5656.00 10,500.00
Large Feature Comic 16(1/41?)-1940 Sunday strips-r in B&W
323.00 970.00 2260.00 4200.00
Large Feature Comic 20('41)-Comic Paint Book, r-single panels from Large Feature #16 at top of each pg. to color; daily strip-r across bottom of each pg. 400.00 1200.00 2800.00 5200.00
Four Color 9('42)- "Finds Pirate Gold"; 64 pgs. by Carl Barks & Jack Hannah (pgs. 1,2,5,12-40 are by Barks, his 1st Donald Duck comic book art work; © 8/17/42) 615.00 1845.00 4300.00 8000.00
Four Color 29(9/43)- "Mummy's Ring" by Barks; reprinted in Uncle Scrooge & Donald Duck #1('65), W. D. Comics Digest #44('73) & Donald Duck Advs. #14 492.00 1476.00 3444.00 6400.00

GD25 FN65 NM94

Four Color 62(1/45)- "Frozen Gold"; 52 pgs. by Barks, reprinted in The Best of W.D. Comics & Donald Duck Advs. #4 154.00 462.00 2000.00
Four Color 108(1946)- "Terror of the River"; 52 pgs. by Carl Barks; reprinted in Gladstone Comic Album #2 112.00 335.00 1450.00
Four Color 147(5/47)-in "Volcano Valley" by Barks 77.00 231.00 1000.00
Four Color 159(8/47)-in "The Ghost of the Grotto";52 pgs. by Carl Barks; reprinted in Best of Uncle Scrooge & Donald Duck #1 ('66) & The Best of W.D. Comics & D.D. Advs. #9; two Barks stories
62.00 185.00 800.00
Four Color 178(12/47)-1st app. Uncle Scrooge by Carl Barks; reprinted in Gold Key Christmas Parade #3 & The Best of Walt Disney Comics
92.00 277.00 1200.00
Four Color 189(6/48)-by Carl Barks; reprinted in Best of Donald Duck & Uncle Scrooge #1('64) & D.D. Advs. #19 58.00 173.00 750.00
Four Color 199(10/48)-by Carl Barks; mentioned in Love and Death; r/in Gladstone Comic Album #5 64.00 190.00 825.00
Four Color 203(12/48)-by Barks; reprinted as Gold Key Christmas Parade #4
43.00 129.00 560.00
Four Color 223(4/49)-by Barks; reprinted as Best of Donald Duck #1 & Donald Duck Advs. #3 62.00 185.00 800.00
Four Color 238(8/49)-in "Voodoo Hoodoo" by Barks 43.00 129.00 560.00
Four Color 256(12/49)-by Barks; reprinted in Best of Donald Duck & Uncle Scrooge #2('67), Gladstone Comic Album #16 & W.D. Comics Digest 44('73)
33.00 99.00 425.00
Four Color 263(2/50)-Two Barks stories; r-in D.D. #278
31.00 92.00 400.00
Four Color 275(5/50), 282(7/50), 291(9/50), 300(11/50)-All by Carl Barks; 275, 282 reprinted in W.D. Comics Digest #44('73). #275 r/in Gladstone Comic Album #10. #291 r/in D. Duck Advs. #16 29.00 87.00 375.00
Four Color 308(1/51), 318(3/51)-by Barks; #318-reprinted in W.D. Comics Digest #34 & D.D. Advs. #2,19 25.00 75.00 325.00
Four Color 328(5/51)-by Carl Barks 27.00 81.00 350.00
Four Color 339(7-8/51), 379-2nd Uncle Scrooge-c; art not by Barks.
6.00 18.00 60.00
Four Color 348(9-10/51), 356,394-Barks-c only 15.00 45.00 160.00
Four Color 367(1-2/52)-by Barks; reprinted as Gold Key Christmas Parade #2 & #8 25.00 75.00 320.00
Four Color 408(7-8/52), 422(9-10/52)-All by Carl Barks. #408-r-in Best of Donald Duck & Uncle Scrooge #1('64) & Gladstone Comic Album #13
25.00 75.00 320.00
26(11-12/52)-In "Trick or Treat" (Barks-a, 36pgs.) 1st story r-in Walt Disney Digest #16 & Gladstone C.A. #23 25.00 76.00 330.00
27-30-Barks-c only 10.00 30.00 110.00
31-44,47-50 4.50 13.50 50.00
45-Barks-a (6 pgs.) 11.00 34.00 125.00
46- "Secret of Hondorica" by Barks, 24 pgs.; reprinted in Donald Duck #98 & 154 18.00 55.00 200.00
51-Barks-a,1/2 pg. 4.50 13.50 50.00
52- "Lost Peg-Leg Mine" by Barks, 10 pgs. 12.00 35.00 130.00
53,55-59 3.60 11.00 40.00
54- "Forbidden Valley" by Barks, 26 pgs. (10¢ & 15¢ versions exist)
12.00 37.00 135.00
60- "Donald Duck & the Titanic Ants" by Barks, 20 pgs. plus 6 more pgs.
12.00 37.00 135.00
61-67,69,70 3.00 9.00 32.00
68-Barks-a, 5 pgs. 9.00 29.00 105.00
71-Barks-r, 1/2 pg. 3.00 9.00 32.00
72-78,80,82-97,99,100: 96-Donald Duck Album 3.00 9.00 32.00
79,81-Barks-a, 1pg. 3.00 9.00 32.00
98-Reprints #46 (Barks) 3.00 9.00 32.00
101-133: 102-Super Goof. 112-1st Moby Duck 1.80 5.50 20.00
134-Barks-r/#52 & WDC&S 194 1.80 5.50 20.00
135-Barks-r/WDC&S 198, 19 pgs. 1.80 5.50 20.00
136-153,155,156,158 1.20 3.60 12.00
154-Barks-r(#46) 1.50 4.50 15.00
157,159,160,164: 157-Barks-r(#45). 159-Reprints/WDC&S #192 (10 pgs.). 160-Barks-r(#26). 164-Barks-r(#79) 1.20 3.60 12.00
161-163,165-173,175-187,189-191: 187-Barks r/#68.
.90 2.70 8.00
174,188: 174-r/4-Color #394. 1.00 3.00 10.00
192-Barks-r(40 pgs.) from Donald Duck #60 & WDC&S #226,234 (52 pgs.)
1.00 3.00 10.00
193-200,202-207,209-211,213-216 5.00
201,208,212: 201-Barks-r/Christmas Parade #26, 16pgs. 208-Barks-r/#60 (6 pgs.). 212-Barks-r/WDC&S #130 5.00
217-219: 217 has 216 on-c. 219-Barks-r/WDC&S #106,107, 10 pgs. ea.
.85 2.60 7.00
220,221,223,224 1.60 4.80 16.00
222-(8-12/80)-Only distr. in Whitman 3-pack 7.50 22.50 75.00
225-228: 228-Barks-r/F.C. #275. 1.00 3.00 10.00
229-240: 229-Barks-r/F.C. #282. 230-Barks-r/ #52 & WDC&S #194
.85 2.60 7.00
241-245 1.20 3.60 12.00
246-(1st Gladstone issue)-Barks-r/FC #422 1.50 4.50 15.00
247-249,251: 248,249-Barks-r/DD #54 & 26. 251-Barks-r/1945 Firestone
1.00 3.00 10.00
250-($1.50, 68 pgs.)-Barks-r/4-Color #9 1.20 3.60 12.00
252-279: 254-Barks-r/FC #328. 256-Barks-r/FC #147. 257-($1.50, 52 pgs.)-Barks-r/Vacaction Parade #1. 261-Barks-r/FC #300. 275-Kelly-r/FC #92. 278-($1.95, 68 pgs.)-Rosa-a; Barks-r/FC #263. 279-($1.95, 68 pgs.)-Rosa-c; Barks-r/MOC #4 5.00
280, 286: 280 (#1, 2nd Series). 286-Rosa-a. 5.00
281,282,284 4.00
283,285,287-294: 283-Don Rosa-a, part-c & scripts 2.00
286 ($2.95, 68 pgs.)-Happy Birthday, Donald 3.00
295-301: 295-Begin $1.50-c 2.00
302-304: 302-Begin $1.95-c 2.00
Mini-Comic #1(1976)-(3-1/4x6-1/2"); r/D.D. #150 6.00

NOTE: ***Carl Barks** wrote all issues he illustrated, but #117, 126, 138 contain his script only. Issues 4-Color #189, 199, 203, 223, 238, 256, 263, 275, 282, 308, 348, 356, 367, 394, 408, 422, 26-30, 35, 44, 46, 52, 55, 57, 60, 65, 70-73, 77-80, 83, 101, 103, 105, 106, 111, 126, 246r, 266r, 268r, 271r, 275r, 278r(F.C. 263) all have **Barks** covers. **Barks** r-263-267, 269-278-282, 284, 285. #96 titled "Comic Album", #99-"Christmas Album". New art issues (not reprints)-106-46, 148-63, 167, 169, 170, 172, 173, 175, 178, 179, 196, 209, 223, 225, 236. **Taliaferro** daily news-*

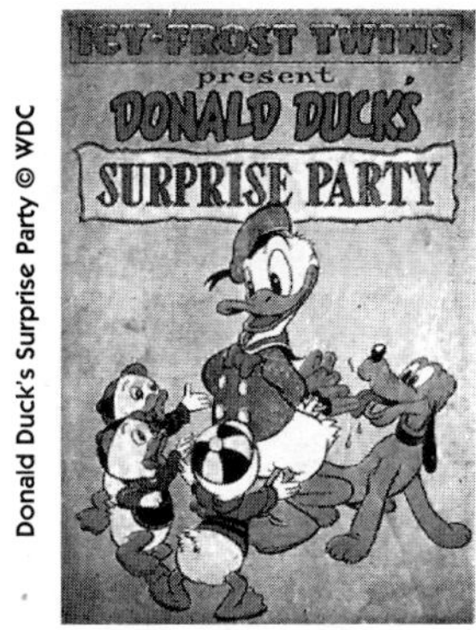

Donald Duck's Surprise Party © WDC

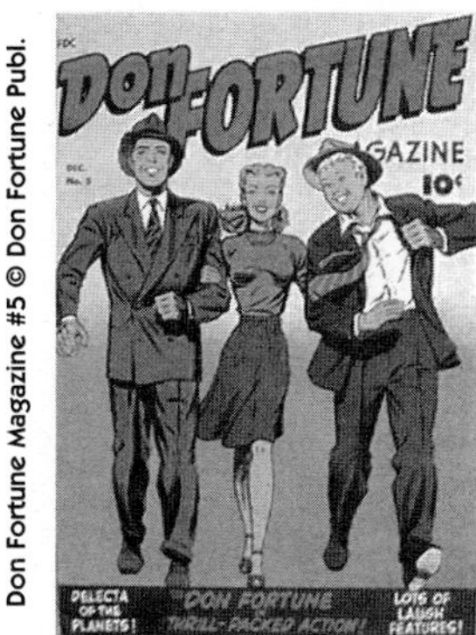

Don Fortune Magazine #5 © Don Fortune Publ.

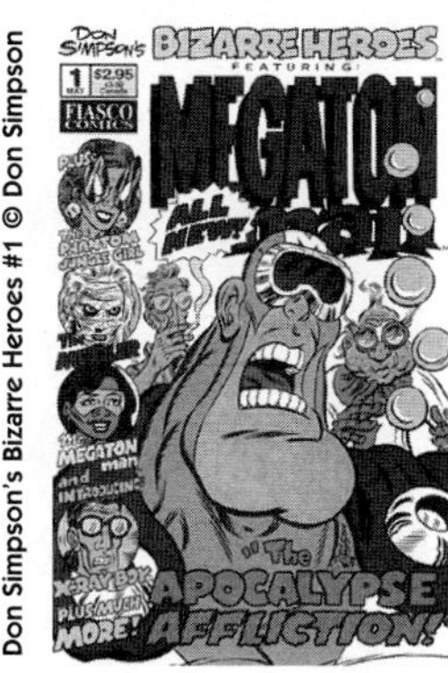

Don Simpson's Bizarre Heroes #1 © Don Simpson

GD25 FN65 NM94

paper strips #258-260, 264, 284, 285; Sunday strips #247, 280-283.

DONALD DUCK
K. K. Publications: 1944 (Christmas giveaway, paper-c, 16 pgs.)(2 versions)
nn-Kelly cover reprint 65.00 195.00 650.00

DONALD DUCK ALBUM (See Comic Album No. 1,3 & Duck Album)
Dell Publishing Co./Gold Key: 5-7/59 - F.C. No. 1239, 10-12/61; 1962; 8/63 - No. 2, Oct, 1963
Four Color 995 (#1) 5.00 15.00 55.00
Four Color 1182, 01204-207 (1962-Dell) 3.60 11.00 40.00
Four Color 1099,1140,1239-Barks-c 5.50 16.50 60.00
1(8/63-Gold Key)-Barks-c 5.00 15.00 55.00
2(10/63) 3.60 11.00 40.00

DONALD DUCK AND THE BOYS (Also see Story Hour Series)
Whitman Publishing Co.: 1948 (5-1/4x5-1/2", 100pgs., hard-c; art & text)
845-(49) new illos by Barks based on his Donald Duck 10-pager in WDC&S #74, Expanded text not written by Barks; Cover not by Barks 48.00 143.00 475.00
(Prices vary widely on this book)

DONALD DUCK AND THE CHRISTMAS CAROL
Whitman Publishing Co.: 1960 (A Little Golden Book, 6-3/8"x7-5/8", 28 pgs.)
nn-Story book pencilled by Carl Barks with the intended title "Uncle Scrooge's Christmas Carol." Finished art adapted by Norman McGary. (Rare)-Reprinted in Uncle Scrooge in Color. 100.00

DONALD DUCK AND THE RED FEATHER
Red Feather Giveaway: 1948 (8-1/2x11", 4 pgs., B&W)
nn 14.00 42.00 105.00

DONALD DUCK BEACH PARTY (Also see Dell Giants)
Gold Key: Sept, 1965 (12¢)
1(#10158-509)-Barks-r/WDC&S #45; painted-c 5.50 16.50 60.00

DONALD DUCK BOOK (See Story Hour Series)

DONALD DUCK COMICS DIGEST
Gladstone Publishing: Nov, 1986 - No. 5, July, 1987 ($1.25/$1.50, 96 pgs.)
1,3: 1-Barks-c/a-r .85 2.60 7.00
2,4,5: 4,5-$1.50-c 4.00

DONALD DUCK FUN BOOK (See Dell Giants)

DONALD DUCK IN DISNEYLAND (See Dell Giants)

DONALD DUCK IN "THE LITTERBUG"
Keep America Beautiful: 1963 (5x7-1/4", 16 pgs., soft-c) (Disney giveaway)
nn 3.20 9.60 32.00

DONALD DUCK MARCH OF COMICS (See March of Comics #4,20,41,56,69,263)

DONALD DUCK MERRY CHRISTMAS (See Dell Giant No. 53)

DONALD DUCK PICNIC PARTY (See Picnic Party listed under Dell Giants)

DONALD DUCK "PLOTTING PICNICKERS" (Also see Ludwig Von Drake & Mickey Mouse)
Fritos Giveaway: 1962 (3-1/4x7", soft-c, 16 pgs.) (Disney)
nn 4.50 13.50 45.00

DONALD DUCK'S SURPRISE PARTY
Walt Disney Productions: 1948 (16 pgs.) (Giveaway for Icy Frost Twins Ice Cream Bars)
nn-(Rare)-Kelly-c/a 314.00 943.00 2200.00

DONALD DUCK TELLS ABOUT KITES (See Kite Fun Book)

DONALD DUCK, THIS IS YOUR LIFE (Disney, TV)
Dell Publishing Co.: No. 1109, Aug-Oct, 1960
Four Color 1109-Gyro flashback to WDC&S #141; origin Donald Duck (1st told) 14.00 41.00 150.00

GD25 FN65 NM94

DONALD DUCK XMAS ALBUM (See regular Donald Duck No. 99)

DONALD IN MATHMAGIC LAND (Disney)
Dell Publishing Co.: No. 1051, Oct-Dec, 1959 - No. 1198, May-July, 1961
Four Color 1051 (#1)-Movie 8.00 25.00 90.00
Four Color 1198-Reprint of above 5.50 16.50 60.00

DONATELLO, TEENAGE MUTANT NINJA TURTLE
Mirage Studios: Aug, 1986 ($1.50, B&W, one-shot, 44 pgs.)
1 1.20 3.00

DONDI
Dell Publishing Co.: No. 1176, Mar-May, 1961 - No. 1276, Dec, 1961
Four Color 1176 (#1)-Movie; origin, photo-c 3.60 11.00 40.00
Four Color 1276 1.80 5.50 20.00

DON FORTUNE MAGAZINE
Don Fortune Publishing Co.: Aug, 1946 - No. 6, Feb, 1947
1-Delecta of the Planets by C. C. Beck in all 19.00 56.00 140.00
2 11.00 32.00 80.00
3-6: 3-Bondage-c 9.30 28.00 65.00

DONKEY KONG (See Blip #1)

DONNA MATRIX
Reactor, Inc.: Aug, 1993 ($2.95, 52 pgs.)
1-Computer generated-c/a by Mike Saenz; 3-D effects 3.00

DONNA MIA
Dark Fantasy Productions: Oct, 1995 -No. 2, Sept, 1996 ($3.95/$4.95, limited series, mature)
1,2-($4.95): 1-Kaluta-c-red foil; fold-out centerfold. 2-Kaluta blue foil-c; nudity 5.00
1,2-($3.95): Kaluta-c on both. 2-Nudity 4.00

DONNA MIA
Avatar Press: Jan, 1997 - Present ($3.00/$3.95, B&W, mature)
1, 0(10/97)-($3.00) 3.00
1-($5.00)-Nude Edition 5.00
2,3-($3.95) 4.00
2-($4.95)-Foil Edition 5.00

DONNA MIA GIANT SIZE
Avatar Press: May, 1997 - Present ($3.95, B&W, limited series, mature)
1,2 3.95

DON NEWCOMBE
Fawcett Publications: 1950 (Baseball)
nn-Photo-c 39.00 116.00 290.00

DON SIMPSON'S BIZARRE HEROES (Also see Megaton Man)
Fiasco Comics: May, 1990 - Present ($2.50/$2.95, B&W)
1-10 2.50
0,11-17: 0-Begin $2.95-c; r/Bizarre Heroes #1. 17-(9/96)-Indicia also reads Megaton Man #0; intro Megaton Man and the Fiascoverse to new readers 3.00

DON'T GIVE UP THE SHIP
Dell Publishing Co.: No. 1049, Aug, 1959
Four Color 1049-Movie, Jerry Lewis photo-c 6.40 19.00 70.00

DON WINSLOW OF THE NAVY
Merwil Publishing Co.: Apr, 1937 - No. 2, May, 1937 (96 pgs.)(A pulp/comic book cross; stapled spine)
GD25 FN65 VF82
V1#1-Has 16 pgs. comics in color. Captain Colorful & Jupiter Jones by Sheldon Mayer; complete Don Winslow novel 567.00 1700.00 3700.00
2-Sheldon Mayer-a 112.00 336.00 950.00

DON WINSLOW OF THE NAVY (See Crackajack Funnies, Famous Feature Stories, Popular Comics & Super Book #5,6)

Doom 2099 #21 © MAR

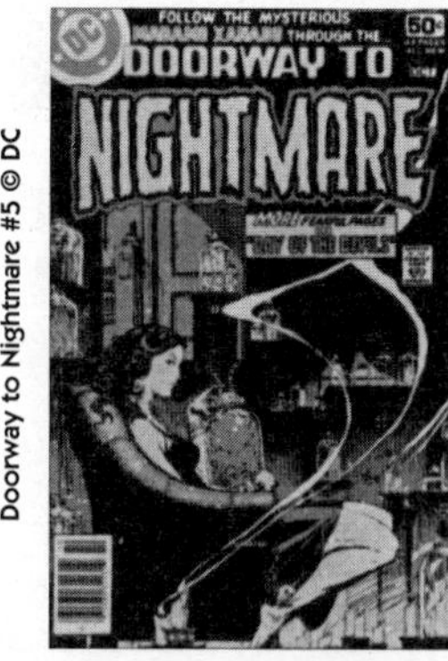

Doorway to Nightmare #5 © DC

Dorothy Lamour #2 © FOX

Dell Publishing Co.: No. 2, Nov, 1939 - No. 22, 1941

Four Color 2 (#1)-Rare 118.00 354.00 1300.00
Four Color 22 28.00 85.00 310.00

DON WINSLOW OF THE NAVY (See TV Teens; Movie, Radio, TV) (Fightin' Navy No. 74 on)
Fawcett Publications/Charlton No. 70 on: 2/43 - #64, 12/48; #65, 1/51 - #69, 9/51; #70, 3/55 - #73, 9/55

	GD25	FN65	NM94
1-(68 pgs.)-Captain Marvel on cover	94.00	282.00	800.00
2	46.00	138.00	390.00
3	37.00	111.00	280.00
4-6: 6-Flag-c	28.00	84.00	210.00
7-10: 8-Last 68 pg. issue?	20.00	60.00	150.00
11-20	16.00	48.00	120.00
21-40	10.00	30.00	75.00
41-64: 51,60-Singapore Sal (villain) app. 64-(12/48)	9.30	28.00	65.00
65(1/51)-Flying Saucer attack; photo-c	11.00	32.00	80.00
66 - 69(9/51): All photo-c. 66-sci-fi story	11.00	32.00	80.00
70(3/55)-73: 70-73 r-/#26,58 & 59	7.85	23.50	55.00

DOOM FORCE SPECIAL
DC Comics: July, 1992 ($2.95, 68 pgs., one-shot, mature) (X-Force parody)

1-Grant Morrison scripts; Simonson, Steacy, & others-a; Giffen/Mignola-c. 3.00

DOOM PATROL, THE (Formerly My Greatest Adventure No. 1-85; see Brave and the Bold, DC Special Blue Ribbon Digest 19, Official... Index & Showcase No. 94-96)
National Periodical Publications: No. 86, 3/64 - No. 121, 9-10/68; No. 122, 2/73 - No. 124, 6-7/73

86-1 pg. origin (#86-121 are 12¢ issues) 9.00 27.00 90.00
87-99: 88-Origin The Chief. 91-Intro. Mento. 99-Intro. Beast Boy (later becomes the Changeling in New Teen Titans 6.50 19.50 65.00
100-Origin Beast Boy; Robot-Maniac series begins (12/65) 7.00 21.00 70.00
101-110: 102-Challengers of the Unknown app. 105-Robot-Maniac series ends. 106-Negative Man begins (origin) 3.00 9.00 30.00
111-120 2.50 7.50 20.00
121-Death of Doom Patrol; Orlando-c. 6.50 19.50 65.00
122-124: All reprints 1.00 3.00 8.00

DOOM PATROL
DC Comics (Vertigo imprint #64 on): Oct, 1987 - No, 87, Feb, 1995 (75¢/$1.00/$1.50/$1.75/$1.95, new format)

1-75¢-c begins. 2.00
2-18: 3-1st app. Lodestone. 4-1st app. Karma. 8,15,16-Art Adams-c(i). 10-$1.00-c begins. 18-Invasion tie-in. 1.00
19-(2/89)-Grant Morrison scripts begin, ends #63; 1st app Crazy Jane; $1.50-c & new format begins. 4.00
20-25 2.50
26-30: 29-Superman app. 30-Night Breed fold-out 3.00
31-40: 35-1st app. of Flex Mentallo (cameo). 36-1st full app. of Flex Mentallo. 39-World Without End preview. 2.00
41-49,51-56,58-60: 42-Origin of Flex Mentallo 2.00
50,57 ($2.50, 52 pgs.) 2.50
61-65: 61-$1.75-c begins; photo-c. 63-(1/93). 2.00
66-87: 66-$1.95-c begins. 70-Photo-c. 73-Death cameo (2 panels) 2.00
...And Suicide Squad 1 (3/88, $1.50, 52 pgs.)-Wraparound-c 1.60
Annual 1 (1988, $1.50, 52 pgs.) 1.60
Annual 2 (1994, $3.95, 68 pgs.)-Children's Crusade tie-in. 4.00
NOTE: ***Simon Bisley*** *painted c-26-48, 55-58.* ***Bolland*** *c-64, 75.* ***Dringenberg*** *a-42(p).* ***Steacy*** *a-53.*

DOOM PATROL (See Tangent Comics/ Doom Patrol)

DOOMSDAY
DC Comics: 1995 ($3.95, one-shot)

1-Year One story by Jurgens, L. Simonson, Ordway, and Gil Kane; Darkseid, Superman app. 4.00

DOOMSDAY + 1 (Also see Charlton Bullseye)
Charlton Comics: July, 1975 - No. 6, June, 1976; No. 7, June, 1978 - No. 12, May, 1979

1: #1-5 are 25¢ issues 1.20 3.60 12.00
2-6: 4-Intro Lor. 5-Ditko-a(1 pg.) 6-Begin 30¢ issues .85 2.60 7.00
V3#7-12 (reprints #1-6) 4.00
5 (Modern Comics reprint, 1977) 3.00
NOTE: ***Byrne*** *c/a-1-12; Painted covers-2-7.*

DOOMSDAY SQUAD, THE
Fantagraphics Books: Aug, 1986 - No. 7, 1987 ($2.00)

1-7: Byrne-a in all. 1-3-New Byrne-c. 3-Usagi Yojimbo app. (1st in color).4-N Adams-c. 5-7-Gil Kane-c 2.00

DOOM'S IV
Image Comics (Extreme): July, 1994 - No.4, Oct, 1994 ($2.50, limited series)

1-4-Liefeld story 2.50
1,2-Two alternate Liefeld-c each, 4 covers form 1 picture 5.00

DOOM 2099 (See Marvel Comics Presents #118 & 2099: World of Tomorrow)
Marvel Comics: Jan, 1993 - No. 44, Aug, 1996 ($1.25/$1.50/$1.95)

1-($1.75)-Metallic foil stamped-c 2.00
1-2nd printing 1.75
2-16: 14-Ron Lim-c(p) 1.25
17-24, 26-28: 17-Begin $1.50-c; bound-in trading card sheet 1.50
25 ($2.25, 52 pgs.) 3.25
25 ($2.95, 52pgs.) Foil embossed cover 3.00
29-44: 29-Begin $2.95-c. 40-Namor & Doctor Strange app. 41-Daredevil app., Namor-c/app. 44-Intro The Emissary; story contin'd in 2099: World of Tomorrow. 2.00
29 ($3.50)-acetate-c. 3.50

DOORWAY TO NIGHTMARE (See Cancelled Comic Cavalcade)
DC Comics: Jan-Feb, 1978 - No. 5, Sept-Oct, 1978

1-5-Madame Xanadu in all. 4-Craig-a 5.00
NOTE: ***Kaluta*** *covers on all. Merged into The Unexpected with No. 190.*

DOPEY DUCK COMICS (Wacky Duck No. 3) (See Super Funnies)
Timely Comics (NPP): Fall, 1945 - No. 2, Apr, 1946

1,2-Casper Cat, Krazy Krow 17.00 50.00 125.00

DORK
Slave Labor: June, 1993 - Present ($2.50/$2.75/$2.95, B&W, mature)

1,2: Evan Dorkin-c/a/scripts in all. 2.75
3,4-$2.75-c 2.75
5-$2.95-c 2.95
1,2-(2nd printing, $2.75): 1-(8/95). 2-(1/96)-Reads 2nd Print on bottom inside-c 1.10 2.75

DOROTHY LAMOUR (Formerly Jungle Lil)(Stage, screen, radio)
Fox Features Syndicate: No. 2, June, 1950 - No. 3, Aug, 1950

2,3-Wood-a(3) each, photo-c 23.00 68.00 170.00

DOT AND DASH AND THE LUCKY JINGLE PIGGIE
Sears Roebuck Co.: 1942 (Christmas giveaway, 12 pgs.)

nn-Contains a war stamp album and a punch out Jingle Piggie bank 5.70 17.00 40.00

DOT DOTLAND (Formerly Little Dot Dotland)
Harvey Publications: No. 62, Sept, 1974 - No. 63, Nov, 1974

62,63 4.00

DOTTY (...& Her Boy Friends)(Formerly Four Teeners; Glamorous Romances No. 41 on)
Ace Magazines (A. A. Wyn): No. 35, June, 1948 - No. 40, May, 1949

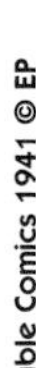

Double Comics 1941 © EP

Double Dragon #4 © Technos Japan Corp.

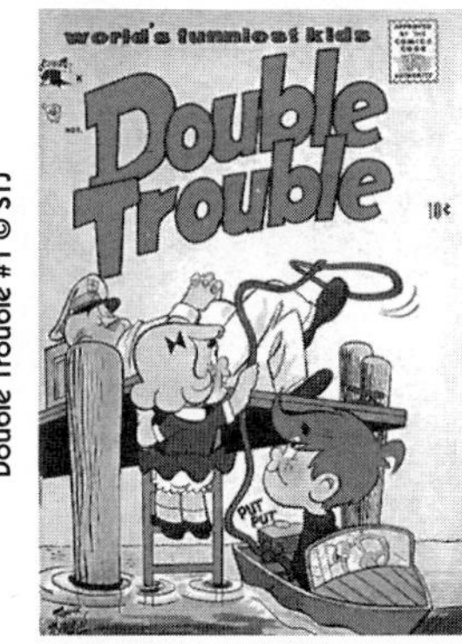

Double Trouble #1 © STJ

	GD25	FN65	NM94
35-Teen-age	5.70	17.00	35.00
36,38-40	3.60	9.00	18.00
37-Transvestism story	4.00	10.00	20.00

DOTTY DRIPPLE (Horace & Dotty Dripple No. 25 on)
Magazine Ent.(Life's Romances)/Harvey No. 3 on: 1946 - No. 24, June, 1952
(Also see A-1 No. 3-8, 10)

	GD25	FN65	NM94
A-1 #1 (1pg. D. Dripple; Mr. Ex, Bush Berry, Rocky, Lew Loyal (20 pgs.)	9.30	28.00	70.00
1 (nd) (10¢)	5.70	17.00	40.00
2	4.00	12.00	20.00
3-10: 3,4-Powell-a	2.40	6.00	12.00
11-24	1.60	4.00	8.00

DOTTY DRIPPLE AND TAFFY
Dell Publishing Co.: No. 646, Sept, 1955 - No. 903, May, 1958

	GD25	FN65	NM94
Four Color 646 (#1)	2.75	8.00	30.00
Four Color 691,718,746,801,903	1.80	5.50	20.00

DOUBLE ACTION COMICS
National Periodical Publications: No. 2, Jan, 1940 (68 pgs., B&W)

2-Contains original stories(?); pre-hero DC contents; same cover as Adventure No. 37. (six known copies) (not an ashcan)
Estimated value.... 12,000.00

NOTE: *The cover to this book was probably reprinted from Adventure #37. #1 exists as an ash can copy with B&W cover; contains a coverless comic on inside with 1st & last page missing.*

DOUBLE COMICS
Elliot Publications: 1940 - 1944 (132 pgs.)

	GD25	FN65	NM94
1940 issues; Masked Marvel-c & The Mad Mong vs. The White Flash covers known	188.00	564.00	1600.00
1941 issues; Tornado Tim-c, Nordac-c, & Green Light covers known	135.00	405.00	1150.00
1942 issues	103.00	310.00	875.00
1943,1944 issues	82.00	246.00	700.00

NOTE: *Double Comics consisted of an almost endless combination of pairs of remaindered, unsold issues of comics representing most publishers and usually mixed publishers in the same book; e.g., a Captain America with a Silver Streak, or a Feature with a Detective, etc., could appear inside the same cover. The actual contents would have to determine its price. Prices listed are for average contents. Any containing rare origin or first issues are worth much more. Covers also vary in same year. Value would be approximately 50 percent of contents.*

DOUBLE-CROSS (See The Crusaders)

DOUBLE-DARE ADVENTURES
Harvey Publications: Dec, 1966 - No. 2, Mar, 1967 (35¢/25¢, 68 pgs.)

	GD25	FN65	NM94
1-Origin Bee-Man, Glowing Gladiator, & Magic-Master; Simon/Kirby-a (last S&K art as a team?)	4.50	13.50	45.00
2-Williamson/Crandall-a; r/Alarming Adv. #3('63)	3.50	10.50	35.00

NOTE: ***Powell** a-1. **Simon/Sparling** c-1, 2.*

DOUBLE DRAGON
Marvel Comics: July, 1991 - No. 6, Dec, 1991 ($1.00, limited series)

	GD25	FN65	NM94
1-6: Based on video game. 2-Art Adams-c			1.00

DOUBLE EDGE
Marvel Comics: Alpha, 1995; Omega, 1995 ($4.95, limited series)

	GD25	FN65	NM94
Alpha ($4.95)- Punisher story, Nick Fury app.			5.00
Omega ($4.95)-Punisher, Daredevil, Ghost Rider app. Death of Nick Fury			5.00

DOUBLE IMPACT (Double Impact Blondage #3 & Double Impact Buttshots #6 on cover only)
High Impact Studios: Mar, 1995 - No. 7, 1996 ($3.95/$2.95/$3.00)

	GD25	FN65	NM94
0 (1997, $2.95)			3.00
0 ($9.95)-Nude Edition	1.00	3.00	10.00
1 (Chromium-c.)-Intro Jazz & China.			4.00
1 (Rainbow-c.)	1.20	3.60	12.00
2-7 (Regular-c.): 4-variant-c. w/no logo exists. 5-fold out back-c. 6-3 variant-c exist. 7-Intro Nikki Blade.			3.00
2 ($9.95) Nude-c;.polybagged & signed	1.00	3.00	10.00
2,3 (Nude-c.) (limited to 5000)	1.00	3.00	10.00
3-"Blondage" variant-c		2.00	6.00
3-($14.95) "Blondage Deluxe"; polybagged & signed	1.50	4.50	15.00
4-"Bad Boy Arizona" variant-c		2.00	6.00
7-Gold (1,000 copies); gold foil logo		2.00	6.00
San Diego Special ('95, limited to 5000)	1.00	3.00	10.00
San Diego Special ('96, limited to 1000)		2.00	6.00
San Diego Special Nude Ed. ('96, limited to 1000)	1.50	4.50	15.00

DOUBLE IMPACT
High Impact Studios: V2#1, 1996 - Present ($3.00)

	GD25	FN65	NM94
V2#1-3-Wraparound-c. 3-Three-c			3.00
1-($4.00)-Deluxe Edition; wraparound-foil-c			3.00
1-Wraparound, prism, foil-c			5.00
1-Gold foil logo			3.00
1-($14.95) Swedish Erotica	1.50	4.50	15.00
1-Variant-c			3.00
2-($10.00)-Nude Ed.; suicide-c	1.00	3.00	10.00

DOUBLE IMPACT/HELLINA (See Hellina/Double Impact)
High Impact Studios: Mar, 1996 ($3.00, one-shot)

	GD25	FN65	NM94
1			3.00
1-($9.95) Nude Edition	1.00	3.00	10.00

DOUBLE LIFE OF PRIVATE STRONG, THE
Archie Publications/Radio Comics: June, 1959 - No. 2, Aug, 1959

	GD25	FN65	NM94
1-Origin & re-intro The Shield; Simon & Kirby-c/a, their re-entry into the super-hero genre; intro./1st app. The Fly; 1st S.A. super-hero for Archie Publ.	48.00	144.00	575.00
2-S&K-c/a; Tuska-a; The Fly app. (2nd or 3rd?)	32.00	96.00	320.00

DOUBLE TALK (Also see Two-Faces)
Feature Publications: No date (1962?) (32 pgs., full color, slick-c)
Christian Anti-Communism Crusade (Giveaway)

	GD25	FN65	NM94
nn-Sickle with blood-c	10.00	30.00	75.00

DOUBLE TROUBLE
St. John Publishing Co.: Nov, 1957 - No. 2, Jan-Feb, 1958

	GD25	FN65	NM94
1,2: Tuffy & Snuffy by Frank Johnson; dubbed "World's Funniest Kids"	4.25	13.00	28.00

DOUBLE TROUBLE WITH GOOBER
Dell Publishing Co.: No. 417, Aug, 1952 - No. 556, May, 1954

	GD25	FN65	NM94
Four Color 417	2.25	6.75	25.00
Four Color 471,516,556	1.85	5.50	15.00

DOUBLE UP
Elliott Publications: 1941 (Pocket size, 200 pgs.)

	GD25	FN65	NM94
1-Contains rebound copies of digest sized issues of Pocket Comics, Speed Comics, & Spitfire Comics	69.00	208.00	590.00

DOVER & CLOVER (See All Funny & More Fun Comics #93)

DOVER BOYS (See Adventures of the...)

DOVER THE BIRD
Famous Funnies Publishing Co.: Spring, 1955

	GD25	FN65	NM94
1-Funny animal; code approved	5.00	15.00	30.00

DOWN WITH CRIME
Fawcett Publications: Nov, 1952 - No. 7, Nov, 1953

	GD25	FN65	NM94
1	25.00	76.00	190.00
2,4,5: 2,4-Powell-a in each. 5-Bondage-c	13.00	38.00	95.00
3-Used in **POP**, pg. 106; "H is for Heroin" drug story	13.00	40.00	100.00
6,7: 6-Used in **POP**, pg. 80	10.00	30.00	75.00

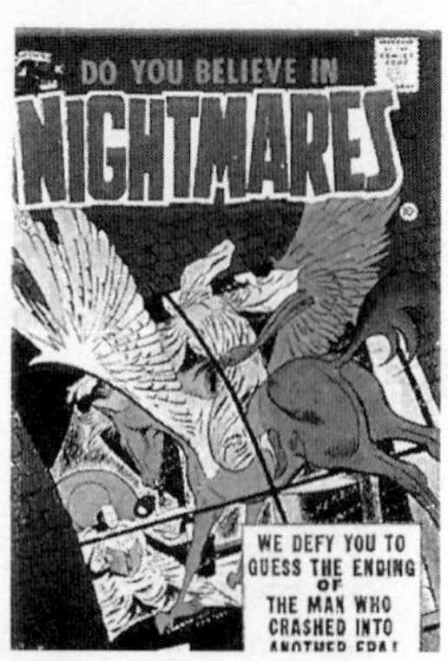

Do You Believe in Nightmares #1 © STJ

Dracula: Lord Of The Undead #1 © MAR

The Dragon: Blood & Guts #3 © Erik Larsen

	GD25	FN65	NM94

DO YOU BELIEVE IN NIGHTMARES?
St. John Publishing Co.: Nov, 1957 - No. 2, Jan, 1958

1-Mostly Ditko-c/a	40.00	120.00	340.00
2-Ayers-a	22.00	66.00	165.00

D.P. 7
Marvel Comics Group (New Universe): Nov, 1986 - No. 32, June, 1989 (26 on: $1.50)

1-20			1.25
21-32			2.00
Annual #1 (11/87)-Intro. The Witness			1.25

NOTE: ***Williamson*** *a-9i, 11i; c-9i.*

DRACULA (See Bram Stoker's Dracula, Giant-Size..., Little Dracula, Marvel Graphic Novel, Requiem for Dracula, Spider-Man Vs...., Tomb of... & Wedding of...; also see Movie Classics under Universal Presents as well as Dracula)

DRACULA (See Movie Classics for #1)(Also see Frankenstein & Werewolf)
Dell Publ. Co.: No. 2, 11/66 - No. 4, 3/67; No. 6, 7/72 - No. 8, 7/73 (No #5)

2-Origin & 1st app. Dracula (11/66) (super hero)	2.40	7.00	26.00
3,4: 4-Intro. Fleeta ('67)	2.00	6.00	16.00
6-('72)-r/#2 w/origin	1.75	5.25	14.00
7,8-r/#3, #4	1.25	3.75	10.00

DRACULA (Magazine)
Warren Publishing Co.: 1979 (120 pgs., full color)

Book 1-Maroto art; Spanish material translated into English	3.80	11.50	40.00

DRACULA CHRONICLES
Topps Comics: Apr, 1995 - No. 3, June, 1995 ($2.50, limited series)

1-3-Linsner-c			2.50

DRACULA LIVES! (Magazine)(Also see Tomb of Dracula)
Marvel Comics Group: 1973(no month) - No. 13, July, 1975 (75¢, B&W) (76 pgs.)

1-Boris painted-c	3.20	9.50	34.00
2 (7/73)-1st time origin Dracula; Adams, Starlin-a	2.40	7.00	26.00
3-1st app. Robert E. Howard's Soloman Kane; Adams-c/a	2.20	6.50	24.00
4,5: 4-Ploog-a. 5(V2#1)-Bram Stoker's Classic Dracula adapt. begins	1.60	4.80	16.00
6-9: 6-8-Bram Stoker adapt. 9-Bondage-c	1.80	5.40	18.00
10 (1/75)-16 pg. Lilith solo (1st?)	2.20	6.50	24.00
11-13: 11-21 pg. Lilith solo sty. 12-31 pg. Dracula sty	1.80	5.40	18.00
Annual 1(Summer, 1975, $1.25, 92 pgs.)-Morrow painted-c; 6 Dracula stys. 25 pgs. Adams-a(r)	2.00	6.00	20.00

NOTE: ***N. Adams*** *a-2, 3i, 10i, Annual 1r(2, 3i).* ***Alcala*** *a-9.* ***Buscema*** *a-3p, 6p, Annual 1p.* ***Colan*** *a(p)-1, 2, 5, 6, 8.* ***Evans*** *a-7.* ***Gulacy*** *a-9.* ***Heath*** *a-1r, 13.* ***Pakula*** *a-6r. Sutton a-13.* ***Weiss*** *r-Annual 1p. 4* ***Dracula*** *stories each in 1, 609; 3* ***Dracula*** *stories each in 2, 4, 5,, 13.*

DRACULA: LORD OF THE UNDEAD
Marvel Comics: Dec, 1998 - No. 3, Dec, 1998 ($2.99, limited series)

1-3-Olliffe & Palmer-a			3.00

DRACULA: RETURN OF THE IMPALER
Slave Labor Graphics: July, 1993 - No. 4, Oct, 1994 ($2.95, limited series)

1-4			3.00

DRACULA VERSUS ZORRO
Topps Comics: Oct, 1993 - No. 2, Nov, 1993 ($2.95, limited series)

1,2: 1-Spot varnish & red foil-c. 2-Polybagged w/16 pg. Zorro #0			3.00

DRACULA: VLAD THE IMPALER (Also see Bram Stoker's Dracula)
Topps Comics: Feb, 1993 - No. 3, Apr, 1993 ($2.95, limited series)

1-3-Polybagged with 3 trading cards each; Maroto-c/a			3.00

DRAFT, THE
Marvel Comics: 1988 ($3.50, one-shot, squarebound)

1-Sequel to "The Pitt"			3.50

DRAG 'N' WHEELS (Formerly Top Eliminator)
Charlton Comics: No. 30, Sept, 1968 - No. 59, May, 1973

30	3.20	9.60	32.00
31-40-Scot Jackson begins	2.50	7.50	24.00
41-50	2.25	6.75	18.00
51-59: Scot Jackson	1.00	3.00	10.00
Modern Comics Reprint 58('78)			4.00

DRAGON, THE (Also see The Savage Dragon)
Image Comics (Highbrow Ent.): Mar, 1996 - No. 5, July, 1996 (99¢, lim. series)

1-5: Reprints Savage Dragon limited series w/new story & art. 5-Youngblood app; includes 5 pg. Savage Dragon story from 1984			1.00

DRAGON, THE: BLOOD & GUTS (Also see The Savage Dragon)
Image Comics (Highbrow Entertainment): Mar, 1995 - No. 3, May, 1995 ($2.50, limited series)

1-3: Jason Pearson-c/a/scripts			2.50

DRAGON CHIANG
Eclipse Books: 1991 ($3.95, B&W, squarebound, 52 pgs.)

nn -Timothy Truman-c/a(p)			4.00

DRAGONFLIGHT
Eclipse Books: Feb, 1991 - No. 3, 1991 ($4.95, 52 pgs.)

Book One - Three: Adapts 1968 novel			5.00

DRAGONFLY (See Americomics #4)
Americomics: Sum, 1985 - No. 8, 1986 ($1.75/$1.95)

1			3.00
2-8			2.00

DRAGONFORCE
Aircel Publishing: 1988 - No. 13, 1989 ($2.00)

1-Dale Keown-c/a/scripts in #1-12			4.00
2-13: 13-No Keown-a			2.00
...Chronicles Book 1-5 ($2.95, B&W, 60 pgs.): Dale Keown-r/Dragonring & Dragonforce			3.00

DRAGONHEART (Movie)
Topps Comics: May, 1996 - No. 2, June, 1996 ($2.95/$4.95, limited series)

1-($2.95, 24 pgs.)-Adaptation of the film; Hildebrandt Bros-c; Lim-a.			3.00
2-($4.95, 64 pgs.)			5.00

DRAGONLANCE (Also see TSR Worlds)
DC Comics: Dec, 1988 - No. 34, Sept, 1991 ($1.25/$1.50, Mando paper)

1-Based on TSR game			2.00
2			1.50
3-15: 6-Begin $1.50-c			1.50
16-34: 25-Begin $1.75-c. 30-32-Kaluta-c			1.80
Annual 1 (1990, $2.95, 68 pgs.)			3.00

DRAGON LINES
Marvel Comics (Epic Comics/Heavy Hitters): May, 1993 - No. 4, Aug, 1993 ($1.95, limited series)

1-($2.50)-Embossed-c; Ron Lim-c/a in all			2.50
2-4			2.00

DRAGON LINES: WAY OF THE WARRIOR
Marvel Comics (Epic Comics/ Heavy Hitters): Nov, 1993 - No. 2, Jan, 1994 ($2.25, limited series)

1,2-Ron Lim-c/a(p)			2.25

DRAGONQUEST
Silverwolf Comics: Dec, 1986 - No. 2, 1987 ($1.50, B&W, 28 pgs.)

1,2-Tim Vigil-c/a in all			1.50

DRAGONRING

Drakuun #1 © DH

Dreadstar #56 © FC

The Dreaming #24 © DC

GD25 FN65 NM94

Aircel Publishing: 1986 - V2#15, 1988 ($1.70/$2.00, B&W/color)

1 — 2.00
2-6: 6-Last B&W issue — 2.00
V2#1-($2.00, color) — 2.00
2-15 — 1.80

DRAGON'S CLAWS
Marvel UK, Ltd.: July, 1988 - No. 10, Apr, 1989 ($1.25/$1.50/$1.75, British)

1-4: 2-Begin $1.50-c. 3-Death's Head 1 pg. strip on back-c (1st app.). 4-Silhouette of Death's Head on last pg. — 1.50
5-1st full app. new Death's Head; begin $1.75-c — 1.75
6-10 — 1.75

DRAGONSLAYER (Movie)
Marvel Comics Group: October, 1981 - No. 2, Nov, 1981

1,2-Paramount Disney movie adaptation — 1.50

DRAGON'S STAR 2
Caliber Press: 1994 ($2.95, B&W)

1 — 3.00

DRAGON STRIKE
Marvel Comics: Feb, 1994 ($1.25)

1-Based on TSR role playing game — 1.25

DRAGOON WELLS MASSACRE
Dell Publishing Co.: No. 815, June, 1957

Four Color 815-Movie, photo-c — 7.00 — 22.00 — 80.00

DRAGSTRIP HOTRODDERS (World of Wheels No. 17 on)
Charlton Comics: Sum, 1963; No. 2, Jan, 1965 - No. 16, Aug, 1967

1 — 4.00 — 12.00 — 40.00
2-5 — 2.80 — 8.40 — 28.00
6-16 — 2.50 — 7.50 — 22.00

DRAKUUN
Dark Horse Comics: Feb, 1997 - Present ($2.95, B&W, manga)

1-6- Johji Manabe-s/a in all. Rise of the Dragon Princess series — 2.95
7-12-Revenge of Gustav. — 2.95
13-17-Shadow of the Warlock — 2.95

DRAMA
Sirius: June, 1994 ($2.95, mature)

1-1st full color Dawn app. in comics — 2.00 — 6.00 — 20.00
1-Limited edition (1400 copies); signed & numbered; fingerprint authenticity — 4.50 — 13.50 — 50.00

NOTE: *Dawn's 1st full color app. was a pin-up in Amazing Heroes' Swimsuit Special #5.*

DRAMA OF AMERICA, THE
Action Text: 1973 ($1.95, 224 pgs.)

1- "Students' Supplement to History" — 3.00

DREADLANDS (Also see Epic)
Marvel Comics (Epic Comics): 1992 - No. 4, 1992 ($3.95, lim. series, 52 pgs.)

1-4: Stiff-c — 4.00

DREADSTAR
Marvel Comics (Epic Comics)/First Comics No. 27 on: Nov, 1982 - No. 64, Mar, 1991

1-5,8-64: 1-Starlin-a begins — 2.00
6,7-1st app. Interstellar Toybox; 8pgs. ea.; Wrightson-a — 3.00
Annual 1 (12/83)-r/The Price — 3.00

DREADSTAR
Malibu Comics (Bravura): Apr, 1994 - No.6, Jan, 1995 ($2.50, limited series)

1-6-Peter David scripts: 1,2-Starlin-c — 2.50

NOTE: *Issues 1-6 contain Bravura stamps.*

DREADSTAR AND COMPANY
Marvel Comics (Epic Comics): July, 1985 - No. 6, Dec, 1985

1-6: 1,3,6-New Starlin-a: 2-New Wrightson-c; reprints of Dreadstar series. — 1.00

DREAM ANGEL
Angel Entertainment: No. 0, Fall, 1996 - No. 1, Winter, 1997 ($2.95, B&W)

0,1: Deodato Studios-c — 3.00
0,1-($5.95) Deluxe Ed.; foil-c — 6.00
0,1-($10.00) Nude-c — 10.00
0,1-($10.00) Deodato Studios Nude-c — 10.00

DREAM ANGEL: THE QUANTUM DREAMER
Angel Entertainment: No. 0, Winter, 1997 - No. 2, Spring, 1997 ($2.95, B&W)

0-2 — 3.00

DREAM BOOK OF LOVE (Also see A-1 Comics)
Magazine Enterprises: No. 106, June-July, 1954 - No. 123, Oct-Nov, 1954

A-1 106 (#1)-Powell, Bolle-a; Montgomery Clift, Donna Reed photo-c — 9.50 — 28.50 — 72.00
A-1-114 (#2)-Guardineer, Bolle-a; Piper Laurie, Victor Mature photo-c — 8.50 — 26.00 — 60.00
A-1 123 (#3)-Movie photo-c — 7.15 — 21.50 — 50.00

DREAM BOOK OF ROMANCE (Also see A-1 Comics)
Magazine Enterprises: No. 92, 1954 - No. 124, Oct-Nov, 1954

A-1 92 (#5)-Guardineer-a; photo-c — 9.30 — 28.00 — 65.00
A-1 101 (#6)(4-6/54)-Marlon Brando photo-c; Powell, Bolle, Guardineer-a — 16.00 — 48.00 — 120.00
A-1 109 (#7)(7-8/54)-Powell-a; movie photo-c — 7.15 — 21.50 — 50.00
A-1 110 (#8)(1/54)-Movie photo-c — 7.15 — 21.50 — 50.00
A-1 124 (#8)(10-11/54) — 7.15 — 21.50 — 50.00

DREAMERY, THE
Eclipse Comics: Dec, 1986 - No. 14, Feb, 1989 ($2.00, B&W, Baxter paper)

1-14: 2-7-Alice In Wonderland adapt. — 2.00

DREAMING, THE (See Sandman, 2nd Series)
DC Comics (Vertigo): June, 1996 - Present ($2.50)

1-McKean-c on all.; LaBan scripts & Snejbjerg-a — 4.00
2-30: 2,3-LaBan scripts & Snejbjerg-a. 4-7-Hogan scripts; Parkhouse-a. 8-Zulli-a. 9-11-Talbot-s/Taylor-a(p) — 2.50
31-($3.95) Art by various — 3.95
32,33 — 2.50
...Beyond The Shores of Night TPB ('97, $19.95) r/#1-8 — 19.95
...Special (7/98, $5.95, one-shot) Trial of Cain — 5.95

DREAM OF LOVE
I. W. Enterprises: 1958 (Reprints)

1,2,8: 1-r/Dream Book of Love #1; Bob Powell-a. 2-r/Great Lover's Romances #10. 8-Great Lover's Romances #1; also contains 2 Jon Juan stories by Siegel & Schomburg; Kinstler-c. — 1.50 — 4.50 — 12.00
9-Kinstler-c; 1pg. John Wayne interview & Frazetta illo from John Wayne Adv. Comics #2 — 1.25 — 3.75 — 10.00

DREAM TEAM (See Battlezones: Dream Team 2)
Malibu Comics (Ultraverse): July, 1995 ($4.95, one-shot)

1-Pin-ups teaming up Marvel & Ultraverse characters by various artists including Allred, Hamner, Romita, Darrow, Balent, Quesada & Palmiotti. — 5.00

DREAMWALKER
Caliber Comics (Tapestry): Dec, 1996 - Present ($2.95, B&W)

1-5-Jenni Gregory-c/s/a — 2.95

DRIFT FENCE (See Zane Grey 4-Color 270)

DRIFT MARLO
Dell Publishing Co.: May-July, 1962 - No. 2, Oct-Dec, 1962

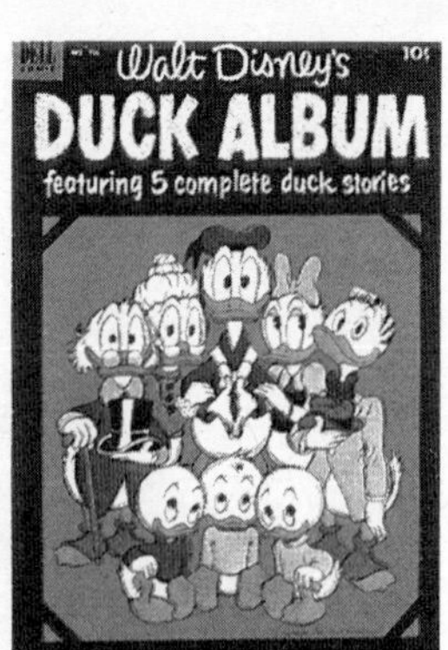

Duck Album Four Color #450 © WDC

Duckman #1 (Topps) © Paramount

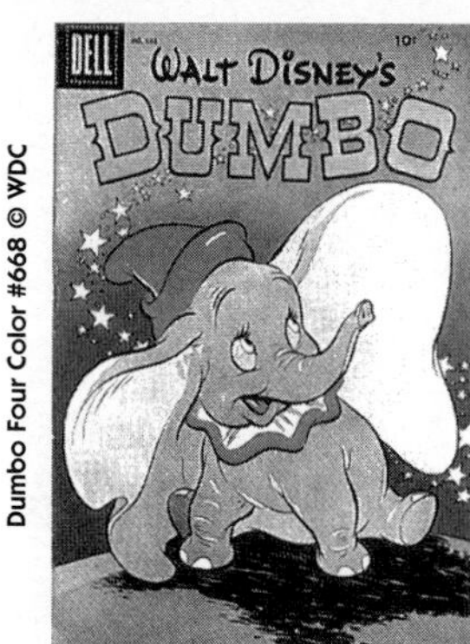

Dumbo Four Color #668 © WDC

GD25 FN65 NM94

01-232-207(#1), 2(12-232-212) 2.90 8.70 32.00

DRISCOLL'S BOOK OF PIRATES
David McKay Publ. (Not reprints): 1934 (B&W, hardcover; 124 pgs, 7x9")
nn-By Montford Amory 19.00 56.00 140.00

DROIDS (Also see Dark Horse Comics)
Marvel Comics (Star Comics): April, 1986 - No. 8, June, 1987
(Based on Saturday morning cartoon)
1-R2D2 & C-3PO from Star Wars app. in all 1.20 3.60 12.00
2,5,7,8 1.10 3.30 11.00
3,4,6 .90 2.70 9.00
NOTE: ***Romita** a-3p. **Williamson** a-2i, 5i, 7i, 8i. **Sinnott** a-3i.*

DROOPY (see Tom & Jerry #60)

DROOPY (Tex Avery's...)
Dark Horse Comics: Oct, 1995 - No. 3, Dec, 1995 ($2.50, limited series)
1-3: Characters created by Tex Avery; painted-c 2.50

DROPSIE AVENUE: THE NEIGHBORHOOD
Kitchen Sink Press: June, 1995 ($15.95/$24.95, B&W)
nn-Will Eisner (softcover) 1.60 4.80 16.00
nn-Will Eisner (hardcover) 2.25 6.80 25.00

DROWNED GIRL, THE
DC Comics (Piranha Press): 1990 ($5.95, 52 pgs, mature)
nn 2.00 6.00

DRUG WARS
Pioneer Comics: 1989 ($1.95)
1-Grell-c 2.00

DRUID
Marvel Comics: May, 1995 - No. 4, Aug, 1995 ($2.50, limited series)
1-4: Warren Ellis scripts. 2.50

DRUM BEAT
Dell Publishing Co.: No. 610, Jan, 1955
Four Color 610-Movie, Alan Ladd photo-c 9.00 27.00 100.00

DRUMS OF DOOM
United Features Syndicate: 1937 (25¢)(Indian)(Text w/color illos.)
nn-By Lt. F.A. Methot; Golden Thunder app.; Tip Top Comics ad in comic; nice-c
29.00 88.00 220.00

DRUNKEN FIST
Jademan Comics: Aug, 1988 - No. 54, Jan, 1993 ($1.50/$1.95, 68 pgs.)
1-8-($1.50) 1.50
9-54-($1.95) 2.00

DUCK ALBUM (See Donald Duck Album)
Dell Publishing Co.: No. 353, Oct, 1951 - No. 840, Sept, 1957
Four Color 353 (#1)-Barks-c; 1st Uncle Scrooge-c (also appears on back-c).
8.25 25.00 90.00
Four Color 450-Barks-c 5.50 16.50 60.00
Four Color 492,531,560,586,611,649,686 4.50 13.50 50.00
Four Color 726,782,840 4.50 13.50 50.00

DUCKMAN
Dark Horse Comics: Sept, 1990 ($1.95, B&W, one-shot)
1-Story & art by Everett Peck 2.00

DUCKMAN
Topps Comics: Nov, 1994 - No. 5, May, 1995; No. 0, Feb, 1996 ($2.50)
0 (2/96, $2.95, B&W)-r/Duckman #1 from Dark Horse Comics 3.00
1-5: 1-w/ coupon #A for Duckman trading card. 2-w/Duckman 1st season episode guide 2.50

DUCKMAN: THE MOB FROG SAGA

GD25 FN65 NM94

Topps Comics: Nov, 1994 - No. 3, Feb, 1995 ($2.50, limited series)
1-3: 1-w/coupon #B for Duckman tradiing card, S. Shaw!-c 1.00 2.50

DUCKTALES
Gladstone Publ.: Oct, 1988 - No. 13, May, 1990 (1,2,9-11: $1.50; 3-8: 95¢)
1-Barks-r 6.00
2-11: Barks-r 4.00
12,13 ($1.95, 68 pgs.)-Barks-r; 12-r/F.C. #495 5.00

DUCKTALES (TV)
Disney Comics: June, 1990 - No. 18, Nov, 1991 ($1.50)
1-All new stories 3.00
2-18 2.00
The Movie nn (1990, $7.95, 68 pgs.)-Graphic novel adapting animated movie
.90 2.70 9.00

DUDLEY (Teen-age)
Feature/Prize Publications: Nov-Dec, 1949 - No. 3, Mar-Apr, 1950
1-By Boody Rogers 13.00 40.00 100.00
2,3 9.30 28.00 65.00

DUDLEY DO-RIGHT (TV)
Charlton Comics: Aug, 1970 - No. 7, Aug, 1971 (Jay Ward)
1 8.00 23.00 85.00
2-7 5.50 16.50 60.00

DUKE OF THE K-9 PATROL
Gold Key: Apr, 1963
1 (10052-304) 2.75 8.00 30.00

DUMBO (Disney; see Movie Comics, & Walt Disney Showcase #12)
Dell Publishing Co.: No. 17, 1941 - No. 668, Jan, 1958
Four Color 17 (#1)-Mickey Mouse, Donald Duck, Pluto app.
164.00 492.00 1800.00
Large Feature Comic 19 ('41)-Part-r 4-Color 17 236.00 708.00 2600.00
Four Color 234 ('49) 9.00 27.00 100.00
Four Color 668 (12/55)-1st of two printings. Dumbo on-c with starry sky. Reprints Four Color 234? same-c as 234 7.00 22.00 80.00
Four Color 668 (1/58)-2nd printing. Same cover altered with Timothy Mouse added. Same contents as above 5.50 16.50 60.00

DUMBO (Walt Disney's..., The Flying Elephant)
Weatherbird Shoes/Ernest Kern Co.(Detroit): 1941 (K.K. Publ. Giveaway)
nn-16 pgs., 9x10" (Rare) 42.00 127.00 340.00
nn-52 pgs., 5-1/2x8-1/2", slick cover in color; B&W interior; half text, half reprints 4-Color No. 17 25.00 74.00 185.00

DUMBO COMIC PAINT BOOK (See Dumbo, Large Feature Comic No. 19)

DUMBO WEEKLY
Walt Disney Prod.: 1942 (Premium supplied by Diamond D-X Gas Stations)
1 47.00 142.00 400.00
2-16 17.00 50.00 125.00
Binder only 325.00
NOTE: *A cover and binder came separate at gas stations. Came with membership card.*

DUNC AND LOO (#1-3 titled "Around the Block with Dunc and Loo")
Dell Publishing Co.: Oct-Dec, 1961 - No. 8, Oct-Dec, 1963
1 8.75 26.50 95.00
2 5.50 16.50 60.00
3-8 4.00 12.00 45.00
NOTE: *Written by **John Stanley; Bill Williams** art.*

DUNE (Movie)
Marvel Comics: Apr, 1985 - No. 3, June, 1985
1-3-r/Marvel Super Special; movie adaptation 1.50

DUNG BOYS, THE
Kitchen Sink Press: 1996 - No. 3, 1996 ($2.95, B&W, limited series)

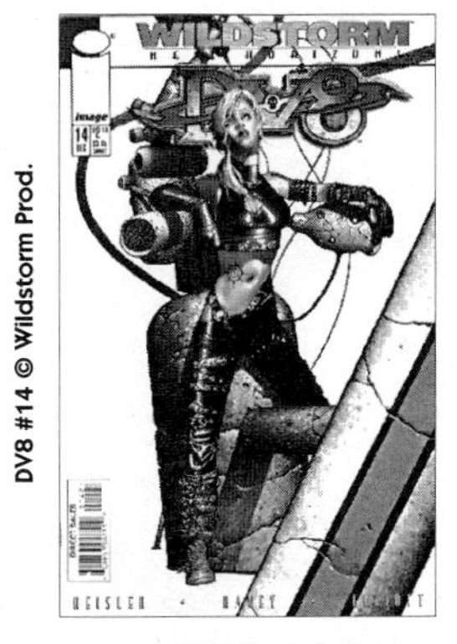

DV8 #14 © Wildstorm Prod.

DELL
15¢
The Life Story of a Great American
DWIGHT D.
EISENHOWER

Dwight D. Eisenhower 01-237-912 © DELL

Dynamic Comics #1 © CHES

GD25 FN65 NM94

1-3 3.00

DURANGO KID, THE (Also see Best of the West, Great Western & White Indian) (Charles Starrett starred in Columbia's Durango Kid movies)
Magazine Enterprises: Oct-Nov, 1949 - No. 41, Oct-Nov, 1955 (All 36 pgs.)

1-Charles Starrett photo-c; Durango Kid & his horse Raider begin; Dan Brand & Tipi (origin) begin by Frazetta & continue through #16 65.00 195.00 550.00
2-Starrett photo-c. 33.00 100.00 250.00
3-5-All have Starrett photo-c. 31.00 94.00 235.00
6-10: 7-Atomic weapon-c/story 17.00 50.00 125.00
11-16-Last Frazetta issue 11.00 34.00 85.00
17-Origin Durango Kid 17.00 50.00 125.00
18-Fred Meagher-a on Dan Brand begins 9.30 28.00 70.00
19-30: 19-Guardineer-c/a(3) begins, end #41. 23-Intro. The Red Scorpion 9.30 28.00 70.00
31-Red Scorpion returns 9.30 28.00 65.00
32-41-Bolle/Frazettaish-a (Dan Brand; true in later issues?) 9.30 28.00 65.00

NOTE: *#6, 8, 14, 15 contain **Frazetta** art not reprinted in White Indian. **Ayers** c-18. **Guardineer** a(3)-19-41; c-19-41. **Fred Meagher** a-18-29 at least.*

DURANGO KID, THE
AC Comics: 1990 - #2, 1990 ($2.50, half-color)

1-Starrett photo front/back-c; Guardineer-r 2.50
2-($2.75, B&W)-Starrett photo-c; White Indian-r by Frazetta; Guardineer-r (50th anniversary of films) 2.75

DUSTCOVERS: THE COLLECTED SANDMAN COVERS 1989-1997
DC Comics (Vertigo): 1997 ($39.95, Hardcover)

Reprints Dave McKean's Sandman covers with Gaiman text 39.95
Softcover (1998, $24.95) 24.95

DUSTY STAR
Image Comics (Desperado Studios): Apr, 1997 - Present ($2.95, B&W)

0,1-Pruett-s/Robinson-a 3.95

DV8 (See Gen 13)
Image Comics (WildStorm Productions): Aug, 1996 - Present ($2.50)

1/2 1.00 3.00 10.00
1-Warren Ellis scripts & Humberto Ramos-c/a(p) 5.00
NOTE: Seven variant-c exist based on the seven deadly sins
1-Jim Lee variant-c 2.00 6.00
1-Each of the six variant-c not by Jim Lee 4.50
2-4: 3-No Ramos-a 4.50
5-24: 14-Regular-c 2.50
14-Variant-c by Charest 2.50
14-($3.50) Voyager Pack w/Danger Girl preview 7.50
Annual 1 (1/98, $2.95) 3.00
Rave-(7/96, $1.75)-Ramos-c; pinups & interviews 4.50

DV8 VS. BLACK OPS
Image Comics (WildStorm): Oct, 1997 - No. 3, Dec, 1997 ($2.50, lim. series)

1-3-Bury-s/Norton-a 2.50

DWIGHT D. EISENHOWER
Dell Publishing Co.: December, 1969

01-237-912 - Life story 2.00 6.00 22.00

DYNABRITE COMICS
Whitman Publishing Co.: 1978 - 1979 (69¢, 10x7-1/8", 48 pgs., cardboard-c) (Blank inside covers)

11350 - Walt Disney's Mickey Mouse & the Beanstalk (4-C 157). 11350-1 - Mickey Mouse Album (4-C 1057,1151,1246). 11351 - Mickey Mouse & His Sky Adventure (4-C 214, 343). 11352 - Donald Duck (4-C 408, Donald Duck 45,52)-Barks-a. 11352-1 - Donald Duck (4-C 318, 10 pg. Barks/WDC&S 125,128)-Barks-c(r). 11353 - Daisy Duck's Diary (4-C 1055,1150) Barks-a. 11354 - Goofy: A Gaggle of Giggles. 11354-1 - Super Goof Meets Super Thief. 11355 - Uncle Scrooge (Barks-a/U.S. 12,33). 11355-1 - Uncle Scrooge (Barks-a/U.S. 13,16) - Barks-c(r). 11356 - (?). 11357 - Star Trek (r/-Star Trek 33,41). 11358 - Star Trek (r/-Star Trek 34,36). 11359 - Bugs Bunny-r. 11360 - Winnie the Pooh Fun and Fantasy (Disney-r). 11361 - Gyro Gearloose & the Disney Ducks (r/4-C 1047,1184)-Barks-c(r)
each.... 3.00

DYNAMIC ADVENTURES
I. W. Enterprises: No. 8, 1964 - No. 9, 1964

8-Kayo Kirby-r by Baker?/Fight Comics 53. 2.25 6.75 18.00
9-Reprints Avon's "Escape From Devil's Island"; Kinstler-c 2.50 7.50 20.00
nn (no date)-Reprints Risks Unlimited with Rip Carson, Senorita Rio; r/Fight #53 2.25 6.75 18.00

DYNAMIC CLASSICS (See Cancelled Comic Cavalcade)
DC Comics: Sept-Oct, 1978 (44 pgs.)

1-Neal Adams Batman, Simonson Manhunter-r 4.00

DYNAMIC COMICS (No #4-7)
Harry 'A' Chesler: Oct, 1941 - No. 3, Feb, 1942; No. 8, Mar, 1944 - No. 25, May, 1948

1-Origin Major Victory by Charles Sultan (reprinted in Major Victory #1), Dynamic Man & Hale the Magician; The Black Cobra only app.; Major Victory & Dynamic Man begin 147.00 441.00 1250.00
2-Origin Dynamic Boy & Lady Satan; intro. The Green Knight & sidekick Lance Cooper 68.00 204.00 575.00
3-1st small logo, resumes with #10 56.00 168.00 475.00
8-Dan Hastings, The Echo, The Master Key, Yankee Boy begin; Yankee Doodle Jones app.; hypo story 56.00 168.00 475.00
9-Mr. E begins; Mac Raboy-c 59.00 177.00 500.00
10-Small logo begins 44.00 132.00 375.00
11-16: 15-The Sky Chief app. 16-Marijuana story 41.00 122.00 325.00
17(1/46)-Illustrated in **SOTI**, "The children told me what the man was going to do with the hot poker," but Wertham saw this in Crime Reporter #2 50.00 150.00 425.00
18,19,21,22,25: 21-Dinosaur-c; new logo 32.00 96.00 240.00
20-Bare-breasted woman-c 44.00 132.00 375.00
23,24-(68 pgs.): 23-Yankee Girl app. 33.00 100.00 250.00
I.W. Reprint #1,8('64): 1-r/#23. 8-Exist? 2.50 7.50 22.00

NOTE: ***Kinstler** c-IW #1. **Tuska** art in many issues, #3, 9, 11, 12, 16, 19. Bondage c-16.*

DYNAMITE (Becomes Johnny Dynamite No. 10 on)
Comic Media/Allen Hardy Publ.: May, 1953 - No. 9, Sept, 1954

1-Pete Morisi-a; Don Heck-c; r-as Danger #6 16.00 48.00 120.00
2 9.30 28.00 65.00
3-Marijuana story; Johnny Dynamite (1st app.) begins by Pete Morisi(c/a); Heck text-a; man shot in face at close range 11.00 32.00 80.00
4-Injury-to-eye, prostitution; Morisi-c/a 12.00 36.00 90.00
5-9-Morisi-c/a in all. 7-Prostitute story plus reprints 8.50 26.00 60.00

DYNAMO (Also see Tales of Thunder & T.H.U.N.D.E.R. Agents)
Tower Comics: Aug, 1966 - No. 4, June, 1967 (25¢)

1-Crandall/Wood, Ditko/Wood-a; Weed series begins; NoMan & Lightning cameos; Wood-c/a 5.25 15.75 52.00
2-4: Wood-c/a in all 3.60 10.80 36.00

NOTE: ***Adkins/Wood** a-2. **Ditko** a-4?. **Tuska** a-2, 3.*

DYNAMO JOE (Also see First Adventures & Mars)
First Comics: May, 1986 - No. 15, Jan, 1988 (#12-15: $1.75)

1-15: 4-Cargonauts begin 1.50
Special 1(1/87)-Mostly-r/Mars 1.50

DYNOMUTT (TV)(See Scooby-Doo (3rd series))
Marvel Comics Group: Nov, 1977 - No. 6, Sept, 1978 (Hanna-Barbera)

1-The Blue Falcon, Scooby Doo in all 1.20 3.60 12.00
2-6-All newsstand only 1.00 3.00 10.00

EAGLE, THE (1st Series) (See Science Comics & Weird Comics #8)
Fox Features Syndicate: July, 1941 - No. 4, Jan, 1942

1-The Eagle begins; Rex Dexter of Mars app. by Briefer; all issues feature

Earth Man On Venus nn © AVON

Easter With Mother Goose Four Color #103 © Oskar Lebeck

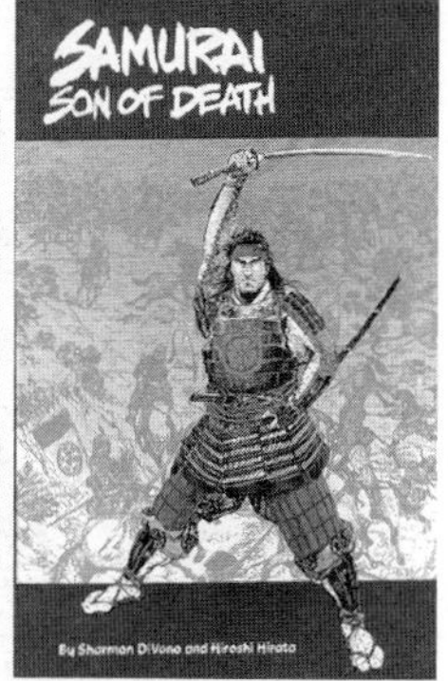

Eclipse Graphic Album Series #14 © Sharman DiVono & Hiroshi Hirata

	GD25	FN65	NM94
German war covers	165.00	495.00	1400.00
2-The Spider Queen begins (origin)	77.00	231.00	650.00
3,4: 3-Joe Spook begins (origin)	62.00	186.00	525.00

EAGLE (2nd Series)
Rural Home Publ.: Feb-Mar, 1945 - No. 2, Apr-May, 1945

	GD25	FN65	NM94
1-Aviation stories	32.00	96.00	240.00
2-Lucky Aces	20.00	60.00	150.00

NOTE: ***L. B. Cole** c/a in each.*

EAGLE
Crystal Comics/Apple Comics #17 on: Sept, 1986 - No. 23, 1989 ($1.50/1.75/1.95, B&W)

	GD25	FN65	NM94
1			2.00
1-Signed and limited			2.75
2-23: 12-Double size origin issue ($2.50)			1.50

EAGLES DARE
Aager comics, Inc.: Aug, 1994 - Present? ($1.95, B&W, limited series)

	GD25	FN65	NM94
1,2			2.00

EARTH MAN ON VENUS (An...) (Also see Strange Planets)
Avon Periodicals: 1951

	GD25	FN65	NM94
nn-Wood-a (26 pgs.); Fawcette-c	109.00	327.00	925.00

EARTHWORM JIM (TV, cartoon)
Marvel Comics: Dec, 1995 - No. 3, Feb, 1996 ($2.25)

	GD25	FN65	NM94
1-3: Based on video game and toys			2.25

EARTH X
Marvel Comics/Wizard Press: 1997 (Wizard supplement)

	GD25	FN65	NM94
nn-Alex Ross sketchbook of Marvel future; painted-c			5.00

EASTER BONNET SHOP (See March of Comics No. 29)

EASTER WITH MOTHER GOOSE
Dell Publishing Co.: No. 103, 1946 - No. 220, Mar, 1949

	GD25	FN65	NM94
Four Color 103 (#1)-Walt Kelly-a	17.00	52.00	190.00
Four Color 140 ('47)-Kelly-a	14.00	42.00	155.00
Four Color 185 ('48),220-Kelly-a	12.00	35.00	130.00

EAST MEETS WEST
Innovation Publishing: Apr, 1990 - No. 2, 1990 ($2.50, limited series, mature)

	GD25	FN65	NM94
1,2: 1-Stevens part-i; Redondo-c(i). 2-Stevens-c(i); 1st app. Cheech & Chong in comics			2.50

EAT RIGHT TO WORK AND WIN
Swift & Company: 1942 (16 pgs.) (Giveaway)

	GD25	FN65	NM94
Blondie, Henry, Flash Gordon by Alex Raymond, Toots & Casper, Thimble Theatre(Popeye), Tillie the Toiler, The Phantom, The Little King, & Bringing up Father - original strips just for this book -(in daily strip form which shows what foods we should eat and why)	30.00	90.00	240.00

E. C. CLASSIC REPRINTS
East Coast Comix Co.: May, 1973 - No. 12, 1976 (E. C. Comics reprinted in color minus ads)

	GD25	FN65	NM94
1-The Crypt of Terror #1 (Tales from the Crypt #46)	1.00	3.00	10.00
2-Weird Science #15('52)		2.00	6.00
3-12: 3-Shock SuspenStories #12. 4-Haunt of Fear #12. 5-Weird Fantasy #13 ('52). 6-Crime SuspenStories #25. 7-Vault of Horror #26. 8-Shock SuspenStories #6. 9-Two-Fisted Tales #34. 10-Haunt of Fear #23. 11-Weird Science #12(#1). 12-Shock SuspenStories #2			5.00

EC CLASSICS
Russ Cochran : Aug, 1985 - No. 12, 1986? (High quality paper; each-r 8 stories in color) (#2-12 were resolicited in 1990)($4.95, 56 pgs., 8x11")

	GD25	FN65	NM94
1-12: 1-Tales From the Crypt. 2-Weird Science. 3-Two-Fisted Tales. 4-Shock SuspenStories. 5-Weird Fantasy. 6-Vault of Horror. 7-Weird Science-Fantasy (r/23,24). 8-Crime SuspensStories. 9-Haunt of Fear. 10-Panic (r/1,2). 11-Tales From the Crypt (r/23,24). 12-Weird Science (r/20,22)		2.00	6.00

ECHO OF FUTUREPAST
Pacific Comics/Continuity Com.: May, 1984 - No. 9, Jan, 1986 ($2.95, 52 pgs.)

	GD25	FN65	NM94
1-9: Neal Adams-c/a in all?			3.50

NOTE: ***N. Adams** a-1-6,7i,9i; c-1-3, 5p,7i,8,9i. **Golden** a-1-6 (Bucky O'Hare); c-6. **Toth** a-6,7.*

ECLIPSE GRAPHIC ALBUM SERIES
Eclipse Comics: Oct, 1978 - 1989 (8-1/2x11") (B&W #1-5)

	GD25	FN65	NM94
1-Sabre (10/78, B&W, 1st print.); Gulacy-a; 1st direct sale graphic novel	1.20	3.60	12.00
1-Sabre (2nd printing, 1/79)	.90	2.70	8.00
1-Sabre (3rd printing, $5.95)		2.00	6.00
2-Night Music (11/79, B&W)-Russell-a	.90	2.70	9.00
3-Detectives, Inc. (5/80, B&W, $6.95)-Rogers-a	.90	2.70	8.00
4-Stewart The Rat (1980, B&W)-G. Colan-a	.90	2.70	8.00
5-The Price (10/81, B&W)-Starlin-a	1.40	4.20	14.00
6-I Am Coyote (11/84, color)-Rogers-c/a	.90	2.70	9.00
7-The Rocketeer (9/85, color)-Dave Stevens-a (r/chapters 1-5)(see Pacific Presents & Starslayer); has 7 pgs. new-a	1.00	3.00	10.00
7-The Rocketeer (2nd print, $7.95)	.90	2.70	8.00
7-The Rocketeer (3rd print, 1991, $8.95)	.90	2.70	9.00
7-The Rocketeer, signed & limited HC	5.50	16.50	60.00
7-The Rocketeer, hard-c (1986, $19.95)	2.00	6.00	20.00
7-The Rocketeer, unsigned HC (3rd, $32.95)	3.00	9.00	33.00
8-Zorro In Old California ('86, color)	1.00	3.00	10.00
8-Hardcover	1.40	4.20	14.00
9-Sacred And The Profane ('86)-Steacy-a	1.60	4.80	16.00
9-Hardcover ($24.95)	2.25	6.80	25.00
10-Somerset Holmes ('86, $15.95)-Adults, soft-c	1.60	4.80	16.00
10-Hardcover ($24.95)	2.25	6.80	25.00
11-Floyd Farland, Citizen of the Future ('87, $3.95, B&W)			5.00
12-Silverheels ('87, $7.95, color)	.90	2.70	8.00
12-Hardcover ($14.95)	1.50	4.50	15.00
12-Hardcover, signed & #'d ($24.95)	2.25	6.80	25.00
13-The Sisterhood of Steel ('87, $8.95, color)	.90	2.70	9.00
14-Samurai, Son of Death ('87, $4.95, B&W)			5.00
14-Samurai, Son of Death ($3.95, 2nd printing)			4.00
15-Twisted Tales (11/87, color)-Dave Stevens-c		2.00	6.00
16-See Airfighters Classics #1			5.00
17-Valkyrie, Prisoner of the Past ('88, $3.95, color)			4.00
18-See Airfighters Classics #2			5.00
19-Scout: The Four Monsters ('88, $14.95, color)-r/Scout #1-7; soft-c	1.50	4.50	15.00
20-See Airfighters Classics #3			5.00
21-XYR-Multiple ending comic ('88, $3.95, B&W)			4.00
22-Alien Worlds #1 (5/88, $3.95, 52 pgs.)-Nudity		2.00	6.00
23-See Airfighters Classics #4			5.00
24-Heartbreak ($4.95, B&W)			5.00
25-Alex Toth's Zorro Vol. 1 ($10.95, B&W)	1.20	3.60	12.00
26-Alex Toth's Zorro Vol. 2 ($10.95, B&W)	1.20	3.60	12.00
27-Fast Fiction (She) ($5.95, B&W)		2.00	6.00
28-Miracleman Book I ($5.95)	.90	2.70	8.00
29-Real Love: The Best of the Simon and Kirby Romance Comics (10/88, $12.95)	1.30	3.90	13.00
30-Brought To Light; Alan Moore scripts (1989)	1.10	3.30	11.00
30-Limited hardcover ed. ($29.95)	2.70	8.00	30.00
31-Pigeons From Hell by R. E. Howard (11/88)	.90	2.70	9.00
31-Signed & Limited Edition ($29.95)	2.90	8.70	32.00
32-Teenaged Dope Slaves and Reform School Girls	1.10	3.30	11.00
33-Bogie	1.10	3.30	11.00
34-Air Fighters Classics #5	1.10	3.30	11.00
35-Rael: Into The Shadow of the Sun	.90	2.70	8.00
36-Dr. Watchstop: Adventures in Time and Space	.90	2.70	9.00

Eddie Campbell's Bacchus #35 © Eddie Campbell

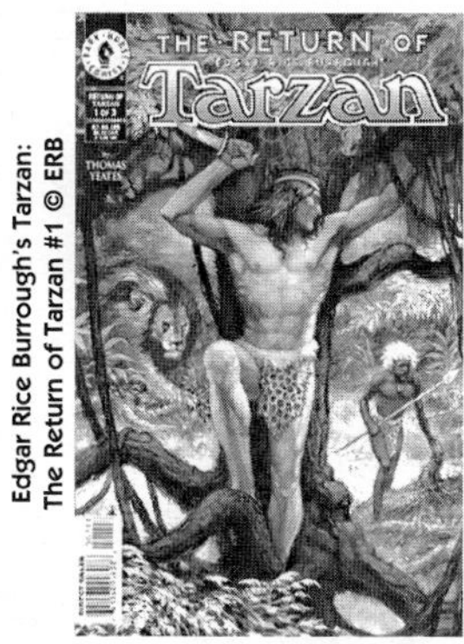

Edgar Rice Burrough's Tarzan: The Return of Tarzan #1 © ERB

Eerie #1 © WP

GD25 FN65 NM94

ECLIPSE MAGAZINE (Becomes Eclipse Monthly)
Eclipse Publishing: May, 1981 - No. 8, Jan, 1983 ($2.95, B&W, magazine)

1-8: 1-1st app. Cap'n Quick and a Foozle by Rogers, Ms. Tree by Beatty, and Dope by Trina Robbins. 2-1st app. I Am Coyote by Rogers. 7-1st app. Masked Man by Boyer — 4.00

NOTE: ***Colan*** *a-3, 5, 8.* ***Golden*** *c/a-2.* ***Gulacy*** *a-6, c-1, 6.* ***Kaluta*** *c/a-5.* ***Mayerik*** *a-2, 3.* ***Rogers*** *a-1-8.* ***Starlin*** *a-1.* ***Sutton*** *a-6.*

ECLIPSE MONTHLY
Eclipse Comics: Aug, 1983 - No. 10, Jul, 1984 (Baxter paper, $2.00/$1.50/$1.75)

1-3: ($2.00, 52 pgs.)-Cap'n Quick and a Foozle by Rogers, Static by Ditko, Dope by Trina Robbins, Rio by Doug Wildey, The Masked Man by Boyer begin. 3-Ragamuffins begins — 2.00
4-10: 4-8-$1.50-c. 9,10-$1.75-c — 1.80

NOTE: ***Boyer*** *c-6.* ***Ditko*** *a-1-3.* ***Rogers*** *a-1-4; c-2, 4, 7.* ***Wildey*** *a-1, 2, 5, 9, 10; c-5, 10.*

ECLIPSO (See Brave and the Bold #64, House of Secrets #61 & Phantom Stranger, 1987)
DC Comics: Nov, 1992 - No. 18, Apr, 1994 ($1.25)

1-14: 1-Giffen plots/breakdowns begin. 10-Darkseid app. — 1.25
15-18: 15-Begin $1.50-c; Creeper in #3-6,9,11-13. 18-Spectre-c/s — 1.50
Annual 1 (1993, $2.50, 68 pgs.)-Intro Prism — 2.50

ECLIPSO: THE DARKNESS WITHIN
DC Comics: July, 1992 - No. 2, Oct, 1992 ($2.50, 68 pgs.)

1-With purple gem attached to-c — 2.50
1-Without gem; Superman, Creeper app. — 2.50
2-Concludes Eclipso storyline from annuals — 2.50

E. C. 3-D CLASSICS (See Three Dimensional...)

ECTOKID (See Razorline)
Marvel Comics: Sept, 1993 - No. 9, May, 1994 ($1.75/$1.95)

1-($2.50)-Foil embossed-c; created by C. Barker — 2.50
2-8: 2-Origin. 5-Saint Sinner x-over — 1.75
9-Begin $1.95-c — 2.00
...: Unleashed! 1 (10/94, $2.95, 52 pgs.) — 3.00

ED "BIG DADDY" ROTH'S RATFINK COMIX (Also see Ratfink)
World of Fandom/ Ed Roth: 1991 - No. 3, 1991 ($2.50)

	GD25	FN65	NM94
1-3: Regular Ed.	1.00	3.00	10.00
1-Limited double cover	1.00	3.00	10.00

EDDIE CAMPBELL'S BACCHUS
Eddie Campbell Comics: May, 1995 - Present ($2.95, B&W)

1-Cerebus app. — 4.00
1-2nd printing (5/97) — 3.00
2-39: 9-Alex Ross back-c. — 3.00
Doing The Islands With Bacchus ('97, $17.95) — 17.95
Earth, Water, Air & Fire ('98, $9.95) — 9.95
The Eyeball Kid ('98, $8.50) — 8.50

EDDIE STANKY (Baseball Hero)
Fawcett Publications: 1951 (New York Giants)

	GD25	FN65	NM94
nn-Photo-c	29.00	88.00	220.00

EDEN MATRIX, THE
Adhesive Comics: 1994 ($2.95)

1,2-Two variant-c; alternate-c on inside back-c — 3.00

EDGAR BERGEN PRESENTS CHARLIE McCARTHY
Whitman Publishing Co. (Charlie McCarthy Co.): No. 764, 1938 (36 pgs.; 15x10-1/2"; in color)

	GD25	FN65	NM94
764	65.00	194.00	550.00

EDGAR RICE BURROUGHS' TARZAN: A TALE OF MUGAMBI
Dark Horse Comics: 1995 ($2.95, one-shot)

1 — 3.00

EDGAR RICE BURROUGHS' TARZAN: IN THE LAND THAT TIME FORGOT AND THE POOL OF TIME
Dark Horse Comics: 1996 ($12.95, trade paperback)

nn-r/Russ Manning-a — 13.00

EDGAR RICE BURROUGHS' TARZAN: THE LOST ADVENTURE
Dark Horse Comics: Jan, 1995 - No. 4, Apr, 1995 ($2.95, B&W, limited series)

1-4: ERB's last Tarzan story, adapted by Joe Lansdale — 3.00
Hardcover (12/95, $19.95) — 20.00
Limited Edition Hardcover ($99.95)-signed & numbered — 100.00

EDGAR RICE BURROUGHS' TARZAN: THE RETURN OF TARZAN
Dark Horse Comics: May, 1997 - No. 3, July, 1997 ($2.95, limited series)

1-3: — 2.95

EDGE
Malibu Comics (Bravura): July, 1994 - No. 3, Apr, 1995 ($2.50, unfinished limited series)

1-3-S. Grant-story & Gil Kane-c/a; w/Bravura stamp — 2.50

EDGE OF CHAOS
Pacific Comics: July, 1983 - No. 3, Jan, 1984 (Limited series)

1-3-Morrow c/a; all contain nudity — 2.00

EDWARD'S SHOES GIVEAWAY
Edward's Shoe Store: 1954 (Has clown on cover)

Contains comic with new cover. Many combinations possible. Contents determines price, 50-60 percent of original. (Similar to Comics From Weatherbird & Free Comics to You)

ED WHEELAN'S JOKE BOOK STARRING FAT & SLAT (See Fat & Slat)

EERIE (Strange Worlds No. 18 on)
Avon Per.: No. 1, Jan, 1947; No. 1, May-June, 1951 - No. 17, Aug-Sept, 1954

	GD25	FN65	NM94
1(1947)-1st horror comic; Kubert, Fugitani-a; bondage-c	240.00	720.00	2400.00
1(1951)-Reprints story from 1947 #1	50.00	150.00	425.00
2-Wood-c/a; bondage-c	56.00	168.00	475.00
3-Wood-c; Kubert, Wood/Orlando-a	56.00	168.00	475.00
4,5-Wood-c	44.00	132.00	375.00
6,8,13,14: 8-Kinstler-a; bondage-c; Phantom Witch Doctor story	25.00	75.00	185.00
7-Wood/Orlando-c; Kubert-a	39.00	117.00	300.00
9-Kubert-a; Check-c	29.00	86.00	215.00
10,11: 10-Kinstler-a. 11-Kinstlerish-a by McCann	23.00	68.00	170.00
12-Dracula story from novel, 25 pgs.	29.00	86.00	220.00
15-Reprints No. 1('51) minus-c(bondage)	18.00	54.00	135.00
16-Wood-a r-/No. 2	20.00	60.00	150.00
17-Wood/Orlando & Kubert-a; reprints #3 minus inside & outside Wood-c	25.00	74.00	185.00

NOTE: ***Hollingsworth*** *a-9-11; c-10, 11.*

EERIE
I. W. Enterprises: 1964

	GD25	FN65	NM94
I.W. Reprint #1('64)-Wood-c(r); r-story/Spook #1	2.80	8.40	28.00
I.W. Reprint #2,6,8: 8-Dr. Drew by Grandenetti from Ghost #9	2.50	7.50	22.00
I.W. Reprint #9-r/Tales of Terror #1(Toby); Wood-c	3.00	9.00	30.00

EERIE (Magazine)(See Warren Presents)
Warren Publ. Co.: No. 1, Sept, 1965; No. 2, Mar, 1966 - No. 139, Feb, 1983

1-24 pgs., black & white, small size (5-1/4x7-1/4"), low distribution; cover from inside back cover of Creepy No. 2; stories reprinted from Creepy No. 7, 8. At least three different versions exist.

First Printing - B&W, 5-1/4" wide x 7-1/4" high, evenly trimmed. On page 18, panel 5, in the upper left-hand corner, the large rear view of a bald headed man blends into solid black and is unrecognizable. Overall printing quality is poor. — 25.00 — 75.00 — 250.00

Second Printing - B&W, 5-1/4x7-1/4", with uneven, untrimmed edges (if one of these were trimmed evenly, the size would be less than as indicated). The figure of the bald headed man on page 18, panel 5 is clear and discernible. The staples have a 1/4" blue stripe.

Eerie #60 © WP

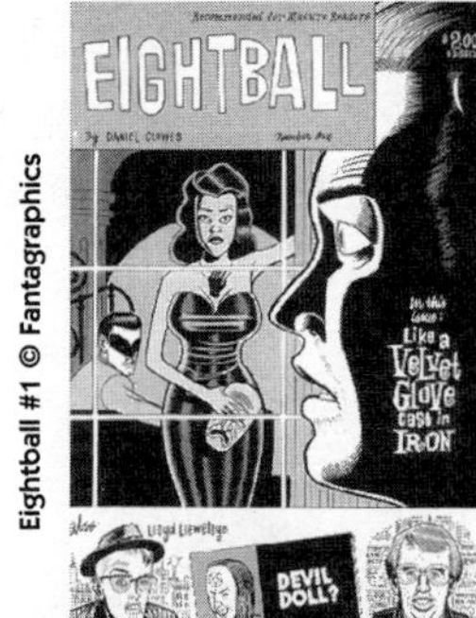

Eightball #1 © Fantagraphics

80 Page Giant #8 © DC

	GD25	FN65	NM94
	9.50	28.50	95.00

Other unauthorized reproductions for comparison's sake would be practically worthless. One known version was probably shot off a first printing copy with some loss of detail; the finer lines tend to disappear in this version which can be determined by looking at the lower right-hand corner of page one, first story. The roof of the house is shaded with straight lines. These lines are sharp and distinct on original, but broken on this version.

NOTE: ***The Overstreet Comic Book Price Guide*** *recommends that, before buying a 1st issue, you consult an expert.*

	GD25	FN65	NM94
2-Frazetta-c (also #3,5,7,8)	6.00	18.00	60.00
3-Frazetta-c & half pg. ad (rerun in #4)	4.60	13.80	46.00
4-10: 4-Frazetta-a (1/2 pg. ad). 5,7,8-Frazetta-c. 9-Headlight-c	2.50	7.50	22.00
11-16,18-20	2.25	6.75	18.00
17 (scarce)	7.50	22.50	75.00
21,22,24,25: 25-Steranko-c	2.50	7.50	24.00
23-Frazetta-c	3.60	10.80	36.00
26-30	1.60	4.80	16.00
31-38,40,43-45	2.00	6.00	20.00
39,41: 39-1st Dax. 41 (scarce)	2.20	6.50	24.00
42,51-('73 & '74 Annuals). 51-Color poster insert	2.20	6.50	24.00
46-50,52,53: 46-Dracula series by Sutton begins	1.20	3.60	12.00
54,55-Color Spirit story by Eisner, reprints sections 12/21/47 & 6/16/46	1.60	4.80	16.00
56-60,62,68,69,72,77: All have an 8 pg. slick color insert., 60-Summer Giant (9/74, $1.25)	1.60	4.80	16.00
61,63-67,70,71,73-76,78: 78-The Mummy-r	1.00	3.00	10.00
79,80-Origin Darklon the Mystic by Starlin (1st app.)	1.20	3.60	12.00
81,83-94,96-129: 84-All sports issue	.90	2.70	9.00
82-1st app. The Rook	2.00	6.00	20.00
95-The Rook & Vampirella team-up	1.20	3.60	12.00
130-Vampirella-c/story	1.20	3.60	12.00
131-139 (lower distr.)	1.20	3.60	12.00
Year Book 1970, 1971-Reprints in both	2.70	8.00	30.00
Year Book 1972-Reprints	2.70	8.00	30.00

NOTE: *The above books contain art by many good artists:* ***N. Adams, Brunner, Corben, Craig (Taycee), Crandall, Ditko, Eisner, Evans, Jeff Jones, Krenkel, McWilliams, Morrow, Orlando, Ploog, Severin, Starlin, Torres, Toth, Williamson, Wood,*** *and* ***Wrightson****; covers by* ***Bode', Corben, Davis, Frazetta, Morrow,*** *and* ***Orlando. Frazetta*** *c-2, 3, 7, 8, 23. Annuals from 1973-on are included in regular numbering. 1970-74 Annuals are complete reprints. Annuals from 1975-on are in the format of the regular issues.*

EERIE ADVENTURES (Also see Weird Adventures)
Ziff-Davis Publ. Co.: Winter, 1951 (Painted-c)

	GD25	FN65	NM94
1-Powell-a(2), McCann-a; used in **SOTI;** bondage-c; Krigstein back-c	34.00	102.00	255.00

NOTE: *Title dropped due to similarity to Avon's Eerie & legal action.*

EERIE TALES (Magazine)
Hastings Associates: 1959 (Black & White)

	GD25	FN65	NM94
1-Williamson, Torres, Tuska-a, Powell(2), & Morrow(2)-a	9.30	28.00	65.00

EERIE TALES
Super Comics: 1963-1964

	GD25	FN65	NM94
Super Reprint No. 10,11,12,18: 10('63)-r/Spook #27. Purple Claw in #11,12 ('63); #12-r/Avon's Eerie #1('51)-Kida-r	2.00	6.00	16.00
15-Wolverton-a, Spacehawk-r/Blue Bolt Weird Tales #113; Disbrow-a	4.00	12.00	40.00

EGBERT
Arnold Publications/Quality Comics Group: Spring, 1946 - No. 20, 1950

	GD25	FN65	NM94
1-Funny animal; intro Egbert & The Count	17.00	50.00	125.00
2	9.30	28.00	65.00
3-10	5.70	17.00	35.00
11-20	4.00	12.00	24.00

EGON
Dark Horse Comics: Jan, 1998 - No.2, Feb, 1998 ($2.95, limited series)

	GD25	FN65	NM94
1,2-Horley-painted-c			2.95

EGYPT
DC Comics (Vertigo): Aug, 1995 - No.7, Feb, 1996 ($2.50, lim. series, mature)

	GD25	FN65	NM94
1-7: Milligan scripts in all.			2.50

EH! (...Dig This Crazy Comic) (From Here to Insanity No. 8 on)
Charlton Comics: Dec, 1953 - No. 7, Nov-Dec, 1954 (Satire)

	GD25	FN65	NM94
1-Davisish-c/a by Ayers, Woodish-a by Giordano; Atomic Mouse app.	28.00	84.00	210.00
2-Ayers-c/a	17.00	52.00	130.00
3,5,7	15.00	44.00	110.00
4,6: Sexual innuendo-c. 6-Ayers-a	16.00	48.00	120.00

EIGHTBALL
Fantagraphics Books: Oct, 1989 - Present ($2.75/$2.95/$3.95, semi-annually, mature)

	GD25	FN65	NM94
1 (1st printing)	1.00	3.00	10.00
2-7 ($2.75)	.85	2.60	7.00
8 ($2.95)			5.00
9,10,11,13-15 ($2.95)			3.00
12 ($2.75)			2.75
16-19 ($3.95): 17-(8/96)			4.00

EIGHTH WONDER, THE
Dark Horse Comics: Nov, 1997 ($2.95, one-shot)

	GD25	FN65	NM94
nn-Reprints stories from Dark Horse Presents #85-87			2.95

EIGHT IS ENOUGH KITE FUN BOOK (See Kite Fun Book)

80 PAGE GIANT (...Magazine No. 2-15)
National Periodical Publications: 8/64 - No. 15, 10/65; No. 16, 11/65 - No. 89, 7/71 (25¢)(All reprints) (#1-56: 84 pgs.; #57-89: 68 pgs.)

	GD25	FN65	NM94
1-Superman Annual; originally planned as Superman Annual #9 (8/64)	35.00	105.00	470.00
2-Jimmy Olsen	19.25	58.00	280.00
3,4: 3-Lois Lane. 4-Flash-G.A.-r; Infantino-a	15.00	45.00	220.00
5-Batman; has Sunday newspaper strip; Catwoman-r; Batman's Life Story-r (25th anniversary special)	15.00	45.00	220.00
6-Superman	12.50	37.50	180.00
7-Sgt. Rock's Prize Battle Tales; Kubert-c/a	13.00	39.00	185.00
8-More Secret Origins-origins of JLA, Aquaman, Robin, Atom, & Superman; Infantino-a	28.00	85.00	400.00
9-11: 9-Flash (r/Flash #106,117,123 & Showcase #14); Infantino-a. 10-Superboy. 11-Superman; all Luthor issue	11.25	33.75	165.00
12-Batman; has Sunday newspaper strip	11.25	33.75	165.00
13,14: 13-Jimmy Olsen. 14-Lois Lane	11.25	33.75	165.00
15-Superman and Batman; Joker-c/story	11.25	33.75	165.00

Continued as part of regular series under each title in which that particular book came out, a Giant being published instead of the regular size. Issues No. 16 to No. 89 are listed for your information. See individual titles for prices.
16-JLA #39 (11/65), 17-Batman #176, 18-Superman #183, 19-Our Army at War #164, 20-Action #334, 21-Flash #160, 22-Superboy #129, 23-Superman #187, 24-Batman #182, 25-Jimmy Olsen #95, 26-Lois Lane #68, 27-Batman #185, 28-World's Finest #161, 29-JLA #48, 30-Batman #187, 31-Superman #193, 32-Our Army at War #177, 33-Action #347, 34-Flash #169, 35-Superboy #138, 36-Superman #197, 37-Batman #193, 38-Jimmy Olsen #104, 39-Lois Lane #77, 40-World's Finest #170, 41-JLA #58, 42-Superman #202, 43-Batman #198, 44-Our Army at War #190, 45-Action #360, 46-Flash #178, 47-Superboy #147, 48-Superman #207, 49-Batman #203, 50-Jimmy Olsen #113, 51-Lois Lane #86, 52-World's Finest #179, 53-JLA #67, 54-Superman #212, 55-Batman #208, 56-Our Army at War #203, 57-Action #373, 58-Flash #187, 59-Superboy #156, 60-Superman #217, 61-Batman #213, 62-Jimmy Olsen #122, 63-Lois Lane #95, 64-World's Finest #188, 65-JLA #76, 66-Superman #222, 67-Batman #218, 68-Our Army at War #216, 69-Adventure #390, 70-Flash #196, 71-Superboy #165, 72-Superman #227, 73-Batman #223, 74-Jimmy Olsen #131, 75-Lois Lane #104, 76-World's Finest #197, 77-JLA #85, 78-Superman #232, 79-Batman #228, 80-Our Army at War #229, 81-Adventure #403, 82-Flash #205, 83-Superboy #174, 84-Superman #239, 85-Batman #233, 86-Jimmy Olsen #140, 87-Lois Lane #113, 88-World's Finest #206, 89-JLA #93.

87TH PRECINCT (TV)
Dell Publishing Co.: Apr-June, 1962 - No. 2, July-Sept, 1962

Elektra #17 © MAR

Elementals #6 © Comico

Elflord #4 (Warp) © Barry Blair & Colin Chin

	GD25	FN65	NM94
Four Color 1309(#1)-Krigstein-a	9.00	27.00	100.00
2	7.00	22.00	80.00

EL BOMBO COMICS
Standard Comics/Frances M. McQueeny: 1946

	GD25	FN65	NM94
nn(1946)	9.30	28.00	70.00
1(no date)	9.30	28.00	70.00

EL CID
Dell Publishing Co.: No. 1259, 1961

	GD25	FN65	NM94
Four Color 1259-Movie, photo-c	6.40	19.00	70.00

EL DIABLO (See All-Star Western #2 & Weird Western Tales #12)
DC Comics: Aug, 1989 - No. 16, Jan, 1991 ($1.50-$1.75, color)

	GD25	FN65	NM94
1 ($2.50, 52pgs.)-Masked hero			2.50
2-6 ($1.50)			1.50
7-11: 7-Begin $1.75-c			1.80
12-16: 12-Begin $2.00-c			2.00

EL DORADO (See Movie Classics)

ELECTRIC UNDERTOW (See Strikeforce Morituri: Electric Undertow)

ELECTRIC WARRIOR
DC Comics: May, 1986 - No. 18, Oct, 1987 ($1.50, Baxter paper)

	GD25	FN65	NM94
1-18			1.50

ELEKTRA (Also see Daredevil #319-325)
Marvel Comics: Mar, 1995 - No. 4, June, 1995 ($2.95, limited series)

	GD25	FN65	NM94
1-4-Embossed-c; Scott McDaniel-a			3.00

ELEKTRA (Also see Daredevil)
Marvel Comics: Nov, 1996 - No. 19, Jun, 1998 ($1.95)

	GD25	FN65	NM94
1-Peter Milligan scripts; Deodato-c/a			4.00
1-Variant-c		2.00	6.00
2			2.50
3-8, -1(7/97): Dr. Strange-c/app.			2.00
9-19: 9-Begin $1.99-c. 10-Logan-c/app.			2.00
.../Cyblade (Image, 3/97,$2.95) Devil's Reign pt. 7			3.00

ELEKTRA: ASSASSIN (Also see Daredevil)
Marvel Comics (Epic Comics): Aug, 1986 - No. 8, June, 1987 (Limited series, mature)

	GD25	FN65	NM94
1-Miller scripts in all; Sienkiewicz-c/a.		2.00	6.00
2			4.50
3-7			3.50
8			5.50
Signed & numbered hardcover (Graphitti Designs, $39.95, 2000 print run)-reprints 1-8			50.00

ELEKTRA LIVES AGAIN (Also see Daredevil)
Marvel Comics (Epic Comics): 1990 ($24.95, oversize, hardcover, 76 pgs.) (Produced by Graphitti Designs)

	GD25	FN65	NM94
nn-Frank Miller-c/a/scripts; Lynn Varley painted-a; Matt Murdock & Bullseye app.; Elektra dies			25.00

ELEKTRA MEGAZINE
Marvel Comics: Nov, 1996 - No. 2, Dec, 1996 ($3.95, 96 pgs., reprints, limited series)

	GD25	FN65	NM94
1,2: Reprints Frank Miller's Elektra stories in Daredevil			4.00

ELEKTRA SAGA, THE
Marvel Comics Group: Feb, 1984 - No. 4, June, 1984 ($2.00, limited series, Baxter paper)

	GD25	FN65	NM94
1-4-r/Daredevil 168-190; Miller-c/a			3.00

ELEMENTALS, THE (See The Justice Machine & Morningstar Spec.)
Comico The Comic Co. : June, 1984 - No. 29, Sept, 1988; V2#1, Mar, 1989 - No. 28, 1994? ($1.50/$2.50, Baxter paper); V3#1, Dec, 1995 - No. 3 ($2.95)

	GD25	FN65	NM94
1-Willingham-c/a, 1-8			3.00
2			2.00
3-10: 9-Bissette-a(p). 10-Photo-c			2.00
11-29			1.50
V2#1-28: 1-3-$1.95-c. 4-Begin $2.50-c. 16-1st app. Strike Force America. 18-Prelude to Avalon mini-series. 37-Prequel to Strike Force America series			2.00
V3#1-3: 1-Daniel-a(p), bagged w/gaming card.			2.00
Lingerie (5/96, $2.95)			3.00
Special 1 (3/86)-Willingham-a(p)			1.75
Special 2 (1/89, $1.95)			2.00

ELEMENTALS: GHOST OF A CHANCE
Comico: Dec, 1995 ($5.95, graphic novel)

	GD25	FN65	NM94
nn-Ross-c.		2.00	6.00

ELEMENTALS: HOW THE WAR WAS WON
Comico: June, 1996 - No. 2, Aug, 1996 ($2.95, limited series)

	GD25	FN65	NM94
1,2-Tony Daniel-a			2.95
1-Variant-c; no logo			2.95

ELEMENTALS: SEX SPECIAL
Comico: May, 1997 - No. 2, June, 1997 ($2.95, limited series)

	GD25	FN65	NM94
1-Tony Daniel, Jeff Moy-a			2.95
2-Robb Phipps, Adam McDaniel-a			2.95

ELEMENTALS: SWIMSUIT SPECTACULAR 1996
Comico: June, 1996 ($2.95, one-shot)

	GD25	FN65	NM94
1-pin-ups by various			2.95
1-Variant-c; no logo			2.95

ELEMENTALS: THE VAMPIRE'S REVENGE
Comico: June, 1996 - No. 2 Aug, 1996 ($2.95, limited series)

	GD25	FN65	NM94
1,2-Willingham-s			2.95
1-Variant-c; no logo			2.95

1111 (ELEVEN ELEVEN)
Crusade Entertainment: Oct, 1996 ($2.95, B&W, one-shot)

	GD25	FN65	NM94
1-Wrightson-c/a			3.00

ELEVEN OR ONE
Sirius: Apr, 1995 ($2.95)

	GD25	FN65	NM94
1-Linsner-c/a	.90	2.70	8.00
1-(6/96) 2nd printing			3.00

ELFLORD
Aircel Publ.: 1986 - No. 6, Oct, 1989 ($1.70, B&W); V2#1- V2#31, 1995 ($2.00)

	GD25	FN65	NM94
1			2.00
1,2-2nd printings			1.50
2,3			2.00
4-6: Last B&W issue			1.60
V2#1-Color-a begins			2.00
2-20			1.60
21-Double size ($4.95)			5.00
22-30: 22-New cast. 25-Begin B&W, $1.95-c			1.75

ELFLORD
Warp Graphics: Jan, 1997-No.4, Apr, 1997 ($2.95, B&W, mini-series)

	GD25	FN65	NM94
1-4			2.95

ELFLORD (CUTS LOOSE) (Vol. 2)
Warp Graphics: Sept, 1997 - Present ($2.95, B&W, mini-series)

	GD25	FN65	NM94
1-7			2.95

ELFLORD: DRAGON'S EYE
Night Wynd Enterprises: 1993 ($2.50, B&W)

	GD25	FN65	NM94
1			2.50

ELFLORD: THE RETURN
Mad Monkey Press: 1996 ($6.95, magazine size)

Elfquest #1 © Barry Blair & Colin Chin

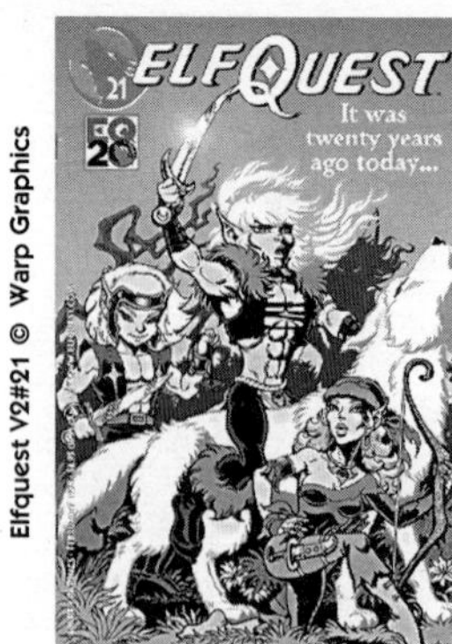

Elfquest V2#21 © Warp Graphics

Elfquest: Blood of Ten Chiefs #9 © Warp Graphics

	GD25	FN65	NM94
1	.85	2.60	7.00

ELFQUEST (Also see Fantasy Quarterly & Warp Graphics Annual)
Warp Graphics, Inc.: No. 2, Aug, 1978 - No. 21, Feb, 1985 (All magazine size) No. 1, Apr, 1979

NOTE: ***Elfquest*** was originally published as one of the stories in **Fantasy Quarterly** #1. When the publisher went out of business, the creative team, Wendy and Richard Pini, formed WaRP Graphics and continued the series, beginning with **Elfquest** #2. **Elfquest** #1, which reprinted the story from **Fantasy Quarterly**, was published about the same time **Elfquest** #4 was released. Thereafter, most issues were reprinted as demand warranted, until Marvel announced it would reprint the entire series under its Epic imprint (Aug., 1985).

	GD25	FN65	NM94
1(4/79)-Reprints Elfquest story from Fantasy Quarterly No. 1			
1st printing ($1.00-c)	2.20	6.25	22.00
2nd printing ($1.25-c)	.90	2.70	9.00
3rd printings ($1.50-c)			3.00
4th printing; different-c ($1.50-c)			1.50
2(8/78)-5: 1st printings ($1.00-c)	1.40	4.20	14.00
2nd printings ($1.25-c)			4.00
3rd & 4th printings ($1.50-c)(all 4th prints 1989)			2.50
6-9: 1st printings ($1.25-c)		2.00	6.00
2nd printings ($1.50-c)			3.50
3rd printings ($1.50-c)			1.50
10-14: ($1.50-c); 16-8pg. preview of A Distant Soil			4.00
10-14: 2nd printings ($1.50)			1.50
15-21 (only one printing)			4.00

ELFQUEST
Marvel Comics (Epic Comics): Aug, 1985 - No. 32, Mar, 1988

1-Reprints in color the Elfquest epic by Warp Graphics 3.00
2-32 1.50

ELFQUEST
Warp Graphics: 1989 - No. 4, 1989 ($1.50, B&W)

1-4: Reprints original Elfquest series 1.50

ELFQUEST (Volume 2)
Warp Graphics: V2#1, May, 1996 - Present ($4.95, B&W)

V2#1-30: 1,3,5,8,10,12,13,18,21,23,25-Wendy Pini-c 5.00

ELFQUEST: BLOOD OF TEN CHIEFS
Warp Graphics: July, 1993 - No. 20, Sept, 1995 ($2.00/$2.50)

1-15-By Richard & Wendy Pini 2.25
16-20: 16-Begin $2.50-c 2.50

ELFQUEST:HIDDEN YEARS
Warp Graphics: May, 1992 - No. 29, Mar, 1996 ($2.00/$2.25)

1-7- 2.25
8-29: 8-Begin $2.25-c 2.50

ELFQUEST:JINK
Warp Graphics: Nov, 1994 - No. 12, Feb, 1996 ($2.25/$2.50)

1-3-W. Pini and John Byrne collaborate on Back-c 2.25
4-12: 4-Begin $2.50-c 2.50

ELFQUEST: KAHVI
Warp Graphics: Oct, 1995 - No. 6, Mar, 1996 ($2.25, B&W)

1-6 2.25

ELFQUEST: KINGS CROSS
Warp Graphics: Nov, 1997 - No. 2, Dec, 1997 ($2.95, B&W, limited series)

1,2 2.95

ELFQUEST: KINGS OF THE BROKEN WHEEL
Warp Graphics: June, 1990 - No. 9, Feb, 1992 ($2.00, B&W) (3rd Elfquest saga)

1-9: By Richard & Wendy Pini; 1-Color insert 2.00
1-2nd printing 2.00

ELFQUEST: METAMORPHOSIS
Warp Graphics: Apr, 1996 ($2.95, B&W, one-shot)

GD25 FN65 NM94

1 3.00

ELFQUEST: NEW BLOOD (...Summer Special on-c #1 only)
WaRP Graphics: Aug, 1992 - No. 35, Jan, 1996 ($2.00/$2.25/$2.50, color/B&W, bi-monthly)

1-($3.95, 68 pgs.)-Byrne-a/scripts (16 pgs.) 4.00
2-17: Barry Blair-a in all 2.25
18-26,35: 18-Begin $2.25-c 2.25
27-34: 27 begin $2.50-c. 2.50

ELFQUEST: SHARDS
Warp Graphics: Aug, 1994 - No. 16, Mar, 1996 ($2.25/$2.50)

1-8 2.25
9-16:9-Begin $2.50-c 2.50

ELFQUEST: SIEGE AT BLUE MOUNTAIN
WaRP Graphics/Apple Comics: Mar, 1987 - No. 8, Dec, 1988 ($1.75/$1.95, B&W, limited series)

1-Staton-a(i) in all; 2nd Elfquest saga 4.00
1-2nd printing 2.00
2 3.00
2,3-2nd printings 1.75
3-8 2.00

ELFQUEST: THE REBELS
Warp Graphics: Nov, 1994 - No. 12, Mar, 1996 ($2.25/$2.50, B&W/color)

1-3 2.25
4-12: 4-Begin $2.50-c 2.50

ELFQUEST: TWO-SPEAR
Warp Graphics: Oct, 1995 - No. 5, Feb, 1996 ($2.25, B&W)

1-5 2.25

ELFQUEST: WAVE DANCERS
Warp Graphics: Dec, 1993 - No. 6, Mar, 1996 ($2.00/$2.25)

1,2: 1-Foil-c & poster 2.50
3-6: 3-Begin 2.25-c 2.25
Special 1 ($2.95) 3.00

ELFQUEST: WORLDPOOL
Warp Graphics: July, 1997 ($2.95, B&W, one-shot)

1 Richard Pini-s/Barry Blair-a 2.95

ELF-THING
Eclipse Comics: March, 1987 ($1.50, B&W, one-shot)

1 1.50

ELIMINATOR (Also see The Solution #16 & The Night Man #16)
Malibu Comics (Ultraverse): Apr, 1995 - No. 3, Jul, 1995 ($2.95/$2.50, lim. series)

0-Mike Zeck-a in all 3.00
1-3-($2.50): 1-1st app. Siren 2.50
1-($3.95)-Black cover edition 4.00

ELIMINATOR FULL COLOR SPECIAL
Eternity Comics: Oct, 1991 ($2.95, one-shot)

1-Dave Dorman painted-c 3.00

ELLA CINDERS (See Comics On Parade, Comics Revue #1,4, Famous Comics Cartoon Book, Giant Comics Editions, Sparkler Comics, Tip Top & Treasury of Comics)

ELLA CINDERS
United Features Syndicate: 1938 - 1940

	GD25	FN65	NM94
Single Series 3(1938)	38.00	114.00	285.00
Single Series 21(#2 on-c, #21 on inside), 28('40)	32.00	96.00	240.00

ELLA CINDERS
United Features Syndicate: Mar, 1948 - No. 5, Mar, 1949

	GD25	FN65	NM94
1-(#2 on cover)	11.00	34.00	85.00

Elmer Fudd Four Color #470 © Warner Bros.

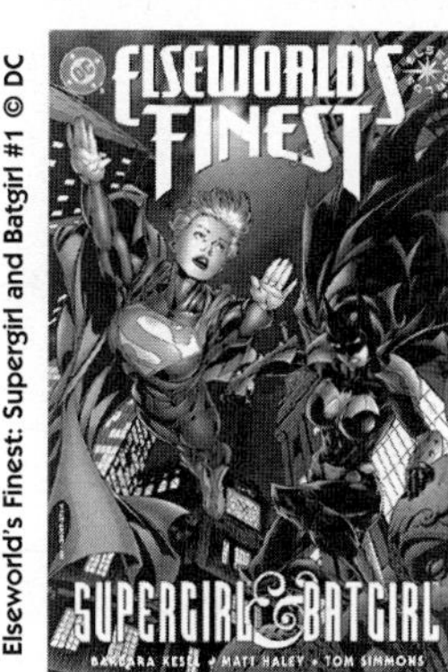

Elseworld's Finest: Supergirl and Batgirl #1 © DC

E-Man #2 © CC

GD25 FN65 NM94

2 7.15 21.50 50.00
3-5 5.70 17.00 35.00

ELLERY QUEEN
Superior Comics Ltd.: May, 1949 - No. 4, Nov, 1949

1-Kamen-c; L.B. Cole-a; r-in Haunted Thrills 43.00 129.00 365.00
2-4: 3-Drug use stories(2) 35.00 104.00 260.00
NOTE: *Iger shop art in all issues.*

ELLERY QUEEN (TV)
Ziff-Davis Publishing Co.: 1-3/52 (Spring on-c) - No. 2, Summer/52 (Saunders painted-c)

1-Saunders-c 41.00 122.00 325.00
2-Saunders bondage, torture-c 35.00 104.00 260.00

ELLERY QUEEN (Also see Crackajack Funnies No. 23)
Dell Publishing Co.: No. 1165, Mar-May, 1961 - No.1289, Apr, 1962

Four Color 1165 (#1)- 10.50 31.50 115.00
Four Color 1243 (11-1/61-61), 1289 8.75 26.50 95.00

ELMER FUDD (Also see Camp Comics, Daffy, Looney Tunes #1 & Super Book #10, 22)
Dell Publishing Co.: No. 470, May, 1953 - No. 1293, Mar-May, 1962

Four Color 470 (#1) 4.50 13.50 50.00
Four Color 558,628,689('56) 3.20 9.50 35.00
Four Color 725,783,841,888,938,977,1032,1081,1131,1171,1222,1293('62) 2.20 6.50 24.00

ELMO COMICS
St. John Publishing Co.: Jan, 1948 (Daily strip-r)

1-By Cecil Jensen 8.50 26.00 60.00

ELONGATED MAN (See Flash #112 & Justice League of America #105)
DC Comics: Jan, 1992 - No. 4, Apr, 1992 ($1.00, limited series)

1-4: 3-The Flash app. 1.00

ELRIC (Of Melnibone)(See First Comics Graphic Novel #6 & Marvel Graphic Novel #2)
Pacific Comics: Apr, 1983 - No. 6, Apr, 1984 ($1.50, Baxter paper)

1-6: Russell-c/a(i) in all 1.50

ELRIC
Topps Comics: 1996 ($2.95, one-shot)

0--One Life: Russell-c/a; adapts Neil Gaiman's short story "One Life--Furnished in Early Moorcock." 3.00

ELRIC, SAILOR ON THE SEAS OF FATE
First Comics: June, 1985 - No. 7, June, 1986 ($1.75, limited series)

1-7: Adapts Michael Moorcock's novel 2.00

ELRIC, STORMBRINGER
Dark Horse Comics/Topps Comics: 1997 - No. 7, 1997($2.95, limited series)

1-7: Russell-c/s/a; adapts Michael Moorcock's novel 2.95

ELRIC: THE BANE OF THE BLACK SWORD
First Comics: Aug, 1988 - No. 6, June, 1989 ($1.75/$1.95, limited series)

1-6: Adapts Michael Moorcock's novel 2.00

ELRIC: THE VANISHING TOWER
First Comics: Aug, 1987 - No. 6, June, 1988 ($1.75, limited series)

1-6: Adapts Michael Moorcock's novel 1.80

ELRIC: WEIRD OF THE WHITE WOLF
First Comics: Oct, 1986 - No. 5, June, 1987 ($1.75, limited series)

1-5: Adapts Michael Moorcock's novel 1.80

EL SALVADOR - A HOUSE DIVIDED
Eclipse Comics: March, 1989 ($2.50, B&W, Baxter paper, stiff-c, 52 pgs.)

1-Gives history of El Salvador 2.50

GD25 FN65 NM94

ELSEWHERE PRINCE, THE (Moebius' Airtight Garage)
Marvel Comics (Epic): May, 1990 - No. 6, Oct, 1990 ($1.95, limited series)

1-6: Moebius scripts & back-up-a in all 2.00

ELSEWORLD'S FINEST
DC Comics: 1997 - No. 2, 1997 ($4.95, limited series)

1,2: Elseworld's story-Superman & Batman in the 1920's 4.95

ELSEWORLD'S FINEST: SUPERGIRL & BATGIRL
DC Comics: 1998 ($5.95, one-shot)

1-Haley-a 6.00

ELSIE THE COW
D. S. Publishing Co.: Oct-Nov, 1949 - No. 3, July-Aug, 1950

1-(36 pgs.) 21.00 64.00 160.00
2,3 16.00 48.00 120.00
Borden's cheese comic picture bk ("40, giveaway) 16.00 48.00 120.00
Borden Milk Giveaway-(16 pgs., nn) (3 ishs, 1957) 12.00 36.00 90.00
Elsie's Fun Book(1950; Borden Milk) 12.00 36.00 90.00
Everyday Birthday Fun With... (1957; 20 pgs.)(100th Anniversary); Kubert-a 12.00 36.00 90.00

ELSON'S PRESENTS
DC Comics: 1981 (100 pgs., no cover price)

Series 1-6: Repackaged 1981 DC comics; 1-DC Comics Presents #29, Flash #303, Batman #331. 2-Superman #335, Ghosts #96, Justice League of America #186. 3-New Teen Titans #3, Secrets of Haunted House #32, Wonder Woman #275. 4-Secrets of the LSH #1, Brave & the Bold #170, New Adv. of Superboy #13. 5-LSH #271, Green Lantern #136, Super Friends #40. 6-Action #515, Mystery in Space #115, Detective #498 4.00

ELVEN (Also see Prime)
Malibu Comics (Ultraverse): Oct, 1994 - No. 4, Feb, 1995 ($2.50, lim. series)

0 ($2.95)-Prime app. 3.00
1-4: 2,4-Prime app. 3-Primevil app. 2.50
1-Limited Foil Edition- no price on cover 3.00

ELVIRA MISTRESS OF THE DARK
Marvel Comics: Oct, 1988 ($2.00, B&W, magazine size)

1-Movie adaptation 4.00

ELVIRA MISTRESS OF THE DARK
Claypool Comics (Eclipse): May, 1993 - Present ($2.50, B&W)

1-Austin-a(i). Spiegle-a 5.00
2-6: Spiegle-a 3.00
7-62-Photo-c: 2.50

ELVIRA'S HOUSE OF MYSTERY
DC Comics: Jan, 1986 - No. 11, Jan, 1987

1-($1.50) 3.00
2-10: 9-Photo-c 2.00
11-Dave Stevens-c 3.00
Special 1 (3/87, $1.25) 2.00

ELVIS MANDIBLE, THE
DC Comics (Piranha Press): 1990 ($3.50, 52 pgs., B&W, mature)

nn 3.50

ELVIS PRESLEY (See Career Girl Romances #32, Go-Go, Howard Chaykin's American Flagg #10, Humbug #8, I Love You #60 & Young Lovers #18)

E-MAN
Charlton Comics: Oct, 1973 - No. 10, Sept, 1975 (Painted-c No. 7-10)

1-Origin & 1st app. E-Man; Staton c/a in all 1.40 4.20 14.00
2-4: 2,4-Ditko-a. 3-Howard-a 2.00 6.00
5-Miss Liberty Belle app. by Ditko 5.00
6-10: Early Byrne-a in all (#6 is 1/75). 6-Disney parody. 8-Full-length story; Nova begins as E-Man's partner .90 2.70 8.00

Embrace #1 © Everette Hartsoe

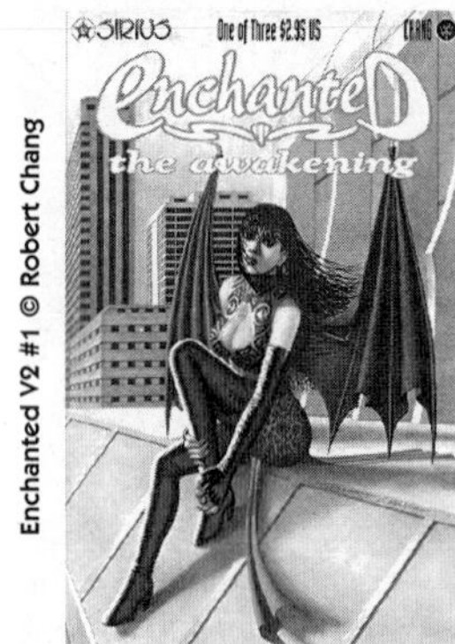

Enchanted V2 #1 © Robert Chang

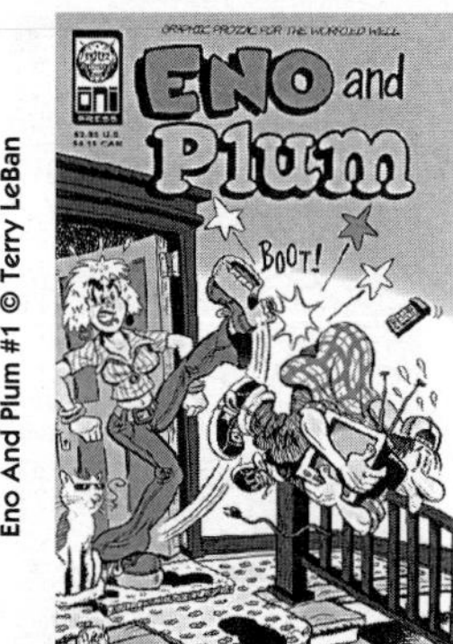

Eno And Plum #1 © Terry LeBan

	GD25	FN65	NM94

1-4,9,10(Modern Comics reprints, '77) 4.00
NOTE: *Killjoy app.-No. 2, 4. Liberty Belle app.-No. 5. Rog 2000 app.-No. 6, 7, 9, 10. Travis app.-No. 3.* ***Tom Sutton*** *a-1.*

E-MAN
Comico: Sept, 1989 ($2.75, one-shot, no ads, high quality paper)
1-Staton-c/a; Michael Mauser story 2.80

E-MAN
Comico: V4#1, Jan, 1990 - No. 3, Mar, 1990 ($2.50, limited series)
1-3: Staton-c/a 2.50

E-MAN
Alpha Productions: Oct, 1993 ($2.75)
V5#1-Staton-c/a; 20th anniversary issue 2.75

E-MAN COMICS (Also see Michael Mauser & The Original E-Man)
First Comics: Apr, 1983 - No. 25, Aug, 1985 ($1.00/$1.25, direct sales only)
1-25: 2-X-Men satire. 3-X-Men/Phoenix satire. 6-Origin retold. 8-Cutey Bunny app. 10-Origin Nova Kane. 24-Origin Michael Mauser 1.00
NOTE: ***Staton*** *a-1-5, 6-25p; c-1-25.*

E-MAN RETURNS
Alpha Productions: 1994 ($2.75, B&W)
1-Joe Staton-c/a(p) 2.75

EMBRACE
London Night Studios: Nov, 1996 ($3.00)
1-Photo-c(Carmen Electra) 3.00
1-($5.00)-NC-17 Edition 5.00

EMBRACE: HUNGER OF THE FLESH
London Night Studios: July, 1997 - No. 3 ($3.00, limited series)
1-3 3.00
1-3-($6.00)-Nude Edition 6.00

EMERALD DAWN
DC Comics: 1991 ($4.95, trade paperback)
nn-Reprints Green Lantern: Emerald Dawn #1-6 5.00

EMERALD DAWN II (See Green Lantern...)

EMERGENCY (Magazine)
Charlton Comics: June, 1976 - No. 4, Jan, 1977 (B&W)

	GD25	FN65	NM94
1-Neal Adams-c/a; Heath, Austin-a	1.00	3.00	10.00
2,3: 2-N. Adams-c. 3-N. Adams-a.		2.00	6.00
4-Alcala-a			5.00

EMERGENCY (TV)
Charlton Comics: June, 1976 - No. 4, Dec, 1976

	GD25	FN65	NM94
1-Staton-c; Byrne-a (22 pages)	.90	2.70	9.00
2-4: 2-Staton-c		2.00	6.00

EMERGENCY DOCTOR
Charlton Comics: Summer, 1963 (one-shot)

	GD25	FN65	NM94
1	2.50	7.50	22.00

EMIL & THE DETECTIVES (See Movie Comics)

EMMA PEEL & JOHN STEED (See The Avengers)

EMPEROR'S NEW CLOTHES, THE
Dell Publishing Co.: 1950 (10¢, 68 pgs., 1/2 size, oblong)

	GD25	FN65	NM94
nn - (Surprise Books series)	2.00	6.00	18.00

EMPIRE STRIKES BACK, THE (See Marvel Comics Super Special #16 & Marvel Special Edition)

EMPTY LOVE STORIES
Slave Labor Graphics: Nov, 1994 - Present ($2.95, B&W)
1,2: Steve Darnall scripts in all. 1-Alex Ross-c. 2-(8/96)-Mike Allred-c 3.00

ENCHANTED
Sirius Entertainment: 1997 - No. 3 ($2.50, B&W, limited series)
1-3-Robert Chang-s/a 2.50

ENCHANTED (Volume 2)
Sirius Entertainment: 1998 - No. 3 ($2.95, limited series)
1-Robert Chang-s/a 2.95

ENCHANTED APPLES OF OZ, THE (See First Comics Graphic Novel #5)

ENCHANTER
Eclipse Comics: Apr, 1987 - No. 3, Aug. 1987 ($2.00, B&W, limited series)
1-3 2.00

ENCHANTING LOVE
Kirby Publishing Co.: Oct, 1949 - No. 6, July, 1950 (All 52 pgs.)

	GD25	FN65	NM94
1-Photo-c	11.00	32.00	80.00
2-Photo-c; Powell-a	6.00	18.00	42.00
3,4,6: 3-Jimmy Stewart photo-c	5.70	17.00	38.00
5-Ingels-a, 9 pgs.; photo-c	13.00	38.00	95.00

ENCHANTMENT VISUALETTES (Magazine)
World Editions: Dec, 1949 - No. 5, Apr, 1950 (Painted c-1)

	GD25	FN65	NM94
1-Contains two romance comic strips each	13.00	38.00	95.00
2	9.30	28.00	70.00
3-5	8.50	26.00	60.00

ENEMY
Dark Horse Comics: May, 1994 - No. 5, Sept, 1994 ($2.50, limited series)
1-5 2.50

ENEMY ACE SPECIAL (Also see Our Army at War #151, Showcase #57, 58 & Star Spangled War Stories #138)
DC Comics: 1990 ($1.00, one-shot)
1-Kubert-r/Our Army #151,153; c-r/Showcase 57 3.00

ENIGMA
DC Comics (Vertigo): Mar, 1993 - No. 8, Oct, 1993 ($2.50, limited series)
1-8: Milligan scripts 2.50
Trade paperback ($19.95)-reprints 20.00

ENO AND PLUM (Also see Cud Comics)
Oni Press: Mar, 1998 ($2.95, B&W)
1-Terry LaBan-s/c/a 3.00

ENSIGN O'TOOLE (TV)
Dell Publishing Co.: Aug-Oct, 1963 - No. 2, 1964

	GD25	FN65	NM94
1,2	1.80	5.50	20.00

ENSIGN PULVER (See Movie Classics)

EPIC
Marvel Comics (Epic Comics): 1992 - Book 4, 1992 ($4.95, lim. series, 52 pgs.)
Book One-Four: 2-Dorman painted-c 5.00
NOTE: *Alien Legion in #3. Cholly & Flytrap by* ***Burden****(scripts) &* ***Suydam****(art) in 3, 4. Dinosaurs in #4. Dreadlands in #1. Hellraiser in #1. Nightbreed in #2. Sleeze Brothers in #2. Stalkers in #1-4. Wild Cards in #1-4.*

EPIC ILLUSTRATED (Magazine)
Marvel Comics Group: Spring, 1980 - No. 34, Dec, 1985 ($2.00/$2.50, B&W/color, mature)

	GD25	FN65	NM94
1-Frazetta-c			4.00
2-18: 12-Wolverton Spacehawk-r edited & recolored w/article on him. 13-Bladerunner preview by Williamson. 14-Elric of Melnibone by Russell; Revenge of the Jedi preview. 15-Vallejo-c & interview; 1st Dreadstar story (cont'd in Dreadstar #1). 16-B. Smith-c/a(2).			4.00
19-30: 20-The Sacred & the Profane begins by Ken Steacy. 26-Galactus series begins; Cerebus the Aardvark story by Dave Sim27-Groo. 28-Cerebus app.		2.00	6.00
31-33	.90	2.70	9.00
34	1.60	4.80	16.00

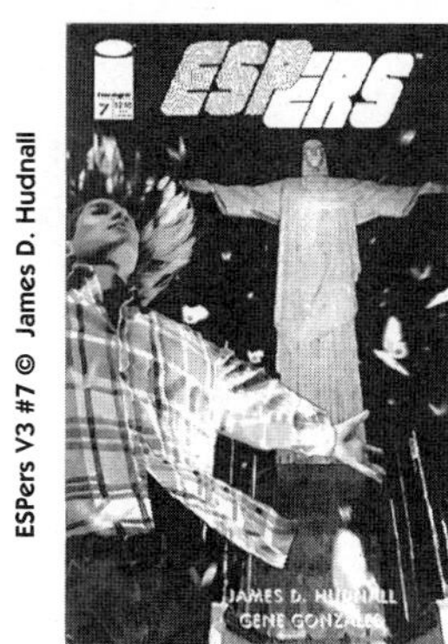

ESPers V3 #7 © James D. Hudnall

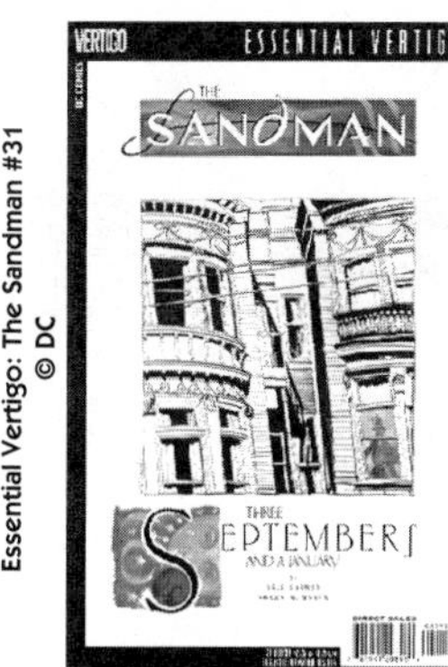

Essential Vertigo: The Sandman #31 © DC

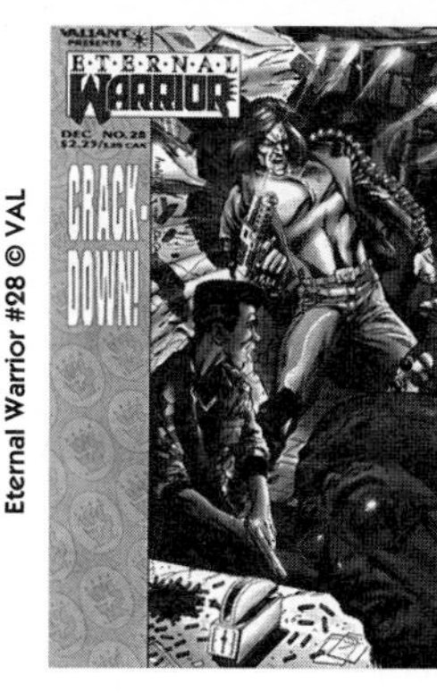

Eternal Warrior #28 © VAL

GD25 FN65 NM94

NOTE: ***N. Adams*** *a-7; c-6.* ***Austin*** *a-15-20i.* ***Bode*** *a-19, 23, 27r.* ***Bolton*** *a-7, 10-12, 15, 18, 22-25; c-10, 18, 22, 23.* ***Boris*** *c/a-15.* ***Brunner*** *c-12.* ***Buscema*** *a-1p, 9p, 11-13p.* ***Byrne/Austin*** *a-26-34.* ***Chaykin*** *a-2; c-8.* ***Conrad*** *a-2-5, 7-9, 25-34; c-17.* ***Corben*** *a-15; c-2.* ***Frazetta*** *c-1.* ***Golden*** *a-3r.* ***Gulacy*** *c/a-3.* ***Jeff Jones*** *c-25.* ***Kaluta*** *a-17r, 21, 24r, 26; c-4, 28.* ***Nebres*** *a-1.* ***Reese*** *a-12.* ***Russell*** *a-2-4, 9, 14, 33; c-14.* ***Simonson*** *a-17.* ***B. Smith*** *c/a-7, 16.* ***Starlin*** *a-1-9, 14, 15, 34.* ***Steranko*** *c-19.* ***Williamson*** *a-13, 27, 34.* ***Wrightson*** *a-13p, 22, 25, 27, 34; c-30.*

EPIC LITE
Marvel Comics (Epic Comics): Sept, 1991 ($3.95, 52 pgs., one-shot)
1-Bob the Alien, Normalman by Valentino 4.00

EPICURUS THE SAGE
DC Comics (Piranha Press): Vol. 1, 1991 - Vol. 2, 1991 ($9.95, 8-1/8x10-7/8")
Volume 1,2-Sam Kieth-c/a 1.00 3.00 10.00

EPSILON WAVE
Independent Comics/Elite Comics No. 5 on: Oct, 1985 - V2#2, 1987 ($1.50/$1.25/$1.75)
1-4: 1-3-($1.50)-Seadragon app. 4-$1.25-c 1.50
5-8: 5-8-$1.75-c. 6-Seadragon app. 1.75
V2#1,2 (B&W) 1.60

ERADICATOR
DC Comics: Aug, 1996 - No. 3, Oct, 1996 ($1.75, limited series)
1-3: Superman app. 1.75

ERNIE COMICS (Formerly Andy Comics #21; All Love Romances #26 on)
Current Books/Ace Periodicals: No. 22, Sept, 1948 - No. 25, Mar, 1949
nn (9/48,11/48; #22,23)-Teenage humor 5.70 17.00 35.00
24,25 4.15 12.50 25.00

ESCAPADE IN FLORENCE (See Movie Comics)

ESCAPE FROM DEVIL'S ISLAND
Avon Periodicals: 1952
1-Kinstler-c; r/as Dynamic Adventures #9 32.00 96.00 240.00

ESCAPE FROM FEAR
Planned Parenthood of America: 1956, 1962, 1969 (Giveaway, 8 pgs. full color) (On birth control)
1956 edition 8.75 26.25 65.00
1962 edition 4.50 13.50 45.00
1969 edition 2.50 7.50 22.00

ESCAPE FROM THE PLANET OF THE APES (See Power Record Comics)

ESCAPE TO WITCH MOUNTAIN (See Walt Disney Showcase No. 29)

ESPERS (Also see Interface)
Eclipse Comics: July, 1986 - No. 5, Apr, 1987 ($1.25/$1.75, Mando paper)
1-3 ($1.25)-James Hudnall story & David Lloyd-a. 1.30
4,5 ($1.75) 1.80

ESPERS
Halloween Comics: V2#1, 1996 - No. 6, 1997 ($2.95, B&W) (1st Halloween Comics series)
V2#1-6: James D. Hudnall scripts 3.00
Undertow TPB ('98, $14.95) r/#1-6 14.95

ESPERS
Image Comics: V3#1, 1997 - Present ($2.95, B&W, limited series)
V3#1-7: James D. Hudnall scripts 2.95
Black Magic TPB ('98, $14.95) r/#1-4 14.95

ESPIONAGE (TV)
Dell Publishing Co.: May-July, 1964 - No. 2, Aug-Oct, 1964
1,2 2.00 6.00 22.00

ESSENTIAL FANTASTIC FOUR
Marvel Comics: 1998 (B&W reprints)
V1-Reprints FF #1-20, Annual #1; new Alan Davis-c 14.95

GD25 FN65 NM94

ESSENTIAL SPIDER-MAN
Marvel Comics: 1996 - Present (B&W reprints)
V1-Reprints AF #15, Amaz. S-M #1-20, Ann. #1 1.30 3.90 13.00
V1-($14.95) 2nd printing 14.95
V2-Reprints Amazing Spider-Man #21-43, Annual #2,3 12.95
V3-Reprints Amazing Spider-Man #44-68 12.95

ESSENTIAL VERTIGO: THE SANDMAN
DC Comics (Vertigo): Aug, 1996 - Present ($1.95/$2.25, reprints)
1-13,15-25: Reprints Sandman, 2nd series 2.00
14-($2.95) 3.00
26-31: 26-Begin $2.25-c 2.25

ESSENTIAL VERTIGO: SWAMP THING
DC Comics: Nov, 1996 - No. 24, Oct, 1998 ($1.95/$2.25,B&W, reprints)
1-9: Reprints Alan Moore's Swamp Thing stories 2.00
10,11,13-24-($2.25) 2.25
12-($3.50) r/Annual #2 3.50

ESSENTIAL X-MEN
Marvel Comics: 1996 - Present (B&W reprints)
V1 1.30 3.90 13.00
V2-Reprints 12.95
V3-Reprints Uncanny X-Men #145-161, Ann. #3-5 14.95

ETC
DC Comics (Piranha Press): 1989 - No. 5, 1990 ($4.50, 60 pgs., mature)
Book 1-5: Conrad scripts/layouts in all 4.50

ETERNAL BIBLE, THE
Authentic Publications: 1946 (Large size) (16 pgs. in color)
1 12.00 36.00 90.00

ETERNALS, THE
Marvel Comics Group: July, 1976 - No. 19, Jan, 1978
1-(Regular 25¢ edition)-Origin & 1st app. Eternals .85 2.60 7.00
1-(30¢-c, limited distribution) 2.20 6.50 24.00
2-(Regular 25¢ edition)-1st app. Ajak & The Celestials 3.00
2-(30¢-c, limited distribution) 1.20 3.60 12.00
3-19: 14,15-Cosmic powered Hulk-c/story 3.00
Annual 1(10/77) 3.00
NOTE: ***Kirby*** *c/a(p) in all.*

ETERNALS, THE
Marvel Comics: Oct, 1985 - No. 12, Sept, 1986 (Maxi-series, mando paper)
1,12 ($1.25, 52 pgs.): 12-Williamson-a(i) 1.25
2-11-(75¢) 1.00

ETERNALS: THE HEROD FACTOR
Marvel Comics: Nov, 1991 ($2.50, 68 pgs.)
1 2.50

ETERNAL WARRIOR (See Solar #10 & 11)
Valiant/Acclaim Comics (Valiant): Aug, 1992 - No. 50, Mar, 1996 ($2.25/$2.50)
1-Unity x-over; Miller-c; origin Eternal Warrior & Aram (Armstrong) 3.00
1-Gold logo 5.00
1-Gold foil logo 2.00 6.00
2-8: 2-Unity x-over; Simonson-c. 3-Archer & Armstrong x-over. 4-1st app. Bloodshot (last pg. cameo); see Rai #0 for 1st full app.; Cowan-c. 5-2nd full app. Bloodshot (12/92; see Rai #0). 6,7: 6-2nd app. Master Darque. 8-Flip book w/Archer & Armstrong #8 2.00
9-25,27-37: 9-1st Book of Geomancer. 14-16-Bloodshot app. 18-Doctor Mirage cameo. 19-Doctor Mirage app. 22-W/bound-in trading card. 25-Archer & Armstrong app.; cont'd from A&A #25 2.00
26-($2.75, 44 pgs.)-Flip book w/Archer & Armstrong 2.75
35-50: 35-Double-c; $2.50-c begins. 50-Geomancer app. 2.50

Everything Happens to Harvey #2 © DC

Evil Ernie #1 © Chaos!

Evil Ernie: Destroyer #7 © Chaos!

	GD25	FN65	NM94
Special 1 (2/96, $2.50)-Art Holcomb script			2.50
Yearbook 1 (1993, $3.95), 2(1994, $3.95)			4.00

ETERNAL WARRIORS: BLACKWORKS
Acclaim Comics (Valiant Heroes): Mar, 1998 ($3.50, one-shot)

	GD25	FN65	NM94
1			3.50

ETERNAL WARRIORS: DIGITAL ALCHEMY
Acclaim Comics (Valiant Heroes): Vol. 2, Sep, 1997 ($3.95, one-shot, 64 pgs.)

	GD25	FN65	NM94
Vol. 2-Holcomb-s/Eaglesham-a(p)			3.95

ETERNAL WARRIORS: FIST AND STEEL
Acclaim Comics (Valiant): May, 1996 - No. 2, June, 1996 ($2.50, lim. series)

	GD25	FN65	NM94
1,2: Geomancer app. in both. 1-Indicia reads "June." 2-Bo Hampton-a			2.50

ETERNAL WARRIORS: TIME AND TREACHERY
Acclaim Comics (Valiant Heroes): Vol. 1, Jun, 1997 ($3.95, one-shot, 48 pgs.)

	GD25	FN65	NM94
Vol. 1-Reintro Aram, Archer, Ivar the Timewalker, & Gilad the Warmaster; 1st app. Shalla Redburn; Art Holcomb script			4.00

ETERNITY SMITH
Renegade Press: Sept, 1986 - No. 5, May, 1987 ($1.25/$1.50, 36 pgs.)

	GD25	FN65	NM94
1 ($1.25)-1st app. Eternity Smith			1.30
2-5 ($1.50): 5-Death of Jasmine			1.50

ETERNITY SMITH
Hero Comics: Sept, 1987 - No. 9, 1988 ($1.95)

	GD25	FN65	NM94
V2#1-9: 8-Indigo begins			2.00

ETTA KETT
King Features Syndicate/Standard: No. 11, Dec, 1948 - No. 14, Sept, 1949

	GD25	FN65	NM94
11-Teenage	7.15	21.50	50.00
12-14	5.35	16.00	32.00

EUDAEMON, THE (See Dark Horse Presents #72-74)
Dark Horse Comics: Aug, 1993 - No. 3, Nov, 1993 ($2.50, limited series)

	GD25	FN65	NM94
1-3: Nelson-a, painted-c & scripts			2.50

EUROPA AND THE PIRATE TWINS
Powder Monkey Productions: Oct, 1996 - No. 2, ($2.50, B&W, limited series)

	GD25	FN65	NM94
1,2: Two covers			3.00

EVANGELINE (Also see Primer)
Comico/First Comics V2#1 on/Lodestone Publ.:
1984 - #2, 6/84; V2#1, 5/87 - V2#12, Mar, 1989 (Baxter paper)

	GD25	FN65	NM94
1,2, V2#1 (5/87) - 12			2.00
Special #1 (1986, $2.00)-Lodestone Publ.			2.00

EVA THE IMP
Red Top Comic/Decker: 1957 - No. 2, Nov, 1957

	GD25	FN65	NM94
1,2	3.20	8.00	16.00

EVEL KNIEVEL
Marvel Comics Group (Ideal Toy Corp.): 1974 (Giveaway, 20 pgs.)

	GD25	FN65	NM94
nn-Contains photo on inside back-c	2.20	6.25	22.00

EVERYBODY'S COMICS (See Fox Giants)

EVERYMAN, THE
Marvel Comics (Epic Comics): Nov, 1991 ($4.50, one-shot, 52 pgs.)

	GD25	FN65	NM94
1-Mike Allred-a	.85	2.60	7.00

EVERYTHING HAPPENS TO HARVEY
National Periodical Publications: Sept-Oct, 1953 - No. 7, Sept-Oct, 1954

	GD25	FN65	NM94
1	21.00	64.00	160.00
2	12.00	36.00	90.00
3-7	9.30	28.00	70.00

EVERYTHING'S ARCHIE
Archie Publications: May, 1969 - No. 157, Sept, 1991 (Giant issues No. 1-20)

	GD25	FN65	NM94
1-(68 pages)	6.50	19.50	65.00
2-(68 pages)	4.50	13.50	45.00
3-5-(68 pages)	3.20	9.60	32.00
6-13-(68 pages)	2.20	6.50	24.00
14-31-(52 pages)	1.40	4.20	14.00
32 (7/74)-50 (8/76)	.90	2.70	8.00
51-80 (12/79),100 (4/82)		2.00	6.00
81-99			4.00
101-120			5.00
121-157: 142,148-Gene Colan-a			2.00

EVERYTHING'S DUCKY (Movie)
Dell Publishing Co.: No. 1251, 1961

	GD25	FN65	NM94
Four Color 1251	3.60	11.00	40.00

EVIL ERNIE
Eternity Comics: Dec, 1991 - No. 5, 1992 ($2.50, B&W, limited series)

	GD25	FN65	NM94
1-1st app. Lady Death by Steven Hughes (12,000 print run); Lady Death app. in all issues	4.50	13.50	50.00
2,3: 2-1st Lady Death-c. 2,3-(7,000 print run)	2.70	8.00	30.00
4-(8,000 print run)	2.25	6.80	25.00
5	2.00	6.00	20.00
Special Edition 1	2.70	8.00	30.00
Youth Gone Wild! ($9.95, trade paperback)-r/#1-5	1.00	3.00	10.00
Youth Gone Wild! Director's Cut ($4.95)-Limited to 15,000 copies, shows the making of the comic			5.00

EVIL ERNIE (Monthly series)
Chaos! Comics: July, 1998 - Present ($2.95)

	GD25	FN65	NM94
1-6-Pulido & Nutman-s/Brewer-a			3.00
1-($10.00) Premium Ed.			10.00

EVIL ERNIE: BADDEST BATTLES
Chaos! Comics: Jan, 1997 ($1.50, one-shot)

	GD25	FN65	NM94
1-Pin-ups			1.50
1-Variant-c			2.00

EVIL ERNIE: DESTROYER
Chaos! Comics: Oct, 1997 - No. 9, Jun, 1998 ($2.95, limited series)

	GD25	FN65	NM94
Preview ($2.50)			2.50
1-9-Flip cover			2.95

EVIL ERNIE: THE RESURRECTION
Chaos! Comics: 1993 - No. 4, 1994 (Limited series)

	GD25	FN65	NM94
1	1.50	4.50	15.00
1A-Gold	3.80	11.50	40.00
2-4	1.00	3.00	10.00

EVIL ERNIE: REVENGE
Chaos! Comics: Oct, 1994 - No.4, Feb, 1995 ($2.95, limited series)

	GD25	FN65	NM94
1: 1-Glow-in-the-dark-c; Lady Death app. 1-3-flip book w. Kilzone Preview (series of 3)		2.00	6.00
1-Commemorative-(4000 print run)	1.50	4.50	15.00
2-4			5.00
Trade paperback (10/95, $12.95)			13.00

EVIL ERNIE: STRAIGHT TO HELL
Chaos! Comics: Oct, 1995 - No. 5, May, 1996 ($2.95, limited series)

	GD25	FN65	NM94
1-5: 1-fold-out-c			3.00
1-($19.95) Chromium Ed.	1.50	4.50	15.00
3-Chastity Chase Cover-(4000 print run)	2.00	6.00	20.00
Special Edition (10,000)	2.25	6.80	25.00

EVIL ERNIE VS. THE MOVIE MONSTERS
Chaos! Comics: Mar, 1997 ($2.95, one-shot)

	GD25	FN65	NM94
1			3.00

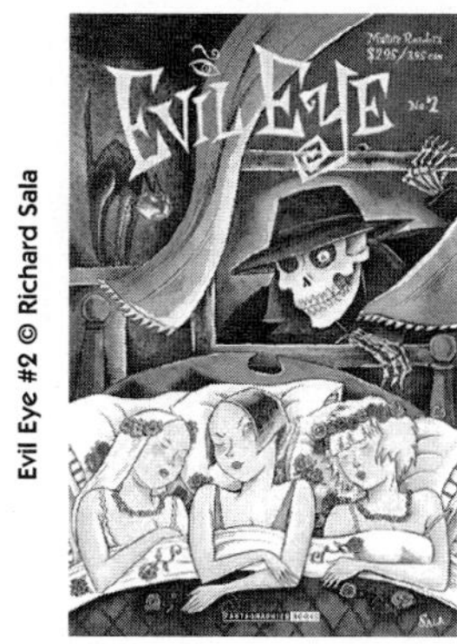

Evil Eye #2 © Richard Sala

Excalibur #125 © MAR

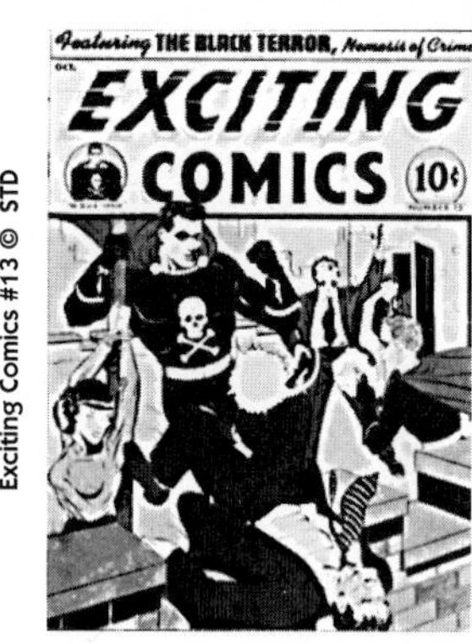

Exciting Comics #13 © STD

GD25 FN65 NM94

1-Variant-"Chaos-Scope•Terror Vision" card stock-c 5.00

EVIL ERNIE VS. THE SUPER HEROES
Chaos! Comics: Aug, 1995 ($2.95, one-shot)

1-Lady Death poster 3.00
1-Foil-c variant (limited to 10,000) 2.25 6.80 25.00
1-Limited Edition (1000) 2.00 6.00 20.00

EVIL EYE
Fantagraphics Books: June, 1998 - Present ($2.95, B&W)

1,2-Richard Sala-s/a 1.20 3.00

EWOKS (Star Wars) (TV) (See Star Comics Magazine)
Marvel Comics (Star Comics): June, 1985 - No. 14, Jul, 1987 (75¢/$1.00)

1,10: 10-Williamson-a (From Star Wars) .90 2.70 8.00
2-9,11-14: 14-($1.00-c) 2.00 6.00

EXCALIBUR (Also see Marvel Comics Presents #31)
Marvel Comics: Apr, 1988; Oct, 1988 - No. 125, Oct, 1998 ($1.50/$1.75/$1.99)

Special Edition nn (The Sword is Drawn)(4/88, $3.25)-1st Excalibur comic .80 2.40 6.50
Special Edition nn (4/88)-no price on-c (scarce) 1.20 3.60 12.00
Special Edition nn (2nd print, 10/88, $3.50) 2.00
Special Edition nn (3rd print, 12/89, 4.50) 2.00
...The Sword is Drawn (Apr, 1992, $4.95) 3.00
1($1.50, 10/88)-X-Men spin-off; Nightcrawler, Shadowcat(Kitty Pryde), Capt. Britain, Phoenix & Meggan begin 5.00
2 2.50
3,4 2.00
5-10 2.00
11-15: 10,11-Rogers/Austin-a 2.00
16-23: 19-Austin-i. 21-Intro Crusader X. 22-Iron Man x-over 1.50
24-40,42-49,51-70,72-74,76: 32-($1.50). 24-John Byrne app. in story; $1.75-c begins. 26-Ron Lim-c/a. 27-B. Smith-a(p). 37-Dr. Doom & Iron Man app. 49-Neal Adams c-swipe. 52,57-X-Men (Cyclops, Wolverine) app. 53-Spider-Man-c/story. 58-X-Men (Wolverine, Gambit, Cyclops, etc.)-c/story. 61-Phoenix returns. 68-Starjammers-c/story 1.50
41-X-Men (Wolverine) app.; Cable cameo 2.00
50-($2.75, 56 pgs.)-New logo 2.75
71-($3.95, 52 pgs.)-Hologram on-c; 30th anniversary 4.00
75-($3.50, 52 pgs.)-Holo-grafx foil-c 4.00
75-($2.25, 52 pgs.)-Regular edition 2.25
77-81,83-86: 77-Begin $1.95-c; bound-in trading card sheet. 83-86-Deluxe edition. 86-1st app. Pete Wisdom 2.00
82-($2.50)-Newsstand edition 2.50
82-($3.50)-Enhanced edition 3.50
83-86-($1.50)-Standard edition 1.50
87-89,91-99,101-110, -1(7/97): 87-Return from Age of Apocalypse. 92-Colossus-c/app. 94-Days of Future Tense 95-X-Man-c/app. 96-Sebastian Shaw & the Hellfire Club app. 99-Onslaught app. 101-Onslaught tie-in. 102-w/card insert. 103-Last Warren Ellis scripts; Belasco app. 109-Spiral-c/app. 2.00
90-($2.95)-double-sized 3.00
100-($2.95)-Onslaught tie-in; wraparound-c 3.50
111-124: 111-Begin $1.99-c, wraparound-c. 119-Calafiore-a 2.00
125-($2.99) Wedding of Capt. Britain and Meggan 3.00
Annual 1 (1993, $2.95)-1st app. Khaos 3.00
Annual 2 (1994, $2.95, 68 pgs.)-X-Men & Psylocke app. 3.00
...Air Apparent nn (12/91, $4.95)-Simonson-c 4.00
...Mojo Mayhem nn (12/89, $4.50)-Art Adams/Austin-c/a 4.00
...: The Possession nn (7/91, $2.95, 52 pgs.) 2.50
...: XX Crossing (7/92, 5/92-inside, $2.50)-vs. The X-Men 2.00

EXCITING COMICS
Nedor/Better Publications/Standard Comics: Apr, 1940 - No. 69, Sept, 1949

GD25 FN65 NM94

1-Origin & 1st app. The Mask, Jim Hatfield, Sgt. Bill King, Dan Williams begin; early Robot-c (see Smash #1) 316.00 950.00 3000.00
2-The Sphinx begins; The Masked Rider app.; Son of the Gods begins, ends #8 141.00 423.00 1200.00
3-Robot-c 94.00 282.00 800.00
4-6 62.00 186.00 525.00
7,8 50.00 150.00 425.00
9-Origin/1st app. of The Black Terror & sidekick Tim, begin series (5/41) (Black Terror c-9-52,54,55) 680.00 2040.00 6800.00
10-2nd app. Black Terror 224.00 675.00 1900.00
11 112.00 336.00 950.00
12,13 74.00 222.00 625.00
14-Last Sphinx, Dan Williams 50.00 150.00 425.00
15-The Liberator begins (origin) 53.00 160.00 450.00
16-20: 20-The Mask ends 43.00 129.00 350.00
21,23-25: 25-Robot-c 39.00 117.00 290.00
22-Origin The Eaglet; The American Eagle begins 44.00 132.00 375.00
26,27,29,30: 26-Schomburg-c begin 46.00 138.00 390.00
28-(Scarce) Crime Crusader begins, ends #58 53.00 160.00 450.00
31-38: 35-Liberator ends, not in 31-33 42.00 126.00 340.00
39-Origin Kara, Jungle Princess 49.00 147.00 420.00
40-50: 42-The Scarab begins. 45-Schomburg Robot-c. 49-Last Kara, Jungle Princess. 50-Last American Eagle 46.00 138.00 390.00
51-Miss Masque begins (1st app.) 52.00 156.00 440.00
52-54: Miss Masque ends. 53-Miss Masque-c 43.00 129.00 360.00
55-58: 55-Judy of the Jungle begins (origin), ends #69; 1 pg. Ingels-a; Judy of the Jungle c-56-66. 56-58: All airbrush-c 46.00 138.00 390.00
59-Frazetta art in Caniff style; signed Frank Frazeta (one t), 9 pgs. 46.00 138.00 390.00
60-66: 60-Rick Howard, the Mystery Rider begins. 66-Robinson/Meskin-a 42.00 126.00 340.00
67-69-All western covers 16.00 48.00 120.00

NOTE: ***Schomburg (Xela)** c-26-68; airbrush c-57-66. Black Terror by **R. Moreira**-#65. **Roussos** a-62. Bondage-c 9, 12, 13, 20, 23, 25, 30, 59.*

EXCITING ROMANCES
Fawcett Publications: 1949 (nd); No. 2, Spring, 1950 - No. 5, 10/50; No. 6 (1951, nd); No. 7, 9/51 -No. 14, 1/53

1(1949) 11.00 34.00 85.00
2,4,5-(1950) 6.50 19.50 45.00
3-Wood-a 11.00 34.00 85.00
6-14 5.70 17.00 35.00

NOTE: ***Powell** a-8-10. **Marcus Swayze** a-5, 6, 9. Photo c-1-7, 10-12.*

EXCITING ROMANCE STORIES (See Fox Giants)

EXCITING WAR (Korean War)
Standard Comics (Better Publ.): No. 5, Sept, 1952 - No. 8, May, 1953; No. 9, Nov, 1953

5 6.70 20.00 45.00
6,7,9 4.15 12.50 25.00
8-Toth-a 6.70 20.00 45.00

EXCITING X-PATROL
Marvel Comics (Amalgam): June, 1997 ($1.95, one-shot)

1-Barbara Kesel-s/ Bryan Hitch-a 1.95

EXILES (Also see Break-Thru)
Malibu Comics (Ultraverse): Aug, 1993 - No. 4, Nov, 1993 ($1.95)

1,2,4: 1,2-Bagged copies of each exist. 2-Gustovich-c. 4-Team dies; story cont'd in Break-Thru #1 2.00
3-($2.50, 40 pgs.)-Rune flip-c/story by B. Smith (3 pgs.) 2.50
1-Holographic-c edition .90 2.70 8.00

EXILES (All New, The) (2nd Series) (Also see Black September)
Malibu Comics (Ultraverse): Sept, 1995 - V2#11, Aug, 1996 ($1.50)

Infinity (9/95, $1.50)-Intro new team including Marvel's Juggernaut & Reaper.

Exploits of Daniel Boone #6 © QUA

Exposed #4 © D.S. Publishing

Factor X #4 © MAR

GD25 FN65 NM94

1.50
Infinity (2000 signed) 1.00 3.00 10.00
V2#1 (2000 signed) 1.00 3.00 10.00
V2#1-4,6-11: 1-(10/95, 64 pgs.)-Reprint of Ultraforce V2#1 follows lead story. 2-1st app. Hellblade. 8-Intro Maxis. 11-Vs. Maxis; Ripfire app.; cont'd in Ultraforce #12 1.50
V2#5-($2.50) Juggernaut returns to the Marvel Universe. 2.50

EXILES VS THE X-MEN
Malibu Comics (Ultraverse): Oct, 1995 (one-shot)

0-Limited Super Premium Edition; signed w/certificate; gold foil logo 1.00 3.00 10.00
0-Limited Premium Edition 1.50 4.50 15.00

EX-MUTANTS
Malibu Comics: Nov, 1992 - No. 18, Apr, 1994 ($1.95/$2.25/$2.50)

1-10 2.00
11-14 ($2.25): 11-Polybagged w/Skycap 2.25
15-18 ($2.50) 2.50

EXORCISTS (See The Crusaders)

EXOSQUAD (TV)
Topps Comics: No. 0, Jan, 1994 ($1.25)

0-($1.00, 20 pgs.)-1st app.; Staton-a(p); wraparound-c 1.00

EXOTIC ROMANCES (Formerly True War Romances)
Quality Comics Group (Comic Magazines): No. 22, Oct, 1955-No. 31, Nov, 1956

22 7.85 23.50 55.00
23-26,29 4.25 13.50 28.00
27,31-Baker-c/a 11.00 32.00 80.00
28,30-Baker-a 9.30 28.00 65.00

EXPLOITS OF DANIEL BOONE
Quality Comics Group: Nov, 1955 - No. 6, Oct, 1956

1-All have Cuidera-c(i) 23.00 70.00 175.00
2 15.00 44.00 110.00
3-6 12.00 36.00 90.00

EXPLOITS OF DICK TRACY (See Dick Tracy)

EXPLORER JOE
Ziff-Davis Comic Group (Approved Comics): Win, 1951 - No. 2, Oct-Nov, 1952

1-2: Saunders painted covers; 2-Krigstein-a 11.00 32.00 80.00

EXPLORERS OF THE UNKNOWN (See Archie Giant Series #587, 599)
Archie Comics: June, 1990 - No. 6, Apr, 1991 ($1.00)

1-6: Featuring Archie and the gang 3.00

EXPOSED (...True Crime Cases; ...Cases in the Crusade Against Crime #5-9)
D. S. Publishing Co.: Mar-Apr, 1948 - No. 9, July-Aug, 1949

1 19.00 56.00 140.00
2-Giggling killer story with excessive blood; two injury-to-eye panels; electrocution panel 22.00 66.00 165.00
3,8,9 9.30 28.00 65.00
4-Orlando-a 9.30 28.00 70.00
5-Breeze Lawson, Sky Sheriff by E. Good 9.30 28.00 65.00
6-Ingels-a; used in **SOTI**, illo. "How to prepare an alibi" 33.00 100.00 250.00
7-Illo. in **SOTI**, "Diagram for housebreakers;" used by N.Y. Legis. Committee 33.00 100.00 250.00

EXTRA!
E. C. Comics: Mar-Apr, 1955 - No. 5, Nov-Dec, 1955

1-Not code approved 12.50 38.00 125.00
2-5 8.50 25.50 85.00

NOTE: *Craig, Crandall, Severin art in all.*

EXTRA COMICS
Magazine Enterprises: 1948 (25¢, 3 comics in one)

1-Giant; consisting of rebound ME comics. Two versions known; (1)-Funnyman by Siegel & Shuster, Space Ace, Undercover Girl, Red Fox by L.B. Cole, Trail Colt & (2)-All Funnyman 45.00 135.00 385.00

EXTREME
Image Comics (Extreme Studios): Aug, 1993 (Giveaway)

0 2.00

EXTREME DESTROYER
Image Comics (Extreme Studios): Jan, 1996 ($2.50)

Prologue 1-Polybagged w/card; Liefeld-c 2.50
Epilogue 1-Liefeld-c 2.50

EXTREME JUSTICE
DC Comics: No. 0, Jan, 1995 - No. 18, July, 1996 ($1.50/$1.75)

0-4 1.75
5-18: 5-Begin $1.75-c 2.00

EXTREMELY YOUNGBLOOD
Image Comics (Extreme Studios): Sept, 1996 ($3.50, one-shot)

1 3.50

EXTREME SACRIFICE
Image Comics (Extreme Studios): Jan, 1995 ($2.50, limited series)

Prelude (#1)-Liefeld wraparound-c; polybagged w/ trading card 2.50
Epilogue (#2)-Liefeld wraparound-c; polybagged w/trading card 2.50
Trade paperback (6/95, $16.95)-Platt-a 17.00

EXTREME SUPER CHRISTMAS SPECIAL
Image Comics (Extreme Studios): Dec, 1994 ($2.95, one-shot)

1 3.00

EXTREMIST, THE
DC Comics (Vertigo): Sept, 1993 - No. 4, Dec, 1993 ($1.95, limited series)

1-4-Peter Milligan scripts; McKeever-c/a 2.50
1-Platinum Edition 1.00 3.00 10.00

EYE OF THE STORM
Rival Productions: Dec, 1994 - No. 7, June, 1995? ($2.95)

1-7: Computer generated comic 3.00

FACE
DC Comics (Vertigo): Jan, 1995 ($4.95, one-shot)

1 5.00

FACE, THE (Tony Trent, the Face No. 3 on) (See Big Shot Comics)
Columbia Comics Group: 1941 - No. 2, 1941?

1-The Face; Mart Bailey-c 79.00 237.00 675.00
2-Bailey-c 47.00 141.00 400.00

FACTOR X
Marvel Comics: Mar, 1995 - No. 4, July, 1995 ($1.95, limited series)

1-Age of Apocalypse 3.00
2-4 2.00

FACULTY FUNNIES
Archie Comics: June, 1989 - No. 5, May, 1990 (75¢/95¢ #2 on)

1-5: 1,2-The Awesome Four app. 3.00

FAFHRD AND THE GREY MOUSER (Also see Sword of Sorcery & Wonder Woman #202)
Marvel Comics: Oct, 1990 - No. 4, 1991 ($4.50, 52 pgs., squarebound)

1-4: Mignola/Williamson-a; Chaykin scripts 4.50

FAIRY TALE PARADE (See Famous Fairy Tales)
Dell Publishing Co.: June-July, 1942 - No. 121, Oct, 1946 (Most by Walt Kelly)

Falcon #3 © MAR

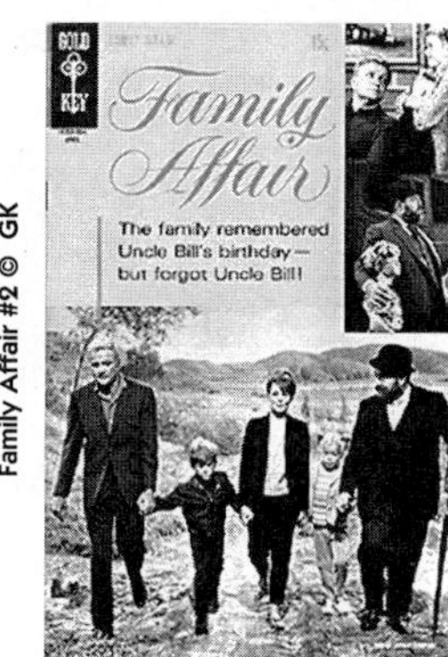

Family Affair #2 © GK

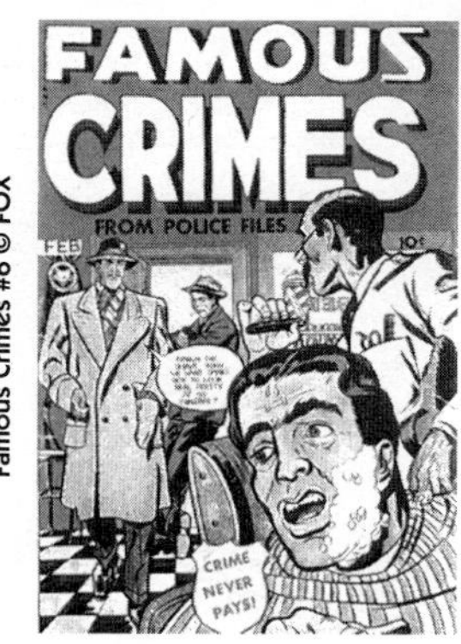

Famous Crimes #6 © FOX

	GD25	FN65	NM94
1-Kelly-a begins	118.00	355.00	1300.00
2(8-9/42)	50.00	150.00	550.00
3-5 (10-11/42 - 2-4/43)	35.00	104.00	380.00
6-9 (5-7/43 - 11-1/43-44)	26.00	79.00	290.00
Four Color 50('44),69('45), 87('45)	24.00	71.00	260.00
Four Color 104,114('46)-Last Kelly issue	17.00	52.00	190.00
Four Color 121('46)-Not by Kelly	10.00	30.00	110.00

NOTE: *#1-9, 4-Color #50, 69 have* ***Kelly*** *c/a; 4-Color #87, 104, 114-****Kelly*** *art only. #9 has a redrawn version of The Reluctant Dragon. This series contains all the classic fairy tales from Jack In The Beanstalk to Cinderella.*

FAIRY TALES
Ziff-Davis Publ. Co. (Approved Comics): No. 10, Apr-May, 1951 - No. 11, June-July, 1951

	GD25	FN65	NM94
10,11-Painted-c	16.00	48.00	120.00

FAITH
Lightning Entertainment: July, 1997 - Present ($2.95, B&W)

	GD25	FN65	NM94
1			2.95

FAITHFUL
Marvel Comics/Lovers' Magazine: Nov, 1949 - No. 2, Feb, 1950 (52 pgs.)

	GD25	FN65	NM94
1,2-Photo-c	7.85	23.50	55.00

FALCON (See Marvel Premiere #49)(Also see Avengers #181 & Captain America #117 & 133)
Marvel Comics Group: Nov, 1983 - No. 4, Feb, 1984 (Mini-series)

	GD25	FN65	NM94
1-4: 1-Paul Smith-c/a(p). 2-Paul Smith-c			1.50

FALLEN ANGEL ON THE WORLD OF MAGIC: THE GATHERING
Acclaim (Armada): May, 1996 ($5.95, one-shot)

	GD25	FN65	NM94
1-Nancy Collins story.		2.00	6.00

FALLEN ANGELS
Marvel Comics Group: April, 1987 - No. 8, Nov, 1987 (Limited series)

	GD25	FN65	NM94
1			2.00
2-8			1.40

FALLING IN LOVE
Arleigh Pub. Co./National Per. Pub.: Sept-Oct, 1955 - No. 143, Oct-Nov, 1973

	GD25	FN65	NM94
1	33.00	100.00	250.00
2	16.00	48.00	120.00
3-10	9.30	28.00	70.00
11-20	7.15	21.50	50.00
21-40	5.70	17.00	35.00
41-47: 47-Last 10¢ issue?	4.25	13.00	26.00
48-70	2.25	6.75	18.00
71-99,108: 108-Wood-a (4 pgs., 7/69)	1.75	5.25	14.00
100	2.50	7.50	25.00
101-107,109-124	1.25	3.75	10.00
134-143	1.10	3.30	9.00
125-133: 52 pgs.	2.50	7.50	20.00

NOTE: ***Colan*** *c/a-75, 81. 52 pgs.-#125-133.*

FALLING MAN, THE
Image Comics: Feb, 1998 - Present ($2.95)

	GD25	FN65	NM94
1-McCorkindale-s/Hester-a			2.95

FALL OF THE HOUSE OF USHER, THE (See A Corben Special & Spirit section 8/22/48)

FALL OF THE ROMAN EMPIRE (See Movie Comics)

FAMILY AFFAIR (TV)
Gold Key: Feb, 1970 - No. 4, Oct, 1970 (25¢)

	GD25	FN65	NM94
1-With pull-out poster; photo-c	4.00	12.00	45.00
1-With poster missing	1.80	5.50	20.00
2-4: 3,4-Photo-c	2.20	6.50	24.00

FAMILY FUNNIES
Parents' Magazine Institute: No. 9, Aug-Sept, 1946

	GD25	FN65	NM94
9	4.00	11.00	22.00

FAMILY FUNNIES (Tiny Tot Funnies No. 9)
Harvey Publications: Sept, 1950 - No. 8, Apr, 1951

	GD25	FN65	NM94
1-Mandrake (has over 30 King Feature strips)	7.15	21.50	50.00
2-Flash Gordon, 1 pg.	5.70	17.00	35.00
3-8: 4,5,7-Flash Gordon, 1 pg.	5.00	15.00	30.00
1(Black & white)	3.60	9.00	18.00

FAMILY MAN
DC Comics (Paradox Press): 1995 - No. 3, 1995 ($4.95, B&W, digest-size, limited series)

	GD25	FN65	NM94
1-3			5.00

FAMOUS AUTHORS ILLUSTRATED (See Stories by...)

FAMOUS COMICS (Also see Favorite Comics)
Zain-Eppy/United Features Syndicate: No date; Mid 1930's (24 pgs., paper-c)

	GD25	FN65	NM94
nn-Reprinted from 1933 & 1934 newspaper strips in color; Joe Palooka, Hairbreadth Harry, Napoleon, The Nebbs, etc. (Many different versions known)	43.00	129.00	350.00

FAMOUS COMICS
King Features Synd. (Whitman Pub. Co.): 1934 (100 pgs., daily newspaper-r) (3-1/2x8-1/2"; paper cover) (came in a box)

	GD25	FN65	NM94
684(#1)-Little Jimmy, Katzenjammer Kids, & Barney Google	31.00	92.00	230.00
684(#2)-Polly, Little Jimmy, Katzenjammer Kids	31.00	92.00	230.00
684(#3)-Little Annie Rooney, Polly and her Pals, Katzenjammer Kids	31.00	92.00	230.00
....Box price....	29.00	86.00	215.00

FAMOUS COMICS CARTOON BOOKS
Whitman Publishing Co.: 1934 (8x7-1/4", 72 pgs., B&W hard-c, daily strip-r)

	GD25	FN65	NM94
1200-The Captain & the Kids (1st app?); Dirks reprints credited to Bernard Dibble	25.00	76.00	190.00
1202-Captain Easy (1st app?) & Wash Tubbs by Roy Crane; 2 slightly different versions of cover exist	31.00	92.00	230.00
1203-Ella Cinders (1st app?)	25.00	74.00	185.00
1204-Freckles & His Friends (1st app?)	22.00	66.00	165.00

NOTE: *Called Famous Funnies Cartoon Books inside.*

FAMOUS CRIMES
Fox Features Syndicate/M.S. Dist. No. 51,52: June, 1948 - No. 19, Sept, 1950; No. 20, Aug, 1951; No. 51, 52, 1953

	GD25	FN65	NM94
1-Blue Beetle app. & crime story-r/Phantom Lady #16	43.00	129.00	360.00
2-Has woman dissolved in acid; lingerie-c/panels	35.00	104.00	260.00
3-Injury-to-eye story used in **SOTI**, pg. 112; has two electrocution stories	41.00	124.00	330.00
4-6	17.00	52.00	130.00
7- "Tarzan, the Wyoming Killer" used in **SOTI**, pg. 44; drug trial/possession story	35.00	106.00	265.00
8-20: 17-Morisi-a	13.00	38.00	95.00
51(nd, 1953)	13.00	38.00	95.00
52	6.70	20.00	45.00

FAMOUS FAIRY TALES
K. K. Publ. Co.: 1942; 1943 (32 pgs.); 1944 (16 pgs.) (Giveaway, soft-c)

	GD25	FN65	NM94
1942-Kelly-a	39.00	117.00	300.00
1943-r-/Fairy Tale Parade No. 2,3; Kelly-a	30.00	90.00	225.00
1944-Kelly-a	27.00	80.00	200.00

FAMOUS FEATURE STORIES
Dell Publishing Co.: 1938 (7-1/2x11", 68 pgs.)

1-Tarzan, Terry & the Pirates, King of the Royal Mtd., Buck Jones, Dick Tracy, Smilin' Jack, Dan Dunn, Don Winslow, G-Man, Tailspin Tommy, Mutt & Jeff,

Famous First Edition V2 #F-6 Hardcover © DC

Famous Funnies #54 © EAS

Famous Funnies #207 © EAS

GD25 FN65 NM94

Little Orphan Annie reprints - all illustrated text 62.00 185.00 525.00

FAMOUS FIRST EDITION (See Limited Collectors' Edition)
National Periodical Publications/DC Comics: ($1.00, 10x13-1/2", 72 pgs.) (No.6-8, 68 pgs.) 1974 - No. 8, Aug-Sept, 1975; C-61, 1979

C-26-Action Comics #1; gold ink outer-c 2.70 8.00 30.00
C-28-Detective #27; silver ink outer-c 5.00 15.00 55.00
C-28-Hardbound edition 21.00 63.00 210.00
C-30-Sensation #1(1974); bronze ink outer-c 2.70 8.00 30.00
F-4-Whiz Comics #2(#1)(10-11/74)-Cover not identical to original (dropped "Gangway for Captain Marvel" from cover); gold ink on outer-c 2.70 8.00 30.00
F-5-Batman #1(F-6 inside); silver ink on outer-c 4.00 12.00 45.00
V2#F-6-Wonder Woman #1 2.70 8.00 30.00
F-7-All-Star Comics #3 1.60 4.80 16.00
F-8-Flash Comics #1(8-9/75) 1.60 4.80 16.00
V8#C-61-Superman #1(1979, $2.00) 1.60 4.80 16.00
Hardbound editions (w/dust jackets $5.00 extra) (Lyle Stuart, Inc.)
C-26,C-30,F-4,F-6 known 16.00 48.00 160.00

Warning: The above books are almost **exact** reprints of the originals that they represent except for the Giant-Size format. None of the originals are Giant-Size. The first five issues and C-61 were printed with two covers. Reprint information can be found on the outside cover, but not on the inside cover which was reprinted exactly like the original (inside and out).

FAMOUS FUNNIES
Eastern Color: 1933 - No. 218, July, 1955

GD25 FN65 VF82 NM94

A Carnival of Comics (probably the second comic book), 36 pgs., no date given, no publisher, no number; contains strip reprints of The Bungle Family, Dixie Dugan, Hairbreadth Harry, Joe Palooka, Keeping Up With the Jones, Mutt & Jeff, Reg'lar Fellers, S'Matter Pop, Strange As It Seems, and others. This book was sold by M. C. Gaines to Wheatena, Milk-O-Malt, John Wanamaker, Kinney Shoe Stores, & others to be given away as premiums and radio give-aways (1933). 760.00 2280.00 4560.00 8000.00

Series 1-(Very rare)(nd-early 1934)(68 pgs.) No publisher given (Eastern Color PrintingCo.); sold in chain stores for 10¢. 35,000 print run. Contains Sunday strip reprints of Mutt & Jeff, Reg'lar Fellers, Nipper, Hairbreadth Harry, Strange As It Seems, Joe Palooka, Dixie Dugan, The Nebbs, Keeping Up With the Jones, and others. Inside front and back covers and pages 1-16 of Famous Funnies Series 1, #s 49-64 reprinted from **Famous Funnies**, **A Carnival of Comics**, and most of pages 17-48 reprinted from **Funnies on Parade**. This was the first comic book sold. 3000.00 9000.00 15,000.00 22,000.00

No. 1 (Rare)(7/34-on stands 5/34) - Eastern Color Printing Co. First monthly newsstand comic book. Contains Sunday strip reprints of Toonerville Folks, Mutt & Jeff, Hairbreadth Harry, S'Matter Pop, Nipper, Dixie Dugan, The Bungle Family, Connie, Ben Webster, Tailspin Tommy, The Nebbs, Joe Palooka, & others. 2215.00 6645.00 11,075.00 15,500.00

GD25 FN65 VF82

2 (Rare, 9/34) 450.00 1350.00 3000.00
3-Buck Rogers Sunday strip-r by Rick Yager begins, ends #218; not in #191-208; 1st comic book app. of Buck Rogers; the number of the 1st strip reprinted is pg. 190, Series No. 1 583.00 1750.00 3800.00
4 183.00 550.00 1200.00
5-1st Christmas-c on a newsstand comic 150.00 450.00 975.00
6-10 108.00 324.00 700.00

GD25 FN65 NM94

11,12,18-Four pgs. of Buck Rogers in each issue, completes stories in Buck Rogers #1 which lacks these pages. 18-Two pgs. of Buck Rogers reprinted in Daisy Comics #1 95.00 287.00 625.00
13-17,19,20: 14-Has two Buck Rogers panels missing. 17-2nd Christmas-c on a newsstand comic (12/35) 73.00 219.00 475.00
21,23-30: 27-(10/36)-War on Crime begins (4 pgs.); 1st true crime in comics (reprints); part photo-c. 29-X-Mas-c (12/36) 52.00 157.00 340.00
22-Four pgs. of Buck Rogers needed to complete stories in Buck Rogers #1 56.00 170.00 375.00
31,33,34,36,37,39,40: 33-Careers of Baby Face Nelson & John Dillinger traced 40.00 120.00 260.00
32-(3/37) 1st app. the Phantom Magician (costume hero) in Advs. of Patsy 43.00 130.00 280.00
35-Two pgs. Buck Rogers omitted in Buck Rogers #2 43.00 130.00 280.00

GD25 FN65 NM94

38-Full color portrait of Buck Rogers 39.00 117.00 270.00
41-60: 41,53-X-Mas-c. 55-Last bottom panel, pg. 4 in Buck Rogers redrawn in Buck Rogers #3 28.00 84.00 185.00
61,63,64,66,67,69,70 18.00 54.00 135.00
62,65,68-Two pgs. Kirby-a "Lightnin' & the Lone Rider". 65-X-Mas-c 21.00 64.00 160.00
71,73,77-80: 77-X-Mas-c. 80-(3/41)-Buck Rogers story continues from Buck Rogers #5 13.00 40.00 100.00
72-Speed Spaulding begins by Marvin Bradley (artist), ends #88. This series was written by Edwin Balmer & Philip Wylie (later appeared as film & book "When Worlds Collide") 14.00 42.00 105.00
74-76-Two pgs. Kirby-a in all 13.00 40.00 100.00
81-Origin & 1st app. Invisible Scarlet O'Neil (4/41); strip begins #82, ends #167; 1st non-funny-c (Scarlet O'Neil) 10.00 30.00 75.00
82-Buck Rogers-c 13.00 40.00 100.00
83-87,90: 86-Connie vs. Monsters on the Moon-c (sci/fi). 87 has last Buck Rogers full page-r. 90-Bondage-c 10.00 30.00 75.00
88-Buck Rogers in "Moon's End" by Calkins, 2 pgs.(not reprints). Beginning with #88, all Buck Rogers pgs. have rearranged panels 11.00 32.00 80.00
89-Origin & 1st app. Fearless Flint, the Flint Man 11.00 32.00 80.00
91-93,95,96,98-99,101,103-110: 105-Series 2 begins (Strip Page #1) 9.30 28.00 70.00
94-Buck Rogers in "Solar Holocaust" by Calkins, 3 pgs.(not reprints) 10.00 30.00 75.00
97-War Bond promotion, Buck Rogers by Calkins, 2 pgs.(not reprints) 10.00 30.00 75.00
100-1st comic to reach #100; 100th Anniversary cover features 11 major Famous Funnies characters, including Buck Rogers 10.00 30.00 75.00
102-Chief Wahoo vs. Hitler,Tojo & Mussolini-c (1/43)24.00 72.00 180.00
111-130 (5/45): 113-X-Mas-c 7.15 21.50 50.00
131-150 (1/47): 137-Strip page No. 110 omitted 5.70 17.00 35.00
151-162,164-168 5.00 15.00 30.00
163-St. Valentine's Day-c 5.70 17.00 38.00
169,170-Two text illos. by Williamson, his 1st comic book work 9.30 28.00 65.00
171-180: 171-Strip pgs. 227,229,230, Series 2 omitted. 172-Strip Pg. 232 omitted 4.25 13.00 28.00
181-190: Buck Rogers ends with start of strip pg. 302, Series 2. 190-Oaky Doaks-c/story 4.25 13.00 28.00
191-197,199,201,203,206-208: No Buck Rogers. 191-Barney Carr, Space detective begins, ends #192. 4.15 12.50 25.00
198,202,205-One pg. Frazetta ads; no B. Rogers 4.25 13.00 28.00
200-Frazetta 1 pg. ad 4.25 13.00 28.00
204-Used in **POP**, pg. 79,99; war-c begin, end #208 5.00 15.00 30.00
209-Buck Rogers begins (12/53) with strip pg. 480, Series 2; Frazetta-c 79.00 237.00 675.00
210-216: Frazetta-c. 211-Buck Rogers ads by Anderson begins, ends #217. #215-Contains B. Rogers strip pg. 515-518, series 2 followed by pgs. 179-181, Series 3 79.00 237.00 675.00
217,218-B. Rogers ends with pg. 199, Series 3. 218-Wee Three-c/story 4.25 13.00 28.00

NOTE: ***Rick Yager*** *did the Buck Rogers Sunday strips reprinted in Famous Funnies. The Sundays were formerly done by Russ Keaton and Lt. Dick Calkins did the dailies, but would sometimes assist Yager on a panel or two from time to time. Strip No. 169 is Yager's first full Buck Rogers page. Yager did the strip until 1958 when* ***Murphy Anderson*** *took over.* ***Tuska*** *art from 4/26/59 - 1965. Virtually every panel was rewritten for Famous Funnies. Not identical to the original Sunday page. The Buck Rogers reprints run continuously through Famous Funnies issue No. 190 (Strip No. 302) with no break in story line. The story line has no continuity after No. 190. The Buck Rogers newspaper strips came out in four series: Series 1, 3/30/30 - 9/21/41 (No. 1 - 600); Series 2, 9/28/41 -10/21/51 (No. 1 -525)(Strip No. 110-1/2 (1/2 pg.) published in only a few newspapers); Series 3, 10/28/51 -2/9/58 (No. 100-428)(No No.1-99); Series 4, 2/16/58 - 6/13/65 (No numbers, dates only).* ***Everett*** *c-85, 86.* ***Moulton*** *a-100. Chief Wahoo c-93, 97, 102, 116, 136, 139, 151. Dickie Dare c-83, 88. Fearless Flint c-89. Invisible Scarlet O'Neil c-81, 87, 95, 121(part), 132. Scorchy Smith c-84, 90.*

FAMOUS FUNNIES

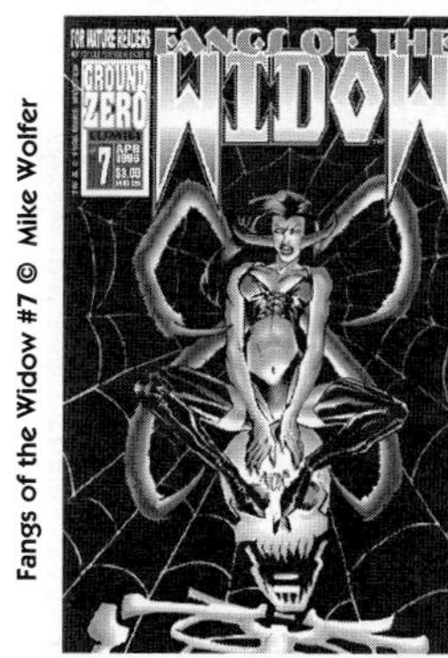

Fangs of the Widow #7 © Mike Wolfer

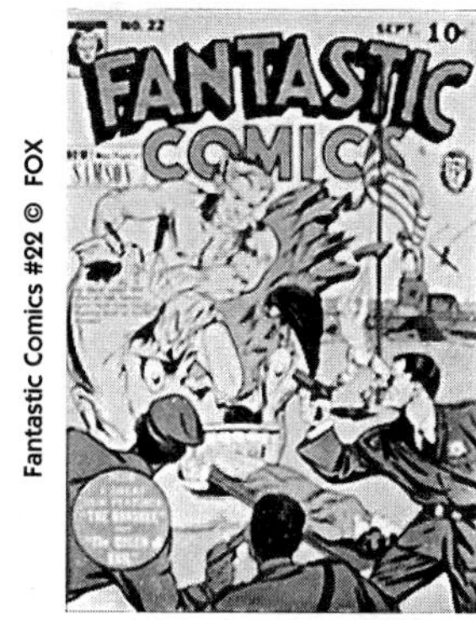

Fantastic Comics #22 © FOX

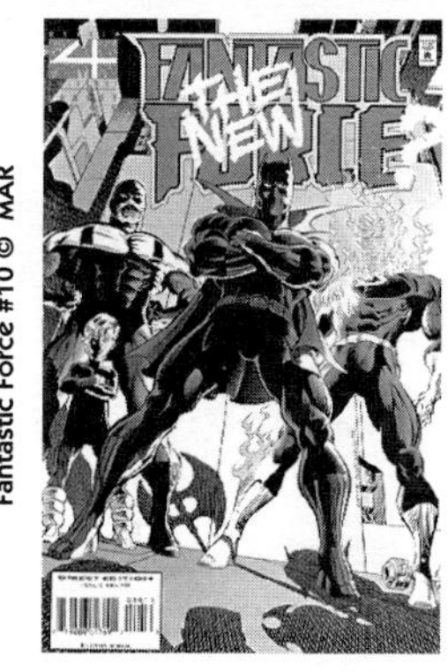

Fantastic Force #10 © MAR

	GD25	FN65	NM94

Super Comics: 1964

Super Reprint Nos. 15-18:17-r/Double Trouble #1. 18-Space Comics #? — 1.50 — 4.50 — 12.00

FAMOUS GANG BOOK OF COMICS (Becomes Donald & Mickey Merry Christmas 1943 on)
Firestone Tire & Rubber Co.: Dec, 1942 (Christmas giveaway, 32 pgs., paper-c)

	GD25	FN65	NM94
nn-(Rare)-Porky Pig, Bugs Bunny, Mary Jane & Sniffles, Elmer Fudd; r/Looney Tunes	60.00	180.00	600.00

FAMOUS GANGSTERS (Crime on the Waterfront No. 4)
Avon Periodicals/Realistic No. 3: Apr, 1951 - No. 3, Feb, 1952

	GD25	FN65	NM94
1-Capone, Dillinger; c-/Avon paperback #329	32.00	96.00	240.00
2-Dillinger Machine Gun Killer; Wood-c/a (1 pg.); r/Saint #7 & retitled "Mike Strong"	32.00	96.00	240.00
3-Lucky Luciano & Murder, Inc; c-/Avon paperback #66	32.00	96.00	240.00

FAMOUS INDIAN TRIBES
Dell Publishing Co.: July-Sept, 1962; No. 2, July, 1972

	GD25	FN65	NM94
12-264-209(#1) (The Sioux)	.90	1.80	10.00
2(7/72)-Reprints above			2.00

FAMOUS STARS
Ziff-Davis Publ. Co.: Nov-Dec, 1950 - No. 6, Spring, 1952 (All have photo-c)

	GD25	FN65	NM94
1-Shelley Winters, Susan Peters, Ava Gardner, Shirley Temple; Jimmy Stewart & Shelley Winters photo-c; Whitney-a	27.00	80.00	200.00
2-Betty Hutton, Bing Crosby, Colleen Townsend, Gloria Swanson; Betty Hutton photo-c; Everett-a(2)	19.00	56.00	140.00
3-Farley Granger, Judy Garland's ordeal, Alan Ladd; Farley Granger & Judy Garland photo-c; Whitney-a	18.00	54.00	135.00
4-Al Jolson, Bob Mitchum, Ella Raines, Richard Conte, Vic Damone; Bob Mitchum photo-c; Crandall-a, 6pgs.	16.00	48.00	120.00
5-Liz Taylor, Betty Grable, Esther Williams, George Brent, Mario Lanza; Liz Taylor photo-c; Krigstein-a	21.00	64.00	160.00
6-Gene Kelly, Hedy Lamarr, June Allyson, William Boyd, Janet Leigh, Gary Cooper; Gene Kelly photo-c	14.00	42.00	105.00

FAMOUS STORIES (...Book No. 2)
Dell Publishing Co.: 1942 - No. 2, 1942

	GD25	FN65	NM94
1,2: 1-Treasure Island. 2-Tom Sawyer	27.00	80.00	200.00

FAMOUS TV FUNDAY FUNNIES
Harvey Publications: Sept, 1961 (25¢ Giant)

	GD25	FN65	NM94
1-Casper the Ghost, Baby Huey, Little Audrey	3.60	10.80	36.00

FAMOUS WESTERN BADMEN (Formerly Redskin)
Youthful Magazines: No. 13, Dec, 1952 - No. 15, Apr, 1953

	GD25	FN65	NM94
13-Redskin story	11.00	32.00	80.00
14,15: 15-The Dalton Boys story	7.85	23.50	55.00

FANGS OF THE WIDOW
London Night/Ground Zero #5 on: Sep, 1995 - No. 14, Jun, 1997 ($3.00, B&W)

	GD25	FN65	NM94
1-14: 5-1st Ground Zero issue			3.00
1-Platinum			3.00

FANTASTIC (Formerly Captain Science; Beware No. 10 on)
Youthful Magazines: No. 8, Feb, 1952 - No. 9, Apr, 1952

	GD25	FN65	NM94
8-Capt. Science by Harrison; decapitation, shrunken head panels	32.00	96.00	240.00
9-Harrison-a	23.00	68.00	170.00

FANTASTIC ADVENTURES
Super Comics: 1963 - 1964 (Reprints)

	GD25	FN65	NM94
9,10,12,15,16,18: 9-r/? 10-r/He-Man #2(Toby). 11-Disbrow-a. 12-Unpublished Chesler material? 15-r/Spook #23. 16-r/Dark Shadows #2(Steinway); Briefer-a.18-r/Superior Stories #1	2.50	7.50	20.00
11-Wood-a; r/Blue Bolt #118	3.50	10.50	35.00
17-Baker-a(2) r/Seven Seas #6	3.50	10.50	35.00

FANTASTIC COMICS
Fox Features Syndicate: Dec, 1939 - No. 23, Nov, 1941

	GD25	FN65	NM94
1-Intro/origin Samson; Stardust, The Super Wizard, Sub Saunders (by Kiefer), Space Smith, Capt. Kidd begin	389.00	1167.00	3700.00
2-Powell text illos	188.00	564.00	1600.00
3-Classic Lou Fine Robot-c; Powell text illos	700.00	2100.00	4800.00
4,5: Last Lou Fine-c	153.00	459.00	1300.00
6,7-Simon-c	115.00	345.00	975.00
8-10: 10-Intro/origin David, Samson's aide	82.00	246.00	700.00
11-17,19,20,22: 16-Stardust ends. 22-Hitler-c	68.00	204.00	575.00
18-1st app. Black Fury & sidekick Chuck; ends #23	71.00	213.00	600.00
21,23: 21-The Banshee begins(origin); ends #23; Hitler-c. 22-Likeness of Hitler as furnace on cover. 23-Origin The Gladiator	71.00	213.00	600.00

*NOTE: **Lou Fine** c-1-5. **Tuska** a-3-5, 8. Bondage c-6, 8, 9. Issue #11 has indicia to Mystery Men Comics #15. All issues feature Samson covers.*

FANTASTIC COMICS (Fantastic Fears #1-9; Becomes Samson #12)
Ajax/Farrell Publ.: No. 10, Nov-Dec, 1954 - No. 11, Jan-Feb, 1955

	GD25	FN65	NM94
10 (#1)	15.00	44.00	110.00
11-Robot-c	17.00	52.00	130.00

FANTASTIC FABLES
Silverwolf Comics: Feb, 1987 - No. 2, 1987 ($1.50, 28 pgs., B&W)

	GD25	FN65	NM94
1,2: 1-Tim Vigil-a (6 pgs.). 2-Tim Vigil-a (7 pgs.)			1.50

FANTASTIC FEARS (Formerly Captain Jet) (Fantastic Comics #10 on)
Ajax/Farrell Publ.: No. 7, May, 1953 - No. 9, Sept-Oct, 1954

	GD25	FN65	NM94
7(#1, 5/53)-Tales of Stalking Terror	35.00	104.00	260.00
8(#2, 7/53)	22.00	66.00	165.00
3,4	16.00	48.00	120.00
5-(1-2/54)-Ditko story (1st drawn) is written by Bruce Hamilton; r-in Weird V2#8 (1st pro work for Ditko but Daring Love #1 was published 1st)	66.00	198.00	560.00
6-Decapitation-girl's head w/paper cutter (classic)	39.00	118.00	315.00
7(5-6/54), 9(9-10/54)	16.00	48.00	120.00
8(7-8/54)-Contains story intended for Jo-Jo; name changed to Kaza; decapitation story	18.00	54.00	135.00

FANTASTIC FORCE
Marvel Comics: Nov, 1994 - No. 18, Apr, 1996 ($1.75)

	GD25	FN65	NM94
1-($2.50)-Foil wraparound-c; intro Fantastic Force w/Huntara, Delvor, Psi-Lord & Vibraxas			2.50
2-18: 13-She-Hulk app.			1.75

FANTASTIC FOUR (See America's Best TV..., Fireside Book Series, Giant-Size..., Giant Size Super-Stars, Marvel Collectors Item Classics, Marvel Milestone Edition, Marvel's Greatest, Marvel Treasury Edition, Marvel Triple Action, Official Marvel Index to... & Power Record Comics)

FANTASTIC FOUR
Marvel Comics Group: Nov, 1961 - No. 416, Sept, 1996 (Created by Stan Lee & Jack Kirby)

	GD25	FN65	VF82	NM94
1-Origin & 1st app. The Fantastic Four (Reed Richards: Mr. Fantastic, Johnny Storm: The Human Torch, Sue Storm: The Invisible Girl, & Ben Grimm: The Thing–Marvel's 1st super-hero group since the G.A.; 1st app. S.A. Human Torch); origin/1st app. The Mole Man.	740.00	2220.00	7400.00	19,000.00

	GD25	FN65	NM94
1-Golden Record Comic Set Reprint (1966)-cover not identical to original	16.00	48.00	160.00
with Golden Record	24.00	72.00	240.00
2-Vs. The Skrulls (last 10¢ issue)	240.00	720.00	3600.00

3-Fantastic Four don costumes & establish Headquarters; brief 1pg. origin; intro The Fantasti-Car; Human Torch drawn w/two left hands on-c

Fantastic Four #15 © MAR

Fantastic Four #113 © MAR

Fantastic Four #259 © MAR

GD25 FN65 NM94

165.00 495.00 2300.00

GD25 FN65 VF82 NM94

4-1st S. A. Sub-Mariner app. (5/62) 200.00 600.00 1300.00 2800.00
5-Origin & 1st app. Doctor Doom 215.00 645.00 1400.00 3000.00

GD25 FN65 NM94

6-Sub-Mariner, Dr. Doom team up; 1st Marvel villain team-up (2nd S.A. Sub-Mariner app. 125.00 375.00 1500.00
7-10: 7-1st app. Kurrgo. 8-1st app. Puppet-Master & Alicia Masters. 9-3rd Sub-Mariner app. 10-Stan Lee & Jack Kirby app. in story 64.00 192.00 770.00
11-Origin/1st app. The Impossible Man (2/63) 54.00 162.00 650.00
12-Fantantic Four Vs. The Hulk (1st meeting); 1st Hulk x-over & ties w/Amazing Spider-Man #1 as 1st Marvel x-over; (3/63) 92.00 275.00 1100.00
13-Intro. The Watcher; 1st app. The Red Ghost 41.00 123.00 480.00
14-19: 14-Sub-Mariner x-over. 15-1st app. Mad Thinker. 16-1st Ant-Man x-over (7/63); Wasp cameo. 18-Origin/1st app. The Super Skrull. 19-Intro. Rama-Tut; Stan Lee & Jack Kirby cameo 29.00 87.00 290.00
20-Origin/1st app. The Molecule Man 31.00 93.00 310.00
21-Intro. The Hate Monger; 1st Sgt. Fury x-over (12/63) 21.00 63.00 210.00
22-24: 22-Sue Storm gains more powers 14.00 42.00 140.00
25,26-The Hulk vs. The Thing (their 1st battle). 25-3rd Avengers x-over (1st time w/Capt. America)(cameo, 4/64); 2nd S.A. app. Cap (takes place between Avengers #4 & 5. 26-4th Avengers x-over 35.00 105.00 390.00
27-1st Doctor Strange x-over (6/64) 16.00 48.00 160.00
28-Early X-Men x-over (7/64); same date as X-Men #6 24.00 72.00 240.00
29,30: 30-Intro. Diablo 10.50 32.00 105.00
31-40: 31-Early Avengers x-over (10/64). 33-1st app. Attuma; part photo-c. 35-Intro/1st app. Dragon Man. 36-Intro/1st app. Madam Medusa & the Frightful Four (Sandman, Wizard, Paste Pot Pete). 39-Wood inks on Daredevil (early x-over) 9.00 27.00 90.00
41-44,47: 41-43-Frightful Four app. 44-Intro. Gorgon.6.00 18.00 60.00
45,46: 45-Intro/1st app. The Inhumans (c/story, 12/65); also see Incredible Hulk Special #1 & Thor #146, & 147. 46-1st Black Bolt-c (Kirby) & 1st full app. 7.00 21.00 70.00
48-Partial origin/1st app. The Silver Surfer & Galactus (3/66) by Lee & Kirby; Galactus cameo in last panel; 1st of 3 part story. 71.00 213.00 850.00
49-2nd app. Silver Surfer & Galactus 24.00 72.00 240.00
50-Silver Surfer battles Galactus 26.00 78.00 260.00
51,54: 54-Inhumans cameo 4.80 14.40 48.00
52-1st app. The Black Panther (7/66) 9.50 28.50 95.00
53-Origin & 2nd app. The Black Panther 8.50 25.50 85.00
55-Thing battles Silver Surfer; 4th app. Silver Surfer 8.00 24.00 80.00
56-60: Silver Surfer x-over. 59,60-Inhumans cameos 5.50 16.50 55.00
61-65,68-70: 61-Silver Surfer cameo; Sandman-c/s 4.20 12.60 42.00
66-Begin 2 part origin of Him (Warlock); does not app. (9/67) 9.50 28.50 95.00
67-Origin/1st app. Him (Warlock); 1 pg. cameo; see Thor #165,166 for 1st full app. 10.50 32.00 105.00
71,73,78-80: 73-Spider-Man, D.D., Thor x-over; cont'd from Daredevil #38 3.50 10.50 35.00
72-Silver Surfer-c/story (pre-dates Silver Surfer #1) 4.20 12.60 42.00
74-77: Silver Surfer app.(#77 is same date/S.S. #1) 4.00 12.00 40.00
81-88: 81-Crystal joins & dons costume. 82,83-Inhumans app. 84-87-Dr. Doom app. 88-Last 12¢ issue 2.50 7.60 28.00
89-99,101: 94-Intro. Agatha Harkness. 2.20 6.25 23.00
100 (7/70) 7.25 22.00 80.00
102,103: Fantastic Four vs. Sub-Mariner 2.25 6.80 25.00
104-111: 104-Magneto-c/story. 108-Last Kirby issue (not in #103-107). 110-reg. version w/green faces 1.60 4.80 16.00

GD25 FN65 NM94

110-Variant-c w/flesh color faces and green Thing. Common version shows green faces. 2.50 7.40 27.00
112-Hulk Vs. Thing (7/71) 4.50 13.50 50.00
113-115: 115-Last 15¢ issue 1.40 4.20 14.00
116-120: 116-(52 pgs.) .90 2.70 9.00
121-123-Silver Surfer-c/stories. 122,123-Galactus 1.40 4.20 14.00
124,125,127,129-149: 129-Intro. Thundra. 130-Sue leaves F.F. 131-Quicksilver app. 132-Medusa joins. 133-Thundra Vs. Thing. 142-Kirbyish-a by Buckler begins. 143-Dr. Doom-c/story. 147-Sub-Mariner .85 2.60 7.00
126-Origin F.F. retold; cover swipe of F.F. #1 1.00 3.00 10.00
128-Four pg. insert of F.F. Friends & Foes 1.00 3.00 10.00
150-Crystal & Quicksilver's wedding 1.10 3.30 11.00
151-154,158-160: 151-Origin Thundra. 159-Medusa leaves; Sue rejoins 2.00 6.00
155-157: Silver Surfer in all .85 2.60 7.00
161-168,172,174-180: 164-The Crusader (old Marvel Boy) revived (origin #165); 1st app.Frankie Raye. 168-170-Cage app. 176-Re-intro Impossible Man; Marvel artists app. 180-r/#101 by Kirby 3.50
169-171,173-(Regular 25¢ edition)(4-6/75,8/75) 3.50
169-171,173-(30¢-c, limited distribution) 1.40 4.20 14.00
181-199: 189-G.A. Human Torch app. & origin retold. 190,191-Fantastic Four break up 3.00
200-(11/78, 52 pgs.)-F.F. re-united vs. Dr. Doom 3.50
201-208,219,222-231: 207-Human Torch vs. Spider-Man-c/story. 211-1st app. Terrax 2.00
209-216,218,220,221-Byrne-a. 209-1st Herbie the Robot. 220-Brief origin 2.50
217-Dazzler app. by Byrne 3.00
232-Byrne-a begins 3.00
233-235,237-249,251-260: All Byrne-a. 238-Origin Frankie Raye. 244-Frankie Raye becomes Nova, Herald of Galactus. 252-Reads sideways; Annihilus app.; contains skin "Tattooz" decals 3.00
236-20th Anniversary issue(11/81, 68 pgs., $1.00)-Brief origin F.F.; Byrne-c/a(p); new Kirby-a(p) 3.00
250-(52 pgs)-Spider-Man x-over; Byrne-a; Skrulls impersonate New X-Men 3.00
261-285: 261-Silver Surfer. 262-Origin Galactus; Byrne writes & draws himself into story. 264-Swipes-c of F.F. #1. 274-Spider-Man's alien costume app. (4th app., 1/85, 2 pgs.) 2.50
286-2nd app. X-Factor continued from Avengers #263; story continues in X-Factor #1 3.00
287-295: 292-Nick Fury app. 293-Last Byrne-a 2.00
296-($1.50)-Barry Smith-c/a; Thing rejoins 3.00
297-318,320-330: 300-Johnny Storm & Alicia Masters wed. 306-New team begins (9/87). 311-Re-intro The Black Panther. 312-X-Factor x-over. 327-Mr. Fantastic & Invisible Girl return 2.00
319-Double size 2.50
331-346,351-357,359,360: 334-Simonson-c/scripts begin. 337-Simonson-a begins. 342-Spider-Man cameo. 356-F.F. vs. The New Warriors; Paul Ryan-c/a begins. 360-Last $1.00-c 1.50
347-Ghost Rider, Wolverine, Spider-Man, Hulk-c/stories thru #349; Arthur Adams-c/a(p) in each 3.00
347-Gold 2nd printing 2.00
348,349 2.25
348-Gold 2nd printing 1.50
350-($1.50, 52 pgs.)-Dr. Doom app. 3.00
358-(11/91, $2.25, 88 pgs.)-30th anniversary issue; gives history of F.F.; die cut-c; Art Adams back-up story-a 2.25
361-368,370,372-374,376-380,382-386: 362-Spider-Man app. 367-Wolverine app. (brief). 370-Infinity War x-over; Thanos & Magus app. 374-Secret Defenders (Ghost Rider, Hulk, Wolverine) x-over 1.50
369-Infinity War x-over; Thanos app. 2.50
371-All white embossed-c ($2.00) 4.00
371-All red 2nd printing ($2.00) 2.50

Fantastic Four #391 © MAR

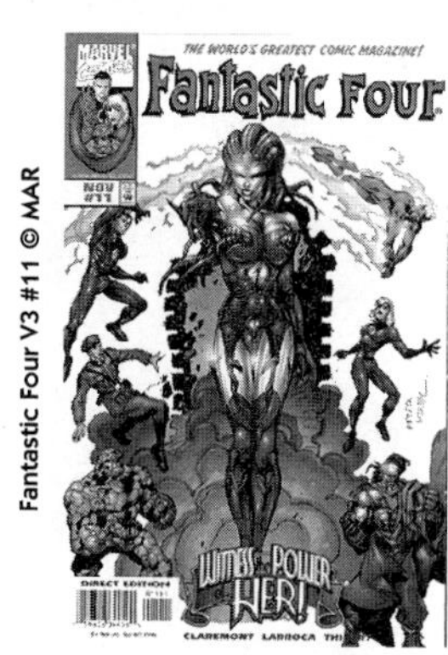

Fantastic Four V3 #11 © MAR

Fantastic Four: Fireworks #1 © MAR

GD25 FN65 NM94

375-($2.95, 52 pgs.)-Holo-grafx foil-c; ann. issue 3.00
381-Death of Reed Richards (Mister Fantastic) & Dr. Doom 3.00
387-Newsstand ed. ($1.25) 1.25
387-($2.95)-Collector's Ed. w/Die-cut foil-c 3.00
388-393, 395-397: 388-Begin $1.50-c; bound-in trading card sheet 1.50
394 ($2.95)-Polybagged w/16 pg. Marvel Action Hour book and acetate print; pink logo 3.00
398,399-Rainbow Foil-c 2.50
400-Rainbow-Foil-c 3.50
401-415: 401,402-Atlantis Rising. 407,408-Return of Reed Richards. 411-Inhumans app. 414-Galactus vs. Hyperstorm. 415-Onslaught tie-in; X-Men app. 1.50
416-($2.50)-Onslaught tie-in; Dr. Doom app.; wraparound-c 2.50
Annual 1('63)-Origin F.F.; Ditko-i 50.00 150.00 600.00
Annual 2('64)-Dr. Doom origin & c/story 31.00 93.00 325.00
Annual 3('65)-Reed & Sue wed; r/#6,11 12.00 36.00 120.00
Special 4(11/66)-G.A. Torch x-over (1st S.A. app.) & origin retold; r/#25,26 (Hulk vs. Thing); Torch vs. Torch battle 7.00 21.00 70.00
Special 5(11/67)-New art; Intro. Psycho-Man; early Black Panther, Inhumans & Silver Surfer (1st solo story) app. 9.00 27.00 90.00
Special 6(11/68)-Intro. Annihilus; birth of Franklin Richards; new 48 pg. movie length epic; last non-reprint annual 4.50 13.50 45.00
Special 7(11/69)-r/F.F. #1-5; Marvel staff photos 2.50 7.50 22.00
Special 8-10: All reprints. 8(12/70)-F.F. vs. Sub-Mariner plus gallery of F.F. foes. 9(12/71). 10('73) 1.40 4.20 14.00
Annual 11-14: 11(1976)-New art begins again. 12(1978). 13(1978). 14(1979) 5.00
Annual 15-21: 15(1980). 16(1981). 17(1983)-Byrne-c/a. 18(1984). 19(1985). 20(1987). 21(1988)-Evolutionary War x-over 3.00
Annual 22-24 (1989-91, $2.00, 68 pgs.): 22-Atlantis Attacks x-over; Sub-Mariner & The Avengers app.; Buckler-a. 23-Byrne-c; Guice-p. 24-2 pg. origin recap of Fantastic Four; Guardians of the Galaxy x-over 2.50
Annual 25(1992, $2.25, 68 pgs.)-Moondragon story 2.25
Annual 26,27('93,'94, $2.95, 68 pgs.). 26-Bagged w/card 3.00
Special Edition 1(5/84)-r/Annual #1; Byrne-c/a 2.50
...: Monsters Unleashed nn (1992, $5.95)-r/F.F. #347-349 w/new Arthur Adams-c 2.00 6.00
...: Nobody Gets Out Alive (1994, $15.95) TPB r/ #387-392 16.00
Giveaway (nn, 1981, 32pgs., Young Model Builders Club) 2.00

NOTE: ***Arthur Adams** c/a-347-349p. **Austin** c(i)-232-236, 238, 240-242, 250i, 286i. **Buckler** c-168. **John Buscema** a(p)-107, 108(w/**Kirby** & **Romita**),109-130, 132, 134-141, 160, 173-175, 202, 296-309p, Annual 11, 13; c(p)-107-122, 124-129, 133-139, 202, Annual 12p, Special 10. **Byrne** a-209-218p, 220p, 221p, 232-265, 266i, 267-273, 274-293p, Annual 17, 19; c-211-214p, 220p, 232-236p, 237, 238p, 239, 240-242p, 243-249, 250p, 251-267, 269-277, 278-281p, 283p, 284, 285, 286p, 288-293, Annual 17, 18. **Ditko** a-13i, 14i(w/**Kirby**-p), Annual 16. **G. Kane** c-150p, 160p. **Kirby** a-1-102p, 108, 180r, 189r, 236p, Special 1-10; c-1-101, 164, 167, 171-177, 180, 181, 190, 200, Annual 11, Special 1-7, 9. **Marcos** a-Annual 14i. **Mooney** a-118i, 152i. **Perez** a(p)-164-167, 170-172, 176-178, 184-188, 191p, 192p. Annual 14p, 15p; c(p)-183-188, 191, 192, 194-197. **Simonson** a-337-341, 343, 344p, 345p, 346, 350p, 352-354; c-212, 334-341, 342p, 343-346, 350, 353, 354. **Steranko** c-130-132p. **Williamson** c-357i.*

FANTASTIC FOUR (Volume Two)
Marvel Comics: V2#1, Nov, 1996 - No. 13, Nov, 1997 ($2.95/$1.95/$1.99) (Produced by WildStorm Productions)

1-($2.95)-Reintro Fantastic Four; Jim Lee-c/a; Brandon Choi scripts; Mole Man app. 4.00
1-($2.95)-Variant-c 2.00 6.00
2-Begin $1.95-c; Namor-c/app. 3.00
3-9: 3-Avengers-c/app. 4-Two covers; Dr. Doom cameo 3.00
10,11,13: All $1.99-c. 13-"World War 3"-pt. 1, x-over w/Image 2.00
12-($2.99) "Heroes Reunited"-pt. 1 3.00

FANTASTIC FOUR (Volume Three)
Marvel Comics: V3#1, Jan, 1998 - Present ($2.99/$1.99)

1-($2.99)-Heroes Return; Lobdell-s/Davis & Farmer-a 4.00
1-Alternate Heroes Return-c 7.00
2,3-($1.95): 2-Two covers 3.00

GD25 FN65 NM94

4-($2.99)-Claremont-s/Larroca-a begin; Silver Surfer c/app. 3.00
5-11: 6-Heroes For Hire app. 9-Spider-Man-c/app. 2.00
12-($2.99) Wraparound-c by Larroca 2.99
13,14-Ronan-c/app. 1.99
...'98 Annual ($3.50) Immonen-a 3.50

FANTASTIC FOUR: ATLANTIS RISING
Marvel Comics: June, 1995 - No. 2, July, 1995 ($3.95, limited series)

1,2: Acetate-c 4.00
Collector's Preview (5/95, $2.25, 52 pgs.) 2.25

FANTASTIC FOUR: FIREWORKS
Marvel Comics: Jan, 1999 - No. 3, Mar, 1999 ($2.99, limited series)

1-Remix; Jeff Johnson-a 2.99

FANTASTIC FOUR INDEX (See Official...)

FANTASTIC FOUR ROAST
Marvel Comics Group: May, 1982 (75¢, one-shot, direct sales)

1-Celebrates 20th anniversary of F.F.#1; X-Men, Ghost Rider & many others cameo; Golden, Miller, Buscema, Rogers, Byrne, Anderson art; Hembeck/Austin-c 4.00

FANTASTIC FOUR: THE LEGEND
Marvel Comics: Oct, 1996 ($3.95, one-shot)

1-Tribute issue 4.00

FANTASTIC FOUR 2099
Marvel Comics: Jan, 1996 - No. 8, Aug, 1996 ($3.95/$1.95)

1-($3.95)-Chromium-c; X-Nation preview 4.00
2-8: 4-Spider-Man 2099-c/app. 5-Doctor Strange app. 7-Thibert-c 2.00

NOTE: ***Williamson** a-1i; c-1i.*

FANTASTIC FOUR UNLIMITED
Marvel Comics: Mar, 1993 - No. 12, Dec, 1995 ($3.95, 68 pgs.)

1-12: 1-Black Panther app. 4-Thing vs. Hulk. 5-Vs. The Frightful Four. 6-Vs. Namor. 7, 9-12-Wraparound-c 4.00

FANTASTIC FOUR UNPLUGGED
Marvel Comics: Sept, 1995 - No. 6, Aug 1996 (99¢, bi-monthly)

1-6 1.00

FANTASTIC FOUR VS. X-MEN
Marvel Comics: Feb, 1987 - No. 4, June, 1987 (Limited series)

1 3.00
2-4: 4-Austin-a(i) 2.00

FANTASTIC GIANTS (Formerly Konga #1-23)
Charlton Comics: V2#24, Sept, 1966 (25¢, 68 pgs.)

V2#24-Special Ditko issue; origin Konga & Gorgo reprinted plus two new Ditko stories 5.50 16.50 55.00

FANTASTIC TALES
I. W. Enterprises: 1958 (no date) (Reprint, one-shot)

1-Reprints Avon's "City of the Living Dead" 2.80 8.40 28.00

FANTASTIC VOYAGE (See Movie Comics)
Gold Key: Aug, 1969 - No. 2, Dec, 1969

1,2 (TV) 3.20 9.50 35.00

FANTASTIC VOYAGES OF SINDBAD, THE
Gold Key: Oct, 1965 - No. 2, June, 1967

1,2-Painted-c 4.00 12.00 45.00

FANTASTIC WORLDS
Standard Comics: No. 5, Sept, 1952 - No. 7, Jan, 1953

5-Toth, Anderson-a 31.00 92.00 230.00
6-Toth-c/a 26.00 78.00 195.00
7 17.00 50.00 125.00

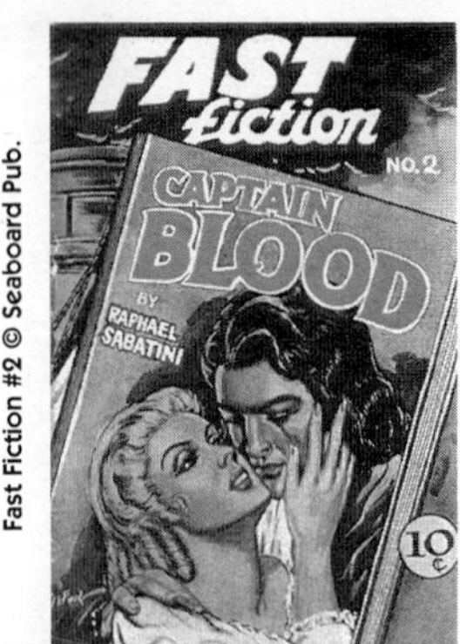

Fast Fiction #2 © Seaboard Pub.

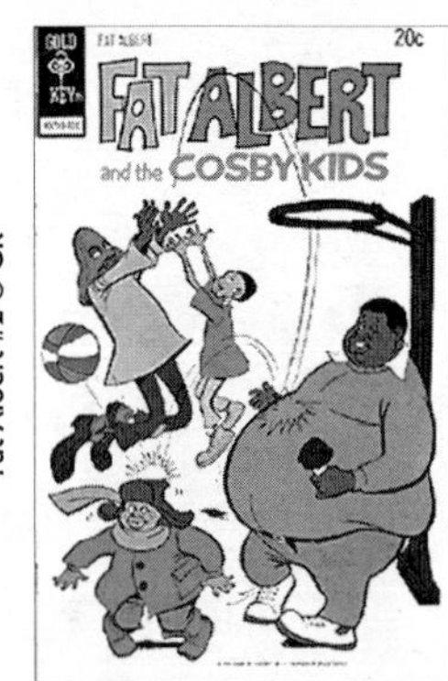

Fat Albert #2 © GK

Fathom #1 © Michael Turner

GD25 FN65 NM94

FANTASY FEATURES
Americomics: 1987 - No. 2, 1987 ($1.75)
1,2 .70 1.80

FANTASY MASTERPIECES (Marvel Super Heroes No. 12 on)
Marvel Comics Group: Feb, 1966 - No. 11, Oct, 1967; V2#1, Dec, 1979 - No. 14, Jan, 1981
1-Photo of Stan Lee (12¢-c #1,2) 5.00 15.00 50.00
2-r/1st Fin Fang Foom from Strange Tales #89 2.50 7.50 25.00
3-8: 3-G.A. Capt. America-r begin, end #11; 1st 25¢ Giant; Colan-r. 3-6-Kirby-c (p). 4-Kirby-c(p)(i). 7-Begin G.A. Sub-Mariner, Torch-r/M. Mystery. 8-Torch battles the Sub-Mariner-r/Marvel Mystery #9 2.50 7.50 25.00
9-Origin Human Torch-r/Marvel Comics #1 3.00 9.00 30.00
10,11: 10-r/origin & 1st app. All Winners Squad from All Winners #19. 11-r/origin of Toro (H.T. #1) & Black Knight #1 2.50 7.50 25.00
V2#1(12/79, 75¢, 52 pgs.)-r/origin Silver Surfer from Silver Surfer #1 with editing plus reprints cover; J. Buscema-a 2.00
2-14-Reprints Silver Surfer #2-14 w/covers 1.50
NOTE: ***Buscema*** *c-V2#7-9(in part).* ***Ditko*** *r-1-3, 7, 9.* ***Everett*** *r-1,7-9.* ***Matt Fox*** *r-9i.* ***Kirby*** *r-1-11; c(p)-3, 4i, 5, 6.* ***Starlin*** *r-8-13. Some direct sale V2#14's had a 50¢ cover price. #3-11 contain Capt. America-r/Capt. America #3-10. #7-11 contain G.A.Human Torch & Sub-Mariner-r.*

FANTASY QUARTERLY (Also see Elfquest)
Independent Publishers Syndicate: Spring, 1978 (B&W) (2nd printing exist?)
1-1st app. Elfquest; Dave Sim-a (6 pgs.) 4.50 13.50 50.00

FANTOMAN (Formerly Amazing Adventure Funnies)
Centaur Publications: No. 2, Aug, 1940 - No. 4, Dec, 1940
2-The Fantom of the Fair, The Arrow, Little Dynamite-r begin; origin The Ermine by Filchock; Fantoman app. in 2-4; Burgos, J. Cole, Ernst, Gustavson-a 112.00 336.00 950.00
3,4: Gustavson-r. 4-Red Blaze story 94.00 282.00 800.00

FAREWELL MOONSHADOW (See Moonshadow)
DC Comics (Vertigo): Jan, 1997 ($7.95, one-shot)
nn-DeMatteis-s/Muth-c/a 8.00

FARGO KID (Formerly Justice Traps the Guilty)(See Feature Comics #47
Prize Publications: V11#3(#1), June-July, 1958 - V11#5, Oct-Nov, 1958
V11#3(#1)-Origin Fargo Kid, Severin-c/a; Williamson-a(2); Heath-a 17.00 50.00 125.00
V11#4,5-Severin-c/a 11.00 32.00 80.00

FARMER'S DAUGHTER, THE
Stanhall Publ./Trojan Magazines: Feb-Mar, 1954 - No. 3, June-July, 1954; No. 4, Oct, 1954
1-Lingerie, nudity panel 17.00 52.00 130.00
2-4(Stanhall) 11.00 34.00 85.00

FASHION IN ACTION
Eclipse Comics: Aug, 1986 - Feb, 1987 (Baxter paper)
Summer Special 1 ($1.75)-Snyder III-c/a 1.80
Winter Special 1 (2/87, $2.00)-Snyder III-c/a 2.00

FASTEST GUN ALIVE, THE (Movie)
Dell Publishing Co.: No. 741, Sept, 1956 (one-shot)
Four Color 741-Photo-c 6.40 19.00 70.00

FAST FICTION (...Action) (Stories by Famous Authors Illustrated #6 on)
Seaboard Publ./Famous Authors Ill.: Oct, 1949 - No. 5, Mar, 1950 (All have Kiefer-c)(48 pgs.)
1-Scarlet Pimpernel; Jim Lavery-c/a 35.00 104.00 260.00
2-Captain Blood; H. C. Kiefer-c/a 32.00 96.00 240.00
3-She, by Rider Haggard; Vincent Napoli-a 40.00 120.00 320.00
4-(1/50, 52 pgs.)-The 39 Steps; Lavery-c/a 25.00 74.00 185.00
5-Beau Geste; Kiefer-c/a 25.00 74.00 185.00
NOTE: ***Kiefer*** *a-2, 5; c-2, 3,5.* ***Lavery*** *c/a-1, 4.* ***Napoli*** *a-3.*

GD25 FN65 NM94

FAST FORWARD
DC Comics (Piranha Press): 1992 - No. 3, 1993 ($4.95, 68 pgs.)
1-3: 1-Morrison scripts; McKean-c/a. 3-Sam Kieth-a 5.00

FAST WILLIE JACKSON
Fitzgerald Periodicals, Inc.: Oct, 1976 - No. 7, 1977
1-7 1.00

FAT ALBERT (...& the Cosby Kids) (TV)
Gold Key: Mar, 1974 - No. 29, Feb, 1979
1 1.80 5.50 20.00
2-10 1.25 3.75 10.00
11-29 1.00 3.00 8.00

FATALE (Also see Powers That Be #1 & Shadow State #1,2)
Broadway Comics: Jan, 1996 - No. 6, Aug, 1996 ($2.50)
1-6: J.G. Jones-c/a in all 2.50
Preview Edition 1 (11/95, B&W) 2.50

FAT AND SLAT (Ed Wheelan) (Becomes Gunfighter No. 5 on)
E. C. Comics: Summer, 1947 - No. 4, Spring, 1948
1-Intro/origin Voltage, Man of Lightning; "Comics" McCormick, the World's No. 1 Comic Book Fan begins, ends #4 28.00 84.00 210.00
2-4: 4-Comics McCormick-c feature 20.00 60.00 150.00

FAT AND SLAT JOKE BOOK
All-American Comics (William H. Wise): Summer, 1944 (52 pgs., one-shot)
nn-by Ed Wheelan 23.00 68.00 170.00

FATE (See Hand of Fate & Thrill-O-Rama)

FATE
DC Comics: Oct, 1994 - No. 22, Sept, 1996 ($1.95/$2.25)
0-7 2.00
8-22: 8-Begin $2.25-c. 11-14-Alan Scott (Sentinel) app. 10,14-Zatanna app. 21-Phantom Stranger app. 22-Spectre app. 2.25

FATHER & SON
Kitchen Sink: July, 1995 ($2.75, B&W, limited series)
1-Jeff NIcholson-s/a 2.75

FATHER OF CHARITY
Catechetical Guild Giveaway: No date (32 pgs.; paper cover)
nn 2.40 6.00 12.00

FATHOM
Comico: May, 1987 - No. 3, July, 1987 ($1.50, limited series)
1-3 1.50

FATHOM
Image Comics (Top Cow Prod.): Aug, 1998 - Present ($2.50)
Preview 10.00
0-Wizard supplement 8.00
1-Turner-s/a; three covers; alternate story pages 5.00
1-Wizard World Ed. 30.00
2,3 2.50

FATIMA...CHALLENGE TO THE WORLD
Catechetical Guild: 1951, 36 pgs. (15¢)
nn (not same as 'Challenge to the World') 2.40 6.00 12.00

FATMAN, THE HUMAN FLYING SAUCER
Lightning Comics(Milson Publ. Co.): April, 1967 - No. 3, Aug-Sept, 1967 (68 pgs.) (Written by Otto Binder)
1-Origin/1st app. Fatman & Tinman by Beck 4.50 13.50 45.00
2-C. C. Beck-a 3.00 9.00 30.00
3-(Scarce)-Beck-a 5.00 15.00 50.00

FAULTLINES

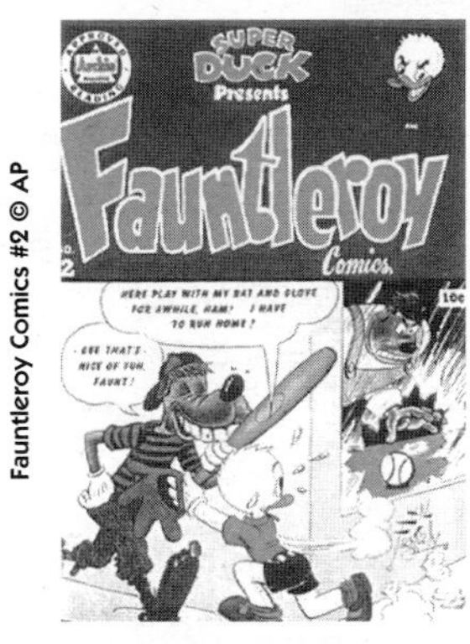

Fauntleroy Comics #2 © AP

Fawcett Movie Comic #9 © FAW

Fear #3 © MAR

GD25 FN65 NM94 | GD25 FN65 NM94

DC Comics (Vertigo): May, 1997 - No. 6, Oct, 1997 ($2.50, limited series)
1-6-Lee Marrs-s/Bill Koeb-a in all 2.50

FAUNTLEROY COMICS (Super Duck Presents...)
Close-Up/Archie Publications: 1950; No. 2, 1951; No. 3, 1952
1-Super Duck-c/stories by Al Fagaly in all 7.15 21.50 50.00
2,3 5.00 15.00 30.00

FAUST
Northstar Publishing/Rebel Studios #7 on: 1989 - No 11, 1997 ($2.00/$2.25, B&W, mature themes)
1-Decapitation-c; Tim Vigil-c/a in all; Begin $2.00-c 3.90 11.70 42.00
1-2nd printing 1.00 3.00 10.00
1-3rd & 4th printing 3.00
2 2.70 8.00 30.00
2-2nd & 3rd printings 3.00
3-Begin $2.25-c 2.00 6.00 20.00
3-2nd printing 3.00
4 .90 2.70 9.00
5-10: 7-Begin Rebel Studios series .85 2.60 7.00
5-2nd printing 3.00
11-($2.25) 2.25

FAVORITE COMICS (Also see Famous Comics)
Grocery Store Giveaway (Diff. Corp.) (detergent): 1934 (36 pgs.)
Book 1-The Nebbs, Strange As It Seems, Napoleon, Joe Palooka, Dixie Dugan, S'Matter Pop, Hairbreadth Harry, etc. reprints 70.00 210.00 600.00
Book 2,3 47.00 141.00 400.00

FAWCETT MINIATURES (See Mighty Midget)
Fawcett Publications: 1946 (3-3/4x5", 12-24 pgs.) (Wheaties giveaways)
Captain Marvel "And the Horn of Plenty"; Bulletman story 13.00 38.00 95.00
Captain Marvel "& the Raiders From Space"; Golden Arrow story 13.00 38.00 95.00
Captain Marvel Jr. "The Case of the Poison Press!" Bulletman story 13.00 38.00 95.00
Delecta of the Planets; C. C. Beck art; B&W inside; 12 pgs.; 3 printing variations (coloring) exist 21.00 64.00 160.00

FAWCETT MOTION PICTURE COMICS (See Motion Picture Comics)

FAWCETT MOVIE COMIC
Fawcett Publications: 1949 - No. 20, Dec, 1952 (All photo-c)
nn- "Dakota Lil"; George Montgomery & Rod Cameron (1949) 29.00 86.00 215.00
nn- "Copper Canyon"; Ray Milland & Hedy Lamarr (1950) 22.00 66.00 165.00
nn- "Destination Moon" (1950) 70.00 212.00 600.00
nn- "Montana"; Errol Flynn & Alexis Smith (1950) 22.00 66.00 165.00
nn- "Pioneer Marshal"; Monte Hale (1950) 22.00 66.00 165.00
nn- "Powder River Rustlers"; Rocky Lane (1950) 33.00 100.00 250.00
nn- "Singing Guns"; Vaughn Monroe, Ella Raines & Walter Brennan (1950) 19.00 58.00 145.00
7- "Gunmen of Abilene"; Rocky Lane; Bob Powell-a (1950) 25.00 74.00 185.00
8- "King of the Bullwhip"; Lash LaRue; Bob Powell-a (1950) 37.00 112.00 280.00
9- "The Old Frontier"; Monte Hale; Bob Powell-a(2/51; mis-dated 2/50) 23.00 70.00 175.00
10- "The Missourians"; Monte Hale (4/51) 23.00 70.00 175.00
11- "The Thundering Trail"; Lash LaRue (6/51) 31.00 92.00 230.00
12- "Rustlers on Horseback"; Rocky Lane (8/51) 25.00 74.00 185.00
13- "Warpath"; Edmond O'Brien & Forrest Tucker (10/51) 16.00 48.00 120.00
14- "Last Outpost"; Ronald Reagan (12/51) 39.00 116.00 290.00
15-(Scarce)- "The Man From Planet X"; Robert Clark; Schaffenberger-a (2/52) 194.00 582.00 1650.00
16- "10 Tall Men"; Burt Lancaster 13.00 38.00 95.00
17- "Rose of Cimarron"; Jack Buetel & Mala Powers 10.00 30.00 75.00
18- "The Brigand"; Anthony Dexter & Anthony Quinn; Schaffenberger-a 10.00 30.00 75.00
19- "Carbine Williams"; James Stewart; Costanza-a; James Stewart photo-c 11.00 34.00 85.00
20- "Ivanhoe"; Robert Taylor & Liz Taylor photo-c 17.00 50.00 125.00

FAWCETT'S FUNNY ANIMALS (No. 1-26, 80-on titled "Funny Animals"; becomes Li'l Tomboy No. 92 on?)
Fawcett Publications/Charlton Comics No. 84 on: 12/42 - #79, 4/53; #80, 6/53 - #83, 12?/53; #84, 4/54 - #91, 2/56
1-Capt. Marvel on cover; intro. Hoppy The Captain Marvel Bunny, cloned from Capt. Marvel; Billy the Kid & Willie the Worm begin 52.00 156.00 440.00
2-Xmas-c 29.00 88.00 220.00
3-5: 3-Spirit of '43-c 18.00 54.00 135.00
6,7,9,10 12.00 36.00 90.00
8-Flag-c 13.00 38.00 95.00
11-20: 14-Cover is a 1944 calendar 9.30 28.00 70.00
21-40: 25-Xmas-c. 26-St. Valentines Day-c 6.00 18.00 42.00
41-87,90,91 5.35 16.00 32.00
87-89(10-54-2/55)-Merry Mailman ish (TV/Radio)-part photo-c 6.00 18.00 42.00
NOTE: *Marvel Bunny in all issues to at least No. 68 (not in 49-54).*

FAZE ONE FAZERS
Americomics (AC Comics): 1986 - No. 4, Sept, 1986 (Limited series)
1-4 1.50

F.B.I., THE
Dell Publishing Co.: Apr-June, 1965
1-Sinnott-a 2.25 6.75 18.00

F.B.I. STORY, THE (Movie)
Dell Publishing Co.: No. 1069, Jan-Mar, 1960
Four Color 1069-Toth-a; James Stewart photo-c 10.00 30.00 110.00

FEAR (Adventure into...)
Marvel Comics Group: Nov, 1970 - No. 31, Dec, 1975
1-Fantasy & Sci-Fi-r in early issues; Giant size 2.20 6.50 24.00
2-6: All Giant size 1.60 4.80 16.00
7-9 1.20 3.60 12.00
10-Man-Thing begins (10/72, 4th app.), ends #19; see Savage Tales #1 for 1st app.; 1st solo series; Chaykin/Morrow-c/a; 2.20 6.50 22.00
11,12: 11-N. Adams-c. 12-Starlin/Buckler-a .90 2.70 9.00
13,14,16-18: 17-Origin/1st app. Wundarr .85 2.60 7.00
15-1st full-length Man-Thing story (8/73) .90 2.70 9.00
19-Intro. Howard the Duck; Val Mayerik-a (12/73) 2.00 6.00 20.00
20-Morbius, the Living Vampire begins, ends #31; has history recap of Morbius with X-Men & Spider-Man 1.80 5.40 18.00
21-23,25 2.00 6.00
24-Blade-c/sty 1.70 5.10 17.00
26-31 4.00
NOTE: ***Bolle** a-13i. **Brunner** c-15-17. **Buckler** a-11p, 12i. **Chaykin** a-10i. **Colan** a-23r. **Craig** a-10p. **Ditko** a-6-8r. **Evans** a-30. **Everett** a-9, 10i, 21r. **Gulacy** a-20p. **Heath** a-12r. **Heck** a-8r, 13r. **Gil Kane** a-21p; c(p)-20, 21, 23-28, 31. **Kirby** a-8r, 9r. **Maneely** a-24r. **Mooney** a-11i, 26r. **Morrow** a-11i. **Paul Reinman** a-14r. **Robbins** a(p)-25-27, 31. **Russell** a-23p, 24p. **Severin** c-8. **Starlin** c-12p.*

FEARBOOK
Eclipse Comics: April, 1986 ($1.75, one-shot, mature)
1-Scholastic Mag- r; Bissette-a 1.80

FEAR IN THE NIGHT (See Complete Mystery No. 3)

FEARLESS FAGAN

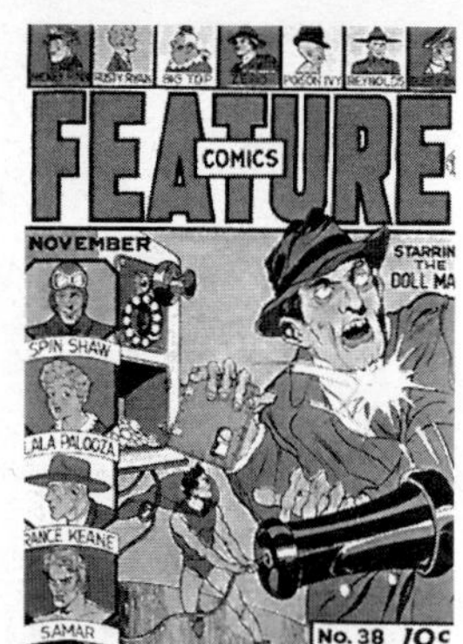

Feature Comics #38 © QUA

Feature Films #3 © DC

Feature Presentations Magazine #6 © FOX

GD25 FN65 NM94

Dell Publishing Co.: No. 441, Dec, 1952 (one-shot)

Four Color 441 3.00 9.00 35.00

FEATURE BOOK (Dell) (See Large Feature Comic)

FEATURE BOOKS (Newspaper-r, early issues)
David McKay Publications: May, 1937 - No. 57, 1948 (B&W)
(Full color, 68 pgs. begin #26 on)

Note: See individual alphabetical listings for prices

nn-Popeye & the Jeep (#1, 100 pgs.); reprinted as Feature Books #3(Very Rare; only 3 known copies, 1-VF, 2-in low grade)
nn-Dick Tracy (#1)-Reprinted as Feature Book #4 (100 pgs.) & in part as 4-Color #1 (Rare, less than 10 known copies)

NOTE: *Above books were advertised together with different covers from Feat. Books #3 & 4.*

1-King of the Royal Mtd. (#1)
2-Popeye (6/37) by Segar
3-Popeye (7/37) by Segar; same as nn issue but a new cover added
4-Dick Tracy (8/37)-Same as nn issue but a new cover added
5-Popeye (9/37) by Segar
6-Dick Tracy (10/37)
7-Little Orphan Annie (#1, 11/37) (Rare)-Reprints strips from 12/31/34 to 7/17/35
8-Secret Agent X-9 (12/37) -Not by Raymond
9-Dick Tracy (1/38)
10-Popeye (2/38)
11-Little Annie Rooney (#1, 3/38)
12-Blondie (#1) (4/38) (Rare)
13-Inspector Wade (5/38)
14-Popeye (6/38) by Segar
15-Barney Baxter (#1) (7/38)
16-Red Eagle (8/38)
17-Gangbusters (#1, 9/38) (1st app.)
18,19-Mandrake
20-Phantom (#1, 12/38)
21-Lone Ranger
22-Phantom
23-Mandrake
24-Lone Ranger (1941)
25-Flash Gordon (#1)-Reprints not by Raymond
26-Prince Valiant (1941)-Hal Foster -c/a; newspaper strips reprinted, pgs. 1-28,30-63; color & 68 pg. issues begin; Foster cover is only original comic book artwork by him
27-29,31,34-Blondie
30-Katzenjammer Kids (#1, 1942)
32,35,41,44-Katzenjammer Kids
33(nn)-Romance of Flying; World War II photos
36('43),38,40('44),42,43, 45,47-Blondie
37-Katzenjammer Kids; has photo & biog. of Harold H.Knerr(1883-1949) who took over strip from Rudolph Dirks in 1914
39-Phantom
46-Mandrake in the Fire World-(58 pgs.)
48-Maltese Falcon by Dashiell Hammett('46)
49,50-Perry Mason; based on Gardner novels
51,54-Rip Kirby; Raymond-c/s; origin-#51
52,55-Mandrake
53,56,57-Phantom

NOTE: *All Feature Books through #25 are over-sized 8-1/2x11-3/8" comics with color covers and black and white interiors. The covers are rough, heavy stock. The page counts, including covers, are as follows: nn, #3, 4-100 pgs.; #1, 2-52 pgs.; #5-25 are all 76 pgs. #33 was found in bound set from publisher.*

FEATURE COMICS (Formerly Feature Funnies)
Quality Comics Group: No. 21, June, 1939 - No. 144, May, 1950

21-The Clock, Jane Arden & Mickey Finn continue from Feature Funnies 52.00 156.00 440.00
22-26: 23-Charlie Chan begins (8/39, 1st app.) 39.00 117.00 310.00
26-(nn, nd)-Cover in one color, (10¢, 36 pgs.; issue No. blanked out. Two variations exist, each contain half of the regular #26) 12.00 36.00 90.00
27-(Rare)-Origin/1st app. Doll Man by Eisner (scripts) & Lou Fine (art); Doll Man begins, ends #139 300.00 900.00 3000.00
28-2nd app. Doll Man by Lou Fine 141.00 423.00 1200.00
29,30: 30-1st Doll Man-c 82.00 246.00 700.00
31-Last Clock & Charlie Chan issue (4/40); Charlie Chan moves to Big Shot #1 following month (5/40) 65.00 195.00 550.00
32-37: 32-Rusty Ryan & Samar begin. 34-Captain Fortune app. 37-Last Fine Doll Man 47.00 141.00 400.00

Note: *A 15¢ Canadian version of Feature Comics #37, made in the US, exists.*

38-41: 38-Origin the Ace of Space. 39-Origin The Destroying Demon, ends #40; X-Mas-c. 40-Bruce Blackburn in costume 40.00 120.00 320.00

GD25 FN65 NM94

42,43,45-50: 42-USA, the Spirit of Old Glory begins. 46-Intro. Boyville Brigadiers in Rusty Ryan. 47-Fargo Kid begins. 48-USA ends 29.00 88.00 220.00
44-Doll Man by Crandall begins, ends #63; Crandall-a(2) 41.00 122.00 325.00
51-60: 56-Marijuana story in Swing Sisson strip. 57-Spider Widow begins. 60-Raven begins, ends #71 22.00 66.00 165.00
61-68 (5/43) 20.00 60.00 150.00
69,70-Phantom Lady x-over in Spider Widow 22.00 66.00 165.00
71-80,100: 71-Phantom Lady x-over. 72-Spider Widow ends 15.00 46.00 115.00
81-99 13.00 38.00 95.00
101-144: 139-Last Doll Man & last Doll Man-c. 140-Intro. Stuntman Stetson (Stuntman Stetson c-140-144) 10.00 30.00 75.00

NOTE: ***Celardo** a-37-43. **Crandall** a-44-60, 62, 63-on(most). **Gustavson** a-(Rusty Ryan)- 32-134. **Powell** a-34, 64-73. The Clock c-25, 28, 29. Doll Man c-30, 32, 34, 36, 38, 40, 42, 44, 46, 48, 50, 52, 54, 56, 58, 60, 62, 64, 66, 68, 70, 72, 74, 77-139. Joe Palooka c-21, 24, 27.*

FEATURE FILMS
National Periodical Publ.: Mar-Apr, 1950 - No. 4, Sept-Oct, 1950 (All photo-c)

1- "Captain China" with John Payne, Gail Russell, Lon Chaney & Edgar Bergen 59.00 178.00 500.00
2- "Riding High" with Bing Crosby 62.00 187.00 525.00
3- "The Eagle & the Hawk" with John Payne, Rhonda Fleming & D. O'Keefe 59.00 178.00 500.00
4- "Fancy Pants"; Bob Hope & Lucille Ball 62.00 187.00 525.00

FEATURE FUNNIES (Feature Comics No. 21 on)
Harry 'A' Chesler: Oct, 1937 - No. 20, May, 1939

1(V9#1-indicia)-Joe Palooka, Mickey Finn (1st app.), The Bungles, Jane Arden, Dixie Dugan (1st app.), Big Top, Ned Brant, Strange As It Seems, & Off the Record strip reprints begin 316.00 950.00 2100.00
2-The Hawk app. (11/37); Goldberg-c 145.00 437.00 950.00
3-Hawks of Seas begins by Eisner, ends #12; The Clock begins; Christmas-c 112.00 337.00 725.00
4,5 83.00 250.00 550.00
6-12: 11-Archie O'Toole by Bud Thomas begins, ends #22 62.00 187.00 425.00
13-Espionage, Starring Black X begins by Eisner, ends #20 70.00 210.00 475.00
14-20 50.00 150.00 350.00

NOTE: *Joe Palooka covers 1, 6, 9, 12, 15, 18.*

FEATURE PRESENTATION, A (Feature Presentations Magazine #6) (Formerly Women in Love) (Also see Startling Terror Tales #11)
Fox Features Syndicate: No. 5, April, 1950

5(#1)-Black Tarantula 38.00 114.00 285.00

FEATURE PRESENTATIONS MAGAZINE (Formerly A Feature Presentation #5; becomes Feature Stories Magazine #3 on)
Fox Features Syndicate: No. 6, July, 1950

6(#2)-Moby Dick; Wood-c 27.00 80.00 200.00

FEATURE STORIES MAGAZINE (Formerly Feature Presentations Mag. #6)
Fox Features Syndicate: No. 3, Aug, 1950 - No. 4, Oct, 1950

3-Jungle Lil, Zegra stories; bondage-c 28.00 84.00 210.00
4 22.00 66.00 165.00

FEDERAL MEN COMICS (See Adventure Comics #32, The Comics Magazine, New Adventure Comics, New Book of Comics, New Comics & Star Spangled Comics #91)
Gerard Publ. Co.: No. 2, 1945 (DC reprints from 1930's)

2-Siegel & Shuster-a; cover redrawn from Detective #9; spanking panel 32.00 96.00 240.00

FELICIA HARDY: THE BLACK CAT
Marvel Comics: July, 1994 - No. 4, Oct, 1994 ($1.50, limited series)

Felicia Hardy, The Black Cat #2 © MAR

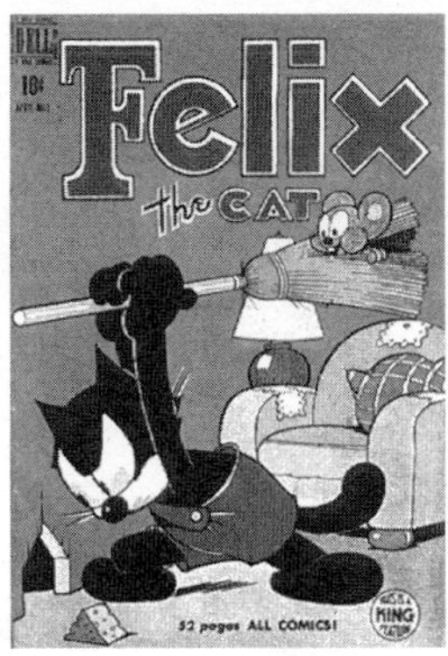

Felix The Cat #14 © KING

Femforce #90 © AC Comics

GD25 FN65 NM94

1-4: 1,4-Spider-Man app. 1.50

FELIX'S NEPHEWS INKY & DINKY
Harvey Publications: Sept, 1957 - No. 7, Oct, 1958

	GD25	FN65	NM94
1-Cover shows Inky's left eye with 2 pupils	7.85	23.50	55.00
2-7	4.25	13.00	26.00

NOTE: ***Messmer*** *art in 1-6.* ***Oriolo*** *a-1-7.*

FELIX THE CAT (See Cat Tales 3-D, The Funnies, March of Comics #24,36, 51, New Funnies & Popular Comics)
Dell Publ. No. 1-19/Toby No. 20-61/Harvey No. 62-118/Dell No. 1-12:
1943 - No. 118, Nov, 1961; Sept-Nov, 1962 - No. 12, July-Sept, 1965

	GD25	FN65	NM94
Four Color 15	65.00	194.00	710.00
Four Color 46('44)	38.00	115.00	420.00
Four Color 77('45)	36.00	107.00	390.00
Four Color 119('46)-All new stories begin	30.00	89.00	325.00
Four Color 135('46)	22.00	65.00	240.00
Four Color 162(9/47)	16.00	49.00	180.00
1(2-3/48)(Dell)	25.00	75.00	275.00
2	14.00	42.00	150.00
3-5	11.00	33.00	120.00
6-19(2-3/51-Dell)	8.00	23.00	85.00
20-30,32,33,36,38-61(6/55)-All Messmer issues.(Toby): 28-(2/52)-Some copies have #29 on cover, #28 on inside (Rare in high grade)	19.00	57.00	210.00
31,34,35-No Messmer-a; Messmer-c only 31,34	6.25	19.00	70.00
37-(100 pgs., 25 ¢, 1/15/53, X-Mas-c, Toby; daily & Sunday-r (rare)	41.00	123.00	450.00
62(8/55)-80,100 (Harvey)	3.80	11.50	40.00
81-99	3.20	9.50	34.00
101-118(11/61): 101-117-Reprints. 118-All new-a	2.20	6.50	24.00
12-269-211(#1, 9-11/62)(Dell)-No Messmer	3.50	10.50	38.00
2-12(7-9/65)(Dell, TV)-No Messmer	2.50	7.50	28.00
3-D Comic Book 1(1953-One Shot, 25¢)-w/glasses	34.00	103.00	290.00
Summer Annual nn ('53, 25¢, 100 pgs., Toby)-Daily & Sunday-r	38.00	113.00	390.00
Winter Annual 2 ('54, 25¢, 100 pgs., Toby)-Daily & Sunday-r	38.00	113.00	390.00

(Special note: Despite the covers on Toby 37 and the Summer Annual above proclaiming "all new stories," they were actually reformatted newspaper strips)

NOTE: ***Otto Messmer*** *went to work for Universal Film as an animator in 1915 and then worked for the Pat Sullivan animation studio in 1916. He created a black cat in the cartoon short, Feline Follies in 1919 that became known as Felix in the early 1920s. The Felix Sunday strip began Aug. 14, 1923 and continued until Sept. 19, 1943 whjen* ***Messmer*** *took the character to Dell (Western Publishing) and began doing Felix comic books, first adapting strips to the comic format. The first all new Felix comic was Four Color #119 in 1946 (#4 in the Dell run). The daily Felix was begun on May 9, 1927 by another artist, but by the following year,* ***Messmer*** *did it too. King Features took the daily away from* ***Messmer*** *in 1954 and he began to do some of his most dynamic art for Toby Press. The daily was continued by* ***Joe Oriolo*** *who drew it until it was discontinued Jan. 9, 1967.* ***Oriolo*** *was* ***Messmer's*** *assistant for many years and inked some of* ***Messmer's*** *pencils through the Toby run, as well as doing some of the stories by himself. Though* ***Messmer*** *continued to work for Harvey, his contirubitons were limited, and no all* ***Messmer*** *stories appeared after the Toby run until some early Toby reprints were published in the 1990s Harvey revival of the title. 4-Color No. 15, 46, 77 and the Toby Annuals are all daily or Sunday newspaper reprints from the 1930's-1940's drawn by* ***Otto Messmer****. #101-r/#64; 102-r/#65; 103-r/#67; 104-117-r/#68-81.* ***Messmer****-a in all Dell/Toby/Harvey issues except #31, 34, 35, 97, 98, 100, 118.* ***Oriolo*** *a-20, 31-on.*

FELIX THE CAT (Also see The Nine Lives of...)
Harvey Comics/Gladstone: Sept, 1991 - No. 7, Jan, 1993 ($1.25/$1.50, bi-monthly)

1: 1950s-r/Toby issues by Messmer begins. 1-Inky and Dinky back-up story (produced by Gladstone) 3.00
2-7, Big Book V2#1 (9/92, $1.95, 52 pgs.) 2.00

FELIX THE CAT AND FRIENDS
Felix Comics: 1992 - No. 4, 1992 ($1.95)

1-Contains Felix trading cards 3.00
2-4 2.00

FELIX THE CAT & HIS FRIENDS (Pat Sullivan's...)
Toby Press: Dec, 1953 - No. 3, 1954 (Indicia title for #2&3 as listed)

	GD25	FN65	NM94
1 (Indicia title, "Felix and His Friends," #1 only)	27.00	80.00	200.00
2-3	17.00	50.00	125.00

FELIX THE CAT DIGEST MAGAZINE
Harvey Comics: July, 1992 ($1.75, digest-size, 98 pgs.)

1-Felix, Richie Rich stories 4.00

FELIX THE CAT KEEPS ON WALKIN'
Hamilton Comics: 1991 ($15.95, 8-1/2"x11", 132 pgs.)

nn-Reprints 15 Toby Press Felix the Cat and Felix and His Friends stories in new computer color 1.60 4.80 16.00

FEM FANTASTIQUE
AC Comics: Aug, 1988 ($1.95, B&W)

V2#1-By Bill Black; Betty Page pin-up 2.50

FEMFORCE (Also see Untold Origin of the Femforce)
Americomics: Apr, 1985 - No. 109 (1.75/1.95/2.25/2.75/2.95, B&W #16-56)

1-Black-a in most; Nightveil, Ms. Victory begin 1.00 3.00 10.00
2 4.00
3-30: 12-15-$1.95-c. 16-19-2.25-c. 20-Begin $2.50-c, 44 pgs. 25-Origin/1st app. new Ms. Victory. 28-Colt leaves. 29,30-Camilla-r by Mayo from Jungle Comics 3.00
31-35,37-49,51-87: 31-Begin $2.75-c. 44-Contains mini-comic insert, Catman & Kitten #0. 51-Photo-c from movie. 57-Begin color issues.64-Re-intro Black Phantom. 3.00
36 (2.95, 52 pgs.) 3.00
50 (2.95, 52 pgs.)-Contains flexi-disc; origin retold; most AC characters app. 3.00
88-99: 88-Begin $2.95-c. 95-Photo-c 3.00
100-($3.95) 3.95
100-($6.90)-Polybagged 6.90
101-109-($4.95) 4.95
Special 1 (Fall, '84)(B&W, 52pgs.)-1st app. Ms. Victory, She-Cat, Blue Bulleteer, Rio Rita & Lady Luger 2.00
Bad Girl Backlash-(12/95, $5.00) 5.00
Frightbook 1 ('92, $2.95, B&W)-Halloween special 3.00
In the House of Horror 1 ('89, 2.50, B&W) 2.50
Night of the Demon 1 ('90, 2.75, B&W) 2.75
Out of the Asylum Special 1 ('87, B&W, $1.95) 2.00
Pin-Up Portfolio 2.00

FEMFORCE UP CLOSE
AC Comics: Apr, 1992 - No. 4, 1993 ($2.75, quarterly)

1-4: 1-Stars Nightveil; inside f/c photo from Femforce movie. 2-Stars Stardust. 3-Stars Dragonfly. 4-Stars She-Cat 2.75

FERDINAND THE BULL (See Mickey Mouse Magazine V4#3)
Dell Publishing Co.: 1938 (10¢, large size, some color w/rest B&W)

nn 17.00 50.00 125.00

FERRET
Malibu Comics: Sept, 1992; May, 1993 - No. 10, Feb, 1994 ($1.95)

1-(1992, one-shot) 2.00
1-($2.50)-Completely die-cut cover 2.50
2-4-($2.50)-Collector's Edition w/poster 2.50
2-4-($1.95)-Newsstand Edition w/different-c 2.00
5-8-($2.25): 5-Polybagged w/Skycap 2.25
9,10: 9-Begin $2.50-c 2.50

FEUD
Marvel Comics (Epic Comics/Heavy Hitters): July, 1993 - No. 4, Oct, 1993 ($1.95, limited series)

1-($2.50)-Embossed-c 2.50
2-4 2.00

Fight Against Crime #12 © Story Comics

Fight Comics #7 © FH

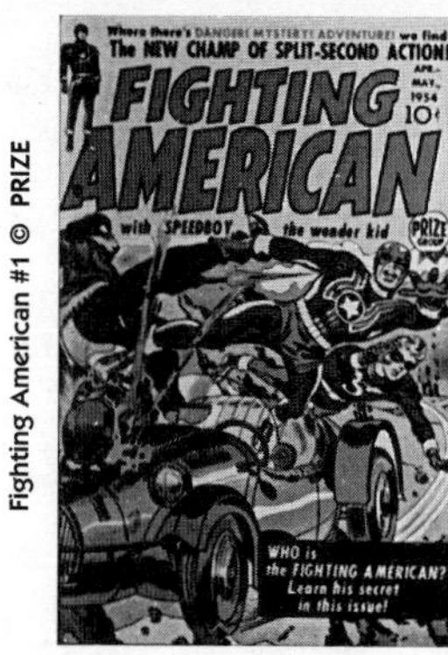

Fighting American #1 © PRIZE

FIBBER McGEE & MOLLY (Radio)(Also see A-1 Comics)
Magazine Enterprises: No. 25, 1949 (one-shot)

	GD25	FN65	NM94
A-1 25	8.50	26.00	60.00

55 DAYS AT PEKING (See Movie Comics)

FICTION ILLUSTRATED
Byron Press Publ.: 1976

	GD25	FN65	NM94
1,3: 1-Schlomo Raven; Sutton-a. 3-Chandler; new Steranko-a	1.20	3.60	12.00
2 (128 pgs.)-Starfawn; Stephen Fabian-a	.90	2.70	9.00

FIGHT AGAINST CRIME (Fight Against the Guilty #22, 23)
Story Comics: May, 1951 - No. 21, Sept, 1954

	GD25	FN65	NM94
1-True crime stories #1-4	28.00	84.00	210.00
2	15.00	45.00	110.00
3,5: 5-Frazetta-a, 1 pg.; content change to horror & suspense	11.00	32.00	80.00
4-Drug story "Hopped Up Killers"	11.00	34.00	85.00
6,7: 6-Used in **POP**, pgs. 83,84	10.00	30.00	70.00
8-Last crime format issue	9.30	28.00	65.00

NOTE: *No. 9-21 contain violent, gruesome stories with blood, dismemberment, decapitation, E.C. style plot twists and several E.C. swipes. Bondage c-4, 6, 18, 19.*

	GD25	FN65	NM94
9-11,13	25.00	76.00	190.00
12-Morphine drug story "The Big Dope"	27.00	80.00	200.00
14-Tothish art by Ross Andru; electrocution-c	25.00	76.00	190.00
15-B&W & color illos in **POP**	24.00	72.00	180.00
16-E.C. story swipe/Haunt of Fear #19; Tothish-a by Ross Andru; bondage-c	28.00	84.00	210.00
17-Wildey E.C. swipe/Shock SuspenStories #9; knife through neck-c (1/54)	28.00	84.00	210.00
18,19: 19-Bondage/torture-c	25.00	76.00	190.00
20-Decapitation cover; contains hanging, ax murder, blood & violence	43.00	129.00	350.00
21-E.C. swipe	21.00	64.00	160.00

NOTE: ***Cameron** a-4, 5, 8. **Hollingsworth** a-3-7, 9, 10, 13. **Wildey** a-6, 15, 16.*

FIGHT AGAINST THE GUILTY (Formerly Fight Against Crime)
Story Comics: No. 22, Dec, 1954 - No. 23, Mar, 1955

	GD25	FN65	NM94
22-Tothish-a by Ross Andru; Ditko-a; E.C. story swipe; electrocution-c (Last pre-code)	22.00	66.00	165.00
23-Hollingsworth-a	17.00	50.00	125.00

FIGHT COMICS
Fiction House Magazines: Jan, 1940 - No. 83, 11/52; No. 84, Wint, 1952-53; No. 85, Spring, 1953; No. 86, Summer, 1954

	GD25	FN65	NM94
1-Origin Spy Fighter, Starring Saber; Jack Dempsey life story; Shark Brodie & Chip Collins begin; Fine-c; Eisner-a	235.00	705.00	2000.00
2-Joe Louis life story; Fine/Eisner-c	100.00	300.00	850.00
3-Rip Regan, the Power Man begins (3/40)	71.00	213.00	600.00
4,5: 4-Fine-c	59.00	177.00	500.00
6-10: 6,7-Powell-c	44.00	132.00	375.00
11-14: Rip Regan ends	41.00	123.00	325.00
15-1st app. Super American plus-c (10/41)	53.00	159.00	450.00
16-Captain Fight begins (12/41); Spy Fighter ends	53.00	159.00	450.00
17,18: Super American ends	43.00	129.00	350.00
19-Captain Fight ends; Senorita Rio begins (6/42, origin & 1st app.); Rip Carson, Chute Trooper begins	43.00	129.00	350.00
20	37.00	112.00	280.00
21-30	25.00	76.00	190.00
31-Decapitation-c	24.00	72.00	180.00
32-Tiger Girl begins (6/44, 1st app.?)	23.00	70.00	175.00
33-50: 44-Capt. Fight returns. 48-Used in Love and Death by Legman. 49-Jungle-c begin, end #81	21.00	64.00	160.00
51-Origin Tiger Girl; Patsy Pin-Up app.	36.00	108.00	270.00
52-60,62-64-Last Baker issue	17.00	50.00	125.00
61-Origin Tiger Girl retold	21.00	64.00	160.00
65-78: 78-Used in **POP**, pg. 99	15.00	46.00	115.00
79-The Space Rangers app.	15.00	46.00	115.00
80-85: 81-Last jungle-c. 82-85-War-c/stories	13.00	40.00	100.00
86-Two Tigerman stories by Evans-r/Rangers Comics #40,41; Moreira-r/ Rangers Comics #45	13.00	40.00	100.00

NOTE: *Bondage covers, Lingerie, headlights panels are common. Captain Fight by **Kamen**-51-66. Kayo Kirby by **Baker**-#43-64, 67(not by Baker). Senorita Rio by **Kamen**-#57-64; by **Grandenetti**-#65, 66. Tiger Girl by **Baker**-#36-60, 62-64; **Eisner** c-1-3, 5, 10, 11. **Kamen** a-54?, 57? **Tuska** a-1, 5, 8, 10, 21, 29, 34. **Whitman** c-73-84. **Zolnerwich** c-16, 17, 22. Power Man c-5, 6, 9. Super American c-15-17. Tiger Girl c-49-81.*

FIGHT FOR FREEDOM
National Assoc. of Mfgrs./General Comics: 1949, 1951 (Giveaway, 16 pgs.)

	GD25	FN65	NM94
nn-Dan Barry-c/a; used in **POP**, pg. 102	5.70	17.00	35.00

FIGHT FOR LOVE
United Features Syndicate: 1952 (no month)

	GD25	FN65	NM94
nn-Abbie & Slats newspaper-r	8.50	26.00	60.00

FIGHTING AIR FORCE (See United States Fighting Air Force)

FIGHTIN' AIR FORCE (Formerly Sherlock Holmes?; Never Again? War and Attack #54 on)
Charlton Comics: No. 3, Feb, 1956 - No. 53, Feb-Mar, 1966

	GD25	FN65	NM94
V1#3	5.70	17.00	35.00
4-10	4.00	10.00	20.00
11(3/58, 68 pgs.)	5.00	15.00	30.00
12 (100 pgs.)	6.50	19.50	45.00
13-30: 13,24-Glanzman-a. 24-Glanzman-c	2.25	6.75	18.00
31-50: 50-American Eagle begins	1.75	5.25	14.00
51-53	1.25	3.75	10.00

FIGHTIN' ARMY (Formerly Soldier and Marine Comics) (See Captain Willy Schultz)
Charlton Comics: No. 16, 1/56 - No. 127, 12/76; No. 128, 9/77 - No. 172, 11/84

	GD25	FN65	NM94
16	5.70	17.00	40.00
17-19,21-23,25-30	4.00	10.00	20.00
20-Ditko-a	5.35	16.00	32.00
24 (3/58, 68 pgs.)	5.00	15.00	30.00
31-45	2.00	6.00	16.00
46-60	1.50	4.50	12.00
61-74	.90	2.70	8.00
75-1st The Lonely War of Willy Schultz	1.00	3.00	10.00
76-80: 76-92-The Lonely War of Willy Schultz. 79-Devil Brigade	.90	2.70	8.00
81-88,91,93-99: 82,83-Devil Brigade	.85	2.60	7.00
89,90,92-Ditko-a	1.00	3.00	10.00
100	1.00	3.00	10.00
101-127		2.00	6.00
128-140			4.00
141-172			3.00
108(Modern Comics-1977)-Reprint			4.00

NOTE: ***Aparo** c-154. **Glanzman** a-77-88. **Montes/Bache** a-48, 49, 51, 69, 75, 76, 170r.*

FIGHTING AMERICAN
Headline Publ./Prize (Crestwood): Apr-May, 1954 - No. 7, Apr-May, 1955

	GD25	FN65	NM94
1-Origin & 1st app. Fighting American & Speedboy (Capt. America & Bucky clones); S&K-c/a(3); 1st super hero satire series	153.00	459.00	1300.00
2-S&K-a(3)	74.00	222.00	625.00
3,4-S&K-a(3)	58.00	174.00	490.00
5-S&K-a(2); Kirby/?-a	58.00	174.00	490.00
6-Origin-r (4 pgs.) plus 2 pgs. by S&K	55.00	165.00	470.00
7-Kirby-a	49.00	147.00	420.00

NOTE: ***Simon** & **Kirby** covers on all. 6 is last pre-code issue.*

FIGHTING AMERICAN
Harvey Publications: Oct, 1966 (25¢)

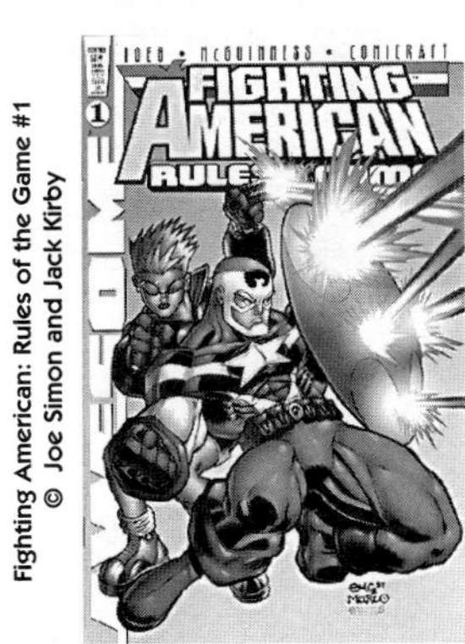

Fighting American: Rules of the Game #1 © Joe Simon and Jack Kirby

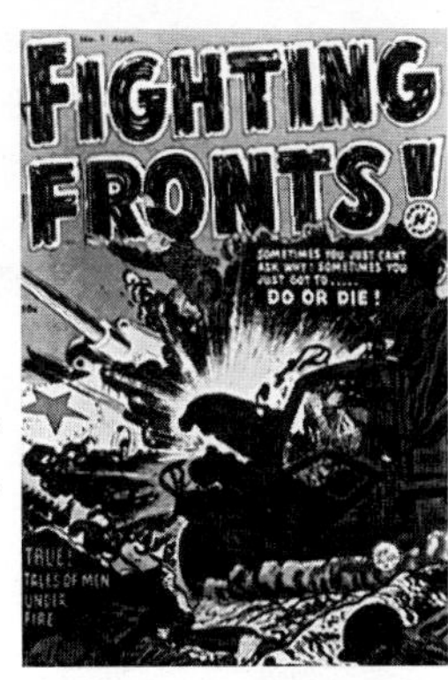

Fighting Fronts #1 © HARV

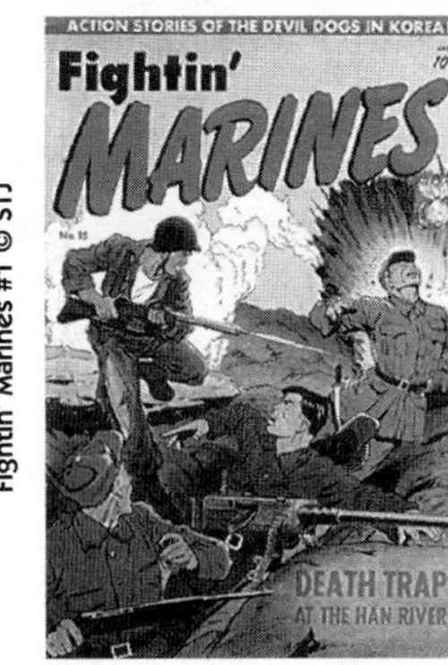

Fightin' Marines #1 © STJ

GD25 FN65 NM94

1-Origin Fighting American & Speedboy by S&K-r; S&K-c/a(3); 1 pg. Neal Adams ad 3.50 10.50 35.00

FIGHTING AMERICAN
DC Comics: Feb, 1994 - No. 6, 1994 ($1.50, limited series)
1-6 1.50

FIGHTING AMERICAN (Vol. 3)
Awesome Entertainment: Aug, 1997 - No. 2, Oct, 1997 ($2.50)
Preview-Agent America (pre-lawsuit) .85 2.60 7.00
1-Four covers by Liefeld, Churchill, Platt, McGuiness 2.50
1-Platinum Edition 10.00
1-Comic Cavalcade Edition 4.00
1-Gold foil Edition 10.00
2-Platt-c 2.50
2-Liefeld variant-c 2.50
2-American Ent. Spice Ed. 4.00

FIGHTING AMERICAN: DOGS OF WAR
Awesome-Hyperwerks: Sept, 1998 - Present ($2.50)
Limited Convention Special (7/98, B&W) Platt-a 2.50
1-Starlin-s/Platt-a/c 2.50

FIGHTING AMERICAN: RULES OF THE GAME
Awesome Entertainment: Nov, 1997 - No. 3, Mar, 1998 ($2.50, lim. series)
1-Loeb-s/McGuinness-a/c 2.50
1-Liefeld SPICE variant-c 3.00
1-Liefeld Fighting American & cast variant-c 2.50
1-Dynamic Forces Ed.; McGuinness-c 3.00
2,3: 2-Flip book with Swat! preview 2.50

FIGHTING CARAVANS (See Zane Grey 4-Color 632)

FIGHTING DANIEL BOONE
Avon Periodicals: 1953
nn-Kinstler-c/a, 22 pgs. 17.00 50.00 125.00
I.W. Reprint #1-Reprints #1 above; Kinstler-c/a; Lawrence/Alascia-a 2.00 6.00 16.00

FIGHTING DAVY CROCKETT (Formerly Kit Carson)
Avon Periodicals: No. 9, Oct-Nov, 1955
9-Kinstler-c 8.50 26.00 60.00

FIGHTIN' FIVE, THE (Fightin' 5 #40 on?; formerly Space War) (Also see The Peacemaker)
Charlton Comics: July, 1964 - No. 41, Jan, 1967; No. 42, Oct, 1981 - No. 49, Dec, 1982
V2#28-Origin & 1st app. Fightin' Five; Montes/Bache-a begins 3.80 11.40 38.00
29-39,41 2.25 6.75 18.00
40-Peacemaker begins (1st app.) 3.80 11.40 38.00
41-Peacemaker (2nd app.) 2.60 7.80 26.00
42-49: Reprints 4.00

FIGHTING FRONTS!
Harvey Publications: Aug, 1952 - No. 5, Jan, 1953
1 6.50 19.50 45.00
2-Extreme violence; Nostrand/Powell-a 8.50 26.00 60.00
3-5: 3-Powell-a 4.25 13.00 26.00

FIGHTING INDIAN STORIES (See Midget Comics)

FIGHTING INDIANS OF THE WILD WEST!
Avon Periodicals: Mar, 1952 - No. 2, Nov, 1952
1-Geronimo, Chief Crazy Horse, Chief Victorio, Black Hawk begin; Larsen-a; McCann-a(2) 13.00 38.00 95.00
2-Kinstler-c & inside-c only; Larsen, McCann-a 9.30 28.00 65.00
100 Pg. Annual (1952, 25¢)-Contains three comics rebound; Geronimo, Chief Crazy Horse, Chief Victorio; Kinstler-c 26.00 78.00 195.00

GD25 FN65 NM94

FIGHTING LEATHERNECKS
Toby Press: Feb, 1952 - No. 6, Dec, 1952
1- "Duke's Diary"; full pg. pin-ups by Sparling 11.00 34.00 85.00
2- "Duke's Diary" 9.30 28.00 65.00
3-5- "Gil's Gals"; full pg. pin-ups 9.30 28.00 65.00
6-(Same as No. 3-5?) 6.50 19.50 45.00

FIGHTING MAN, THE (War)
Ajax/Farrell Publications(Excellent Publ.): May, 1952 - No. 8, July, 1953
1 9.30 28.00 70.00
2 5.35 16.00 32.00
3-8 4.25 13.00 28.00
Annual 1 (1952, 25¢, 100 pgs.) 19.00 58.00 145.00

FIGHTIN' MARINES (Formerly The Texan; also see Approved Comics)
St. John(Approved Comics)/Charlton Comics No. 14 on:
No. 15, 8/51 - No. 12, 3/53; No. 14, 5/55 - No. 132, 11/76; No. 133, 10/77 - No. 176, 9/84 (No #13?) (Korean war #1-3)
15(#1)-Matt Baker c/a "Leatherneck Jack"; slightly large size; Fightin' Texan No. 16 & 17? 37.00 110.00 275.00
2-1st Canteen Kate by Baker; slightly large size; partial Baker-c 39.00 116.00 290.00
3-9,11-Canteen Kate by Baker; Baker c-#2,3,5-11; 4-Partial Baker-c 20.00 60.00 150.00
10-Matt Baker-c 7.85 23.50 55.00
12-No Baker-a; Last St. John issue? 4.00 11.00 22.00
14 (5/55; 1st Charlton issue; formerly?)-Canteen Kate by Baker; all stories reprinted from #2 15.00 46.00 115.00
15-Baker-c 6.50 19.50 45.00
16,18-20-Not Baker-c 4.00 10.00 20.00
17-Canteen Kate by Baker 11.00 32.00 80.00
21-24 4.00 10.00 20.00
25-(68 pgs.)(3/58)-Check-a? 6.00 18.00 42.00
26-(100 pgs.)(8/58)-Check-a(5) 9.30 28.00 65.00
27-50 1.50 4.50 12.00
51-81: 78-Shotgun Harker & the Chicken series begin 1.25 3.75 10.00
82-(100 pgs.) 2.50 7.50 25.00
83-100 .90 2.70 8.00
101-121 5.00
122-(1975) Pilot issue for "War" title (Fightin' Marines Presents War) .90 2.70 8.00
123-140 4.00
141-176 3.00
120(Modern Comics reprint, 1977) 3.00

NOTE: *No. 14 & 16 (CC) reprint St. John issues; No. 16 reprints St. John insignia on cover.* ***Colan*** *a-3, 7.* ***Glanzman*** *c/a-92, 94.* ***Montes/Bache*** *a-48, 53, 55, 64, 65, 72-74, 77-83, 176r.*

FIGHTING MARSHAL OF THE WILD WEST (See The Hawk)

FIGHTIN' NAVY (Formerly Don Winslow)
Charlton Comics: No. 74, 1/56 - No. 125, 4-5/66; No. 126, 8/83 - No. 133, 10/84
74 3.20 9.60 32.00
75-81 2.20 6.60 22.00
82-Sam Glanzman-a 2.15 6.50 17.00
83-(100 pgs.) 3.00 9.00 30.00
84-99 1.75 5.25 14.00
100 2.00 6.00 16.00
101-UFO story 1.75 5.25 14.00
102-105,106-125('66) 1.40 4.15 11.00
126-133 (1984) 3.00

NOTE: ***Montes/Bache*** *a-109.* ***Glanzman*** *a-82, 92, 96, 98, 100, 131r.*

FIGHTING PRINCE OF DONEGAL, THE (See Movie Comics)

FIGHTIN' TEXAN (Formerly The Texan & Fightin' Marines?)
St. John Publishing Co.: No. 16, Sept, 1952 - No. 17, Dec, 1952

Fighting Yank #1 © Nedor

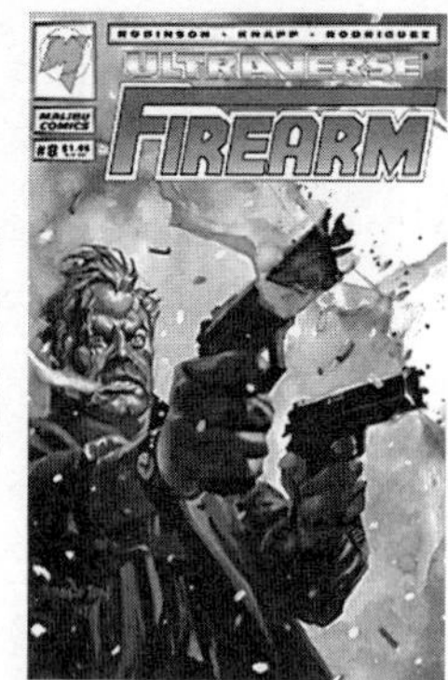

Firearm #8 © MAL

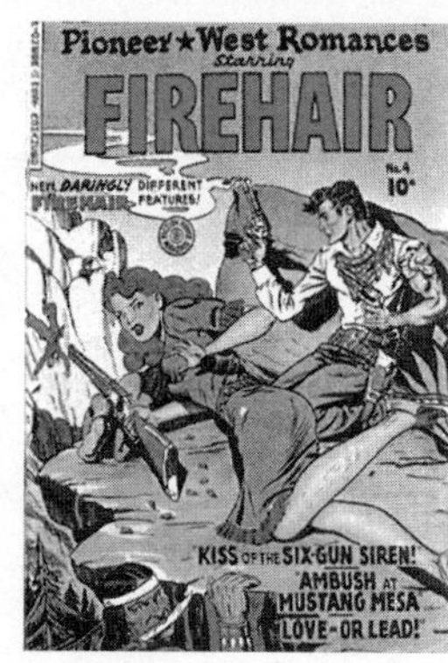

Firehair Comics #4 © FH

GD25 FN65 NM94

16,17: Tuska-a each. 17-Cameron-c/a 6.00 18.00 42.00

FIGHTING UNDERSEA COMMANDOS (See Undersea Fighting...)
Avon Periodicals: May, 1952 - No. 5, April, 1953 (U.S. Navy frogmen)

1-Cover title is Undersea Fighting... #1 only 10.00 30.00 75.00
2 7.15 21.50 50.00
3-5: 1,3-Ravielli-c. 4-Kinstler-c 6.50 19.50 45.00

FIGHTING WAR STORIES
Men's Publications/Story Comics: Aug, 1952 - No. 5, 1953

1 7.15 21.50 50.00
2-5 4.25 13.00 28.00

FIGHTING YANK (See America's Best Comics & Startling Comics)
Nedor/Better Publ./Standard: Sept, 1942 - No. 29, Aug, 1949

1-The Fighting Yank begins; Mystico, the Wonder Man app; bondage-c 188.00 564.00 1600.00
2 82.00 246.00 700.00
3,4: 4-Schomburg-c begin 62.00 186.00 525.00
5-10: 7-Grim Reaper app. 8,10-Bondage/torture-c 47.00 141.00 400.00
11-20: 11-The Oracle app. 12-Hirohito bondage-c. 15-Bondage/torture-c. 18-The American Eagle app. 42.00 126.00 335.00
21,23,24: 21-Kara, Jungle Princess app. 24-Miss Masque app. 39.00 117.00 310.00
22-Miss Masque-c/story 44.00 132.00 370.00
25-Robinson/Meskin-a; strangulation, lingerie panel; The Cavalier app. 44.00 132.00 370.00
26-29: All-Robinson/Meskin-a. 28-One pg. Williamson-a 39.00 117.00 310.00

NOTE: *Schomburg (Xela) c-4-29; airbrush-c 28, 29. Bondage c-1, 4, 8, 10, 11, 12, 15, 17.*

FIGHTMAN
Marvel Comics: June, 1993 ($2.00, one-shot, 52 pgs.)

1 2.00

FIGHT THE ENEMY
Tower Comics: Aug, 1966 - No. 3, Mar, 1967 (25¢, 68 pgs.)

1-Lucky 7 & Mike Manly begin 2.50 7.50 25.00
2-Boris Vallejo, McWilliams-a 2.50 7.50 20.00
3-Wood-a (1/2 pg.); McWilliams, Bolle-a 2.50 7.50 20.00

FILM FUNNIES
Marvel Comics (CPC): Nov, 1949 - No. 2, Feb, 1950 (52 pgs.)

1-Krazy Krow, Wacky Duck 16.00 48.00 120.00
2-Wacky Duck 12.00 36.00 90.00

FILM STARS ROMANCES
Star Publications: Jan-Feb, 1950 - No. 3, May-June, 1950 (True life stories of movie stars)

1-Rudy Valentino & Gregory Peck stories; L. B. Cole-c; lingerie panels 39.00 117.00 300.00
2-Liz Taylor/Robert Taylor photo-c & true life story 32.00 96.00 240.00
3-Douglas Fairbanks story; photo-c 22.00 66.00 165.00

FINAL CYCLE, THE
Dragon's Teeth Productions: July, 1987 - No. 4, 1988 (Limited series)

1-4 2.00

FINAL NIGHT, THE (See DC related titles and Parallax: Emerald Night)
DC Comics: Nov, 1996 - No. 4, Nov, 1996 ($1.95, weekly limited series)

1-3: Kesel-s/Immonen-a(p) in all. 3.00
4-Parallax's final acts 5.00
Preview 1.00
TPB-(1998, $12.95) r/#1-4, Parallax: Emerald Night #1, and preview 12.95

FIRE
Caliber Press: 1993 - No. 2, 1993 ($2.95, B&W, limited series, 52 pgs.)

1,2-Photo-c 3.00

FIRE AND BLAST
National Fire Protection Assoc.: 1952 (Giveaway, 16 pgs., paper-c)

nn-Mart Baily A-Bomb-c; about fire prevention 15.00 44.00 110.00

FIREARM (Also see Codename: Firearm, Freex #15, Night Man #4 & Prime #10)
Malibu Comics (Ultraverse): Sept, 1993 - No. 18, Mar, 1995 ($1.95/$2.50)

0 ($14.95)-Came w/ video containing 1st half of story (comic contains 2nd half); 1st app. Duet 1.50 4.50 15.00
1,3-6: 1-James Robinson scripts begin; Cully Hamner-a; Howard Chaykin-c; 1st app Alec Swan. 3-Intro The Sportsmen; Chaykin-c. 4-Break-Thru x-over; Chaykin-c. 5-1st app. Ellen (Swan's girlfriend); 2 pg. origin of Prime. 6-Prime app. (story cont'd in Prime #10); Brereton-c 2.00
1-($2.50)-Newsstand edition polybagged w/card 2.50
1-Ultra Limited silver foil-c 5.00
2 ($2.50, 44 pgs.)-Hardcase app.;Chaykin-c; Rune flip-c/story by B. Smith (3 pgs.) 2.50
7-10,12-17: 12-The Rafferty Saga begins, ends #18; 1st app. Rafferty 15-Night Man & Freex app. 17-Swan marries Ellen 2.00
11-($3.50, 68 pgs.)-Flip book w/Ultraverse Premiere #5 3.50
18-Death of Rafferty; Chaykin-c 2.50

NOTE: ***Brereton** c-6. **Chaykin** c-1-4, 14, 16, 18. **Hamner** a-1-4. **Herrera** a-12. **James Robinson** scripts-0-18.*

FIRE BALL XL5 (See Steve Zodiac & The ...)

FIREBRAND (Also see Showcase '96 #4)
DC Comics: Feb, 1996 - No. 9, Oct, 1996 ($1.75)

1-9: Brian Augustyn scripts; Velluto-c/a in all. 9-Daredevil #319-c/swipe 1.75

FIRE CHIEF AND THE SAFE OL' FIREFLY, THE
National Board of Fire Underwriters: 1952 (16 pgs.) (Safety brochure given away at schools) (produced by American Visuals Corp.)(Eisner)

nn-(Rare) Eisner-c/a 50.00 150.00 400.00

FIRE FROM HEAVEN
Image Comics (WildStorm Productions): Mar, 1996 ($2.50)

1,2-Moore-s 2.50

FIREHAIR COMICS (Formerly Pioneer West Romances #3-6; also see Rangers Comics)
Fiction House Magazines (Flying Stories): Winter/48-49; No. 2, Wint/49-50; No. 7, Spr/51 - No. 11, Spr/52

1-Origin Firehair 49.00 147.00 440.00
2 24.00 71.00 190.00
7-11 15.50 47.00 125.00
I.W. Reprint 8-(nd)-Kinstler-c; reprints Rangers #57; Dr. Drew story by Grandenetti 2.50 7.50 25.00

FIRESIDE BOOK SERIES
Simon and Schuster: 1974 - 1980 (130-260pgs.), Square bound, color

Amazing Spider-Man, The, 1979, 130pgs., $3.95, Bob Larkin-c
Hardcover 7.00 21.00 70.00
Softcover 4.20 12.60 42.00
America At War–The Best of DC War Comics, 1979, $6.95, 260pgs, Joe Kubert-c.
Hardcover 7.00 21.00 70.00
Softcover 4.50 13.50 50.00
Bring On The Bad Guys (origins of the Marvel Comics Villains, 1976, $6.95, 260pgs.); Romita-c
Hardcover 6.00 17.50 65.00
Softcover 4.20 12.60 42.00
Captain America, Sentinel of Liberty, 1979, 130pgs., $12.95
Hardcover 5.00 15.00 55.00
Softcover 2.90 8.70 32.00
Doctor Strange Master of the Mystic Arts, 1980, 130pgs.
Hardcover 6.00 17.50 65.00

Firestorm, The Nuclear Man #82 © DC

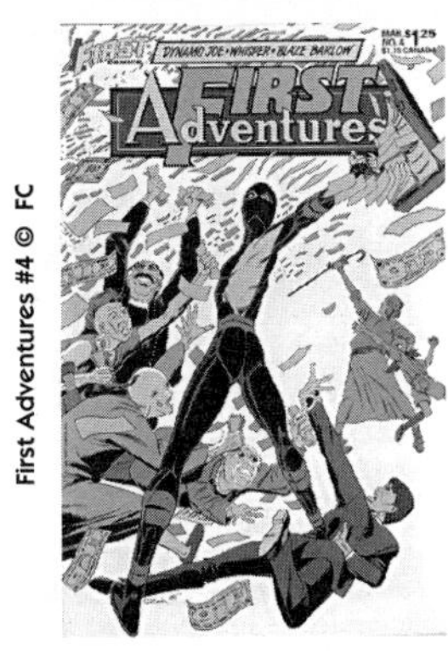

First Adventures #4 © FC

First Issue Special #13 © DC

GD25 FN65 NM94

	GD25	FN65	NM94
Softcover	4.20	12.60	42.00
Fantastic Four, The, 1979, 130pgs.			
Hardcover	5.00	15.00	55.00
Softcover	2.90	8.70	32.00
Heart Throbs–The Best of DC Romance Comics, 1979, 260pgs., $6.,95			
Hardcover	13.00	38.00	140.00
Softcover	8.00	24.00	90.00
Marvel's Greatest Superhero Battles, 1978, 260pgs., $6.95, Romita-c			
Hardcover	9.00	27.00	100.00
Softcover	5.00	15.00	55.00
Mysteries in Space, 1980, $7,95, Anderson-c. Reprints DC science fiction stories			
Softcover	2.90	8.70	32.00
Origins of Marvel Comics, 1974, 260pgs., $5.95. Reprints covers & origins of key Marvel books & characters			
Hardcover	5.00	15.00	55.00
Softcover	2.90	8.70	32.00
Silver Surfer, The, 1978, 130pgs., $4.95, Norem-c			
Hardcover	6.00	17.50	65.00
Softcover	4.20	12.60	42.00
Son of Origins of Marvel Comics, 1975, 260pgs., $6.95, Romita-c. Reprints many covers & origins of Marvel characters			
Hardcover	5.00	15.00	55.00
Softcover	2.90	8.70	32.00
Superhero Women, The–Featuring the fabulous females of Marvel Comics, 1977, 260pgs., $6.95, Romita-c			
Hardcover	7.25	22.00	80.00
Softcover	4.50	13.50	50.00

Note: Prices listed are for 1st printings. Later printings are worth 30% less.

FIRESTAR
Marvel Comics Group: Mar, 1986 - No. 4, June, 1986 (75¢)(From Spider-Man TV series)

1-X-Men & New Mutants app. 3.00
2-Wolverine-c (not real Wolverine?); Art Adams-a(p) 3.00
3,4: 3-Art Adams/Sienkiewicz-c. 4-B. Smith-c 2.00

FIRESTONE (See Donald And Mickey Merry Christmas)

FIRESTORM (See Cancelled Comic Cavalcade, DC Comics Presents, Flash #289, The Fury of... & Justice League of America #179)
DC Comics: March, 1978 - No. 5, Oct-Nov, 1978

1,5: 1-Origin & 1st app. 2.00 6.00
2-4: 2-Origin Multiplex. 3-Origin & 1st app. Killer Frost. 4-1st app. Hyena 4.00

FIRESTORM, THE NUCLEAR MAN (Formerly Fury of Firestorm)
DC Comics: No. 65, Nov, 1987 - No. 100, Aug, 1990

65-99: 66-1st app. Zuggernaut; Firestorm vs. Green Lantern. 71-Death of Capt. X. 67,68-Millennium tie-ins. 83-1st new look 1.00
100-($2.95, 68 pgs.) 3.00
Annual 5 (10/87)-1st app. new Firestorm 1.25

FIRST ADVENTURES
First Comics: Dec, 1985 - No. 5, Apr, 1986 ($1.25)

..1-5: Blaze Barlow, Whisper & Dynamo Joe in all 1.30

FIRST AMERICANS, THE
Dell Publishing Co.: No. 843, Sept, 1957

Four Color 843-Marsh-a 8.00 25.00 90.00

FIRST CHRISTMAS, THE (3-D)
Fiction House Magazines (Real Adv. Publ. Co.): 1953 (25¢, 8-1/4x10-1/4", oversize)(Came w/glasses)

nn-(Scarce)-Kelly Freas painted-c; Biblical theme, birth of Christ; Nativity-c 30.00 90.00 225.00

FIRST COMICS GRAPHIC NOVEL
First Comics: Jan, 1984 - No. 20? (52pgs./176 pgs., high quality paper)

	GD25	FN65	NM94
1-Beowulf ($5.95)	.85	2.60	7.00
1-2nd printing ($6.95)	.85	2.60	7.00
2-Time Beavers ($5.95)	.85	2.60	7.00
3($11.95, 100 pgs.)-American Flagg! Hard Times (2nd printing exists)	1.40	4.20	14.00
4-Nexus ($6.95)-r/B&W 1-3	1.00	3.00	10.00
5-The Enchanted Apples of Oz ($7.95, 52 pgs.)-Intro by Harlan Ellison (1986)	.90	2.70	9.00
6-Elric of Melnibone ($14.95, 176 pgs.)-Reprints with new color	1.60	4.80	16.00
7-The Secret Island Of Oz ($7.95)	.90	2.70	9.00
8-Teenage Mutant Ninja Turtles Book I ($9.95, 132 pgs.)-r/TMNT #1-3 in color w/12 pgs. new-a; origin	1.00	3.00	10.00
9-Time 2: The Epiphany by Chaykin (11/86, $7.95, 52pgs. - indicia says #8)	.90	2.70	8.00
10-Teenage Mutant Ninja Turtles Book II ($9.95)-r/TMNT #4-6 in color	1.00	3.00	10.00
11-Sailor On The Sea of Fate ($14.95)	1.50	4.50	15.00
nn-Time 2: The Satisfaction of Black Mariah (9/87)	.90	2.70	8.00
12-American Flagg! Southern Comfort (10/87, $11.95)	1.20	3.60	12.00
13-The Ice King Of Oz ($7.95)	.90	2.70	8.00
14-Teenage Mutant Ninja Turtles Book III ($9.95)-r/TMNT #7,8 in color plus new 12 pg. story	1.00	3.00	10.00
15-Hex Breaker: Badger ($7.95, 68 pgs.)	.90	2.70	8.00
16-The Forgotten Forest of Oz ($8.95)	.90	2.70	9.00
17-Mazinger (68 pgs., $8.95)	.90	2.70	9.00
18-Teenage Mutant Ninja Turtles Book IV ($9.95)-r/TMNT #10,11 plus 3 pg. fold-out	1.00	3.00	10.00
19-The Original Nexus Graphic Novel ($7.95, 104 pgs.)-Reprints First Comics Graphic Novel #4 ($7.95)	.90	2.70	9.00
20-American Flagg!: State of the Union; r/A.F. 7-9 ($11.95, 96 pgs.)	1.40	4.20	14.00

NOTE: *Most or all issues have been reprinted.*

1ST FOLIO (The Joe Kubert School Presents...)
Pacific Comics: Mar, 1984 ($1.50, one-shot)

1-Joe Kubert-c/a(2 pgs.); Adam & Andy Kubert-a 1.50

1ST ISSUE SPECIAL
National Periodical Publications: Apr, 1975 - No. 13, Apr, 1976 (Tryout series)

1,5,6: 1-Intro. Atlas; Kirby-c/a/script. 5-Manhunter; Kirby-c/a/script. 6-Dingbats 5.00
2,7,9,12: 2-Green Team (see Cancelled.Comic Cavalcade). 7-The Creeper by Ditko (c/a). 9-Dr. Fate; Kubert-c. 12-Origin/1st app. "Blue" Starman (2nd app. in Starman, 2nd Series #3); Kubert-c. 2.00 6.00
3,4,10,11: 3-Metamorpho by Ramona Fradon. 4-Lady Cop. 10-The Outsiders. 11-Code Name: Assassin; Grell-c. 4.00
8,13: 8-Origin/1st app. The Warlord; Grell-c/a (11/75). 13-Return of the New Gods; Darkseid app.; 1st new costume Orion; predates New Gods #12 by more than a year 1.00 3.00 10.00

FIRST KISS
Charlton Comics: Dec, 1957 - No. 40, Jan, 1965

	GD25	FN65	NM94
V1#1	3.20	9.60	32.00
V1#2-10	2.50	7.50	20.00
11-40	1.40	4.15	11.00

FIRST LOVE ILLUSTRATED
Harvey Publications(Home Comics)(True Love): 2/49 - No. 9, 6/50; No. 10, 1/51 - No. 86, 3/58; No. 87, 9/58 - No. 88, 11/58; No. 89, 11/62, No. 90, 2/63

	GD25	FN65	NM94
1-Powell-a(2)	15.00	44.00	110.00
2-Powell-a	7.85	23.50	55.00
3-"Was I Too Fat To Be Loved" story	7.85	23.50	55.00
4-10	5.35	16.00	32.00

11-30: 13-"I Joined a Teen-age Sex Club" story. 30-Lingerie panel

Firstman #1 © Andy Smith

Fish Police #1 © Steve Moncuse

The Flash #107 (1st Series) © DC

	GD25	FN65	NM94
	4.00	12.00	24.00
31-34,37,39-49: 49-Last pre-code (2/55)	3.60	9.00	18.00
35-Used in **SOTI**, illo "The title of this comic book is First Love"	16.00	48.00	120.00
36-Communism story, "Love Slaves"	4.25	13.00	28.00
38-Nostrand-a	5.70	17.00	35.00
50-90	2.00	6.00	16.00

NOTE: ***Disbrow*** *a-13.* ***Orlando*** *c-87.* ***Powell*** *a-1, 3-5, 7, 10, 11, 13-17, 19-24, 26-29, 33,35-41, 43, 45, 46, 50, 54, 55, 57, 58, 61-63, 65, 71-73, 76, 79r, 82, 84, 88.*

FIRSTMAN
Image Comics: June, 1997 ($2.50)

1 Snyder-s/ Andy Smith-a 2.50

FIRST MEN IN THE MOON (See Movie Comics)

FIRST ROMANCE MAGAZINE
Home Comics(Harvey Publ.)/True Love: 8/49 - #6, 6/50; #7, 6/51 - #50, 2/58; #51, 9/58 - #52, 11/58

	GD25	FN65	NM94
1	12.00	36.00	90.00
2	6.85	21.00	48.00
3-5	5.70	17.00	38.00
6-10	5.00	15.00	30.00
11-20	4.00	11.00	22.00
21-27,29-32: 32-Last pre-code issue (2/55)	3.60	9.00	18.00
28-Nostrand-a(Powell swipe)	5.00	15.00	30.00
33-52	2.80	7.00	14.00

NOTE: ***Powell*** *a-1-5, 8-10, 14, 18, 20-22, 24, 25, 28, 36, 46, 48, 51.*

FIRST TRIP TO THE MOON (See Space Adventures No. 20)

FISH POLICE (Inspector Gill of the...#2, 3)
Fishwrap Productions/Comico V2#5-17/Apple Comics #18 on: Dec, 1985 - No. 11, Nov, 1987 ($1.50, B&W); V2#5, April, 1988 - V2#17, May, 1989 ($1.75, color) No. 18, Aug, 1989 - No. 26, Dec, 1990 ($2.25, B&W)

1-11 1.50
1(5/86),2-2nd print 1.50
V2#5-17-(Color): V2#5-11. 12-17, new-a 2.50
18-26 ($2.25-c, B&W) 18-Origin Inspector Gill 2.00
Special 1($2.50, 7/87, Comico) 2.50
Graphic Novel: The Hairball Saga (r/1-4, color) 4.00

FISH POLICE
Marvel Comics: V2#1, Oct, 1992 - No. 6, Mar, 1993 ($1.25)

V2#1-6: 1-Hairballs Saga begins; r/#1 (1985) 1.25

5-STAR SUPER-HERO SPECTACULAR (See DC Special Series No. 1)

FLAME, THE (See Big 3 & Wonderworld Comics)
Fox Features Synd.: Sum, 1940 - No. 8, Jan, 1942 (#1,2: 68 pgs; #3-8: 44 pgs.)

	GD25	FN65	NM94
1-Flame stories reprinted from Wonderworld #5-9; origin The Flame; Lou Fine-a (36 pgs.), r/Wonderworld #3,10	306.00	918.00	2600.00
2-Fine-a(2); Wing Turner by Tuska	118.00	354.00	1000.00
3-8: 3-Powell-a	79.00	237.00	675.00

FLAME, THE (Formerly Lone Eagle)
Ajax/Farrell Publications (Excellent Publ.): No. 5, Dec-Jan, 1954-55 - No. 3, April-May, 1955

	GD25	FN65	NM94
5(#1)-1st app. new Flame	39.00	116.00	290.00
2,3	25.00	76.00	190.00

FLAMING CARROT (...Comics #6? on; see Anything Goes, Cerebus, Teenage Mutant Ninja Turtles/Flaming Carrot Crossover & Visions)
Aardvark-Vanaheim/Renegade Press #6-17/Dark Horse #18 on: 5/84 - No. 5, 1/85; No. 6, 3/85 - Present? ($1.70/$2.00, B&W)

	GD25	FN65	NM94
1-Bob Burden story/art	3.80	11.50	40.00
2	2.00	6.00	20.00
3	1.40	4.20	14.00
4-6	1.00	3.00	10.00
7-9	.85	2.60	7.00
10-12			5.00
13-15			3.00
15-Variant without cover price			5.00
16-20: 18-1st Dark Horse issue			3.00
21-23,25: 25-Contains trading cards; TMNT app.			2.00
24-(2.50, 52 pgs.)-10th anniversary issue			2.50
26-28: 26-Begin $2.25-c. 26,27-Teenage Mutant Ninja Turtles x-over. 27-Todd McFarlane-c			2.25
29-31-(2.50-c)			2.50
Annual 1(1/97, $5.00)			5.00
... :The Wild Shall Wild Remain (1997, $17.95, TPB) r/#4-11			17.95

FLAMING CARROT COMICS (Also see Junior Carrot Patrol)
Killian Barracks Press: Summer-Fall, 1981 ($1.95, one shot) (Lg size, 8-1/2x11")

1-Bob Burden-c/a/scripts; serially numbered to 6500 4.50 13.50 50.00

FLAMING LOVE
Quality Comics Group (Comic Magazines): Dec, 1949 - No. 6, Oct, 1950 (Photo covers #2-6) (52 pgs.)

	GD25	FN65	NM94
1-Ward-c/a (9 pgs.)	33.00	98.00	245.00
2	14.00	42.00	105.00
3-Ward-a (9 pgs.); Crandall-a	23.00	68.00	170.00
4-6: 4-Gustavson-a	12.00	36.00	90.00

FLAMING WESTERN ROMANCES (Formerly Target Western Romances)
Star Publications: No. 3, Mar-Apr, 1950

3-Robert Taylor, Arlene Dahl photo on-c with biographies inside; L. B. Cole-c 35.00 104.00 260.00

FLARE (Also see Champions for 1st app. & League of Champions)
Hero Comics/Hero Graphics Vol. 2 on: Nov, 1988 - No. 3, Jan, 1989 ($2.75, color, 52 pgs); V2#1, Nov, 1990 - No. 7, Nov, 1991 ($2.95/$3.50, color, mature, 52 pgs.);V2#8, Oct, 1992 - No. 16, Feb, 1994 ($3.50/$3.95, B&W, 36 pgs.)

1-3 2.75
V2#1-3,16 ($2.95) 3.00
V2#4-6,8-10: 4-Begin $3.50-c. 5-Eternity Smith returns. 6-Intro The Tigress 3.50
V2#7,11-15 ($3.95) 4.00
Annual 1(1992, $4.50, B&W, 52 pgs.)-Champions-r 4.50

FLARE ADVENTURES
Hero Graphics: Feb, 1992 - No. 12, 1993? ($3.50/$3.95)

1 (90¢, color, 20 pgs.) .90
2-7 ($3.50)-Flip books w/Champions Classics 3.50
8-12 ($3.95)-Flip books w/Champions Classics 4.00

FLASH, THE (See Adventure, The Brave and the Bold, Crisis On Infinite Earths, DC Comics Presents, DC Special, DC Special Series, DC Super-Stars, Green Lantern, Impulse, Justice League of America, Showcase, Super Team Family, & World's Finest)

FLASH, THE (1st Series)(Formerly Flash Comics)(See Showcase #4,8,13,14)
National Periodical Publ./DC: No. 105, Feb-Mar, 1959 - No. 350, Oct, 1985

	GD25	FN65	VF82	NM94
105-(2-3/59)-Origin Flash(retold), & Mirror Master (1st app.)	306.00	917.00	2450.00	5500.00

	GD25	FN65	NM94
106-Origin Grodd & Pied Piper; Flash's 1st visit to Gorilla City; begin Grodd the Super Gorilla trilogy (Scarce)	117.00	350.00	1400.00
107-Grodd trilogy, part 2	63.00	189.00	750.00
108-Grodd trilogy ends	54.00	162.00	650.00
109-2nd app. Mirror Master	41.00	123.00	480.00
110-Intro/origin The Weather Wizard & Kid Flash who later becomes Flash in Crisis On Infinite Earths #12; begin Kid Flash trilogy, ends #112 (also in #114,116,118)	100.00	300.00	1200.00

The Flash #129 (1st Series) © DC

The Flash #233 (1st Series) © DC

The Flash #104 (2nd Series) © DC

GD25 FN65 NM94

111-2nd Kid Flash tryout; Cloud Creatures 31.00 93.00 350.00
112-Origin & 1st app. Elongated Man (4-5/60); also apps. in #115,119,130 38.00 114.00 420.00
113-Origin & 1st app. Trickster 31.00 93.00 350.00
114-Captain Cold app. (see Showcase #8) 26.00 78.00 260.00
115,116,118-120: 119-Elongated Man marries Sue Dearborn. 120-Flash & Kid Flash team-up for 1st time 20.00 60.00 200.00
117-Origin & 1st app. Capt. Boomerang; 1st & only S.A. app. Winky Blinky & Noddy 27.00 81.00 270.00
121,122: 122-Origin & 1st app. The Top 15.00 45.00 150.00
123-(9/61)-Re-intro. Golden Age Flash; origins of both Flashes; 1st mention of an Earth II where DC G. A. heroes live 100.00 300.00 1200.00
124-Last 10¢ issue 12.50 38.00 125.00
125-128,130: 127-Return of Grodd-c/story. 128-Origin & 1st app. Abra Kadabra 12.00 36.00 120.00
129-2nd G.A. Flash x-over; J.S.A. cameo in flashback (1st S.A. app. G.A. Green Lantern, Hawkman, Atom, Black Canary & Dr. Mid-Nite) 28.00 84.00 280.00
131-136,138,140: 130-(7/62)-1st Gauntlet of Super-Villains (Mirror Master, Capt. Cold, The Top, Capt. Boomerang & Trickster). 131-Early Green Lantern x-over (9/62). 135-1st app. of Kid Flash's yellow costume (3/63). 136-1st Dexter Miles. 140-Origin & 1st app. Heat Wave 10.00 30.00 100.00
137-G.A. Flash x-over; J.S.A. cameo (1st S.A. app.)(1st real app. since 2-3/51); 1st S.A. app. Vandal Savage & Johnny Thunder; JSA team decides to re-form 40.00 120.00 400.00
139-Origin & 1st app. Prof. Zoom 11.00 33.00 110.00
141-150: 142-Trickster app. 8.50 25.50 85.00
151-Engagement of Barry Allen & Iris West; G.A. Flash vs. The Shade. 10.50 32.00 105.00
152-159 6.00 18.00 60.00
160-(80-Pg. Giant G-21); G.A. Flash & Johnny Quick-r 8.50 25.50 85.00
161-168,170: 165-Barry Allen weds Iris West. 167-New facts about Flash's origin. 168-Green Lantern-c/story. 170-Dr. Mid-Nite, Dr. Fate, G.A. Flash x-over 5.50 16.50 55.00
169-(80-Pg. Giant G-34)-New facts about origin 8.50 25.50 85.00
171-174,176,177,179,180: 171-JLA, Green Lantern, Atom flashbacks. 173-G.A. Flash x-over. 174-Barry Allen reveals I.D. to wife. 179-(5/68)-Flash travels to Earth-Prime and meets DC editor Julie Schwartz; 1st unnamed app. Earth-Prime (See Justice League of America #123 for 1st named app. & 3rd app. overall) 5.00 15.00 50.00
175-2nd Superman/Flash race (12/67) (See Superman #199 & World's Finest #198,199); JLA cameo; gold kryptonite used (on J'onn J'onzz impersonating Superman) 14.00 42.00 140.00
178-(80-Pg. Giant G-46) 7.00 21.00 70.00
181-186,188-195,197-199: 186-Re-intro. Sargon 3.00 9.00 30.00
187,196: (68-Pg. Giants G-58, G-70) 4.80 14.40 48.00
200 3.60 10.80 36.00
201-204,206,207: 201-New G.A. Flash story. 206-Elongated Man begins 1.80 5.40 18.00
205-(68-Pg. Giant G-82) 3.20 9.60 35.00
208-213-(52 pg.): 211-G.A. Flash origin-r/#104. 213-Reprints #137 2.00 6.00 20.00
214-DC 100 Page Super Spectacular DC-11; origin Metal Men-r/Showcase #37; never before pubbed G.A. Flash story. (see DC 100 pg. Super Spec. #11 for price) - - -
215 (52 pgs.)-Flash-r/Showcase #4; G.A. Flash x-over, reprinted in #216 2.50 7.50 28.00
216,220: 220-1st app. Turtle since Showcase #4 1.80 5.40 18.00
217-219: Neal Adams-a in all. 217-Green Lantern/Green Arrow series begins (9/72); 2nd G.L. & G.A. team-up series (see Green Lantern #76). 219-Last Green Arrow 2.20 6.50 24.00
221-225,227,228,230,231,233: 222-G. Lantern x-over. 228-(7-8/74)-Flash writer Cary Bates travels to Earth-One & meets Flash, Iris Allen & Trickster; 2nd unnamed app. Earth-Prime (See Justice League of America #123 for 1st named app. & 3rd app. overall) 1.00 3.00 10.00
226-Neal Adams-p 1.25 3.75 12.00
229,232-(100 pg. issues)-G.A. Flash-r & new-a 2.50 7.50 28.00
234-288,290: 235-Green Lantern x-over. 243-Death of The Top. 245-Origin The Floronic Man in Green Lantern back-up, ends #246. 246-Last Green Lantern. 250-Intro Golden Glider. 256-Death of The Top retold. 265-267-(44 pgs.). 267-Origin of Flash's uniform. 270-Intro The Clown. 275,276-Iris West Allen dies. 286-Intro/origin Rainbow Raider 2.00 6.00
289-1st Perez DC art (Firestorm); new Firestorm back-up series begins (9/80), ends #304 .85 2.60 7.00
291-299,301-305: 291-1st app. Saber-Tooth (villain). 295-Gorilla Grodd-c/story. 298-Intro/origin new Shade. 301-Atomic bomb-c. 303-The Top returns. 304-Intro/origin Colonel Computron; 305-G.A. Flash x-over 4.00
300-(52 pgs.)-Origin Flash retold; 25th ann. issue 5.00
306-Dr. Fate by Giffen begins, ends #313 3.00
307-349: 307-313-Giffen-a. 309-Origin Flash retold. 318-323-Creeper back-ups. 323,324-Two part Flash vs. Flash story. 324-Death of Reverse Flash (Professor Zoom). 328-Iris West Allen's death retold. 344-Origin Kid Flash 2.50
350-Double size ($1.25) 5.00
Annual 1(10-12/63, 84 pgs.)-Origin Elongated Man & Kid Flash-r; origin Grodd; G.A. Flash-r 36.00 108.00 395.00

NOTE: **N. Adams** *c-194, 195, 203, 204, 206-208, 211, 213, 215, 226p, 246.* **M. Anderson** *c-165, a(i)-195, 200-204, 206-208.* **Austin** *a-233i, 234i, 246i.* **Buckler** *a-271p, 272p; c(p)-247-250, 252, 253p, 255, 256p, 258, 262, 265-267, 269-271.* **Giffen** *a-306-313p; c-310p, 315.* **Giordano** *a-226i.* **Sid Greene** *a-167-174i, 229i(r).* **Grell** *a-237p, 238p, 240-243p; c-236.* **Heck** *a-198p.* **Infantino/Anderson** *a-135. c-135, 170-174, 192, 200, 201, 328-330.* **Infantino/Giella** *c-105-112, 163, 164, 166-168.* **G. Kane** *a-195p, 197-199p, 229r, 232r; c-197-199, 312p.* **Kubert** *a-108p, 215i(r); c-189-191.* **Lopez** *c-272.* **Meskin** *a-229r, 232r.* **Perez** *a-289-293p; c-293.* **Starlin** *a-294-296p.* **Staton** *c-263p, 264p. Green Lantern x-over-131, 143, 168, 171, 191.*

FLASH (2nd Series)(See Crisis on Infinite Earths #12 and Justice League Europe)
DC Comics: June, 1987 - Present (75¢/$1.00/$1.50/$1.75/$1.95/$1.99)

1-Guice-c/a begins; New Teen Titans app. 4.00
2,3: 3-Intro. Kilgore 2.50
4-10: 5-Intro. Speed McGee. 7-1st app. Blue Trinity. 8,9-Millennium tie-ins. 9-1st app. The Chunk 2.50
11-65: 12-Free extra 16 pg. Dr. Light story. 19-Free extra 16 pg. Flash story. 28-Capt. Cold app. 29-New Phantom Lady app. 40-Dr. Alchemy app. 50-($1.75, 52 pgs.). 62-Flash: Year One begins, ends #65. 65-Last $1.00-c 2.00
66-78,80-84: 66-Aquaman app. 69,70-Green Lantern app. 70-Gorilla Grodd story ends. 73-Re-intro Barry Allen & begin saga ("Barry Allen's" true ID revealed in #78). 76-Re-intro of Max Mercury (Quality Comics' Quicksilver), not in uniform until #77. 80-Regular ed. 81,82-Nightwing & Starfire app. 84-Razer app. 2.00
79-($2.50, 68 pgs.)-Barry Allen saga ends 2.75
80-($2.50)-Foil-c edition 2.75
0,85-91,93-99,101: 85-Begin $1.50-c. 94-Zero Hour. 95-"Terminal Velocity" begins, ends #100. 96,98,99-Kobra app. 97-Origin Max Mercury; Chillblaine app. 3.00
92-1st Impulse 1.00 3.00 10.00
100 ($2.50)-Newstand edition; Kobra & JLA app. 3.00
100 ($3.50)-Foil-c edition; Kobra & JLA app. 4.00
102-131: 102-Mongul app.; begin-$1.75-c. 105-Mirror Master app. 107-Shazam app. 108-"Dead Heat" begins; 1st app. Savitar. 109-"Dead Heat" Pt. 2 (cont'd in Impulse #10). 110-"Dead Heat" Pt. 4 (cont'd in Impulse #11). 111-"Dead Heat" finale; Savitar disappears into the Speed Force; John Fox cameo (2nd app.). 112-"Race Against Time" begins, ends #118; re-intro John Fox; intro new Chillblaine. 113-Tornado Twins app. 119-Final Night x-over 127-129-Rogue's Gallery & Neron. 128,129-JLA-app. 130-Morrison & Millar-s begin 2.00
132-140: 132-Begin $1.95-c. 135-GL & GA app. 1.95
141-144: 141-Begin $1.99-c. 142-Wally marries Linda; Waid returns.

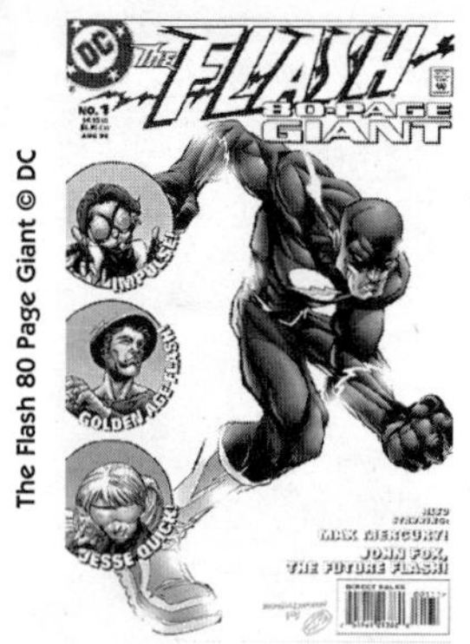

The Flash 80 Page Giant © DC

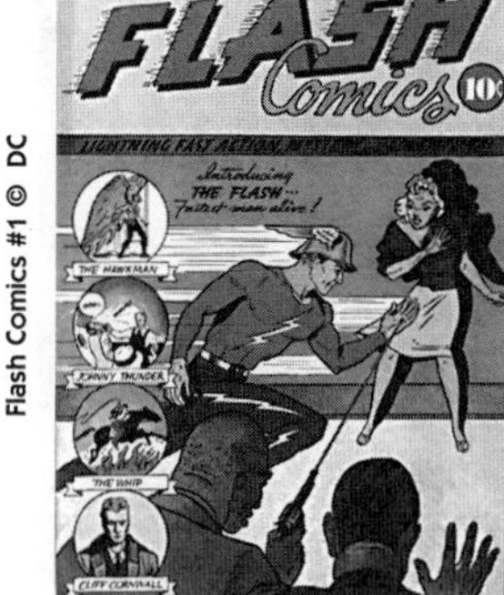

Flash Comics #1 © DC

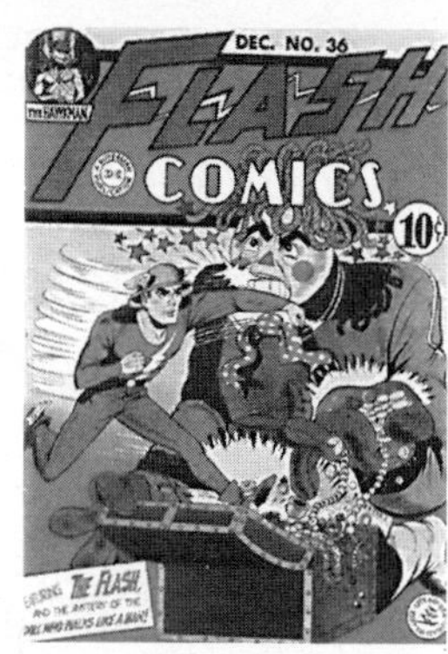

Flash Comics #36 © DC

GD25 FN65 NM94

144-Cobalt Blue origin 1.99
#1,000,000 (11/98) 853rd Century x-over 2.00
Annual 1 (1987, $1.25) .80 2.00
Annual 2, 3: 2-(1988, $1.50) 3-(1989, $1.75, 68 pgs.)-Gives history of G.A., S.A., & Modern Age Flash in text. 1.75
Annual 4 (1991, $2.00, 68 pgs.)-Armaggedon 2001 2.00
Annual 5 (1992, $2.50, 68 pgs.)-Eclipso-c/story 2.50
Annual 6 (1993, $2.50, 68 pgs.) 2.50
Annual 7 (1994, $2.95)-Elseworlds story 3.00
Annual 8 (1995, $3.50)-Year One story 3.50
Annual 9 (1996, $2.95)-Legends of the Dead Earth story; J.H. Williams-a(p); Mick Gray-a(i) 3.00
Annual 10 (1997, $3.95)-Pulp Heroes stories 4.00
Annual 11 (1998, $2.95)-Ghosts; Wrightson-c 2.95
...80-Page Giant (8/98, $4.95) Flash family stories by Waid, Byrne, Millar, and others; Mhan-c 5.00
...Plus 1 (1/1997, $2.95)-Nightwing-c/app. 2.95
...Secret Files 1 (11/97, $4.95, one-shot) Origin-s & pin-ups 4.95
Special 1 (1990, $2.95, 84 pgs.)-50th anniversary issue; Kubert-c; 1st Flash story by Mark Waid; 1st app. John Fox (27th Century Flash) 3.00
TV Special 1 (1991, $3.95, 76 pgs.)-Photo-c plus behind the scenes photos of TV show; Saltares-a, Byrne scripts 4.00
Terminal Velocity (1996, $12.95, TPB)-r/#95-100. 13.00
The Return of Barry Allen (1996, $12.95, TPB)-r/#74-79. 13.00

NOTE: ***Guice*** *a-1-9p, 11p, Annual 1p; c-1-9p, Annual 1p.* ***Perez*** *c-15-17, Annual 2i.* ***Travest Charest*** *c/a-Annual 5p.*

FLASH, THE (See Tangent Comics/ The Flash)

FLASH/ GREEN LANTERN: FASTER FRIENDS (See Green Lantern/Flash...)
DC Comics: No. 2, 1997 ($4.95, continuation of Green Lantern/Flash: Faster Friends #1)

2-Waid/Augustyn-s 5.00

FLASH SPECTACULAR, THE (See DC Special Series No. 11)

FLASH COMICS (Whiz Comics No. 2 on)
Fawcett Publications: Jan, 1940 (12 pgs., B&W, regular size)
(Not distributed to newsstands; printed for in-house use)

NOTE: *Whiz Comics #2 was preceded by two books,* ***Flash Comics*** *and* ***Thrill Comics****, both dated Jan, 1940, (12 pgs, B&W, regular size) and were not distributed. These two books are identical except for the title, and were sent out to major distributors as ad copies to promote sales. It is believed that the complete 68 page issue of Fawcett's* ***Flash*** *and* ***Thrill Comics*** *#1 was finished and ready for publication with the January date. Since DC Comics was also about to publish a book with the same date and title, Fawcett hurriedly printed up the black and white version of* ***Flash Comics*** *to secure copyright before DC. The inside covers are blank, with the covers and inside pages printed on a high quality uncoated paper stock.The eight page origin story of Captain Thunder is composed of pages 1-7 and 13 of the Captain Marvel story essentially as they appeared in the first issue of* ***Whiz Comics****. The balloon dialogue on page thirteen was relettered to tie the story into the end of page seven in* ***Flash*** *and* ***Thrill Comics*** *to produce a shorter version of the origin story for copyright purposes. Obviously, DC acquired the copyright and Fawcett dropped* ***Flash*** *as well as* ***Thrill*** *and came out with* ***Whiz Comics*** *a month later. Fawcett never used the cover to* ***Flash*** *and* ***Thrill*** *#1, designing a new cover for* ***Whiz Comics****. Fawcett also must have discovered that Captain Thunder had already been used by another publisher (Captain Terry Thunder by Fiction House). All references to Captain Thunder were relettered to Captain Marvel before appearing in* ***Whiz****.*

1 (nn on-c, #1 on inside)-Origin & 1st app. Captain Thunder. Eight copies of Flash and three copies of Thrill exist. All 3 copies of Thrill sold in 1986 for between $4,000-$10,000 each. A NM copy of Thrill sold in 1987 for $12,000. A vg copy of Thrill sold in 1987 for $9000 cash; another copy sold in 1987 for $2000 cash, $10,000 trade; cover by Leo O'Mealia

FLASH COMICS (The Flash No. 105 on) (Also see All-Flash)
National Periodical Publ./All-American: Jan, 1940 - No. 104, Feb, 1949

GD25 FN65 VF82 NM94

1-The Flash (origin/1st app.) by Harry Lampert, Hawkman (origin/1st app.) by Gardner Fox, The Whip, & Johnny Thunder (origin/1st app.) by Stan Asch; Cliff Cornwall by Moldoff, Flash Picture Novelets (later Minute Movies w/#12) begin; Moldoff (Shelly) cover; 1st app. Shiera Sanders who later becomes Hawkgirl, #24; reprinted in Famous First Edition (on sale 11/10/39); The Flash-c 5180.00 15,545.00 31,080.00 57,000.00

1-Reprint, Oversize 13-1/2x10". **WARNING:** This comic is an exact reprint of the original except for its size. DC published it in 1974 with a second cover titling it as a Famous First Edition. There have been many reported cases of the outer cover being removed and the interior sold as the original edition. The reprint with the new outer cover removed is practically worthless. See Famous First Edition for value.

GD25 FN65 NM94

2-Rod Rian begins, ends #11; Hawkman-c 600.00 1800.00 6000.00
3-King Standish begins (1st app.), ends #41 (called The King #16-37,39-41); E.E. Hibbard-a begins on Flash 450.00 1350.00 4500.00
4-Moldoff (Shelly) Hawkman begins; The Whip-c 360.00 1080.00 3600.00
5-The King-c 316.00 948.00 3000.00
6-2nd Flash-c (alternates w/Hawkman #6 on) 410.00 1230.00 4100.00
7-2nd Hawkman-c; 1st Moldoff Hawkman-c 360.00 1080.00 3600.00
8-New logo begins; classic Moldoff Flash-c 259.00 777.00 2200.00
9,10: 9-Moldoff Hawkman-c; 10-Classic Moldoff Flash-c 274.00 822.00 2600.00
11-13,15-20: 12-Les Watts begins; "Sparks" #16 on. 17-Last Cliff Cornwall 171.00 513.00 1450.00
14-World War II cover 206.00 618.00 1750.00
21-23: 21-Classic Hawkman-c 147.00 441.00 1250.00
24-Shiera becomes Hawkgirl (12/41); see All-Star Comics #5 for 1st app. 176.00 528.00 1500.00
25-28,30: 28-Last Les Sparks. 103.00 309.00 875.00
29-Ghost Patrol begins (origin/1st app.), ends #104. 115.00 345.00 975.00
31,33-Classic Hawkman-c. 33-Origin Shade 94.00 282.00 800.00
32,34-40 91.00 273.00 775.00
41-50 82.00 246.00 700.00
51-61: 52-1st computer in comics, c/s (4/44). 59-Last Minute Movies. 61-Last Moldoff Hawkman 74.00 222.00 625.00
62-Hawkman by Kubert begins 91.00 273.00 775.00
63-70: 66-68-Hop Harrigan in all. 70-Mutt & Jeff app. 68.00 204.00 575.00
71-85: 80-Atom begins, ends #104 68.00 204.00 575.00
86-Intro. The Black Canary in Johnny Thunder (8/47); see All-Star #38. 224.00 672.00 1900.00
87,88,90: 87-Intro. The Foil. 88-Origin Ghost. 103.00 309.00 875.00
89-Intro villain The Thorn 118.00 354.00 1000.00
91,93-99: 98-Atom & Hawkman don new costumes 118.00 353.00 975.00
92-1st solo Black Canary plus-c; rare in Mint due to black ink smearing on white-c 263.00 790.00 2500.00
100 (10/48),103(Scarce)-52 pgs. each 253.00 760.00 2400.00
101,102(Scarce) 212.00 636.00 1800.00
104-Origin The Flash retold (Scarce) 580.00 1740.00 5800.00

NOTE: ***Irwin Hasen*** *a-Wheaties Giveaway. c-97, Wheaties Giveaway.* ***E.E. Hibbard*** *c-6, 12, 20, 24, 26, 28, 30, 44, 46, 48, 50, 62, 66, 68, 69, 72, 74, 76, 78, 80, 82.* ***Infantino*** *a-86p, 90, 93-95, 99-104; c-90, 92, 93, 97, 99, 101, 103.* ***Kinstler*** *a-87, 89(Hawkman); c-87.* ***Chet Kozlak*** *c-77, 79, 81.* ***Krigstein*** *a-94.* ***Kubert*** *a-62-76, 83, 85, 86, 88-104; c-63, 65, 67, 70, 71, 73, 75, 83, 85, 86, 88, 89, 91, 94, 96, 98, 100, 104.* ***Moldoff*** *a-3; c-3, 7-11, 13-17, plus odd #'s 19-61.* ***Martin Naydell*** *c-52, 54, 56, 58, 60, 64, 84.*

FLASH COMICS
National Periodical Publications: 1946 (6-1/2x8-1/4", 32 pgs.)
(Wheaties Giveaway)

nn-Johnny Thunder, Ghost Patrol, The Flash & Kubert Hawkman app.; Irwin Hasen-c/a 300.00 1100.00 -

NOTE: *All known copies were taped to Wheaties boxes and are never found in mint condition. Copies with light tape residue bring the listed prices in all grades*

FLASH DIGEST, THE (See DC Special Series #24)

FLASH GORDON (See Defenders Of The Earth, Eat Right to Work..., Giant Comic Album, King Classics, King Comics, March of Comics #118, 133, 142, The Phantom #18, Street Comix & Wow Comics, 1st series)

FLASH GORDON
Dell Publishing Co.: No. 25, 1941; No. 10, 1943 - No. 512, Nov, 1953

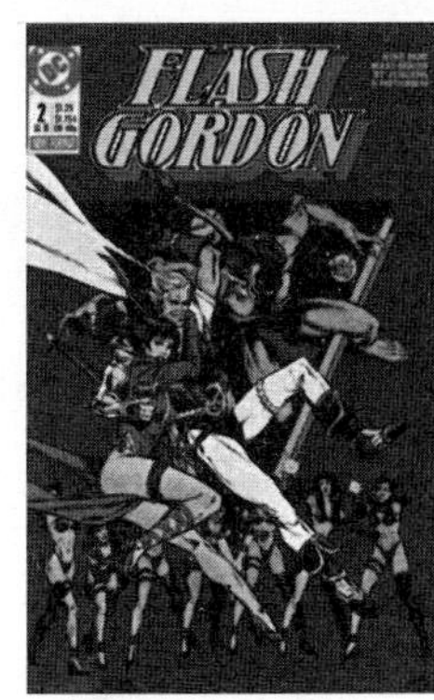

Flash Gordon #2 © DC

Flat-Top #1 © HARV

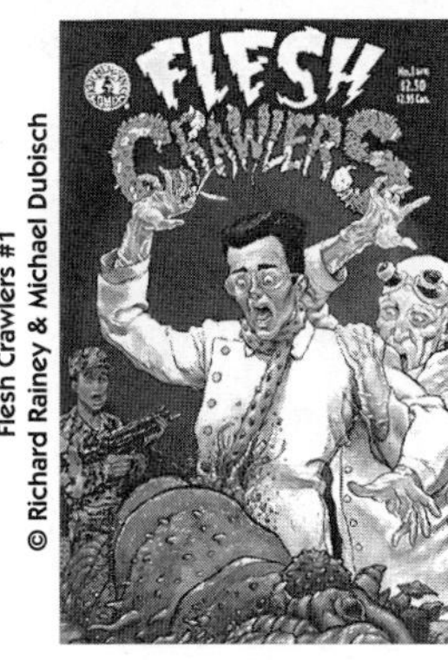

Flesh Crawlers #1
© Richard Rainey & Michael Dubisch

	GD25	FN65	NM94
Feature Books 25 (#1)(1941))-r-not by Raymond	68.00	204.00	750.00
Four Color 10(1943)-by Alex Raymond; reprints "The Ice Kingdom"	75.00	225.00	825.00
Four Color 84(1945)-by Alex Raymond; reprints "The Fiery Desert"	35.00	105.00	385.00
Four Color 173,190: 190-Bondage-c	12.00	37.00	135.00
Four Color 204,247	9.00	29.00	105.00
Four Color 424-Painted-c	8.00	23.00	85.00
2(5-7/53-Dell)-Painted-c; Evans-a?	4.50	13.50	50.00
Four Color 512-Painted-c	4.50	13.50	50.00
Macy's Giveaway(1943)-(Rare)-20 pgs.; not by Raymond	52.00	157.00	470.00

FLASH GORDON (See Tiny Tot Funnies)
Harvey Publications: Oct, 1950 - No. 4, April, 1951

1-Alex Raymond-a; bondage-c; reprints strips from 7/14/40 to 12/8/40	27.00	81.00	200.00
2-Alex Raymond-a; r/strips 12/15/40-4/27/41	19.00	57.00	140.00
3,4-Alex Raymond-a; 3-bondage-c; r/strips 5/4/41-9/21/41. 4-r/strips 10/24/37-3/27/38	17.00	51.00	130.00

5-(Rare)-Small size-5-1/2x8-1/2"; B&W; 32 pgs.; Distributed to some mail subscribers only. Estimated value $200.00–$300.00
(Also see All-New No. 15, Boy Explorers No. 2, and Stuntman No. 3)

FLASH GORDON
Harvey Comics: 1951 (16 pgs. in color, regular size, paper-c)
(Gordon Bread giveaway)

1,2: 1-r/strips 10/24/37 - 2/6/38. 2-r/strips 7/14/40 - 10/6/40; Reprints by Raymond each....	1.50	4.50	10.00

NOTE: *Most copies have brittle edges.*

FLASH GORDON
Gold Key: June, 1965

1 (1947 reprint)-Painted-c	3.60	11.00	40.00

FLASH GORDON (Also see Comics Reading Libraries)
King #1-11/Charlton #12-18/Gold Key #19-23/Whitman #28 on:
9/66 - #11, 12/67; #12, 2/69 - #18, 1/70; #19, 10-11/78 - #37, 3/82
(Painted covers No. 19-30, 34)

1-1st S.A. app Flash Gordon; Williamson c/a(2); E.C. swipe/Incredible S.F. #32; Mandrake story	3.50	10.50	35.00
1-8: 1-Army giveaway(1968)("Complimentary" on cover)(Same as regular #1 minus Mandrake story & back-c). 2-Bolle, Gil Kane-c; Mandrake story. 3-Williamson-c. 4-Secret Agent X-9 begins, Williamson-c/a(3). 5-Williamson-c/a(2). 6,8-Crandall-a. 7-Raboy-a (last in comics?). 8-Secret Agent X-9-r	2.50	7.50	20.00
9,10-Raymond-r. 10-Buckler's 1st pro work (11/67)	2.25	6.75	18.00
11-Crandall-a	2.50	7.50	20.00
12-Crandall-c/a	2.50	7.50	20.00
13-Jeff Jones-a (15 pgs.)	2.50	7.50	20.00
14-17: 17-Brick Bradford story	1.25	3.75	10.00
18-Kaluta-a (3rd pro work?)(see Teen Confessions)	1.75	5.25	14.00
19(9/78, G.K.), 20-26			4.00
27-29		2.00	6.00
30 (10/80) (scarce)	1.20	3.60	12.00
30 (7/81; re-issue).			4.00
31-33 (Bagged 3-pack): Movie adaptation; Williamson-a.			10.00
31-33-single issues			4.00
34-37: Movie adaptation		2.00	6.00

NOTE: ***Aparo** a-8. **Bolle** a-21, 22. **Boyette** a-14-18. **Briggs** c-10. **Buckler** a-10. **Crandall** c-6. **Estrada** a-3. **Gene Fawcette** a-29, 30, 34, 37. **McWilliams** a-31-33, 36.*

FLASH GORDON
DC Comics: June, 1988 - No. 9, Holiday, 1988-'89 ($1.25, mini-series)

1-9: 1,5-Painted-c			1.25

FLASH GORDON
Marvel Comics: June, 1995 - No. 2, July, 1995 ($2.95, limited series)

	GD25	FN65	NM94
1,2: Schultz scripts; Williamson-a			3.00

FLASH GORDON THE MOVIE
Western Publishing Co.: 1980 (8-1/4 x 11", $1.95, 68 pgs.)

11294-Williamson-c/a; adapts movie	1.00	3.00	10.00
13743-Hardback edition	1.50	4.50	15.00

FLAT-TOP
Mazie Comics/Harvey Publ.(Magazine Publ.) No. 4 on: 11/53 - No. 3, 5/54; No. 4, 3/55 - No. 7, 9/55

1-Teenage; Flat-Top, Mazie, Mortie & Stevie begin	5.00	15.00	30.00
2,3	3.60	9.00	18.00
4-7	2.80	7.00	14.00

FLESH & BLOOD
Brainstorm Comics: Dec, 1995 ($2.95, B&W, mature)

1-Balent-c; foil-c.			3.00

FLESH AND BONES
Upshot Graphics (Fantagraphics Books): June, 1986 - No. 4, Dec, 1986 (Limited series)

1-Dalgoda by Fujitake in all			2.50
2-4 Alan Moore scripts (r) in all			2.00

FLESH CRAWLERS
Kitchen Sink Press: Aug, 1993 - No. 3, 1995 ($2.50, B&W, limited series, mature)

1-3			2.50

FLEX MENTALLO (Man of Muscle Mystery) (See Doom Patrol, 2nd Series)
DC Comics (Vertigo): Jun, 1996 - No. 4, Sept, 1996 ($2.50, lim. series, mature)

1: Grant Morrison scripts & Frank Quitely-c/a. in all			5.00
2-4			3.50

FLINTSTONE KIDS, THE (TV) (See Star Comics Digest)
Star Comics/Marvel Comics #5 on: Aug, 1987 - No. 11, Apr, 1989

1-11			2.50

FLINTSTONES, THE (TV)(See Dell Giant #48 for No. 1)
Dell Publ. Co./Gold Key No. 7 (10/62) on: No. 2, Nov-Dec, 1961 - No. 60, Sept, 1970 (Hanna-Barbera)

2-2nd app. (TV show debuted on 9/30/60)	9.00	27.00	100.00
3-6(7-8/62): 2-5: 15¢. 6-Begin 12¢ issues	6.00	18.00	65.00
7 (10/62; 1st GK)	6.00	18.00	65.00
8-10: Mr. & Mrs. J. Evil Scientist begin?	4.50	13.50	50.00
11-1st app. Pebbles (6/63)	7.75	23.50	85.00
12-15,17-20	3.50	10.50	38.00
16-1st app. Bamm-Bamm (1/64)	6.75	20.50	75.00
21-23,25-30	3.00	9.00	32.00
24-1st app. The Grusomes	5.00	15.00	55.00
31,32,35-40: 31-Xmas-c. 39-Reprints	2.75	8.00	30.00
33-Meet Frankenstein & Dracula.	2.90	8.70	32.00
34-1st app. The Great Gazoo	5.00	15.00	55.00
41-60: 45-Last 12¢ issue	2.50	7.50	28.00
At N. Y. World's Fair('64)-J.W. Books(25¢)-1st printing; no date on-c (29¢ version exists, 2nd print?)	4.00	12.00	45.00
At N. Y. World's Fair (1965 on-c; re-issue). NOTE: Warehouse find in 1984	1.00	3.00	12.00
Bigger & Boulder 1(#30013-211) (Gold Key Giant, 11/62, 25¢, 84 pgs.)	7.25	22.00	80.00
Bigger & Boulder 2-(1966, 25¢)-Reprints B&B No. 1	6.00	18.00	65.00
...With Pebbles & Bamm Bamm (100 pgs., G.K.)-30028-511 (paper-c, 25¢) (11/65)	6.50	20.00	80.00

NOTE: *(See Comic Album #16, Bamm-Bamm & Pebbles Flintstone, Dell Giant 48, Golden Comics Digest, March of Comics #229, 243, 271, 289, 299, 317, 327, 341, Pebbles Flintstone, Top Comics #2-4, and Whitman Comic Books.)*

The Flintstones and the Jetsons #12 © H-B

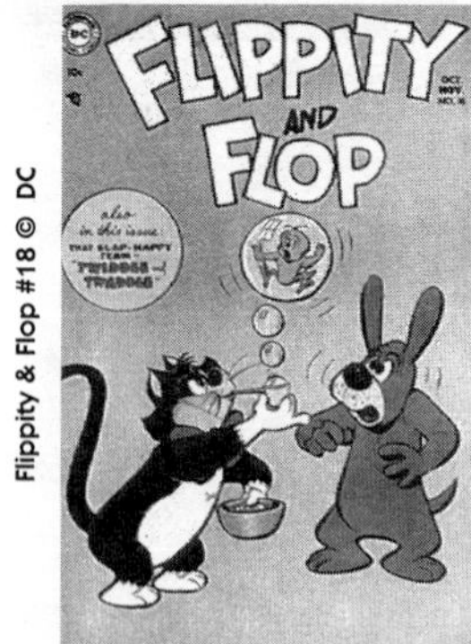

Flippity & Flop #18 © DC

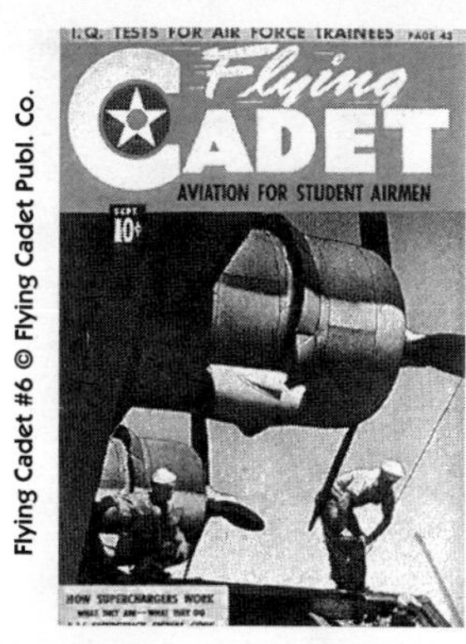

Flying Cadet #6 © Flying Cadet Publ. Co.

FLINTSTONES, THE (TV)(...& Pebbles)
Charlton Comics: Nov, 1970 - No. 50, Feb, 1977 (Hanna-Barbera)

	GD25	FN65	NM94
1	5.00	15.00	55.00
2	2.70	8.00	30.00
3-7,9,10	2.20	6.25	22.00
8- "Flintstones Summer Vacation" (Summer, 1971, 52 pgs.)	5.00	15.00	55.00
11-20,36: 36-Mike Zeck illos (early work)	2.00	6.00	20.00
21-35,38-41,43-50:	1.50	4.50	15.00
37,42: 37-Byrne text illos (early work; see Nightmare #20). 42-Byrne-a (2 pgs.)	2.20	6.25	22.00

(Also see Barney & Betty Rubble, Dino, The Great Gazoo, & Pebbles & Bamm-Bamm)

FLINTSTONES, THE (TV)(See Yogi Bear, 3rd series) (Newsstand sales only)
Marvel Comics Group: October, 1977 - No. 9, Feb, 1979 (Hanna-Barbera)

	GD25	FN65	NM94
1	1.20	3.60	12.00
2,3,5-9: Yogi Bear app.	1.00	3.00	10.00
4-The Jetsons app.	1.60	4.80	16.00

FLINTSTONES, THE (TV)
Harvey Comics: Sept, 1992 - No. 13, Jun, 1994 ($1.25/$1.50) (Hanna-Barbera)

	GD25	FN65	NM94
V2#1-13: 5-Begin $1.50-c			2.00
...Big Book 1,2 (11/92, 3/93; both $1.95, 52 pgs.)			3.00
...Giant Size 1-3 (10/92, 4/93, 11/93; $2.25, 68 pgs.)			3.00

FLINTSTONES, THE (TV)
Archie Publications: Sept, 1995 - No. 22, June, 1997 ($1.50)

	GD25	FN65	NM94
1-22			2.00

FLINTSTONES AND THE JETSONS, THE (TV)
DC Comics: Aug, 1997 - Present ($1.75/$1.95)

	GD25	FN65	NM94
1-4			1.75
5-13: 5-Begin $1.95-c			1.95
14-18-($1.99)			1.99

FLINTSTONES CHRISTMAS PARTY, THE (See The Funtastic World of Hanna-Barbera No. 1)

FLIP
Harvey Publications: April, 1954 - No. 2, June, 1954 (Satire)

	GD25	FN65	NM94
1,2-Nostrand-a each. 2-Powell-a	20.00	60.00	150.00

FLIPPER (TV)
Gold Key: Apr, 1966 - No. 3, Nov, 1967 (All have photo-c)

	GD25	FN65	NM94
1	4.50	13.50	50.00
2,3	3.00	9.00	35.00

FLIPPITY & FLOP
National Per. Publ. (Signal Publ. Co.): 12-1/51-52 - No. 46, 8-10/59; No. 47, 9-11/60

	GD25	FN65	NM94
1-Sam dog & his pets Flippity The Bird and Flop The Cat begin; Twiddle and Twaddle begin	24.00	72.00	180.00
2	13.00	40.00	100.00
3-5	11.00	32.00	80.00
6-10	9.30	28.00	70.00
11-20: 20-Last precode (3/55)	8.30	25.00	58.00
21-47	6.85	21.00	48.00

FLOATERS
Dark Horse Comics: Sept, 1993 - No. 5, Jan, 1994 ($2.50, B&W, lim. series)

	GD25	FN65	NM94
1-5			2.50

FLOOD RELIEF
Malibu Comics (Ultraverse): Jan, 1994 (36 pgs.)(Ordered thru mail w/$5.00 to Red Cross)

	GD25	FN65	NM94
1-Hardcase, Prime & Prototype app.			5.00

FLOYD FARLAND (See Eclipse Graphic Album Series #11)

FLY, THE (Also see Adventures of..., Blue Ribbon Comics & Flyman)
Archie Enterprises, Inc.: May, 1983 - No. 9, Oct, 1984

	GD25	FN65	NM94
1-9: 1-Mr. Justice app; origin Shield. 2-Flygirl app.			2.00

NOTE: *Buckler a-1, 2. Ditko a-2-9; c-4-8p. Nebres c-3, 4, 5i, 6, 7i. Steranko c-1, 2.*

FLY, THE
Impact Comics (DC): Aug, 1991 - No. 17, Dec, 1992 ($1.00)

	GD25	FN65	NM94
1-17: 4-Vs. The Black Hood. 9-Trading card inside			1.00
Annual 1 ('92, $2.50, 68 pgs.)-Impact trading card			2.50

FLYBOY (Flying Cadets)(Also see Approved Comics)
Ziff-Davis Publ. Co. (Approved): Spring, 1952 - No. 4, 1953

	GD25	FN65	NM94
1-Saunders painted-c	16.00	48.00	120.00
2-(10-11/52)-Saunders painted-c	11.00	34.00	85.00
3,4-Saunders painted-c	9.30	28.00	65.00

FLYING ACES (Aviation stories)
Key Publications: July, 1955 - No. 5, Mar, 1956

	GD25	FN65	NM94
1	4.25	13.00	28.00
2-5: 2-Trapani-a	4.00	10.00	20.00

FLYING A'S RANGE RIDER, THE (TV)(See Western Roundup under Dell Giants)
Dell Publishing Co.: #404, 6-7/52; #2, June-Aug, 1953 - #24, Aug, 1959 (All photo-c)

	GD25	FN65	NM94
Four Color 404(#1)-Titled "The Range Rider"	10.00	30.00	110.00
2	6.00	18.00	65.00
3-10	4.50	13.50	50.00
11-16,18-24	4.00	12.00	45.00
17-Toth-a	5.25	16.00	58.00

FLYING CADET (WW II Plane Photos)
Flying Cadet Publ. Co.; Jan, 1943 - V2#8, 1947 (Half photos, half comics)

	GD25	FN65	NM94
V1#1-Painted-c	11.00	34.00	85.00
2	5.70	17.00	40.00
3-9 (Two #6's, Sept. & Oct.): 5,6a,6b-Photo-c	5.70	17.00	35.00
V2#1-7(#10-16)	4.25	13.00	28.00
8(#17)-Bare-breasted woman-c	15.00	46.00	115.00

FLYING COLORS 10th ANNIVERSARY SPECIAL
Flying Colors Comics: Fall 1998 ($2.95, one-shot)

	GD25	FN65	NM94
1-Dan Brereton-c; pin-ups by Jim Lee and Jeff Johnson			2.95

FLYIN' JENNY
Pentagon Publ. Co./Leader Enterprises #2: 1946 - No. 2, 1947 (1945 strip-r)

	GD25	FN65	NM94
nn-Marcus Swayze strip-r (entire insides)	11.00	34.00	85.00
2-Baker-c; Swayze strip reprints	13.00	38.00	95.00

FLYING MODELS
H-K Publ. (Health-Knowledge Publs.): V61#3, May, 1954 (5¢, 16 pgs.)

	GD25	FN65	NM94
V61#3 (Rare)	6.50	19.50	45.00

FLYING NUN (TV)
Dell Publishing Co.: Feb, 1968 - No. 4, Nov, 1968

	GD25	FN65	NM94
1-Sally Field photo-c	3.90	11.50	42.00
2-4: 2-Sally Field photo-c	2.50	7.50	28.00

FLYING NURSES (See Sue & Sally Smith...)

FLYING SAUCERS
Avon Periodicals/Realistic: 1950; 1952; 1953

	GD25	FN65	NM94
1(1950)-Wood-a, 21 pgs.; Fawcette-c	64.00	192.00	575.00
nn(1952)-Cover altered plus 2 pgs. of Wood-a not in original	41.00	122.00	325.00
nn(1953)-Reprints above	31.00	94.00	235.00

FLYING SAUCERS (Comics)
Dell Publishing Co.: April, 1967 - No. 4, Nov, 1967; No. 5, Oct, 1969

	GD25	FN65	NM94
1	2.60	7.80	26.00
2-5	2.25	6.75	18.00

Foodini #2 © HOKE

Foolkiller #4 © MAR

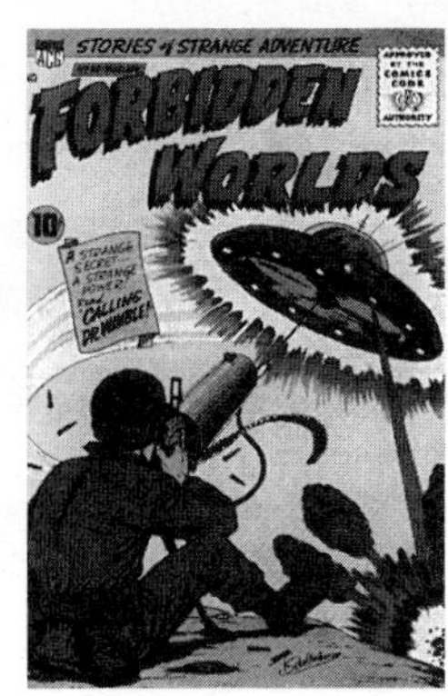

Forbidden Worlds #86 © ACG

GD25 FN65 NM94

FLY MAN (Formerly Adventures of The Fly; Mighty Comics #40 on)
Mighty Comics Group (Radio Comics) (Archie):
No. 32, July, 1965 - No. 39, Sept, 1966 (Also see Mighty Crusaders)

32,33-Comet, Shield, Black Hood, The Fly & Flygirl x-over. 33-Re-intro Wizard, Hangman (1st S.A. appearances) 3.00 9.00 30.00
34-36: 34-Shield begins. 35-Origin Black Hood. 36-Hangman x-over in Shield; re-intro. & origin of Web (1st S.A. app.) 2.50 7.50 20.00
37-39: 37-Hangman, Wizard x-over in Flyman; last Shield issue. 38-Web story. 39-Steel Sterling story (1st S.A. app.) 2.50 7.50 20.00

FOES
Ram Comics: 1989 - No. 3, 1989 ($1.95, limited series)

1-3 2.00

FOLLOW THE SUN (TV)
Dell Publishing Co.: May-July, 1962 - No. 2, Sept-Nov, 1962 (Photo-c)

01-280-207(No.1), 12-280-211(No.2) 3.60 11.00 40.00

FOODANG
Continum Comics: July, 1994 ($1.95, B&W, bi-monthly)

1 2.00

FOODINI (TV)(The Great...; see Jingle Dingle & Pinhead &...)
Continental Publ. (Holyoke): March, 1950 - No. 5, 1950 (All have 52 pgs.)

1-Based on TV puppet show (very early TV comic) 16.00 48.00 120.00
2-Jingle Dingle begins 9.30 28.00 65.00
3-5: 4-(8/50) 7.15 21.50 50.00

FOOEY (Magazine) (Satire)
Scoff Publishing Co.: Feb, 1961 - No. 4, May, 1961

1 5.70 17.00 40.00
2-4 4.25 13.00 26.00

FOOFUR (TV)
Marvel Comics (Star Comics)/Marvel No. 5 on: Aug, 1987 - No. 6, Jun, 1988

1-6 1.50

FOOLKILLER (Also see The Amazing Spider-Man #225, The Defenders #73 Man-Thing #3 & Omega the Unknown #8)
Marvel Comics: Oct, 1990 - No. 10, Oct, 1991 ($1.75, limited series)

1-10: 1-Origin 3rd Foolkiller; Greg Salinger app; DeZuniga-a(i) in 1-4. 8-Spider-Man x-over 1.75

FOOTBALL THRILLS (See Tops In Adventure)
Ziff-Davis Publ. Co.: Fall-Winter, 1951-52 - No. 2, Fall, 1952
(Edited by "Red" Grange)

1-Powell a(2); Saunders painted-c; Red Grange, Jim Thorpe stories 26.00 78.00 195.00
2-Saunders painted-c 17.00 50.00 125.00

FOOT SOLDIERS, THE
Dark Horse Comics: Jan, 1996 - No. 4, Apr, 1996 ($2.95, limited series)

1-4: Jim Krueger story & Michael Avon Oeming-a. in all. 1-Alex Ross-c. 4-John K. Snyder, III-c. 3.00

FOOT SOLDIERS, THE (Volume Two)
Image Comics: Sept, 1997 - Present ($2.95, limited series)

1-5: 1-Yeowell-a. 2-McDaniel, Hester, Sienkiewicz, Giffen-a 2.95

FOR A NIGHT OF LOVE
Avon Periodicals: 1951

nn-Two stories adapted from the works of Emile Zola; Astarita, Ravielli-a; Kinstler-c 25.00 76.00 190.00

FORBIDDEN KNOWLEDGE: ADVENTURE BEYOND THE DOORWAY TO SOULS WITH RADICAL DREAMER (Also see Radical Dreamer)
Mark's Giant Economy Size Comics: 1996 ($3.50, B&W, one-shot, 48 pgs.)

nn-Max Wrighter app.; Wheatley-c/a/script; painted infinity-c 3.50

GD25 FN65 NM94

FORBIDDEN LOVE
Quality Comics Group: Mar, 1950 - No. 4, Sept, 1950 (52 pgs.)

1-(Scarce)-Classic photo-c; Crandall-a 60.00 180.00 510.00
2,3-(Scarce)-Photo-c 31.00 93.00 230.00
4-(Scarce)-Ward/Cuidera-a; photo-c 35.00 105.00 260.00

FORBIDDEN LOVE (See Dark Mansion of...)

FORBIDDEN PLANET
Innovation Publishing: May, 1992 - No. 4, 1992 ($2.50, limited series)

1-4: Adapts movie; painted-c 2.50

FORBIDDEN TALES OF DARK MANSION (Formerly Dark Mansion of Forbidden Love #1-4)
National Periodical Publ.: No. 5, May-June, 1972 - No. 15, Feb-Mar, 1974

5-(52 pgs.) 2.40 7.00 26.00
6-10 1.40 4.20 14.00
11-15: 13-Kane/Howard-a 1.20 3.60 12.00

NOTE: ***N. Adams*** *c-9.* ***Alcala*** *a-9-11, 13.* ***Chaykin*** *a-7,15.* ***Evans*** *a-14.* ***Heck*** *a-5.* ***Kaluta*** *a-7i, 8-12; c-7, 8, 13.* ***G. Kane*** *a-13.* ***Kirby*** *a-6.* ***Nino*** *a-8, 12, 15.* ***Redondo*** *a-14.*

FORBIDDEN WORLDS
American Comics Group: 7-8/51 - No. 34, 10-11/54; No. 35, 8/55 - No. 145, 8/67 (No. 1-5: 52 pgs.; No. 6-8: 44 pgs.)

1-Williamson/Frazetta-a (10 pgs.) 112.00 338.00 975.00
2 56.00 168.00 480.00
3-Williamson/Orlando-a (7 pgs.); Wood (2 panels); Frazetta (1 panel) 58.00 176.00 490.00
4 31.00 94.00 240.00
5-Krenkel/Williamson-a (8 pgs.) 45.00 136.00 385.00
6-Harrison/Williamson-a (8 pgs.) 40.00 120.00 330.00
7,8,10: 7-1st monthly issue 24.00 71.00 180.00
9-A-Bomb explosion story 26.00 79.00 200.00
11-20 17.00 49.00 125.00
21-33: 24-E.C. swipe by Landau 11.50 34.00 85.00
34(10-11/54)(Scarce)(becomes Young Heroes #35 on)-Last pre-code issue; A-Bomb explosion story 11.50 34.00 85.00
35(8/55)-Scarce 10.00 30.00 70.00
36-62 7.50 22.50 50.00
63,69,76,78-Williamson-a in all; w/Krenkel #69 8.35 25.00 55.00
64,66-68,70-72,74,75,77,79-85,87-90 6.35 19.00 42.00
65- "There's a New Moon Tonight" listed in #114 as holding 1st record fan mail response 7.50 22.50 50.00
73-1st app. Herbie by Ogden Whitney 31.00 94.00 235.00
86-Flying saucer-c by Schaffenberger 6.50 19.50 45.00
91-93,95-100 2.80 8.40 28.00
94-Herbie (2nd app.) 6.00 18.00 60.00
101-109,111-113,115,117-120 2.50 7.50 22.00
110,114,116-Herbie app. 114-1st Herbie-c; contains list of editor's top 20 ACG stories. 116-Herbie goes to Hell 4.00 12.00 40.00
121-123 2.50 7.50 22.00
124-Magic Agent app. 2.50 7.50 25.00
125-Magic Agent app.; intro. & origin Magicman series, ends #141 3.50 10.50 35.00
126-130 2.60 7.80 26.00
131-139: 133-Origin/1st app. Dragonia in Magicman (1-2/66); returns in #138. 136-Nemesis x-over in Magicman 2.50 7.50 24.00
140-Mark Midnight app. by Ditko 2.80 8.40 28.00
141-145 2.00 6.00 16.00

NOTE: ***Buscema*** *a-75, 79, 81, 82, 140r.* ***Cameron*** *a-5.* ***Disbrow*** *a-10.* ***Ditko*** *a-137p, 138, 140.* ***Landau*** *a-24, 27-29, 31-34, 48, 86r, 96, 143-45.* ***Lazarus*** *a-18, 23, 24, 57.* ***Moldoff*** *a-27, 31, 139r.* ***Reinman*** *a-93.* ***Whitney*** *a-115, 116, 137; c-40, 46, 57, 60, 68, 78, 79, 90, 93, 94, 100, 102, 103, 106-108, 114, 129.*

FORCE, THE (See The Crusaders)

FORCE OF BUDDHA'S PALM THE
Jademan Comics: Aug, 1988 - No. 55, Feb, 1993 ($1.50/$1.95, 68 pgs.)

Force Works #11 © MAR

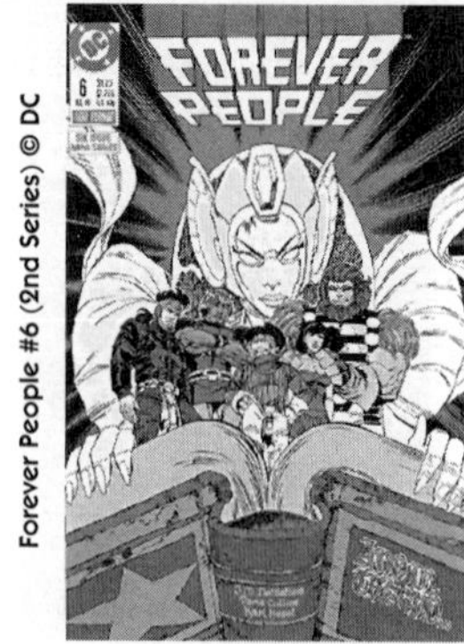

Forever People #6 (2nd Series) © DC

Four Color (Series 1) #9 © NY News Synd.

GD25 FN65 NM94

1-8 ($1.50)-Kung Fu stories 1.50
9-55 ($1.95) 2.00

FORCE WORKS
Marvel Comics: July, 1994 - No. 22, Apr, 1996 ($1.50)

1-($3.95)-Fold-out pop-up-c; Iron Man, Wonder Man, Spider-Woman,U.S. Agent & Scarlet Witch (new costume) 4.00
2-11, 13-22: 5-Blue logo version & pink logo version. 9-Intro Dreamguard. 13-Avengers app. 1.50
5-Pink logo ($2.95)-polybagged w/ 16pg. Marvel Action Hour Preview & acetate print 3.00
12 ($2.50)-Flip book w/War Machine. 2.50

FORD ROTUNDA CHRISTMAS BOOK (See Christmas at the Rotunda)

FOREIGN INTRIGUES (Formerly Johnny Dynamite; becomes Battlefield Action #16 on)
Charlton Comics: No. 13, 1956 - No. 15, Aug, 1956

13-15-Johnny Dynamite continues 5.35 16.00 32.00

FOREMOST BOYS (See 4Most)

FOREST FIRE (Also see Smokey The Bear)
American Forestry Assn.(Commerical Comics): 1949 (dated-1950) (16 pgs., paper-c)

nn-Intro/1st app. Smokey The Forest Fire Preventing Bear; created by Rudy Wendelein; Wendelein/Sparling-a; 'Carter Oil Co.' on back-c of original 16.00 48.00 120.00

FOR ETERNITY
Antarctic Press: July, 1997 - No. 4, Jan, 1998 ($2.95, B&W)

1-4 2.95

FOREVER DARLING (Movie)
Dell Publishing Co.: No. 681, Feb, 1956

Four Color 681-w/Lucille Ball & Desi Arnaz; photo-c 10.00 30.00 110.00

FOREVER PEOPLE, THE
National Periodical Publications: Feb-Mar, 1971 - No. 11, Oct-Nov, 1972 (Fourth World)

1-1st app. Forever People; Superman x-over; Kirby-c/a begins; 1st full app. Darkseid (3rd anywhere, 3 weeks before New Gods #1); Darkseid storyline begins, ends #8(app. in 1-4,6,8; cameos in 5,11) 3.20 9.60 35.00
2-5: 4-G.A. reprints begin, end #9 2.00 6.00 20.00
6-11: 9,10-Deadman app. 1.00 3.00 10.00

NOTE: *Kirby c/a(p)-1-11; #4-9 contain Sandman reprints from Adventure #85, 84, 75, 80, 77, 74 in that order. #1-3, 10-11 are 36pgs; #4-9 are 52pgs.*

FOREVER PEOPLE
DC Comics: Feb, 1988 - No. 6, July, 1988 ($1.25, limited series)

1-6 1.25

FOR GIRLS ONLY
Bernard Bailey Enterprises: Nov, 1953 (100 pgs., digest size)

1-Half comic book, half magazine 11.50 34.00 80.00

FORGOTTEN FOREST OF OZ, THE (See First Comics Graphic Novel #16)

FORGOTTEN REALMS (Also see Avatar & TSR Worlds)
DC Comics: Sept, 1989 - No. 25, Sept, 1991 ($1.50/$1.75)

1-Based on TSR role-playing game 2.00
2,3 2.00
4-10 1.80
11-15 1.50
16-25: 16-Begin $1.75-c. 18-Avatar story 1.80
Annual 1 (1990, $2.95, 68 pgs.) 3.00

FORGOTTEN STORY BEHIND NORTH BEACH, THE
Catechetical Guild: No date (8 pgs., paper-c)

nn 2.40 6.00 12.00

GD25 FN65 NM94

FORLORN RIVER (See Zane Grey Four Color 395)

FOR LOVERS ONLY (Formerly Hollywood Romances)
Charlton Comics: No. 60, Aug, 1971 - No. 87, Nov, 1976

60 2.25 6.80 25.00
61-72,74-87 .90 2.70 9.00
73-Spanking scene-c/story 1.50 4.50 15.00

40 BIG PAGES OF MICKEY MOUSE
Whitman Publ. Co.: No. 945, Jan, 1936 (10-1/4x12-1/2", 44 pgs., cardboard-c)

945-Reprints Mickey Mouse Magazine #1, but with a different cover; ads were eliminated and some illustrated stories had expanded text. The book is 3/4" shorter than Mickey Mouse Mag. #1, but the reprints are the same size (Rare) 150.00 450.00 1200.00

48 FAMOUS AMERICANS
J. C. Penney Co. (Cpr. Edwin H. Stroh): 1947 (Giveaway) (Half-size in color)

nn-Simon & Kirby-a 10.00 30.00 75.00

FOR YOUR EYES ONLY (See James Bond...)

FOUR COLOR
Dell Publishing Co.: Sept?, 1939 - No. 1354, Apr-June, 1962 (Series I are all 68 pgs.)

NOTE: *Four Color only appears on issues #19-25, 1-99,101. Dell Publishing Co. filed these as Series I, #1-25, and Series II, #1-1354. Issues beginning with #710? were printed with and without ads on back cover. Issues without ads are worth more.*

SERIES I:	GD25	FN65	VF82	NM94
1(nn)-Dick Tracy	590.00	1775.00	3540.00	6500.00

	GD25	FN65	NM94
2(nn)-Don Winslow of the Navy (#1) (Rare) (11/39?)	118.00	354.00	1300.00
3(nn)-Myra North (1/40?)	70.00	210.00	775.00
4-Donald Duck by Al Taliaferro (1940)(Disney)(3/40?)	808.00	2423.00	10,500.00
(Prices vary widely on this book)			
5-Smilin' Jack (#1) (5/40?)	54.00	162.00	595.00
6-Dick Tracy (Scarce)	134.00	400.00	1470.00
7-Gang Busters	33.00	98.00	360.00
8-Dick Tracy	67.00	200.00	735.00
9-Terry and the Pirates-r/Super #9-29	54.00	161.00	590.00
10-Smilin' Jack	49.00	146.00	535.00
11-Smitty (#1)	34.00	101.00	370.00
12-Little Orphan Annie; reprints strips from 12/19/37 to 6/4/38	45.00	135.00	495.00
13-Walt Disney's Reluctant Dragon('41)-Contains 2 pgs. of photos from film; 2 pg. foreword to Fantasia by Leopold Stokowski; Donald Duck, Goofy, Baby Weems & Mickey Mouse (as the Sorcerer's Apprentice) app. (Disney)	147.00	443.00	1625.00
14-Moon Mullins (#1)	33.00	98.00	360.00
15-Tillie the Toiler (#1)	32.00	95.00	360.00

	GD25	FN65	VF82
16-Mickey Mouse (#1) (Disney) by Gottfredson	654.00	1961.00	9000.00

	GD25	FN65	NM94
17-Walt Disney's Dumbo, the Flying Elephant (#1)(1941)-Mickey Mouse, Donald Duck, & Pluto app. (Disney)	164.00	492.00	1800.00
18-Jiggs and Maggie (#1)(1936-38-r)	36.00	109.00	400.00
19-Barney Google and Snuffy Smith (#1)-(1st issue with Four Color on the cover)	36.00	106.00	390.00
20-Tiny Tim	27.00	80.00	295.00
21-Dick Tracy	57.00	170.50	625.00
22-Don Winslow	28.00	85.00	310.00
23-Gang Busters	26.00	77.00	280.00
24-Captain Easy	39.00	118.00	435.00
25-Popeye (1942)	66.00	197.00	720.00

Four Color #25 © Walter Lantz Prod.

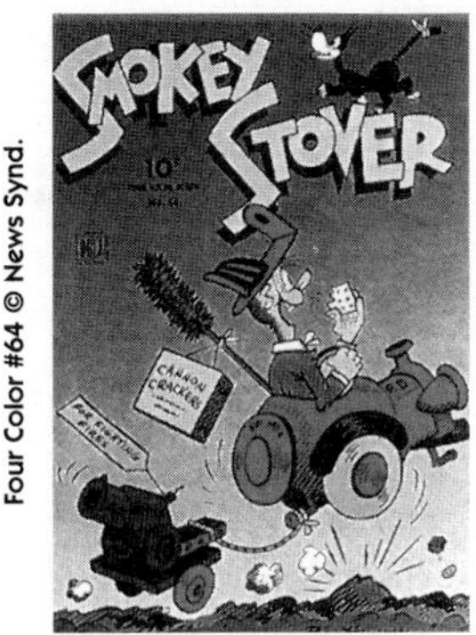

Four Color #64 © News Synd.

Four Color #75 © Gene Autry

	GD25	FN65	NM94
SERIES II:			
1-Little Joe (1942)	42.00	125.00	460.00
2-Harold Teen	24.00	71.00	270.00
3-Alley Oop (#1)	45.00	135.00	495.00
4-Smilin' Jack	40.00	121.00	445.00
5-Raggedy Ann and Andy (#1)	46.00	139.00	510.00
6-Smitty	20.00	60.00	220.00
7-Smokey Stover (#1)	30.00	90.00	330.00
8-Tillie the Toiler	21.00	63.00	230.00

	GD25	FN65	VF82	NM94
9-Donald Duck Finds Pirate Gold, by Carl Barks & Jack Hannah (Disney) (© 8/17/42)	615.00	1845.00	4300.00	8000.00

	GD25	FN65	NM94
10-Flash Gordon by Alex Raymond; reprinted from "The Ice Kingdom"	75.00	225.00	825.00
11-Wash Tubbs	27.00	80.00	295.00
12-Walt Disney's Bambi (#1)	50.00	150.00	550.00
13-Mr. District Attorney (#1)-See The Funnies #35 for 1st app.	27.00	82.00	300.00
14-Smilin' Jack	32.00	97.00	355.00
15-Felix the Cat (#1)	65.00	194.00	710.00
16-Porky Pig (#1)(1942)- "Secret of the Haunted House"	72.00	215.00	790.00
17-Popeye	48.00	143.50	535.00
18-Little Orphan Annie's Junior Commandos; Flag-c; reprints strips from 6/14/42 to 11/21/42	36.00	107.00	390.00
19-Walt Disney's Thumper Meets the Seven Dwarfs (Disney); reprinted in Silly Symphonies	51.00	153.00	560.00
20-Barney Baxter	24.50	73.50	270.00
21-Oswald the Rabbit (#1)(1943)	46.00	139.00	510.00
22-Tillie the Toiler	16.00	49.00	180.00
23-Raggedy Ann and Andy	35.00	104.00	380.00
24-Gang Busters	26.00	77.00	280.00
25-Andy Panda (#1) (Walter Lantz)	45.00	135.00	495.00
26-Popeye	48.00	143.00	535.00
27-Walt Disney's Mickey Mouse and the Seven Colored Terror	77.00	232.00	850.00
28-Wash Tubbs	20.00	59.00	215.00

	GD25	FN65	VF82	NM94
29-Donald Duck and the Mummy's Ring, by Carl Barks (Disney) (9/43)	492.00	1477.00	3446.00	6400.00

	GD25	FN65	NM94
30-Bambi's Children (1943)-Disney	50.00	150.00	550.00
31-Moon Mullins	17.00	50.00	185.00
32-Smitty	14.00	44.00	160.00
33-Bugs Bunny "Public Nuisance #1"	105.00	315.00	1150.00
34-Dick Tracy	39.00	116.00	425.00
35-Smokey Stover	16.00	47.00	170.00
36-Smilin' Jack	21.00	64.00	235.00
37-Bringing Up Father	18.00	55.00	200.00
38-Roy Rogers (#1, © 4/44)-1st western comic with photo-c	182.00	546.00	2000.00
39-Oswald the Rabbit (1944)	33.00	98.00	360.00
40-Barney Google and Snuffy Smith	21.00	63.00	230.00
41-Mother Goose and Nursery Rhyme Comics (#1)-All by Walt Kelly	21.00	63.00	230.00
42-Tiny Tim (1934-r)	16.00	47.00	170.00
43-Popeye (1938-'42-r)	30.00	89.00	325.00
44-Terry and the Pirates (1938-r)	37.00	112.00	410.00
45-Raggedy Ann	28.00	85.00	310.00
46-Felix the Cat and the Haunted Castle	38.00	115.00	420.00
47-Gene Autry (copyright 6/16/44)	39.00	117.00	425.00
48-Porky Pig of the Mounties by Carl Barks (7/44)	91.00	273.00	1000.00
49-Snow White and the Seven Dwarfs (Disney)	56.00	169.00	620.00

	GD25	FN65	NM94
50-Fairy Tale Parade-Walt Kelly art (1944)	24.00	71.00	260.00
51-Bugs Bunny Finds the Lost Treasure	34.00	102.00	370.00
52-Little Orphan Annie; reprints strips from 6/18/38 to 11/19/38	28.00	85.00	310.00
53-Wash Tubbs	14.00	44.00	160.00
54-Andy Panda	29.00	86.00	315.00
55-Tillie the Toiler	12.00	37.00	135.00
56-Dick Tracy	31.00	93.00	340.00
57-Gene Autry	36.00	109.00	400.00
58-Smilin' Jack	21.00	64.00	235.00
59-Mother Goose and Nursery Rhyme Comics-Kelly-c/a	18.00	53.00	195.00
60-Tiny Folks Funnies	13.00	40.00	145.00
61-Santa Claus Funnies(11/44)-Kelly art	22.00	67.00	245.00
62-Donald Duck in Frozen Gold, by Carl Barks (Disney) (1/45)	154.00	462.00	2000.00
63-Roy Rogers; color photo-all 4 covers	44.00	134.00	490.00
64-Smokey Stover	11.00	34.00	125.00
65-Smitty	11.00	34.00	125.00
66-Gene Autry	36.00	109.00	400.00
67-Oswald the Rabbit	16.00	48.00	175.00
68-Mother Goose and Nursery Rhyme Comics, by Walt Kelly	18.00	53.00	195.00
69-Fairy Tale Parade, by Walt Kelly	24.00	71.00	260.00
70-Popeye and Wimpy	24.00	72.00	265.00
71-Walt Disney's Three Caballeros, by Walt Kelly (© 4/45)-(Disney)	75.00	225.00	825.00
72-Raggedy Ann	24.00	71.00	260.00
73-The Gumps (#1)	11.00	33.00	120.00
74-Marge's Little Lulu (#1)	91.00	273.00	1000.00
75-Gene Autry and the Wildcat	28.00	85.00	315.00
76-Little Orphan Annie; reprints strips from 2/28/40 to 6/24/40	23.00	70.00	255.00
77-Felix the Cat	36.00	107.00	390.00
78-Porky Pig and the Bandit Twins	22.00	65.00	240.00
79-Walt Disney's Mickey Mouse in The Riddle of the Red Hat by Carl Barks (8/45)	95.00	286.00	1050.00
80-Smilin' Jack	14.00	42.00	155.00
81-Moon Mullins	9.00	27.00	100.00
82-Lone Ranger	40.00	120.00	435.00
83-Gene Autry in Outlaw Trail	29.00	87.00	315.00
84-Flash Gordon by Alex Raymond-Reprints from "The Fiery Desert"	35.00	105.00	385.00
85-Andy Panda and the Mad Dog Mystery	14.50	43.50	160.00
86-Roy Rogers; photo-c	33.00	99.00	360.00
87-Fairy Tale Parade by Walt Kelly; Dan Noonan-c	24.00	71.00	260.00
88-Bugs Bunny's Great Adventure (Sci/fi)	19.00	57.00	210.00
89-Tillie the Toiler	12.00	37.00	135.00
90-Christmas with Mother Goose by Walt Kelly (11/45)	16.00	49.00	180.00
91-Santa Claus Funnies by Walt Kelly (11/45)	16.00	49.00	180.00
92-Walt Disney's The Wonderful Adventures Of Pinocchio (1945); Donald Duck by Kelly, 16 pgs. (Disney)	55.00	164.00	600.00
93-Gene Autry in The Bandit of Black Rock	25.00	74.00	270.00
94-Winnie Winkle (1945)	11.00	33.00	120.00
95-Roy Rogers Comics; photo-c	33.00	98.00	360.00
96-Dick Tracy	22.00	67.00	245.00
97-Marge's Little Lulu (1946)	43.00	130.00	475.00
98-Lone Ranger, The	29.00	87.00	315.00
99-Smitty	9.00	29.00	105.00
100-Gene Autry Comics; photo-c	25.00	74.00	270.00
101-Terry and the Pirates	25.00	74.00	270.00

NOTE: *No. 101 is last issue to carry "Four Color" logo on cover; all issues beginning with No. 100 are marked "...O. S." (One Shot) which can be found in the bottom left-hand panel on the first page; the numbers following "O. S." relate to the year/month issued.*

Four Color #120 © Marjorie H. Buell

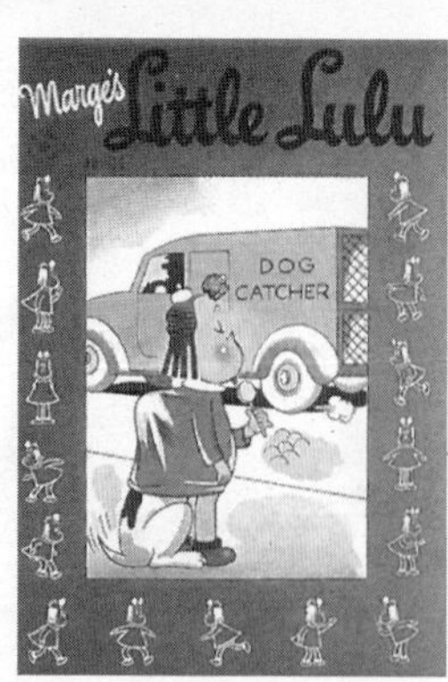

Four Color #167 © Lone Ranger, Inc.

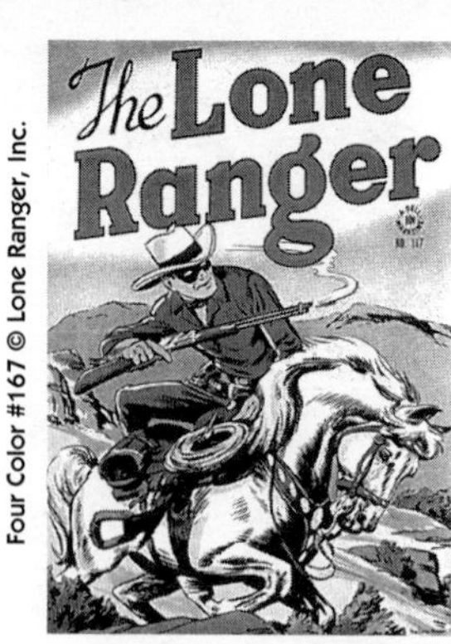

Four Color #200 © Warner Bros.

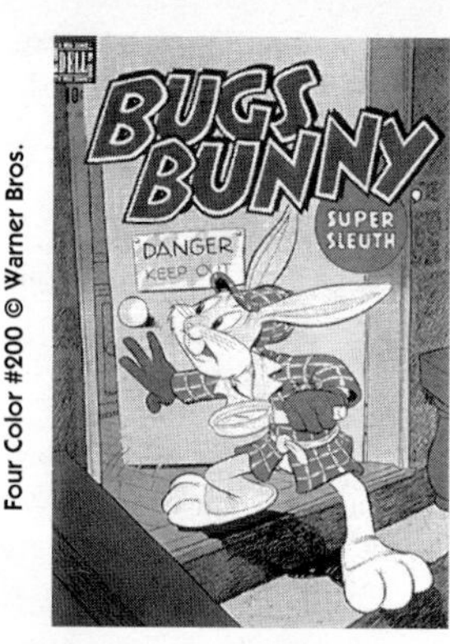

	GD25	FN65	NM94
102-Oswald the Rabbit-Walt Kelly art, 1 pg.	14.00	41.00	150.00
103-Easter with Mother Goose by Walt Kelly	17.00	52.00	190.00
104-Fairy Tale Parade by Walt Kelly	17.00	52.00	190.00
105-Albert the Alligator and Pogo Possum (#1) by Kelly (4/46)	63.00	189.00	690.00
106-Tillie the Toiler	9.00	27.00	100.00
107-Little Orphan Annie; reprints strips from 11/16/42 to 3/24/43	19.00	58.00	215.00
108-Donald Duck in The Terror of the River, by Carl Barks (Disney) (© 4/16/46)	112.00	335.00	1450.00
109-Roy Rogers Comics; photo-c	24.00	72.00	265.00
110-Marge's Little Lulu	31.00	93.00	340.00
111-Captain Easy	13.00	40.00	145.00
112-Porky Pig's Adventure in Gopher Gulch	13.00	38.00	140.00
113-Popeye; all new Popeye stories begin	12.00	35.00	130.00
114-Fairy Tale Parade by Walt Kelly	17.00	52.00	190.00
115-Marge's Little Lulu	31.00	93.00	340.00
116-Mickey Mouse and the House of Many Mysteries (Disney)	21.00	64.00	235.00
117-Roy Rogers Comics; photo-c	17.00	51.00	185.00
118-Lone Ranger, The	29.00	87.00	315.00
119-Felix the Cat; all new Felix stories begin	30.00	89.00	325.00
120-Marge's Little Lulu	27.00	81.00	295.00
121-Fairy Tale Parade-(not Kelly)	10.00	30.00	110.00
122-Henry (#1) (10/46)	12.00	35.00	130.00
123-Bugs Bunny's Dangerous Venture	14.00	42.00	155.00
124-Roy Rogers Comics; photo-c	17.00	51.00	185.00
125-Lone Ranger, The	20.00	59.00	215.00
126-Christmas with Mother Goose by Walt Kelly (1946)	13.00	38.00	140.00
127-Popeye	12.00	35.00	130.00
128-Santa Claus Funnies- "Santa & the Angel" by Gollub; "A Mouse in the House" by Kelly	13.00	38.00	140.00
129-Walt Disney's Uncle Remus and His Tales of Brer Rabbit (#1) (1946)-Adapted from Disney movie "Song of the South"	26.00	79.00	290.00
130-Andy Panda (Walter Lantz)	9.00	27.00	100.00
131-Marge's Little Lulu	27.00	81.00	295.00
132-Tillie the Toiler (1947)	9.00	27.00	100.00
133-Dick Tracy	19.00	57.00	210.00
134-Tarzan and the Devil Ogre; Marsh-c/a	59.00	177.00	650.00
135-Felix the Cat	22.00	65.00	240.00
136-Lone Ranger, The	20.00	59.00	215.00
137-Roy Rogers Comics; photo-c	17.00	51.00	185.00
138-Smitty	8.00	25.00	90.00
139-Marge's Little Lulu (1947)	25.00	75.00	275.00
140-Easter with Mother Goose by Walt Kelly	14.00	42.00	155.00
141-Mickey Mouse and the Submarine Pirates (Disney)	18.00	55.00	200.00
142-Bugs Bunny and the Haunted Mountain	14.00	42.00	155.00
143-Oswald the Rabbit & the Prehistoric Egg	8.00	25.00	90.00
144-Roy Rogers Comics (1947)-Photo-c	17.00	51.00	185.00
145-Popeye	12.00	35.00	130.00
146-Marge's Little Lulu	25.00	75.00	275.00
147-Donald Duck in Volcano Valley, by Carl Barks (Disney) (5/47)	77.00	231.00	1000.00
148-Albert the Alligator and Pogo Possum by Walt Kelly (5/47)	56.00	168.00	615.00
149-Smilin' Jack	9.00	27.00	100.00
150-Tillie the Toiler (6/47)	8.00	25.00	90.00
151-Lone Ranger, The	16.00	48.00	175.00
152-Little Orphan Annie; reprints strips from 1/2/44 to 5/6/44	13.00	38.00	140.00
153-Roy Rogers Comics; photo-c	14.00	44.00	160.00
154-Walter Lantz Andy Panda	9.00	27.00	100.00
155-Henry (7/47)	7.00	22.00	80.00
156-Porky Pig and the Phantom	9.00	27.00	100.00
157-Mickey Mouse & the Beanstalk (Disney)	18.00	55.00	200.00
158-Marge's Little Lulu	25.00	75.00	275.00
159-Donald Duck in the Ghost of the Grotto, by Carl Barks (Disney) (8/47)	62.00	185.00	800.00
160-Roy Rogers Comics; photo-c	14.00	44.00	160.00
161-Tarzan and the Fires Of Tohr; Marsh-c/a	50.00	150.00	550.00
162-Felix the Cat (9/47)	16.00	49.00	180.00
163-Dick Tracy	15.00	45.00	165.00
164-Bugs Bunny Finds the Frozen Kingdom	14.00	42.00	155.00
165-Marge's Little Lulu	25.00	75.00	275.00
166-Roy Rogers Comics (52 pgs.)-Photo-c	14.00	44.00	160.00
167-Lone Ranger, The	16.00	48.00	175.00
168-Popeye (10/47)	12.00	35.00	130.00
169-Woody Woodpecker (#1)- "Manhunter in the North"; drug use story	13.00	40.00	145.00
170-Mickey Mouse on Spook's Island (11/47)(Disney)-reprinted in Mickey Mouse #103	14.00	44.00	160.00
171-Charlie McCarthy (#1) and the Twenty Thieves	23.00	68.00	250.00
172-Christmas with Mother Goose by Walt Kelly (11/47)	13.00	38.00	140.00
173-Flash Gordon	12.00	37.00	135.00
174-Winnie Winkle	6.40	19.00	70.00
175-Santa Claus Funnies by Walt Kelly (1947)	13.00	38.00	140.00
176-Tillie the Toiler (12/47)	8.00	25.00	90.00
177-Roy Rogers Comics-(36 pgs.); Photo-c	14.00	44.00	160.00
178-Donald Duck "Christmas on Bear Mountain" by Carl Barks; 1st app. Uncle Scrooge (Disney)(12/47)	92.00	277.00	1200.00
179-Uncle Wiggily (#1)-Walt Kelly-c	14.00	44.00	160.00
180-Ozark Ike (#1)	9.00	27.00	100.00
181-Walt Disney's Mickey Mouse in Jungle Magic	14.00	44.00	160.00
182-Porky Pig in Never-Never Land (2/48)	9.00	27.00	100.00
183-Oswald the Rabbit (Lantz)	8.00	25.00	90.00
184-Tillie the Toiler	8.00	25.00	90.00
185-Easter with Mother Goose by Walt Kelly (1948)	12.00	35.00	130.00
186-Walt Disney's Bambi (4/48)-Reprinted as Movie Classic Bambi #3 (1956)	15.50	46.50	170.00
187-Bugs Bunny and the Dreadful Dragon	9.50	28.50	105.00
188-Woody Woodpecker (Lantz, 5/48)	9.00	27.00	100.00
189-Donald Duck in The Old Castle's Secret, by Carl Barks (Disney) (6/48)	58.00	173.00	750.00
190-Flash Gordon ('48)	12.00	37.00	135.00
191-Porky Pig to the Rescue	9.00	27.00	100.00
192-The Brownies (#1)-by Walt Kelly (7/48)	11.00	33.00	120.00
193-M.G.M. Presents Tom and Jerry (#1)(1948)	13.00	38.00	140.00
194-Mickey Mouse in The World Under the Sea (Disney)-Reprinted in Mickey Mouse #101	14.00	44.00	160.00
195-Tillie the Toiler	5.50	16.50	60.00
196-Charlie McCarthy in The Haunted Hide-Out; part photo-c	16.00	47.00	170.00
197-Spirit of the Border (#1) (Zane Grey) (1948)	11.00	32.00	115.00
198-Andy Panda	9.00	27.00	100.00
199-Donald Duck in Sheriff of Bullet Valley, by Carl Barks; Barks draws himself on wanted poster, last page; used in Love & Death (Disney) (10/48)	64.00	190.00	825.00
200-Bugs Bunny, Super Sleuth (10/48)	9.50	28.50	105.00
201-Christmas with Mother Goose by W. Kelly	11.00	33.00	120.00
202-Woody Woodpecker	5.75	17.00	63.00
203-Donald Duck in the Golden Christmas Tree, by Carl Barks (Disney) (12/48)	43.00	129.00	560.00
204-Flash Gordon (12/48)	9.00	29.00	105.00
205-Santa Claus Funnies by Walt Kelly	12.00	35.00	130.00
206-Little Orphan Annie; reprints strips from 11/10/40 to 1/11/41			

Four Color #246 © Zane Grey, Inc.

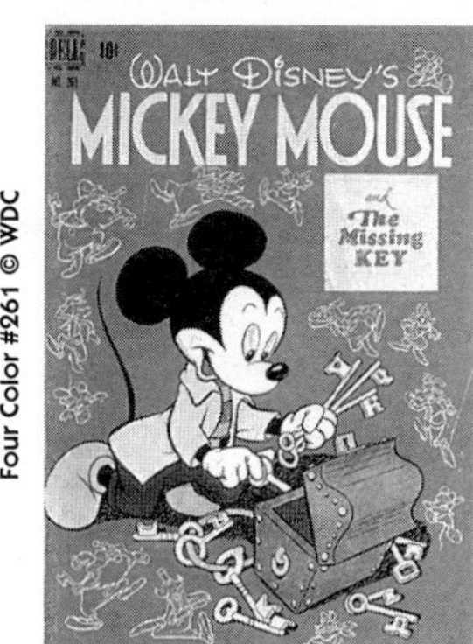

Four Color #261 © WDC

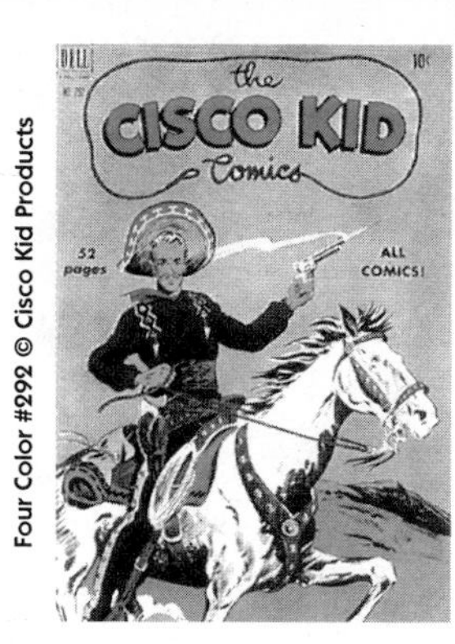

Four Color #292 © Cisco Kid Products

	GD25	FN65	NM94
	7.00	20.00	75.00
207-King of the Royal Mounted (#1) (12/48)	14.00	41.00	150.00
208-Brer Rabbit Does It Again (Disney) (1/49)	11.00	32.00	115.00
209-Harold Teen	3.60	11.00	40.00
210-Tippie and Cap Stubbs	3.60	11.00	40.00
211-Little Beaver (#1)	7.00	20.00	75.00
212-Dr. Bobbs	3.60	10.80	40.00
213-Tillie the Toiler	5.50	16.50	60.00
214-Mickey Mouse and His Sky Adventure (2/49)(Disney)-Reprinted in Mickey Mouse #105	13.00	38.00	140.00
215-Sparkle Plenty (Dick Tracy-r by Gould)	9.00	27.00	100.00
216-Andy Panda and the Police Pup (Lantz)	6.00	19.00	68.00
217-Bugs Bunny in Court Jester	9.50	28.50	105.00
218-3 Little Pigs and the Wonderful Magic Lamp (Disney) (3/49)(#1)	11.00	33.00	120.00
219-Swee'pe	8.00	25.00	90.00
220-Easter with Mother Goose by Walt Kelly	12.00	35.00	130.00
221-Uncle Wiggily-Walt Kelly cover in part	9.00	27.00	100.00
222-West of the Pecos (Zane Grey)	5.50	16.50	60.00
223-Donald Duck "Lost in the Andes" by Carl Barks (Disney-4/49) (square egg story)	62.00	185.00	800.00
224-Little Iodine (#1), by Hatlo (4/49)	8.00	25.00	90.00
225-Oswald the Rabbit (Lantz)	5.00	15.00	55.00
226-Porky Pig and Spoofy, the Spook	7.00	22.00	80.00
227-Seven Dwarfs (Disney)	10.00	30.00	110.00
228-Mark of Zorro, The (#1) (1949)	20.00	60.00	220.00
229-Smokey Stover	4.50	13.50	50.00
230-Sunset Pass (Zane Grey)	5.50	16.50	60.00
231-Mickey Mouse and the Rajah's Treasure (Disney)	13.00	38.00	140.00
232-Woody Woodpecker (Lantz, 6/49)	5.75	17.00	63.00
233-Bugs Bunny, Sleepwalking Sleuth	9.50	28.50	105.00
234-Dumbo in Sky Voyage (Disney)	9.00	27.00	100.00
235-Tiny Tim	3.60	11.00	40.00
236-Heritage of the Desert (Zane Grey) (1949)	5.50	16.50	60.00
237-Tillie the Toiler	5.50	16.50	60.00
238-Donald Duck in Voodoo Hoodoo, by Carl Barks (Disney) (8/49)	43.00	129.00	560.00
239-Adventure Bound (8/49)	4.25	13.00	48.00
240-Andy Panda (Lantz)	6.00	19.00	68.00
241-Porky Pig, Mighty Hunter	7.00	22.00	80.00
242-Tippie and Cap Stubbs	2.75	8.00	30.00
243-Thumper Follows His Nose (Disney)	9.00	27.00	100.00
244-The Brownies by Walt Kelly	10.00	30.00	110.00
245-Dick's Adventures (9/49)	4.50	13.50	50.00
246-Thunder Mountain (Zane Grey)	3.60	11.00	40.00
247-Flash Gordon	9.00	29.00	105.00
248-Mickey Mouse and the Black Sorcerer (Disney)	13.00	38.00	140.00
249-Woody Woodpecker in the "Globetrotter" (10/49)	5.75	17.00	63.00
250-Bugs Bunny in Diamond Daze; used in **SOTI**, pg. 309	11.00	33.00	120.00
251-Hubert at Camp Moonbeam	3.60	11.00	40.00
252-Pinocchio (Disney)-not by Kelly; origin	9.00	27.00	100.00
253-Christmas with Mother Goose by W. Kelly	11.00	33.00	120.00
254-Santa Claus Funnies by Walt Kelly; Pogo & Albert story by Kelly (11/49)	12.00	35.00	130.00
255-The Ranger (Zane Grey) (1949)	3.60	11.00	40.00
256-Donald Duck in "Luck of the North" by Carl Barks (Disney) (12/49)-Shows #257 on inside	33.00	99.00	425.00
257-Little Iodine	6.40	19.00	70.00
258-Andy Panda and the Balloon Race (Lantz)	6.00	19.00	68.00
259-Santa and the Angel (Gollub art-condensed from #128) & Santa at the Zoo (12/49)-two books in one	3.60	11.00	40.00
260-Porky Pig, Hero of the Wild West (12/49)	7.00	22.00	80.00
261-Mickey Mouse and the Missing Key (Disney)	13.00	38.00	140.00
262-Raggedy Ann and Andy	6.40	19.00	70.00
263-Donald Duck in "Land of the Totem Poles" by Carl Barks (Disney) (2/50)-Has two Barks stories	31.00	92.00	400.00
264-Woody Woodpecker in the Magic Lantern (Lantz)	5.75	17.00	63.00
265-King of the Royal Mounted (Zane Grey)	7.00	22.00	80.00
266-Bugs Bunny on the "Isle of Hercules" (2/50)-Reprinted in Best of Bugs Bunny #1	8.00	25.00	90.00
267-Little Beaver; Harmon-c/a	3.50	11.00	38.00
268-Mickey Mouse's Surprise Visitor (1950) (Disney)	12.00	35.00	130.00
269-Johnny Mack Brown (#1)-Photo-c	21.00	62.00	225.00
270-Drift Fence (Zane Grey) (3/50)	3.60	11.00	40.00
271-Porky Pig in Phantom of the Plains	7.00	22.00	80.00
272-Cinderella (Disney) (4/50)	9.00	27.00	100.00
273-Oswald the Rabbit (Lantz)	5.00	15.00	55.00
274-Bugs Bunny, Hare-brained Reporter	8.00	25.00	90.00
275-Donald Duck in "Ancient Persia" by Carl Barks (Disney) (5/50)	29.00	87.00	375.00
276-Uncle Wiggily	7.00	22.00	80.00
277-Porky Pig in Desert Adventure (5/50)	7.00	22.00	80.00
278-Bill Elliott Comics (#1)-Photo-c	12.00	35.00	130.00
279-Mickey Mouse and Pluto Battle the Giant Ants (Disney); reprinted in Mickey Mouse #102 & 245	9.00	27.00	100.00
280-Andy Panda in The Isle Of Mechanical Men (Lantz)	6.00	19.00	68.00
281-Bugs Bunny in The Great Circus Mystery	8.00	25.00	90.00
282-Donald Duck and the Pixilated Parrot by Carl Barks (Disney) (© 5/23/50)	29.00	87.00	375.00
283-King of the Royal Mounted (7/50)	7.00	22.00	80.00
284-Porky Pig in The Kingdom of Nowhere	7.00	22.00	80.00
285-Bozo the Clown & His Minikin Circus (#1) (TV)	17.00	51.00	190.00
286-Mickey Mouse in The Uninvited Guest (Disney	9.00	27.00	100.00
287-Gene Autry's Champion in The Ghost Of Black Mountain; photo-c	8.50	25.50	95.00
288-Woody Woodpecker in Klondike Gold (Lantz)	5.75	17.00	63.00
289-Bugs Bunny in "Indian Trouble"	8.00	25.00	90.00
290-The Chief (#1) (8/50)	4.50	13.50	50.00
291-Donald Duck in "The Magic Hourglass" by Carl Barks (Disney) (9/50)	29.00	87.00	375.00
292-The Cisco Kid Comics (#1)	22.00	66.00	240.00
293-The Brownies-Kelly-c/a	10.00	30.00	110.00
294-Little Beaver	3.50	11.00	38.00
295-Porky Pig in President Porky (9/50)	7.00	22.00	80.00
296-Mickey Mouse in Private Eye for Hire (Disney)	9.00	27.00	100.00
297-Andy Panda in The Haunted Inn (Lantz, 10/50)	6.00	19.00	68.00
298-Bugs Bunny in Sheik for a Day	8.00	25.00	90.00
299-Buck Jones & the Iron Horse Trail (#1)	11.00	34.00	125.00
300-Donald Duck in "Big-Top Bedlam" by Carl Barks (Disney) (11/50)	29.00	87.00	375.00
301-The Mysterious Rider (Zane Grey)	3.60	11.00	40.00
302-Santa Claus Funnies (11/50)	3.60	11.00	40.00
303-Porky Pig in The Land of the Monstrous Flies	4.50	13.50	50.00
304-Mickey Mouse in Tom-Tom Island (Disney) (12/50)	7.00	22.00	80.00
305-Woody Woodpecker (Lantz)	3.00	10.00	36.00
306-Raggedy Ann	4.50	13.50	50.00
307-Bugs Bunny in Lumber Jack Rabbit	7.00	20.00	75.00
308-Donald Duck in "Dangerous Disguise" by Carl Barks (Disney) (1/51)	25.00	75.00	325.00
309-Betty Betz' Dollface and Her Gang (1951)	4.50	13.50	50.00
310-King of the Royal Mounted (1/51)	5.50	16.50	60.00

Four Color #323 © KING

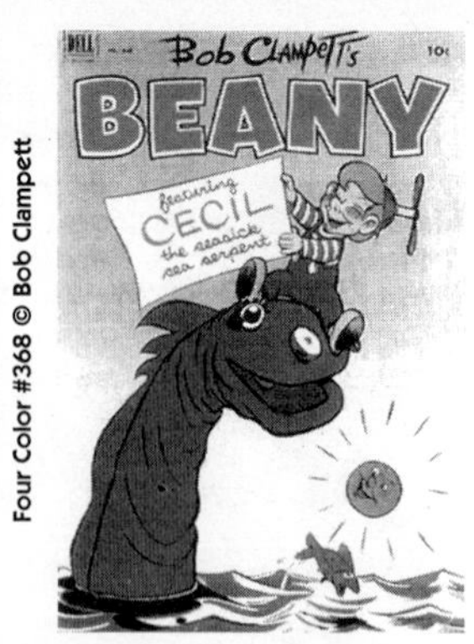

Four Color #368 © Bob Clampett

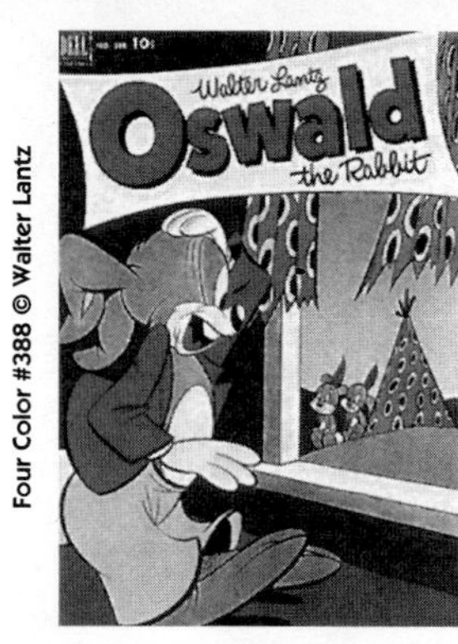

Four Color #388 © Walter Lantz

	GD25	FN65	NM94
311-Porky Pig in Midget Horses of Hidden Valley	4.50	13.50	50.00
312-Tonto (#1)	9.00	27.00	100.00
313-Mickey Mouse in The Mystery of the Double-Cross Ranch (#1) (Disney) (2/51)	7.00	22.00	80.00

Note: Beginning with the above comic in 1951 Dell/Western began adding #1 in small print on the covers of several long running titles with the evident intention of switching these titles to their own monthly numbers, but when the conversions were made, there was no connection. It is thought that the post office may have stepped in and decreed the sequences should commence as though the first four colors printed had each begun with number one, or the first issues sold by subscription. Since the regular series' numbers don't correctly match to the numbers of earlier issues published, it's not known whether or not the numbering was in error.

	GD25	FN65	NM94
314-Ambush (Zane Grey)	3.60	11.00	40.00
315-Oswald the Rabbit (Lantz)	4.00	12.00	45.00
316-Rex Allen (#1)-Photo-c; Marsh-a	13.00	38.00	140.00
317-Bugs Bunny in Hair Today Gone Tomorrow (#1)	7.00	20.00	75.00
318-Donald Duck in "No Such Varmint" by Carl Barks (#1)-Indicia shows #317 (Disney, © 1/23/51)	25.00	75.00	325.00
319-Gene Autry's Champion; painted-c	3.60	11.00	40.00
320-Uncle Wiggily (#1)	7.00	22.00	80.00
321-Little Scouts (#1) (3/51)	2.75	8.00	30.00
322-Porky Pig in Roaring Rockets (#1 on-c)	4.50	13.50	50.00
323-Susie Q. Smith (#1) (3/51)	3.00	9.00	35.00
324-I Met a Handsome Cowboy (3/51)	8.00	25.00	90.00
325-Mickey Mouse in The Haunted Castle (#2) (Disney) (4/51)	7.00	22.00	80.00
326-Andy Panda (#1) (Lantz)	3.75	11.50	40.00
327-Bugs Bunny and the Rajah's Treasure (#2)	7.00	20.00	75.00
328-Donald Duck in Old California (#2) by Carl Barks-Peyote drug use issue (Disney) (5/51)	27.00	81.00	350.00
329-Roy Roger's Trigger (#1)(5/51)-Photo-c	11.00	32.00	120.00
330-Porky Pig Meets the Bristled Bruiser (#2)	4.50	13.50	50.00
331-Alice in Wonderland (Disney) (1951)	13.75	41.50	150.00
332-Little Beaver	3.50	11.00	38.00
333-Wilderness Trek (Zane Grey) (5/51)	3.60	11.00	40.00
334-Mickey Mouse and Yukon Gold (Disney) (6/51)	7.00	22.00	80.00
335-Francis the Famous Talking Mule (#1, 6/51)-1st Dell non animated movie comic (all issues based on movie)	7.00	22.00	80.00
336-Woody Woodpecker (Lantz)	3.00	10.00	36.00
337-The Brownies-not by Walt Kelly	3.00	10.00	36.00
338-Bugs Bunny and the Rocking Horse Thieves	7.00	20.00	75.00
339-Donald Duck and the Magic Fountain-not by Carl Barks (Disney) (7-8/51)	6.00	18.00	60.00
340-King of the Royal Mounted (7/51)	5.50	16.50	60.00
341-Unbirthday Party with Alice in Wonderland (Disney) (7/51)	13.75	41.50	150.00
342-Porky Pig the Lucky Peppermint Mine; r/in Porky Pig #3	3.60	11.00	40.00
343-Mickey Mouse in The Ruby Eye of Homar-Guy-Am (Disney)-Reprinted in Mickey Mouse #104	5.50	16.50	60.00
344-Sergeant Preston from Challenge of The Yukon (#1) (TV)	11.00	33.00	120.00
345-Andy Panda in Scotland Yard (8-10/51) (Lantz)	3.75	11.50	40.00
346-Hideout (Zane Grey)	3.60	11.00	40.00
347-Bugs Bunny the Frigid Hare (8-9/51)	7.00	20.00	75.00
348-Donald Duck "The Crocodile Collector"; Barks-c only (Disney) (9-10/51)	15.00	45.00	160.00
349-Uncle Wiggily	5.50	16.50	60.00
350-Woody Woodpecker (Lantz)	3.00	10.00	36.00
351-Porky Pig & the Grand Canyon Giant (9-10/51)	3.60	11.00	40.00
352-Mickey Mouse in The Mystery of Painted Valley (Disney)	5.50	16.50	60.00
353-Duck Album (#1)-Barks-c (Disney)	8.00	24.00	90.00
354-Raggedy Ann & Andy	4.50	13.50	50.00
355-Bugs Bunny Hot-Rod Hare	7.00	20.00	75.00
356-Donald Duck in "Rags to Riches"; Barks-c only	15.00	45.00	160.00
357-Comeback (Zane Grey)	2.75	8.00	30.00
358-Andy Panda (Lantz) (11-1/52)	3.75	11.50	40.00
359-Frosty the Snowman (#1)	7.00	22.00	80.00
360-Porky Pig in Tree of Fortune (11-12/51)	3.60	11.00	40.00
361-Santa Claus Funnies	3.60	11.00	40.00
362-Mickey Mouse and the Smuggled Diamonds (Disney)	5.50	16.50	60.00
363-King of the Royal Mounted	4.50	13.50	50.00
364-Woody Woodpecker (Lantz)	3.00	9.00	34.00
365-The Brownies-not by Kelly	3.00	10.00	36.00
366-Bugs Bunny Uncle Buckskin Comes to Town (12-1/52)	7.00	20.00	75.00
367-Donald Duck in "A Christmas for Shacktown" by Carl Barks (Disney) (1-2/52)	25.00	75.00	320.00
368-Bob Clampett's Beany and Cecil (#1)	25.00	75.00	275.00
369-The Lone Ranger's Famous Horse Hi-Yo Silver (#1); Silver's origin	8.00	25.00	90.00
370-Porky Pig in Trouble in the Big Trees	3.60	11.00	40.00
371-Mickey Mouse in The Inca Idol Case (1952) (Disney)	5.50	16.50	60.00
372-Riders of the Purple Sage (Zane Grey)	2.75	8.00	30.00
373-Sergeant Preston (TV)	6.40	19.00	70.00
374-Woody Woodpecker (Lantz)	3.00	9.00	34.00
375-John Carter of Mars (E. R. Burroughs)-Jesse Marsh-a; origin	23.00	68.00	250.00
376-Bugs Bunny, "The Magic Sneeze"	7.00	20.00	75.00
377-Susie Q. Smith	2.75	8.00	30.00
378-Tom Corbett, Space Cadet (#1) (TV)-McWilliams-a	16.00	48.00	175.00
379-Donald Duck in "Southern Hospitality"; Not by Barks (Disney)	6.00	18.00	60.00
380-Raggedy Ann & Andy	4.50	13.50	50.00
381-Marge's Tubby (#1)	18.00	54.00	195.00
382-Snow White and the Seven Dwarfs (Disney)-origin; partial reprint of 4-Color #49 (Movie)	10.00	30.00	110.00
383-Andy Panda (Lantz)	3.00	9.00	32.00
384-King of the Royal Mounted (3/52)(Zane Grey)	4.50	13.50	50.00
385-Porky Pig in The Isle of Missing Ships (3-4/52)	3.60	11.00	40.00
386-Uncle Scrooge (#1)-by Carl Barks (Disney) in "Only a Poor Old Man" (3/52)	86.00	259.00	950.00
387-Mickey Mouse in High Tibet (Disney) (4-5/52)	5.50	16.50	60.00
388-Oswald the Rabbit (Lantz)	4.00	12.00	45.00
389-Andy Hardy Comics (#1)	2.75	8.00	30.00
390-Woody Woodpecker (Lantz)	3.00	9.00	34.00
391-Uncle Wiggily	5.50	16.50	60.00
392-Hi-Yo Silver	4.00	12.00	45.00
393-Bugs Bunny	7.00	20.00	75.00
394-Donald Duck in Malayalaya-Barks-c only (Disney)	15.00	45.00	160.00
395-Forlorn River(Zane Grey)-First Nevada (5/52)	2.75	8.00	30.00
396-Tales of the Texas Rangers(#1)(TV)-Photo-c	10.00	30.00	110.00
397-Sergeant Preston of the Yukon (TV) (5/52)	6.40	19.00	70.00
398-The Brownies-not by Kelly	3.00	10.00	36.00
399-Porky Pig in The Lost Gold Mine	3.60	11.00	40.00
400-Tom Corbett, Space Cadet (TV)-McWilliams-c/a	9.00	27.00	100.00
401-Mickey Mouse and Goofy's Mechanical Wizard (Disney) (6-7/52)	3.60	11.00	40.00
402-Mary Jane and Sniffles	7.00	22.00	80.00
403-Li'l Bad Wolf (Disney) (6/52)(#1)	6.40	19.00	70.00
404-The Range Rider (#1) (TV)-Photo-c	10.00	30.00	110.00

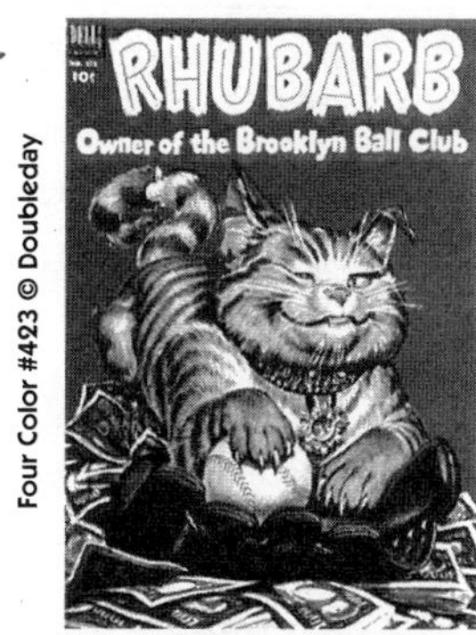

Four Color #423 © Doubleday

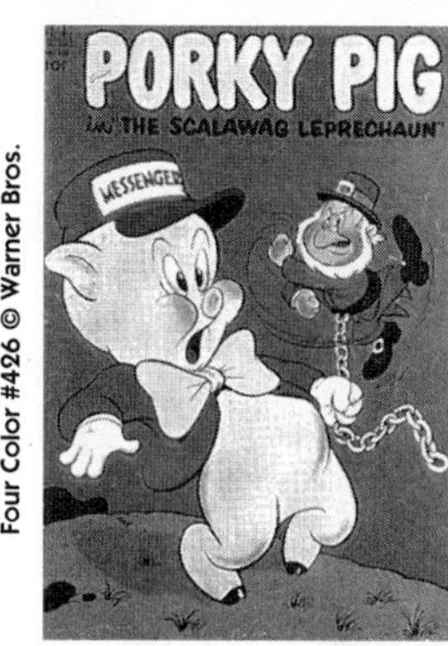

Four Color #426 © Warner Bros.

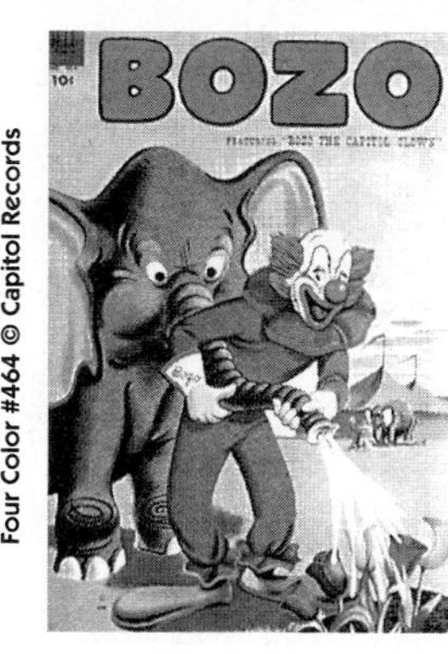

Four Color #464 © Capitol Records

	GD25	FN65	NM94
405-Woody Woodpecker (Lantz) (6-7/52)	3.00	9.00	34.00
406-Tweety and Sylvester (#1)	7.00	22.00	80.00
407-Bugs Bunny, Foreign-Legion Hare	5.50	16.50	60.00
408-Donald Duck and the Golden Helmet by Carl Barks (Disney) (7-8/52)	25.00	75.00	320.00
409-Andy Panda (7-9/52)	3.00	9.00	32.00
410-Porky Pig in The Water Wizard (7/52)	3.60	11.00	40.00
411-Mickey Mouse and the Old Sea Dog (Disney) (8-9/52)	3.60	11.00	40.00
412-Nevada (Zane Grey)	2.75	8.00	30.00
413-Robin Hood (Disney-Movie) (8/52)-Photo-c (1st Disney movie four color book)	10.00	30.00	110.00
414-Bob Clampett's Beany and Cecil (TV)	16.00	47.00	170.00
415-Rootie Kazootie (#1) (TV)	10.00	30.00	110.00
416-Woody Woodpecker (Lantz)	3.00	9.00	34.00
417-Double Trouble with Goober (#1) (8/52)	2.25	6.75	25.00
418-Rusty Riley, a Boy, a Horse, and a Dog (#1)-Frank Godwin-a (strip reprints) (8/52)	3.60	11.00	40.00
419-Sergeant Preston (TV)	6.40	19.00	70.00
420-Bugs Bunny in The Mysterious Buckaroo (8-9/52)	5.50	16.50	60.00
421-Tom Corbett, Space Cadet(TV)-McWilliams-a	9.00	27.00	100.00
422-Donald Duck and the Gilded Man, by Carl Barks (Disney) (9-10/52) (#423 on inside)	25.00	75.00	320.00
423-Rhubarb, Owner of the Brooklyn Ball Club (The Millionaire Cat) (#1)-Painted cover	4.50	13.50	50.00
424-Flash Gordon-Test Flight in Space (9/52)	8.00	23.00	85.00
425-Zorro, the Return of	11.00	34.00	125.00
426-Porky Pig in The Scalawag Leprechaun	3.60	11.00	40.00
427-Mickey Mouse and the Wonderful Whizzix (Disney) (10-11/52)-Reprinted in Mickey Mouse #100	3.60	11.00	40.00
428-Uncle Wiggily	3.60	11.00	40.00
429-Pluto in "Why Dogs Leave Home" (Disney) (10/52)(#1)	8.00	23.00	85.00
430-Marge's Tubby, the Shadow of a Man-Eater	10.00	31.00	115.00
431-Woody Woodpecker (10/52) (Lantz)	3.00	9.00	34.00
432-Bugs Bunny and the Rabbit Olympics	5.50	16.50	60.00
433-Wildfire (Zane Grey) (11-1/52-53)	2.75	8.00	30.00
434-Rin Tin Tin "In Dark Danger" (#1) (TV) (11/52)-Photo-c	14.00	41.00	150.00
435-Frosty the Snowman (11/52)	3.60	11.00	40.00
436-The Brownies-not by Kelly (11/52)	3.00	9.00	32.00
437-John Carter of Mars (E. R. Burroughs)-Marsh-a	14.00	44.00	160.00
438-Annie Oakley (#1) (TV)	14.00	41.00	150.00
439-Little Hiawatha (Disney) (12/52)j(#1)	4.50	13.50	50.00
440-Black Beauty (12/52)	2.75	8.00	30.00
441-Fearless Fagan	3.00	9.00	35.00
442-Peter Pan (Disney) (Movie)	8.00	25.00	90.00
443-Ben Bowie and His Mountain Men (#1)	5.50	16.50	60.00
444-Marge's Tubby	10.00	31.00	115.00
445-Charlie McCarthy	4.50	13.50	50.00
446-Captain Hook and Peter Pan (Disney)(Movie)(1/53)	8.00	25.00	90.00
447-Andy Hardy Comics	2.25	6.75	25.00
448-Bob Clampett's Beany and Cecil (TV)	16.00	47.00	170.00
449-Tappan's Burro (Zane Grey) (2-4/53)	2.75	8.00	30.00
450-Duck Album; Barks-c (Disney)	5.50	16.50	60.00
451-Rusty Riley-Frank Godwin-a (strip-r) (2/53)	2.75	8.00	30.00
452-Raggedy Ann & Andy (1953)	4.50	13.50	50.00
453-Susie Q. Smith (2/53)	2.75	8.00	30.00
454-Krazy Kat Comics; not by Herriman	3.00	9.00	35.00
455-Johnny Mack Brown Comics(3/53)-Photo-c	5.00	15.00	55.00
456-Uncle Scrooge Back to the Klondike (#2) by Barks (3/53) (Disney)	57.00	170.00	625.00
457-Daffy (#1)	8.00	25.00	90.00
458-Oswald the Rabbit (Lantz)	2.90	8.70	32.00
459-Rootie Kazootie (TV)	6.40	19.00	70.00
460-Buck Jones (4/53)	4.50	13.50	50.00
461-Marge's Tubby	9.00	27.00	100.00
462-Little Scouts	1.35	4.00	15.00
463-Petunia (4/53)	3.00	9.00	35.00
464-Bozo (4/53)	8.00	25.00	90.00
465-Francis the Famous Talking Mule	4.50	13.50	50.00
466-Rhubarb, the Millionaire Cat; painted-c	3.60	11.00	40.00
467-Desert Gold (Zane Grey) (5-7/53)	2.75	8.00	30.00
468-Goofy (#1) (Disney)	11.00	34.00	125.00
469-Beetle Bailey (#1) (5/53	9.00	27.00	100.00
470-Elmer Fudd	4.50	13.50	50.00
471-Double Trouble with Goober	1.85	5.50	15.00
472-Wild Bill Elliott (6/53)-Photo-c	3.60	11.00	40.00
473-Li'l Bad Wolf (Disney) (6/53)(#2)	3.60	11.00	40.00
474-Mary Jane and Sniffles	6.40	19.00	70.00
475-M.G.M.'s The Two Mouseketeers (#1)	6.40	19.00	70.00
476-Rin Tin Tin (TV)-Photo-c	7.00	22.00	80.00
477-Bob Clampett's Beany and Cecil (TV)	16.00	47.00	170.00
478-Charlie McCarthy	4.50	13.50	50.00
479-Queen of the West Dale Evans (#1)-Photo-c	21.00	63.00	230.00
480-Andy Hardy Comics	2.25	6.75	25.00
481-Annie Oakley And Tagg (TV)	8.00	23.00	85.00
482-Brownies-not by Kelly	3.00	9.00	32.00
483-Little Beaver (7/53)	2.75	8.00	30.00
484-River Feud (Zane Grey) (8-10/53)	2.75	8.00	30.00
485-The Little People-Walt Scott (#1)	5.50	16.50	60.00
486-Rusty Riley-Frank Godwin strip-r	2.75	8.00	30.00
487-Mowgli, the Jungle Book (Rudyard Kipling's)	5.00	15.00	55.00
488-John Carter of Mars (Burroughs)-Marsh-a; painted-c	14.00	48.00	160.00
489-Tweety and Sylvester	3.50	10.50	38.00
490-Jungle Jim (#1)	5.50	16.50	60.00
491-Silvertip (#1) (Max Brand)-Kinstler-a (8/53)	7.00	22.00	80.00
492-Duck Album (Disney)	4.50	13.50	50.00
493-Johnny Mack Brown; photo-c	5.00	15.00	55.00
494-The Little King (#1)	9.00	27.00	100.00
495-Uncle Scrooge (#3) (Disney)-by Carl Barks (9/53)	43.00	130.00	475.00
496-The Green Hornet; painted-c	23.00	68.00	250.00
497-Zorro (Sword of…)-Kinstler-a	12.00	37.00	135.00
498-Bugs Bunny's Album (9/53)	4.50	13.50	50.00
499-M.G.M.'s Spike and Tyke (#1) (9/53)	2.75	8.00	30.00
500-Buck Jones	4.50	13.50	50.00
501-Francis the Famous Talking Mule	3.60	11.00	40.00
502-Rootie Kazootie (TV)	6.40	19.00	70.00
503-Uncle Wiggily (10/53)	3.60	11.00	40.00
504-Krazy Kat; not by Herriman	3.00	9.00	35.00
505-The Sword and the Rose (Disney) (10/53)(Movie)-Photo-c	8.00	25.00	90.00
506-The Little Scouts	1.35	4.00	15.00
507-Oswald the Rabbit (Lantz)	3.00	9.00	32.00
508-Bozo (10/53)	8.00	25.00	90.00
509-Pluto (Disney) (10/53)	4.50	13.50	50.00
510-Son of Black Beauty	2.75	8.00	30.00
511-Outlaw Trail (Zane Grey)-Kinstler-a	3.60	11.00	40.00
512-Flash Gordon (11/53)	4.50	13.50	50.00
513-Ben Bowie and His Mountain Men	2.75	8.00	30.00
514-Frosty the Snowman (11/53)	3.60	11.00	40.00
515-Andy Hardy	2.25	6.75	25.00
516-Double Trouble With Goober	1.85	5.50	15.00
517-Chip 'N' Dale (#1) (Disney)	7.00	22.00	80.00

Four Color #529 © Steven Slesinger

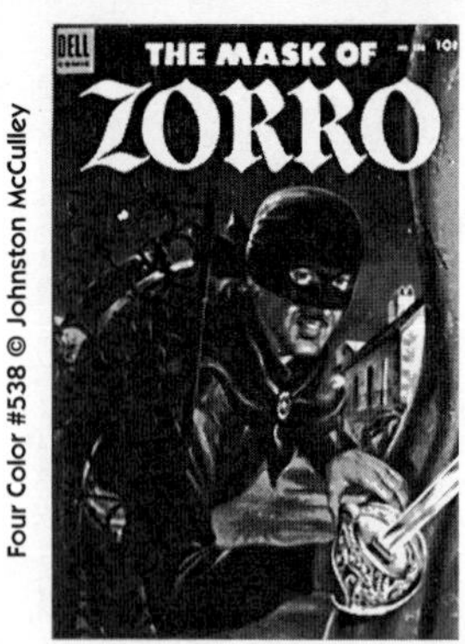

Four Color #538 © Johnston McCulley

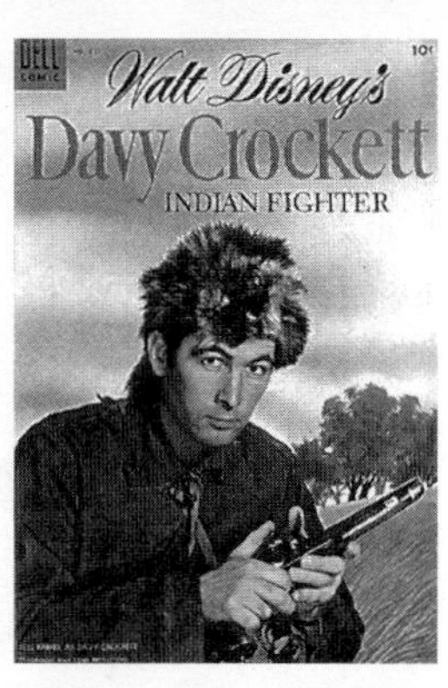

Four Color #631 © WDC

	GD25	FN65	NM94
518-Rivets (11/53)	2.25	6.75	25.00
519-Steve Canyon (#1)-Not by Milton Caniff	8.00	25.00	90.00
520-Wild Bill Elliott-Photo-c	3.60	11.00	40.00
521-Beetle Bailey (12/53)	4.50	13.50	50.00
522-The Brownies	3.00	9.00	32.00
523-Rin Tin Tin (TV)-Photo-c (12/53)	7.00	22.00	80.00
524-Tweety and Sylvester	3.50	10.50	38.00
525-Santa Claus Funnies	3.60	11.00	40.00
526-Napoleon	1.80	5.50	20.00
527-Charlie McCarthy	4.50	13.50	50.00
528-Queen of the West Dale Evans; photo-c	9.50	28.50	105.00
529-Little Beaver	2.75	8.00	30.00
530-Bob Clampett's Beany and Cecil (TV) (1/54)	16.00	51.00	170.00
531-Duck Album (Disney)	4.50	13.50	50.00
532-The Rustlers (Zane Grey) (2-4/54)	2.75	8.00	30.00
533-Raggedy Ann and Andy	4.50	13.50	50.00
534-Western Marshal(Ernest Haycox's)-Kinstler-a	4.50	13.50	50.00
535-I Love Lucy (#1) (TV) (2/54)-Photo-c	48.00	143.00	525.00
536-Daffy (3/54)	4.00	12.00	45.00
537-Stormy, the Thoroughbred... (Disney-Movie) on top 2/3 of each page; Pluto story on bottom 1/3 of each page (2/54)	2.75	8.00	30.00
538-The Mask of Zorro; Kinstler-a	12.00	37.00	135.00
539-Ben and Me (Disney) (3/54)	3.00	9.00	32.00
540-Knights of the Round Table (3/54) (Movie)-Photo-c	6.40	19.00	70.00
541-Johnny Mack Brown; photo-c	5.00	15.00	55.00
542-Super Circus Featuring Mary Hartline (TV) (3/54)	6.40	19.00	70.00
543-Uncle Wiggily (3/54)	3.60	11.00	40.00
544-Rob Roy (Disney-Movie)-Manning-a; photo-c	7.00	22.00	80.00
545-The Wonderful Adventures of Pinocchio-Partial reprint of 4-Color #92 (Disney-Movie)	6.40	19.00	70.00
546-Buck Jones	4.50	13.50	50.00
547-Francis the Famous Talking Mule	3.60	11.00	40.00
548-Krazy Kat; not by Herriman (4/54)	2.75	8.00	30.00
549-Oswald the Rabbit (Lantz)	3.00	9.00	32.00
550-The Little Scouts	1.35	4.00	15.00
551-Bozo (4/54)	8.00	25.00	90.00
552-Beetle Bailey	4.50	13.50	50.00
553-Susie Q. Smith	2.75	8.00	30.00
554-Rusty Riley (Frank Godwin strip-r)	2.75	8.00	30.00
555-Range War (Zane Grey)	2.75	8.00	30.00
556-Double Trouble With Goober (5/54)	1.85	5.50	15.00
557-Ben Bowie and His Mountain Men	2.75	8.00	30.00
558-Elmer Fudd (5/54)	3.20	9.50	35.00
559-I Love Lucy (#2) (TV)-Photo-c	30.00	89.00	325.00
560-Duck Album (Disney) (5/54)	4.50	13.50	50.00
561-Mr. Magoo (5/54)	11.00	33.00	120.00
562-Goofy (Disney)(#2)	6.40	19.00	70.00
563-Rhubarb, the Millionaire Cat (6/54)	3.60	11.00	40.00
564-Li'l Bad Wolf (Disney)(#3)	3.60	11.00	40.00
565-Jungle Jim	2.75	8.00	30.00
566-Son of Black Beauty	2.75	8.00	30.00
567-Prince Valiant (#1)-By Bob Fuje (Movie)-Photo-c	10.00	30.00	110.00
568-Gypsy Colt (Movie) (6/54)	3.60	11.00	40.00
569-Priscilla's Pop	2.75	8.00	30.00
570-Bob Clampett's Beany and Cecil (TV)	16.00	47.00	170.00
571-Charlie McCarthy	4.50	13.50	50.00
572-Silvertip (Max Brand) (7/54); Kinstler-a	3.60	11.00	40.00
573-The Little People by Walt Scott	3.00	9.00	35.00
574-The Hand of Zorro; Kinstler-a	12.00	38.00	135.00
575-Annie Oakley and Tagg (TV)-Photo-c	8.00	23.00	85.00
576-Angel (#1) (8/54)	2.25	6.75	25.00

	GD25	FN65	NM94
577-M.G.M.'s Spike and Tyke	1.80	5.50	20.00
578-Steve Canyon (8/54)	4.50	13.50	50.00
579-Francis the Famous Talking Mule	3.60	11.00	40.00
580-Six Gun Ranch (Luke Short-8/54)	2.75	8.00	30.00
581-Chip 'N' Dale (#2) (Disney)	4.50	13.50	50.00
582-Mowgli Jungle Book (Kipling) (8/54)	3.60	11.00	40.00
583-The Lost Wagon Train (Zane Grey)	2.75	8.00	30.00
584-Johnny Mack Brown-Photo-c	5.00	15.00	55.00
585-Bugs Bunny's Album	4.50	13.50	50.00
586-Duck Album (Disney)	4.50	13.50	50.00
587-The Little Scouts	1.35	4.00	15.00
588-King Richard and the Crusaders (Movie) (10/54) Matt Baker-a; photo-c	9.00	27.00	100.00
589-Buck Jones	4.50	13.50	50.00
590-Hansel and Gretel; partial photo-c	5.50	16.50	60.00
591-Western Marshal(Ernest Haycox's)-Kinstler-a	4.50	13.50	50.00
592-Super Circus (TV)	5.50	16.50	60.00
593-Oswald the Rabbit (Lantz)	3.00	9.00	32.00
594-Bozo (10/54)	8.00	25.00	90.00
595-Pluto (Disney)	2.75	8.00	30.00
596-Turok, Son of Stone (#1)	55.00	164.00	600.00
597-The Little King	4.50	13.50	50.00
598-Captain Davy Jones	3.60	11.00	40.00
599-Ben Bowie and His Mountain Men	2.75	8.00	30.00
600-Daisy Duck's Diary (#1) (Disney) (11/54)	6.00	18.00	65.00
601-Frosty the Snowman	3.60	11.00	40.00
602-Mr. Magoo and Gerald McBoing-Boing	11.00	33.00	120.00
603-M.G.M.'s The Two Mouseketeers	3.60	11.00	40.00
604-Shadow on the Trail (Zane Grey)	2.75	8.00	30.00
605-The Brownies-not by Kelly (12/54)	3.00	9.00	32.00
606-Sir Lancelot (not TV)	6.40	19.00	70.00
607-Santa Claus Funnies	3.60	11.00	40.00
608-Silvertip- "Valley of Vanishing Men" (Max Brand)-Kinstler-a	3.60	11.00	40.00
609-The Littlest Outlaw (Disney-Movie) (1/55)-Photo-c	5.50	16.50	60.00
610-Drum Beat (Movie); Alan Ladd photo-c	9.00	27.00	100.00
611-Duck Album (Disney)	4.50	13.50	50.00
612-Little Beaver (1/55)	2.75	8.00	30.00
613-Western Marshal (Ernest Haycox's) (2/55)-Kinstler-a	4.50	13.50	50.00
614-20,000 Leagues Under the Sea (Disney) (Movie) (2/55)-Painted-c	9.00	27.00	100.00
615-Daffy	4.00	12.00	45.00
616-To the Last Man (Zane Grey)	2.75	8.00	30.00
617-The Quest of Zorro	11.00	34.00	125.00
618-Johnny Mack Brown; photo-c	5.00	15.00	55.00
619-Krazy Kat; not by Herriman	2.75	8.00	30.00
620-Mowgli Jungle Book (Kipling)	3.60	11.00	40.00
621-Francis the Famous Talking Mule (4/55)	2.75	8.00	30.00
622-Beetle Bailey	4.50	13.50	50.00
623-Oswald the Rabbit (Lantz)	2.00	6.00	22.00
624-Treasure Island(Disney-Movie)(4/55)-Photo-c	9.00	27.00	90.00
625-Beaver Valley (Disney-Movie)	5.50	16.50	60.00
626-Ben Bowie and His Mountain Men	2.75	8.00	30.00
627-Goofy (Disney) (5/55)	6.40	19.00	70.00
628-Elmer Fudd	3.20	9.50	35.00
629-Lady and the Tramp with Jock (Disney)	6.00	18.00	65.00
630-Priscilla's Pop	2.75	8.00	30.00
631-Davy Crockett, Indian Fighter (#1) (Disney) (5/55) (TV)-Fess Parker photo-c	17.00	51.00	185.00
632-Fighting Caravans (Zane Grey)	2.75	8.00	30.00
633-The Little People by Walt Scott (6/55)	3.00	9.00	35.00
634-Lady and the Tramp Album (Disney) (6/55)	3.65	11.00	40.00

Four Color #673 © Tie-Ups Co.

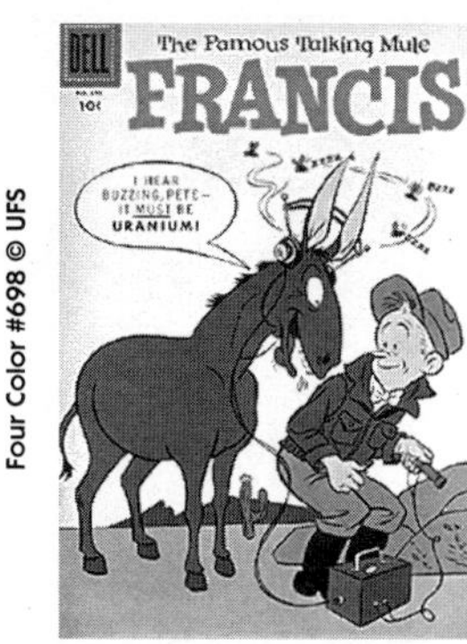

Four Color #698 © UFS

Four Color #720 © CBS

	GD25	FN65	NM94
635-Bob Clampett's Beany and Cecil (TV)	16.00	47.00	170.00
636-Chip 'N' Dale (Disney)	4.50	13.50	50.00
637-Silvertip (Max Brand)-Kinstler-a	3.60	11.00	40.00
638-M.G.M.'s Spike and Tyke (8/55)	1.80	5.50	20.00
639-Davy Crockett at the Alamo (Disney) (7/55) (TV)-Fess Parker photo-c	13.00	40.00	145.00
640-Western Marshal(Ernest Haycox's)-Kinstler-a	4.50	13.50	50.00
641-Steve Canyon (1955)-by Caniff	4.50	13.50	50.00
642-M.G.M.'s The Two Mouseketeers	3.60	11.00	40.00
643-Wild Bill Elliott; photo-c	2.75	8.00	30.00
644-Sir Walter Raleigh (5/55)-Based on movie "The Virgin Queen"; photo-c	5.50	16.50	60.00
645-Johnny Mack Brown; photo-c	5.00	15.00	55.00
646-Dotty Dripple and Taffy (#1)	2.75	8.00	30.00
647-Bugs Bunny's Album (9/55)	4.50	13.50	50.00
648-Jace Pearson of the Texas Rangers (TV)-Photo-c	4.50	13.50	50.00
649-Duck Album (Disney)	4.50	13.50	50.00
650-Prince Valiant; by Bob Fuje	5.50	16.50	60.00
651-King Colt (Luke Short) (9/55)-Kinstler-a	2.75	8.00	30.00
652-Buck Jones	2.75	8.00	30.00
653-Smokey the Bear (#1) (10/55)	9.00	27.00	100.00
654-Pluto (Disney)	2.75	8.00	30.00
655-Francis the Famous Talking Mule	2.75	8.00	30.00
656-Turok, Son of Stone (#2) (10/55)	32.00	96.00	350.00
657-Ben Bowie and His Mountain Men	2.75	8.00	30.00
658-Goofy (Disney)	6.40	19.00	70.00
659-Daisy Duck's Diary (Disney)(#2)	5.00	15.00	55.00
660-Little Beaver	2.75	8.00	30.00
661-Frosty the Snowman	3.60	11.00	40.00
662-Zoo Parade (TV)-Marlin Perkins (11/55)	4.00	12.00	45.00
663-Winky Dink (TV)	7.00	22.00	80.00
664-Davy Crockett in the Great Keelboat Race (TV) (Disney) (11/55)-Fess Parker photo-c	12.00	37.00	135.00
665-The African Lion (Disney-Movie) (11/55)	4.50	13.50	50.00
666-Santa Claus Funnies	3.60	11.00	40.00
667-Silvertip and the Stolen Stallion (Max Brand) (12/55)-Kinstler-a	3.60	11.00	40.00
668-Dumbo (Disney) (12/55)-First of two printings. Dumbo on cover with starry sky. Reprints 4-Color #234?; same-c as #234	7.00	22.00	80.00
668-Dumbo (Disney) (1/58)-Second printing. Same cover altered, with Timothy Mouse added. Same contents as above	5.50	16.50	60.00
669-Robin Hood (Disney-Movie) (12/55)-Reprints #413 plus-c; photo-c	4.50	13.50	50.00
670-M.G.M's Mouse Musketeers (#1) (1/56)-Formerly the Two Mouseketeers	2.75	8.00	30.00
671-Davy Crockett and the River Pirates (TV) (Disney) (12/55)-Jesse Marsh-a; Fess Parker photo-c	12.00	37.00	135.00
672-Quentin Durward (1/56) (Movie)-Photo-c	5.50	16.50	60.00
673-Buffalo Bill, Jr. (#1) (TV)-James Arness photo-c	5.75	17.00	63.00
674-The Little Rascals (#1) (TV)	6.40	19.00	70.00
675-Steve Donovan, Western Marshal (#1) (TV)-Kinstler-a; photo-c	7.00	22.00	80.00
676-Will-Yum!	1.80	5.50	20.00
677-Little King	4.50	13.50	50.00
678-The Last Hunt (Movie)-Photo-c	6.40	19.00	70.00
679-Gunsmoke (#1) (TV)-Photo-c	14.00	44.00	160.00
680-Out Our Way with the Worry Wart (2/56)	1.80	5.50	20.00
681-Forever Darling (Movie) with Lucille Ball & Desi Arnaz (2/56)-; photo-c	10.00	30.00	110.00
682-When Knighthood Was in Flower (Disney-Movie)-Reprint of #505; Renamed the Sword & the Rose for the novel; photo-c	6.40	19.00	70.00
683-Hi and Lois (3/56)	2.25	6.75	25.00
684-Helen of Troy (Movie)-Buscema-a; photo-c	10.00	30.00	110.00

	GD25	FN65	NM94
685-Johnny Mack Brown; photo-c	5.00	15.00	55.00
686-Duck Album (Disney)	4.50	13.50	50.00
687-The Indian Fighter (Movie)-Kirk Douglas photo-c	7.00	22.00	80.00
688-Alexander the Great (Movie) (5/56)-Buscema-a; photo-c	6.00	19.00	68.00
689-Elmer Fudd (3/56)	3.20	9.50	35.00
690-The Conqueror (Movie) - John Wayne photo-c	14.00	44.00	160.00
691-Dotty Dripple and Taffy	1.80	5.50	20.00
692-The Little People-Walt Scott	3.00	9.00	35.00
693-Song of the South (Disney) (1956)-Partial reprint of #129	8.00	25.00	90.00
694-Super Circus (TV)-Photo-c	5.50	16.50	60.00
695-Little Beaver	2.75	8.00	30.00
696-Krazy Kat; not by Herriman (4/56)	2.75	8.00	30.00
697-Oswald the Rabbit (Lantz)	2.00	6.00	22.00
698-Francis the Famous Talking Mule (4/56)	2.75	8.00	30.00
699-Prince Valiant-by Bob Fuje	5.50	16.50	60.00
700-Water Birds and the Olympic Elk (Disney-Movie) (4/56)	4.50	13.50	50.00
701-Jiminy Cricket (#1) (Disney) (5/56)	8.00	25.00	90.00
702-The Goofy Success Story (Disney)	6.40	19.00	70.00
703-Scamp (#1) (Disney)	8.00	25.00	90.00
704-Priscilla's Pop (5/56)	2.75	8.00	30.00
705-Brave Eagle (#1) (TV)-Photo-c	5.50	16.50	60.00
706-Bongo and Lumpjaw (Disney) (6/56)	4.50	13.50	50.00
707-Corky and White Shadow (Disney) (5/56)-Mickey Mouse Club (TV); photo-c	6.40	19.00	70.00
708-Smokey the Bear	4.50	13.50	50.00
709-The Searchers (Movie) - John Wayne photo-c	24.00	71.00	260.00
710-Francis the Famous Talking Mule	2.75	8.00	30.00
711-M.G.M's Mouse Musketeers	1.80	5.50	20.00
712-The Great Locomotive Chase (Disney-Movie) (9/56)-Photo-c	6.40	19.00	70.00
713-The Animal World (Movie) (8/56)	2.75	8.00	30.00
714-Spin and Marty (#1) (TV) (Disney)-Mickey Mouse Club (6/56); photo-c	11.00	33.00	120.00
715-Timmy (8/56)	2.75	8.00	30.00
716-Man in Space (Disney)(A science feature from Tomorrowland)	8.00	25.00	90.00
717-Moby Dick (Movie)-Gregory Peck photo-c	8.00	25.00	90.00
718-Dotty Dripple and Taffy	1.80	5.50	20.00
719-Prince Valiant; by Bob Fuje (8/56)	5.50	16.50	60.00
720-Gunsmoke (TV)-James Arness photo-c	7.00	20.00	75.00
721-Captain Kangaroo (TV)-Photo-c	13.00	40.00	145.00
722-Johnny Mack Brown-Photo-c	5.00	15.00	55.00
723-Santiago (Movie)-Kinstler-a (9/56); Alan Ladd photo-c	10.00	30.00	110.00
724-Bugs Bunny's Album	3.60	11.00	40.00
725-Elmer Fudd (9/56)	2.20	6.50	24.00
726-Duck Album (Disney) (9/56)	4.50	13.50	50.00
727-The Nature of Things (TV) (Disney)-Jesse Marsh-a	4.50	13.50	50.00
728-M.G.M's Mouse Musketeers	1.80	5.50	20.00
729-Bob Son of Battle (11/56)	2.75	8.00	30.00
730-Smokey Stover	3.50	11.00	38.00
731-Silvertip and The Fighting Four (Max Brand)-Kinstler-a	3.60	11.00	40.00
732-Zorro, the Challenge of (10/56)	11.00	34.00	125.00
733-Buck Jones	2.75	8.00	30.00
734-Cheyenne (#1) (TV) (10/56)-Clint Walker photo-c	16.00	47.00	170.00
735-Crusader Rabbit (#1) (TV)	31.00	93.00	340.00
736-Pluto (Disney)	2.75	8.00	30.00
737-Steve Canyon-Caniff-a	4.50	13.50	50.00

Four Color #762 © United Artists

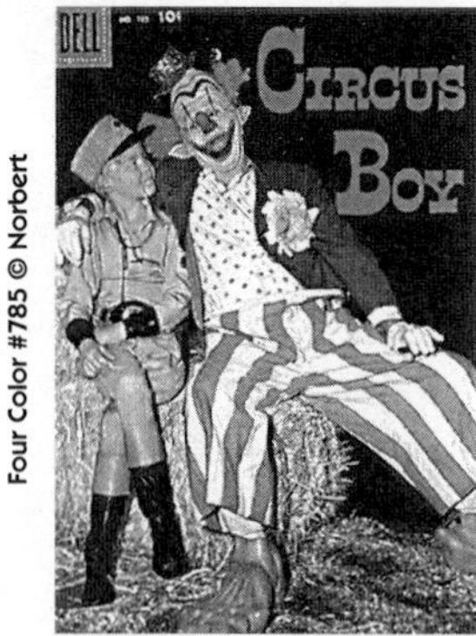

Four Color #785 © Norbert

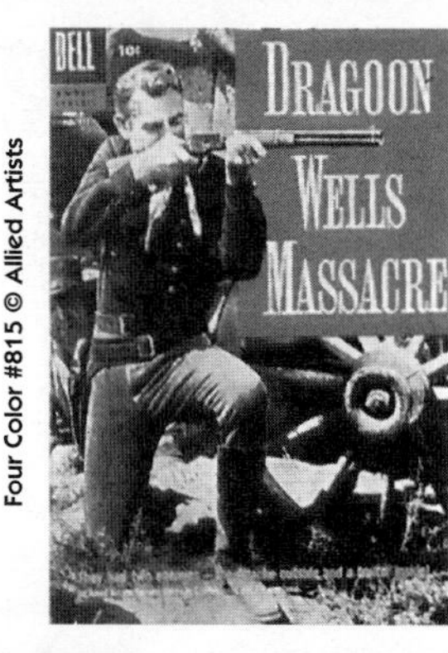

Four Color #815 © Allied Artists

	GD25	FN65	NM94
738-Westward Ho, the Wagons (Disney-Movie)-Fess Parker photo-c	7.00	22.00	80.00
739-Bounty Guns (Luke Short)-Drucker-a	2.75	8.00	30.00
740-Chilly Willy (#1) (Walter Lantz)	3.60	11.00	40.00
741-The Fastest Gun Alive (Movie)(9/56)-Photo-c	6.40	19.00	70.00
742-Buffalo Bill, Jr. (TV)-Photo-c	4.00	12.00	45.00
743-Daisy Duck's Diary (Disney) (11/56)	5.00	15.00	55.00
744-Little Beaver	2.75	8.00	30.00
745-Francis the Famous Talking Mule	2.75	8.00	30.00
746-Dotty Dripple and Taffy	1.80	5.50	20.00
747-Goofy (Disney)	6.40	19.00	70.00
748-Frosty the Snowman (11/56)	3.00	9.00	35.00
749-Secrets of Life (Disney-Movie)-Photo-c	3.60	11.00	40.00
750-The Great Cat Family (Disney-TV/Movie)-Pinocchio & Alice app.	5.50	16.50	60.00
751-Our Miss Brooks (TV)-Photo-c	7.00	22.00	80.00
752-Mandrake, the Magician	9.00	27.00	100.00
753-Walt Scott's Little People (11/56)	3.00	9.00	35.00
754-Smokey the Bear	4.50	13.50	50.00
755-The Littlest Snowman (12/56)	3.00	10.00	36.00
756-Santa Claus Funnies	3.60	11.00	40.00
757-The True Story of Jesse James (Movie)-Photo-c	9.00	27.00	100.00
758-Bear Country (Disney-Movie)	4.50	13.50	50.00
759-Circus Boy (TV)-The Monkees' Mickey Dolenz photo-c (12/56)	10.00	32.00	115.00
760-The Hardy Boys (#1) (TV) (Disney)-Mickey Mouse Club; photo-c	10.00	30.00	110.00
761-Howdy Doody (TV) (1/57)	9.00	27.00	100.00
762-The Sharkfighters (Movie) (1/57); Buscema-a; photo-c	7.00	22.00	80.00
763-Grandma Duck's Farm Friends (#1) (Disney)	6.40	19.00	70.00
764-M.G.M's Mouse Musketeers	1.80	5.50	20.00
765-Will-Yum!	1.80	5.50	20.00
766-Buffalo Bill, Jr. (TV)-Photo-c	4.00	12.00	45.00
767-Spin and Marty (TV) (Disney)-Mickey Mouse Club (2/57)	9.00	27.00	100.00
768-Steve Donovan, Western Marshal (TV)-Kinstler-a; photo-c	5.50	16.50	60.00
769-Gunsmoke (TV)-James Arness photo-c	7.00	20.00	75.00
770-Brave Eagle (TV)-Photo-c	2.75	8.00	30.00
771-Brand of Empire (Luke Short)(3/57)-Drucker-a	2.75	8.00	30.00
772-Cheyenne (TV)-Clint Walker photo-c	7.00	20.00	75.00
773-The Brave One (Movie)-Photo-c	4.50	13.50	50.00
774-Hi and Lois (3/57)	1.80	5.50	20.00
775-Sir Lancelot and Brian (TV)-Buscema-a; photo-c	7.00	22.00	80.00
776-Johnny Mack Brown; photo-c	5.00	15.00	55.00
777-Scamp (Disney) (3/57)	5.50	16.50	60.00
778-The Little Rascals (TV)	3.80	11.50	42.00
779-Lee Hunter, Indian Fighter (3/57)	3.60	11.00	40.00
780-Captain Kangaroo (TV)-Photo-c	11.00	34.00	125.00
781-Fury (#1) (TV) (3/57)-Photo-c	7.00	22.00	80.00
782-Duck Album (Disney)	4.50	13.50	50.00
783-Elmer Fudd	2.20	6.50	24.00
784-Around the World in 80 Days (Movie) (2/57)-Photo-c	5.75	17.00	63.00
785-Circus Boy (TV) (4/57)-The Monkees' Mickey Dolenz photo-c	10.00	30.00	110.00
786-Cinderella (Disney) (3/57)-Partial-r of #272	5.50	16.50	60.00
787-Little Hiawatha (Disney) (4/57)(#2)	3.60	11.00	40.00
788-Prince Valiant; by Bob Fuje	5.50	16.50	60.00
789-Silvertip-Valley Thieves (Max Brand) (4/57)-Kinstler-a	3.60	11.00	40.00

	GD25	FN65	NM94
790-The Wings of Eagles (Movie) (John Wayne)-Toth-a; John Wayne photo-c; 10 & 15¢ editions exist	14.00	44.00	160.00
791-The 77th Bengal Lancers (TV)-Photo-c	6.40	19.00	70.00
792-Oswald the Rabbit (Lantz)	2.00	6.00	22.00
793-Morty Meekle	1.80	5.50	20.00
794-The Count of Monte Cristo (5/57) (Movie)-Buscema-a	8.00	25.00	90.00
795-Jiminy Cricket (Disney)(#2)	5.50	16.50	60.00
796-Ludwig Bemelman's Madeleine and Genevieve	2.75	8.00	30.00
797-Gunsmoke (TV)-Photo-c	7.00	20.00	75.00
798-Buffalo Bill, Jr. (TV)-Photo-c	4.00	12.00	45.00
799-Priscilla's Pop	2.75	8.00	30.00
800-The Buccaneers (TV)-Photo-c	6.40	19.00	70.00
801-Dotty Dripple and Taffy	1.80	5.50	20.00
802-Goofy (Disney) (5/57)	6.40	19.00	70.00
803-Cheyenne (TV)-Clint Walker photo-c	7.00	20.00	75.00
804-Steve Canyon-Caniff-a (1957)	4.50	13.50	50.00
805-Crusader Rabbit (TV)	24.00	72.00	260.00
806-Scamp (Disney) (6/57)	5.50	16.50	60.00
807-Savage Range (Luke Short)-Drucker-a	2.75	8.00	30.00
808-Spin and Marty (TV)(Disney)-Mickey Mouse Club; photo-c	9.00	27.00	100.00
809-The Little People (Walt Scott)	3.00	9.00	35.00
810-Francis the Famous Talking Mule	2.25	6.75	25.00
811-Howdy Doody (TV) (7/57)	9.00	27.00	100.00
812-The Big Land (Movie); Alan Ladd photo-c	9.00	27.00	100.00
813-Circus Boy (TV)-The Monkees' Mickey Dolenz photo-c	10.00	30.00	110.00
814-Covered Wagons, Ho! (Disney)-Donald Duck (TV) (6/57); Mickey Mouse app.	4.50	13.50	50.00
815-Dragoon Wells Massacre (Movie)-photo-c	7.00	22.00	80.00
816-Brave Eagle (TV)-photo-c	2.75	8.00	30.00
817-Little Beaver	2.75	8.00	30.00
818-Smokey the Bear (6/57)	4.50	13.50	50.00
819-Mickey Mouse in Magicland (Disney) (7/57)	3.00	9.00	35.00
820-The Oklahoman (Movie)-Photo-c	9.00	27.00	100.00
821-Wringle Wrangle (Disney)-Based on movie "Westward Ho, the Wagons"; Marsh-a; Fess Parker photo-c	7.00	22.00	80.00
822-Paul Revere's Ride with Johnny Tremain (TV) (Disney)-Toth-a	9.00	27.00	100.00
823-Timmy	1.80	5.50	20.00
824-The Pride and the Passion (Movie) (8/57)-Frank Sinatra & Cary Grant photo-c	8.00	25.00	90.00
825-The Little Rascals (TV)	3.80	11.50	42.00
826-Spin and Marty and Annette (TV) (Disney)-Mickey Mouse Club; Annette Funicello photo-c	23.00	68.00	250.00
827-Smokey Stover (8/57)	3.50	11.00	38.00
828-Buffalo Bill, Jr. (TV)-Photo-c	4.00	12.00	45.00
829-Tales of the Pony Express (TV) (8/57)-Painted-c	3.60	11.00	40.00
830-The Hardy Boys (TV) (Disney)-Mickey Mouse Club (8/57); photo-c	9.00	27.00	100.00
831-No Sleep 'Til Dawn (Movie)-Karl Malden photo-c	5.50	16.50	60.00
832-Lolly and Pepper (#1)	2.75	8.00	30.00
833-Scamp (Disney) (9/57)	5.50	16.50	60.00
834-Johnny Mack Brown; photo-c	5.00	15.00	55.00
835-Silvertip-The False Rider (Max Brand)	3.60	11.00	40.00
836-Man in Flight (Disney) (TV) (9/57)	6.40	19.00	70.00
837-All-American Athlete Cotton Woods	2.75	8.00	30.00
838-Bugs Bunny's Life Story Album (9/57)	3.60	11.00	40.00
839-The Vigilantes (Movie)	6.40	19.00	70.00
840-Duck Album (Disney) (9/57)	4.50	13.50	50.00
841-Elmer Fudd	2.20	6.50	24.00
842-The Nature of Things (Disney-Movie) ('57)-Jesse Marsh-a (TV series)	4.50	13.50	50.00

Four Color #846 © Loew's Inc

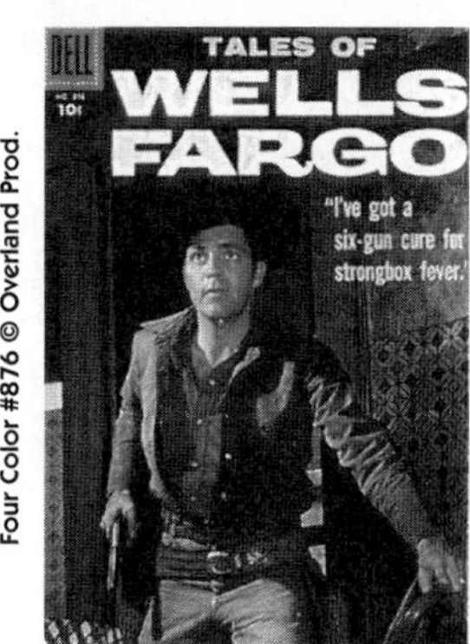

Four Color #876 © Overland Prod.

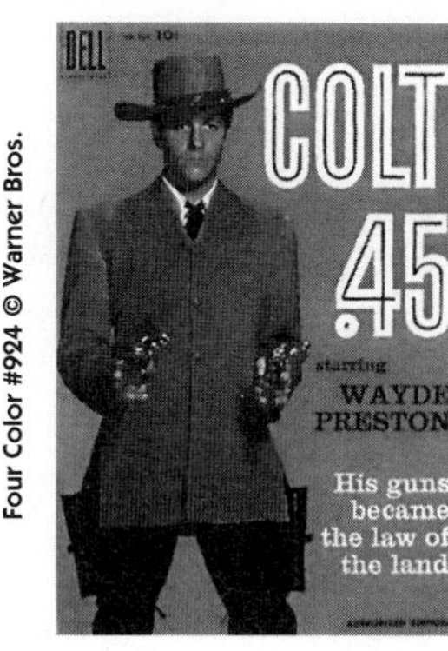

Four Color #924 © Warner Bros.

	GD25	FN65	NM94
843-The First Americans (Disney) (TV)-Marsh-a	8.00	25.00	90.00
844-Gunsmoke (TV)-Photo-c	7.00	21.00	75.00
845-The Land Unknown (Movie)-Alex Toth-a	11.00	34.00	125.00
846-Gun Glory (Movie)-by Alex Toth; photo-c	9.00	27.00	100.00
847-Perri (squirrels) (Disney-Movie)-Two different covers published	4.50	13.50	50.00
848-Marauder's Moon (Luke Short)	3.60	11.00	40.00
849-Prince Valiant; by Bob Fuje	5.50	16.50	60.00
850-Buck Jones	2.75	8.00	30.00
851-The Story of Mankind (Movie) (1/58)-Hedy Lamarr & Vincent Price photo-c	6.40	19.00	70.00
852-Chilly Willy (2/58) (Lantz)	2.75	8.00	30.00
853-Pluto (Disney) (10/57)	2.75	8.00	30.00
854-The Hunchback of Notre Dame (Movie)-Photo-c	12.00	35.00	130.00
855-Broken Arrow (TV)-Photo-c	5.00	15.00	54.00
856-Buffalo Bill, Jr. (TV)-Photo-c	4.00	12.00	45.00
857-The Goofy Adventure Story (Disney) (11/57)	6.40	19.00	70.00
858-Daisy Duck's Diary (Disney) (11/57)	4.00	12.00	45.00
859-Topper and Neil (TV) (11/57)	3.60	11.00	40.00
860-Wyatt Earp (#1) (TV)-Manning-a; photo-c	10.00	30.00	110.00
861-Frosty the Snowman	3.00	9.00	35.00
862-The Truth About Mother Goose (Disney-Movie) (11/57)	6.40	19.00	70.00
863-Francis the Famous Talking Mule	2.25	6.75	25.00
864-The Littlest Snowman	3.00	10.00	36.00
865-Andy Burnett (TV) (Disney) (12/57)-Photo-c	9.00	27.00	100.00
866-Mars and Beyond (Disney-TV)(A science feature from Tomorrowland)	8.00	25.00	90.00
867-Santa Claus Funnies	3.60	11.00	40.00
868-The Little People (12/57)	3.00	9.00	35.00
869-Old Yeller (Disney-Movie)-Photo-c	4.50	13.50	50.00
870-Little Beaver (1/58)	2.75	8.00	30.00
871-Curly Kayoe	1.80	5.50	20.00
872-Captain Kangaroo (TV)-Photo-c	11.00	34.00	125.00
873-Grandma Duck's Farm Friends (Disney)	4.50	13.50	50.00
874-Old Ironsides (Disney-Movie with Johnny Tremain) (1/58)	5.50	16.50	60.00
875-Trumpets West (Luke Short) (2/58)	2.75	8.00	30.00
876-Tales of Wells Fargo (#1)(TV)(2/58)-Photo-c	9.00	27.00	100.00
877-Frontier Doctor with Rex Allen (TV)-Alex Toth-a; Rex Allen photo-c	9.00	27.00	100.00
878-Peanuts (#1)-Schulz-c only (2/58)	14.00	41.00	150.00
879-Brave Eagle (TV) (2/58)-Photo-c	2.75	8.00	30.00
880-Steve Donovan, Western Marshal-Drucker-a (TV)-Photo-c	3.60	11.00	40.00
881-The Captain and the Kids (2/58)	2.75	8.00	30.00
882-Zorro (Disney)-1st Disney issue; by Alex Toth (TV) (2/58); photo-c	16.00	49.00	180.00
883-The Little Rascals (TV)	3.80	11.50	42.00
884-Hawkeye and the Last of the Mohicans (TV) (3/58); photo-c	6.40	19.00	70.00
885-Fury (TV) (3/58)-Photo-c	5.50	16.50	60.00
886-Bongo and Lumpjaw (Disney) (3/58)	3.80	11.50	40.00
887-The Hardy Boys (Disney) (TV)-Mickey Mouse Club (1/58)-Photo-c	9.00	27.00	100.00
888-Elmer Fudd (3/58)	2.20	6.50	24.00
889-Clint and Mac (Disney) (TV) (3/58)-Alex Toth-a; photo-c	12.00	37.00	135.00
890-Wyatt Earp (TV)-by Russ Manning; photo-c	7.00	20.00	75.00
891-Light in the Forest (Disney-Movie) (3/58)-Fess Parker photo-c	7.30	22.00	80.00
892-Maverick (#1) (TV) (4/58)-James Garner photo-c	25.00	75.00	275.00
893-Jim Bowie (TV)-Photo-c	4.50	13.50	50.00

	GD25	FN65	NM94
894-Oswald the Rabbit (Lantz)	2.00	6.00	22.00
895-Wagon Train (#1) (TV) (3/58)-Photo-c	11.00	33.00	120.00
896-The Adventures of Tinker Bell (Disney)	8.00	24.00	85.00
897-Jiminy Cricket (Disney)	5.50	16.50	60.00
898-Silvertip (Max Brand)-Kinstler-a (5/58)	3.60	11.00	40.00
899-Goofy (Disney) (5/58)	3.60	11.00	40.00
900-Prince Valiant; by Bob Fuje	5.50	16.50	60.00
901-Little Hiawatha (Disney)	3.60	11.00	40.00
902-Will-Yum!	1.80	5.50	20.00
903-Dotty Dripple and Taffy	1.80	5.50	20.00
904-Lee Hunter, Indian Fighter	2.75	8.00	30.00
905-Annette (Disney) (TV) (5/58)-Mickey Mouse Club; Annette Funicello photo-c	26.00	78.00	285.00
906-Francis the Famous Talking Mule	2.25	6.75	25.00
907-Sugarfoot (#1) (TV)Toth-a; photo-c	12.00	37.00	135.00
908-The Little People and the Giant-Walt Scott (5/58)	3.00	9.00	35.00
909-Smitty	1.80	5.50	20.00
910-The Vikings (Movie)-Buscema-a; Kirk Douglas photo-c	8.00	25.00	90.00
911-The Gray Ghost (TV)-Photo-c	8.00	25.00	90.00
912-Leave It to Beaver (#1) (TV)-Photo-c	17.00	52.00	190.00
913-The Left-Handed Gun (Movie) (7/58); Paul Newman photo-c	10.00	30.00	110.00
914-No Time for Sergeants (Movie)-Andy Griffith photo-c; Toth-a	9.00	27.00	100.00
915-Casey Jones (TV)-Alan Hale photo-c	4.50	13.50	50.00
916-Red Ryder Ranch Comics (7/58)	2.75	8.00	30.00
917-The Life of Riley (TV)-Photo-c	11.00	33.00	120.00
918-Beep Beep, the Roadrunner (#1) (7/58)-Published with two different back covers	9.00	27.00	95.00
919-Boots and Saddles (#1) (TV)-Photo-c	7.00	22.00	80.00
920-Zorro (Disney) (TV) (6/58)Toth-a; photo-c	11.00	34.00	125.00
921-Wyatt Earp (TV)-Manning-a; photo-c	7.00	20.00	75.00
922-Johnny Mack Brown by Russ Manning; photo-c	6.00	18.00	65.00
923-Timmy	1.80	5.50	20.00
924-Colt .45 (#1) (TV) (8/58)-W. Preston photo-c	9.00	27.00	100.00
925-Last of the Fast Guns (Movie) (8/58)-Photo-c	6.40	19.00	70.00
926-Peter Pan (Disney)-Reprint of #442	3.60	11.00	40.00
927-Top Gun (Luke Short) Buscema-a	2.75	8.00	30.00
928-Sea Hunt (#1) (9/58) (TV)-Lloyd Bridges photo-c	11.00	33.00	120.00
929-Brave Eagle (TV)-Photo-c	2.75	8.00	30.00
930-Maverick (TV) (7/58)-James Garner photo-c	10.00	30.00	110.00
931-Have Gun, Will Travel (#1) (TV)-Photo-c	14.00	41.00	150.00
932-Smokey the Bear (His Life Story)	4.50	13.50	50.00
933-Zorro (Disney, 9/58) (TV)-Alex Toth-a; photo-c	11.00	34.00	125.00
934-Restless Gun (#1) (TV)-Photo-c	11.00	32.00	120.00
935-King of the Royal Mounted	2.75	8.00	30.00
936-The Little Rascals (TV)	3.80	11.50	42.00
937-Ruff and Reddy (#1) (9/58) (TV) (1st Hanna-Barbera comic book)	12.00	36.00	130.00
938-Elmer Fudd (9/58)	2.20	6.50	24.00
939-Steve Canyon - not by Caniff	4.50	13.50	50.00
940-Lolly and Pepper (10/58)	1.80	5.50	20.00
941-Pluto (Disney) (10/58)	2.75	8.00	30.00
942-Pony Express (TV)	3.60	11.00	40.00
943-White Wilderness (Disney-Movie) (10/58)	5.50	16.50	60.00
944-The 7th Voyage of Sinbad (Movie) (9/58)-Buscema-a; photo-c	12.00	35.00	130.00
945-Maverick (TV)-James Garner/Jack Kelly photo-c	10.00	30.00	110.00
946-The Big Country (Movie)-Photo-c	6.40	19.00	70.00
947-Broken Arrow (TV)-Photo-c (11/58)	4.00	12.00	45.00

Four Color #970 © Warner Bros.

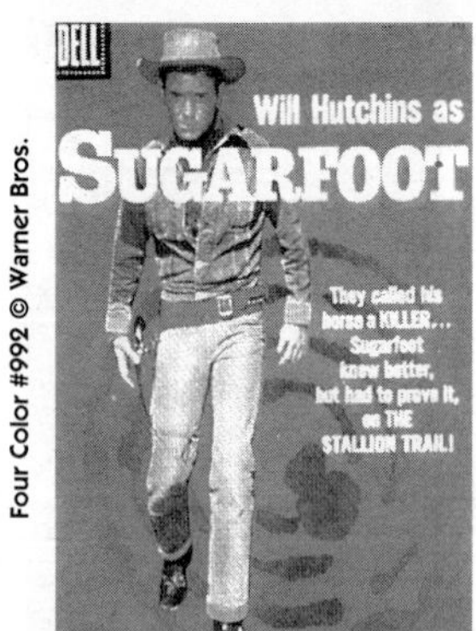

Four Color #992 © Warner Bros.

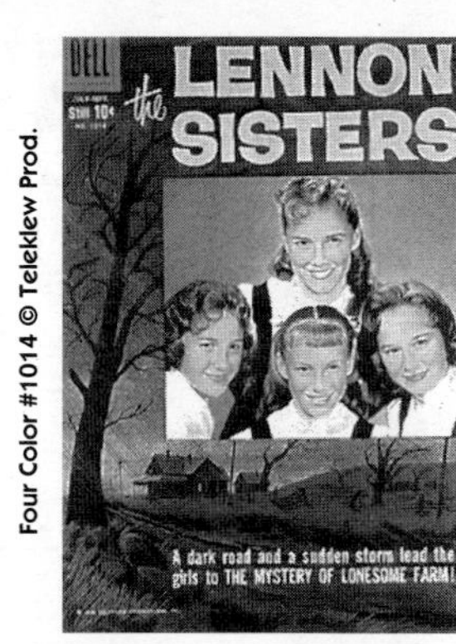

Four Color #1014 © Teleklew Prod.

	GD25	FN65	NM94
948-Daisy Duck's Diary (Disney) (11/58)	4.00	12.00	45.00
949-High Adventure(Lowell Thomas')(TV)-Photo-c	5.50	13.50	50.00
950-Frosty the Snowman	3.00	9.00	35.00
951-The Lennon Sisters Life Story (TV)-Toth-a, 32 pgs.; photo-c	13.00	40.00	145.00
952-Goofy (Disney) (11/58)	3.60	11.00	40.00
953-Francis the Famous Talking Mule	2.25	6.75	25.00
954-Man in Space-Satellites (TV)	6.40	19.00	70.00
955-Hi and Lois (11/58)	1.80	5.50	20.00
956-Ricky Nelson (#1) (TV)-Photo-c	18.00	55.00	200.00
957-Buffalo Bee (#1) (TV)	9.00	27.00	100.00
958-Santa Claus Funnies	3.00	9.00	35.00
959-Christmas Stories-(Walt Scott's Little People) (1951-56 strip reprints)	3.00	9.00	35.00
960-Zorro (Disney) (TV) (12/58)-Toth art; photo-c	11.00	34.00	125.00
961-Jace Pearson's Tales of the Texas Rangers (TV)-Spiegle-a; photo-c	4.00	12.00	45.00
962-Maverick (TV) (1/59)-James Garner/Jack Kelly photo-c	10.00	30.00	110.00
963-Johnny Mack Brown; photo-c	5.00	15.00	55.00
964-The Hardy Boys (TV) (Disney) (1/59)-Mickey Mouse Club; photo-c	9.00	27.00	100.00
965-Grandma Duck's Farm Friends (Disney)(1/59)	3.60	11.00	40.00
966-Tonka (starring Sal Mineo; Disney-Movie)-Photo-c	7.00	22.00	80.00
967-Chilly Willy (2/59) (Lantz)	2.75	8.00	30.00
968-Tales of Wells Fargo (TV)-Photo-c	8.00	25.00	90.00
969-Peanuts (2/59)	10.00	30.00	110.00
970-Lawman (#1) (TV)-Photo-c	12.00	36.00	130.00
971-Wagon Train (TV)-Photo-c	6.00	18.00	65.00
972-Tom Thumb (Movie)-George Pal (1/59)	9.00	27.00	100.00
973-Sleeping Beauty and the Prince(Disney)(5/59)	11.00	33.00	120.00
974-The Little Rascals (TV) (3/59)	3.80	11.50	42.00
975-Fury (TV)-Photo-c	5.50	16.50	60.00
976-Zorro (Disney) (TV)-Toth-a; photo-c	11.00	34.00	125.00
977-Elmer Fudd (3/59)	2.20	6.50	24.00
978-Lolly and Pepper	1.80	5.50	20.00
979-Oswald the Rabbit (Lantz)	2.00	6.00	22.00
980-Maverick (TV) (4-6/59)-James Garner/Jack Kelly photo-c	10.00	30.00	110.00
981-Ruff and Reddy (TV) (Hanna-Barbera)	8.00	24.00	85.00
982-The New Adventures of Tinker Bell (TV) (Disney)	7.00	22.00	80.00
983-Have Gun, Will Travel (TV) (4-6/59)-Photo-c	9.00	27.00	95.00
984-Sleeping Beauty's Fairy Godmothers (Disney)	8.00	25.00	90.00
985-Shaggy Dog (Disney-Movie)-Photo-all four covers; Annette on back-c(5/59)	6.40	19.00	70.00
986-Restless Gun (TV)-Photo-c	8.00	24.00	85.00
987-Goofy (Disney) (7/59)	3.60	11.00	40.00
988-Little Hiawatha (Disney)	3.60	11.00	40.00
989-Jiminy Cricket (Disney) (5-7/59)	5.50	16.50	60.00
990-Huckleberry Hound (#1)(TV)(Hanna-Barbera); 1st app. Huck, Yogi Bear, & Pixie & Dixie & Mr. Jinx	11.00	33.00	120.00
991-Francis the Famous Talking Mule	2.25	6.75	25.00
992-Sugarfoot (TV)-Toth-a; photo-c	11.00	34.00	125.00
993-Jim Bowie (TV)-Photo-c	4.50	13.50	50.00
994-Sea Hunt (TV)-Lloyd Bridges photo-c	8.00	25.00	85.00
995-Donald Duck Album (Disney) (5-7/59)(#1)	5.00	15.00	55.00
996-Nevada (Zane Grey)	2.75	8.00	30.00
997-Walt Disney Presents-Tales of Texas John Slaughter (#1) (TV) (Disney)-Photo-c; photo of W. Disney inside-c	6.40	19.00	70.00
998-Ricky Nelson (TV)-Photo-c	18.00	55.00	200.00
999-Leave It to Beaver (TV)-Photo-c	14.00	44.00	160.00
1000-The Gray Ghost (TV) (6-8/59)-Photo-c	8.00	25.00	90.00

	GD25	FN65	NM94
1001-Lowell Thomas' High Adventure (TV) (8-10/59)-Photo-c	4.50	13.50	50.00
1002-Buffalo Bee (TV)	6.00	18.00	65.00
1003-Zorro (TV) (Disney)-Toth-a; photo-c	11.00	34.00	125.00
1004-Colt .45 (TV) (6-8/59)-Photo-c	7.00	20.00	75.00
1005-Maverick (TV)-James Garner/Jack Kelly photo-c	10.00	30.00	110.00
1006-Hercules (Movie)-Buscema-a; photo-c	9.00	27.00	100.00
1007-John Paul Jones (Movie)-Robert Stack photo-c	5.00	15.00	50.00
1008-Beep Beep, the Road Runner (7-9/59)	4.40	13.00	48.00
1009-The Rifleman (#1) (TV)-Photo-c	22.00	65.00	240.00
1010-Grandma Duck's Farm Friends (Disney)-by Carl Barks	12.00	37.00	135.00
1011-Buckskin (#1) (TV)-Photo-c	6.40	19.00	70.00
1012-Last Train from Gun Hill (Movie) (7/59)-Photo-c	8.00	24.00	90.00
1013-Bat Masterson (#1) (TV) (8/59)-Gene Barry photo-c	11.00	34.00	125.00
1014-The Lennon Sisters (TV)-Toth-a; photo-c	13.00	40.00	145.00
1015-Peanuts-Schulz-c	10.00	30.00	110.00
1016-Smokey the Bear Nature Stories	2.75	8.00	30.00
1017-Chilly Willy (Lantz)	2.75	8.00	30.00
1018-Rio Bravo (Movie)(6/59)-John Wayne; Toth-a; John Wayne, Dean Martin & Ricky Nelson photo-c	18.00	55.00	200.00
1019-Wagon Train (TV)-Photo-c	6.00	18.00	65.00
1020-Jungle Jim-McWilliams-a	2.25	6.75	25.00
1021-Jace Pearson's Tales of the Texas Rangers (TV)-Photo-c	4.00	12.00	45.00
1022-Timmy	1.80	5.50	20.00
1023-Tales of Wells Fargo (TV)-Photo-c	8.00	25.00	90.00
1024-Darby O'Gill and the Little People (Disney-Movie)-Toth-a; photo-c	9.00	27.00	100.00
1025-Vacation in Disneyland (8-10/59)-Carl Barks-a(24pgs.) (Disney)	18.00	55.00	200.00
1026-Spin and Marty (TV) (Disney) (9-11/59)-Mickey Mouse Club; photo-c	7.00	22.00	80.00
1027-The Texan (#1)(TV)-Photo-c	8.00	25.00	90.00
1028-Rawhide (#1) (TV) (9-11/59)-Clint Eastwood photo-c; Tufts-a	22.00	65.00	240.00
1029-Boots and Saddles (TV) (9/59)-Photo-c	4.50	13.50	50.00
1030-Spanky and Alfalfa, the Little Rascals (TV)	3.80	11.50	42.00
1031-Fury (TV)-Photo-c	5.50	16.50	60.00
1032-Elmer Fudd	2.20	6.50	24.00
1033-Steve Canyon-not by Caniff; photo-c	4.50	13.50	50.00
1034-Nancy and Sluggo Summer Camp (9-11/59)	3.25	10.00	36.00
1035-Lawman (TV)-Photo-c	6.40	19.00	70.00
1036-The Big Circus (Movie)-Photo-c	5.50	16.50	60.00
1037-Zorro (Disney) (TV)-Tufts-a; Annette Funicello photo-c	14.00	44.00	160.00
1038-Ruff and Reddy (TV)(Hanna-Barbera)(1959)	8.00	24.00	85.00
1039-Pluto (Disney) (11-1/60)	2.75	8.00	30.00
1040-Quick Draw McGraw (#1) (TV) (Hanna-Barbera) (12-2/60)	13.00	39.00	140.00
1041-Sea Hunt (TV) (10-12/59)-Toth-a; Lloyd Bridges photo-c	8.00	25.00	90.00
1042-The Three Chipmunks (Alvin, Simon & Theodore) (#1) (TV) (10-12/59)	5.00	15.00	55.00
1043-The Three Stooges (#1)-Photo-c	18.00	55.00	200.00
1044-Have Gun, Will Travel (TV)-Photo-c	9.00	27.00	95.00
1045-Restless Gun (TV)-Photo-c	8.00	24.00	85.00
1046-Beep Beep, the Road Runner (11-1/60)	4.40	13.00	48.00
1047-Gyro Gearloose (#1) (Disney)-All Barks-c/a	18.00	55.00	200.00
1048-The Horse Soldiers (Movie) (John Wayne)-Sekowsky-a; painted cover featuring John Wayne	13.00	38.00	140.00
1049-Don't Give Up the Ship (Movie) (8/59)-Jerry Lewis photo-c			

Four Color #1052 © Loews Inc.

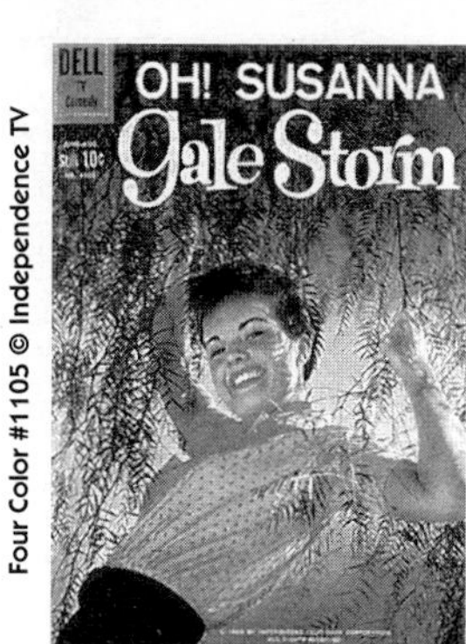

Four Color #1105 © Independence TV

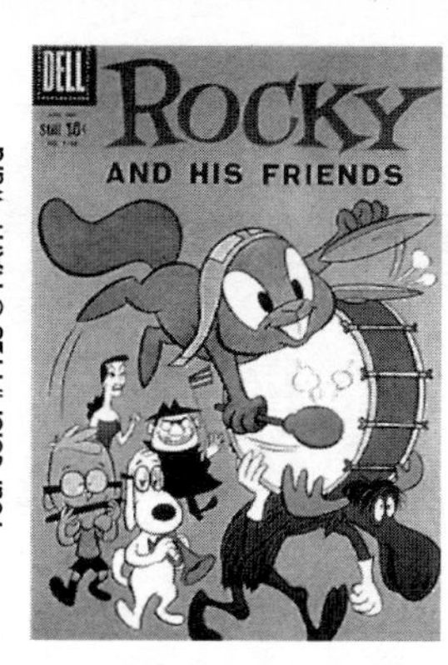

Four Color #1128 © P.A.T. -Ward

	GD25	FN65	NM94
	6.40	19.00	70.00
1050-Huckleberry Hound (TV) (Hanna-Barbera) (10-12/59)	8.00	24.00	85.00
1051-Donald in Mathmagic Land (Disney-Movie)	8.00	25.00	90.00
1052-Ben-Hur (Movie) (11/59)-Manning-a	9.00	27.00	100.00
1053-Goofy (Disney) (11-1/60)	3.60	11.00	40.00
1054-Huckleberry Hound Winter Fun (TV) (Hanna-Barbera) (12/59)	8.00	24.00	85.00
1055-Daisy Duck's Diary (Disney)-by Carl Barks (11-1/60)	9.00	27.00	100.00
1056-Yellowstone Kelly (Movie)-Clint Walker photo-c	5.00	15.00	54.00
1057-Mickey Mouse Album (Disney)	2.75	8.00	30.00
1058-Colt .45 (TV)-Photo-c	7.00	20.00	75.00
1059-Sugarfoot (TV)-Photo-c	8.00	25.00	90.00
1060-Journey to the Center of the Earth (Movie)-Pat Boone & James Mason photo-c	11.00	33.00	120.00
1061-Buffalo Bee (TV)	6.00	18.00	65.00
1062-Christmas Stories (Walt Scott's Little People strip-r)	3.00	9.00	35.00
1063-Santa Claus Funnies	3.00	9.00	35.00
1064-Bugs Bunny's Merry Christmas (12/59)	3.60	11.00	40.00
1065-Frosty the Snowman	3.00	9.00	35.00
1066-77 Sunset Strip (#1) (TV)-Toth-a (1-3/60)-Efrem Zimbalist, Jr. & Edd "Kookie" Byrnes photo-c	11.00	33.00	120.00
1067-Yogi Bear (#1) (TV) (Hanna-Barbera)	11.00	32.00	115.00
1068-Francis the Famous Talking Mule	2.25	6.75	25.00
1069-The FBI Story (Movie)-Toth-a; James Stewart photo on-c	10.00	30.00	110.00
1070-Solomon and Sheba (Movie)-Sekowsky-a; photo-c	9.00	27.00	100.00
1071-The Real McCoys (#1) (TV) (1-3/60)-Toth-a; Walter Brennan photo-c	9.00	27.00	100.00
1072-Blythe (Marge's)	4.50	13.50	50.00
1073-Grandma Duck's Farm Friends-Barks-c/a (Disney)	12.00	37.00	135.00
1074-Chilly Willy (Lantz)	2.75	8.00	30.00
1075-Tales of Wells Fargo (TV)-Photo-c	8.00	25.00	90.00
1076-The Rebel (#1) (TV)-Sekowsky-a; photo-c	10.00	30.00	110.00
1077-The Deputy (#1) (TV)-Buscema-a; Henry Fonda photo-c	12.00	35.00	130.00
1078-The Three Stooges (2-4/60)-Photo-c	10.00	30.00	110.00
1079-The Little Rascals (TV) (Spanky & Alfalfa)	3.80	11.50	42.00
1080-Fury (TV) (2-4/60)-Photo-c	5.50	16.50	60.00
1081-Elmer Fudd	2.20	6.50	24.00
1082-Spin and Marty (Disney) (TV)-Photo-c	7.00	22.00	80.00
1083-Men into Space (TV)-Anderson-a; photo-c	4.50	13.50	50.00
1084-Speedy Gonzales	3.60	11.00	40.00
1085-The Time Machine (H.G. Wells) (Movie) (3/60)-Alex Toth-a; Rod Taylor photo-c	14.00	44.00	160.00
1086-Lolly and Pepper	1.80	5.50	20.00
1087-Peter Gunn (TV)-Photo-c	9.00	27.00	100.00
1088-A Dog of Flanders (Movie)-Photo-c	3.60	11.00	40.00
1089-Restless Gun (TV)-Photo-c	8.00	23.00	85.00
1090-Francis the Famous Talking Mule	2.25	6.75	25.00
1091-Jacky's Diary (4-6/60)	3.60	11.00	40.00
1092-Toby Tyler (Disney-Movie)-Photo-c	5.50	16.50	60.00
1093-MacKenzie's Raiders (Movie/TV)-Richard Carlson photo-c from TV show	5.50	16.50	60.00
1094-Goofy (Disney)	3.60	11.00	40.00
1095-Gyro Gearloose (Disney)-All Barks-c/a	10.00	30.00	110.00
1096-The Texan (TV)-Rory Calhoun photo-c	7.00	22.00	80.00
1097-Rawhide (TV)-Manning-a; Clint Eastwood photo-c	14.00	41.00	150.00
1098-Sugarfoot (TV)-Photo-c	8.00	25.00	90.00

	GD25	FN65	NM94
1099-Donald Duck Album (Disney) (5-7/60)-Barks-c	5.50	16.50	60.00
1100-Annette's Life Story (Disney-Movie) (5/60)-Annette Funicello photo-c	21.00	63.00	230.00
1101-Robert Louis Stevenson's Kidnapped (Disney-Movie) (5/60); photo-c	5.50	16.50	60.00
1102-Wanted: Dead or Alive (#1) (TV) (5-7/60); Steve McQueen photo-c	12.00	37.00	125.00
1103-Leave It to Beaver (TV)-Photo-c	14.00	44.00	160.00
1104-Yogi Bear Goes to College (TV) (Hanna-Barbera) (6-8/60)	7.00	20.00	75.00
1105-Gale Storm (Oh! Susanna) (TV)-Toth-a; photo-c	12.00	35.00	130.00
1106-77 Sunset Strip(TV)(6-8/60)-Toth-a; photo-c	9.00	27.00	100.00
1107-Buckskin (TV)-Photo-c	5.50	16.50	60.00
1108-The Troubleshooters (TV)-Keenan Wynn photo-c	4.50	13.50	50.00
1109-This Is Your Life, Donald Duck (Disney) (TV) (8-10/60)-Gyro flashback to WDC&S #141; origin Donald Duck (1st told)	14.00	41.00	150.00
1110-Bonanza (#1) (TV) (6-8/60)-Photo-c	34.00	102.00	375.00
1111-Shotgun Slade (TV)-Photo-c	5.50	16.50	60.00
1112-Pixie and Dixie and Mr. Jinks (#1) (TV) (Hanna-Barbera) (7-9/60)	7.00	20.00	75.00
1113-Tales of Wells Fargo (TV)-Photo-c	8.00	25.00	90.00
1114-Huckleberry Finn (Movie) (7/60)-Photo-c	4.50	13.50	50.00
1115-Ricky Nelson (TV)-Manning-a; photo-c	14.00	41.00	150.00
1116-Boots and Saddles (TV) (8/60)-Photo-c	4.50	13.50	50.00
1117-Boy and the Pirates (Movie)-Photo-c	5.50	16.50	60.00
1118-The Sword and the Dragon (Movie) (6/60)-Photo-c	7.00	22.00	80.00
1119-Smokey the Bear Nature Stories	2.75	8.00	30.00
1120-Dinosaurus (Movie)-Painted-c	6.40	19.00	70.00
1121-Hercules Unchained (Movie) (8/60)-Crandall/Evans-a	9.00	27.00	100.00
1122-Chilly Willy (Lantz)	2.75	8.00	30.00
1123-Tombstone Territory (TV)-Photo-c	9.00	27.00	100.00
1124-Whirlybirds (#1) (TV)-Photo-c	8.00	25.00	90.00
1125-Laramie (#1) (TV)-Photo-c; G. Kane/Heath-a	9.00	27.00	100.00
1126-Sundance (TV) (8-10/60)-Earl Holliman photo-c	5.50	16.50	60.00
1127-The Three Stooges-Photo-c (8-10/60)	10.00	30.00	110.00
1128-Rocky and His Friends (#1) (TV) (Jay Ward) (8-10/60)	36.00	109.00	400.00
1129-Pollyanna (Disney-Movie)-Hayley Mills photo-c	7.00	22.00	80.00
1130-The Deputy (TV)-Buscema-a; Henry Fonda photo-c	9.00	27.00	100.00
1131-Elmer Fudd (9-11/60)	2.20	6.50	24.00
1132-Space Mouse (Lantz) (8-10/60)	3.60	11.00	40.00
1133-Fury (TV)-Photo-c	5.50	16.50	60.00
1134-Real McCoys (TV)-Toth-a; photo-c	9.00	27.00	100.00
1135-M.G.M.'s Mouse Musketeers (9-11/60)	1.80	5.50	20.00
1136-Jungle Cat (Disney-Movie)-Photo-c	5.50	16.50	60.00
1137-The Little Rascals (TV)	3.80	11.50	42.00
1138-The Rebel (TV)-Photo-c	8.00	25.00	90.00
1139-Spartacus (Movie) (11/60)-Buscema-a; Kirk Douglas photo-c	12.00	35.00	130.00
1140-Donald Duck Album (Disney)-Barks-c	5.50	16.50	60.00
1141-Huckleberry Hound for President (TV) (Hanna-Barbera) (10/60)	7.00	22.00	80.00
1142-Johnny Ringo (TV)-Photo-c	6.40	19.00	70.00
1143-Pluto (Disney) (11-1/61)	2.75	8.00	30.00
1144-The Story of Ruth (Movie)-Photo-c	9.00	27.00	100.00
1145-The Lost World (Movie)-Gil Kane-a; photo-c; 1 pg. Conan Doyle biography by Torres	10.00	30.00	110.00

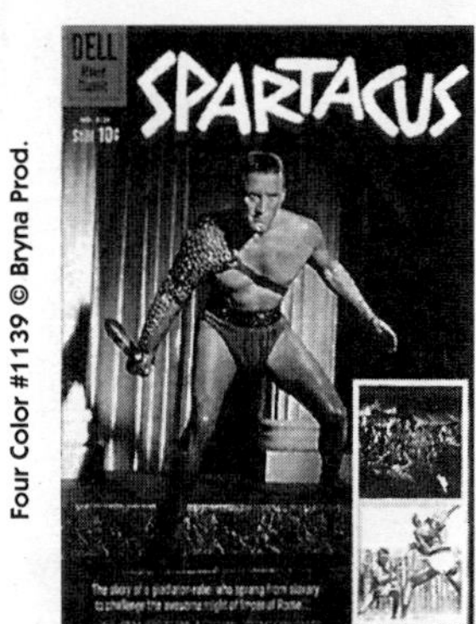

Four Color #1139 © Bryna Prod.

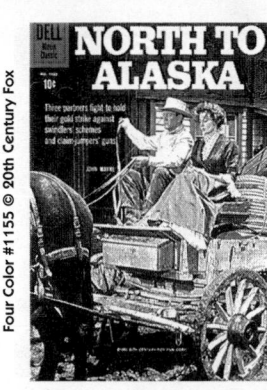

Four Color #1155 © 20th Century Fox

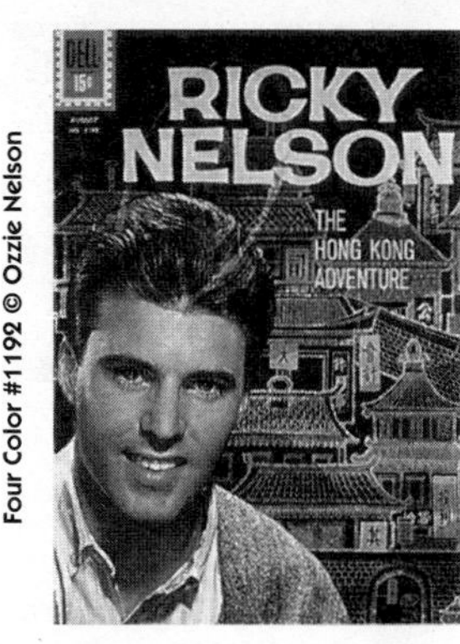

Four Color #1192 © Ozzie Nelson

	GD25	FN65	NM94
1146-Restless Gun (TV)-Photo-c; Wildey-a	8.00	24.00	85.00
1147-Sugarfoot (TV)-Photo-c	8.00	25.00	90.00
1148-I Aim at the Stars-the Wernher Von Braun Story (Movie) (11-1/61)-Photo-c	6.40	19.00	70.00
1149-Goofy (Disney) (11-1/61)	3.60	11.00	40.00
1150-Daisy Duck's Diary (Disney) (12-1/61) by Carl Barks	9.00	27.00	100.00
1151-Mickey Mouse Album (Disney) (11-1/61)	2.75	8.00	30.00
1152-Rocky and His Friends (TV) (Jay Ward) (12-2/61)	23.00	68.00	250.00
1153-Frosty the Snowman	3.00	9.00	35.00
1154-Santa Claus Funnies	3.00	9.00	35.00
1155-North to Alaska (Movie)-John Wayne photo-c	16.00	47.00	170.00
1156-Walt Disney Swiss Family Robinson (Movie) (12/60)-Photo-c	6.40	19.00	70.00
1157-Master of the World (Movie) (7/61)	4.50	13.50	50.00
1158-Three Worlds of Gulliver (2 issues exist with different covers) (Movie)-Photo-c	6.00	18.00	65.00
1159-77 Sunset Strip (TV)-Toth-a; photo-c	9.00	27.00	100.00
1160-Rawhide (TV)-Clint Eastwood photo-c	14.00	41.00	150.00
1161-Grandma Duck's Farm Friends (Disney) by Carl Barks (2-4/61)	12.00	37.00	135.00
1162-Yogi Bear Joins the Marines (TV) (Hanna-Barbera) (5-7/61)	7.00	20.00	75.00
1163-Daniel Boone (3-5/61); Marsh-a	4.50	13.50	50.00
1164-Wanted: Dead or Alive (TV)-Steve McQueen photo-c	9.00	27.00	100.00
1165-Ellery Queen (#1) (3-5/61)	10.00	32.00	115.00
1166-Rocky and His Friends (TV) (Jay Ward)	23.00	68.00	250.00
1167-Tales of Wells Fargo (TV)-Photo-c	7.00	22.00	80.00
1168-The Detectives (TV)-Robert Taylor photo-c	9.00	27.00	100.00
1169-New Adventures of Sherlock Holmes	14.00	44.00	160.00
1170-The Three Stooges (3-5/61)-Photo-c	10.00	30.00	110.00
1171-Elmer Fudd	2.20	6.50	24.00
1172-Fury (TV)-Photo-c	5.50	16.50	60.00
1173-The Twilight Zone (#1) (TV) (5/61)-Crandall/Evans-c/a; Crandall tribute to Ingles	18.00	55.00	200.00
1174-The Little Rascals (TV)	2.90	8.70	32.00
1175-M.G.M.'s Mouse Musketeers (3-5/61)	1.80	5.50	20.00
1176-Dondi (Movie)-Origin; photo-c	3.60	11.00	40.00
1177-Chilly Willy (Lantz) (4-6/61)	2.75	8.00	30.00
1178-Ten Who Dared (Disney-Movie) (12/60)-Painted-c; cast member photo on back-c	6.40	19.00	70.00
1179-The Swamp Fox (TV) (Disney)-Leslie Nielson photo-c	8.00	25.00	90.00
1180-The Danny Thomas Show (TV)-Toth-a; photo-c	14.00	44.00	160.00
1181-Texas John Slaughter (TV) (Disney) (4-6/61)-Photo-c	6.40	19.00	70.00
1182-Donald Duck Album (Disney) (5-7/61)	3.60	11.00	40.00
1183-101 Dalmatians (Disney-Movie) (3/61)	9.00	27.00	100.00
1184-Gyro Gearloose; All Barks-c/a (Disney) (5-7/61) Two variations exist	10.00	30.00	110.00
1185-Sweetie Pie	2.75	8.00	30.00
1186-Yak Yak (#1) by Jack Davis (2 versions - one minus 3-pg. Davis-c/a)	7.00	22.00	80.00
1187-The Three Stooges (6-8/61)-Photo-c	10.00	30.00	110.00
1188-Atlantis, the Lost Continent (Movie) (5/61)-Photo-c	9.00	27.00	100.00
1189-Greyfriars Bobby (Disney-Movie) (11/61)-Photo-c (scarce)	6.40	19.00	70.00
1190-Donald and the Wheel (Disney-Movie) (11/61); Barks-c	6.40	19.00	70.00
1191-Leave It to Beaver (TV)-Photo-c	14.00	44.00	160.00
1192-Ricky Nelson (TV)-Manning-a; photo-c	14.00	41.00	150.00
1193-The Real McCoys (TV) (6-8/61)-Photo-c	8.00	25.00	90.00
1194-Pepe (Movie) (4/61)-Photo-c	1.80	5.50	20.00
1195-National Velvet (#1) (TV)-Photo-c	5.50	16.50	60.00
1196-Pixie and Dixie and Mr. Jinks (TV) (Hanna-Barbera) (7-9/61)	5.00	15.00	55.00
1197-The Aquanauts (TV) (5-7/61)-Photo-c	6.25	19.00	70.00
1198-Donald in Mathmagic Land (Disney-Movie)-Reprint of #1051	5.50	16.50	60.00
1199-The Absent-Minded Professor (Disney-Movie) (4/61)-Photo-c	6.40	19.00	70.00
1200-Hennessey (TV) (8-10/61)-Gil Kane-a; photo-c	5.50	16.50	60.00
1201-Goofy (Disney) (8-10/61)	3.60	11.00	40.00
1202-Rawhide (TV)-Clint Eastwood photo-c	14.00	41.00	150.00
1203-Pinocchio (Disney) (3/62)	4.50	13.50	50.00
1204-Scamp (Disney)	3.00	9.00	35.00
1205-David and Goliath (Movie) (7/61)-Photo-c	5.50	16.50	60.00
1206-Lolly and Pepper (9-11/61)	1.80	5.50	20.00
1207-The Rebel (TV)-Sekowsky-a; photo-c	8.00	25.00	90.00
1208-Rocky and His Friends (Jay Ward) (TV)	23.00	68.00	250.00
1209-Sugarfoot (TV)-Photo-c (10-12/61)	8.00	25.00	90.00
1210-The Parent Trap (Disney-Movie) (8/61)-Hayley Mills photo-c	8.00	25.00	90.00
1211-77 Sunset Strip (TV)-Manning-a; photo-c	8.00	25.00	90.00
1212-Chilly Willy (Lantz) (7-9/61)	2.75	8.00	30.00
1213-Mysterious Island (Movie)-Photo-c	8.00	25.00	90.00
1214-Smokey the Bear	2.75	8.00	30.00
1215-Tales of Wells Fargo (TV) (10-12/61)-Photo-c	7.00	22.00	80.00
1216-Whirlybirds (TV)-Photo-c	7.00	22.00	80.00
1218-Fury (TV)-Photo-c	5.50	16.50	60.00
1219-The Detectives (TV)-Robert Taylor & Adam West photo-c	7.00	22.00	80.00
1220-Gunslinger (TV)-Photo-c	8.00	25.00	90.00
1221-Bonanza (TV) (9-11/61)-Photo-c	16.00	49.00	180.00
1222-Elmer Fudd (9-11/61)	2.20	6.50	24.00
1223-Laramie (TV)-Gil Kane-a; photo-c	5.50	16.50	60.00
1224-The Little Rascals (TV) (10-12/61)	2.90	8.70	32.00
1225-The Deputy (TV)-Henry Fonda photo-c	9.00	27.00	100.00
1226-Nikki, Wild Dog of the North (Disney-Movie) (9/61)-Photo-c	4.50	13.50	50.00
1227-Morgan the Pirate (Movie)-Photo-c	7.00	22.00	80.00
1229-Thief of Baghdad (Movie)-Crandall/Evans-a; photo-c	6.00	18.00	65.00
1230-Voyage to the Bottom of the Sea (#1) (Movie)-Photo insert on-c	9.00	27.00	100.00
1231-Danger Man (TV) (9-11/61)-Patrick McGoohan photo-c	10.00	30.00	110.00
1232-On the Double (Movie)	3.60	11.00	40.00
1233-Tammy Tell Me True (Movie) (1961)	5.50	16.50	60.00
1234-The Phantom Planet (Movie) (1961)	6.40	19.00	70.00
1235-Mister Magoo (#1) (12-2/62)	9.00	27.00	100.00
1235-Mister Magoo (3-5/65) 2nd printing; reprint of 12-2/62 issue	5.50	16.50	60.00
1236-King of Kings (Movie)-Photo-c	7.00	22.00	80.00
1237-The Untouchables (#1) (TV)-Not by Toth; photo-c	22.00	65.00	240.00
1238-Deputy Dawg (TV)	10.00	30.00	110.00
1239-Donald Duck Album (Disney) (10-12/61)-Barks-c	5.50	16.50	60.00
1240-The Detectives (TV)-Tufts-a; Robert Taylor photo-c	7.00	22.00	80.00
1241-Sweetie Pie	2.75	8.00	30.00
1242-King Leonardo and His Short Subjects (#1) (TV) (11-1/62)	13.00	38.00	140.00

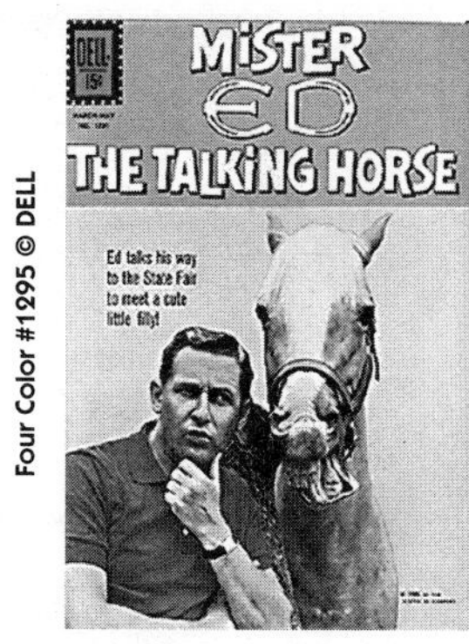

Four Color #1295 © DELL

Four Color #1308 © Videocraft

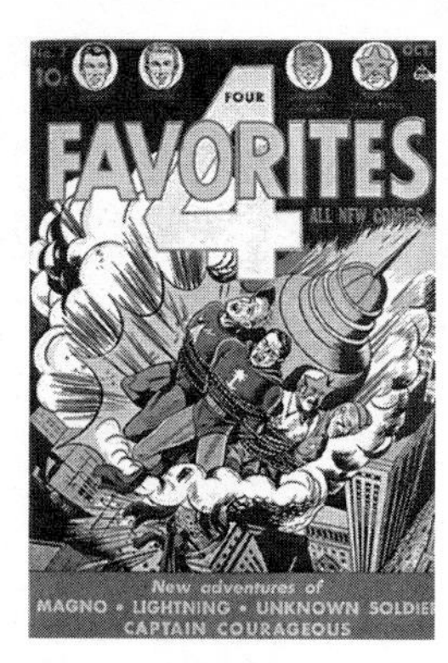

Four Favorites #7 © ACE

	GD25	FN65	NM94
1243-Ellery Queen	9.00	27.00	95.00
1244-Space Mouse (Lantz) (11-1/62)	3.60	11.00	40.00
1245-New Adventures of Sherlock Holmes	14.00	44.00	160.00
1246-Mickey Mouse Album (Disney)	2.75	8.00	30.00
1247-Daisy Duck's Diary (Disney) (12-2/62)	4.00	12.00	45.00
1248-Pluto (Disney)	2.75	8.00	30.00
1249-The Danny Thomas Show (TV)-Manning-a; photo-c	14.00	44.00	160.00
1250-The Four Horsemen of the Apocalypse (Movie)-Photo-c	6.40	19.00	70.00
1251-Everything's Ducky (Movie) (1961)	3.60	11.00	40.00
1252-The Andy Griffith Show (TV)-Photo-c; 1st show aired 10/3/60	30.00	90.00	330.00
1253-Space Man (#1) (1-3/62)	6.40	19.00	70.00
1254- "Diver Dan" (#1) (TV) (2-4/62)-Photo-c	4.50	13.50	50.00
1255-The Wonders of Aladdin (Movie) (1961)	5.75	17.00	63.00
1256-Kona, Monarch of Monster Isle (#1) (2-4/62)-Glanzman-a	5.50	16.50	60.00
1257-Car 54, Where Are You? (#1) (TV) (3-5/62)-Photo-c	6.40	19.00	70.00
1258-The Frogmen (#1)-Evans-a	6.40	19.00	70.00
1259-El Cid (Movie) (1961)-Photo-c	6.40	19.00	70.00
1260-The Horsemasters (TV, Movie) (Disney) (12-2/62)-Annette Funicello photo-c	11.00	33.00	120.00
1261-Rawhide (TV)-Clint Eastwood photo-c	14.00	41.00	150.00
1262-The Rebel (TV)-Photo-c	8.00	25.00	90.00
1263-77 Sunset Strip (TV) (12-2/62)-Manning-a; photo-c	8.00	25.00	90.00
1264-Pixie and Dixie and Mr. Jinks (TV) (Hanna-Barbera)	5.00	15.00	55.00
1265-The Real McCoys (TV)-Photo-c	8.00	25.00	90.00
1266-M.G.M.'s Spike and Tyke (12-2/62)	1.65	5.00	18.00
1267-Gyro Gearloose; Barks-c/a, 4 pgs. (Disney) (12-2/62)	7.00	20.00	75.00
1268-Oswald the Rabbit (Lantz)	2.00	6.00	22.00
1269-Rawhide (TV)-Clint Eastwood photo-c	14.00	41.00	150.00
1270-Bullwinkle and Rocky (#1) (TV) (Jay Ward) (3-5/62)	18.00	55.00	200.00
1271-Yogi Bear Birthday Party (TV) (Hanna-Barbera) (11/61)	4.50	13.50	50.00
1272-Frosty the Snowman	3.00	9.00	35.00
1273-Hans Brinker (Disney-Movie)-Photo-c (2/62)	5.50	16.50	60.00
1274-Santa Claus Funnies (12/61)	3.00	9.00	35.00
1275-Rocky and His Friends (TV) (Jay Ward)	23.00	68.00	250.00
1276-Dondi	1.80	5.50	20.00
1278-King Leonardo and His Short Subjects (TV)	13.00	38.00	140.00
1279-Grandma Duck's Farm Friends (Disney)	3.60	11.00	40.00
1280-Hennessey (TV)-Photo-c	5.50	16.50	60.00
1281-Chilly Willy (Lantz) (4-6/62)	2.75	8.00	30.00
1282-Babes in Toyland (Disney-Movie) (1/62); Annette Funicello photo-c	11.00	34.00	125.00
1283-Bonanza (TV) (2-4/62)-Photo-c	16.00	49.00	180.00
1284-Laramie (TV)-Heath-a; photo-c	5.50	16.50	60.00
1285-Leave It to Beaver (TV)-Photo-c	14.00	44.00	160.00
1286-The Untouchables (TV)-Photo-c	16.00	47.00	170.00
1287-Man from Wells Fargo (TV)-Photo-c	5.00	15.00	55.00
1288-Twilight Zone (TV) (4/62)-Crandall/Evans-c/a	11.00	32.00	115.00
1289-Ellery Queen	9.00	27.00	95.00
1290-M.G.M.'s Mouse Musketeers	1.80	5.50	20.00
1291-77 Sunset Strip (TV)-Manning-a; photo-c	8.00	25.00	90.00
1293-Elmer Fudd (3-5/62)	2.20	6.50	24.00
1294-Ripcord (TV)	6.40	19.00	70.00
1295-Mister Ed, the Talking Horse (#1) (TV) (3-5/62)-Photo-c	12.00	35.00	130.00
1296-Fury (TV) (3-5/62)-Photo-c	5.50	16.50	60.00
1297-Spanky, Alfalfa and the Little Rascals (TV)	2.75	8.00	30.00
1298-The Hathaways (TV)-Photo-c	3.60	11.00	40.00
1299-Deputy Dawg (TV)	10.00	30.00	110.00
1300-The Comancheros (Movie) (1961)-John Wayne photo-c	14.00	44.00	160.00
1301-Adventures in Paradise (TV) (2-4/62)	3.60	11.00	40.00
1302-Johnny Jason, Teen Reporter (2-4/62)	2.75	8.00	30.00
1303-Lad: A Dog (Movie)-Photo-c	2.75	8.00	30.00
1304-Nellie the Nurse (3-5/62)-Stanley-a	6.40	19.00	70.00
1305-Mister Magoo (3-5/62)	9.00	27.00	100.00
1306-Target: The Corruptors (#1) (TV) (3-5/62)-Photo-c	5.00	15.00	55.00
1307-Margie (TV) (3-5/62)	3.60	11.00	40.00
1308-Tales of the Wizard of Oz (TV) (3-5/62)	11.00	32.00	115.00
1309-87th Precinct (#1) (TV) (4-6/62)-Krigstein-a; photo-c	9.00	27.00	100.00
1310-Huck and Yogi Winter Sports (TV) (Hanna-Barbera) (3/62)	8.00	24.00	85.00
1311-Rocky and His Friends (TV) (Jay Ward)	23.00	68.00	250.00
1312-National Velvet (TV)-Photo-c	2.75	8.00	30.00
1313-Moon Pilot (Disney-Movie)-Photo-c	6.40	19.00	70.00
1328-The Underwater City (Movie) (1961)-Evans-a; photo-c	6.40	19.00	70.00
1329-See Gyro Gearloose #01329-207			
1330-Brain Boy (#1)-Gil Kane-a	12.00	37.00	135.00
1332-Bachelor Father (TV)	7.00	22.00	80.00
1333-Short Ribs (4-6/62)	4.50	13.50	50.00
1335-Aggie Mack (4-6/62)	2.75	8.00	30.00
1336-On Stage; not by Leonard Starr	3.60	11.00	40.00
1337-Dr. Kildare (#1) (TV) (4-6/62)-Photo-c	8.00	25.00	90.00
1341-The Andy Griffith Show (TV) (4-6/62)-Photo-c	30.00	90.00	330.00
1348-Yak Yak (#2)-Jack Davis-c/a	7.00	22.00	80.00
1349-Yogi Bear Visits the U.N. (TV) (Hanna-Barbera) (1/62)-Photo-c	9.00	27.00	100.00
1350-Comanche (Disney-Movie)(1962)-Reprints 4-Color #966 (title change from "Tonka" to "Comanche") (4-6/62)-Sal Mineo photo-c	4.50	13.50	50.00
1354-Calvin & the Colonel (#1) (TV) (4-6/62)	7.00	22.00	80.00

NOTE: *Missing numbers probably do not exist.*

4-D MONKEY, THE (Adventures of... #? on)
Leung's Publications: 1988 - No. 11, 1990 ($1.80/$2.00, 52 pgs.)

1-Karate Pig, Ninja Flounder & 4-D Monkey (48 pgs., centerfold is a Christmas card)	1.80
2-4 (52 pgs.)	1.80
5-11 ($2.00-c)	2.00

FOUR FAVORITES (Crime Must Pay the Penalty No. 33 on)
Ace Magazines: Sept, 1941 - No. 32, Dec, 1947

	GD25	FN65	NM94
1-Vulcan, Lash Lightning (formerly Flash Lightning in Sure-Fire), Magno the Magnetic Man & The Raven begin; flag-c	118.00	354.00	1000.00
2-The Black Ace only app.	47.00	141.00	400.00
3-Last Vulcan	42.00	126.00	340.00
4,5: 4-The Raven & Vulcan end; Unknown Soldier begins (see Our Flag), ends #28. 5-Captain Courageous begins (5/42), ends #28 (moves over from Captain Courageous #6); not in #6	39.00	117.00	300.00
6-8: 6-The Flag app.; Mr. Risk begins (7/42)	35.00	105.00	260.00
9-Kurtzman-a (Lash Lightning); robot-c	39.00	117.00	300.00
10-Classic Kurtzman-c/a (Magno & Davey)	43.00	129.00	350.00
11-Kurtzman-a; Hitler, Mussolini, Hirohito-c; L.B. Cole-a; Unknown Soldier by Kurtzman	43.00	129.00	350.00
12-L.B. Cole-a	28.00	84.00	210.00
13-20: 18,20-Palais-c/a	23.00	69.00	170.00
21-No Unknown Soldier; The Unknown app.	17.00	51.00	125.00

4Most V3 #3 © Premium Service

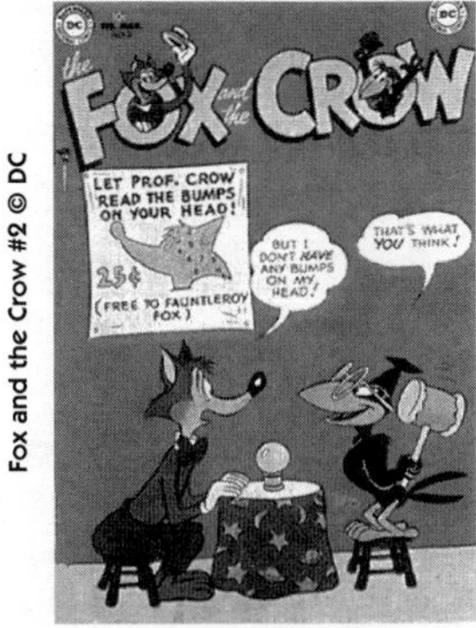

Fox and the Crow #2 © DC

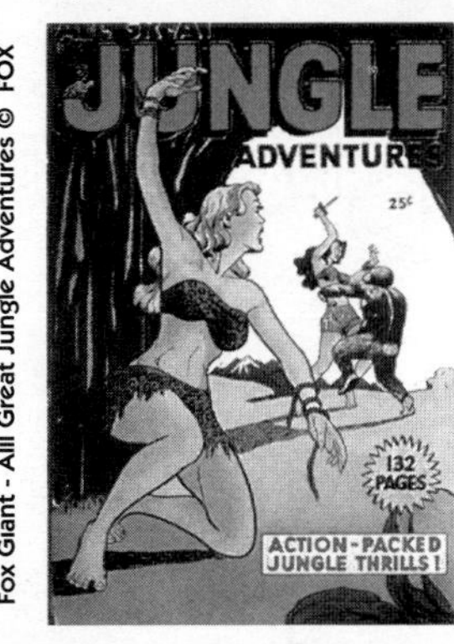

Fox Giant - All Great Jungle Adventures © FOX

GD25 FN65 NM94

22-26: 22-Captain Courageous drops costume. 23-Unknown Soldier drops costume. 25-29-HapHazard app. 26-Last Magno 17.00 51.00 125.00
27-32: 30-Funny-c begin (teen humor), end #32 11.00 33.00 85.00
NOTE: ***Dave Berg*** *c-5.* ***Jim Mooney*** *a-6; c-1-3.* ***Palais*** *a-18-20; c-18-25. Torture chamber c-5.*

FOUR HORSEMEN, THE (See The Crusaders)

FOUR HORSEMEN OF THE APOCALYPSE, THE (Movie)
Dell Publishing Co.: No. 1250, Jan-Mar, 1962 (one-shot)

Four Color 1250-Photo-c 6.40 19.00 70.00

4MOST (Foremost Boys No. 32-40; becomes Thrilling Crime Cases #41 on)
Novelty Publications/Star Publications No. 37-on:
Winter, 1941-42 - V8#5(#36), 9-10/49; #37, 11-12/49 - #40, 4-5/50

V1#1-The Target by Sid Greene, The Cadet & Dick Cole begin with origins retold; produced by Funnies Inc.; quarterly issues begin, end V6#3 106.00 318.00 900.00
2-Last Target (Spr/42) 44.00 132.00 370.00
3-Dan'l Flannel begins; flag-c 39.00 117.00 300.00
4-1pg. Dr. Seuss (signed) (Aut/42) 33.00 100.00 250.00
V2#1-3 11.00 33.00 80.00
4-Hitler, Tojo & Mussolini app. as pumpkins on-c 16.00 48.00 120.00
V3#1-4 10.00 30.00 75.00
V4#1-4: 2-Walter Johnson-c 7.85 23.50 55.00
V5#1-4: 1-The Target & Targeteers app. 6.50 19.50 45.00
V6#1-4 6.50 19.50 45.00
5-L. B. Cole-c 15.00 45.00 110.00
V7#1,3,5, V8#1, 37 6.50 19.50 45.00
2,4,6-L. B. Cole-c. 6-Last Dick Cole 15.00 45.00 110.00
V8#2,3,5-L. B. Cole-c/a 16.00 48.00 120.00
4-L. B. Cole-a 10.00 30.00 75.00
38-40: 38-Johnny Weismuller (Tarzan) life story & Jim Braddock (boxer) life story. 38-40-L.B. Cole-c. 40-Last White Rider 13.00 39.00 100.00
Accepted Reprint 38-40 (nd): 40-r/Johnny Weismuller life story; all have L.B. Cole-c 7.15 21.50 50.00

FOUR-STAR BATTLE TALES
National Periodical Publications: Feb-Mar, 1973 - No. 5, Nov-Dec, 1973

1-reprints begin 2.00 6.00 20.00
2-5 1.20 3.60 12.00
NOTE: ***Drucker*** *r-1, 3-5.* ***Heath*** *r-2, 5; c-1.* ***Krigstein*** *r-5.* ***Kubert*** *r-4; c-2.*

FOUR STAR SPECTACULAR
National Periodical Publications: Mar-Apr, 1976 - No. 6, Jan-Feb, 1977

1 .90 2.70 8.00
2-6: Reprints in all. 2-Infinity cover 5.00
NOTE: *All contain DC Superhero reprints. #1 has 68 pgs.; #2-6, 52 pgs.. #1, 4-Hawkman app.; #2-Kid Flash app.; #3-Green Lantern app; #2, 4, 5-Wonder Woman, Superboy app; #5-Green Arrow, Vigilante app; #6-Blackhawk G.A.-r.*

FOUR TEENERS (Formerly Crime Must Pay The Penalty; Dotty No. 35 on)
A. A. Wyn: No. 34, April, 1948 (52 pgs.)

34-Teen-age comic; Dotty app.; Curly & Jerry continue from Four Favorites 5.00 15.00 30.00

FOURTH WORLD GALLERY, THE (Jack Kirby's...)
DC Comics: 1996 (9/96) ($3.50, one-shot)

nn-Pin-ups of Jack Kirby's Fourth World characters (New Gods, Forever People & Mister Miracle) by John Byrne, Rick Burchett, Dan Jurgens, Walt Simonson & others 3.50

FOX AND THE CROW (Stanley & His Monster No. 109 on) (See Comic Cavalcade & Real Screen Comics)
National Periodical Publications: Dec-Jan, 1951-52 - No. 108, Feb-Mar, 1968

1 94.00 282.00 800.00
2(Scarce) 45.00 135.00 380.00
3-5 32.00 96.00 240.00
6-10 23.00 69.00 170.00

GD25 FN65 NM94

11-20 16.00 48.00 120.00
21-30: 22-Last precode issue (2/55) 11.00 33.00 80.00
31-40 9.30 28.00 65.00
41-60 5.50 16.50 55.00
61-80 3.40 10.20 34.00
81-94: 94-(11/65)-The Brat Finks begin 2.50 7.50 25.00
95-Stanley & His Monster begins (origin & 1st app) 3.20 9.60 32.00
96-99,101-108 1.75 5.25 14.00
100 (10-11/66) 2.25 6.75 18.00
NOTE: *Many covers by* ***Mort Drucker.***

FOX AND THE HOUND, THE (Disney)(Movie)
Whitman Publishing Co.: Aug, 1981 - No. 3, Oct, 1981

11292(#1),2,3-Based on animated movie 4.00

FOXFIRE (See The Phoenix Resurrection)
Malibu Comics (Ultraverse): Feb, 1996 - No. 4, May, 1996 ($1.50)

1-4: Sludge, Ultraforce app. 4-Punisher app. 1.50

FOX GIANTS (Also see Giant Comics Edition)
Fox Features Syndicate: 1944 - 1950 (25¢, 132 - 196 pgs.)

Album of Crime nn(1949, 132p) 39.00 117.00 310.00
Album of Love nn(1949, 132p) 37.00 110.00 275.00
All Famous Crime Stories nn('49, 132p) 39.00 117.00 310.00
All Good Comics 1(1944, 132p)(R.W. Voigt)-The Bouncer, Purple Tigress, Rick Evans, Puppeteer, Green Mask; Infinity-c 36.00 108.00 270.00
All Great nn(1944, 132p)-Capt. Jack Terry, Rick Evans, Jaguar Man 36.00 108.00 270.00
All Great nn(Chicago Nite Life News)(1945, 132p)-Green Mask, Bouncer, Puppeteer, Rick Evans, Rocket Kelly 39.00 116.00 290.00
All-Great Confessions nn(1949, 132p) 34.00 102.00 255.00
All Great Crime Stories nn('49, 132p) 39.00 117.00 310.00
All Great Jungle Adventures nn('49, 132p) 43.00 129.00 365.00
All Real Confession Magazine 3 (3/49, 132p) 34.00 102.00 255.00
All Real Confession Magazine 4 (4/49, 132p) 34.00 102.00 255.00
All Your Comics 1(1944, 132p)-The Puppeteer, Red Robbins, & Merciless the Sorcerer 37.00 112.00 280.00
Almanac Of Crime nn(1948, 148p)-Phantom Lady 43.00 129.00 355.00
Almanac Of Crime 1(1950, 132p) 39.00 117.00 310.00
Book Of Love nn(1950, 132p) 33.00 98.00 245.00
Burning Romances 1(1949, 132p) 39.00 117.00 300.00
Crimes Incorporated nn(1950, 132p) 37.00 112.00 280.00
Daring Love Stories nn(1950, 132p) 33.00 98.00 245.00
Everybody's Comics 1(1944, 50¢, 196p)-The Green Mask, The Puppeteer, The Bouncer, Rocket Kelly, Rick Evans 39.00 117.00 310.00
Everybody's Comics 1(1946, 196p)-Green Lama, The Puppeteer 32.00 96.00 240.00
Everybody's Comics 1(1946, 196p)-Same as 1945 Ribtickler 25.00 74.00 185.00
Everybody's Comics nn(1947, 132p)-Jo-Jo, Purple Tigress, Cosmo Cat, Bronze Man 31.00 94.00 235.00
Exciting Romance Stories nn(1949, 132p) 33.00 98.00 245.00
Famous Love nn(1950, 132p) 33.00 98.00 245.00
Intimate Confessions nn(1950, 132p) 33.00 100.00 250.00
Journal Of Crime nn(1949, 132p) 39.00 117.00 310.00
Love Problems nn(1949, 132p) 34.00 102.00 255.00
Love Thrills nn(1950, 132p) 34.00 102.00 255.00
March of Crime nn('48, 132p)-Female w/rifle-c 37.00 112.00 280.00
March of Crime nn('49, 132p)-Cop w/pistol-c 37.00 112.00 280.00
March of Crime nn(1949, 132p)-Coffin & man w/machine-gun-c 37.00 112.00 280.00
Revealing Love Stories nn(1950, 132p) 33.00 100.00 250.00
Ribtickler nn(1945, 50¢, 196p)-Chicago Nite Life News; Marvel Mutt, Cosmo Cat, Flash Rabbit, The Nebbs app. 30.00 90.00 225.00
Romantic Thrills nn(1950, 132p) 33.00 98.00 245.00
Secret Love nn(1949, 132p) 33.00 98.00 245.00

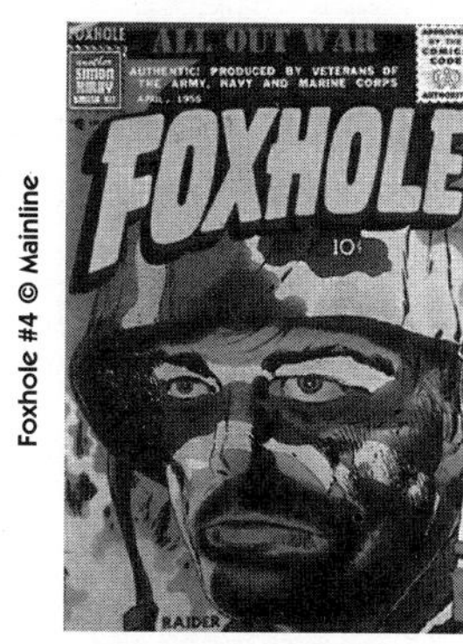

Foxhole #4 © Mainline

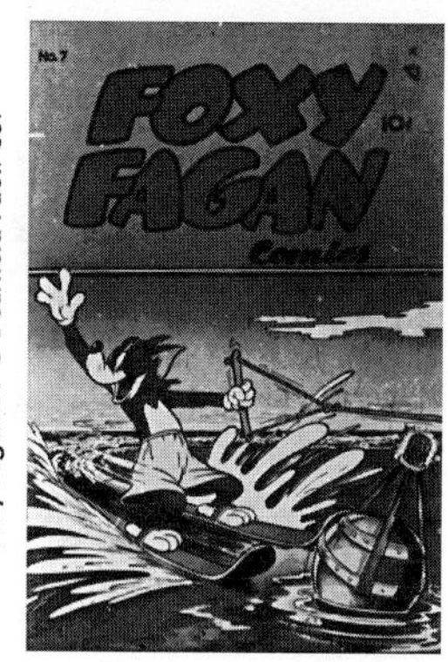

Foxy Fagan #7 © Dearfield Publ. Co.

Frankenstein Comics #25 © PRIZE

	GD25	FN65	NM94
Secret Love Stories nn(1949, 132p)	33.00	98.00	245.00
Strange Love nn(1950, 132p)-Photo-c	39.00	117.00	295.00
Sweetheart Scandals nn(1950, 132p)	33.00	98.00	245.00
Teen-Age Love nn(1950, 132p)	33.00	98.00	245.00
Throbbing Love nn(1950, 132p)-Photo-c; used in **POP**, pg. 107	39.00	116.00	290.00
Truth About Crime nn(1949, 132p)	39.00	117.00	310.00
Variety Comics 1(1946, 132p)-Blue Beetle, Jungle Jo	33.00	100.00	250.00
Variety Comics nn(1950, 132p)-Jungle Jo, My Secret Affair(w/Harrison/ Wood-a), Crimes by Women & My Story	33.00	98.00	245.00
Western Roundup nn('50, 132p)-Hoot Gibson; Cody of the Pony Express app.	36.00	108.00	270.00

NOTE: *Each of the above usually contain four remaindered Fox books minus covers. Since these missing covers often had the first page of the first story, most Giants therefore are incomplete. Approximate values are listed. Books with appearances of Phantom Lady, Rulah, Jo-Jo, etc. could bring more.*

FOXHOLE (Becomes Never Again #8?)
Mainline/Charlton No. 5 on: 9-10/54 - No. 4, 3-4/55; No. 5, 7/55 - No. 7, 3/56

	GD25	FN65	NM94
1-Classic Kirby-c	33.00	100.00	250.00
2-Kirby-c/a(2); Kirby scripts based on his war time experiences	23.00	70.00	175.00
3-5-Kirby-c only	13.00	38.00	95.00
6-Kirby-c/a(2)	21.00	62.00	155.00
7	5.70	17.00	35.00
Super Reprints #10-12,15-18: 10-r/? 11,12,18-r/Foxhole #1,2,3. 15,16-r/ United States Marines #5,8. 17-r/Monty Hall #?	1.50	4.50	12.00

NOTE: ***Kirby** a(r)-Super #11, 12. **Powell** a(r)-Super #15, 16. Stories by actual veterans.*

FOX KIDS FUNHOUSE (TV)
Acclaim Books: 1997 - Present ($4.50, digest size)

1-The TIck 4.50

FOXY FAGAN COMICS (Funny Animal)
Dearfield Publishing Co.: Dec, 1946 - No. 7, Summer, 1948

	GD25	FN65	NM94
1-Foxy Fagan & Little Buck begin	11.00	32.00	80.00
2	5.70	17.00	40.00
3-7: 6-Rocket ship-c	5.35	16.00	32.00

FRACTURED FAIRY TALES (TV)
Gold Key: Oct, 1962 (Jay Ward)

	GD25	FN65	NM94
1 (10022-210)-From Bullwinkle TV show	10.00	30.00	110.00

FRAGGLE ROCK (TV)
Marvel Comics (Star Comics)/Marvel V2#1 on: Apr, 1985 - No. 8, Sept, 1986; V2#1, Apr, 1988 - No. 6, Sept, 1988

1-8 (75¢) 3.00
V2#1-6-($1.00): Reprints 1st series 1.50

FRANCIS, BROTHER OF THE UNIVERSE
Marvel Comics Group: 1980 (75¢, 52 pgs., one-shot)

nn-Buscema/Marie Severin-a; story of Francis Bernadone celebrating his 800th birthday in 1982 2.00

FRANCIS THE FAMOUS TALKING MULE (All based on movie)
Dell Publishing Co.: No. 335 (#1), June, 1951 - No. 1090, March, 1960

	GD25	FN65	NM94
Four Color 335 (#1)	7.00	22.00	80.00
Four Color 465	4.50	13.50	50.00
Four Color 501,547,579	3.60	11.00	40.00
Four Color 621,655,698,710,745	2.75	8.00	30.00
Four Color 810,863,906,953,991,1068,1090	2.25	6.75	25.00

FRANK
Nemesis Comics (Harvey): Apr (Mar inside), 1994 - No. 4, 1994 ($1.75/$2.50, limited series)

1-4-($2.50, direct sale): 1-Foil-c Edition 2.50
1-4-($1.75)-Newsstand Editions; Cowan-a in all 1.75

FRANK
Fantagraphics Books: Sept, 1996 ($2.95, B&W)

1-Woodring-c/a/scripts 3.00

FRANK BUCK (Formerly My True Love)
Fox Features Syndicate: No. 70, May, 1950 - No. 3, Sept, 1950

	GD25	FN65	NM94
70-Wood a(p)(3 stories)-Photo-c	30.00	90.00	225.00
71-Wood-a (9 pgs.); photo/painted-c	15.00	45.00	115.00
3: 3-Photo/painted-c	12.00	36.00	90.00

NOTE: *Based on "Bring 'Em Back Alive" TV show.*

FRANKENSTEIN (See Dracula, Movie Classics & Werewolf)
Dell Publishing Co.: Aug-Oct, 1964; No. 2, Sept, 1966 - No. 4, Mar, 1967

	GD25	FN65	NM94
1(12-283-410)(1964)	4.00	12.00	45.00
2-Intro. & origin super-hero character (9/66)	2.50	7.50	28.00
3,4	1.50	4.50	16.00

FRANKENSTEIN (The Monster of...; also see Monsters Unleashed #2, Power Record Comics, Psycho & Silver Surfer #7)
Marvel Comics Group: Jan, 1973 - No. 18, Sept, 1975

	GD25	FN65	NM94
1-Ploog-c/a begins, ends #6	2.70	8.00	30.00
2	2.00	6.00	20.00
3-5	1.50	4.50	15.00
6,7,10: 7-Dracula cameo	1.00	3.00	10.00
8,9-Dracula c/sty. 9-Death of Drucula	2.40	7.00	26.00
11-17	.85	2.60	7.00
18-Wrightson-c(i)	1.00	3.00	10.00

NOTE: ***Adkins** c-17i. **Buscema** a-7-10p. **Ditko** a-12r. **G. Kane** c-15p. **Orlando** a-8r. **Ploog** a-1-3, 4p, 5p, 6; c-1-6. **Wrightson** c-18i.*

FRANKENSTEIN COMICS (Also See Prize Comics)
Prize Publ. (Crestwood/Feature): Sum, 1945 - V5#5(#33), Oct-Nov, 1954

	GD25	FN65	NM94
1-Frankenstein begins by Dick Briefer (origin); Frank Sinatra parody	91.00	273.00	775.00
2	46.00	138.00	390.00
3-5	36.00	108.00	270.00
6-10: 7-S&K a(r)/Headline Comics. 8(7-8/47)-Superman satire	31.00	92.00	230.00
11-17(1-2/49)-11-Boris Karloff parody-c/story. 17-Last humor issue	26.00	78.00	195.00
18(3/52)-New origin, horror series begins	37.00	110.00	275.00
19,20(V3#4, 8-9/52)	22.00	66.00	165.00
21(V3#5), 22(V3#6)	19.00	58.00	145.00
23(V4#1) - #28(V4#6)	19.00	58.00	145.00
29(V5#1) - #33(V5#5)	19.00	58.00	145.00

NOTE: ***Briefer** c/a-all. **Meskin** a-21, 29.*

FRANKENSTEIN/DRACULA WAR, THE
Topps Comics: Feb, 1995 - No. 3, May, 1995 ($2.50, limited series)

1-3 2.50

FRANKENSTEIN, JR. (...& the Impossibles) (TV)
Gold Key: Jan, 1966 (Hanna-Barbera)

	GD25	FN65	NM94
1-Super hero (scarce)	9.00	27.00	100.00

FRANKENSTEIN: OR THE MODERN PROMETHEUS
Caliber Press: 1994 ($2.95, one-shot)

1 3.00

FRANK FRAZETTA FANTASY ILLUSTRATED (Magazine)
Quantum Cat Entertainment: Spring 1998 - Present ($5.95, quarterly)

1-Anthology; art by Corben, Horley, Jusko 6.00
1-Linsner variant-c 8.00
2-Battle Chasers by Madureira; Harris-a 8.00
2-Madureira Battle Chasers variant-c 12.00

FRANK FRAZETTA'S THUN'DA TALES

Freckles and His Friends #5 © STD

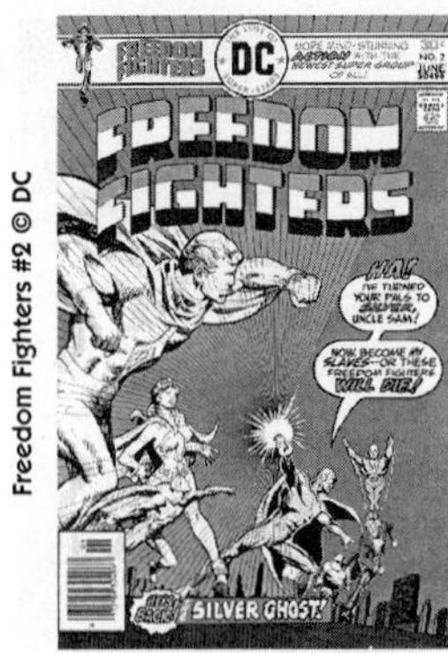

Freedom Fighters #2 © DC

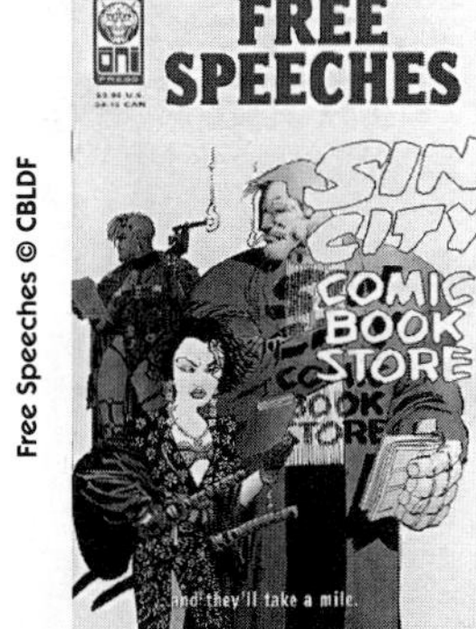

Free Speeches © CBLDF

GD25 FN65 NM94

Fantagraphics Books: 1987 ($2.00, one-shot)

1-Frazetta-r 2.00

FRANK FRAZETTA'S UNTAMED LOVE (Also see Untamed Love)
Fantagraphics Books: Nov, 1987 ($2.00, one-shot)

..1-Frazetta-r from 1950's romance comics 2.00

FRANKIE COMICS (...& Lana No. 13-15) (Formerly Movie Tunes; becomes Frankie Fuddle No. 16 on)
Marvel Comics (MgPC): No. 4, Wint, 1946-47 - No. 15, June, 1949

4-Mitzi, Margie, Daisy app. 11.00 32.00 80.00
5-9 6.50 19.50 45.00
10-15: 13-Anti-Wertham editorial 5.70 17.00 35.00

FRANKIE DOODLE (See Sparkler, both series)
United Features Syndicate: No. 7, 1939

Single Series 7 28.00 84.00 210.00

FRANKIE FUDDLE (Formerly Frankie & Lana)
Marvel Comics: No. 16, Aug, 1949 - No. 17, Nov, 1949

16,17 5.70 17.00 35.00

FRANK LUTHER'S SILLY PILLY COMICS (See Jingle Dingle...)
Children's Comics (Maltex Cereal): 1950 (10¢)

1-Characters from radio, records, & TV 5.35 16.00 32.00

FRANK MERRIWELL AT YALE (Speed Demons No. 5 on?)
Charlton Comics: June, 1955 - No. 4, Jan, 1956 (Also see Shadow Comics)

1 5.00 15.00 30.00
2-4 4.00 12.00 24.00

FRANTIC (Magazine) (See Ratfink & Zany)
Pierce Publishing Co.: Oct, 1958 - V2#2, Apr, 1959 (Satire)

V1#1 7.15 21.50 50.00
2 5.70 17.00 40.00
V2#1,2: 1-Burgos-a, Severin-c/a; Powell-a? 5.00 15.00 30.00

FREAK FORCE (Also see Savage Dragon)
Image Comics (Highbrow Ent.): Dec, 1993 - No. 18, July, 1995 ($1.95/$2.50)

1-7-Superpatriot & Mighty Man in all; Erik Larsen scripts in all. 4-Vanguard app. 2.00
8-18: 8-Begin $2.50-c. 9-Cyberforce-c & app. 13-Variant-c 2.50

FREAK FORCE (Also see Savage Dragon)
Image Comics: Apr, 1997 - No. 3, July, 1997 ($2.95)

1-3-Larsen-s 2.95

FRECKLES AND HIS FRIENDS (See Crackajack Funnies, Famous Comics Cartoon Book, Honeybee Birdwhistle... & Red Ryder)

FRECKLES AND HIS FRIENDS
Standard Comics/Argo: No. 5, 11/47 - No. 12, 8/49; 11/55 - No. 4, 6/56

5-Reprints 5.70 17.00 40.00
6-12-Reprints. 7-9-Airbrush-c (by Schomburg?). 11-Lingerie panels 4.25 13.00 26.00

NOTE: *Some copies of No. 8 & 9 contain a printing oddity. The negatives were elongated in the engraving process, probably to conform to page dimensions on the filler pages. Those pages only look normal when viewed at a 45 degree angle.*

1(Argo,'55)-Reprints (NEA Service) 4.25 13.00 28.00
2-4 4.00 10.00 20.00

FREDDY (Formerly My Little Margie's Boy Friends) (Also see Blue Bird)
Charlton Comics: V2#12, June, 1958 - No. 47, Feb, 1965

V2#12 2.50 7.50 22.00
13-15 1.85 5.50 15.00
16-47 1.25 3.75 10.00
Schiff's Shoes Presents... #1 (1959)-Giveaway 1.00 3.00 8.00

FREDDY
Dell Publishing Co.: May-July, 1963 - No. 3, Oct-Dec, 1964

1 2.50 7.50 20.00
2,3 1.50 4.50 12.00

FREDDY KRUEGER'S A NIGHTMARE ON ELM STREET
Marvel Comics: Oct, 1989 - No. 2, Dec, 1989 ($2.25, B&W, movie adaptation)

1,2: Origin Freddy Krueger; Buckler/Alcala-a 2.30

FREDDY'S DEAD: THE FINAL NIGHTMARE
Innovation Publishing: Oct, 1991 - No. 3, Dec 1991 ($2.50, color mini-series, adapts movie)

..1-3: Dismukes (film poster artist) painted-c 2.50

FRED HEMBECK DESTROYS THE MARVEL UNIVERSE
Marvel Comics: July, 1989 ($1.50, one-shot)

1-Punisher app.; Staton-i (5 pgs.) 1.50

FRED HEMBECK SELLS THE MARVEL UNIVERSE
Marvel Comics: Oct, 1990 ($1.25, one-shot)

1-Punisher, Wolverine parodies; Hembeck/Austin-c 1.25

FREE COMICS TO YOU FROM... (name of shoe store) (Has clown on cover & another with a rabbit) (Like comics from Weather Bird & Edward's Shoes)
Shoe Store Giveaway: Circa 1956, 1960-61

Contains a comic bound with new cover - several combinations possible; some Harvey titles known. Contents determines price.

FREEDOM AGENT (Also see John Steele)
Gold Key: Apr, 1963 (12¢)

1 (10054-304)-Painted-c 2.50 7.50 28.00

FREEDOM FIGHTERS (See Justice League of America #107,108)
National Periodical Publ./DC Comics: Mar-Apr, 1976 - No. 15, July-Aug, 1978

1-Uncle Sam, The Ray, Black Condor, Doll Man, Human Bomb, & Phantom Lady begin (all former Quality characters) .85 2.60 7.00
2-9: 4,5-Wonder Woman x-over. 7-1st app. Crusaders 5.00
10-15: 10-Origin Doll Man; Cat-Man-c/story (4th app; 1st revival since Det. #325). 11-Origin The Ray. 12-Origin Firebrand. 13-Origin Black Condor. 14-Batgirl & Batwoman app. 15-Batgirl & Batwoman app.; origin Phantom Lady 2.00 6.00

NOTE: ***Buckler** c-5-11p, 13p, 14p.*

FREEDOM TRAIN
Street & Smith Publications: 1948 (Giveaway)

nn-Powell-c w/mailer 17.00 50.00 125.00

FREE SPEECHES
Oni Press: Aug, 1998 ($2.95, one-shot)

1-Speeches against comic censorship; Frank Miller-c 3.00

FREEX
Malibu Comics (Ultraverse): July, 1993 - No. 18, Mar, 1995 ($1.95)

1-3,5-14,16-18: 1-Polybagged w/trading card. 2-Some were polybagged w/card. 6-Nightman-c/story. 7-2 pg. origin Hardcase by Zeck. 17-Rune app. 2.00
1-Holographic-c edition .90 2.70 8.00
1-Ultra 5,000 limited silver ink-c 5.00
4-($2.50, 48 pgs.)-Rune flip-c/story by B. Smith (3 pgs.); 3 pg. Night Man preview 2.50
15 ($3.50)-w/Ultraverse Premiere #9 flip book; Alec Swan & Rafferty app. 3.50
Giant Size 1 (1994, $2.50)-Prime app. 2.50

NOTE: ***Simonson** c-1.*

FRENZY (Magazine) (Satire)
Picture Magazine: Apr, 1958 - No. 6, Mar, 1959

1 7.85 23.50 55.00
2-6 5.70 17.00 36.00

FRIDAY FOSTER

The Friendly Ghost, Casper #5 © HARV

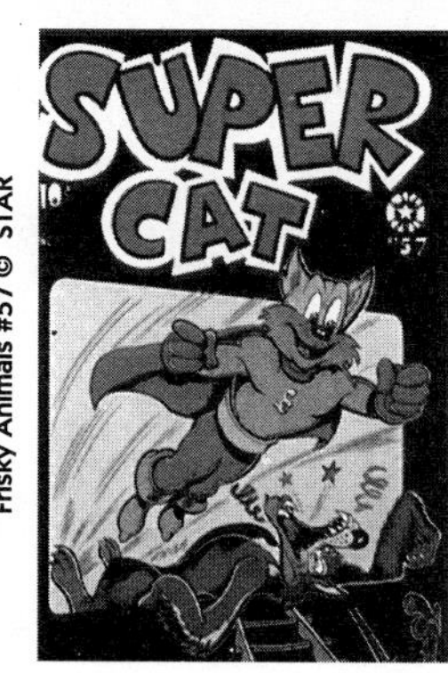

Frisky Animals #57 © STAR

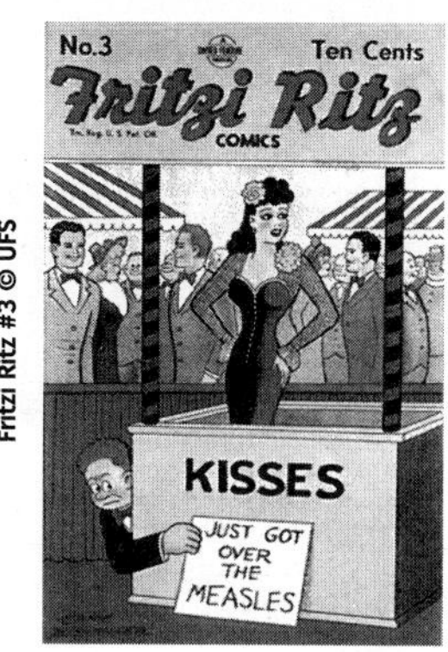

Fritzi Ritz #3 © UFS

Dell Publishing Co.: October, 1972

	GD25	FN65	NM94
1	2.00	6.00	22.00

FRIENDLY GHOST, CASPER, THE (Becomes Casper... #254 on)
Harvey Publications: Aug, 1958 - No. 224, Oct, 1982; No. 225, Oct, 1986 - No. 253, June, 1990

	GD25	FN65	NM94
1-Infinity-c	24.00	72.00	240.00
2	11.00	33.00	110.00
3-10: 6-X-Mas-c	5.50	16.50	55.00
11-20: 18-X-Mas-c	3.80	11.40	38.00
21-30	2.20	6.60	22.00
31-50	2.00	6.00	16.00
51-70,100: 54-X-Mas-c	1.75	5.25	14.00
71-99	1.50	4.50	12.00
101-130	1.25	3.75	10.00
131-159	1.10	3.30	9.00
160-163: All 52 pg. Giants	1.50	4.50	12.00
164-200		2.00	5.00
201-237: 173,179,185-Cub Scout Specials. 230-X-mas-c. 232-Valentine's-c			4.00
238-253: 238-Begin $1.00-c. 238,244-Halloween-c. 243-Last new material			2.00
American Dental Assoc. giveaway-Small size (1967, 16 pgs.)	2.50	7.50	20.00

FRIENDS OF MAXX (Also see Maxx)
Image Comics (I Before E): Apr, 1996 ($2.95)

	GD25	FN65	NM94
1-Featuring Dude Japan; Sam Kieth-c/a/scripts			3.00

FRIGHT
Atlas/Seaboard Periodicals: June, 1975 (Aug on inside)

	GD25	FN65	NM94
1-Origin The Son of Dracula; Frank Thorne-c/a			3.00

FRIGHT NIGHT
Now Comics: Oct, 1988 - No. 22, 1990 ($1.75)

	GD25	FN65	NM94
1-22: 1,2 Adapts movie. 8, 9-Evil Ed horror photo-c from movie			1.75

FRIGHT NIGHT II
Now Comics: 1989 ($3.95, 52 pgs.)

	GD25	FN65	NM94
1-Adapts movie sequel			4.00

FRISKY ANIMALS (Formerly Frisky Fables; Super Cat #56 on)
Star Publications: No. 44, Jan, 1951 - No. 55, Sept, 1953

	GD25	FN65	NM94
44-Super Cat; L.B. Cole	19.00	57.00	140.00
45-Classic L. B. Cole-c	27.00	81.00	200.00
46-51,53-55: Super Cat. 54-Super Cat-c begin	17.00	51.00	130.00
52-L. B. Cole-c/a, 3 1/2 pgs.; X-Mas-c	19.00	57.00	140.00

NOTE: *All have* ***L. B. Cole****-c. No. 47-No Super Cat.* ***Disbrow*** *a-49, 52.* ***Fago*** *a-51.*

FRISKY ANIMALS ON PARADE (Formerly Parade Comics; becomes Superspook)
Ajax-Farrell Publ. (Four Star Comic Corp.): Sept, 1957 - No. 3, Dec-Jan, 1957-1958

	GD25	FN65	NM94
1-L. B. Cole-c	16.00	48.00	120.00
2-No L. B. Cole-c	6.50	19.50	45.00
3-L. B. Cole-c	13.00	40.00	100.00

FRISKY FABLES (Frisky Animals No. 44 on)
Premium Group/Novelty Publ./Star Publ. V5#4 on: Spring, 1945 - No. 43, Oct, 1950

	GD25	FN65	NM94
V1#1-Funny animal; Al Fago-c/a #1-38	17.00	52.00	130.00
2,3(Fall & Winter, 1945)	8.50	26.00	60.00
V2#1(#4, 4/46) - 9,11,12(#15, 3/47): 4-Flag-c	6.00	18.00	42.00
10-Christmas-c	6.85	21.00	48.00
V3#1(#16, 4/47) - 12(#27, 3/48): 4-Flag-c. 7,9-Infinity-c. 10-X-Mas-c	5.70	17.00	35.00
V4#1(#28, 4/48) - 7(#34, 2-3/49)	5.70	17.00	35.00
V5#1(#35, 4-5/49) - 4(#38, 10-11/49)	5.70	17.00	35.00
39-43-L. B. Cole-c; 40-X-mas-c	19.00	56.00	140.00
Accepted Reprint No. 43 (nd); L.B. Cole-c	6.50	19.50	45.00

FRITZI RITZ (See Comics On Parade, Single Series #5, 1(reprint), Tip Top & United Comics)

FRITZI RITZ (United Comics No. 8-26)
United Features Synd./St. John No. 37?-55/Dell No. 56 on: Fall, 1948 - No. 7, 1949; No. 27, 3-4/53 - No. 36, 9-10/54; No. 42, 1/55; No. 43, 6/56 - No. 55, 9-11/57; No. 56, 12-2/57-58 - No. 59, 9-11/58

	GD25	FN65	NM94
nn(1948)-Special Fall issue; by Ernie Bushmiller	13.00	40.00	100.00
2	7.15	21.50	50.00
3-7(1949): 6-Abbie & Slats app.	5.70	17.00	40.00
27-29(1953): 29-Five pg. Abbie & Slats; 1 pg. Mamie by Russell Patterson	5.00	15.00	30.00
30-59: 31-Peanuts by Schulz (1st app.?, 11-12/53). 36-1 pg. Mamie by Patterson	4.25	13.00	28.00

NOTE: *Abbie & Slats in #6,7, 27-31. Li'l Abner in #33, 35, 36. Peanuts in #31, 43, 58, 59.*

FROGMAN COMICS
Hillman Periodicals: Jan-Feb, 1952 - No. 11, May, 1953

	GD25	FN65	NM94
1	11.00	32.00	80.00
2	5.70	17.00	40.00
3,4,6-11: 4-Meskin-a	5.35	16.00	32.00
5-Krigstein-a	5.70	17.00	40.00

FROGMEN, THE
Dell Publishing Co.: No. 1258, Feb-Apr, 1962 - No. 11, Nov-Jan, 1964-65 (Painted-c)

	GD25	FN65	NM94
Four Color 1258(#1)-Evans-a	6.40	19.00	70.00
2,3-Evans-a; part Frazetta inks in #2,3	4.50	13.50	50.00
4,6-11	2.25	6.75	25.00
5-Toth-a	3.00	9.00	35.00

FROM BEYOND THE UNKNOWN
National Periodical Publications: 10-11/69 - No. 25, 11-12/73

	GD25	FN65	NM94
1	4.00	12.00	40.00
2-10	2.25	6.75	18.00
7-11: (64 pgs.) 7-Intro Col. Glenn Merrit	2.50	7.50	20.00
12-17: (52 pgs.) 13-Wood-a(i)(r)	2.00	6.00	16.00
18-25: Star Rovers-r begin #18,19. Space Museum in #23-25	1.50	4.50	12.00

NOTE: ***N. Adams*** *c-3, 6, 8, 9.* ***Anderson*** *c-2, 4, 5, 10, 11i, 15-17, 22; reprints-3, 4, 6-8, 10, 11, 13-16, 24, 25.* ***Infantino*** *r-1-5, 7-19, 23-25; c-11p.* ***Kaluta*** *c-18, 19.* ***Gil Kane*** *a-9r.* ***Kubert*** *c-1, 7, 12-14.* ***Toth*** *a-2r.* ***Wood*** *a-13i. Photo c-22.*

FROM DUSK TILL DAWN (Movie)
Big Entertainment: 1996 ($4.95, one-shot)

	GD25	FN65	NM94
nn-Adaptation of the film; Brereton-c			5.00
nn-($9.95)Deluxe Ed. w/ new material	1.00	3.00	10.00

FROM HERE TO INSANITY (Satire) (Formerly Eh! #1-7)
(See Frantic & Frenzy)
Charlton Comics: No. 8, Feb, 1955 - V3#1, 1956

	GD25	FN65	NM94
8	13.00	40.00	100.00
9	11.00	34.00	85.00
10-Ditko-c/a (3 pgs.)	19.00	56.00	140.00
11,12-All Kirby except 4 pgs.	25.00	76.00	190.00
V3#1(1956)-Ward-c/a(2) (signed McCartney); 5 pgs. Wolverton-a; 3 pgs. Ditko-a; magazine format (cover says "Crazy, Man, Crazy" and becomes Crazy, Man, Crazy with V2#2)	37.00	112.00	280.00

FROM THE PIT
Fantagor Press: 1994 ($4.95, one-shot, mature)

	GD25	FN65	NM94
1-R. Corben-a; HP Lovecraft back-up story			5.00

FRONTIER DAYS
Robin Hood Shoe Store (Brown Shoe): 1956 (Giveaway)

Frontier Fighters #3 © DC

Frontline Combat #4 © WMG

Full Metal Fiction #6 © Everette Hartsoe

	GD25	FN65	NM94
1	3.20	8.00	16.00

FRONTIER DOCTOR (TV)
Dell Publishing Co.: No. 877, Feb, 1958 (one-shot)

	GD25	FN65	NM94
Four Color 877-Toth-a, Rex Allen photo-c	9.00	27.00	100.00

FRONTIER FIGHTERS
National Periodical Publications: Sept-Oct, 1955 - No. 8, Nov-Dec, 1956

	GD25	FN65	NM94
1-Davy Crockett, Buffalo Bill (by Kubert), Kit Carson begin (Scarce)	51.00	154.00	435.00
2	40.00	120.00	310.00
3-8	36.00	107.00	270.00

NOTE: *Buffalo Bill by* ***Kubert*** *in all.*

FRONTIER ROMANCES
Avon Periodicals/I. W.: Nov-Dec, 1949 - No. 2, Feb-Mar, 1950 (Painted-c)

	GD25	FN65	NM94
1-Used in **SOTI**, pg. 180(General reference) & illo. "Erotic spanking in a western comic book"	43.00	129.00	360.00
2 (Scarce)-Woodish-a by Stallman	33.00	100.00	250.00
I.W. Reprint #1-Reprints Avon's #1	3.50	10.50	35.00
I.W. Reprint #9-Reprints ?	2.50	7.50	22.00

FRONTIER SCOUT: DAN'L BOONE (Formerly Death Valley; The Masked Raider No. 14 on)
Charlton Comics: No. 10, Jan, 1956 - No. 13, Aug, 1956; V2#14, Mar, 1965

	GD25	FN65	NM94
10	8.50	26.00	60.00
11-13(1956)	5.35	16.00	32.00
V2#14(3/65)	4.00	10.00	20.00

FRONTIER TRAIL (The Rider No. 1-5)
Ajax/Farrell Publ.: No. 6, May, 1958

	GD25	FN65	NM94
6	4.25	13.00	26.00

FRONTIER WESTERN
Atlas Comics (PrPl): Feb, 1956 - No. 10, Aug, 1957

	GD25	FN65	NM94
1	17.00	52.00	130.00
2,3,6-Williamson-a, 4 pgs. each	12.00	36.00	90.00
4,7,9,10: 10-Check-a	7.15	21.50	50.00
5-Crandall, Baker, Davis-a; Williamson text illos	11.00	32.00	80.00
8-Crandall, Morrow, & Wildey-a	7.15	21.50	50.00

NOTE: ***Baker*** *a-9.* ***Colan*** *a-2, 6.* ***Drucker*** *a-3, 4.* ***Heath*** *c-5.* ***Maneely*** *c/a-2, 7, 9.* ***Maurera*** *a-2.* ***Romita*** *a-7.* ***Severin*** *c-6, 8, 10.* ***Tuska*** *a-2.* ***Wildey*** *a-5, 8. Ringo Kid in No. 4.*

FRONTLINE COMBAT
E. C. Comics: July-Aug, 1951 - No. 15, Jan, 1954

	GD25	FN65	NM94
1-Severin/Kurtzman-a	49.00	147.00	490.00
2	31.00	92.00	275.00
3	22.00	66.00	200.00
4-Used in **SOTI**, pg. 257; contains "Airburst" by Kurtzman which is his personal all-time favorite story	20.00	60.00	180.00
5	18.00	53.00	160.00
6-10	14.00	43.00	130.00
11-15	10.50	32.00	95.00

NOTE: ***Davis*** *a-in all; c-11, 12.* ***Evans*** *a-10-15.* ***Heath*** *a-1.* ***Kubert*** *a-14.* ***Kurtzman*** *a-1-5; c-1-9.* ***Severin*** *a-5-7, 9, 13, 15.* ***Severin/Elder*** *a-2-11; c-10.* ***Toth*** *a-8, 12.* ***Wood*** *a-1-4, 6-10, 12-15; c-13-15. Special issues: No. 7 (Iwo Jima), No. 9 (Civil War), No. 12 (Air Force).*
(Canadian reprints known; see Table of Contents.)

FRONTLINE COMBAT
Russ Cochran/Gemstone Publishing: Aug, 1995 - Present ($2.00/$2.50)

	GD25	FN65	NM94
1-4-E.C. reprints in all			2.00
5-14-($2.50)			2.50

FRONT PAGE COMIC BOOK
Front Page Comics (Harvey): 1945

	GD25	FN65	NM94
1-Kubert-a; intro. & 1st app. Man in Black by Powell; Fuje-c	35.00	104.00	260.00

FROST AND FIRE (See DC Science Fiction Graphic Novel)

FROSTY THE SNOWMAN
Dell Publishing Co.: No. 359, Nov, 1951 - No. 1272, Dec-Feb?/1961-62

	GD25	FN65	NM94
Four Color 359 (#1)	7.00	22.00	80.00
Four Color 435	3.60	11.00	40.00
Four Color 514,601,661	3.60	11.00	40.00
Four Color 748,861,950,1065,1153,1272	3.00	9.00	35.00

FRUITMAN SPECIAL
Harvey Publications: Dec, 1969 (68 pgs.)

	GD25	FN65	NM94
1-Funny super hero	2.00	6.00	20.00

F-TROOP (TV)
Dell Publishing Co.: Aug, 1966 - No. 7, Aug, 1967 (All have photo-c)

	GD25	FN65	NM94
1	8.00	25.00	90.00
2-7	5.00	15.00	55.00

FUGITIVES FROM JUSTICE
St. John Publishing Co.: Feb, 1952 - No. 5, Oct, 1952

	GD25	FN65	NM94
1	17.00	52.00	130.00
2-Matt Baker-r/Northwest Mounties #2; Vic Flint strip reprints begin	18.00	54.00	135.00
3-Reprints panel from Authentic Police Cases that was used in **SOTI** with changes; Tuska-a	18.00	54.00	135.00
4	7.85	23.50	55.00
5-Last Vic Flint-r; bondage-c	9.50	28.75	72.00

FUGITOID
Mirage Studios: 1985 (B&W, magazine size, one-shot)

	GD25	FN65	NM94
1-Ties into Teenage Mutant Ninja Turtles #5			3.00

FULL COLOR COMICS
Fox Features Syndicate: 1946

	GD25	FN65	NM94
nn	11.00	32.00	80.00

FULL METAL FICTION
London Night Studios: Mar, 1997 - Present ($3.95, B&W, mature)

	GD25	FN65	NM94
1-8-Anthology: 1-Razor			3.95

FULL OF FUN
Red Top (Decker Publ.)(Farrell)/I. W. Enterprises: Aug, 1957 - No. 2, Nov, 1957; 1964

	GD25	FN65	NM94
1(1957)-Funny animal; Dave Berg-a	5.70	17.00	35.00
2-Reprints Bingo, the Monkey Doodle Boy	4.00	11.00	22.00
8-I.W. Reprint('64)	1.25	3.75	10.00

FUN AT CHRISTMAS (See March of Comics No. 138)

FUN CLUB COMICS (See Interstate Theatres...)

FUN COMICS (Formerly Holiday Comics #1-8; Mighty Bear #13 on)
Star Publications: No. 9, Jan, 1953 - No. 12, Oct, 1953

	GD25	FN65	NM94
9-(25¢ Giant)-L. B. Cole X-Mas-c; X-Mas issue	19.00	56.00	140.00
10-12-L. B. Cole-c. 12-Mighty Bear-c/story	16.00	48.00	120.00

FUNDAY FUNNIES (See Famous TV..., and Harvey Hits No. 35,40)

FUN-IN (TV)(Hanna-Barbera)
Gold Key: Feb, 1970 - No. 10, Jan, 1972; No. 11, 4/74 - No. 15, 12/74

	GD25	FN65	NM94
1-Dastardly & Muttley in Their Flying Machines; Perils of Penelope Pitstop in #1-4; It's the Wolf in all	4.50	13.50	50.00
2-4,6-Cattanooga Cats in 2-4	2.25	6.75	26.00
5,7-Motormouse & Autocat, Dastardly & Muttley in both; It's the Wolf in #7	2.75	8.00	30.00
8,10-The Harlem Globetrotters, Dastardly & Muttley in #10	2.25	6.75	24.00
9-Where's Huddles?, Dastardly & Muttley, Motormouse & Autocat app.	2.75	8.00	30.00
11-15: 11-Butch Cassidy. 12,15-Speed Buggy. 13-Hair Bear Bunch. 14-Inch High Private Eye	1.65	5.00	18.00

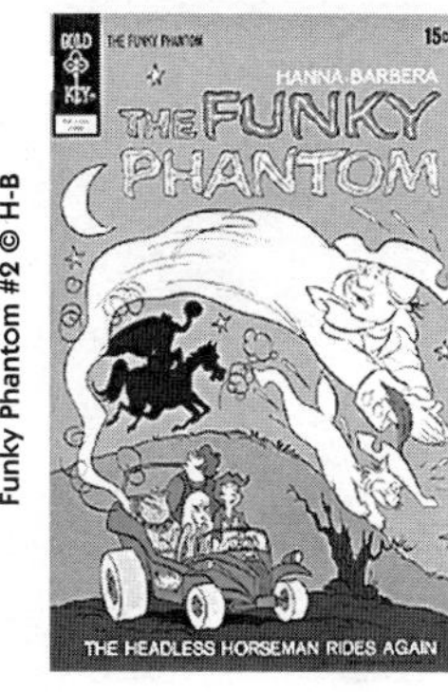

Funky Phantom #2 © H-B

The Funnies #4 © DELL

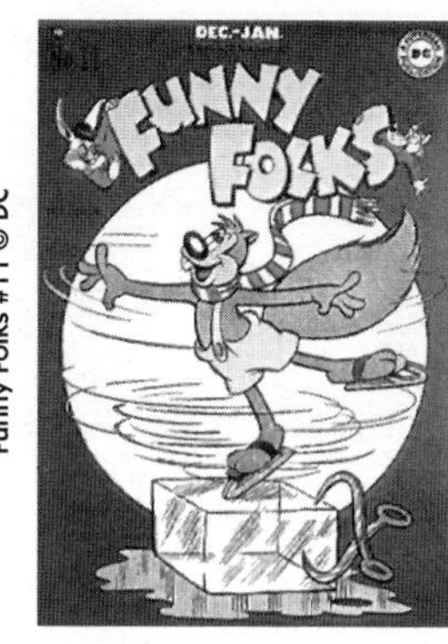

Funny Folks #11 © DC

GD25 FN65 NM94

FUNKY PHANTOM, THE (TV)
Gold Key: Mar, 1972 - No. 13, Mar, 1975 (Hanna-Barbera)

	GD25	FN65	NM94
1	3.60	11.00	40.00
2-5	1.80	5.50	20.00
6-13	1.40	4.20	14.00

FUNLAND
Ziff-Davis (Approved Comics): No date (1940s) (25¢)

	GD25	FN65	NM94
nn-Contains games, puzzles, cut-outs, etc.	13.00	40.00	100.00

FUNLAND COMICS
Croyden Publishers: 1945

	GD25	FN65	NM94
1-Funny animal	13.00	40.00	100.00

FUNNIES, THE (New Funnies No. 65 on)
Dell Publishing Co.: Oct, 1936 - No. 64, May, 1942

	GD25	FN65	NM94
1-Tailspin Tommy, Mutt & Jeff, Alley Oop (1st app?), Capt. Easy (1st app.), Don Dixon begin	325.00	975.00	2300.00
2-Scribbly by Mayer begins (1st app.)	137.00	412.00	925.00
3	110.00	330.00	700.00
4,5: 4-Christmas-c	83.00	249.00	575.00
6-10	62.00	187.00	425.00
11-20: 16-Christmas-c	56.00	170.00	380.00
21-29: 25-Crime Busters by McWilliams(4pgs.)	44.00	132.00	290.00
30-John Carter of Mars (origin/1st app.) begins by Edgar Rice Burroughs; Warner Bros.' Bosko-c (4/39)	106.00	318.00	900.00
31-44: 33-John Coleman Burroughs art begins on John Carter. 34-Last funny-c. 35-(9/39)-Mr. District Attorney begins; based on radio show	65.00	195.00	550.00
45-Origin/1st app. Phantasmo, the Master of the World (Dell's 1st super-hero, 7/40) & his sidekick Whizzer McGee	59.00	177.00	500.00
46-50: 46-The Black Knight begins, ends #62	43.00	129.00	360.00
51-56-Last ERB John Carter of Mars	41.00	122.00	325.00
57-Intro. & origin Captain Midnight (7/41)	165.00	495.00	1400.00
58-60: 58-Captain Midnight-c begin, end #63	68.00	204.00	575.00
61-Andy Panda begins by Walter Lantz	56.00	168.00	475.00
62,63: 63-Last Captain Midnight-c; bondage-c	56.00	168.00	475.00
64-Format change; Oswald the Rabbit, Felix the Cat, Li'l Eight Ball app.; origin & 1st app. Woody Woodpecker in Oswald; last Capt. Midnight; Oswald, Andy Panda, Li'l Eight Ball-c	88.00	264.00	750.00

NOTE: ***Mayer*** *c-26, 48.* ***McWilliams*** *art in many issues on "Rex King of the Deep". Alley Oop c-17, 20. Captain Midnight c-57(i/2), 58-63. John Carter c-35-37, 40. Phantasmo c-45-56, 57(1/2), 58-61(part). Rex King c-38, 39, 42. Tailspin Tommy c-41.*

FUNNIES ANNUAL, THE
Avon Periodicals: 1959 ($1.00, approx. 7x10", B&W; tabloid-size)

	GD25	FN65	NM94
1-(Rare)-Features the best newspaper comic strips of the year: Archie, Snuffy Smith, Beetle Bailey, Henry, Blondie, Steve Canyon, Buz Sawyer, The Little King, Hi & Lois, Popeye, & others. Also has a chronological history of the comics from 2000 B.C. to 1959.	41.00	122.00	325.00

FUNNIES ON PARADE (Premium)
Eastern Color Printing Co.: 1933 (Probably the 1st comic book)
(36 pgs., slick cover) No date or publisher listed

	GD25	FN65	VF82	NM94
nn-Contains Sunday page reprints of Mutt & Jeff, Joe Palooka, Hairbreadth Harry, Reg'lar Fellers, Skippy, & others (10,000 print run). This book was printed for Proctor & Gamble to be given away & came out before Famous Funnies or Century of Comics.	1000.00	3000.00	6000.00	11,000.00

FUNNY ANIMALS (See Fawcett's Funny Animals)
Charlton Comics: Sept, 1984 - No. 2, Nov, 1984

	GD25	FN65	NM94
1,2-Atomic Mouse-r			1.00

FUNNYBONE (... The Laugh-Book of Comical Comics)
La Salle Publishing Co.: 1944 (25¢, 132 pgs.)

	GD25	FN65	NM94
nn	25.00	74.00	185.00

GD25 FN65 NM94

FUNNY BOOK (...Magazine for Young Folks) (Hocus Pocus No. 9)
Parents' Magazine Press (Funny Book Publishing Corp.):
Dec, 1942 - No. 9, Aug-Sept, 1946 (Comics, stories, puzzles, games)

	GD25	FN65	NM94
1-Funny animal; Alice In Wonderland app.	12.00	36.00	90.00
2-Gulliver in Giant-Land	6.50	19.50	45.00
3-9: 4-Advs. of Robin Hood. 9-Hocus-Pocus strip	5.35	16.00	32.00

FUNNY COMICS
Modern Store Publ.: 1955 (7¢, 5x7", 36 pgs.)

	GD25	FN65	NM94
1-Funny animal	1.60	4.00	8.00

FUNNY COMIC TUNES (See Funny Tunes)

FUNNY FABLES
Decker Publications (Red Top Comics): Aug, 1957 - V2#2, Nov, 1957

	GD25	FN65	NM94
V1#1	4.00	12.00	24.00
V2#1,2	3.20	8.00	16.00

FUNNY FILMS (Features funny animal characters from films)
American Comics Group(Michel Publ./Titan Publ.): Sept-Oct, 1949 - No. 29, May-June, 1954 (No. 1-4: 52 pgs.)

	GD25	FN65	NM94
1-Puss An' Boots, Blunderbunny begin	17.00	50.00	125.00
2	9.30	28.00	65.00
3-10: 3-X-Mas-c	5.70	17.00	40.00
11-20	5.00	15.00	30.00
21-29	4.00	10.50	21.00

FUNNY FOLKS (Hollywood... on cover only No. 16-26; becomes Hollywood Funny Folks No. 27 on)
National Periodical Publications: April-May, 1946 - No. 26, June-July, 1950 (52 pgs., #16 on)

	GD25	FN65	NM94
1-Nutsy Squirrel begins (1st app.) by Rube Grossman	39.00	116.00	290.00
2	17.00	52.00	130.00
3-5: 4-1st Nutsy Squirrel-c	13.00	38.00	95.00
6-10: 6,9-Nutsy Squirrel-c begin	9.30	28.00	70.00
11-26: 16-Begin 52 pg. issues (10-11/48)	8.50	26.00	60.00

NOTE: ***Sheldon Mayer*** *a-in some issues.* ***Post*** *a-18. Christmas c-12.*

FUNNY FROLICS
Timely/Marvel Comics (SPI): Summer, 1945 - No. 5, Dec, 1946

	GD25	FN65	NM94
1-Sharpy Fox, Puffy Pig, Krazy Krow	19.00	56.00	140.00
2	10.00	30.00	75.00
3,4	7.85	23.50	55.00
5-Kurtzman-a	9.30	28.00	65.00

FUNNY FUNNIES
Nedor Publishing Co.: April, 1943 (68 pgs.)

	GD25	FN65	NM94
1-Funny animals; Peter Porker app.	17.00	50.00	125.00

FUNNYMAN (Also see Cisco Kid Comics & Extra Comics)
Magazine Enterprises: Dec, 1947; No. 1, Jan, 1948 - No. 6, Aug, 1948

	GD25	FN65	NM94
nn(12/47)-Prepublication B&W undistributed copy by Siegel & Shuster-(5-3/4x8"), 16 pgs.; Sold at auction in 1997 for $575.00			
1-Siegel & Shuster-a in all; Dick Ayers 1st pro work (as assistant) on 1st few issues	37.00	110.00	275.00
2	23.00	70.00	175.00
3-6	20.00	60.00	150.00

FUNNY MOVIES (See 3-D Funny Movies)

FUNNY PAGES (Formerly The Comics Magazine)
Comics Magazine Co./Ultem Publ.(Chesler)/Centaur Publications:
No. 6, Nov, 1936 - No. 42, Oct, 1940

	GD25	FN65	NM94
V1#6 (nn, nd)-The Clock begins (2 pgs., 1st app.), ends #11; The Clock is the 1st masked comic book hero	153.00	460.00	1300.00
(Estimated up to 10 total copies exist; prices vary widely on this book)			
7-11	65.00	195.00	550.00

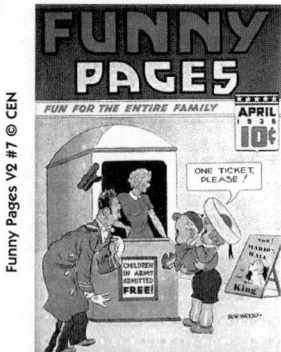

Funny Pages V2 #7 © CEN

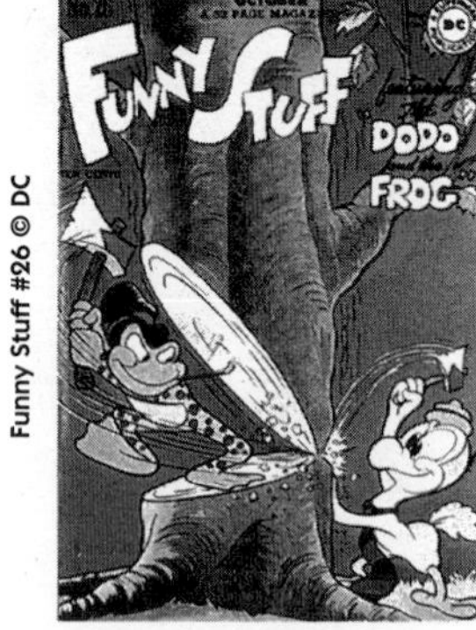

Funny Stuff #26 © DC

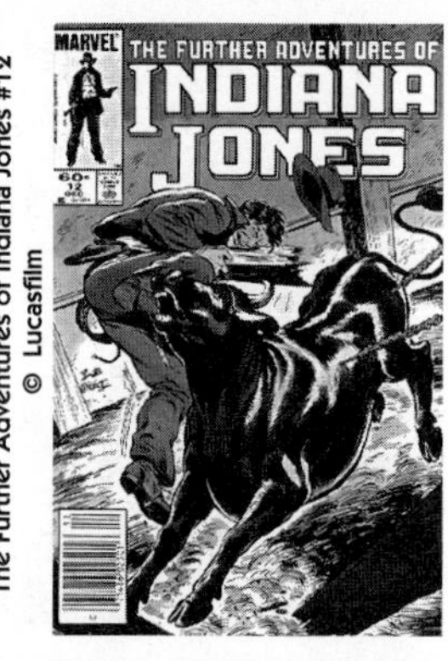

The Further Adventures of Indiana Jones #12 © Lucasfilm

	GD25	FN65	NM94
V2#1 (9/37)(V2#2 on-c; V2#1 in indicia)	44.00	132.00	375.00
V2#2 (10/37)(V2#3 on-c; V2#2 in indicia)	44.00	132.00	375.00
3(11/37)-5	44.00	132.00	375.00
6(1st Centaur, 3/38)	77.00	231.00	650.00
7-9	52.00	156.00	440.00
10(Scarce, 9/38)-1st app. of The Arrow by Gustavson (Blue costume)	235.00	705.00	2000.00
11,12	94.00	282.00	800.00
V3#1-6: 6,8-Last funny covers	91.00	273.00	775.00
7-1st Arrow-c (9/39)	164.00	492.00	1400.00
8,9: 9-Tarpe Mills jungle-c	94.00	282.00	800.00
10-2nd Arrow-c	135.00	405.00	1150.00
V4#1(1/40, Arrow-c)-(Rare)-The Owl & The Phantom Rider app.; origin Mantoka, Maker of Magic by Jack Cole. Mad Ming begins, ends #42; Tarpe Mills-a	164.00	492.00	1400.00
35-Classic Arrow-c	164.00	492.00	1400.00
36-38-Mad Ming-c	91.00	273.00	775.00
39-42-Arrow-c. 42-Last Arrow	124.00	372.00	1050.00

NOTE: *Biro c-V2#9.* ***Burgos*** *c-V3#10.* ***Jack Cole*** *a-V2#3, 7, 8, 10, 11, V3#2, 6, 9, 10, V4#1, 37; c-V3#2, 4.* ***Eisner*** *a-V1#7, 8?, 10.* ***Ken Ernst*** *a-V1#7, 8.* ***Everett*** *a-V2#11 (illos).* ***Filchock*** *c-V2#10, V3#6.* ***Gill Fox*** *a-V2#11.* ***Sid Greene*** *a-39.* ***Guardineer*** *a-V2#2, 3, 5.* ***Gustavson*** *a-V2#5, 11, 12, V3#1-10, 35, 38-42; c-V3#7, 35, 39-42.* ***Bob Kane*** *a-V3#1.* ***McWilliams*** *a-V2#12, V3#1, 3-6.* ***Tarpe Mills*** *a-V3#8-10, V4#1; c-V3#9.* ***Ed Moore Jr.*** *a-V2#12.* ***Schwab*** *c-V3#1.* ***Bob Wood*** *a-V2#2, 3, 8, 11, V3#6, 9, 10; c-V2#6, 7. Arrow c-V3#7, 10, V4#1, 35, 40-42.*

FUNNY PICTURE STORIES (Comic Pages V3#4 on)
Comics Magazine Co./Centaur Publications: Nov, 1936 - V3#3, May, 1939

	GD25	FN65	NM94
V1#1-The Clock begins (c-feature)(see Funny Pages for 1st app.)	263.00	789.00	2500.00
2	91.00	273.00	775.00
3-9: 4-Eisner-a; X-Mas-c. 7-Racial humor-c	65.00	195.00	550.00
V2#1 (9/37; V1#10 on-c; V2#1 in indicia)-Jack Strand begins	43.00	129.00	360.00
2 (10/37; V1#11 on-c; V2#2 in indicia)	43.00	129.00	360.00
3-5: 4-Xmas-c	40.00	120.00	320.00
6-(1st Centaur, 3/38)	71.00	213.00	600.00
7-11	40.00	120.00	320.00
V3#1-3	39.00	117.00	290.00
Laundry giveaway (16-20 pgs., 1930s)-slick-c	25.00	75.00	190.00

NOTE: ***Biro*** *c-V2#1, 8, 9, 11.* ***Guardineer*** *a-V1#11; c-V2#6, V3#5.* ***Bob Wood*** *c/a-V1#11, V2#2; c-V2#3, 5.*

FUNNY STUFF (Becomes The Dodo & the Frog No. 80)
All-American/National Periodical Publications No. 7 on: Summer, 1944 - No. 79, July-Aug, 1954 (#1-7 are quarterly)

	GD25	FN65	NM94
1-The Three Mouseketeers (ends #28) & The "Terrific Whatzit" begin; Sheldon Mayer-a	82.00	246.00	700.00
2-Sheldon Mayer-a	41.00	123.00	330.00
3-5: 3-Flash parody. 5-All Mayer-a/scripts issue	28.00	84.00	210.00
6-10 10-(6/46)	19.00	57.00	140.00
11-17,19,20: 20-1st Dodo & the Frog-c (4/47)	14.00	42.00	105.00
18-The Dodo & the Frog (2/47, 1st app?) begin?; X-Mas-c	25.00	75.00	185.00
21,23-30: 24-Infinity-c	9.30	28.00	70.00
22-Superman cameo	39.00	117.00	300.00
31-79: 70-1st Bo Bunny by Mayer & begins	7.50	22.50	52.00

NOTE: ***Mayer*** *a-1-8, 55, ,57, 58, 61, 62, 64, 65, 68, 70, 72, 74-79; c-2, 5, 6, 8.*

FUNNY STUFF
National Periodical Publications (Wheaties Giveaway): 1946 (6-1/2x8-1/4")

	GD25	FN65	NM94
nn-(Scarce)-Dodo & the Frog, Three Mouseketeers, etc.; came taped to Wheaties box; never found in better than fine	100.00	300.00	-

FUNNY STUFF STOCKING STUFFER
DC Comics: Mar, 1985 ($1.25, 52 pgs.)

	GD25	FN65	NM94
1-Almost every DC funny animal featured			1.25

FUNNY 3-D
Harvey Publications: December, 1953 (25¢, came with 2 pair of glasses)

	GD25	FN65	NM94
1-Shows cover in 3-D on inside	10.00	30.00	75.00

FUNNY TUNES (Animated Funny Comic Tunes No. 16-22; Funny Comic Tunes No. 23, on covers only; formerly Krazy Komics #15; Oscar No. 24 on)
U.S.A. Comics Magazine Corp. (Timely): No. 16, Summer, 1944 - No. 23, Fall, 1946

	GD25	FN65	NM94
16-Silly Seal, Ziggy Pig, Krazy Krow begin	11.00	34.00	85.00
17 (Fall/44)-Becomes Gay Comics #18 on?	9.30	28.00	65.00
18-22: 21-Super Rabbit app.	7.15	21.50	50.00
23-Kurtzman-a	9.30	28.00	65.00

FUNNY TUNES (Becomes Space Comics #4 on)
Avon Periodicals: July, 1953 - No. 3, Dec-Jan, 1953-54

	GD25	FN65	NM94
1-Space Mouse, Peter Rabbit, Merry Mouse, Spotty the Pup, Cicero the Cat begin; all continue in Space Comics	8.50	26.00	60.00
2,3	5.70	17.00	38.00

FUNNY WORLD
Marbak Press: 1947 - No. 3, 1948

	GD25	FN65	NM94
1-The Berrys, The Toodles & other strip-r begin	6.50	19.50	45.00
2,3	5.70	17.00	35.00

FUNTASTIC WORLD OF HANNA-BARBERA, THE (TV)
Marvel Comics Group: Dec, 1977 - No. 3, June, 1978 ($1.25, oversized)

	GD25	FN65	NM94
1-3: 1-The Flintstones Christmas Party(12/77). 2-Yogi Bear's Easter Parade(3/78). 3-Laff-a-lympics(6/78)	2.90	8.70	32.00

FUN TIME
Ace Periodicals: Spring, 1953; No. 2, Sum, 1953; No. 3(nn), Fall, 1953; No. 4, Wint, 1953-54

	GD25	FN65	NM94
1-(25¢, 100 pgs.)-Funny animal	7.85	23.50	55.00
2-4 (All 25¢, 100 pgs.)	11.00	34.00	85.00

FUN WITH SANTA CLAUS (See March of Comics No. 11, 108, 325)

FURTHER ADVENTURES OF CYCLOPS AND PHOENIX (Also see Adventures of Cyclops and Phoenix, Uncanny X-Men & X-Men)
Marvel Comics: June, 1996 - No. 4, Sept, 1996 ($1.95, limited series)

	GD25	FN65	NM94
1-4: Origin of Mr. Sinister; Peter Milligan scripts; John Paul Leon-c/a(p). 2-4-Apocalypse app.			2.00
Trade Paperback (1997, $14.99) r/1-4			14.99

FURTHER ADVENTURES OF INDIANA JONES, THE (Movie) (Also see Indiana Jones and the Last Crusade & Indiana Jones and the Temple of Doom)
Marvel Comics Group: Jan, 1983 - No. 34, Mar, 1986

	GD25	FN65	NM94
1-34: 1-Byrne/Austin-a; Austin-c. 2-Byrne/Austin-c/a			1.50

NOTE: ***Austin*** *a-1i, 2i, 6i, 9i; c-1, 2i, 6i, 9i.* ***Byrne*** *a-1p, 2p; c-2p.* ***Chaykin*** *a-6p; c-6p, 8p-10p.* ***Ditko*** *a-21p, 25-28, 34.* ***Golden*** *c-24, 25.* ***Simonson*** *c-9. Painted c-14.*

FURTHER ADVENTURES OF NYOKA, THE JUNGLE GIRL, THE (See Nyoka)
AC Comics: 1988 - No. 5, 1989 ($1.95, color; $2.25/$2.50, B&W)

	GD25	FN65	NM94
1,2 ($1.95)-Bill Black-a plus reprints			2.00
3,4 ($2.25, B&W); 3-Photo-c. 4-Krigstein-r			2.30
5 ($2.50, B&W)-Reprints plus movie photos			2.50

FURY (Straight Arrow's Horse...) (See A-1 No. 119)

FURY (TV) (See March Of Comics #200)
Dell Publishing Co./Gold Key: No. 781, Mar, 1957 - Nov, 1962 (All photo-c)

	GD25	FN65	NM94
Four Color 781	7.00	22.00	80.00
Four Color 885,975,1031,1080,1133,1172,1218,1296, 01292-208(#1-'62)	5.50	16.50	60.00
10020-211(11/62-G.K.)	5.50	16.50	60.00

FURY
Marvel Comics: May, 1994 ($2.95, one-shot)

	GD25	FN65	NM94
1-Ironman, Red Skull, FF, Hatemonger, Logan, Scorpio app.; Origin Nick Fury			3.00

Fury / Agent 13 #1 © MAR

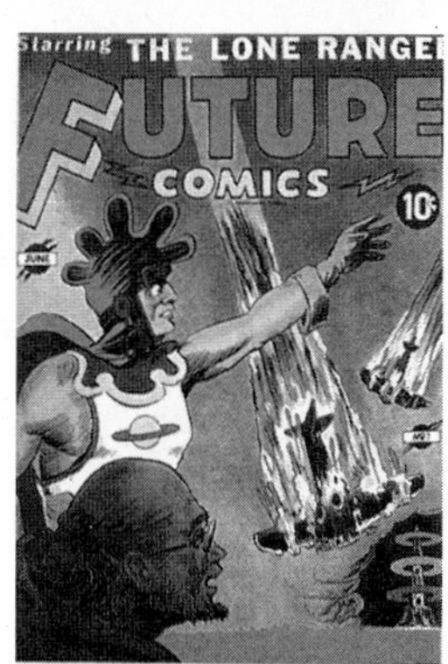

Future Comics #1 © DMP

Gambit #2 © MAR

GD25 FN65 NM94

FURY/ AGENT 13
Marvel Comics: June, 1998 - No. 2, July, 1998 ($2.99, limited series)
1,2-Nick Fury returns 3.00

FURY OF FIRESTORM, THE (Becomes Firestorm The Nuclear Man #65 on) (Also see Firestorm)
DC Comics: June, 1982 - No. 64, Oct, 1987 (75¢ on)
1-Intro The Black Bison; brief origin 2.00
2-64: 4-JLA x-over. 17-1st app. Firehawk. 21-Death of Killer Frost. 22-Origin. 23-Intro. Byte. 24-(6/84)-1st app. Blue Devil & Bug (origin); origin Byte. 34-1st app./origin Killer Frost II. 39-Weasel's ID revealed 41,42-Crisis x-over. 48-Intro. Moonbow. 53-Origin/1st app. Silver Shade. 55,56-Legends x-over. 58-1st app./origin Parasite 1.00
61-Test cover variant; Superman logo 2.25 6.80 25.00
Annual 1-4: 1(1983), 2(1984), 3(1985), 4(1986) 1.25
NOTE: ***Colan*** *a-19p, Annual 4p.* ***Giffen*** *a-Annual 4p.* ***Gil Kane*** *c-30.* ***Nino*** *a-37.* ***Tuska*** *a-(p)-17, 18, 32, 45.*

FURY OF HELLINA (Also see Hellina)
Lightning Comics: Jan, 1995 ($2.75, B&W)
1 2.75

FURY OF SHIELD
Marvel Comics: Apr, 1995 - No. 4, July, 1995 ($2.50/$1.95, limited series)
1 ($2.50)-Foil-c 2.50
2-4: 4-Bagged w/ decoder 2.00

FUSION
Eclipse Comics: Jan, 1987 - No. 17, Oct, 1989 ($2.00, B&W, Baxter paper)
1-17: 11-The Weasel Patrol begins (1st app.?) 2.00

FUTURE COMICS
David McKay Publications: June, 1940 - No. 4, Sept, 1940
1-(6/40, 64 pgs.)-Origin The Phantom (4 pgs.); The Lone Ranger (8 pgs.) & Saturn Against the Earth (4 pgs.) begin 224.00 672.00 1900.00
2 106.00 318.00 900.00
3,4 88.00 264.00 750.00

FUTURETECH
Mushroom Comics: Jan, 1996 ($2.50, limited series)
1-Flipbook w/SWARM 2.50

FUTURE WORLD COMICS
George W. Dougherty: Summer, 1946 - No. 2, Fall, 1946
1,2: H. C. Kiefer-c; preview of the World of Tomorrow 23.00 70.00 175.00

FUTURE WORLD COMIX (Warren Presents...)
Warren Publications: Sept, 1978
1-Corben, Morrow, Nino, Sutton-a; Todd-c .90 2.70 9.00

FUTURIANS, THE (See Marvel Graphic Novel #9)
Lodestone Publishing/Eternity Comics: Sept, 1985 - No. 3, 1985 ($1.50)
1-3: Indicia title "Dave Cockrum's..." 1.50
Graphic Novel 1 ($9.95, Eternity)-r/#1-3, plus never published #4 issue 1.00 3.00 10.00

G-8 (See G-Eight)

GABBY (Formerly Ken Shannon) (Teen humor)
Quality Comics Group: No. 11, Jul, 1953; No. 2, Sep, 1953 - No. 9, Sep, 1954
11(#1)(7/53) 6.50 19.50 45.00
2 4.25 13.00 28.00
3-9 4.00 10.00 20.00

GABBY GOB (See Harvey Hits No. 85, 90, 94, 97, 100, 103, 106, 109)

GABBY HAYES ADVENTURE COMICS
Toby Press: Dec, 1953
1-Photo-c 13.00 40.00 100.00

GD25 FN65 NM94

GABBY HAYES WESTERN (Movie star) (See Monte Hale, Real Western Hero & Western Hero)
Fawcett Publications/Charlton Comics No. 51 on: Nov, 1948 - No. 50, Jan, 1953; No. 51, Dec, 1954 - No. 59, Jan, 1957
1-Gabby & his horse Corker begin; photo front/back-c begin 47.00 142.00 400.00
2 23.00 68.00 170.00
3-5 15.00 46.00 115.00
6-10: 9-Young Falcon begins 13.00 38.00 95.00
11-20: 19-Last photo back-c 10.00 30.00 75.00
21-49: 20,22,24,26,28,29-(52 pgs.) 7.85 23.50 55.00
50-(1/53)-Last Fawcett issue; last photo-c? 9.30 28.00 65.00
51-(12/54)-1st Charlton issue; photo-c 9.30 28.00 65.00
52-59(1955-57): 53,55-Photo-c. 58-Swayze-a 5.35 16.00 32.00
Quaker Oats Giveaway nn's(#1-5, 1951, 2-1/2x7") (Kagran Corp.)-...In Tracks of Guilt, ...In the Fence Post Mystery, ...In the Accidental Sherlock, ... In the Frame-Up, ...In the Double Cross Brand known 9.30 28.00 70.00

GAGS
United Features Synd./Triangle Publ. No. 9 on: July, 1937 - V3#10, Oct, 1944 (13-3/4x10-3/4")
1(7/37)-52 pgs.; 20 pgs. Grin & Bear It, Fellow Citizen 5.70 17.00 35.00
V1#9 (36 pgs.) (7/42) 4.00 11.00 22.00
V3#10 3.60 9.00 18.00

GALACTIC GUARDIANS
Marvel Comics: July, 1994 - No. 4, Oct, 1994 ($1.50, limited series)
1-4 1.50

GALACTIC WAR COMIX (Warren Presents... on cover)
Warren Publications: December, 1978
nn-Wood, Williamson-r .90 2.70 9.00

GALLANT MEN, THE (TV)
Gold Key: Oct, 1963 (Photo-c)
1(1008-310)-Manning-a 2.25 6.75 18.00

GALLEGHER, BOY REPORTER (Disney, TV)
Gold Key: May, 1965
1(10149-505)-Photo-c 1.50 4.50 12.00

GAMBIT (See X-Men #266 & X-Men Annual #14)
Marvel Comics: Dec, 1993 - No. 4, Mar, 1994 ($2.00, limited series)
1-($2.50)-Lee Weeks-c/a in all; gold foil stamped-c. 5.00
1 (Gold) 1.50 4.50 15.00
2-4 3.00

GAMBIT
Marvel Comics: Sept, 1997 - No. 4, Dec, 1997 ($2.50, limited series)
1-4-Janson-a/ Mackie & Kavanagh-s 2.50

GAMBIT AND THE X-TERNALS
Marvel Comics: Mar, 1995 - No. 4, July, 1995 ($1.95, limited series)
1-Age of Apocalyse 3.00
2-4 2.00

GAMEBOY (Super Mario covers on all)
Valiant: 1990 - No. 5 ($1.95, coated-c)
1-5: 3,4-Layton-c. 4-Morrow-a. 5-Layton-c(i) 4.00

GAMERA
Dark Horse Comics: Aug, 1996 - No. 4, Nov, 1996 ($2.95, limited series)
1-4 3.00

GAMMARAUDERS
DC Comics: Jan, 1989 - No. 10, Dec, 1989 ($1.25/$1.50/$2.00)

Gangland #2 © DC

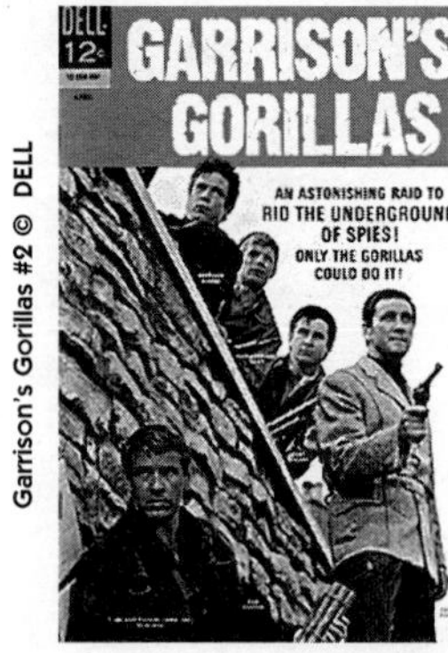

Garrison's Gorillas #2 © DELL

Geisha #2 © Andi Watson

	GD25	FN65	NM94
1-10-Based on TSR game			2.00

GAMORRA SWIMSUIT SPECIAL
Image Comics (WildStorm Productions): June, 1996 ($2.50, one-shot)

	GD25	FN65	NM94
1-Campbell wraparound-c; pinups			2.50

GANDY GOOSE (Movies/TV)(See All Surprise, Giant Comics Edition #5A &10, Paul Terry's Comics & Terry-Toons)
St. John Publ. Co./Pines No. 5,6: Mar, 1953 - No. 5, Nov, 1953; No. 5, Fall, 1956 - No. 6, Sum/58

	GD25	FN65	NM94
1-All St. John issues are pre-code	8.50	26.00	60.00
2	4.25	13.00	28.00
3-5(1953)(St. John)	4.00	12.00	24.00
5,6(1956-58)(Pines)-CBS Televison Presents...	3.60	9.00	18.00

GANG BUSTERS (See Popular Comics #38)
David McKay/Dell Publishing Co.: 1938 - 1943

	GD25	FN65	NM94
Feature Books 17(McKay)('38)-1st app.	48.00	144.00	525.00
Large Feature Comic 10('39)-(Scarce)	48.00	144.00	525.00
Large Feature Comic 17('41)	29.00	87.00	315.00
Four Color 7(1940)	33.00	98.00	360.00
Four Color 23,24('42-43)	26.00	77.00	280.00

GANG BUSTERS (Radio/TV)(Gangbusters #14 on)
National Periodical Publications: Dec-Jan, 1947-48 - No. 67, Dec-Jan, 1958-59 (No. 1-23: 52 pgs.)

	GD25	FN65	NM94
1	74.00	222.00	630.00
2	37.00	111.00	275.00
3-5	25.00	75.00	190.00
6-10: 9-Dan Barry-a. 9,10-Photo-c	20.00	60.00	150.00
11-13-Photo-c	17.00	51.00	125.00
14,17-Frazetta-a, 8 pgs. each. 14-Photo-c	35.00	105.00	260.00
15,16,18-20	12.00	36.00	90.00
21-25,27-30	11.00	33.00	80.00
26-Kirby-a	12.00	36.00	90.00
31-44: 44-Last Pre-code (2-3/55)	9.30	28.00	70.00
45-67	7.85	23.50	55.00

NOTE: ***Barry** a-6, 8, 10. **Drucker** a-51. **Moreira** a-48, 50, 59. **Roussos** a-8.*

GANGLAND
DC Comics (Vertigo): Jun, 1998 - No. 4, Sept, 1998 ($2.95, limited series)

	GD25	FN65	NM94
1-4:Crime anthology by various. 2-Corben-a			3.00

GANGSTERS AND GUN MOLLS
Avon Per./Realistic Comics: Sept, 1951 - No. 4, June, 1952 (Painted c-1-3)

	GD25	FN65	NM94
1-Wood-a, 1 pg; c-/Avon paperback #292	41.00	124.00	330.00
2-Check-a, 8 pgs.; Kamen-a; Bonnie Parker story	32.00	96.00	240.00
3-Marijuana mentioned; used in **POP**, pg. 84,85	29.00	86.00	215.00
4-Syd Shores-c	23.00	70.00	175.00

GANGSTERS CAN'T WIN
D. S. Publishing Co.: Feb-Mar, 1948 - No. 9, June-July, 1949 (All 52 pgs?)

	GD25	FN65	NM94
1-True crime stories	27.00	82.00	205.00
2	13.00	38.00	95.00
3-6: 4-Acid in face story	11.00	32.00	80.00
7-9	9.30	28.00	65.00

NOTE: ***Ingles** a-5, 6. **McWilliams** a-5, 7. **Reinman** c-6.*

GANG WORLD
Standard Comics: No. 5, Nov, 1952 - No. 6, Jan, 1953

	GD25	FN65	NM94
5-Bondage-c	16.00	48.00	120.00
6	13.00	38.00	95.00

GARGOYLE (See The Defenders #94)
Marvel Comics Group: June, 1985 - No. 4, Sept, 1985 (75¢, limited series)

	GD25	FN65	NM94
1-4: 1-Wrightson-c; character from Defenders			1.00

GARGOYLES (TV cartoon)
Marvel Comics: Feb, 1995 - No. 17, June, 1996 ($2.50)

	GD25	FN65	NM94
1-17: Based on animated series			2.50

GARRISON'S GORILLAS (TV)
Dell Publishing Co.: Jan, 1968 - No. 4, Oct, 1968; No. 5, Oct, 1969 (Photo-c)

	GD25	FN65	NM94
1	3.20	9.60	35.00
2-5: 5-Reprints #1	2.10	6.20	23.00

GARY GIBSON COMICS (Donut club membership)
National Dunking Association: 1950 (Included in donut box with pin and card)

	GD25	FN65	NM94
1-Western soft-c, 16 pgs.; folded into the box	2.50	7.50	20.00

GASM
Stories, Layouts & Press, Inc.: Nov, 1977 - nn(No. 4), Jun, 1978 (B&W/color)

	GD25	FN65	NM94
1-Mark Wheatley-s/a; Gene Day-s/a; Workman-a	1.80	5.40	18.00
nn(#2, 2/78) Day-s/a; Wheatley-a; Workman-a	1.20	3.60	12.00
nn(#3, 4/78) Day-s/a; Wheatley-a; Corben-a	1.80	5.40	18.00
nn(#4, 6/78) Hempel-a; Howarth-a; Corben-a	2.00	6.00	20.00

GASOLINE ALLEY (Top Love Stories No. 3 on?)
Star Publications: Sept-Oct, 1950 - No. 2, Dec, 1950 (Newspaper-r)

	GD25	FN65	NM94
1-Contains 1 pg. intro. history of the strip (The Life of Skeezix); reprints 15 scenes of highlights from 1921-1935, plus an adventure from 1935 and 1936 strips; a 2-pg. filler is included on the life of the creator Frank King, with photo of the cartoonist.	19.00	56.00	140.00
2-(1936-37 reprints)-L. B. Cole-c	23.00	68.00	170.00

(See Super Book No. 21)

GASP!
American Comics Group: Mar, 1967 - No. 4, Aug, 1967 (12¢)

	GD25	FN65	NM94
1	2.80	8.40	28.00
2-4	2.00	6.00	16.00

GAY COMICS (Honeymoon No. 41)
Timely Comics/USA Comic Mag. Co. No. 18-24: Mar, 1944 (no month); No. 18, Fall, 1944 - No. 40, Oct, 1949

	GD25	FN65	NM94
1-Wolverton's Powerhouse Pepper; Tessie the Typist begins; 1st app. Willie (one shot)	42.00	126.00	335.00
18-(Formerly Funny Tunes #17?)-Wolverton-a	24.00	72.00	180.00
19-29: Wolverton-a in all. 21,24-6 pg., 7 pg. Powerhouse Pepper; additional 2 pg. story in 24). 23-7 pg Wolverton story & 2 two pg stories(total of 11pgs.). 24,29-Kurtzman-a (24-"Hey Look"(2))	19.00	57.00	140.00
30,33,36,37-Kurtzman's "Hey Look"	8.50	26.00	60.00
31-Kurtzman's "Hey Look" (1), Giggles 'N' Grins (1-1/2)	8.50	26.00	60.00
32,35,38-40: 35-Nellie The Nurse begins?	6.50	19.50	45.00
34-Three Kurtzman's "Hey Look"	9.30	28.00	65.00

GAY COMICS (Also see Smile, Tickle, & Whee Comics)
Modern Store Publ.: 1955 (7¢, 5x7-1/4", 52 pgs.)

	GD25	FN65	NM94
1	1.20	3.00	6.00

GAY PURR-EE (See Movie Comics)

GAZILLION
Image Comics: Nov, 1998 ($2.50, one-shot)

	GD25	FN65	NM94
1-Howard Shum-s/ Keron Grant-a			2.50

GEEK, THE (See Brother Power... & Vertigo Visions)

G-8 AND HIS BATTLE ACES
Gold Key: Oct, 1966

	GD25	FN65	NM94
1 (10184-610)-Painted-c	2.80	8.40	30.00

G-8 AND HIS BATTLE ACES
Blazing Comics: 1991 ($1.50, one-shot)

	GD25	FN65	NM94
1-Glanzman-a; Truman-c			1.50

NOTE: *Flip book format with "The Spider's Web" #1 on other side w/**Glanzman**-a, **Truman**-c.*

GEISHA
Oni Press: Sept, 1998 - No. 4 ($2.95, limited series)

Gemini Blood #5 © DC

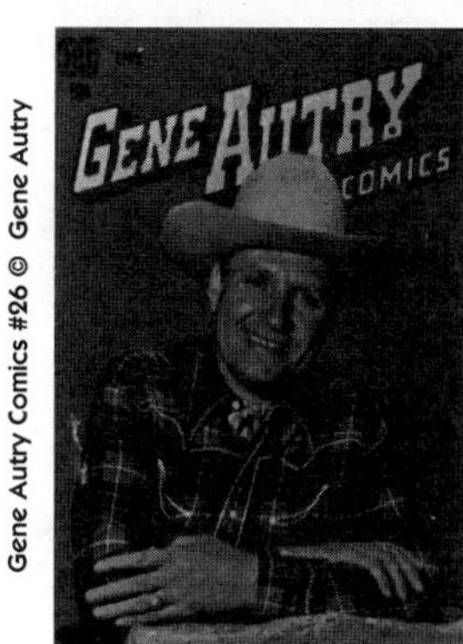

Gene Autry Comics #26 © Gene Autry

Generation X #35 © MAR

GD25 FN65 NM94

1-3-Andi Watson-s/a. 2-Adam Warren-c 2.95

GEM COMICS
Spotlight Publishers: Apr, 1945 (52 pgs)

1-Little Mohee, Steve Strong app.; Jungle bondage-c
24.00 72.00 180.00

GEMINI BLOOD
DC Comics (Helix): Sept, 1996 - No. 9, May, 1997 ($2.25, limited series)

1-9:5-Simonson-c 2.25

GENE AUTRY (See March of Comics No. 25, 28, 39, 54, 78, 90, 104, 120, 135, 150 & Western Roundup under Dell Giants)

GENE AUTRY COMICS (Movie, Radio star; singing cowboy)
Fawcett Publications: 1941 (On sale 12/31/41) - No. 10, 1943 (68 pgs.) (Dell takes over with No. 11)

	GD25	FN65	NM94
1 (Rare)-Gene Autry & his horse Champion begin	700.00	2100.00	7000.00
2-(1942)	124.00	372.00	1050.00
3-5: 3-(11/1/42)	85.00	255.00	725.00
6-10	71.00	213.00	600.00

GENE AUTRY COMICS (...& Champion No. 102 on)
Dell Publishing Co.: No. 11, 1943 - No. 121, Jan-Mar, 1959 (TV - later issues)

	GD25	FN65	NM94
11 (1943, 60 pgs.)-Continuation of Fawcett series; photo back-c	52.00	157.00	575.00
12 (2/44, 60 pgs.)	48.00	143.00	525.00
Four Color 47(1944, 60 pgs.)	39.00	117.00	425.00
Four Color 57(11/44),66('45)(52 pgs. each)	36.00	109.00	400.00
Four Color 75,83('45, 36 pgs. each)	29.00	87.00	315.00
Four Color 93,100('45-46, 36 pgs. each): 100-Photo-c	25.00	74.00	270.00
1(5-6/46, 52 pgs.)	40.00	120.00	440.00
2(7-8/46)-Photo-c begin, end #111	22.00	66.00	240.00
3-5: 4-Intro Flapjack Hobbs	16.00	48.00	175.00
6-10	13.00	38.00	140.00
11-20: 20-Panhandle Pete begins	11.00	33.00	120.00
21-29(36pgs.)	8.00	24.00	90.00
30-40(52pgs.)	6.75	20.50	75.00
41-56(52pgs.)	5.50	16.50	60.00
57-66(36pgs.): 58-X-mas-c	4.00	12.00	45.00
67-80(52pgs.)	4.00	12.00	45.00
81-90(52pgs.): 82-X-mas-c. 87-Blank inside-c	3.20	9.60	35.00
91-99(36pgs. No. 91-on). 94-X-mas-c	2.50	7.50	28.00
100	2.90	8.70	32.00
101-111-Last Gene Autry photo-c	2.40	7.00	26.00
112-121-All Champion painted-c, most by Savitt	2.00	6.00	22.00
...Adventure Comics And Play-Fun Book ('47)-32 pgs., 8x6-1/2"; games, comics, magic (Pillsbury premium)	21.00	63.00	230.00
Quaker Oats Giveaway(1950)-2-1/2x6-3/4"; 5 different versions; "Death Card Gang", "Phantoms of the Cave", "Riddle of Laughing Mtn.", "Secret of Lost Valley", "Bond of the Broken Arrow" (came in wrapper) each...	8.50	26.50	95.00
3-D Giveaway(1953)-Pocket-size; 5 different	9.00	27.00	100.00

NOTE: *Photo back covers 4-18, 20-45, 48-65.* ***Manning*** *a-118.* ***Jesse Marsh*** *art: 4-Color No. 66, 75, 93, 100, No. 1-25, 27-37, 39, 40.*

GENE AUTRY'S CHAMPION (TV)
Dell Publ. Co.: No. 287, 8/50; No. 319, 2/51; No. 3, 8-10/51 - No. 19, 8-10/55

	GD25	FN65	NM94
Four Color 287(#1)('50, 52pgs.)-Photo-c	8.50	26.50	95.00
Four Color 319(#2, '51), 3: 2-Painted-c begin, most by Sam Savitt	3.60	11.00	40.00
4-19: 19-Last painted-c	2.75	8.00	30.00

GENE AUTRY TIM (Formerly Tim) (Becomes Tim in Space)
Tim Stores: 1950 (Half-size) (B&W Giveaway)

nn-Several issues (All Scarce) 11.00 32.00 80.00

GENE DOGS
Marvel Comics UK: Oct, 1993 - No. 4, Jan, 1994 ($1.75, limited series)

1-($2.75)-Polybagged w/4 trading cards 2.75
2-4: 2-Vs. Genetix 1.75

GENERAL DOUGLAS MACARTHUR
Fox Features Syndicate: 1951

nn-True life story 17.00 52.00 130.00

GENERIC COMIC, THE
Marvel Comics Group: Apr, 1984 (one-shot)

1 2.00

GENERATION HEX
DC Comics (Amalgam): June, 1997 ($1.95, one-shot)

1-Milligan-s/ Pollina & Morales-a 1.95

GENERATION NEXT
Marvel Comics: Mar, 1995 - No. 4, June, 1995 ($1.95, limited series)

1-Age of Apocalypse; Scott Lobdell scripts & Chris Bachalo-c/a 5.00
2-4 3.00

GENERATION X (See Gen 13/ Generation X)
Marvel Comics: Oct, 1994 - Present ($1.50/$1.95/$1.99)

	GD25	FN65	NM94
Collectors Preview ($1.75)			2.00
"Ashcan" Edition			1.00
1/2 (San Diego giveaway)	.85	2.60	7.00
1-($3.95)-Wraparound chromium-c; Scott Lobdell scripts & Chris Bachalo-a begins.	.85	2.60	7.00
2-($1.95)-Deluxe edition, Bachalo-a			3.00
3,4-($1.95)-Deluxe Edition; Bachalo-a			3.00
2-4-Standard Edition; Bachalo-a			2.00
5-24, 26-28, -1(7/97): 5-Returns from "Age of Apocalypse," begin $1.95-c. 6-Bachalo-a(p) ends, returns #17. 7-Roger Cruz-a(p). 10-Omega Red-c/app. 13,14-Bishop-app. 17-Stan Lee app. (Stan Lee scripts own dialogue); Bachalo/Buckingham-a; Onslaught update. 18-Toad cameo. 20-Franklin Richards app; Howard the Duck cameo. 21-Howard the Duck app. 22-Nightmare app.			2.00
25-($2.99)-Wraparound-c. Black Tom, Howard the Duck app.			3.00
29-47: 29-Begin $1.99-c, "Operation Zero Tolerance". 33-Hama-s. 38-Dodson-a begins. 40-Penance ID revealed			1.99
'95 Special-($3.95)			4.00
'96 Special-($2.95)-Wraparound-c; Jeff Johnson-c/a			3.00
'97 Special-($2.99)-Wraparound-c;			2.99
'98 Annual-($3.50)-vs. Dracula			3.50
...Underground Special 1 (5/98, $2.50, B&W)			2.50

GENERATION X/ GEN 13 (Also see Gen 13/ Generation X)
Marvel Comics: 1997 ($3.99, one-shot)

1-Robinson-s/Larroca-a(p) 4.00

GENE RODDENBERRY'S LOST UNIVERSE
Tekno Comix: Apr, 1995 - No. 6, Dec, 1995 ($1.95)

0 (11/95, $2.25) 2.25
1-3-w/ bound-in game piece & trading card 2.00
4-6: 4-bound-in trading card 2.00

GENE RODDENBERRY'S XANDER IN LOST UNIVERSE
Tekno Comix: Dec, 1995 - No. 8, July, 1996 ($2.25)

1-8: 1-5-Jae Lee-c. 4-Polybagged. 8-Includes Pt. 5 of The Big Bang x-over. 2.25

GENESIS (See DC related titles)
DC Comics: Oct, 1997 - No. 4, Oct, 1997 ($1.95, weekly limited series)

1-4: Byrne-s/Wagner-a(p) in all. 2.00

GENESIS: THE #1 COLLECTION (WildStorm Archives)
WildStorm Productions: 1998 ($9.99, TPB, B&W)

Gen 12 #1 © Wildstorm Prod.

Gen 13 #9 © Wildstorm Prod.

Gen 13: Magical Drama Queen Roxy #2 (variant cover) © Wildstorm Prod.

nn-Reprints #1 issues of WildStorm titles and pin-ups 10.00

GENETIX
Marvel Comics UK: Oct, 1993 - No. 6, Mar, 1994 ($1.75, limited series)

1-($2.75)-Polybagged w/4 cards; Dark Guard app. 2.75
2-6: 2-Intro Tektos. 4-Vs. Gene Dogs 1.75

GENSAGA
Entity Comics: 1995 ($2.50/$6.75, one-shot)

1 2.50
1 ($6.75)-bagged w/PC Game .85 2.60 6.75

GEN 12 (Also see Gen 13 and Team 7)
Image Comics (WildStorm Productions): Feb, 1998 - No. 5, June, 1998 ($2.50, limited series)

1-5: 1-Team 7 & Gen 13 app.; wraparound-c 2.50

GEN 13 (Also see Wild C.A.T.S. #1 & Deathmate Black #2)
Image Comics (WildStorm Productions): Feb, 1994 - No. 5, July 1994 ($1.95, limited series)

0 (8/95, $2.50)-Ch. 1 w/Jim Lee-p; Ch.4 w/Charest-p 4.00
1/2 1.50 4.50 15.00
1-($2.50)-Created by Jim Lee 2.00 6.00 20.00
1-2nd printing 3.00
1-"3-D" Edition (9/97, $4.95)-w/glasses 4.95
2-($2.50) 1.50 4.50 15.00
3-Pitt-c & story 1.00 3.00 10.00
4-Pitt-c & story; wraparound-c .90 2.70 8.00
5 5.00
5-Alternate Portacio-c; see Deathblow #5 1.00 3.00 10.00
...Collected Edition ('94, $12.95)-r/#1-5 .85 2.60 7.00
...Rave ($1.50, 3/95)-wraparound-c 2.00

NOTE: *Issues 1-4 contain coupons redeemable for the ashcan edition of Gen 13 #0. Price listed is for a complete book.*

GEN 13
Image Comics (WildStorm Productions): Mar, 1995 - Present ($2.50)

1-A (Charge)-Campbell/Gardner-c .85 2.60 7.00
1-B (Thumbs Up)-Campbell/Gardner-c .85 2.60 7.00
1-C (Lil' GEN 13)-Art Adams-c 1.00 3.00 10.00
1-D (Barbari-GEN)-Simon Bisley-c 1.00 3.00 10.00
1-E (Your Friendly Neighborhood Grunge)-John Cleary-c 1.00 3.00 10.00
1-F (GEN 13 Goes Madison Ave.)-MIchael Golden-c 1.00 3.00 10.00
1-G (Lin-GEN-re)-Michael Lopez-c 1.20 3.60 12.00
1-H (GEN-et Jackson)-Jason Pearson-c 1.20 3.60 12.00
1-I (That's the way we became GEN 13)-Campbell/Gibson-c 1.00 3.00 10.00
1-J (All Dolled Up)-Campbell/McWeeney-c 1.00 3.00 10.00
1-K (Verti-GEN)-Joe Dunn-c 1.00 3.00 10.00
1-L (Picto-Fiction) 1.20 3.60 12.00
1-M (Do it Yourself Cover) 1.00 3.00 10.00
1-"3-D" Edition (2/98, $4.95)-w/glasses 5.00
2 ($1.95, Newsstand)-WildStorm Rising Pt. 4; bound-in card 2.00
2-12: 2-($2.50, Direct Market)-WildStorm Rising Pt. 4, bound-in card. 6,7-Jim Lee-c/a(p). 9-Ramos-a. 10-Fire From Heaven Pt. 3. 11-Fire From Heaven Pt. 9 3.00
11-($4.95)-Special European Tour Edition; chromium-c 25.00
13A,13B,13C-($1.30, 13 pgs.): 13A-Archie & Friends app. 13B-Bone-c/app.; Teenage Mutant Ninja Turtles, Madman, Spawn & Jim Lee app. 1.50
14-20: 20-Last Campbell-a 2.50
21-24 2.50
25-($3.50)-Two covers by Campbell and Charest 3.50
25-($3.50)-Voyager Pack w/Danger Girl preview 3.50
26-36: 26-Arcudi-s/Frank-a begins. 33-Flip book w/Planetary preview

34-Back-up story by Art Adams 2.50
Annual 1 (1997, $2.95) Ellis-s/ Dillon-c/a. 2.95
...Archives (4/98, $12.99) B&W reprints of mini-series, #0,1/2,1-13ABC; includes cover gallery and sourcebook 13.00
...European Vacation ($6.95, trade paperback) r/6,7 6.95
...Lost in Paradise ($6.95, trade paperback) r/3-5 6.95
...#13 A,B&C Collected Edition ($6.95, TPB) r/#13A,B&C 6.95
Variant Collection-Four editions (all 13 variants w/Chromium variant-limited, signed) 21.00 61.00 225.00

GEN 13 BOOTLEG
Image Comics (WildStorm): Nov, 1996 - No. 20, Jul, 1998 ($2.50)

1-Alan Davis-a; alternate costumes-c 3.00
1-Team falling variant-c 2.00 6.00
2-7: 2-Alan Davis-a. 5,6-Terry Moore-s. 7-Robinson-s/Scott Hampton-a. 3.00
8-10-Adam Warren-s/a .85 2.60 7.00
11-17,19,20: 11,12-Lopresti-s/a & Simonson-s. 13-Wieringo-s/a. 14-Mariotte-s/Phillips-a. 15,16-Strnad-s/Shaw-a 2.50
18-Altieri-s/a(p)/c 2.50
18-Variant-c by Bruce Timm 4.00
Annual 1 (2/98, $2.95) Ellis-s/Dillon-c/a 1.20 3.00
... Grunge: The Movie (12/97, $9.95) r/#8-10, Warren-c 1.00 3.00 10.00
...Vol. 1 TPB (10/98, $11.95) r/#1-4 11.95

GEN 13/ GENERATION X (Also see Generation X / Gen 13)
Image Comics (WildStorm Publications): July, 1997 ($2.95, one-shot)

1-Choi-s/ Art Adams-p/Garner-i. Variant covers by Adams/Garner and Campbell/McWeeney 3.00
1-($4.95) 3-D Edition w/glasses; Campbell-c 5.00

GEN 13 INTERACTIVE
Image Comics (WildStorm): Oct, 1997 - No. 3, Dec, 1997 ($2.50, lim. series)

1-3-Internet voting used to determine storyline 2.50

GEN 13/ MAXX
Image Comics (WildStorm Publications): Dec, 1995 ($3.50, one-shot)

1-Wm. Messner-Loebs story, 1st Tomm Coker-c/a. 3.50

GEN 13 : MAGICAL DRAMA QUEEN ROXY
Image Comics (WildStorm): Oct, 1998 - No. 3, Dec, 1998 ($3.50, lim. series)

1-3-Adam Warren-s/c/a; manga style 3.50
1-($6.95) Dynamic Forces Ed. w/Varaint Warren-c 6.95
2-Variant-c by Hiroyuki Utatane 3.50

GEN 13 /MONKEYMAN & O'BRIEN
Image Comics (WildStorm): Jun, 1998 - No. 2, July, 1998 ($2.50, lim. series)

1,2-Art Adams-s/a(p); 1-Two covers 2.50
1-($4.95) Chromium-c 10.00
1-($6.95) Dynamic Forces Ed. 10.00

GEN 13: ORDINARY HEROES
Image Comics (WildStorm Publications): Feb, 1996 - No. 2, July, 1996 ($2.50, limited series)

1-Adam Hughes-c/a/scripts 3.00

GEN 13 3-D SPECIAL
Image Comics (WildStorm Publications): 1997 ($4.95, one-shot)

1-Art Adams-s/a(p) 4.95

GEN 13: THE UNREAL WORLD
Image Comics (WildStorm Productions): July, 1996 ($2.95, one-shot)

1-Humberto Ramos-c/a 3.00

GEN 13: 'ZINE
Image Comics (WildStorm Productions): Dec, 1996 ($1.95, B&W, digest size)

1-Campbell/Garner-c 2.00

GENTLE BEN (TV)

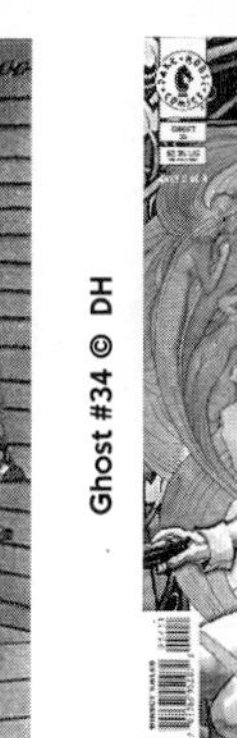

Georgie Comics #3 © MAR

Ghost #34 © DH

Ghost in the Shell #1 © DH

	GD25	FN65	NM94

Dell Publishing Co.: Feb, 1968 - No. 5, Oct, 1969 (All photo-c)

1	2.50	7.50	28.00
2-5: 5-Reprints #1	1.40	4.20	16.00

GEOMANCER (Also see Eternal Warrior: Fist & Steel)
Valiant: Nov, 1994 - No. 8, June, 1995 ($3.75/$2.25)

1 ($3.75)-Chromium wraparound-c; Eternal Warrior app.			3.75
2-8			2.25

GEORGE OF THE JUNGLE (TV)(See America's Best TV Comics)
Gold Key: Feb, 1969 - No. 2, Oct, 1969 (Jay Ward)

1	11.25	34.00	125.00
2	8.00	24.00	85.00

GEORGE PAL'S PUPPETOONS (Funny animal puppets)
Fawcett Publications: Dec, 1945 - No. 18, Dec, 1947; No. 19, 1950

1-Captain Marvel-c	39.00	117.00	300.00
2	20.00	60.00	150.00
3-10	12.00	36.00	90.00
11-19	10.00	30.00	75.00

GEORGIE COMICS (...& Judy Comics #20-35?; see All Teen & Teen Comics)
Timely Comics/GPI No. 1-34: Spr, 1945 - No. 39, Oct, 1952 (#1-3 are quarterly)

1-Dave Berg-a	20.00	60.00	150.00
2	9.30	28.00	70.00
3-5,7,8	7.85	23.50	55.00
6-Georgie visits Timely Comics	10.00	30.00	75.00
9,10-Kurtzman's "Hey Look" (1 & ?); Margie app.	8.50	26.00	60.00
11,12: 11-Margie, Millie app.	5.70	17.00	38.00
13-Kurtzman's "Hey Look", 3 pgs.	7.15	21.50	50.00
14-Wolverton-a(1 pg.); Kurtzman's "Hey Look"	8.50	26.00	60.00
15,16,18-20	5.35	16.00	32.00
17,29-Kurtzman's "Hey Look", 1 pg.	6.50	19.50	45.00
21-24,27,28,30-39: 21-Anti-Wertham editorial	4.25	13.00	28.00
25-Painted-c by classic pin-up artist Peter Driben	7.15	21.50	50.00
26-Logo design swipe from Archie Comics	5.35	16.00	32.00

GERALD McBOING-BOING AND THE NEARSIGHTED MR. MAGOO (TV)
(Mr. Magoo No. 6 on)
Dell Publishing Co.: Aug-Oct, 1952 - No. 5, Aug-Oct, 1953

1	8.00	25.00	90.00
2-5	6.40	19.00	70.00

GERONIMO (See Fighting Indians of the Wild West!)
Avon Periodicals: 1950 - No. 4, Feb, 1952

1-Indian Fighter; Maneely-a; Texas Rangers-r/Cowpuncher #1; Fawcette-c	16.00	48.00	120.00
2-On the Warpath; Kit West app.; Kinstler-c/a	10.00	30.00	70.00
3-And His Apache Murderers; Kinstler-c/a(2); Kit West-r/Cowpuncher #6	10.00	30.00	70.00
4-Savage Raids of; Kinstler-c & inside front-c; Kinstlerish-a by McCann(3)	8.50	26.00	60.00

GERONIMO JONES
Charlton Comics: Sept, 1971 - No. 9, Jan, 1973

1	1.10	3.30	11.00
2-9		2.00	6.00
Modern Comics Reprint #7('78)			3.50

GETALONG GANG, THE (TV)
Marvel Comics (Star Comics): May, 1985 - No. 6, Mar, 1986

1-6: Saturday morning TV stars			2.00

GET LOST
Mikeross Publications/New Comics: Feb-Mar, 1954 - No. 3, June-July, 1954 (Satire)

1-Andru/Esposito-a in all?	25.00	76.00	190.00
2-Andru/Esposito-c; has 4 pg. E.C. parody featuring "The Sewer Keeper"	18.00	54.00	135.00
3-John Wayne 'Hondo' parody	14.00	42.00	105.00
1,2 (10,12/87-New Comics)-B&W r-original			1.00

GET SMART (TV)
Dell Publ. Co.: June, 1966 - No. 8, Sept, 1967 (All have Don Adams photo-c)

1	8.50	26.50	95.00
2-Ditko-a	5.50	16.50	60.00
3-8: 3-Ditko-a(p)	5.00	15.00	55.00

GHOST (...Comics #9)
Fiction House Magazines: 1951(Winter) - No. 11, Summer, 1954

1-Most covers by Whitman	57.00	171.00	485.00
2-Ghost Gallery & Werewolf Hunter stories	31.00	92.00	230.00
3-9: 3,6,7,9-Bondage-c. 9-Abel, Discount-a	25.00	76.00	190.00
10,11-Dr. Drew by Grandenetti in each, reprinted from Rangers; 11-Evans-r/Rangers #39; Grandenetti-r/Rangers #49	24.00	72.00	180.00

GHOST (See Comic's Greatest World)
Dark Horse Comics: Apr, 1995 - No. 36, Apr, 1998 ($2.50/$2.95)

1-Adam Hughes-a	.90	2.70	8.00
2,3-Hughes-a			4.00
4-24: 4-Barb Wire app. 5,6-Hughes-c. 12-Ghost/Hellboy preview. 15,21-X app. 18,19-Barb Wire app.			2.50
25-($3.50)-48 pgs. special			3.50
26-36: 26-Begin $2.95-c. 29-Flip book w/Timecop. 33-36-Jade Cathedral; Harris painted-c			2.95
Special 1 (7/94, $3.95, 48 pgs.)	.85	2.60	7.00
Special 2 (6/98, $3.95) Barb Wire app.			3.95
...Nocturnes (1996, $9.95, trade paperback)-r/#1-3 & 5			10.00
...Stories (1995, $9.95, trade paperback)-r/Early Ghost app.			10.00

GHOST (Volume 2)
Dark Horse Comics: Sept, 1998 - Present ($2.95)

1,2-Ryan Benjamin-c/Zanier-a			2.95

GHOST AND THE SHADOW
Dark Horse Comics: Dec, 1995 ($2.95, one-shot)

1-Moench scripts			3.00

GHOST/HELLBOY
Dark Horse Comics: May, 1996 - No. 2, June, 1996 ($2.50, limited series)

1,2: Mike Mignola-c/scripts & breakdowns; Scott Benefiel finished-a			2.50

GHOST BREAKERS (Also see Racket Squad in Action, Red Dragon & (CC) Sherlock Holmes Comics)
Street & Smith Publications: Sept, 1948 - No. 2, Dec, 1948 (52 pgs.)

1-Powell-c/a(3); Dr. Neff (magician) app.	38.00	114.00	285.00
2-Powell-c/a(2); Maneely-a	30.00	90.00	225.00

GHOSTBUSTERS (TV) (Also, see Real...and Slimer)
First Comics: Feb, 1987 - No. 6, Aug, 1987 ($1.25)

1-6: Based on new animated TV series			1.30

GHOSTBUSTERS II
Now Comics: Oct, 1989 - No. 3, Dec, 1989 ($1.95, mini-series)

1-3: Movie Adaptation			2.00

GHOST CASTLE (See Tales of...)

GHOSTDANCING
DC Comics (Vertigo): Mar, 1995 - No. 6, Sept, 1995 ($1.95, limited series)

1-6: Case-c/a			2.00

GHOST IN THE SHELL (Manga)
Dark Horse: Mar, 1995 - No. 8, Oct, 1995 ($3.95, B&W/color, lim. series)

1	2.25	6.75	25.00
2	2.50	7.60	28.00

Ghostly Haunts #44 © CC

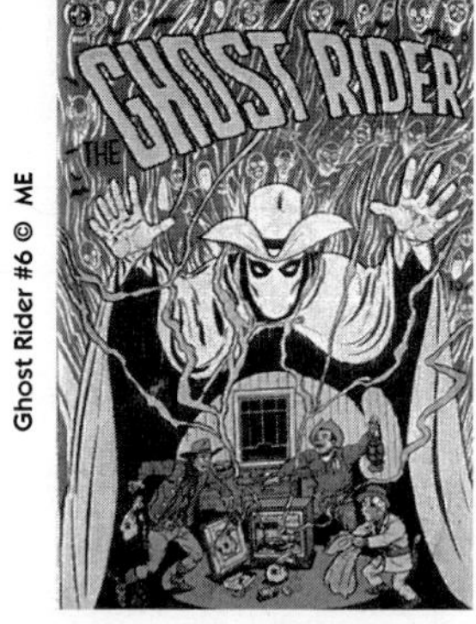

Ghost Rider #6 © ME

Ghost Rider #7 © MAR

GD25 FN65 NM94

3 1.50 4.50 15.00
4-8 1.00 3.00 10.00

GHOSTLY HAUNTS (Formerly Ghost Manor)
Charlton Comics: #20, 9/71 - #53, 12/76; #54, 9/77 - #55, 10/77; #56, 1/78 - #58, 4/78

20 1.20 3.60 12.00
21-40: 27-Dr. Graves x-over. 32-New logo. 33-Back to old logo. 39-Origin & 1st app. Destiny Fox .90 2.70 9.00
41-58: .85 2.60 7.00
40,41(Modern Comics-r, 1977, 1978) 3.00
NOTE: ***Ditko*** *a-22-25, 27, 28, 31-34, 36-41, 43-48, 50, 52, 54, 56r; c-22-27, 29, 30, 33-37, 47, 54, 56.* ***Glanzman*** *a-20.* ***Howard*** *a-27, 30, 35, 40-43, 48, 54, 57.* ***Kim*** *a-38, 41, 57.* ***Larson*** *a-48, 50.* ***Newton*** *c/a-42.* ***Staton*** *a-32, 35; c-28, 46.* ***Sutton*** *c-33, 37, 39, 41.*

GHOSTLY TALES (Formerly Blue Beetle No. 50-54)
Charlton Comics: No. 55, 4-5/66 - No. 124, 12/76; No. 125, 9/77 - No. 169, 10/84

55-Intro. & origin Dr. Graves 2.60 7.80 26.00
56-70-Dr. Graves ends 1.75 5.25 14.00
71-100 .90 2.70 9.00
101-124: 107-Sutton, Wood-a. 114-Newton-a .85 2.60 7.00
125-169 4.00
NOTE: ***Aparo*** *a-65, 66, 68, 72, 141r, 142r; c-71, 72, 74-76, 81, 146r.* ***Ditko*** *a-55-58, 60, 61, 67, 69-73, 75-90, 92-95, 97, 99-118, 120-122, 125r, 126r, 131-133r, 136-141r, 143r, 144r, 152, 155, 161, 163; c-67, 69, 73, 77, 78, 83, 84, 86-90, 92-97, 99, 102, 109, 111, 118, 120-122, 125, 131-133, 163.* ***Glanzman*** *a-167.* ***Howard*** *a-95, 98, 99, 108, 117, 129; c-98, 107, 120, 121, 161.* ***Larson*** *a-117, 119.* ***Morisi*** *a-83, 84, 86.* ***Newton*** *a-114; c-115(painted).* ***Palais*** *a-61.* ***Staton*** *a-161; c-117.* ***Sutton*** *a-106, 107, 111-114, 127, 130; c-100, 106, 110, 113(painted).* ***Wood*** *a-107.*

GHOSTLY WEIRD STORIES (Formerly Blue Bolt Weird)
Star Publications: No. 120, Sept, 1953 - No. 124, Sept, 1954

120-Jo-Jo-r 31.00 92.00 230.00
121-124: 121-Jo-Jo-r. 122-The Mask-r/Capt. Flight #5; Rulah-r; has 1pg. story 'Death and the Devil Pills'-r/Western Outlaws #17. 123-Jo-Jo; Disbrow-a(2). 124-Torpedo Man 26.00 78.00 195.00
NOTE: ***Disbrow*** *a-120-124.* ***L. B. Cole*** *covers-all issues (#122 is a sci-fi cover).*

GHOST MANOR (Ghostly Haunts No. 20 on)
Charlton Comics: July, 1968 - No. 19, July, 1971

1 2.50 7.50 22.00
2-5 1.75 5.25 14.00
6-12,17: 17-Morisi-a 1.25 3.75 10.00
13-16,18,19-Ditko-a; c-15,18,19 1.50 4.50 12.00

GHOST MANOR (2nd Series)
Charlton Comics: Oct, 1971-No. 32, Dec, 1976; No. 33, Sept, 1977-No. 77, 11/84

1 2.20 6.25 22.00
2-7,9,10 1.10 3.30 11.00
8-Wood-a 1.30 3.90 13.00
11-17 .85 2.60 7.00
18-30: 18-Newton's 1st pro art. 19,20,22-Newton-a. 19,28-Nudity panels. 21-E-Man, Blue Beetle, Capt. Atom cameos. 1.00 3.00 10.00
31-39, 41-56 .85 2.60 7.00
40-Torture & drug use. .90 2.70 9.00
57-Wood, Ditko, Howard-a .90 2.70 9.00
58-77: 77-Aparo-r/Space Adventures V3#60 (Paul Mann) 5.00
19 (Modern Comics reprint, 1977) 3.00
NOTE: ***Ditko*** *a-4, 8, 10, 11(2), 13, 14, 18, 20-22, 24-26, 28, 29, 31, 37r, 38r, 40r, 42-44r, 46r, 47, 51r, 52r, 54r, 57, 60, 62(4), 64r, 71; c-2-7, 9-11, 14-16, 28, 31, 37, 38, 42, 43, 46, 47, 51, 52, 60, 62, 64.* ***Howard*** *a-4, 8, 12, 17, 19-21, 31, 41, 45, 57.* ***Newton*** *a-18-20, 22, 64; c-22.* ***Staton*** *a-13, 38, 44, 45.* ***Sutton*** *a-19, 23, 25, 45;c-8, 18.*

GHOST RIDER (See A-1 Comics, Best of the West, Black Phantom, Bobby Benson, Great Western, Red Mask & Tim Holt)
Magazine Enterprises: 1950 - No. 14, 1954
NOTE: *The character was inspired by Vaughn Monroe's "Ghost Riders in the Sky", and Disney's movie "The Headless Horseman".*

GD25 FN65 NM94

1(A-1 #27)-Origin Ghost Rider 62.00 186.00 525.00
2-5: 2(A-1 #29), 3(A-1 #31), 4(A-1 #34), 5(A-1 #37)-All Frazetta-c only 53.00 159.00 450.00
6,7: 6(A-1 #44)-Loco weed story, 7(A-1 #51) 23.00 69.00 175.00
8,9: 8(A-1 #57)-Drug use story, 9(A-1 #69) 21.00 62.00 155.00
10(A-1 #71)-Vs. Frankenstein 21.00 62.00 155.00
11-14: 11(A-1 #75). 12(A-1 #80)-Bondage-c; one-eyed Devil-c. 13(A-1 #84). 14(A-1 #112) 17.00 52.00 130.00
NOTE: ***Dick Ayers*** *art in all; c-1, 6-14.*

GHOST RIDER, THE (See Night Rider & Western Gunfighters)
Marvel Comics Group: Feb, 1967 - No. 7, Nov, 1967 (Western hero)(12¢)

1-Origin & 1st app. Ghost Rider; Kid Colt-reprints begin 5.00 15.00 50.00
2 3.00 9.00 30.00
3-7: 6-Last Kid Colt-r; All Ayers-c/a(p) 2.50 7.50 22.00

GHOST RIDER (See The Champions, Marvel Spotlight #5, Marvel Team-Up #15, 58, Marvel Treasury Edition #18, Marvel Two-In-One #8, The Original Ghost Rider & The Original Ghost Rider Rides Again)
Marvel Comics Group: Sept, 1973 - No. 81, June, 1983 (Super-hero)

1-Johnny Blaze, the Ghost Rider begins; 1st app. Daimon Hellstrom (Son of Satan) in cameo 5.00 15.00 55.00
2-1st full app. Daimon Hellstrom; gives glimpse of costume (1 panel); story continues in Marvel Spotlight #12 2.00 6.00 20.00
3-5: 3-Ghost Rider gets new cycle; Son of Satan app. 1.20 3.60 12.00
6-10: 10-Reprints origin/1st app. from Marvel Spotlight #5; Ploog-a .90 2.70 9.00
11-18: 18-Spider-Man-c & app. 2.00 6.00
19-(Regular 25¢ edition)(8/76) 2.00 6.00
19-(30¢-c, limited distribution) 2.20 6.50 24.00
20-Daredevil x-over; ties into D.D. #138; Byrne-a .90 2.70 8.00
21-30: 22-1st app. Enforcer. 29,30-Vs. Dr. Strange 3.50
31-34,36-49 3.00
35-Death Race classic; Starlin-c/a/sty 2.00 6.00
50-Double size 5.00
51-67,69-76,78-80: 80-Brief origin recap 3.00
68,77-Origin retold 4.00
81-Death of Ghost Rider (Demon leaves Blaze) 5.00
NOTE: ***Anderson*** *c-64p.* ***Infantino*** *a(p)-43, 44, 51.* ***G. Kane*** *a-21p; c(p)-1, 2, 4, 5, 8, 9, 11-13, 19, 20, 24, 25.* ***Kirby*** *c-21-23.* ***Mooney*** *a-2-9p, 30i.* ***Nebres*** *c-26i.* ***Newton*** *a-23i.* ***Perez*** *c-26p.* ***Shores*** *a-2i.* ***J. Sparling*** *a-62p, 64p, 65p.* ***Starlin*** *a(p)-35.* ***Sutton*** *a-1p, 44i, 64i, 65i, 66, 67i.* ***Tuska*** *a-13p, 14p, 16p.*

GHOST RIDER (Volume 2) (Also see Doctor Strange/Ghost Rider Special, Marvel Comics Presents & Midnight Sons Unlimited)
Marvel Comics (Midnight Sons imprint #44 on): V2#1, May, 1990 - No. 93, Feb, 1998 ($1.50/$1.75/$1.95)

1-($1.95, 52 pgs.)-Origin/1st app. new Ghost Rider; Kingpin app. 2.00 6.00
1-2nd printing (not gold) 2.00
2,3,5: 3-Kingpin app. 5-Punisher app.; Jim Lee-c 3.00
4-Scarcer 4.00
5-Gold background 2nd printing 2.00
6-Punisher app. 2.00
7-10: 9-X-Factor app. 10-Reintro Johnny Blaze on the last pg. 1.50
11-14: 11-Stroman-c/a(p). 12,13-Dr. Strange x-over cont'd in D.S. #28. 13-Painted-c. 14-Johnny Blaze vs. Ghost Rider; origin recap 1st Ghost Rider (Blaze) 1.50
15-Glow in the dark-c; begin $1.75-c 2.00
15-Gold background 2nd printing 1.50
16,17-Spider-Man/Hobgoblin-c/story 1.50
18-24,29,30,32-39: 18-Painted-c by Nelson. 29-Wolverine-c/story. 32-Dr. Strange x-over; Johnny Blaze app. 34-Williamson-a(i). 36-Daredevil app. 37-Archangel app. 1.50

Ghost Rider V2 #52 © MAR

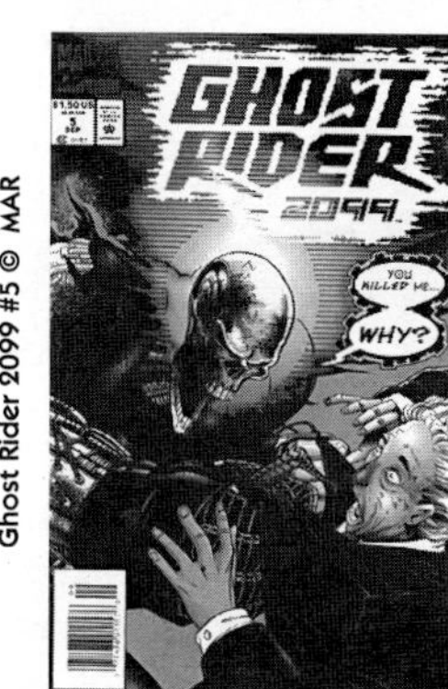

Ghost Rider 2099 #5 © MAR

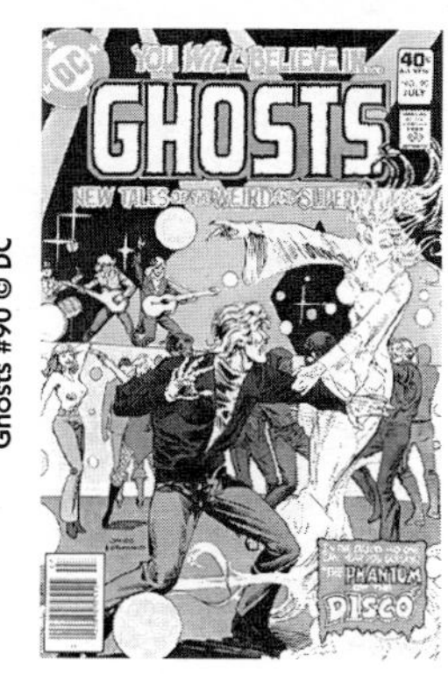

Ghosts #90 © DC

GD25 FN65 NM94

25-27: 25-($2.75)-Contains pop-up scene insert. 26,27-X-Men x-over; Lee/Williams-c on both — 2.75
28-($2.50, 52 pgs.)-Polybagged w/poster; part 1 of Rise of the Midnight Sons storyline (see Ghost Rider/Blaze #1) — 2.50
31-($2.50, 52 pgs.)-Polybagged w/poster; part 6 of Rise of the Midnight Sons — 2.50
40-Outer-c is Darkhold envelope made of black parchment w/gold ink; Midnight Massacre; Demogoblin app. — 2.25
41-48: 41-Lilith & Centurious app.; begin $1.75-c. 41-43-Neon ink-c. 43-Has free extra 16 pg. insert on Siege of Darkness. 44,45-Siege of Darkness parts 2 & 10. 44-Spot varnish-c. 46-Intro new Ghost Rider. 48-Spider-Man app. — 1.75
49,51-60,62-78: 49-Begin $1.95-c; bound-in trading card sheet; Hulk app. 55-Werewolf by Night app. 65-Punisher app. 67,68-Gambit app. 68-Wolverine app. 73,74-Blaze, Vengeance app. 78-New costume. — 2.00
50-($2.50, 52 pgs.)-Regular edition — 2.50
50-($2.95, 52 pgs.)-Collectors ed. die cut foil-c — 3.00
61-($2.50) — 2.50
75-83: 75-Begin $1.50-c. 76-Vs. Vengeance. 77-Dr. Strange-c/app. 78-Dr. Strange app. — 1.50
84-86, -1(7/97): 84-Begin $1.95-c — 2.00
87-92,94: 87-Begin $1.99-c. 94-Final issue — 2.00
93-($2.99)-Saltares & Texeira-a — 3.00
Annual 1 (1993, $2.95, 68 pgs.)-Bagged w/card — 3.00
Annual 2 (1994, $2.95, 68 pgs.) — 3.00
...And Cable 1 (9/92, $3.95, stiff-c, 68 pgs.)-Reprints Marvel Comics Presents #90-98 w/new Kieth-c — 4.00

NOTE: ***Andy & Joe Kubert** c/a-28-31. **Quesada** c-21. **Williamson** a(i)-33-35; c-33i.*

GHOST RIDER/BALLISTIC
Marvel Comics: Feb, 1997 ($2.95, one-shot)

1-Devil's Reign pt. 3 — 2.95

GHOST RIDER/BLAZE: SPIRITS OF VENGEANCE (Also see Blaze)
Marvel Comics (Midnight Sons imprint #17 on): Aug, 1992 - No. 23, June, 1994 ($1.75)

1-($2.75, 52 pgs.)-Polybagged w/poster; part 2 of Rise of the Midnight Sons storyline; Adam Kubert-c/a begins — 2.75
2-11,14-21: 4-Art Adams & Joe Kubert-p. 5,6-Spirits of Venom parts 2 & 4 cont'd from Web of Spider-Man #95,96 w/Demogoblin. 14-17-Neon ink-c. 15-Intro Blaze's new costume & power. 17,18-Siege of Darkness parts 8 & 13. 17-Spot varnish-c — 1.75
12-($2.95)-Glow-in-the-dark-c — 3.00
13-($2.25)-Outer-c is Darkhold envelope made of black parchment w/gold ink; Midnight Massacre x-over — 2.25
22,23: 22-Begin $1.95-c; bound-in trading card sheet — 2.00

NOTE: ***Adam & Joe Kubert** c-7, 8. **Adam Kubert/Steacy** c-6. **J. Kubert** a-13p(6 pgs.)*

GHOST RIDER/CAPTAIN AMERICA: FEAR
Marvel Comics: Oct, 1992 ($5.95, 52 pgs.)

nn-Wraparound gatefold-c; Williamson inks — 2.00 — 6.00

GHOST RIDER 2099
Marvel Comics: May, 1994 - No. 25, May, 1996 ($1.50/$1.95)

1 ($2.25)-Collector's Edition w/prismatic foil-c — 2.00
1 ($1.50)-Regular Edition; bound-in trading card sheet — 1.50
2-12: 7-Spider-Man 2099 app. — 1.50
13-24 ($1.95) — 2.00
25 ($2.95) — 3.00

GHOST RIDER, WOLVERINE, PUNISHER: THE DARK DESIGN
Marvel Comics: Dec, 1994 ($5.95, one-shot)

nn-Gatefold-c — 2.00 — 6.00

GHOST RIDER; WOLVERINE; PUNISHER: HEARTS OF DARKNESS
Marvel Comics: Dec, 1991 ($4.95, one-shot, 52 pgs.)

GD25 FN65 NM94

1-Double gatefold-c; John Romita, Jr.-c/a(p) — 5.00

GHOSTS (Ghost No. 1)
National Periodical Publications/DC Comics: Sept-Oct, 1971 - No. 112, May, 1982 (No. 1-5: 52 pgs.)

	GD25	FN65	NM94
1-Aparo-a	7.25	22.00	80.00
2-Wood-a(i)	3.80	11.50	40.00
3-5	2.70	8.00	30.00
6-10	1.80	5.40	18.00
11-20	1.20	3.60	12.00
21-39	.90	2.70	9.00
40-68 pgs.	1.60	4.80	16.00
41-60		2.00	6.00
61-96			4.00
97-99-The Spectre vs. Dr. 13 by Aparo. 97,98-Spectre-c by Aparo.	.90	2.70	8.00
100-Infinity-c			4.00
101-112			3.00

NOTE: ***B. Baily** a-77. **Buckler** c-99, 100. **J. Craig** a-108. **Ditko** a-77, 111. **Giffen** a-104p, 106p, 111p. **Glanzman** a-2. **Golden** a-88. **Infantino** a-8. **Kaluta** c-7, 93, 101. **Kubert** a-8; c-89, 105-108, 111. **Mayer** a-111. **McWilliams** a-99. **Win Mortimer** a-89, 91, 94. **Nasser/Netzer** a-97. **Newton** a-92p, 94p. **Nino** a-35, 37, 57. **Orlando** a-74i; c-80. **Redondo** a-8, 13, 45. **Sparling** a(p)-90, 93, 94. **Spiegle** a-103, 105. **Tuska** a-2i. Dr. 13, the Ghostbreaker back-ups in 95-99, 101.*

GHOSTS SPECIAL (See DC Special Series No. 7)

GHOST STORIES (See Amazing Ghost Stories)

GHOST STORIES
Dell Publ. Co.: Sept-Nov, 1962; No. 2, Apr-June, 1963 - No. 37, Oct, 1973

	GD25	FN65	NM94
12-295-211(#1)-Written by John Stanley	4.00	12.00	40.00
2	2.50	7.50	20.00
3-10: Two No. 6's exist with different c/a(12-295-406 & 12-295-503) #12-295-503 is actually #9 with indicia to #6	2.00	6.00	16.00
11-20	1.50	4.50	12.00
21-37	1.10	3.30	9.00

NOTE: *#21-34, 36, 37 all reprint earlier issues.*

GHOUL TALES (Magazine)
Stanley Publications: Nov, 1970 - No. 5, July, 1971 (52 pgs.) (B&W)

	GD25	FN65	NM94
1-Aragon pre-code reprints; Mr. Mystery as host; bondage-c	5.00	15.00	55.00
2,3: 2-(1/71)Reprint/Climax #1. 3-(3/71)	2.40	7.00	26.00
4-(5/71)Reprints story "The Way to a Man's Heart" used in **SOTI**	3.50	10.50	38.00
5-ACG reprints	2.00	6.00	20.00

NOTE: *No. 1-4 contain pre-code Aragon reprints.*

GIANT BOY BOOK OF COMICS (Also see Boy Comics)
Newsbook Publications (Gleason): 1945 (240 pgs., hard-c)

	GD25	FN65	NM94
1-Crimebuster & Young Robin Hood; Biro-c	82.00	247.00	700.00

GIANT COMIC ALBUM
King Features Syndicate: 1972 (59¢, 11x14", 52 pgs., B&W, cardboard-c)

Newspaper reprints: Little Iodine, Katzenjammer Kids, Henry, Mandrake the Magician ('59 Falk), Popeye, Beetle Bailey, Barney Google, Blondie, Flash Gordon ('68-69 Dan Barry), & Snuffy Smith

	GD25	FN65	NM94
each...	2.40	7.00	26.00

GIANT COMICS
Charlton Comics: Summer, 1957 - No. 3, Winter, 1957 (25¢, 100 pgs.)

	GD25	FN65	NM94
1-Atomic Mouse, Hoppy app.	19.00	56.00	140.00
2,3: 2-Romance. 3-Christmas Book; Atomic Mouse, Atomic Rabbit, Li'l Genius, Li'l Tomboy & Atom the Cat stories	13.00	40.00	100.00

NOTE: *The above may be rebound comics; contents could vary.*

GIANT COMICS (See Wham-O Giant Comics)

GIANT COMICS EDITION (See Terry-Toons) (Also see Fox Giants)
St. John Publishing Co.: 1947 - No. 17, 1950 (25¢, 100-164 pgs.)

Giant Comics Edition #15 © STJ

Giant-Size Conan #3 © MAR

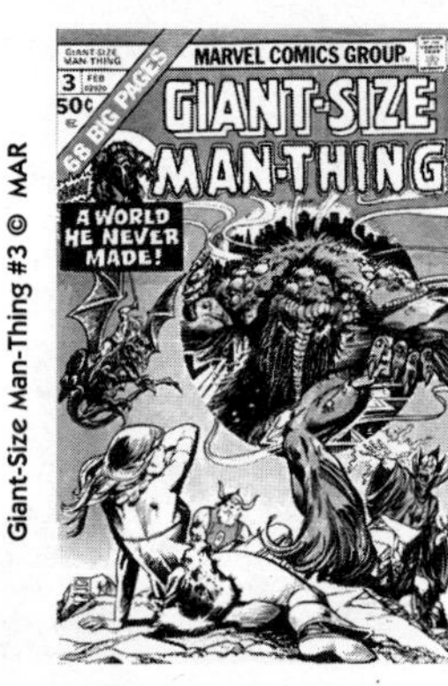

Giant-Size Man-Thing #3 © MAR

GD25 FN65 NM94

1-Mighty Mouse 42.00 126.00 420.00
2-Abbie & Slats 19.50 58.00 195.00
3-Terry-Toons Album; 100 pgs. 32.00 96.00 320.00
4-Crime comics; contains Red Seal No. 16, used & illo. in **SOTI** 49.00 147.00 490.00
5-Police Case Book (4/49, 132 pgs.)-Contents varies; contains remaindered St. John books - some volumes contain 5 copies rather than 4, with 160 pages; Matt Baker-c 46.00 138.00 460.00
5A-Terry-Toons Album (132 pgs.)-Mighty Mouse, Heckle & Jeckle, Gandy Goose & Dinky stories 29.00 87.00 290.00
6-Western Picture Stories; Baker-c/a(3); Tuska-a; The Sky Chief, Blue Monk, Ventrilo app., 132 pgs. 44.00 132.00 440.00
7-Contains a teen-age romance plus 3 Mopsy comics 26.00 78.00 260.00
8-The Adventures of Mighty Mouse (10/49) 29.00 87.00 290.00
9-Romance and Confession Stories; Kubert-a(4); Baker-a; photo-c (132 pgs.) 46.00 138.00 460.00
10-Terry-Toons Album (132 pgs.)-Mighty Mouse, Heckle & Jeckle, Gandy Goose stories 29.00 87.00 290.00
11-Western Picture Stories-Baker-c/a(4); The Sky Chief, Desperado, & Blue Monk app.; another version with Son of Sinbad by Kubert (132 pgs.) 42.00 126.00 420.00
12-Diary Secrets; Baker prostitute-c; 4 St. John romance comics; Baker-a 75.00 225.00 750.00
13-Romances; Baker, Kubert-a 39.00 117.00 395.00
14-Mighty Mouse Album (132 pgs.) 29.00 87.00 290.00
15-Romances (4 love comics)-Baker-c 43.00 129.00 430.00
16-Little Audrey; Abbott & Costello, Casper 29.00 87.00 290.00
17(nn)-Mighty Mouse Album (nn, no date, but did follow No. 16); 100 pgs. on cover but has 148 pgs. 29.00 87.00 290.00

NOTE: *The above books contain remaindered comics and contents could vary with each issue. No. 11, 12 have part photo magazine insides.*

GIANT COMICS EDITIONS
United Features Syndicate: 1940's (132 pgs.)

1-Abbie & Slats, Abbott & Costello, Jim Hardy, Ella Cinders, Iron Vic, Gordo, & Bill Bumlin 35.00 104.00 260.00
2-Jim Hardy, Ella Cinders, Elmo & Gordo 26.00 78.00 195.00

NOTE: *Above books contain rebound copies; contents can vary.*

GIANT GRAB BAG OF COMICS (See Archie All-Star Specials under Archie Comics)

GIANTS (See Thrilling True Story of the Baseball...)

GIANT-SIZE...
Marvel Comics Group: May, 1974 - Dec, 1975 (35/50¢, 52/68 pgs.)
(Some titles quarterly) (Scarce in strict NM or better due to defective cutting, gluing and binding; warping, splitting and off-center pages are common)

Avengers 1(8/74)-New-a plus G.A. H. Torch-r; 1st modern app. The Whizzer; 1st & only modern app. Miss America 1.25 4.00 16.00
Avengers 2,3: 2(11/74)-Death of the Swordsman. 3(2/75) .75 2.50 10.00
Avengers 4,5: 4(6/75)-Vision marries Scarlet Witch. 5(12/75)-Reprints Avengers Special #1 .75 2.50 10.00
Captain America 1(12/75)-r/stories T.O.S. 59-63 by Kirby (#63 reprints origin) 1.50 4.50 16.50
Captain Marvel 1(12/75)-r/Capt. Marvel #17, 20 by Gil Kane (p) 1.00 3.00 12.00
Chillers 1(6/74, 52 pgs)-Curse of Dracula; origin/1st app. Lilith, Dracula's daughter; Heath-r, Colan-c/a(p); becomes Giant-Size Dracula #2 on 2.00 6.00 24.00
Chillers 1(2/75, 50¢, 68 pgs.)-Alacala-a 1.25 4.00 14.00
Chillers 2(5/75)-All-r; Everett-r from Advs. into Weird Worlds .75 2.50 10.00
Chillers 3(8/75)-Wrightson-c(new)/a(r); Colan, Kirby, Smith-r 1.00 3.00 12.00
Conan 1(9/74)-B. Smith-r/#3; start adaptation of Howard's "Hour of the Dragon" (ends #4); 1st app. Belit; new-a begins 1.25 4.00 15.00
Conan 2(12/74)-B. Smith-r/#5; Sutton-a(i)(#1 also); Buscema-c 1.00 3.00 12.00
Conan 3-5: 3(4/75)-B. Smith-r/#6; Sutton-a(i). 4(6/75)-B. Smith-r/#7. 5(1975)-B. Smith-r/#14,15; Kirby-c .75 2.50 10.00
Creatures 1(5/74, 52 pgs.)-Werewolf app; 1st app. Tigra (formerly Cat); Crandall-r; becomes Giant-Size Werewolf w/#2 1.50 4.50 18.00
Daredevil 1(1975) 1.00 3.00 12.00
Defenders 1(7/74)-Silver Surfer app.; Starlin-a; Ditko, Everett & Kirby reprints 1.75 5.50 22.00
Defenders 2(10/74, 68 pgs.)-New G. Kane-c/a(p); Son of Satan app.; Sub-Mariner-r by Everett; Ditko-r/Strange Tales #119 (Dr. Strange); Maneely-r. 1.00 3.00 12.00
Defenders 3-5: 3(1/75)-1st app. Korvac.; Newton, Starlin-a; Ditko, Everett-r. 4(4/75)-Ditko, Everett-r; G. Kane-c. 5-(7/75)-Guardians app. .75 2.50 10.00
Doc Savage 1(1975, 68 pgs.)-r/#1,2; Mooney-r .75 2.50 10.00
Doctor Strange 1(11/75)-Reprints stories from Strange Tales #164-168; Lawrence, Tuska-r 1.00 3.00 12.00
Dracula 2(9/74, 50¢)-Formerly Giant-Size Chillers 1.00 3.00 12.00
Dracula 3(12/74)-Fox-r/Uncanny Tales #6 .75 2.50 10.00
Dracula 4(3/75)-Ditko-r(2) .75 2.50 10.00
Dracula 5(6/75)-1st Byrne art at Marvel 2.00 6.00 24.00
Fantastic Four 2-4: 2(8/74)-Formerly Giant-Size Super-Stars; Ditko-r. 3(11/74). 4(2/75)-1st Madrox; 2-4-All have Buscema-a 1.25 4.00 15.00
Fantastic Four 5,6: 5(5/75)-All-r; Kirby, G. Kane-r. 6(10/75)-All-r; Kirby-r 1.00 3.00 12.00
Hulk 1(1975) r/Hulk Special #1 1.75 5.50 20.00
Invaders 1(6/75, 50¢, 68 pgs.)-Origin; G.A. Sub-Mariner-r/Sub-Mariner #1; intro Master Man 1.00 3.00 12.00
Iron Man 1(1975)-Ditko reprint 1.25 4.00 16.00
Kid Colt 1-3: 1(1/75). 2(4/75). 3(7/75)-new Ayers-a 3.00 9.00 36.00
Man-Thing 1(8/74)-New Ploog-c/a (25 pgs.); Ditko-r/Amazing Adv. #11; Kirby-r/Strange Tales Ann. #2 & T.O.S. #15; (#1-5 all have new Man-Thing stories, pre-hero-r & are 68 pgs.) 1.25 4.00 16.00
Man-Thing 2,3: 2(11/74)-Buscema-c/a(p); Kirby, Powell-r. 3(2/75)-Alcala-a; Ditko, Kirby, Sutton-r; Gil Kane-c .75 2.50 10.00
Man-Thing 4,5: 4(5/75)-Howard the Duck by Brunner-c/a; Ditko-r. 5(8/75)-Howard the Duck by Brunner (p); Dracaula cameo in Howard the Duck; Buscema-a(p); Sutton-a(i); G. Kane-c 1.25 4.00 16.00
Marvel Triple Action 1,2: 1(5/75). 2(7/75) 1.00 3.00 12.00
Master of Kung Fu 1(9/74)-Russell-a; Yellow Claw-r in #1-4; Gulacy-a in #1,2 1.25 4.00 16.00
Master of Kung Fu 2(12/74)-r/Yellow Claw #1 .75 2.50 10.00
Master of Kung Fu 3(3/75)-Gulacy-a .75 2.50 10.00
Master of Kung Fu 4(6/75) .75 2.50 10.00
Power Man 1(1975) .75 2.50 10.00
Spider-Man 1(7/74)-Kirby/Ditko, Byrne-r plus new-a (Dracula-c/story) 3.25 10.00 40.00
Spider-Man 2,3: 2(10/74). 3(1/75)-Byrne-r 2.00 6.00 24.00
Spider-Man 4(4/75)-3rd Punisher app.; Byrne, Ditko-r 6.00 18.00 72.00
Spider-Man 5,6: 5(7/75)-Byrne-r. 6(9/75) 1.25 4.00 16.00
Super-Heroes Featuring Spider-Man 1(6/74, 35¢, 52 pgs.)-Spider-Man vs. Man-Wolf; Morbius, the Living Vampire app.; Ditko-r; G. Kane-a(p); Spidey villains app. 4.00 12.00 48.00
Super-Stars 1(5/74, 35¢, 52 pgs.)-Fantastic Four; Thing vs. Hulk; Kirbyish-c/a by Buckler/Sinnott; F.F. villains profiled; becomes Giant-Size Fantastic Four #2 on 1.75 5.50 22.00
Super-Villain Team-Up 1(3/75, 68 pgs.)-Craig-r(i) (Also see Fantastic Four #6 for 1st super-villain team-up) 1.00 3.00 12.00
Super-Villain Team-Up 2(6/75, 68 pgs.)-Dr. Doom, Sub-Mariner app.; Spider-Man-r/Amazing Spider-Man #8 by Ditko; Sekowsky-a(p) .75 2.50 10.00

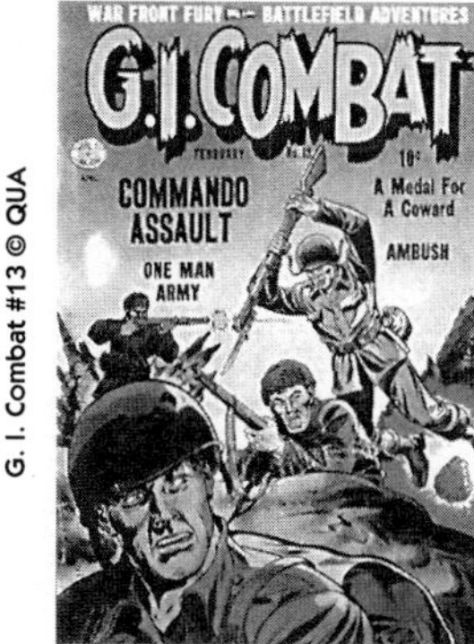

G. I. Combat #13 © QUA

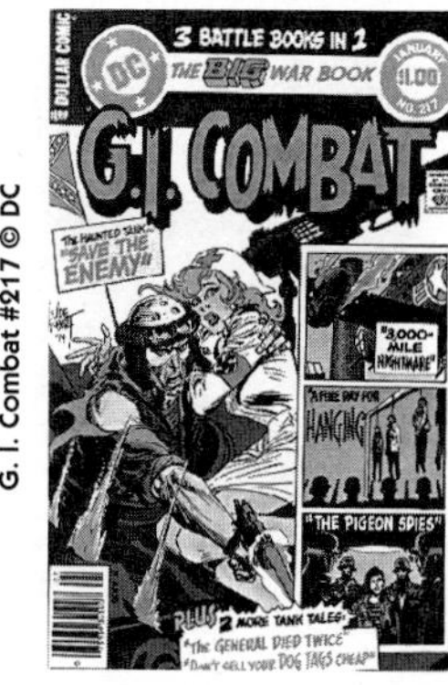

G. I. Combat #217 © DC

Gifts of the Night #1 © Paul Chadwick & John Bolton

GD25 FN65 NM94

Thor 1(7/75) 1.00 3.00 12.00
Werewolf 2(10/74, 68 pgs.)-Formerly Giant-Size Creatures; Ditko-r; Frankenstein app. 1.00 3.00 12.00
Werewolf 3,5: 3(1/75, 68 pgs.). 5(7/75, 68 pgs.) 1.00 3.00 12.00
Werewolf 4(4/75, 68 pgs.)-Morbius the Living Vampire app. 1.25 4.00 16.00
X-Men 1(Summer, 1975, 50¢, 68 pgs.)-1st app. new X-Men; intro Nightcrawler, Storm, Colossus & Thunderbird; 2nd full app. Wolverine after Incredible Hulk #181 40.00 120.00 480.00
X-Men 2(11/75)-N. Adams-r (51 pgs) 4.50 13.50 54.00

GIANT SPECTACULAR COMICS (See Archie All-Star Special under Archie Comics)

GIANT SUMMER FUN BOOK (See Terry-Toons...)

G. I. COMBAT
Quality Comics Group: Oct, 1952 - No. 43, Dec, 1956

1-Crandall-c; Cuidera a-1-43i 53.00 159.00 450.00
2 26.00 78.00 195.00
3-5,10-Crandall-c/a 24.00 72.00 180.00
6-Crandall-a 21.00 64.00 160.00
7-9 17.00 52.00 130.00
11-20 13.00 38.00 95.00
21-31,33,35-43: 41-1st S.A. issue 11.00 32.00 80.00
32-Nuclear attack-c/story "Atomic Rocket Assault" 13.00 40.00 100.00
34-Crandall-a 11.00 34.00 85.00

G. I. COMBAT (See DC Special Series #22)
National Periodical Publ./DC Comics: No. 44, Jan, 1957 - No. 288, Mar, 1987

44-Grey tone-c 44.00 132.00 440.00
45 24.00 72.00 240.00
46-50 18.00 54.00 180.00
51-Grey tone-c 17.00 51.00 170.00
52-54,59,60 14.50 44.00 145.00
55-minor Sgt. Rock prototype by Finger 14.50 44.00 145.00
56-Sgt. Rock prototype by Kanigher/Kubert 14.50 44.00 145.00
57,58-Pre-Sgt. Rock Easy Co. stories 14.50 44.00 145.00
61-65,69-74 10.00 30.00 100.00
67-1st Tank Killer 13.50 40.00 135.00
68-(1/59) Introduces "The Rock", Sgt. Rock prototype by Kanigher/Kubert; once considered his actual 1st app. (see Our Army at War #82,83) 22.50 68.00 225.00
75-80: 75-Greytone-c begin, end #109 10.50 32.00 105.00
81,82,84-86 8.00 24.00 80.00
83-1st Big Al, Little Al, & Charlie Cigar 10.50 32.00 105.00
87-1st Haunted Tank; series begins 40.00 120.00 450.00
88-2nd Haunted Tank 15.00 45.00 150.00
89-91: 90-Last 10¢ issue. 91-1st Haunted Tank-c 8.50 25.50 85.00
92-99 7.00 21.00 70.00
100,108: 108-1st Sgt. Rock x-over 8.00 24.00 80.00
101-107 5.80 17.50 58.00
109-Grey tone-c 6.00 18.00 60.00
110-113,115-120: 113-Grey tone-c 4.50 13.50 45.00
114-Origin Haunted Tank 10.00 30.00 100.00
121-137,139,140: 121-1st app. Sgt. Rock's father. 136-Last 12¢ issue 2.50 7.50 25.00
138-Intro. The Losers (Capt. Storm, Gunner/Sarge, Johnny Cloud) in Haunted Tank (10-11/69) 6.50 19.50 65.00
141-143 1.25 3.75 10.00
144-148 (68pgs.) 1.75 5.25 14.00
149,151-154 (52 pgs.)- 151-Capt. Storm story. 151,153-Medal of Honor series by Maurer 1.25 3.75 10.00
150-Ice Cream Soldier story (tells how he got his name); Death of Haunted Tank-c/s 2.25 6.75 18.00
155-170,200 1.00 3.00 8.00
171-199 1.00 2.80 7.00
201-210 ($1.00 size) 1.00 3.00 8.00
211-230 ($1.00 size) 2.00 5.00
231-259 ($1.00 size).232-Origin Kana the Ninja. 244-Death of Slim Stryker; 1st app. The Mercenaries. 246-(76 pgs., $1.50)-30th Anniversary issue. 257-Intro. Stuart's Raiders 4.00
260-281: 260-Begin $1.25, 52 pg. issues, end #281. 264-Intro Sgt. Bullet; origin Kana. 269-Intro. The Bravos of Vietnam 3.00
282-288 (75¢): 282-New advs. begin 4.00

NOTE: ***N. Adams** c-168, 201, 202. **Check** a-168, 173. **Drucker** a-48, 61, 63, 66, 71, 72, 76, 134, 140, 141, 144, 147, 148, 153. **Evans** a-135, 138, 158, 164, 166, 201, 202, 204, 205, 215, 256. Giffen a-267. **Glanzman** a-most issues. **Kubert/Heath** a-most issues; **Kubert** covers most issues. **Morrow** a-159-161(2 pgs.). **Redondo** a-189, 240i, 243i. **Sekowsky** a-162p. **Severin** a-147, 152, 154. **Simonson** c-169. **Thorne** a-152, 156. **Wildey** a-153. Johnny Cloud app.-112, 115, 120. Mlle. Marie app.-123, 132, 200. Sgt. Rock app.-111-113, 115, 120, 125, 141, 146, 147, 149, 200. USS Stevens by **Glanzman**-145, 150-153, 157. **Grandenetti** c-44-48.*

G. I. COMICS (Also see Jeep & Overseas Comics)
Giveaways: 1945 - No. 73?, 1946 (Distributed to U. S. Armed Forces)

1-73-Contains Prince Valiant by Foster, Blondie, Smilin' Jack, Mickey Finn, Terry & the Pirates, Donald Duck, Alley Oop, Moon Mullins & Capt. Easy strip reprints (at least 73 issues known to exist) 4.25 13.00 28.00

GIDGET (TV)
Dell Publishing Co.: Apr, 1966 - No. 2, Dec, 1966

1-Sally Field photo-c 8.00 24.00 90.00
2 5.50 16.50 60.00

GIFT (See The Crusaders)

GIFT COMICS
Fawcett Publications: 1942 - No. 4, 1949 (50¢/25¢, 324 pgs./152 pgs.)

1-Captain Marvel, Bulletman, Golden Arrow, Ibis the Invincible, Mr. Scarlet, & Spy Smasher begin; not rebound, remaindered comics, printed at same time as originals; 50¢-c & 324 pgs. begin, end #3. 230.00 690.00 2300.00
2-Commando Yank, Phantom Eagle, others app. 150.00 450.00 1500.00
3 100.00 300.00 1000.00
4-(25¢, 152 pgs.)-The Marvel Family, Captain Marvel, etc.; each issue can vary in contents 62.50 187.50 625.00

GIFTS FROM SANTA (See March of Comics No. 137)

GIFTS OF THE NIGHT
DC Comics (Vertigo): Feb, 1999 - No. 4, May, 1999 ($2.95, limited series)

1-4-Bolton-c/a; Chadwick-s 2.95

GIGGLE COMICS (Spencer Spook No. 100) (Also see Ha Ha Comics)
Creston No.1-63/American Comics Group No. 64 on; Oct, 1943 - No. 99, Jan-Feb, 1955

1-Funny animal 28.00 84.00 210.00
2 13.00 40.00 100.00
3-5: Ken Hultgren-a begins? 10.00 30.00 75.00
6-10: 9-1st Superkatt (6/44) 8.50 26.00 60.00
11-20 6.00 18.00 42.00
21-40: 32-Patriotic-c. 37,61-X-Mas-c. 39-St. Valentine's Day-c 5.70 17.00 35.00
41-54,56-59,61-99: 95-Spencer Spook begins? 5.00 15.00 30.00
55,60-Milt Gross-a 5.70 17.00 38.00

G-I IN BATTLE (G-I No. 1 only)
Ajax-Farrell Publ./Four Star: Aug, 1952 - No. 9, July, 1953; Mar, 1957 - No. 6, May, 1958

1 8.50 26.00 60.00
2 5.00 15.00 30.00
3-9 4.15 12.50 25.00
Annual 1(1952, 25¢, 100 pgs.) 23.00 68.00 170.00
1(1957-Ajax) 5.70 17.00 35.00
2-6 4.00 11.00 22.00

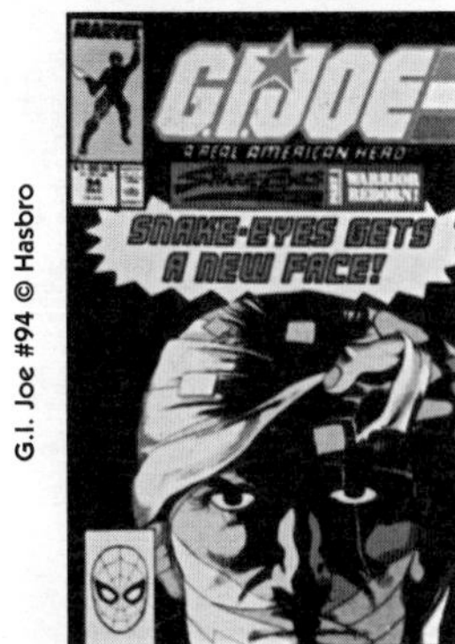

G.I. Joe #94 © Hasbro

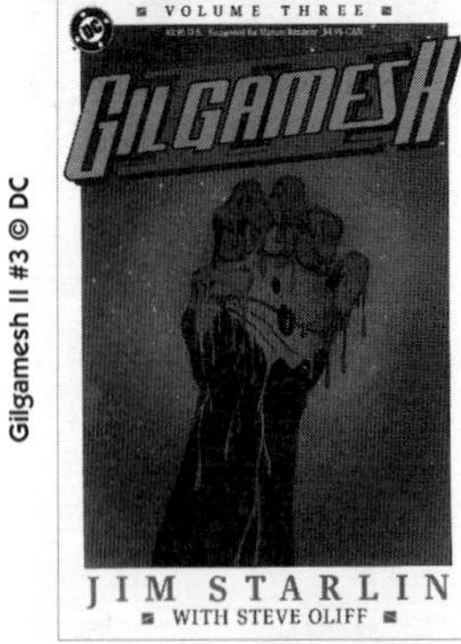

Gilgamesh II #3 © DC

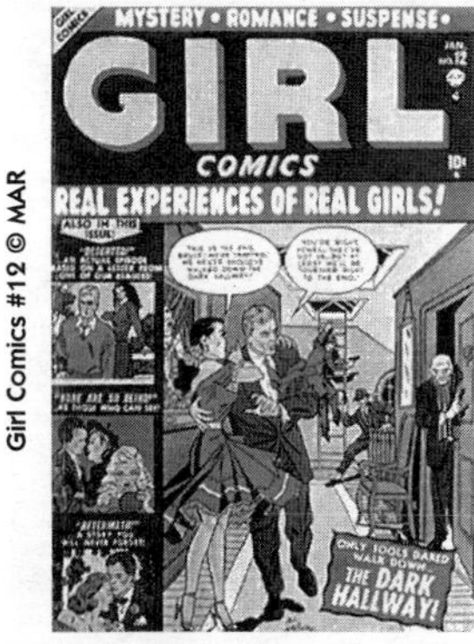

Girl Comics #12 © MAR

G. I. JANE
Stanhall/Merit No. 11: May, 1953 - No. 11, Mar, 1955 (Misdated 3/54)

	GD25	FN65	NM94
1-PX Pete begins; Bill Williams-c/a	10.00	30.00	75.00
2-7(5/54)	5.70	17.00	38.00
8-10(12/54, Stanhall)	5.00	15.00	30.00
11 (3/55, Merit)	4.15	12.50	25.00

G. I. JOE (Also see Advs. of..., Showcase #53, 54 & The Yardbirds)
Ziff-Davis Publ. Co. (Korean War): No. 10, 1950; No. 11, 4-5/51 - No. 51, 6/57 (52pgs.: 10-14,6-17?)

	GD25	FN65	NM94
10(#1, 1950)-Saunders painted-c begin	11.00	34.00	85.00
11-14(#2-5, 10/51): 11-New logo. 12-New logo	7.85	23.50	55.00
V2#6(12/51)-17-(11/52; Last 52 pgs.?)	7.15	21.50	50.00
18-(25¢, 100 pg. Giant, 12-1/52-53)	17.00	52.00	130.00
19-30: 20-22,24,28-31-The Yardbirds app.	5.70	17.00	40.00
31-47,49-51	5.70	17.00	35.00
48-Atom bomb story	5.70	17.00	40.00

NOTE: ***Powell*** *a-V2#7, 8, 11.* ***Norman Saunders*** *painted c-10-14, V2#6-14, 26, 30, 31, 35, 38, 39.* ***Tuska*** *a-7. Bondage c-29, 35, 38.*

G. I. JOE (America's Movable Fighting Man)
Custom Comics: 1967 (5-1/8x8-3/8", 36 pgs.)

	GD25	FN65	NM94
nn-Schaffenberger-a; based on Hasbro toy	2.50	7.50	20.00

G.I. JOE
Dark Horse Comics: Dec, 1995 - No. 4, Apr, 1996 ($1.95, limited series)

	GD25	FN65	NM94
1-4: Mike W. Barr scripts. 1,2-Miller-c. 3-Simonson-c			2.00

G.I. JOE
Dark Horse Comics: V2#1, June, 1996 - V2#4, Sept, 1996 ($2.50)

	GD25	FN65	NM94
V2#1-4: Mike W. Barr scripts. 4-Painted-c			2.50

G. I. JOE AND THE TRANSFORMERS
Marvel Comics Group: Jan, 1987 - No. 4, Apr, 1987 (Limited series)

	GD25	FN65	NM94
1-4			3.00

G. I. JOE, A REAL AMERICAN HERO (...Starring Snake-Eyes on-c #135 on)
Marvel Comics Group: June, 1982 - No. 155, Dec, 1994

	GD25	FN65	NM94
1-Printed on Baxter paper; based on Hasbro toy		2.00	6.00
2-Printed on reg. paper		2.00	6.00
3-10			4.00
11-20: 11-Intro Airborne			3.00
21,22,26,27: 26,27-Origin Snake-Eyes parts 1 & 2			3.00
23-25,28-30			2.50
31-80: 33-New headquarters. 60-Todd McFarlane-a			1.25
81-120: 110-1st Ron Garney-a			2.00
121-155: 135-138-($1.75)-Polybagged w/trading card. 139-142-New Transformers app. 144-Origin Snake-Eyes			2.50
All 2nd printings			1.00
Special Treasury Edition (1982)-r/#1	1.00	3.00	10.00
Yearbook 1 (3/85)-r/#1; Golden-c			3.00
Yearbook 2 (3/86)-Golden-c/a , 3(3/87, 68 pgs.)			3.00
Yearbook 4 (2/88)			2.00

NOTE: ***Garney*** *a(p)-110.* ***Golden*** *c-23, 29, 34, 36.* ***Heath*** *a-24.* ***Rogers*** *a(p)-75, 77-82, 84, 86; c-77.*

G. I. JOE COMICS MAGAZINE
Marvel Comics Group: Dec, 1986 - No. 13, 1988 ($1.50, digest-size)

	GD25	FN65	NM94
1-13: G.I. Joe-r			3.00

G.I. JOE EUROPEAN MISSIONS (Action Force in indicia)
Marvel Comics Ltd. (British): Jun, 1988 - No. 15, Dec, 1989 ($1.50/$1.75)

	GD25	FN65	NM94
1-11: Reprints Action Force			2.00
12-15-($1.75)			1.75

G. I. JOE ORDER OF BATTLE, THE
Marvel Comics Group: Dec, 1986 - No. 4, Mar, 1987 (limited series)

	GD25	FN65	NM94
1-4			1.50

G. I. JOE SPECIAL MISSIONS (Indicia title: Special Missions)
Marvel Comics Group: Oct, 1986 - No. 28, Dec, 1989 ($1.00)

	GD25	FN65	NM94
1-28			1.00

G. I. JUNIORS (See Harvey Hits No. 86,91,95,98,101,104,107,110,112,114,116,118,120,122)

GILGAMESH II
DC Comics: 1989 - No. 4, 1989 ($3.95, limited series, prestige format, mature)

	GD25	FN65	NM94
1-4: Starlin-c/a/scripts			4.00

GIL THORP
Dell Publishing Co.: May-July, 1963

	GD25	FN65	NM94
1-Caniffish-a	2.50	7.50	28.00

GINGER
Archie Publications: 1951 - No. 10, Summer, 1954

	GD25	FN65	NM94
1-Teenage humor	10.00	30.00	100.00
2-(1952)	5.50	16.50	55.00
3-6: 6-(Sum/53)	4.00	12.00	40.00
7-10-Katy Keene app.	6.00	18.00	60.00

GINGER FOX (Also see The World of Ginger Fox)
Comico: Sept, 1988 - No. 4, Dec, 1988 ($1.75, limited series)

	GD25	FN65	NM94
1-4: 1-4-part photo-c			1.75

G.I. R.A.M.B.O.T.
Wonder Color Comics/Pied Piper #2: Apr, 1987 - No. 2? ($1.95)

	GD25	FN65	NM94
1,2: 2-Exist?			2.00

GIRL
DC Comics (Vertigo Verite): Jul, 1996 - No. 3, 1996 ($2.50, lim. series, mature)

	GD25	FN65	NM94
1-3: Peter Milligan scripts; Fegredo-c/a			2.50

GIRL COMICS (Becomes Girl Confessions No. 13 on)
Marvel/Atlas Comics(CnPC): Oct, 1949 - No. 12, Jan, 1952 (#1-4: 52 pgs.)

	GD25	FN65	NM94
1-Photo-c	17.00	50.00	125.00
2-Kubert-a; photo-c	10.00	30.00	75.00
3-Everett-a; Liz Taylor photo-c	13.00	40.00	100.00
4-11: 4-Photo-c. 10-12-Sol Brodsky-c	7.85	23.50	55.00
12-Krigstein-a; Al Hartley-c	9.30	28.00	65.00

GIRL CONFESSIONS (Formerly Girl Comics)
Atlas Comics (CnPC/ZPC): No. 13, Mar, 1952 - No. 35, Aug, 1954

	GD25	FN65	NM94
13-Everett-a	9.30	28.00	70.00
14,15,19,20	6.00	18.00	42.00
16-18-Everett-a	7.50	22.50	52.00
21-35: Robinson-a	4.25	13.00	28.00

GIRL CRAZY
Dark Horse Comics: May, 1996 - No. 3, July, 1996 ($2.95, B&W, limited series)

	GD25	FN65	NM94
1-3: Gilbert Hernandez-a/scripts.			3.00

GIRL FROM U.N.C.L.E., THE (TV) (Also see The Man From...)
Gold Key: Jan, 1967 - No. 5, Oct, 1967

	GD25	FN65	NM94
1-McWilliams-a; Stephanie Powers photo front/back-c & pin-ups (no ads, 12¢)	8.20	24.60	90.00
2-5-Leonard Swift-Courier No. 5	5.50	16.50	60.00

GIRLS' FUN & FASHION MAGAZINE (Formerly Polly Pigtails)
Parents' Magazine Institute: V5#44, Jan, 1950 - V5#48, Sept., 1950

	GD25	FN65	NM94
V5#44	4.25	13.00	26.00
45-48	3.20	8.00	16.00

GIRLS IN LOVE
Fawcett Publications: May, 1950 - No. 2, July, 1950

	GD25	FN65	NM94
1,2-Photo-c	8.50	26.00	60.00

GIRLS IN LOVE (Formerly G. I. Sweethearts No. 45)
Quality Comics Group: No. 46, Sept, 1955 - No. 57, Dec, 1956

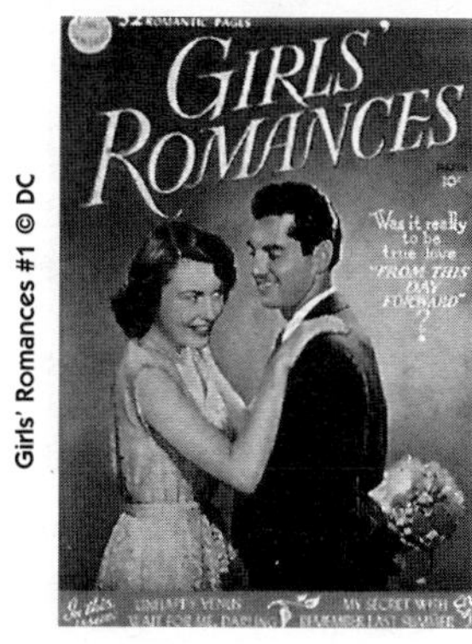

Girls' Romances #1 © DC

The Girl Who Would Be Death #1 © DC

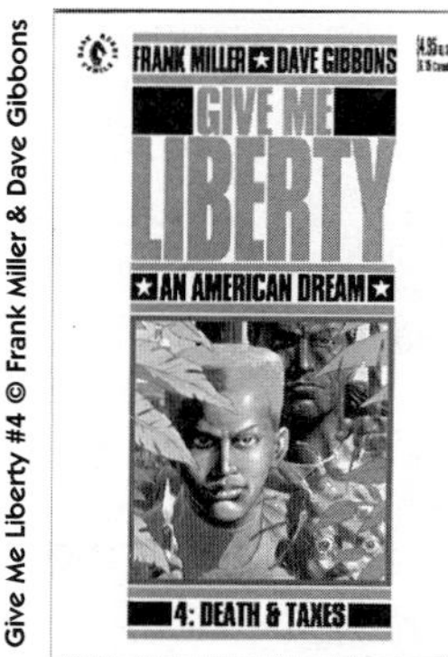

Give Me Liberty #4 © Frank Miller & Dave Gibbons

	GD25	FN65	NM94
46	5.70	17.00	38.00
47-53,55,56	4.25	13.00	26.00
54- 'Commie' story	5.00	15.00	30.00
57-Matt Baker-c/a	6.50	19.50	45.00

GIRLS IN WHITE (See Harvey Comics Hits No. 58)

GIRLS' LIFE (Patsy Walker's Own Magazine For Girls!)
Atlas Comics (BFP): Jan, 1954 - No. 6, Nov, 1954

	GD25	FN65	NM94
1	8.30	25.00	58.00
2-Al Hartley-c	5.35	16.00	32.00
3-6	4.25	13.00	26.00

GIRLS' LOVE STORIES
National Comics(Signal Publ. No. 9-65/Arleigh No. 83-117): Aug-Sept, 1949 - No. 180, Nov-Dec, 1973 (No. 1-13: 52 pgs.)

	GD25	FN65	NM94
1-Toth, Kinstler-a, 8 pgs. each; photo-c	47.00	141.00	395.00
2-Kinstler-a?	28.00	84.00	210.00
3-10: 1-9-Photo-c. 7-Infantino-c(p)	18.00	54.00	135.00
11-20	14.00	42.00	105.00
21-33: 21-Kinstler-a. 33-Last pre-code (1-2/55)	8.50	25.50	60.00
34-50	6.60	20.00	46.00
51-70	4.50	13.50	45.00
71-99: 83-Last 10¢ issue	3.00	9.00	30.00
100	3.50	10.50	35.00
101-146: 113-117-April O'Day app.	2.50	7.50	22.00
147-151- "Confessions" serial	2.00	6.00	16.00
152-160,171-179	1.50	4.50	12.00
161-170 (52 pgs.)	2.50	7.50	24.00
180 Last issue	2.50	7.50	20.00

GIRLS' ROMANCES
National Periodical Publ.(Signal Publ. No. 7-79/Arleigh No. 84): Feb-Mar, 1950 - No. 160, Oct, 1971 (No. 1-11: 52 pgs.)

	GD25	FN65	NM94
1-Photo-c	45.00	135.00	385.00
2-Photo-c; Toth-a	27.00	80.00	200.00
3-10: 3-6-Photo-c	18.00	54.00	135.00
11,12,14-20	13.00	38.00	95.00
13-Toth-c	13.00	40.00	100.00
21-31: 31-Last pre-code (2-3/55)	7.85	23.50	55.00
32-50	4.50	13.50	45.00
51-99: 80-Last 10¢ issue	3.00	9.00	30.00
100	3.50	10.50	35.00
101-108,110-120	2.50	7.50	20.00
109-Beatles-c/story	10.00	30.00	100.00
121-133,135-140	2.00	6.00	16.00
134-Neal Adams-c (splash pg. is same as-c)	2.80	8.40	28.00
141-158	1.50	4.50	12.00
159,160-52 pgs.	2.50	7.50	22.00

GIRL WHO WOULD BE DEATH, THE
DC Comics (Vertigo) Dec, 1998 - No. 4, March, 1999 ($2.50, lim. series)

	GD25	FN65	NM94
1,2-Kiernan-s/Ormston-a			2.50

G. I. SWEETHEARTS (Formerly Diary Loves; Girls In Love #46 on)
Quality Comics Group: No. 32, June, 1953 - No. 45, May, 1955

	GD25	FN65	NM94
32	5.70	17.00	38.00
33-45: 44-Last pre-code (3/55)	4.25	13.00	26.00

G.I. TALES (Formerly Sgt. Barney Barker No. 1-3)
Atlas Comics (MCI): No. 4, Feb, 1957 - No. 6, July, 1957

	GD25	FN65	NM94
4-Severin-a(4)	6.00	18.00	42.00
5	5.00	15.00	30.00
6-Orlando, Powell, & Woodbridge-a	5.35	16.00	32.00

GIVE ME LIBERTY (Also see Dark Horse Presents Fifth Anniversary Special, Dark Horse Presents #100-4, Happy Birthday Martha Washington, Martha Washington Goes to War, Martha Washington Stranded In Space & San Diego Comicon Comics #2)
Dark Horse Comics: June, 1990 - No. 4, 1991 ($4.95, limited series, 52 pgs.)

	GD25	FN65	NM94
1-4: 1st app. Martha Washington; Frank Miller scripts, Dave Gibbons-c/a in all.			5.00

G. I. WAR BRIDES
Superior Publishers Ltd.: Apr, 1954 - No. 8, June, 1955

	GD25	FN65	NM94
1	6.00	18.00	42.00
2	4.00	12.00	24.00
3-8: 4-Kamenesque-a; lingerie panels	4.00	10.00	20.00

G. I. WAR TALES
National Periodical Publications: Mar-Apr, 1973 - No. 4, Oct-Nov, 1973

	GD25	FN65	NM94
1-Reprints in all; dinosaur-c/s	1.60	4.80	16.00
2-N. Adams-a(r)	1.40	4.20	14.00
3,4: 4-Krigstein-a(r)	1.20	3.60	12.00

NOTE: *Drucker a-3r, 4r. Heath a-4r. Kubert a-2, 3; c-4r.*

GIZMO (Also see Domino Chance)
Chance Ent.: May-June, 1985 (B&W, one-shot)

	GD25	FN65	NM94
1			3.00

GIZMO
Mirage Studios: 1986 - No. 6, July, 1987 ($1.50, B&W)

	GD25	FN65	NM94
1-6			1.50

GLADSTONE COMIC ALBUM
Gladstone: 1987 - No. 28, 1990 ($5.95/$9.95, 8-1/2x11")(All Mickey Mouse albums are by Gottfredson)

	GD25	FN65	NM94
1-10: 1-Uncle Scrooge; Barks-r; Beck-c. 2-Donald Duck; r/F.C. #108 by Barks. 3-Mickey Mouse-r by Gottfredson. 4-Uncle Scrooge; r/F.C. #456 by Barks w/ unedited story. 5-Donald Duck Advs.; r/F.C. #199. 6-Uncle Scrooge-r by Barks. 7-Donald Duck-r by Barks. 8-Mickey Mouse-r. 9-Bambi; r/F.C. #186? 10-Donald Duck Advs.; r/F.C. #275	.85	2.60	7.00
11-20: 11-Uncle Scrooge; r/U.S. #4. 12-Donald And Daisy; r/F.C. #1055, WDC&S. 13-Donald Duck Advs.; r/F.C. #408. 14-Uncle Scrooge; Barks-r/ U.S #21. 15-Donald And Gladstone; Barks-r. 16-Donald Duck Advs.; r/F.C. #238. 17-Mickey Mouse strip-r (The World of Tomorrow, The Pirate Ghost Ship). 18-Donald Duck and the Junior Woodchucks; Barks-r. 19-Uncle Scrooge; r/U.S. #12; Rosa-c. 20-Uncle Scrooge; r/F.C. #386; Barks-c/a(r)	.85	2.60	7.00
21-25: 21-Donald Duck Family; Barks-c/a(r). 22-Mickey Mouse strip-r. 23-Donald Duck; Barks-r/D.D. #26 w/unedited story. 24-Uncle Scrooge; Barks-r; Rosa-c. 25-D. Duck; Barks-c/a-r/F.C. #367	.85	2.60	7.00
26-28: All have $9.95-c. 26-Mickey and Donald; Gottfredson-c/a(r). 27-Donald Duck; r/WDC&S by Barks; Barks painted-c. 28-Uncle Scrooge & Donald Duck; Rosa-c/a (4 stories)	1.10	3.30	11.00
Special 1 (1989, $9.95)-Donald Duck Finds Pirate Gold; r/F.C. #9	1.10	3.30	11.00
Special 2 (1989, $8.95)-Uncle Scrooge and Donald Duck; Barks-r/Uncle Scrooge #5; Rosa-c	1.00	3.00	10.00
Special 3 (1989, $8.95)-Mickey Mouse strip-r	1.00	3.00	10.00
Special 4 (1989, $11.95)-Uncle Scrooge; Rosa-c/a-r/Son of the Sun from U.S. #219 plus Barks-r/U.S.	1.30	3.90	13.00
Special 5 (1990, $11.95)-Donald Duck Advs.; Barks-r/F.C. #282 & 422 plus Barks painted-c	1.30	3.90	13.00
Special 6 (1990, $12.95)-Uncle Scrooge; Barks-c/a-r/Uncle Scrooge	1.40	4.20	14.00
Special 7 (1990, $13.95)-Mickey Mouse; Gottfredson strip-r	1.50	4.50	15.00

GLADSTONE COMIC ALBUM (2nd Series)(Also see The Original Dick Tracy)
Gladstone Publishing: 1990 ($5.95, 8-1/2 x 11," stiff-c, 52 pgs.)

	GD25	FN65	NM94
1,2-The Original Dick Tracy. 2-Origin of the 2-way wrist radio.		2.00	6.00

Glory #3 © Rob Liefeld

Goddess #1 © Garth Ennis & Phil Winslade

Gog (Villains) #1 © DC

GD25 FN65 NM94

3-D Tracy Meets the Mole-r by Gould ($6.95). .90 2.70 8.00

GLAMOROUS ROMANCES (Formerly Dotty)
Ace Magazines (A. A. Wyn): No. 41, July, 1949 - No. 90, Oct, 1956 (Photo-c 68-90)

41-Dotty app. 6.00 18.00 42.00
42-72,74-80: 44-Begin 52 pg. issues. 45,50-61-Painted-c. 80-Last pre-code (2/55) 4.25 13.00 26.00
73-L.B. Cole-r/All Love #27 5.00 15.00 30.00
81-90 4.00 11.00 22.00

GLOBAL FORCE
Silverline Comics: 1987 - No. 2 ($1.95)

1,2 2.00

GLORY
Image Comics (Extreme Studios)/Maximum Press: Mar, 1995 - No. 22, Apr, 1997 ($2.50)

0-Deodato-c/a 2.50
1-(3/95)-Deodato-a 3.00
1A-Variant-c 2.00 6.00
2-11,13-22: 5-Bagged w/Youngblood gaming card. 7,8-Deodato-c/a(p). 8-Babewatch x-over. 9-Cruz-c; Extreme Destroyer Pt. 5; polybagged w/card. 10-Angela-c/app. 11-Deodato-c. 2.50
4-Variant-c by Quesada & Palmiotti 5.00
12-($3.50)-Photo-c 3.50
Trade Paperback (1995, $9.95)-r/#1-4 10.00

GLORY & FRIENDS BIKINI FEST
Image Comics (Extreme): Sept, 1995 - No. 2, Oct, 1995 ($2.50, limited series)

1,2: 1-Photo-c; centerfold photo; pin-ups 2.50

GLORY & FRIENDS CHRISTMAS SPECIAL
Image Comics (Extreme Studios): Dec, 1995 ($2.50, one-shot)

1-Deodato-c 2.50

GLORY & FRIENDS LINGIRIE SPECIAL
Image Comics (Extreme Studios): Sept, 1995 ($2.95, one-shot)

1-Pin-ups w/photos; photo-c; varant-c exists 3.00

GLORY/ANGELA: ANGELS IN HELL (See Angela/Glory: Rage of Angels)
Image Comics (Extreme Studios): Apr, 1996 ($2.50, one-shot)

1-Flip book w/Darkchylde #1 2.50

GLORY/AVENGELYNE
Image Comics (Extreme Studios): Oct, 1995 ($3.95, one-shot)

1-Chromium-c 4.00
1-Regular-c 4.00

GLORY/CELESTINE: DARK ANGEL
Image Comics/Maximum Press (Extreme Studios): Sept, 1996 - No. 3, Nov, 1996 ($2.50, limited series)

1-3 2.50

GNOME MOBILE, THE (See Movie Comics)

GOBBLEDYGOOK
Mirage Studios: 1984 - No. 2, 1984 (B&W)(1st Mirage comics, published at same time)

1,2-(24 pgs.)-1st Teenage Mutant Ninja Turtles 19.00 57.00 210.00

GOBBLEDYGOOK
Mirage Studios: Dec, 1986 ($3.50, B&W, one-shot, 100 pgs.)

1-New 8 pg. TMNT story plus a Donatello/Michaelangelo 7 pg. story & a Gizmo story; Corben-i(r)/TMNT #7 4.00

GOBLIN, THE
Warren Publishing Co.: June, 1982 - No. 4, Dec, 1982 (Magazine, $2.25)

1-The Gremlin app; Golden-a(p) 1.50 4.50 15.00

GD25 FN65 NM94

2-4: 2-1st Hobgoblin 1.00 3.00 10.00

GODDESS
DC Comics (Vertigo): June, 1995 - No. 8, Jan, 1996 ($2.95, limited series)

1-Garth Ennis scripts; Phil Winslade-c/a in all 2.00 6.00
2-8 4.00

GODFATHERS, THE (See The Crusaders)

GOD IS
Spire Christian Comics (Fleming H. Revell Co.): 1973, 1975 (35-49¢)

nn-By Al Hartley 3.00

GOD'S COUNTRY (Also see Marvel Comics Presents)
Marvel Comics: 1994 ($6.95)

nn-P. Craig Russell-a; Colossus story; r/Marvel Comics Presents #10-17 .85 2.60 7.00

GODS FOR HIRE
Hot Comics: Dec, 1986 - No. 3 ($1.50)

1-3: Barry Crain-c/a(p) 1.50

GOD'S HEROES IN AMERICA
Catechetical Guild Educational Society: 1956 (nn) (25¢/35¢, 68 pgs.)

307 2.00 5.00 10.00

GOD'S SMUGGLER (Religious)
Spire Christian Comics/Fleming H. Revell Co.: 1972 (39¢/40¢)

..1-Two variations exist 3.00

GODWHEEL
Malibu Comics (Ultraverse): No. 0, Jan, 1995 - No. 3, Feb, 1995 ($2.50, limited series)

0-3: 0-Flip-c. 1-1st app. of Primevil; Thor cameo (1 panel). 3-Perez-a in Chapter 3, Thor app. 2.50

GODZILLA (Movie)
Marvel Comics : August, 1977 - No. 24, July, 1979 (Based on movie series)

1-(Regular 30¢ edition)-Mooney-i .85 2.60 7.00
1-(35¢-c, limited distribution) 2.25 6.80 25.00
2-(Regular 30¢ edition)-Tuska-i. 4.00
2-(35¢-c, limited distribution) 1.30 3.90 13.00
3- Champions app.(w/o Ghost Rider) .90 2.70 8.00
4-10: 4,5-Sutton-a 4.00
11-24: 14-Shield app. 20-F.F. app. 21,22-Devil Dinosaur app. 3.00

GODZILLA (Movie)
Dark Horse Comics: May, 1988 - No. 6, 1988 ($1.95, B&W, limited series) (Based on movie series)

1 5.00
2-6 3.00
...Collection (1990, $10.95)-r/1-6 with new-c 1.10 3.30 11.00
...Color Special 1 (Sum, 1992, $3.50, color, 44 pgs.)-Arthur Adams wrap-around-c/a & part scripts 4.00
...King Of The Monsters Special (8/87, $1.50)-Origin; Bissette-c/a 3.00
...Vs. Barkley nn (12/93, $2.95, color)-Dorman painted-c 3.00

GODZILLA (King of the Monsters) (Movie)
Dark Horse Comics: May, 1995 - No. 16, Sept, 1996 ($2.50) (Based on movies)

0-16: 0-r/Dark Horse Comics #10,11. 1-3-Kevin Maguire scripts. 3-8-Art Adams-c 4.00
...Vs. Hero Zero ($2.50) 2.50

GOG (VILLAINS) (See Kingdom Come)
DC Comics: Feb, 1998 ($1.95, one-shot)

1-Waid-s/Ordway-a(p)/Pearson-c 3.00

GO-GO

Golden Age #4 © DC

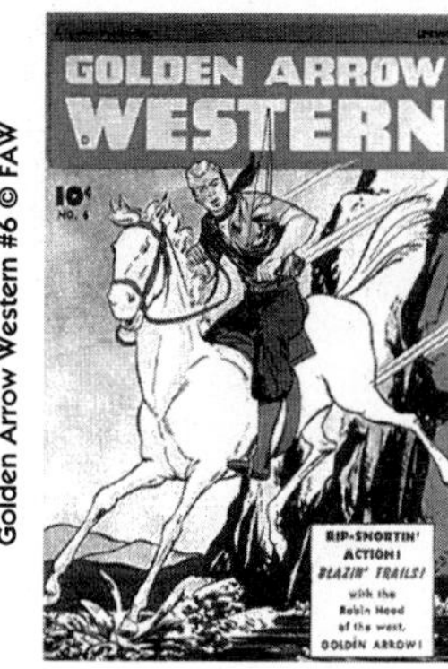

Golden Arrow Western #6 © FAW

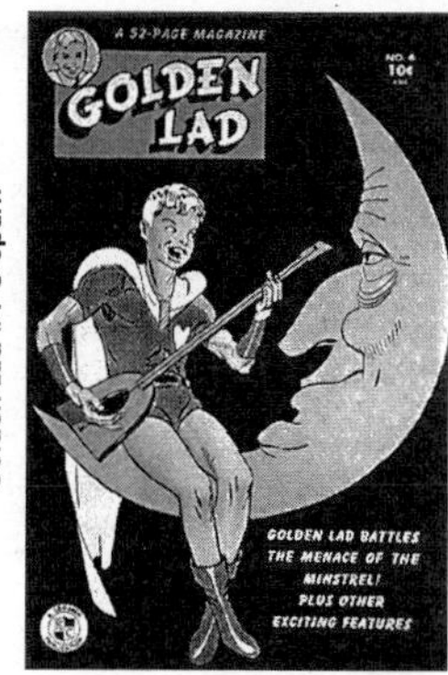

Golden Lad #4 © Spark

GD25 FN65 NM94

Charlton Comics: June, 1966 - No. 9, Oct, 1967

1-Miss Bikini Luv begins; Rolling Stones, Beatles, Elvis, Sonny & Cher, Bob Dylan, Sinatra, parody; Herman's Hermits pin-ups; D'Agostino-c/a in #1-8 — 5.25 15.75 52.00
2-Ringo Starr, David McCallum & Beatles photos on cover; Beatles story and photos — 5.25 15.75 52.00
3,4: 3-Blooperman begins, ends #6; 1 pg. Batman & Robin satire; full pg. photo pin-ups Lovin' Spoonful & The Byrds — 2.80 8.40 28.00
5-7,9: 5 (2/67)-Super Hero & TV satire by Jim Aparo & Grass Green begins; Aparo's 1st published work. 6-8-Aparo-a. 6-Petula Clark photo-c. 7-Photo of Brian Wilson of Beach Boys on-c & Beach Boys photo inside f/b-c. 9-Aparo-c/a. — 2.80 8.40 28.00
8-Monkees photo on-c & photo inside f/b-c — 3.00 9.00 30.00

GO-GO AND ANIMAL (See Tippy's Friends...)

GOING STEADY (Formerly Teen-Age Temptations)
St. John Publ. Co.: No. 10, Dec, 1954 - No. 13, June, 1955; No. 14, Oct, 1955

10(1954)-Matt Baker-c/a — 17.00 52.00 130.00
11(2/55, last precode), 12(4/55)-Baker-c — 9.30 28.00 70.00
13(6/55)-Baker-c/a — 12.00 36.00 90.00
14(10/55)-Matt Baker-c/a, 25 pgs. — 14.00 42.00 105.00

GOING STEADY (Formerly Personal Love)
Prize Publications/Headline: V3#3, Feb, 1960 - V3#6, Aug, 1960; V4#1, Sept-Oct, 1960

V3#3-6, V4#1 — 2.00 6.00 16.00

GOING STEADY WITH BETTY (Becomes Betty & Her Steady No. 2)
Avon Periodicals: Nov-Dec, 1949

1 — 12.00 36.00 90.00

GOLDEN AGE, THE
DC Comics (Elseworlds): 1993 - No. 4, 1994 ($4.95, limited series)

1-4: James Robinson scripts; Paul Smith-c/a; gold foil embossed-c. — 2.00 6.00
Trade Paperback (1995, $19.95) — 20.00

GOLDEN ARROW (See Fawcett Miniatures, Mighty Midget & Whiz Comics)

GOLDEN ARROW (...Western No. 6)
Fawcett Publications: Spring, 1942 - No. 6, Spring, 1947 (68 pgs.)

1-Golden Arrow begins — 71.00 213.00 640.00
2-(1943) — 36.00 108.00 300.00
3-5: 3-(Win/45-46). 4-(Spr/46). 5-(Fall/46) — 26.00 80.00 210.00
6-Krigstein-a — 29.00 86.00 230.00
...Well Known Comics (1944; 12 pgs.; 8-1/2x10-1/2"; paper-c; glued binding)-Bestmaid/Samuel Lowe giveaway; printed in green — 7.15 21.50 50.00

GOLDEN COMICS DIGEST
Gold Key: May, 1969 - No. 48, Jan, 1976

NOTE: *Whitman editions exist of many titles and are generally valued the same.*

1-Tom & Jerry, Woody Woodpecker, Bugs Bunny — 2.90 8.70 32.00
2-Hanna-Barbera TV Fun Favorites; Space Ghost, Flintstones, Atom Ant, Jetsons, Yogi Bear, Banana Splits, others app. — 3.80 11.50 40.00
3-Tom & Jerry, Woody Woodpecker — 1.60 4.80 16.00
4-Tarzan; Manning & Marsh-a — 3.20 9.50 35.00
5,8-Tom & Jerry, W. Woodpecker, Bugs Bunny — 1.40 4.20 14.00
6-Bugs Bunny — 1.40 4.20 14.00
7-Hanna-Barbera TV Fun Favorites — 2.20 6.25 22.00
9-Tarzan — 3.20 9.50 35.00
10,12-17: 10-Bugs Bunny. 12-Tom & Jerry, Bugs Bunny, W. Woodpecker Journey to the Sun. 13-Tom & Jerry. 14-Bugs Bunny Fun Packed Funnies. 15-Tom & Jerry, Woody Woodpecker, Bugs Bunny. 16-Woody Woodpecker Cartoon Special. 17-Bugs Bunny — 1.40 4.20 14.00
11-Hanna-Barbera TV Fun Favorites — 2.20 6.25 22.00
18-Tom & Jerry; Barney Bear-r by Barks — 1.60 4.80 16.00
19-Little Lulu — 2.70 8.00 30.00
20-22: 20-Woody Woodpecker Falltime Funtime. 21-Bugs Bunny Showtime. 22-Tom & Jerry Winter Wingding — 1.40 4.20 14.00
23-Little Lulu & Tubby Fun Fling — 2.70 8.00 30.00
24-26,28: 24-Woody Woodpecker Fun Festival. 25-Tom & Jerry. 26-Bugs Bunny Halloween Hulla-Boo-Loo; Dr. Spektor article, also #25. 28-Tom & Jerry — 1.30 3.90 13.00
27-Little Lulu & Tubby in Hawaii — 2.20 6.50 24.00
29-Little Lulu & Tubby — 2.20 6.50 24.00
30-Bugs Bunny Vacation Funnies — 1.30 3.90 13.00
31-Turok, Son of Stone; r/4-Color #596,656; c-r/#9 — 2.70 8.00 30.00
32-Woody Woodpecker Summer Fun — 1.30 3.90 13.00
33,36: 33-Little Lulu & Tubby Halloween Fun; Dr. Spektor app. 36-Little Lulu & Her Friends — 2.70 8.00 30.00
34,35,37-39: 34-Bugs Bunny Winter Funnies. 35-Tom & Jerry Snowtime Funtime. 37-Woody Woodpecker County Fair. 39-Bugs Bunny Summer Fun — 1.30 3.90 13.00
38-The Pink Panther — 1.60 4.80 16.00
40,43: 40-Little Lulu & Tubby Trick or Treat; all by Stanley. 43-Little Lulu in Paris — 2.70 8.00 30.00
41,42,44,47: 41-Tom & Jerry Winter Carnival. 42-Bugs Bunny. 44-Woody Woodpecker Family Fun Festival. 47-Bugs Bunny — 1.10 3.30 11.00
45-The Pink Panther — 1.60 4.80 16.00
46-Little Lulu & Tubby — 2.20 6.50 24.00
48-The Lone Ranger — 1.60 4.80 16.00

NOTE: *#1-30, 164 pgs.; #31 on, 132 pgs..*

GOLDEN LAD
Spark Publications: July, 1945 - No. 5, June, 1946 (#4, 5: 52 pgs.)

1-Origin & 1st app. Golden Lad & Swift Arrow; Sandusky and the Senator begins — 62.00 186.00 525.00
2-Mort Meskin-c/a — 32.00 96.00 240.00
3,4-Mort Meskin-c/a — 28.00 84.00 210.00
5-Origin/1st Golden Girl; Shaman & Flame app. — 33.00 100.00 250.00

NOTE: *All have* ***Robinson,*** *and* ***Roussos*** *art plus* ***Meskin*** *covers and art.*

GOLDEN LEGACY
Fitzgerald Publishing Co.: 1966 - 1972 (Black History) (25¢)

1-Toussaint L'Ouverture (1966), 2-Harriet Tubman (1967), 3-Crispus Attucks & the Minutemen (1967), 4-Benjamin Banneker (1968), 5-Matthew Henson (1969), 6-Alexander Dumas & Family (1969), 7-Frederick Douglass, Part 1 (1969), 8-Frederick Douglass, Part 2 (1970), 9-Robert Smalls (1970), 10-J. Cinque & the Amistad Mutiny (1970), 11-Men in Action: White, Marshall J. Wilkins (1970), 12-Black Cowboys (1972), 13-The Life of Martin Luther King, Jr. (1972), 14-The Life of Alexander Pushkin (1971), 15-Ancient African Kingdoms (1972), 16-Black Inventors (1972)
each.... — 1.00 3.00 8.00
1-10,12,13,15,16(1976)-Reprints — 2.40 6.00

GOLDEN LOVE STORIES (Formerly Golden West Love)
Kirby Publishing Co.: No. 4, April, 1950

4-Powell-a; Glenn Ford/Janet Leigh photo-c — 13.00 38.00 95.00

GOLDEN PICTURE CLASSIC, A
Western Printing Co. (Simon & Shuster): 1956-1957 (Text stories w/illustrations in color; 100 pgs. each)

CL-401: Treasure Island — 7.15 21.50 50.00
CL-402: Tom Sawyer — 6.00 18.00 42.00
CL-403: Black Beauty — 6.00 18.00 42.00
CL-404: Little Women — 6.00 18.00 42.00
CL-405: Heidi — 6.00 18.00 42.00
CL-406: Ben Hur — 4.25 13.00 28.00
CL-407: Around the World in 80 Days — 4.25 13.00 28.00
CL-408: Sherlock Holmes — 5.70 17.00 35.00
CL-409: The Three Musketeers — 4.25 13.00 28.00
CL-410: The Merry Advs. of Robin Hood — 4.25 13.00 28.00
CL-411: Hans Brinker — 5.70 17.00 35.00

Golden West Love #1 © Kirby Publ.

Goofy Four Color #468 © WDC

Goofy Comics #9 © STD

	GD25	FN65	NM94
CL-412: The Count of Monte Cristo	5.70	17.00	35.00

(Both soft & hardcover editions are valued the same)

NOTE: *Recent research has uncovered new information. Apparently #s 1-6 were issued in 1956 and #7-12 in 1957. But they can be found in five different series listings: CL-1 to CL-12 (softbound); CL-401 to CL-412 (also softbound); CL-101 to CL-112 (hardbound); plus two new series discoveries: A Golden Reading Adventure, publ. by Golden Press; edited down to 60 pages and reduced in size to 6x9"; only #s discovered so far are #381 (CL-4), #382 (CL-6) & #387 (CL-3). They have no reorder list and some have covers different from GPC. There have also been found British hardbound editions of GPC with dust jackets. Copies of all five listed series vary from scarce to very rare. Some editions of some series have not yet been found at all.*

GOLDEN PICTURE STORY BOOK
Racine Press (Western): Dec, 1961 (50¢, Treasury size, 52 pgs.) (All are scarce)

	GD25	FN65	NM94
ST-1-Huckleberry Hound (TV)	18.50	55.00	185.00
ST-2-Yogi Bear (TV)	18.50	55.00	185.00
ST-3-Babes in Toyland (Walt Disney's...)-Annette Funicello photo-c	22.00	66.00	220.00
ST-4-(...of Disney Ducks)-Walt Disney's Wonderful World of Ducks (Donald Duck, Uncle Scrooge, Donald's Nephews, Grandma Duck, Ludwig Von Drake, & Gyro Gearloose stories)	22.00	66.00	220.00

GOLDEN RECORD COMIC (See Amazing Spider-Man #1, Avengers #4, Fantastic Four #1, Journey Into Mystery #83)

GOLDEN STORY BOOKS
Western Printing Co. (Simon & Shuster): 1949 (Heavy covers, digest size, 128 pgs.) (Illustrated text in color)

	GD25	FN65	NM94
7-Walt Disney's Mystery in Disneyville, a book-length adventure starring Donald and Nephews, Mickey and Nephews, and with Minnie, Daisy and Goofy. Art by Dick Moores & Manuel Gonzales (scarce)	23.00	69.00	185.00
10-Bugs Bunny's Treasure Hunt, a book-length adventure starring Bugs & Porky Pig, with Petunia Pig & Nephew, Cicero. Art by Tom McKimson (scarce)	15.00	45.00	120.00

GOLDEN WEST LOVE (Golden Love Stories No. 4)
Kirby Publishing Co.: Sept-Oct, 1949 - No. 3, Feb, 1950 (All 52 pgs.)

	GD25	FN65	NM94
1-Powell-a in all; Roussos-a; painted-c	17.00	52.00	130.00
2,3: Photo-c	12.00	36.00	90.00

GOLDEN WEST RODEO TREASURY (See Dell Giants)

GOLDILOCKS (See March of Comics No. 1)

GOLDILOCKS & THE THREE BEARS
K. K. Publications: 1943 (Giveaway)

	GD25	FN65	NM94
nn	9.30	28.00	70.00

GOLD KEY CHAMPION
Gold Key: Mar, 1978 - No. 2, May, 1978 (50¢, 52pgs.)

	GD25	FN65	NM94
1-Space Family Robinson; half-r		2.00	6.00
2-Mighty Samson; half-r		2.00	6.00

GOLD KEY SPOTLIGHT
Gold Key: May, 1976 - No. 11, Feb, 1978

	GD25	FN65	NM94
1-Tom, Dick & Harriet	.85	2.60	7.00
2-5,7,10,11: 2-Wacky Advs. of Cracky. 3-Wacky Witch. 4-Tom, Dick & Harriet. 5-Wacky Advs. of Cracky. 7-Wacky Witch & Greta Ghost 10-O. G. Whiz. 11-Tom, Dick & Harriet			5.00
6,8,9: 6-Dagar the Invincible; Santos-a; origin Demonomicon. 8-The Occult Files of Dr. Spektor, Simbar, Lu-sai; Santos-a. 9-Tragg	.85	2.60	7.00

GOLD MEDAL COMICS
Cambridge House: 1945 (25¢, one-shot, 132 pgs.)

	GD25	FN65	NM94
nn-Captain Truth by Fugitani, Crime Detector, The Witch of Salem, Luckyman, others app.	24.00	72.00	180.00

GOMER PYLE (TV)
Gold Key: July, 1966 - No. 3, Jan, 1967

	GD25	FN65	NM94
1-Photo front/back-c	6.25	19.00	70.00
2,3	4.50	13.50	50.00

GON
DC Comics (Paradox Press): July, 1996 - No. 4, Oct, 1996 ($5.95, B&W, digest-size, limited series)

	GD25	FN65	NM94
1-4: Misadventures of baby dinosaur; Tanaka-c/a/scripts in all		2.00	6.00

GON COLOR SPECTACULAR
DC Comics (Paradox Press): 1998 ($5.95, square-bound)

	GD25	FN65	NM94
nn-Tanaka-c/a/scripts			5.95

GON SWIMMIN'
DC Comics (Paradox Press): 1997 ($6.95, B&W, digest-size)

	GD25	FN65	NM94
nn-Tanaka-c/a/scripts in all			6.95

GOODBYE, MR. CHIPS (See Movie Comics)

GOOD GIRL ART QUARTERLY
AC Comics: Summer, 1990 - No. 16, 1992? (B&W/color, 52 pgs.)

	GD25	FN65	NM94
1,3-16 ($3.50)-All have one new story (often FemForce) & rest reprints by Baker, Ward & other "good girl" artists			3.50
2 ($3.95)			4.00

GOOD GUYS, THE
Defiant: Nov, 1993 - No. 9, July, 1994 ($2.50/$3.25/$3.50)

	GD25	FN65	NM94
1-($3.50, 52 pgs.)-Glory x-over from Plasm			3.50
2,3,5-9: 9-Pre-Schism issue			2.50
4-($3.25, 52 pgs.)			3.25

GOOFY (Disney)(See Dynabrite Comics, Mickey Mouse Magazine V4#7, Walt Disney Showcase #35 & Wheaties)
Dell Publishing Co.: No. 468, May, 1953 - Sept-Nov, 1962

	GD25	FN65	NM94
Four Color 468 (#1)	11.00	34.00	125.00
Four Color 562,627,658,702,747,802,857	6.40	19.00	70.00
Four Color 899,952,987,1053,1094,1149,1201	3.60	11.00	40.00
12-308-211(Dell, 9-11/62)	3.60	11.00	40.00

GOOFY ADVENTURES
Disney Comics: June, 1990 - No. 17, 1991 ($1.50)

	GD25	FN65	NM94
1-17: Most new stories. 2-Joshua Quagmire-a w/free poster. 7-WDC&S-r plus new-a. 9-Gottfredson-r. 14-Super Goof story. 15-All Super Goof issue. 17-Gene Colan-a(p)			1.50

GOOFY ADVENTURE STORY (See Goofy No. 857)

GOOFY COMICS (Companion to Happy Comics)(Not Disney)
Nedor Publ. Co. No. 1-14/Standard No. 14-48: June, 1943 - No. 48, 1953 (Animated Cartoons)

	GD25	FN65	NM94
1-Funny animal; Oriolo-c	24.00	72.00	180.00
2	12.00	36.00	90.00
3-10	9.30	28.00	70.00
11-19	7.15	21.50	50.00
20-35-Frazetta text illos in all	9.30	28.00	65.00
36-48	5.75	17.00	35.00

GOOFY SUCCESS STORY (See Goofy No. 702)

GOOSE (Humor magazine)
Cousins Publ. (Fawcett): Sept, 1976 - No. 3, 1976 (75¢, 52 pgs., B&W)

	GD25	FN65	NM94
1-Nudity in all	1.80	5.40	18.00
2,3: 2-Fonz-c/s; Lone Ranger story. 3-Wonder Woman, King Kong, Six Million Dollar Man stories	1.20	3.60	12.00

GORDO (See Comics Revue No. 5 & Giant Comics Edition)

GORGO (Based on M.G.M. movie) (See Return of...)
Charlton Comics: May, 1961 - No. 23, Sept, 1965

	GD25	FN65	NM94
1-Ditko-a, 22 pgs.	20.00	60.00	200.00
2,3-Ditko-c/a	10.00	30.00	100.00
4-10: 4-Ditko-c	6.00	18.00	60.00

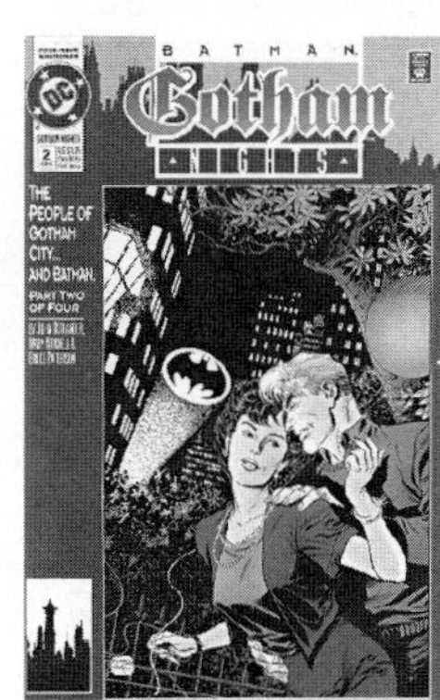

Gotham Nights #2 © DC

Great Action Comics #8 © I.W. Ent.

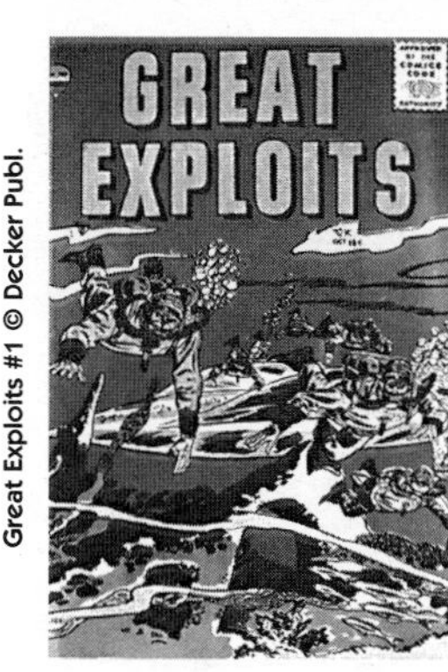

Great Exploits #1 © Decker Publ.

GD25 FN65 NM94

11,13-16-Ditko-a 5.00 15.00 50.00
12,17-23: 12-Reptisaurus x-over; Montes/Bache-a-No. 17-23. 20-Giordano-c 2.50 7.50 25.00
Gorgo's Revenge('62)-Becomes Return of... 4.20 12.60 42.00

GOSPEL BLIMP, THE
Spire Christian Comics (Fleming H. Revell Co.): 1973,1974 (35¢/39¢, 36 pgs.)
nn 5.00

G.O.T.H.
Verotik: Dec, 1995 - No. 3, June, 1996 ($2.95, limited series, mature)
1-3: Danzig scripts; Liam Sharpe-a. 3.00

GOTHAM BY GASLIGHT (A Tale of the Batman)(See Batman: Master of...)
DC Comics: 1989 ($3.95, one-shot, squarebound, 52 pgs.)
nn-Mignola/Russell-a; intro by Robert Bloch 4.00

GOTHAM NIGHTS (See Batman: Gotham Nights II)
DC Comics: Mar, 1992 - No. 4, June, 1992 ($1.25, limited series)
1-4: Featuring Batman 1.25

GOTHIC ROMANCES
Atlas/Seaboard Publ.: Dec, 1974 (75¢, B&W, magazine, 76 pgs.)
1-Text w/ illos by N. Adams, Chaykin, Heath (2 pgs. ea.); painted cover 3.35 10.00 40.00

GOTHIC TALES OF LOVE (Magazine)
Marvel Comics: Apr, 1975 - No. 2, Jun, 1975 (B&W, 76 pgs.)
1,2-painted-c/a 2.70 8.00 30.00

GOVERNOR & J. J., THE (TV)
Gold Key: Feb, 1970 - No. 3, Aug, 1970 (Photo-c)
1 2.75 8.00 30.00
2,3 2.00 6.00 22.00

GRACKLE, THE
Acclaim Comics: Jan, 1997 - No. 4, Apr, 1997 ($2.95, B&W)
1-4: Mike Baron scripts & Paul Gulacy-c/a. 1-4-Doublecross 3.00

GRAFIK MUZIK
Caliber Press: Dec, 1989 - No. 3, May, 1990 ($2.95, 52 pgs.)
1-3: Mike Allred-c/a/scripts 3.00

GRANDMA DUCK'S FARM FRIENDS(See Walt Disney's C&S 293 & Wheaties)
Dell Publishing Co.: No. 763, Jan, 1957 - No. 1279, Feb, 1962 (Disney)
Four Color 763 (#1) 6.40 19.00 70.00
Four Color 873 4.50 13.50 50.00
Four Color 965,1279 3.60 11.00 40.00
Four Color 1010,1073,1161-Barks-a; 1073,1161-Barks c/a 12.00 37.00 135.00

GRAND PRIX (Formerly Hot Rod Racers)
Charlton Comics: No. 16, Sept, 1967 - No. 31, May, 1970
16-Features Rick Roberts 2.50 7.50 24.00
17-20 2.25 6.75 18.00
21-31 1.75 5.25 14.00

GRAVEDIGGERS
Acclaim Comics: Nov, 1996 - No. 4, Feb, 1997 ($2.95, B&W)
1-4: Moretti scripts 3.00

GRAVESTONE
Malibu Comics: July, 1993 - No. 7, Feb, 1994 ($2.25)
1-6: 3-Polybagged w/Skycap 2.25
7-($2.50) 2.50

GRAVE TALES (Also see Maggots)
Hamilton Comics: Oct, 1991 - No. 3, Feb, 1992 ($3.95, B&W, mag., 52 pgs.)
1-Staton-c/a .90 2.70 8.00

GD25 FN65 NM94

2,3: 2-Staton-a; Morrow-c 2.00 6.00

GRAY GHOST, THE
Dell Publishing Co.: No. 911, July, 1958; No. 1000, June-Aug, 1959
Four Color 911 (#1)-Photo-c 8.00 25.00 90.00
Four Color 1000-Photo-c 8.00 25.00 90.00

GREASE MONKEY
Image Comics: Jan, 1998 - Present ($2.95, B&W)
1,2-Tim Eldred-s/a 2.95

GREAT ACTION COMICS
I. W. Enterprises: 1958 (Reprints with new covers)
1-Captain Truth reprinted from Gold Medal #1 2.50 7.50 20.00
8,9-Reprints Phantom Lady #15 & 23 8.00 24.00 80.00

GREAT AMERICAN COMICS PRESENTS - THE SECRET VOICE
Peter George 4-Star Publ./American Features Syndicate: 1945 (10¢)
1-Anti-Nazi; "What Really Happened to Hitler" 24.00 72.00 180.00

GREAT AMERICAN WESTERN, THE
AC Comics: 1987 - No. 4, 1990? ($1.75/$2.95/$3.50, B&W with some color)
1($1.75)-Western-r plus Bill Black-a 1.80
2,3 ($2.95) 2-Tribute to ME comics; Durango Kid photo-c 3-Tribute to Tom Mix plus Roy Rogers, Durango Kid; Billy the Kid-r by Severin; photo-c 3.00
4 ($3.50, 52 pgs., 16 pgs. color)-Tribute to Lash LaRue; photo-c & interior photos; Fawcett-r 3.50
...Presents 1 (1991, $5.00) New Sunset Carson; film history 5.00

GREAT CAT FAMILY, THE (Disney-TV/Movie)
Dell Publishing Co.: No. 750, Nov, 1956 (one-shot)
Four Color 750-Pinocchio & Alice app. 5.50 16.50 60.00

GREAT COMICS
Great Comics Publications: Nov, 1941 - No. 3, Jan, 1942
1-Origin/1st app. The Great Zarro; Madame Strange & Guy Gorham, Wizard of Science & The Great Zarro begin 112.00 336.00 950.00
2-Buck Johnson, Jungle Explorer app.; X-Mas-c 56.00 168.00 475.00
3-Futuro Takes Hitler to Hell-c/s; "The Lost City" movie story (starring William Boyd); continues in Choice Comics #3 129.00 388.00 1100.00

GREAT COMICS
Novack Publishing Co./Jubilee Comics/Barrel O' Fun: 1945
1-(Novack)-The Defenders, Capt. Power app.; L. B. Cole-c 37.00 112.00 280.00
1-(Jubilee)-Same cover; Boogey Man, Satanas, & The Sorcerer & His Apprentice 25.00 76.00 190.00
1-(Barrel O' Fun)-L. B. Cole-c; Barrel O' Fun overprinted in indicia; Li'l Cactus, Cuckoo Sheriff (humorous) 17.00 50.00 125.00

GREAT DOGPATCH MYSTERY (See Mammy Yokum & the...)

GREATEST BATMAN STORIES EVER TOLD, THE (See Batman)

GREATEST JOKER STORIES EVER TOLD, THE (See Batman)

GREAT EXPLOITS
Decker Publ./Red Top: Oct, 1957
1-Krigstein-a(2) (re-issue on cover); reprints Daring Advs. #6 by Approved Comics 6.50 19.50 45.00

GREAT FOODINI, THE (See Foodini)

GREAT GAZOO, THE (The Flintstones)(TV)
Charlton Comics: Aug, 1973 - No. 20, Jan, 1977 (Hanna-Barbera)
1 2.20 6.25 22.00
2-10 1.20 3.60 12.00
11-20 .90 2.70 8.00

GREAT GRAPE APE, THE (TV)(See TV Stars #1)
Charlton Comics: Sept, 1976 - No. 2, Nov, 1976 (Hanna-Barbera)

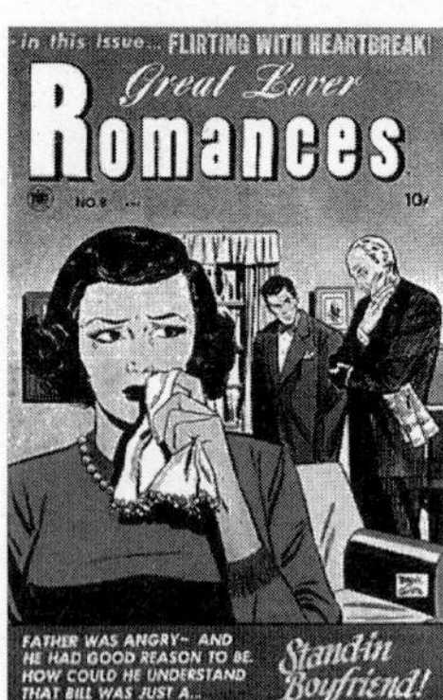

Great Lover Romances #8 © TOBY

Green Arrow #4 © DC

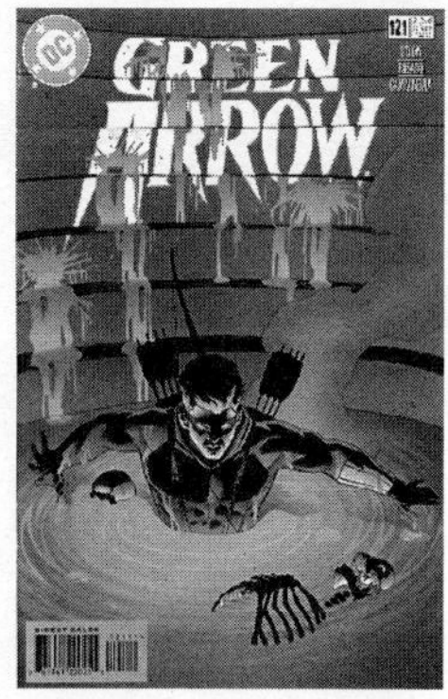

Green Arrow #121 © DC

GD25 FN65 NM94

1 1.40 4.20 14.00
2 .90 2.70 9.00

GREAT LOCOMOTIVE CHASE, THE (Disney)
Dell Publishing Co.: No. 712, Sept, 1956 (one-shot)

Four Color 712-Movie, photo-c 6.40 19.00 70.00

GREAT LOVER ROMANCES (Young Lover Romances #4,5)
Toby Press (Photo-c #1-5, 10 ,13, 15, 17) (no #4, 5): 3/51; #2, 1951(nd); #3, 1952 (nd); #6, Oct?, 1952 - No. 22, May, 1955

1-Jon Juan story-r/Jon Juan #1 by Schomburg; Dr. Anthony King app. 14.00 42.00 105.00
2-Jon Juan, Dr. Anthony King app. 7.50 22.50 52.00
3,7,9-14,16-22: 10-Rita Hayworth photo-c. 17-Rita Hayworth & Aldo Ray photo-c 5.00 15.00 30.00
6-Kurtzman-a (10/52) 7.85 23.50 55.00
8-Five pgs. of "Pin-Up Pete" by Sparling 7.85 23.50 55.00
15-Liz Taylor photo-c 9.30 28.00 65.00

GREAT PEOPLE OF GENESIS, THE
David C. Cook Publ. Co.: No date (Religious giveaway, 64 pgs.)

nn-Reprint/Sunday Pix Weekly 2.40 6.00 12.00

GREAT RACE, THE (See Movie Classics)

GREAT SACRAMENT, THE
Catechetical Guild: 1953 (Giveaway, 36 pgs.)

nn 2.40 6.00 12.00

GREAT SCOTT SHOE STORE (See Bulls-Eye)

GREAT WEST (Magazine)
M. F. Enterprises: 1969 (B&W, 52 pgs.)

V1#1 2.40 6.00

GREAT WESTERN
Magazine Enterprises: No. 8, Jan-Mar, 1954 - No. 11, Oct-Dec, 1954

8(A-1 93)-Trail Colt by Guardineer; Powell Red Hawk-r/Straight Arrow begins, ends #11; Durango Kid story 19.00 56.00 140.00
9(A-1 105), 11(A-1 127)-Ghost Rider, Durango Kid app. in each. 9-Red Mask-c, but no app. 11.00 32.00 80.00
10(A-1 113)-The Calico Kid by Guardineer-r/Tim Holt #8; Straight Arrow, Durango Kid app. 11.00 32.00 80.00
I.W. Reprint #1,2 9: 1,2-r/Straight Arrow #36,42. 9-r/Straight Arrow #? 2.25 6.75 18.00
I.W. Reprint #8-Origin Ghost Rider(r/Tim Holt #11); Tim Holt app.; Bolle-a 2.50 7.50 22.00

NOTE: ***Guardineer*** *c-8.* ***Powell*** *a(r)-8-11 (from Straight Arrow).*

GREEN ARROW (See Action #440, Adventure, Brave & the Bold, DC Super Stars #17, Detective #521, Flash #217, Green Lantern #76, Justice League of America #4, Leading, More Fun #73 (1st app.), Showcase '95 #9 & World's Finest Comics)

GREEN ARROW
DC Comics: May, 1983 - No. 4, Aug, 1983 (limited series)

1-Origin; Speedy cameo; Mike W. Barr scripts, Trevor Von Eeden-c/a. 3.00
2-4 2.00

GREEN ARROW
DC Comics: Feb, 1988 - No. 137, Oct, 1998 ($1.00/$1.50/$1.95/$2.25/$2.50) (Painted-c #1-3)

1-Mike Grell scripts begin, ends #80 3.00
2 2.25
3-49,51-74,76-86: 27,28-Warlord app. 35-38-Co-stars Black Canary; Bill Wray-i. 40-Grell-a. 47-Begin $1.50-c. 63-No longer has mature readers on-c. 63-66-Shado app. 68-Last $1.50-c. 81-Aparo-a begins, ends #100; Nuklon app. 82-Intro & death of Rival. 83-Huntress-c/story. 84-Deathstroke cameo. 85-Deathstroke-c/app. 86-Catwoman-c/story w/Jim Balent layouts 2.00

GD25 FN65 NM94

50,75-($2.50, 52 pgs.): Anniversary issues. 75-Arsenal (Roy Harper) & Shado app. 2.50
0,87-96: 87-$1.95-c begins. 88-Guy Gardner, Martian Manhunter, & Wonder Woman-c/app.; Flash-c. 89-Anarky app. 90-(9/94)-Zero Hour tie-in. 0-(10/94)-1st app. Connor Hawke; Aparo-a(p). 91-(11/94). 93-1st app. Camorouge. 95-Hal Jordan cameo. 96-Intro new Force of July; Hal Jordan (Parallax) app; Oliver Queen learns that Connor Hawke is his son 2.00
97-99,102-109: 97-Begin $2.25-c; no Aparo-a. 97-99-Arsenal app. 102,103-Underworld Unleashed x-over. 104-GL(Kyle Rayner)-c/app. 105-Robin-c/app. 107-109-Thorn app. 109-Lois Lane cameo; Weeks-c. 2.50
100-($3.95)-Foil-c; Superman app. 4.00
101-Apparent death of Oliver Queen; Superman app. 2.00 6.00
110,111-GL x-over. 110-Intro Hatchet. 2.25
112-124: 114-Final Night. 115-117-Black Canary & Oracle app. 2.25
125-($3.50, 48 pgs)-GL x-over cont. in GL #92 3.50
126-137: 126-Begin $2.50-c. 130-GL & Flash x-over. 132,133-JLA app. 134,135-Brotherhood of the Fist pts. 1,5. 136-Hal Jordan-c/app. 137-Last issue; Superman app. 2.50
#1,000,000 (11/98) 853rd Century x-over 2.50
Annual 1 (1988, $2.00)-No Grell scripts 2.00
Annual 2 (1989, $2.50, 68pgs.)-No Grell scripts; recaps origin Green Arrow, Speedy, Black Canary & others 2.50
Annual 3 (1990, $2.95, 68pgs.)-Bill Wray-a 3.00
Annual 4 (1991, $2.95, 68pgs.)-50th anniversary issue 3.00
Annual 5 (1992, $3.00, 68pgs.)-Batman, Eclipso app. 3.00
Annual 6 (1993, $3.50, 68pgs.)-Bloodlines; Hook app. 3.50
Annual 7 (1995, $3.95)-Year One story 4.00

NOTE: ***Aparo*** *a-0, 81-85, 86 (partial),87p, 88p, 91-95, 96i, 98-100p, 109p; c-81,98-100p.* ***Austin*** *c-96i.* ***Balent*** *layouts-86.* ***Burchett*** *c-91-95.* ***Campanella*** *a-100-108i, 110-113i; c-99i, 101-108i,110-113i.* ***Denys Cowan*** *a-39p, 41-43p, 47p, 48p, 60p; c-41-43.* ***Damaggio*** *a(p)-97p, 100-108p, 110-112p; c-97-99p, 101-108p, 110-113p.* ***Mike Grell*** *c-1-4, 10p, 11, 39, 40, 44, 45, 47-80, Annual 4, 5.* ***Nasser/Netzer*** *a-89, 96.* ***Sienkiewicz*** *a-109i.* ***Springer*** *a-67, 68.* ***Weeks*** *c-109.*

GREEN ARROW: THE LONG BOW HUNTERS
DC Comics: Aug, 1987 - No. 3, Oct, 1987 ($2.95, limited series, mature)

1-Grell-c/a in all 4.00
1,2-2nd printings 3.00
2,3 3.00
Trade paperback (1989, $12.95)-r/#1-3 13.00

GREEN ARROW: THE WONDER YEAR
DC Comics: Feb, 1993 - No. 4, May, 1993 ($1.75, limited series)

1-4: Mike Grell-a(p)/scripts & Gray Morrow-a(i) 1.75

GREEN BERET, THE (See Tales of...)

GREEN CANDLES
DC Comics (Paradox Press): Sept, 1995 - No. 3, Dec, 1995 ($5.95, B&W, limited series, digest size)

1-3 2.00 6.00

GREEN GIANT COMICS (Also see Colossus Comics)
Pelican Publ. (Funnies, Inc.): 1940 (No price on cover; distributed in New York City only)

GD25 FN65 VF82 NM94

1-Dr. Nerod, Green Giant, Black Arrow, Mundoo & Master Mystic app.; origin Colossus (Rare) 900.00 2700.00 5400.00 8500.00

NOTE: *The idea for this book came from George Kapitan. Printed by Moreau Publ. of Orange, N.J. as an experiment to see if they could profitably use the idle time of their 40-page Hoe color press. The experiment failed due to the difficulty of obtaining good quality color registration and Mr. Moreau believes the book never reached the stands. The book has no price or date which lends credence to this. Contains five pages reprinted from Motion Picture Funnies Weekly.*

GREEN GOBLIN
Marvel Comics: Oct, 1995 - No. 13, Oct, 1996 ($2.95/$1.95)

1-($2.95)-Scott McDaniel-c/a begins, ends #7; foil-c 3.00
2-13: 2-Begin $1.95-c. 4-Hobgoblin-c/app; Thing app. 6-Daredevil-c/app.

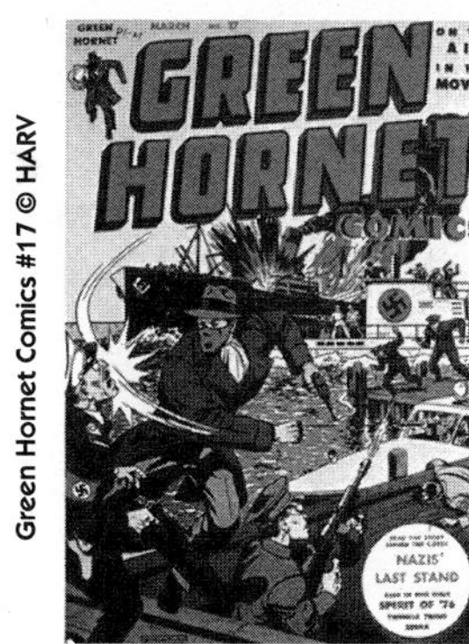

Green Hornet Comics #17 © HARV

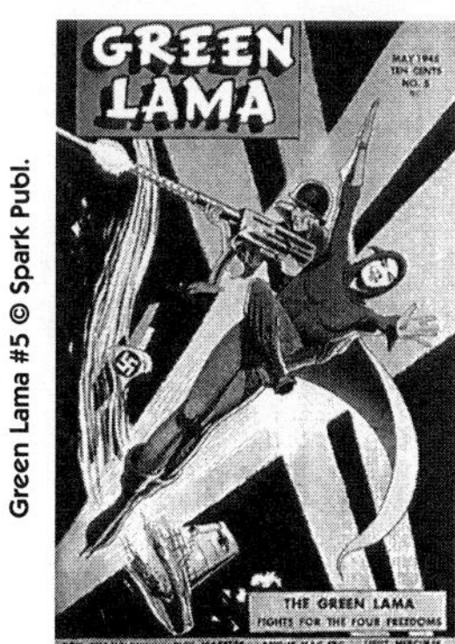

Green Lama #5 © Spark Publ.

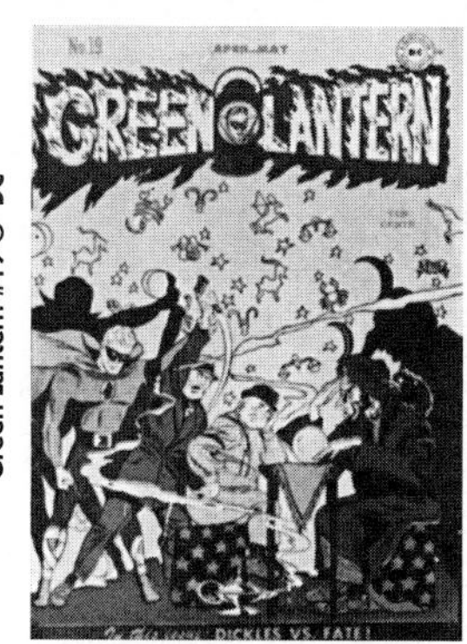

Green Lantern #19 © DC

GD25 FN65 NM94

8-Darrick Robertson-a; McDaniel-c. 10-Arcade app. 12,13-Onslaught x-over. 13-Green Goblin quits; Spider-Man app. 2.00

GREENHAVEN
Aircel Publishing: 1988 - No. 3, 1988 ($2.00, limited series, 28 pgs.)

1-3 2.00

GREEN HORNET, THE (TV)
Dell Publishing Co./Gold Key: Sept, 1953; Feb, 1967 - No. 3, Aug, 1967

Four Color 496-Painted-c. 23.00 68.00 250.00
1-All have Bruce Lee photo-c 19.00 57.00 210.00
2,3 13.00 40.00 145.00

GREEN HORNET, THE (Also see Kato of the... & Tales of the...)
Now Comics: Nov, 1989 - No. 14, Feb, 1991 ($1.75)
V2#1, Sept, 1991 - V2#39, Dec, 1994 ($1.95)

1 ($2.95, double-size)-Steranko painted-c; G.A. Green Hornet 3.00
1-2nd printing ('90, $3.95)-New Butler-c 4.00
2 2.00
3-8: 5-Death of original (1930s) Green Hornet. 6-Dave Dorman painted-c 2.00
9-14: 11-Snyder-c 2.00
V2#1-11,13-21,24-26,28-30,32-37,39: 1-Butler painted-c. 9-Mayerik-c 2.00
12-($2.50)-Color Green Hornet button polybagged inside 2.50
22,23-($2.95)-Bagged w/color hologravure card 3.00
27-($2.95)-Newsstand ed. polybagged w/multi-dimensional card (1993 Anniversary Special on cover) 3.00
27-($2.95)-Direct Sale ed. polybagged w/multi-dimensional card; cover variations 3.00
31,38: 31-($2.50)-Polybagged w/trading card 2.50
1-($2.50)-Polybagged w/button (same as #12) 2.50
2,3-($1.95)-Same as #13 & 14 2.00
Annual 1 (12/92, $2.50) 2.50
Annual 1994 (10/94, $2.95) 3.00

GREEN HORNET: SOLITARY SENTINEL, THE
Now Comics: Dec, 1992 - No. 3, 1993 ($2.50, limited series)

1-3 2.50

GREEN HORNET COMICS (...Racket Buster #44) (Radio, movies)
Helnit Publ. Co.(Holyoke) No. 1-6/Family Comics(Harvey) No. 7-on:
Dec, 1940 - No. 47, Sept, 1949 (See All New #13,14)(Early issues: 68 pgs.)

1-1st app. Green Hornet & Kato; origin of Green Hornet on inside front-c; intro the Black Beauty (Green Hornet's car); painted-c 400.00 1200.00 4000.00
2-Early issues based on radio adventures 147.00 441.00 1250.00
3 118.00 354.00 1000.00
4-6: 6-(8/41) 91.00 273.00 775.00
7 (6/42)-Origin The Zebra & begins; Robin Hood, Spirit of '76, Blonde Bomber & Mighty Midgets begin; new logo 80.00 240.00 680.00
8,10 69.00 207.00 585.00
9-Kirby-c 86.00 258.00 730.00
11,12-Mr. Q in both 68.00 204.00 575.00
13-1st Nazi-c; shows Hitler poster on-c 71.00 213.00 600.00
14-20 49.00 147.00 420.00
21-23,25-30 40.00 120.00 340.00
24-Sci-Fi-c 43.00 129.00 360.00
31-The Man in Black Called Fate begins (11-12/45, early app.) 43.00 129.00 360.00
32-36 39.00 117.00 290.00
37-Shock Gibson app. by Powell; S&K Kid Adonis reprinted from Stuntman #3 39.00 117.00 300.00
38-Shock Gibson, Kid Adonis app. 39.00 117.00 290.00
39-Stuntman story by S&K 44.00 132.00 370.00
40,41 28.00 84.00 210.00

GD25 FN65 NM94

42-47-Kerry Drake in all. 45-Boy Explorers on-c only. 46- "Case of the Marijuana Racket" cover/story; Kerry Drake app. 28.00 84.00 210.00

NOTE: *Fuje a-23, 24, 26. Henkle c-7-9. Kubert a-20, 30. Powell a-7-10, 12, 14, 16-21, 30, 31(2), 32(3), 33, 34(3), 35, 36, 37(2), 38. Robinson a-27. Schomburg c-15, 17-23. Kirbyish c-7, 15. Bondage c-8, 14, 18, 26, 36.*

GREEN JET COMICS, THE (See Comic Books, Series 1)

GREEN LAMA (Also see Comic Books, Series 1, Daring Adventures #17 & Prize Comics #7)
Spark Publications/Prize No. 7 on: Dec, 1944 - No. 8, Mar, 1946

1-Intro. Lt. Hercules & The Boy Champions; Mac Raboy-c/a #1-8 115.00 345.00 975.00
2-Lt. Hercules borrows the Human Torch's powers for one panel 68.00 204.00 575.00
3,6,8: 7-X-mas-c; Raboy craft tint-c/a 54.00 162.00 460.00
4-Dick Tracy take-off in Lt. Hercules story by H. L. Gold (sci-fiction writer) 54.00 162.00 460.00
5-Lt. Hercules story; Little Orphan Annie, Smilin' Jack & Snuffy Smith take-off (5/45) 54.00 162.00 460.00
7-X-mas-c; Raboy craft tint-c/a (note: a small quantity of NM copies surfaced) 41.00 123.00 330.00

NOTE: *Robinson a-3-5, 8. Roussos a-8. Formerly a pulp hero who began in 1940.*

GREEN LANTERN (1st Series) (See All-American, All Flash Quarterly, All Star Comics, The Big All-American & Comic Cavalcade)
National Periodical Publications/All-American: Fall, 1941 - No. 38, May-June, 1949 (#1-18 are quarterly)

	GD25	FN65	VF82	NM94
1-Origin retold; classic Purcell-c	2,300.00	6,900.00	13,800.00	27,000.00

	GD25	FN65	NM94
2-1st book-length story	580.00	1740.00	5800.00
3-Classic German war-c by Mart Nodell	410.00	1230.00	4100.00
4-Green Lantern & Doiby Dickles join the Army	316.00	950.00	3000.00
5	229.00	687.00	1950.00
6,8: 8-Hop Harrigan begins; classic-c	182.00	546.00	1550.00
7-Robot-c.	200.00	600.00	1700.00
9,10: 10-Origin/1st app. Vandal Savage	165.00	495.00	1400.00
11-17,19,20: 12-Origin/1st app. Gambler	126.00	378.00	1070.00
18-Christmas-c	138.00	414.00	1175.00
21-26,28-30: 30-Origin/1st app. Streak the Wonder Dog by Toth (2-3/48)	115.00	345.00	975.00
27-Origin/1st app. Sky Pirate	118.00	354.00	1000.00
31-35: 35-Kubert-c. 35-38-New logo	97.00	291.00	825.00
36-38: 37-Sargon the Sorcerer app.	118.00	354.00	1000.00

NOTE: *Book-length stories #2-7. Mayer/Moldoff c-9. Mayer/Purcell c-8. Purcell c-1. Mart Nodell c-2, 3, 7. Paul Reinman c-11, 12, 15-22. Toth a-28, 30, 31, 34-38; c-28, 30, 34p, 36-38p. Cover to #8 says Fall while the indicia says Summer Issue. Streak the Wonder Dog c-30 (w/Green Lantern), 34, 36, 38.*

GREEN LANTERN (See Action Comics Weekly, Adventure Comics, Brave & the Bold, DC Special, DC Special Series, Flash, Guy Gardner, Guy Gardner Reborn, Justice League of America, Parallax: Emerald Night, Showcase, Showcase '93 #12 & Tales of The...Corps)

GREEN LANTERN (2nd Series)(Green Lantern Corps #206 on)
(See Showcase #22-24)
National Periodical Publ./DC Comics: 7-8/60 - No. 89, 4-5/72; No. 90, 8-9/76 - No. 205, 10/86

	GD25	FN65	VF82	NM94
1-(7-8/60)-Origin retold; Gil Kane-c/a continues; 1st app. Guardians of the Universe	190.00	570.00	1250.00	2700.00

	GD25	FN65	NM94
2-1st Pieface	58.00	174.00	700.00
3-Contains readers poll	36.00	108.00	400.00
4,5: 5-Origin/1st app. Hector Hammond	31.00	93.00	310.00
6-Intro Tomar-Re the alien G.L.	29.00	87.00	290.00
7-Origin/1st app. Sinestro (7-8/61)	25.00	75.00	250.00
8-10: 8-1st 5700 A.D. story; grey tone-c. 9-1st Jordan Brothers; last 10¢ issue	22.00	66.00	220.00
11,12	15.00	45.00	150.00

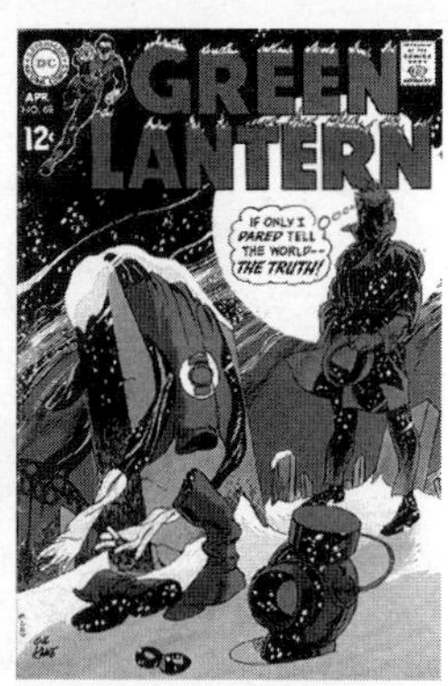

Green Lantern #68 (2nd Series) © DC

Green Lantern #110 (2nd Series) © DC

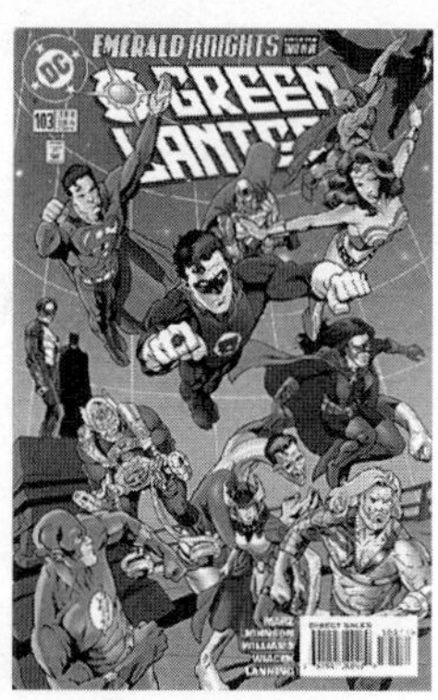

Green Lantern #103 (3rd Series) © DC

GD25 FN65 NM94

13-Flash x-over 18.00 54.00 180.00
14-20: 14-Origin/1st app. Sonar. 16-Origin & 1st app. Star Sapphire. 20-Flash x-over 13.00 39.00 130.00
21-30: 21-Origin & 1st app. Dr. Polaris. 23-1st Tattooed Man. 24-Origin & 1st app. Shark. 29-JLA cameo; 1st Blackhand 11.00 33.00 110.00
31-39: 37-1st app. Evil Star (villain) 9.00 27.00 90.00
40-1st app. Crisis (10/65); 2nd solo G.A. Green Lantern in Silver Age (see Showcase #55); origin The Guardians; Doiby Dickles app. 40.00 120.00 475.00
41-44,46-50: 42-Zatanna x-over. 43-Flash x-over 7.00 21.00 70.00
45-2nd S.A. app. G.A. Green Lantern in title (6/66) 13.00 39.00 130.00
51,53-58 5.25 15.75 52.00
52-G.A. Green Lantern x-over 7.50 22.50 75.00
59-1st app. Guy Gardner (3/68) 19.00 57.00 190.00
60,62-69: 69-Wood inks; last 12 cent issue 3.50 10.50 35.00
61-G.A. Green Lantern x-over 5.00 15.00 50.00
70-75 2.20 6.60 24.00
76-(4/70)-Begin Green Lantern/Green Arrow series (by Neal Adams #76-89) ends #122 (see Flash #217 for 2nd series) 16.00 48.00 175.00
77 4.75 14.00 52.00
78-80 3.80 11.50 42.00
81-84: 82-Wrightson-i(1 pg.). 83-G.L. reveals i.d. to Carol Ferris. 84-N. Adams/ Wrightson-a(22 pgs.); last 15¢-c; partial photo-c 3.50 10.50 38.00
85,86-(52 pgs.)-Anti-drug issues. 86-G.A. Green Lantern-r; Toth-a 4.75 14.00 52.00
87-(52 pgs.): 2nd app. Guy Gardner (cameo); 1st app. John Stewart (12-1/ 71-72) (becomes 3rd Green Lantern in #182) 2.90 8.70 32.00
88-(2-3/72, 52 pgs.)-Unpubbed G.A. Green Lantern story; Green Lantern-r/ Showcase #23. N. Adams-c/a (1 pg.) 1.40 4.20 14.00
89-(4-5/72, 52 pgs.)-G.A. Green Lantern-r; Green Lantern & Green Arrow move to Flash #217 (2nd team-up series) 2.00 6.00 20.00
90 (8-9/76)-Begin 3rd Green Lantern/Green Arrow team-up series; Mike Grell-c/a begins, ends #111 1.10 3.30 11.00
91-99 2.00 6.00
100-(1/78, Giant)-1st app. Air Wave II 1.20 3.60 12.00
101-111,113-115,117-119: 107-1st Tales of the G.L. Corps story. 108-110-(44 pgs)-G.A. Green Lantern back-ups in each. 111-Origin retold; G.A. Green Lantern app. 4.50
112-G.A. Green Lantern origin retold 1.10 3.30 11.00
116-1st app. Guy Gardner as a G.L. (5/79) 2.50 7.40 27.00
120,121,124-135,138-140,142-149: 130-132-Tales of the G.L. Corps. 132-Adam Strange series begins, ends 147. 142,143-Omega Men app.; Perez-c. 144-Omega Men cameo. 148-Tales of the G.L. Corps begins, ends #173 2.50
122-Last Green Lantern/Green Arrow team-up 2.50
123-Green Lantern back to solo action; 2nd app. Guy Gardner as Green Lantern 4.00
136,137-1st app. Citadel; Space Ranger app. 2.50
141-1st app. Omega Men (6/81) 2.50
150-Anniversary issue, 52 pgs.; no G.L. Corps 3.00
151-170: 159-Origin Evil Star. 160,161-Omega Men app. 2.00
171-193,196-199,201-205: (75¢ cover). 181-Hal Jordan resigns as G.L. 182-John Stewart becomes new G.L.; origin recap of Hal Jordan as G.L. 185-Origin new G.L. (John Stewart).188-I.D. revealed; Alan Moore back-up scripts. 191-Re-intro Star Sapphire (cameo). 192-Re-intro Star Sapphire (1st full app.). 194,198-Crisis x-over. 199-Hal Jordan returns as a member of G.L. Corps (3 G.L.s now). 201-Green Lantern Corps begins (is cover title, says premiere issue) 2.00
194-Hal Jordan/Guy Gardner battle; Guardians choose Guy Gardner to become new Green Lantern 3.00
195-Guy Gardner becomes Green Lantern; Crisis x-over .85 2.60 7.00
200-Double-size 2.50
Annual 1 (Listed as Tales Of The...)

GD25 FN65 NM94

Annual 2,3 (See Green Lantern Corps Annual #2,3)
Special 1 (1988), 2 (1989)-(Both $1.50, 52 pgs.) 2.00
NOTE: ***N. Adams*** *a-76, 77-87p, 89; c-63, 76-89.* ***M. Anderson*** *a-137i.* ***Austin*** *a-93i, 94i, 171i.* ***Chaykin*** *c-196.* ***Greene*** *a-39-49i, 58-63i; c-54-58i.* ***Grell*** *a-90-106, 108-111; c-90-106, 108-112.* ***Heck*** *a-120-122p.* ***Infantino*** *a-137p, 145-147p, 151, 152p.* ***Gil Kane*** *a-1-49p, 50-57, 58-61p, 68-75p, 85p(r), 87p(r), 88p(r), 156, 177, 184p; c-1-52, 54-61p, 67-75, 123, 154, 156, 165-171, 177, 184.* ***Newton*** *a-148p, 149p, 181.* ***Perez*** *c-132p, 141-144.* ***Sekowsky*** *a-65p, 170p.* ***Simonson*** *c-200.* ***Sparling*** *a-63p.* ***Starlin*** *c-129, 133.* ***Staton*** *a-117p, 123-127p, 128, 129-131p, 132-139, 140p, 141-146, 147p, 148-150, 151-155p; c-107p, 117p, 135(i), 136p, 145p, 146, 147, 148-152p, 155p.* ***Toth*** *a-86r, 171p.* ***Tuska*** *a-166-168p, 170p.*

GREEN LANTERN (3rd Series)
DC Comics: June, 1990 - Present ($1.00/$1.25/$1.50/$1.75/$1.95/$1.99)

1-Hal Jordan, John Stewart & Guy Gardner return; Batman app. 3.00
2,3 2.00
4-8 1.25
9-12-Guy Gardner solo story 2.50
13-($1.75, 52 pgs.) 2.00
14-18,20-24,26: 18-Guy Gardner solo story. 26-Last $1.00-c 1.00
19-($1.75, 52 pgs.)-50th anniversary issue; Mart Nodell (original G.A. artist) part-p on G.A. Gr. Lantern; G. Kane-c 1.75
25-($1.75, 52 pgs.)-Hal Jordan/Guy Gardner battle 2.00
27-45,47: 30,31-Gorilla Grodd-c/story(see Flash #69). 38,39-Adam Strange-c/ story. 42-Deathstroke-c/s. 47-Green Arrow x-over 1.25
46-Superman app. cont'd in Superman #82 5.00
48,49: 48-Emerald Twilight part 1; begin $1.50-c 5.00
50-($2.95, 52 pgs.)-Glow-in-the-dark-c 2.00 6.00
0, 51-62: 51-1st app. New Green Lantern (Kyle Rayner) with new costume. 53-Superman-c/story. 55-(9/94)-Zero Hour. 0-(10/94). 56-(11/94) 2.00
63,64-Kyle Rayner vs. Hal Jordan. 5.00
65-92: 63-Begin $1.75-c. 65-New Titans app. 66,67-Flash app. 71-Batman & Robin app. 72-Shazam!-c/app. 73-Wonder Woman-c/app. 73-75-Adam Strange app. 76,77-Green Arrow x-over. 80-Final Night x-over. 81-(Regular Edition)-Memorial for Hal Jordan (Parallax); most DC heroes app. 87-JLA app. 91-Genesis x-over. 92-Green Arrow x-over. 2.00
81-($3.95, Deluxe Edition)-Embossed prism-c 5.00
93-97: 93-Begin $1.95-c; Deadman app. 94-Superboy app. 95-Starlin-a(p). 2.00
98,99-Legion of Super-Heroes-c/app. 2.50
100-($2.95) Two covers (Jordan & Rayner); vs. Sinestro 5.00
101-106: Hal Jordan-c/app. 103-Begin $1.99-c; JLA-c/app. 104-Green Arrow-c/app. 105,106-Parallax app. 3.00
107-109: 107-Jade becomes a Green Lantern 1.99
#1,000,000 (11/98) 853rd Century x-over 2.00
Annual 1 (1992, $2.50, 68 pgs.)-Eclipso app. 2.50
Annual 2 (1993, $2.50, 68 pgs.)-Intro Nightblade 2.50
Annual 3 (1994, $2.95)-Elseworlds story 3.00
Annual 4 (1995, $3.50)-Year One story 3.50
Annual 5 (1996, $2.95)-Legends of the Dead Earth 3.00
Annual 6 (1997, $3.95)-Pulp Heroes story 3.95
Annual 7 (1998, $2.95)-Ghosts; Wrightson-c 2.95
...80 Page Giant (12/98, $4.95) Stories by various 4.95
...3-D #1 (12/98, $3.95) Jeanty-a 3.95
...: A New Dawn TPB (1998, $9.95)-r/#50-55 9.95
...: Emerald Knights TPB (1998, $12.95)-r/Hal Jordan's return 12.95
...: Emerald Twilight nn (1994, $5.95)-r/#48-50 6.00
...: Ganthet's Tale nn (1992, $5.95, 68 pgs.)-Silver foil stamped logo;Larry Niven scripts; Byrne-c/a 6.00
.../Green Arrow Collection, Vol. 2-r/Gl #84-87,89 & Flash #217-219 & GL/GA #5-7 by O'Neil/Adams/Wrightson 13.00
...Plus 1 (12/1996, $2.95)-The Ray & Polaris-c/app. 2.95
...Secret Files 1 (7/98, $4.95) Origin stories & profiles 5.00
...The Road Back nn (1992, $8.95)-r/1-8 w/covers 9.00
NOTE: ***Staton*** *a(p)-9-12; c-9-12.*

Green Lantern Annual #1, 1963 © DC

Green Lantern: Mosaic #15 © DC

Grendel #11 © Matt Wagner

GD25 FN65 NM94

GREEN LANTERN (See Tangent Comics/ Green Lantern)

GREEN LANTERN ANNUAL NO. 1, 1963
DC Comics: 1998 ($4.95, one-shot)

1-Reprints Golden Age & Silver Age stories in 1963-style 80 pg. Giant format; new Gil Kane sketch art 5.00

GREEN LANTERN CORPS, THE (Formerly Green Lantern; see Tales of...)
DC Comics: No. 206, Nov, 1986 - No. 224, May, 1988

206-223: 220,221-Millennium tie-ins 1.00
224-Double-size last issue 1.50
...Corps Annual 2 (12/86)-Formerly Tales of ...Annual #1; Alan Moore scripts 2.00
...Corps Annual 3 (8/87)-Indicia says Green Lantern Annual #3; Moore scripts; Byrne-a 2.00

NOTE: ***Austin** a-Annual 3i. **Gil Kane** a-223, 224p; c-223, 224, Annual 2. **Russell** a-Annual 3i. **Staton** a-207-213p, 217p, 221p, 222p, Annual 3; c-207-213p, 217p, 221p, 222p. **Willingham** a-213p, 219p, 220p, 218p, 219p, Annual 2, 3p; c-218p, 219p.*

GREEN LANTERN CORPS QUARTERLY
DC Comics: Summer, 1992 - No. 8, Spring, 1994 ($2.50/$2.95, 68 pgs.)

1-5: 1-G.A. Green Lantern story; Staton-a(p). 2-G.A. G.L.-c/story; Austin-c(i); Gulacy-a(p). 3-G.A. G.L. story. 4-Austin-i 2.50
6-8: 6-Begin $2.95-c. 7-Painted-c; Tim Vigil-a. 8-Lobo-c/s 3.00

GREEN LANTERN: EMERALD DAWN (Also see Emerald Dawn)
DC Comics: Dec, 1989 - No. 6, May, 1990 ($1.00, limited series)

1-Origin retold; Giffen plots in all 2.00
2-6 1.50

GREEN LANTERN: EMERALD DAWN II (Emerald Dawn II #1 & 2)
DC Comics: Apr, 1991 - No. 6, Sept, 1991 ($1.00, limited series)

1 1.25
2-6 1.00

GREEN LANTERN/FLASH: FASTER FRIENDS (See Flash/Green Lantern...)
DC Comics: 1997 ($4.95, limited series)

1-Marz-s 4.95

GREEN LANTERN GALLERY
DC Comics: Dec, 1996 ($3.50, one-shot)

1-Wraparound-c; pin-ups by various 3.50

GREEN LANTERN/GREEN ARROW (Also see The Flash #217)
DC Comics: Oct, 1983 - No. 7, April, 1984 (52-60 pgs.)

1 Reprints Green Lantern #76,77 3.00
2-7: Reprints Green Lantern #78-89 2.50

NOTE: ***Neal Adams** r-1-7; c-1-4. **Wrightson** r-4, 5.*

GREEN LANTERN: MOSAIC (Also see Cosmic Odyssey #2)
DC Comics: June, 1992 - No. 18, Nov, 1993 ($1.25)

1-18: Featuring John Stewart. 1-Painted-c by Cully Hamner 1.25

GREEN LANTERN/SENTINEL: HEART OF DARKNESS
DC Comics: Mar, 1998 - No. 3, May, 1998 ($1.95, limited series)

1-3-Marz-s/Pelletier-a 2.00

GREEN LANTERN/SILVER SURFER: UNHOLY ALLIANCES
DC Comics: 1995 ($4.95, one-shot)(Prelude to DC Versus Marvel)

nn-Hal Jordan app. 5.00

GREEN MASK, THE (See Mystery Men)
Summer, 1940 - No. 9, 2/42; No. 10, 8/44 - No. 11, 11/44;
Fox Features Syndicate: V2#1, Spring, 1945 - No. 6, 10-11/46

	GD25	FN65	NM94
V1#1-Origin The Green Mask & Domino; reprints/Mystery Men #1-3,5-7; Lou Fine-c	305.00	915.00	2900.00
2-Zanzibar The Magician by Tuska	115.00	345.00	975.00
3-Powell-a; Marijuana story	74.00	222.00	625.00
4-Navy Jones begins, ends #6	59.00	177.00	500.00
5	47.00	141.00	400.00
6-The Nightbird begins, ends #9; bondage/torture-c	40.00	120.00	320.00
7-9: 9(2/42)-Becomes The Bouncer #10(nn) on? & Green Mask #10 on	35.00	105.00	260.00
10,11: 10-Origin One Round Hogan & Rocket Kelly	26.00	78.00	195.00
V2#1	20.00	60.00	150.00
2-6	18.00	54.00	135.00

GREEN PLANET, THE
Charlton Comics: 1962 (one-shot) (12¢)

nn-Giordano-c; sci-fi 5.50 16.50 55.00

GREEN TEAM (See Cancelled Comic Cavalcade & 1st Issue Special)

GREETINGS FROM SANTA (See March of Comics No. 48)

GRENDEL (Also see Primer #2 and Mage)
Comico: Mar, 1983 - No. 3, Feb, 1984 ($1.50, B&W)(#1 has indicia to Skrog #1)

1-Origin Hunter Rose 9.00 27.00 100.00
2,3: 2-Origin Argent 7.25 22.00 80.00

GRENDEL
Comico: Oct, 1986 - No. 40, Feb, 1991 ($1.50/$1.95/$2.50, mature)

	GD25	FN65	NM94
1	.85	2.60	7.00
1,2: 2nd printings			2.00
2			4.00
3-10: 4-Dave Stevens-c(i)			3.00
11-15: 13-15-Ken Steacy-c			3.00
16-Re-intro Mage (series begins, ends #19)			4.00
17-32: 18-26-$1.75-c; 27-32-$1.95-c. 24-25, 27-28,30-31-Snyder-c/a; 26,29-Snyder-i			3.00
33-($2.75, 44 pgs.)			3.00
34-40: 34-Begin $2.50 cover price			3.00
Devil by the Deed (Graphic Novel, 10/86, $5.95, 52 pgs.)-r/Grendel back-ups/ Mage 6-14; Alan Moore intro.	.85	2.60	7.00
Devil's Legacy ($14.95, 1988, Graphic Novel)	1.50	4.50	15.00
Devil's Vagary (10/87, B&W & red)-No price; included in Comico Collection	1.20	3.60	12.00

GRENDEL CLASSICS
Dark Horse Comics: July, 1995 - Aug, 1995 ($3.95, limited series, mature)

1,2-reprints; new Wagner-c 4.00

GRENDEL CYCLE
Dark Horse Comics: Oct, 1995 ($5.95, one shot)

1-nn-history of Grendel by M. Wagner & others 2.00 6.00

GRENDEL: DEVIL BY THE DEED
Dark Horse Comics: July, 1993 ($3.95, one shot, spot varnish-c)

1-nn-M. Wagner-c/a/scripts; r/Grendel back-ups from Mage #6-14 4.00
Reprint (12/97, $3.95) w/pin-ups by various 4.00

GRENDEL: DEVIL QUEST
Dark Horse Comics: Nov, 1995 ($4.95, one shot)

1-nn-Prequel to Batman/Grendel II; M. Wagner story & art; r/back-up story from Grendel Tales series. 5.00

GRENDEL: DEVILS AND DEATHS
Dark Horse Comics: Oct, 1994 - Nov, 1994 ($2.95, limited series, mature)

1,2 (10/94-11/94, $2.95, mature) 3.00

GRENDEL TALES: DEVIL'S CHOICES
Dark Horse Comics: Mar, 1995 - Jun, 1995 ($2.95, limited series, mature)

1-4 3.00

GRENDEL TALES: FOUR DEVILS, ONE HELL
Dark Horse Comics: Aug, 1993 - Jan, 1994 ($2.95, limited series, mature)

Grendel: War Child #5 © Matt Wagner

Grifter & The Mask #1 © DH/Wildstorm Prod.

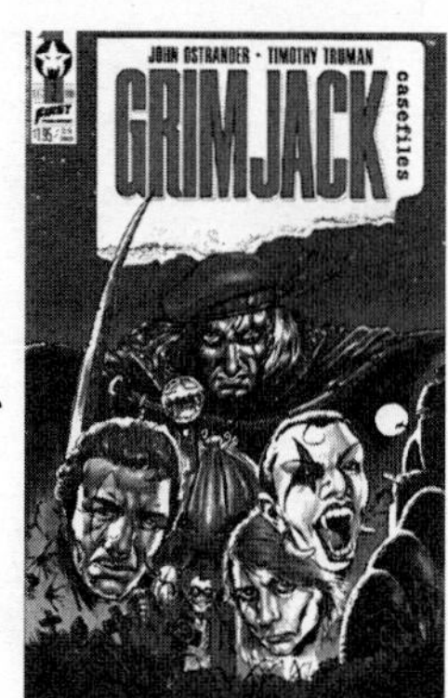

Grimjack #2 © FC

GD25 FN65 NM94

1-6-Wagner painted-c 3.00
TPB (12/94, $17.95) r/#1-6 18.00

GRENDEL TALES: HOMECOMING
Dark Horse Comics: Dec, 1994 - Feb, 1995 ($2.95, limited series, mature)
1-3 3.00

GRENDEL TALES: THE DEVIL IN OUR MIDST
Dark Horse Comics: May, 1994 - Sep, 1995 ($2.95, limited series, mature)
1-5-Wagner painted-c. in all 3.00

GRENDEL TALES: THE DEVIL MAY CARE
Dark Horse Comics: Dec, 1995 - 1996 ($2.95, limited series, mature)
1-6-Terry LaBan scripts. 5-Batman/Grendel II preview 3.00

GRENDEL TALES: THE DEVIL'S APPRENTICE
Dark Horse Comics: Sept, 1997 - No. 3, Nov, 1997 ($2.95, lim. series, mature)
1-3 3.00

GRENDEL TALES: THE DEVIL'S HAMMER
Dark Horse Comics: Feb, 1994 - Apr, 1994 ($2.95, limited series, mature)
1-3 3.00

GRENDEL: WAR CHILD
Dark Horse Comics: Aug, 1992 - No. 10, 1993 ($2.50, limited series, mature)
1-9: 1-4-Bisley painted-c; Wagner-i & scripts in all 2.50
10-($3.50, 52 pgs.) Wagner-c 3.50
Limited Edition Hardcover ($99.95) 100.00

GREYFRIARS BOBBY (Disney)(Movie)
Dell Publishing Co.: No. 1189, Nov, 1961 (one-shot)
Four Color 1189-Photo-c (scarce) 6.40 19.20 70.00

GREYLORE
Sirius: 12/85 - No. 5, Sept, 1986 ($1.50/$1.75, high quality paper)
1-5: Bo Hampton-a in all 1.50

GRIFFIN, THE
DC Comics: 1991 - No. 6, 1992 ($4.95, limited series, 52 pgs.)
Book 1-6: Matt Wagner painted-c 5.00

GRIFTER (Also see Team 7 & WildC.A.T.S)
Image Comics (WildStorm Prod.): May, 1995 - No. 10, Mar, 1996 ($1.95)
1 ($1.95, Newsstand)-WildStorm Rising Pt. 5 2.50
1 ($2.50, Direct Market)-WildStorm Rising Pt. 5, bound-in trading card 3.00
2-10 2.00

GRIFTER
Image Comics (WildStorm Prod.): V2#1, July, 1996 - No. 14, Aug, 1997 ($2.50)
V2#1-14: Steven Grant scripts 2.50

GRIFTER AND THE MASK
Dark Horse Comics: Sept, 1996 - No. 2, Oct, 1996 ($2.50, limited series) (1st Dark Horse Comics/Image x-over)
1,2: Steve Seagle scripts 2.50

GRIFTER/BADROCK (Also see WildC.A.T.S & Youngblood)
Image Comics (Extreme Studios): Oct, 1995 - No.2, Nov, 1995 ($2.50, unfinished limited series)
1,2: 2-Flip book w/Badrock #2 2.50

GRIFTER: ONE SHOT
Image Comics (WildStorm Productions): Jan, 1995 ($4.95, one-shot)
1-Flip-c 5.50

GRIFTER/SHI
Image Comics (WildStorm Productions): Apr, 1996 - No. 2, May, 1996 ($2.95, limited series)
1,2: 1-Jim Lee-c/a(p); Travis Charest-a(p). 2-Billy Tucci-c/a(p); Travis Charest-a(p) 3.00

GRIM GHOST, THE
Atlas/Seaboard Publ.: Jan, 1975 - No. 3, July, 1975
1-3: 1-Origin. 3-Heath-c 3.00

GRIMJACK (Also see Demon Knight & Starslayer)
First Comics: Aug, 1984 - No. 81, Apr, 1991 ($1.00/$1.95/$2.25)
1-John Ostrander scripts & Tim Truman-c/a begins. 2.00
2-25: 20-Sutton-c/a begins. 22-Bolland-a. 1.50
26-2nd color Teenage Mutant Ninja Turtles 2.00
27-74,76-81 (Later issues $1.95, $2.25): 30-Dynamo Joe x-over; 31-Mandrake-c/a begins. 73,74-Kelley Jones-a 1.25
75-($5.95, 52 pgs.)-Fold-out map; coated stock 2.00 6.00
NOTE: *Truman c/a-1-17.*

GRIMJACK CASEFILES
First Comics: Nov, 1990 - No. 5, Mar, 1991 ($1.95, limited series)
1-5 Reprints 1st stories from Starslayer #10 on 2.00

GRIMM'S GHOST STORIES (See Dan Curtis)
Gold Key/Whitman No. 55 on: Jan, 1972 - No. 60, June, 1982 (Painted-c #1-42,44,46-56)
1 2.20 6.25 22.00
2-5,8: 5,8-Williamson-a 1.10 3.30 11.00
6,7,9,10 .90 2.70 8.00
11-20 2.00 6.00
21-42,45-54: 32,34-Reprints. 45-Photo-c 4.00
43,44,55-60: 43,44-(52 pgs.). 43-Photo-c. 59-Williamson-a(r/#8) 2.00 6.00
Mini-Comic No. 1 (3-1/4x6-1/2", 1976) 5.00
NOTE: *Reprints-#32?, 34?, 39, 43, 44, 47?, 53; 56-60(1/3).* ***Bolle*** *a-8, 17, 22-25, 27, 29(2), 33, 35, 41, 43r, 45(2), 48(2), 50, 52.* ***Celardo*** *a-17, 26, 28p, 30, 31, 43(2), 45.* ***Lopez*** *a-24, 25.* ***McWilliams*** *a-33, 44r, 48, 54(2), 57, 58.* ***Win Mortimer*** *a-31, 33, 49, 51, 55, 56, 58(2), 59, 60.* ***Roussos*** *a-25, 30.* ***Sparling*** *a-23, 24, 28, 30, 31, 33, 43r, 44, 45, 51(2), 52, 56, 58, 59(2), 60.* ***Spiegle*** *a-44.*

GRIN (The American Funny Book) (Satire)
APAG House Pubs: Nov, 1972 - No. 3, April, 1973 (Magazine, 52 pgs.)
1-Parodies-Godfather, All in the Family 1.80 5.40 18.00
2,3 1.20 3.60 12.00

GRIN & BEAR IT (See Gags)
Dell Publishing Co.: No. 28, 1941
Large Feature Comic 28 8.00 25.00 90.00

GRIPS (Extreme violence)
Silverwolf Comics: Sept, 1986 - No. 4, Dec, 1986 ($1.50, B&W, mature)
1-Tim Vigil-c/a in all 4.00
2-4 3.00

GRIT GRADY (See Holyoke One-Shot No. 1)

GROO (Sergio Aragones'...)
Image Comics: Dec, 1994 - No. 12, Dec, 1995 ($1.95)
1-12: 2-Indicia reads #1, Jan, 1995; Aragones-c/a in all 2.00

GROO (Sergio Aragones'...)
Dark Horse Comics: Jan, 1998 - No. 4, Apr, 1998 ($2.95)
1-4: Aragones-c/a in all 3.00

GROO CARNIVAL, THE
Marvel Comics (Epic Comics): Dec, 1991 ($8.95, trade paperback)
nn-Reprints Groo #9-12 by Aragones .90 2.70 9.00

GROO CHRONICLES, THE (Sergio Aragones)
Marvel Comics (Epic Comics): June, 1989 - No. 6, Feb, 1990 ($3.50)
Book 1-6: Reprints early Pacific issues 3.50

Groo The Wanderer #116 © Sergio Aragonés

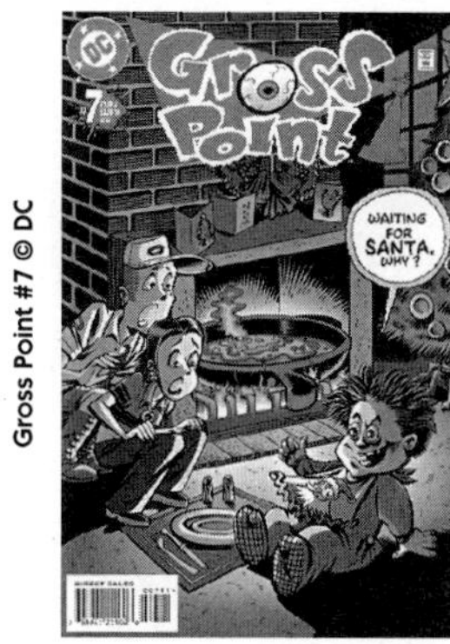

Gross Point #7 © DC

Guardians of the Galaxy #55 © MEG

GD25 FN65 NM94

GROO SPECIAL
Eclipse Comics: Oct, 1984 ($2.00, 52 pgs., Baxter paper)

1-Aragones-c/a 1.40 4.20 14.00

GROO THE WANDERER (See Destroyer Duck #1, Marvel Graphic Novel #32 & & Starslayer #5)
Pacific Comics: Dec, 1982 - No. 8, Apr, 1984

1-Aragones-c/a(p) in all; Aragones biog., photo 1.50 4.50 15.00
2 1.00 3.00 10.00
3-8: 5-Deluxe paper (1.00-c) .90 2.70 9.00

GROO THE WANDERER (Sergio Aragones'...)
Marvel Comics (Epic Comics): March, 1985 - No. 120, Jan, 1995

1-Aragones-c/a in all .85 2.60 7.00
2 4.50
3-10 3.50
11-20 2.75
21-30 2.25
31-86: 50-($1.50, double size) 1.60
87-99,101-120: 87-Begin $2.25, direct sale only, high quality paper issues 3.50
100-($2.95, 52 pgs.) 5.00
Marvel Graphic Novel 32: Death of Groo 1.20 3.60 12.00
Death of Groo 2nd printing ($5.95) 6.00
Groo Garden, The (4/94, $10.95)-r/25-28 1.10 3.30 11.00

GROOVY (Cartoon Comics - not CCA approved)
Marvel Comics Group: March, 1968 - No. 3, July, 1968

1-Monkees, Ringo Starr, Sonny & Cher, Mamas & Papas photos 6.50 19.50 65.00
2,3 4.50 13.50 45.00

GROSS POINT
DC Comics: Aug, 1997 - No. 14, Aug, 1998 ($2.50)

1-Waid/Augustyn-s 3.00
2-14 2.50

GROUP LARUE, THE
Innovation Publishing: 1989 - No. 4, 1990 ($1.95, mini-series)

1-4-By Mike Baron 2.00

GUADALCANAL DIARY (See American Library)

GUARDIANS OF JUSTICE & THE O-FORCE
Shadow Comics: 1990 (no date) ($1.50, 7-1/2 x10-1/4)

1-Super-hero group 1.50

GUARDIANS OF METROPOLIS
DC Comics: Nov, 1995 - Feb, 1995 ($1.50, limited series)

1-4: 1-Superman & Granny Goodness app. 1.50

GUARDIANS OF THE GALAXY (Also see The Defenders #26, Marvel Presents #3, Marvel Super-Heroes #18, Marvel Two-In-One #5)
Marvel Comics: June, 1990 - No. 62, July, 1995 ($1.00/$1.25)

1-16: 1-Valentino-c/a(p) begin. 2-Zeck-c(i). 5-McFarlane-c(i). 7-Intro Malevolence (Mephisto's daughter); Perez-c(i). 8-Intro Rancor (descendant of Wolverine) in cameo. 9-1st full app. Rancor; Rob Liefeld-c(i). 10-Jim Lee-c(i). 13,14-1st app. Spirit of Vengeance (futuristic Ghost Rider). 14-Spirit of Vengeance vs. The Guardians. 15-Starlin-c(i). 16-($1.50, 52 pgs.)-Starlin-c(i) 2.00
17-23,26-38,40-47: 17-20-31st century Punishers storyline. 20-Last $1.00-c. 21-Rancor app. 22-Reintro Starhawk. 26-Origin retold. 27-28-Infinity War x-over; 27-Inhumans app. 43-Intro Wooden (son of Thor) 1.25
24-Silver Surfer-c/story; Ron Lim-c 2.00
25-($2.50)-Prism foil-c; Silver Surfer/Galactus-c/s 2.50
25-($2.50)-Without foil-c; newsstand edition 2.50
39-($2.95, 52 pgs.)-Embossed & holo-grafx foil-c; Dr. Doom vs. Rancor 3.00
48,49,51-62: 48-$1.50-c begins; bound-in trading card sheet 1.50
50-($2.00, 52 pgs.)-Newsstand edition 2.00
50-($2.95, 52 pgs.)-Collectors ed. w/foil embossed-c 3.00
Annual 1 (1991, $2.00, 68 pgs.)-2 pg. origin 2.00
Annual 2 (1992, $2.25, 68 pgs.)-Spirit of Vengeance-c/story 2.25
Annual 3 (1993, $2.95, 68 pgs.)-Bagged w/card 3.00
Annual 4 (1994, $2.95) 3.00

GUERRILLA WAR (Formerly Jungle War Stories)
Dell Publishing Co.: No. 12, July-Sept, 1965 - No. 14, Mar, 1966

12-14 1.75 5.25 14.00

GUFF
Dark Horse Comics: Apr, 1998 ($1.95, B&W)

1-Flip book; Aragonés-c 1.95

GUILTY (See Justice Traps the Guilty)

GULF FUNNY WEEKLY (Gulf Comic Weekly No. 1-4)
Gulf Oil Company (Giveaway): 1933 - No. 422, 5/23/41 (in full color; 4 pgs.; tabloid size to 2/3/39; 2/10/39 on, regular comic book size)(early issues undated)

1 59.00 177.00 500.00
2-5 20.00 60.00 150.00
6-30 10.00 30.00 75.00
31-100 7.85 23.50 55.00
101-196 5.70 17.00 35.00
197-Wings Winfair begins(1/29/37); by Fred Meagher beginning in 1938 25.00 76.00 190.00
198-300 (Last tabloid size) 13.00 40.00 100.00
301-350 (Regular size) 7.15 21.50 50.00
351-422 5.70 17.00 35.00

GULLIVER'S TRAVELS
Macy's Department Store: 1939, small size

nn-Christmas giveaway 10.00 30.00 75.00

GULLIVER'S TRAVELS (See Dell Jr. Treasury No. 3)
Dell Publishing Co.: Sept-Nov, 1965 - No. 3, May, 1966

1 4.00 12.25 45.00
2,3 3.20 9.50 35.00

GUMBY'S SUMMER FUN SPECIAL
Comico: July, 1987 ($2.50)

1-Art Adams-c/a; B. Burden scripts 3.00

GUMBY'S WINTER FUN SPECIAL
Comico: Dec, 1988 ($2.50, 44 pgs.)

1-Art Adams-c/a 3.00

GUMPS, THE (See Merry Christmas..., Popular & Super Comics)
Dell Publ. Co./Bridgeport Herald Corp.: No. 73, 1945; Mar-Apr, 1947 - No. 5, Nov-Dec, 1947

Four Color 73 (Dell)(1945) 11.00 33.00 120.00
1 (3-4/47) 13.00 40.00 100.00
2-5 9.30 28.00 65.00

GUNFIGHTER (Fat & Slat #1-4) (Becomes Haunt of Fear #15 on)
E. C. Comics (Fables Publ. Co.): No. 5, Sum, 1948 - No. 14, Mar-Apr, 1950

5,6-Moon Girl in each 39.00 117.00 360.00
7-14: 14-Bondage-c 30.00 90.00 250.00

NOTE: ***Craig** & **H. C. Kiefer** art in most issues. **Craig** c-5, 6, 13, 14. **Feldstein/Craig** a-10. **Feldstein** a-7-11. **Harrison/Wood** a-13, 14. **Ingels** a-5-14; c-7-12.*

GUNFIGHTERS, THE
Super Comics (Reprints): 1963 - 1964

10-12,15,16,18: 10,11-r/Billy the Kid #s? 12-r/The Rider #5(Swift Arrow).

Gunfire #5 © DC

Gun Runner #1 © MAR

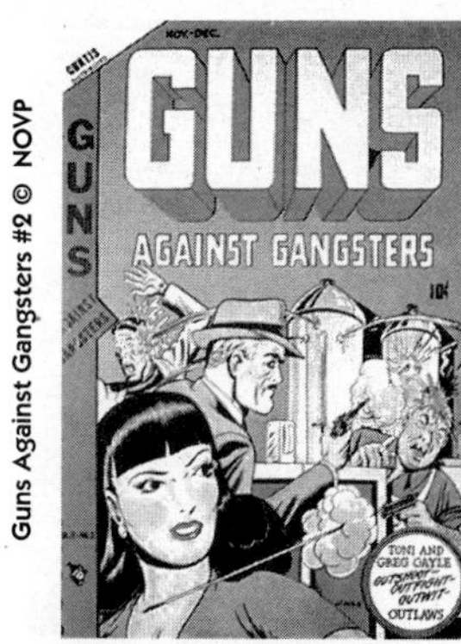

Guns Against Gangsters #2 © NOVP

15-r/Straight Arrow #42; Powell-r. 16-r/Billy the Kid #?(Toby). 18-r/ The Rider #3; Severin-c 1.40 4.15 11.00

GUNFIGHTERS, THE (Formerly Kid Montana)
Charlton Comics: No. 51, 10/66 - No. 52, 10/67; No. 53, 6/79 - No. 85, 7/84

51,52 2.00 6.00 16.00
53,54,56:53,54-Williamson/Torres-r/Six Gun Heroes #47,49. 56-Williamson/ Severin-c; Severin-r/Sheriff of Tombstone #1 5.00
55,57-85: . 85-S&K-r/1955 Bullseye 3.00

GUNFIRE (See Deathstroke Annual #2 & Showcase 94 #1,2)
DC Comics: May, 1994 - No. 13, June, 1995 ($1.75)

1-4: 2-Ricochet-c/story. 5-(9/94) 1.75
5,0,6-12: 0-(10/94). 6-(11/94). 2.00
13-$2.25-c begins. 2.25

GUN GLORY (Movie)
Dell Publishing Co.: No. 846, Oct, 1957 (one-shot)

Four Color 846-Toth-a, photo-c. 9.00 27.00 100.00

GUNHAWK, THE (Formerly Whip Wilson)(See Wild Western)
Marvel Comics/Atlas (MCI): No. 12, Nov, 1950 - No. 18, Dec, 1951
(Also see Two-Gun Western #5)

12 16.00 48.00 120.00
13-18: 13-Tuska-a. 16-Colan-a. 18-Maneely-c 11.00 34.00 85.00

GUNHAWKS (Gunhawk No. 7)
Marvel Comics Group: Oct, 1972 - No. 7, October, 1973

1,6: 1-Reno Jones, Kid Cassidy; Shores-c/a(p). 6-Kid Cassidy dies 1.20 3.60 12.00
2-5,7: 7-Reno Jones solo .90 2.70 9.00

GUNHED
Vix Comics: 1990 - No. 3, 1991? ($4.95, 7-1/8 x 9-1/8, 52 pgs., bi-monthly)

1-3: Japanese sci-fi based on 1991 movie 5.00

GUNMASTER (Becomes Judo Master #89 on)
Charlton Comics: 9/64 - No. 4, 1965; No. 84, 7/65 - No. 88, 3-4/66; No. 89, 10/67

V1#1 2.50 7.50 24.00
2-4 2.00 6.00 16.00
V5#84-86: 84-Formerly Six-Gun Heroes 2.25 6.75 18.00
V5#87-89 1.50 4.50 12.00
NOTE: *Vol. 5 was originally cancelled with #88 (3-4/66). #89 on, became Judo Master, then later in 1967, Charlton issued #89 as a Gunmaster one-shot.*

GUN RUNNER
Marvel Comics UK: Oct, 1993 - No. 6, Mar, 1994 ($1.75, limited series)

1-($2.75)-Polybagged w/4 trading cards; Spirits of Vengeance app. 2.75
2-6: 2-Ghost Rider & Blaze app. 1.75

GUNS AGAINST GANGSTERS (True-To-Life Romances #8 on)
Curtis Publications/Novelty Press: Sept-Oct, 1948 - No. 6, July-Aug, 1949; V2#1, Sept-Oct, 1949 - No. 2, 11-12/49

1-Toni & Greg Gayle begins by Schomburg; L.B. Cole-c 30.00 90.00 225.00
2-L.B. Cole-c 22.00 66.00 165.00
3-6, V2#1,2: 6-Toni Gayle-c 19.00 58.00 145.00
NOTE: ***L. B. Cole** c-1-6, V2#1, 2; a-1, 2, 3(2), 4-6.*

GUNSLINGER
Dell Publishing Co.: No. 1220, Oct-Dec, 1961 (one-shot)

Four Color 1220-Photo-c 8.00 25.00 90.00

GUNSLINGER (Formerly Tex Dawson...)
Marvel Comics Group: No. 2, Apr, 1973 - No. 3, June, 1973

2,3 1.20 3.60 12.00

GUNSMITH CATS: BAD TRIP (Manga)
Dark Horse Comics: Jun, 1998 - No. 6, Nov, 1998 ($2.95, B&W, lim. series)

1-6 2.95

GUNSMITH CATS: GOLDIE VS. MISTY (Manga)
Dark Horse Comics: Nov, 1997 - No. 7, May, 1998 ($2.95, B&W, limited series)

1-7 2.95

GUNSMITH CATS: THE RETURN OF GRAY (Manga)
Dark Horse Comics: Aug, 1996 - No. 7, Feb, 1997 ($2.95, B&W, limited series)

1-7 3.00

GUNSMITH CATS: SHADES OF GRAY (Manga)
Dark Horse Comics: May, 1997 - No. 5, Sept, 1997 ($2.95, B&W, limited series)

1-5 3.00

GUNSMOKE (Blazing Stories of the West)
Western Comics (Youthful Magazines): Apr-May, 1949 - No. 16, Jan, 1952

1-Gunsmoke & Masked Marvel begin by Ingels; Ingels bondage-c 39.00 117.00 300.00
2-Ingels-c/a(2) 25.00 76.00 190.00
3-Ingels bondage-c/a 20.00 60.00 150.00
4-6: Ingels-c 15.00 46.00 115.00
7-10 9.30 28.00 65.00
11-16: 15,16-Western/horror stories 7.15 21.50 50.00
NOTE: ***Stallman** a-11, 14. **Wildey** a-15, 16.*

GUNSMOKE (TV)
Dell Publishing Co./Gold Key (All have James Arness photo-c): No. 679, Feb, 1956 - No. 27, June-July, 1961; Feb, 1969 - No. 6, Feb, 1970

Four Color 679(#1) 15.00 45.00 160.00
Four Color 720,769,797,844 (#2-5) 6.80 21.00 75.00
6(11-1/57-58), 7 6.80 21.00 75.00
8,9,11,12-Williamson-a in all, 4 pgs. each 7.50 23.50 85.00
10-Williamson/Crandall-a, 4 pgs. 7.50 23.50 85.00
13-27 6.00 18.00 65.00
Gunsmoke Film Story (11/62-G.K. Giant) No. 30008-211 (scarce) 18.00 55.00 200.00
1 (Gold Key) 4.50 13.50 50.00
2-6('69-70) 2.20 6.50 24.00

GUNSMOKE TRAIL
Ajax-Farrell Publ./Four Star Comic Corp.: June, 1957 - No. 4, Dec, 1957

1 8.50 26.00 60.00
2-4 5.70 17.00 35.00

GUNSMOKE WESTERN (Formerly Western Tales of Black Rider)
Atlas Comics No. 32-35(CPS/NPI); Marvel No. 36 on: No. 32, Dec, 1955 - No. 77, July, 1963

32-Baker & Drucker-a 14.00 42.00 105.00
33,35,36-Williamson-a in each: 5,6 & 4 pgs. plus Drucker-a #33. 33-Kinstler-a? 11.00 34.00 85.00
34-Baker-a, 4 pgs.; Kirby-c 9.30 28.00 70.00
37-Davis-a(2); Williamson text illo 9.30 28.00 65.00
38,39: 39-Williamson text illo (unsigned) 7.15 21.50 50.00
40-Williamson/Mayo-a (4 pgs.) 8.50 26.50 60.00
41,42,45,46,48,49,52-54,57,58,60: 49,52-Kid from Texas story. 57-1st Two Gun Kid by Severin. 60-Sam Hawk app. in Kid Colt 5.35 16.00 32.00
43,44-Torres-a 5.75 17.00 35.00
47-Kirby-a 5.70 17.00 38.00
50-Kirby, Crandall-a 6.50 19.50 45.00
51,59-Kirby-a 5.70 17.00 38.00
55,56-Matt Baker-a 5.70 17.00 40.00
61-Crandall-a 5.70 17.00 40.00
62-67,69,71,73,77-Kirby-a 3.20 9.60 32.00

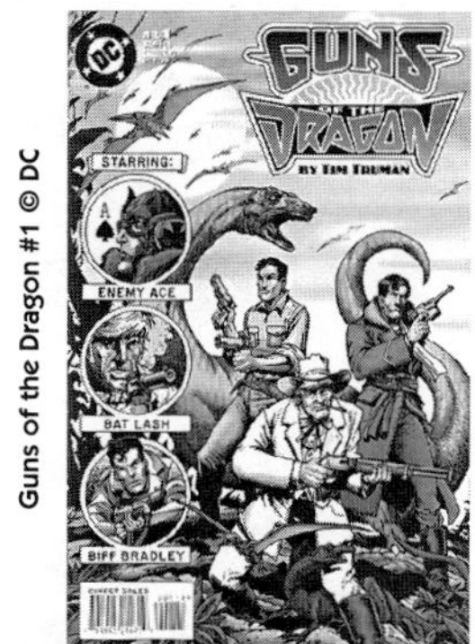

Guns of the Dragon #1 © DC

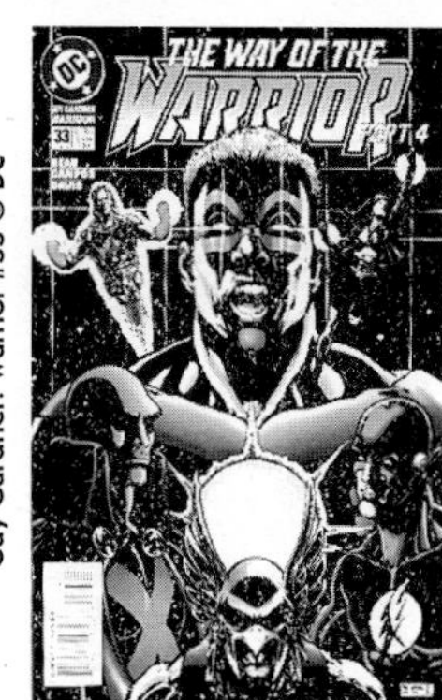

Guy Gardner: Warrior #33 © DC

The Hammer #3 © Kelley Jones

	GD25	FN65	NM94
68,70,74-76	2.80	8.40	28.00
72-Origin Kid Colt	3.20	9.60	32.00

NOTE: *Colan a-35-37, 39, 72, 76.* ***Davis*** *a-37, 52, 54, 55; c-50, 54.* ***Ditko*** *a-66; c-56p.* ***Drucker*** *a-.32-34.* ***Heath*** *c-33.* ***Jack Keller*** *a-35, 40, 60, 72; c-72.* ***Kirby*** *a-47, 50, 51, 59, 62(3), 63-67, 69, 71, 73, 77; c-56(w/****Ditko****),57, 58, 60, 61(w/****Ayers****), 62, 63, 66, 68, 69, 71-77.* ***Robinson*** *a-35.* ***Severin*** *a-35, 59-61; c-34, 35, 39, 42, 43.* ***Tuska*** *a-34.* ***Wildey*** *a-10, 37, 42, 56, 57. Kid Colt in all. Two-Gun Kid in No. 57, 59, 60-63. Wyatt Earp in No. 45, 48, 49, 52, 54, 55, 58.*

GUNS OF FACT & FICTION (Also see A-1 Comics)
Magazine Enterprises: No. 13, 1948 (one-shot)

	GD25	FN65	NM94
A-1 13-Used in **SOTI**, pg. 19; Ingels & J. Craig-a	27.00	80.00	200.00

GUNS OF THE DRAGON
DC Comics: Oct, 1998 - No. 4, Jan, 1999 ($2.50, limited series)

1-4-DCU in the 1920's; Enemy Ace & Bat Lash app. 2.50

GUN THAT WON THE WEST, THE
Winchester-Western Division & Olin Mathieson Chemical Corp.: 1956 (Giveaway, 24 pgs.)

	GD25	FN65	NM94
nn-Painted-c	5.00	15.00	30.00

GUY GARDNER (Guy Gardner: Warrior #17 on)(Also see Green Lantern #59)
DC Comics: Oct, 1992 - No. 44, July, 1996 ($1.25/$1.50/$1.75)

1-24,0,26-30: 1-Staton-c/a(p) begins. 6-Guy vs. Hal Jordan. 8-Vs. Lobo-c/story. 15-JLA x-over, begin $1.50-c. 18-Begin 4-part Emerald Fallout story; splash page x-over GL #50. 18-21-Vs. Hal Jordan. 24-(9/94)-Zero Hour. 0-(10/94) 1.50
25 (11/94, $2.50, 52 pgs.) 2.50
29 ($2.95)-Gatefold-c 3.00
29-Variant-c (Edward Hopper's Nighthawks) 1.50
31-44: 31-$1.75-c begins. 40-Gorilla Grodd-c/app. 44-Parallax-app. (1 pg.) 1.75
Annual 1 (1995, $3.50)-Year One story 3.50
Annual 2 (1996, $2.95)-Legends of the Dead Earth story 3.00

GUY GARDNER REBORN
DC Comics: 1992 - Book 3, 1992 ($4.95, limited series)

1-3: Staton-c/a(p). 1-Lobo-c/cameo. 2,3-Lobo-c/s 5.00

GYPSY COLT
Dell Publishing Co.: No. 568, June, 1954 (one-shot)

	GD25	FN65	NM94
Four Color 568--Movie	3.60	11.00	40.00

GYRO GEARLOOSE (See Dynabrite Comics, Walt Disney's C&S #140 & Walt Disney Showcase #18)
Dell Publishing Co.: No. 1047, Nov-Jan/1959-60 - May-July, 1962 (Disney)

	GD25	FN65	NM94
Four Color 1047 (No. 1)-All Barks-c/a	18.00	55.00	200.00
Four Color 1095,1184-All by Carl Barks	10.00	30.00	110.00
Four Color 1267-Barks c/a, 4 pgs.	7.00	20.00	75.00
01329-207 (#1, 5-7/62)-Barks-c only (intended as 4-Color 1329?)	5.00	15.00	55.00

HACKER FILES, THE
DC Comics: Aug, 1992 - No. 12, July, 1993 ($1.95)

1-12: 1-Sutton-a(p) begins; computer generated-c 2.00

HAGAR THE HORRIBLE (See Comics Reading Libraries)

HA HA COMICS (Teepee Tim No. 100 on; also see Giggle Comics)
Scope Mag.(Creston Publ.) No. 1-80/American Comics Group: Oct, 1943 - No. 99, Jan, 1955

	GD25	FN65	NM94
1-Funny animal	28.00	84.00	210.00
2	13.00	40.00	100.00
3-5: Ken Hultgren-a begins?	10.00	30.00	75.00
6-10	8.50	26.00	60.00
11-20: 14-Infinity-c	6.00	18.00	42.00
21-40	5.70	17.00	35.00
41-94,96-99: 49-X-Mas-c	5.00	15.00	30.00
95-3-D effect-c	13.00	38.00	95.00

HAIR BEAR BUNCH, THE (TV) (See Fun-In No. 13)
Gold Key: Feb, 1972 - No. 9, Feb, 1974 (Hanna-Barbera)

	GD25	FN65	NM94
1	2.70	8.00	30.00
2-9	1.60	4.80	16.00

HALLELUJAH TRAIL, THE (See Movie Classics)

HALL OF FAME FEATURING THE T.H.U.N.D.E.R. AGENTS
JC Productions(Archie Comics Group): May, 1983 - No. 3, Dec, 1983

1-3: Thunder Agents-r(Crandall, Tuska, Wood-a) 2.00

HALLOWEEN HORROR
Eclipse Comics: Oct, 1987 (Seduction of the Innocent #7)($1.75)

1-Pre-code horror-r 1.80

HALLOWEEN MEGAZINE
Marvel Comics: Dec, 1996 ($3.95, one-shot, 96 pgs.)

1-Reprints Tomb of Dracula 4.00

HALO, AN ANGEL'S STORY
Sirius Entertainment: Apr, 1996 - No. 4, Sept, 1996 ($2.95, limited series)

1-4: Knowles-c/a/scripts 3.00
TPB ($12.95) r/#1-4 12.95

HALO JONES (See The Ballad of...)

HAMMER, THE
Dark Horse Comics: Oct, 1997 - No. 4, Jan, 1998 ($2.95, limited series)

1-4-Kelley Jones-s/c/a 3.00
...: Uncle Alex (8/98, $2.95) 2.95

HAMMERLOCKE
DC Comics: Sept, 1992 - No. 9, May, 1993 ($1.75, limited series)

1-($2.50, 52 pgs.)-Chris Sprouse-c/a in all 2.50
2-9 1.75

HAMMER OF GOD (Also see Nexus)
First Comics: Feb, 1990 - No. 4, May, 1990 ($1.95, limited series)

1-4 2.00

HAMMER OF GOD: BUTCH
Dark Horse Comics: May, 1994 - No. 4, Aug, 1994 ($2.50, limited series)

1-3 2.50

HAMMER OF GOD: PENTATHLON
Dark Horse Comics: Jan, 1994 ($2.50, one shot)

1-character from Nexus 2.50

HAMMER OF GOD: SWORD OF JUSTICE
First Comics: Feb 1991 - Mar 1991 ($4.95, lim. series, squarebound, 52 pgs.)

V2#1,2 5.00

HANDBOOK OF THE CONAN UNIVERSE, THE
Marvel Comics: June, 1985 ($1.25, one-shot)

1-Kaluta-c. 1.25

HAND OF FATE (Formerly Men Against Crime)
Ace Magazines: No. 8, Dec, 1951 - No. 26, March, 1955 (Weird/horror stories) (Two #25's)

	GD25	FN65	NM94
8-Surrealistic text story	32.00	96.00	240.00
9,10	18.00	54.00	135.00
11-18,20,22,23	14.00	42.00	105.00
19-Bondage, hypo needle scenes	16.00	48.00	120.00
21-Necronomicon story; drug belladonna used	18.00	54.00	135.00
24-Electric chair-c	23.00	68.00	170.00
25a(11/54), 25b(12/54)-Both have Cameron-a	11.00	34.00	85.00
26-Nostrand-a; exist?	14.00	42.00	105.00

NOTE: ***Cameron*** *a-9, 10, 19-25a, 25b; c-13.* ***Sekowsky*** *a-8, 9, 13, 14.*

HAND OF FATE

Hangman Comics #7 © MLJ

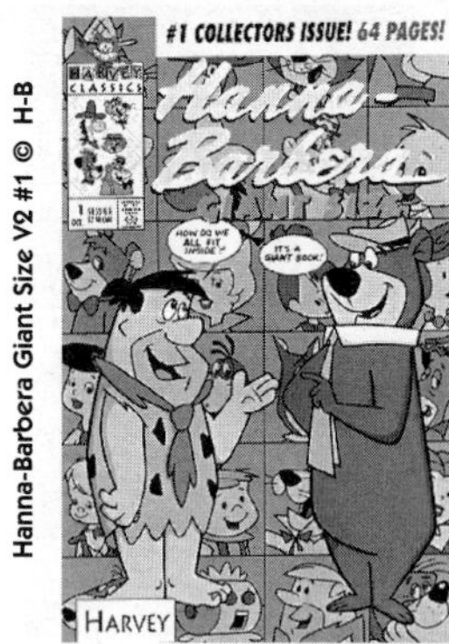

Hanna-Barbera Giant Size V2 #1 © H-B

Hap Hazard Comics #3 © ACE

Eclipse Comics: Feb, 1988 - No. 3, Apr, 1988 ($1.75/$2.00, Baxter paper)

1,2 1.75
3-$2.00-c; B&W 2.00

HANDS OF THE DRAGON
Seaboard Periodicals (Atlas): June, 1975

1-Origin; Mooney inks 4.00

HANGMAN COMICS (Special Comics No. 1; Black Hood No. 9 on)
(Also see Flyman, Mighty Comics, Mighty Crusaders & Pep Comics)
MLJ Magazines: No. 2, Spring, 1942 - No. 8, Fall, 1943

2-The Hangman, Boy Buddies begin 159.00 476.00 1350.00
3-Beheading splash pg.; 1st Nazi war-c 106.00 318.00 900.00
4-8: 5-1st Jap war-c. 8-2nd app. Super Duck (ties w/Jolly Jingles #11) 94.00 282.00 800.00

NOTE: ***Fuje** a-7(3), 8(3); c-3. **Reinman** c/a-3. Bondage c-3. **Sahle** c-6.*

HANK
Pentagon Publishing Co.: 1946

nn-Coulton Waugh's newspaper reprint 6.00 18.00 42.00

HANNA-BARBERA (See Golden Comics Digest No. 2, 7, 11)

HANNA-BARBERA ALL-STARS
Archie Publications: Oct, 1995 - No. 6, Sept, 1996 ($1.50, bi-monthly)

1-6 2.00

HANNA-BARBERA BAND WAGON (TV)
Gold Key: Oct, 1962 - No. 3, Apr, 1963

1-Giant, 84 pgs. 1-Augie Doggie & Lippy the Lion app. (pre-#1's) 11.25 34.00 125.00
2-Giant, 84 pgs. 8.75 26.50 95.00
3-Regular size; Mr. & Mrs. J. Evil Scientist app. (pre-#1) & Snagglepuss app. 6.00 18.00 65.00

HANNA-BARBERA GIANT SIZE
Harvey Comics: Oct, 1992 - No. 3 ($2.25, 68 pgs.)

V2#1-3:Flintstones, Yogi Bear, Magilla Gorilla, Huckleberry Hound, Quick Draw McGraw, Yakky Doodle & Chopper, Jetsons & others 3.00

HANNA-BARBERA HI-ADVENTURE HEROES (See Hi-Adventure...)

HANNA-BARBERA PARADE (TV)
Charlton Comics: Sept, 1971 - No. 10, Dec, 1972

1 6.00 18.00 65.00
2,4-10 2.90 8.70 32.00
3-(52 pgs.)- "Summer Picnic" 4.50 13.50 50.00

NOTE: *No. 4 (1/72) went on sale late in 1972 with the January 1973 issues.*

HANNA-BARBERA PRESENTS
Archie Publications: Nov, 1995 - Present ($1.50, bi-monthly)

1-6: 2-Wacky Races. 4-Quick Draw McGraw & Magilla Gorilla. 5-A Pup Named Scooby-Doo 1.50

HANNA-BARBERA SPOTLIGHT (See Spotlight)

HANNA-BARBERA SUPER TV HEROES (TV)
Gold Key: Apr, 1968 - No. 7, Oct, 1969 (Hanna-Barbera)

1-The Birdman, The Herculoids(ends #6; not in #2), Moby Dick, Young Samson & Goliath(ends #2,4), and The Mighty Mightor begin; Spiegle-a in all 14.50 43.00 160.00
2-The Galaxy Trio app.; Shazzan begins; 12 & 15 cent versions exist 10.00 30.00 110.00
3,6,7-The Space Ghost app. 9.50 28.00 105.00
4,5 8.75 26.50 95.00

HANNA-BARBERA TV FUN FAVORITES (See Golden Comics Digest #2,7,11)

HANNA-BARBERA (TV STARS) (See TV Stars)

HANS BRINKER (Disney)
Dell Publishing Co.: No. 1273, Feb, 1962 (one-shot)

Four Color 1273-Movie, photo-c 5.50 16.50 60.00

HANS CHRISTIAN ANDERSEN
Ziff-Davis Publ. Co.: 1953 (100 pgs., Special Issue)

nn-Danny Kaye (movie)-Photo-c; fairy tales 15.00 44.00 110.00

HANSEL & GRETEL
Dell Publishing Co.: No. 590, Oct, 1954 (one-shot)

Four Color 590-Partial photo-c 5.50 16.50 60.00

HANSI, THE GIRL WHO LOVED THE SWASTIKA
Spire Christian Comics (Fleming H. Revell Co.): 1973, 1976 (39¢/49¢)

nn .90 2.70 8.00

HAP HAZARD COMICS (Real Love No. 25 on)
Ace Magazines (Readers' Research): Summer, 1944 - No. 24, Feb, 1949
(#1-6 are quarterly issues)

1 11.00 34.00 85.00
2 6.00 18.00 42.00
3-10 5.00 15.00 30.00
11-13,15-24 4.00 12.00 24.00
14-Feldstein-c (4/47) 6.85 21.00 48.00

HAP HOPPER (See Comics Revue No. 2)

HAPPIEST MILLIONAIRE, THE (See Movie Comics)

HAPPINESS AND HEALING FOR YOU (Also see Oral Roberts'...)
Commercial Comics: 1955 (36 pgs., slick cover) (Oral Roberts Giveaway)

nn 7.85 23.50 55.00

NOTE: *The success of this book prompted Oral Roberts to go into the publishing business himself to produce his own material.*

HAPPI TIM (See March of Comics No. 182)

HAPPY BIRTHDAY MARTHA WASHINGTON (Also see Give Me Liberty, Martha Washington Goes To War, & Martha Washington Stranded In Space)
Dark Horse Comics: Mar, 1995 ($2.95, one-shot)

1-Miller script; Gibbons-c/a 3.00

HAPPY COMICS (Happy Rabbit No. 41 on)
Nedor Publ./Standard Comics (Animated Cartoons): Aug, 1943 - No. 40, Dec, 1950 (Companion to Goofy Comics)

1-Funny animal 24.00 72.00 180.00
2 12.00 36.00 90.00
3-10 8.50 26.00 60.00
11-19 6.00 18.00 42.00
20-31,34-37-Frazetta text illos in all (2 in #34&35, 3 in #27,28,30). 27-Al Fago-a 7.85 23.50 55.00
32-Frazetta-a, 7 pgs. plus 2 text illos; Roussos-a 17.00 52.00 130.00
33-Frazetta-a(2), 6 pgs. each (Scarce) 24.00 72.00 180.00
38-40 4.25 13.00 28.00

HAPPY DAYS (TV)(See Kite Fun Book)
Gold Key: Mar, 1979 - No. 6, Feb, 1980

1-Photo-c of TV cast .90 2.70 8.00
2-6 5.00

HAPPY HOLIDAY (See March of Comics No. 181)

HAPPY HOULIHANS (Saddle Justice No. 3 on; see Blackstone, The Magician Detective)
E. C. Comics: Fall, 1947 - No. 2, Winter, 1947-48

1-Origin Moon Girl (same date as Moon Girl #1) 36.00 108.00 320.00
2 20.00 60.00 170.00

HAPPY JACK
Red Top (Decker): Aug, 1957 - No. 2, Nov, 1957

V1#1,2 4.00 10.00 20.00

Harbinger #14 © Voyager Comm.

Hardcore Station #1 © Jim Starlin

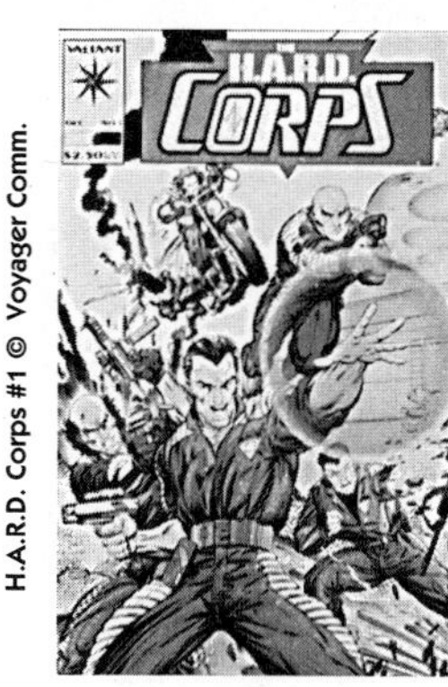

H.A.R.D. Corps #1 © Voyager Comm.

GD25 FN65 NM94

HAPPY JACK HOWARD
Red Top (Farrell)/Decker: 1957

nn-Reprints Handy Andy story from E. C. Dandy Comics #5, renamed "Happy Jack" 4.00 12.00 24.00

HAPPY RABBIT (Formerly Happy Comics)
Standard Comics (Animated Cartoons): No. 41, Feb, 1951 - No. 48, Apr, 1952

41-Funny animal 5.00 15.00 30.00
42-48 4.00 10.00 20.00

HARBINGER (Also see Unity)
Valiant: Jan, 1992 - No. 41, June, 1995 ($1.95/$2.50)

0-(Advance) 3.00
1-1st app. 2.50
2,3 2.00
4-Low print run 2.50
5-10: 8,9-Unity x-overs. 8-Miller-c. 9-Simonson-c. 10-1st app. H.A.R.D Corps (10/92) 2.00
11-16: 14-1st app. Stronghold 2.00
17-24,26-41: 18-Intro Screen. 19-1st app. Stunner. 22-Archer & Armstrong app. 24-Cover similar to #1. 26-Intro New Harbingers. 29-Bound-in trading card. 30-H.A.R.D. Corps app. 32-Eternal Warrior app. 33-Dr. Eclipse app. 2.00
25-($3.50, 52 pgs.)-Harada vs. Sting 2.00
...Files 1,2 (8/94,2/95 $2.50) 2.00
Trade paperback nn (11/92, $9.95)-Reprints #1-4 & comes polybagged with a copy of Harbinger #0 w/new-c. 10.00
NOTE: *Issues 1-6 have coupons with origin of Harada and are redeemable for Harbinger #0 .*

HARD BOILED
Dark Horse Comics: Sept, 1990 - No. 3, 1992 ($4.95/$5.95, 8 1/2x11", lim. ser.)

1-($4.95)-Miller scripts; Darrow-c/a; sexually explicit & violent 2.00 6.00
2,3-($5.95) .85 2.60 7.00
TPB (5/93, $15.95) 2.00 6.00 16.00
Big Damn Hard Boiled (12/97, $29.95, B&W) r/#1-3 30.00

HARDCASE (See Break Thru, Flood Relief & Ultraforce, 1st Series)
Malibu Comics (Ultraverse): June, 1993 - No. 26, Aug, 1995 ($1.95/$2.50)

1-Intro Hardcase; Dave Gibbons-c; has coupon for Ultraverse Premiere #0; Jim Callahan-a(p) begin, ends #3 2.00
1-With coupon missing 1.00
1-Platinum Edition 2.50
1-Holographic Cover Edition; 1st full-c holograph tied w/Prime 1 & Strangers 1 4.00
1-Ultra Limited silver foil-c 2.50
2,3-Callahan-a 2.50
2-($2.50)-Newsstand edition bagged w/trading card 2.50
4,6-15, 17-19: 4-Strangers app. 7-Break-Thru x-over. 8-Solution app. 9-Vs. Turf. 12-Silver foil logo, wraparound-c. 17-Prime app. 2.00
5-($2.50, 48 pgs.)-Rune flip-c/story by B. Smith (3 pgs.) 2.50
16 ($3.50, 68 pgs.)-Rune pin-up 3.50
20-26: 20-$2.50-c begins. 23-Loki app. 2.50
NOTE: ***Perez** a-8(2); c-20i.*

HARDCORE STATION
DC Comics: July, 1998 - No. 6, Dec, 1998 ($2.50, limited series)

1-6-Starlin-s/a(p). 3-Green Lantern-c/app. 5,6-JLA-c/app. 2.50

H.A.R.D. CORPS, THE (See Harbinger #10)
Valiant: Dec, 1992 - No. 30, Feb, 1995 ($2.25) (Harbinger spin-off)

1-(Advance) 3.00
1-($2.50)-Gatefold-c by Jim Lee & Bob Layton 2.50
1-Gold variant 3.00
2-6: 5-Bloodshot-c/story cont'd from Bloodshot #3 2.25
5-Variant edition; came w/Comic Defense System 2.50
7-30: 10-Turok app. 17-vs. Armorines. 18-Bound-in trading card. 20-Harbinger app. 2.25

HARDWARE
DC Comics (Milestone): Apr, 1993 - No. 50, Apr, 1997 ($1.50/$1.75/$2.50)

1-($2.95)-Collector's Edition polybagged w/poster & trading card (direct sale only) 3.00
1-Platinum Edition 5.00
1-15,17-19: 11-Shadow War x-over. 11,14-Simonson-c. 12-Buckler-a(p). 17-Worlds Collide Pt. 2. 18-Simonson-c; Worlds Collide Pt. 9. 15-1st Humberto Ramos DC work 1.50
16-($3.95, 52 pgs.)-Collector's Edition w/gatefold 2nd cover by Byrne; new armor; Icon app. 4.00
16-($2.50, 52 pgs.)-Newsstand Edition 2.50
20-24, 26-28: 20-Begin $1.75-c begins 1.75
25-($2.95, 52 pgs.) 3.00
29-49: 29-Begin $2.50-c. 49-Moebius-c 2.50
50-($3.95, 52 pgs) 3.95

HARDY BOYS, THE (Disney
Dell Publ. Co.: No. 760, Dec, 1956 - No. 964, Jan, 1959 (Mickey Mouse Club)

Four Color 760 (#1)-Photo-c 10.00 30.00 110.00
Four Color 830(8/57), 887(1/58), 964-Photo-c 9.00 27.00 100.00

HARDY BOYS, THE (TV)
Gold Key: Apr, 1970 - No. 4, Jan, 1971

1 3.00 9.00 32.00
2-4 2.00 6.00 22.00

HARI KARI (See The Death of Hari Kari)
Blackout Comics: No. 0, 1995 -No. 1, 1995 ($2.95)

0,1: Both have pin-ups. 1-Variant-c. 3.00
1-($9.95)-Commemorative Ed. -New-c; foil stamped; 2,500 copies. 1.00 3.00 10.00

...BLOODSHED 1997 ($2.95)
1-Virkaitis-s 3.00
1-($9.95)-Variant-c 1.00 3.00 10.00

...GOES HOLLYWOOD 1998 ($2.95)
1-Movie parody pin-ups 2.95
1-($9.95)-Variant-c 9.95

...LIVE & UNTAMED No. 0, 1996 ($2.95, one-shot)
0-w/photo layout 3.00
0-($9.95)-Variant-c 1.00 3.00 10.00

...POSSESSED BY EVIL 1997($2.95, B&W, one-shot)
1 3.00

...PRIVATE GALLERY No. 0, Feb, 1996 ($2.95, one-shot)
0-pin-ups 3.00
0-($9.95)-Commemorative Ed. 1.00 3.00 10.00

...REBIRTH 1996 ($2.95, one-shot)
1-Virkaitis-s 3.00
1-($9.95)-Variant Edition 1.00 3.00 10.00

...: RESURRECTION 1997 ($2.95, one-shot)
1-Virkaitis-s 3.00
1-($9.95)-Nude variant Edition 1.00 3.00 10.00

...: SEXY SUMMER RAMPAGE 1997 ($2.95, one-shot)
1-Pin-ups 3.00
1-($9.95)-Variant Edition 1.00 3.00 10.00

...: THE BEGINNING 1996 ($2.95)
1-Origin 3.00

... THE DIARY OF KARI SUN 1997 ($2.95, one-shot)
1/2-Text w/art 3.00
1/2-($9.95) Variant-c 1.00 3.00 10.00

Harlem Globetrotters #10 © GK

Harvey Comics Hits #56 © HARV

Harvey Hits #2 © HARV

...: THE SILENCE OF EVIL No. 0, 1996 ($2.95, bi-monthly)

	GD25	FN65	NM94
0			3.00

HARLAN ELLISON'S DREAM CORRIDOR
Dark Horse Comics: Mar, 1995 - No. 5, July, 1995 ($2.95, anthology)

	GD25	FN65	NM94
1-5: Adaptation of Ellison stories. 1-4-Byrne-a.			3.00
Special (1/95, $4.95)			5.00
Trade paperback-(1996, $18.95, 192 pgs)-r/#1-5 & Special #1			19.00

HARLAN ELLISON'S DREAM CORRIDOR QUARTERLY
Dark Horse Comics: V2#1, Aug, 1996 ($5.95, anthology, squarebound)

	GD25	FN65	NM94
V2#1-Adaptations of Ellison's stories w/new material; Neal Adams-a		2.00	6.00

HARLEM GLOBETROTTERS (TV) (See Fun-In No. 8, 10)
Gold Key: Apr, 1972 - No. 12, Jan, 1975 (Hanna-Barbera)

	GD25	FN65	NM94
1	2.00	6.00	22.00
2-5	1.40	4.20	14.00
6-12	1.00	3.00	10.00

NOTE: *#4, 8, and 12 contain 16 extra pages of advertising.*

HAROLD TEEN (See Popular Comics, & Super Comics)
Dell Publishing Co.: No. 2, 1942 - No. 209, Jan, 1949

	GD25	FN65	NM94
Four Color 2	24.50	73.50	270.00
Four Color 209	3.60	11.00	40.00

HARRIERS
Entity Comics: June, 1995 - No. 3, 1995 ($2.50)

	GD25	FN65	NM94
1-Foil-c; polybagged w/PC game			3.00
1-3 ($2.50)			2.50

HARROWERS, THE (See Clive Barker's...)

HARSH REALM
Harris Comics: 1994 ($2.95, one-shot)

	GD25	FN65	NM94
1-4: Painted-c			3.00

HARVEY
Marvel Comics: Oct, 1970; No. 2, 12/70; No. 3, 6/72 - No. 6, 12/72

	GD25	FN65	NM94
1	6.00	17.50	65.00
2-6	3.80	11.50	40.00

HARVEY COLLECTORS COMICS (Richie Rich Collectors Comics #10 on, cover title only)
Harvey Publ.: Sept, 1975 - No. 15, Jan, 1978; No. 16, Oct, 1979 (52 pgs.)

	GD25	FN65	NM94
1-Reprints Richie Rich #1,2	1.00	3.00	10.00
2-10: 7-Splash pg. shows-c to Friendly Ghost Casper #1		2.00	6.00
11-16: 16-Sad Sack-r			4.00

NOTE: *All reprints: Casper-#2, 7, Richie Rich-#1, 3, 5, 6, 8-15, Sad Sack-#16. Wendy-#4. #6 titled 'Richie Rich...'on inside.*

HARVEY COMICS HITS (Formerly Joe Palooka #50)
Harvey Publications: No. 51, Oct, 1951 - No. 62, Apr, 1953

	GD25	FN65	NM94
51-The Phantom	25.00	76.00	190.00
52-Steve Canyon's Air Power(Air Force sponsored)	11.00	32.00	80.00
53-Mandrake the Magician	19.00	56.00	140.00
54-Tim Tyler's Tales of Jungle Terror	10.00	30.00	75.00
55-Love Stories of Mary Worth	5.70	17.00	35.00
56-The Phantom; bondage-c	21.00	64.00	160.00
57-Rip Kirby Exposes the Kidnap Racket; entire book by Alex Raymond	13.00	40.00	100.00
58-Girls in White (nurses stories)	5.35	16.00	32.00
59-Tales of the Invisible featuring Scarlet O'Neil	9.30	28.00	65.00
60-Paramount Animated Comics #1 (9/52) (3rd app. Baby Huey); 2nd Harvey app. Baby Huey & Casper the Friendly Ghost (1st in Little Audrey #25 (8/52)); 1st app. Herman & Catnip (c/story) & Buzzy the Crow	36.00	108.00	270.00
61-Casper the Friendly Ghost #6 (3rd Harvey Casper, 10/52)-Casper-c	39.00	116.00	290.00
62-Paramount Animated Comics #2; Herman & Catnip, Baby Huey & Buzzy the Crow	12.00	36.00	90.00

HARVEY COMICS LIBRARY
Harvey Publications: Apr, 1952 - No. 2, 1952

	GD25	FN65	NM94
1-Teen-Age Dope Slaves as exposed by Rex Morgan, M.D.; drug propaganda story; used in **SOTI,** pg. 27	77.00	231.00	650.00
2-Dick Tracy Presents Sparkle Plenty in "Blackmail Terror"	16.00	48.00	120.00

HARVEY COMICS SPOTLIGHT
Harvey Comics: Sept, 1987 - No. 4, Mar, 1988 (75¢/$1.00)

	GD25	FN65	NM94
1-New material; begin 75¢, ends #3; Sand Sack			3.00
2-4: 2,4-All new material. 2-Baby Huey. 3-Little Dot; contains reprints w/5 pg. new story. 4-$1.00-c; Little Audrey			2.00

NOTE: No. 5 was advertised but not published.

HARVEY HITS
Harvey Publications: Sept, 1957 - No. 122, Nov, 1967

	GD25	FN65	NM94
1-The Phantom	22.00	66.00	220.00
2-Rags Rabbit (10/57)	2.50	7.50	24.00
3-Richie Rich (11/57)-r/Little Dot; 1st book devoted to Richie Rich; see Little Dot for 1st app.	60.00	180.00	725.00
4-Little Dot's Uncles (12/57)	12.50	38.00	125.00
5-Stevie Mazie's Boy Friend (1/58)	2.00	6.00	16.00
6-The Phantom (2/58); Kirby-c; 2pg. Powell-a	16.00	48.00	160.00
7-Wendy the Good Little Witch (3/58, pre-dates Wendy #1; 1st book devoted to Wendy)	15.00	45.00	150.00
8-Sad Sack's Army Life; George Baker-c	5.00	15.00	50.00
9-Richie Rich's Golden Deeds; reprints (2nd book devoted to Richie Rich)	32.00	96.00	350.00
10-Little Lotta's Lunch Box	8.50	25.50	85.00
11-Little Audrey Summer Fun (7/58)	6.50	18.00	65.00
12-The Phantom; Kirby-c; 2pg. Powell-a (8/58)	13.00	39.00	130.00
13-Little Dot's Uncles (9/58); Richie Rich 1pg.	8.50	25.50	85.00
14-Herman & Katnip (10/58, TV/movies)	2.50	7.50	20.00
15-The Phantom (12/58)-1 pg. origin	13.00	39.00	130.00
16-Wendy the Good Little Witch (1/59); Casper app.	8.50	25.50	85.00
17-Sad Sack's Army Life (2/59)	4.20	12.60	42.00
18-Buzzy & the Crow	2.50	7.50	22.00
19-Little Audrey (4/59)	3.80	11.40	38.00
20-Casper & Spooky	5.00	15.00	50.00
21-Wendy the Witch	5.00	15.00	50.00
22-Sad Sack's Army Life	3.50	10.50	35.00
23-Wendy the Witch (8/59)	5.00	15.00	50.00
24-Little Dot's Uncles (9/59); Richie Rich 1pg.	6.50	19.50	65.00
25-Herman & Katnip (10/59)	2.00	6.00	16.00
26-The Phantom (11/59)	10.50	32.00	105.00
27-Wendy the Good Little Witch (12/59)	4.50	13.50	45.00
28-Sad Sack's Army Life (1/60)	2.50	7.50	22.00
29-Harvey-Toon (No.1)('60); Casper, Buzzy	3.20	9.60	32.00
30-Wendy the Witch (3/60)	5.00	15.00	50.00
31-Herman & Katnip (4/60)	1.50	4.50	12.00
32-Sad Sack's Army Life (5/60)	2.25	6.75	18.00
33-Wendy the Witch (6/60)	5.00	15.00	50.00
34-Harvey-Toon (7/60)	2.25	6.75	18.00
35-Funday Funnies (8/60)	1.50	4.50	12.00
36-The Phantom (1960)	9.00	27.00	90.00
37-Casper & Nightmare	3.50	10.50	35.00
38-Harvey-Toon	2.25	6.75	18.00
39-Sad Sack's Army Life (12/60)	2.25	6.75	18.00
40-Funday Funnies (1/61)	1.25	3.75	10.00
41-Herman & Katnip	1.50	4.50	12.00
42-Harvey-Toon (3/61)	1.75	5.25	14.00
43-Sad Sack's Army Life (4/61)	2.00	6.00	16.00
44-The Phantom (5/61)	8.50	25.50	85.00

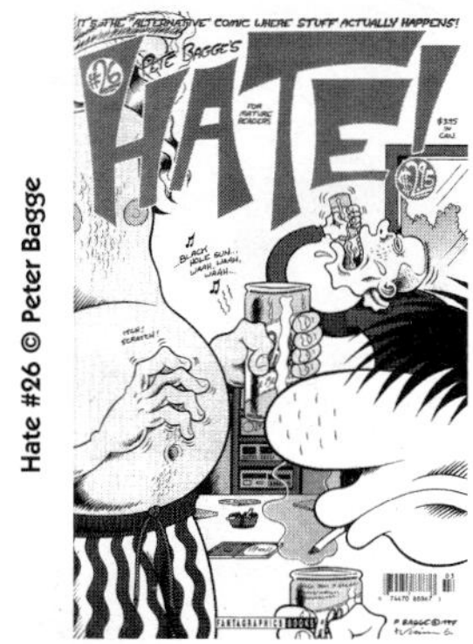

Hate #26 © Peter Bagge

Haunted #38 © CC

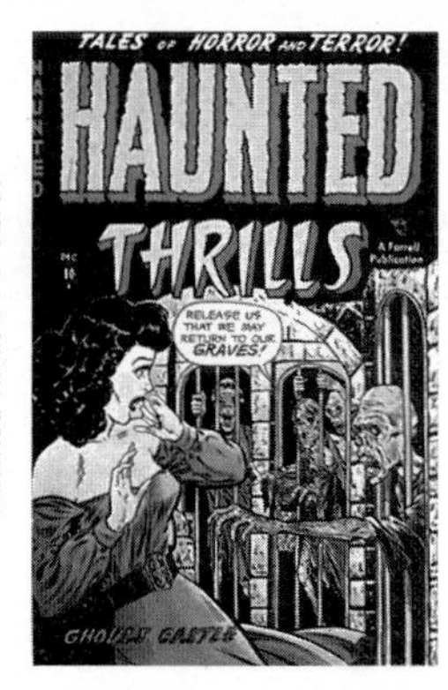

Haunted Thrills #4 © AJAX

	GD25	FN65	NM94
45-Casper & Nightmare	3.00	9.00	30.00
46-Harvey-Toon (7/61)	1.50	4.50	12.00
47-Sad Sack's Army Life (8/61)	2.00	6.00	16.00
48-The Phantom (9/61)	8.50	25.50	85.00
49-Stumbo the Giant (1st app. in Hot Stuff)	7.50	22.50	75.00
50-Harvey-Toon (11/61)	1.50	4.50	12.00
51-Sad Sack's Army Life (12/61)	2.00	6.00	16.00
52-Casper & Nightmare	3.00	9.00	30.00
53-Harvey-Toons (2/62)	1.25	3.75	10.00
54-Stumbo the Giant	3.50	10.50	35.00
55-Sad Sack's Army Life (4/62)	2.00	6.00	16.00
56-Casper & Nightmare	2.60	7.80	26.00
57-Stumbo the Giant	3.50	10.50	35.00
58-Sad Sack's Army Life	2.00	6.00	16.00
59-Casper & Nightmare (7/62)	2.60	7.80	26.00
60-Stumbo the Giant (9/62)	3.50	10.50	35.00
61-Sad Sack's Army Life	1.75	5.25	14.00
62-Casper & Nightmare	2.50	7.50	22.00
63-Stumbo the Giant	3.00	9.00	30.00
64-Sad Sack's Army Life (1/63)	1.75	5.25	14.00
65-Casper & Nightmare	2.50	7.50	22.00
66-Stumbo The Giant (3/63)	3.00	9.00	30.00
67-Sad Sack's Army Life (4/63)	1.75	5.25	14.00
68-Casper & Nightmare	2.50	7.50	22.00
69-Stumbo the Giant (6/63)	3.00	9.00	30.00
70-Sad Sack's Army Life (7/63)	1.75	5.25	14.00
71-Casper & Nightmare (8/63)	2.00	6.00	16.00
72-Stumbo the Giant	3.00	9.00	30.00
73-Little Sad Sack (10/63)	1.75	5.25	14.00
74-Sad Sack's Muttsy... (11/63)	1.75	5.25	14.00
75-Casper & Nightmare	2.00	6.00	16.00
76-Little Sad Sack	1.75	5.25	14.00
77-Sad Sack's Muttsy...	1.75	5.25	14.00
78-Stumbo the Giant (3/64); JFK caricature	3.00	9.00	30.00
79-87: 79-Little Sad Sack (4/64). 80-Sad Sack's Muttsy... (5/64). 81-Little Sad Sack. 82-Sad Sack's Muttsy... 83-Little Sad Sack(8/64). 84-Sad Sack's Muttsy... 85-Gabby Gob (#1)(10/64). 86-G. I. Juniors (#1)(11/64). 87-Sad Sack's Muttsy... (12/64)	1.75	5.25	14.00
88-Stumbo the Giant (1/65)	3.00	9.00	30.00
89-122: 89-Sad Sack's Muttsy... 90-Gabby Gob. 91-G. I. Juniors. 92-Sad Sack's Muttsy... (5/65). 93-Sadie Sack (6/65). 94-Gabby Gob. 95-G. I. Juniors (8/65). 96-Sad Sack's Muttsy... (9/65). 97-Gabby Gob (10/65). 98-G. I. Juniors (11/65). 99-Sad Sack's Muttsy... (12/65). 100-Gabby Gob(1/66). 101-G. I. Juniors (2/66). 102-Sad Sack's Muttsy... (3/66). 103-Gabby Gob. 104- G. I. Juniors. 105-Sad Sack's Muttsy... 106-Gabby Gob (7/66). 107-G. I. Juniors (8/66). 108-Sad Sack's Muttsy... 109-Gabby Gob. 110-G. I. Juniors (11/66). 111-Sad Sack's Muttsy... (12/66). 112-G. I. Juniors. 113-Sad Sack's Muttsy... 114-G. I. Juniors. 115-Sad Sack's Muttsy... 116-G. I. Juniors (5/67). 117-Sad Sack's Muttsy... 118-G. I. Juniors. 119-Sad Sack's Muttsy... (8/67). 120-G. I. Juniors (9/67). 121-Sad Sack's Muttsy... (10/67). 122-G. I. Juniors (11/67)	1.00	3.00	8.00

HARVEY HITS COMICS
Harvey Publications: Nov, 1986 - No. 6, Oct, 1987

	GD25	FN65	NM94
1-Little Lotta, Little Dot, Wendy & Baby Huey			3.00
2-6: 3-Xmas-c			2.00

HARVEY POP COMICS (Teen Humor)
Harvey Publications: Oct, 1968 - No. 2, Nov, 1969 (Both are 68 pg. Giants)

	GD25	FN65	NM94
1-The Cowsills	4.20	13.20	42.00
2-Bunny	3.50	10.50	35.00

HARVEY 3-D HITS (See Sad Sack)

HARVEY-TOON (...S) (See Harvey Hits No. 29, 34, 38, 42, 46, 50, 53)

HARVEY WISEGUYS (...Digest #? on)
Harvey Comics: Nov, 1987; #2, Nov, 1988; #3, Apr, 1989 - No. 4, Nov, 1989 (98 pgs., digest-size, $1.25/$1.75)

	GD25	FN65	NM94
1,2: 1-Hot Stuff, Spooky, etc. 2 (68 pgs.)			3.00
3,4			2.50

HATARI (See Movie Classics)

HATE
Fantagraphics Books: Spr, 1990 - No. 30, 1998 ($2.50/$2.95, B&W/color)

	GD25	FN65	NM94
1	2.00	6.00	20.00
2-3	1.50	4.50	15.00
4-10	.90	2.70	8.00
11-15			4.00
16-29: 16-$2.95-c & color begins			3.00
30-($3.95) Last issue			4.00
Buddy Go Home! (1997, $16.95) r/Buddy stories in color			16.95
Hate-Ball Special Edition ($3.95, giveaway)-reprints			4.00
Hate Jamboree (10/98, $4.50) old & new cartoons			4.50

HATHAWAYS, THE (TV)
Dell Publishing Co.: No. 1298, Feb-Apr, 1962 (one-shot)

	GD25	FN65	NM94
Four Color 1298-Photo-c	3.60	11.00	40.00

HAUNTED (See This Magazine Is Haunted)

HAUNTED (Baron Weirwulf's Haunted Library on-c #21 on)
Charlton Comics: 9/71 - No. 30, 11/76; No. 31, 9/77 - No. 75, 9/84

	GD25	FN65	NM94
1-All Ditko issue	1.80	5.40	18.00
2-5	1.20	3.60	12.00
6-20	.90	2.70	9.00
21-1st Baron Weirwulf; Newton-c/a	1.20	3.60	12.00
22-40	.85	2.60	7.00
41-60: 51-Reprints #1			5.00
61-75: 64,75-Reprints			3.00

NOTE: ***Aparo*** *c-45.* ***Ditko*** *a-1-8, 11-16, 18, 23, 24, 28, 30, 34r, 36r, 39-42r, 47r, 49-51r, 57, 60, 74. c-1-7, 11, 13, 14, 16, 30, 41, 47, 49-51, 74.* ***Howard*** *a-6, 9, 18, 22, 25, 32.* ***Kim*** *a-9, 19.* ***Morisi*** *a-13.* ***Newton*** *a-17, 21, 59r; c-21, 22(painted).* ***Staton*** *a-11, 12, 18, 21, 22, 30, 33, 35, 38; c-18, 33.* ***Sutton*** *a-10, 17, 20-22, 31, 35, 37, 38; c-15, 17, 18, 23(painted), 24(painted), 64r. #49 reprints Tales of the Mysterious Traveler #4.*

HAUNTED LOVE
Charlton Comics: Apr, 1973 - No. 11, Sept, 1975

	GD25	FN65	NM94
1-Tom Sutton-a (16 pgs.)	2.70	8.00	30.00
2,3, 6-11	1.20	3.60	12.00
4,5-Ditko-a	1.50	4.50	15.00
Modern Comics #1(1978)	.90	2.70	8.00

NOTE: ***Howard*** *a-8i.* ***Kim*** *a-7-9.* ***Newton*** *c-8, 9.* ***Staton*** *a-1-6.* ***Sutton*** *a-1, 3-5, 10, 11.*

HAUNTED THRILLS (Tales of Horror and Terror)
Ajax/Farrell Publications: June, 1952 - No. 18, Nov-Dec, 1954

	GD25	FN65	NM94
1-r/Ellery Queen #1	38.00	114.00	285.00
2-L. B. Cole-a r-/Ellery Queen #1	24.00	72.00	180.00
3-5: 3-Drug use story	21.00	64.00	160.00
6-10,12: 7-Hitler story.	17.00	52.00	130.00
11-Nazi death camp story	19.00	56.00	140.00
13,16-18: 18-Lingerie panels	15.00	44.00	110.00
14-Jesus Christ apps. in story by Webb	15.00	44.00	110.00
15-Jo-Jo-r	15.00	44.00	110.00

NOTE: ***Kamenish*** *art in most issues.* ***Webb*** *a-12.*

HAUNT OF FEAR (Formerly Gunfighter)
E. C. Comics: No. 15, May-June, 1950 - No. 28, Nov-Dec, 1954

	GD25	FN65	NM94
15(#1, 1950)(Scarce)-1st app. Old Witch	230.00	690.00	2200.00
16	90.00	270.00	850.00
17-Origin of Crypt of Terror, Vault of Horror, & Haunt of Fear; used in **SOTI**, pg. 43; last pg. Ingels-a used by N.Y. Legis. Comm.; story "Monster Maker" based on Frankenstein	90.00	270.00	850.00
4	60.00	180.00	575.00
5-Injury-to-eye panel, pg. 4 of Wood story	45.00	135.00	425.00

Haunt of Fear #8 © WMG

Hawk and Dove #9 (3rd Series) © DC

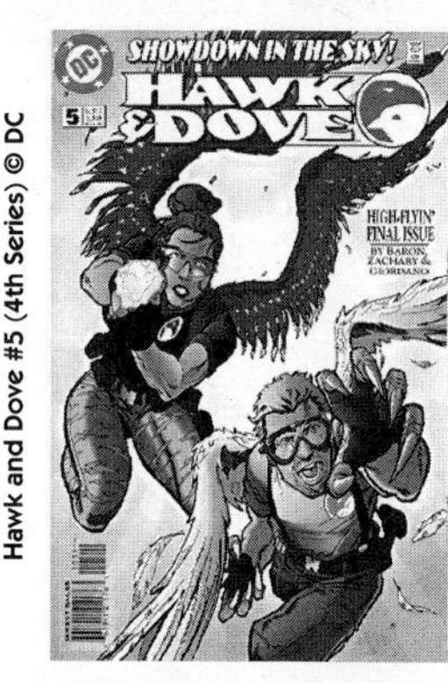

Hawk and Dove #5 (4th Series) © DC

	GD25	FN65	NM94
6-10: 8-Shrunken head cover. 10-Ingels biog.	34.00	102.00	290.00
11-13,15-18: 11-Kamen biog. 12-Feldstein biog. 16,18-Ray Bradbury adaptations. 18-Ray Bradbury biography	25.00	75.00	220.00
14-Origin Old Witch by Ingels	36.00	108.00	320.00
19-Used in **SOTI**, ill. "A comic book baseball game" & Senate investigation on juvenile delinq. bondage/decapitation-c	34.00	102.00	290.00
20-Feldstein-r/Vault of Horror #12	23.00	69.00	200.00
21,22,25,27: 27-Cannibalism story; Wertham cameo	16.00	48.00	140.00
23-Used in **SOTI**, pg. 241	16.00	48.00	140.00
24-Used in Senate Investigative Report, pg.8	16.00	48.00	140.00
26-Contains anti-censorship editorial, 'Are you a Red Dupe?'	16.00	48.00	140.00
28-Low distribution	16.00	48.00	150.00

NOTE: *(Canadian reprints known; see Table of Contents).* ***Craig*** *a-15-17, 5, 7, 10, 12, 13; c-15-17, 5-7.* ***Crandall*** *a-20, 21, 26, 27.* ***Davis*** *a-4-26, 28.* ***Evans*** *a-15-19, 22-25, 27.* ***Feldstein*** *a-15-17, 20; c-4, 8-10.* ***Ingels*** *a-16, 17, 4-28; c-11-28.* ***Kamen*** *a-16, 4, 6, 7, 9-11, 13-19, 21-28.* ***Krigstein*** *a-28.* ***Kurtzman*** *a-15(#1), 17(#3).* ***Orlando*** *a-9, 12.* ***Wood*** *a-15, 16, 4-6.*

HAUNT OF FEAR, THE
Gladstone Publishing: May, 1991 - No. 2, July, 1991 ($2.00, 68 pgs.)

1,2: 1-Ghastly Ingels-c(r); 2-Craig-c(r)			2.50

HAUNT OF FEAR
Russ Cochran/Gemstone Publ.: Sept, 1991 - No. 5, 1992 ($2.00, 68 pgs.); Nov, 1992 - Present ($1.50/$2.00/$2.50)

1-Ingels-c(r)			2.50
2-5			2.00
1-3: 1-3-r/HOF #15-17 with original-c			1.50
4-15: 4,5-r/HOF #4,5 with original-c			2.00
16-25			2.50
Annual 1- r/#1-5			8.95
Annual 2- r/#6-10			9.95
Annual 3- r/#11-15			10.95
Annual 4- r/#16-20			10.50
Annual 5- r/#21-25			13.50

HAUNT OF HORROR, THE (Digest)
Marvel Comics: Jun, 1973 - No. 2, Aug, 1973 (164 pgs.)

1-Morrow painted skull-c	2.00	6.00	20.00
2-Kelly Freas painted bondage-c	1.50	4.50	15.00

HAUNT OF HORROR, THE (Magazine)
Cadence Comics Publ. (Marvel): May, 1974 - No. 5, Jan, 1975 (75¢) (B&W)

1	1.20	3.60	12.00
2,4: 2-Origin & 1st app. Gabriel the Devil Hunter; Satana begins. 4-Neal Adams-a	.90	2.70	9.00
3,5: 5-Evans-a(2)	.85	2.60	7.00

NOTE: ***Alcala*** *a-2.* ***Colan*** *a-2p.* ***Heath*** *r-1.* ***Krigstein*** *r-3.* ***Reese*** *a-1.* ***Simonson*** *a-1.*

HAVE GUN, WILL TRAVEL (TV)
Dell Publishing Co.: No. 931, 8/58 - No. 14, 7-9/62 (All Richard Boone photo-c)

Four Color 931 (#1)	14.00	42.00	150.00
Four Color 983,1044 (#2,3)	8.50	25.50	95.00
4 (1-3/60) - 14	7.00	21.00	75.00

HAVOK & WOLVERINE - MELTDOWN (See Marvel Comics Presents #24)
Marvel Comics (Epic Comics): Mar, 1989 - No. 4, Oct, 1989 ($3.50, mini-series, squarebound, mature)

1-4: Violent content			3.50

HAWAIIAN EYE (TV)
Gold Key: July, 1963 (Troy Donahue, Connie Stevens photo-c)

1 (10073-307)	4.00	12.00	45.00

HAWAIIAN ILLUSTRATED LEGENDS SERIES
Hogarth Press: 1975 (B&W)(Cover printed w/blue, yellow, and green)

1-Kalelealuaka, the Mysterious Warrior			1.20
2,3(Exist?)			1.00

HAWK, THE (Also see Approved Comics #1, 7 & Tops In Adventure)
Ziff-Davis/St. John Publ. Co. No. 4 on: Wint/51 - No. 3, 11-12/52; No. 4, 1953 - No. 12, 5/55 (Painted c-1-4)

1-Anderson-a	19.00	56.00	140.00
2 (Sum, '52)-Kubert, Infantino-a	10.00	30.00	75.00
3-7,11: 11-Buckskin Belle & The Texan app.	8.50	26.00	60.00
8-Reprints #3 w/different-c by Baker	10.00	30.00	75.00
9-Baker-c/a; Kubert-a(r)/#2	10.00	30.00	75.00
10-Baker-c/a; r/one story from #2	10.00	30.00	75.00
12-Baker-c/a; Buckskin Belle app.	10.00	30.00	75.00
3-D 1(11/53, 25¢)-Came w/glasses; Baker-c	31.00	94.00	230.00

NOTE: ***Baker*** *c-8-12.* ***Larsen*** *a-10.* ***Tuska*** *a-1, 9, 12. Painted c-1, 4, 7.*

HAWK AND THE DOVE, THE (See Showcase #75 & Teen Titans) (1st series)
National Periodical Publications: Aug-Sept, 1968 - No. 6, June-July, 1969

1-Ditko-c/a	5.50	16.50	55.00
2-6: 5-Teen Titans cameo	3.80	11.40	38.00

NOTE: ***Ditko*** *c/a-1, 2.* ***Gil Kane*** *a-3p, 4p, 5, 6p; c-3-6.*

HAWK AND DOVE (2nd Series)
DC Comics: Oct, 1988 - No. 5, Feb, 1989 ($1.00, limited series)

1-Rob Liefeld-c/a(p) in all			3.00
2-5			2.00
Trade paperback ('93, $9.95)-Reprints #1-5			10.00

HAWK AND DOVE
DC Comics: June, 1989 - No. 28, Oct, 1991 ($1.00)

1-28			1.00
Annual 1 (1990, $2.00)-Liefeld pin-up			2.00
Annual 2 (1991)-Armageddon 2001 x-over			2.00

HAWK AND DOVE
DC Comics: Nov, 1997 - No.5, Mar, 1998 ($2.50, limited series)

1-5-Baron-s/Zachary & Giordano-a			2.50

HAWK AND WINDBLADE (See Elflord)
Warp Graphics: Aug, 1997 - No.2, Sept, 1997 ($2.95, limited series)

1,2-Blair-s/Chan-c/a			2.95

HAWKEYE (See The Avengers #16 & Tales Of Suspense #57)
Marvel Comics Group: Sept, 1983 - No. 4, Dec, 1983 (limited series)

1-4: Mark Gruenwald-a/scripts. 1-Origin Hawkeye. 3-Origin Mockingbird. 4-Hawkeye & Mockingbird elope			1.50

HAWKEYE
Marvel Comics: Jan, 1994 - No. 4, Apr, 1994 ($1.75, limited series)

1-4			1.75

HAWKEYE & THE LAST OF THE MOHICANS (TV)
Dell Publishing Co.: No. 884, Mar, 1958 (one-shot)

Four Color 884-Photo-c	6.40	19.00	70.00

HAWKEYE: EARTH'S MIGHTIEST MARKSMAN
Marvel Comics: Oct, 1998 ($2.99, one-shot)

1-Justice and Firestar app.; DeFalco-s			3.00

HAWKMAN (See Atom & Hawkman, The Brave & the Bold, DC Comics Presents, Detective, Flash Comics, Hawkworld, Justice League of America #31, Mystery in Space, Shadow War Of..., Showcase, & World's Finest #256)

HAWKMAN (1st Series) (Also see The Atom #7 & Brave & the Bold #34-36, 42-44, 51)
National Periodical Publications: Apr-May, 1964 - No. 27, Aug-Sept, 1968

1-(4-5/64)-Anderson-c/a begins, ends #21	44.00	132.00	540.00
2	19.00	57.00	190.00
3,5	12.00	36.00	120.00
4-Origin & 1st app. Zatanna (10-11/64)	16.00	48.00	160.00

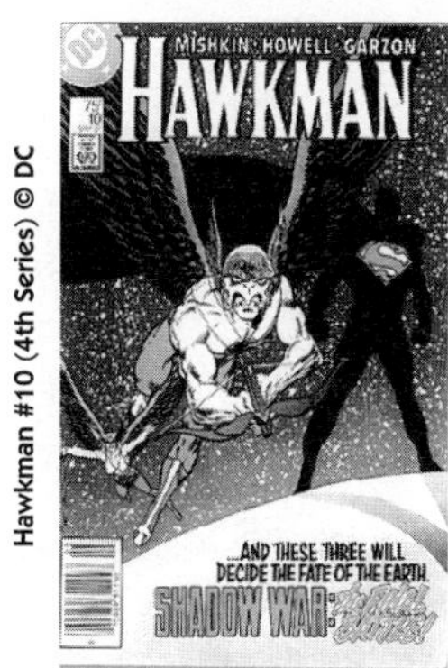

Hawkman #10 (4th Series) © DC

Headline Comics #8 © PRIZE

Heartbreakers #3 © Paul Guinan & Anina Bennett

GD25 FN65 NM94

6 10.00 30.00 100.00
7 9.00 27.00 90.00
8-10: 9-Atom cameo; Hawkman & Atom learn each other's I.D.; 2nd app. Shadow Thief 7.50 22.50 75.00
11-15 5.60 17.00 56.00
16-27: 18-Adam Strange x-over (cameo #19). 25-G.A. Hawkman-r by Moldoff. 27-Kubert-c 4.50 13.50 45.00

HAWKMAN (2nd Series)
DC Comics: Aug, 1986 - No. 17, Dec, 1987

1-17: 10-Byrne-c 1.00
Special #1 (1986, $1.25) 1.50
Trade paperback (1989, $19.95)-r/Brave and the Bold #34-36,42-44 by Kubert; Kubert-c 20.00

HAWKMAN (4th Series)(See both Hawkworld limited & ongoing series)
DC Comics: Sept, 1993 - No. 33, July, 1996 ($1.75/$1.95/$2.25)

1-($2.50)-Gold foil embossed-c; storyline cont'd from Hawkworld ongoing series; new costume & powers. 2.50
2-11: 2-Green Lantern x-over. 3-Airstryke app. 4,6-Wonder Woman app. 1.75
12,13,0,14-20: 12-Begin $1.95-c. 13-(9/94)-Zero Hour. 0-(10/94). 14-(11/94). 15-Aquaman-c & app. 2.00
21-33: 21-Begin $2.25-c, 23-Wonder Woman app. 25-Kent Williams-c. 29,30-Chaykin-c. 32-Breyfogle-c 2.25
Annual 1 (1993, $2.50, 68 pgs.)-Bloodlines Earthplague 2.50
Annual 2 (1995, $3.95)-Year One story 4.00

HAWKMOON: THE JEWEL IN THE SKULL
First Comics: May, 1986 - No. 4, Nov, 1986 ($1.75, limited series, Baxter paper)

1-4: Adapts novel by Michael Moorcock 2.00

HAWKMOON: THE MAD GOD'S AMULET
First Comics: Jan, 1987 - No. 4, July, 1987 ($1.75, limited series, Baxter paper)

1-4: Adapts novel by Michael Moorcock 2.00

HAWKMOON: THE RUNESTAFF
First Comics: Jun, 1988 -No. 4, Dec, 1988 ($1.75-$1.95, lim. series, Baxter paper)

1-4: ($1.75) Adapts novel by Michael Moorcock. 3,4 ($1.95) 2.00

HAWKMOON: THE SWORD OF DAWN
First Comics : Sept, 1987 - No. 4, Mar, 1988 ($1.75, lim. series, Baxter paper)

1-4: Dorman painted-c; adapts Moorcock novel 2.00

HAWKWORLD
DC Comics: 1989 - No. 3, 1989 ($3.95, prestige format, limited series)

Book 1-Tim Truman story & art in all; Hawkman dons new costume; reintro Byth. 4.00
Books 2,3 4.00

HAWKWORLD (3rd Series)
DC Comics: June, 1990 - No. 32, Mar, 1993 ($1.50/$1.75)

1-Hawkman spin-off; story cont'd from limited series. 2.50
2-32: 15,16-War of the Gods x-over. 22-J'onn J'onzz app. 1.75
Annual 1-3 ('90-'92, $2.95, 68 pgs.) 3.00
Annual 2-2nd printing with silver ink-c 3.00
NOTE: ***Truman*** *a-30-32; c-27-32, Annual 1.*

HAWTHORN-MELODY FARMS DAIRY COMICS
Everybody's Publishing Co.: No date (1950's) (Giveaway)

nn-Cheerie Chick, Tuffy Turtle, Robin Koo Koo, Donald & Longhorn Legends 1.60 4.00 8.00

HAYWIRE
DC Comics: Oct, 1988 - No. 13, Sept, 1989 ($1.25, mature)

1-13 1.30

HAZARD
Image Comics (WildStorm Prod.): June, 1996 - No. 7, Nov, 1996 ($1.75)

1-7: 1-Intro Hazard; Jeff Mariotte scripts begin; Jim Lee-c(p) 1.75

HEADBUSTERS
Antarctic Press: Oct, 1998 ($2.95, B&W)

1-Mallette-s 2.95

HEADHUNTERS
Image Comics: Apr, 1997 - No. 3, June, 1997 ($2.95, B&W)

1-3: Chris Marrinan-s/a 2.95

HEADLINE COMICS (...For the American Boy) (...Crime No. 32-39)
Prize Publications: Feb, 1943 - No. 22, Nov-Dec, 1946; No. 23, 1947 - No. 77, Oct, 1956

1-Junior Rangers-c/stories begin; Yank & Doodle x-over in Junior Rangers (Junior Rangers are Uncle Sam's nephews) 40.00 120.00 320.00
2 19.00 56.00 140.00
3-Used in **POP**, pg. 84 15.00 44.00 110.00
4-7,9,10: 4,9,10-Hitler stories in each 13.00 38.00 95.00
8-Classic Hitler-c 32.00 96.00 240.00
11,12 10.00 30.00 75.00
13-15-Blue Streak in all 11.00 34.00 85.00
16-Origin & 1st app. Atomic Man (11-12/45) 21.00 64.00 160.00
17,18,20,21: 21-Atomic Man ends (9-10/46) 11.00 32.00 80.00
19-S&K-a 24.00 72.00 180.00
22-Last Junior Rangers; Kiefer-c 7.85 23.50 55.00
23,24: (All S&K-a). 23-Valentine's Day Massacre story; content changes to true crime. 24-Dope-crazy killer story 23.00 68.00 170.00
25-35-S&K-c/a. 25-Powell-a 21.00 64.00 160.00
36-S&K-a; photo-c begin 16.00 48.00 120.00
37-1 pg. S&K, Severin-a; rare Kirby photo-c app. 16.00 48.00 120.00
38,40-Meskin-a 5.70 17.00 38.00
39,41,42,46-48,50,52-55: 41-J. Edgar Hoover 26th Anniversary Issue with photo on-c 4.25 13.00 28.00
43,49-Meskin-a 5.00 15.00 30.00
44-S&K-c; Severin/Elder, Meskin-a 9.30 28.00 70.00
45-Kirby-a 7.85 23.50 55.00
51-Kirby-c 5.35 16.00 32.00
56-S&K-a 9.30 28.00 70.00
57-77: 72-Meskin-c/a(i) 4.00 12.00 22.00
NOTE: ***Hollingsworth*** *a-30. Photo c-36-43.* ***H. C. Kiefer*** *c-12-16, 22. Atomic Man c-17-19.*

HEADMAN
Innovation Publishing: 1990 ($2.50, mature)

1-Sci/fi 2.50

HEAP, THE
Skywald Publications: Sept, 1971 (52 pgs.)

1-Kinstler-r/Strange Worlds #8 1.50 4.50 15.00

HEART AND SOUL
Mikeross Publications: April-May, 1954 - No. 2, June-July, 1954

1,2 5.70 17.00 35.00

HEARTBREAKERS (Also see Dark Horse Presents)
Dark Horse Comics: Apr, 1996 - No. 4, July, 1996 ($2.95, limited series)

1-4: 1-W/paper doll & pin-up. 2-Ross pin-up. 3-Evan Dorkin pin-ups. 4-Brereton-c; Matt Wagner pin-up 3.00
...Superdigest (7/98, $9.95, digest-size) new stories 9.95

HEARTLAND (See Hellblazer)
DC Comics (Vertigo): Mar, 1997 ($4.95, one-shot, mature)

1-Garth Ennis-s/Steve Dillon-c/a 2.00 6.00

HEART OF DARKNESS
Hardline Studios: 1994 ($2.95)

1-Brereton-c 3.00

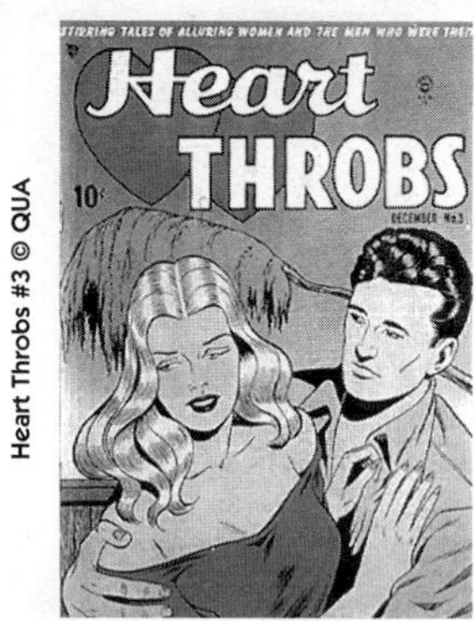

Heart Throbs #3 © QUA

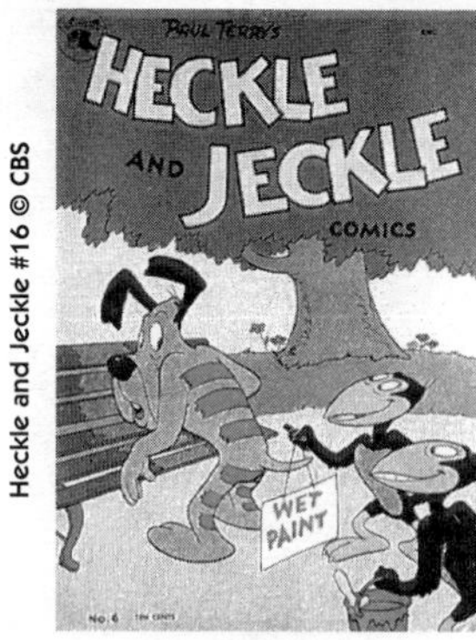

Heckle and Jeckle #16 © CBS

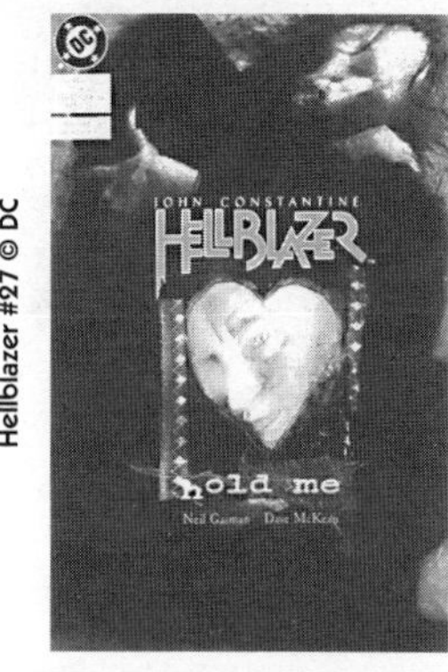

Hellblazer #27 © DC

HEART OF THE BEAST, THE
DC Comics (Vertigo): 1994 ($19.95, hardcover, mature)

	GD25	FN65	NM94
1-Dean Motter scripts			20.00

HEARTS OF DARKNESS (See Ghost Rider; Wolverine; Punisher: Hearts of...)

HEART THROBS (Love Stories No. 147 on)
Quality Comics/National Periodical #47(4-5/57) on (Arleigh #48-101): 8/49 - No. 8, 10/50; No. 9, 3/52 - No. 146, Oct, 1972

	GD25	FN65	NM94
1-Classic Ward-c, Gustavson-a, 9 pgs.	36.00	108.00	270.00
2-Ward-c/a (9 pgs); Gustavson-a	21.00	64.00	160.00
3-Gustavson-a	6.85	21.00	48.00
4,6,8-Ward-a, 8-9 pgs.	11.00	32.00	80.00
5,7	5.00	15.00	30.00
9-Robert Mitchum, Jane Russell photo-c	7.50	22.50	52.00
10,15-Ward-a	8.75	26.25	62.00
11-14,16-20: 12 (7/52)	4.15	12.50	25.00
21-Ward-c	7.50	22.50	52.00
22,23-Ward-a(p)	5.70	17.00	36.00
24-33: 33-Last pre-code (3/55)	4.00	11.50	23.00
34-39,41-46 (12/56; last Quality issue)	3.80	9.50	19.00
40-Ward-a; r-7 pgs./#21	5.70	17.00	34.00
47-(4-5/57; 1st DC issue)	22.00	66.00	220.00
48-60	7.50	22.50	75.00
61-70	5.00	15.00	50.00
71-99: 74-Last 10 cent issue	4.00	12.00	40.00
100	5.00	15.00	50.00
101-The Beatles app. on-c	12.00	36.00	120.00
102-119: 102-123-(Serial)-Three Girls, Their Lives, Their Loves	2.50	7.50	20.00
120-Neal Adams-c	3.50	10.50	35.00
121-132,143-146	1.40	4.20	14.00
133-142-(52 pgs.)	2.20	6.25	22.00

NOTE: ***Gustavson** a-8. **Tuska** a-128. Photo c-4, 5, 8-10, 15, 17.*

HEART THROBS - THE BEST OF DC ROMANCE COMICS (See Fireside Book Series)

HEART THROBS
DC Comics (Vertigo): Jan, 1999 - No. 4, Apr, 1999 ($2.95, lim. series)

	GD25	FN65	NM94
1-4-Romance anthology. 1-Timm-c			2.95

HEATHCLIFF (See Star Comics Magazine)
Marvel Comics (Star Comics)/Marvel Comics No. 23 on: Apr, 1985 - No. 56, Feb, 1991 (#16-on, $1.00)

	GD25	FN65	NM94
1-56: Post-a most issues. 43-X-Mas issue. 47-Batman parody (Catman vs. the Soaker)			2.00
Annual 1 ('87)			2.00

HEATHCLIFF'S FUNHOUSE
Marvel Comics (Star Comics)/Marvel No. 6 on: May, 1987 - No. 10, 1988

	GD25	FN65	NM94
1-10			2.00

HEAVY HITTERS
Marvel Comics (Epic Comics): 1993 ($3.75, 68 pgs.)

	GD25	FN65	NM94
1-Bound w/trading card; Lawdog, Feud, Alien Legion, Trouble With Girls, & Spyke			3.75

HECKLE AND JECKLE (See Blue Ribbon, Giant Comics Edition #5A & 10, Paul Terry's, Terry-Toons Comics)
St. John Publ. Co. No. 1-24/Pines No. 25 on: 10/51 - No. 24, 10/55; No. 25, Fall/56 - No. 34, 6/59

	GD25	FN65	NM94
1-Funny animal	23.00	70.00	175.00
2	12.00	36.00	90.00
3-5	9.30	28.00	70.00
6-10	6.50	19.50	45.00
11-20	5.70	17.00	35.00
21-34: 25-Begin CBS Television Presents on-c	4.25	13.00	26.00

HECKLE AND JECKLE (TV) (See New Terrytoons)
Gold Key/Dell Publ. Co.: 11/62 - No. 4, 8/63; 5/66; No. 2, 10/66; No. 3, 8/67

	GD25	FN65	NM94
1 (11/62; Gold Key)	5.50	16.50	60.00
2-4	2.40	7.00	26.00
1 (5/66; Dell)	2.90	8.70	32.00
2,3	2.20	6.50	24.00

(See March of Comics No. 379, 472, 484)

HECKLE AND JECKLE 3-D
Spotlight Comics: 1987 - No. 2?, 1987 ($2.50)

	GD25	FN65	NM94
1,2			3.00

HECTIC PLANET
Slave Labor Graphics 1998 ($12.95/$14.95)

	GD25	FN65	NM94
Book One ($12.95) Reprints Dorkin-s/a from Pirate Corp$ Vol. 1			12.95
Book Two ($14.95) Reprints Dorkin-s/a from Pirate Corp$ Vol. 2			14.95

HECTOR COMICS (The Keenest Teen in Town)
Key Publications: Nov, 1953 - No. 3, 1954

	GD25	FN65	NM94
1-Teen humor	4.00	11.00	22.00
2,3	2.80	7.00	14.00

HECTOR HEATHCOTE (TV)
Gold Key: Mar, 1964

	GD25	FN65	NM94
1 (10111-403)	6.00	18.00	65.00

HECTOR THE INSPECTOR (See Top Flight Comics)

HEDY DEVINE COMICS (Formerly All Winners #21? or Teen #22?(6/47); Hedy of Hollywood #36 on; also see Annie Oakley, Comedy & Venus)
Marvel Comics (RCM)/Atlas #50: No. 22, Aug, 1947 - No. 50, Sept, 1952

	GD25	FN65	NM94
22-1st app. Hedy Devine (also see Joker #32)	15.00	44.00	110.00
23,24,27-30: 23-Wolverton-a, 1 pg; Kurtzman's "Hey Look", 2 pgs. 24,27-30-"Hey Look" by Kurtzman, 1-3 pgs.	14.00	42.00	105.00
25-Classic "Hey Look" by Kurtzman, "Optical Illusion"	15.00	44.00	110.00
26- "Giggles 'n' Grins" by Kurtzman	9.30	28.00	70.00
31-34,36-50: 32-Anti-Wertham editorial	7.15	21.50	50.00
35-Four pgs. "Rusty" by Kurtzman	11.00	34.00	85.00

HEDY-MILLIE-TESSIE COMEDY (See Comedy Comics)

HEDY WOLFE (Also see Patsy & Hedy & Miss America Magazine V1#2)
Atlas Publishing Co. (Emgee): Aug, 1957

	GD25	FN65	NM94
1-Patsy Walker's rival; Al Hartley-c	9.30	28.00	65.00

HEE HAW (TV)
Charlton Press: July, 1970 - No. 7, Aug, 1971

	GD25	FN65	NM94
1	2.40	7.00	26.00
2-7	1.80	5.40	18.00

HEIDI (See Dell Jr. Treasury No. 6)

HELEN OF TROY (Movie)
Dell Publishing Co.: No. 684, Mar, 1956 (one-shot)

	GD25	FN65	NM94
Four Color 684-Buscema-a, photo-c	10.00	30.00	110.00

HELLBLAZER (John Constantine) (See Saga of Swamp Thing #37) (Also see Books of Magic limited series)
DC Comics (Vertigo #63 on): Jan, 1988 - Present ($1.25/$1.50/$1.95/$2.25)

	GD25	FN65	NM94
1-(44 pgs.)-John Constantine; McKean-c thru #21	1.50	4.50	15.00
2-5	.90	2.70	9.00
6-10: 9-X-over w/Swamp Thing #76. 9,10-Swamp Thing cameo			5.00
11-20: 19-Sandman app.			4.00
21-26,28-30: 22-Williams-c. 24-Contains bound-in Shocker movie poster. 25,26-Grant Morrison scripts.			3.00
27-Neil Gaiman scripts; Dave McKean-a; fold-out guide to Nightbreed	.90	2.70	8.00
31-39: 36-Preview of World Without End.			3.00

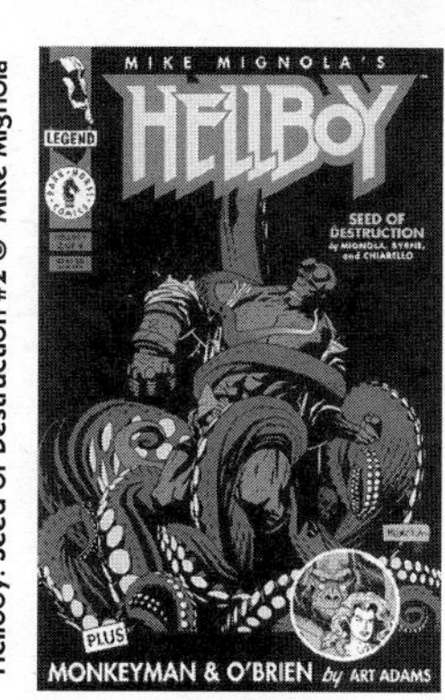

Hellboy: Seed of Destruction #2 © Mike Mignola

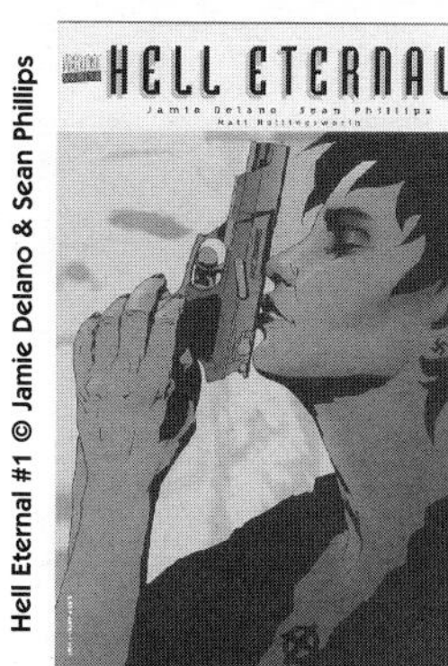

Hell Eternal #1 © Jamie Delano & Sean Phillips

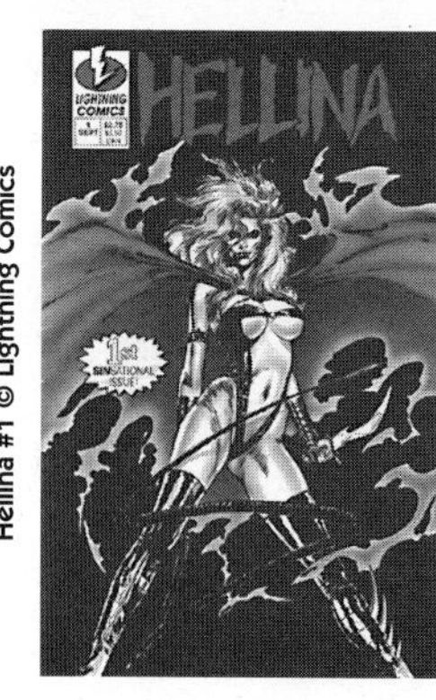

Hellina #1 © Lightning Comics

GD25 FN65 NM94

40-($2.25, 52 pgs.)-Dave McKean-a & colors; preview of Kid Eternity 3.50
41-Ennis scripts begin; ends #83 2.00 6.00
42-49: 44-Begin $1.75-c. 44,45-Sutton-a(i) 4.00
50-($3.00, 52 pgs.) 5.00
51-65: 52-Glenn Fabry painted-c begin. 62-Special Death insert by McKean. 63-Silver metallic ink on-c 4.50
66-74,76-88: 66-Begin $1.95-c. 77-Totleben-c. 84-Sean Phillips-c/a begins; Delano story. 85-88-Eddie Campbell story. 4.50
75-($2.95, 52 pgs.) 4.50
89-99,101-119: 89-Paul Jenkins scripts begin; begin $2.25-c. 108-Adlard-a 4.50
100 ($3.50, 48 pgs.) 4.50
120 ($3.50, 48 pgs.) 4.00
121-128 2.50
129-133: 129-Ennis-s; begin $2.50-c 2.50
Annual 1 (1989, $2.95, 68 pgs.)-Bryan Talbot's 1st work in American comics 5.00
Special 1 (1993, $3.95, 68 pgs.)-Ennis story; w/pin-ups. 1.00 3.00 10.00
...Dangerous Habits (1997, $14.95, TPB) r/#41-46 15.00
...Fear and Loathing (1997, $14.95, TPB) r/#62-67 15.00
...Tainted Love (1998, $16.95, TPB) r/#68-71, Vertigo Jam #1 and Hellblazer Special #1 16.95

NOTE: ***Alcala*** *a-8i, 9i, 18-22i.* ***Gaiman*** *scripts-27.* ***McKean*** *a-27,40; c-1-21.* ***Sutton*** *a-44i, 45i.* ***Talbot*** *a-Annual 1.*

HELLBLAZER/THE BOOKS OF MAGIC
DC Comics (Vertigo): Dec, 1997 - No. 2, Jan, 1998 ($2.50, mini-series)
1,2-John Constantine and Tim Hunter 2.50

HELLBOY (Also see Dark Horse Presents, John Byrne's Next Men. San Diego Comic Con #2, Danger Unlimited #4, Gen[13] #13B, Ghost/Hellboy, & Savage Dragon)

HELLBOY: ALMOST COLOSSUS
Dark Horse Comics (Legend): Jun, 1997 - No. 2, Jul, 1997 ($2.95, lim. series)
1,2-Mignola-s/a 3.50

HELLBOY CHRISTMAS SPECIAL
Dark Horse Comics: Dec, 1997 ($3.95, one-shot)
nn-Christmas stories by Mignola, Gianni, Darrow, Purcell 4.00

HELLBOY, JR., HALLOWEEN SPECIAL
Dark Horse Comics: Oct, 1997 ($3.95, one-shot)
nn-"Harvey" style renditions of Hellboy characters; Bill Wray, Mike Mignola & various-s/a; wraparound-c by Wray 4.00

HELLBOY: SEED OF DESTRUCTION
Dark Horse Comics (Legend): Mar, 1994 - No. 4, Jun, 1994 ($2.50, lim. series)
1-4-Mignola-c/a w/Byrne scripts; Monkeyman & O'Brien back-up story (origin) by Art Adams. 1.60 4.00
Trade paperback (1994, $17.95)-collects all four issues plus r/Hellboy's 1st app. in San Diego Comic Con #2 & pin-ups 18.00
Limited edition hardcover (1995, $99.95)-includes everything in trade paperback plus additional material. 100.00

HELLBOY: THE CORPSE AND THE IRON SHOES
Dark Horse Comics (Legend): Jan, 1996 ($2.95, one-shot)
nn-Mignola-c/a/scripts; reprints "The Corpse" serial from Capitol City's Advance Comics catalog w/new story 3.00

HELLBOY: THE WOLVES OF ST. AUGUST
Dark Horse Comics (Legend): 1995 ($4.95, squarebound, one-shot)
nn-Mignola--c/a/scripts; r/Dark Horse Presents #88-91 with additional story. 5.00

HELLBOY: WAKE THE DEVIL (Sequel to Seed of Destruction)
Dark Horse Comics (Legend): Jun, 1996 - No. 5, Oct, 1996 ($2.95, lim. series)
1-5: Mignola-c/a & scripts; The Monstermen back-up story by Gary Gianni 3.00
TPB (1997, $17.95) r/#1-5 17.95

HELLCOP
Image Comics (Avalon Studios): Aug, 1998 - Present ($2.50)
1,2: 1-(Oct. on-c) Casey-s 2.50

HELL ETERNAL
DC Comics (Vertigo Verité): 1998 ($6.95, squarebound, one-shot)
1-Delano-s/Phillips-a 6.95

HELLHOUNDS (...: Panzer Cops #3-6)
Dark Horse Comics: 1994 - No. 6, July, 1994 ($2.50, B&W, limited series)
1,3-5: 1-Hamner-c. 3-(4/94) 2.50
2,6-($2.95, 52 pgs.): 2-Joe Phillips-c 3.00

HELLHOUND, THE REDEMPTION QUEST
Marvel Comics (Epic Comics): Dec, 1993 - No. 4, Mar, 1994 ($2.25, limited series, coated stock)
1-4 2.25

HELLINA
Lightning Comics: Sept, 1994 ($2.75/$9.95, B&W, one-shot)
1-Origin; pin-up gallery 3.00
1 ($9.95)-Nude Edition 10.00

HELLINA/CATFIGHT Oct, 1995 ($2.75, B&W, one-shot)
1 2.75
1 ($9.95)-Nude Edition 10.00
1 (1997, $2.95)-Encore Edition 3.00

HELLINA: CHRISTMAS IN HELL Dec, 1996 ($2.95, B&W, one-shot)
1, 1b 3.00
1 ($9.95)-Nude edition; polybagged. 10.00
1 ($9.95)-Platinum edition 10.00
1 ($29.95)-Platinum Nude edition 30.00

HELLINA/CYNDER Sept, 1997 ($2.95, B&W, one-shot)
1,1B-($2.95)-Abrams-c 2.95
1A,1B-($9.95)-Nude Edition; polybagged 9.95

HELLINA/DOUBLE IMPACT Feb, 1996 ($3.00, one-shot)
1, 1b: 1b-Cleary-c. 3.00
1 ($9.95)-Nude Edition; polybagged. 10.00

HELLINA: GENESIS Apr, 1996 ($3.50, B&W, one-shot)
1-polybagged w/poster 3.50
1 ($9.95)-Nude Edition 10.00
1 ($20.00)-Platinum Edition 20.00

HELLINA: HEART OF THORNS July, 1996 - No. 2, Sept, 1996 ($2.75/$3.00, limited series)
1-Flip book w/Moxi story 3.00
1,2A,2B-($9.95): All Nude Editions 10.00
2A,2B 2.75
2-($9.95)-Platinum Edition 10.00

HELLINA: HELLBORN Dec, 1997 - No. 2, Feb, 1998 ($2.95, B&W)
1,2-Christina Z. -s 3.00
1,2-($9.95)-Nude Edition 10.00

HELLINA: HELL'S ANGEL Nov, 1996 - No. 2, Dec, 1996 ($2.75, B&W)
1,2-($2.75) 2.75
1,2-($9.95)-Nude Edition 10.00

HELLINA: IN THE FLESH Aug, 1997 ($2.95, B&W, one-shot)
1a,1b-($2.95) 2.95
1a,1b-($9.95)-Nude Edition 9.95

HELLINA: KISS OF DEATH July, 1995 ($2.75/$9.95/$20.00, B&W)
1 3.00
1 ($9.95)-Nude Edition 10.00
1 ($20.00)-Gold Edition 20.00

Hellshock #3 © Jae Lee

Hellstorm: Prince of Lies #5 © MAR

Herbie #21 © ACG

GD25 FN65 NM94

1,1b (Mar, 1997, $2.95)-Encore Edition 2.95

HELLINA:NAKED DESIRE May, 1997 ($2.95, B&W, one-shot)
1 2.95

HELLINA:NIRA X Aug, 1996 ($2.95, color, one-shot)
1a,1b-($2.95) 3.00
1-($9.95)-Commemorative Edition 10.00

HELLINA:THE RELIC June, 1997 ($2.95, B&W, one-shot)
1 2.95

HELLINA:SKYBOLT TOYZ Aug, 1997 ($1.50, B&W, one-shot)
1,1b-($1.50)-Reprint of Hellina: Wicked Ways 1.50

HELLINA: TAKING BACK THE NIGHT Apr, 1995 ($2.75, B&W, one-shot)
1 3.00
1 ($9.95)-Nude Edition 10.00

HELLINA: WICKED WAYS Nov, 1995 ($2.75/$9.95, B&W, one-shot)
1,1b: 1b-Trent Kaniuga-c; polybagged. 2.75
1-($9.95)-Nude Edition 10.00
1a (Apr, 1997, $2.95)-Encore Edition 2.95

HELLO, I'M JOHNNY CASH
Spire Christian Comics (Fleming H. Revell Co.): 1976 (39/49¢)
nn 3.00

HELL ON EARTH (See DC Science Fiction Graphic Novel)

HELLO PAL COMICS (Short Story Comics)
Harvey Publications: Jan, 1943 - No. 3, May, 1943 (Photo-c)
1-Rocketman & Rocketgirl begin; Yankee Doodle Jones app.; Mickey Rooney photo-c 56.00 168.00 475.00
2-Charlie McCarthy photo-c (scarce) 47.00 141.00 400.00
3-Bob Hope photo-c 46.00 138.00 390.00

HELLRAISER/NIGHTBREED – JIHAD (Also see Clive Barker's...)
Epic Comics (Marvel Comics): 1991 - Book 2, 1991 ($4.50, 52 pgs.)
Book 1,2 4.50

HELL-RIDER (Magazine)
Skywald Publications: Aug, 1971 - No. 2, Oct, 1971 (B&W)
1-Origin & 1st app.; Butterfly & Wildbunch begins 3.50 10.50 38.00
2 2.40 7.00 26.00
NOTE: *#3 advertised in Psycho #5 but did not come out.* ***Buckler*** *a-1, 2.* ***Morrow*** *c-3.*

HELL'S ANGEL (Becomes Dark Angel #6 on)
Marvel Comics UK: July, 1992 - No. 5, Nov, 1993 ($1.75)
1-5: X-Men (Wolverine, Cyclops)-c/stories. 1-Origin. 3-Jim Lee cover swipe 1.75

HELLSHOCK
Image Comics: July, 1994 - No. 4, Nov, 1994 ($1.95, limited series)
1-4-Jae Lee-c/a & scripts. 4-variant-c. 2.00

HELLSHOCK
Image Comics: Jan, 1997 - No.2, Feb, 1997 ($2.95/$2.50, limited series)
1-($2.95)-Jae Lee-c/s/a, Villarrubia-painted-a 2.95
2-($2.50) 2.50

HELLSHOCK BOOK THREE: THE SCIENCE OF FAITH
Image Comics: Jan, 1998 ($2.50)
1-Jae Lee-c/s/a, Villarrubia-painted-a 2.50

HELLSTORM: PRINCE OF LIES (See Ghost Rider #1 & Marvel Spotlight #12)
Marvel Comics: Apr, 1993 - No. 21, Dec, 1994 ($2.00)
1-($2.95)-Parchment-c w/red thermographic ink 3.00
2-21: 14-Bound-in trading card sheet. 18-P. Craig Russell-c 2.00

HE-MAN (See Masters Of The Universe)

HE-MAN (Also see Tops In Adventure)
Ziff-Davis Publ. Co. (Approved Comics): Fall, 1952
1-Kinstler painted-c; Powell-a 13.00 38.00 95.00

HE-MAN
Toby Press: May, 1954 - No. 2, July, 1954 (Painted-c by B. Safran)
1 12.00 36.00 90.00
2 9.30 28.00 70.00

HENNESSEY (TV)
Dell Publishing Co.: No. 1200, Aug-Oct, 1961 - No. 1280, Mar-May, 1962
Four Color 1200-Gil Kane-a, photo-c 5.50 16.50 60.00
Four Color 1280-Photo-c 5.50 16.50 60.00

HENRY (Also see Little Annie Rooney)
David McKay Publications: 1935 (52 pgs.) (Daily B&W strip reprints)(10"x10" cardboard-c)
1-By Carl Anderson 33.00 100.00 250.00

HENRY (See King Comics & Magic Comics)
Dell Publishing Co.: No. 122, Oct, 1946 - No. 65, Apr-June, 1961
Four Color 122-All new stories begin 12.00 35.00 130.00
Four Color 155 (7/47) 7.00 22.00 80.00
1 (1-3/48)-All new stories 7.00 22.00 80.00
2 3.25 10.00 36.00
3-10 3.00 9.00 32.00
11-20: 20-Infinity-c 1.80 5.50 20.00
21-30 1.50 4.50 16.00
31-40 1.10 3.30 10.00
41-65 1.00 3.00 8.00

HENRY (See Giant Comic Album and March of Comics No. 43, 58, 84, 101, 112, 129, 147, 162, 178, 189)

HENRY ALDRICH COMICS (TV)
Dell Publishing Co.: Aug-Sept, 1950 - No. 22, Sept-Nov, 1954
1-Part series written by John Stanley; Bill Williams-a 7.00 22.00 80.00
2 3.60 11.00 40.00
3-5 3.00 9.00 35.00
6-10 2.50 7.50 28.00
11-22 1.80 5.50 20.00
Giveaway (16 pgs., soft-c, 1951)-Capehart radio 2.00 6.00 22.00

HENRY BREWSTER
Country Wide (M.F. Ent.): Feb, 1966 - V2#7, Sept, 1967 (All 25¢ Giants)
1 1.50 4.50 12.00
2-6(12/66)-Powell-a in most 1.00 3.00 8.00
V2#7 2.40 6.00

HEPCATS
Antarctic Press: Nov, 1996 - Present ($2.95, B&W)
0-12-Martin Wagner-c/s/a: 0-color 3.00
0-($9.95) CD Edition 10.00

HERBIE (See Forbidden Worlds & Unknown Worlds)
American Comics Group: April-May, 1964 - No. 23, Feb, 1967 (All 12¢)
1-Whitney-c/a in most issues 15.00 45.00 150.00
2-4 8.00 24.00 80.00
5-Beatles, Dean Martin, F. Sinatra app. 9.50 28.50 95.00
6,7,9,10 6.00 18.00 60.00
8-Origin & 1st app. The Fat Fury 7.50 22.50 75.00
11-23: 14-Nemesis & Magicman app. 17-r/2nd Herbie from Forbidden Worlds #94. 23-r/1st Herbie from F.W. #73 4.50 13.50 45.00

HERBIE
Dark Horse Comics: Oct, 1992 - No. 12, 1993 ($2.50, limited series)
1-6: Whitney-r plus new-c/a. 1-Byrne-c/a & scripts. 3-Bob Burden-c/a. 4-Art Adams-c 2.50

HERBIE GOES TO MONTE CARLO, HERBIE RIDES AGAIN (See Walt Disney

Hercules: The Legendary Journeys #3 © MCA Television

Here's Howie Comics #5 © DC

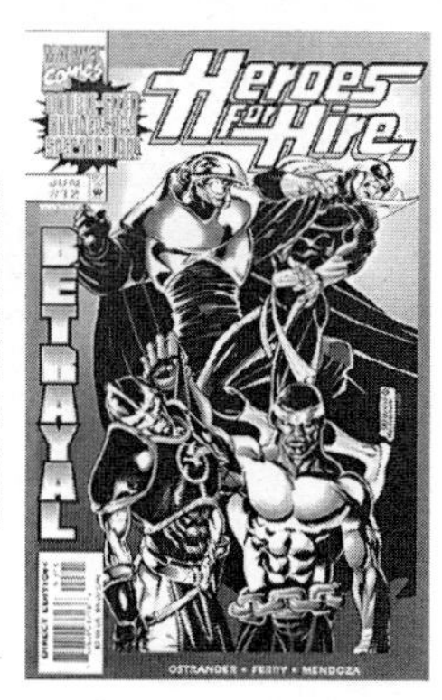

Heroes For Hire #12 © MAR

GD25 FN65 NM94

Showcase No. 24, 41)

HERCULES (See Hit Comics #1-21, Journey Into Mystery Annual, Marvel Graphic Novel #37, Marvel Premiere #26 & The Mighty...)

HERCULES
Charlton Comics: Oct, 1967 - No. 13, Sept, 1969; Dec, 1968

1-Thane of Bagarth begins; Glanzman-a in all 2.25 6.75 18.00
2-7,9-13: 1-5,7,9,10-Aparo-a 1.50 4.50 12.00
8-(Low distribution)(12/68, 35¢, B&W); magazine format; new Hercules story plus-r story/#1; Thane-r/#1-3 4.00 12.00 40.00
Modern Comics reprint 10('77), 11('78) 2.00 5.00

HERCULES (Prince of Power) (Also see The Champions)
Marvel Comics Group: V1#1, 9/82 - V1#4, 12/82; V2#1, 3/84 - V2#4, 6/84 (color, both limited series)

1-4: Layton-c/a. 1.60
V2#1-4: Layton-c/a. 4-Death of Zeus. 1.00
NOTE: *Layton a-1, 2, 3p, 4p, V2#1-4; c-1-4, V2#1-4.*

HERCULES: HEART OF CHAOS
Marvel Comics: Aug, 1997 - No. 3, Oct, 1997 ($2.50, limited series)

1-3-DeFalco-s, Frenz-a 2.50

HERCULES: OFFICIAL COMICS MOVIE ADAPTION
Acclaim Books: 1997 ($4.50, digest size)

nn-Adaption of the Disney animated movie 4.50

HERCULES: THE LEGENDARY JOURNEYS (TV)
Topps Comics: June, 1996 - No. 5, Oct, 1996 ($2.95)

1-2: 1-Golden-c. 3.00
3-Xena-c/app. .85 2.60 7.00
3-Variant-c 1.50 4.50 15.00
4,5: Xena-c/app. 5.00

HERCULES UNBOUND
National Periodical Publications: Oct-Nov, 1975 - No. 12, Aug-Sept, 1977

1-Wood-i begins 5.00
2-12: 7-Adams ad. 10-Atomic Knights x-over 3.00
NOTE: ***Buckler** c-7p. **Layton** inks-No. 9, 10. **Simonson** a-7-10p, 11, 12; c- 8p, 9-12. **Wood** a-1-8i; c-7i, 8i.*

HERCULES (...Unchained #1121) (Movie)
Dell Publishing Co.: No. 1006, June-Aug, 1959 - No.1121, Aug, 1960

Four Color 1006-Buscema-a, photo-c 9.00 27.00 100.00
Four Color 1121-Crandall/Evans-a 9.00 27.00 100.00

HERE COMES SANTA (See March of Comics No. 30, 213, 340)

HERE COME THE BIG PEOPLE
Event Comics: Oct, 1997 ($2.95, one-shot)

1-Trace Beaulieu-s/Conner & Palmiotti-c/a; variant-c by Darrow 2.95

HERE IS SANTA CLAUS
Goldsmith Publishing Co. (Kann's in Washington, D.C.): 1930s (16 pgs., 8 in color) (stiff paper covers)

nn 9.30 28.00 65.00

HERE'S HOW AMERICA'S CARTOONISTS HELP TO SELL U.S. SAVINGS BONDS
Harvey Comics: 1950? (16 pgs., giveaway, paper cover)

Contains: Joe Palooka, Donald Duck, Archie, Kerry Drake, Red Ryder, Blondie & Steve Canyon 15.00 44.00 110.00

HERE'S HOWIE COMICS
National Periodical Publications: Jan-Feb, 1952 - No. 18, Nov-Dec, 1954

1 20.00 60.00 150.00
2 10.00 30.00 75.00
3-5: 5-Howie in the Army issues begin (9-10/52) 7.15 21.50 50.00
6-10 5.70 17.00 40.00
11-18 5.35 16.00 32.00

HERETIC, THE
Dark Horse Comics (Blanc Noir): Nov, 1996 - No. 4, Mar, 1997 ($2.95, limited series)

1-4:-w/back-up story 3.00

HERITAGE OF THE DESERT (See Zane Grey, 4-Color 236)

HERMAN & KATNIP (See Harvey Comics Hits #60 & 62, Harvey Hits #14,25,31,41 & Paramount Animated Comics #1)

HERMES VS. THE EYEBALL KID
Dark Horse Comics: Dec, 1994 - No. 3,Feb, 1995 ($2.95, B&W, limited series)

1-3: Eddie Campbell-c/a/scripts 3.00

HERO (Warrior of the Mystic Realms)
Marvel Comics: May, 1990 - No. 6, Oct, 1990 ($1.50, limited series)

1-6: 1-Portachio-i 1.50

HERO ALLIANCE, THE
Sirius Comics: Dec, 1985 - No. 2, Sept, 1986 (B&W)

1,2: 2-($1.50) 1.50
Special Edition 1 (7/86, color) 1.50

HERO ALLIANCE
Wonder Color Comics: May, 1987 ($1.95)

1-Ron Lim-a 2.00

HERO ALLIANCE
Innovation Publishing: V2#1, Sept, 1989 - V2#17, Nov, 1991 ($1.95, 28 pgs.)

V2#1-17: 1,2-Ron Lim-a 2.00
Annual 1 (1990, $2.75, 36 pgs.)-Paul Smith-c/a 2.80
Special 1 (1992, $2.50, 32 pgs.)-Stuart Immonen-a (10 pgs.) 2.50

HERO ALLIANCE: END OF THE GOLDEN AGE
Innovation Publishing: July, 1989 - No. 3, Aug, 1989 ($1.75, bi-weekly limited series)

1-3: Bart Sears & Ron Lim-c/a; reprints & new-a 1.80

HEROES (Also see Shadow Cabinet & Static)
DC Comics (Milestone): May, 1996 - No. 6, Nov, 1996 ($2.50, limited series)

1-6: 1-Intro Heroes (Iota, Donner, Blitzen, Starlight, Payback & Static) 2.50

HEROES AGAINST HUNGER
DC Comics: 1986 ($1.50; one-shot for famine relief)

1-Superman, Batman app.; Neal Adams-c(p); includes many artists work; Jeff Jones assist (2 pg.) on B. Smith-a 2.50

HEROES ALL CATHOLIC ACTION ILLUSTRATED
Heroes All Co.: 1943 - V6#5, Mar 10, 1948 (paper covers)

V1#1,2-(16 pgs., 8x11") 15.00 44.00 110.00
V2#1(1/44)-3(3/44)-(16 pgs., 8x11") 12.00 36.00 90.00
V3#1(1/45)-10(12/45)-(16 pgs., 8x11") 11.00 32.00 80.00
V4#1-35 (12/20/46)-(16 pgs.) 9.30 28.00 65.00
V5#1(1/10/47)-8(2/28/47)-(16 pgs.) 7.15 21.50 50.00
V5#9(3/7/47)-20(11/25/47)-(32 pgs.) 7.15 21.50 50.00
V6#1(1/10/48)-5(3/10/48)-(32 pgs.) 7.15 21.50 50.00

HEROES FOR HIRE
Marvel Comics: July, 1997 - Present ($2.99/$1.99)

1-($2.99)-Wraparound cover 5.00
2-11: 2-Variant cover. 7-Thunderbolts app. 9-Punisher-c/app. 10,11 Deadpool-c/app. 3.00
12-($2.99) 3.00
13-19: 18,19-Wolverine-c/app. 2.00
.../Quicksilver '98 Annual ($2.99) Siege of Wundagore pt.5 3.00

HEROES FOR HOPE STARRING THE X-MEN

Heroes Reborn: The Return #3 © MAR

Heroic Comics #4 © EAS

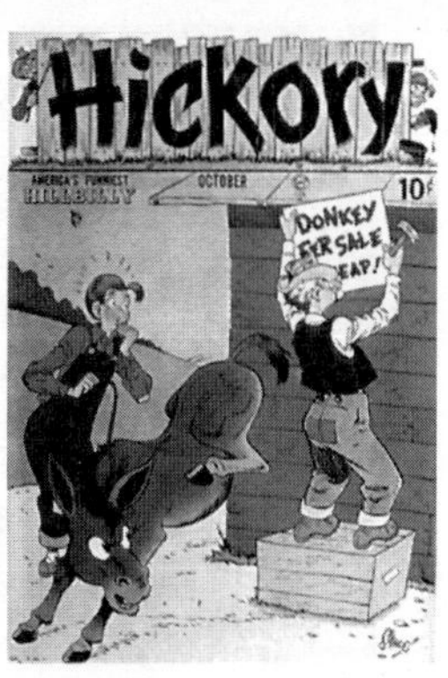

Hickory #1 © QUA

GD25 FN65 NM94

Marvel Comics Group: Dec, 1985 ($1.50, one-shot, 52pgs., proceeds donated to famine relief)

1-Stephen King scripts; Byrne, Miller, Corben-a; Wrightson/J. Jones-a (3 pgs.); Art Adams-c; Starlin back-c 4.00

HEROES, INC. PRESENTS CANNON
Wally Wood/CPL/Gang Publ. No. 2: 1969 - No. 2, 1976 (Sold at Army PX's)

nn-Ditko, Wood-a; Wood-c; Reese-a(p) 1.50 4.50 12.00
2-Wood-c; Ditko, Byrne, Wood-a; 8-1/2x10-1/2"; B&W; $2.00 2.25 6.75 18.00

NOTE: *First issue not distributed by publisher; 1,800 copies were stored and 900 copies were stolen from warehouse. Many copies have surfaced in recent years.*

HEROES OF THE WILD FRONTIER (Formerly Baffling Mysteries)
Ace Periodicals: No. 27, Jan, 1956 - No. 2, Apr, 1956

27(#1),2-Davy Crockett, Daniel Boone, Buffalo Bill 4.25 13.00 26.00

HEROES REBORN: THE RETURN
Marvel Comics: Dec, 1997 - No. 4 ($2.50, weekly mini-series)

1-4-Avengers, Fantastic Four, Iron Man & Captain America rejoin regular Marvel Universe; Peter David-s/Larocca-c/a 2.50
1-4-Variant-c for each 3.00
1/2-Wizard offer .90 2.70 9.00
Return of the Heroes TPB ('98, $14.95) r/#1-4 14.95

HERO FOR HIRE (Power Man No. 17 on; also see Cage)
Marvel Comics Group: June, 1972 - No. 16, Dec, 1973

1-Origin & 1st app. Luke Cage; Tuska-a(p) 3.20 9.50 35.00
2-Tuska-a(p) 1.20 3.60 12.00
3-5: 3-1st app. Mace. 4-1st app. Phil Fox of the Bugle .90 2.70 9.00
6-10: 8,9-Dr. Doom app. 9-F.F. app. 2.00 6.00
11-16: 14-Origin retold. 15-Everett Subby-r('53). 16-Origin Stilletto; death of Rackham 5.00

HERO HOTLINE (1st app. in Action Comics Weekly #637)
DC Comics: April, 1989 - No. 6, Sept, 1989 ($1.75, limited series)

1-6: Super-hero humor; Schaffenberger-i .90 1.80

HEROIC ADVENTURES (See Adventures)

HEROIC COMICS (Reg'lar Fellers...#1-15; New Heroic #41 on)
Eastern Color Printing Co./Famous Funnies(Funnies, Inc. No. 1): Aug, 1940 - No. 97, June, 1955

1-Hydroman (origin) by Bill Everett, The Purple Zombie (origin) & Mann of India by Tarpe Mills begins (all 1st apps.) 135.00 405.00 1150.00
2 64.00 192.00 540.00
3,4 43.00 129.00 350.00
5,6 37.00 112.00 280.00
7-Origin & 1st app. Man O'Metal (1 pg.) 40.00 120.00 315.00
8-10: 10-Lingerie panels 27.00 80.00 200.00
11,13: 13-Crandall/Fine-a 25.00 76.00 190.00
12-Music Master (origin/1st app.) begins by Everett, ends No. 31; last Purple Zombie & Mann of India 28.00 84.00 210.00
14,15-Hydroman x-over in Rainbow Boy. 14-Origin & 1st app. Rainbow Boy (super hero). 15-1st app. Downbeat 27.00 80.00 200.00
16-20: 16-New logo. 17-Rainbow Boy x-over in Hydroman. 19-Rainbow Boy x-over in Hydroman & vice versa 19.00 56.00 140.00
21-30:25-Rainbow Boy x-over in Hydroman. 28-Last Man O'Metal. 29-Last Hydroman 12.00 36.00 90.00
31,34,38 4.00 12.00 24.00
32,36,37-Toth-a (3-4 pgs. each) 5.70 17.00 38.00
33,35-Toth-a (8 & 9 pgs.) 5.70 17.00 40.00
39-42-Toth, Ingels-a 5.70 17.00 40.00
43,46,47,49-Toth-a (2-4 pgs.). 47-Ingels-a 5.00 15.00 30.00
44,45,50-Toth-a (6-9 pgs.) 5.70 17.00 35.00
48,53,54 4.00 11.00 22.00

GD25 FN65 NM94

51-Williamson-a 5.70 17.00 38.00
52-Williamson-a (3 pg. story) 4.25 13.00 28.00
55-Toth-c/a 5.35 16.00 32.00
56-60-Toth-c. 60-Everett-a 4.25 13.00 28.00
61-Everett-a 4.00 11.00 22.00
62,64-Everett-c/a 4.15 12.50 25.00
63-Everett-c 3.60 9.00 18.00
65-Williamson/Frazetta-a; Evans-a (2 pgs.) 6.50 19.50 45.00
66,75,94-Frazetta-a (2 pgs. each) 4.15 12.50 25.00
67,73-Frazetta-a (4 pgs. each) 5.00 15.00 30.00
68,74,76-80,84,85,88-93,95-97: 95-Last pre-code 3.60 9.00 18.00
69,72-Frazetta-a (6 & 8 pgs. each); 1st (?) app. Frazetta Red Cross ad 6.50 19.50 45.00
70,71,86,87-Frazetta, 3-4 pgs. each; 1 pg. ad by Frazetta in #70 4.15 12.50 25.00
81,82-Frazetta art (1 pg. each): 81-1st (?) app. Frazetta Boy Scout ad (tied w/ Buster Crabbe #9 3.60 9.00 18.00
83-Frazetta-a (1/2 pg.) 3.60 9.00 18.00

NOTE: ***Evans** a-64, 65. **Everett** a-(Hydroman-c/a-No. 1-9), 44, 60-64; c-1-9, 62-64. **Harvey Fuller** c-28-35. **Sid Greene** a-38-43, 46. **Guardineer** a-42(3), 43, 44, 45(2), 49(3), 50, 60, 61(2), 65, 67(2) 70-72. **Ingels** c-41. **Kiefer** a-46, 48; c-19-22, 24, 44, 46, 48, 51-53, 65, 67-69, 71-74, 76, 77, 79, 80, 82, 85, 86, 88, 89, 94, 95. **Mort Lawrence** a-45. **Tarpe Mills** a-2(2), 3(2), 10. **Ed Moore** a-49, 52-54, 56-63, 65-69, 72-74, 76, 77. **H.G. Peter** a-58-74, 76, 77, 87. **Paul Reinman** a-49. **Rico** a-31. Captain Tootsie by **Beck**-31, 32. Painted-c #16 on. Hydroman c-1-11. Music Master c-12, 13, 15. Rainbow Boy c-14.*

HERO ZERO (Also see Comics' Greatest World & Godzilla Versus Hero Zero)
Dark Horse Comics: Sept, 1994 ($2.50)

0 2.50

HEX (Replaces Jonah Hex)
DC Comics: Sept, 1985 - No. 18, Feb, 1987 (Story cont'd from Jonah Hex # 92)

1-10,14-18: 1-Hex in post-atomic war world; origin. 6-Origin Stiletta 2.00
11-13: All contain future Batman storyline. 13-Intro The Dogs of War (origin #15) 2.50

NOTE: ***Giffen** a(p)-15-18; c(p)-15,17,18. **Texeira** a-1, 2p, 3p, 5-7p, 9p, 11-14p; c(p)-1, 2, 4-7, 12.*

HEXBREAKER (See First Comics Graphic Novel #15)

HEY THERE, IT'S YOGI BEAR (See Movie Comics)

HI-ADVENTURE HEROES (TV)
Gold Key: May, 1969 - No. 2, Aug, 1969 (Hanna-Barbera)

1-Three Musketeers, Gulliver, Arabian Knights 4.00 12.00 45.00
2-Three Musketeers, Micro-Venture, Arabian Knights 3.20 9.60 35.00

HI AND LOIS
Dell Publishing Co.: No. 683, Mar, 1956 - No. 955, Nov, 1958

Four Color 683 (#1) 2.25 6.75 25.00
Four Color 774(3/57),955 1.80 5.50 20.00

HI AND LOIS
Charlton Comics: Nov, 1969 - No. 11, July, 1971

1 1.80 5.40 18.00
2-11 1.00 3.00 10.00

HICKORY (See All Humor Comics)
Quality Comics Group: Oct, 1949 - No. 6, Aug, 1950

1-Sahl-c/a in all; Feldstein?-a 13.00 40.00 100.00
2 7.15 21.50 50.00
3-6 6.50 19.50 45.00

HIDDEN CREW, THE (See The United States Air Force Presents:...)

HIDE-OUT (See Zane Grey, Four Color No. 346)

HIDING PLACE, THE
Spire Christian Comics (Fleming H. Revell Co.): 1973 (39¢/49¢)

nn 4.00

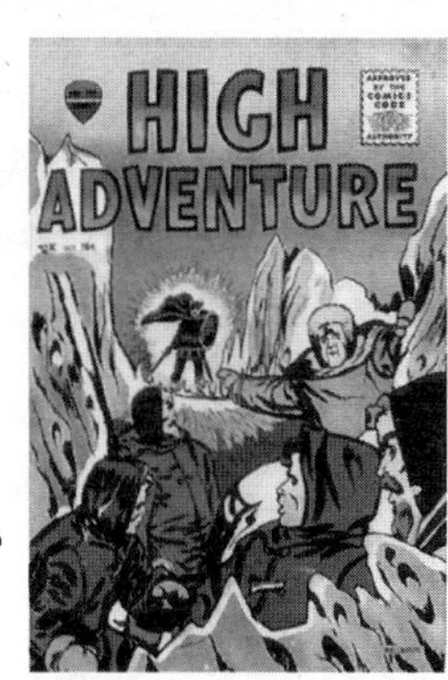

High Adventure #1 © Decker Pub.

Hi-School Romance #2 © HARV

Hit Comics #52 © QUA

	GD25	FN65	NM94
HIGH ADVENTURE			
Red Top(Decker) Comics (Farrell): Oct, 1957			
1-Krigstein-r from Explorer Joe (re-issue on-c)	4.25	13.00	26.00
HIGH ADVENTURE (TV)			
Dell Publishing Co.: No. 949, Nov, 1958 - No. 1001, Aug-Oct, 1959 (Lowell Thomas)			
Four Color 949 (#1)-Photo-c	4.50	13.50	50.00
Four Color 1001-Lowell Thomas'...(#2)	4.50	13.50	50.00
HIGH CHAPPARAL (TV)			
Gold Key: Aug, 1968 (Photo-c)			
1 (10226-808)-Tufts-a	4.00	12.00	45.00
HIGH SCHOOL CONFIDENTIAL DIARY (Confidential Diary #12 on)			
Charlton Comics: June, 1960 - No. 11, Mar, 1962			
1	3.20	9.60	32.00
2-11	2.25	6.75	18.00
HIGH VOLTAGE			
Blackout Comics: 1996 ($2.95)			
0-Mike Baron-s			3.00
HI-HO COMICS			
Four Star Publications: nd (2/46?) - No. 3, 1946			
1-Funny Animal; L. B. Cole-c	31.00	92.00	230.00
2,3: 2-L. B. Cole-c	17.00	50.00	125.00
HI-JINX (Teen-age Animal Funnies)			
La Salle Publ. Co./B&I Publ. Co. (American Comics Group)/Creston: 1945; July-Aug, 1947 - No. 7, July-Aug, 1948			
nn-(© 1945, 25 cents, 132 Pgs.)(La Salle)	18.00	53.00	132.00
1-Teen-age, funny animal	13.00	40.00	100.00
2,3	8.50	26.00	60.00
4-7-Milt Gross. 4-X-Mas-c	11.00	34.00	85.00
HI-LITE COMICS			
E. R. Ross Publishing Co.: Fall, 1945			
1-Miss Shady	14.00	42.00	105.00
HILLBILLY COMICS			
Charlton Comics: Aug, 1955 - No. 4, July, 1956 (Satire)			
1-By Art Gates	6.50	19.50	45.00
2-4	4.25	13.00	28.00
HILLY ROSE'S SPACE ADVENTURES			
Astro Comics: May, 1995 - Present ($2.95, B&W)			
1	1.00	3.00	10.00
2			4.00
3-9			3.00
Trade Paperback (1996, $12.95)-r/#1-5			13.00
HIP-IT-TY HOP (See March of Comics No. 15)			
HI-SCHOOL ROMANCE (...Romances No. 41 on)			
Harvey Publ./True Love(Home Comics): Oct, 1949 - No. 5, June, 1950; No. 6, Dec, 1950 - No. 73, Mar, 1958; No. 74, Sept, 1958 - No. 75, Nov, 1958			
1-Photo-c	12.00	36.00	90.00
2-Photo-c	6.85	21.00	48.00
3-9: 3,5-Photo-c	5.35	16.00	32.00
10-Rape story	6.85	21.00	48.00
11-20	3.80	9.50	19.00
21-31	3.20	8.00	16.00
32- "Unholy passion" story	5.35	16.00	32.00
33-36: 36-Last pre-code (2/55)	3.00	7.50	15.00
37-75	2.20	5.50	11.00

NOTE: ***Powell*** *a-1-3, 5, 8, 12-16, 18, 21-23, 25-27, 30-34, 36, 37, 39, 45-48, 50-52, 57, 58, 60, 64, 65, 67, 69.*

	GD25	FN65	NM94
HI-SCHOOL ROMANCE DATE BOOK			
Harvey Publications: Nov, 1962 - No. 3, Mar, 1963 (25¢ Giants)			
1-Powell, Baker-a	2.80	8.40	28.00
2,3	2.00	6.00	16.00
HIS NAME IS SAVAGE (Magazine format)			
Adventure House Press: June, 1968 (35¢, 52 pgs.)			
1-Gil Kane-a	3.50	10.50	35.00
HI-SPOT COMICS (Red Ryder No. 1 & No. 3 on)			
Hawley Publications: No. 2, Nov, 1940			
2-David Innes of Pellucidar; art by J. C. Burroughs; written by Edgar Rice Burroughs	103.00	309.00	875.00
HISTORY OF THE DC UNIVERSE (Also see Crisis on Infinite Earths)			
DC Comics: Sept, 1986 - No. 2, Nov, 1986 ($2.95, limited series)			
1,2: 1-Perez-c/a			3.00
Limited Edition hardcover	3.20	9.50	35.00
HITCHHIKERS GUIDE TO THE GALAXY (See Life, the Universe and Everything & Restaraunt at the End of the Universe)			
DC Comics: 1993 - No. 3, 1993 ($4.95, limited series)			
1-3: Adaptation of Douglas Adams book			5.00
TPB (1997, $14.95) r/#1-3			15.00
HIT COMICS			
Quality Comics Group: July, 1940 - No. 65, July, 1950			
1-Origin/1st app. Neon, the Unknown & Hercules; intro. The Red Bee; Bob & Swab, Blaze Barton, the Strange Twins, X-5 Super Agent, Casey Jones & Jack & Jill (ends #7) begin	520.00	1560.00	5200.00
2-The Old Witch begins, ends #14	229.00	687.00	1950.00
3-Casey Jones ends; transvestism story "Jack & Jill"	206.00	618.00	1750.00
4-Super Agent (ends #17), & Betty Bates (ends #65) begin; X-5 ends	182.00	546.00	1550.00
5-Classic Lou Fine cover	442.00	1326.00	4200.00
6-10: 10-Old Witch by Crandall (4 pgs.); 1st work in comics (4/41)	165.00	495.00	1400.00
11-Classic cover	112.00	336.00	950.00
12-17: 13-Blaze Barton ends. 17-Last Neon; Crandall Hercules in all; Last Lou Fine-c	103.00	309.00	875.00
18-Origin & 1st app. Stormy Foster, the Great Defender (12/41); The Ghost of Flanders begins; Crandall-c	115.00	345.00	975.00
19,20	94.00	282.00	800.00
21-24: 21-Last Hercules. 24-Last Red Bee & Strange Twins	88.00	264.00	750.00
25-Origin & 1st app. Kid Eternity and begins by Moldoff (12/42); 1st app. The Keeper (Kid Eternity's aide)	141.00	423.00	1200.00
26-Blackhawk x-over in Kid Eternity	88.00	264.00	750.00
27-29	43.00	129.00	360.00
30,31- "Bill the Magnificent" by Kurtzman, 11 pgs. in each	41.00	122.00	325.00
32-40: 32-Plastic Man x-over. 34-Last Stormy Foster	23.00	68.00	170.00
41-50	15.00	46.00	115.00
51-60-Last Kid Eternity	14.00	42.00	105.00
61-63-Crandall-c/a; 61-Jeb Rivers begins	15.00	44.00	110.00
64,65-Crandall-a	14.00	42.00	105.00

NOTE: ***Crandall*** *a-11-17(Hercules), 23, 24(Stormy Foster); c-18-20, 23, 24.* ***Fine*** *c-1-14, 16, 17(most).* ***Ward*** *c-33. Bondage c-7, 64. Hercules c-3, 10-17. Jeb Rivers c-61-65. Kid Eternity c-25-60 (w/Keeper-28-34, 36, 39-43, 45-55). Neon the Unknown c-2, 4, 8, 9. Red Bee c-1, 5-7. Stormy Foster c-18-24.*

HITLER'S ASTROLOGER (See Marvel Graphic Novel #35)

HITMAN (Also see Bloodbath #2, Batman Chronicles #4 & The Demon Annual #2)
DC Comics: May, 1996 - Present ($2.25)

Hitman #29 © DC

The Hobbit #1 © ECL

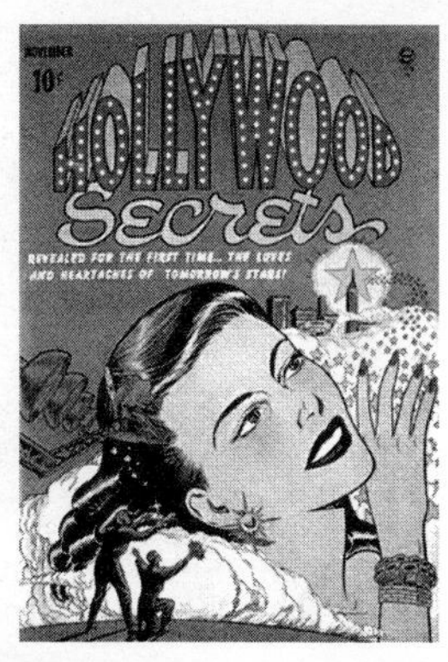

Hollywood Secrets #1 © QUA

GD25 FN65 NM94

1-Garth Ennis-s & John McCrea-c/a begin; Batman app. 1.00 3.00 10.00

2-Joker-c;Two Face, Mad Hatter, Batman app. .90 2.70 8.00

3-Batman-c/app.; Joker app 5.00

4-10: 4-1st app. Nightfist. 8-Final Night x-over. 10-GL cameo 4.00

11-20: 11,12-GL-c/app. 15-20-"Ace of Killers". 16-18-Catwoman app. 17-19-Demon-app 1.20 3.00

21-29 2.25

30-33: 30-Begin $2.50-c 2.50

#1,000,000 (11/98) Hitman goes to the 853rd Century 2.50

Annual 1 (1997, $3.95) Pulp Heroes 3.95

TPB-(1997, $9.95) r/Hitman #1-3, Demon Ann. #2, Batman Chronicles #4 10.00

10,000 Bullets TPB ('98, $9.95) r/#4-8 10.00

HI-YO SILVER (See Lone Ranger's Famous Horse... and also see The Lone Ranger and March of Comics No. 215)

HOBBIT, THE
Eclipse Comics: 1989 - No. 3, 1990 ($4.95, squarebound, 52 pgs.)

Book 1-3: Adapts novel (#1has a 2nd printing) 5.00

HOCUS POCUS (Formerly Funny Book)
Parents' Magazine Press: No. 9, Aug-Sept, 1946

9 4.25 13.00 28.00

HOGAN'S HEROES (TV)
Dell Publishing Co.: June, 1966 - No. 8, Sept, 1967; No. 9, Oct, 1969

1: #1-7 photo-c 6.75 20.50 75.00

2,3-Ditko-a(p) 4.25 13.00 48.00

4-9: 9-Reprints #1 2.90 8.70 32.00

HOKUM & HEX (See Razorline)
Marvel Comics (Razorline): Sept, 1993 - No. 9, May, 1994 ($1.75/$1.95)

1-($2.50)-Foil embossed-c; by Clive Barker 2.50

2-8: 5-Hyperkind x-over 1.75

9-($1.95) 2.00

HOLIDAY COMICS
Fawcett Publications: 1942 (25¢, 196 pgs.)

1-Contains three Fawcett comics plus two page portrait of Captain Marvel; Capt. Marvel, Nyoka #1, & Whiz. Not rebound, remaindered comics; printed at the same time as originals 140.00 420.00 1400.00

HOLIDAY COMICS (Becomes Fun Comics #9-12)
Star Publications: Jan, 1951 - No. 8, Oct, 1952

1-Funny animal contents (Frisky Fables) in all; L. B. Cole X-Mas-c 29.00 87.00 220.00

2-Classic L. B. Cole-c 32.00 96.00 240.00

3-8: 5,8-X-Mas-c; all L.B. Cole-c 20.00 60.00 150.00

Accepted Reprint 4 (nd)-L.B. Cole-c 8.50 26.00 60.00

HOLIDAY DIGEST
Harvey Comics: 1988 ($1.25, digest-size)

1 5.00

HOLIDAY PARADE (Walt Disney's...)
W. D. Publications (Disney): Winter, 1990-91(no yr. given) - No. 2, Winter, 1990-91 ($2.95, 68 pgs.)

1-Reprints 1947 Firestone by Barks plus new-a 3.00

2-Barks-r plus other stories 3.00

HOLI-DAY SURPRISE (Formerly Summer Fun)
Charlton Comics: V2#55, Mar, 1967 (25¢ Giant)

V2#55 2.50 7.50 20.00

HOLLYWOOD COMICS
New Age Publishers: Winter, 1944 (52 pgs.)

1-Funny animal 15.00 44.00 110.00

GD25 FN65 NM94

HOLLYWOOD CONFESSIONS
St. John Publishing Co.: Oct, 1949 - No. 2, Dec, 1949

1-Kubert-c/a (entire book) 21.00 64.00 160.00

2-Kubert-c/a (entire book) (Scarce) 31.00 92.00 230.00

HOLLYWOOD DIARY
Quality Comics Group: Dec, 1949 - No. 5, July-Aug, 1950

1-No photo-c 16.00 48.00 120.00

2-Photo-c 10.00 30.00 75.00

3-5-Photo-c. 5-June Allyson/Peter Lawford photo-c 8.50 26.00 60.00

HOLLYWOOD FILM STORIES
Feature Publications/Prize: April, 1950 - No. 4, Oct, 1950 (All photo-c; "Fumetti" type movie comic)

1-June Allyson photo-c 16.00 48.00 120.00

2-4: 2-Lizabeth Scott photo-c. 3-Barbara Stanwick photo-c. 4-Betty Hutton photo-c 12.00 36.00 90.00

HOLLYWOOD FUNNY FOLKS (Formerly Funny Folks; Becomes Nutsy Squirrel #61 on)
National Periodical Publ.: No. 27, Aug-Sept, 1950 - No. 60, July-Aug, 1954

27 12.00 36.00 90.00

28-40 8.50 26.00 60.00

41-60 7.15 21.50 50.00

NOTE: ***Sheldon Mayer** a-27-35, 37-40, 43-46, 48-51, 53, 56, 57, 60.*

HOLLYWOOD LOVE DOCTOR (See Doctor Anthony King...)

HOLLYWOOD PICTORIAL (...Romances on cover)
St. John Publishing Co.: No. 3, Jan, 1950

3-Matt Baker-a; photo-c 20.00 60.00 150.00
(Becomes a movie magazine - Hollywood Pictorial Western with No. 4.)

HOLLYWOOD ROMANCES (Formerly Brides In Love; becomes For Lovers Only #60 on)
Charlton Comics: V2#46, 11/66; #47, 10/67; #48, 11/68;V3#49,11/69-V3#59, 6/71

V2#46-Rolling Stones-c/story 7.00 21.00 70.00

V2#47-V3#59: 56- "Born to Heart Break" begins 1.00 3.00 8.00

HOLLYWOOD SECRETS
Quality Comics Group: Nov, 1949 - No. 6, Sept, 1950

1-Ward-c/a (9 pgs.) 27.00 80.00 200.00

2-Crandall-a, Ward-c/a (9 pgs.) 18.00 54.00 135.00

3-6: All photo-c. 5-Lex Barker (Tarzan)-c 9.30 28.00 65.00

...of Romance, I.W. Reprint #9; r/#2 above w/Kinstler-c 1.50 4.50 12.00

HOLLYWOOD SUPERSTARS
Marvel Comics (Epic Comics): Nov, 1990 - No. 5, Apr, 1991 ($2.25)

1-($2.95, 52 pgs.)-Spiegle-c/a in all; Aragones-a, inside front-c plus 2-4 pgs. 3.00

2-5 ($2.25) 2.30

HOLO-MAN (See Power Record Comics)

HOLYOKE ONE-SHOT
Holyoke Publishing Co. (Tem Publ.): 1944 - No. 10, 1945 (All reprints)

1-Grit Grady (on cover only), Miss Victory, Alias X (origin)-All reprints from Captain Fearless 8.50 26.00 60.00

2-Rusty Dugan (Corporal); Capt. Fearless (origin), Mr. Miracle (origin) app. 8.50 26.00 60.00

3-Miss Victory; r/Crash #4; Cat Man (origin), Solar Legion by Kirby app.; Miss Victory on cover only (1945) 19.00 58.00 145.00

4-Mr. Miracle; The Blue Streak app. 7.15 21.50 50.00

5-U.S. Border Patrol Comics (Sgt. Dick Carter of the...), Miss Victory (story matches cover to #3), Citizen Smith, & Mr. Miracle app. 8.50 26.00 60.00

6-Capt. Fearless, Alias X, Capt. Stone (splash used as-c to #10); Diamond

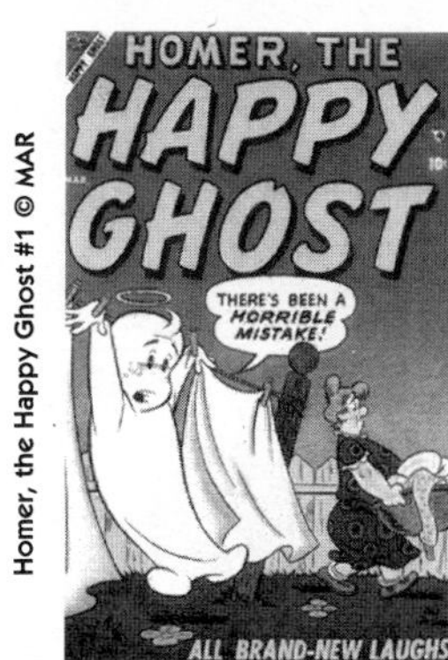

Homer, the Happy Ghost #1 © MAR

Hong On The Range #1 © Flypaper Press

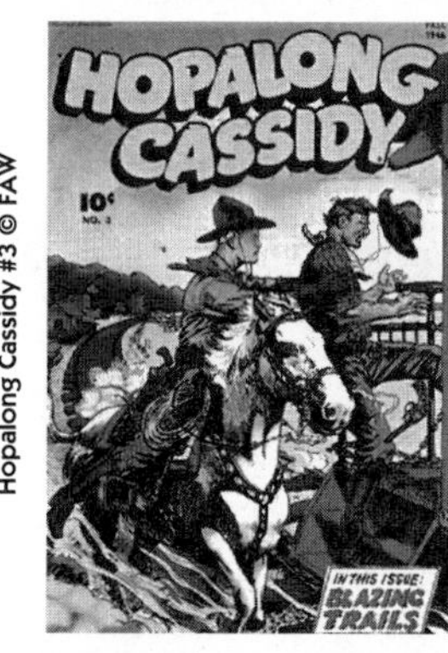

Hopalong Cassidy #3 © FAW

GD25 FN65 NM94

Jim & Rusty Dugan (splash from cover of #2) 7.15 21.50 50.00
7-Secret Agent Z-2, Strong Man, Blue Streak (story matches cover to #8); Reprints from Crash #2 8.50 26.00 60.00
8-Blue Streak, Strong Man (story matches cover to #7)-Crash reprints 7.15 21.50 50.00
9-Citizen Smith, The Blue Streak, Solar Legion by Kirby & Strongman, the Perfect Human app.; reprints from Crash #4 & 5; Citizen Smith on cover only-from story in #5 (1944-before #3) 12.00 36.00 90.00
10-Captain Stone; r/Crash; Solar Legion by S&K 12.00 36.00 90.00

HOMER COBB (See Adventures of...)

HOMER HOOPER
Atlas Comics: July, 1953 - No. 4, Dec, 1953

1-Teenage humor 7.50 22.50 52.00
2-4 5.70 17.00 35.00

HOMER, THE HAPPY GHOST (See Adventures of...)
Atlas(ACI/PPI/WPI)/Marvel: 3/55 - No. 22, 11/58; V2#1, 11/69 - V2#5, 7/70

V1#1-Dan DeCarlo-c/a begins, ends #22 13.00 38.00 95.00
2-1st code approved issue 7.15 21.50 50.00
3-10 5.70 17.00 38.00
11-22 5.00 15.00 30.00
V2#1 (11/69) 8.00 24.00 80.00
2-4 4.00 12.00 40.00
V2#5 (7/70)(Exist?) 15.00 45.00 150.00

HOME RUN (Also see A-1 Comics)
Magazine Enterprises: No. 89, 1953 (one-shot)

A-1 89 (#3)-Powell-a; Stan Musial photo-c 10.00 30.00 75.00

HOMICIDE (Also see Dark Horse Presents)
Dark Horse Comics: Apr, 1990 ($1.95, B&W, one-shot)

1-Detective story 2.00

HOMICIDE: TEARS OF THE DEAD
Chaos! Comics: Apr, 1997 ($2.95, one-shot)

1-Brom-c 2.95
1-Premium Ltd. Ed. w/wraparound-c 2.95

HONEYBEE BIRDWHISTLE AND HER PET PEPI (Introducing...)
Newspaper Enterprise Assoc.: 1969 (Giveaway, 24 pgs., B&W, slick cover)

nn-Contains Freckles newspaper strips with a short biography of Henry Fornhals (artist) & Fred Fox (writer) of the strip 4.00 12.00 40.00

HONEYMOON (Formerly Gay Comics)
A Lover's Magazine(USA) (Marvel): No. 41, Jan, 1950

41-Photo-c; article by Betty Grable 7.85 23.50 55.00

HONEYMOONERS, THE (TV)
Lodestone: Oct, 1986 ($1.50)

1-Photo-c 1.50

HONEYMOONERS, THE (TV)
Triad Publications: Sept, 1987 - No. 13? ($2.00)

1-13 2.00

HONEYMOON ROMANCE
Artful Publications (Canadian): Apr, 1950 - No. 2, July, 1950 (25¢, digest size)

1,2-(Rare) 32.00 96.00 240.00

HONEY WEST (TV)
Gold Key: Sept, 1966 (Photo-c)

1 (10186-609) 9.50 28.50 105.00

HONG KONG PHOOEY (TV)
Charlton Comics: June, 1975 - No. 9, Nov, 1976 (Hanna-Barbera)

1 3.20 9.50 35.00
2 1.80 5.40 18.00

GD25 FN65 NM94

3-9 1.20 3.60 12.00

HONG ON THE RANGE
Image/Flypaper Press: Dec, 1997 - No. 3, Feb, 1998 ($2.50, lim. series)

1-3: Wu-s/Lafferty-a 2.50

HOODED HORSEMAN, THE (Also see Blazing West)
American Comics Group (Michel Publ.): No. 21, 1-2/52 - No. 27, 1-2/53; No. 18, 12-1/54-55 - No. 27, 6-7/56

21(1-2/52)-Hooded Horseman, Injun Jones continue 13.00 38.00 95.00
22 8.50 26.00 60.00
23-25,27(1-2/53) 6.50 19.50 45.00
26-Origin/1st app. Cowboy Sahib by L. Starr 9.30 28.00 70.00
18(11-12/54)(Formerly Out of the Night) 8.50 26.00 60.00
19-Last precode (1-2/55) 5.70 17.00 40.00
20-Origin Johnny Injun 7.15 21.50 50.00
21-24,26,27(6-7/56) 5.70 17.00 40.00
25-Cowboy Sahib on cover only; Hooded Horseman i.d. revealed 6.50 19.50 45.00

NOTE: *Whitney c/a-21('52), 20-22.*

HOODED MENACE, THE (Also see Daring Adventures)
Realistic/Avon Periodicals: 1951 (one-shot)

nn-Based on a band of hooded outlaws in the Pacific Northwest, 1900-1906; reprinted in Daring Advs. #15 42.00 127.00 340.00

HOODS UP
Fram Corp.: 1953 (15¢, distributed to service station owners, 16 pgs.)

1-(Very Rare; only 2 known); Eisner-c/a in all. 44.00 132.00 375.00
2-6-(Very Rare; only 1 known of #3; 4, 2 known of #2) 44.00 132.00 375.00

NOTE: *Convertible Connie gives tips for service stations, selling Fram oil filters.*

HOOK (Movie)
Marvel Comics: Early Feb, 1992 - No. 4, Late Mar, 1992 ($1.00, limited series)

1-4: Adapts movie; Vess-c; 1-Morrow-a(p) 1.00
nn (1991, $5.95, 84 pgs.)-Contains #1-4; Vess-c 2.00 6.00
1 (1991, $2.95, magazine, 84 pgs.)-Contains #1-4; Vess-c (same cover as nn issue) 3.00

HOOT GIBSON'S WESTERN ROUNDUP (See Western Roundup under Fox Giants)

HOOT GIBSON WESTERN (Formerly My Love Story)
Fox Features Syndicate: No. 5, May, 1950 - No. 3, Sept, 1950

5,6(#1,2): 5-Photo-c. 6-Photo/painted-c 24.00 72.00 180.00
3-Wood-a; painted-c 26.00 78.00 195.00

HOPALONG CASSIDY (Also see Bill Boyd Western, Master Comics, Real Western Hero, Six Gun Heroes & Western Hero; Bill Boyd starred as H. Cassidy in the movies; H. Cassidy in movies, radio & TV)
Fawcett Publications: Feb, 1943; No. 2, Summer, 1946 - No. 85, Nov, 1953

1 (1943, 68 pgs.)-H. Cassidy & his horse Topper begin (on sale 1/8/43)-Captain Marvel app. on-c 420.00 1260.00 4600.00
2-(Sum, '46) 71.00 213.00 640.00
3,4: 3-(Fall, '46, 52 pgs. begin) 32.00 96.00 290.00
5- "Mad Barber" story mentioned in **SOTI**, pgs. 308,309; photo-c 27.00 80.00 240.00
6-10: 8-Photo-c 22.00 63.00 200.00
11-19: 11,13-19-Photo-c 17.00 50.00 150.00
20-29 (52 pgs.)-Painted/photo-c 13.00 39.00 115.00
30,31,33,34,37-39,41 (52 pgs.)-Painted-c 10.00 30.00 75.00
32,40 (36pgs.)-Painted-c 9.30 28.00 65.00
35,42,43,45 (52 pgs.)-Photo-c 9.30 28.00 70.00
36,44,48 (36 pgs.)-Photo-c 8.50 25.50 60.00
46,47,49-51,53,54,56 (52 pgs.)-Photo-c 9.30 28.00 70.00
52,55,57-70 (36 pgs.)-Photo-c 7.15 21.50 50.00
71-84-Photo-c 5.70 17.00 38.00

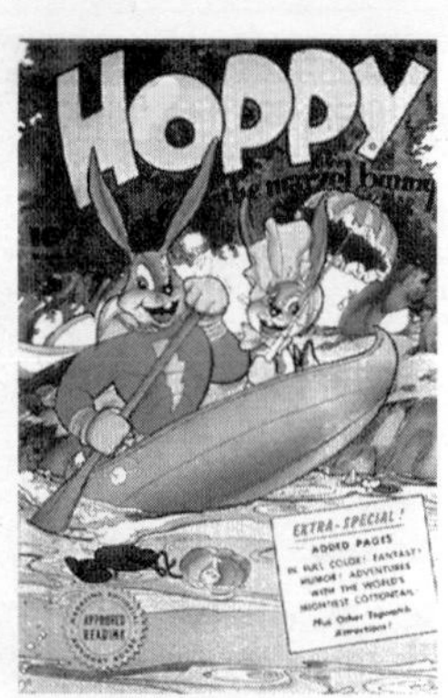

Hoppy The Marvel Bunny #4 © FAW

Horrific #7 © Comic Media

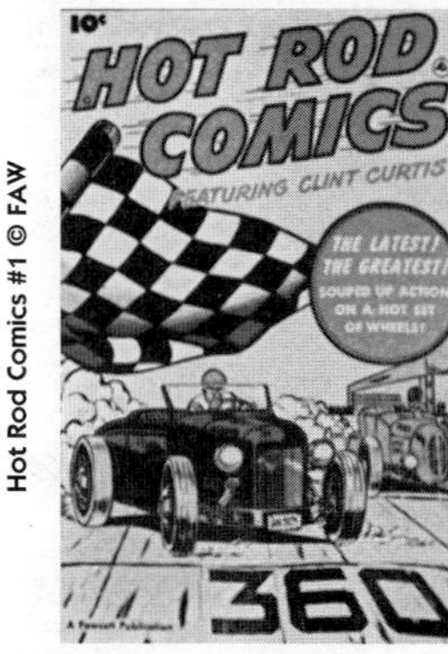

Hot Rod Comics #1 © FAW

85-Last Fawcett issue; photo-c 7.15 21.50 50.00
NOTE: *Line-drawn c-1-4, 6, 7, 9, 10, 12.*
Grape Nuts Flakes giveaway (1950,9x6") 13.00 39.00 95.00
...& the Mad Barber (1951 Bond Bread giveaway)-7x5"; used in **SOTI**, pgs. 308,309 20.00 60.00 150.00
...Meets the Brend Brothers Bandits (1951 Bond Bread giveaway, color, paper-c, 16pgs. 3-1/2x7")-Fawcett Publ. 9.30 28.00 70.00
...Strange Legacy (1951 Bond Bread giveaway) 9.30 28.00 70.00
White Tower Giveaway (1946, 16pgs., paper-c) 9.30 28.00 70.00
... & The 5 Men of Evil (AC Comics, 1991, $12.95) r/newspaper strips and Fawcett story "Signature of Death" 12.95

HOPALONG CASSIDY (TV)
National Periodical Publications: No. 86, Feb, 1954 - No. 135, May-June, 1959 (All-36 pgs.)

86-Gene Colan-a begins, ends #117; photo covers continue 35.00 106.00 265.00
87 20.00 60.00 150.00
88-91: 91-1 pg. Superboy-sty (6/54) 13.00 40.00 100.00
92-99 (98 has #93 on-c; last precode issue, 2/55). 95-Reversed photo-c to #52. 98-Reversed photo-c to #61. 99-Reversed photo-c to #60 11.00 33.00 85.00
100-Same cover as #50 13.00 39.00 95.00
101-108: 105-Same photo-c as #54. 107-Same photo-c as #51. 108-Last photo-c 6.50 19.50 65.00
109-135: 118-Gil Kane-a begins. 123-Kubert-a (2 pgs.). 124-Painted-c 5.50 16.50 55.00

HOPE SHIP
Dell Publishing Co.: June-Aug, 1963

1 1.10 3.30 9.00

HOPPY THE MARVEL BUNNY (See Fawcett's Funny Animals)
Fawcett Publications: Dec, 1945 - No. 15, Sept, 1947

1 27.00 80.00 200.00
2 13.00 38.00 95.00
3-15: 7-Xmas-c 11.00 32.00 80.00
...Well Known Comics (1944,8-1/2x10-1/2", paper-c) Bestmaid/Samuel Lowe (printed in red or blue) 6.85 21.00 48.00

HORACE & DOTTY DRIPPLE (Dotty Dripple No. 1-24)
Harvey Publications: No. 25, Aug, 1952 - No. 43, Oct, 1955

25-43 2.00 5.00 10.00

HORIZONTAL LIEUTENANT, THE (See Movie Classics)

HOROBI
Viz Premiere Comics: 1990 - No. 8, 1990 ($3.75, B&W, mature readers, 84 pgs.) V2#1, 1990 - No. 7, 1991 ($4.25, B&W, 68 pgs.)

1-8: Japanese manga 4.00
Part Two, #1-7 4.50

HORRIFIC (Terrific No. 14 on)
Artful/Comic Media/Harwell/Mystery: Sept, 1952 - No. 13, Sept, 1954

1 33.00 100.00 250.00
2 17.00 52.00 130.00
3-Bullet in head-c 31.00 92.00 230.00
4,5,7,9,10: 4-Shrunken head-c. 7-Guillotine-c 13.00 38.00 95.00
6-Jack The Ripper story 14.00 42.00 105.00
8-Origin & 1st app. The Teller (E.C. parody) 17.00 52.00 130.00
11-13: 11-Swipe/Witches Tales #6,27; Devil-c 11.00 32.00 80.00
NOTE: ***Don Heck** a-8; c-3-13. **Hollingsworth** a-4. **Morisi** a-8. **Palais** a-5, 7-12.*

HORROR FROM THE TOMB (Mysterious Stories No. 2 on)
Premier Magazine Co.: Sept, 1954

1-Woodbridge/Torres, Check-a; The Keeper of the Graveyard is host 33.00 98.00 245.00

HORRORIST, THE (Also see Hellblazer)
DC Comics (Vertigo): Dec, 1995 - No. 2, Jan, 1996 ($5.95, lim. series, mature)

1,2: Jamie Delano scripts, David Lloyd-c/a; John Constantine (Hellblazer) app. 2.00 6.00

HORRORS, THE (Formerly Startling Terror Tales #10)
Star Publications: No. 11, Jan, 1953 - No. 15, Apr, 1954

11-Horrors of War; Disbrow-a(2) 23.00 70.00 175.00
12-Horrors of War; color illo in **POP** 22.00 66.00 165.00
13-Horrors of Mystery; crime stories 21.00 62.00 155.00
14,15-Horrors of the Underworld; crime stories 22.00 66.00 165.00
NOTE: *All have **L. B. Cole** covers; a-12. **Hollingsworth** a-13. **Palais** a-13r.*

HORROR TALES (Magazine)
Eerie Publications: V1#7, 6/69 - V6#6, 12/74; V7#1, 2/75; V7#2, 5/76 - V8#5, 1977; V9#3, 8/78; (V1-V6: 52 pgs.; V7, V8#2: 112 pgs.; V8#4 on: 68 pgs.) (No V5#3, V8#1,3)

V1#7 3.20 9.50 35.00
V1#8,9 2.20 6.50 24.00
V2#1-6('70), V3#1-6('71) 2.00 6.00 20.00
V4#1-3,5-7('72) 2.00 6.00 20.00
V4#4-LSD story reprint/Weird V3#5 2.70 8.00 30.00
V5#1,2,4,5(6/73),5(10/73),6(12/73),V6#1-6('74),V7#1,2,4('76),V7#3('76)-Giant issue,V8#2,4,5('77) 2.20 6.50 24.00
V9#1-3(11/78, $1.50) 2.50 7.60 28.00
NOTE: *Bondage-c-V6#1, 3, V7#2.*

HORSE FEATHERS COMICS
Lev Gleason Publ.: Nov, 1945 - No. 4, July(Summer on-c), 1948 (52 pgs.)

1-Wolverton's Scoop Scuttle, 2 pgs. 17.00 50.00 125.00
2 8.50 26.00 60.00
3,4: 3-(5/48) 5.70 17.00 40.00

HORSEMAN
Crusade Comics/Kevlar Studios: Mar, 1996 - No. 2, Jan, 1997 ($2.95)

0-1st Kevlar Studios issue. 3.00
1-(3/96)-Crusade issue; Shi-c/app. 3.00
1-(11/96),2-(1/97)-Kevlar Studios 3.00

HORSEMASTERS, THE (Disney)(TV, Movie)
Dell Publishing Co.: No. 1260, Dec-Feb, 1961/62

Four Color 1260-Annette Funicello photo-c 11.00 33.00 120.00

HORSE SOLDIERS, THE
Dell Publishing Co.: No. 1048, Nov-Jan, 1959/60 (John Wayne movie)

Four Color 1048-Painted-c, Sekowsky-a 13.00 38.00 140.00

HORSE WITHOUT A HEAD, THE (See Movie Comics)

HOT DOG
Magazine Enterprises: June-July, 1954 - No. 4, Dec-Jan, 1954-55

1(A-1 #107) 6.00 18.00 42.00
2,3(A-1 #115),4(A-1 #136) 5.00 15.00 30.00

HOT DOG (See Jughead's Pal, Hotdog)

HOTEL DEPAREE - SUNDANCE (TV)
Dell Publishing Co.: No. 1126, Aug-Oct, 1960 (one-shot)

Four Color 1126-Earl Holliman photo-c 5.50 16.50 60.00

HOT ROD AND SPEEDWAY COMICS
Hillman Periodicals: Feb-Mar, 1952 - No. 5, Apr-May, 1953

1 23.00 68.00 170.00
2-Krigstein-a 17.00 50.00 125.00
3-5 9.30 28.00 65.00

HOT ROD COMICS (...Featuring Clint Curtis) (See XMas Comics)
Fawcett Publications: Nov, 1951 (no month given) - V2#7, Feb, 1953

nn (V1#1)-Powell-c/a in all 27.00 80.00 200.00

Hot Rods and Racing Cars #8 © CC

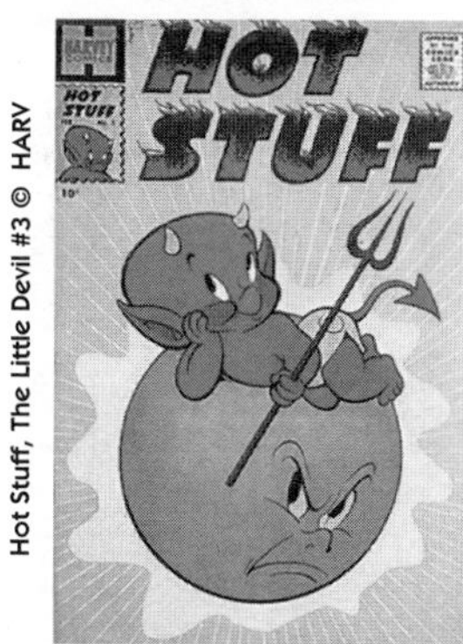

Hot Stuff, The Little Devil #3 © HARV

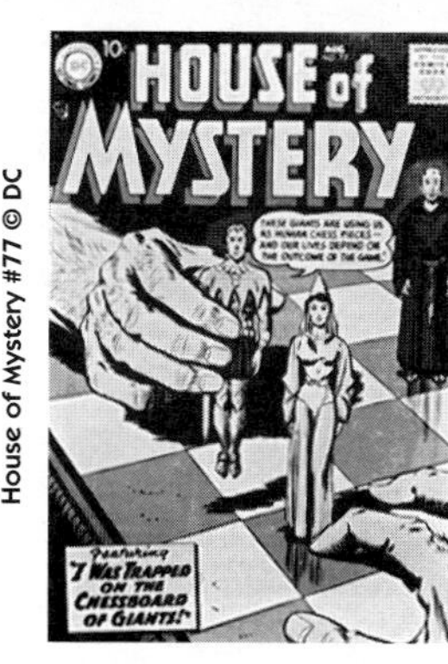

House of Mystery #77 © DC

	GD25	FN65	NM94
2 (4/52)	15.00	46.00	115.00
3-6, V2#7	11.00	32.00	80.00

HOT ROD KING (Also see Speed Smith the Hot Rod King)
Ziff-Davis Publ. Co.: Fall, 1952

	GD25	FN65	NM94
1-Giacoia-a; Saunders painted-c	23.00	68.00	170.00

HOT ROD RACERS (Grand Prix No. 16 on)
Charlton Comics: Dec, 1964 - No. 15, July, 1967

	GD25	FN65	NM94
1	6.50	19.50	65.00
2-5	4.00	12.00	40.00
6-15	2.80	8.40	28.00

HOT RODS AND RACING CARS
Charlton Comics (Motor Mag. No. 1): Nov, 1951 - No. 120, June, 1973

	GD25	FN65	NM94
1-Speed Davis begins; Indianapolis 500 story	24.00	72.00	180.00
2	12.00	36.00	90.00
3-10	8.50	26.00	60.00
11-20	6.50	19.50	45.00
21-34,36-40	5.70	17.00	35.00
35 (6/58, 68 pgs.)	7.85	23.50	55.00
41-60	4.00	12.00	28.00
61-80	2.50	7.50	20.00
81-100	1.85	5.50	15.00
101-120	1.50	4.50	12.00

HOT SHOT CHARLIE
Hillman Periodicals: 1947 (Lee Elias)

	GD25	FN65	NM94
1	7.15	21.50	50.00

HOT SHOTS: AVENGERS
Marvel Comics: Oct, 1995 ($2.95, one-shot)

	GD25	FN65	NM94
nn-pin-ups			3.00

HOTSPUR
Eclipse Comics: Jun, 1987 - No. 3, Sep, 1987 ($1.75, lim. series, Baxter paper)

	GD25	FN65	NM94
1-3			1.80

HOT STUFF (See Stumbo Tinytown)
Harvey Comics: V2#1, Sept, 1991 - No. 12, June, 1994 ($1.00)

	GD25	FN65	NM94
V2#1-Stumbo back-up story			3.00
2-12 ($1.50)			2.00
...Big Book 1 (11/92), 2 (6/93) (Both $1.95, 52 pgs.)			3.00

HOT STUFF CREEPY CAVES
Harvey Publications: Nov, 1974 - No. 7, Nov, 1975

	GD25	FN65	NM94
1	2.20	6.25	22.00
2-7	1.20	3.60	12.00

HOT STUFF DIGEST
Harvey Comics: July, 1992 - No. 5, Nov, 1993 ($1.75, digest-size)

	GD25	FN65	NM94
V2#1-Hot Stuff, Stumbo, Richie Rich stories			3.50
2-5			2.00

HOT STUFF GIANT SIZE
Harvey Comics: Oct, 1992 - No. 3, Oct, 1993 ($2.25, 68 pgs.)

	GD25	FN65	NM94
V2#1-Hot Stuff & Stumbo stories			3.50
2,3			2.50

HOT STUFF SIZZLERS
Harvey Publications: July, 1960 - No. 59, Mar, 1974; V2#1, Aug, 1992

	GD25	FN65	NM94
1: 84 pgs. begin, ends #5; Hot Stuff, Stumbo begin	11.00	33.00	110.00
2-5	4.80	14.40	48.00
6-10: 6-68 pgs. begin, ends #45	3.00	9.00	30.00
11-20	2.40	7.20	24.00
21-45	1.60	4.80	16.00
46-52: 52 pgs. begin	1.20	3.60	12.00
53-59	1.00	3.00	8.00
V2#1-(8/92, $1.25)-Stumbo back-up			3.00

HOT STUFF, THE LITTLE DEVIL (Also see Devil Kids & Harvey Hits)
Harvey Publications (Illustrated Humor): 10/57 - No. 141, 7/77; No. 142, 2/78 - No. 164, 8/82; No. 165, 10/86 - No. 171, 11/87; No. 172, 11/88; No. 173, Sept, 1990 - No. 177, 1/91

	GD25	FN65	NM94
1	31.50	94.00	315.00
2-1st app. Stumbo the Giant (12/57)	16.00	48.00	160.00
3-5	12.00	36.00	120.00
6-10	7.00	21.00	70.00
11-20	5.00	15.00	50.00
21-40	3.00	9.00	30.00
41-60	1.80	5.40	18.00
61-80	1.40	4.20	14.00
81-105	1.00	3.00	10.00
106-112: All 52 pg. Giants	1.60	4.80	16.00
113-125		2.00	5.00
126-141			3.00
142-177: 172-177-($1.00)			2.00
Shoestore Giveaway('63)	1.20	3.60	12.00

HOT WHEELS (TV)
National Periodical Publications: Mar-Apr, 1970 - No. 6, Jan-Feb, 1971

	GD25	FN65	NM94
1	7.25	22.00	80.00
2,4,5	3.20	9.50	35.00
3-Neal Adams-c	3.80	11.50	40.00
6-Neal Adams-c/a	5.00	15.00	55.00

NOTE: ***Toth*** *a-1p, 2-5; c-1p, 5.*

HOURMAN (See Adventure Comics #48)

HOUSE OF MYSTERY (See Brave and the Bold #93, Elvira's House of Mystery, Limited Collectors' Edition & Super DC Giant)

HOUSE OF MYSTERY, THE
National Periodical Publications/DC Comics: Dec-Jan, 1951-52 - No. 321, Oct, 1983 (No. 199-203: 52 pgs.)

	GD25	FN65	NM94
1	193.00	581.00	1650.00
2	84.00	253.00	725.00
3	62.00	187.00	540.00
4,5	47.00	141.00	410.00
6-10	40.00	120.00	310.00
11-15	34.00	101.00	250.00
16(7/53)-25	25.00	75.00	190.00
26-35(2/55)-Last pre-code issue; 30-Woodish-a	19.00	56.00	150.00
36-50: 50-Text story of Orson Welles' War of the Worlds broadcast	12.50	38.00	125.00
51-60: 55-1st S.A. issue	10.00	30.00	100.00
61,63,65,66,70,72,76,85-Kirby-a	10.00	30.00	100.00
62,64,67-69,71,73-75,77-83,86-99	8.00	24.00	80.00
84-Prototype of Negative Man (Doom Patrol)	12.50	38.00	125.00
100 (7/60)	9.00	27.00	90.00
101-116: 109-Toth, Kubert-a. 116-Last 10¢ issue	7.00	21.00	70.00
117-130: 117-Swipes-c to HOS #20. 120-Toth-a	6.50	19.50	65.00
131-142	5.25	15.75	52.00
143-J'onn J'onzz, Manhunter begins (6/64), ends #173; story continues from Detective #326	23.50	70.00	235.00
144	12.50	38.00	125.00
145-155,157-159: 149-Toth-a. 155-The Human Hurricane app. (12/65), Red Tornado prototype. 158-Origin/1st app. Diabolu Idol-Head in J'onn J'onzz	8.50	25.50	85.00
156-Robby Reed begins (origin/1st app.), ends #173	11.00	33.00	110.00
160-(7/66)-Robby Reed becomes Plastic Man in this issue only; 1st S.A. app. Plastic Man; intro Marco Xavier (Martian Manhunter) & Vulture Crime Organization; ends #173	13.00	39.00	130.00
161-173: 169-Origin/1st app. Gem Girl	6.00	18.00	60.00

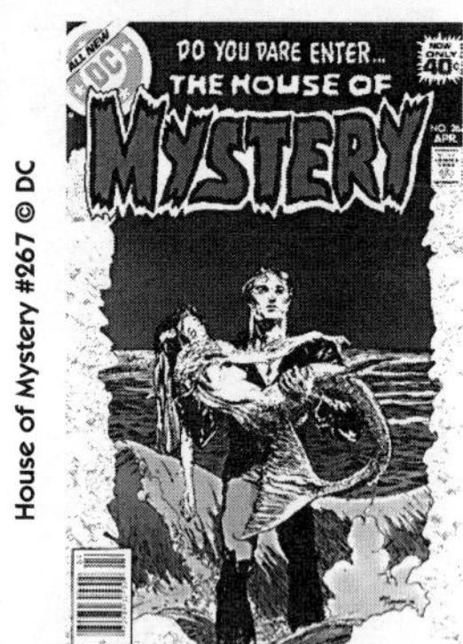

House of Mystery #267 © DC

House of Secrets #106 © DC

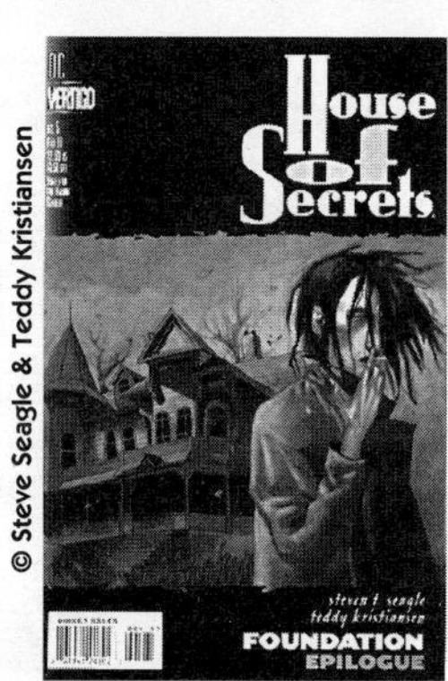

House of Secrets #5
© Steve Seagle & Teddy Kristiansen

	GD25	FN65	NM94
174-Mystery format begins.	4.20	12.60	42.00
175-177: 176-1st app. Cain (HOM host)	2.80	8.40	28.00
178-Neal Adams-a (2/68)	3.50	10.50	35.00
179-N. Adams/Orlando, Wrightson-a (1st pro work, 3 pgs.)	6.50	19.50	65.00
180,181,183: Wrightson-a (3,10, & 3 pgs.). 180-Last 12¢ issue; Kane/ Wood-a(2). 183-Wood-a	2.80	8.40	28.00
182-Toth-a	2.50	7.50	20.00
184-Kane/Wood, Toth-a	1.80	5.40	18.00
185-Williamson/Kaluta-a; Howard-a (3 pgs.)	2.20	6.50	24.00
186-N. Adams-c/a; Wrightson-a (10 pgs.)	2.20	6.50	24.00
187,190: Adams-c. 187-Toth-a. 190-Toth-a(r)	1.40	4.20	14.00
188-Wrightson-a (8 & 3pgs.); Adams-c	2.20	6.50	24.00
189,192,197: Adams-c; 189-Wood-a(i)	1.60	4.80	16.00
191-Wrightson-a (8 & 3pgs.); Adams-c	2.00	6.00	20.00
193-Wrightson-c	1.60	4.80	16.00
194-Wrightson-c; 52 pgs begin, end #203; Toth,Kirby-a	2.00	6.00	20.00
195: Wrightson-c. Swamp creature story by Wrightson similar to Swamp Thing (10 pgs.)(10/71)	2.20	6.50	24.00
196,198	1.60	4.80	16.00
199-Adams-c; Wood-a(8pgs.); Kirby-a	1.80	5.40	18.00
200-(25¢, 52 pgs.)-One third-r (3/72)	2.00	6.00	20.00
201-203-(25¢, 52 pgs.)-One third-r	1.80	5.40	18.00
204-Wrightson-c/a, 9 pgs.	1.60	4.80	16.00
205,206,208,210,212,215,216,218	.90	2.70	8.00
207-Wrightson c/a; Starlin, Redondo-a	1.40	4.20	14.00
209,211,213,214,217,219-Wrightson-c	.90	2.70	9.00
220,222,223		2.00	6.00
221-Wrightson/Kaluta-a(8 pgs.)	1.40	4.20	14.00
224-Wrightson-r from Spectre #9; Dillin/Adams-r from House of Secrets #82; begin 100 pg. issues; Phantom Stranger-r.	2.70	8.00	30.00
225,227-(100 pgs.): 225-Spectre app.	2.70	8.00	30.00
226-Wrightson/Redondo-a Phantom Stranger-r	2.70	8.00	30.00
228-N. Adams inks; Wrightson-r	2.70	8.00	30.00
229-Wrightson-a(r); Toth-r; last 100 pg. issue.	2.70	8.00	30.00
230,232-235,237-250			4.00
231,236-Wrightson-c	.90	2.70	8.00
236-Ditko-a(p); N. Adams-i; Wrightson-c	.90	2.70	8.00
251-254-(84 pgs.)-Adams-c. 251-Wood-a	.90	2.70	8.00
255,256-(84 pgs.)-Wrightson-c	.90	2.70	9.00
257-259-(84 pgs.)	.90	2.70	9.00
260			5.00
261-270			4.00
271-289: 282-(68 pgs.)-Has extra story "The Computers That Saved Metropolis" Radio Shack giveaway by Jim Starlin			3.75
290-1st "I, Vampire"	.90	2.70	8.00
291-299			4.00
300,319,321: Death of "I, Vampire"		2.00	6.00
301-318-"I, Vampire"			3.75
320			4.00
Welcome to the House of Mystery (7/98, $5.95) reprints stories with new framing story by Gaiman and Aragonés		2.00	6.00

NOTE: ***Neal Adams*** *a-236i; c-175-192, 197, 199, 251-254.* ***Alcala*** *a-209, 217, 219, 224, 227.* ***M. Anderson*** *a-212; c/a-37.* ***Aparo*** *a-209.* ***Aragones*** *a-185, 186, 194, 196, 200, 202, 229, 251.* ***Baily*** *a-279p.* ***Cameron*** *a-76, 79.* ***Colan*** *a-202r.* ***Craig*** *a-263, 275, 295, 300.* ***Dillin/Adams*** *r-224.* ***Ditko*** *a-236p, 247, 254, 258, 276; c-277.* ***Drucker*** *a-37.* ***Evans*** *c-218.* ***Fraden*** *a-251.* ***Giffen*** *a-284.* ***Giunta*** *a-199, 227r.* ***Golden*** *a-257, 259.* ***Heath*** *a-194r; c-203.* ***Howard*** *a-182, 185, 187, 196, 229r, 247i, 254, 279i.* ***Kaluta*** *a-195, 200, 250r; c-200-202, 210, 212, 233, 260, 261, 263, 265, 267, 268, 273, 276, 284, 287, 288, 293-295, 300, 302, 304, 305, 309-319, 321.* ***Bob Kane*** *a-84.* ***Gil Kane*** *a-196p, 253p, 300p.* ***Kirby*** *a-194r, 199r; c-65, 76, 78, 79, 85.* ***Kubert*** *c-282, 283, 285, 286, 289-292, 297-299, 301, 303, 306-308.* ***Maneely*** *a-68, 227r.* ***Mayer*** *a-317p.* ***Meskin*** *a-52-144 (most), 195r, 224r, 229r; c-63, 66, 124, 127.* ***Mooney*** *a-24, 159, 160.* ***Moreira*** *a-3, 4, 20-50, 58, 59, 62, 68, 77, 79, 90, 108, 113, 123, 201r, 228; c-4-28, 44, 47, 50, 54, 59, 62, 64, 68, 70, 73.* ***Morrow*** *a-192, 196, 255, 320i.* ***Mortimer*** *a-204(3 pgs.).* ***Nasser*** *a-276.* ***Newton*** *a-259, 272.* ***Nino*** *a-204, 212, 213, 220, 224, 225, 245, 250, 252-256, 283.* ***Orlando*** *a-175(2 pgs.), 178, 240i; c-240, 258p, 262, 264p, 270p, 271, 272, 274, 275, 278, 296i.* ***Redondo*** *a-194, 195, 197, 202, 203, 207, 211, 214, 217, 219, 226, 227, 229, 235, 241, 287(layout), 302p, 303i, 308; c-229.* ***Reese*** *a-195, 200, 205i.* ***Rogers*** *a-254, 274, 277.* ***Roussos*** *a-65, 84, 224i.* ***Sekowsky*** *a-282p.* ***Sparling*** *a-203.* ***Starlin*** *a-207(2 pgs.), 282p; c-281.* ***Leonard Starr*** *a-9.* ***Staton*** *a-300p.* ***Sutton*** *a-189, 271, 290, 291, 293, 295, 297-299, 302, 303, 306-309, 310-313i, 314.* ***Tuska*** *a-293p, 294p, 316p.* ***Wrightson*** *c-193-195, 204, 207, 209, 211, 213, 214, 217, 219, 221, 231, 236, 255, 256; r-224.*

HOUSE OF SECRETS (Combined with The Unexpected after #154)
National Periodical Publications/DC Comics: 11-12/56 - No. 80, 9-10/66; No. 81, 8-9/69 - No. 140, 2-3/76; No. 141, 8-9/76 - No. 154, 10-11/78

	GD25	FN65	NM94
1-Drucker-a; Moreira-c	100.00	300.00	1200.00
2-Moreira-a	39.00	117.00	440.00
3-Kirby-c/a	32.00	96.00	360.00
4-Kirby-a	27.00	82.00	275.00
5-7	17.50	52.00	175.00
8-Kirby-a	21.00	63.00	215.00
9-11: 11-Lou Cameron-a (unsigned)	15.50	47.00	155.00
12-Kirby-c/a; Lou Cameron-a	16.50	50.00	165.00
13-15: 14-Flying saucer-c	11.50	34.00	115.00
16-20	10.00	30.00	100.00
21,22,24-30	9.50	28.50	95.00
23-1st app. Mark Merlin & begin series (8/59)	10.50	32.00	105.00
31-50: 48-Toth-a. 50-Last 10¢ issue	7.50	22.50	75.00
51-60: 58-Origin Mark Merlin	7.00	21.00	70.00
61-First Eclipso (7-8/63) and begin series	16.50	50.00	165.00
62	8.00	24.00	80.00
63-65,67-Toth-a on Eclipso (see Brave and the Bold #64)	6.50	19.50	65.00
66-1st Eclipso-c (also #67,70,78,79); Toth-a	8.50	25.50	85.00
68-80: 73-Mark Merlin becomes Prince Ra-Man (1st app.). 76-Prince Ra-Man vs. Eclipso. 80-Eclipso, Prince Ra-Man end	6.50	19.50	65.00
81-Mystery format begins; 1st app. Abel (HOS host)	4.50	13.50	45.00
82-84: 82-Neal Adams-c(i)	2.50	7.50	20.00
85,87,90: 85-N. Adams-a(i). 87-Wrightson & Kaluta-a. 90-Buckler (early work)/ N. Adams-a(i)	3.00	9.00	33.00
86,88,89,91	2.20	6.25	22.00
92-1st app. Swamp Thing-c/story (8 pgs.)(6-7/71) by Berni Wrightson(p) w/JeffJones/Kaluta/Weiss ink assists; classic-c.	39.00	118.00	470.00
93,95,97,98-(52 pgs.)-Wrightson-c	1.80	5.40	18.00
94,96-Wrightson-c. 94-Wrightson-a(i);96-Wood-a	2.00	6.00	20.00
99-Wrightson splash pg.	1.60	4.80	16.00
100-Wrightson-c	2.20	6.25	22.00
101,102,104,105,108-120	1.00	3.00	10.00
103,106,107-Wrightson-c	1.40	4.20	14.00
121-133	.85	2.60	7.00
134-136,139-Wrightson-a	.90	2.70	8.00
137,138,141-154			5.00
140-1st solo origin of the Patchworkman (see Swamp Thing #3)	1.70	5.10	17.00

NOTE: ***Neal Adams*** *c-81, 82, 84-88, 90, 91.* ***Alcala*** *a-104-107.* ***Anderson*** *a-91. Aparo a-93, 97, 105.* ***B. Bailey*** *a-107.* ***Cameron*** *a-13, 15.* ***Colan*** *a-63.* ***Ditko*** *a-139p, 148.* ***Elias*** *a-58.* ***Evans*** *a-118.* ***Finlay*** *a-7r(Real Fact?).* ***Glanzman*** *a-91.* ***Golden*** *a-151.* ***Heath*** *a-31.* ***Heck*** *a-85.* ***Kaluta*** *a-87, 98, 99; c-98, 99, 101, 102, 105, 149, 151, 154.* ***Bob Kane*** *a-18, 21.* ***G. Kane*** *a-85p.* ***Kirby*** *c-3, 11, 12.* ***Kubert*** *a-39.* ***Meskin*** *a-2-68 (most), 94r; c-55-60.* ***Moreira*** *a-7, 8, 51, 54, 102-104, 106, 108, 113, 116, 118, 121, 123, 127; c-1, 2, 4-10, 13-20.* ***Morrow*** *a-86, 89, 90; c-89, 146-148.* ***Nino*** *a-101, 103, 106, 109, 115, 117, 126, 128, 131, 147, 153.* ***Redondo*** *a-95, 99, 102, 104p, 113, 116, 134, 136, 139, 140.* ***Reese*** *a-85.* ***Severin*** *a-91.* ***Starlin*** *c-150.* ***Sutton*** *a-154.* ***Toth*** *a-63-67, 83, 93r, 94r, 96r-98r, 123.* ***Tuska*** *a-90, 104.* ***Wrightson*** *a-134; c-92-94, 96, 100, 103, 106, 107, 135, 136, 139.*

HOUSE OF SECRETS
DC Comics (Vertigo): Oct, 1996 - No. 25, Dec, 1998 ($2.50) (Creator-owned series)

	GD25	FN65	NM94
1-Steven Seagle-s/Kristiansen-c/a.			4.00
2-4			3.00
5-25: 5,7-Kristiansen-c/a. 6-Fegrado-a			2.50
TPB-(1997, $14.95) r/1-5			14.95

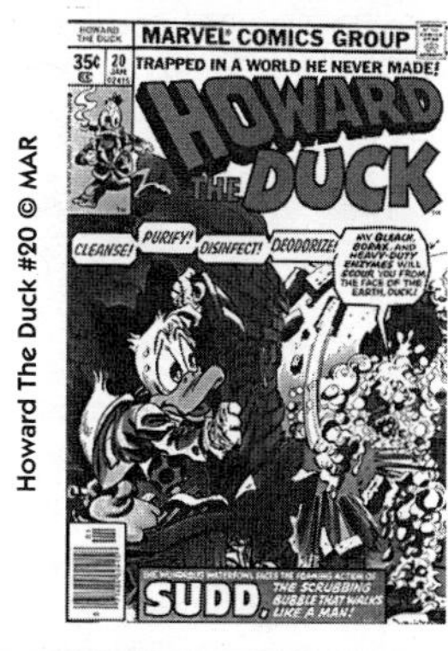

Howard The Duck #20 © MAR

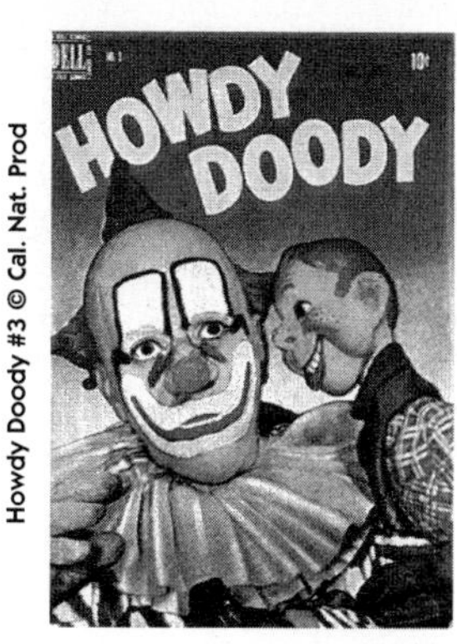

Howdy Doody #3 © Cal. Nat. Prod

H.R. Pufnstuf #2 © GK

GD25 FN65 NM94

HOUSE OF TERROR (3-D)
St. John Publishing Co.: Oct, 1953 (25¢, came w/glasses)

	GD25	FN65	NM94
1-Kubert, Baker-a	31.00	92.00	230.00

HOUSE OF YANG, THE (See Yang)
Charlton Comics: July, 1975 - No. 6, June, 1976; 1978

	GD25	FN65	NM94
1-Sanho Kim-a in all		2.00	6.00
2-6			4.00
Modern Comics #1,2(1978)			3.00

HOUSE II: THE SECOND STORY
Marvel Comics: Oct, 1987 (One-shot)

	GD25	FN65	NM94
1-Adapts movie			2.00

HOWARD CHAYKIN'S AMERICAN FLAGG (See American Flagg!)
First Comics: V2#1, May, 1988 - V2#12, Apr, 1989 ($1.75/$1.95, Baxter paper)

	GD25	FN65	NM94
V2#1-5: ($1.75)-Chaykin-c(p) in all			1.75
6-9,11,12: ($1.95)			2.00
10-Elvis Presley photo-c			3.00

HOWARD THE DUCK (See Bizarre Adventures #34, Crazy Magazine, Fear, Man-Thing, Marvel Treasury Edition & Sensational She-Hulk #14-17)
Marvel Comics Group: Jan, 1976 - No. 31, May, 1979; No. 32, Jan, 1986; No. 33, Sept, 1986

	GD25	FN65	NM94
1-Brunner-c/a; Spider-Man x-over (low distr.)	1.00	3.00	10.00
2-Brunner-c/a (low distr.)			4.00
3-(Regular 25¢ edition)-Buscema-a(p), (7/76)			3.00
3-(30¢-c, limited distribution)	1.20	3.60	12.00
4,5			3.00
6-11: 8-Howard The Duck for president. 9-1st Sgt. Preston Dudley of RCMP. 10-Spider-Man-c/sty			2.00
12-1st app. Kiss (cameo, 3/77)	.90	2.70	8.00
13-Kiss app. (1st full story, 6/77); Daimon Hellstrom app. plus cameo of Howard as Son of Satan	1.20	3.60	12.00
14-32: 14-Howard as Son of Satan-c/story; Son of Satan app. 16-Album issue; 3 pgs. comics. 22,23-Man-Thing-c/stories; Star Wars parody. 30,32-P. Smith-a			2.00
33-(9/86)			3.00
Annual 1(1977, 52 pgs.)-Mayerik-a			3.00

NOTE: ***Austin*** *c-29i.* ***Bolland*** *c-33.* ***Brunner*** *a-1p, 2p; c-1, 2.* ***Buckler*** *c-3p.* ***Buscema*** *a-3p.* ***Colan*** *a(p)-4-15, 17-20, 24-27, 30, 31; c(p)-4-31, Annual 1p.* ***Leialoha*** *a-1-13i; c(i)-3-5, 8-11.* ***Mayerik*** *a-22, 23, 33.* ***Paul Smith*** *a-30p, 32. Man-Thing app. in #22, 23.*

HOWARD THE DUCK (Magazine)
Marvel Comics Group: Oct, 1979 - No. 9, Mar, 1981 (B&W, 68 pgs.)

	GD25	FN65	NM94
1			5.00
2,3,5-9: 3-Xmas issue. 7-Has poster by Byrne			3.50
4-Beatles, John Lennon, Elvis, Kiss & Devo cameos; Hitler app.			5.00

NOTE: ***Buscema*** *a-4p.* ***Colan*** *a-1-5p, 7-9p.* ***Jack Davis*** *c-3.* ***Golden*** *a(p)-1, 5, 6(51pgs.).* ***Rogers*** *a-7, 8.* ***Simonson*** *a-7.*

HOWARD THE DUCK HOLIDAY SPECIAL
Marvel Comics: Feb, 1997 ($2.50, one-shot)

	GD25	FN65	NM94
1-Wraparound-c; Hama-s			2.50

HOWARD THE DUCK: THE MOVIE
Marvel Comics Group: Dec, 1986 - No. 3, Feb, 1987 (Limited series)

	GD25	FN65	NM94
1-3: Movie adaptation; r/Marvel Super Special			1.00

HOW BOYS AND GIRLS CAN HELP WIN THE WAR
The Parents' Magazine Institute: 1942 (10¢, one-shot)

	GD25	FN65	NM94
1-All proceeds used to buy war bonds	22.00	66.00	165.00

HOWDY DOODY (TV)(See Jackpot of Fun-- & Poll Parrot)
Dell Publishing Co.: 1/50 - No. 38, 7-9/56; No. 761, 1/57; No. 811, 7/57

	GD25	FN65	NM94
1-(Scarce)-Photo-c; 1st TV comic	82.00	246.00	900.00
2-Photo-c	35.00	104.00	380.00
3-5: All photo-c	19.00	57.00	210.00
6-Used in **SOTI**, pg. 309; painted-c begin	16.00	48.00	175.00
7-10	13.00	40.00	145.00
11-20: 13-X-Mas-c	10.50	31.00	115.00
21-38, Four Color 761,811	9.00	27.00	100.00

HOW IT BEGAN
United Features Syndicate: No. 15, 1939 (one-shot)

	GD25	FN65	NM94
Single Series 15	29.00	88.00	220.00

HOW SANTA GOT HIS RED SUIT (See March of Comics No. 2)

HOW STALIN HOPES WE WILL DESTROY AMERICA
Joe Lowe Co. (Pictorial News): 1951 (Giveaway, 16 pgs.)

	GD25	FN65	NM94
nn	46.00	138.00	390.00

HOW THE WEST WAS WON (See Movie Comics)

HOW TO DRAW FOR THE COMICS
Street and Smith: No date (1942?) (10¢, 64 pgs., B&W & color, no ads)

	GD25	FN65	NM94
nn-Art by Winsor McCay, George Marcoux (Supersnipe artist), Vernon Greene (The Shadow artist), Jack Binder(with biog.), Thorton Fisher, Jon Small, & Jack Farr; has biographies of each artist	24.00	72.00	180.00

H. P. LOVECRAFT'S CTHULHU
Millennium Publications: Dec, 1991 - No. 3, May, 1992 ($2.50, limited series)

	GD25	FN65	NM94
1-3: 1-Contains trading cards on thin stock			2.50

H. R. PUFNSTUF (TV) (See March of Comics #360)
Gold Key: Oct, 1970 - No. 8, July, 1972

	GD25	FN65	NM94
1-Photo-c (all have photo-c?)	16.00	49.00	190.00
2-8	8.00	25.00	95.00

HUBERT AT CAMP MOONBEAM
Dell Publishing Co.: No. 251, Oct, 1949 (one shot)

	GD25	FN65	NM94
Four Color 251	3.60	11.00	40.00

HUCK & YOGI JAMBOREE (TV)
Dell Publishing Co.: Mar, 1961 ($1.00, 6-1/4x9", 116 pgs., cardboard-c, high quality paper) (B&W original material)

	GD25	FN65	NM94
nn	7.50	22.50	90.00

HUCK & YOGI WINTER SPORTS (TV)
Dell Publishing Co.: No. 1310, Mar, 1962 (Hanna-Barbara) (one-shot)

	GD25	FN65	NM94
Four Color 1310	8.50	25.50	85.00

HUCK FINN (See The New Adventures of... & Power Record Comics)

HUCKLEBERRY FINN (Movie)
Dell Publishing Co.: No. 1114, July, 1960

	GD25	FN65	NM94
Four Color 1114-Photo-c	4.50	13.50	50.00

HUCKLEBERRY HOUND (See Dell Giant #31,44, Golden Picture Story Book, Kite Fun Book, March of Comics #199, 214, 235, Spotlight #1 & Whitman Comic Books)

HUCKLEBERRY HOUND (TV)
Dell/Gold Key No. 18 (10/62) on: No. 990, 5-7/59 - No. 43, 10/70 (Hanna-Barbera)

	GD25	FN65	NM94
Four Color 990(#1)-1st app. Huckleberry Hound, Yogi Bear, & Pixie & Dixie & Mr. Jinx	11.00	33.00	120.00
Four Color 1050,1054 (12/59)	7.75	23.50	85.00
3(1-2/60) - 7 (9-10/60)	7.30	22.00	80.00
Four Color 1141 (10/60)	7.30	22.00	80.00
8-10	5.25	16.00	58.00
11,13-17 (6-8/62)	3.60	11.00	40.00
12-1st Hokeywolf	4.50	13.50	50.00
18,19 (84pgs.; 18-20 titled ...Chuckleberry Tales)	7.25	22.00	80.00
20-Titled Chuckleberry Tales	2.75	8.00	35.00
21-30	2.75	8.00	30.00
31-43: 37-Reprints	2.00	6.00	22.00

HUCKLEBERRY HOUND (TV)

Hulk 2099 #2 © MAR

Human Fly #13 © MAR

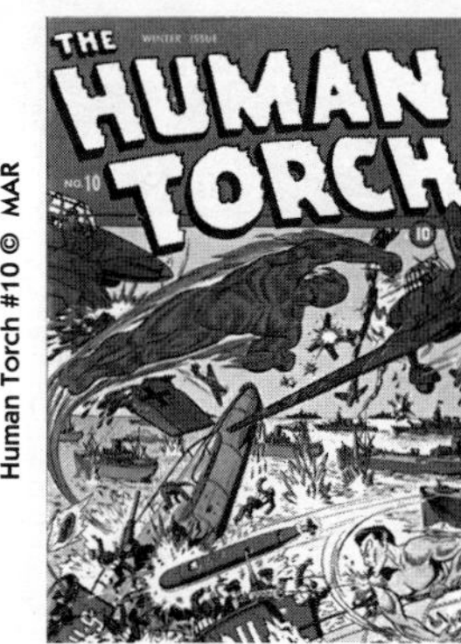

Human Torch #10 © MAR

Charlton Comics: Nov, 1970 - No. 8, Jan, 1972 (Hanna-Barbera)

	GD25	FN65	NM94
1	3.20	9.50	35.00
2-8	2.00	6.00	20.00

HUEY, DEWEY, & LOUIE (See Donald Duck, 1938 for 1st app. Also see Mickey Mouse Magazine V4#2, V5#7 & Walt Disney's Junior Woodchucks Limited Series)

HUEY, DEWEY, & LOUIE BACK TO SCHOOL (See Dell Giant #22, 35, 49 & Dell Giants)

HUEY, DEWEY, AND LOUIE JUNIOR WOODCHUCKS (Disney)
Gold Key No. 1-61/Whitman No. 62 on: Aug, 1966 - No. 81, 1984 (See Walt Disney's Comics & Stories #125)

	GD25	FN65	NM94
1	4.50	13.50	50.00
2,3(12/68)	2.70	8.00	30.00
4,5(4/70)-r/two WDC&S D.Duck stys by Barks	2.50	7.50	28.00
6-17	2.25	6.75	25.00
18,27-30	1.50	4.50	16.00
19-23,25-New storyboarded scripts by Barks, 13-25 pgs. per issue	2.30	7.00	26.00
24,26: 26-r/Barks Donald Duck WDC&S stories	1.50	4.50	16.00
31-57,60,61: 35,41-r/Barks J.W. scripts	.80	2.40	8.00
58,59: 58-r/Barks Donald Duck WDC&S stories	1.00	3.00	10.00
62-64 (Whitman)	.90	2.70	9.00
65-(9/80), 66 (Pre-pack? scarce)	1.40	4.20	15.00
67 (1/81),68	1.10	3.30	12.00
69-74	1.00	3.00	10.00
75-81 (all #90183; pre-pack?; nd, nd code; scarce)	1.10	3.30	12.00

HUGGA BUNCH (TV)
Marvel Comics (Star Comics): Oct, 1986 - No. 6, Aug, 1987

	GD25	FN65	NM94
1-6			2.00

HULK (Magazine)(Formerly The Rampaging Hulk)(Also see The Incredible Hulk)
Marvel Comics: No. 10, Aug., 1978 - No. 27, June, 1981 ($1.50)

	GD25	FN65	NM94
10-Bill Bixby interview	.90	2.70	8.00
11-Moon Knight begins, ends 20		2.00	6.00
12-15: Moon Knight stories. 12-Lou Ferrigno interview			4.00
16,19,21,22,24-27: 24-Part color, Lou Ferrigno interview. 25-Part color. 26,27-are B&W			3.00
17,18,20: Moon Knight stories			3.50
23-Last full color issue; Banner is attacked			3.50

NOTE: ***Alcala*** *a(i)-15, 17-20, 22, 24-27.* ***Buscema*** *a-23; c-26.* ***Chaykin*** *a-21-25.* ***Colan*** *a(p)-11, 19, 24-27.* ***Jusko*** *painted c-12.* ***Nebres*** *a-16.* ***Severin*** *a-19i. Moon Knight by* ***Sienkiewicz*** *in 13-15, 17, 18, 20.* ***Simonson*** *a-27; c-23. Dominic Fortune appears in #21-24.*

HULK: FUTURE IMPERFECT
Marvel Comics: Jan, 1993 - No. 2, Dec, 1992 (In error) ($5.95, 52 pgs., square-bound, limited series)

	GD25	FN65	NM94
1,2: Embossed-c; Peter David story & George Perez-c/a. 1-1st app. Maestro.	.85	2.60	7.00

HULK/ PITT
Marvel Comics: 1997 ($5.99, one-shot)

	GD25	FN65	NM94
1 David-s/Keown-c/a		2.00	6.00

HULK 2099
Marvel Comics: Dec, 1994 - No. 10, Sept, 1995 ($1.50/$1.95)

	GD25	FN65	NM94
1 ($2.50)-Green foil-c			2.50
2-6: 2-A. Kubert-c			1,50
7-10: 7-begin $1.95-c			2.00

HUMAN FLY
I.W. Enterprises/Super: 1963 - 1964 (Reprints)

	GD25	FN65	NM94
I.W. Reprint #1-Reprints Blue Beetle #44('46)	1.50	4.50	12.00
Super Reprint #10-R/Blue Beetle #46('47)	1.50	4.50	12.00

HUMAN FLY, THE
Marvel Comics Group: Sept, 1977 - No. 19, Mar, 1979

	GD25	FN65	NM94
1-Origin; Spider-Man x-over			3.00
2-Ghost Rider app.			4.00
3-19: 9-Daredevil x-over; Byrne-c(p)			1.80

NOTE: ***Austin*** *c-4i, 9i.* ***Elias*** *a-1, 3p, 4p, 7p, 10-12p, 15p, 18p, 19p.* ***Layton*** *c-19.*

HUMAN TARGET SPECIAL (TV)
DC Comics: Nov, 1991 ($2.00, 52 pgs., one-shot)

	GD25	FN65	NM94
1			2.00

HUMAN TORCH, THE (Red Raven #1)(See All-Select, All Winners, Marvel Mystery, Men's Adventures, Mystic Comics (2nd series), Sub-Mariner, USA & Young Men)
Timely/Marvel Comics (TP 2,3/TCI 4-9/SePI 10/SnPC 11-25/CnPC 26-35/Atlas Comics (CPC 36-38)): No. 2, Fall, 1940 - No. 15, Spring, 1944; No. 16, Fall, 1944 - No. 35, Mar, 1949 (Becomes Love Tales #36 on); No. 36, April, 1954 - No. 38, Aug, 1954

	GD25	FN65	VF82	NM94
2(#1)-Intro & Origin Toro; The Falcon, The Fiery Mask, Mantor the Magician, & Microman only app.; Human Torch by Burgos, Sub-Mariner by Everett begin (origin of each in text)	1900.00	5700.00	11,400.00	21,000.00

	GD25	FN65	NM94
3(#2)-40pg. H.T. story; H.T. & S.M. battle over who is best artist in text-Everett or Burgos	430.00	1290.00	4300.00
4(#3)-Origin The Patriot in text; last Everett Sub-Mariner; Sid Greene-a	330.00	990.00	3300.00
5(#4)-The Patriot app; Angel x-over in Sub-Mariner (Summer, 1941); 1st Nazi war-c this title	263.00	790.00	2500.00
5-Human Torch battles Sub-Mariner (Fall, '41); 60 pg. story	380.00	1140.00	3800.00
6,9	176.00	528.00	1500.00
7-1st Japanese war-c	188.00	564.00	1600.00
8-Human Torch battles Sub-Mariner; 52 pg. story; Wolverton-a, 1 pg.	274.00	822.00	2600.00
10-Human Torch battles Sub-Mariner, 45 pg. story; Wolverton-a, 1 pg.	235.00	700.00	2000.00
11,13-15: 14-1st Atlas Globe logo (Winter, 1943-44; see All Winners #11 also)	141.00	423.00	1200.00
12-classic-c	218.00	654.00	1850.00
16-20: 20-Last War issue	100.00	300.00	850.00
21,22,24-30:	94.00	282.00	800.00
23 (Sum/46)-Becomes Junior Miss 24? Classic Schomburg Robot-c	109.00	327.00	925.00
31-Namora x-over in Sub-Mariner (also #30); last Toro	79.00	237.00	675.00
32-Sungirl, Namora app.; Sungirl-c	79.00	237.00	675.00
33-Capt. America x-over	82.00	246.00	700.00
34-Sungirl solo	74.00	222.00	625.00
35-Captain America & Sungirl app. (1949)	82.00	246.00	700.00
36-38(1954)-Sub-Mariner in all	79.00	237.00	675.00

NOTE: ***Ayers*** *Human Torch in 36(3).* ***Brodsky*** *c-25, 31-33?, 37, 38.* ***Burgos*** *c-36.* ***Everett*** *a-1-3, 27, 28, 30, 37, 38.* ***Powell*** *a-36(Sub-Mariner).* ***Schomburg*** *c-1-3, 5-8, 10-23.* ***Sekowsky*** *c-28, 34?, 35?* ***Shores*** *c-24, 26, 27, 29, 30.* ***Mickey Spillane*** *text 4-6. Bondage c-2, 12, 19.*

HUMAN TORCH, THE (Also see Avengers West Coast, Fantastic Four, The Invaders, Saga of the Original... & Strange Tales #101)
Marvel Comics Group: Sept, 1974 - No. 8, Nov, 1975

	GD25	FN65	NM94
1: 1-8-r/stories from Strange Tales #101-108	1.20	3.60	12.00
2-8: 1st H.T. title since G.A. 7-vs. Sub-Mariner	.85	2.60	7.00

NOTE: *Golden Age & Silver Age Human Torch-r #1-8.* ***Ayers*** *r-6, 7.* ***Kirby/Ayers*** *r-1-5, 8.*

HUMBUG (Satire by Harvey Kurtzman)
Humbug Publications: Aug, 1957 - No. 9, May, 1958; No. 10, June, 1958; No. 11, Oct, 1958

	GD25	FN65	NM94
1-Wood-a (intro pgs. only)	24.00	72.00	180.00
2	11.00	34.00	85.00
3-9: 8-Elvis in Jailbreak Rock	9.30	28.00	70.00
10,11-Magazine format. 10-Photo-c	13.00	38.00	95.00

Huntress #17 (1st Series) © DC

Hyperkind #2 © MAR

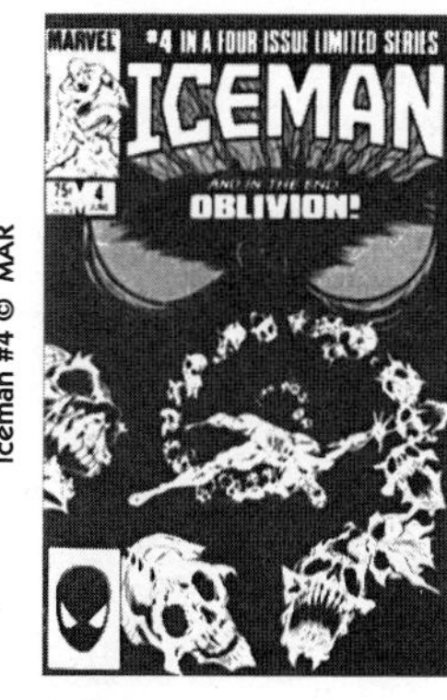

Iceman #4 © MAR

GD25 FN65 NM94

Bound Volume(#1-9)(extremely rare) 59.00 177.00 500.00
NOTE: ***Davis*** *a-1-11.* ***Elder*** *a-2-4, 6-9, 11.* ***Heath*** *a-2, 4-8, 10.* ***Jaffee*** *a-2, 4-9.* ***Kurtzman*** *a-11.*

HUMDINGER (Becomes White Rider and Super Horse #3 on?)
Novelty Press/Premium Group: May-June, 1946 - V2#2, July-Aug, 1947

1-Jerkwater Line, Mickey Starlight by Don Rico, Dink begin 28.00 84.00 210.00
2 12.00 36.00 90.00
3-6, V2#1,2 8.50 26.00 60.00

HUMONGOUS MAN
Alternative Press (Ikon Press): Sept, 1997 -Present ($2.25, B&W)

1-3-Stepp & Harrison-c/s/a. 2.25

HUMOR (See All Humor Comics)

HUMPHREY COMICS (Joe Palooka Presents...; also see Joe Palooka)
Harvey Publications: Oct, 1948 - No. 22, Apr, 1952

1-Joe Palooka's pal (r); (52 pgs.)-Powell-a 10.00 30.00 75.00
2,3: Powell-a 5.70 17.00 35.00
4-Boy Heroes app.; Powell-a 5.70 17.00 40.00
5-8,10: 5,6-Powell-a. 7-Little Dot app. 4.25 13.00 26.00
9-Origin Humphrey 5.70 17.00 35.00
11-22 4.00 10.00 20.00

HUNCHBACK OF NOTRE DAME, THE
Dell Publishing Co.: No. 854, Oct, 1957 (one shot)

Four Color 854-Movie, photo-c 12.00 35.00 130.00

HUNK
Charlton Comics: Aug, 1961 - No. 11, 1963

1 2.60 7.80 26.00
2-11 1.60 4.85 13.00

HUNTED (Formerly My Love Memoirs)
Fox Features Syndicate: No. 13, July, 1950 - No. 2, Sept, 1950

13(#1)-Used in **SOTI**, pg. 42 & illo. "Treating police contemptuously" (lower left); Hollingsworth bondage-c 29.00 88.00 220.00
2 13.00 38.00 95.00

HUNTER'S HEART
DC Comics: June, 1995 - No. 3, Aug, 1995 ($5.95, B&W, limited series)

1-3 2.00 6.00

HUNTRESS, THE (See All-Star Comics #69, Batman Family, Brave & the Bold #62, DC Super Stars #17, Detective #652, Infinity, Inc. #1, Sensation Comics #68 & Wonder Woman #271)
DC Comics: Apr, 1989 - No. 19, Oct, 1990 ($1.00, mature)

1-19: Staton-c/a(p) in all. 17-19-Batman-c/stories 1.25

HUNTRESS, THE
DC Comics: June, 1994 - No. 4, Sept, 1994 ($1.50, limited series)

1-4-Netzer-c/a: 2-Batman app. 1.75

HURRICANE COMICS
Cambridge House: 1945 (52 pgs.)

1-(Humor, funny animal) 19.00 56.00 140.00

HURRICANE KIDS, THE (Also See Magic Morro, The Owl, Popular Comics #45)
R.S. Callender: 1941 (Giveaway, 7-1/2x5-1/4", soft-c)

nn-Will Ely-a. 8.50 26.00 60.00

HYBRIDS
Continunity Comics: Jan, 1994 ($2.50, one-shot)

1-Neal Adams-c(p) & part-a(i); embossed-c. 2.50

HYBRIDS DEATHWATCH 2000
Continuity Comics: Apr, 1993 - No. 5, Aug, 1993 ($2.50)

0-(Giveaway)-Foil-c; Neal Adams-c(i) & plots (also #1,2) 2.50
1-5: 1-Polybagged w/card; die-cut-c. 2-Thermal-c. 3-Polybagged w/card; indestructible-c; Adams plot. 4,5-Valeria She-Bat; origin Hybrids; Adams-c(p) 2.50

GD25 FN65 NM94

HYBRIDS ORIGIN
Continunity Comics: 1993 - No. 5, 1994? ($2.50)

1-5: 2,3-Neal Adams-c. 4,5-Valeria the She-Bat app. Adams-c(i) 2.50

HYDE-25
Harris Publications: Apr, 1995 ($2.95, one-shot)

0-coupon for poster; r/Vampirella's 1st app. 3.00

HYDROMAN (See Heroic Comics)

HYPERKIND (See Razorline)
Marvel Comics: Sept, 1993 - No. 9, May, 1994 ($1.75/$1.95)

1-($2.50)-Foil embossed-c; by Clive Barker 2.50
2-8 1.75
9-($1.95) 2.00

HYPERKIND UNLEASED
Marvel Comics: Aug, 1994 ($2.95, 52 pgs., one-shot)

1 3.00

HYPER MYSTERY COMICS
Hyper Publications: May, 1940 - No. 2, June, 1940 (68 pgs.)

1-Hyper, the Phenomenal begins; Calkins-a 176.00 528.00 1500.00
2 94.00 282.00 800.00

HYPERSONIC
Dark Horse Comics: Nov, 1997 - No. 4, Feb, 1998 ($2.95, limited series)

1-4: Abnett & White/Erskine-a 3.00

I AIM AT THE STARS (Movie)
Dell Publishing Co.: No. 1148, Nov-Jan/1960-61 (one-shot)

Four Color 1148-The Werner Von Braun Sty-photo-c 6.40 19.00 70.00

I AM COYOTE (See Eclipse Graphic Album Series & Eclipse Magazine #2)

I AM LEGEND
Eclipse Books: 1991 - No. 4, 1991 ($5.95, B&W, squarebound, 68 pgs.)

1-4: Based on 1954 novel 2.00 6.00

IBIS, THE INVINCIBLE (See Fawcett Miniatures, Mighty Midget & Whiz)
Fawcett Publications: 1943 (Feb) - #2, 1943; #3, Wint, 1945 - #5, Fall, 1946; #6, Spring, 1948

1-Origin Ibis; Raboy-c; on sale 1/2/43 153.00 460.00 1300.00
2-Bondage-c 77.00 231.00 650.00
3-Wolverton-a #3-6 (4 pgs. each) 62.00 186.00 525.00
4-6: 5-Bondage-c 43.00 129.00 360.00
NOTE: ***Mac Raboy*** *c(p)-3-5.* ***Shaffenberger*** *c-6.*

I-BOTS (See Isaac Asimov's I-BOTS)

ICE AGE ON THE WORLD OF MAGIC: THE GATHERING (See Magic The Gathering)

ICE KING OF OZ, THE (See First Comics Graphic Novel #13)

ICEMAN (Also see The Champions & X-Men #94)
Marvel Comics Group: Dec, 1984 - No. 4, June, 1985 (Limited series)

1 1.50
2,4 1.50
3-The Defenders, Champions (Ghost Rider) & the original X-Men x-over 2.00
NOTE: ***Zeck*** *c-1-4.*

ICON
DC Comics (Milestone): May, 1993 - No. 42, Feb, 1997($1.50/$1.75/$2.50)

1-($2.95)-Collector's Edition polybagged w/poster & trading card (direct sale only) 3.00
1-14: 9-Simonson-c 1.50
15-24,26: 15-Begin $1.75-c. 15,16-Worlds Collide Pt. 4 & 11. 15-Superboy app.

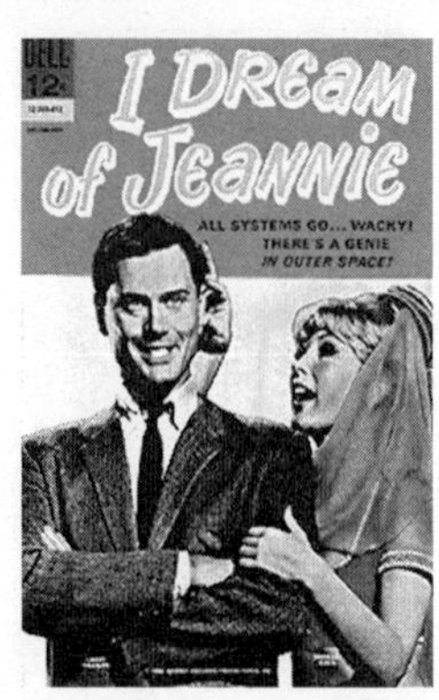

I Dream of Jeannie #2 © DELL

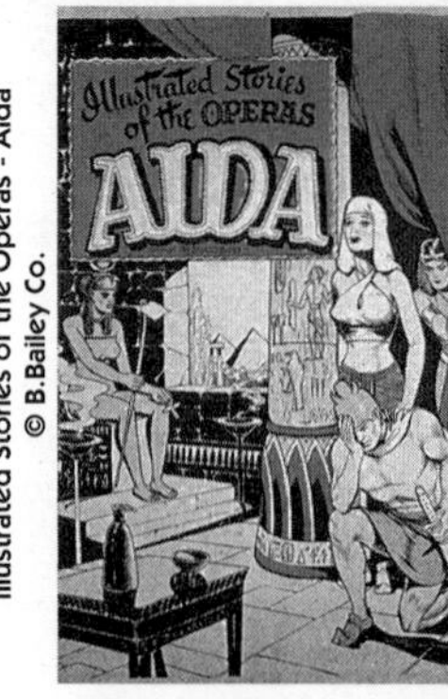

Illustrated Stories of the Operas - Aida © B.Bailey Co.

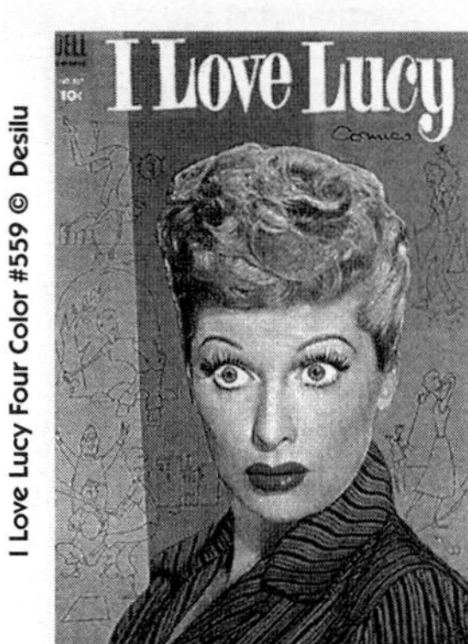

I Love Lucy Four Color #559 © Desilu

GD25 FN65 NM94

16-Superman-c/story 1.75
25-($2.95, 52 pgs.) 3.00
27-30,32-42: Begin $2.50-c. 40-Vs. Blood Syndicate 2.50
31-(99¢) 1.00

IDAHO
Dell Publishing Co.: June-Aug, 1963 - No. 8, July-Sept, 1965

1 2.00 6.00 16.00
2-8: 5-7-Painted-c 1.10 3.30 9.00

IDEAL (... a Classical Comic) (2nd Series) (Love Romances No. 6 on)
Timely Comics: July, 1948 - No. 5, March, 1949 (Feature length stories)

1-Antony & Cleopatra 30.00 90.00 225.00
2-The Corpses of Dr. Sacotti 27.00 82.00 205.00
3-Joan of Arc; used in **SOTI**, pg. 308 'Boer War' 24.00 72.00 180.00
4-Richard the Lion-hearted; titled "...the World's Greatest Comics"; The Witness app. 40.00 120.00 310.00
5-Ideal Love & Romance; change to love; photo-c 15.00 44.00 110.00

IDEAL COMICS (1st Series) (Willie Comics No. 5 on)
Timely Comics (MgPC): Fall, 1944 - No. 4, Spring, 1946

1-Funny animal; Super Rabbit in all 17.00 52.00 130.00
2 11.00 32.00 80.00
3,4 10.00 30.00 75.00

IDEAL LOVE & ROMANCE (See Ideal, A Classical Comic)

IDEAL ROMANCE (Formerly Tender Romance)
Key Publ.: No. 3, April, 1954 - No. 8, Feb, 1955 (Diary Confessions No. 9 on)

3-Bernard Baily-c 6.00 18.00 42.00
4-8: 4,5-B. Baily-c 4.00 11.50 23.00

IDOL
Marvel Comics (Epic Comics): 1992 - No. 3, 1992 ($2.95, mini-series, 52 pgs.)

Book 1-3 3.00

I DREAM OF JEANNIE (TV)
Dell Publishing Co.: Apr, 1965 - No. 2, Dec, 1966 (Photo-c)

1-Barbara Eden photo-c, each 14.00 42.00 155.00
2 11.00 33.00 120.00

IF THE DEVIL WOULD TALK
Roman Catholic Catechetical Guild/Impact Publ.: 1950; 1958 (32 pgs.; paper cover; in full color)

nn-(Scarce)-About secularism (20-30 copies known to exist); very low distribution 65.00 195.00 550.00
1958 Edition-(Impact Publ.); art & script changed to meet church criticism of earlier edition; 80 plus copies known to exist 30.00 90.00 225.00
Black & White version of nn edition; small size; only 4 known copies exist 27.00 81.00 200.00

NOTE: *The original edition of this book was printed and killed by the Guild's board of directors. It is believed that a very limited number of copies were distributed. The 1958 version was a complete bomb with very limited, if any, circulation. In 1979, 11 original, 4 1958 reprints, and 4 B&W's surfaced from the Guild's old files in St. Paul, Minnesota.*

ILLUMINATOR
Marvel Comics/Nelson Publ.: 1993 - No. 4, 1993 ($4.99/$2.95, 52 pgs.)

1,2-($4.99) 5.00
3,4 3.00

ILLUSTRATED GAGS
United Features Syndicate: No. 16, 1940

Single Series 16 14.00 42.00 105.00

ILLUSTRATED LIBRARY OF..., AN (See Classics Illustrated Giants)

ILLUSTRATED STORIES OF THE OPERAS
Baily (Bernard) Publ. Co.: 1943 (16 pgs.; B&W) (25 cents) (cover-B&W & red)

nn-(Rare)-Faust (part-r in Cisco Kid #1) 50.00 150.00 425.00
nn-(Rare)-Aida 50.00 150.00 425.00
nn-(Rare)-Carmen; Baily-a 50.00 150.00 425.00
nn-(Rare)-Rigoleito 50.00 150.00 425.00

ILLUSTRATED STORY OF ROBIN HOOD & HIS MERRY MEN, THE
(See Classics Giveaways, 12/44)

ILLUSTRATED TARZAN BOOK, THE (See Tarzan Book)

I LOVED (Formerly Rulah; Colossal Features Magazine No. 33 on)
Fox Features Syndicate: No. 28, July, 1949 - No. 32, Mar, 1950

28 7.85 23.50 55.00
29-32 5.70 17.00 35.00

I LOVE LUCY
Eternity Comics : 6/90 - No. 6, 1990;V2#1, 11/90 - No. 6, 1991 ($2.95, B&W, mini-series)

1-6: Reprints 1950s comic strip; photo-c 3.00
Book II #1-6: Reprints comic strip; photo-c 3.00
...In Full Color 1 (1991, $5.95, 52 pgs.)-Reprints I Love Lucy Comics #4,5,8,16; photo-c with embossed logo (2 versions exist, one with pgs. 18 & 19 reversed, the other corrected) 2.00 6.00
...In 3-D 1 (1991, $3.95, w/glasses)-Reprints I Love Lucy Comics; photo-c sealed in plastic bag 4.00

I LOVE LUCY COMICS (TV) (Also see The Lucy Show)
Dell Publishing Co.: No. 535, Feb, 1954 - No. 35, Apr-June, 1962 (All have Lucille Ball photo-c)

Four Color 535(#1) 48.00 143.00 525.00
Four Color 559(#2, 5/54) 30.00 89.00 325.00
3 (8-10/54) - 5 17.00 52.00 190.00
6-10 14.00 41.00 150.00
11-20 10.00 30.00 110.00
21-35 8.00 23.00 85.00

I LOVE YOU
Fawcett Publications: June, 1950 (one-shot)

1-Photo-c 12.00 36.00 90.00

I LOVE YOU (Formerly In Love)
Charlton Comics: No. 7, 9/55 - No. 121, 12/76; No. 122, 3/79 - No. 130, 5/80

7-Kirby-c; Powell-a 7.50 22.50 75.00
8-10 2.80 8.40 28.00
11-16,18-20 2.20 6.60 22.00
17-(68 pg. Giant) 5.00 15.00 50.00
21-25,27-50 2.50 7.50 20.00
26-No Torres-a 1.85 5.50 15.00
51-59 1.50 4.50 12.00
60-(1/66)-Elvis Presley line drawn c/story 12.00 36.00 120.00
61-85 1.00 3.00 8.00
86-110 2.00 6.00
111-130 4.00

I, LUSIPHER (Becomes Poison Elves, 1st series #8 on)
Mulehide Graphics: 1991 - No. 7, 1992 (B&W, magazine size)

1-Drew Hayes-c/a/scripts 7.00 21.00 75.00
2,4,5 4.00 12.25 45.00
3-Low print run 9.00 27.00 100.00
6,7 3.80 11.50 40.00
Poison Elves: Requiem For An Elf (Sirius Ent., 6/96, $14.95, trade paperback)-Reprints I, Lusiphur #1,2 as text, and 3-6 15.00

I'M A COP
Magazine Enterprises: 1954 - No. 3, 1954?

1(A-1 #111)-Powell-c/a in all 13.00 40.00 100.00
2(A-1 #126), 3(A-1 #128) 7.15 21.50 50.00

IMAGE GRAPHIC NOVEL
Image Int.: 1984 ($6.95)(Advertised as Pacific Comics Graphic Novel #1)

1-The Seven Samuroid; Brunner-c/a .85 2.60 7.00

Impact #1 © WMG

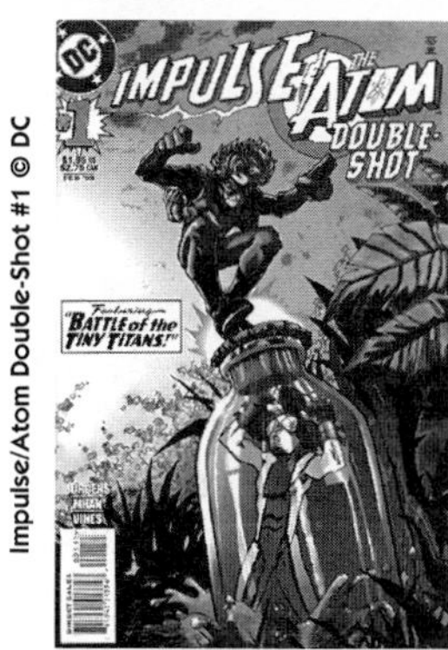

Impulse/Atom Double-Shot #1 © DC

Incredible Hulk #102 © MAR

GD25 FN65 NM94

IMAGES OF A DISTANT SOIL
Image Comics: Feb, 1997 ($2.95, B&W, one-shot)
1-Sketches by various 2.95

IMAGES OF SHADOWHAWK (Also see Shadowhawk)
Image Comics: Sept, 1993 - No. 3, 1994 ($1.95, limited series)
1-3: Keith Giffen-c/a; Trencher app. 2.00

IMAGE ZERO
Image Comics: 1993 (Received through mail w/coupons from Image books)
0-Savage Dragon, StormWatch, Shadowhawk, Strykeforce; 1st app. Troll; 1st app. McFarlane's Freak, Blotch, Sweat and Bludd 5.00

I'M DICKENS - HE'S FENSTER (TV)
Dell Publishing Co.: May-July, 1963 - No. 2, Aug-Oct, 1963 (Photo-c)
1,2 4.00 12.00 45.00

I MET A HANDSOME COWBOY
Dell Publishing Co.: No. 324, Mar, 1951
Four Color 324 8.00 25.00 90.00

IMMORTAL DOCTOR FATE, THE
DC Comics: Jan, 1995 - No. 3, Mar, 1985 ($1.25, limited series)
1-3: 1-Simonson-c/a. 2-Giffen-c/a(p) 1.30

IMMORTALIS (See Mortigan Goth: Immortalis)

IMMORTAL II
Image Comics: Apr, 1997 - No. 5, Feb, 1998 ($2.50, B&W&Grey, lim. series)
1-5: 1-B&W w/ color pull-out poster 2.50

IMPACT
E. C. Comics: Mar-Apr, 1955 - No. 5, Nov-Dec, 1955
1-Not code approved 13.00 40.00 125.00
2 8.50 26.00 80.00
3-5: 4-Crandall-a 7.00 21.00 65.00
NOTE: ***Crandall** a-1-4. **Davis** a-2-4; c-1-5. **Evans** a-1, 4, 5. **Ingels** a-in all. **Kamen** a-3. **Krigstein** a-1, 5. **Orlando** a-2, 5.*

IMPACT CHRISTMAS SPECIAL
DC Comics (Impact Comics): 1991 ($2.50, 68 pgs.)
1-Gift of the Magi by Infantino/Rogers; The Black Hood, The Fly, The Jaguar, & The Shield stories 2.50

IMPOSSIBLE MAN SUMMER VACATION SPECTACULAR, THE
Marvel Comics: Aug, 1990; No. 2, Sept, 1991 ($2.00, 68 pgs.) (See Fantastic Four#11)
1-Spider Man, Quasar, Dr. Strange, She-Hulk, Punisher & Dr. Doom stories; Barry Crain, Guice-a; Art Adams-c(i) 2.00
2-Ka Zar & Thor app.; Cable Wolverine-c app. 2.00

IMPERIAL GUARD
Marvel Comics: Jan, 1997 - No. 3, Mar, 1997 ($1.95, limited series)
1-3: Augustyn-s in all; 1-Wraparound-c 1.95

IMPULSE (See Flash #92, 2nd Series for 1st app.) (Also see Young Justice)
DC Comics: Apr, 1995 - Present ($1.50/$1.75/$1.95/$2.25)
1-Mark Waid scripts & Humberto Ramos-c/a(p) begin; brief retelling of origin .90 2.70 8.00
2-4: 3-Begin $1.75-c. 4.00
5-9: 9-XS from Legion (Impulse's cousin) comes to the 20th Century, returns to the 30th Century in #12. 3.00
10-12:10-Dead Heat Pt. 3 (cont'd in Flash #110). 11-Dead Heat Pt. 4 (cont'd in Flash #111); Johnny Quick dies. 5.00
13-25: 14-Trickster app. 17-Zatanna-c/app. 21-Legion-c/app. 22-Jesse Quick-c/app. 24-Origin; Flash app. 25-Last Ramos-a. 2.00
26-31: 26-Rousseau-a(p) begins. 28-1st new Arrowette (see World's Finest #113). 30-Genesis x-over. .75 1.75
32-40: 32-Begin $1.95-c 1.95
41-45: 41-Begin $2.25-c; Arrowette-c/app. 2.25
#1,000,000 (11/98) John Fox app. 2.25
Annual 1 (1996, $2.95)-Legends of the Dead Earth; Parobeck-a 3.00
Annual 2 (1997, $3.95)-Pulp Heroes stories; Orbik painted-c 4.00
.../Atom Double-Shot 1(2/98, $1.95) Jurgens-s/Mhan-a 2.00
...Plus(9/97, $2.95) w/Gross Out (Scare Tactics)-c/app. 3.00
...Reckless Youth (1997, $14.95, TPB) r/Flash #92-94, Impulse #1-6 14.95

INCAL, THE
Marvel Comics (Epic): Nov, 1988 - No. 3, Jan, 1989 ($10.95/$12.95, mature)
1,3: Moebius-c/a in all; sexual content 1.10 3.30 11.00
2-($12.95) 1.30 3.90 13.00

INCOMPLETE DEATH'S HEAD (Also see Death's Head)
Marvel Comics UK: Jan, 1993 - No. 12, Dec, 1993 ($1.75, limited series)
1-($2.95, 56 pgs.)-Die-cut cover 3.00
2-11: 2-Re-intro original Death's Head. 3-Original Death's Head vs. Dragon's Claws 1.75
12-($2.50, 52 pgs.)-She Hulk app. 2.50

INCREDIBLE HULK, THE (See Aurora, The Avengers #1, The Defenders #1, Giant-Size..., Hulk, Marvel Collectors Item Classics, Marvel Comics Presents #26, Marvel Fanfare, Marvel Treasury Edition, Power Record Comics, Rampaging Hulk, She-Hulk & 2099 Unlimited)

INCREDIBLE HULK, THE
Marvel Comics: May, 1962 - No. 6, Mar, 1963; No. 102, Apr, 1968 - No. 474, Mar, 1999

	GD25	FN65	VF82	NM94
1-Origin & 1st app. (skin is grey colored); Kirby pencils begin, end #5	545.00	1635.00	4900.00	12,000.00
2-1st green skinned Hulk; Kirby/Ditko-a	145.00	435.00	1085.00	2300.00
3-Origin retold; 1st app. Ringmaster & Hercules (9/62)	95.00	285.00	665.00	1400.00
4,5: 4-Brief origin retold	85.00	255.00	595.00	1300.00
6-Intro. Teen Brigade; all Ditko-a	125.00	375.00	875.00	1900.00

	GD25	FN65	NM94
102 (Formerly Tales to Astonish)-Origin retold; story continued from Tales to Astonish #101	12.50	37.50	150.00
103	6.80	20.50	68.00
104-Rhino app.	6.20	18.75	62.00
105-108: 105-1st Missing Link. 107-Mandarin app.(9/68). 108-Mandarin & Nick Fury app. (10/68).	5.20	15.75	52.00
109,110: 109-Ka-Zar app.	3.50	10.50	35.00
111-117: 117-Last 12 cent issue	2.90	8.70	29.00
118-Hulk vs. Sub-Mariner	2.60	7.80	26.00
119-121,123-125	2.00	6.00	20.00
122-Hulk battles Thing (12/69)	3.40	10.20	37.00
126-1st Barbara Norriss (Valkyrie)	2.20	6.25	22.00
127-139: 131-Hulk vs. Iron Man; 1st Jim Wilson, Hulk's new sidekick. 136-1st Xeron, The Star-Slayer	1.25	3.75	12.00
140-Written by Harlan Ellison; 1st Jarella, Hulk's love	1.75	5.25	17.00
141-1st app. Doc Samson (7/71)	2.80	8.40	31.00
142-144,146-161: 149-1st app. The Inheritor. 155-1st app. Shaper. 158-Warlock cameo(12/72). 161-The Mimic dies; Beast app.		2.00	6.00
145-(52 pgs.)-Origin retold	.90	2.70	8.00
162-1st app. The Wendigo (4/73); Beast app.	.85	2.60	7.00
163-171,173-175: 163-1st app. The Gremlin. 164-1st Capt. Omen & Colonel John D. Armbruster. 166-1st Zzzax. 168-1st The Harpy; nudity panels of Betty Brant. 169-1st app. Bi-Beast		2.00	5.00
165-Variant w/4 extra pgs. of ads on slick paper(7/73)	1.00	2.80	10.00
172-X-Men cameo; origin Juggernaut retold	1.10	3.30	11.00
176-Warlock cameo (2 panels only); same date as Strange Tales #178 (6/74)		2.00	6.00
177-1st actual death of Warlock (last panel only)	.90	2.70	8.00
178-Rebirth of Warlock	1.00	3.00	10.00

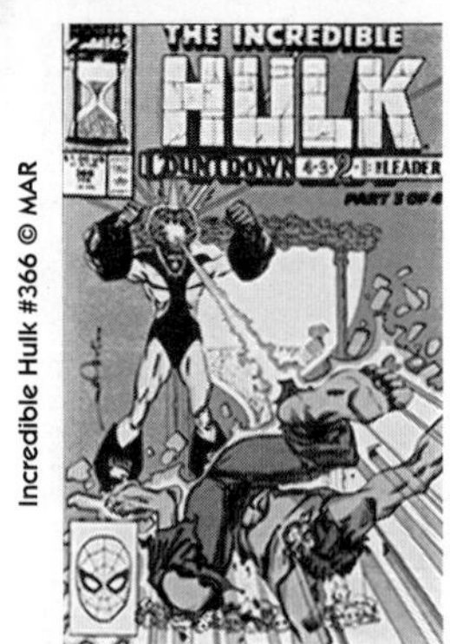

Incredible Hulk #366 © MAR

Incredible Hulk #466 © MAR

Incredible Hulk Annual #2 © MAR

GD25 FN65 NM94

179-No Warlock 4.00
180-(10/74)-1st app. Wolverine (cameo last pg.) 5.50 16.50 60.00
181-(11/74)-1st full Wolverine story 40.00 120.00 465.00
182-Wolverine cameo; see Giant-Size X-Men #1 for next app.; 1st Crackajack Jackson 5.50 16.50 60.00
183-199: 185-Death of Col. Armbruster 4.00
200-Silver Surfer app.; anniversary issue 2.00 6.00 20.00
201-240: 201-Conan swipe-c/sty. 212-1st app. The Constrictor. 227-Original Avengers app. 232-Capt. America x-over from C.A. #230. 233-Marvel Man app. 234-(4/79)-1st app. Quasar (formerly Marvel Man & changes name to Quasar) 3.50
241-249,251-299: 243-Cage app. 271-Rocket Raccoon app. 272-Sasquatch & Wendigo app.; Wolverine & Alpha Flight cameo in flashback. 278,279-Most Marvel characters app. (Wolverine in both). 279-X-Men & Alpha Flight cameos. 282-284-She-Hulk app. 293-F.F. app. 2.50
250-Giant size; Silver Surfer app. .85 2.60 7.00
300-(11/84, 52 pgs.)-Spider-Man app in new black costume on-c & 2 pg. cameo 2.50
301-313: 312-Origin Hulk retold 2.50
314-Byrne-c/a begins, ends #319 4.00
315-319: 319-Bruce Banner & Betty Talbot wed 2.50
320-323,325,327-329 2.50
324-1st app. Grey Hulk since #1 (c-swipe of #1) .90 2.70 8.00
326-Grey vs. Green Hulk 2.00
330-1st McFarlane issue (4/87); death of Thunderbolt Ross 1.00 3.00 10.00
331-Grey Hulk series begins 1.00 3.00 10.00
332-334,336-339: 336,337-X-Factor app. .85 2.60 7.00
335-No McFarlane-a 2.50
340-Hulk battles Wolverine by McFarlane 1.50 4.50 15.00
341-344 4.00
345-($1.50, 52 pgs.) 4.00
346-Last McFarlane issue 4.00
347-349,351-358,360-366: 347-1st app. Marlo 1.50
350-Hulk/Thing battle 4.00
359-Wolverine app. (illusion only) 1.50
367-1st Dale Keown-a on Hulk (3/90) .85 2.60 7.00
368-Sam Kieth-c/a, 1st app. Pantheon 4.00
369,370-Dale Keown-c/a. 370,371-Original Defenders app. 3.50
371,373-376: Keown-c/a. 376-Green vs. Grey Hulk 3.50
372-Green Hulk app.; Keown-c/a .85 2.60 7.00
377-1st all new Hulk; fluorescent-c; Keown-c/a .90 2.70 8.00
377-Fluorescent green logo 2nd printing 3.50
378,380,389: No Keown-a. 380-Doc Samson app. 1.50
379-Keown-a 3.50
381-388,390-392-Keown-a. 385-Infinity Gauntlet x-over. 389-Last $1.00-c. 392-X-Factor app. 3.50
393-($2.50, 72 pgs.)-30th anniversary issue; green foil stamped-c; swipes-c to #1; has pin-ups of classic battles; Keown-c/a 3.50
393-2nd printing 2.50
394-397: 394-No Keown-c/a; intro Trauma. 395,396-Punisher-c/stories; Keown-c/a. 397-Begin "Ghost of the Past" 4-part sty; Keown c/a 2.00
398,399: 398-Last Keown-c/a 2.00
400-($2.50, 68 pgs.)-Holo-grafx foil-c & r/TTA #63 2.50
400-2nd printing-Different color foil-c 1.50
401-416: 402-Return of Doc Samson 1.50
417-424: 417-Begin $1.50-c; Rick Jones' bachelor party; Hulk returns from "Future Imperfect"; bound-in trading card sheet. 418-(Regular edition)-Rick Jones marries Marlo; includes cameo apps of various Marvel characters as well as DC's Death & Peter David. 420-Death of Jim Wilson 1.50
418-($2.50)-Collector's Edition w/gatefold die-cut-c 2.50
425 ($2.25, 52 pgs.) 2.25
425 ($3.50, 52 pgs.)-Holographic-c 3.50

GD25 FN65 NM94

426-434, 436-442: 426-Begin $1.95-c. 427, 428-Man-Thing app. 431,432-Abomination app. 434-Funeral for Nick Fury. 436-Ghosts of the Future begins, ends #440. 439-Hulk becomes Maestro, Avengers app. 440-Thor-c/app. 441,442-She-Hulk-c/app. 442-Molecule Man app. 2.00
435 ($2.50)-Rhino-app; excerpt from "What Savage Beast" 2.50
443-448: 443-Begin $1.50-c; re-app. of Hulk. 444-Cable-c/app.; "Onslaught". 445-"Onslaught". 446-w/card insert. 447-Begin Deodato-c/a(p) 1.50
447-Variant cover 3.00
449-Thunderbolts-c/app. 4.00
450-($2.95)-Thunderbolts app.; 2 stories; Heroes Reborn-c/app. 3.00
451-454, -1(7/97):($1.95) 2.00
455-465: 455-Begin $1.99-c, X-Men-c/app. 460-Bruce Banner returns. 464-Silver Surfer-c/app. 2.00
466,467: Betty dies. 467-Last Peter David-s/Kubert-a 2.00
468-473: 468-Casey-s/Pulido-a begin 2.00
474-($2.99) Last issue; Abomination app. 2.99
Special 1 (10/68, 25¢, 68 pg.)-New 51 pg. story, Hulk battles The Inhumans (early app.); Steranko-c. 7.00 21.00 70.00
Special 2 (10/69, 25¢, 68 pg.)-Origin retold 4.50 13.50 45.00
Special 3 (1/71, 25¢, 68 pg.) 1.50 4.50 15.00
Special 4 (1/72) 1.50 4.50 15.00
Annual 5 (1976) .90 2.70 8.00
Annual 6 (1977) 5.00
Annual 7 (1978)-Byrne/Layton-c/a; Iceman & Angel app. in book-length story 5.00
Annual 8 ('79)-Book-length Sasquatch-c/sty 4.00
Annual 9-17: 9('80). 10('81). 11('82)-Doc Samson back-up by Miller(p)(5 pgs.); Spider-Man & Avengers app. Buckler-a(p). 12 ('83). 13('84). 14('85). 15('86). 16('90, $2.00, 68 pgs.)-She-Hulk app. 17(1991, $2.00)-Origin retold 3.00
Annual 18 (1992, $2.25, 68 pgs.)-Return of the Defenders, Pt. I; no Keown-c/a 2.25
Annual 19 (1993, $2.95, 68 pgs.)-Bagged w/card 3.00
Annual 20 (1994, $2.95, 68 pgs.) 3.00
...'97 ($2.99) Pollina-c 2.99
...And Wolverine 1 (10/86, $2.50)-r/1st app. #180-181 1.00 3.00 10.00
...: Beauty and the Behemoth ('98, $19.95, TPB) r/Bruce & Betty stories 19.95
...Ground Zero ('95, $12.95) r/#340-346 1.30 3.90 13.00
...Hercules Unleashed (10/96, $2.50) David-s/Deodato-c/a 2.50
.../Sub-Mariner "98 Annual ($2.99) 3.00
...Versus Quasimodo 1 (3/83, one-shot)-Based on Saturday morning cartoon 3.00
...Versus Venom 1 (4/94, $2.50, one-shot)-Embossed-c; red foil logo 2.75
(Also see titles listed under **Hulk**)

NOTE: ***Adkins*** *a-111-116i.* ***Austin*** *a(i)-350, 351, 353, 354; c-302i, 350i.* ***Ayers*** *a-3-5i.* ***Buckler*** *a-Annual 5; c-252.* ***John Buscema*** *c-202p.* ***Byrne*** *a-314-319p; c-314-316, 318, 319, 359, Annual 14i.* ***Colan*** *c-363.* ***Ditko*** *a-2i, 6, 249, Annual 2r(5), 3r, 9p; c-2i, 6, 235, 249.* ***Everett*** *c-133i.* ***Golden*** *c-248, 251.* ***Kane*** *c(p)-193, 194, 196, 198.* ***Dale Keown*** *a(p)-367, 369-377, 379, 381-388, 390-393, 395-398; c-369-377p, 381, 382p, 384, 385, 386, 387p, 388, 390p, 391-393, 395p, 396, 397p, 398.* ***Kirby*** *a-1-5p, Special 2, 3p, Annual 5p; c-1-5, Annual 5.* ***McFarlane*** *a-330-334p, 336-339p, 340-343, 344-346p; c-330p, 340p, 341-343, 344p, 345, 346p.* ***Mignola*** *c-302, 305, 313.* ***Miller*** *c-258p, 261, 264, 268.* ***Mooney*** *a-230p, 287i, 288i.* ***Powell*** *a-Special 3r(2).* ***Romita*** *a-Annual 17p.* ***Severin*** *a(i)-108-110, 131-133, 141-151, 153-155; c(i)-109, 110, 132, 142, 144-155.* ***Simonson*** *c-283, 364-367.* ***Starlin*** *a-222p; c-217.* ***Staton*** *a(i)-187-189, 191-209.* ***Tuska*** *a-102i, 105i, 106i, 218p.* ***Williamson*** *a-310i; c-310i, 311i.* ***Wrightson*** *c-197.*

INCREDIBLE MR. LIMPET, THE (See Movie Classics)

INCREDIBLE SCIENCE FICTION (Formerly Weird Science-Fantasy)
E. C. Comics: No. 30, July-Aug, 1955 - No. 33, Jan-Feb, 1956

30,33: 33-Story-r/Weird Fantasy #18 30.00 90.00 270.00
31-Williamson/Krenkel-a, Wood-a(2) 32.00 96.00 280.00
32-Williamson/Krenkel-a 32.00 96.00 280.00

NOTE: ***Davis*** *a-30, 32, 33; c-30-32.* ***Krigstein*** *a-in all.* ***Orlando*** *a-30, 32, 33("Judgement Day" reprint).* ***Wood*** *a-30, 31, 33; c-33.*

INCREDIBLE SCIENCE FICTION (Formerly Weird Science-Fantasy)

Indiana Jones and the Fate of Atlantis #1 © Lucasfilm

Indian Chief #23 © DELL

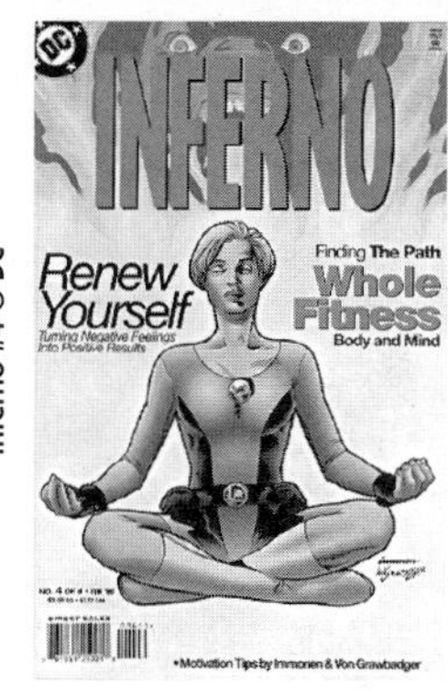

Inferno #4 © DC

GD25 FN65 NM94

Russ Cochran/Gemstone Publ.: No. 8, Aug, 1994 - No. 11, May, 1995 ($2.00)
8-11: Reprints #30-33 of E.C. series 2.00

INDEPENDENCE DAY (Movie)
Marvel Comics: No. 0, June, 1996 - No. 2, Aug, 1996 ($1.95, limited series)
0-Special Edition; photo-c 5.00
0-2 2.00

INDEPENDENT VOICES
Peregrine Entertainment: Sept, 1998 ($1.95, B&W)
1-Sampler of Indy titles for CBLDF 1.95

INDIANA JONES AND THE ARMS OF GOLD
Dark Horse Comics: Feb, 1994 - May, 1994 ($2.50, limited series)
1-4 2.50

INDIANA JONES AND THE FATE OF ATLANTIS
Dark Horse Comics: Mar, 1991 - Sep, 1991 ($2.50, limited series)
1-4-Dorman painted-c on all; contain trading cards (#1 has a 2nd printing, 10/91) 2.50

INDIANA JONES AND THE GOLDEN FLEECE
Dark Horse Comics: Jun, 1994 - July, 1994 ($2.50, limited series)
1,2 2.50

INDIANA JONES AND THE IRON PHOENIX
Dark Horse Comics: Dec, 1994 - Mar, 1995 ($2.50, limited series)
1-4 2.50

INDIANA JONES AND THE LAST CRUSADE
Marvel Comics: 1989 - No. 4, 1989 ($1.00, limited series, movie adaptation)
1-4: Williamson-i assist 1.00
1-(1989, $2.95, B&W mag., 80 pgs.) 3.00

INDIANA JONES AND THE SHRINE OF THE SEA DEVIL
Dark Horse Comics: Sep, 1994 ($2.50, one shot)
1-Gary Gianni-a 2.50

INDIANA JONES AND THE SPEAR OF DESTINY
Dark Horse Comics: Apr, 1995 - Aug, 1995 ($2.50, limited series)
1-4 2.50

INDIANA JONES: THUNDER IN THE ORIENT
Dark Horse Comics: Sep, 1993 - 1994 ($2.50, limited series)
1-6: Dan Barry story & art in all; 1-Dorman painted-c 2.50

INDIANA JONES AND THE TEMPLE OF DOOM
Marvel Comics Group: Sept, 1984 - No. 3, Nov, 1984 (Movie adaptation)
1-3-r/Marvel Super Special; Guice-a 1.00

INDIAN BRAVES (Baffling Mysteries No. 5 on)
Ace Magazines: March, 1951 - No. 4, Sept, 1951
1-Green Arrowhead begins, ends #3 9.30 28.00 70.00
2 5.70 17.00 35.00
3,4 4.25 13.00 28.00
I.W. Reprint #1 (nd)-r/Indian Braves #4 1.50 4.50 12.00

INDIAN CHIEF (White Eagle...) (Formerly The Chief, Four Color 290)
Dell Publ. Co.: No. 3, July-Sept, 1951 - No. 33, Jan-Mar, 1959 (All painted-c)
3 3.00 9.00 35.00
4-11: 6-White Eagle app. 2.50 7.50 28.00
12-1st White Eagle(10-12/53)-Not same as earlier character 3.00 9.00 35.00
13-29 1.80 5.50 20.00
30-33-Buscema-a 2.00 6.00 22.00

INDIAN CHIEF (See March of Comics No. 94, 110, 127, 140, 159, 170, 187)

INDIAN FIGHTER, THE (Movie)
Dell Publishing Co.: No. 687, May, 1956 (one-shot)
Four Color 687-Kirk Douglas photo-c 7.00 22.00 80.00

INDIAN FIGHTER
Youthful Magazines: May, 1950 - No. 11, Jan, 1952
1 10.00 30.00 75.00
2-Wildey-a/c(bondage) 6.50 19.50 45.00
3-11: 3,4-Wildey-a 5.00 15.00 30.00
NOTE: ***Walter Johnson*** *c-1, 3, 4, 6.* ***Palais*** *a-10.* ***Stallman*** *a-7.* ***Wildey*** *a-2-4; c-2, 5.*

INDIAN LEGENDS OF THE NIAGARA (See American Graphics)

INDIANS
Fiction House Magazines (Wings Publ. Co.): Spring, 1950 - No. 17, Spring, 1953 (1-8: 52 pgs.)
1-Manzar The White Indian, Long Bow & Orphan of the Storm begin 24.00 72.00 180.00
2-Starlight begins 12.00 36.00 90.00
3-5: 5-17-Most-c by Whitman 10.00 30.00 75.00
6-10 8.50 26.00 60.00
11-17 7.15 21.50 50.00

INDIANS OF THE WILD WEST
I. W. Enterprises: Circa 1958? (no date) (Reprints)
9-Kinstler-c; Whitman-a; r/Indians #? 1.75 5.25 14.00

INDIANS ON THE WARPATH
St. John Publishing Co.: No date (Late 40s, early 50s) (132 pgs.)
nn-Matt Baker-c; contains St. John comics rebound. Many combinations possible 27.00 80.00 200.00

INDIAN TRIBES (See Famous Indian Tribes)

INDIAN WARRIORS (Formerly White Rider and Super Horse; becomes Western Crime Cases #9)
Star Publications: No. 7, June, 1951 - No. 8, Sept, 1951
7-White Rider & Superhorse continue; "Last of the Mohicans" serial begins; L.B. Cole-c 15.00 44.00 110.00
8-L. B. Cole-c 13.00 40.00 100.00
3-D 1(12/53, 25¢)-Came w/glasses; L. B. Cole-c 39.00 116.00 290.00
Accepted Reprint(nn)(inside cover shows White Rider & Superhorse #11)-r/cover to #7; origin White Rider &...;. L. B. Cole-c 5.35 16.00 32.00
Accepted Reprint #8 (nd); L.B. Cole-c (r-cover to #8) 5.35 16.00 32.00

INDOORS-OUTDOORS (See Wisco)

INDOOR SPORTS
National Specials Co.: nd (6x9", 64 pgs., B&W-r, hard-c)
nn-By Tad 5.00 15.00 30.00

INDUSTRIAL GOTHIC
DC Comics (Vertigo): Dec, 1995 - No. 5, Apr, 1996 ($2.50, limited series)
1-5: Ted McKeever-c/a/scripts 2.50

INFERIOR FIVE, THE (Inferior 5 #11, 12) (See Showcase #62, 63, 65)
National Periodical Publications (#1-10: 12¢): 3-4/67 - No. 10, 9-10/68; No. 11, 8-9/72 - No. 12, 10-11/72
1-(3-4/67)-Sekowsky-a(p); 4th app. 3.850 7.50 22.00
3-12: 4-Thor app. 6-Stars DC staff. 10-Superman x-over; F.F., Spider-Man & Sub-Mariner app. 11,12-Orlando-c/a; both r/Showcase #62,63 2.00 6.00 16.00

INFERNO
Caliber Comics: 1995 - No. 5 ($2.95, B&W)
1-5 3.00

INFERNO (See Legion of Super-Heroes)
DC Comics: Oct, 1997 - No. 4, Feb, 1998 ($2.50, limited series)
1-4-Immonen-s/c/a 2.50

INFINITY CRUSADE
Marvel Comics: June, 1993 - No. 6, Nov, 1993 ($2.50, limited series, 52 pgs.)

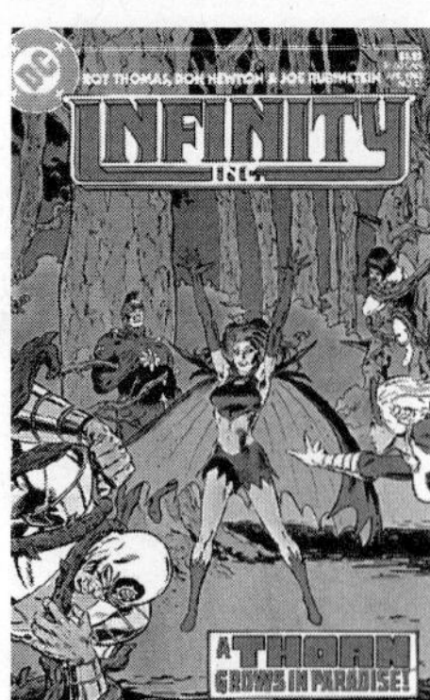

Infinity, Inc. #13 © DC

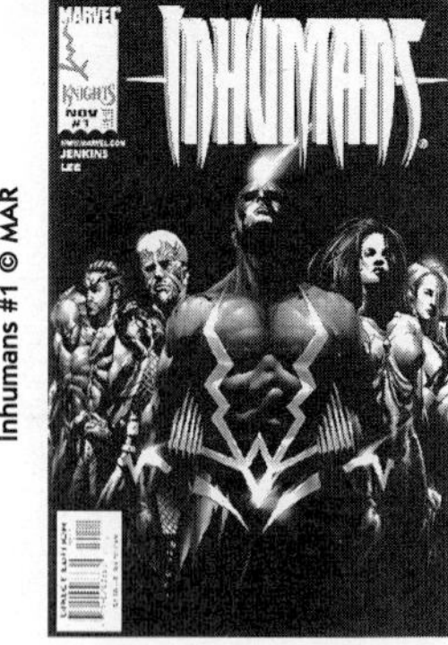

Inhumans #1 © MAR

Interface#4 © James D. Hudnall

GD25 FN65 NM94

1-6: By Jim Starlin & Ron Lim 2.50

INFINITY GAUNTLET (The... #2 on; see Infinity Crusade, The Infinity War & Warlock & the Infinity Watch)
Marvel Comics: July, 1991 - No. 6, Dec, 1991 ($2.50, limited series)

1-6:Thanos-c/stories in all; Starlin scripts in all; 5,6-Ron Lim-c/a 2.50
NOTE: ***Lim*** *a-3p(part), 5p, 6p; c-5i, 6i.* ***Perez*** *a-1-3p, 4p(part); c-1(painted), 2-4, 5i, 6i.*

INFINITY, INC. (See All-Star Squadron #25)
DC Comics: Mar, 1984 - No. 53, Aug, 1988 ($1.25, Baxter paper, 36 pgs.)

1-Brainwave, Jr., Fury, The Huntress, Jade, Northwind, Nuklon, Obsidian, Power Girl, Silver Scarab & Star Spangled Kid begin 1.50
2-5: 2-Dr. Midnite, G.A. Flash, W. Woman, Dr. Fate, Hourman, Green Lantern, Wildcat app. 5-Nudity panels 1.20
6-13,38-49,51-53: 46,47-Millennium tie-ins 1.20
14-Todd McFarlane-a (5/85, 2nd full story) .90 2.70 8.00
15-37-McFarlane-a (20,23,24: 5 pgs. only; 33: 2 pgs.); 18-24-Crisis x-over. 21-Intro new Hourman & Dr. Midnight. 26-New Wildcat app. 31-Star Spangled Kid becomes Skyman. 32-Green Fury becomes Green Flame. 33-Origin Obsidian. 35-1st modern app. G.A. Fury 3.00
50 ($2.50, 52 pgs.) 2.50
Annual 1,2: 1(12/85)-Crisis x-over. 2('88, $2.00) 2.00
Special 1 (1987, $1.50) 1.50
NOTE: ***Kubert*** *r-4.* ***McFarlane*** *a-14-37p, Annual 1p; c(p)-14-19, 22, 25, 26, 31-33, 37, Annual 1.* ***Newton*** *a-12p, 13p(last work 4/85).* ***Tuska*** *a-11p. JSA app. 3-10.*

INFINITY WAR, THE (Also see Infinity Gauntlet & Warlock and the Infinity...)
Marvel Comics: June, 1992 - No. 6, Nov, 1992 ($2.50, mini-series)

1-Starlin scripts, Lim-c/a(p), Thanos app. in all 2.50
2-6: All have wraparound gatefold covers 2.50

INFORMER, THE
Feature Television Productions: April, 1954 - No. 5, Dec, 1954

1-Sekowsky-a begins 9.30 28.00 65.00
2 6.00 18.00 42.00
3-5 5.70 17.00 38.00

IN HIS STEPS
Spire Christian Comics (Fleming H. Revell Co.): 1973, 1977 (39/49¢)

nn 5.00

INHUMANOIDS, THE (TV)
Marvel Comics (Star Comics): Jan, 1987 - No. 4, July 1987

1-4: Based on Hasbro toys 2.00

INHUMANS, THE (See Amazing Adventures, Fantastic Four #54 & Special #5, Incredible Hulk Special #1, Marvel Graphic Novel & Thor #146)
Marvel Comics Group: Oct, 1975 - No. 12, Aug, 1977

1: #1-4,6 are 25¢ issues .90 2.70 8.00
2-12: 9-Reprints Amazing Adventures #1,2('70). 12-Hulk app. 4.00
Special 1(4/90, $1.50, 52 pgs.)-F.F. cameo 2.00
NOTE: ***Buckler*** *c-2-4p, 5.* ***Gil Kane*** *a-5-7p; c-1p, 7p, 8p.* ***Kirby*** *a-9r.* ***Mooney*** *a-11i.* ***Perez*** *a-1-4p, 8p.*

INHUMANS (Marvel Knights)
Marvel Comics: Nov, 1998 - No. 12, ($2.99, limited series)

1-Jae Lee-c/a; Paul Jenkins-s 3.00
1-($6.95) DF Edition; Jae Lee variant-c 7.00
2,3: 2-Two covers by Lee and Darrow 3.00

INHUMANS: THE GREAT REFUGE
Marvel Comics: May, 1995 ($2.95, one-shot)

1 3.00

INKY & DINKY (See Felix's Nephews...)

IN LOVE (...Magazine on-c; I Love You No. 7 on)
Mainline/Charlton No. 5 (5/55)-on: Aug-Sept, 1954 - No. 6, July, 1955 ('Adult Reading' on-c)

GD25 FN65 NM94

1-Simon & Kirby-a; book-length novel in all issues 29.00 88.00 220.00
2-S&K-a 17.00 52.00 130.00
3,4-S&K-a. 3-Last pre-code (12-1/54-55) 14.00 42.00 105.00
5-S&K-c only 7.50 22.50 52.00
6-No S&K-a 4.25 13.00 26.00

IN LOVE WITH JESUS
Catechetical Educational Society: 1952 (Giveaway, 36 pgs.)

nn 4.00 10.00 20.00

INNOVATION SPECTACULAR
Innovation Publishing: 1991 - No. 2, 1991 ($2.95, squarebound, 100 pgs.)

1,2: Contains rebound comics w/o covers 3.00

INNOVATION SUMMER FUN SPECIAL
Innovation Publishing: 1991 ($3.50, B&W/color, squarebound)

1-Contains rebound comics (Power Factory) 3.50

INSANE
Dark Horse Comics: Feb, 1988 - No. 2? ($1.75, B&W)

1,2: 1-X-Men, Godzilla parodies. 2-Concrete 1.80

IN SEARCH OF THE CASTAWAYS (See Movie Comics)

INSIDE CRIME (Formerly My Intimate Affair)
Fox Features Syndicate (Hero Books): No. 3, July, 1950 - No. 2, Sept, 1950

3-Wood-a (10 pgs.); L. B. Cole-c 24.00 72.00 180.00
2-Used in **SOTI**, pg. 182,183; r/Spook #24 19.00 56.00 140.00
nn(no publ. listed, nd) 7.50 22.50 52.00

INSPECTOR, THE (TV) (Also see The Pink Panther)
Gold Key: July, 1974 - No. 19, Feb, 1978

1 2.00 6.00 20.00
2-5 1.20 3.60 12.00
6-9 .90 2.70 9.00
10-19: 11-Reprints 2.00 6.00

INSPECTOR GILL OF THE FISH POLICE (See Fish Police)

INSPECTOR WADE
David McKay Publications: No. 13, May, 1938

Feature Books 13 18.50 56.00 185.00

INSTANT PIANO
Dark Horse Comics: Aug, 1994 - No. 4, Feb, 1995 ($3.95, B&W, bimonthly, mature)

1-4 4.00

INTERFACE
Marvel Comics (Epic Comics): Dec, 1989 - No. 8, Dec, 1990 ($1.95, mature, coated paper)

1-5: Continued from 1st ESPers series; painted-c/a 2.00
6-8: 6-Begin $2.25-c .90 2.30
Espers: Interface TPB ('98, $16.95) r/#1-6 16.95

INTERNATIONAL COMICS (...Crime Patrol No. 6)
E. C. Comics: Spring, 1947 - No. 5, Nov-Dec, 1947

1-Schaffenberger-a begins, ends #4 44.00 142.00 440.00
2 32.00 96.00 310.00
3-5 28.00 84.00 260.00

INTERNATIONAL CRIME PATROL (Formerly International Comics #1-5; becomes Crime Patrol No. 7 on)
E. C. Comics: No. 6, Spring, 1948

6-Moon Girl app. 46.00 138.00 450.00

INTERSTATE THEATRES' FUN CLUB COMICS
Interstate Theatres: Mid 1940's (10¢ on cover) (B&W cover) (Premium)

Cover features MLJ characters looking at a copy of Top-Notch Comics, but contains an early Detective Comic on inside; many combinations possible 5.70 17.00 36.00

Intimate Confessions #8 © REAL

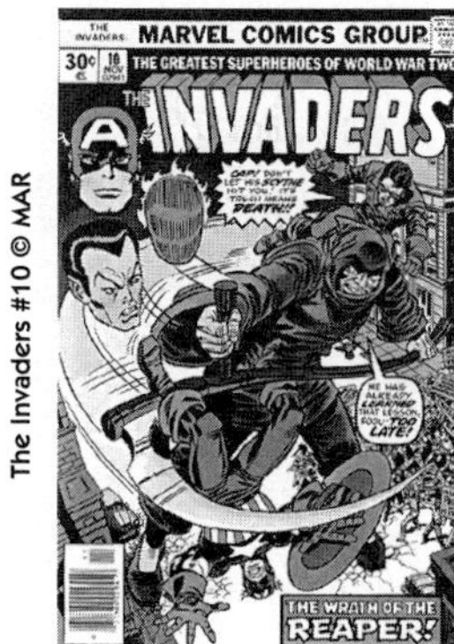

The Invaders #10 © MAR

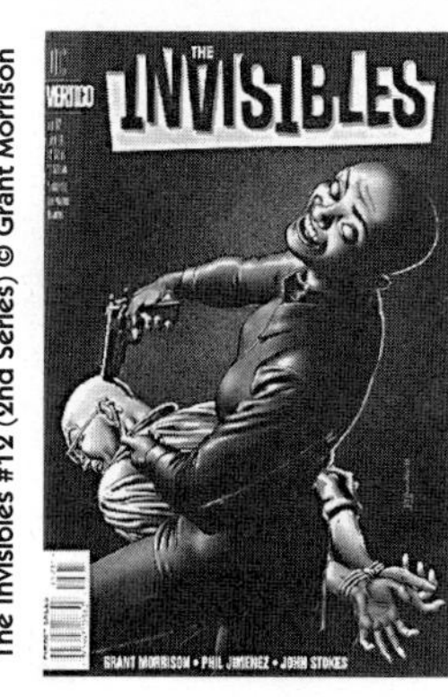

The Invisibles #12 (2nd Series) © Grant Morrison

GD25 FN65 NM94

IN THE DAYS OF THE MOB (Magazine)
Hampshire Dist. Ltd. (National): Fall, 1971 (B&W)

1-Kirby-a; John Dillinger wanted poster inside 7.00 21.00 70.00

IN THE PRESENCE OF MINE ENEMIES
Spire Christian Comics/Fleming H. Revell Co.: 1973 (35/49¢)

nn 1.00

INTIMATE
Charlton Comics: Dec, 1957 - No. 3, May, 1958

1-3 2.80 7.00 14.00

INTIMATE CONFESSIONS (See Fox Giants)

INTIMATE CONFESSIONS
Realistic Comics: July-Aug, 1951 - No. 7, Aug, 1952; No. 8, Mar, 1953 (All painted-c)

1-Kinstler-c/a; c/Avon paperback #222 64.00 192.00 540.00
2 16.00 48.00 120.00
3-c/Avon paperback #250; Kinstler-c/a 19.00 56.00 140.00
4-6,8: 4-c/Avon paperback #304; Kinstler-c. 6-c/Avon paperback #120. 8-c/Avon paperback #375; Kinstler-a 16.00 48.00 120.00
7-Spanking panel 16.00 48.00 120.00

INTIMATE CONFESSIONS
I. W. Enterprises/Super Comics: 1964

I.W. Reprint #9,10 1.50 4.50 12.00
Super Reprint #12,18 1.50 4.50 12.00

INTIMATE LOVE
Standard Comics: No. 5, 1950 - No. 28, Aug, 1954

5 5.70 17.00 40.00
6-8-Severin/Elder-a 5.70 17.00 40.00
9 4.00 11.00 22.00
10-Jane Russell, Robert Mitchum photo-c 6.50 19.50 45.00
11-18,20,23,25,27,28 3.00 7.50 15.00
19,21,22,24,26-Toth-a 5.35 16.00 32.00

NOTE: ***Celardo*** *a-8, 10.* ***Colletta*** *a-23.* ***Moreira*** *a-13(2). Photo-c-6, 7, 10, 12, 14, 15, 18-20, 24, 26, 27.*

INTIMATE SECRETS OF ROMANCE
Star Publications: Sept, 1953 - No. 2, Apr, 1954

1,2-L. B. Cole-c 14.00 42.00 105.00

INTRIGUE
Quality Comics Group: Jan, 1955

1-Horror; Jack Cole reprint/Web of Evil 25.00 76.00 190.00

INTRUDER
TSR, Inc.: 1990 - No. 10, 1991 ($2.95, 44 pgs.)

1-10 3.00

INVADERS, THE (TV)
Gold Key: Oct, 1967 - No. 4, Oct, 1968 (All have photo-c)

1-Spiegle-a in all 9.00 26.00 95.00
2-4 6.40 19.00 70.00

INVADERS, THE (Also see The Avengers #71 & Giant-Size Invaders)
Marvel Comics Group: August, 1975 - No. 40, May, 1979; No. 41, Sept, 1979

1-Captain America & Bucky, Human Torch & Toro, & Sub-Mariner begin; cont'd. from Giant Size Invaders #1; #1-7 are 25¢ issues 1.50 4.50 15.00
2-5,7-10: 2-1st app. Brain-Drain. 3-Battle issue; Cap vs. Namor vs. Torch; intro U-Man. 7-Intro Baron Blood & intro/1st app. Union Jack; Human Torch origin retold. 8-Union Jack-c/story. 9-Origin Baron Blood. 10-G.A. Capt. America-r/C.A #22 2.00 6.00
6-(Regular 25¢ edition)(7/76) Liberty Legion app 2.00 6.00
6-(30¢-c, limited distribution) 2.20 6.50 24.00
11-19: 11-Origin Spitfire; intro The Blue Bullet. 14-1st app. The Crusaders. 16-Re-intro The Destroyer. 17-Intro Warrior Woman. 18-Re-intro The Destroyer w/new origin. 19-Hitler-c/story 4.00
20-Reprints origin/1st app. Sub-Mariner from Motion Picture Funnies Weekly with color added & brief write-up about MPFW; 1st app. new Union Jack II .90 2.70 8.00
21-(Regular 30¢ edition)-r/Marvel Mystery #10 (battle issue) 4.00
21-(35¢-c, limited distribution) 1.60 4.80 16.00
22-30,34-40: 22-New origin Toro. 24-r/Marvel Mystery #17 (team-up issue; all-r). 25-All new-a begins. 28-Intro new Human Top & Golden Girl. 29-Intro Teutonic Knight. 34-Mighty Destroyer joins. 35-The Whizzer app. 3.00
31-Frankenstein-c/sty 2.00 6.00
32,33-Thor app. 5.00
41-Double size last issue 2.00 6.00
Annual 1 (9/77)-Schomburg, Rico stories (new); Schomburg-c/a (1st for Marvel in 30 years); Avengers app.; re-intro The Shark & The Hyena .90 2.70 8.00

NOTE: ***Buckler*** *a-5.* ***Everett*** *r-20('39), 21(1940), 24, Annual 1.* ***Gil Kane*** *c(p)-13, 17, 18, 20-27.* ***Kirby*** *c(p)-3-12, 14-16, 32, 33.* ***Mooney*** *a-5i, 16, 22.* ***Robbins*** *a-1-4, 6-9, 10(3 pg.), 11-15, 17-21, 23, 25-28; c-28.*

INVADERS (See Namor, the Sub-Mariner #12)
Marvel Comics Group: May, 1993 - No. 4, Aug, 1993 ($1.75, limited series)

1-4 1.75

INVADERS FROM HOME
DC Comics (Piranha Press): 1990 - No. 6, 1990 ($2.50, mature)

1-6 2.50

INVASION
DC Comics: Holiday, 1988-'89 - No. 3, Jan, 1989 ($2.95, lim. series, 84 pgs.)

1-3:1-McFarlane/Russell-a. 2-McFarlane/Russell & Giffen/Gordon-a 3.00

INVINCIBLE FOUR OF KUNG FU & NINJA
Leung Publications: April, 1988 - No. 6, 1989 ($2.00)

1-($2.75) 2.75
2-6: 2-Begin $2.00-c 2.00

INVISIBLE BOY (See Approved Comics)

INVISIBLE MAN, THE (See Superior Stories #1 & Supernatural Thrillers #2)

INVISIBLES, THE (1st Series)
DC Comics (Vertigo): Sept, 1994 - No. 25, Oct, 1996 ($1.95/$2.50, mature)

1-($2.95, 52 pgs.)-Intro King Mob, Ragged Robin, Boy, Lord Fanny & Dane (Jack Frost); Grant Morrison scripts in all 3.50
2-8: 4-Includes bound-in trading cards. 5-1st app. Orlando; brown paper-c 2.00
9-25: 9-Begin $2.50-c. 10-Intro Jim Crow. 13-15-Origin Lord Fanny. 19-Origin King Mob; polybagged. 20-Origin Boy. 21-Mister Six revealed. 25-Intro Division X 2.50
Say You Want A Revolution (1996, $17.50, TPB)-r/#1-8 17.50

NOTE: ***Buckingham*** *a-25p.* ***Rian Hughes*** *c-1, 5.* ***Phil Jimenez*** *a-17p-19p.* ***Paul Johnson*** *a-16, 21.* ***Sean Phillips*** *c-2-4, 6-25.* ***Weston*** *a-10p.* ***Yeowell*** *a-1p-4p, 22p-24p.*

INVISIBLES, THE (2nd Series)
DC Comics (Vertigo): V2#1, Feb, 1997 - No. 22, Feb, 1999 ($2.50, mature)

1-Intro Jolly Roger; Grant Morrison scripts, Phil Jimenez-a, & Brian Bolland-c begins 4.00
2-22: 9,14-Weston-a 2.50
Bloody Hell in America TPB ('98, $12.95) r/#1-4 13.00

INVISIBLE SCARLET O'NEIL (Also see Famous Funnies #81 & Harvey Comics Hits #59)
Famous Funnies (Harvey): Dec, 1950 - No. 3, Apr, 1951
(2-3 pgs. of Powell-a in each issue.)

1 11.00 34.00 85.00
2,3 9.30 28.00 65.00

Iron Fist (3rd Series) #1 © MAR

Iron Man #61 © MAR

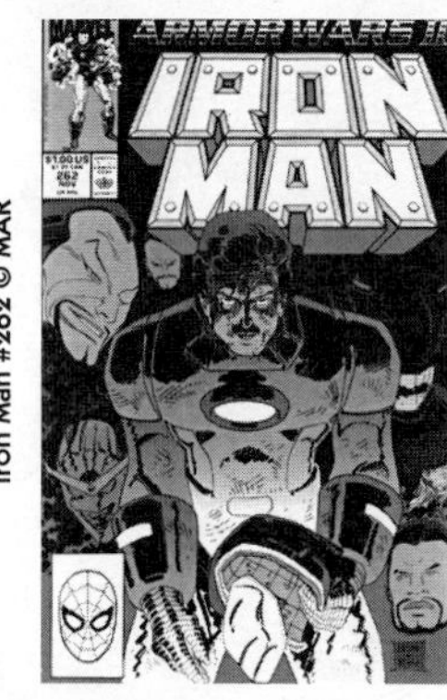

Iron Man #262 © MAR

IRON CORPORAL, THE (See Army War Heroes #22)
Charlton Comics: No. 23, Oct, 1985 - No. 25, Feb, 1986

23-25: Glanzman-a(r) 1.00

IRON FIST (See Deadly Hands of Kung Fu, Marvel Premiere & Power Man)
Marvel Comics: Nov, 1975 - No. 15, Sept, 1977

	GD25	FN65	NM94
1-Iron Fist battles Iron Man (#1-6: 25¢)	2.50	7.60	28.00
2	1.80	5.40	18.00
3-10: 8-Origin retold	1.20	3.60	12.00
4,5-(Regular 25¢ edition)(4,6/76)	1.20	3.60	12.00
4,5-(30¢-c, limited distribution)	4.40	13.00	48.00
11-13: 12-Capt. America app.	.90	2.70	8.00
14-1st app. Sabretooth (8/77)(see Power Man)	8.00	24.00	90.00
15-(Regular 30¢ ed.) X-Men app., Byrne-a	3.20	9.50	35.00
15-(35¢-c, limited distribution)	9.00	27.00	100.00

NOTE: *Adkins a-8p, 10i, 13i; c-8i. Byrne a-1-15p; c-8p, 15p. G. Kane c-4-6p. McWilliams a-1i.*

IRON FIST
Marvel Comics: Sept, 1996 - No. 2, Oct, 1996 ($1.50, limited series)

1,2 3.00

IRON FIST
Marvel Comics: Jul, 1998 - No. 3, Sept, 1998 ($2.50, limited series)

1-3: Jurgens-s/Guice-a 2.50

IRONHAND OF ALMURIC (Robert E. Howard's...)
Dark Horse Comics: Aug, 1991 - No. 4, 1991 ($2.00, B&W, mini-series)

1-4: 1-Conrad painted-c 2.00

IRON HORSE (TV)
Dell Publishing Co.: March, 1967 - No. 2, June, 1967

1,2-Dale Robertson photo covers 1.75 5.25 14.00

IRONJAW (Also see The Barbarians)
Atlas/Seaboard Publ.: Jan, 1975 - No. 4, July, 1975

1-1st app. Iron Jaw; Neal Adams-c; Sekowsky-a(p) 4.00
2-4: 2-Neal Adams-c. 4-Origin 3.00

IRON LANTERN
Marvel Comics (Amalgam): June, 1997 ($1.95, one-shot)

1-Kurt Busiek-s/Paul Smith & Al Williamson-a 2.00

IRON MAN (Also see The Avengers #1, Giant-Size..., Marvel Collectors Item Classics, Marvel Double Feature, Marvel Fanfare & Tales of Suspense #39)
Marvel Comics: May, 1968 - No. 332, Sept, 1996

	GD25	FN65	NM94
1-Origin; Colan-c/a(p); story continued from Iron Man & Sub-Mariner #1	27.00	81.00	325.00
2	11.00	33.00	110.00
3	6.00	18.00	60.00
4,5	5.00	15.00	50.00
6-10: 9-Iron Man battles green Hulk-like android	4.00	12.00	40.00
11-15: 15-Last 12¢ issue	2.50	7.50	24.00
16-20	1.80	5.40	18.00
21-24,26-42: 22-Death of Janice Cord. 27-Intro Fire Brand. 33-1st app. Spymaster. 35-Nick Fury & Daredevil x-over. 42-Last 15¢ issue	1.30	3.90	13.00
25-Iron Man battles Sub-Mariner	1.50	4.50	15.00
43-Intro The Guardsman; 25¢ giant	1.30	3.90	13.00
44-46,48-50: 43-Giant-Man back-up by Ayers. 44-Ant-Man by Tuska. 46-The Guardsman dies. 50-Princess Python app.	1.00	3.00	10.00
47-Origin retold; Barry Smith-a(p)	1.30	3.90	13.00
51-53: 53-Starlin part pencils	.85	2.60	7.00
54-Iron Man battles Sub-Mariner; 1st app. Moondragon (1/73) as Madame MacEvil; Everett part-c	1.50	4.50	15.00
55-1st app. Thanos (cameo), Drax the Destroyer, Mentor, Starfox & Kronos (2/73); Starlin-c/a	7.00	21.00	75.00
56-Starlin-a	1.50	4.50	15.00
57-67,69,70: 59-Firebrand returns. 65-Origin Dr. Spectrum. 66-Iron Man vs. Thor. 67-Last 20¢ issue		2.00	6.00
68-Sunfire & Unicorn app.; origin retold; Starlin-c	.85	2.60	7.00
71-99: 72-Cameo portraits of N. Adams, 73-Rename Stark Industries to Stark International; Brunner. 76-r/#9. 86-1st app. Blizzard. 87-Origin Blizzard. 88-Thanos app. 89-Daredevil app.; last 25¢ issue. 96-1st app. new Guardsman			4.00
100-(7/77)-Starlin-c	1.00	3.00	10.00
101-117: 101-Intro DreadKnight. 109-1st app. new Crimson Dynamo; 1st app. Vanguard. 110-Origin Jack of Hearts retold; death of Count Nefaria. 114-Avengers app.			4.00
118-Byrne-a(p); 1st app. Jim Rhodes		2.00	6.00
119,120,123-128-Tony Stark treated for alcohol problem. 120,121-Sub-Mariner x-over. 125-Ant-Man app.			3.50
121,122,129-149: 122-Origin. 131,132-Hulk x-over			3.00
150-Double size			4.00
151-168: 152-New armor. 161-Moon Knight app. 167-Tony Stark alcohol problem starts again			2.50
169-New Iron Man (Jim Rhodes replaces Tony Stark)			4.50
170			3.00
171			2.50
172-199: 172-Captain America x-over. 186-Intro Vibro. 190-Scarlet Witch app. 191-198-Tony Stark returns as original Iron Man. 192-Both Iron Men battle			2.00
200-(11/85, $1.25, 52 pgs.)-Tony Stark returns as new Iron Man (red & white armor) thru #230			3.00
201-224: 213-Intro new Dominic Fortune. 214-Spider-Woman apps. in new black costume (1/87)			2.00
225-Double size ($1.25)			3.00
226-243,245-249: 228-vs. Capt. America. 231-Intro new Iron Man. 233-Ant-Man app. 234-Spider-Man x-over. 243-Tony Stark loses use of legs. 247-Hulk x-over			2.00
244-($1.50, 52 pgs.)-New Armor makes him walk			3.00
250-($1.50, 52 pgs.)-Dr. Doom-c/story			2.00
251-274,276-281,283,285-287,289,291-299: 258-277-Byrne scripts. 271-Fin Fang Foom app. 276-Black Widow-c/story; last $1.00-c. 281-1st app. ;War Machine (cameo). 283-2nd full app. War Machine			2.00
275-($1.50, 52 pgs.)			2.00
282-1st full app. War Machine (7/92)			5.00
284-Death of Iron Man (Tony Stark)			3.00
288-($2.50, 52pg.)-Silver foil stamped-c; Iron Man's 350th app. in comics			2.50
290-($2.95, 52pg.)-Gold foil stamped-c; 30th ann.			3.00
300-($3.95, 68 pgs.)-Collector's Edition w/embossed foil-c; anniversary issue; War Machine-c/story			4.00
300-($2.50, 68 pgs.)-Newsstand Edition			2.50
301-303: 302-Venom-c/story (cameo #301)			1.50
304-316,318-324,326-332: 304-Begin $1.50-c; bound-in trading card sheet; Thunderstrike-c/story. 310-Orange logo. 312-w/bound-in Power Ranger Card. 319-Prologue to "The Crossing." 326-New Tony Stark; Pratt-c. 330-War Machine & Stockpile app; return of Morgan Stark. 332-Onsalught x-over			1.50
310 ($2.95)-Polybagged w/ 16 pg. Marvel Action Hour preview & acetate print; white logo.			3.00
317 ($2.50)-Flip book			2.50
325-($2.95)-Wraparound-c			3.00
Special 1(8/70)-Sub-Mariner x-over; Everett-c	2.00	6.00	20.00
Special 2(11/71)-r/TOS #81,82,91 (all-r)	.90	2.70	9.00
Annual 3(1976)-Man-Thing app.			4.00
King Size 4(8/77)-The Champions (w/Ghost Rider) app.; Newton-a(i)			3.00
Annual 5-9: 5(1982)-New-a. 6(1983)-New Iron Man (J. Rhodes) app. 7(1984). 8(1986)-X-Factor app. 9(1987)			2.25

Annual 10(1989, $2.00, 68 pgs.)-Atlantis Attacks x-over; P. Smith-a; Layton/

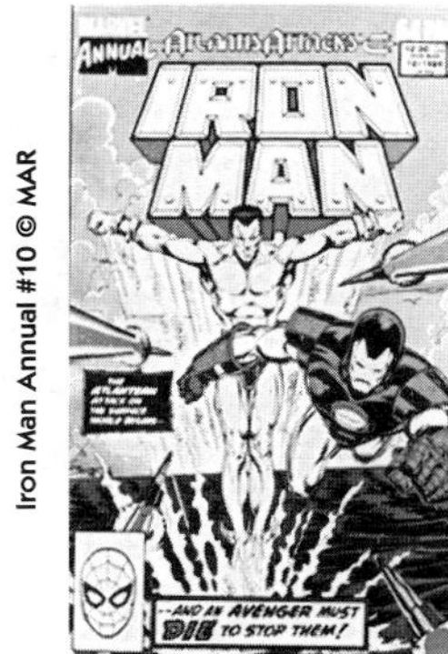

Iron Man Annual #10 © MAR

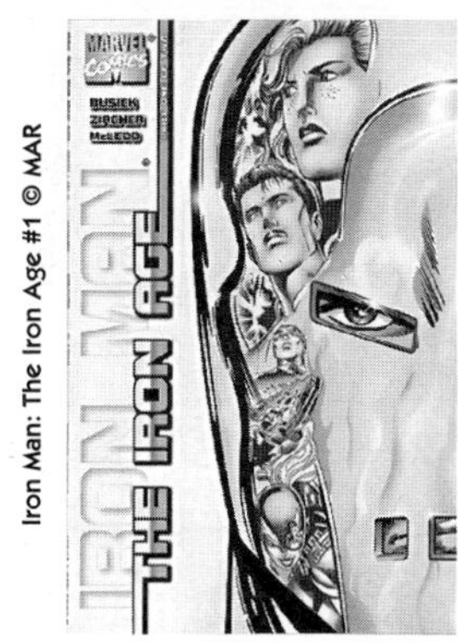

Iron Man: The Iron Age #1 © MAR

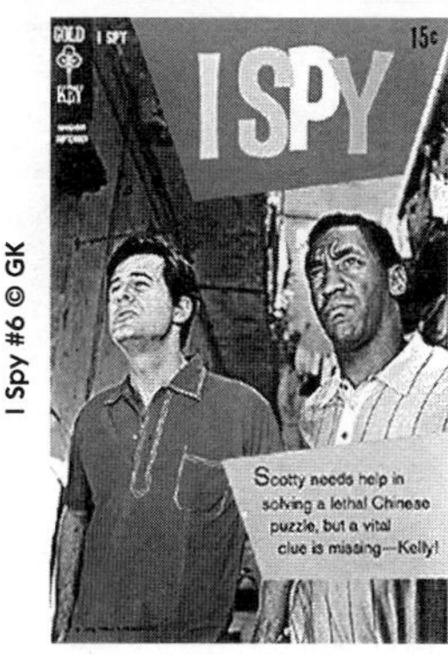

I Spy #6 © GK

GD25 FN65 NM94

Guice-a; Sub-Mariner app. 2.50
Annual 11,12 ($2.00, 68 pgs.): 11-(1990)-Origin of Mrs. Arbogast by Ditko (p&i). 12-(1991)-1 pg. origin recap; Ant-Man back-up story 2.00
Annual 13 (1992, $2.25, 68 pgs.)-Darkhawk & Avengers West Coast app.; Colan/Williamson-a 2.25
Annual 14 (1993, $2.95, 68 pgs.)-Bagged w/card 3.00
Annual 15 (1994, $2.95, 68 pgs.) 3.00
Manual 1 (1993, $1.75)-Operations handbook 1.75
Graphic Novel: Crash (1988, $12.95, Adults, 72 pgs)-Computer generated art & color; violence & nudity 1.30 3.90 13.00
...Collector's Preview 1(11/94, $1.95)-wraparound-c; text & illos-no comics. 2.00
...Vs. Dr. Doom (12/94, $12.95)-r/#149-150, 249,250. J-Bell-c 1.30 3.90 13.00

NOTE: **Austin** *c-105i, 109-111i, 151i.* **Byrne** *a-118p; c-109p, 197, 253.* **Colan** *a-1p, 253, Special 1p(3); c-1p.* **Craig** *a-1i, 2-4, 5-13i, 14, 15-19i, 24p, 25p, 26-28i; c-2-4.* **Ditko** *a-160p.* **Everett** *c-29.* **Guice** *a-233-241p.* **G. Kane** *c(p)-52-54, 63, 67, 72-75, 77-79, 88, 98.* **Kirby** *a-Special 1p; c-13, 80p, 90, 92-95.* **Mooney** *a-40i, 43i, 47i.* **Perez** *c-103p.* **Simonson** *c-Annual 8.* **B. Smith** *a-232p, 243i; c-232.* **P. Smith** *a-159p, 245p, Annual 10p; c-159.* **Starlin** *a-53p(part), 55p, 56p; c-55p, 160, 163.* **Tuska** *a-5-13p, 15-23p, 24i, 32p, 38-46p, 48-54p, 57-61p, 63-69p, 70-72p, 78p, 86-92p, 95-106p, Annual 4p.* **Wood** *a-Special 1i.*

IRON MAN (The Invincible...) (Volume Two)
Marvel Comics: Nov, 1996 - No. 13, Nov, 1997 ($2.95/$1.95/$1.99) (Produced by WildStorm Productions)

V2#1-Heroes Reborn begins; Scott Lobdell scripts & Whilce Portacio-c/a begin; new origin Iron Man & Hulk 3.00
1-Variant-c 4.00
2,3: 2-Hulk app. 3-Fantastic Four app. 3.00
4-10-($1.95): 4-Two covers. 6-Fantastic Four app.; Industrial Revolution; Hulk app. 7-Return of Rebel. 2.00
11-($1.99) Dr. Doom-c/app. 2.00
12-($2.99) "Heroes Reunited"-pt. 3; Hulk-c/app. 3.00
13-($1.99) "World War 3"-pt. 3, x-over w/Image 2.00

IRON MAN (The Invincible...) (Volume Three)
Marvel Comics: Feb, 1998 - Present ($2.99/$1.99)

V3#1-($2.99)-Follows Heroes Return; Busiek scripts & Chen-c/a begin; Deathsquad app. 3.00
1-Alternate Ed. .85 2.60 7.00
2-12-($1.99): 2-Two covers. 6-Black Widow-c/app. 7-Warbird-c/app. 8-Black Widow app. 9-Mandarin returns 2.00
13-($2.99) battles the Controller 2.99

IRON MAN & SUB-MARINER
Marvel Comics Group: Apr, 1968 (12¢, one-shot) (Pre-dates Iron Man #1 & Sub-Mariner #1)

1-Iron Man story by Colan/Craig continued from Tales of Suspense #99 & continued in Iron Man #1; Sub-Mariner story by Colan continued from Tales to Astonish #101 & continued in Sub-Mariner #1; Colan/Everett-c 10.00 30.00 100.00

IRON MAN: THE IRON AGE
Marvel Comics: Aug, 1998 - No. 2, Sept, 1998 ($5.99, limited series)

1,2-Busiek-s; flashback story from gold armor days 2.00 6.00

IRON MAN: THE LEGEND
Marvel Comics: Sept, 1996 ($3.95, one-shot)

1-Tribute issue 4.50

IRON MAN 2020 (Also see Machine Man limited series)
Marvel Comics: June, 1994 ($5.95, one-shot)

nn 2.00 6.00

IRON MAN/X-O MANOWAR: HEAVY METAL (See X-O Manowar/Iron Man: In Heavy Metal)
Marvel Comics: Sept, 1996 ($2.50, one-shot) (1st Marvel/Valiant x-over)

1-Pt. II of Iron Man/X-O Manowar x-over; Fabian Nicieza scripts; 1st app. Rand Banion 2.50

IRON MARSHALL
Jademan Comics: July, 1990 - No. 32, Feb, 1993 ($1.75, plastic coated-c)

1-32: Kung Fu stories. 1-Poster centerfold 1.80

IRON VIC (See Comics Revue No. 3 & Giant Comics Editions)
United Features Syndicate/St. John Publ. Co.: 1940; Aug, 1947 - No. 3, 1947

Single Series 22 29.00 88.00 220.00
2,3(St. John) 7.15 21.50 50.00

IRONWOLF
DC Comics: 1986 ($2.00, one shot)

1-r/Weird Worlds 8-10; Chaykin story & art 2.00

IRONWOLF: FIRES OF THE REVOLUTION (See Weird Worlds #8-10)
DC Comics: 1992 ($29.95, hardcover)

nn-Chaykin/Moore story, Mignola-a w/Russell inks. 2.70 8.00 30.00

ISAAC ASIMOV'S I-BOTS
Tekno Comix: Dec, 1995 - No. 7, May, 1996 ($1.95)

1-7: 1-6-Perez-c/a. 2-Chaykin variant-c exists. 3-Polybagged. 7-Lady Justice-c/app. 2.00

ISAAC ASIMOV'S I-BOTS
BIG Entertainment: V2#1, June, 1996 - Present ($2.25)

V2#1-9: 1-Lady Justice-c/app. 6-Gil Kane-c 2.25

ISIS (TV) (Also see Shazam)
National Per.l Publ./DC Comics: Oct-Nov, 1976 - No. 8, Dec-Jan, 1977-78

1-Wood inks .90 2.70 8.00
2-8: 5-Isis new look. 7-Origin 4.00

ISLAND AT THE TOP OF THE WORLD (See Walt Disney Showcase #27)

ISLAND OF DR. MOREAU, THE (Movie)
Marvel Comics Group: Oct, 1977 (52 pgs.)

1-Gil Kane-c 3.00

I SPY (TV)
Gold Key: Aug, 1966 - No. 6, Sept, 1968 (All have photo-c)

1-Bill Cosby, Robert Culp photo covers 22.00 66.00 240.00
2-6: 3,4-McWilliams-a 13.00 39.00 140.00

IS THIS TOMORROW?
Catechetical Guild: 1947 (One Shot) (3 editions) (52 pgs.)

1-Theme of communists taking over the USA; (no price on cover) Used in **POP**, pg. 102 13.00 38.00 95.00
1-(10¢ on cover) 17.00 52.00 130.00
1-Has blank circle with no price on cover 19.00 56.00 140.00
Black & White advance copy titled "Confidential" (52 pgs.)-Contains script and art edited out of the color edition, including one page of extreme violence showing mob nailing a Cardinal to a door; (only two known copies) 39.00 117.00 300.00

NOTE: *The original color version first sold for 10 cents. Since sales were good, it was later printed as a giveaway. Approximately four million in total were printed. The two black and white copies listed plus two other versions as well as a full color untrimmed version surfaced in 1979 from the Guild's old files in St. Paul, Minnesota.*

IT! (See Astonishing Tales No. 21-24 & Supernatural Thrillers No. 1)

ITCHY & SCRATCHY COMICS (Simpson's TV show)
Bongo Comics: 1993 - No. 3, 1993 ($1.95)

1-($2.25)-Bound-in jumbo poster 2.50
2 2.00
3-($2.25)-w/decoder screen trading card 2.25
Holiday Special ('94, $1.95) 2.00

IT REALLY HAPPENED
William H. Wise No. 1,2/Standard (Visual Editions): 1944 - No. 11, Oct, 1947

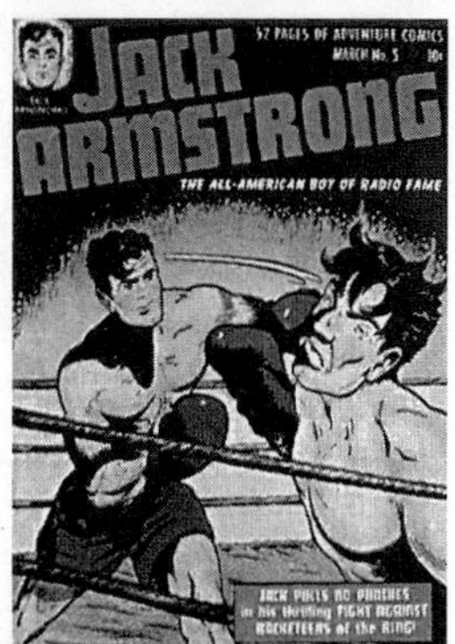

Jack Armstrong #5 © PMI

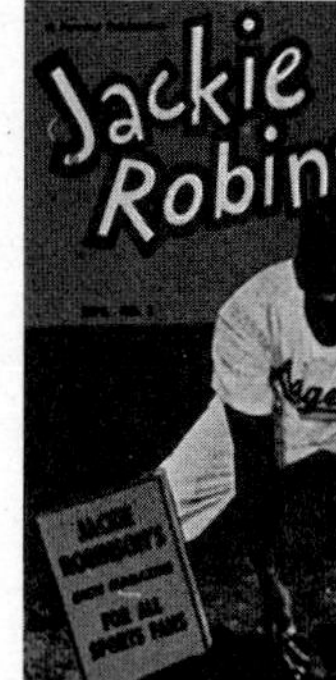

Jackie Robinson #3 © FAW

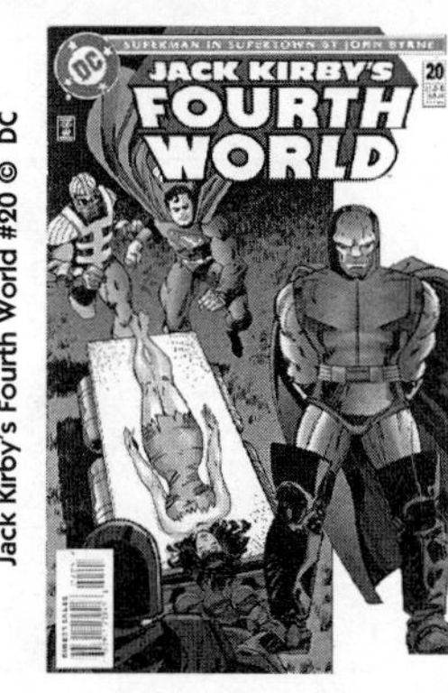

Jack Kirby's Fourth World #20 © DC

	GD25	FN65	NM94
1-Kit Carson & Ben Franklin stories	16.00	48.00	120.00
2	9.30	28.00	65.00
3,4,6,9,11: 6-Joan of Arc story. 9-Captain Kidd & Frank Buck stories	7.15	21.50	50.00
5-Lou Gehrig & Lewis Carroll stories	12.00	36.00	90.00
7-Teddy Roosevelt story	7.15	21.50	50.00
8-Story of Roy Rogers	14.00	42.00	105.00
10-Honus Wagner & Mark Twain stories	10.00	30.00	75.00

NOTE: ***Guardineer** a-7(2), 8(2), 11. **Schomburg** c-1-7, 9-11.*

IT RHYMES WITH LUST (Also see Bold Stories & Candid Tales)
St. John Publishing Co.: 1950 (Digest size, 128 pgs.)

	GD25	FN65	NM94
nn (Rare)-Matt Baker & Ray Osrin-a	47.00	141.00	400.00

IT'S ABOUT TIME (TV)
Gold Key: Jan, 1967

	GD25	FN65	NM94
1 (10195-701)-Photo-c	3.00	9.00	35.00

IT'S A DUCK'S LIFE
Marvel Comics/Atlas(MMC): Feb, 1950 - No. 11, Feb, 1952

	GD25	FN65	NM94
1-Buck Duck, Super Rabbit begin	12.00	36.00	90.00
2	6.00	18.00	42.00
3-11	5.35	16.00	32.00

IT'S FUN TO STAY ALIVE
National Automobile Dealers Association: 1948 (Giveaway, 16 pgs., heavy stock paper)

	GD25	FN65	NM94
Featuring: Bugs Bunny, The Berrys, Dixie Dugan, Elmer, Henry, Tim Tyler, Bruce Gentry, Abbie & Slats, Joe Jinks, The Toodles, & Cokey; all art copyright 1946-48 drawn especially for this book.	16.00	48.00	120.00

IT'S GAMETIME
National Periodical Publications: Sept-Oct, 1955 - No. 4, Mar-Apr, 1956

	GD25	FN65	NM94
1-(Scarce)-Infinity-c; Davy Crockett app. in puzzle	65.00	195.00	550.00
2,3 (Scarce): 2-Dodo & The Frog	50.00	150.00	425.00
4 (Rare)	53.00	159.00	450.00

IT'S LOVE, LOVE, LOVE
St. John Publishing Co.: Nov, 1957 - No. 2, Jan, 1958 (10¢)

	GD25	FN65	NM94
1,2	4.15	12.50	25.00

IVANHOE (See Fawcett Movie Comics No. 20)

IVANHOE
Dell Publishing Co.: July-Sept, 1963

	GD25	FN65	NM94
1 (12-373-309)	2.25	6.75	25.00

IWO JIMA (See Spectacular Features Magazine)

JACE PEARSON OF THE TEXAS RANGERS (Radio/TV)(4-Color #396 is titled Tales of the Texas Rangers; ...'s Tales of ... #11-on)(See Western Roundup under Dell Giants)
Dell Publishing Co.: No. 396, 5/52 - No. 1021, 8-10/59 (No #10) (All-Photo-c)

	GD25	FN65	NM94
Four Color 396 (#1)	10.00	30.00	110.00
2(5-7/53) - 9(2-4/55)	5.50	16.50	60.00
Four Color 648(#10, 9/55)	4.50	13.50	50.00
11(11-2/55-56) - 14,17-20(6-8/58)	4.00	12.00	45.00
15,16-Toth-a	4.50	13.50	50.00
Four Color 961, 1021: 961--Spiegle-a	4.00	12.00	45.00

NOTE: *Joel McCrea photo c-1-9, F.C. 648 (starred on radio show only); Willard Parker photo c-11-on (starred on TV series).*

JACK & JILL VISIT TOYTOWN WITH ELMER THE ELF
Butler Brothers (Toytown Stores): 1949 (Giveaway, 16 pgs., paper cover)

	GD25	FN65	NM94
nn	3.60	9.00	18.00

JACK ARMSTRONG (Radio)(See True Comics)
Parents' Institute: Nov, 1947 - No. 9, Sept, 1948; No. 10, Mar, 1949 - No. 13, Sept, 1949

	GD25	FN65	NM94
1-(Scarce) (odd size)	40.00	120.00	320.00
2	17.00	52.00	130.00
3-5	13.00	38.00	95.00
6-13: 7-Vic Hardy's Crime Lab begins?	10.00	30.00	75.00
12-Premium version(distr. in Chicago only); Free printed on upper right-c; no price (Rare)	17.00	50.00	125.00

JACK HUNTER
Blackthorne Publishing: July, 1987 - No. 3 ($1.25)

	GD25	FN65	NM94
1-3			1.25

JACKIE CHAN'S SPARTAN X
Topps Comics: May, 1997 - No. 3 ($2.95, limited series)

	GD25	FN65	NM94
1-3-Michael Golden-s/a; variant photo-c			3.00

JACKIE CHAN'S SPARTAN X: HELL BENT HERO FOR HIRE
Image Comics (Little Eva Ink): Mar, 1998 - Present ($2.95, B&W)

	GD25	FN65	NM94
1-3-Michael Golden-s/a: 1-variant photo-c			2.95

JACKIE GLEASON (TV) (Also see The Honeymooners)
St. John Publishing Co.: 1948 - No. 2, 1948; Sept, 1955 - No. 4, Dec, 1955?

	GD25	FN65	NM94
1(1948)	65.00	195.00	550.00
2(1948)	49.00	147.00	420.00
1(1955)(TV)-Photo-c	53.00	159.00	450.00
2-4	39.00	117.00	300.00

JACKIE GLEASON AND THE HONEYMOONERS (TV)
National Periodical Publications: June-July, 1956 - No. 12, Apr-May, 1958

	GD25	FN65	NM94
1-1st app. Ralph Kramden	77.00	231.00	650.00
2	49.00	147.00	420.00
3-11	40.00	120.00	315.00
12 (Scarce)	54.00	162.00	460.00

JACKIE JOKERS (Became Richie Rich &...)
Harvey Publications: March, 1973 - No. 4, Sept, 1973 (#5 was advertised, but not published)

	GD25	FN65	NM94
1-1st app.	1.80	5.40	18.00
2-4: 2-President Nixon app.	.90	2.70	8.00

JACKIE ROBINSON (Famous Plays of...) (Also see Negro Heroes #2 & Picture News #4)
Fawcett Publications: May, 1950 - No. 6, 1952 (Baseball hero) (All photo-c)

	GD25	FN65	NM94
nn	77.00	231.00	650.00
2	48.00	144.00	410.00
3-6	41.00	122.00	325.00

JACK IN THE BOX (Formerly Yellowjacket Comics #1-10; becomes Cowboy Western Comics #17 on)
Frank Comunale/Charlton Comics No. 11 on: Feb, 1946; No. 11, Oct, 1946 - No. 16, Nov-Dec, 1947

	GD25	FN65	NM94
1-Stitches, Marty Mouse & Nutsy McKrow	11.00	34.00	85.00
11-Yellowjacket (early Charlton comic)	15.00	44.00	110.00
12,14,15	5.70	17.00	40.00
13-Wolverton-a	18.00	54.00	135.00
16-12 pg. adapt. of Silas Marner; Kiefer-a	9.30	28.00	65.00

JACK KIRBY'S FOURTH WORLD (See New Gods, 3rd Series)
DC Comics: Mar, 1997 - No. 20, Oct, 1998 ($1.95/$2.25)

	GD25	FN65	NM94
1-18: 1-Byrne-a/scripts & Simonson-c begin; story cont'd from New Gods, 3rd Series #15; retells "The Pact" (New Gods, 1st Series #7); 1st DC app. Thor (cameo). 2-Thor vs. Big Barda; "Apokolips Then" back-up begins; Kirby-c/swipe (Thor #126) 8-Genesis x-over. 10-Simonson-s/a 13-Simonson back-up story			2.00
19,20-($2.25). 20-Superman-c/app.			2.25

JACK KIRBY'S SECRET CITY SAGA
Topps Comics (Kirbyverse): No. 0, Apr, 1993; No. 1, May, 1993 - No. 4, Aug, 1993 ($2.95, limited series)

The Jaguar #1 © AP

Jaguar God #3 © Verotik

Jane Arden #1 © UFS

GD25 FN65 NM94

0-(No cover price, 20 pgs.)-Simonson-c/a 2.00
1-4-Bagged w/3 trading cards; Ditko-c/a: 1-Ditko/Art Adams-c. 2-Ditko/Byrne-c; has coupon for Pres. Clinton holo-foil trading card. 3-Dorman poster; has coupon for Gore holo-foil trading card. 4-Ditko/Perez-c 3.00
NOTE: *Issues #1-4 contain coupons redeemable for Kirbychrome version of #1*

JACK KIRBY'S SILVER STAR (Also see Silver Star)
Topps Comics (Kirbyverse): Oct, 1993 ($2.95)(Intended as a 4-issue limited series)
1-Silver ink-c; Austin-c/a(i); polybagged w/3 cards 3.00

JACK KIRBY'S TEENAGENTS (See Satan's Six)
Topps Comics (Kirbyverse): Aug, 1993 - No. 3, Oct, 1993 ($2.95)(Intended as a 4-issue limited series)
1-3: Polybagged with/3 trading cards; 1-3-Austin-c(i): 3-Liberty Project app. 3.00

JACK OF HEARTS (Also see The Deadly Hands of Kung Fu #22 & Marvel Premiere #44)
Marvel Comics Group: Jan, 1984 - No. 4, Apr, 1984 (60¢, limited series)
1-4 1.00

JACKPOT COMICS (Jolly Jingles #10 on)
MLJ Magazines: Spring, 1941 - No. 9, Spring, 1943
1-The Black Hood, Mr. Justice, Steel Sterling & Sgt. Boyle begin; Biro-c 259.00 777.00 2200.00
2-S. Cooper-c 115.00 318.00 975.00
3-Hubbell-c 85.00 255.00 725.00
4-Archie begins (Win/41; on sale 12/41)-(also see Pep Comics #22); 1st app. Mrs. Grundy, the principal; Novick-c 280.00 840.00 2800.00
5-Hitler-c by Montana; 1st definitive Mr. Weatherbee; 1st app. Reggie in 1 panel cameo 124.00 372.00 1050.00
6-9: 6,7-Bondage-c by Novick. 8,9-Sahle-c 91.00 273.00 775.00

JACKPOT OF FUN COMIC BOOK
DCA Food Ind.: 1957, giveaway
nn-Features Howdy Doody 6.50 19.50 45.00

JACK Q FROST (See Unearthly Spectaculars)

JACK THE GIANT KILLER (See Movie Classics)

JACK THE GIANT KILLER (New Adventures of...)
Bimfort & Co.: Aug-Sept, 1953
V1#1-H. C. Kiefer-c/a 19.00 56.00 140.00

JACKY'S DIARY
Dell Publishing Co.: No. 1091, Apr-June, 1960 (one-shot)
Four Color 1091 3.60 11.00 40.00

JADEMAN COLLECTION
Jademan Comics: Dec, 1989 - No. 3, 1990 ($2.50, plastic coated-c, 68 pgs.)
1-3: 1-Wraparound-c w/fold-out poster 2.50

JADEMAN KUNG FU SPECIAL
Jademan Comics: 1988 ($1.50, 64 pgs.)
1 1.50

JAGUAR, THE (Also see The Adventures of...)
Impact Comics (DC): Aug, 1991 - No. 14, Oct, 1992 ($1.00)
1-14: 4-The Black Hood x-over. 7-Sienkiewicz-c. 9-Contains Crusaders trading card 1.00
Annual 1 (1992, $2.50, 68 pgs.)-With trading card 2.50

JAGUAR GOD
Verotik: Mar, 1995 - Present ($2.95, mature)
0 (2/96, $3.50)-Embossed Frazetta-c; Bisley-a; w/pin-ups. 3.50
1-Frazetta-c. 2.00 6.00
2-Frazetta-c 5.00
3-6: 3-Bisley-c. 4-Emond-c 4.00
7-($2.95)-Frazetta-c 2.95

JAKE THRASH
Aircel Publishing: 1988 - No. 3, 1988 ($2.00)
1-3 2.00

JAM, THE (...Urban Adventure)
Slave Labor Nos. 1-5/Dark Horse Comics Nos. 6-8/Caliber Comics No. 9 on: Nov, 1989 - Present ($1.95/$2.50/$2.95, B&W)
1-5-Bernie Mireault-c/a/scripts 2.00
6-7: 6-1st Dark Horse issue; begin $2.50-c. 2.50
8-13: 8-Begin $2.95-c. 9-1st Caliber issue 3.00

JAMBOREE
Round Publishing Co.: Feb, 1946(no mo. given) - No. 3, Apr, 1946
1-Funny animal 20.00 60.00 150.00
2,3 12.00 36.00 90.00

JAMES BOND 007: A SILENT ARMAGEDDON
Dark Horse Comics/Acme Press: Mar, 1993 - Apr 1993 (limited series)
1,2 3.50

JAMES BOND 007: GOLDENEYE (Movie)
Topps Comics: Jan, 1996 ($2.95, unfinished limited series of 3)
1-Movie adaptation; Stelfreeze-c 3.00

JAMES BOND 007: SERPENT'S TOOTH
Dark Horse Comics/Acme Press: July 1992 - Aug 1992 ($4.95, limited series)
1-3-Paul Gulacy-c/a 5.00

JAMES BOND 007: SHATTERED HELIX
Dark Horse Comics: Jun 1994 - July 1994 ($2.50, limited series)
1,2 3.00

JAMES BOND 007: THE QUASIMODO GAMBIT
Dark Horse Comics: Jan 1995 - May 1995 ($3.95, limited series)
1-3 4.50

JAMES BOND FOR YOUR EYES ONLY
Marvel Comics Group: Oct, 1981 - No. 2, Nov, 1981
1,2-Movie adapt.; r/Marvel Super Special #19 1.50

JAMES BOND JR. (TV)
Marvel Comics: Jan, 1992 - No. 12, Dec, 1992 (#1: $1.00, #2-on: $1.25)
1-12: Based on animated TV show 1.25

JAMES BOND: LICENCE TO KILL (See Licence To Kill)

JAMES BOND: PERMISSION TO DIE
Eclipse Comics/ACME Press: 1989 - No. 3, 1991 ($3.95, limited series, squarebound, 52 pgs.)
1-3: Mike Grell-c/a/scripts in all. 3-($4.95) 5.00

JAM, THE: SUPER COOL COLOR INJECTED TURBO ADVENTURE #1 FROM HELL!
Comico: May, 1988 ($2.50, 44 pgs., one-shot)
1 2.50

JANE ARDEN (See Feature Funnies & Pageant of Comics)
St. John (United Features Syndicate): Mar, 1948 - No. 2, June, 1948
1-Newspaper reprints 15.00 45.00 105.00
2 11.00 33.00 75.00

JANN OF THE JUNGLE (Jungle Tales No. 1-7)
Atlas Comics (CSI): No. 8, Nov, 1955 - No. 17, June, 1957
8(#1) 26.00 78.00 195.00
9,11-15 14.00 42.00 105.00
10-Williamson/Colletta-c 15.00 44.00 110.00
16,17-Williamson/Mayo-a(3), 5 pgs. each 16.00 48.00 120.00
NOTE: ***Everett** c-15-17. **Heck** a-8, 15, 17. **Maneely** c-11. **Shores** a-8.*

Jay & Silent Bob #3 © View Askew Prod.

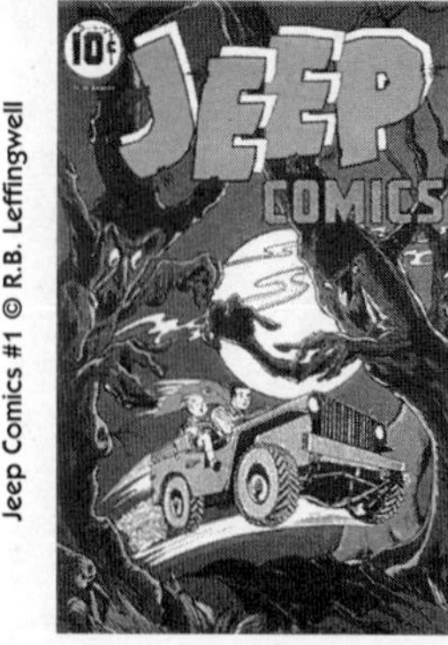

Jeep Comics #1 © R.B. Leffingwell

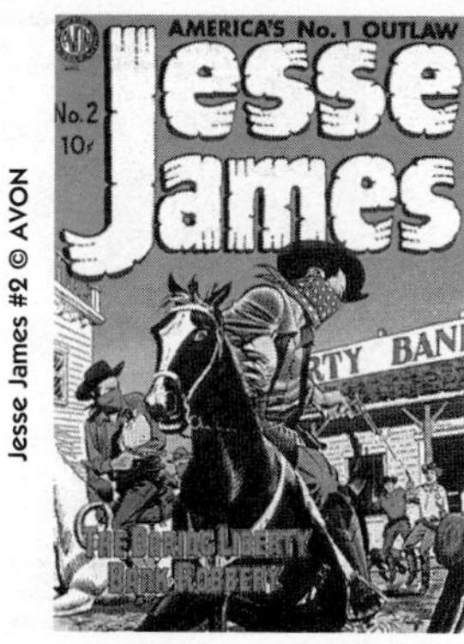

Jesse James #2 © AVON

	GD25	FN65	NM94

JAR OF FOOLS
Penny Dreadful Press: 1994 ($5.95, B&W)

1-Jason Lutes-c/a/scripts		2.00	6.00

JAR OF FOOLS
Black Eye Productions: 1994 - No. 2, 1994 ($6.95, B&W)

1,2: 1-Reprints of earlier ed. Jason Lutes-c/a/scripts	.85	2.60	7.00

JASON & THE ARGONAUTS (See Movie Classics)

JASON GOES TO HELL: THE FINAL FRIDAY (Movie)
Topps Comics: July, 1993 - No. 3, Sept, 1993 ($2.95, limited series)

1-3: Adaptation of film. 1-Glow-in-the-dark-c			3.00

JASON'S QUEST (See Showcase #88-90)

JASON VS. LEATHERFACE
Topps Comics: Oct, 1995 - No. 3, Jan, 1996 ($2.95, limited series)

1-3: Collins scripts; Bisley-c			3.00

JAWS 2 (See Marvel Comics Super Special, A)

JAY & SILENT BOB (See Clerks & Oni Double Feature)
Oni Press: July, 1998 - No. 4 ($2.95, B&W, limited series)

1-Kevin Smith-s/Fegredo-a; photo-c			6.00
1-Quesada & Palmiotti-c			6.00
1-2nd & 3rd printings			3.00
2,3: 3-Flip-c by Jaime Hernandez			3.00

JAZZ (Also see Double Impact)
High Impact Studios: Mar, 1996 - No. 3, June, 1996 ($3.00, B&W, bi-monthly, limited series)

1-3			3.00
1-Gold foil logo (1000 print run)	2.00	6.00	20.00
2-($9.95)-Deluxe Edition; photo-c	1.00	3.00	10.00
3-Variant-c (1000 print run)	1.00	3.00	10.00

JCP FEATURES
J.C. Productions (Archie): Feb, 1982-c; Dec, 1981-indicia ($2.00, one-shot, B&W)

1-T.H.U.N.D.E.R. Agents; Black Hood by Morrow & Neal Adams; 2 pgs. S&K-a from Fly #1		2.00	6.00

JEANIE COMICS (Formerly All Surprise; Cowgirl Romances #28)
Marvel Comics/Atlas(CPC): No. 13, April, 1947 - No. 27, Oct, 1949

13-Mitzi, Willie begin	13.00	40.00	100.00
14,15	10.00	30.00	75.00
16-Used in Love and Death by Legman; Kurtzman's "Hey Look"	13.00	39.00	95.00
17-19,22-Kurtzman's "Hey Look", (1-3 pgs. each)	10.00	30.00	65.00
20,21,23-27	7.15	21.50	50.00

JEEP COMICS (Also see G.I. Comics and Overseas Comics)
R. B. Leffingwell & Co.: Winter, 1944 - No. 3, Mar-Apr, 1948

1-Capt. Power, Criss Cross & Jeep & Peep (costumed) begin	39.00	116.00	290.00
2	25.00	74.00	185.00
3-L. B. Cole dinosaur-c	37.00	112.00	280.00
1-46(Giveaways)-Strip reprints in all; Tarzan, Flash Gordon, Blondie, The Nebbs, Little Iodine, Red Ryder, Don Winslow, The Phantom, Johnny Hazard, Katzenjammer Kids; distr. to U.S. Armed Forces from 1945-1946	4.00	10.00	20.00

JEFF JORDAN, U.S. AGENT
D. S. Publishing Co.: Dec, 1947 - Jan, 1948

1	11.00	32.00	80.00

JEMM, SON OF SATURN
DC Comics: Sept, 1984 - No. 12, Aug, 1985 (Maxi-series, mando paper)

1-12: 3-Origin			1.00

NOTE: ***Colan** a-1-12p; c-1-5, 7-12p.*

JERRY DRUMMER (Formerly Soldier & Marine V2#9)
Charlton Comics: V2#10, Apr, 1957 - V3#12, Oct, 1957

V2#10, V3#11,12: 11-Whitman-c/a	4.25	13.00	28.00

JERRY IGER'S... (All titles, Blackthorne/First)(Value: cover or less)

JERRY LEWIS (See The Adventures of...)

JESSE JAMES (The True Story Of..., also seeThe Legend of...)
Dell Publishing Co.: No. 757, Dec, 1956 (one shot)

Four Color 757-Movie, photo-c	9.00	27.00	100.00

JESSE JAMES (See Badmen of the West & Blazing Sixguns)
Avon Periodicals: 8/50 - No. 9, 11/52; No. 15, 10/53 - No. 29, 8-9/56

1-Kubert Alabam-r/Cowpuncher #1	15.00	44.00	110.00
2-Kubert-a(3)	12.00	36.00	90.00
3-Kubert Alabam-r/Cowpuncher #2	11.00	32.00	80.00
4,9-No Kubert	5.35	16.00	32.00
5,6-Kubert Jesse James-a(3); 5-Wood-a(1pg.)	11.00	32.00	80.00
7-Kubert Jesse James-a(2)	9.30	28.00	65.00
8-Kinstler-a(3)	6.00	18.00	42.00
15-Kinstler-r/#3	4.25	13.00	28.00
16-Kinstler-r/#3 & story-r/Butch Cassidy #1	5.00	15.00	30.00
17-19,21: 17-Jesse James-r/#4; Kinstler-c idea from Kubert splash in #6. 18-Kubert Jesse James-r/#5. 19-Kubert Jesse James-r/#6. 21-Two Jesse James-r/#4, Kinstler-r/#4	4.00	12.00	24.00
20-Williamson/Frazetta-a; r/Chief Vic. Apache Massacre; Kubert Jesse James-r/#6; Kit West story by Larsen	11.00	34.00	85.00
22,23-No Kubert	4.00	12.00	24.00
24-New McCarty strip by Kinstler; Kinstler-r	4.00	11.00	22.00
25-New McCarty Jesse James strip by Kinstler; Jesse James-r/#7,9	4.00	11.00	22.00
26,27-New McCarty Jesse James strip plus a Kinstler/McCann Jesse James-r	4.00	11.00	22.00
28,29: 28-Reprints most of Red Mountain, Featuring Quantrells Raiders	4.00	11.00	22.00
Annual nn (1952; 25¢, 100 pgs.)- "...Brings Six-Gun Justice to the West"- 3 earlier issues rebound; Kubert, Kinstler-a(3)	25.00	74.00	185.00

NOTE: *Mostly reprints #10 on. **Fawcette** c-1, 2. **Kida** a-5. **Kinstler** a-3, 4, 7-9, 15r, 16r(2), 21-27; c-3, 4, 9, 17-27. Painted c-5-8. 22 has 2 stories r/Sheriff Bob Dixon's Chuck Wagon #1 with name changed to Sheriff Bob Trent.*

JESSE JAMES
Realistic Publications: July, 1953

nn-Reprints Avon's #1; same-c, colors different	8.50	26.00	60.00

JEST (Formerly Snap; becomes Kayo #12)
Harry 'A' Chesler: No. 10, 1944; No. 11, 1944

10-Johnny Rebel & Yankee Boy app. in text	13.00	38.00	95.00
11-Little Nemo in Adventure Land	13.00	38.00	95.00

JESTER
Harry 'A' Chesler: No. 10, 1945

10	11.00	32.00	80.00

JESUS
Spire Christian Comics (Fleming H. Revell Co.): 1979 (49¢)

nn			5.00

JET (See Jet Powers)

JET ACES
Fiction House Magazines: 1952 - No. 4, 1953

1	11.00	32.00	80.00
2-4	7.15	21.50	50.00

JET DREAM (...and Her Stunt-Girl Counterspies)(See The Man from Uncle #7)

The Jetsons #36 © H-B

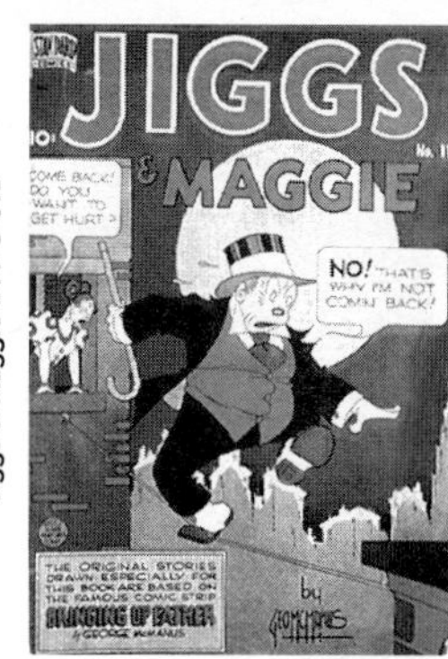

Jiggs & Maggie #11 © STD

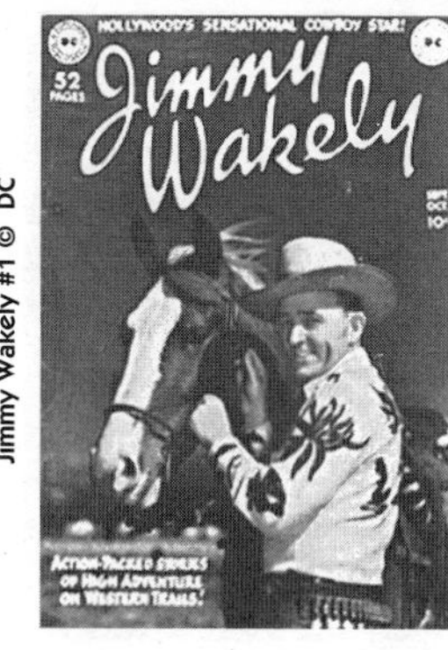

Jimmy Wakely #1 © DC

	GD25	FN65	NM94

Gold Key: June, 1968 (12¢)

1-Painted-c	2.70	8.00	30.00

JET FIGHTERS (Korean War)
Standard Magazines: No. 5, Nov, 1952 - No. 7, Mar, 1953

5,7-Toth-a. 5-Toth-c	10.00	30.00	75.00
6-Celardo-a	5.00	15.00	30.00

JET POWER
I.W. Enterprises: 1963

I.W. Reprint 1,2-r/Jet Powers #1,2	2.60	7.80	26.00

JET POWERS (American Air Forces No. 5 on)
Magazine Enterprises: 1950 - No. 4, 1951

1(A-1 #30)-Powell-c/a begins	29.00	86.00	215.00
2(A-1 #32)	21.00	62.00	155.00
3(A-1 #35)-Williamson/Evans-a	34.00	102.00	255.00
4(A-1 #38)-Williamson/Wood-a; "The Rain of Sleep" drug story	34.00	102.00	255.00

JET PUP (See 3-D Features)

JETSONS, THE (TV) (See March of Comics #276, 330, 348 & Spotlight #3)
Gold Key: Jan, 1963 - No. 36, Oct, 1970 (Hanna-Barbera)

1	21.00	62.00	225.00
2	10.50	31.50	115.00
3-10	8.20	24.60	90.00
11-20	5.40	16.20	60.00
21-36	4.50	13.50	50.00

JETSONS, THE (TV) (Also see Golden Comics Digest)
Charlton Comics: Nov, 1970 - No. 20, Dec, 1973 (Hanna-Barbera)

1	6.00	17.50	65.00
2	2.90	8.70	32.00
3-10	2.40	7.00	26.00
11-20	1.60	4.80	16.00

JETSONS, THE (TV)
Harvey Comics: V2#1, Sept, 1992 - No. 5, Nov, 1993 ($1.25/$1.50) (Hanna-Barbera)

V2#1-5			2.00
...Big Book V2#1,2,3 ($1.95, 52 pgs.): 1-(11/92). 2-(4/93). 3-(7/93)			3.00
...Giant Size 1,2,3 ($2.25, 68 pgs): 1-(10/92). 2-(4/93). 3-(10/93)			3.00

JETSONS, THE (TV)
Archie Comics: Sept, 1995 - No. 17, Aug, 1996 ($1.50)

1-17			1.50

JETTA OF THE 21ST CENTURY
Standard Comics: No. 5, Dec, 1952 - No. 7, Apr, 1953 (Teen-age Archie type)

5	20.00	60.00	150.00
6,7: 6-Robot-c	11.00	34.00	85.00

JEZEBEL JADE (Hanna-Barbara)
Comico: Oct, 1988 - No. 3, Dec, 1988 ($2.00, mini-series)

1-3: Johnny Quest spin-off			2.00

JIGGS & MAGGIE
Dell Publishing Co.: No. 18, 1941 (one shot)

Four Color 18 (#1)-(1936-38-r)	36.00	109.00	400.00

JIGGS & MAGGIE
Standard Comics/Harvey Publications No. 22 on: No. 11, 1949(June) - No. 21, 2/53; No. 22, 4/53 - No. 27, 2-3/54

11	9.30	28.00	70.00
12-15,17-21	5.70	17.00	35.00
16-Wood text illos.	6.50	19.50	45.00
22-25,27: 22-24-Little Dot app.	4.25	13.00	28.00
26-Four pgs. partially in 3-D	12.00	36.00	90.00

NOTE: *Sunday page reprints by McManus loosely blended into story continuity. Based on Bringing Up Father strip. Advertised on covers as "All New."*

JIGSAW (Big Hero Adventures)
Harvey Publ. (Funday Funnies): Sept, 1966 - No. 2, Dec, 1966 (36 pgs.)

1-Origin & 1st app.; Crandall-a (5 pgs.)	1.75	5.25	14.00
2-Man From S.R.A.M.	1.25	3.75	10.00

JIGSAW OF DOOM (See Complete Mystery No. 2)

JIM BOWIE (Formerly Danger; Black Jack No. 20 on)
Charlton Comics: No. 15, 1955? - No. 19, Apr, 1957

15	5.70	17.00	40.00
16-19	4.25	13.00	28.00

JIM BOWIE (TV, see Western Tales)
Dell Publishing Co.: No. 893, Mar, 1958 - No. 993, May-July, 1959

Four Color 893 (#1), 993-Photo-c	4.50	13.50	50.00

JIM DANDY
Dandy Magazine (Lev Gleason): May, 1956 - No. 3, Sept, 1956 (Charles Biro)

1-Biro-c	6.00	18.00	42.00
2,3	4.25	13.00	26.00

JIM HARDY (See Giant Comics Eds., Sparkler & Treasury of Comics #2 & 5)
United Features Syndicate/Spotlight Publ.: 1939; 1942; 1947 - No. 2, 1947

Single Series 6 ('39)	39.00	116.00	290.00
Single Series 27('42)	31.00	92.00	230.00
1('47)-Spotlight Publ.	11.00	34.00	85.00
2	7.15	21.50	50.00

JIM HARDY
Spotlight/United Features Synd.: 1944 (25¢, 132 pgs.) (Tip Top, Sparkler-r)

nn-Origin Mirror Man; Triple Terror app.	37.00	112.00	280.00

JIMINY CRICKET (Disney,, see Mickey Mouse Mag. V5#3 & Walt Disney Showcase #37)
Dell Publishing Co.: No. 701, May, 1956 - No. 989, May-July, 1959

Four Color 701	8.00	25.00	90.00
Four Color 795, 897, 989	5.50	16.50	60.00

JIMMY DURANTE (Also see A-1 Comics)
Magazine Enterprises: No. 18, 1949 - No. 20, 1949

A-1 18,20-Photo-c	39.00	117.00	300.00

JIMMY OLSEN (See Superman's Pal...)

JIMMY WAKELY (Cowboy movie star)
National Per. Publ.: Sept-Oct, 1949 - No. 18, July-Aug, 1952 (1-13: 52pgs.)

1-Photo-c, 52 pgs. begin; Alex Toth-a; Kit Colby Girl Sheriff begins	94.00	282.00	800.00
2-Toth-a	43.00	129.00	350.00
3,6,7-Frazetta-a in all, 3 pgs. each; Toth-a in all. 7-Last photo-c	43.00	129.00	360.00
4-Frazetta-a (3 pgs.); Kurtzman "Pot-Shot Pete", 1 pg; Toth-a	43.00	129.00	360.00
5,8-15,18-Toth-a; 12,14-Kubert-a (3 & 2 pgs.)	35.00	105.00	260.00
16,17	29.00	87.00	220.00

NOTE: ***Gil Kane** c-10-19p.*

JIM RAY'S AVIATION SKETCH BOOK
Vital Publishers: Mar-Apr, 1946 - No. 2, May-June, 1946

1,2-Picture stories about planes and pilots	23.00	68.00	170.00

JIM SOLAR (See Wisco/Klarer)

JINGLE BELLS (See March of Comics No. 65)

JINGLE BELLS CHRISTMAS BOOK
Montgomery Ward (Giveaway): 1971 (20 pgs., B&W inside, slick-c)

Jinx V2 #5 © Brian Michael Bendis

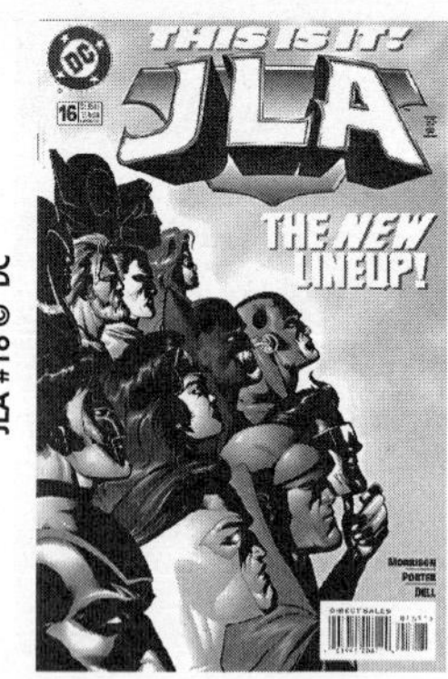

JLA #16 © DC

JLA: The Nail #3 © DC

GD25 FN65 NM94

nn 2.00

JINGLE DINGLE CHRISTMAS STOCKING COMICS (See Foodini #2)
Stanhall Publications: V2#1, 1951 (no date listed) (25¢, 100 pgs.; giant-size) (Publ. annually)

V2#1-Foodini & Pinhead, Silly Pilly plus games & puzzles 14.00 42.00 105.00

JINGLE JANGLE COMICS (Also see Puzzle Fun Comics)
Eastern Color Printing Co.: Feb, 1942 - No. 42, Dec, 1949

1-Pie-Face Prince of Old Pretzleburg, Jingle Jangle Tales by George Carlson, Hortense, & Benny Bear begin 39.00 117.00 300.00
2,3-No Pie-Face Prince 18.00 54.00 135.00
4-Pie-Face Prince cover 18.00 54.00 135.00
5 16.00 48.00 120.00
6-10: 8-No Pie-Face Prince 13.00 40.00 100.00
11-15 10.00 30.00 75.00
16-30: 17,18-No Pie-Face Prince. 30-XMas-c 8.50 26.00 60.00
31-42: 36,42-Xmas-c 7.15 21.50 50.00

NOTE: ***George Carlson*** *a-(2) in all except No. 2, 3, 8; c-1-6.* ***Carlson*** *1 pg. puzzles in 9, 10, 12-15, 18, 20.* ***Carlson*** *illustrated a series of Uncle Wiggily books in 1930's.*

JING PALS
Victory Publishing Corp.: Feb, 1946 - No. 4, Aug?, 1946 (Funny animal)

1-Wishing Willie, Puggy Panda & Johnny Rabbit begin 11.00 34.00 85.00
2-4 6.00 18.00 42.00

JINKS, PIXIE, AND DIXIE (See Kite Fun Book & Whitman Comic Books)

JINX
Caliber Press: 1996 - No. 7, 1996 ($2.95, B&W, 32 pgs.)

1-7: Brian Michael Bendis-c/a/scripts. 2-Photo-c 3.00

JINX (Volume 2)
Image Comics: 1997 - Present ($2.95, B&W, bi-monthly)

1-4: Brian Michael Bendis-c/a/scripts. 3.00
5-($3.95) Brereton-c 4.00
...Buried Treasures ('98, $3.95) short stories 4.00
...Confessions ('98, $3.95) short stories 4.00
TPB (1997, $10.95) r/Vol 1,#1-4 10.95

JINX: TORSO
Image Comics: 1998 - Present ($3.95, B&W)

1,2-Brian Michael Bendis & Marc Andreyko-s/Bendis-a 3.95

JLA (See Justice League of America)
DC Comics: Jan, 1997 - Present ($1.95/$1.99)

1-Morrison-s/Porter & Dell-a. The Hyperclan app. 1.80 5.40 18.00
2 2.00 6.00 20.00
3,4 1.50 4.50 15.00
5-Membership drive; Tomorrow Woman app. 1.00 3.00 10.00
6-9: 8-Green Arrow joins. .85 2.60 7.00
10-14: 10-Rock of Ages begins. 11-Joker and Luthor-c/app. 2.50
15-($2.95) Rock of Ages concludes 4.00
16-20: 16-New members join; Prometheus app. 17,20-Jorgensen-a. 18-21-Waid-s. 20,21-Adam Strange c/app. 2.00
22-25: 22-Begin $1.99-c; Sandman (Daniel) app. 1.99
#1,000,000 (11/98)853rd Century x-over 2.00
Annual 1 (1997, $3.95) Pulp Heroes; Augustyn-s/Olivetti & Ha-a 4.00
Annual 2 (1998, $2.95) Ghosts; Wrightson-c 2.95
...80-Page Giant 1 (7/98, $4.95) stories & art by various 5.00
Gallery (1997, $2.95) pin-ups by various; Quitely-c 3.00
...In Crisis Secret Files 1 (11/98, $4.95) recap of JLA in DC x-overs 5.00
American Dreams (1998, $7.95, TPB) r/#5-9 7.95
New World Order (1997, $5.95, TPB) r/#1-4 5.95
Rock of Ages (1998, $9.95, TPB) r/#10-15 9.95
Strength in Numbers (1998, $12.95, TPB) r/#16-23, Secret Files #2 and Prometheus #1 12.95

GD25 FN65 NM94

JLA PARADISE LOST
DC Comics: Jan, 1998 - No. 3, Mar, 1998 ($1.95, limited series)

1-3-Millar-s/Olivetti-a 2.00

JLA SECRET FILES
DC Comics: Sept, 1997 - Present ($4.95)

1-Standard Ed. w/origin-s & pin-ups 5.00
1-Collector's Ed. w/origin-s & pin-ups; cardstock-c 2.00 6.00
2-(8/98) origin-s of JLA #16's newer members 5.00

JLA: THE NAIL (Elseworlds)
DC Comics: Aug, 1998 - No. 3, Oct, 1998 ($4.95, prestige format)

1-3-JLA in a world without Superman; Alan Davis-s/a(p) 5.00
TPB ('98, $12.95) r/series w/new Davis-c 12.95

JLA / TITANS
DC Comics: Dec, 1998 - No. 3, Feb, 1999 ($2.95, limited series)

1-3-Grayson-s; P. Jimenez-c/a 3.00

JLA: TOMORROW WOMAN (Girlfrenzy)
DC Comics: June, 1998 ($1.95, one-shot)

1-Peyer-s; story takes place during JLA #5 2.50

JLA/ WILDC.A.T.S
DC Comics: 1997 ($5.95, one-shot, prestige format)

1-Morrison-s/Semeiks & Conrad-a 2.00 6.00

JLA/ WORLD WITHOUT GROWN-UPS (See Young Justice)
DC Comics: Aug, 1998 - No. 2, Sept, 1998 ($4.95, prestige format)

1,2-JLA, Robin, Impulse & Superboy app.; Ramos & McKone-a 5.00
TPB ('98, $9.95) r/series & Young Justice: The Secret #1 9.95

JLA: YEAR ONE
DC Comics: Jan, 1998 - No. 12, Dec, 1998 ($2.95/$1.95, limited series)

1-($2.95)-Waid & Augustyn-s/Kitson-a 3.00
2-8-($1.95): 5-Doom Patrol-c/app. 7-Superman app. 2.00
9-11 ($1.99) 2.00
12-($2.95) 3.00

JLX
DC Comics (Amalgam): Apr, 1996 ($1.95, one-shot)

1-Mark Waid scripts 2.00

JLX UNLEASHED
DC Comics (Amalgam): June, 1997 ($1.95, one-shot)

1-Priest-s/ Oscar Jimenez & Rodriquez/a 1.95

JOAN OF ARC (Also see A-1 Comics & Ideal a Classical Comic)
Magazine Enterprises: No. 21, 1949 (one shot)

A-1 21-Movie adaptation; Ingrid Bergman photo-covers & interior photos; Whitney-a 25.00 75.00 185.00

JOAN OF ARC
Catechetical Guild (Topix) (Giveaway): No date (28 pgs.)

nn 9.30 28.00 65.00

NOTE: *Unpublished version exists which came from the Guild's files.*

JOE COLLEGE
Hillman Periodicals: Fall, 1949 - No. 2, Wint, 1950 (Teen-age humor, 52 pgs.)

1,2: Powell-a; 1-Briefer-a 9.30 28.00 65.00

JOE JINKS
United Features Syndicate: No. 12, 1939

Single Series 12 26.00 78.00 195.00

JOE LOUIS (See Fight Comics #2, Picture News #6 & True Comics #5)
Fawcett Publications: Sept, 1950 - No. 2, Nov, 1950 (Photo-c) (Boxing champ) (See Dick Cole #10)

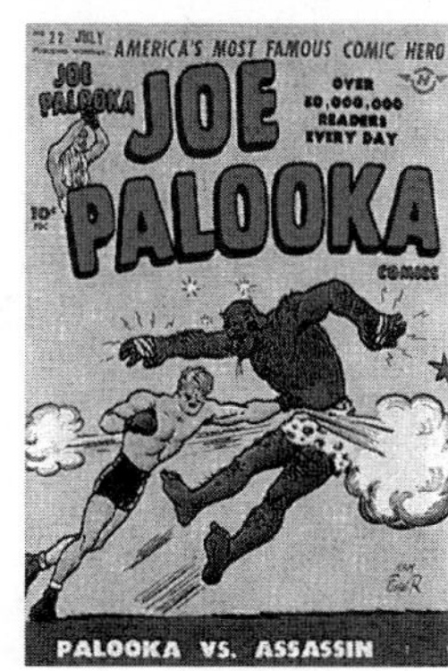

Joe Palooka #22 © CCG

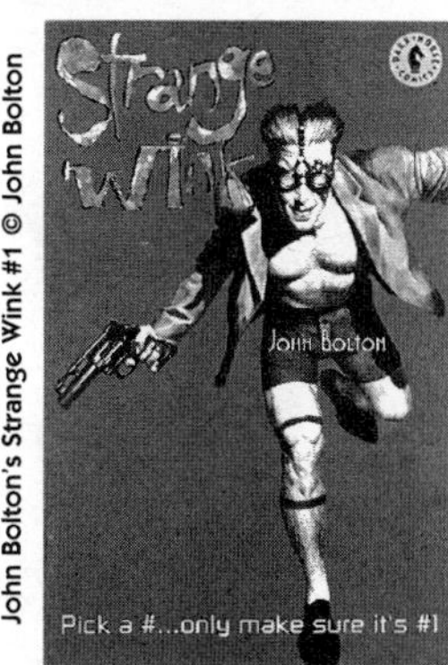

John Bolton's Strange Wink #1 © John Bolton

John Byrne's Next Men #29 © John Byrne

GD25 FN65 NM94

1-Photo-c; life story 49.00 147.00 420.00
2-Photo-c 36.00 108.00 270.00

JOE PALOOKA (1st Series)(Also see Big Shot Comics, Columbia Comics & Feature Funnies)
Columbia Comic Corp. (Publication Enterprises): 1942 - No. 4, 1944

1-1st to portray American president; gov't permission required
68.00 204.00 575.00
2 (1943)-Hitler-c 42.00 127.00 340.00
3,4: 3-Nazi Sub-c 29.00 88.00 220.00

JOE PALOOKA (2nd Series) (Battle Adv. #68-74; ...Advs. #75, 77-81, 83-85, 87; Champ of the Comics #76, 82, 86, 89-93) (See All-New)
Harvey Publications: Nov, 1945 - No. 118, Mar, 1961

1 42.00 126.00 335.00
2 20.00 60.00 150.00
3,4,6,7-1st Flyin' Fool, ends #25 12.00 36.00 90.00
5-Boy Explorers by S&K (7-8/46) 18.00 54.00 135.00
8-10 9.30 28.00 70.00
11-14,16-20: 19-Freedom Train-c 7.85 23.50 55.00
15-Origin & 1st app. Humphrey (12/47); Super heroine Atoma app. by Powell 12.00 36.00 90.00
21-26,28-30: 30-Nude female painting 5.70 17.00 40.00
27-1st app. Little Max? (12/48) 7.15 21.50 50.00
31-61: 35-Little Max-c/story. 36-Humphrey story. 39-Humphrey & Little Max begin (12/49). 41-Bing Crosby photo on-c. 44-Palooka marries Ann Howe. 50-(11/51)-Becomes Harvey Comics Hits #51 5.00 15.00 30.00
62-S&K Boy Explorers-r 5.70 17.00 38.00
63-80: 66,67-'Commie' torture story 4.15 12.50 25.00
81-99,101-115 4.00 11.00 22.00
100 4.35 13.00 26.00
116-S&K Boy Explorers-r (Giant, '60) 5.70 17.00 38.00
117,118-Giants 5.35 16.00 32.00
...Body Building Instruction Book (1958 B&M Sports Toy giveaway, 16pgs., 5-1/4x7")-Origin 8.50 26.00 60.00
...Fights His Way Back (1945 Giveaway, 24 pgs.) Family Comics
16.00 48.00 120.00
...in Hi There! (1949 Red Cross giveaway, 12 pgs., 4-3/4x6")
7.85 23.50 55.00
...in It's All in the Family (1945 Red Cross giveaway, 16 pgs., regular size)
9.30 28.00 70.00
...**Visits the Lost City** nn (1945)(One Shot)(50¢)-164 page continuous story strip reprint. Has biography & photo of Ham Fisher; possibly the single longest comic book story published (159 pgs.?) 130.00 390.00 1300.00

*NOTE: **Nostrand/Powell** a-73. **Powell** a-7, 8, 10, 12, 14, 17, 19, 26-45, 47-53, 70, 73 at least. Black Cat text stories #8, 12, 13, 19.*

JOE PSYCHO & MOO FROG
Goblin Studios: 1996 - Present ($2.50, B&W)

1-5: 4-Two covers 2.50
...Full Color Extravagarbonzo ($2.95, color) 2.95

JOE YANK (Korean War)
Standard Comics (Visual Editions): No. 5, Mar, 1952 - No. 16, 1954

5-Toth, Celardo, Tuska-a 5.70 17.00 40.00
6-Toth, Severin/Elder-a 7.15 21.50 50.00
7 4.15 12.50 25.00
8-Toth-c 5.70 17.00 38.00
9-16: 9-Andru-c. 12-Andru-a 4.00 11.00 24.00

JOHN BOLTON'S HALLS OF HORROR
Eclipse Comics: June, 1985 - No. 2, June, 1985 ($1.75, limited series)

1,2-British-r; Bolton-c/a 1.80

JOHN BOLTON'S STRANGE WINK
Dark Horse Comics: Mar, 1998 - No. 3, May, 1998 ($2.95, B&W, limited series)

1-3-Anthology; Bolton-s/c/a 3.00

GD25 FN65 NM94

JOHN BYRNE'S NEXT MEN (See Dark Horse Presents #54)
Dark Horse Comics (Legend imprint #19 on): Jan, 1992 - No. 30, Dec, 1994 ($2.50, mature)

1-Silver foil embossed-c; Byrne-c/a/scripts in all 5.00
1-4: 1-2nd printing with gold ink logo 3.00
0-(2/92)-r/chapters 1-4 from DHP w/new Byrne-c 2.00
5-20,22-30: 7-10-MA #1-4 mini-series on flip side. 16-Origin of Mark IV. 17-Miller-c. 19-22-Faith storyline. 23-26-Power storyline. 27-30-Lies storyline Pt. 1-4. 2.50
21-1st Hellboy 4.00
...Parallel, Book 2 ($16.95)-TPB; r/#7-12 17.00
...Fame, Book 3($16.95)-TPB r/#13-18 17.00
...Faith, Book 4($14.95)-TPB r/#19-22 15.00

*NOTE: Issues 1 through 6 contain certificates redeemable for an exclusive Next Men trading card set by Byrne. Prices are for complete books. **Cody** painted c-23-26. **Mignola** a-21(part); c-21.*

JOHN CARTER OF MARS (See The Funnies & Tarzan #207)
Dell Publishing Co.: No. 375, Mar-May, 1952 - No. 488, Aug-Oct, 1953 (Edgar Rice Burroughs)

Four Color 375 (#1)-Origin; Jesse Marsh-a 23.00 68.00 250.00
Four Color 437, 488-Painted-c 14.00 44.00 160.00

JOHN CARTER OF MARS
Gold Key: Apr, 1964 - No. 3, Oct, 1964

1(10104-404)-r/4-Color #375; Jesse Marsh-a 4.50 13.50 50.00
2(407), 3(410)-r/4-Color #437 & 488; Marsh-a 3.20 9.50 35.00

JOHN CARTER OF MARS
House of Greystroke: 1970 (10-1/2x16-1/2", 72 pgs., B&W, paper-c)

1941-42 Sunday strip-r; John Coleman Burroughs-a 2.00 6.00 20.00

JOHN CARTER, WARLORD OF MARS (Also see Weird Worlds)
Marvel Comics: June, 1977 - No. 28, Oct, 1979

1,18: 18-Frank Miller-a(p)(1st publ. Marvel work) 3.00
2-17,19-28: 1-Origin. 11-Origin Dejah Thoris 2.00
Annuals 1-3: 1(1977). 2(1978). 3(1979)-All 52 pgs. with new book-length stories 2.00

*NOTE: **Austin** c-24i. **Gil Kane** a-1-10p; c-1p, 2p, 3, 4-9p, 10, 15p, Annual 1p. **Layton** a-17i. **Miller** c-25, 26p. **Nebres** a-2-4i, 8-16i; c(i)-6-9, 11-22, 25, Annual 1. **Perez** c-24p. **Simonson** a-15p. **Sutton** a-7i.*

JOHN F. KENNEDY, CHAMPION OF FREEDOM
Worden & Childs: 1964 (no month) (25¢)

nn-Photo-c 5.00 15.00 50.00

JOHN F. KENNEDY LIFE STORY
Dell Publishing Co.: Aug-Oct, 1964; Nov, 1965; June, 1966 (12¢)

12-378-410-Photo-c 3.20 9.50 35.00
12-378-511 (reprint, 11/65) 2.00 6.00 22.00
12-378-606 (reprint, 6/66) 1.80 5.50 20.00

JOHN FORCE (See Magic Agent)

JOHN HIX SCRAP BOOK, THE
Eastern Color Printing Co. (McNaught Synd.): Late 1930's (no date) (10¢, 68 pgs., regular size)

1-Strange As It Seems (resembles Single Series books)
32.00 96.00 240.00
2-Strange As It Seems 23.00 70.00 175.00

JOHN JAKES' MULKON EMPIRE
Tekno Comix: Sept, 1995 - No. 6, Feb, 1996 ($1.95)

1-6 2.00

JOHN LAW DETECTIVE(See Smash Comics #3)
Eclipse Comics: April, 1983 ($1.50, Baxter paper)

1-Three Eisner stories originally drawn in 1948 for the never published John Law #1; original cover pencilled in 1948 & inked in 1982 by Eisner
2.00

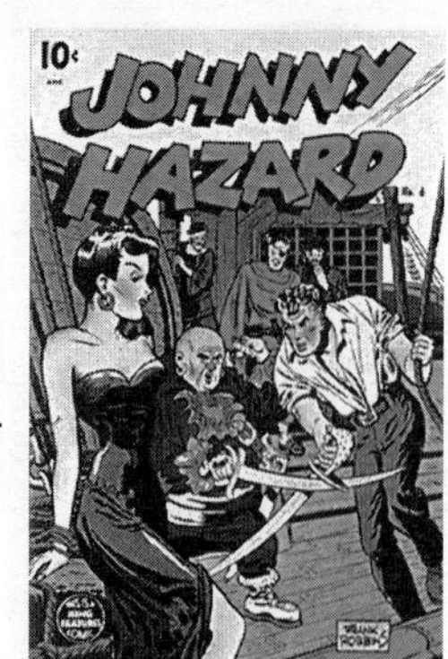

Johnny Hazard #6 © STD

Johnny The Homicidal Maniac #3 © Jhonen Vasquez

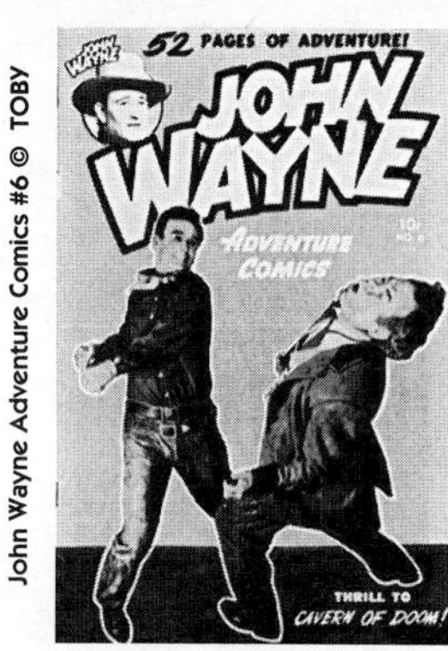

John Wayne Adventure Comics #6 © TOBY

JOHNNY APPLESEED (See Story Hour Series)

JOHNNY CASH (See Hello, I'm...)

JOHNNY DANGER (See Movie Comics, 1946)
Toby Press: 1950 (Based on movie serial)

	GD25	FN65	NM94
1-Photo-c; Sparling-a	15.00	44.00	110.00

JOHNNY DANGER PRIVATE DETECTIVE
Toby Press: Aug, 1954 (Reprinted in Danger #11 by Super)

	GD25	FN65	NM94
1-Photo-c; Opium den story	11.00	34.00	85.00

JOHNNY DYNAMITE (Formerly Dynamite #1-9; Foreign Intrigues #13 on)
Charlton Comics: No. 10, June, 1955 - No. 12, Oct, 1955

	GD25	FN65	NM94
10-12	6.50	19.50	45.00

JOHNNY DYNAMITE
Dark Horse Comics: Sept, 1994 - Dec, 1994 ($2.95, B&W & red, limited series)

	GD25	FN65	NM94
1-4: Max Allan Collins scripts in all.			3.00

JOHNNY HAZARD
Best Books (Standard Comics) (King Features): No. 5, Aug, 1948 - No. 8, May, 1949; No. 35, date?

	GD25	FN65	NM94
5-Strip reprints by Frank Robbins (c/a)	12.00	36.00	90.00
6,8-Strip reprints by Frank Robbins	9.30	28.00	70.00
7-New art, not Robbins	7.15	21.50	50.00
35	7.15	21.50	50.00

JOHNNY JASON (...Teen Reporter)
Dell Publishing Co.: Feb-Apr, 1962 - No. 2, June-Aug, 1962

	GD25	FN65	NM94
Four Color 1302, 2(01380-208)	2.75	8.00	30.00

JOHNNY JINGLE'S LUCKY DAY
American Dairy Assoc.: 1956 (16 pgs.; 7-1/4x5-1/8") (Giveaway) (Disney)

	GD25	FN65	NM94
nn	4.00	12.00	24.00

JOHNNY LAW, SKY RANGER
Good Comics (Lev Gleason): Apr, 1955 - No. 3, Aug, 1955; No. 4, Nov, 1955

	GD25	FN65	NM94
1-Edmond Good-c/a	7.15	21.50	50.00
2-4	5.00	15.00	30.00

JOHNNY MACK BROWN (TV western star; see Western Roundup under Dell Giants)
Dell Publishing Co.: No. 269, Mar, 1950 - No. 963, Feb, 1959 (All Photo-c)

	GD25	FN65	NM94
Four Color 269(#1)(3/50, 52pgs.)-Johnny Mack Brown & his horse Rebel begin; photo front/back-c begin; Marsh-a in #1-9	21.00	62.00	225.00
2(10-12/50, 52pgs.)	10.00	30.00	110.00
3(1-3/51, 52pgs.)	8.00	24.00	90.00
4-10 (9-11/52)(36pgs.)	5.00	15.00	55.00
Four Color 455,493,541,584,618	5.00	15.00	55.00
Four Color 645,685,722,776,834,963	5.00	15.00	55.00
Four Color 922-Manning-a	5.50	16.50	60.00

JOHNNY NEMO
Eclipse Comics: Sept, 1985 - No. 3, Feb, 1986 (Mini-series)

	GD25	FN65	NM94
1,2-($1.75)			1.80
3-($2.00)			2.00

JOHNNY PERIL (See Comic Cavalcade #15, Danger Trail #5, Sensation Comics #107 & Sensation Mystery)

JOHNNY RINGO (TV)
Dell Publishing Co.: No. 1142, Nov-Jan, 1960/61 (one shot)

	GD25	FN65	NM94
Four Color 1142-Photo-c	6.40	19.00	70.00

JOHNNY STARBOARD (See Wisco)

JOHNNY THE HOMICIDAL MANIAC
Slave Labor Graphics: Aug, 1995 - No. 7, Jan, 1997 ($2.95, B&W, lim. series)

	GD25	FN65	NM94
1-Jhonen Vasquez-c/s/a	3.80	11.50	40.00
1-Signed & numbered edition	2.25	6.80	25.00
2,3: 2-(11/95). 3-(2/96)	1.20	3.60	12.00
4-7: 4-(5-96). 5-(8/96)			5.00
Hardcover-($29.95) r/#1-7			29.95
TPB-($19.95)			19.95

JOHNNY THUNDER
National Periodical Publications: Feb-Mar, 1973 - No. 3, July-Aug, 1973

	GD25	FN65	NM94
1-Johnny Thunder & Nighthawk-r. in all	1.10	3.30	11.00
2,3: 2-Trigger Twins app.	.90	2.70	8.00

NOTE: *All contain 1950s DC reprints from All-American Western.* **Drucker** *r-2, 3.* **G. Kane** *r-2, 3.* **Moriera** *r-1.* **Toth** *r-1, 3; c-1r, 3r. Also see All-American, All-Star Western, Flash Comics, Western Comics, World's Best & World's Finest.*

JOHN PAUL JONES
Dell Publishing Co.: No. 1007, July-Sept, 1959 (one-shot)

	GD25	FN65	NM94
Four Color 1007-Movie, Robert Stack photo-c	4.50	13.50	50.00

JOHN STEED & EMMA PEEL (See The Avengers, Gold Key series)

JOHN STEELE SECRET AGENT (Also see Freedom Agent)
Gold Key: Dec, 1964

	GD25	FN65	NM94
1-Freedom Agent	8.00	23.00	85.00

JOHN WAYNE ADVENTURE COMICS (Movie star; See Big Tex, Oxydol-Dreft, Tim McCoy, & With The Marines...#1)
Toby Press: Winter, 1949-50 - No. 31, May, 1955 (Photo-c: 1-12,17,25-on)

	GD25	FN65	NM94
1 (36pgs.)-Photo-c begin (1st time in comics on-c)	135.00	405.00	1150.00
2 (4/50, 36pgs.)-Williamson/Frazetta-a(2) 6 & 2 pgs. (one story-r/Billy the Kid #1); photo back-c	55.00	165.00	470.00
3 (36pgs.)-Williamson/Frazetta-a(2), 16 pgs. total; photo back-c	55.00	165.00	470.00
4 (52pgs.)-Williamson/Frazetta-a(2), 16 pgs. total	55.00	165.00	470.00
5 (52pgs.)-Kurtzman-a-(Alfred "L" Newman in Potshot Pete)	43.00	129.00	350.00
6 (52pgs.)-Williamson/Frazetta-a (10 pgs.); Kurtzman-a "Pot-Shot Pete", (5 pgs.); & "Genius Jones", (1 pg.)	52.00	156.00	440.00
7 (52pgs.)-Williamson/Frazetta-a (10 pgs.)	42.00	126.00	340.00
8 (36pgs.)-Williamson/Frazetta-a(2) (12 & 9 pgs.)	52.00	156.00	440.00
9-11: Photo western-c	33.00	98.00	245.00
12,14-Photo war-c. 12-Kurtzman-a(2 pg.) "Genius"	33.00	98.00	245.00
13,15: 13,15-Line-drawn-c begin, end #24	29.00	88.00	220.00
16-Williamson/Frazetta-r/Billy the Kid #1	31.00	92.00	230.00
17-Photo-c	32.00	96.00	240.00
18-Williamson/Frazetta-a (r/#4 & 8, 19 pgs.)	35.00	104.00	260.00
19-24: 23-Evans-a?	26.00	78.00	195.00
25-Photo-c resume; end #31; Williamson/Frazetta-r/Billy the Kid #3	35.00	104.00	260.00
26-28,30-Photo-c	30.00	90.00	225.00
29,31-Williamson/Frazetta-a in each (r/#4, 2)	32.00	96.00	240.00

NOTE: *Williamsonish art in later issues by* **Gerald McCann.**

JO-JO COMICS (...Congo King #7-29; My Desire #30 on)
(Also see Fantastic Fears and Jungle Jo)
Fox Feature Syndicate: 1945 - No. 29, July, 1949 (Two No.7's; no #13)

	GD25	FN65	NM94
nn(1945)-Funny animal, humor	13.00	40.00	100.00
2(Sum,'46)-6(4-5/47): Funny animal. 2-Ten pg. Electro story (Fall/46)	7.15	21.50	50.00
7(7/47)-Jo-Jo, Congo King begins (1st app.); Bronze Man & Purple Tigress app.	74.00	222.00	625.00
7(#8) (9/47)	54.00	162.00	455.00
8-10(#9-11): 8-Tanee begins	43.00	129.00	355.00
11,12(#12,13),14,16: 11,16-Kamen bondage-c	40.00	120.00	315.00
15-Cited by Dr. Wertham in 5/47 Saturday Review of Literature	41.00	123.00	325.00
17-Kamen bondage-c	41.00	123.00	325.00
18-20	40.00	120.00	315.00
21-29: 21-Hollingsworth-a(4 pgs.; 23-1 pg.)	36.00	108.00	270.00

NOTE: *Many bondage-c/a by* **Baker/Kamen/Feldstein/Good.** *No. 7's have Princesses*

The Joker #6 © DC

Jonah Hex #4 (mini-series) © DC

Jonny Double #1 © DC

GD25 FN65 NM94

Gwenna, Geesa, Yolda, & Safra before settling down on Tanee.

JO-JOY (The Adventures of...)
W. T. Grant Dept. Stores: 1945 - 1953 (Christmas gift comic, 16 pgs., 7-1/16x10-1/4")

1945-53 issues 4.35 13.00 26.00

JOKEBOOK COMICS DIGEST ANNUAL (...Magazine No. 5 on)
Archie Publications: Oct, 1977 - No. 13, Oct, 1983 (Digest Size)

1(10/77)-Reprints; Neal Adams-a 1.20 3.60 12.00
2(4/78)-5 .90 2.70 8.00
6-11 2.00 6.00

JOKER, THE (See Batman #1, Batman: The Killing Joke, Brave & the Bold, Detective, Greatest Joker Stories & Justice League Annual #2)
National Periodical Publications: May, 1975 - No. 9, Sept-Oct, 1976

1-Two-Face app. 2.25 6.80 25.00
2,3: 3-The Creeper app. 1.20 3.60 12.00
4-9: 4-Green Arrow-c/sty. 6-Sherlock Holmes-c/sty. 7-Lex Luthor-c/story. 8-Scarecrow-c/story. 9-Catwoman-c/story 1.00 3.00 10.00

JOKER, THE (See Tangent Comics/ The Joker)

JOKER COMICS (Adventures Into Terror No. 43 on)
Timely/Marvel Comics No. 36 on (TCI/CDS): Apr, 1942 - No. 42, Aug, 1950

1-(Rare)-Powerhouse Pepper (1st app.) begins by Wolverton; Stuporman app. from Daring Comics 200.00 600.00 1700.00
2-Wolverton-a; 1st app. Tessie the Typist & begin series 74.00 222.00 625.00
3-5-Wolverton-a 47.00 141.00 400.00
6-10-Wolverton-a. 6-Tessie-c begin 37.00 110.00 275.00
11-20-Wolverton-a 29.00 86.00 215.00
21,22,24-27,29,30-Wolverton cont'd. & Kurtzman's "Hey Look" in #23-27 25.00 74.00 185.00
23-1st "Hey Look" by Kurtzman; Wolverton-a 27.00 80.00 200.00
28,32,34,37-41: 28-Millie the Model begins. 32-Hedy begins. 41-Nellie the Nurse app. 6.85 21.00 48.00
31-Last Powerhouse Pepper; not in #28 17.00 50.00 125.00
33,35,36-Kurtzman's "Hey Look" 9.30 28.00 70.00
42-Only app. 'Patty Pinup,' clone of Millie the Model 8.30 25.00 58.00

JOKER: DEVIL'S ADVOCATE
DC Comics: 1996 ($24.95/$12.95, one-shot)

nn-(Hardcover)-Dixon scripts/Nolan & Hanna-a 25.00
nn-(Softcover) 13.00

JOLLY CHRISTMAS, A (See March of Comics No. 269)

JOLLY CHRISTMAS BOOK (See Christmas Journey Through Space)
Promotional Publ. Co.: 1951; 1954; 1955 (36 pgs.; 24 pgs.)

1951-(Woolworth giveaway)-slightly oversized; no slick cover; Marv Levy-c/a 5.70 17.00 40.00
1954-(Hot Shoppes giveaway)-regular size-reprints 1951 issue; slick cover added; 24 pgs.; no ads 5.70 17.00 40.00
1955-(J. M. McDonald Co. giveaway)-reg. size 5.00 15.00 30.00

JOLLY COMICS
Four Star Publishing Co.: 1947

1 7.85 23.50 55.00

JOLLY JINGLES (Formerly Jackpot Comics)
MLJ Magazines: No. 10, Sum, 1943 - No. 16, Wint, 1944/45

10-Super Duck begins (origin & 1st app.); Woody The Woodpecker begins (not same as Lantz character) 32.00 96.00 240.00
11 (Fall, '43)-2nd Super Duck(see Hangman #8) 16.00 48.00 120.00
12-Hitler-c 15.00 44.00 110.00
13-16: 13-Sahle-c. 15-Vigoda-c 9.30 28.00 70.00

JONAH HEX (See All-Star Western, Hex and Weird Western Tales)

GD25 FN65 NM94

National Periodical Pub./DC Comics: Mar-Apr, 1977 - No. 92, Aug, 1985

1 3.80 11.50 42.00
2-4,9: 9-Wrightson-c. 1.60 4.80 16.00
5,6,10: 5-Rep 1st app. from All-Star Western #10 1.20 3.60 12.00
7,8-Explains Hex's face disfigurement (origin) 1.60 4.80 16.00
11-20: 12-Starlin-c .85 2.60 7.00
21-50: 31,32-Origin retold 4.00
51-91: 89-Mark Texeira-a. 92-Story contd in Hex #1 3.50
92 1.00 3.00 10.00

NOTE: ***Ayers** a(p)-35-37, 40, 41, 44-53, 56, 58-82. **Buckler** a-11; c-11, 13-16. **Kubert** c-43-46. **Morrow** a-90-92; c-10. **Spiegle(Tothish)** a-34, 38, 40, 49, 52. **Texeira** a-89p. Batlash back-ups in 49, 52. El Diablo back-ups in 48, 56-60, 73-75. Scalphunter back-ups in 40, 41, 45-47.*

JONAH HEX AND OTHER WESTERN TALES (Blue Ribbon Digest)
DC Comics: Sept-Oct, 1979 - No. 3, Jan-Feb, 1980 (100 pgs.)

1-3: 1-Origin Scalphunter-r, Ayers/Evans, Neal Adams-a.; painted-c. 2-Weird Western Tales-r; Neal Adams, Toth, Aragones-a. 3-Outlaw-r, Scalphunter-r; Gil Kane, Wildey-a .85 2.60 7.00

JONAH HEX: RIDERS OF THE WORM AND SUCH
DC Comics (Vertigo): Mar, 1995 - No. 5, July, 1995 ($2.95, limited series)

1-5-Lansdale story, Truman -a 3.00

JONAH HEX SPECTACULAR (See DC Special Series No. 16)

JONAH HEX: TWO-GUN MOJO
DC Comics (Vertigo): Aug, 1993 - No. 5, Dec, 1993 ($2.95, limited series)

1-Lansdale scripts in all;Truman/Glanzman-a in all w/Truman-c 4.00
1-Silver ink edition with no price on cover .90 2.70 8.00
2-5 3.00
TPB-(1994, $12.95) r/#1-5 1.30 3.90 13.00

JONESY (Formerly Crack Western)
Comic Favorite/Quality Comics Group: No. 85, Aug, 1953; No. 2, Oct, 1953 - No. 8, Oct, 1954

85(#1)-Teen-age humor 5.70 17.00 35.00
2 4.00 12.00 24.00
3-8 3.20 8.00 16.00

JON JUAN (Also see Great Lover Romances)
Toby Press: Spring, 1950

1-All Schomburg-a (signed Al Reid on-c); written by Siegel; used in **SOTI**, pg. 38 (Scarce) 53.00 159.00 450.00

JONNI THUNDER (...A.K.A. Thunderbolt)
DC Comics: Feb, 1985 - No. 4, Aug, 1985 (75¢, limited series)

1-4: 1-Origin & 1st app. 1.00

JONNY DEMON
Dark Horse Comics: May, 1994 - No. 3, July, 1994 ($2.50, limited series)

1-3 2.50

JONNY DOUBLE
DC Comics (Vertigo): Sept, 1998 - No. 4, Dec, 1998 ($2.95, limited series)

1-4-Azzarello-s 2.95

JONNY QUEST (TV)
Gold Key: Dec, 1964 (Hanna-Barbera)

1 (10139-412) 31.00 93.00 340.00

JONNY QUEST (TV)
Comico: June 1986 - No. 31, Dec, 1988 ($1.50/$1.75)(Hanna-Barbera)

1 5.00
2,3,5: 3,5-Dave Stevens-c 3.00
4,6-14 1.50
15-31: 15-Begin $1.75-c. 30-Adapts TV episode 2.00
Special 1(9/88, $1.75), 2(10/88, $1.75) 2.50

*NOTE: **M. Anderson** a-9. **Mooney** a-Special 1. **Pini** a-2. **Quagmire** a-31p. **Rude** a-1; c-2i. **Sienkiewicz** c-11. **Spiegle** a-7, 12, 21; c-21 **Staton** a-2i, 11p. **Steacy** c-8. **Stevens** a-4i; c-3,5.*

Jon Sable, Freelance #23 © First Comics

Journey Into Mystery #86 © MAR

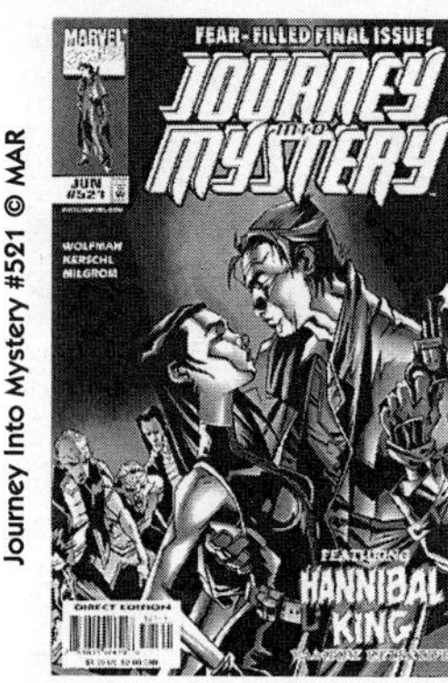

Journey Into Mystery #521 © MAR

GD25 FN65 NM94

Wildey a-1, c-1, 7, 12. Williamson a-4i; c-4i.

JONNY QUEST CLASSICS (TV)
Comico: May, 1987 - No. 3, July, 1987 ($2.00) (Hanna-Barbera)

1-3: Wildey-c/a; 3-Based on TV episode 2.50

JON SABLE, FREELANCE (Also see Mike Grell's Sable & Sable)
First Comics: 6/83 - No. 56, 2/88 (#1-17, $1; #18-33, $1.25, #34-on, $1.75)

1-Mike Grell-c/a/scripts 3.50
2-5: 3-5-Origin, parts 1-3 2.50
6-10: 6-Origin, part 4 2.00
11-20: 11-1st app. of Maggie the Cat. 14-Mando paper begins. 16-Maggie the Cat. app. 1.80
21-33: 25-30-Shatter app. 1.50
34-56: 34-Deluxe format begins ($1.75) 1.75

NOTE: Aragones a-33; c-33(part). Grell a-1-43;c-1-52, 53p, 54-56.

JOSEPH & HIS BRETHREN (See The Living Bible)

JOSIE (She's... #1-16) (...& the Pussycats #45 on) (See Archie Giant Series Magazine #528, 540, 551, 562, 571, 584, 597, 610, 622)
Archie Publications/Radio Comics: Feb, 1963; No. 2, Aug, 1963 - No. 106, Oct, 1982

	GD25	FN65	NM94
1	14.50	44.00	145.00
2	7.50	22.50	75.00
3-5	4.50	13.50	45.00
6-10	3.00	9.00	32.00
11-20	2.50	7.50	22.00
21, 23-30	1.60	4.80	16.00
22 (9/66)-Mighty Man & Mighty (Josie Girl) app.	2.80	8.40	28.00
31-44	1.75	5.25	14.00
45 (12/69)-Josie and the Pussycats begins (Hanna Barbera TV cartoon)	3.00	9.00	30.00
46-54	1.60	4.80	16.00
55-74 (2/74)(52pg. issues)	1.20	3.60	12.00
75-90(8/76)	.85	2.60	7.00
91-99,101-106			5.00
100 (10/79)	.90	2.70	8.00

JOSIE & THE PUSSYCATS (TV)
Archie Comics: 1993 - No. 2, 1994 ($2.00, 52 pgs.)(Published annually)

1,2-Bound-in pull-out poster in each. 2-(Spr/94) 2.50

JOURNAL OF CRIME (See Fox Giants)

JOURNEY
Aardvark-Vanaheim #1-14/Fantagraphics Books #15-on: 1983 - No. 14, 9/84; No. 15, 4/85 - No. 27, 7/86 (B&W)

1 4.00
2 2.00
3-27: 20-Sam Kieth-a 1.25

JOURNEY INTO FEAR
Superior-Dynamic Publications: May, 1951 - No. 21, Sept, 1954

	GD25	FN65	NM94
1-Baker-r(2)	50.00	150.00	425.00
2	35.00	104.00	260.00
3,4	29.00	88.00	220.00
5-10,15: 15-Used in **SOTI**, pg. 389	20.00	60.00	150.00
11-14,16-21	19.00	56.00	140.00

NOTE: *Kamenish 'headlight'-a most issues. Robinson a-10.*

JOURNEY INTO MYSTERY (1st Series) (Thor Nos. 126-502)
Atlas(CPS No. 1-48/AMI No. 49-68/Marvel No. 69 (6/61) on): 6/52 - No. 48, 8/57; No. 49, 11/58 - No. 125, 2/66; 503, 11/96 - No. 521, June, 1998

	GD25	FN65	NM94
1-Weird/horror stories begin	260.00	780.00	2650.00
2	90.00	270.00	800.00
3,4	68.00	206.00	600.00
5-11	44.00	132.00	390.00
12-20,22: 15-Atomic explosion panel. 22-Davisesque-a; last pre-code issue (2/55)	38.00	116.00	310.00
21-Kubert-a; Tothish-a by Andru	40.00	120.00	315.00
23-32,35-38,40: 24-Torres?-a. 38-Ditko-a	24.00	71.00	190.00
33-Williamson-a; Ditko-a (his 1st for Atlas?)	26.00	77.00	210.00
34,39: 34-Krigstein-a. 39-1st S.A. issue; Wood-a	24.00	73.00	195.00
41-Crandall-a; Frazettaesque-a by Morrow	17.00	51.00	170.00
42,48-Torres-a	17.00	51.00	170.00
43,44-Williamson/Mayo-a in both	18.00	54.00	180.00
45,47,52,53	16.00	48.00	160.00
46-Torres & Krigstein-a	17.00	51.00	170.00
49-Matt Fox, Check-a	17.00	51.00	170.00
50,54: 50-Davis-a. 54-Williamson-a	16.00	48.00	160.00
51-Kirby/Wood-a	19.00	57.00	190.00
55-61,63-65,67-69,71,72,74,75: 74-Contents change to Fantasy. 75-Last 10¢ issue	16.50	50.00	165.00
62-Prototype ish. (The Hulk); 1st app. Xemnu (Titan) called "The Hulk"	22.50	68.00	225.00
66-Prototype ish. (The Hulk)-Return of Xemnu "The Hulk"	22.50	68.00	225.00
70-Prototype ish. (The Sandman)(7/61); similar to Spidey villain	22.50	68.00	225.00
73-Story titled "The Spider" where a spider is exposed to radiation & gets powers of a human and shoots webbing; a reverse prototype of Spider-Man's origin	32.00	96.00	320.00
76,77,80-82: 80-Anti-communist propaganda story	13.00	39.00	130.00
78-The Sorceror (Dr. Strange prototype) app. (3/62)	22.00	66.00	220.00
79-Prototype issue. (Mr. Hyde)	19.00	57.00	190.00

	GD25	FN65	VF82	NM94
83-Origin & 1st app. The Mighty Thor by Kirby (8/62) and begin series; Thor-c also begin	275.00	825.00	2063.00	4400.00

	GD25	FN65	NM94
83-Reprint from the Golden Record Comic Set	9.00	27.00	90.00
with the record (1966)	16.00	48.00	160.00
84-2nd app. Thor	79.00	238.00	950.00
85-1st app. Loki & Heimdall; Odin cameo (1 panel)	48.00	144.00	575.00
86-1st full app. Odin	34.00	102.00	375.00
87-89: 89-Origin Thor retold	26.00	78.00	260.00
90-No Kirby-a	14.50	44.00	145.00
91,92,94-96-Sinnott-a	12.50	38.00	125.00
93,97-Kirby-a; Tales of Asgard series begins #97 (origin which concludes in #99)	15.50	47.00	155.00
98-100-Kirby/Heck-a. 98-Origin/1st app. The Human Cobra. 99-1st app. Surtur & Mr. Hyde	11.00	33.00	110.00
101-108,110: 101-(2/64)-2nd Avengers x-over (w/o Capt. America); see Tales Of Suspense #49 for 1st x-over. 102-Intro Sif. 103-1st app. Enchantress. 105-109-Ten extra pgs. Kirby-a in each. 107-1st app. Grey Gargoyle. 108-(9/64)-Early Dr. Strange & Avengers x-over	8.00	24.00	80.00
109-Magneto-c & app. (1st x-over, 10/64)	11.00	33.00	110.00
111,113,114,116-125: 113-Origin Loki. 114-Origin/1st app. Absorbing Man. 118-1st app. Destroyer. 119-Intro Hogun, Fandrall, Volstagg. 124-Hercules-c/story	7.00	21.00	70.00
112-Thor Vs. Hulk (1/65). 112-Origin Loki	18.00	54.00	180.00
115-Origin Loki	9.00	27.00	90.00
503-507: 503-(11/96, $1.50)-The Lost Gods begin; Tom DeFalco scripts & Deodato Studios-c/a. 505-Spider-Man-c/app.			1.50
508-510, -1(7/97)-($1.95): 509-Loki-c/app.		.80	2.00
511-521: 511-Begin $1.99-c. 514-516-Shang-Chi		.80	2.00
Annual 1(1965, 25¢, 72 pgs.)-New Thor vs. Hercules(1st app.)-c/story (see Incredible Hulk #3); Kirby-c/a; r/#85,93,95,97	15.50	47.00	155.00

NOTE: *Ayers a-14, 39, 64i, 71i, 74i, 80i. Bailey a-43. Briefer a-5, 12. Cameron a-35. Check a-17. Colan a-23, 81; c-14. Ditko a-33, 38, 50-96; c-58, 67, 71, 88i. Kirby/Ditko a-50-83. Everett a-20, 48; c-4-7, 9, 36, 37, 39-42, 44, 45, 47. Forte a-19, 35, 40, 53. Heath a-4-6, 11, 14; c-1, 8,*

Journey Into Mystery #2 (2nd Series) © MAR

Judge Dredd #12 © Eagle

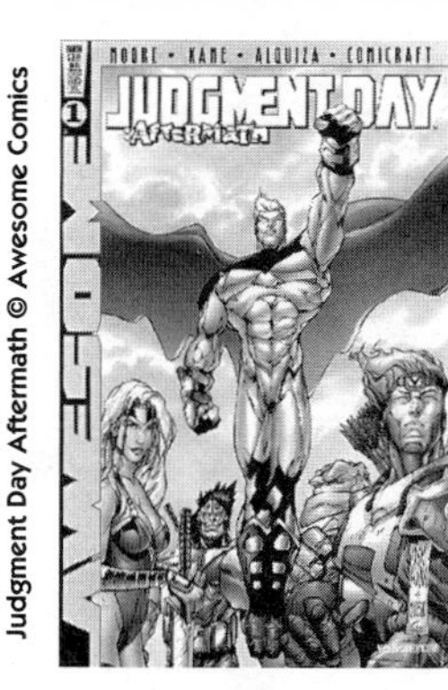

Judgment Day Aftermath © Awesome Comics

GD25 FN65 NM94

*11, 15, 51. **Heck** a-53, 73. **Kirby** a(p)-51, 52, 56, 57, 60, 62, 64, 66, 69, 71-74, 76, 79, 80-89, 93, 97, 98, 100(w/**Heck**), 101-125; c-50-57, 59-66, 68-70, 72-82, 88(w/**Ditko**), 83 & 84(w/**Sinnott**), 85-96(w/**Ayers**), 97-152p. **Leiber/Fox** a-93, 98-102. **Maneely** c-20-22. **Morisi** a-42. **Morrow** a-41, 42. **Orlando** a-30, 45, 57. **Mac Pakula** (Tothish) a-9, 35, 41. **Powell** a-20, 27, 34. **Reinman** a-39, 87, 92, 96i. **Robinson** a-9. **Roussos** a-39. **Robert Sale** a-14. **Severin** a-27; c-30. **Sinnott** a-41; c-50. **Tuska** a-11. **Wildey** a-16.*

JOURNEY INTO MYSTERY (2nd Series)
Marvel Comics: Oct, 1972 - No. 19, Oct, 1975

1-Robert Howard adaptation; Starlin/Ploog-a 1.40 4.20 14.00
2-5: 2,3,5-Bloch adapt. 4-H. P. Lovecraft adapt. .90 2.70 8.00
6-19: Reprints 3.00

NOTE: ***N. Adams** a-2i. **Ditko** r-7, 10, 12, 14, 15, 19; c-10. **Everett** r-9, 14. **G. Kane** a-1p, 2p; c-1-3p. **Kirby** r-7, 13, 18, 19; c-7. **Mort Lawrence** r-2. **Maneely** r-3. **Orlando** r-16. **Reese** a-1, 2i. **Starlin** a-1p, 3p. **Torres** r-16. **Wildey** r-9, 14.*

JOURNEY INTO UNKNOWN WORLDS (Formerly Teen)
Atlas Comics (WFP): No. 36, 9/50 - No. 38, 2/51; No. 4, 4/51 - No. 59, 8/57

36(#1)-Science fiction/weird; "End Of The Earth" c/story
188.00 564.00 1600.00
37(#2)-Science fiction; "When Worlds Collide" c/story; Everett-c/a; Hitler story
88.00 264.00 750.00
38(#3)-Science fiction 72.00 213.00 615.00
4-6,8,10-Science fiction/weird 45.00 135.00 385.00
7-Wolverton-a "Planet of Terror", 6 pgs; electric chair c-inset/story
75.00 225.00 640.00
9-Giant eyeball story 53.00 160.00 450.00
11,12-Krigstein-a 38.00 114.00 285.00
13,16,17,20 29.00 87.00 215.00
14-Wolverton-a "One of Our Graveyards Is Missing", 4 pgs; Tuska-a
56.00 168.00 475.00
15-Wolverton-a "They Crawl by Night", 5 pgs.; 2 pg. Maneely s/f story
56.00 168.00 475.00
18,19-Matt Fox-a 33.00 100.00 245.00
21-33: 21-Decapitation-c. 24-Sci/fic story. 26-Atom bomb panel. 27-Sid Check-a. 33-Last pre-code (2/55) 22.00 66.00 165.00
34-Kubert, Torres-a 16.00 48.00 120.00
35-Torres-a 15.00 45.00 110.00
36-42 14.00 42.00 105.00
43,44: 43-Krigstein-a. 44-Davis-a 14.00 42.00 105.00
45,55,59-Williamson-a in all; with Mayo #55,59. 55-Crandall-a
14.00 42.00 105.00
46,47,49,52,56-58 12.00 36.00 90.00
48,53-Crandall-a (4 pgs. #48). 48-Check-a 14.00 42.00 105.00
50-Davis, Crandall-a 14.00 42.00 105.00
51-Ditko, Wood-a 15.00 45.00 110.00
54-Torres-a 12.00 36.00 90.00

NOTE: ***Ayers** a-24, 43. **Berg** a-38(#3), 43. **Lou Cameron** a-33. **Colan** a-37(#2), 6, 17, 19, 20, 23, 39. **Ditko** a-45, 51. **Drucker** a-35, 58. **Everett** a-37(#2), 11, 14, 41, 55, 56; c-37(#2), 11, 13, 14, 17, 22, 47, 48, 50, 53-55, 59. **Forte** a-49. **Fox** a-21i. **Heath** a-36(#1), 4, 6-8, 17, 20, 22, 36i; c-18. **Keller** a-15. **Mort Lawrence** a-38, 39. **Maneely** a-7, 8, 15, 16, 22, 49, 58; c-19, 25, 52. **Morrow** a-48. **Orlando** a-44, 57. **Pakula** a-36. **Powell** a-42, 53, 54. **Reinman** a-8. **Rico** a-21. **Robert Sale** a-24, 49. **Sekowsky** a-4, 5, 9. **Severin** a-38, 51; c-38, 48i, 56. **Sinnott** a-9, 21, 24. **Tuska** a-38(#3), 14. **Wildey** a-25, 43, 44.*

JOURNEY OF DISCOVERY WITH MARK STEEL (See Mark Steel)

JOURNEY TO THE CENTER OF THE EARTH (Movie)
Dell Publishing Co.: No. 1060, Nov-Jan, 1959/60 (one-shot)

Four Color 1060-Pat Boone & James Madson photo-c 11.00 33.00 120.00

J2 (Also see A-Next and Juggernaut)
Marvel Comics: Oct, 1998 - Present ($1.99)

1-Juggernaut's son; Lim-a 2.00
2-4: 2-Two covers; X-People app. 3-J2 battles the Hulk 1.99

JUDE, THE FORGOTTEN SAINT
Catechetical Guild Education Soc.: 1954 (16 pgs.; 8x11"; full color; paper-c)

nn 2.00 5.00 10.00

GD25 FN65 NM94

JUDGE COLT
Gold Key: Oct, 1969 - No. 4, Sept, 1970

1 1.00 3.00 8.00
2-4 2.00 5.00

JUDGE DREDD (...Classics #62 on; also see Batman - Judge Dredd, Dredd Rules, The Law of Dredd & 2000 A.D. Monthly)
Eagle Comics/IPC Magazines Ltd./Quality Comics #34-35, V2#1-37/ Fleetway #38 on: Nov, 1983 - No. 35, 1986; V2#1, Oct, 1986 - No. 77, 1993

1-Bolland-c/a 2.00 6.00
2-35 2.50
V2#1-77: 1-('86)-New look begins. 20-Begin $1.50-c. 21/22, 23/24-Two issue numbers in one. 28-1st app. Megaman (super-hero). 39-Begin $1.75-c. 51-Begin $1.95-c. 53-Bolland-a. 57-Reprints 1st published Judge Dredd story 2.00
Special 1 2.00

NOTE: ***Bolland** a-1-6, 8, 10; c-1-10, 15. **Guice** c-V2#23/24, 26, 27.*

JUDGE DREDD (3rd Series)
DC Comics: Aug, 1994 - No. 18, Jan, 1996 ($1.95)

1-11 2.00
12-18: 12-Begin $2.25-c 2.25
nn ($5.95)-Movie adaptation, Sienkiewicz-c 2.00 6.00

JUDGE DREDD'S CRIME FILE
Eagle Comics: Aug, 1989 - No. 6, Feb, 1986 ($1.25, limited series)

1-6: 1-Byrne-a 2.00

JUDGE DREDD: LEGENDS OF THE LAW
DC Comics: Dec, 1994 - No. 13, Dec, 1995 ($1.95)

1-7: 1-5-Dorman-c 2.00
8-13: 8-Begin $2.25-c 2.25

JUDGE DREDD: THE EARLY CASES
Eagle Comics: Feb, 1986 - No. 6, Jul, 1986 ($1.25, Mega-series, Mando paper)

1-6: 2000 A.D.-r 1.50

JUDGE DREDD: THE JUDGE CHILD QUEST (Judge Child in indicia)
Eagle Comics: Aug, 1984 - No. 5, Oct, 1984 ($1.25, Lim. series, Baxter paper)

1-5: 2000A.D.-r; Bolland-c/a 1.50

JUDGE DREDD: THE MEGAZINE
Fleetway/Quality: 1991 - Present ($4.95, stiff-c, squarebound, 52 pgs.)

1-3 5.00

JUDGEMENT DAY
Lightning Comics: Sept, 1993 - No. 8, Apr, 1994 ($2.95)

1-($3.50)-Red foil-c 3.50
1-Gold Prism Edition 3.00
1-Purple-c Edition 3.00
2-8: 2-Polybagged with trading card. 7-Origin 3.00

JUDGE PARKER
Argo: Feb, 1956 - No. 2, 1956

1-Newspaper strip reprints 5.35 16.00 32.00
2 4.00 11.00 22.00

JUDGMENT DAY
Awesome Entertainment: June, 1997 - No. 3, Oct, 1997 ($2.50, limited series)

1 Alpha-Moore-s/Liefeld-c/a(p) flashback art by various in all 2.50
1-Variant cover by Dave Gibbons 2.50
2 Omega 2.50
2-Variant cover by Dave Gibbons 2.50
3 Final Judgment 2.50
3-Variant cover by Dave Gibbons 2.50
...Aftermath-($3.50) Moore-s/Kane-a; Youngblood, Glory, New Men, Maximage Allies and Spacehunter short stoiries 3.50
...Aftermath-Variant cover by Dave Gibbons 3.50

Judy Canova #1 © FOX

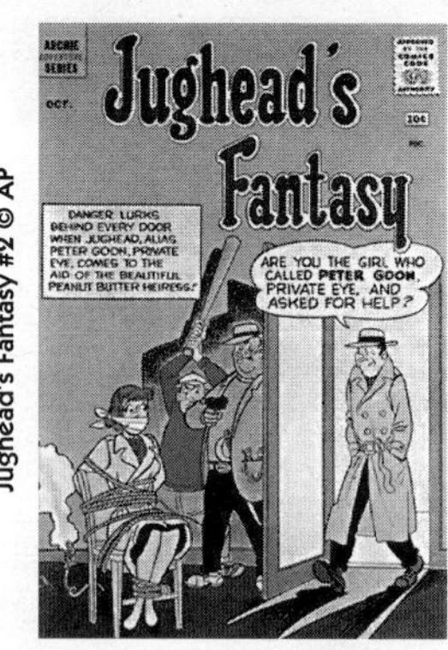

Jughead's Fantasy #2 © AP

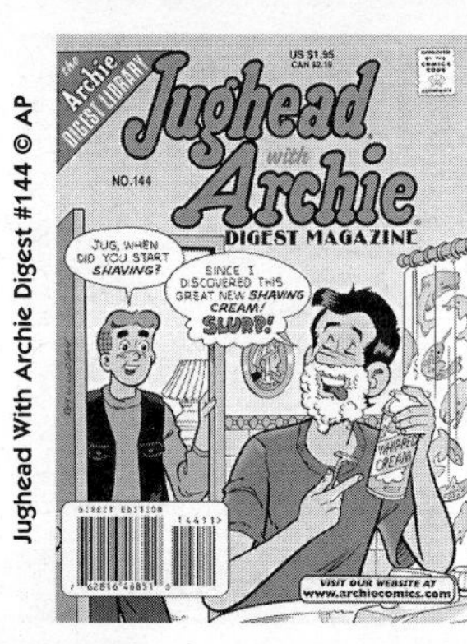

Jughead With Archie Digest #144 © AP

	GD25	FN65	NM94

JUDGMENT PAWNS
Antarctic Press: Feb, 1997 ($2.95, one-shot)

1			2.95

JUDO JOE
Jay-Jay Corp.: Aug, 1953 - No. 3, Dec, 1953 (Judo lessons in each issue)

1-Drug ring story	7.50	22.50	48.00
2,3: 3-Hypo needle story	5.35	16.00	32.00

JUDOMASTER (Gun Master #84-89) (Also see Crisis on Infinite Earths, Sarge Steel #6 & Special War Series)
Charlton Comics: No. 89, May-June, 1966 - No. 98, Dec, 1967 (Two No. 89's)

89-3rd app. Judomaster	2.60	8.40	28.00
90,92-98: 93-Intro. Tiger	2.50	7.50	22.00
91-Sarge Steel begins	2.60	7.80	26.00
93,94,96,98 (Modern Comics reprint, 1977)			4.00

NOTE: ***Morisi*** *Thunderbolt #90. #91 has 1 pg. biography on writer/artist Frank McLaughlin.*

JUDY CANOVA (Formerly My Experience) (Stage, screen, radio)
Fox Features Syndicate: No. 23, May, 1950 - No. 3, Sept, 1950

23(#1)-Wood-c,a(p)?	17.00	51.00	130.00
24-Wood-a(p)	18.00	54.00	135.00
3-Wood-c; Wood/Orlando-a	20.00	60.00	150.00

JUDY GARLAND (See Famous Stars)

JUDY JOINS THE WAVES
Toby Press: 1951 (For U.S. Navy)

nn	5.35	16.00	32.00

JUGGERNAUT (See X-Men)
Marvel Comics: Apr, 1997 ($2.99, one-shot)

1-Kelly-s/ Rouleau-a			3.00

JUGHEAD (Formerly Archie's Pal...)
Archie Publications: No. 127, Dec, 1965 - No. 352, June, 1987

127-130	2.50	7.50	22.00
131,133,135-160(9/68)	2.25	6.75	18.00
132,134: 132-Shield-c; The Fly & Black Hood app.; Shield cameo. 134-Shield-c	2.50	7.50	24.00
161-180	1.75	5.25	14.00
181-199	1.00	3.00	10.00
200(1/'72)	1.20	3.60	12.00
201-240(5/75)	.85	2.60	7.00
241-270(11/77)			5.00
271-299			4.00
300(5/80)			5.00
301-320(1/82): 300-Anniversary issue; infinity-c			3.00
321-352			2.00

JUGHEAD (2nd Series)(Becomes Archie's Pal Jughead Comics #46 on)
Archie Enterprises: Aug, 1987 - No. 45, May, 1993 (.75/$1.00/$1.25)

1			4.00
2-10			3.00
11-45: 4-X-Mas issue. 17-Colan-c/a			2.00

JUGHEAD AS CAPTAIN HERO (See Archie as Purehear the Powerful, Archie Giant Series Magazine #142 & Life With Archie)
Archie Publications: Oct, 1966 - No. 7, Nov, 1967

1-Super hero parody	4.50	13.50	45.00
2	3.20	9.60	32.00
3-7	2.50	7.50	22.00

JUGHEAD JONES COMICS DIGEST, THE (...Magazine No. 10-64; Jughead Jones Digest Magazine #65)
Archie Publ.: June, 1977 - No. 98 ($1.35/$1.50/$1.75, digest-size, 128 pgs.)

1-Neal Adams-a; Capt. Hero-r	2.00	6.00	20.00
2(9/77)-Neal Adams-a	1.60	4.80	16.00
3-10: 7-Origin Jaguar-r; N. Adams-a.	1.00	3.00	10.00
11-20: 13-r/1957 Jughead's Folly	.85	2.60	7.00
21-50			5.00
51-70			4.00
71-98			2.00

JUGHEAD'S BABY TALES
Archie Comics: Spring, 1994 ($2.00, 52 pgs.)

1-Bound-in pull-out poster			3.00

JUGHEAD'S DINER
Archie Comics: Apr, 1990 - No. 7, Apr, 1991 ($1.00)

1			3.00
2-7			2.00

JUGHEAD'S DOUBLE DIGEST (...Magazine #5)
Archie Comics: Oct, 1989 - Present ($2.25/$2.50/$2.75/$2.79/$2.95, 256 pgs.)

1	.90	2.70	8.00
2-10: 2,5-Capt. Hero stories		2.00	6.00
11-25			4.00
26-48			2.75
49-57			2.95

JUGHEAD'S EAT-OUT COMIC BOOK MAGAZINE (See Archie Giant Series Magazine No. 170)

JUGHEAD'S FANTASY
Archie Publications: Aug, 1960 - No. 3, Dec, 1960

1	16.00	48.00	160.00
2	10.50	32.00	105.00
3	9.50	28.50	95.00

JUGHEAD'S FOLLY
Archie Publications (Close-Up): 1957 (36 pgs.)(one-shot)

1-Jughead a la Elvis (Rare) (1st reference to Elvis in comics?)	43.00	129.00	360.00

JUGHEAD'S JOKES
Archie Publications: Aug, 1967 - No. 78, Sept, 1982
(No. 1-8, 38 on: reg. size; No. 9-23: 68 pgs.; No. 24-37: 52 pgs.)

1	5.50	16.50	55.00
2	3.00	9.00	30.00
3-8	2.50	7.50	20.00
9,10 (68 pgs.)	2.50	7.50	22.00
11-23(4/71) (68 pgs.)	1.60	4.80	16.00
24-37(1/74) (52 pgs.)	1.40	4.20	14.00
38-50(9/76)		2.00	6.00
51-78			3.00

JUGHEAD'S PAL HOT DOG (See Laugh #14 for 1st app.)
Archie Comics: Jan, 1990 - No. 5, Oct, 1990 ($1.00)

1			3.00
2-5			2.00

JUGHEAD'S SOUL FOOD
Spire Christian Comics (Fleming H. Revell Co.): 1979 (49 cents)

nn	.85	2.60	7.00

JUGHEAD'S TIME POLICE
Archie Comics: July, 1990 - No. 6, May, 1991 ($1.00, bi-monthly)

1			3.00
2-6: Colan a-3-6p; c-3-6			2.00

JUGHEAD WITH ARCHIE DIGEST (...Plus Betty & Veronica & Reggie Too No. 1,2; ...Magazine #33-?, 101-on; ...Comics Digest Mag.)
Archie Publ.: Mar, 1974 - Present (Digest; $1.00/$1.25/$1.35/$1.50/$1.75/$1.95)

1	4.00	12.25	45.00
2	2.50	7.60	28.00
3-10	1.60	4.80	16.00

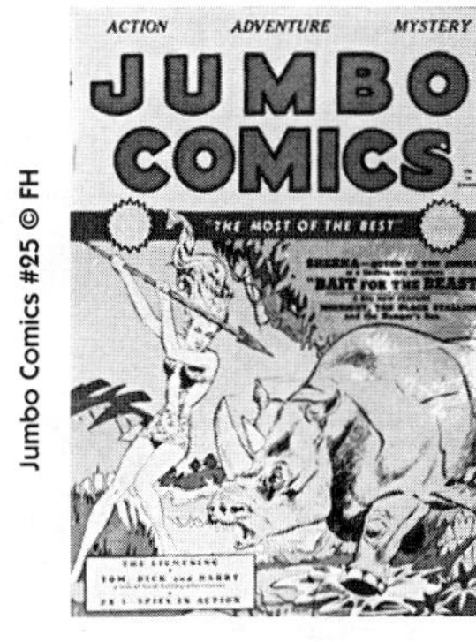

Jumbo Comics #25 © FH

Jungle Action #3 © ATL

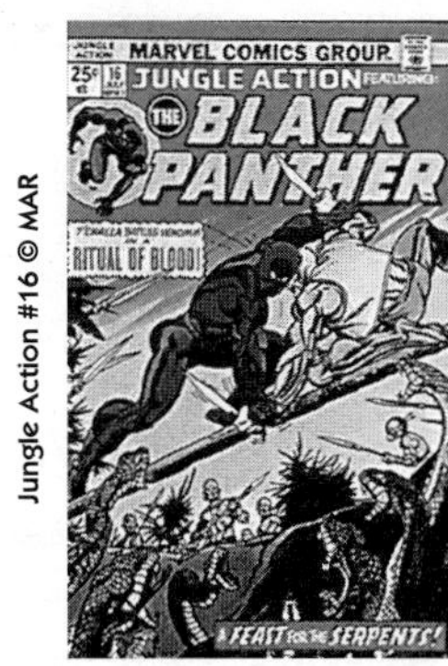

Jungle Action #16 © MAR

GD25 FN65 NM94

11-20: Capt. Hero-r in #14-16; Pureheart the Powerful #18,21,22; Capt. Pureheart #17,19 1.00 3.00 10.00
21-50: 29-The Shield-r. 30-The Fly-r .85 2.60 7.00
51-99 5.00
100 .85 2.60 7.00
101-121 3.00
122-137-($1.75) 1.75
138-146-($1.95) 1.95

JUKE BOX COMICS
Famous Funnies: Mar, 1948 - No. 6, Jan, 1949

1-Toth-c/a; Hollingsworth-a 39.00 117.00 300.00
2-Transvestism story 24.00 72.00 180.00
3-6: 3-Peggy Lee story. 4-Jimmy Durante line drawn-c. 6-Features Desi Arnaz plus Arnaz line drawn-c 18.00 54.00 135.00

JUMBO COMICS (Created by S.M. Iger)
Fiction House Magazines (Real Adv. Publ. Co.): Sept, 1938 - No. 167, Mar, 1953 (No. 1-3: 68 pgs.; No. 4-8: 52 pgs.)(No. 1-8 oversized-10-1/2x14-1/2"; black & white) GD25 FN65 VF82

1-(Rare)-Sheena Queen of the Jungle(1st app.) by Meskin, Hawks of the Seas (The Hawk #10 on; see Feature Funnies #3) by Eisner, The Hunchback by Dick Briefer (ends #8), Wilton of the West (ends #24), Inspector Dayton (ends #67) & ZX-5 (ends #140) begin; 1st comic art by Jack Kirby (Count of Monte Cristo & Wilton of the West); Mickey Mouse appears (1 panel) with brief biography of Walt Disney; 1st app. Peter Pupp by Bob Kane. Note: Sheena was created by Iger for publication in England as a newspaper strip. The early issues of Jumbo contain Sheena strip-r; mutiple panel-c 1,2,7 1500.00 4500.00 16,500.00
2-(Rare)-Origin Sheena. Diary of Dr. Hayward by Kirby (also #3) plus 2 other stories; contains strip from Universal Film featuring Edgar Bergen & Charlie McCarthy plus-c (preview of film) 540.00 1620.00 5400.00
3-Last Kirby issue 380.00 1140.00 3800.00
4-(Scarce)-Origin The Hawk by Eisner; Wilton of the West by Fine (ends #14)(1st comic work); Count of Monte Cristo by Fine (ends #15); The Diary of Dr. Hayward by Fine (cont'd #8,9) 360.00 1080.00 3600.00
5-Christmas-c 316.00 948.00 3000.00
6-8-Last B&W issue. #8 was a 1939 N. Y. World's Fair Special Edition; Frank Buck's Jungleland story 274.00 822.00 2600.00
9-Stuart Taylor begins by Fine (ends #140); Fine-c; 1st color issue (8-9/39)-1st Sheena (jungle) cover; 8-1/4x10-1/4" (oversized in width only) 256.00 768.00 2300.00

GD25 FN65 NM94

10-Regular size 68 pg. issues begin; Sheena dons new costume w/ origin costume; Stuart Taylor sci/fi-c; classic Lou Fine-c. 153.00 459.00 1300.00
11-13: 12-The Hawk-c by Eisner. 13-Eisner-c 112.00 336.00 950.00
14-Intro. Lightning (super-hero) on-c only 116.00 348.00 990.00
15,17-20: 15-1st Lightning story and begins, ends #41. 17-Lightning part-c 69.00 207.00 590.00
16-Lightning-c 88.00 264.00 750.00
21-30: 22-1st Tom, Dick & Harry; origin The Hawk retold. 25-Midnight the Black Stallion begins, ends #65 55.00 165.00 465.00
31-40: 31-(9/41)-1st app. Mars God of War in Stuart Taylor story (see Planet Comics #15. 35-Shows V2#11 (correct number does not appear) 44.00 132.00 375.00
41-50: 42-Ghost Gallery begins, ends #167 39.00 117.00 300.00
51-60: 52-Last Tom, Dick & Harry 32.00 96.00 240.00
61-70: 68-Sky Girl begins, ends #130; not in #79 25.00 74.00 185.00
71-93,95-99: 89-ZX5 becomes a private eye. 19.00 56.00 140.00
94-Used in Love and Death by Legman 20.00 60.00 150.00
100 19.00 58.00 145.00
101-140,150-158 15.00 44.00 110.00
141-149-Two Sheena stories. 141-Long Bow, Indian Boy begins, ends #160 15.00 44.00 110.00

GD25 FN65 NM94

155-Used in **POP**, pg. 98 15.00 44.00 110.00
159-163: Space Scouts serial in all. 160-Last jungle-c (6/52). 161-Ghost Gallery covers begin, end #167. 163-Suicide Smith app. 13.00 40.00 100.00
164-The Star Pirate begins, ends #165 13.00 40.00 100.00
165-167: 165,167-Space Rangers app. 13.00 40.00 100.00
NOTE: *Bondage covers, negligee panels, torture, etc. are common in this series. Hawks of the Seas, Inspector Dayton, Spies in Action, Sports Shorts, & Uncle Otto by Eisner, #1-7. Hawk by* ***Eisner****-#10-15.* ***Eisner*** *c-1-8, 12-14. 1pg. Patsy pin-ups in 92-97, 99-101. Sheena by* ***Meskin****-#1, 4; by* ***Powell****-#2, 3, 5-28;* ***Powell*** *c-14, 16, 17, 19.* ***Powell/Eisner*** *c-15. Sky Girl by* ***Matt Baker****-#69-78, 80-130. ZX-5 & Ghost Gallery by* ***Kamen****-#90-130.* ***Bailey*** *a-3-8.* ***Briefer*** *a-1-8, 10.* ***Fine*** *a-14; c-9-11.* ***Kamen*** *a-101, 105, 123, 132; c-105, 121-145.* ***Bob Kane*** *a-1-8.* ***Whitman*** *c-146-167(most). Jungle c-9, 13, 15, 17 on.*

JUMPING JACKS PRESENTS THE WHIZ KIDS
Jumping Jacks Stores giveaway: 1978 (In 3-D) with glasses (4 pgs.)

nn 1.00

JUNGLE ACTION
Atlas Comics (IPC): Oct, 1954 - No. 6, Aug, 1955

1-Leopard Girl begins by Al Hartley (#1,3); Jungle Boy by Forte; Maneely-a in all 32.00 96.00 240.00
2-(3-D effect cover) 34.00 102.00 255.00
3-6: 3-Last precode (2/55) 20.00 60.00 150.00
NOTE: ***Maneely*** *c-1, 2, 5, 6.* ***Romita*** *a-3, 6.* ***Shores*** *a-3, 6; c-3, 4?.*

JUNGLE ACTION (...& Black Panther #18-21?)
Marvel Comics Group: Oct, 1972 - No. 24, Nov, 1976

1-Lorna, Jann-r (All reprints in 1-4) 1.40 4.20 14.00
2-4 .90 2.70 8.00
5-Black Panther begins (r/Avengers #62) 1.60 4.80 16.00
6,7,9,10: 6-new stories begin; 9-Contains pull-out centerfold ad by Mark Jewelers 2.00 6.00
8-Origin Black Panther .90 2.70 8.00
11-18: 4.00
19-21,23,24: 19-23-KKK x-over. 23-r/#22. 24-1st Wind Eagle; sty contd in Marvel Premiere #51-#53 3.00
22-(Regular 25¢ edition)(7/76) 3.00
22-(30¢-c, limited distribution) 1.20 3.60 12.00
NOTE: ***Buckler*** *a-6-9p, 22; c-8p, 12p.* ***Buscema*** *a-5p; c-22.* ***Byrne*** *c-23.* ***Gil Kane*** *a-8p; c-2, 4, 10p, 11p, 13-17, 19, 24.* ***Kirby*** *c-18.* ***Maneely*** *r-1.* ***Russell*** *a-13i.* ***Starlin*** *c-3p.*

JUNGLE ADVENTURES
Super Comics: 1963 - 1964 (Reprints)

10,12,15: 10-r/Terrors of the Jungle #4 & #10(Rulah). 12-r/Zoot #14(Rulah).15-r/ Kaanga from Jungle #152 & Tiger Girl 3.00 9.00 30.00
17-All Jo-Jo reprints 3.00 9.00 30.00
18-Reprints/White Princess of the Jungle #1; no Kinstler-a; origin of both White Princess & Cap'n Courage 3.00 9.00 30.00

JUNGLE ADVENTURES
Skywald Comics: Mar, 1971 - No. 3, June, 1971 (25¢, 52 pgs.)

1-Zangar origin; reprints of Jo-Jo, Blue Gorilla(origin)/White Princess #3, Kinstler-r/White Princess #2 1.40 4.20 14.00
2-Zangar, Sheena-r/Sheena #17 & Jumbo #162, Jo-Jo, origin Slave Girl Princess-r 1.00 3.00 10.00
3-Zangar, Jo-Jo, White Princess-r, Rulah 1.00 3.00 10.00

JUNGLE BOOK (See King Louie and Mowgli, Movie Comics, Mowgli..., Walt Disney Showcase #45 & Walt Disney's The Jungle Book)

JUNGLE BOOK FUN BOOK, THE (Disney)
Baskin Robbins: 1978

nn-Ice Cream giveaway 1.50 4.50 12.00

JUNGLE CAT (Disney)
Dell Publishing Co.: No. 1136, Sept-Nov, 1960 (one shot)

Four Color 1136-Movie, photo-c 5.50 16.50 60.00

JUNGLE COMICS
Fiction House Magazines: 1/40 - No. 157, 3/53; No. 158, Spr, 1953 - No. 163,

Jungle Comics #31 © FH

Jungle Jim #14 © STD

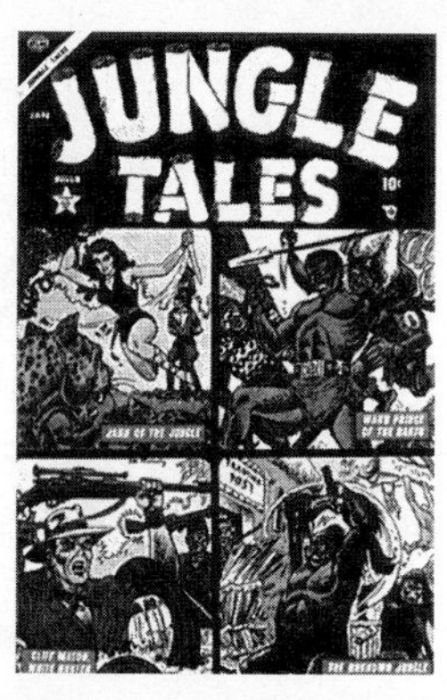

Jungle Tales #3 © MAR

GD25 FN65 NM94

Summer, 1954

1-Origin The White Panther, Kaanga, Lord of the Jungle, Tabu, Wizard of the Jungle; Wambi, the Jungle Boy, Camilla & Capt. Terry Thunder begin (all 1st app.). Lou Fine-c 350.00 1050.00 3500.00
2-Fantomah, Mystery Woman of the Jungle begins, ends #51; The Red Panther begins, ends #26 135.00 400.00 1150.00
3,4 115.00 345.00 975.00
5-Classic Eisner-c 124.00 372.00 1050.00
6-10: 7,8-Powell-c 66.00 198.00 560.00
11-20: 13-Tuska-c 46.00 138.00 395.00
21-30: 25-Shows V2#1 (correct number does not appear). #27-New origin Fantomah, Daughter of the Pharoahs; Camilla dons new costume 41.00 124.00 330.00
31-40 31.00 92.00 230.00
41,43-50 27.00 80.00 200.00
42-Kaanga by Crandall, 12 pgs. 29.00 88.00 220.00
51-60 25.00 74.00 185.00
61-70: 67-Cover swipes Crandall splash pg. in #42 20.00 60.00 150.00
71-80: 79-New origin Tabu 18.00 54.00 135.00
81-97,99,101-110 16.00 48.00 120.00
98-Used in **SOTI**, pg. 185 & illo "In ordinary comic books, there are pictures within pictures for children who know how to look;" used by N.Y. Legis. Comm. 29.00 86.00 215.00
100 20.00 60.00 150.00
111-163: 104-In Camilla story villain is Dr. Wertham. 118-Clyde Beatty app. 135-Desert Panther begins in Terry Thunder (origin), not in #137; ends (dies) #138. 139-Last 52 pg. issue. 141-Last Tabu. 143,145-Used in **POP**, pg. 99. 151-Last Camilla & Terry Thunder. 152-Tiger Girl begins. 158-Last Wambi; Sheena app. 15.00 44.00 110.00
I.W. Reprint #1,9: 1-r/? 9-r/#151 2.60 7.80 26.00

NOTE: *Bondage covers, negligee panels, torture, etc. are common to this series. Camilla by* ***Fran Hopper****-#70-92; by* ***Baker****-#69, 100-113, 115, 116; by* ***Lubbers****-#97-99 by* ***Tuska****-#63, 65. Kaanga by* ***John Celardo****-#80-113; by* ***Larsen****-#71, 75-79; by* ***Moreira****-#58, 60, 61, 63-70, 72-74; by* ***Tuska****-#37, 62; by* ***Whitman****-#114-163. Tabu by* ***Larsen****-#59-75, 82-92; by* ***Whitman****-#93-115. Terry Thunder by* ***Hopper****-#71, 72; by* ***Celardo****-#78, 79; by* ***Lubbers****-#80-85. Tiger Girl-r by* ***Baker****-#152, 153, 155-157, 159. Wambi by* ***Baker****-#62-67, 74.* ***Astarita*** *c-45, 46.* ***Celardo*** *a-78; c-98-113.* ***Crandall*** *c-67 from splash pg.* ***Eisner*** *c-2, 5, 6.* ***Fine*** *c-1.* ***Larsen*** *a-65, 66, 71, 72, 74, 75, 79, 83, 84, 87-90.* ***Moriera*** *c-43, 44.* ***Morisi*** *a-51.* ***Powell*** *c-7, 8.* ***Sultan*** *c-3, 4.* ***Tuska*** *c-13.* ***Whitman*** *c-132-163(most).* ***Zolnerowich*** *c-11, 12, 18-41.*

JUNGLE COMICS
Blackthorne Publishing: May, 1988 - No.4 ($2.00, B&W/color)

1-4: 1-Dave Stevens-c; B. Jones scripts in all. 2-B&W-a begins 2.00

JUNGLE GIRL (See Lorna, the...)

JUNGLE GIRL (Nyoka, Jungle Girl No. 2 on)
Fawcett Publications: Fall, 1942 (one-shot)(No month listed)

1-Bondage-c; photo of Kay Aldridge who played Nyoka in movie serial app. on-c. Adaptation of the classic Republic movie serial Perils of Nyoka. 1st comic to devote entire contents to a movie serial adaptation 100.00 300.00 850.00

JUNGLE GIRLS
AC Comics: 1989 - No. 16, 1993 (B&W)

1-($1.95)-New story & "good girl" reprints 2.00
2-($2.25)-New story & "good girl" reprints 2.25
3-16: 3,4,10,13-16-New story & g.g. reprints. 5-9,11,12-All g.g. reprints (Baker, Powell, Lubbers, others) 2.50

JUNGLE JIM (Also see Ace Comics)
Standard Comics (Best Books): No. 11, Jan, 1949 - No. 20, Apr, 1951

11 7.50 22.50 52.00
12-20 5.00 15.00 30.00

JUNGLE JIM
Dell Publishing Co.: No. 490, 8/53 - No. 1020, 8-10/59 (Painted-c)

GD25 FN65 NM94

Four Color 490(#1) 5.50 16.50 60.00
Four Color 565(#2, 6/54) 2.75 8.00 30.00
3(10-12/54)-5 2.50 7.50 28.00
6-19(1-3/59) 2.25 6.75 25.00
Four Color 1020(#20) 2.25 6.75 25.00

JUNGLE JIM
King Features Syndicate: No. 5, Dec, 1967

5-Reprints Dell #5; Wood-c 1.50 4.50 12.00

JUNGLE JIM (Continued from Dell series)
Charlton Comics: No. 22, Feb, 1969 - No. 28, Feb, 1970 (#21 was an overseas edition only)

22-Dan Flagg begins; Ditko/Wood-a 2.50 7.50 25.00
23-26: 23-Last Dan Flagg; Howard-c. 24-Jungle People begin 2.00 6.00 16.00
27,28: 27-Ditko/Howard-a. 28-Ditko-a 2.50 7.50 20.00

NOTE: *Ditko cover of #22 reprints story panels*

JUNGLE JO
Fox Feature Syndicate (Hero Books): Mar, 1950 - No. 6, Mar, 1951

nn-Jo-Jo blanked out, leaving Congo King; came out after Jo-Jo #29 (intended as Jo-Jo #30?) 35.00 105.00 265.00
1-Tangi begins; part Wood-a 40.00 120.00 320.00
2 31.00 93.00 230.00
3-6 30.00 90.00 225.00

JUNGLE LIL (Dorothy Lamour #2 on; also see Feature Stories Magazine)
Fox Feature Syndicate (Hero Books): April, 1950

1 33.00 100.00 245.00

JUNGLE TALES (Jann of the Jungle No. 8 on)
Atlas Comics (CSI): Sept, 1954 - No. 7, Sept, 1955

1-Jann of the Jungle 32.00 96.00 240.00
2-7: 3-Last precode (1/55) 22.00 66.00 165.00

NOTE: ***Heath*** *c-5.* ***Heck*** *a-6, 7.* ***Maneely*** *a-2; c-1, 3.* ***Shores*** *a-5-7; c-4, 6.* ***Tuska*** *a-2.*

JUNGLE TALES OF CAVEWOMAN
Basement Comics: 1998 ($2.95, B&W)

1-Budd Root-s/a 3.00

JUNGLE TALES OF TARZAN
Charlton Comics: Dec, 1964 - No. 4, July, 1965

1 4.20 12.60 42.00
2-4 3.20 9.60 32.00

NOTE: ***Giordano*** *c-3p.* ***Glanzman*** *a-1-3.* ***Montes/Bache*** *a-4.*

JUNGLE TERROR (See Harvey Comics Hits No. 54)

JUNGLE THRILLS (Formerly Sports Thrills; Terrors of the Jungle #17 on)
Star Publications: No. 16, Feb, 1952; Dec, 1953; No. 7, 1954

16-Phantom Lady & Rulah story-reprint/All Top No. 15; used in **POP**, pg. 98,99; L. B. Cole-c 44.00 132.00 370.00
3-D 1(12/53, 25¢)-Came w/glasses; Jungle Lil & Jungle Jo appear; L. B. Cole-c 46.00 138.00 395.00
7-Titled 'Picture Scope Jungle Adventures;' (1954, 36 pgs, 15¢)-3-D effect c/stories; story & coloring book; Disbrow-a/script; L.B. Cole-c 43.00 129.00 355.00

JUNGLE TWINS, THE (Tono & Kono)
Gold Key/Whitman No. 18: Apr, 1972 - No. 17, Nov, 1975; No. 18, May, 1982

1 1.20 3.60 12.00
2-5 6.00
6-18: 18-Reprints 4.00

NOTE: *UFO c/story No. 13. Painted-c No. 1-17.* ***Spiegle*** *c-18.*

JUNGLE WAR STORIES (Guerrilla War No. 12 on)
Dell Publishing Co.: July-Sept, 1962 - No. 11, Apr-June, 1965 (Painted-c)

01-384-209 (#1) 2.50 7.50 22.00

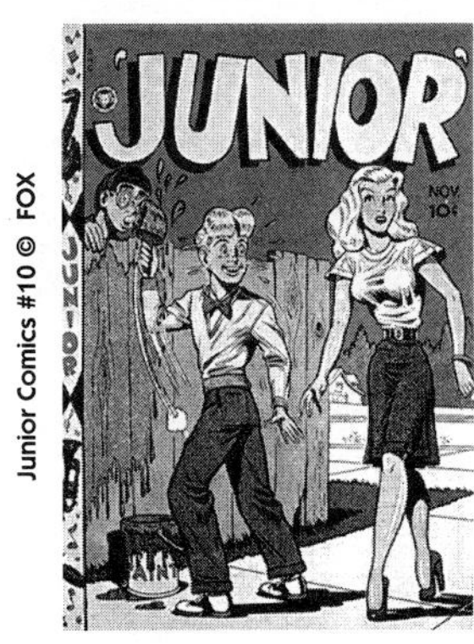

Junior Comics #10 © FOX

Jurassic Park: Raptors Hijack #2 © Universal

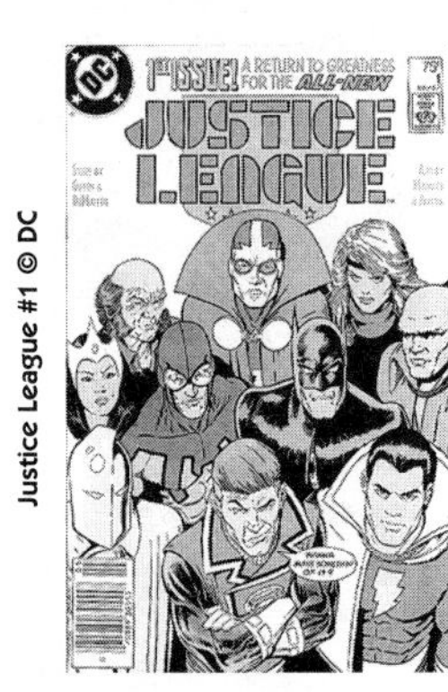

Justice League #1 © DC

GD25 FN65 NM94

2-11 2.00 6.00 16.00

JUNIE PROM (Also see Dexter Comics)
Dearfield Publishing Co.: Winter, 1947-48 - No. 7, Aug, 1949

1-Teen-age 10.00 30.00 75.00
2 5.70 17.00 40.00
3-7 4.25 13.00 28.00

JUNIOR CARROT PATROL (Jr. Carrot Patrol #2)
Dark Horse Comics: May, 1989; No. 2, Nov, 1990 ($2.00, B&W)

1,2-Flaming Carrot spin-off. 1-Bob Burden-c(i) 2.00

JUNIOR COMICS (Formerly Li'l Pan; becomes Western Outlaws with #17)
Fox Feature Syndicate: No. 9, Sept, 1947 - No. 16, July, 1948

9-Feldstein-c/a; headlights-c 68.00 203.00 575.00
10-16-Feldstein-c/a; headlights-c on all 61.00 182.00 515.00

JUNIOR FUNNIES (Formerly Tiny Tot Funnies No. 9)
Harvey Publ. (King Features Synd.): No. 10, Aug, 1951 - No. 13, Feb, 1952

10-Partial reprints in all; Blondie, Dagwood, Daisy, Henry, Popeye, Felix, Katzenjammer Kids 3.60 9.00 18.00
11-13 3.20 8.00 16.00

JUNIOR HOPP COMICS
Stanmor Publ.: Feb, 1952 - No. 3, July, 1952

1-Teenage humor 7.15 21.50 50.00
2,3: 3-Dave Berg-a 4.25 13.00 28.00

JUNIOR MEDICS OF AMERICA, THE
E. R. Squire & Sons: No. 1359, 1957 (15¢)

1359 2.80 7.00 14.00

JUNIOR MISS
Timely/Marvel (CnPC): Wint, 1944; No. 24, Apr, 1947 - No. 39, Aug, 1950

1-Frank Sinatra & June Allyson life story 23.00 68.00 170.00
24-Formerly The Human Torch #23? 10.00 30.00 75.00
25-38: 29,31,34-Cindy-c/stories (others?) 5.70 17.00 38.00
39-Kurtzman-a 7.85 23.50 55.00
NOTE: *Painted-c 35-37. 35, 37-all romance. 36, 38-mostly teen humor.*

JUNIOR PARTNERS (Formerly Oral Roberts' True Stories)
Oral Roberts Evangelistic Assn.: No. 120, Aug, 1959 - V3#12, Dec, 1961

120(#1) 3.20 9.60 32.00
2(9/59) 2.50 7.50 22.00
3-12(7/60) 1.75 5.25 14.00
V2#1(8/60)-5(12/60) 1.10 3.30 9.00
V3#1(1/61)-12 1.00 2.80 7.00

JUNIOR TREASURY (See Dell Junior...)

JUNIOR WOODCHUCKS GUIDE (Walt Disney's...)
Danbury Press: 1973 (8-3/4"x5-3/4", 214 pgs., hardcover)

nn-Illustrated text based on the long-standing J.W. Guide used by Donald Duck's nephews Huey, Dewey & Louie by Carl Barks. The guidebook was a popular plot devise to enable the nephews to solve problems facing their uncle or Scrooge McDuck (scarce) 3.20 9.50 35.00

JUNIOR WOODCHUCKS LIMITED SERIES (Walt Disney's...)
W. D. Publications (Disney): July, 1991 - No. 4, Oct, 1991 ($1.50, limited series; new & reprint-a)

1-4: 1-The Beagle Boys app.; Barks-r 1.50

JUNIOR WOODCHUCKS (See Huey, Dewey & Louie...)

JUNK CULTURE
DC Comics (Vertigo): July, 1997 - No. 2, Aug, 1997 ($2.50, limited series)

1,2: Ted McKeever-s/a in all 2.50

JURASSIC JANE
London Night Studios: Apr, 1997 - No. 7 ($3.00, B&W)

1-7 3.00
1-7-($6.00)-Variant nude-c 2.00 6.00

JURASSIC PARK
Topps Comics: 6/93 - No. 4, 8/93; #5, 10/94 - #10, 2/95

1-($2.50)-Newsstand Edition; Kane/Perez-a in all; 1-4: movie adaptation 3.00
1-($2.95)-Collector's Ed.; polybagged w/3 cards 4.00
1-Amberchrome Edition w/no price or ads .85 2.60 7.00
2-4-($2.50)-Newsstand Edition 2.50
2,3-($2.95)-Collector's Ed.; polybagged w/3 cards 3.00
4-($2.95)-Collector's Ed.; polybagged w/1 of 4 different action hologram trading card; Gil Kane/Perez-a 3.00
5-10: 5-becomes Advs. of 2.00
Annual 1 ($3.95, 5/95) 4.00
Trade paperback (1993, $9.95)-r/#1-4; bagged w/#0 1.00 3.00 10.00

JURASSIC PARK: RAPTOR
Topps Comics: Nov, 1993 - No. 2, Dec, 1993 ($2.95, limited series)

1,2: 1-Bagged w/3 trading cards & Zorro #0; Golden c-1,2 3.00

JURASSIC PARK: RAPTORS ATTACK
Topps Comics: Mar, 1994 - No. 4, June, 1994 ($2.50, limited series)

1-4-Michael Golden-c/frontispiece 2.50

JURASSIC PARK: RAPTORS HIJACK
Topps Comics: July, 1994 - No. 4, Oct, 1994 ($2.50, limited series)

1-4: Michael Golden-c/front piece 2.50

JUSTICE
Marvel Comics Group (New Universe): Nov, 1986 - No. 32, June, 1989

1-32: 26-32-$1.50-c 1.00

JUSTICE COMICS (Formerly Wacky Duck; Tales of Justice #53 on)
Marvel/Atlas Comics (NPP 7-9,4-19/CnPC 20-23/MjMC 24-38/Male 39-52: No. 7, Fall/47 - No. 9, 6/48; No. 4, 8/48 - No. 52, 3/55

7(#1, 1947) 23.00 70.00 175.00
8(#2)-Kurtzman-a "Giggles 'n' Grins" (3) 16.00 48.00 120.00
9(#3, 6/48) 15.00 44.00 110.00
4 13.00 40.00 100.00
5-9: 8-Anti-Wertham editorial 11.00 34.00 85.00
10-15-Photo-c 9.30 28.00 65.00
16-30 7.15 21.50 50.00
31-40,42-52: 35-Gene Colan-a. 48-Last precode; Pakula & Tuska-a. 6.50 19.50 45.00
41-Electrocution-c 13.00 38.00 95.00
NOTE: ***Heath** a-24. **Maneely** c-44, 52. **Pakula** a-43, 45, 48. **Louis Ravielli** a-39. **Robinson** a-22, 25, 41. **Shores** c-7(#1), 8(#2)? **Tuska** a-48. **Wildey** a-52.*

JUSTICE: FOUR BALANCE
Marvel Comics: Sept, 1994 - No. 4, Dec, 1994 ($1.75, limited series)

1-4: 1-Thing & Firestar app. 1.75

JUSTICE, INC. (The Avenger) (Pulp)
National Periodical Publications: May-June, 1975 - No. 4, Nov-Dec, 1975

1-McWilliams-a, Kubert-c; origin 5.00
2-4: 2-4-Kirby-a(p), c-2,3p. 4-Kubert-c 4.00
NOTE: *Adapted from Kenneth Robeson novel, creator of Doc Savage.*

JUSTICE, INC. (Pulp)
DC Comics: 1989 - No. 2, 1989 ($3.95, 52 pgs., squarebound, mature)

1,2: Re-intro The Avenger; Andrew Helfer scripts & Kyle Baker-c/a 4.00

JUSTICE LEAGUE (...International #7-25; ...America #26 on)
DC Comics: May, 1987 - No. 113, Aug, 1996 (Also see Legends #6)

1-Batman, Green Lantern (Guy Gardner), Blue Beetle, Mr. Miracle, Capt. Marvel & Martian Manhunter begin 4.00

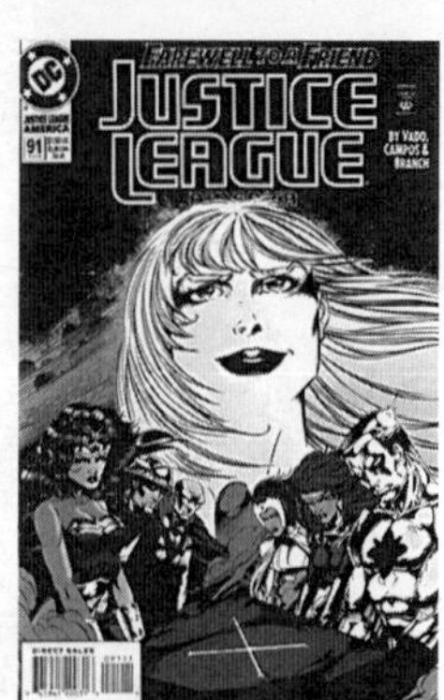

Justice League America #91 © DC

Justice League Europe #28 © DC

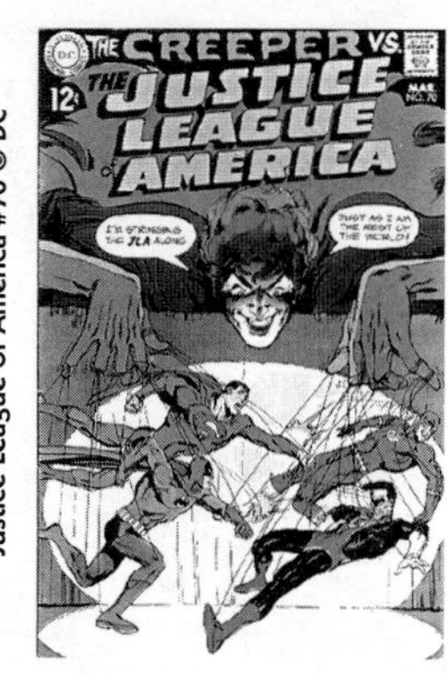

Justice League of America #70 © DC

GD25 FN65 NM94

2 3.00
3-Regular-c (white background) 2.00
3-Limited-c (yellow background, Superman logo) 2.00 6.00 20.00
4-6: 4-Booster Gold joins. 5-Origin Gray Man; Batman vs. Guy Gardner; Creeper app. 2.50
7-($1.25, 52 pgs.)-Capt. Marvel & Dr. Fate resign; Capt. Atom & Rocket Red join 2.00
8-10: 9,10-Millennium x-over 1.50
11-23: 16-Bruce Wayne-c/story. 18-21-Lobo app. 1.25
24-($1.50)-1st app. Justice League Europe 1.75
25-49,51-62: 31,32-Justice League Europe x-over. 58-Lobo app. 61-New team begins; swipes-c to JLA #1(10-11/60). 62-Last $1.00-c 1.25
50-($1.75, 52 pgs.) 1.75
63-68,72-82: 80-Intro new Booster Gold. 82,83-Guy Gardner-c/stories 1.25
69-Doomsday tie-in; takes place between Superman: The Man of Steel #18 & Superman #74 4.00
69,70-2nd printings 1.25
70-Funeral for a Friend part 1; red 3/4 outer-c 2.50
70-Newsstand version w/o outer-c 1.50
71-Direct sales version w/black outer-c 2.00
71-Newsstand version w/o outer-c 1.25
83-92: 83-$1.50-c begins. 92-(9/94)-Zero Hour x-over; Triumph app 1.50
0-(10/94)-New team begins (Hawkman, Wonder Woman, Metamorpho, Flash, Nuklon, Crimson Fox, Obsidian & Fire) 1.50
93-99: 93-(11/94) 1.50
100 ($3.95)-Foil-c; 52 pgs. 4.00
100 ($2.95)-Newstand 3.00
101-113: 101-$1.75-c begins. 113-Flash, Green Lantern & Hawkman app 1.75
Annual 1-5 (1987-1991): 2-Joker-c/story; Batman cameo. 5-Armageddon 2001 x-over; Silver ink 2nd printing 2.00
Annual 6,7 (1992,1993, $2.50, 68 pgs.):7-Bloodlines x-over 2.50
Annual 8 (1994, $2.95, 68 pgs.)-Elseworlds story 3.00
Annual 9 (1995, $3.50)-Year One story 3.50
Annual 10 (1996, $2.95)-Legends of the Dead Earth 3.00
Special 1 (1990, $1.50, 52 pgs.)-Giffen plots 1.50
Special 2 (1991, $2,95, 52 pgs.)-Staton-a(p) 3.00
Spectacular 1 (1992, $1.50, 52 pgs.)-Intro new JLI & JLE teams; ties into JLI #61 & JLE #37 1.50
A New Beginning Trade Paperback (1989, $12.95)-r/#1-7 13.00
NOTE: ***Anderson** c-61i. **Austin** a-1i, 60i; c-1i. **Giffen** a-13; c-21p. **Guice** a-62i. **Maguire** a-1-12, 16-19, 22, 23. **Russell** a-Annual 1i; c-54i. **Willingham** a-30p, Annual 2.*

JUSTICE LEAGUE: A MIDSUMMER'S NIGHTMARE
DC Comics: Sept, 1996 - No. 3, Nov, 1996 ($2.95, limited series, 38 pgs.)
1-3: Re-establishes Superman, Batman, Green Lantern, The Martian Manhunter, Flash, Aquaman & Wonder Woman as the Justice League; Mark Waid & Fabian Nicieza co-scripts; Jeff Johnson & Darick Robertson-a(p); Kevin Maguire-c. 5.00
TPB-(1997, $8.95) r/1-3 8.95

JUSTICE LEAGUE EUROPE (Justice League International #51 on)
DC Comics: Apr, 1989 - No. 68, Sept., 1994 (75¢/ $1.00/$1.25/$1.50)
1-Giffen plots in all, breakdowns in #1-8,13-30; Justice League #1-c/swipe 2.00
2-49,51-57: 5-Begin $1.00-c. 7-9-Batman app. 7,8-JLA x-over. 8,9-Superman app. 12-Metal Men app. 20-22-Rogers-c/a(p). 33,34-Lobo vs. Despero. 37-New team begins; swipes-c to JLA #9; see JLA Spectacular. 1.25
50-($2.50, 68 pgs.)-Battles Sonar 2.50
58-68: 58-$1.50-c begins. 68-Zero Hour x-over; Triumph joins Justice League Task Force (See JLTF #17) 1.50
Annual 1 (1990, $2.00, 68 pgs.)-Return of the Global Guardians; Giffen plots/ breakdowns 2.00

GD25 FN65 NM94

Annual 2 (1991, $2.00, 68pgs.)-Armageddon 2001; Giffen-a(p); Rogers-a(p); Golden-a(i) 2.00
Annual 3 (1992, $2.50, 68 pgs.)-Eclipso app. 2.50
Annual 4 (1993, $2.50, 68 pgs.)-Intro Lionheart 2.50
Annual 5 (1994, $2.95)-Elseworlds story 3.00
NOTE: ***Phil Jimenez** a-68p. **Rogers** c/a-20-22. **Sears** a-1-12, 14-19, 23-29; c-1-10, 12, 14-19, 23-29.*

JUSTICE LEAGUE INTERNATIONAL (See Justice League Europe)

JUSTICE LEAGUE OF AMERICA (See Brave & the Bold #28-30, Mystery In Space #75 & Official... Index)
National Periodical Publ./DC Comics: Oct-Nov, 1960 - No. 261, Apr, 1987 (#91-99,139-157: 52 pgs.)

	GD25	FN65	VF82	NM94
1-(10-11/60)-Origin & 1st app. Despero; Aquaman, Batman, Flash, Green Lantern, J'onn J'onzz, Superman & Wonder Woman continue from Brave and the Bold	227.00	680.00	1475.00	3400.00

	GD25	FN65	NM94
2	56.00	168.00	667.00
3-Origin/1st app. Kanjar Ro (see Mystery in Space #75)(scarce in high grade due to black-c)	46.00	138.00	560.00
4-Green Arrow joins JLA	34.00	102.00	380.00
5-Origin & 1st app. Dr. Destiny	29.00	87.00	290.00
6-8,10: 6-Origin & 1st app. Prof. Amos Fortune. 7-(10-11/61)-Last 10¢ issue. 10-(3/62)-Origin & 1st app. Felix Faust; 1st app. Lord of Time.	25.00	75.00	250.00
9-(2/62)-Origin JLA (1st origin)	34.00	102.00	380.00
11-15: 12-(6/62)-Origin & 1st app. Dr. Light. 13-(8/62)-Speedy app. 14-(9/62)-Atom joins JLA.	17.00	51.00	170.00
16-20: 17-Adam Strange flashback	14.50	44.00	145.00
21-(8/63)-"Crisis on Earth-One"; re-intro. of JSA in this title (see Flash #129) (1st S.A. app. Hourman & Dr. Fate)	28.00	84.00	280.00
22- "Crisis on Earth-Two"; JSA x-over (story continued from #21)	26.00	78.00	260.00
23-28: 24-Adam Strange app. 27-Robin app.	9.50	28.50	95.00
29-JSA x-over; 1st S.A. app. Starman; "Crisis on Earth-Three"	13.00	39.00	130.00
30-JSA x-over	10.50	32.00	105.00
31-Hawkman joins JLA, Hawkgirl cameo (11/64)	8.50	25.50	85.00
32-Intro & Origin Brain Storm	6.00	18.00	60.00
33,35,36,40,41: 40-3rd S.A. Penguin app. 41-Intro & origin The Key	5.00	15.00	50.00
34-Joker-c/story	5.50	16.50	55.00
37,38-JSA x-over (1st S.A. app. Mr. Terrific #37). 37-1st S.A. app. Mr. Terrific; Batman cameo. 38-"Crisis on Earth-A"	8.50	25.50	85.00
39-Giant G-16; r/B&B #28,30 & JLA #5	9.00	27.00	90.00
42-45: 42-Metamorpho app. 43-Intro. Royal Flush Gang	4.00	12.00	40.00
46-JSA x-over; 1st S.A. app. Sandman; 3rd S.A. app. of G.A. Spectre (8/66)	9.00	27.00	90.00
47-JSA x-over; 4th S.A. app of G.A. Spectre.	4.50	13.50	45.00
48-Giant G-29; r/JLA #2,3 & B&B #29	5.00	15.00	50.00
49-54,57,59,60	3.80	11.40	38.00
55-Intro. Earth 2 Robin (1st G.A. Robin in S.A.)	5.20	15.60	52.00
56-JLA vs. JSA (1st G.A. Wonder Woman in S.A.)	3.50	10.50	35.00
58-Giant G-41; r/JLA #6,8,1	4.80	14.40	48.00
61-63,66,68-72: 69-Wonder Woman quits. 71-Manhunter leaves. 72-Last 12¢ issue	2.80	8.40	28.00
64,65-JSA story. 64-(8/68)-Origin/1st app. S.A. Red Tornado	3.20	9.60	32.00
67-Giant G-53; r/JLA #4,14,31	4.20	12.60	42.00
73-1st S.A. app. of G.A. Superman; 1st app. of S. A. Black Canary	3.00	9.00	30.00
74-Black Canary joins; 1st meeting of G.A. & S.A. Superman.	2.50	7.50	22.00

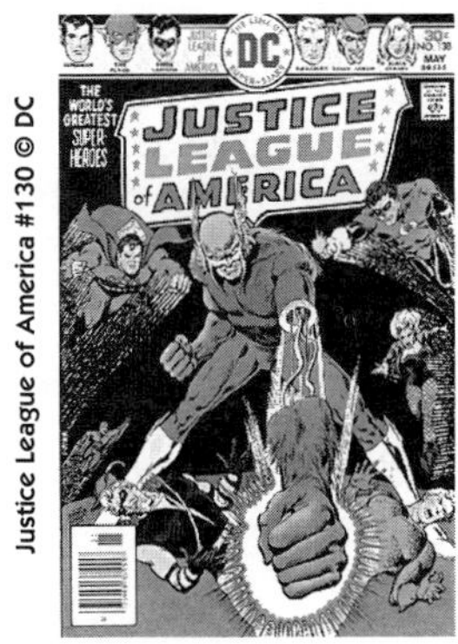

Justice League of America #130 © DC

Justice League International Quarterly #16 © DC

Justice Society of America #5 (1st Series) © DC

GD25 FN65 NM94

75-2nd app. Green Arrow in new costume (see Brave & the Bold #85) 2.50 7.50 20.00
76-Giant G-65 3.50 9.00 35.00
77-80: 78-Re-intro Vigilante (1st S.A. app?) 1.80 5.40 18.00
81-84,86-90: 82-1st S.A. app. of G.A. Batman (cameo). 83-Death of Spectre. 1.80 5.40 18.00
85,93-(Giant G-77,G-89; 68 pgs.) 2.50 7.60 28.00
91,92: 91-1st meeting of the G.A. & S.A. Robin; begin 25¢, 52 pgs. issues, ends #99. 92-S. A. Robin tries on costume that is similar to that of G.A. Robin in All Star Comics #58. 1.80 5.40 18.00
94-Reprints 1st Sandman story (Adv. #40) & origin/1st app. Starman (Adv. #61); Deadman x-over; N. Adams-a (4 pgs.) 7.25 22.00 80.00
95-Origin Dr. Fate & Dr. Midnight reprint (from More Fun #67, All-American #25) 2.50 7.50 27.00
96-Origin Hourman (Adv. #48); Wildcat-r 2.50 7.50 27.00
97-Origin JLA retold; Sargon, Starman-r 2.20 6.25 22.00
98,99: 98-G.A. Sargon, Starman-r. 99-G.A. Sandman, Atom-r; last 52 pg. issue 2.20 6.25 22.00
100-(8/72)-1st meeting of G.A. & S.A. W. Woman 2.90 8.70 32.00
101,102: JSA x-overs. 102-Red Tornado dies 1.40 4.20 14.00
103-106,109: 103-Phantom Stranger joins. 105-Elongated Man joins. 106-New Red Tornado joins. 109-Hawkman resigns 1.00 3.00 10.00
107,108-G.A. Uncle Sam, Black Condor, The Ray, Dollman, Phantom Lady & The Human Bomb (JSA) x-over, 1st S.A. app. 1.20 3.60 12.00
110-116: All 100 pgs. 111-JLA vs. Injustice Gang; Shining Knight, Green Arrow-r. 112-Amazo app; Crimson Avenger, Vigilante-r; origin Starman-r/Adv. #81. 115-Martian Manhunter app. 2.20 6.25 22.00
117-134: 117-Hawkman rejoins. 120,121-Adam Strange app.123-(10/75)-1st named app. Earth-Prime (3rd app. overall) (See Flash; 1st Series #179 & 228); DC editor Julie Schwartz & JLA writers Cary Bates & Elliot S! Maggin appear in story as themselves. 123,124-JLA/JSA app. 125-Two-Face-c/story. 126-Two-Face app. 128-Wonder Woman rejoins. 129-Destruction of Red Tornado 5.00
135-136: 135-137-G.A. Bulletman, Bulletgirl, Spy Smasher, Mr. Scarlet, Pinky & Ibis x-over, 1st S.A. appearances .90 2.70 8.00
137-Superman battles G.A. Capt. Marvel 1.00 3.00 10.00
138,158-190: 138-Adam Strange app. w/c by Neal Adams; 1st app. Green Lantern of the 73rd Century. 158-160-(44 pgs.). 161-Zatanna joins & new costume. 171-Mr. Terrific murdered. 178-Cover similar to #1; J'onn J'onzz app. 179-Firestorm joins. 181-Green Arrow leaves JLA 4.00
139-157-(52 pgs.): 139-Adam Strange app.144-Origin retold; origin J'onn J'onzz. 145-Red Tornado resurrected. 147,148-Legion x-over. 2.00 6.00
191-199: 192,193-Real origin Red Tornado. 193-1st app. All-Star Squadron as free 16 pg. insert 2.25
200 ($1.50, Anniversary issue, 76pgs.)-JLA origin retold; Green Arrow rejoins; Bolland, Broderick, Aparo, Giordano, Gil Kane, Infantino, Kubert-a; Perez-c/a. 4.00
201-250: 203-Intro/origin new Royal Flush Gang. 207,208-JSA, JLA, & All-Star Squadron team-up. 219,220-True origin Black Canary. 228-Re-intro Martian Manhunter. 228-230-War of the Worlds storyline; JLA Satellite destroyed by Martians. 233-Story cont'd from Annual #2. 243-Aquaman leaves. 244,245-Crisis x-over. 250-Batman rejoins 2.00
251-259: 253-Origin Despero. 258-Death of Vibe. 258-261-Legends x-over 1.25
260-Death of Steel 4.00
261-Last issue 2.00 6.00
Annual 1(1983) 2.75
Annual 2(1984)-Intro new J.L.A. (Aquaman, Martian Manhunter, Steel, Gypsy, Vixen, Vibe, Elongated Man, & Zatanna) 2.00
Annual 3(1985)-Crisis x-over 2.00

NOTE: ***Neal Adams*** *c-63, 66, 67, 70, 74, 79, 81, 82, 86-89, 91, 92, 94, 96-98, 138, 139.* ***M. Anderson*** *c-1-4, 6, 7, 10, 12-14.* ***Aparo*** *a-200.* ***Austin*** *a-200i.* ***Baily*** *a-96r.* ***Bolland*** *a-200.* ***Buckler*** *c-158, 163, 164.* ***Burnley*** *r-94, 98, 99.* ***Greene*** *a-46-61i, 64-73i, 110i(r).* ***Grell*** *c-117, 122.* ***Kaluta*** *c-154p.* ***Gil Kane*** *a-200.* ***Krigstein*** *a-96(r/Sensation #84).* ***Kubert*** *a-200; c-72, 73.* ***Nino*** *a-228i, 230i.* ***Orlando*** *c-151i.* ***Perez*** *a-184-186p, 192-197p, 200p; c-184p, 186, 192-195, 196p, 197p, 199, 200, 201p, 202, 203-205p, 207-209, 212-215, 217, 219, 220.* ***Reinman*** *r-97.* ***Roussos*** *a-62i.* ***Sekowsky*** *a-37, 38, 44-63p, 110-112p(r); c-46-48p, 51p.* ***Sekowsky/Anderson*** *c-5, 8, 9, 11, 15.* ***B. Smith*** *c-185i.* ***Starlin*** *c-178-180, 183, 185p.* ***Staton*** *a-244p; c-157p, 244p.* ***Toth*** *r-110.* ***Tuska*** *a-153, 228p, 241-243p. JSA x-overs-21, 22, 29, 30, 37, 38, 46, 47, 55, 56, 64, 65, 73, 74, 82, 83, 91, 92, 100, 101, 102, 107, 108, 110, 113, 115, 123, 124, 135-137, 147, 148, 159, 160, 171, 172, 183-185, 195-197, 207-209, 219, 220, 231, 232, 244.*

GD25 FN65 NM94

JUSTICE LEAGUE QUARTERLY (...International Quarterly #6 on)
DC Comics: Winter, 1990-91 - No. 17, Winter, 1994 ($2.95/$3.50, 84 pgs.)

1-6: 1-Intro The Conglomerate (Booster Gold, Praxis, Gypsy, Vapor, Echo, Maxi-Man, & Reverb); Justice League #1-c/swipe. 1,2-Giffen plots/breakdowns. 3-Giffen plot; 72 pg. story. 4-Rogers/Russell-a in back-up. 5,6-Waid scripts 3.00
7-12,14-17: 8,17-Global Guardians app. 12-Waid script 3.50
13-Linsner-c 5.00

NOTE: ***Phil Jimenez*** *a-17p.* ***Sprouse*** *a-1p.*

JUSTICE LEAGUE TASK FORCE
DC Comics: June, 1993 - No. 37, Aug, 1996 ($1.25/$1.50/$1.75)

1-7: Aquaman, Nightwing, Flash, J'onn J'onzz, & Gypsy form team. 5,6-Knight-quest tie-ins (new Batman cameo #5, 1 pg.) 1.25
8-16: 8-$1.50-c begins. 15-Triumph cameo. 16-(9/94)-Zero Hour x-over; Triumph app. 1.50
0,17-23: 0-(10/94). 17-(11/94)-Triumph becomes part of Justice League Task Force (See JLE #68) 1.50
24-37: 24-$1.75-c begins, 26-Impulse app. 35-Warlord app. 37-Triumph quits team 1.75

JUSTICE MACHINE, THE
Noble Comics: June, 1981 - No. 5, Nov, 1983 ($2.00, nos. 1-3 are mag. size)

1-Byrne-c(p) 2.25 6.80 25.00
2-Austinpc(i) 1.50 4.50 15.00
3 1.00 3.00 10.00
4,5 5.00
Annual 1 (1/84, 68 pgs.)(published by Texas Comics); 1st app. The Elementals; Golden-c(p) 4.00

JUSTICE MACHINE (Also see The New Justice Machine)
Comico/Innovation Publishing: Jan, 1987 - No. 29, May 1989 ($1.50/$1.75)

1-29 1.50
Annual 1(6/89, $2.50, 36 pgs.)-Last Comico ish. 2.50
Summer Spectacular 1 ('89, $2.75)-Innovation Publ.; Byrne/Gustovich cover 2.75

JUSTICE MACHINE, THE
Innovation Publishing: 1990 - No. 4, 1990 ($1.95/$2.25, deluxe format, mature)

1-4: Gustovich-c/a in all 2.25

JUSTICE MACHINE FEATURING THE ELEMENTALS
Comico: May, 1986 - No. 4, Aug, 1986 ($1.50, limited series)

1-4 1.50

JUSTICE RIDERS
DC Comics: 1997 ($5.95, one-shot, prestige format)

1-Elseworlds; Dixon-s/Williams & Gray-a 2.00 6.00

JUSTICE SOCIETY OF AMERICA (See Adventure #461 & All-Star #3)
DC Comics: April, 1991 - No. 8, Nov, 1991 ($1.00, limited series)

1-8: 1-Flash. 2-Black Canary. 3-Green Lantern. 4-Hawkman. 5-Flash/Hawkman. 6-Green Lantern/Black Canary. 7-JSA 1.00

JUSTICE SOCIETY OF AMERICA (Also see Last Days of the... Special)
DC Comics: Aug, 1992 - No. 10, May, 1993 ($1.25)

1-10 1.25

JUSTICE TRAPS THE GUILTY (Fargo Kid V11#3 on)
Prize/Headline Publications: Oct-Nov, 1947 - V11#2(#92), Apr-May, 1958 (True FBI Cases)

V2#1-S&K-c/a; electrocution-c 47.00 142.00 400.00

Ka'a'nga Comics #3 © FH

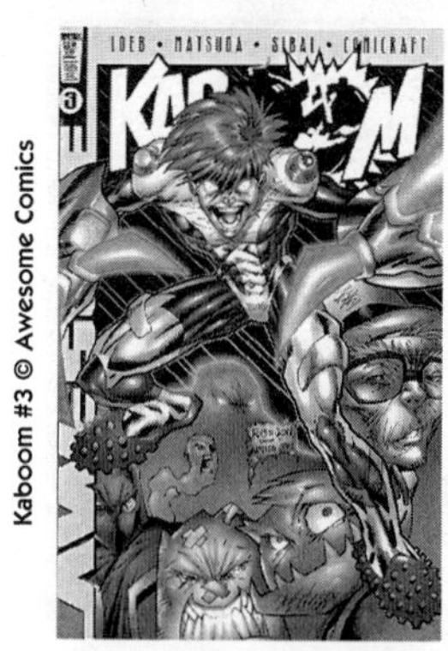

Kaboom #3 © Awesome Comics

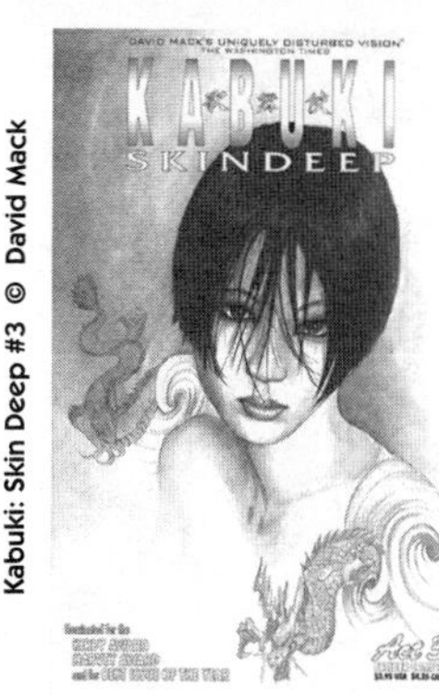

Kabuki: Skin Deep #3 © David Mack

	GD25	FN65	NM94
2-S&K-c/a	29.00	88.00	220.00
3-5-S&K-c/a	27.00	82.00	205.00
6-S&K-c/a; Feldstein-a	29.00	88.00	220.00
7,9-S&K-c/a. 7-9-V2#1-3 in indicia; #7-9 on-c	23.00	70.00	175.00
8,10-Krigstein-a; S&K-c. 10-S&K-a	26.00	78.00	195.00
11,18,19-S&K-c	11.00	32.00	80.00
12,14-17,20-No S&K. 14-Severin/Elder-a (8pg.)	5.70	17.00	38.00
13-Used in **SOTI**, pg. 110-111	8.00	24.00	55.00
21,30-S&K-c/a	9.30	28.00	65.00
22,23,27-S&K-c	6.50	19.50	45.00
24-26,28,29,31-50: 28-Kirby-c. 32-Meskin story	4.25	13.00	28.00
51-55,57,59-70	4.15	12.50	25.00
56-Ben Oda, Joe Simon, Joe Genola, Mort Meskin & Jack Kirby app. in police line-up on classic-c	5.70	17.00	40.00
58-Illo. in **SOTI**, "Treating police contemptuously" (top left); text on heroin	17.00	51.00	170.00
71-92: 76-Orlando-a	4.00	10.00	22.00

NOTE: ***Bailey** a-12, 13. **Elder** a-8. **Kirby** a-19p. **Meskin** a-22, 27, 63, 64; c-45, 46. **Robinson/Meskin** a-5, 19. **Severin** a-8, 11p. Photo c-12, 15-17.*

JUST MARRIED
Charlton Comics: January, 1958 - No. 114, Dec, 1976

	GD25	FN65	NM94
1	5.00	15.00	50.00
2	3.00	9.00	30.00
3-10	2.50	7.50	20.00
11-30	1.50	4.50	15.00
31-50	1.20	3.30	12.00
51-70	.90	2.70	9.00
71-90		2.00	6.00
91-114			5.00

JUSTY
Viz Comics: Dec 6, 1988 - No. 9, 1989 ($1.75, B&W, bi-weekly mini-series)

	GD25	FN65	NM94
1-9: Japanese manga			1.80

KA'A'NGA COMICS (...Jungle King)(See Jungle Comics)
Fiction House Magazines (Glen-Kel Publ. Co.): Spring, 1949 - No. 20, Summer, 1954

	GD25	FN65	NM94
1-Ka'a'nga, Lord of the Jungle begins	46.00	138.00	390.00
2 (Winter, '49-'50)	25.00	76.00	190.00
3,4	18.00	54.00	135.00
5-Camilla app.	13.00	40.00	100.00
6-10: 7-Tuska-a. 9-Tabu, Wizard of the Jungle app. 10-Used in **POP**, pg. 99	11.00	34.00	85.00
11-15: 15-Camilla-r by Baker/Jungle #106	9.30	28.00	70.00
16-Sheena app.	10.00	30.00	75.00
17-20	9.30	28.00	65.00
I.W. Reprint #1,8: 1-r/#18; Kinstler-c. 8-r/#10	2.50	7.50	20.00

NOTE: ***Celardo** c-1. **Whitman** c-8-20(most).*

KABOOM
Awesome Entertainment: Sept, 1997 - No. 3, Nov, 1997 ($2.50)

	GD25	FN65	NM94
1-Matsuda-a/Loeb-s; 4 covers exist (Matsuda, Sale, Pollina and McGuinness)			2.50
1-Dynamic Forces Edition			2.50
2-Regular			2.50
2-Alicia Watcher variant-c			3.00
2-Gold logo variant -c			2.50
3-Liefeld-c			2.50
3-Matsuda-c			2.50
3-Dynamic Forces Ed.			5.00
Prelude			4.00
Prelude Gold Edition			7.50

KABUKI
Caliber Press: Nov, 1994 ($3.50, B&W)

	GD25	FN65	NM94
1-Intro Kabuki	.85	2.60	7.00
Color Special (1/96, $2.95)-Mack-c/a/scripts; pin-ups by Tucci, Harris & Quesada			5.00
Gallery (8/95, $2.95)- pinups from Mack, Paul Pope, Tim Bradstreet & others.			3.00

KABUKI
Image Comics: Oct, 1997 - Present ($2.95, color)

	GD25	FN65	NM94
1-David Mack-c/s/a			4.00
1-($10.00)-Dynamic Forces Edition	1.00	3.00	10.00
2-6			2.95
...Images (6/98, $4.95) r/#1 with new pin-ups			5.00
...Reflections (7/98, $4.95) new story plus art techniques			5.00

KABUKI: CIRCLE OF BLOOD
Caliber Press: Jan, 1995 - No. 6, Nov, 1995 ($2.95, B&W)

	GD25	FN65	NM94
1-David Mack story/a in all		2.00	6.00
2-6: 3-#1on inside indicia.			3.00
6-Variant-c			3.00
TPB ($16.95) r/#1-6, intro. by Steranko			16.95
TPB (1997, $17.95) Image Edition-r/#1-6, intro. by Steranko			17.95
TPB ($24.95) Deluxe Edition			24.95

KABUKI: DANCE OF DEATH
London Night Studios: Jan, 1995 ($3.00, B&W, one-shot)

	GD25	FN65	NM94
1-David Mack-c/a/scripts	.90	2.70	8.00

KABUKI: DREAMS
Image Comics: Jan, 1998 ($4.95, TPB)

	GD25	FN65	NM94
nn-Reprints Color Special & Dreams of the Dead			5.00

KABUKI: DREAMS OF THE DEAD
Caliber: July, 1996 ($2.95, one-shot)

	GD25	FN65	NM94
nn-David Mack-c/a/scripts			3.00

KABUKI FAN EDITION
Gemstone Publ./Caliber: Feb, 1997 (mail-in offer, one-shot)

	GD25	FN65	NM94
nn-David Mack-c/a/scripts			4.00

KABUKI: FEAR THE REAPER
Caliber: Nov, 1994 ($3.50, B&W, one-shot)

	GD25	FN65	NM94
nn-David Mack-c/a/scripts	.90	2.70	8.00

KABUKI: MASKS OF THE NOH
Caliber: May, 1996 - No. 4, Feb, 1997 ($2.95, limited series)

	GD25	FN65	NM94
1-4: 1-Three-c (1A-Quesada, 1B-Buzz, &1C-Mack). 3-Terry Moore pin-up			3.00
TPB-(4/98, $10.95) r/#1-4; intro by Terry Moore			10.95

KABUKI: SKIN DEEP
Caliber Comics: Oct, 1996 - No. 3, May, 1997 ($2.95)

	GD25	FN65	NM94
1-3:David Mack-c/a/scripts. 2-Two-c (1-Mack, 1-Ross)			3.00
TPB-(5/98, $9.95) r/#1-3; intro by Alex Ross			9.95

KAMANDI: AT EARTH'S END
DC Comics: June, 1993 - No. 6, Nov, 1993 ($1.75, limited series)

	GD25	FN65	NM94
1-6: Elseworlds storyline			1.75

KAMANDI, THE LAST BOY ON EARTH (Also see Alarming Tales #1, Brave and the Bold #120 & 157 & Cancelled Comic Cavalcade)
National Periodical Publ./DC Comics: Oct-Nov, 1972 - 59, Sept-Oct, 1978

	GD25	FN65	NM94
1-Origin & 1st app. Kamandi	2.70	8.00	30.00
2	1.80	5.40	18.00
3-5: 4-Intro. Prince Tuftan of the Tigers	.90	2.70	8.00
6-10		2.00	6.00
11-20			5.00
21-28,30,31,33-40: 24-Last 20¢ issue. 31-Intro Pyra.			4.00
29,32: 29-Superman x-over. 32-(68 pgs.)-r/origin from #1 plus one new story; 4			

Kaos Moon #4 © David Boller

Karate Kid #6 © DC

Katy Keene #37 © AP

	GD25	FN65	NM94
pg. biog. of Jack Kirby with B&W photos		2.00	6.00
41-57			3.00
58-(44 pgs.)-Karate Kid x-over from LSH		2.00	6.00
59-(44 pgs.)-Cont'd in B&B #157; The Return of Omac back-up by Starlin-c/a(p)		2.00	6.00

NOTE: ***Ayers*** *a(p)-48-59 (most).* ***Giffen*** *a-44p, 45p.* ***Kirby*** *a-1-40p; c-1-33.* ***Kubert*** *c-34-41.* ***Nasser*** *a-45p, 46p.* ***Starlin*** *a-59p; c-57, 59p.*

KAMUI (Legend Of...#2 on)
Eclipse Comics/Viz Comics: May 12, 1987 - No. 37, Nov. 15, 1988 ($1.50, B&W, bi-weekly)

	GD25	FN65	NM94
1-37: 1-3 have 2nd printings			1.50

KAOS MOON (Also see Negative Burn #34)
Caliber Comics: 1996 - No. 4, 1997 ($2.95, B&W)

	GD25	FN65	NM94
1-4-David Boller-s/a			3.00
3,4-Limited Alternate-c			5.00
3,4-Gold Alternate-c			8.00
Full Circle TPB ($5.95) r/#1,2		2.00	6.00

KARATE KID (See Action, Adventure, Legion of Super-Heroes, & Superboy)
National Periodical Publications/DC Comics: Mar-Apr, 1976 - No. 15, July-Aug, 1978 (Legion spin-off)

	GD25	FN65	NM94
1,15: 1-Meets Iris Jacobs; Estrada/Staton-a. 15-Continued into Kamandi #58		2.00	6.00
2-14: 2-Major Disaster app. 14-Robin x-over			4.00

NOTE: ***Grell*** *c-1-4, 5p, 6p, 7, 8.* ***Staton*** *a-1-9i. Legion x-over-No. 1, 2, 4, 6, 10, 12, 13. Princess Projectra x-over-#8, 9.*

KASCO KOMICS
Kasko Grainfeed (Giveaway): 1945; No. 2, 1949 (Regular size, paper-c)

	GD25	FN65	NM94
1(1945)-Similar to Katy Keene; Bill Woggon-a; 28 pgs.; 6-7/8x9-7/8"	15.00	44.00	110.00
2(1949)-Woggon-c/a	11.50	34.00	85.00

KATHY
Standard Comics: Sept, 1949 - No. 17, Sept, 1955

	GD25	FN65	NM94
1-Teen-age	7.85	23.50	55.00
2-Schomburg-c	5.70	17.00	35.00
3-5	4.00	11.00	22.00
6-17: 17-Code approved	3.00	7.50	15.00

KATHY (The Teenage Tornado)
Atlas Comics/Marvel (ZPC): Oct, 1959 - No. 27, Feb, 1964

	GD25	FN65	NM94
1-Teen-age	5.00	15.00	50.00
2	2.50	7.50	25.00
3-15	2.00	6.00	16.00
16-27	1.10	3.30	9.00

KAT KARSON
I. W. Enterprises: No date (Reprint)

	GD25	FN65	NM94
1-Funny animals	1.25	3.75	10.00

KATO OF THE GREEN HORNET (Also see The Green Hornet)
Now Comics: Nov, 1991 - No. 4, Feb, 1992 ($2.50, mini-series)

	GD25	FN65	NM94
1-4: Brent Anderson-c/a			2.50

KATY AND KEN VISIT SANTA WITH MISTER WISH
S. S. Kresge Co. : 1948 (Giveaway, 16 pgs., paper-c)

	GD25	FN65	NM94
nn	4.25	13.00	26.00

KATY KEENE (Also see Kasco Komics, Laugh, Pep, Suzie, & Wilbur)
Archie Publ./Close-Up/Radio Comics: 1949 - No. 4, 1951; No. 5, 3/52 - No. 62, Oct, 1961 (50-53-Adventures of...on-c)

	GD25	FN65	NM94
1-Bill Woggon-c/a begins; swipes-c to Mopsy #1	88.00	265.00	750.00
2-(1950)	44.00	132.00	375.00
3-5: 3-(1951). 4-(1951)	37.00	112.00	280.00
6-10	31.00	92.00	230.00
11,13-21: 21-Last pre-code issue (3/55)	26.00	78.00	195.00
12-(Scarce)	29.00	88.00	220.00
22-40	16.00	48.00	140.00
41-62: 54-Wedding Album plus wedding pin-up. 62-Robot-c	13.00	39.00	110.00
Annual 1('54, 25¢)-All new stories; last pre-code	43.00	129.00	350.00
Annual 2-6('55-59, 25¢)-All new stories	26.00	78.00	195.00
3-D 1(1953, 25¢, large size)-Came w/glasses	38.00	114.00	285.00
Charm 1(9/58)-Woggon-c/a; new stories, and cut-outs	25.00	74.00	185.00
Glamour 1(1957)-Puzzles, games, cut-outs	25.00	74.00	185.00
Spectacular 1('56)	25.00	74.00	185.00

NOTE: *Debby's Diary in #45, 47-49, 52, 57.*

KATY KEENE COMICS DIGEST MAGAZINE
Close-Up, Inc. (Archie Ent.): 1987 - No. 10, July, 1990 ($1.25/$1.35/$1.50, digest size)

	GD25	FN65	NM94
1	.85	2.60	7.00
2-10			4.00

KATY KEENE FASHION BOOK MAGAZINE
Radio Comics/Archie Publications: 1955 - No. 13, Sum, '56 - N. 23, Wint, '58-59 (nn 3-10)

	GD25	FN65	NM94
1-Bill Woggon-c/a	40.00	120.00	350.00
2	26.00	78.00	195.00
11-18: 18-Photo Bill Woggon	19.00	57.00	140.00
19-23	16.00	48.00	110.00

KATY KEENE HOLIDAY FUN (See Archie Giant Series Magazine No. 7, 12)

KATY KEENE PINUP PARADE
Radio Comics/Archie Publications: 1955 - No. 15, Summer, 1961 (25¢) (Cut-out & missing pages are common)

	GD25	FN65	NM94
1-Cut-outs in all?; last pre-code issue	40.00	120.00	350.00
2-(1956)	24.00	72.00	175.00
3-5: 3-(1957)	21.00	63.00	155.00
6-10,12-14: 8-Mad parody. 10-Bill Woggon photo	15.00	45.00	130.00
11-Story of how comics get CCA approved, narrated by Katy	19.00	57.00	170.00
15(Rare)-Photo artist & family	36.00	108.00	320.00

KATY KEENE SPECIAL (Katy Keene #7 on; see Laugh Comics Digest)
Archie Ent.: Sept, 1983 - No. 33, 1990 (Later issues published quarterly)

	GD25	FN65	NM94
1-Woggon-r; new Woggon-c			4.00
2-33: 3-Woggon-r			2.00

KATZENJAMMER KIDS, THE (See Captain & the Kids & Giant Comic Album)
David McKay Publ./Standard No. 12-21(Spring/'50 - 53)/Harvey No. 22, 4/53 on: 1945-1946; Summer, 1947 - No. 27, Feb-Mar, 1954

	GD25	FN65	NM94
Feature Books 30	15.00	46.00	115.00
Feature Books 32,35('45),41,44('46)	14.00	42.00	105.00
Feature Book 37-Has photos & biography of Harold Knerr	15.00	46.00	115.00
1(1947)-All new stories begin	15.00	46.00	115.00
2	7.85	23.50	55.00
3-11	5.70	17.00	35.00
12-14(Standard)	4.35	13.00	26.00
15-21(Standard)	4.00	11.00	22.00
22-25,27(Harvey): 22-24-Henry app.	4.00	10.00	20.00
26-Half in 3-D	17.00	52.00	130.00

KAYO (Formerly Bullseye & Jest; becomes Carnival Comics)
Harry 'A' Chesler: No. 12, Mar, 1945

	GD25	FN65	NM94
12-Green Knight, Capt. Glory, Little Nemo (not by McCay)	13.00	38.00	95.00

KA-ZAR (Also see Marvel Comics #1, Savage Tales #6 & X-Men #10)
Marvel Comics Group: Aug, 1970 - No. 3, Mar, 1971 (Giant-Size, 68 pgs.)

Ka-Zar V2 #16 © MAR

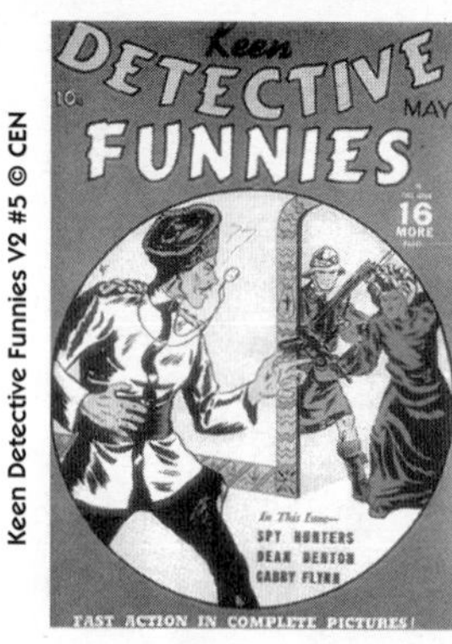

Keen Detective Funnies V2 #5 © CEN

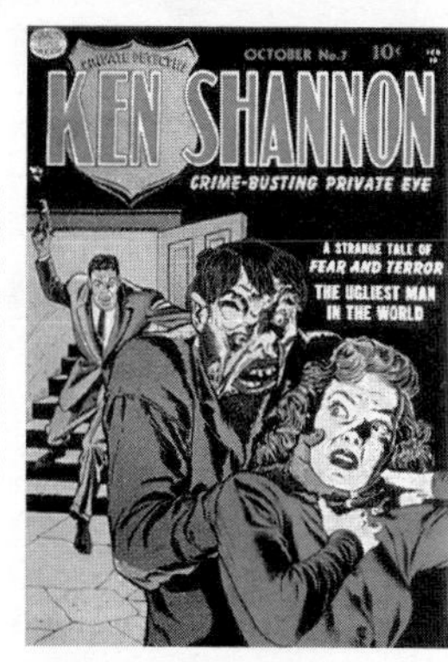

Ken Shannon #7 © QUA

GD25 FN65 NM94

1-Reprints earlier Ka-Zar stories; Avengers x-over in Hercules; Daredevil, X-Men app.; hidden profanity-c 2.50 7.50 22.00
2,3-Daredevil-r. 2-r/Daredevil #13 w/Kirby layouts; Ka-Zar origin, Angel-r from X-Men by Tuska. 3-Romita & Heck-a (no Kirby) 2.00 6.00 16.00
NOTE: ***Buscema*** *r-2.* ***Colan*** *a-1p(r).* ***Kirby*** *c/a-1, 2. #1-Reprints X-Men #10 & Daredevil #24*

KA-ZAR
Marvel Comics Group: Jan, 1974 - No. 20, Feb, 1977 (Regular Size)

1 .85 2.60 7.00
2-Shanna 5.00
3-10 4.00
11-16,18-20 3.00
17-(Regular 25¢ edition)(8/76) 3.00
17-(30¢-c, limited distribution) 1.20 3.60 12.00
NOTE: ***Alcala*** *a-6i, 8i.* ***Brunner*** *c-4.* ***J. Buscema*** *a-6-10p; c-1, 5, 7.* ***Heath*** *a-12.* ***G. Kane*** *c(p)-3, 5, 8-11, 15, 20.* ***Kirby*** *c-12p.* ***Reinman*** *a-1p.*

KA-ZAR (Volume 2)
Marvel Comics: May, 1997 - No. 20, Dec, 1998 ($1.95/$1.99)

1-Waid-s/Andy Kubert-c/a. thru #4 3.00
1-2nd printing; new cover 2.00
2,4: 2-Two-c 2.00
3-Alpha Flight #1 preview 3.00
5-13: 5-Begin $1.99-c. 8-Includes Spider-Man Cybercomic CD-ROM. 9-11-Thanos app. 13-Lopresti-a 2.00
14-($2.99) Last Waid/Kubert issue; flip book with 2nd story previewing new creative team of Priest-s/Martinez & Rodriguez-a 3.00
15-20: 15-Priest-s/Martinez & Rodriguez-a begin; Punisher app. 2.00
'97 Annual ($2.99)-Wraparound-c 3.00

KA-ZAR OF THE SAVAGE LAND
Marvel Comics: Feb, 1997 ($2.50, one-shot)

1-Wraparound-c 2.50

KA-ZAR: SIBLING RIVALRY
Marvel Comics: July, 1997 ($1.95, one-shot)

-1-Flashback story w/Alpha Flight #1 preview 2.00

KA-ZAR THE SAVAGE (See Marvel Fanfare)
Marvel Comics Group: Apr, 1981 - No. 34, Oct, 1984 (Regular size) (Mando paper #10 on)

1 2.00
2-34: 11-Origin Zabu. 12-One of two versions with panel missing on page 10. 20-Kraven the Hunter-c/story (also apps. in #21). 21-23, 25,26-Spider-Man app. 26-Photo-c. 1.25
12-Version with panel on pg. 10 (1600 printed) 4.00
29-Double size; Ka-Zar & Shanna wed 2.00
NOTE: ***B. Anderson*** *a-1-15p, 18, 19; c-1-17, 18p, 20(back).* ***G. Kane*** *a(back-up)-11, 12, 14.*

KEEN DETECTIVE FUNNIES (Formerly Detective Picture Stories?)
Centaur Publications: No. 8, July, 1938 - No. 24, Sept, 1940

V1#8-The Clock continues-r/Funny Picture Stories #1; Roy Crane-a (1st?) 176.00 528.00 1500.00
9-Tex Martin by Eisner; The Gang Buster app. 74.00 222.00 625.00
10,11: 11-Dean Denton story (begins?) 65.00 195.00 550.00
V2#1,2-The Eye Sees by Frank Thomas begins; ends #23(Not in V2#3&5). 2-Jack Cole-a 59.00 177.00 500.00
3-6: 3-TNT Todd begins. 4-Gabby Flynn begins. 5,6-Dean Denton story 56.00 168.00 475.00
7-The Masked Marvel by Ben Thompson begins (7/39, 1st app.)(scarce) 176.00 528.00 1500.00
8-Nudist ranch panel w/four girls 68.00 204.00 575.00
9-11 62.00 186.00 525.00
12(12/39)-Origin The Eye Sees by Frank Thomas; death of Masked Marvel's sidekick ZL 76.00 228.00 650.00
V3#1,2 59.00 177.00 500.00
18,19,21,22: 18-Bondage/torture-c 59.00 177.00 500.00
20-Classic Eye Sees-c by Thomas 79.00 237.00 675.00
23,24: 23-Air Man begins (intro). 23,24-Air Man-c 76.00 228.00 650.00
NOTE: ***Burgos*** *a-V2#2.* ***Jack Cole*** *a-V2#2.* ***Eisner*** *a-10, V2#6r.* ***Ken Ernst*** *a-V2#4-7, 9, 10, 19, 21; c-V2#4.* ***Everett*** *a-V2#6, 7, 9, 11, 12, 20.* ***Guardineer*** *a-V2#5, 66.* ***Gustavson*** *a-V2#4-6.* ***Simon*** *c-V3#1.* ***Thompson*** *c-V2#7, 9, 10, 22.*

KEEN KOMICS
Centaur Publications: V2#1, May, 1939 - V2#3, Nov, 1939

V2#1(Large size)-Dan Hastings (s/f), The Big Top, Bob Phantom the Magician, The Mad Goddess app. 85.00 255.00 725.00
V2#2(Reg. size)-The Forbidden Idol of Machu Picchu; Cut Carson by Burgos begins 55.00 165.00 465.00
V2#3-Saddle Sniffl by Jack Cole, Circus Pays, Kings Revenge app. 55.00 165.00 465.00
NOTE: ***Binder*** *a-V2#2.* ***Burgos*** *a-V2#2, 3.* ***Ken Ernst*** *a-V2#3.* ***Gustavson*** *a-V2#2.* ***Jack Cole*** *a-V2#3.*

KEEN TEENS (Girls magazine)
Life's Romances Publ./Leader/Magazine Ent.: 1945 - No. 6, Aug-Sept, 1947

nn (#1)-14 pgs. Claire Voyant (cont'd. in other nn issue) movie photos, Dotty Dripple, Gertie O'Grady & Sissy; Van Johnson, Frank Sinatra photo-c 22.00 66.00 165.00
nn (#2, 1946)-16 pgs. Claire Voyant & 16 pgs. movie photos 22.00 66.00 165.00
3-6: 4-Glenn Ford photo-c. 5-Perry Como-c 7.15 21.50 50.00

KELLYS, THE (Formerly Rusty Comics; Spy Cases No. 26 on)
Marvel Comics (HPC): No. 23, Jan, 1950 - No. 25, June, 1950 (52 pgs.)

23-Teenage 10.00 30.00 75.00
24,25: 24-Margie app. 7.50 22.50 45.00

KELVIN MACE
Vortex Publications: 1986 - No. 2, 1986 ($2.00, B&W)

1,2: 1-(B&W). 2-(Color) 2.00
1-2nd print (1/87, $1.75) 1.75

KEN MAYNARD WESTERN (Movie star)(See Wow Comics, 1936)
Fawcett Publ.: Sept, 1950 - No. 8, Feb, 1952 (All 36 pgs; photo front/back-c)

1-Ken Maynard & his horse Tarzan begin 53.00 160.00 450.00
2 35.00 104.00 260.00
3-8: 6-Atomic bomb explosion panel 27.00 80.00 200.00

KEN SHANNON (Becomes Gabby #11 on) (Also see Police Comics #103)
Quality Comics Group: Oct, 1951 - No. 10, Apr, 1953 (A private eye)

1-Crandall-a 33.00 98.00 245.00
2-Crandall c/a(2) 27.00 80.00 200.00
3-5-Crandall-a. 3-Horror-c 18.00 54.00 135.00
6-Crandall-c/a; "The Weird Vampire Mob"-c/s 20.00 60.00 150.00
7-Crandall-a 15.00 44.00 110.00
8,9: 8-Opium den drug use story 14.00 42.00 105.00
10-Crandall-c 15.00 44.00 110.00
NOTE: ***Crandall/Cuidera*** *c-1-10.* ***Jack Cole*** *a-1-9. #1-15 published after title change to Gabby.*

KEN STUART
Publication Enterprises: Jan, 1949 (Sea Adventures)

1-Frank Borth-c/a 8.00 24.00 56.00

KENT BLAKE OF THE SECRET SERVICE (Spy)
Marvel/Atlas Comics(20CC): May, 1951 - No. 14, July, 1953

1-Injury to eye, bondage, torture; Brodsky-c 16.00 48.00 120.00
2-Drug use w/hypo scenes; Brodsky-c 11.00 34.00 85.00
3-14: 8-R.Q. Sale-a (2 pgs.) 6.85 21.00 48.00
NOTE: ***Heath*** *c-5, 7, 8.* ***Infantino*** *c-12.* ***Maneely*** *c-3.* ***Sinnott*** *a-2(3).* ***Tuska*** *a-8(3pg.).*

KENTS, THE
DC Comics: Aug, 1997 - No. 12, July, 1998 ($2.50, limited series)

1-8-Ostrander-s/Truman & Bair-a. 2.50
9-12-Ostrander-s/Mandrake-a 2.50

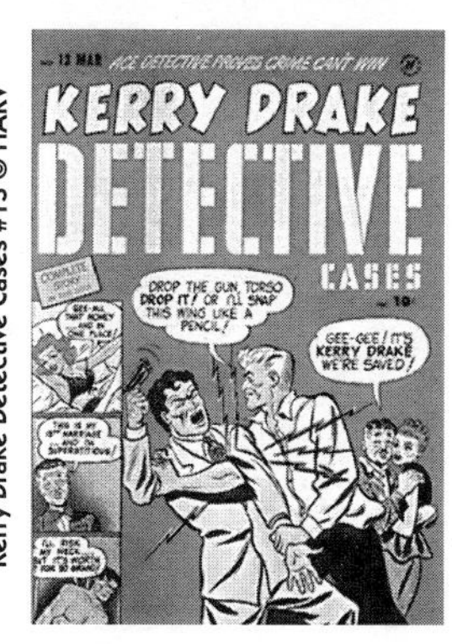

Kerry Drake Detective Cases #13 © HARV

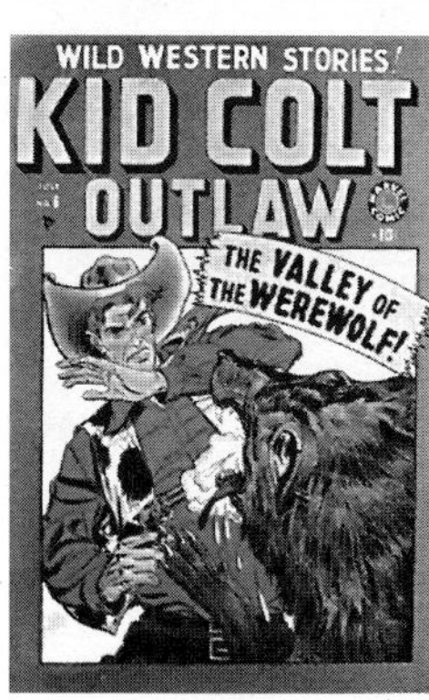

Kid Colt Outlaw #6 © Z-D

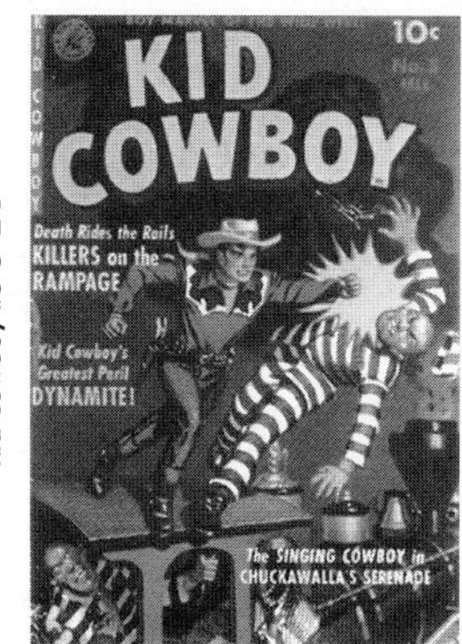

Kid Cowboy #5 © Z-D

GD25 FN65 NM94

KERRY DRAKE (Also see A-1 Comics)
Life's Romances Publ. nn/Argo: 1944; Jan, 1956 - No. 2, March, 1956

nn- (A-1 Comics on-c)(1944)Kerry Drake, Johnny Devildog, Rocky, Streamer Kelly (Slightly large size) 23.00 68.00 170.00
1,2-Newspaper-r 6.50 19.50 45.00

KERRY DRAKE DETECTIVE CASES (...Racket Buster No. 32,33)
(Also see Chamber of Clues & Green Hornet Comics #42-47)
Life's Romances/Com/Magazine Ent. No.1-5/Harvey No.6 on: 1944 - No. 5, 1944; No. 6, Jan, 1948 - No. 33, Aug, 1952

nn(1944)(A-1 Comics)(slightly over-size) 24.00 72.00 180.00
2 15.00 44.00 110.00
3-5(1944) 12.00 36.00 90.00
6,8(1948): Lady Crime by Powell. 8-Bondage-c 7.15 21.50 50.00
7-Kubert-a; biog of Andriola (artist) 9.30 28.00 65.00
9,10-Two-part marijuana story; Kerry smokes marijuana in #10 12.00 36.00 90.00
11-15 6.50 19.50 45.00
16-30 5.35 16.00 32.00
31-33 5.70 17.00 36.00
...in the Case of the Sleeping City-(1951-Publishers Synd.)-16 pg. giveaway for armed forces; paper cover 4.25 13.00 26.00
NOTE: ***Andiola** c-6-9. **Berg** a-5. **Powell** a-10-23, 28, 29.*

KEWPIES
Will Eisner Publications: Spring, 1949

1-Feiffer-a; Kewpie Doll ad on back cover 41.00 122.00 325.00

KEY COMICS
Consolidated Magazines: Jan, 1944 - No. 5, Aug, 1946

1-The Key, Will-O-The-Wisp begin 35.00 104.00 260.00
2 (3/44) 17.00 52.00 130.00
3,4: 4-(5/46)-Origin John Quincy The Atom (begins); Walter Johnson c-3-5 15.00 44.00 110.00
5-4pg. Faust Opera adaptation; Kiefer-a; back-c advertises "Masterpieces Illustrated" by Lloyd Jacquet after he left Classic Comics (no copies of Masterpieces Illustrated known) 20.00 60.00 150.00

KEY COMICS
Key Clothing Co./Peterson Clothing: 1951 - 1956 (32 pgs.) (Giveaway)
Contains a comic from different publishers bound with new cover. Cover changed each year. Many combinations possible. Distributed in Nebraska, Iowa, & Kansas. Contents would determine price, 40-60 percent of original.

KEY RING COMICS
Dell Publishing Co.: 1941 (16 pgs.; two colors) (sold 5 for 10¢)

1-Sky Hawk, 1-Viking Carter, 1-Features Sleepy Samson, 1-Origin Greg Gilday-r/War Comics #2, 1-Radior (Super hero) 4.15 12.50 25.00
NOTE: *Each book has two holes in spine to put in binder.*

KICKERS, INC.
Marvel Comics Group: Nov, 1986 - No. 12, Oct, 1987

1-12 1.00

KID CARROTS
St. John Publishing Co.: September, 1953

1-Funny animal 5.35 16.00 32.00

KID COLT OUTLAW (Kid Colt #1-4; ...Outlaw #5-on)(Also see All Western Winners, Best Western, Black Rider, Giant-Size..., Two-Gun Kid, Two-Gun Western, Western Winners, Wild Western, Wisco)
Marvel Comics(LCC) 1-16; Atlas(LMC) 17-102; Marvel 103-on: 8/48 - No. 139, 3/68; No. 140, 11/69 - No. 229, 4/79

1-Kid Colt & his horse Steel begin. 82.00 247.00 700.00
2 40.00 120.00 320.00
3-5: 4-Anti-Wertham editorial; Tex Taylor app. 5-Blaze Carson app. 32.00 96.00 240.00
6-8: 6-Tex Taylor app; 7-Nimo the Lion begins, ends #10 21.00 64.00 160.00
9,10 (52 pgs.) 21.00 64.00 160.00
11-Origin 25.00 74.00 185.00
12-20 16.00 48.00 120.00
21-32 13.00 38.00 95.00
33-45: Black Rider in all 10.00 30.00 75.00
46,47,49,50 8.50 26.00 60.00
48-Kubert-a 9.30 28.00 65.00
51-53,55,56 6.85 21.00 48.00
54-Williamson/Maneely-c 7.85 23.50 55.00
57-60,66: 4-pg. Williamson-a in all. 59-Reprints Rawhide Kid #79; Colan text illo 6.00 18.00 60.00
61-63,67-78,80-86: 70-Severin-c. 73-Maneely-c. 86-Kirby-a(r). 3.50 10.50 35.00
64,65-Crandall-a 4.00 12.00 40.00
79,87: 79-Origin retold. 87-Davis-a(r) 4.00 12.00 40.00
88,89-Williamson-a in both (4 pgs.). 89-Redrawn Matt Slade #2 4.50 13.50 45.00
90-99,101: 91-Kirby/Ayers-c. 95-Kirby/Ayers-c/story. 101-Last 10¢ issue 2.50 7.50 24.00
100 3.20 9.60 32.00
101-109,111-120: 114-(1/64)-2nd app. Iron Mask 2.50 7.50 20.00
110-(5/63)-1st app. Iron Mask (Iron Man type villain) 2.50 7.50 24.00
121-129,133-140: 121-Rawhide Kid x-over. 125-Two-Gun Kid x-over 140-Reprints begin 1.40 4.20 14.00
130-132 (68 pgs.)-one new story each. 130-Origin 2.20 6.50 24.00
141-155,157-160: (later issues all-r) 1.20 3.60 12.00
156-Giant; reprints 1.80 5.40 18.00
161-180,200: 170-Origin retold. 1.20 3.60 12.00
181-199 1.00 3.00 10.00
201-229: 229-Rawhide Kid-r .85 2.60 7.00
...Album (no date; 1950's; Atlas Comics)-132 pgs.; random binding, cardboard cover, B&W stories; contents can vary (Rare) 69.00 207.00 585.00
NOTE: ***Ayers** a-many. **Colan** a-52, 53; c(p)-223, 228, 229. **Crandall** a-140r, 167r. **Everett** a-90, 137i, 225i(r). **Heath** a-8(2); c-34, 35, 39, 44, 46, 48, 49, 57, 64. **Heck** a-135, 139. **Jack Keller** a-25(2), 26-68(3-4), 78, 94p, 98, 99, 108, 110, 130, 132, 140-150r. **Kirby** a-86r, 93, 96, 119, 176(part); c-87, 92-95, 97, 99-112, 114-117, 121-123, 197r; w/**Ditko** c-89. **Maneely** a-12, 68, 81; c-17, 19, 40-43, 47, 52, 53, 62, 65, 68, 78, 81, 142r, 150r. **Morrow** a-173r, 216r. **Rico** a-13, 18. **Severin** c-58, 59, 143, 148, 149i. **Shores** a-39, 41-43, 143r; c-1-10(most), 24. **Sutton** a-136, 137p, 225p(r). **Wildey** a-47, 54, 82, 144r. **Williamson** r-147, 170, 172, 216. **Woodbridge** a-64, 81. Black Rider in #33-45, 74, 86. Iron Mask in #110, 114, 121, 127. Sam Hawk in #84, 101, 111, 121, 146, 174, 181, 188.*

KID COWBOY (Also see Approved Comics #4 & Boy Cowboy)
Ziff-Davis Publ./St. John (Approved Comics): 1950 - No. 14, 1954
(Painted covers #1-10, 14)

1-Lucy Belle & Red Feather begin 12.00 36.00 90.00
2-Maneely-c 7.85 23.50 55.00
3-14: 5-Berg-a. 14-Code approved 6.50 19.50 45.00

KID DEATH & FLUFFY HALLOWEEN SPECIAL
Event Comics: Oct, 1997 ($2.95, B&W, one-shot)

1-Variant-c by Cebollero & Quesada/Palmiotti 2.95

KID DEATH & FLUFFY SPRING BREAK SPECIAL
Event Comics: July, 1996 ($2.50, B&W, one-shot)

1-Quesada & Palmiotti-c/scripts 2.50

KIDDIE KAPERS
Kiddie Kapers Co., 1945/Decker Publ. (Red Top-Farrell): 1945?(nd); Oct, 1957; 1963 - 1964

1(nd, 1945-46?, 36 pgs.)-Infinity-c; funny animal 5.70 17.00 40.00
1(10/57)(Decker)-Little Bit-r from Kiddie Karnival 4.00 12.00 24.00
Super Reprint #7, 10('63), 12, 14('63), 15,17('64), 18('64): 10, 14-r/Animal Adventures #1. 15-Animal Adventures #? 17-Cowboys 'N' Injuns #? 1.00 3.00 8.00

KIDDIE KARNIVAL

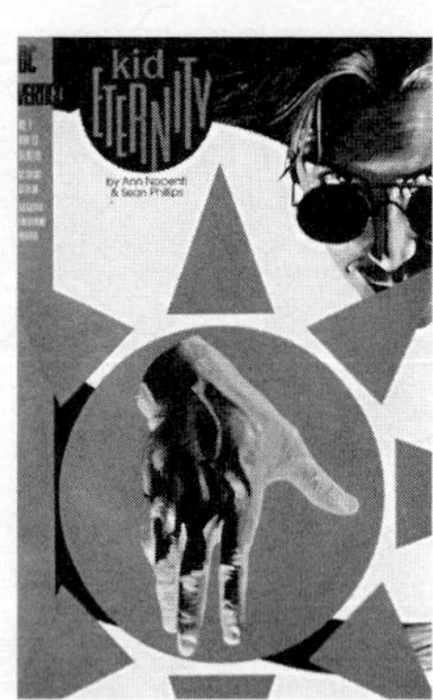

Kid Eternity #1 (Vertigo series) © DC

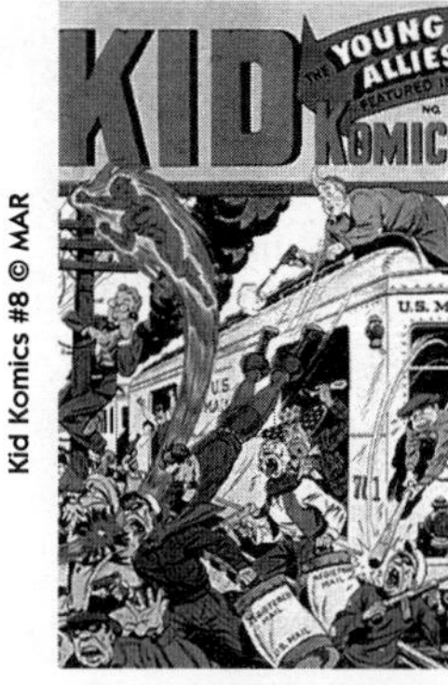

Kid Komics #8 © MAR

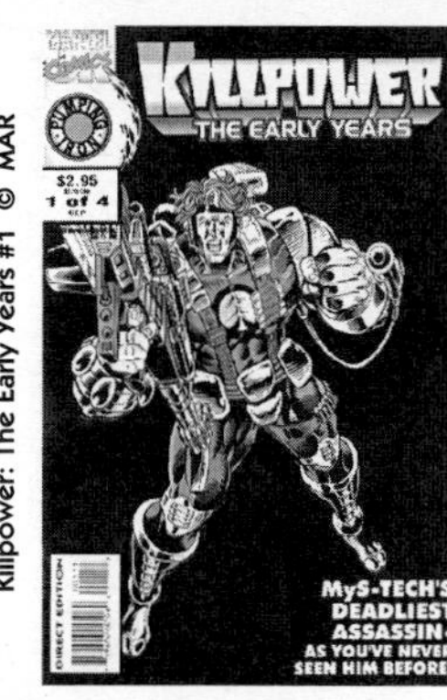

Killpower: The Early Years #1 © MAR

	GD25	FN65	NM94

Ziff-Davis Publ. Co. (Approved Comics): 1952 (25¢, 100 pgs.) (One Shot)

nn-Rebound Little Bit #1,2; painted-c	32.00	96.00	240.00

KID ETERNITY (Becomes Buccaneers) (See Hit Comics)
Quality Comics Group: Spring, 1946 - No. 18, Nov, 1949

1	74.00	221.00	625.00
2	36.00	108.00	270.00
3-Mac Raboy-a	39.00	117.00	295.00
4-10	21.00	64.00	160.00
11-18	16.00	48.00	120.00

KID ETERNITY
DC Comics: 1991 - No. 3, Nov, 1991 ($4.95, limited series)

1-3: Grant Morrison scripts 5.00

KID ETERNITY
DC Comics (Vertigo): May, 1993 - No. 16, Sept, 1994 ($1.95, mature)

1-16: 1-Gold ink-c. 6-Photo-c. All Sean Phillips-c/a except #15 (Phillips-c/i only) 2.00

KID FROM DODGE CITY, THE
Atlas Comics (MMC): July, 1957 - No. 2, Sept, 1957

1-Don Heck-c	7.85	23.50	55.00
2-Everett-c	5.35	16.00	32.00

KID FROM TEXAS, THE (A Texas Ranger)
Atlas Comics (CSI): June, 1957 - No. 2, Aug, 1957

1-Powell-a; Severin-c	8.50	26.00	60.00
2	5.35	16.00	32.00

KID KOKO
I. W. Enterprises: 1958

Reprint #1,2-(r/M.E.'s Koko & Kola #4, 1947)	1.00	3.00	8.00

KID KOMICS (Kid Movie Komics No. 11)
Timely Comics (USA 1,2/FCI 3-10): Feb, 1943 - No. 10, Spring, 1946

1-Origin Captain Wonder & sidekick Tim Mullrooney, & Subbie; intro the Sea-Going Lad, Pinto Pete, & Trixie Trouble; Knuckles & Whitewash Jones (from Young Allies) app.; Wolverton-a (7 pgs.)	326.00	978.00	3100.00
2-The Young Allies, Red Hawk, & Tommy Tyme begin; last Captain Wonder & Subbie	150.00	450.00	1275.00
3-The Vision, Daredevils & Red Hawk app.	115.00	345.00	975.00
4-The Destroyer begins; Sub-Mariner app.; Red Hawk & Tommy Tyme end	97.00	291.00	825.00
5,6: 5-Tommy Tyme begins, ends #10	75.00	225.00	640.00
7-10: 7,10-The Whizzer app. Destroyer not in #7,8. 10-Last Destroyer, Young Allies & Whizzer	68.00	204.00	575.00

NOTE: ***Brodsky** c-5. **Schomburg** c-2-4, 6-10. **Shores** c-1. Captain Wonder c-1, 2. The Young Allies c-3-10.*

KID MONTANA (Formerly Davy Crockett Frontier Fighter; The Gunfighters No. 51 on)
Charlton Comics: V2#9, Nov, 1957 - No. 50, Mar, 1965

V2#9	4.00	12.00	40.00
10,13: 13-Williamson-a	3.00	9.00	30.00
11,12,14-20	2.50	7.50	20.00
21-35	1.50	4.50	12.00
36-50	1.00	3.00	8.00

NOTE: *Title change to Montana Kid on cover only #44 & 45; remained Kid Montana on inside.*

KID MOVIE KOMICS (Formerly Kid Komics; Rusty Comics #12 on)
Timely Comics: No. 11, Summer, 1946

11-Silly Seal & Ziggy Pig; 2 pgs. Kurtzman "Hey Look" plus 6 pg. "Pigtales" story	22.00	66.00	165.00

KIDNAPPED (Robert Louis Stevenson's...also see Movie Comics)(Disney)
Dell Publishing Co.: No. 1101, May, 1960

Four Color 1101-Movie, photo-c	5.50	16.50	60.00

KIDNAP RACKET (See Harvey Comics Hits No. 57)

KID SLADE GUNFIGHTER (Formerly Matt Slade...)
Atlas Comics (SPI): No. 5, Jan, 1957 - No. 8, July, 1957

5-Maneely, Roth, Severin-a in all; Maneely-c	10.00	30.00	75.00
6,8-Severin-c	5.70	17.00	38.00
7-Williamson/Mayo-a, 4 pgs.	8.50	26.00	60.00

KID SUPREME (See Supreme)
Image Comics (Extreme Studios): Mar, 1996 - No. 3, July, 1996 ($2.50)

1-3: Fraga-a/scripts. 3-Glory-c/app. 2.50

KID ZOO COMICS
Street & Smith Publications: July, 1948 (52 pgs.)

1-Funny Animal	23.00	68.00	170.00

KILLER (...Tales By Timothy Truman)
Eclipse Comics: March, 1985 ($1.75, one-shot, Baxter paper)

1-Timothy Truman-c/a 1.75

KILLER INSTINCT (Video game)
Acclaim Comics: June, 1996 - Present ($2.50, limited series)

1-6: 1-Bart Sears-a(p). 4-Special #1. 5-Special #2. 6-Special #3 2.50

KILLERS, THE
Magazine Enterprises: 1947 - No. 2, 1948 (No month)

1-Mr. Zin, the Hatchet Killer; mentioned in **SOTI**, pgs. 179,180; used by N.Y. Legis. Comm.; L. B. Cole-c	85.00	254.00	720.00
2-(Scarce)-Hashish smoking story; "Dying, Dying, Dead" drug story; Whitney, Ingels-a; Whitney hanging-c	74.00	222.00	630.00

KILLING JOKE, THE (See Batman: The Killing Joke under Batman one-shots)

KILLPOWER: THE EARLY YEARS
Marvel Comics UK: Sept, 1993 - No. 4, Dec, 1993 ($1.75, mini-series)

1-($2.95)-Foil embossed-c 3.00
2-4: 2-Genetix app. 3-Punisher app. 1.75

KILLRAZOR
Image Comics (Top Cow Productions): Aug, 1995 ($2.50, one-shot)

1 2.50

KILL YOUR BOYFRIEND
DC Comics (Vertigo): June, 1995 ($4.95, one-shot)

1-Grant Morrison story	.90	2.70	8.00
1($5.95, 1998) 2nd printing			5.95

KILROY (Volume 2)
Caliber Press: 1998 ($2.95, B&W)

1-Pruett-s 2.95

KILROY IS HERE
Caliber Press: 1995 ($2.95, B&W)

1-10 3.00

KILROYS, THE
B&I Publ. Co. No. 1-19/American Comics Group: June-July, 1947 - No. 54, June-July, 1955

1	20.00	60.00	150.00
2	10.00	30.00	75.00
3-5: 5-Gross-a	7.85	23.50	55.00
6-10: 8-Milt Gross's Moronica	5.70	17.00	40.00
11-20: 14-Gross-a	5.70	17.00	35.00
21-30	4.25	13.00	26.00
31-47,50-54	4.00	12.00	24.00
48,49-(3-D effect-c/stories)	15.00	46.00	115.00

KILROY: THE SHORT STORIES
Caliber Press: 1995 ($2.95, B&W)

1 3.00

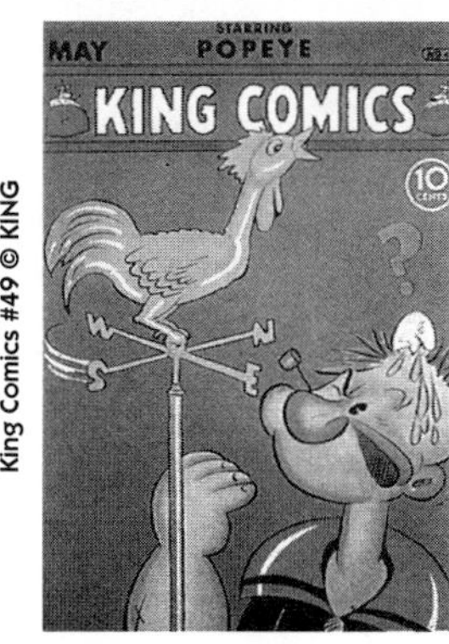

King Comics #49 © KING

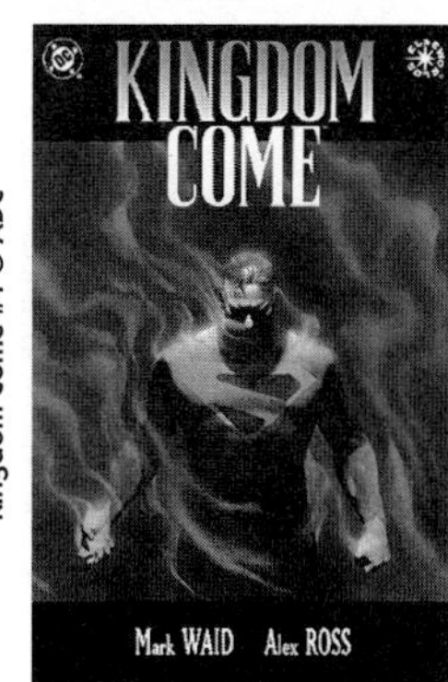

Kingdom Come #4 © ADC

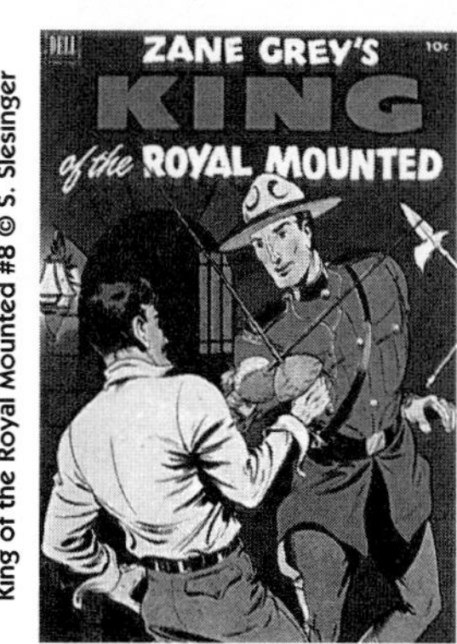

King of the Royal Mounted #8 © S. Slesinger

GD25 FN65 NM94

KINDRED, THE
Image Comics (WildStorm Productions): Mar, 1994 - No. 4, July, 1995 ($1.95, limited series)

1-($2.50)-Grifter & Backlash app. in all; bound-in trading card 2.50
2,3-($1.95) 2.00
2-Variant-c 5.00
3-Alternate-c by Portacio, see Deathblow #5 4.00
4-($2.50) 2.50
Trade paperback (2/95, $9.95) 10.00
NOTE: ***Booth*** *c/a-1-4. The first four issues contain coupons redeemable for a Jim Lee Grifter/Backlash print.*

KING ARTHUR AND THE KNIGHTS OF JUSTICE
Marvel Comics UK: Dec, 1993 - No. 3, Feb, 1994 ($1.25, limited series)

1-3: TV adaptation 1.25

KING CLASSICS
King Features : 1977 (36 pgs., cardboard-c)
(Printed in Spain for U.S. distr.)

1-Connecticut Yankee, 2-Last of the Mohicans, 3-Moby Dick, 4-Robin Hood, 5-Swiss Family Robinson, 6-Robinson Crusoe, 7-Treasure Island, 8-20,000 Leagues, 9-Christmas Carol, 10-Huck Finn, 11-Around the World in 80 Days, 12-Davy Crockett, 13-Don Quixote, 14-Gold Bug, 15-Ivanhoe, 16-Three Musketeers, 17-Baron Munchausen, 18-Alice in Wonderland, 19-Black Arrow, 20-Five Weeks in a Balloon, 21-Great Expectations, 22-Gulliver's Travels, 23-Prince & Pauper, 24-Lawrence of Arabia (Originals, 1977-78)
each.... .90 2.70 9.00
Reprints (1979; HRN-24) 2.00 6.00
NOTE: *The first eight issues were not numbered. Issues No. 25-32 were advertised but not published. The 1977 originals have HRN 32a; the 1978 originals have HRN 32b.*

KING COLT (See Luke Short's Western Stories)

KING COMICS (Strip reprints)
David McKay Publications/Standard #156-on: 4/36 - No. 155, 11-12/49; No. 156, Spr/50 - No. 159, 2/52 (Winter on-c)

	GD25	FN65	VF82
1-1st app. Flash Gordon by Alex Raymond; Brick Bradford (1st app.), Popeye, Henry (1st app.) & Mandrake the Magician (1st app.) begin; Popeye-c begin	1125.00	3375.00	7400.00
(Estimated up to 25 total copies exist, none in NM/Mint)			
	GD25	**FN65**	**NM94**
2	329.00	987.00	2300.00
3	214.00	642.00	1500.00
4	164.00	492.00	1150.00
5	121.00	363.00	850.00
6-10: 9-X-Mas-c	86.00	258.00	600.00
11-20	67.00	200.00	470.00
21-30: 21-X-Mas-c	49.00	147.00	340.00
31-40: 33-Last Segar Popeye	39.00	117.00	270.00
41-50: 46-Little Lulu, Alvin & Tubby app. as text illos by Marge Buell. 50-The Lone Ranger begins	31.00	92.00	230.00
51-60: 52-Barney Baxter begins?	21.00	64.00	160.00
61-The Phantom begins	19.00	58.00	145.00
62-80: 76-Flag-c. 79-Blondie begins	16.00	48.00	120.00
81-99	13.00	38.00	95.00
100	15.00	46.00	115.00
101-114: 114-Last Raymond issue (1 pg.); Flash Gordon by Austin Briggs begins, ends #155	11.00	34.00	85.00
115-145: 117-Phantom origin retold	9.30	28.00	65.00
146,147-Prince Valiant in both	7.15	21.50	50.00
148-155: 155-Flash Gordon ends (11-12/49)	7.15	21.50	50.00
156-159: 156-New logo begins (Standard)	6.50	19.50	45.00

NOTE: *Marge Buell text illos in No. 24-46 at least.*

KING CONAN (Conan The King No. 20 on)
Marvel Comics Group: Mar, 1980 - No. 19, Nov, 1983 (52 pgs.)

1 3.50
2-19: 4-Death of Thoth Amon. 7-1st Paul Smith-a, 1 pg. pin-up (9/81) 1.75
NOTE: ***J. Buscema*** *a-1-9p, 17p; c(p)-1-5, 7-9, 14, 17.* ***Kaluta*** *c-19.* ***Nebres*** *a-17i, 18, 19i.* ***Severin*** *c-18.* ***Simonson*** *c-6.*

KINGDOM COME
DC Comics (Elseworlds): 1996 - No. 4, 1996 ($4.95, painted limited series)

1- Mark Waid scripts & Alex Ross-painted c/a in all; tells the last days of the DC Universe; 1st app. Magog. 1.20 3.60 12.00
2-4: 2-Superman forms new Justice League. 3-Return of Capt. Marvel 1.00 3.00 10.00
Deluxe Slipcase Edition-($89.95) w/Revelations companion book, 12 new story pages, foil stamped covers, signed and numbered 120.00
Hardcover Edition-($29.95)-Includes 12 new story pages and artwork from Revelations, new cover artwork with gold foil inlay 35.00
Hardcover 2nd printing 29.95
Softcover Edition-($14.95)-Includes 12 new story pages and artwork from Revelations, new cover artwork 14.95

KING KONG (See Movie Comics)

KING LEONARDO & HIS SHORT SUBJECTS (TV)
Dell Publishing Co./Gold Key: Nov-Jan, 1961-62 - No. 4, Sept, 1963

Four Color 1242,1278	13.00	38.00	140.00
01390-207(5-7/62)(Dell)	10.00	30.00	110.00
1 (10/62)	10.50	32.00	115.00
2-4	8.25	25.00	90.00

KING LOUIE & MOWGLI (See Jungle Book under Movie Comics)
Gold Key: May, 1968 (Disney)

1 (#10223-805)-Characters from Jungle Book 1.80 5.40 20.00

KING OF DIAMONDS (TV)
Dell Publishing Co.: July-Sept, 1962

01-391-209-Photo-c 3.00 9.00 32.00

KING OF KINGS (Movie)
Dell Publishing Co.: No. 1236, Oct-Nov, 1961

Four Color 1236-Photo-c 7.00 22.00 80.00

KING OF THE BAD MEN OF DEADWOOD
Avon Periodicals: 1950 (See Wild Bill Hickok #16)

nn-Kinstler-c; Kamen/Feldstein-r/Cowpuncher #2 13.50 41.00 100.00

KING OF THE ROYAL MOUNTED (See Famous Feature Stories, King Comics, Red Ryder #3 & Super Book #2, 6)

KING OF THE ROYAL MOUNTED (Zane Grey's...)
David McKay/Dell Publishing Co.: No. 1, May, 1937; No. 9, 1940; No. 207, Dec, 1948 - No. 935, Sept-Nov, 1958

Feature Books 1 (5/37)(McKay)	61.00	184.00	675.00
Large Feature Comic 9 (1940)	33.00	100.00	365.00
Four Color 207(#1, 12/48)	14.00	41.00	150.00
Four Color 265,283	7.00	22.00	80.00
Four Color 310,340	5.50	16.50	60.00
Four Color 363,384, 8(6-8/52)-10	4.50	13.50	50.00
11-20	3.00	9.00	35.00
21-28(3-5/58), Four Color 935(9-11/58)	2.75	8.00	30.00

NOTE: *4-Color No. 207, 265, 283, 310, 340, 363, 384 are all newspaper reprints with* ***Jim Gary*** *art. No. 8 on are all Dell originals. Painted c-No. 9-on.*

KINGPIN
Marvel Comics: Nov, 1997 ($5.99, squarebound, one-shot)

nn-Spider-Man & Daredevil vs. Kingpin; Stan Lee-s/ John Romita Sr.-a 2.00 6.00

KING RICHARD & THE CRUSADERS
Dell Publishing Co.: No. 588, Oct, 1954

Four Color 588-Movie, Matt Baker-a, photo-c 9.00 27.00 100.00

KINGS OF THE NIGHT
Dark Horse Comics: 1990 - No. 2, 1990 ($2.25, limited series)

1,2-Robert E. Howard adaptation; Bolton-c 2.25

KISS The Psycho Circus #12 © KISS Catalog

Kitty Pryde, Agent of S.H.I.E.L.D. #3 © MAR

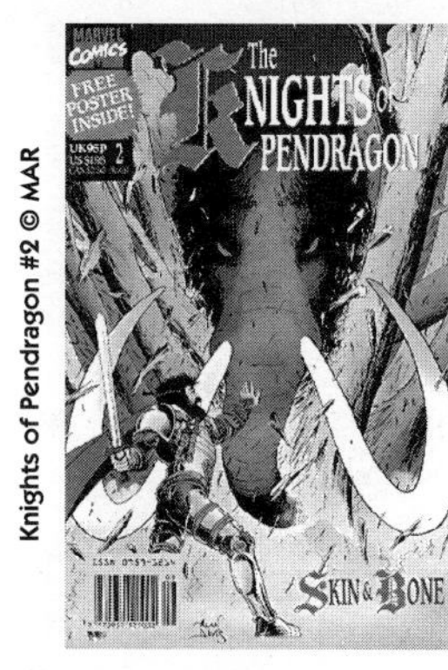

Knights of Pendragon #2 © MAR

	GD25	FN65	NM94

KING SOLOMON'S MINES (Movie)
Avon Periodicals: 1951

nn (#1 on 1st page)	35.00	104.00	260.00

KING TIGER & MOTORHEAD
Dark Horse Comics: Aug, 1996 - No. 2, Sept, 1996 ($2.95, limited series)

1,2: Chichester scripts			3.00

KIPLING, RUDYARD (See Mowgli, The Jungle Book)

KISS (See Crazy Magazine, Howard the Duck #12, 13, Marvel Comics Super Special #1, 5, Rock Fantasy Comics #10 & Rock N' Roll Comics #9)

KISS: THE PSYCHO CIRCUS
Image Comics: Aug, 1997 - Present ($1.95/$2.25)

1-Holguin-s/Medina-a(p)	1.00	3.00	10.00
1-2nd & 3rd printings			2.50
2		2.00	6.00
3,4: 4-Photo-c			4.00
5-8: 5-Begin $2.25-c			3.00
9-14			2.25
Book 1 TPB ('98, $12.95) r/#1-6			12.95
...Magazine 1 ($6.95) r/#1-3 plus interviews			6.95

KISSYFUR (TV)
DC Comics: 1989 (Sept.) ($2.00, 52 pgs., one-shot)

1-Based on Saturday morning cartoon			2.50

KIT CARSON (Formerly All True Detective Cases No. 4; Fighting Davy Crockett No. 9; see Blazing Sixguns & Frontier Fighters)
Avon Periodicals: 1950; No. 2, 8/51 - No. 3, 12/51; No. 5, 11-12/54 - No. 8, 9/55 (No #4)

nn(#1) (1950)- "...Indian Scout" ; r-Cowboys 'N' Injuns #?	12.00	36.00	90.00
2(8/51)	7.85	23.50	55.00
3(12/51)- "...Fights the Comanche Raiders"	6.50	19.50	45.00
5-6,8(11-12/54-9/55): 5-Formerly All True Detective Cases (last pre-code); titled "...and the Trail of Doom"	6.00	18.00	42.00
7-McCann-a?	6.50	19.50	45.00
I.W. Reprint #10('63)-r/Kit Carson #1; Severin-c	1.75	5.25	14.00

NOTE: ***Kinstler** c-1-3, 5-8.*

KIT CARSON & THE BLACKFEET WARRIORS
Realistic: 1953

nn-Reprint; Kinstler-c	7.85	23.50	55.00

KITE FUN BOOK
Pacific, Gas & Electric/Sou. California Edison/Florida Power & Light: 1954 - 1981 (16pgs, 5x7-1/4", soft-c)

1954-Donald Duck Tells About Kites-Fla. Power, S.C.E. & version with label issues-Barks pencils-8 pgs.; inks-7 pgs. (Rare)	400.00	1200.00	2800.00
1954-Donald Duck Tells About Kites-P.G.&E. issue -7th page redrawn changing middle 3 panels to show P.G.&E. in story line; (All Barks; last page Barks pencils only) Scarce	247.00	741.00	2100.00
1954-Pinocchio Learns About Kites (Disney)	43.00	129.00	350.00
1955-Brer Rabbit in "A Kite Tail" (Disney)	31.00	93.00	230.00
1956-Woody Woodpecker (Lantz)	13.00	38.00	95.00
1957-?			
1958-Tom And Jerry (M.G.M.)	7.85	23.50	55.00
1960-Porky Pig (Warner Bros.)	4.00	12.00	40.00
1960-Bugs Bunny (Warner Bros.)	4.00	12.00	40.00
1961-Huckleberry Hound (Hanna-Barbera)	5.00	15.00	50.00
1962-Yogi Bear (Hanna-Barbera)	3.20	9.60	32.00
1963-Rocky and Bullwinkle (TV)(Jay Ward)	9.50	28.50	95.00
1963-Top Cat (TV)(Hanna-Barbera)	4.00	12.00	40.00
1964-Magilla Gorilla (TV)(Hanna-Barbera)	3.50	10.50	35.00
1965-Jinks, Pixie and Dixie (TV)(Hanna-Barbera)	2.50	7.50	25.00
1965-Tweety and Sylvester (Warner); S.C.E. version with Reddy Kilowatt app.	1.10	3.30	9.00
1966-Secret Squirrel (Hanna-Barbera); S.C.E. version with Reddy Kilowatt app.	6.00	18.00	60.00
1967-Beep! Beep! The Road Runner (TV)(Warner)	2.25	6.75	18.00
1968-Bugs Bunny (Warner Bros.)	2.50	7.50	20.00
1969-Dastardly and Muttley (TV)(Hanna-Barbera)	3.50	10.50	35.00
1970-Rocky and Bullwinkle (TV)(Jay Ward)	6.50	19.50	65.00
1971-Beep! Beep! The Road Runner (TV)(Warner)	1.85	5.50	15.00
1972-The Pink Panther (TV)	1.25	3.75	10.00
1973-Lassie (TV)	2.60	7.80	26.00
1974-Underdog (TV)	2.00	6.00	16.00
1975-Ben Franklin		2.40	6.00
1976-The Brady Bunch (TV)	2.25	6.00	18.00
1977-Ben Franklin		2.40	6.00
1977-Popeye	1.50	4.50	12.00
1978-Happy Days (TV)	1.50	4.50	12.00
1979-Eight is Enough (TV)	1.50	4.50	12.00
1980-The Waltons (TV, released in 1981)	1.50	4.50	12.00

KIT KARTER
Dell Publishing Co.: May-July, 1962

1	2.00	6.00	22.00

KITTY
St. John Publishing Co.: Oct, 1948

1-Teenage; Lily Renee-c/a	5.70	17.00	40.00

KITTY PRYDE, AGENT OF S.H.I.E.L.D. (Also see Excalibur)
Marvel Comics: Dec, 1997 - No. 3, Feb, 1998 ($2.50, limited series)

1-3-Hama-s			2.50

KITTY PRYDE AND WOLVERINE (Also see Uncanny X-Men & X-Men)
Marvel Comics Group: Nov, 1984 - No. 6, Apr, 1985 (Limited series)

1-Characters from X-Men			2.00
2-6			1.50

KLARER GIVEAWAYS (See Wisco)

KNIGHTHAWK
Acclaim Comics (Windjammer): Sept, 1995 - No. 6, Nov, 1995 ($2.50, lim. series)

1-6: 6-origin			2.50

KNIGHTMARE
Antarctic Press: July, 1994 - May, 1995 ($2.75, B&W, mature readers)

1-6			2.75

KNIGHTMARE
Image Comics (Extreme Studios): Feb, 1995 - No. 5, June, 1995 ($2.50)

0 ($3.50)			3.50
1-5: 5-Flip book w/Warcry			2.50
4-Quesada & Palmiotti variant-c			4.00

KNIGHTS OF PENDRAGON, THE (Also see Pendragon)
Marvel Comics Ltd.: July, 1990 - No. 18, Dec, 1991 ($1.95)

1-18: 1-Capt. Britain app. 2,8-Free poster inside. 9,10-Bolton-c. 11,18-Iron Man app.			2.00

KNIGHTS OF THE ROUND TABLE
Dell Publishing Co.: No. 540, Mar, 1954

Four Color 540-Movie, photo-c	6.40	19.00	70.00

KNIGHTS OF THE ROUND TABLE
Pines Comics: No. 10, April, 1957

10	4.00	11.00	22.00

KNIGHTS OF THE ROUND TABLE
Dell Publishing Co.: Nov-Jan, 1963-64

1 (12-397-401)-Painted-c	2.25	6.75	25.00

Knight Watchman #1 © Gary Carlson

Knuckles #18 © SEGA

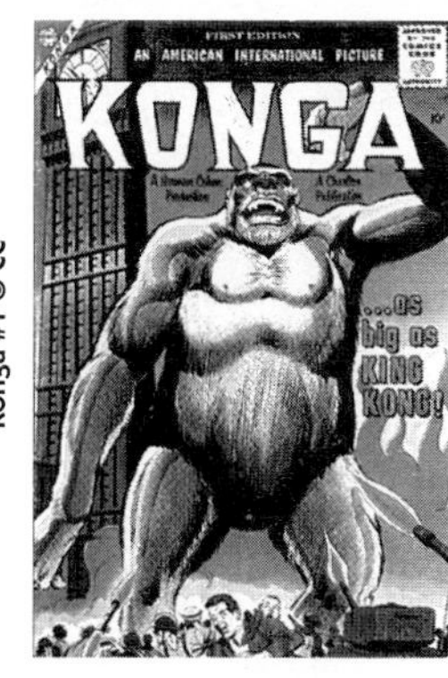

Konga #1 © CC

GD25 FN65 NM94

KNIGHTSTRIKE (Also see Operation: Knightstrike)
Image Comics (Extreme Studios): Jan, 1996 ($2.50)
1-Rob Liefeld & Eric Stephenson story; Extreme Destroyer Part 6. 2.50

KNIGHT WATCHMAN (See Big Bang & Dr. Weird)
Image Comics: June, 1998 - No. 4, Oct, 1998 ($2.95, B&W, limited series)
1-4-Ben Torres-c/a 3.00

KNIGHT WATCHMAN: GRAVEYARD SHIFT
Caliber Press: 1994 ($2.95, B&W)
1,2-Ben Torres-a 1.20 3.00

KNOCK KNOCK (...Who's There?)
Whitman Publ./Gerona Publications: No. 801, 1936 (52 pgs.) (8x9", B&W)
801-Joke book; Bob Dunn-a 5.70 17.00 35.00

KNOCKOUT ADVENTURES
Fiction House Magazines: Winter, 1953-54
1-Reprints Fight Comics #53 w/Rip Carson-c/s 12.00 36.00 90.00

KNOW YOUR MASS
Catechetical Guild: No. 303, 1958 (35¢, 100 Pg. Giant) (Square binding)
303-In color 3.60 9.00 18.00

KNUCKLES
Archie Publications: Apr, 1997 - Present ($1.50/$1.75)
1-7 1.50
8-20: 8-Begin $1.75-c 1.75

KNUCKLES' CHAOTIX
Archie Publications: Jan, 1996 ($2.00, annual)
1 2.00

KOBALT
DC Comics (Milestone): June, 1994 - No. 16, Sept, 1995 ($1.75/$2.50)
1-12: 1-Byrne-c. 4-Intro Page 1.75
13-16 ($2.50): 16-Kent Williams-c 2.50

KOBRA (See DC Special Series No. 1)
National Periodical Publications: Feb-Mar, 1976 - No. 7, Mar-Apr, 1977
1-1st app.; Kirby-a redrawn by Marcos; only 25¢ issue 5.00
2-7: (All 30¢ issues) 3-Giffen-a 3.00
NOTE: ***Austin** a-3i. **Buckler** a-5p; c-5p. **Kubert** c-4. **Nasser** a-6p, 7; c-7.*

KOKEY KOALA (...and the Magic Button)
Toby Press: May, 1952
1 9.30 28.00 65.00

KOKO AND KOLA (Also see A-1 Comics #16 & Tick Tock Tales)
Com/Magazine Enterprises: Fall, 1946 - No. 5, May, 1947; No. 6, 1950
1-Funny animal 9.30 28.00 65.00
2-X-Mas-c 5.70 17.00 35.00
3-6: 6(A-1 28) 4.25 13.00 28.00

KO KOMICS
Gerona Publications: Oct, 1945
1-The Duke of Darkness & The Menace (hero) 53.00 159.00 450.00

KOMIC KARTOONS
Timely Comics (EPC): Fall, 1945 - No. 2, Winter, 1945
1,2-Andy Wolf, Bertie Mouse 17.00 50.00 125.00

KOMIK PAGES (Formerly Snap; becomes Bullseye #11)
Harry 'A' Chesler, Jr. (Our Army, Inc.): Apr, 1945 (All reprints)
10(#1 on inside)-Land O' Nod by Rick Yager (2 pgs.), Animal Crackers, Foxy GrandPa, Tom, Dick & Mary, Cheerio Minstrels, Red Starr plus other 1-2 pg. strips; Cole-a 20.00 60.00 150.00

GD25 FN65 NM94

KONA (...Monarch of Monster Isle)
Dell Publishing Co.: Feb-Apr, 1962 - No. 21, Jan-Mar, 1967 (Painted-c)
Four Color 1256 (#1) 5.50 16.50 60.00
2-10: 4-Anak begins 2.00 6.00 23.00
11-21 1.65 5.50 18.00
NOTE: ***Glanzman** a-all issues.*

KONGA (Fantastic Giants No. 24) (See Return of...)
Charlton Comics: 1960; No. 2, Aug, 1961 - No. 23, Nov, 1965
1(1960)-Based on movie; Giordano-c 22.00 66.00 220.00
2-Giordano-c; no Ditko-a 9.00 27.00 90.00
3-5 9.00 27.00 90.00
6-15 6.50 19.50 65.00
16-23 4.00 12.00 40.00
NOTE: ***Ditko** a-1, 3-15; c-4, 6-9. **Glanzman** a-12. **Montes** & **Bache** a-16-23.*

KONGA'S REVENGE (Formerly Return of...)
Charlton Comics: No. 2, Summer, 1963 - No. 3, Fall, 1964; Dec, 1968
2,3: 2-Ditko-c/a 4.80 14.40 48.00
1(12/68)-Reprints Konga's Revenge #3 2.50 7.50 24.00

KONG THE UNTAMED
National Periodical Publications: June-July, 1975 - V2#5, Feb-Mar, 1976
1-1st app. Kong; Wrightson-c; Alcala-a 2.00 6.00
2-5: 2-Wrightson-c. 2,3-Alcala-a 3.50

KOOKIE
Dell Publishing Co.: Feb-Apr, 1962 - No. 2, May-July, 1962 (15 cents)
1,2: Written by John Stanley; Bill Williams-a 7.00 21.00 70.00

KOOSH KINS
Archie Comics: Oct, 1991 - No. 3, Feb, 1992 ($1.00, bi-monthly, limited series)
1-3 1.00
NOTE: *No. 4 was planned, but cancelled.*

K. O. PUNCH, THE (Also see Lucky Fights It Through)
E. C. Comics: 1948 (Educational giveaway)
nn-Feldstein-splash; Kamen-a 83.00 250.00 750.00

KORAK, SON OF TARZAN (Edgar Rice Burroughs)(See Tarzan #139)
Gold Key: Jan, 1964 - No. 45, Jan, 1972 (Painted-c No. 1-?)
1-Russ Manning-a 4.50 13.50 50.00
2-11-Russ Manning-a 2.50 7.50 28.00
12-21: 12,13-Warren Tufts-a. 14-Jon of the Kalahari ends. 15-Mabu, Jungle Boy begins. 21-Manning-a 1.80 5.40 20.00
22-30 1.20 3.60 14.00
31-45 .90 2.70 9.00

KORAK, SON OF TARZAN (Tarzan Family #60 on; see Tarzan #230)
National Periodical Publications: V9#46, May-June, 1972 - V12#56, Feb-Mar, 1974; No. 57, May-June, 1975 - No. 59, Sept-Oct, 1975 (Edgar Rice Burroughs)
46-(52 pgs.)-Carson of Venus begins (origin), ends #56; Pellucidar feature; Weiss-a 1.00 3.00 10.00
47-59: 49-Origin Korak retold 4.00
NOTE: ***Kaluta** a-46-56. All have covers by **Joe Kubert**. **Manning** strip reprints-No. 57-59. **Frank Thorn** a-46-51.*

KOREA MY HOME (Also see Yalta to Korea)
Johnstone and Cushing: nd (1950s)
nn-Anti-communist; Korean War 23.00 68.00 170.00

KORG: 70,000 B. C. (TV)
Charlton Publications: May, 1975 - No. 9, Nov, 1976 (Hanna-Barbera)
1-Boyette-c/a 1.10 3.30 11.00
2-Painted-c; Byrne text illos 1.20 3.60 12.00
3-9 .90 2.70 8.00

KORNER KID COMICS
Four Star Publications: 1947

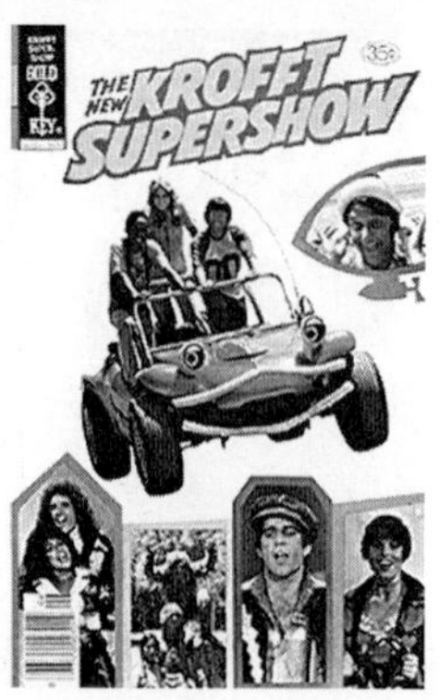

Krofft Supershow #3 © Krofft

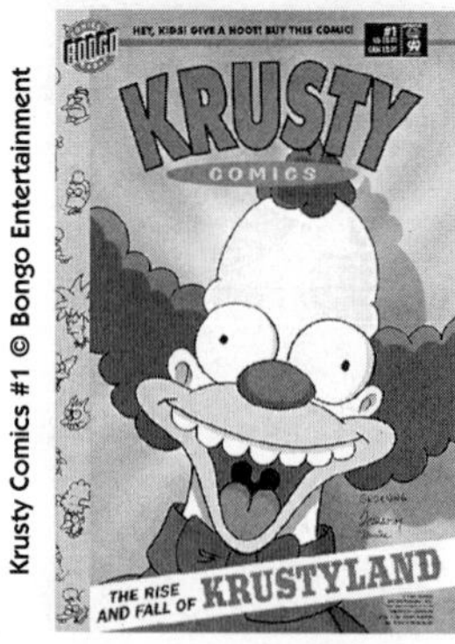

Krusty Comics #1 © Bongo Entertainment

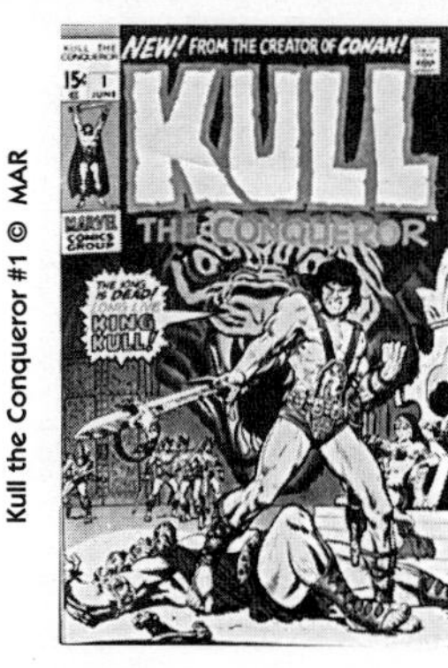

Kull the Conqueror #1 © MAR

GD25 FN65 NM94

1 5.70 17.00 40.00

KRAZY KAT
Holt: 1946 (Hardcover)

Reprints daily & Sunday strips by Herriman 53.00 160.00 450.00
dust jacket only 43.00 130.00 350.00

KRAZY KAT (See Ace Comics & March of Comics No. 72, 87)

KRAZY KAT COMICS (...& Ignatz the Mouse early issues)
Dell Publ. Co./Gold Key: May-June, 1951 - F.C. #696, Apr, 1956; Jan, 1964 (None by Herriman)

1(1951) 6.40 19.00 70.00
2-5 (#5, 8-10/52) 3.60 11.00 40.00
Four Color 454,504 3.00 9.00 35.00
Four Color 548,619,696 (4/56) 2.75 8.00 30.00
1(10098-401)(1/64-Gold Key)(TV) 2.75 8.00 30.00

KRAZY KOMICS (1st Series) (Cindy Comics No. 27 on)
Timely Comics (USA No. 1-21/JPC No. 22-26): July, 1942 - No. 26, Spr, 1947 (Also see Ziggy Pig)

1-Toughy Tomcat, Ziggy Pig (by Jaffee) & Silly Seal begin
46.00 138.00 390.00
2 23.00 68.00 170.00
3-8,10 16.00 48.00 120.00
9-Hitler parody 17.00 52.00 130.00
11,13,14 11.00 32.00 80.00
12-Timely's entire art staff drew themselves into a Creeper story
21.00 62.00 155.00
15-(8-9/44)-Becomes Funny Tunes #16; has "Super Soldier" by Pfc. Stan Lee
11.00 32.00 80.00
16-24,26: 16-(10-11/44). 26-Super Rabbit-c/story 9.30 28.00 65.00
25-Wacky Duck-c/story & begin; Kurtzman-a (6pgs.) 11.00 32.00 80.00

KRAZY KOMICS (2nd Series)
Timely/Marvel Comics: Aug, 1948 - No. 2, Nov, 1948

1-Wolverton (10 pgs.) & Kurtzman (8 pgs.)-a; Eustice Hayseed begins (Li'l Abner swipe) 37.00 110.00 275.00
2-Wolverton-a (10 pgs.); Powerhouse Pepper cameo
27.00 80.00 200.00

KRAZY KROW (Also see Dopey Duck, Film Funnies, Funny Frolics & Movie Tunes)
Marvel Comics (ZPC): Summer, 1945 - No. 3, Wint, 1945/46

1 15.00 44.00 110.00
2,3 10.00 30.00 75.00
I.W. Reprint #1('57), 2('58), 7 1.75 5.25 14.00

KRAZYLIFE (Becomes Nutty Life #2)
Fox Feature Syndicate: 1945 (no month)

1-Funny animal 12.00 36.00 90.00

KREE/SKRULL WAR STARRING THE AVENGERS, THE
Marvel Comics: Sept, 1983 - No. 2, Oct, 1983 ($2.50, 68 pgs., Baxter paper)

1,2 2.50
NOTE: ***Neal Adams** p-1r, 2. **Buscema** a-1r, 2r. **Simonson** a-1p; c-1p.*

KRIM-KO KOMICS
Krim-ko Chocolate Drink: 5/18/35 - No. 6, 6/22/35; 1936 - 1939 (weekly)

1-(16 pgs., soft-c, Dairy giveaways)-Tom, Mary & Sparky Advs. by Russell Keaton, Jim Hawkins by Dick Moores, Mystery Island! by Rick Yager begin
13.00 40.00 100.00
2-6 (6/22/35) 9.30 28.00 70.00
Lola, Secret Agent; 184 issues, 4 pg. giveaways - all original stories
each.... 6.00 18.00 42.00

KROFFT SUPERSHOW (TV)
Gold Key: Apr, 1978 - No. 6, Jan, 1979

1-Photo-c 2.00 6.00
2-6: 6-Photo-c 5.00

KRULL
Marvel Comics Group: Nov, 1983 - No. 2, Dec, 1983

1,2-Adaptation of film; r/Marvel Super Special. 1-Photo-c from movie
1.00

KRUSTY COMICS (TV)(See Simpsons Comics)
Bongo Comics: 1995 - No. 3, 1995 ($2.25, limited series)

1-3 2.50

KRYPTON CHRONICLES
DC Comics: Sept, 1981 - No. 3, Nov, 1981

1-3: 1-Buckler-c(p) 1.00

KULL AND THE BARBARIANS
Marvel Comics: May, 1975 - No. 3, Sept, 1975 ($1.00, B&W, magazine, 84 pgs.)

1-Andru/Wood-r/Kull #1; 2 pgs. Neal Adams; Gil Kane(p), Marie & John Severin-a(r); Krenkel text illo. .90 2.70 8.00
2-Red Sonja by Chaykin begins; Soloman Kane by Weiss/N. Adams; Gil Kane-a. 5.00
3-Origin Red Sonja by Chaykin; N. Adams-a; Solomon Kane app. 4.00

KULL THE CONQUEROR (...the Destroyer #11 on; see Conan #1, Creatures on the Loose #10, Marvel Preview, Monsters on the Prowl)
Marvel Comics Group: June, 1971 - No. 2, Sept, 1971; No. 3, July, 1972 - No. 15, Aug, 1974; No. 16, Aug, 1976 - No. 29, Oct, 1978

1-Andru/Wood-a; 2nd app. & origin Kull; 15¢ issue 2.20 6.50 24.00
2-5: 2-3rd Kull app. Last 15¢ iss. 3-13: 20¢ issues 1.00 3.00 10.00
6-10 .85 2.60 7.00
11-15: 11-15-Ploog-a. 14,15: 25¢ issues 5.00
16-(Regular 25¢ edition)(8/76) 4.00
16-(30¢-c, limited distribution) 1.60 4.80 16.00
17-29 2.50
NOTE: *No. 1, 2, 7-9, 11 are based on Robert E. Howard stories. **Alcala** a-17p, 18-20i; c-24. **Ditko** a-12r, 15r. **Gil Kane** c-15p, 21. **Nebres** a-22i-27i; c-25i, 27i. **Ploog** c-11, 12p, 13. **Severin** a-2-9i; c-2-10i, 19. **Starlin** c-14.*

KULL THE CONQUEROR
Marvel Comics Group: Dec, 1982 - No. 2, Mar, 1983 (52 pgs., Baxter paper)

1,2: 1-Buscema-a(p) 2.50

KULL THE CONQUEROR (No. 9,10 titled "Kull")
Marvel Comics Group: 5/83 - No. 10, 6/85 (52 pgs., Baxter paper)

V3#1-10: Buscema-a in #1-3,5-10 1.50
NOTE: Bolton a-4. Golden painted c-3-8. Guice a-4p. Sienkiewicz a-4; c-2.

KUNG FU (See Deadly Hands of..., & Master of...)

KUNG FU FIGHTER (See Richard Dragon...)

KURT BUSIEK'S ASTRO CITY
Image Comics (Juke Box Productions): Aug, 1995 - No. 6, Jan, 1996 ($2.25, limited series)

1-Kurt Busiek scripts, Brent Anderson-a & Alex Ross front & back-c begins; 1st app. Samaritan & Honor Guard (Cleopatra, MHP, Beautie, The Black Rapier, Quarrel & N-Forcer) 1.20 3.60 12.00
2-6: 2-1st app. The Silver Agent, The Old Soldier, & the "original" Honor Guard (Max O'Millions, Starwoman, the "original" Cleopatra, the "original" N-Forcer, the Bouncing Beatnik, Leopardman & Kitkat). 3-1st app. Jack-in-the-Box & The Deacon. 4-1st app. Winged Victory (cameo), The Hanged Man & The First Family. 5-1st app. Crackerjack, The Astro City Irregulars, Nightingale & Sunbird. 6-Origin Samaritan; 1st full app Winged Victory
1.00 3.00 10.00
Life In The Big City-(8/96, $19.95, trade paperback)-r/Image Comics limited series w/sketchbook & cover gallery; Ross-c 20.00
Life In The Big City-(8/96, $49.95, hardcover, 1000 print run)-r/Image Comics limited series w/sketchbook & cover gallery; Ross-c 50.00

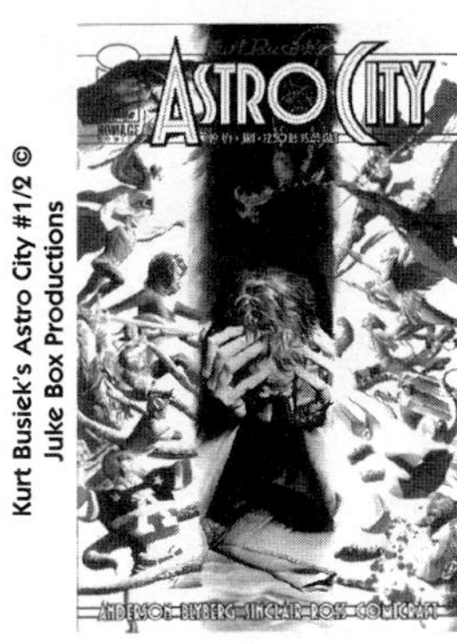

Kurt Busiek's Astro City #1/2 © Juke Box Productions

Lady Death #1 © Chaos!

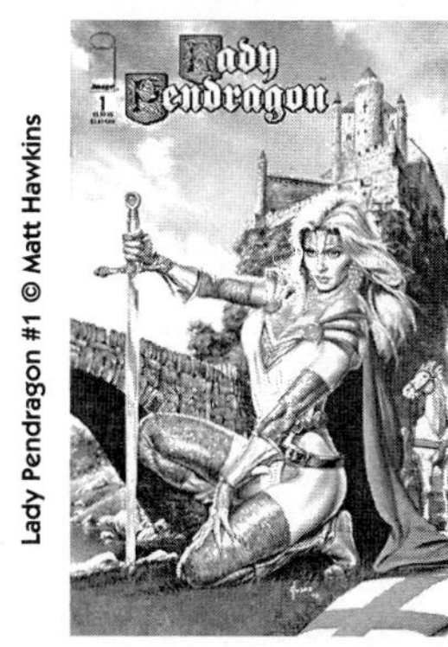

Lady Pendragon #1 © Matt Hawkins

GD25 FN65 NM94

KURT BUSIEK'S ASTRO CITY
Image Comics (Homage Comics): V2#1, Sept, 1996 - Present ($2.50) (1st Homage Comics series)
1/2-(10/96)-The Hanged Man story; 1st app. The All-American & Slugger, The Lamplighter, The Time-Keeper & Eterneon 1.00 3.00 10.00
1/2-(1/98) 2nd printing w/new cover 2.50
1- Kurt Busiek scripts, Alex Ross-c, Brent Anderson-p & Will Blyberg-i begin; intro The Gentleman, Thunderhead & Helia. 1.00 3.00 10.00
1-(12/97, $4.95) "3-D Edition" w/glasses 5.00
2-Origin The First Family; Astra story .85 2.60 7.00
3-5: 4-1st app. The Crossbreed, Ironhorse, Glue Gun & The Confessor (cameo) 2.00 6.00
6-10 5.00
11-14 2.50
TPB-($19.95) Ross-c, r/#4-9, #1/2 w/sketchbook 20.00
Family Album TPB ($19.95) r/#1-3,10-13 19.95

LABMAN
Image Comics: Nov, 1996 ($3.50, one-shot)
1-Allred-c 4.00

LABOR IS A PARTNER
Catechetical Guild Educational Society: 1949 (32 pgs., paper-c)
nn-Anti-communism 18.00 54.00 135.00
Confidential Preview-(8-1/2x11", B&W, saddle stitched)-only one known copy; text varies from color version, advertises next book on secularism (If the Devil Would Talk) 33.00 100.00 250.00

LABYRINTH
Marvel Comics Group: Nov, 1986 - No. 3, Jan, 1987 (Limited series)
1-3: David Bowie movie adaptation; r/Marvel Super Special #40 1.50

LA COSA NOSTROID (See Scud: The Disposible Assassin)
Fireman Press: Mar, 1996 - Present ($2.95, B&W)
1-9-Dan Harmon-s/Rob Schrab-c/a 3.00

LAD: A DOG (Movie)
Dell Publishing Co.: 1961 - No. 2, July-Sept, 1962
Four Color 1303, 2 2.75 8.00 30.00

LADY AND THE TRAMP (Disney, See Dell Giants & Movie Comics)
Dell Publishing Co.: No. 629, May, 1955 - No. 634, June, 1955
Four Color 629 (#1)-..with Jock 6.00 18.00 65.00
Four Color 634-...Album 3.65 11.00 40.00

LADY AND THE TRAMP IN "BUTTER LATE THAN NEVER"
American Dairy Assoc. (Premium): 1955 (16 pgs., 5x7-1/4", soft-c) (Disney)
nn 10.00 30.00 75.00

LADY COP (See 1st Issue Special)

LADY DEATH (See Evil Ernie)
Chaos! Comics: Jan, 1994 - No. 3, Mar, 1994 ($2.75, limited series)
1/2: S. Hughes-c/a in all 1.00 3.00 10.00
1/2 Gold 1.50 4.50 15.00
1/2 Velvet 1.00 3.00 10.00
1/2 Signed Limited Edition 1.60 4.80 16.00
1-($3.50)-Chromium-c 2.25 6.80 25.00
1-Commemorative 2.00 6.00 20.00
1-(9/96, $2.95) "Encore Presentation"; r/#1 3.00
2 1.20 3.60 12.00
3 .90 2.70 8.00
...And The Women of Chaos! Gallery #1 (11/96, $2.25) pin-ups by various 2.25
...Death Becomes Her #0 (11/97, $2.95) Hughes-c/a 3.00
...FAN Edition: All Hallow's Eve #1 (1/97, mail-in) 2.00 6.00
...In Lingerie #1 (8/95, $2.95) pin-ups, wraparound-c 3.00

GD25 FN65 NM94

...In Lingerie #1-Leather Edition (10,000) 1.60 4.80 16.00
...In Lingerie #1-Micro Premium Edition; Lady Demon-c (2,000) 4.00 12.25 45.00
...Swimsuit Special #1-($2.50)-Wraparound-c 3.00
...Swimsuit Special #1-Red velvet-c 1.60 4.80 16.00
...: The Reckoning (7/94, $6.95)-r/#1-3 .85 2.60 7.00
...: The Reckoning (8/95, $12.95)- new printing including Lady Death 1/2 & Swimsuit Special #1 1.30 3.90 13.00

LADY DEATH (Ongoing series)
Chaos! Comics: Feb, 1998 - Present ($2.95)
1-4: Pulido-s/S. Hughes-c/a 3.00
5-8-Deodato-a 3.00
9-11-Hughes-a 2.95
...Retribution (8/98, $2.95) Jadsen-a 2.95
...Retribution Premium Ed. 10.00

LADY DEATH: THE CRUCIBLE
Chaos! Comics: Nov, 1996 - No. 6, Oct, 1997 ($3.50/$2.95, limited series)
1/2 4.00
1/2 Cloth Edition .90 2.70 8.00
1-Wraparound silver foil embossed-c 4.00
1-($19.95)-Leather Edition 1.20 3.60 12.00
2-6-($2.95) 3.00

LADY DEATH: THE ODYSSEY
Chaos! Comics: Apr, 1996 - No. 4, Aug, 1996 ($3.50/$2.95)
1-($1.50)-Sneak Peek Preview 1.50
1-($1.50)-Sneak Peek Preview Micro Premium Edition (2500 print run) 1.50 4.50 15.00
1-($3.50)-Embossed, wraparound goil foil-c 2.00 6.00
1-Black Onyx Edition (200 print run) 8.00 24.00 90.00
1-($19.95)-Premium Edition (10,000 print run) 1.60 4.80 16.00
2-4-($2.95) 3.00

LADY DEATH II: BETWEEN HEAVEN & HELL
Chaos! Comics: Mar, 1995 - No. 4, July, 1995 ($3.50, limited series)
1-Chromium wraparound-c; Evil Ernie cameo .90 2.70 8.00
1-Commemorative (4,000) 2.25 6.80 25.00
1-Black Velvet-c 2.25 6.80 25.00
1-Gold 1.60 4.80 16.00
1-"Refractor" edition (5,000) 2.90 8.70 32.00
2-4 3.00
4-Lady Demon variant-c 1.20 3.60 12.00
Trade paperback-($12.95)-r/#1-4 13.00

LADY FOR A NIGHT (See Cinema Comics Herald)

LADY JUSTICE (See Neil Gaiman's...)

LADY LUCK (Formerly Smash #1-85) (Also see Spirit Sections #1)
Quality Comics Group: No. 86, Dec, 1949 - No. 90, Aug, 1950
86(#1) 73.00 219.00 620.00
87-90 56.00 168.00 475.00

LADY PENDRAGON
Maximum Press: Mar, 1996 ($2.50)
1-Matt Hawkins script 2.50

LADY PENDRAGON
Image Comics: Nov, 1998 - Present ($2.50)
1-Matt Hawkins-s/Stinsman-a 2.50
1-($6.95) DF Ed. with variant-c by Jusko 6.95

LADY RAWHIDE
Topps Comics: July, 1995 - No. 5, Mar, 1996 ($2.95, bi-monthly, limited series)
1-5: Don McGregor scripts & Mayhew-a. in all. 2-Stelfreeze-c. 3-Hughes-c. 4-Golden-c. 5-Julie Bell-c. 2.00
Special Edition 1 (6/95, $3.95)-Reprints 2.00

Lana #7 © MAR

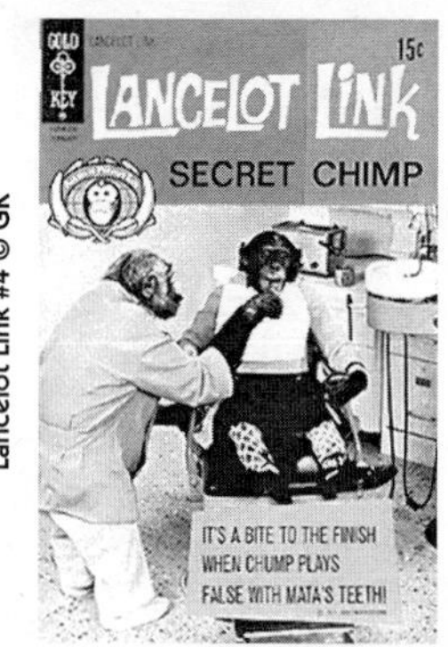

Lancelot Link #4 © GK

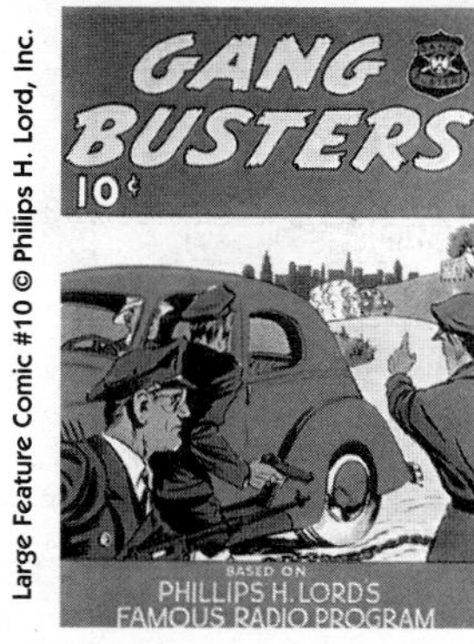

Large Feature Comic #10 © Philips H. Lord, Inc.

LADY RAWHIDE (Volume 2)
Topps Comics: Oct, 1996 -No. 5, June, 1997 ($2.95, limited series)

	GD25	FN65	NM94
1-5: 1-Julie Bell-c.			2.00

LADY SUPREME (See Asylum)(Also see Supreme & Kid Supreme)
Image Comics (Extreme): May, 1996 - No. 2, June, 1996 ($2.50, limited series)

	GD25	FN65	NM94
1,2-Terry Moore -s: 1-Terry Moore-c. 2-Flip book w/Newmen preview			2.50

LAFF-A-LYMPICS (TV)(See The Funtastic World of Hanna-Barbera)
Marvel Comics: Mar, 1978 - No. 13, Mar, 1979 (Newsstand sales only)

	GD25	FN65	NM94
1-Yogi Bear, Scooby Doo, Pixie & Dixie, etc.	1.20	3.60	12.00
2-8	1.00	3.00	10.00
9-13: 11-Jetsons x-over; 1 pg. illustrated bio of Mighty Mightor, Herculoids, Shazzan, Galaxy Trio & Space Ghost	1.40	4.20	14.00

LAFFY-DAFFY COMICS
Rural Home Publ. Co.: Feb, 1945 - No. 2, Mar, 1945

	GD25	FN65	NM94
1,2-Funny animal	7.15	21.50	50.00

LANA (Little Lana No. 8 on)
Marvel Comics (MjMC): Aug, 1948 - No. 7, Aug, 1949 (Also see Annie Oakley)

	GD25	FN65	NM94
1-Rusty, Millie begin	15.00	44.00	110.00
2-Kurtzman's "Hey Look" (1); last Rusty	10.00	30.00	70.00
3-7: 3-Nellie begins	7.00	21.00	45.00

LANCELOT & GUINEVERE (See Movie Classics)

LANCELOT LINK, SECRET CHIMP (TV)
Gold Key: Apr, 1971 - No. 8, Feb, 1973

	GD25	FN65	NM94
1-Photo-c	2.90	8.70	32.00
2-8: 2-Photo-c	1.80	5.40	20.00

LANCELOT STRONG (See The Shield)

LANCE O'CASEY (See Mighty Midget & Whiz Comics)
Fawcett Publications: Spring, 1946 - No. 3, Fall, 1946; No. 4, Summer, 1948

	GD25	FN65	NM94
1-Captain Marvel app. on-c	29.00	88.00	220.00
2	19.00	56.00	140.00
3,4	13.00	38.00	95.00

NOTE: *The cover for the 1st issue was done in 1942 but was not published until 1946. The cover shows 68 pages but actually has only 36 pages.*

LANCER (TV)(Western)
Gold Key: Feb, 1969 - No. 3, Sept, 1969 (All photo-c)

	GD25	FN65	NM94
1	2.40	7.00	26.00
2,3	1.80	5.40	20.00

LAND OF NOD, THE
Dark Horse Comics: July, 1997 - Present ($2.95, B&W)

	GD25	FN65	NM94
1-3-Jetcat; Jay Stephens-s/a			2.95

LAND OF OZ
Arrow Comics: 1998 - Present ($2.95, B&W)

	GD25	FN65	NM94
1-Bishop-s/Bryan-s/a			2.95

LAND OF THE GIANTS (TV)
Gold Key: Nov, 1968 - No. 5, Sept, 1969 (All have photo-c)

	GD25	FN65	NM94
1	4.50	13.50	50.00
2-5	2.70	8.00	30.00

LAND OF THE LOST COMICS (Radio)
E. C. Comics: July-Aug, 1946 - No. 9, Spring, 1948

	GD25	FN65	NM94
1	28.00	84.00	210.00
2	19.00	56.00	140.00
3-9	15.00	44.00	110.00

LAND UNKNOWN, THE (Movie)
Dell Publishing Co.: No. 845, Sept, 1957

	GD25	FN65	NM94
Four Color 845-Alex Toth-a	11.00	34.00	125.00

LA PACIFICA
DC Comics (Paradox Press): 1994/1995 ($4.95, B&W, limited series, digest size, mature readers)

	GD25	FN65	NM94
1-3			5.00

LARAMIE (TV)
Dell Publishing Co.: Aug, 1960 - July, 1962 (All photo-c)

	GD25	FN65	NM94
Four Color 1125-Gil Kane/Heath-a	9.00	27.00	100.00
Four Color 1223,1284, 01-418-207 (7/62)	5.50	16.50	60.00

LAREDO (TV)
Gold Key: June, 1966

	GD25	FN65	NM94
1 (10179-606)-Photo-c	2.70	8.00	30.00

LARGE FEATURE COMIC (Formerly called Black & White in previous guides)
Dell Publishing Co.: 1939 - No. 13, 1943

Note: See individual alphabetical listings for prices

1 (Series I)-Dick Tracy Meets the Blank
3-Heigh-Yo Silver! The Lone Ranger (text & ill.)(76 pgs.); also exists as a Whitman #710; based on radio
6-Terry & the Pirates & The Dragon Lady; reprints dailies from 1936
8-Dick Tracy the Racket Buster
9-King of the Royal Mounted (Zane Grey's...)
10-(Scarce)-Gang Busters (No. appears on inside front cover); first slick cover (based on radio program)
13-Dick Tracy and Scottie of Scotland Yard
15-Dick Tracy and the Kidnapped Princes
17-Gang Busters (1941)
18-Phantasmo (see The Funnies #45)
20-Donald Duck Comic Paint Book (rarer than #16) (Disney)
21,22: 21-Private Buck. 22-Nuts & Jolts
24-Popeye in "Thimble Theatre" by Segar
26-Smitty
28-Grin and Bear It
30-Tillie the Toiler
2-Winnie Winkle (#1)
3-Dick Tracy
4-Tiny Tim (#1)
6-Terry and the Pirates; Caniff-a
8-Bugs Bunny (#1)('42)
9-Bringing Up Father
10-Popeye (Thimble Theatre)
11-Barney Google and Snuffy Smith
13-(nn)-1001 Hours Of Fun; puzzles & games; by A. W. Nugent. This book was bound as #13 with Large Feature Comics in publisher's files
2-Terry and the Pirates (#1)
4-Dick Tracy Gets His Man
5-Tarzan of the Apes (#1) by Harold Foster (origin); reprints 1st Tarzan dailies from 1929
7-(Scarce, 52 pgs.)-Hi-Yo Silver the Lone Ranger to the Rescue; also exists as a Whitman #715, based on radio program
11-Dick Tracy Foils the Mad Doc Hump
12-Smilin' Jack; no number on-c
14-Smilin' Jack Helps G-Men Solve a Case!
16-Donald Duck; 1st app. Daisy Duck on back cover (6/41-Disney)
19-Dumbo Comic Paint Book (Disney); partial-r from 4-Color #17
23-The Nebbs
25-Smilin' Jack-1st issue to show title on-c
27-Terry and the Pirates; Caniff-c/a
29-Moon Mullins
1 (Series II)-Peter Rabbit by Harrison Cady; arrival date-3/27/42
5-Toots and Casper
7-Pluto Saves the Ship (#1) (Disney)-Written by Carl Barks, Jack Hannah, & Nick George (Barks' 1st comic book work)
12-Private Buck

NOTE: *The Black & White Feature Books are oversized 8-1/2x11-3/8" comics with color covers and black and white interiors. The first nine issues all have rough, heavy stock covers and, except for #7, all have 76 pages, including covers. #7 and #10-on all have 52 pages. Beginning with #10 the covers are slick and thin and, because of their size, are difficult to handle without damaging. For this reason, they are seldom found in fine to mint condition. The paper stock, unlike Wow #1 and Capt. Marvel #1, is itself not unstable ...just thin.*

LARRY DOBY, BASEBALL HERO
Fawcett Publications: 1950 (Cleveland Indians)

	GD25	FN65	NM94
nn-Bill Ward-a; photo-c	66.00	198.00	560.00

LARRY HARMON'S LAUREL AND HARDY (...Comics)

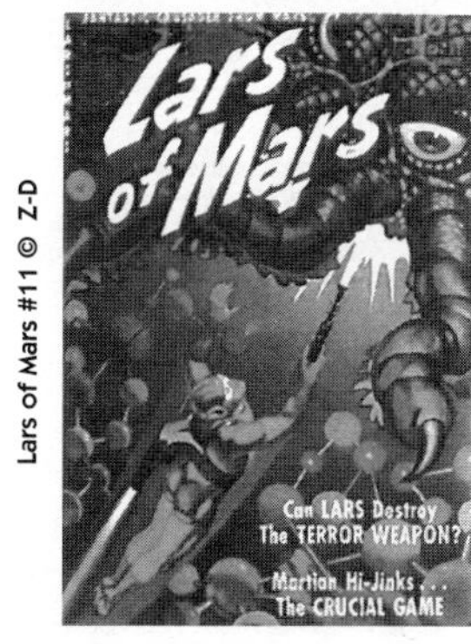

Lars of Mars #11 © Z-D

Lassie #3 © MGM

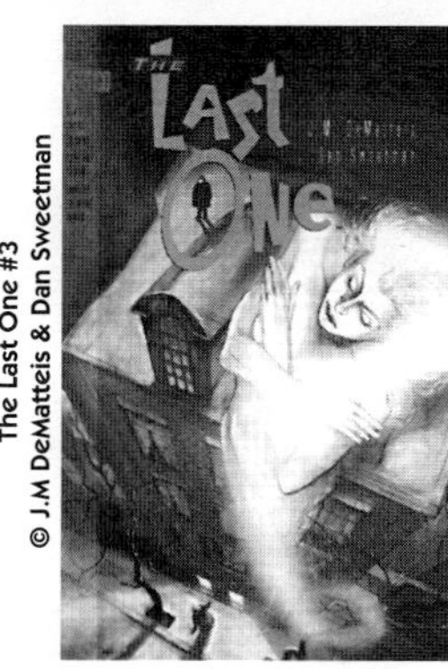

The Last One #3
© J.M DeMatteis & Dan Sweetman

GD25 FN65 NM94

National Periodical Publ.: July-Aug, 1972 (Digest advertised, not published)

	GD25	FN65	NM94
1	5.50	16.50	60.00

LARS OF MARS
Ziff-Davis Publishing Co.: No. 10, Apr-May, 1951 - No. 11, July-Aug, 1951 (Painted-c) (Created by Jerry Siegel, editor)

	GD25	FN65	NM94
10-Origin; Anderson-a(3) in each; robot-c	68.00	203.00	575.00
11-Gene Colan-a	53.00	159.00	450.00

LARS OF MARS 3-D
Eclipse Comics: Apr, 1987 ($2.50)

	GD25	FN65	NM94
1-r/Lars of Mars #10,11 in 3-D plus new story			2.50
2-D limited edition (B&W, 100 copies)			4.00

LASER ERASER & PRESSBUTTON (See Axel Pressbutton & Miracle Man 9)
Eclipse Comics: Nov, 1985 - No. 6, 1987 (95¢/$2.50, limited series)

	GD25	FN65	NM94
1-6: 5,6-(95¢)			1.00
...In 3-D 1 (8/86, $2.50)			2.50
2-D 1 (B&W, limited to 100 copies signed & numbered)			2.50

LASH LARUE WESTERN (Movie star; king of the bullwhip)(See Fawcett Movie Comic, Motion Picture Comics & Six-Gun Heroes)
Fawcett Publications: Sum, 1949 - No. 46, Jan, 1954 (36pgs., 1-7,9,13,16-on)

	GD25	FN65	NM94
1-Lash & his horse Black Diamond begin; photo front/back-c begin	94.00	282.00	800.00
2(11/49)	41.00	123.00	325.00
3-5	37.00	111.00	275.00
6,7,9: 6-Last photo back-c; intro. Frontier Phantom (Lash's twin brother)	28.00	84.00	210.00
8,10 (52pgs.)	29.00	87.00	220.00
11,12,14,15 (52pgs.)	20.00	60.00	150.00
13,16-20 (36pgs.)	17.00	52.00	125.00
21-30: 21-The Frontier Phantom app.	15.00	44.00	110.00
31-45	13.00	38.00	95.00
46-Last Fawcett issue & photo-c	13.00	40.00	100.00

LASH LARUE WESTERN (Continues from Fawcett series)
Charlton Comics: No. 47, Mar-Apr, 1954 - No. 84, June, 1961

	GD25	FN65	NM94
47-Photo-c	17.00	50.00	125.00
48	12.00	36.00	90.00
49-60	9.30	28.00	65.00
61-66,69,70: 52-r/#8; 53-r/#22	8.50	26.00	60.00
67,68-(68 pgs.). 68-Check-a	9.30	28.00	65.00
71-83	5.70	17.00	40.00
84-Last issue	7.15	21.50	50.00

LASH LARUE WESTERN
AC Comics: 1990 ($3.50, 44 pgs) (24 pgs. of color, 16 pgs. of B&W)

	GD25	FN65	NM94
1-Photo covers; r/Lash #6; r/old movie posters			3.50
Annual 1 (1990, $2.95, B&W, 44 pgs.)-Photo covers			3.00

LASSIE (TV)(M-G-M's... #1-36; see Kite Fun Book)
Dell Publ. Co./Gold Key No. 59 (10/62) on: June, 1950 - No. 70, July, 1969

	GD25	FN65	NM94
1 (52 pgs.)-Photo-c; inside lists One Shot #282 in error	13.00	39.00	140.00
2-Painted-c begin	5.50	16.50	60.00
3-10	3.50	10.50	38.00
11-19: 12-Rocky Langford (Lassie's master) marries Gerry Lawrence. 15-1st app. Timbu	2.50	7.50	28.00
20-22-Matt Baker-a	3.00	9.00	32.00
23-38,40: 33-Robinson-a.	2.00	6.00	22.00
39-1st app. Timmy as Lassie picks up her TV family	3.60	11.00	40.00
	2.00	6.00	22.00
41-58	1.80	5.50	20.00
59 (10/62)-1st Gold Key	3.00	9.00	34.00
60-70: 63-Last Timmy (10/63). 64-r/#19. 65-Forest Ranger Corey Stuart begins, ends #69. 70-Forest Rangers Bob Ericson & Scott Turner app. (Lassie's new masters)	2.00	6.00	22.00
11193(1978, $1.95, 224 pgs., Golden Press)-Baker-r (92 pgs.)	1.60	4.80	16.00
The Adventures of... nn-(Red Heart Dog Food giveaway, 1949)-16 pgs, soft-c; 1st app. Lassie in comics	16.50	50.00	165.00

NOTE: *Photo c-57, 63. (See March of Comics #210, 217, 230, 254, 266, 278, 296, 308, 324, 334, 346, 358, 370, 381, 394, 411, 432)*

LAST AMERICAN, THE
Marvel Comics (Epic): Dec, 1990 - No. 4, March, 1991 ($2.25, mini-series)

	GD25	FN65	NM94
1-4: Alan Grant scripts			2.25

LAST AVENGERS STORY, THE (Last Avengers #1)
Marvel Comics: Nov, 1995 - No. 2, Dec, 1995 ($5.95, painted, limited series) (Alterniverse)

	GD25	FN65	NM94
1,2: Peter David story; acetate-c in all. 1-New team (Hank Pym, Wasp, Human Torch, Cannonball, She-Hulk, Hotshot, Bombshell, Tommy Maximoff, Hawkeye, & Mockingbird) forms to battle Ultron 59, Kang the Conqueror, The Grim Reaper & Oddball		2.00	6.00

LAST DAYS OF THE JUSTICE SOCIETY SPECIAL
DC Comics: 1986 ($2.50, one-shot, 68 pgs.)

	GD25	FN65	NM94
1-62 pg. JSA story plus unpubbed G.A. pg.			3.00

LAST GENERATION, THE
Black Tie Studios: 1986 - No. 5, 1989 ($1.95, B&W, high quality paper)

	GD25	FN65	NM94
1-5			2.00
Book 1 (1989, $6.95)-By Caliber Press	.85	2.60	7.00

LAST HUNT, THE
Dell Publishing Co.: No. 678, Feb, 1956

	GD25	FN65	NM94
Four Color 678-Movie, photo-c	6.40	19.00	70.00

LAST KISS
ACME Press (Eclipse): 1988 ($3.95, B&W, squarebound, 52 pgs.)

	GD25	FN65	NM94
1-One story adapts E.A. Poe's The Black Cat			4.00

LAST OF THE COMANCHES (Movie) (See Wild Bill Hickok #28)
Avon Periodicals: 1953

	GD25	FN65	NM94
nn-Kinstler-c/a, 21pgs.; Ravielli-a	13.00	39.00	95.00

LAST OF THE ERIES, THE (See American Graphics)

LAST OF THE FAST GUNS, THE
Dell Publishing Co.: No. 925, Aug, 1958

	GD25	FN65	NM94
Four Color 925-Movie, photo-c	6.40	19.00	70.00

LAST OF THE MOHICANS (See King Classics & White Rider and...)

LAST OF THE VIKING HEROES, THE (Also see Silver Star #1)
Genesis West Comics: Mar, 1987 - No. 12 ($1.50/$1.95)

	GD25	FN65	NM94
1-4: 4-Intro The Phantom Force			1.50
1-Signed edition ($1.50)			1.50
5A,5B,6-12: 5A-Kirby/Stevens-c. 5B,6 ($1.95). 7-Art Adams-c. 8-Kirby back-c. 9,10,12-($2.50)			2.00
Summer Special 1-3: 1-(1988)-Frazetta-c & illos. 2(1990, $2.50)-A TMNT app. 3 (1991, $2.50)-Teenage Mutant Ninja Turtles			2.50
Summer Special 1-Signed edition (sold for $1.95)			2.00

NOTE: ***Art Adams** c-7. **Byrne** c-3. **Kirby** c-1p, 5p. **Perez** c-2i. **Stevens** c-5Ai.*

LAST ONE, THE
DC Comics (Vertigo): July, 1993 - No. 6, Dec, 1993 ($2.50, lim. series, mature)

	GD25	FN65	NM94
1-6			2.50

LAST STARFIGHTER, THE
Marvel Comics Group: Oct, 1984 - No. 3, Dec, 1984 (75¢, movie adaptation)

	GD25	FN65	NM94
1-3: r/Marvel Super Special; Guice-c			1.00

LAST TEMPTATION, THE

Laugh Comics #35 © AP

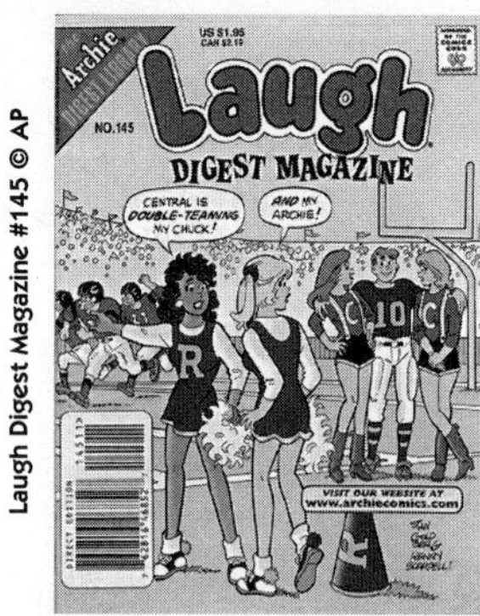

Laugh Digest Magazine #145 © AP

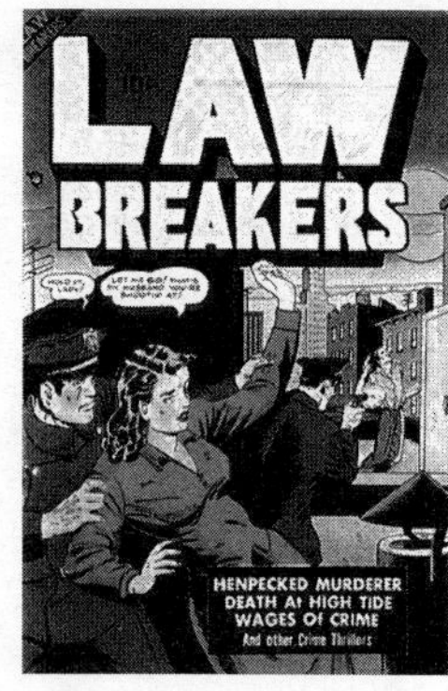

Lawbreakers #2 © CC

	GD25	FN65	NM94

Marvel Comics: 1994 - No. 3, 1994 ($4.95, limited series)

	GD25	FN65	NM94
1-3-Alice Cooper story; Neil Gaiman scripts; McKean-c; Zulli-a: 1-Two covers.			5.00

LAST TRAIN FROM GUN HILL
Dell Publishing Co.: No. 1012, July, 1959

	GD25	FN65	NM94
Four Color 1012-Movie, photo-c	8.00	25.00	90.00

LATEST ADVENTURES OF FOXY GRANDPA (See Foxy Grandpa)

LATEST COMICS (Super Duper No. 3?)
Spotlight Publ./Palace Promotions (Jubilee): Mar, 1945 - No. 2, 1945?

	GD25	FN65	NM94
1-Super Duper	13.00	38.00	95.00
2-Bee-29 (nd); Jubilee in indicia blacked out	10.00	30.00	75.00

LAUGH
Archie Enterprises: June, 1987 - No. 29, Aug, 1991 (75¢/$1.00)

	GD25	FN65	NM94
V2#1			4.00
2-10,14,24: 5-X-Mas issue. 14-1st app. Hot Dog. 24-Re-intro Super Duck			3.00
11-13,15-23,25-29: 19-X-Mas issue			1.50

LAUGH COMICS (Teenage) (Formerly Black Hood #9-19) (Laugh #226 on)
Archie Publications (Close-Up): No. 20, Fall, 1946 - No. 400, Apr, 1987

	GD25	FN65	NM94
20-Archie begins; Katy Keene & Taffy begin by Woggon; Suzie & Wilbur also begin; Archie covers begin	56.00	168.00	475.00
21-23,25	31.00	92.00	230.00
24- "Pipsy" by Kirby (6 pgs.)	32.00	96.00	240.00
26-30	15.00	45.00	115.00
31-40	11.00	32.00	85.00
41-60: 41,54-Debbi by Woggon	7.15	21.50	50.00
61-80: 67-Debbi by Woggon	5.70	17.00	38.00
81-99	3.00	9.00	30.00
100	3.50	10.50	35.00
101-126: 125-Debbi app.	2.50	7.50	20.00
127-144: Super-hero app. in all (see note)	2.50	7.50	25.00
145-156,158-160	2.50	7.50	20.00
157-Josie app.(4/64)	2.60	7.80	26.00
161-165,167-180	2.00	6.00	16.00
166-Beatles-c (1/65)	3.40	10.20	34.00
181-199	1.50	4.50	12.00
200 (12/67)	2.00	6.00	16.00
201-240(3/71)	1.00	3.00	10.00
241-280(7/74)	.85	2.60	7.00
281-299			5.00
300(3/76)		2.00	6.00
301-340 (7/79)			3.00
341-370 (1/82)			2.50
371-380,385-399			2.00
381-384,400: 381-384-Katy Keene app.; by Woggon-381,382			2.50

NOTE: *The Fly app. in 128, 129, 132, 134, 138, 139. Flygirl app. in 136, 137, 143. Flyman app. in 137. The Jaguar app. in 127, 130, 131, 133, 135, 140-142, 144. Josie app. in 145, 160, 164. Katy Keene app. in 20-125, 129, 130, 133. Many issues contain paper dolls.* ***Al Fagaly*** *c-20-29.* ***Montana*** *c-33, 36, 37, 42.* ***BillVigoda*** *c-30, 50.*

LAUGH COMICS DIGEST (...Magazine #23-89; Laugh Digest Mag. #90 on)
Archie Publ. (Close-Up No. 1, 3 on): 8/74; No. 2, 9/75; No. 3, 3/76 - Present (Digest-size)

	GD25	FN65	NM94
1-Neal Adams-a	2.70	8.00	30.00
2,7,8,19-Neal Adams-a	1.80	5.40	18.00
3-6,9,10	1.20	3.60	12.00
11-18,20	1.00	3.00	10.00
21-40	.85	2.60	7.00
41-80			5.00
81-99			4.00
100			5.00
101-138			2.50
139-146: 139-Begin $1.95-c			1.95

NOTE: *Katy Keene in 23, 25, 27, 32-38, 40, 45-48, 50. The Fly-r in 19, 20. The Jaguar-r in 25, 27. Mr. Justice-r in 21. The Web-r in 23.*

LAUGH COMIX (Formerly Top Notch Laugh; Suzie Comics No. 49 on)
MLJ Magazines: No. 46, Summer, 1944 - No. 48, Winter, 1944-45

	GD25	FN65	NM94
46-Wilbur & Suzie in all; Harry Sahle-c	19.00	56.00	140.00
47,48: 47-Sahle-c. 48-Bill Vigoda-c	13.00	40.00	100.00

LAUGH-IN MAGAZINE (TV)(Magazine)
Laufer Publ. Co.: Oct, 1968 - No. 12, Oct, 1969 (50¢) (Satire)

	GD25	FN65	NM94
V1#1	3.50	10.50	35.00
2-12	2.50	7.50	25.00

LAUREL & HARDY (See Larry Harmon's... & March of Comics No. 302, 314)

LAUREL AND HARDY (...Comics)
St. John Publ. Co.: 3/49 - No. 3, 9/49; No. 26, 11/55 - No. 28, 3/56 (No #4-25)

	GD25	FN65	NM94
1	59.00	177.00	500.00
2	39.00	116.00	290.00
3	26.00	78.00	195.00
26-28 (Reprints)	15.00	44.00	110.00

LAUREL AND HARDY (TV)
Dell Publishing Co.: Oct, 1962 - No. 4, Sept-Nov, 1963

	GD25	FN65	NM94
12-423-210 (8-10/62)	4.00	12.00	45.00
2-4 (Dell)	2.90	8.70	32.00

LAUREL AND HARDY (Larry Harmon's...)
Gold Key: Jan, 1967 - No. 2, Oct, 1967

	GD25	FN65	NM94
1-Photo back-c	4.00	12.00	40.00
2	2.75	8.00	30.00

LAW AGAINST CRIME (Law-Crime on cover)
Essenkay Publishing Co.: April, 1948 - No. 3, Aug, 1948 (Real Stories from Police Files)

	GD25	FN65	NM94
1-(#1-3 are half funny animal, half crime stories)-L. B. Cole-c/a in all; electrocution-c	57.00	171.00	485.00
2-L. B. Cole-c/a	42.00	126.00	360.00
3-Used in **SOTI**, pg. 180,181 & illo "The wish to hurt or kill couples in lovers' lanes;" reprinted in All-Famous Crime #9	55.00	164.00	465.00

LAW AND ORDER
Maximum Press: Sept, 1995 - No. 2, 1995 ($2.50, unfinished limited series)

	GD25	FN65	NM94
1,2			2.50

LAWBREAKERS (...Suspense Stories No. 10 on)
Law and Order Magazines (Charlton): Mar, 1951 - No. 9, Oct-Nov, 1952

	GD25	FN65	NM94
1	27.00	80.00	200.00
2	14.00	42.00	105.00
3,5,6,8,9	10.00	30.00	75.00
4- "White Death" junkie story	13.00	38.00	85.00
7- "The Deadly Dopesters" drug story	13.00	38.00	85.00

LAWBREAKERS ALWAYS LOSE!
Marvel Comics (CBS): Spring, 1948 - No. 10, Oct, 1949

	GD25	FN65	NM94
1-2pg. Kurtzman-a, "Giggles 'n' Grins"	28.00	84.00	210.00
2	14.00	42.00	105.00
3-5: 4-Vampire story	11.00	32.00	80.00
6(2/49)-Has editorial defense against charges of Dr. Wertham	11.00	34.00	85.00
7-Used in **SOTI**, illo "Comic-book philosophy"	25.00	75.00	185.00
8-10: 9,10-Photo-c	10.00	30.00	75.00

NOTE: ***Brodsky*** *c-4, 5.* ***Shores*** *c-1-3, 6-8.*

LAWBREAKERS SUSPENSE STORIES (Formerly Lawbreakers; Strange Suspense Stories No. 16 on)
Capitol Stories/Charlton Comics: No. 10, Jan, 1953 - No. 15, Nov, 1953

	GD25	FN65	NM94
10	23.00	70.00	175.00

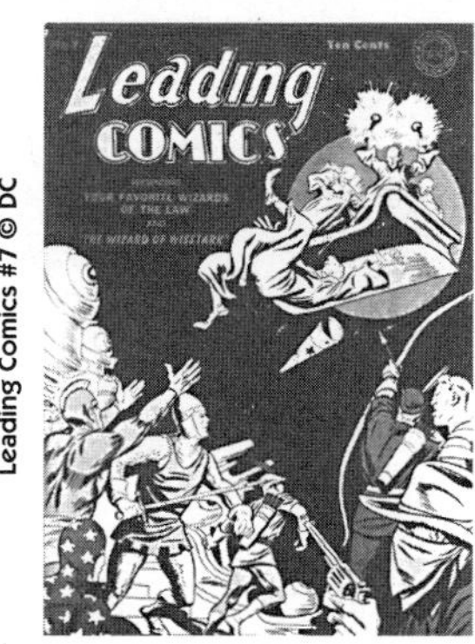

Leading Comics #7 © DC

Leave it to Chance #11 © James Robinson & Paul Smith

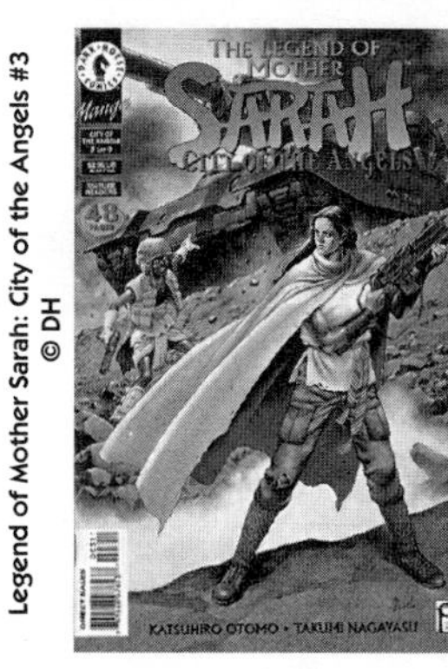

Legend of Mother Sarah: City of the Angels #3 © DH

GD25 FN65 NM94

11 (3/53)-Severed tongues-c/story & woman negligee scene
68.00 204.00 575.00
12-14: 13-Giordana-c begin, end #15 11.00 32.00 80.00
15-Acid-in-face-c/story; hands dissolved in acid sty 35.00 105.00 260.00

LAW-CRIME (See Law Against Crime)

LAWDOG
Marvel Comics (Epic Comics): May, 1993 - No. 10, Feb, 1993 ($3.50)
1-10 1.50

LAWDOG/GRIMROD: TERROR AT THE CROSSROADS
Marvel Comics (Epic Comics): Sept, 1993 ($3.50)
1 3.50

LAWMAN (TV)
Dell Publishing Co.: No. 970, Feb, 1959 - No. 11, Apr-June, 1962 (All photo-c)
Four Color 970(#1) 12.00 36.00 130.00
Four Color 1035('60), 3(2-4/60)-Toth-a 6.40 19.00 70.00
4-11 4.50 13.50 50.00

LAW OF DREDD, THE (Also see Judge Dredd)
Quality Comics/Fleetway #8 on: 1989 - No. 33, 1992 ($1.50/$1.75)
1-8 ($1.50)-Bolland a-1-6,8,10-12,14(2 pg),15,19 1.50
9-20,24-28: 9-Begin $1.75-c 1.75
21-23,29-33)$1.95-c) 2.00

LAWRENCE (See Movie Classics)

LAZARUS CHURCHYARD
Tundra Publishing: June, 1992 - No. 3, 1992 ($3.95, 44 pgs., coated stock)
1-3 4.00

LEADING COMICS (...Screen Comics No. 42 on)
National Periodical Publications: Winter, 1941-42 - No. 41, Feb-Mar, 1950
1-Origin The Seven Soldiers of Victory; Crimson Avenger, Green Arrow & Speedy, Shining Knight, The Vigilante, Star Spangled Kid & Stripesy begin; The Dummy (Vigilante villain) 1st app. 337.00 1011.00 3200.00
2-Meskin-a;Fred Ray-c 135.00 405.00 1150.00
3 112.00 336.00 950.00
4,5 79.00 237.00 675.00
6-10 71.00 213.00 600.00
11-14(Spring, 1945): 13-Robot-c 50.00 150.00 425.00
15-(Sum,'45)-Contents change to funny animal 24.00 72.00 180.00
16-22,24-30: 16-Nero Fox-c begin, end #22 10.00 30.00 75.00
23-1st app. Peter Porkchops by Otto Feur & begins 22.00 66.00 175.00
31,32,34-41: 34-41-Leading Screen... on-c only 9.30 28.00 65.00
33-(Scarce) 18.00 54.00 135.00
NOTE: ***Rube Grossman**-a(Peter Porkchops)-most #15-on; c-15-41. **Post** a-23-37, 39, 41.*

LEADING SCREEN COMICS (Formerly Leading Comics)
National Periodical Publ.: No. 42, Apr-May, 1950 - No. 77, Aug-Sept, 1955
42-Peter Porkchops-c/stories continue 9.30 28.00 65.00
43-77 7.85 23.50 55.00
NOTE: ***Grossman** a-most. **Mayer** a-45-48, 50, 54-57, 60, 62-74, 75(3), 76, 77.*

LEAGUE OF CHAMPIONS, THE (Also see The Champions)
Hero Graphics: Dec, 1990 - No. 12, 1992 ($2.95, 52 pgs.)
1-12: 1-Flare app. 2-Origin Malice 3.00

LEAGUE OF JUSTICE
DC Comics (Elseworlds): 1996 - No. 2, 1996 ($5.95, 48 pgs., squarebound)
1,2: Magic-based alternate DC Universe story; Giordano-i 2.00 6.00

LEATHERFACE
Arpad Publishing: May (April on-c), 1991 - No. 4, May, 1992 ($2.75, painted-c)
1-Based on Texas Chainsaw movie; Dorman-c 4.00
2-4 3.00

LEATHERNECK THE MARINE (See Mighty Midget Comics)

GD25 FN65 NM94

LEAVE IT TO BEAVER (TV)
Dell Publishing Co.: No. 912, June, 1958; May-July, 1962 (All photo-c)
Four Color 912 17.00 52.00 190.00
Four Color 999,1103,1191,1285, 01-428-207 14.00 44.00 160.00

LEAVE IT TO BINKY (Binky No. 72 on) (Super DC Giant) (No. 1-22: 52 pgs.)
National Periodical Publications: 2-3/48 - #60, 10/58; #61, 6-7/68 - #71, 2-3/70 (Teen-age humor)
1-Lucy wears Superman costume 31.00 92.00 230.00
2 15.00 46.00 115.00
3,4 9.30 28.00 65.00
5-Superman cameo 15.00 44.00 110.00
6-10 7.85 23.50 55.00
11-14,16-22: Last 52pg. issue 6.50 19.50 45.00
15-Scribbly story by Mayer 9.30 28.00 65.00
23-28,30-45: 45-Last pre-code (2/55) 4.25 13.00 28.00
29-Used in **POP**, pg. 78 5.00 15.00 30.00
46-60: 60-(10/58) 2.50 7.50 22.00
61 (6-7/68) 4.00 12.00 40.00
62-69 2.50 7.50 22.00
70-7pg. app. Bus Driver who looks like Ralph from Honeymooners
3.20 9.00 32.00
71-Last issue 2.60 7.80 26.00
NOTE: ***Aragones**-a-61, 62, 67. **Drucker** a-28. **Mayer** a-1, 2, 15. Created by **Mayer**.*

LEAVE IT TO CHANCE
Homage Comics: Sept, 1996 - Present ($2.50)
1-Intro Chance Falconer & St. George; James Robinson scripts & Paul Smith-c/a begins 1.00 3.00 10.00
2 .90 2.70 8.00
3 1.00 3.00 10.00
4-7 4.00
8-11: 8-Begin $2.95-c 3.00
Shaman's Rain TPB (1997, $9.95) r/#1-4 1.00 3.00 10.00

LEE HUNTER, INDIAN FIGHTER
Dell Publishing Co.: No. 779, Mar, 1957; No. 904, May, 1958
Four Color 779 (#1) 3.60 11.00 40.00
Four Color 904 2.75 8.00 30.00

LEFT-HANDED GUN, THE (Movie)
Dell Publishing Co.: No. 913, July, 1958
Four Color 913-Paul Newman photo-c 10.00 30.00 110.00

LEGACY
Majestic Entertainment: Oct, 1993 - No. 2, Nov, 1993; No. 0, 1994 ($2.25)
1-2: 1-Glow-in-the-dark-c 2.25
0-Platinum 3.00

LEGEND OF CUSTER, THE (TV)
Dell Publishing Co.: Jan, 1968
1-Wayne Maunder photo-c 1.80 5.50 20.00

LEGEND OF JESSE JAMES, THE (TV)
Gold Key: Feb, 1966
10172-602-Photo-c 1.80 5.50 20.00

LEGEND OF KAMUI, THE (See Kamui)

LEGEND OF LOBO, THE (See Movie Comics)

LEGEND OF MOTHER SARAH (Manga)
Dark Horse Comics: Apr, 1995 - No. 8, Nov, 1995 ($2.50, limited series)
1-8: Katsuhiro Otomo scripts 2.50

LEGEND OF MOTHER SARAH: CITY OF THE ANGELS (Manga)
Dark Horse Comics: Oct, 1996 - Present ($3.95, B&W, limited series)
1(10/96), 2(12/97),3-9: Otomo scripts 4.00

Legend of the Elflord #1 © Davdez

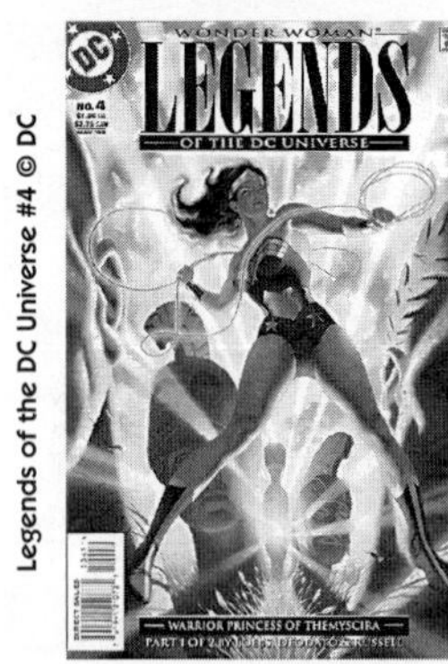

Legends of the DC Universe #4 © DC

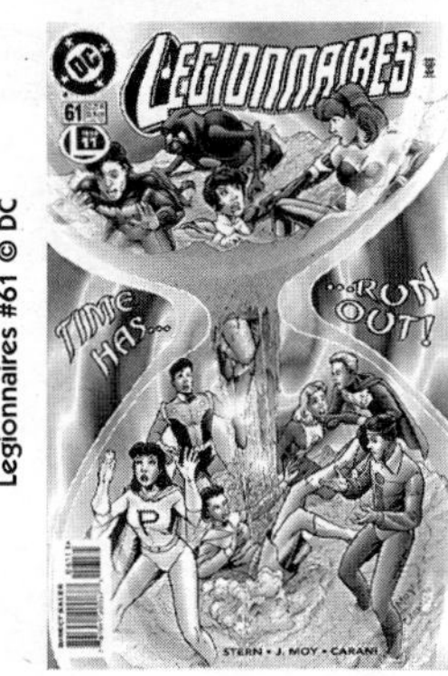

Legionnaires #61 © DC

GD25 FN65 NM94

LEGEND OF MOTHER SARAH: CITY OF THE CHILDREN (Manga)
Dark Horse Comics: Jan, 1996 - No. 7, July, 1996 ($3.95, B&W, limited series)
1-7: Otomo scripts 4.00

LEGEND OF SUPREME
Image Comics (Extreme): Dec, 1994 - No. 3, Feb, 1995 ($2.50, limited series)
1-3 2.50

LEGEND OF THE ELFLORD
DavDez Arts: July, 1998 - Present ($2.95)
1-Barry Blair & Colin Chin-s/a 3.00

LEGEND OF THE SHIELD, THE
DC Comics (Impact Comics): July, 1991 - No. 16, Oct, 1992 ($1.00)
1-16: 6,7-The Fly x-over. 12-Contains trading card 1.00
Annual 1 (1992, $2.50, 68 pgs.)-Snyder-a; w/trading card 2.50

LEGEND OF WONDER WOMAN, THE
DC Comics: May, 1986 - No. 4, Aug, 1986 (75¢, limited series)
1-4 1.00

LEGEND OF YOUNG DICK TURPIN, THE (Disney)(TV)
Gold Key: May, 1966
1 (10176-605)-Photo/painted-c 1.80 5.50 20.00

LEGEND OF ZELDA, THE (Link: The Legend... in indicia)
Valiant Comics: 1990 - No. 4, 1990 ($1.95, coated stiff-c)
V2#1, 1990 - No. 5, 1990 ($1.50)
1-4: 4-Layton-c(i) 5.00
V2#1-5 3.50

LEGENDS
DC Comics: Nov, 1986 - No. 6, Apr, 1987 (75¢, limited series)
1-6: 1-Byrne-c/a(p) in all; 1st app. new Capt. Marvel. 3-1st app. new Suicide Squad; death of Blockbuster. 6-1st app. new Justice League 1.00

LEGENDS OF DANIEL BOONE, THE (...Frontier Scout)
National Periodical Publications: Oct-Nov, 1955 - No. 8, Dec-Jan, 1956-57

	GD25	FN65	NM94
1 (Scarce)-Nick Cardy c-1-8	54.00	162.00	460.00
2 (Scarce)	42.00	126.00	335.00
3-8 (Scarce)	39.00	117.00	295.00

LEGENDS OF KID DEATH AND FLUFFY
Event Comics: Feb, 1997 ($2.95, B&W, one-shot)
1-Five covers 3.00

LEGENDS OF LUXURA
Brainstorm Comics: 1996 ($2.95, B&W)
1-3:1-Lindo-c. 3-Regular -c & nude-c 3.00

LEGENDS OF NASCAR, THE
Vortex Comics: Nov, 1990 - No. 14, 1992? (#1 3rd printing (1/91) says 2nd printing inside)
1-Bill Elliott biog.; Trimpe-a ($1.50) 5.00
1-2nd printing (11/90, $2.00) 2.00
1-3rd print; contains Maxx racecards ($3.00) 3.00
2-Richard Petty ($2.00) 4.00
3-14: 3-Ken Schrader (7/91). 4-Bobby Allison; Spiegle-a(p); Adkins part-i. 5-Sterling Marlin. 6-Bill Elliott. 7-Junior Johnson; Spiegle-c/a. 8-Benny Parsons; Heck-a 2.50
1-13-Hologram cover versions. 2-Hologram shows Bill Elliott's car by mistake (all are numbered & limited) 5.00
2-Hologram corrected version 5.00
Christmas Special ($5.95) 2.00 6.00

LEGENDS OF THE DARK CLAW
DC Comics (Amalgam): Apr, 1996 ($1.95)
1-Jim Balent-c/a 3.00

LEGENDS OF THE DARK KNIGHT (See Batman: ...)

LEGENDS OF THE DC UNIVERSE
DC Comics: Feb, 1998 - Present ($1.95/$1.99)
1-3-Superman; Robinson-s/Semeiks-a/Orbik-painted-c 2.00
4,5-Wonder Woman; Deodato-a/Rude painted-c 2.00
6-13: 7,8-GL/GA, O'Neil-s. 8-Begin $1.99-c. 10,11-Batgirl; Dodson-a. 12,13-Justice League 2.00
... 80 Page Giant 1 (9/98, $4.95) Stories and art by various incl. Ditko, Perez Gibbons, Mumy; Joe Kubert-c 4.95
... 3-D Gallery (12/98, $2.95) Pin-ups w/glasses 2.95

LEGENDS OF THE LEGION (See Legion of Super-Heroes)
DC Comics: Feb, 1998 - No. 4, May, 1998 ($2.25, limited series)
1-4:1-Origin-s of Ultra Boy. 2-Spark. 3-Umbra. 4-Star Boy 2.25

LEGENDS OF THE STARGRAZERS (See Vanguard Illustrated #2)
Innovation Publishing: Aug, 1989 - No. 6, 1990 ($1.95, limited series, mature)
1-6: 1-Redondo part inks 2.00

LEGENDS OF THE WORLD'S FINEST (See World's Finest)
DC Comics: 1994 - No. 3, 1994 ($4.95, squarebound, limited series)
1-3: Simonson scripts; Brereton-c/a; embossed foil logos 5.00
TPB-(1995, $14.95) r/#1-3 15.00

L.E.G.I.O.N. (The # to right of title represents year of print)(Also see Lobo & R.E.B.E.L.S.)
DC Comics: Feb, 1989 - No. 70, Sept, 1994 ($1.50/$1.75)
1-Giffen plots/breakdowns in #1-12 1.75
2-22,24-47: 3-Lobo app. #3 on. 4-1st Lobo-c this title. 5-Lobo joins L.E.G.I.O.N. 13-Lar Gand app. 16-Lar Gand joins L.E.G.I.O.N., leaves #19. 28-Giffen-c(p). 31-Capt. Marvel app. 35-L.E.G.I.O.N. '92 begins 1.50
23-($2.50, 52 pgs.)-L.E.G.I.O.N. '91 begins 2.50
48,49,51-69: 48-Begin $1.75-c. 63-L.E.G.I.O.N. '94 begins; Superman x-over 1.75
50-($3.50, 68 pgs.) 3.50
70-($2.50, 52 pgs.)-Zero Hour 2.50
Annual 1-3 (1990-1992, $2.95, 68 pgs.): 1-Lobo, Superman app. 2-Alan Grant scripts 3.00
Annual 4 (1993, $3.50, 68 pgs.) 3.50
Annual 5 (1994, $3.50, 68 pgs.)-Elseworlds story; Lobo app. 3.50
NOTE: ***Alan Grant*** *scripts in #1-39, 51, Annual 1, 2.*

LEGIONNAIRES (See Legion of Super-Heroes #40, 41 & Showcase 95 #6)
DC Comics: Apr, 1992 - Present ($1.25/$1.50/$2.25)
1-8: 1-Chris Sprouse-c/a; polybagged w/SkyBox trading card 1.50
9-18: 9-Begin $1.50-c. 11-Kid Quantum joins. 18-(9/94)-Zero Hour 1.50
..0-(10/94)-Restart of Legion continuity 2.00
19(11/94) -25 1.50
26-$1.75-c 1.75
27-49: 27-Begin $2.25-c. 37-Valor (Lar Gand) becomes M'onel (5/96). 43-Legion tryouts; reintro Princess Projectra, Shadow Lass & others 47-Forms one cover image with LSH #91 2.25
50-($3.95) Pullout poster by Davis/Farmer 4.00
51-63: 52-Shrinking Violet becomes LeViathan. 60-Karate Kid & Kid Quantum join. 61-Silver Age & 70's Legion app. 2.25
64-68: 64-Begin $2.50-c 2.50
#1,000,000 (11/98) Sean Phillips-a 2.50
Annual 1 (1994, $2.95)-Elseworlds story 3.00
Annual 2 (1995, $3.95)-Year One story 4.00
Annual 3 (1996, $2.95)-Legends of the Dead Earth story 3.00

LEGIONNAIRES THREE
DC Comics: Jan, 1986 - No. 4, May, 1986 (75¢, limited series)

Legion of Super-Heroes #301 © DC

Legion of Super-Heroes #8 (4th series) © DC

Lenore #2 © Roman Dirge

	GD25	FN65	NM94

1-4 1.00

LEGION OF MONSTERS (Also see Marvel Premiere #28 & Marvel Preview #8)
Marvel Comics Group: Sept, 1975 ($1.00, B&W, magazine, 76 pgs.)

1-Origin & 1st app. Legion of Monsters; Neal Adams-c; Morrow-a; origin & only app. The Manphibian; Frankenstein by Mayerik; Bram Stoker's Dracula adaptation; Reese-a; painted-c (#2 was advertised with Morbius & Satana, but was never published) 1.80 5.40 18.00

LEGION OF NIGHT, THE
Marvel Comics: Oct, 1991 - No. 2, Oct, 1991 ($4.95, 52 pgs.)

1,2-Whilce Portacio-c/a(p) 5.00

LEGION OF SUBSTITUTE HEROES SPECIAL (See Adventure Comics #306)
DC Comics: July, 1985 ($1.25, one-shot, 52 pgs.)

1-Giffen-c/a(p) 1.25

LEGION OF SUPER-HEROES (See Action, Adventure, All New Collectors Edition, Legionnaires, Legends of the Legion, Limited Collectors Edition, Secrets of the..., Superboy & Superman)
National Periodical Publications: Feb, 1973 - No. 4, July-Aug, 1973

1-Legion & Tommy Tomorrow reprints begin 1.60 4.80 16.00
2-4: 2-Forte-r. 3-r/Adv. #340. Action #240. 4-r/Adv. #341, Action #233; Mooney-r .90 2.70 9.00

LEGION OF SUPER-HEROES, THE (Formerly Superboy and...; Tales of The Legion No. 314 on)
DC Comics: No. 259, Jan, 1980 - No. 313, July, 1984

259(#1)-Superboy leaves Legion 5.00
260-270: 265-Contains 28 pg. insert "Superman & the TRS-80 Computer"; origin Tyroc; Tyroc leaves Legion 3.00
271-284,291-293: 272-Blok joins; origin; 20pg. insert-Dial 'H' For Hero. 277-Intro Reflecto. 280-Superboy re-joins legion. 282-Origin Reflecto. 283-Origin Wildfire 2.00
285-290:285,286-Giffen back up sty. 287-Giffen-a on Legion begins. 290-294-Great Darkness saga 3.00
294-Double size (52 pgs.) 2.50
295-299,301-305: 297-Origin retold. 298-Free 16pg. Amethyst preview 1.75
300-(68 pgs., Mando paper)-Anniversary issue; has c/a by almost everyone at DC 3.00
306-313 (75¢): 306-Brief origin Star Boy 1.25
Annual 1(1982, 52 pgs.)-Giffen-c/a; 1st app./origin new Invisible Kid who joins Legion 2.50
Annual 2,3: 2(1983, 52 pgs.)-Giffen-c; Karate Kid & Princess Projectra wed & resign. 3(1984, 52 pgs.) 1.75
...The Great Darkness Saga (1989, $17.95, 196 pgs.)-r/LSH #287,290-294 & Annual #3; Giffen-c/a 1.80 5.40 18.00

NOTE: ***Aparo** c-282, 283, 300(part). **Austin** c-268i. **Buckler** c-273p, 274p, 276p. **Colan** a-311p. **Ditko** a(p)-267, 268, 272, 274, 276, 281. **Giffen** a-285-313p, Annual 1p; c-287p, 288p, 289, 290p, 291p, 292, 293, 294-299p, 300, 301-313p, Annual 1p, 2p. **Perez** c-268p, 277-280, 281p. **Starlin** a-265. **Staton** a-259p, 260p, 280. **Tuska** a-308p.*

LEGION OF SUPER-HEROES (3rd Series) (Reprinted in Tales of the Legion)
DC Comics: Aug, 1984 - No. 63, Aug, 1989 ($1.25/$1.75, deluxe format)

1-Silver ink logo 2.00
2-10: 4-Death of Karate Kid. 5-Death of Nemesis Kid 1.50
11-14: 12-Cosmic Boy, Lightning Lad, & Saturn Girl resign. 14-Intro new members: Tellus, Sensor Girl, Quislet 1.25
15-18: 15-17-Crisis tie-ins. 18-Crisis x-over 1.50
19-25: 25-Sensor Girl i.d. revealed as Princess Projectra 1.25
26-36,39-44: 35-Saturn Girl rejoins. 40-$1.75-c. price begins. 42,43-Millennium tie-ins. 44-Origin Quislet. 1.25
37,38-Death of Superboy 1.10 3.30 11.00
45 ($2.95, 68 pgs.)-Anniversary issue 3.00
46-49,51-62 1.25
50-Double size, $2.50 2.50
63-Final issue 1.50
Annual 1 (10/85, 52 pgs.)-Crisis tie-in 1.75
Annual 2,3: 2 (1986, 52 pgs.). 3 (1987, $2.25, 52 pgs.) 2.25
Annual 4 (1988, $2.50, 52 pgs.) 2.50

NOTE: *Byrne c-36p. **Giffen** a(p)-1, 2, 50-55, 57-63, Annual 1p, 2; c-1-5p, 54p, Annual 1. **Orlando** a-6p. **Steacy** c-45-50, Annual 3.*

LEGION OF SUPER-HEROES (4th Series)
DC Comics: Nov, 1989 - Present ($1.75/$1.95/$2.25)

1-Giffen-c/a(p)/scripts begin (4 pg.-a only #18) 1.75
2-49,51-53,55-58: 4-Mon-El (Lar Gand) destroys Time Trapper, changes reality. 5-Alt. reality story where Mordru rules all; Ferro Lad app. 6-1st app. of Laurel Gand (Lar Gand's cousin). 8-Origin. 13-Free poster by Giffen show ing new costumes. 15-(2/91)-1st reference of Lar Gand as Valor. 21-24-Lobo & Darkseid storyline. 26-New map of headquarters. 34-Six pg. preview of Timber Wolf mini-series. 40-Minor Legionnaires app. 41-(3/93)-Intro SW6 Legionnaires 1.75
50-($3.50, 68 pgs.) 3.50
54-($2.95)-Die-cut & foil stamped-c 3.00
59-61: 59-Begin $1.95-c. 61-(9/94)-Zero Hour 2.00
0,62-68: 0-(10/94). 62-(11/94) 2.00
69-99: 69-Begin $2.25-c. 75-XS travels back to the 20th Century (cont'd in Impulse #9). 77-Origin of Brainiac 5. 81-Reintro Sun Boy. 85-Half of the Legion sent to the 20th century, Superman-c/app. 86-Final Night. 87-Deadman-c/app. 88-Impulse-c/app. Adventure Comics #247 cover swipe. 91-Forms one cover image with Legionnaires #47. 96-Wedding of Ultra Boy and Apparition. 99-Robin, Impulse, Superboy app. 2.25
100-($5.95, 96 pgs.)-Legionnaires return to the 30th Century; gatefold-c; 5 stories-art by Simonson, Davis and others 2.00 6.00
101-107: 101-Armstrong-a(p) begins. 105-Legion past & present vs. Time Trapper 2.25
108-111: 108-Begin $2.50-c. 109-Moder-a. 110-Thunder joins 2.50
#1,000,000 (11/98) Giffen-a 2.50
Annual 1-5 (1990-1994, $3.50, 68 pgs.): 4-Bloodlines. 5-Elseworlds story 3.50
Annual 6 (1995,$3.95)-Year One story 4.00
Annual 7 (1996, $3.50, 48 pgs.)-Legends of the Dead Earth story; intro 75th Century Legion of Super-Heroes; Wildfire app. 3.50
Legion: Secret Files 1 (1/98, $4.95) Retold origin & pin-ups 5.00

NOTE: ***Giffen** a-1-24; breakdowns-26-32, 34-36; c-1-7, 8(part), 9-24. **Brandon Peterson** a(p)-15(1st for DC), 16, 18, Annual 2(54 pgs.); c-Annual 2p. **Swan/Anderson** c-8(part).*

LEGION: SCIENCE POLICE (See Legion of Super-Heroes)
DC Comics: Aug, 1998 - No. 4, Nov, 1998 ($2.25, limited series)

1-4-Ryan-a 2.25

LEMONADE KID, THE (See Bobby Benson's B-Bar-B Riders)
AC Comics: 1990 ($2.50, 28 pgs.)

1-Powell-c(r); Red Hawk-r by Powell; Lemonade Kid-r/Bobby Benson by Powell (2 stories) 2.50

LENNON SISTERS LIFE STORY, THE
Dell Publishing Co.: No. 951, Nov, 1958 - No. 1014, Aug, 1959

Four Color 951 (#1)-Toth-a, 32pgs, photo-c 13.00 40.00 145.00
Four Color 1014-Toth-a, photo-c 13.00 40.00 145.00

LENORE
Slave Labor Graphics: Feb, 1998 - Present ($2.95, B&W)

1-Roman Dirge-s/a 4.00
2,3 2.95

LEONARD NIMOY'S PRIMORTALS
Tekno Comix: Mar, 1995 - No. 15, May, 1996 ($1.95)

1-15: Concept by Leonard Nimoy & Isaac Asimov 1-3-w/bound-in game piece & trading card. 4-w/Teknophage Steel Edition coupon. 13,14-Art Adams-c. 15-Simonson-c 2.00

LEONARD NIMOY'S PRIMORTALS

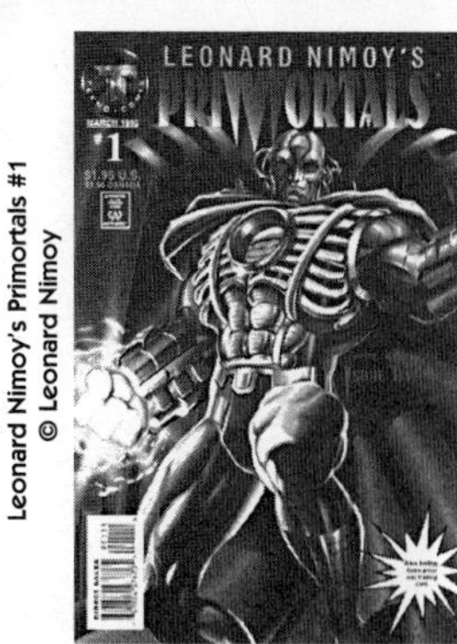

Leonard Nimoy's Primortals #1 © Leonard Nimoy

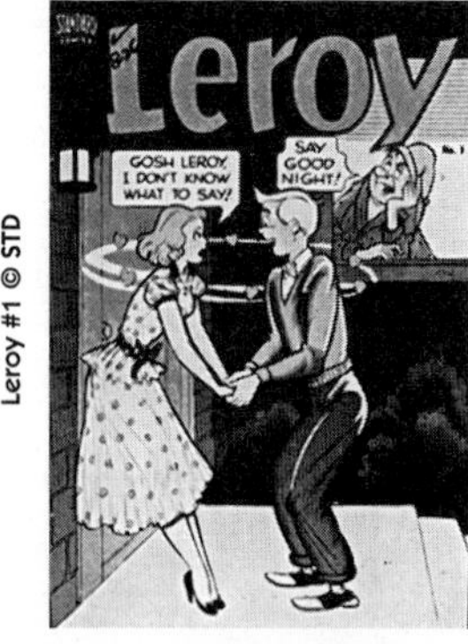

Leroy #1 © STD

Liberty Comics #11 © Green Publ. Co.

BIG Entertainment: V2#0, June, 1996 - No. 8, Feb, 1997 ($2.25)

	GD25	FN65	NM94
V2#0-8: 0-Includes Pt. 9 of "The Big Bang" x-over. 0,1-Simonson-c. 3-Kelley Jones-c			2.25

LEONARD NIMOY'S PRIMORTALS ORIGINS
Tekno Comix: Nov, 1995 - No. 2, Dec, 1995 ($2.95, limited series)

	GD25	FN65	NM94
1,2: Nimoy scripts; Art Adams-c; polybagged			3.00

LEONARDO (Also see Teenage Mutant Ninja Turtles)
Mirage Studios: Dec, 1986 ($1.50, B&W, one-shot)

	GD25	FN65	NM94
1			2.00

LEO THE LION
I. W. Enterprises: No date(1960s) (10¢)

	GD25	FN65	NM94
1-Reprint	1.10	3.30	9.00

LEROY (Teen-age)
Standard Comics: Nov, 1949 - No. 6, Nov, 1950

	GD25	FN65	NM94
1	5.70	17.00	40.00
2-Frazetta text illo.	5.00	15.00	30.00
3-6: 3-Lubbers-a	4.00	12.00	24.00

LETHAL (Also see Brigade)
Image Comics (Extreme Studios): Feb, 1996 ($2.50, unfinished limited series)

	GD25	FN65	NM94
1-Marat Mychaels-c/a.			2.50

LETHAL FOES OF SPIDER-MAN (Sequel to Deadly Foes of Spider-Man)
Marvel Comics: Sept, 1993 - No. 4, Dec, 1993 ($1.75, limited series)

	GD25	FN65	NM94
1-4			1.75

LETHAL STRYKE
London Night Studios: June, 1995 - No. 3, 1995 ($3.00)

	GD25	FN65	NM94
0-(8/95, $5.95)-Collector's ed.		2.00	6.00
1/2, 1-3: 1-polybagged w/card			3.00
Annual 1-(1996, $3.00)			3.00
Annual 1-Platinum Edition			10.00
Trade paperback-(1996, $12.95)-r/#(1/2)-3			12.95

LETHAL STRYKE/DOUBLE IMPACT: LETHAL IMPACT
London Night Studios: May, 1996 ($3.00, one-shot)

	GD25	FN65	NM94
1-Hartsoe/Lyon-a(p)			3.00
1-Natural Born Killers Edition		2.00	6.00

LETHARGIC LAD
Crusade Ent.: June, 1996 - No. 3, Sept, 1996 ($2.95, B&W, limited series)

	GD25	FN65	NM94
1-3: 3-Alex Ross-c/swipe (Kingdom Come)			3.00

LETHARGIC LAD ADVENTURES
Crusade Ent./Destination Ent.#3 on: Oct, 1997 - Present ($2.95, B&W)

	GD25	FN65	NM94
1-7-Hyland-s/a			3.00

LET'S PRETEND (CBS radio)
D. S. Publishing Co.: May-June, 1950 - No. 3, Sept-Oct, 1950

	GD25	FN65	NM94
1	13.00	38.00	95.00
2,3	10.00	30.00	75.00

LET'S READ THE NEWSPAPER
Charlton Press: 1974

	GD25	FN65	NM94
nn-Features Quincy by Ted Sheares			5.00

LET'S TAKE A TRIP (TV) (CBS Television Presents)
Pines Comics: Spring, 1958

	GD25	FN65	NM94
1-Marv Levy-c/a	4.00	11.00	22.00

LETTERS TO SANTA (See March of Comics No. 228)

LEX LUTHOR: THE UNAUTHORIZED BIOGRAPHY
DC Comics: 1989 ($3.95, 52 pgs., one-shot, squarebound)

	GD25	FN65	NM94
1-Painted-c; Clark Kent app.			4.00

LIBERTY COMICS (Miss Liberty No. 1)
Green Publishing Co.: No. 4, 1945 - No. 15, July, 1946 (MLJ & other reprints)

	GD25	FN65	NM94
4	13.00	38.00	95.00
5 (5/46)-The Prankster app; Starr-a	11.00	34.00	85.00
10-Hangman & Boy Buddies app.; Suzie & Wilbur begin; reprints Hangman story from Hangman #8	15.00	46.00	115.00
11(V2#2, 1/46)-Wilbur in women's clothes	13.00	38.00	95.00
12-Black Hood & Suzie app.	13.00	40.00	100.00
14,15-Patty of Airliner; Starr-a in both	8.50	26.00	60.00

LIBERTY GUARDS
Chicago Mail Order: No date (1946?)

	GD25	FN65	NM94
nn-Reprints Man of War #1 with cover of Liberty Scouts #1; Gustavson-c	29.00	86.00	250.00

LIBERTY PROJECT, THE
Eclipse Comics: June, 1987 - No. 8, May, 1988 ($1.75, color, Baxter paper)

	GD25	FN65	NM94
1-8: 6-Valkyrie app.			1.80

LIBERTY SCOUTS (See Liberty Guards & Man of War)
Centaur Publications: No. 2, June, 1941 - No. 3, Aug, 1941

	GD25	FN65	NM94
2(#1)-Origin The Fire-Man, Man of War; Vapo-Man & Liberty Scouts begin; intro Liberty Scouts; Gustavson-c/a in both	115.00	344.00	975.00
3(#2)-Origin & 1st app. The Sentinel	85.00	256.00	725.00

LICENCE TO KILL (James Bond 007) (Movie)
Eclipse Comics: 1989 ($7.95, slick paper, 52 pgs.)

	GD25	FN65	NM94
nn-Movie adaptation; Timothy Dalton photo-c	.90	2.70	8.00
Limited Hardcover ($24.95)	2.25	6.80	25.00

LIDSVILLE (TV)
Gold Key: Oct, 1972 - No. 5, Oct, 1973

	GD25	FN65	NM94
1-Photo-c	2.90	8.70	32.00
2-5	1.70	5.10	18.00

LIEUTENANT, THE (TV)
Dell Publishing Co.: April-June, 1964

	GD25	FN65	NM94
1-Photo-c	1.70	5.10	18.00

LIEUTENANT BLUEBERRY (Also see Blueberry)
Marvel Comics (Epic Comics): 1991 - No. 3, 1991 (Graphic novel)

	GD25	FN65	NM94
1,2 ($8.95)-Moebius-a in all	.90	2.70	9.00
3 ($14.95)	1.50	4.50	15.00

LT. ROBIN CRUSOE, U.S.N. (See Movie Comics & Walt Disney Showcase #26)

LIFE OF CAPTAIN MARVEL, THE
Marvel Comics Group: Aug, 1985 - No. 5, Dec, 1985 ($2.00, Baxter paper)

	GD25	FN65	NM94
1-5: 1-All reprint Starlin issues of Iron Man #55, Capt. Marvel #25-34 plus Marvel Feature #12 (all with Thanos). 4-New Thanos back-c by Starlin			2.00

LIFE OF CHRIST, THE
Catechetical Guild Educational Society: No. 301, 1949 (35¢, 100 pgs.)

	GD25	FN65	NM94
301-Reprints from Topix(1949)-V5#11,12	5.70	17.00	40.00

LIFE OF CHRIST: THE CHRISTMAS STORY, THE
Marvel Comics/Nelson: Feb, 1993 ($2.99, slick stock)

	GD25	FN65	NM94
nn			4.00

LIFE OF CHRIST: THE EASTER STORY, THE
Marvel Comics/Nelson: 1993 ($2.99, slick stock)

	GD25	FN65	NM94
nn			3.00

LIFE OF CHRIST VISUALIZED
Standard Publishers: 1942 - No. 3, 1943

	GD25	FN65	NM94
1-3: All came in cardboard case	5.00	15.00	30.00
With case.....	8.50	26.00	60.00

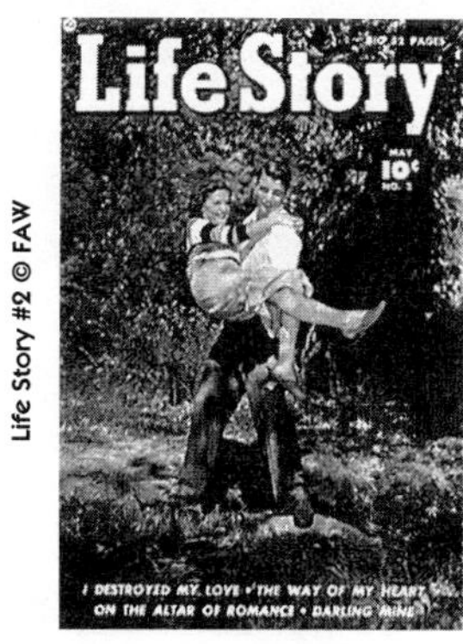

Life Story #2 © FAW

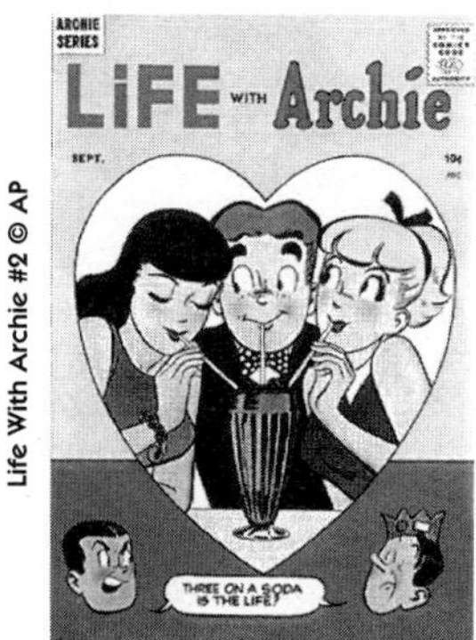

Life With Archie #2 © AP

Lillith #1 © Ben Y. Dunn

	GD25	FN65	NM94
LIFE OF CHRIST VISUALIZED			
The Standard Publ. Co.: 1946? (48 pgs. in color)			
nn	2.80	7.00	14.00
LIFE OF ESTHER VISUALIZED			
The Standard Publ. Co.: No. 2062, 1947 (48 pgs. in color)			
2062	3.20	8.00	16.00
LIFE OF JOSEPH VISUALIZED			
The Standard Publ. Co.: No. 1054, 1946 (48 pgs. in color)			
1054	2.80	7.00	14.00
LIFE OF PAUL (See The Living Bible)			
LIFE OF POPE JOHN PAUL II, THE			
Marvel Comics Group: Jan, 1983 ($1.50/$1.75)			
1			3.00
LIFE OF RILEY, THE (TV)			
Dell Publishing Co.: No. 917, July, 1958			
Four Color 917-Photo-c	11.00	33.00	120.00
LIFE OF THE BLESSED VIRGIN			
Catechetical Guild (Giveaway): 1950 (68pgs.) (square binding)			
nn-Contains "The Woman of the Promise" & "Mother of Us All" rebound	4.15	12.50	25.00
LIFE'S LIKE THAT			
Croyden Publ. Co.: 1945 (25¢, B&W, 68 pgs.)			
nn-Newspaper Sunday strip-r by Neher	5.70	17.00	35.00
LIFE STORIES OF AMERICAN PRESIDENTS (See Dell Giants)			
LIFE STORY			
Fawcett Publications: Apr, 1949 - V8#46, Jan, 1953; V8#47, Apr, 1953 (All have photo-c?)			
V1#1	11.00	32.00	80.00
2	5.35	16.00	32.00
3-6	4.25	13.00	28.00
V2#7-12	4.25	13.00	28.00
V3#13-Wood-a	11.00	34.00	85.00
V3#14-18, V4#19-24, V5#25-30, V6#31-35	4.00	12.00	24.00
V6#36- "I sold drugs" on-c	5.00	15.00	30.00
V7#37,40-42, V8#44,45	3.00	7.50	15.00
V7#38, V8#43-Evans-a	4.25	13.00	28.00
V7#39-Drug Smuggling & Junkie story	4.15	12.50	25.00
V8#46,47 (Scarce)	4.15	12.50	25.00
NOTE: ***Powell*** *a-13, 23, 24, 26, 28, 30, 32, 39.* ***Marcus Swayze*** *a-1-3, 10-12, 15, 16, 20, 21, 23-25, 31, 35, 37, 40, 44, 46.*			
LIFE, THE UNIVERSE AND EVERYTHING (See Hitchhikers Guide to the Galaxy & Restaurant at the End of the Universe)			
DC Comics: 1996 - No. 3, 1996 ($6.95, squarebound, limited series)			
1-3: Adaptation of novel by Douglas Adams.	.85	2.60	7.00
LIFE WITH ARCHIE			
Archie Publications: Sept, 1958 - No. 285, July, 1991			
1	27.00	81.00	270.00
2-(9/59)	13.00	39.00	130.00
3-5: 3-(7/60)	9.00	27.00	90.00
6-10	6.00	18.00	60.00
11-20	4.00	12.00	40.00
21(7/63)-30	3.00	9.00	30.00
31-41	2.50	7.50	22.00
42-Pureheart begins (1st app.-c/s, 10/65)	5.00	15.00	50.00
43,44	3.00	9.00	30.00
45(1/66) 1st Man From R.I.V.E.R.D.A.L.E.	3.80	11.40	38.00
46-49: 46-Origin Pureheart	2.50	7.50	20.00
50-United Three begin: Pureheart (Archie), Superteen (Betty), Captain Hero (Jughead)	2.50	7.50	25.00
51-59: 59-Pureheart ends	2.50	7.50	25.00
60-Archie band begins	3.00	9.00	30.00
61-66: 61-Man From R.I.V.E.R.D.A.L.E.-c/s	2.25	6.75	18.00
67-80	1.20	3.60	12.00
81-99	1.00	3.00	10.00
100 (8/70)	1.60	4.80	16.00
101-112, 114-130(2/73), 139(11/73)-Archie Band c/s	.90	2.70	8.00
113-Sabrina & Salem app.	1.20	3.60	12.00
131,134-138,140-146,148-161,164-170(6/76)		2.00	6.00
132,133,147,163-all horror-c/s	.90	2.70	8.00
162-UFO c/s	.90	2.70	9.00
171,173-175,177-184,186,189,191-194,196			4.00
172,185,197			5.00
176(12/76)-1st app. Capt. Archie of Starship Rivda, in 24th century c/s; 1st app. Stella the Robot	.90	2.70	8.00
187,188,195,198,199-all horror-c/s			5.00
190-1st Dr. Doom-c/s			5.00
200 (12/78) Maltese Pigeon-s		2.00	6.00
201-203,205-237,239,240: 208-Reintro Veronica.			3.00
204-Flying saucer-c/s			5.00
238-(9/83)-25th anniversary issue; Ol' Betsy (jalopy) replaced			3.00
241-278,280-284: 250-Comic book convention-s			2.00
279,285: 279-Intro Mustang Sally ($1.00, 7/90)			3.00
NOTE: ***Gene Colan*** *a-272-279, 285, 286.*			
LIFE WITH MILLIE (Formerly A Date With Millie) (Modeling With Millie #21 on)			
Atlas/Marvel Comics Group: No. 8, Dec, 1960 - No. 20, Dec, 1962			
8-Teenage	6.00	18.00	60.00
9-11	4.00	12.00	40.00
12-20	3.00	9.00	30.00
LIFE WITH SNARKY PARKER (TV)			
Fox Feature Syndicate: Aug, 1950			
1-Early TV comic; photo-c from TV puppet show	22.00	66.00	175.00
LIGHT AND DARKNESS WAR, THE			
Marvel Comics (Epic Comics): Oct, 1988 - No. 6, Dec, 1989 ($1.95, lim. series)			
1-6			2.00
LIGHT FANTASTIC, THE (Terry Pratchett's)			
Innovation Publishing: June, 1992 - No. 4, Sept, 1992 ($2.50, mini-series)			
1-4: Adapts 2nd novel in Discworld series			2.50
LIGHT IN THE FOREST (Disney)			
Dell Publishing Co.: No. 891, Mar, 1958			
Four Color 891-Movie, Fess Parker photo-c	7.30	22.00	80.00
LIGHTNING COMICS (Formerly Sure-Fire No. 1-3)			
Ace Magazines: No. 4, Dec, 1940 - No. 13(V3#1), June, 1942			
4-Characters continue from Sure-Fire	88.00	264.00	750.00
5,6: 6-Dr. Nemesis begins	58.00	174.00	490.00
V2#1-6: 2- "Flash Lightning" becomes "Lash..."	46.00	138.00	390.00
V3#1-Intro. Lightning Girl & The Sword	46.00	138.00	390.00
NOTE: ***Anderson*** *a-V2#6.* ***Mooney*** *c-V1#5, 6, V2#1-6, V3#1. Bondage c-V2#6. Lightning-c on all.*			
LIGHTNING COMICS PRESENTS			
Lightning Comics: May, 1994 ($3.50)			
1-Red foil-c distributed by Diamond Distributors			3.50
1-Black/yellow/blue-c distrib. by Capital Distributors			3.50
1-Red/yellow-c distributed by H. World			3.50
1-Platinum			3.50
LI'L (See Little)			
LILLITH (See Warrior Nun...)			
Antarctic Press: Sept, 1996 - No. 3, Feb, 1997 ($2.95, limited series)			

Limited Collectors' Edition #C-32 © DC

Linda #2 © AJAX

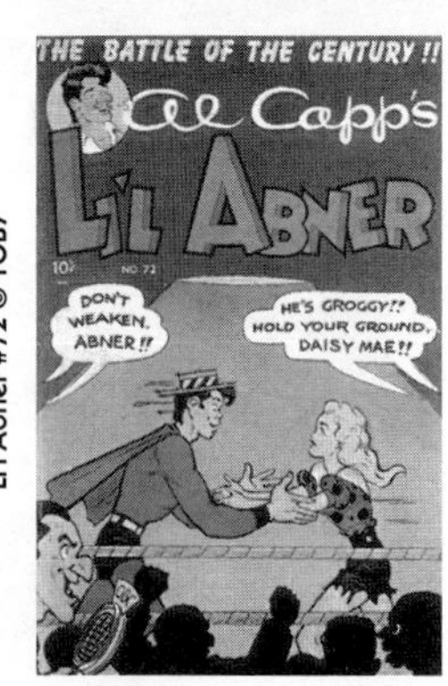

Li'l Abner #72 © TOBY

	GD25	FN65	NM94
1-3: 1-Variant-c			2.95

LIMITED COLLECTORS' EDITION (See Famous First Edition, Marvel Treasury #28, Rudolph the Red Nosed Reindeer & Superman Vs. The Amazing Spider-Man; becomes All-New Collectors' Edition)
National Periodical Publications/DC Comics:
(#21-34,51-59: 84 pgs.; #35-41: 68 pgs.; #42-50: 60 pgs.)
nn, 12/72: C-21, Summer, 1973 - No. C-59, 1978 ($1.00) (10x13-1/2")

	GD25	FN65	NM94
nn(C-20)-Rudolph (12/72) (scarce)	21.00	61.00	225.00
C-21: Shazam (TV); r/Captain Marvel Jr. #11 by Raboy; C.C. Beck-c, biog. & photo	2.25	6.80	25.00
C-22: Tarzan; complete origin reprinted from #207-210; all Kubert-c/a; Joe Kubert biography & photo inside	2.00	6.00	20.00
C-23: House of Mystery; Wrightson, N. Adams/Orlando, G. Kane/Wood, Toth, Aragones, Sparling reprints	2.70	8.00	30.00
C-24: Rudolph The Red-nosed Reindeer	7.00	21.00	70.00
C-25: Batman; Neal Adams-c/a(r); G.A. Joker-r; Batman/Enemy Ace-r; has photos from TV show	3.20	9.50	35.00
C-26: See Famous First Edition C-26 (same contents)			
C-27: Shazam (TV); G.A. Capt. Marvel & Mary Marvel-r; Beck-r	2.00	6.00	20.00
C-29: Tarzan; reprints "Return of Tarzan" from #219-223 by Kubert; Kubert-c	2.00	6.00	20.00
C-31: Superman; origin-r; N. Adams-a; photos of George Reeves from 1950s TV show on inside b/c; Burnley, Boring-r	2.00	6.00	20.00
C-32: Ghosts (new-a)	2.70	8.00	30.00
C-33: Rudolph The Red-nosed Reindeer(new-a)	5.50	16.50	60.00
C-34: Christmas with the Super-Heroes; unpublished Angel & Ape story by Oksner & Wood; Batman & Teen Titans-r	1.80	5.40	18.00
C-35: Shazam (TV); photo cover features TV's Captain Marvel, Jackson Bostwick; Beck-r; TV photos inside b/c	1.50	4.50	15.00
C-36: The Bible; all new adaptation beginning with Genesis by Kubert, Redondo & Mayer; Kubert-c	1.50	4.50	15.00
C-37: Batman; r-1946 Sundays; inside b/c photos of Batman TV show villains (all villain issue; r/G.A. Joker, Catwoman, Penguin, Two-Face, & Scarecrow stories plus 1946 Sundays-r)	2.20	6.25	22.00
C-38: Superman; 1 pg. N. Adams; part photo-c; photos from TV show on inside back-c	1.50	4.50	15.00
C-39: Secret Origins of Super-Villains; N. Adams-i(r); collection reprints 1950's Joker origin, Luthor origin from Adv. Comics #271, Capt. Cold origin from Showcase #8 among others; G.A. Batman-r; Beck-r.	1.50	4.50	15.00
C-40: Dick Tracy by Gould featuring Flattop; newspaper-r from 12/21/43 - 5/17/44; biog. of Chester Gould	1.50	4.50	15.00
C-41: Super Friends (TV); JLA-r(1965); Toth-c/a	1.80	5.40	18.00
C-42: Rudolph	4.00	12.25	45.00
C-43: Christmas with the Super-Heroes; Wrightson, S&K, Neal Adams-a	1.60	4.80	16.00
C-44: Batman; N. Adams-p(r) & G.A.-r; painted-c	1.60	4.80	16.00
C-45: More Secret Origins of Super-Villains; Flash-r/#105; G.A. Wonder Woman & Batman/Catwoman-r	1.60	4.80	16.00
C-46: Justice League of America(1963-r); 3 pgs. Toth-a	1.60	4.80	16.00
C-47: Superman Salutes the Bicentennial (Tomahawk interior); 2 pgs. new-a	1.60	4.80	16.00
C-48: Superman Vs. The Flash (Superman/Flash race); swipes-c to Superman #199; r/Superman #199 & Flash #175; 6 pgs. Neal Adams-a	1.80	5.40	18.00
C-49: Superboy & the Legion of Super-Heroes	1.80	5.40	18.00
C-50: Rudolph The Red-nosed Reindeer	4.00	12.25	45.00
C-51: Batman; Neal Adams-c/a	1.80	5.40	18.00
C-52: The Best of DC; Neal Adams-c/a; Toth, Kubert-a	1.60	4.80	16.00
C-57: Welcome Back, Kotter-r(TV)(5/78)	1.80	5.40	18.00
C-59: Batman's Strangest Cases; N. Adams-r; Wrightson-r/Swamp Thing #7; N. Adams/Wrightson-c	1.60	4.80	16.00

NOTE: *All-r with exception of some special features and covers.* ***Aparo*** *a-52r; c-37.* ***Grell*** *c-49.* ***Infantino*** *a-25, 39, 44, 45, 52.* ***Bob Kane*** *r-25.* ***Robinson*** *r-25, 44.* ***Sprang*** *r-44. Issues #21-31, 35-39, 45, 48 have back cover cut-outs.*

LINDA (Everybody Loves...) (Phantom Lady No. 5 on)
Ajax-Farrell Publ. Co.: Apr-May, 1954 - No. 4, Oct-Nov, 1954

	GD25	FN65	NM94
1-Kamenish-a	13.00	40.00	100.00
2-Lingerie panel	11.00	32.00	80.00
3,4	8.50	26.00	60.00

LINDA CARTER, STUDENT NURSE
Atlas Comics (AMI): Sept, 1961 - No. 9, Jan, 1963

	GD25	FN65	NM94
1-Al Hartley-c	3.50	10.50	35.00
2-9	2.50	7.50	25.00

LINDA LARK
Dell Publishing Co.: Oct-Dec, 1961 - No. 8, Aug-Oct, 1963

	GD25	FN65	NM94
1	2.25	6.75	20.00
2-8	1.10	3.30	12.00

LINUS, THE LIONHEARTED (TV)
Gold Key: Sept, 1965

	GD25	FN65	NM94
1 (10155-509)	7.25	22.00	80.00

LION, THE (See Movie Comics)

LION OF SPARTA (See Movie Classics)

LIPPY THE LION AND HARDY HAR HAR (TV)
Gold Key: Mar, 1963 (12¢) (See Hanna-Barbera Band Wagon #1)

	GD25	FN65	NM94
1 (10049-303)	8.00	24.00	90.00

LI'L ABNER (See Comics on Parade, Sparkle, Sparkler Comics, Tip Top Comics & Tip Topper)
United Features Syndicate: 1939 - 1940

	GD25	FN65	NM94
Single Series 4 ('39)	64.00	191.00	540.00
Single Series 18 ('40) (#18 on inside, #2 on-c)	53.00	159.00	450.00

LI'L ABNER (Al Capp's; continued from Comics on Parade #58)
Harvey Publ. No. 61-69 (2/49)/Toby Press No. 70 on: No. 61, Dec, 1947 - No. 97, Jan, 1955 (See Oxydol-Dreft)

	GD25	FN65	NM94
61(#1)-Wolverton & Powell-a	31.00	92.00	230.00
62-65: 63-The Wolf Girl app. 65-Powell-a	18.00	54.00	135.00
66,67,69,70	15.00	46.00	115.00
68-Full length Fearless Fosdick-c/story	17.00	50.00	125.00
71-74,76,80	12.00	36.00	90.00
75,77-79,86,91-All with Kurtzman art; 91-r/#77	15.00	46.00	115.00
81-85,87-90,92-94,96,97: 93-reprints #71	11.00	32.00	80.00
95-Full length Fearless Fosdick story	13.00	40.00	100.00
...& the Creatures from Drop-Outer Space-nn (Job Corps giveaway; 36 pgs., in color)(entire book by Frank Frazetta)	27.00	82.00	205.00
...Joins the Navy (1950) (Toby Press Premium)	10.00	30.00	75.00
...by Al Capp Giveaway (Circa 1955, nd)	10.00	30.00	75.00

LI'L ABNER
Toby Press: 1951

	GD25	FN65	NM94
1	15.00	46.00	115.00

LI'L ABNER'S DOGPATCH (See Al Capp's...)

LISA COMICS (TV)(See Simpsons Comics)
Bongo Comics: 1995 ($2.25)

	GD25	FN65	NM94
1-Lisa in Wonderland			2.25

LITTLE AL OF THE F.B.I.
Ziff-Davis Publications: No. 10, 1950 (no month) - No. 11, Apr-May, 1951 (Saunders painted-c)

	GD25	FN65	NM94
10(1950)	13.00	40.00	100.00
11(1951)	11.00	32.00	80.00

Little Ambrose #1 © AP

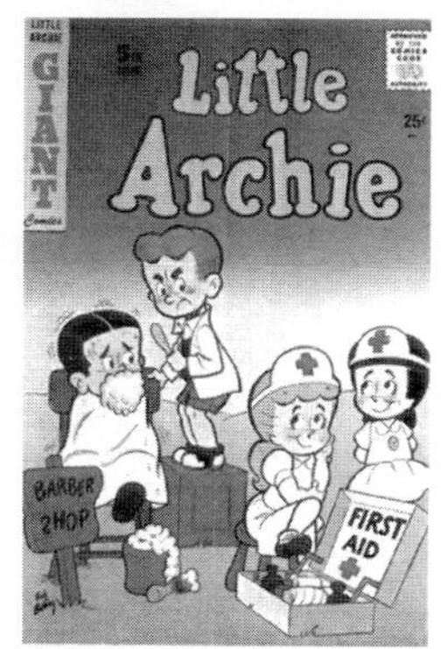

Little Archie #5 © AP

Little Audrey #27 © HARV

	GD25	FN65	NM94

LITTLE AL OF THE SECRET SERVICE
Ziff-Davis Publications: No. 10, 7-8/51; No, 2, 9-10/51; No. 3, Winter, 1951 (Saunders painted-c)

	GD25	FN65	NM94
10(#1)-Spanking panels (2)	15.00	44.00	110.00
2,3	11.00	32.00	80.00

LITTLE ALONZO
Macy's Dept. Store: 1938 (B&W, 5-1/2x8-1/2")(Christmas giveaway)

	GD25	FN65	NM94
nn-By Ferdinand the Bull's Munro Leaf	7.15	21.50	50.00

LITTLE AMBROSE
Archie Publications: September, 1958

	GD25	FN65	NM94
1-Bob Bolling-c	13.00	38.00	95.00

LITTLE ANGEL
Standard (Visual Editions)/Pines: No. 5, Sept, 1954; No. 6, Sept, 1955 - No. 16, Sept, 1959

	GD25	FN65	NM94
5-Last pre-code issue	5.70	17.00	38.00
6-16	4.00	12.00	24.00

LITTLE ANNIE ROONEY (Also see Henry)
David McKay Publ.: 1935 (25¢, B&W dailies, 48 pgs.)(10"x10", cardboard-c)

	GD25	FN65	NM94
Book 1-Daily strip-r by Darrell McClure	33.00	100.00	250.00

LITTLE ANNIE ROONEY (See King Comics & Treasury of Comics)
David McKay/St. John/Standard: 1938; Aug, 1948 - No. 3, Oct, 1948

	GD25	FN65	NM94
Feature Books 11 (McKay, 1938)	33.00	100.00	250.00
1 (St. John)	11.00	32.00	80.00
2,3	6.50	19.50	45.00

LITTLE ARCHIE (The Adventures of... #13-on) (See Archie Giant Series Mag. #527, 534, 538, 545, 549, 556, 560, 566, 570, 583, 594, 596, 607, 609, 619)
Archie Publications: 1956 - No. 180, Feb, 1983 (Giants No. 3-84)

	GD25	FN65	NM94
1-(Scarce)	48.00	144.00	575.00
2 (1957)	23.00	69.00	230.00
3-5: 3-(1958)-Bob Bolling-c & giant issues begin	12.00	36.00	120.00
6-10	9.00	27.00	90.00
11-22 (84 pgs.)	5.50	16.50	55.00
23-39 (68 pgs.)	3.20	9.60	32.00
40 (Fall/66)-Intro. Little Pureheart-c/s (68 pgs.)	4.00	12.00	40.00
41,44-Little Pureheart (68 pgs.)	3.00	9.00	30.00
42-Intro The Little Archies Band, ends #66 (68 pgs.)	3.80	14.40	38.00
43-1st Boy From R.I.V.E.R.D.A.L.E. (68 pgs.)	3.00	9.00	30.00
45-58	2.50	7.50	22.00
59-Little Sabrina begins	5.00	15.00	50.00
60-66	2.50	7.50	22.00
67(9/71)-84: 84-Last 52pg. Giant-Size (2/74)	1.20	3.60	12.00
85-99	.85	2.60	7.00
100	1.00	3.00	10.00
101-112,114-116,118-129			5.00
113-Halloween Special issue(12/76)	.85	2.60	7.00
117-Donny Osmond-c cameo	.85	2.60	7.00
130-UFO cover (5/78)	.85	2.60	7.00
131-150(1/80), 180(Last issue, 2/83)			4.00
151-179			3.00
...In Animal Land 1 (1957)	11.50	34.00	115.00
...In Animal Land 17 (Winter, 1957-58)-19 (Summer,1958)-Formerly Li'l Jinx	6.00	18.00	60.00

NOTE: *Little Archie Band app. 42-66. Little Sabrina in 59-78,80-180*

LITTLE ARCHIE CHRISTMAS SPECIAL (See Archie Giant Series #581)

LITTLE ARCHIE COMICS DIGEST ANNUAL (...Magazine #5 on)
Archie Publications: 10/77 - No. 48, 5/91 (Digest-size, 128 pgs., later issues $1.35-$1.50)

	GD25	FN65	NM94
1(10/77)-Reprints	1.60	4.80	16.00
2(4/78)-Neal Adams-a	1.40	4.20	14.00
3(11/78)-The Fly-r by S&K; Neal Adams-a	1.40	4.20	14.00
4(4/79) - 10	1.00	3.00	10.00
11-20	.85	2.60	7.00
21-30: 28-Christmas-c			5.00
31-48: 40,46-Christmas-c			4.00

NOTE: *Little Archie, Little Jinx, Little Jughead & Little Sabrina in most issues.*

LITTLE ARCHIE DIGEST MAGAZINE
Archie Comics: July, 1991 - Present ($1.50/$1.79/$1.89, digest size, bi-annual)

	GD25	FN65	NM94
V2#1			4.00
2-10			3.00
11-20			1.75
21-25: 21-Begin $1.95-c			1.95

LITTLE ARCHIE MYSTERY
Archie Publications: Aug, 1963 - No. 2, Oct, 1963 (12¢ issues)

	GD25	FN65	NM94
1	10.00	30.00	100.00
2	5.00	15.00	50.00

LITTLE ASPIRIN (See Little Lenny & Wisco)
Marvel Comics (CnPC): July, 1949 - No. 3, Dec, 1949 (52 pgs.)

	GD25	FN65	NM94
1-Oscar app.; Kurtzman-a (4 pgs.)	13.00	40.00	100.00
2-Kurtzman-a (4 pgs.)	8.50	26.00	60.00
3-No Kurtzman-a	5.00	15.00	30.00

LITTLE AUDREY (Also see Playful...)
St. John Publ.: Apr, 1948 - No. 24, May, 1952

	GD25	FN65	NM94
1-1st app. Little Audrey	39.00	116.00	290.00
2	19.00	56.00	140.00
3-5	12.00	36.00	90.00
6-10	8.50	26.00	60.00
11-20: 16-X-Mas-c	5.70	17.00	40.00
21-24	5.35	16.00	32.00

LITTLE AUDREY (See Harvey Hits #11, 19)
Harvey Publications: No. 25, Aug, 1952 - No. 53, April, 1957

	GD25	FN65	NM94
25-(Paramount Pictures Famous Star... on-c); 1st Harvey Casper and Baby Huey (1 month earlier than Harvey Comic Hits #60(9/52))	10.00	30.00	100.00
26-30: 26-28-Casper app.	5.00	15.00	50.00
31-40: 32-35-Casper app.	4.00	12.00	40.00
41-53	2.50	7.50	25.00
...Clubhouse 1 (9/61, 68 pg. Giant)-New stories & reprints	7.00	21.00	70.00

LITTLE AUDREY
Harvey Comics: Aug, 1992 - No. 8, July, 1993 ($1.25/$1.50)

	GD25	FN65	NM94
V2#1			3.00
2-8			2.00

LITTLE AUDREY (...Yearbook)
St. John Publishing Co.: 1950 (50¢, 260 pgs.)

	GD25	FN65	NM94
Contains 8 complete 1949 comics rebound; Casper, Alice in Wonderland, Little Audrey, Abbott & Costello, Pinocchio, Moon Mullins, Three Stooges (from Jubilee), Little Annie Rooney app. (Rare)	57.00	171.00	570.00

(Also see All Good & Treasury of Comics)

NOTE: *This book contains remaindered St. John comics; many variations possible.*

LITTLE AUDREY & MELVIN (Audrey & Melvin No. 62)
Harvey Publications: May, 1962 - No. 61, Dec, 1973

	GD25	FN65	NM94
1	7.50	22.50	75.00
2-5	3.60	10.80	36.00
6-10	2.60	7.80	26.00
11-20	1.80	5.40	18.00
21-40: 22-Richie Rich app.	1.20	3.60	12.00
41-50,55-61	.90	2.70	8.00
51-54: All 52 pg. Giants	1.20	3.60	12.00

Little Dot #20 © HARV

Little Eva #1 © STJ

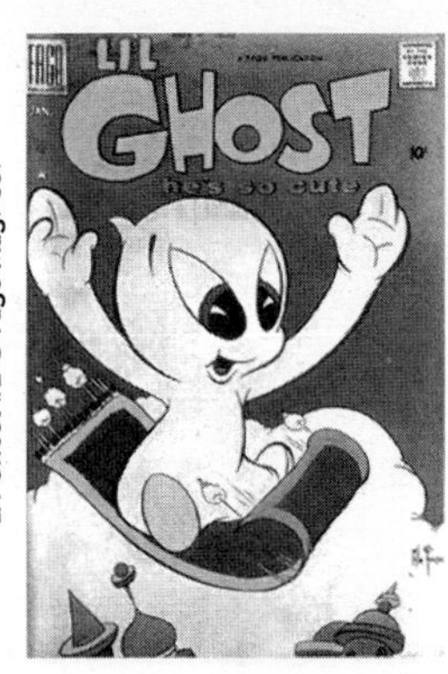

Li'l Ghost #2 © Fago Mag. Co.

LITTLE AUDREY TV FUNTIME
Harvey Publ.: Sept, 1962 - No. 33, Oct, 1971 (#1-31: 68 pgs.; #32,33: 52 pgs.)

	GD25	FN65	NM94
1-Richie Rich app.	6.50	19.50	65.00
2,3: Richie Rich app.	4.50	13.50	45.00
4,5: 5-25¢ & 35¢ issues exist	3.40	10.20	34.00
6-10	2.00	6.00	20.00
11-20	1.20	3.60	12.00
21-33	1.00	3.00	10.00

LITTLE BAD WOLF (Disney; seeWalt Disney's C&S #52, Walt Disney Showcase #21 & Wheaties)
Dell Publishing Co.: No. 403, June, 1952 - No. 564, June, 1954

	GD25	FN65	NM94
Four Color 403 (#1)	6.40	19.00	70.00
Four Color 473 (6/53), 564	3.60	11.00	40.00

LITTLE BEAVER
Dell Publishing Co.: No. 211, Jan, 1949 - No. 870, Jan, 1958 (All painted-c)

	GD25	FN65	NM94
Four Color 211('49)-All Harman-a	7.00	20.00	75.00
Four Color 267,294,332(5/51)	3.50	11.00	38.00
3(10-12/51)-8(1-3/53)	3.00	9.00	35.00
Four Color 483(8-10/53),529	2.75	8.00	30.00
Four Color 612,660,695,744,817,870	2.75	8.00	30.00

LITTLE BIT
Jubilee/St. John Publishing Co.: Mar, 1949 - No. 2, June, 1949

	GD25	FN65	NM94
1,2	5.00	15.00	30.00

LITTLE DOT (See Humphrey, Li'l Max, Sad Sack, and Tastee-Freez Comics)
Harvey Publications: Sept, 1953 - No. 164, Apr, 1976

	GD25	FN65	NM94
1-Intro./1st app. Richie Rich & Little Lotta	85.00	255.00	850.00
2-1st app. Freckles & Pee Wee (Richie Rich's poor friends)	35.00	105.00	350.00
3	22.00	66.00	220.00
4	16.00	48.00	160.00
5-Origin dots on Little Dot's dress	22.00	66.00	220.00
6-Richie Rich, Little Lotta, & Little Dot all on cover; 1st Richie Rich cover featured	20.00	60.00	200.00
7-10: 9-Last pre-code issue (1/55)	12.00	36.00	120.00
11-20	8.00	24.00	80.00
21-40	4.20	12.60	42.00
41-60	2.20	6.60	22.00
61-80	1.60	4.80	16.00
81-100	1.20	3.60	12.00
101-141	.80	2.40	8.00
142-145: All 52 pg. Giants	1.40	4.20	14.00
146-164			5.00
Shoe store giveaway 2	3.80	11.40	38.00

NOTE: *Richie Rich & Little Lotta in all.*

LITTLE DOT
Harvey Comics: Sept, 1992 - No. 7, June, 1994 ($1.25/$1.50)

	GD25	FN65	NM94
V2#1-Little Dot, Little Lotta, Richie Rich in all			3.00
2-7 ($1.50)			2.00

LITTLE DOT DOTLAND (Dot Dotland No. 62, 63)
Harvey Publications: July, 1962 - No. 61, Dec, 1973

	GD25	FN65	NM94
1-Richie Rich begins	8.50	25.50	85.00
2,3	4.20	12.60	42.00
4,5	3.60	10.80	36.00
6-10	2.40	7.20	24.00
11-20	1.80	5.40	18.00
21-30	1.00	3.00	10.00
31-50,55-61	.80	2.40	8.00
51-54: All 52 pg. Giants	1.40	4.20	14.00

LITTLE DOT'S UNCLES & AUNTS (See Harvey Hits No. 4, 13, 24)
Harvey Enterprises: Oct, 1961; No. 2, Aug, 1962 - No. 52, Apr, 1974

	GD25	FN65	NM94
1-Richie Rich begins; 68 pgs. begin	10.00	30.00	100.00
2,3	5.50	16.50	55.00
4,5	3.60	10.80	36.00
6-10	2.40	7.20	24.00
11-20	2.00	6.00	20.00
21-37: Last 68 pg. issue	1.60	4.80	16.00
38-52: All 52 pg. Giants	1.40	4.20	14.00

LITTLE DRACULA
Harvey Comics: Jan, 1992 - No. 3, May, 1992 ($1.25, quarterly, mini-series)

	GD25	FN65	NM94
1-3			2.00

LITTLE EVA
St. John Publishing Co.: May, 1952 - No. 31, Nov, 1956

	GD25	FN65	NM94
1	11.00	34.00	85.00
2	6.00	18.00	42.00
3-5	4.25	13.00	28.00
6-10	4.00	10.00	20.00
11-31	3.60	9.00	18.00
3-D 1,2(10/53, 11/53, 25¢)-Both came w/glasses. 1-Infinity-c	17.00	52.00	130.00
I.W. Reprint #1-3,6-8: 1-r/Little Eva #28. 2-r/Little Eva #29. 3-r/Little Eva #24	1.00	3.00	8.00
Super Reprint #10,12('63),14,16,18('64): 18-r/Little Eva #25.	1.00	3.00	8.00

LITTLE FIR TREE, THE
W. T. Grant Co. : nd (1942) (8-1/2x11") (12 pgs. with cover, color & B&W, heavy paper) (Christmas giveaway)

nn-Story by Hans Christian Anderson; 8 pg. Kelly-r/Santa Claus Funnies (not signed); X-Mas-c
(One copy in Mint sold for $1750.00 in 1986 & another copy in VF sold for $1000.00 in 1991)

LI'L GENIUS (Summer Fun No. 54) (See Blue Bird & Giant Comics #3)
Charlton Comics: 1954 - No. 52, 1/65; No. 53, 10/65; No. 54, 10/85 - No. 55, 1/86

	GD25	FN65	NM94
1	8.50	26.00	60.00
2	5.00	15.00	30.00
3-15,19,20	4.00	10.00	20.00
16,17-(68 pgs.)	5.70	17.00	35.00
18-(100 pgs., 10/58)	7.85	23.50	55.00
21-35	2.25	6.75	18.00
36-53	1.50	4.50	12.00
54,55			3.00

LI'L GHOST
St. John Publ. Co./Fago No. 1 on: Feb, 1958; Nov?, 1958 - No. 3, Mar, 1959

	GD25	FN65	NM94
1(St. John)	6.50	19.50	45.00
1(Fago)-Al Fago-c/a begins	5.00	15.00	30.00
2,3: 2-(1/59)	4.00	11.00	22.00

LITTLE GIANT COMICS
Centaur Publications: 7/38 - No. 3, 10/38; No. 4, 2/39 (132 pgs.) (6-3/4x4-1/2")

	GD25	FN65	NM94
1-B&W with color-c; stories, puzzles, magic	53.00	160.00	450.00
2,3-B&W with color-c	46.00	138.00	390.00
4 (6-5/8x9-3/8")(68 pgs., B&W inside)	47.00	141.00	400.00

NOTE: ***Filchock** c-2, 4. **Gustavson** a-1. **Pinajian** a-4. **Bob Wood** a-1.*

LITTLE GIANT DETECTIVE FUNNIES
Centaur Publ.: Oct, 1938 - No. 4, Jan, 1939 (6-3/4x4-1/2", 132 pgs., B&W)

	GD25	FN65	NM94
1-B&W with color-c	62.00	186.00	525.00
2,3	46.00	138.00	390.00
4(1/39, B&W; color-c; 68 pgs., 6-1/2x9-1/2")-Eisner-r	49.00	147.00	420.00

LITTLE GIANT MOVIE FUNNIES
Centaur Publ.: Aug, 1938 - No. 2, Oct, 1938 (6-3/4x4-1/2", 132 pgs., B&W)

	GD25	FN65	NM94
1-Ed Wheelan's "Minute Movies" reprints	62.00	186.00	525.00

Li'l Jinx #12 © AP

Little Lotta #6 © HARV

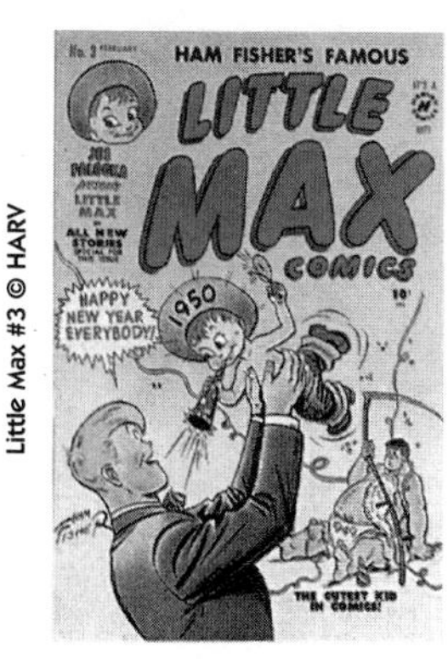

Little Max #3 © HARV

	GD25	FN65	NM94
2-Ed Wheelan's "Minute Movies" reprints	46.00	138.00	390.00

LITTLE GROUCHO (...the Red-Headed Tornado; ...Grouchy No. 2)
Reston Publ. Co.: No. 16; Feb-Mar, 1955 - No. 2, June-July, 1955 (See Tippy Terry)

	GD25	FN65	NM94
16, 1 (2-3/55)	6.50	19.50	45.00
2(6-7/55)	5.00	15.00	30.00

LITTLE HIAWATHA (Disney; see Walt Disney's C&S #143)
Dell Publishing Co.: No. 439, Dec, 1952 - No. 988, May-July, 1959

	GD25	FN65	NM94
Four Color 439 (#1)	4.50	13.50	50.00
Four Color 787 (4/57), 901 (5/58), 988	3.60	11.00	40.00

LITTLE IKE
St. John Publishing Co.: April, 1953 - No. 4, Oct, 1953

	GD25	FN65	NM94
1	7.85	23.50	55.00
2	5.00	15.00	30.00
3,4	4.00	12.00	24.00

LITTLE IODINE (See Giant Comic Album)
Dell Publ. Co.: No. 224, 4/49 - No. 257, 1949: 3-5/50 - No. 56, 4-6/62 (1-4-52pgs.)

	GD25	FN65	NM94
Four Color 224-By Jimmy Hatlo	8.00	25.00	90.00
Four Color 257	6.40	19.00	70.00
1(3-5/50)	8.00	25.00	90.00
2-5	3.00	10.00	36.00
6-10	2.50	7.50	27.00
11-20	1.65	5.00	18.00
21-30: 27-Xmas-c	1.50	4.50	16.00
31-40	1.40	4.20	12.00
41-56	1.10	3.30	9.00

LITTLE JACK FROST
Avon Periodicals: 1951

	GD25	FN65	NM94
1	7.15	21.50	50.00

LI'L JINX (Little Archie in Animal Land #17) (Also see Pep Comics #62)
Archie Publications: No. 11, Nov, 1956 - No. 16, Sept, 1957

	GD25	FN65	NM94
11-By Joe Edwards	9.30	28.00	70.00
12(1/57)-16	7.15	21.50	50.00

LI'L JINX (See Archie Giant Series Magazine No. 223)

LI'L JINX CHRISTMAS BAG (See Archie Giant Series Mag. No. 195, 206, 219)

LI'L JINX GIANT LAUGH-OUT (See Archie Giant Series Mag. No. 176, 185)
Archie Publications: No. 33, Sept, 1971 - No. 43, Nov, 1973 (52 pgs.)

	GD25	FN65	NM94
33-43 (52 pgs.)	1.20	3.60	12.00

LITTLE JOE (See Popular Comics & Super Comics)
Dell Publishing Co.: No. 1, 1942

	GD25	FN65	NM94
Four Color 1	42.00	125.00	460.00

LITTLE JOE
St. John Publishing Co.: Apr, 1953

	GD25	FN65	NM94
1	4.00	10.00	20.00

LI'L KIDS (Also see Li'l Pals)
Marvel Comics Group: 8/70 - No. 2, 10/70; No. 3, 11/71 - No. 12, 6/73

	GD25	FN65	NM94
1	3.80	11.50	40.00
2-9	2.20	6.25	22.00
10-12-Calvin app.	2.50	7.60	28.00

LITTLE KING
Dell Publishing Co.: No. 494, Aug, 1953 - No. 677, Feb, 1956

	GD25	FN65	NM94
Four Color 494 (#1)	9.00	27.00	100.00
Four Color 597, 677	4.50	13.50	50.00

LITTLE KLINKER
Little Klinker Ventures: Nov, 1960 (20 pgs.) (slick cover)
(Montgomery Ward Giveaway)

	GD25	FN65	NM94
nn	1.50	4.50	12.00

LITTLE LANA (Formerly Lana)
Marvel Comics (MjMC): No. 8, Nov, 1949; No. 9, Mar, 1950

	GD25	FN65	NM94
8,9	6.00	18.00	42.00

LITTLE LENNY
Marvel Comics (CDS): June, 1949 - No. 3, Nov, 1949

	GD25	FN65	NM94
1-Little Aspirin app.	9.30	28.00	65.00
2,3	5.35	16.00	32.00

LITTLE LIZZIE
Marvel Comics (PrPl)/Atlas (OMC): 6/49 - No. 5, 4/50; 9/53 - No. 3, Jan, 1954

	GD25	FN65	NM94
1	10.00	30.00	75.00
2-5	6.00	18.00	42.00
1 (9/53, 2nd series by Atlas)-Howie Post-c	6.85	21.00	48.00
2,3	5.35	16.00	32.00

LITTLE LOTTA (See Harvey Hits No. 10)
Harvey Publications: 11/55 - No. 110, 11/73; No. 111, 9/74 - No. 120, 5/76
V2#1, Oct, 1992 - No. 4, July, 1993 ($1.25)

	GD25	FN65	NM94
1-Richie Rich (r) & Little Dot begin	30.00	90.00	300.00
2,3	13.00	39.00	130.00
4,5	7.00	21.00	70.00
6-10	6.00	18.00	60.00
11-20	3.80	11.40	38.00
21-40	2.40	7.20	24.00
41-60	2.00	6.00	20.00
61-80: 62-1st app. Nurse Jenny	1.60	4.80	16.00
81-99	1.00	3.00	10.00
100-103: All 52 pg. Giants	1.40	4.20	14.00
104-120	.70	2.10	7.00
V2#1-4 (1992-93)			2.00

NOTE: *No. 121 was advertised, but never released.*

LITTLE LOTTA FOODLAND
Harvey Publications: 9/63 - No. 14, 10/67; No. 15, 10/68 - No. 29, Oct, 1972

	GD25	FN65	NM94
1-Little Lotta, Little Dot, Richie Rich, 68 pgs. begin	10.50	32.00	105.00
2,3	6.50	19.50	65.00
4,5	4.50	13.50	45.00
6-10	3.20	9.60	32.00
11-20	2.20	6.60	22.00
21-26: 26-Last 68 pg. issue	1.80	5.40	18.00
27,28: Both 52 pgs.	1.60	4.80	16.00
29-(36 pgs.)	.90	2.70	9.00

LITTLE LULU (Formerly Marge's...)
Gold Key 207-257/Whitman 258 on: No. 207, Sept, 1972 - No. 268, April, 1984

	GD25	FN65	NM94
207,209,220-Stanley-r. 207-1st app. Henrietta	.90	2.70	8.00
208,210-219: 208-1st app. Snobbly, Wilbur's brother		2.00	6.00
221-240,242-249, 250(r/#166), 251-254(r/#206)			4.00
241,263-Stanley-r			5.00
255-257(Gold Key): 256-r/#212			3.00
258,259,262,264,265 (Whitman)			4.00
260,261	.85	2.60	7.00
266-268 (All #90028 on-c; no date, no date code; 3-pack?: 268-Stanley-r)	.85	2.60	7.00

LITTLE MARY MIXUP (See Comics On Parade)
United Features Syndicate: No. 10, 1939, - No. 26, 1940

	GD25	FN65	NM94
Single Series 10, 26	31.00	92.00	230.00

LITTLE MAX COMICS (Joe Palooka's Pal; see Joe Palooka)
Harvey Publications: Oct, 1949 - No. 73, Nov, 1961

	GD25	FN65	NM94
1-Infinity-c; Little Dot begins; Joe Palooka on-c	15.00	46.00	115.00
2-Little Dot app.; Joe Palooka on-c	8.50	25.50	60.00
3-Little Dot app.; Joe Palooka on-c	5.70	17.00	40.00

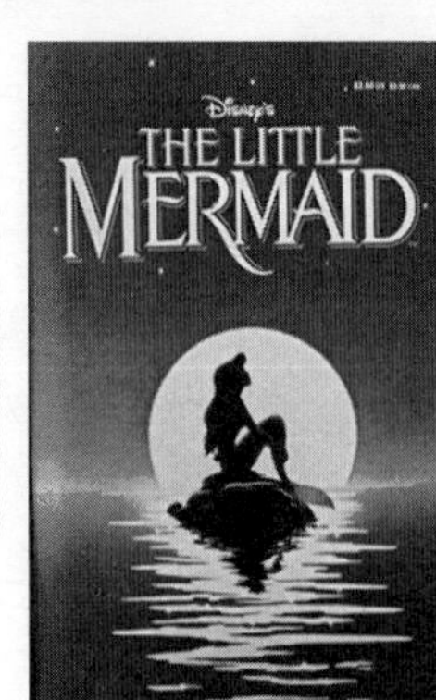

The Little Mermaid © WDC

Little Miss Muffet #12 © STD

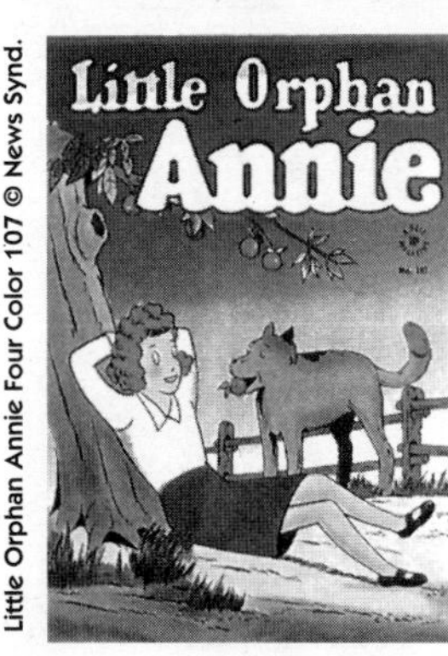

Little Orphan Annie Four Color 107 © News Synd.

	GD25	FN65	NM94
4-10: 5-Little Dot app., 1pg.	4.25	13.00	26.00
11-20	4.00	12.00	20.00
21-73: 23-Little Dot app. 38-r/#20. 63-65,67-73-Include new five pg. Richie Rich stories 70-73-Little Lotta app.	1.50	4.50	15.00

LI'L MENACE
Fago Magazine Co.: Dec, 1958 - No. 3, May, 1959

	GD25	FN65	NM94
1-Peter Rabbit app.	6.00	18.00	42.00
2-Peter Rabbit (Vincent Fago's)	5.35	16.00	32.00
3	4.25	13.00	28.00

LITTLE MERMAID, THE (Walt Disney's...; also see Disney's...)
W. D. Publications (Disney): 1990 (no date given)($5.95, no ads, 52 pgs.)

	GD25	FN65	NM94
nn-Adapts animated movie	.85	2.60	7.00
nn-Comic version ($2.50)			3.00

LITTLE MERMAID, THE
Disney Comics: 1992 - No. 4, 1992 ($1.50, mini-series)

	GD25	FN65	NM94
1-4: Based on movie			2.00
1-4: 2nd printings sold at Wal-Mart w/different-c			2.00

LITTLE MISS MUFFET
Best Books (Standard Comics)/King Features Synd.: No. 11, Dec, 1948 - No. 13, March, 1949

	GD25	FN65	NM94
11-Strip reprints; Fanny Cory-c/a	6.50	19.50	45.00
12,13-Strip reprints; Fanny Cory-c/a	5.00	15.00	30.00

LITTLE MISS SUNBEAM COMICS
Magazine Enterprises/Quality Bakers of America: June-July, 1950 - No. 4, Dec-Jan, 1950-51

	GD25	FN65	NM94
1	13.00	38.00	95.00
2-4	7.15	21.50	50.00
...Advs. In Space ('55)	5.00	15.00	30.00
Bread Giveaway 1-4(Quality Bakers, 1949-50)-14 pgs. each	4.25	13.00	26.00
Bread Giveaway (1957,61; 16pgs, reg. size)	4.00	12.00	24.00

LITTLE MONSTERS, THE (See March of Comics #423, Three Stooges #17)
Gold Key: Nov, 1964 - No. 44, Feb, 1978

	GD25	FN65	NM94
1	4.00	12.00	45.00
2	2.00	6.00	22.00
3-10	1.80	5.40	18.00
11-20	1.40	4.20	14.00
21-30	1.00	3.00	10.00
31-44: 20,34-39,43-Reprints	.85	2.60	7.00

LITTLE MONSTERS (Movie)
Now Comics: 1989 - No. 6, June, 1990 ($1.75)

	GD25	FN65	NM94
..1-6: Photo-c from movie			1.80

LITTLE NEMO (See Cocomalt, Future Comics, Help, Jest, Kayo, Punch, Red Seal, & Superworld; most by Winsor McCay Jr., son of famous artist) (Other McCay books: see Little Sammy Sneeze & Dreams of the Rarebit Fiend)

LITTLE NEMO (...in Slumberland)
McCay Features/Nostalgia Press('69): 1945 (11x7-1/4", 28 pgs., B&W)

	GD25	FN65	NM94
1905 & 1911 reprints by Winsor McCay	7.85	23.50	55.00
1969-70 (Exact reprint)	2.00	5.00	10.00

LITTLE ORPHAN ANNIE (See Annie, Famous Feature Stories, Marvel Super Special, Merry Christmas..., Popular Comics, Super Book #7, 11, 23 & Super Comics)

LITTLE ORPHAN ANNIE
David McKay Publ./Dell Publishing Co.: No. 7, 1937 - No. 3, Sept-Nov, 1948; No. 206, Dec, 1948

	GD25	FN65	NM94
Feature Books(McKay) 7-(1937) (Rare)	77.00	231.00	850.00
Four Color 12(1941)	45.00	135.00	495.00
Four Color 18(1943)-Flag-c	36.00	107.00	390.00
Four Color 52(1944)	28.00	85.00	310.00
Four Color 76(1945)	23.00	70.00	255.00
Four Color 107(1946)	19.00	58.00	215.00
Four Color 152(1947)	13.00	38.00	140.00
1(3-5/48)-r/strips from 5/7/44 to 7/30/44	13.00	38.00	140.00
2-r/strips from 7/21/40 to 9/9/40	9.00	26.00	95.00
3-r/strips from 9/10/40 to 11/9/40	9.00	26.00	95.00
Four Color 206(12/48)	7.00	20.00	75.00
Junior Commandos Giveaway (same-c as 4-Color #18, K.K. Publ.)(Big Shoe Store); same back cover as '47 Popped Wheat giveaway; 16 pgs; flag-c; r/strips 9/7/42-10/10/42	27.00	81.00	215.00
Popped Wheat Giveaway ('47)-16 pgs. full color; reprints strips from 5/3/40 to 6/20/40	2.00	5.00	10.00
Quaker Sparkies Giveaway (1940)	15.50	47.00	125.00
Quaker Sparkies Giveaway (1941, full color, 20 pgs.); "LOA and the Rescue"; r/strips 4/13/39-6/21/39 & 7/6/39-7/17/39. "LOA and the Kidnappers"; r/strips 11/28/38-1/28/39	13.00	39.00	105.00
Quaker Sparkies Giveaway (1942, full color, 20 pgs.); "LOA and Mr. Gudge"; r/strips 2/13/38-3/21/38 & 4/18/37-5/30/37. "LOA and the Great Am"	11.30	34.00	90.00

LI'L PALS (Also see Li'l Kids)
Marvel Comics Group: Sept, 1972 - No. 5, May, 1973

	GD25	FN65	NM94
1	2.70	8.00	30.00
2-5	1.80	5.40	18.00

LI'L PAN (Formerly Rocket Kelly; becomes Junior Comics with #9)
Fox Features Syndicate: No. 6, Dec-Jan, 1946-47 - No. 8, Apr-May, 1947 (Also see Wotalife Comics)

	GD25	FN65	NM94
6	7.15	21.50	50.00
7,8: 7-Atomic bomb story; robot-c	5.70	17.00	35.00

LITTLE PEOPLE
Dell Publishing Co.: No. 485, Aug-Oct, 1953 - No. 1062, Dec, 1959 (Walt Scott's)

	GD25	FN65	NM94
Four Color 485 (#1)	5.50	16.50	60.00
Four Color 573(7/54), 633(6/55)	3.00	9.00	35.00
Four Color 692(3/56),753(11/56),809(7/57),868(12/57),908(5/58), 959(12/58), 1062	3.00	9.00	35.00
Four Color 1024-Darby O'Gill &...-Movie, Toth-a, photo-c	9.00	27.00	100.00

LITTLE RASCALS
Dell Publishing Co.: No. 674, Jan, 1956 - No. 1297, Mar-May, 1962

	GD25	FN65	NM94
Four Color 674 (#1)	6.40	19.00	70.00
Four Color 778(3/57),825(8/57)	3.75	11.50	42.00
Four Color 883(3/58),936(9/58),974(3/59),1030(9/59),1079(2-4/60),1137 (9-11/60)	3.75	11.50	42.00
Four Color 1174(3-5/61),1224(10-12/61),1297	3.00	9.00	32.00

LI'L RASCAL TWINS (Formerly Nature Boy)
Charlton Comics: No. 6, 1957 - No. 18, Jan, 1960

	GD25	FN65	NM94
6-Li'l Genius & Tomboy in all	5.00	15.00	30.00
7-18: 7-Timmy the Timid Ghost app.	3.20	8.00	16.00

LITTLE ROQUEFORT COMICS (See Paul Terry's Comics #105)
St. John Publishing Co.(all pre-code)/Pines No. 10: June, 1952 - No. 9, Oct, 1953; No. 10, Summer, 1958

	GD25	FN65	NM94
1-By Paul Terry	8.50	26.00	60.00
2	4.25	13.00	28.00
3-10: 10-CBS Television Presents on-c	4.00	11.00	22.00

LITTLE SAD SACK (See Harvey Hits No. 73, 76, 79, 81, 83)
Harvey Publications: Oct, 1964 - No. 19, Nov, 1967

	GD25	FN65	NM94
1-Richie Rich app. on cover only	3.50	10.50	35.00
2-10	2.00	6.00	20.00
11-19	1.60	4.80	16.00

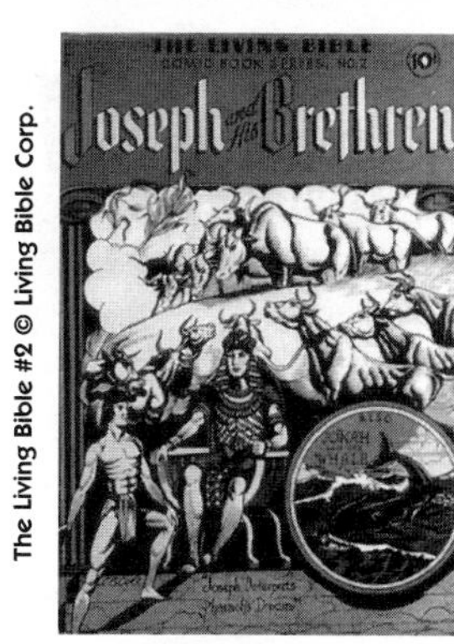

The Living Bible #2 © Living Bible Corp.

Lobo #50 © DC

Lobo In the Chair #1 © DC

	GD25	FN65	NM94
LITTLE SCOUTS			
Dell Publishing Co.: No. 321, Mar, 1951 - No. 587, Oct, 1954			
Four Color #321 (#1, 3/51)	2.75	8.00	30.00
2(10-12/51) - 6(10-12/52)	1.35	4.00	15.00
Four Color #462,506,550,587	1.35	4.00	15.00
LITTLE SHOP OF HORRORS SPECIAL (Movie)			
DC Comics: Feb, 1987 ($2.00, 68 pgs.)			
1-Colan-c/a			2.00
LITTLE SPUNKY			
I. W. Enterprises: No date (1963?) (10¢)			
1-r/Frisky Fables #1	1.10	3.30	9.00
LITTLE STOOGES, THE (The Three Stooges' Sons)			
Gold Key: Sept, 1972 - No. 7, Mar, 1974			
1-Norman Maurer cover/stories in all	2.00	6.00	22.00
2-7	1.10	3.30	12.00
LITTLEST OUTLAW (Disney)			
Dell Publishing Co.: No. 609, Jan, 1955			
Four Color 609-Movie, photo-c	5.50	16.50	60.00
LITTLEST SNOWMAN, THE			
Dell Publishing Co.: No. 755, 12/56; No. 864, 12/57; 12-2/1963-64			
Four Color #755,864, 1(1964)	3.00	10.00	36.00
LI'L TOMBOY (Formerly Fawcett's Funny Animals; see Giant Comics #3)			
Charlton Comics: V14#92, Oct, 1956; No. 93, Mar, 1957 - No. 107, Feb, 1960			
V14#92	4.25	13.00	26.00
93-107: 97-Atomic Bunny app.	4.00	10.00	20.00
LITTLE TREE THAT WASN'T WANTED, THE			
W. T. Grant Co. (Giveaway): 1960, (Color, 28 pgs.)			
nn-Christmas giveaway	1.50	4.50	12.00
LI'L WILLIE COMICS (Formerly & becomes Willie Comics #22 on)			
Marvel Comics (MgPC): No. 20, July, 1949 - No. 21, Sept, 1949			
20,21: 20-Little Aspirin app.	6.00	18.00	42.00
LITTLE WOMEN (See Power Record Comics)			
LIVE IT UP			
Spire Christian Comics (Fleming H. Revell Co.): 1973, 1976 (39-49 cents)			
nn			4.00
LIVING BIBLE, THE			
Living Bible Corp.: Fall, 1945 - No. 3, Spring, 1946			
1-The Life of Paul; all have L. B. Cole-c	35.00	106.00	265.00
2-Joseph & His Brethren; Jonah & the Whale	22.00	66.00	165.00
3-Chaplains At War (classic-c)	35.00	106.00	265.00
LOBO			
Dell Publishing Co.: Dec, 1965; No. 2, Oct, 1966			
1,2-1st black character to have his own title.	2.25	6.75	18.00
LOBO (Also see Action #650, Adventures of Superman, Demon (2nd series), Justice League, L.E.G.I.O.N., Mister Miracle, Omega Men #3 & Superman #41)			
DC Comics: Nov, 1990 - No. 4, Feb, 1991 ($1.50, color, limited series)			
1-(99¢)-Giffen plots/Breakdowns in all			1.00
1-2nd printing			1.00
2-Legion '89 spin-off			1.00
3,4: 1-4 have Bisley painted covers & art			1.00
...: Blazing Chain of Love 1 (9/92, $1.50)-Denys Cowan-c/a; Alan Grant scripts			1.50
...Convention Special 1 (1993, $1.75)			1.75
...Paramilitary Christmas Special 1 (1991, $2.39, 52 pgs.)-Bisley-c/a			2.40
...: Portrait of a Victim 1 (1993, $1.75)			1.75

	GD25	FN65	NM94
LOBO (Also see Showcase '95 #9)			
DC Comics: Dec, 1993 - Present ($1.75/$1.95/$2.25/$2.50, mature)			
1 ($2.95)-Foil enhanced-c; Alan Grant scripts begin			3.50
2-7-Alan Grant scripts			1.75
0,8,-15: 8-Begin $1.95-c. 9-(9/94). 0-(10/94)-Origin retold			2.00
16-54: 16-Begin $2.25-c. 50-Lobo vs. the DCU			2.25
55-58: 55-Begin $2.50-c. 58-Giffen-a			2.50
#1,000,000 (11/98) 853rd Century x-over			2.50
Annual 1 (1993, $3.50, 68 pgs.)-Bloodlines x-over			3.50
Annual 2 (1994, $3.50)-21 artists (20 listed on-c); Alan Grant script; Elseworlds story			2.00
Annual 3 (1995, $3.95)-Year One story			4.00
...Big Babe Spring Break Special (Spr, '95, $1.95)-Balent-a			2.00
...Bounty Hunting for Fun and Profit ('95)-Bisley-c			5.00
...Chained (5/97, $2.50)-Alan Grant story			2.50
.../Deadman: The Brave And The Bald (2/95, $3.50)			3.50
.../Demon: Helloween (12/96, $2.25)-Giarrano-a			2.25
...Fragtastic Voyage 1 ('97, $5.95)-Mejia painted-c/a		2.00	6.00
...Gallery (9/95, $3.50)-pin-ups.			3.50
...In the Chair 1 (8/94, $1.95, 36 pgs.)			2.00
...I Quit-(12/95, $2.25)			2.25
.../Judge Dredd ('95, $4.95).			5.00
...Lobocop 1 (2/94, $1.95)-Alan Grant scripts; painted-c			2.00
LOBO: A CONTRACT ON GAWD			
DC Comics: Apr, 1994 - July, 1994 ($1.75, mini-series, mature)			
1-4: Alan Grant scripts. 3-Groo cameo			1.75
LOBO: DEATH AND TAXES			
DC Comics: Oct, 1996 - No. 4, Jan, 1997 ($2.25, mini-series)			
1-4-Giffen/Grant scripts			2.25
LOBO GOES TO HOLLYWOOD			
DC Comics: Aug, 1996 ($2.25, one shot)			
1-Grant scripts			2.25
LOBO: INFANTICIDE			
DC Comics: Oct, 1992 - Jan, 1993 ($1.50, mini-series, mature)			
1-4-Giffen-c/a; Alan Grant scripts			1.50
LOBO/ MASK			
DC Comics: Feb, 1997 - No.2, Mar, 1997 ($5.95, limited series)			
1,2			5.95
LOBO'S BACK			
DC Comics: May, 1992 - No. 4, Nov, 1992 ($1.50, mini-series, mature)			
1-4: 1-Has 3 outer covers. Bisley painted-c 1,2; a-1-3. 3-Sam Kieth-c; all have Giffen plots/breakdown & Grant scripts			1.50
Trade paperback (1993, $9.95)-r/1-4			10.00
LOBO THE DUCK			
DC Comics (Amalgam): June, 1997 ($1.95, one-shot)			
1-Alan Grant-s/Val Semeiks & Ray Kryssing-a			1.95
LOBO: UNAMERICAN GLADIATORS			
DC Comics: Jun, 1993 - Sep, 1993 ($1.75, mini-series, mature)			
1-4-Mignola-c; Grant/Wagner scripts			1.75
LOCKE!			
Blackthorne Publishing: 1987 - No. 3, ($1.25, limited series)			
1-3			1.25
LOCO (Magazine) (Satire)			
Satire Publications: Aug, 1958 - V1#3, Jan, 1959			
V1#1-Chic Stone-a	6.50	19.50	45.00
V1#2,3-Severin-a, 2 pgs. Davis; 3-Heath-a	5.70	17.00	35.00
LOGAN: PATH OF THE WARLORD			

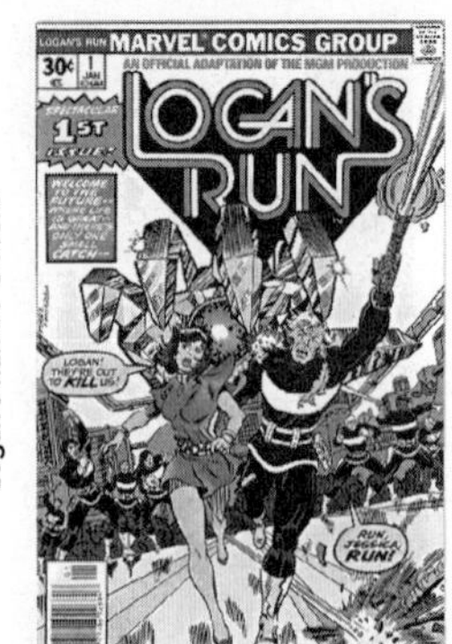

Logan's Run #1 © MGM

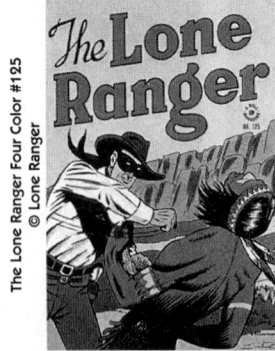

The Lone Ranger Four Color #125 © Lone Ranger

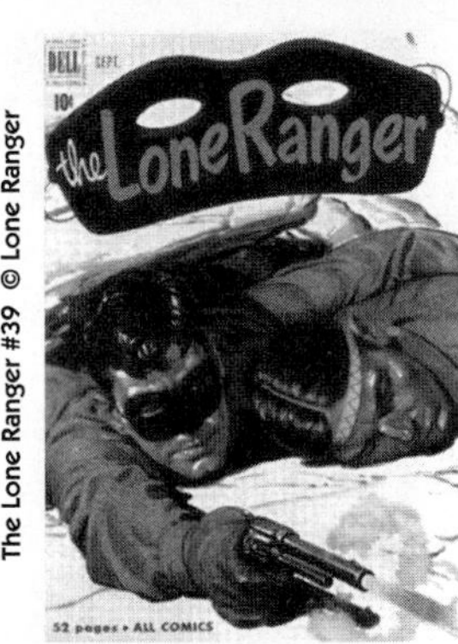

The Lone Ranger #39 © Lone Ranger

	GD25	FN65	NM94

Marvel Comics: Feb, 1996 ($5.95, one-shot)

	GD25	FN65	NM94
1-John Paul Leon-a		2.00	6.00

LOGAN: SHADOW SOCIETY
Marvel Comics: 1996 ($5.95, one-shot)

	GD25	FN65	NM94
1		2.00	6.00

LOGAN'S RUN
Marvel Comics Group: Jan, 1977 - No. 7, July, 1977

	GD25	FN65	NM94
1: 1-5-Based on novel & movie			4.00
2-5,7: 6,7-New stories adapted from novel			3.00
6-1st Thanos (also see Iron Man #55) solo story (back-up) by Zeck (6/77)	.90	2.70	8.00

NOTE: **Austin** *a-6i.* **Gulacy** *c-6.* **Kane** *c-7p.* **Perez** *a-1-5p; c-1-5p.* **Sutton** *a-6p, 7p.*

LOIS & CLARK, THE NEW ADVENTURES OF SUPERMAN
DC Comics: 1994 ($9.95, one-shot)

	GD25	FN65	NM94
1-r/Man of Steel #2, Superman Annual 1, Superman #9 & 11, Action #600 & 655, Adventures of Superman #445, 462 & 466	1.00	3.00	10.00

LOIS LANE (Also see Daring New Adventures of Supergirl, Showcase #9,10 & Superman's Girlfriend...)
DC Comics: Aug, 1986 - No. 2, Sept, 1986 ($1.50, 52 pgs.)

	GD25	FN65	NM94
1,2-Morrow-c/a in each			1.50

LOLLY AND PEPPER
Dell Publishing Co.: No. 832, Sept, 1957 - July, 1962

	GD25	FN65	NM94
Four Color 832(#1)	2.75	8.00	30.00
Four Color 940,978,1086,1206	1.80	5.50	20.00
01-459-207 (7/62)	1.80	5.50	20.00

LOMAX (See Police Action)

LONDON NIGHT LINGERIE SPECIAL
London Night Studios: 1996 ($3.00/$10.00, one-shot)

	GD25	FN65	NM94
1-($3.00)-"Nice" Edition; JJ North photo-c			3.00
1-($10.00)-"Naughty" Edition; JJ North naughty photo-c			10.00

LONDON'S DARK
Escape/Titan: 1989 ($8.95, B&W, graphic novel)

	GD25	FN65	NM94
nn-James Robinson script; Paul Johnson-c/a	.90	2.70	9.00

LONE EAGLE (The Flame No. 5 on)
Ajax/Farrell Publications: Apr-May, 1954 - No. 4, Oct-Nov, 1954

	GD25	FN65	NM94
1	10.00	30.00	75.00
2-4: 3-Bondage-c	6.50	19.50	45.00

LONELY HEART (Formerly Dear Lonely Hearts; Dear Heart #15 on)
Ajax/Farrell Publ. (Excellent Publ.): No. 9, Mar, 1955 - No. 14, Feb, 1956

	GD25	FN65	NM94
9-Kamenesque-a; (Last precode)	7.85	21.00	55.00
10-14	5.00	15.00	30.00

LONE RANGER, THE (See Ace Comics, Aurora, Dell Giants,Future Comics, Golden Comics Digest #48, King Comics, Magic Comics & March of Comics #165, 174, 193, 208, 225, 238, 310, 322, 338, 350)

LONE RANGER, THE
Dell Publishing Co.: No. 3, 1939 - No. 167, Feb, 1947

	GD25	FN65	NM94
Large Feature Comic 3(1939)-Heigh-Yo Silver; text with illus. by Robert Weisman; also exists as a Whitman #710	95.00	285.00	950.00
Large Feature Comic 7(1939)-Illustr. by Henry Vallely; Hi-Yo Silver the Lone Ranger to the Rescue; also exists as a Whitman #715	90.00	270.00	900.00
Feature Book 21(1940), 24(1941)	65.00	195.00	650.00
Four Color 82(1945)	40.00	120.00	435.00
Four Color 98(1945),118(1946)	29.00	87.00	315.00
Four Color 125(1946),136(1947)	19.50	58.00	215.00
Four Color 151,167(1947)	16.00	48.00	175.00

LONE RANGER, THE (Movie, radio & TV; Clayton Moore starred as Lone Ranger in the movies; No. 1-37: strip reprints)(See Dell Giants)
Dell Publishing Co.: Jan-Feb, 1948 - No. 145, May-July, 1962

	GD25	FN65	NM94
1 (36 pgs.)-The Lone Ranger, his horse Silver, companion Tonto & his horse Scout begin	57.00	170.00	625.00
2 (52 pgs. begin, end #41)	26.00	78.00	290.00
3-5	20.00	60.00	215.00
6,7,9,10	16.50	50.00	180.00
8-Origin retold; Indian back-c begin, end #35	20.00	60.00	220.00
11-20: 11- "Young Hawk" Indian boy serial begins, ends #145	10.00	30.00	110.00
21,22,24-31: 51-Reprint. 31-1st Mask logo	8.75	26.50	95.00
23-Origin retold	11.00	33.00	120.00
32-37: 32-Painted-c begin. 36-Animal photo back-c begin, end #49. 37-Last newspaper-r issue; new outfit	6.75	20.50	75.00
38-41 (All 52 pgs.) 38-Paul S. Newman-s (wrote most of the stories #38-on)	6.25	18.50	68.00
42-50 (36 pgs.)	5.00	15.00	54.00
51-74 (52 pgs.): 56-One pg. origin story of Lone Ranger & Tonto. 71-Blank inside-c	5.00	15.00	54.00
75,77-99: 79-X-mas-c	4.00	12.00	45.00
76-Flag-c	5.00	15.00	55.00
100	5.75	17.00	63.00
101-111: Last painted-c	4.25	13.00	48.00
112-Clayton Moore photo-c begin, end #145	15.00	45.00	165.00
113-117	8.50	26.50	95.00
118-Origin Lone Ranger, Tonto, & Silver retold; Special anniversary issue	22.00	66.00	240.00
119-140: 139-Fran Striker-s	7.25	22.00	80.00
141-145	8.50	26.50	95.00
Cheerios Giveaways (1954, 16 pgs., 2-1/2x7", soft-c) #1- "The Lone Ranger, His Mask & How He Met Tonto". #2- "The Lone Ranger & the Story of Silver" each....	14.00	42.00	105.00
Doll Giveaways (Gabriel Ind.)(1973, 3-1/4x5")- "The Story of The Lone Ranger" & "The Carson City Bank Robbery"	1.20	3.60	12.00
How the Lone Ranger Captured Silver Book(1936)-Silvercup Bread giveaway	47.00	141.00	400.00
...In Milk for Big Mike (1955, Dairy Association giveaway), soft-c; 5x7-1/4", 16 pgs.	13.00	40.00	100.00
Merita Bread giveaway (1954, 16 pgs., 5x7-1/4")- "How to Be a Lone Ranger Health & Safety Scout"	15.00	44.00	110.00

NOTE: **Hank Hartman** *painted c(signed)-65, 66, 70, 75, 82; unsigned-64?, 67-69?, 71, 72, 73?, 74?, 76-78, 80, 81, 83-91, 92?, 93-111.* **Ernest Nordli** *painted c(signed)-42, 50, 52, 53, 56, 59, 60; unsigned-39-41, 44-49, 51, 54, 55, 57, 58, 61-63?*

LONE RANGER, THE
Gold Key (Reprints in #13-20): 9/64 - No. 16, 12/69; No. 17, 11/72; No. 18, 9/74 - No. 28, 3/77

	GD25	FN65	NM94
1-Retells origin	4.00	12.00	45.00
2	2.00	6.00	22.00
3-10: Small Bear-r in #6-12	1.65	4.80	18.00
11-17	1.10	3.30	12.00
18-28	.85	2.60	7.00
Golden West 1(30029-610, 10/66)-Giant; r/most Golden West #3 including Clayton Moore photo front/back-c	6.00	18.00	65.00
Legend of The Lone Ranger (1969, 16 pgs., giveaway)-Origin The Lone Ranger	1.40	4.20	15.00

LONE RANGER AND TONTO, THE
Topps Comics: Aug, 1994 - No. 4, Nov, 1994 ($2.50, limited series)

	GD25	FN65	NM94
1-4: 3-Origin of Lone Ranger; Tonto leaves; Lansdale story, Truman-c/a in all.			2.50
1-4: Silver logo	1.00	3.00	10.00
Trade paperback (1/95, $9.95)			10.00

LONE RANGER COMICS, THE
Lone Ranger, Inc. : Book 1, 1939(inside) (shows 1938 on-c) (52 pgs. in color;

The Lone Ranger's Famous Horse Hi-Yo Silver #4 © Lone Ranger, Inc.

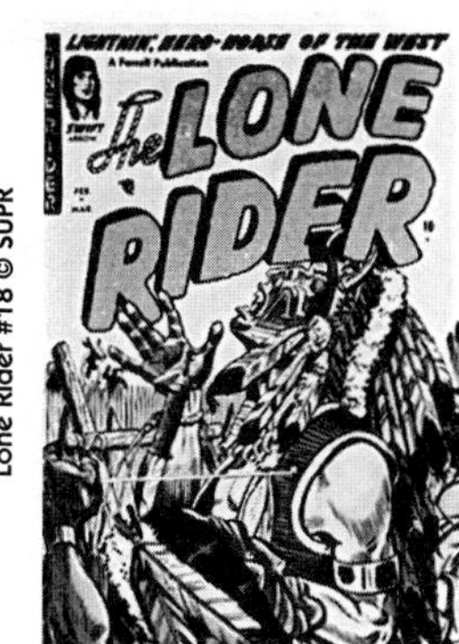

Lone Rider #18 © SUPR

Looney Tunes #4 (3rd Series) © Warner Bros.

	GD25	FN65	NM94

regular size) (Ice cream mail order)	GD25	FN65	VF82
Book 1-(Scarce)-The first western comic devoted to a single character; not by Vallely	800.00	2400.00	4200.00

LONE RANGER'S COMPANION TONTO, THE (TV)
Dell Publishing Co.: No. 312, Jan, 1951 - No. 33, Nov-Jan/58-59 (All painted-c)

	GD25	FN65	NM94
Four Color 312(#1, 1/51)	9.00	27.00	100.00
2(8-10/51),3: (#2 titled "Tonto")	4.50	13.50	50.00
4-10	4.00	12.00	45.00
11-20	3.00	9.00	32.00
21-33	2.00	6.00	22.00

NOTE: ***Ernest Nordli** painted c(signed)-2, 7; unsigned-3-6, 8-11, 12?, 13, 14, 18?, 22-24? See Aurora Comic Booklets.*

LONE RANGER'S FAMOUS HORSE HI-YO SILVER, THE (TV)
Dell Publishing Co.: No. 369, Jan, 1952 - No. 36, Oct-Dec, 1960 (All painted-c, most by Sam Savitt)

	GD25	FN65	NM94
Four Color 369(#1)-Silver's origin as told by The Lone Ranger	8.00	25.00	90.00
Four Color 392(#2, 4/52)	4.00	12.00	45.00
3(7-9/52)-10(4-6/52)	3.00	10.00	36.00
11-36	2.50	7.50	27.00

LONE RIDER (Also see The Rider)
Superior Comics(Farrell Publ.): Apr, 1951 - No. 26, Jul, 1955 (#3-on: 36 pgs.)

	GD25	FN65	NM94
1 (52 pgs.)-The Lone Rider & his horse Lightnin' begin; Kamenish-a begins	17.00	52.00	130.00
2 (52 pgs.)-The Golden Arrow begins (origin)	9.30	28.00	65.00
3-6: 6-Last Golden Arrow	7.85	23.50	55.00
7-Golden Arrow becomes Swift Arrow; origin of his shield	9.30	28.00	65.00
8-Origin Swift Arrow	10.00	30.00	75.00
9,10	6.85	21.00	48.00
11-14	5.70	17.00	35.00
15-Golden Arrow origin-r from #2, changing name to Swift Arrow	6.50	19.50	45.00
16-20,22-26: 23-Apache Kid app.	5.70	17.00	35.00
21-3-D effect-c	12.00	36.00	90.00

LONE WOLF AND CUB
First Comics: May, 1987 - No. 45, Apr, 1991 ($1.95-$3.25, B&W, deluxe size)

	GD25	FN65	NM94
1			2.00
1-2nd print, 3rd print			1.50
2			2.00
2-2nd print			1.50
3-25: 6-72 pgs. origin ish. 8-$2.50-c begins			2.50
26-30,33 ($2.95)			2.50
31,32,34-38,40,42-45 ($3.25): 40,42-Ploog-c			3.25
39-($5.95, 120 pgs.)-Ploog-c		2.00	6.00
41-($3.95, 84 pgs.)-Ploog-c			4.00
Deluxe Edition ($19.95, B&W)	2.00	6.00	20.00

NOTE: ***Miller** c-1-12p; intro 1-12. **Sienkiewicz** c-13-24. **Matt Wagner** c-25-30.*

LONG BOW (...Indian Boy)(See Indians & Jumbo Comics #141)
Fiction House Mag. (Real Adventures Publ.): 1951 - No. 9, Wint, 1952/53

	GD25	FN65	NM94
1-Most covers by Maurice Whitman	13.00	40.00	100.00
2	9.30	28.00	65.00
3-9	7.15	21.50	50.00

LONG HOT SUMMER, THE
DC Comics (Milestone): Jul, 1995 - No. 3, Sept, 1995 ($2.95/$2.50, lim. series)

	GD25	FN65	NM94
1 ($2.95)			3.00
2,3 ($2.50)			2.50

LONG JOHN SILVER & THE PIRATES (Formerly Terry & the Pirates)
Charlton Comics: No. 30, Aug, 1956 - No. 32, March, 1957 (TV)

	GD25	FN65	NM94
30-32: Whitman-c	7.85	23.50	55.00

LONGSHOT (Also see X-Men, 2nd Series #10)
Marvel Comics: Sept, 1985 - No. 6, Feb, 1986 (60¢, limited series)

	GD25	FN65	NM94
1-Arthur Adams/Whilce Portacio-c/a in all		2.00	6.00
2-5: 4-Spider-Man app.			5.00
6-Double size		2.00	6.00
Trade Paperback (1989, $16.95)-r/#1-6			17.00

LONGSHOT
Marvel Comics: Feb, 1998 ($3.99, one-shot)

	GD25	FN65	NM94
1-DeMatteis-s/Zulli-a			4.00

LOOKERS
Avatar Press: Feb, 1997 - Present ($3.00, B&W)

	GD25	FN65	NM94
1			3.00

LOONEY TUNES (2nd Series) (TV)
Gold Key/Whitman: April, 1975 - No. 47, July, 1984

	GD25	FN65	NM94
1 -Reprints	2.00	6.00	20.00
2-10: 2,4-reprints	1.20	3.60	12.00
11-20: 16-reprints	.85	2.60	7.00
21-30			5.00
31,32,36-42			3.50
33-35('80) (Whitman, scarce)	.85	2.60	7.00
43,44 (low distribution)			5.00
45-47 (All #90296 on-c; nd, nd code, pre-pack?)		2.00	6.00

LOONEY TUNES (3rd Series) (TV)
DC Comics: Apr, 1994 - Present ($1.50/$1.75/$1.95)

	GD25	FN65	NM94
1-22: 1-Marvin Martian-c/sty; Bugs Bunny, Roadrunner, Daffy, Tweety begin			1.50
23-34-($1.75-c)			1.75
35-43-($1.95-c)			1.95
44-48-($1.99-c)			1.99

LOONEY TUNES AND MERRIE MELODIES COMICS ("Looney Tunes" #166 (8/55) on)(Also see Porky's Duck Hunt)
Dell Publishing Co.: 1941 - No. 246, July-Sept, 1962

	GD25	FN65	VF82	NM94
1-Porky Pig, Bugs Bunny, Daffy Duck, Elmer Fudd, Mary Jane & Sniffles, Pat Patsy and Pete begin (1st comic book app. of each). Bugs Bunny story by Win Smith (early Mickey Mouse artist)	864.00	2592.00	5184.00	10,000.00

	GD25	FN65	NM94
2 (11/41)	135.00	405.00	1350.00
3-Kandi the Cave Kid begins by Walt Kelly; also in #4-6,8,11,15	115.00	345.00	1150.00
4-Kelly-a	98.00	294.00	975.00
5-Bugs Bunny The Super-Duper Rabbit story (1st funny animal super hero, 3/42; also see Coo Coo); Kelly-a	88.00	264.00	875.00
6,8-Kelly-a	65.00	195.00	650.00
7,9,10: 9-Painted-c. 10-Flag-c	48.00	144.00	480.00
11,15-Kelly-a; 15-X-Mas-c	48.00	144.00	480.00
12-14,16-19	34.00	102.00	340.00
20-25: Pat, Patsy & Pete by Walt Kelly in all	30.00	90.00	300.00
26-30	21.50	64.00	215.00
31-40: 33-War bond-c. 39-X-Mas-c	17.50	53.00	175.00
41-50	13.00	39.00	140.00
51-60	9.00	27.00	100.00
61-80	6.00	18.00	65.00
81-99: 87-X-Mas-c	4.00	12.25	45.00
100	5.00	15.00	55.00
101-120	3.20	9.60	35.00
121-150	2.70	8.00	30.00
151-200: 159-X-Mas-c	1.60	4.80	18.00
201-240	1.20	3.60	14.00

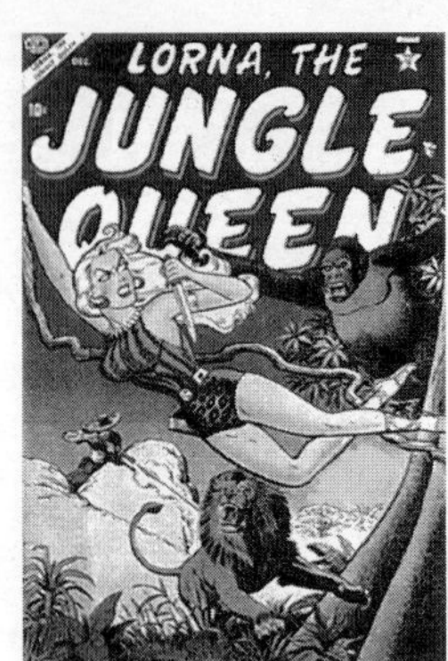

Lorna, The Jungle Queen #4 © MAR

Lost in Space #1 © New Line

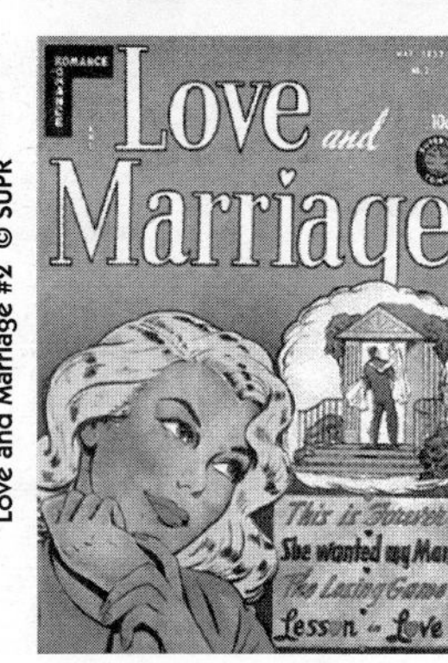

Love and Marriage #2 © SUPR

GD25 FN65 NM94

241-246 1.60 4.80 18.00

LOONY SPORTS (Magazine)
3-Strikes Publishing Co.: Spring, 1975 (68 pgs.)

1-Sports satire .90 2.70 8.00

LOOSE CANNON (Also see Action Comics Annual #5 & Showcase '94 #5)
DC Comics: June, 1995 - No. 4, Sept, 1995 ($1.75, limited series)

1-4: Adam Pollina-a. 1-Superman app. 1.75

LOOY DOT DOPE
United Features Syndicate: No. 13, 1939

Single Series 13 25.00 76.00 190.00

LORD JIM (See Movie Comics)

LORD PUMPKIN
Malibu Comics (Ultraverse): Oct, 1994 ($2.50, one-shot)

0-Two covers 2.50

LORD PUMPKIN/NECROMANTRA
Malibu Comics (Ultraverse): Apr, 1995 - No. 4, July, 1995 ($2.95, limited series, flip book)

1-4 3.00

LORDS OF MISRULE
Dark Horse Comics: Jan, 1997 - No. 6, Jun, 1997 ($2.95, B&W, limited series)

1-6: 1-Wraparound-c 2.95

LORDS OF THE ULTRA-REALM
DC Comics: June, 1986 - No. 6, Nov, 1986 (Mini-series)

1 2.00
2-6 1.75
Special 1(12/87, $2.25) 2.25

LORNA THE JUNGLE GIRL (...Jungle Queen #1-5)
Atlas Comics (NPI 1/OMC 2-11/NPI 12-26): July, 1953 - No. 26, Aug, 1957

1-Origin & 1st app. 32.00 96.00 240.00
2-Intro. & 1st app. Greg Knight 16.00 48.00 120.00
3-5 13.00 40.00 100.00
6-11: 11-Last pre-code (1/55) 11.00 32.00 80.00
12-17,19-26: 14-Colletta & Maneely-c 8.50 26.00 60.00
18-Williamson/Colletta-c 9.30 28.00 70.00
NOTE: ***Brodsky*** *c-1-3, 5, 9.* ***Everett*** *c-21, 23-26.* ***Heath*** *c-6, 7.* ***Maneely*** *c-12, 15.* ***Romita*** *a-20, 22, 24, 26.* ***Shores*** *a-14-16, 24, 26; c-11, 13, 16.* ***Tuska*** *a-6.*

LOSERS SPECIAL (See Our Fighting Forces #123)(Also see G.I. Combat & Our Fighting Forces)
DC Comics: Sept, 1985 ($1.25, one-shot)

1-Capt. Storm, Gunner & Sarge; Crisis x-over 1.30

LOST, THE
Chaos! Comics: Dec, 1997 - No. 2 ($2.95, B&W, unfinished limited series)

1,2-Andreyko-script: 1-Russell back-c 2.95

LOST CONTINENT
Eclipse Int'l: Sept, 1990 - No. 6, 1991 ($3.50, B&W, squarebound, 60 pgs.)

1-6: Japanese story translated to English 3.50

LOST HEROES
Davdez Arts: Mar, 1998 - Present ($2.95)

0-3-Rob Prior-s/painted-a 2.95

LOST IN SPACE (TV)(Also see Space Family Robinson)
Innovation Publishing: Aug, 1991 - No. 12, Jan, 1993 ($2.50, limited series)

1-12: Bill Mumy (Will Robinson) scripts in #1-9. 9-Perez-c 2.50
1,2-Special Ed.; r/#1,2 plus new art & new-c 2.50
Annual 1,2 (1991, 1992, $2.95, 52 pgs.) 3.00

LOST IN SPACE (Movie)
Dark Horse Comics: Apr, 1998 - No. 3, July, 1998 ($2.95, limited series)

GD25 FN65 NM94

1-3-Continuation of movie; Erskine-c 3.00

LOST IN SPACE: PROJECT ROBINSON (TV)
Innovation Publishing: Nov, 1993 ($2.50, limited series intended)

1-Takes place after #12 2.50

LOST IN SPACE: VOYAGE TO THE BOTTOM OF THE SOUL
Innovation Publishing: No. 13, Aug, 1993 - No. 18, 1994 ($2.50, limited series)

13(V1#1, $2.95)-Embossed silver logo edition; Bill Mumy scripts begin; painted-c 2.50
13(V1#1, $4.95)-Embossed gold logo edition bagged w/poster 5.00
14-18: Painted-c 2.50
NOTE: *Originally intended to be a 12 issue limited series.*

LOST PLANET
Eclipse Comics: 5/87 - No. 5, 2/88; No. 6, 3/89 (Mini-series, Baxter paper)

1,2 ($1.75)-Bo Hampton-c/a in all 1.80
3-6 ($2.00) 2.00

LOST WAGON TRAIN, THE (See Zane Grey Fou r Color 583)

LOST WORLD, THE
Dell Publishing Co.: No. 1145, Nov-Jan, 1960-61

Four Color 1145-Movie, Gil Kane-a, photo-c; 1pg. Conan Doyle biography by Torres 10.00 30.00 110.00

LOST WORLD, THE (See Jurassic Park)
Topps Comics: May, 1997 - No. 4, Aug, 1997 ($2.95, limited series)

1-4-Movie adaption 2.95

LOST WORLDS (Weird Tales of the Past and Future)
Standard Comics: No. 5, Oct, 1952 - No. 6, Dec, 1952

5- "Alice in Terrorland" by Alex Toth; J. Katz-a 37.00 112.00 280.00
6-Toth-a 31.00 92.00 230.00

LOTS 'O' FUN COMICS
Robert Allen Co.: 1940's? (5¢, heavy stock, blue covers)

nn-Contents can vary; Felix, Planet Comics known; contents would determine value. Similar to Up-To-Date Comics. Remainders - re-packaged.

LOU GEHRIG (See The Pride of the Yankees)

LOVE ADVENTURES (Actual Confessions #13)
Marvel (IPS)/Atlas Comics (MPI): Oct, 1949; No. 2, Jan, 1950; No. 3, Feb, 1951 - No. 12, Aug, 1952

1-Photo-c 12.00 36.00 90.00
2-Powell-a; Tyrone Power, Gene Tierney photo-c 12.00 36.00 90.00
3-8,10-12: 8-Robinson-a 6.00 18.00 42.00
9-Everett-a 6.85 21.00 48.00

LOVE AND MARRIAGE
Superior Comics Ltd.: Mar, 1952 - No. 16, Sept, 1954

1 10.00 30.00 75.00
2 5.70 17.00 38.00
3-10 4.25 13.00 26.00
11-16 4.00 11.50 23.00
I.W. Reprint #1,2,8,11,14: 8-r/Love and Marriage #3. 11-r/Love and Marriage #11. 1.10 3.30 9.00
Super Reprint #10('63),15,17('64):15-Love and Marriage #? 1.10 3.30 9.00
NOTE: *All issues have* ***Kamenish*** *art.*

LOVE AND ROCKETS
Fantagraphics Books: July, 1982 - No. 50, May, 1996 ($2.95/$2.50/$4.95, B&W, mature)

1-B&W-c (6/82, $2.95; small size, publ. by Hernandez Bros.)(800 printed) 2.70 8.00 30.00
1 (Fall, '82; color-c) 2.50 7.60 28.00
1-2nd & 3rd printing 3.00
2 1.00 3.00 10.00

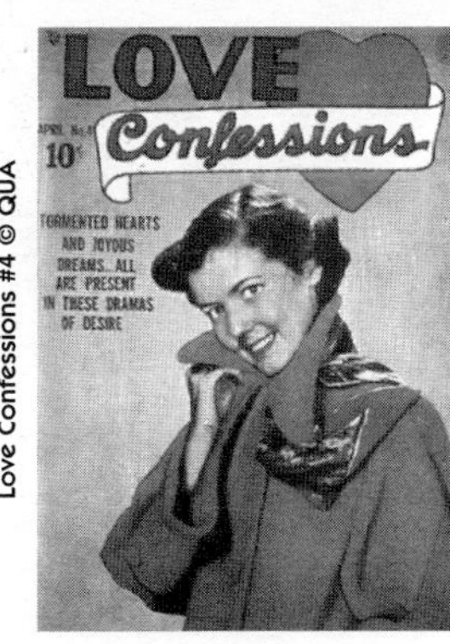

Love Confessions #4 © QUA

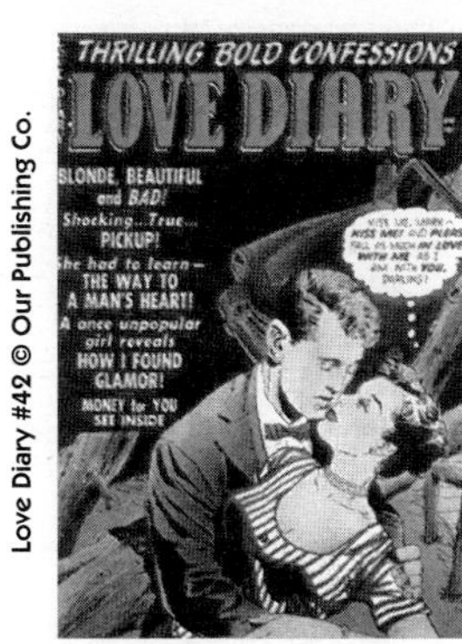

Love Diary #42 © Our Publishing Co.

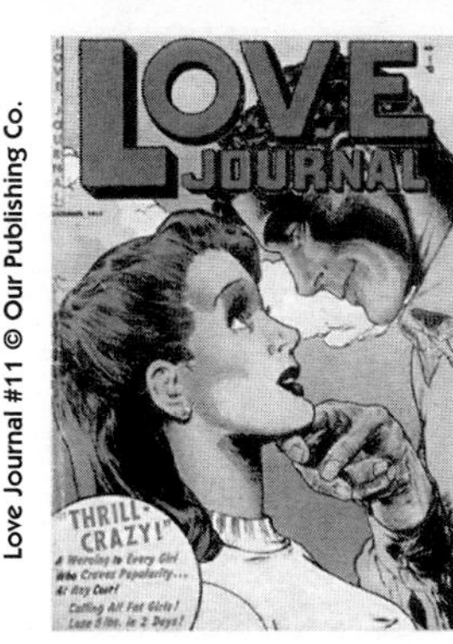

Love Journal #11 © Our Publishing Co.

	GD25	FN65	NM94
2-11, 29-31: 2nd printings ($2.50)			2.50
3-5	.85	2.60	7.00
6-10			4.50
11-49: 30 ($2.95, 52 pgs.). 31-on: $2.50-c			3.50
50-($4.95)			4.00

LOVE AND ROMANCE
Charlton Comics: Sept, 1971 - No. 24, Sept, 1975

	GD25	FN65	NM94
1	1.80	5.40	18.00
2-10	1.00	3.00	10.00
11-24		2.00	6.00

LOVE AT FIRST SIGHT
Ace Magazines (RAR Publ. Co./Periodical House): Oct, 1949 - No. 43, Nov, 1956 (Photo-c: 21-42)

	GD25	FN65	NM94
1-Painted-c	11.00	32.00	80.00
2-Painted-c	5.70	17.00	40.00
3-10: 4-Painted-c	4.25	13.00	26.00
11-20	4.00	11.50	23.00
21-33: 33-Last pre-code	3.40	8.50	17.00
34-43	2.60	6.50	13.00

LOVE BUG, THE (See Movie Comics)

LOVE CLASSICS
A Lover's Magazine/Marvel: Nov, 1949 - No. 2, Feb, 1950 (Photo-c, 52 pgs.)

	GD25	FN65	NM94
1,2: 2-Virginia Mayo photo-c; 30 pg. story "I Was a Small Town Flirt"	11.00	32.00	80.00

LOVE CONFESSIONS
Quality Comics: Oct, 1949 - No. 54, Dec, 1956 (Photo-c: 3,4,6,7,9,11-18,21)

	GD25	FN65	NM94
1-Ward-c/a, 9 pgs; Gustavson-a	25.00	76.00	190.00
2-Gustavson-a; Ward-c	11.00	32.00	80.00
3	5.70	17.00	40.00
4-Crandall-a	7.85	23.50	55.00
5-Ward-a, 7 pgs.	10.00	30.00	70.00
6,7,9,11-13,15,16,18: 7-Van Johnson photo-c. 8-Robert Mitchum & Jane Russell photo-c	4.15	12.50	25.00
8,10-Ward-a(2 stories in #10)	10.00	30.00	70.00
14,17,19,22-Ward-a; 17-Faith Domerque photo-c	8.35	25.00	58.00
20-Ward-a(2)	10.00	30.00	70.00
21,23-28,30-38,40-42: Last precode, 4/55	3.40	8.50	17.00
29-Ward-a	8.00	24.00	56.00
39-Matt Baker-a	5.70	17.00	35.00
43,44,46-48,50-54: 47-Ward-c?	3.00	7.50	15.00
45-Ward-a	4.25	13.00	28.00
49-Baker-c/a	6.00	18.00	42.00

LOVE DIARY
Our Publishing Co./Toytown/Patches: July, 1949 - No. 48, Oct, 1955 (Photo-c: 1-24,27-29) (52 pgs. #1-11?)

	GD25	FN65	NM94
1-Krigstein-a	13.00	40.00	100.00
2,3-Krigstein & Mort Leav-a in each	10.00	30.00	65.00
4-8	4.25	13.00	28.00
9,10-Everett-a	5.70	17.00	34.00
11-20: 16- Mort Leav-a, 3 pg. Baker-sty. Leav-a	4.00	12.00	24.00
21-30,32-48: 45-Leav-a. 47-Last precode(12/54)	4.00	10.00	20.00
31-John Buscema headlights-c	4.25	13.00	26.00

LOVE DIARY (Diary Loves #2 on; title change due to previously published title)
Quality Comics Group: Sept, 1949

	GD25	FN65	NM94
1-Ward-c/a, 9 pgs.	25.00	76.00	190.00

LOVE DIARY
Charlton Comics: July, 1958 - No. 102, Dec, 1976

	GD25	FN65	NM94
1	6.50	19.50	45.00
2	5.00	15.00	30.00
3-5,7-10: 10-Photo-c	4.00	10.00	20.00
6-Torres-a	5.00	15.00	30.00
11-20: 20-Photo-c	1.85	5.50	15.00
21-40	1.60	4.85	13.00
41-60	.90	2.70	9.00
61-80,100-102	.85	2.60	7.00
81-99		2.00	6.00

LOVE DOCTOR (See Dr. Anthony King...)

LOVE DRAMAS (True Secrets No. 3 on?)
Marvel Comics (IPS): Oct, 1949 - No. 2, Jan, 1950

	GD25	FN65	NM94
1-Jack Kamen-a; photo-c	14.00	42.00	105.00
2	11.00	32.00	80.00

LOVE EXPERIENCES (Challenge of the Unknown No. 6)
Ace Periodicals (A.A. Wyn/Periodical House): Oct, 1949 - No. 5, June, 1950; No. 6, Apr, 1951 - No. 38, June, 1956

	GD25	FN65	NM94
1-Painted-c	9.30	28.00	70.00
2	5.00	15.00	30.00
3-5: 5-Painted-c	4.00	11.00	22.00
6-10	3.40	8.50	17.00
11-30: 30-Last pre-code (2/55)	2.60	6.50	13.00
31-38: 38-Indicia date-6/56; c-date-8/56	2.20	5.50	11.00

NOTE: ***Anne Brewster*** *a-15. Photo c-4, 15-35, 38.*

LOVE JOURNAL
Our Publishing Co.: No. 10, Oct, 1951 - No. 25, July, 1954

	GD25	FN65	NM94
10	8.50	25.00	60.00
11-25: 19-Mort Leav-a	5.00	15.00	30.00

LOVELAND
Mutual Mag./Eye Publ. (Marvel): Nov, 1949 - No. 2, Feb, 1950 (52 pgs.)

	GD25	FN65	NM94
1,2-Photo-c	8.00	24.00	56.00

LOVE LESSONS
Harvey Comics/Key Publ. No. 5: Oct, 1949 - No. 5, June, 1950

	GD25	FN65	NM94
1-Metallic silver-c printed over the cancelled covers of Love Letters #1; indicia title is "Love Letters"	11.00	32.00	80.00
2-Powell-a; photo-c	5.35	16.00	32.00
3-5: 3-Photo-c	4.25	13.00	26.00

LOVE LETTERS (10/49, Harvey; advertised but never published; covers were printed before cancellation and were used as the cover to Love Lessons #1)

LOVE LETTERS (Love Secrets No. 32 on)
Quality Comics: 11/49 - #6, 9/50; #7, 3/51 - #31, 6/53; #32, 2/54 - #51, 12/56

	GD25	FN65	NM94
1-Ward-c, Gustavson-a	20.00	60.00	150.00
2-Ward-c, Gustavson-a	16.00	48.00	120.00
3-Gustavson-a	11.00	32.00	80.00
4-Ward-a, 9 pgs.	15.00	44.00	110.00
5-8,10	4.25	13.00	28.00
9-One pg. Ward "Be Popular with the Opposite Sex"; Robert Mitchum photo-c	5.70	17.00	40.00
11-Ward-r/Broadway Romances #2 & retitled	6.00	18.00	42.00
12-15,18-20	4.00	12.00	24.00
16,17-Ward-a; 16-Anthony Quinn photo-c. 17-Jane Russell photo-c	8.75	26.25	62.00
21-29	4.00	11.00	22.00
30,31(6/53)-Ward-a	5.70	17.00	36.00
32(2/54)-39: 38-Crandall-a. 39-Last precode (4/55)	3.20	8.00	16.00
40-48	2.60	6.50	13.00
49,50-Baker-a	6.00	18.00	42.00
51-Baker-c	5.00	15.00	30.00

NOTE: *Photo-c on most 3-28.*

LOVE LIFE
P. L. Publishing Co.: Nov, 1951

	GD25	FN65	NM94
1	7.15	21.50	50.00

Lovers' Lane #4 © LEV

Love Secrets #2 © QUA

Love Trails #1 © MAR

	GD25	FN65	NM94

LOVELORN (Confessions of the Lovelorn #52 on)
American Comics Group (Michel Publ./Regis Publ.): Aug-Sept, 1949 - No. 51, July, 1954 (No. 1-26: 52 pgs.)

	GD25	FN65	NM94
1	12.00	36.00	90.00
2	6.35	19.00	44.00
3-10	5.00	15.00	30.00
11-20,22-48: 18-Drucker-a(2 pgs.). 46-Lazarus-a	4.00	12.00	24.00
21-Prostitution story	5.70	17.00	35.00
49-51-Has 3-D effect-c/stories	13.00	40.00	100.00

LOVE MEMORIES
Fawcett Publications: 1949 (no month) - No. 4, July, 1950 (All photo-c)

	GD25	FN65	NM94
1	11.00	32.00	80.00
2-4: 2-(Win/49-50)	6.00	18.00	42.00

LOVE MYSTERY
Fawcett Publications: June, 1950 - No. 3, Oct, 1950 (All photo-c)

	GD25	FN65	NM94
1-George Evans-a	18.00	54.00	135.00
2,3-Evans-a. 3-Powell-a	15.00	44.00	110.00

LOVE PROBLEMS (See Fox Giants)

LOVE PROBLEMS AND ADVICE ILLUSTRATED (see True Love...)

LOVE ROMANCES (Formerly Ideal #5)
Timely/Marvel/Atlas(TCI No. 7-71/Male No. 72-106): No. 6, May, 1949 - No. 106, July, 1963

	GD25	FN65	NM94
6-Photo-c	11.00	32.00	80.00
7-Photo-c; Kamen-a	6.85	21.00	48.00
8-Kubert-a; photo-c	7.15	21.50	50.00
9-20: 9-12-Photo-c	5.20	15.50	32.00
21,24-Krigstein-a	6.50	19.50	45.00
22,23,25-35,37,39,40	4.25	13.00	28.00
36,38-Krigstein-a	5.70	17.00	40.00
41-44,46,47: Last precode (2/55)	4.25	13.00	28.00
45,57-Matt Baker-a	5.70	17.00	40.00
48,50-52,54-56,58-74	2.50	7.50	22.00
49,53-Toth-a, 6 & ? pgs.	4.00	12.00	40.00
75,77,82-Matt Baker-a	3.80	11.40	38.00
76,78-81,84,86-95: Last 10¢ issue? 80-Heath-c	2.50	7.50	22.00
83-Kirby-c, Severin-a	3.80	11.40	38.00
85,96-Kirby-c/a	4.20	12.60	42.00
97,100-104	2.50	7.50	20.00
98-Kirby-a(4)	6.00	18.00	60.00
99,105,106-Kirby-a	3.80	11.40	38.00

NOTE: ***Anne Brewster** a-67, 72. **Colletta** a-37, 40, 42, 44, 67(2); c-42, 44, 49, 54, 80. **Everett** c-70. **Heath** a-87. **Kirby** c-80, 85, 88. **Robinson** a-29.*

LOVERS (Formerly Blonde Phantom)
Marvel Comics No. 23,24/Atlas No. 25 on (ANC): No. 23, May, 1949 - No. 86, Aug?, 1957

	GD25	FN65	NM94
23-Photo-c begin, end #28	11.00	32.00	80.00
24-Tothish plus Robinson-a	5.70	17.00	38.00
25,30-Kubert-a; 7, 10 pgs.	6.00	18.00	42.00
26-29,31-36,39,40	4.25	13.00	28.00
37,38-Krigstein-a	7.00	21.00	45.00
41-Everett-a(2)	5.70	17.00	38.00
42,44-65: 65-Last pre-code (1/55)	4.25	13.00	26.00
43-Frazetta 1 pg. ad	4.15	12.50	25.00
66,68-86	4.00	11.00	22.00
67-Toth-a	5.00	15.00	30.00

NOTE: ***Anne Brewster** a-86. **Colletta** a-54, 59, 62, 64, 65, 69, 85; c-61, 64, 65, 75. **Heath** a-61. **Maneely** a-57. **Powell** a-27, 30. **Robinson** a-54, 56.*

LOVERS' LANE
Lev Gleason Publications: Oct, 1949 - No. 41, June, 1954 (No. 1-18: 52 pgs.)

	GD25	FN65	NM94
1-Biro-c	8.30	25.00	58.00
2-Biro-c	5.00	15.00	30.00
3-20: 3,4-Painted-c. 20-Frazetta 1 pg. ad	4.00	11.00	22.00
21-38,40,41	3.00	7.50	15.00
39-Story narrated by Frank Sinatra	4.25	13.00	28.00

NOTE: ***Briefer** a-6, 21. **Fuje** a-4, 16; c-many. **Guardineer** a-1. **Kinstler** c-41. **Tuska** a-6. Painted c-3-18. Photo c-19-22, 26-28.*

LOVE SCANDALS
Quality Comics: Feb, 1950 - No. 5, Oct, 1950 (Photo-c #2-5) (All 52 pgs.)

	GD25	FN65	NM94
1-Ward-c/a, 9 pgs.	22.00	66.00	165.00
2,3: 2-Gustavson-a	8.00	24.00	56.00
4-Ward-a, 18 pgs; Gil Fox-a	18.00	54.00	135.00
5-C. Cuidera-a; tomboy story "I Hated Being a Woman"	8.00	24.00	56.00

LOVE SECRETS
Marvel Comics(IPC): Oct, 1949 - No. 2, Jan, 1950 (52 pgs., photo-c)

	GD25	FN65	NM94
1	11.00	32.00	80.00
2	7.15	21.50	50.00

LOVE SECRETS (Formerly Love Letters #31)
Quality Comics Group: No. 32, Aug, 1953 - No. 56, Dec, 1956

	GD25	FN65	NM94
32	7.15	21.50	50.00
33,35-39	4.15	12.50	25.00
34-Ward-a	8.00	24.00	52.00
40-Matt Baker-c	5.70	17.00	35.00
41-43: 43-Last precode (3/55)	4.00	12.00	24.00
44,47-50,53,54	3.20	8.00	16.00
45,46-Ward-a. 46-Baker-a	6.00	18.00	42.00
51,52-Ward(r). 52-r/Love Confessions #17	4.25	13.00	28.00
55,56: 55-Baker-a. 56-Baker-c	5.35	16.00	32.00

LOVE STORIES (Formerly My Love Affair #5)
Fox Feature Syndicate: No. 6, 1950 - No. 12, 1951

	GD25	FN65	NM94
6,8-Wood-a	16.00	48.00	120.00
7,9-12	7.15	21.50	50.00

LOVE STORIES (Formerly Heart Throbs)
National Periodical Publ.: No. 147, Nov, 1972 - No. 152, Oct-Nov, 1973

	GD25	FN65	NM94
147-152	1.20	3.60	12.00

LOVE STORIES OF MARY WORTH (See Harvey Comics Hits #55 & Mary Worth)
Harvey Publications: Sept, 1949 - No. 5, May, 1950

	GD25	FN65	NM94
1-1940's newspaper reprints-#1-4	5.70	17.00	38.00
2	5.00	15.00	30.00
3-5: 3-Kamen/Baker-a?	5.00	15.00	30.00

LOVE SUCKS
Ace Comics: 1995; Oct, 1996 - Present ($2.95, B&W)

	GD25	FN65	NM94
1-(1995) Hynes-s/Juch-a			3.00
1-(10/96) Santiago-s/Juch-a			3.00
2-5			2.95

LOVE TALES (Formerly The Human Torch #35)
Marvel/Atlas Comics (ZPC No. 36-50/MMC No. 67-75): No. 36, 5/49 - No. 58, 8/52; No. 59, date? - No. 75, Sept, 1957

	GD25	FN65	NM94
36-Photo-c	11.00	32.00	80.00
37	6.35	19.00	42.00
38-44,46-50: 39-41-Photo-c	5.00	15.00	30.00
45-Powell-a	5.35	16.00	32.00
51,69-Everett-a	5.70	17.00	34.00
52-Krigstein-a	5.70	17.00	34.00
53-60: 60-Last pre-code (2/55)	4.00	11.50	23.00
61-68,70-75: 75-Brewster, Cameron, Colletta-a	3.00	7.50	15.00

LOVE THRILLS (See Fox Giants)

LOVE TRAILS (Western romance)
A Lover's Magazine (CDS)(Marvel): Dec, 1949 - No. 2, Mar, 1950 (52 pgs.)

Lucky Duck #7 © STD

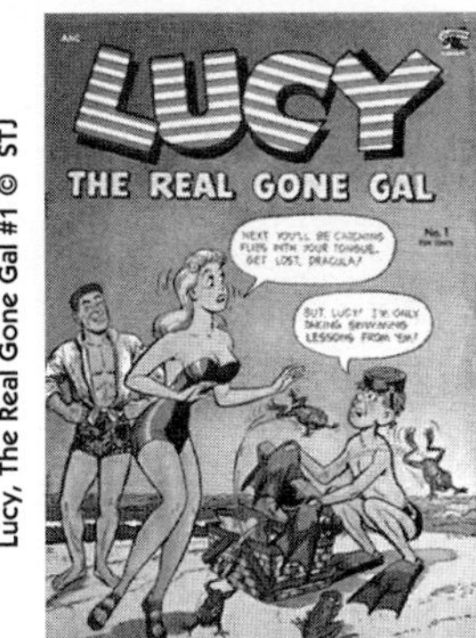

Lucy, The Real Gone Gal #1 © STJ

Lyndon B. Johnson © DELL

GD25 FN65 NM94 GD25 FN65 NM94

1,2: 1-Photo-c 11.00 32.00 80.00

LOWELL THOMAS' HIGH ADVENTURE (See High Adventure)

LT. (See Lieutenant)

LUBA
Fantographics Books: Feb, 1998 - Present ($2.95, B&W, mature)

1,2-Gilbert Hernandez-s/a 2.95

LUCIFER'S HAMMER (Larry Niven & Jerry Pournelle's...)
Innovation Publishing: Nov, 1993 - No. 6, 1994 ($2.50, painted, limited series)

1-6: Adaptatin of novel, painted-c & art 2.50

LUCKY COMICS
Consolidated Magazines: Jan, 1944; No. 2, Sum, 1945 - No. 5, Sum, 1946

1-Lucky Starr & Bobbie begin 17.00 50.00 125.00
2-5: 5-Devil-c by Walter Johnson 9.30 28.00 70.00

LUCKY DUCK
Standard Comics (Literary Ent.): No. 5, Jan, 1953 - No. 8, Sept, 1953

5-Funny animal; Irving Spector-a 9.30 28.00 70.00
6-8-Irving Spector-a 7.85 23.50 55.00
NOTE: Harvey Kurtzman tried to hire Spector for Mad #1.

LUCKY FIGHTS IT THROUGH (Also see The K. O. Punch)
Educational Comics: 1949 (Giveaway, 16 pgs. in color, paper-c)

nn-(Very Rare)-1st Kurtzman work for E. C.; V.D. prevention
111.00 333.00 1000.00
nn-Reprint in color (1977) 2.00
NOTE: *Subtitled "The Story of That Ignorant, Ignorant Cowboy". Prepared for Communications Materials Center, Columbia University.*

LUCKY "7" COMICS
Howard Publishers Ltd.: 1944 (No date listed)

1-Pioneer, Sir Gallagher, Dick Royce, Congo Raider, Punch Powers; bondage-c 29.00 88.00 220.00

LUCKY STAR (Western)
Nation Wide Publ. Co.: 1950 - No. 7, 1951; No. 8, 1953 - No. 14, 1955 (5x7-1/4"; full color, 5¢)

nn (#1)-(5¢, 52 pgs.)-Davis-a 9.30 28.00 70.00
2,3-(5¢, 52 pgs.)-Davis-a 6.50 19.50 45.00
4-7-(5¢, 52 pgs.)-Davis-a 5.70 17.00 40.00
8-14-(36 pgs.) 5.00 15.00 30.00
Given away with Lucky Star Western Wear by the Juvenile Mfg. Co.
4.00 10.00 20.00

LUCY SHOW, THE (TV) (Also see I Love Lucy)
Gold Key: June, 1963 - No. 5, June, 1964 (Photo-c: 1,2)

1 12.25 37.00 135.00
2 6.25 19.00 70.00
3-5: Photo back c-1,2,4,5 5.50 16.50 60.00

LUCY, THE REAL GONE GAL (Meet Miss Pepper #5 on)
St. John Publishing Co.: June, 1953 - No. 4, Dec, 1953

1-Negligee panels 9.30 28.00 70.00
2 5.70 17.00 38.00
3,4: 3-Drucker-a 5.00 15.00 30.00

LUDWIG BEMELMAN'S MADELEINE & GENEVIEVE
Dell Publishing Co.: No. 796, May, 1957

Four Color 796 2.75 8.00 30.00

LUDWIG VON DRAKE (TV)(Disney)(See Walt Disney's C&S #256)
Dell Publishing Co.: Nov-Dec, 1961 - No. 4, June-Aug, 1962

1 6.00 18.00 65.00
2-4 4.00 12.00 45.00
...Fish Stampede (1962, Fritos giveaway)-16 pgs., 3-1/4x7", soft-c; also see Donald Duck & Mickey Mouse 5.35 16.00 32.00

LUFTWAFFE: 1946 (Volume 1)
Antarctic Press: July, 1996 - No.4, Jan, 1997 ($2.95, B&W, limited series)

1-4-Ben Dunn & Ted Nomura-s/a 3.00
...Special 3.00

LUFTWAFFE: 1946 (Volume 2)
Antarctic Press: Mar, 1997 - Present ($2.95, B&W, limited series)

1-10: 8-Reviews Tigers of Terra series 3.00
Annual 1 (4/98, $2.95)-Reprints early Nomura pages 3.00
...Color Special (4/98) 3.00
...Technical Manual 1 (2/98, $3.95) 4.00

LUGER
Eclipse Comics: Oct, 1986 - No. 3, Feb, 1987 ($1.75, miniseries, Baxter paper)

1-3: Bruce Jones scripts; Yeates-c/a 1.80

LUKE CAGE (See Cage & Hero for Hire)

LUKE SHORT'S WESTERN STORIES
Dell Publishing Co.: No. 580, Aug, 1954 - No. 927, Aug, 1958

Four Color 580(8/54), 651(9/55)-Kinstler-a 2.75 8.00 30.00
Four Color 739,771,807,875,927 2.75 8.00 30.00
Four Color 848 3.60 11.00 40.00

LUNATIC FRINGE, THE
Innovation Publishing: July, 1989 - No. 2, 1989 ($1.75, deluxe format)

1,2 1.80

LUNATICKLE (Magazine) (Satire)
Whitstone Publ.: Feb, 1956 - No. 2, Apr, 1956

1,2-Kubert-a 3.60 9.00 18.00

LUNATIK
Marvel Comics: Dec, 1995 - No. 3, Feb, 1996 ($1.95, limited series)

1-3 2.00

LUST FOR LIFE
Slave Labor Graphics: Feb, 1997 - No. 4, Jan, 1998 ($2.95, B&W)

1-4: 1-Jeff Levin-s/a 3.00

LYCANTHROPE LEO
Viz Communications: 1994 - No. 7($2.95, B&W, limited series, 44 pgs.)

1-7 3.00

LYNCH (See Gen 13)
Image Comics (WildStorm Productions): May, 1997 ($2.50, one-shot)

1-Helmut-c/app. 2.50

LYNCH MOB
Chaos! Comics: June, 1994 - No. 4, Sept, 1994 ($2.50, limited series)

1-4 2.50
1-Special edition full foil-c 5.00

LYNDON B. JOHNSON
Dell Publishing Co.: Mar, 1965

12-445-503-Photo-c 2.25 6.75 18.00

M
Eclipse Books: 1990 - No. 4, 1991 ($4.95, painted, 52 pgs.)

1-Adapts movie; contains flexi-disc ($5.95) 2.00 6.00
2-4 5.00

MACHINE, THE
Dark Horse Comics: Nov, 1994 - Feb, 1995 ($2.50, color)

1-4 2.50

MACHINE MAN (Also see 2001, A Space Odyssey)
Marvel Comics Group: Apr, 1978 - No. 9, Dec, 1978; No. 10, Aug, 1979 - No. 19, Feb, 1981

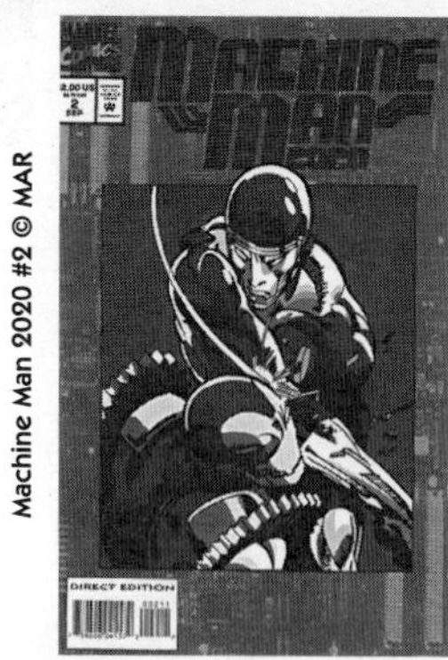

Machine Man 2020 #2 © MAR

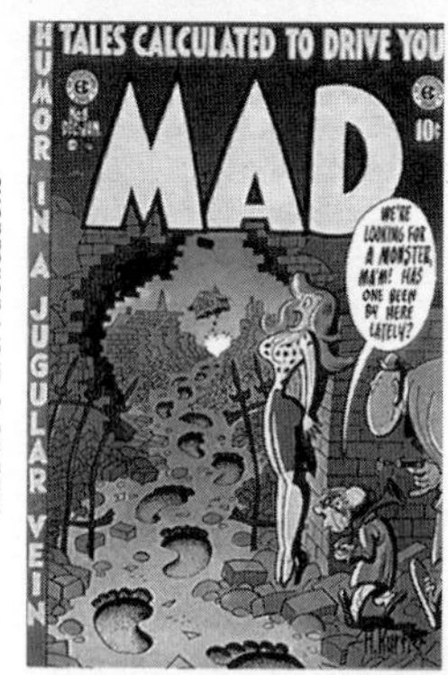

Mad #8 © E.C. Publications

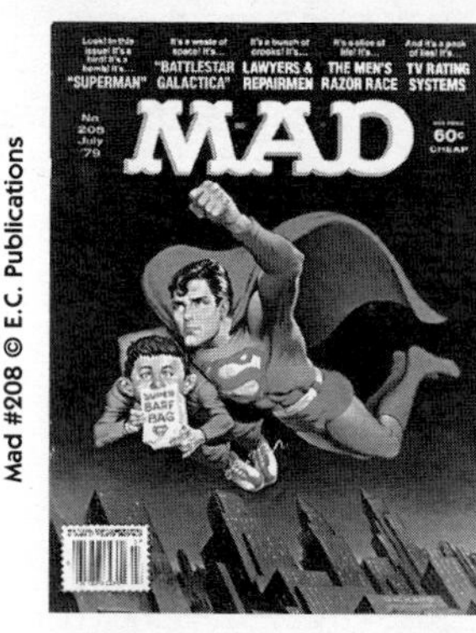

Mad #208 © E.C. Publications

GD25 FN65 NM94

1-Jack Kirby-c/a/scripts begin; end #9 4.00
2-17: 10-Marv Wolfman scripts & Ditko-a begins 2.00
18-Wendigo, Alpha Flight-ties into X-Men #140 1.25
19-Intro/1st app. Jack O'Lantern (Macendale), later becomes 2nd Hobgoblin .90 2.70 9.00

NOTE: ***Austin*** *c-7i, 19i.* ***Buckler*** *c-17p, 18p.* ***Byrne*** *c-14p.* ***Ditko*** *a-10-19; c-10-13, 14i, 15, 16.* ***Kirby*** *a-1-9p; c-1-5, 7-9p.* ***Layton*** *c-7i.* ***Miller*** *c-19p.* ***Simonson*** *c-6.*

MACHINE MAN
Marvel Comics Group: Oct, 1984 - No. 4, Jan, 1985 (Limited-series)

1-Barry Smith-c/a(i) & colors in all 1.50
2-4 1.25
.../Bastion '98 Annual ($2.99) wraparound-c 3.00

MACHINE MAN 2020
Marvel Comics: Aug, 1994 - Nov, 1994 ($2.00, 52 pgs., limited series)

1-4: Reprints Machine Man limited series; Barry Windsor-Smith-c/i(r) 2.00

MACK BOLAN: THE EXECUTIONER (Don Pendleton's...)
Innovation Publishing: July, 1993 ($2.50)

1-3-($2.50) 2.50
1-($3.95)-Indestructible Cover Edition 4.00
1-($2.95)-Collector's Gold Edition; foil stamped 3.00
1-($3.50)-Double Cover Edition; red foil outer-c 3.50

MACKENZIE'S RAIDERS (Movie, TV)
Dell Publishing Co.: No. 1093, Apr-June, 1960

Four Color 1093-Richard Carlson photo-c from TV show 5.50 16.50 60.00

MACO TOYS COMIC
Maco Toys/Charlton Comics: 1959 (Giveaway, 36 pgs.)

1-All military stories featuring Maco Toys 1.25 3.75 10.00

MACROSS (Becomes Robotech: The Macross Saga #2 on)
Comico: Dec, 1984 ($1.50)(Low print run)

1-Early manga app. 2.00 6.00 20.00

MACROSS II
Viz Select Comics: 1992 - No. 10, 1993 ($2.75, B&W, limited series)

1-10: Based on video series 2.75

MAD (Tales Calculated to Drive You...)
E. C. Comics (Educational Comics): Oct-Nov, 1952 - Present (No. 24 on are magazine format) (Kurtzman editor No. 1-28, Feldstein No. 29 - No. ?)

1-Wood, Davis, Elder start as regulars 470.00 2700.00 5400.00
2-Dick Tracy cameo 120.00 360.00 1200.00
3,4: 3-Stan Lee mentioned. 4-Reefer mention story "Flob Was a Slob" by Davis; Superman parody 74.00 222.00 720.00
5-Low distr.; W.M. Gaines biog. 124.00 372.00 1200.00
6-11: 6-Popeye cameo. 7,8- "Hey Look" reprints by Kurtzman. 11-Wolverton-a; Davis story was-r/Crime Suspenstories #12 w/new Kurtzman dialogue 55.00 165.00 540.00
12-15: 15,18-Pot Shot Pete-r by Kurtzman 44.00 132.00 425.00
16-23(5/55): 18-Alice in Wonderland by Jack Davis. 21-1st app. Alfred E. Neuman on-c in fake ad. 22-All by Elder plus photo-montages by Kurtzman. 23-Special cancel announcement 37.00 111.00 325.00
24(7/55)-1st magazine issue (25¢); Kurtzman logo & border on-c; 1st "What? Me Worry?" on-c; 2nd printing exists 88.00 264.00 800.00
25-Jaffee starts as regular writer 37.00 111.00 330.00
26,27: 27-Jaffee starts as story artist; new logo 34.00 102.00 270.00
28-Last issue edited by Kurtzman; (three cover variations exist with different wording on contents banner on lower right of cover; value of each the same) 31.00 93.00 250.00
29-Kamen-a; Don Martin starts as regular; Feldstein editing begins 31.00 93.00 250.00
30-1st A. E. Neuman cover by Mingo; last Elder-a; Bob Clarke starts as regular; Disneyland & Elvis Presley spoof 43.00 130.00 390.00
31-Freas starts as regular; last Davis-a until #99 25.00 75.00 200.00
32,33: 32-Orlando, Drucker, Woodbridge start as regulars; Wood back-c. 33-Orlando back-c 23.00 70.00 180.00
34-Berg starts as regular 19.00 56.00 150.00
35-Mingo wraparound-c; Crandall-a 19.00 56.00 150.00
36-40 12.00 36.00 95.00
41-50 10.00 30.00 80.00
51-60: 60-Two Clarke-c; Prohias starts as regular 8.00 24.00 65.00
61-70: 64-Rickard starts as regular. 68-Martin-c 6.00 18.00 50.00
71-80: 76-Aragones starts as regular 4.00 12.00 40.00
81-90: 86-1st Fold-in. 89-One strip by Walt Kelly. 90-Frazetta back-c; Beatles app. 3.50 10.50 35.00
91-100: 91-Jaffee starts as story artist. 99-Davis-a resumes 3.00 9.00 30.00
101-104,106-120: 101-Infinity-c. 106-Frazetta back-c 2.50 7.50 25.00
105-Batman TV show take-off 3.20 9.60 32.00
121-140: 121-Beatles app. 122-Ronald Reagan photo inside; Drucker & Mingo-c. 128-Last Orlando. 130-Torres begins as reg. 131-Reagan photo back-c. 135,139-Davis-c 2.00 6.00 16.00
141-170: 165-Martin-c. 169-Drucker-c 1.75 5.25 14.00
171-200: 182-Bob Jones starts as regular. 186-Star Trek take-off. 187-Harry North starts as regular. 196-Star Wars take-off 1.40 4.15 11.00
201-250: 203-Star Wars take-off. 204-Hulk TV show take-off. 208-Superman movie take-off. 245- Last Rikard-a. 2.00 6.00
251-300: 256-Last issue edited by Feldstein. 274-Last Martin-a. 284-Roger Rabbit-c/story. 289-Batman movie parody. 291-TMNT-c only. 299-Simpson's-c/story 4.00
301-379: 306-TMNT III movie parody. 308-Terminator parody. 311-Addams Family-c/story. 314-Batman Returns-c/story. 315-Tribute to William Gaines. 316-Photo-c. 322-Batman animated series parody. 338-Frazetta-c. 347-Broken Arrow & Mission Impossible parody. 350-Polybagged w/CD Rom disc. 358-X-Files. 2.50
300-303 (1/91-6/91)-Special Hussein Asylum Editions; only distributed to the troops in the Middle East (see Mad Super Spec.) 5.00

NOTE: ***Aragones*** *c-210, 293.* ***Davis*** *c-2, 27, 135, 139, 173, 178, 212, 213, 219, 246, 260, 296, 308.* ***Drucker*** *c-122, 169, 176, 225, 234, 264, 266, 274, 280, 285, 297, 299, 303, 314, 315, 321.* ***Elder*** *c-5, 259, 261, 268.* ***Elder/Kurtzman*** *a-258-274.* ***Jules Feiffer*** *a(r)-42.* ***Freas*** *c-39-59, 62-67, 69-70, 72, 74.* ***Heath*** *a-14, 27.* ***Jaffee*** *c-199, 217, 224, 258.* ***Kamen*** *a-29.* ***Krigstein*** *a-12, 17, 24, 26.* ***Kurtzman*** *c-1, 3, 4, 6-10, 13, 16, 18.* ***Martin*** *c-68, 165, 229.* ***Mingo*** *c-30-37, 61, 71, 75-80, 82-114, 117-124, 126, 129, 131, 133, 134, 136, 140, 143-148, 150-162, 164, 166-168, 171, 172, 174, 175, 177, 179, 181, 183, 185, 198, 206, 209, 211, 214, 218, 221, 222, 300.* ***John Severin*** *a-1-6, 9, 10.* ***Wolverton*** *c-11; a-11, 17, 29, 31, 36, 40, 82, 137.* ***Wood*** *a-24-45, 59; c-26, 28, 29.* ***Woodbridge*** *a-43. Issues 1-23 are 36 pgs.; 24-28 are 58 pgs.; 29 on are 52 pgs.*

MAD (See Mad Follies, ...Special, More Trash from..., and The Worst from...)

MAD ABOUT MILLIE (Also see Millie the Model)
Marvel Comics Group: April, 1969 - No. 17, Dec, 1970

1-Giant issue 5.00 15.00 50.00
2,3 (Giants) 3.50 10.50 35.00
4-10 2.50 7.50 20.00
11-16: 16-r 2.00 6.00 16.00
17 (Exist?) 4.00 12.00 40.00
Annual 1(11/71) 2.50 7.50 20.00

MADAME XANADU
DC Comics: July, 1981 ($1.00, no ads, 36 pgs.)

1-Marshall Rogers-a(25 pgs.); Kaluta-c/a(2pgs.); pin-up of Madame Xanadu 3.00

MADBALLS
Star Comics/Marvel Comics #9 on: Sept, 1986 - No. 3, Nov, 1986; No. 4, June, 1987 - No. 10, June, 1988

1-10: Based on toys. 9-Post-a 3.00

MAD DISCO

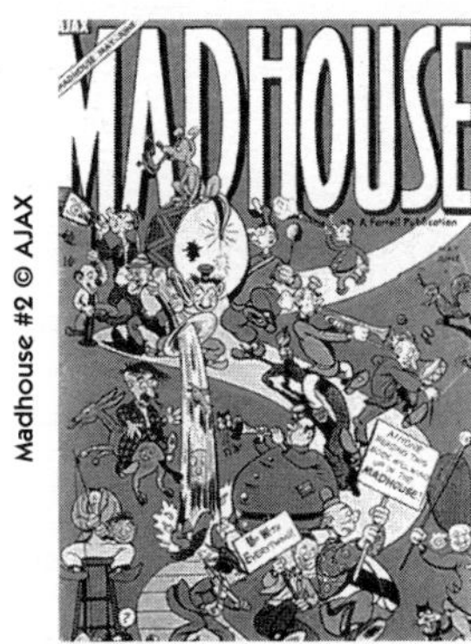

Madhouse #2 © AJAX

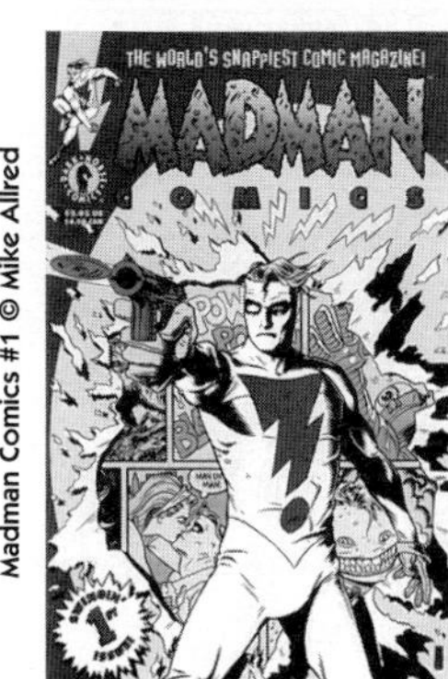

Madman Comics #1 © Mike Allred

Mad Super Special #108 © E.C. Publications

	GD25	FN65	NM94
E.C. Comics: 1980 (one-shot, 36 pgs.)			
1-Includes 30 minute flexi-disc of Mad disco music	1.50	4.50	15.00

MAD DOGS
Eclipse Comics: Feb, 1992 - No. 3, July, 1992 ($2.50, B&W, limited series)

1-3			2.50

MAD 84 (Mad Extra)
E.C. Comics: 1984 (84 pgs.)

1		2.00	6.00

MAD FOLLIES (Special)
E. C. Comics: 1963 - No. 7, 1969

nn(1963)-Paperback book covers	23.00	70.00	255.00
2(1964)-Calendar	17.00	50.00	190.00
3(1965)-Mischief Stickers	13.00	40.00	140.00
4(1966)-Mobile; Frazetta-r/back-c Mad #90	10.00	30.00	110.00
5(1967)-Stencils	6.80	20.00	75.00
6(1968)-Mischief Stickers	6.80	20.00	75.00
7(1969)-Nasty Cards	6.80	20.00	75.00

(If bonus is missing, issue is half price)
NOTE: ***Clarke** c-4. **Frazetta** r-4, 6 (1 pg. ea.). **Mingo** c-1-3. **Orlando** a-5.*

MAD HATTER, THE (Costumed Hero)
O. W. Comics Corp.: Jan-Feb, 1946; No. 2, Sept-Oct, 1946

1-Freddy the Firefly begins; Giunta-c/a	71.00	212.00	600.00
2-Has ad for E.C.'s Animal Fables #1	37.00	112.00	280.00

MADHOUSE
Ajax/Farrell Publ. (Excellent Publ./4-Star): 3-4/54 - No. 4, 9-10/54; 6/57 - No. 4, Dec?, 1957

1(1954)	25.00	76.00	190.00
2,3	14.00	42.00	105.00
4-Surrealistic-c	22.00	66.00	165.00
1(1957, 2nd series)	11.00	32.00	80.00
2-4	7.50	22.50	52.00

MAD HOUSE (Formerly Madhouse Glads; ...Comics #104? on)
Red Circle Productions/Archie Publications: No. 95, 9/74 - No. 97, 1/75; No. 98, 8/75 - No. 130, 10/82

95,96-Horror stories through #97	.90	2.70	9.00
97-Intro. Henry Hobson; Morrow, Thorne-a		2.00	6.00
98,99,101-130-Satire/humor stories. 110-Sabrina app.,1pg.			5.00
100		2.00	6.00
Annual 8(1970-71)-Formerly Madhouse Ma-ad Annual;Sabrina app. (6 pgs.)	1.80	5.40	18.00
Annual 9- 12(1974-75): 11-Wood-a(r)	1.20	3.60	12.00
...Comics Digest 1('75-76)	1.50	4.50	15.00
2- 8(8/82)(...Mag. #5 on)-Sabrina in many	1.00	3.00	10.00

NOTE: ***B. Jones** a-96. **McWilliams** a-97. **Morrow** a-96, 97; c-95-97. **Wildey** a-95, 96. See Archie Comics Digest #1, 13.*

MADHOUSE GLADS (Formerly ...Ma-ad; Madhouse #95 on)
Archie Publ.: No. 73, May, 1970 - No. 94, Aug, 1974 (No. 78-92: 52 pgs.)

73-77,93,94: 74-1 pg. Sabrina	.90	2.70	8.00
78-92 (52 pgs.)	1.20	3.60	12.00

MADHOUSE MA-AD (...Jokes #67-70; ...Freak-Out #71-74)
(Formerly Archie's Madhouse) (Becomes Madhouse Glads #73 on)
Archie Publications: No. 67, April, 1969 - No. 72, Jan, 1970

67-71: 70-1 pg. Sabrina	1.00	3.00	10.00
72-6 pgs. Sabrina	1.40	4.20	14.00
...Annual 7(1969-70)-Formerly Archie's Madhouse Annual; becomes Madhouse Annual; 6 pgs. Sabrina	2.00	6.00	20.00

MADMAN (See Creatures of the Id #1)
Tundra Publishing: Mar, 1992 - No. 3, 1992 ($3.95, duotone, high quality, limited series, 52 pgs.)

1-Mike Allred-c/a in all	1.40	4.20	14.00
1-2nd printing			5.00
2,3	1.00	3.00	10.00

MADMAN ADVENTURES
Tundra Publishing: 1992 - No. 3, 1993 ($2.95, limited series)

1-Mike Allred-c/a in all	1.00	3.00	10.00
2,3	.85	2.60	7.00

MADMAN COMICS
Dark Horse Comics (Legend No. 2 on): Apr, 1994 - Present ($2.95, bi-monthly)

1-Allred-c/a; F. Miller back-c.		2.00	6.00
2-3: 3-Alex Toth back-c.			4.00
4-12: 4-Dave Stevens back-c. 6,7-Miller/Darrow's Big Guy app. 6-Bruce Timm back-c. 7-Darrow back-c. 8-Origin?; Bagge back-c. 10-Allred/Ross-c; Ross back-c. 11-Frazetta back-c			3.50
Ltd. Ed. Slipcover (1997, $99.95, signed and numbered) w/Vol.1 & Vol. 2. Vol.1- reprints #1-5; Vol. 2- reprints #6-10			100.00
Yearbook '95 (1996, $17.95, TPB)-r/#1-5, intro by Teller			18.00
Volume 2 ($17.95, TPB) r/#6-10			18.00

MADMAN / THE JAM
Dark Horse Comics: Jul, 1998 - No. 2, Aug, 1998 ($2.95, mini-series)

1,2-Allred & Mireault-s/a			2.95

MAD MONSTER PARTY (See Movie Classics)

MADNESS IN MURDERWORLD
Marvel Comics: 1989 (Came with computer game from Paragon Software)

V1#1-Starring The X-Men			1.00

MADRAVEN HALLOWEEN SPECIAL
Hamilton Comics: Oct, 1995 ($2.95, one-shot)

nn-Morrow-a			3.00

MAD SPECIAL (...Super Special)
E. C. Publications, Inc.: Fall, 1970 - Present (84 - 116 pgs.)
(If bonus is missing, issue is half price)

Fall 1970(#1)-Bonus-Voodoo Doll; contains 17 pgs. new material	7.50	22.50	75.00
Spring 1971(#2)-Wall Nuts; 17 pgs. new material	4.50	13.50	45.00
3-Protest Stickers	4.50	13.50	45.00
4-8: 4-Mini Posters. 5-Mad Flag. 6-Mad Mischief Stickers. 7-Presidential candidate posters, Wild Shocking Message posters. 8-TV Guise	3.80	11.40	38.00
9(1972)-Contains Nostalgic Mad #1 (28 pgs.)	2.80	8.40	28.00
10,11,13: 10-Nonsense Stickers (Don Martin). 11-33-1/3 RPM record. 13-Sickie Stickers; 3 pgs. Wolverton-r/Mad #137	2.50	7.50	25.00
12-Contains Nostalgic Mad #2 (36 pgs.); Davis, Wolverton-a	2.50	7.50	25.00
14-Vital Message posters & Art Depreciation paintings	1.60	4.80	16.00
15-Contains Nostalgic Mad #3 (28 pgs.)	1.80	5.40	18.00
16,17,19,20: 16-Mad-hesive Stickers. 17-Don Martin posters. 20-Martin Stickers	1.60	4.80	16.00
18-Contains Nostalgic Mad #4 (36 pgs.)	1.60	4.80	16.00
21,24-Contains Nostalgic Mad #5 (28 pgs.) & #6 (28 pgs.)	1.60	4.80	16.00
22,23,25,27,29,30: 22-Diplomas. 23-Martin Stickers. 25-Martin Posters.27-Mad Shock-Sticks. 29-Mad Collectable-Correctables Posters. 30-The Movies	1.00	3.00	10.00
26-Has 33-1/3 RPM record	1.40	4.20	14.00
28-Contains Nostalgic Mad #7 (36 pgs.)	1.00	3.00	10.00
31-50: 32-Contains Nostalgic Mad #8. 36-Has 96 pgs. of comic book & comic strip spoofs: titles "The Comics" on-c	1.00	3.00	10.00
51-70	.90	2.70	8.00

Mage #6 © Matt Wagner

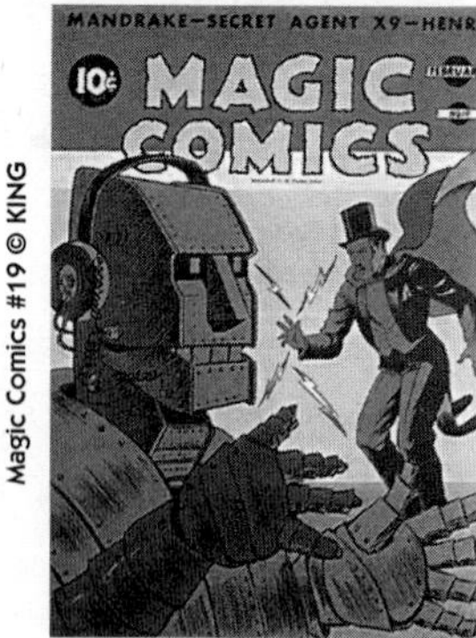

Magic Comics #19 © KING

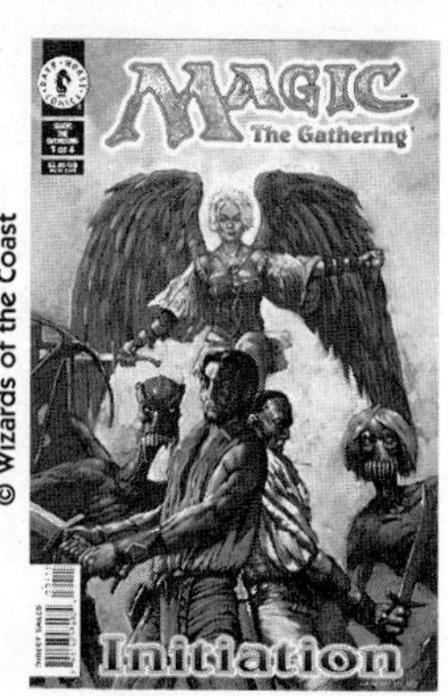

Magic: The Gathering: Gerrard's Quest #1 © Wizards of the Coast

GD25 FN65 NM94

71-88,90-100: 71-Batman parodies-r by Wood, Drucker. 72-Wolverton-c r-from 1st panel in Mad #11; Wolverton-s r/new dialogue. 83-All Star Trek spoof issue 2.00 6.00
76-(Fall, 1991)-Special Hussein Asylum Edition; distributed only to the troops in the Middle East (see Mad #300-303) 2.00 6.00
89-($3.95)-Polybagged w/1st of 3 Spy vs. Spy hologram trading cards (direct sale only issue)(other cards came w/card set) 2.00 6.00
101-135: 117-Sci-Fi parodies-r. 4.00
NOTE: *#28-30 have no number on cover.* ***Freas*** *c-76.* ***Mingo*** *c-9, 11, 15, 19, 23.*

MAGE (The Hero Discovered...; also see Grendel #16)
Comico: Feb, 1984 (no month) - No. 15, Dec, 1986 ($1.50, Mando paper)

	GD25	FN65	NM94
1-Comico's 1st color comic	1.00	3.00	10.00
2		2.00	6.00
3-5: 3-Intro Edsel			4.00
6-Grendel begins (1st in color)	2.25	6.80	25.00
7-1st new Grendel story	1.20	3.60	12.00
8-14: 13-Grendel dies. 14-Grendel story ends		2.00	6.00
15-$2.95, Double size w/pullout poster		2.00	6.00
Volume 1 TPB (10/98, $5.95) r/#1,2			5.95

MAGE (The Hero Defined)
Image Comics: July, 1997 - Present ($2.50)

	GD25	FN65	NM94
1-Matt Wagner-c/s/a in all			3.00
1-"3-D Editon" (2/98, $4.95) w/glasses			5.00
2-9			2.50
0-(7/97, $5.00) American Ent. Ed.			5.00
Volume 1 TPB ('98, $9.95) r/#1-4			9.95

MAGGIE AND HOPEY COLOR SPECIAL (See Love and Rockets)
Fantagraphics Books: May, 1997 ($3.50, one-shot)

1 3.50

MAGGIE THE CAT (Also see Jon Sable, Freelance #11 & Shaman's Tears #12)
Image Comics (Creative Fire Studio): Jan, 1996 - No. 2, Feb, 1996 ($2.50, unfinished limited series)

1,2: Mike Grell-c/a/scripts 2.50

MAGIC AGENT (See Forbidden Worlds & Unknown Worlds)
American Comics Group: Jan-Feb, 1962 - No. 3, May-June, 1962

	GD25	FN65	NM94
1-Origin & 1st app. John Force	2.50	7.50	22.00
2,3	2.00	6.00	16.00

MAGIC COMICS
David McKay Publications: Aug, 1939 - No. 123, Nov-Dec, 1949

	GD25	FN65	NM94
1-Mandrake the Magician, Henry, Popeye , Blondie, Barney Baxter, Secret Agent X-9 (not by Raymond), Bunky by Billy DeBeck & Thornton Burgess text stories illustrated by Harrison Cady begin; Henry covers begin	300.00	900.00	2100.00
2	100.00	300.00	700.00
3	77.00	232.00	525.00
4	66.00	200.00	450.00
5	50.00	150.00	340.00
6-10: 8-11,21-Mandrake/Henry-c	41.00	125.00	280.00
11-16,18,20: 12-Mandrake-c begin.	36.00	108.00	250.00
17-The Lone Ranger begins	38.00	114.00	260.00
19-Robot-c	41.00	125.00	290.00
21-30: 25-Only Blondie-c. 26-Dagwood-c begin	20.00	60.00	160.00
31-40: 36-Flag-c	14.50	45.00	115.00
41-50	11.30	34.00	90.00
51-60	10.00	30.00	80.00
61-70	7.85	23.50	55.00
71-99	6.00	18.00	42.00
100	7.15	23.50	55.00
101-106,109-123: 123-Last Dagwood-c	5.70	17.00	38.00
107,108-Flash Gordon app; not by Raymond	6.00	18.00	42.00

GD25 FN65 NM94

MAGICA DE SPELL (See Walt Disney Showcase #30)

MAGIC FLUTE, THE (See Night Music #9-11)

MAGIC MORRO (Also see Super Comics #21, The Owl, & The Hurricane Kids)
K. K. Publications: 1941 (7-1/2x5-1/4, giveaway, soft-c)

	GD25	FN65	NM94
nn-Ken Ernst-a.	11.00	34.00	85.00

MAGIC OF CHRISTMAS AT NEWBERRYS, THE
E. S. London: 1967 (Giveaway) (B&W, slick-c, 20 pgs.)

nn 2.40 6.00

MAGIC PRIEST (See Warrior Nun)
Antarctic Press: June, 1998 - Present ($2.95, B&W)

1-Lyga-s 3.00

MAGIC SWORD, THE (See Movie Classics)

MAGIC THE GATHERING
Acclaim Comics (Armada)

...ANTIQUITIES WAR, Nov, 1995 - Feb, 1996 ($2.50, limited series)
1-4-Paul Smith-a(p). 1-Pratt-c. 2.50

...ARABIAN NIGHTS, Dec, 1995 - Jan, 1996 ($2.50, limited series)
1,2 2.50

...COLLECTION ,1995 ($4.95, limited series)
1,2-polybagged 5.00

...CONVOCATIONS, 1995 ($2.50, one shot)
1-nn-pin-ups 2.50

...ELDER DRAGONS ,1995 ($2.50, limited series)
1,2-Doug Wheatley-a 2.50

...FALLEN ANGEL ,1995 ($5.95, one shot)
nn 2.00 6.00

...FALLEN EMPIRES ,Sep, 1995 - Oct, 1995 ($2.75, limited series)
1,2 2.75
...Collection ($4.95)-polybagged 5.00

...HOMELANDS ,1995 ($5.95, one shot)
nn-polybagged w/card; Hildebrandts-c 2.00 6.00

... ICE AGE (On The World of...) ,July, 1995 - Nov, 1995 ($2.50, limited series)
1-4: 1,2-bound-in Magic Card. 3,4-bound-in insert 2.50

...LEGEND OF JEDIT OJANEN, 1996 ($2.50, limited series)
1,2 2.50

...NIGHTMARE, 1995 ($2.50, one shot)
1 2.50

...THE SHADOW MAGE, July, 1995 - Oct, 1995 ($2.50, limited series)
1-4--polybagged w/Magic The Gathering card 2.50
...Collection 1,2 (1995, $4.95)-Trade paperback; polybagged 5.00

...SHANDALAR ,1996 ($2.50, limited series)
1,2 2.50

...WAYFARER ,Nov, 1995 - Feb, 1996 ($2.50, limited series)
1-5 2.50

MAGIC: THE GATHERING: GERRARD'S QUEST
Dark Horse Comics: Mar, 1998 - No. 4, June, 1998 ($2.95, limited series)

1-4: Grell-s/Mhan-a 3.00

MAGIK (Illyana and Storm Limited Series)
Marvel Comics Group: Dec, 1983 - No. 4, Mar, 1984 (60¢, limited series)

1-4: 1-Characters from X-Men; Inferno begins; X-Men cameo (Buscema pencils in #1,2; c-1p. 2-4: 2-Nightcrawler app. & X-Men cameo 2.00

MAGILLA GORILLA (TV) (See Kite Fun Book)
Gold Key: May, 1964 - No. 10, Dec, 1968 (Hanna-Barbera)

	GD25	FN65	NM94
1	8.00	23.50	85.00

Magnus, Robot Fighter #31 © VAL

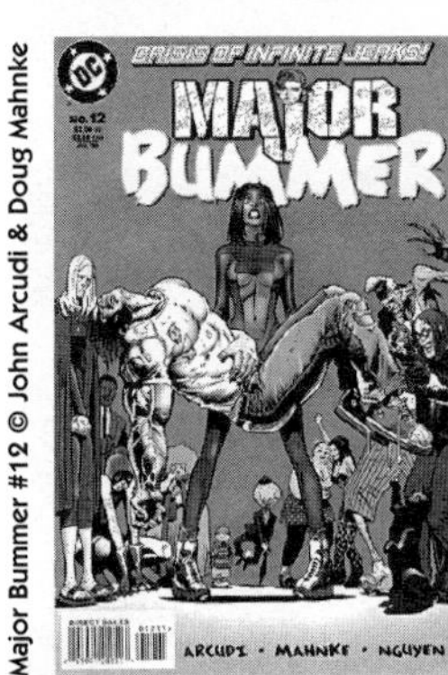

Major Bummer #12 © John Arcudi & Doug Mahnke

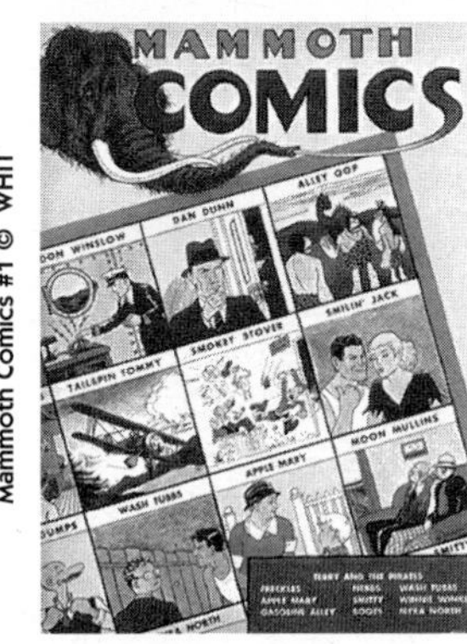

Mammoth Comics #1 © WHIT

GD25 FN65 NM94

2,4-10 4.50 13.50 50.00
3-Vs. Yogi Bear for President 5.50 16.50 60.00

MAGILLA GORILLA (TV)(See Spotlight #4)
Charlton Comics: Nov, 1970 - No. 5, July, 1971 (Hanna-Barbera)

1 3.20 9.50 35.00
2-5 2.20 6.25 22.00

MAGNETIC MEN FEATURING MAGNETO
Marvel Comics (Amalgam): June, 1997 ($1.95, one-shot)

1-Tom Peyer-s/Barry Kitson & Dan Panosian-a 2.00

MAGNETO (See X-Men #1)
Marvel Comics: nd (Sept, 1993) (Giveaway) (one-shot)

0-Embossed foil-c by Sienkiewicz; r/Classic X-Men #19 & 12 by John Bolton 5.00

MAGNETO
Marvel Comics: Nov, 1996 - No. 4, Feb, 1997 ($1.95, limited series)

1-4: Peter Milligan scripts & Kelley Jones-a(p) 2.00

MAGNETO AND THE MAGNETIC MEN
Marvel Comics (Amalgam): Apr, 1996 ($1.95, one-shot)

1-Jeff Matsuda-a(p) 2.00

MAGNUS, ROBOT FIGHTER (...4000 A.D.)(See Doctor Solar)
Gold Key: Feb, 1963 - No. 46, Jan, 1977 (All painted covers except #5)

1-Origin & 1st app. Magnus; Aliens (1st app.) series begins 20.00 60.00 220.00
2,3 9.00 27.00 100.00
4-10: 10-Simonson fan club illo (5/65, 1st-a?) 5.00 15.00 55.00
11-20 2.90 8.70 32.00
21,24-28: 28-Aliens ends 2.00 6.00 22.00
22,23: 22-Origin-r/#1 2.20 6.60 24.00
29-46-Mostly reprints 1.00 3.00 10.00

NOTE: ***Manning** a-1-22, 28-43(r). **Spiegle** a-23, 44r.*

MAGNUS ROBOT FIGHTER (Also see Vintage Magnus)
Valiant/Acclaim Comics: May, 1991 - No. 64, Feb, 1996 ($1.75/$1.95/$2.25/$2.50)

1-Nichols/Layton-c/a; 1-8 have trading cards 2.00
2-5: 4-Rai cameo. 5-Origin & 1st full app. Rai (10/91); 5-8 are in flip book format and back-c & half of book are Rai #1-4 mini-series 2.00
6-8: 6-1st Solar x-over. 7-Magnus vs. Rai-c/story; 1st X-O Armor. 8-Begin $1.95-c 2.00
0-Origin issue; Layton-a; ordered through mail w/coupons from 1st 8 issues plus 50¢; B. Smith trading card 3.00
0-Sold thru comic shops without trading card 2.00
9-11: 11-Last $1.95-c 2.00
12-(3.25, 44 pgs.)-Turok-c/story (1st app. in Valiant universe, 5/92); has 8 pg. Magnus story insert 5.00
13-20,22-24,26-48, 50-63: 14-1st app. Isak. 15,16-Unity x-overs. 15-Miller-c. 16-Birth of Magnus. 24-Story cont'd in Rai & the Future Force #9. 33-Timewalker app.36-Bound-in trading cards. 37-Rai & Starwatchers app. 44-Bound-in sneak peek card 2.25
21-New direction & new logo; Reese inks 2.25
21-Gold ink variant 4.00
25-($2.95)-Embossed silver foil-c; new costume 3.00
49, 64 ($2.50): 64-Magnus dies? 2.50
...Invasion (1994, $9.95)-r/Rai #1-4 & Magnus #5-8 1.00 3.00 10.00
Yearbook (1994, $3.95, 52 pgs.) 4.00

NOTE: ***Ditko/Reese** a-18. **Layton** a(i)-5; c-6-9i, 25; back(i)-5-8. **Reese** a(i)-22, 25, 28; c(i)-22, 24, 28. **Simonson** c-16. Prices for issues 1-8 are for trading cards and coupons intact.*

MAGNUS ROBOT FIGHTER
Acclaim Comics (Valiant Heroes): V2#1, May, 1997 - No. 17 ($2.50)

1-17: 1-Reintro Magnus; Donavon Wylie (X-O Manowar) cameo; Tom Peyer scripts & Mike McKone-c/a begin; painted variant-c exists 2.50

GD25 FN65 NM94

MAGNUS ROBOT FIGHTER 4000 A.D.
Valiant: 1990 - No. 2?, 1991 ($7.95, high quality paper, card stock-c, 96 pgs.)

1,2: Russ Manning-r in all. 1-Origin .90 2.70 8.00

MAGNUS ROBOT FIGHTER/NEXUS
Valiant/Dark Horse Comics: Dec, 1993 - No. 2, Apr, 1994 ($2.95, lim. series)

1,2: Steve Rude painted-c & pencils in all 3.00

MAID OF THE MIST (See American Graphics)

MAI, THE PSYCHIC GIRL
Eclipse Comics: May, 1987 - No. 28, July, 1989 ($1.50, B&W, bi-weekly, 44pgs.)

1-28 1.30
1,2-2nd print 1.20

MAJOR BUMMER
DC Comics: Aug, 1997 - No. 15, Oct, 1998 ($2.50)

1-Origin and 1st app. Major Bummer 3.00
2-15 2.50

MAJOR HOOPLE COMICS (See Crackajack Funnies)
Nedor Publications: nd (Jan, 1943)

1-Mary Worth, Phantom Soldier app. by Moldoff 36.00 108.00 270.00

MAJOR INAPAK THE SPACE ACE
Magazine Enterprises (Inapac Foods): 1951 (20 pgs.) (Giveaway)

1-Bob Powell-c/a 2.00

NOTE: *Many warehouse copies surfaced in 1973.*

MAJOR VICTORY COMICS (Also see Dynamic Comics)
H. Clay Glover/Service Publ./Harry 'A' Chesler: 1944 - No. 3, Summer, 1945

1-Origin Major Victory (patriotic hero) by C. Sultan (reprint from Dynamic #1); 1st app. Spider Woman 49.00 147.00 420.00
2-Dynamic Boy app. 36.00 108.00 270.00
3-Rocket Boy app. 31.00 92.00 230.00

MALIBU ASHCAN: RAFFERTY (See Firearm #12)
Malibu Comics (Ultraverse): Nov, 1994 (99¢, B&W w/color-c; one-shot)

1-Previews "The Rafferty Saga" storyline in Firearm; Chaykin-c. 1.00

MALTESE FALCON
David McKay Publications: No. 48, 1946

Feature Books 48-by Dashiell Hammett 64.00 191.00 540.00

MALU IN THE LAND OF ADVENTURE
I. W. Enterprises: 1964 (See White Princess of Jungle #2)

1-r/Avon's Slave Girl Comics #1; Severin-c 4.00 12.00 40.00

MAMMOTH COMICS
Whitman Publishing Co.(K. K. Publ.): 1938 (84 pgs.) (B&W, 8-1/2x11-1/2")

1-Alley Oop, Terry & the Pirates, Dick Tracy, Little Orphan Annie, Wash Tubbs, Moon Mullins, Smilin' Jack, Tailspin Tommy, Don Winslow, Dan Dunn, Smokey Stover & other reprints 147.00 441.00 1250.00

MAMMY YOKUM & THE GREAT DOGPATCH MYSTERY
Toby Press: 1951 (Giveaway)

nn-Li'l Abner 17.00 50.00 125.00
nn-Reprint (1956) 4.25 13.00 28.00

MAN AGAINST TIME
Image Comics (Motown Machineworks): May, 1996 - No. 3, June, 1996 ($2.25, limited series)

1-3: 1-Simonson-c. 2,3,-Leon-c. 2.25

MAN-BAT (See Batman Family, Brave & the Bold, & Detective #400)
National Periodical Publications/DC Comics: Dec-Jan, 1975-76 - No. 2, Feb-Mar, 1976; Dec, 1984

1-Ditko-a(p); Aparo-c; Batman app.; 1st app. She-Bat?

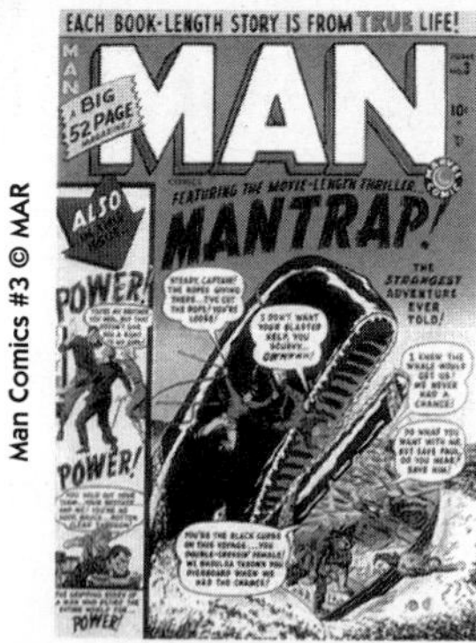

Man Comics #3 © MAR

Man From U.N.C.L.E. #13 © GK

Manhunter #3 © DC

GD25 FN65 NM94

.90 2.70 8.00
2-Aparo-c 2.00 6.00
1 (12/84)-N. Adams-r(3)/Det.(Vs. Batman on-c) 4.00

MAN-BAT
DC Comics: Feb, 1996 - No. 3, Apr, 1996 ($2.25, limited series)
1-3: Dixon scripts in all. 2-Killer Croc-c/app. 2.25

MAN CALLED A-X, THE
Malibu Comics (Bravura): Nov, 1994 - No. 4, Jun, 1995 ($2.95, limited series)
0-4: Marv Wolfman scripts & Shawn McManus-c/a. 0-(2/95). 1-"1A" on cover 3.00

MAN CALLED A-X, THE
DC Comics: Oct, 1997 - No. 8, May, 1998 ($2.50)
1-8: Marv Wolfman scripts & Shawn McManus-c/a. 2.50

MAN COMICS
Marvel/Atlas Comics (NPI): Dec, 1949 - No. 28, Sept, 1953 (#1-6: 52 pgs.)
1-Tuska-a 19.00 56.00 140.00
2-Tuska-a 10.00 30.00 75.00
3-6 8.50 26.00 60.00
7,8 7.85 23.50 55.00
9-13,15: 9-Format changes to war 5.70 17.00 35.00
14-Henkel (3 pgs.); Pakula-a 6.50 19.50 45.00
16-21,23-28: 28-Crime issue (Bob Brant) 5.00 15.00 30.00
22-Krigstein-a, 5 pgs. 6.50 19.50 45.00
NOTE: ***Berg** a-14, 15, 19. **Colan** a-9, 21. **Everett** a-8, 22; c-22, 25. **Heath** a-11, 17, 21. Kubertish a-by **Bob Brown**-3. **Maneely** a-11; c-10, 11. **Reinman** a-11. **Robinson** a-7, 10, 14. **Robert Sale** a-9, 11. **Sinnott** a-22, 23. **Tuska** a-14, 23.*

MANDRAKE THE MAGICIAN (See Defenders Of The Earth, 123, 46, 52, 55, Giant Comic Album, King Comics, Magic Comics, The Phantom #21, Tiny Tot Funnies & Wow Comics, '36)

MANDRAKE THE MAGICIAN (See Harvey Comics Hits #53)
David McKay Publ./Dell/King Comics (All 12¢): 1938 - 1948; Sept, 1966 - No. 10, Nov, 1967 (Also see Four Color #752)
Feature Books 18,19,25 (1938) 43.00 130.00 425.00
Feature Books 46 39.00 116.00 290.00
Feature Books 52,55 31.00 92.00 230.00
Four Color 752 (11/56) 9.00 27.00 100.00
1-Begin S.O.S. Phantom, ends #3 3.20 9.60 32.00
2-7,9: 4-Girl Phantom app. 5-Flying Saucer-c/story. 5,6-Brick Bradford app. 7-Origin Lothar. 9-Brick Bradford app. 1.80 5.40 18.00
8-Jeff Jones-a (4 pgs.) 2.80 8.40 28.00
10-Rip Kirby app.; Raymond-a (14 pgs.) 2.80 8.40 28.00

MANDRAKE THE MAGICIAN
Marvel Comics: Apr, 1995 - No. 2, May, 1995 ($2.95, unfinished limited series)
1,2: Mike Barr scripts 3.00

MAN-EATING COW (See Tick #7,8)
New England Comics: July, 1992 - No. 10, 1994? ($2.75, B&W, limited series)
1-10 3.00
Man-Eating Cow Bonanza (6/96, $4.95, 128 pgs.)-r/#1-4. 5.00

MAN FROM ATLANTIS (TV)
Marvel Comics: Feb, 1978 - No. 7, Aug, 1978
1-(84 pgs.)-Sutton-a(p), Buscema-c; origin & cast photos 3.00
2-7 2.00

MAN FROM PLANET X, THE
Planet X Productions: 1987 (no price;probably unlicensed)
1-Reprints Fawcett Movie Comic 1.00

MAN FROM U.N.C.L.E., THE (TV) (Also see The Girl From Uncle)
Gold Key: Feb, 1965 - No. 22, Apr, 1969 (All photo-c)
1 14.00 42.00 155.00
2-Photo back c-2-8 8.00 23.00 85.00

GD25 FN65 NM94

3-10: 7-Jet Dream begins (1st app., also see Jet Dream) (all new stories) 5.00 15.00 55.00
11-22: 21,22-Reprint #10 & 7 4.00 12.00 45.00

MAN FROM U.N.C.L.E., THE (TV)
Entertainment Publishing: 1987 - No. 11 ($1.50/$1.75, B&W)
1-7 ($1.50), 8-11 ($1.75) 2.00

MAN FROM WELLS FARGO (TV)
Dell Publishing Co.: No. 1287, Feb-Apr, 1962 - May-July, 1962 (Photo-c)
Four Color 1287, #01-495-207 5.00 15.00 55.00

MANGA SHI (See Tomoe)
Crusade Entertainment: Aug, 1996 ($2.95)
1-Printed backwards (manga-style) 3.00

MANGA SHI 2000
Crusade Entertainment: Feb, 1997 - No. 3, June, 1997 ($2.95, mini-series)
1-3: 1-Two covers 3.00

MANGA ZEN (Also see Zen Intergalactic Ninja)
Zen Comics (Fusion Studios): 1996 - No. 3, 1996 ($2.50, B&W)
1-3 2.50

MANGAZINE
Antarctic Press: Aug, 1985 - No. 4, Sept, 1986 (B&W)
1-Soft paper-c 2.00 6.00 20.00
2 1.50 4.50 15.00
3,4 1.00 3.00 10.00

MANGLE TANGLE TALES
Innovation Publishing: 1990 ($2.95, deluxe format)
1-Intro by Harlan Ellison 3.00

MANHUNT! (Becomes Red Fox #15 on)
Magazine Enterprises: Oct, 1947 - No. 14, 1953
1-Red Fox by L. B. Cole, Undercover Girl by Whitney, Space Ace begin (1st app.); negligee panels 43.00 129.00 360.00
2-Electrocution-c 35.00 106.00 265.00
3-6 30.00 90.00 225.00
7-10: 7-Space Ace ends. 8-Trail Colt begins (intro/1st app., 5/48) by Guardineer; Trail Colt-c. 10-G. Ingels-a 27.00 80.00 200.00
11(8/48)-Frazetta-a, 7 pgs.; The Duke, Scotland Yard begin 37.00 112.00 270.00
12 19.00 58.00 145.00
13(A-1 #63)-Frazetta, r-/Trail Colt #1, 7 pgs. 34.00 102.00 255.00
14(A-1 #77)-Bondage/hypo-c; last L. B. Cole Red Fox; Ingels-a 27.00 82.00 205.00
NOTE: ***Guardineer** a-1-5; c-8. **Whitney** a-2-14; c-1-6, 10. Red Fox by **L. B. Cole**-#1-14. #15 was advertised but came out as Red Fox #15. Bondage c-6.*

MANHUNTER (See Adventure #58, 73, Brave & the Bold, Detective Comics, 1st Issue Special, House of Mystery #143 and Justice League of America)
DC Comics: 1984 ($2.50, 76 pgs; high quality paper)
1-Simonson-c/a(r)/Detective; Batman app. 2.50

MANHUNTER
DC Comics: July, 1988 - No. 24, Apr, 1990 ($1.00)
1-24: 8,9-Flash app. 9-Invasion. 17-Batman-c/sty 1.00

MANHUNTER
DC Comics: No. 0, Nov, 1994 - No. 12, Nov, 1995 ($1.95/$2.25)
0-7 2.00
8-12: 8-Begin $2.25-c 2.25

MAN IN BLACK (See Thrill-O-Rama) (Also see All New Comics, Front Page, Green Hornet #31, Strange Story & Tally-Ho Comics)
Harvey Publications: Sept, 1957 - No. 4, Mar, 1958
1-Bob Powell-c/a 13.00 38.00 95.00

Man of War #8 © MAL

Man-Thing V3 #6 © MAR

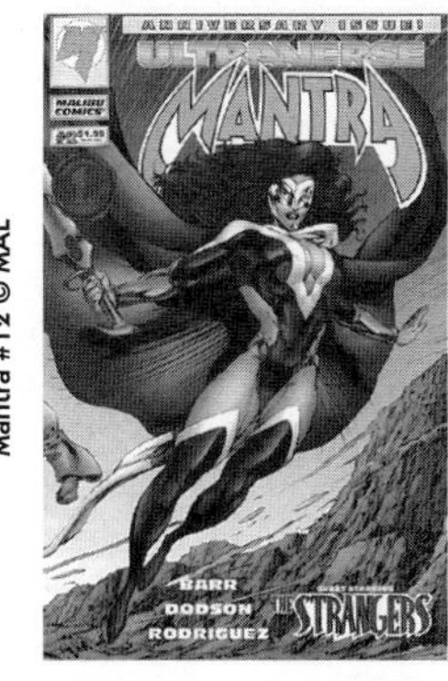

Mantra #12 © MAL

GD25 FN65 NM94

2-4: Powell-c/a 11.00 32.00 80.00

MAN IN BLACK
Lorne-Harvey Publications (Recollections): 1990 - No. 2, July, 1991 (B&W)

1,2 2.00

MAN IN FLIGHT (Disney, TV)
Dell Publishing Co.: No. 836, Sept, 1957

Four Color 836 6.40 19.00 70.00

MAN IN SPACE (Disney, TV, see Dell Giant #27)
Dell Publishing Co.: No. 716, Aug, 1956 - No. 954, Nov, 1958

Four Color 716-A science feat. from Tomorrowland 8.00 25.00 90.00
Four Color 954-Satellites 6.40 19.00 70.00

MAN OF PEACE, POPE PIUS XII
Catechetical Guild: 1950 (See Pope Pius XII... & To V2#8)

nn-All Powell-a 4.25 13.00 26.00

MAN OF STEEL, THE (Also see Superman: The Man of Steel)
DC Comics: 1986 (June release) - No. 6, 1986 (75¢, limited series)

1-Silver logo; Byrne-c/a/scripts in all; origin 3.00
1-Alternate-c for newsstand sales 3.00
1-Distr. to toy stores by So Much Fun 3.00
2-6: 2-Intro. Lois Lane, Jimmy Olsen. 3-Intro/origin Magpie; Batman-c/story. 4-Intro. new Lex Luthor 3.00
1-6-Silver Editions (1993, $1.95)-r/1-6 3.00
...The Complete Saga nn-Contains #1-6, given away in contest 3.00
Limited Edition, softcover 2.70 8.00 30.00

NOTE: *Issues 1-6 were released between Action #583 (9/86) & Action #584 (1/87) plus Superman #423 (9/86) & Advs. of Superman #424 (1/87).*

MAN OF THE ATOM (See Solar, Man of the Atom Vol. 2)

MAN OF WAR (See Liberty Guards & Liberty Scouts)
Centaur Publications: Nov, 1941 - No. 2, Jan, 1942

1-The Fire-Man, Man of War, The Sentinel, Liberty Guards, & Vapo-Man begin; Gustavson-c/a; Flag-c 141.00 423.00 1200.00
2-Intro The Ferret; Gustavson-c/a 109.00 327.00 925.00

MAN OF WAR
Eclipse Comics: Aug, 1987 - No. 3, Feb, 1988 ($1.75, Baxter paper)

1-3: Bruce Jones scripts 1.80

MAN OF WAR (See The Protectors)
Malibu Comics: 1993 - No, 8, Feb, 1994 ($1.95/$2.50/$2.25)

1-5 ($1.95)-Newsstand Editions w/different-c 2.00
1-5 ($2.50)-Collector's Editions w/poster 2.50
6-8 ($2.25): 6-Polybagged w/Skycap. 8-Vs. Rocket Rangers 2.25

MAN O' MARS
Fiction House Magazines: 1953; 1964

1-Space Rangers; Whitman-c 37.00 110.00 275.00
I.W. Reprint #1-r/Man O'Mars #1 & Star Pirate; Murphy Anderson-a 4.20 12.60 42.00

MANTECH ROBOT WARRIORS
Archie Enterprises, Inc.: Sept, 1984 - No. 4, Apr, 1985 (75¢)

1-4: Ayers-c/a(p). 1-Buckler-c(i) .80

MAN-THING (See Fear, Giant-Size..., Marvel Comics Presents, Marvel Fanfare, Monsters Unleashed, Power Record Comics & Savage Tales)
Marvel Comics Group: Jan, 1974 - No. 22, Oct, 1975; V2#1, Nov, 1979 - V2#11, July, 1981

1-Howard the Duck(2nd app.) cont'd/Fear #19 1.60 4.80 16.00
2 .90 2.70 9.00
3-1st app. original Foolkiller .85 2.60 7.00
4-Origin Foolkiller; last app. 1st Foolkiller 5.00
5-11-Ploog-a. 11-Foolkiller cameo (flashback) 4.00
12-22: 19-1st app. Scavenger. 20-Spidey cameo. 21-Origin Scavenger, Man-Thing. 22-Howard the Duck cameo 3.00
V2#1(1979) - 11 2.00

NOTE: ***Alcala** a-14. **Brunner** c-1. J. **Buscema** a-12p, 13p, 16p. **Gil Kane** c-4p, 10p, 12-20p, 21. **Mooney** a-17, 18, 19p, 20-22, V2#1-3p. **Ploog** Man-Thing-5p, 6p, 7, 8, 9-11p; c-5, 6, 8, 9, 11. **Sutton** a-13i. No. 19 says #10 in indicia.*

MAN-THING (Volume Three, continues in Strange Tales #1 (9/98))
Marvel Comics: Dec, 1997 - No. 8, July, 1998 ($2.99)

1-8-DeMatteis-s/Sharp-a. 2-Two covers. 6-Howard the Duck-c/app. 7,8-Namor-c/app. 3.00

MANTRA
Malibu Comics (Ultraverse): July, 1993 - No. 24, Aug, 1995 ($1.95/$2.50)

1-Polybagged w/trading card & coupon 2.00
1-Newsstand edition w/o trading card or coupon 2.00
1-Full cover holographic edition 1.50 4.50 15.00
1-Ultra-limited silver foil-c 2.00 6.00
2,3,5,6: 3-Intro Warstrike & Kismet. 6-Break-Thru x-over 2.25
2-($2.50- Newsstand edition bagged w/card 2.50
4-($2.50, 48 pgs.)-Rune flip-c/story by B. Smith (3 pgs.) 2.50
7-9,11-17: 7-Prime app.; origin Prototype by Jurgens/Austin (2 pgs.). 11-New costume. 17-Intro NecroMantra & Pinnacle; prelude to Godwheel. 2.00
10-($3.50, 68 pgs.)-Flip-c w/Ultraverse Premiere #2 3.50
18-24: 18-Begin $2.50-c 2.50
Giant Size 1 (7/94, $2.50, 44 pgs.) 2.50
...Spear of Destiny 1,2 (4/95, $2.50, 36pgs.) 2.50

MANTRA (2nd Series) (Also See Black September)
Malibu Comics (Ultraverse): Infinity, Sept, 1995 - No. 7, Apr, 1996 ($1.50)

Infinity (9/95, $1.50)-Black September x-over, Intro new Mantra. 1.50
1-7: 1-(10/95). 5-Return of Eden (original Mantra). 6,7-Rush app. 1.50

MAN WITH THE X-RAY EYES, THE (See X,... under Movie Comics)

MANY GHOSTS OF DR. GRAVES, THE (Doctor Graves #73 on)
Charlton Comics: 5/67 - No. 60, 12/76; No. 61, 9/77 - No. 62, 10/77; No. 63, 2/78 - No. 65, 4/78; No. 66, 6/81 - No. 72, 5/82

1-Palais-a; early issues 12¢-c 2.50 7.50 24.00
2-10 1.50 4.50 12.00
11-20 1.10 3.30 9.00
21-44 2.00 6.00
46-72: 47,49-Newton-a 5.00
45-1st Newton comic work (8 pgs.); new logo .90 2.70 9.00
Modern Comics Reprint 12,25 (1978) 4.00

NOTE: ***Aparo** a-4, 5, 7, 8, 66r, 69r; c-8, 14, 19, 66r, 67r. **Byrne** c-54. **Ditko** a-1, 7, 9, 11-13, 15-18, 20-22, 24, 26, 27, 35, 37, 38, 40-44, 47, 48, 51-54, 58, 60r-65r, 70, 72; c-11-13, 16-18, 22, 24, 26-35, 38, 40, 55, 58, 62-65. **Howard** a-45i; c-48. **Morisi** a-13, 14, 23, 26. **Newton** a-45, 47p, 49p; c-49, 52. **Sutton** a-42, 49; c-42, 44, 45; painted c-53.*

MANY LOVES OF DOBIE GILLIS (TV)
National Periodical Publications: May-June, 1960 - No. 26, Oct, 1964

1-Most covers by Bob Oskner 23.00 69.00 230.00
2-5 12.50 38.00 125.00
6-10 8.50 25.50 85.00
11-26: 20-Drucker-a 7.50 22.50 75.00

MARAUDER'S MOON (See Luke Short, Four Color #848)

MARCH OF COMICS (Boys' and Girls'...#3-353)
K. K. Publications/Western Publishing Co.: 1946 - No. 488, April, 1982 (#1-4 are not numbered) (K.K. Giveaway) (Founded by Sig Feuchtwanger)

Early issues were full size, 32 pages, and were printed with and without an extra cover of slick stock, just for the advertiser. The binding was stapled if the slick cover was added; otherwise, the pages were glued together at the spine. Most 1948 - 1951 issues were full size,24 pages, pulp covers. Starting in 1952 they were half-size and 32 pages with slick covers.1959 and later issues had only 16 pages plus covers. 1952 -1959 issues read oblong; 1960 and later issues read upright. All have new stories except where noted.

nn (#1, 1946)-Goldilocks; Kelly back-c (16 pgs., stapled)

March of Comics #20 © WDC

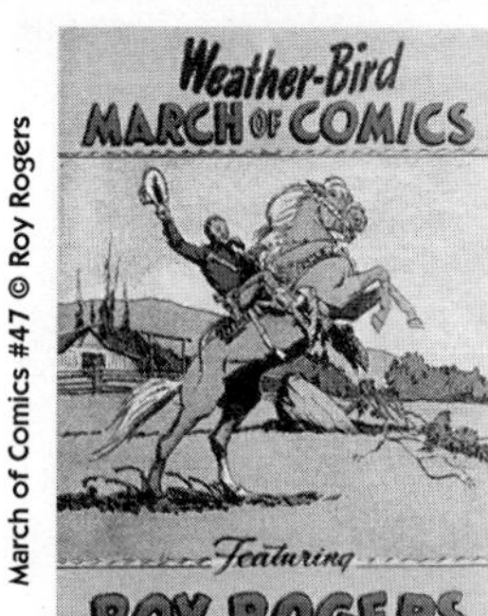

March of Comics #47 © Roy Rogers

March of Comics #70 © MGM

	GD25	FN65	NM94
	36.00	107.00	250.00
nn (#2, 1946)-How Santa Got His Red Suit; Kelly-a (11 pgs., r/4-Color #61 from 1944) (16pgs., stapled)	36.00	107.00	250.00
nn (#3, 1947)-Our Gang (Walt Kelly)	46.00	137.00	340.00
nn (#4)-Donald Duck by Carl Barks, "Maharajah Donald", 28 pgs.; Kelly-c? (Disney)	857.00	2571.00	7000.00
5-Andy Panda (Walter Lantz)	21.50	64.00	150.00
6-Popular Fairy Tales; Kelly-c; Noonan-a(2)	25.00	75.00	175.00
7-Oswald the Rabbit	24.00	71.00	165.00
8-Mickey Mouse, 32 pgs. (Disney)	71.00	215.00	500.00
9(nn)-The Story of the Gloomy Bunny	11.00	33.00	75.00
10-Out of Santa's Bag	10.00	30.00	70.00
11-Fun With Santa Claus	8.35	25.00	55.00
12-Santa's Toys	8.35	25.00	55.00
13-Santa's Surprise	8.35	25.00	55.00
14-Santa's Candy Kitchen	8.35	25.00	55.00
15-Hip-It-Ty Hop & the Big Bass Viol	8.35	25.00	50.00
16-Woody Woodpecker (1947)(Walter Lantz)	16.00	47.00	110.00
17-Roy Rogers (1948)	29.00	86.00	200.00
18-Popular Fairy Tales	13.00	39.00	90.00
19-Uncle Wiggily	11.00	33.00	75.00
20-Donald Duck by Carl Barks, "Darkest Africa", 22 pgs.; Kelly-c (Disney)	500.00	1500.00	4000.00
21-Tom and Jerry	13.00	39.00	90.00
22-Andy Panda (Lantz)	11.50	34.00	80.00
23-Raggedy Ann & Andy; Kerr-a	17.00	49.00	115.00
24-Felix the Cat, 1932 daily strip reprints by Otto Messmer	27.00	81.00	190.00
25-Gene Autry	27.00	81.00	190.00
26-Our Gang; Walt Kelly	26.00	79.00	185.00
27-Mickey Mouse; r/in M. M. #240 (Disney)	50.00	150.00	350.00
28-Gene Autry	26.00	79.00	185.00
29-Easter Bonnet Shop	5.85	17.50	40.00
30-Here Comes Santa	5.35	16.00	32.00
31-Santa's Busy Corner	5.35	16.00	32.00
32-No book produced			
33-A Christmas Carol (12/48)	5.35	16.00	32.00
34-Woody Woodpecker	11.50	34.00	80.00
35-Roy Rogers (1948)	29.00	86.00	200.00
36-Felix the Cat(1949); by Messmer; 1934 daily strip-r	24.00	71.00	165.00
37-Popeye	18.00	54.00	125.00
38-Oswald the Rabbit	10.00	30.00	58.00
39-Gene Autry	26.00	79.00	185.00
40-Andy and Woody	10.00	30.00	58.00
41-Donald Duck by Carl Barks, "Race to the South Seas", 22 pgs.; Kelly-c	500.00	1500.00	3500.00
42-Porky Pig	10.00	30.00	65.00
43-Henry	8.00	24.00	48.00
44-Bugs Bunny	11.00	33.00	75.00
45-Mickey Mouse (Disney)	39.00	116.00	270.00
46-Tom and Jerry	11.00	33.00	75.00
47-Roy Rogers	25.00	75.00	175.00
48-Greetings from Santa	4.25	13.00	26.00
49-Santa Is Here	4.25	13.00	26.00
50-Santa Claus' Workshop (1949)	4.25	13.00	26.00
51-Felix the Cat (1950) by Messmer	19.00	58.00	135.00
52-Popeye	15.00	45.00	105.00
53-Oswald the Rabbit	10.00	30.00	58.00
54-Gene Autry	23.00	69.00	160.00
55-Andy and Woody	8.70	26.00	52.00
56-Donald Duck; not by Barks; Barks art on back-c (Disney)	36.00	109.00	255.00
57-Porky Pig	8.70	26.00	60.00

	GD25	FN65	NM94
58-Henry	6.35	19.00	38.00
59-Bugs Bunny	10.00	30.00	65.00
60-Mickey Mouse (Disney)	35.00	105.00	245.00
61-Tom and Jerry	8.70	26.00	52.00
62-Roy Rogers	24.00	71.00	165.00
63-Welcome Santa (1/2-size, oblong)	4.25	13.00	26.00
64(nn)-Santa's Helpers (1/2-size, oblong)	4.25	13.00	26.00
65(nn)-Jingle Bells (1950) (1/2-size, oblong)	4.25	13.00	26.00
66-Popeye (1951)	13.00	39.00	90.00
67-Oswald the Rabbit	8.50	25.50	52.00
68-Roy Rogers	21.50	64.00	150.00
69-Donald Duck; Barks-a on back-c (Disney)	31.00	94.00	220.00
70-Tom and Jerry	8.00	24.00	48.00
71-Porky Pig	8.50	25.50	52.00
72-Krazy Kat	10.00	30.00	65.00
73-Roy Rogers	19.00	56.00	130.00
74-Mickey Mouse (1951)(Disney)	29.00	86.00	200.00
75-Bugs Bunny	8.70	26.00	52.00
76-Andy and Woody	8.00	24.00	48.00
77-Roy Rogers	18.00	54.00	125.00
78-Gene Autry (1951); last regular size issue	17.00	51.00	120.00
79-Andy Panda (1952, 5x7" size)	4.25	13.00	28.00
80-Popeye	11.50	34.00	80.00
81-Oswald the Rabbit	5.00	15.00	30.00
82-Tarzan; Lex Barker photo-c	19.00	58.00	135.00
83-Bugs Bunny	6.70	20.00	40.00
84-Henry	4.00	12.00	24.00
85-Woody Woodpecker	4.00	12.00	24.00
86-Roy Rogers	13.50	41.00	95.00
87-Krazy Kat	8.70	26.00	52.00
88-Tom and Jerry	5.70	17.00	34.00
89-Porky Pig	4.00	12.00	24.00
90-Gene Autry	13.00	39.00	90.00
91-Roy Rogers & Santa	13.00	39.00	90.00
92-Christmas with Santa	4.00	10.00	20.00
93-Woody Woodpecker (1953)	4.00	12.00	24.00
94-Indian Chief	10.00	30.00	70.00
95-Oswald the Rabbit	4.00	12.00	24.00
96-Popeye	10.00	30.00	68.00
97-Bugs Bunny	5.70	17.00	34.00
98-Tarzan; Lex Barker photo-c	21.00	62.00	145.00
99-Porky Pig	4.00	12.00	24.00
100-Roy Rogers	10.70	32.00	75.00
101-Henry	4.00	11.00	22.00
102-Tom Corbett (TV)('53, early app).; painted-c	17.00	49.00	115.00
103-Tom and Jerry	4.00	12.00	24.00
104-Gene Autry	11.00	33.00	75.00
105-Roy Rogers	11.00	33.00	75.00
106-Santa's Helpers	4.00	11.00	22.00
107-Santa's Christmas Book - not published			
108-Fun with Santa (1953)	4.00	11.00	22.00
109-Woody Woodpecker (1954)	4.00	11.00	22.00
110-Indian Chief	5.70	17.00	34.00
111-Oswald the Rabbit	4.00	11.00	22.00
112-Henry	4.00	10.00	20.00
113-Porky Pig	4.00	11.00	22.00
114-Tarzan; Russ Manning-a	21.00	62.00	145.00
115-Bugs Bunny	4.25	13.00	28.00
116-Roy Rogers	11.00	33.00	75.00
117-Popeye	10.00	30.00	68.00
118-Flash Gordon; painted-c	13.50	41.00	95.00
119-Tom and Jerry	4.00	11.00	22.00
120-Gene Autry	11.00	33.00	75.00
121-Roy Rogers	11.00	33.00	75.00

March of Comics #125 © ERB

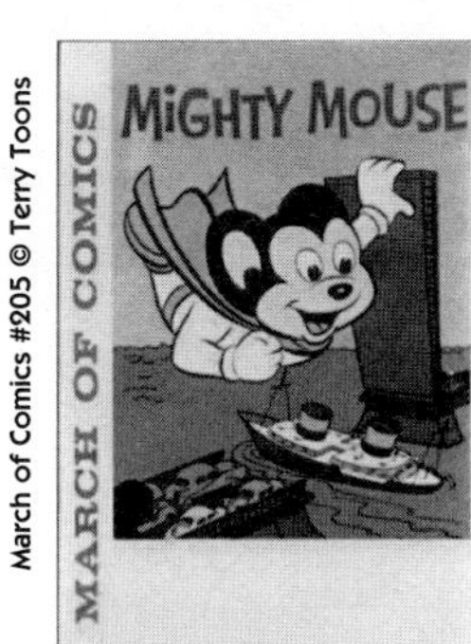

March of Comics #205 © Terry Toons

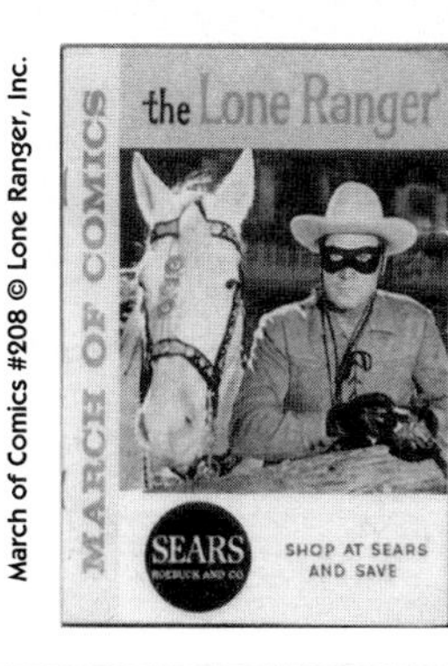

March of Comics #208 © Lone Ranger, Inc.

	GD25	FN65	NM94
122-Santa's Surprise (1954)	3.60	9.00	18.00
123-Santa's Christmas Book	3.60	9.00	18.00
124-Woody Woodpecker (1955)	4.00	10.00	20.00
125-Tarzan; Lex Barker photo-c	19.00	58.00	135.00
126-Oswald the Rabbit	4.00	10.00	20.00
127-Indian Chief	5.70	17.00	35.00
128-Tom and Jerry	4.00	10.00	20.00
129-Henry	3.40	8.50	17.00
130-Porky Pig	4.00	10.00	20.00
131-Roy Rogers	11.00	33.00	75.00
132-Bugs Bunny	4.00	12.00	24.00
133-Flash Gordon; painted-c	12.00	36.00	85.00
134-Popeye	8.00	24.00	48.00
135-Gene Autry	10.00	30.00	68.00
136-Roy Rogers	10.00	30.00	68.00
137-Gifts from Santa	2.80	7.00	14.00
138-Fun at Christmas (1955)	2.80	7.00	14.00
139-Woody Woodpecker (1956)	4.00	10.00	20.00
140-Indian Chief	5.70	17.00	35.00
141-Oswald the Rabbit	4.00	10.00	20.00
142-Flash Gordon	12.00	36.00	85.00
143-Porky Pig	4.00	10.00	20.00
144-Tarzan; Russ Manning-a; painted-c	18.00	54.00	125.00
145-Tom and Jerry	4.00	10.00	20.00
146-Roy Rogers; photo-c	11.00	33.00	75.00
147-Henry	3.00	7.50	15.00
148-Popeye	8.00	24.00	48.00
149-Bugs Bunny	4.00	11.00	22.00
150-Gene Autry	10.00	30.00	68.00
151-Roy Rogers	10.00	30.00	68.00
152-The Night Before Christmas	2.80	7.00	14.00
153-Merry Christmas (1956)	2.80	7.00	14.00
154-Tom and Jerry (1957)	4.00	10.00	20.00
155-Tarzan; photo-c	18.00	54.00	125.00
156-Oswald the Rabbit	4.00	10.00	20.00
157-Popeye	6.70	20.00	40.00
158-Woody Woodpecker	4.00	10.00	20.00
159-Indian Chief	5.70	17.00	35.00
160-Bugs Bunny	4.00	11.00	22.00
161-Roy Rogers	10.00	30.00	58.00
162-Henry	3.00	7.50	15.00
163-Rin Tin Tin (TV)	7.50	22.50	50.00
164-Porky Pig	4.00	10.00	20.00
165-The Lone Ranger	10.00	30.00	65.00
166-Santa and His Reindeer	2.80	7.00	14.00
167-Roy Rogers and Santa	10.00	30.00	58.00
168-Santa Claus' Workshop (1957)	2.80	7.00	14.00
169-Popeye (1958)	6.70	20.00	40.00
170-Indian Chief	5.70	17.00	35.00
171-Oswald the Rabbit	3.60	9.00	18.00
172-Tarzan	13.50	41.00	95.00
173-Tom and Jerry	3.60	9.00	18.00
174-The Lone Ranger	10.00	30.00	65.00
175-Porky Pig	3.60	9.00	18.00
176-Roy Rogers	9.15	27.00	55.00
177-Woody Woodpecker	3.60	9.00	18.00
178-Henry	3.00	7.50	15.00
179-Bugs Bunny	3.60	9.00	18.00
180-Rin Tin Tin (TV)	6.50	19.50	45.00
181-Happy Holiday	2.00	5.00	10.00
182-Happi Tim	3.20	8.00	16.00
183-Welcome Santa (1958)	2.40	6.00	12.00
184-Woody Woodpecker (1959)	3.20	8.00	16.00
185-Tarzan; photo-c	13.00	39.00	90.00
186-Oswald the Rabbit	3.20	8.00	16.00
187-Indian Chief	5.35	16.00	32.00
188-Bugs Bunny	3.20	8.00	16.00
189-Henry	2.80	7.00	14.00
190-Tom and Jerry	3.20	8.00	16.00
191-Roy Rogers	8.35	25.00	50.00
192-Porky Pig	3.20	8.00	16.00
193-The Lone Ranger	10.00	30.00	60.00
194-Popeye	5.85	17.50	35.00
195-Rin Tin Tin (TV)	6.00	18.00	40.00
196-Sears Special - not published			
197-Santa Is Coming	2.40	6.00	12.00
198-Santa's Helpers (1959)	2.40	6.00	12.00
199-Huckleberry Hound (TV)(1960, early app.)	7.15	21.50	50.00
200-Fury (TV)	5.35	16.00	32.00
201-Bugs Bunny	3.20	8.00	16.00
202-Space Explorer	9.15	27.50	55.00
203-Woody Woodpecker	2.80	7.00	14.00
204-Tarzan	10.00	30.00	70.00
205-Mighty Mouse	6.35	19.00	38.00
206-Roy Rogers; photo-c	8.35	25.00	50.00
207-Tom and Jerry	2.80	7.00	14.00
208-The Lone Ranger; Clayton Moore photo-c	12.00	36.00	85.00
209-Porky Pig	2.80	7.00	14.00
210-Lassie (TV)	6.35	19.00	38.00
211-Sears Special - not published			
212-Christmas Eve	2.40	6.00	12.00
213-Here Comes Santa (1960)	2.40	6.00	12.00
214-Huckleberry Hound (TV)(1961)	6.00	18.00	40.00
215-Hi Yo Silver	6.00	18.00	40.00
216-Rocky & His Friends (TV)(1961); predates Rocky and His Fiendish Friends #1 (see Four Color #1128)	10.00	30.00	70.00
217-Lassie (TV)	5.70	17.00	35.00
218-Porky Pig	2.80	7.00	14.00
219-Journey to the Sun	5.35	16.00	32.00
220-Bugs Bunny	3.20	8.00	16.00
221-Roy and Dale; photo-c	7.50	22.50	45.00
222-Woody Woodpecker	2.80	7.00	14.00
223-Tarzan	10.00	30.00	70.00
224-Tom and Jerry	2.80	7.00	14.00
225-The Lone Ranger	7.50	22.50	45.00
226-Christmas Treasury (1961)	2.40	6.00	12.00
227-Sears Special - not published?			
228-Letters to Santa (1961)	2.40	6.00	12.00
229-The Flintstones (TV)(1962); early app.; predates 1st Flintstones Gold Key issue (#7)	10.00	30.00	70.00
230-Lassie (TV)	5.00	15.00	30.00
231-Bugs Bunny	3.20	8.00	16.00
232-The Three Stooges	10.00	30.00	65.00
233-Bullwinkle (TV) (1962, very early app.)	11.00	32.00	75.00
234-Smokey the Bear	4.00	10.00	20.00
235-Huckleberry Hound (TV)	6.00	18.00	40.00
236-Roy and Dale	5.85	17.50	35.00
237-Mighty Mouse	4.70	14.00	28.00
238-The Lone Ranger	7.50	22.50	45.00
239-Woody Woodpecker	2.80	7.00	14.00
240-Tarzan	9.15	27.50	60.00
241-Santa Claus Around the World	2.00	5.00	10.00
242-Santa's Toyland (1962)	2.00	5.00	10.00
243-The Flintstones (TV)(1963)	9.15	27.50	55.00
244-Mister Ed (TV); early app.; photo-c	5.85	17.50	35.00
245-Bugs Bunny	3.20	8.00	16.00
246-Popeye	4.35	13.00	26.00
247-Mighty Mouse	4.70	14.00	28.00

March of Comics #280 © WEST

March of Comics #290 © WEST

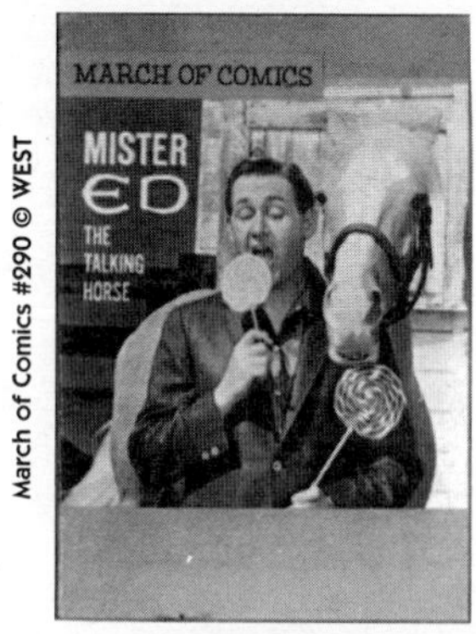

March of Comics #364 © H-B

	GD25	FN65	NM94
248-The Three Stooges	10.00	30.00	65.00
249-Woody Woodpecker	2.80	7.00	14.00
250-Roy and Dale	5.85	17.50	35.00
251-Little Lulu & Witch Hazel	14.00	43.00	100.00
252-Tarzan; painted-c	9.15	27.50	55.00
253-Yogi Bear (TV)	7.15	21.50	50.00
254-Lassie (TV)	5.35	16.00	32.00
255-Santa's Christmas List	2.40	6.00	12.00
256-Christmas Party (1963)	2.40	6.00	12.00
257-Mighty Mouse	4.70	14.00	28.00
258-The Sword in the Stone (Disney)	9.15	27.50	55.00
259-Bugs Bunny	3.20	8.00	16.00
260-Mister Ed (TV)	4.70	14.00	28.00
261-Woody Woodpecker	2.80	7.00	14.00
262-Tarzan	8.35	25.00	50.00
263-Donald Duck; not by Barks (Disney)	10.00	30.00	65.00
264-Popeye	4.35	13.00	26.00
265-Yogi Bear (TV)	5.70	17.00	35.00
266-Lassie (TV)	4.15	12.50	25.00
267-Little Lulu; Irving Tripp-a	11.50	34.00	80.00
268-The Three Stooges	10.00	30.00	60.00
269-A Jolly Christmas	2.00	5.00	10.00
270-Santa's Little Helpers	2.00	5.00	10.00
271-The Flintstones (TV)(1965)	9.15	27.50	60.00
272-Tarzan	8.35	25.00	50.00
273-Bugs Bunny	3.20	8.00	16.00
274-Popeye	4.35	13.00	26.00
275-Little Lulu; Irving Tripp-a	10.00	30.00	65.00
276-The Jetsons (TV)	16.00	47.00	110.00
277-Daffy Duck	3.20	8.00	16.00
278-Lassie (TV)	4.15	12.50	25.00
279-Yogi Bear (TV)	5.70	17.00	35.00
280-The Three Stooges; photo-c	10.00	30.00	60.00
281-Tom and Jerry	2.40	6.00	12.00
282-Mister Ed (TV)	4.70	14.00	28.00
283-Santa's Visit	2.40	6.00	12.00
284-Christmas Parade (1965)	2.40	6.00	12.00
285-Astro Boy (TV); 2nd app. Astro Boy	41.00	122.00	300.00
286-Tarzan	7.50	22.50	45.00
287-Bugs Bunny	3.20	8.00	16.00
288-Daffy Duck	2.80	7.00	14.00
289-The Flintstones (TV)	8.50	26.00	60.00
290-Mister Ed (TV); photo-c	4.00	12.00	24.00
291-Yogi Bear (TV)	5.00	15.00	30.00
292-The Three Stooges; photo-c	10.00	30.00	60.00
293-Little Lulu; Irving Tripp-a	9.15	27.50	55.00
294-Popeye	4.35	13.00	26.00
295-Tom and Jerry	2.40	6.00	12.00
296-Lassie (TV); photo-c	4.00	11.00	22.00
297-Christmas Bells	2.40	6.00	12.00
298-Santa's Sleigh (1966)	2.40	6.00	12.00
299-The Flintstones (TV)(1967)	8.50	26.00	60.00
300-Tarzan	7.50	22.50	45.00
301-Bugs Bunny	2.80	7.00	14.00
302-Laurel and Hardy (TV); photo-c	5.00	15.00	30.00
303-Daffy Duck	2.00	5.00	10.00
304-The Three Stooges; photo-c	9.15	27.50	55.00
305-Tom and Jerry	2.00	5.00	10.00
306-Daniel Boone (TV); Fess Parker photo-c	5.85	17.50	40.00
307-Little Lulu; Irving Tripp-a	7.50	22.50	45.00
308-Lassie (TV); photo-c	4.00	11.00	22.00
309-Yogi Bear (TV)	4.25	13.00	28.00
310-The Lone Ranger; Clayton Moore photo-c	12.00	36.00	85.00
311-Santa's Show	2.40	6.00	12.00

	GD25	FN65	NM94
312-Christmas Album (1967)	2.40	6.00	12.00
313-Daffy Duck (1968)	2.00	5.00	10.00
314-Laurel and Hardy (TV)	4.70	14.00	28.00
315-Bugs Bunny	2.80	7.00	14.00
316-The Three Stooges	7.50	22.50	45.00
317-The Flintstones (TV)	7.15	21.50	50.00
318-Tarzan	6.70	20.00	40.00
319-Yogi Bear (TV)	4.25	13.00	28.00
320-Space Family Robinson (TV); Spiegle-a	14.00	43.00	100.00
321-Tom and Jerry	2.00	5.00	10.00
322-The Lone Ranger	6.70	20.00	40.00
323-Little Lulu; not by Stanley	4.35	13.00	26.00
324-Lassie (TV); photo-c	4.00	11.00	22.00
325-Fun with Santa	2.40	6.00	12.00
326-Christmas Story (1968)	2.40	6.00	12.00
327-The Flintstones (TV)(1969)	7.15	21.50	50.00
328-Space Family Robinson (TV); Spiegle-a	14.00	43.00	100.00
329-Bugs Bunny	2.80	7.00	14.00
330-The Jetsons (TV)	11.50	34.00	80.00
331-Daffy Duck	2.00	5.00	10.00
332-Tarzan	5.35	16.00	32.00
333-Tom and Jerry	2.00	5.00	10.00
334-Lassie (TV)	4.00	10.00	20.00
335-Little Lulu	4.35	13.00	26.00
336-The Three Stooges	7.50	22.50	45.00
337-Yogi Bear (TV)	4.25	13.00	28.00
338-The Lone Ranger	6.70	20.00	40.00
339-(Was not published)			
340-Here Comes Santa (1969)	2.40	6.00	12.00
341-The Flintstones (TV)	7.15	21.50	50.00
342-Tarzan	5.35	16.00	32.00
343-Bugs Bunny	2.40	6.00	12.00
344-Yogi Bear (TV)	4.15	12.50	25.00
345-Tom and Jerry	2.00	5.00	10.00
346-Lassie (TV)	4.00	10.00	20.00
347-Daffy Duck	2.00	5.00	10.00
348-The Jetsons (TV)	10.00	30.00	70.00
349-Little Lulu; not by Stanley	4.00	11.00	22.00
350-The Lone Ranger	5.00	15.00	30.00
351-Beep-Beep, the Road Runner (TV)	2.80	7.00	14.00
352-Space Family Robinson (TV); Spiegle-a	14.00	43.00	100.00
353-Beep-Beep, the Road Runner (1971) (TV)	2.80	7.00	14.00
354-Tarzan (1971)	4.70	14.00	28.00
355-Little Lulu; not by Stanley	4.00	11.00	22.00
356-Scooby Doo, Where Are You? (TV)	7.15	21.50	50.00
357-Daffy Duck & Porky Pig	2.00	5.00	10.00
358-Lassie (TV)	4.00	10.00	20.00
359-Baby Snoots	2.80	7.00	14.00
360-H. R. Pufnstuf (TV); photo-c	7.15	21.50	50.00
361-Tom and Jerry	2.00	5.00	10.00
362-Smokey the Bear (TV)	2.00	5.00	10.00
363-Bugs Bunny & Yosemite Sam	2.40	6.00	12.00
364-The Banana Splits (TV); photo-c	5.70	17.00	40.00
365-Tom and Jerry (1972)	2.00	5.00	10.00
366-Tarzan	4.35	13.00	26.00
367-Bugs Bunny & Porky Pig	2.40	6.00	12.00
368-Scooby Doo (TV)(4/72)	5.70	17.00	40.00
369-Little Lulu; not by Stanley	3.60	9.00	18.00
370-Lassie (TV); photo-c	4.00	10.00	20.00
371-Baby Snoots	2.40	6.00	12.00
372-Smokey the Bear (TV)	2.00	5.00	10.00
373-The Three Stooges	6.70	20.00	40.00
374-Wacky Witch	2.00	5.00	10.00
375-Beep-Beep & Daffy Duck (TV)	2.00	5.00	10.00

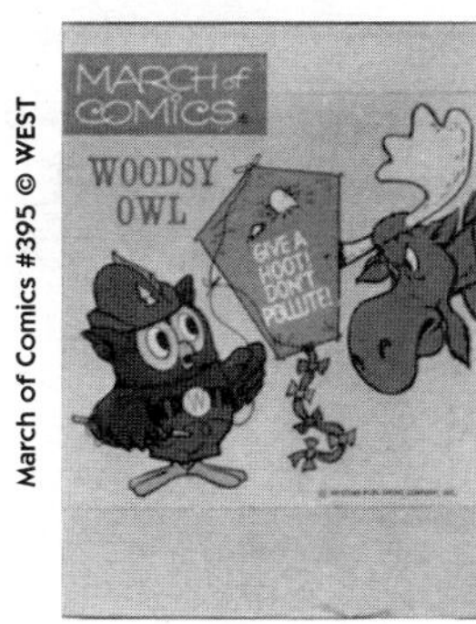

March of Comics #395 © WEST

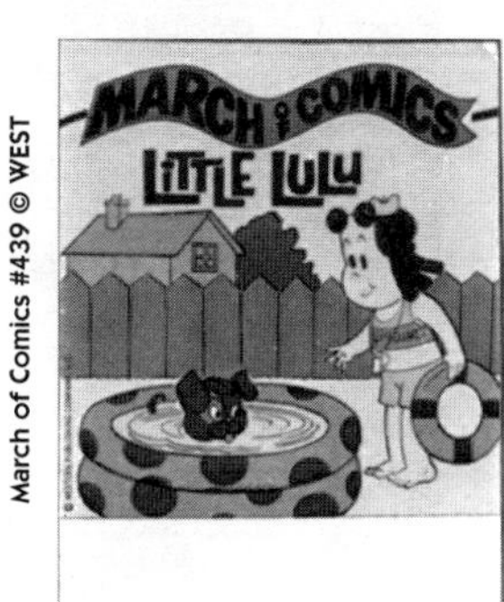

March of Comics #439 © WEST

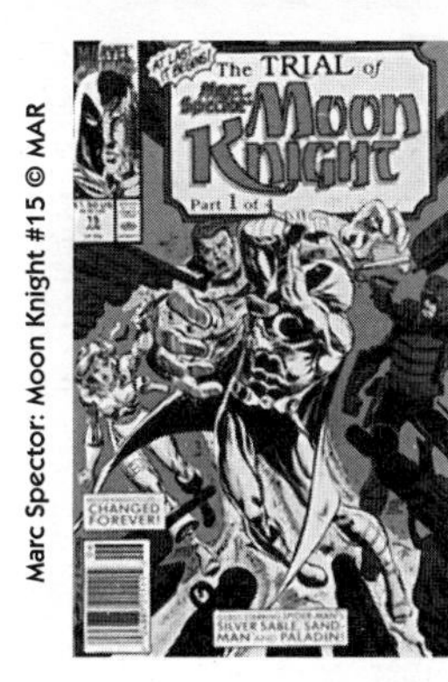

Marc Spector: Moon Knight #15 © MAR

	GD25	FN65	NM94
376-The Pink Panther (1972) (TV)	2.80	7.00	14.00
377-Baby Snoots (1973)	2.40	6.00	12.00
378-Turok, Son of Stone; new-a	16.00	47.00	110.00
379-Heckle & Jeckle New Terrytoons (TV)	2.00	5.00	10.00
380-Bugs Bunny & Yosemite Sam	2.00	5.00	10.00
381-Lassie (TV)	3.20	8.00	16.00
382-Scooby Doo, Where Are You? (TV)	5.00	15.00	30.00
383-Smokey the Bear (TV)	1.60	4.00	8.00
384-Pink Panther (TV)	2.00	5.00	10.00
385-Little Lulu	3.00	7.50	15.00
386-Wacky Witch	1.60	4.00	8.00
387-Beep-Beep & Daffy Duck (TV)	1.60	4.00	8.00
388-Tom and Jerry (1973)	1.60	4.00	8.00
389-Little Lulu; not by Stanley	3.00	7.50	15.00
390-Pink Panther (TV)	1.60	4.00	8.00
391-Scooby Doo (TV)	4.15	12.50	25.00
392-Bugs Bunny & Yosemite Sam	1.20	3.00	6.00
393-New Terrytoons (Heckle & Jeckle) (TV)	1.20	3.00	6.00
394-Lassie (TV)	2.40	6.00	12.00
395-Woodsy Owl	1.20	3.00	6.00
396-Baby Snoots	1.60	4.00	8.00
397-Beep-Beep & Daffy Duck (TV)	1.20	3.00	6.00
398-Wacky Witch	1.20	3.00	6.00
399-Turok, Son of Stone; new-a	13.00	39.00	90.00
400-Tom and Jerry	1.20	3.00	6.00
401-Baby Snoots (1975) (r/#371)	1.60	4.00	8.00
402-Daffy Duck (r/#313)	1.00	2.50	5.00
403-Bugs Bunny (r/#343)	1.20	3.00	6.00
404-Space Family Robinson (TV)(r/#328)	10.00	30.00	70.00
405-Cracky	1.00	2.50	5.00
406-Little Lulu (r/#355)	2.40	6.00	12.00
407-Smokey the Bear (TV)(r/#362)	1.20	3.00	6.00
408-Turok, Son of Stone; c-r/Turok #20 w/changes; new-a	9.30	28.00	65.00
409-Pink Panther (TV)	1.00	2.50	5.00
410-Wacky Witch	.80	2.00	4.00
411-Lassie (TV)(r/#324)	2.40	6.00	12.00
412-New Terrytoons (1975) (TV)	.80	2.00	4.00
413-Daffy Duck (1976)(r/#331)	.80	2.00	4.00
414-Space Family Robinson (r/#328)	9.30	28.00	65.00
415-Bugs Bunny (r/#329)	.80	2.00	4.00
416-Beep-Beep, the Road Runner (r/#353)(TV)	.80	2.00	4.00
417-Little Lulu (r/#323)	2.40	6.00	12.00
418-Pink Panther (r/#384) (TV)	.80	2.00	4.00
419-Baby Snoots (r/#377)	1.00	2.50	5.00
420-Woody Woodpecker	.80	2.00	4.00
421-Tweety & Sylvester	.80	2.00	4.00
422-Wacky Witch (r/#386)	.80	2.00	4.00
423-Little Monsters	1.00	2.50	5.00
424-Cracky (12/76)	.80	2.00	4.00
425-Daffy Duck	.80	2.00	4.00
426-Underdog (TV)	5.00	15.00	30.00
427-Little Lulu (r/#335)	1.60	4.00	8.00
428-Bugs Bunny	.60	1.50	3.00
429-The Pink Panther (TV)	.60	1.50	3.00
430-Beep-Beep, the Road Runner (TV)	.60	1.50	3.00
431-Baby Snoots	.80	2.00	4.00
432-Lassie (TV)	1.20	3.00	6.00
433-437: 433-Tweety & Sylvester. 434-Wacky Witch. 435-New Terrytoons (TV). 436-Wacky Advs. of Cracky. 437-Daffy Duck	.60	1.50	3.00
438-Underdog (TV)	4.15	12.50	25.00
439-Little Lulu (r/#349)	1.60	4.00	8.00
440-442,444-446: 440-Bugs Bunny. 441-The Pink Panther (TV). 442-Beep-Beep, the Road Runner (TV). 444-Tom and Jerry. 445-Tweety and Sylvester. 446-Wacky Witch	.60	1.50	3.00
443-Baby Snoots	.80	2.00	4.00
447-Mighty Mouse	1.20	3.00	6.00
448-455,457,458: 448-Cracky. 449-Pink Panther (TV). 450-Baby Snoots 451-Tom and Jerry. 452-Bugs Bunny. 453-Popeye. 454-Woody Woodpecker. 455-Beep-Beep, the Road Runner (TV). 457-Tweety & Sylvester. 458-Wacky Witch	.60	1.50	3.00
456-Little Lulu (r/#369)	1.20	3.00	6.00
459-Mighty Mouse	1.20	3.00	6.00
460-466: 460-Daffy Duck. 461-The Pink Panther (TV). 462-Baby Snoots. 463-Tom and Jerry. 464-Bugs Bunny. 465-Popeye. 466-Woody Woodpecker	.60	1.50	3.00
467-Underdog (TV)	4.00	10.00	20.00
468-Little Lulu (r/#385)	.80	2.00	4.00
469-Tweety & Sylvester	.60	1.50	3.00
470-Wacky Witch	.60	1.50	3.00
471-Mighty Mouse	.80	2.50	5.00
472-474,476-478: 472-Heckle & Jeckle(12/80). 473-Pink Panther(1/81)(TV). 474-Baby Snoots. 476-Bugs Bunny. 477-Popeye. 478-Woody Woodpecker	.60	1.50	3.00
475-Little Lulu (r/#323)	.80	2.00	4.00
479-Underdog (TV)	3.00	7.50	15.00
480-482: 480-Tom and Jerry. 481-Tweety and Sylvester. 482-Wacky Witch	.60	1.50	3.00
483-Mighty Mouse	.80	2.00	5.00
484-487: 484-Heckle & Jeckle. 485-Baby Snoots. 486-The Pink Panther (TV). 487-Bugs Bunny	.60	1.50	3.00
488-Little Lulu (4/82) (r/#335)	.80	2.00	4.00

MARCH OF CRIME (Formerly My Love Affair #1-6) (See Fox Giants)
Fox Features Synd.: No. 7, July, 1950 - No. 2, Sept, 1950; No. 3, Sept, 1951

	GD25	FN65	NM94
7(#1)(7/50)-True crime stories; Wood-a	35.00	106.00	265.00
2(9/50)-Wood-a (exceptional)	33.00	100.00	250.00
3(9/51)	15.00	44.00	110.00

MARCO POLO
Charlton Comics Group: 1962 (Movie classic)

	GD25	FN65	NM94
nn (Scarce)-Glanzman-c/a (25 pgs.)	9.50	28.50	95.00

MARC SPECTOR: MOON KNIGHT (Also see Moon Knight)
Marvel Comics: June, 1989 - No. 60, Mar, 1994 ($1.50/$1.75, direct sales)

	NM94
1-21: 4-Intro new Midnight. 8,9-Punisher app. 15-Silver Sable app. 20-Guice-c. 21-23-Cowan-c(p). 19-21-Spider-Man & Punisher app.	2.00
22-24,26-31,34: 34-Last $1.50-c	1.75
25-($2.50, 52 pgs.)-Ghost Rider app.	2.50
32,33,35-38: 32,33-Hobgoblin II (Macendale) & Spider-Man (in black costume) app. 35-38-Punisher story	2.00
39-49,51-54: 42-44-Infinity War x-over. 46-Demogoblin app. 51,53-Gambit app.	1.75
50-($2.95, 56 pgs.)-Special die-cut cover	3.00
55-New look & Stephen Platt-c/a begin	2.50
56,57-Platt-c/a. 57-Spider-Man-c/story	2.50
58-60: 58,59-S. Platt-c only. 60-S.Platt-c/a; Moon Knight dies.	2.00
...: Divided We Fall ($4.95, 52 pgs.)	5.00
Special 1 (1992, $2.50)	2.50

NOTE: *Heath c/a-4. Platt c-a*

MARGARET O'BRIEN (See The Adventures of...)

MARGE'S LITTLE LULU (Little Lulu #207 on)
Dell Publishing Co./Gold Key #165-206: No. 74, 6/45 - No. 164, 7-9/62; No. 165, 10/62 - No. 206, 8/72

Marjorie Henderson Buell, born in Philadelphia, Pa., in 1904, created Little Lulu, a cartoon character that appeared weekly in the Saturday Evening Post from Feb. 23, 1935 through Dec. 30, 1944. She was not responsible for any of the comic books. **John Stanley** did pencils only on all Little Lulu comics through at least #135 (1959). He did pencils and inks on Four Color #74 & 97. **Irving Tripp** began inking stories from #1 on, and remained the comic's illustrator throughout its entire run. **Stanley** did storyboards (layouts), pencils, and scripts in all cases and inking only on

Marge's Little Lulu #1 © Marjorie H. Buell

Marge's Tubby #22 © Marjorie H. Buell

Marines In Battle #2 © ATLAS

GD25 FN65 NM94

covers. His word balloons were written in cursive. **Tripp** and occasionally other artists at Western Publ. in Poughkeepsie, N.Y. blew up the pencilled pages, inked the blowups, and lettered them. **Arnold Drake** did storyboards, pencils and scripts starting with #197 (1970) on, amidst reprinted issues. **Buell** sold her rights exclusively to Western Publ. in Dec., 1971. The earlier issues had to be approved by **Buell** prior to publication.

Four Color 74('45)-Intro Lulu, Tubby & Alvin 91.00 273.00 1000.00
Four Color 97(2/46) 43.00 130.00 475.00
(Above two books are all John Stanley - cover, pencils, and inks.)
Four Color 110('46)-1st Alvin Story Telling Time; 1st app. Willy 31.00 93.00 340.00
Four Color 115-1st app. Boys' Clubhouse 31.00 93.00 340.00
Four Color 120, 131: 120-1st app. Eddie 26.00 80.00 295.00
Four Color 139('47),146,158 25.00 75.00 275.00
Four Color 165 (10/47)-Smokes doll hair & has wild hallucinations. 1st Tubby detective story 25.00 75.00 275.00
1(1-2/48)-Lulu's Diary feature begins 52.00 157.00 575.00
2-1st app. Gloria; 1st Tubby story in a L.L. comic; 1st app. Miss Feeny 26.00 80.00 295.00
3-5 24.00 72.00 265.00
6-10: 7-1st app. Annie; Xmas-c 17.00 53.00 195.00
11-20: 18-X-Mas-c. 19-1st app. Wilbur. 20-1st app. Mr. McNabbem 15.00 46.00 170.00
21-30: 26-r/F.C. 110. 30-Xmas-c 12.00 37.00 135.00
31-38,40: 35-1st Mumday story 11.00 33.00 120.00
39-Intro. Witch Hazel in "That Awful Witch Hazel" 12.00 35.00 130.00
41-60: 42-Xmas-c. 45-2nd Witch Hazel app. 49-Gives Stanley & others credit 10.00 30.00 110.00
61-80: 63-1st app. Chubby (Tubby's cousin). 68-1st app. Prof. Cleff. 78-Xmas-c. 80-Intro. Little Itch (2/55) 7.00 20.00 75.00
81-99: 90-Xmas-c 5.00 15.00 55.00
100 5.50 16.50 60.00
101-130: 123-1st app. Fifi 4.50 13.50 50.00
131-164: 135-Last Stanley-p 3.60 11.00 40.00
165-Giant; ...in Paris ('62) 11.00 33.00 120.00
166-Giant; ...Christmas Diary (1962 - '63) 11.00 33.00 120.00
167-169 3.20 9.50 35.00
170,172,175,176,178-196,198-200-Stanley-r. 182-1st app. Little Scarecrow Boy 1.60 4.80 16.00
171,173,174,177,197 1.00 3.00 10.00
201,203,206-Last issue to carry Marge's name .90 2.70 8.00
202,204,205-Stanley-r 1.20 3.60 12.00
...& Tubby in Japan (12¢)(5-7/62) 01476-207 6.00 18.00 65.00
...Summer Camp 1(8/67-G.K.-Giant) '57-58-r 4.00 12.00 45.00
...Trick 'N' Treat 1(12¢)(12/62-Gold Key) 5.00 15.00 55.00

NOTE: *See Dell Giant Comics #23, 29, 36, 42, 50, & Dell Giants for annuals. All Giants not by Stanley from L.L. on Vacation (7/54) on. Irving Tripp a-#1-on. Christmas c-7, 18, 30, 42, 78, 90, 126, 166, 250. Summer Camp issues #173, 177, 181, 189, 197, 201, 206.*

MARGE'S LITTLE LULU (See Golden Comics Digest #19, 23, 27, 29, 33, 36, 40, 43, 46, & March of Comics #251, 267, 275, 293, 307, 323, 335, 349, 355, 369, 385, 406, 417, 427, 439, 456, 468, 475, 488)

MARGE'S TUBBY (Little Lulu)(See Dell Giants)
Dell Publishing Co./Gold Key: No. 381, Aug, 1952 - No. 49, Dec-Feb, 1961-62

Four Color 381(#1)-Stanley script; Irving Tripp-a 17.00 53.00 195.00
Four Color 430,444-Stanley-a 10.00 30.00 115.00
Four Color 461 (4/53)-1st Tubby & Men From Mars story; Stanley-a 9.00 26.00 100.00
5 (7-9/53)-Stanley-a 7.00 20.00 80.00
6-10 5.50 16.50 60.00
11-20 4.00 12.00 45.00
21-30 3.00 9.00 32.00
31-49 2.50 7.40 27.00
...& the Little Men From Mars No. 30020-410(10/64-G.K.)-25¢, 68 pgs. 7.00 21.00 75.00

NOTE: ***John Stanley** did all storyboards & scripts through at least #35 (1959). **Lloyd White** did all art except F.C. 381, 430, 444, 461 & #5.*

MARGIE (See My Little...)

MARGIE (TV)
Dell Publ. Co.: No. 1307, Mar-May, 1962 - No. 2, July-Sept, 1962 (Photo-c)

Four Color 1307(#1), 2 3.60 11.00 40.00

MARGIE COMICS (Formerly Comedy Comics; Reno Browne #50 on)
(Also see Cindy Comics & Teen Comics)
Marvel Comics (ACI): No. 35, Winter, 1946-47 - No. 49, Dec, 1949

35 11.00 34.00 85.00
36-38,42,45,47-49 6.50 19.50 45.00
39,41,43(2),44,46-Kurtzman's "Hey Look" 9.30 28.00 65.00
40-Three "Hey Looks", three "Giggles 'n' Grins" by Kurtzman 10.00 30.00 75.00

MARINES (See Tell It to the...)

MARINES ATTACK
Charlton Comics: Aug, 1964 - No. 9, Feb-Mar, 1966

1-Glanzman-a begins 2.50 7.50 20.00
2-9 1.50 4.50 12.00

MARINES AT WAR (Formerly Tales of the Marines #4)
Atlas Comics (OPI): No. 5, Apr, 1957 - No. 7, Aug, 1957

5-7 5.70 17.00 38.00

NOTE: ***Colan** a-5. **Drucker** a-5. **Everett** a-5. **Maneely** a-5. **Orlando** a-7. **Severin** c-5.*

MARINES IN ACTION
Atlas News Co.: June, 1955 - No. 14, Sept, 1957

1-Rock Murdock, Boot Camp Brady begin 8.50 25.50 60.00
2-14 5.70 17.00 38.00

NOTE: ***Berg** a-2, 8, 9, 11, 14. **Heath** c-2, 9. **Maneely** c-1. **Severin** a-4; c-7-11, 14.*

MARINES IN BATTLE
Atlas Comics (ACI No. 1-12/WPI No. 13-25): Aug, 1954 - No. 25, Sept, 1958

1-Heath-c; Iron Mike McGraw by Heath; history of U.S. Marine Corps. begins 15.00 44.00 110.00
2-Heath-c 8.50 26.00 60.00
3-6,8-10: 4-Last precode (2/55) 6.00 18.00 42.00
7-Kubert/Moskowitz-a (6 pgs.) 7.00 21.00 48.00
11-16,18-21,24 5.70 17.00 38.00
17-Williamson-a (3 pgs.) 8.00 24.00 55.00
22,25-Torres-a 6.00 18.00 42.00
23-Crandall-a; Mark Murdock app. 7.00 21.00 48.00

NOTE: ***Berg** a-22. **G. Colan** a-22, 23. **Drucker** a-6. **Everett** a-4, 15; c-21. **Heath** c-1, 2, 4. **Maneely** c-23, 24. **Orlando** a-14. **Pakula** a-6, 23. **Powell** a-16. **Severin** a-22; c-12. **Sinnott** a-23. **Tuska** a-15.*

MARINE WAR HEROES (Charlton Premiere #19 on)
Charlton Comics: Jan, 1964 - No. 18, Mar, 1967

1-Montes/Bache-c/a 2.50 7.50 20.00
2-18: 14,18-Montes/Bache-a 1.50 4.50 12.00

MARK, THE (Also see Mayhem)
Dark Horse Comics: Dec, 1993 - No. 4, Mar, 1994 ($2.50, limited series)

1-4 2.50

MARK HAZZARD: MERC
Marvel Comics Group: Nov, 1986 - No. 12, Oct, 1987 (75¢)

1-12: Morrow-a .80
Annual 1 (11/87, $1.25) 1.25

MARK OF ZORRO (See Zorro, Four Color #228)

MARKSMAN, THE (Also see Champions)
Hero Comics: Jan, 1988 - No. 5, 1988 ($1.95)

1-5: 1-Rose begins. 1-3-Origin The Marksman 2.00
Annual 1 ('88, $2.75, 52pgs)-Champions app. 2.80

MARK STEEL
American Iron & Steel Institute: 1967, 1968, 1972 (Giveaway) (24 pgs.)

The Marriage of Hercules and Xena #1 © Universal

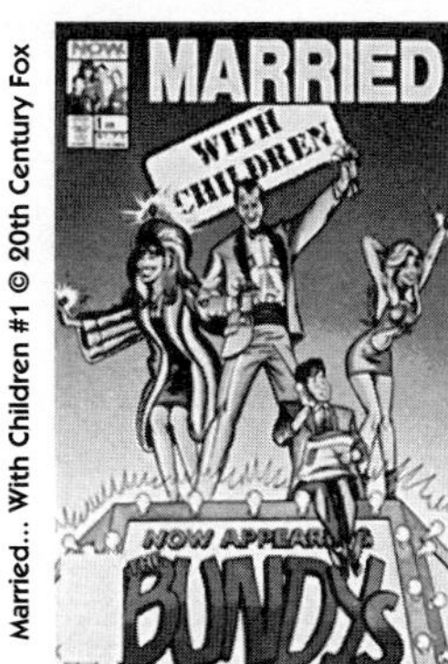

Married... With Children #1 © 20th Century Fox

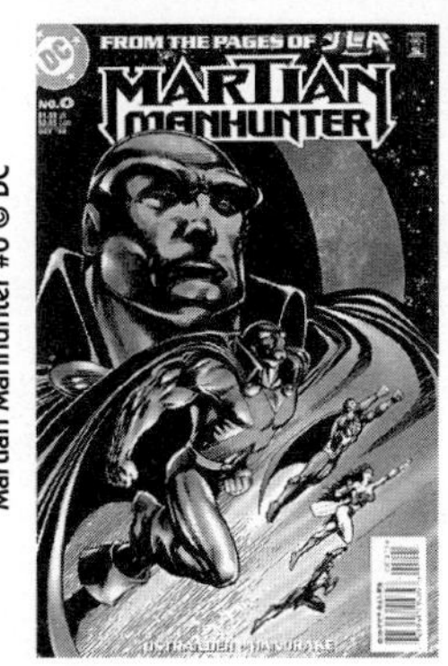

Martian Manhunter #0 © DC

	GD25	FN65	NM94
1967,1968- "Journey of Discovery with..."; Neal Adams art	2.25	6.75	18.00
1972- "...Fights Pollution"; N. Adams-a	.90	2.70	9.00

MARK TRAIL
Standard Magazines (Hall Syndicate)/Fawcett Publ. No. 5: Oct, 1955; No. 5, Summer, 1959

	GD25	FN65	NM94
1(1955)-Sunday strip-r	5.70	17.00	35.00
5(1959)	4.00	10.00	20.00
...Adventure Book of Nature 1 (Summer, 1958, 25¢, Pines)-100 pg. Giant; Special Camp Issue; contains 78 Sunday strip-r	7.85	23.50	55.00

MARMADUKE MONK
I. W. Enterprises/Super Comics: No date; 1963 (10¢)

	GD25	FN65	NM94
I.W. Reprint 1 (nd)	1.00	3.00	8.00
Super Reprint 14 (1963)-r/Monkeyshines Comics #?	1.00	3.00	8.00

MARMADUKE MOUSE
Quality Comics Group (Arnold Publ.): Spring, 1946 - No. 65, Dec, 1956 (Early issues: 52 pgs.)

	GD25	FN65	NM94
1-Funny animal	15.00	44.00	110.00
2	7.85	23.50	55.00
3-10	5.70	17.00	40.00
11-30	5.00	15.00	30.00
31-65: Later issues are 36 pgs.	4.00	12.00	24.00
Super Reprint #14(1963)	1.50	4.50	12.00

MARRIAGE OF HERCULES AND XENA, THE
Topps Comics: July, 1998 ($2.95, one-shot)

1-Photo-c; Lopresti-a; Alex Ross pin-up 3.00
1-Alex Ross painted-c 3.00
1-Gold foil logo-c 5.00

MARRIED ... WITH CHILDREN (TV)
Now Comics: June, 1990 - No. 7, Feb, 1991(12/90 inside) ($1.75)
V2#1, Sept, 1991 - No. 12, 1992 ($1.95)

1-7: Based on Fox TV show. 2-Photo-c 1.75
1,2-2nd printing ($1.75) 1.75
V2#1-12: 1,4,5,9-Photo-c 1.75
...Buck's Tale (6/94, $1.95) 2.00
...1994 Annual nn (2/94, $2.50, 52 pgs.)-Flip book format 2.50
Special 1 (7/92, $1.95)-Kelly Bundy photo-c/poster 2.00

MARRIED ... WITH CHILDREN: KELLY BUNDY
Now Comics: Aug, 1992 - No. 3, Oct, 1992 ($1.95, limited series)

1-3: Kelly Bundy photo-c & poster in each 2.00

MARRIED ... WITH CHILDREN: QUANTUM QUARTET
Now Comics: Oct, 1993 - No. 4, 1994, ($1.95, limited series)

1-4: Fantastic Four parody 2.00

MARRIED ... WITH CHILDREN: 2099
Now Comics: June, 1993 - No. 3, Aug, 1993 ($1.95, limited series)

1-3 2.00

MARS
First Comics: Jan, 1984 - No. 12, Jan, 1985 ($1.00, Mando paper)

nn: 1-12: Marc Hempel & Mark Wheatley story & art. 2-The Black Flame begins. 10-Dynamo Joe begins 1.00

MARS & BEYOND (Disney, TV)
Dell Publishing Co.: No. 866, Dec, 1957

	GD25	FN65	NM94
Four Color 866-A Science feat. from Tomorrowland	8.00	25.00	90.00

MARS ATTACKS
Topps Comics: May, 1994 - No. 5, Sept, 1994 ($2.95, limited series)

	GD25	FN65	NM94
1-5-Giffen story; flip books			4.00
Special Edition	1.20	3.60	12.00

Trade paperback (12/94, $12.95)-r/limited series plus new 8 pg. story 13.00

MARS ATTACKS
Topps Comics: V2#1, 8/95 - V2#3, 10/95; V2#4, 1/96 - No. 7, 5/96($2.95, bi-monthly #6 on)

V2#1-7: 1-Counterstrike storyline begins. 4-(1/96). 5-(1/96). 5,7-Brereton-c. 6-(3/96)-Simonson-c. 7-Story leads into Baseball Special #1 3.00
Baseball Special 1 (6/96, $2.95)-Bisley-c. 3.00

MARS ATTACKS HIGH SCHOOL
Topps Comics: May, 1997 - No. 2, Sept, 1997 ($2.95, B&W, limited series)

1,2-Stelfreeze-c 3.00

MARS ATTACKS IMAGE
Topps Comics: Dec, 1996 - No. 4, Mar, 1997 ($2.50, limited series)

1-4-Giffen-s/Smith/Sienkiewicz-a 2.50

MARS ATTACKS THE SAVAGE DRAGON
Topps Comics: Dec, 1996 - No. 4, Mar, 1997 ($2.95, limited series)

1-4: 1--w/bound-in card 3.00

MARSHAL BLUEBERRY (See Blueberry)
Marvel Comics (Epic Comics): 1991 (14.95, graphic novel)

	GD25	FN65	NM94
1-Moebius-a	1.50	4.50	15.00

MARSHAL LAW (Also see Crime And Punishment: Marshall Law...)
Marvel Comics (Epic Comics): Oct, 1987 - No. 6, May, 1989 ($1.95, mature)

1-6 2.00

M.A.R.S. PATROL TOTAL WAR (Formerly Total War #1,2)
Gold Key: No. 3, Sept, 1966 - No. 10, Aug, 1969 (All-Painted-c except #7)

	GD25	FN65	NM94
3-Wood-a; aliens invade USA	4.80	14.40	48.00
4-10	2.50	7.50	24.00

MARTHA WASHINGTON (Also see Dark Horse Presents Fifth Anniversary Special, Dark Horse Presents #100-4, Give Me Liberty, Happy Birthday Martha Washington & San Diego Comicon Comics #2)

MARTHA WASHINGTON GOES TO WAR
Dark Horse Comics (Legend): May, 1994 - No. 5, Sep, 1994 ($2.95, lim. series)

1-5-Miller scripts; Gibbons-c/a 3.00
TPB ($17.95) r/#1-5 17.95

MARTHA WASHINGTON SAVES THE WORLD
Dark Horse Comics: Dec, 1997 - No. 3, Feb, 1998 ($2.95/$3.95, lim. series)

1,2-Miller scripts; Gibbons-c/a in all 3.00
3-($3.95) 4.00

MARTHA WASHINGTON STRANDED IN SPACE
Dark Horse Comics (Legend): Nov, 1995 ($2.95, one-shot)

nn-Miller-s/Gibbons-a; Big Guy app. 3.00

MARTHA WAYNE (See The Story of...)

MARTIAN MANHUNTER (See Detective Comics & Showcase '95 #9)
DC Comics: May, 1988 - No. 4, Aug,. 1988 ($1.25, limited series)

1-4: 1,4-Batman app. 2-Batman cameo 1.25
Special 1-(1996, $3.50) 3.50

MARTIAN MANHUNTER (See JLA)
DC Comics: No. 0, Oct, 1998 - Present ($1.99)

0-Origin retold; Ostrander-s/Mandrake-c/a 2.00
1-3: 1-(12/98) 2.00
#1,000,000 (11/98) 853rd Century x-over 2.00
Annual 1 (1998, $2.95) Ghosts; Wrightson-c 3.00

MARTIAN MANHUNTER: AMERICAN SECRETS
DC Comics: 1992 - Book Three, 1992 ($4.95, limited series, prestige format)

1-3: Barreto-a 5.00

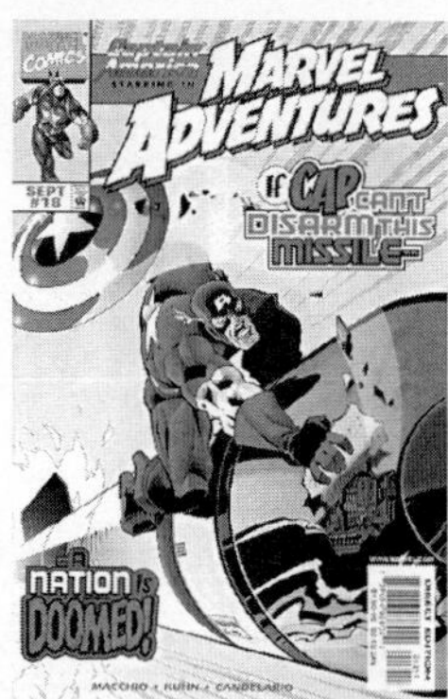

Marvel Adventures #18 © MAR

Marvel Collectible Classics #4 © MAR

Marvel Comics Presents #43 © MAR

GD25 FN65 NM94

MARTIN KANE (William Gargan as... Private Eye)(Stage/Screen/Radio/TV)
Fox Features Syndicate (Hero Books): No. 4, June, 1950 - No. 2, Aug, 1950 (Formerly My Secret Affair)

4(#1)-True crime stories; Wood-c/a(2); used in **SOTI**, pg. 160; photo back-c 25.00 76.00 190.00
2-Wood/Orlando story, 5 pgs; Wood-a(2) 20.00 60.00 150.00

MARTY MOUSE
I. W. Enterprises: No date (1958?) (10¢)

1-Reprint 1.25 3.75 10.00

MARVEL ACTION HOUR FEATURING IRON MAN (TV cartoon)
Marvel Comics: Nov, 1994 - No. 8, June, 1995 ($1.50/$2.95)

1-8: Based on cartoon series 1.50
1 ($2.95)-Polybagged w/16 pg Marvel Action Hour Preview & acetate print 3.00

MARVEL ACTION HOUR FEATURING THE FANTASTIC FOUR (TV cartoon)
Marvel Comics: Nov, 1994 - No. 8, June, 1995 ($1.50/$2.95)

1-8: Based on cartoon series 1.50
1-($2.95)-Polybagged w/ 16 pg. Marvel Action Hour Preview & acetate print 3.00

MARVEL ACTION UNIVERSE (TV cartoon)
Marvel Comics: Jan, 1989 ($1.00, one-shot)

1-r/Spider-Man And His Amazing Friends 1.00

MARVEL ADVENTURES
Marvel Comics: Apr, 1997 - No. 18, Sept, 1998 ($1.50)

1-18-"Animated style": 1,4,7-Hulk-c/app. 2,11-Spider-Man. 3,8,15-X-Men. 5-Spider-Man & X-Men. 6-Spider-Man & Human Torch. 9,12-Fantastic Four. 10,16-Silver Surfer. 13-Spider-Man & Silver Surfer. 14-Hulk & Dr. Strange 18-Capt. America 1.50

MARVEL ADVENTURES STARRING DAREDEVIL (...Adventure #3 on)
Marvel Comics Group: Dec, 1975 - No. 6, Oct, 1976

1 .90 2.70 8.00
2-6-r/Daredevil #22-27 by Colan 4.00

MARVEL AND DC PRESENT FEATURING THE UNCANNY X-MEN AND THE NEW TEEN TITANS
Marvel Comics/DC Comics: 1982 ($2.00, 68 pgs., one-shot, Baxter paper)

1-3rd app. Deathstroke the Terminator; Darkseid app.; Simonson/Austin-c/a 1.50 4.50 15.00

MARVEL BOY (Astonishing #3 on; see Marvel Super Action #4)
Marvel Comics (MPC): Dec, 1950 - No. 2, Feb, 1951

1-Origin Marvel Boy by Russ Heath 82.00 247.00 700.00
2-Everett-a 64.00 191.00 540.00

MARVEL CHILLERS (Also see Giant-Size Chillers)
Marvel Comics Group: Oct, 1975 - No. 7, Oct, 1976 (All 25¢ issues)

1-Intro. Modred the Mystic, ends #2; Kane-c(p) 2.00 6.00
2,4,5,7: 4-Kraven app. 5,6-Red Wolf app. 7-Kirby-c; Tuska-p 4.00
3-Tigra, the Were-Woman begins (origin), ends #7 (see Giant-Size Creatures #1). Chaykin/Wrightson-c. 1.00 3.00 10.00
6-Byrne-a(p); Buckler-c(p) 5.00
NOTE: ***Bolle** a-1. **Buckler** c-2.*

MARVEL CLASSICS COMICS SERIES FEATURING... (Also see Pendulum Illustrated Classics)
Marvel Comics Group: 1976 - No. 36, Dec, 1978 (52 pgs., no ads)

1-Dr. Jekyll and Mr. Hyde 1.20 3.60 12.00
2-10,28: 28-1st Golden-c/a; Pit and the Pendulum .90 2.70 9.00
11-27,29-36 .85 2.60 7.00
NOTE: ***Adkins** c-1i, 4i, 12i. **Alcala** a-34i; c-34. **Bolle** a-35. **Buscema** c-17p, 19p, 26p. **Golden** c/a-28. **Gil Kane** c-1-16p, 21p, 22p, 24p, 32p. **Nebres** a-5; c-24i. **Nino** a-2, 8, 12. **Redondo** a-1, 9. No. 1-12 were reprinted from Pendulum Illustrated Classics.*

GD25 FN65 NM94

MARVEL COLLECTIBLE CLASSICS: AVENGERS
Marvel Comics: 1998 ($10.00, reprints with chromium wraparound-c)

1-Reprints Avengers Vol.3, #1; Perez-c 10.00

MARVEL COLLECTIBLE CLASSICS: X-MEN
Marvel Comics: 1998 ($10.00, reprints with chromium wraparound-c)

1-Reprints (Uncanny) X-Men #1 & 2; Adam Kubert-c 10.00
2-Reprints Uncanny X-Men #141 & 142; Byrne-c 10.00
3-Reprints (Uncanny) X-Men #137; Larroca-c 10.00
4-Reprints X-Men #25; Andy Kubert-c 10.00
5-Reprints Giant Size X-Men #1; Gary Frank-c 10.00

MARVEL COLLECTOR'S EDITION
Marvel Comics: 1992 (Ordered thru mail with Charleston Chew candy wrapper)

1-Flip-book format; Spider-Man, Silver Surfer, Wolverine (by Sam Kieth), & Ghost Rider stories; Wolverine back-c by Kieth 3.00

MARVEL COLLECTOR'S EDITION: X-MEN
Marvel Comics: 1993 (3-3/4x6-1/2")

1-4-Pizza Hut giveaways 3.00

MARVEL COLLECTORS' ITEM CLASSICS (Marvel's Greatest #23 on)
Marvel Comics Group(ATF): Feb, 1965 - No. 22, Aug, 1969 (25¢, 68 pgs.)

1-Fantastic Four, Spider-Man, Thor, Hulk, Iron Man-r begin 6.35 19.00 70.00
2 (4/66) 3.15 9.50 35.00
3,4 2.50 7.50 28.00
5-10 2.00 6.00 22.00
11-22: 22-r/The Man in the Ant Hill/TTA #27 1.50 4.50 16.00
NOTE: *All reprints; **Ditko**, **Kirby** art in all.*

MARVEL COMICS (Marvel Mystery Comics #2 on)
Timely Comics (Funnies, Inc.): Oct, Nov, 1939

NOTE: The first issue was originally dated October 1939. Most copies have a black circle stamped over the date (on cover and inside) with "November" printed over it. However, some copies do not have the November overprint and could have a higher value. Most No. 1's have printing defects, i.e., tilted pages which caused trimming into the panels usually on right side and bottom. Covers exist with and without gloss finish.

GD25 FN65 VF82 NM94

1-Origin Sub-Mariner by Bill Everett(1st newsstand app.); 1st 8 pgs. were produced for Motion Picture Funnies Weekly #1 which was probably not distributed outside of advance copies; intro Human Torch by Carl Burgos, Kazar the Great (1st Tarzan clone), & Jungle Terror(only app.); intro. The Angel by Gustavson, The Masked Raider & his horse Lightning (ends #12); cover by sci/fi pulp illustrator Frank R. Paul 10,500.00 31,500.00 63,000.00 115,000.00

MARVEL COMICS PRESENTS
Marvel Comics (Midnight Sons imprint #143 on): Early Sept, 1988 - No. 175, Feb, 1995 ($1.25/$1.50/$1.75, bi-weekly)

GD25 FN65 NM94

1-Wolverine by Buscema in #1-10 2.00 6.00
2-5 3.00
6-10: 6-Sub-Mariner app. 10-Colossus begins 2.50
11-32,34-37: 17-Cyclops begins. 19-1st app. Damage Control. 24-Havok begins. 25-Origin/1st app. Nth Man. 26-Hulk begins by Rogers. 29-Quasar app. 31-Excalibur begins by Austin (i). 32-McFarlane-a(p). 37-Devil-Slayer app. 1.50
33-Capt. America; Jim Lee-a 2.75
38-Wolverine begins by Buscema; Hulk app. 3.00
39-47,51-53: 39-Spider-Man app. 46-Liefeld Wolverine-c. 51-53-Wolverine by Rob Liefeld 2.50
48-50-Wolverine & Spider-Man team-up by Erik Larsen-c/a. 48-Wasp app. 49, 50-Savage Dragon prototype app. by Larsen. 50-Silver Surfer. 50-53-Comet Man; Bill Mumy scripts 3.00
54-61-Wolverine/Hulk story: 54-Werewolf by Night begins; The Shroud by Ditko. 58-Iron Man by Ditko. 59-Punisher 3.00
62-Deathlok & Wolverine stories 3.00

Marvel Comics Presents #157 © MAR

Marvel Comics Super Special #24 © MAR

Marvel Family #13 © FAW

GD25 FN65 NM94

63-Wolverine 2.50
64-71-Wolverine/Ghost Rider 8-part story. 70-Liefeld Ghost Rider/ Wolverine-c 2.50
72-Begin 13-part Weapon-X story (Wolverine origin) by B. Windsor-Smith (prologue) 4.00
73-Weapon-X part 1; Black Knight, Sub-Mariner 3.00
74-Weapon-X part 2; Black Knight, Sub-Mariner 2.50
75-80: 76-Death's Head story. 77-Mr. Fantastic story. 78-Iron Man by Steacy 80,81-Capt. America by Ditko/Austin 2.50
81-84: 81-Daredevil by Rogers/Williamson. 82-Power Man. 83-Human Torch by Ditko(a&scripts); $1.00-c direct, $1.25 newsstand. 84-Last Weapon-X (24 pg. conclusion) 2.25
85-Begin 8-part Wolverine story by Sam Keith (c/a); 1st Kieth-a on Wolverine; begin 8-part Beast story by Jae Lee(p) with Liefeld part pencils #85,86; 1st Jae Lee-a (assisted w/Liefeld, 1991) 4.50
86-89-Wolverine, Beast stories continue 2.50
90-Begin 8-part Ghost Rider & Cable story, ends #97; begin flip book format with two covers 3.00
91-94: 93-Begin 6-part Wolverine story, ends #98 2.00
95-98: 95-Begin $1.50-c. 98-Begin 2-part Ghost Rider story 1.50
99,101-107,112-116: 99-Spider-Man story. 101-Begin 6-part Ghost Rider/Dr. Strange story & begin 8-part Wolverine/Nightcrawler story by Colan/ Williamson; Punisher story. 107-Begin 6-part Ghost Rider/Werewolf by Night story. 112-Demogoblin story by Colan/Williamson; Pip the Troll story w/Starlin scripts & Gamora cameo. 113-Begin 6-part Giant-Man & begin 6-part Ghost Rider/Iron Fist stories 1.50
100-Full-length Ghost Rider/Wolverine story by Sam Keith w/Tim Vigil assists; anniversary issue, non flip-book 1.50
108-111: 108-Begin 4 part Thanos story; Starlin scripts. 109-Begin 8 part Wolverine/Typhoid Mary story. 111-Iron Fist 1.50
117-Preview of Ravage 2099 (1st app.); begin 6 part Wolverine/Venom story w/Kieth-a 1.50
118-Preview of Doom 2099 (1st app.) 1.50
119-142,147-152: 119-Begin Ghost Rider/Cloak & Dagger story by Colan. 120,136,138-Spider-Man. 123-Begin 8-part Ghost Rider/Typhoid Mary story; begin 4-part She Hulk story; begin 8-partWolverine/Lynx story. 125-Begin 6-part Iron Fist story. 129-Jae Lee back-c. 130-Begin 6-part Ghost Rider/ Cage story. 131-Begin 6-part Ghost Rider/Cage story. 132-Begin 5-part Wolverine story. 133-136-Iron Fist vs. Sabretooth. 136-Daredevil. 137-Begin 6-part Wolverine story & 6-part Ghost Rider story. 147-Begin 2-part Vengeance-c/story w/new Ghost Rider. 149-Vengeance-c/story w/new Ghost Rider. 150-Silver ink-c; begin 2-part Bloody Mary story w/Typhoid Mary, Wolverine, Daredevil, new Ghost Rider; intro Steel Raven. 152-Begin 4-part Wolverine, 4-part War Machine, 4-part Vengeance, 3-part Moon Knight stories; same date as War Machine #1 .70 1.75
143-146: ($1.75)-Siege of Darkness parts 3,6,11,14; all have spot-varnished covers. 143-Ghost Rider/Scarlet Witch; intro new Werewolf. 144-Begin 2-part Morbius story. 145-Begin 2-part Nightstalkers story. .70 1.75
153-175: 153-$1.75-c begins. 153-155-Bound-in Spider-Man trading card sheet .70 1.75
...Colossus: God's Country (1994, $6.95) r/#10-17 1.00 2.80 7.00
...Mini Comic Giveaway (1988, 4 1/4 x 6 1/4, 20 pgs.)(4 different issues)
nn-Alf 2.00 6.00
nn-Flintstone Kids .90 2.70 8.00
nn-Spider-Man-reprints Amazing Spider-Man #1 1.00 3.00 10.00
nn-X-Men-reprints X-Men #53; B. Smith-a 1.00 3.00 10.00

NOTE: ***Austin** a-31-37i; c(i)-48, 50, 99, 122. **Buscema** a-1-10, 38-47; c-6. **Byrne** a-79; c-71. **Colan** a(p)-36, 37. **Colan/Williamson** a-101-108. **Ditko** a-7p, 10, 56p, 58, 80, 81, 83. **Guice** a-62. **Sam Kieth** a-85-92, 117-122; c-85-98, 99p, 100-108, 117, 118, 120-122; back c-109-113, 117. **Jae Lee** c-129(back). **Liefeld** a-51, 52, 53p(2), 85p; c-46, 70. **McFarlane** c-32. **Mooney** a-73. **Rogers** a-26, 38, 46i, 81p. **Russell** a-10i; c-4i. **Saltares** a-8p(early), 38-45p. **Simonson** c-1. **B. Smith** a-72-84; c-72-84. **P. Smith** c-34. **Sparling** a-33. **Starlin** a-89i. **Staton** a-74. **Steacy** a-78. **Sutton** a-101-105. **Williamson** c-62i. Two Gun Kid by **Gil Kane** in #116, 122.*

MARVEL COMICS SUPER SPECIAL, A (Marvel Super Special #5 on)
Marvel Comics: Sept, 1977 - No. 41(?), Nov, 1986 (nn 7) ($1.50, magazine)

GD25 FN65 NM94

1-Kiss, 40 pgs. comics plus photos & features; Simonson-a(p); also see Howard the Duck #12; ink contains real KISS blood 9.00 27.00 100.00
2-Conan (1978) .90 2.70 9.00
3-Close Encounters of the Third Kind (1978); Simonson-a .85 2.60 7.00
4-The Beatles Story (1978)-Perez/Janson-a; has photos & articles 2.50 7.60 28.00
5-Kiss (1978)-Includes poster 9.00 27.00 100.00
6-Jaws II (1978) .85 2.60 7.00
7-Sgt. Pepper; Beatles movie adaptation; withdrawn from U.S. distribution
8-Battlestar Galactica; tabloid size ($1.50, 1978); adapts TV show 1.40 4.20 14.00
8-Modern-r of tabloid size; scarce 2.50 7.60 28.00
8-Battlestar Galactica; publ. in regular magazine format; low distribution ($1.50, 8-1/2x11") 1.40 4.20 14.00
9-Conan .85 2.60 7.00
10-Star-Lord 5.00
11-13-Weirdworld begins #11; 25 copy special press run of each with gold seal and signed by artists (Proof quality), Spring-June, 1979 7.25 22.00 80.00
11-13-Weirdworld (regular issues): 11-Fold-out centerfold 5.00
14-Miller-c(p); adapts movie "Meteor." 5.00
15-Star Trek with photos & pin-ups($1.50) 5.00
15-With $2.00 price (scarce); the price was changed at tail end of a 200,000 press run .85 2.60 7.00
16-20 (Movie adaptations): 16-Empire Strikes Back; Williamson-a. 17-Xanadu. 18-Raiders of the Lost Ark. 19-For Your Eyes Only (James Bond). 20-Dragonslayer 5.00
21-30 (Movie adaptations): 21-Conan. 22-Bladerunner; Williamson-a; Steranko-c. 23-Annie. 24-The Dark Crystal. 25-Rock and Rule-w/photos; artwork is from movie. 26-Octopussy (James Bond). 27-Return of the Jedi. 28-Krull; photo-c. 29-Tarzan of the Apes (Greystoke movie). 30-Indiana Jones and the Temple of Doom 5.00
31-41: 31-The Last Star Fighter. 32-The Muppets Take Manhattan. 33-Buckaroo Banzai. 34-Sheena. 35-Conan The Destroyer. 36-Dune. 37-2010. 38-Red Sonja. 39-Santa Claus:The Movie. 40-Labyrinth. 41-Howard The Duck 2.00 6.00

NOTE: ***J. Buscema** a-1, 2, 9, 11-13, 18p, 21, 35, 40; c-11(part), 12. **Chaykin** a-9, 19p; c-18, 19. **Colan** a(p)-6, 10, 14. **Morrow** a-34; c-1i, 34. **Nebres** a-11. **Spiegle** a-29. **Stevens** a-27. **Williamson** a-27. #22-28 contain photos from movies.*

MARVEL DOUBLE FEATURE
Marvel Comics Group: Dec, 1973 - No. 21, Mar, 1977

1-Capt. America, Iron Man-r/T.O.S. begin 1.00 3.00 10.00
2-10: 3-Last 20¢ issue 2.00 6.00
11-16,20,21 4.00
17-Story-r/Iron Man & Sub-Mariner #1; last 25ç issue 4.00
18,19-Colan/Craig-r from Iron Man #1 in both 5.00

NOTE: ***Colan** r-1-19p. **Craig** r-17-19i. **G. Kane** r-15p; c-15p. **Kirby** r-1-16p, 20, 21; c-17-20.*

MARVEL FAMILY (Also see Captain Marvel Adventures No. 18)
Fawcett Publications: Dec, 1945 - No. 89, Jan, 1954

1-Origin Captain Marvel, Captain Marvel Jr., Mary Marvel, & Uncle Marvel retold; origin/1st app. Black Adam 135.00 406.00 1150.00
2-The 3 Lt. Marvels & Uncle Marvel app. 64.00 192.00 540.00
3 44.00 132.00 375.00
4,5 39.00 117.00 310.00
6-10: 7-Shazam app. 33.00 100.00 250.00
11-20 25.00 75.00 185.00
21-30 19.00 57.00 145.00
31-40 17.00 51.00 125.00
41-46,48-50 13.00 39.00 95.00
47-Flying Saucer-c/story (5/50) 18.00 48.00 135.00
51-76,79,80,82-89: 79-Horror satire-c 12.00 36.00 90.00
77-Communist Threat-c 19.00 53.00 145.00
78,81-Used in **POP**, pg. 92,93. 13.00 40.00 100.00

Marvel Fanfare #10 (1st Series) © MAR

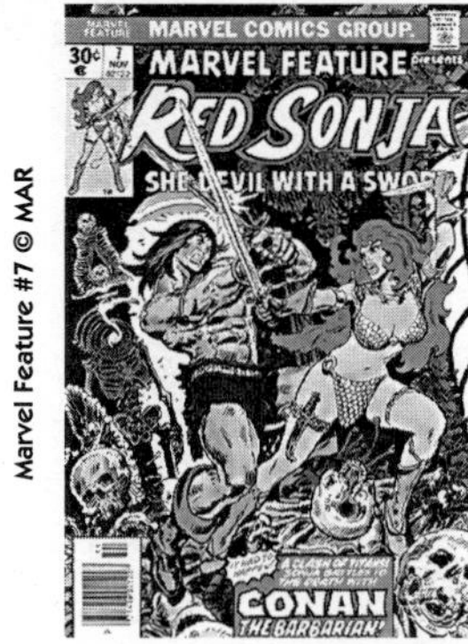

Marvel Feature #7 © MAR

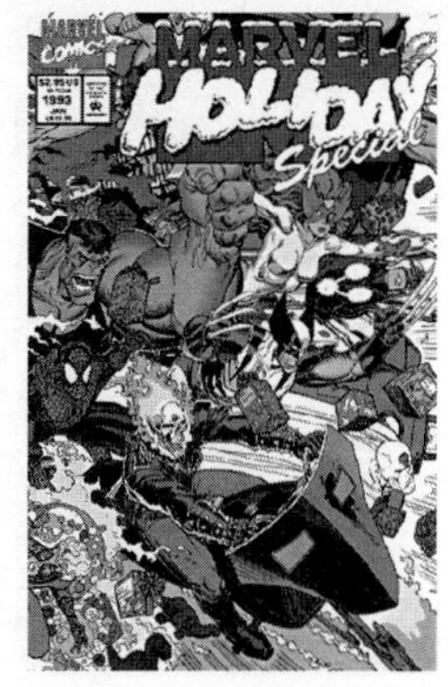

Marvel Holiday Special 1993 © MAR

GD25 FN65 NM94

MARVEL FANFARE (1st Series)
Marvel Comics Group: March, 1982 - No. 60, Jan, 1992 ($1.25/$2.25, slick paper, direct sales)

1-Spider-Man/Angel team-up; 1st Paul Smith-a (1st full story; see King Conan #7); Daredevil app. 5.00
2-Spider-Man, Ka-Zar, The Angel. F.F. origin retold 4.00
3,4-X-Men & Ka-Zar. 4-Deathlok, Spidey app. 3.00
5-Dr. Strange, Capt. America 2.50
6-15: 6-Spider-Man, Scarlet Witch. 7-Incredible Hulk; D.D. back-up(also 15). 8-Dr. Strange; Wolf Boy begins. 9-Man-Thing. 10-13-Black Widow. 14-The Vision. 15-The Thing by Barry Smith, c/a 2.25
16-32,34-50: 16,17-Skywolf. 16-Sub-Mariner back-up. 17-Hulk back-up. 18-Capt. America by Miller. 19-Cloak and Dagger. 20-Thing/Dr. Strange. 21-Thing/Dr. Strange/Hulk. 22,23-Iron Man vs. Dr. Octopus. 24-26-Weird-world. 24-Wolverine back-up. 27-Daredevil/Spider-Man. 28-Alpha Flight. 29-Hulk. 30-Moon Knight. 31,32-Captain America. 34-37-Warriors Three. 38-Moon Knight/Dazzler. 39-Moon Knight/Hawkeye. 40-Angel/Rogue & Storm. 41-Dr. Strange. 42-Spider-Man. 43-Sub-Mariner/Human Torch. 44-Iron Man vs. Dr. Doom by Ken Steacy. 45-All pin-up issue by Steacy, Art Adams & others. 46-Fantastic Four. 47-Hulk. 48-She-Hulk/Vision. 49-Dr. Strange/Nick Fury. 50-X-Factor; begin $2.25-c 2.25
33-X-Men, Wolverine app.; Punisher pin-up 2.50
51-($2.95, 52 pgs.)-Silver Surfer; Fantastic Four & Capt. Marvel app.; 51,52-Colan/Williamson back-up (Dr. Strange) 3.00
52,53: 52-54-Black Knight; 53-Iron Man back up 2.25
54,55-Wolverine back-ups. 55-Power Pack 2.50
56-60: 56-59-Shanna the She-Devil. 58-Vision & Scarlet Witch back-up. 60-Black Panther/Rogue/Daredevil stories 2.25

NOTE: ***Art Adams** c-13. **Austin** a-1i, 4i, 33i, 38i; c-8i, 33i. **Buscema** a-51p. **Byrne** a-1p, 29, 48; c-29. **Chiodo** painted c-56-59. **Colan** a-51p. **Cowan/Simonson** c/a-60. **Golden** a-1, 2, 4p, 47; c-1, 2, 47. **Infantino** c/a(p)-8. **Gil Kane** a-8-11p. **Miller** a-18; c-1(Back-c), 18. **Perez** a-10, 11p, 12, 13p; c-10-13p. **Rogers** a-5p; c-5p. **Russell** a-5i, 6i, 8-11i, 43i; c-5i, 6. **Paul Smith** a-1p, 4p, 32, 60; c-4p. **Staton** c/a-50(p). **Williamson** a-30i, 51i.*

MARVEL FANFARE (2nd Series)
Marvel Comics: Sept, 1996 - No. 6, Feb, 1997 (99¢)

1-6: 1-Capt. America & The Falcon-c/story; Deathlok app. 2-Wolverine & Hulk-c/app. 3-Ghost Rider & Spider-Man-c/app. 5-Longshot-c/app. 6-Sabretooth, Power Man, & Iron Fist-c/app 1.00

MARVEL FEATURE (See Marvel Two-In-One)
Marvel Comics Group: Dec, 1971 - No. 12, Nov, 1973 (1,2: 25¢ giants)(#1-3: quarterly)

1-Origin/1st app. The Defenders (Sub-Mariner, Hulk & Dr. Strange); see Sub-Mariner #34,35 for prequel; Dr. Strange solo story (predates D.S. #1) plus 1950s Sub-Mariner-r; Neal Adams-c 9.00 27.00 100.00
2-2nd app. Defenders; 1950s Sub-Mariner-r 5.00 15.00 55.00
3-Defenders ends 3.50 10.50 38.00
4-Re-intro Antman (1st app. since 1960s), begin series; brief origin; Spider-Man app. 1.60 4.80 16.00
5-7,9,10: 6-Wasp app. & begins team-ups. 9-Iron Man app. 10-Last Antman .85 2.60 7.00
8-Origin Antman & Wasp-r/TTA #44. 1.20 3.60 12.00
10-(7/73)-Variant w/4 extra pgs. ads on slick paper 2.00 6.00
11-Thing vs. Hulk; 1st Thing solo book (9/73); origin Fantastic Four retold 2.20 6.50 24.00
12-Thing/Iron Man; early Thanos app.; occurs after Capt. Marvel #33; Starlin-a(p) 1.20 3.60 12.00

NOTE: ***Bolle** a-9i. **Everett** a-1i, 3i. **Hartley** r-10. **Kane** c-3p, 7p. **Russell** a-7-10p. **Starlin** a-8, 11, 12; c-8.*

MARVEL FEATURE (Also see Red Sonja)
Marvel Comics: Nov, 1975 - No. 7, Nov, 1976 (Story cont'd in Conan #68)

1-Red Sonja begins (pre-dates Red Sonja #1); adapts Howard short story; Adams-r/Savage Sword of Conan #1 5.00
2,3,6: Thorne-c/a in #2-7 3.00

GD25 FN65 NM94

4,5-(Regular 25¢ edition)(5,7/76) 3.00
4,5-(30¢-c, limited distribution) 1.20 3.60 12.00
7-Battles Conan 2.00 6.00

MARVEL FRONTIER COMICS UNLIMITED
Marvel Frontier Comics: Jan, 1994 ($2.95, 68 pgs.)

1-Dances with Demons, Immortalis, Children of the Voyager, Evil Eye, The Fallen stories 3.00

MARVEL FUMETTI BOOK
Marvel Comics Group: Apr, 1984 ($1.00, one-shot)

1-All photos; Stan Lee photo-c; Art Adams touch-ups 3.00

MARVEL FUN & GAMES
Marvel Comics Group: 1979/80 (color comic for kids)

1-Games, puzzles, etc. (beware marked pages) 2.00 6.00
2-10,12,13 4.00
11-X-Men-c 2.00 6.00

MARVEL GRAPHIC NOVEL
Marvel Comics Group (Epic Comics): 1982 - No. 38, 1990? ($5.95/$6.95)

1-Death of Captain Marvel (2nd Marvel graphic novel); Capt. Marvel battles Thanos by Jim Starlin (c/a/scripts) 2.00 6.00 20.00
1 (2nd & 3rd printings) 5.00
2-Elric: The Dreaming City 1.40 4.20 14.00
3-Dreadstar; Starlin-c/a, 52 pgs. 1.40 4.20 14.00
4-Origin/1st app. The New Mutants (1982) 1.40 4.20 14.00
4,5-2nd printings 5.50
5-X-Men; book-length story (1982) 1.60 4.80 16.00
6-18: 6-The Star Slammers. 7-Killraven. 8-Super Boxers; Byrne scripts. 9-The Futurians. 10-Heartburst. 11-Void Indigo. 12-The Dazzler. 13-Starstruck. 14-The Swords Of The Swashbucklers. 15-The Raven Banner (Asgard). 16-The Aladdin Effect. 17-Revenge Of The Living Monolith. 18-She Hulk .90 2.70 8.00
19-21,23-31: 19-The Witch Queen of Acheron (Conan). 20-Greenberg the Vampire. 21-Marada the She-Wolf. 23-Dr. Strange. 24-Love and War (Daredevil); Miller scripts. 25-Alien Legion. 26-Dracula. 27-Avengers (Emperor Doom). 28-Conan the Reaver. 29-The Big Chance (Thing vs. Hulk). 30-A Sailor's Story. 31-Wolfpack. .90 2.70 9.00
22-Amaz. Spider-Man in Hooky by Wrightson 1.40 4.20 14.00
32-Death of Groo 1.40 4.20 14.00
32-2nd printing ($5.95) .85 2.60 7.00
33,34,36,37: 33-Thor. 34-Predator & Prey (Cloak & Dagger). 36-Willow (movie adapt.). 37-Hercules .90 2.70 9.00
35-Hitler's Astrologer (The Shadow, $12.95, hard-c) 1.50 4.50 15.00
35-Soft-c reprint (1990, $10.95) 1.10 3.30 11.00
38-Silver Surfer (Judgement Day)($14.95) 1.50 4.50 15.00
nn-Arena by Bruce Jones ($5.95) 2.00 6.00
nn-Black Widow Coldest War .90 2.70 9.00
nn-Inhumans (1988, $7.95)-Williamson-i .90 2.70 9.00
nn-Last of the Dragons (1988, $6.95) .85 2.60 7.00
nn-Who Framed Roger Rabbit (1989, $6.95) 1.00 3.00 10.00
nn-Roger Rabbit In The Resurrection Of Doom (1989, $8.95) 1.00 3.00 10.00

NOTE: ***Aragones** a-27, 32. **Buscema** a-38. **Byrne** c/a-18. **Heath** a-35i. **Kaluta** a-13, 35p; c-13. **Miller** a-24p. **Simonson** a-6; c-6. **Starlin** c/a-1,3. **Williamson** a-34. **Wrightson** c-29i.*

MARVEL-HEROES & LEGENDS
Marvel Comics: Oct, 1996; 1997 ($2.95)

nn-Wraparound-c 3.00
...1997 ($2.99) -Original Avengers story 3.00

MARVEL HOLIDAY SPECIAL
Marvel Comics: No. 1, 1991 ($2.25, 84 pgs.); nn, Jan, 1993 ($2.95, 68 pgs.)

1-X-Men, Fantastic Four, Punisher, Thor, Capt. America, Ghost Rider, Capt. Ultra, Spidey stories; Art Adams-c/a 2.25
nn (1/93)-Wolverine, Thanos (by Starlin/Lim/Austin) 3.00

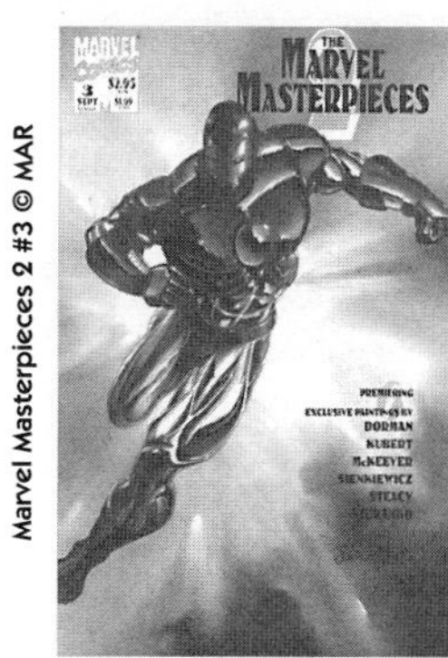

Marvel Masterpieces 2 #3 © MAR

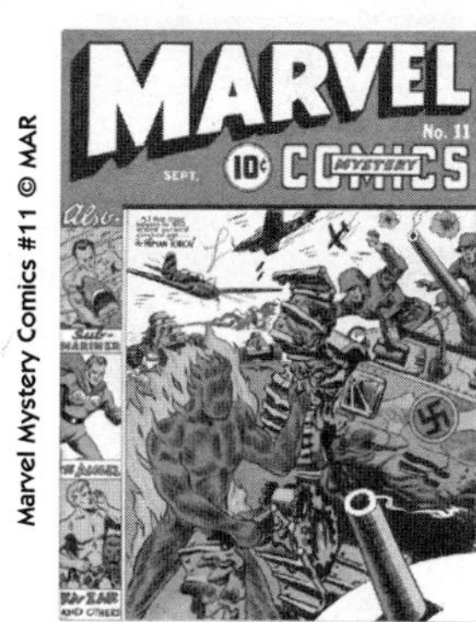

Marvel Mystery Comics #11 © MAR

Marvel Mystery Comics #37 © MAR

GD25 FN65 NM94

nn (1994)-Capt. America, X-Men, Silver Surfer 3.00
...1996-Spider-Man by Waid & Olliffe; X-Men, Silver Surfer 3.00
NOTE: *Art Adams c-'93. Golden a-'93. Perez c-'94.*

MARVEL ILLUSTRATED: SWIMSUIT ISSUE (See Marvel Swimsuit Spec.)
Marvel Comics: 1991 ($3.95, magazine, 52 pgs.)

V1#1-Parody of Sports Illustrated swimsuit issue; Mary Jane Parker centerfold pin-up by Jusko; 2nd print exists 2.00 6.00

MARVEL KNIGHTS (See Black Panther, Daredevil, Inhumans, & Punisher)
Marvel Comics: 1998 (Previews for upcoming series)

Sketchbook-Wizard suppl.; Quesada & Palmiotti-c 2.50
Tourbook-($2.99) Interviews and art previews 3.00

MARVEL MASTERPIECES COLLECTION, THE
Marvel Comics: May, 1993 - No. 4, Aug, 1993 ($2.95, coated paper, lim. series)

1-4-Reprints Marvel Masterpieces trading cards w/ new Jusko paintings in in each; Jusko painted-c/a 3.00

MARVEL MASTERPIECES 2 COLLECTION, THE
Marvel Comics: July, 1994 - No. 3, Sept, 1994 ($2.95, limited series)

1-3: 1-Kaluta-c; r/trading cards; new Steranko centerfold 3.00

MARVEL MILESTONE EDITION
Marvel Comics: 1991 - 1995 ($2.95, coated stock)(r/originals with original ads w/silver ink-c)

....: X-Men #1-Reprints X-Men #1 (1991) 3.00
....: Giant Size X-Men #1-(1991, $3.95, 68 pgs.) 4.00
....: Fantastic Four #1 (11/91) 3.00
....: Incredible Hulk #1 (3/92, says 3/91 by error) 3.00
....: Amazing Fantasy #15 (3/92) 3.00
....: Fantastic Four #5 (11/92) 3.00
....: Amazing Spider-Man #129 (11/92) 3.00
....: Iron Man #55 (11/92) 3.00
....: Iron Fist #14 (11/92) 3.00
....: Amazing Spider-Man #1 (1/93) 3.00
....: Amazing Spider-Man #1 (1/93) variation- no price on-c 5.00
....: Tales of Suspense #39 (3/93) 3.00
....: Avengers #1 (9/93) 3.00
....: X-Men #9 (10/93) 3.00
....: Avengers #16 (10/93) 3.00
....:Amazing Spider-Man #149 (11/94, $2.95) 3.00
....:X-Men #28 (11/94, $2.95) 3.00
....:Captain America #1 (3/95, $3.95) 4.00
....:Amazing Spider-Man #3 (3/95, $2.95) 3.00
....:Avengers #4 (3/95, $2.95) 3.00
....:Strange Tales-r/Dr. Strange stories from #110, 111, 114, & 115 3.00

MARVEL MINI-BOOKS
Marvel Comics Group: 1966 (50 pgs., B&W; 5/8x7/8") (6 different issues) (Smallest comics ever published)

Captain America, Millie the Model, Spider-Man, Sgt. Fury, Hulk, Thor 5.50 16.50 55.00
NOTE: *Each came in six different color covers, usually one color: Pink, yellow, green, etc.*

MARVEL MOVIE PREMIERE (Magazine)
Marvel Comics Group: Sept, 1975 (B&W, one-shot)

1-Burroughs' "The Land That Time Forgot" adapt. .90 2.70 8.00

MARVEL MOVIE SHOWCASE FEATURING STAR WARS
Marvel Comics Group: Nov, 1982 - No. 2, Dec, 1982 ($1.25, 68 pgs.)

1,2-Star Wars movie adaptation; reprints Star Wars #1-6 by Chaykin; 1-Reprints-c to Star Wars #1. 2-Stevens-r 3.00

MARVEL MOVIE SPOTLIGHT FEATURING RAIDERS OF THE LOST ARK
Marvel Comics Group: Nov, 1982 ($1.25, 68 pgs.)

1-Edited-r/Raiders of the Lost Ark #1-3; Buscema-c/a(p); movie adaptation 1.25

GD25 FN65 NM94

MARVEL MYSTERY COMICS (Formerly Marvel Comics) (Becomes Marvel Tales No. 93 on)
Timely /Marvel Comics (TP #2-17/TCI #18-54/MCI #55-92): No. 2, Dec, 1939 - No. 92, June, 1949

GD25 FN65 VF82 NM94

2-American Ace begins, ends #3; Human Torch (blue costume) by Burgos, Sub-Mariner by Everett continue; 2 pg. origin recap of Human Torch 1818.00 5455.00 11,817.00 20,000.00
3-New logo from Marvel pulp begins 860.00 2580.00 5160.00 8600.00
4-Intro. Electro, the Marvel of the Age (ends #19), The Ferret, Mystery Detective (ends #9); 1st Sub-Mariner-c by Schomburg; 1st Nazi war-c on a comic book & 1st German flag (Swastika) on-c of a comic (2/40) 700.00 2100.00 4200.00 7000.00
5 Classic Schomburg-c (Scarce) 1365.00 4100.00 8200.00 15,000.00
6,7: 6-Gustavson Angel story 480.00 1440.00 2880.00 4200.00
8-1st Human Torch & Sub-Mariner battle(6/40) 700.00 2100.00 4200.00 7000.00
9-(Scarce)-Human Torch & Sub-Mariner battle (cover/story); 1st Television in comics?; classic-c 1500.00 4500.00 9000.00 18,000.00

GD25 FN65 NM94

10-Human Torch & Sub-Mariner battle, conclusion; Terry Vance, the Schoolboy Sleuth begins, ends #57 490.00 1470.00 4900.00
11 274.00 822.00 2600.00
12-Classic Kirby-c 316.00 950.00 3000.00
13-Intro. & 1st app. The Vision by S&K (11/40); Sub-Mariner dons new costume, ends #15 360.00 1080.00 3600.00
14-16: 14-Shows-c to Human Torch #1 on-c (12/40). 15-S&K Vision, Gustavson Angel story 206.00 618.00 1750.00
17-Human Torch/Sub-Mariner team-up by Burgos/Everett; pin-up on back-c; shows-c to Human Torch #2 on-c 229.00 687.00 1950.00
18 182.00 546.00 1550.00
19-Origin Toro in text; shows-c to Sub-Mariner #1 on-c 200.00 600.00 1700.00
20-Origin The Angel in text 200.00 600.00 1700.00
21-Intro. & 1st app. The Patriot (7/41); not in #46-48; pin-up on back-c 182.00 546.00 1550.00
22-25: 23-Last Gustavson Angel; origin The Vision in text. 24-Injury-to-eye story 159.00 477.00 1350.00
26-30: 27-Ka-Zar ends; last S&K Vision who battles Satan. 28-Jimmy Jupiter in the Land of Nowhere begins, ends #48; Sub-Mariner vs. The Flying Dutchman. 30-1st Japanese war-c 147.00 441.00 1250.00
31-Sub-Mariner by Everett ends, resumes #84 129.00 387.00 1100.00
32-1st app. The Boboes 129.00 387.00 1100.00
33,35-40: 37-Hitler-c. 40-Zeppelin-c 129.00 387.00 1100.00
34-Everett, Burgos, Martin Goodman, Funnies, Inc. office appear in story & battles Hitler; last Burgos Human Torch 147.00 441.00 1250.00
41-43,45-48: 46-Hitler-c. 48-Last Vision; flag-c 109.00 327.00 925.00
44-Classic Super Plane-c 109.00 327.00 925.00
49-Origin Miss America 147.00 441.00 1250.00
50-Mary becomes Miss Patriot (origin) 115.00 345.00 975.00
51-60: 53-Bondage-c. 60-Last Japanese war-c 100.00 300.00 850.00
61,62,64-Last German war-c 94.00 282.00 800.00
63-Classic Hitler War-c; The Villainess Cat-Woman only app. 103.00 309.00 875.00
65,66-Last Japanese War-c 94.00 282.00 800.00
67-75: 74-Last Patriot. 75-Young Allies begin 85.00 255.00 725.00
76-78: 76-Ten Chapter Miss America serial begins, ends #85 85.00 255.00 725.00
79-New cover format; Super Villains begin on cover; last Angel 88.00 264.00 750.00
80-1st app. Capt. America in Marvel Comics 112.00 336.00 950.00
81-Captain America app. 85.00 255.00 725.00
82-Origin & 1st app. Namora (5/47); 1st Sub-Mariner/Namora team-up; Captain America app. 212.00 636.00 1800.00

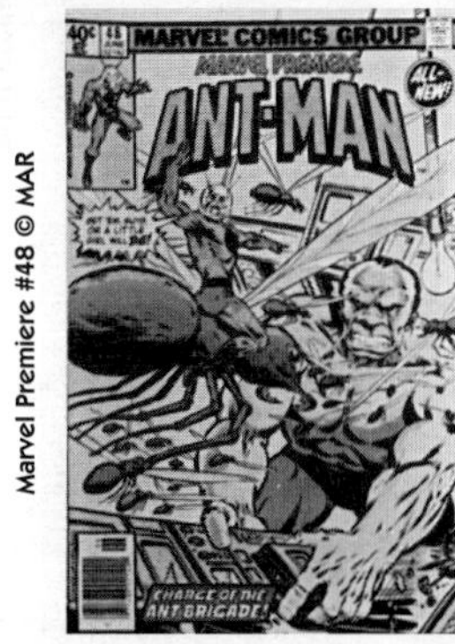

Marvel Premiere #48 © MAR

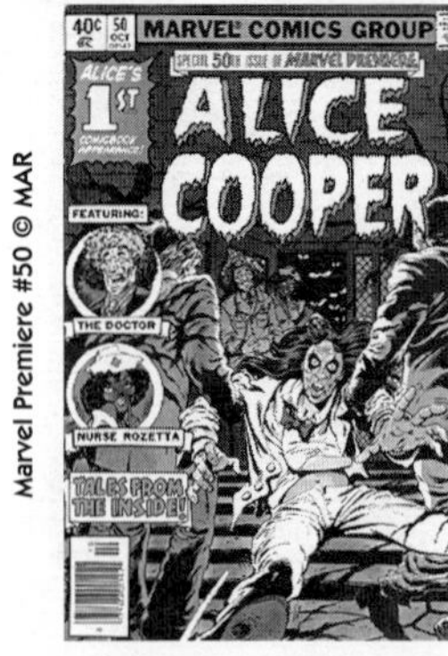

Marvel Premiere #50 © MAR

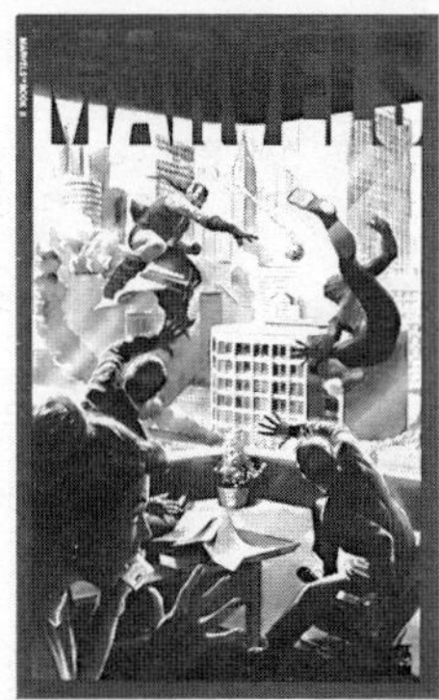
Marvels #0 © MAR

GD25 FN65 NM94

83,85: 83-Last Young Allies. 85-Last Miss America; Blonde Phantom app. 79.00 237.00 675.00
84-Blonde Phantom begins (on-c of #84,88,89); Sub-Mariner by Everett begins; Captain America app. 112.00 336.00 950.00
86-Blonde Phantom i.d. revealed; Captain America app.; last Bucky app. 90.00 270.00 765.00
87-1st Capt. America/Golden Girl team-up 96.00 288.00 815.00
88-Golden Girl, Namora, & Sun Girl (1st in Marvel Comics) x-over; Captain America, Blonde Phantom app.; last Toro 91.00 273.00 775.00
89-1st Human Torch/Sun Girl team-up; 1st Captain America solo; Blonde Phantom app. 90.00 270.00 765.00
90-Blonde Phantom un-masked; Captain America app. 96.00 288.00 815.00
91-Capt. America app.; Blonde Phantom & Sub-Mariner end; early Venus app. (4/49) 96.00 288.00 815.00
92-Feature story on the birth of the Human Torch and the death of Professor Horton (his creator); 1st app. The Witness in Marvel Comics; Captain America app. 229.00 687.00 1950.00
132 Pg. issue, B&W, 25¢ (1943-44)-printed in N. Y.; square binding, blank inside covers; has Marvel No. 33-c in color; contains Capt. America #18 & Marvel Mystery Comics #33; same contents as Captain America Annual

GD25 FN65 VF82

(Less than 5 copies known to exist) 2667.00 8000.00 16,000.00

NOTE: ***Brodsky*** *c-49, 72, 86, 88-92.* ***Crandall*** *a-26i.* ***Everett*** *c-7-9, 27, 84.* ***Gabrielle*** *c-30-32.* ***Schomburg*** *c-3-11, 13-29, 33-36, 39-48, 50-59, 63-69, 74, 76, 132 pg. issue.* ***Shores*** *c-37, 38, 75p, 77, 78p, 79p, 80, 81p, 82-84, 85p, 87p.* ***Sekowsky*** *c-73. Bondage covers-3, 4, 7, 12, 28, 29, 49, 50, 52, 56, 57, 58, 59, 65. Angel c-2, 3, 8, 12. Remember Pearl Harbor issues-#30-32.*

MARVEL NO-PRIZE BOOK, THE (The Official... on-c)
Marvel Comics Group: Jan, 1983 (one-shot, direct sales only)

GD25 FN65 NM94

1-Golden-c 2.00

MARVEL PREMIERE
Marvel Comics Group: April, 1972 - No. 61, Aug, 1981 (A tryout book for new characters)

1-Origin Warlock (pre-#1) by Gil Kane/Adkins; origin Counter-Earth; Hulk & Thor cameo (#1-14 are 20¢-c) 2.70 8.00 30.00
2-Warlock ends; Kirby Yellow Claw-r 1.50 4.50 15.00
3-Dr. Strange series begins (pre #1, 7/72), B. Smith-c/a(p) 2.20 6.50 24.00
4-Smith/Brunner-a .90 2.70 9.00
5-9: 8-Starlin-c/a(p) 5.50
10-Death of the Ancient One .90 2.70 8.00
11-14: 11-Dr. Strange origin-r by Ditko. 14-Last Dr. Strange (3/74), gets own title 3 months later 4.50
15-Origin/1st app. Iron Fist (5/74), ends #25 4.50 13.50 50.00
16-2nd app. Iron Fist; origin cont'd from #15; Hama's 1st Marvel-a 1.50 4.50 15.00
17-24: Iron Fist in all 1.00 3.00 10.00
25-1st Byrne Iron Fist (moves to own title next) 1.50 4.50 15.00
26-Hercules. 3.00
27-Satana 2.00 6.00
28-Legion of Monsters (Ghost Rider, Man-Thing, Morbius, Werewolf) 1.20 3.60 12.00
29-49,51-56,61: 29,30-The Liberty Legion. 29-1st modern app. Patriot. 31-1st app. Woodgod; last 25¢ issue. 32-1st app. Monark Starstalker. 33,34-1st color app. Solomon Kane (Robert E. Howard adaptation "Red Shadows". 35-Origin/1st app. 3-D Man. 36,37-3-D Man. 38-1st Weirdworld. 39,40-Torpedo. 41-1st Seeker 3000! 42-Tigra. 43-Paladin. 44-Jack of Hearts (1st solo book, 10/78). 45,46-Man-Wolf. 47-Origin/1st app. new Ant-Man. 48-Ant-Man. 49-The Falcon (1st solo book, 8/79). 51-53-Black Panther. 54-1st Caleb Hammer. 55-Wonder Man. 56-1st color app. Dominic Fortune. 61-Star Lord 2.00
50-1st app. Alice Cooper; co-plotted by Alice .90 2.70 9.00
57-Dr. Who (2nd U.S. app.-see Movie Classics) 3.00
58-60-Dr. Who 2.25

NOTE: ***N. Adams*** *(Crusty Bunkers) part inks-10, 12, 13.* ***Austin*** *a-50i, 56i; c-46i, 50i, 56i, 58.* ***Brunner*** *a-4i, 6p, 9-14p; c-9-14.* ***Byrne*** *a-47p, 48p.* ***Chaykin*** *a-32-34; c-32, 33, 56.* ***Giffen*** *a-31p, 44p; c-44.* ***Gil Kane*** *a(p)-1, 2, 15; c(p)-1, 2, 15, 16, 22-24, 27, 36, 37.* ***Kirby*** *c-26, 29-31, 35.* ***Layton*** *a-47i, 48i; c-47.* ***McWilliams*** *a-25i.* ***Miller*** *c-49p, 53p, 58p.* ***Nebres*** *a-44i; c-38i.* ***Nino*** *a-38i.* ***Perez*** *c/a-38p, 45p, 46p.* ***Ploog*** *a-38; c-5-7.* ***Russell*** *a-7p.* ***Simonson*** *a-60(2pgs.); c-57.* ***Starlin*** *a-8p; c-8.* ***Sutton*** *a-41, 43, 50p, 61; c-50p, 61. #57-60 published w/two different prices on-c.*

MARVEL PRESENTS
Marvel Comics: October, 1975 - No. 12, Aug, 1977 (#1-5 are 25¢ issues)

1,2: 1-Origin & 1st app. Bloodstone. 2-Origin Bloodstone continued; Kirby-c 5.00
3-Guardians of the Galaxy (1st solo book, 2/76) begins, ends #12 .90 2.70 7.50
4-7,9-12: 9,10-Origin Starhawk 5.00
8-r/story from Silver Surfer #2 plus 4 pgs. new-a 2.00 6.00

NOTE: ***Austin*** *a-6i.* ***Buscema*** *r-8p.* ***Chaykin*** *a-5p.* ***Kane*** *c-1p.* ***Starlin*** *layouts-10.*

MARVEL PREVIEW (Magazine) (Bizarre Adventures #25 on)
Marvel Comics: Feb (no month), 1975 - No. 24, Winter, 1980 (B&W) ($1.00)

1-Man-Gods From Beyond the Stars; Crusty Bunkers (Neal Adams)-a(i) & cover; Nino-a .90 2.70 9.00
2-1st origin The Punisher (see Amaz. Spider-Man #129 & Classic Punisher); 1st app. Dominic Fortune; Morrow-c 5.50 16.50 60.00
3,8,10: 3-Blade the Vampire Slayer. 8-Legion of Monsters; Morbius app. 10-Thor the Mighty; Starlin frontispiece 1.00 3.00 10.00
4,5: 4-Star-Lord & Sword in the Star (origins & 1st app.). 5,6-Sherlock Holmes. .90 2.70 8.00
6,9: 6-Sherlock Holmes; N. Adams frontispiece. 9-Man-God; origin Star Hawk, ends #20 5.00
7-Satana, Sword in the Star app. .85 2.60 7.00
11,16,19: 11-Star-Lord; Byrne-a; Starlin frontispiece. 16-Masters of Terror. 19-Kull. 4.00
12-15,17,18,20-24: 12-Haunt of Horror. 14,15-Star-Lord. 14-Starlin painted-c. 16-Masters of Terror. 17-Blackmark by G. Kane (see SSOC #1-3). 18-Star-Lord. 20-Bizarre Advs. 21-Moon Knight (Spr/80)-Predates Moon Knight #1; The Shroud by Ditko. 22-King Arthur. 23-Bizarre Advs.; Miller-a. 24-Debut Paradox 3.00

NOTE: ***N. Adams*** *(C. Bunkers) r-20i.* ***Buscema*** *a-22, 23.* ***Byrne*** *a-11.* ***Chaykin*** *a-20r; c-20 (new).* ***Colan*** *a-8, 16p(3), 18p, 23p; c-16p.* ***Elias*** *a-18.* ***Giffen*** *a-7.* ***Infantino*** *a-14p.* ***Kaluta*** *a-12; c-15.* ***Miller*** *a-23.* ***Morrow*** *a-8i; c-2-4.* ***Perez*** *a-20p.* ***Ploog*** *a-8.* ***Starlin*** *c-13, 14. Nudity in some issues*

MARVEL RIOT
Marvel Comics: Dec, 1995 ($1.95, one-shot)

1-"Age of Apocalypse" spoof; Lobdell script 2.00

MARVELS
Marvel Comics: Jan, 1994 - No. 4, Apr, 1994 ($5.95, painted lim. series)
No. 1 (2nd Printing), Apr, 1996 - No. 4 (2nd Printing), July, 1996 ($2.95)

1-4: Kurt Busiek scripts & Alex Ross painted-c/a in all; double-c w/acetate overlay .90 2.70 8.00
Marvel Classic Collectors Pack ($11.90)-Issues #1 & 2 boxed (1st printings). 1.20 3.60 12.00
0-(8/94, $2.95)-no acetate overlay. 4.00
1-4-(2nd printing): r/original limited series w/o acetate overlay 3.00
Hardcover (1994, $59.95)-r/#0-4; w/intros by Stan Lee, John Romita, Sr., Kurt Busiek & Scott McCloud. 59.95
Trade paperback ($19.95) 19.95

MARVEL SAGA, THE
Marvel Comics Group: Dec, 1985 - No. 25, Dec, 1987

1 1.50
2-25 1.00

NOTE: ***Williamson*** *a(i)-9, 10; c(i)-7, 10-12, 14, 16.*

MARVEL'S GREATEST COMICS (Marvel Collectors' Item Classics #1-22)

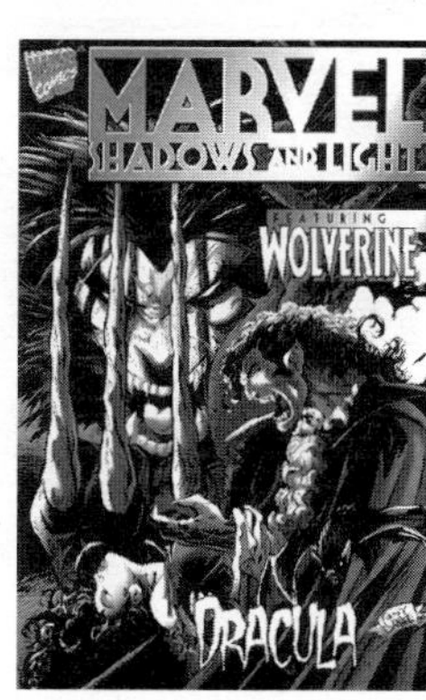

Marvel: Shadows and Light #1 © MAR

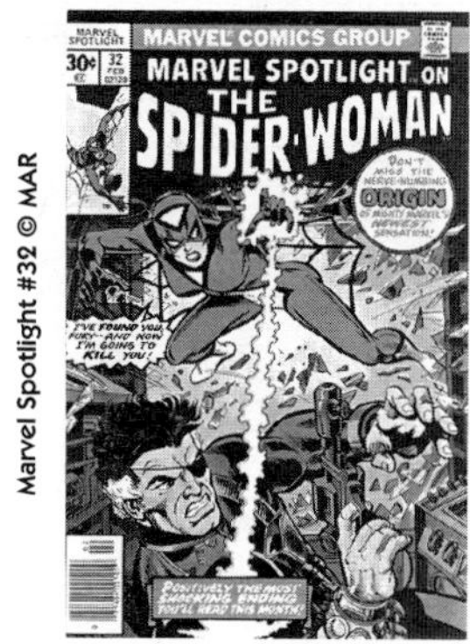

Marvel Spotlight #32 © MAR

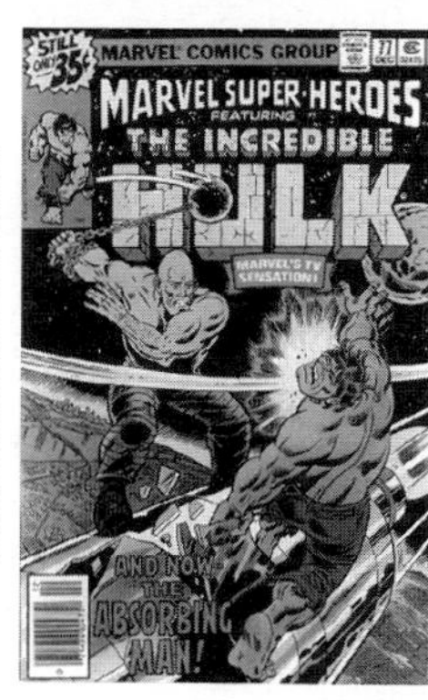

Marvel Super-Heroes #77 © MAR

GD25 FN65 NM94

Marvel Comics Group: No. 23, Oct, 1969 - No. 96, Jan, 1981

23-34 (Giants). Begin Fantastic Four-r/#30s?-116 1.40 4.20 14.00
35-37-Silver Surfer-r/Fantastic Four #48-50 .85 2.60 7.00
38-50: 42-Silver Surfer-r/F.F.(others?) 5.00
51-96 2.50

NOTE: *Dr. Strange, Fantastic Four, Iron Man, Watcher-#23, 24. Capt. America, Dr. Strange, Iron Man, Fantastic Four-#25-28. Fantastic Four-#38-96.* ***Buscema*** *r-85-92; c-87-92r.* ***Ditko*** *r-23-28.* ***Kirby*** *r-23-82; c-75, 77p, 80p. #81 reprints Fantastic Four #100.*

MARVEL'S GREATEST SUPERHERO BATTLES (See Fireside Book Series)

MARVEL: SHADOWS AND LIGHT
Marvel Comics: Feb, 1997 ($2.95, B&W, one-shot)

1-Tony Daniel-c 3.00

MARVELS OF SCIENCE
Charlton Comics: March, 1946 - No. 4, June, 1946

1-A-Bomb story 19.00 56.00 140.00
2-4 11.00 34.00 85.00

MARVEL SPECIAL EDITION FEATURING... (Also see Special Collectors' Ed.)
Marvel Comics Group: 1975 - 1978 (84 pgs.) (Oversized)

1-The Spectacular Spider-Man ($1.50); r/Amazing Spider-Man #6,35, Annual 1; Ditko-a(r) 1.20 3.60 12.00
1-Star Wars (1977, $1.00); r/Star Wars #1-3 1.00 3.00 10.00
2-Star Wars (1978, $1.00); r/Star Wars #4-6 1.00 3.00 10.00
3-Star Wars ('78, $2.50, 116pgs.); r/S. Wars #1-6 1.00 3.00 10.00
3-Close Encounters of the Third Kind (1978, $1.50, 56 pgs.)-Movie adaptation; Simonson-a(p) 1.00 3.00 10.00
V2#2(Spring, 1980, $2.00, oversized)- "Star Wars: The Empire Strikes Back"; r/Marvel Comics Super Special #16 2.00 6.00 20.00

NOTE: ***Chaykin*** *c/a(r)-1(1977), 2, 3.* ***Stevens*** *a(r)-2i, 3i.* ***Williamson*** *a(r)-V2#2.*

MARVEL SPECTACULAR
Marvel Comics Group: Aug, 1973 - No. 19, Nov, 1975

1-Thor-r from mid-sixties begin by Kirby .85 2.60 7.00
2-10 4.00
11-19 3.00

MARVELS: PORTRAITS
Marvel Comics: Mar, 1995 - No. 4, June, 1995 ($2.95, limited series)

1-4:Different artists renditions of Marvel characters 3.00

MARVEL SPOTLIGHT (...& Son of Satan #19, 20, 23, 24)
Marvel Comics Group: Nov, 1971 - No. 33, Apr, 1977; V2#1, July, 1979 - V2#11, Mar, 1981 (A try-out book for new characters)

1-Origin Red Wolf (western hero)(1st solo book, pre-#1); Wood inks, Neal Adams-c; only 15¢ issue 2.20 6.25 22.00
2-(25¢, 52 pgs.)-Venus-r by Everett; origin/1st app. Werewolf By Night (begins) by Ploog; N. Adams-c 9.00 27.00 100.00
3,4: 4-Werewolf By Night ends (6/72); gets own title 9/72 2.70 8.00 30.00
5-Origin/1st app. Ghost Rider (8/72) & begins 6.00 17.50 65.00
6-8: 6-Origin G.R. retold. 8-Last Ploog issue 2.70 8.00 30.00
9-11-Last Ghost Rider (gets own title next mo.) 2.00 6.00 20.00
12-Origin & 2nd full app. The Son of Satan (10/73); story cont'd from Ghost Rider #2 & into #3; series begins, ends #24 2.00 6.00 20.00
12-Variant w/4 extra pgs. of ads on slick paper plus a Mark Jeweler pull-out centerfold ad 2.20 6.50 24.00
13-21,23,24: 13-Partial origin Son of Satan. 14-Last 20¢ issue. 24-Last Son of Satan (10/75); gets own title 12/75 2.00 6.00
22-Ghost Rider-c & cameo (5 panels) 2.00 6.00
25,27,30,31: 25-Sinbad; contains pull-out Mark Jewelers ad. 27-Sub-Mariner. 30-The Warriors Three. 31-Nick Fury 3.00
26-Scarecrow 5.00
28-1st solo Moon Knight app., (6/76) 1.20 3.60 12.00
29-(Regular 25¢ edition)(8/76) Moon Knight app.; last 25¢ issue 1.20 3.60 12.00
29-(30¢-c, limited distribution) 4.40 13.00 48.00
32-1st app./partial origin Spider-Woman (2/77); Nick Fury app. 1.20 3.60 12.00
33-Deathlok; 1st app. Devil-Slayer 5.00
V2#1-7,9-11: 1-4-Capt. Marvel. 5-Dragon Lord. 6,7-StarLord; origin #6. 9-11-Capt. Universe (see Micronauts #8) 2.00
8-Capt. Marvel; Miller-c/a(p) 3.00

NOTE: ***Austin*** *c-V2#2i, 8.* ***J. Buscema*** *c/a-30p.* ***Chaykin*** *a-31; c-26, 31.* ***Colan*** *a-18p, 19p.* ***Ditko*** *a-V2#4, 5, 9-11; c-V2#4, 9-11.* ***Kane*** *c-21p, 32p.* ***Kirby*** *c-29p.* ***McWilliams*** *a-20i.* ***Miller*** *a-V2#8p; c(p)-V2#2, 5, 7, 8.* ***Mooney*** *a-8i, 10i, 14p, 15, 16p, 17p, 24p, 27, 32i.* ***Nasser*** *a-33p.* ***Ploog*** *a-2-5, 6-8p; c-3-9.* ***Romita*** *c-13.* ***Sutton*** *a-9-11p, V2#6, 7. #29-25¢ & 30¢ issues exist.*

MARVEL SUPER ACTION (Magazine)
Marvel Comics Group: Jan, 1976 (B&W, 76 pgs.)

1-Origin/2nd app. Dominic Fortune(see Marv. Preview); early Punisher app.; Weird World & The Huntress; Evans, Ploog-a 3.50 10.50 38.00

MARVEL SUPER ACTION
Marvel Comics Group: May, 1977 - No. 37, Nov, 1981

1-Reprints Capt. America #100 by Kirby .85 2.60 7.00
2,3,5-13: r/Capt. America #101,102,103-111. 11-Origin-r. 12,13-Classic Steranko-c/a(r) 4.00
4-Marvel Boy-r(origin)/M. Boy #1 4.00
14-20: r/Avengers #55,56, Annual 2, others 3.00
21-37: 30-r/Hulk #6 from U.K. 2.00

NOTE: ***Buscema*** *a(r)-14p, 15p; c-18-20, 22, 35r-37.* ***Everett*** *a-4.* ***Heath*** *a-4r.* ***Kirby*** *r-1-3, 5-11.* ***B. Smith*** *a-27r, 28r.* ***Steranko*** *a(r)-12p, 13p; c-12r, 13r.*

MARVEL SUPER HERO CONTEST OF CHAMPIONS
Marvel Comics Group: June, 1982 - No. 3, Aug, 1982 (Limited series)

1-3: Features nearly all Marvel characters currently appearing in their comics; 1st Marvel limited series 4.00

MARVEL SUPER HEROES
Marvel Comics Group: October, 1966 (25¢, 68 pgs.) (1st Marvel one-shot)

1-r/origin Daredevil from D.D. #1; r/Avengers #2; G.A. Sub-Mariner-r/Marvel Mystery #8 (Human Torch app.). 6.00 18.00 70.00

MARVEL SUPER-HEROES (Formerly Fantasy Masterpieces #1-11)
(Also see Giant-Size Super Heroes) (#12-20: 25¢, 68 pgs.)
Marvel Comics: No. 12, 12/67 - No. 31, 11/71; No. 32, 9/72 - No. 105, 1/82

12-Origin & 1st app. Capt. Marvel of the Kree; G.A. Human Torch, Destroyer, Capt. America, Black Knight, Sub-Mariner-r (#12-20 all contain new stories and reprints) 5.50 16.50 60.00
13-2nd app. Capt. Marvel; G.A. Black Knight, Torch, Vision, Capt. America, Sub-Mariner-r 2.70 8.00 30.00
14-Amazing Spider-Man (5/68, new-a by Andru/Everett); G.A. Sub-Mariner, Torch, Mercury (1st Kirby-a at Marvel), Black Knight, Capt. America reprints 5.50 16.50 60.00
15-Black Bolt cameo in Medusa (new-a); Black Knight, Sub-Mariner, Black Marvel, Capt. America-r 2.25 6.80 25.00
16-Origin & 1st app. S. A. Phantom Eagle; G.A. Torch, Capt. America, Black Knight, Patriot, Sub-Mariner-r 2.25 6.80 25.00
17-Origin Black Knight (new-a); G.A. Torch, Sub-Mariner-r; reprint from All-Winners Squad #21 (cover & story) 2.25 6.80 25.00
18-Origin/1st app. Guardians of the Galaxy (1/69); G.A. Sub-Mariner, All-Winners Squad-r 2.50 7.50 30.00
19-Ka-Zar (new-a); G.A. Torch, Marvel Boy, Black Knight, Sub-Mariner reprints; Smith-c(p); Tuska-a(r) 1.20 3.60 12.00
20-Doctor Doom (5/69); r/Young Men #24 w/-c 1.80 5.40 20.00
21-31: All-r issues. 21-X-Men, Daredevil, Iron Man-r begin, end #31. 31-Last Giant issue 1.20 3.60 10.00
32-50: 32-Hulk/Sub-Mariner-r begin from TTA. 4.00
51-105: 56-r/origin Hulk/Inc. Hulk #102; Hulk-r begin 2.00

NOTE: ***Austin*** *a-104.* ***Colan*** *a(p)-12, 13, 15, 18; c-12, 13, 15, 18.* ***Everett*** *a-14i(new); r-14, 15i, 18, 19, 33; c-85(r). New* ***Kirby*** *c-22, 27, 54.* ***Maneely*** *r-14, 15, 19.* ***Severin*** *r-83-85i, 100-102; c-100-102r.* ***Starlin*** *c-47.* ***Tuska*** *a-19p. Black Knight-r by* ***Maneely*** *in 12-16, 19. Sub-Mariner-r by* ***Everett*** *in 12-20.*

Marvel Super-Heroes #12 © MAR

Marvel Tales #96 © MAR

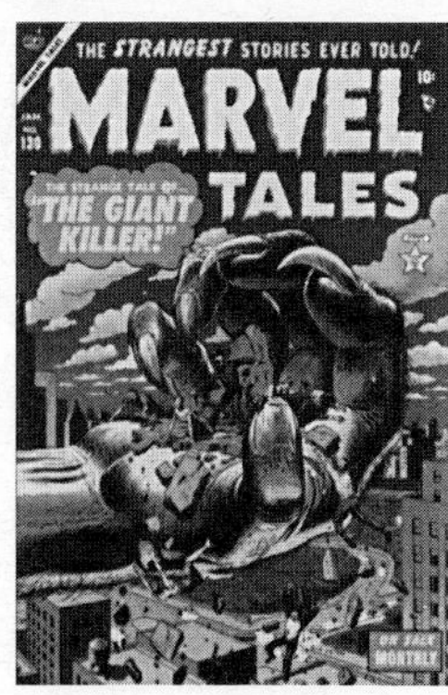

Marvel Tales #130 © MAR

MARVEL SUPER-HEROES
Marvel Comics: May, 1990 - V2#15, Oct, 1993 ($2.95/$2.25/$2.50, quarterly, 68-84 pgs.)

1-Moon Knight, Hercules, Black Panther, Magik, Brother Voodoo, Speedball (by Ditko) & Hellcat; Hembeck-a 3.00
2,4,5: 2-Summer Special(7/90); Rogue, Speedball (by Ditko), Iron Man, Falcon, Tigra & Daredevil. 4-Spider-Man/Nick Fury, Daredevil, Speedball, Wonder Man, Spitfire & Black Knight; Byrne-c. 5-Thor, Dr. Strange, Thing & She-Hulk; Speedball by Ditko(p) 2.25
V2#3-Retells origin Capt. America w/new facts; Blue Shield, Capt. Marvel, Speedball, Wasp; Hulk by Ditko/Rogers 2.25
V2#6-9: 6-8-$2.25-c. 6,7-X-Men, Cloak & Dagger, The Shroud (by Ditko) & Marvel Boy in each. 8-X-Men, Namor & Iron Man (by Ditko); Larsen-c. 9-W.C Avengers, Iron Man app.; Kieth-c(p); begin $2.50-c 2.25
V2#10-Ms. Marvel/Sabretooth-c/story (intended for Ms. Marvel #24; shows-c to #24); Namor, Vision, Scarlet Witch stories 2.50
V2#11,12 ($2.50): 11-Original Ghost Rider-c/story; Giant-Man, Ms. Marvel stories. 12-Dr. Strange, Falcon, Iron Man 2.50
V2#13-15 ($2.75, 84 pgs.): 13-All Iron Man issue; 30th anniversary. 15-Iron Man/Thor/Volstagg/Dr. Druid 2.75

MARVEL SUPER-HEROES MEGAZINE
Marvel Comics: Oct, 1994 - No. 6, Mar, 1995 ($2.95, 100 pgs.)

1-6: 1-r/FF #232, DD #159, Iron Man #115, Incred. Hulk #314 3.00

MARVEL SUPER-HEROES SECRET WARS (See Secret Wars II)
Marvel Comics Group: May, 1984 - No. 12, Apr, 1985 (limited series)

1 3.00
1-3-2nd printings (sold in multi-packs) 1.00
2-7,9-12: 6-The Wasp dies. 7-Intro. new Spider-Woman. 12-($1.00, 52 pgs.) 2.00
8-Spider-Man's new black costume explained as alien costume (1st app. Venom as alien costume) 1.50 4.50 15.00
NOTE: *Zeck a-1-12; c-13, 8-12.*

MARVEL SUPER SPECIAL, A (See Marvel Comics Super...)

MARVEL SWIMSUIT SPECIAL (Also see Marvel Illustrated...)
Marvel Comics: 1992 - No. 4, 1995 ($3.95/$4.50, magazine, 52 pgs.)

1-Silvestri-c; pin-ups by many artists 4.00
2-4: 2-Jusko painted-c; all pin-ups. 3-Hughes-c 4.50

MARVEL TAILS STARRING PETER PORKER THE SPECTACULAR SPIDER-HAM (Also see Peter Porker...)
Marvel Comics Group: Nov, 1983 (one-shot)

1-Peter Porker, the Spectacular Spider-Ham, Captain Americat, Goose Rider, Hulk Bunny app. 1.50

MARVEL TALES (Formerly Marvel Mystery Comics #1-92)
Marvel/Atlas Comics (MCI): No. 93, Aug, 1949 - No. 159, Aug, 1957

93-Horror/weird stories begin 115.00 345.00 1000.00
94-Everett-a 82.00 247.00 700.00
95,96,99,101,103,105: 95-New logo 54.00 162.00 460.00
97-Sun Girl, 2 pgs; Kirbyish-a; one story used in N.Y. State Legislative document 67.00 201.00 570.00
98-Krigstein-a 58.00 173.00 490.00
100 58.00 173.00 490.00
102-Wolverton-a "The End of the World", (6 pgs.) 80.00 240.00 680.00
104-Wolverton-a "Gateway to Horror", (6 pgs.) 76.00 229.00 650.00
106,107-Krigstein-a. 106-Decapitation story 45.00 136.00 385.00
108-120: 118-Hypo-c/panels in End of World story. 120-Jack Katz-a 35.00 104.00 260.00
121,123-131: 128-Flying Saucer-c. 131-Last precode (2/55) 28.00 84.00 210.00
122-Kubert-a 29.00 86.00 215.00
132,133,135-141,143,145 17.00 52.00 130.00
134-Krigstein, Kubert-a; flying saucer-c 19.00 56.00 140.00
142-Krigstein-a 17.00 52.00 130.00
144-Williamson/Krenkel-a, 3 pgs. 17.00 52.00 130.00
146,148-151,154-156,158: 150-1st S.A. issue. 156-Torres-a 13.00 40.00 100.00
147-Ditko-a 16.00 48.00 120.00
152-Wood, Morrow-a 16.00 48.00 120.00
153-Everett End of World c/story 17.00 52.00 130.00
157,159-Krigstein-a 14.00 42.00 105.00
NOTE: ***Andru** a-103. **Briefer** a-118. **Check** a-147. **Colan** a-105, 107, 118, 120, 121, 127, 131. **Drucker** a-127, 135, 141, 146, 150. **Everett** a-98, 104, 106(2), 108(2), 131, 148, 151, 153, 155; c-107, 109, 111, 112, 114, 117, 127, 143, 147-151, 153, 155, 156. **Forte** a-119, 125, 130. **Heath** a-110, 113, 118, 119; c-104-106, 110, 130. **Gil Kane** a-117. **Lawrence** a-130. **Maneely** a-111, 126, 129; c-108, 116, 120, 129, 152. **Mooney** a-114. **Morisi** a-153. **Morrow** a-150, 152, 156. **Orlando** a-149, 151, 157. **Pakula** a-119, 121, 135, 144, 150, 152, 156. **Powell** a-136, 137, 150, 154. **Ravielli** a-117. **Rico** a-97, 99. **Romita** a-108. **Sekowsky** a-96-98. **Shores** a-110; c-96. **Sinnott** a-105, 116. **Tuska** a-114. **Whitney** a-107. **Wildey** a-126, 138.*

MARVEL TALES (...Annual #1,2; ...Starring Spider-Man #123 on)
Marvel Comics Group (NPP earlier issues): 1964 - No. 291, Nov, 1994 (No. 1-32: 72 pgs.)

1-Reprints origins of Spider-Man/Amazing Fantasy #15, Hulk/Inc. Hulk#1, Ant-Man/T.T.A. #35, Giant Man/T.T.A. #49, Iron Man/T.O.S. #39,48, Thor/J.I.M. #83 & r/Sgt. Fury #1 25.00 76.00 265.00
2 ('65)-r/X-Men #1(origin), Avengers #1(origin), origin Dr. Strange-r/Strange Tales #115 & origin Hulk(Hulk #3) 8.00 24.00 85.00
3 (7/66)-Spider-Man, Strange Tales (H. Torch), Journey into Mystery (Thor), Tales to Astonish (Ant-Man)-r begin (r/Strange Tales #101) 3.70 11.00 40.00
4,5 2.50 7.50 27.00
6-8,10: 10-Reprints 1st Kraven/Amaz. S-M #15 2.00 6.00 18.00
9-r/Amazing Spider-Man #14 w/cover 2.50 7.50 22.00
11-32: 11-Spider-Man battles Daredevil-r/Amaz. Spider-Man #16. 13-Origin Marvel Boy-r/M. Boy #1. 22-Green Goblin-c/story-r/Amaz. Spider-Man #27. 30-New Angel story. 32-Last 72 pg. issue 1.50 4.50 16.00
33-50: 33-(52 pgs.,)-Kraven-r. 34-Begin regular size issues 5.00
51-67,69,71-105: 75-Origin Spider-Man-r. 77-79-Drug issues-r/A. Spider-Man #96-98. 98-Death of Gwen Stacy-r/A. Spider-Man #121 (Green Goblin). 99-Death Green Goblin-r/A. Spider-Man #122. 100-(52 pgs.)-New Hawkeye/Two Gun Kid story. 101-105-All Spider-Man-r 3.00
68,70-(Regular 25¢ edition)(6,8/76) 3.00
68,70-(30¢-c, limited distribution) 1.20 3.60 12.00
106-r/1st Punisher-Amazing Spider-Man #129 4.00
107-133-All Spider-Man-r. 111,112-r/Spider-Man #134,135 (Punisher). 113, 114-r/Spider-Man #136,137(Green Goblin). 126-128-r/clone story from Amazing Spider-Man #149-151 2.00
134-136-Dr. Strange-r begin; SpM stories continue. 134-Dr. Strange-r/ Strange Tales #110 2.00
137-Origin-r Dr. Strange; shows original unprinted-c & origin Spider-Man/ Amazing Fantasy #15 3.00
137-Nabisco giveaway 2.00 6.00
138-Reprints all Amazing Spider-Man #1; begin reprints of Spider-Man with covers similar to originals 3.00
139-144: r/Amazing Spider-Man #2-7 2.00
145-191,193-199: Spider-Man-r continue w/#8 on. 149-Contains skin "Tattooz" decals. 150-($1.00, 52pgs.)-r/Spider-Man Annual 1(Kraven app.). 153-r/1st Kraven/Spider-Man #15. 155-r/2nd Green Goblin/Spider-Man #17. 161,164,165-Gr. Goblin-c/stories-r/Spider-Man #23,26,27. 178,179-Green Goblin-c/story-r/Spider-Man #39,40. 187,189-Kraven-r. 191-($1.50, 68 pgs.)-r/Spider-Man #96-98. 193-Byrne-r/Marvel Team-Up begin w/scripts 2.00
192-($1.25, 52 pgs.)-r/Spider-Man #121,122 2.00
200-Double size ($1.25)-Miller-c & r/Annual #14 1.50
201-208,210-222: 208-Last Byrne-r. 210,211-r/Spidey #134,135. 212,213-r/ Giant-Size Spidey #4. 213-r/1st solo Silver Surfer story/F.F. Annual #5. 214, 215-r/Spidey #161,162. 222-Reprints origin Punisher/Spectacular Spider-Man #83; last Punisher reprint 1.00

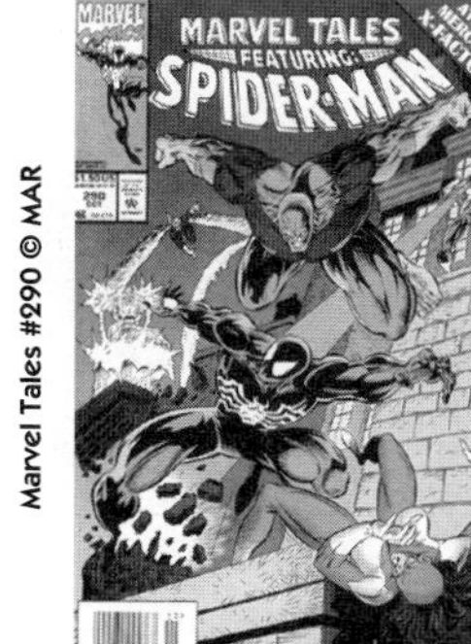

Marvel Tales #290 © MAR

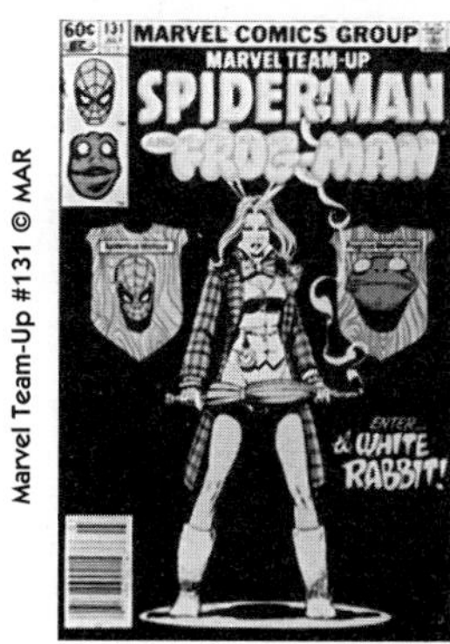

Marvel Team-Up #131 © MAR

Marvel Team-Up #8 (2nd Series) © MAR

GD25 FN65 NM94

209-Reprints 1st app. The Punisher/Amazing Spider-Man #129; Punisher reprints begin, end #222 1.75

223-McFarlane-c begins, end #239 1.50

224-249,251,252,254-257: 233-Spider-Man/X-Men team-ups begin; r/X-Men #35. 234-r/Marvel Team-Up #4. 235,236-r/M. Team-Up Annual #1. 237, 238-r/M. Team-Up #150. 239,240-r/M. Team-Up #38,90(Beast). 242-r/M. Team-Up #89. 243-r/M. Team-Up #117(Wolverine). 251-r/Spider-Man #100 (Green Goblin-c/story). 252-r/1st app. Morbius/Amaz. Spider-Man #101. 254-r/M. Team-Up #15(Ghost Rider); new painted-c. 255,256-Spider-Man & Ghost Rider-r/Marvel Team-Up #58,91. 257-Hobgoblin-r begin(r/Amazing Spider-Man #238); last $1.00-c 1.00

250-($1.50, 52pgs.)-r/1st Karma/M. Team-Up #100 1.50

253-($1.50, 52 pgs.)-r/Amaz. S-M #102 1.50

258-289: 258-261-r/A. Spider-Man #239,249-251(Hobgoblin). 262,263-r/Marv. Team-Up #53,54. 262-New X-Men vs. Sunstroke story. 263-New Woodgod origin story. 264,265-r/A. Spider-Man Annual 5. 266-273-Reprints alien costume stories/A. S-M 252-259. 277-r/1st Silver Sable/A. S-M 265. 283-r/ A. S-M 275 (Hobgoblin). 284-r/A. S-M 276 (Hobgoblin) 1.25

285-variant w/Wonder-Con logo on c-no price-giveaway 1.00

286-($2.95)-p/bagged w/16 page insert & animation print 3.00

290, 291: 290-Begin $1.50-c 1.50

NOTE: *All contain reprints; some have new art. #89-97-r/Amazing Spider-Man #110-118; #98-136-r/#121-159; #137-150-r/Amazing Fantasy #15, #1-12 & Annual 1; #151-167-r/#13-28 & Annual 2; #168-186-r/#29-46.* ***Austin*** *a-100i; c-272i, 273i.* ***Byrne*** *a(r)-193-198p, 201-208p.* ***Ditko*** *a-1-30, 83, 100, 137-155.* ***G. Kane*** *a-71, 81, 98-101p, 249r; c-125-127p, 130p, 137-155.* ***Sam Kieth*** *c-255, 262, 263.* ***Ron Lim*** *c-266p-281p, 283p-285p.* ***McFarlane*** *c-223-239.* ***Mooney*** *a-63, 95-97i, 103(i).* ***Nasser*** *a-100p.* ***Nebres*** *a-242i.* ***Perez*** *c-259-261.* ***Rogers*** *c-240, 241, 243-252.*

MARVEL TEAM-UP (See Marvel Treasury Edition #18 & Official Marvel Index To...) (Replaced by Web of Spider-Man)
Marvel Comics Group: March, 1972 - No. 150, Feb, 1985
NOTE: *Spider-Man team-ups in all but Nos. 18, 23, 26, 29, 32, 35, 97, 104, 105, 137.*

1-Human Torch 9.00 27.00 100.00

2-Human Torch 2.90 8.70 32.00

3-Spider-Man/Human Torch vs. Morbius (part 1); 3rd app. of Morbius (7/72) 3.20 9.50 35.00

4-Spider-Man/X-Men vs. Morbius (part 2 of story); 4th app. of Morbius 3.80 11.50 40.00

5-10: 5-Vision. 6-Thing. 7-Thor. 8-The Cat (4/73, came out between The Cat #3 & 4). 9-Iron Man. 10-H-T 1.50 4.50 15.00

11,13,14,16-20: 11-Inhumans. 13-Capt. America. 14-Sub-Mariner. 16-Capt. Marvel. 17-Mr. Fantastic. 18-H-T/Hulk. 19-Ka-Zar. 20-Black Panther; last 20¢ issue .90 2.70 8.00

12-Werewolf (8/73, 1 month before Werewolf #1). 1.80 5.40 18.00

15-1st Spider-Man/Ghost Rider team-up (11/73) 2.00 6.00 20.00

21-30: 21-Dr. Strange. 22-Hawkeye. 23-H-T/Iceman (X-Men cameo). 24-Brother Voodoo. 25-Daredevil. 26-H-T/Thor. 27-Hulk. 28-Hercules. 29-H-T/Iron Man. 30-Falcon 4.00

31-45,47-50: 31-Iron Fist. 32-H-T/Son of Satan. 33-Nighthawk. 34-Valkyrie. 35-H-T/Dr. Strange. 36-Frankenstein. 37-Man-Wolf. 38-Beast. 39-H-T. 40-Sons of the Tiger/H-T. 41-Scarlet Witch. 42-The Vision. 43-Dr. Doom; retells origin. 44-Moondragon. 45-Killraven. 47-Thing. 48-Iron Man; last 25¢ issue. 49-Dr. Strange; Iron Man app. 50-Iron Man; Dr. Strange app. 3.50

46-Spider-Man/Deathlok team-up 2.00 6.00

51,52,56,57: 51-Iron Man; Dr. Strange app. 52-Capt. America. 56-Daredevil. 57-Black Widow 2.50

53-Hulk; Woodgod & X-Men app., 1st Byrne-a on X-Men (1/77) 2.00 6.00 20.00

54,59,60: 54-Hulk; Woodgod app. 59-Yellowjacket/The Wasp. 60-The Wasp (Byrne-a in all) 4.00

55-Warlock-c/story; Byrne-a 5.00

58-Ghost Rider 4.00

61-70: All Byrne-a; 61-H-T. 62-Ms. Marvel; last 30¢ issue. 63-Iron Fist. 64-Daughters of the Dragon. 65-Capt. Britain (1st U.S. app.). 66-Capt. Britain; 1st app. Arcade. 67-Tigra; Kraven the Hunter app. 68-Man-Thing. 69-Havok (from X-Men). 70-Thor 3.00

71-74,76-78,80: 71-Falcon. 72-Iron Man. 73-Daredevil. 74-Not Ready for Prime Time Players (Belushi). 76-Dr. Strange. 77-Ms. Marvel. 78-Wonder Man. 80-Dr. Strange/Clea; last 35¢ issue 2.00

75,79: Byrne-a(p). 75-Power Man; Cage app. 79-Mary Jane Watson as Red Sonja; Clark Kent cameo (1 panel, 3/79) 3.00

81-Death of Satana 4.00

82-85,87,88,90,92-99: 82-Black Widow. 83-Nick Fury. 84-Shang-Chi. 92-Hawkeye. 93-Werewolf by Night. 94-Spider-Man vs. The Shroud. 95-Mockingbird (intro.); Nick Fury app. 96-Howard the Duck; last 40¢ issue. 97-Spider-Woman/Hulk. 98-Black Widow. 99-Machine Man. 85-Shang-Chi/ Black Widow/Nick Fury. 87-Black Panther. 88-Invisible Girl. 90-Beast 2.00

86-Guardians of the Galaxy 3.00

89-Nightcrawler (from X-Men) 3.00

91-Ghost Rider 3.00

100-(Double-size)-Fantastic Four/Storm/Black Panther; origin/1st app. Karma, one of the New Mutants; origin Storm; X-Men x-over; Miller-c/a(p); Byrne-a (on X-Men app. only) 4.00

101-116: 101-Nighthawk(Ditko-a). 102-Doc Samson. 103-Ant-Man. 104-Hulk/ Ka-Zar. 105-Hulk/Powerman/Iron Fist. 106-Capt. America. 107-She-Hulk. 108-Paladin; Dazzler cameo. 109-Dazzler; Paladin app. 110-Iron Man. 111-Devil-Slayer. 112-King Kull; last 50¢ issue. 113-Quasar. 114-Falcon. 115-Thor. 116-Valkyrie 1.50

117-Wolverine-c/story .85 2.60 7.00

118-140,142-149: 118-Professor X; Wolverine app. (4 pgs.); X-Men cameo. 119-Gargoyle. 120-Dominic Fortune. 121-Human Torch. 122-Man-Thing. 123-Daredevil. 124-The Beast. 125-Tigra. 126-Hulk & Powerman/Son of Satan. 127-The Watcher. 128-Capt. America; Spider-Man/Capt. America photo-c. 129-The Vision. 130-Scarlet Witch. 131-Frogman. 132-Mr. Fantastic. 133-Fantastic Four. 134-Jack of Hearts. 135-Kitty Pryde; X-Men cameo. 136-Wonder Man. 137-Aunt May/Franklin Richards. 138-Sandman. 139-Nick Fury. 140-Black Widow. 142-Capt. Marvel. 143-Starfox. 144-Moon Knight. 145-Iron Man. 146-Nomad. 147-Human Torch; SpM back to old costume. 148-Thor. 149-Cannonball 1.50

141-Daredevil; SpM/Black Widow app. (Spidey in new black costume; ties w/ Amaz. S-M #252 for 1st black costume) 3.00

150-X-Men ($1.00, double-size); B. Smith-c 4.00

Annual 1(1976)-SpM/X-Men (early app.) 1.50 4.50 15.00

Annuals 2-7: 2(1979)-SpM/Hulk. 3(1980)-Hulk/Power Man/Machine Man/Iron Fist; Miller-c(p). 4(1981)-SpM/Daredevil/Moon Knight/Power Man/Iron Fist; brief origins of each; Miller-c; Miller scripts on Daredevil. 5(1982)-SpM/The Thing/Scarlet Witch/Dr. Strange/Quasar. 6(1983)-SpM/New Mutants (early app.), Cloak & Dagger. 7(1984)-Alpha Flight; Byrne-c(i) 2.00

NOTE: ***Art Adams*** *c-141p.* ***Austin*** *a-79i; c-76i, 79i, 96i, 101i, 112i, 130i.* ***Bolle*** *a-9i.* ***Byrne*** *a(p)-53-55, 59-70, 75, 79, 100; c-68p, 70p, 72p, 75, 76p, 79p, 129i, 133i.* ***Colan*** *a-87p.* ***Ditko*** *a-101.* ***Kane*** *a(p)-4-6, 13, 14, 16-19, 23; c(p)-4, 13, 14, 17-19, 23, 25, 26, 32-35, 37, 41, 44, 45, 47, 53, 54.* ***Miller*** *a-100p; c-95p, 99p, 100p, 102p, 106.* ***Mooney*** *a-2i, 7i, 8, 10p, 11p, 16i, 24-31p, 72, 93i, Annual 5i.* ***Nasser*** *a-89p; c-101p.* ***Simonson*** *c-99i, 148.* ***Paul Smith*** *c-131, 132.* ***Starlin*** *c-27.* ***Sutton*** *a-93p. "H-T" means Human Torch; "SpM" means Spider-Man; "S-M" means Sub-Mariner.*

MARVEL TEAM-UP (2nd Series)
Marvel Comics: Sept, 1997 - No. 11, July, 1998 ($1.99)

1-7: 1-Spider-Man team-ups begin, Generation x-app. 2-Hercules-c/app.; two covers. 3-Sandman. 4-Man-Thing. 7-Blade 2.00

8-11: 8-Namor team-ups begin, Dr. Strange app. 9-Capt. America. 10-Thing. 11-Iron Man 2.00

MARVEL TREASURY EDITION
Marvel Comics Group: 1974; #2, Dec, 1974 - #28, 1981 ($1.50/$2.50, 100 pgs., oversized, new-a &-r)(Also see Amazing Spider-Man, The, Marvel Spec. Ed. Feat.--, Savage Fists of Kung Fu, Superman Vs., & 2001, A Space Odyssey)

1-Spectacular Spider-Man; story-r/Marvel Super-Heroes #14; Romita-c/a(r); G. Kane, Ditko-r; Green Goblin/Hulk-r 3.00 9.00 33.00

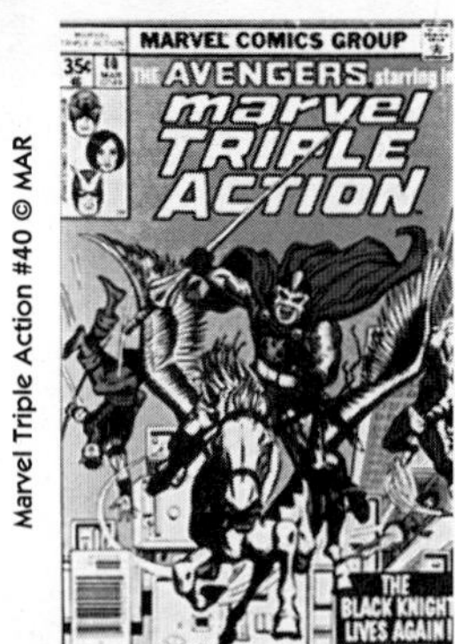

Marvel Triple Action #40 © MAR

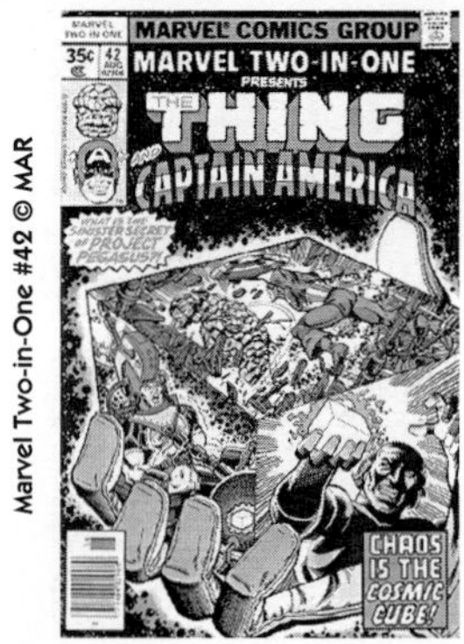

Marvel Two-in-One #42 © MAR

Marvel Universe #1 © MAR

GD25 FN65 NM94

1-1,000 numbered copies signed by Stan Lee & John Romita on front-c & sold thru mail for $5.00; these were the1st 1,000 copies off the press 10.00 30.00 110.00
2-10: 2-Fantastic Four-r/F.F. 6,11,48-50(Silver Surfer). 3-The Mighty Thor-r/ Thor #125-130. 4-Conan the Barbarian; Barry Smith-c/a(r)/Conan #11. 5-The Hulk (origin-r/Hulk #3). 6-Dr. Strange. 7-Mighty Avengers. 8-Giant Superhero Holiday Grab-Bag; Spider-Man, Hulk, Nick Fury. 9-Giant; Super-hero Team-up. 10-Thor; r/Thor #154-157 1.60 4.80 16.00
11-25,27: 11-Fantastic Four. 12-Howard the Duck (r/#H. the Duck #1 & G.S. Man-Thing #4,5) plus new Defenders story. 13-Giant Super-Hero Holiday Grab-Bag. 14-The Sensational Spider-Man; r/1st Morbius from Amazing S-M #101,102 plus #100 & r/Not Brand Echh #6. 15-Conan; B. Smith, Neal Adams-i; r/Conan #24. 16-The Defenders (origin) & Valkyrie; r/Defenders #1,4,13,14. 17-The Hulk. 18-The Astonishing Spider-Man; r/Spider-Man's 1st team-ups with Iron Fist, The X-Men, Ghost Rider & Werewolf by Night; inside back-c has photos from 1978 Spider-Man TV show. 19-Conan the Barbarian. 20-Hulk. 21-Fantastic Four. 22-Spider-Man. 23-Conan. 24-Rampaging Hulk. 25-Spider-Man vs. The Hulk. 27-Spider-Man 1.20 3.60 12.00
26-The Hulk; 6 pg. new Wolverine/Hercules-s 1.20 3.60 12.00
28-Spider-Man/Superman; (origin of each) 1.80 5.40 18.00
NOTE: *Reprints-2, 3, 5, 7-9, 13, 14, 16, 17.* ***Neal Adams*** *a(i)-6, 15.* ***Brunner*** *a-6, 12; c-6.* ***Buscema*** *a-15, 19, 28; c-28.* ***Colan*** *a-6r; c-12p.* ***Ditko*** *a-1, 6.* ***Gil Kane*** *c-16p.* ***Kirby*** *a-2, 10, 11; c-7.* ***Perez*** *a-26.* ***Romita*** *c-1, 5.* ***B. Smith*** *a-4, 15, 19; c-4, 19.*

MARVEL TREASURY OF OZ FEATURING THE MARVELOUS LAND OF OZ
Marvel Comics Group: 1975 ($1.50, oversized) (See MGM's Marvelous…)
1-Buscema-a; Romita-c 1.25 3.75 14.00

MARVEL TREASURY SPECIAL (Also see 2001: A Space Odyssey)
Marvel Comics Group: 1974; 1976 ($1.50, oversized, 84 pgs.)
Vol. 1-Spider-Man, Torch, Sub-Mariner, Avengers "Giant Superhero Holiday Grab-Bag"; Wood, Colan/Everett, plus 2 Kirby-r; reprints Hulk vs. Thing from Fantastic Four #25,26 1.25 3.75 14.00
Vol. 1-... Featuring Captain America's Bicentennial Battles (6/76)-Kirby-a; B. Smith inks, 11 pgs. 1.80 5.50 20.00

MARVEL TRIPLE ACTION (See Giant-Size…)
Marvel Comics Group: Feb, 1972 - No. 24, Mar, 1975; No. 25, Aug, 1975 - No. 47, Apr, 1979
1-(25¢ giant, 52 pgs.)-Dr. Doom, Silver Surfer, The Thing begin, end #4 ('66 reprints from Fantastic Four) 1.50 4.50 15.00
2-5 .90 2.70 8.00
6-10 5.00
11-20 3.00
21-47: 45-r/X-Men #45. 46-r/Avengers #53(X-Men) 2.00
NOTE: *#5-44, 46, 47 reprint Avengers #11 thru ?. #40-r/Avengers #48(1st Black Knight).* ***Buscema*** *a(r)-35p, 36p, 38p, 39p, 41, 42, 43p, 44p, 46p, 47p.* ***Ditko*** *a-2r; c-47.* ***Kirby*** *a(r)-1-4p.* ***Starlin*** *c-7.* ***Tuska*** *a(r)-40p, 43i, 46i, 47i. #2 through at least #17 are 20¢-c.*

MARVEL TWO-IN-ONE (…Featuring … #82? on; also see The Thing)
Marvel Comics Group: January, 1974 - No. 100, June, 1983
1-Thing team-ups begin; Man-Thing 3.50 10.50 38.00
2-4: 2-Sub-Mariner; last 20¢ issue. 3-Daredevil. 4-Capt. America 1.20 3.60 12.00
5-Guardians of the Galaxy (9/74, 2nd app.?) 1.20 3.60 12.00
6-Dr. Strange (11/74) 1.20 3.60 12.00
7,9,10 2.00 6.00
8-Early Ghost Rider app. (3/75) .85 2.60 7.00
11-14,17-20: 13-Power Man. 14-Son of Satan (early app.). 17-Spider-Man. 18-Last 25¢ issue 4.00
15,16-(Regular 25¢ edition)(5-6/76) 4.00
15,16-(30¢-c, limited distribution) 1.60 4.80 16.00
21-26,29,31-40: 29-Master of Kung Fu; Spider-Woman cameo. 31-33-Spider-Woman. 39-Vision 3.00
27-Deathlok 4.00
28-(Regular 30¢ edition)(6/77) 3.00

GD25 FN65 NM94

28-(35¢-c, limited distribution) 1.20 3.60 12.00
30-2nd full app. Spider-Woman (see Marvel Spotlight #32 for 1st app.) 5.00
41,42,44-49: 42-Capt. America. 45-Capt. Marvel. 46-Thing battles Hulk-c/story 3.00
43,50,53,55-Byrne-a(p). 53-Quasar(7/79, 2nd app.) 2.50
51-The Beast, Nick Fury, Ms. Marvel; Miller-p 3.00
52-Moon Knight app. 3.00
54-Death of Deathlok: Byrne-a .90 2.70 7.50
56-60,64-68,70-79,81,82: 60-Intro. Impossible Woman. 68-Angel. 71-1st app. Maelstrom. 75-Avengers (52 pgs.). 76-Iceman 2.00
61-63: 61-Starhawk (from Guardians); "The Coming of Her" storyline begins, ends #63; cover similar to F.F. #67 (Him-c). 62-Moondragon; Thanos & Warlock cameo in flashback; Starhawk app. 63-Warlock?; Warlock revived shortly; Starhawk & Moondragon app. 2.00
69-Guardians of the Galaxy 3.00
80-Ghost Rider 3.00
83,84: 83-Sasquatch. 84-Alpha Flight app. 2.00
85-99: 90-Spider-Man. 93-Jocasta dies. 96-X-Men-c & cameo 2.00
100-Double size, Byrne scripts 2.00
Annual 1 (1976, 52 pgs.)-Thing/Liberty Legion 2.00
Annual 2(1977, 52 pgs.)-Thing/Spider-Man; 2nd death of Thanos; end of Thanos saga; Warlock app.; Starlin-c/a 1.00 3.00 10.00
Annual 3,4 (1978-79, 52 pgs.): 3-Nova. 4-Black Bolt 2.00
Annual 5-7 (1980-82, 52 pgs.): 5-Hulk. 6-1st app. American Eagle. 7-The Thing/ Champion; Sasquatch, Colossus app.; X-Men cameo (1 pg.) 2.00
NOTE: ***Austin*** *c(i)-42, 54, 56, 58, 61, 63, 66.* ***John Buscema*** *a-30p, 45; c-30p.* ***Byrne*** *(p)-43, 50, 53-55; c-43, 53p, 56p, 98i, 99i.* ***Gil Kane*** *a-1p, 2p; c(p)-1-3, 9, 11, 14, 28.* ***Kirby*** *c-10, 12, 19p, 20, 25, 27.* ***Mooney*** *a-18i, 38i, 90i.* ***Nasser*** *a-70p.* ***Perez*** *a(p)-56-58, 60, 64, 65; c(p)-32, 33, 42, 50-52, 54, 55, 57, 58, 61-66, 70.* ***Roussos*** *a-Annual 1i.* ***Simonson*** *c-43i, 97p, Annual 6i.* ***Starlin*** *c-6, Annual 1.* ***Tuska*** *a-6p.*

MARVEL UNIVERSE (See Official Handbook Of The…)

MARVEL UNIVERSE
Marvel Comics: June, 1998 - No. 7, Dec, 1998 ($2.99/$1.99)
1-($2.99)-Invaders stories from WW2; Stern-s 3.00
2,3-($1.99): 2-Two covers 2.00
4-7-Monster Hunters; Manley-a/Stern-s 2.00

MARVEL VERSUS DC (See DC Versus Marvel) (Also see Amazon, Assassins, Bruce Wayne: Agent of S.H.I.E.L.D., Bullets & Bracelets, Doctor Strangefate, JLX, Legend of the Dark Claw, Magneto & The Magnetic Men, Speed Demon, Spider-Boy, Super Soldier, & X-Patrol)
Marvel Comics: No. 2, 1996 - No. 3, 1996 ($3.95, limited series)
2,3: 2-Peter David script. 3-Ron Marz script; Dan Jurgens-a(p). 1st app. of Super Soldier, Spider-Boy, Dr. Doomsday, Doctor Strangefate, The Dark Claw, Nightcreeper, Amazon, Wraith & others. Storyline continues in Amalgam books. 4.00

MARVEL X-MEN COLLECTION, THE
Marvel Comics: Jan, 1994 - No. 3, Mar, 1994 ($2.95, limited series)
1-3-r/X-Men trading cards by Jim Lee 3.00

MARVEL - YEAR IN REVIEW (Magazine)
Marvel Comics: 1989 - No. 3, 1991 (52 pgs.)
1-3: 1-McFarlane Spider-Man-c. 2-Capt. America-c. 3-X-Men/Wolverine-c 2.00 6.00

MARVIN MOUSE
Atlas Comics (BPC): September, 1957
1-Everett-c/a; Maneely-a 10.00 30.00 75.00

MARY JANE & SNIFFLES (See Looney Tunes)
Dell Publishing Co.: No. 402, June, 1952 - No. 474, June, 1953
Four Color 402 (#1) 7.00 22.00 80.00
Four Color 474 6.40 19.00 70.00

MARY MARVEL COMICS (Monte Hale #29 on) (Also see Captain Marvel #18, Marvel Family, Shazam, & Wow Comics)

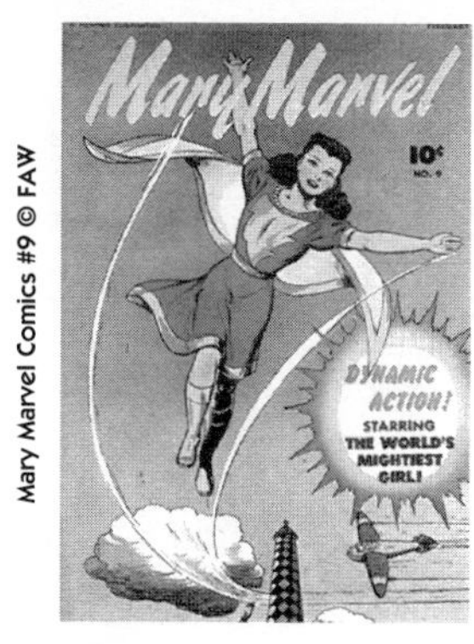

Mary Marvel Comics #9 © FAW

Mask / Marshall Law #1 © DH

Masked Man #12 © ECL

	GD25	FN65	NM94
Fawcett Publications: Dec, 1945 - No. 28, Sept, 1948			
1-Captain Marvel introduces Mary on-c; intro/origin Georgia Sivana	165.00	494.00	1400.00
2	65.00	194.00	550.00
3,4: 3-New logo	43.00	129.00	360.00
5-8: 8-Bulletgirl x-over in Mary Marvel; X-Mas-c	33.00	100.00	250.00
9,10	29.00	88.00	220.00
11-20	19.00	58.00	145.00
21-28: 28-Western-c	17.00	50.00	125.00

MARY POPPINS (See Movie Comics & Walt Disney Showcase No. 17)

MARY'S GREATEST APOSTLE (St. Louis Grignion de Montfort)
Catechetical Guild (Topix) (Giveaway): No date (16 pgs.; paper cover)

	GD25	FN65	NM94
nn	2.80	7.00	14.00

MARY SHELLEY'S FRANKENSTEIN
Topps Comics: Oct, 1994 - Jan, 1995 ($2.95, limited series)

	GD25	FN65	NM94
1-4-polybagged w/3 trading cards			3.00
1-4 ($2.50)-Newstand ed.			2.50

MARY WORTH (See Harvey Comics Hits #55 & Love Stories of...)
Argo: March, 1956 (Also see Romantic Picture Novelettes)

	GD25	FN65	NM94
1	5.70	17.00	40.00

MASK (TV)
DC Comics: Dec, 1985 - No. 4, Mar, 1986; Feb, 1987 - No. 9, Oct, 1987

	GD25	FN65	NM94
1-Sat. morning TV show.			2.00
2-4			1.40
1-(2nd series)			1.20
2-9			.90

MASK, THE
Dark Horse Comics: Aug, 1991 - No. 4, Oct, 1991; No. 0, Dec, 1991 ($2.50, 36 pgs., limited series)

	GD25	FN65	NM94
1-4: 1-1st app. Lt. Kellaway as The Mask	.85	2.60	7.00
0-(12/91, B&W, 56 pgs.)-r/Mayhem #1-4			5.00
...: HUNT FOR GREEN OCTOBER July, 1995 - Oct, 1995 ($2.50, lim. series)			
1-4-Evan Dorkin scripts			2.50
.../ MARSHALL LAW Feb, 1998 - No. 2, Mar, 1998 ($2.95, lim. series)			
1,2-Mills-s/O'Neill-a			3.00
...: OFFICIAL MOVIE ADAPTATION July, 1994 - Aug, 1994 ($2.50, lim. series)			
1,2			2.50
... RETURNS Oct, 1992 - No. 4, Mar, 1993 ($2.50, limited series)			
1-4			4.00
... SOUTHERN DISCOMFORT Mar, 1996 - No. 4, July, 1996 ($2.50, lim. series)			
1-4			2.50
... STRIKES BACK Feb, 1995 - No. 5, Jun, 1995 ($2.50, limited series)			
1-5			2.50
... SUMMER VACATION July, 1995 ($10.95, one shot, hard-c)			
1-nn-Rick Geary-c/a	1.10	3.30	11.00
... TOYS IN THE ATTIC Aug, 1998 - No. 4, Nov, 1998 ($2.95, limited series)			
1-4-Fingerman-s			2.95
... VIRTUAL SURREALITY July, 1997 ($2.95, one shot)			
nn-Mignola, Aragonés, and others-s/a		1.20	3.00
... WORLD TOUR Dec, 1995 - No. 4, Mar, 1996 ($2.50, limited series)			
1-4: 3-X & Ghost-c/app.		1.00	2.50

MASK COMICS
Rural Home Publ.: Feb-Mar, 1945 - No. 2, Apr-May, 1945; No. 2, Fall, 1945

	GD25	FN65	NM94
1-Classic L. B. Cole Satan-c/a; Palais-a	224.00	672.00	1900.00
2-(Scarce)-Classic L. B. Cole Satan-c; Black Rider, The Boy Magician, & The Collector app.	147.00	441.00	1250.00
2-(Fall, 1945)-No publ.-same as regular #2; L. B. Cole-c	112.00	336.00	950.00

MASKED BANDIT, THE
Avon Periodicals: 1952

	GD25	FN65	NM94
nn-Kinstler-a	13.00	39.00	95.00

MASKED MAN, THE
Eclipse Comics: 12/84 - #10, 4/86; #11, 10/87; #12, 4/88 ($1.75/$2.00, color/B&W #9 on, Baxter paper)

	GD25	FN65	NM94
1-Origin retold			2.00
2-12: 3-Origin Aphid-Man; begin $2.00-c			1.80

MASKED MARVEL (See Keen Detective Funnies)
Centaur Publications: Sept, 1940 - No. 3, Dec, 1940

	GD25	FN65	NM94
1-The Masked Marvel begins	150.00	450.00	1275.00
2,3: 2-Gustavson, Tarpe Mills-a	100.00	300.00	850.00

MASKED PILOT, THE (See Popular Comics #43)
R.S. Callender: 1939 (7-1/2x5-1/4", 16 pgs., premium, non-slick-c)

	GD25	FN65	NM94
nn-Bob Jenney-a	9.30	28.00	70.00

MASKED RAIDER, THE (Billy The Kid #9 on; Frontier Scout, Daniel Boone #10-13) (Also see Blue Bird)
Charlton Comics: June, 1955 - No. 8, July, 1957; No. 14, Aug, 1958 - No. 30, June, 1961

	GD25	FN65	NM94
1-Masked Raider & Talon the Golden Eagle begin; painted-c	9.30	28.00	70.00
2	5.70	17.00	40.00
3-8: 8-Billy The Kid app.	4.25	13.00	28.00
14,16-30: 22-Rocky Lane app.	4.00	11.00	22.00
15-Williamson-a, 7 pgs.	4.25	13.00	28.00

MASKED RANGER
Premier Magazines: Apr, 1954 - No. 9, Aug, 1955

	GD25	FN65	NM94
1-The Masked Ranger, his horse Streak, & The Crimson Avenger (origin) begin, end #9; Woodbridge/Frazetta-a	36.00	108.00	270.00
2,3	11.00	32.00	80.00
4-8-All Woodbridge-a. 5-Jesse James by Woodbridge. 6-Billy The Kid by Woodbridge. 7-Wild Bill Hickok by Woodbridge. 8-Jim Bowie's Life Story	12.00	36.00	90.00
9-Torres-a; Wyatt Earp by Woodbridge; Says Death of Masked Ranger on-c	13.00	38.00	95.00

NOTE: ***Check*** *a-1.* ***Woodbridge*** *c/a-1, 4-9.*

MASK OF DR. FU MANCHU, THE (See Dr. Fu Manchu)
Avon Periodicals: 1951

	GD25	FN65	NM94
1-Sax Rohmer adapt.; Wood-c/a (26 pgs.); Hollingsworth-a	79.00	237.00	675.00

MASK OF ZORRO, THE
Image Comics: Aug, 1998 - No. 4, Nov, 1998 ($2.95, limited series)

	GD25	FN65	NM94
1-4-Movie adapt. Photo variant-c			2.95

MASQUE OF THE RED DEATH (See Movie Classics)

MASTER COMICS (Combined with Slam Bang Comics #7 on)
Fawcett Publications: Mar, 1940 - No. 133, Apr, 1953 (No. 1-6: oversized issues) (#1-3: 15¢, 52 pgs.; #4-6: 10¢, 36 pgs.; #7-Begin 68 pg. issues)

	GD25	FN65	VF82	NM94
1-Origin & 1st app. Master Man; The Devil's Dagger, El Carim, Master of Magic, Rick O'Say, Morton Murch, White Rajah, Shipwreck Roberts, Frontier Marshal, Streak Sloan, Mr. Clue begin (all features end #6)	680.00	2040.00	4080.00	6800.00

	GD25	FN65	NM94
2	188.00	564.00	1600.00
3-5	147.00	441.00	1250.00
6-Last Master Man	147.00	441.00	1250.00

NOTE: *#1-6 rarely found in near mint to mint condition due to large-size format.*

Master Comics #30 © FAW

Master Comics #93 © FAW

Master of Kung-Fu #125 © MAR

GD25 FN65 NM94

7-(10/40)-Bulletman, Zoro, the Mystery Man (ends #22), Lee Granger, Jungle King, & Buck Jones begin; only app. The War Bird & Mark Swift & the Time Retarder; Zoro, Lee Granger, Jungle King & Mark Swift all continue from Slam Bang; Bulletman moves from Nickel 247.00 741.00 2100.00
8-The Red Gaucho (ends #13), Captain Venture (ends #22) & The Planet Princess begin 129.00 387.00 1100.00
9,10: 10-Lee Granger ends 103.00 309.00 875.00
11-Origin & 1st app. Minute-Man (2/41) 229.00 687.00 1950.00
12 115.00 345.00 975.00
13-Origin & 1st app. Bulletgirl; Hitler-c 176.00 528.00 1500.00
14-16: 14-Companions Three begins, ends #31 94.00 282.00 800.00
17-20: 17-Raboy-a on Bulletman begins. 20-Captain Marvel cameo app. in Bulletman 88.00 264.00 750.00

GD25 FN65 VF82 NM94

21-(12/41; Scarce)-Captain Marvel & Bulletman team up against Capt. Nazi; origin & 1st app. Capt. Marvel Jr's most famous nemesis Captain Nazi who will cause creation of Capt. Marvel Jr. in Whiz #25. Part I of trilogy origin of Capt. Marvel Jr.; 1st Mac Raboy-c for Fawcett; Capt. Nazi-c
440.00 1320.00 2640.00 4400.00
22-(1/42)-Captain Marvel Jr. moves over from Whiz #25 & teams up with Bulletman against Captain Nazi; part III of trilogy origin of Capt. Marvel Jr. & his 1st cover and adventure 400.00 1200.00 2400.00 4000.00

GD25 FN65 NM94

23-Capt. Marvel Jr. c/stories begin (1st solo story); fights Capt. Nazi by himself.
239.00 717.00 2150.00
24,25 87.00 261.00 740.00
26-28,30-Captain Marvel Jr. vs. Capt. Nazi. 30-Flag-c
79.00 237.00 675.00
29-Hitler & Hirohito-c 88.00 264.00 750.00
31,32: 32-Last El Carim & Buck Jones; intro Balbo, the Boy Magician in El Carim story; classic Eagle-c by Raboy 57.00 169.00 480.00
33-Balbo, the Boy Magician (ends #47), Hopalong Cassidy (ends #49) begins
57.00 169.00 480.00
34-Capt. Marvel Jr. vs. Capt. Nazi-c/story 63.00 189.00 535.00
35 56.00 168.00 480.00
36-40: 40-Flag-c 51.00 153.00 435.00
41-(8/43)-Bulletman, Capt. Marvel Jr. & Bulletgirl x-over in Minute-Man; only app.Crime Crusaders Club (Capt. Marvel Jr., Minute-Man, Bulletman & Bulletgirl) 56.00 168.00 480.00
42-47,49: 47-Hitler becomes Corpl. Hitler Jr. 49-Last Minute-Man
36.00 108.00 270.00
48-Intro. Bulletboy; Capt. Marvel cameo in Minute-Man
40.00 120.00 315.00
50-Intro Radar & Nyoka the Jungle Girl & begin series (5/44); Radar also intro in Captain Marvel #35 (same date); Capt. Marvel x-over in Radar; origin Radar; Capt. Marvel & Capt. Marvel, Jr. introduce Radar on-c
37.00 112.00 280.00
51-58 19.00 56.00 140.00
59-62: Nyoka serial "Terrible Tiara" in all; 61-Capt. Marvel Jr. 1st meets Uncle Marvel 21.00 64.00 160.00
63-80 15.00 44.00 110.00
81,83-87,89-91,95-99: 88-Hopalong Cassidy begins (ends #94). 95-Tom Mix begins (ends #133) 13.00 38.00 95.00
82,88,92-94-Krigstein-a 14.00 42.00 105.00
100 13.00 40.00 100.00
101-106-Last Bulletman 12.00 36.00 90.00
107-131 11.00 32.00 80.00
132-B&W and color illos in **POP** 11.00 34.00 85.00
133-Bill Battle app. 16.00 48.00 120.00

NOTE: ***Mac Raboy*** *a-15-39, 40(part), 42, 58. c-21-49, 51, 52, 54, 56, 58, 68(part), 69(part). Bulletman c-7-11, 13(half), 15, 18(part), 19, 20, 21(w/Capt. Marvel & Capt. Nazi), 22(w/Capt. Marvel, Jr.). Capt. Marvel, Jr. c-23-133. Master Man c-1-6. Minute Man c-12, 13(half), 14, 16, 17, 18(part).*

MASTER DARQUE
Acclaim Comics (Valiant): Feb, 1998 ($3.95)

1-Manco-a/Christina Z.-s 3.95

MASTER DETECTIVE
Super Comics: 1964 (Reprints)

17-r/Criminals on the Loose V4 #2; r/Young King Cole #?; McWilliams-r
1.10 3.30 9.00

MASTER OF KUNG FU (Formerly Special Marvel Edition; see Deadly Hands of Kung Fu & Giant-Size...)
Marvel Comics Group: No. 17, April, 1974 - No. 125, June, 1983

17-Starlin-a; intro Black Jack Tarr; 3rd Shang-Chi (ties w/Deadly Hands #1)
1.70 5.10 17.00
18-20: 19-Man-Thing-c/story .90 2.70 9.00
21-23,25-30 5.50
24-Starlin, Simonson-a .85 2.60 7.00
31-50: 33-1st Leiko Wu. 43-Last 25¢ issue 4.00
51-99 3.50
100-Double size 4.50
101-117,119-124 3.00
118,125-Double size issues 4.00
Annual 1(4/76)-Iron Fist app. .85 2.60 7.00

NOTE: ***Austin*** *c-63i, 74i.* ***Buscema*** *c-44p.* ***Gulacy*** *a(p)-18-20, 22, 25, 29-31, 33-35, 38, 39, 40(p&i), 42-50, 53r(#20); c-51, 55, 64, 67.* ***Gil Kane*** *c(p)-20, 38, 39, 42, 45, 59, 63.* ***Nebres*** *c-73i.* ***Starlin*** *a-17p, 24; c-54.* ***Sutton*** *a-42i. #53 reprints #20.*

MASTER OF KUNG-FU: BLEEDING BLACK
Marvel Comics: Feb, 1991 ($2.95, 84 pgs., one-shot)

1-The Return of Shang-Chi 3.00

MASTER OF THE WORLD
Dell Publishing Co.: No. 1157, July, 1961

Four Color 1157-Movie 4.50 13.50 50.00

MASTERS OF TERROR (Magazine)
Marvel Comics Group: July, 1975 - No. 2, Sept, 1975 (B&W) (All reprints)

1-Brunner, Barry Smith-a; Morrow/Steranko-c; Starlin-a(p); Gil Kane-a
1.00 3.00 10.00
2-Reese, Kane, Mayerik-a; Adkins/Steranko-c .90 2.70 9.00

MASTERS OF THE UNIVERSE
DC Comics: Dec, 1982 - No. 3, Feb, 1983 (Mini-series)

1-3: 2-Origin He-Man & Ceril 1.00

NOTE: ***Alcala*** *a-1i,, 2i.* ***Tuska*** *a-1-3p; c-1-3p. #2 has 75 & 95 cent cover price.*

MASTERS OF THE UNIVERSE (Comic Album)
Western Publishing Co.: 1984 (8-1/2x11", $2.95, 64 pgs.)

11362-Based on Mattel toy & cartoon 2.00 6.00

MASTERS OF THE UNIVERSE
Star Comics/Marvel #7 on: May 1986 - No. 12, March, 1988 (75¢/$1.00)

1-12: 8-Begin $1.00-c 1.00
The Motion Picture (11/87, $2.00)-Tuska-p 2.00

MASTERWORKS SERIES OF GREAT COMIC BOOK ARTISTS, THE
Sea Gate Dist./DC Comics: May, 1983 - No. 3, Dec, 1983 (Baxter paper)

1-3: 1,2-Shining Knight by Frazetta r-/Adventure. 2-Tomahawk by Frazetta-r. 3-Wrightson-c/a(r) 2.00

MATT SLADE GUNFIGHTER (Kid Slade Gunfighter #5 on; See Western Gunfighters)
Atlas Comics (SPI): May, 1956 - No. 4, Nov, 1956

1-Intro Matt & horse Eagle; Williamson/Torres-a 17.00 50.00 125.00
2-Williamson-a 9.30 28.00 70.00
3,4 7.85 23.50 55.00

NOTE: ***Maneely*** *a-1, 3, 4; c-1, 2, 4.* ***Roth*** *a-2-4.* ***Severin*** *a-1, 3, 4.* ***Maneely*** *c/a-1.*

MAVERICK (TV)
Dell Publishing Co.: No. 892, 4/58 - No. 19, 4-6/62 (All have photo-c)

Four Color 892 (#1)-James Garner photo-c begin 25.00 75.00 275.00

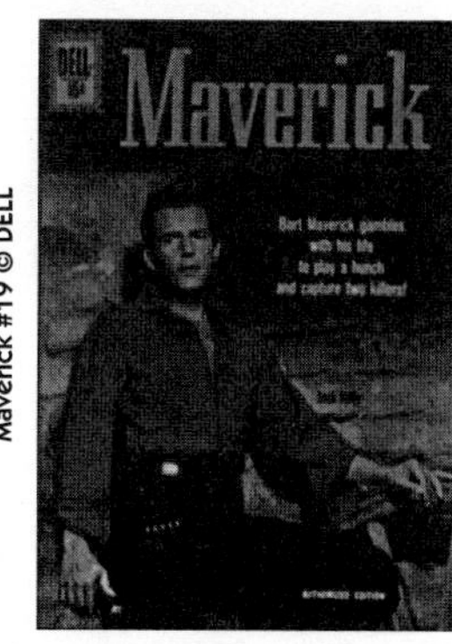

Maverick #19 © DELL

Maxx #1 3-D Edition © I Before E

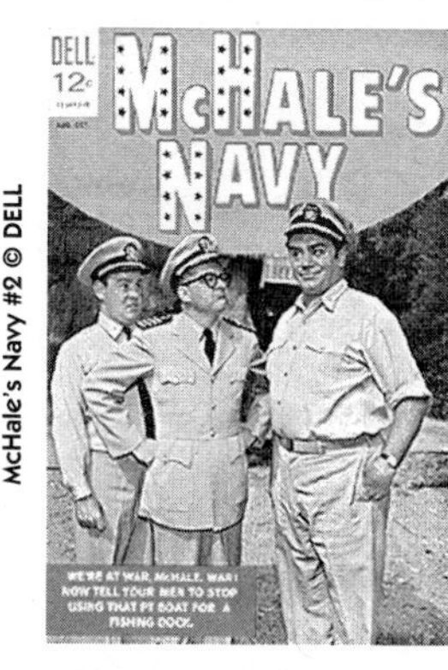

McHale's Navy #2 © DELL

	GD25	FN65	NM94
Four Color 930,945,962,980,1005 (6-8/59): 945-James Garner/Jack Kelly photo-c begin	10.00	30.00	110.00
7 (10-12/59) - 14: Last Garner/Kelly-c	8.00	23.00	85.00
15-18: Jack Kelly/Roger Moore photo-c	6.50	19.50	72.00
19-Jack Kelly photo-c	6.50	19.50	72.00

MAVERICK (See X-Men)
Marvel Comics: Jan, 1997 ($2.95, one-shot)

	GD25	FN65	NM94
1-Hama-s			3.00

MAVERICK (See X-Men)
Marvel Comics: Sept, 1997 - No. 12, Aug, 1998 ($2.99/$1.99)

	GD25	FN65	NM94
1-($2.99)-Wraparound-c.			3.00
2-11-($1.99): 2-Two covers. 4-Wolverine. 6,7-Sabretooth app.			2.00
12-($2.99) Battles Omega Red			3.00

MAVERICK MARSHAL
Charlton Comics: Nov, 1958 - No. 7, May, 1960

	GD25	FN65	NM94
1	5.00	15.00	30.00
2-7	4.00	10.00	20.00

MAVERICKS
Daggar Comics Group: Jan, 1994 - No. 5, 1994 (#1-$2.75, #2-5-$2.50)

	GD25	FN65	NM94
1-5: 1-Bronze. 1-Gold. 1-Silver			2.50

MAX BRAND (See Silvertip)

MAXIMAGE
Image Comics (Extreme Studios): Dec, 1995 - No. 7, June 1996 ($2.50)

	GD25	FN65	NM94
1-7: 1-Liefeld-c. 2-Extreme Destroyer Pt. 2; polybagged w/card. 4-Angela & Glory-c/app.			2.50

MAXIMUM MANGA
London Knight Studios: Nov, 1997 ($4.95, B&W, bi-monthy)

	GD25	FN65	NM94
1-Anthology w/Jurassic Jane, Demonique, CYJAX and others			4.95

MAXX (Also see Darker Image, Primer #5, & Friends of Maxx)
Image Comics (I Before E): Mar, 1993 - Present ($1.95)

	GD25	FN65	NM94
1/2	1.00	3.00	10.00
1/2 (Gold)			25.00
1-Sam Kieth-c/a/scripts			4.00
1-Glow-in-the-dark variant	1.50	4.50	15.00
1-"3-D Edition" (1/98, $4.95) plus new back-up story			5.00
2-12: 6-Savage Dragon cameo(1 pg.). 7,8-Pitt-c & story			2.50
13-16			2.50
17-35: 21-Alan Moore-s			2.00

MAYA (See Movie Classics)
Gold Key: Mar, 1968

	GD25	FN65	NM94
1 (10218-803)(TV)	1.65	4.90	18.00

MAYHEM
Dark Horse Comics: May, 1989 - No. 4, Sept, 1989 ($2.50, B&W, 52 pgs.)

	GD25	FN65	NM94
1- 4-part Stanley Ipkiss/Mask story begins; Mask-c	1.00	3.00	10.00
2-4: 2-Mask 1/2 back-c. 4-Mask-c	.90	2.70	8.00

MAZE AGENCY, THE
Comico/Innovation Publ. #8 on: Dec, 1988 - No. 20, 1991 ($1.95-$2.50, color)

	GD25	FN65	NM94
1-6,8-15 ($1.95): 9-Ellery Queen app.			2.00
7,16-20: 7 ($2.50)-Last Comico issue			2.50
Annual 1 (1990, $2.75)-Ploog-c; Spirit tribute ish			2.80
Special 1 (1989, $2.75)-Staton-p (Innovation)			2.80

MAZE AGENCY, THE (Vol. 2)
Caliber Comics: July, 1997 - Present ($2.95, B&W)

	GD25	FN65	NM94
1-3: 1-Barr-s/Gonzales-a(p). 3-Hughes-c			3.00

MAZIE (...& Her Friends) (See Flat-Top, Mortie, Stevie & Tastee-Freez)
Mazie Comics(Magazine Publ.)/Harvey Publ. No. 13-on: 1953 - #12, 1954; #13, 12/54 - #22, 9/56; #23, 9/57 - #28, 8/58

	GD25	FN65	NM94
1-(Teen-age)-Stevie's girlfriend	5.70	17.00	40.00
2	4.00	10.00	20.00
3-10	3.00	7.50	15.00
11-28	2.00	5.00	10.00

MAZIE
Nation Wide Publishers: 1950 - No. 7, 1951 (5¢) (5x7-1/4"-miniature)(52 pgs.)

	GD25	FN65	NM94
1-Teen-age	12.00	36.00	90.00
2-7	6.50	19.50	45.00

MAZINGER (See First Comics Graphic Novel #17)

'MAZING MAN
DC Comics: Jan, 1986 - No. 12, Dec, 1986

	GD25	FN65	NM94
1-12: 7,8-Hembeck-a. 12-Dark Knight part-c by Miller			.80
Special 1 ('87), 2 (4/88), 3 ('90)-All $2.00, 52pgs.			2.00

McCRORY'S CHRISTMAS BOOK
Western Printing Co: 1955 (36 pgs., slick-c) (McCrory Stores Corp. giveaway)

	GD25	FN65	NM94
nn-Painted-c	3.60	9.00	18.00

McCRORY'S TOYLAND BRINGS YOU SANTA'S PRIVATE EYES
Promotional Publ. Co.: 1956 (16 pgs.) (Giveaway)

	GD25	FN65	NM94
nn-Has 9 pg. story plus 7 pgs. toy ads	2.80	7.00	14.00

McCRORY'S WONDERFUL CHRISTMAS
Promotional Publ. Co.: 1954 (20 pgs., slick-c) (Giveaway)

	GD25	FN65	NM94
nn	3.60	9.00	18.00

McHALE'S NAVY (TV) (See Movie Classics)
Dell Publ. Co.: May-July, 1963 - No. 3, Nov-Jan, 1963-64 (All have photo-c)

	GD25	FN65	NM94
1	5.00	15.00	55.00
2,3	4.00	12.00	45.00

McKEEVER & THE COLONEL (TV)
Dell Publishing Co.: Feb-Apr, 1963 - No. 3, Aug-Oct, 1963

	GD25	FN65	NM94
1-Photo-c	5.00	15.00	55.00
2,3	3.80	11.50	40.00

McLINTOCK (See Movie Comics)

MD
E. C. Comics: Apr-May, 1955 - No. 5, Dec-Jan, 1955-56

	GD25	FN65	NM94
1-Not approved by code	10.00	30.00	100.00
2-5	7.50	22.50	75.00

NOTE: ***Crandall, Evans, Ingels, Orlando** art in all issues; **Craig** c-1-5.*

M.D. GEIST
CPM Comics: 1995 - No. 3, 1995 (Limited series)

	GD25	FN65	NM94
1-3			3.00

M.D. GEIST DATA ALBUM
CPM Comics: June, 1996 ($9.95, trade paperback)

	GD25	FN65	NM94
1			10.00

M.D. GEIST: GROUND ZERO
CPM Comics: Mar, 1996 - No. 3, May, 1996 ($2.95, limited series)

	GD25	FN65	NM94
1-3			3.00

MEASLES
Fantagraphics Books: Christmas 1998 - Present ($2.95, B&W, quarterly)

	GD25	FN65	NM94
1-Anthology; Venus-s by Hernandez			2.95

MEAT CAKE
Iconografix: 1992 (B&W)

	GD25	FN65	NM94
1			1.00

MEAT CAKE
Fantagraphics Books: No. 1, Oct, 1993 - No. 5 (B&W)

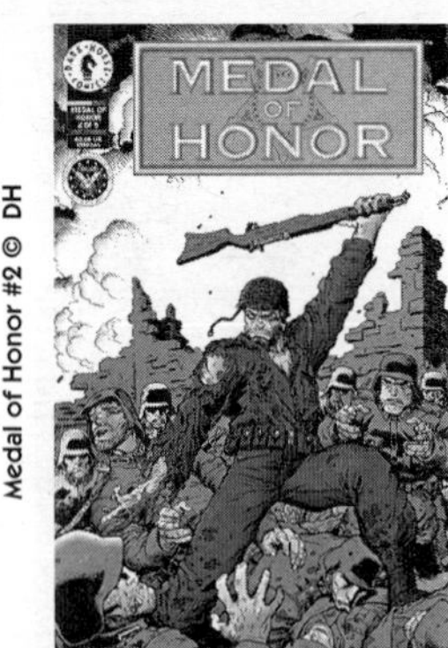

Medal of Honor #2 © DH

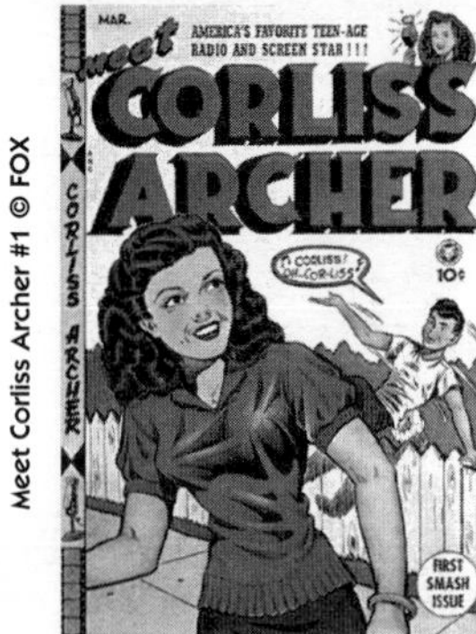

Meet Corliss Archer #1 © FOX

Megaton #5 © Gary S. Carlson

0-8: 3-Sal Buscema-a. 0 (1996)-reprints Meat Cake #1 from Iconographix. 2.50

MECHA (Also see Mayhem)
Dark Horse Comics: June, 1987 - No. 6, 1988 ($1.50/$1.95, color/B&W)

1-6: 1,2 ($1.95, color), 3,4-($1.75, B&W), 5,6-($1.50, B&W) 2.00

MECHANIC, THE
Image Comics: 1998 ($5.95, one-shot, squarebound)

1-Chiodo-painted art; Peterson-s 2.00 6.00
1-($10.00) DF Alternate Cover Ed. 10.00

MECHA SPECIAL
Dark Horse Comics: May, 1995 ($2.95, one-shot)

1 3.00

MEDAL FOR BOWZER, A
American Visuals: 1966 (8 pgs.)

nn-Eisner-c/script 21.00 63.00 210.00

MEDAL OF HONOR COMICS
A. S. Curtis: Spring, 1946

1-War stories 9.30 28.00 70.00

MEDAL OF HONOR SPECIAL
Dark Horse Comics: 1994 ($2.50, one-shot)

1-Kubert-c/a (first story) 2.50

MEDIA STARR
Innovation Publ.: July, 1989 - No. 3, Sept, 1989 ($1.95, mini-series, 28pgs.)

1-3: Deluxe format 2.00

MEDIEVAL SPAWN/WITCHBLADE
Image Comics (Top Cow Productions): May, 1996 - No. 3, June, 1996 ($2.95, limited series)

1-Garth Ennis scripts in all 1.20 3.60 12.00
1-Platinum foil-c (500 copies from Pittsburgh Con) 40.00
1-Gold 15.00
1-ETM Exclusive Edition; gold foil logo 10.00
2 1.20 3.60 12.00
3 1.00 3.00 10.00
TPB ($9.95) r/#1-3 10.00

MEET ANGEL (Formerly Angel & the Ape)
National Periodical Publications: No. 7, Nov-Dec, 1969

7-Wood-a(i) 1.85 5.50 15.00

MEET CORLISS ARCHER (Radio/Movie)(My Life #4 on)
Fox Features Syndicate: Mar, 1948 - No. 3, July, 1948

1-(Teen-age)-Feldstein-c/a; headlight-c 59.00 177.00 500.00
2-Feldstein-c only 46.00 138.00 390.00
3-Part Feldstein-c only 43.00 129.00 350.00
NOTE: *No. 1-3 used in Seduction of the Innocent, pg. 39.*

MEET HERCULES (See Three Stooges)

MEET HIYA A FRIEND OF SANTA CLAUS
Julian J. Proskauer/Sundial Shoe Stores, etc.: 1949 (18 pgs.?, paper-c)-(Giveaway)

nn 5.70 17.00 35.00

MEET MERTON
Toby Press: Dec, 1953 - No. 4, June, 1954

1-(Teen-age)-Dave Berg-c/a 6.00 18.00 42.00
2-Dave Berg-c/a 4.25 13.00 26.00
3,4-Dave Berg-c/a 4.00 12.00 24.00
I.W. Reprint #9 1.00 3.00 8.00
Super Reprint #11('63), 18 1.00 3.00 8.00

MEET MISS BLISS (Becomes Stories Of Romance #5 on)
Atlas Comics (LMC): May, 1955 - No. 4, Nov, 1955

1-Al Hartley-c/a 11.00 32.00 80.00
2-4 6.50 19.50 45.00

MEET MISS PEPPER (Formerly Lucy, The Real Gone Gal)
St. John Publishing Co.: No. 5, April, 1954 - No. 6, June, 1954

5-Kubert/Maurer-a 17.00 52.00 130.00
6-Kubert/Maurer-a; Kubert-c 14.00 42.00 105.00

MEET THE NEW POST GAZETTE SUNDAY FUNNIES
Pittsburgh Post Gazette: 3/12/49 (7-1/4x10-1/4", 16 pgs., paper-c)
Commercial Comics (insert in newspaper)
Dick Tracy by Gould, Gasoline Alley, Terry & the Pirates, Brenda Starr, Buck Rogers by Yager, The Gumps, Peter Rabbit by Fago, Superman, Funnyman by Siegel & Shuster, The Saint, Archie, & others done especially for this book. A fine copy sold at auction in 1985 for $276.00.
Estimated value.... $300 – $800

MEGAHURTZ
Image Comics: Aug, 1997 - No. 3, Oct, 1997 ($2.95, B&W)

1-3-St. Pierre-s 3.00

MEGALITH DEATHWATCH 2000 (Megalith #3 on)
Continuity: Apr, 1993 - No. 9, Mar, 1994 ($2.50)

0-Foil-c; no c-price, giveaway; Adams plot 2.50
1-3-Bagged w/card: 1-Gatefold-c by Nebres; Adams plot. 2-Fold-out-c; Adams plot. 3-Indestructible-c 2.50
4-9-Embossed-c: 4-Adams/Nebres-c; Adams part-i. 5-Sienkiewicz-i. 6-Adams part-i. 7-Adams-c(p); Adams plot 2.50

MEGATON (A super hero)
Megaton Publ.: Nov, 1983; No. 2, Oct, 1985 - No. 8, Aug, 1987 (B&W)

1-($2.00, 68 pgs.)-Erik Larsen's 1st pro work; Vanguard by Larsen begins (1st app.), ends #4; 1st app. Megaton, Berzerker, & Ethrian; Guice-c/a(p); Gustovich-a(p) in #1,2 1.20 3.60 12.00
2-($2.00, 68 pgs.)-The Dragon cameo (1 pg.) by Larsen (later The Savage Dragon in Image Comics); Guice-c/a(p) 2.00 6.00
3-(44 pgs.)-1st full app. Savage Dragon-c/story by Larsen; 1st comic book work by Angel Medina (pin-up) 1.60 4.80 16.00
4-(52 pgs.)-2nd full app. Savage Dragon by Larsen; 4,5-Wildman by Grass Green 1.10 3.30 11.00
5-1st Liefeld published-a (inside f/c, 6/86) 2.00 6.00
6,7: 6-Larsen-c 4.00
8-1st Liefeld story-a (7 pg. super hero story) plus 1 pg. Youngblood ad 2.00 6.00
...Explosion (6/87, 16 pg. color giveaway)-1st app. Youngblood by Rob Liefeld (2 pg. spread); shows Megaton heroes 2.00 6.00 20.00
...Holiday Special 1 (1994, $2.95, color, 40 pgs., publ. by Entity Comics)-Gold foil logo; bagged w/Kelley Jones card; Vanguard, Megaton plus shows unpublished-c to 1987 Youngblood #1 by Liefeld/Ordway 3.00
NOTE: *Copies of Megaton Explosion were also released in early 1992 all signed by Rob Liefeld and were made available to retailers.*

MEGATON MAN (See Don Simpson's Bizarre Heroes)
Kitchen Sink Enterprises: Nov, 1984 - No. 10, 1986

1-10 2.00
1-2nd printing (1989) 2.00
...Meets The Uncategorizable X-Thems 1 (4/89, $2.00) 2.00

MEGATON MAN VS. FORBIDDEN FRANKENSTEIN
Fiasco Comics: Apr, 1996 ($2.95, B&W, one-shot)

1-Intro The Tomb Team (Forbidden Frankenstein, Drekula, Bride of the Monster, & Moon Wolf). 3.00

MEL ALLEN SPORTS COMICS (The Voice of the Yankees)
Standard Comics: No. 5, Nov, 1949; No. 6, June, 1950

5(#1 on inside)-Tuska-a 19.00 56.00 140.00
6(#2)-Lou Gehrig story 13.00 38.00 95.00

MELTING POT
Kitchen Sink Press: Dec, 1993 - No. 4, Sept, 1994 ($2.95)

Menace #11 © ATLAS

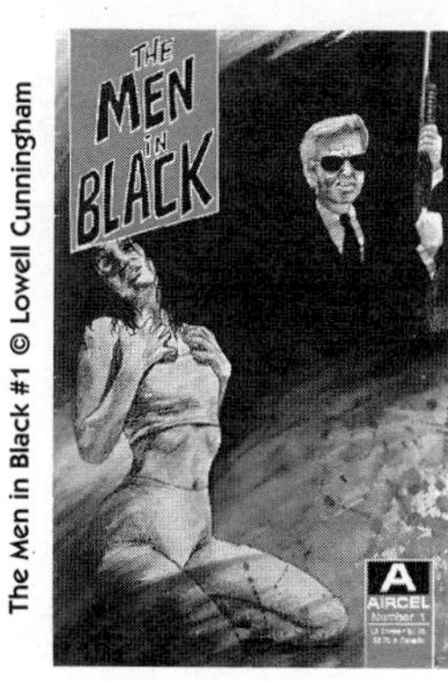

The Men in Black #1 © Lowell Cunningham

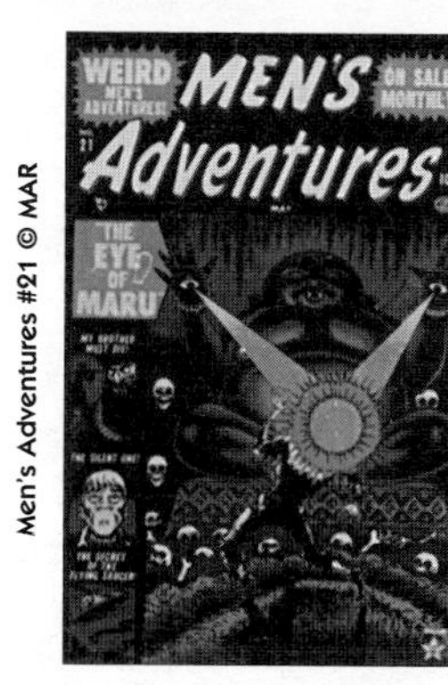

Men's Adventures #21 © MAR

GD25 FN65 NM94

1-4: Bisley-painted-c 3.00

MELVIN MONSTER (See Peter, the Little Pest)
Dell Publishing Co.: Apr-June, 1965 - No. 10, Oct, 1969

1-By John Stanley 10.00 30.00 110.00
2-10-All by Stanley. #10-r/#1 7.00 20.00 75.00

MELVIN THE MONSTER (Dexter The Demon #7)
Atlas Comics (HPC): July, 1956 - No. 6, July, 1957

1-Maneely-c/a 11.00 32.00 80.00
2-6: 4-Maneely-c/a 7.15 21.50 50.00

MENACE
Atlas Comics (HPC): Mar, 1953 - No. 11, May, 1954

1-Horror & sci/fi stories begin; Everett-c/a 54.00 162.00 460.00
2-Post-atom bomb disaster by Everett; anti-Communist propaganda/torture scenes; Sinnott sci/fi story "Rocket to the Moon" 39.00 117.00 310.00
3,4,6-Everett-a. 4-Sci/fi story "Escape to the Moon". 6-Romita sci/fi story "Science Fiction" 32.00 96.00 240.00
5-Origin & 1st app. The Zombie by Everett (reprinted in Tales of the Zombie #1)(7/53); 5-Sci/fi story "Rocket Ship" 43.00 129.00 350.00
7,8,10,11: 7-Frankenstein story. 8-End of world story; Heath 3-D art(3 pgs.). 10-H-Bomb panels 23.00 68.00 170.00
9-Everett-a r-in Vampire Tales #1 27.00 80.00 200.00

NOTE: ***Brodsky*** *c-7, 8, 11.* ***Colan*** *a-6; c-9.* ***Everett*** *a-1-6, 9; c-1-6.* ***Heath*** *a-1-8; c-10.* ***Katz*** *a-11.* ***Maneely*** *a-3, 5, 7-9.* ***Powell*** *a-11.* ***Romita*** *a-3, 6, 8, 11.* ***Shelly*** *a-10.* ***Shores*** *a-7.* ***Sinnott*** *a-2, 7.* ***Tuska*** *a-1, 2, 5.*

MENACE
Awesome-Hyperwerks: Nov, 1998 - Present ($2.50)

1-Jada Pinkett Smith-s/Fraga-a 2.50

MEN AGAINST CRIME (Formerly Mr. Risk; Hand of Fate #8 on)
Ace Magazines: No. 3, Feb, 1951 - No. 7, Oct, 1951

3-Mr. Risk app. 8.50 26.00 60.00
4-7: 4-Colan-a; entire book-r as Trapped! #4. 5-Meskin-a 5.70 17.00 35.00

MEN, GUNS, & CATTLE (See Classics Illustrated Special Issue)

MEN IN ACTION (Battle Brady #10 on)
Atlas Comics (IPS): April, 1952 - No. 9, Dec, 1952 (War stories)

1-Berg, Reinman-a 13.00 38.00 95.00
2 7.85 23.50 55.00
3-6,8,9: 3-Heath-c/a 5.70 17.00 40.00
7-Krigstein-a; Heath-c 8.50 26.00 60.00

NOTE: ***Brodsky*** *c-1, 4-6.* ***Maneely*** *c-5.* ***Pakula*** *a-1, 6.* ***Robinson*** *c-8.* ***Shores*** *c-9.*

MEN IN ACTION
Ajax/Farrell Publications: April, 1957 - No. 9, 1958

1 6.50 19.50 45.00
2 4.25 13.00 26.00
3-9 4.00 11.00 22.00

MEN IN BLACK, THE (1st series)
Aircel Comics (Malibu): Jan, 1990 - No. 3 Mar, 1990 ($2.25, B&W, lim. series)

1-Cunningham-s/a in all 4.50 13.50 50.00
2 3.80 11.50 40.00
3 2.70 8.00 30.00
Graphic Novel (Jan, 1991) r/#1-3 2.00 6.00 20.00

MEN IN BLACK (2nd series)
Aircel Comics (Malibu): May, 1991 - No. 3, Jul, 1991 ($2.50, B&W, lim. series)

1-Cunningham-s/a in all 2.25 6.80 25.00
2 1.50 4.50 15.00
3 1.00 3.00 10.00

MEN IN BLACK: FAR CRY
Marvel Comics: Aug, 1997 ($3.99, color, one-shot)

1-Cunningham-s 4.00

MEN IN BLACK: RETRIBUTION
Marvel Comics: Dec, 1997 ($3.99, color, one-shot)

1-Cunningham-s; continuation of the movie 4.00

MEN IN BLACK: THE MOVIE
Marvel Comics: Oct, 1997 ($3.99, one-shot, movie adaption)

1-Cunningham-s 4.00

MEN INTO SPACE
Dell Publishing Co.: No. 1083, Feb-Apr, 1960

Four Color 1083-Anderson-a, photo-c 4.50 13.50 50.00

MEN OF BATTLE (Also see New Men of Battle)
Catechetical Guild: V1#5, March, 1943 (Hardcover)

V1#5-Topix reprints 4.00 10.00 20.00

MEN OF COURAGE
Catechetical Guild: 1949

Bound Topix comics-V7#2,4,6,8,10,16,18,20 4.00 10.00 20.00

MEN OF WAR
DC Comics, Inc.: August, 1977 - No. 26, March, 1980 (#9,10: 44 pgs.)

1-Enemy Ace, Gravedigger (origin #1,2) begin 2.00 6.00
2-4,8-10,12-14,19,20: All Enemy Ace stories. 4-1st Dateline Frontline. 9-Unknown Soldier app. 4.00
5-7,11,15-18,21-25: 17-1st app. Rosa 3.00
26-Sgt. Rock & Easy Co.-c/s 2.00 6.00

NOTE: ***Chaykin*** *a-9, 10, 12-14, 19, 20.* ***Evans*** *c-25.* ***Kubert*** *c-2-23, 24p, 26.*

MEN'S ADVENTURES (Formerly True Adventures)
Marvel/Atlas Comics (CCC): No. 4, Aug, 1950 - No. 28, July, 1954

4(#1)(52 pgs.) 27.00 80.00 200.00
5-Flying Saucer story 17.00 50.00 125.00
6-8: 7-Buried alive story. 8-Sci/fic story 14.00 42.00 105.00
9-20: All war format 9.30 28.00 70.00
21,22,24-26: All horror format. 25-Shrunken head-c 13.00 40.00 100.00
23-Crandall-a; Fox-a(i); horror format 15.00 46.00 115.00
27,28-Human Torch & Toro-c/stories; Captain America & Sub-Mariner stories in each (also see Young Men #24-28) 90.00 271.00 750.00

NOTE: ***Ayers*** *a-27(H. Torch).* ***Berg*** *a-15, 16.* ***Brodsky*** *c-4-9, 11, 12, 16-18, 24.* ***Burgos*** *c-27, 28(Human Torch).* ***Colan*** *a-14, 19.* ***Everett*** *a-10, 14, 22, 25, 28; c-14, 21-23.* ***Heath*** *a-8, 11, 24; c-13, 20, 26.* ***Lawrence*** *a-23; 27(Captain America).* ***Maneely*** *a-24; c-10, 15.* ***Mac Pakula*** *a-15, 25.* ***Post*** *a-23.* ***Powell*** *a-27(Sub-Mariner).* ***Reinman*** *a-11, 12.* ***Robinson*** *c-19.* ***Romita*** *a-22.* ***Shores*** *c-25.* ***Sinnott*** *a-21.* ***Tuska*** *a-24. Adventure-#4-8; War-#9-20; Weird/Horror-#21-26.*

MEN WHO MOVE THE NATION
Publisher unknown: (Giveaway) (B&W)

nn-Neal Adams-a 4.25 13.00 26.00

MENZ INSANA
DC Comics (Vertigo): 1997 ($7.95, one-shot)

nn-Fowler-s/Bolton painted art .90 2.70 8.00

MEPHISTO VS... (See Silver Surfer #3)
Marvel Comics Group: Apr, 1987 - No. 4, July, 1987 ($1.50, mini-series)

1-4: 1-Fantastic Four; Austin-i. 2-X-Factor. 3-X-Men. 4-Avengers 1.75

MERC (See Mark Hazzard: Merc)

MERCHANTS OF DEATH
Acme Press (Eclipse): Jul, 1988 - No. 4, Nov, 1988 ($3.50, B&W/16 pgs. color, 44pg. mag.)

1-4: 4-Toth-c 3.50

MERCY
DC Comics (Vertigo): 1993 ($5.95, 68 pgs., mature)

nn 2.00 6.00

MERLIN JONES AS THE MONKEY'S UNCLE (See Movie Comics and The

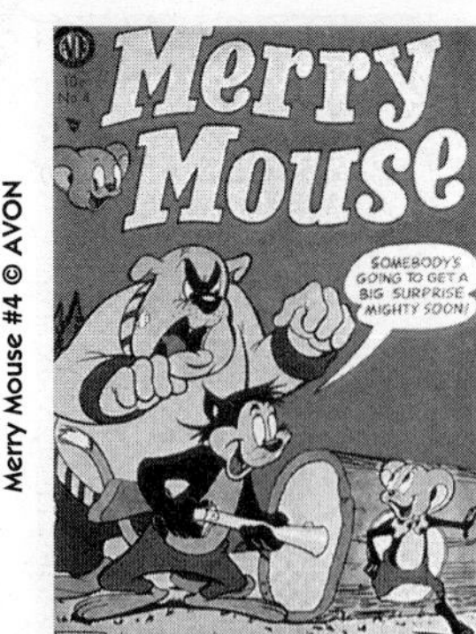

Merry Mouse #4 © AVON

Metal Men #1 © DC

Metropolis S.C.U. #1 © DC

Misadventures of... under Movie Comics)

MERRILL'S MARAUDERS (See Movie Classics)

MERRY CHRISTMAS (See A Christmas Adventure, Donald Duck..., Dell Giant #39, & March of Comics #153)

MERRY CHRISTMAS, A
K. K. Publications (Child Life Shoes): 1948 (Giveaway)

nn 4.25 13.00 26.00

MERRY CHRISTMAS
K. K. Publications (Blue Bird Shoes Giveaway): 1956 (7-1/4x5-1/4")

nn 2.40 6.00 12.00

MERRY CHRISTMAS FROM MICKEY MOUSE
K. K. Publications: 1939 (16 pgs.) (Color & B&W) (Shoe store giveaway)

nn-Donald Duck & Pluto app.; text with art (Rare); c-reprint/Mickey Mouse Mag. V3#3 (12/37)(Rare) 222.00 667.00 2000.00

MERRY CHRISTMAS FROM SEARS TOYLAND (See Santa's Christmas Comic)
Sears Roebuck Giveaway: 1939 (16 pgs.) (Color)

nn-Dick Tracy, Little Orphan Annie, The Gumps, Terry & the Pirates 94.00 282.00 800.00

MERRY COMICS
Carlton Publishing Co.: Dec, 1945 (No cover price)

nn-Boogeyman app. 17.00 50.00 125.00

MERRY COMICS
Four Star Publications: 1947

1 11.00 34.00 85.00

MERRY-GO-ROUND COMICS
LaSalle Publ. Co./Croyden Publ./Rotary Litho.: 1944 (25¢, 132 pgs.); 1946; 9-10/47 - No. 2, 1948

nn(1944)(LaSalle)-Funny animal; 29 new features 15.00 44.00 110.00
21 5.70 17.00 35.00
1(1946)(Croyden)-Al Fago-c; funny animal 7.85 23.50 55.00
V1#1,2(1947-48; 52 pgs.)(Rotary Litho. Co. Ltd., Canada); Ken Hultgren-a 5.70 17.00 40.00

MERRY MAILMAN (See Fawcett's Funny Animals #87-89)

MERRY MOUSE (Also see Funny Tunes & Space Comics)
Avon Periodicals: June, 1953 - No. 4, Jan-Feb, 1954

1-1st app.; funny animal; Frank Carin-c/a 7.15 21.50 50.00
2-4 5.00 15.00 30.00

META-4
First Comics: Feb, 1991 - No. 4, 1991 ($2.25)

1-($3.95, 52pgs.) 4.00
2-4 2.25

METAL MEN (See Brave & the Bold, DC Comics Presents, and Showcase #37-40)
National Periodical Publications/DC Comics: 4-5/63 - No. 41, 12-1/69-70; No. 42, 2-3/73 - No. 44, 7-8/73; No. 45, 4-5/76 - No. 56, 2-3/78

1-(4-5/63)-5th app. Metal Men 40.00 120.00 450.00
2 15.00 45.00 150.00
3-5 9.00 27.00 90.00
6-10 6.00 18.00 60.00
11-20: 12-Beatles cameo (12/65) 4.50 13.50 45.00
21-26,28-30: 21-Batman, Robin & Flash x-over 3.50 10.50 32.00
27-Origin Metal Men retold 4.50 13.50 45.00
31-41(1968-70): 38-Last 12¢ issue. 41-Last 15¢ 2.50 7.50 20.00
42-44(1973)-Reprints 1.00 3.00 10.00
45('76)-49-Simonson-a in all: 48,49-Re-intro Eclipso 2.00 6.00
50-56: 50-Part-r. 54,55-Green Lantern x-over 2.00 6.00

NOTE: ***Andru/Esposito*** *c-1-29.* ***Aparo*** *c-53-56.* ***Giordano*** *c-45, 46.* ***Kane*** *a-30, 31p; c-31.* ***Simonson*** *a-45-49; c-47-52.* ***Staton*** *a-50-56.*

METAL MEN
DC Comics: Oct, 1993 - No. 4, Jan, 1994 ($1.25, mini-series)

1-($2.50)-Multi-colored foil-c 2.50
2-4: 2-Origin 1.25

METAL MEN (See Tangent Comics/ Metal Men)

METAMORPHO (See Action Comics #413, Brave & the Bold #57,58, 1st Issue Special,& World's Finest #217)
National Periodical Publications: July-Aug, 1965 - No. 17, Mar-Apr, 1968 (All 12¢ issues)

1-(7-8/65)-3rd app. Metamorpho 9.50 28.50 95.00
2,3 5.00 15.00 50.00
4-6 3.50 10.50 35.00
7-9 3.00 9.00 30.00
10-Origin & 1st app. Element Girl (1-2/67) 3.50 10.50 35.00
11-17 2.50 7.50 20.00

NOTE: ***Ramona Fraden*** *a-B&B 57, 58, 1-4.* ***Orlando*** *a-5, 6; c-5-9, 11.* ***Sal Trapani*** *a-7-16.*

METAMORPHO
DC Comics: Aug, 1993 - No. 4, Nov, 1993 ($1.50, mini-series)

1-4 1.50

METAPHYSIQUE
Malibu Comics (Bravura): Apr, 1995 - No. 6, Oct, 1995 ($2.95, limited series)

1-6: Norm Breyfogle-c/a/scripts 3.00

METEOR COMICS
L. L. Baird (Croyden): Nov, 1945

1-Captain Wizard, Impossible Man, Race Wilkins app.; origin Baldy Bean, Capt. Wizard's sidekick; bare-breasted mermaids story 35.00 106.00 265.00

METEOR MAN
Marvel Comics: Aug, 1993 - No. 6, Jan, 1994 ($1.25, limited series)

1-6: 1-Polybagged w/button & rap newspaper. 4-Night Thrasher-c/story. 6-Terry Austin-c(i) 1.25

METROPOL (See Ted McKeever's...)

METROPOL A.D. (See Ted McKeever's...)

METROPOLIS S.C.U. (Also see Showcase '96 #1)
DC Comics: Nov, 1995 - No. 4, Feb, 1996 ($1.50, limited series)

1-4:1-Superman-c & app. 1.50

MEZZ: GALACTIC TOUR 2494 (Also See Nexus)
Dark Horse Comics: May, 1994 ($2.50, one-shot)

1 2.50

MGM'S MARVELOUS WIZARD OF OZ (See Marvel Treasury of Oz)
Marvel Comics Group/National Periodical Publications: 1975 ($1.50, 84 pgs.; oversize)

1-Adaptation of MGM's movie; J. Buscema-a 4.00

M.G.M'S MOUSE MUSKETEERS (Formerly M.G.M.'s The Two Mouseketeers)
Dell Publishing Co.: No. 670, Jan, 1956 - No. 1290, Mar-May, 1962

Four Color 670 (#4) 2.75 8.00 30.00
Four Color 711,728,764 1.80 5.50 20.00
8 (4-6/57) - 21 (3-5/60) 1.65 5.00 18.00
Four Color 1135,1175,1290 1.80 5.50 20.00

M.G.M.'S SPIKE AND TYKE (also see Tom & Jerry #79)
Dell Publishing Co.: No. 499, Sept, 1953 - No. 1266, Dec-Feb, 1961-62

Four Color 499 (#1) 2.75 8.00 30.00
Four Color 577,638 1.80 5.50 20.00
4(12-2/55-56)-10 1.65 5.00 18.00
11-24(12-2/60-61) 1.50 4.50 15.00

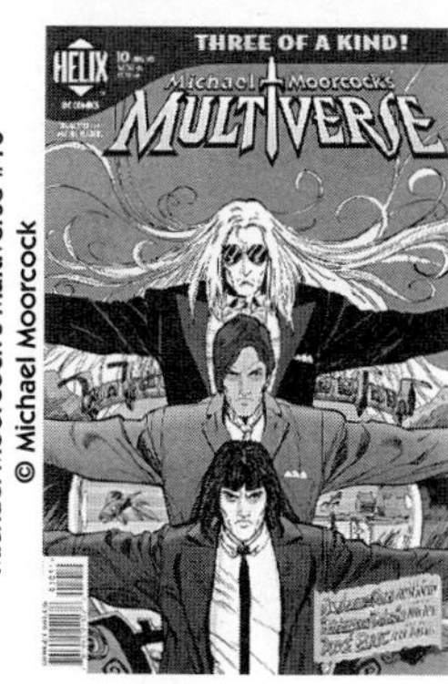

Michael Moorcock's Multiverse #10 © Michael Moorcock

Mickey Finn #5 © McNaught Synd.

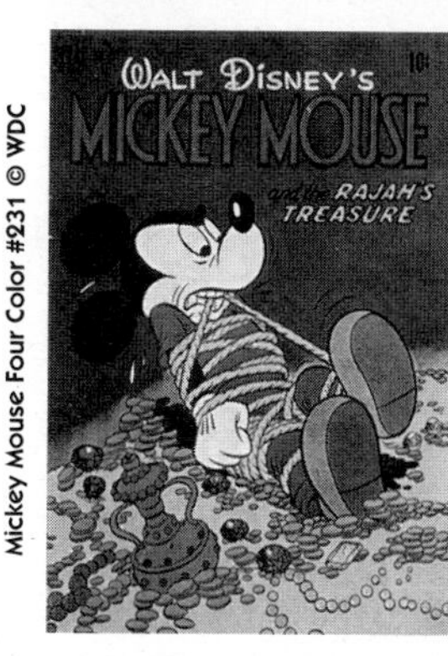

Mickey Mouse Four Color #231 © WDC

	GD25	FN65	NM94
Four Color 1266	1.65	5.00	18.00

M.G.M.'S THE TWO MOUSKETEERS
Dell Publishing Co.: No. 475, June, 1953 - No. 642, July, 1955

	GD25	FN65	NM94
Four Color 475 (#1)	6.40	19.00	70.00
Four Color 603 (11/54), 642	3.60	11.00	40.00

MICHAELANGELO CHRISTMAS SPECIAL (See Teenage Mutant Ninja Turtles Christmas Special)

MICHAELANGELO, TEENAGE MUTANT NINJA TURTLE
Mirage Studios: 1986 (One shot) ($1.50, B&W)

	GD25	FN65	NM94
1			3.00
1-2nd printing ('89, $1.75)-Reprint plus new-a			2.00

MICHAEL MOORCOCK'S MULTIVERSE
DC Comics (Helix): Nov, 1997 - No. 12, Oct, 1998 ($2.50, limited series)

	GD25	FN65	NM94
1-12: Simonson, Reeve & Ridgway-a			2.50

MICKEY AND DONALD (See Walt Disney's...)

MICKEY AND DONALD IN VACATIONLAND (See Dell Giant No. 47)

MICKEY & THE BEANSTALK (See Story Hour Series)

MICKEY & THE SLEUTH (See Walt Disney Showcase #38, 39, 42)

MICKEY FINN (Also see Big Shot Comics #74 & Feature Funnies)
Eastern Color 1-4/McNaught Synd. #5 on (Columbia)/Headline V3#2:
Nov?, 1942 - V3#2, May, 1952

	GD25	FN65	NM94
1	27.00	82.00	205.00
2	13.00	40.00	100.00
3-Charlie Chan story	9.30	28.00	70.00
4	7.15	21.50	50.00
5-10	5.70	17.00	38.00
11-15(1949): 12-Sparky Watts app.	4.25	13.00	28.00
V3#1,2(1952)	4.00	11.00	22.00

MICKEY MALONE
Hale Nass Corp.: 1936 (Color, punchout-c) (B&W-a on back)

	GD25	FN65	VF82
nn-1pg. of comics	125.00	250.00	400.00

MICKEY MANTLE (See Baseball's Greatest Heroes #1)

MICKEY MOUSE (See Adventures of Mickey Mouse, The Best of Walt Disney Comics, Cheerios giveaways, Donald and ..., Dynabrite Comics, 40 Big Pages..., Gladstone Comic Album, Merry Christmas From..., Walt Disney's Mickey and Donald, Walt Disney's Comics & Stories, Walt Disney's..., & Wheaties)

MICKEY MOUSE (...Secret Agent #107-109; Walt Disney's... #148-205?)
(See Dell Giants for annuals) (#204 exists from both G.K. & Whitman)
Dell Publ. Co./Gold Key #85-204/Whitman #204-218/Gladstone #219 on:
#16, 1941 - #84, 7-9/62; #85, 11/62 - #218, 7/84; #219, 10/86 - #256, 4/90

	GD25	FN65	VF82
Four Color 16(1941)-1st Mickey Mouse comic book; "...vs. the Phantom Blot" by Gottfredson	654.00	1961.00	9000.00

	GD25	FN65	NM94
Four Color 27(1943)- "7 Colored Terror"	77.00	232.00	850.00
Four Color 79(1945)-By Carl Barks (1 story)	95.00	286.00	1050.00
Four Color 116(1946)	21.00	64.00	235.00
Four Color 141,157(1947)	18.00	55.00	200.00
Four Color 170,181,194('48)	14.00	44.00	160.00
Four Color 214('49),231,248,261	13.00	38.00	140.00
Four Color 268-Reprints/WDC&S #22-24 by Gottfredson ("Surprise Visitor")	12.00	35.00	130.00
Four Color 279,286,296	9.00	27.00	100.00
Four Color 304,313(#1),325(#2),334	7.00	22.00	80.00
Four Color 343,352,362,371,387	5.50	16.50	60.00
Four Color 401,411,427(10-11/52)	3.60	11.00	40.00
Four Color 819-Mickey Mouse in Magicland	3.00	9.00	35.00
Four Color 1057,1151,1246(1959-61)-Album	2.75	8.00	30.00
28(12-1/52-53)-32,34	2.25	6.75	26.00
33-(Exists with 2 dates, 10-11/53 & 12-1/54)	2.25	6.75	26.00
35-50	1.80	5.40	20.00
51-73,75-80	1.40	4.20	14.00
74-Story swipe "The Rare Stamp Search" from 4-Color #422- "The Gilded Man"	1.60	4.80	16.00
81-99: 93,95-titled "Mickey Mouse Club Album"	1.40	4.20	14.00
100-105: Reprint 4-Color #427,194,279,170,343,214 in that order	1.40	4.20	14.00
106-120	1.20	3.60	12.00
121-130	1.00	3.00	10.00
131-146	.90	2.70	8.00
147,148: 147-Reprints "The Phantom Fires" from WDC&S #200-202.148-Reprints "The Mystery of Lonely Valley" from WDC&S #208-210	.90	2.70	8.00
149-158			5.00
159-Reprints "The Sunken City" from WDC&S #205-207		2.60	7.00
160-170: 162-170-r			4.00
171-178,180-203: 200-r/Four Color #371			4.00
179-(52 pgs.)		.80	2.00
204-(Whitman or G.K.), 205,206		2.00	6.00
207(8/80), 209(pre-pack?)	1.00	3.00	10.00
208-(8-12/80)-Only distr. in Whitman 3-pack	1.60	4.80	18.00
210(2/81),211-214		2.00	6.00
215-218	.90	2.70	8.00
219-1st Gladstone issue; The Seven Ghosts serial-r begins by Gottfredson	1.50	4.50	15.00
220,221	.90	2.70	8.00
222-225: 222-Editor-in Grief strip-r			3.00
226-230			3.00
231-243,245-254: 240-r/March of Comics #27. 245-r/F.C. #279. 250-r/F.C. #248			3.00
244 (1/89, $2.95, 100 pgs.)-Squarebound 60th anniversary issue; gives history of Mickey			4.00
245, 256: 245-r/F.C. #279. 256-$1.95, 68 pgs.			4.00
255 ($1.95, 68 pgs.)			2.00

NOTE: *Reprints #195-197, 198(2/3), 199(1/3), 200-208, 211(1/2), 212, 213, 215(1/3), 216-on.* ***Gottfredson*** *Mickey Mouse serials in #219-239, 241-244, 246-249, 251-253, 255.*

	GD25	FN65	NM94
Album 01-518-210(Dell), 1(10082-309)(9/63-Gold Key)	1.60	4.80	16.00
...& Goofy "Bicep Bungle"(1952, 16 pgs., 3-1/4x7") Fritos giveaway, soft-c (also see Donald Duck & Ludwig Von Drake)	5.70	17.00	35.00
...& Goofy Explore Business(1978)			4.00
...& Goofy Explore Energy(1976-1978, 36 pgs.); Exxon giveaway in color; regular size			4.00
...& Goofy Explore Energy Conservation(1976-1978)-Exxon			4.00
...& Goofy Explore The Universe of Energy(1985, 20 pgs.); Exxon giveaway in color; regular size			3.00
...Club 1(1/64-Gold Key)(TV)	2.40	7.20	26.00
Mini Comic 1(1976)(3-1/4x6-1/2")-Reprints 158		2.00	6.00
New Mickey Mouse Club Fun Book 11190 (Golden Press, 1977, $1.95, 224 pgs.)	1.60	4.80	16.00
The Perils of Mickey nn (1993, 5-1/4x7-1/4", 16 pgs.)-Nabisco giveaway w/ games, Nabisco coupons & 6 pgs. of stories; Phantom Blot app.			2.00
Surprise Party 1(30037-901, G.K.)(1/69)-40th Anniversary (see Walt Disney Showcase #47)	2.20	6.50	24.00
Surprise Party 1(1979)-r/1969 issue			5.00

MICKEY MOUSE
Whitman Publishing Co.: c. 1933-1934 (10"x8-3/4", 34 pgs., cardboard-c)

	GD25	FN65	NM94
948-1932 & 1933 Sunday strips in color, printed from the same plates as Mickey Mouse Book #3 by David McKay, but only pages 5-17 & 32-48 (including all of the "Wolf Barker" continuity)	131.00	395.00	1050.00

NOTE: Some copies bound with back cover upside down. Variance doesn't affect value. Same art appears on front and back covers of all copies. Height of Whitman reissue of McKay book trimmed 1/2 inch.

Mickey Mouse Adventures #1 © WDC

Mickey Mouse Magazine #6 © WDC

Mickey Mouse Magazine V4 #2 © WDC

GD25 FN65 NM94

MICKEY MOUSE ADVENTURES
Disney Comics: June, 1990 - No. 18, Nov, 1991 ($1.50)

1-18: 1-Bradbury, Murry-r/M.M. #45,73 plus new-a. 2-Begin all new stories. 8-Byrne-c. 9-Fantasia 50th ann. issue w/new adapt. of movie. 10-r/F.C. #214 — 1.50

MICKEY MOUSE CLUB MAGAZINE (See Walt Disney...)

MICKEY MOUSE COMICS DIGEST
Gladstone: 1986 - No. 5, 1987 (96 pgs.)

	GD25	FN65	NM94
1,2 ($1.25)	.85	2.60	7.00
3-5 ($1.50)			4.00

MICKEY MOUSE IN COLOR
Another Rainbow/Pantheon: 1988 (Deluxe, 13"x17", hard-c, $250.00) (Trade, 9-7/8"x11-1/2", hard-c, $39.95)

	GD25	FN65	NM94
Deluxe limited edition of 3,000 copies signed by Floyd Gottfredson and Carl Barks, designated as the "Official Mickey Mouse 60th Anniversary" book. Mickey Sunday and daily reprints, plus Barks "Riddle of the Red Hat" from Four Color #79. Comes with 45 r.p.m. record interview with Gottfredson and Barks. 240 pgs.	23.00	68.00	250.00
Deluxe, limited to 100 copies, as above, but with a unique colored pencil original drawing of Mickey Mouse by Carl Barks. Add value of art to book price.			750.00
Pantheon trade edition, edited down & without Barks, 192 pgs.	3.80	11.50	40.00

MICKEY MOUSE MAGAZINE
Walt Disney Productions: V1#1, Jan, 1933 - V1#9, Sept, 1933 (5-1/4x7-1/4")
No. 1-3 published by Kamen-Blair (Kay Kamen, Inc.)

(Scarce)-Distributed by dairies and leading stores through their local theatres. First few issues had 5¢ listed on cover, later ones had no price.

	GD25	FN65	VF82
V1#1	357.00	1071.00	3200.00
2-9	117.00	350.00	950.00

MICKEY MOUSE MAGAZINE
Walt Disney Productions: V1#1, 11/33 - V2#12, 10/35 (Mills giveaways issued by different dairies)

	GD25	FN65	NM94
V1#1	133.00	400.00	1200.00
2-12: 2-X-Mas issue	44.00	132.00	375.00
V2#1-12: 2-X-Mas issue. 4-St. Valentine-c	34.00	101.00	255.00

MICKEY MOUSE MAGAZINE (Becomes Walt Disney's Comics & Stories)
K. K. Publ./Western Publishing Co.: Summer, 1935 (June-Aug, indicia) - V5#12, Sept, 1940; V1#1-5, V3#11,12, V4#1-3 are 44 pgs; V2#3-100 pgs; V5#12-68 pgs; rest are 36 pgs.(No V3#1, V4#6)

	GD25	FN65	VF82	NM94
V1#1 (Large size, 13-1/4x10-1/4"; 25¢)-Contains puzzles, games, cels, stories & comics of Disney characters. Promotional magazine for Disney cartoon movies and paraphernalia	1100.00	3300.00	7150.00	11000.00

Note: *Some copies were autographed by the editors & given away with all early one year subscriptions.*

	GD25	FN65	VF82
2 (Size change, 11-1/2x8-1/2"; 10/35; 10¢)-High quality paper begins; Messmer-a	131.00	395.00	1100.00
3,4: 3-Messmer-a	72.00	216.00	575.00
5-1st Donald Duck solo-c; 2nd cover app. ever; last 44 pg. & high quality paper issue	81.00	244.00	650.00
6-9: 6-36 pg. issues begin; Donald becomes editor. 8-2nd Donald solo-c. 9-1st Mickey/Minnie-c	64.00	193.00	525.00
10-12, V2#1,2: 11-1st Pluto/Mickey-c; Donald fires himself and appoints Mickey as editor	61.00	182.00	475.00
V2#3-Special 100 pg. Christmas issue (25¢); Messmer-a; Donald becomes editor of Wise Quacks	287.00	862.00	2300.00
4-Mickey Mouse Comics & Roy Ranger (adventure strip) begin; both end V2#9; Messmer-a	54.00	160.00	420.00

	GD25	FN65	NM94
5-Ted True (adventure strip, ends V2#9) & Silly Symphony Comics (ends V3#3) begin	43.00	130.00	330.00
6-9: 6-1st solo Minnie-c. 6-9-Mickey Mouse Movies cut-out in each	43.00	130.00	330.00
10-1st full color issue; Mickey Mouse (by Gottfredson; ends V3#12) & Silly Symphony (ends V3#3) full color Sunday-r, Peter The Farm Detective (ends V5#8) & Ole Of The North (ends V3#3) begins	67.00	200.00	550.00
11-13: 12-Hiawatha-c & feature story	43.00	130.00	330.00
V3#2-Big Bad Wolf Halloween-c	52.00	155.00	420.00
3 (12/37)-1st app. Snow White & The Seven Dwarfs (before release of movie)(possibly 1st in print); Mickey X-Mas-c	90.00	270.00	675.00
4 (1/38)-Snow White & The Seven Dwarfs serial begins (on stands before release of movie); Ducky Symphony (ends V3#11) begins	72.00	215.00	550.00
5-1st Snow White & Seven Dwarfs-c (St. Valentine's Day)	93.00	280.00	700.00
6-Snow White serial ends; Lonesome Ghosts app. (2 pp.)	50.00	150.00	390.00
7-Seven Dwarfs Easter-c	49.00	145.00	375.00
8-10: 9-Dopey-c. 10-1st solo Goofy-c	40.00	120.00	310.00
11,12 (44 pgs; 8 more pgs. color added). 11-Mickey the Sheriff serial (ends V4#3) & Donald Duck strip-r (ends V3#12) begin. Color feature on Snow White's Forest Friends	43.00	130.00	330.00
V4#1 (10/38; 44 pgs.)-Brave Little Tailor-c/feature story, nominated for Academy Award; Bobby & Chip by Otto Messmer (ends V4#2) & The Practical Pig (ends V4#2) begin	43.00	130.00	330.00
2 (44 pgs.)-1st Huey, Dewey & Louie-c	44.00	132.00	340.00
3 (12/38, 44 pgs.)-Ferdinand The Bull-c/feature story, Academy Award winner; Mickey Mouse & The Whalers serial begins, ends V4#12	43.00	130.00	330.00
4-Spotty, Mother Pluto strip-r begin, end V4#8	40.00	120.00	310.00
5-St. Valentine's day-c. 1st Pluto solo-c	47.00	141.00	360.00
7 (3/39)-The Ugly Duckling-c/feature story, Academy Award winner	43.00	130.00	330.00
7 (4/39)-Goofy & Wilbur The Grasshopper classic-c/feature story from 1st Goofy solo cartoon movie; Timid Elmer begins, ends V5#5	43.00	130.00	330.00
8-Big Bad Wolf-c from Practical Pig movie poster; Practical Pig feature story	43.00	130.00	330.00
9-Donald Duck & Mickey Mouse Sunday-r begin; The Pointer feature story, nominated for Academy Award	43.00	130.00	330.00
10-Classic July 4th drum & fife-c; last Donald Sunday-r	54.00	160.00	440.00
11-1st slick-c; last over-sized issue	40.00	120.00	310.00
12 (9/39; format change, 10-1/4x8-1/4")-1st full color, cover to cover issue; Donald's Penguin-c/feature story	48.00	145.00	390.00
V5#1-Black Pete-c; Officer Duck-c/feature story; Autograph Hound feature story; Robinson Crusoe serial begins	48.00	145.00	375.00
2-Goofy-c; 1st app. Pinocchio (cameo)	64.00	195.00	500.00
3 (12/39)-Pinocchio Christmas-c (Before movie release). 1st app. Jiminy Cricket; Pinocchio serial begins	72.00	215.00	560.00
4,5: 5-Jiminy Cricket-c; Pinocchio serial ends; Donald's Dog Laundry feature story	48.00	145.00	375.00
6-Tugboat Mickey feature story; Rip Van Winkle feature begins, ends V5#8	47.00	140.00	360.00
7-2nd Huey, Dewey & Louie-c	47.00	140.00	360.00
8-Last magazine size issue; 2nd solo Pluto-c; Figaro & Cleo feature story	48.00	144.00	370.00
9 (6/40; change to comic book size)-Jiminy Cricket feature story; Donald-c & Sunday-r begin	52.00	155.00	400.00
10-Special Independence Day issue	52.00	155.00	400.00
11-Hawaiian Holiday & Mickey's Trailer feature stories; last 36 pg. issue	52.00	155.00	400.00

Mickey Mouse Magazine V5 #12 © WDC

Mickey Spillane's Mike Danger #6 © Mickey Spillane

Micronauts #15 © MAR

GD25 FN65 NM94

12 (Format change)-The transition issue (68 pgs.) becoming a comic book. With only a title change to follow, becomes Walt Disney's Comics & Stories #1 with the next issue 411.00 1233.00 3700.00
V4#1 (Giveaway) 38.00 114.00 265.00
NOTE: *Otto Messmer-a is in many issues of the first two-three years. The following story titles and issues have gags created by **Carl Barks:** V4#3(12/38)-'Donald's Better Self' & 'Donald's Golf Game;' V4#4(1/39)-'Donald's Lucky Day;' V4#7(3/39)-'Hockey Champ;' V4#7(4/39)-'Donald's Cousin Gus;' V4#9(6/39)-'Sea Scouts;' V4#12(9/39)-'Donald's Penguin;' V5#9 (6/40)-'Donald's Vacation;' V5#10(7/40)-'Bone Trouble;' V5#12(9/40)-'Window Cleaners.'*

MICKEY MOUSE MARCH OF COMICS (See March of Comics #8,27,45,60,74)

MICKEY MOUSE'S SUMMER VACATION (See Story Hour Series)

MICKEY MOUSE SUMMER FUN (See Dell Giants)

MICKEY SPILLANE'S MIKE DANGER
Tekno Comix: Sept, 1995 - No. 11, May, 1996 ($1.95)
1-11: 1-Frank Miller-c. 7-polybagged; Simonson-c. 8,9-Simonson-c. 2.00

MICKEY SPILLANE'S MIKE DANGER
Big Entertainment: V2#1, June, 1996 - No. 10, Apr, 1997 ($2.25)
V2#1-10: Max Allan Collins scripts 2.25

MICROBOTS, THE
Gold Key: Dec, 1971 (one-shot)
1 (10271-112) 1.40 4.20 14.00

MICRONAUTS (Toys)
Marvel Comics Group: Jan, 1979 - No. 59, Aug, 1984 (Mando paper #53 on)
1-Intro/1st app. Baron Karza 2.20
2-5 1.20
6-36,39-59: 7-Man-Thing app. 8-1st app. Capt. Universe (8/79). 9-1st app. Cilicia. 13-1st app. Jasmine. 15-Death of Microtron. 15-17-Fantastic Four app. 17-Death of Jasmine. 20-Ant-Man app. 21-Microverse series begins. 25-Origin Baron Karza. 25-29-Nick Fury app. 27-Death of Biotron. 34,35-Dr. Strange app. 35-Double size; origin Microverse; intro Death Squad. 40-Fantastic Four app. 57-(52 pgs.). 59-Golden painted-c 1.00
37-Nightcrawler app.; X-Men cameo (2 pgs.) 2.00
38-First direct sale 1.60
nn-Reprints #1-3; blank UPC; diamond on top 3.00
Annual 1(12/79)-Ditko-c/a 2.50
Annual 2(10/80)-Ditko-c/a 2.00
NOTE: *#38-on distributed only through comic shops. **N. Adams** c-7i. **Chaykin** a-13-18p. **Ditko** a-39p. **Giffen** a-36p, 37p(part). **Golden** a-1-12p; c-2-7p, 8-23, 24p, 38, 39, 59. **Guice** a-48-58p; c-49-58. **Gil Kane** a-38, 40-45p; c-40-45. **Layton** c-33-37. **Miller** c-31.*

MICRONAUTS (Toys)
Marvel Comics Group: Oct, 1984 - No. 20, May, 1986
V2#1-20 .75
NOTE: ***Kelley Jones** a-1; c-1, 6. **Guice** a-4p; c-2p.*

MICRONAUTS SPECIAL EDITION
Marvel Comics Group: Dec, 1983 - No. 5, Apr, 1984 ($2.00, limited series, Baxter paper)
1-5: r-/original series 1-12; Guice-c(p)-all 2.00

MIDGET COMICS (Fighting Indian Stories)
St. John Publishng Co.: Feb, 1950 - No. 2, Apr, 1950 (5-3/8x7-3/8", 68 pgs.)
1-Fighting Indian Stories; Matt Baker-c 16.00 48.00 120.00
2-Tex West, Cowboy Marshal (also in #1) 7.85 23.50 55.00

MIDNIGHT (See Smash Comics #18)

MIDNIGHT
Ajax/Farrell Publ. (Four Star Comic Corp.): Apr, 1957 - No. 6, June, 1958
1-Reprints from Voodoo & Strange Fantasy with some changes 11.00 32.00 80.00
2-6 6.50 19.50 45.00

MIDNIGHT EYE
Viz Premiere Comics: 1991 - No. 6, 1992 ($4.95, 44 pgs., mature)
1-6: Japanese stories translated into English 5.00

MIDNIGHT MEN
Marvel Comics (Epic Comics/Heavy Hitters): June, 1993 - No. 4, Sept, 1993 ($2.50/$1.95, limited series)
1-($2.50)-Embossed-c; Chaykin-c/a & scripts in all. 2.50
2-4 2.00

MIDNIGHT MYSTERY
American Comics Group: Jan-Feb, 1961 - No. 7, Oct, 1961
1-Sci/Fi story 7.50 22.50 75.00
2-7: 7-Gustavson-a 4.00 12.00 40.00
NOTE: ***Reinman** a-1, 3. **Whitney** a-1, 4-6; c-1-3, 5, 7.*

MIDNIGHT SONS UNLIMITED
Marvel Comics (Midnight Sons imprint #4 on): Apr, 1993 - No. 9, May, 1995 ($3.95, 68 pgs.)
1-9: Blaze, Darkhold (by Quesada #1), Ghost Rider, Morbius & Nightstalkers in all. 1-Painted-c. 3-Spider-Man app. 4-Siege of Darkness part 17; new Dr. Strange & new Ghost Rider app.; spot varnish-c 4.00
NOTE: ***Sears** a-2.*

MIDNIGHT TALES
Charlton Press: Dec, 1972 - No. 18, May, 1976
V1#1 1.50 4.50 15.00
2-10 .90 2.70 8.00
11-18: 11-14-Newton-a(p) 2.00 6.00
12,17(Modern Comics reprint, 1977) 4.00
NOTE: ***Adkins** a-12i, 13i. **Ditko** a-12. **Howard** (Wood imitator) a-1-15, 17, 18; c-1-18. **Don Newton** a-11-14p. **Staton** a-1, 3-11, 13. **Sutton** a-3-10.*

MIGHTY ATOM, THE (...& the Pixies #6) (Formerly The Pixies #1-5)
Magazine Enterprises: No. 6, 1949; Nov, 1957 - No. 6, Aug-Sept, 1958
6(1949-M.E.)-no month (1st Series) 4.25 13.00 28.00
1-6(2nd Series)-Pixies-r 3.20 8.00 16.00
I.W. Reprint #1(nd) 2.40 6.00
Giveaway(1959, '63, Whitman)-Evans-a 1.00 3.00 8.00
Giveaway ('64r, '65r, '66r, '67r, '68r, '73r, '76r)-Evans-r? 2.00

MIGHTY BEAR (Formerly Fun Comics; becomes Unsane #15)
Star Publ. No. 13,14/Ajax-Farrell (Four Star): No. 13, Jan, 1954 - No. 14, Mar, 1954; 9/57 - No. 3, 2/58
13,14-L. B. Cole-c 14.00 42.00 105.00
1-3('57-58)Four Star; becomes Mighty Ghost #4 4.00 12.00 24.00

MIGHTY COMICS (...Presents) (Formerly Flyman)
Radio Comics (Archie): No. 40, Nov, 1966 - No. 50, Oct, 1967 (All 12¢ issues)
40-Web 2.50 7.50 24.00
41-50: 41-Shield, Black Hood. 42-Black Hood. 43-Shield, Web & Black Hood. 44-Black Hood, Steel Sterling & The Shield. 45-Shield & Hangman; origin Web retold. 46-Steel Sterling, Web & Black Hood. 47-Black Hood & Mr. Justice. 48-Shield & Hangman; Wizard x-over in Shield. 49-Steel Sterling & Fox; Black Hood x-over in Steel Sterling. 50-Black Hood & Web; Inferno x-over in Web 2.50 7.50 20.00
NOTE: ***Paul Reinman** a-40-50.*

MIGHTY CRUSADERS, THE (Also see Adventures of the Fly, The Crusaders & Fly Man)
Mighty Comics Group (Radio Comics): Nov, 1965 - No. 7, Oct, 1966 (All 12¢)
1-Origin The Shield 4.00 12.00 40.00
2-Origin Comet 2.50 7.50 24.00
3-Origin Fly-Man 2.50 7.50 20.00
4-1st S.A. app. Fireball, Inferno & Fox; Firefly, Web, Bob Phantom, Blackjack, Hangman, Zambini, Kardak, Steel Sterling, Mr. Justice, Wizard, Capt. Flag, Jaguar x-over 2.50 7.50 22.00
5-Intro. Ultra-Men (Fox, Web, Capt. Flag) & Terrific Three (Jaguar, Mr. Justice, Steel Sterling) 2.50 7.50 20.00

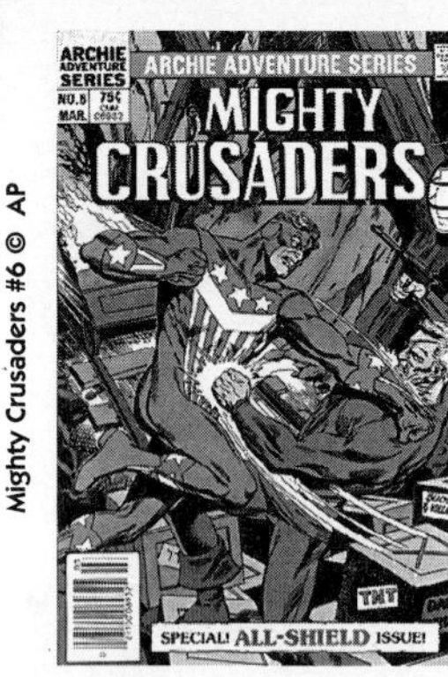
Mighty Crusaders #6 © AP

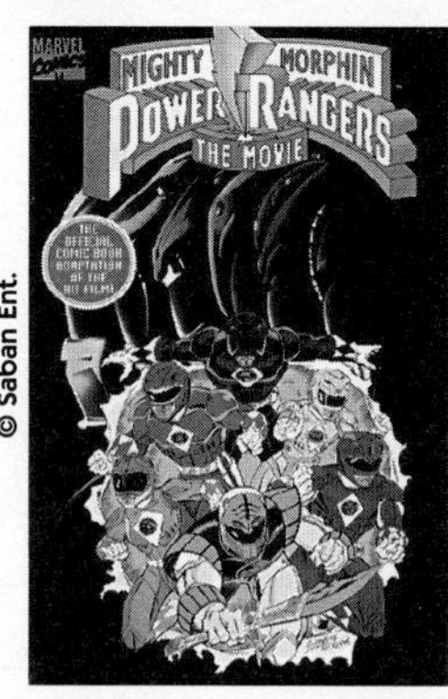
Mighty Morphin' Power Rangers: The Movie © Saban Ent.

Mighty Mouse #20 © Terry Toons

GD25 FN65 NM94

6,7: 7-Steel Sterling feature; origin Fly-Girl 2.50 7.50 20.00
NOTE: ***Reinman*** *a-6.*

MIGHTY CRUSADERS, THE (All New Advs. of...#2)
Red Circle Prod./Archie Ent. No. 6 on: Mar, 1983 - No. 13, Sept, 1985 ($1.00, 36 pgs, Mando paper)

1-Origin Black Hood, The Fly, Fly Girl, The Shield, The Wizard, The Jaguar, Pvt. Strong & The Web. 2.00
2-13: 2-Mister Midnight begins. 4-Darkling replaces Shield. 5-Origin Jaguar, Shield begins. 7-Untold origin Jaguar 1.50
NOTE: ***Buckler*** *a-1-3, 4i, 5p, 7p, 8i, 9i; c-1-10p.*

MIGHTY GHOST (Formerly Mighty Bear #1-3)
Ajax/Farrell Publ.: No. 4, June, 1958

4 4.00 11.00 22.00

MIGHTY HERCULES, THE (TV)
Gold Key: July, 1963 - No. 2, Nov, 1963

1,2(10072-307, 10072-311) 14.00 41.00 150.00

MIGHTY HEROES, THE (TV) (Funny)
Dell Publishing Co.: Mar, 1967 - No. 4, July, 1967

1-Also has a 1957 Heckle & Jeckle-r 13.00 40.00 145.00
2-4: 4-Has two 1958 Mighty Mouse-r 9.00 27.00 100.00

MIGHTY HEROES
Spotlight Comics: 1987 (B&W, one-shot)

1-Heckle & Jeckle backup 1.00

MIGHTY HEROES
Marvel Comics: Jan, 1998 ($2.99, one-shot)

1-Origin of the Mighty Heroes 3.00

MIGHTY MARVEL WESTERN, THE
Marvel Comics Group (LMC earlier issues): Oct, 1968 - No. 46, Sept, 1976 (#1-14: 68 pgs.; #15,16: 52 pgs.)

1-Begin Kid Colt, Rawhide Kid, Two-Gun Kid-r 3.20 9.60 32.00
2-16: (2-14-68 pgs./ 15,16-52 pgs.) 2.00 6.00 20.00
17-20 1.10 3.30 11.00
21-30,32,37: 24-Kid Colt-r end. 25-Matt Slade-r begin. 32-Origin-r/Rawhide Kid #23; Williamson-r/Kid Slade #7. 37-Williamson, Kirby-r/Two-Gun Kid 51 .90 2.70 9.00
31,33-36,38-46: 31-Baker-r. .85 2.60 7.00
NOTE: ***Jack Davis*** *a(r)-21-24.* ***Keller*** *r-1-13, 22.* ***Kirby*** *a(r)-1-3, 6, 9, 12-14, 16, 26, 29, 32, 36, 41, 43, 44; c-29.* ***Maneely*** *a(r)-22.* ***Severin*** *c-3i, 9. No Matt Slade-#43.*

MIGHTY MIDGET COMICS, THE (Miniature)
Samuel E. Lowe & Co.: No date; circa 1942-1943 (Sold 2 for 5¢, B&W and red, 36 pgs, approx. 5x4")

Bulletman #11(1943)-r/cover/Bulletman #3 16.00 48.00 120.00
Captain Marvel Adventures #11 16.00 48.00 120.00
Captain Marvel #11 (Same as above except for full color ad on back cover; this issue was glued to cover of Captain Marvel #20 and is not found in fine-mint condition) 233.00 700.00 –
Captain Marvel Jr. #11 (Same-c as Master #27 16.00 48.00 120.00
Captain Marvel Jr. #11 (Same as above except for full color ad on back-c; this issue was glued to cover of Captain Marvel #21 and is not found in fine-mint condition) 242.00 725.00 –
Golden Arrow #11 15.00 44.00 110.00
Ibis the Invincible #11(1942)-Origin; reprints cover to Ibis #1 (Predates Fawcett's Ibis the Invincible #1). 16.00 48.00 120.00
Spy Smasher #11(1942) 16.00 48.00 120.00
NOTE: *The above books came in a box called "box full of books" and was distributed with other Samuel Lowe puzzles, paper dolls, coloring books, etc. They are not titled Mighty Midget Comics. All have a war bond seal on back cover which is otherwise blank. These books came in a "Mighty Midget" flat cardboard counter display rack.*
Balbo, the Boy Magician #12 (1943)-1st book devoted entirely to character. 6.50 19.50 45.00
Bulletman #12 11.00 34.00 85.00
Commando Yank #12 (1943)-Only comic devoted entirely to character. 8.50 26.00 60.00
Dr. Voltz the Human Generator (1943)-Only comic devoted entirely to character. 6.50 19.50 45.00
Lance O'Casey #12 (1943)-1st comic devoted entirely to character (Predates Fawcett's Lance O'Casey #1). 6.50 19.50 45.00
Leatherneck the Marine (1943)-Only comic devoted entirely to character. 6.50 19.50 45.00
Minute Man #12 11.00 34.00 85.00
Mister "Q" (1943)-Only comic devoted entirely to character. 6.50 19.50 45.00
Mr. Scarlet and Pinky #12 (1943)-Only comic devoted entirely to character. 9.30 28.00 70.00
Pat Wilton and His Flying Fortress (1943)-1st comic devoted entirely to character. 6.50 19.50 45.00
The Phantom Eagle #12 (1943)-Only comic devoted entirely to character. 7.15 21.50 50.00
State Trooper Stops Crime (1943)-Only comic devoted entirely to character. 6.50 19.50 45.00
Tornado Tom (1943)-Origin, r/from Cyclone #1-3; only comic devoted entirely to character. 6.50 19.50 45.00

MIGHTY MORPHIN' POWER RANGERS: THE MOVIE (Also see Saban's Mighty Morphin' Power Rangers)
Marvel Comics: Sept, 1995 ($3.95, one-shot)

nn-adaptation of movie 4.00

MIGHTY MOUSE (See Adventures of..., Dell Giant #43, Giant Comics Edition, March of Comics #205, 237, 247, 257, 447, 459, 471, 483, Oxydol-Dreft, Paul Terry's, & Terry-Toons Comics)

MIGHTY MOUSE (1st Series)
Timely/Marvel Comics (20th Century Fox): Fall, 1946 - No. 4, Summer, 1947

1 103.00 309.00 875.00
2 47.00 141.00 400.00
3,4 37.00 110.00 275.00

MIGHTY MOUSE (2nd Series) (Paul Terry's... #62-71)
St. John Publishing Co./Pines No. 68 (3/56) on (TV issues #72 on): Aug, 1947 - No. 67, 11/55; No. 68, 3/56 - No. 83, 6/59

5(#1) 35.00 104.00 260.00
6-10 17.00 52.00 130.00
11-19 11.00 32.00 80.00
20 (11/50) - 25-(52 pg. editions) 8.50 26.00 60.00
20-25-(36 pg. editions) 7.15 21.50 50.00
26-37: 35-Flying saucer-c 5.70 17.00 40.00
38-45-(100 pgs.) 16.00 48.00 120.00
46-83: 62-64,67-Painted-c. 82-Infinity-c 5.70 17.00 38.00
Album 1(10/52, 25¢, 100 pgs., St. John)-Gandy Goose app. 25.00 76.00 190.00
Album 2,3(11/52 & 12/52, St. John) (100 pgs.) 20.00 60.00 150.00
Fun Club Magazine 1(Fall, 1957-Pines, 25¢, 100 pgs.) (CBS TV)-Tom Terrific, Heckle & Jeckle, Dinky Duck, Gandy Goose 14.00 42.00 105.00
Fun Club Magazine 2-6(Winter, 1958-Pines) 9.30 28.00 65.00
3-D 1-(1st printing-9/53, 25¢)(St. John)-Came w/glasses; stiff covers; says World's First! on-c; 1st 3-D comic 27.00 80.00 200.00
3-D 1-(2nd printing-10/53, 25¢)-Came w/glasses; slick, glossy covers, slightly smaller 24.00 72.00 180.00
3-D 2,3(11/53, 12/53, 25¢)-(St. John)-With glasses 23.00 68.00 170.00

MIGHTY MOUSE (TV)(3rd Series)(Formerly Adventures of Mighty Mouse)
Gold Key/Dell Publ. Co. No. 166-on: No. 161, Oct, 1964 - No. 172, Oct, 1968

161(10/64)-165(9/65)-(Becomes Adventures of... No. 166 on) 3.50 10.50 38.00
166(3/66), 167(6/66)-172 2.40 7.00 26.00

Mike Grell's Sable #8 © First Publ., Inc.

Military Comics #38 © QUA

Millennium Fever #3 © Nick Abadzis & Duncan Fegredo

GD25 FN65 NM94

MIGHTY MOUSE (TV)
Spotlight Comics: 1987 - No. 2, 1987 ($1.50, color)
1,2-New stories 1.50
...And Friends Holiday Special (11/87, $1.75) 1.75

MIGHTY MOUSE (TV)
Marvel Comics: Oct, 1990 - No. 10, July, 1991 ($1.00)(Based on Sat. cartoon)
1-10: 1-Dark Knight-c parody. 2-10: 3-Intro Bat-Bat; Byrne-c. 4,5-Crisis-c/story parodies w/Perez-c. 6-Spider-Man-c parody. 7-Origin Bat-Bat 1.00

MIGHTY MOUSE ADVENTURE MAGAZINE
Spotlight Comics: 1987 ($2.00, B&W, 52 pgs., magazine size, one-shot)
1-Deputy Dawg, Heckle & Jeckle backup stories 3.00

MIGHTY MOUSE ADVENTURES (Adventures of... #2 on)
St. John Publishing Co.: November, 1951
1 31.00 92.00 230.00

MIGHTY MOUSE ADVENTURE STORIES (Paul Terry's... on-c only)
St. John Publishing Co.: 1953 (50¢, 384 pgs.)
nn-Rebound issues 41.00 124.00 330.00

MIGHTY MUTANIMALS (See Teenage Mutant Ninja Turtles Adventures #19)
May, 1991 - No. 3, July, 1991 ($1.00, limited series)
Archie Comics: Apr, 1992 - Present ($1.25)
1-3: 1-Story cont'd from TMNT Advs. #19 1.00
1-8 (1992): 7-1st app. Merdude 1.25

MIGHTY SAMSON (Also see Gold Key Champion)
Gold Key: 7/64 - #20, 11/69; #21, 8/72; #22, 12/73 - #31, 3/76; #32, 8/82 (Painted c-1-31)
1-Origin/1st app.; Thorne-a begins 6.25 19.00 70.00
2-5 3.20 9.50 35.00
6-10: 7-Tom Morrow begins, ends #20 2.00 6.00 22.00
11-20 1.60 4.80 16.00
21-31: 21,22-r 1.00 2.80 10.00
32-r .85 2.60 7.00

MIGHTY THOR (See Thor)

MIKE BARNETT, MAN AGAINST CRIME (TV)
Fawcett Publications: Dec, 1951 - No. 6, Oct, 1952
1 16.00 48.00 120.00
2 9.30 28.00 70.00
3,4,6 8.50 26.00 60.00
5- "Market for Morphine" cover/story 10.00 30.00 75.00

MIKE DANGER (See Mickey Spillane's...)

MIKE DEODATO'S...
Caliber Comics
...FALLOUT 3000 ,1996 ($2.95, B&W, one-shot)
1 3.00
...JONAS ,1996 ($2.95, B&W, magazine size)
1 3.00
...PRIME CUTS ,1996 ($2.95, B&W, magazine size)
1 3.00
...PROTHEUS ,1996 - No. 2, 1996 ($2.95, B&W, limited series)
1,2 3.00
...RAMTHAR ,1996 ($2.95, B&W, one-shot)
1 3.00
...RAZOR NIGHTS ,1996 ($2.95, B&W, one-shot)
1 3.00

MIKE GRELL'S SABLE (Also see Jon Sable & Sable)
First Comics: Mar, 1990 - No. 10, Dec, 1990 ($1.75)
1-10: r/Jon Sable Freelance #1-10 by Grell 1.80

MIKE MIST MINUTE MIST-ERIES (See Ms. Tree/Mike Mist in 3-D)
Eclipse Comics: April, 1981 ($1.25, B&W, one-shot)
1 1.25

MIKE SHAYNE PRIVATE EYE
Dell Publishing Co.: Nov-Jan, 1962 - No. 3, Sept-Nov, 1962
1 2.20 6.60 24.00
2,3 1.50 4.50 15.00

MILITARY COMICS (Becomes Modern Comics #44 on)
Quality Comics Group: Aug, 1941 - No. 43, Oct, 1945
GD25 FN65 VF82 NM94
1-Origin/1st app. Blackhawk by C. Cuidera (Eisner scripts); Miss America, The Death Patrol by Jack Cole (also #2-7,27-30), & The Blue Tracer by Guardineer; X of the Underground, The Yankee Eagle, Q-Boat & Shot & Shell, Archie Atkins, Loops & Banks by Bud Ernest (Bob Powell)(ends #13) begin 780.00 2340.00 4680.00 7800.00
GD25 FN65 NM94
2-Secret War News begins (by McWilliams #2-16); Cole-a; new uniform with yellow circle & hawk's head for Blackhawk 229.00 687.00 1950.00
3-Origin/1st app. Chop Chop 194.00 582.00 1650.00
4 153.00 459.00 1300.00
5-The Sniper begins; Miss America in costume #4-7 129.00 387.00 1100.00
6-9: 8-X of the Underground begins (ends #13). 9-The Phantom Clipper begins (ends #16) 97.00 291.00 825.00
10-Classic Eisner-c 100.00 300.00 850.00
11-Flag-c 76.00 228.00 650.00
12-Blackhawk by Crandall begins, ends #22 100.00 300.00 850.00
13-15: 14-Private Dogtag begins (ends #83) 74.00 222.00 625.00
16-20: 16-Blue Tracer ends. 17-P.T. Boat begins 65.00 195.00 550.00
21-31: 22-Last Crandall Blackhawk. 23-Shrunken head-c. 27-Death Patrol revived 56.00 168.00 475.00
32-43 49.00 147.00 420.00
NOTE: ***Berg** a-6. **Al Bryant** c-31-34, 38, 40-43. **J. Cole** a-1-3, 27-32. **Crandall** a-12-22; c-13-20. **Cuidera** c-2-9. **Eisner** c-1, 2(part), 9, 10. **Kotsky** c-21-29, 35, 37, 39. **McWilliams** a-2-16. **Powell** a-1-13. **Ward** Blackhawk-30, 31(15 pgs. each); c-30.*

MILK AND CHEESE (Also see Cerebus Bi-Weekly #20)
Slave Labor: 1991 - Present ($2.50, B&W)
1-Evan Dorkin story & art in all. 6.25 19.00 70.00
1-2nd-6th printings 4.00
2-"Other #1" 3.80 11.50 40.00
2-reprint 3.00
3-"Third #1" 2.70 8.00 35.00
4-"Fourth #1", 5-"First Second Issue" 1.50 4.50 15.00
6-"#666" .85 2.60 7.00
7 .85 2.60 7.00
NOTE: *Multiple printings of all issues exist and are worth cover price unless listed here.*

MILLENNIUM
DC Comics: Jan, 1988 - No. 8, Feb, 1988 (Weekly limited series)
1-Staton c/a(p) begins 2.50
2-8 1.60

MILLENNIUM FEVER
DC Comics (Vertigo): Oct, 1995 - No.4, Jan, 1996 ($2.50, limited series)
1-4: Duncan Fegredo-c/a 2.50

MILLENNIUM INDEX
Independent Comics Group: Mar, 1988 - No. 2, Mar, 1988 ($2.00)
1,2 2.00

MILLIE, THE LOVABLE MONSTER
Dell Publishing Co.: Sept-Nov, 1962 - No. 6, Jan, 1973
12-523-211, 2(8-10/63)-Bill Woggon c/a 3.00 9.00 35.00
3(8-10/64) 2.25 6.75 26.00

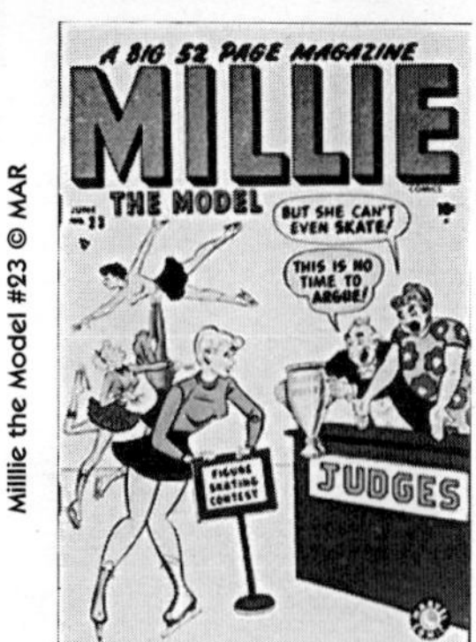

Millie the Model #23 © MAR

The Minx #1 © Peter Milligan & Sean Phillips

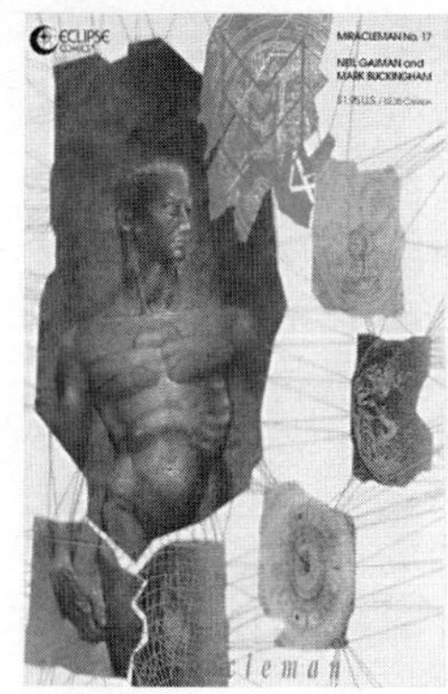

Miracleman #17 © ECL

4(7/72), 5(10/72), 6(1/73) 1.40 4.20 14.00
NOTE: ***Woggon** a-3-6; c-3-6. 4 reprints 1; 5 reprints 2; 6 reprints 3.*

MILLIE THE MODEL (See Comedy Comics, A Date With..., Joker Comics #28, Life With..., Mad About..., Marvel Mini-Books, Misty & Modeling With...)
Marvel/Atlas/Marvel Comics(CnPC #1)(SPI/Male/VPI):1945 - No. 207, Dec, 1973

1-Origin 62.00 185.00 525.00
2 (10/46)-Millie becomes The Blonde Phantom to sell Blonde Phantom perfume; a pre-Blonde Phantom app. (see All-Select #11, Fall, 1946) 37.00 110.00 275.00
3-7: 4-7-Willie app. 7-Willie smokes extra strong tobacco 23.00 68.00 170.00
8,10-Kurtzman's "Hey Look". 8-Willie & Rusty app. 23.00 68.00 170.00
9-Powerhouse Pepper by Wolverton, 4 pgs. 27.00 80.00 200.00
11-Kurtzman-a, "Giggles 'n' Grins" 16.00 48.00 120.00
12,15,17-20: 12-Rusty & Hedy Devine app. 11.00 32.00 80.00
13,14,16-Kurtzman's "Hey Look". 13-Hedy Devine app. 12.00 36.00 90.00
21-30 7.85 23.50 55.00
31-60 4.00 12.00 40.00
61-99 2.80 8.40 28.00
100 3.50 10.50 35.00
101-130: 107-Jack Kirby app. in story 2.50 7.50 24.00
131-153: 141-Groovy Gears-c/s 2.50 7.50 20.00
154-New Millie begins (10/67) 2.80 8.40 28.00
155-190 2.25 6.75 18.00
191-199,201-206: 192-(52 pgs.) 1.85 5.50 15.00
200,207(Last issue) 2.50 7.50 20.00
(Beware: cut-up pages are common in all Annuals)
Annual 1(1962)-Early Marvel annual (2nd?) 15.00 45.00 150.00
Annual 2(1963) 12.00 36.00 120.00
Annual 3-5 (1964-1966) 6.50 19.50 65.00
Annual 6-10(1967-11/71) 5.00 15.00 50.00
Queen-Size 11(9/74), 12(1975) 4.00 12.00 40.00
NOTE: ***Dan DeCarlo** a-18-93.*

MILLION DOLLAR DIGEST (Richie Rich... #23 on; also see Richie Rich...)
Harvey Publications: 11/86 - No. 7, 11/87; No. 8, 4/88 - No. 34, Nov, 1994 ($1.25/$1.75, digest size)

1-8: 8-(68 pgs.) 1.25
9-34: 9-Begin $1.75-c. 14-May not exist 1.75

MILT GROSS FUNNIES (Also see Picture News #1)
Milt Gross, Inc. (ACG?): Aug, 1947 - No. 2, Sept, 1947

1,2 11.00 32.00 80.00

MILTON THE MONSTER & FEARLESS FLY (TV)
Gold Key: May, 1966

1 (10175-605) 9.00 27.00 100.00

MINIMUM WAGE
Fantagraphics Books: V1#1, July, 1995 ($9.95, B&W, graphic novel, mature) V2#1, 1995 - Present ($2.95, B&W, mature)

V1#1-Bob Fingerman story & art 1.00 3.00 10.00
V2#1-9($2.95): Bob Fingerman story & art. 2-Kevin Nowlan back-c. 4-w/pin-ups. 5-Mignola back-c 3.00
Book Two TPB ('97, $12.95) r/V2#1-5 12.95

MINUTE MAN (See Master Comics & Mighty Midget Comics)
Fawcett Publications: Summer, 1941 - No. 3, Spring, 1942 (68 pgs.)

1 147.00 441.00 1250.00
2,3 94.00 267.00 800.00

MINUTE MAN
Sovereign Service Station giveaway: No date (16 pgs., B&W, paper-c blue & red)
nn-American history 2.40 6.00

MINUTE MAN ANSWERS THE CALL, THE

GD25 FN65 NM94

By M. C. Gaine: 1942 (4 pgs.) (Giveaway inserted in Jr. JSA Membership Kit)
nn-Sheldon Moldoff-a 10.00 30.00 75.00

MINX, THE
DC Comics (Vertigo): Oct, 1998 - Present ($2.50)

1-5-Milligan-s/Phillips-c/a 2.50

MIRACLE COMICS
Hillman Periodicals: Feb, 1940 - No. 4, Mar, 1941

1-Sky Wizard Master of Space, Dash Dixon, Man of Might, Pinkie Parker, Dusty Doyle, The Kid Cop, K-7, Secret Agent, The Scorpion, & Blandu, Jungle Queen begin; Masked Angel only app. (all 1st app.) 153.00 459.00 1300.00
2 76.00 228.00 650.00
3,4: 3-Bill Colt, the Ghost Rider begins. 4-The Veiled Prophet & Bullet Bob (by Burnley) app. 69.00 207.00 585.00

MIRACLEMAN
Eclipse Comics: Aug, 1985 - No. 15, Nov, 1988; No. 16, Dec, 1989 - No. 24, 1994

1-r/British Marvelman series; Alan Moore scripts in #1-16 5.00
1-Gold & Silver editions 4.00
2-12: 8-Airboy preview. 9,10-Origin Miracleman. 9-Shows graphic scenes of childbirth. 10-Snyder-c 4.00
13-15-($1.75) 4.00
16-18-($1.95): 17-"The Golden Age" begins, ends #22. Dave McKean-c begins, end #22; Neil Gaiman scripts in #17-24 4.00
19-24-($2.50); 23-"The Silver Age" begins. 23,24-B. Smith-c. 4.00
3-D 1 (12/85) 3.00
The Golden Age (1997, $12.99, TPB) r/#17-22 13.00
NOTE: ***Chaykin** c-3. **Gulacy** c-7. **McKean** c-17-22. **B. Smith** c-23, 24. **Starlin** c-4. **Totleben** a-11-13; c-9, 11-13. **Truman** c-6.*

MIRACLEMAN: APOCRYPHA
Eclipse Comics: Nov, 1991 - No. 3, Feb, 1992 ($2.50, limited series)

1-3: 1-Stories by Neil Gaiman, Mark Buckingham, Alex Ross & others. 3-Stories by James Robinson, Kelley Jones, Matt Wagner, Neil Gaiman, Mark Buckingham & others 2.50

MIRACLEMAN FAMILY
Eclipse Comics: May, 1988 - No. 2, Sept, 1988 ($1.95, lim. series, Baxter paper)

1,2: 2-Gulacy-c 2.00

MIRACLE OF THE WHITE STALLIONS, THE (See Movie Comics)

MIRACLE ON BROADWAY
Broadway Comics: Dec, 1995 (Giveaway)

1-Ernie Colon-c/a; Jim Shooter &Co. story; 1st known digitally printed comic book; 1st app. Spire & Knights on Broadway (1150 print run) 20.00
NOTE: *Miracle on Broadway was a limited edition comic given to 1100 VIPs in the entertainment industry for the 1995 Holiday Season.*

MIRACLE SQUAD, THE
Upshot Graphics (Fantagraphics Books): Aug, 1986 - No. 4, 1987 ($2.00)

1-4 2.00

MIRACLE SQUAD: BLOOD AND DUST, THE
Apple Comics: Jan, 1989 - No. 4, July, 1989 ($1.95, B&W, limited series)

1-4 2.00

MIRRORWORLD: RAIN
NetCo Partners (Big Ent.): Feb, 1997 - No. 0, Apr, 1997 ($3.25, limited series)

0,1-Tad Williams-s 3.25

MISADVENTURES OF MERLIN JONES, THE (See Movie Comics & Merlin Jones as the Monkey's Uncle under Movie Comics)

MISS AMERICA COMICS (Miss America Magazine #2 on; also see Blonde Phantom & Marvel Mystery Comics)
Marvel Comics (20CC): 1944 (one-shot)

1-2 pgs. pin-ups 135.00 406.00 1150.00

Miss America Magazine #3 © MAR

Miss Fury Comics #2 © TCI

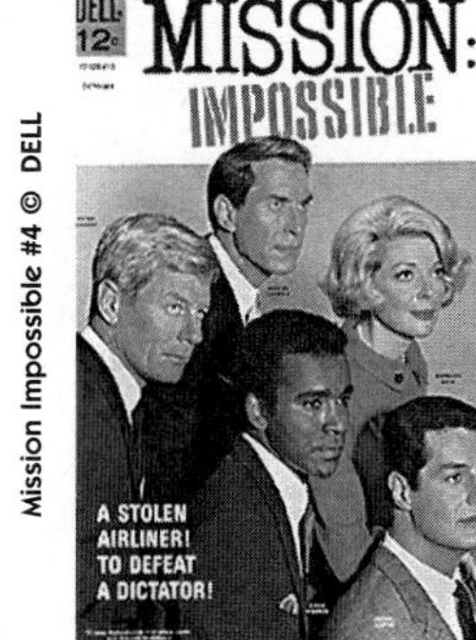

Mission Impossible #4 © DELL

	GD25	FN65	NM94
MISS AMERICA MAGAZINE (Formerly Miss America; Miss America #51 on) **Miss America Publ. Corp./Marvel/Atlas (MAP):** V1#2, Nov, 1944 - No. 93, Nov, 1958			
V1#2-Photo-c of teenage girl in Miss America costume; Miss America, Patsy Walker (intro.) comic stories plus movie reviews & stories; intro. Buzz Baxter & Hedy Wolfe; 1 pg. origin Miss America	112.00	335.00	950.00
3-5-Miss America & Patsy Walker stories	43.00	129.00	350.00
6-Patsy Walker only	9.30	28.00	70.00
V2#1(4/45)-6(9/45)-Patsy Walker continues	5.70	17.00	35.00
V3#1(10/45)-6(4/46)	5.70	17.00	35.00
V4#1(5/46),2,5(9/46)	5.35	16.00	32.00
V4#3(7/46)-Liz Taylor photo-c	7.85	23.50	55.00
V4#4 (8/46; 68 pgs.)	5.00	15.00	30.00
V4#6 (10/46; 92 pgs.)	5.00	15.00	30.00
V5#1(11/46)-6(4/47), V6#1(5/47)-3(7/47)	5.00	15.00	30.00
V7#1(8/47)-14,16-23(#56, 6/49)	4.25	13.00	26.00
V7#15-All comics	5.35	16.00	32.00
V7#24(#57, 7/49)-Kamen-a (becomes Best Western #58 on?)	5.00	15.00	30.00
V7#25(8/49), 27-44(3/52), VII,nn(5/52)	4.00	12.00	24.00
V7#26(9/49)-All comics	5.00	15.00	30.00
V1,nn(7/52)-V1,nn(1/53)(#46-49)	4.00	12.00	24.00
V7#50(Spring '53), V1#51-V7?#54(7/53)	4.00	12.00	24.00
55-93	4.00	12.00	24.00

NOTE: *Photo-c #1, 4, V2#1, 4, 5, V3#5, V4#3, 4, 6, V7#15, 16, 24, 26, 34, 37, 38. Painted c-3.* ***Powell*** *a-V7#31.*

	GD25	FN65	NM94
MISS BEVERLY HILLS OF HOLLYWOOD (See Adventures of Bob Hope) **National Periodical Publ.:** Mar-Apr, 1949 - No. 9, July-Aug, 1950 (52 pgs.)			
1 (Meets Alan Ladd)	52.00	155.00	440.00
2-William Holden photo on-c	39.00	117.00	315.00
3-5: 2-9-Part photo-c. 5-Bob Hope photo on-c	33.00	100.00	250.00
6,7,9: 6-Lucille Ball photo on-c	31.00	93.00	235.00
8-Reagan photo on-c	36.00	108.00	285.00

NOTE: *Beverly meets Alan Ladd in #1, Eve Arden #2, Betty Hutton #4, Bob Hope #5.*

	GD25	FN65	NM94
MISS CAIRO JONES **Croyden Publishers:** 1945			
1-Bob Oksner daily newspaper-r (1st strip story); lingerie panels	18.00	54.00	135.00
MISS FURY COMICS (Newspaper strip reprints) **Timely Comics (NPI 1/CmPI 2/MPC 3-8):** Winter, 1942-43 - No. 8, Winter, 1946 (Published quarterly)			
1-Origin Miss Fury by Tarpe' Mills (68 pgs.) in costume w/pin-ups	274.00	821.00	2600.00
2-(60 pgs.)-In costume w/pin-ups	141.00	423.00	1200.00
3-(60 pgs.)-In costume w/pin-ups; Hitler-c	115.00	345.00	975.00
4-(52 pgs.)-In costume, 2 pgs. w/pin-ups	88.00	264.00	750.00
5-(52 pgs.)-In costume w/pin-ups	79.00	237.00	675.00
6-(52 pgs.)-Not in costume in inside stories, w/pin-ups	74.00	220.00	625.00
7,8-(36 pgs.)-In costume 1 pg. each; no pin-ups	68.00	204.00	575.00

NOTE: ***Schomburg*** *c-1, 5, 6.*

	GD25	FN65	NM94
MISS FURY **Adventure Comics:** 1991 - No. 4, 1991 ($2.50, limited series)			
1-4: 1-Origin; granddaughter of original Miss Fury			2.50
1-Limited ed. ($4.95)			5.00
MISSION IMPOSSIBLE (TV) **Dell Publ. Co.:** May, 1967 - No. 4, Oct, 1968; No. 5, Oct, 1969 (All have photo-c)			
1	7.50	22.50	90.00
2-5: 5-Reprints #1	5.00	15.00	60.00
MISSION IMPOSSIBLE (Movie) **Marvel Comics (Paramount Comics):** May, 1996 ($2.95, one-shot) (1st Paramount Comics book)			
1-Liefeld-c & back-up story			3.00
MISS LIBERTY (Becomes Liberty Comics) **Burten Publishing Co.:** 1945 (MLJ reprints)			
1-The Shield & Dusty, The Wizard, & Roy, the Super Boy app.; r/Shield-Wizard #13	26.00	78.00	195.00
MISS MELODY LANE OF BROADWAY (See The Adventures of Bob Hope) **National Periodical Publ.:** Feb-Mar, 1950 - No. 3, June-July, 1950 (52 pgs.)			
1-Movie stars photos app. on all-c.	53.00	159.00	450.00
2,3: 3-Ed Sullivan photo on-c.	38.00	114.00	285.00
MISS PEACH **Dell Publishing Co.:** Oct-Dec, 1963; 1969			
1-Jack Mendelsohn-a/script	6.40	19.00	70.00
...Tells You How to Grow (1969; 25¢)-Mel Lazarus-a; also given away (36 pgs.)	3.60	11.00	40.00
MISS PEPPER (See Meet Miss Pepper)			
MISS SUNBEAM (See Little Miss...)			
MISS VICTORY (See Captain Fearless #1,2, Holyoke One-Shot #3, Veri Best Sure Fire & Veri Best Sure Shot Comics)			
MISTER AMERICA **Endeavor Comics:** Apr, 1994 - No. 2, May, 1994 ($2.95, limited series)			
1,2			3.00
MR. & MRS. BEANS **United Features Syndicate:** No. 11, 1939			
Single Series 11	31.00	92.00	230.00
MR. & MRS. J. EVIL SCIENTIST (TV)(See The Flintstones & Hanna-Barbera Band Wagon #3) **Gold Key:** Nov, 1963 - No. 4, Sept, 1966 (Hanna-Barbera, all 12¢)			
1-From The Flintstones	7.00	22.00	80.00
2-4	4.50	13.50	50.00
MR. ANTHONY'S LOVE CLINIC (Based on radio show) **Hillman Periodicals:** Nov, 1949 - No. 5, Apr-May, 1950 (52 pgs.)			
1-Photo-c	11.00	32.00	80.00
2	6.85	21.00	48.00
3-5: 5-Photo-c	5.70	17.00	38.00
MISTER BLANK **Amaze Ink:** No. 0, Jan, 1996 - Present ($1.75/$2.95, B&W)			
0-($1.75, 16 pgs.) Origin of Mr. Blank			2.00
1-7-($2.95) Chris Hicks-s/a			3.00
MR. BUG GOES TO TOWN (See Cinema Comics Herald) **K.K. Publications:** 1941 (Giveaway, 52 pgs.)			
nn-Cartoon movie (scarce)	53.00	159.00	450.00
MR. DISTRICT ATTORNEY (Radio/TV) **National Per. Publ.:** Jan-Feb, 1948 - No. 67, Jan-Feb, 1959 (1-23: 52 pgs.)			
1-Howard Purcell c-5-23 (most)	90.00	270.00	775.00
2	40.00	120.00	340.00
3-5	30.00	90.00	230.00
6-10	23.00	69.00	180.00
11-20	18.00	54.00	140.00
21-43: 43-Last pre-code (1-2/55)	13.50	41.00	95.00
44-67	11.00	33.00	75.00
MR. DISTRICT ATTORNEY (SeeThe Funnies #35) **Dell Publishing Co.:** No. 13, 1942			
Four Color 13-See The Funnies #35 for 1st app.	27.00	82.00	300.00
MISTER E (Also see Books of Magic limited series)			

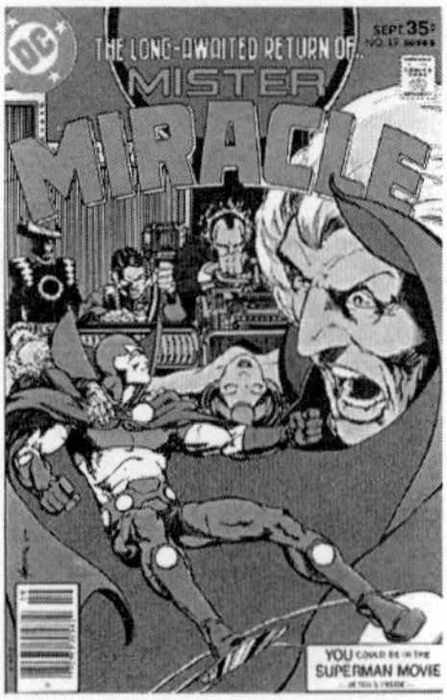

Mister Miracle #19 © DC

Mr. Mxyzptlk (Villains) #1 © DC

Mister Mystery #12 © Media Publ.

GD25 FN65 NM94

DC Comics: Jun, 1991- No. 4, Sept, 1991($1.75, limited series)

1-4-Snyder III-c/a; follow-up to Books of Magic limited series 2.00

MISTER ED, THE TALKING HORSE (TV)
Dell Publishing Co./Gold Key: Mar-May, 1962 - No. 6, Feb, 1964 (All photo-c; photo back-c: 1-6)

	GD25	FN65	NM94
Four Color 1295	12.00	35.00	130.00
1(11/62) (Gold Key)-Photo-c	9.00	27.00	100.00
2-6: Photo-c	5.00	15.00	55.00

(See March of Comics #244, 260, 282, 290)

MR. HERO, THE NEWMATIC MAN (See Neil Gaiman's...)

MR. MAGOO (TV) (The Nearsighted..., ...& Gerald McBoing Boing 1954 issues; formerly Gerald McBoing-Boing And ...)
Dell Publishing Co.: No. 6, Nov-Jan, 1953-54; 5/54 - 3-5/62; 9-11/63 - 3-5/65

	GD25	FN65	NM94
6	11.00	33.00	120.00
Four Color 561(5/54),602(11/54)	11.00	33.00	120.00
Four Color 1235(#1, 12-2/62),1305(#2, 3-5/62)	9.00	27.00	100.00
3(9-11/63) - 5	8.00	23.00	85.00
Four Color 1235(12-536-505)(3-5/65)-2nd Printing	5.50	16.50	60.00

MISTER MIRACLE (1st series) (See Cancelled Comic Cavalcade)
National Periodical Publications/DC Comics: 3-4/71 - V4#18, 2-3/74; V5#19, 9/77 - V6#25, 8-9/78; 1987 (Fourth World)

	GD25	FN65	NM94
1-1st app. Mr. Miracle (#1-3 are 15¢)	2.70	8.00	30.00
2,3	1.60	4.80	16.00
4-8: 4-Boy Commandos-r begin; all 52 pgs.	2.20	6.25	22.00
9,10: 9-Origin Mr. Miracle; Darkseid cameo	1.00	3.00	10.00
11-18: 15-Intro/1st app. Shilo Norman. 18-Barda & Scott Free wed; New Gods app. & Darkseid cameo; Last Kirby issue.	1.00	3.00	10.00
19-25 (1977-78)		2.00	6.00
Special 1(1987, $1.25, 52 pgs.)			3.00
Jack Kirby's Mister Miracle TPB ('98, $12.95) B&W&Grey-toned reprint of #1-10; David Copperfield intro.			12.95

NOTE: ***Austin*** *a-19i.* ***Ditko*** *a-6r.* ***Golden*** *a-23-25p; c-25p.* ***Heath*** *a-24i, 25i; c-25i.* ***Kirby*** *a(p)/c-1-18.* ***Nasser*** *a-19i.* ***Rogers*** *a-19-22p; c-19, 20p, 21p, 22-24. 4-8 contain* ***Simon & Kirby*** *Boy Commandos reprints from Detective 82,76, Boy Commandos 1, 3 & Detective 64 in that order.*

MISTER MIRACLE (2nd Series) (See Justice League)
DC Comics: Jan, 1989 - No. 28, June, 1991 ($1.00)

1-28: 13,14-Lobo app. 22-1st new Mr. Miracle w/new costume 1.00

MISTER MIRACLE (3rd Series)
DC Comics: Apr, 1996 - No. 7, Oct, 1996 ($1.95)

1-7: 2-Vs. JLA. 6-Simonson-c 2.00

MR. MIRACLE (See Capt. Fearless #1 & Holyoke One-Shot #4)

MR. MONSTER (1st Series)(Doc Stearn... #7 on; See Airboy-Mr. Monster Special, Dark Horse Presents, Super Duper Comics & Vanguard Illustrated #7)
Eclipse Comics: Jan, 1985 - No. 10, June, 1987 ($1.75, Baxter paper)

	GD25	FN65	NM94
1-1st story-r from Vanguard Ill. #7(1st app.)			2.50
2-Dave Stevens-c			1.75
3-10: 3-Alan Moore scripts; Wolverton-r/Weird Mysteries #5. 6-Ditko-r/Fantastic Fears #5 plus new Giffen-a 10 6-D issue			1.75

MR. MONSTER
Dark Horse Comics: Feb, 1988 - No. 8, July, 1991 ($1.75, B&W)

	GD25	FN65	NM94
1-7			1.75
8-($4.95, 60 pgs.)-Origins conclusion			5.00

MR. MONSTER ATTACKS! (Doc Stearn...)
Tundra Publ.: Aug, 1992 - No. 3, Oct, 1992 ($3.95, limited series, 32 pgs.)

1-3: Michael T. Gilbert-a/scripts; Gilbert/Dorman painted-c 4.00

MR. MONSTER PRESENTS (CRACK-A-BOOM!)
Caliber Comics: 1997 - No. 3, 1997 ($2.95, B&W&Red, limited series)

1-3: Michael T. Gilbert-a/scripts: 1-Wraparound-c 1.20 3.00

GD25 FN65 NM94

MR. MONSTER'S SUPER-DUPER SPECIAL
Eclipse Comics: May, 1986 - No. 8, July, 1987

	GD25	FN65	NM94
1-(5/86)...3-D High Octane Horror #1			3.00
1-(5/86)...2-D version, 100 copies	1.20	3.60	12.00
2-(8/86)...High Octane Horror #1, 3-(9/86)...True Crime #1, 4-(11/86)...True Crime #2, 5-(1/87)...Hi-Voltage Super Science #1, 6-(3/87)...High Shock Schlock #1, 7-(5/87)...High Shock Schlock #2, 8-(7/87)...Weird Tales Of The Future #1			3.00

NOTE: ***Jack Cole*** *r-3, 4.* ***Evans*** *a-2r.* ***Kubert*** *a-1r.* ***Powell*** *a-5r.* ***Wolverton*** *a-2r, 7r, 8r.*

MR. MONSTER VS. GORZILLA
Image Comics: July, 1998 ($2.95, one-shot)

1- Michael T. Gilbert-a 3.00

MR. MUSCLES (Formerly Blue Beetle #18-21)
Charlton Comics: No. 22, Mar, 1956; No. 23, Aug, 1956

	GD25	FN65	NM94
22,23	5.70	17.00	38.00

MR. MXYZPTLK (VILLAINS)
DC Comics: Feb, 1998 ($1.95, one-shot)

1-Grant-s/Morgan-a/Pearson-c 2.00

MISTER MYSTERY (Tales of Horror and Suspense)
Mr. Publ. (Media Publ.) No. 1-3/SPM Publ./Stanmore (Aragon): Sept, 1951 - No. 19, Oct, 1954

	GD25	FN65	NM94
1-Kurtzmanesque horror story	69.00	207.00	585.00
2,3-Kurtzmanesque story. 3-Anti-Wertham edit.	46.00	138.00	390.00
4,6: Bondage-c; 6-Torture	46.00	138.00	390.00
5,8,10	43.00	129.00	350.00
7- "The Brain Bats of Venus" by Wolverton; partially re-used in Weird Tales of the Future #7	92.00	277.00	785.00
9-Nostrand-a	43.00	129.00	350.00
11-Wolverton "Robot Woman" story/Weird Mysteries #2, cut up, rewritten & partially redrawn	64.00	191.00	540.00
12-Classic injury to eye-c	92.00	277.00	785.00
13,14,17,19: 17-Severed heads-c. 19-Reprints	29.00	88.00	220.00
15- "Living Dead" junkie story	29.00	88.00	220.00
16-Bondage-c	29.00	88.00	220.00
18- "Robot Woman" by Wolverton reprinted from Weird Mysteries #2; decapitation, bondage-c	49.00	146.00	415.00

NOTE: ***Andru*** *a-1, 2p, 3p.* ***Andru/Esposito*** *c-1-3.* ***Baily*** *c-10-18(most).* ***Mortellaro*** *c-5-7. Bondage c-7. Some issues have graphic dismemberment scenes.*

MR. PUNCH
DC Comics (Vertigo): 1994 ($24.95, one-shot)

	GD25	FN65	NM94
nn (Hard-c)-Gaiman scripts; McKean-c/a	2.25	6.80	25.00
nn (Soft-c)	1.50	4.50	15.00

MISTER Q (See Mighty Midget Comics & Our Flag Comics #5)

MR. RISK (Formerly All Romances; Men Against Crime #3 on)(Also see Our Flag Comics & Super-Mystery Comics)
Ace Magazines: No. 7, Oct, 1950 - No. 2, Dec, 1950

	GD25	FN65	NM94
7,2	6.50	19.50	45.00

MR. SCARLET & PINKY (See Mighty Midget Comics)

MR. T AND THE T-FORCE
Now Comics: June, 1993 - No. 10, May, 1994 ($1.95, color)

	GD25	FN65	NM94
1-10-Newsstand editions: 1-7-polybagged with photo trading card in each. 1,2-Neal Adams-c/a(p). 3-Dave Dorman painted-c			2.00
1-10-Direct Sale editions polybagged w/line drawn trading cards. 1-Contains gold foil trading card by Neal Adams			2.00

MISTER UNIVERSE (Professional wrestler)
Mr. Publications Media Publ. (Stanmor, Aragon): July, 1951; No. 2, Oct, 1951 - No. 5, April, 1952

	GD25	FN65	NM94
1	18.00	54.00	135.00
2- "Jungle That Time Forgot", (24 pg. story); Andru/Esposito-c			

Mitzi Romances #8 © MAR

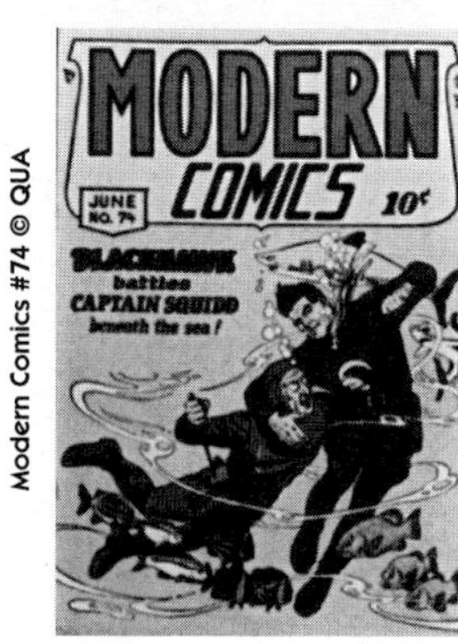

Modern Comics #74 © QUA

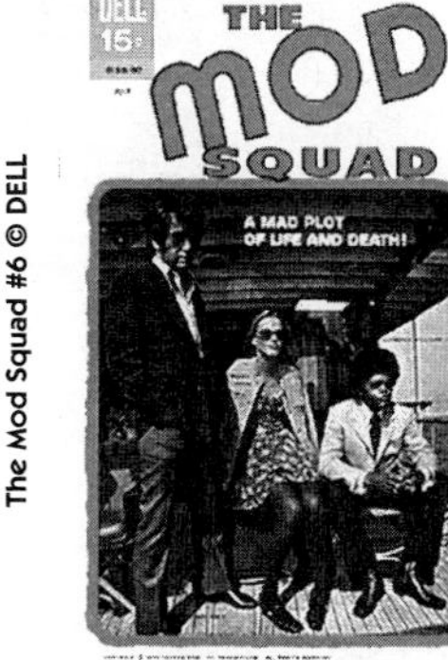

The Mod Squad #6 © DELL

	GD25	FN65	NM94
	11.00	34.00	85.00
3-Marijuana story	11.00	34.00	85.00
4,5- "Goes to War" cover/stories	8.50	26.00	60.00

MISTER X (See Vortex)
6/84 - No. 14, 8/88 ($1.50/$2.25, direct sales, coated paper)
Mr. Publications/Vortex Comics/Caliber V3#1 on: V2#1, Apr, 1989 - V2#12, Mar, 1990 ($2.00/$2.50, B&W, newsprint) V3#1, 1996 - Present ($2.95, B&W)

	GD25	FN65	NM94
1			3.00
2			2.50
3-14: 11-Dave McKean story & art (6 pgs.)			2.00
V2#1-11 (Second Coming, $2.00, B&W): 1-Four different covers. 10-Photo-c			2.00
V2#12 ($2.50)			2.50
V3#1-3(2.95, B&W): 1-1st Caliber issue			3.00
Return of… ($11.95, graphic novel)-r/1-4	1.20	3.60	12.00
Return of… ($34.95, hardcover limited edition)-r/1-4	3.20	9.50	35.00
Special (no date, 1990?)			2.00

MISTY
Marvel Comics (Star Comics): Dec, 1985 - No. 6, May, 1986 (Limited series)

	GD25	FN65	NM94
1-6: Millie The Model's niece		.80	2.00

MITZI COMICS (Becomes Mitzi's Boy Friend #2 on)(See All Teen)
Timely Comics: Spring, 1948 (one-shot)

	GD25	FN65	NM94
1-Kurtzman's "Hey Look" plus 3 pgs. "Giggles 'n' Grins"	18.00	54.00	135.00

MITZI'S BOY FRIEND (Formerly Mitzi Comics; becomes Mitzi's Romances)
Marvel Comics (TCI): No. 2, June, 1948 - No. 7, April, 1949

	GD25	FN65	NM94
2	9.30	28.00	65.00
3-7	6.85	21.00	48.00

MITZI'S ROMANCES (Formerly Mitzi's Boy Friend)
Timely/Marvel Comics (TCI): No. 8, June, 1949 - No. 10, Dec, 1949

	GD25	FN65	NM94
8-Becomes True Life Tales #8 (10/49) on?	9.30	28.00	65.00
9,10: 10-Painted-c	6.85	21.00	48.00

MOBFIRE
DC Comics (Vertigo): Dec, 1994 - No. 6, May, 1995 ($2.50, limited series)

	GD25	FN65	NM94
1-6			2.50

MOBY DICK (See Feature Presentations #6, and King Classics)
Dell Publishing Co.: No. 717, Aug, 1956

	GD25	FN65	NM94
Four Color 717-Movie, Gregory Peck photo-c	8.00	25.00	90.00

MOBY DUCK (See Donald Duck #112 & Walt Disney Showcase #2,11)
Gold Key (Disney): Oct, 1967 - No. 11, Oct, 1970; No. 12, Jan, 1974 - No. 30, Feb, 1978

	GD25	FN65	NM94
1	1.80	5.40	18.00
2-5	1.00	3.00	10.00
6-11	.85	2.60	7.00
12-30: 21,30-r			4.00

MODEL FUN (With Bobby Benson)
Harle Publications: No. 3, Winter, 1954-55 - No. 5, July, 1955

	GD25	FN65	NM94
3-Bobby Benson	5.70	17.00	38.00
4,5-Bobby Benson	4.00	12.00	24.00

MODELING WITH MILLIE (Formerly Life With Millie)
Atlas/Marvel Comics (Male Publ.): No. 21, Feb, 1963 - No. 54, June, 1967

	GD25	FN65	NM94
21	7.00	21.00	70.00
22-30	4.00	12.00	40.00
31-54	2.50	7.50	28.00

MODERN COMICS (Formerly Military Comics #1-43)
Quality Comics Group: No. 44, Nov, 1945 - No. 102, Oct, 1950

	GD25	FN65	NM94
44-Blackhawk continues	47.00	141.00	400.00
45-52: 49-1st app. Fear, Lady Adventuress	38.00	114.00	285.00
53-Torchy by Ward begins (9/46)	39.00	118.00	315.00
54-60: 55-J. Cole-a	31.00	94.00	235.00
61-77,79,80: 73-J. Cole-a	28.00	84.00	210.00
78-1st app. Madame Butterfly	31.00	94.00	235.00
81-99,101: 82,83-One pg. J. Cole-a. 83-The Spirit app.; last 52 pg. issue? 99-Blackhawks on the moon-c/story	28.00	84.00	210.00
100	28.00	84.00	210.00
102-(Scarce)-J. Cole-a; Spirit by Eisner app.	33.00	98.00	245.00

NOTE: ***Al Bryant*** *c-44-51, 54, 55, 66, 69.* ***Jack Cole*** *a-55, 73.* ***Crandall*** *Blackhawk-#46, 47, 50, 51, 54, 56, 58-60, 64, 67-70, 73, 74, 76-78, 80-83; c-60-65, 67, 68, 70-95.* ***Crandall/Cuidera*** *c-56-59, 96-102.* ***Gustavson*** *a-47.* ***Ward*** *Blackhawk-#52, 53, 55 (15 pgs. each). Torchy in #53-102; by* ***Ward*** *only in #53-89(9/49); by* ***Gil Fox*** *#93, 102.*

MODERN LOVE
E. C. Comics: June-July, 1949 - No. 8, Aug-Sept, 1950

	GD25	FN65	NM94
1	46.00	138.00	440.00
2-Craig/Feldstein-c	36.00	108.00	320.00
3-Spanking panel	32.00	96.00	270.00
4-6 (Scarce): 4-Bra/panties panels	43.00	129.00	400.00
7,8	35.00	105.00	290.00

NOTE: ***Craig*** *a-3.* ***Feldstein*** *a-in most issues; c-1, 2i, 3-8.* ***Harrison*** *a-4.* ***Iger*** *a-6-8.* ***Ingels*** *a-1, 2, 4-7.* ***Palais*** *a-5.* ***Wood*** *a-7.* ***Wood/Harrison*** *a-5-7. (Canadian reprints known; see Table of Contents.)*

MOD LOVE
Western Publishing Co.: 1967 (50¢, 36 pgs.)

	GD25	FN65	NM94
1	2.60	7.80	26.00

MODNIKS, THE
Gold Key: Aug, 1967 - No. 2, Aug, 1970

	GD25	FN65	NM94
10206-708(#1)	2.50	7.50	22.00
2	1.75	5.25	14.00

MOD SQUAD (TV)
Dell Publishing Co.: Jan, 1969 - No. 3, Oct, 1969 - No. 8, April, 1971

	GD25	FN65	NM94
1-Photo-c	4.50	13.50	50.00
2-4: 2-4-Photo-c	2.90	8.70	32.00
5-8: 8-Photo-c; Reprints #2	2.40	7.00	26.00

MOD WHEELS
Gold Key: Mar, 1971 - No. 19, Jan, 1976

	GD25	FN65	NM94
1	2.50	7.50	22.00
2-9	1.85	5.50	15.00
10-19: 11,15-Extra 16 pgs. ads	1.25	3.75	10.00

MOE & SHMOE COMICS
O. S. Publ. Co.: Spring, 1948 - No. 2, Summer, 1948

	GD25	FN65	NM94
1	6.50	19.50	45.00
2	5.35	16.00	32.00

MOEBIUS (Graphic novel)
Marvel Comics (Epic Comics): Oct, 1987 - No. 6, 1988; No. 7, 1990; No. 8, 1991 ($9.95, 8x11", mature)

	GD25	FN65	NM94
1,2,4-6,8: (#2, 2nd printing, $9.95)	1.00	3.00	10.00
3,7: 3-(1st & 2nd printings, $12.95)	1.30	3.90	13.00
0 (1990, $12.95)	1.30	3.90	13.00
Moebius I-Signed & numbered hard-c ($45.95, Graphitti Designs, 1,500 copies printed)-r/#1-3	4.20	12.50	46.00

MOEBIUS COMICS
Caliber: May, 1996 - No. 6 ($2.95, B&W)

	GD25	FN65	NM94
1-6: Moebius-c/a. 1-William Stout-a			3.00

MOEBIUS: THE MAN FROM CIGURI
Dark Horse Comics: 1996 ($7.95, digest-size)

	GD25	FN65	NM94
nn-Moebius-c/a	.90	2.70	8.00

MOLLY MANTON'S ROMANCES (Romantic Affairs #3)

Molly O'Day #1 © AVON

Monkeyman and O'Brien #2 © Art Adams

Monte Hale Western #32 © FAW

	GD25	FN65	NM94

Marvel Comics (SePI): Sept, 1949 - No. 2, Dec, 1949 (52 pgs.)

1-Photo-c (becomes Blaze the Wonder Collie #2 (10/49) on? & Molly Manton's Romances #2	11.00	32.00	80.00
2-Titled "Romances of…"; photo-c	8.00	24.00	56.00

MOLLY O'DAY (Super Sleuth)
Avon Periodicals: February, 1945 (1st Avon comic)

1-Molly O'Day, The Enchanted Dagger by Tuska (r/Yankee #1), Capt'n Courage, Corporal Grant app.	42.00	127.00	340.00

MONKEES, THE (TV)(Also see Circus Boy, Groovy, Not Brand Echh #3, Teen-Age Talk, Teen Beam & Teen Beat)
Dell Publishing Co.: March, 1967 - No. 17, Oct, 1969 (#1-4,6,7,9,10,12,15,16 have photo-c)

1-Photo-c	8.00	25.00	90.00
2-6,7,9,10,12,15,16: All photo-c	5.00	15.00	55.00
8,11,13,14,17-No photo-c: 17-Reprints #1	3.50	11.00	38.00

MONKEY AND THE BEAR, THE
Atlas Comics (ZPC): Sept, 1953 - No. 3, Jan, 1954

1-Howie Post-c/a in all; funny animal	6.00	18.00	42.00
2,3	4.15	12.50	25.00

MONKEYMAN AND O'BRIEN (Also see Dark Horse Presents #80, 100-5, Gen13/..., Hellboy: Seed of Destruction, & San Diego Comic Con #2)
Dark Horse Comics (Legend): Jul, 1996 - No. 3, Sept, 1996 ($2.95, lim. series)

1-3: New stories; Art Adams-c/a/scripts			3.50
nn-(2/96, $2.95)-r/back-up stories from Hellboy: Seed of Destruction; Adams-c/a/scripts			3.50

MONKEYSHINES COMICS
Ace Periodicals/Publishers Specialists/Current Books/Unity Publ.: Summer, 1944 - No. 27, July, 1949

1-Funny animal	9.30	28.00	70.00
2-(Aut/44)	5.70	17.00	35.00
3-10: 3-(Win/44)	4.25	13.00	28.00
11-17,19-27: 23,24-Fago-c/a	4.00	12.00	24.00
18-Frazetta-a	5.35	16.00	32.00

MONKEY'S UNCLE, THE (See Merlin Jones As... under Movie Comics)

MONROES, THE (TV)
Dell Publishing Co.: Apr, 1967

1-Photo-c	2.00	6.00	22.00

MONSTER
Fiction House Magazines: 1953 - No. 2, 1953

1-Dr. Drew by Grandenetti; reprint from Rangers Comics #48; Whitman-c	42.00	127.00	340.00
2-Whitman-c	33.00	100.00	250.00

MONSTER CRIME COMICS (Also see Crime Must Stop)
Hillman Periodicals: Oct, 1952 (15¢, 52 pgs.)

1 (Scarce)	82.00	247.00	700.00

MONSTER HOWLS (Magazine)
Humor-Vision: December, 1966 (Satire) (35¢, 68 pgs.)

1	4.00	12.00	40.00

MONSTER HUNTERS
Charlton Comics: Aug, 1975 - No. 9, Jan, 1977; No. 10, Oct, 1977 - No. 18, Feb, 1979

1-Howard-a; Newton-c.	1.50	4.50	15.00
2-Ditko-a	1.20	3.60	12.00
3-10	.90	2.70	9.00
11-13,15-18		2.00	6.00
14-Special all-Ditko issue	1.20	3.60	12.00
1,2 (Modern Comics reprints, 1977)			3.00

NOTE: ***Ditko*** *a-2, 6, 8, 10, 13-15r, 18r; c-13-15, 18.* ***Howard*** *a-1, 3, 17; r-13.* ***Morisi*** *a-1.* ***Staton*** *a-1, 13.* ***Sutton*** *a-2, 4; c-2, 4; r-16-18.* ***Zeck*** *a-4-9. Reprints in #12-18.*

	GD25	FN65	NM94

MONSTER MADNESS (Magazine)
Marvel Comics: 1972 - #3, 1973 (60¢, B&W)

1-3: Stories by "Sinister" Stan Lee	2.20	6.25	22.00

MONSTER MAN
Image Comics (Action Planet): Sept, 1997 ($2.95, B&W)

1-Mike Manley-c/s/a			3.00

MONSTER MATINEE
Chaos! Comics: Oct, 1997 - No. 3, Oct, 1997 ($2.50, limited series)

1-3: pin-ups			2.50

MONSTER MENACE
Marvel Comics: Dec, 1993 - No. 4, Mar, 1994 ($1.25, limited series)

1-4: Pre-code Atlas horror reprints.			2.00

NOTE: ***Ditko****-r &* ***Kirby****-r in all.*

MONSTER OF FRANKENSTEIN (See Frankenstein)

MONSTERS ON THE PROWL (Chamber of Darkness #1-8)
Marvel Comics Group (No. 13,14: 52 pgs.): No. 9, 2/71 - No. 27, 11/73; No. 28, 6/74 - No. 30, 10/74

9-Barry Smith inks	2.00	6.00	20.00
10-12,15,17-30	.90	2.70	8.00
13,14-52 pgs.	1.60	4.80	16.00
16-(4/72)-King Kull 4th app.; Severin-c	1.20	3.60	12.00

NOTE: ***Ditko*** *r-5, 9, 14, 16.* ***Gil Kane*** *c-7.* ***Kirby*** *r-10-17, 21, 23, 25, 27, 28, 30; c-9, 25.* ***Kirby/Ditko*** *r-14, 17-20, 22, 24, 26, 29.* ***Reinman*** *r-5.* ***Marie/John Severin*** *a-16(Kull). 9-13, 15 contain one new story. Woodish art by* ***Reese****-11. King Kull created by Robert E. Howard.*

MONSTERS TO LAUGH WITH (Magazine) (Becomes Monsters Unlimited #4)
Marvel Comics Group: 1964 - No. 3, 1965 (B&W)

1-Humor by Stan Lee	5.00	15.00	50.00
2,3	3.00	9.00	30.00

MONSTERS UNLEASHED (Magazine)
Marvel Comics Group: July, 1973 - No. 11, Apr, 1975; Summer, 1975 (B&W)

1-Soloman Kane sty; Werewolf app.	2.40	7.00	26.00
2-4: 2-The Frankenstein Monster begins, ends #10. 3-Neal Adams-c/a; The Man-Thing begins (origin-r); Son of Satan preview. 4-Intro. Satana, the Devil's daughter; Werewolf app.	2.20	6.25	22.00
5-7: Werewolf in all. 5-Man-Thing. 7-Williamson-a(r)	1.20	3.60	12.00
8-11: 8-Man-Thing; N. Adams-r. 9-Man-Thing; Wendigo app. 10-Origin Tigra	1.50	4.50	15.00
Annual 1 (Summer,1975, 92 pgs.)-Kane-a	1.40	4.20	14.00

NOTE: ***Boris*** *c-2, 6.* ***Brunner*** *a-2; c-11.* ***J. Buscema*** *a-2p, 4p, 5p.* ***Colan*** *a-1, 4r.* ***Davis*** *a-3r.* ***Everett*** *a-2r.* ***G. Kane*** *a-3.* ***Krigstein*** *r-4.* ***Morrow*** *a-3; c-1.* ***Perez*** *a-8.* ***Ploog*** *a-6.* ***Reese*** *a-1, 2.* ***Tuska*** *a-3p.* ***Wildey*** *a-1r.*

MONSTERS UNLIMITED (Magazine) (Formerly Monsters To Laugh With)
Marvel Comics Group: No. 4, 1965 - No. 7, 1966 (B&W)

4-7	2.50	7.50	25.00

MONTANA KID, THE (See Kid Montana)

MONTE HALE WESTERN (Movie star; Formerly Mary Marvel #1-28; also see Fawcett Movie Comic, Motion Picture Comics, Picture News #8, Real Western Hero, Six-Gun Heroes, Western Hero & XMas Comics)
Fawcett Publ./Charlton No. 83 on: No. 29, Oct, 1948 - No. 88, Jan, 1956

29-(#1, 52 pgs.)-Photo-c begin, end #82; Monte Hale & his horse Pardner begin	44.00	132.00	370.00
30-(52 pgs.)-Big Bow and Little Arrow begin, end #34; Captain Tootsie by Beck	23.00	68.00	170.00
31-36,38-40-(52 pgs.): 34-Gabby Hayes begins, ends #80. 39-Captain Tootsie by Beck	17.00	50.00	125.00
37,41,45,49-(36 pgs.)	11.00	34.00	85.00
42-44,46-48,50-(52 pgs.): 47-Big Bow & Little Arrow app.			

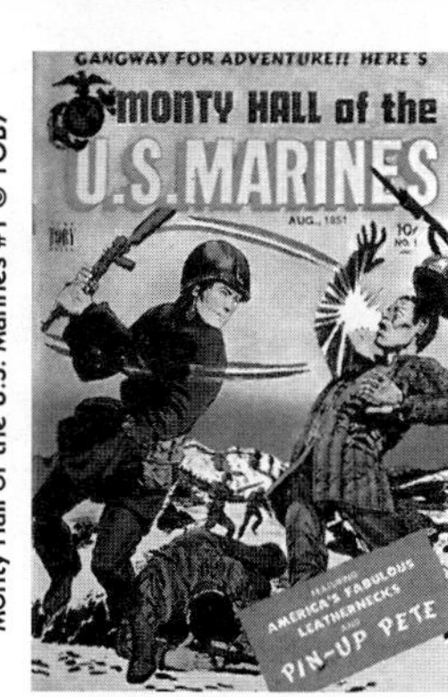

Monty Hall of the U.S. Marines #1 © TOBY

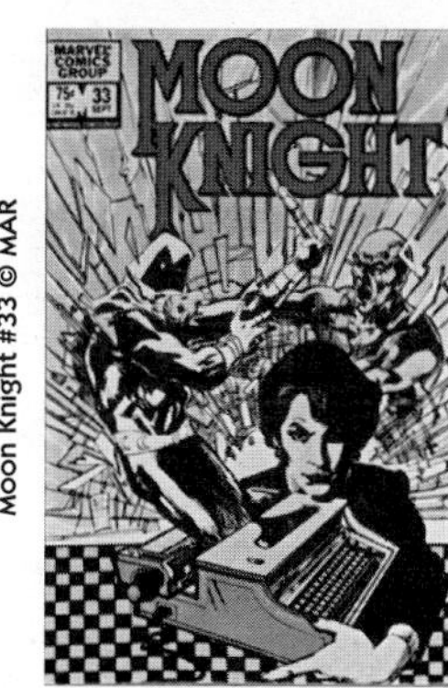

Moon Knight #33 © MAR

Moonshadow #7 © J.M. DeMatteis & Jon J. Muth

	GD25	FN65	NM94
	12.00	36.00	90.00
51,52,54-56,58,59-(52 pgs.)	9.30	28.00	70.00
53,57-(36 pgs.): 53-Slim Pickens app.	7.85	23.50	55.00
60-81: 36 pgs. #60-on. 80-Gabby Hayes ends	7.85	23.50	55.00
82-Last Fawcett issue (6/53)	9.30	28.00	70.00
83-1st Charlton issue (2/55); B&W photo back-c begin. Gabby Hayes returns, ends #86	11.00	32.00	80.00
84 (4/55)	8.50	26.00	60.00
85-86	7.85	23.50	55.00
87-Wolverton-r, 1/2 pg.	8.50	26.00	60.00
88-Last issue	8.50	26.00	60.00

NOTE: ***Gil Kane*** *a-33?, 34? Rocky Lane -1 pg. (Carnation ad)-38, 40, 41, 43, 44, 46, 55.*

MONTY HALL OF THE U.S. MARINES (See With the Marines...)
Toby Press: Aug, 1951 - No. 11, Apr, 1953

	GD25	FN65	NM94
1	9.30	28.00	65.00
2	5.70	17.00	36.00
3-5	5.35	16.00	32.00
6-11	4.25	13.00	28.00

NOTE: *Full page pin-ups (Pin-Up Pete) by* ***Jack Sparling*** *in #1-9.*

MOON, A GIRL...ROMANCE, A (Becomes Weird Fantasy #13 on; formerly Moon Girl #1-8)
E. C. Comics: No. 9, Sept-Oct, 1949 - No. 12, Mar-Apr, 1950

	GD25	FN65	NM94
9-Moon Girl cameo; spanking panel	55.00	165.00	475.00
10,11	40.00	120.00	360.00
12-(Scarce)	60.00	180.00	490.00

NOTE: ***Feldstein, Ingels*** *art in all.* ***Feldstein*** *c-9-12.* ***Wood/Harrison*** *a-10-12. Canadian reprints known; see Table of Contents.*

MOON GIRL AND THE PRINCE (#1) (Moon Girl #2-6; Moon Girl Fights Crime #7, 8; becomes A Moon, A Girl, Romance #9 on)(Also see Animal Fables #7 and Happy Houlihans)
E. C. Comics: Fall, 1947 - No. 8, Summer, 1949

	GD25	FN65	NM94
1-Origin Moon Girl (see Happy Houlihans #1)	70.00	210.00	700.00
2	36.00	108.00	360.00
3,4: 4-Moon Girl vs. a vampire	31.00	93.00	310.00
5-E.C.'s 1st horror story, "Zombie Terror"	80.00	240.00	800.00
6-8 (Scarce): 7-Origin Star (Moongirl's sidekick)	39.00	117.00	390.00

NOTE: ***Craig*** *a-2, 5.* ***Moldoff*** *a-1-8; c-2-6.* ***Wheelan's*** *Fat and Slat app. in #3, 4, 6. #2 & #3 are 52 pgs., #4 on, 36 pgs. Canadian reprints known; (see Table of Contents.)*

MOON KNIGHT (Also see The Hulk, Marc Spector..., Marvel Preview #21, Marvel Spotlight & Werewolf by Night #32)
Marvel Comics Group: Nov, 1980 - No. 38, Jul, 1984 (Mando paper #33 on)

	NM94
1-Origin resumed in #4; begin Sienkiewicz-c/a	3.00
2-34,36-38: 4-Intro Midnight Man. 16-The Thing app. 25-Double size	1.50
35-($1.00, 52 pgs.)-X-men app.; F.F. cameo	1.50

NOTE: ***Austin*** *c-27i, 31i.* ***Cowan*** *a-16; c-16, 17.* ***Kaluta*** *c-36-38; back c-35.* ***Miller*** *c-9, 12p, 13p, 15p, 27p.* ***Ploog*** *back c-35.* ***Sienkiewicz*** *a-1-15, 17-20, 22-26, 28-30, 33i, 36(4), 37; c-1-5, 7, 8, 10, 11, 14-16, 18-26, 28-30, 31p, 33, 34.*

MOON KNIGHT
Marvel Comics Group: June, 1985 - V2#6, Dec, 1985

V2#1-6: 1-Double size; new costume. 6-Sienkiewicz painted-c. 1.00

MOON KNIGHT
Marvel Comics: Jan, 1998 - No. 4, Apr, 1998 ($2.50, limited series)

1-4-Moench-s/Edwards-c/a 2.50

MOON KNIGHT (Volume 3)
Marvel Comics: Jan, 1999 - No. 4, Apr, 1999 ($2.99, limited series)

1-4-Moench-s/Texeira-a(p) 2.99

MOON KNIGHT: DIVIDED WE FALL
Marvel Comics: 1992 ($4.95, 52 pgs.)

nn-Denys Cowan-c/a(p) 5.00

MOON KNIGHT SPECIAL
Marvel Comics: Oct, 1992 ($2.50, 52 pgs.)

1-Shang Chi, Master of Kung Fu-c/story 2.50

MOON KNIGHT SPECIAL EDITION
Marvel Comics Group: Nov, 1983 - No. 3, Jan, 1984 ($2.00, limited series, Baxter paper)

1-3: Reprints from Hulk mag. by Sienkiewicz 2.00

MOON MULLINS (See Popular Comics, Super Book #3 & Super Comics)
Dell Publishing Co.: 1941 - 1945

	GD25	FN65	NM94
Four Color 14(1941)	33.00	98.00	360.00
Large Feature Comic 29(1941)	24.00	71.00	260.00
Four Color 31(1943)	17.00	50.00	185.00
Four Color 81(1945)	9.00	27.00	100.00

MOON MULLINS
Michel Publ. (American Comics Group): Dec-Jan, 1947-48 - No. 8, 1949 (52 pgs)

	GD25	FN65	NM94
1-Alternating Sunday & daily strip-r	19.00	56.00	140.00
2	9.30	28.00	70.00
3-8: 8-...Featuring Kayo on-c	7.85	23.50	55.00

NOTE: ***Milt Gross*** *a-2-6, 8.* ***Frank Willard*** *r-all.*

MOON PILOT
Dell Publishing Co.: No. 1313, Mar-May, 1962

	GD25	FN65	NM94
Four Color 1313-Movie, photo-c	6.40	19.00	70.00

MOONSHADOW (Also see Farewell, Moonshadow)
Marvel Comics (Epic Comics): 5/85 - #12, 2/87 ($1.50/$1.75, mature) (1st fully painted comic book)

	GD25	FN65	NM94
1-Origin; J. M. DeMatteis scripts & Jon J. Muth painted-c/a.			5.00
2-12: 11-Origin			3.00
Trade paperback (1987?)-r/#1-12			14.00
Signed & numbered hard-c ($39.95, 1,200 copies)-r/#1-12	7.00	21.00	75.00

MOONSHADOW
DC Comics (Vertigo): Oct, 1994 - No. 12, Aug, 1995 ($2.25/$2.95)

	GD25	FN65	NM94
1-11: Reprints Epic series.			2.50
12 ($2.95)-w/expanded ending			3.00
The Complete Moonshadow TPB ('98, $39.95) r/#1-12 and Farewell Moonshadow; new Muth painted-c	3.80	11.50	40.00

MOON-SPINNERS, THE (See Movie Comics)

MOPSY (See Pageant of Comics & TV Teens)
St. John Publ. Co.: Feb, 1948 - No. 19, Sept, 1953

	GD25	FN65	NM94
1-Part-r; reprints "Some Punkins" by Neher	16.00	47.00	110.00
2	10.00	30.00	60.00
3-10(1953): 8-Lingerie panels	7.50	22.50	45.00
11-19: 19-Lingerie-c	6.35	19.00	38.00

NOTE: *#1, 3-6, 13, 18, 19 have paper dolls.*

MORBID ANGEL
London Night Studios: Oct, 1995 ($3.00, B&W)

1-Hartsoe-c 3.00

MORBID ANGEL
London Night Studios: July, 1996 - No. 3, Jan, 1997 ($3.00, limited series)

	NM94
1/2-($9.95)-Angel Tear Edition; foil logo	10.00
1-3	3.00
1-Penance-c	4.00
...-To Hell and Back-(10/96, $3.00, B&W)	3.00

MORBIUS REVISITED
Marvel Comic: Aug, 1993 - No. 5, Dec, 1993 ($1.95, mini-series)

1-5-Reprints Fear #27-31 2.00

MORBIUS: THE LIVING VAMPIRE (Also see Amazing Spider-Man #101,

Morbius: The Living Vampire #25 © MAR

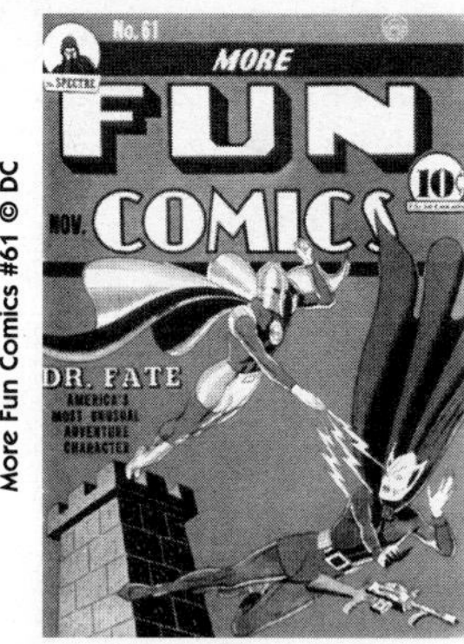

More Fun Comics #61 © DC

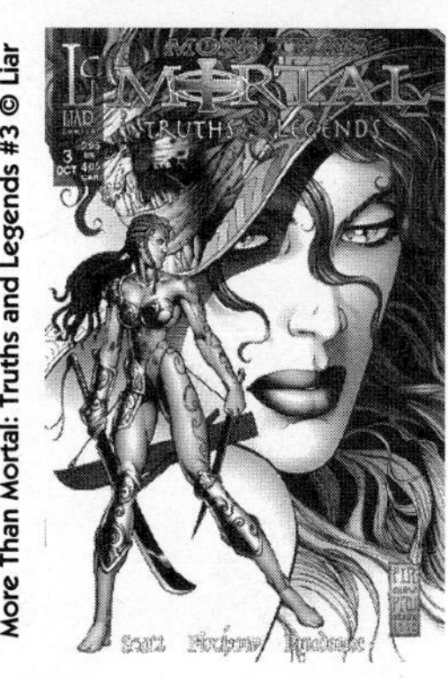

More Than Mortal: Truths and Legends #3 © Liar

102, Fear #20, Marvel Team-Up #3, 4, Midnight Sons Unl. & Vampire Tales)
Marvel Comics (Midnight Sons imprint #16 on): Sept, 1992 - No. 32, Apr, 1995 ($1.75/$1.95)

1-($2.75, 52 pgs.)-Polybagged w/poster; Ghost Rider & Johnny Blaze x-over (part 3 of Rise of the Midnight Sons) 3.00
2-5: 3,4-Vs. Spider-Man-c/story 2.00
6-11,13-20: 15-Ghost Rider app. 16-Spot varnish-c. 16,17-Siege of Darkness parts 5 &13. 18-Deathlok app. 1.75
12-($2.25)-Outer-c is a Darkhold envelope made of black parchment w/gold ink; Midnight Massacre x-over 2.25
21-24,26-32: 21-Begin $1.95-c; bound-in Spider-Man trading card sheet; S-M app. 2.00
25-($2.50, 52 pgs.)-Gold foil logo 2.50

MORE FUN COMICS (Formerly New Fun Comics #1-6)
National Periodical Publications: No. 7, Jan, 1936 - No. 127, Nov-Dec, 1947 (No. 7,9-11: paper-c) — **GD25 FN65 VF82**

7(1/36)-Oversized, paper-c; 1 pg. Kelly-a 723.00 2170.00 4700.00
8(2/36)-Oversized (10x12"), slick-c; 1 pg. Kelly-a 723.00 2170.00 4700.00
9(3-4/36)(Very rare, 1st comic-sized issue)-Last multiple panel-c 892.00 2675.00 5800.00
10,11(7/36): 10-Last Henri Duval by Siegel & Shuster. 11-1st "Calling All Cars" by Siegel & Shuster; new classic logo begins 508.00 1525.00 3300.00
12(8/36)-Slick-c begin 400.00 1200.00 2600.00
V2#1(9/36, #13) 370.00 1110.00 2400.00
2(10/36, #14)-Dr. Occult in costume (1st in color)(Superman proto-type; 1st DC appearance) continues from The Comics Magazine, ends #17 1770.00 5300.00 11,500.00
V2#3(11/36, #15), 16(V2#4), 17(V2#5): 16-Cover numbering begins; Xmas-c; last Superman tryout issue 708.00 2123.00 4600.00
18-20(V2#8, 5/37) 277.00 831.00 1800.00

GD25 FN65 NM94

21(V2#9)-24(V2#12, 9/37) 275.00 825.00 1850.00
25(V3#1, 10/37)-27(V3#3, 12/37): 27-Xmas-c 275.00 825.00 1850.00
28-30: 30-1st non-funny cover 245.00 735.00 1650.00
31-Has ad for Action #1 261.00 785.00 1750.00
32-35: 32-Last Dr. Occult 245.00 735.00 1650.00
36-40: 36-(10/38)-The Masked Ranger & sidekick Pedro begins; Ginger Snap by Bob Kane (2 pgs.; 1st-a?). 39-Xmas-c 245.00 735.00 1650.00
41-50: 41-Last Masked Ranger 187.00 560.00 1250.00
51-The Spectre app. (in costume) in one panel ad at end of Buccaneer story 723.00 2170.00 4700.00

GD25 FN65 VF82 NM94

52-(2/40)-Origin/1st app. The Spectre (in costume splash panel only), part 1 by Bernard Baily (parts 1 & 2 written by Jerry Siegel; Spectre's costume changes color from purple & blue to green & grey; last Wing Brady 4000.00 12,000.00 24,000.00 48,000.00
53-Origin The Spectre (in costume at end of story), part 2; Capt. Desmo begins 2460.00 7380.00 16,000.00 32,000.00
54-The Spectre in costume; last King Carter; classic-c 820.00 2460.00 4920.00 8400.00
55-(Scarce, 5/40)-Dr. Fate begins (Intro & 1st app.); last Bulldog Martin 1046.00 3138.00 6800.00 11,500.00

GD25 FN65 NM94

56-Congo Bill begins (6/40), 1st app.; 1st Dr. Fate-c (classic), origin continues. 430.00 1290.00 4300.00
57-60 295.00 885.00 2800.00
61,65: 61-Classic Dr. Fate-c. 65-Classic Spectre-c 274.00 821.00 2600.00
62-64,66: 63-Last St. Bob Neal. 64-Lance Larkin begins. 271.00 812.00 2300.00

GD25 FN65 VF82 NM94

67-(5/41)-Origin (1st) Dr. Fate; last Congo Bill & Biff Bronson (C.B. continues in Action Comics #37 (6/41) 630.00 1890.00 3780.00 6300.00

GD25 FN65 NM94

68-70: 68-Clip Carson begins. 70-Last Lance Larkin 212.00 635.00 1800.00

GD25 FN65 VF82 NM94

71-Origin & 1st app. Johnny Quick by Mort Weisinger (9/41); sci/fi-c 490.00 1470.00 2940.00 4900.00

GD25 FN65 NM94

72-Dr. Fate's new helmet; last Sgt. Carey, Sgt. O'Malley & Captain Desmo; German submarine-c (only German war-c) 176.00 529.00 1500.00

GD25 FN65 VF82 NM94

73-Origin & 1st app. Aquaman (11/41) by Paul Norris; intro. Green Arrow & Speedy 955.00 2865.00 5730.00 10,500.00

GD25 FN65 NM94

74-2nd Aquaman 211.00 633.00 1900.00
75-77: 76-Last Clip Carson; Johnny Quick (by Meskin #76-97) begins, ends #107. 77-Last Dr. Fate cover 189.00 567.00 1700.00
78-80: 78-Green Arrow-c begin 189.00 567.00 1700.00
81-88,90: 81-Last large logo. 82-1st small logo. 84-Only Japanese war-c. 87-Last Radio Squad 106.00 318.00 950.00
89-Origin Green Arrow & Speedy Team-up 122.00 366.00 1100.00
91-99: 91-1st bi-monthly issue. 93-Dover & Clover begin (1st app., 9-10/43). 97-Kubert-a. 98-Last Dr. Fate 75.00 225.00 675.00
100-Lat Green Arrow-c 106.00 318.00 950.00

GD25 FN65 VF82 NM94

101-Origin & 1st app. Superboy (1-2/45)(not by Siegel & Shuster); last Spectre issue 700.00 2100.00 4200.00 7000.00

GD25 FN65 NM94

102-2nd Superboy app. 115.00 344.00 975.00
103-3rd Superboy app. 88.00 265.00 750.00
104-1st Superboy-c 76.00 228.00 650.00
105-107: 107-Last Johnny Quick & Superboy 74.00 221.00 625.00
108-120: 108-Genius Jones begins (3-4/46; cont'd from Adventure Comics #102) 20.00 60.00 150.00
121-124,126: 121-123,126-Post-c (Jimminy-c) 15.00 44.00 110.00
125-Superman on cover 68.00 204.00 575.00
127-(Scarce)-Post-c/a 31.00 92.00 230.00

NOTE: *All issues are scarce to rare. Cover features: The Spectre-#52-55, 57-60, 62-67. Dr. Fate-#56, 61, 68-76. The Green Arrow & Speedy-#77-85, 88-97, 99, 101 (w/Dover & Clover-#98, 103). Johnny Quick-#86, 87, 100. Dover & Clover-#102, (104, 106 w/Superboy), 107, 108(w/Genius Jones), 110, 112, 114, 117, 119. Genius Jones-#109, 111, 113, 115, 118, 120.* ***Baily*** *a-45, 52-on; c-52-55, 57-60, 62-67.* ***Al Capp*** *a-45(signed Koppy).* ***Ellsworth*** *c-7.* ***Creig Flessel*** *c-30, 31, 35-48(most).* ***Guardineer*** *c-47, 49, 50.* ***Kiefer*** *a-20.* ***Meskin*** *c-86, 87, 100?* ***Moldoff*** *c-51.* ***George Papp*** *c-77-85.* ***Post*** *c-121-127.* ***Vincent Sullivan*** *c-8-28, 32-34.*

MORE SEYMOUR (See Seymour My Son)
Archie Publications: Oct, 1963

1 1.50 4.50 12.00

MORE THAN MORTAL
Liar Comics: June, 1997 - No. 4, Apr, 1998 ($2.95, limited series)

1-Blue forest background-c 4.00
1-Variant-c 5.00
1-White-c 1.00 3.00 10.00
1-2nd printing; purple sky cover 3.00
2-4: 3-Silvestri-c 3.00
4-Variant-c by Randy Queen 4.00

MORE THAN MORTAL SAGAS
Liar Comics: Aug, 1998 - Present ($2.95)

1,2-Painted art by Romano 2.95
1-Variant-c by Linsner 8.00
2-Variant-c by Firchow 3.00

MORE THAN MORTAL TRUTHS AND LEGENDS
Liar Comics: Aug, 1998 - Present ($2.95)

1-3 2.95

MORE TRASH FROM MAD (Annual)
E. C. Comics: 1958 - No. 12, 1969

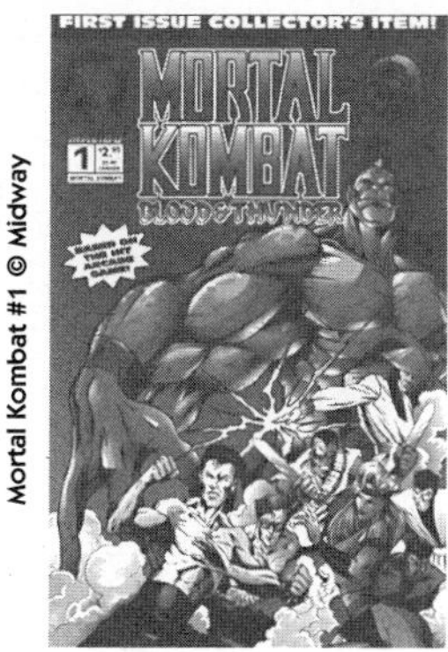

Mortal Kombat #1 © Midway

Mother Goose and Nursery Rhyme Comics Four Color #68 © Oskar Lebeck

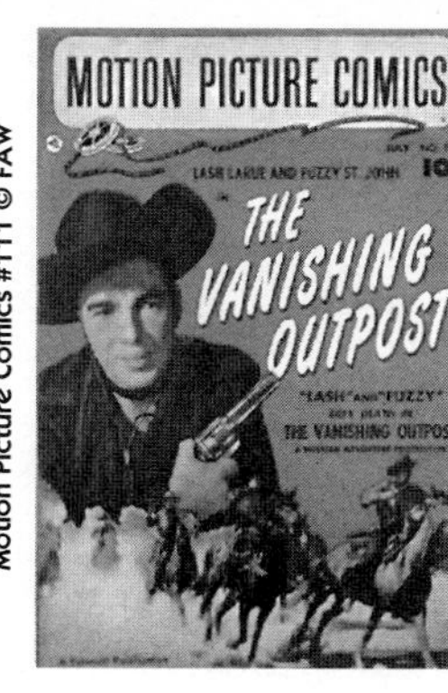

Motion Picture Comics #111 © FAW

	GD25	FN65	NM94
(Note: Bonus missing = half price)			
nn(1958)-8 pgs. color Mad reprint from #20	17.50	52.00	185.00
2(1959)-Market Product Labels	12.00	36.00	130.00
3(1960)-Text book covers	11.00	33.00	120.00
4(1961)-Sing Along with Mad booklet	11.00	33.00	120.00
5(1962)-Window Stickers; r/from Mad #39	7.50	22.50	80.00
6(1963)-TV Guise booklet	8.50	25.50	90.00
7(1964)-Alfred E. Neuman commemorative stamps	6.00	18.00	65.00
8(1965)-Life size poster-Alfred E. Neuman	4.00	12.00	45.00
9,10(1966-67)-Mischief Sticker	3.50	10.50	38.00
11(1968)-Campaign poster & bumper sticker	3.50	10.50	38.00
12(1969)-Pocket medals	3.50	10.50	38.00

NOTE: ***Kelly Freas** c-1, 2, 4. **Mingo** c-3, 5-9, 12.*

MORGAN THE PIRATE (Movie)
Dell Publishing Co.: No. 1227, Sept-Nov, 1961

	GD25	FN65	NM94
Four Color 1227-Photo-c	7.00	22.00	80.00

MORLOCK 2001
Atlas/Seaboard Publ.: Feb, 1975 - No. 3, July, 1975

	GD25	FN65	NM94
1,2: 1-(Super-hero)-Origin & 1st app.			3.00
3-Ditko/Wrightson-a; origin The Midnight Man & The Midnight Men			5.00

MORNINGSTAR SPECIAL
Comico: Apr, 1990 ($2.50)

	GD25	FN65	NM94
1-From the Elementals; Willingham-c/a/scripts			2.50

MORRIGAN
Dimension X: Aug, 1993 ($2.75, B&W)

	GD25	FN65	NM94
1-Foil stamped-c			2.75

MORRIGAN
Sirius Entertainment: 1997 ($2.95, limited series)

	GD25	FN65	NM94
1-Tenuta-c/a			2.95

MORTAL KOMBAT
Malibu Comics: July, 1994 - No. 6, Dec, 1994 ($2.95)

	GD25	FN65	NM94
1-6: 1-Two variant covers exist			3.00
1-Limited edition gold foil embossed-c			4.00
0 (12/94), Special Edition 1 (11/94)			3.00
Tournament Edition (12/94, $3.95)			4.00
Tournament Edition II (1995, $3.95)			4.00
...: **BARAKA** ,June, 1995 ($2.95, one-shot)			
1			3.00
...: **BATTLEWAVE** ,Feb, 1995 - No. 6, July, 1995 ($2.95)			
1-6			3.00
...: **GORO, PRINCE OF PAIN** ,Sept, 1994 - No. 3, Nov, 1994 ($2.95)			
1-3			3.00
...: **KITANA AND MILEENA** ,Aug, 1995 ($2.95, one-shot)			
1			3.00
...: **KUNG LAO** ,July, 1995 ($2.95, one shot)			
1			3.00
...: **RAYDON & KANO** ,Mar, 1995 - No. 3, May, 1995 ($2.95)			
1-3			3.00
...: **U.S. SPECIAL FORCES** ,Jan, 1995 - No. 2, Feb, 1995 ($3.50)			
1,2			3.50

MORTIE (Mazie's Friend; also see Flat-Top)
Magazine Publishers: Dec, 1952 - No. 4, June, 1953?

	GD25	FN65	NM94
1	5.85	17.50	40.00
2-4	4.00	10.00	22.00

MORTIGAN GOTH: IMMORTALIS (See Marvel Frontier Comics Unlimited)
Marvel Comics: Sept, 1993 - No. 4, Mar, 1994 ($1.95, mini-series)

	GD25	FN65	NM94
1-($2.95)-Foil-c			3.00
2-4			2.00

MORT THE DEAD TEENAGER
Marvel Comics: Nov, 1993 - No. 4, Mar, 1994 ($1.75, mini-series)

	GD25	FN65	NM94
1-4			1.75

MORTY MEEKLE
Dell Publishing Co.: No. 793, May, 1957

	GD25	FN65	NM94
Four Color 793	1.80	5.50	20.00

MOSES & THE TEN COMMANDMENTS (See Dell Giants)

MOTHER GOOSE AND NURSERY RHYME COMICS (See Christmas With Mother Goose)
Dell Publishing Co.: No. 41, 1944 - No. 862, Nov, 1957

	GD25	FN65	NM94
Four Color 41-Walt Kelly-c/a	21.00	63.00	230.00
Four Color 59, 68-Kelly c/a	18.00	53.00	195.00
Four Color 862-The Truth About..., Movie (Disney)	6.40	19.00	70.00

MOTHER OF US ALL
Catechetical Guild Giveaway: 1950? (32 pgs.)

	GD25	FN65	NM94
nn	2.00	5.00	10.00

MOTHER TERESA OF CALCUTTA
Marvel Comics Group: 1984

	GD25	FN65	NM94
1-(52 pgs.) No ads			2.00

MOTION PICTURE COMICS (See Fawcett Movie Comics)
Fawcett Publications: No. 101, 1950 - No. 114, Jan, 1953 (All-photo-c)

	GD25	FN65	NM94
101- "Vanishing Westerner"; Monte Hale (1950)	27.00	82.00	205.00
102- "Code of the Silver Sage"; Rocky Lane (1/51)	25.00	76.00	190.00
103- "Covered Wagon Raid"; Rocky Lane (3/51)	25.00	76.00	190.00
104- "Vigilante Hideout"; Rocky Lane (5/51)-Book length Powell-a	25.00	76.00	190.00
105- "Red Badge of Courage"; Audie Murphy; Bob Powell-a (7/51)	31.00	92.00	230.00
106- "The Texas Rangers"; George Montgomery (9/51)	26.00	78.00	195.00
107- "Frisco Tornado"; Rocky Lane (11/51)	23.00	68.00	170.00
108- "Mask of the Avenger"; John Derek	16.00	48.00	120.00
109- "Rough Rider of Durango"; Rocky Lane	23.00	70.00	175.00
110- "When Worlds Collide"; George Evans-a (5/52); Williamson & Evans drew themselves in story; (also see Famous Funnies No. 72-88)	85.00	256.00	725.00
111- "The Vanishing Outpost"; Lash LaRue	28.00	84.00	210.00
112- "Brave Warrior"; Jon Hall & Jay Silverheels	15.00	46.00	115.00
113- "Walk East on Beacon"; George Murphy; Schaffenberger-a	11.00	32.00	80.00
114- "Cripple Creek"; George Montgomery (1/53)	12.00	36.00	90.00

MOTION PICTURE FUNNIES WEEKLY (Amazing Man #5 on?)
First Funnies, Inc.: 1939 (Giveaway)(B&W, 36 pgs.)
No month given; last panel in Sub-Mariner story dated 4/39
(Also see Colossus, Green Giant & Invaders No. 20)

	GD25	FN65	NM94
1-Origin & 1st printed app. Sub-Mariner by Bill Everett (8 pgs.); Fred Schwab-c; reprinted in Marvel Mystery #1 with color added over the craft tint which was used to shade the black & white version; Spy Ring, American Ace (reprinted in Marvel Mystery #3) app. (Rare)-only eight (8) known copies,one near mint with white pages, the rest with brown pages.	2600.00	5500.00	15,000.00
Covers only to #2-4 (set)			500.00

NOTE: The only eight known copies (with a ninth suspected) were discovered in 1974 in the estate of the deceased publisher. Covers only to issues No. 2-4 were also found which evidently were printed in advance along with #1. #1 was to be distributed only through motion picture movie houses. However, it is believed that only advanced copies were sent out and the motion picture houses not going for the idea. Possible distribution at local theaters in Boston suspected. The last panel of Sub-Mariner contains a rectangular box with "Continued Next Week" printed in it. When reprinted in Marvel Mystery, the box was left in with lettering omitted.

MOTORHEAD (See Comic's Greatest World)
Dark Horse Comics: Aug, 1995 - No. 6, Jan, 1996 ($2.50)

Movie Classics - The Incredible Mr. Limpet © DELL

Movie Classics - Mad Monster Party © DELL

Movie Classics - McHale's Navy © DELL

GD25 FN65 NM94

1-6: Bisley-c on all. 1-Predator app. 2.50
Special 1 (3/94, $3.95, 52pgs.)-Jae Lee-c; Barb Wire, The Machine & Wolf Gang app. 4.00

MOTORMOUTH (... & Killpower #7? on)
Marvel Comics UK: June, 1992 - No. 12, May, 1993 ($1.75)

1-13: 1,2-Nick Fury app. 3-Punisher-c/story. 5,6-Nick Fury & Punisher app. 6-Cable cameo. 7-9-Cable app. 1.80

MOUNTAIN MEN (See Ben Bowie)

MOUSE MUSKETEERS (See M.G.M.'s...)

MOUSE ON THE MOON, THE (See Movie Classics)

MOVIE CLASSICS
Dell Publishing Co.: Jan, 1963 - Dec, 1969

(Before 1963, most movie adaptations were part of the 4-Color series)
(Disney movie adaptations after 1970 are in Walt Disney Showcase)

Around the World Under the Sea 12-030-612 (12/66) 2.50 7.50 25.00
Bambi 3(4/56)-Disney; r/4-Color #186 3.00 9.00 30.00
Battle of the Bulge 12-056-606 (6/66) 2.80 8.40 28.00
Beach Blanket Bingo 12-058-509 5.50 16.50 55.00
Bon Voyage 01-068-212 (12/62)-Disney; photo-c 3.00 9.00 30.00
Castilian, The 12-110-401 2.80 8.40 28.00
Cat, The 12-109-612 (12/66) 2.20 6.60 22.00
Cheyenne Autumn 12-112-506 (4-6/65) 5.00 15.00 50.00
Circus World, Samuel Bronston's 12-115-411; John Wayne app.; John Wayne photo-c 9.00 27.00 90.00
Countdown 12-150-710 (10/67)-James Caan photo-c 2.80 8.40 28.00
Creature, The 1 (12-142-302) (12-2/62-63) 5.00 15.00 50.00
Creature, The 12-142-410 (10/64) 3.00 9.00 30.00
David Ladd's Life Story 12-173-212 (10-12/62)-Photo-c 6.50 19.50 65.00
Die, Monster, Die 12-175-603 (3/66)-Photo-c 3.80 11.40 38.00
Dirty Dozen 12-180-710 (10/67) 3.50 10.50 35.00
Dr. Who & the Daleks 12-190-612 (12/66)-Peter Cushing photo-c; 1st U.S. app. of Dr. Who 9.00 27.00 90.00
Dracula 12-231-212 (10-12/62) 4.50 13.50 45.00
El Dorado 12-240-710 (10/67)-John Wayne; photo-c 11.50 34.00 115.00
Ensign Pulver 12-257-410 (8-10/64) 2.40 7.20 24.00
Frankenstein 12-283-305 (3-5/63) 4.50 13.50 45.00
Great Race, The 12-299-603 (3/66)-Natallie Wood, Tony Curtis photo-c 3.50 10.50 35.00
Hallelujah Trail, The 12-307-602 (2/66) (Shows 1/66 inside); Burt Lancaster, Lee Remick photo-c 4.00 12.00 40.00
Hatari 12-340-301 (1/63)-John Wayne 7.00 21.00 70.00
Horizontal Lieutenant, The 01-348-210 (10/62) 2.40 7.20 24.00
Incredible Mr. Limpet, The 12-370-408; Don Knotts photo-c 3.00 9.00 30.00
Jack the Giant Killer 12-374-301 (1/63) 7.00 21.00 70.00
Jason & the Argonauts 12-376-310 (8-10/63)-Photo-c 8.50 25.50 85.00
Lancelot & Guinevere 12-416-310 (10/63) 4.50 13.50 45.00
Lawrence 12-426-308 (8/63)-Story of Lawrence of Arabia; movie ad on back-c; not exactly like movie 4.50 13.50 45.00
Lion of Sparta 12-439-301 (1/63) 2.80 8.40 28.00
Mad Monster Party 12-460-801 (9/67)-Based on Kurtzman's screenplay 4.80 14.40 48.00
Magic Sword, The 01-496-209 (9/62) 4.50 13.50 45.00
Masque of the Red Death 12-490-410 (8-10/64)-Vincent Price photo-c 4.50 13.50 45.00
Maya 12-495-612 (12/66)-Clint Walker & Jay North part photo-c 3.50 10.50 35.00
McHale's Navy 12-500-412 (10-12/64) 3.50 10.50 35.00
Merrill's Marauders 12-510-301 (1/63)-Photo-c 2.40 7.20 24.00
Mouse on the Moon, The 12-530-312 (10/12/63)-Photo-c 3.00 9.00 30.00
Mummy, The 12-537-211 (9-11/62) 2 versions with different back-c 5.00 15.00 50.00
Music Man, The 12-538-301 (1/63) 2.40 7.20 24.00
Naked Prey, The 12-545-612 (12/66)-Photo-c 5.00 15.00 50.00
Night of the Grizzly, The 12-558-612 (12/66)-Photo-c 3.00 9.00 30.00
None But the Brave 12-565-506 (4-6/65) 5.00 15.00 50.00
Operation Bikini 12-597-310 (10/63)-Photo-c 2.80 8.40 28.00
Operation Crossbow 12-590-512 (10-12/65) 2.80 8.40 28.00
Prince & the Pauper, The 01-654-207 (5-7/62)-Disney 3.00 9.00 30.00
Raven, The 12-680-309 (9/63)-Vincent Price photo-c 4.00 12.00 40.00
Ring of Bright Water 01-701-910 (10/69) (inside shows #12-701-909) 3.00 9.00 30.00
Runaway, The 12-707-412 (10-12/64) 2.50 7.50 25.00
Santa Claus Conquers the Martians #? (1964)-Photo-c 6.00 18.00 60.00
Santa Claus Conquers the Martians 12-725-603 (3/66, 12¢)-Reprints 1964 issue; photo-c 5.00 15.00 50.00
Another version given away with a Golden Record, SLP 170, nn, no price (3/66)-Complete with record 13.00 39.00 130.00
Six Black Horses 12-750-301 (1/63)-Photo-c 2.80 8.40 28.00
Ski Party 12-743-511 (9-11/65)-Frankie Avalon photo-c 4.00 12.00 40.00
Smoky 12-746-702 (2/67) 2.50 7.50 25.00
Sons of Katie Elder 12-748-511 (9-11/65); John Wayne app.; photo-c 12.00 36.00 120.00
Tales of Terror 12-793-302 (2/63)-Evans-a 3.00 9.00 30.00
Three Stooges Meet Hercules 01-828-208 (8/62)-Photo-c 7.50 22.50 75.00
Tomb of Ligeia 12-830-506 (4-6/65) 3.00 9.00 30.00
Treasure Island 01-845-211 (7-9/62)-Disney; r/4-Color #624 2.80 8.40 28.00
Twice Told Tales (Nathaniel Hawthorne) 12-840-401 (11-1/63-64); Vincent Price photo-c 3.80 11.40 38.00
Two on a Guillotine 12-850-506 (4-6/65) 2.40 7.20 24.00
Valley of Gwangi 01-880-912 (12/69) 8.00 24.00 80.00
War Gods of the Deep 12-900-509 (7-9/65) 2.60 7.80 26.00
War Wagon, The 12-533-709 (9/67); John Wayne app. 7.50 22.50 75.00
Who's Minding the Mint? 12-924-708 (8/67) 2.40 7.20 24.00
Wolfman, The 12-922-308 (6-8/63) 3.50 10.50 35.00
Wolfman, The 1(12-922-410)(8-10/64)-2nd printing; r/#12-922-308 3.00 9.00 30.00
Zulu 12-950-410 (8-10/64)-Photo-c 7.00 21.00 70.00

MOVIE COMICS (See Cinema Comics Herald & Fawcett Movie Comics)

MOVIE COMICS
National Periodical Publications/Picture Comics: April, 1939 - No. 6, Sept-Oct, 1939 (Most all photo-c)

1- "Gunga Din", "Son of Frankenstein", "The Great Man Votes", "Fisherman's Wharf", & "Scouts to the Rescue" part 1; Wheelan "Minute Movies" begin 284.00 852.00 2700.00
2- "Stagecoach", "The Saint Strikes Back", "King of the Turf", "Scouts to the Rescue" part 2, "Arizona Legion", Andy Devine photo-c 206.00 618.00 1750.00
3- "East Side of Heaven", "Mystery in the White Room", "Four Feathers", "Mexican Rose" with Gene Autry, "Spirit of Culver", "Many Secrets", "The Mikado" 147.00 441.00 1250.00
4- "Captain Fury", Gene Autry in "Blue Montana Skies", "Streets of N.Y." with Jackie Cooper, "Oregon Trail" part 1 with Johnny Mack Brown, "Big Town Czar" with Barton MacLane, & "Star Reporter" with Warren Hull 115.00 345.00 975.00
5- "The Man in the Iron Mask", "Five Came Back", "Wolf Call", "The Girl & the

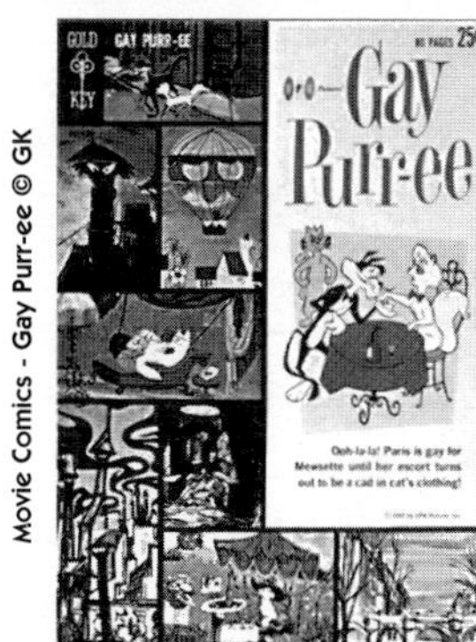

Movie Comics - Gay Purr-ee © GK

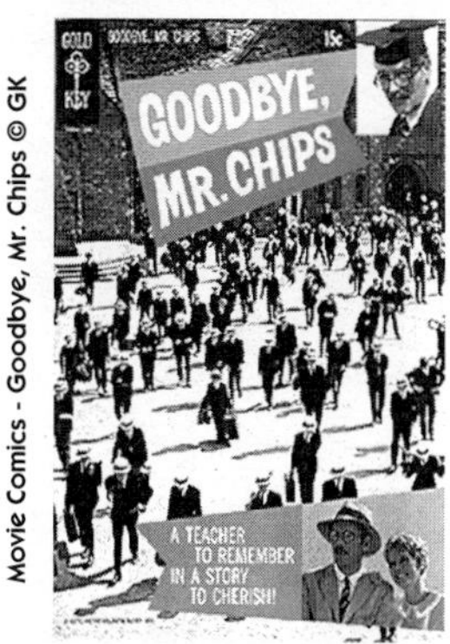

Movie Comics - Goodbye, Mr. Chips © GK

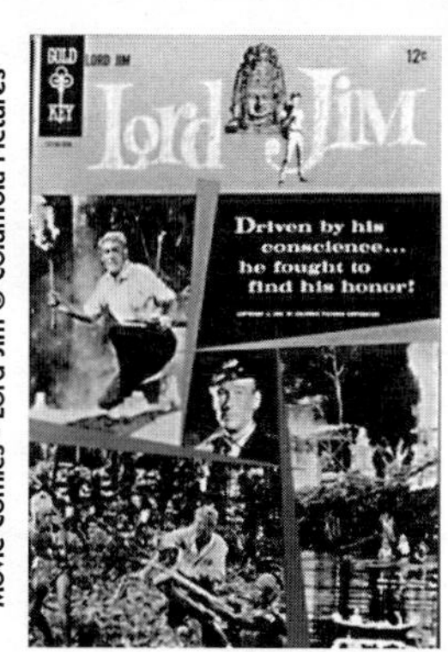

Movie Comics - Lord Jim © Columbia Pictures

GD25 FN65 NM94

Gambler", "The House of Fear", "The Family Next Door", "Oregon Trail" part 2 — 129.00 387.00 1100.00
6- "The Phantom Creeps", "Chumps at Oxford", & "The Oregon Trail" part 3; 2nd Robot-c — 165.00 495.00 1400.00

NOTE: *Above books contain many original movie stills with dialogue from movie scripts. All issues are scarce.*

MOVIE COMICS
Fiction House Magazines: Dec, 1946 - No. 4, 1947

1-Big Town (by Lubbers), Johnny Danger begin; Celardo-a; Mitzi of the Movies by Fran Hopper — 49.00 147.00 420.00
2-(2/47)- "White Tie & Tails" with William Bendix; Mitzi of the Movies begins by Matt Baker, ends #4 — 39.00 117.00 315.00
3-(6/47)-Andy Hardy starring Mickey Rooney — 39.00 117.00 315.00
4-Mitzi In Hollywood by Matt Baker; Merton of the Movies with Red Skelton; Yvonne DeCarlo & George Brent in "Slave Girl" — 44.00 132.00 375.00

MOVIE COMICS
Gold Key/Whitman: Oct, 1962 - 1984

Alice in Wonderland 10144-503 (3/65)-Disney; partial reprint of 4-Color #331 — 3.20 9.60 32.00
Aristocats, The 1 (30045-103)(3/71)-Disney; with pull-out poster (25¢) (No poster = half price) — 6.00 18.00 60.00
Bambi 1 (10087-309)(9/63)-Disney; r/4-C #186 — 3.00 9.00 30.00
Bambi 2 (10087-607)(7/66)-Disney; r/4-C #186 — 2.20 6.60 22.00
Beneath the Planet of the Apes 30044-012 (12/70)-with pull-out poster; photo-c (No poster = half price) — 7.00 21.00 70.00
Big Red 10026-211 (11/62)-Disney; photo-c — 2.20 6.60 22.00
Big Red 10026-503 (3/65)-Disney; reprints 10026-211; photo-c — 2.20 6.60 22.00
Blackbeard's Ghost 10222-806 (6/68)-Disney — 2.40 7.20 24.00
Bullwhip Griffin 10181-706 (6/67)-Disney; Manning-a; photo-c — 3.00 9.00 30.00
Captain Sindbad 10077-309 (9/63)-Manning-a; photo-c — 4.80 14.40 48.00
Chitty Chitty Bang Bang 1 (30038-902)(2/69)-with pull-out poster; Disney; photo-c (No poster = half price) — 6.00 18.00 60.00
Cinderella 10152-508 (8/65)-Disney; r/4-C #786 — 2.80 8.40 28.00
Darby O'Gill & the Little People 10251-001(1/70)-Disney; reprints 4-Color #1024 (Toth-a); photo-c — 4.50 13.50 45.00
Dumbo 1 (10090-310)(10/63)-Disney; r/4-C #668 — 2.80 8.40 28.00
Emil & the Detectives 10120-502 (2/65)-Disney; photo-c — 2.60 7.80 26.00
Escapade in Florence 1 (10043-301)(1/63)-Disney; starring Annette Funicello — 7.50 22.50 75.00
Fall of the Roman Empire 10118-407 (7/64); Sophia Loren photo-c — 3.00 9.00 30.00
Fantastic Voyage 10178-702 (2/67)-Wood/Adkins-a; photo-c — 4.50 13.50 45.00
55 Days at Peking 10081-309 (9/63)-Photo-c — 2.80 8.40 28.00
Fighting Prince of Donegal, The 10193-701 (1/67)-Disney — 2.60 7.80 26.00
First Men in the Moon 10132-503 (3/65)-Fred Fredericks-a; photo-c — 2.60 7.80 26.00
Gay Purr-ee 30017-301(1/63, 84 pgs.) — 4.00 12.00 40.00
Gnome Mobile, The 10207-710 (10/67)-Disney — 2.80 8.40 28.00
Goodbye, Mr. Chips 10246-006 (6/70)-Peter O'Toole photo-c — 2.80 8.40 28.00
Happiest Millionaire, The 10221-804 (4/68)-Disney — 2.80 8.40 28.00
Hey There, It's Yogi Bear 10122-409 (9/64)-Hanna-Barbera — 5.50 16.50 55.00
Horse Without a Head, The 10109-401 (1/64)-Disney — 2.60 7.80 26.00
How the West Was Won 10074-307 (7/63)-Tufts-a — 3.00 9.00 30.00
In Search of the Castaways 10048-303 (3/63)-Disney; Hayley Mills photo-c — 6.00 18.00 60.00

GD25 FN65 NM94

Jungle Book, The 1 (6022-801)(1/68-Whitman)-Disney; large size (10x13-1/2"); 59¢ — 5.00 15.00 50.00
Jungle Book, The 1 (30033-803)(3/68, 68 pgs.)-Disney; same contents as Whitman #1 — 3.20 9.60 32.00
Jungle Book, The 1 (6/78, $1.00 tabloid) — 1.60 4.80 16.00
Jungle Book (1984)-r/Giant — 2.00 5.00
Kidnapped 10080-306 (6/63)-Disney; reprints 4-Color #1101; photo-c — 2.80 8.40 28.00
King Kong 30036-809(9/68-68 pgs.)-painted-c — 2.40 7.20 24.00
King Kong nn-Whitman Treasury($1.00, 68 pgs.,1968), same cover as Gold Key issue — 3.80 11.40 38.00
King Kong 11299(#1-786, 10x13-1/4", 68 pgs., $1.00, 1978) — 1.80 5.40 18.00
Lady and the Tramp 10042-301 (1/63)-Disney; r/4-Color #629 — 3.00 9.00 30.00
Lady and the Tramp 1 (1967-Giant; 25¢)-Disney; reprints part of Dell #1 — 4.50 13.50 45.00
Lady and the Tramp 2 (10042-203)(3/72)-Disney; r/4-Color #629 — 1.90 5.70 19.00
Legend of Lobo, The 1 (10059-303)(3/63)-Disney; photo-c — 2.00 6.00 20.00
Lt. Robin Crusoe, U.S.N. 10191-610 (10/66)-Disney; Dick Van Dyke photo-c — 2.00 6.00 20.00
Lion, The 10035-301 (1/63)-Photo-c — 1.80 5.40 18.00
Lord Jim 10156-509 (9/65)-Photo-c — 2.00 6.00 20.00
Love Bug, The 10237-906 (6/69)-Disney; Buddy Hackett photo-c — 2.20 6.60 22.00
Mary Poppins 10136-501 (1/65)-Disney; photo-c — 3.80 11.40 38.00
Mary Poppins 30023-501 (1/65-68 pgs.)-Disney; photo-c — 5.50 16.50 55.00
McLintock 10110-403 (3/64); John Wayne app.; John Wayne & Maureen O'Hara photo-c — 11.00 33.00 110.00
Merlin Jones as the Monkey's Uncle 10115-510 (10/65)-Disney; Annette Funicello front/back photo-c — 4.20 12.60 42.00
Miracle of the White Stallions, The 10065-306 (6/63)-Disney — 2.60 7.80 26.00
Misadventures of Merlin Jones, The 10115-405 (5/64)-Disney; Annette Funicello photo front/back-c — 4.50 13.50 45.00
Moon-Spinners, The 10124-410 (10/64)-Disney; Haley Mills photo-c — 6.00 18.00 60.00
Mutiny on the Bounty 1 (10040-302)(2/63)-Marlon Brando photo-c — 2.80 8.40 28.00
Nikki, Wild Dog of the North 10141-412 (12/64)-Disney; reprints 4-Color #1226 — 2.20 6.60 22.00
Old Yeller 10168-601 (1/66)-Disney; reprints 4-Color #869; photo-c — 2.20 6.60 22.00
One Hundred & One Dalmations 1 (10247-002) (2/70)-Disney; reprints Four Color #1183 — 2.40 7.20 24.00
Peter Pan 1 (10086-309)(9/63)-Disney; reprints Four Color #442 — 2.80 8.40 28.00
Peter Pan 2 (10086-909)(9/69)-Disney; reprints Four Color #442 — 2.00 6.00 20.00
Peter Pan 1 ('83)-r/4-Color #442 — 2.00
P.T. 109 10123-409 (9/64)-John F. Kennedy — 3.50 10.50 35.00
Rio Conchos 10143-503(3/65) — 3.00 9.00 30.00
Robin Hood 10163-506 (6/65)-Disney; reprints Four Color #413 — 2.40 7.20 24.00
Shaggy Dog & the Absent-Minded Professor 30032-708 (8/67-Giant, 68 pgs.) Disney; reprints 4-Color #985,1199 — 4.50 13.50 45.00
Sleeping Beauty 1 (30042-009)(9/70)-Disney; reprints Four Color #973; with pull-out poster (No poster = half price) — 5.50 16.50 55.00
Snow White & the Seven Dwarfs 1 (10091-310)(10/63)-Disney; reprints Four Color #382 — 2.40 7.20 24.00
Snow White & the Seven Dwarfs 10091-709 (9/67)-Disney; reprints

Movie Comics - Toby Tyler © WDC

Movie Love #12 © FF

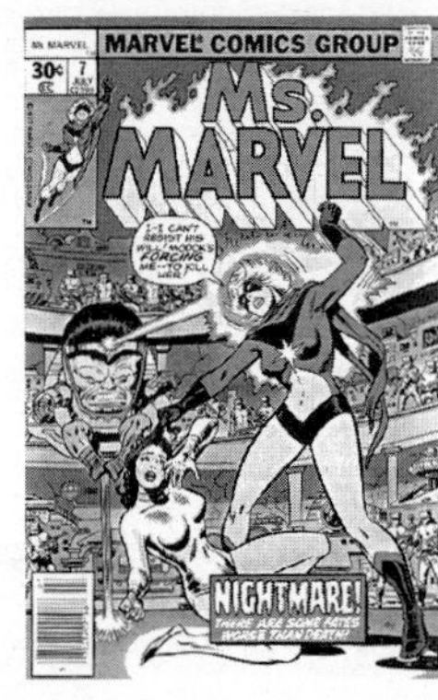

Ms. Marvel #7 © MAR

GD25 FN65 NM94

Four Color #382 2.00 6.00 20.00
Snow White & the Seven Dwarfs 90091-204 (2/84)-Reprints Four Color #382 2.00
Son of Flubber 1 (10057-304)(4/63)-Disney; sequel to "The Absent-Minded Professor" 2.40 7.20 24.00
Summer Magic 10076-309 (9/63)-Disney; Hayley Mills photo-c; Manning-a 6.00 18.00 60.00
Swiss Family Robinson 10236-904 (4/69)-Disney; reprints Four Color #1156; photo-c 2.40 7.20 24.00
Sword in the Stone, The 30019-402 (2/64-Giant, 68 pgs.)-Disney (see March of Comics #258 & Wart and the Wizard 5.00 15.00 50.00
That Darn Cat 10171-602 (2/66)-Disney; Hayley Mills photo-c 5.50 16.50 55.00
Those Magnificent Men in Their Flying Machines 10162-510 (10/65); photo-c 2.60 7.80 26.00
Three Stooges in Orbit 30016-211 (11/62-Giant, 32 pgs.)-All photos from movie; stiff-photo-c 8.50 25.50 85.00
Tiger Walks, A 10117-406 (6/64)-Disney; Torres?, Tufts-a; photo-c 3.60 10.80 36.00
Toby Tyler 10142-502 (2/65)-Disney; reprints Four Color #1092; photo-c 2.40 7.20 24.00
Treasure Island 1 (10200-703)(3/67)-Disney; reprints Four Color #624; photo-c 2.20 6.60 22.00
20,000 Leagues Under the Sea 1 (10095-312)(12/63)-Disney; reprints Four Color #614 2.40 7.20 24.00
Wonderful Adventures of Pinocchio, The 1 (10089-310)(10/63)-Disney; reprints Four Color #545 (see Wonderful Advs. of...) 2.80 8.40 28.00
Wonderful Adventures of Pinocchio, The 10089-109 (9/71)-Disney; reprints Four Color #545 2.20 6.60 22.00
Wonderful World of the Brothers Grimm 1 (10008-210)(10/62) 3.50 10.50 35.00
X, the Man with the X-Ray Eyes 10083-309 (9/63)-Ray Milland photo on-c 6.20 18.60 62.00
Yellow Submarine 35000-902 (2/69-Giant, 68 pgs.)-With pull-out poster; The Beatles cartoon movie 22.00 66.00 220.00
Without poster 6.00 18.00 60.00

MOVIE LOVE (Also see Personal Love)
Famous Funnies: Feb, 1950 - No. 22, Aug, 1953 (All photo-c)

1-Dick Powell, Evelyn Keyes, & Mickey Rooney photo-c 10.50 32.00 85.00
2-Myrna Loy photo-c 6.00 18.00 42.00
3-7,9: 6-Ricardo Montalban photo-c. 9-Gene Tierney, John Lund, Glenn Ford, & Rhonda Fleming photo-c. 5.70 17.00 35.00
8-Williamson/Frazetta-a, 6 pgs. 30.00 90.00 240.00
10-Frazetta-a, 6 pgs. 34.00 102.00 270.00
11,14-16: 14-Janet Leigh photo-c 5.00 15.00 30.00
12-Dean Martin & Jerry Lewis photo-c (12/51, pre-dates Advs. of Dean Martin & Jerry Lewis comic) 6.00 18.00 42.00
13-Ronald Reagan photo-c with 1 pg. biog. 17.00 51.00 135.00
17-Leslie Caron & Ralph Meeker photo-c; 1 pg. Frazetta ad 5.00 15.00 30.00
18-22: 19-John Derek photo-c. 21-Paul Henreid & Patricia Medina photo-c. 22-John Payne & Coleen Gray photo-c 4.15 13.00 28.00
NOTE: *Each issue has a full-length movie adaptation with photo covers.*

MOVIE THRILLERS (Movie)
Magazine Enterprises: 1949

1-Adaptation of "Rope of Sand" w/Burt Lancaster; Burt Lancaster photo-c 27.00 81.00 205.00

MOVIE TOWN ANIMAL ANTICS (Formerly Animal Antics; becomes Raccoon Kids #52 on)
National Periodical Publ.: No. 24, Jan-Feb, 1950 - No. 51, July-Aug, 1954

24-Raccoon Kids continue 10.00 30.00 75.00
25-51 9.30 28.00 65.00

GD25 FN65 NM94

NOTE: ***Sheldon Mayer*** *a-28-33, 35, 37-41, 43, 44, 47, 49-51.*

MOVIE TUNES COMICS (Formerly Animated...; Frankie No. 4 on)
Marvel Comics (MgPC): No. 3, Fall, 1946

3-Super Rabbit, Krazy Krow, Silly Seal & Ziggy Pig 10.00 30.00 75.00

MOWGLI JUNGLE BOOK (Rudyard Kipling's...)
Dell Publ. Co.: No. 487, Aug-Oct, 1953 - No. 620, Apr, 1955

Four Color 487 (#1) 5.00 15.00 55.00
Four Color 582 (8/54), 620 3.60 11.00 40.00

MOXI
Lightning Comics: July, 1996 ($3.00)

1-Flip book w/Hellina; two covers 3.00
1-($9.95)-Commemorative Edition; polybagged 10.00

MOXI'S FRIENDS...BOBBY JOE & NITRO
Lightning Comics: Sept, 1996 ($2.75, B&W, one-shot)

1-Regular Edition 2.75
1($9.95)-Commemorative Edition 10.00

MOXI: STRANGE DAZE
Lightning Comics: Nov, 1996 ($2.75, B&W, one-shot)

1, 1b-Regular Edition 2.75
1($9.95)-Platinum Edition 10.00

MR. (See Mister)

MS. CYANIDE & ICE
Blackout Comics: June, 1995 - No. 1, 1995 ($2.95, B&W)

0,1 3.00

MS. FORTUNE
Image Comics: Jan, 1998 ($2.95, B&W, one-shot)

1-Chris Marrinan-s/a 2.95

MS. MARVEL (Also see The Avengers #183)
Marvel Comics Group: Jan, 1977 - No. 23, Apr, 1979

1-1st app. Ms. Marvel; Scorpion app. in #1,2 4.00
2-Origin 2.50
3-10: 5-Vision app. 10-Last 30¢ issue 2.00
11-15,19-23: 19-Capt. Marvel app. 20-New costume. 23-Vance Astro (leader of the Guardians) app. 1.50
16,17-Mystique cameo .90 2.70 8.00
18-1st full Mystique; Avengers x-over 1.20 3.60 12.00
NOTE: ***Austin*** *c-14i, 16i, 17i, 22i.* ***Buscema*** *a-1-3p; c(p)-2, 4, 6, 7, 15.* ***Infantino*** *a-14p, 19p.* ***Gil Kane*** *c-8.* ***Mooney*** *a-4-8p, 13p, 15-18p.* ***Starlin*** *c-12.*

MS. MYSTIC
Pacific Comics: Oct, 1982 - No. 2, Feb, 1984 ($1.00/$1.50)

1-Origin; intro Erth, Ayre, Fyre & Watr; Neal Adams-c/a/script 1.50
2 ($1.50)-N. Adams-c/a/script 1.50

MS. MYSTIC
Continunity Comics: V2#1, Oct, 1993 - V2#9, 1994 ($2.50)

V2#1-9: 1-Adams-c(i)/part-i. 2-4-Embossed-c. 2-Nebres part-i. 3-Adams-c(i)/plot. 4-Adams-c(p)/plot 2.50

MS. MYSTIC DEATHWATCH 2000 (Ms. Mystic #3)
Continuity: May, 1993 - No. 3, Aug, 1993 ($2.50)

1-Bagged w/card; Adams-c & plot 2.50
2-Bagged w/card; Adams plot 2.50
3-Bagged w/card; wraparound indestructible-c by Golden/Cory; Adams plot 2.50

MS. TREE QUARTERLY / SPECIAL
DC Comics: Summer, 1990 -No. 10, 1992 ($3.95/$3.50, 84 pgs, mature)

1-Midnight story; Batman text story, Grell-a. 4.00
2-9: 2,3-Midnight stories; The Butcher text stories. 4.00
10 ($3.50) 3.50

Muktuk Wolfsbreath: Hard-Boiled Shaman #1 © Terry Laban & Steve Parkhouse

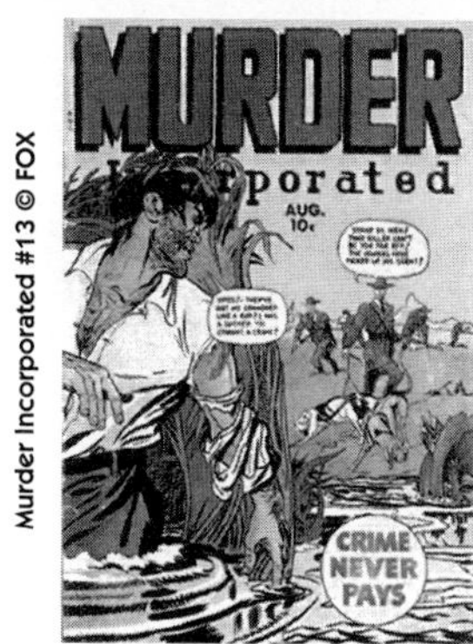

Murder Incorporated #13 © FOX

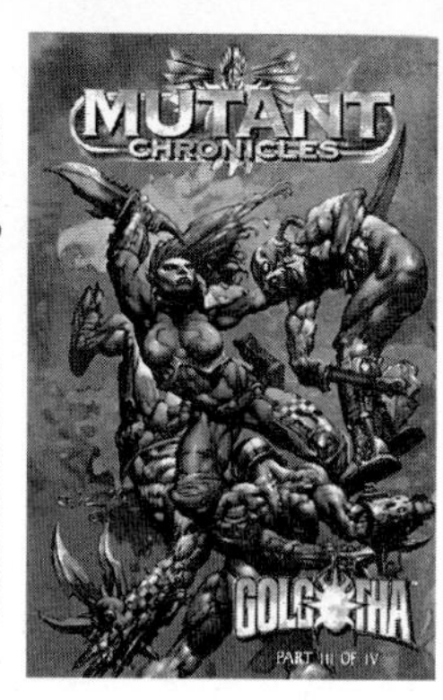

Mutant Chronicles V1 #3 © Target Games

GD25 FN65 NM94

NOTE: ***Cowan** c-2. **Grell** c-1, 6. **Infantino** a-8.*

MS. TREE'S THRILLING DETECTIVE ADVS (Ms. Tree #4 on; also see The Best of Ms. Tree)(Baxter paper #4-9)
Eclipse Comics/Aardvark-Vanaheim 10-18/Renegade Press 19 on: 2/83 - #9, 7/84; #10, 8/84 - #18, 5/85; #19, 6/85 - #50, 6/89

1 — 2.00
2-8: 2-Schythe begins — 1.80
9-Last Eclipse & last color issue — 1.80
10-49: 10,11-2-tone; ($1.70; $2.00 #34 on) — 1.80
50-Contains flexi-disc ($3.95, 52pgs.) — 4.00
Summer Special 1 (8/86) — 3.00
1950s 3-D Crime (7/87, no glasses)-Johnny Dynamite in 3-D — 2.50
Mike Mist in 3-D (8/85)-With glasses — 3.00

NOTE; ***Miller** pin-up 1-4. Johnny Dynamite-r begin #36 by **Morisi**.*

MS. VICTORY SPECIAL(Also see Capt. Paragon & Femforce)
Americomics: Jan, 1985 (nd)

1 — 1.70

MUGGSY MOUSE (Also see Tick Tock Tales)
Magazine Enterprises: 1951 - No. 3, 1951; No. 4, 1954 - No. 5, 1954; 1963

	GD25	FN65	NM94
1(A-1 #33)	5.70	17.00	35.00
2(A-1 #36)-Racist-c	7.15	21.50	50.00
3(A-1 #39), 4(A-1 #95), 5(A-1 #99)	4.00	10.00	20.00
Super Reprint #14(1963)	1.00	2.80	7.00
I.W. Reprint #1,2 (nd)	1.00	2.80	7.00

MUGGY-DOO, BOY CAT
Stanhall Publ.: July, 1953 - No. 4, Jan, 1954

	GD25	FN65	NM94
1-Funny animal; Irving Spector-a	5.70	17.00	40.00
2-4	4.25	13.00	28.00
Super Reprint #12('63), 16('64)	1.00	2.80	7.00

MUKTUK WOLFSBREATH: HARD-BOILED SHAMAN
DC Comics (Vertigo): Aug, 1998 - No. 3, Oct, 1998 ($2.50)

1-3-Terry LaBan-s/Steve Parkhouse-a — 2.50

MULLKON EMPIRE (See John Jake's...)

MUMMY, THE (See Universal Presents... under Dell Giants & Movie Classics)

MUNDEN'S BAR ANNUAL
First Comics: Apr, 1988; 1989 ($2.95/$5.95)

	GD25	FN65	NM94
1-($2.95)-r/from Grimjack; Fish Police story			3.00
2-($5.95)-Teenage Mutant Ninja Turtles app.		2.00	6.00

MUNSTERS, THE (TV)
Gold Key: Jan, 1965 - No. 16, Jan, 1968 (All photo-c)

	GD25	FN65	NM94
1 (10134-501)	17.00	52.00	200.00
2	8.00	25.00	95.00
3-5	6.40	19.00	75.00
6-16	5.50	16.50	65.00

MUNSTERS, THE (TV)
TV Comics!: Aug, 1997 - Present ($2.95, B&W)

	GD25	FN65	NM94
1-4-All have photo-c			3.00
1,4-($7.95)-Variant-c	.90	2.70	8.00
2-Variant-c w/Beverly Owens as Marilyn			3.00
Special Comic Con Ed. (7/97, $9.95)	1.00	3.00	10.00

MUPPET BABIES, THE (TV)(See Star Comics Magazine)
Marvel Comics (Star Comics)/Marvel #18 on: Aug, 1985 - No. 26, July, 1989 (Children's book)

1-13 (75¢) — .75
14-26 ($1.00) — 1.00

MUPPETS TAKE MANHATTAN, THE
Marvel Comics (Star Comics): Nov, 1984 - No. 3, Jan, 1985

1-3-Movie adapt. r-/Marvel Super Special — .60

MURCIELAGA, SHE-BAT
Heroic Publishing: Jan, 1993 - No. 2, 1993 (B&W)

1-($1.50, 28 pgs.) — 1.50
2-($2.95, 36 pgs.)-Coated-c — 3.00

MURDER CAN BE FUN
Slave Labor Graphics: Feb, 1996 - Present ($2.95, B&W)

1-11: 1-Dorkin-c. 2-Vasquez-c. — 3.00

MURDER INCORPORATED (My Private Life #16 on)
Fox Feature Syndicate: 1/48 - No. 15, 12/49; (2 No.9's); 6/50 - No. 3, 8/51

	GD25	FN65	NM94
1 (1st Series); 1,2 have 'For Adults Only' on-c	43.00	129.00	360.00
2-Electrocution story	35.00	104.00	260.00
3-7,9(4/49),10(5/49),11-15	19.00	56.00	140.00
8-Used in **SOTI**, pg. 160	21.00	62.00	155.00
9(3/49)-Possible use in **SOTI**, pg. 145; r/Blue Beetle #56('48)	19.00	58.00	145.00
5(#1, 6/50)(2nd Series)-Formerly My Desire #4; bondage-c.	13.00	40.00	100.00
2(8/50)-Morisi-a	12.00	36.00	90.00
3(8/51)-Used in **POP**, pg. 81; Rico-a; lingerie-c/panels	13.00	40.00	100.00

MURDEROUS GANGSTERS
Avon Per./Realistic No. 3 on: Jul, 1951; No. 2, Dec, 1951 - No. 4, Jun, 1952

	GD25	FN65	NM94
1-Pretty Boy Floyd, Leggs Diamond; 1 pg. Wood-a	39.00	116.00	290.00
2-Baby-Face Nelson; 1 pg. Wood-a; painted-c	24.00	72.00	180.00
3-Painted-c	19.00	56.00	140.00
4- "Murder by Needle" drug story; Mort Lawrence-a; Kinstler-c	24.00	72.00	180.00

MURDER TALES (Magazine)
World Famous Publications: V1#10, Nov, 1970 - V1#11, Jan, 1971 (52 pgs.)

	GD25	FN65	NM94
V1#10-One pg. Frazetta ad	2.50	7.60	28.00
11-Guardineer-r; bondage-c	1.80	5.40	18.00

MUSHMOUSE AND PUNKIN PUSS (TV)
Gold Key: September, 1965 (Hanna-Barbera)

	GD25	FN65	NM94
1 (10153-509)	8.00	24.00	90.00

MUSIC MAN, THE (See Movie Classics)

MUTANT CHRONICLES (Video game)
Acclaim Comics (Armada): May, 1996 - No. 4, Aug, 1996 ($2.95, lim. series)

1-4: Simon Bisley-c on all — 3.00
Sourcebook (#5) — 3.00

MUTANT MISADVENTURES OF CLOAK AND DAGGER, THE (Becomes Cloak and Dagger #14 on)
Marvel Comics: Oct, 1988 - No. 19, Aug, 1991 ($1.25/$1.50)

1-8,10-18: 1-$.25-c. X-Factor app. 2-Begin $1.50-c. 9,10-Painted-c. 12-Dr. Doom app. 14-Begin new direction. 16-18-Spider-Man x-over. 18-Infinity Gauntlet x-over; Thanos cameo; Ghost Rider app. — 1.50
9-($2.50, 52 pgs.)-The Avengers x-over — 2.50
19-($2.50, 52 pgs.)-Origin Cloak & Dagger — 2.50

NOTE: ***Austin** a-12i; c(i)-4, 12, 13; scripts-all. **Russell** a-2i. **Williamson** a-14i-16i; c-15i.*

MUTANTS & MISFITS
Silverline Comics (Solson): 1987 - No. 3, 1987 ($1.95)

1-3 — 2.00

MUTANTS VS. ULTRAS
Malibu Comics (Ultraverse): Nov, 1995 ($6.95, one-shot)

	GD25	FN65	NM94
1-r/Exiles vs. X-Men, NIght Man vs. Wolverine, Prime vs. Hulk	.85	2.60	7.00

MUTANT X (See X-Factor)

Mutant X #1 © MAR

Mutt and Jeff #23 © DC

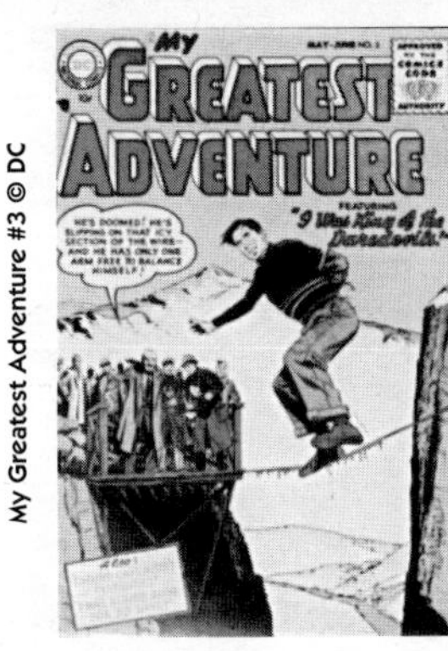

My Greatest Adventure #3 © DC

Marvel Comics: Nov, 1998 - Present ($2.99/$1.99)

	GD25	FN65	NM94
1-($2.99) Alex Summers with alternate world's X-Men			3.00
2-4-($1.99): 2-Two covers			2.00

MUTATIS
Marvel Comics (Epic Comics): 1992 - No. 3, 1992 ($2.25, mini-series)

	GD25	FN65	NM94
1-3: Painted-c			2.25

MUTINY (Stormy Tales of the Seven Seas)
Aragon Magazines: Oct, 1954 - No. 3, Feb, 1955

	GD25	FN65	NM94
1	14.00	42.00	105.00
2,3: 2-Capt. Mutiny. 3-Bondage-c	11.00	32.00	80.00

MUTINY ON THE BOUNTY (See Classics Illustrated #100 & Movie Comics)

MUTT AND JEFF (See All-American, All-Flash #18, Cicero's Cat, Comic Cavalcade, Famous Feature Stories, The Funnies, Popular & Xmas Comics)
All American/National 1-103(6/58)/Dell 104(10/58)-115 (10-12/59)/ Harvey 116(2/60)-148: Summer, 1939 (nd) - No. 148, Nov, 1965

	GD25	FN65	NM94
1(nn)-Lost Wheels	121.00	363.00	1150.00
2(nn)-Charging Bull (Summer, 1940, nd; on sale 6/20/40)	66.00	200.00	625.00
3(nn)-Bucking Broncos (Summer, 1941, nd)	47.00	141.00	450.00
4(Winter, '41), 5(Summer, '42)	42.00	126.00	400.00
6-10	20.00	60.00	185.00
11-20: 20-X-Mas-c	13.00	39.00	115.00
21-30	9.00	27.00	85.00
31-50: 32-X-Mas-c	7.00	21.00	60.00
51-75-Last Fisher issue. 53-Last 52 pgs.	6.00	18.00	45.00
76-99,101-103: 76-Last precode issue(1/55)	3.20	10.00	32.00
100	3.80	11.40	38.00
104-148: 116-131-Richie Rich app.	2.20	6.60	22.00
...Jokes 1-3(8/60-61, Harvey)-84 pgs.; Richie Rich in all; Little Dot in #2,3	3.00	9.00	30.00
...New Jokes 1-4(10/63-11/65, Harvey)-68 pgs.; Richie Rich in #1-3; Stumbo in #1	2.00	6.00	20.00

NOTE: *Most all issues by* ***Al Smith****. Issues from 1963 on have* ***Fisher*** *reprints. Clarification: early issues signed by Fisher are mostly drawn by Smith.*

MY BROTHERS' KEEPER
Spire Christian Comics (Fleming H. Revell Co.): 1973 (35/49¢, 36 pgs.)

	GD25	FN65	NM94
nn			4.00

MY CONFESSIONS (My Confession #7&8; formerly Western True Crime; A Spectacular Feature Magazine #11)
Fox Feature Syndicate: No. 7, Aug, 1949 - No. 10, Jan-Feb, 1950

	GD25	FN65	NM94
7-Wood-a (10 pgs.)	18.00	54.00	135.00
8,9: 8-Harrison/Wood-a (19 pgs.). 9-Wood-a	16.00	48.00	120.00
10	8.00	24.00	56.00

MY DATE COMICS (Teen-age)
Hillman Periodicals: July, 1947 - V1#4, Jan, 1948 (2nd Romance comic; see Young Romance)

	GD25	FN65	NM94
1-S&K-c/a	29.00	88.00	220.00
2-4-S&K-c/a; Dan Barry-a	19.00	58.00	145.00

MY DESIRE (Formerly Jo-Jo Comics; becomes Murder, Inc. #5 on)
Fox Feature Syndicate: No. 30, Aug, 1949 - No. 4, April, 1950

	GD25	FN65	NM94
30(#1)	11.00	34.00	85.00
31 (#2, 10/49),3(2/50),4	7.85	23.50	55.00
31 (Canadian edition)	5.70	17.00	35.00
32(12/49)-Wood-a	15.00	46.00	115.00

MY DIARY (Becomes My Friend Irma #3 on?)
Marvel Comics (A Lovers Mag.): Dec, 1949 - No. 2, Mar, 1950

	GD25	FN65	NM94
1,2-Photo-c	11.00	34.00	85.00

MY DOG TIGE (Buster Brown's Dog)
Buster Brown Shoes: 1957 (Giveaway)

	GD25	FN65	NM94
nn	4.00	12.00	24.00

MY EXPERIENCE (Formerly All Top; becomes Judy Canova #23 on)
Fox Feature Syndicate: No. 19, Sept, 1949 - No. 22, Mar, 1950

	GD25	FN65	NM94
19-Wood-a	19.00	58.00	145.00
20	8.00	24.00	56.00
21-Wood-a(2)	19.00	58.00	145.00
22-Wood-a (9 pgs.)	16.00	48.00	120.00

MY FAVORITE MARTIAN (TV)
Gold Key: 1/64; No.2, 7/64 - No. 9, 10/66 (No. 1,3-9 have photo-c)

	GD25	FN65	NM94
1-Russ Manning-a	12.00	37.00	133.00
2	6.00	18.00	65.00
3-9	5.00	15.00	55.00

MY FRIEND IRMA (Radio/TV) (Formerly My Diary? and/or Western Life Romances?)
Marvel/Atlas Comics (BFP): No. 3, June, 1950 - No. 47, Dec, 1954; No. 48, Feb, 1955

	GD25	FN65	NM94
3-Dan DeCarlo-a in all; 52 pgs. begin, end ?	11.00	34.00	85.00
4-Kurtzman-a (10 pgs.)	15.00	44.00	110.00
5- "Egghead Doodle" by Kurtzman (4 pgs.)	11.00	32.00	80.00
6,8-10: 9-paper dolls, 1 pg; Millie app. (5 pgs.)	7.15	21.50	50.00
7-One pg. Kurtzman-a	7.15	21.50	50.00
11-23: 23-One pg. Frazetta-a	5.00	15.00	30.00
24-48: 41,48-Stan Lee & Dan DeCarlo app.	4.15	12.50	25.00

MY GIRL PEARL
Atlas Comics: 4/55 - #4, 10/55; #5, 7/57 - #6, 9/57; #7, 8/60 - #11, ?/61

	GD25	FN65	NM94
1-Dan DeCarlo-c/a in #1-6	11.00	32.00	80.00
2	5.70	17.00	40.00
3-6	4.15	12.50	25.00
7-11	2.50	7.50	20.00

MY GREATEST ADVENTURE (Doom Patrol #86 on)
National Periodical Publications: Jan-Feb, 1955 - No. 85, Feb, 1964

	GD25	FN65	NM94
1-Before CCA	120.00	360.00	1200.00
2	45.00	135.00	550.00
3-5	32.00	96.00	355.00
6-10: 6-Science fiction format begins	31.00	93.00	310.00
11-15: 12-1st S.A. issue	21.00	63.00	210.00
16-18: Kirby-a in all. 18-Kirby-c	23.00	69.00	230.00
19,22-25	18.00	54.00	180.00
20,21,28-Kirby-a	21.00	63.00	210.00
26,27,29,30	13.00	39.00	130.00
31-40	10.50	32.00	105.00
41-61: 58,60,61-Toth-a; Last 10¢ issue	8.00	24.00	80.00
62-79: 77-Toth-a; Robotman prototype	4.50	13.50	45.00
80-(6/63)-Intro/origin Doom Patrol and begin series; origin & 1st app. Negative Man, Elasti-Girl & S.A. Robotman	33.00	100.00	370.00
81-85: 81,85-Toth-a	15.00	45.00	150.00

NOTE: ***Anderson*** *a-42.* ***Cameron*** *a-24.* ***Colan*** *a-77.* ***Meskin*** *a-25, 26, 32, 39, 45, 50, 56, 57, 61, 64, 70, 73, 74, 76, 79; c-76.* ***Moreira*** *a-11, 12, 15, 17, 20, 23, 25, 27, 37, 40-43, 46, 48, 55-57, 59, 60, 62-65, 67, 69, 70; c-1-4, 7-10.* ***Roussos*** *c/a-71-73.* ***Wildey*** *a-32.*

MY GREATEST THRILLS IN BASEBALL
Mission of California: Date? (16 pg. Giveaway)

	GD25	FN65	NM94
nn-By Mickey Mantle	49.00	147.00	420.00

MY GREAT LOVE (Becomes Will Rogers Western #5)
Fox Feature Syndicate: Oct, 1949 - No. 4, Apr, 1950

	GD25	FN65	NM94
1	11.00	34.00	85.00
2-4	6.50	19.50	45.00

MY INTIMATE AFFAIR (Inside Crime #3)
Fox Feature Syndicate: Mar, 1950 - No. 2, May, 1950

My Little Margie #9 © CC

My Love Affair #1 © FOX

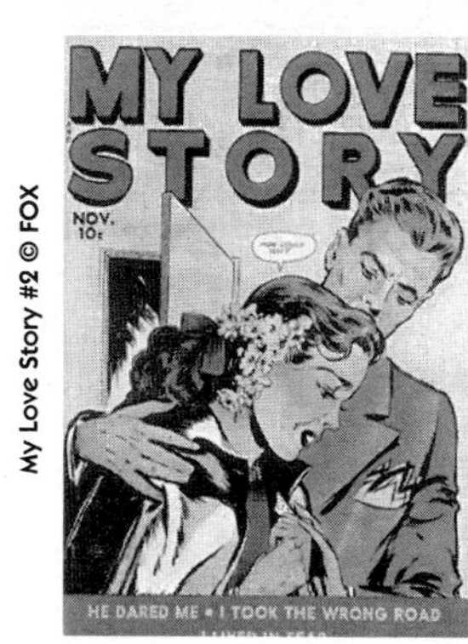

My Love Story #2 © FOX

	GD25	FN65	NM94
1	11.00	34.00	85.00
2	6.50	19.50	45.00

MY LIFE (Formerly Meet Corliss Archer)
Fox Feature Syndicate: No. 4, Sept, 1948 - No. 15, July, 1950

	GD25	FN65	NM94
4-Used in **SOTI**, pg. 39; Kamen/Feldstein-a	33.00	100.00	250.00
5-Kamen-a	17.00	52.00	130.00
6-Kamen/Feldstein-a	18.00	54.00	135.00
7-Wood-a; wash cover	16.00	48.00	120.00
8,9,11-15	6.85	21.00	48.00
10-Wood-a	15.00	44.00	110.00

MY LITTLE MARGIE (TV)
Charlton Comics: July, 1954 - No. 54, Nov, 1964

	GD25	FN65	NM94
1-Photo front/back-c	27.00	80.00	200.00
2-Photo front/back-c	12.00	36.00	90.00
3-7,10	7.15	21.50	50.00
8,9-Infinity-c	7.85	23.50	55.00
11-14: Part-photo-c (#13, 8/56)	6.50	19.50	45.00
15-19	3.20	9.60	32.00
20-(25¢, 100 pg. issue)	7.50	22.50	75.00
21-39-Last 10¢ issue?	2.80	8.40	28.00
40-53	2.50	7.50	22.00
54-Beatles on cover; lead story spoofs the Beatle haircut craze of the 1960's	12.50	38.00	125.00

NOTE: *Doll cut-outs in 32, 33, 40, 45, 50.*

MY LITTLE MARGIE'S BOY FRIENDS (TV) (Freddy V2#12 on)
Charlton Comics: Aug, 1955 - No. 11, Apr?, 1958

	GD25	FN65	NM94
1-Has several Archie swipes	11.00	32.00	80.00
2	6.50	19.50	45.00
3-11	5.00	15.00	30.00

MY LITTLE MARGIE'S FASHIONS (TV)
Charlton Comics: Feb, 1959 - No. 5, Nov, 1959

	GD25	FN65	NM94
1	10.00	30.00	75.00
2-5	5.70	17.00	40.00

MY LOVE (Becomes Two Gun Western #5 (11/50) on?)
Marvel Comics (CLDS): July, 1949 - No. 4, Apr, 1950 (All photo-c)

	GD25	FN65	NM94
1	11.00	32.00	80.00
2,3	6.85	21.00	48.00
4-Betty Page photo-c (see Cupid #2)	25.00	76.00	190.00

MY LOVE
Marvel Comics Group: Sept, 1969 - No. 39, Mar, 1976

	GD25	FN65	NM94
1	2.70	8.00	30.00
2-9: 4-6-Colan-a	1.50	4.50	15.00
10-Williamson-r/My Own Romance #71; Kirby-a	2.00	6.00	20.00
11-13,15-20	1.40	4.20	14.00
14-(52 pgs.)-Woodstock-c/sty; Morrow-c/a; Kirby/Colletta-r	2.40	7.00	26.00
21,22,24-38: 38-Reprints	1.00	3.00	10.00
23-Steranko-r/Our Love Story #5	1.60	4.80	16.00
39-Last issue; reprints	1.40	4.20	14.00
Special(12/71)(52 pgs.)	2.20	6.50	24.00

NOTE: ***John Buscema** a-1-7, 10, 22r(2), 24r, 25r, 29r, 34r, 36r, 37r, Spec. (r)(4); c-13, 15, 25, 27, Spec. **Colan** a-16,22,24r,35r,39r. **Colan/Everett** a-13, 15, 16, 27(r/#13). **Kirby** a-(r)-14,28.*

MY LOVE AFFAIR (March of Crime #7 on)
Fox Feature Syndicate: July, 1949 - No. 6, May, 1950

	GD25	FN65	NM94
1	11.00	34.00	85.00
2	6.85	21.00	48.00
3-6-Wood-a. 5-(3/50)-Becomes Love Stories #6	15.00	44.00	110.00

MY LOVE LIFE (Formerly Zegra)
Fox Feature Synd.: No. 6, June, 1949 - No. 13, Aug, 1950; No. 13, Sept, 1951

	GD25	FN65	NM94
6-Kamenish-a	13.00	40.00	100.00
7-13	6.85	21.00	48.00
13 (9/51)	6.00	18.00	42.00

MY LOVE MEMOIRS (Formerly Women Outlaws; Hunted #13 on)
Fox Feature Syndicate: No. 9, Nov, 1949 - No. 12, May, 1950

	GD25	FN65	NM94
9,11,12-Wood-a	14.00	42.00	105.00
10	6.85	21.00	48.00

MY LOVE SECRET (Formerly Phantom Lady; Animal Crackers #31)
Fox Feature Syndicate/M. S. Distr.: No. 24, June, 1949 - No. 30, June, 1950; No. 53, 1954

	GD25	FN65	NM94
24-Kamen/Feldstein-a	13.00	40.00	100.00
25-Possible caricature of Wood on-c?	7.85	23.50	55.00
26,28-Wood-a	13.00	40.00	100.00
27,29,30: 30-Photo-c	6.00	18.00	42.00
53-(Reprint, M.S. Distr.) 1954? nd given; formerly Western Thrillers; becomes Crimes by Women #54; photo-c	4.25	13.00	26.00

MY LOVE STORY (Hoot Gibson Western #5 on)
Fox Feature Syndicate: Sept, 1949 - No. 4, Mar, 1950

	GD25	FN65	NM94
1	11.00	34.00	85.00
2	6.85	21.00	48.00
3,4-Wood-a	15.00	44.00	110.00

MY LOVE STORY
Atlas Comics (GPS): April, 1956 - No. 9, Aug, 1957

	GD25	FN65	NM94
1	9.30	28.00	65.00
2	5.00	15.00	30.00
3-Matt Baker-a	6.85	21.00	48.00
4-6,8,9	4.25	13.00	28.00
7-Matt Baker, Toth-a	6.85	21.00	48.00

NOTE: ***Brewster** a-3. **Colletta** a-1(2), 3, 4(2), 5; c-3.*

MY NAME IS CHAOS
DC Comics: 1992 - No. 4, 1992 ($4.95, limited series, 52 pgs.)

	GD25	FN65	NM94
Book 1-4: Tom Veitch scripts; painted-c			5.00

MY NAME IS HOLOCAUST
DC Comics: May, 1995 - No. 5, Sept, 1995 ($2.50, limited series)

	GD25	FN65	NM94
1-5			2.50

MY ONLY LOVE
Charlton Comics: July, 1975 - No. 9, Nov, 1976

	GD25	FN65	NM94
1	1.20	3.60	12.00
2,4-9	.90	2.70	8.00
3-Toth-a	1.00	3.00	10.00

MY OWN ROMANCE (Formerly My Romance; Teen-Age Romance #77 on)
Marvel/Atlas (MjPC/RCM No. 4-59/ZPC No. 60-76): No. 4, Mar, 1949 - No. 76, July, 1960

	GD25	FN65	NM94
4-Photo-c	11.00	34.00	85.00
5-10: 5,6,8-10-Photo-c	5.70	17.00	40.00
11-20: 14-Powell-a	5.35	16.00	32.00
21-42: 42-Last precode (2/55)	5.00	15.00	30.00
43-54,56-60	2.50	7.50	22.00
55-Toth-a	3.00	9.00	30.00
61-70,72-76	2.25	6.75	18.00
71-Williamson-a	3.20	9.60	32.00

NOTE: ***Brewster** a-59. **Colletta** a-45(2), 48, 50, 55, 57(2), 59; c-58i, 59, 61. **Everett** a-25; c-58p. **Morisi** a-18. **Orlando** a-61. **Romita** a-36. **Tuska** a-10.*

MY PAL DIZZY (See Comic Books, Series I)

MY PAST (...Confessions) (Formerly Western Thrillers)
Fox Feature Syndicate: No. 7, Aug, 1949 - No. 11, Apr, 1950 (Crimes Inc. #12)

	GD25	FN65	NM94
7	11.00	34.00	85.00
8-10	6.85	21.00	48.00
11-Wood-a	14.00	42.00	105.00

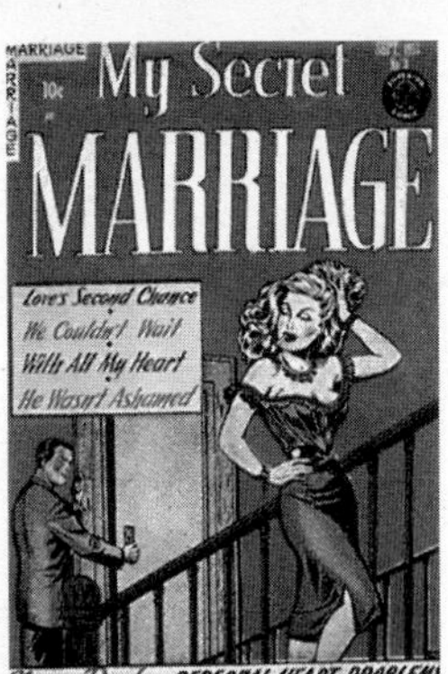

My Secret Marriage #3 © SUPR

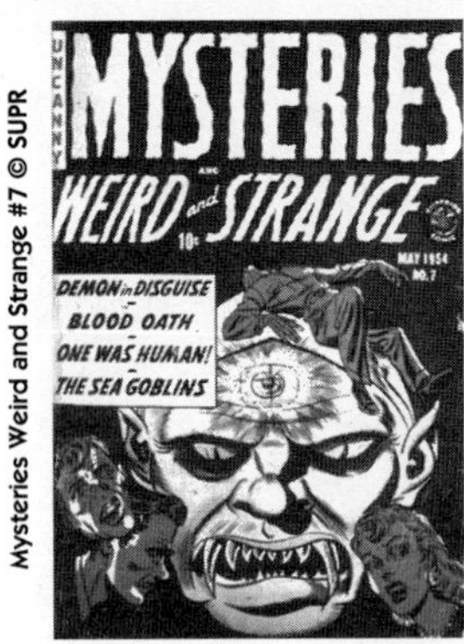

Mysteries Weird and Strange #7 © SUPR

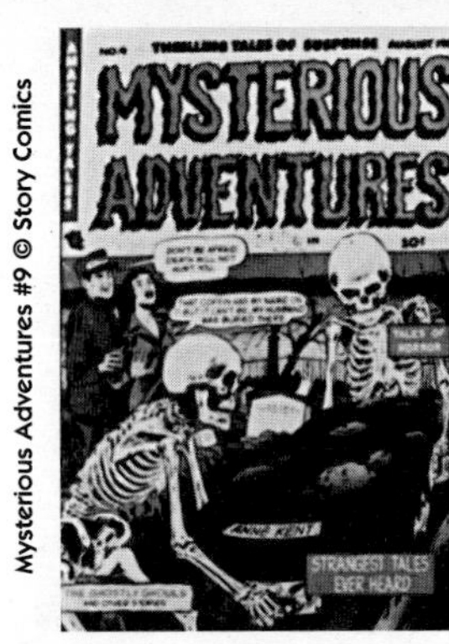

Mysterious Adventures #9 © Story Comics

	GD25	FN65	NM94

MY PERSONAL PROBLEM
Ajax/Farrell/Steinway Comic: 11/55; No. 2, 2/56; No. 3, 9/56 - No. 4, 11/56; 10/57 - No. 3, 5/58

1	6.85	21.00	48.00
2-4	5.00	15.00	30.00
1-3('57-'58)-Steinway	4.15	12.50	25.00

MY PRIVATE LIFE (Formerly Murder, Inc.; becomes Pedro #18)
Fox Feature Syndicate: No. 16, Feb, 1950 - No. 17, April, 1950

16,17	9.50	28.75	72.00

MYRA NORTH (See The Comics, Crackajack Funnies & Red Ryder)
Dell Publishing Co.: No. 3, Jan, 1940

Four Color 3	71.00	212.00	775.00

MY REAL LOVE
Standard Comics: No. 5, June, 1952 (Photo-c)

5-Toth-a, 3 pgs.; Tuska, Cardy, Vern Greene-a	11.00	32.00	80.00

MY ROMANCE (Becomes My Own Romance #4 on)
Marvel Comics (RCM): Sept, 1948 - No. 3, Jan, 1949

1	11.00	34.00	85.00
2,3: 2-Anti-Wertham editorial (11/48)	6.85	21.00	48.00

MY ROMANTIC ADVENTURES (Formerly Romantic Adventures)
American Comics Group: No. 68, 8/56 - No. 115, 12/60; No. 116, 7/61 - No. 138, 3/64

68	6.50	19.50	45.00
69-85	4.00	12.00	24.00
86-Three pg. Williamson-a (2/58)	5.70	17.00	38.00
87-100	2.00	6.00	16.00
101-138	1.25	3.75	10.00

NOTE: ***Whitney** art in most issues.*

MY SECRET (Becomes Our Secret #4 on)
Superior Comics, Ltd.: Aug, 1949 - No. 3, Oct, 1949

1	11.00	32.00	80.00
2,3	7.15	21.50	50.00

MY SECRET AFFAIR (Becomes Martin Kane #4)
Hero Book (Fox Feature Syndicate): Dec, 1949 - No. 3, April, 1950

1-Harrison/Wood-a (10 pgs.)	16.00	48.00	120.00
2-Wood-a (poor)	11.00	32.00	80.00
3-Wood-a	14.00	42.00	105.00

MY SECRET CONFESSION
Sterling Comics: September, 1955

1-Sekowsky-a	6.85	21.00	48.00

MY SECRET LIFE (Formerly Western Outlaws; Romeo Tubbs #26 on)
Fox Feature Syndicate: No. 22, July, 1949 - No. 27, May, 1950

22	9.30	28.00	65.00
23,26-Wood-a, 6 pgs.	14.00	42.00	105.00
24,25,27	5.70	17.00	40.00

NOTE: *The title was changed to Romeo Tubbs after #25 even though #26 & 27 did come out.*

MY SECRET LIFE (Formerly Young Lovers; Sue & Sally Smith #48)
Charlton Comics: No. 19, Aug, 1957 - No. 47, Sept, 1962

19	2.50	7.50	20.00
20-35	1.25	3.75	10.00
36-47: 44-Last 10¢ issue	1.00	2.80	7.00

MY SECRET MARRIAGE
Superior Comics, Ltd.: May, 1953 - No. 24, July, 1956

1	9.30	28.00	65.00
2	5.00	15.00	30.00
3-24	4.00	11.00	22.00
I.W. Reprint #9		2.00	6.00

NOTE: *Many issues contain **Kamenish** art.*

MY SECRET ROMANCE (Becomes A Star Presentation #3)
Hero Book (Fox Feature Syndicate): Jan, 1950 - No. 2, March, 1950

1	11.00	32.00	80.00
2-Wood-a	14.00	42.00	105.00

MY SECRET STORY (Formerly Captain Kidd #25; Sabu #30 on)
Fox Feature Syndicate: No. 26, Oct, 1949 - No. 29, April, 1950

26	11.00	34.00	85.00
27-29	6.85	21.00	48.00

MYS-TECH WARS
Marvel Comics UK: Mar, 1993 - No. 4, June, 1993 ($1.75, mini-series)

1-4: 1-Gatefold-c			1.75

MYSTERIES (...Weird & Strange)
Superior/Dynamic Publ. (Randall Publ. Ltd.): May, 1953 - No. 11, Jan, 1955

1	29.00	88.00	220.00
2-A-Bomb blast story	16.00	48.00	120.00
3-9,11	14.00	42.00	105.00
10-Kamenish-c/a reprinted from Strange Mysteries #2; cover is from a panel in Strange Mysteries #2	14.00	42.00	105.00

MYSTERIES IN SPACE (See Fireside Book Series)

MYSTERIES OF SCOTLAND YARD (Also see A-1 Comics)
Magazine Enterprises: No. 121, 1954 (one shot)

A-1 121-Reprinted from Manhunt (5 stories)	14.00	42.00	105.00

MYSTERIES OF UNEXPLORED WORLDS (See Blue Bird) (Becomes Son of Vulcan V2#49 on)
Charlton Comics: Aug, 1956; No. 2, Jan, 1957 - No. 48, Sept, 1965

1	31.00	92.00	230.00
2-No Ditko	11.00	34.00	85.00
3,4,8,9 Ditko-a. 3-Diko c/a (4). 4-Ditko c/a (2).	22.00	66.00	165.00
5-7,10,11: 5,6-Ditko-c/a (all). 7-(2/58, 68 pgs.); Ditko-a(4). 10-Ditko-c/a(4). 11-Ditko-c/a(3); signed J. Kotdi	24.00	72.00	180.00
12,19,21-24,26-Ditko-a. 12-Ditko sty (3); Baker story "The Charm Bracelet."	16.00	48.00	120.00
13-18,20	5.35	16.00	32.00
25,27-30	2.50	7.50	22.00
31-45	1.85	5.50	15.00
46(5/65)-Son of Vulcan begins (origin/1st app.)	3.20	9.60	32.00
47,48	2.00	6.00	16.00

NOTE: ***Ditko** c-3-6, 10, 11, 19, 21-24. Covers to #19, 21-24 reprint story panels.*

MYSTERIOUS ADVENTURES
Story Comics: Mar, 1951 - No. 24, Mar, 1955; No. 25, Aug, 1955

1-All horror stories	42.00	127.00	340.00
2	23.00	70.00	175.00
3,4,6,10	20.00	60.00	150.00
5-Bondage-c	23.00	70.00	175.00
7-Daggar in eye panel	33.00	98.00	245.00
8-Eyeball story	35.00	104.00	260.00
9-Extreme violence	27.00	80.00	200.00
11(12/52)-Used in **SOTI**, pg. 84	27.00	80.00	200.00
12,13	23.00	70.00	175.00
14-E.C. Old Witch swipe	22.00	66.00	165.00
15-21: 18-Used in Senate Investigative report, pgs. 5,6; E.C. swipe/TFTC #35; The Coffin-Keeper & Corpse (hosts). 20-Used by Wertham in the Senate hearings. 21-Bondage/beheading-c	32.00	96.00	240.00
22- "Cinderella" parody	23.00	68.00	170.00
23-Disbrow-a (6 pgs.); E.C. swipe "The Mystery Keeper's Tale" (host) and "Mother Ghoul's Nursery Tale"	23.00	68.00	170.00
24,25	17.00	52.00	130.00

NOTE: ***Tothish** art by **Ross Andru**-#22, 23. **Bache** a-8. **Cameron** a-5-7. **Harrison** a-12. **Hollingsworth** a-3-8, 12. **Schaffenberger** a-24, 25. **Wildey** a-15, 17.*

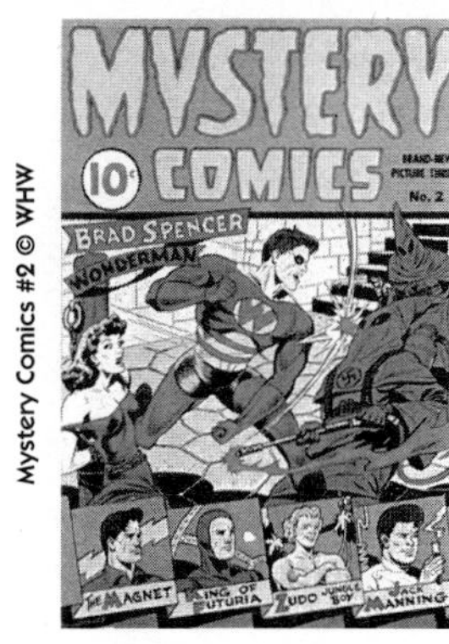

Mystery Comics #2 © WHW

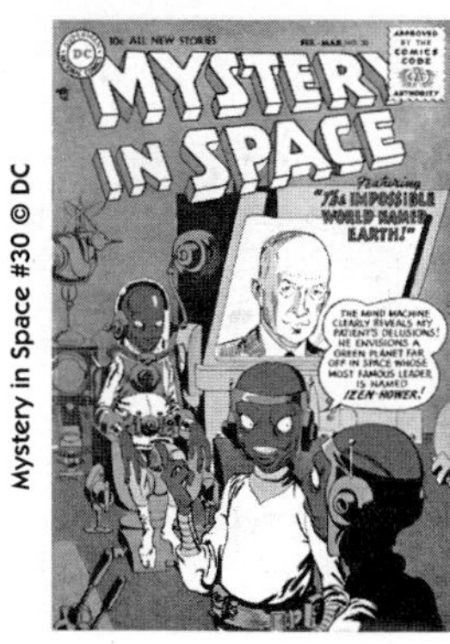

Mystery in Space #30 © DC

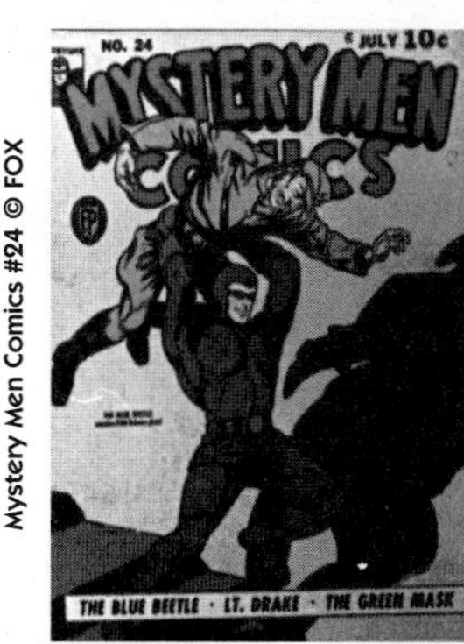

Mystery Men Comics #24 © FOX

GD25 FN65 NM94

MYSTERIOUS ISLAND
Dell Publishing Co.: No. 1213, July-Sept, 1961

Four Color 1213-Movie, photo-c 8.00 25.00 90.00

MYSTERIOUS ISLE
Dell Publishing Co.: Nov-Jan, 1963/64 (Jules Verne)

1 2.00 6.00 16.00

MYSTERIOUS RIDER, THE (See Zane Grey, 4-Color 301)

MYSTERIOUS STORIES (Formerly Horror From the Tomb #1)
Premier Magazines: No. 2, Dec-Jan, 1954-1955 - No. 7, Dec, 1955

2-Woodbridge-c; last pre-code issue 32.00 96.00 240.00
3-Woodbridge-c/a 22.00 66.00 165.00
4-7: 5-Cinderella parody. 6-Woodbridge-c 21.00 62.00 155.00
NOTE: ***Hollingsworth** a-2, 4.*

MYSTERIOUS SUSPENSE
Charlton Comics: Oct, 1968 (12¢)

1-Return of the Question by Ditko (c/a) 5.00 15.00 50.00

MYSTERIOUS TRAVELER (See Tales of the...)

MYSTERIOUS TRAVELER COMICS (Radio)
Trans-World Publications: Nov, 1948

1-Powell-c/a(2); Poe adaptation, "Tell Tale Heart" 49.00 148.00 420.00

MYSTERY COMICS
William H. Wise & Co.: 1944 - No. 4, 1944 (No months given)

1-The Magnet, The Silver Knight, Brad Spencer, Wonderman, Dick Devins, King of Futuria, & Zudo the Jungle Boy begin (all 1st app.); Schomburg-c on all 91.00 274.00 775.00
2-Bondage-c 59.00 177.00 500.00
3-Lance Lewis, Space Detective begins (1st app.); Robot-c 53.00 160.00 450.00
4(V2#1 inside) 53.00 160.00 450.00

MYSTERY COMICS DIGEST
Gold Key: Mar, 1972 - No. 26, Oct, 1975

1-Ripley's Believe It or Not; reprint of Ripley's #1 origin Ra-Ka-Tep the Mummy; Wood-a 2.90 8.70 32.00
2-9: 2-Boris Karloff Tales of Mystery; Wood-a; 1st app. Werewolf Count Wulfstein 3-Twilight Zone (TV); Crandall, Toth & George Evans-a; 1st app. Tragg & Simbar the Lion Lord; (2) Crandall/Frazetta-r/Twilight Zone #1 4-Ripley's Believe It or Not; 1st app. Baron Tibor, the Vampire. 5-Boris Karloff Tales of Mystery; 1st app. Dr. Spektor. 6-Twilight Zone (TV); 1st app. U.S. Marshal Reid & Sir Duane; Evans-r. 7-Ripley's Believe It or Not; origin The Lurker in the Swamp; 1st app. Duroc. 8-Boris Karloff Tales of Mystery; McWilliams-r; Orlando-r. 9-Twilight Zone (TV); Williamson, Crandall, McWilliams-a; 2nd Tragg app.;Torres, Evans, Heck/Tuska-r 2.00 6.00 20.00
10-26: 10,13-Ripley's Believe It or Not: 13-Orlando-r. 11,14-Boris Karloff Tales of Mystery. 14-1st app. Xorkon. 12,15-Twilight Zone (TV). 16,19,22,25-Ripley's Believe It or Not. 17-Boris Karloff Tales of Mystery; Williamson-r; Orlando-r. 18,21,24-Twilight Zone (TV). 20,23,26-Boris Karloff Tales of Mystery 1.40 4.20 14.00
NOTE: *Dr. Spektor app.-#5, 10-12, 21. Durak app.-#15. Duroc app.-#14 (later called Durak). King George 1st app.-#8.*

MYSTERY IN SPACE (Also see Fireside Book Series)
National Periodical Publ.: 4-5/51 - No. 110, 9/66; No. 111, 9/80 - No. 117, 3/81 (#1-3: 52 pgs.)

1-Frazetta-a, 8 pgs.; Knights of the Galaxy begins, ends #8 200.00 600.00 2600.00
2 83.00 250.00 1000.00
3 67.00 200.00 800.00
4,5 54.00 162.00 650.00
6-10: 7-Toth-a 45.00 135.00 540.00

GD25 FN65 NM94

11-15: 13-Toth-a 34.00 102.00 380.00
16-18,20-25: Interplanetary Insurance feature by Infantino in all. 21-1st app. Space Cabbie. 24-Last pre-code issue 31.00 93.00 340.00
19-Virgil Finlay-a 33.00 100.00 370.00
26-40: 26-Space Cabbie feature begins. 34-1st S.A. issue 28.00 84.00 280.00
41-52: 47-Space Cabbie feature ends 21.00 63.00 210.00

GD25 FN65 VF82 NM94

53-Adam Strange begins (8/59, 10pg. sty); robot-c 133.00 400.00 800.00 1600.00

GD25 FN65 NM94

54 37.00 111.00 410.00
55-Grey tone-c 28.00 84.00 280.00
56-60: 59-Kane/Anderson-a 20.00 60.00 200.00
61-71: 61-1st app. Adam Strange foe Ulthoon. 62-1st app. A.S. foe Mortan. 63-Origin Vandor. 66-Star Rovers begin (1st app.). 68-1st app. Dust Devils (6/61). 69-1st Mailbag. 70-2nd app. Dust Devils. 71-Last 10¢ issue 15.50 47.00 155.00
72-74,76-80 11.00 33.00 110.00
75-JLA x-over in Adam Strange (5/62)(sequel to JLA #3) 23.50 70.00 235.00
81-86 7.50 22.50 75.00
87-(11/63)-Adam Strange/Hawkman double feat begins; 3rd Hawkman tryout series 18.50 55.00 185.00
88-Adam Strange & Hawkman stories 16.50 50.00 165.00
89-Adam Strange & Hawkman stories 15.50 47.00 155.00
90-Adam Strange & Hawkman team-up for 1st time (3/64); Hawkman moves to own title next month 17.50 52.00 175.00
91-103: 91-End Infantino art on Adam Strange; double-length Adam Strange story. 92-Space Ranger begins (6/64), ends #103. 92-94,96,98-Space Ranger-c. 94,98-Adam Strange/Space Ranger team-up. 102-Adam Strange ends (no Space Ranger). 103-Origin Ultra, the Multi-Alien; last Space Ranger 3.50 10.50 35.00
104-110: 110-(9/66)-Last 12¢ issue 2.50 7.50 22.00
V17#111(9/80)-117: 117-Newton-a(3 pgs.) 5.00
NOTE: ***Anderson** a-2, 4, 8-10, 12-17, 19, 45-48, 51, 57, 59i, 61-64, 70, 76, 87-91; c-9, 10, 15-25, 87, 89, 105-108, 110. **Aparo** a-111. **Austin** a-112i. **Bolland** a-115. **Craig** a-114, 116. **Ditko** a-111, 114-116. **Drucker** a-13, 14. **Elias** a-98, 102, 103. **Golden** a-113p. **Sid Greene** a-78, 91. **Infantino** a-1-8, 11, 14-25, 27-46, 48, 49, 51, 53-91, 103, 117; c-60-86, 88, 90, 91, 105, 107. **Gil Kane** a-14p, 15p, 18p, 19p, 26p, 29-59p(most), 100-102; c-52, 101. **Kubert** a-113; c-111-115. **Moriera** c-27, 28. **Rogers** a-111. **Sekowsky** a-52. **Simon & Kirby** a-4(2 pgs.). **Spiegle** a-111, 114. **Starlin** c-116. **Sutton** a-112. **Tuska** a-115p, 117p.*

MYSTERY MEN COMICS
Fox Features Syndicate: Aug, 1939 - No. 31, Feb, 1942

1-Intro. & 1st app. The Blue Beetle, The Green Mask, Rex Dexter of Mars by Briefer, Zanzibar by Tuska, Lt. Drake, D-13-Secret Agent by Powell, Chen Chang, Wing Turner, & Captain Denny Scott 940.00 2820.00 9400.00
2-Robot & sci/fi-c (2nd Robot-c w/Movie #6) 274.00 822.00 2600.00
3 (10/39)-Classic Lou Fine-c 330.00 990.00 3300.00
4,5: 4-Capt. Savage begins (11/39) 218.00 654.00 1850.00
6-Tuska-c 182.00 546.00 1550.00
7-1st Blue Beetle-c app. 218.00 654.00 1850.00
8-Lou Fine-c 194.00 582.00 1650.00
9-The Moth begins; Lou Fine-c 97.00 291.00 825.00
10-12: All Joe Simon-c. 10-Wing Turner by Kirby; Simon-c. 11-Intro. Domino 85.00 255.00 725.00
13-Intro. Lynx & sidekick Blackie (8/40) 56.00 168.00 475.00
14-18 54.00 162.00 455.00
19-Intro. & 1st app. Miss X (ends #21) 55.00 165.00 470.00
20-31: 26-The Wraith begins 49.00 147.00 415.00
NOTE: ***Briefer** a-1-15, 20, 24; c-9. **Cuidera** a-22. **Lou Fine** c-1-5,8,9. **Powell** a-1-15, 24. **Simon** c-10-12. **Tuska** a-1-16, 22, 24, 27; c-6. Bondage-c 1, 3, 7, 8, 25, 27-29, 31. Blue Beetle c-7, 8, 10-31. D-13 Secret Agent c-6. Green Mask c-1, 3-5. Rex Dexter of Mars c-2, 9.*

MYSTERY PLAY, THE
DC Comics (Vertigo): 1994 ($19.95, one-shot)

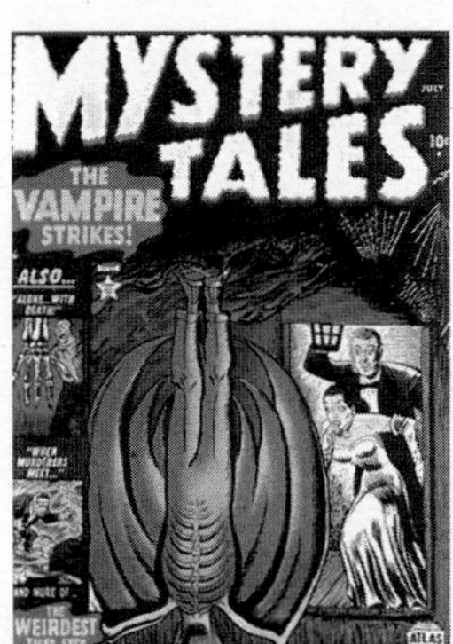

Mystery Tales #3 © MAR

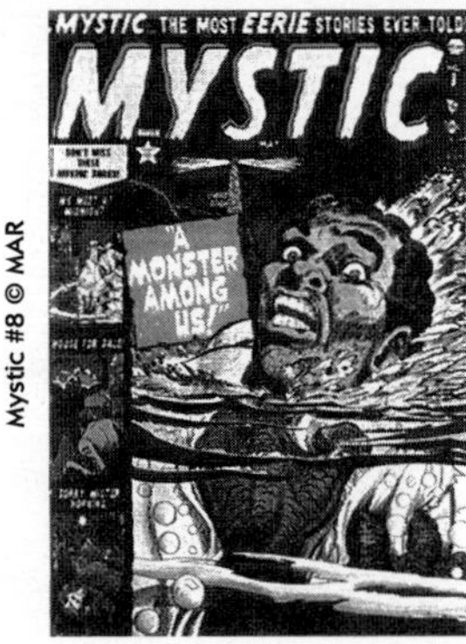

Mystic #8 © MAR

Mythography #8 © Bardic Press

GD25 FN65 NM94

nn-Hardcover-Morrison-s/Muth-painted art 25.00
Softcover ($9.95)-New Muth cover 9.95

MYSTERY TALES
Atlas Comics (20CC): Mar, 1952 - No. 54, Aug, 1957

1-Horror/weird stories in all 71.00 212.00 600.00
2-Krigstein-a 39.00 117.00 310.00
3-10: 6-A-Bomb panel. 10-Story similar to "The Assassin" from Shock SuspenStories 32.00 96.00 240.00
11,13-21: 14-Maneely s/f story. 20-Electric chair issue. 21-Matt Fox-a; decapitation story 23.00 70.00 175.00
12,22: 12-Matt Fox-a. 22-Forte/Matt Fox-c; a(i) 25.00 74.00 185.00
23-26 (2/55)-Last precode issue 18.00 54.00 135.00
27,29-35,37,38,41-43,48,49: 43-Morisi story contains Frazetta art swipes from Untamed Love 14.00 42.00 105.00
28,36,39,40,45: 28-Jack Katz-a. 36,39-Krigstein-a. 40,45-Ditko-a (#45 is 3 pgs. only) 15.00 44.00 110.00
44,46,47,51: 44,51-Williamson/Krenkel-a 16.00 48.00 120.00
46-Williamson/Krenkel-a; Crandall text illos 16.00 48.00 120.00
47-Crandall, Ditko, Powell-a 16.00 48.00 120.00
50-Torres, Morrow-a 15.00 44.00 110.00
52,53 13.00 40.00 100.00
54-Crandall, Check-a 14.00 42.00 105.00

NOTE: ***Ayers** a-18, 49, 52. **Berg** a-17, 51. **Colan** a-1, 3, 18, 35, 43. **Colletta** a-18. **Drucker** a-41. **Everett** a-2, 29, 33, 35, 41; c-8-11, 14, 38, 39, 41, 43, 44, 46, 48-51, 53. **Fass** a-16. **Forte** a-21, 22, 45, 46. **Matt Fox** a-12?, 21, 22; c-22. **Heath** a-3; c-3, 15, 17, 26. **Heck** a-25. **Kinstler** a-15. **Mort Lawrence** a-26, 32, 34. **Maneely** a-1, 9, 14, 22; c-12, 23, 24, 27. **Mooney** a-3, 40. **Morisi** a-43, 49, 52. **Morrow** a-50. **Orlando** a-51. **Pakula** a-16. **Powell** a-21, 29, 37, 38, 47. **Reinman** a-1, 14, 17. **Robinson** a-7p, 42. **Romita** a-37. **Roussos** a-4, 44. **R.Q. Sale** a-45, 46, 49. **Severin** c-52. **Shores** a-17, 45. **Tuska** a-10, 12, 14. **Whitney** a-2. **Wildey** a-37.*

MYSTERY TALES
Super Comics: 1964

Super Reprint #16,17('64): 16-r/Tales of Horror #2. 17-r/Eerie #14(Avon), 18-Kubert-r/Strange Terrors #4 1.75 5.25 14.00

MYSTIC (3rd Series)
Marvel/Atlas Comics (CLDS 1/CSI 2-21/OMC 22-35/CSI 35-61): March, 1951 - No. 61, Aug, 1957

1-Atom bomb panels; horror/weird stories in all 75.00 226.00 640.00
2 43.00 129.00 350.00
3-Eyes torn out 37.00 110.00 275.00
4- "The Devil Birds" by Wolverton (6 pgs.) 63.00 189.00 535.00
5,7-10 27.00 80.00 200.00
6- "The Eye of Doom" by Wolverton (7 pgs.) 63.00 189.00 535.00
11-20: 16-Bondage/torture c/story 23.00 70.00 175.00
21-25,27-36-Last precode (3/55). 25-E.C. swipe 18.00 54.00 135.00
26-Atomic War, severed head stories 19.00 56.00 140.00
37-51,53-57,61: 57-Story "Trapped in the Ant-Hill" (1957) is very similar to "The Man in the Ant Hill" in TTA #27 15.00 44.00 110.00
52-Wood-a; Crandall-a? 17.00 50.00 125.00
58,59-Krigstein-a 15.00 46.00 115.00
60-Williamson/Mayo-a (4 pgs.) 15.00 46.00 115.00

NOTE: ***Andru** a-23, 25. **Ayers** a-35, 53; c-8. **Berg** a-49. **Cameron** a-49, 51. **Check** a-31, 60. **Colan** a-3, 7, 12, 21, 37, 60. **Colletta** a-29. **Drucker** a-46, 52, 56. **Everett** a-8, 9, 17, 40, 44, 57; c-13, 18, 21, 42, 47, 49, 51-55, 57-59, 61. **Forte** a-35, 52, 58. **Fox** a-24i. **Al Hartley** a-35. **Heath** a-10; c-10, 20, 22, 23, 25, 30. **Infantino** a-12. **Kane** a-8, 24p. **Jack Katz** a-31, 33. **Mort Law.rence** a-19, 37. **Maneely** a-22, 24, 58; c-7, 15, 28, 29, 31. **Moldoff** a-29. **Morisi** a-48, 49, 52. **Morrow** a-51. **Orlando** a-57, 61. **Pakula** a-52, 57, 59. **Powell** a-52, 54-56. **Robinson** a-5. **Romita** a-11, 15. **R.Q. Sale** a-35, 53, 58. **Sekowsky** a-1, 2, 4, 5. **Severin** c-56, 60. **Tuska** a-15. **Whitney** a-33. **Wildey** a-28, 30. **Ed Win** a-17, 20. Canadian reprints known-title 'Startling.'*

MYSTICAL TALES
Atlas Comics (CCC 1/EPI 2-8): June, 1956 - No. 8, Aug, 1957

1-Everett-c/a 39.00 117.00 310.00
2,4: 2-Berg-a 21.00 64.00 160.00
3,5: 3,4-Crandall-a. 5-Williamson-a (4 pgs.) 22.00 66.00 165.00
6-Torres, Krigstein-a 21.00 62.00 155.00

GD25 FN65 NM94

7-Bolle, Forte, Torres, Orlando-a 20.00 60.00 150.00
8-Krigstein, Check-a 18.00 54.00 135.00

NOTE: ***Everett** a-1; c-1-4, 6, 7. **Orlando** a-1, 2, 7. **Pakula** a-3. **Powell** a-1, 4.*

MYSTIC COMICS (1st Series)
Timely Comics (TPI 1-5/TCI 8-10): March, 1940 - No. 10, Aug, 1942

GD25 FN65 VF82 NM94

1-Origin The Blue Blaze, The Dynamic Man, & Flexo the Rubber Robot; Zephyr Jones, 3X's & Deep Sea Demon app.; The Magician begins (all 1st app.); c-from Spider pulp V18#1, 6/39 1090.00 3272.00 6540.00 12,000.00

GD25 FN65 NM94

2-The Invisible Man & Master Mind Excello begin; Space Rangers, Zara of the Jungle, Taxi Taylor app. 326.00 978.00 3100.00
3-Origin Hercules, who last appears in #4 253.00 760.00 2400.00
4-Origin The Thin Man & The Black Widow; Merzak the Mystic app.; last Flexo, Dynamic Man, Invisible Man & Blue Blaze (some issues have date sticker on cover; others have July w/August overprint in silver color); Roosevelt assassination-c 274.00 822.00 2600.00
5-(3/41)-Origin The Black Marvel, The Blazing Skull, The Sub-Earth Man, Super Slave & The Terror; The Moon Man & Black Widow app.; 5-German war-c begin, end #10 253.00 760.00 2400.00
6-(10/41)-Origin The Challenger & The Destroyer (1st app.?; also see All-Winners #2, Fall, 1941) 270.00 810.00 2700.00
7-The Witness begins (12/41, origin & 1st app.); origin Davey & the Demon; last Black Widow; Hitler opens his trunk of terror-c by Simon & Kirby (classic-c) 280.00 840.00 2800.00
8,9: 9-Gary Gaunt app.; last Black Marvel, Mystic & Blazing Skull; Hitler-c 165.00 495.00 1400.00
10-Father Time, World of Wonder, & Red Skeleton app.; last Challenger & Terror 165.00 495.00 1400.00

NOTE: ***Gabrielle** c-8-10. **Kirby/Schomburg** c-6. **Rico** a-9(2). **Schomburg** a-1-4; c-1-5. **Sekowsky** a-9. **Sekowsky/Klein** a-8(Challenger). Bondage c-1, 2, 9.*

MYSTIC COMICS (2nd Series)
Timely Comics (ANC): Oct, 1944 - No. 3, Win, 1944-45; No. 4, Mar, 1945

1-The Angel, The Destroyer, The Human Torch, Terry Vance the Schoolboy Sleuth, & Tommy Tyme begin 194.00 582.00 1650.00
2-(Fall/44)-Last Human Torch & Terry Vance; bondage/hypo-c 100.00 300.00 850.00
3-Last Angel (two stories) & Tommy Tyme 97.00 291.00 825.00
4-The Young Allies-c & app.; Schomburg-c 91.00 273.00 775.00

MYSTIC EDGE (Manga)
Antarctic Press: Oct, 1998 ($2.95, one-shot)

1-Ryan Kinnaird-s/a/c 2.95

MYSTIQUE & SABRETOOTH (Sabretooth and Mystique on-c)
Marvel Comics: Dec, 1996 - No. 4, Mar, 1997 ($1.95, limited series)

1-4: Characters from X-Men 2.00

MY STORY (...True Romances in Pictures #5,6) (Formerly Zago)
Hero Books (Fox Features Syndicate): No. 5, May, 1949 - No. 12, Aug, 1950

5-Kamen/Feldstein-a 16.00 48.00 120.00
6-8,11,12: 12-Photo-c 8.00 24.00 56.00
9,10-Wood-a 15.00 44.00 110.00

MYTHOGRAPHY
Bardic Press: Sept, 1996 - Present ($3.95, B&W, anthology)

1-3: 1-Drew Hayes-s/a .85 2.60 7.00
4,5,7-($4.25) 4.25
6,8-($3.95) 4.00

MYTHOS: THE FINAL TOUR
DC Comics/Vertigo: Dec, 1996 - No. 3, Feb, 1997 ($5.95, limited series)

1-3: 1-Ney Rieber-s/Amaro-a. 2-Snejbjerg-a; Constantine-app. 3-Kristiansen-a; Black Orchid-app. 2.00 6.00

MY TRUE LOVE (Formerly Western Killers #64; Frank Buck #70 on)

The 'Nam #65 © MAR

Namor, The Sub-Mariner #52 © MAR

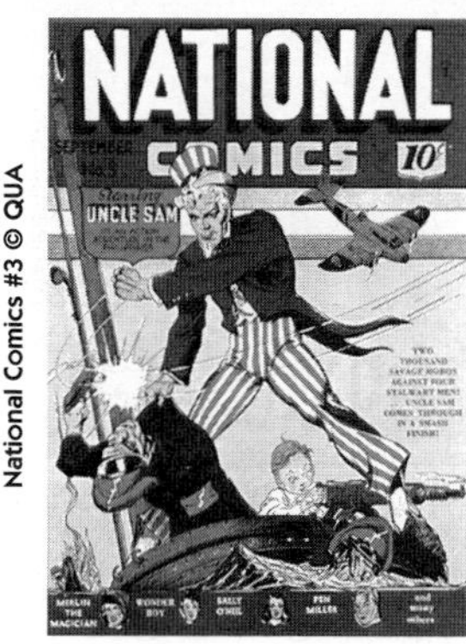

National Comics #3 © QUA

Fox Features Syndicate: No. 65, July, 1949 - No. 69, March, 1950

	GD25	FN65	NM94
65	11.00	34.00	85.00
66,68,69: 69-Morisi-a	7.50	22.50	52.00
67-Wood-a	15.00	45.00	110.00

NAKED PREY, THE (See Movie Classics)

'NAM, THE (See Savage Tales #1, 2nd series & Punisher Invades...)
Marvel Comics Group: Dec, 1986 - No. 84, Sept, 1993

	GD25	FN65	NM94
1-Golden a(p)/c begins, ends #13			1.50
1 (2nd printing)			1.00
2-7: 7-Golden-a (2 pgs.)			1.50
8-64: 32-Death R. Kennedy. 52,53-Frank Castle (The Punisher) app. 52,53-Gold 2nd printings. 58-Silver logo			1.25
65-74,76-84: 65-Heath-c/a; begin $1.75-c. 67-69-Punisher 3 part story. 70-Lomax scripts begin			1.50
75-($2.25, 52 pgs.)			2.25
Trade Paperback 1,2: 1-r/#1-4. 2-r/#5-8			4.50

'NAM MAGAZINE, THE
Marvel Comics: Aug, 1988 - No. 10, May, 1989 ($2.00, B&W, 52pgs.)

	GD25	FN65	NM94
1-10: Each issue reprints 2 of the comic		.80	2.00

NAMELESS, THE
Image Comics: May, 1997 - No. 5, Sept, 1997 ($2.95, B&W)

	GD25	FN65	NM94
1-5: Pruett/Hester-s/a			3.00

NAMORA (See Marvel Mystery Comics #82 & Sub-Mariner Comics)
Marvel Comics (PrPl): Fall, 1948 - No. 3, Dec, 1948

	GD25	FN65	NM94
1-Sub-Mariner x-over in Namora; Namora by Everett(2), Sub-Mariner by Rico (10 pgs.)	194.00	582.00	1650.00
2-The Blonde Phantom & Sub-Mariner story; Everett-a	112.00	336.00	950.00
3-(Scarce)-Sub-Mariner app.; Everett-a	112.00	336.00	950.00

NAMOR, THE SUB-MARINER (See Prince Namor & Sub-Mariner)
Marvel Comics: Apr, 1990 - No. 62, May, 1995 ($1.00/$1.25/$1.50)

	GD25	FN65	NM94
1-Byrne-c/a/scripts in 1-25 (scripts only #26-32)			3.00
2-5: 5-Iron Man app.			1.50
6-11: 8,10,16-Re-intro Iron Fist (8-cameo only)			1.25
12-($1.50, 52 pgs.)-Re-intro. The Invaders			1.75
13-22: 18-Punisher cameo (1 panel); 21-23,25-Wolverine cameos. 22-Last $1.00-c. 22,23-Iron Fist app.			1.00
23-25: 24-Namor vs. Wolverine			1.25
26-New look for Namor w/new costume; 1st Jae Lee-c/a this title (5/92) & begins			3.00
27-30: 28-Iron Fist-c/story			2.00
31-36,38-49: 31-Dr. Doom-c/story. 33,34-Iron Fist cameo. 35-New Tiger Shark-c/story. 48-The Thing app.			1.25
37-($2.00)-Aqua holo-grafx foil-c			2.25
50-($1.75, 52 pgs.)-Newsstand edition; w/bound-in S-M trading card sheet (both versions)			1.75
50-($2.95, 52 pgs.)-Collector edition w/foil-c			3.00
51-62: 51-Begin $1.50-c			1.50
Annual 1 (1991, $2.00, 68 pgs.)-3 pg. origin recap			2.00
Annual 2 (1992, $2.25, 68 pgs.)-Return/Defenders			2.25
Annual 3 (1993, $2.95, 68 pgs.)-Bagged w/card			3.00
Annual 4 (1994, $2.95, 68 pgs.)-Painted-c			3.00

NOTE: *Jae Lee a-26-30p, 31-37, 38p, 39, 40; c-26-40.*

NANCY AND SLUGGO (See Comics On Parade & Sparkle Comics)
United Features Syndicate: No. 16, 1949 - No. 23, 1954

	GD25	FN65	NM94
16(#1)	6.50	19.50	45.00
17-23	4.25	13.00	28.00

NANCY & SLUGGO (Nancy #146-173; formerly Sparkler Comics)
St. John/Dell #146-187/Gold Key #188 on: No. 121, Apr, 1955-No. 192, Oct, 1963

	GD25	FN65	NM94
121(4/55)(St. John)	5.70	17.00	35.00
122-145(7/57)(St. John)	4.25	13.00	26.00
146(9/57)-Peanuts begins, ends #192 (Dell)	3.50	11.00	38.00
147-161 (Dell)	2.75	8.00	30.00
162-165,177-180-John Stanley-a	6.40	19.00	70.00
166-176-Oona & Her Haunted House series; Stanley-a	7.00	22.00	80.00
181-187(3-5/62)(Dell)	2.90	8.70	32.00
188(10/62)-192 (Gold Key)	3.25	10.00	36.00
Four Color 1034(9-11/59)-Summer Camp	3.25	10.00	36.00

(See Dell Giant #34, 45 & Dell Giants)

NANNY AND THE PROFESSOR (TV)
Dell Publishing Co.: Aug, 1970 - No. 2, Oct, 1970 (Photo-c)

	GD25	FN65	NM94
1(01-546-008), 2	2.75	8.00	30.00

NAPOLEON
Dell Publishing Co.: No. 526, Dec, 1953

	GD25	FN65	NM94
Four Color 526	1.80	5.50	20.00

NAPOLEON & SAMANTHA (See Walt Disney Showcase No. 10)

NAPOLEON & UNCLE ELBY (See Clifford McBride's...)
Eastern Color Printing Co.: July, 1942 (68 pgs.) (One Shot)

	GD25	FN65	NM94
1	36.00	108.00	270.00
1945-American Book-Strafford Press (128 pgs.) (8x10-1/2"; B&W reprints; hardcover)	12.00	36.00	90.00

NARRATIVE ILLUSTRATION, THE STORY OF THE COMICS
M.C. Gaines: Summer, 1942 (32 pgs., 7-1/4"x10", B&W w/color inserts)

nn-16pgs. text with illustrations of ancient art, strips and comic covers; 4 pg. WWII War Bond promo, "The Minute Man Answers the Call" color comic drawn by Shelly and a special 8-page color comic insert of "The Story of Saul" from Picture Stories from the Bible #1 or soon to appear in PS #1. Insert has special title page indicating it was No. 10 of a Sunday newspaper supplement insert series that had already run in a New England "Sunday Herald." (very rare; only two known copies.) Estimated value... 1,100.00

NATHANIEL DUSK
DC Comics: Feb, 1984 - No. 4, May, 1984 ($1.25, mini-series, direct sales, Baxter paper)

	GD25	FN65	NM94
1-4: 1-Intro/origin; Gene Colan-c/a in all			1.25

NATHANIEL DUSK II
DC Comics: Oct, 1985 - No. 4, Jan, 1986 ($2.00, mini-series, Baxter paper)

	GD25	FN65	NM94
1-4: Gene Colan-c/a in all			2.00

NATIONAL COMICS
Quality Comics Group: July, 1940 - No. 75, Nov, 1949

	GD25	FN65	NM94
1-Uncle Sam begins (1st app.); origin sidekick Buddy by Eisner; origin Wonder Boy & Kid Dixon; Merlin the Magician (ends #45); Cyclone, Kid Patrol, Sally O'Neil Policewoman, Pen Miller (by Klaus Nordling; ends #22), Prop Powers (ends #26), & Paul Bunyan (ends #22) begin	440.00	1320.00	4400.00
2	200.00	600.00	1700.00
3-Last Eisner Uncle Sam	141.00	423.00	1200.00
4-Last Cyclone	112.00	336.00	950.00
5-(11/40)-Quicksilver begins (1st app.)(3rd w/lightning speed?); origin Uncle Sam; bondage-c	126.00	378.00	1075.00
6,8-11: 8-Jack & Jill begins (ends #22). 9-Flag-c	112.00	336.00	950.00
7-Classic Lou Fine-c	176.00	528.00	1500.00
12	85.00	255.00	725.00
13-16-Lou Fine-a	76.00	228.00	650.00
17,19-22: 22-Last Pen Miller (moves to Crack #23)	56.00	168.00	475.00
18-(12/41)-Shows orientals attacking Pearl Harbor; on stands one month before actual event	103.00	309.00	875.00
23-The Unknown & Destroyer 171 begin	58.00	174.00	490.00
24-Japanese War-c	55.00	165.00	470.00

National Comics #43 © QUA

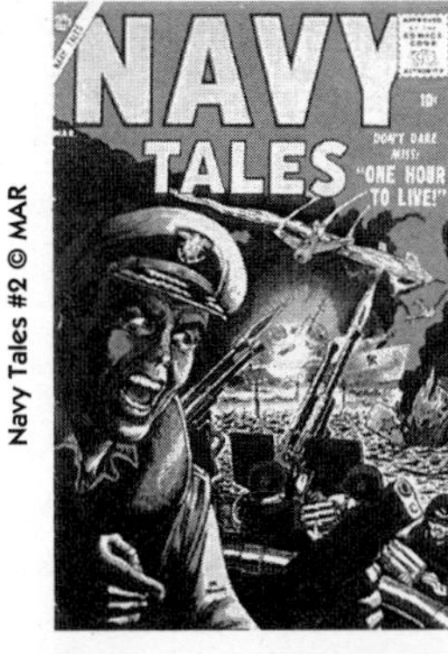

Navy Tales #2 © MAR

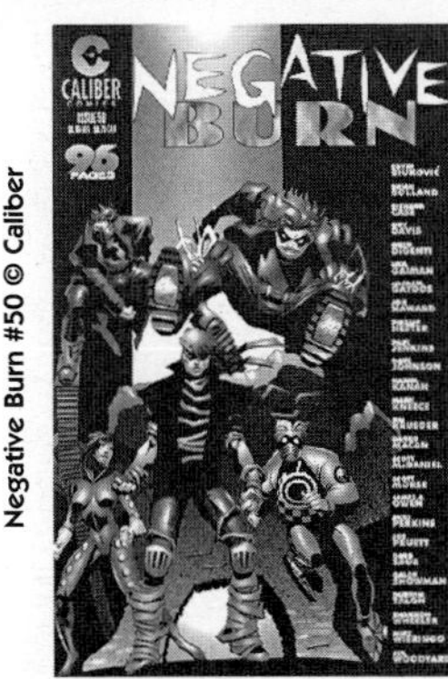

Negative Burn #50 © Caliber

	GD25	FN65	NM94
25,26,28,30: 26-Wonder Boy ends	41.00	124.00	330.00
27-G-2 the Unknown begins (ends #46)	41.00	124.00	330.00
29-Origin The Unknown	41.00	124.00	330.00
31-33: 33-Chic Carter begins (ends #47)	39.00	117.00	300.00
34-40: 35-Last Kid Patrol. 39-Hitler-c	31.00	92.00	230.00
41-50: 42-The Barker begins (1st app?, 5/44); The Barker covers begin. 48-Origin The Whistler	19.00	56.00	140.00
51-Sally O'Neil by Ward, 8 pgs. (12/45)	25.00	74.00	185.00
52-60	15.00	46.00	115.00
61-67: 67-Format change; Quicksilver app.	11.00	34.00	85.00
68-75: The Barker ends	9.30	28.00	65.00

NOTE: ***Cole** Quicksilver-13; Barker-43; c-43, 46, 47, 49-51. **Crandall** Uncle Sam-11-13 (with **Fine**), 25, 26; c-24-26, 30-33, 43. **Crandall** Paul Bunyan-10-13. **Fine** Uncle Sam-13 (w/**Crandall**), 17, 18; c-1-14, 16, 18, 21. **Gill Fox** c-69-74. **Guardineer** Quicksilver-27, 35. **Gustavson** Quicksilver-14-26. **McWilliams** a-23-28, 55, 57. Uncle Sam c-1-41. Barker c-42-75.*

NATIONAL CRUMB, THE (Magazine-Size)
Mayfair Publications: August, 1975 (52 pgs., B&W) (Satire)

	GD25	FN65	NM94
1-Grandenetti-c/a, Ayers-a	1.00	3.00	10.00

NATIONAL VELVET (TV)
Dell Publishing Co./Gold Key: May-July, 1961 - No. 2, Mar, 1963 (All photo-c)

	GD25	FN65	NM94
Four Color 1195 (#1)	5.50	16.50	60.00
Four Color 1312	2.75	8.00	30.00
01-556-207, 12-556-210 (Dell)	2.75	8.00	30.00
1(12/62), 2(3/63) (Gold Key)	3.20	9.50	35.00

NATION OF SNITCHES
Piranha Press (DC): 1990 ($4.95, color, 52 pgs.)

	GD25	FN65	NM94
nn			5.00

NATURE BOY (Formerly Danny Blaze; Li'l Rascal Twins #6 on)
Charlton Comics: No. 3, March, 1956 - No. 5, Feb, 1957

	GD25	FN65	NM94
3-Origin; Blue Beetle story; Buscema-c/a	20.00	60.00	150.00
4,5	15.00	44.00	110.00

NOTE: ***John Buscema** a-3, 4p, 5; c-3. **Powell** a-4.*

NATURE OF THINGS (Disney, TV/Movie)
Dell Publishing Co.: No. 727, Sept, 1956 - No. 842, Sept, 1957

	GD25	FN65	NM94
Four Color 727 (#1), 842-Jesse Marsh-a	4.50	13.50	50.00

NAUSICAA OF THE VALLEY OF WIND
Viz Comics: 1988 - No. 7, 1989; 1989 - No. 4, 1990 ($2.50, B&W, 68pgs.)

	GD25	FN65	NM94
Book 1-7: ($2.50) 1-Contains Moebius poster			2.50
Part II, Book 1-3 ($2.95)			3.00
Part II, Book 4 ($3.25)			3.25

NAVY ACTION (Sailor Sweeney #12-14)
Atlas Comics (CDS): Aug, 1954 - No. 11, Apr, 1956; No. 15, 1/57 - No. 18, 8/57

	GD25	FN65	NM94
1-Powell-a	14.00	42.00	105.00
2-Lawrence-a	8.00	24.00	55.00
3-11: 4-Last precode (2/55)	5.70	17.00	35.00
15-18	5.00	15.00	30.00

NOTE: ***Berg** a-7, 9. **Colan** a-8. **Drucker** a-7, 17. **Everett** a-3, 7, 16; c-16, 17. **Heath** c-1, 2, 6. **Maneely** a-7, 8, 18; c-9, 11. **Pakula** a-2, 3, 9. **Reinman** a-17.*

NAVY COMBAT
Atlas Comics (MPI): June, 1955 - No. 20, Oct, 1958

	GD25	FN65	NM94
1-Torpedo Taylor begins by Don Heck	14.00	42.00	105.00
2	8.00	24.00	55.00
3-10	5.70	17.00	35.00
11,13,15,16,18-20	5.35	16.00	32.00
12-Crandall-a	7.85	23.50	55.00
14-Torres-a	5.70	17.00	40.00
17-Williamson-a, 4 pgs.; Torres-a	5.70	17.00	42.00

NOTE: ***Berg** a-10, 11. **Colan** a-11. **Drucker** a-7. **Everett** a-3, 20; c-8 & 9 w/**Tuska**, 10, 13-16. **Heck** a-11(2). **Maneely** c-1, 6, 11, 17. **Morisi** a-8. **Pakula** a-7. **Powell** a-20.*

NAVY HEROES
Almanac Publishing Co.: 1945

	GD25	FN65	NM94
1-Heavy in propaganda	9.30	28.00	70.00

NAVY: HISTORY & TRADITION
Stokes Walesby Co./Dept. of Navy: 1958 - 1961 (nn) (Giveaway)

	GD25	FN65	NM94
1772-1778, 1778-1782, 1782-1817, 1817-1865, 1865-1936, 1940-1945: 1772-1778-16 pg. in color	4.25	13.00	28.00
1861: Naval Actions of the Civil War: 1865-36 pg. in color; flag-c	4.25	13.00	28.00

NAVY PATROL
Key Publications: May, 1955 - No. 4, Nov, 1955

	GD25	FN65	NM94
1	5.70	17.00	35.00
2-4	4.00	10.00	20.00

NAVY TALES
Atlas Comics (CDS): Jan, 1957 - No. 4, July, 1957

	GD25	FN65	NM94
1-Everett-c; Berg, Powell-a	12.00	36.00	90.00
2-Williamson/Mayo-a(5 pgs); Crandall-a	11.00	32.00	80.00
3,4-Reinman-a; Severin-c. 4-Crandall-a	9.50	28.75	72.00

NOTE: ***Colan** a-4. **Maneely** c-2. **Sinnott** a-4.*

NAVY TASK FORCE
Stanmor Publications/Aragon Mag. No. 4-8: Feb, 1954 - No. 8, April, 1956

	GD25	FN65	NM94
1	6.35	19.00	40.00
2	4.00	11.00	22.00
3-8: #8-r/Navy Patrol #1	3.60	9.00	18.00

NAVY WAR HEROES
Charlton Comics: Jan, 1964 - No. 7, Mar-Apr, 1965

	GD25	FN65	NM94
1	2.50	7.50	22.00
2-7	1.75	5.25	14.00

NAZA (Stone Age Warrior)
Dell Publishing Co.: Nov-Jan, 1963-64 - No. 9, March, 1966

	GD25	FN65	NM94
12-555-401 (#1)-Painted-c	3.00	9.00	32.00
2-9: 2-4-Painted-c	2.50	7.50	22.00

NAZZ, THE
DC Comics: 1990 - No. 4, 1991 ($4.95, 52 pgs., mature)

	GD25	FN65	NM94
1-4			5.00

NEBBS, THE (Also see Crackajack Funnies)
Dell Publishing Co./Croydon Publishing Co.: 1941; 1945

	GD25	FN65	NM94
Large Feature Comic 23(1941)	13.00	40.00	145.00
1(1945, 36 pgs.)-Reprints	10.00	30.00	75.00

NECROMANCER: THE GRAPHIC NOVEL
Marvel Comics (Epic Comics): 1989 ($8.95)

	GD25	FN65	NM94
nn	.90	2.70	9.00

NEGATIVE BURN
Caliber : 1993 - No. 50, 1997 ($2.95, B&W, anthology)

	GD25	FN65	NM94
1,2,4-12,26-30,32-35: Anthology by various including Bolland, Burden, Doran, Gaiman, Moebius, Moore, & Pope			4.00
3-Bone story	2.00	6.00	20.00
13-Strangers in Paradise story	2.00	6.00	20.00
25,31,36-47-($3.95): 25-Gaiman, Moore & Pope			4.00
48,49-($4.95)			4.95
50-($6.95, 96 pgs.)-Gaiman, Robinson, Bolland			6.95

NEGRO (See All-Negro)

NEGRO HEROES (Calling All Girls, Real Heroes, & True Comics reprints)
Parents' Magazine Institute: Spring, 1947 - No. 2, Summer, 1948

	GD25	FN65	NM94
1	74.00	221.00	625.00
2-Jackie Robinson-c/story	79.00	238.00	675.00

NEGRO ROMANCE (Negro Romances #4)

Neil Gaiman's Wheel of Worlds #0 © Big Ent. Inc.

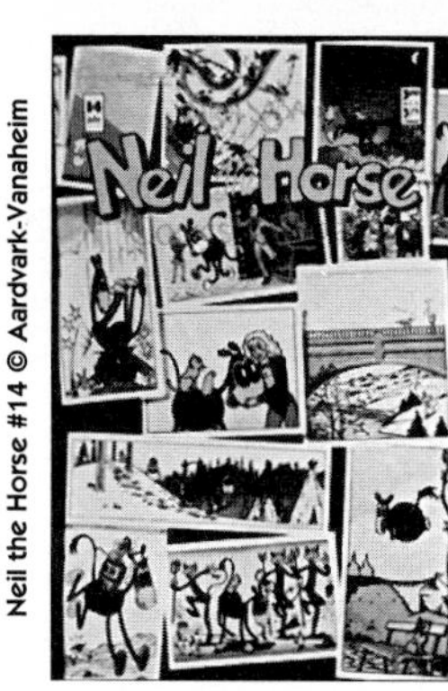
Neil the Horse #14 © Aardvark-Vanaheim

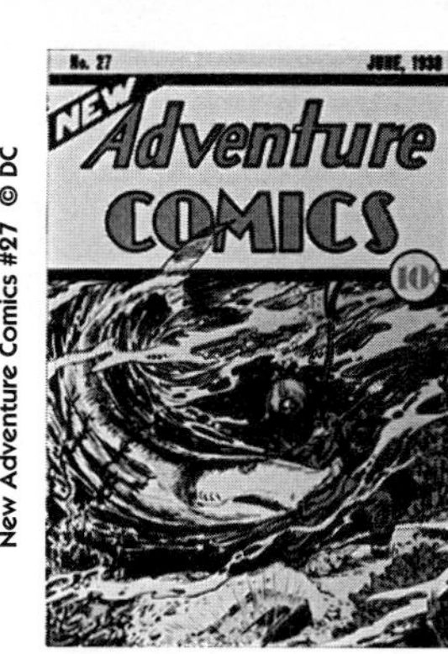

New Adventure Comics #27 © DC

GD25 FN65 NM94

Fawcett Publications: June, 1950 - No. 3, Oct, 1950 (All photo-c)

	GD25	FN65	NM94
1-Evans-a	97.00	291.00	825.00
2,3	77.00	230.00	650.00

NEGRO ROMANCES (Formerly Negro Romance; Romantic Secrets #5 on)
Charlton Comics: No. 4, May, 1955

	GD25	FN65	NM94
4-Reprints Fawcett #2	60.00	180.00	510.00

NEIL GAIMAN AND CHARLES VESS' STARDUST
DC Comics (Vertigo): 1997 - No. 4, 1998 ($5.95/$6.95, square-bound, lim. series)

	GD25	FN65	NM94
1-3: Gaiman text with Vess paintings in all		2.00	6.00
4-($6.95)	.85	2.60	7.00

NEIL GAIMAN'S LADY JUSTICE
Tekno Comix: Sept, 1995 - No. 11, May, 1996 ($1.95/$2.25)

	GD25	FN65	NM94
1-($2.25)-Sienkiewicz-c; pin-ups			2.25
1-5-($1.95): Brereton-c in all.			2.00
6-11: 6-Begin $2.25-c. 7-polybagged. 11-Includes The Big Bang Pt. 7			2.25

NEIL GAIMAN'S LADY JUSTICE
BIG Entertainment: V2#1, June, 1996 - No. 9, Feb, 1997 ($2.25)

	GD25	FN65	NM94
V2#1-9: Dan Brereton-c on all. 6-8-Dan Brereton script			2.25

NEIL GAIMAN'S MR. HERO-THE NEWMATIC MAN
Tekno Comix: Mar, 1995 - No. 17, May, 1996 ($1.95/$2.25)

	GD25	FN65	NM94
1-Intro Mr. Hero & Teknophage; bound-in game piece and trading card			2.50
2-11: 4-w/Steel edition Neil Gaiman's Teknophage #1 coupon			2.00
12-17: 12-Begin $2.25-c. 13-polybagged.			2.25

NEIL GAIMAN'S MR. HERO-THE NEWMATIC MAN
BIG Entertainment: V2#1, June, 1996 ($2.25)

	GD25	FN65	NM94
V2#1-Teknophage destroys Mr. Hero; includes The Big Bang Pt. 10			2.25

NEIL GAIMAN'S PHAGE-SHADOWDEATH
BIG Entertainment: June, 1996 - No. 6, Nov, 1996 ($2.25, limited series)

	GD25	FN65	NM94
1-6: Bryan Talbot-c & scripts in all. 1-1st app. Orlando Holmes			2.25

NEIL GAIMAN'S TEKNOPHAGE
Tekno Comix: Aug, 1995 - No. 10, Mar, 1996 ($1.95/$2.25)

	GD25	FN65	NM94
1-6-Rick Veitch scripts & Bryan Talbot-c/a.			2.00
1-Steel Edition			5.00
7-10: Paul Jenkins scripts in all. 7-$2.25-c begins. 8-polybagged			2.25

NEIL GAIMAN'S WHEEL OF WORLDS
Tekno Comix: Apr, 1995 - No. 1, May, 1996 ($2.95/$3.25)

	GD25	FN65	NM94
0-1st app. Lady Justice; 48 pgs.; bound-in poster			3.00
0-Regular edition			2.00
1 ($3.25, 5/96)-Bruce Jones scripts; Lady Justice & Teknophage app.; computer-generated photo-c.			3.25

NEIL THE HORSE (See Charlton Bullseye #2)
Aardvark-Vanaheim #1-10/Renegade Press #11 on: 2/83 - No. 10, 12/84; No. 11, 4/85 - #15, 1985 (B&W)

	GD25	FN65	NM94
1($1.40)			2.00
1-2nd print			1.50
2-13: 13-Double size; 11,13-w/paperdolls			2.00
14,15: Double size ($3.00). 15 is a flip book(2-c)			3.00

NELLIE THE NURSE (Also see Gay Comics & Joker Comics)
Marvel/Atlas Comics (SPI/LMC): 1945 - No. 36, Oct, 1952; 1957

	GD25	FN65	NM94
1-(1945)	33.00	100.00	250.00
2-(Spring/46)	16.00	48.00	120.00
3,4: 3-New logo (9/46)	12.00	36.00	90.00
5-Kurtzman's "Hey Look" (3); Georgie app.	14.00	42.00	105.00
6-8,10: 7,8-Georgie app. 10-Millie app.	11.00	32.00	80.00
9-Wolverton-a (1 pg.); Mille the Model app.	11.00	34.00	85.00
11,14-16,18-Kurtzman's "Hey Look"	12.00	36.00	90.00
12- "Giggles 'n' Grins" by Kurtzman	11.00	32.00	80.00
13,17,19,20: 17-Annie Oakley app.	8.00	24.00	55.00
21-27,29,30	6.35	19.00	44.00
28-Mr. Nexdoor-r (3 pgs.) by Kurtzman/Rusty #22	7.00	21.00	48.00
31-36: 36-Post-c	5.70	17.00	38.00
1('57)-Leading Mag. (Atlas)-Everett-a, 20 pgs	7.00	21.00	48.00

NELLIE THE NURSE
Dell Publishing Co.: No. 1304, Mar-May, 1962

	GD25	FN65	NM94
Four Color 1304-Stanley-a	6.40	19.00	70.00

NEMESIS THE WARLOCK (Also see Spellbinders)
Eagle Comics: Sept, 1984 - No. 7, Mar, 1985 (limited series, Baxter paper)

	GD25	FN65	NM94
1-7: 2000 A.D. reprints			1.50

NEMESIS THE WARLOCK
Quality Comics/Fleetway Quality #2 on: 1989 - No. 19, 1991 ($1.95, B&W)

	GD25	FN65	NM94
1-19			2.00

NEURO JACK
BIG Entertainment Interactive: Aug, 1996 ($2.25)

	GD25	FN65	NM94
1-Digital art			2.25

NEUTRO
Dell Publishing Co.: Jan, 1967

	GD25	FN65	NM94
1-Jack Sparling-c/a (super hero)	2.40	7.00	26.00

NEVADA (See Zane Grey's Four Color 412, 996 & Zane Grey's Stories of the West #1)

NEVADA
DC Comics (Vertigo): May, 1998 - No. 6, Oct, 1998 ($2.50, limited series)

	GD25	FN65	NM94
1-6-Gerber-s/Winslade-c/a			2.50

NEVER AGAIN (War stories; becomes Soldier & Marine V2#9)
Charlton Comics: Aug, 1955 - No. 2, Oct?, 1955; No. 8, July, 1956 (No #3-7)

	GD25	FN65	NM94
1	6.50	19.50	45.00
2-(Becomes Fightin' Air Force #3), 8-(Formerly Foxhole?)	4.25	13.00	26.00

NEW ADVENTURE COMICS (Formerly New Comics; becomes Adventure Comics #32 on; V1#12 indicia says NEW COMICS #12)
National Periodical Publications: V1#12, Jan, 1937 - No. 31, Oct, 1938

	GD25	FN65	VF82	NM94
V1#12-Federal Men by Siegel & Shuster continues; Jor-L mentioned; Whitney Ellsworth-c begin, end #14	483.00	1450.00	3000.00	-
V2#1(2/37, #13)-(Rare)	450.00	1350.00	2800.00	-
V2#2 (#14)	400.00	1200.00	2500.00	-

	GD25	FN65		NM94
15(V2#3)-20(V2#8): 15-1st Adventure logo; Creig Flessel-c begin, end #31. 16-1st non-funny cover. 17-Nadir, Master of Magic begins, ends #30	350.00	1050.00	1750.00	2450.00
21(V2#9),22(V2#10, 2/37): 22-X-Mas-c	320.00	960.00	1600.00	2250.00
23-31	270.00	810.00	1350.00	1900.00

NEW ADVENTURE OF WALT DISNEY'S SNOW WHITE AND THE SEVEN DWARFS, A (See Snow White Bendix Giveaway)

NEW ADVENTURES OF ABRAHAM LINCOLN, THE
Image Comics (Homage): 1998 ($19.95, one-shot)

	GD25	FN65	NM94
1-Scott McCloud-s/computer art	2.00	6.00	20.00

NEW ADVENTURES OF CHARLIE CHAN, THE (TV)
National Periodical Publications: May-June, 1958 - No. 6, Mar-Apr, 1959

	GD25	FN65	NM94
1 (Scarce)-Gil Kane/Sid Greene-a in all	59.00	177.00	500.00
2 (Scarce)	42.00	127.00	340.00
3-6 (Scarce)-Greene/Giella-a	37.00	112.00	280.00

New Adventures of Superboy #5 © DC

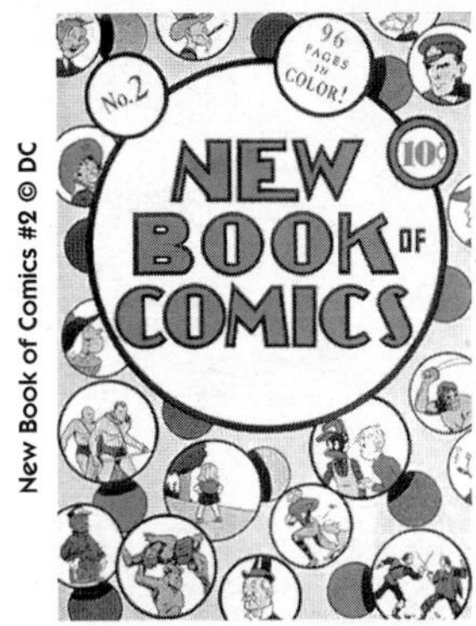

New Book of Comics #2 © DC

New Funnies #76 © DELL

GD25 FN65 NM94

NEW ADVENTURES OF HUCK FINN, THE (TV)
Gold Key: December, 1968 (Hanna-Barbera)

1- "The Curse of Thut"; part photo-c 2.90 8.70 32.00

NEW ADVENTURES OF PETER PAN (Disney)
Western Publishing Co.: 1953 (5x7-1/4", 36 pgs.) (Admiral giveaway)

nn 9.30 28.00 70.00

NEW ADVENTURES OF PINOCCHIO (TV)
Dell Publishing Co.: Oct-Dec, 1962 - No. 3, Sept-Nov, 1963

12-562-212(#1) 8.00 24.00 90.00
2,3 5.50 16.50 60.00

NEW ADVENTURES OF ROBIN HOOD (See Robin Hood)

NEW ADVENTURES OF SHERLOCK HOLMES (Also see Sherlock Holmes)
Dell Publishing Co.: No. 1169, Mar-May, 1961 - No. 1245, Nov-Jan, 1961/62

Four Color 1169(#1), 1245 14.00 44.00 160.00

NEW ADVENTURES OF SPEED RACER
Now Comics: Dec, 1993 - No. 7, 1994? ($1.95)

1-7 2.00
0-(Premiere)-3-D cover 3.00

NEW ADVENTURES OF SUPERBOY, THE (Also see Superboy)
DC Comics: Jan, 1980 - No. 54, June, 1984

1-54: 7-Has extra story "The Computers That Saved Metropolis" by Starlin (Radio Shack giveaway w/indicia). 11-Superboy gets new power. 14-Lex Luthor app. 15-Superboy gets new parents. 28-Dial "H" For Hero begins, ends #49. 45-47-1st app. Sunburst. 48-Begin 75¢-c. 50-Legion app. 1.00

NOTE: ***Buckler** a-9p; c-36p. **Giffen** a-50; c-50. 40i. **Gil Kane** c-32p, 33p, 35, 39, 41-49. **Miller** c-51. **Starlin** a-7. Krypto back-ups in 17, 22. Superbaby in 11, 14, 19, 24.*

NEW ADVENTURES OF THE PHANTOM BLOT, THE (See The Phantom Blot)

NEW AMERICA
Eclipse Comics: Nov, 1987 - No. 4, Feb, 1988 ($1.75, Baxter paper)

1-4: Scout limited series 1.80

NEW ARCHIES, THE (TV)
Archie Comic Publications: Oct, 1987 - No. 22, May, 1990 (75¢)

1 4.00
2-10: 3-Xmas issue 3.00
11-22: 17-22 (95¢-$1.00): 21-Xmas issue 2.00

NEW ARCHIES DIGEST (TV)(...Comics Digest Magazine #4?-10; ...Digest Magazine #11 on)
Archie Comics: May, 1988 - No. 14, July, 1991 ($1.35/$1.50, quarterly)

1 5.00
2-14: 6-Begin $1.50-c 3.00

NEW BOOK OF COMICS (Also see Big Book Of Fun)
National Periodical Publ.: 1937; No. 2, Spring, 1938 (100 pgs. each) (Reprints)

GD25 FN65 VF82 NM94

1(Rare)-1st regular size comic annual; 2nd DC annual; contains r/New Comics #1-4 & More Fun #9; r/Federal Men (8 pgs.), Henri Duval (1 pg.), & Dr. Occult in costume (1 pg.) by Siegel & Shuster; Moldoff, Sheldon Mayer (15 pgs.)-a 1833.00 5500.00 12,000.00 –

GD25 FN65 VF82 NM94

2-Contains-r/More Fun #15 & 16; r/Dr. Occult in costume (a Superman prototype), & Calling All Cars (4 pgs.) by Siegel & Shuster 916.00 2750.00 6000.00 –

NEW COMICS (New Adventure #12 on)
National Periodical Publ.: 12/35 - No. 11, 12/36 (No. 1-6: paper cover) (No. 1-5: 84 pgs.)

GD25 FN65 VF82 NM94

V1#1-Billy the Kid, Sagebrush 'n' Cactus, Jibby Jones, Needles, The Vikings, Sir Loin of Beef, Now-When I Was a Boy, & other 1-2 pg. strips; 2 pgs. Kelly art(1st)-(Gulliver's Travels); Sheldon Mayer-a(1st)(2 2pg. strips); Vincent Sullivan-c(1st) 2417.00 7250.00 16,000.00 –

2-1st app. Federal Men by Siegel & Shuster & begins (also see The Comics Magazine #2); Mayer, Kelly-a (Rare)(1/36) 916.00 2750.00 6000.00 –

3-6: 3,4-Sheldon Mayer-a which continues in The Comics Magazine #1. 3-Vincent Sullivan-c. 4-Dickens' "A Tale of Two Cities" adaptation begins. 5-Junior Federal Men Club; Kiefer-a. 6- "She" adaptation begins 550.00 1650.00 3500.00 –

7-11: 11-Christmas-c 433.00 1300.00 2800.00 –

NOTE: *#1-6 rarely occur in mint condition. **Whitney Ellsworth** c-4-11.*

NEW DEFENDERS (See Defenders)

NEW DNAGENTS, THE (Formerly DNAgents)
Eclipse Comics: V2#1, Oct, 1985 - V2#17, Mar, 1987 (Whole #s 25-40; Mando paper)

V2#1-12: 1-Origin recap. 7-Begin 95 cent-c. 9,10-Airboy preview 1.00
13-17 ($1.25) 1.25
3-D 1 (1/86, $2.25) 2.25
2-D 1 (1/86)-Limited ed. (100 copies) 4.00

NEWFORCE (Also see Newmen)
Image Comics (Extreme Studios): Jan, 1996-No. 4, Apr, 1996 ($2.50, lim. series)

1-4: 1-"Extreme Destroyer" Pt. 8; polybagged w/gaming card. 4-Newforce disbands. 2.50

NEW FUN COMICS (More Fun #7 on; see Big Book of Fun Comics)
National Periodical Publications: Feb, 1935 - No. 6, Oct, 1935 (10x15", No. 1-4,: slick-c) (No. 1-5: 36 pgs; 40 pgs. No. 6)

GD25 FN65 VF82 NM94

V1#1 (1st DC comic); 1st app. Oswald The Rabbit; Jack Woods (cowboy) begins 6170.00 18,500.00 38,000.00 –
2(3/35)-(Very Rare) 2590.00 7750.00 16,500.00 –
3-5(8/35): 3-Don Drake on the Planet Soro-c/story (sci/fi, 4/35). 5-Soft-c 1300.00 3900.00 8000.00 –
6(10/35)-1st Dr. Occult by Siegel & Shuster (Leger & Reuths); last "New Fun" title. "New Comics" #1 begins in Dec. which is reason for title change to More Fun; Henri Duval (ends #10) by Siegel & Shuster begins; paper-c 2917.00 8750.00 18,500.00 –

NEW FUNNIES (The Funnies #1-64; Walter Lantz...#109 on; New TV... #259, 260, 272, 273; TV Funnies #261-271)
Dell Publishing Co.: No. 65, July, 1942 - No. 288, Mar-Apr, 1962

GD25 FN65 NM94

65(#1)-Andy Panda in a world of real people, Raggedy Ann & Andy, Oswald the Rabbit (with Woody Woodpecker x-overs), Li'l Eight Ball & Peter Rabbit begin 61.00 184.00 675.00
66-70: 66-Felix the Cat begins. 67-Billy & Bonnie Bee by Frank Thomas begins. 69-Kelly-a (2 pgs.); The Brownies begin (not by Kelly) 28.00 85.00 315.00
71-75: 72-Kelly illos. 75-Brownies by Kelly? 17.00 52.00 190.00
76-Andy Panda (Carl Barks & Pabian-a); Woody Woodpecker x-over in Oswald ends 91.00 273.00 1000.00
77,78: 77-Kelly-c. 78-Andy Panda in a world with real people ends 17.00 52.00 190.00
79-81 12.00 37.00 135.00
82-Brownies by Kelly begins; Homer Pigeon begins 13.00 40.00 145.00
83-85-Brownies by Kelly in ea. 83-X-mas-c. 85-Woody Woodpecker, 1 pg. strip begins 13.00 40.00 145.00
86-90: 87-Woody Woodpecker stories begin 9.50 29.00 105.00
91-99 6.00 17.50 65.00
100 (6/45) 6.40 19.00 70.00
101-110 3.60 11.00 40.00
111-120: 119-X-Mas-c 3.00 9.00 35.00
121-150: 131,143-X-Mas-c 2.75 8.00 30.00
151-200: 155-X-Mas-c. 168-X-Mas-c. 182-Origin & 1st app. Knothead &

New Gods #10 (2nd Series) © DC

Newmen #3 © Rob Liefeld

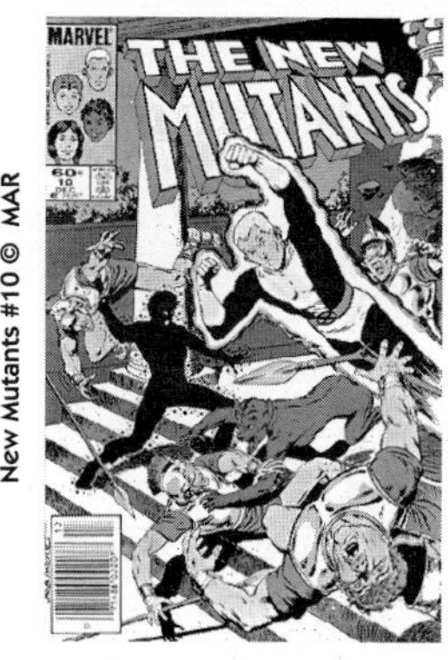

New Mutants #10 © MAR

GD25 FN65 NM94

Splinter. 191-X-Mas-c 1.80 5.50 20.00
201-240 1.20 3.60 12.00
241-288: 270,271-Walter Lantz c-app. 281-1st story swipes/WDC&S #100 .90 2.70 8.00

NOTE: *Early issues written by* ***John Stanley.***

NEW GODS, THE (1st Series)(New Gods #12 on)(See Adventure #459, DC Graphic Novel #4, 1st Issue Special #13 & Super-Team Family)
National Periodical Publications/DC Comics: 2-3/71 - V2#11, 10-11/72; V3#12, 7/77 - V3#19, 7-8/78 (Fourth World)

1-Intro/1st app. Orion; 4th app. Darkseid (cameo; 3 weeks after Forever People #1) (#1-3 are 15¢ issues) 4.50 13.50 50.00
2-Darkseid-c/story (2nd full app., 4-5/71) 2.50 7.60 28.00
3-1st app. Black Racer 2.00 6.00 20.00
4-9: (25¢, 52 pg. giants): 4-Darkseid cameo; origin Manhunter-r. 5,7,8-Young Gods feature. 7-Darkseid app. (2-3/72); origin Orion; 1st origin of all New Gods as a group. 9-1st app. Forager 1.40 4.20 14.00
10,11: 11-Last Kirby issue. .90 2.70 9.00
12-19: Darkseid storyline w/minor apps. 12-New costume Orion (see 1st Issue Special #13 for 1st new costume). 19-Story continued in Adventure Comics #459,460 5.00
Jack Kirby's New Gods TPB ('98, $11.95, B&W&Grey) r/#1-11 plus cover gallery of original series and "84 reprints 1.20 3.60 12.00

NOTE: *#4-9(25¢, 52 pgs.) contain Manhunter-r by* ***Simon*** *&* ***Kirby*** *from Adventure #73, 74, 75, 76, 77, 78 with covers in that order.* ***Adkins*** *i-12-14, 17-19.* ***Buckler*** *a(p)-15.* ***Kirby*** *c/a-1-11p.* ***Newton*** *a(p)-12-14, 16-19.* ***Starlin*** *c-17.* ***Staton*** *c-19p.*

NEW GODS (Also see DC Graphic Novel #4)
DC Comics: May, 1984 - No. 6, Nov, 1984 ($2.00, Baxter paper)

1-5: New Kirby-c; r/New Gods #1-10. 2.50
6-Reprints New Gods #11 w/48 pgs of new Kirby story & art; leads into DC Graphic Novel #4 2.00 6.00

NEW GODS (2nd Series)
DC Comics: Feb, 1989 - No. 28, Aug, 1991 ($1.50)

1-28 2.00

NEW GODS (3rd Series) (Becomes Jack Kirby's Fourth World) (Also see Showcase '94 #1 & Showcase '95 #7)
DC Comics: Oct, 1995 - No. 15, Feb, 1997 ($1.95)

1-11,13-15: 9-Giffen-a(p). 10,11-Superman app. 13-Takion, Mr. Miracle & Big Barda app. 13-15-Byrne-a(p)/scripts & Simonson-c. 15-Apokolips merged w/ New Genesis; story cont'd in Jack Kirby's Fourth World 2.00
12-(11/96, 99¢)-Byrne-a(p)/scripts & Simonson-c begin; Takion cameo; indicia reads October 1996 1.00
...Secret Files 1 (9/98, $4.95) Origin-s 4.95

NEW GUARDIANS, THE
DC Comics: Sept, 1988 - No. 12, Sept, 1989 ($1.25)

1-($2.00, 52pgs)-Staton-c/a in #1-9 2.00
2-12 1.25

NEW HEROIC (See Heroic)

NEW JUSTICE MACHINE, THE (Also see The Justice Machine)
Innovation Publishing: 1989 - No. 3, 1989 ($1.95, limited series)

1-3 2.00

NEW KIDS ON THE BLOCK, THE (Also see Richie Rich and...)
Harvey Comics: Dec, 1990 -1991 ($1.25)

1-5 2.00
...**Backstage Pass** 1(12/90) - 5 **Chillin'** 1(12/90) - 5: 1-Photo-c...**Comics Tour** '90/91 1 (12/90) - 5 **Hanging Tough** 1 (2/91) - 3 **Live** 1 (2/91) - 3 **Magic Summer Tour** 1 (Fall/90, one-shot) **Step By Step** 1 (Fall/90, one-shot) **Valentine Girl** 1 (Fall/90, one-shot)-Photo-c 2.00

NEW LOVE (See Love & Rockets)
Fantagraphics Books: Aug, 1996 - No. 6, Dec, 1997 ($2.95, B&W, lim. series)

GD25 FN65 NM94

1-6: Gilbert Hernandez-s/a 3.00

NEWMAN
Image Comics (Extreme Studios): Jan, 1996 - No. 4, Apr, 1996 ($2.50, lim. series)

1-4: 1-Extreme Destroyer Pt. 3; polybagged w/card. 4-Shadowhunt tie-in; Eddie Collins becomes new Shadowhawk 2.50

NEWMEN (becomes The Adventures Of The...#22)
Image Comics (Extreme Studios): Apr, 1994 - No. 20, Nov, 1995; No. 21, Nov, 1996 ($1.95/$2.50)

1-5: Matsuda-c/a. 1-Liefeld/Matsuda plot 2.00
6-21: 6-(9/94)-Begin $2.50-c. 10-Polybagged w/trading card. 11-Polybagged. 20-Variant-c; Babewatch! x-over. 21-(11/96)-Series relaunch; Chris Sprouse-a begins; pin-up 2.50
16-Quesada & Palmiotti variant-c 3.00
TPB-(1996, $12.95) r/#1-4 w/pin-ups 13.00

NEW MEN OF BATTLE, THE
Catechetical Guild: 1949 (nn) (Carboard-c)

nn(V8#1-3,5,6)-192 pgs.; contains 5 issues of Topix rebound 5.70 17.00 35.00
nn(V8#7-V8#11)-160 pgs.; contains 5 iss. of Topix 5.70 17.00 35.00

NEW MUTANTS, THE (See Marvel Graphic Novel #4 for 1st app.)(Also see X-Force & Uncanny X-Men #167)
Marvel Comics Group: Mar, 1983 - No. 100, Apr, 1991

1 4.00
2,3: 3,4-Ties into X-Men #167 2.50
4-10: 10-1st app. Magma 2.50
11-17,19,20: 13-Kitty Pryde app. 16-1st app. Warpath (w/out costume); see X-Men #193 2.00
18-Intro. new Warlock 3.00
21-Double size; origin new Warlock; newsstand version has cover price written in by Sienkiewicz 3.00
22-24,29,30: 23-25-Cloak & Dagger app. 2.00
25-Legion app. (cameo) 3.00
26-1st full Legion app. 3.00
27,28 2.00
31-58: 35-Magneto intro'd as new headmaster. 43-Portacio-i. 50-Double size. 58-Contains pull-out mutant registration form 2.00
59-Fall of The Mutants begins, ends #61 2.50
60-($1.25, 52 pgs.) 1.50
61-Fall of The Mutants ends 1.50
62,64-72,74-85: 68-Intro Spyder. 76-X-Factor & X-Terminator app. 85-Liefeld-c begin 1.25
63-X-Men & Wolverine clones app.; begin $1.00-c 2.50
73-($1.50, 52 pgs.) 2.00
86-Rob Liefeld-a begins; McFarlane-c(i) swiped from Ditko splash pg.; Cable cameo (last page teaser) 3.00
87-1st full app. Cable (3/90) .90 2.70 8.00
87-2nd printing; gold metallic ink-c ($1.00) 2.00
88-2nd app. Cable 5.00
89-3rd app. Cable 3.00
90,91: 90-New costumes. 90,91-Sabretooth app. 3.00
92-No Liefeld-a; Liefeld-c 2.00
93,94-Cable vs. Wolverine 4.00
95-97-X-Tinction Agenda x-over. 95-Death of new Warlock. 97-Wolverine & Cable-c, but no app. 4.00
95-Gold 2nd printing 2.00
98-1st app. Deadpool, Gideon & Domino (2/91); 2nd Shatterstar (cameo) 4.00
99-1st app. of Feral (of X-Force); Byrne-c/swipe (X-Men, 1st Series #138) 4.00
100-($1.50, 52 pgs.)-1st app. X-Force (cameo) 2.00
100-Gold 2nd printing 1.50
100-Silver ink 3rd printing 1.50

New Talent Showcase #14 © DC

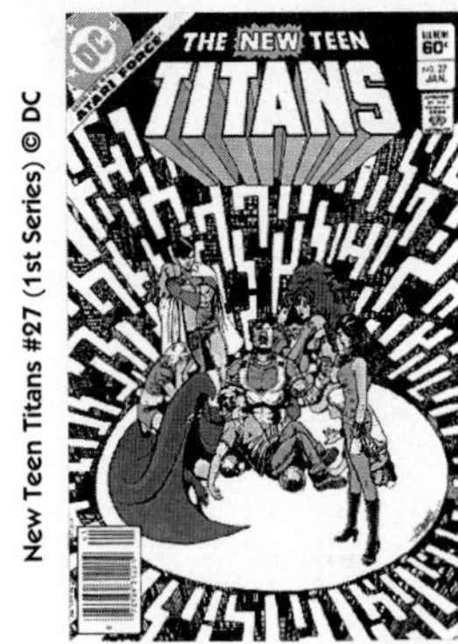

New Teen Titans #27 (1st Series) © DC

New Teen Titans #45 (2nd Series) © DC

GD25 FN65 NM94

Annual 1 (1984) 2.00
Annual 2 (1986, $1.25)-1st Psylocke 5.00
Annual 3 (1987, $1.25) 2.00
Annual 4 (1988, $1.75)-Evolutionary War x-over 2.00
Annual 5 (1989, $2.00, 68 pgs.)-Atlantis Attacks; 1st Liefeld-a on New Mutants 3.00
Annual 6 (1990, $2.00, 68 pgs.)-1st new costumes by Liefeld (3 pgs.); 1st app. (cameo) Shatterstar (of X-Force) 2.00
Annual 7 (1991, $2.00, 68 pgs.)-Liefeld pin-up only; X-Terminators back-up story; 2nd app. X-Force (continued in New Warriors Annual #1) 2.00
Special 1-Special Edition ('85, 68 pgs.)-Ties in w/X-Men Alpha Flight limited series; cont'd in X-Men Annual #9; Art Adams/Austin-a 4.00
Summer Special 1(Sum/90, $2.95, 84 pgs.) 3.00

NOTE: ***Art Adams** c-38, 39. **Austin** c-57i. **Byrne** c/a-75p. **Liefeld** a-86-91p, 93-96p, 98-100, Annual 5p, 6(3 pgs.); c-85-91p, 92, 93p, 94, 95, 96p, 97-100, Annual 5, 6p. **McFarlane** c-85-89i, 93i. **Portacio** a(i)-43. **Russell** a-48i. **Sienkiewicz** a-18-31, 35-38i; c-17-31, 35i, 37i, Annual 1. **Simonson** c-11p. **B. Smith** c-36, 40-48. **Williamson** a(i)-69, 71-73, 78-80, 82, 83; c(i)-69, 72, 73, 78i.*

NEW MUTANTS, THE: TRUTH OR DEATH
Marvel Comics: Nov, 1997 - No. 3, Jan, 1998 ($2.50, limited series)

1-3-Raab-s/Chang-a(p) 2.50

NEW ORDER, THE
CFD Publishing: Nov, 1994 ($2.95)

1 3.00

NEW PEOPLE, THE (TV)
Dell Publishing Co.: Jan, 1970 - No. 2, May, 1970

1,2 1.40 4.20 14.00

NEW ROMANCES
Standard Comics: No. 5, May, 1951 - No. 21, May, 1954

5-Photo-c 9.30 28.00 70.00
6-9: 6-Barbara Bel Geddes, Richard Basehart "Fourteen Hours" photo-c. 7-Ray Milland & Joan Fontaine photo-c. 9-Photo-c from '50s movie 5.70 17.00 35.00
10,14,16,17-Toth-a 6.00 18.00 42.00
11-Toth-a; Liz Taylor, Montgomery Cliff photo-c 11.00 34.00 85.00
12,13,15,18-21 4.15 12.50 25.00

NOTE: ***Celardo** a-9. **Moreira** a-6. **Tuska** a-7, 20. Photo c-5-16.*

NEW SHADOWHAWK, THE (Also see Shadowhawk & Shadowhunt)
Image Comics (Shadowline Ink): June, 1995 - No. 7, Mar, 1996 ($2.50)

1-7: Kurt Busiek scripts in all 2.50

NEW STATESMEN, THE
Fleetway Publications (Quality Comics): 1989 - No. 5, 1990 ($3.95, limited series, mature readers, 52pgs.)

1-5: Futuristic; squarebound; 3-Photo-c 4.00

NEWSTRALIA
Innovation Publishing: July, 1989 - No. 5, 1989 ($1.75, color)(#2 on, $2.25,, B&W)

1,2: Timothy Truman-c/a; Gustovich-i 1.75
3-5 ($2.25, B&W) 2.25

NEW TALENT SHOWCASE (Talent Showcase #16 on)
DC Comics: Jan, 1984 - No. 19, Oct, 1985 (Direct sales only)

1-10: Features new strips & artists .70
11-19 ($1.25): 18-Williamson-c(i) 1.25

NEW TEEN TITANS, THE (See DC Comics Presents 26, Marvel and DC Present & Teen Titans; Tales of the Teen Titans #41 on)
DC Comics: Nov, 1980 - No. 40, Mar, 1984

1-Robin, Kid Flash, Wonder Girl, The Changeling (1st app.), Starfire, The Raven, Cyborg begin; partial origin 2.00 6.00
2-1st app. Deathstroke the Terminator 5.00

GD25 FN65 NM94

3-9: 3-Origin Starfire; Intro The Fearsome Five. 4-Origin continues; J.L.A. app. 6-Origin Raven. 7-Cyborg origin. 8-Origin Kid Flash retold. 9-Minor cameo Deathstroke on last pg. 3.00
10-2nd app. Deathstroke the Terminator (see Marvel & DC Present for 3rd app.); origin Changeling retold 3.00
11-20: 13-Return of Madame Rouge & Capt. Zahl; Robotman revived. 14-Return of Mento; origin Doom Patrol. 15-Death of Madame Rouge & Capt. Zahl; intro. new Brotherhood of Evil. 16-1st app. Captain Carrot (free 16 pg. preview). 18-Return of Starfire. 19-Hawkman teams-up 1.50
21-30: 21-Intro Night Force in free 16 pg. insert; intro Brother Blood. 23-1st app. Vigilante (not in costume), & Blackfire. 24-Omega Men app. 25-Omega Men cameo; free 16 pg. preview Masters of the Universe. 26-1st app. Terra. 27-Free 16 pg. preview Atari Force. 29-The New Brotherhood of Evil & Speedy app. 30-Terra joins the Titans 2.00
31-33,35-38,40: 37-Batman & The Outsiders x-over. 38-Origin Wonder Girl 2.00
34-4th app. Deathstroke the Terminator 3.00
39-Last Dick Grayson as Robin; Kid Flash quits 2.00
Annual 1(11/82)-Omega Men app. 2.00
Annual V2#2(9/83)-1st app. Vigilante in costume 2.00
Annual 3 (See Tales of the Teen Titans Annual #3)
nn(11/83-Keebler Co. Giveaway)-In cooperation with "The President's Drug Awareness Campaign"; came in Presidential envelope w/letter from White House (Nancy Reagan) 1.00
nn-(re-issue of above on Mando paper for direct sales market); American Soft Drink Ind. version; I.B.M. Corp. version 1.00

NOTE: ***Perez** a-1-4p, 6-34p, 37-40p, Annual 1p, 2p; c-1-12, 13-17p, 18-21, 22p, 23p, 24-37, 38, 39(painted), 40, Annual 1, 2.*

NEW TEEN TITANS, THE (Becomes The New Titans #50 on)
DC Comics: Aug, 1984 - No. 49, Nov, 1988 ($1.25/$1.75; deluxe format)

1-New storyline; Perez-c/a begins 3.00
2,3: 2-Re-intro Lilith 2.50
4-10: 5-Death of Trigon. 7-9-Origin Lilith. 8-Intro Kole. 10-Kole joins 2.00
11-19: 13,14-Crisis x-over 1.25
20-Robin (Jason Todd) joins; original Teen Titans return 2.00
21-49: 37-Begin $1.75-c. 38-Infinity, Inc. x-over. 47-Origin of all Titans; Titans (East & West) pin-up by George Perez. 2.00
Annual 1 (9/85)-Intro. Vanguard 2.00
Annual 2 (8/86; $2.50): Byrne c/a(p); origin Brother Blood; intro new Dr. Light 2.50
Annual 3 (11/87)-Intro. Danny Chase 2.25
Annual 4 ('88, $2.50)-Perez-c 2.50

NOTE: ***Buckler** c-10. **Kelley Jones** a-47, Annual 4. **Erik Larsen** a-33. **Orlando** c-33p. **Perez** a-1-5; c-1-7, 19-23, 43. **Steacy** c-47.*

NEW TERRYTOONS (TV)
Dell Publishing Co./Gold Key: 6-8/60 - No. 8, 3-5/62; 10/62 - No. 54, 1/79

1(1960-Dell)-Deputy Dawg, Dinky Duck & Hashimoto-San begin (1st app. of each) 4.50 13.50 50.00
2-8(1962) 2.50 7.60 28.00
1(30010-210)(10/62-Gold Key, 84 pgs.)-Heckle & Jeckle begins 6.00 17.50 65.00
2(30010-301)-84 pgs. 5.00 15.00 55.00
3-10 1.60 4.80 16.00
11-20 1.20 3.60 12.00
21-30 .90 2.70 9.00
31-54 2.00 6.00

NOTE: *Reprints: #4-12, 38, 40, 47. (See March of Comics #379, 393, 412, 435)*

NEW TESTAMENT STORIES VISUALIZED
Standard Publishing Co.: 1946 - 1947

"New Testament Heroes–Acts of Apostles Visualized, Book I"
"New Testament Heroes–Acts of Apostles Visualized, Book II"
"Parables Jesus Told" Set.... 11.00 32.00 80.00

NOTE: *All three are contained in a cardboard case, illustrated on front and info about the set.*

New Titans #120 © DC

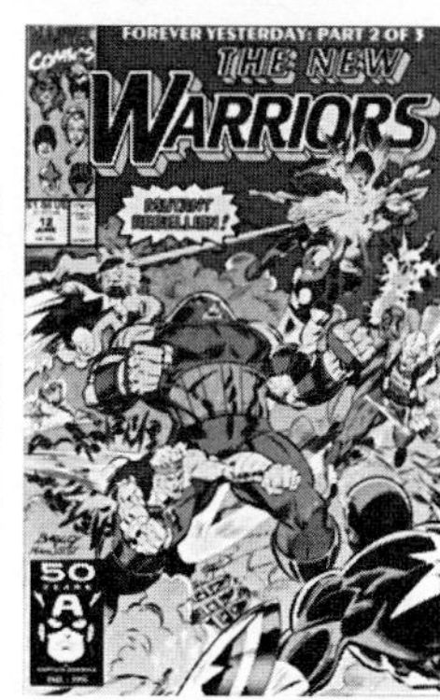

New Warriors #12 © MAR

Nexus #4 © Capital Publ. Inc.

GD25 FN65 NM94

NEW TITANS, THE (Formerly The New Teen Titans)
DC Comics: No. 50, Dec, 1988 - No. 130, Feb, 1996 ($1.75/$2.25)

50-Perez-c/a begins; new origin Wonder Girl 3.00
51-59: 50-55-Painted-c. 55-Nightwing (Dick Grayson) forces Danny Chase to resign; Batman app. in flashback, Wonder Girl becomes Troia 2.25
60-A Lonely Place of Dying Part 2 continues from Batman #440; new Robin tie-in; Timothy Drake app. 4.00
61-A Lonely Place of Dying Part 4 3.00
62-65: Deathstroke the Terminator app. 65-Timothy Drake (Robin) app. 3.00
66-69,71: 71-(44 pgs.)-10th anniversary issue; Deathstroke cameo 2.50
70-1st Deathstroke solo cover/story 2.50
72-79-Deathstroke in all: 74-Intro. Pantha. 79-Terra brought back to life; 1 panel cameo Team Titans (1st app.) 2.50
80-99,101-111: Deathstroke in #80-84,86. 80-2nd full app. Team Titans. 83, 84-Deathstroke kills his son, Jericho. 85-Team Titans app. 86-Deathstroke vs. Nightwing-c/story; last Deathstroke app. 87-New costume Nightwing. 90-92-Parts 2,5,8 Total Chaos (Team Titans) 1.75
100-($3.50, 52 pgs.)-Holo-grafx foil-c 3.50
112-114: 112-Begin $1.95-c. 114-(9/94) 2.00
0,115-121: 0-(10/94). 115-(11/94) 2.00
122-124, 126-130: 122-begin $2.25-c. 130-Perez-c 2.25
125 (3.50)-wraparound-c 3.50
Annual 5,6 (1989, 1990, $3.50, 68 pgs.) 3.50
Annual 7 (1991, $3.50, 68 pgs.)-Armaggedon 2001 x-over; 1st full app. Teen (Team) Titans (new group) 3.50
Annual 8,9 (1992, '93, $3.50, 68 pgs.): 8-Deathstroke app.; Eclipso app. (minor) 3.50
Annual 10 (1994, $3.50, 68 pgs.)-Elseworlds story 3.50
Annual 11 (1995, $3.95)-Year One story 4.00
NOTE: ***Perez** a-50-55p, 57,60p, 58,59,61(layouts); c-50-61, 62-67i, Annual 5i; co-plots-66.*

NEW TV FUNNIES (See New Funnies)

NEW TWO-FISTED TALES, THE
Dark Horse Comics/Byron Preiss: 1993 ($4.95, limited series, 52 pgs.)

1-Kurtzman-r & new-a 5.00
NOTE: ***Eisner** c-1i. **Kurtzman** c-1p, 2.*

NEW WARRIORS, THE (See Thor #411,412)
Marvel Comics: July, 1990 - No. 75, 1996 ($1.00/$1.25/$1.50)

1-Williamson-i; Bagley-c/a(p) in 1-13, Annual 1 3.00
1-Gold 2nd printing (7/91) 1.00
2-5: 1,3-Guice-c(i). 2-Williamson-c/a(i). 2.00
6-10: 7-Punisher cameo (last pg.). 8,9-Punisher app. 2.00
11-14: 14-Darkhawk & Namor x-over 2.00
15-19: 17-Fantastic Four & Silver Surfer x-over. 19-Gideon (of X-Force) app.; last $1.00-c 1.25
20-24,26-46: 28-Intro Turbo & Cardinal. 31-Cannonball & Warpath app. 42-Nova vs. Firelord. 46-Photo-c 1.25
25-($2.50, 52 pgs.)-Die-cut cover 2.50
40-($2.25)-Gold foil collector's edition 2.25
47-49,51-59, 61-75: 47-Begin $1.50-c; bound-in S-M trading card sheet. 52-12 pg. ad insert. 62-Scarlet Spider-c/app. 70-Spider-Man-c/app. 72-Avengers-c/app. 1.50
50-($2.95, 52 pgs.)-Glow in the dark-c 3.00
60 ($2.50) 2.50
Annual 1 (1991, $2.00, 68 pgs.)-Origins all members; 3rd app. X-Force (cont'd from New Mutants Ann. #7 & cont'd in X-Men Ann. #15); x-over before X-Force #1 2.50
Annual 2 (1992, $2.25, 68 pgs.) 2.25
Annual 3 (1993, $2.95, 68 pgs.)-Bagged w/card 3.00
Annual 4 (1994, $2.95, 68 pgs.) 3.00

NEW WAVE, THE
Eclipse Comics: 6/10/86 - No. 13, 3/87 (#1-8: bi-weekly, 20pgs; #9-13: monthly)

GD25 FN65 NM94

1-8 (50 cents): 1-Origin, concludes #5. 6-Origin Megabyte. 8,9-The Heap returns .50
9-13 ($1.50): 13-Synder-c 1.50
Versus the Volunteers 3-D #1,2(4/87): 1-Snyder-c 2.50

NEW WORLD (See Comic Books, series I)

NEW WORLDS
Caliber: 1996 - No. 6 ($2.95, 80 pgs., B&W, anthology)

1-6: 1-Mister X & other stories 3.00

NEW YORK GIANTS (See Thrilling True Story of the Baseball Giants)

NEW YORK STATE JOINT LEGISLATIVE COMMITTEE TO STUDY THE PUBLICATION OF COMICS, THE
N.Y. State Legislative Document: 1951, 1955

This document was referenced by Wertham for **Seduction of the Innocent.** Contains numerous repros from comics showing violence, sadism, torture, and sex.
1955 version (196p, No. 37, 2/23/55)-Sold for $180 in 1986.

NEW YORK WORLD'S FAIR (Also see Big Book of Fun & New Book of Fun)
National Periodical Publ.: 1939, 1940 (100 pgs.; cardboard covers)
(DC's 4th & 5th annuals) GD25 FN65 VF82 NM94

1939-Scoop Scanlon, Superman (blond haired Superman on-c), Sandman, Zatara, Slam Bradley, Ginger Snap by Bob Kane begin; 1st published app. The Sandman (see Adventure #40 for his 1st drawn story); Vincent Sullivan-c; cover background by Guardineer
2000.00 6000.00 13,000.00 24,000.00
(Estimated up to 110 total copies exist, 4 in NM/Mint)
1940-Batman, Hourman, Johnny Thunderbolt, Red, White & Blue & Hanko (by Creig Flessel) app.; Superman, Batman & Robin-c (1st time they all appear together); early Robin app.; 1st Burnley-c/a (per Burnley)
1080.00 3240.00 7020.00 13,000.00
NOTE: *The 1939 edition was published 4/29/39 and released 4/30/39, the day the fair opened, at 25¢, and was first sold only at the fair. Since all other comics were 10¢, it didn't sell. Remaining copies were advertised beginning in the August issues of most DC comics for 25¢, but soon the price was dropped to 15¢. Everyone that sent a quarter through the mail for it received a free Superman #1 or a #2 to make up the dime difference. 15¢ stickers were placed over the 25¢ price. Four variations on the 15¢ stickers are known. The 1940 edition was published 5/11/40 and was priced at 15¢. It was a precursor to World's Best #1.*

NEW YORK: YEAR ZERO
Eclipse Comics: July, 1988 - No. 4, Oct, 1988 ($2.00, B&W, limited series)

1-4 2.00

NEXT MAN
Comico: Mar, 1985 - No. 5, Oct, 1985 ($1.50, color, Baxter paper)

1-5 1.50

NEXT MEN (See John Byrne's...)

NEXT NEXUS, THE
First Comics: Jan, 1989 - No. 4, April, 1989 ($1.95, limited series, Baxter paper)

1-4: Mike Baron scripts & Steve Rude-c/a. 2.00

NEXUS (See First Comics Graphic Novel #4, 19 & The Next Nexus)
Capital Comics/First Comics No. 7 on: June, 1981 - No. 6, Mar, 1984; No. 7, Apr, 1985 - No. 80?, May, 1991
(Direct sales only, 36 pgs.; V2#1('83)-printed on Baxter paper

1-B&W version; mag. size; w/double size poster 1.50 4.50 15.00
1-B&W 1981 limited edition; 500 copies printed and signed; same as above except this version has a 2-pg. poster & a pencil sketch on paperboard by Rude 2.00 6.00 20.00
2-B&W, magazine size 1.20 3.60 12.00
3-B&W, magazine size; contains 33-1/3 rpm record ($2.95 price) .90 2.70 8.00
V2#1-Color version 5.00
2-80: 2-Nexus' origin begins. 50-($3.50, 52 pgs.). 67-Snyder-c/a. 73-Begin $2.25-c 2.50
NOTE: ***Bissette** c-V2#29. **Giffen** c/a-V2#23. **Gulacy** c-1 (B&W), 2(B&W). **Mignola** c/a-V2#28. **Rude** c-3(B&W), V2#1-22, 24-27, 33-36, 39-42, 45-48, 50, 58-60, 75; a-1-3, V2#1-7, 8-16p, 18-*

Nickel Comics #2 © FAW

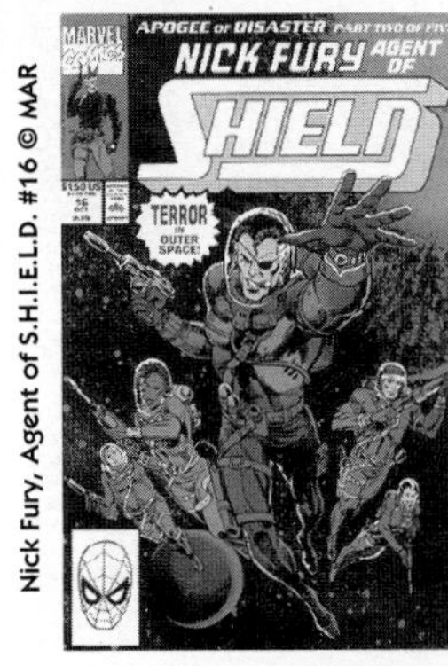

Nick Fury, Agent of S.H.I.E.L.D. #16 © MAR

Nighthawk #1 © MAR

	GD25	FN65	NM94

22p, 24-27p, 33-36p, 39-42p, 45-48p, 50, 58, 59p, 60. ***Paul Smith*** *a-V2#37, 38, 43, 44, 51-55p; c-V2#37, 38, 43, 44, 51-55.*

NEXUS: ALIEN JUSTICE
Dark Horse Comics: Dec, 1992 - No. 3, Feb, 1993 ($3.95, limited series)

1-3: Mike Baron scripts & Steve Rude-c/a 4.00

NEXUS: EXECUTIONER'S SONG
Dark Horse Comics: June, 1996 - No. 4, Sept, 1996 ($2.95, limited series)

1-4: Mike Baron scripts & Steve Rude-c/a 3.00

NEXUS FILES
First Comics: 1989 ($4.50, color/16pgs. B&W, one-shot, squarebound, 52pgs.)

1-New Rude-a; info on Nexus 4.50

NEXUS: GOD CON
Dark Horse Comics: Apr, 1997 - No. 2, May, 1997 ($2.95, limited series)

1,2-Baron-s/Rude-c/a 3.00

NEXUS LEGENDS
First Comics: May, 1989 - No. 23, Mar, 1991 ($1.50, Baxter paper)\

1-23: R/1-3(Capital) & early First Comics issues w/new Rude covers #1-6,9,10 1.50

NEXUS MEETS MADMAN (...Special)
Dark Horse Comics: May, 1996 ($2.95, one-shot)

nn-Mike Baron & Mike Allred scripts, Steve Rude-c/a. 3.00

NEXUS: NIGHTMARE IN BLUE
Dark Horse Comics: July, 1997 - No. 4, Oct, 1997 ($2.50, limited series)

1-4: 1,2,4-Adam Hughes-c 2.50

NEXUS: THE LIBERATOR
Dark Horse Comics: Aug, 1992 - No. 4, Nov, 1992 ($2.95, limited series)

1-4 3.00

NEXUS: THE ORIGIN
Dark Horse Comics: July, 1996 ($3.95, one-shot)

nn-Mike Baron- scripts, Steve Rude-c/a. 4.00

NEXUS: THE WAGES OF SIN
Dark Horse Comics: Mar, 1995 - No. 4, June, 1995 ($2.95, limited series)

1-4 3.00

NICKEL COMICS
Dell Publishing Co.: 1938 (Pocket size - 7-1/2x5-1/2")(132 pgs.)

	GD25	FN65	NM94
1- "Bobby & Chip" by Otto Messmer, Felix the Cat artist. Contains some English reprints	59.00	176.00	500.00

NICKEL COMICS
Fawcett Publications: May, 1940 - No. 8, Aug, 1940 (36 pgs.; Bi-Weekly; 5¢)

	GD25	FN65	NM94
1-Origin/1st app. Bulletman	337.00	1011.00	3200.00
2	112.00	336.00	950.00
3	82.00	246.00	700.00
4-The Red Gaucho begins	72.00	216.00	615.00
5-8: 8-World's Fair-c; Bulletman moved to Master Comics #7 in October	66.00	198.00	565.00

NOTE: ***Beck*** *c-5-8.* ***Jack Binder*** *c-1-4. Bondage c-5. Bulletman c-1-8.*

NICK FURY, AGENT OF SHIELD (See Fury, Marvel Spotlight #31 & Shield)
Marvel Comics Group: 6/68 - No. 15, 11/69; No. 16, 11/70 - No. 18, 3/71

	GD25	FN65	NM94
1	6.50	19.50	65.00
2-4: 4-Origin retold	3.50	10.50	35.00
5-Classic-c	4.00	12.00	40.00
6,7: 7-Salvador Dali painting swipe	2.50	7.50	24.00
8-11,13: 9-Hate Monger begins, ends #11. 10-Smith layouts/pencil. 11-Smith-c. 13-1st app. Super-Patriot; last 12¢ issue	1.50	4.50	12.00
12-Smith-c/a	1.85	5.50	15.00
14-Begin 15¢ issues	1.10	3.30	9.00
15-1st app. & death of Bullseye-c/story(11/69); Nick Fury shot & killed	4.50	13.50	45.00
16-18-(25¢, 52 pgs.)-r/Str. Tales #135-143	1.00	3.00	10.00

NOTE: ***Adkins*** *a-3i.* ***Craig*** *a-10i.* ***Sid Greene*** *a-12i.* ***Kirby*** *a-16-18r.* ***Springer*** *a-4, 6, 7, 8p, 9, 10p, 11; c-8, 9.* ***Steranko*** *a(p)-1-3, 5; c-1-7.*

NICK FURY AGENT OF SHIELD (Also see Strange Tales #135)
Marvel Comics: Dec, 1983 - No. 2, Jan, 1984 (2.00, 52 pgs., Baxter paper)

1,2-r/Nick Fury #1-4; new Steranko-c 2.00

NICK FURY, AGENT OF S.H.I.E.L.D.
Marvel Comics: Sept, 1989 - No. 47, May, 1993 ($1.50/$1.75)

V2#1-26: 10-Capt. America app. 13-Return of The Yellow Claw. 15-Fantastic Four app. 1.50
27-29-Wolverine-c/stories 2.00
30-47: 30,31-Deathlok app. 32-Begin $1.75-c. 36-Cage app. 37-Woodgod c/story. 38-41-Flashes back to pre-Shield days after WWII. 44-Capt. America-c/s. 45-Viper-c/s. 46-Gideon x-over 1.75

NOTE: ***Alan Grant*** *scripts-11.* ***Guice*** *a(p)-20-23, 25, 26; c-20-28.*

NICK FURY VS. S.H.I.E.L.D.
Marvel Comics: June, 1988 - No. 6, Nov, 1988 ($3.50, 52 pgs, deluxe format)

1-Steranko-c 4.00
2-(Low print run) Sienkiewicz-c 4.00
3-6 3.00

NICK HALIDAY (Thrill of the Sea)
Argo: May, 1956

	GD25	FN65	NM94
1-Daily & Sunday strip-r by Petree	6.50	19.50	45.00

NIGHT AND THE ENEMY (Graphic Novel)
Comico: 1988 (8-1/2x11") ($11.95, color, 80 pgs.)

	GD25	FN65	NM94
1-Harlan Ellison scripts/Ken Steacy-c/a; r/Epic Illustrated & new-a (1st and 2nd printings)	1.20	3.60	12.00
1-Limited edition ($39.95)	3.80	11.50	40.00

NIGHT BEFORE CHRISTMAS, THE (See March of Comics No. 152)

NIGHT BEFORE CHRISTMASK, THE
Dark Horse Comics: Nov, 1994 ($9.95, one-shot)

	GD25	FN65	NM94
nn-Hardcover book; Rick Geary -c/a	1.00	3.00	10.00

NIGHTBREED (See Clive Barker's Nightbreed)

NIGHTCRAWLER
Marvel Comics Group: Nov, 1985 - No. 4, Feb, 1986 (Mini-series from X-Men)

1-4: 1-Cockrum-c/a 2.00

NIGHT FORCE, THE (See New Teen Titans #21)
DC Comics: Aug, 1982 - No. 14, Sept, 1983 (60¢)

1 3.00
2-14: 13-Origin Baron Winter. 14-Nudity panels 2.00

NOTE: ***Colan*** *c/a-1-14p.* ***Giordano*** *c-1i, 2i, 4i, 5i, 7i, 12i.*

NIGHT FORCE
DC Comics: Dec, 1996 - No. 12, Nov, 1997 ($2.25)

1-12: 1-3-Wolfman-s/Anderson-a(p). 8-"Convergence" part 2 2.25

NIGHT GLIDER
Topps Comics (Kirbyverse): April, 1993 ($2.95, one-shot)

1-Kirby c-1, Heck-a; polybagged w/Kirbychrome trading card 3.00

NIGHTHAWK
Marvel Comics: Sept, 1998 - No. 3, Nov, 1998 ($2.99, mini-series)

1-3-Krueger-s; Daredevil app. 3.00

NIGHTINGALE, THE
Henry H. Stansbury Once-Upon-A-Time Press, Inc.: 1948 (10¢, 7-1/4x10-1/4", 14 pgs., 1/2 B&W)

(Very Rare)-Low distribution; distributed to Westchester County & Bronx, N.Y. only; used in **Seduction of the Innocent**, pg. 312,313 as the 1st and only "good" comic book ever published.

The Night Man #8 © MAL

Nightmare #1 © Z-D

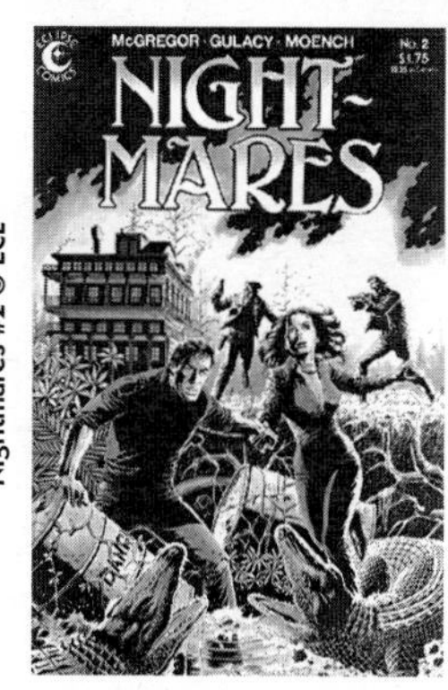

Nightmares #2 © ECL

	GD25	FN65	NM94

Ill. by Dong Kingman; 1,500 words of text, printed on high quality paper & no word balloons. Copyright registered 10/22/48, distributed week of 12/5/48. (By Hans Christian Andersen)
Estimated value........ $200

NIGHT MAN, THE (See Sludge #1)
Malibu Comics (Ultraverse): Oct, 1993 - No. 23, Aug, 1995 ($1.95/$2.50)

1-($2.50, 48 pgs.)-Rune flip-c/story by B. Smith (3 pgs.)			2.50
1-Ultra-Limited silver foil-c			8.00
2-15, 17: 3-Break-Thru x-over; Freex app. 4-Origin Firearm (2 pgs.) by Chaykin. 6-TNTNT app. 8-1st app. Teknight			2.00
16 ($3.50)-flip book (Ultraverse Premiere #11)			3.50
...:The Pilgrim Conundrum Saga (1/95, $3.95, 68 pgs.)-Strangers app.			4.00
18-23: 22-Loki-c/a			2.50
Infinity ($1.50)			1.50
...Vs. Wolverine #0-Kelley Jones-c; mail in offer	1.00	3.00	10.00

*NOTE: **Zeck** a-16.*

NIGHT MAN, THE
Malibu Comics (Ultraverse): Sept, 1995 - No.4, Dec, 1995 ($1.50, lim. series)

1-4: Post Black September storyline 1.50

NIGHT MAN, THE /GAMBIT
Malibu Comics (Ultraverse): Mar, 1996 - No. 3, May, 1996 ($1.95, lim. series)

0-Limited Premium Edition 5.00
1-3: David Quinn scripts in all. 3-Rhiannon discovered to be The Night Man's mother 2.00

NIGHTMARE
Ziff-Davis (Approved Comics)/St. John No. 3,4: Summer, 1952 - No. 3, Winter, 1952, 53 (Painted-c)

1-1 pg. Kinstler-a; Tuska-a(2)	46.00	138.00	390.00
2-Kinstler-a-Poe's "Pit & the Pendulum"	36.00	108.00	270.00
3-Kinstler-a	29.00	86.00	215.00

NIGHTMARE (Weird Horrors #1-9) (Amazing Ghost Stories #14 on)
St. John Publishing Co.: No. 10, Dec, 1953 - No. 13, Aug, 1954

10-Reprints Ziff-Davis Weird Thrillers #2 w/new Kubert-c plus 2 pgs. Kinstler-a; Anderson, Colan & Toth-a	46.00	138.00	390.00
11-Krigstein-a; painted-c; Poe adapt., "Hop Frog"	36.00	108.00	270.00
12-Kubert bondage-c; adaptation of Poe's "The Black Cat"; Cannibalism story	31.00	92.00	230.00
13-Reprints Z-D Weird Thrillers #3 with new cover; Powell-a(2), Tuska-a; Baker-c	23.00	70.00	175.00

NIGHTMARE (Magazine)
Skywald Publishing Corp.: Dec, 1970 - No. 23, Feb, 1975 (B&W, 68 pgs.)

1-Everett-a	5.00	15.00	55.00
2-5: 4-Decapitation story	2.50	7.50	27.00
6-Kaluta-a; Jeff Jones photo & interview	2.50	7.50	27.00
7,10	2.00	6.00	20.00
8,9: 8-Features E. C. movie "Tales From the Crypt"; reprints some E.C. comics panels. 9-Wrightson-a	2.50	7.50	27.00
11-20: 12-Excessive gore, severed heads. 20-Byrne's 1st artwork (8/74); sev ered head-c	1.80	5.40	18.00
21-23: 21-(1974 Summer Special)-Kaluta-a. 22-Tomb of Horror issue. 23-(1975 Winter Special)	2.50	7.50	22.00
Annual 1(1972)-B. Jones-a	2.40	7.00	26.00
Winter Special 1(1973)	2.00	6.00	20.00
Yearbook nn(1974)-B. Jones, Reese, Wildey-a	2.00	6.00	20.00

NOTE: ***Adkins** a-5. **Boris** c-2, 3, 5 (#4 is not by Boris). **Buckler** a-3, 15. **Byrne** a-20p. **Everett** a-4, 5, 12. **Jeff Jones** a-6, 21r(Psycho #6); c-6. **Katz** a-5. **Reese** a-4, 5. **Wildey** a-4, 5, 6, 21, '74 Yearbook.*

NIGHTMARE (Alex Nino's)
Innovation Publishing: 1989 ($1.95)

1-Alex Nino-a 2.00

NIGHTMARE
Marvel Comics: Dec, 1994 - No. 4, Mar, 1995 ($1.95, limited series)

1-4 2.00

NIGHTMARE & CASPER (See Harvey Hits #71) (Casper & Nightmare #6 on) (See Casper The Friendly Ghost #19)
Harvey Publications: Aug, 1963 - No. 5, Aug, 1964 (25¢)

1-All reprints?	5.50	16.50	55.00
2-5: All reprints?	3.20	9.60	32.00

NIGHTMARE ON ELM STREET, A (See Freddy Krueger's...)

NIGHTMARES (See Do You Believe in Nightmares)

NIGHTMARES
Eclipse Comics: May, 1985 - No. 2, May, 1985 ($1.75, Baxter paper)

1,2 1.75

NIGHTMARE THEATER
Chaos! Comics: Nov, 1997 - No. 4, Nov, 1997 ($2.50, mini-series)

1-4-Horror stories by various; Wrightson-a 2.50

NIGHTMARK: BLOOD & HONOR
Alpha Productions: 1994 - No. 3, 1994 ($2.50, B&W, mini-series)

1,2 2.50

NIGHTMARK MYSTERY SPECIAL
Alpha Productions: Jan, 1994 ($2.50, B&W)

1 2.50

NIGHTMASK
Marvel Comics Group: Nov, 1986 - No. 12, Oct, 1987

1-12 .75

NIGHT MASTER
Silverwolf: Feb, 1987 ($1.50, B&W)

1-Tim Vigil-c/a 1.50

NIGHT MUSIC (See Eclipse Graphic Album Series, The Magic Flute)
Eclipse Comics: Dec, 1984 - No. 11, 1990 ($1.75/$3.95/$4.95, Baxter paper)

1-7: 3-Russell's Jungle Book adapt. 4,5-Pelleas And Melisande (double titled) 6-Salome' (double titled). 7-Red Dog #1 1.75
8-($3.95) Ariane and Bluebeard 4.00
9-11-($4.95) The Magic Flute; Russell adapt. 5.00

NIGHT NURSE
Marvel Comics Group: Nov, 1972 - No. 4, May, 1973

1	8.00	24.00	90.00
2-4	5.50	16.50	60.00

NIGHT OF MYSTERY
Avon Periodicals: 1953 (no month) (one-shot)

nn-1 pg. Kinstler-a, Hollingsworth-c	38.00	114.00	285.00

NIGHT OF THE GRIZZLY, THE (See Movie Classics)

NIGHTRAVEN: THE COLLECTED STORIES
Marvel Comics UK, Ltd.: 1991 ($9.95, graphic novel)

nn-Bolton-r/British Hulk mag.; David Lloyd-c/a	1.00	3.00	10.00

NIGHT RIDER (Western)
Marvel Comics Group: Oct, 1974 - No. 6, Aug, 1975

1: 1-6 reprint Ghost Rider #1-6 (#1-origin)	1.00	3.00	10.00
2-6	.85	2.60	7.00

NIGHT'S CHILDREN: THE VAMPIRE
Millenium: July, 1995 - No. 2, Aug, 1995 ($2.95, B&W)

1,2: Wendy Snow-Lang story & art 3.00

NIGHTSHADE
No Mercy Comics: Aug, 1997 ($2.50)

1-Mark Williams-s/a 2.50

Nights into Dreams #6 © SEGA

Nightwing & Huntress #1 © DC

Ninjak #7 © VAL

GD25 FN65 NM94

NIGHTS INTO DREAMS (Based on video game)
Archie Comics: Feb, 1998 -No. 6, Oct, 1998 ($1.75, limited series)

1-6 — 1.75

NIGHTSTALKERS (Also see Midnight Sons Unlimited)
Marvel Comics (Midnight Sons #14 on): Nov, 1992 - No. 18, Apr, 1994 ($1.75)

1-($2.75, 52 pgs.)-Polybagged w/poster; part 5 of Rise of the Midnight Sons storyline; Garney/Palmer-c/a begins; Hannibal King, Blade & Frank Drake begin (see Tomb of Dracula for & Dr. Strange) — 2.75
2-9,11-18: 5-Punisher app. 7-Ghost Rider app. 8,9-Morbius app. 14-Spot varnish-c. 14,15-Siege of Darkness Pts 1 & 9 — 1.75
10-($2.25)-Outer-c is a Darkhold envelope made of black parchment w/gold ink; Midnight Massacre part 1 — 2.25

NIGHT THRASHER (Also see The New Warriors)
Marvel Comics: Aug, 1993 - No. 21, Apr, 1995 ($1.75/$1.95)

1-($2.95, 52 pgs.)-Red holo-grafx foil-c; origin — 3.00
2-9: 2-Intro Tantrum. 3-Gideon (of X-Force) app. — 1.75
10-21: 10-Begin $1.95-c; bound-in trading card sheet; Iron Man app. 15-Hulk app. — 2.00

NIGHT THRASHER: FOUR CONTROL
Marvel Comics: Oct, 1992 - No. 4, Jan, 1993 ($2.00, limited series)

1-4: 1-Hero from New Warriors. 2-Intro Tantrum. 3-Gideon (of X-Force) app. — 2.00

NIGHTVEIL (Also see Femforce)
Americomics/AC Comics: Nov, 1984 - No. 7, 1985 ($1.75)

1-7 — 2.00
...'s Cauldron Of Horror 1 (1989, B&W)-Kubert, Powell, Wood-r plus new Nightveil story — 2.50
...'s Cauldron Of Horror 2 (1990, $2.95, B&W, 44pgs)-Pre-code horror-r by Kubert & Powell — 3.00
Special 1 ('88, $1.95)-Kaluta-c — 2.00
One Shot ('96, $5.95)-Flip book w/ Colt — 6.00

NIGHTWATCH
Marvel Comics: Apr, 1994 - No. 12, Mar, 1995 ($1.50)

1-($2.95)-Collectors edition; foil-c; Ron Lim-c/a begins; Spider-Man app. — 3.00
1-($1.50)-Regular edition — 1.50
2-12: 2-Bound-in S-M trading card sheet; 5,6-Venom-c & app. 7,11-Cardiac app. — 1.50

NIGHTWING (Also see New Teen Titans, New Titans, Showcase '93 #11,12, Tales of the New Teen Titans & Teen Titans Spotlight)
DC Comics: Sept, 1995 - No. 4, Dec, 1995 ($2.25, limited series)

1-Dennis O'Neil story/Greg Land-a in all — 2.00 — 6.00
2-4 — 5.00
...: Alfred's Return (7/95, $3.50) Giordano-a — 5.00
...Ties That Bind (1997, $12.95, TPB) r/mini-series & Alfred's Return — 12.95

NIGHTWING
DC Comics: Oct, 1996 - Present ($1.95/$1.99)

1-Chuck Dixon scripts & Scott McDaniel-c/a — 1.20 — 3.60 — 12.00
2 — .90 — 2.70 — 9.00
3 — .85 — 2.60 — 7.00
4,5 — 5.00
6-10: 6-Robin-c/app. — 4.00
11-23: 13-15-Batman app. 19,20-Cataclysm pts. 2,11. 23-Green Arrow app. — 2.00
24-29: 24-Begin $1.99-c. 26-29-Huntress-c/app. — 2.00
#1,000,000 (11/98) teams with future Batman — 2.00
Annual 1(1997, $3.95) Pulp Heroes — 4.00
...A Knight in Blüdhaven (1998, $14.95, TPB) r/#1-8 — 14.95
Wizard 1/2 (Mail offer) — 5.00

GD25 FN65 NM94

NIGHTWING (See Tangent Comics/ Nightwing)

NIGHTWING AND HUNTRESS
DC Comics: May, 1998 - No. 4, Aug, 1998 ($1.95, limited series)

1-4-Grayson-s/Land & Sienkiewicz-a — 2.00

NIGHTWINGS (See DC Science Fiction Graphic Novel)

NIKKI, WILD DOG OF THE NORTH (Disney, see Movie Comics)
Dell Publishing Co.: No. 1226, Sept, 1961

Four Color 1226-Movie, photo-c — 4.50 — 13.50 — 50.00

1963
Image Comics (Shadowline Ink): Apr, 1993 - No. 6, Oct, 1993 ($1.95, lim. series)

1-6: Alan Moore scripts; Veitch, Bissette & Gibbons-a(p) — 2.00
1-Gold — 4.00

NOTE: ***Bissette** a-2-4; **Gibbons** a-1i, 2i, 6i; c-2.*

1984 (Magazine) (1994 #11 on)
Warren Publishing Co.: June, 1978 - No. 10, Jan, 1980 ($1.50)

1-Nino-a in all — 1.50 — 4.50 — 15.00
2-10 — 1.00 — 3.00 — 10.00

NOTE: ***Alacla** a-1-3, 5i. **Corben** a-1-8; c-1, 2. **Thorne** a-7-10. **Wood** a-1, 2, 5i.*

1994 (Formerly 1984) (Magazine)
Warren Publishing Co.: No. 11, Feb, 1980 - No. 29, Feb, 1983

11-29: 27-The Warhawks return — .90 — 2.70 — 8.00

NOTE: ***Corben** c-26. **Nino** a-11-19, 20(2), 21, 25, 26, 28; c-21. **Redondo** c-20. **Thorne** a-11-14, 17-21, 25, 26, 28, 29.*

NINE VOLT
Image Comics (Top Cow Productions): July, 1997 - No. 4, Oct, 1997 ($2.50)

1-4 — 2.50

NINJA HIGH SCHOOL (1st series)
Antarctic Press: 1986 - No. 3, Aug, 1987 (B&W)

1-Ben Dunn-s/c/a; early Manga series — 1.60 — 4.80 — 16.00
2,3 — 1.00 — 3.00 — 10.00

NINJAK (See Bloodshot #6, 7 & Deathmate)
Valiant/Acclaim Comics (Valiant) No. 16 on: Feb, 1994 - No. 26, Nov. 1995 ($2.25/$2.50)

1 ($3.50)-Chromium-c; Quesada-c/a(p) in #1-3 — 3.50
1-Gold — 4.00
2-13: 3-Batman, Spawn & Random (from X-Factor) app. as costumes at party (cameo). 4-w/bound-in trading card. 5,6-X-O app. — 2.25
0,00,14-26: 14-(4/95)-Begin $2.50-c. 0-(6/95, $2.50). 00-(6/95, $2.50) — 2.50
Yearbook 1 (1994, $3.95) — 3.00

NINJAK
Acclaim Comics (Valiant Heroes): V2#1, Mar, 1997 -No. 12, Feb, 1998 ($2.50)

V2#1-12: 1-Intro new Ninjak; 1st app. Brutakon; Kurt Busiek scripts begin; painted variant-c exists. 2-1st app. Karnivor & Zeer. 3-1st app. Gigantik, Shurikai, & Nixie. 4-Origin; 1st app. Yasuiti Motomiya; intro The Dark Dozen; Colin King (original Ninjak) cameo. 9-Copycat-c — 2.50

NINTENDO COMICS SYSTEM (Also see Adv. of Super Mario Brothers)
Valiant Comics: Feb, 1990 - No. 9, Oct, 1991 ($4.95, card stock-c, 68pgs.)

1-Featuring Game Boy, Super Mario, Clappwall — 2.00 — 6.00
2-4: 3-Layton-c — 3.00
5-8-Super Mario Bros. — 5.00
9-Dr. Mario 1st app. — 2.00 — 6.00

NIRA X
Entity Comics

...: ANIME No. 0, Mar, 1997 ($2.75,one-shot)
0a,0b-Manga Swimsuit Edition — 2.75

...: CYBERANGEL Dec, 1994 - No. 4, 1995 ($2.95, limited series)

Nocturnals #1 © Daniel Brereton

Nomad V2 #4 © MAR

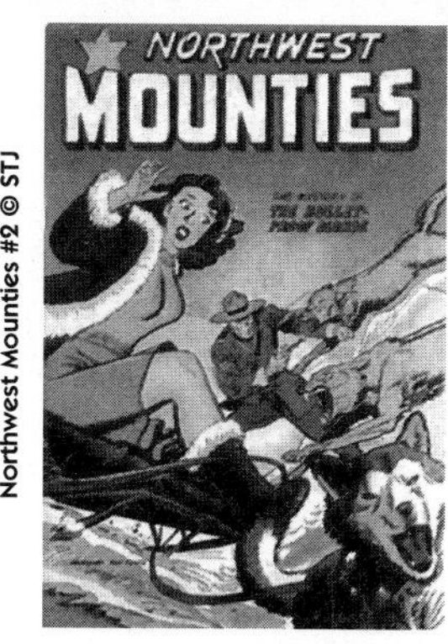

Northwest Mounties #2 © STJ

GD25 FN65 NM94

1-Foil logo 3.00
2-4 ($2.50) 2.50
4-($6.95)-bagged w/PC Game 7.00

...: CYBERANGEL SERIES II 1995 - No. 4, 1995 ($2.50, limited series)
1-4 2.50

...: CYBERANGEL SERIES III 1995 - No. 3, 1995 ($2.50/$2.95, limited series)
1,2-($2.50) 2.50
3-($2.95) 3.00
1-($6.95)-Bagged w/PC Game 7.00

...-CYNDER: ENDANGERED SPECIES Feb, 1996 ($2.95, one-shot)
1-Maus-a(p)/scripts 3.00
1-($12.95)-Commemorative 13.00

...: EXODUS 1997 - No. 2, 1997 ($3.00, limited series)
0-2-Wraparound-c 3.00
0-2-($4.95) Nude-c 4.95

...: HEATWAVE July, 1997 ($3.75, one-shot)
1-Wraparound chromium-c 3.75

...: HELLINA Aug, 1996 ($2.95, one-shot)
1-Two covers (1 gold foil & 1 red foil) 3.00
1-($12.95)-Platinum Edition; polybagged w/certificate 13.00

...: SHOOT FIRST Dec, 1997 ($3.00, one-shot)
1-Maus-a(p)/scripts 3.00
1-($4.95) Nude-c 4.95

...: SOUL SKURGE Nov, 1996 - No. 2, Dec, 1996 ($2.75, B&W, limited series)
1,2 2.75

... UNLIMITED SERIES No. 0, Mar, 1996 - No. 4, Aug, 1996 ($2.75, B&W)
0-4 2.75
Annual 1-($2.75) 2.75

NOAH'S ARK
Spire Christian Comics/Fleming H. Revell Co.: 1973 (35/49¢)
nn-By Al Hartley 1.00

NOBODY (Amado, Cho & Adlard's...)
Oni Press: Nov, 1998 - No. 4, Feb, 1999 ($2.95. B&W, mini-series)
1-4 2.95

NOCTURNALS, THE
Malibu Comics (Bravura): Jan, 1995 - No. 6, Aug, 1995 ($2.95, limited series)
1-6: Dan Brereton painted-c/a & scripts 3.00
1-Glow-in-the-Dark premium edition 5.00
Black Planet TPB ('98, $19.95, Oni Press) r/#1-6 19.95

NOCTURNALS, THE :WITCHING HOUR
Dark Horse Comics: May 1998 ($4.95, one-shot)
1-Brereton-s/painted-a; reprints DHP stories + 8 new pgs. 5.00

NOCTURNE
Marvel Comics: June, 1995 - No. 4, Sept. 1995 ($1.50, limited series)
1-4 1.50

NO ESCAPE (Movie)
Marvel Comics: June, 1994 - No. 3, Aug, 1994 ($1.50)
1-3: Based on movie 1.50

NOMAD (See Captain America #180)
Marvel Comics: Nov, 1990 - No. 4, Feb, 1991 ($1.50, limited series)
1-4: 1,4-Captain America app. 1.50

NOMAD
Marvel Comics: V2#1, May, 1992 - No. 25, May, 1994 ($1.75)
V2#1-($2.00)-Has gatefold-c w/map/wanted poster 2.50
2-5: 4-Deadpool x-over. 5-Punisher vs. Nomad-c/story 1.80
6-25: 6-Punisher & Daredevil-c/story cont'd in Punisher War Journal #48. 7-Gambit-c/story. 10-Red Wolf app. 21-Man-Thing-c/story. 25-Bound-in trading card sheet 1.75

NOMAN (See Thunder Agents)
Tower Comics: Nov, 1966 - No. 2, March, 1967 (25¢, 68 pgs.)
1-Wood/Williamson-c; Lightning begins; Dynamo cameo; Kane-a(p) & Whitney-a 6.00 18.00 60.00
2-Wood-c only; Dynamo x-over; Whitney-a 4.00 12.00 40.00

NONE BUT THE BRAVE (See Movie Classics)

NOODNIK COMICS (See Pinky the Egghead)
Comic Media/Mystery/Biltmore: Dec, 1953; No. 2, Feb, 1954 - No. 5, Aug, 1954
3-D(1953, 25¢; Comic Media)(#1)-Came w/glasses 30.00 90.00 225.00
2-5 5.70 17.00 35.00

NORMALMAN (See Cerebus the Aardvark #55, 56)
Aardvark-Vanaheim/Renegade Press #6 on: Jan, 1984 - No. 12, Dec, 1985 ($1.70/$2.00)
1-5 ($1.70, color)-Jim Valentino-c/a in all 1.70
6-12 ($2.00, B&W): 10-Cerebus cameo; Sim-a (2 pgs.) 2.00
...3-D 1 (Annual, 1986, $2.25) 2.25

NORMALMAN-MEGATON MAN SPECIAL
Image Comics: Aug, 1994 ($2.50, color)
1 2.50

NORTH AVENUE IRREGULARS (See Walt Disney Showcase #49)

NORTHSTAR
Marvel Comics: Apr, 1994 - No. 4, July, 1994 ($1.75, mini-series)
1-4: Character from Alpha Flight 1.75

NORTH TO ALASKA
Dell Publishing Co.: No. 1155, Dec, 1960
Four Color 1155-Movie, John Wayne photo-c 16.00 47.00 170.00

NORTHWEST MOUNTIES (Also see Approved Comics #12)
Jubilee Publications/St. John: Oct, 1948 - No. 4, July, 1949
1-Rose of the Yukon by Matt Baker; Walter Johnson-a; Lubbers-c 42.00 126.00 335.00
2-Baker-a; Lubbers-c. Ventrilo app. 34.00 102.00 255.00
3-Bondage-c, Baker-a; Sky Chief, K-9 app. 35.00 105.00 260.00
4-Baker-c/a(2 pgs.); Blue Monk & The Desperado app. 35.00 105.00 260.00

NO SLEEP 'TIL DAWN
Dell Publishing Co.: No. 831, Aug, 1957
Four Color 831-Movie, Karl Malden photo-c 5.50 16.50 60.00

NOT BRAND ECHH (Brand Echh #1-4; See Crazy, 1973)
Marvel Comics Group (LMC): Aug, 1967 - No. 13, May, 1969 (1st Marvel parody book)
1: 1-8 are 12¢ issues 3.20 9.60 32.00
2-4: 3-Origin Thor, Hulk & Capt. America; Monkees, Alfred E. Neuman cameo. 4-X-Men app. 2.50 7.50 20.00
5-8: 5-Origin/intro. Forbush Man. 7-Origin Fantastical-4 & Stuporman. 8-Beatles cameo; X-Men satire 2.50 7.50 20.00
9-13 (25¢, 68 pgs., all Giants) 9-Beatles cameo. 10-All-r; The Old Witch, Crypt Keeper & Vault Keeper cameos. 12,13-Beatles cameo 2.60 7.80 26.00

NOTE: ***Colan*** *a(p)-4, 5, 8, 9, 13.* ***Everett*** *a-1i.* ***Kirby*** *a(p)-1, 3, 5-7, 10r; c-1p.* ***J. Severin*** *a-1; c-3, 6-8, 11.* ***M. Severin*** *a-1-13; c-2, 9, 10, 12, 13.* ***Sutton*** *a-3, 4, 5i, 6i, 8, 9, 10r, 11-13; c-5. Archie satire in #9. Avengers satire in #8, 12.*

NOTHING CAN STOP THE JUGGERNAUT
Marvel Comics: 1989 ($3.95)
1-r/Amazing Spider-Man #229 & 230 4.00

NO TIME FOR SERGEANTS (TV)

Nova #9 © MAR

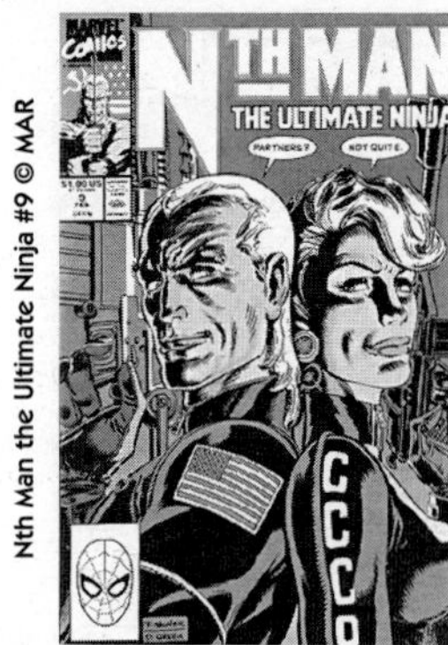

Nth Man the Ultimate Ninja #9 © MAR

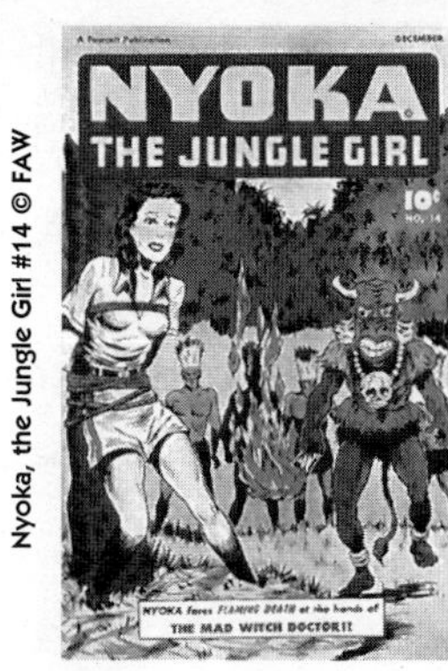

Nyoka, the Jungle Girl #14 © FAW

	GD25	FN65	NM94
Dell Publ. Co.: No. 914, July, 1958; Feb-Apr, 1965 - No. 3, Aug-Oct, 1965			
Four Color 914 (Movie)-Toth-a; Andy Griffith photo-c	9.00	27.00	100.00
1(2-4/65)-3 (TV): Photo-c	3.60	11.00	40.00

NOVA (The Man Called... No. 22-25)(See New Warriors)
Marvel Comics Group: Sept, 1976 - No. 25, May, 1979

	GD25	FN65	NM94
1-Origin/1st app. Nova			4.00
2-11: 4-Thor x-over			3.00
12-Spider-Man x-over			2.50
13-(Regular 30¢ edition)(9/77) Intro Crime-Buster.			3.00
13-(35¢-c, limited distribution)	1.20	3.60	12.00
14-24: 14-Last 30¢ issue. 18-Yellow Claw app. 19-Wally West (Kid Flash) cameo			3.00
25-Last issue			4.00

NOTE: ***Austin** c-21i, 23i. **John Buscema** a(p)-1-3, 8, 21; c-1p, 2, 15. **Infantino** a(p)-15-20, 22-25; c-17-20, 21p, 23p, 24p. **Kirby** c-4p, 5, 7. **Nebres** c-25i. **Simonson** a-23i.*

NOVA
Marvel Comics: Jan, 1994 - June, 1995 ($1.75/$1.95)
(Started as 4-part mini-series)

	GD25	FN65	NM94
1-($2.95, 52 pgs.)-Collector's Edition w/gold foil-c; new costume for Nova			3.00
1-($2.25, 52 pgs.)-Newsstand Edition w/o foil-c			2.25
2-4: 3-Spider-Man-c/story. 5-Stan Lee app.			1.75
5-18: 5-Begin $1.95-c; bound-in card sheet. 13-Firestar & Night Thrasher app.14-Darkhawk			2.00

NOW AGE ILLUSTRATED (See Pendulum Illustrated Classics)

NOW AGE BOOKS ILLUSTRATED (See Pendulum Illustrated Classics)

NTH MAN THE ULTIMATE NINJA (See Marvel Comics Presents 25)
Marvel Comics: Aug, 1989 - No. 16, Sept, 1990 ($1.00)

	GD25	FN65	NM94
1-7,9-16-Ninja mercenary			1.00
8-Dale Keown's 1st Marvel work (1/90, pencils)			2.00

NUCLEUS (Also see Cerebus)
Heiro-Graphic Publications: May, 1979 ($1.50, B&W, adult fanzine)

	GD25	FN65	NM94
1-Contains "Demonhorn" by Dave Sim; early app. of Cerebus The Aardvark (4 pg. story)	2.90	8.70	32.00

NUKLA
Dell Publishing Co.: Oct-Dec, 1965 - No. 4, Sept, 1966

	GD25	FN65	NM94
1-Origin & 1st app. Nukla (super hero)	2.70	8.00	30.00
2,3	1.80	5.40	18.00
4-Ditko-a, c(p)	2.50	7.60	28.00

NURSE BETSY CRANE (Formerly Teen Secret Diary)
Charlton Comics: V2#12, Aug, 1961 - V2#27, Mar, 1964 (See Soap Opera Romances)

	GD25	FN65	NM94
V2#12-27	1.50	4.50	12.00

NURSE HELEN GRANT (See The Romances of...)

NURSE LINDA LARK (See Linda Lark)

NURSERY RHYMES
Ziff-Davis Publ. Co. (Approved Comics): No. 10, July-Aug, 1951 - No. 2, Winter, 1951 (Painted-c)

	GD25	FN65	NM94
10 (#1), 2: 10-Howie Post-a	13.00	38.00	95.00

NURSES, THE (TV)
Gold Key: April, 1963 - No. 3, Oct, 1963 (Photo-c: #1,2)

	GD25	FN65	NM94
1	2.40	7.00	26.00
2,3	1.80	5.40	18.00

NUTS! (Satire)
Premiere Comics Group: March, 1954 - No. 5, Nov, 1954

	GD25	FN65	NM94
1-Hollingsworth-a	25.00	74.00	185.00
2,4,5: 5-Capt. Marvel parody	17.00	52.00	130.00
3-Drug "reefers" mentioned	17.00	52.00	130.00

NUTS (Magazine) (Satire)
Health Knowledge: Feb, 1958 - No. 2, April, 1958

	GD25	FN65	NM94
1	6.50	19.50	45.00
2	5.70	17.00	35.00

NUTS & JOLTS
Dell Publishing Co.: No. 22, 1941

	GD25	FN65	NM94
Large Feature Comic 22	9.00	26.00	95.00

NUTSY SQUIRREL (Formerly Hollywood Funny Folks)(See Comic Cavalcade)
National Periodical Publications: #61, 9-10/54 - #69, 1-2/56; #70, 8-9/56 - #71, 10-11/56; #72, 11/57

	GD25	FN65	NM94
61-Mayer-a; Grossman-a in all	12.00	36.00	90.00
62-72: Mayer a-62,65,67-72	8.50	26.00	60.00

NUTTY COMICS
Fawcett Publications: Winter, 1946 (Funny animal)

	GD25	FN65	NM94
1-Capt. Kidd story; 1 pg. Wolverton-a	11.00	32.00	80.00

NUTTY COMICS
Home Comics (Harvey Publications): 1945 - No. 8, June-July, 1947

	GD25	FN65	NM94
nn-Helpful Hank, Bozo Bear & others (funny animal)	6.50	19.50	45.00
2-4	4.25	13.00	28.00
5-8: 5-Rags Rabbit begins(1st app.); infinity-c	4.00	11.00	22.00

NUTTY LIFE (Formerly Krazy Life #1; becomes Wotalife Comics #3 on)
Fox Features Syndicate: No. 2, Summer, 1946

	GD25	FN65	NM94
2	7.85	23.50	55.00

NYOKA, THE JUNGLE GIRL (Formerly Jungle Girl; see The Further Adventures of..., Master Comics #50 & XMas Comics)
Fawcett Publications: No. 2, Winter, 1945 - No. 77, June, 1953 (Movie serial)

	GD25	FN65	NM94
2	49.00	148.00	420.00
3	28.00	84.00	210.00
4,5	24.00	72.00	180.00
6-10	17.00	52.00	130.00
11,13,14,16-18-Krigstein-a: 17-Sam Spade ad by Lou Fine	17.00	52.00	130.00
12,15,19,20	15.00	46.00	115.00
21-30: 25-Clayton Moore photo-c?	9.30	28.00	70.00
31-40	7.85	23.50	55.00
41-50	6.00	18.00	42.00
51-60	5.35	16.00	32.00
61-77	4.25	13.00	28.00

NOTE: *Photo-c from movies 25, 30-70, 72, 75-77. Bondage c-4, 5, 7, 8, 14, 24.*

NYOKA, THE JUNGLE GIRL (Formerly Zoo Funnies; Space Adventures #23 on)
Charlton Comics: No. 14, Nov, 1955 - No. 22, Nov, 1957

	GD25	FN65	NM94
14	8.50	25.50	60.00
15-22	6.00	18.00	42.00

OAKLAND PRESS FUNNYBOOK, THE
The Oakland Press: 9/17/78 - 4/13/80 (16 pgs.) (Weekly)
Full color in comic book form; changes to tabloid size 4/20/80-on

	GD25	FN65	NM94
Contains Tarzan by Manning, Marmaduke, Bugs Bunny, etc. (low distribution); 9/23/79 - 4/13/80 contain Buck Rogers by Gray Morrow & Jim Lawrence			2.00

OAKY DOAKS (See Famous Funnies #190)
Eastern Color Printing Co.: July, 1942 (One Shot)

	GD25	FN65	NM94
1	30.00	90.00	225.00

OBIE
Store Comics: 1953 (6¢)

	GD25	FN65	NM94
1			5.00

The Official Handbook of the Marvel Universe #2 © MAR

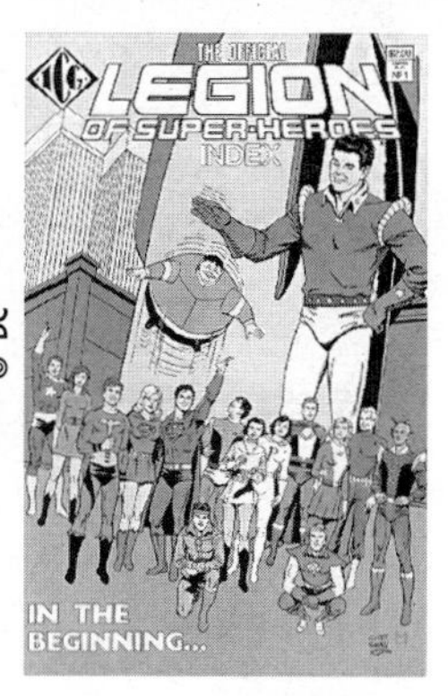

The Official Legion of Super-Heroes Index #1 © DC

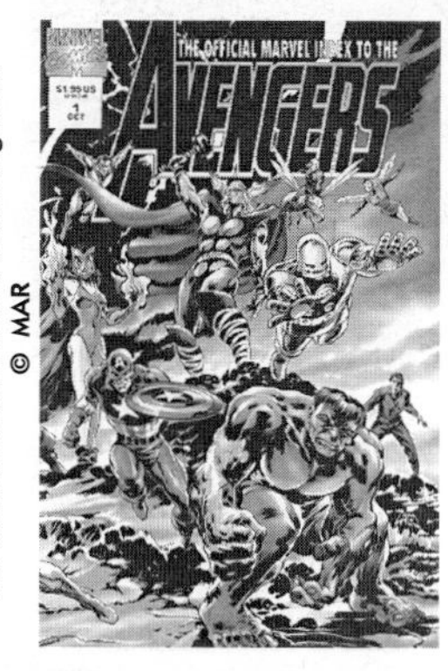

The Official Marvel Index to the Avengers #1 © MAR

GD25 FN65 NM94

OBLIVION
Comico: Aug, 1995 - No. 3, May, 1996 ($2.50)

1-3: 1-Art Adams-c. 2-(1/96)-Polybagged w/gaming card. 3-(5/96)-Darrow-c — 2.50

OBNOXIO THE CLOWN (Character from Crazy Magazine)
Marvel Comics Group: April, 1983 (one-shot)

1-Vs. the X-Men — 1.00

OCCULT FILES OF DR. SPEKTOR, THE
Gold Key/Whitman No. 25: Apr, 1973 - No. 24, Feb, 1977; No. 25, May, 1982 (Painted-c #1-24)

	GD25	FN65	NM94
1-1st app. Lakota; Baron Tibor begins	2.00	6.00	22.00
2-5	1.00	3.00	8.00
6-10: 8-Dracula app.		2.40	6.00
11-13,15-25: 11-1st app. Spektor as Werewolf. 23-Dr. Solar app. 25-Reprints			4.00
14-Dr. Solar app.	1.50	4.50	15.00
9(Modern Comics reprint, 1977)(exist?)	1.80	5.50	20.00

NOTE: *Also see Dan Curtis, Golden Comics Digest 33, Gold Key Spotlight, Mystery Comics Digest 5, & Spine Tingling Tales.*

ODELL'S ADVENTURES IN 3-D (See Adventures in 3-D)

OFFCASTES
Marvel Comics (Epic Comics/Heavy Hitters): July, 1993 - No. 3, Sept, 1993 ($1.95, limited series)

1-3: Mike Vosburg-c/a/scripts in all — 2.00

OFFICIAL CRISIS ON INFINITE EARTHS INDEX, THE
Independent Comics Group (Eclipse): Mar, 1986 ($1.75)

1 — 1.75

OFFICIAL CRISIS ON INFINITE EARTHS CROSSOVER INDEX, THE
Independent Comics Group (Eclipse): July, 1986 ($1.75)

1-Perez-c. — 1.75

OFFICIAL DOOM PATROL INDEX, THE
Independent Comics Group (Eclipse): Feb, 1986 - No. 2, Mar, 1986 ($1.50, limited series)

1,2: Byrne-c. — 1.50

OFFICIAL HANDBOOK OF THE CONAN UNIVERSE (See Handbook of...)

OFFICIAL HANDBOOK OF THE MARVEL UNIVERSE, THE
Marvel Comics Group: Jan, 1983 - No. 15, May, 1984 (Limited series)

	NM94
1-Lists Marvel heroes & villains (letter A)	3.00
2 (B-C)	2.50
3-5: 3-(C-D). 4-(D-G). 5-(H-J)	2.00
6-9: 6-(K-L). 7-(M). 8-(N-P); Punisher-c. 9-(Q-S)	1.50
10-15: 10-(S). 11-(S-U). 12-(V-Z); Wolverine-c. 13,14-Book of the Dead. 15-Weaponry catalogue	1.25

NOTE: ***Bolland** a-8. **Byrne** c/a(p)-1-14; c-15p. **Grell** a-6, 9. **Kirby** a-1, 3. **Layton** a-2, 5, 7. **Mignola** a-3, 4, 5, 6, 8, 12. **Miller** a-4-6, 8, 10. **Nebres** a-3, 4, 8. **Redondo** a-3, 4, 8, 13, 14. **Simonson** a-1, 4, 6-13. **Paul Smith** a-1-12. **Starlin** a-5, 7, 8, 10, 13, 14. **Steranko** a-8p. **Zeck**-2-14.*

OFFICIAL HANDBOOK OF THE MARVEL UNIVERSE, THE
Marvel Comics Group: Dec, 1985 - No. 20, Feb, 1988 ($1.50, maxi-series)

	NM94
V2#1-Byrne-c	3.00
2-5: 2,3-Byrne-c	2.00
6-10	1.50
11-20	1.50
Trade paperback Vol. 1-10 ($6.95)	7.00

NOTE: ***Art Adams** a-7, 8, 11, 12, 14. **Bolland** a-8, 10, 13. **Buckler** a-1, 3, 5, 10. **Buscema** a-1, 5, 8, 9, 10, 13, 14. **Byrne** a-1-14; c-1-11. **Ditko** a-1, 2, 4, 6, 7, 11, 13. a-7, 11. **Mignola** a-2, 4, 9, 11, 13. **Miller** a-2, 4, 12. **Simonson** a-1, 2, 4-13, 15. **Paul Smith** a-1-5, 7-12, 14. **Starlin** a-6, 8, 9, 12, 16. **Zeck** a-1-4, 6, 7, 9-14, 16.*

OFFICIAL HANDBOOK OF THE MARVEL UNIVERSE, THE
Marvel Comics: July, 1989 - No. 8, Mid-Dec, 1990 ($1.50, lim. series, 52 pgs.)

V3#1-8: 1-McFarlane-a(2 pgs.) — 1.50

OFFICIAL HAWKMAN INDEX, THE
Independent Comics Group: Nov, 1986 - No. 2, Dec, 1986 ($2.00)

1,2 — 2.00

OFFICIAL JUSTICE LEAGUE OF AMERICA INDEX, THE
Independent Comics Group (Eclipse): April, 1986 - No. 8, Mar, 1987 ($2.00, Baxter paper)

1-8: 1,2-Perez-c. — 4.00

OFFICIAL LEGION OF SUPER-HEROES INDEX, THE
Independent Comics Group (Eclipse): Dec, 1986 - No. 5, 1987 ($2.00, limited series)(No Official in Title #2 on)

1-5: 4-Mooney-c — 4.00

OFFICIAL MARVEL INDEX TO MARVEL TEAM-UP
Marvel Comics Group: Jan, 1986 - No. 6, 1986 ($1.25, limited series)

1-6 — 2.00

OFFICIAL MARVEL INDEX TO THE AMAZING SPIDER-MAN
Marvel Comics Group: Apr, 1985 - No. 9, Dec, 1985 ($1.25, limited series)

	NM94
1 ($1.00)-Byrne-c.	2.50
2-9: 5,6,8,9-Punisher-c.	2.00

OFFICIAL MARVEL INDEX TO THE AVENGERS, THE
Marvel Comics: Jun, 1987 - No. 7, Aug, 1988 ($2.95, limited series)

1-7 — 4.00

OFFICIAL MARVEL INDEX TO THE AVENGERS, THE
Marvel Comics: V2#1, Oct, 1994 - V2#6, 1995 ($1.95, limited series)

	FN65	NM94
V2#1-#6	.80	2.00

OFFICIAL MARVEL INDEX TO THE FANTASTIC FOUR
Marvel Comics Group: Dec, 1985 - No. 12, Jan, 1987 ($1.25, limited series)

1-12: 1-Byrne-c — 2.00

OFFICIAL MARVEL INDEX TO THE X-MEN, THE
Marvel Comics: May, 1987 - No. 7, July, 1988 ($2.95, limited series)

1-7 — 4.00

OFFICIAL MARVEL INDEX TO THE X-MEN, THE
Marvel Comics: V2#1, Apr, 1994 - V2#5, 1994 ($1.95, limited series)

V2#1-5: 1-Covers X-Men #1-51. 2-Covers #52-122,Special #1,2,Giant-Size #1,2. 3-Byrne-c; covers #123-177, Annuals 3-7, Spec. Ed. #1. 4-Covers Uncanny X-Men #178-234, Annuals 8-12. 5-Covers #235-287, Annuals 13-15 — 2.00

OFFICIAL SOUPY SALES COMIC (See Soupy Sales)

OFFICIAL TEEN TITANS INDEX, THE
Indep. Comics Group (Eclipse): Aug, 1985 - No. 5, 1986 ($1.50, lim. series)

1-5 — 2.00

OFFICIAL TRUE CRIME CASES (Formerly Sub-Mariner #23; All-True Crime Cases #26 on)
Marvel Comics (OCI): No. 24, Fall, 1947 - No. 25, Winter, 1947-48

	GD25	FN65	NM94
24(#1)-Burgos-a; Syd Shores-c	20.00	60.00	150.00
25-Syd Shores-c; Kurtzman's "Hey Look"	16.00	48.00	120.00

OF SUCH IS THE KINGDOM
George A. Pflaum: 1955 (15¢, 36 pgs.)

	GD25	FN65	NM94
nn-Reprints from 1951 Treasure Chest	2.40	6.00	12.00

O.G. WHIZ (See Gold Key Spotlight #10)
Gold Key: 2/71 - No. 6, 5/72; No. 7, 5/78 - No. 11, 1/79 (No. 7: 52 pgs.)

	GD25	FN65	NM94
1,2-John Stanley scripts	5.00	15.00	55.00
3-6(1972)	2.50	7.50	28.00

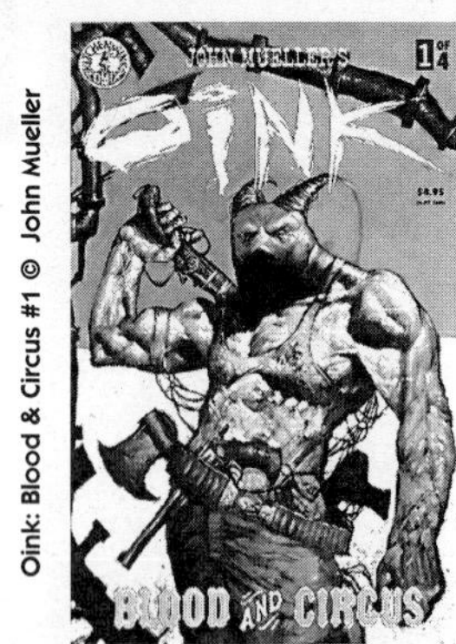

Oink: Blood & Circus #1 © John Mueller

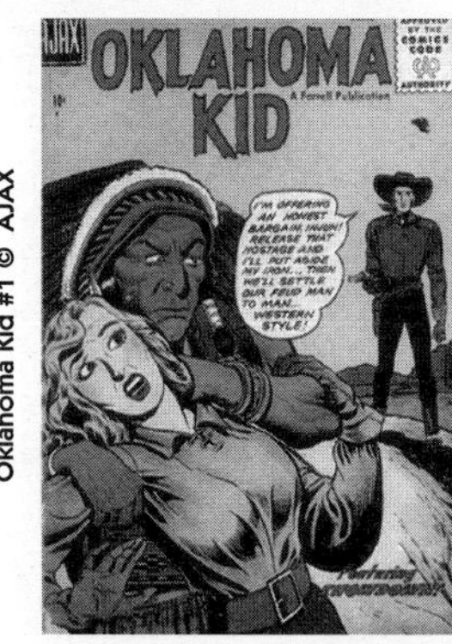

Oklahoma Kid #1 © AJAX

The Omen #1 © Chaos!

GD25 FN65 NM94

7-11(1978-79)-Part-r: 9-Tubby app. 1.50 4.50 12.00

OH, BROTHER! (Teen Comedy)
Stanhall Publ.: Jan, 1953 - No. 5, Oct, 1953
1-By Bill Williams 5.70 17.00 35.00
2-5 4.00 11.00 22.00

OH MY GODDESS! (Manga)
Dark Horse Comics: Aug, 1994 - No. 6, Jan, 1995($2.50, B&W, limited series)
1-6 4.00
... PART II Feb, 1995 - No. 9, Sept, 1995 ($2.50, B&W, limited series)
1-9 3.00
... PART III Nov, 1995 - No. 11, Sept, 1996 ($2.95, B&W, lim. series)
1-11 3.00
... PART IV Dec, 1996 - No. 8, July, 1997 ($2.95, B&W, limited series)
1-8 3.00
... PART V Sept, 1997 - Present ($2.95, B&W, limited series)
1,2,5,8: 5-Ninja Master pt. 1 3.00
3,4,6,7,10-12-($3.95, 48 pgs.) 10-Fallen Angel. 11-Play The Game 4.00
9-($3.50) "It's Lonely At The Top" 1.40 3.50

OH SUSANNA (TV)
Dell Publishing Co.: No. 1105, June-Aug, 1960 (Gale Storm)
Four Color 1105-Toth-a, photo-c 12.00 35.00 130.00

OINK: BLOOD AND CIRCUS
Kitchen Sink: 1998 - No. 4, July, 1998 ($4.95, limited series)
1-4-John Mueller-s/a 5.00

OKAY COMICS
United Features Syndicate: July, 1940
1-Captain & the Kids & Hawkshaw the Detective reprints 39.00 117.00 310.00

O.K. COMICS
United Features Syndicate/Hit Publications: July, 1940 - No. 2, Oct, 1940
1-Little Giant (w/super powers), Phantom Knight, Sunset Smith, & The Teller Twins begin 65.00 194.00 550.00
2 (Rare)-Origin Mister Mist by Chas. Quinlan 65.00 194.00 550.00

OKLAHOMA KID
Ajax/Farrell Publ.: June, 1957 - No. 4, 1958
1 8.50 26.00 60.00
2-4 5.70 17.00 35.00

OKLAHOMAN, THE
Dell Publishing Co.: No. 820, July, 1957
Four Color 820-Movie, photo-c 9.00 27.00 100.00

OKTANE
Dark Horse Comics: Aug, 1995 - Nov, 1995($2.50, color, limited series)
1-4-Gene Ha-a 2.50

OLD GLORY COMICS
Chesapeake & Ohio Railway: 1944 (Giveaway)
nn-Capt. Fearless reprint 5.70 17.00 35.00

OLD IRONSIDES (Disney)
Dell Publishing Co.: No. 874, Jan, 1958
Four Color 874-Movie w/Johnny Tremain 5.50 16.50 60.00

OLD YELLER (Disney, see Movie Comics, and Walt Disney Showcase #25)
Dell Publishing Co.: No. 869, Jan, 1958
Four Color 869-Movie, photo-c 4.50 13.50 50.00

OMAC (One Man Army; ...Corps. #4 on; also see Kamandi #59 & Warlord) (See Cancelled Comic Cavalcade)

GD25 FN65 NM94

National Periodical Publications: Sept-Oct, 1974 - No. 8, Nov-Dec, 1975
1-Origin .90 2.70 8.00
2-8: 8-2 pg. Neal Adams ad 4.00
NOTE: ***Kirby*** *a-1-8p; c-1-7p.* ***Kubert*** *c-8.*

OMAC: ONE MAN ARMY CORPS
DC Comics: 1991 - No. 4, 1991 ($3.95, B&W, mini-series, mature, 52 pgs.)
Book One - Four: John Byrne-c/a & scripts 4.00

O'MALLEY AND THE ALLEY CATS
Gold Key: April, 1971 - No. 9, Jan, 1974 (Disney)
1 1.60 4.80 16.00
2-9 1.00 3.00 10.00

OMEGA ELITE
Blackthorne Publishing: 1987 ($1.25)
1-Starlin-c 1.25

OMEGA MEN, THE (See Green Lantern #141)
DC Comics: Dec, 1982 - No. 38, May, 1986 ($1.00/$1.50; Baxter paper)
1 1.50
2,4,6-8,11-18,21-36,38: 2-Origin Broot. 7-Origin The Citadel. 26,27-Alan Moore scripts. 30-Intro new Primus. 31-Crisis x-over. 34,35-Teen Titans x-over 1.00
3-1st app. Lobo (5 pgs.)(6/83); Lobo-c 3.00
5,9-2nd & 3rd app. Lobo (cameo, 2 pgs. each) 2.00
10-1st full Lobo story 3.00
19-Lobo cameo 1.50
20-2nd full Lobo story 3.00
37-1st solo Lobo story (8 pg. back-up by Giffen) 2.00
Annual 1(11/84, 52 pgs.), 2(11/85) 1.50
NOTE: ***Giffen*** *c/a-1-6p.* ***Morrow*** *a-24r.* ***Nino*** *c/a-16, 21; a-Annual 1i.*

OMEGA THE UNKNOWN
Marvel Comics Group: March, 1976 - No. 10, Oct, 1977
1-1st app. Omega 4.00
2-(Regular 25¢ edition)-Hulk-c/story. 4.00
2-(30¢-c, limited distribution) 1.60 4.80 16.00
3,8: 3-Electro-c/story. 8-1st app. 2nd Foolkiller (Greg Salinger), 1 panel only (cameo) 4.00
4-7,10 3.00
9-(Regular 30¢ edition)(7/77)-1st full app. 2nd Foolkiller 4.00
9-(35¢-c, limited distribution) 1.60 4.80 16.00
NOTE: ***Kane*** *c(p)-3, 5, 8, 9.* ***Mooney*** *a-1-3, 4p, 5, 6p, 7, 8i, 9, 10.*

OMEN
Northstar Publishing: 1989 - No. 3, 1989 ($2.00, B&W, mature)
1-Tim Vigil-c/a in all .90 2.70 8.00
1, (2nd printing), 2,3 2.00
2,3 5.00

OMEN, THE
Chaos! Comics: May, 1998 - No. 5, Sept, 1998 ($2.95, limited series)
1-5: 1-Six covers 2.95
...: Vexed (10/98, $2.95) Chaos! characters appear 2.95

OMNI MEN
Blackthorne Publishing: 1987 - No. 3, 1987 ($1.25)
1-3 1.25

ONE, THE
Marvel Comics (Epic Comics): July, 1985 - No. 6, Feb, 1986 (Limited series, mature)
1-6: Post nuclear holocaust super-hero. 2-Intro The Other 1.50

ONE-ARM SWORDSMAN, THE
Victory Prod./Lueng's Publ. #4 on: 1987 - No. 12, 1990 ($2.75/$1.80, 52pgs.)
1-3 ($2.75) 2.75

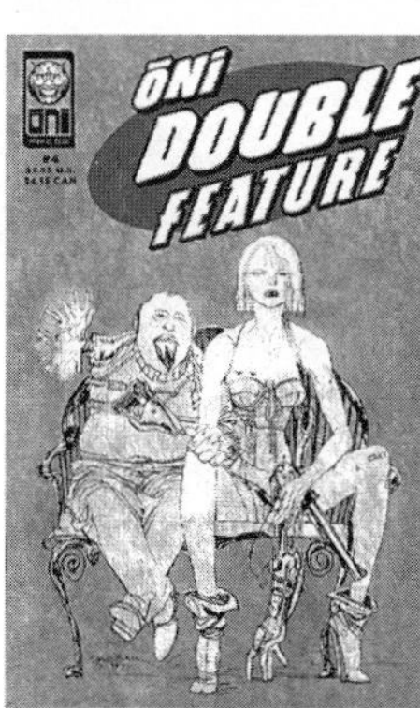

Oni Double Feature #4 © Oni Press

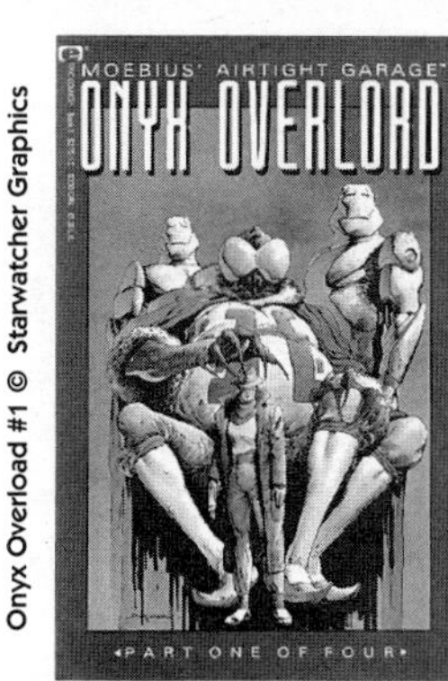

Onyx Overload #1 © Starwatcher Graphics

Operation Peril #8 © ACG

	GD25	FN65	NM94
4-12: 4-6-$1.80-c. 7-12-$2.00-c			1.80

ONE HUNDRED AND ONE DALMATIANS (Disney, see Cartoon Tales, Movie Comics, and Walt Disney Showcase #9, 51)
Dell Publishing Co.: No. 1183, Mar, 1961

Four Color 1183-Movie	9.00	27.00	100.00

101 DALMATIONS (Movie)
Disney Comics: 1991 (52 pgs., graphic novel)

nn-($4.95, direct sales)-r/movie adaptation & more			5.00
1-($2.95, newsstand edition)			3.00

101 WAYS TO END THE CLONE SAGA (See Spider-Man)
Marvel Comics: Jan, 1997 ($2.50, one-shot)

1			2.50

100 PAGES OF COMICS
Dell Publishing Co.: 1937 (Stiff covers, square binding)

101(Found on back cover)-Alley Oop, Wash Tubbs, Capt. Easy, Og Son of Fire, Apple Mary, Tom Mix, Dan Dunn, Tailspin Tommy, Doctor Doom	138.00	415.00	1175.00

100 PAGE SUPER SPECTACULAR (See DC 100 Page...)

100% TRUE?
DC Comics (Paradox Press): Summer 1996 - Present ($4.95, B&W)

1,2-Reprints stories from various Paradox Press books.			5.00

$1,000,000 DUCK (See Walt Disney Showcase #5)

ONE MILLION YEARS AGO (Tor #2 on)
St. John Publishing Co.: Sept, 1953

1-Origin & 1st app. Tor; Kubert-c/a; Kubert photo inside front cover	17.00	52.00	130.00

ONE SHOT (See Four Color...)

1001 HOURS OF FUN
Dell Publishing Co.: No. 13, 1943

Large Feature Comic 13 (nn)-Puzzles & games; by A.W. Nugent. This book was bound as #13 w/Large Feature Comics in publisher's files	24.00	72.00	180.00

ONE TRICK RIP OFF, THE (See Dark Horse Presents)

ONI DOUBLE FEATURE (See Clerks: The Comic Book and Jay & Silent Bob)
Oni Press: Jan, 1998 - Present ($2.95, B&W)

1-Jay & Silent Bob; Kevin Smith-s/Matt Wagner-a	.90	2.70	8.00
1-2nd printing		1.20	3.00
2-10: 2,3-Paul Pope-s/a. 3,4-Nixey-s/a. 4,5-Sienkewicz-s/a. 6,7-Gaiman-s. 9-Bagge-c			3.00

ONIGAMI (See Warrior Nun Areala: Black & White)
Antarctic Press: Apr, 1998 - No. 3, July, 1998 ($2.95, B&W, limited series)

1-3-Michel Lacombe-s/a			2.95

ONSLAUGHT: EPILOGUE
Marvel Comics: Feb, 1997 ($2.95, one-shot)

1-Hama-s/Green-a; Xavier-c; Bastion-app.			3.00

ONSLAUGHT: MARVEL
Marvel Comics: Oct, 1996 ($3.95, one-shot)

1-Conclusion to Onslaught x-over; wraparound-c	.85	2.60	7.00

ONSLAUGHT: X-MEN
Marvel Comics: Aug, 1996 ($3.95, one-shot)

1-Mark Waid & Scott Lobdell script; Fantastic Four & Avengers app.; Xavier as Onslaught			5.00
1-Variant-c	1.20	3.60	12.00

ON STAGE
Dell Publishing Co.: No. 1336, Apr-June, 1962

	GD25	FN65	NM94
Four Color 1336-Not by Leonard Starr	3.60	11.00	40.00

ON THE AIR
NBC Network Comic: 1947 (Giveaway, paper-c)

nn-(Rare)	23.00	70.00	175.00

ON THE DOUBLE (Movie)
Dell Publishing Co.: No. 1232, Sept-Nov, 1961

Four Color 1232	3.60	11.00	40.00

ON THE ROAD WITH ANDRAE CROUCH
Spire Christian Comics (Fleming H. Revell): 1973, 1977 (39¢)

nn			3.00

ON THE SPOT (Pretty Boy Floyd...)
Fawcett Publications: Fall, 1948

nn-Pretty Boy Floyd photo on-c; bondage-c	29.00	86.00	215.00

ONYX OVERLORD
Marvel Comics (Epic): Oct, 1992 - No. 4, Jan, 1993 ($2.75, mini-series)

1-4: Moebius scripts			2.75

OPEN SPACE
Marvel Comics: Mid-Dec, 1989 - No. 4, Aug, 1990 ($4.95, bi-monthly, 68 pgs.)

1-4: 1-Bill Wray-a; Freas-c			5.00

OPERATION BIKINI (See Movie Classics)
OPERATION BUCHAREST (See The Crusaders)
OPERATION CROSSBOW (See Movie Classics)

OPERATION: KNIGHTSTRIKE (See Knightstrike)
Image Comics (Extreme Studios): May, 1995 - No.3, July, 1995 ($2.50)

1-3			2.50

OPERATION PERIL
American Comics Group (Michel Publ.): Oct-Nov, 1950 - No. 16, Apr-May, 1953 (#1-5: 52 pgs.)

1-Time Travelers, Danny Danger (by Leonard Starr) & Typhoon Tyler (by Ogden Whitney) begin	33.00	100.00	250.00
2-War-c	20.00	60.00	150.00
3-War-c; horror story	18.00	52.00	130.00
4,5-Sci/fi-c/story	19.00	56.00	140.00
6-10: 6,8,9,10-Sci/fi-c. 6-Dinosaur-c. 7-Sabretooth-c	15.00	44.00	110.00
11,12-War-c; last Time Travelers	11.00	32.00	80.00
13-16: All war format	7.50	22.50	52.00

NOTE: ***Starr** a-2, 5. **Whitney** a-1, 2, 5-10, 12; c-1, 3, 5, 8, 9.*

OPERATION: STORMBREAKER
Acclaim Comics (Valiant Heroes): Aug, 1997 ($3.95, one-shot)

1-Waid/Augustyn-s, Braithwaite-a			3.95

OPTIC NERVE
Drawn and Quarterly: Apr, 1995 - Present ($2.95, bi-annual)

1,2: Adrian Tomine-c/a/scripts in all			5.00
3-5			3.00
32 Stories-($9.95, trade paperback)-r/Optic Nerve mini-comics			10.00
32 Stories-($29.95, hardcover)-r/Optic Nerve mini-comics; signed & numbered			30.00

ORAL ROBERTS' TRUE STORIES (Junior Partners #120 on)
TelePix Publ. (Oral Roberts' Evangelistic Assoc./Healing Waters): 1956 (no month) - No. 119, 7/59 (15¢)(No. 102: 25¢)

V1#1(1956)-(Not code approved)- "The Miracle Touch"	18.00	54.00	135.00
102-(Only issue approved by code, 10/56) "Now I See"	11.00	32.00	80.00
103-119: 115-(114 on inside)	7.15	21.50	50.00

NOTE: *Also see Happiness & Healing For You.*

Original E-Man & Michael Mauser #6 © FC

Original Ghost Rider #12 © MAR

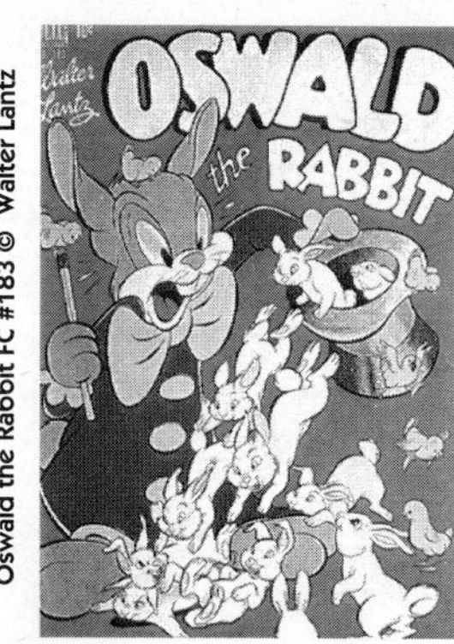

Oswald the Rabbit FC #183 © Walter Lantz

GD25 FN65 NM94

ORANGE BIRD, THE
Walt Disney Educational Media Co.: No date (1980) (36 pgs.; in color; slick cover)

nn-Included with educational kit on foods 1.00
...in Nutrition Adventures nn (1980) .60
...and the Nutrition Know-How Revue nn (1983) .60

ORBIT
Eclipse Books:1990 - No. 3, 1990 ($4.95, 52 pgs., squarebound)

1-3: Reprints from Isaac Asimov's Science Fiction Magazine; 1-Dave Stevens-c, Bolton-a. 3-Bolton-c/a, Yeates-a 5.00

ORIENTAL HEROES
Jademan Comics: Aug, 1988 - No. 55, Feb, 1993 ($1.50/$1.95, 68pgs.)

1-9 ($1.50) 1.50
10-55 ($1.95) 2.00

ORIGINAL ASTRO BOY, THE
Now Comics: Sept, 1987 - No. 19, 1989 ($1.50/$1.75)

1-All have Ken Steacy painted-c/a 2.00
2,3: 3-Begin $1.75-c 1.75
4-19 1.50

ORIGINAL BLACK CAT, THE
Recollections: Oct. 6, 1988 - No. 9, 1992 ($2.00, limited series)

1-9: Elias-r; 1-Bondage-c. 2-M. Anderson-c 2.00

ORIGINAL DICK TRACY, THE
Gladstone Publishing: Sept, 1990 - No. 5, 1991 ($1.95, bi-monthly, 68pgs.)

1-5: 1-Vs. Pruneface. 2-& the Evil influence; begin $2.00-c 2.00

NOTE: *#1 reprints strips 7/16/43 - 9/30/43. #2 reprints strips 12/1/46 - 2/2/47. #3 reprints 8/31/46 - 11/14/46. #4 reprints 9/17/45 - 12/23/45. #5 reprints 6/10/46 - 8/28/46.*

ORIGINAL DOCTOR SOLAR, MAN OF THE ATOM, THE
Valiant: Apr, 1995 ($2.95, one-shot)

1-Reprints Doctor Solar, Man of the Atom #1,5; Bob Fugitani-r; Paul Smith-c; afterword by Seaborn Adamson 3.00

ORIGINAL E-MAN AND MICHAEL MAUSER, THE
First Comics: Oct, 1985 - No. 7, April, 1986 ($1.75, Baxter paper)

1-Has r-/Charlton's E-Man, Vengeance Squad 2.00
2-6: 2-Shows #4 in indicia by mistake 1.80
7 ($2.00, 44pgs.)-Staton-a 2.00

ORIGINAL GHOST RIDER, THE
Marvel Comics: July, 1992 - No. 20, Feb, 1994 ($1.75)

1-20: 1-7-r/Marvel Spotlight #5-11 by Ploog w/new-c. 3-New Phantom Rider (former Night Rider) back-ups begin by Ayers. 4-Quesada-c(p). 8-Ploog-c. 8,9-r/Ghost Rider #1,2. 10-r/Marvel Spotlight #12. 11-18,20-r/Ghost Rider #3-12. 19-r/Marvel Two-in-One #8 1.75

ORIGINAL GHOST RIDER RIDES AGAIN, THE
Marvel Comics: July, 1991 - No. 7, Jan, 1992, ($1.50, limited series, 52 pgs.)

1-Reprints Ghost Rider #68(origin),69 w/covers 1.50
2-7: Reprints G.R. #70-81 w/covers 1.50

ORIGINAL MAGNUS ROBOT FIGHTER, THE
Valiant: Apr, 1995 ($2.95, one-shot)

1-Reprints Magnus, Robot Fighter 4000 #2; Russ Manning-r; Rick Leonardi-c; afterword by Seaborn Adamson 3.00

ORIGINAL NEXUS GRAPHIC NOVEL (See First Comics Graphic Novel #19)

ORIGINAL SHIELD, THE
Archie Enterprises, Inc.: Apr, 1984 - No. 4, Oct, 1984

1-4: 1,2-Origin Shield; Ayers p-1-4, Nebres c-1,2 1.00

ORIGINAL SWAMP THING SAGA, THE (See DC Special Series #2, 14, 17, 20)

GD25 FN65 NM94

ORIGINAL TUROK, SON OF STONE, THE
Valiant: Apr, 1995 - No. 2, May, 1995 ($2.95, limited series)

1,2: 1-Reprints Turok, Son of Stone #24,25,42; Alberto Gioletti-r; Rags Morales-c; afterword by Seaborn Adamson. 2-Reprints Turok, Son of Stone #24,33; Gioletti-r; Mike McKone-c 3.00

ORIGIN OF GALACTUS (See Fantastic Four #48-50)
Marvel Comics: Feb, 1996 ($2.50, one-shot)

1-Lee & Kirby reprints w/pin-ups 2.50

ORIGIN OF THE DEFIANT UNIVERSE, THE
Defiant Comics: Feb, 1994 ($1.50, 20 pgs., one-shot)

1-David Lapham, Adam Pollina & Alan Weiss-a; Weiss-c 1.50

NOTE: *The comic was originally published as Defiant Genesis and was distributed at the 1994 Philadelphia ComicCon.*

ORIGINS OF MARVEL COMICS (See Fireside Book Series)

ORION (Manga)
Dark Horse Comics: Sept, 1992 - No. 6, July, 1993 ($2.95/$3.95, B&W, bimonthly, limited series)

1,2,6-($3.95, squarebound): 1-Masamune Shirow-c/a/s in all 4.00
4,5-($2.95) 3.00

OSBORNE JOURNALS (See Spider-Man titles)
Marvel Comics: Feb, 1997 ($2.95, one-shot)

1-Hotz-c/a 2.95

OSCAR COMICS (Formerly Funny Tunes; Awful...#11 & 12) (Also see Cindy Comics)
Marvel Comics: No. 24, Spring, 1947 - No. 10, Apr, 1949; No. 13, Oct, 1949

	GD25	FN65	NM94
24(#1, Spring, 1947)	12.00	36.00	90.00
25(#2, Sum, 1947)-Wolverton-a plus Kurtzman's "Hey Look"	15.00	46.00	115.00
26(#3)-Same as regular #3 except #26 was printed over in black ink with #3 appearing on-c below the over print	9.30	28.00	65.00
3-9,13: 8-Margie app.	9.30	28.00	65.00
10-Kurtzman's "Hey Look"	11.00	32.00	80.00

OSWALD THE RABBIT (Also see New Fun Comics #1)
Dell Publishing Co.: No. 21, 1943 - No. 1268, 12-2/61-62 (Walter Lantz)

	GD25	FN65	NM94
Four Color 21(1943)	46.00	139.00	510.00
Four Color 39(1943)	33.00	98.00	360.00
Four Color 67(1944)	16.00	48.00	175.00
Four Color 102(1946)-Kelly-a, 1 pg.	14.00	41.00	150.00
Four Color 143,183	8.00	25.00	90.00
Four Color 225,273	5.00	15.00	55.00
Four Color 315,388	4.00	12.00	45.00
Four Color 458,507,549,593	2.90	8.70	32.00
Four Color 623,697,792,894,979,1268	2.00	6.00	22.00

OSWALD THE RABBIT (See The Funnies, March of Comics #7, 38, 53, 67, 81, 95, 111, 126, 141, 156, 171, 186, New Funnies & Super Book #8, 20)

OTHERS, THE
Image Comics (Shadowline Ink): 1995 - No. 3, 1995 ($2.50)

0 ($1.00)-16 pg. preview 1.00
1-3 2.50

OTIS GOES TO HOLLYWOOD
Dark Horse Comics: Apr, 1997 - No.2, May, 1997 ($2.95, B&W, mini-series)

1,2-Fingerman-c/s/a 3.00

OUTCAST, THE
Valiant: Dec, 1995 ($2.50, one-shot)

1-Breyfogle-a. 2.50

OUR ARMY AT WAR (Becomes Sgt. Rock #302 on; also see Army At War)
National Periodical Publications: Aug, 1952 - No. 301, Feb, 1977

Our Army at War #8 © DC

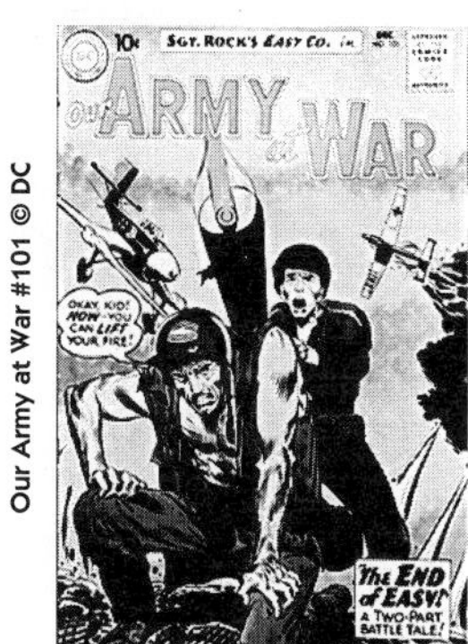

Our Army at War #101 © DC

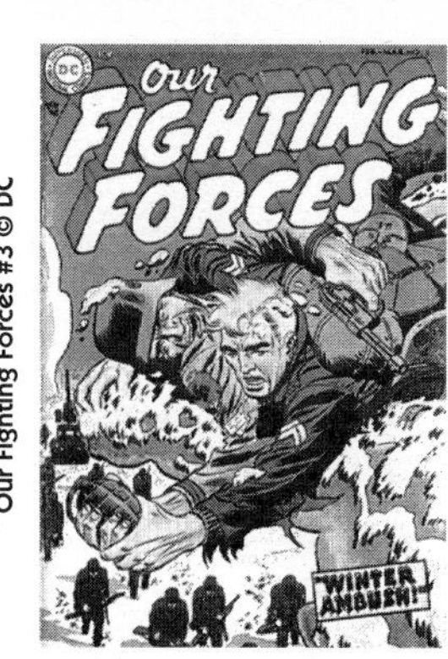

Our Fighting Forces #3 © DC

	GD25	FN65	NM94
1	117.00	351.00	1400.00
2	54.00	162.00	650.00
3,4: 4-Krigstein-a	43.00	129.00	475.00
5-7	36.00	108.00	390.00
8-11,14-Krigstein-a	33.00	100.00	360.00
12,15-20	28.00	84.00	280.00
13-Krigstein-c/a; flag-c	34.00	102.00	370.00
21-31: Last precode (2/55)	19.00	57.00	190.00
32-40	16.00	48.00	160.00
41-60: 51-1st S.A. issue	13.50	40.00	135.00
61-70: 67-Minor Sgt. Rock prototype	11.50	34.00	115.00
71-80	9.50	28.50	95.00

	GD25	FN65	VF82	NM94
81- (4/59)-Sgt. Rocky of Easy Co. app. by Andru & Esposito; (the last Sgt. Rock prototype)	177.00	531.00	900.00	2300.00
82-1st Sgt. Rock app., in name only, in Easy Co. story (6 panels) by Kanigher & Drucker	41.00	123.00	246.00	500.00
83-(6/59)-1st true Sgt. Rock app. in "The Rock and the Wall" by Kubert & Kanigher; (most similar to prototype in G.I. Combat #68)	100.00	300.00	600.00	1200.00

	GD25	FN65	NM94
84-Kubert-c	23.00	69.00	230.00
85-Origin & 1st app. Ice Cream Soldier	32.00	96.00	320.00
86,87-Early Sgt. Rock; Kubert-a	22.00	66.00	220.00
88-1st Sgt. Rock-c; Kubert-c/a	24.00	72.00	240.00
89	20.00	60.00	200.00
90-Kubert-c/a; How Rock got his stripes	26.00	78.00	260.00
91-All-Sgt. Rock issue; Grandenetti-c/Kubert-a	45.00	135.00	550.00
92,94,96-99: 97-Regular Kubert-c begin	13.50	40.00	135.00
93-1st Zack Nolan	14.50	44.00	145.00
95,100: 95-1st app. Bulldozer	14.50	44.00	145.00
101,105,108,113,115: 101-1st app. Buster. 105-1st app. Junior. 113-1st app. Wildman & Jackie Johnson. 115-Rock revealed as orphan; 1st x-over Mlle. Marie. 1st Sgt. Rock's battle family	10.00	30.00	100.00
102-104,106,107,109,110,114,116-120: 104-Nurse Jane-c/s. 109-Pre Easy Co. Sgt. Rock-s. 118-Sunny injured	9.00	27.00	90.00
111-1st app. Wee Willie & Sunny	10.00	30.00	100.00
112-Classic Easy Co. roster-c	11.00	33.00	110.00
121-125,130-133,135-139,141-150: 138-1st Sparrow. 141-1st Shaker. 147,148-Rock becomes a General	5.50	16.50	55.00
126,129,134: 126-1st app. Canary; grey tone-c	6.00	18.00	60.00
127-2nd all-Sgt. Rock issue; 1st app. Little Sure	7.00	21.00	70.00
128-Training & origin Sgt. Rock; 1st Sgt. Krupp	20.00	60.00	200.00
140-3rd all-Sgt. Rock issue	6.00	18.00	60.00
151-Intro. Enemy Ace by Kubert (2/65)	30.00	90.00	300.00
152-4th all-Sgt. Rock issue	5.00	15.00	50.00
153-2nd app. Enemy Ace (4/65)	13.50	41.00	135.00
154,156,157,159-161,165-167: 157-2 pg. pin-up: 159-1st Nurse Wendy Winston-c/s. 165-2nd Iron Major	4.50	13.50	45.00
155-3rd app. Enemy Ace (6/65)(see Showcase)	9.00	27.00	90.00
158-Origin & 1st app. Iron Major(9/65), formerly Iron Captain	5.50	16.50	55.00
162,163-Viking Prince x-over in Sgt. Rock	5.00	15.00	50.00
164-Giant G-19	8.00	24.00	80.00
168-1st Unknown Soldier app.; referenced in Star-Spangled War Stories #157; (Sgt. Rock x-over) (6/66)	8.00	24.00	80.00
169,170	4.20	12.60	42.00
171-176,178-181: 171-1st Mad Emperor	3.20	9.60	32.00
177-(80 pg. Giant G-32)	5.00	15.00	50.00
182,183,186-Neal Adams-a. 186-Origin retold	4.00	12.00	40.00
184,185,187,188,193-195,197-199: 184-Wee Willie dies	3.00	9.00	30.00
189,191,192,196: 189-Intro. The Teen-age Underground Fighters of Unit 3. 196-Hitler cameo	3.00	9.00	30.00
190-(80 pg. Giant G-44)	4.50	13.50	45.00
200-12 pg. Rock story told in verse; Evans-a	3.50	10.50	35.00
201-Krigstein-r/#14	2.25	6.75	18.00
202,204-215: 204,205-All reprints; no Sgt. Rock	2.25	6.75	18.00
203-(80 pg. Giant G-56)-All-r, Sgt. Rock story	4.00	12.00	40.00
216,229-(80 pg. Giants G-68, G-80): 216-Has G-58 on-c by mistake	4.00	12.00	40.00
217-219: 218-1st U.S.S. Stevens	1.50	4.50	15.00
220-Classic dinosaur/Sgt. Rock-c/s	1.80	5.40	18.00
221-228,230-234: 231-Intro/death Rock's brother	1.40	4.20	14.00
235-239,241: 52 pg. Giants	1.80	5.40	18.00
240-Neal Adams-a; 52 pg. Giant	2.40	7.00	26.00
242-Also listed as **DC 100 Page Super Spectacular #9**; see for price			-
243-246: 244-(52 pgs.) no Adams-a	1.60	4.80	16.00
247-250,254-268,270: 247-Joan of Arc	1.10	3.30	11.00
251-253-Return of Iron Major	1.20	3.60	12.00
269,275-(100 pgs.)	2.50	7.60	28.00
271-274,276-279: 273-Crucifixion-c	1.10	3.30	11.00
280-(68 pgs.)-200th app. Sgt. Rock; reprints Our Army at War #81,83	2.00	6.00	20.00
281-299,301: 295-Bicentennial cover	1.00	3.00	10.00
300-Sgt. Rock-s by Kubert (2/77)	1.20	3.60	12.00

*NOTE **Alcala** a-251. **Drucker** a-27, 67, 68, 79, 82, 83, 96, 164, 177, 203, 212, 243r, 244, 269r, 275r, 280r. **Evans** a-165-175, 200, 266, 269, 270, 274, 276, 278, 280. **Glanzman** a-218, 220, 222, 223, 225, 227, 230-232, 238-241, 244, 247, 248, 256-259, 261, 265-267, 271, 282, 283, 298. **Grandenetti** c-91. **Grell** a-287. **Heath** a-50, 164, & most 176-281. **Kubert** a-38, 59, 67, 68 & most issues from 83-165, 233, 236, 267, 275, 300; c-84, 280. **Maurer** a-233, 237, 239, 240, 45, 280, 284, 288, 290, 291, 295. **Severin** a-236, 252, 265, 267, 269r, 272. **Toth** a-235, 241, 254. **Wildey** a-283-285, 287p. **Wood** a-249.*

OUR FIGHTING FORCES

National Per. Publ./DC Comics: Oct-Nov, 1954 - No. 181, Sept-Oct, 1978

	GD25	FN65	NM94
1-Grandenetti-c/a	75.00	225.00	790.00
2	34.00	102.00	370.00
3-Kubert-c; last precode issue (3/55)	31.00	93.00	315.00
4,5	24.00	72.00	240.00
6-9: 7-1st S.A. issue	20.50	63.00	205.00
10-Wood-a	21.50	65.00	215.00
11-20: 20-Grey tone-c (4/57)	16.00	48.00	160.00
21-30	11.00	33.00	110.00
31-40	10.50	32.00	105.00
41-Unknown Soldier tryout	12.50	38.00	125.00
42-44	9.00	27.00	90.00
45-Gunner & Sarge begins, end #94	30.00	90.00	300.00
46	12.50	38.00	125.00
47	9.00	27.00	90.00
48,50	7.00	21.00	70.00
49-1st Pooch	10.00	30.00	100.00
51-64: 51-Grey tone-c. 64-Last 10¢ issue	6.50	19.50	65.00
65-70	4.50	13.50	45.00
71-80: 71-Grey tone-c	2.60	7.80	26.00
81-90	2.50	7.50	24.00
91-98: 95-Devil-Dog begins, ends #98.	2.00	6.00	16.00
99-Capt. Hunter begins, ends #106	2.50	7.50	22.00
100	2.50	7.50	20.00
101-105,107-122: 116-Mlle. Marie app. 121-Intro. Heller	1.60	4.80	16.00
106-Hunters Hellcats begin	1.80	5.40	18.00
123-Losers (Capt. Storm, Gunner & Sarge, Johnny Cloud) begin	3.20	9.50	35.00
124-132	1.40	4.20	14.00
133-137 (Giants). 134-Toth-a	1.60	4.80	16.00
138-150: 146-Toth-a	1.00	3.00	10.00
151-162-Kirby a(p)	1.40	4.20	14.00
163-180	.90	2.70	8.00
181-Last issue	1.00	3.00	10.00

Our Gang Comics #2 © Loew's, Inc.

OUR GANG COMICS
OUR GANG · BARNEY BEAR
TOM & JERRY · FLIP & DIP · PETE SMITH

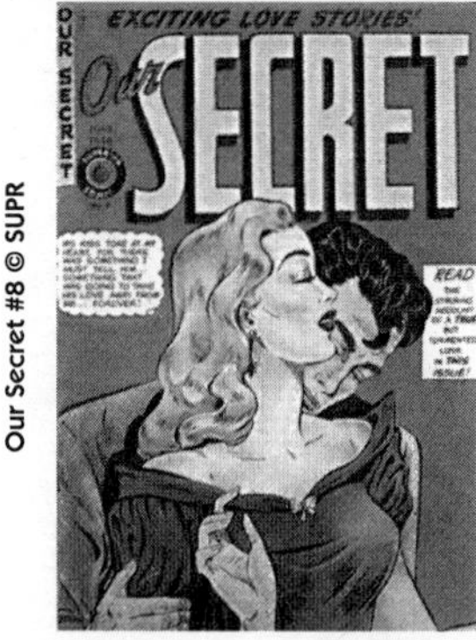

Our Secret #8 © SUPR

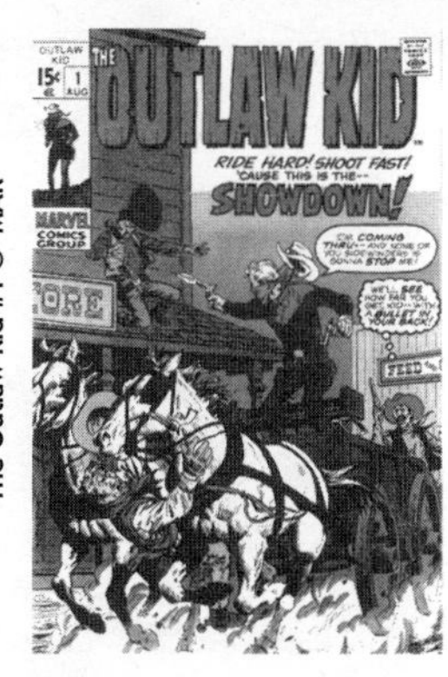

The Outlaw Kid #1 © MAR

GD25 FN65 NM94

NOTE: **N. Adams** c-147. **Drucker** a-28, 37, 39, 42-44, 49, 53, 133r. **Evans** a-149, 164-174, 177-181. **Glanzman** a-125-128, 132, 134, 138-141, 143, 144. **Heath** a-2, 16, 18, 28, 41, 44, 49, 114, 135-138r; c-51. **Kirby** a-151-162p; c-152-159. **Kubert** c/a in many issues. **Maurer** a-135. **Redondo** a-166. **Severin** a-123-130, 131i, 132-150.

OUR FIGHTING MEN IN ACTION (See Men In Action)

OUR FLAG COMICS
Ace Magazines: Aug, 1941 - No. 5, April, 1942

1-Captain Victory, The Unknown Soldier (intro.) & The Three Cheers begin
194.00 582.00 1650.00
2-Origin The Flag (patriotic hero); 1st app? 97.00 291.00 825.00
3-5: 5-Intro & 1st app. Mr. Risk 78.00 234.00 665.00
NOTE: **Anderson** a-1, 4. **Mooney** a-1, 2; c-2.

OUR GANG COMICS (With Tom & Jerry #39-59; becomes Tom & Jerry #60 on; based on film characters)
Dell Publishing Co.: Sept-Oct, 1942 - No. 59, June, 1949

1-Our Gang & Barney Bear by Kelly, Tom & Jerry, Pete Smith, Flip & Dip, The Milky Way begin (all 1st app.) 82.00 246.00 900.00
2-Benny Burro begins (#2 by Kelly) 41.00 123.00 450.00
3-5 27.00 82.00 300.00
6-Bumbazine & Albert only app. by Kelly 41.00 123.00 450.00
7-No Kelly story 21.00 63.00 230.00
8-Benny Burro begins by Barks 52.00 157.00 575.00
9-Barks-a(2): Benny Burro & Happy Hound; no Kelly story
47.00 142.00 520.00
10-Benny Burro by Barks 34.00 101.00 370.00
11-1st Barney Bear & Benny Burro by Barks (5-6/44); Happy Hound by Barks
47.00 142.00 520.00
12-20 21.00 63.00 230.00
21-30: 30-X-Mas-c 14.00 41.00 150.00
31-36-Last Barks issue 9.00 29.00 105.00
37-40 5.50 16.50 60.00
41-50 4.00 12.00 45.00
51-57 3.20 9.50 35.00
58,59-No Kelly art or Our Gang stories 2.70 8.00 30.00
NOTE: **Barks** art in part only. **Barks** did not write Barney Bear stories #30-34. (See March of Comics #3, 26). Early issues have photo back-c.

OUR LADY OF FATIMA
Catechetical Guild Educational Society: 3/11/55 (15¢) (36 pgs.)

395 4.00 10.00 20.00

OUR LOVE (True Secrets #3 on? or Romantic Affairs #3 on?)
Marvel Comics (SPC): Sept, 1949 - No. 2, Jan, 1950

1-Photo-c 11.00 32.00 80.00
2-Photo-c 6.85 21.00 48.00

OUR LOVE STORY
Marvel Comics Group: Oct, 1969 - No. 38, Feb, 1976

1 2.70 8.00 30.00
2-4,6-12 1.60 4.80 16.00
5-Steranko-a 4.00 12.25 45.00
13-)(10/71, 52 pg.s) 2.25 6.80 25.00
14-New story by Gary Fredrich & Tarpe' Mills 1.80 5.40 18.00
15-20,27:27-Colan/Everett-a(r?); Kirby/Colletta-r 1.20 3.60 12.00
21-26,28-37: .90 2.70 9.00
38-Last issue 1.40 4.20 14.00
NOTE: **J. Buscema** a-1-3, 5-7, 9, 13r, 16r, 19r(2), 21r, 22r(2), 23r, 34r, 35r; c-11, 13, 16, 22, 23, 24, 27, 35. **Colan** a-3-6, 21r(#6), 22r, 23r(#3), 24r(#4), 27; c-19. **Katz** a-17. **Maneely** a-13r. **Romita** a-13r. **Weiss** a-16, 17, 29r(#17).

OUR MISS BROOKS
Dell Publishing Co.: No. 751, Nov, 1956

Four Color 751-Photo-c 7.00 22.00 80.00

OUR SECRET (Exciting Love Stories)(Formerly My Secret)
Superior Comics Ltd.: No. 4, Nov, 1949 - No. 8, Jun, 1950

GD25 FN65 NM94

4-Kamen-a; spanking scene 15.00 44.00 110.00
5,6,8 8.00 24.00 55.00
7-Contains 9 pg. story intended for unpublished Ellery Queen #5; lingerie panels 10.00 30.00 65.00

OUTBREED 999
Blackout Comics: May, 1994 - No. 6, 1994 ($2.95)

1-6: 4-1st app. of Extreme Violet in 7 pg. backup story
3.00

OUTCASTS
DC Comics: Oct, 1987 - No. 12, Sept, 1988 ($1.75, limited series)

1-12: John Wagner & Alan Grant scripts in all 1.80

OUTER LIMITS, THE (TV)
Dell Publishing Co.: Jan-Mar, 1964 - No. 18, Oct, 1969 (Most painted-c)

1 9.00 27.00 100.00
2 5.00 15.00 55.00
3-10 4.00 12.25 45.00
11-18: 17-Reprints #1. 18-r/#2 2.90 8.70 32.00

OUTER SPACE (Formerly This Magazine Is Haunted, 2nd Series)
Charlton Comics: No. 17, May, 1958 - No. 25, Dec, 1959; Nov, 1968

17-Williamson/Wood style art; not by them (Sid Check?)
11.00 34.00 85.00
18-20-Ditko-a 17.00 52.00 130.00
21-25: 21-Ditko-c 10.00 30.00 75.00
V2#1(11/68)-Ditko-a, Boyette-c 3.50 10.50 35.00

OUTER SPACE BABES, THE
Silhouette Studios: Feb, 1994 ($2.95)

V3#1 3.00

OUTLANDERS (Manga)
Dark Horse Comics: Dec, 1988 - No. 33, Sep,1991 ($2.00-$2.50, B&W, 44pgs.)

1-7: Japanese Sci-fi manga 2.00
8-21 ($2.25) 2.25
22-33 ($2.50) 2.50

OUTLAW (See Return of the...)

OUTLAW FIGHTERS
Atlas Comics (IPC): Aug, 1954 - No. 5, Apr, 1955

1-Tuska-a 11.00 32.00 80.00
2-5: 5-Heath-c/a, 7 pgs. 6.85 21.00 48.00
NOTE: **Heath** c/a-5. **Maneely** c-2. **Pakula** a-2. **Reinman** a-2. **Tuska** a-1, 2.

OUTLAW KID, THE (1st Series; see Wild Western)
Atlas Comics (CCC No. 1-11/EPI No. 12-29): Sept, 1954 - No. 19, Sept, 1957

1-Origin; The Outlaw Kid & his horse Thunder begin; Black Rider app.
22.00 66.00 165.00
2-Black Rider app. 11.00 32.00 80.00
3-7,9: 3-Wildey-a(3) 9.30 28.00 70.00
8-Williamson/Woodbridge-a, 4 pgs. 10.00 30.00 75.00
10-Williamson-a 9.30 28.00 70.00
11-17,19: 13-Baker text illo. 15-Williamson text illo (unsigned)
6.50 19.50 45.00
18-Williamson/Mayo-a 7.85 23.50 55.00
NOTE: **Berg** a-4, 7, 13. **Maneely** c-1-3, 5-8, 11-13, 15, 16, 18. **Pakula** a-3. **Severin** c-10, 17, 19. **Shores** a-1. **Wildey** a-1(3), 2-8, 10, 11, 12(4), 13(4), 15-19(4 each); c-4.

OUTLAW KID, THE (2nd Series)
Marvel Comics Group: Aug, 1970 - No. 30, Oct, 1975

1-Reprints; 1-Orlando-r, Wildey-r(3) 1.80 5.40 18.00
2,3,9,10: 2-Reps. 3,9-Williamson-a(r). 10-Origin 1.40 4.20 14.00
4-7 1.20 3.60 12.00
8-Double size; Crandall-r 1.80 5.40 18.00
11-20: new-a in #10-16 .90 2.70 9.00
21-30: 27-Origin-r/#10 .85 2.60 7.00

Out of the Shadows #7 © STD

Out of the Vortex #8 © DH

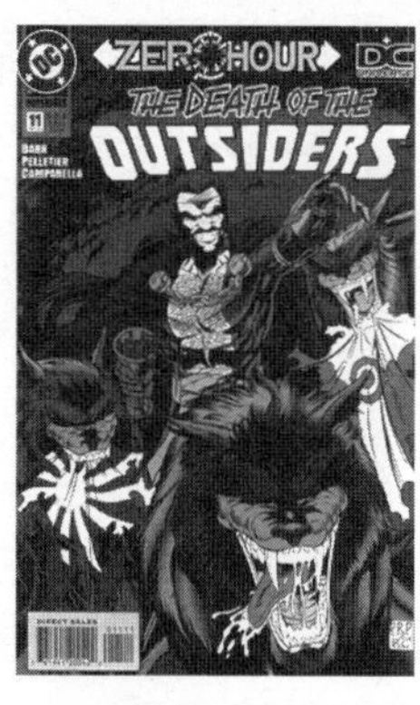

Outsiders #11 © DC

GD25 FN65 NM94

NOTE: *Ayers a-10, 27r. Berg a-7, 25r. Everett a-2(2 pgs.). Gil Kane c-10, 11, 15, 27r, 28. Roussos a-10i, 27i(r). Severin c-1, 9, 20, 25. Wildey r-1-4, 6-9, 19-22, 25, 26. Williamson a-28r. Woodbridge/Williamson a-9r.*

OUTLAWS
D. S. Publishing Co.: Feb-Mar, 1948 - No. 9, June-July, 1949

1-Violent & suggestive stories 28.00 84.00 210.00
2-Ingels-a; Baker-a 27.00 82.00 205.00
3,5,6: 3-Not Frazetta. 5-Sky Sheriff by Good app. 6-McWilliams-a 12.00 36.00 90.00
4-Orlando-a 14.00 42.00 105.00
7,8-Ingels-a in each 21.00 62.00 155.00
9-(Scarce)-Frazetta-a (7 pgs.) 43.00 129.00 345.00
NOTE: *Another #3 was printed in Canada with **Frazetta** art "Prairie Jinx," 7 pgs.*

OUTLAWS, THE (Formerly Western Crime Cases)
Star Publishing Co.: No. 10, May, 1952 - No. 13, Sep, 1953; No. 14, Apr, 1954

10-L. B. Cole-c 16.00 48.00 120.00
11-14-L. B. Cole-c. 14-Reprints Western Thrillers #4 (Fox) w/new L.B. Cole-c; Kamen, Feldstein-r 12.00 36.00 90.00

OUTLAWS
DC Comics: Sept, 1991 - No. 8, Apr, 1992 ($1.95, limited series)

1-8: Post-apocalyptic Robin Hood. 2.00

OUTLAWS OF THE WEST (Formerly Cody of the Pony Express #10)
Charlton Comics: No. 11, 7/57 - No. 81, 5/70; No. 82, 7/79 - No. 88, 4/80

11 6.50 19.50 45.00
12,13,15-17,19,20 4.00 12.00 24.00
14-(68 pgs., 2/58) 6.50 19.50 45.00
18-Ditko-a 7.85 23.50 55.00
21-30 2.25 6.75 18.00
31-50: 34-Gunmaster app. 1.75 5.25 14.00
51-53,55-63,65-67,69,70 1.50 4.50 12.00
54,64,68: 54-Kid Montana app. 64-Captain Doom begins (1st app.). 68-Kid Montana series begins 1.50 4.50 12.00
71-79: 73-Origin & 1st app. The Sharp Shooter, last app. #74. 75-Last Capt. Doom 1.10 3.30 9.00
80,81-Ditko-a 1.50 4.50 12.00
82-88 3.00
64,79(Modern Comics-r, 1977, '78) 3.00

OUTLAWS OF THE WILD WEST
Avon Periodicals: 1952 (25¢, 132 pgs.) (4 rebound comics)

1-Wood back-c; Kubert-a (3 Jesse James-r) 28.00 84.00 210.00

OUTLAW TRAIL (See Zane Grey 4-Color 511)

OUT OF SANTA'S BAG (See March of Comics #10)

OUT OF THE NIGHT (The Hooded Horseman #18 on)
Amer. Comics Group (Creston/Scope): Feb-Mar, 1952 - No. 17, Oct-Nov, 1954

1-Williamson/LeDoux-a (9 pgs.) 54.00 162.00 460.00
2-Williamson-a (5 pgs.) 44.00 132.00 365.00
3,5-10: 9-Sci/Fic story 23.00 68.00 170.00
4-Williamson-a (7 pgs.) 40.00 120.00 300.00
11-17: 13-Nostrand-a? 17-E.C. Wood swipe 17.00 50.00 125.00
NOTE: *Landau a-14, 16, 17. Shelly a-12.*

OUT OF THE PAST A CLUE TO THE FUTURE
E. C. Comics (Public Affairs Comm.): 1946? (16 pgs.) (paper cover)

nn-Based on public affairs pamphlet "What Foreign Trade Means to You" 22.00 66.00 165.00

OUT OF THE SHADOWS
Standard Comics/Visual Editions: No. 5, July, 1952 - No. 14, Aug, 1954

5-Toth-p; Moreira, Tuska-a; Roussos-c 42.00 126.00 340.00
6-Toth/Celardo-a; Katz-a(2) 31.00 93.00 230.00
7-Jack Katz-c/a(2) 21.00 63.00 155.00

GD25 FN65 NM94

8,10: 8-Katz shrunken head-c. 10-Sekowsky-a 16.00 48.00 120.00
9-Crandall-a(2) 21.00 63.00 155.00
11-Toth-a, 2 pgs.; Katz-a; Andru-c 21.00 63.00 155.00
12-Toth/Peppe-a(2); Katz-a 30.00 90.00 225.00
13-Cannabalism story; Sekowsky-a; Roussos-c 22.00 66.00 165.00
14-Toth-a 22.00 66.00 165.00

OUT OF THE VORTEX (Comics' Greatest World:... #1-4)
Dark Horse Comics: Oct., 1993 - No. 12, Oct, 1994 ($2.00, limited series)

1-11: 1-Foil logo. 4-Dorman-c(p). 6-Hero Zero x-over 2.00
12 ($2.50) 2.50
NOTE: *Art Adams c-7. Golden c-8. Mignola c-2. Simonson c-3. Zeck c-10.*

OUT OF THIS WORLD
Charlton Comics: Aug, 1956 - No. 16, Dec, 1959

1 20.00 60.00 150.00
2 11.00 33.00 75.00
3-6-Ditko-c/a (3) each 25.00 76.00 190.00
7-(2/58, 15¢, 68 pgs.)-Ditko-c/a(4) 25.00 76.00 190.00
8-(5/58, 15¢, 68 pgs.)-Ditko-a(2) 21.00 64.00 160.00
9,10,12,16-Ditko-a 17.00 52.00 130.00
11-Ditko c/a (3) 19.00 56.00 140.00
13-15 8.00 24.00 50.00
NOTE: *Ditko c-3-12, 16. Reinman a-10.*

OUT OF THIS WORLD (...Adventures #2)
Avon Periodicals: June, 1950; No. 2, Dec, 1950 (25¢ pulp)

1-Kubert-a(2) (one reprinted/Eerie #1, 1947) plus Crom the Barbarian by Gardner Fox & John Giunta (origin); Fawcette-c 54.00 162.00 460.00
2-Kubert-a plus The Spider God of Akka by Gardner Fox & John Giunta. pulp magazine w/comic insert 42.00 126.00 335.00
NOTE: *Out of This World Adventures is a sci-fi pulp magazine w/32 pgs. of color comics.*

OUT OUR WAY WITH WORRY WART
Dell Publishing Co.: No. 680, Feb, 1956

Four Color 680 1.80 5.50 20.00

OUTPOSTS
Blackthorne Publishing: June, 1987 - No. 4, 1987 ($1.25)

1-4: 1-Kaluta-c(p) 1.25

OUTSIDERS, THE
DC Comics: Nov, 1987 - No. 28, Feb, 1988

1 1.50
2-28: 18-26-Batman returns. 21-Intro. Strike Force Kobra; 1st app. Clayface IV 22-E.C. parody; Orlando-a. 21- 25-Atomic Knight app. 27,28-Millennium tie-ins. 1.00
Annual 1 (12/86, $2.50) 2.00
Special 1 (7/87, $1.50) 1.50
NOTE: *Aparo a-1-7, 9-14, 17-22, 25, 26; c-1-7, 9-14, 17, 19-26. Byrne a-11. Bolland a-6, 18; c-16. Ditko a-13p. Erik Larsen a-24, 27 28; c-27, 28. Morrow a-12.*

OUTSIDERS
DC Comics: Nov, 1993 - No. 24, Nov, 1995 ($1.75/$1.95/$2.25)

1-Alpha; Travis Charest-c 1.75
1-Omega; Travis Charest-c 1.75
2-9: 5-Atomic Knight app. 8-New Batman-c/story 1.75
10,11: 10-Begin $1.95-c. 11-(9/94)-Zero Hour 2.00
0,12-18: 0-(10/94).12-(11/94). 2.00
19-24: 19-Begin $2.25-c. 21-Darkseid cameo. 22-New Gods app. 2.25

OUTSTANDING AMERICAN WAR HEROES
The Parents' Institute: 1944 (16 pgs., paper-c)

nn-Reprints from True Comics 4.00 12.00 24.00

OVERSEAS COMICS (Also see G.I. Comics & Jeep Comics)
Giveaway (Distributed to U.S. Armed Forces): 1944 - No. 105?, 1946 (7-1/4x10-1/4"; 16 pgs. in color)

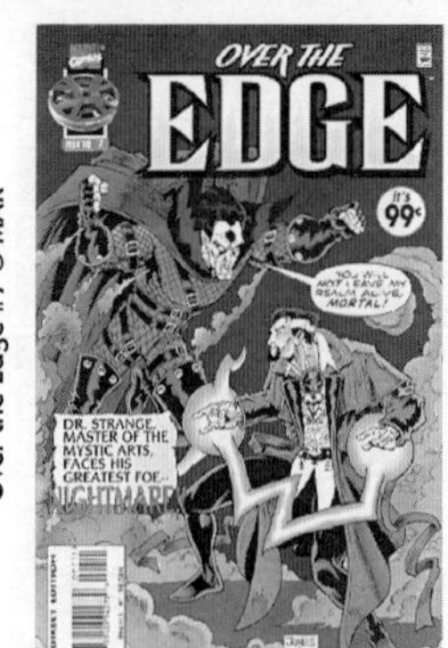

Over the Edge #7 © MAR

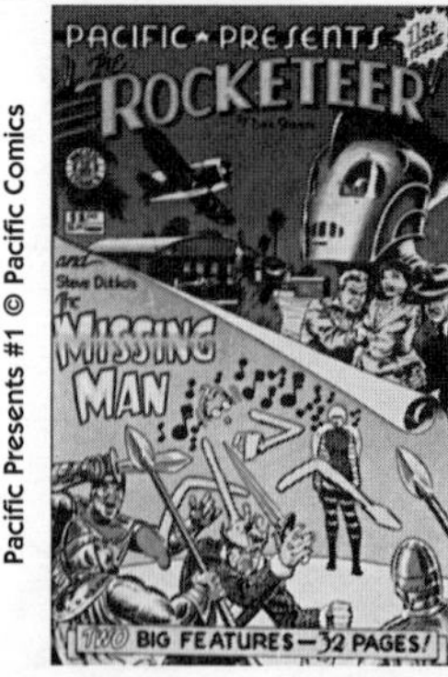

Pacific Presents #1 © Pacific Comics

Pakkin's Land: Quest for Kings #4 © Gary and Rhoda Shipman

23-105-Bringing Up Father (by McManus), Popeye, Joe Palooka, Dick Tracy, Superman, Gasoline Alley, Buz Sawyer, Li'l Abner, Blondie, Terry & the Pirates, Out Our Way 5.00 15.00 30.00

OVER THE EDGE
Marvel Comics: Nov, 1995 - No. 10, Aug, 1996 (99¢)

1-10: 1,6,10-Daredevil-c/story. 2,7-Dr. Strange-c/story. 3-Hulk-c/story. 4,9-Ghost Rider-c/story. 5-Punisher-c/story. 8-Elektra-c/story 1.00

OWL, THE (See Crackajack Funnies #25 & Popular Comics #72)(Also see The Hurricane Kids & Magic Morro
Western Pub. Co./R.S. Callender: 1940 (Giveaway)(7-1/2x5-1/4")(Soft-c, color)

nn-Frank Thomas-a 17.00 52.00 130.00

OWL, THE (See Crackajack Funnies #25 & Popular Comics #72)
Gold Key: April, 1967; No. 2, April, 1968

1,2-Written by Jerry Siegel; '40s super hero 2.90 8.75 35.00

OXYDOL-DREFT
Oxydol-Dreft: 1950 (Set of 6 pocket-size giveaways; distributed through the mail as a set) (Scarce)

1-3: 1-Li'l Abner. 2-Daisy Mae. 3-Shmoo 9.30 28.00 70.00
4-John Wayne; Williamson/Frazetta-c from John Wayne #3 15.00 44.00 110.00
5-Archie 10.00 30.00 75.00
6-Terrytoons Mighty Mouse 9.30 28.00 70.00
NOTE: *Set is worth more with original envelope.*

OZ (See First Comics Graphic Novel, Marvel Treaury Of Oz & MGM's Marvelous...)

OZ
Caliber Press: 1994 - 1997 ($2.95, B&W)

0-22 4.00
1 ($5.95)-Limited Edition; double-c 6.00
...Specials: Freedom Fighters. Lion. Scarecrow. Tin Man 3.00

OZARK IKE
Dell Publishing Co./Standard Comics B11 on: Feb, 1948; Nov, 1948 - No. 24, Dec, 1951; No. 25, Sept, 1952

Four Color 180(1948-Dell) 9.00 27.00 100.00
B11, B12, 13-15 7.15 21.50 50.00
16-25 5.70 17.00 38.00

OZ: DAEMONSTORM
Caliber Press: 1997 ($3.95, B&W, one-shot)

1 4.00

OZ: ROMANCE IN RAGS
Caliber Press: 1996 ($2.95, B&W, limited series)

1-3 3.00
...Special 3.00

OZ SQUAD
Brave New Worlds/Patchwork Press: 1992 - No. 4, 1994 ($2.50/$2.75, B&W)

1-3 2.50
4-Patchwork Press 2.75

OZ SQUAD
Patchwork Press: Dec, 1995 - No. 10, 1996 ($2.95, B&W)

1 ($3.95) 4.00
2-10 3.00

OZ: STRAW AND SORCERY
Caliber Press: 1997 ($2.95, B&W, limited series)

1-3 3.00

OZ-WONDERLAND WARS, THE
DC Comics: Jan, 1986 - No. 3, March, 1986 (Mini-series)

1-3-Capt Carrot app. 3.00

GD25 FN65 NM94

OZZIE & BABS (TV Teens #14 on)
Fawcett Publications: Dec, 1947 - No. 13, Fall, 1949

1-Teen-age 7.15 21.50 50.00
2 4.25 13.00 26.00
3-13 4.00 10.00 20.00

OZZIE & HARRIET (See The Adventures of...)

PACIFIC COMICS GRAPHIC NOVEL (See Image Graphic Novel)

PACIFIC PRESENTS (Also see Starslayer #2, 3)
Pacific Comics: Oct, 1982 - No. 2, Apr, 1983; No. 3, Mar, 1984 - No. 4, Jun, 1984

1-Chapter 3 of The Rocketeer; Stevens-c/a 2.00 6.00
2-Chapter 4 of The Rocketeer (4th app.); nudity; Stevens-c/a 5.00
3,4: 3-1st app. Vanity 2.00
NOTE: ***Conrad** a-3, 4; c-3. **Ditko** a-1-3; c-1(1/2). **Dave Stevens** a-1, 2; c-1(1/2), 2.*

PACT, THE
Image Comics: Feb, 1994 - No. 3, June, 1994 ($1.95, limited series)

1-3: Valentino co-scripts & layouts 2.00

PADRE OF THE POOR
Catechetical Guild: nd (Giveaway) (16 pgs., paper-c)

nn 3.00 7.50 15.00

PAGEANT OF COMICS (See Jane Arden & Mopsy)
Archer St. John: Sept, 1947 - No. 2, Oct, 1947

1-Mopsy strip-r 7.85 23.50 55.00
2-Jane Arden strip-r 7.85 23.50 55.00

PAINKILLER JANE
Event Comics: June, 1997 - Present ($3.95/$2.95)

1-Augustyn/Waid-s/Leonardi/Palmiotti-a, variant-c 4.00
2-5: Two covers (Quesada, Leonardi) 3.00

PAINKILLER JANE / HELLBOY
Event Comics: Aug, 1998 ($2.95, one-shot)

1-Leonardi & Palmiotti-a 2.95

PAINKILLER JANE VS. THE DARKNESS
Event Comics: Apr, 1997 ($2.95, one-shot)

1-Ennis-s; four variant-c 3.50

PAKKIN'S LAND
Caliber Comics (Tapestry): 1996 - No. 6 ($2.95, B&W)

1-Gary and Rhoda Shipman-s/a 1.50 4.50 15.00
2,3 1.00 3.00 10.00
1-3-2nd printing 3.00
4-6,0 2.00 6.00

PAKKIN'S LAND: FORGOTTEN DREAMS
Caliber Comics: Apr, 1998 - No. 4 ($2.95, B&W)

1-4-Gary and Rhoda Shipman-s/a 3.00

PAKKIN'S LAND: QUEST FOR KINGS
Caliber Comics: Aug, 1997 - No. 6, Mar, 1998 ($2.95, B&W)

1-Gary and Rhoda Shipman-s/a; Jeff Smith var-c 4.00
2-6 3.00

PANCHO VILLA
Avon Periodicals: 1950

nn-Kinstler-c 21.00 64.00 160.00

PANDEMONIUM
Chaos! Comics: Sept, 1998 ($2.95, one-shot)

1-Al Rio-c 2.95

PANDORA
Avatar Press: Jan, 1997 - No. 2, Feb, 1997 ($3.00, B&W, limited series)

0,1,2: 1-Lindo-c 3.00

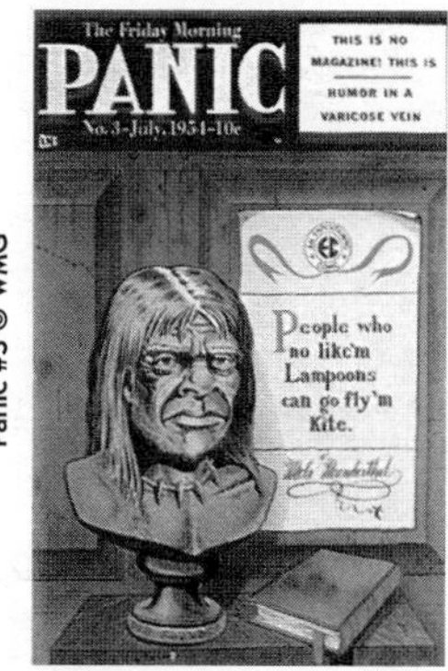

Panic #3 © WMG

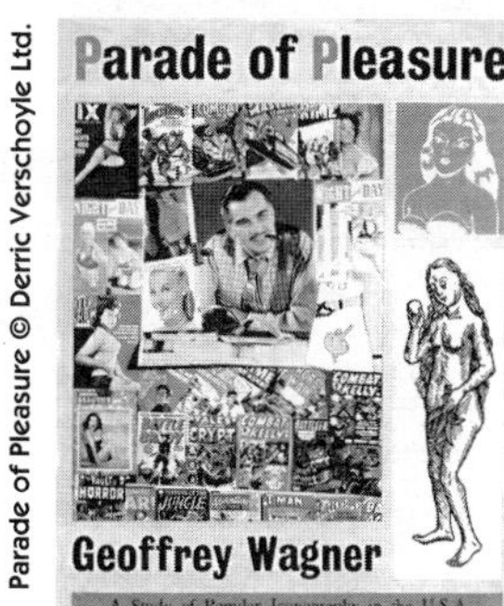

Parade of Pleasure
Geoffrey Wagner
A Study of Popular Iconography in the U.S.A.

Parade of Pleasure © Derric Verschoyle Ltd.

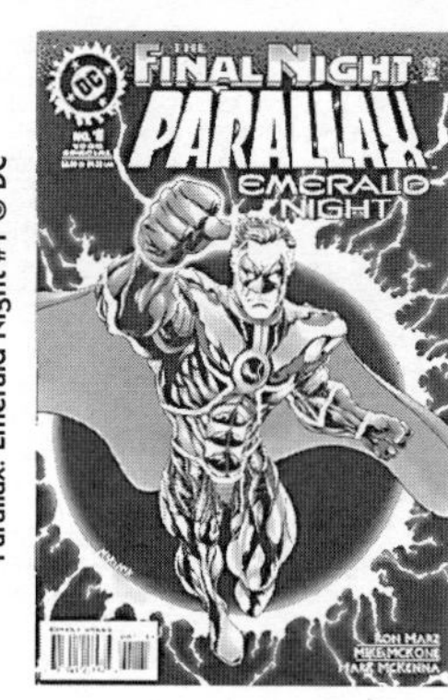

Parallax: Emerald Night #1 © DC

GD25 FN65 NM94

...Demonography (5/97, $3.00) 3.00

PANDORA PIN-UP
Avatar Press: July, 1997 ($3.00, B&W, one-shot)
1-($3.00)-Regular ed. 3.00
1-($4.95)-Nude ed. 5.00

PANDORA/WIDOW
Avatar Press: Sept, 1997 ($3.95, B&W, one-shot)
1-($3.95)-Regular ed. 3.95
1-($4.95)-Nude ed. 4.95
1-($25.00)-Leather ed. 25.00

PANHANDLE PETE AND JENNIFER (TV) (See Gene Autry #20)
J. Charles Laue Publishing Co.: July, 1951 - No. 3, Nov, 1951
1 8.50 26.00 60.00
2,3 5.70 17.00 40.00

PANIC (Companion to Mad)
E. C. Comics (Tiny Tot Comics): Feb-Mar, 1954 - No. 12, Dec-Jan, 1955-56
1-Used in Senate Investigation hearings; Elder draws entire E. C. staff; Santa Claus & Mickey Spillane parody 20.00 60.00 200.00
2 9.00 27.00 90.00
3,4: 3-Senate Subcommittee parody; Davis draws Gaines, Feldstein & Kelly, 1 pg.; Old King Cole smokes marijuana. 4-Infinity-c; John Wayne parody 8.00 24.00 80.00
5-11: 8-Last pre-code issue (5/55). 9-Superman, Smilin' Jack & Dick Tracy app. on-c; has photo of Walter Winchell on-c 7.50 22.50 75.00
12 (Low distribution; thousands were destroyed) 9.00 27.00 90.00
NOTE: ***Davis** a-1-12; c-12. **Elder** a-1-12. **Feldstein** c-1-3, 5. **Kamen** a-1. **Orlando** a-1-9. **Wolverton** c-4, panel-3. **Wood** a-2-9, 11, 12.*

PANIC (Magazine) (Satire)
Panic Publ.: July, 1958 - No. 6, July, 1959; V2#10, Dec, 1965 - V2#12, 1966
1 9.30 28.00 70.00
2-6 5.70 17.00 35.00
V2#10-12: Reprints earlier issues 2.50 7.50 25.00
NOTE: ***Davis** a-3(2 pgs.), 4, 5, 10; c-10. **Elder** a-5. **Powell** a-V2#10, 11. **Torres** a-1-5. **Tuska** a-V2#11.*

PANIC
Gemstone Publishing: March, 1997 - Present ($2.50, quarterly)
1-8: E.C. reprints 2.50

PANTHA: HAUNTED PASSION
Harris Comics: May, 1997 ($2.95, B&W, one-shot)
1-r/Vampirella #30,31 3.00

PARADAX (Also see Strange Days)
Eclipse Comics: 1986 (one-shot)
1 2.00

PARADAX
Vortex Comics: April, 1987 - No. 2, Aug, 1987 ($1.75, mature)
1,2-Nudity, adult language 1.80

PARADE (See Hanna-Barbera...)

PARADE COMICS (Frisky Animals on Parade #2 on)
Ajax/Farrell Publ. (World Famous Publ.): Sept, 1957
1 5.70 17.00 35.00
NOTE: *Cover title: Frisky Animals on Parade.*

PARADE OF PLEASURE
Derric Verschoyle Ltd., London, England: 1954 (192 pgs.) (Hardback book)
By Geoffrey Wagner. Contains section devoted to the censorship of American comic books with illustrations in color and black and white. (Also see **Seduction of the Innocent**). Distributed in USA by Library Publishers, N. Y. 39.00 118.00 275.00
with dust jacket.... 70.00 212.00 600.00

GD25 FN65 NM94

PARADOX
Dark Visions Publ: June, 1994 - No. 2, Aug, 1994 ($2.95, B&W, mature)
1,2: 1-Linsner-c. 2-Boris-c. 3.00

PARALLAX: EMERALD NIGHT (See Final Night)
DC Comics: Nov, 1996 ($2.95, one-shot, 48 pgs.)
1-Final Night tie-in; Green Lantern (Kyle Rayner) app. 4.00

PARAMOUNT ANIMATED COMICS (See Harvey Comics Hits #60, 62)
Harvey Publications: No. 3, Feb, 1953 - No. 22, July, 1956
3-Baby Huey, Herman & Katnip, Buzzy the Crow begin 18.00 54.00 135.00
4-6 7.85 23.50 55.00
7-Baby Huey becomes permanent cover feature; cover title becomes Baby Huey with #9 17.00 52.00 130.00
8-10: 9-Infinity-c 7.15 21.50 50.00
11-22 5.75 17.00 35.00

PARENT TRAP, THE (Disney)
Dell Publishing Co.: No. 1210, Oct-Dec, 1961
Four Color 1210-Movie, Haley Mills photo-c 8.00 25.00 90.00

PARODY
Armour Publishing: Mar, 1977 - No. 3, Aug, 1977 (B&W humor magazine)
1 1.40 4.20 14.00
2,3: 2-King Kong, Happy Days. 3-Charlie's Angels, Rocky 1.00 3.00 10.00

PAROLE BREAKERS
Avon Periodicals/Realistic #2 on: Dec, 1951 - No. 3, July, 1952
1(#2 on inside)-r-c/Avon paperback #283 (painted) 39.00 116.00 290.00
2-Kubert-a; r-c/Avon paperback #114 (photo-c) 27.00 81.00 200.00
3-Kinstler-c 25.00 75.00 185.00

PARTRIDGE FAMILY, THE (TV)(Also see David Cassidy)
Charlton Comics: Mar, 1971 - No. 21, Dec, 1973
1 4.00 12.25 45.00
2-4,6-10 2.00 6.00 20.00
5-Partridge Family Summer Special (52 pgs.); The Shadow, Lone Ranger, Charlie McCarthy, Flash Gordon, Hopalong Cassidy, Gene Autry & others app. 5.00 15.00 55.00
11-21 1.60 4.80 16.00

PARTS UNKNOWN
Eclipse Comics/FX: July, 1992 - No. 4, Oct, 1992 ($2.50, B&W, mature)
1-4: All contain FX gaming cards 2.50

PASSION, THE
Catechetical Guild: No. 394, 1955
394 3.60 9.00 18.00

PASSOVER (See Avengelyne)
Maximum Press: Dec, 1996 ($2.99, one-shot)
1 3.00

PAT BOONE (TV)(Also see Superman's Girlfriend Lois Lane #9)
National Per. Publ.: Sept-Oct, 1959 - No. 5, May-Jun, 1960 (All have photo-c)
1 41.00 122.00 320.00
2-5: 3-Fabian, Connie Francis & Paul Anka photos on-c. 4-Previews "Journey To The Center Of The Earth". 4-Johnny Mathis & Bobbie Darin photos on-c. 5-Dick Clark & Frankie Avalon photos on-c 33.00 100.00 250.00

PATCHES
Rural Home/Patches Publ. (Orbit): Mar-Apr, 1945 - No. 11, Nov, 1947
1-L. B. Cole-c 31.00 92.00 230.00
2 11.00 34.00 85.00
3,4,6,8-11: 6-Henry Aldrich story. 8-Smiley Burnette-c/s (6/47); pre-dates Smiley Burnette #1. 9-Mr. District Attorney story (radio). Leav/Keigstein-a

Patsy and Hedy #7 © MAR

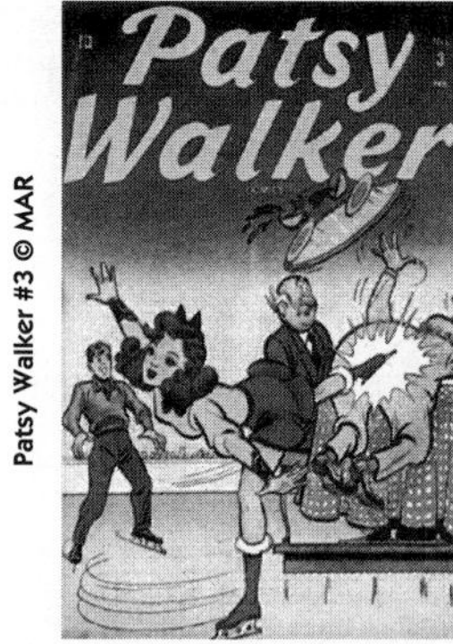

Patsy Walker #3 © MAR

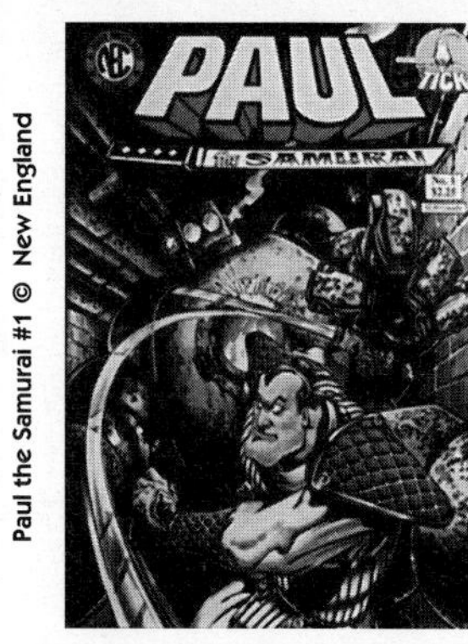

Paul the Samurai #1 © New England

	GD25	FN65	NM94
(16 pgs.). 9-11-Leav-c. 10-Jack Carson (radio) c/story; Leav-c. 11-Red Skelton story	10.00	30.00	80.00
5-Danny Kaye-c/story; L.B. Cole-c.	16.00	48.00	120.00
7-Hopalong Cassidy-c/story	13.00	40.00	100.00

PATHWAYS TO FANTASY
Pacific Comics: July, 1984

	GD25	FN65	NM94
1-Barry Smith-c/a; Jeff Jones-a (4 pgs.)			2.00

PATORUZU (See Adventures of...)

PATSY & HEDY (Teenage)(Also see Hedy Wolfe)
Atlas Comics/Marvel (GPI/Male): Feb, 1952 - No. 110, Feb, 1967

	GD25	FN65	NM94
1-Patsy Walker & Hedy Wolfe; Al Jaffee-c	17.00	52.00	130.00
2	9.30	28.00	70.00
3-10: 3,8-Al Jaffee-c	7.15	21.50	50.00
11-20	5.70	17.00	36.00
21-40	4.25	13.00	28.00
41-60	2.50	7.50	22.00
61-80: 88-Lingerie panel	2.00	6.00	16.00
81-87,89-99,101-110	1.75	5.25	14.00
100	2.00	6.00	16.00
Annual 1(1963)-Early Marvel annual	8.00	24.00	80.00

PATSY & HER PALS (Teenage)
Atlas Comics (PPI): May, 1953 - No. 29, Aug, 1957

	GD25	FN65	NM94
1-Patsy Walker	15.00	44.00	110.00
2	7.85	23.50	55.00
3-10	6.50	19.50	45.00
11-29: 24-Everett-c	5.35	16.00	32.00

PATSY WALKER (See All Teen, A Date With Patsy, Girls' Life, Miss America Magazine, Patsy & Hedy, Patsy & Her Pals & Teen Comics)
Marvel/Atlas Comics (BPC): 1945 (no month) - No. 124, Dec, 1965

	GD25	FN65	NM94
1-Teenage	42.00	127.00	340.00
2	20.00	60.00	150.00
3,4,6-10	15.00	46.00	115.00
5-Injury-to-eye-c; spanking panel	18.00	54.00	135.00
11,12,15,16,18	10.00	30.00	75.00
13,14,17,19-22-Kurtzman's "Hey Look"	11.00	32.00	80.00
23,24	7.85	23.50	55.00
25-Rusty by Kurtzman; painted-c	11.00	32.00	80.00
26-29,31: 26-31: 52 pgs.	6.50	19.50	45.00
30(52 pgs.)-Egghead Doodle by Kurtzman (1 pg.)	7.85	23.50	55.00
32-57: Last precode (3/55)	4.25	13.00	26.00
58-80	2.50	7.50	20.00
81-99: 92,98-Millie x-over	2.00	6.00	16.00
100	2.50	7.50	20.00
101-124	1.75	5.25	14.00
Fashion Parade 1(1966, 68 pgs.) (Beware cut-out & marked pages)	6.00	18.00	60.00

NOTE: *Painted c-25-28. Anti-Wertham editorial in #21. Georgie app. in #8, 11. Millie app. in #10, 92, 98. Mitzi app. in #11. Rusty app. in #12, 25. Willie app. in #12.* ***Al Jaffee*** *c-57, 58.*

PAT THE BRAT (Adventures of Pipsqueak #34 on)
Archie Publications (Radio): June, 1953; Summer, 1955 - No. 4, 5/56; No. 15, 7/56 - No. 33, 7/59

	GD25	FN65	NM94
nn(6/53)	11.00	32.00	80.00
1(Summer, 1955)	7.15	21.50	50.00
2-4-(5/56) (#5-14 not published)	5.00	15.00	30.00
15-(7/56)-33	2.25	6.75	18.00

PAT THE BRAT COMICS DIGEST MAGAZINE
Archie Publications: October, 1980

	GD25	FN65	NM94
1-Li'l Jinx & Super Duck app.	1.20	3.60	12.00

PATTY CAKE
Permanent Press: Mar, 1995 - No. 9, Jul, 1996 ($2.95, B&W)

	GD25	FN65	NM94
1-9: Scott Roberts-s/a			4.00

PATTY CAKE
Caliber Press (Tapestry): Oct, 1996 - No. 3, Apr, 1997 ($2.95, B&W)

	GD25	FN65	NM94
1-3: Scott Roberts-s/a			3.00
...Christmas (12/96)			3.00

PATTY CAKE & FRIENDS
Slave Labor Graphics: Nov, 1997 - Present ($2.95, B&W)

	GD25	FN65	NM94
Here There Be Monsters (10/97)			3.00
1-7: Scott Roberts-s/a			3.00

PATTY POWERS (Formerly Della Vision #3)
Atlas Comics: No. 4, Oct, 1955 - No. 7, Oct, 1956

	GD25	FN65	NM94
4	7.15	21.50	50.00
5-7	4.15	12.50	25.00

PAT WILTON (See Mighty Midget Comics)

PAUL
Spire Christian Comics (Fleming H. Revell Co.): 1978 (49¢)

	GD25	FN65	NM94
nn			4.00

PAULINE PERIL (See The Close Shaves of...)

PAUL REVERE'S RIDE (TV, Disney, see Walt Disney Showcase #34)
Dell Publishing Co.: No. 822, July, 1957

	GD25	FN65	NM94
Four Color 822-w/Johnny Tremain, Toth-a	9.00	27.00	100.00

PAUL TERRY'S ADVENTURES OF MIGHTY MOUSE (See Adventures of...)

PAUL TERRY'S COMICS (Formerly Terry-Toons Comics; becomes Adventures of Mighty Mouse No. 126 on)
St. John Publishing Co.: No. 85, Mar, 1951 - No. 125, May, 1955

	GD25	FN65	NM94
85,86-Same as Terry-Toons #85, & 86 with only a title change; published at same time?; Mighty Mouse, Heckle & Jeckle & Gandy Goose continue from Terry-Toons	9.30	28.00	70.00
87-99	6.00	18.00	42.00
100	7.15	21.50	50.00
101-104,107-125: 121,122,125-Painted-c	5.70	17.00	40.00
105,106-Giant Comics Edition (25¢, 100 pgs.) (9/53 & ?). 105-Little Roquefort-c/story	16.00	48.00	120.00

PAUL TERRY'S HOW TO DRAW FUNNY CARTOONS
Terrytoons, Inc. (Giveaway): 1940's (14 pgs.) (Black & White)

	GD25	FN65	NM94
nn-Heckle & Jeckle, Mighty Mouse, etc.	11.00	34.00	85.00

PAUL TERRY'S MIGHTY MOUSE (See Mighty Mouse)

PAUL TERRY'S MIGHTY MOUSE ADVENTURE STORIES (See Mighty Mouse Adventure Stories)

PAUL THE SAMURAI (See The Tick #4)
New England Comics: July, 1992 - No. 6, July, 1993 ($2.75, B&W)

	GD25	FN65	NM94
1-6			2.75

PAWNEE BILL
Story Comics (Youthful Magazines?): Feb, 1951 - No. 3, July, 1951

	GD25	FN65	NM94
1-Bat Masterson, Wyatt Earp app.	10.00	30.00	75.00
2,3: 3-Origin Golden Warrior; Cameron-a	6.00	18.00	42.00

PAY-OFF (This Is the..., ...Crime, ...Detective Stories)
D. S. Publishing Co.: July-Aug, 1948 - No. 5, Mar-Apr, 1949 (52 pgs.)

	GD25	FN65	NM94
1-True Crime Cases #1,2	20.00	60.00	150.00
2	12.00	36.00	90.00
3-5-Thrilling Detective Stories	11.00	32.00	80.00

PEACEMAKER, THE (Also see Fightin' Five)
Charlton Comics: V3#1, Mar, 1967 - No. 5, Nov, 1967 (All 12¢ cover price)

	GD25	FN65	NM94
1-Fightin' Five begins	3.20	9.60	32.00
2,3,5	2.25	6.75	18.00
4-Origin The Peacemaker	3.00	9.00	30.00

Peanuts #2 © UFS

Penny #1 © AVON

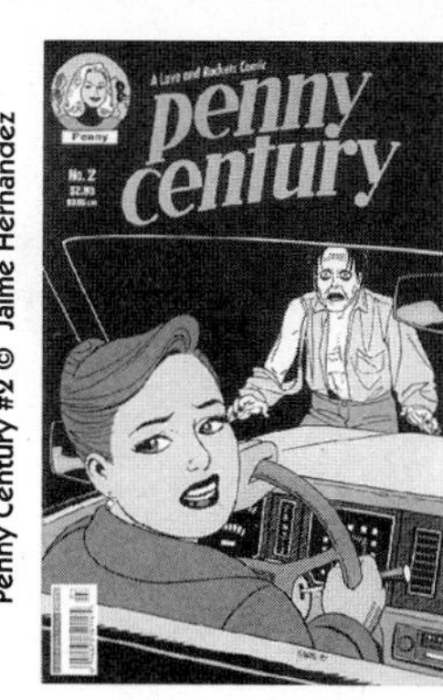

Penny Century #2 © Jaime Hernandez

GD25 FN65 NM94

1,2(Modern Comics reprint, 1978) 3.00

PEACEMAKER (Also see Crisis On Infinite Earths & Showcase '93 #7,9,10)
DC Comics: Jan, 1988 - No. 4, Apr, 1988 ($1.25, limited series)

1-4 1.25

PEANUTS (Charlie Brown) (See Fritzi Ritz, Nancy & Sluggo, Tip Top, Tip Topper & United Comics)
Dell Publishing Co./Gold Key: 1953-54; No. 878, 2/58 - No. 13, 5-7/62; 5/63 - No. 4, 2/64

1(1953-54)-Reprints United Features' Strange As It Seems, Willie, Ferdnand 11.00 33.00 120.00
Four Color 878(#1) 14.00 41.00 150.00
Four Color 969,1015('59) 10.00 30.00 110.00
4(2-4/60) 8.00 23.00 85.00
5-13 5.50 16.50 60.00
1(Gold Key, 5/63) 10.50 31.00 115.00
2-4 6.25 18.50 70.00

PEBBLES & BAMM BAMM (TV) (See Cave Kids #7, 12)
Charlton Comics: Jan, 1972 - No. 36, Dec, 1976 (Hanna-Barbera)

1-From the Flintstones; "Teen Age..." on cover 4.00 12.00 45.00
2-10 2.00 6.00 22.00
11-20 1.60 4.80 16.00
21-36 1.20 3.60 12.00

PEBBLES & BAMM BAMM (TV)
Harvey Comics: Nov, 1993 - No. 3, Mar, 1994 ($1.50) (Hanna-Barbera)

V2#1-3 3.00
...Giant Size 1 (10/93, $2.25, 68 pgs.)("Summer Special" on-c) 3.00

PEBBLES FLINTSTONE (TV) (See The Flintstones #11)
Gold Key: Sept, 1963 (Hanna-Barbera)

1 (10088-309)-Early Pebbles app. 8.50 26.00 95.00

PEDRO (Formerly My Private Life #17; also see Romeo Tubbs)
Fox Features Syndicate: No. 18, June, 1950 - No. 2, Aug, 1950?

18(#1)-Wood-c/a(p) 19.00 58.00 145.00
2-Wood-a? 15.00 44.00 110.00

PEE-WEE PIXIES (See The Pixies)

PELLEAS AND MELISANDE (See Night Music #4, 5)

PENALTY (See Crime Must Pay the...)

PENDRAGON (Knights of... #5 on; also see Knights of...)
Marvel Comics UK, Ltd.: July, 1992 - No. 15, Sept, 1993 ($1.75)

1-15: 1-4-Iron Man app. 6-8-Spider-Man app. 1.75

PENDULUM ILLUSTRATED BIOGRAPHIES
Pendulum Press: 1979 (B&W)

19-355x-George Washington/Thomas Jefferson, 19-3495-Charles Lindbergh/Amelia Earhart, 19-3509-Harry Houdini/Walt Disney, 19-3517-Davy Crockett/Daniel Boone-Redondo-a, 19-3525-Elvis Presley/Beatles, 19-3533-Benjamin Franklin/Martin Luther King Jr, 19-3541-Abraham Lincoln/Franklin D. Roosevelt, 19-3568-Marie Curie/Albert Einstein-Redondo-a, 19-3576-Thomas Edison/Alexander Graham Bell-Redondo-a, 19-3584-Vince Lombardi/Pele, 19-3592-Babe Ruth/Jackie Robinson, 19-3606-Jim Thorpe/Althea Gibson

Softback 1.50
Hardback 4.50

NOTE: *Above books still available from publisher.*

PENDULUM ILLUSTRATED CLASSICS (Now Age Illustrated)
Pendulum Press: 1973 - 1978 (75¢, 62pp, B&W, 5-3/8x8")
(Also see Marvel Classics)

64-100x(1973)-Dracula-Redondo art, 64-131x-The Invisible Man-Nino art, 64-0968-Dr. Jekyll and Mr. Hyde-Redondo art, 64-1005-Black Beauty, 64-1010-Call of the Wild, 64-1020-Frankenstein, 64-1025-Hucklebury Finn, 64-1030-Moby Dick-Nino-a, 64-1040-Red Badge of Courage, 64-1045-The Time Machine-Nino-a, 64-1050-Tom Sawyer, 64-1055-Twenty Thousand Leagues Under the Sea, 64-1069-Treasure Island, 64-1328(1974)-Kidnapped, 64-1336-Three Musketeers-Nino art, 64-1344-A Tale of Two Cities, 64-1352-Journey to the Center of the Earth, 64-1360-The War of the Worlds-Nino-a, 64-1379-The Greatest Advs. of Sherlock Holmes-Redondo art, 64-1387-Mysterious Island, 64-1395-Hunchback of Notre Dame, 64-1409-Helen Keller-story of my life, 64-1417-Scarlet Letter, 64-1425-Gulliver's Travels, 64-2618(1977)-Around the World in Eighty Days, 64-2626-Captains Courageous, 64-2634-Connecticut Yankee, 64-2642-The Hound of the Baskervilles, 64-2650-The House of Seven Gables, 64-2669-Jane Eyre, 64-2677-The Last of the Mohicans, 64-2685-The Best of O'Henry, 64-2693-The Best of Poe-Redondo-a, 64-2707-Two Years Before the Mast, 64-2715-White Fang, 64-2723-Wuthering Heights, 64-3126(1978)-Ben Hur-Redondo art, 64-3134-A Christmas Carol, 64-3142-The Food of the Gods, 64-3150-Ivanhoe, 64-3169-The Man in the Iron Mask, 64-3177-The Prince and the Pauper, 64-3185-The Prisoner of Zenda, 64-3193-The Return of the Native, 64-3207-Robinson Crusoe, 64-3215-The Scarlet Pimpernel, 64-3223-The Sea Wolf, 64-3231-The Swiss Family Robinson, 64-3851-Billy Budd, 64-386x-Crime and Punishment, 64-3878-Don Quixote, 64-3886-Great Expectations, 64-3894-Heidi, 64-3908-The Iliad, 64-3916-Lord Jim, 64-3924-The Mutiny on Board H.M.S. Bounty, 64-3932-The Odyssey, 64-3940-Oliver Twist, 64-3959-Pride and Prejudice, 64-3967-The Turn of the Screw

Softback 1.45
Hardback 4.50

NOTE: *All of the above books can be ordered from the publisher; some were reprinted as Marvel Classic Comics #1-12. In 1972 there was another brief series of 12 titles which contained Classics Ill. artwork. They were entitled* ***Now Age Books*** *Illustrated, but can be easily distinguished from later series by the small Classics Illustrated logo at the top of the front cover. The format is the same as the later series. The 48 pg. C.I. art was stretched out to make 62 pgs. After Twin Circle Publ. terminated the Classics Ill. series in 1971, they made a one year contract with Pendulum Press to print these twelve titles of C.I. art. Pendulum was unhappy with the contract, and at the end of 1972 began their own art series, utilizing the talents of the Filipino artist group. One detail which makes this rather confusing is that when they redid the art in 1973, they gave it the same identifying no. as the 1972 series. All 12 of the 1972 C.I. editions have new covers, taken from internal art panels. In spite of their recent age, all of the 1972 C.I. series are very rare. Mint copies would fetch at least $50. Here is a list of the 1972 series, with C.I. title no. counterpart:*

64-1005 (CI#60-A2) 64-1010 (CI#91) 64-1015 (CI-Jr #503) 64-1020 (CI#26)
64-1025 (CI#19-A2) 64-1030 (CI#5-A2) 64-1035 (CI#169) 64-1040 (CI#98)
64-1045 (CI#133) 64-1050 (CI#50-A2) 64-1055 (CI#47) 64-1060 (CI-Jr#535)

PENDULUM ILLUSTRATED ORIGINALS
Pendulum Press: 1979 (In color)

94-4254-Solarman: The Beginning (See Solarman) 3.00

PENDULUM'S ILLUSTRATED STORIES
Pendulum Press: 1990 - No. 72, 1990? (No cover price ($4.95), squarebound, 68 pgs.)

1-72: Reprints Pendulum Ill. Classics series 5.00

PENNY
Avon Comics: 1947 - No. 6, Sept-Oct, 1949 (Newspaper reprints)

1-Photo & biography of creator 10.00 30.00 75.00
2-5 6.50 19.50 45.00
6-Perry Como photo on-c 7.15 21.50 50.00

PENNY CENTURY (See Love and Rockets)
Fantagraphics Books: Dec, 1997 - Present ($2.95, B&W, mini-series)

1-3-Jaime Hernandez-s/a 3.00

PENTHOUSE COMIX
General Media Int.: 1994 - No. 33, July, 1998 ($4.95, bimonthly, magazine, mature)

1 1.20 3.60 12.00
2,3 .90 2.70 8.00
4-25: 15-Corben-c. 16-Dorman-c. 17-Manara-c. 20-Chiodo-c. 21,23-Boris-c 24-Scott Hampton-c 5.00
26-33-Comic-sized 4.95

PENTHOUSE MAX
General Media International: July, 1996 - No. 3 ($4.95, magazine, mature)

1-3: 1-Giffen, Sears, Maguire-a. 2-Political satire. 3-Mr. Monster-c/app.; Dorman-c 2.00 6.00

PENTHOUSE MEN'S ADVENTURE COMIX
General Media International: 1995 - No. 7, 1996 ($4.95, magazine, mature)

1-7 (Magazine Size): 1-Boris-c 2.00 6.00
1-5 (Comic Size): 1-Boris-c 2.00 6.00

Pep Comics #13 © AP

Pep Comics #48 © AP

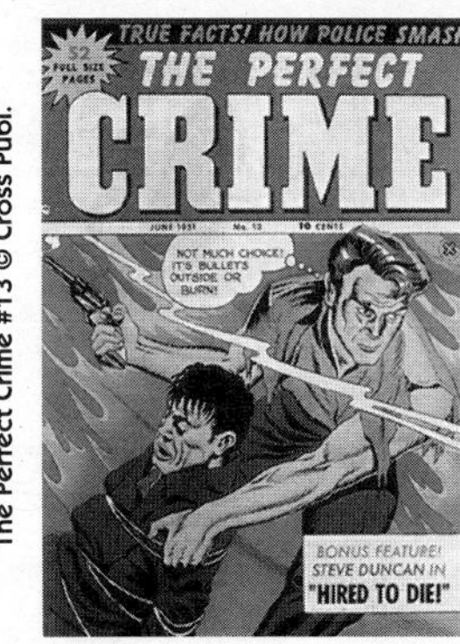

The Perfect Crime #13 © Cross Publ.

PEP COMICS (See Archie Giant Series #576, 589, 601, 614, 624)
MLJ Magazines/Archie Publications No. 56 (3/46) on: Jan, 1940 - No. 411, Mar, 1987

	GD25	FN65	VF82	NM94
1-Intro. The Shield (1st patriotic hero) by Irving Novick; origin & 1st app. The Comet by Jack Cole, The Queen of Diamonds & Kayo Ward; The Rocket, The Press Guardian (The Falcon #1 only), Sergeant Boyle, Fu Chang, & Bentley of of Scotland Yard; Robot-c; Shield-c begin	660.00	1980.00	3960.00	6800.00

	GD25	FN65	NM94
2-Origin The Rocket	188.00	564.00	1600.00
3	135.00	405.00	1150.00
4-Wizard cameo	112.00	336.00	950.00
5-Wizard cameo in Shield story	112.00	336.00	950.00
6-10: 8-Last Cole Comet; no Cole-a in #6,7	85.00	255.00	725.00
11-Dusty, Shield's sidekick begins (1st app.); last Press Guardian, Fu Chang	91.00	273.00	775.00
12-Origin & 1st app. Fireball (2/41); last Rocket & Queen of Diamonds; Danny in Wonderland begins	112.00	336.00	950.00
13-15	71.00	213.00	600.00
16-Origin Madam Satan; blood drainage-c	112.00	336.00	950.00
17-Origin/1st app. The Hangman (7/41); death of The Comet; Comet is revealed as Hangman's brother	274.00	822.00	2600.00
18-21: 20-Last Fireball. 21-Last Madam Satan	71.00	213.00	600.00

	GD25	FN65	VF82	NM94
22-Intro. & 1st app. Archie, Betty, & Jughead(12/41); (also see Jackpot)	910.00	2730.00	5460.00	10,000.00

	GD25	FN65	NM94
23	118.00	354.00	1000.00
24,25: 24-Coach Kleets app. (unnamed until Archie #94); bondage/torture-c. 25-1st app. Archie's jalopy; 1st skinny Mr. Weatherbee prototype	97.00	291.00	825.00
26-1st app. Veronica Lodge (4/42)	135.00	405.00	1150.00
27-30: 29-Origin Shield retold; 30-Capt. Commando begins; bondage/torture-c; 1st Miss Grundy (definitive version); see Jackpot #4	79.00	237.00	675.00
31-35: 31-MLJ offices & artists are visited in Sgt. Boyle story; 1st app. Mr. Lodge. 32-Shield dons new costume. 34-Bondage/Hypo-c. 33-Pre-Moose tryout (see Jughead #1)	62.00	186.00	525.00
36-1st Archie-c (2/43) w/Shield & Hangman	141.00	423.00	1200.00
37-40	46.00	138.00	390.00
41-50: 41-Archie-c begin. 47-Last Hangman issue; infinity-c. 48-Black Hood begins (5/44); ends #51,59,60	33.00	100.00	250.00
51-60: 52-Suzie begins. 56-Last Capt. Commando. 59-Black Hood not in costume; spanking & lingerie panels; Archie dresses as his aunt; Suzie ends. 60-Katy Keene begins(3/47), ends #154	23.00	68.00	170.00
61-65-Last Shield. 62-1st app. Li'l Jinx (7/47)	19.00	56.00	140.00
66-80: 66-G-Man Club becomes Archie Club (2/48); Nevada Jones by Bill Woggon. 78-1st app. Dilton	11.00	34.00	85.00
81-99	9.30	28.00	65.00
100	11.00	32.00	80.00
101-130	5.00	15.00	30.00
131(2/59)-149(9/61)	2.50	7.50	20.00
150-160-Super-heroes app. in each (see note). 150 (10/61?)-2nd or 3rd app. The Jaguar? 152-157-Sci/Fi-c. 157-Li'l Jinx story	2.80	8.40	28.00
161(3/63)-167,169-180	2.00	6.00	16.00
168-.(1/64)-Jaguar app	2.50	7.50	20.00
181(5/65)-199: 192-UFO-c. 198-Giantman-c(only)	1.75	5.25	14.00
200(12/66)	2.50	7.50	20.00
201-217,219-226,228-240(4/70)	1.00	3.00	10.00
218,227-Archies Band-c only	1.20	3.60	12.00
241-270(10/72)	1.00	3.00	10.00
271-299: 298-Josie and the Pussycats-c	.85	2.60	7.00
300(4/75)	.90	2.70	9.00
301-340(8/78)			4.00
341-382			3.00
383(4/82),393(3/84): 383-Marvelous Maureen begins (Sci/fi). 393-Thunderbunny begins			4.00
384-392,394-399,401-410			2.00
400(5/85),411: 400-Story featuring Archie staff (DeCarlo-a)			4.00

NOTE: ***Biro*** *a-2, 4, 5.* ***Jack Cole*** *a-1-5, 8.* ***Al Fagaly*** *c-55-72.* ***Fuje*** *a-39, 45, 47; c-34.* ***Meskin*** *a-2, 4, 5, 11(2).* ***Montana*** *c-30, 32, 33, 36, 73-87(most).* ***Novick*** *c-1-28, 29(w/****Schomburg****), 31i.* ***Harry Sahle*** *c-35, 39-50.* ***Schomburg*** *c-38.* ***Bob Wood*** *a-2, 4-6, 11. The Fly app. in 151, 154, 160. Flygirl app. in 153, 155, 156, 158. Jaguar app. in 150, 152, 157, 159, 168. Katy Keene by* ***Bill Woggon*** *in many later issues. Bondage c-7, 12, 13, 15, 18, 21, 31, 32. Cover features: Shield #1-16; Shield/Hangman #17-27, 29-41; Hangman #28. Archie #36, 41-on.*

PEPE
Dell Publishing Co.: No. 1194, Apr, 1961

	GD25	FN65	NM94
Four Color 1194-Movie, photo-c	1.80	5.50	20.00

PERFECT CRIME, THE
Cross Publications: Oct, 1949 - No. 33, May, 1953 (#2-12, 52 pgs.)

	GD25	FN65	NM94
1-Powell-a(2)	25.00	75.00	185.00
2 (4/50)	14.00	42.00	105.00
3-10: 7-Steve Duncan begins, ends #30. 10-Flag-c	12.00	36.00	90.00
11-Used in **SOTI**, pg. 159	14.00	42.00	105.00
12-14	11.00	32.00	80.00
15- "The Most Terrible Menace" 2 pg. drug editorial	11.00	34.00	85.00
16,17,19-25,27-29,31-33	8.50	25.50	60.00
18-Drug cover, heroin drug propaganda story, plus 2 pg. anti-drug editorial	18.00	54.00	135.00
26-Drug-c with hypodermic; drug propaganda story	19.00	57.00	140.00
30-Strangulation cover	19.00	58.00	145.00

NOTE: ***Powell*** *a-No. 1, 2, 4.* ***Wildey*** *a-1, 5. Bondage c-11.*

PERFECT LOVE
Ziff-Davis(Approved Comics)/St. John No. 9 on: #10, 8-9/51 (cover date; 5-6/51 indicia date); #2, 10-11/51 - #10, 12/53

	GD25	FN65	NM94
10(#1)(8-9/51)-Painted-c	16.00	48.00	120.00
2(10-11/51)	11.00	32.00	80.00
3,5-7: 3-Painted-c. 5-Photo-c	7.85	23.50	55.00
4,8 (Fall, 1952)-Kinstler-a; last Z-D issue	8.50	26.00	60.00
9,10 (10/53, 12/53, St. John): 9-Painted-c. 10-Photo-c	7.15	21.50	50.00

PERG (Also see Hellina)
Lightning Comics: Oct, 1993 - No. 8, May, 1994 ($2.95)

	GD25	FN65	NM94
1-($3.50)-Flip-c is glow-in-the-dark by Saltares			3.50
1-4: Platinum Editions			3.00
2-8: 4-Origin Perg. 7-Blue & Pink cover versions			3.00

PERRI (Disney)
Dell Publishing Co.: No. 847, Jan, 1958

	GD25	FN65	NM94
Four Color 847-Movie, w/2 diff-c publ.	4.50	13.50	50.00

PERRY MASON
David McKay Publications: No. 49, 1946 - No. 50, 1946

	GD25	FN65	NM94
Feature Books 49, 59-Based on Gardner novels	21.00	64.00	160.00

PERRY MASON MYSTERY MAGAZINE (TV)
Dell Publishing Co.: June-Aug, 1964 - No. 2, Oct-Dec, 1964

	GD25	FN65	NM94
1,2: 2-Raymond Burr photo-c	2.50	7.50	24.00

PERSONAL LOVE (Also see Movie Love)
Famous Funnies: Jan, 1950 - No. 33, June, 1955

	GD25	FN65	NM94
1-Photo-c	14.00	42.00	105.00
2-Kathryn Grayson & Mario Lanza photo-c	7.85	23.50	55.00
3-7,10: 7-Robert Walker & Joanne Dru photo-c. 10-Loretta Young & Joseph Cotton photo-c	6.00	18.00	42.00
8,9: 8-Esther Williams & Howard Keel photo-c. 9-Debra Paget & Louis Jourdan photo-c	6.50	19.50	45.00

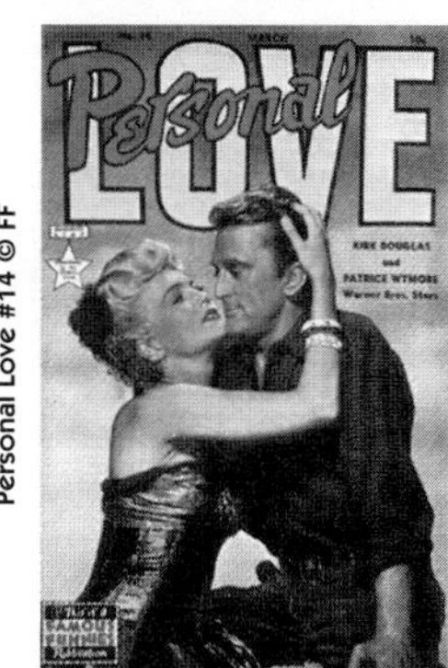

Personal Love #14 © FF

Peter Parker: Spider-Man V2 #1 © MAR

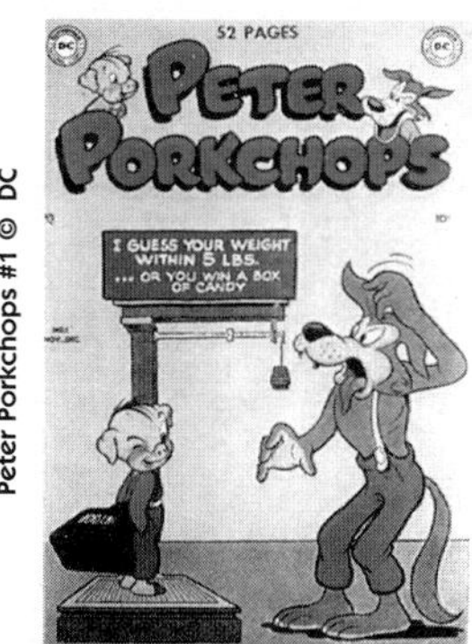

Peter Porkchops #1 © DC

	GD25	FN65	NM94
11-Toth-a; Glenn Ford & Gene Tierney photo-c	9.30	28.00	65.00
12,16,17-One pg. Frazetta each. 17-Rock Hudson & Yvonne DeCarlo photo-c	6.00	18.00	42.00
13-15,18-23: 12-Jane Greer & William Lundigan photo-c. 14-Kirk Douglas photo-c. 15-Dale Robertson & Joanne Dru photo-c. 18-Gregory Peck & Susan Hayworth photo-c. 19-Anthony Quinn & Suzan Ball photo-c. 20-Robert Wagner & Kathleen Crowley photo-c. 21-Roberta Peters & Byron Palmer photo-c. 22-Dale Robertson photo-c. 23-Rhonda Fleming-c	5.70	17.00	35.00
24,27,28-Frazetta-a in each (8,8&6 pgs.). 27-Rhonda Fleming & Fernando Lamas photo-c. 28,30-Mitzi Gaynor photo-c	32.00	96.00	240.00
25-Frazetta-a (tribute to Betty Page, 7 pg. story); Tyrone Power/Terry Moore photo-c from "King of the Khyber Rifles"	32.00	96.00	240.00
26,29,30,33: 26-Constance Smith & Byron Palmer photo-c. 29-Charlton Heston & Nicol Morey photo-c. 30-Johnny Ray & Mitzi Gaynor photo-c. 33-Dana Andrews & Piper Laurie photo-c	5.35	16.00	32.00
31-Marlon Brando & Jean Simmons photo-c; last pre-code (2/55)	7.85	23.50	55.00
32-Classic Frazetta-a (8 pgs.); Kirk Douglas & Bella Darvi photo-c	43.00	129.00	360.00

NOTE: *All have photo-c. Many feature movie stars.* ***Everett*** *a-5, 9, 10, 24.*

PERSONAL LOVE (Going Steady V3#3 on)
Prize Publ. (Headline): V1#1, Sept, 1957 - V3#2, Nov-Dec, 1959

	GD25	FN65	NM94
V1#1	6.50	19.50	45.00
2	4.25	13.00	26.00
3-6(7-8/58)	4.25	13.00	24.00
V2#1(9-10/58)-V2#6(7-8/59)	4.00	10.00	20.00
V3#1-Wood?/Orlando-a	4.25	13.00	28.00
2	3.60	9.00	18.00

PETER CANNON - THUNDERBOLT (See Crisis on Infinite Earths)(Also see Thunderbolt)
DC Comics: Sept, 1992 - No. 12, Aug, 1993 ($1.25)

	GD25	FN65	NM94
1-12			1.25

PETER COTTONTAIL
Key Publications: Jan, 1954; Feb, 1954 - No. 2, Mar, 1954 (Says 3/53 in error)

	GD25	FN65	NM94
1(1/54)-Not 3-D	5.70	17.00	40.00
1(2/54)-(3-D, 25¢)-Came w/glasses; written by Bruce Hamilton	19.00	58.00	145.00
2-Reprints 3-D #1 but not in 3-D	5.00	15.00	30.00

PETER GUNN (TV)
Dell Publishing Co.: No. 1087, Apr-June, 1960

	GD25	FN65	NM94
Four Color 1087-Photo-c	9.00	27.00	100.00

PETER PAN (Disney) (See Hook, Movie Classics & Comics, New Adventures of... & Walt Disney Showcase #36)
Dell Publishing Co.: No. 442, Dec, 1952 - No. 926, Aug, 1958

	GD25	FN65	NM94
Four Color 442 (#1)-Movie	8.00	25.00	90.00
Four Color 926-Reprint of 442	3.60	11.00	40.00

PETER PAN
Disney Comics: 1991 ($5.95, graphic novel, 68 pgs.)(Celebrates video release)

	GD25	FN65	NM94
nn-r/Peter Pan Treasure Chest from 1953	.85	2.60	7.00

PETER PANDA
National Periodical Publications: Aug-Sept, 1953 - No. 31, Aug-Sept, 1958

	GD25	FN65	NM94
1-Grossman-c/a in all	37.00	112.00	280.00
2	17.00	50.00	125.00
3-10: 9-Robot-c	13.00	38.00	95.00
11-31	9.30	28.00	65.00

PETER PAN TREASURE CHEST (See Dell Giants)

PETER PARKER (See The Spectacular Spider-Man)

PETER PARKER: SPIDER-MAN
Marvel Comics: Jan, 1999 - Present ($2.99/$1.99)

	GD25	FN65	NM94
1-Mackie-s/Romita Jr.-a; wraparound-c			3.00
1-($6.95) DF Edition w/variant cover by the Romitas			6.95
2,3-($1.99): 2-Two covers; Thor app.			2.00

PETER PAT
United Features Syndicate: No. 8, 1939

	GD25	FN65	NM94
Single Series 8	29.00	88.00	222.00

PETER PAUL'S 4 IN 1 JUMBO COMIC BOOK
Capitol Stories (Charlton): No date (1953)

	GD25	FN65	NM94
1-Contains 4 comics bound; Space Adventures, Space Western, Crime & Justice, Racket Squad in Action	37.00	110.00	275.00

PETER PENNY AND HIS MAGIC DOLLAR
American Bankers Association, N. Y. (Giveaway): 1947 (16 pgs.; paper-c; regular size)

	GD25	FN65	NM94
nn-(Scarce)-Used in **SOTI**, pg. 310, 311	16.00	48.00	120.00
Diff. version (7-1/4x11")-redrawn, 16 pgs., paper-c	9.30	28.00	65.00

PETER PIG
Standard Comics: No. 5, May, 1953 - No. 6, Aug, 1953

	GD25	FN65	NM94
5,6	5.00	15.00	30.00

PETER PORKCHOPS (See Leading Comics #23)
National Periodical Publications: 11-12/49 - No. 61, 9-11/59; No. 62, 10-12/60 (1-11: 52 pgs.)

	GD25	FN65	NM94
1	30.00	90.00	225.00
2	15.00	44.00	110.00
3-10: 6- "Peter Rockets to Mars!" c/story	11.00	32.00	80.00
11-30	8.50	26.00	60.00
31-62	7.15	21.50	50.00

NOTE: ***Otto Feur*** *a-all.* ***Sheldon Mayer*** *a-30-38, 40-44, 46-52, 61.*

PETER PORKER, THE SPECTACULAR SPIDER-HAM
Star Comics (Marvel): May, 1985 - No. 17, Sept, 1987 (Also see Marvel Tails)

	GD25	FN65	NM94
1-Michael Golden-c			2.00
2-17: 12-Origin/1st app. Bizarro Phil. 13-Halloween issue			1.00

NOTE: *Back-up features: 2-X-Bugs. 3-Iron Mouse. 4-Croctor Strange. 5-Thrr, Dog of Thunder.*

PETER POTAMUS (TV)
Gold Key: Jan, 1965 (Hanna-Barbera)

	GD25	FN65	NM94
1	8.00	23.00	85.00

PETER RABBIT (See New Funnies #65 & Space Comics)
Dell Publishing Co.: No. 1, 1942

	GD25	FN65	NM94
Large Feature Comic 1	36.00	107.00	385.00

PETER RABBIT (Adventures of...; New Advs. of... #9 on)(Also see Funny Tunes & Space Comics)
Avon Periodicals: 1947 - No. 34, Aug-Sept, 1956

	GD25	FN65	NM94
1(1947)-Reprints 1943-44 Sunday strips; contains a biography & drawing of Cady	31.00	92.00	230.00
2 (4/48)	23.00	68.00	170.00
3 ('48) - 6(7/49)-Last Cady issue	20.00	60.00	150.00
7-10(1950-8/51): 9-New logo	5.35	16.00	32.00
11(11/51)-34('56)-Avon's character	4.00	11.00	22.00
...Easter Parade (1952, 25¢, 132 pgs.)	14.00	42.00	105.00
...Jumbo Book (1954-Giant Size, 25¢)-Jesse James by Kinstler (6 pgs.); space ship-c	19.00	58.00	145.00

PETER RABBIT
Fago Magazine Co.: 1958

	GD25	FN65	NM94
1	6.70	20.00	40.00

PETER RABBIT 3-D
Eternity Comics: April, 1990 ($2.95, with glasses; sealed in plastic bag)

	GD25	FN65	NM94
1-By Harrison Cady (reprints)			3.00

Petticott Junction #2 © DELL

The Phantom #73 © KING

Phantom Lady #14 © FOX

PETER, THE LITTLE PEST (#4 titled Petey)
Marvel Comics Group: Nov, 1969 - No. 4, May, 1970

	GD25	FN65	NM94
1	3.80	11.50	40.00
2-4-r-Dexter the Demon & Melvin the Monster	2.70	8.00	30.00

PETER WHEAT (The Adventures of...)
Bakers Associates Giveaway: 1948 - 1956? (16 pgs. in color) (paper covers)

	GD25	FN65	NM94
nn(No.1)-States on last page, end of 1st Adventure of...; Kelly-a	28.00	84.00	210.00
nn(4 issues)-Kelly-a	18.00	54.00	135.00
6-10-All Kelly-a	13.00	38.00	95.00
11-20-All Kelly-a	11.00	32.00	80.00
21-35-All Kelly-a	9.30	28.00	65.00
36-66	6.00	18.00	42.00
...Artist's Workbook ('54, digest size)	6.00	18.00	42.00
...Four-In-One Fun Pack (Vol. 2, '54), oblong, comics w/puzzles	7.85	23.50	55.00
...Fun Book ('52, 32 pgs., paper-c, B&W & color, 8-1/2x10-3/4")-Contains cut-outs, puzzles, games, magic & pages to color	10.00	30.00	75.00

NOTE: ***Al Hubbard** art #36 on; written by Del Connell.*

PETER WHEAT NEWS
Bakers Associates: 1948 - No. 30, 1950 (4 pgs. in color)

	GD25	FN65	NM94
Vol. 1-All have 2 pgs. Peter Wheat by Kelly	23.00	70.00	175.00
2-10	13.00	40.00	100.00
11-20	7.15	21.50	50.00
21-30	5.70	17.00	35.00

NOTE: *Early issues have no date & **Kelly** art.*

PETE'S DRAGON (See Walt Disney Showcase #43)

PETE THE PANIC
Stanmor Publications: November, 1955

	GD25	FN65	NM94
nn-Code approved	4.00	11.00	22.00

PETEY (See Peter, the Little Pest)

PETTICOAT JUNCTION (TV)
Dell Publ. Co.: Oct-Dec, 1964 - No. 5, Oct-Dec, 1965 (#1-3, 5 have photo-c)

	GD25	FN65	NM94
1	5.50	16.50	60.00
2-5	4.00	12.25	45.00

PETUNIA (Also see Looney Tunes and Porky Pig)
Dell Publishing Co.: No. 463, Apr, 1953

	GD25	FN65	NM94
Four Color 463	3.00	9.00	35.00

PHAGE (See Neil Gaiman's Teknophage & Neil Gaiman's Phage-Shadowdeath)

PHANTACEA
McPherson Publishing Co.: Sept, 1977 - No. 6, Summer, 1980 (B&W)

	GD25	FN65	NM94
1-Early Dave Sim-a (32 pgs.)	2.50	7.60	28.00
2-Dave Sim-a(10 pgs.)	1.80	5.40	18.00
3,5: 3-Flip-c w/Damnation Bridge	1.00	3.00	10.00
4,6: 4-Gene Day-a	1.40	4.20	14.00

PHANTASMO (See The Funnies #45)
Dell Publishing Co.: No. 18, 1941

	GD25	FN65	NM94
Large Feature Comic 18	24.00	71.00	260.00

PHANTOM, THE
David McKay Publishing Co.: 1939 - 1949

	GD25	FN65	NM94
Feature Books 20	61.00	183.00	675.00
Feature Books 22	52.00	156.00	570.00
Feature Books 39	45.00	135.00	380.00
Feature Books 53,56,57	38.00	114.00	285.00

PHANTOM, THE (See Ace Comics, Defenders Of The Earth, Eat Right to Work and Win, Future Comics, Harvey Comics Hits #51,56, Harvey Hits #1, 6, 12, 15, 26, 36, 44, 48, & King Comics)

PHANTOM, THE (nn 29-Published overseas only) (Also see Comics Reading Library)
Gold Key(#1-17)/King(#18-28)/Charlton(#30 on): Nov, 1962 - No. 17, Jul, 1966; No. 18, Sept, 1966 - No. 28, Dec, 1967; No. 30, Feb, 1969 - No. 74, Jan, 1977

	GD25	FN65	NM94
1-Manning-a; origin revealed on inside-c. & back-c.	13.00	39.00	130.00
2-King, Queen & Jack begins, ends #11	6.00	17.50	65.00
3-10	4.50	13.50	50.00
11-17: 12-Track Hunter begins	3.80	11.50	40.00
18-Flash Gordon begins; Wood-a	3.25	10.00	36.00
19,20-Flash Gordon ends (both by Gil Kane)	2.40	7.00	26.00
21-24,26,27: 21-Mandrake begins. 20,24-Girl Phantom app. 26-Brick Bradford app.	2.40	7.00	26.00
25-Jeff Jones-a(4 pgs.); 1 pg. Williamson ad	2.40	7.00	26.00
28(nn)-Brick Bradford app.	2.00	6.00	22.00
30-40: 36,39-Ditko-a	1.60	4.80	16.00
41-66: 46-Intro. The Piranha. 62-Bolle-c	1.40	4.20	14.00
67-Origin retold	1.40	4.20	14.00
68-73-Newton-c/a	.90	2.70	9.00
74-Classic flag-c by Newton; Newton-a;	1.40	4.20	14.00

NOTE: ***Aparo** a-31-34, 36-38; c-31-38, 60, 61. Painted c-1-17.*

PHANTOM, THE
DC Comics: May, 1988 - No. 4, Aug, 1988 ($1.25, mini-series)

	GD25	FN65	NM94
1-4: Orlando-c/a in all			1.50

PHANTOM, THE
DC Comics: Mar, 1989 - No. 13, Mar, 1990 ($1.50)

	GD25	FN65	NM94
1-13: 1-Brief origin			1.50

PHANTOM, THE
Wolf Publishing: 1992 - No. 8, 1993? ($2.25)

	GD25	FN65	NM94
1-8		.90	2.25

PHANTOM BLOT, THE (#1 titled New Adventures of...)
Gold Key: Oct, 1964 - No. 7, Nov, 1966 (Disney)

	GD25	FN65	NM94
1 (Meets The Beagle Boys)	4.00	12.25	45.00
2-1st Super Goof	3.80	11.50	40.00
3-7	2.20	6.50	24.00

PHANTOM EAGLE (See Mighty Midget, Marvel Super Heroes #16 & Wow #6)

PHANTOM FORCE
Image Comics/Genesis West #0, 3-7: 12/93 - #2, 1994; #0, 3/94; #3, 5/94 - #8, 10/94 ($2.50/$3.50, limited series)

	GD25	FN65	NM94
0 (3/94, $2.50)-Kirby/Jim Lee-c; Kirby-p pgs. 1,5,24-29.			2.50
1 (12/93, $2.50)-Polybagged w/trading card; Kirby Liefeld-c; Kirby plots/pencils w/inks by Liefeld, McFarlane, Jim Lee, Silvestri, Larsen, Williams, Ordway & Miki.			2.50
2 ($3.50)-Kirby-a(p); Kirby/Larson-c			3.50
3-8: 3-(5/94, $2.50)-Kirby/McFarlane-c 4-(5/94)-Kirby-c(p). 5-(6/94)			2.50

PHANTOM GUARD
Image Comics (WildStorm Productions): Oct, 1997 - Present ($2.50)

	GD25	FN65	NM94
1-6: 1-Two covers			2.50
1-($3.50)-Voyager Pack w/Wildcore preview			3.50

PHANTOM LADY (1st Series) (My Love Secret #24 on) (Also see All Top, Daring Adventures, Freedom Fighters, Jungle Thrills, & Wonder Boy)
Fox Features Syndicate: No. 13, Aug, 1947 - No. 23 Apr, 1949

	GD25	FN65	NM94
13(#1)-Phantom Lady by Matt Baker begins (1st app.); The Blue Beetle story	333.00	1000.00	3000.00
14(#2)-Not Baker-c	219.00	657.00	1750.00
15-P.L. injected with experimental drug	219.00	657.00	1750.00
16-Negligee-c, panels; true crime stories begin	219.00	657.00	1750.00
17-Classic bondage cover; used in **SOTI**, illo "Sexual stimulation by combining 'headlights' with the sadist's dream of tying up a woman"	467.00	1400.00	4200.00
18,19	150.00	450.00	1250.00

Phantom Stranger #1 © DC

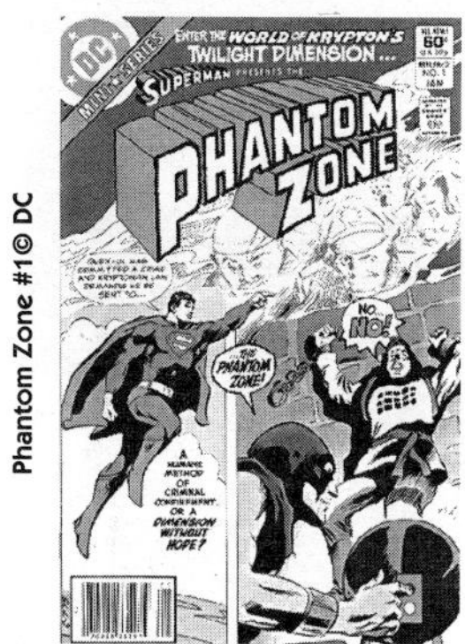

Phantom Zone #1© DC

Pictorial Romances #4 © STJ

GD25 FN65 NM94

20-22 116.00 348.00 925.00
23-Bondage-c 123.00 370.00 1050.00
NOTE: *Matt Baker a-in all; c-13, 15-21. Kamen a-22, 23.*

PHANTOM LADY (2nd Series) (See Terrific Comics) (Formerly Linda)
Ajax/Farrell Publ.: V1#5, Dec-Jan, 1954/1955 - No. 4, June, 1955

V1#5(#1)-By Matt Baker 94.00 282.00 800.00
V1#2-Last pre-code 76.00 228.00 625.00
3,4-Red Rocket. 3-Heroin story 61.00 183.00 490.00

PHANTOM LADY
Verotik Publications: 1994 ($9.95)

1-Reprints G. A. stories from Phantom Lady and All Top Comics; Adam Hughes-c 9.95

PHANTOM PLANET, THE
Dell Publishing Co.: No. 1234, 1961

Four Color 1234-Movie 6.40 19.00 70.00

PHANTOM STRANGER, THE (1st Series)(See Saga of Swamp Thing)
National Periodical Publications: Aug-Sept, 1952 - No. 6, June-July, 1953

1(Scarce)-1st app. 171.00 513.00 1450.00
2 (Scarce) 100.00 300.00 800.00
3-6 (Scarce) 87.00 262.00 700.00

PHANTOM STRANGER, THE (2nd Series) (See Showcase #80)
National Periodical Publications: May-June, 1969 - No. 41, Feb-Mar, 1976

1-2nd S.A. app. P. Stranger; only 12¢ issue 7.50 22.50 75.00
2,3 3.00 9.00 30.00
4-1st new look Phantom Stranger; N. Adams-a 3.50 10.50 35.00
5-7 2.50 7.50 22.00
8-14: 14-Last 15¢ issue 1.80 5.40 18.00
15-19: All 25¢ giants (52 pgs.) 1.70 5.10 17.00
20-Dark Circle begins, ends #24. 1.50 4.50 15.00
21,22 .90 2.70 9.00
23-Spawn of Frankenstein begins by Kaluta 1.80 5.40 18.00
24,25,27-30-Last Spawn of Frankenstein 1.20 3.60 12.00
26- Book-length story featuring Phantom Stranger, Dr.13 & Spawn of Frankenstein 1.40 4.20 14.00
31-The Black Orchid begins (6-7/74). 1.80 5.40 18.00
32,34-38: 34-Last 20¢ issue (#35 on are 25¢) .90 2.70 9.00
33-Deadman-c/story 1.00 3.00 10.00
39-41-Deadman app. 1.40 4.20 14.00
NOTE: ***N. Adams** a-4; c-3-19. **Anderson** a-4, 5i. **Aparo** a-7-17, 19-26; c-20-24, 33-41. **B. Bailey** a-27-30. **DeZuniga** a-12-16, 18, 19, 21, 22, 31, 34. **Grell** a-33. **Kaluta** a-23-25; c-26. **Meskin** r-15, 16, 18, 19. **Redondo** a-32, 35, 36. **Sparling** a-20. **Starr** a-17r. **Toth** a-15r. Black Orchid by **Carrilo**-38-41. Dr. 13 solo in-13, 18, 19, 20, 21, 34. Frankenstein by **Kaluta**-23-25; by **Baily**-27-30. No Black Orchid-33, 34, 37.*

PHANTOM STRANGER (See Justice League of America #103)
DC Comics: Oct, 1987 - No. 4, Jan, 1988 (75¢, limited series)

1-Mignola/Russell-c/a & Eclipso app. in all 2.00
2-4: 3,4-Eclipso-c 1.25

PHANTOM STRANGER (See Vertigo Visions-The Phantom Stranger)

PHANTOM: THE GHOST WHO WALKS
Marvel Comics: Feb, 1995 - No. 3, Apr, 1995 ($2.95, limited series)

1-3 3.00

PHANTOM 2040 (TV cartoon)
Marvel Comics: May, 1995 - No. 4, Aug, 1995 ($1.50)

1-4-Based on animated series 1.50

PHANTOM WITCH DOCTOR (Also see Durango Kid #8 & Eerie #8)
Avon Periodicals: 1952

1-Kinstler-c/a (7 pgs.) 41.00 123.00 330.00

PHANTOM ZONE, THE (See Adventure #283 & Superboy #100, 104)
DC Comics: January, 1982 - No. 4, April, 1982

1-Superman app. in all 1.10
2-4: Batman, Green Lantern app. 1.35
NOTE: ***Colan** a-1-4p; c-1-4p. **Giordano** c-1-4i.*

PHAZE
Eclipse Comics: Apr, 1988 - No. 2, Oct, 1988 ($2.25)

1,2: 1-Sienkiewicz-c. 2-Gulacy painted-c 2.25

PHIL RIZZUTO (Baseball Hero)(See Sport Thrills, Accepted reprint)
Fawcett Publications: 1951 (New York Yankees)

nn-Photo-c 58.00 174.00 490.00

PHOENIX
Atlas/Seaboard Publ.: Jan, 1975 - No. 4, Oct, 1975

1-Origin 4.00
2-4: 3-Origin & only app. The Dark Avenger. 4-New origin/costume The Protector (formerly Phoenix) 3.00
NOTE: ***Infantino** appears in #1, 2. **Austin** a-3i. **Thorne** c-3.*

PHOENIX (...The Untold Story)
Marvel Comics Group: April, 1984 ($2.00, one-shot)

1-Byrne/Austin-r/X-Men #137 with original unpublished ending 1.00 3.00 10.00

PHOENIX RESURRECTION, THE
Malibu Comics (Ultraverse): 1995 - 1996 ($3.95)

Genesis #1 (12/95)-X-Men app; wraparound-c 4.00
Revelations #1 (12/95)-X-Men app; wraparound-c 4.00
Aftermath #1 (1/96)-X-Men app. 4.00
0-($1.95)-r/series 2.00
0-American Entertainment Ed. 4.00

PICNIC PARTY (See Dell Giants)

PICTORIAL CONFESSIONS (Pictorial Romances #4 on)
St. John Publishing Co.: Sept, 1949 - No. 3, Dec, 1949

1-Baker-c/a(3) 25.00 74.00 185.00
2-Baker-a; photo-c 16.00 48.00 120.00
3-Kubert, Baker-a; part Kubert-c 16.00 48.00 120.00

PICTORIAL LOVE STORIES (Formerly Tim McCoy)
Charlton Comics: No. 22, Oct, 1949 - No. 26, July, 1950 (all photo-c)

22-26: All have "Me-Dan Cupid". 25-Fred Astaire-c 17.00 50.00 125.00

PICTORIAL LOVE STORIES
St. John Publishing Co.: October, 1952

1-Baker-c 23.00 70.00 175.00

PICTORIAL ROMANCES (Formerly Pictorial Confessions)
St. John Publ. Co.: No. 4, Jan, 1950; No. 5, Jan, 1951 - No. 24, Mar, 1954

4-Baker-a; photo-c 24.00 72.00 180.00
5,10-All Matt Baker issues. 5-Reprints all stories from #4 w/new Baker-c 18.00 54.00 135.00
6-9,12,13,15,16-Baker-c, 2-3 stories 13.00 40.00 100.00
11-Baker-c/a(3); Kubert-r/Hollywood Confessions #1 14.00 42.00 105.00
14,21-24: Baker-c/a each. 21,24-Each has signed story by Estrada 11.00 34.00 85.00
17-20(7/53, 25¢, 100 pgs.): Baker-c/a; each has two signed stories by Estrada 23.00 70.00 175.00
NOTE: ***Matt Baker** art in most issues. **Estrada** a-17-20(2), 21, 24.*

PICTURE NEWS
Lafayette Street Corp.: Jan, 1946 - No. 10, Jan-Feb, 1947

1-Milt Gross begins, ends No. 6; 4 pg. Kirby-a; A-Bomb-c/story 35.00 106.00 265.00
2-Atomic explosion panels; Frank Sinatra/Perry Como story 17.00 52.00 130.00
3-Atomic explosion panels; Frank Sinatra, June Allyson, Benny Goodman

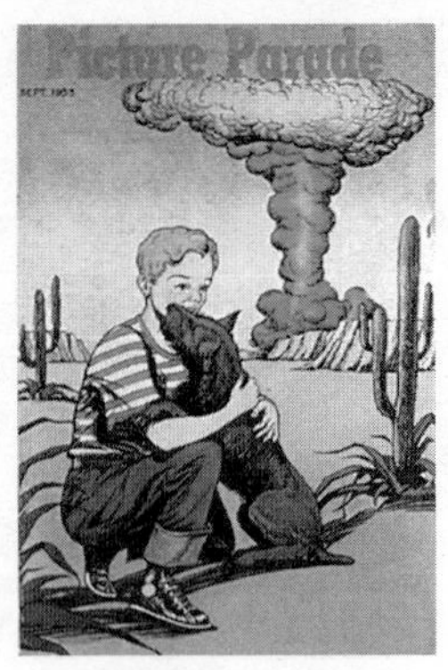

Picture Parade #1 © GIL

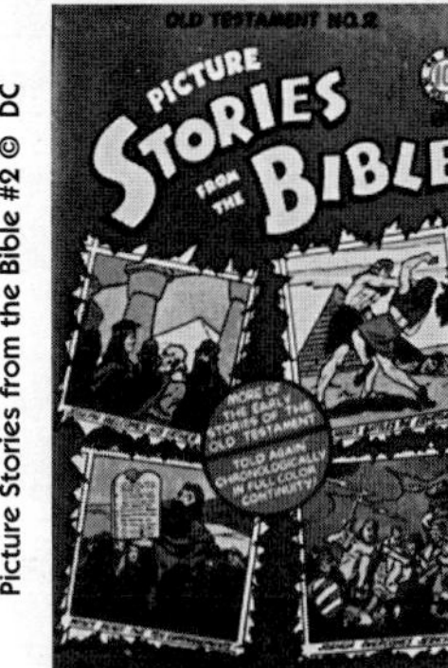

Picture Stories from the Bible #2 © DC

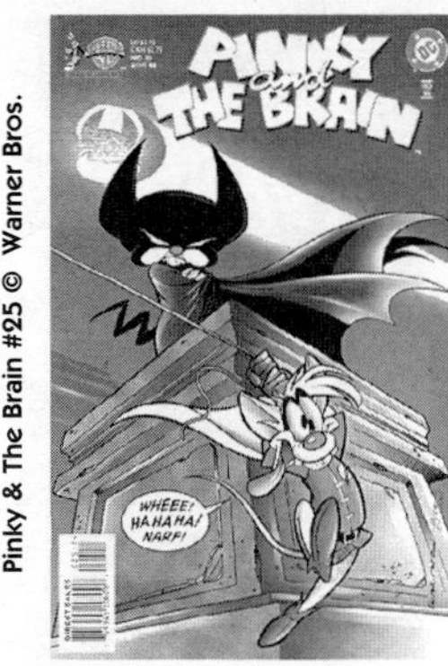

Pinky & The Brain #25 © Warner Bros.

stories 14.00 42.00 105.00
4-Atomic explosion panels; "Caesar and Cleopatra" movie adapt. w/Claude Raines & Vivian Leigh; Jackie Robinson story 17.00 52.00 130.00
5-7: 5-Hank Greenberg story. 6-Joe Louis-c/story 11.00 32.00 80.00
8-Monte Hale story (9-10/46; 1st?) 12.00 36.00 90.00
9-A-Bomb story; "Crooked Mile" movie adaptation; Joe DiMaggio story 12.00 36.00 90.00
10-Dick Quick; A-Bomb story; Krigstein, Gross-a 12.00 36.00 90.00

PICTURE PARADE (Picture Progress #5 on)
Gilberton Company (Also see A Christmas Adventure): Sept, 1953 - V1#4, Dec, 1953 (28 pgs.)

V1#1-Andy's Atomic Adventures; A-bomb blast-c; (Teachers version distributed to schools exists) 16.00 48.00 120.00
2-Around the World with the United Nations 9.30 28.00 70.00
3-Adventures of the Lost One(The American Indian), 4-A Christmas Adventure (r-under same title in 1969) 9.30 28.00 70.00

PICTURE PROGRESS (Formerly Picture Parade)
Gilberton Corp.: V1#5, Jan, 1954 - V3#2, Oct, 1955 (28-36 pgs.)

V1#5-9,V2#1-9: 5-News in Review 1953. 6-The Birth of America. 7-The Four Seasons. 8-Paul Revere's Ride. 9-The Hawaiian Islands(5/54). V2#1-The Story of Flight(9/54). 2-Vote for Crazy River(The Meaning of Elections). 3-Louis Pasteur. 4-The Star Spangled Banner. 5-News in Review 1954. 6-Alaska: The Great Land. 7-Life in the Circus. 8-The Time of the Cave Man. 9-Summer Fun(5/55) 5.35 16.00 32.00
V3#1,2: 1-The Man Who Discovered America. 2-The Lewis & Clark Expedition 5.35 16.00 32.00

PICTURE SCOPE JUNGLE ADVENTURES (See Jungle Thrills)

PICTURE STORIES FROM AMERICAN HISTORY
National/All-American/E. C. Comics: 1945 - No. 4, Sum, 1947 (#1,2: 10¢, 56 pgs.; #3,4: 15¢, 52 pgs.)

1 25.00 76.00 190.00
2-4 21.00 64.00 160.00

PICTURE STORIES FROM SCIENCE
E.C. Comics: Spring, 1947 - No. 2, Fall, 1947

1-(15¢) 25.00 76.00 190.00
2-(10¢) 23.00 70.00 175.00

PICTURE STORIES FROM THE BIBLE (See Narrative Illustration, the Story of the Comics by M.C. Gaines)
National/All-American/E.C. Comics: 1942 - No. 4, Fall, 1943; 1944-46

1-4('42-Fall, '43)-Old Testament (DC) 20.00 60.00 150.00
Complete Old Testament Edition, (12/43-DC, 50¢, 232 pgs.);-1st printing; contains #1-4; 2nd - 8th (1/47) printings exist; later printings by E.C. 24.00 72.00 180.00
Complete Old Testament Edition (1945-publ. by Bible Pictures Ltd.)-232 pgs., hardbound, in color with dust jacket 24.00 72.00 180.00

NOTE: *Both Old and New Testaments published in England by Bible Pictures Ltd. in hardback, 1943, in color, 376 pgs. (2 vols.: O.T. 232 pgs. & N.T. 144 pgs.), and were also published by Scarf Press in 1979 (Old Test., $9.95) and in 1980 (New Test., $7.95)*

1-3(New Test.; 1944-46, DC)-52 pgs. ea. 15.00 44.00 110.00
The Complete Life of Christ Edition (1945, 25¢, 96 pgs.)-Contains #1&2 of the New Testament Edition 20.00 60.00 150.00
1,2(Old Testament-r in comic book form)(E.C., 1946; 52 pgs.) 15.00 44.00 110.00
1(DC),2(AA),3(EC)(New Testament-r in comic book form)(E.C., 1946; 52 pgs.) 15.00 44.00 110.00
Complete New Testament Edition (1946-E.C., 50¢, 144 pgs.)-Contains #1-3 20.00 60.00 150.00

NOTE: *Another British series entitled* ***The Bible Illustrated*** *from 1947 has recently been discovered, with the same internal artwork. This eight edition series (5-OT, 3-NT) is of particular interest to Classics Ill. collectors because it exactly copied the C.I. logo format. The British publisher was Thorpe & Porter, who in 1951 began publishing the British Classics Ill. series. All editions of The Bible Ill. have new British painted covers. While this market is still new, and not all editions have as yet been found, current market value is about the same as the first U.S. editions of Picture Stories From The Bible.*

GD25 FN65 NM94

PICTURE STORIES FROM WORLD HISTORY
E.C. Comics: Spring, 1947 - No. 2, Summer, 1947 (52, 48 pgs.)

1-(15¢) 25.00 76.00 190.00
2-(10¢) 23.00 70.00 175.00

PINHEAD
Marvel Comics (Epic Comics): Dec, 1993 - No. 6, May, 1994 ($2.50)

1-($2.95)-Embossed foil-c by Kelley Jones; Intro Pinhead & Disciples (Snakeoil, Hangman, Fan Dancer & Dixie) 3.00
2-6 2.50

PINHEAD & FOODINI (TV)(Also see Foodini & Jingle Dingle Christmas...)
Fawcett Publications: July, 1951 - No. 4, Jan, 1952 (Early TV comic)

1-(52 pgs.)-Photo-c; based on TV puppet show 28.00 84.00 210.00
2,3-Photo-c 13.00 40.00 100.00
4 11.00 32.00 80.00

PINHEAD VS. MARSHALL LAW (Law in Hell)
Marvel Comics (Epic): Nov, 1993 - No. 2, Dec, 1993 ($2.95, lim. series)

1,2: 1-Embossed red foil-c. 2-Embossed silver foil-c 3.00

PINK DUST
Kitchen Sink Press: 1998 ($3.50, B&W, mature)

1-J. O'Barr-s/a 3.50

PINK PANTHER, THE (TV)(See The Inspector & Kite Fun Book)
Gold Key #1-70/Whitman #71-87: April, 1971 - No. 87, 1984

1-The Inspector begins 3.80 11.50 40.00
2-5 1.80 5.40 18.00
6-10 1.40 4.20 14.00
11-30: Warren Tufts-a #16-on 1.00 3.00 10.00
31-60 .90 2.70 8.00
61-70 5.00
71-74,81-83 .85 2.60 7.00
75(8/80),76-80(pre-pack?) 1.00 3.00 10.00
84-87(All #90266 on-c, no date or date code) .90 2.70 8.00
Mini-comic No. 1(1976)(3-1/4x6-1/2") 2.00 6.00

NOTE: *Pink Panther began as a movie cartoon. (See Golden Comics Digest #38, 45 and March of Comics #376, 384, 390, 409, 418, 429, 441, 449, 461, 473, 486); #37, 72, 80-85 contain reprints.*

PINK PANTHER SUPER SPECIAL (TV)
Harvey Comics: Oct, 1993 ($2.25, 68 pgs.)

V2#1-The Inspector & Wendy Witch stories also 3.00

PINK PANTHER, THE
Harvey Comics: Nov, 1993 - No. 9, July, 1994 ($1.50)

V2#1-9 2.00

PINKY & THE BRAIN (See Animaniacs)
DC Comics: July, 1996 - No. 27, Nov, 1998 ($1.75/$1.95/$1.99)

1-17 1.75
18-25-($1.95) 1.95
26,27-($1.99) 1.99
Christmas Special (1/96, $1.50) 1.50

PINKY LEE (See Adventures of...)

PINKY THE EGGHEAD
I.W./Super Comics: 1963 (Reprints from Noodnik)

I.W. Reprint #1,2(nd) 1.00 3.00 8.00
Super Reprint #14-r/Noodnik Comics #4 1.00 3.00 8.00

PINOCCHIO (See 4-Color #92, 252, 545, 1203, Mickey Mouse Mag. V5#3, Movie Comics under Wonderful Advs. of..., New Advs. of..., Thrilling Comics #2, Walt Disney Showcase, Walt Disney's..., Wonderful Advs. of..., & World's Greatest Stories #2)

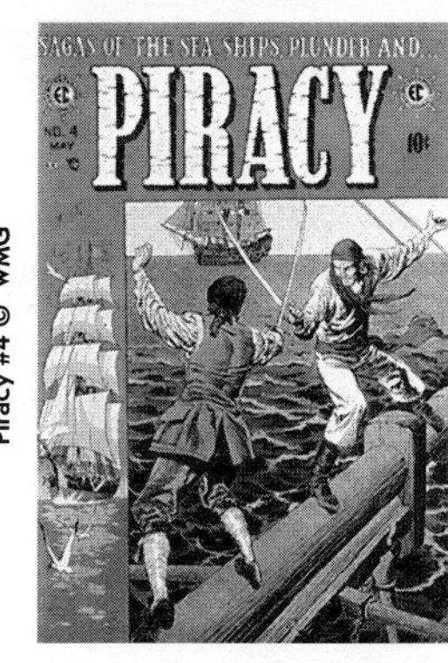

Piracy #4 © WMG

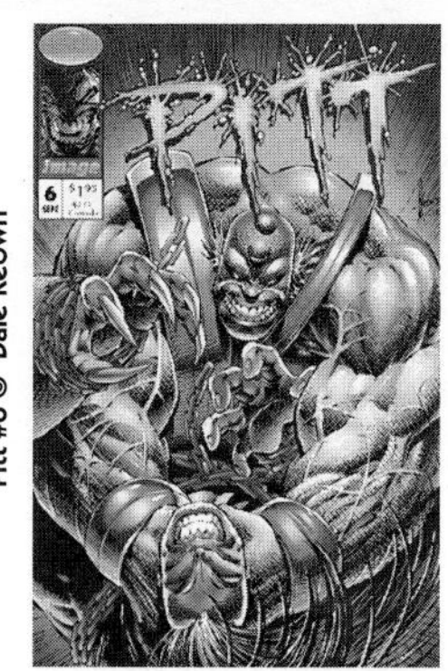

Pitt #6 © Dale Keown

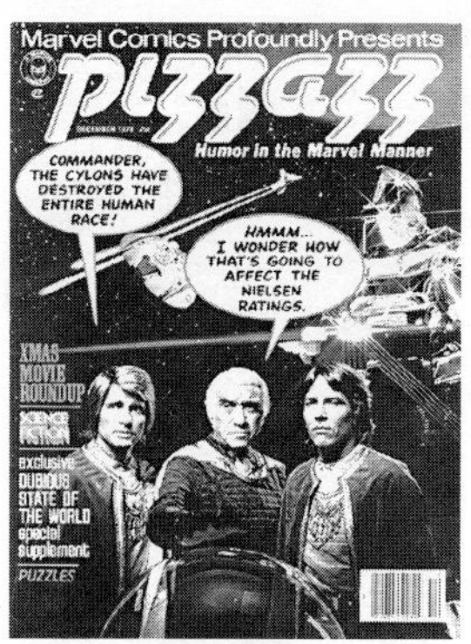

Pizzazz #15 © MAR

GD25 FN65 NM94

Dell Publishing Co.: No. 92, 1945 - No. 1203, Mar, 1962 (Disney)
Four Color 92-The Wonderful Adventures of...; 16 pg. Donald Duck story ; entire book by Kelly 55.00 164.00 600.00
Four Color 252 (10/49)-Origin, not by Kelly 9.00 27.00 100.00
Four Color 545 (3/54)-The Wonderful Advs. of...; part-r of 4-Color #92; Disney-movie 6.40 19.00 70.00
Four Color 1203 (3/62) 4.50 13.50 50.00

PINOCCHIO
Cocomalt/Montgomery Ward Co.: 1940 (10 pgs.; giveaway, linen-like paper)
nn-Cocomalt edition 15.00 46.00 115.00
nn-store edition 12.00 36.00 90.00

PINOCCHIO AND THE EMPEROR OF THE NIGHT
Marvel Comics: Mar, 1988 ($1.25, 52 pgs.)
1-Adapts film 1.25

PINOCCHIO LEARNS ABOUT KITES (See Kite Fun Book)

PIN-UP PETE (Also see Great Lover Romances & Monty Hall...)
Toby Press: 1952
1-Jack Sparling pin-ups 16.00 48.00 120.00

PIONEER MARSHAL (See Fawcett Movie Comics)

PIONEER PICTURE STORIES
Street & Smith Publications: Dec, 1941 - No. 9, Dec, 1943
1-The Legless Air Ace begins 25.00 76.00 190.00
2 -True life story of Errol Flynn 13.00 38.00 95.00
3-9 11.00 32.00 80.00

PIONEER WEST ROMANCES (Firehair #1,2,7-11)
Fiction House Magazines: No. 3, Spring, 1950 - No. 6, Winter, 1950-51
3-(52 pgs.)-Firehair continues 18.00 54.00 135.00
4-6 18.00 54.00 135.00

PIPSQUEAK (See The Adventures of...)

PIRACY
E. C. Comics: Oct-Nov, 1954 - No. 7, Oct-Nov, 1955
1-Williamson/Torres-a 22.00 66.00 200.00
2-Williamson/Torres-a 13.00 40.00 125.00
3-7 11.00 33.00 105.00
*NOTE: **Crandall** a-in all; c-2-4. **Davis** a-1, 2, 6. **Evans** a-3-7; c-7. **Ingels** a-3-7. **Krigstein** a-3-5, 7; c-5, 6. **Wood** a-1, 2; c-1.*

PIRACY
Gemstone Publishing: March, 1998 - No. 7, Sept, 1998 ($2.50)
1-7: E.C. reprints 2.50
Annual 1 ($10.95) Collects #1-4 10.95
Annual 2 ($7.95) Collects #5-7 7.95

PIRANA (See The Phantom #46 & Thrill-O-Rama #2, 3)

PIRATE CORP$, THE (See Hectic Planet)
Eternity Comics/Slave Labor Graphics: 1987 - No. 5, 1988 ($1.95)
1-5: 3-Color begins 2.00
Special 1 ('89, $1.95, B&W)-Slave Labor Publ. 2.00

PIRATE CORP$, THE (Volume 2)
Slave Labor Graphics: 1989 - No. 4, 1992 ($1.95)
1-4-Dorkin-s/a 2.00

PIRATE OF THE GULF, THE (See Superior Stories #2)

PIRATES COMICS
Hillman Periodicals: Feb-Mar, 1950 - No. 4, Aug-Sept, 1950 (All 52 pgs.)
1 21.00 64.00 160.00
2-Dave Berg-a 15.00 44.00 110.00
3,4-Berg-a 14.00 42.00 105.00

PIRATES OF DARK WATER, THE

GD25 FN65 NM94

Marvel Comics: Nov, 1991 - No. 9, Aug, 1992 ($1.95)
1-9: 9-Vess-c 2.00

P.I.'S: MICHAEL MAUSER AND MS. TREE, THE
First Comics: Jan, 1985 - No. 3, May, 1985 ($1.25, limited series)
1-3: Staton-c/a(p) 1.25

PITT, THE (Also see The Draft & The War)
Marvel Comics: Mar, 1988 ($3.25, 52 pgs., one-shot)
1-Ties into Starbrand, D.P.7 3.50

PITT (See Youngblood #4 & Gen 13 #3,#4)
Image Comics #1-9/Full Bleed #1/2,10-on: Jan, 1993 - Present ($1.95, intended as a four part limited series)
1/2-(12/95)-1st Full Bleed issue 5.00
1-Dale Keown-c/a. 1-1st app. The Pitt 5.00
2,4: Dale Keown-c/a 5.00
3 (Low distribution) 5.00
5-13: All Dale Keown-c/a. 10 (1/96)-Indicia reads "January 1995" 4.00
14-16: 14-Begin $2.50-c, pullout poster 3.00
17-19 2.50
TPB-(1997, $9.95) r/#1/2, 1-4 1.00 3.00 10.00

PITT CREW
Full Bleed Studios: Aug, 1998 - Present ($2.50, one-shot)
1,2: 1-Richard Pace-s/Ken Lashley-a. 2-Scott Lee-a 2.50

PITT IN THE BLOOD
Full Bleed Studios: Aug, 1996 ($2.50, one-shot)
nn-Richard Pace-a/script 2.50

PIUS XII MAN OF PEACE
Catechetical Guild: No date (12 pgs.; 5-1/2x8-1/2") (B&W)
nn-Catechetical Guild Giveaway 4.00 12.00 24.00

PIXIE & DIXIE & MR. JINKS (TV)(See Jinks, Pixie, and Dixie & Whitman Comic Books)
Dell Publishing Co./Gold Key: July-Sept, 1960 - Feb, 1963 (Hanna-Barbera)
Four Color 1112 6.75 21.00 75.00
Four Color 1196,1264 5.00 15.00 55.00
01-631-207 (Dell, 7/62), 1(2/63-Gold Key) 5.00 15.00 55.00

PIXIE PUZZLE ROCKET TO ADVENTURELAND
Avon Periodicals: Nov, 1952
1 11.00 32.00 80.00

PIXIES, THE (Advs. of...)(The Mighty Atom and ...#6 on)(See A-1 Comics #16)
Magazine Enterprises: Winter, 1946 - No. 4, Fall?, 1947; No. 5, 1948
1-Mighty Atom 5.70 17.00 40.00
2-5-Mighty Atom 4.00 11.00 22.00
I.W. Reprint #1(1958), 8-(Pee-Wee Pixies), 10-I.W. on cover, Super on inside 1.10 3.30 9.00

PIZZAZZ
Marvel Comics: Oct, 1977 - No. 16, Jan, 1979 (slick-color kids mag. w/puzzles, games, comics)
1-Star Wars photo-c/article; origin Tarzan; KISS 2.00 6.00 20.00
2-Spider-Man-c 1.20 3.60 12.00
3-8: 3-Close Encounters-c. 4-Alice Cooper. 7-James Bond. 8-TV Spider-Man photo-c/article 1.20 3.60 12.00
9-14: 10-Sgt. Pepper-c. 12-Battlestar Galactica-c; Spider-Man app. 13-TV Hulk-c/sty .90 2.70 8.00
15,16: 15-Battlestar Galactica-c/sty. 16-Movie Superman photo-c/sty. 1.00 3.00 10.00
NOTE: **Star Wars** comics in all. **Tarzan** comics, 1pg.-#1-8. 1pg. "Hey Look" by Kurtzman #12-16.

PLANET COMICS

Planet Comics #7 © FH

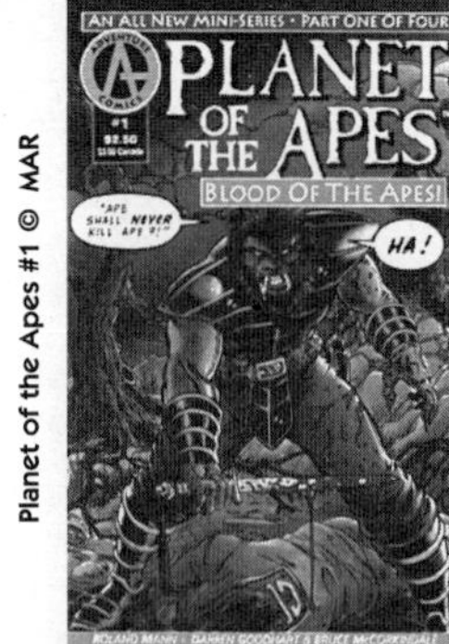

Planet of the Apes #1 © MAR

Plastic Man #4 © QUA

Fiction House Magazines: 1/40 - No. 62, 9/49; No. 63, Wint, 1949-50; No. 64, Spring, 1950; No. 65, 1951(nd); No. 66-68, 1952(nd); No. 69, Wint, 1952-53; No. 70-72, 1953(nd); No. 73, Winter, 1953-54

	GD25	FN65	VF82	NM94
1-Origin Auro, Lord of Jupiter by Briefer (ends #61); Flint Baker & The Red Comet begin; Eisner/Fine-c	900.00	2700.00	5400.00	9000.00

	GD25	FN65	NM94
2-Lou Fine-c (Scarce)	340.00	1020.00	3400.00
3-Eisner-c	253.00	760.00	2400.00
4-Gale Allen and the Girl Squadron begins	224.00	672.00	1900.00
5,6-(Scarce): 5-Eisner/Fine-c	212.00	636.00	1800.00
7-12: 8-Robot-c. 12-The Star Pirate begins	176.00	528.00	1500.00
13-14: 13-Reff Ryan begins	129.00	387.00	1100.00
15-(Scarce)-Mars, God of War begins (11/41); see Jumbo Comics #31 for 1st app.	259.00	777.00	2200.00
16-20,22	118.00	354.00	1000.00
21-The Lost World & Hunt Bowman begin	121.00	363.00	1025.00
23-26: 26-Space Rangers begin (9/43), end #71	112.00	336.00	950.00
27-30	91.00	273.00	775.00
31-35: 33-Origin Star Pirates Wonder Boots, reprinted in #52. 35-Mysta of the Moon begins, ends #62	76.00	228.00	650.00
36-45: 38-1st Mysta of the Moon-c. 41-New origin of "Auro, Lord of Jupiter". 42-Last Gale Allen. 43-Futura begins	68.00	204.00	575.00
46-60: 48-Robot-c. 53-Used in **SOTI**, pg. 32	53.00	160.00	450.00
61-68,70: 61-Last 68 pg. issue. 64,70-Robot-c. 65-70-All partial-r of earlier issues. 70-r/stories from #41	41.00	122.00	325.00
69-Used in **POP**, pgs. 101,102	41.00	122.00	325.00
71-73-No series stories. 71-Space Rangers strip	32.00	96.00	240.00
I.W. Reprint #1(nd)-r/#70; cover-r from Attack on Planet Mars	6.00	18.00	60.00
I.W. Reprint #8 (r/#72), 9-r/#73	6.00	18.00	60.00

NOTE: ***Anderson*** *a-33-38, 40-51 (Star Pirate).* ***Matt Baker*** *a-53-59 (Mysta of the Moon).* ***Celardo*** *c-12.* ***Bill Discount*** *a-71 (Space Rangers).* ***Elias*** *c-70.* ***Evans*** *a-46-49 (Auro, Lord of Jupiter), 50-64 (Lost World).* ***Fine*** *c-2, 5.* ***Hopper*** *a-31, 35 (Gale Allen), 41, 42, 48, 49 (Mysta of the Moon).* ***Ingels*** *a-24-31 (Lost World), 56-61 (Auro, Lord of Jupiter).* ***Lubbers*** *a-44-47 (Space Rangers); c-40, 41.* ***Moriera*** *a-43, 44 (Mysta of the Moon.* ***Renee*** *a-40-49 (Lost World); c-33, 35, 39.* ***Tuska*** *a-30 (Star Pirate).* ***M. Whitman*** *a-50-52 (Mysta of the Moon), 53-58 (Star Pirate); c-71-73.* ***Starr*** *a-59.* ***Zolnerwich*** *c-10. 13-25. Bondage c-53.*

PLANET COMICS
Blackthorne Publishing: Apr, 1988 - No. 3 (2.00, color/B&W #3)

1-3: New stories. 1-Dave Stevens-c 2.00

PLANET OF THE APES (Magazine) (Also see Adventures on the… & Power Record Comics)
Marvel Comics Group: Aug, 1974 - No. 29, Feb, 1977 (B&W) (Based on movies)

	GD25	FN65	NM94
1-Ploog-a	2.20	6.50	24.00
2-Ploog-a	1.20	3.60	12.00
3-10	.90	2.70	9.00
11-20 (uncommon)	1.00	3.00	10.00
21-29 (low distribution)	1.40	4.20	14.00

NOTE: ***Alcala*** *a-7-11, 17-22, 24.* ***Ploog*** *a-1-4, 6, 8, 11, 13, 14, 19.* ***Sutton*** *a-11, 12, 15, 17, 19, 20, 23, 24, 29.* ***Tuska*** *a-1-6.*

PLANET OF THE APES
Adventure Comics: Apr, 1990 - No. 24, 1992 ($2.50, B&W)

1-New movie tie-in; comes w/outer-c (3 colors) 5.00
1-Limited serial numbered edition ($5.00) 5.00
1-2nd printing (no outer-c, $2.50) 2.50
2-24 2.50
Annual 1 ($3.50) 3.50
...Urchak's Folly 1-4 ($2.50, mini-series) 2.50

PLANET OF VAMPIRES
Seaboard Publications (Atlas): Feb, 1975 - No. 3, July, 1975

1-Neal Adams-c(i); 1st Broderick c/a(p) 4.00
2,3: 2-Neal Adams-c. 3-Heath-c/a 3.00

PLANET TERRY
Marvel Comics (Star Comics)/Marvel: April, 1985 - No. 12, March, 1986 (Children's comic)

1-12 2.00

PLASM (See Warriors of Plasm)
Defiant Comics: June, 1993

0-Came bound into Diamond Previews V3#6 (6/93); price is for complete Previews with comic still attached 3.00
0-Comic only removed from Previews 2.00

PLASMER
Marvel Comics UK: Nov, 1993 - No. 4, Feb, 1994 ($1.95, limited series)

1-($2.50)-Polybagged w/4 trading cards 2.50
2-4: Capt. America & Silver Surfer app. 2.00

PLASTIC FORKS
Marvel Comis (Epic Comics): 1990 - No. 5, 1990 ($4.95, 68 pgs., limited series, mature)

Book 1-5: Squarebound 5.00

PLASTIC MAN (Also see Police Comics & Smash Comics #17)
Vital Publ. No. 1,2/Quality Comics No. 3 on: Sum, 1943 - No. 64, Nov, 1956

	GD25	FN65	NM94
nn(#1)- "In The Game of Death"; Skull-c; Jack Cole-c/a begins; ends-#64?	353.00	1060.00	3000.00
nn(#2, 2/44)- "The Gay Nineties Nightmare"	147.00	441.00	1250.00
3 (Spr, '46)	91.00	273.00	775.00
4 (Sum, '46)	74.00	222.00	625.00
5 (Aut, '46)	62.00	186.00	525.00
6-10	50.00	150.00	425.00
11-20	44.00	132.00	375.00
21-30: 26-Last non-r issue?	39.00	117.00	300.00
31-40: 40-Used in POP, pg. 91	30.00	90.00	225.00
41-64: 53-Last precode issue. 54-Robot-c	25.00	76.00	190.00
Super Reprint 11,16,18: 11('63)-r/#16. 16-r/#18 & #21; Cole-a. 18('64)-Spirit-r by Eisner from Police #95	4.00	12.00	40.00

NOTE: ***Cole*** *r-44, 49, 56, 58, 59 at least.* ***Cuidera*** *c-32-64i.*

PLASTIC MAN (See DC Special #15 & House of Mystery #160)
National Periodical Publications/DC Comics: 11-12/66 - No. 10, 5-6/68; V4#11, 2-3/76 - No. 20, 10-11/77

	GD25	FN65	NM94
1-Real 1st app. Silver Age Plastic Man (House of Mystery #160 is actually tryout); Gil Kane-c/a; 12¢ issues begin	6.00	17.50	65.00
2-5: 4-Infantino-c; Mortimer-a	2.70	8.00	30.00
6-10('68): 7-G.A. Plastic Man & Woozy Winks (1st S.A. app.) app.; origin retold. 10-Sparling-a; last 12¢ issue	1.80	5.40	18.00
V4#11('76)-20: 11-20-Fradon-p. 17-Origin retold			5.00

PLASTIC MAN
DC Comics: Nov, 1988 - No. 4, Feb, 1989 ($1.00, mini-series)

1-4: 1-Origin; Woozy Winks app. 1.00

PLASTRON CAFE
Mirage Studios: Dec, 1992 - No. 4, July, 1993 ($2.25, B&W)

1-4: 1-Teenage Mutant Ninja Turtles app.; Kelly Freas-c. 2-Hildebrandt painted-c. 4-Spaced & Alien Fire stories .90 2.25

PLAYFUL LITTLE AUDREY (TV)(Also see Little Audrey #25)
Harvey Publications: 6/57 - No. 110, 11/73; No. 111, 8/74 - No. 121, 4/76

	GD25	FN65	NM94
1	19.00	57.00	190.00
2	10.00	30.00	100.00
3-5	7.00	21.00	70.00
6-10	4.50	13.50	45.00
11-20	3.00	9.00	30.00
21-40	2.00	6.00	20.00
41-60	1.60	4.80	16.00
61-80	1.20	3.60	12.00

Plop #13 © DC

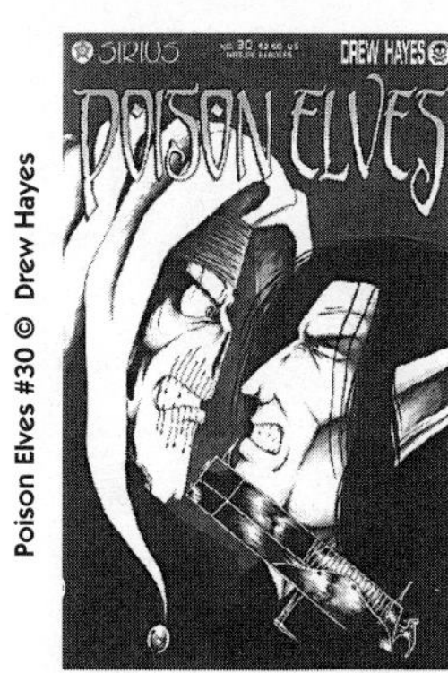

Poison Elves #30 © Drew Hayes

Police Academy #3 © MAR

	GD25	FN65	NM94
81-99	.90	2.70	9.00
100-52 pg. Giant	1.40	4.20	14.00
101-103: 52 pg. Giants	1.20	3.60	12.00
104-121		2.00	6.00
...In 3-D (Spring, 1988, $2.25, Blackthorne #66)			3.00

PLOP! (Also see The Best of DC #60)
National Periodical Publications: Sept-Oct, 1973 - No. 24, Nov-Dec, 1976

1,5: 1-Sergio Aragonés-a; 1,5-Wrightson-a	1.80	5.40	18.00
2-20	.90	2.70	9.00
21-24 (52 pgs.). 23-No Aragonés-a (52 pgs.)	1.40	4.20	14.00

NOTE: ***Alcala** a-1-3. **Anderson** a-5. **Aragonés** a-1-22, 24. **Ditko** a-16p. **Evans** a-1. **Mayer** a-1. **Orlando** a-21, 22; c-21. **Sekowsky** a-5, 6p. **Toth** a-11. **Wolverton** r-4, 22-24(1 pg.ea.); c-1-12, 14, 17, 18. **Wood** a-14, 16i, 18-24; c-13, 15, 16, 19.*

PLUTO (See Cheerios Premiums, Four Color #537, Mickey Mouse Magazine, Walt Disney Showcase #4, 7, 13, 20, 23, 33 & Wheaties)
Dell Publ. Co.: No. 7, 1942; No. 429, 10/52 - No. 1248, 11-1/61-62 (Disney)

Large Feature Comic 7(1942)-Written by Carl Barks, Jack Hannah, & Nick George (Barks' 1st comic book work)	105.00	315.00	1150.00
Four Color 429 (#1)	8.00	23.00	85.00
Four Color 509	4.50	13.50	50.00
Four Color 595,654,736,853	2.75	8.00	30.00
Four Color 941,1039,1143,1248	2.75	8.00	30.00

POCAHONTAS
Pocahontas Fuel Company (Coal): 1941 - No. 2, 1942

nn(#1), 2	11.00	32.00	80.00

POCKET COMICS (Becomes Super Duper #5?; also see Double Up)
Harvey Publications: Aug, 1941 - No. 4, Jan, 1942 (Pocket size; 100 pgs.) (1st Harvey comic)

1-Origin & 1st app. The Black Cat, Cadet Blakey the Spirit of '76, The Red Blazer, The Phantom, Sphinx, & The Zebra; Phantom Ranger, British Agent #99, Spin Hawkins, Satan, Lord of Evil begin (1st app. of each); Simon-c/a in #1-3	85.00	255.00	725.00
2-Black Cat on-c #2-4	58.00	174.00	490.00
3,4	44.00	132.00	370.00

POE
Cheese Comics: Sept, 1996 - No. 6, Apr, 1997 ($2.00, B&W)

1-6-Jason Asala-s/a			2.00

POE
Sirius Entertainment (Dogstar Press): Oct, 1997 - Present ($2.50, B&W)

1-12-Jason Asala-s/a			2.50

POGO PARADE (See Dell Giants)

POGO POSSUM (Also see Animal Comics & Special Delivery)
Dell Publishing Co.: No. 105, 4/46 - No. 148, 5/47; 10-12/49 - No. 16, 4-6/54

Four Color 105(1946)-Kelly-c/a	63.00	189.00	690.00
Four Color 148-Kelly-c/a	56.00	168.00	615.00
1-(10-12/49)-Kelly-c/a in all	47.00	142.00	515.00
2	38.00	114.00	415.00
3-5	26.00	78.00	280.00
6-10: 10-Infinity-c	21.00	63.00	235.00
11-16: 11-X-Mas-c	17.00	50.00	185.00

NOTE: *#1-4, 9-13: 52 pgs.; #5-8, 14-16: 36 pgs.*

POINT BLANK
Acme Press (Eclipse): May, 1989 - No. 2, 1989 ($2.95, B&W, magazine)

1,2-European-r			3.00

POISON ELVES (Formerly I, Lusiphur)
Mulehide Graphics: No. 8, 1993- No. 20, 1995 (B&W, magazine/comic size, mature readers)

8-Drew Hayes-c/a/scripts.	2.70	8.00	30.00
9-11: 11-1st comic size issue	2.70	8.00	30.00
12,14,16,20	2.00	6.00	20.00
13,15-scarce	3.80	11.50	40.00
15-2nd print			4.00
17-19	2.20	6.50	24.00
...Desert of the Third Sin-(1997, $14.95, TPB)-r/#13-18			15.00
...Patrons-($4.95, TPB)-r/#19,20			5.00
...Traumatic Dogs-(1996, $14.95,TPB)-Reprints I, Lusiphur #7, Poison Elves #8-12			15.00

POISON ELVES (See I, Lusiphur)
Sirius Entertainment: June, 1995 - Present ($2.50, B&W, mature readers)

1-Linsner-c; Drew Hayes-a/scripts in all.	1.40	4.20	14.00
1-2nd print			3.00
2-24: 12-Purple Marauder-c/app.			4.00
25-($2.95)			3.00
26-40			2.50
... FAN Edition #1 mail-in offer; Drew Hayes-c/s/a	1.20	3.60	12.00

POIZON
London Night Studios: Oct, 1995 - Present ($3.00)

0,1/2-3: 1/2-Razor-c/app. 1-Razor & Stryke app.; wraparound-c. 2-Razor & Stryke app. 3-Razor-c/app.			3.00
0-($5.00) Nude photo-c			5.00
0-Gothchik Edition			5.00
1-($5.95)-Necro-Nude Edition		2.00	6.00
1-Purple Reign Edition			5.00
1-($15.00)-Green Death Edition; in green envelope w/certificate			15.00

POIZON: CADILLACS AND GREEN TOMATOES
London Night Studios: 1997 - Present ($3.00)

1-3			3.00
1-3-($6.00) Nude photo-c			6.00

POLICE ACADEMY (TV)
Marvel Comics: Nov, 1989 - No. 6, Feb, 1990 ($1.00)

1-6: Based on TV cartoon; Post-c/a(p) in all			1.00

POLICE ACTION
Atlas News Co.: Jan, 1954 - No. 7, Nov, 1954

1-Violent-a by Robert Q. Sale	17.00	51.00	130.00
2	9.30	28.00	65.00
3-7: 7-Powell-a	7.85	23.50	55.00

NOTE: ***Ayers** a-4, 5. **Colan** a-1. **Forte** a-1, 2. **Mort Lawrence** a-5. **Maneely** a-3; c-1, 5. **Reinman** a-6, 7.*

POLICE ACTION
Atlas/Seaboard Publ.: Feb, 1975 - No. 3, June, 1975

1-3: 1-Lomax, N.Y.P.D., Luke Malone begin; McWilliams-a. 2-Origin Luke Malone, Manhunter			3.00

NOTE: ***Ploog** art in all. **Sekowsky/McWilliams** a-1-3. **Thorne** c-3.*

POLICE AGAINST CRIME
Premiere Magazines: April, 1954 - No. 9, Aug, 1955

1-Disbrow-a; extreme violence (man's face slashed with knife); Hollingsworth-a	20.00	60.00	150.00
2-Hollingsworth-a	11.00	32.00	80.00
3-9	9.30	28.00	65.00

POLICE BADGE #479 (Formerly Spy Thrillers #1-4)
Atlas Comics (PrPI): No. 5, Sept, 1955

5-Maneely-c/a (6 pgs.)	9.30	28.00	65.00

POLICE CASE BOOK (See Giant Comics Editions)

POLICE CASES (See Authentic... & Record Book of...)

POLICE COMICS
Quality Comics Group (Comic Magazines): Aug, 1941 - No. 127, Oct, 1953

1-Origin/1st app. Plastic Man by Jack Cole (r-in DC Special #15), The Human

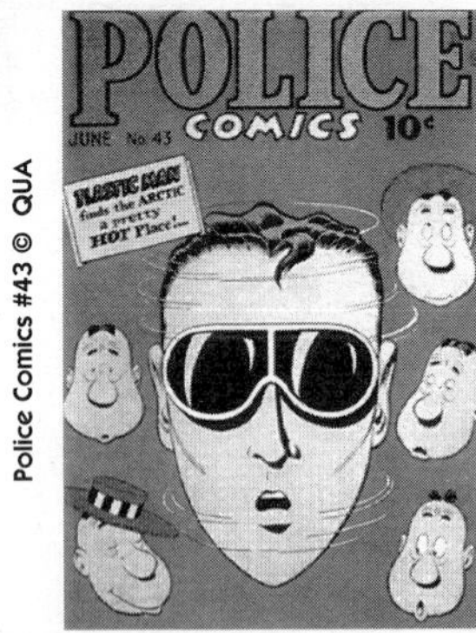

Police Comics #43 © QUA

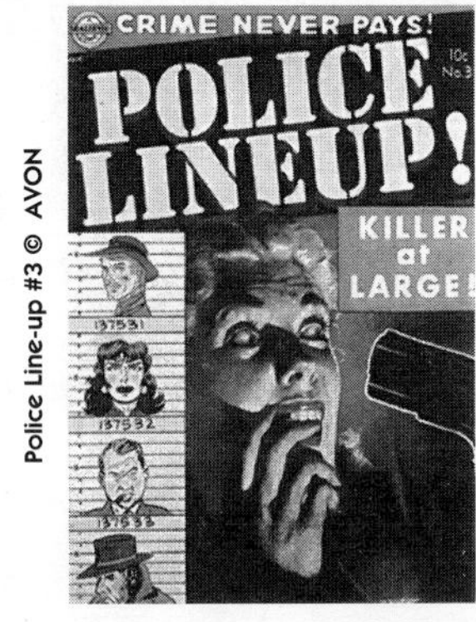

Police Line-up #3 © AVON

Polly Pigtails #1 © PMI

GD25 FN65 NM94

Bomb by Gustavson, & No. 711; intro. Chic Carter by Eisner, The Firebrand by Reed Crandall, The Mouthpiece by Guardineer, Phantom Lady, & The Sword; Firebrand-c 1-4 620.00 1860.00 6200.00
2-Plastic Man smuggles opium 265.00 790.00 2250.00
3 182.00 546.00 1550.00
4 171.00 513.00 1450.00
5-Plastic Man-c begin; Plastic Man forced to smoke marijuana; Plastic Man covers begin, end #102 150.00 450.00 1275.00
6,7 138.00 414.00 1175.00
8-Manhunter begins (origin/1st app.) (3/42) 165.00 495.00 1400.00
9,10 115.00 345.00 975.00
11-The Spirit strip reprints begin by Eisner (origin-strip #1); 1st comic book app. The Spirit & 1st cover app. (9/42) 188.00 564.00 1600.00
12-Intro. Ebony 115.00 345.00 975.00
13-Intro. Woozy Winks; last Firebrand 115.00 345.00 975.00
14-19: 15-Last No. 711; Destiny begins 82.00 246.00 700.00
20-The Raven x-over in Phantom Lady; features Jack Cole himself 82.00 246.00 700.00
21,22: 21-Raven & Spider Widow x-over in Phantom Lady (cameo in #22) 68.00 204.00 575.00
23-30: 23-Last Phantom Lady. 24-26-Flatfoot Burns by Kurtzman in all 62.00 186.00 525.00
31-41: 37-1st app. Candy by Sahle & begins (12/44). 41-Last Spirit-r by Eisner 43.00 129.00 360.00
42,43-Spirit-r by Eisner/Fine 39.00 117.00 290.00
44-Fine Spirit-r begin, end #88,90,92 33.00 100.00 250.00
45-50: 50-(#50 on-c, #49 on inside, 1/46) 33.00 100.00 250.00
51-60: 58-Last Human Bomb 28.00 84.00 210.00
61-88: 63-(Some issues have #65 printed on cover, but #63 on inside) Kurtzman-a, 6 pgs. 21.00 63.00 160.00
89,91,93-No Spirit stories 19.00 57.00 140.00
90,92-Spirit by Fine 23.00 69.00 175.00
94-99,101,102: Spirit by Eisner in all; 101-Last Manhunter. 102-Last Spirit & Plastic Man by Jack Cole 29.00 87.00 220.00
100 36.00 108.00 270.00
103-Content change to crime; Ken Shannon & T-Man begin (1st app. of each, 12/50) 21.00 63.00 160.00
104-111,114-127: Crandall-a most issues (not in 104,105,122,125-127). 109-Atomic bomb story 17.00 51.00 125.00
112-Crandall-a 17.00 51.00 125.00
113-Crandall-c/a(2), 9 pgs. each 17.00 52.00 130.00

NOTE: *Most Spirit stories signed by Eisner are not by him; all are reprints.* ***Cole*** *c-17, 19-21, 24-26, 28-31, 36-38, 40-42, 45-48, 65-68, 69, 73, 75.* ***Crandall*** *Firebrand-1-8. Spirit by* ***Eisner*** *1-41, 94-102; by* ***Eisner/Fine****-42, 43; by* ***Fine****-44-88, 90, 92. 103, 109.* ***Al Bryant*** *c-33, 34.* ***Cole*** *c-17-32, 35-102(most).* ***Crandall*** *c-13, 14.* ***Crandall/Cuidera*** *c-105-127.* ***Eisner*** *c-4i.* ***Gill Fox*** *c-1-3, 4p, 5-12, 15. Bondage c-103, 109, 125.*

POLICE LINE-UP
Avon Periodicals/Realistic Comics #3,4: Aug, 1951 - No. 4, July, 1952 (Painted-c #1-3)

1-Wood-a, 1 pg. plus part-c; spanking panel-r/Saint #5 35.00 104.00 260.00
2-Classic story "The Religious Murder Cult", drugs, perversion; r/Saint #5; c-r/Avon paperback #329 25.00 74.00 185.00
3-Kubert-a(r?)/part-c; Kinstler-a (inside-c only) 18.00 54.00 135.00
4 18.00 54.00 135.00

POLICE TRAP (Public Defender In Action #7 on)
Mainline #1-4/Charlton #5,6: 8-9/54 - No. 4, 2-3/55; No. 5, 7/55 - No. 6, 9/55

1-S&K covers-all issues; Meskin-a; Kirby scripts 25.00 74.00 185.00
2-4 15.00 44.00 110.00
5,6-S&K-c/a 21.00 62.00 155.00

POLICE TRAP
Super Comics: No. 11, 1963; No. 16-18, 1964

Reprint #11,16-18: 11-r/Police Trap #3. 16-r/Justice Traps the Guilty #? 17-r/Inside Crime #3 & r/Justice Traps The Guilty #83; 18-r/Inside Crime #3 1.10 3.30 9.00

POLL PARROT
Poll Parrot Shoe Store/International Shoe
K. K. Publications (Giveaway): 1950 - No. 4, 1951; No. 2, 1959 - No. 16, 1962

1 ('50)-Howdy Doody; small size 12.00 36.00 90.00
2-4('51)-Howdy Doody 9.30 28.00 70.00
2('59)-16('62): 2-The Secret of Crumbley Castle. 5-Bandit Busters. 7-The Make-Believe Mummy. 8-Mixed Up Mission('60). 10-The Frightful Flight. 11-Showdown at Sunup. 12-Maniac at Mubu Island. 13-...and the Runaway Genie. 14-Bully for You. 15-Trapped In Tall Timber. 16-...& the Rajah's Ruby('62) 2.25 6.75 18.00

POLLY & HER PALS (See Comic Monthly #1)

POLLYANNA (Disney)
Dell Publishing Co.: No. 1129, Aug-Oct, 1960

Four Color 1129-Movie, Haley Mills photo-c 7.00 22.00 80.00

POLLY PIGTAILS (Girls' Fun & Fashion Magazine #44 on)
Parents' Magazine Institute/Polly Pigtails: Jan, 1946 - V4#43, Oct-Nov, 1949

1-Infinity-c; photo-c 9.30 28.00 65.00
2-Photo-c 5.35 16.00 32.00
3-5: 3,4-Photo-c 4.00 12.00 24.00
6-10: 7-Photo-c 4.00 10.00 20.00
11-30: 22-Photo-c 2.80 7.00 14.00
31-43 2.40 6.00 12.00

PONY EXPRESS (See Tales of the...)

PONYTAIL
Dell Publishing Co./Charlton No. 13 on: 7-9/62 - No. 12, 10-12/65; No. 13, 11/69 - No. 20, 1/71

12-641-209(#1) 2.00 6.00 22.00
2-12 1.40 4.20 14.00
13-20 .90 2.70 9.00

POP COMICS
Modern Store Publ.: 1955 (36 pgs.; 5x7"; in color) (7¢)

1-Funny animal 5.00

POPEYE (See Comic Album #7, 11, 15, Comics Reading Libraries, Eat Right to Work and Win, Giant Comic Album, King Comics, Kite Fun Book, Magic Comics, March of Comics #37, 52, 66, 80, 96, 117, 134, 148, 157, 169, 194, 246, 264, 274, 294, 453, 465, 477 & Wow Comics, 1st series)

POPEYE (See Thimble Theatre)
David McKay Publications: 1935 (25¢; 52 pgs.; B&W) (By Segar)

1-Daily strip serial reprints- "The Gold Mine Thieves" 59.00 177.00 590.00
2-Daily strip-r 46.00 138.00 460.00

NOTE: *Popeye first entered Thimble Theatre in 1929.*

POPEYE
David McKay Publications: 1937 - 1939 (All by Segar)

Feature Books nn (100 pgs.) (Very Rare) 545.00 1635.00 6000.00
Feature Books 2 (52 pgs.) 61.00 184.00 675.00
Feature Books 3 (100 pgs.)-r/nn issue with a new-c 57.00 170.00 625.00
Feature Books 5,10 (76 pgs.) 52.00 157.00 575.00
Feature Books 14 (76 pgs.) (Scarce) 61.00 184.00 675.00

POPEYE (Strip reprints through 4-Color #70)
Dell #1-65/Gold Key #66-80/King #81-92/Charlton #94-138/Gold Key #139-155/Whitman #156 on: 1941 - 1947; #1, 2-4/48 - #65, 7-9/62; #66, 10/62 - #80, 5/66; #81, 8/66 - #92, 12/67; #94, 2/69 - #138, 1/77; #139, 5/78 - #171, 7/84 (no #93,160,161)

Large Feature Comic 24('41)-Half by Segar 50.00 150.00 550.00
Four Color 25('41)-by Segar 66.00 197.00 720.00
Large Feature Comic 10('43) 42.00 125.00 460.00

Popeye #4 © KING

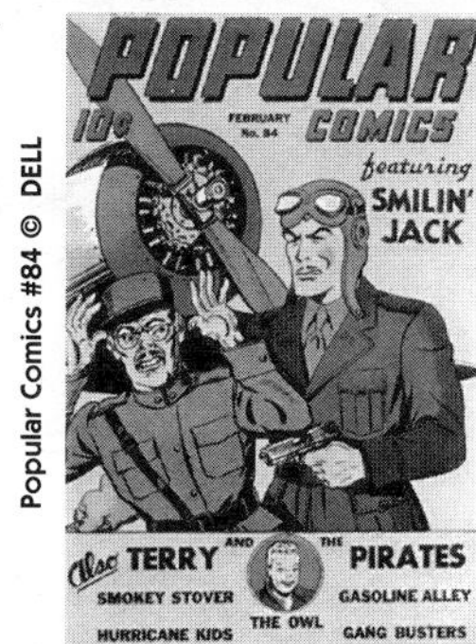

Popular Comics #84 © DELL

Popular Romance #7 © STD

	GD25	FN65	NM94
Four Color 17('43),26('43)-by Segar	48.00	143.00	535.00
Four Color 43('44)	30.00	89.00	325.00
Four Color 70('45)-Title: ...& Wimpy	24.00	72.00	265.00
Four Color 113('46-original strips begin),127,145('47),168	12.00	35.00	130.00
1(2-4/48)(Dell)-All new stories continue	26.00	77.00	280.00
2	13.00	38.00	140.00
3-10: 5-Popeye on moon w/rocket-c	11.00	32.00	115.00
11-20	9.00	27.00	100.00
21-40	7.00	22.00	80.00
41-45,47-50	5.00	15.00	55.00
46-Origin Swee' Pee	7.00	22.00	80.00
51-60	4.50	13.50	50.00
61-65 (Last Dell issue)	3.60	11.00	40.00
66,67-Both 84 pgs. (Gold Key)	5.00	15.00	55.00
68-80	2.00	6.00	22.00
81-92,94-100 (no #93)	1.45	4.40	16.00
101-130	1.00	3.00	10.00
131-155: 144-50th Anniversary issue			5.00
156,157,162-167(Whitman) (no #160,161,168)	.85	2.60	7.00
158(9/80),159(11/80)-pre-pack?	1.00	3.00	10.00
169-171: 169(#168 on-c). All #90069 on-c; pre-pack?	.90	2.70	8.00
Bold Detergent giveaway (Same as regular issue #94)		1.20	3.00
Quaker Cereal premium (1989, 16pp, small size,4 diff.)(Popeye & the Time Machine,--On Safari, --& Big Foot, --vs. Bluto)	1.50	4.50	12.00

NOTE: *Reprints-#145, 147, 149, 151, 153, 155, 157, 163-68(1/3), 170.*

POPEYE
Charlton (King Features) (Giveaway): 1972 - 1974 (36 pgs. in color)

E-1 to E-15 (Educational comics)			5.00
nn-Popeye Gettin' Better Grades-4 pgs. used as intro. to above giveaways (in color)			5.00

POPEYE
Harvey Comics: Nov, 1993 - No. 7, Aug, 1994 ($1.50)

V2#1-7			1.50
...Summer Special V2#1-(10/93, $2.25, 68 pgs.)-Sagendorf-r & others			2.25

POPEYE CARTOON BOOK
The Saalfield Publ. Co.: 1934 (8-1/2x13", 40 pgs., cardboard-c)

2095-(Rare)-1933 strip reprints in color by Segar; each page contains a vertical half of a Sunday strip, so the continuity reads row by row completely across each double page spread. If each page is read by itself, the continuity makes no sense. Each double page spread reprints one complete Sunday page (from 1933)	200.00	600.00	1600.00
12 Page Version	88.00	262.00	700.00

POPEYE SPECIAL
Ocean Comics: Summer, 1987 - No. 2, Sept, 1988 ($1.75/$2.00)

1-Origin ($1.75)			1.75
2 ($2.00)			2.00

POPPLES (TV, movie)
Star Comics (Marvel): Dec, 1986 - No. 5, Aug, 1987

1-3-Based on toys			.70
4,5 ($1.00)			1.00

POPPO OF THE POPCORN THEATRE
Fuller Publishing Co. (Publishers Weekly): 10/29/55 - No. 13, 1956 (weekly)

1	6.85	21.00	48.00
2-5	5.00	15.00	30.00
6-13	4.00	12.00	24.00

NOTE: *By **Charles Biro**. 10¢ cover, given away by supermarkets such as IGA.*

POP-POP COMICS
R. B. Leffingwell Co.: No date (Circa 1945) (52 pgs.)

	GD25	FN65	NM94
1-Funny animal	9.30	28.00	65.00

POPSICLE PETE FUN BOOK (See All-American Comics #6)
Joe Lowe Corp.: 1947, 1948

nn-36 pgs. in color; Sammy 'n' Claras, The King Who Couldn't Sleep & Popsicle Pete stories, games, cut-outs	7.85	23.50	55.00
Adventure Book ('48)-Has Classics ad with checklist to HRN #343 (Great Expectations #43)	6.50	19.50	45.00

POPULAR COMICS
Dell Publishing Co.: Feb, 1936 - No. 145, July-Sept, 1948

	GD25	FN65	VF82
1-Dick Tracy (1st comic book app.), Little Orphan Annie, Terry & the Pirates, Gasoline Alley, Don Winslow (1st app.), Harold Teen, Little Joe, Skippy, Moon Mullins, Mutt & Jeff, Tailspin Tommy, Smitty, Smokey Stover, Winnie Winkle & The Gumps begin (all strip-r)	566.00	1700.00	3700.00
(Estimated up to 90 total copies exist, 4 in NM/Mint)			
2	183.00	550.00	1250.00
3	145.00	437.00	925.00
4,5: 5-Tom Mix begins	119.00	357.00	770.00
6-10: 6,8,9-Scribbly app. 8,9-, Reglar Fellers app.	91.00	275.00	585.00

	GD25	FN65	NM94
11-20: 12-X-Mas-c	78.00	234.00	490.00
21-27: 27-Last Terry & the Pirates, Little Orphan Annie, & Dick Tracy	54.00	162.00	350.00
28-37: 28-Gene Autry app. 31,32-Tim McCoy app. 35-Christmas-c; Tex Ritter app.	45.00	137.00	300.00
38-43: Tarzan in text only. 38-(4/39)-Gang Busters (Radio, 2nd app.) & Zane Grey's Tex Thorne begins? 43-The Masked Pilot app.; 1st non-funny-c?	36.00	108.00	320.00
44,45: 45-Hurricane Kid-c	28.00	84.00	210.00
46-Origin/1st app. Martan, the Marvel Man(12/39)	39.00	117.00	300.00
47-50	27.00	80.00	200.00
51-Origin The Voice (The Invisible Detective) strip begins (5/40)	28.00	84.00	210.00
52-59: 52-Robot-c. 55-End of World story	21.00	64.00	160.00
60-Origin/1st app. Professor Supermind and Son (2/41)	23.00	68.00	170.00
61-71: 63-Smilin' Jack begins	17.00	52.00	130.00
72-The Owl & Terry & the Pirates begin (2/42); Smokey Stover reprints begin	39.00	116.00	290.00
73-75	22.00	68.00	170.00
76-78-Capt. Midnight in all (see The Funnies #57)	32.00	96.00	240.00
79-85-Last Owl	20.00	60.00	150.00
86-99: 98-Felix the Cat, Smokey Stover-r begin	15.00	44.00	110.00
100	16.00	48.00	120.00
101-130	9.30	28.00	65.00
131-145: 142-Last Terry & the Pirates	8.50	26.00	60.00

NOTE: *Martan, the Marvel Man c-47-49, 52, 57-59. Professor Supermind c-60-63, 64(1/2), 65, 66. The Voice c-53.*

POPULAR FAIRY TALES (See March of Comics #6, 18)

POPULAR ROMANCE
Better-Standard Publications: No. 5, Dec, 1949 - No. 29, July, 1954

5	7.85	23.50	55.00
6-9: 7-Palais-a; lingerie panels	5.35	16.00	32.00
10-Wood-a (2 pgs.)	6.85	21.00	48.00
11,12,14-16,18-21,28,29	4.25	13.00	28.00
13,17-Severin/Elder-a (3&8 pgs.)	5.35	16.00	32.00
22-27-Toth-a	6.85	21.00	48.00

NOTE: *All have photo-c. **Tuska** art in most issues.*

POPULAR TEEN-AGERS (Secrets of Love) (School Day Romances #1-4)
Star Publications: No. 5, Sept, 1950 - No. 23, Nov, 1954

5-Toni Gay, Midge Martin & Eve Adams continue from School Day Romances; Ginger Bunn (formerly Ginger Snapp & becomes Honey Bunn #6 on) begins;

Portia Prinz of the Glamazons #1 © ECL

Power & Glory #4 © MAL

Power Man #49 © MAR

	GD25	FN65	NM94
all features end #8	28.00	84.00	210.00
6-8 (7/51)-Honey Bunn begins; all have L. B. Cole-c; 6-Negligee panels	25.00	74.00	185.00
9-(...Romances; 1st romance issue, 10/51)	14.00	42.00	105.00
10-(...Secrets of Love thru #23)	14.00	42.00	105.00
11,16,18,19,22,23	11.00	34.00	85.00
12,13,17,20,21-Disbrow-a	13.00	38.00	95.00
14-Harrison/Wood-a; 2 spanking scenes	18.00	54.00	130.00
15-Wood?, Disbrow-a	15.00	46.00	115.00
Accepted Reprint 5,6 (nd); L.B. Cole-c	5.70	17.00	40.00

NOTE: *All have **L. B. Cole** covers.*

PORKY PIG (See Bugs Bunny &..., Kite Fun Book, Looney Tunes, March of Comics #42, 57, 71, 89, 99, 113, 130, 143, 164, 175, 192, 209, 218, 367, and Super Book #6, 18, 30)

PORKY PIG (...& Bugs Bunny #40-69)
Dell Publishing Co./Gold Key No. 1-93/Whitman No. 94 on: No. 16, 1942 - No. 81, Mar-Apr, 1962; Jan, 1965 - No. 109, July, 1984

	GD25	FN65	NM94
Four Color 16(#1, 1942)	72.00	215.00	790.00
Four Color 48(1944)-Carl Barks-a	91.00	273.00	1000.00
Four Color 78(1945)	22.00	65.00	240.00
Four Color 112(7/46)	13.00	38.00	140.00
Four Color 156,182,191('49)	9.00	27.00	100.00
Four Color 226,241('49),260,271,277,284,295	7.00	22.00	80.00
Four Color 303,311,322,330: 322-Sci/fi-c/story	4.50	13.50	50.00
Four Color 342,351,360,370,385,399,410,426	3.60	11.00	40.00
25 (11-12/52)-30	2.75	8.00	30.00
31-40	1.50	4.50	16.00
41-60	1.40	4.20	15.00
61-81(3-4/62)	1.30	3.90	14.00
1(1/65-Gold Key)(2nd Series)	3.20	9.50	35.00
2,4,5-r/4-Color 226,284 & 271 in that order	2.00	6.00	22.00
3,6-10: 3-r/Four Color #342	1.30	3.90	14.00
11-30	1.00	3.00	10.00
31-54	.90	2.70	8.00
55-70			5.00
71-93(Gold Key)			3.00
94-96			4.00
97(9/80),98,99-pre-pack?	.90	2.70	8.00
100	.85	2.60	7.00
101-105			4.00
106-109 (All #90140 on-c, no date or date code)	.85	2.60	7.00

NOTE: *Reprints-#1-8, 9-35(2/3); 36-46, 58, 67, 69-74, 76, 78, 102-109(1/3-1/2).*

PORKY PIG'S DUCK HUNT
Saalfield Publishing Co.: 1938 (12pgs.)(large size)(heavy linen-like paper)

	GD25	FN65	NM94
2178-1st app. Porky Pig & Daffy Duck by Leon Schlesinger. Illustrated text story book written in verse.1st book ever devoted to these characters. (see Looney Tunes #1 for their 1st comic book app.)	59.00	176.00	500.00

PORKY'S BOOK OF TRICKS
K. K. Publications (Giveaway): 1942 (8-1/2x5-1/2", 48 pgs.)

	GD25	FN65	NM94
nn-7 pg. comic story, text stories, plus games & puzzles	39.00	117.00	300.00

PORTIA PRINZ OF THE GLAMAZONS
Eclipse Comics: Dec, 1986 - No. 6, Oct, 1987 ($2.00, B&W, Baxter paper)

	GD25	FN65	NM94
1-6			2.00

POST GAZETTE (See Meet the New...)

POWDER RIVER RUSTLERS (See Fawcett Movie Comics)

POWER & GLORY (See American Flagg! & Howard Chaykin's American Flagg!
Malibu Comics (Bravura): Feb, 1994 - No. 4, May, 1994 ($2.50, limited series, mature)

	GD25	FN65	NM94
1A, 1B-By Howard Chaykin; w/Bravura stamp			2.50
1-Newsstand ed. (polybagged w/children's warning on bag), Gold ed., Silver-foil ed., Blue-foil ed.(print run of 10,000), Serigraph ed. (print run of 3,000)-($2.95)-Howard Chaykin-c/a begin			3.00
2-4-Contains Bravura stamp			2.50
Holiday Special (Win '94, $2.95)			3.00

POWER COMICS
Holyoke Publ. Co./Narrative Publ.: 1944 - No. 4, 1945

	GD25	FN65	NM94
1-L. B. Cole-c	124.00	372.00	1050.00
2-Hitler, Hirohito-c (scarce)	124.00	372.00	1050.00
3-Classic L.B. Cole-c; Dr. Mephisto begins?	135.00	405.00	1150.00
4-L.B. Cole-c; Miss Espionage app. #3,4; Leav-a	124.00	372.00	1050.00

POWER COMICS
Power Comics Co.: 1977 - No. 5, Dec, 1977 (B&W)

	GD25	FN65	NM94
1- "A Boy And His Aardvark" by Dave Sim; first Dave Sim aardvark (not Cerebus)	1.00	3.00	10.00
1-Reprint (3/77, black-c)			5.00
2-Cobalt Blue by Gustovich		2.00	6.00
3-5: 3-Nightwitch. 4-Northern Light. 5-Bluebird		2.00	6.00

POWER COMICS
Eclipse Comics (Acme Press): Mar, 1988 - No. 4, Sept, 1988 ($2.00, B&W, mini-series)

	GD25	FN65	NM94
1-4: Bolland, Gibbons-r in all			2.00

POWER FACTOR
Wonder Color Comics: May, 1987 - No. 2, 1987 ($1.95)

	GD25	FN65	NM94
1,2: Super team. 2-Infantino-c			2.00

POWER FACTOR
Innovation Publishing: Oct, 1990 - No. 3, 1991 ($1.95/$2.25)

	GD25	FN65	NM94
1-Reprints 1st story plus new-a			2.00
2,3: 2-Begin $2.25-c; r/2nd story plus new-a. 3-Infantino-a			2.25

POWER GIRL (See All-Star #58, Infinity, Inc., Showcase #97-99)
DC Comics: June, 1988 - No. 4, Sept, 1988 ($1.00, color, limited series)

	GD25	FN65	NM94
1-4			1.00

POWERHOUSE PEPPER COMICS (See Gay Comics, Joker Comics & Tessie the Typist)
Marvel Comics (20CC): No. 1, 1943; No. 2, May, 1948 - No. 5, Nov, 1948

	GD25	FN65	NM94
1-(60 pgs.)-Wolverton-a in all; c-2,3	135.00	405.00	1150.00
2	74.00	222.00	625.00
3,4	68.00	204.00	575.00
5-(Scarce)	81.00	273.00	690.00

POWER LINE
Marvel Comics (Epic Comics): May, 1988 - No. 8, Sept, 1989 ($1.25/$1.50)

	GD25	FN65	NM94
1-3: 2-Williamson-i. 3-Austin-i, Dr. Zero app.			1.25
4-8: 4-Begin $1.50-c. 4-7-Morrow-a. 8-Williamson-i			1.50

POWER LORDS
DC Comics: Dec, 1983 - No. 3, Feb, 1984 (Limited series, Mando paper)

	GD25	FN65	NM94
1-3: Based on Revell toys			.80

POWER MAN (Formerly Hero for Hire; ...& Iron Fist #68 on; see Cage & Giant-Size...)
Marvel Comics Group: No. 17, Feb, 1974 - No. 125, Sept, 1986

	GD25	FN65	NM94
17-Luke Cage continues; Iron Man app.		2.00	6.00
18-20: 18-Last 20¢ issue			5.00
21-30			4.00
31-Part Neal Adams-i		2.00	6.00
32-46: 34-Last 25¢ issue. 36-r/Hero For Hire #12. 41-1st app. Thunderbolt. 45-Starlin-c.			3.00
47-Barry Smith-a			5.00
48-50-Byrne-a(p); 48-Power Man/Iron Fist 1st meet. 50-Iron Fist joins Cage	.85	2.60	7.00
51-56,58-60: 58-Intro El Aguila			2.00
57-New X-Men app. (6/79)	.90	2.70	9.00

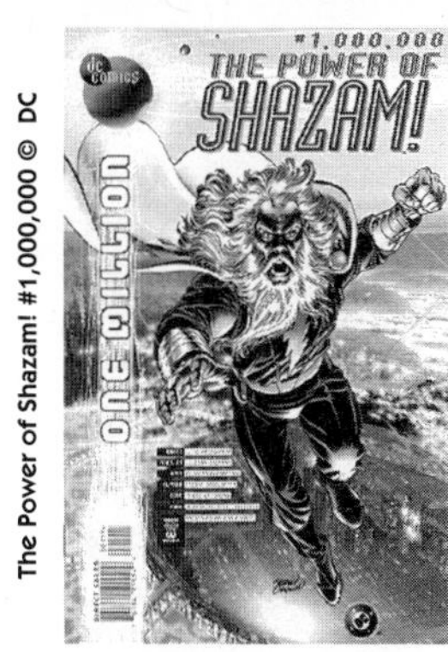

The Power of Shazam! #1,000,000 © DC

Power Pack #62 © MAR

Preacher #37 © Garth Ennis & Steve Dillon

GD25 FN65 NM94

61-65,67-77,79-83,85-124: 75-Double size. 77-Daredevil app. 87-Moon Knight app. 90-Unus app. 109-The Reaper app. 100-Double size; origin K'un L'un 1.00
66-2nd app. Sabretooth (see Iron Fist #14) 2.00 6.00 20.00
78-3rd app. Sabretooth (cameo under cloak) .90 2.70 8.00
84-4th app. Sabretooth .90 2.70 8.00
125-Double size; death of Iron Fist 2.00
Annual 1(1976)-Punisher cameo in flashback 5.00
NOTE: **Austin** c-102i. **Byrne** a-48-50; c-102, 104, 106, 107, 112-116. **Kane** c(p)-24, 25, 28, 48. **Miller** a-68, 76(2 pgs.); c-66-68, 70-74, 80i. **Mooney** a-38i, 53i, 55i. **Nebres** a-76p. **Nino** a-42i, 43i. **Perez** a-27. **B. Smith** a-47i. **Tuska** a(p)-17, 20, 24, 26, 28, 29, 36, 47. Painted c-75, 100.

POWER OF PRIME
Malibu Comics (Ultraverse): July, 1995 - No. 4, Nov, 1995 ($2.50, lim. series)
1-4 2.50

POWER OF SHAZAM!, THE (See SHAZAM!)
DC Comics: 1994 (Painted graphic novel) (Prequel to new series)
Hardcover-($19.95)-New origin of Shazam!; Ordway painted-c/a & script 2.25 6.80 25.00
Softcover-($7.50) 7.50
Softcover-($9.95)-New-c. 1.20 3.60 12.00

POWER OF SHAZAM!, THE
DC Comics: Mar, 1995 - No. 47, Mar, 1999 ($1.50/$1.75/$1.95/$2.50)
1-Jerry Ordway scripts begin 3.00
2-10,20-22: 4-Begin $1.75-c. 6:Re-intro of Capt. Nazi. 8-Re-intro of Spy Smasher, Bulletman & Minuteman; Swan-a (7 pgs.). 20-Superman-c/app.; "Final Night.". 21-Plastic Man-c/app. 22-Batman-c/app. 2.50
11-19,23-31: 11-Re-intro of Ibis, Swan-a(2 pgs.). 14-Gil Kane-a(p). 2.00
32-41: 32-Begin $1.95-c. 35,36-Crossover w/Starman #39,40. 38-41-Mr. Mind. 2.00
43-47: 43-Begin $2.50-c; Bulletman app. 45-JLA-c/app. 2.50
#1,000,000 (11/98) 853rd Century x-over; Ordway-c/s/a 2.50
Annual 1 (1996, $2.95)-Legends of the Dead Earth story; Jerry Ordway-c; Mike Manley-a 4.00

POWER OF STRONGMAN, THE (Also see Strongman)
AC Comics: 1989 ($2.95)
1-Powell G.A.-r 3.00

POWER OF THE ATOM (See Secret Origins #29)
DC Comics: Aug, 1988 - No. 18, Nov, 1989 ($1.00)
1-18: 6-Chronos returns; Byrne-p. 9-JLI app. 1.00

POWER PACHYDERMS
Marvel Comics: Sept, 1989 ($1.25, one-shot)
1-Elephant super-heroes; parody of X-Men, Elektra, & 3 Stooges 1.30

POWER PACK
Marvel Comics Group: Aug, 1984 - No. 62, Feb, 1991
1-($1.00, 52 pgs.)-Origin & 1st app. Power Pack 1.00
2-18,20-26,28,30-45,47-62 1.00
19-(52 pgs.)-Cloak & Dagger, Wolverine app. 2.00
27-Mutant massacre; Wolverine & Sabretooth app. 2.00
29-Spider-Man & Hobgoblin app. 2.00
46-Punisher app. 2.00
...Holiday Special 1 (2/92, $2.25, 68 pgs.) 2.25
NOTE: **Austin** scripts-53. **Mignola** c-20. **Morrow** a-51. **Spiegle** a-55i. **Williamson** a(i)-43, 50, 52.

POWER RANGERS ZEO (TV)(Saban's...)(Also see Saban's Mighty Morphin Power Rangers)
Image Comics (Extreme Studios): Aug, 1996 ($2.50)
1-Based on TV show 2.50

POWER RECORD COMICS
Marvel Comics/Power Records: 1974 - 1978 ($1.49, 7x10" comics, 20 pgs. with 45 R.P.M. record)
PR10-Spider-Man-r/from #124,125; Man-Wolf app. PR11-Hulk-r. PR12-Captain America-r/#168. PR13-Fantastic Four-r/#126. PR14-Frankenstein-Ploog-r/#1. PR15-Tomb of Dracula-Colan-r/#2. PR16-Man-Thing-Ploog-r/#5. PR17-Werewolf By Night-Ploog-r/Marvel Spotlight #2. PR18-Planet of the Apes-r. PR19-Escape From the Planet of the Apes-r. PR20-Beneath the Planet of the Apes-r. PR21-Battle for the Planet of the Apes-r. PR24-Spider-Man II-New-a begins. PR25-Star Trek "Passage to Moauv". PR26-Star Trek "Crier in Emptiness." PR27-Batman "Stacked Cards"; N. Adams-a(p). PR28-Superman "Alien Creatures". PR29-Space: 1999 "Breakaway". PR30-Batman; N. Adams-r/Det.(7 pgs.). PR31-Conan-N. Adams-a; reprinted in Conan #116. PR32-Space: 1999 "Return to the Beginning". PR33-Superman-G.A. origin, Buckler-a(p). PR34-Superman. PR35-Wonder Woman-Buckler-a(p). PR36-Holo-Man. PR37-Robin Hood. PR39-Huckleberry Finn. PR40-Davy Crockett. PR41-Robinson Crusoe. PR42-20,000 Leagues Under the Sea. PR46-Star Trek "The Robot Masters". PR47-Little Women
With record; each... 1.40 4.20 14.00

POWERS THAT BE (Becomes Star Seed No.7 on)
Broadway Comics: Nov, 1995 - No. 6, June, 1996 ($2.50)
1-5: 1-Intro of Fatale & Star Seed. 2.50
6-Begin $2.95-c. 3.00
Preview Editions 1-3 (9/95 - 11/95, B&W) 2.50

POW MAGAZINE (Bob Sproul's) (Satire Magazine)
Humor-Vision: Aug, 1966 - No. 3, Feb, 1967 (30¢)
1-3: 2-Jones-a. 3-Wrightson-a 3.00 9.00 30.00

PREACHER
DC Comics (Vertigo): Apr, 1995 - Present ($2.50, mature)
nn-Preview 3.80 11.50 40.00
1 ($2.95)-Ennis scripts, Dillon-a & Fabry-c in all; 1st app. Jesse, Tulip, & Cassidy 2.70 8.00 30.00
2,3: 2-1st app. Saint of Killers. 2.25 6.80 25.00
4,5,12: 12-Polybagged w/videogame w/Ennis text 1.50 4.50 15.00
6-11,13-15: 13-Hunters storyline begins; ends #17 1.00 3.00 10.00
16-20: 19-Saint of Killers app.; begin "Crusaders", ends #24 .85 2.60 7.00
21-25: 21-24-Saint of Killers app. 25-Origin of Cassidy. 5.00
26-40 4.00
41-46 2.50
Dixie Fried ($14.95, 1998, TPB)-r/#27-33, Special: Cassidy 14.95
Gone To Texas ($14.95, 1996, TPB)-r/#1-7; Fabry-c 15.00
Proud Americans ($14.95, 1997, TPB)-r/#18-26; Fabry-c 15.00
Until the End of the World ($14.95, 1996, TPB)-r/#8-17; Fabry-c 15.00

PREACHER SPECIAL: CASSIDY: BLOOD & WHISKEY
DC Comics (Vertigo): 1998 ($5.95, one-shot)
1-Ennis-scripts/Fabry-c /Dillon-a 2.00 6.00

PREACHER SPECIAL: ONE MAN'S WAR
DC Comics (Vertigo): Mar, 1998 ($4.95, one-shot)
1-Ennis-scripts/Fabry-c /Snelbjerg-a 5.00

PREACHER SPECIAL: SAINT OF KILLERS
DC Comics (Vertigo): Aug, 1996 - No. 4, Nov, 1996 ($2.50, lim. series, mature)
1,2: Ennis-scripts/Fabry-c/Pugh-a 4.00
1-Signed & numbered 25.00
3,4-Ezquerra-a 3.00

PREACHER SPECIAL: THE GOOD OLD BOYS
DC Comics (Vertigo): Aug, 1997 ($4.95, one-shot, mature)
1-Ennis-scripts/Fabry-c /Esquerra-a 5.00

PREACHER SPECIAL: THE STORY OF YOU-KNOW-WHO
DC Comics (Vertigo): Dec, 1996 ($4.95, one-shot, mature)
1-Ennis-scripts/Fabry-c/Case-a 5.00

PREDATOR (Also see Aliens Vs. ..., Batman vs. ..., Dark Horse Comics, & Dark Horse Presents)
Dark Horse Comics: June, 1989 - No. 4, Mar, 1990 ($2.25, limited series)
1-Based on movie; 1st app. Predator 2.00 6.00

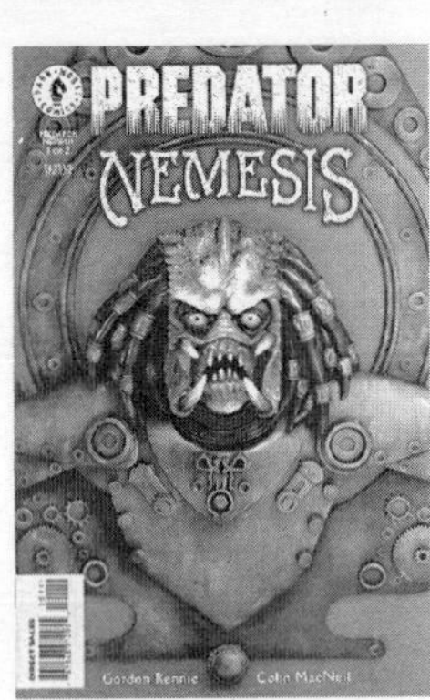

Predator: Nemesis #2 © 20th Century Fox

Predator vs. Magnus Robot Fighter #2 © 20th Century Fox/VAL

Prime #10 © MAL

GD25 FN65 NM94

1-2nd printing 4.00
2 5.00
3,4 3.00
Trade paperback (1990, $12.95)-r/#1-4 13.00

PREDATOR: BAD BLOOD
Dark Horse Comics: Dec, 1993 - No. 4, 1994 ($2.50, limited series)
1-4 2.50

PREDATOR: BIG GAME
Dark Horse Comics: Mar, 1991 - No. 4, June, 1991 ($2.50, limited series)
1: 1-3-Contain 2 Dark Horse trading cards 3.00
2-4 2.75

PREDATOR BLOODY SANDS OF TIME
Dark Horse Comics: Feb, 1992 - No. 2, Feb, 1992 ($2.50, limited series)
1,2-Dan Barry-c/a(p)/scripts 2.50

PREDATOR: CAPTIVE
Dark Horse Comics: Apr, 1998 ($2.95, one-shot)
1 3.00

PREDATOR COLD WAR
Dark Horse Comics: Sept, 1991 - No. 4, Dec, 1991 ($2.50, limited series)
1-4: All have painted-c 2.50

PREDATOR: DARK RIVER
Dark Horse Comics: July, 1996 - No.4, Oct, 1996 ($2.95, limited series)
1-4: Miran Kim-c 3.00

PREDATOR: HELL & HOT WATER
Dark Horse Comics: Apr, 1997 - No. 3, June, 1997 ($2.95, limited series)
1-3 3.00

PREDATOR: HELL COME A WALKIN'
Dark Horse Comics: Feb, 1998 - No. 2, Mar, 1998 ($2.95, limited series)
1,2-Predator at the Civil War 3.00

PREDATOR: INVADERS FROM THE FOURTH DIMENSION
Dark Horse Comics: July, 1994 ($3.95, one-shot, 52 pgs.)
1 4.00

PREDATOR: JUNGLE TALES
Dark Horse Comics: Mar, 1995 ($2.95, one-shot)
1-r/Dark Horse Comics 3.00

PREDATOR: KINDRED
Dark Horse Comics: Dec, 1996 - No. 4, Mar, 1997 ($2.50, limited series)
1-4 2.50

PREDATOR: NEMESIS
Dark Horse Comics: Dec, 1997 - No. 2, Jan, 1998 ($2.95, limited series)
1,2-Predator in Victorian England; Taggart-c 3.00

PREDATOR: PRIMAL
Dark Horse Comics: July, 1997 - No. 2, Aug, 1997 ($2.95, limited series)
1,2 2.95

PREDATOR: RACE WAR (See Dark Horse Presents #67)
Dark Horse Comics: Feb, 1993 - No. 4, Oct, 1993 ($2.50, color, limited series)
1-4-Dorman painted-c #1-4 2.50
0-(4/93) 2.50

PREDATOR: STRANGE ROUX
Dark Horse Comics: Nov, 1996 ($2.95, one-shot)
1 3.00

PREDATOR 2
Dark Horse Comics: Feb, 1991 - No. 2, June, 1991 ($2.50, limited series)
1-Adapts movie; 2 trading cards inside; photo-c 2.50
2-Photo-c; w/2 trading cards inside 2.50

PREDATOR VS. JUDGE DREDD
Dark Horse Comics: Oct, 1997 - No. 3 ($2.50, limited series)
1-3-Wagner-s/Alcatena-a/Bolland-c 2.50

PREDATOR VS. MAGNUS ROBOT FIGHTER
Dark Horse/Valiant: Oct, 1992 - No. 2, 1993 ($2.95, limited series)
(1st Dark Horse/Valiant x-over)
1 (Regular)-Barry Smith-c; Lee Weeks-a in both 3.00
1 (Platinum edition, 11/92)-Barry Smith-c 5.00
2-Contains 2 bound-in trading cards; Barry Smith-c. 3.00

PREHISTORIC WORLD (See Classics Illustrated Special Issue)

PREMIERE (See Charlton Premiere)

PRESTO KID, THE (See Red Mask)

PRETTY BOY FLOYD (See On the Spot)

PREZ (See Cancelled Comic Cavalcade & Supergirl #10)
National Periodical Publications: Aug-Sept, 1973 - No. 4, Feb-Mar, 1974
1-Origin; Joe Simon scripts 1.65 4.80 16.00
2-4 1.00 3.00 10.00

PRICE, THE (See Eclipse Graphic Album Series)

PRIDE & JOY
DC Comics (Vertigo): July, 1997 - No. 4, Oct, 1997 (2.50, limited series)
1-4-Ennis-s 2.50

PRIDE AND THE PASSION, THE
Dell Publishing Co.: No. 824, Aug, 1957
Four Color 824-Movie, Frank Sinatra & Cary Grant photo-c
8.00 25.00 90.00

PRIDE OF THE YANKEES, THE (See Real Heroes & Sport Comics)
Magazine Enterprises: 1949 (The Life of Lou Gehrig)
nn-Photo-c; Ogden Whitney-a 71.00 212.00 600.00

PRIEST (Also see Asylum)
Maximum Press: Aug, 1996 - No. 2, Oct, 1996 ($2.99)
1,2 3.00

PRIMAL FORCE
DC Comics: No. 0, Oct, 1994 - No. 14, Dec, 1995 ($1.95/$2.25)
0-8: Red Tornado, Golem, Jack O'Lantern, Meridian & Silver Dragon
2.00
9-14: 9-begin $2.25-c 2.25

PRIMAL MAN (See The Crusaders)

PRIMAL RAGE
Sirius Entertainment: 1996 ($2.95)
1-Dark One-c; based of video game 3.00

PRIME (See Break-Thru, Flood Relief & Ultraforce)
Malibu Comics (Ultraverse): June, 1993 - No. 26, Aug, 1995 ($1.95/$2.50)
1-1st app. Prime; has coupon for Ultraverse Premiere #0 2.00
1-With coupon missing 1.50
1-Full cover holographic edition; 1st of kind w/Hardcase #1 & Strangers #1
2.00
1-Ultra 5,000 edition w/silver ink-c 2.00
2-Polybagged w/card & coupon for U. Premiere #0 2.00
3,4-Prototype app. 4-Direct sale w/o card 2.75
4-($2.50)-Newsstand ed. polybagged w/card 2.50
5-($2.50, 48 pgs.)-Rune flip-c/story part B by Barry Smith; see Sludge #1 for 1st app. Rune; 3-pg. Night Man preview 2.50
6-11,14-19: 6-Bill & Chelsea Clinton app. 7-Break-Thru x-over. 8-Mantra app.; 2-pg. origin Freex by Simonson. 10-Firearm app.15-Intro Papa Verite; Perez-c/a. 16-Intro Turbo Charge 2.00
12-($3.50, 68 pgs.)-Flip book w/Ultraverse Premiere #3; silver foil logo

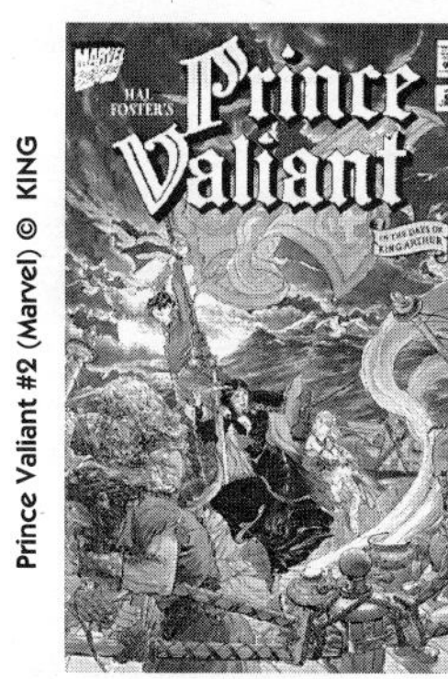

Prince Valiant #2 (Marvel) © KING

Prison Break #4 © AVON

Prize Comics #2 © PRIZE

	GD25	FN65	NM94
			3.50
13-($2.95, 52 pgs.)-Variant covers			3.00
20-26: 20-$2.50-c begins.)			2.50
...: Gross and Disgusting 1 (10/94, $3.95)-Boris-c; "Annual" on cover, published monthly in indicia			4.00
...Month "Ashcan" (8/94, 75¢)-Boris-c			.75
... Time: A Prime Collection (1994, $9.95)-r/1-4	1.00	3.00	10.00
...Vs. The Incredible Hulk (1995)-mail away limited edition	1.00	3.00	10.00
...Vs. The Incredible Hulk Premium edition	1.00	3.00	10.00
...Vs. The Incredible Hulk Super Premium edition	1.50	4.50	15.00

NOTE: ***Perez** a-15; c-15, 16.*

PRIME (Also see Black September)
Malibu Comics (Ultraverse): Infinity, Sept, 1995 - V2#15, Dec, 1996 ($1.50)

Infinity, V2#1-8: Post Black September storyline. 6-8-Solitaire app. 9-Breyfogle-c/a. 10-12-Ramos-c. 15-Lord Pumpkin app.			1.50
Infinity Signed Edition (2,000 printed)			5.00

PRIME/CAPTAIN AMERICA
Malibu Comics: Mar, 1996 ($3.95, one-shot)

1-Norm Breyfogle-a			4.00

PRIMER (Comico...)
Comico: Oct (no month), 1982 - No. 6, Feb, 1984 (B&W)

1 (52 pgs.)			5.00
2-1st app. Grendel & Argent by Wagner	11.00	33.00	120.00
3,4			5.00
5-1st Sam Kieth art in comics ('83) & 1st The Maxx	3.80	11.50	40.00
6-Intro & 1st app. Evangeline			4.00

PRIMORTALS (Leonard Nimoy's...)

PRIMUS (TV)
Charlton Comics: Feb, 1972 - No. 7, Oct, 1972

1-Staton-a in all	1.20	3.60	12.00
2-7: 6-Drug propaganda story	.90	2.70	8.00

PRINCE NAMOR, THE SUB-MARINER (Also see Namor ...)
Marvel Comics Group: Sept, 1984 - No. 4, Dec, 1984 (Limited-series)

1			1.80
2-4			1.20

PRINCE NIGHTMARE
Aaaargh! Associated Artists: 1987 ($2.95, 68pgs.)

Book 1			3.00

PRINCE VALIANT (See Ace Comics, Comics Reading Libraries, & King Comics #146, 147)
David McKay Publ./Dell: No. 26, 1941; No. 67, June, 1954 - No. 900, May, 1958

Feature Books 26 ('41)-Harold Foster-c/a; newspaper strips reprinted, pgs. 1-28,30-63; color & 68 pgs; Foster cover is only original comic book artwork by him	66.00	198.00	725.00
Four Color 567 ((6/54)(#1)-By Bob Fuje-Movie, photo-c	10.00	30.00	110.00
Four Color 650 (9;55), 699 (4/56), 719 (8/56),-Fuje-a	5.50	16.50	60.00
Four Color 788 (4/57), 849 (1/58), 900-Fuje-a	5.50	16.50	60.00

PRINCE VALIANT
Marvel Comics: Dec, 1994 - No. 4, Mar, 1995 ($3.95, limited series)

1-4; Kaluta-c in all.			4.00

PRINCE VANDAL
Triumphant Comics: Nov, 1993 - Apr?, 1994 ($2.50)

1-6: 1,2-Triumphant Unleashed x-over		1.00	2.50

PRINCESS SALLY (Video game)
Archie Publications: Apr, 1995 - No. 3, June, 1995 ($1.50, limited series)

1-3: Spin-off from Sonic the Hedgehog			3.00

PRIORITY: WHITE HEAT
AC Comics: 1986 - No. 2, 1986 ($1.75, mini-series)

	GD25	FN65	NM94
1,2-Bill Black-a			1.75

PRISCILLA'S POP
Dell Publishing Co.: No. 569, June, 1954 - No. 799, May, 1957

Four Color 569 (#1)	2.75	8.00	30.00
Four Color 630 (5/55), 704 (5/56), 799	2.75	8.00	30.00

PRISON BARS (See Behind...)

PRISON BREAK!
Avon Per./Realistic No. 3 on: Sept, 1951 - No. 5, Sept, 1952 (Painted c-3)

1-Wood-c & 1 pg.; has-r/Saint #7 retitled Michael Strong Private Eye	39.00	117.00	290.00
2-Wood-c; Kubert-a; Kinstler inside front-c	25.00	75.00	190.00
3-Orlando, Check-a; c-/Avon paperback 179	22.00	66.00	165.00
4,5: 4-Kinstler-c & inside f/c; Lawrence, Lazarus-a. 5-Kinstler-c; Infantino-a	19.00	57.00	140.00

PRISONER, THE (TV)
DC Comics: 1988 - No. 4, 1989 ($3.50, squarebound, mini-series)

1-4 (Books a-d)			3.50

PRISON RIOT
Avon Periodicals: 1952

1-Marijuana Murders-1 pg. text; Kinstler-c; 2 Kubert illos on text pages	25.00	74.00	185.00

PRISON TO PRAISE
Logos International: 1974 (35¢)

nn-True Story of Merlin R. Carothers			5.00

PRIVATE BUCK
Dell Publishing Co.: No. 21, 1941 - No. 12, 1942

Large Feature Comic 21 (#1)(1941)(Series I)	9.00	26.00	95.00
Large Feature Comic 22 (1941)(Series I), 12 (1942)(Series II)	9.00	26.00	95.00

PRIVATEERS
Vanguard Graphics: Aug, 1987 - No. 2, 1987 ($1.50)

1,2			1.50

PRIVATE EYE (Cover title: Rocky Jorden...#6-8)
Atlas Comics (MCI): Jan, 1951 - No. 8, March, 1952

1-Cover title: Crime Cases... #1-5	18.00	54.00	135.00
2,3-Tuska c/a(3)	11.00	32.00	80.00
4-8	9.30	28.00	65.00

NOTE: ***Henkel** a-6(3), 7; c-7. **Sinnott** a-6.*

PRIVATE EYE (See Mike Shayne...)

PRIVATE SECRETARY
Dell Publishing Co.: Dec-Feb, 1962-63 - No. 2, Mar-May, 1963

1,2	2.50	7.50	20.00

PRIVATE STRONG (See The Double Life of...)

PRIZE COMICS (...Western #69 on) (Also see Treasure Comics)
Prize Publications: March, 1940 - No. 68, Feb-Mar, 1948

1-Origin Power Nelson, The Futureman & Jupiter, Master Magician; Ted O'Neil, Secret Agent M-11, Jaxon of the Jungle, Bucky Brady & Storm Curtis begin (1st app. of each)	194.00	582.00	1650.00
2-The Black Owl begins (1st app.)	91.00	273.00	775.00
3,4: 4-Robot-c	79.00	237.00	675.00
5,6: Dr. Dekkar, Master of Monsters app. in each	74.00	222.00	625.00
7-(Scarce)-Black Owl by S&K; origin/1st app. Dr. Frost & Frankenstein; The Green Lama, Capt. Gallant, The Great Voodini & Twist Turner begin; 1st app. The Green Lama (12/40)	150.00	450.00	1275.00
8,9-Black Owl & Ted O'Neil by S&K	81.00	243.00	690.00

Prize Comics Western #79 © PRIZE

Prometheus (Villains) #1 © DC

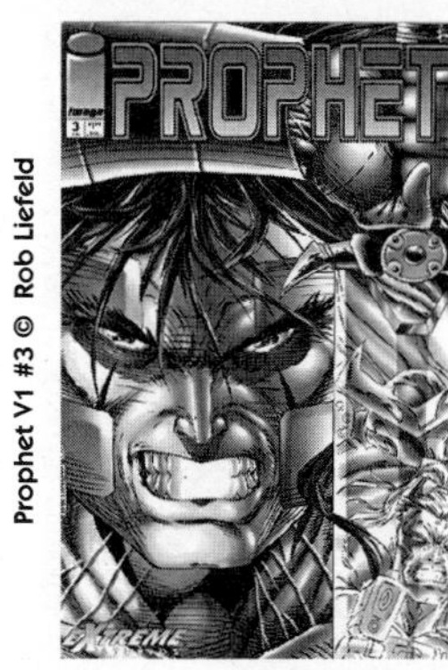

Prophet V1 #3 © Rob Liefeld

GD25 FN65 NM94

10-12,14-20: 11-Origin Bulldog Denny. 16-Spike Mason begins 58.00 174.00 490.00
13-Yank & Doodle begin (8/41, origin/1st app.) 65.00 195.00 550.00
21-24 42.00 127.00 340.00
25-30 25.00 76.00 190.00
31-33 21.00 62.00 155.00
34-Origin Airmale, Yank & Doodle; The Black Owl joins army, Yank & Doodle's father assumes Black Owl's role 25.00 74.00 185.00
35-36,38-40: 35-Flying Fist & Bingo begin 17.00 50.00 125.00
37-Intro. Stampy, Airmale's sidekick; Hitler-c 25.00 74.00 185.00
41-50: 45-Yank & Doodle learn Black Owl's I.D. (their father). 48-Prince Ra begins 13.00 38.00 95.00
51-62,64,67,68: 53-Transvestism story. 55-No Frankenstein. 57-X-Mas-c. 64-Black Owl retires 11.00 34.00 85.00
63-Simon & Kirby c/a 13.00 40.00 100.00
65,66-Frankenstein-c by Briefer 12.00 36.00 90.00

NOTE: ***Briefer** a 7-on; c-65, 66. **J. Binder** a-16; c-21-29. **Guardineer** a-62. **Kiefer** c-62. **Palais** c-68. **Simon & Kirby** c-63, 75, 83.*

PRIZE COMICS WESTERN (Formerly Prize Comics #1-68)
Prize Publications (Feature): No. 69(V7#2), Apr-May, 1948 - No. 119, Nov-Dec, 1956 (No. 69-84: 52 pgs.)

69(V7#2) 13.00 38.00 95.00
70-75: 74-Kurtzman-a (8 pgs.) 11.00 32.00 80.00
76-Randolph Scott photo-c; "Canadian Pacific" movie adaptation 12.00 36.00 90.00
77-Photo-c; Severin/Elder, Mart Bailey-a; "Streets of Laredo" movie adaptation 11.00 32.00 80.00
78-Photo-c; S&K-a, 10 pgs.; Severin, Mart Bailey-a; "Bullet Code", & "Roughshod" movie adaptations 16.00 48.00 120.00
79-Photo-c; Kurtzman-a, 8 pgs.; Severin/Elder, Severin, Mart Bailey-a; "Stage To Chino" movie adaptation w/George O'Brien 16.00 48.00 120.00
80,81-Photo-c; Severin/Elder-a(2) 11.00 34.00 85.00
82-Photo-c; 1st app. The Preacher by Mart Bailey; Severin/Elder-a(3) 11.00 34.00 85.00
83,84 9.30 28.00 70.00
85-1st app. American Eagle by John Severin & begins (V9#6, 1-2/51) 23.00 68.00 170.00
86,101-105 11.00 32.00 80.00
87-99,110,111-Severin/Elder-a(2-3) each 11.00 34.00 85.00
100 13.00 38.00 95.00
106-108,112 8.50 26.00 60.00
109-Severin/Williamson-a 11.00 32.00 80.00
113-Williamson/Severin-a(2)/Frazetta? 11.00 34.00 85.00
114-119: Drifter series in all; by Mort Meskin #114-118 6.50 19.50 45.00

NOTE: ***Fass** a-81. **Severin & Elder** c-84-99. **Severin** a-72, 75, 77-79, 83-86, 96, 97, 100-105; c-92,100-109(most), 110-119. **Simon & Kirby** c-75, 83.*

PRIZE MYSTERY
Key Publications: May, 1955 - No. 3, Sept, 1955

1 7.85 23.50 55.00
2,3 6.00 18.00 42.00

PROFESSIONAL FOOTBALL (See Charlton Sport Library)

PROFESSOR COFFIN
Charlton Comics: No. 19, Oct, 1985 - No. 21, Feb, 1986

19-21: Wayne Howard-a(r) 3.00

PROFESSOR OM
Innovation Publishing: May, 1990 - No. 2, 1990 ($2.50, limited series)

1,2-East Meets West spin-off 2.50

PROFESSOR XAVIER AND THE X-MEN (Also see X-Men, 1st series)
Marvel Comics: Nov, 1995 - No. 18 (99¢)

1-18: Stories featuring the Original X-Men. 2-vs. The Blob. 5-Vs. the Original Brotherhood of Evil Mutants. 10-Vs The Avengers 1.00

GD25 FN65 NM94

PROJECT A-KO (Manga)
Malibu Comics: Mar, 1994 - No. 4, June, 1994 ($2.95)

1-4-Based on anime film 3.00

PROJECT A-KO 2 (Manga)
CPM Comics: May, 1995 - No. 3, Aug, 1995 ($2.95, limited series)

1-3 3.00

PROJECT A-KO VERSUS THE UNIVERSE (Manga)
CPM Comics: Oct, 1995 - No. 5, June, 1996 ($2.95, limited series, bi-monthly)

1-5 3.00

PROJECT: HERO
Vanguard Graphics (Canadian): Aug, 1987 ($1.50)

1 1.50

PROMETHEUS (VILLAINS) (See JLA #16,17)
DC Comics: Feb, 1998 ($1.95, one-shot)

1-Origin & 1st app.; Morrison-s/Pearson-c 3.00

PROPELLERMAN
Dark Horse Comics: Jan, 1993 - No. 8, Mar, 1994 ($2.95, limited series)

1-8: 2,4,8-Contain 2 trading cards 3.00

PROPHET (See Youngblood #2)
Image Comics (Extreme Studios): Oct, 1993 - No. 10, 1995 ($1.95)

1-($2.50)-Liefeld/Panosian-c/a; 1st app. Mary McCormick; Liefeld scripts in 1-4; #1-3 contain coupons for Prophet #0 2.00
1-Gold foil embossed-c edition rationed to dealers 5.00
2-4: 2-Liefeld-c(p). 3-1st app. Judas. 4-1st app. Omen; Black and White Pt. 3 by Thibert 2.00
4-Alternate-c by Stephen Platt 2.00
5,6-Platt-c/a 2.00
0-(7/94, $2.50)-San Diego Comic Con ed. (2200 copies) 3.00
7-10: 7-(9/94, $2.50)-Platt-c/a. 8-Bloodstrike app. 10-Polybagged w/trading card; Platt-c. 2.50

PROPHET
Image Comics (Extreme Studios): V2#1, Aug, 1995 - No. 8 ($3.50)

V2#1-8: Dixon scripts in all. 1-4-Platt-a. 1-Boris-c; F. Miller variant-c. 4-Newmen app. 5,6-Wraparound-c 2.50
Annual 1 (9/95, $2.50)-Bagged w/Youngblood gaming card; Quesada-c 2.50
Babewatch Special 1 (12/95, $2.50)-Babewatch tie-in 2.50
1995 San Diego Edition-B&W preview of V2#1. 3.00
TPB-(1996, $12.95) r/#1-7 13.00

PROPHET/CABLE
Image Comics (Extreme): Jan, 1997 - No. 2, Mar, 1997 ($3.50, limited series)

1,2-Liefeld-c/a: 2-#1 listed on cover 3.50

PROPHET/CHAPEL: SUPER SOLDIERS
Image Comics (Extreme): May, 1996 - No. 2, June, 1996 ($2.50, limited series)

1,2: 1-Two covers exist 2.50
1-San Diego Edition; B&W-c 2.50

PROTECTORS (Also see The Ferret)
Malibu Comics: Sept, 1992 - No. 20, May, 1994 ($1.95-$2.50/$2.25/$2.50)

1-12 ($2.50, direct sale)-With poster & diff-c: 1-Origin; has 3/4 outer-c 2.50
1-12 ($1.95, newsstand)-Without poster 2.00
13-16 ($2.25): 13-Polybagged w/Skycap 2.25
17-20: 17-Begin $2.50-c 2.50

PROTOTYPE (Also see Flood Relief & Ultraforce)
Malibu Comics (Ultraverse): Aug, 1993 - No. 18, Feb, 1995 ($1.95/$2.50)

1,2 2.00

Prototype #10 © MAL

Psyba-Rats #2 © DC

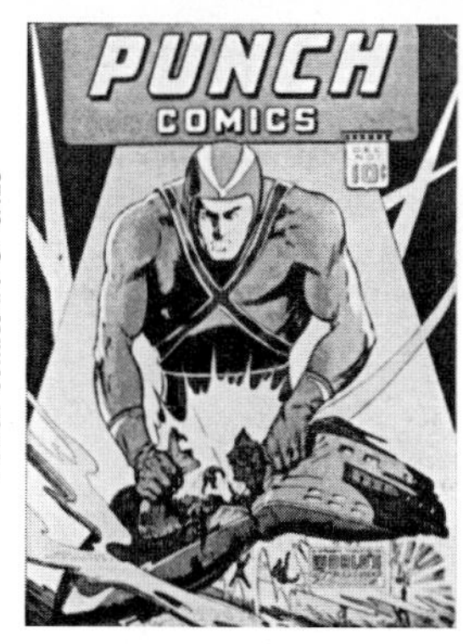

Punch Comics #1 © CHES

GD25 FN65 NM94

1-Holo-c 5.00
1-Ultra Limited silver foil-c 4.00
3-($2.50, 48 pgs.)-Rune flip-c/story by B. Smith (3 pgs.) 2.50
4-12: 4-Intro Wrath. 5-Break-Thru & Strangers x-over. 6-Arena cameo. 7,8-Arena-c/story. 12-(7/94) 2.00
0-(8/94,$ 2.50, 44 pgs.) 2.50
13 (8/94, $3.50)-Flip book(Ultraverse Premiere #6) 3.50
14-17: 14-(10/94) 2.00
18 ($2.50) 2.50
Giant Size 1 (10/94, $2.50, 44 pgs.) 2.50

PROWLER (Also see Revenge of the...)
Eclipse Comics: July, 1987 - No. 4, Oct, 1987 ($1.75)

1-4: Snyder-c/a. 3,4-Origin 1.80

PROWLER, THE
Marvel Comics: Nov, 1994 ($1.75)

1-4: 1-Spider-Man app. 1.75

PROWLER IN "WHITE ZOMBIE", THE
Eclipse Comics: Oct, 1988 ($2.00, B&W, Baxter paper)

1-Adapts Bela Lugosi movie White Zombie 2.00

PRUDENCE & CAUTION (Also see Dogs of War & Warriors of Plasm)
Defiant: May, 1994 - No. 2, June, 1994 ($3.50/$2.50)(Spanish versions exist)

1-($3.50, 52 pgs.)-Chris Claremont scripts in all 3.50
2-($2.50) 2.50

PRYDE AND WISDOM (Also see Excalibur)
Marvel Comics: Sept, 1996 - No. 3, Nov, 1996 ($1.95, limited series)

1-3: Warren Ellis scripts; Terry Dodson & Karl Story-c/a 2.00

PSI-FORCE
Marvel Comics Group: Nov, 1986 - No. 32, June, 1989 (75¢/$1.50)

1-32: 11-13-Williamson-i 1.25
Annual 1 (10/87) 1.25

PSI-JUDGE ANDERSON
Fleetway Publications (Quality): 1989 - No. 15, 1990 ($1.95, B&W)

1-15 2.50

PSI-LORDS
Valiant: Sept, 1994 - No. 10, June, 1995 ($2.25)

1-($3.50)-Chromium wraparound-c 3.50
1-Gold 4.00
2-10: 3-Chaos Effect Epsilon Pt. 2 2.25

PSYBA-RATS (Also see Showcase '94 #3,4)
DC Comics: Apr, 1995-No. 3, June, 1995 ($2.50, limited series)

1-3 2.50

PSYCHO (Magazine)
Skywald Publ. Corp.: Jan, 1971 - No. 24, Mar, 1975 (68 pgs.; B&W) (No #22?)

	GD25	FN65	NM94
1-All reprints	4.40	13.00	48.00
2-Origin & 1st app. The Heap, & Frankenstein series by Adkins	2.90	8.70	32.00
3-10	2.20	6.25	22.00
11-20: 13-Cannabalism; 3 pgs of Christopher Lee as Dracula photos. 18-Injury to eye-c. 20-Severed Head-c	1.60	4.80	16.00
21-24: 24-1975 Winter Special	2.00	6.00	20.00
Annual 1(1972)(68 pgs.)	2.40	7.00	26.00
Fall Special (1974)-Reese, Wildey-a(r)	2.00	6.00	20.00
Winter Special 1 (1975)-Dave Sim scripts	2.00	6.00	20.00
Yearbook(1974-nn)-Everett, Reese-a	2.20	6.25	22.00

NOTE: ***Boris** c-3, 5. **Buckler** a-2, 4, 5. **Gene Day** a-24. **Everett** a-3-6. **B. Jones** a-4. **Jeff Jones** a-6, 7, 9; c-12. **Kaluta** a-13. **Katz/Buckler** a-3. **Kim** a-24. **Morrow** a-1. **Reese** a-5. **Dave Sim** a-24. **Sutton** a-3. **Wildey** a-5.*

PSYCHOANALYSIS
E. C. Comics: Mar-Apr, 1955 - No. 4, Sept-Oct, 1955

	GD25	FN65	NM94
1-All Kamen-c/a; not approved by code	15.00	45.00	140.00
2-4-Kamen-c/a in all	11.00	33.00	110.00

PSYCHOBLAST
First Comics: Nov, 1987 - No. 9, July, 19898 ($1.75)

1-9 1.80

PSYCHONAUTS
Marvel Comics (Epic Comics): Oct, 1993 - No. 4, Jan, 1994 ($4.95, lim. series)

1-4: American/Japanese co-produced comic 5.00

PSYLOCKE & ARCHANGEL CRIMSON DAWN
Marvel Comics: Aug, 1997 - No. 4, Nov, 1997 ($2.50, limited series)

1-4-Raab-s/Larroca-a(p) 2.50

P.T. 109 (See Movie Comics)

PUBLIC DEFENDER IN ACTION (Formerly Police Trap)
Charlton Comics: No. 7, Mar, 1956 - No. 12, Oct, 1957

	GD25	FN65	NM94
7	7.85	23.50	55.00
8-12	5.70	17.00	35.00

PUBLIC ENEMIES
D. S. Publishing Co.: 1948 - No. 9, June-July, 1949

	GD25	FN65	NM94
1-True Crime Stories	20.00	60.00	150.00
2-Used in **SOTI**, pg. 95	19.00	56.00	140.00
3-5: 5-Arrival date of 10/1/48	11.00	32.00	80.00
6,8,9	10.00	30.00	75.00
7-McWilliams-a; injury to eye panel	11.00	32.00	80.00

PUDGY PIG
Charlton Comics: Sept, 1958 - No. 2, Nov, 1958

	GD25	FN65	NM94
1,2	2.50	7.50	20.00

PUMA BLUES
Aardvark One International/Mirage Studios #21 on: 1986 - No. 26, 1990 ($1.70-$1.75, B&W)

1-19, 21-26: 1-1st & 2nd printings. 25,26-$1.75-c 2.00
20 ($2.25)-By Alan Moore, Miller, Grell, others 2.50
Trade Paperback (12/88, $14.95) 14.95

PUMPKINHEAD: THE RITES OF EXORCISM (Movie)
Dark Horse Comics: 1993 - No. 2, 1993 ($2.50, limited series)

1,2: Based on movie; painted-c by McManus 2.50

PUNCH & JUDY COMICS
Hillman Per.: 1944; No. 2, Fall, 1944 - V3#2, 12/47; V3#3, 6/51 - V3#9, 12/51

	GD25	FN65	NM94
V1#1-(60 pgs.)	17.00	52.00	130.00
2	10.00	30.00	75.00
3-12(7/46)	7.85	23.50	55.00
V2#1(8/49),3-9	5.00	15.00	30.00
V2#2,10-12, V3#1-Kirby-a(2) each	19.00	56.00	140.00
V3#2-Kirby-a	17.00	52.00	130.00
3-9	5.00	15.00	30.00

PUNCH COMICS
Harry 'A' Chesler: 12/41; #2, 2/42; #9, 7/44 - #19, 10/46; #20, 7/47 - #23, 1/48

	GD25	FN65	NM94
1-Mr. E, The Sky Chief, Hale the Magician, Kitty Kelly begin	112.00	336.00	950.00
2-Captain Glory app.	75.00	225.00	640.00
9-Rocketman & Rocket Girl & The Master Key begin	62.00	186.00	525.00
10-Sky Chief app.; J. Cole-a; Master Key-r/Scoop #3	52.00	156.00	440.00
11-Origin Master Key-r/Scoop #1; Sky Chief, Little Nemo app.; Jack Cole-a; Fineish art by Sultan	49.00	147.00	420.00
12-Rocket Boy & Capt. Glory app; classic Skull-c	100.00	300.00	850.00

The Punisher #33 © MAR

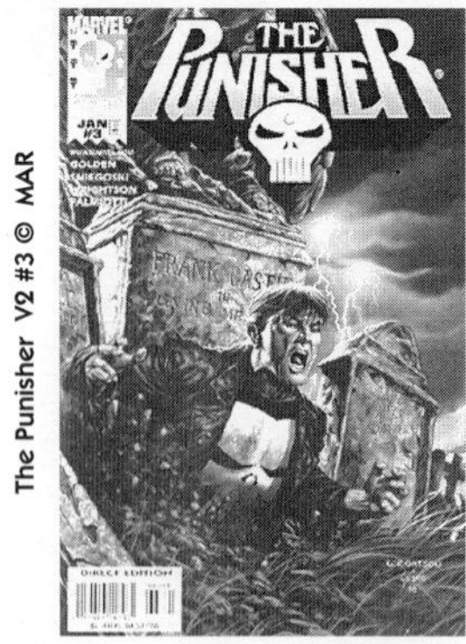

The Punisher V2 #3 © MAR

The Punisher Magazine #4 © MAR

GD25 FN65 NM94

13-Cover has list of 4 Chesler artists' names on tombstone 52.00 156.00 440.00
14-17,19: 46.00 138.00 390.00
18-Bondage-c; hypodermic panels 55.00 165.00 470.00
20-Unique cover with bare-breasted women 76.00 228.00 650.00
21-Hypo needle story 46.00 138.00 390.00
22,23-Little Nemo-not by McCay. 22-Intro Baxter (teenage) 25.00 76.00 190.00

PUNCHY AND THE BLACK CROW
Charlton Comics: No. 10, Oct, 1985 - No. 12, Feb, 1986

10-12: Al Fago funny animal-r 1.00

PUNISHER (See Amazing Spider-Man #129, Blood and Glory, Captain America #241, Classic Punisher, Daredevil #182-184, 257, Daredevil and the..., Ghost Rider V2#5, 6, Marc Spector #8 & 9, Marvel Preview #2, Marvel Super Action, Marvel Tales, Power Pack #46, Spectacular Spider-Man #81-83, 140, 141, 143 & new Strange Tales #13 & 14)

PUNISHER (The...)
Marvel Comics Group: Jan, 1986 - No. 5, May, 1986 (Limited series)

1-Double size 5.00
2 3.00
3-5 1.50
Trade Paperback (1988)-r/#1-5 11.00
NOTE: *Zeck a-1-4; c-1-5.*

PUNISHER (The...)
Marvel Comics: July, 1987 - No. 104, July, 1995

V2#1 4.00
2-9: 7-Last 75¢ issue. 8-Portacio/Williams-c/a begins, ends #18. 9-Scarcer, low distribution 2.00
10-Daredevil app.; ties in w/Daredevil #257 3.00
11-15: 13-18-Kingpin app. 2.00
16-20: 19-Stroman-c/a. 20-Portacio-c(p) 2.00
21-24,26-40: 24-1st app. Shadowmasters 1.50
25,50:($1.50, 52 pgs.). 25-Shadowmasters app. 1.50
41-49 ($1.25) 1.25
51-59: 57-Photo-c; came w/outer-c (newsstand ed. w/o outer-c). 59-Punisher is severely cut & has skin grafts (has black skin); last $1.00-c 1.00
60-74,76-85,87-89: 60-Begin $1.25-c. 60-62-Luke Cage app. 62-Punisher back to white skin. 68-Tarantula-c/story. 85-Prequel to Suicide Run Pt. 0. 87,88-Suicide Run Pt. 6 & 9 1.00
75-($2.75, 52 pgs.)-Embossed silver foil-c 2.75
86-($2.95, 52 pgs.)-Embossed & foil stamped-c; Suicide Run part 3 3.00
90-99, 101-104: 90-Begin $1.50-c; bound-in card sheet. 99-Cringe app. 102-Bullseye. 1.50
100-($2.95, 68 pgs.) 3.00
100-($3.95, 68 pgs.)-Foil cover 4.00
"Ashcan" edition (75¢)-Joe Kubert-c .75
Annual 1 (1988)-Evolutionary War x-over 2.00
Annual 2 (1989, $2.00, 68 pgs.)-Atlantis Attacks x-over; Jim Lee-a(p) (back-up story, 6 pgs.); Moon Knight app. 2.00
Annual 3,4 ('90, '91, $2.00, 68 pgs.): 4-Golden-c(p) 2.00
Annual 5 (1992, $2.25, 68 pgs.) 2.25
Annual 6 (1993, $2.95, 68 pgs.)-Bagged w/card 3.00
Annual 7 (1994, $2.95)-Rapido app. 3.00
...: A Man Named Frank (1994, $6.95, TPB) .85 2.60 7.00
...and Wolverine in African Saga nn (1989, $5.95, 52 pgs.)-Reprints Punisher War Journal #6 & 7; Jim Lee-c/a(r) 4.00
Back to School Special 1 (11/92, $2.95, 68 pgs.) 3.00
Back to School Special 2 (10/93, $2.95, 68 pgs.) 3.00
Back to School Special 3 (10/94, $2.95) 3.00
.../Batman: Deadly Knights (10/94, $4.95) 5.00
...Bloodlines nn (1991, $5.95, 68 pgs.) 2.00 6.00
...: Die Hard in the Big Easy nn ('92, $4.95, 52 pgs.) 5.00
...: Empty Quarter nn ('94, $6.95) .85 2.60 7.00
...G-Force nn (1992, $4.95, 52 pgs.)-Painted-c 5.00
...Holiday Special 1 (1/93, $2.95, 52 pgs.)-Foil-c 3.00
...Holiday Special 2 (1/94, $2.95, 68 pgs.) 3.00
...Holiday Special 3 (1/95, $2.95, 68 pgs.) 3.00
...Invades the 'Nam: Final Invasion nn (2/94, $6.95)-J. Kubert-c & chapter break art; reprints The 'Nam #84 & unpublished #85,86 .85 2.60 7.00
...Meets Archie (8/94, $3.95, 52 pgs.)-Die cut-c; no ads; same contents as Archie Meets The Punisher 4.00
...Movie Special 1 (6/90, $5.95, 68 pgs.) 2.00 6.00
...: No Escape nn (1990, $4.95, 52 pgs.)-New-a 5.00
...The Prize nn (1990, $4.95, 68 pgs.)-New-a 5.00
Summer Special 1 (8/91, $2.95, 52 pgs.)-No ads 3.00
Summer Special 2 (8/92, $2.50, 52 pgs.)-Bisley painted-c; Austin-a(i) 2.50
Summer Special 3 (8/93, $2.50, 52 pgs.)-No ads 2.50
Summer Special 4 (7/94, $2.95, 52 pgs.) 3.00
NOTE: ***Austin** c(i)-47, 48. **Cowan** c-39. **Golden** c-50, 85, 86, 100. **Heath** a-26, 27, 89, 90; c-26, 27. **Quesada** c-56p, 62p. **Sienkiewicz** c-Back to School 1.**Stroman** a-76p(9 pgs.). **Williamson** a(i)-25, 60-62i, 64-70, 74, Annual 5; c(i)-62, 65-68.*

PUNISHER (Also see Double Edge)
Marvel Comics: Nov, 1995 - No. 18, Apr, 1997 ($2.95/$1.95/$1.50)

1 ($2.95)-Ostrander scripts begin; foil-c. 3.00
2-8: 7-Vs. S.H.I.E.L.D. 2.00
9-18: 9-Begin $1.50-c. 11-"Onslaught." 12-17-X-Cutioner-c/app. 17-Daredevil, Spider-Man-c/app. 1.50

PUNISHER (Marvel Knights)
Marvel Comics: Nov, 1998 - No. 4, Feb, 1999 ($2.99, limited series)

1-Wrightson-a; Wrightson & Jusko-c 3.00
1-($6.95) DF Edition; Jae Lee variant-c 6.95
2-4 3.00

PUNISHER AND WOLVERINE: DAMAGING EVIDENCE (See Wolverine and...)

PUNISHER ARMORY, THE
Marvel Comics: 7/90 ($1.50); No. 2, 6/91; No. 3, 4/92 - 10/94($1.75/$2.00)

1($1.50)-r/weapons pgs. from War Journal; Jim Lee-c 1.50
2 ($1.75)-Jim Lee-c 2.00
3-10 ($2.00): All new material. 3-Jusko painted-c 2.00

PUNISHER KILLS THE MARVEL UNIVERSE
Marvel Comics: Nov, 1995 ($5.95, one-shot)

1-Garth Ennis script 6.00

PUNISHER MAGAZINE, THE
Marvel Comics: Oct, 1989 - No. 16, Nov, 1990 ($2.25, B&W, Magazine, 52 pgs.)

1-3: 1-r/Punisher #1('86). 2,3-r/Punisher 2-5 2.25
4-16: 4-7-r/Punisher V2#1-8. 4-Chiodo-c. 8-r/Punisher #10 & Daredevil #257; Portacio & Lee-r. 14-r/Punisher War Journal #1,2 w/new Lee-c. 16-r/Punisher W. J. #3,8 2.25
NOTE: ***Chiodo** painted c-4, 7, 16. **Jusko** painted c-6, 8. **Jim Lee** r-8, 14-16; c-14. **Portacio/ Williams** r-7-12.*

PUNISHER MOVIE COMIC
Marvel Comics: Nov, 1989 - No. 3, Dec, 1989 ($1.00, limited series)

1-3: Movie adaptation 1.25
1 (1989, $4.95, squarebound)-contains #1-3 5.00

PUNISHER: ORIGIN OF MICRO CHIP, THE
Marvel Comics: July, 1993 - No. 2, Aug, 1993 ($1.75, limited series)

1,2 1.75

PUNISHER: P.O.V.
Marvel Comics: 1991 - No. 4, 1991 ($4.95, painted, limited series, 52 pgs.)

1-4: Starlin scripts & Wrightson painted-c/a in all. 2-Nick Fury app. 5.00

PUNISHER: THE GHOSTS OF INNOCENTS
Marvel Comics: Jan, 1993 - No. 2, Jan, 1993 ($5.95, 52 pgs.)

Punisher War Journal #31 © MAR

Purgatori #1 © Chaos!

Quantum & Woody #12 © Acclaim

GD25 FN65 NM94

1,2-Starlin scripts 2.00 6.00

PUNISHER 2099 (See Punisher War Journal #50)
Marvel Comics: Feb, 1993 - No. 34, Nov, 1995 ($1.25/$1.50/$1.95)

1-($1.75)-Foil stamped-c 2.00
1-($1.75)-Second printing 1.75
2-15: 13-Spider-Man 2099 x-over; Ron Lim-c(p) 1.25
16-24, 26,27: 16-Begin $1.50-c; bound-in card sheet 1.50
25 ($2.95, 52 pgs.)-Deluxe edition; embossed foil-cover 3.00
25 ($2.25, 52 pgs.) 2.25
28-34: 28-Begin $1.95-c 2.00

PUNISHER WAR JOURNAL, THE
Marvel Comics: Nov, 1988 - No. 80, July, 1995 ($1.50/$1.75/$1.95)

1-Origin The Punisher; Matt Murdock cameo; Jim Lee inks begin 3.00
2-5: 2,3-Daredevil x-over; Jim Lee-c(i). 4-Jim Lee c/a begins. 2.00
6-Two part Wolverine story begins 2.00
7-Wolverine-c, story ends 1.50
8-12,17-19: 19-Last Jim Lee-c/a 1.50
13-16,20-22: No Jim Lee-a. 13-Lee-c only. 13-15-Heath-i. 14,15-Spider-Man x-over 1.50
23-28,31-49,51-60,62,63,65: 23-Begin $1.75-c. 31-Andy & Joe Kubert art. 36-Photo-c. 47,48-Nomad/Daredevil-c/stories; see Nomad. 57,58-Daredevil & Ghost Rider-c/stories. 62,63-Suicide Run Pt. 4 & 7 1.00
29,30-Ghost Rider app. 1.50
50-($2.95, 52 pgs.)-Preview of Punisher 2099 (1st app.); embossed-c. 3.00
61-($2.95, 52 pgs.)-Embossed foil cover; Suicide Run Pt. 1 3.00
64-($2.95, 52 pgs.)-Die-cut-c; Suicide Run Pt. 10 3.00
64-($2.25, 52 pgs.)-Regular cover edition 2.25
66-74. 76-80: 66-Begin $1.95-c; bound-in card sheet 2.00
75 ($2.50, 52 pgs.) 2.50

NOTE: ***Golden*** *c-25-30, 40, 61, 62.* ***Jusko*** *painted c-31, 32.* ***Jim Lee*** *a-1i-3i, 4p-13p, 17p-19p; c-2i, 3i, 4p-15p, 17p, 18p, 19p. Painted c-40.*

PUNISHER: WAR ZONE, THE
Marvel Comics: Mar, 1992 - No. 41, July, 1995 ($1.75/$1.95)

1-($2.25, 40 pgs.)-Die cut-c; Romita, Jr.-c/a begins 2.25
2 2.00
3-22,24,26: 8-Last Romita, Jr.-c/a. 19-Wolverine app. 24-Suicide Run Pt. 5 1.75
23-($2.95, 52 pgs.)-Enbossed foil-c; Suicide Run part 2; Buscema-a(part) 3.00
25-($2.25, 52 pgs.)-Suicide Run part 8; painted-c 2.25
27-41: 27-Begin 1.95-c; bound-in card sheet 2.00
Annual 1 (1993, $2.95, 68 pgs.)-Bagged w/card; John Buscema-a 3.00
Annual 2 (1994, $2.95, 68 pgs.) 3.00

NOTE: ***Golden*** *c-23.* ***Romita, Jr.*** *c/a-1-8.*

PUNISHER: YEAR ONE
Marvel Comics: Dec, 1994 - No. 4, Apr, 1995 ($2.50, limited series)

1-4 2.50

PUNX
Acclaim (Valiant): Nov, 1995 - No. 3, Jan, 1996 ($2.50, unfinished lim. series)

1-3: Giffen story & art in all. 2-Satirizes Scott McCloud's Understanding Comics 2.50
(Manga) Special 1 (3/96, $2.50)-Giffen scripts 2.50

PUPPET COMICS
George W. Dougherty Co.: Spring, 1946 - No. 2, Summer, 1946

1,2-Funny animal 9.30 28.00 65.00

PUPPETOONS (See George Pal's...)

PURE OIL COMICS (Also see Salerno Carnival of Comics, 24 Pages of Comics, & Vicks Comics)
Pure Oil Giveaway: Late 1930's (24 pgs., regular size, paper-c)

GD25 FN65 NM94

nn-Contains 1-2 pg. strips; i.e., Hairbreadth Harry, Skyroads, Buck Rogers by Calkins & Yager, Olly of the Movies, Napoleon, S'Matter Pop, etc. 39.00 117.00 300.00
Also a 16 pg. 1938 giveaway w/Buck Rogers 36.00 108.00 270.00

PURGATORI
Chaos! Comics: Prelude #-1, 5/96 ($1.50, 16 pgs.); 1996 - No. 3 Dec, 1996 ($3.50/$2.95, limited series)

Prelude #-1-Brian Pulido story; Jim Balent-c/a; contains sketches & interviews. 1.50
1-($3.50)-Wraparound cover; red foil embossed-c; Jim Balent-a 7.00
1-($19.95)-Premium Edition (1000 print run) 2.00 6.00 20.00
2-($3.00)-Wraparound-c 3.00
2-Variant-c 5.00
...The Dracula Gambit-($2.95) 3.00
...The Dracula Gambit Sketchbook-($2.95) 3.00
...The Vampire's Myth 1-($19.95) Premium ed. (10,000) 2.00 6.00 20.00

PURGATORI
Chaos! Comics: Oct, 1998 - Present ($2.95)

1-3-Quinn-s/Rio-c/a. 2-Lady Death-c 2.95

PURGE
ANIA/U.P. Comics: Aug, 1993 ($1.95, unfinished limited series)

1 2.00

PURPLE CLAW, THE (Also see Tales of Horror)
Minoan Publishing Co./Toby Press: Jan, 1953 - No. 3, May, 1953

1-Origin; horror/weird stories in all 25.00 75.00 190.00
2,3: 1-3 r-in Tales of Horror #9-11 19.00 57.00 140.00
I.W. Reprint #8-Reprints #1 2.50 7.50 22.00

PUSSYCAT (Magazine)
Marvel Comics Group: Oct, 1968 (B&W reprints from Men's magazines)

1-(Scarce)-Ward, Everett, Wood-a; Everett-c 15.50 47.00 155.00

PUZZLE FUN COMICS (Also see Jingle Jangle)
George W. Dougherty Co.: Spring, 1946 - No. 2, Summer, 1946 (52 pgs.)

1-Gustavson-a 19.00 58.00 145.00
2 13.00 40.00 100.00

NOTE: *#1 & 2('46) each contain a* ***George Carlson*** *cover plus a 6 pg. story "Alec in Fumbleland"; also many puzzles in each.*

QUACK!
Star Reach Productions: July, 1976 - No. 6, 1977? ($1.25, B&W)

1-Brunner-c/a on Duckaneer (Howard the Duck clone); Dave Stevens, Gilbert, Shaw-a 1.60 4.80 16.00
1-2nd printing (10/76) 3.00
2,4-6: 2-Newton the Rabbit Wonder by Aragones/Leialoha; Gilbert, Shaw-a; Leialoha-c. 6-Brunner-a (Duckeneer); Gilbert-a .85 2.60 7.00
3-The Beavers by Dave Sim begin, end #5; Gilbert, Shaw-a; Sim/Leialoha-c .90 2.70 9.00

QUADRANT
Quadrant Publications: 1983 - No. 8, 1986 (B&W, nudity, adults)

1-Peter Hsu-c/a in all 4.00
2 3.00
3-8 2.00

QUAKER OATS (Also see Cap'n Crunch)
Quaker Oats Co.: 1965 (Giveaway) (2-1/2x5-1/2") (16 pgs.)

"Plenty of Glutton", starring Quake & Quisp; 2.50 7.50 20.00
"Lava Come-Back", "Kite Tale" 4.00

QUANTUM & WOODY
Acclaim Comics: June, 1997 - No. 17 ($2.50)

1-17: 1-1st app.; two covers. 6-Copycat-c. 9-Troublemakers app. 2.50
The Director's Cut TPB ('97, $7.95) r/#1-4 plus extra pages 7.95

Quantum Leap #1 © Innovation Publ.

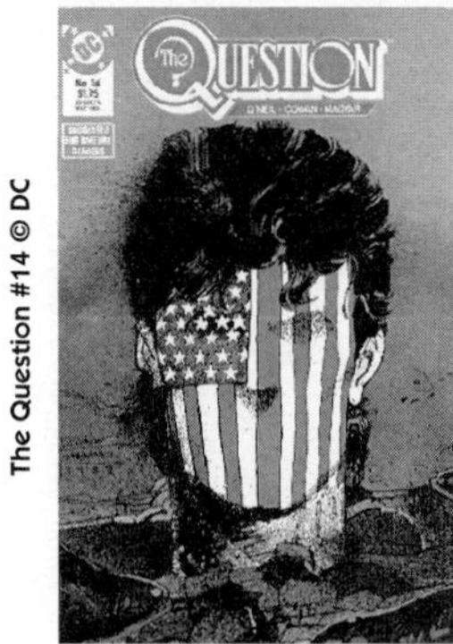

The Question #14 © DC

Quicksilver #10 © MAR

GD25 FN65 NM94

QUANTUM LEAP (TV) (See A Nightmare on Elm Street)
Innovation Publishing: Sept, 1991 - No. 12, Jun, 1993 ($2.50, painted-c)

1-12: Based on TV show; all have painted-c. 8-Has photo gallery 2.50
Special Edition 1 (10/92)-r/#1 w/8 extra pgs. of photos & articles 2.50
Time and Space Special 1 (#13) ($2.95)-Foil logo 3.00

QUASAR (See Avengers #302, Captain America #217, Incredible Hulk #234, Marvel Team-Up #113 & Marvel Two-in-One #53)
Marvel Comics: Oct, 1989 - No. 60, Jul, 1994 ($1.00/$1.25, Direct sales #17 on)

1-Origin; formerly Marvel Boy/Marvel Man 2.00
2-5: 3-Human Torch app. 1.50
6-Venom cameo (2 pgs.) 2.00
7-Cosmic Spidey app. 2.50
8-15,18-24: 11-Excalibur x-over. 14-McFarlane-c. 20-Fantastic Four app. 23-Ghost Rider x-over 1.20
16-($1.50, 52 pgs.) 1.50
17-Flash parody (Buried Alien) 2.00
25-($1.50, 52 pgs.)-New costume Quasar 1.50
26-Infinity Gauntlet x-over; Thanos-c/story 2.00
27-Infinity Gauntlet x-over 1.50
28-30: 30-Thanos cameo in flashback; last $1.00-c 1.00
31-49,51-60: 31-Begin $1.25-c; D.P. 7 guest stars. 38-40-Infinity War x-overs. 38-Battles Warlock. 39-Thanos-c & cameo. 40-Thanos app. 42-Punisher-c/story. 53-Warlock & Moondragon app. 58-w/bound-in card sheet 1.25
50-($2.95, 52 pgs.)-Holo-grafx foil-c; Silver Surfer, Man-Thing, Ren & Stimpy app. 3.00
Special #1-3 ($1.25, newsstand)-Same as #32-34 1.25

QUEEN OF THE WEST, DALE EVANS (TV)(See Dale Evans Comics, Roy Rogers & Western Roundup under Dell Giants)
Dell Publ. Co.: No. 479, 7/53 - No. 22, 1-3/59 (All photo-c; photo back c-4-8,15)

	GD25	FN65	NM94
Four Color 479(#1, '53)	21.00	63.00	230.00
Four Color 528(#2, '54)	9.00	28.00	105.00
3,4: 3(4-6/54)-Toth-a. 4-Toth, Manning-a	8.00	23.00	85.00
5-10-Manning-a. 5-Marsh-a	6.00	18.00	65.00
11,19,21-No Manning 21-Tufts-a	4.40	13.00	48.00
12-18,20,22-Manning-a	5.25	16.00	58.00

QUENTIN DURWARD
Dell Publishing Co.: No. 672, Jan, 1956

Four Color 672-Movie, photo-c 5.50 16.50 60.00

QUESTAR ILLUSTRATED SCIENCE FICTION CLASSICS
Golden Press: 1977 (224 pgs.) ($1.95)

11197-Stories by Asimov, Sturgeon, Silverberg & Niven; Starstream-r 2.20 6.25 22.00

QUEST FOR CAMELOT
DC Comics: July, 1998 ($4.95)

1-Movie adaption 4.95

QUEST FOR DREAMS LOST (Also see Word Warriors)
Literacy Volunteers of Chicago: July 4, 1987 ($2.00, B&W, 52 pgs.)(Proceeds donated to help illiteracy)

1-Teenage Mutant Ninja Turtles by Eastman/Laird, Trollords, Silent Invasion, The Realm, Wordsmith, Reacto Man, Eb'nn, Aniverse 2.00

QUESTION, THE (See Americomics, Blue Beetle (1967), Charlton Bullseye & Mysterious Suspense)

QUESTION, THE (Also see Showcase '95 #3)
DC Comics: Feb, 1987 - No. 36, Mar, 1990 ($1.50)

1-36: Denny O'Neil scripts in all 1.50
Annual 1 (1988, $2.50) 2.50
Annual 2 (1989, $3.50) 3.50

QUESTION QUARTERLY, THE
DC Comics: Summer, 1990 - No. 5, Spring, 1992 ($2.50, 52pgs.)

1-5 2.50
NOTE: ***Cowan*** *a-1, 2, 4, 5; c-1-3, 5.* ***Mignola*** *a-5i.* ***Quesada*** *a-3-5.*

QUESTION RETURNS, THE
DC Comics: Feb, 1997 ($3.50, one-shot)

1-Brereton-c 3.50

QUESTPROBE
Marvel Comics: 8/84; No. 2, 1/85; No. 3, 11/85 (lim. series)

1-3: 1-The Hulk app. by Romita. 2-Spider-Man; Mooney-a(i). 3-Human Torch & Thing 1.00

QUICK-DRAW McGRAW (TV) (Hanna-Barbera)(See Whitman Comic Books)
Dell Publishing Co./Gold Key No. 12 on: No. 1040, 12-2/59-60 - No. 11, 7-9/62; No. 12, 11/62; No. 13, 2/63; No. 14, 4/63; No. 15, 6/69
(1st show aired 9/29/59)

	GD25	FN65	NM94
Four Color 1040(#1)	13.00	39.00	140.00
2(4-6/60)-4,6: 2-Augie Doggie & Snooper & Blabber stories (8 pgs. each); pre-dates both of their #1 issues. 4-Augie Doggie & Snooper & Blabber stories.	7.00	21.00	75.00
5-1st Snagglepuss app.; last 10¢ issue	8.00	23.00	85.00
7-11	5.00	15.00	55.00
12,13-Title change to ...Fun-Type Roundup (84pgs.)	8.00	23.00	85.00
14,15	4.00	12.00	45.00

QUICK-DRAW McGRAW (TV)(See Spotlight #2)
Charlton Comics: Nov, 1970 - No. 8, Jan, 1972 (Hanna-Barbera)

	GD25	FN65	NM94
1	3.80	11.50	42.00
2-8	2.20	6.50	24.00

QUICKSILVER (See Avengers)
Marvel Comics: Nov, 1997 - No. 13, Nov, 1998 ($2.99/$1.99)

1-($2.99)-Peyer-s/Casey Jones-a; wraparound-c 3.00
2-11: 2-Two covers-variant by Golden. 4-6-Inhumans app. 2.00
12-($2.99) Siege of Wundagore pt. 4 3.00
13-Magneto-c/app.; last issue 2.00

QUICK-TRIGGER WESTERN (...Action #12; Cowboy Action #5-11)
Atlas Comics (ACI #12/WPI #13-19): No. 12, May, 1956 - No. 19, Sept, 1957

	GD25	FN65	NM94
12-Baker-a	13.00	38.00	95.00
13-Williamson-a, 5 pgs.	12.00	36.00	90.00
14-Everett, Crandall, Torres-a; Heath-c	11.00	32.00	80.00
15-Torres, Crandall-a	9.30	28.00	65.00
16-Orlando, Kirby-a	8.50	26.00	60.00
17,18: 18-Baker-a	8.50	26.00	60.00
19	6.50	19.50	45.00

NOTE: ***Ayers*** *a-17.* ***Colan*** *a-16.* ***Maneely*** *a-15, 17; c-15, 18.* ***Morrow*** *a-18.* ***Powell*** *a-14.* ***Severin*** *a-19; c-12, 13, 16, 17, 19.* ***Shores*** *a-16.* ***Tuska*** *a-17.*

QUINCY (See Comics Reading Libraries)

Q-UNIT
Harris Comics: Dec, 1993 ($2.95)

1-($2.95)-Polybagged w/trading card version 1.2 3.00

RABID
FantaCo Enterprises: 1994 ($5.95, B&W)

1 2.00 6.00

RACCOON KIDS, THE (Formerly Movietown Animal Antics)
National Periodical Publications (Arleigh No. 63,64):
No. 52, Sept-Oct, 1954 - No. 64, Nov, 1957

	GD25	FN65	NM94
52-Doodles Duck by Mayer	13.00	40.00	100.00
53-64: 53-62-Doodles Duck by Mayer	9.30	28.00	70.00

RACE FOR THE MOON
Harvey Publications: Mar, 1958 - No. 3, Nov, 1958

1-Powell-a(5); 1/2-pg. S&K-a; cover redrawn from Galaxy Science Fiction

Rack & Pain: Killers #4 © Brian Pulido

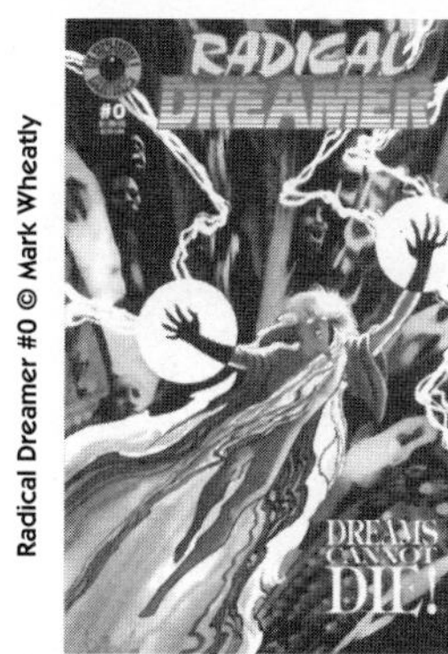

Radical Dreamer #0 © Mark Wheatly

Rai #5 © VAL

	GD25	FN65	NM94
pulp (5/53)	11.50	34.00	80.00
2-Kirby/Williamson-c(r)/a(3); Kirby-p 7 more stys	24.00	71.00	165.00
3-Kirby/Williamson-c/a(4); Kirby-p 6 more stys	25.00	75.00	175.00

RACE OF SCORPIONS
Dark Horse Comics: 1990 - No. 2, 1990 ($4.50/$4.95, 52pgs.)

	GD25	FN65	NM94
1-r/stories from Dark Horse Presents #23-27			4.50
2-($4.95-c); r/Dark Horse Presents			5.00

RACER-X
Now Comics: 8/88 - No. 11, 8/89; V2#1, 9/89 - V2#10, 1990 ($1.75)

	GD25	FN65	NM94
0-Deluxe ($3.50)			3.50
1 (9/88) - 11, V2#1-10			1.80

RACK & PAIN
Dark Horse Comics: Mar, 1994 - No. 4, June, 1994 ($2.50, limited series)

	GD25	FN65	NM94
1-4: Brian Pulido scripts in all. 1-Greg Capullo-c			3.00

RACK & PAIN: KILLERS
Chaos! Comics: Sept, 1996 - No. 4, Jan, 1997 ($2.95, limited series)

	GD25	FN65	NM94
1-4: Reprints Dark Horse series; Jae Lee-c			3.00

RACKET SQUAD IN ACTION
Capitol Stories/Charlton Comics: May-June, 1952 - No. 29, Mar, 1958

	GD25	FN65	NM94
1	24.00	72.00	180.00
2-4,6: 3,4,6-Dr. Neff, Ghost Breaker app.	12.00	36.00	90.00
5-Dr. Neff, Ghost Breaker app; headlights-c	19.00	56.00	140.00
7-10: 10-Explosion-c	11.00	32.00	80.00
11-Ditko-c/a	24.00	72.00	180.00
12-Ditko explosion-c (classic); Shuster-a(2)	41.00	124.00	330.00
13-Shuster-c(p)/a.	9.30	28.00	65.00
14-Marijuana story "Shakedown"	11.00	32.00	80.00
15-28	8.50	26.00	60.00
29-(15¢, 68 pgs.)	9.30	28.00	65.00

RADIANT LOVE (Formerly Daring Love #1)
Gilmor Magazines: No. 2, Dec, 1953 - No. 6, Aug, 1954

	GD25	FN65	NM94
2	6.00	18.00	42.00
3-6	4.25	13.00	26.00

RADICAL DREAMER
Blackball Comics: No. 0, May, 1994 - No. 4, Nov, 1994 ($1.99, bi-monthly) (1st poster format comic)

	GD25	FN65	NM94
0-2-($1.99, poster format): 0-1st app. Max Wrighter			2.00
3,4-($2.50)			2.50

RADICAL DREAMER
Mark's Giant Economy Size Comics: V2#1, June, 1995 - V2#6, Feb, 1996 ($2.95, B&W, limited series)

	GD25	FN65	NM94
V2#1-6			3.00
Prime (5/96, $2.95)			3.00
Dreams Cannot Die!-(1996, $20.00, softcover)-Collects V1#0-4 & V2#1-6; intro by Kurt Busiek; afterward by Mark Waid			20.00
Dreams Cannot Die!-(1996, $60.00, hardcover)-Signed & limited edition; collects V1#0-4 & V2#1-6; intro by Kurt Busiek; afterward by Mark Waid			60.00

RADIOACTIVE MAN (Simpsons TV show)
Bongo Comics: 1993 - No. 6, 1994 ($1.95/$2.25, limited series)

	GD25	FN65	NM94
1-($2.95)-Glow-in-the-dark-c; bound-in jumbo poster; origin Radioactive Man; (cover dated Nov. 1952)			3.25
2-Says #88 on-c & inside & dated May 1962; cover parody of Atlas Kirby monster-c; Superior Squad app.; origin Fallout Boy			2.00
3-($1.95)-Cover "dated" Aug 1972 #216			2.00
4-($2.25)-Cover "dated" Oct 1980 #412; w/trading card			2.25
5-($2.25)-Cover "dated" Jan 1986 #679; w/trading card			2.25
6-($2.25)-Cover "dated" Jan 1995 #1000			2.25
Colossal #1-($4.95)			4.95

RAGAMUFFINS
Eclipse Comics: Jan, 1985 ($1.75, one shot)

	GD25	FN65	NM94
1-Eclipse Magazine-r, w/color			1.80

RAGGEDY ANN AND ANDY (See Dell Giants, March of Comics #23 & New Funnies)
Dell Publishing Co.: No. 5, 1942 - No. 533, 2/54; 10-12/64 - No. 4, 3/66

	GD25	FN65	NM94
Four Color 5(1942)	46.00	139.00	510.00
Four Color 23(1943)	35.00	104.00	380.00
Four Color 45(1943)	28.00	85.00	310.00
Four Color 72(1945)	24.00	71.00	260.00
1(6/46)-Billy & Bonnie Bee by Frank Thomas	25.00	75.00	275.00
2,3: 3-Egbert Elephant by Dan Noonan begins	13.00	38.00	140.00
4-Kelly-a, 16 pgs.	14.00	41.00	150.00
5-10: 7-Little Black Sambo, Black Mumbo & Black Jumbo only app; Christmas-c	10.00	30.00	110.00
11-21: 21-Alice In Wonderland cover/story	8.00	25.00	90.00
22-27,29-39(8/49), Four Color 262(1/50): 34-"...In Candyland"	6.40	19.00	70.00
28-Kelly-c	7.00	22.00	80.00
Four Color 306,354,380,452,533	4.50	13.50	50.00
1(10-12/64-Dell)	2.70	8.00	30.00
2,3(10-12/65), 4(3/66)	1.80	5.40	18.00

NOTE: ***Kelly** art ("Animal Mother Goose")-#1-34, 36, 37; c-28. Peterkin Pottle by **John Stanley** in 32-38.*

RAGGEDY ANN AND ANDY
Gold Key: Dec, 1971 - No. 6, Sept, 1973

	GD25	FN65	NM94
1	2.50	7.50	22.00
2-6	1.50	4.50	12.00

RAGGEDY ANN & THE CAMEL WITH THE WRINKLED KNEES (See Dell Jr. Treasury #8)

RAGMAN (See Batman Family #20, The Brave & The Bold #196 & Cancelled Comic Cavalcade)
National Per. Publ./DC Comics No. 5: Aug-Sept, 1976 - No. 5, Jun-Jul, 1977

	GD25	FN65	NM94
1-Origin & 1st app.		2.00	6.00
2-5: 2-Origin ends; Kubert-c. 4-Drug use story			4.00

NOTE: ***Kubert** a-4, 5; c-1-5. **Redondo** studios a-1-4.*

RAGMAN (2nd Series)
DC Comics: Oct, 1991 - No. 8, May, 1992 ($1.50, limited series)

	GD25	FN65	NM94
1-Giffen plots/breakdowns			2.00
2-8: 3-Origin. 8-Batman-c/story			1.50

RAGMAN: CRY OF THE DEAD
DC Comics: Aug, 1993 - No. 6, Jan, 1994 ($1.75, limited series)

	GD25	FN65	NM94
1-6: Joe Kubert-c			1.75

RAGMOP
Image Comics: Sept, 1997 - Present ($2.95, B&W)

	GD25	FN65	NM94
1,2-Rob Walton-c/s/a			2.95

RAGS RABBIT (Formerly Babe Ruth Sports #10 or Little Max #10?; also see Harvey Hits #2, Harvey Wiseguys & Tastee Freez)
Harvey Publications: No. 11, June, 1951 - No. 18, March, 1954 (Written & drawn for little folks)

	GD25	FN65	NM94
11-(See Nutty Comics #5 for 1st app.)	4.00	11.00	22.00
12-18	3.60	9.00	18.00

RAI (Rai and the Future Force #9-23) (See Magnus #5-8)
Valiant: Mar, 1992 - No. 0, Oct, 1992; No. 9, May, 1993 - No. 33, Jun, 1995 ($1.95/$2.25)

	GD25	FN65	NM94
1,2-Valiant's 1st original character			2.00
3,4: 4-Low print run; last $1.95-c			2.00
5-8: 6,7-Unity x-overs. 7-Death of Rai			2.00

0-(11/92)-Origin/1st app. new Rai (Rising Spirit) & 1st full app. & partial origin

Ramar of the Jungle #1 © CC

The Rampaging Hulk #5 © MAR

Rangers Comics #10 © FH

	GD25	FN65	NM94
Bloodshot; also see Eternal Warrior #4; tells future of all characters			2.00
9-($2.50)-Gatefold-c; story cont'd from Magnus #24; Magnus, Eternal Warrior & X-O app.			2.50
10-33: 15-Manowar Armor app. 17-19-Magnus x-over. 21-1st app. The Starwatchers (cameo); bound-in trading card. 22-Death of Rai. 26-Chaos Effect Epsilon Pt. 3			2.25

NOTE: ***Layton*** *c-2i, 9i.* ***Miller*** *c-6.* ***Simonson*** *c-7.*

RAIDERS OF THE LOST ARK (Movie)
Marvel Comics Group: Sept, 1981 - No. 3, Nov, 1981 (Movie adaptation)

1-r/Marvel Comics Super Special #18			1.50
2,3			1.00

NOTE: ***Buscema*** *a(p)-1-3; c(p)-1.* ***Simonson*** *a-3i; scripts-1-3.*

RAINBOW BRITE AND THE STAR STEALER
DC Comics: 1985

nn-Movie adaptation			3.00

RALPH KINER, HOME RUN KING
Fawcett Publications: 1950 (Pittsburgh Pirates)

nn-Photo-c; life story	52.00	155.00	440.00

RALPH SNART ADVENTURES
Now Comics: June, 1986 - V2#9, 1987; V3#1 - #26, Feb, 1991; V4#1, 1992 - #4, 1992

1-($1.00, B&W)			1.00
2,3			1.25
V2#1 (11/86, B&W) - 7; 8,9-color			1.50
V3#1-23,25,26: 1 (9/88, $1.75)-Color series begins			1.75
24-($2.50)-3-D issue			2.50
V4#1-3-Direct sale versions w/cards			2.50
V4#1-3-Newsstand versions w/random cards			2.00
Book 1	.90	2.70	8.00
3-D Special (11/92, $3.50)-Complete 12-card set w/3-D glasses			3.50

RAMAR OF THE JUNGLE (TV)
Toby Press No. 1/Charlton No. 2 on: 1954 (no month); No. 2, Sept, 1955 - No. 5, Sept, 1956

1-Jon Hall photo-c; last pre-code issue	17.00	51.00	130.00
2-5: 2-Jon Hall photo-c	12.00	36.00	90.00

RAMM
Megaton Comics: May, 1987 - No. 2, Sept, 1987 ($1.50, B&W)

1,2-Both have 1 pg. Youngblood ad by Liefeld			1.50

RAMPAGING HULK (The Hulk #10 on; see Marvel Treasury Edition)
Marvel Comics Group: Jan, 1977 - No. 9, June, 1978 ($1.00, B&W magazine)

1-Bloodstone story	1.00	3.00	10.00
2-Old X-Men app; origin old & new X-Men in text w/Cockrum illos	.90	2.70	9.00
3-9: 7-Man-Thing story. 9-Thor vs. Hulk battle; Shanna the She-Devil story.		2.00	6.00

NOTE: ***Alcala*** *a-1-3i, 5i, 8i.* ***Buscema*** *a-1.* ***Giffen*** *a-4.* ***Nino*** *a-4i.* ***Simonson*** *a-1-3p.* ***Starlin*** *a-4(w/**Nino**), 7; c-4, 5, 7.*

RAMPAGING HULK
Marvel Comics: Aug, 1998 - No. 6, Jan, 1999 ($2.99/$1.99)

1-($2.99) Flashback stories of Savage Hulk; Leonardi-a			3.00
2-6-($1.99): 2-Two covers			2.00

RANDOLPH SCOTT (Movie star)(See Crack Western #67, Prize Comics Western #76, Western Hearts #8, Western Love #1 & Western Winners #7)

RANGE BUSTERS
Fox Features Syndicate: Sept, 1950 - No. 8, 1951

1	16.00	48.00	120.00
2	10.00	30.00	75.00
3-8	8.50	26.00	60.00

RANGE BUSTERS (Formerly Cowboy Love?; Wyatt Earp, Frontier Marshall #11 on)
Charlton Comics: No. 8, May, 1955 - No. 10, Sept, 1955

8	5.70	17.00	40.00
9,10	4.25	13.00	28.00

RANGELAND LOVE
Atlas Comics (CDS): Dec, 1949 - No. 2, Mar, 1950 (52 pgs.)

1-Robert Taylor & Arlene Dahl photo-c	13.00	40.00	100.00
2-Photo-c	11.00	34.00	85.00

RANGER, THE (See Zane Grey, Four Color #255)

RANGE RIDER, THE (TV)(See Flying A's...)

RANGE ROMANCES
Comic Magazines (Quality Comics): Dec, 1949 - No. 5, Aug, 1950 (#5: 52 pg)

1-Gustavson-c/a	22.00	66.00	165.00
2-Crandall-c/a; "spanking" scene	29.00	86.00	215.00
3-Crandall, Gustavson-a; photo-c	19.00	56.00	140.00
4-Crandall-a; photo-c	16.00	48.00	120.00
5-Gustavson-a; Crandall-a(p); photo-c	16.00	48.00	120.00

RANGERS COMICS (...of Freedom #1-7)
Fiction House Magazines: 10/41 - No. 67, 10/52; No. 68, Fall, 1952; No. 69, Winter, 1952-53 (Flying stories)

1-Intro. Ranger Girl & The Rangers of Freedom; ends #7, cover app. only #5	194.00	582.00	1650.00
2	71.00	213.00	600.00
3	59.00	177.00	500.00
4,5	53.00	160.00	450.00
6-10: 8-U.S. Rangers begin	43.00	129.00	350.00
11,12-Commando Rangers app.	41.00	122.00	325.00
13-Commando Ranger begins-not same as Commando Rangers	39.00	117.00	300.00
14-20	33.00	100.00	250.00
21-Intro/origin Firehair (begins, 2/45)	37.00	110.00	275.00
22-30: 23-Kazanda begins, ends #28. 28-Tiger Man begins (origin/1st app., 4/46), ends #46. 30-Crusoe Island begins, ends #40	25.00	76.00	190.00
31-40: 33-Hypodermic panels	21.00	64.00	160.00
41-46: 41-Last Werewolf Hunter	17.00	50.00	125.00
47-56- "Eisnerish" Dr. Drew by Grandenetti. 48-Last Glory Forbes. 53-Last 52 pg. issue. 55-Last Sky Rangers	17.00	50.00	125.00
57-60-Straight Dr. Drew by Grandenetti	13.00	38.00	95.00
61,62,64-66: 64-Suicide Smith begins	11.00	34.00	85.00
63-Used in **POP**, pgs. 85, 99	11.00	34.00	85.00
67-69: 67-Space Rangers begin, end #69	11.00	34.00	85.00

NOTE: *Bondage, discipline covers, lingerie panels are common. Crusoe Island by* ***Larsen****-#30-36. Firehair by* ***Lubbers****-#30-49. Glory Forbes by* ***Baker****-#36-45, 47; by* ***Whitman****-#34, 35. I Confess in #41-53. Jan of the Jungle in #42-58. King of the Congo in #49-53. Tiger Man by* ***Celardo****-#30-39.* ***M. Anderson*** *a-30?* ***Baker*** *a-36-38, 42, 44.* ***John Celardo*** *a-34, 36-39.* ***Lee Elias*** *a-21-28.* ***Evans*** *a-19, 38-46, 48-52.* ***Hopper*** *a-25, 26.* ***Ingels*** *a-13-16.* ***Larsen*** *a-34.* ***Bob Lubbers*** *a-30-38, 40-44; c-40-45.* ***Moreira*** *a-41-47.* ***Tuska*** *a-16, 17, 19, 22.* ***M. Whitman*** *c-61-66.* ***Zolnerwich*** *c-1-17.*

RANGO (TV)
Dell Publishing Co.: Aug, 1967

1-Tim Conway photo-c	1.65	5.00	18.00

RAPHAEL (See Teenage Mutant Ninja Turtles)
Mirage Studios: 1985 ($1.50, 7-1/2x11", B&W w/2 color cover, one-shot)

1-1st Turtles one-shot spin-off; contains 1st drawing of the Turtles as a group from 1983			3.00
1-2nd printing (11/87); new-c & 8 pgs. art			2.00

RASCALS IN PARADISE
Dark Horse Comics: Aug, 1994 - No. 3, Dec, 1994 ($3.95, magazine size)

1-3-Jim Silke-a/story			4.00

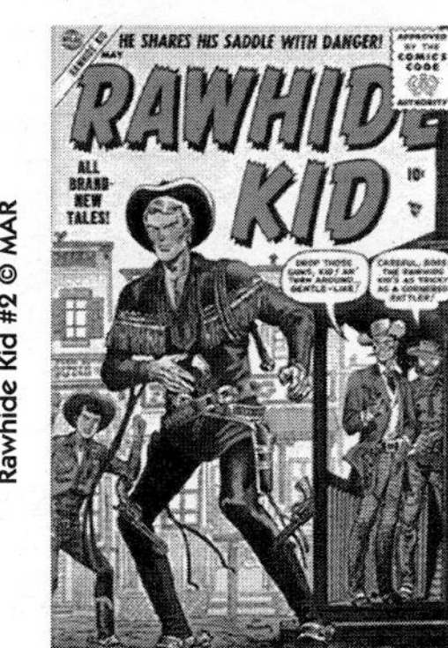

Rawhide Kid #2 © MAR

The Ray #1 © DC

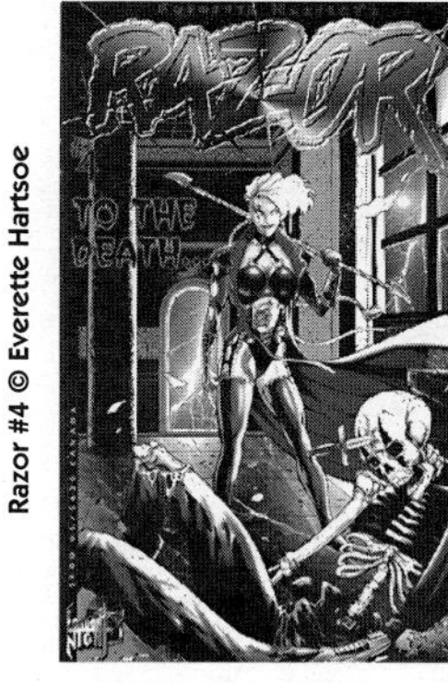

Razor #4 © Everette Hartsoe

GD25 FN65 NM94

Trade paperback-($16.95)-r/#1-3 17.00

RATFINK (See Frantic, Zany, & Ed "Big Daddy" Roth's Ratfink Comix)
Canrom, Inc.: Oct, 1964

1-Woodbridge-a 2.60 7.80 26.00

RAT PATROL, THE (TV)
Dell Publishing Co.: Mar, 1967 - No. 5, Nov, 1967; No. 6, Oct, 1969

1-Christopher George photo-c 6.00 18.00 60.00
2-6: 3-6-Photo-c 3.50 10.50 35.00

RAVAGE 2099 (See Marvel Comics Presents #117)
Marvel Comics: Dec, 1992 - No. 33, Aug, 1995($1.25/$1.50)

1-($1.75)-Gold foil stamped-c; Stan Lee scripts 1.75
1-($1.75)-2nd printing 1.75
2,3 1.75
4-17: 5-Last Ryan-c. 6-Last Ryan-a. 14-Punisher 2099 x-over. 15-Ron Lim-c(p) 1.25
18-24, 26-30: 18-Begin $1.50-c; bound-in card sheet 1.50
25 ($2.25, 52 pgs.) 2.25
25 ($2.95, 52 pgs.)-Silver foil embossed-c 3.00
31-33: 31-Begin $1.95-c 2.00

RAVEN, THE (See Movie Classics)

RAVEN CHRONICLES
Caliber (New Worlds): 1995 - Present ($2.95, B&W)

1-15: 10-Flip book w/Wordsmith #6. 15-Flip book w/High Caliber #4 3.00

RAVENING, THE
Avatar Press: June, 1997 - No. 2 ($3.00, B&W, limited series)

1,2 3.00

RAVENS AND RAINBOWS
Pacific Comics: Dec, 1983 (Baxter paper)(Reprints fanzine work in color)

1-Jeff Jones-c/a(r); nudity scenes 1.50

RAWHIDE (TV)
Dell Publishing Co./Gold Key: Sept-Nov, 1959 - June-Aug, 1962; July, 1963 - No. 2, Jan, 1964

Four Color 1028 (#1) 22.00 65.00 240.00
Four Color 1097,1160,1202,1261,1269 14.00 41.00 150.00
01-684-208(8/62-Dell) 12.00 35.00 130.00
1(10071-307, G.K.), 2-(12¢) 11.00 32.00 120.00
NOTE: *All have Clint Eastwood photo-c.* ***Tufts*** *a-1028.*

RAWHIDE KID
Atlas/Marvel Comics (CnPC No. 1-16/AMI No. 17-30): 3/55 - No. 16, 9/57; No. 17, 8/60 - No. 151, 5/79

1-Rawhide Kid, his horse Apache & sidekick Randy begin; Wyatt Earp app.; #1 was not code approved; Maneely splash pg. 74.00 221.00 625.00
2 33.00 100.00 250.00
3-5 23.00 68.00 170.00
6-10: 7-Williamson-a (4 pgs.) 17.00 52.00 130.00
11-16: 16-Torres-a 14.00 42.00 105.00
17-Origin by Jack Kirby; Kirby-a begins 21.00 63.00 210.00
18-21,24-30 10.00 30.00 100.00
22-Monster-c/story by Kirby/Ayers 12.00 36.00 120.00
23-Origin retold by Jack Kirby 15.00 45.00 150.00
31-35,40: 31,32-Kirby-a. 33-35-Davis-a. 34-Kirby-a. 35-Intro & death of The Raven. 40-Two-Gun Kid x-over. 8.00 24.00 80.00
36,37,39,41,42-No Kirby. 42-1st Larry Lieber issue 7.00 21.00 70.00
38-Red Raven-c/story; Kirby-c (2/64). 9.00 27.00 90.00
43-Kirby-a (beware: pin-up often missing) 8.00 24.00 80.00
44,46: 46-Toth-a. 46-Doc Holliday-c/s 6.00 18.00 60.00
45-Origin retold, 17 pgs. 8.00 24.00 80.00
47-49,51-60 3.20 9.50 32.00
50-Kid Colt x-over; vs. Rawhide Kid 3.80 11.40 38.00
61-70: 64-Kid Colt story. 66-Two-Gun Kid story. 67-Kid Colt story 2.80 8.40 28.00
71-78,80-83,85 2.00 6.00 16.00
79,84,86,95: 79-Williamson-a(r). 84,86: Kirby-a. 86-Origin-r; Williamson-r/Ringo Kid #13 (4 pgs.) 2.50 7.50 20.00
87-91,94,96-99: 90-Kid Colt app. 1.40 4.20 14.00
92,93 (52 pg.Giants). 92-Kirby-a 2.20 6.50 24.00
100 (6/72)-Origin retold & expanded 1.80 5.40 18.00
101-120: 115-Last new story 1.00 3.00 10.00
121-151 .90 2.70 8.00
Special 1(9/71, 25¢, 68 pgs.)-All Kirby/Ayers-r 2.20 6.50 24.00
NOTE: ***Ayers*** *a-13, 14, 16.* ***Colan*** *a-5, 35, 37; c-145p, 148p, 149p.* ***Davis*** *a-125r.* ***Everett*** *a-54i, 65, 66, 88, 96i, 148i(r).* ***Gulacy*** *c-147.* ***Heath*** *c-4.* ***G. Kane*** *c-101, 144.* ***Keller*** *a-5, 144r.* ***Kirby*** *a-17-32, 34, 42, 43, 84, 86, 92, 109r, 112r, 137r, Spec. 1; c-17-35, 37, 38, 40, 41, 43-47, 137r.* ***Maneely*** *c-1, 2, 5, 6, 14.* ***Morisi*** *a-13.* ***Morrow/Williamson*** *r-111.* ***Roussos*** *r-146i, 147i, 149-151i.* ***Severin*** *a-16; c-8, 13.* ***Sutton*** *a-93.* ***Torres*** *a-99r.* ***Tuska*** *a-14.* ***Wildey*** *r-146-151(Outlaw Kid).* ***Williamson*** *r-79, 86, 95.*

RAWHIDE KID
Marvel Comics Group: Aug, 1985 - No. 4, Nov, 1985 (Mini-series)

1-4 2.00

RAY, THE (See Freedom Fighters & Smash Comics #14)
DC Comics: Feb, 1992 - No. 6, July, 1992 ($1.00, mini-series)

1-Sienkiewicz-c; Joe Quesada-a(p) in 1-5 2.00 6.00
2 3.50
3: 3-6-Quesada-c(p) 3.00
4-6: 6-Quesada layouts only 2.50
...In a Blaze of Power (1994, $12.95)-r/#1-6 w/new Quesada-c 13.00

RAY, THE
DC Comics: May, 1994 - No. 28, Oct, 1996 ($1.75/$1.95/$2.25)

1-3: 1,2-Quesada-c(p); Superboy app. 1.75
1-($2.95)-Collectors Edition w/different Quesada-c; embossed foil-c 3.00
4,5: 4-Begin $1.95-c. 5-(9/94) 2.00
0,6-12: 0-(10/94) 2.00
13-24, 26-28: 13-Begin $2.25-c 2.25
25-($3.50)-Future Flash (Bart Allen)-c/app; double size 3.50
Annual 1 ($3.95, 68 pgs.)-Superman app. 4.00

RAY BRADBURY COMICS
Topps Comics: Feb, 1993 - V4#1, June, 1994 ($2.95)

1-5-Polybagged w/3 trading cards each. 1-All dinosaur issue; Corben-a; Williamson/Torres/Krenkel-r/Weird Science-Fantasy #25. 3-All dinosaur issue; Steacy painted-c; Stout-a 3.00
Special Edition 1 (1994, $2.95)-The Illustrated Man 3.00
...Special: Tales of Horror #1 ($2.50) 2.50
...Trilogy of Terror V3#1 (5/94, $2.50) 2.50
...Martian Chronicles V4#1 (6/94, $2.50)-Steranko-c 2.50
NOTE: ***Kelley Jones*** *a-Trilogy of Terror V3#1.* ***Kaluta*** *a-Martian Chronicles V4#1.* ***Kurtzman/Matt Wagner*** *c-2.* ***McKean*** *c-4.* ***Mignola*** *a-4.* ***Wood*** *a-Trilogy of Terror V3#1r.*

RAZOR
London Night Studios: May, 1992 - Present ($3.95, B&W, mature)

0 (5/92, $3.95)-Direct market 1.50 4.50 15.00
0 (4/95, $3.00)-London Night edition 3.50
1/2 (4/95, mail-in offer)-1st Poizon; Linsner-c 5.00
1 (8/92, $2.50)-Fathom Press 1.50 4.50 15.00
1-2nd printing 3.50
2 ($2.95)-J. O'Barr-c 1.20 3.60 12.00
2-Limited editions in red & blue 1.40 4.20 14.00
2-Platinum; no price on cover 1.40 4.20 14.00
3-($3.95)-Jim Balent-c 2.00 6.00
3-w/poster insert .85 2.60 7.00
4-Vigil-c 4.00
4-w/poster insert 5.00
5-Linsner-c .85 2.60 7.00

Razor #50 © Everette Hartsoe

Real Clue Crime Stories V2 #8 © HILL

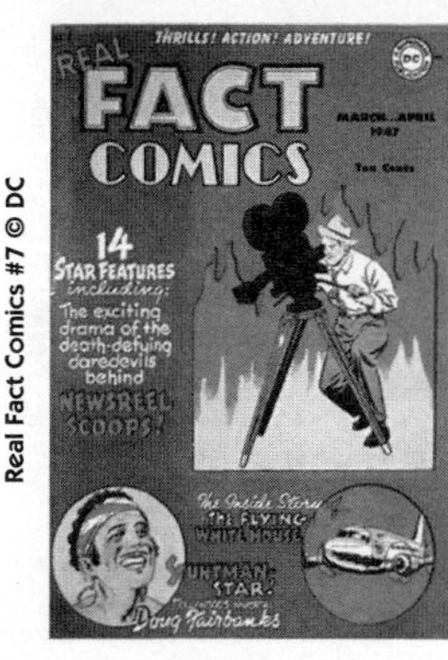

Real Fact Comics #7 © DC

GD25 FN65 NM94

5-Platinum 1.20 3.60 12.00
6,7 3.00
8-10: 10-1st app. Stryke 3.00
11-31, 33, 34:11,12 -Rituals Pt. 1 & 2. 21-Rose & Gunn app. 25-Photo-c 3.00
25-Uncut ($10.00)-Nude Edition; double-c .85 2.60 7.00
32-($3.50) 3.50
32-($5.00)-Nude Edition; Nude-c 5.00
35-49 3.00
40-Uncut ($6.00)-Nude Edition 2.00 6.00
50-Uncut-Four covers incl. Tony Dainel 3.00
Annual 1 (1993, $2.95)-1st app. Shi 2.70 8.00 30.00
Annual 1-Gold (1200 printed) 2.70 8.00 30.00
Annual 2 (Late 1994, $3.00) 3.50
.../Cry No More 1-($3.95)-Origin Razor; variant-c exists 4.00
.../Embrace nn-($3.00)-Variant photo-c(Carmen Electra) 3.00
...Pictorial 1-(10/97, $5.00) 5.00
.../Shi Special 1 (7/94, $3.00) .85 2.60 7.00
.../Switchblade Symphony 1-($3.95)-Hartsoe-s 4.00
...: Swimsuit Special-painted-c 3.00
.../Warrior Nun Areala-Faith-(5/96, $3.95) 4.00
.../Warrior Nun Areala-Faith-(5/96, $3.95)-Virgin-c .85 2.60 7.00

RAZOR AND THE LADIES OF LONDON NIGHT
London Night Studios: March, 1997 ($3.95, one-shot, mature)
1-Photo-c & insides 3.95

RAZOR: ARCHIVES
London Night Studios: May, 1997 - Present ($3.95/$5.00, mature)
1-($3.95) 3.95
2-5-($5.00) 5.00

RAZOR: BURN
London Night Studios: 1994 - No. 5, 1994 ($3.00, limited series, mature)
1-5 3.00
TPB-($14.95) r/ #1-5 15.00

RAZOR/DARK ANGEL: THE FINAL NAIL
Boneyard Press #1/London Night Studios #2: June, 1994 -No. 2, June, 1994 ($2.95, B&W, limited series, mature)
1,2 3.00

RAZOR• DEEP CUTS
London Night Studios: Sept, 1997 ($5.00, one-shot, mature)
1-Photo-c & insides 5.00
1-($10.00)-Nude Edition; Photo-c & insides 10.00

RAZOR/MORBID ANGEL: SOUL SEARCH
London Night Studios: Sept, 1996 - No. 3, 1997 ($3.00, limited series, mature)
1-3 3.00

RAZOR: THE SUFFERING
London Night Studios: 1994 - No. 3, 1995 ($2.95, limited series, mature)
1-3 ($2.95): 2-(9/94) 3.00
1-($3.00)-Director's Cut 3.00
1-Platinum 7.00
Trade paperback-($12.95) 13.00

RAZOR: TORTURE
London Night Studios: 1995 - No. 6, 1995 ($3.00, limited series, mature)
0-($3.95)-Wraparound, chromium-c; polybagged w/card; alternate-c exists? 4.00
1-6 ($3.00): 3-Error & corrected issues exist 3.00

RAZOR: VOLUME TWO
London Night Studios: Oct, 1996 - Present ($3.95/$3.00, mature)
1-Wraparound foil-c; Quinn-s 3.95
2-7-($3.00):3-Error & corrected issues exist 3.00

RAZORLINE
Marvel Comics: Sept, 1993 (75¢, one-shot)
1-Clive Barker super-heroes: Ectokid, Hokum & Hex, Hyperkind & Saint Sinner (all 1st app.) 1.00

REAL ADVENTURE COMICS (Action Adventure #2 on)
Gillmor Magazines: Apr, 1955
1 4.25 13.00 28.00

REAL ADVENTURES OF JONNY QUEST, THE
Dark Horse Comics: Sept, 1996 - No. 12, Sept, 1997 ($2.95)
1-12 3.00

REAL CLUE CRIME STORIES (Formerly Clue Comics)
Hillman Periodicals: V2#4, June, 1947 - V8#3, May, 1953
V2#4(#1)-S&K c/a(3); Dan Barry-a 40.00 120.00 320.00
5-7-S&K c/a(3-4). 7-Iron Lady app. 31.00 93.00 235.00
8-12 8.50 26.00 60.00
V3#1-8,10-12, V4#1-3,5-8,11,12 7.15 21.50 50.00
V3#9-Used in **SOTI**, pg. 102 10.00 30.00 75.00
V4#4-S&K-a 11.00 32.00 80.00
V4#9,10-Krigstein-a 8.50 26.00 60.00
V5#1-5,7,8,10,12 5.70 17.00 38.00
6,9,11-Krigstein-a 7.85 23.50 55.00
V6#1-5,8,9,11 5.35 16.00 32.00
6,7,10,12-Krigstein-a. 10-Bondage-c 7.15 21.50 50.00
V7#1-3,5-11, V8#1-3: V7#6-1 pg. Frazetta ad "Prayer" - 1st app.? 5.35 16.00 32.00
4,12-Krigstein-a 7.15 21.50 50.00
NOTE: ***Barry** a-9, 10; c-V2#8. **Briefer** a-V6#6. **Fuje** a- V2#7(2), 8, 11. **Infantino** a-V2#8; c-V2#11. **Lawrence** a-V3#8, V5#7. **Powell** a-V4#11, 12. V5#4, 5, 7 are 68 pgs.*

REAL EXPERIENCES (Formerly Tiny Tessie)
Atlas Comics (20CC): No. 25, Jan, 1950
25-Virginia Mayo photo-c from movie "Red Light" 5.70 17.00 38.00

REAL FACT COMICS
National Periodical Publications: Mar-Apr, 1946 - No. 21, July-Aug, 1949
1-S&K-c/a; Harry Houdini story; Just Imagine begins (not by Finlay); Fred Ray-a 53.00 159.00 450.00
2-S&K-a; Rin-Tin-Tin & P. T. Barnum stories 39.00 117.00 300.00
3-H.G. Wells, Lon Chaney stories; 1st DC letter column 33.00 100.00 250.00
4-Virgil Finlay-a on 'Just Imagine' begins, ends #12 (2 pgs. each); Jimmy Stewart & Jack London stories; Joe DiMaggio 1 pg. biography 39.00 117.00 300.00
5-Batman/Robin-c taken from cover of Batman #9; 5 pg. story about creation of Batman & Robin; Tom Mix story 165.00 494.00 1400.00
6-Origin & 1st app. Tommy Tomorrow by Finlay (1-2/47); Flag-c; 1st writing by Harlan Ellison (letter column, non-professional); "First Man to Reach Mars" epic-c/story 103.00 309.00 875.00
7-(No. 6 on inside)-Roussos-a; D. Fairbanks sty. 17.00 50.00 125.00
8-2nd app. Tommy Tomorrow by Finlay (5-6/47) 56.00 168.00 475.00
9-S&K-a; Glenn Miller, Indianapolis 500 stories 27.00 80.00 200.00
10-Vigilante by Meskin (based on movie serial); 4 pg. Finlay s/f story 25.00 74.00 185.00
11,12: 11-Annie Oakley, G-Men stories; Kinstler-a 14.00 42.00 105.00
13-Dale Evans and Tommy Tomorrow-c/stories 47.00 141.00 400.00
14,17,18: 14-Will Rogers story 13.00 38.00 95.00
15-Nuclear explosion part-c ("Last War on Earth" story); Clyde Beatty story 17.00 50.00 125.00
16-Tommy Tomorrow app.; 1st Planeteers? 43.00 129.00 350.00
19-Sir Arthur Conan Doyle story 15.00 44.00 110.00
20-Kubert-a, 4 pgs; Daniel Boone story 16.00 48.00 120.00
21-Kubert-a, 2 pgs; Kit Carson story 13.00 38.00 95.00

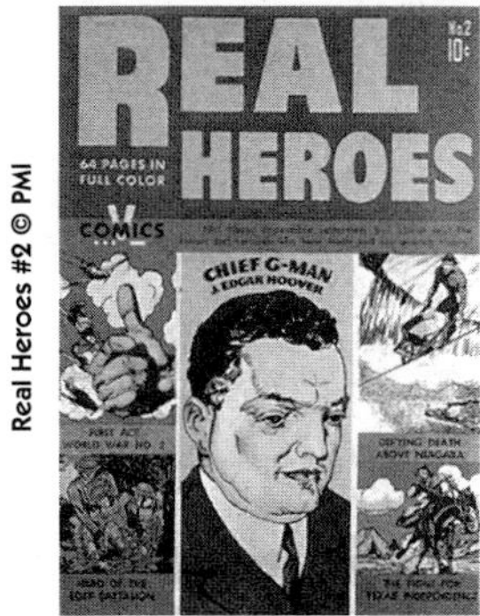

Real Heroes #2 © PMI

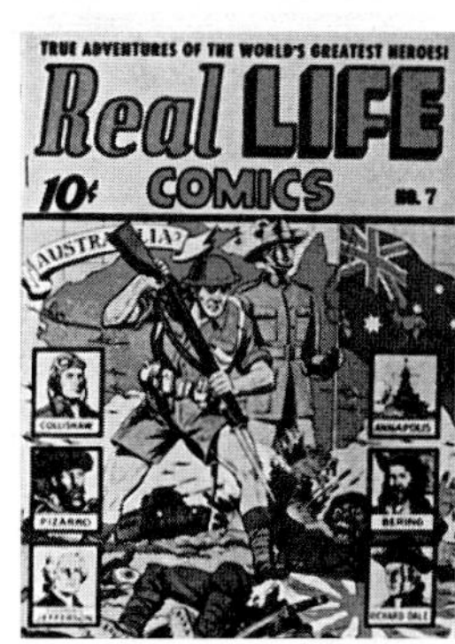

Real Life Comics #7 © STD

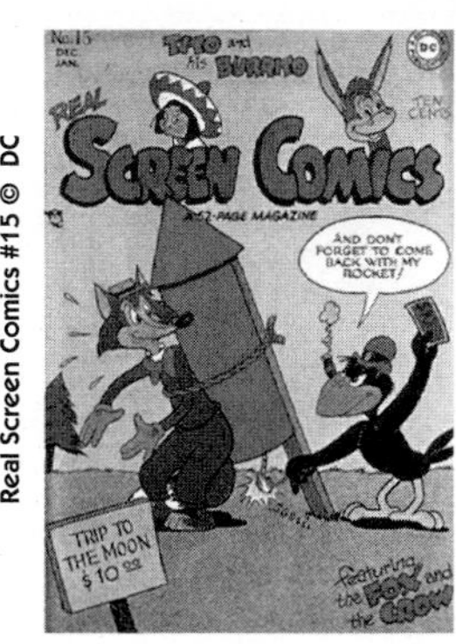

Real Screen Comics #15 © DC

	GD25	FN65	NM94

NOTE: ***Barry** c-16. **Virgil Finlay** c-6, 8. **Meskin** c-10. **Roussos** a-1-4, 6.*

REAL FUN OF DRIVING!!, THE
Chrysler Corp.: 1965, 1967 (Regular size)

	GD25	FN65	NM94
nn-Schaffenberger-a (12 pgs.)			3.00

REAL FUNNIES
Nedor Publishing Co.: Jan, 1943 - No. 3, June, 1943

	GD25	FN65	NM94
1-Funny animal, humor; Black Terrier app. (clone of The Black Terror)	28.00	84.00	210.00
2,3	13.00	40.00	100.00

REAL GHOSTBUSTERS, THE (Also see Slimer)
Now Comics: Aug, 1988 - No. 32, 1991 ($1.75/$1.95)

	GD25	FN65	NM94
1-32: 1-Based on Ghostbusters movie. 30-Begin $1.95-c			1.95

REAL HEROES COMICS
Parents' Magazine Institute: Sept, 1941 - No. 16, Oct, 1946

	GD25	FN65	NM94
1-Roosevelt-c/story	28.00	84.00	210.00
2-J. Edgar Hoover-c/story	12.00	36.00	90.00
3-5,7-10: 4-Churchill, Roosevelt stories	10.00	30.00	75.00
6-Lou Gehrig-c/story	17.00	50.00	125.00
11-16: 13-Kiefer-a	6.50	19.50	45.00

REAL HIT
Fox Features Publications: 1944 (Savings Bond premium)

	GD25	FN65	NM94
1-Blue Beetle-r	16.00	48.00	120.00

NOTE: *Two versions exist, with and without covers. The coverless version has the title, No. 1 and price printed at top of splash page.*

REALISTIC ROMANCES
Realistic Comics/Avon Periodicals: July-Aug, 1951 - No. 17, Aug-Sept, 1954 (No #9-14)

	GD25	FN65	NM94
1-Kinstler-a; c-/Avon paperback #211	18.00	54.00	135.00
2	8.50	26.00	60.00
3,4	6.85	21.00	48.00
5,8-Kinstler-a	7.15	21.50	50.00
6-c-/Diversey Prize Novels #6; Kinstler-a	8.30	25.00	58.00
7-Evans-a?; c-/Avon paperback #360	8.30	25.00	58.00
15,17: 17-Kinstler-c	6.50	19.50	45.00
16-Kinstler marijuana story-r/Romantic Love #6	8.30	25.00	58.00
I.W. Reprint #1,8,9: #1-r/Realistic Romances #4; Astarita-a. 9-r/Women To Love #1	1.10	3.30	9.00

NOTE: ***Astarita** a-2-4, 7, 8, 17. Photo c-1, 2. Painted c-3, 4.*

REAL LIFE COMICS
Nedor/Better/Standard Publ./Pictorial Magazine No. 13: Sept, 1941 - No. 59, Sept, 1952

	GD25	FN65	NM94
1-Uncle Sam-c/story; Daniel Boone story	43.00	129.00	360.00
2	20.00	60.00	150.00
3-Hitler cover	47.00	142.00	400.00
4,5: 4-Story of American flag "Old Glory"	13.00	38.00	95.00
6-10: 6-Wild Bill Hickok story	12.00	36.00	90.00
11-20: 17-Albert Einstein story	10.00	30.00	75.00
21-23,25,26,28-30: 29-A-Bomb story	8.50	26.00	60.00
24-Story of Baseball (Babe Ruth)	13.00	40.00	100.00
27-Schomburg A-Bomb-c; story of A-Bomb	13.00	40.00	100.00
31-33,35,36,42-44,48,49: 49-Baseball issue	6.50	19.50	45.00
34,37-41,45-47: 34-Jimmy Stewart story. 37-Story of motion pictures; Bing Crosby story. 38-Jane Froman story. 39- "1,000,000 A.D." story. 40-Bob Feller story. 41-Jimmie Foxx story; "Home Run" Baker story. 45-Story of Olympic games; Burl Ives & Kit Carson story. 46-Douglas Fairbanks Jr. & Sr. story. 47-George Gershwin story	8.50	26.00	60.00
50-Frazetta-a (5 pgs.)	22.00	66.00	165.00
51-Jules Verne "Journey to the Moon" by Evans	15.00	46.00	115.00
52-Frazetta-a (4 pgs.); Severin/Elder-a(2); Evans-a	24.00	72.00	180.00
53-57-Severin/Elder-a. 54-Bat Masterson-c/story	10.00	30.00	75.00
58-Severin/Elder-a(2)	11.00	32.00	80.00
59-1 pg. Frazetta; Severin/Elder-a	9.30	28.00	70.00

NOTE: *Some issues had two titles. **Guardineer** a-40(2), 44. **Meskin** a-52. **Roussos** a-50. **Schomburg** c-1, 2, 4, 5, 7, 11, 13-21, 23, 24, 26, 28, 30-32, 34-40, 42, 44-47, 55. **Tuska** a-53. Photo-c 5, 6.*

REAL LIFE SECRETS (Real Secrets #2 on)
Ace Periodicals: Sept, 1949 (one-shot)

	GD25	FN65	NM94
1-Painted-c	7.85	23.50	55.00

REAL LIFE STORY OF FESS PARKER (Magazine)
Dell Publishing Co.: 1955

	GD25	FN65	NM94
1	9.00	27.00	90.00

REAL LIFE TALES OF SUSPENSE (See Suspense)

REAL LOVE (Formerly Hap Hazard)
Ace Periodicals (A. A. Wyn): No. 25, April, 1949 - No. 76, Nov, 1956

	GD25	FN65	NM94
25	9.30	28.00	70.00
26	5.70	17.00	38.00
27-L. B. Cole-a	9.30	28.00	65.00
28-35	4.25	13.00	28.00
36-66: 66-Last pre-code (2/55)	4.00	11.00	24.00
67-76	1.75	5.25	15.00

NOTE: *Photo c-50-76. Painted c-46.*

REALM, THE
Arrow Comics/WeeBee Comics #13/Caliber Press #14 on: Feb, 1986 - No. 21, 1991 ($1.50/$1.95/$2.50, B&W)

	GD25	FN65	NM94
1-16: 4-1st app. Deadworld (9/86). 13-Begin $1.95-c			1.50
17-21: 17-Begin $2.50-c			2.50
Book 1 ($4.95, B&W)			5.00

REAL McCOYS, THE (TV)
Dell Publ. Co.: No. 1071, 1-3/60 - 5-7/1962 (All have Walter Brennan photo-c)

	GD25	FN65	NM94
Four Color 1071,1134-Toth-a in both	9.00	27.00	100.00
Four Color 1193,1265	8.00	25.00	90.00
01-689-207 (5-7/62)	7.00	22.00	80.00

REAL SCREEN COMICS (#1 titled Real Screen Funnies; TV Screen Cartoons #129-138)
National Periodical Publications: Spring, 1945 - No. 128, May-June, 1959 (#1-40: 52 pgs.)

	GD25	FN65	NM94
1-The Fox & the Crow, Flippity & Flop, Tito & His Burrito begin	94.00	282.00	800.00
2	44.00	132.00	375.00
3-5	29.00	88.00	220.00
6-10 (2-3/47)	19.00	58.00	145.00
11-20 (10-11/48): 13-The Crow x-over in Flippity & Flop	15.00	44.00	110.00
21-30 (6-7/50)	11.00	32.00	80.00
31-50	9.30	28.00	70.00
51-99	7.15	21.50	50.00
100	7.85	23.50	55.00
101-128	5.70	17.00	38.00

REAL SECRETS (Formerly Real Life Secrets)
Ace Periodicals: No. 2, Nov, 1950 - No. 5, May, 1950

	GD25	FN65	NM94
2-Painted-c	7.85	23.50	55.00
3-5: 3-Photo-c	5.35	16.00	32.00

REAL SPORTS COMICS (All Sports Comics #2 on)
Hillman Periodicals: Oct-Nov, 1948 (52 pgs.)

	GD25	FN65	NM94
1-Powell-a (12 pgs.)	35.00	104.00	260.00

REAL WAR STORIES
Eclipse Comics: July, 1987; No. 2, Jan, 1991 ($2.00, 52 pgs.)

	GD25	FN65	NM94
1-Bolland-a(p), Bissette-a, Totleben-a(i); Alan Moore scripts (2nd printing exists, 2/88)			2.00

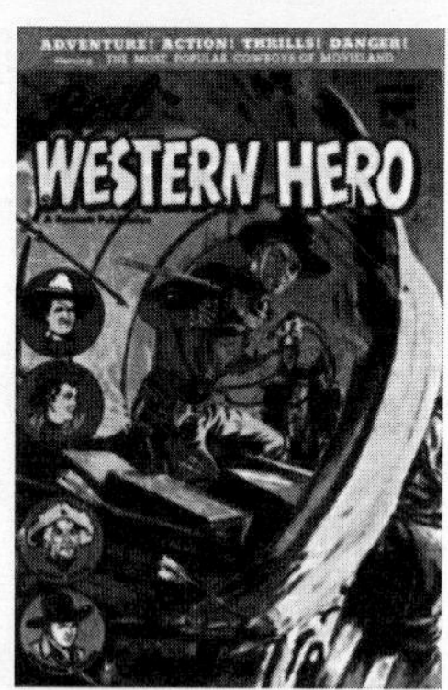

Real Western Hero #74 © FAW

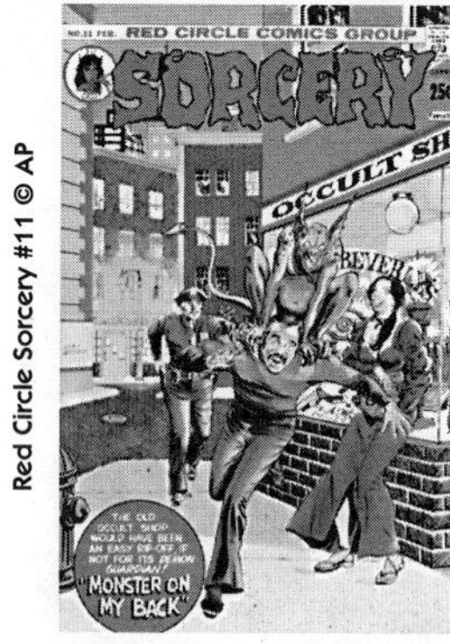

Red Circle Sorcery #11 © AP

Red Dragon Comics #5 (2nd Series) © Condé Nast

GD25 FN65 NM94

2-($4.95) 5.00

REAL WESTERN HERO (Formerly Wow #1-69; Western Hero #76 on)
Fawcett Publications: No. 70, Sept, 1948 - No. 75, Feb, 1949 (All 52 pgs.)

70(#1)-Tom Mix, Monte Hale, Hopalong Cassidy, Young Falcon begin 32.00 96.00 240.00
71-75: 71-Gabby Hayes begins. 71,72-Captain Tootsie by Beck. 75-Big Bow and Little Arrow app. 20.00 60.00 150.00
NOTE: *Painted/photo c-70-73; painted c-74, 75.*

REAL WEST ROMANCES
Crestwood Publishing Co./Prize Publ.: 4-5/49 - V1#6, 3/50; V2#1, Apr-May, 1950 (All 52 pgs. & photo-c)

V1#1-S&K-a(p) 19.00 56.00 140.00
2-Spanking panel 11.00 32.00 80.00
3-Kirby-a(p) only 11.00 32.00 80.00
4-S&K-a; Whip Wilson, Reno Browne photo-c 16.00 48.00 120.00
5-Audie Murphy, Gale Storm photo-c; S&K-a 15.00 44.00 110.00
6-Produced by S&K, no S&K-a; Robert Preston & Cathy Downs photo-c 11.00 32.00 80.00
V2#1-Kirby-a(p) 9.30 28.00 65.00
NOTE: ***Meskin** a-V1#5, 6. **Severin/Elder** a-V1#3-6, V2#1. **Meskin** a-V1#6. **Leonard Starr** a-1-3. Photo-c V1#1-6, V2#1.*

RE-ANIMATOR IN FULL COLOR
Adventure Comics: Oct, 1991 - No. 3, 1992 ($2.95, mini-series)

1-3: Adapts horror movie. 1-Dorman painted-c 3.00

REAP THE WILD WIND (See Cinema Comics Herald)

REBEL, THE (TV)
Dell Publishing Co.: No. 1076, Feb-Apr, 1960 - No. 1262, Dec-Feb, 1961-62

Four Color 1076 (#1)-Sekowsky-a, photo-c 10.00 30.00 110.00
Four Color 1138 (9-11/60), 1207 (9-11/61), 1262-Photo-c 8.00 25.00 90.00

R.E.B.E.L.S. '94 (Becomes R.E.B.E.L.S. '95 & R.E.B.E.L.S. '96)
DC Comics: No. 0, Oct, 1994 - No. 17, Mar, 1996 ($1.95/$2.25)

0-7 2.00
8-17: 8-$2.25-c begins. 15-R.E.B.E.L.S '96 begins. 2.25

REBEL SWORD (Manga)
Dark Horse Comics: Oct, 1994 - No. 6, Feb, 1995 ($2.50, B&W)

1-6 2.50

RECORD BOOK OF FAMOUS POLICE CASES
St. John Publishing Co.: 1949 (25¢, 132 pgs.)

nn-Kubert-a(3); r/Son of Sinbad; Baker-c 33.00 100.00 250.00

RED ARROW
P. L. Publishing Co.: May-June, 1951 - No. 3, Oct, 1951

1 8.50 26.00 60.00
2,3 6.50 19.50 45.00

RED BALL COMIC BOOK
Parents' Magazine Institute: 1947 (Red Ball Shoes giveaway)

nn-Reprints from True Comics 2.40 6.00 12.00

RED BAND COMICS
Enwil Associates: Feb, 1945 - No. 4, May, 1945

1 31.00 92.00 230.00
2-Origin Bogeyman & Santanas; c-reprint/#1 25.00 74.00 185.00
3,4-Captain Wizard app. in both (1st app.); each has identical contents/cover 22.00 66.00 165.00

REDBLADE
Dark Horse Comics: Apr, 1993 - No. 3, July, 1993 ($2.50, mini-series)

1-3: 1-Double gatefold-c 2.50

RED CIRCLE COMICS
Rural Home Publications (Enwil): Jan, 1945 - No. 4, April, 1945

1-The Prankster & Red Riot begin 29.00 88.00 220.00
2-Starr-a; The Judge (costumed hero) app. 23.00 70.00 175.00
3,4-Starr-c/a. 3-The Prankster not in costume 18.00 54.00 135.00
4-(Dated 4/45)-Leftover covers to #4 were later restapled over early 1950s coverless comics; variations in the coverless comics used are endless; Woman Outlaws, Dorothy Lamour, Crime Does Not Pay, Sabu, Diary Loves, Love Confessions & Young Love V3#3 known 11.00 32.00 80.00

RED CIRCLE SORCERY (Chilling Adventures in Sorcery #1-5)
Red Circle Prod. (Archie): No. 6, Apr, 1974 - No. 11, Feb, 1975 (All 25¢ iss.)

6-9,11: 8-Only app. The Cobra 5.00
10-Wood-a(i) .85 2.60 7.00
NOTE: ***Chaykin** a-6, 10. **B. Jones** a-7(w/**Wrightson, Kaluta, J. Jones**). **McWilliams** a-10(2 & 3 pgs.). **Mooney** a-11p. **Morrow** a-6-8, 9(text illos), 10, 11i; c-6-11. **Thorne** a-8, 10. **Toth** a-8, 9.*

RED DOG (See Night Music #7)

RED DRAGON
Comico: June, 1996 ($2.95)

1-Bisley-c 3.00

RED DRAGON COMICS (1st Series) (Formerly Trail Blazers; see Super Magician V5#7, 8)
Street & Smith Publications: No. 5, Jan, 1943 - No. 9, Jan, 1944

5-Origin Red Rover, the Crimson Crimebuster; Rex King, Man of Adventure, Captain Jack Commando, & The Minute Man begin; text origin Red Dragon; Binder-c 88.00 264.00 750.00
6-Origin The Black Crusader & Red Dragon (3/43); 1st story app. Red Dragon & 1st cover (classic-c) 171.00 513.00 1450.00
7-Classic-c 115.00 345.00 975.00
8-The Red Knight app. 62.00 186.00 525.00
9-Origin Chuck Magnon, Immortal Man 62.00 186.00 525.00

RED DRAGON COMICS (2nd Series)(See Super Magician V2#8)
Street & Smith Publications: Nov, 1947 - No. 6, Jan, 1949; No. 7, July, 1949

1-Red Dragon begins; Elliman, Nigel app.; Edd Cartier-c/a 79.00 237.00 675.00
2-Cartier-c 58.00 174.00 490.00
3-1st app. Dr. Neff Ghost Breaker by Powell; Elliman, Nigel app. 49.00 147.00 415.00
4-Cartier c/a 64.00 192.00 540.00
5-7 39.00 117.00 290.00
NOTE: ***Maneely** a-5, 7. **Powell** a-2-7; c-3, 5, 7.*

REDDY GOOSE
International Shoe Co. (Western Printing): No #, 1958?; No. 2, Jan, 1959 - No. 16, July, 1962 (Giveaway)

nn (#1) 4.00 12.00 40.00
2-16 2.50 7.50 21.00

REDDY KILOWATT (5¢) (Also see Story of Edison)
Educational Comics (E. C.): 1946 - No. 2, 1947; 1956 - 1960 (no month) (16 pgs., paper-c)

nn-Reddy Made Magic (1946, 5¢) 9.30 28.00 70.00
nn-Reddy Made Magic (1958) 5.35 16.00 32.00
2-Edison, the Man Who Changed the World (3/4" smaller than #1) (1947, 5¢) 9.30 28.00 70.00
...Comic Book 2 (1954)- "Light's Diamond Jubilee" 6.50 19.50 40.00
...Comic Book 2 (1958, 16 pgs.)- "Wizard of Light" 5.35 16.00 32.00
...Comic Book 3 (1956, 8 pgs.)- "The Space Kite"; Orlando story; regular size 5.35 16.00 32.00
...Comic Book 3 (1960, 8 pgs.)- "The Space Kite"; Orlando story; regular size 4.25 13.00 28.00
NOTE: *Several copies surfaced in 1979.*

REDDY MADE MAGIC
Educational Comics (E. C.): 1956, 1958 (16 pgs., paper-c)

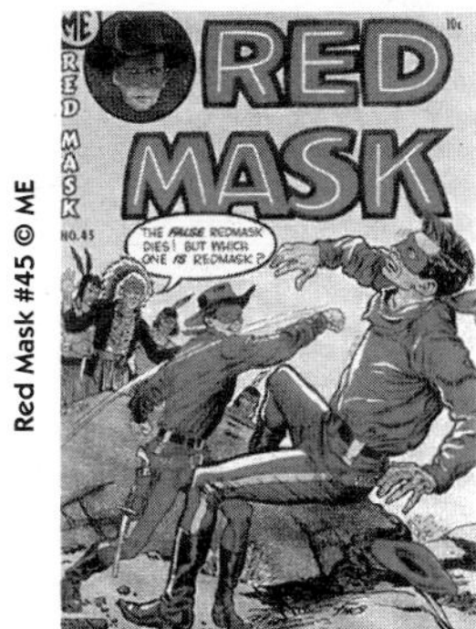

Red Mask #45 © ME

"Red" Rabbit Comics #7 © Dearfield Pub.

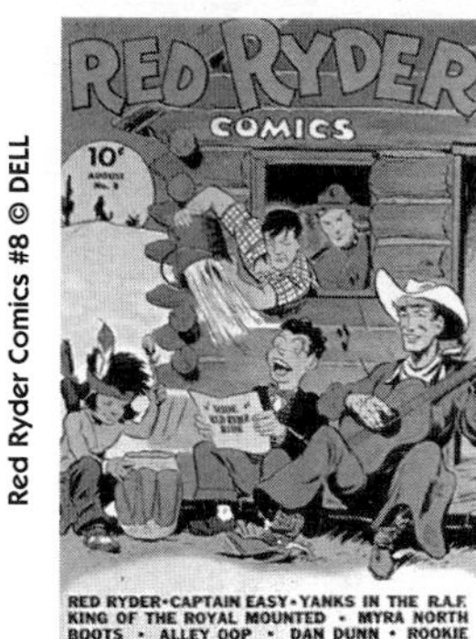

Red Ryder Comics #8 © DELL

GD25 FN65 NM94

1-Reddy Kilowatt-r (splash panel changed) 6.85 21.00 48.00
1 (1958 edition) 5.00 15.00 30.00

RED EAGLE
David McKay Publications: No. 16, Aug, 1938

Feature Books 16 16.00 46.00 170.00

REDEYE (See Comics Reading Libraries)

RED FOX (Formerly Manhunt! #1-14; also see Extra Comics)
Magazine Enterprises: No. 15, 1954

15(A-1 #108)-Undercover Girl story; L.B. Cole-c/a (Red Fox); r-from Manhunt; Powell-a 16.00 48.00 120.00

RED FURY
High Impact Entertainment: 1997 ($2.95, B&W)

1 2.95

RED GOOSE COMIC SELECTIONS (See Comic Selections)

RED HAWK (See A-1 Comics, Bobby Benson's ..#14-16 & Straight Arrow #2)
Magazine Enterprises: No. 90, 1953

A-1 90-Powell-c/a 10.00 30.00 75.00

RED ICEBERG, THE
Impact Publ. (Catechetical Guild): 1960 (10¢, 16 pgs., Communist propaganda)

nn-(Rare)- 'We The People' back-c 27.00 81.00 270.00
2nd version- 'Impact Press' back-c 30.00 90.00 300.00
3rd version-"Explains comic" back-c 30.00 90.00 300.00
NOTE: *This book was the Guild's last anti-communist propaganda book and had very limited circulation. 3 - 4 copies surfaced in 1979 from the defunct publisher's files. Other copies do turn up.*

RED MASK (Formerly Tim Holt; see Best Comics, Blazing Six-Guns)
Magazine Enterprises No. 42-53/Sussex No. 54 (M.E. on-c): No. 42, June-July, 1954 - No. 53, May, 1956; No. 54, Sept, 1957

42-Ghost Rider by Ayers continues, ends #50; Black Phantom continues; 3-D effect c/stories begin 19.00 56.00 140.00
43-3-D effect-c/stories 17.00 50.00 125.00
44-50: 3-D effect stories only. 47-Last pre-code issue. 50-Last Ghost Rider 15.00 46.00 115.00
51-The Presto Kid begins by Ayers (1st app.); Presto Kid-c begins, ends #54; last 3-D effect story 15.00 46.00 115.00
52-Origin The Presto Kid 15.00 46.00 115.00
53,54-Last Black Phantom 11.00 34.00 85.00
I.W. Reprint #1 (r-/#52). 2 (nd, r/#51 w/diff.-c). 3, 8 (nd; Kinstler-c); 8-r/Red Mask #52 2.50 7.50 20.00
NOTE: ***Ayers** art on Ghost Rider & Presto Kid. **Bolle** art in all (Red Mask); c-43, 44, 49. **Guardineer** a-52. Black Phantom in #42-44, 47-50, 53, 54.*

REDMASK OF THE RIO GRANDE
AC Comics: 1990 ($2.50, 28pgs.)(Has photos of movie posters)

1-Bolle-c/a(r); photo inside-c 2.50

RED MOUNTAIN FEATURING QUANTRELL'S RAIDERS (Movie)(Also see Jesse James #28)
Avon Periodicals: 1952

nn-Alan Ladd; Kinstler-c 24.00 72.00 180.00

"RED" RABBIT COMICS
Dearfield Comic/J. Charles Laue Publ. Co.: Jan, 1947 - No. 22, Aug-Sep, 1951

1 10.00 30.00 75.00
2 5.70 17.00 40.00
3-10 5.00 15.00 30.00
11-17,19-22 4.15 12.50 25.00
18-Flying Saucer-c (1/51) 5.70 17.00 38.00

RED RAVEN COMICS (Human Torch #2 on)(Also see X-Men #44 & Sub-Mariner #26, 2nd series)
Timely Comics: August, 1940 GD25 FN65 VF82 NM94

1-Origin & 1st app. Red Raven; Comet Pierce & Mercury by Kirby, The Human Top & The Eternal Brain; intro. Magar, the Mystic & only app.; Kirby-c (his 1st signed work) 1000.00 3000.00 6000.00 10,000.00

RED ROCKET 7
Dark Horse Comics: Aug, 1997 - No. 7, June, 1998 ($3.95, square format, limited series)

1-7-Mike Allred-c/s/a 4.00

RED RYDER COMICS (Hi Spot #2)(Movies, radio)(See Crackajack Funnies)
Hawley Publ. No. 1/Dell Publishing Co.(K.K.) No. 3 on: 9/40; No. 3, 8/41 - No. 5, 12/41; No. 6, 4/42 - No. 151, 4-6/57

GD25 FN65 NM94

1-Red Ryder, his horse Thunder, Little Beaver & his horse Papoose strip reprints begin by Fred Harman; 1st meeting of Red & Little Beaver; Harman line-drawn-c #1-85 250.00 750.00 2500.00
3-(Scarce)-Alley Oop, King of the Royal Mtd., Capt. Easy, Freckles & His Friends, Myra North, Dan Dunn strip-r begin 84.00 252.00 925.00
4-6: 6-1st Dell issue (4/42) 40.00 120.00 440.00
7-10 33.00 98.00 360.00
11-20 23.00 68.00 250.00
21-32-Last Alley Oop, Dan Dunn, Capt. Easy, Freckles 14.00 44.00 160.00
33-40 (52 pgs.) 9.00 27.00 100.00
41 (52 pgs.)-Rocky Lane photo back-c; photo back-c begin, end #57 9.00 29.00 105.00
42-46 (52 pgs.): 46-Last Red Ryder strip-r 8.00 23.00 85.00
47-53 (52 pgs.): 47-New stories on Red Ryder begin. 49,52-Harmon photo back-c 6.40 19.00 70.00
54-57 (36 pgs.) 5.00 15.00 54.00
58-73 (36 pgs.): 59-Harmon photo back-c. 73-Last King of the Royal Mtd; strip-r by Jim Gary 5.00 15.00 54.00
74-85,93 (52 pgs.)-Harman line-drawn-c 5.00 15.00 54.00
86-92 (52 pgs.)-Harman painted-c 5.00 15.00 54.00
94-96 (36 pgs.)-Harman painted-c 3.60 11.00 40.00
97,98,107,108 (36 pgs.)-Harman line-drawn-c 3.60 11.00 40.00
99,101-106 (36 pgs.)-Jim Bannon Photo-c 3.60 11.00 40.00
100 (36 pgs.)-Bannon photo-c 4.00 12.00 45.00
109-118 (52 pgs.)-Harman line-drawn-c 3.20 9.50 35.00
119-129 (52 pgs.): 119-Painted-c begin, not by Harman, end #151 2.90 8.70 32.00
130-144 (#130 on have 36 pgs.) 2.70 8.00 30.00
145-148: 145-Title change to Red Ryder Ranch Magazine with photos 2.40 7.00 26.00
149-151: 149-Title changed to Red Ryder Ranch Comics 2.40 7.00 26.00
Four Color 916 (7/58) 2.75 8.00 30.00
Buster Brown Shoes Giveaway (1941, color, soft-c, 32 pgs.) 25.00 74.00 185.00
Red Ryder Super Book Of Comics 10 (1944; paper-c; 32 pgs.; blank back-c)-Magic Morro app. 25.00 74.00 185.00
Red Ryder Victory Patrol-nn(1943, 32 pgs.)(Langendorf bread; includes cutout "Rodeomatic" decoder, order coupon for "Magic V-Badge", cut-out membership card and membership certificate comic book) 425.00 1275.00 3600.00
Red Ryder Victory Patrol-nn(1944, 32 pgs.)-r-/#43,44; comic has a paper-c & is stapled inside a triple cardboard fold-out-c; contains membership card, decoder, map of R.R. home range, etc. Herky app. (Langendorf Bread give-away; sub-titled 'Super Book of Comics')(Rare) 378.00 1133.00 3400.00
Wells Lamont Corp. giveaway (1950)-16 pgs. in color; regular size; paper-c; 1941-r 23.00 68.00 170.00
NOTE: ***Fred Harman** a-1-99; c-1-98, 107-118. Don Red Barry, Allan Rocky Lane, Wild Bill Elliott & Jim Bannon starred as Red Ryder in the movies. Robert Blake starred as Little Beaver.*

RED RYDER PAINT BOOK
Whitman Publishing Co.: 1941 (8-1/2x11-1/2", 148 pgs.)

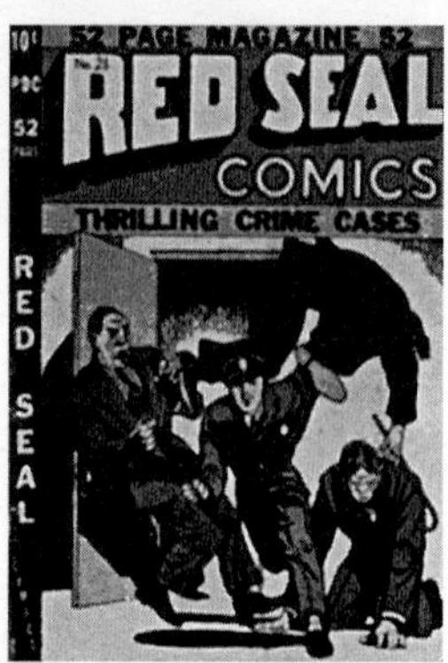

Red Seal Comics #21 © SUPR

Re-Gex #1 © Awesome-Hyperwerks

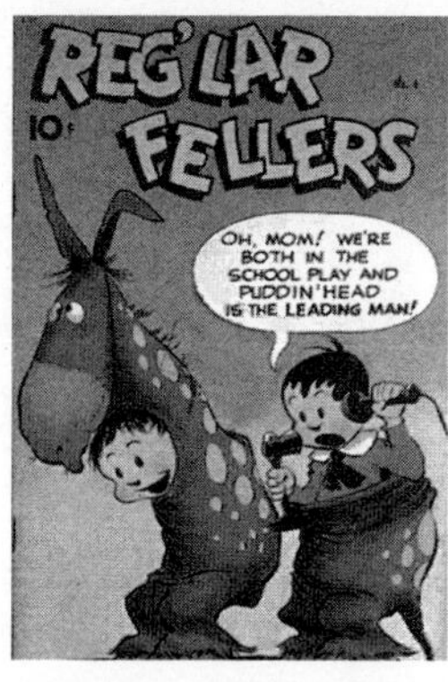

Reg'lar Fellers #6 © STD

GD25 FN65 NM94

nn-Reprints 1940 daily strips 65.00 194.00 550.00

RED SEAL COMICS (Formerly Carnival Comics, and/or Spotlight Comics?)
Harry 'A' Chesler/Superior Publ. No. 19 on: No. 14, 10/45 - No. 18, 10/46; No. 19, 6/47 - No. 22, 12/47

14-The Black Dwarf begins (continued from Spotlight?); Little Nemo app; bondage/hypo-c; Tuska-a 62.00 186.00 525.00
15-Torture story; funny-c 42.00 127.00 340.00
16-Used in **SOTI**, pg. 181, illo "Outside the forbidden pages of de Sade, you find draining a girl's blood only in children's comics;" drug club story r-later in Crime Reporter #1; Veiled Avenger & Barry Kuda app; Tuska-a; funny-c 53.00 159.00 450.00
17-Lady Satan, Yankee Girl & Sky Chief app; Tuska-a 42.00 127.00 340.00
18,20-Lady Satan & Sky Chief app. 42.00 127.00 340.00
19-No Black Dwarf (on-c only); Zor, El Tigre app. 37.00 112.00 280.00
21-Lady Satan & Black Dwarf app. 29.00 87.00 220.00
22-Zor, Rocketman app. (68 pgs.) 29.00 87.00 220.00

REDSKIN (Thrilling Indian Stories)(Famous Western Badmen #13 on)
Youthful Magazines: Sept, 1950 - No. 12, Oct, 1952

1-Walter Johnson-a (7 pgs.) 12.00 36.00 90.00
2 9.00 27.00 60.00
3-12: 3-Daniel Boone story. 6-Geronimo story 7.50 22.50 50.00
NOTE: ***Walter Johnson** c-3, 4. **Palais** a-11. **Wildey** a-5, 11. Bondage c-6, 12.*

RED SONJA (Also see Conan #23, Kull & The Barbarians, Marvel Feature & Savage Sword Of Conan #1)
Marvel Comics Group: 1/77 - No. 15, 5/79; V1#1, 2/83 - V2#2, 3/83; V3#1, 8/83 - V3#4, 2/84; V3#5, 1/85 - V3#13, 5/86

1-Created by Robert E. Howard 2.00 6.00
2-10: 5-Last 30¢ issue 4.00
11-15, V1#1,V2#2: 14-Last 35¢ issue 3.00
V3#1-4 ($1.00, 52 pgs.) 2.00
5-13 (65-75¢) 1.50
NOTE: ***Brunner** c-12-14. **J. Buscema** a(p)-12, 13, 15; c-V#1. **Nebres** a-V3#3i(part). **N. Redondo** a-8i, V3#2i, 3i. **Simonson** a-V3#1. **Thorne** c/a-1-11.*

RED SONJA: SCAVENGER HUNT
Marvel Comics: Dec, 1995 ($2.95, one-shot)

1 3.00

RED SONJA: THE MOVIE
Marvel Comics Group: Nov, 1985 - No. 2, Dec, 1985 (Limited series)

1,2-Movie adapt-r/Marvel Super Spec. #38 .80

RED TORNADO (See All-American #20 & Justice League of America #64)
DC Comics: July, 1985 - No. 4, Oct, 1985 (Limited series)

1-4: Kurt Busiek scripts in all. 1-3-Superman cameos. 1,3-Batman cameos 1.00

RED WARRIOR
Marvel/Atlas Comics (TCI): Jan, 1951 - No. 6, Dec, 1951

1-Red Warrior & his horse White Wing; Tuska-a 13.00 39.00 105.00
2-Tuska-c 8.50 26.00 60.00
3-6: 4-Origin White Wing. 6-Maneely-c 7.15 21.50 50.00

RED WOLF (See Avengers #80 & Marvel Spotlight #1)
Marvel Comics Group: May, 1972 - No. 9, Sept, 1973

1-(Western hero); Gil Kane/Severin-c; Shores-a 1.40 4.20 14.00
2-9: 2-Kane-c; Shores-a. 6-Tuska-r in back-up. 7-Red Wolf as super hero begins. 9-Origin sidekick, Lobo (wolf) .90 2.70 8.00

REESE'S PIECES
Eclipse Comics: Oct, 1985 - No.2, Oct, 1985 ($1.75, Baxter paper)

1,2-B&W-r in color 1.80

REFORM SCHOOL GIRL!
Realistic Comics: 1951

GD25 FN65 NM94

nn-Used in **SOTI**, pg. 358, & cover ill. with caption "Comic books are supposed to be like fairy tales" 115.00 345.00 975.00
(Prices vary widely on this book)
NOTE: *The cover and title originated from a digest-sized book published by Diversey Publishing Co. of Chicago in 1948. The original book "House of Fury", Doubleday, came out in 1941. The girl's real name which appears on the cover of the digest and comic is Marty Collins, Canadian model and ice skating star who posed for this special color photograph for the Diversey novel.*

REGENTS ILLUSTRATED CLASSICS
Prentice Hall Regents, Englewood Cliffs, NJ 07632: 1981 (Plus more recent reprintings) (48 pgs., B&W-a with 14 pgs. of teaching helps)

NOTE: *This series contains Classics Ill. art, and was produced from the same illegal source as **Cassette Books.** But when Twin Circle sued to stop the sale of the Cassette Books, they decided to permit this series to continue. This series was produced as a teaching aid. The 20 title series is divided into four levels based upon number of basic words used therein. There is also a teacher's manual for each level. All of the titles are still available from the publisher for about $5 each retail. The number to call for mail order purchases is (201)767-5937. Almost all of the issues have new covers taken from some interior art panel. Here is a list of the series by Regents ident. no. and the Classics Ill. counterpart.*

16770(CI#24-A2)18333(CI#3-A2)21668(CI#13-A2)32224(CI#21)33051(CI#26)
35788(CI#84)37153(CI#16)44460(CI#19-A2)44808(CI#18-A2)52395(CI#4-A2)
58627(CI#5-A2)60067(CI#30)68405(CI#23-A1)70302(CI#29)78192(CI#7-A2)
78193(CI#10-A2)79679(CI#85)92046(CI#1-A2)93062(CI#64)93512(CI#25)

RE: GEX
Awesome-Hyperwerks: Sept, 1998 - Present ($2.50)

Preview (7/98) Wizard Con Edition 3.00
1-Loeb-s/Liefeld-a/c 2.50

REGGIE (Formerly Archie's Rival...; Reggie & Me #19 on)
Archie Publications: No. 15, Sept, 1963 - No. 18, Nov, 1965

15(9/63), 16(10/64), 17(8/65), 18(11/65) 4.00 12.00 40.00
NOTE: *Cover title No. 15 & 16 is Archie's Rival Reggie.*

REGGIE AND ME (Formerly Reggie)
Archie Publ.: No. 19, Aug, 1966 - No. 126, Sept, 1980 (No. 50-68: 52 pgs.)

19-Evilheart app. 2.60 7.80 26.00
20-23-Evilheart app.; with Pureheart #22 2.25 6.75 18.00
24-40(3/70) 1.00 3.00 10.00
41-49(7/71) .90 2.70 8.00
50(9/71)-68 (1/74, 52 pgs.) 1.20 3.60 12.00
69-99 5.00
100(10/77) .90 2.70 8.00
101-126 4.00

REGGIE'S JOKES (See Reggie's Wise Guy Jokes)

REGGIE'S REVENGE!
Archie Comic Publications, Inc.: Spring, 1994 - No. 3 ($2.00, 52 pgs.) (Published semi-annually)

1-Bound-in pull-out poster 3.00
2,3 2.00

REGGIE'S WISE GUY JOKES
Archie Publications: Aug, 1968 - No. 60, Jan, 1982 (#5-28 are Giants)

1 3.60 10.80 36.00
2-4 1.75 5.25 14.00
5-16 (1/71)(68 pg. Giants) 2.00 6.00 20.00
17-28 (52 pg. Giants) 1.40 4.20 14.00
29-40(1/77) 2.00 6.00
41-60 4.00

REGISTERED NURSE
Charlton Comics: Summer, 1963

1-r/Nurse Betsy Crane & Cynthia Doyle 2.00 6.00 16.00

REG'LAR FELLERS
Visual Editions (Standard): No. 5, Nov, 1947 - No. 6, Mar, 1948

5,6 6.85 21.00 48.00

REG'LAR FELLERS HEROIC (See Heroic Comics)

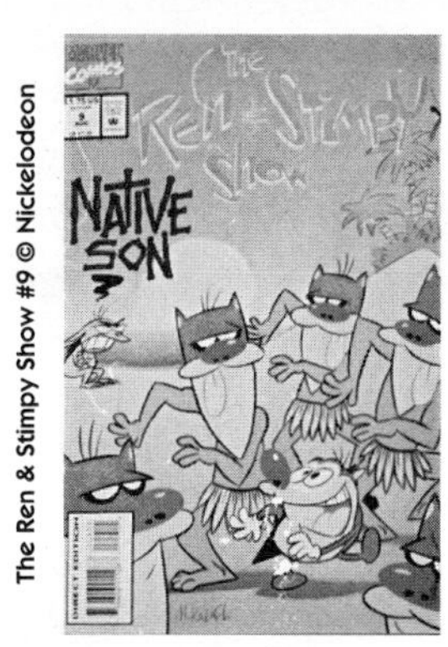

The Ren & Stimpy Show #9 © Nickelodeon

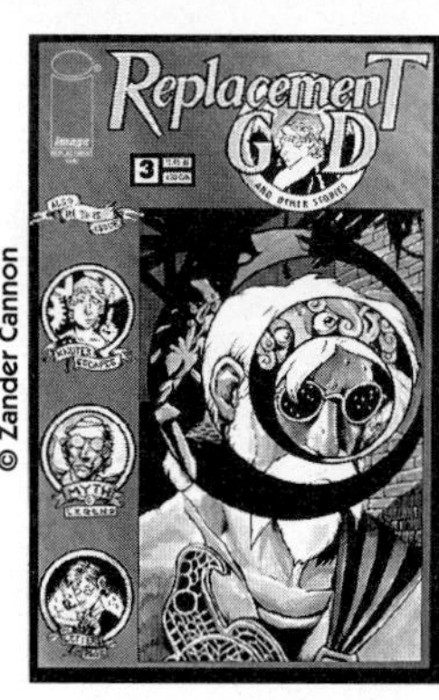

Replacement God #3 (2nd Series) © Zander Cannon

Resurrection Man #17 © DC

REGULATORS
Image Comics: June, 1995 - No. 3, Aug, 1995 ($2.50)

1-3: Kurt Busiek scripts 2.50

REID FLEMING, WORLD'S TOUGHEST MILKMAN
Eclipse Comics/ Deep Sea Comics: 8/86; V2#1, 12/86 - V2#3, 12/88; V2#4, 11/89; V2#5, 11/90 (B&W)

1 (3rd print, large size, 8/86, $2.50) 2.50
1-4th & 5th printings ($2.50) 2.50
V2#1 (10/86, regular size, $2.00) 2.00
1-2nd print, 3rd print ($2.00, 2/89) 2.00
2-8 , V2#2-2nd & 3rd printings, V2#4-2nd printing, V2#5 ($2.00) 2.00

RELUCTANT DRAGON, THE (Walt Disney's...)
Dell Publishing Co.: No. 13, 1940

Four Color 13-Contains 2 pgs. of photos from film; 2 pg. foreword to Fantasia by Leopold Stokowski; Donald Duck, Goofy, Baby Weems & Mickey Mouse (as the Sorcerer's Apprentice) app. 147.00 443.00 1625.00

REMEMBER PEARL HARBOR
Street & Smith Publications: 1942 (68 pgs.) (Illustrated story of the battle)

nn-Uncle Sam-c; Jack Binder-a 41.00 124.00 330.00

REN & STIMPY SHOW, THE (TV) (Nicklodeon cartoon characters)
Marvel Comics: Dec, 1992 - No. 44, July, 1996 ($1.75/$1.95)

1-($2.25)-Polybagged w/scratch & sniff Ren or Stimpy air fowler (equal amounts of each were made) 3.00
1-2nd printing; different dialogue on-c 2.00
1-3rd printing; yet different dialogue on-c 2.00
2,3 2.00
4-6: 4-Muddy Mudskipper back-up. 5-Bill Wray painted-c. 6-Spider-Man vs. Powdered Toast Man 2.00
7-17: 12-1st solo back-up story w/Tank & Brenner 1.75
18-44: 18-Begin $1.95-c; Powered Toast Man app. 2.00
25($2.95) Deluxe edition w/die cut cover 3.00
...Don't Try This at Home (3/94, $12.95, TPB)-r/#9-12 13.00
...Eenteractive Special ('95, $2.95) 3.00
...Holiday Special 1994 (2/95, $2.95, 52 pgs.) 3.00
...Pick of the Litter nn (1993, $12.95, TPB)-r/#1-4 13.00
...Radio Daze (11/95, $1.95) 2.00
...Running Joke nn (1993, $12.95, TPB)-r/#1-4 plus new-a 13.00
...Seeck Little Monkeys (1/95, $12.95)-r/#17-20 13.00
...Special 2 (7/94, $2.95, 52 pgs.) 3.00
...Special 3 (10/94, $2.95, 52 pgs.)-Choose adventure 3.00
...Special: Around the World in a Daze ($2.95) 3.00
...Special: Four Swerks (1/95, $2.95, 52 pgs.)-FF #1 cover swipe; cover reads "Four Swerks w/5 pg. coloring book." 3.00
...Special: Powdered Toast Man 1 (4/94, $2.95, 52 pgs.) 3.00
...Special: Powdered Toast Man's Cereal Serial (4/95, $2.95) 3.00
...Special: Sports (10/95, $2.95) 3.00
...Tastes Like Chicken nn (11/93,$12.95,TPB)-r/#5-8 13.00
...Your Pals (1994, $12.95, TPB)-r/#13-16 13.00

RENFIELD
Caliber Press: 1994 - No. 3, 1995 ($2.95, B&W, limited series)

1-3 3.00

RENO BROWNE, HOLLYWOOD'S GREATEST COWGIRL (Formerly Margie Comics; Apache Kid #53 on; also see Western Hearts, Western Life Romances & Western Love)
Marvel Comics (MPC): No. 50, April, 1950 - No. 52, Sept, 1950 (52 pgs.)

50-Reno Browne photo-c on all 29.00 88.00 220.00
51,52 24.00 73.00 180.00

REPLACEMENT GOD
Amaze Ink: June, 1995 - No. 8 ($2.95, B&W)

1-8-Zander Cannon-s/a 3.00

REPLACEMENT GOD
Image Comics: May, 1997 - Present ($2.95, B&W)

1-Flip book w/"Knute's Escapes", r/original series 2.95
2-Flip book w/"Harris Thermidor" 2.95
3-5: 3-Flip book w/"Myth and Legend" 2.95

REPTILICUS (Becomes Reptisaurus #3 on)
Charlton Comics: Aug, 1961 - No. 2, Oct, 1961

1 (Movie) 11.50 34.00 115.00
2 7.00 21.00 70.00

REPTISAURUS (Reptilicus #1,2)
Charlton Comics: V2#3, Jan, 1962 - No. 8, Dec, 1962; Summer, 1963

V2#3-8: 8-Montes/Bache-c/a 4.50 13.50 45.00
Special Edition 1 (Summer, 1963) 4.00 12.00 40.00

REQUIEM FOR DRACULA
Marvel Comics: Feb, 1993 ($2.00, 52 pgs.)

nn-r/Tomb of Dracula #69,70 by Gene Colan 2.00

RESCUERS, THE (See Walt Disney Showcase #40)

RESTAURANT AT THE END OF THE UNIVERSE, THE (See Hitchhiker's Guide to the Galaxy & Life, the Universe & Everything)
DC Comics: 1994 - No. 3, 1994 ($6.95, limited series)

1-3 .85 2.60 7.00

RESTLESS GUN (TV)
Dell Publishing Co.: No. 934, Sept, 1958 - No. 1146, Nov-Jan, 1960-61

Four Color 934 (#1)-Photo-c 11.00 33.00 120.00
Four Color 986 (5/59), 1045 (11-1/60), 1089 (3/60), 1146-Wildey-a; all photo-c 8.00 23.00 85.00

RESURRECTION MAN
DC Comics: May, 1997 - Present ($2.50)

1-Lenticular disc on cover .90 2.70 8.00
2-JLA app. 1.00 3.75 10.00
3-5 2.00 6.00
6-10: 6-Genesis-x-over. 7-Batman app. 10-Hitman-c/app. 5.00
11-17: 16,17-Supergirl x-over 3.00
18-21: 18-Deadman & Phantom Stranger-c/app. 21-JLA-c/app 2.50
#1,000,000 (11/98) 853rd Century x-over 2.50

RETIEF (Keith Laumer's)
Adventure Comics (Malibu): Dec, 1989 - Vol. 2, No.6, ($2.25, B&W)

1-6 2.25
Vol. 2, #1-6 2.25
Vol. 3 (...of The CDT) #1-6 2.50
...and The Warlords #1-6 2.50
...of The CDT #1-6 2.50
...: Diplomatic Immunity #1 (4/91) 2.50
...: Giant Killer #1 (9/91) 2.50
...: Crime & Punishment #1 (11/91) 2.50

RETURN FROM WITCH MOUNTAIN (See Walt Disney Showcase #44)

RETURN OF GORGO, THE (Formerly Gorgo's Revenge)
Charlton Comics: No. 2, Aug, 1963; No. 3, Fall, 1964 (12¢)

2,3-Ditko-c/a; based on M.G.M. movie 6.00 18.00 60.00

RETURN OF KONGA, THE (Konga's Revenge #2 on)
Charlton Comics: 1962

nn 5.50 16.50 55.00

RETURN OF MEGATON MAN
Kitchen Sink Press: July, 1988 - No. 3, 1988 ($2.00, limited series)

1-3: Simpson-c/a 2.00

RETURN OF THE OUTLAW

Rex Allen Comics #2 © DELL

Ribit! #1 © Comico

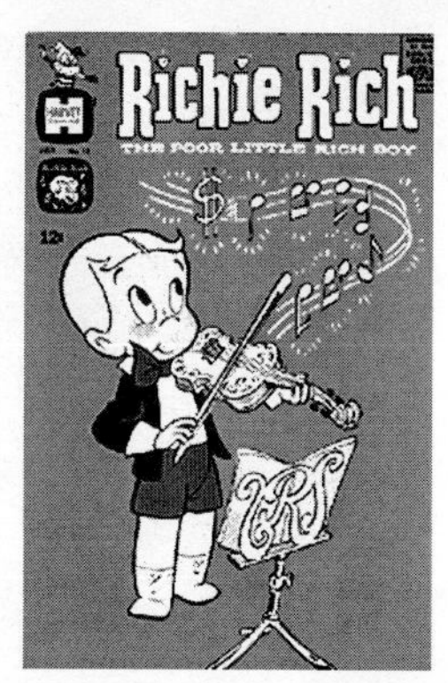

Richie Rich #18 © HARV

GD25 FN65 NM94

Toby Press (Minoan): Feb, 1953 - No. 11, 1955

1-Billy the Kid 7.85 23.50 55.00
2 5.00 15.00 30.00
3-11 4.00 12.00 24.00

RETURN TO JURASSIC PARK
Topps Comics: Apr, 1995 - No. 9, Feb, 1996 ($2.50/$2.95)

1,2 2.50
3-9: 3-Begin $2.95-c. 9-Artist's Jam issue 3.00

RETURN TO THE AMALGAM AGE OF COMICS: THE MARVEL COMICS COLLECTION
Marvel Comics: 1997 ($12.95, TPB)

nn-Reprints Amalgam one-shots: Challengers of the Fantastic #1, The Exciting X-Patrol #1, Iron Lantern# 1, The Magnetic Men Featuring Magneto #1, Spider-Boy Team-Up #1 & Thorion of the New Asgods #1 12.95

REVEALING LOVE STORIES (See Fox Giants)

REVEALING ROMANCES
Ace Magazines: Sept, 1949 - No. 6, Aug, 1950

1 7.85 23.50 55.00
2 4.25 13.00 28.00
3-6 4.00 11.00 22.00

REVENGE OF THE PROWLER (Also see The Prowler)
Eclipse Comics: Feb, 1988 - No. 4, June, 1988 ($1.75/$1.95)

1,3,4: 1-$1.75. 3,4-$1.95-c; Snyder III-a(p) 2.00
2 ($2.50)-Contains flexi-disc 2.50

REVENGERS FEATURING MEGALITH
Continuity Comics: Sept, 1985; 1987 - No. 6, 1988 ($2.00, Baxter paper)

1 (1985)-Origin; Neal Adams-c/a, scripts 2.00
1 (1987, newsstand)- 6 2.00

REX ALLEN COMICS (Movie star)(Also see Four Color #877 & Western Roundup under Dell Giants)
Dell Publ. Co.: No. 316, Feb, 1951 - No. 31, Dec-Feb, 1958-59 (All-photo-c)

Four Color 316(#1)(52 pgs.)-Rex Allen & his horse Koko begin; Marsh-a 13.00 38.00 140.00
2 (9-11/51, 36 pgs.) 8.00 23.00 85.00
3-10 5.50 16.50 60.00
11-20 4.50 13.50 50.00
21-23,25-31 4.00 12.00 45.00
24-Toth-a 5.00 15.00 55.00

NOTE: ***Manning** a-20, 27-30. Photo back-c F.C. #316, 2-12, 20, 21.*

REX DEXTER OF MARS (See Mystery Men Comics)
Fox Features Syndicate: Fall, 1940 (68 pgs.)

1-Rex Dexter, Patty O'Day, & Zanzibar (Tuska-a) app.; Briefer-c/a 171.00 512.00 1450.00

REX HART (Formerly Blaze Carson; Whip Wilson #9 on)
Timely/Marvel Comics (USA): No. 6, Aug, 1949 - No. 8, Feb, 1950 (All photo-c)

6-Rex Hart & his horse Warrior begin; Black Rider app; Captain Tootsie by Beck 25.00 74.00 185.00
7,8: 18 pg. Thriller in each. 8-Blaze the Wonder Collie app. in text 17.00 50.00 125.00

REX MORGAN, M.D. (Also see Harvey Comics Library)
Argo Publ.: Dec, 1955 - No. 3, Apr?, 1956

1-r/Rex Morgan daily newspaper strips & daily panel-r of "These Women" by D'Alessio & "Timeout" by Jeff Keate 10.00 30.00 75.00
2,3 7.15 21.50 50.00

REX THE WONDER DOG (See The Adventures of...)

RHUBARB, THE MILLIONAIRE CAT
Dell Publishing Co.: No. 423, Sept-Oct, 1952 - No. 563, June, 1954

Four Color 423 (#1) 4.50 13.50 50.00
Four Color 466(5/53),563 3.60 11.00 40.00

RIB
Dilemma Productions: Oct, 1995 - April, 1996 ($1.95, B&W)

Ashcan, 1 2.00

RIB
Bookmark Productions: 1996 ($2.95, B&W)

1-Sakai-c; Andrew Ford-s/a 3.00

RIB
Caliber Comics: May, 1997 - No. 5, 1998 ($2.95, B&W)

1-5: 1-"Beginnings" pts. 1 & 2 3.00

RIBIT!
Comico: Jan, 1989 - No. 4, April?, 1989 ($1.95, limited series)

1-4: Frank Thorne-c/a/scripts 2.00

RIBTICKLER (Also see Fox Giants)
Fox Feature Synd./Green Publ. (1957)/Norlen (1959): 1945 - No. 9, Aug, 1947; 1957; 1959

1-Funny animal 13.00 38.00 90.00
2-(1946) 6.50 19.50 45.00
3-9: 3,7-Cosmo Cat app. 5.70 17.00 35.00
3,7,8 (Green Publ.-1957) 2.00 6.00 16.00
3,7,8 (Norlen Mag.-1959) 2.00 6.00 16.00

RICHARD DRAGON, KUNG-FU FIGHTER (See The Batman Chronicles #5, Brave & the Bold, & The Question)
National Periodical Publ./DC Comics: Apr-May, 1975 - No. 18, Nov-Dec, 1977

1-3: 1-Intro Richard Dragon, Ben Stanley & O-Sensei; 1st app. Barney Ling; adaptation of Jim Dennis novel "Dragon's Fists" begins, ends #4. 2-Intro Carolyn Woosan; Starlin/Weiss-c/a; bondage-c. 3-Kirby-a(p); Giordano bondage-c .85 2.60 7.00
4-8-Wood inks. 4-Carolyn Woosan dies. 5-1st app. Lady Shiva 5.00
9-13,15-18: 9-Ben Stanley becomes Ben Turner; intro Preying Mantis. 16-1st app. Prof Ojo. 18-1st app. Ben Turner as The Bronze Tiger 3.50
14-"Spirit of Bruce Lee" .85 2.60 7.00

NOTE: ***Buckler** a-14. c-15, 18. **Chua** c-13. **Estrada** a-9, 13-18. **Estrada/Abel** a-10-12. **Estrada/Wood** a-4-8. **Giordano** c-1, 3-11. **Weiss** a-2(partial) c-2i.*

RICHARD THE LION-HEARTED (See Ideal a Classical Comic)

RICHIE RICH (See Harvey Collectors Comics, Harvey Hits, Little Dot, Little Lotta, Little Sad Sack, Million Dollar Digest, Mutt & Jeff, Super Richie, and 3-D Dolly)

RICHIE RICH (...the Poor Little Rich Boy) (See Harvey Hits #3, 9)
Harvey Publ.: Nov, 1960 - #218, Oct, 1982; #219, Oct, 1986 - #254, Jan, 1991

1-(See Little Dot for 1st app.) 140.00 420.00 1400.00
2 47.50 142.00 475.00
3-5 27.00 81.00 270.00
6-10: 8-Christmas-c 16.50 50.00 165.00
11-20 10.00 30.00 100.00
21-30 8.00 24.00 80.00
31-40 6.00 18.00 60.00
41-50 4.50 13.50 45.00
51-55,57-60: 59-Buck, prototype of Dollar the Dog 3.20 9.60 32.00
56-1st app. Super Richie 4.00 12.00 40.00
61-64,66-80: 71-Nixon & Robert Kennedy caricatures 2.00 6.00 20.00
65-1st app. Dollar the Dog 2.50 7.50 25.00
81-99 1.40 4.20 14.00
100(12/70)-1st app. Irona the robot maid 1.80 5.40 18.00
101-111,117-120 1.00 3.00 10.00
112-116: All 52 pg. Giants 1.60 4.80 16.00
121-140: 137-1st app. Mr. Cheepers .85 2.60 7.00
141-160: 145-Infinity-c. 155-3rd app. The Money Monster 5.00
161-180 3.00

Richie Rich #212 © HARV

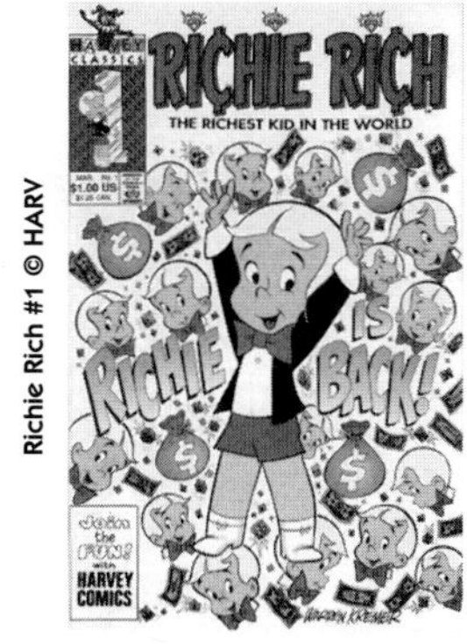

Richie Rich #1 © HARV

Richie Rich and Cadbury #16 © HARV

	GD25	FN65	NM94
181-199			4.00
200		2.00	6.00
201-218: 210-Stone-Age Riches app			3.00
219-254: 237-Last original material			2.00

RICHIE RICH
Harvey Comics: Mar, 1991 - No. 28, Nov, 1994 ($1.00, bi-monthly)

	GD25	FN65	NM94
1			3.00
2-28: Reprints best of Richie Rich			2.00
Giant Size 1-4 (10/91-10/93, $2.25, 68 pgs.)			3.00

RICHIE RICH ADVENTURE DIGEST MAGAZINE
Harvey Comics: 1992 - No. 7, Sept, 1994 ($1.25, quarterly, digest-size)

	GD25	FN65	NM94
1-7			4.00

RICHIE RICH AND...
Harvey Comics: Oct, 1987 - No. 11, May, 1990 ($1.00)

	GD25	FN65	NM94
1-Professore Keenbean			4.00
2-11: 2-Casper. 3-Dollar the Dog. 4-Cadbury. 5 Mayda Munny. 6-Irona. 7-Little Dot. 8-Professor Keenbean. 9-Little Audrey. 10-Mayda Munny. 11-Cadbury.			2.00

RICHIE RICH AND BILLY BELLHOPS
Harvey Publications: Oct, 1977 (52 pgs., one-shot)

	GD25	FN65	NM94
1	.90	2.70	9.00

RICHIE RICH AND CADBURY
Harvey Publ.: 10/77; #2, 9/78 - #23, 7/82; #24, 7/90 - #29, 1/91 (1-10: 52pgs.)

	GD25	FN65	NM94
1-(52 pg. Giant)	1.20	3.60	12.00
2-10-(52 pg. Giant)	.90	2.70	8.00
11-23			4.00
24-29: 24-Begin $1.00-c			2.00

RICHIE RICH AND CASPER
Harvey Publications: Aug, 1974 - No. 45, Sept, 1982

	GD25	FN65	NM94
1	2.20	6.25	22.00
2-5	1.20	3.60	12.00
6-10: 10-Xmas-c	.90	2.70	8.00
11-20			5.00
21-45: 22-Xmas-c			3.00

RICHIE RICH AND DOLLAR THE DOG (See Richie Rich #65)
Harvey Publications: Sept, 1977 - No. 24, Aug, 1982 (#1-10: 52 pgs.)

	GD25	FN65	NM94
1-(52 pg. Giant)	1.00	3.00	10.00
2-10-(52 pg. Giant)	.85	2.60	7.00
11-24			3.00

RICHIE RICH AND DOT
Harvey Publications: Oct, 1974 (one-shot)

	GD25	FN65	NM94
1	1.60	4.80	16.00

RICHIE RICH AND GLORIA
Harvey Publications: Sept, 1977 - No. 25, Sept, 1982 (#1-11: 52 pgs.)

	GD25	FN65	NM94
1-(52 pg. Giant)	1.00	3.00	10.00
2-11-(52 pg. Giant)	.85	2.60	7.00
12-25			3.00

RICHIE RICH AND HIS GIRLFRIENDS
Harvey Publications: April, 1979 - No. 16, Dec, 1982

	GD25	FN65	NM94
1-(52 pg. Giant)	1.00	3.00	10.00
2-(52 pg. Giant)	.85	2.60	7.00
3-10			4.00
11-16			3.00

RICHIE RICH AND HIS MEAN COUSIN REGGIE
Harvey Publications: April, 1979 - No. 3, 1980 (50¢) (#1,2: 52 pgs.)

	GD25	FN65	NM94
1	.90	2.70	9.00
2-3:			6.00

NOTE: *No. 4 was advertised, but never released.*

RICHIE RICH AND JACKIE JOKERS (Also see Jackie Jokers)
Harvey Publications: Nov, 1973 - No. 48, Dec, 1982

	GD25	FN65	NM94
1: 52 pg. Giant; contains material from unpublished Jackie Jokers #5	2.90	8.70	32.00
2,3-(52 pg. Giants). 2-R.R. & Jackie 1st meet	2.00	6.00	20.00
4,5	1.20	3.60	12.00
6-10	.90	2.70	8.00
11-20: 11-1st app. Kool Katz		2.00	6.00
21-25,27-40			4.00
26-Star Wars parody		2.00	6.00
41-48			3.00

RICHIE RICH AND PROFESSOR KEENBEAN
Harvey Comics: Sept, 1990 - No. 2, Nov, 1990 ($1.00)

	GD25	FN65	NM94
1,2			2.00

RICHIE RICH AND THE NEW KIDS ON THE BLOCK
Harvey Publications: Feb, 1991 - No. 3, June, 1991 ($1.25, bi-monthly)

	GD25	FN65	NM94
1-3: 1,2-New Richie Rich stories			2.00

RICHIE RICH AND TIMMY TIME
Harvey Publications: Sept, 1977 (50¢, 52 pgs, one-shot)

	GD25	FN65	NM94
1	.90	2.70	9.00

RICHIE RICH BANK BOOKS
Harvey Publications: Oct, 1972 - No. 59, Sept, 1982

	GD25	FN65	NM94
1	3.50	10.50	38.00
2-5: 2-2nd app. The Money Monster	2.20	6.25	22.00
6-10	1.40	4.20	14.00
11-20: 18-Super Richie app.	.90	2.70	9.00
21-30		2.00	6.00
31-40			4.00
41-59			3.00

RICHIE RICH BEST OF THE YEARS
Harvey Publications: Oct, 1977 - No. 6, June, 1980 (128 pgs., digest-size)

	GD25	FN65	NM94
1(10/77)-Reprints	1.00	3.00	10.00
2-6(11/79-6/80, 95¢). #2(10/78)-Rep.. #3(6/79, 75¢)	.85	2.60	7.00

RICHIE RICH BIG BOOK
Harvey Publications: Nov, 1992 - No. 2, May, 1993 ($1.50, 52 pgs.)

	GD25	FN65	NM94
1,2			3.00

RICHIE RICH BIG BUCKS
Harvey Publications: Apr, 1991 - No. 8, July, 1992 ($1.00, bi-monthly)

	GD25	FN65	NM94
1-8			2.00

RICHIE RICH BILLIONS
Harvey Publications: Oct, 1974 - No. 48, Oct, 1982 (#1-33: 52 pgs.)

	GD25	FN65	NM94
1	2.70	8.00	30.00
2-5	1.60	4.80	16.00
6-10	1.00	3.00	10.00
11-20	.90	2.70	8.00
21-33			5.00
34-48: 35-Onion app.			3.00

RICHIE RICH CASH
Harvey Publications: Sept, 1974 - No. 47, Aug, 1982

	GD25	FN65	NM94
1-1st app. Dr. N-R-Gee	2.70	8.00	30.00
2-5	1.60	4.80	16.00
6-10	1.20	3.60	12.00
11-20	.90	2.70	8.00
21-30			5.00
31-47: 33-Dr. Blemish app.			3.00

RICHIE RICH CASH MONEY
Harvey Comics: May, 1992 - No. 2, Aug, 1992 ($1.25)

Richie Rich Diamonds #4 © HARV

Richie Rich Fortunes #5 © HARV

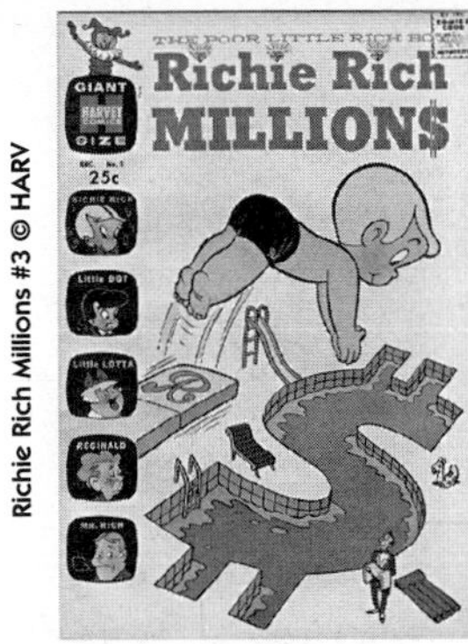

Richie Rich Millions #3 © HARV

GD25 FN65 NM94

1,2 2.00

RICHIE RICH, CASPER & WENDY NATIONAL LEAGUE
Harvey Publications: June, 1976 (52 pgs.)

1 (Released-3/76 with 6/76 date) 1.20 3.60 12.00
1 (6/76)-2nd version w/San Francisco Giants & KTVU 2 logos; has "Compliments of Giants and Straw Hat Pizza" on-c 1.20 3.60 12.00
1-Variants for other 11 NL teams, similar to Giants version but with different ad on inside front-c 1.20 3.60 12.00

RICHIE RICH COLLECTORS COMICS (See Harvey Collectors Comics)

RICHIE RICH DIAMONDS
Harvey Publications: Aug, 1972 - No. 59, Aug, 1982 (#1, 23-45: 52 pgs.)

1-(52 pg. Giant) 4.00 12.25 45.00
2-5 2.00 6.00 20.00
6-10 1.20 3.60 12.00
11-22 .90 2.70 8.00
23-30 5.00
31-45: 39-r/Origin Little Dot 4.00
46-50 3.00
51-59 2.00

RICHIE RICH DIGEST
Harvey Publications: Oct, 1986 - No. 42, Oct, 1994 ($1.25/$1.75, digest-size)

1 2.00 6.00
2-20 4.00
21-42 3.00

RICHIE RICH DIGEST STORIES (...Magazine #?-on)
Harvey Publications: Oct, 1977 - No., 17, Oct, 1982 (75¢/95¢, digest-size)

1-Reprints 1.00 3.00 10.00
2-10: Reprints 2.00 6.00
11-17: Reprints 4.00

RICHIE RICH DIGEST WINNERS
Harvey Publications: Dec, 1977 - No. 16, Sept, 1982 (75¢/95¢, 132 pgs., digest-size)

1 1.00 3.00 10.00
2-5 2.00 6.00
6-16 4.00

RICHIE RICH DOLLARS & CENTS
Harvey Publications: Aug, 1963 - No. 109, Aug, 1982 (#1-43: 68 pgs.; 44-60, 71-94: 52 pgs.)

1: (#1-64 are all reprint issues) 15.00 45.00 150.00
2 7.00 21.00 70.00
3-5: 5-r/1st app. of R.R. from Little Dot #1 4.50 13.50 45.00
6-10 3.00 9.00 30.00
11-20 2.60 7.80 26.00
21-30: 25-r/1st app. Nurse Jenny (Little Lotta #62) 2.25 6.75 18.00
31-43: 43-Last 68 pg. issue 1.40 4.20 14.00
44-60: All 52 pgs. 1.20 3.60 12.00
61-71 2.00 6.00
72-94: All 52 pgs. .90 2.70 9.00
95-109: 100-Anniversary issue 3.00

RICHIE RICH FORTUNES
Harvey Publications: Sept, 1971 - No. 63, July, 1982 (#1-15: 52 pgs.)

1 4.00 12.25 45.00
2-5 2.20 6.50 24.00
6-10 1.40 4.20 14.00
11-15: 11-r/1st app. The Onion 1.00 3.00 10.00
16-30 5.00
31-40 3.00
41-63: 62-Onion app. 2.00

RICHIE RICH GEMS
Harvey Publications: Sept, 1974 - No. 43, Sept, 1982

1 2.50 7.60 28.00
2-5 1.40 4.20 14.00
6-10 1.00 3.00 10.00
11-20 2.00 6.00
21-30 4.00
31-43: 36-Dr. Blemish, Onion app. 38-1st app. Stone-Age Riches 3.00

RICHIE RICH GOLD AND SILVER
Harvey Publications: Sept, 1975 - No. 42, Oct, 1982 (#1-27: 52 pgs.)

1 2.20 6.25 22.00
2-5 1.20 3.60 12.00
6-10 .90 2.70 9.00
11-27 .85 2.60 7.00
28-42: 34-Stone-Age Riches app. 3.00

RICHIE RICH GOLD NUGGETS DIGEST
Harvey Publications: Feb., 1991 - No. 4, June, 1991 ($1.75, digest-size)

1 3.00
2-4 1.75

RICHIE RICH HOLIDAY DIGEST MAGAZINE (...Digest #4)
Harvey Publications: Jan, 1980 - #3, Jan, 1982; #4, 3/88; #5, 2/89 (annual)

1-X-Mas-c .90 2.70 8.00
2-5: 2,3: All X-Mas-c. 4-(3/88, $1.25), 5-(2/89, $1.75) 5.00

RICHIE RICH INVENTIONS
Harvey Publications: Oct, 1977 - No. 26, Oct, 1982 (#1-11: 52 pgs.)

1 1.00 3.00 10.00
2-5 .85 2.60 7.00
6-11 5.00
12-26 3.00

RICHIE RICH JACKPOTS
Harvey Publications: Oct, 1972 - No. 58, Aug, 1982 (#41-43: 52 pgs.)

1 4.00 12.25 45.00
2-5 2.20 6.25 22.00
6-10 1.40 4.20 14.00
11-20: 16-Super Richie app. .90 2.70 9.00
21-30 2.00 6.00
31-40,44-50: 37-Caricatures of Frank Sinatra, Dean Martin, Sammy Davis, Jr. 45-Dr. Blemish app. 5.00
41-43 (52 pgs.) .85 2.60 7.00
51-58 3.00

RICHIE RICH MILLION DOLLAR DIGEST (...Magazine #?-on)(See Million Dollar Digest)
Harvey Publications: Oct, 1980 - No. 10, Oct, 1982 ($1.50)

1 .90 2.70 8.00
2-10 5.00

RICHIE RICH MILLIONS
Harvey Publ.: 9/61; #2, 9/62 - #113, 10/82 (#1-48: 68 pgs.; 49-64, 85-97: 52 pgs.)

1: (#1-3 are all reprint issues) 18.00 54.00 180.00
2 9.50 28.50 95.00
3-10: All other giants are new & reprints. 5-1st 15 pg. Richie Rich story 7.50 22.50 75.00
11-20 3.80 11.40 38.00
21-30 2.80 8.40 28.00
31-48: 31-1st app. The Onion. 48-Last 68 pg. Giant 1.80 5.40 18.00
49-64: 52 pg. Giants 1.20 3.60 12.00
65-67,69-84: 74-1st app. Mr. Woody; Super Richie app. .85 2.60 7.00
68- 1st Super Richie-c (11/74) 1.40 4.20 14.00
85-97: 52 pg. Giants .90 2.70 9.00
98,99 4.00
100 2.00 6.00
101-113 3.00

Richie Rich Success Stories #6 © HARV

The Rider #2 © AJAX

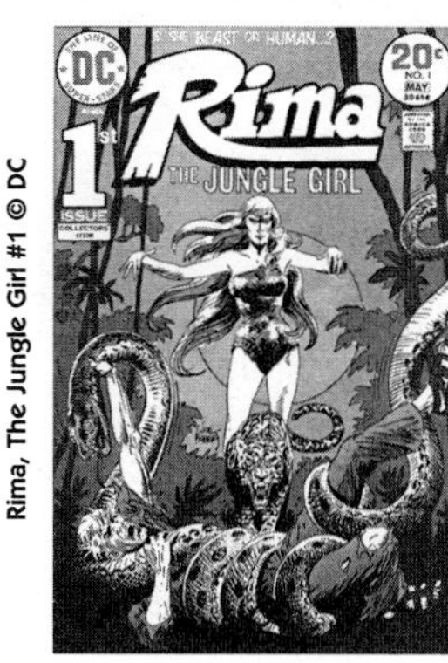

Rima, The Jungle Girl #1 © DC

RICHIE RICH MONEY WORLD
Harvey Publications: Sept, 1972 - No. 59, Sept, 1982

	GD25	FN65	NM94
1-(52 pg. Giant)-1st app. Mayda Munny	4.00	12.25	45.00
2-5: 2-Super Richie app.	1.80	5.40	18.00
6-10: 9,10-Richie Rich mistakenly named Little Lotta on covers	1.20	3.60	12.00
11-20: 16,20-Dr. N-R-Gee	.85	2.60	7.00
21-30			5.00
31-50			4.00
51-59			3.00
Digest 1 (2/91, $1.75)			4.00
2-8 (12/93, $1.75)			1.75

RICHIE RICH PROFITS
Harvey Publications: Oct, 1974 - No. 47, Sept, 1982

	GD25	FN65	NM94
1	2.90	8.70	32.00
2-5	1.40	4.20	14.00
6-10: 10-Origin of Dr. N-R-Gee	.90	2.70	9.00
11-20: 15-Christmas-c		2.00	6.00
21-30			4.00
31-47			3.00

RICHIE RICH RELICS
Harvey Comics: Jan, 1988 - No.4, Feb, 1989 (75¢/$1.00, reprints)

	GD25	FN65	NM94
1-4			3.00

RICHIE RICH RICHES
Harvey Publications: July, 1972 - No. 59, Aug, 1982 (#1, 2, 41-45: 52 pgs.)

	GD25	FN65	NM94
1-(52 pg. Giant)-1st app. The Money Monster	4.00	12.25	45.00
2-(52 pg. Giant)	2.20	6.25	22.00
3-5	1.40	4.20	14.00
6-10	1.00	3.00	10.00
11-20: 17-Super Richie app. (3/75)	.85	2.60	7.00
21-40			5.00
41-45: 52 pg. Giants	.85	2.60	7.00
46-59: 56-Dr. Blemish app.			3.00

RICHIE RICH SUCCESS STORIES
Harvey Publications: Nov, 1964 - No. 105, Sept, 1982 (#1-38: 68 pgs., 39-55, 67-90: 52 pgs.)

	GD25	FN65	NM94
1	16.00	48.00	160.00
2-5	7.50	22.50	75.00
6-10	4.00	12.00	40.00
11-20	3.50	10.50	35.00
21-30: 27-1st Penny Van Dough (8/69)	2.50	7.50	22.00
31-38: 38-Last 68 pg. Giant	1.80	5.40	18.00
39-55-(52 pgs.): 44-Super Richie app.	1.40	4.20	14.00
56-66	.85	2.60	7.00
67-90: 52 pgs.	.90	2.70	8.00
91-105: 91-Onion app. 101-Dr. Blemish app.			3.00

RICHIE RICH SUMMER BONANZA
Harvey Comics: Oct, 1991 ($1.95, one-shot, 68 pgs.)

	GD25	FN65	NM94
1-Richie Rich, Little Dot, Little Lotta			3.00

RICHIE RICH TREASURE CHEST DIGEST (...Magazine #3)
Harvey Publications: Apr, 1982 - No. 3, Aug, 1982 (95¢, Digest Mag.) (#4 advertised but not publ.)

	GD25	FN65	NM94
1		2.00	6.00
2,3			4.00

RICHIE RICH VACATION DIGEST
Harvey Comics: Oct, 1991; Oct, 1992; Oct, 1993 ($1.75, digest-size)

	GD25	FN65	NM94
1			3.00
1-(10/92)			3.00
1-(10/93)			3.00

RICHIE RICH VACATIONS DIGEST
Harvey Publ.: 11/77; No. 2, 10/78 - No. 7, 10/81; No. 8, 8/82; (Digest, 132 pgs.)

	GD25	FN65	NM94
1-Reprints	1.00	3.00	10.00
2-8		2.00	6.00

RICHIE RICH VAULT OF MYSTERY
Harvey Publications: Nov, 1974 - No. 47, Sept, 1982

	GD25	FN65	NM94
1	2.20	6.25	22.00
2-10	1.20	3.60	12.00
11-20	.85	2.60	7.00
21-30			4.00
31-47			3.00

RICHIE RICH ZILLIONZ
Harvey Publ.: Oct, 1976 - No. 33, Sept, 1982 (#1-4: 68 pgs.; #5-18: 52 pgs.)

	GD25	FN65	NM94
1	2.00	6.00	20.00
2-4: 4-Last 68 pg. Giant	1.20	3.60	12.00
5-10	.85	2.60	7.00
11-18: 18-Last 52 pg. Giant			5.00
19-33			2.50

RICK GEARY'S WONDERS AND ODDITIES
Dark Horse Comics: Dec, 1988 ($2.00, B&W, one-shot)

	GD25	FN65	NM94
1			2.00

RICKY
Standard Comics (Visual Editions): No. 5, Sept, 1953

	GD25	FN65	NM94
5-Teenage humor	4.00	12.00	24.00

RICKY NELSON (TV)(See Sweethearts V2#42)
Dell Publishing Co.: No. 956, Dec, 1958 - No. 1192, June, 1961 (All photo-c)

	GD25	FN65	NM94
Four Color 956,998	18.00	55.00	200.00
Four Color 1115	14.00	41.00	150.00
Four Color 1192-Manning-a	14.00	41.00	150.00

RIDER, THE (Frontier Trail #6; also see Blazing Sixguns I.W. Reprint #10, 11)
Ajax/Farrell Publ. (Four Star Comic Corp.): Mar, 1957 - No. 5, 1958

	GD25	FN65	NM94
1-Swift Arrow, Lone Rider begin	9.30	28.00	70.00
2-5	5.70	17.00	35.00

RIDERS OF THE PURPLE SAGE (See Zane Grey & Four Color #372)

RIFLEMAN, THE (TV)
Dell Publ. Co./Gold Key No. 13 on: No. 1009, 7-9/59 - No. 12, 7-9/62; No. 13, 11/62 - No. 20, 10/64

	GD25	FN65	NM94
Four Color 1009 (#1)	22.00	65.00	240.00
2 (1-3/60)	11.00	33.00	120.00
3-Toth-a (4 pgs.)	12.00	35.00	130.00
4,5,7-10	9.00	27.00	100.00
6-Toth-a (4 pgs.)	9.00	27.00	100.00
11-20	7.00	20.00	75.00

NOTE: ***Warren Tufts** a-2-9. All have Chuck Connors photo-c. Photo back c-13-15.*

RIMA, THE JUNGLE GIRL
National Periodical Publications: Apr-May, 1974 - No. 7, Apr-May, 1975

	GD25	FN65	NM94
1-Origin, part 1 (#1-5: 20¢; 6,7: 25¢)	.85	2.60	7.00
2-4-Origin, parts 2-4			4.00
5-6			4.00
7-Origin & only app. Space Marshal	.90	2.70	8.00

NOTE: ***Kubert** c-1-7. **Nino** a-1-7. **Redondo** a-1-7.*

RING OF BRIGHT WATER (See Movie Classics)

RING OF THE NIBELUNG, THE
DC Comics: 1989 - No. 4, 1990 ($4.95, squarebound, 52 pgs., mature readers)

	GD25	FN65	NM94
1-4: Adapts novel, Gil Kane-c/a			5.00

RINGO KID, THE (2nd Series)
Marvel Comics Group: Jan, 1970 - No. 23, Nov, 1973; No. 24, Nov, 1975 - No.

The Ringo Kid #19 (2nd Series) © MAR

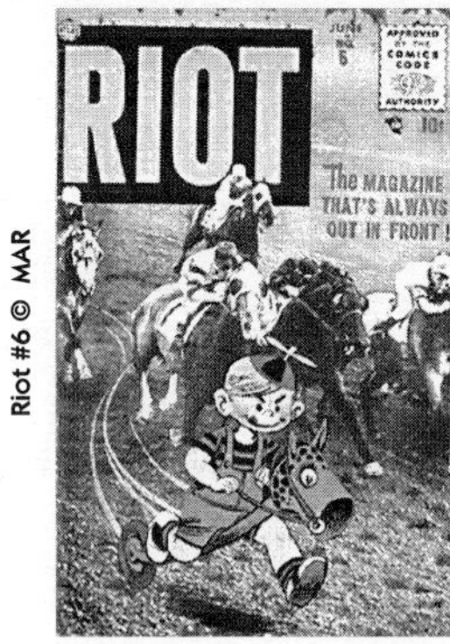

Riot #6 © MAR

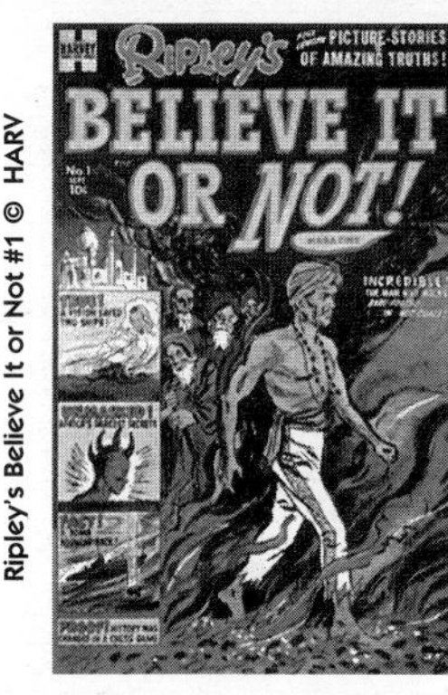

Ripley's Believe It or Not #1 © HARV

	GD25	FN65	NM94
30, Nov, 1976			
1-Williamson-a r-from #10, 1956.	2.00	6.00	20.00
2-11: 2-Severin-c	1.20	3.60	12.00
12 (Giant)	1.80	5.40	18.00
13-20: 13-Wildey-r. 20-Williamson-r/#1	.90	2.70	9.00
21-30	.85	2.60	7.00

RINGO KID WESTERN, THE (1st Series) (See Wild Western & Western Trails)
Atlas Comics (HPC)/Marvel Comics: Aug, 1954 - No. 21, Sept, 1957

	GD25	FN65	NM94
1-Origin; The Ringo Kid begins	25.00	76.00	190.00
2-Black Rider app.; origin/1st app. Ringo's Horse Arab	13.00	38.00	95.00
3-5	8.50	26.00	60.00
6-8-Severin-a(3) each	9.30	28.00	70.00
9,11,12,14-21: 12-Orlando-a (4 pgs.)	6.50	19.50	45.00
10,13-Williamson-a (4 pgs.)	7.15	21.50	50.00

NOTE: ***Berg** a-8. **Maneely** a-1-5, 15, 16(text illos only), 17(4), 18, 20, 21; c-1-6, 8, 13, 15-18, 20. **J. Severin** c-10, 11. **Sinnott** a-1. **Wildey** a-16-18.*

RIN TIN TIN (See March of Comics #163,180,195)

RIN TIN TIN (TV) (...& Rusty #21 on; see Western Roundup under Dell Giants)
Dell Publishing Co./Gold Key: Nov, 1952 - No. 38, May-July, 1961; Nov, 1963 (All Photo-c)

	GD25	FN65	NM94
Four Color 434 (#1)	14.00	41.00	150.00
Four Color 476,523	7.00	22.00	80.00
4(3-5/54)-10	5.50	16.50	60.00
11-20	5.00	15.00	55.00
21-38: 36-Toth-a (4 pgs.)	3.60	11.00	40.00
... & Rusty 1 (11/63-Gold Key)	5.00	15.00	55.00

RIO (Also see Eclipse Monthly)
Comico: June, 1987 ($8.95, 64 pgs.)

1-Wildey-c/a 9.00

RIO AT BAY
Dark Horse Comics: July, 1992 - No. 2, Aug, 1992 ($2.95, limited series)

1,2-Wildey-c/a 3.00

RIO BRAVO (Movie) (See 4-Color #1018)
Dell Publishing Co.: June, 1959

	GD25	FN65	NM94
Four Color #1018-Toth-a; John Wayne, Dean Martin, & Ricky Nelson photo-c.	18.00	55.00	200.00

RIO CONCHOS (See Movie Comics)

RIOT (Satire)
Atlas Comics (ACI No. 1-5/WPI No. 6): Apr, 1954 - No. 3, Aug, 1954; No. 4, Feb, 1956 - No. 6, June, 1956

	GD25	FN65	NM94
1-Russ Heath-a	25.00	76.00	190.00
2-Li'l Abner satire by Post	19.00	58.00	145.00
3-Last precode (8/54)	17.00	50.00	125.00
4-Infinity-c; Marilyn Monroe "7 Year Itch" movie satire; Mad Rip-off ads	21.00	64.00	160.00
5-Marilyn Monroe, John Wayne parody; part photo-c	22.00	66.00	165.00
6-Lorna of the Jungle satire by Everett; Dennis the Menace satire-c/story; part photo-c	17.00	50.00	125.00

NOTE: ***Berg** a-3. **Burgos** c-1, 2. **Colan** a-1. **Everett** a-1, 4, 6. **Heath** a-1. **Maneely** a-1, 2, 4-6; c-3, 4, 6. **Post** a-1-4. **Reinman** a-2. **Severin** a-4-6.*

RIOT GEAR
Triumphant Comics: Sept, 1993 - No. 11, July, 1994 ($2.50, serially numbered)

	GD25	FN65	NM94
1-11: 1-2nd app. Riot Gear. 2-1st app. Rabin. 3,4-Triumphant Unleashed x-over. 3-1st app. Surzar. 4-Death of Captain Tich			2.50
Violent Past 1,2: 1-(2/94, $2.50)			2.50

R.I.P.
TSR, Inc.:1990 - No. 8, 1991 ($2.95, 44 pgs.)

1-8-Based on TSR game 3.00

RIPCLAW (See Cyberforce)
Image Comics (Top Cow Prod.): Apr, 1995 - No. 3, June, 1995 (Limited series)

	GD25	FN65	NM94
1/2-Gold	1.40	4.20	14.00
1/2-San Diego ed.	1.10	3.30	11.00
1/2-Chicago ed.	1.10	3.30	11.00
1-3: Brandon Peterson-a(p)			2.50

RIPCLAW
Image Comics (Top Cow Prod.): V2#1, Dec, 1995 - No. 6, June, 1996 ($2.50)

	GD25	FN65	NM94
V2#1-6: 5-Medieval Spawn/Witchblade Preview			2.50
Special (10/95, $2.50)			2.50

RIPCORD (TV)
Dell Publishing Co.: Mar-May, 1962

	GD25	FN65	NM94
Four Color 1294	6.40	19.00	70.00

RIPFIRE
Malibu Comics (Ultraverse): No. 0, Apr, 1995 ($2.50, one-shot)

0 2.50

RIP HUNTER TIME MASTER (See Showcase #20, 21, 25, 26 & Time Masters)
National Periodical Publications: Mar-Apr, 1961 - No. 29, Nov-Dec, 1965

	GD25	FN65	NM94
1-(3-4/61)	41.00	123.00	470.00
2	22.50	68.00	225.00
3-5: 5-Last 10¢ issue	13.00	39.00	130.00
6,7-Toth-a in each	9.00	27.00	90.00
8-15	6.50	19.50	65.00
16-20: 20-Hitler c/s	5.50	16.50	55.00
21-29: 29-Gil Kane-c	4.50	13.50	45.00

RIP IN TIME (Also see Teenage Mutant Ninja Turtles #5-7)
Fantagor Press: Aug, 1986 - No.5, 1987 ($1.50, B&W)

1-5: Corben-c/a in all 1.50

RIP KIRBY (Also see Harvey Comics Hits #57, & Street Comix)
David McKay Publications: 1948

	GD25	FN65	NM94
Feature Books 51,54: Raymond-c; 51-Origin	28.00	84.00	225.00

RIPLEY'S BELIEVE IT OR NOT! (See Ace Comics, All-American Comics, Mystery Comics Digest #1, 4, 7, 10, 13, 16, 19, 22, 25)

RIPLEY'S BELIEVE IT OR NOT!
Harvey Publications: Sept, 1953 - No. 4, March, 1954

	GD25	FN65	NM94
1-Powell-a	10.00	30.00	75.00
2-4	7.15	21.50	50.00
J. C. Penney giveaway (1948)	6.50	19.50	45.00

RIPLEY'S BELIEVE IT OR NOT! (Formerly ...True War Stories)
Gold Key: No. 4, April, 1967 - No. 94, Feb, 1980

	GD25	FN65	NM94
4-Photo-c; McWilliams-a	2.20	6.50	24.00
5-Subtitled "True War Stories"; Evans-a; 1st Jeff Jones-a in comics? (2 pgs.)	2.00	6.00	22.00
6-10: 6-McWilliams-a. 10-Evans-a(2)	2.00	6.00	22.00
11-20: 15-Evans-a	1.50	4.50	16.00
21-30	1.20	3.60	12.00
31-38,40-60	.90	2.70	9.00
39-Crandall-a	1.00	3.00	10.00
61-73		2.00	6.00
74,77-83-(52 pgs.)	.90	2.70	9.00
75,76,84-94			4.00
Story Digest Mag. 1(6/70)-4-3/4x6-1/2"	3.20	9.50	35.00

NOTE: ***Evanish** art by **Luiz Dominguez** #22-25, 27, 30, 31, 40. **Jeff Jones** a-5(2 pgs.). **McWilliams** a-65, 66, 70, 89. **Orlando** a-8. **Sparling** c-68. Reprints-74, 77-84, 87 (part); 91, 93 (all). **Williamson, Wood** a-80r/#1.*

RIPLEY'S BELIEVE IT OR NOT! TRUE GHOST STORIES (Becomes ...True War Stories) (See Dan Curtis)

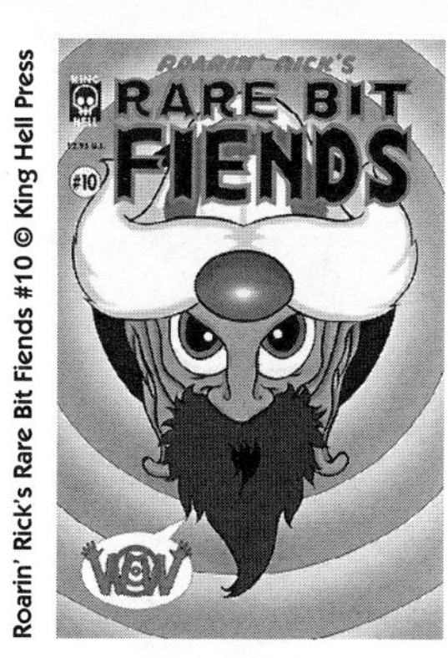

Roarin' Rick's Rare Bit Fiends #10 © King Hell Press

Robin #3 (mini-series) © DC

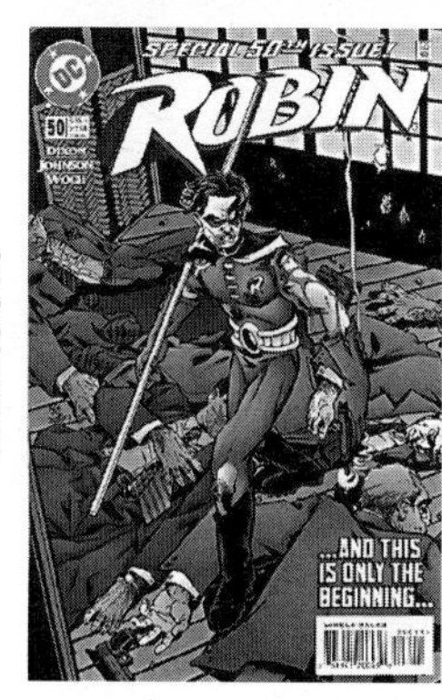

Robin #50 © DC

	GD25	FN65	NM94

Gold Key: June, 1965 - No. 2, Oct, 1966

1-Williamson, Wood & Evans-a; photo-c	4.00	12.00	45.00
2-Orlando, McWilliams-a; photo-c	2.70	8.00	30.00
Mini-Comic 1(1976-3-1/4x6-1/2")		2.00	6.00
11186(1977)-Golden Press; ($1.95, 224 pgs.)-All-r	2.20	6.25	22.00
11401(3/79)-Golden Press; ($1.00, 96 pgs.)-All-r	1.40	4.20	14.00

RIPLEY'S BELIEVE IT OR NOT! TRUE WAR STORIES (Formerly ...True Ghost Stories; becomes Ripley's Believe It or Not! #4 on)
Gold Key: Nov, 1966

1(#3)-No Williamson-a	2.20	6.50	24.00

RIPLEY'S BELIEVE IT OR NOT! TRUE WEIRD
Ripley Enterprises: June, 1966 - No. 2, Aug, 1966 (B&W Magazine)

1,2-Comic stories & text	2.00	6.00	16.00

RIPTIDE
Image Comics: Sep, 1995 - No. 2, Oct, 1995 ($2.50, limited series)

1,2: Rob Liefeld-c — 2.50

RISE OF APOCALYPSE
Marvel Comics: Oct, 1996 - No. 4, Jan, 1997 ($1.95, limited series)

1-4: Adam Pollina-c/a — 2.00

RIVERDALE HIGH (Archie's... #7,8)
Archie Comics: Aug, 1990 - No. 8, Oct, 1991 ($1.00, bi-monthly)

1-8 — 1.00

RIVER FEUD (See Zane Grey & Four Color #484)

RIVETS
Dell Publishing Co.: No. 518, Nov, 1953

Four Color 518	2.25	6.75	25.00

RIVETS (A dog)
Argo Publ.: Jan, 1956 - No. 3, May, 1956

1-Reprints Sunday & daily newspaper strips	4.25	13.00	26.00
2,3	3.60	9.00	18.00

ROACHMILL
Blackthorne Publ.: Dec, 1986 - No. 6, Oct, 1987 ($1.75, B&W)

1-6 — 1.75

ROACHMILL
Dark Horse Comics: May, 1988 - No. 10, Dec, 1990 ($1.75, B&W)

1-10: 10-Contains trading cards — 1.75

ROAD RUNNER (See Beep Beep, the...)

ROADWAYS
Cult Press: May, 1994 ($2.75, B&W, limited series)

1 — 2.75

ROARIN' RICK'S RARE BIT FIENDS
King Hell Press: July, 1994 - Present ($2.95, B&W, mature)

1-21: Rick Veitch-c/a/scripts in all. 20-(5/96). 21-(8/96)-Reads Subtleman #1 on cover — 3.00
Rabid Eye: The Dream Art of Rick Veitch ($14.95, B&W, TPB)-r/#1-8 & the appendix from #12 — 15.00
Pocket Universe (6/96, $14.95, B&W, TPB)-Reprints — 15.00

ROBERT E. HOWARD'S CONAN THE BARBARIAN
Marvel Comics: 1983 ($2.50, 68 pgs., Baxter paper)

1-r/Savage Tales #2,3 by Smith, c-r/Conan #21 by Smith. — 2.50

ROBERT LOUIS STEVENSON'S KIDNAPPED (See Kidnapped)

ROBIN (See Aurora, Detective Comics #38, New Teen Titans, Robin II, Robin III, Robin 3000, Star Spangled Comics #65, Teen Titans & Young Justice)

ROBIN (See Batman #457)
DC Comics: Jan, 1991 - No. 5, May, 1991 ($1.00, limited series)

1-Free poster by N. Adams; Bolland-c on all — 4.00
1-2nd & 3rd printings (without poster) — 1.50
2 — 1.75
2-2nd printing — 1.00
3-5 — 1.50
Annual 1,2 (1992-93, $2.50, 68 pgs.): 1-Grant/Wagner scripts; Sam Kieth-c. 2-Intro Razorsharp; Jim Balent-c(p) — 2.50

ROBIN (See Detective #668)
DC Comics: Nov, 1993 - Present ($1.50/$1.95/$1.99)

1-($2.95)-Collector's edition w/foil embossed-c; 1st app. Robin's car, The Redbird; Azrael as Batman app. — 3.00
1-Newsstand ed. — 1.75
0,2-13,15,16-Regular editions: 3-5-The Spoiler app. 6-The Huntress-c/story cont'd from Showcase '94 #5. 7-Knightquest: The Conclusion w/new Batman (Azrael) vs. Bruce Wayne. 8-KnightsEnd Pt. 5. 9-KnightsEnd Aftermath; Batman-c & app. 10-(9/94)-Zero Hour. 0-(10/94). 11-(11/94) — 1.50
14 ($2.50)-Embossed-c; Troika Pt. 4 — 2.50
14 ($1.50)-Regular edition — 1.50
17-49: 17-Begin $1.95-c. 25-Green Arrow-c/app. 26-Batman app. 27-Contagion Pt. 3; Catwoman-c/app; Penguin & Azrael app. 28-Contagion Pt. 11. 29-Penguin app. 31-Wildcat-c/app. 32-Legacy Pt. 3. 33-Legacy Pt. 7 35-Final Night. 46-Genesis — 2.00
50-($2.95)-Lady Shiva & King Snake app. — 3.00
51-56: 52,53-Cataclysm pt. 7, conclusion. 55-Green Arrow app. — 2.00
57-60: 57-Begin $1.99-c — 1.99
#1,000,000 (11/98) 853rd Century x-over — 2.00
Annual 3-5: 3-(1994, $2.95)-Elseworlds story. 4-(1995, $2.95)-Year One story. 5-(1996, $2.95)-Legends of the Dead Earth story — 3.00
Annual 6 (1997, $3.95)-Pulp Heroes story. — 4.00
.../Argent 1 (2/98, $1.95) Argent (Teen Titans) app. — 2.00
...Plus 1 (12/96, $2.95) Impulse-c/app.; Waid-s — 3.00
...Plus 2 (12/97, $2.95) Fang (Scare Tactics) app. — 3.00

ROBIN: A HERO REBORN
DC Comics: 1991 ($4.95, squarebound, trade paperback)

nn-r/Batman #455-457 & Robin #1-5; Bolland-c — 5.00

ROBIN HOOD (See The Advs. of..., Brave and the Bold, Four Color #413, 669, King Classics, Movie Comics & Power Record Comics)

ROBIN HOOD (...& His Merry Men, The Illustrated Story of...) (See Classic Comics #7 & Classics Giveaways, 12/44)

ROBIN HOOD (New Adventures of...)
Walt Disney Productions: 1952 (Flour giveaways, 5x7-1/4", 36 pgs.)

"New Adventures of Robin Hood", "Ghosts of Waylea Castle", & "The Miller's Ransom" each....	4.25	13.00	26.00

ROBIN HOOD (Adventures of... #7, 8)
Magazine Enterprises (Sussex Pub. Co.): No. 52, Nov, 1955 - No. 6, Jun, 1957

52 (#1)-Origin Robin Hood & Sir Gallant of the Round Table	14.00	42.00	105.00
53 (#2), 3-6: 6-Richard Greene photo-c (TV)	10.00	30.00	75.00
I.W. Reprint #1,2,9: 1-r/#3. 2-r/#4. 9-r/#52 (1963)	1.85	5.50	15.00
Super Reprint #10,15: 10-r/#53. 15-r/#5	1.85	5.50	15.00

NOTE: ***Bolle** a-in all; c-52. **Powell** a-6.*

ROBIN HOOD (Not Disney)
Dell Publishing Co.: May-July, 1963 (one-shot)

1	1.80	5.50	20.00

ROBIN HOOD (Disney)
Western Publishing Co.: 1973 ($1.50, 8-1/2x11", 52 pgs., cardboard-c)

96151- "Robin Hood", based on movie, 96152- "The Mystery of Sherwood Forest", 96153- "In King Richard's Service", 96154- "The Wizard's Ring" each....	1.50	4.50	15.00

ROBIN HOOD

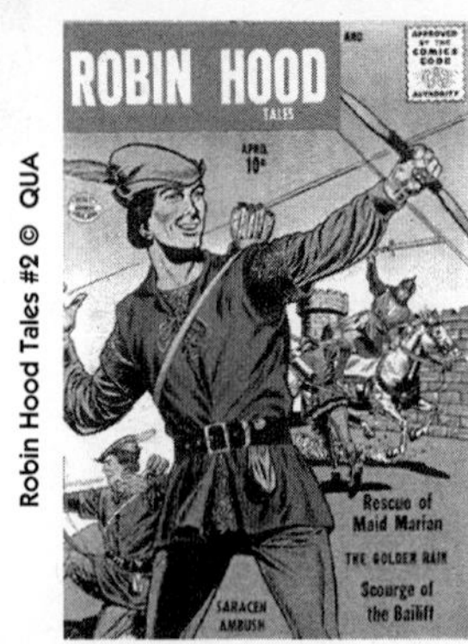

Robin Hood Tales #2 © QUA

Robin II #2 © DC

Robocop #12 © Orion Pictures

	GD25	FN65	NM94

Eclipse Comics: July, 1991 - No. 3, 1991 ($2.50, limited series)

	GD25	FN65	NM94
1-3: Timothy Truman layouts			2.50

ROBIN HOOD AND HIS MERRY MEN (Formerly Danger & Adventure)
Charlton Comics: No. 28, Apr, 1956 - No. 38, Aug, 1958

	GD25	FN65	NM94
28	7.85	23.50	55.00
29-37	5.70	17.00	40.00
38-Ditko-a (5 pgs.); Rocke-c	11.00	34.00	85.00

ROBIN HOOD'S FRONTIER DAYS (...Western Tales, Adventures of... #1)
Shoe Store Giveaway (Robin Hood Stores): No date (Circa 1955) 20 pgs., slick-c (Seven issues?)

	GD25	FN65	NM94
nn	4.25	13.00	28.00
nn-Issues with Crandall-a	6.85	21.00	48.00

ROBIN HOOD TALES (Published by National Periodical #7 on)
Quality Comics Group (Comic Magazines): Feb, 1956 - No. 6, Nov-Dec, 1956

	GD25	FN65	NM94
1-All have Baker/Cuidera-c	29.00	88.00	220.00
2-6-Matt Baker-a	28.00	84.00	210.00

ROBIN HOOD TALES (Cont'd from Quality series)(See Brave & the Bold #5)
National Periodical Publ.: No. 7, Jan-Feb, 1957 - No. 14, Mar-Apr, 1958

	GD25	FN65	NM94
7-All have Andru/Esposito-c	35.00	104.00	260.00
8-14	28.00	84.00	210.00

ROBINSON CRUSOE (See King Classics & Power Record Comics)
Dell Publishing Co.: Nov-Jan, 1963-64

	GD25	FN65	NM94
1	1.20	3.60	12.00

ROBIN II (The Joker's Wild)
DC Comics: Oct, 1991 - No. 4, Dec, 1991 ($1.50, mini-series)

	GD25	FN65	NM94
1-(Direct sales, $1.50)-With 4 different-c; same hologram on each			1.50
1-(Newsstand, $1.00)-No hologram; 1 version			1.00
1-Collector's set ($10.00)-Contains all 5 versions bagged with hologram trading card inside			10.00
2-(Direct sales, $1.50)-With 3 different-c			1.50
2-4-(Newsstand, $1.00)-1 version of each			1.00
2-Collector's set ($8.00)-Contains all 4 versions bagged with hologram trading card inside			8.00
3-(Direct sale, $1.50)-With 2 different-c			1.50
3-Collector's set ($6.00)-Contains all 3 versions bagged with hologram trading card inside			6.00
4-(Direct sales, $1.50)-Only one version			1.50
4-Collector's set ($4.00)-Contains both versions bagged with Bat-Signal hologram trading card			4.00
Multi-pack (All four issues w/hologram sticker)			4.00
Deluxe Complete Set ($30.00)-Contains all 14 versions of #1-4 plus a new hologram trading card; numbered & limited to 25,000; comes with slipcase & 2 acid free backing boards			30.00

ROBIN III: CRY OF THE HUNTRESS
DC Comics: Dec, 1992 - No. 6, Mar, 1993 (Limited series)

	GD25	FN65	NM94
1-6 ($2.50, collector's ed.)-Polybagged w/movement enhanced-c plus mini-poster of newsstand-c by Zeck			2.50
1-6 ($1.25, newsstand ed.): All have Zeck-c			1.25

ROBIN 3000
DC Comics (Elseworlds): 1992 - No. 2, 1992 ($4.95, mini-series, 52 pgs.)

	GD25	FN65	NM94
1,2-Foil logo; Russell-c/a			5.00

ROBOCOP
Marvel Comics: Oct, 1987 ($2.00, B&W, magazine, one-shot)

	GD25	FN65	NM94
1-Movie adaptation			2.00

ROBOCOP (Also see Dark Horse Comics)
Marvel Comics: Mar, 1990 - No. 23, Jan, 1992 ($1.50)

	GD25	FN65	NM94
1-Based on movie			3.00
2-6			2.00
7-23			1.50
nn (7/90, $4.95, 52 pgs.)-r/B&W magazine in color; adapts 1st movie			5.00

ROBOCOP: MORTAL COILS
Dark Horse Comics: Sept, 1993 - No. 4, Dec, 1993 ($2.50, limited series)

	GD25	FN65	NM94
1-4: 1,2-Cago painted-c			2.50

ROBOCOP: PRIME SUSPECT
Dark Horse Comics: Oct, 1992 - No. 4, Jan, 1993 ($2.50, limited series)

	GD25	FN65	NM94
1-4: 1,3-Nelson painted-c. 2,4-Bolton painted-c			2.50

ROBOCOP: ROULETTE
Dark Horse Comics: Dec, 1993 - No. 4, 1994 ($2.50, limited series)

	GD25	FN65	NM94
1-4: 1,3-Nelson painted-c. 2,4-Bolton painted-c			2.50

ROBOCOP 2
Marvel Comics: Aug, 1990 ($2.25, B&W, magazine, 68 pgs.)

	GD25	FN65	NM94
1-Adapts movie sequel			2.25

ROBOCOP 2
Marvel Comics: Aug, 1990; Late Aug, 1990 - #3, Late Sept, 1990 ($1.00, limited series)

	GD25	FN65	NM94
nn-(8/90, $4.95, 68 pgs., color)-Same contents as B&W magazine			5.00
1: #1-3 reprint no number issue			3.00
2,3: 2-Guice-c(i)			1.50

ROBOCOP 3
Dark Horse Comics: July, 1993 - No. 3, Nov, 1993 ($2.50, limited series)

	GD25	FN65	NM94
1-3: Nelson painted-c; Nguyen-a(p)			2.50

ROBOCOP VERSUS THE TERMINATOR
Dark Horse Comics: Sept, 1992 - No. 4, 1992 (Dec.) ($2.50, limited series)

	GD25	FN65	NM94
1-4: Miller scripts & Simonson-c/a in all			2.50
1-Platinum Edition			10.00

NOTE: *All contain a different Robocop cardboard cut-out stand-up.*

ROBO-HUNTER (Also see Sam Slade...)
Eagle Comics: Apr, 1984 - No. 5, 1984 ($1.00)

	GD25	FN65	NM94
1-5-2000 A.D.			1.00

R.O.B.O.T. BATTALION 2050
Eclipse Comics: Mar, 1988 ($2.00, B&W, one-shot)

	GD25	FN65	NM94
1			2.00

ROBOT COMICS
Renegade Press: No. 0, June, 1987 ($2.00, B&W, one-shot)

	GD25	FN65	NM94
0-Bob Burden story & art			2.00

ROBOTECH
Antarctic Press: Mar, 1997 - Present ($2.95)

	GD25	FN65	NM94
1-9			2.95
Annual 1 (4/98, $2.95)			2.95

ROBOTECH: COVERT-OPS
Antarctic Press: Aug, 1998 - No. 2, Sept, 1998 ($2.95, B&W, limited series)

	GD25	FN65	NM94
1,2-Gregory Lane-s/a			2.95

ROBOTECH DEFENDERS
DC Comics: Mar, 1985 - No. 2, Apr, 1985 (Mini-series)

	GD25	FN65	NM94
1,2			1.00

ROBOTECH ESCAPE
Antarctic Press: May, 1998 ($2.95, B&W)

	GD25	FN65	NM94
1			2.95

ROBOTECH IN 3-D (TV)
Comico: Aug, 1987 ($2.50)

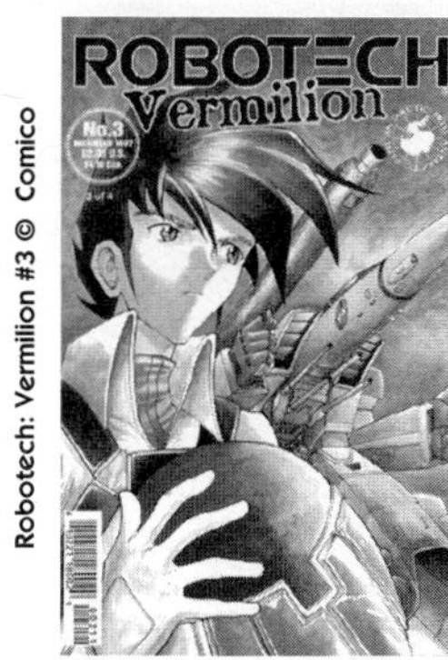

Robotech: Vermilion #3 © Comico

Rocket Comics #2 © HILL

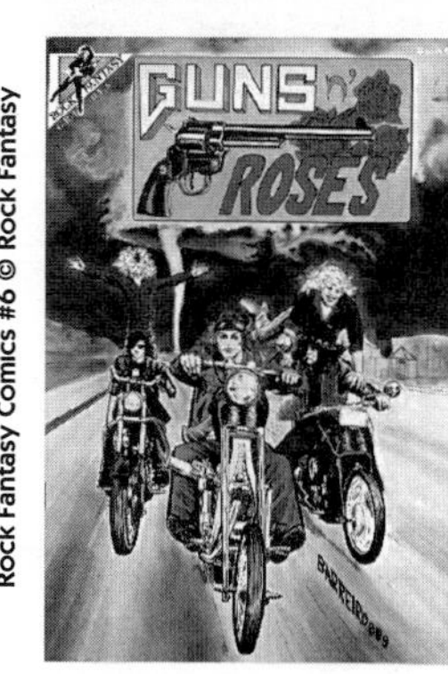

Rock Fantasy Comics #6 © Rock Fantasy

GD25 FN65 NM94

1-Steacy painted-c 2.50

ROBOTECH MASTERS (TV)
Comico: July, 1985 - No. 23, Apr, 1988 ($1.50)

1 2.50
2-23 2.00

ROBOTECH: SENTINELS - RUBICON
Antarctic Press: July, 1998 - Present ($2.95, B&W)

1 2.95

ROBOTECH SPECIAL
Comico: May, 1988 ($2.50, one-shot, 44 pgs.)

1-Steacy wraparound-c; partial photo-c 2.50

ROBOTECH THE GRAPHIC NOVEL
Comico: Aug, 1986 ($5.95, 8-1/2x11", 52pgs.)

1-Origin SDF-1; intro T.R. Edwards, Steacy-c/a; 2nd printing also exists (12/86). 2.00 6.00

ROBOTECH: THE MACROSS SAGA (TV)(Formerly Macross)
Comico: No. 2, Feb, 1985 - No. 36, Feb, 1989 ($1.50)

2-10 2.50
11-36: 12,17-Ken Steacy painted-c. 26-Begin $1.75-c. 35,36-($1.95) 2.00

ROBOTECH: THE NEW GENERATION
Comico: July, 1985 - No. 25, July, 1988

1-25 2.00

ROBOTECH: VERMILION
Antarctic Press: Mar, 1997 - No. 4, ($2.95, B&W, limited series)

1-4 2.95

ROBOTECH: WINGS OF GIBRALTAR
Antarctic Press: Aug, 1998 - No. 2, Sept, 1998 ($2.95, B&W, limited series)

1,2-Lee Duhig-s/a 2.95

ROBOTIX
Marvel Comics: Feb, 1986 (75¢, one-shot)

1-Based on toy 1.00

ROBOTMEN OF THE LOST PLANET (Also see Space Thrillers)
Avon Periodicals: 1952 (Also see Strange Worlds #19)

1-McCann-a (3 pgs.); Fawcette-a 85.00 256.00 725.00

ROB ROY
Dell Publishing Co.: 1954 (Disney-Movie)

Four Color 544-Manning-a, photo-c 7.00 22.00 80.00

ROBYN OF SHERWOOD
Caliber Comics: 1998 - Present ($2.95, B&W)

1-Two covers 2.95

ROCK & ROLL HIGH SCHOOL
Roger Corman's Cosmic Comics: Oct, 1995 ($2.50)

1-Bob Fingerman scripts 2.50

ROCK AND ROLLO (Formerly TV Teens)
Charlton Comics: V2#14, Oct, 1957 - No. 19, Sept, 1958

V2#14-19 4.25 13.00 26.00

ROCK COMICS
Landgraphic Publ.: Jul/Aug, 1979 ($1.25, tabloid size, 28 pgs.)

1-N. Adams-c; Thor(not Marvel's) story by Adams 1.20 3.60 12.00

ROCKET COMICS
Hillman Periodicals: Mar, 1940 - No. 3, May, 1940

1-Rocket Riley, Red Roberts the Electro Man (origin), The Phantom Ranger, The Steel Shark, The Defender, Buzzard Barnes and his Sky Devils, Lefty Larson, & The Defender, the Man with a Thousand Faces begin (1st app. of each); all have Rocket Riley-c 212.00 636.00 1800.00
2,3 109.00 327.00 925.00

ROCKETEER, THE (See Eclipse Graphic Album Series, Pacific Presents & Starslayer)

ROCKETEER ADVENTURE MAGAZINE, THE
Comico/Dark Horse Comics No. 3: July, 1988 ($2.00); No. 2, July, 1989 ($2.75); No. 3, Jan, 1995 ($2.95)

1-(7/88, $2.00)-Dave Stevens-c/a in all; Kaluta back-up-a; 1st app. Jonas (character based on The Shadow) 1.00 3.00 10.00
2-(6/88, $2.75)-Stevens/Dorman painted-c .85 2.60 7.00
3-(1/95, $2.95)-Includes pinups by Stevens, Gulacy, Plunkett, & Mignola 3.00
Volume 2-(9/96, $9.95, magazine size TPB)-Reprints #1-3 10.00

ROCKETEER SPECIAL EDITION, THE
Eclipse Comics: Nov, 1984 ($1.50, Baxter paper)(Chapter 5 of Rocketeer serial)

1-Stevens-c/a; Kaluta back-c; pin-ups inside 1.20 3.60 12.00
NOTE: *Originally intended to be published in Pacific Presents.*

ROCKETEER: THE OFFICIAL MOVIE ADAPTATION, THE
W. D. Publications (Disney): 1991

nn-($5.95, 68 pgs.)-Squarebound deluxe edition 6.00
nn-($2.95, 68 pgs.)-Stapled regular edition 3.00
3-D Comic Book (1991, $7.98, 52 pgs.) 8.00

ROCKET KELLY (See The Bouncer, Green Mask #10); becomes Li'l Pan #6)
Fox Feature Syndicate: 1944; Fall, 1945 - No. 5, Oct-Nov, 1946

nn (1944) 25.00 74.00 185.00
1 25.00 74.00 185.00
2-The Puppeteer app. (costumed hero) 19.00 58.00 145.00
3-5: 5-(#5 on cover, #4 inside) 17.00 52.00 130.00

ROCKETMAN (Strange Fantasy #2 on) (See Hello Pal & Scoop Comics)
Ajax/Farrell Publications: June, 1952 (Strange Stories of the Future)

1-Rocketman & Cosmo 39.00 116.00 290.00

ROCKET RACCOON
Marvel Comics: May, 1995 - No. 4, Aug, 1985 (color, limited series)

1-4: Mignola-a 1.50

ROCKETS AND RANGE RIDERS
Richfield Oil Corp.: May, 1957 (Giveaway, 16 pgs., soft-c)

nn-Toth-a 16.00 48.00 120.00

ROCKET SHIP X
Fox Features Syndicate: September, 1951; 1952

1 54.00 161.00 455.00
1952 (nn, nd, no publ.)-Edited 1951-c 38.00 114.00 285.00

ROCKET TO ADVENTURE LAND (See Pixie Puzzle...)

ROCKET TO THE MOON
Avon Periodicals: 1951

nn-Orlando-c/a; adapts Otis Aldebert Kline's "Maza of the Moon" 88.00 265.00 750.00

ROCK FANTASY COMICS
Rock Fantasy Comics: Dec, 1989 - No. 16?, 1991 ($2.25/$3.00, B&W)(No cover price)

1-Pink Floyd part 1 2.50
1-2nd printing ($3.00-c) 3.00
2,3: 2-Rolling Stones #1. 3-Led Zeppelin #1 3.00
2,3: 2nd printings ($3.00-c, 1/90 & 2/90) 3.00
4-Stevie Nicks Not published
5-Monstrosities of Rock #1; photo back-c 2.50
5-2nd printing ($3.00, 3/90 indicia, 2/90-c) 3.00
6-15,17,18: 6-Guns n' Roses #1 (1st & 2nd printings, 3/90)-Begin $3.00-c. 7-Sex Pistols #1. 8-Alice Cooper; not published. 9-Van Halen #1; photo back-c.

Rocko's Modern Life #1 © Nickelodeon

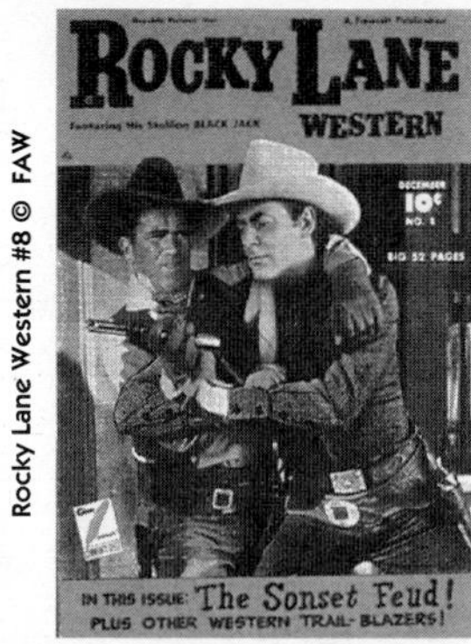

Rocky Lane Western #8 © FAW

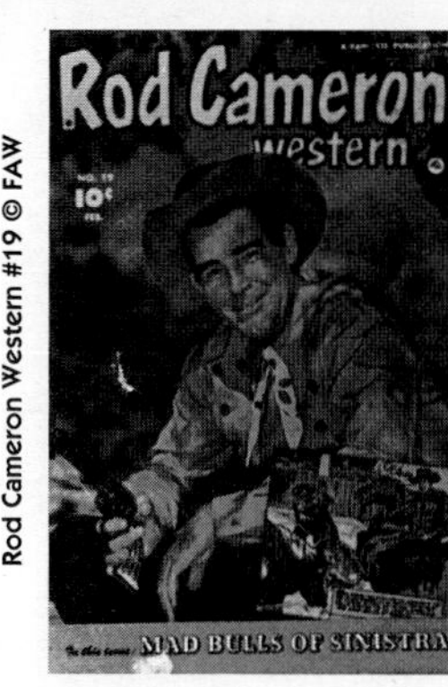

Rod Cameron Western #19 © FAW

GD25 FN65 NM94

10-Kiss #1; photo back-c. 11-Jimi Hendrix #1; wraparound-c 3.00
16-($5.00, 68 pgs.)-The Great Gig in the Sky(Floyd) 5.00

ROCK HAPPENING (Harvey Pop Comics:...)(See Bunny)
Harvey Publications: Sept, 1969 - No. 2, Nov, 1969

1,2: Featuring Bunny 2.50 7.50 24.00

ROCK N' ROLL COMICS
Revolutionary Comics: Jun, 1989 - No. 24, 1992 ($1.50/$1.95, B&W/col. #15 on)

1-Guns N' Roses .90 2.70 8.00
1-2nd thru 6th printings 1.50
1-7th printing (full color w/new-c/a; $1.95) 2.00
2-Metallica 1.00 3.00 10.00
2-2nd thru 6th printings (6th in color) 1.50
3-Bon Jovi (no reprints) .90 2.70 8.00
4-8,10-24: 4-Motley Crue(2nd printing only, 1st destroyed). 5-Def Leppard (2 printings). 6-Rolling Stones(4 printings). 7-The Who(3 printings). 8-Skid Row; not published. 10-Warrant/Whitesnake(2 printings; 1st has 2 diff.-c). 11-Aerosmith (2 printings?). 12-New Kids on the Block(2 printings). 12-3rd printing; rewritten & titled NKOTB Hate Book. 13-Led Zeppelin. 14-Sex Pistols. 15-Poison; 1st color issue. 16-Van Halen. 17-Madonna. 18-Alice Cooper. 19-Public Enemy/2 Live Crew. 20-Queensryche/Tesla. 21-Prince? 22-AC/DC; begin $2.50-c. 23-Living Colour. 24-Anthrax 5.00
9-Kiss 1.00 3.00 10.00
9-2nd & 3rd printings 2.00

NOTE: *Most issues were reprinted except #3. Later reprints are in color. #8 was not released.*

ROCKO'S MODERN LIFE (TV)
Marvel Comics: June, 1994 - No. 7, Dec, 1994 ($1.95) (Nickelodeon cartoon)

1-7 2.00

ROCKY AND HIS FIENDISH FRIENDS (TV)(Bullwinkle)
Gold Key: Oct, 1962 - No. 5, Sept, 1963 (Jay Ward)

1 (25¢, 80 pgs.) 20.00 60.00 220.00
2,3 (25¢, 80 pgs.) 14.00 42.00 155.00
4,5 (Regular size, 12¢) 9.00 29.00 105.00

ROCKY AND HIS FRIENDS (See Kite Fun Book & March of Comics #216)

ROCKY AND HIS FRIENDS (TV)
Dell Publishing Co.: No. 1128, 8-10/60 - No.1311,1962 (Jay Ward)

Four Color #1128 (#1) (8-10/60) 36.00 109.00 400.00
Four Color #1152 (12-2/61), 1166, 1208, 1275, 1311('62) 23.00 68.00 250.00

ROCKY HORROR PICTURE SHOW THE COMIC BOOK, THE
Caliber Press: Jul, 1990 - No. 3, 1990 ($2.95, mini-series, 52 pgs.)(Photo-c #1)

1-Adapts cult film plus photos, etc. 3.00
1-2nd printing 3.00
2,3 3.00
...Collection ($4.95) 5.00

ROCKY JONES SPACE RANGER (See Space Adventures #15-18)

ROCKY JORDEN PRIVATE EYE (See Private Eye)

ROCKY LANE WESTERN (Allan Rocky Lane starred in Republic movies & TV for a short time as Allan Lane, Red Ryder & Rocky Lane) (See Black Jack Fawcett Movie Comics, Motion Picture Comics & Six-Gun Heroes)
Fawcett Publications/Charlton No. 56 on: May, 1949 - No. 87, Nov, 1959

1 (36 pgs.)-Rocky, his stallion Black Jack, & Slim Pickens begin; photo-c begin, end #57; photo back-c 88.00 265.00 750.00
2 (36 pgs.)-Last photo back-c 39.00 117.00 300.00
3-5 (52 pgs.): 4-Captain Tootsie by Beck 25.00 76.00 190.00
6,10 (36 pgs.): 10-Complete western novelette "Badman's Reward" 19.00 56.00 140.00
7-9 (52 pgs.) 20.00 60.00 150.00
11-13,15-17 (52 pgs.): 15-Black Jack's Hitching Post begins, ends #25 15.00 44.00 110.00
14,18 (36 pgs.) 12.00 36.00 90.00
19-21,23,24 (52 pgs.): 20-Last Slim Pickens. 21-Dee Dickens begins, ends #55,57,65-68 12.00 36.00 90.00
22,25-28,30 (36 pgs. begin) 11.00 34.00 85.00
29-Classic complete novel "The Land of Missing Men" with hidden land of ancient temple ruins (r-in #65) 16.00 48.00 120.00
31-40 10.00 30.00 75.00
41-54 9.30 28.00 65.00
55-Last Fawcett issue (1/54) 9.30 28.00 70.00
56-1st Charlton issue (2/54)-Photo-c 16.00 48.00 120.00
57,60-Photo-c 9.30 28.00 70.00
58,59,61-64: 59-61-Young Falcon app. 64-Slim Pickens app. 7.15 21.50 50.00
65-r/#29, "The Land of Missing Men" 8.50 26.00 60.00
66-68: Reprints #30,31,32 7.15 21.50 50.00
69-78,80-86 7.15 21.50 50.00
79-Giant Edition (68 pgs.) 9.30 28.00 70.00
87-Last issue 9.30 28.00 65.00

NOTE: *Complete novels in #10, 14, 18, 22, 25, 30-32, 36, 38, 39, 49. Captain Tootsie in #4, 12, 20. Big Bow and Little Arrow in #11, 28, 63. Black Jack's Hitching Post in #15-25, 64, 73.*

ROCKY LANE WESTERN
AC Comics: 1989 ($2.50, B&W, one-shot?)

1-Photo-c; Giordano reprints 2.50
Annual 1 (1991, $2.95, B&W, 44 pgs.)-photo front/back & inside-c; reprints. 3.00

ROD CAMERON WESTERN (Movie star)
Fawcett Publications: Feb, 1950 - No. 20, Apr, 1953

1-Rod Cameron, his horse War Paint, & Sam The Sheriff begin; photo front/back-c begin 49.00 147.00 415.00
2 24.00 72.00 180.00
3-Novel length story "The Mystery of the Seven Cities of Cibola" 20.00 60.00 150.00
4-10: 9-Last photo back-c 16.00 48.00 120.00
11-19 13.00 38.00 95.00
20-Last issue & photo-c 13.00 40.00 100.00

NOTE: *Novel length stories in No. 1-8, 12-14.*

RODEO RYAN (See A-1 Comics #8)

ROEL
Sirius: Feb, 1997 ($2.95, B&W, one-shot)

1 2.95

ROGAN GOSH
DC Comics (Vertigo): 1994 ($6.95, one-shot)

nn-Peter Milligan scripts .85 2.60 7.00

ROGER DODGER (Also in Exciting Comics #57 on)
Standard Comics: No. 5, Aug, 1952

5-Teen-age 4.15 12.50 25.00

ROGER RABBIT (Also see Marvel Graphic Novel)
Disney Comics: June, 1990 - No. 18, Nov, 1991 ($1.50)

1-18-All new stories 1.50
In 3-D 1 (1992, $2.50)-Sold at Wal-Mart?; w/glasses 2.50

ROGER RABBIT'S TOONTOWN
Disney Comics: Aug, 1991 - No. 5, Dec, 1991 ($1.50)

1-5 1.50

ROGER ZELAZNY'S AMBER: THE GUNS OF AVALON
DC Comics: 1996 - No. 3, 1996 ($6.95, limited series)

1-3: Based on novel .85 2.60 7.00

ROG 2000
Pacific Comics: June, 1982 ($2.95, 44 pgs., B&W, one-shot)

nn-Byrne-c/a (r); 2nd printing (7/82) exists 5.00

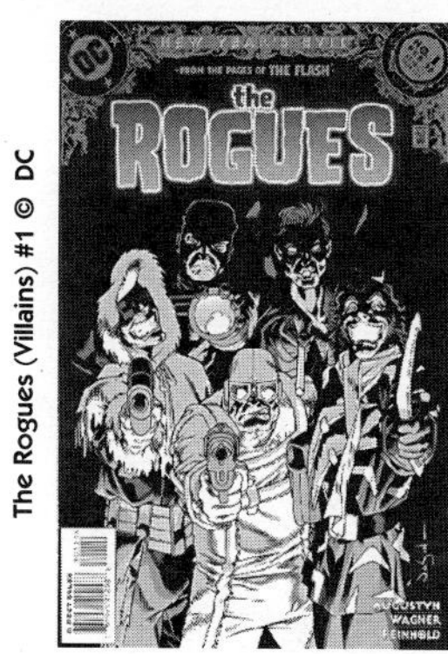

The Rogues (Villains) #1 © DC

ROM #27 © Parker Bros.

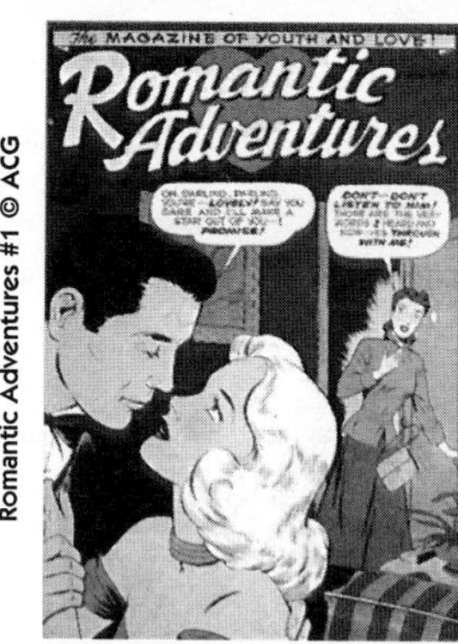

Romantic Adventures #1 © ACG

	GD25	FN65	NM94

ROG 2000
Fantagraphics Books: 1987 - No. 2, 1987 ($2.00, limited series)

	GD25	FN65	NM94
1,2-Byrne-r			2.00

ROGUE
Marvel Comics: Jan, 1995 - No. 4, Apr, 1995 ($2.95, limited series)

	GD25	FN65	NM94
1-4: 1-Gold foil logo			3.50
TPB-($12.95) r/#1-4			13.00

ROGUES GALLERY
DC Comics: 1996 ($3.50, one-shot)

	GD25	FN65	NM94
1-Pinups of DC villains by various artists			3.50

ROGUES, THE (VILLAINS) (See The Flash)
DC Comics: Feb, 1998 ($1.95, one-shot)

	GD25	FN65	NM94
1-Augustyn-s/Pearson-c			2.00

ROGUE TROOPER
Quality Comics/Fleetway Quality #38-on : Oct, 1986 - No. 49, 1991 ($1.25/$1.50/$1.75)

	GD25	FN65	NM94
1-19:($1.25). 6-Double size			1.25
20-38- ($1.50): 21,22,25-27-Guice-c			1.50
39-49 ($1.75): 47,48-Alan Moore scripts			1.75

ROLLING STONES: VOODOO LOUNGE
Marvel Comics: 1995 ($6.95, Prestige format, one-shot)

	GD25	FN65	NM94
nn	1.00	2.80	7.00

ROLY POLY COMIC BOOK
Green Publishing Co.: 1945 - No. 15, 1946 (MLJ reprints)

	GD25	FN65	NM94
1-Red Rube & Steel Sterling begin; Sahle-c	25.00	76.00	190.00
6-The Blue Circle & The Steel Fist app.	13.00	40.00	100.00
10-Origin Red Rube retold; Steel Sterling story (Zip #41)	12.00	36.00	90.00
11,12,14: The Black Hood app. in each. 14-Decapitation-c	15.00	44.00	110.00
15-The Blue Circle & The Steel Fist app.; cover exact swipe from Fox Blue Beetle #1	28.00	84.00	210.00

ROM (Based on toy)
Marvel Comics Group: Dec, 1979 - No. 75, Feb, 1986

	GD25	FN65	NM94
1			3.00
2-16,19-24,26-30: Based on a Parker Bros. toy; 1-Origin/1st app.13-Saga of the Space Knights begins. 19-X-Men cameo. 24-F.F. cameo;Skrulls, Nova & The New Champions app. 26,27-Galactus app.25-Dbl.size			1.95
17,18-X-Men app.			4.00
31-60: 31,32-Brotherhood of Evil Mutants app. 32-X-Men cameo. 34,35-Sub-Mariner app. 41,42-Dr. Strange app. 50-Skrulls app. (52 pgs.). 56,57-Alpha Flight app. 58,59-Ant-Man app.			1.95
61-75: 65-West Coast Avengers & Beta Ray Bill app. 65,66-X-Men app.			2.25
Annual 1,4: 1(1982, 52 pgs.). 4(1985, 52 pgs.)			1.95
Annual 2,3: 2(1983, 52 pgs.). 3(1984, 52 pgs.)			1.95

NOTE: *Austin c-3i, 18i, 61i.* ***Byrne*** *a-74i; c-56, 57, 74.* ***Ditko*** *a-59-75p, Annual 4.* ***Golden*** *c-7-12, 19.* ***Guice*** *a-61i; c-55, 58, 60p, 70p.* ***Layton*** *a-59i, 72i; c-15, 59i, 69.* ***Miller*** *c-2p?, 3p, 17p, 18p.* ***Russell*** *a(i)-64, 65, 67, 69, 71, 75; c-64, 65i, 66, 71i, 75.* ***Severin*** *c-41p.* ***Sienkiewicz*** *a-53i; c-46, 47, 52-54, 68, 71p, Annual 2.* ***Simonson*** *c-18.* ***P. Smith*** *c-59p.* ***Starlin*** *c-67.* ***Zeck*** *c-50.*

ROMANCE (See True Stories of...)

ROMANCE AND CONFESSION STORIES (See Giant Comics Edition)
St. John Publishing Co.: No date (1949) (25¢, 100 pgs.)

	GD25	FN65	NM94
1-Baker-c/a; remaindered St. John love comics	37.00	112.00	280.00

ROMANCE DIARY
Marvel Comics (CDS)(CLDS): Dec, 1949 - No. 2, Mar, 1950

	GD25	FN65	NM94
1,2	11.00	32.00	80.00

ROMANCE OF FLYING, THE
David McKay Publications: 1942

	GD25	FN65	NM94
Feature Books 33 (nn)-WW II photos	12.00	36.00	90.00

ROMANCES OF MOLLY MANTON (See Molly Manton)

ROMANCES OF NURSE HELEN GRANT, THE
Atlas Comics (VPI): Aug, 1957

	GD25	FN65	NM94
1	5.70	17.00	35.00

ROMANCES OF THE WEST (Becomes Romantic Affairs #3?)
Marvel Comics (SPC): Nov, 1949 - No. 2, Mar, 1950 (52 pgs.)

	GD25	FN65	NM94
1-Movie photo-c of Yvonne DeCarlo & Howard Duff (Calamity Jane & Sam Bass)	19.00	58.00	145.00
2-Photo-c	13.00	38.00	95.00

ROMANCE STORIES OF TRUE LOVE (Formerly True Love Problems & Advice Illustrated)
Harvey Publications: No. 45, 5/57 - No. 50, 3/58; No. 51, 9/58 - No. 52, 11/58

	GD25	FN65	NM94
45-51: 45,46,48-50-Powell-a	4.00	11.00	22.00
52-Matt Baker-a	6.00	18.00	42.00

ROMANCE TALES (Formerly Western Winners #6?)
Marvel Comics (CDS): No. 7, Oct, 1949 - No. 9, Mar, 1950 (7,8: photo-c)

	GD25	FN65	NM94
7	11.00	32.00	80.00
8,9: 8-Everett-a	7.85	23.50	55.00

ROMANCE TRAIL
National Periodical Publications: July-Aug, 1949 - No. 6, May-June, 1950 (All photo-c & 52 pgs.)

	GD25	FN65	NM94
1-Kinstler, Toth-a; Jimmy Wakely photo-c	52.00	155.00	440.00
2-Kinstler-a; Jim Bannon photo-c	27.00	80.00	200.00
3-Photo-c; Kinstler, Toth-a	29.00	88.00	220.00
4-Photo-c; Toth-a	22.00	66.00	165.00
5,6: Photo-c on both. 5-Kinstler-a	19.00	58.00	145.00

ROMAN HOLIDAYS, THE (TV)
Gold Key: Feb, 1973 - No. 4, Nov, 1973 (Hanna-Barbera)

	GD25	FN65	NM94
1	2.90	8.70	32.00
2-4	1.80	5.50	20.00

ROMANTIC ADVENTURES (My... #49-67, covers only)
American Comics Group (B&I Publ. Co.): Mar-Apr, 1949 - No. 67, July, 1956 (Becomes My... #68 on)

	GD25	FN65	NM94
1	13.00	40.00	100.00
2	7.15	21.50	50.00
3-10	5.35	16.00	32.00
11-20 (4/52)	4.25	13.00	26.00
21-45,49,51,52: 52-Last Pre-code (2/55)	4.00	11.00	22.00
46-48-3-D effect-c/stories (TrueVision)	9.30	28.00	65.00
50-Classic cover/story "Love of A Lunatic"	7.15	21.50	50.00
53-67	3.00	7.50	15.00

NOTE: *#1-23, 52 pgs.* ***Shelly*** *a-40. Whitney c/art in many issues.*

ROMANTIC AFFAIRS (Formerly Molly Manton's Romances #2 and/or Romances of the West #2 and/or Our Love #2?)
Marvel Comics (SPC): No. 3, Mar, 1950

	GD25	FN65	NM94
3-Photo-c from Molly Manton's Romances #2	7.15	21.50	50.00

ROMANTIC CONFESSIONS
Hillman Periodicals: Oct, 1949 - V3#1, Apr-May, 1953

	GD25	FN65	NM94
V1#1-McWilliams-a	12.00	36.00	90.00
2-Briefer-a; negligee panels	7.15	21.50	50.00
3-12	5.35	16.00	32.00
V2#1,2,4-8,10-12: 2-McWilliams-a	4.25	13.00	28.00
3-Krigstein-a	7.00	21.00	45.00
9-One pg. Frazetta ad	4.25	13.00	28.00
V3#1	4.25	13.00	26.00

ROMANTIC HEARTS

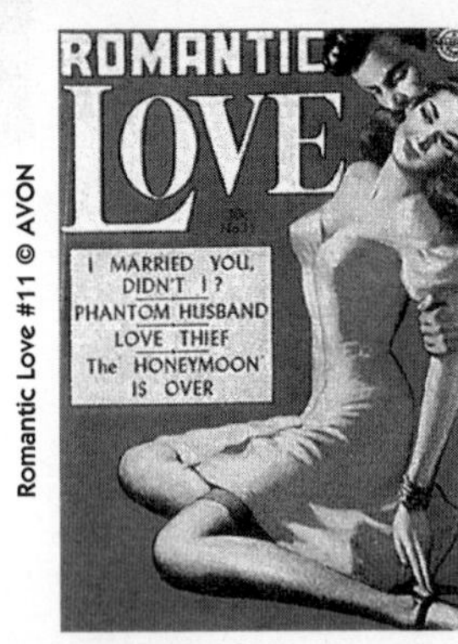

Romantic Love #11 © AVON

Romantic Secrets #1 © FAW

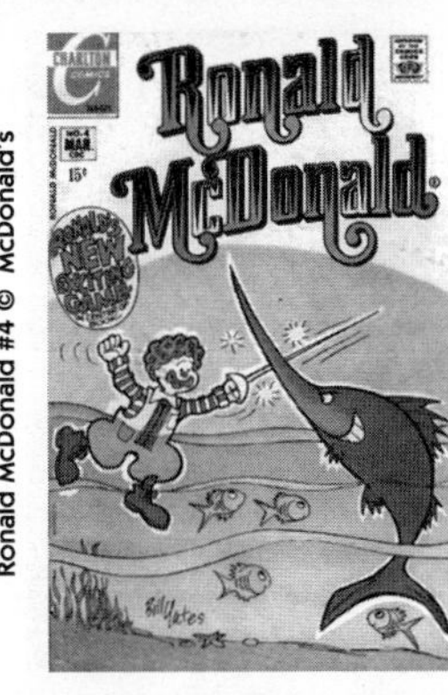

Ronald McDonald #4 © McDonald's

Story Comics/Master/Merit Pubs.: Mar, 1951 - No. 10, Oct, 1952; July, 1953 - No. 12, July, 1955

	GD25	FN65	NM94
1(3/51) (1st Series)	11.00	32.00	80.00
2	5.70	17.00	38.00
3-10: Cameron-a	5.00	15.00	30.00
1(7/53) (2nd Series)-Some say #11 on-c	6.85	21.00	48.00
2	4.15	12.50	25.00
3-12	4.00	11.00	22.00

ROMANTIC LOVE
Avon Periodicals/Realistic (No #14-19): 9-10/49 - #3, 1-2/50; #4, 2-3/51 - #13, 10/52; #20, 3-4/54 - #23, 9-10/54

	GD25	FN65	NM94
1-c-/Avon paperback #252	20.00	60.00	150.00
2-5: 3-c-/paperback Novel Library #12. 4-c-/paperback Diversey Prize Novel #5. 5-c-/paperback Novel Library #34	11.00	34.00	85.00
6- "Thrill Crazy" marijuana story; c-/Avon paperback #207; Kinstler-a	16.00	48.00	120.00
7,8: 8-Astarita-a(2)	10.00	30.00	75.00
9-12: 9-c-/paperback Novel Library #41; Kinstler-a. 10-c-/Avon paperback #212. 11-c-/paperback Novel Library #17; Kinstler-a. 12-c-/paperback Novel Library #13	11.00	34.00	85.00
13,21,22: 22-Kinstler-c	10.00	30.00	75.00
20-Kinstler-c/a	10.00	30.00	75.00
23-Kinstler-c	8.35	25.00	58.00
nn(1-3/53)(Realistic-r)	7.50	22.50	52.00

NOTE: ***Astarita** a-7, 10, 11, 21. Painted c-1-3, 5, 7-11, 13. Photo c-4, 6.*

ROMANTIC LOVE
Quality Comics Group: No. 4, June, 1950

	GD25	FN65	NM94
4 (6/50)(Exist?)	5.70	17.00	35.00
I.W. Reprint #2,3,8: 2-r/Romantic Love #2	1.00	3.00	8.00

ROMANTIC MARRIAGE (Cinderella Love #25 on)
Ziff-Davis/St. John No. 18 on (#1-8: 52 pgs.): #1-3 (1950, no months); #4, 5-6/51 - #17, 9/52; #18, 9/53 - #24, 9/54

	GD25	FN65	NM94
1-Photo-c; Cary Grant/Betsy Drake photo back-c.	16.00	48.00	120.00
2-Painted-c; Anderson-a (also #15)	10.00	30.00	75.00
3-9: 3,4,8,9-Painted-c; 5-7-Photo-c	7.85	23.50	55.00
10-Unusual format; front-c is a painted-c; back-c is a photo-c complete with logo, price, etc.	15.00	44.00	110.00
11-17 13-Photo-c. 15-Signed story by Anderson. 17-(9/52)-Last Z-D issue	7.15	21.50	50.00
18-22,24: 20-Photo-c	7.15	21.50	50.00
23-Baker-c; all stories are reprinted from #15	7.85	23.50	55.00

ROMANTIC PICTURE NOVELETTES
Magazine Enterprises: 1946

	GD25	FN65	NM94
1-Mary Worth-r; Creig Flessel-c	14.00	42.00	105.00

ROMANTIC SECRETS (Becomes Time For Love)
Fawcett/Charlton Comics No. 5 (10/55) on: Sept, 1949 - No. 39, 4/53; No. 5, 10/55 - No. 52, 11/64 (#1-5: photo-c)

	GD25	FN65	NM94
1-(52 pg. issues begin, end #?)	12.00	36.00	90.00
2,3	7.15	21.50	50.00
4,9-Evans-a	7.85	23.50	55.00
5-8,10	5.35	16.00	32.00
11-23	5.00	15.00	30.00
24-Evans-a	5.70	17.00	40.00
25-39('53)	4.00	11.00	22.00
5 (Charlton, 2nd Series)(10/55, formerly Negro Romances #4)	7.15	21.50	50.00
6-10	5.35	16.00	32.00
11-20	2.50	7.50	22.00
21-35: Last 10¢ issue?	2.00	6.00	16.00
36-52('64)	1.50	4.50	12.00

NOTE: ***Bailey** a-20. **Powell** a(1st series)-5, 7, 10, 12, 16, 17, 20, 26, 29, 33, 34, 36, 37. **Sekowsky** a-26. Photo c(1st series)-1-5, 16, 25, 27, 33. **Swayze** a(1st series)-16, 18, 19, 23, 26-28, 31, 32, 39.*

ROMANTIC STORY (Cowboy Love #28 on)
Fawcett/Charlton Comics No. 23 on: 11/49 - #22, Sum, 1953; #23, 5/54 - #27, 12/54; #28, 8/55 - #130, 11/73

	GD25	FN65	NM94
1-Photo-c begin, end #24; 52 pgs. begins	13.00	40.00	100.00
2	7.15	21.50	50.00
3-5	6.00	18.00	42.00
6-14	5.35	16.00	32.00
15-Evans-a	6.00	18.00	42.00
16-22(Sum, '53; last Fawcett issue). 21-Toth-a?	4.00	12.00	24.00
23-39: 26,29-Wood swipes	4.00	12.00	24.00
40-(100 pgs.)	7.85	23.50	55.00
41-50	2.00	6.00	16.00
51-80: 57-Hypo needle story	1.50	4.50	12.00
81-99	.90	2.70	9.00
100	1.20	3.60	12.00
101-130	.85	2.60	7.00

NOTE: ***Jim Aparo** a-94. **Powell** a-7, 8, 16, 20, 30. **Marcus Swayze** a-2, 12, 20, 32.*

ROMANTIC THRILLS (See Fox Giants)

ROMANTIC WESTERN
Fawcett Publications: Winter, 1949 - No. 3, June, 1950 (All Photo-c)

	GD25	FN65	NM94
1	18.00	54.00	135.00
2-(Spr/50)-Williamson, McWilliams-a	18.00	54.00	135.00
3	13.00	38.00	95.00

ROMEO TUBBS (...That Lovable Teenager; formerly My Secret Life)
Fox Feature Syndicate/Green Publ. Co. No. 27: No. 26, 5/50 - No. 28, 7/50; No. 1, 1950; No. 27, 12/52

	GD25	FN65	NM94
26-Teen-age	9.30	28.00	70.00
27-Contains Pedro on inside; Wood-a	13.00	40.00	100.00
28, 1	8.50	26.00	60.00

RONALD McDONALD (TV)
Charlton Press (King Features Synd.): Sept, 1970 - No. 4, March, 1971

	GD25	FN65	NM94
1	4.50	13.50	50.00
2-4	2.70	8.00	30.00

RONIN
DC Comics: July, 1983 - No. 6, Aug, 1984 ($2.50, limited series, 52 pgs.)

	GD25	FN65	NM94
1-Frank Miller-c/a/scripts in all			5.00
2-5			3.00
6-Scarcer; has fold-out poster.	.90	2.70	8.00
Trade paperback (1987, $12.95)-Reprints #1-6			13.00

RONNA
Knight Press: Apr, 1997 ($2.95, B&W, one-shot)

	GD25	FN65	NM94
1-Beau Smith-s			2.95

ROOK (See Eerie Magazine & Warren Presents: The Rook)
Warren Publications: Nov, 1979 - No. 14, April, 1982

	GD25	FN65	NM94
1-Nino-a	1.20	3.60	12.00
2-14: 3,4-Toth-a	.90	2.70	8.00

ROOK
Harris Comics: No. 0, Jun, 1995 - No. 4, 1995 ($2.95)

	GD25	FN65	NM94
0-4: 0-short stories (3) w/preview. 4-Brereton-c.			3.00

ROOKIE COP (Formerly Crime and Justice?)
Charlton Comics: No. 27, Nov, 1955 - No. 33, Aug, 1957

	GD25	FN65	NM94
27	6.85	21.00	48.00
28-33	5.35	16.00	32.00

ROOM 222 (TV)
Dell Publishing Co.: Jan, 1970; No. 2, May, 1970 - No. 4, Jan, 1971

	GD25	FN65	NM94
1	4.00	12.00	42.00

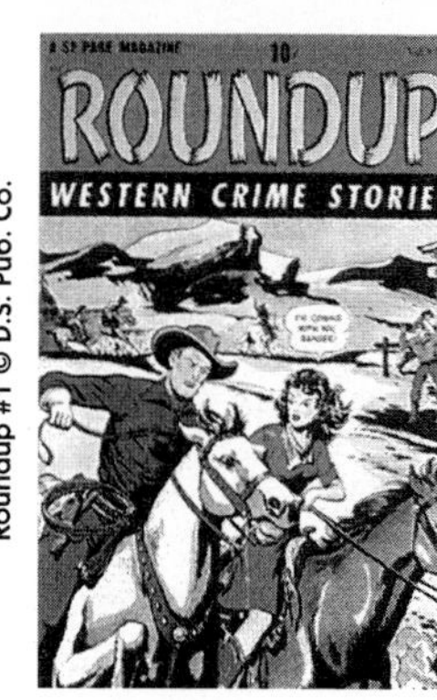

Roundup #1 © D.S. Pub. Co.

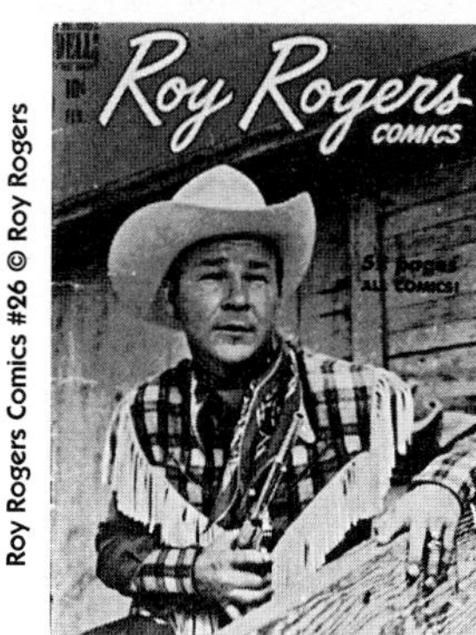

Roy Rogers Comics #26 © Roy Rogers

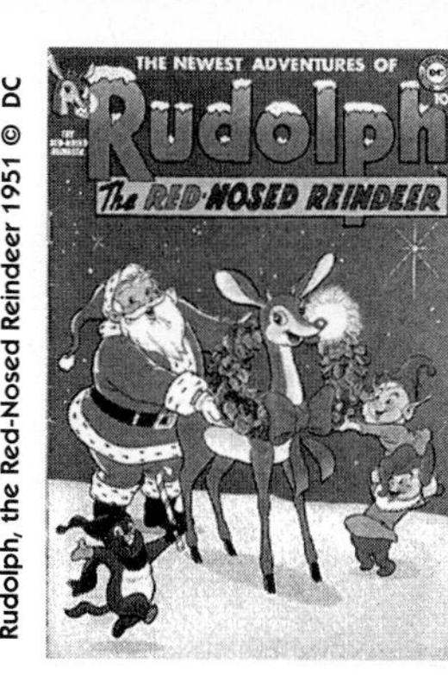

Rudolph, the Red-Nosed Reindeer 1951 © DC

	GD25	FN65	NM94
2-4: 2,4-Photo-c. 3-Marijuana story. 4 r/#1	2.25	6.80	25.00

ROOTIE KAZOOTIE (TV)(See 3-D-ell)
Dell Publishing Co.: No. 415, Aug, 1952 - No. 6, Oct-Dec, 1954

	GD25	FN65	NM94
Four Color 415 (#1)	10.00	30.00	110.00
Four Color 459,502(#2,3)	6.40	19.00	70.00
4(4-6/54)-6	6.40	19.00	70.00

ROOTS OF THE SWAMP THING
DC Comics: July, 1986 - No.5, Nov, 1986 ($2.00, Baxter paper, 52 pgs.)

1-5: r/Swamp Thing #1-10 by Wrightson & House of Mystery-r. 1-new Wrightson-c (2-5 reprinted covers). 2.00

ROSE N'GUNN
Bishop Press: Jan, 1995 - No. 6, May, 1996 ($2.95, B&W, mature)

	GD25	FN65	NM94
1-6			3.00
Creator's Choice ($2.95)-reprints w/pin-ups			3.00

ROSE N'GUNN
London Night Studios: June, 1996 - Aug, 1996 ($3.00, B&W, mature)

	GD25	FN65	NM94
1,2			3.00
1-($6.00)-Blood & Glory Edition		2.00	6.00

ROSWELL: LITTLE GREEN MAN (See Simpsons Comics #19-22)
Bongo Comics: 1996 - Present ($2.95, quarterly)

	GD25	FN65	NM94
1-4			3.50
5			2.95
...Walks Among Us TPB('97, $12.95) r/ #1-3 & Simpsons flip books			12.95

ROUND THE WORLD GIFT
National War Fund (Giveaway): No date (mid 1940's) (4 pgs.)

	GD25	FN65	NM94
nn	11.00	34.00	85.00

ROUNDUP (...Western Crime Stories)
D. S. Publishing Co.: July-Aug, 1948 - No. 5, Mar-Apr, 1949 (All 52 pgs.)

	GD25	FN65	NM94
1-Kiefer-a	17.00	52.00	130.00
2-5: 2-Marijuana drug mention story	11.00	34.00	85.00

ROYAL ROY
Marvel Comics (Star Comics): May, 1985 - No.6, Mar, 1986 (Children's book)

	GD25	FN65	NM94
1-6			1.00

ROY CAMPANELLA, BASEBALL HERO
Fawcett Publications: 1950 (Brooklyn Dodgers)

	GD25	FN65	NM94
nn-Photo-c; life story	52.00	155.00	440.00

ROY ROGERS (See March of Comics #17, 35, 47, 62, 68, 73, 77, 86, 91, 100, 105, 116, 121, 131, 136, 146, 151, 161, 167, 176, 191, 206, 221, 236, 250)

ROY ROGERS AND TRIGGER
Gold Key: Apr, 1967

	GD25	FN65	NM94
1-Photo-c; reprints	3.00	9.00	40.00

ROY ROGERS COMICS (See Western Roundup under Dell Giants)
Dell Publishing Co.: No. 38, 4/44 - No. 177, 12/47 (#38-166: 52 pgs.)

	GD25	FN65	NM94
Four Color 38 (1944)-49 pg. story; photo front/back-c on all 4-Color issues (1st western comic with photo-c)	182.00	546.00	2000.00
Four Color 63 (1945)-Color photos on all four-c	45.00	135.00	490.00
Four Color 86,95 (1945)	33.00	98.00	360.00
Four Color 109 (1946)	24.00	72.00	265.00
Four Color 117,124,137,144	17.00	51.00	185.00
Four Color 153,160,166: 166-48 pg. story	14.50	43.00	160.00
Four Color 177 (36 pgs.)-32 pg. story	14.50	43.00	160.00

ROY ROGERS COMICS (...& Trigger #92(8/55)-on)(Roy starred in Republic movies, radio & TV) (Singing cowboy) (Also see Dale Evans, It Really Happened #8, Queen of the West Dale Evans, & Roy Rogers' Trigger)
Dell Publishing Co.: Jan, 1948 - No. 145, Sept-Oct, 1961 (#1-19: 36 pgs.)

	GD25	FN65	NM94
1-Roy, his horse Trigger, & Chuck Wagon Charley's Tales begin; photo-c begin, end #145	73.00	219.00	800.00
2	24.00	72.00	260.00
3-5	17.00	51.00	185.00
6-10	13.00	39.00	140.00
11-19: 19-Chuck Wagon Charley's Tales ends	9.50	29.00	105.00
20 (52 pgs.)-Trigger feature begins, ends #46	9.50	29.00	105.00
21-30 (52 pgs.)	8.00	25.00	90.00
31-46 (52 pgs.): 37-X-Mas-c	6.25	18.50	70.00
47-56 (36 pgs.): 47-Chuck Wagon Charley's Tales returns, ends #133. 49-X-mas-c. 55-Last photo back-c	4.50	13.50	50.00
57 (52 pgs.)-Heroin drug propaganda story	5.25	16.00	58.00
58-70 (52 pgs.): 58-Heroin drug use/dealing story. 61-X-Mas-c	4.50	13.50	50.00
71-80 (52 pgs.): 73-X-Mas-c	3.80	11.50	40.00
81-91 (36 pgs. #81-on): 85-X-Mas-c	3.25	10.00	36.00
92-99,101-110,112-118: 92-Title changed to Roy Rogers and Trigger (8/55)	3.25	10.00	36.00
100-Trigger feature returns, ends #131	4.75	14.00	52.00
111,119-124-Toth-a	5.00	15.00	55.00
125-131: 125-Toth-a (1 pg.)	3.00	9.00	34.00
132-144-Manning-a. 132-1st Dale Evans-sty by Russ Manning138,144-Dale Evans featured	4.00	12.00	45.00
145-Last issue	5.00	15.00	55.00
...& the Man From Dodge City (Dodge giveaway, 16 pgs., 1954)-Frontier, Inc. (5x7-1/4")	8.00	23.00	85.00
Official Roy Rogers Riders Club Comics (1952; 16 pgs., reg. size, paper-c)	17.00	52.00	190.00

NOTE: ***Buscema** a-74-108(2 stories each). **Manning** a-123, 124, 132-144. **Marsh** a-110. Photo back-c No. 1-9, 11-35, 38-55.*

ROY ROGERS' TRIGGER (TV)
Dell Publishing Co.: No. 329, May, 1951 - No. 17, June-Aug, 1955

	GD25	FN65	NM94
Four Color 329 (#1)-Painted-c	11.00	33.00	120.00
2 (9-11/51)-Photo-c	9.50	29.00	105.00
3-5: 3-Painted-c begin, end #17, most by S. Savitt	4.00	12.00	42.00
6-17: Title merges with Roy Rogers after #17	2.70	8.00	30.00

ROY ROGERS WESTERN CLASSICS
AC Comics: 1989 -No. 4 ($2.95/$3.95, 44pgs.) (24 pgs. color, 16 pgs. B&W)

	GD25	FN65	NM94
1-Dale Evans-r by Manning, Trigger-r by Buscema; photo covers & interior photos by Roy & Dale			3.00
2-Buscema-r (3); photo-c & B&W photos inside			3.00
3,4 ($3.95): 3-Dale Evans-r by Manning; Trigger-r by Buscemaplus other Buscema-r; photo-c.			4.00

RUDOLPH, THE RED NOSED REINDEER (See Limited Collectors' Edition #20, 24, 33, 42, 50)

RUDOLPH, THE RED-NOSED REINDEER
Montgomery Ward: 1939 (2,400,000 copies printed); Dec, 1951 (Giveaway)

	GD25	FN65	NM94
Paper cover-1st app. in print; written by Robert May; ill. by Denver Gillen	11.00	32.00	80.00
Hardcover version	15.00	44.00	110.00
1951 Edition (Has 1939 date)-36 pgs., slick-c printed in red & brown; pulp interior printed in four mixed-ink colors: red, green, blue & brown	6.50	19.50	45.00
1951 Edition with red-spiral promotional booklet printed on high quality stock, 8-1/2"x11", in red & brown, 25 pages composed of 4 fold outs, single sheets and the Rudolph comic book inserted (rare)	45.00	136.00	385.00

RUDOLPH, THE RED-NOSED REINDEER
National Per. Publ.: 1950 - No. 13, Winter, 1962-63 (Issues are not numbered)

	GD25	FN65	NM94
1950 issue (#1); Grossman-c/a begins	17.00	52.00	130.00
1951-53 issues (3 total)	10.00	30.00	75.00
1954/55, 55/56, 56/57	8.50	26.00	60.00
1957/58, 58/59, 59/60, 60/61, 61/62	5.00	15.00	50.00
1962/63 (rare)	9.00	27.00	90.00

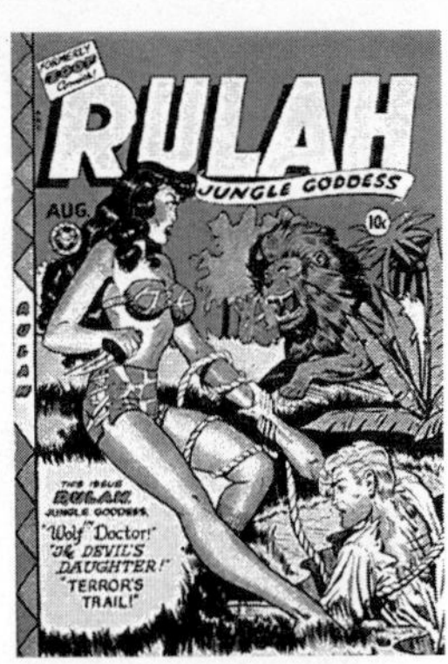

Rulah Jungle Goddess #17 © FOX

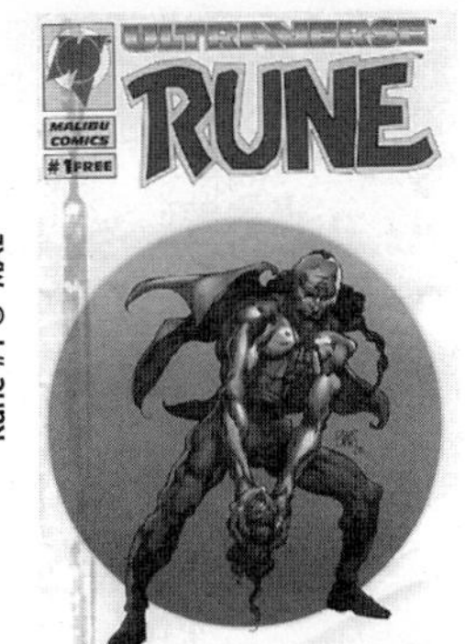

Rune #1 © MAL

Rusty, Boy Detective #2 © LEV

GD25 FN65 NM94

NOTE: *The 1962-63 issue is 84 pages. 9? total issues published. Has games & puzzles also.*

RUFF AND REDDY (TV)
Dell Publ. Co.: No. 937, 9/58 - No. 12, 1-3/62 (Hanna-Barbera)(#9 on: 15¢)

Four Color 937(#1)(1st Hanna-Barbera comic book) 12.00 36.00 130.00
Four Color 981,1038 8.00 23.00 85.00
4(1-3/60)-10: 8-Last 10¢ issue 6.00 18.00 65.00
11,12 6.25 18.50 70.00

RUGGED ACTION (Strange Stories of Suspense #5 on)
Atlas Comics (CSI): Dec, 1954 - No. 4, June, 1955

1-Brodsky-c 11.00 32.00 80.00
2-4: 2-Last precode (2/55) 7.15 21.50 50.00
NOTE: ***Ayers** a-2, 3. **Maneely** c-2, 3. **Severin** a-2.*

RUINS
Marvel Comics (Alterniverse): July, 1995 - No. 2, Sept, 1995 ($5.00, painted, limited series)

1,2: Phil Sheldon from Marvels; Warren Ellis scripts; acetate-c 5.00

RULAH JUNGLE GODDESS (Formerly Zoot; I Loved #28 on) (Also see All Top Comics & Terrors of the Jungle)
Fox Features Syndicate: No. 17, Aug, 1948 - No. 27, June, 1949

17 77.00 231.00 650.00
18-Classic girl-fight interior splash 57.00 171.00 480.00
19,20 52.00 156.00 445.00
21-Used in **SOTI**, pg. 388,389 57.00 171.00 480.00
22-Used in **SOTI**, pg. 22,23 52.00 156.00 445.00
23-27 43.00 129.00 345.00
NOTE: ***Kamen** c-17-19, 21, 22.*

RUNAWAY, THE (See Movie Classics)

RUN BABY RUN
Logos International: 1974 (39¢)

nn-By Tony Tallarico from Nicky Cruz's book 3.00

RUN, BUDDY, RUN (TV)
Gold Key: June, 1967 (Photo-c)

1 (10204-706) 1.80 5.50 20.00

RUNE (See Curse of Rune, Sludge & all other Ultraverse titles for previews)
Malibu Comics (Ultraverse): 1994 - No. 9, Apr, 1995 ($1.95)

0-Obtained by sending coupons from 11 comics; came w/Solution #0, poster, temporary tattoo, card .90 2.70 9.00
1,2,4-9: 1-Barry Windsor-Smith-c/a/stories begin, ends #6. 5-1st app. of Gemini. 6-Prime & Mantra app. 2.00
1-(1/94)-"Ashcan" edition flip book w/Wrath #1 1.00
1-Ultra 5000 Limited silver foil edition .85 2.60 7.00
3-(3/94, $3.50, 68 pgs.)-Flip book w/Ultraverse Premiere #1 3.50
Giant Size 1 ($2.50, 44 pgs.)-B.Smith story & art. 2.50

RUNE (2nd Series)(Formerly Curse of Rune)(See Ultraverse Unlimited #1)
Malibu Comics (Ultraverse): Infinity, Sept, 1995 - V2#7, Apr, 1996 ($1.50)

Infinity, V2#1-7: Infinity-Black September tie-in; black-c & painted-c exist. 1,3-7-Marvel's Adam Warlock app; regular & painted-c exist. 2-Flip book w/"Phoenix Resurrection" Pt. 6. 1.50
...Vs. Venom 1 (12/95, $3.95) 4.00

RUNE: HEARTS OF DARKNESS
Malibu Comics (Ultraverse): Sept, 1996 - No. 3, Nov, 1996 ($1.50, lim. series)

1-3: Doug Moench scripts & Kyle Hotz-c/a; flip books w/6 pg. Rune story by the Pander Bros. 1.50

RUNE/SILVER SURFER
Marvel Comics/Malibu Comics (Ultraverse): Apr, 1995 ($5.95/$2.95, one-shot)

1 ($5.95, direct market)-BWS-c 2.00 6.00
1 ($2.95, newstand)-BWS-c 3.00
1-Collector's limited edition 5.00

GD25 FN65 NM94

RUST
Now Comics: 7/87 - No. 15, 11/88; V2#1, 2/89 - No. 7, 1989 ($1.50/$1.75)

1-3 ($1.50) 1.50
4-11,13-15, V2#1-7 ($1.75) 1.75
12-(8/88, $1.75)-5 pg. preview of The Terminator (1st app.) 1.75

RUST
Caliber Comics: 1996/1997 ($2.95, B&W)

1,2 2.95

RUSTLERS, THE (See Zane Grey Four Color 532)

RUSTY, BOY DETECTIVE
Good Comics/Lev Gleason: Mar-April, 1955 - No. 5, Nov, 1955

1-Bob Wood, Carl Hubbell-a begins 7.15 19.50 50.00
2-5 5.00 15.00 30.00

RUSTY COMICS (Formerly Kid Movie Comics; Rusty and Her Family #21, 22; The Kelleys #23 on; see Millie The Model)
Marvel Comics (HPC): No. 12, Apr, 1947 - No. 22, Sept, 1949

12-Mitzi app. 15.00 46.00 115.00
13 8.50 26.00 60.00
14-Wolverton's Powerhouse Pepper (4 pgs.) plus Kurtzman's "Hey Look" 17.00 52.00 130.00
15-17-Kurtzman's "Hey Look" 13.50 41.00 100.00
18,19 7.15 21.50 50.00
20-Kurtzman-a (5 pgs.) 13.50 41.00 100.00
21,22-Kurtzman-a (17 & 22 pgs.) 18.00 54.00 130.00

RUSTY DUGAN (See Holyoke One-Shot #2)

RUSTY RILEY
Dell Publishing Co.: No. 418, Aug, 1952 - No. 554, April, 1954 (Frank Godwin strip reprints)

Four Color 418 (...a Boy, a Horse, and a Dog #1 3.60 11.00 40.00
Four Color #451(2/53), 486 ('53), 554 2.75 8.00 30.00

SAARI ("The Jungle Goddess")
P. L. Publishing Co.: November, 1951

1 39.00 117.00 300.00

SABAN POWERHOUSE (TV)
Acclaim Books: 1997 - Present ($4.50, digest size)

1,2-Power Rangers, BeetleBorgs, and others 4.50

SABAN PRESENTS POWER RANGERS TURBO VS. BEETLEBORGS METALLIX (TV)
Acclaim Books: 1997 ($4.50, digest size, one-shot)

nn 4.50

SABAN'S MIGHTY MORPHIN POWER RANGERS
Hamilton Comics: Dec, 1994 - No. 6, May, 1995 ($1.95, limited series)

1-6: 1-w/bound-in Power Ranger Barcode Card 2.00

SABAN'S MIGHTY MORPHIN POWER RANGERS (TV)
Marvel Comics: 1995 - No. 8, 1996 ($1.75)

1-8 1.75

SABAN'S NINJA RANGERS
Hamilton Comics: Dec, 1995 - No. 4, Mar, 1995 ($1.95, limited series)

1-4: Flip book w/Saban's V.R. Troopers 2.00

SABAN'S V.R. TROOPERS (See Saban's Ninja Rangers)

SABLE (Formerly Jon Sable, Freelance; also see Mike Grell's...)
First Comics: Mar, 1988 - No. 27, May, 1990 ($1.75/$1.95)

1-27: 10-Begin $1.95-c 1.75

SABRE (See Eclipse Graphic Album Series)

Sabretooth V2 #1 © MAR

Sabrina, the Teen-age Witch #19 © AP

Sad Sack Comics #4 © HARV

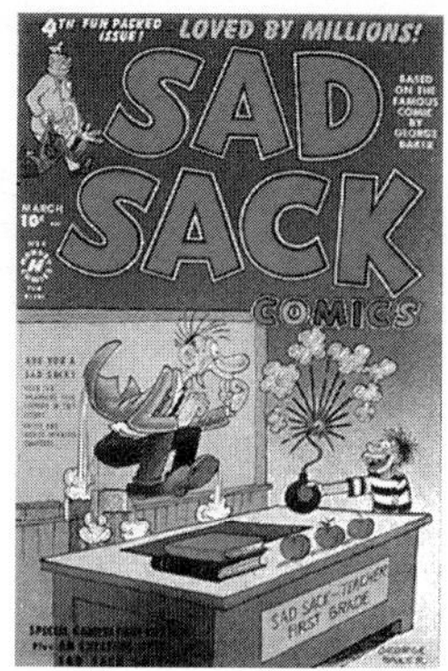

GD25 FN65 NM94

Eclipse Comics: Aug, 1982 - No. 14, Aug, 1985 (Baxter paper #4 on)
1-3 ($1.00): 1-Sabre & Morrigan Tales begin 1.00
4-10 ($1.50): 4-6-Incredible Seven origin 1.50
11,12 ($1.75) 1.75
13,14 ($2.00) 2.00

SABRETOOTH (See Iron Fist, Power Man, X-Factor #10 & X-Men)
Marvel Comics: Aug, 1993 - No. 4, Nov, 1993 ($2.95, lim. series, coated paper)
1-4: 1-Die-cut-c. 3-Wolverine app. 3.00
...Special 1 "In the Red Zone"(1995, $4.95) Chromium wraparound-c 2.00 6.00
V2 #1 (1/98, $5.95, one-shot) Wildchild app. 2.00 6.00
Trade paperback (12/94, $12.95) r/#1-4 13.00

SABRETOOTH AND MYSTIQUE (See Mystique and Sabretooth)

SABRETOOTH CLASSIC
Marvel Comics: May, 1994 - No. 15, July, 1995 ($1.50)
1-15: 1-3-r/Power Man & Iron Fist #66,78,84. 4-r/Spec. S-M #116. 9-Uncanny X-Men #212, 10-r/Uncanny X-Men #213. 11-0r/ Daredevil #238. 12-r/Classic X-Men #10 1.50

SABRINA'S CHRISTMAS MAGIC (See Archie Giant Series Magazine #196, 207, 220, 231, 243, 455, 467, 479, 491, 503, 515)

SABRINA'S HALLOWEEN SPOOOKTACULAR
Archie Publications: 1993 - 1995 ($2.00, 52 pgs.)
1-Neon orange ink-c; bound-in poster 3.00
2,3 2.00

SABRINA, THE TEEN-AGE WITCH (TV)(See Archie Giant Series, Archie's Madhouse 22, Archie's TV..., Chilling Advs. In Sorcery, Little Archie #59)
Archie Publications: April, 1971 - No. 77, Jan, 1983 (52 pg.Giants No. 1-17)

	GD25	FN65	NM94
1-52 pgs. begin, end #17	8.00	23.00	85.00
2-Archie's group x-over	3.80	11.50	40.00
3-5: 3,4-Archie's Group x-over	2.25	6.80	25.00
6-10	2.00	6.00	20.00
11-17(2/74)	1.60	4.80	16.00
18-40(8/77)	.90	2.70	9.00
41-60(6/80)		2.00	6.00
61-77			4.00

SABRINA, THE TEEN-AGE WITCH
Archie Publications: 1996 ($1.50, 32 pgs., one-shot)
1-Updated origin 2.00

SABRINA, THE TEEN-AGE WITCH
Archie Publications: May, 1997 - Present ($1.50/$1.75, 32 pgs)
1-8-Photo-c with Melissa Joan Hart 2.50
9-22: 9-Begin $1.75-c 2.00

SABU, "ELEPHANT BOY" (Movie; formerly My Secret Story)
Fox Features Syndicate: No. 30, June, 1950 - No. 2, Aug, 1950

	GD25	FN65	NM94
30(#1)-Wood-a; photo-c from movie	22.00	66.00	165.00
2-Photo-c from movie; Kamen-a	16.00	48.00	120.00

SACHS & VIOLENS
Marvel Comics (Epic Comics): Nov, 1993 - No. 4, July, 1994 ($2.25, limited series, mature)
1-($2.75)-Embossed-c w/bound-in trading card 2.75
1-($3.50)-Platinum edition (1 for each 10 ordered) 4.00
2-4: Perez-c/a; bound-in trading card: 2-(5/94) 2.25

SACRAMENTS, THE
Catechetical Guild Educational Society: Oct, 1955 (25¢)
304 2.80 7.00 14.00

SACRED AND THE PROFANE, THE (See Eclipse Graphic Album Series #9 & Epic Illustrated #20)

GD25 FN65 NM94

SAD CASE OF WAITING ROOM WILLIE, THE
American Visuals Corp. (For Baltimore Medical Society): (nd, 1950?) (14 pgs. in color; paper covers; regular size)
nn-By Will Eisner (Rare) 43.00 131.00 370.00

SADDLE JUSTICE (Happy Houlihans #1,2) (Saddle Romances #9 on)
E. C. Comics: No. 3, Spring, 1948 - No. 8, Sept-Oct, 1949

	GD25	FN65	NM94
3-The 1st E.C. by Bill Gaines to break away from M. C. Gaines' old Educational Comics format. Craig, Feldstein, H. C. Kiefer, & Stan Asch-a; mentioned in Love and Death	36.00	108.00	300.00
4-1st Graham Ingels-a for E.C.	36.00	108.00	300.00
5-8-Ingels-a in all	35.00	105.00	280.00

NOTE: ***Craig** and **Feldstein** art in most issues. Canadian reprints known; see Table of Contents. **Craig** c-3, 4. **Ingels** c-5-8. #4 contains a biography of **Craig**.*

SADDLE ROMANCES (Saddle Justice #3-8; Weird Science #12 on)
E. C. Comics: No. 9, Nov-Dec, 1949 - No. 11, Mar-Apr, 1950

	GD25	FN65	NM94
9-Ingels-c/a	36.00	108.00	300.00
10-Wood's 1st work at E. C.; Ingels-a; Feldstein-c	36.00	108.00	310.00
11-Ingels-a; Feldstein-c	36.00	108.00	300.00

NOTE: *Canadian reprints known; see Table of Contents. **Wood/Harrison** a-10, 11.*

SADE
Bishop Press/London Night Studios: No. 0, May, 1995 - No. 2, 1996 ($2.95, B&W, mature)
0-2: All Bishop Press issues. 1-Razor app; w/pin-ups 3.00
1($3.00)-London Night Studio's Encore Edition. 3.00
Special 1-Razor app. 3.00
Special 1 ($4.95, limited edition)-Razor app. 5.00

SADE
London Night Studios: June, 1996 - No. 4 ($3.00, B&W, mature)
1-4 3.00
1-Balance of Pain Edition 3.00

SADE AND ROSE & GUNN CONFEDERATE MISTS
Bishop Press: Mar, 1996 ($3.00, B&W, one-shot, mature)
1-w/pin-ups. 3.00

SADIE SACK (See Harvey Hits #93)

SAD SACK AND THE SARGE
Harvey Publications: Sept, 1957 - No. 155, June, 1982

	GD25	FN65	NM94
1	12.00	36.00	120.00
2	5.50	16.50	55.00
3-10	4.00	12.00	40.00
11-20	3.50	10.50	35.00
21-30	2.50	7.50	22.00
31-50	1.75	5.25	14.00
51-70	1.00	3.00	10.00
71-90,97-99	.85	2.60	7.00
91-96: All 52 pg. Giants	1.20	3.60	12.00
100	.90	2.70	9.00
101-120			5.00
121-155			4.00

SAD SACK COMICS (See Harvey Collector's Comics #16, Little Sad Sack, Tastee Freez Comics #4 & True Comics #55)
Harvey Publications/Lorne-Harvey Publications (Recollections) #288 On: Sept, 1949 - No. 287, Oct, 1982; No. 288, 1992 - No. 293?, 1993

	GD25	FN65	NM94
1-Infinity-c; Little Dot begins (1st app.); civilian issues begin, end #21; based on comic strip	40.00	120.00	400.00
2-Flying Fool by Powell	20.00	60.00	200.00
3	11.00	32.00	110.00
4-10	8.00	24.00	80.00
11-21	5.50	16.50	55.00
22-("Back In The Army Again" on covers #22-36); "The Specialist" story about Sad Sack's return to Army	3.50	10.50	35.00

Sad Sack's Funny Friends #1 © HARV

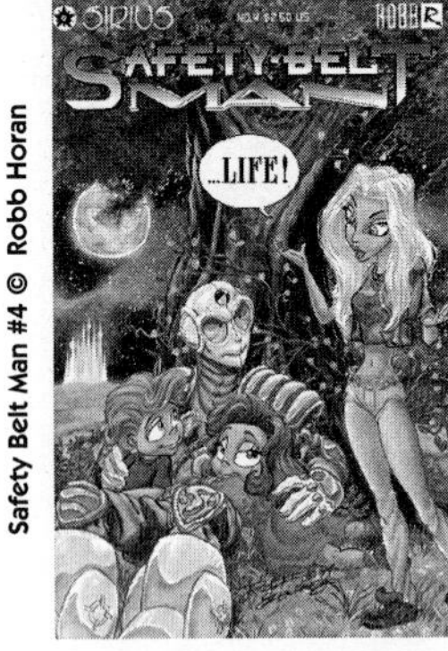

Safety Belt Man #4 © Robb Horan

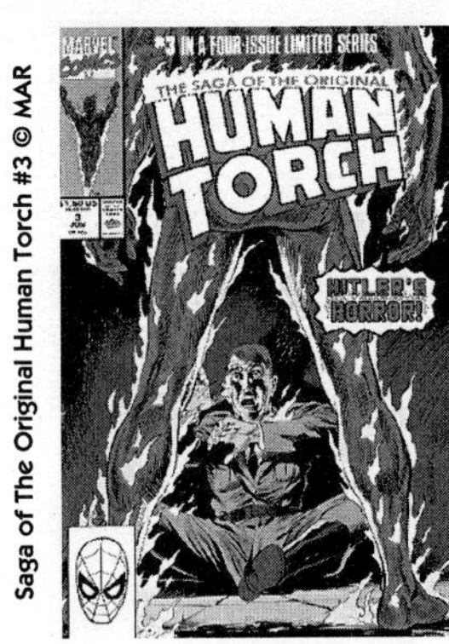

Saga of The Original Human Torch #3 © MAR

	GD25	FN65	NM94
23-50	2.50	7.50	22.00
51-80,100: 62-"The Specialist" reprinted	2.25	6.75	18.00
81-99	1.85	5.50	15.00
101-140	1.20	3.60	12.00
141-170	1.00	3.00	10.00
171-199	.90	2.70	9.00
200	1.00	3.00	10.00
201-222		2.00	6.00
223-228 (25¢ Giants, 52 pgs.)	1.00	3.00	10.00
229-285			4.00
286,287-Limited distribution		2.00	6.00
288,289 ($2.75, 1992): 289-50th anniversary issue			5.00
290-293 ($1.00, 1993, B&W)			3.00
3-D 1 (1/54, 25¢)-Came with 2 pairs of glasses; titled "Harvey 3-D Hits"	16.50	50.00	165.00
Armed Forces Complimentary copies, HD #1-40 (1957-1962)	1.00	2.80	7.00
...At Home for the Holidays 1 (1993, no-c price)-Publ. by Lorne-Harvey' X-Mas issue			2.00

NOTE: *The Sad Sack Comics comic book was a spin-off from a Sunday Newspaper strip launched through John Wheeler's Bell Syndicate. The previous Sunday page and the first 21 comics depicted the Sad Sack in civvies. Unpopularity caused the Sunday page to be discontinued in the early '50s. Meanwhile Sad Sack returned to the Army, by popular demand, in issue No. 22, remaining there ever since. Incidentally, relatively few of the first 21 issues were ever collected and remain scarce due to this.*

SAD SACK FUN AROUND THE WORLD
Harvey Publications: 1974 (no month)

	GD25	FN65	NM94
1-About Great Britain	1.40	4.20	14.00

SAD SACK GOES HOME
Harvey Publications: 1951 (16 pgs. in color, no cover price)

	GD25	FN65	NM94
nn-By George Baker	4.50	13.50	45.00

SAD SACK LAUGH SPECIAL
Harvey Publications: Winter, 1958-59 - No. 93, Feb, 1977 (#1-9: 84 pgs.; #10-60: 68 pgs.; #61-76: 52 pgs.)

	GD25	FN65	NM94
1-Giant 25¢ issues begin	10.00	30.00	100.00
2	5.00	15.00	50.00
3-10	3.50	10.50	35.00
11-30	2.80	8.40	28.00
31-60: 31-1st app. Hi-Fi Tweeter. 60-Last 68 pg. Giant	2.00	6.00	16.00
61-76-(All 52 pg. issues)	1.20	3.60	12.00
77-93		2.00	6.00

SAD SACK NAVY, GOBS 'N' GALS
Harvey Publications: Aug, 1972 - No. 8, Oct, 1973

	GD25	FN65	NM94
1: 52 pg. Giant	1.80	5.40	18.00
2-8	1.00	3.00	10.00

SAD SACK'S ARMY LIFE (See Harvey Hits #8, 17, 22, 28, 32, 39, 43, 47, 51, 55, 58, 61, 64, 67, 70)

SAD SACK'S ARMY LIFE (...Parade #1-57, ...Today #58 on)
Harvey Publications: Oct, 1963 - No. 60, Nov, 1975; No. 61, May, 1976

	GD25	FN65	NM94
1-(68 pg. issues begin)	5.50	16.50	55.00
2-10	2.80	8.40	28.00
11-20	1.50	4.50	15.00
21-34: Last 68 pg. issue	1.20	3.60	12.00
35-51: All 52 pgs.	1.00	3.00	10.00
52-61		2.00	6.00

SAD SACK'S FUNNY FRIENDS (See Harvey Hits #75)
Harvey Publications: Dec, 1955 - No. 75, Oct, 1969

	GD25	FN65	NM94
1	9.00	27.00	90.00
2-10	4.50	13.50	45.00
11-20	2.50	7.50	22.00
21-30	1.40	4.20	14.00
31-50	1.20	3.60	12.00
51-75	1.00	3.00	10.00

SAD SACK'S MUTTSY (See Harvey Hits #74, 77, 80, 82, 84, 87, 89, 92, 96, 99, 102, 105, 108, 111, 113, 115, 117, 119, 121)

SAD SACK USA (...Vacation #8)
Harvey Publications: Nov, 1972 - No. 7, Nov, 1973; No. 8, Oct, 1974

	GD25	FN65	NM94
1	1.50	4.50	15.00
2-8	.90	2.70	8.00

SAD SACK WITH SARGE & SADIE
Harvey Publications: Sept, 1972 - No. 8, Nov, 1973

	GD25	FN65	NM94
1-(52 pg. Giant)	1.80	5.40	18.00
2-8	.90	2.70	8.00

SAD SAD SACK WORLD
Harvey Publ.: Oct, 1964 - No. 46, Dec, 1973 (#1-31: 68 pgs.; #32-38: 52 pgs.)

	GD25	FN65	NM94
1	5.00	15.00	50.00
2-10	2.50	7.50	25.00
11-20	2.00	6.00	20.00
21-31: 31-Last 68 pg. issue	1.80	5.40	18.00
32-39-(All 52 pgs)	1.20	3.60	12.00
40-46	.85	2.60	7.00

SAFEST PLACE IN THE WORLD, THE
Dark Horse Comics: 1993 ($2.50, one-shot)

	GD25	FN65	NM94
1-Steve Ditko-c/a/scripts			2.50

SAFETY-BELT MAN
Sirius Entertainment: June, 1994 - No. 6, 1995 ($2.50, B&W)

	GD25	FN65	NM94
1-Horan-s/Dark One-a/Sprouse-c			3.00
2,3-Warren-c			2.50
4-Linsner back-up story			5.00
5,6-Crilley-a			3.00

SAFETY-BELT MAN ALL HELL
Sirius Entertainment: June, 1996 - No. 6, Mar, 1997 ($2.95, color)

	GD25	FN65	NM94
1-6-Horan-s/Fillbach Bros.-a			3.00

SAGA OF BIG RED, THE
Omaha World-Herald: Sept, 1976 ($1.25) (In color)

	GD25	FN65	NM94
nn-by Win Mumma; story of the Nebraska Cornhuskers (sports)			2.00

SAGA OF CRYSTAR, CRYSTAL WARRIOR, THE
Marvel Comics: May, 1983 - No. 11, Feb, 1985 (Remco toy tie-in)

	GD25	FN65	NM94
1 ($2.00, baxter paper)			2.00
2-5,7-11: 3-Dr. Strange app. 3-11-Golden-c (painted-4,5). 11-Alpha Flight app.			1.00
6-Nightcrawler app; Golden-c.			1.50

SAGA OF RA'S AL GHUL, THE
DC Comics: Jan, 1988 - No. 4, Apr, 1988 ($2.50, limited series)

	GD25	FN65	NM94
1-4-r/N. Adams Batman			2.50

SAGA OF SABAN'S MIGHTY MORPHIN POWER RANGERS (Also see Saban's Mighty Morphin Power Rangers)
Hamilton Comics: 1995 - No. 4, 1995 ($1.95, limited series)

	GD25	FN65	NM94
1-4			2.00

SAGA OF THE SWAMP THING, THE (See Swamp Thing)

SAGA OF THE ORIGINAL HUMAN TORCH
Marvel Comics: Apr, 1990 - No. 4, July, 1990 ($1.50, limited series)

	GD25	FN65	NM94
1-4: 1-Origin; Buckler-c/a(p). 3-Hitler-c			1.50

SAGA OF THE SUB-MARINER, THE
Marvel Comics: Nov, 1988 - No. 12, Oct, 1989 ($1.25/$1.50 #5 on)

	GD25	FN65	NM94
1-12: 9-Original X-Men app.			1.50

Saint Sinner #4 © Clive Barker

Samuree #4 © Continuity Comics

SAN DIEGO COMIC CON COMICS
MARTIN · BYRNE · MILLER · DARROW · CHADWICK · ADAMS
GEARY · GIBBONS · MIGNOLA · WAGNER · ALLRED · O'BARR

San Diego Comic Con Comics #2 © DH

GD25 FN65 NM94

SAILOR ON THE SEA OF FATE (See First Comics Graphic Novel #11)

SAILOR SWEENEY (Navy Action #1-11, 15 on)
Atlas Comics (CDS): No. 12, July, 1956 - No. 14, Nov, 1956

12-14: 12-Shores-a. 13-Severin-c 6.50 19.50 45.00

SAINT, THE (Also see Movie Comics(DC) #2 & Silver Streak #18)
Avon Periodicals: Aug, 1947 - No. 12, Mar, 1952

1-Kamen bondage-c/a 62.00 186.00 525.00
2 39.00 117.00 290.00
3,4: 4-Lingerie panels 29.00 87.00 220.00
5-Spanking panel 36.00 114.00 270.00
6-Miss Fury app. by Tarpe Mills (14 pgs.) 41.00 123.00 325.00
7-c-/Avon paperback #118 23.00 70.00 175.00
8,9(12/50): Saint strip-r in #8-12; 9-Kinstler-c 21.00 62.00 155.00
10-Wood-a, 1 pg; c-/Avon paperback #289 21.00 62.00 155.00
11 14.00 42.00 105.00
12-c-/Avon paperback #123 17.00 49.00 125.00
NOTE: *Lucky Dale, Girl Detective in #1,2,4,6.* **Hollingsworth** *a-4, 6. Painted-c 7, 8, 10-12.*

ST. GEORGE
Marvel Comics (Epic Comics): June, 1988 - No.8, Oct, 1989 ($1.25,/$1.50)

1-8: Sienkiewicz-c 3-begin $1.50-c 1.50

SAINT GERMAINE
Caliber Comics: 1997 - Present ($2.95)

1-8: 1,5-Alternate covers 2.95

SAINT SINNER (See Razorline)
Marvel Comics (Razorline): Oct, 1993 - No. 7, Apr, 1994 ($1.75)

1-($2.50)-Foil embossed-c; created by Clive Barker 2.50
2-7: 5-Ectokid x-over 1.75

ST. SWITHIN'S DAY
Trident Comics: Apr, 1990 ($2.50, one-shot)

1-Grant Morrison scripts 3.00

ST. SWITHIN'S DAY
Oni Press: Mar, 1998 ($2.95, B&W, one-shot)

1-Grant Morrison-s/Paul Grist-a 3.00

SALERNO CARNIVAL OF COMICS (Also see Pure Oil Comics, 24 Pages of Comics, & Vicks Comics)
Salerno Cookie Co.: Late 1930s (Giveaway, 16 pgs, paper-c)

nn-Color reprints of Calkins' Buck Rogers & Skyroads, plus other strips from Famous Funnies 47.00 141.00 400.00

SALOME' (See Night Music #6)

SAM AND MAX, FREELANCE POLICE SPECIAL
Fishwrap Prod./Comico: 1987 ($1.75, B&W); Jan, 1989 ($2.75, 44 pgs.)

1 ($1.75, B&W, Fishwrap) 1.75
2 ($2.75, color, Comico) 2.75

SAM HILL PRIVATE EYE
Close-Up (Archie): 1950 - No. 7, 1951

1 14.00 42.00 105.00
2 8.50 26.00 60.00
3-7 7.85 23.50 55.00

SAM SLADE ROBOHUNTER
Quality Comics: Oct, 1986 - No. 31, 1989 ($1.25/$1.50)

1-19 ($1.25) 1.25
20-31 ($1.50) 1.50

SAMSON (1st Series) (Captain Aero #7 on; see Big 3 Comics)
Fox Features Syndicate: Fall, 1940 - No. 6, Sept, 1941 (See Fantastic Comics)

1-Samson begins, ends #6; Powell-a, signed 'Rensie;' Wing Turner by Tuska app; Fine-c? 188.00 565.00 1600.00

GD25 FN65 NM94

2-Dr. Fung by Powell; Fine-c? 74.00 221.00 625.00
3-Navy Jones app.; Joe Simon-c 58.00 173.00 490.00
4-Yarko the Great, Master Magician begins 49.00 146.00 415.00
5,6: 6-Origin The Topper 41.00 124.00 330.00

SAMSON (2nd Series) (Formerly Fantastic Comics #10, 11)
Ajax/Farrell Publications (Four Star): No. 12, April, 1955 - No. 14, Aug, 1955

12-Wonder Boy 25.00 76.00 190.00
13,14: 13-Wonder Boy, Rocket Man 22.00 66.00 165.00

SAMSON (See Mighty Samson)

SAMSON & DELILAH (See A Spectacular Feature Magazine)

SAMUEL BRONSTON'S CIRCUS WORLD (See Circus World under Movie Comics)

SAMURAI (Also see Eclipse Graphic Album Series #14)
Aircel Publications: 1985 - No. 23, 1987 ($1.70, B&W)

1 3.00
1-2nd & 3rd printings 1.70
2-12,17-23 1.70
2-2nd printing 1.70
13-Dale Keown's 1st published artwork (1987) 5.00
14-16-Dale Keown-a 3.00

SAMURAI
Warp Graphics: May, 1997 - Present ($2.95, B&W)

1 2.95

SAMURAI CAT
Marvel Comics (Epic Comics): June, 1991 - No. 3, Sept, 1991 ($2.25, limited series)

1-3: 3-Darth Vader-c/story parody 2.25

SAMUREE
Continuity Comics: May, 1987 - No. 9, Jan, 1991

1-9 2.00

SAMUREE
Continuity Comics: V2#1, May, 1993 - V2#4, Jan,1994 ($2.50)

V2#1-4-Embossed-c: 2,4-Adams plot, Nebres-i. 3-Nino-c(i) 2.50

SAMUREE
Acclaim Comics (Windjammer): Oct, 1995 - No. 2, Nov,1995 ($2.50, lim. series)

1,2 2.50

SAN DIEGO COMIC CON COMICS
Dark Horse Comics: 1992 - No.4, 1995 (B&W, promo comic for the San Diego Comic Con)

1-(1992)-Includes various characters published from Dark Horse including Concrete, The Mask, RoboCop and others; 1st app. of Sprint from John Byrne's Next Men; art by Quesada, Byrne, Rude, Burden, Moebius & others; pin-ups by Rude, Dorkin, Allred & others; Chadwick-c. 4.00
2-(1993)-Intro of Legend imprint; 1st app. of John Byrne's Danger Unlimited, Mike Mignola's Hellboy, Art Adams' Monkeyman & O'Brien; contains stories featuring Concrete, Sin City, Martha Washington & others; Grendel, Madman, & Big Guy pin-ups; Don Martin-c. 5.00
3-(1994)-Contains stories featuring Barb Wire, The Mask, The Dirty Pair, & Grendel by Matt Wagner; contains pin-ups of Ghost, Predator & Rascals In Paradise; The Mask-c. 4.00
4-(1995)-Contains Sin City story by Miller (3pg.), Star Wars, The Mask, Tarzan, Foot Soldiers; Sin City & Star Wars flip-c 4.00

SANDMAN, THE (1st Series) (Also see Adventure Comics #40, New York World's Fair & World's Finest #3)
National Periodical Publications: Winter, 1974; No. 2, Apr-May, 1975 - No. 6, Dec-Jan, 1975-76

1-1st app. Bronze Age Sandman by Simon & Kirby (last S&K collaboration) . 1.40 4.20 14.00
2-6: 6-Kirby/Wood-c/a 2.00 6.00

Sandman #23 © DC

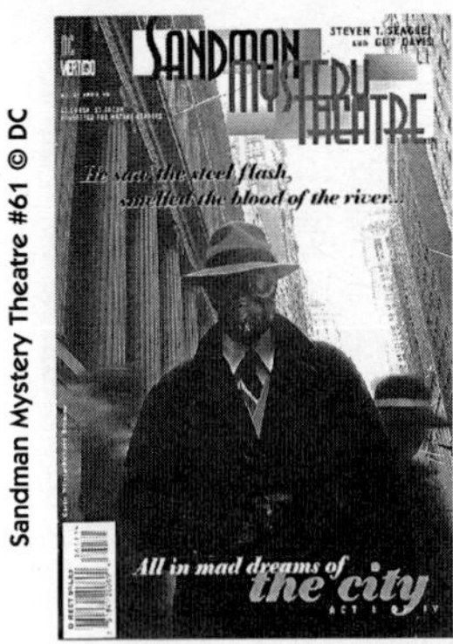

Sandman Mystery Theatre #61 © DC

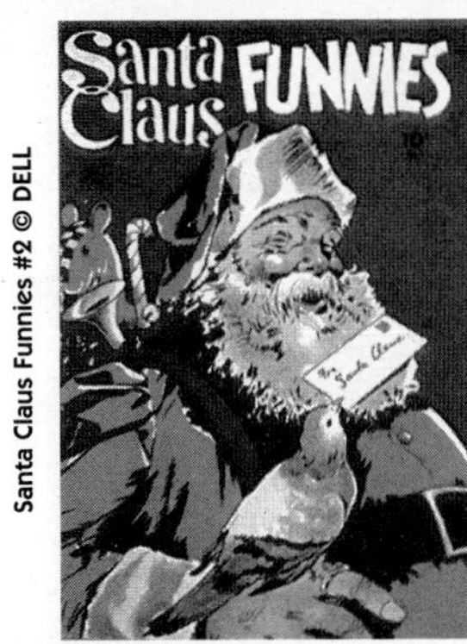

Santa Claus Funnies #2 © DELL

GD25 FN65 NM94

NOTE: ***Kirby** a-1p, 4-6p; c-1-5, 6p.*

SANDMAN (2nd Series) (See Books of Magic, Vertigo Jam & Vertigo Preview)
DC Comics (Vertigo imprint #47 on): Jan, 1989 - No. 75, Mar, 1996 ($1.50/$1.75/$2.50, mature)

1 ($2.00, 52 pgs.)-1st app. Modern Age Sandman (Morpheus); Neil Gaiman scripts begin; Sam Kieth-a(p) in #1-5; Wesley Dodds (G.A. Sandman) cameo. 3.80 11.50 40.00
2-Cain & Abel app. (from HOM & HOS) 1.60 4.80 16.00
3-5: 3-John Constantine app. 1.40 4.20 14.00
6,7 .90 2.70 9.00
8-Death-c/story (1st app.)-Regular ed. has Jeanette Kahn publishorial & American Cancer Society ad w/no indicia on inside front-c; 2.25 6.80 25.00
8-Limited ed. (600+ copies?); has Karen Berger editorial and next issue teaser on inside covers (has indicia) 6.00 17.50 65.00
9-13: 10-Has explaination about #8 mixup; has bound-in Shocker movie poster .90 2.70 8.00
14-($2.50, 52 pgs.)-Bound-in Nightbreed fold-out .90 2.70 8.00
15-20: 16-Photo-c. 17,18-Kelley Jones-a. 19-Vess-a. 5.00
18-Error version w/1st 3 panels on pg. 1 in blue ink 2.00 6.00 20.00
19-Error version w/pages 18 & 20 facing each other 2.00 6.00 20.00
21,23-27: Seasons of Mist storyline. 22-World Without End preview. 24-Kelley Jones/Russell-a 5.00
22-1st Daniel (Later becomes new Sandman) 1.50 4.50 15.00
28-30 3.00
31-35,37-48: 41,44-48-Metallic ink on-c. 48-Cerebus appears as a doll 2.50
36-($2.50, 52 pgs.) 2.50
49,51-53,55: 49-Begin $1.95-c 3.00
50-($2.95, 52 pgs.)-Black-c w/metallic ink by McKean; Russell-a; McFarlane pin-up 4.00
50-($2.95)-Signed & limited (5,000) Treasury Edition with sketch of Neil Gaiman 1.00 3.00 10.00
50-Platinum 25.00
54-Re-intro Prez; Death app.; Belushi, Nixon & Wildcat cameos 4.00
56-68: 57-Metallic ink on c. 65-w/bound-in trading card 4.00
69-Death of Sandman 4.00
70-74: 70-73-Zulli-a. 74-Jon J. Muth-a. 4.00
75-($3.95)-Vess-a. 5.00
Annual 1 (10/94, $3.95) 4.00
Special 1 (1991, $3.50, 68 pgs.)-Glow-in-the-dark-c 3.50
...: A Gallery of Dreams ($2.95)-Intro by N. Gaiman 3.00
...: Preludes & Nocturnes ($29.95, HC)-r/#1-8. 40.00
...: The Doll's House (1990, $29.95, HC)-r/#8-16. 40.00
...: Dream Country ($29.95, HC)-r/#17-20. 30.00
...: Season of Mists ($29.95, Leatherbound HC)-r/#21-28. 50.00
...: A Game of You ($29.95, HC)-r/32-37. 30.00
...: Fables and Reflections ($29.95, HC)-r/Vertigo Preview #1, Sandman Special #1, #29-31, #38-40 & #50. 30.00
...: Brief Lives ($29.95, HC)-r/#41-49. 30.00
...: World's End ($29.95, HC)-r/#51-56. 30.00
...: The Kindly Ones (1996, $34.95, HC)-r/#57-69 & Vertigo Jam#1 35.00
...: The Wake ($29.95, HC)-r/#70-75. 30.00

NOTE: *Multiple printings exist of softcover collections.* ***Bachalo** a-12;* ***Kelley Jones** a-17, 18, 22, 23, 26, 27.* ***Vess** a-19, 75.*

SANDMAN MIDNIGHT THEATRE
DC Comics (Vertigo): Sept, 1995 ($6.95, squarebound, one-shot)

nn-Modern Age Sandman (Morpheus) meets G.A. Sandman; Gaiman & Wagner story; McKean-c; Kristiansen-a .85 2.60 7.00

SANDMAN MYSTERY THEATRE (Also see Sandman (2nd Series) #1)
DC Comics (Vertigo): Apr, 1993 - Present ($1.95/$2.25/$2.50, mature)

1-G.A. Sandman advs. begin; Matt Wagner scripts begin 4.00
2-27: 5-Neon ink logo. 3.00
28-49: 28-Begin $2.25-c. 29-32-Hourman app. 38-Ted Knight (G.A. Starman) app. 42-Jim Corrigan (Spectre) app. 45-48-Blackhawk app. 3.00
50-($3.50, 48 pgs.) w/bonus story of S.A. Sandman, Torres-a 3.50
51-57 2.25
58-69: 58-Begin $2.50 2.50
Annual 1 (10/94, $3.95, 68 pgs.)-Bolton, Ross & others-a. 4.00

SANDS OF THE SOUTH PACIFIC
Toby Press: Jan, 1953

1 19.00 56.00 140.00

SANTA AND HIS REINDEER (See March of Comics #166)

SANTA AND POLLYANNA PLAY THE GLAD GAME
Sales Promotion: Aug, 1960 (16 pgs.) (Disney giveaway)

nn 1.75 5.25 14.00

SANTA AND THE ANGEL (See Dell Junior Treasury #7)
Dell Publishing Co.: Dec, 1949 (Combined w/Santa at the Zoo) (Gollub-a condensed from FC#128)

Four Color 259 3.60 11.00 40.00

SANTA & THE BUCCANEERS
Promotional Publ. Co.: 1959 (Giveaway)

nn-Reprints 1952 Santa & the Pirates 1.25 3.75 10.00

SANTA & THE CHRISTMAS CHICKADEE
Murphy's: 1974 (Giveaway, 20 pgs.)

nn 2.00 6.00

SANTA & THE PIRATES
Promotional Publ. Co.: 1952 (Giveaway)

nn-Marv Levy-c/a 2.80 7.00 14.00

SANTA AT THE ZOO (See Santa And The Angel)

SANTA CLAUS AROUND THE WORLD (See March of Comics #241)

SANTA CLAUS CONQUERS THE MARTIANS (See Movie Classics)

SANTA CLAUS FUNNIES (Also see The Little Fir Tree)
W. T. Grant Co./Whitman Publishing: nd; 1940 (Giveaway, 8x10"; 12 pgs., color & B&W, heavy paper)

nn-(2 versions) 11.00 34.00 85.00

SANTA CLAUS FUNNIES (Also see Dell Giants)
Dell Publishing Co.: Dec?, 1942 - No. 1274, Dec, 1961

nn(#1)(1942)-Kelly-a 36.00 107.00 390.00
2(12/43)-Kelly-a 23.00 70.00 255.00
Four Color 61(1944)-Kelly-a 22.00 67.00 245.00
Four Color 91(1945)-Kelly-a 16.00 49.00 180.00
Four Color 128('46),175('47)-Kelly-a 13.00 38.00 140.00
Four Color 205,254-Kelly-a 12.00 35.00 130.00
Four Color 302,361 3.60 11.00 40.00
Four Color 525,607,666,756,867 3.60 11.00 40.00
Four Color 958,1063,1154,1274 3.00 9.00 35.00

NOTE: *Most issues contain only one Kelly story.*

SANTA CLAUS PARADE
Ziff-Davis (Approved Comics)/St. John Publishing Co.: 1951; No. 2, Dec, 1952; No. 3, Jan, 1955 (25¢)

nn(1951-Ziff-Davis)-116 pgs. (Xmas Special 1,2) 25.00 74.00 185.00
2(12/52-Ziff-Davis)-100 pgs.; Dave Berg-a 19.00 58.00 145.00
V1#3(1/55-St. John)-100 pgs.; reprints-c/#1 17.00 50.00 125.00

SANTA CLAUS' WORKSHOP (See March of Comics #50, 168)

SANTA IS COMING (See March of Comics #197)

SANTA IS HERE (See March of Comics #49)

SANTA ON THE JOLLY ROGER

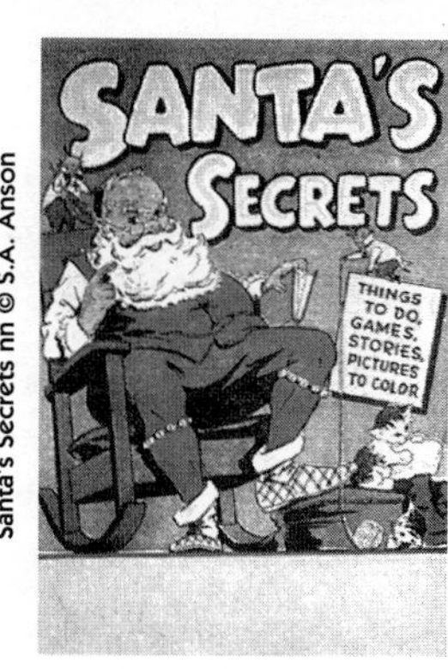

Santa's Secrets nn © S.A. Anson

Satan's Six #1 © Jack Kirby

Savage Combat Tales #2 © Seaboard Periodicals, Inc.

GD25 FN65 NM94

Promotional Publ. Co. (Giveaway): 1965
nn-Marv Levy-c/a 2.40 6.00

SANTA! SANTA!
R. Jackson: 1974 (20 pgs.) (Montgomery Ward giveaway)
nn 4.00

SANTA'S BUSY CORNER (See March of Comics #31)

SANTA'S CANDY KITCHEN (See March of Comics #14)

SANTA'S CHRISTMAS BOOK (See March of Comics #123)

SANTA'S CHRISTMAS COMICS
Standard Comics (Best Books): Dec, 1952 (100 pgs.)
nn-Supermouse, Dizzy Duck, Happy Rabbit, etc. 15.00 44.00 110.00

SANTA'S CHRISTMAS COMIC VARIETY SHOW (See Merry Christmas From Sears Toyland)
Sears Roebuck & Co.: 1943 (24 pgs.)
Contains puzzles & new comics of Dick Tracy, Little Orphan Annie, Moon Mullins, Terry & the Pirates, etc. 47.00 141.00 400.00

SANTA'S CHRISTMAS LIST (See March of Comics #255)

SANTA'S CHRISTMAS TIME STORIES
Premium Sales, Inc.: nd (Late 1940s) (16 pgs., paper-c) (Giveaway)
nn 5.35 16.00 32.00

SANTA'S CIRCUS
Promotional Publ. Co.: 1964 (Giveaway, half-size)
nn-Marv Levy-c/a 1.00 3.00 8.00

SANTA'S FUN BOOK
Promotional Publ. Co.: 1951, 1952 (Regular size, 16 pgs., paper-c) (Murphy's giveaway)
nn 3.00 7.50 15.00

SANTA'S GIFT BOOK
No Publisher: No date (16 pgs.)
nn-Puzzles, games only 2.80 7.00 14.00

SANTA'S HELPERS (See March of Comics #64, 106, 198)

SANTA'S LITTLE HELPERS (See March of Comics #270)

SANTA'S NEW STORY BOOK
Wallace Hamilton Campbell: 1949 (16 pgs., paper-c) (Giveaway)
nn 5.00 15.00 30.00

SANTA'S REAL STORY BOOK
Wallace Hamilton Campbell/W. W. Orris: 1948, 1952 (Giveaway, 16 pgs.)
nn 4.25 13.00 28.00

SANTA'S RIDE
W. T. Grant Co.: 1959 (Giveaway)
nn 1.75 5.25 14.00

SANTA'S RODEO
Promotional Publ. Co.: 1964 (Giveaway, half-size)
nn-Marv Levy-a 1.00 2.80 7.00

SANTA'S SECRETS
Sam B. Anson Christmas giveaway: 1951, 1952? (16 pgs., paper-c)
nn-Has games, stories & pictures to color 3.20 8.00 16.00

SANTA'S SHOW (See March of Comics #311)

SANTA'S SLEIGH (See March of Comics #298)

SANTA'S STORIES
K. K. Publications (Klines Dept. Store): 1953 (Regular size, paper-c)
nn-Kelly-a 16.00 48.00 120.00
nn-Another version (1953, glossy-c, half-size, 7-1/4x5-1/4")-Kelly-a 11.00 32.00 80.00

SANTA'S SURPRISE (See March of Comics #13)

SANTA'S SURPRISE
K. K. Publications: 1947 (Giveaway, 36 pgs., slick-c)
nn 5.35 16.00 32.00

SANTA'S TINKER TOTS
Charlton Comics: 1958
1-Based on "The Tinker Tots Keep Christmas" 2.25 6.75 18.00

SANTA'S TOYLAND (See March of Comics #242)

SANTA'S TOYS (See March of Comics #12)

SANTA'S TOYTOWN FUN BOOK
Promotional Publ. Co.: 1953 (Giveaway)
nn-Marv Levy-c 2.00 5.00 10.00

SANTA'S VISIT (See March of Comics #283)

SANTA THE BARBARIAN
Maximum Press: Dec, 1996 ($2.99, one-shot)
1-Fraga/Mhan-s/a 3.00

SANTIAGO (Movie)
Dell Publishing Co.: Sept, 1956 (Alan Ladd photo-c)
Four Color 723-Kinstler-a 10.00 30.00 110.00

SARGE SNORKEL (Beetle Bailey)
Charlton Comics: Oct, 1973 - No. 17, Dec, 1976
1 1.20 3.60 12.00
2-10 .90 2.70 8.00
11-17 2.00 6.00

SARGE STEEL (Becomes Secret Agent #9 on; also see Judomaster)
Charlton Comics: Dec, 1964 - No. 8, Mar-Apr, 1966 (All 12¢ issues)
1-Origin & 1st app. 2.50 7.50 24.00
2-5,7,8 1.75 5.25 14.00
6-2nd app. Judomaster 2.25 6.75 18.00

SATANIKA
Verotik: Jan, 1995 - No. 3, 1996 ($2.95, limited series, mature)
0-3: Danzig story in all. 0-(7/95)-Frazetta-c; 1-Bisley-c. 2.00 6.00
The Brimstone Trail (1996, $9.95, TPB)-r/#0-2. 10.00

SATANIKA
Verotik: Feb, 1996 - Present ($2.95, mature)
1-9: Danzig story in all. 2-Igrat cameo; indicia reads "Satanika #1." 4,5-nudity-c 3.00

SATANIKA X
Verotik: Feb, 1996 ($4.95, one-shot, mature)
1-Embossed-c. 5.00

SATAN'S SIX
Topps Comics (Kirbyverse): Apr, 1993 - No. 4, July, 1993 ($2.95, lim. series)
1-Polybagged w/Kirbychrome trading card; Kirby/McFarlane-c plus 8 pgs. Kirby-a(p); has coupon for Kirbychrome ed. of Secret City Saga #0 3.00
2-4-Polybagged w/3 cards. 4-Teenagents preview 3.00
NOTE: *Ditko a-1. Miller a-1.*

SATAN'S SIX: HELLSPAWN
Topps Comics (Kirbyverse): June, 1994 - No. 3, July, 1994 ($2.50, lim. series)
1-3: 1-(6/94)-Indicia incorrectly shows "Vol 1 #2". 2-(6/94) 2.50

SAVAGE COMBAT TALES
Atlas/Seaboard Publ.: Feb, 1975 - No. 3, July, 1975
1-3: 1-Sgt. Stryker's Death Squad begins (origin). 2-Only app. Warhawk 4.00

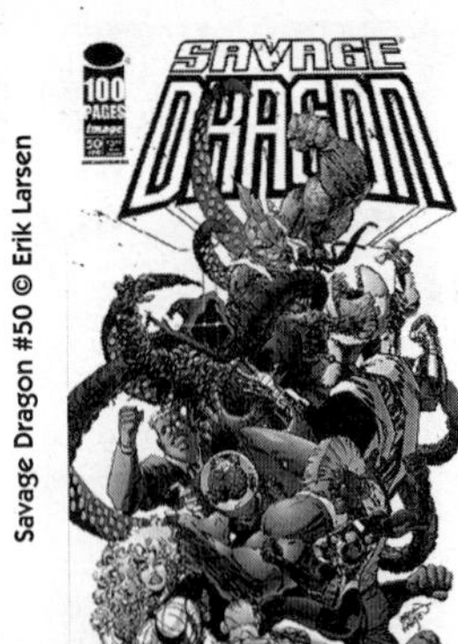

Savage Dragon #50 © Erik Larsen

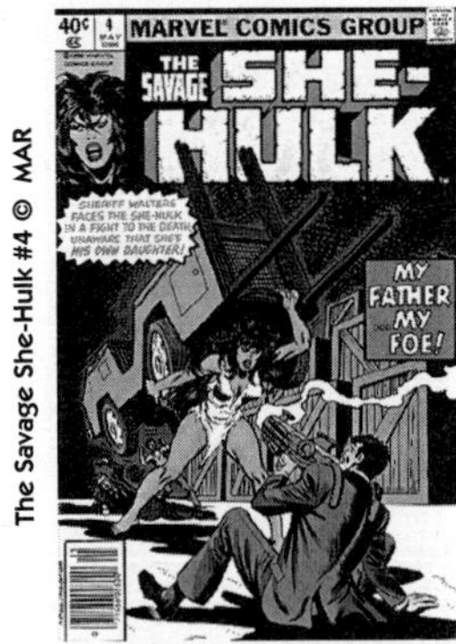

The Savage She-Hulk #4 © MAR

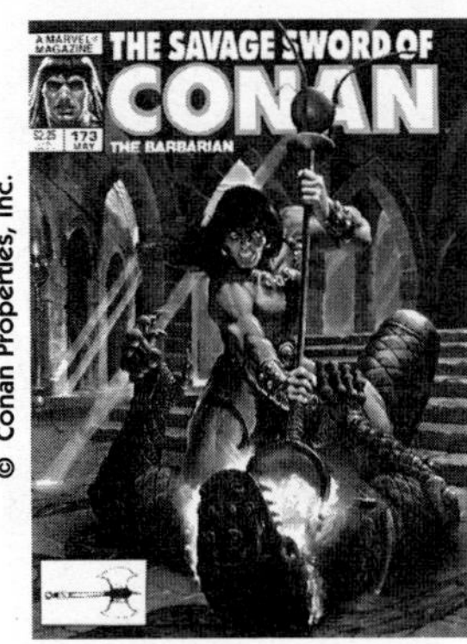

Savage Sword of Conan #173 © Conan Properties, Inc.

GD25 FN65 NM94 | GD25 FN65 NM94

NOTE: ***Buckler** c-3. **McWilliams** a-1-3; c-1. **Sparling** a-1, 3. **Toth** a-2.*

SAVAGE DRAGON, THE (See Megaton #3 & 4)
Image Comics (Highbrow Entertainment): July, 1992 - No. 3, Dec, 1992 ($1.95, limited series)

1-Erik Larsen-c/a/scripts & bound-in poster in all; 4 cover color variations w/4 different posters; 1st Highbrow Entertainment title 3.00
2-Intro SuperPatriot-c/story (10/92) 3.00
3-Contains coupon for Image Comics #0 2.00
3-With coupon missing 1.00
...Vs. Savage Megaton Man 1 (3/93, $1.95)-Larsen & Simpson-c/a. 2.00
TPB-('93, $9.95) r/#1-3 10.00

SAVAGE DRAGON, THE
Image Comics (Highbrow Entertainment): June, 1993 - Present ($1.95/$2.50)

1-Erik Larsen-c/a/scripts 2.00
2,27-(Wondercon Exclusive): 2-($2.95, 52 pgs.)-Teenage Mutant Ninja Turtles-c/story; flip book features Vanguard #0 (See Megaton for 1st app.). 27 (Wondercon Exclusive)-new-c. 2.00
3-7: Erik Larsen-c/a/scripts. 3-Mighty Man back-up story w/Austin-a(i). 4-Flip book w/Ricochet. 5-Mighty Man flip-c & back-up plus poster. 6-Jae Lee poster. 7-Vanguard poster 2.25
8-12,13B,14-15: 8-Deadly Duo poster by Larsen. 13B (6/95)-Larsen story. 15-Dragon poster by Larsen. 2.00
13A,16-24,26,28-30: 13A (10/94)-Jim Lee-c/a; 1st app. Max Cash (Condition Red). 16-$2.50-c begins. 22-TMNT-c/a; Bisley pin-up. 28-Maxx-c/app. 29-Wildstar-c/app. 30-Spawn app. 2.50
25 ($3.95)-variant-c exists. 4.00
27-"Wondercon Exclusive" new-c 3.00
31-49: 31-God vs. The Devil; alternate version exists w/o expletives (has "God Is Good" inside Image logo) 33-Birth of Dragon/Rapture's baby. 34,35-Hellboy-c/app. 2.50
50-($5.95, 100 pgs.) Kaboom and Mighty Man app.; Matsuda back-c; pin-ups by McFarlane, Simonson, Capullo and others 2.00 6.00
51-55: 51-Origin of She-Dragon 2.50
The Fallen TPB (11/97, $12.95) r/#7-11 12.95

SAVAGE DRAGON/DESTROYER DUCK, THE
Image Comics/ Highbrow Entertainment: Nov, 1996 ($3.95, one-shot)

1 4.00

SAVAGE DRAGON/MARSHALL LAW
Image Comics: July, 1997 - No. 2, Aug, 1997 ($2.95, B&W, limited series)

1,2-Pat Mills-s, Kevin O'Neill-a 2.95

SAVAGE DRAGON: SEX & VIOLENCE
Image Comics: Aug, 1997 - No. 2, Sept, 1997 ($2.50, limited series)

1,2-T&M Bierbaum-s, Mays, Lupka, Adam Hughes-a 2.50

SAVAGE DRAGON/TEENAGE MUTANT NINJA TURTLES CROSSOVER
Mirage Studios: Sept, 1993 ($2.75, one-shot)

1-Erik Larsen-c(i) only 2.75

SAVAGE DRAGON: THE RED HORIZON
Image Comics/ Highbrow Entertainment: Feb, 1997 - No. 3 ($2.50, lim. series)

1-3 2.50

SAVAGE FISTS OF KUNG FU
Marvel Comics Group: 1975 (Marvel Treasury)

1-Iron Fist, Shang Chi, Sons of Tiger; Adams, Starlin-a 1.35 4.00 16.00

SAVAGE HENRY
Vortex Comics: Jan, 1987 - No. 16?, 1990 ($1.75/$2.00, B&W, mature)

1-9 ($1.75) 1.75
10-15 ($2.00) 2.00
16-Begin $2.50-c 2.50

SAVAGE HULK, THE (Also see Incredible Hulk)
Marvel Comics: Jan, 1996 ($6.95, one-shot)

1-Bisley-c; David, Lobdell, Wagner, Loeb, Gibbons, Messner-Loebs scripts; McKone, Kieth, Ramos & Sale-a. .85 2.60 7.00

SAVAGE RAIDS OF GERONIMO (See Geronimo #4)

SAVAGE RANGE (See Luke Short, Four Color 807)

SAVAGE RETURN OF DRACULA
Marvel Comics: 1992 ($2.00, 52 pgs.)

1-r/Tomb of Dracula #1,2 by Gene Colan 2.00

SAVAGE SHE-HULK, THE (See The Avengers, Marvel Graphic Novel #18 & The Sensational She-Hulk)
Marvel Comics Group: Feb, 1980 - No. 25, Feb, 1982

1-Origin & 1st app. She-Hulk .85 2.60 7.00
2-10 3.00
11-25: 25-(52 pgs.) 2.25
NOTE: ***Austin** a-25i; c-23i-25i. **J. Buscema** a-1p; c-1, 2p. **Golden** c-8-11.*

SAVAGE SWORD OF CONAN (The... #41 on; ...The Barbarian #175 on)
Marvel Comics Group: Aug, 1974 - No. 235, July, 1995 ($1.00/$1.25/$2.25, B&W magazine, mature)

1-Smith-r; J. Buscema/N. Adams/Krenkel-a; origin Blackmark by Gil Kane (part 1, ends #3); Blackmark's 1st app. in magazine form-r/from paperback) & Red Sonja (3rd app.) 6.50 19.00 70.00
2-Neal Adams-c; Chaykin/N. Adams-a 2.25 6.80 25.00
3-Severin/B. Smith-a; N. Adams-a 1.60 4.80 16.00
4-Neal Adams/Kane-a(r) 1.40 4.20 14.00
5-10: 5-Jeff Jones frontispiece (r) 1.20 3.60 12.00
11-20 1.00 3.00 10.00
21-50: 34-3 pg. preview of Conan newspaper strip. 35-Cover similar to Savage Tales #1. 45-Red Sonja returns; begin $1.25-c .90 2.70 9.00
51-100: 63-Toth frontispiece. 65-Kane-a w/Chaykin/Miller/Simonson/Sherman finishes. 70-Article on movie. 83-Red Sonja-r by Neal Adams from #1 5.00
101-176: 163-Begin $2.25-c. 169-King Kull story. 171-Soloman Kane by Williamson (i). 172-Red Sonja story 3.50
177-235: 179,187,192-Red Sonja app. 190-193-4 part King Kull story. 196, 202-King Kull story. 200-New Buscema-a; Robert E. Howard app. with Conan in story. 204-60th anniversary (1932-92). 211-Rafael Kayanan's 1st Conan-a. 214-Sequel to Red Nails by Robert E. Howard 2.25
Special 1(1975, B&W)-B. Smith-r/Conan #10,13 1.20 3.60 12.00
NOTE: ***N. Adams** a-14p, 60, 83p(r). **Alcala** a-2 ,4, 7, 12, 15-20, 23, 24, 28, 59, 67, 69, 75, 76i, 80i, 82i, 83i, 89, 180i, 184i, 187i, 189i, 216p. **Austin** a-78i. **Boris** painted c-1, 4, 5, 7, 9, 10, 12, 15. **Brunner** a-30; c-8, 30. **Buscema** a-1-5, 7, 10-12, 15-24, 26-28, 31, 32, 36-43, 45, 47-58p, 60-67p, 70, 71-74p, 76-81p, 87-96p, 98, 99-101p, 190-204p; painted c-40. **Chaykin** c-31. **Chiodo** painted c-71, 76, 79, 81, 84, 85, 178. **Conrad** c-215, 217. **Corben** a-4, 16, 29. **Finlay** a-16. **Golden** a-98, 101; c-98, 101, 105, 106, 117, 124, 150. **Kaluta** a-11, 18; c-3, 91, 93. **Gil Kane** a-2, 3, 8, 13r, 29, 47, 64, 65, 67, 85p, 86p. **Rafael Kayanan** a-211-213, 215, 217. **Krenkel** a-9, 11, 14, 16, 24. **Morrow** a-7. **Nebres** a-93i, 101i, 107, 114. **Newton** a-6. **Nino** c/a-6. **Redondo** painted c-48-50, 52, 56, 57, 85i, 90, 96i. **Marie & John Severin** a-Special 1. **Simonson** a-7, 8, 12, 15-17. **Barry Smith** a-7, 16, 24, 82r, Special 1r. **Starlin** c-26. **Toth** a-64. **Williamson** a(i)-162, 171, 186. No. 8 , 10 & 16 contain a Robert E. Howard Conan adaptation.*

SAVAGE TALES (...Featuring Conan #4 on)(Magazine)
Marvel Comics Group: May, 1971; No. 2, 10/73; No. 3, 2/74 - No. 12, Summer, 1975 (B&W)

1-Origin/1st app. The Man-Thing by Morrow; Conan the Barbarian by Barry Smith (1st Conan x-over outside his own title); Femizons by Romita-r/in #3; Ka-Zar story by Buscema 11.00 34.00 125.00
2-B. Smith, Brunner, Morrow, Williamson-a; Wrightson King Kull reprint/ Creatures on the Loose #10 2.70 8.00 30.00
3-B. Smith, Brunner, Steranko, Williamson-a 2.00 6.00 20.00
4,5-N. Adams-c; last Conan (Smith-r/#4) plus Kane/N. Adams-a. 5-Brak the Barbarian begins, ends #8 1.60 4.80 16.00
6-Ka-Zar begins; Williamson-r; N. Adams-c 1.00 3.00 10.00
7-N. Adams-i .90 2.70 8.00

Scarab #3 © DC

Scarlet Crush #2 © Awesome Ent.

Scary Godmother Bloody Valentine Special #1 © Jill Thompson

GD25 FN65 NM94

8-Shanna, the She-Devil app. thru #10; Williamson-r .85 2.60 7.00
9,11 2.00 6.00
10-Neal Adams-a(i), Williamson-r 2.00 6.00
...Featuring Ka-Zar Annual 1 (Summer, '75, B&W)(#12 on inside)-Ka-Zar origin by G. Kane; B. Smith-r/Astonishing Tales 1.20 3.60 12.00

NOTE: ***Boris** c-7, 10. **Buscema** a-5r, 6p, 8p; c-2. **Colan** a-1p. **Fabian** c-8. **Golden** a-1, 4; c-1. **Heath** a-10p, 11p. **Kaluta** c-9. **Maneely** r-2, 4(The Crusader in both). **Morrow** a-1, 2, Annual 1. **Reese** a-2. **Severin** a-1-7. **Starlin** a-5. Robert E. Howard adaptations-1-4.*

SAVAGE TALES
Marvel Comics Group: Nov, 1985 - No. 9, Mar, 1987 ($1.50, B&W, magazine, mature)

1-1st app. The Nam; Golden, Morrow-a 3.00
2-9: 2,7-Morrow-a. 4-2nd Nam story; Golden-a 1.50

SAVANT GARDE (Also see WildC.A.T.S...)
Image Comics/WildStorm Productions: Mar, 1997 - No. 7, Sept, 1997 ($2.50)

1-7 2.50

SAVED BY THE BELL (TV)
Harvey Comics: Mar, 1992 - No. 4, Aug, 1992? ($1.25, limited series)

1-4 1.25
Special 1 (9/92, $1.50)-photo-c 1.50

SCAMP (Walt Disney)(See Walt Disney's Comics & Stories #204)
Dell Publ. Co./Gold Key: No. 703, 5/56 - No. 1204, 8-10/61; 11/67 - No. 45, 1/79

Four Color 703(#1) 8.00 25.00 90.00
Four Color 777,806('57),833 5.50 16.50 60.00
5(3-5/58)-10(6-8/59) 4.50 13.50 50.00
11-16(12-2/60-61), Four Color 1204(1961) 3.00 9.00 35.00
1(12/67-Gold Key)-Reprints begin 3.20 9.50 35.00
2(3/69)-10 1.50 4.50 15.00
11-20 .90 2.70 9.00
21-45 2.40 6.00

NOTE: *New stories-#20(in part), 22-25, 27, 29-31, 34, 36-40, 42-45. New covers-#11, 12, 14, 15, 17-25, 27, 29-31, 34, 36-38.*

SCARAB
DC Comics (Vertigo): Nov, 1993 - No. 8, June, 1994 ($1.95, limited series)

1-8-Glenn Fabry painted-c: 1-Silver ink-c. 2-Phantom Stranger app. 2.00

SCAR FACE (See The Crusaders)

SCARECROW OF ROMNEY MARSH, THE (See W. Disney Showcase #53)
Gold Key: April, 1964 - No. 3, Oct, 1965 (Disney TV Show)

10112-404 (#1) 2.50 7.60 28.00
2,3 1.80 5.40 20.00

SCARECROW (VILLAINS) (See Batman)
DC Comics: Feb, 1998 ($1.95, one-shot)

1-Fegredo-a/Milligan-s/Pearson-c 2.00

SCARE TACTICS
DC Comics: Dec, 1996 - No. 12, Mar, 1998 ($2.25)

1-12: 1-1st app. 2.25

SCARLET O'NEIL (See Harvey Comics Hits #59 & Invisible...)

SCARLET CRUSH
Awesome Entertainment: Jan, 1998 - No. 2, Feb, 1998 ($2.50)

1-Five covers by Liefeld, Stinsman(wraparound), Churchill, Skroce, and Sprouse; Stinsman-s/a(p) 2.50
1-American Entertainment Ed.; Stinsman-c 5.00
2-Three covers by Stinsman, McGuinness & Peterson 2.50

SCARLET SPIDER
Marvel Comics: Nov, 1995 - No. 2, Jan, 1996 ($1.95)

1,2: Replaces Spider-Man 2.00

SCARLET SPIDER UNLIMITED
Marvel Comics: Nov, 1995 ($3.95, one-shot)

GD25 FN65 NM94

1-Replaces Spider-Man Unlimited 4.00

SCARLETT
DC Comics: Jan, 1993 - No. 14, Feb, 1994 (1.75)

1-($2.95) 3.00
2-14 1.75

SCARLET THUNDER
Amaze Ink: Nov, 1995, - Present ($1.50, B&W)

1-3: 3-(5/96) 1.50

SCARLET WITCH (See Avengers #16, Vision &... & X-Men #4)
Marvel Comics: Jan, 1994 - No. 4, Apr, 1994 ($1.75, limited series)

1-4 1.75

SCARY GODMOTHER: BLOODY VALENTINE SPECIAL
Sirius: Feb, 1998 ($3.95,B&W, one-shot)

1-Jill Thompson-s/a; pin-ups by Ross, Mignola, Russell 4.00

SCARY GODMOTHER: HOLIDAY SPOOKTAKULAR
Sirius: Nov, 1998 ($2.95,B&W, one-shot)

1-Thompson-s/a; pin-ups by Brereton, LaBan, Dorkin, Fingerman 3.00

SCARY TALES
Charlton Comics: 8/75 - #9, 1/77; #10, 9/77 - #20, 6/79; #21, 8/80 - #46, 10/84

1-Origin/1st app. Countess Von Bludd, not in #2 1.20 3.60 12.00
2-11: 3-Sutton painted-c .90 2.70 8.00
12-20 2.00 6.00
21-46: 39,46-All reprints. 37,38,40-45-New-a. 38-Mr. Jigsaw app. 5.00
1(Modern Comics reprint, 1977) 4.00

NOTE: ***Adkins** a-31i; c-31i. **Ditko** a-3, 5, 7, 8(2), 11, 12, 14-16r, 18(3)r, 19r, 21r, 30r, 32, 39r; c-5, 11, 14, 18, 30, 32. **Newton** a-31p; c-31p. **Powell** a-18r. **Staton** a-1(2 pgs.), 4, 20r; c-1, 20. **Sutton** a-9; c-4, 9.*

SCATTERBRAIN
Dark Horse Comics: Jun, 1998 - Present ($2.95, limited series)

1-4-Humor anthology by Aragonés, Dorkin, Stevens and others 2.95

SCAVENGERS
Quality Comics: Feb, 1988 - No. 14, 1989 ($1.25/$1.50)

1-7 ($1.25) 1.25
8-14 ($1.50): 9-13-Guice-c 1.50

SCAVENGERS
Triumphant Comics: 1993(nd, July) - No. 11, May, 1994 ($2.50, serially numbered)

1-9: 5,6-Triumphant Unleashed x-over. 9-(3/94) 2.50
0-Retail edition (3/94, $2.50, 36 pgs.) 2.50
0-Giveaway edition (3/94, 20 pgs.) 2.50
0-Coupon redemption edition 2.50
10,11: 10-(4/94) 2.50

SCHOOL DAY ROMANCES (...of Teen-Agers #4; Popular Teen-Agers #5 on)
Star Publications: Nov-Dec, 1949 - No. 4, May-June, 1950 (Teenage)

1-Toni Gayle (later Toni Gay), Ginger Snapp, Midge Martin & Eve Adams begin 23.00 68.00 170.00
2,3: 3-Jane Powell photo on-c & true life story 16.00 48.00 120.00
4-Ronald Reagan photo on-c; L.B. Cole-c 25.00 76.00 190.00

NOTE: *All have **L. B. Cole** covers.*

SCHWINN BICYCLE BOOK (...Bike Thrills, 1959)
Schwinn Bicycle Co.: 1949; 1952; 1959 (10¢)

1949 5.00 15.00 30.00
1952-Believe It or Not facts; comic format; 36 pgs. 4.00 10.00 20.00
1959 2.00 5.00 10.00

SCIENCE COMICS (1st Series)
Fox Features Syndicate: Feb, 1940 - No. 8, Sept, 1940

1-Origin Dynamo (1st app., called Electro in #1), The Eagle (1st app.), & Navy

Science Comics #6 © FOX

Scooby-Doo #6 (DC) © H-B

Scoop Comics #8 © CHES

GD25 FN65 NM94

Jones; Marga, The Panther Woman (1st app.), Cosmic Carson & Perisphere Payne, Dr. Doom begin; bondage/hypo-c; Electro-c 347.00 1042.00 3300.00
2-Lou Fine Dynamo-c 182.00 546.00 1550.00
3-Classic Lou Fine Dynamo-c 153.00 460.00 1300.00
4-Kirby-a; Cosmic Carson-c by Joe Simon 135.00 405.00 1150.00
5-8: 5,8-Eagle-c. 6,7-Dynamo-c 79.00 237.00 670.00
NOTE: *Cosmic Carson by **Tuska**-#1-3; by **Kirby**-#4. **Lou Fine** c-1-3 only.*

SCIENCE COMICS (2nd Series)
Humor Publications (Ace Magazines?): Jan, 1946 - No. 5, 1946
1-Palais-c/a in #1-3; A-Bomb-c 13.00 40.00 100.00
2 7.15 21.50 50.00
3-Feldstein-a (6 pgs.) 13.00 38.00 95.00
4,5: 4-Palais-c 5.70 17.00 38.00

SCIENCE COMICS
Ziff-Davis Publ. Co.: May, 1947 (8 pgs. in color)
nn-Could be ordered by mail for 10¢; like the nn Amazing Adventures (1950) & Boy Cowboy (1950); used to test the market 33.00 100.00 250.00

SCIENCE COMICS (True Science Illustrated)
Export Publication Ent., Toronto, Canada: Mar, 1951
Distr. in U.S. by Kable News Co.
1-Science Adventure stories plus some true science features; man on moon story 7.15 21.50 50.00

SCIENCE FICTION SPACE ADVENTURES (See Space Adventures)

SCOOBY DOO (TV)(...Where are you? #1-16,26; ...Mystery Comics #17-25, 27 on)(See March Of Comics #356, 368, 382, 391)
Gold Key: Mar, 1970 - No. 30, Feb, 1975 (Hanna-Barbera)
1 5.75 17.50 70.00
2-5 3.75 11.50 45.00
6-10 3.00 9.00 35.00
11-20: 11-Tufts-a 2.00 6.00 24.00
21-30 1.50 4.50 18.00

SCOOBY DOO (TV)
Charlton Comics: Apr, 1975 - No. 11, Dec, 1976 (Hanna-Barbera)
1 3.20 9.50 34.00
2-5 2.00 6.00 20.00
6-11 1.40 4.20 14.00

SCOOBY-DOO (TV) (Newsstand sales only)
Marvel Comics Group: Oct, 1977 - No. 9, Feb, 1979 (Hanna-Barbera)
1,6-9: 1-Dyno-Mutt begins 1.20 3.60 12.00
2-5 .90 2.70 9.00

SCOOBY-DOO (TV)
Harvey Comics: Sept, 1992 - No. 3, May, 1993 ($1.25)
V2#1,2 2.00
Big Book 1,2 (11/92, 4/93, $1.95, 52 pgs.) 3.00
Giant Size 1,2 (10/92, 3/93, $2.25, 68 pgs.) 3.00

SCOOBY DOO (TV)
Archie Comics: Oct, 1995 -No. 21, June, 1997 ($1.50)
1-21: 12-Cover by Scooby Doo creative designer Iwao Takamoto 2.00

SCOOBY DOO (TV)
DC Comics: Aug, 1997 - Present ($1.75/$1.95/$1.99)
1-4 2.00
5-13: 5-Begin-$1.95-c 1.95
14-18: 14-Begin $1.99-c 1.99

SCOOP COMICS (Becomes Yankee Comics #4-7, a digest sized cartoon book not listed in this guide; becomes Snap #9)
Harry 'A' Chesler (Holyoke): November, 1941 - No. 3, Mar, 1943; No. 8, 1944
1-Intro. Rocketman & Rocketgirl & begins; origin The Master Key & begins; Dan Hastings begins; Charles Sultan-c/a 115.00 345.00 975.00
2-Rocket Boy begins; injury to eye story (reprinted in Spotlight #3); classic-c 118.00 354.00 1000.00
3-Injury to eye story-r from #2; Rocket Boy 56.00 168.00 480.00
8-Formerly Yankee Comics; becomes Snap 39.00 117.00 300.00

SCOOTER (See Swing With...)

SCOOTER COMICS
Rucker Publ. Ltd. (Canadian): Apr, 1946
1-Teen-age/funny animal 8.50 26.00 60.00

SCORCHED EARTH
Tundra Publishing: Apr, 1991 - No. 6, 1991 ($2.95, stiff-c)
1-6 3.00

SCORE, THE
DC Comics (Piranha Press): 1989 - No. 4, 1990 ($4.95, 52 pgs, squarebound, mature)
Books One - Four 3.00

SCORPION
Atlas/Seaboard Publ.: Feb, 1975 - No. 3, July, 1975
1-Intro.; bondage-c by Chaykin 5.00
2-Chaykin-a w/Wrightson, Kaluta, Simonson assists(p) 5.00
3 3.00
NOTE: ***Chaykin** a-1, 2; c-1. **Colon** c-2. **Craig** c/a-3.*

SCORPION CORPS
Dagger Comics Group: Nov, 1993 - No. 7, May, 1994? ($2.75/$2.50)
1,2-($2.75): 1-Intro Angel Dust, Shellcase, Tork, Feedback & Magnon 2.75
2-Bronze, 2-Gold, 2-Silver 2.75
3-7-($2.50) 2.50

SCORPIO ROSE
Eclipse Comics: Jan, 1983 - No. 2, Oct, 1983 ($1.25, Baxter paper)
1,2: Dr. Orient back-up story begins. 2-origin. 1.25

SCOTLAND YARD (Inspector Farnsworth of)(Texas Rangers in Action #5 on?)
Charlton Comics Group: June, 1955 - No. 4, Mar, 1956
1-Tothish-a 12.00 36.00 90.00
2-4: 2-Tothish-a 10.00 30.00 60.00

SCOUT (See Eclipse Graphic Album #16, New America & Swords of Texas)(Becomes Scout: War Shaman)
Eclipse Comics: Dec, 1985 - No. 24, Oct, 1987($1.75/$1.25, Baxter paper)
1-8,11,12: 11-Monday, the Eliminator begins 1.80
9,10 ($1.25): 9-Airboy preview. 10-Bissette-a 1.25
13-15,17,18,20-24 ($1.75): 15-Swords of Texas 1.80
16-Scout 3-D Special ($2.50) 2.50
16-Scout 2-D Limited Edition 2.50
19-contains flexi-disk ($2.50) 2.50
...Handbook 1 (8/87, $1.75, B&W) 1.75

SCOUT: WAR SHAMAN (Formerly Scout)
Eclipse Comics: Mar, 1988 - No. 16, Dec, 1989 ($1.95)
1-16 2.00

SCREAM (...Comics) (Andy Comics #20 on)
Humor Publications/Current Books(Ace Magazines): Autumn, 1944 - No. 19, Apr, 1948
1-Teenage humor 13.00 40.00 100.00
2 7.15 21.50 50.00
3-16: 11-Racist humor (Indians). 16-Intro. Lily-Belle 5.70 17.00 40.00
17,19 5.00 15.00 30.00
18-Hypo needle story 5.70 17.00 40.00

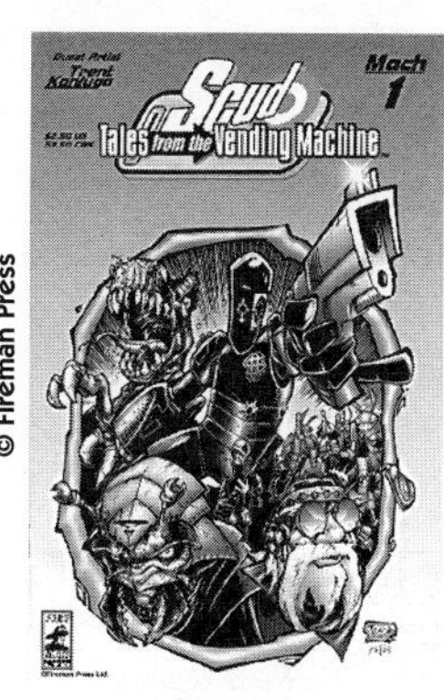

Scud: Tales From the Vending Machine #1 © Fireman Press

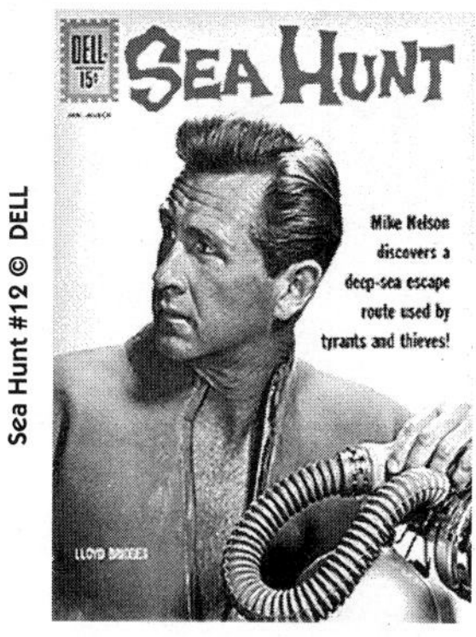

Sea Hunt #12 © DELL

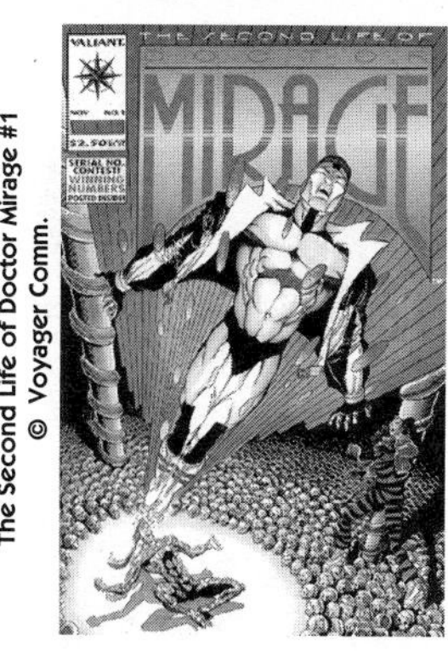

The Second Life of Doctor Mirage #1 © Voyager Comm.

GD25 FN65 NM94

SCREAM
Skywald Publishing Corp.: Aug, 1973 - No. 11, Feb, 1975 (68 pgs., B&W, magazine)

1 2.70 8.00 30.00
2-5: 2-Origin Lady Satan. 3 (12/73)-#3 found on pg. 22
1.60 4.80 16.00
6-8: 6-Origin The Victims 1.20 3.60 12.00
9-11: 9-Severed head-c. 11- "Mr. Poe and the Raven" story
1.60 4.80 16.00

SCREWBALL SQUIRREL
Dark Horse Comics: July, 1995 - No. 3, Sept, 1995 ($2.50, limited series)

1-3: Characters created by Tex Avery 2.50

SCRIBBLY (See All-American Comics, Buzzy, The Funnies, Leave It To Binky & Popular Comics)
National Periodical Publications: 8-9/48 - No. 13, 8-9/50; No. 14, 10-11/51 - No. 15, 12-1/51-52

1-Sheldon Mayer-c/a in all; 52 pgs. begin 88.00 264.00 750.00
2 58.00 174.00 490.00
3-5 46.00 138.00 390.00
6-10 35.00 104.00 260.00
11-15: 13-Last 52 pgs. 31.00 92.00 230.00

SCUD: TALES FROM THE VENDING MACHINE
Fireman Press: 1998 - Present ($2.50, B&W)

1-3: 1-Kaniuga-a. 2-Ruben Martinez-a 2.50

SCUD: THE DISPOSABLE ASSASSIN
Fireman Press: Feb, 1994 - Present ($2.95, B&W)

1 1.20 3.60 12.00
1-2nd printing in color 3.00
2,3 .90 2.70 8.00
4-9 5.00
10-19 3.00
Heavy 3PO ($12.95, TPB) r/#1-4 12.95
Programmed For Damage ($14.95, TPB) r/#5-9 14.95
Solid Gold Bomb ($17.95, TPB) r/#10-15 17.95

SEA DEVILS (See Limited Collectors' Edition #39,45, & Showcase #27-29)
National Periodical Publications: Sept-Oct, 1961 - No. 35, May-June, 1967

1-(9-10/61) 41.00 123.00 500.00
2-Last 10¢ issue 25.00 75.00 250.00
3-Begin 12¢ issues thru #35 16.00 48.00 160.00
4,5 14.50 44.00 145.00
6-10 8.50 25.50 85.00
11,12,14-20 6.00 18.00 60.00
13-Kubert, Colan-a; Joe Kubert app. in story 6.50 19.50 65.00
21-35: 22-Intro. International Sea Devils; origin & 1st app. Capt. X & Man Fish 4.00 12.00 40.00

NOTE: *Heath a-B&B 27-29, 1-10; c-B&B 27-29, 1-10, 14-16.* ***Moldoff*** *a-16i.*

SEA DEVILS (See Tangent Comics/ Sea Devils)

SEADRAGON (Also see the Epsilion Wave)
Elite Comics: May, 1986 - No. 8, 1987 ($1.75)

1-8: 1-1st & 2nd printings exist 1.75

SEA HOUND, THE (Captain Silver's Log Of The...)
Avon Periodicals: 1945 (no month) - No. 2, Sept-Oct, 1945

nn (#1)-29 pg. novel length sty-"The Esmeralda's Treasure"
13.00 40.00 100.00
2 10.00 30.00 75.00

SEA HOUND, THE (Radio)
Capt. Silver Syndicate: No. 3, July, 1949 - No. 4, Sept, 1949

3,4 7.85 23.50 55.00

GD25 FN65 NM94

SEA HUNT (TV)
Dell Publishing Co.: No. 928, 8/58 - No. 1041, 10-12/59; No. 4, 1-3/60 - No. 13, 4-6/62 (All have Lloyd Bridges photo-c)

Four Color 928(#1) 11.00 33.00 120.00
Four Color 994(#2), 4-13: Manning-a #4-6,8-11,13 8.00 23.00 85.00
Four Color 1041(#3)-Toth-a 8.00 25.00 90.00

SEAQUEST (TV)
Nemesis Comics: Mar, 1994 ($2.25)

1-Has 2 diff-c stocks (slick & cardboard); Alcala-i 2.25

SEARCH FOR LOVE
American Comics Group: Feb-Mar, 1950 - No. 2, Apr-May, 1950 (52 pgs.)

1 9.30 28.00 70.00
2,3(6-7/50): 3-Exist? 6.50 19.50 45.00

SEARCHERS, THE (Movie)
Dell Publishing Co.: No. 709, 1956

Four Color 709-John Wayne photo-c 24.00 71.00 260.00

SEARCHERS, THE
Caliber Comics: 1996 - No. 4, 1996 ($2.95, B&W)

1-4 3.00

SEARCHERS, THE : APOSTLE OF MERCY
Caliber Comics: 1997 - No. 2, 1997 ($2.95/$3.95, B&W)

1-($2.95) 3.00
2-($3.95) 4.00

SEARS (See Merry Christmas From...)

SEASON'S GREETINGS
Hallmark (King Features): 1935 (6-1/4x5-1/4", 32 pgs. in color)

nn-Cover features Mickey Mouse, Popeye, Jiggs & Skippy. "The Night Before Christmas" told one panel per page, each panel by a famous artist featuring their character. Art by Alex Raymond, Gottfredson, Swinnerton, Segar, Chic Young, Milt Gross, Sullivan (Messmer), Herriman, McManus, Percy Crosby & others (22 artists in all)
Estimated value... 550.00

SEBASTION O
DC Comics (Vertigo): May, 1993 - No. 3, July, 1993 ($1.95, limited series)

1-3-Grant Morrison scripts 2.00

SECOND LIFE OF DOCTOR MIRAGE, THE (See Shadowman #16)
Valiant: Nov, 1993 - No. 18, May, 1995 ($2.50)

1-18: 1-With bound-in poster. 5-Shadowman x-over. 7-Bound-in trading card 2.50
1-Gold ink logo edition; no price on-c 3.00

SECRET AGENT (Formerly Sarge Steel)
Charlton Comics: V2#9, Oct, 1966; V2#10, Oct, 1967

V2#9-Sarge Steel part-r begins 2.25 6.75 18.00
10-Tiffany Sinn, CIA app. (from Career Girl Romances #39); Aparo-a
1.50 4.50 12.00

SECRET AGENT (TV) (See Four Color #1231)
Gold Key: Nov, 1966; No. 2, Jan, 1968

1-Photo-c 11.00 33.00 115.00
2-Photo-c 7.00 20.00 75.00

SECRET AGENT X-9 (See Flash Gordon #4 by King)
David McKay Publ.: 1934 (Book 1: 84 pgs.; Book 2: 124 pgs.) (8x7-1/2")

Book 1-Contains reprints of the first 13 weeks of the strip by Alex Raymond; complete except for 2 dailies 37.00 111.00 315.00
Book 2-Contains reprints immediately following contents of Book 1, for 20 weeks by Alex Raymond; complete except for two dailies. Note: Raymond mis-dated the last five strips from 6/34, and while the dating sequence is

The Secret Defenders #11 © MEG

Secret Loves #1 © QUA

Secret Origins #5 (3rd series) © DC

GD25 FN65 NM94

confusing, the continuity is correct 36.00 108.00 270.00

SECRET AGENT X-9 (See Magic Comics)
Dell Publishing Co.: Dec, 1937 (Not by Raymond)
Feature Books 8 35.00 104.00 380.00

SECRET AGENT Z-2 (See Holyoke One-Shot No. 7)

SECRET CITY SAGA (See Jack Kirby's Secret City Saga)

SECRET DEFENDERS (Also see The Defenders & Fantastic Four #374)
Marvel Comics: Mar, 1993 - No. 25, Mar, 1995 ($1.75/$1.95)
1-($2.50)-Red foil stamped-c; Dr. Strange, Nomad, Wolverine, Spider Woman & Darkhawk begin 2.50
2-11,13,14: 9-New team w/Silver Surfer, Thunderstrike, Dr. Strange & War Machine. 13-Thanos replaces Dr. Strange as leader; leads into Cosmic Powers limited series; 14-Dr. Druid 1.75
12-($2.50)-Prismatic foil-c 2.50
15-24: 15-Begin $1.95-c.; bound-in card sheet. 18-Giant Man & Iron Fist app. 2.00
25 ($2.50, 52 pgs.) 2.50

SECRET DIARY OF EERIE ADVENTURES
Avon Periodicals: 1953 (25¢ giant, 100 pgs., one-shot)
nn-(Rare)-Kubert-a; Hollingsworth-c; Sid Check back-c 135.00 406.00 1150.00

SECRET FILES
Angel Entertainment: Spring 1997 ($2.95, B&W, limited series)
1 2.95

SECRET HEARTS
National Periodical Publications (Beverly)(Arleigh No. 50-113): 9-10/49 - No. 6, 7-8/50; No. 7, 12-1/51-52 - No. 153, 7/71 (All 52 pgs.)
1-Kinstler-a; photo-c begin, end #6 46.00 138.00 390.00
2-Toth-a (1 pg.); Kinstler-a 25.00 74.00 185.00
3,6 (1950) 21.00 64.00 160.00
4,5-Toth-a 22.00 66.00 165.00
7(12-1/51-52) (Rare) 38.00 114.00 285.00
8-10 (1952) 15.00 44.00 110.00
11-20 12.00 36.00 90.00
21-26: 26-Last precode (2-3/55) 10.00 30.00 75.00
27-40 6.00 18.00 55.00
41-50 3.80 11.40 38.00
51-60 3.00 9.00 30.00
61-75: 75-Last 10¢ issue 2.50 7.50 24.00
76-99,101-109 2.00 6.00 18.00
100 2.50 7.50 24.00
110- "Reach for Happiness" serial begins, ends #138 1.60 4.80 16.00
111-119,121-126 1.40 4.20 14.00
120,134-Neal Adams-c 2.00 6.00 20.00
127 (4/68)-Beatles cameo 2.00 6.00 20.00
128-133,135-140 1.20 3.60 12.00
141,142- "20 Miles to Heartbreak", Chapter 2 & 3 (see Young Love for Chapters 1 & 4); Toth, Colletta-a 1.20 3.60 12.00
143-148,150-153: 144-Morrow-a. 153-Kirby-i 1.00 3.00 10.00
149-Toth-a 1.20 3.60 12.00

SECRET ISLAND OF OZ, THE (See First Comics Graphic Novel)

SECRET LOVE (See Fox Giants & Sinister House of...)

SECRET LOVE
Ajax-Farrell/Four Star Comic Corp. No. 2 on: 12/55 - No. 3, 8/56; 4/57 - No. 5, 2/58; No. 6, 6/58
1(12/55-Ajax, 1st series) 7.85 23.50 55.00
2,3 5.35 16.00 32.00
1(4/57-Ajax, 2nd series) 6.00 18.00 42.00
2-6: 5-Bakerish-a 4.25 13.00 28.00

GD25 FN65 NM94

SECRET LOVES
Comic Magazines/Quality Comics Group: Nov, 1949 - No. 6, Sept, 1950
1-Ward-c 20.00 60.00 150.00
2-Ward-c 17.00 52.00 130.00
3-Crandall-a 11.00 32.00 80.00
4,6 7.15 21.50 50.00
5-Suggestive art "Boom Town Babe"; photo-c 11.00 32.00 80.00

SECRET LOVE STORIES (See Fox Giants)

SECRET MISSIONS (Admiral Zacharia's...)
St. John Publishing Co.: February, 1950
1-Joe Kubert-c; stories of U.S. foreign agents 17.00 52.00 130.00

SECRET MYSTERIES (Formerly Crime Mysteries & Crime Smashers)
Ribage/Merit Publications No. 17 on: No. 16, Nov, 1954 - No. 19, July, 1955
16-Horror, Palais-a; Myron Fass-c 20.00 60.00 150.00
17-19-Horror. 17-Fass-c; mis-dated 3/54? 13.00 38.00 95.00

SECRET ORIGINS (1st Series) (See 80 Page Giant #8)
National Periodical Publications: Aug-Oct, 1961 (Annual) (Reprints)
1-Origin Adam Strange (Showcase #17), Green Lantern (Green Lantern #1), Challengers (partial-r/Showcase #6, 6 pgs. Kirby-a), J'onn J'onzz (Det. #225), The Flash (Showcase #4), Green Arrow (1 pg. text), Superman-Batman team (W. Finest #94), Wonder Woman (Wonder Woman #105) 45.00 135.00 540.00
Replica Edition (1998, $4.95) r/entire book and house ads 5.00

SECRET ORIGINS (2nd Series)
National Periodical Publications: Feb-Mar, 1973 - No. 6, Jan-Feb, 1974; No. 7, Oct-Nov, 1974 (All 20¢ issues) (All origin reprints)
1-Superman(r/1 pg. origin/Action #1, 1st time since G.A.), Batman(Det. #33), Ghost(Flash #88), The Flash(Showcase #4) 2.50 7.50 24.00
2-4: 2-Green Lantern & The Atom(Showcase #22 & 34), Supergirl(Action #252). 3-Wonder Woman(W.W. #1), Wildcat(Sensation #1). 4-Vigilante (Action #42) by Meskin, Kid Eternity(Hit #25) 1.20 3.60 12.00
5-7: 5-The Spectre by Baily (More Fun #52,53). 6-Blackhawk(Military #1) & Legion of Super-Heroes(Superboy #147). 7-Robin(Detective #38), Aquaman (More Fun #73) 1.20 3.60 12.00
NOTE: ***Infantino*** *a-1.* ***Kane*** *a-2.* ***Kubert*** *a-1.*

SECRET ORIGINS (3rd Series)
DC Comics: 4/86 - No. 50, 8/90 (All origins)(52 pgs. #6 on)(#27 on: $1.50)
1-Origin Superman 3.00
2-Blue Beetle 2.00
3-5: 3-Shazam. 4-Firestorm. 5-Crimson Avenger 2.00
6-Halo/G.A. Batman 2.00
7-12,14-26: 7-Green Lantern(Guy Gardner)/G.A. Sandman. 8-Shadow Lass/Doll Man. 9-G.A. Flash/Skyman. 10-Phantom Stranger w/Alan Moore scripts; Legends spin-off. 11-G.A. Hawkman/Power Girl. 12-Challengers of Unknown/G.A. Fury (2nd modern app.). 14-Suicide Squad; Legends spin-off. 15-Spectre/Deadman. 16-G.A. Hourman/Warlord. 17-Adam Strange story by Carmine infantino; Dr. Occult. 18-G.A. Gr. Lantern/The Creeper. 19-Uncle Sam/The Guardian. 20-Batgirl/G.A. Dr. Mid-Nite. 21-Jonah Hex/Black Condor. 22-Manhunters. 23-Floronic Man/Guardians of the Universe. 24-Blue Devil/Dr. Fate. 25-LSH/Atom. 26-Black Lightning/Miss America 2.00
13-Origin Nightwing; Johnny Thunder app. 2.00
27-38,40-44: 27-Zatara/Zatanna. 28-Midnight/Nightshade. 29-Power of the Atom/Mr. America; new 3 pg. Red Tornado story by Mayer (last app. of Scribbly, 8/88). 30-Plastic Man/Elongated Man. 31-JSA. 32-JLA. 33-35-JLI. 36-Poison Ivy by Neil Gaiman & Mark Buckingham/Green Lantern. 37-Legion Of Substitute Heroes/Doctor Light. 38-Green Arrow/Speedy; Grell scripts. 40-All Ape issue. 41-Rogues Gallery of Flash. 42-Phantom Girl/Grim Ghost. 43-Original Hawk & Dove/Cave Carson/Chris KL-99. 44-Batman app.; story based on Det. #40 2.00
39-Animal Man-c/story continued in Animal Man #10; Grant Morrison scripts;

Secret Origins 80-Page Giant #1 © DC

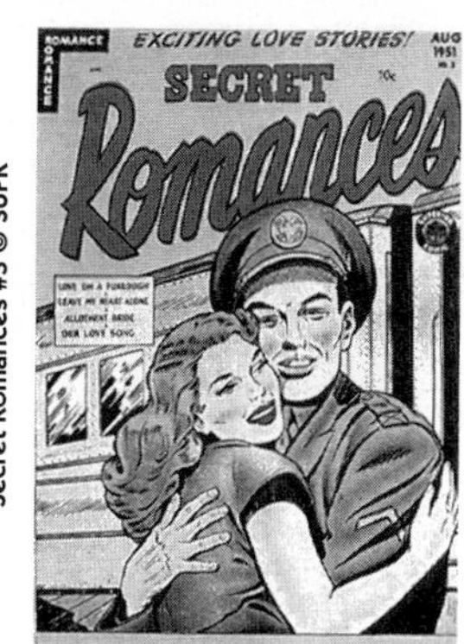
Secret Romances #3 © SUPR

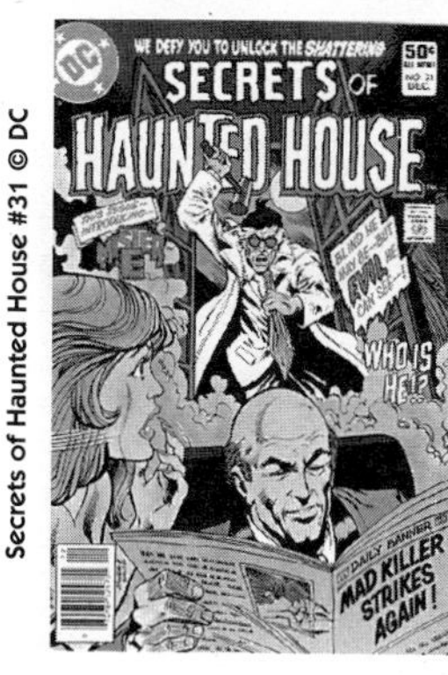
Secrets of Haunted House #31 © DC

GD25 FN65 NM94

Batman app. 2.00
45-49: 45-Blackhawk/El Diablo. 46-JLA/LSH/New Titans. 47-LSH. 48-Ambush Bug/Stanley & His Monster/Rex the Wonder Dog/Trigger Twins. 49-Newsboy Legion/Silent Knight/brief origin Bouncing Boy 2.00
50-($3.95, 100 pgs.)-Batman & Robin in text, Flash of Two Worlds, Johnny Thunder, Dolphin, Black Canary & Space Museum 5.00
Annual 1 (8/87)-Capt. Comet/Doom Patrol 3.00
Annual 2 ('88, $2.00)-Origin Flash II & Flash III 3.00
Annual 3 ('89, $2.95, 84 pgs.)-Teen Titans; 1st app. new Flamebird who replaces original Bat-Girl 3.50
Special 1 (10/89, $2.00)-Batman villains: Penguin, Riddler, & Two-Face; Bolland-c; Sam Kieth-a; Neil Gaiman scripts(2) 3.00

NOTE: ***Art Adams** a-33i(part). **M. Anderson** 8, 19, 21, 25i; c-19(part). **Aparo** c/a-10. **Bissette** c-23. **Bolland** c-7. **Byrne** c/a-Annual 1. **Colan** c/a-5p. **Forte** a-37. **Giffen** a-18p, 44p, 48. **Infantino** a-17, 50p. **Kaluta** c-39. **Gil Kane** a-2, 28; c-2p. **Kirby** c-19(part). **Erik Larsen** a-13. **Mayer** a-29. **Morrow** a-21. **Orlando** a-10. **Perez** a-50i, Annual 3i; c- Annual 3. **Rogers** a-6p. **Russell** a-27i. **Simonson** c-22. **Staton** a-36, 50p. **Steacy** a-35. **Tuska** a-4p, 9p.*

SECRET ORIGINS 80 PAGE GIANT (Young Justice)
DC Comics: Dec, 1998 ($4.95, one-shot)

1-Origin-s of Young Justice members; Ramos-a (Impulse) 4.95

SECRET ORIGINS OF SUPER-HEROES (See DC Special Series #10, 19)

SECRET ORIGINS OF THE WORLD'S GREATEST SUPER-HEROES
DC Comics: 1989 ($4.95, 148 pgs.)

nn-Reprints Superman, JLA.origins; new Batman-o; Bolland-c. 5.50

SECRET ROMANCE
Charlton Comics: Oct, 1968 - No. 41, Nov, 1976; No. 42, Mar, 1979 - No. 48, Feb, 1980

	GD25	FN65	NM94
1-Begin 12¢ issues, ends #?	1.00	3.00	10.00
2-10: 9-Reese-a		2.00	6.00
11-30			4.00
31-48			2.00

NOTE: *Beyond the Stars app.-No. 9, 11, 12, 14.*

SECRET ROMANCES (Exciting Love Stories)
Superior Publications Ltd.: Apr, 1951 - No. 27, July, 1955

	GD25	FN65	NM94
1	11.00	32.00	80.00
2	6.85	21.00	48.00
3-10	5.70	17.00	34.00
11-13,15-18,20-27	4.15	12.50	25.00
14,19-Lingerie panels	5.35	16.00	32.00

SECRET SERVICE (See Kent Blake of the...)

SECRET SIX (See Action Comics Weekly)
National Periodical Publications: Apr-May, 1968 - No. 7, Apr-May, 1969 (12¢)

	GD25	FN65	NM94
1-Origin/1st app.	4.50	13.50	45.00
2-7	2.50	7.50	25.00

SECRET SIX (See Tangent Comics/ Secret Six)

SECRET SOCIETY OF SUPER-VILLAINS
National Per. Publ./DC Comics: May-June, 1976 - No. 15, June-July, 1978

	GD25	FN65	NM94
1-Origin; JLA cameo & Capt. Cold app.	.90	2.70	8.00
2,4,15: 2-Re-intro/origin Capt. Comet; Green Lantern x-over.15-G.A. Atom, Dr. Midnite, & JSA app.			5.50
3,5: 5-Green Lantern, Hawkman x-over; Darkseid app.		2.40	6.50
6-9: 9-Creeper x-over			5.00
10-14: 10-Creeper x-over. 11-Capt. Comet; Orlando-i.			4.00

SECRET SOCIETY OF SUPER-VILLAINS SPECIAL (See DC Special Series #6)

SECRETS OF HAUNTED HOUSE
National Periodical Publications/DC Comics: 4-5/75 - #5, 12-1/75-76; #6, 6-7/77 - #14, 10-11/78; #15, 8/79 - #46, 3/82

	GD25	FN65	NM94
1	2.20	6.25	22.00
2-4	1.00	3.00	10.00
5-Wrightson-c	1.20	3.60	12.00
6-14	.85	2.60	7.00
15-30			5.00
31-Mr. E series begins, ends #41		2.00	6.00
32-43,45,46			3.50
44-Wrightson-c		2.00	6.00

NOTE: ***Aparo** c-7. **Aragones** a-1. **B. Bailey** a-8. **Bissette** a-46. **Buckler** c-32-40p. **Ditko** a-9, 12, 41, 45. **Golden** a-10. **Howard** a-13i. **Kaluta** c-8, 10, 11, 14, 16, 29. **Kubert** c-41, 42. **Sheldon Mayer** a-43p. **McWilliams** a-35. **Nasser** a-24. **Newton** a-30p. **Nino** a-1, 13, 19. **Orlando** c-13, 30, 43, 45i. **N. Redondo** a-4, 5, 29. **Rogers** c-26. **Spiegle** a-31-41. **Wrightson** c-5, 44.*

SECRETS OF HAUNTED HOUSE SPECIAL (See DC Special Series #12)

SECRETS OF LIFE (Movie)
Dell Publishing Co.: 1956 (Disney)

	GD25	FN65	NM94
Four Color 749-Photo-c	3.60	11.00	40.00

SECRETS OF LOVE (See Popular Teen-Agers...)

SECRETS OF LOVE AND MARRIAGE
Charlton Comics: V2#1, Aug, 1956 - V2#25, June, 1961

	GD25	FN65	NM94
V2#1	3.20	9.60	32.00
V2#2-6	2.20	6.60	22.00
V2#7-9-(All 68 pgs.)	3.60	10.80	36.00
10-25	1.75	5.25	14.00

SECRETS OF MAGIC (See Wisco)

SECRETS OF SINISTER HOUSE (Sinister House of Secret Love #1-4)
National Periodical Publ.: No. 5, June-July, 1972 - No. 18, June-July, 1974

	GD25	FN65	NM94
5-(52 pgs.).	2.70	8.00	30.00
6-9: 7-Redondo-a	1.50	4.50	15.00
10-Neal Adams-a(i)	2.20	6.25	22.00
11-18: 15-Redondo-a. 17-Barry-a; early Chaykin 1 pg. strip	.90	2.70	9.00

NOTE: ***Alcala** a-6, 13, 14. **Glanzman** a-7. **Kaluta** c-6, 7. **Nino** a-8, 11-13. Ambrose Bierce adapt.-#14.*

SECRETS OF THE LEGION OF SUPER-HEROES
DC Comics: Jan, 1981 - No. 3, Mar, 1981 (Limited series)

1-3: 1-Origin of the Legion. 2-Retells origins of Brainiac 5, Shrinking Violet, Sun-Boy, Bouncing Boy, Ultra-Boy, Matter-Eater Lad, Mon-El, Karate Kid, & Dream Girl 2.00

SECRETS OF TRUE LOVE
St. John Publishing Co.: Feb, 1958

	GD25	FN65	NM94
1	4.00	12.00	24.00

SECRETS OF YOUNG BRIDES
Charlton Comics: No. 5, Sept, 1957 - No. 44, Oct, 1964; July, 1975 - No. 9, Nov, 1976

	GD25	FN65	NM94
5	3.20	9.60	32.00
6-10: 8-Negligee panel	2.50	7.50	22.00
11-20	2.25	6.75	18.00
21-30: Last 10¢ issue?	1.50	4.50	12.00
31-44(10/64)	1.00	3.00	8.00
1-(2nd series) (7/75)	.90	2.70	8.00
2-9			4.00

SECRET SQUIRREL (TV)(See Kite Fun Book)
Gold Key: Oct, 1966 (12¢) (Hanna-Barbera)

	GD25	FN65	NM94
1	11.35	34.00	125.00

SECRET STORY ROMANCES (Becomes True Tales of Love)
Atlas Comics (TCI): Nov, 1953 - No. 21, Mar, 1956

	GD25	FN65	NM94
1-Everett-a; Jay Scott Pike-c	11.00	32.00	80.00
2	5.70	17.00	40.00
3-11: 11-Last pre-code (2/55)	5.35	16.00	32.00

Seekers into the Mystery #13 © J.M. DeMatteis

Seeker 3000 #1 © MAR

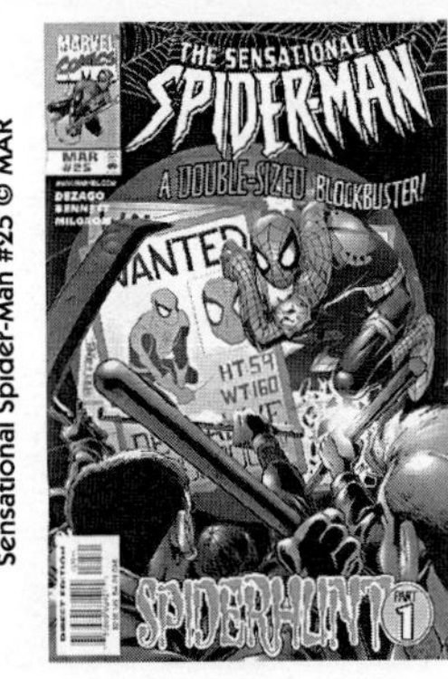

Sensational Spider-Man #25 © MAR

GD25 FN65 NM94

12-21 4.25 13.00 28.00
NOTE: *Colletta a-10, 14, 15, 17, 21; c-10, 14, 17.*

SECRET VOICE, THE (See Great American Comics Presents...)

SECRET WARS II (Also see Marvel Super Heroes...)
Marvel Comics Group: July, 1985 - No. 9, Mar, 1986 (Maxi-series)

1-9: 2-1st app. Boom Boom. 2,8,9-X-Men app. 5,8,9-Spider-Man app. 9-(52 pgs.) 1.00

SECRET WEAPONS
Valiant: Sept, 1993 - No. 21, May, 1995 ($2.25)

1-10,12-21: 3-Reese-a(i). 5-Ninjak app. 9-Bound-in trading card. 12-Bloodshot app. 2.25
11-(Sept. on envelope, Aug on-c, $2.50)-Enclosed in manilla envelope; Blootshot app; intro new team. 2.50

SECTAURS
Marvel Comics: June, 1985 - No. 10?, 1986 (75¢) (Based on Coleco Toys)

1-10 1.00
1-Coleco giveaway; different-c 1.00

SEDUCTION OF THE INNOCENT (Also see New York State Joint Legislative Committee to Study...)
Rinehart & Co., Inc., N. Y.: 1953, 1954 (400 pgs.) (Hardback, $4.00)(Written by Fredric Wertham, M.D.)(Also printed in Canada by Clarke, Irwin & Co. Ltd.)

(1st Version)-with bibliographical note intact (pages 399 & 400)(several copies got out before the comic publishers forced the removal of this page) 47.00 141.00 400.00
Dust jacket only 27.00 80.00 200.00
(1st Version)-without bibliographical note 27.00 80.00 200.00
Dust jacket only 12.00 36.00 90.00
(2nd Version)-Published in England by Kennikat Press, 1954, 399 pgs. has bibliographical page 6.00 17.50 65.00
1972 r-/of 2nd version; 400 pgs. w/bibliography page; Kennikat Press 2.20 6.50 24.00
NOTE: *Material from this book appeared in the November, 1953(Vol.70, pp50-53,214) issue of the **Ladies' Home Journal** under the title "What Parents Don't Know About Comic Books". With the release of this book, Dr. Wertham reveals seven years of research attempting to link juvenile delinquency to comic books. Many illustrations showing excessive violence, sex, sadism, and torture are shown. This book was used at the Kefauver Senate hearings which led to the Comics Code Authority. Because of the influence this book had on the comic industry and the collector's interest in it, we feel this listing is justified. Also see **Parade of Pleasure.***

SEDUCTION OF THE INNOCENT! (Also see Halloween Horror)
Eclipse Comics: Nov, 1985 - 3-D#2, Apr, 1986 ($1.75)

1-6: Double listed under cover title from #7 on 1.80
3-D 1 (10/85, $2.25, 36 pgs.)-contains unpublished Advs. Into Darkness #15 (pre-code);Dave Stevens-c 2.25
2D 1 (100 copy limited signed & numbered edition)(B&W) 5.00
3-D 2 (4/86)-Baker, Toth, Wrightson-c 2.50
2-D 2 (100 copy limited signed & numbered edition)(B&W) 5.00
NOTE: ***Anderson** r-2, 3. **Crandall** c/a(r)-1. **Meskin** c/a(r)-3, 3-D 1. **Moreira** r-2. **Toth** a-1-6r; c-4r. **Tuska** r-6.*

SEEKER
Sky Comics: Apr, 1994 ($2.50, one-shot)

1 2.50

SEEKERS INTO THE MYSTERY
DC Comics (Vertigo): Jan, 1996 - No. 15, Apr, 1997 ($2.50)

1-14: J.M. DeMatteis scripts in all. 1-4-Glenn Barr-a. 5,10-Muth-c/a. 6-9-Zulli-c/a. 11-14-Bolton-c; Jill Thompson-a 2.50
15-($2.95)-Muth-c/a 2.95

SEEKER 3000 (See Marvel Premiere #41)
Marvel Comics: Jun, 1998 - No. 4, Sept, 1998 ($2.99/$2.50, limited series)

1-($2.99)-Set 25 years after 1st app.; wraparound-c 3.00
2-4-($2.50) 2.50

GD25 FN65 NM94

...Premiere 1 (6/98, $1.50) Reprints 1st app. from Marvel Premiere #41; wraparound-c 1.50

SELECT DETECTIVE (Exciting New Mystery Cases)
D. S. Publishing Co.: Aug-Sept, 1948 - No. 3, Dec-Jan, 1948-49

1-Matt Baker-a 22.00 66.00 165.00
2-Baker, McWilliams-a 14.00 42.00 105.00
3 12.00 36.00 90.00

SELF-LOATHING COMICS
Fantagraphics Books: Feb, 1995 ($2.95, B&W)

1,2-Crumb 3.00

SEMPER FI (Tales of the Marine Corp)
Marvel Comics: Dec, 1988- No.9, Aug, 1989 (75¢)

1-9: Severin-c/a 1.00

SENSATIONAL POLICE CASES (Becomes Captain Steve Savage, 2nd Series)
Avon Periodicals: 1952; 1954 - No. 4, July-Aug, 1954

nn-(1952, 25¢, 100 pgs.)-Kubert-a?; Check, Larsen, Lawrence & McCann-a; Kinstler-c 37.00 112.00 280.00
1 (1954)-Exists? 13.00 40.00 100.00
2-4: 2-Kirbyish-a (3-4/54). 4-Reprint/Saint #5; spanking panel 11.00 32.00 80.00
I.W. Reprint #5-(1963?, nd)-Reprints Prison Break #5(1952-Realistic); Infantino-a 2.50 7.50 24.00

SENSATIONAL SHE-HULK, THE (She-Hulk #21-23) (See Savage She-Hulk)
Marvel Comics: V2#1, 5/89 - No. 60, Feb, 1994 ($1.50/$1.75, deluxe format)

V2#1-Byrne-c/a(p)/scripts begin, end #8 3.00
2-8: 3-Spidey. 4-Reintro G.A. Blonde Phantom 2.25
9-49,51-60: 14-17-Howard the Duck app. 21-23-Return of the Blonde Phantom. 22-All Winners Squad app. 25-Thor app. 26-Excalibur app.; Guice-c. 29-Wolverine app. (3 pgs.). 30-Hobgoblin-c & cameo. 31-Byrne-c/a/scripts begin again. 35-Last $1.50-c. 37-Wolverine/Punisher/Spidey-c, but no app. 39-Thing app. 56-War Zone app.; Hulk cameo. 57-Vs. Hulk-c/story. 58-Electro-c/story. 59-Jack O'Lantern app. 2.00
50-($2.95, 52 pgs.)-Embossed green foil-c; Byrne app.; last Byrne-c/a; Austin, Chaykin, Simonson-a; Miller-a(2 pgs.) 3.25
NOTE: ***Dale Keown** a(p)-13, 15-22.*

SENSATIONAL SHE-HULK IN CEREMONY, THE
Marvel Comics: 1989 - No. 2, 1989 ($3.95, squarebound, 52 pgs.)

nn-Part 1, nn-Part 2 4.00

SENSATIONAL SPIDER-MAN
Marvel Comics: Apr, 1989 ($5.95, squarebound, 80 pgs.)

1-r/Amazing Spider-Man Annual #14,15 by Miller & Annual #8 by Kirby & Ditko. 2.00 6.00

SENSATIONAL SPIDER-MAN, THE
Marvel Comics: Jan, 1996 - No. 33, Nov, 1998 ($1.95/$1.99)

0 ($4.95)-Lenticular-c; Jurgens-a/scripts 5.00
1-17, -1(7/97), 18: 2-Kaine & Rhino app. 3-Giant-Man app. 9-Onslaught tie-in; revealed that Peter & Mary Jane's unborn baby is a girl. 11-Revelations. 13-15-Ka-Zar app. 14,15-Hulk app. 16 Begin-$1.99-c 2.00
1-($2.95) variant-c; polybagged w/cassette 3.00
19-24: Living Pharoah app. 22,23-Dr. Strange app. 2.00
25-($2.99) Spiderhunt pt. 1; Normie Osborne kidnapped 3.00
26-33: 26-Nauck-a. 27-Double-c with "The Sensational Hornet #1"; Vulture app. 28-Hornet vs. Vulture. 29,30-Black Cat-c/app. 33-Last issue; Gathering of Five concludes 2.00
'96 Annual ($2.95) 3.00

SENSATION COMICS (Sensation Mystery #110 on)
National Per. Publ./All-American: Jan, 1942 - No. 109, May-June, 1952

GD25 FN65 VF82 NM94

1-Origin Mr. Terrific(1st app.), Wildcat(1st app.), The Gay Ghost, & Little Boy

Sensation Comics #15 © DC

Sgt. Bilko's Pvt. Doberman #11 © DC

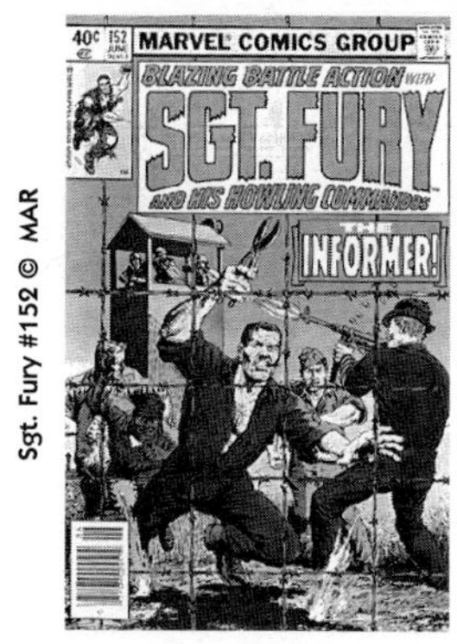

Sgt. Fury #152 © MAR

	GD25	FN65	NM94
Blue; Wonder Woman(cont'd from All Star #8), The Black Pirate begin; intro. Justice & Fair Play Club 1910.00	5730.00	11,460.00	21,000.00

(Estimated up to 150 total copies exist, 7 in NM/Mint)

1-Reprint, Oversize 13-1/2x10". WARNING: This comic is an exact duplicate reprint of the original except for its size. DC published it in 1974 with a second cover titling it as a Famous First Edition. There have been many reported cases of the outer cover being removed and the interior sold as the original edition. The reprint with the new outer cover removed is practically worthless. See Famous First Edition for value.

	GD25	FN65	NM94
2-Etta Candy begins	350.00	1050.00	3500.00
3-W. Woman gets secretary's job	218.00	654.00	1850.00
4-1st app. Stretch Skinner in Wildcat	159.00	477.00	1350.00
5-Intro. Justin, Black Pirate's son	127.00	381.00	1075.00
6-Origin/1st app. Wonder Woman's magic lasso	127.00	381.00	1075.00
7-10	91.00	273.00	775.00
11,12,14-20	82.00	246.00	700.00
13-Hitler, Tojo, Mussolini-c (as bowling pins)	106.00	318.00	900.00
21-30	65.00	195.00	550.00
31-33	49.00	147.00	420.00
34-Sargon, the Sorcerer begins (10/44), ends #36; begins again #52	52.00	156.00	440.00
35-40: 38-X-Mas-c	43.00	129.00	360.00
41-50: 43-The Whip app.	39.00	117.00	310.00
51-60: 51-Last Black Pirate. 56,57-Sargon by Kubert	35.00	105.00	260.00
61-67,69-80: 63-Last Mr. Terrific. 66-Wildcat by Kubert	35.00	105.00	260.00
68-Origin & 1st app.Huntress (8/47)	36.00	108.00	270.00
81-Used in **SOTI**, pg. 33,34; Krigstein-a	36.00	108.00	270.00
82-90: 83-Last Sargon. 86-The Atom app. 90-Last Wildcat	27.00	80.00	200.00
91-Streak begins by Alex Toth	27.00	80.00	200.00
92,93: 92-Toth-a (2 pgs.)	27.00	80.00	200.00
94-1st all girl issue	39.00	117.00	310.00
95-99,101-106: 95-Unmasking of Wonder Woman-c/story. 99-1st app. Astra, Girl of the Future, ends #106. 103-Robot-c. 105-Last 52 pgs. 106-Wonder Woman ends	39.00	116.00	290.00
100-(11-12/50)	49.00	147.00	420.00
107-(Scarce, 1-2/52)-1st mystery issue; Johnny Peril by Toth(p), 8 pgs. & begins; continues from Danger Trail #5 (3-4/51)(see Comic Cavalcade #15 for 1st app.)	59.00	177.00	500.00
108-(Scarce)-Johnny Peril by Toth(p)	47.00	141.00	400.00
109-(Scarce)-Johnny Peril by Toth(p)	59.00	177.00	500.00

NOTE: *Krigstein a-(Wildcat)-81, 83, 84.* ***Moldoff*** *Black Pirate-1-25; Black Pirate not in 34-36, 43-48.* ***Oskner*** *c(i)-89-91, 94-106. Wonder Woman by* ***H. G. Peter****, all issues except #8, 17-19, 21; c-4-7, 9-18, 20-88, 92, 93.* ***Toth*** *a-91, 98; c-107. Wonder Woman c-1-106.*

SENSATION MYSTERY (Formerly Sensation Comics #1-109)
National Periodical Publ.: No. 110, July-Aug, 1952 - No. 116, July-Aug, 1953

	GD25	FN65	NM94
110-Johnny Peril continues	39.00	116.00	290.00
111-116-Johnny Peril in all. 116-M. Anderson-a	39.00	116.00	290.00

NOTE: ***M. Anderson*** *c-110.* ***Colan*** *a-114p.* ***Giunta*** *a-112.* ***G. Kane*** *c(p)-108, 109, 111-115.*

SENTINELS OF JUSTICE, THE (See Americomics & Captain Paragon &...)

SENTRY SPECIAL
Innovation Publishing: 1991 ($2.75, one-shot)(Hero Alliance spin-off)

1-Lost in Space preview (3 pgs.) 2.75

SERAPHIM
Innovation Publishing: May, 1990 ($2.50, mature readers)

1 2.50

SERGEANT BARNEY BARKER (Becomes G. I. Tales #4 on)
Atlas Comics (MCI): Aug, 1956 - No. 3, Dec, 1956

	GD25	FN65	NM94
1-Severin-c/a(4)	17.00	50.00	125.00
2,3: 2-Severin-c/a(4). 3-Severin-c/a(5)	11.00	34.00	85.00

SERGEANT BILKO (Phil Silvers Starring as...) (TV)
National Periodical Publications: May-June, 1957 - No. 18, Mar-Apr, 1960

	GD25	FN65	NM94
1-All have Bob Oskner-c	66.00	198.00	560.00
2	37.00	112.00	280.00
3-5	31.00	92.00	230.00
6-18: 11,12,15,17-Photo-c	25.00	76.00	190.00

SGT. BILKO'S PVT. DOBERMAN (TV)
National Periodical Publications: June-July, 1958 - No. 11, Feb-Mar, 1960

	GD25	FN65	NM94
1-Bob Oskner c-1-4,7,11	33.00	100.00	320.00
2	20.00	60.00	190.00
3-5: 5-Photo-c	14.00	42.00	130.00
6-11: 6,9-Photo-c	10.00	30.00	95.00

SGT. DICK CARTER OF THE U.S. BORDER PATROL (See Holyoke One-Shot)

SGT. FURY (& His Howling Commandos)(See Fury & Special Marvel Edition)
Marvel Comics Group (BPC earlier issues): May, 1963 - No. 167, Dec, 1981

	GD25	FN65	NM94
1-1st app. Sgt. Nick Fury (becomes agent of Shield in Strange Tales #135); Kirby/Ayers-c/a; 1st Dum-Dum Dugan & the Howlers	88.00	264.00	1050.00
2-Kirby-a	29.00	88.00	295.00
3-5: 3-Reed Richards x-over. 4-Death of Junior Juniper. 5-1st Baron Strucker app.; Kirby-a	17.00	51.00	170.00
6-10: 8-Baron Zemo, 1st Percival Pinkerton app. 9-Hitler-c & app. 10-1st app. Capt. Savage (the Skipper)(9/64)	11.00	33.00	110.00
11,12,14-20: 14-1st Blitz Squad. 18-Death of Pamela Hawley	5.50	16.50	55.00
13-Captain America & Bucky app.(12/64); 2nd solo Capt. America x-over outside The Avengers; Kirby-a	28.00	84.00	280.00
21-30: 25-Red Skull app. 27-1st app. Eric Koenig; origin Fury's eye patch	4.00	12.00	40.00
31-50: 34-Origin Howling Commandos. 35-Eric Koenig joins Howlers. 43-Bob Hope, Glen Miller app. 44-Flashback on Howlers 1st mission	2.50	7.50	20.00
51-60	2.25	6.75	18.00
61-80: 64-Capt. Savage & Raiders x-over. 76-Fury's Father app. in WWI story	1.85	5.50	15.00
81-100: 98-Deadly Dozen x-over. 100-Capt. America, Fantastic 4 cameos; Stan Lee, Martin Goodman & others app.	1.50	4.50	12.00
101-120: 101-Origin retold	1.25	3.75	10.00
121-130: 121-123-r/#19-21	1.00	3.00	8.00
131-167: 167-Reprints (from 1963)	1.00	2.80	7.00
Annual 1(1965, 25¢, 72 pgs.)-r/#4,5 & new-a	12.50	38.00	125.00
Special 2(1966)	4.00	12.00	40.00
Special 3(1967)	2.50	7.50	25.00
Special 4(1968)	2.25	6.75	18.00
Special 5-7(1969-11/71)	1.50	4.50	12.00

NOTE: ***Ayers*** *a-8, Annual 1.* ***Ditko*** *a-15i.* ***Gil Kane*** *c-37, 96.* ***Kirby*** *a-1-7, 13p, 167p(r). Special 5; c-1-20, 25, 167p.* ***Severin*** *a-44-46, 48, 162, 164; inks-49-79, Special 4, 6; c-4i, 5, 6, 44, 46, 110, 149i, 155i, 162-166.* ***Sutton*** *a-57p. Reprints in #80, 82, 85, 87, 89, 91, 93, 95, 99, 101, 103, 105, 107, 109, 111, 121-123, 145-155, 167.*

SGT. FURY AND HIS HOWLING DEFENDERS (See The Defenders #147)

SERGEANT PRESTON OF THE YUKON (TV)
Dell Publishing Co.: No. 344, Aug, 1951 - No. 29, Nov-Jan, 1958-59

	GD25	FN65	NM94
Four Color 344(#1)-Sergeant Preston & his dog Yukon King begin; painted-c begin, end #18	11.00	33.00	120.00
Four Color 373,397,419('52)	6.40	19.00	70.00
5(11-1/52-53)-10(2-4/54): 6-Bondage-c.	4.50	13.50	50.00
11,12,14-17	3.60	11.00	40.00
13-Origin Sgt. Preston	4.50	13.50	50.00
18-Origin Yukon King; last painted-c	4.50	13.50	50.00
19-29: All photo-c	6.00	18.00	65.00

SERGEANT PRESTON OF THE YUKON
Quaker Cereals: 1956 (4 comic booklets) (Soft-c, 16 pgs., 7x2-1/2" & 5x2-1/2") Giveaways

Sgt. Rock #355 © DC

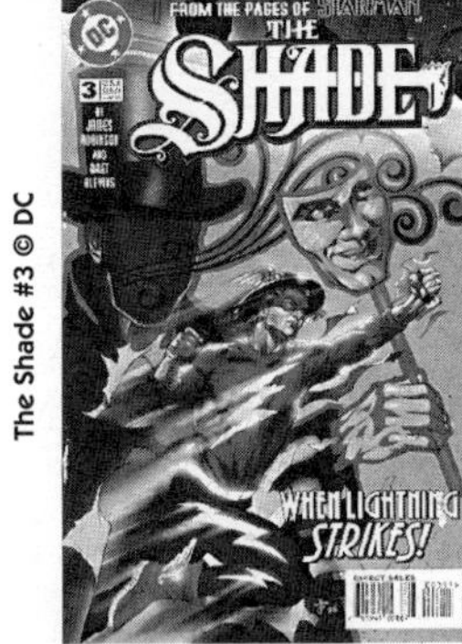

The Shade #3 © DC

Shade, The Changing Man #52 © DC

GD25 FN65 NM94

"How He Found Yukon King", "The Case That Made Him A Sergeant", "How Yukon King Saved Him From The Wolves", "How He Became A Mountie" each... 7.85 23.50 55.00

SGT. ROCK (Formerly Our Army at War; see Brave & the Bold #52 & Showcase #45)
National Periodical Publications/DC Comics: No. 302, Mar, 1977 - No. 422, July, 1988 (See G.I. Combat #108)

302 2.25 6.80 25.00
303-310 1.50 4.50 15.00
311-320: 318-Reprints 1.00 3.00 10.00
321-350 .90 2.70 8.00
351-399,401-421 5.00
400,422: 422-1st Joe, Adam, Andy Kubert-a team .85 2.60 7.00
Annual 2-4: 2(1982)-Formerly Sgt. Rock's Prize Battle Tales #1. 3(1983). 4(1984) 5.00

NOTE: ***Estrada** a-322, 327, 331, 336, 337, 341, 342i. **Glanzman** a-384, 421. **Kubert** a-302, 303, 305r, 306, 328, 351, 356, 368, 373, 422; c-317, 318r, 319-323, 325-333-on, Annual 2, 3. **Severin** a-347. **Spiegle** a-382, Annual 2, 3. **Thorne** a-384. **Toth** a-385r. **Wildey** a-307, 311, 313, 314.*

SGT. ROCK SPECIAL (Sgt. Rock #14 on; see DC Special Series #3)
DC Comics: Oct, 1988 - No. 21, Feb, 1992; No. 1, 1992 ($2.00, quarterly, 52 pgs)

1 2.75
2-8,10-21: All-r; 5-r/1st Sgt. Rock/Our Army at War #81. 7-Tomahawk-r by Thorne. 10-All Rock issue. 11-r/1st Haunted Tank story. 12-All Kubert issue; begins monthly. 13-Dinosaur story by Heath(r). 14-Enemy Ace-r (22 pgs.) by Adams/Kubert. 15-Enemy Ace (22 pgs.) by Kubert. 16-Iron Major-c/story. 16,17-Enemy Ace-r. 19-r/Batman/Sgt. Rock team-up/B&B #108 by Aparo 2.25
9-Enemy Ace-r by Kubert 3.00
1,2: 1 (1992, $2.95, 68 pgs.)-Simonson-c; unpubbed Kubert-a; Glanzman, Russell, Pratt, & Wagner-a 3.50

NOTE: ***Neal Adams** r-1, 8, 14p. **Chaykin** a-2; r-3, 9(2pgs.); c-3. **Drucker** r-6. **Glanzman** r-20. **Golden** a-1. **Heath** a-2; r-5, 9-13, 16, 19, 21. **Krigstein** r-4, 8. **Kubert** r-1-17, 20, 21; c-1p, 2, 8, 14-21. **Miller** r-6p. **Severin** r-3, 6, 10. **Simonson** r-2, 4; c-4. **Thorne** r-7. **Toth** r-2, 8, 11. **Wood** r-4.*

SGT. ROCK SPECTACULAR (See DC Special Series #13)

SGT. ROCK'S PRIZE BATTLE TALES (Becomes Sgt. Rock Annual #2 on; see DC Special Series #18 & 80 Page Giant #7)
National Periodical Publications: Winter, 1964 (Giant - 80 pgs., one-shot)

1-Kubert, Heath-r; new Kubert-c 29.00 87.00 290.00

SGT. STRYKER'S DEATH SQUAD (See Savage Combat Tales)

SERGIO ARAGONES' BOOGEYMAN
Dark Horse Comics: June, 1998 - No. 4, Sept, 1998 ($2.95, B&W, lim. series)

1-4-Aragonés-c/a 2.95

SERGIO ARAGONES DESTROYS DC
DC Comics: June, 1996 ($3.50, one-shot)

1-DC Superhero parody book; Aragonés-c/a; Evanier scripts. 3.50

SERGIO ARAGONES' GROO THE WANDERER (See Groo...)

SERGIO ARAGONES' LOUDER THAN WORDS
Dark Horse Comics: July, 1997 - No. 6, Dec, 1997 ($2.95, B&W, limited series)

1-6-Aragonés-c/a 2.95

SERGIO ARAGONES MASSACRES MARVEL
Marvel Comics: June, 1996 ($3.50, one-shot)

1-Marvel Superhero parody book; Aragonés-c/a; Evanier scripts 3.50

SERRA ANGEL ON THE WORLDS OF MAGIC THE GATHERING
Acclaim Comics (Armada): Aug, 1996 ($5.95, one-shot)

1 2.00 6.00

SERINA

GD25 FN65 NM94

Antarctic Press: Mar, 1996 - No. 3, July, 1996 ($2.95)

1-3: Warrior Nun app. 3.00

SEVEN BLOCK
Marvel Comics (Epic Comics): 1990 ($4.50, one-shot, 52 pgs.)

1 4.50

SEVEN DEAD MEN (See Complete Mystery #1)

SEVEN DWARFS (Also see Snow White)
Dell Publishing Co.: No. 227, 1949 (Disney-Movie)

Four Color #227 10.00 30.00 110.00

SEVEN MILES A SECOND
DC Comics (Vertigo Verité): 1996 ($7.95, one-shot)

nn-Wojnarowicz-s/Romberg-a .90 2.70 8.00

SEVEN SAMUROID, THE (See Image Graphic Novel)

SEVEN SEAS COMICS
Universal Phoenix Features/Leader No. 6: Apr, 1946 - No. 6, 1947(no month)

1-South Sea Girl by Matt Baker, Capt. Cutlass begin; Tugboat Tessie by Baker app. 74.00 222.00 625.00
2-Swashbuckler-c 62.00 186.00 525.00
3,5,6: 3-Six pg. Feldstein-a 56.00 168.00 475.00
4-Classic Baker-c 59.00 177.00 500.00

NOTE: ***Baker** a-1-6; c-3-6.*

1776 (See Charlton Classic Library)

7TH VOYAGE OF SINBAD, THE (Movie)
Dell Publishing Co.: Sept, 1958 (photo-c)

Four Color 944-Buscema-a 12.00 35.00 130.00

77 SUNSET STRIP (TV)
Dell Publ. Co./Gold Key: No. 1066, Jan-Mar, 1960 - No. 2, Feb, 1963 (All photo-c)

Four Color 1066-Toth-a 11.00 33.00 120.00
Four Color 1106,1159-Toth-a 9.00 27.00 100.00
Four Color 1211,1263,1291, 01-742-209(7-9/62)-Manning-a in all 8.00 25.00 90.00
1(11/62-G.K.), 2-Manning-a in each 9.00 27.00 100.00

77TH BENGAL LANCERS, THE (TV)
Dell Publishing Co.: May, 1957

Four Color 791-Photo-c 6.40 19.00 70.00

SEYMOUR, MY SON (See More Seymour)
Archie Publications (Radio Comics): Sept, 1963

1 2.50 7.50 24.00

SHADE, THE (See Starman)
DC Comics: Apr, 1997 - No. 4, July, 1997 ($2.25, limited series)

1-4-Robinson-s/Harris-c: 1-Gene Ha-a. 2-Williams/Gray-a 3-Blevins-a. 4-Zulli-a 4.00

SHADE, THE CHANGING MAN (See Cancelled Comic Cavalcade)
National Per. Publ./DC Comics: June-July, 1977 - No. 8, Aug-Sept, 1978

1-1st app. Shade; Ditko-c/a in all 2.00 6.00
2-8 4.00

SHADE, THE CHANGING MAN (2nd series) (Also see Suicide Squad #16)
DC Comics (Vertigo imprint #33 on): July, 1990 - No.70, 1996 ($1.50/$1.75/$1.95/$2.25, mature)

1-($2.50, 52 pgs.)-Peter Milligan scripts in all 4.00
2-49,51-59: 6-Preview of World Without End. 17-Begin $1.75-c. 33-Metallic ink on-c. 41-Begin $1.95-c. 42-44-John Constantine app. 2.00
50-($2.95, 52 pgs.) 3.50
60-70: 60-begin $2.25-c 2.25

NOTE: ***Bachalo** a-1-9, 11-13, 15-21, 23-26, 33-39, 42-45, 47-50; c-30, 33-39.*

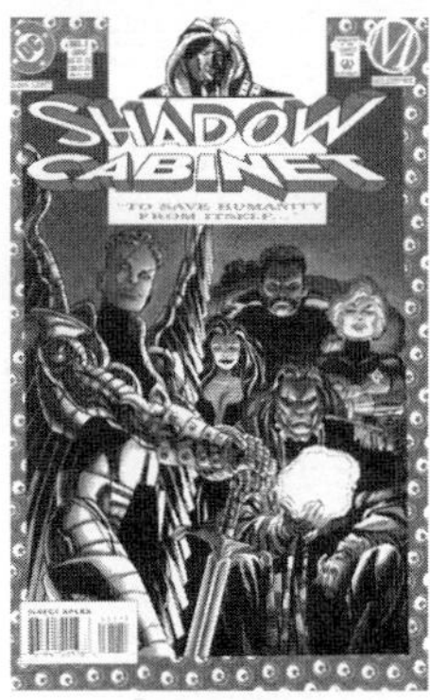

Shadow Cabinet #1 © DC

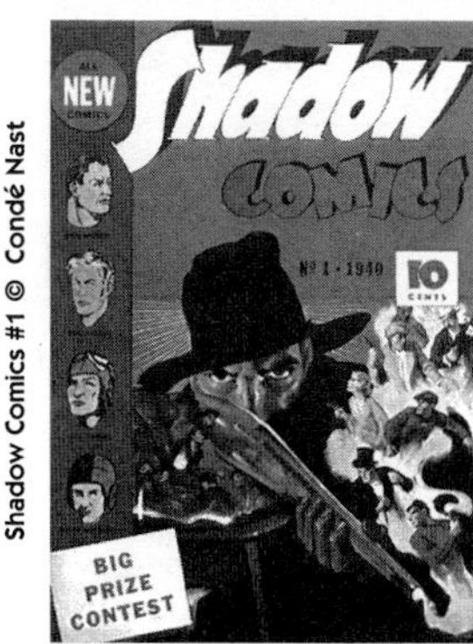

Shadow Comics #1 © Condé Nast

Shadowhawk #13 © Jim Valentino

GD25 FN65 NM94

SHADO: SONG OF THE DRAGON (See Green Arrow #63-66)
DC Comics: 1992 - No. 4, 1992 ($4.95, limited series, 52 pgs.)

Book One - Four: Grell scripts; Morrow-a(i) 5.00

SHADOW, THE (See Batman #253, 259 & Marvel Graphic Novel #35)

SHADOW, THE (Pulp, radio)
Archie Comics (Radio Comics): Aug, 1964 - No. 8, Sept, 1965 (All 12¢)

	GD25	FN65	NM94
1-Jerrry Siegel scripts in all; Shadow-c.	4.50	13.50	45.00
2-8: 2-App. in super-hero costume on-c only; Reinman-a(backup). 3-Superhero begins; Reinman-a (book-length novel). 3,4,6,7-The Fly 1 pg. strips. 4-8-Reinman-a. 5-8-Siegel scripts. 7-Shield app.	2.80	8.40	28.00

SHADOW, THE
National Periodical Publications: Oct-Nov, 1973 - No. 12, Aug-Sept, 1975

	GD25	FN65	NM94
1-Kaluta-a begins	2.20	6.25	22.00
2	1.10	3.30	11.00
3-Kaluta/Wrightson-a	1.40	4.20	14.00
4,6-Kaluta-a ends. 4-Chaykin, Wrightson part-i	.90	2.70	9.00
5,7-12: 11-The Avenger (pulp character) x-over		2.00	6.00

NOTE: ***Craig*** *a-10.* ***Cruz*** *a-10-12.* ***Kaluta*** *a-1, 2, 3p, 4, 6; c-1-4, 6, 10-12.* ***Kubert*** *c-9.* ***Robbins*** *a-5, 7-9; c-5, 7, 8.*

SHADOW, THE
DC Comics: May, 1986 - No. 4, Aug, 1986 (limited series)

1-4: Howard Chaykin art in all 2.50
Blood & Judgement ($12.95)-r/1-4 13.00

SHADOW, THE
DC Comics: Aug, 1987 - No. 19, Jan, 1989 ($1.50)

1-19: Andrew Helfer scripts in all. 1.75
Annual 1 (12/87, $2.25) 2.50
Annual 2 (1988, $2.50)-The Shadow dies; origin retold (story inspired by the movie "Citizen Kane"). 2.75

NOTE: ***Kyle Baker*** *a-7i, 8-19, Annual 2.* ***Chaykin*** *c-Annual 1.* ***Helfer*** *scripts in all.* ***Orlando*** *a-Annual 1.* ***Rogers*** *c/a-7.* ***Sienkiewicz*** *c/a-1-6.*

SHADOW, THE (Movie)
Dark Horse Comics: June, 1994 - No. 2, July, 1994 ($2.50, limited series)

1,2-Adaptation from Universal Pictures film 3.00
NOTE: ***Kaluta*** *c/a-1, 2.*

SHADOW AND DOC SAVAGE, THE
Dark Horse Comics: July, 1995 - No. 2, Aug, 1995 ($2.95, limited series)

1,2 3.50

SHADOW AND THE MYSTERIOUS 3, THE
Dark Horse Comics: Sept, 1994 ($2.95, one-shot)

1-Kaluta co-scripts. 3.00
NOTE: ***Stevens*** *c-1.*

SHADOW CABINET (See Heroes)
DC Comics (Milestone): Jan, 1994 - No. 17, Oct, 1995 ($1.75/$2.50)

0-($2.50, 52 pgs.)-Silver ink-c; Simonson-c 2.50
1-13: 1-Byrne-c 1.75
14-17: 14-begin $2.50-c 2.50

SHADOW COMICS (Pulp, radio)
Street & Smith Publications: Mar, 1940 - V9#5, Aug-Sept, 1949
NOTE: *The Shadow first appeared on radio in 1929 and was featured in pulps beginning in April, 1931, written by Walter Gibson. The early covers of this series were reprinted from the pulp covers.*

	GD25	FN65	NM94
V1#1-Shadow, Doc Savage, Bill Barnes, Nick Carter (radio), Frank Merriwell, Iron Munro, the Astonishing Man begin	390.00	1170.00	3900.00
2-The Avenger begins, ends #6; Capt. Fury only app.	159.00	477.00	1350.00
3(nn-5/40)-Norgil the Magician app.; cover is exact swipe of Shadow pulp from 1/33	112.00	336.00	950.00
4,5: 4-The Three Musketeers begins, ends #8. 5-Doc Savage ends	91.00	273.00	775.00
6,8,9: 9-Norgil the Magician app.	79.00	237.00	675.00
7-Origin/1st app. The Hooded Wasp & Wasplet (11/40); series ends V3#8; Hooded Wasp/Wasplet app. on-c thru #9	87.00	261.00	740.00
10-Origin The Iron Ghost, ends #11; The Dead End Kids begins, ends #14	79.00	237.00	675.00
11-Origin Hooded Wasp & Wasplet retold	79.00	237.00	675.00
12-Dead End Kids app.	62.00	186.00	525.00
V2#1,2(11/41): 2-Dead End Kids story	55.00	165.00	470.00
3-Origin & 1st app. Supersnipe (3/42); series begins; Little Nemo story	79.00	237.00	675.00
4,5: 4,8-Little Nemo story	50.00	150.00	425.00
6-9: 6-Blackstone the Magician story	43.00	131.00	370.00
10-12: 10-Supersnipe app.	43.00	131.00	370.00
V3#1-12: 10-Doc Savage begins, not in V5#5, V6#10-12, V8#4	43.00	129.00	350.00
V4#1-12	40.00	120.00	320.00
V5#1-12	38.00	114.00	285.00
V6#1-11: 9-Intro. Shadow, Jr. (12/46)	33.00	100.00	250.00
12-Powell-c/a; atom bomb panels	38.00	114.00	285.00
V7#1,2,5,7-9,12: 2,5-Shadow, Jr. app.; Powell-a	39.00	118.00	315.00
3,6,11-Powell-c/a	43.00	129.00	345.00
4-Powell-c/a; Atom bomb panels	44.00	131.00	370.00
10(1/48)-Flying Saucer-c/story (2nd of this theme; see The Spirit 9/28/47); Powell-c/a	49.00	147.00	420.00
V8#1-12-Powell-a. 8-Powell Spider-c/a	43.00	129.00	345.00
V9#1,5-Powell-a	39.00	117.00	310.00
2-4-Powell-c/a	43.00	129.00	345.00

NOTE: ***Binder*** *c-V3#1.* ***Powell*** *art in most issues beginning V6#12. Painted c-1-6.*

SHADOWDRAGON
DC Comics: 1995 ($3.50, annual)

Annual 1-Year One story 3.50

SHADOW EMPIRES: FAITH CONQUERS
Dark Horse Comics: Aug, 1994 - No. 4, Nov, 1994 ($2.95, limited series)

1-4 3.00

SHADOWHAWK (See Images of Shadowhawk, New Shadowhawk, Shadowhawk II, Shadowhawk III & Youngblood #2)
Image Comics (Shadowline Ink): Aug, 1992 - No. 4, Mar, 1993; No. 12, Aug, 1994 - No. 18, May, 1995 ($1.95/$2.50)

1-($2.50)-Embossed silver foil stamped-c; Valentino/Liefeld-c; Valentino-c/a/scripts in all; has coupon for Image #0; 1st Shadowline Ink title 2.00
1-With coupon missing 2.00
1-($1.95)-Newsstand version w/o foil stamp 2.00
2-Shadowhawk poster w/McFarlane-i; brief Spawn app.; wraparound-c w/silver ink highlights 2.00
3-($2.50)-Glow-in-the-dark-c 2.50
4-($1.95)-Savage Dragon-c/story; Valentino/Larsen-c 2.00
5-11-(See Shadowhawk II and III)
12,13:12-Cont'd from Shadowhawk III; pull-out poster by Texeira. 13-w/ShadowBone poster; WildC.A.T.s app. 2.00
0 (10/94)-Liefeld c/a/story; ShadowBart poster. 2.00
14-18: 14-(10/94, $2.50)-The Others app. 16-Supreme app. 17-Spawn app.; story cont'd from Badrock & Co. #6. 18-Shadowhawk dies; Savage Dragon & Brigade app. 2.50
Special 1(12/94, $3.50, 52 pgs.)-Silver Age Shadowhawk flip book 3.50
Gallery (4/94, $1.95) 2.00
Out of the Shadows ($19.95)-r/Youngblood #2, Shadowhawk #1-4, Image Zero #0, Operation :Urban Storm (Never published) 20.00
.../Vampirella (2/95, $4.95)-Pt.2 of x-over (See Vampirella/Shadowhawk for Pt. 1) 5.00

NOTE: *Shadowhawk was originally a four issue limited series. The story continued in Shadowhawk II, Shadowhawk III & then became Shadowhawk again with issue #12.*

SHADOWHAWK II (Follows Shadowhawk #4)

Shadowhawk III #2 © Jim Valentino

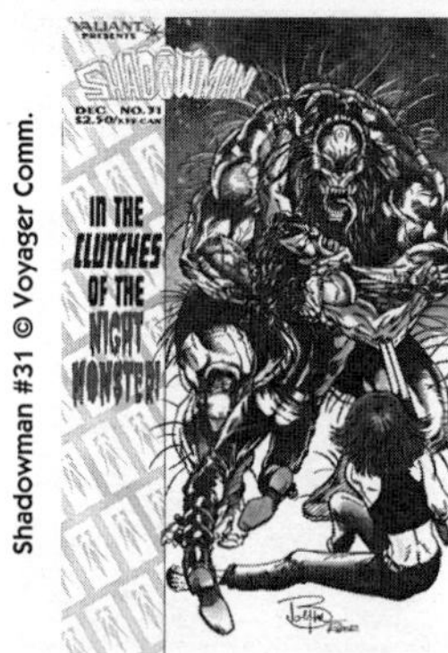

Shadowman #31 © Voyager Comm.

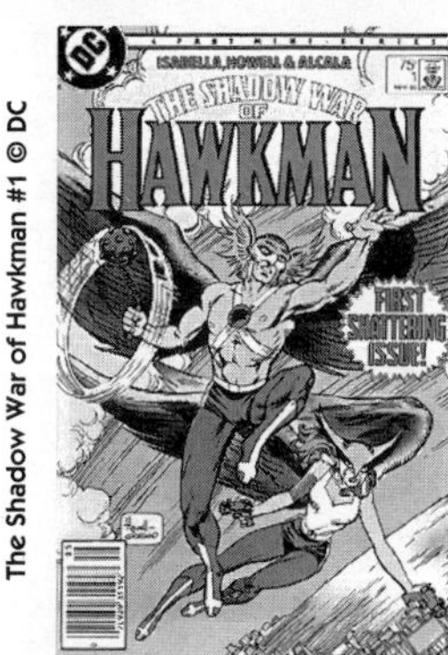

The Shadow War of Hawkman #1 © DC

	GD25	FN65	NM94

Image Comics (Shadowline Ink): V2#1, May, 1993 - V2#3, Aug, 1993 ($3.50/$1.95/$2.95, limited series)

V2#1 ($3.50)-Cont'd from Shadowhawk #4; die-cut mirricard-c 3.50
2 ($1.95)-Foil embossed logo; reveals identity; gold-c variant exists 2.00
3 ($2.95)-Pop-up-c w/Pact ashcan insert 3.00

SHADOWHAWK III (Follows Shadowhawk II #3)
Image Comics (Shadowline Ink): V3#1, Nov, 1993 - V3#4, Mar, 1994 ($1.95, limited series);

V3#1-4: 1-Cont'd from Shadowhawk II; intro Valentine; gold foil & red foil stamped-c variations. 2-(52 pgs.)-Shadowhawk contracts HIV virus; U.S. Male by M. Anderson (p) in free 16 pg.insert. 4-Continues in Shadowhawk #12. 2.00

SHADOWHAWKS OF LEGEND
Image Comics (Shadowline Ink): Nov, 1995 ($4.95, one-shot)

nn-Stories of past Shadowhawks by Kurt Busiek, Beau Smith & Alan Moore. 5.00

SHADOW, THE: HELL'S HEAT WAVE (Movie, pulp, radio)
Dark Horse Comics: Apr, 1995 - No. 3, June, 1995 ($2.95, limited series)

1-3: Kaluta story 3.50

SHADOWHUNT SPECIAL
Image Comics (Extreme Studios): Apr, 1996 ($2.50)

1-Retells origin of past Shadowhawks; Jim Valentino script; Chapel app. 2.50

SHADOW, THE: IN THE COILS OF THE LEVIATHAN (Movie, pulp, radio)
Dark Horse Comics: Oct, 1993 - No. 4, Apr, 1994 ($2.95, limited series)

1-4-Kaluta-c & co-scripter 3.50
Trade paperback (10/94, $13.95)-r/1-4 14.00

SHADOW LADY: DANGEROUS LOVE (Masakazu Katsura's...)
Dark Horse Comics: Oct, 1998 - No. 7 ($2.50, B&W, limited series)

1-Manga by Masakazu Katsura-s/a 2.50

SHADOWLINE SAGA: CRITICAL MASS, A
Marvel Comics (Epic): Jan, 1990 - No. 7, July, 1990 ($4.95, lim. series, 68 pgs)

1-6: Dr. Zero, Powerline, St. George 5.00
7 ($5.95, 84 pgs.)-Morrow-a, Williamson-c(i) 2.00 6.00

SHADOWMAN (See X-O Manowar #4)
Valiant/Acclaim Comics (Valiant): May, 1992 - No. 43, Dec, 1995 ($2.50)

1-Partial origin 3.00
2-5: 3-1st app. Sousa the Soul Eater 3.00
6-15,17: 8-1st app. Master Darque 2.00
16-1st app. Dr. Mirage (8/93) 1.50
18-43: 15-Minor Turok app. 17,18-Archer & Armstrong x-over. 19-Aerosmith-c/story. 23-Dr. Mirage x-over. 24-(4/94). 25-Bound-in trading card. 29-Chaos Effect. 43-Shadowman jumps to his death 2.50
0-($2.50, 4/94)-Regular edition 2.50
0-($3.50)-Wraparound chromium-c edition 3.50
0-Gold 6.00
Yearbook 1 (12/94, $3.95) 4.00

SHADOWMAN
Acclaim Comics (Valiant Heroes): V2#1, Mar, 1997 - No. 20 ($2.50, mature)

V2#1-20: 1-1st app. Zero; Garth Ennis scripts begin, end #4. 2-Zero becomes new Shadowman. 4-Origin; Jack Boniface (original Shadowman) rises from the grave. 5-Jamie Delano scripts begin. 9-Copycat-c 2.50
V2#1-Variant painted cover 2.50

SHADOWMASTERS
Marvel Comics: 10/89 - No.4, 1/90 ($3.95, squarebound, limited series, 52 pgs.)

1-Jim Lee-c; Heath-a(i); story cont'd from Punisher 4.00
2-4: Heath-a(i) 4.00

SHADOW OF THE BATMAN
DC Comics: Dec, 1985 - No. 5, Apr, 1986 ($1.75, limited series)

1-Detective-r (all have wraparound-c) 5.50
2,3,5: 3-Penguin-c & cameo. 5-Clayface app. 3.50
4-Joker-c/story 4.75
NOTE: ***Austin*** *a(new)-2i, 3i; r-2-4i.* ***Rogers*** *a(new)-1, 2p, 3p, 4, 5; r-1-5p; c-1-5.* ***Simonson*** *a-1r.*

SHADOW OF THE TORTURER, THE
Innovation: July, 1991 - No. 3, 1992 ($2.50, limited series)

1-3: Based on Pocket Books novel 2.50

SHADOW ON THE TRAIL (See Zane Grey & Four Color #604)

SHADOW PLAY (Tales of the Supernatural)
Whitman Publications: June, 1982

1-Painted-c 4.00

SHADOW RIDERS
Marvel Comics UK, Ltd.: June, 1993 - No. 4, Sept, 1993 ($1.75, limited series)

1-($2.50)-Embossed-c; Cable-c/story 2.50
2-4-Cable app. 2-Ghost Rider app. 1.75

SHADOWS & LIGHT
Marvel Comics: Feb, 1998 - Present ($2.99, B&W, quarterly)

1-B&W anthology of Marvel characters; art by Ha, Wrightson, Ditko & Stelfreeze; Stelfreeze painted-c 3.00
2-Weeks, Sharp, Starlin, Thompson-a 3.00
3-Buscema, Grindberg, Giffen, Layton-a 3.00

SHADOWS FROM BEYOND (Formerly Unusual Tales)
Charlton Comics: V2#50, October, 1966

V2#50-Ditko-c 2.50 7.50 20.00

SHADOW SLASHER
Pocket Change Comics: No. 0, 1994 - No. 6, 1995? ($2.50, B&W)

0-6 2.50

SHADOW'S FALL
DC Comics (Vertigo): Nov, 1994 - No. 6, Apr, 1995 ($2.95, limited series)

1-6: Van Fleet-c/a in all. 3.00

SHADOW STATE
Broadway Comics: Dec, 1995 - No. 5, Apr, 1996 ($2.50)

1-5: 1,2-Fatale back-up story; Cockrum-a(p) 2.50
Preview Edition 1,2 (10-11/95, $2.50, B&W) 2.50

SHADOW STRIKES!, THE (Pulp, radio)
DC Comics: Sept, 1989 - No.31, May, 1992 ($1.75)

1-18: 5,6-Doc Savage x-over 1.80
19-31: 19-begin $2.00-c. 31-Mignola-c. 2.00
Annual 1 (1989, $3.50, 68 pgs.)-Spiegle a; Kaluta-c 3.50

SHADOW WAR OF HAWKMAN
DC Comics: May, 1985 - No. 4, Aug, 1985 (limited series)

1-4 1.00

SHAGGY DOG & THE ABSENT-MINDED PROFESSOR (See Movie Comics & Walt Disney Showcase #46)(Disney-Movie)
Dell Publ. Co.: No. 985, May, 1959; No. 1199, Apr, 1961

Four Color #985,1199 6.40 19.00 70.00

SHALOMAN
Al Wiesner: Aug, 1988 - Present (B&W)

V1#1-9 1.75
V2#1 2.00
2-4, 6-10 2.50
5 (Color)-Shows Vol 2, No. 4 in indicia 3.00

SHAMAN'S TEARS (Also see Maggie the Cat)

Sharky #4 © Dave Elliot

Shazam! #3 © DC

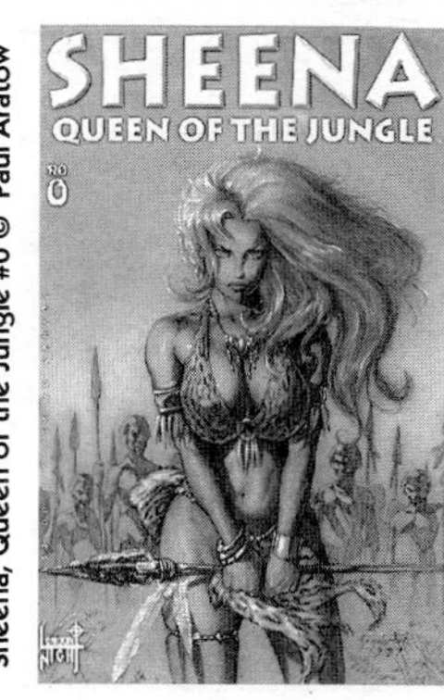

Sheena, Queen of the Jungle #0 © Paul Aratow

	GD25	FN65	NM94

Image Comics (Creative Fire Studio): 5/93 - No. 2, 8/93; No. 3, 11/94 - No. 0, 1/96 ($2.50/$1.95)

0-2: 0-(DEC-c, 1/96)-Last Issue. 1-(5/93)-Embossed red foil stamped-c; Mike Grell-c/a & scripts in all. 2-Cover unfolds into poster (8/93-c, 7/93 inside). 2.50
3-12: 3-Begin $1.95-c. 5-Re-intro Jon Sable. 12-Re-intro Maggie the Cat (1 pg.) 2.00

SHANNA, THE SHE-DEVIL (See Savage Tales #8)
Marvel Comics Group: Dec, 1972 - No. 5, Aug, 1973 (All are 20¢ issues)

	GD25	FN65	NM94
1-1st app. Shanna; Steranko-c; Tuska-a(p)	1.20	3.60	12.00
2-Steranko-c; heroin drug story	.90	2.70	9.00
3-5	.85	2.60	7.00

SHARDS
Ascension Comics: Apr, 1994 ($2.50, B&W, unfinished limited series)

1-Flip-c. 2.50

SHARK FIGHTERS, THE (Movie)
Dell Publishing Co.: Jan, 1957

	GD25	FN65	NM94
Four Color 762-Buscema-a; photo-c	7.00	22.00	80.00

SHARKY
Image Comics: Feb, 1998 - No. 4, 1998 ($2.50, bi-monthly)

1,2: 1-Mask app.; Elliot-s/a. Horley painted-c. 2.50
1-($2.95) "$1,000,000" variant 3.00
2-($2.50) Savage Dragon variant-c 2.50
3,4: 3-Three covers by Horley, Bisley, & Horley/Elliot. 4-Two covers (swipe of Avengers#4 and wraparound) 2.50

SHARP COMICS (Slightly large size)
H. C. Blackerby: Winter, 1945-46 - V1#2, Spring, 1946 (52 pgs.)

	GD25	FN65	NM94
V1#1-Origin Dick Royce Planetarian	37.00	112.00	280.00
2-Origin The Pioneer; Michael Morgan, Dick Royce, Sir Gallagher, Planetarian, Steve Hagen, Weeny and Pop app.	33.00	98.00	245.00

SHARPY FOX (See Comic Capers & Funny Frolics)
I. W. Enterprises/Super Comics: 1958; 1963

	GD25	FN65	NM94
1,2-I.W. Reprint (1958): 2-r/Kiddie Kapers #1	1.00	3.00	8.00
14-Super Reprint (1963)	1.00	3.00	8.00

SHATTER (See Jon Sable #25-30)
First Comics: June, 1985; Dec, 1985 - No. 14, Apr, 1988. ($1.75, Baxter paper/deluxe paper)

1 (6/85)-1st computer gernerated-a in a comic book (1st & 2nd printings) 1.75
1-14: computer-generated-a & lettering in all. 1-(12/85) 1.75

SHATTERED IMAGE
Image Comics (WildStorm Productions): Aug, 1996 - No. 4, Dec, 1996 ($2.50, limited series)

1-4: 1st Image company-wide x-over; Kurt Busiek scripts in all. 1-Tony Daniel-c/a(p). 2-Alex Ross-c/swipe (Kingdom Come) by Ryan Benjamin & Travis Charest 2.50

SHAZAM (See Giant Comics to Color, Limited Collectors' Edition & The Power Of Shazam!)

SHAZAM! (TV)(See World's Finest #253)
National Periodical Publ./DC Comics: Feb, 1973 - No. 35, May-June, 1978

	GD25	FN65	NM94
1-1st revival of original Captain Marvel since G.A. (origin retold), by Beck; Captain Marvel Jr. & Mary Marvel x-over; Superman-c.	1.00	3.00	10.00
2-5: 2-Infinity photo-c.; re-intro Mr. Mind & Tawny. 3-Capt. Marvel-r. (10/46). 4-Origin retold; Capt. Marvel-r. (1949). 5-Capt. Marvel Jr. origin retold; Capt. Marvel-r. (1948, 7 pgs.)			5.00
6,7,9-11: 6-photo-c; Capt. Marvel-r (1950, 6 pgs.). 9-Mr. Mind app. 10-Last C.C. Beck issue. 11-Schaffenberger-a begins.			4.00
8 (100 pgs.) 8-r/Capt. Marvel Jr. by Raboy; origin/C.M. #80; origin Mary Marvel/C.M. #18; origin Mr. Tawny/C.M. #79	2.40	7.00	26.00
12-17-(All 100 pgs.). 15-vs. Lex Luthor & Mr. Mind.	1.80	5.40	18.00
18-30: 21-24-All reprints. 25-1st app. Isis. 26-Sivana app. (10/76). 27-Kid Eternity teams up w/Capt. Marvel. 28-1st S.A. app. of Black Adam. 30-1st DC app. 3 Lt. Marvels.			5.00
31-35: 31-1st DC app. Minuteman. 34-Origin Capt. Nazi & Capt. Marvel Jr. retold		2.00	6.00

NOTE: *Reprints in #1-8, 10, 12-17, 21-24.* ***Beck*** *a-1-10, 12-17r, 21-24r; c-1, 3-9.* ***Nasser*** *c-35p.* ***Newton*** *a-35p.* ***Raboy*** *a-5r, 8r, 17r.* ***Schaffenberger*** *a-11, 14-20, 25, 26, 27p, 28, 29-31p, 33i, 35i; c-20, 22, 23, 25, 26i, 27i, 28-33.*

SHAZAM: THE NEW BEGINNING
DC Comics: Apr, 1987 - No. 4, July, 1987 (Legends spin-off) (Limited series)

1-4: 1-New origin & 1st modern app. Captain Marvel; Marvel Family cameo. 2-4-Sivana & Black Adam app. 1.50

SHEA THEATRE COMICS (Also see Theatre Comics)
Shea Theatre: No date (1940's) (32 pgs.)

	GD25	FN65	NM94
nn-Contains Rocket Comics; MLJ cover in one color	8.50	26.00	60.00

SHE-BAT (See Murcielaga, She-Bat & Valeria the She-Bat)

SHEENA (Movie)
Marvel Comics: Dec, 1984 - No. 2, Feb, 1985 (limited series)

1,2-r/Marvel Comics Super Special #34; Tanya Roberts movie 1.50

SHEENA, QUEEN OF THE JUNGLE (See Jerry Iger's Classic..., Jumbo Comics, & 3-D Sheena)
Fiction House Magazines: Spr, 1942; No. 2, Wint, 1942-43; No. 3, Spr, 1943; No. 4, Fall, 1948; No. 5, Sum, 1949; No. 6, Spr, 1950; No. 7-10, 1950(nd); No. 11, Spr, 1951 - No. 18, Wint, 1952-53 (#1-3: 68 pgs.; #4-7: 52 pgs.)

	GD25	FN65	NM94
1-Sheena begins	212.00	635.00	1800.00
2 (Winter, 1942-43)	94.00	282.00	800.00
3 (Spring, 1943)	71.00	213.00	600.00
4,5 (Fall, 1948, Sum, 1949): 4-New logo; cover swipe from Jumbo #20	43.00	129.00	360.00
6,7 (Spring, 1950, 1950)	39.00	117.00	300.00
8-10(1950 - Win/50, 36 pgs.)	37.00	110.00	275.00
11-18: 15-Cover swipe from Jumbo #43. 18-Used in **POP**, pg. 98	29.00	88.00	220.00
I.W. Reprint #9-r/#18; c-r/White Princess #3	4.20	12.60	42.00

NOTE: ***Baker*** *c-5-10?* ***Whitman*** *c-11-18(most).*

SHEENA-QUEEN OF THE JUNGLE
London Night: Feb, 1998 - Present ($3.00)

0-($3.00)-Hartsoe-s/Sandoval-c 3.00
0-($5.00) Crocodile, Zebra, & Leopard editions 5.00
1-($3.00) 3.00
1-($5.00) Ministry Edition 5.00

SHEENA 3-D SPECIAL (Also see Blackthorne 3-D Series #1)
Eclipse Comics: Jan, 1985 ($2.00)

1-Dave Stevens-c 4.00

SHE-HULK (See The Savage She-Hulk & The Sensational She-Hulk)

SHERIFF BOB DIXON'S CHUCK WAGON (TV) (See Wild Bill Hickok #22)
Avon Periodicals: Nov, 1950

	GD25	FN65	NM94
1-Kinstler-c/a(3)	11.00	34.00	85.00

SHERIFF OF COCHISE, THE (TV)
Mobil: 1957 (16 pgs.) Giveaway

	GD25	FN65	NM94
nn-Shaffenberger-a	3.00	7.50	15.00

SHERIFF OF TOMBSTONE
Charlton Comics: Nov, 1958 - No. 17, Sept, 1961

	GD25	FN65	NM94
V1#1-Giordano-c; Severin-a	6.00	18.00	60.00
2	3.80	11.40	38.00
3-10	2.60	7.80	26.00

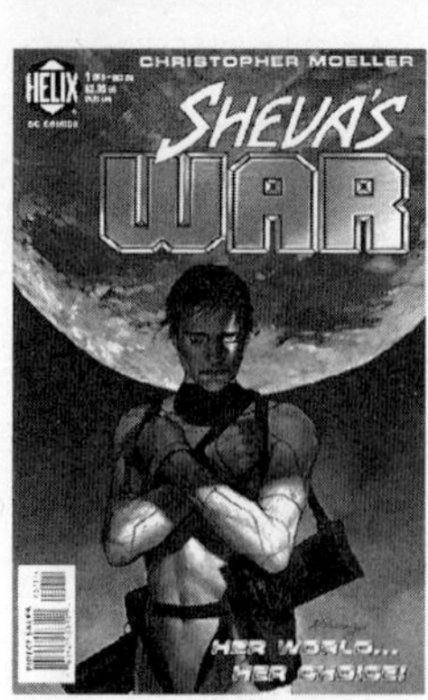

Sheva's War #1 © Christopher Moeller

Shi: Black, White & Red #2 © William Tucci

Shi: The Series #8 © William Tucci

GD25 FN65 NM94

11-17 2.50 7.50 22.00

SHERLOCK HOLMES (See Marvel Preview, New Adventures of..., & Spectacular Stories)

SHERLOCK HOLMES (All New Baffling Adventures of...)(Young Eagle #3 on?)
Charlton Comics: Oct, 1955 - No. 2, Mar, 1956

1-Dr. Neff, Ghost Breaker app. 39.00 117.00 300.00
2 33.00 100.00 250.00

SHERLOCK HOLMES (Also see The Joker)
National Periodical Publications: Sept-Oct, 1975

1-Cruz-a; Simonson-c 1.80 5.40 18.00

SHERRY THE SHOWGIRL (Showgirls #4)
Atlas Comics: July, 1956 - No. 3, Dec, 1956; No. 5, Apr, 1957 - No. 7, Aug, 1957

1-Dan DeCarlo-c/a in all 11.00 34.00 85.00
2 8.50 26.00 60.00
3,5-7 6.00 18.00 42.00

SHE'S JOSIE (See Josie)

SHEVA'S WAR
DC Comics (Helix): Oct, 1998 - No. 5, Feb, 1999 ($2.95, mini-series)

1-5-Christopher Moeller-s/painted-a/c 2.95

SHI (See Razor Annual #1 for 1st app.)

SHI: BLACK, WHITE AND RED
Crusade Comics: Mar, 1998 - No. 2, May, 1998 ($2.95, B&W&Red, mini-series)

1,2-J.G. Jones-painted art 3.00

SHI/CYBLADE: THE BATTLE FOR THE INDEPENDENTS
Crusade Comics: Sept, 1995 ($2.95)

1-Tucci c; features Cerebus, Bone, Hellboy, as well as others. 4.00
1-Silvestri variant-c 1.00 3.00 10.00

SHI/DAREDEVIL: HONOR THY MOTHER (See Daredevil/Shi..)
Crusade Comics: Jan, 1997 ($2.95, one-shot)

1-Flip book 3.00

SHI: EAST WIND RAIN
Crusade Comics: Nov, 1997 - No. 2, Feb, 1998 ($3.50, limited series)

1,2-Shi at WW2 Pearl Harbor 3.50

SHI: FAN EDITIONS
Crusade Comics: 1997

1-3-Two covers polybagged in FAN #19-21 5.00
1-3-Gold editions 10.00

SHI: HEAVEN AND EARTH
Crusade Comics: June, 1997 - No. 4, Apr, 1998 ($2.95)

1-4 3.00
4-($4.95) Pencil-c variant 5.00
Rising Sun Edition-signed by Tucci in FanClub Starter Pack 4.00
"Tora No Shi" variant-c 3.00

SHI: KAIDAN
Crusade Comics: Oct, 1996 ($2.95)

1-Two covers; Tucci-c; Jae Lee wraparound-c 3.00

SHI: MASQUERADE
Crusade Comics: Mar, 1998 ($3.50, one-shot)

1-Painted art by Lago, Texeira, and others 3.50

SHI: NIGHTSTALKERS
Crusade Comics: Sept, 1997 ($3.50, one-shot)

1-Painted art by Val Mayerik 3.50

SHI: REKISHI
Crusade Comics: Jan, 1997 ($2.95)

1-Character bios and story summaries of Shi: The Way of the Warrior told in Detective Joe Labianca's point of view; Christopher Golden script; Tucci-c; J.G. Jones-a; flip book w/Shi: East Wind Rain preview 3.00

SHI: SENRYAKU
Crusade Comics: Aug, 1995 - No. 3, Nov, 1995 ($2.95, limited series)

1-3: 1-Tucci-c; Quesada, Darrow, Sim, Lee, Smith-a. 2-Tucci-c; Silvestri, Balent, Perez, Mack-a. 3-Jusko-c; Hughes, Ramos, Bell, Moore-a. 5.00
1-variant-c (no logo) 1.00 3.00 10.00
Hardcover ($24.95)-r/#1-3; Frazetta-c. 25.00
Trade Paperback ($13.95)-r/#1-3; Frazetta-c. 14.00

SHI: THE ART OF WAR TOURBOOK
Crusade Comics: 1998 ($4.95, one-shot)

1-Blank cover for Convention sketches; early Tucci-a inside 5.00
1-Mexico Edition ($10.00) Mexican flag-c 1.00 3.00 10.00
1-U.K. Edition ($10.00) British flag-c 1.00 3.00 10.00

SHI: THE SERIES
Crusade Comics: Aug, 1997 - Present ($2.95, color #1-10, B&W #11)

1-10 3.00
11-13: 11-B&W. 12-Color; Lau-a 3.00

SHI: THE WAY OF THE WARRIOR
Crusade Comics: Mar, 1994 - No. 12, Apr, 1997 ($2.50/$2.95)

1/2 .90 2.70 8.00
1 2.00 6.00 20.00
1-Commemorative ed., B&W, new-c; given out at 1994 San Diego Comic Con 3.80 11.50 40.00
1-Fan appreciation edition -r/#1 3.00
1-Fan appreciation edition (variant) 1.80 5.40 18.00
2 1.20 3.60 12.00
2-Commemorative edition (3,000) 3.80 11.50 40.00
2-Fan appreciation edition -r/#2 4.00
3 1.00 3.00 10.00
4-6: 4-Silvestri poster 4.00
5-Silvestri variant-c 1.20 3.60 12.00
5-Gold edition 50.00
6-Tomoe #1 variant-c 1.20 3.60 12.00
6-Fan appreciation edition 3.00
7-Tomoe app. 4.00
8-12: 8-Begin $2.95-c 3.00
8-Signed Edition-(5000) 5.00
Trade paperback (1995, $12.95)-r/#1-4 13.00
Trade paperback (1995, $14.95)-r/#1-4 revised; Julie Bell-c 15.00

SHI/ VAMPIRELLA
Crusade Comics: Oct, 1997 ($2.95, one-shot)

1-Ellis-s/Lau-a 5.00

SHI VS. TOMOE
Crusade Comics: Aug, 1996 ($3.95, one-shot)

1-Tucci-a/scripts; wraparound foil-c 4.00
1-(6/96, $5.00. B&W)-Preview Ed.; sold at San Diego Comic Con 5.00

S.H.I.E.L.D. (Nick Fury & His Agents of...) (Also see Nick Fury)
Marvel Comics Group: Feb, 1973 - No. 5, Oct, 1973 (All 20¢ issues)

1-Steranko-c 1.00 3.00 10.00
2-5: 2-Steranko flag-c. 1-5 all contain-r from Str. Tales #146-155. 3-5-are cover-r; 3-Kirby/Steranko-c(r). 4-Steranko-c(r) 2.00 6.00
NOTE: ***Buscema** a-3p(r). **Kirby** layouts 1-5; c-3 (w/**Steranko**). **Steranko** a-3r, 4r(2).*

SHIELD, THE (Becomes Shield-Steel Sterling #3; #1 titled Lancelot Strong; also see Advs. of the Fly, Double Life of Private Strong, Fly Man, Mighty Comics, The Mighty Crusaders, The Original... & Pep Comics #1)

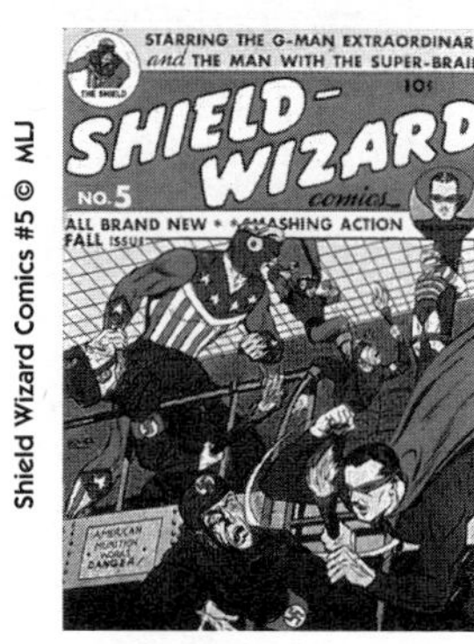

Shield Wizard Comics #5 © MLJ

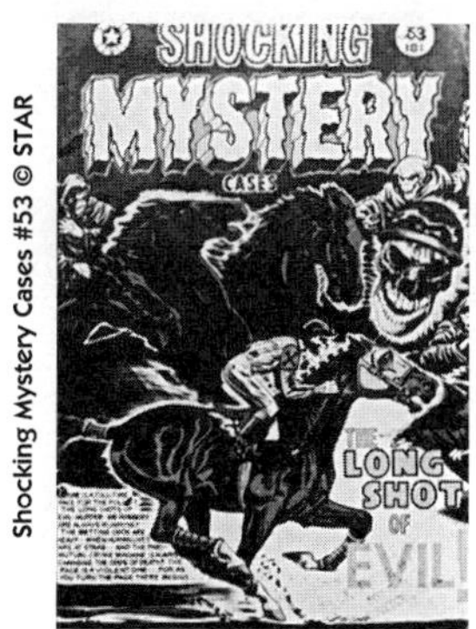

Shocking Mystery Cases #53 © STAR

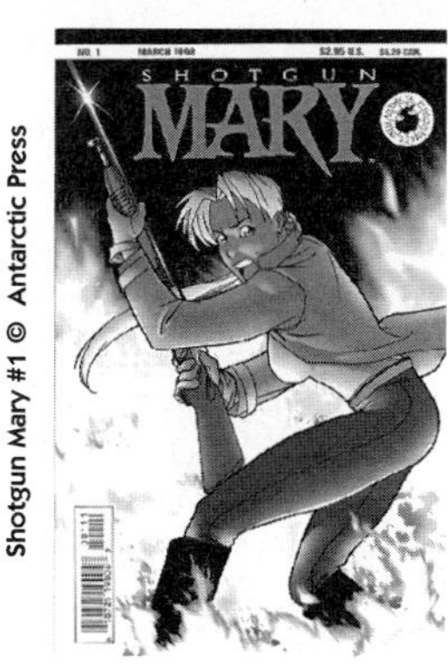

Shotgun Mary #1 © Antarctic Press

GD25 FN65 NM94

Archie Enterprises, Inc.: June, 1983 - No. 2, Aug, 1983

1,2: Steel Sterling app. 1.00

SHIELD-STEEL STERLING (Formerly The Shield)
Archie Enterprises, Inc.: No. 3, Dec, 1983 (Becomes Steel Sterling No. 4)

3-Nino-a 1.00

SHIELD WIZARD COMICS (Also see Pep Comics & Top-Notch Comics)
MLJ Magazines: Summer, 1940 - No. 13, Spring, 1944

1-(V1#5 on inside)-Origin The Shield by Irving Novick & The Wizard by Ed Ashe, Jr; Flag-c 358.00 1074.00 3400.00
2-(Winter/40)-Origin The Shield retold; Wizard's sidekick, Roy the Super Boy begins (see Top-Notch #8 for 1st app.) 171.00 513.00 1450.00
3,4 109.00 327.00 925.00
5-Dusty, the Boy Detective begins 97.00 291.00 825.00
6-8: 6-Roy the Super Boy begins. 7-Shield dons new costume (Summer, 1942); S & K-c? 88.00 264.00 750.00
9-13: 13-Bondage-c 74.00 222.00 625.00

NOTE: ***Bob Montana** c-13. **Novick** c-1-6,8-11. **Harry Sahle** c-12.*

SHINING KNIGHT (See Adventure Comics #66)

SHIP AHOY
Spotlight Publishers: Nov, 1944 (52 pgs.)

1-L. B. Cole-c 15.00 44.00 110.00

SHIP OF FOOLS
Image Comics: Aug, 1997 - Present ($2.95, B&W)

0-3-Glass-s/Oeming-a 3.00

SHIPWRECKED! (Disney-Movie)
Disney Comics: 1990 ($5.95, graphic novel, 68 pgs.)

nn-adaptation; Spiegle-a 2.00 6.00

SHMOO (See Al Capp's... & Washable Jones &...)

SHOCK (Magazine)
Stanley Publ.: May, 1969 - V3#4, Sept, 1971 (B&W reprints from horror comics)

V1#1-Cover-r/Weird Tales of the Future #7 by Bernard Baily; r/Weird Chills #1 3.20 9.50 35.00
2-Wolverton-r/Weird Mysteries 5; r-Weird Mysteries #7 used in **SOTI**; cover reprints cover to Weird Chills #1 2.90 8.70 32.00
3,5,6 2.00 6.00 20.00
4-Harrison/Williamson-r/Forbid. Worlds #6 2.20 6.50 24.00
V2#2, V1#8, V2#4-6(1/71), V3#1-4: V2#4-Cover swipe from Weird Mysteries #6 1.80 5.40 18.00

NOTE: ***Disbrow** r-V2#4; Bondage c-V1#4, V2#6, V3#1.*

SHOCK DETECTIVE CASES (Formerly Crime Fighting Detective)
(Becomes Spook Detective Cases No. 22)
Star Publications: No. 20, Sept, 1952 - No. 21, Nov, 1952

20,21-L.B. Cole-c; based on true crime cases 18.00 54.00 135.00

NOTE: ***Palais** a-20. No. 21-Fox-r.*

SHOCK ILLUSTRATED (...Adult Crime Stories; Magazine format)
E. C. Comics: Sept-Oct, 1955 - No. 3, Spring, 1956 (Adult Entertainment on-c #1,2)(All 25¢)

1-All by Kamen; drugs, prostitution, wife swapping 7.15 21.50 50.00
2-Williamson-a redrawn from Crime SuspenStories #13 plus Ingels, Crandall, Evans & part Torres-i; painted-c 8.50 26.00 60.00
3-Only 100 known copies bound & given away at E.C. office; Crandall, Evans-a; painted-c; shows May, 1956 on-c 78.00 234.00 700.00

SHOCKING MYSTERY CASES (Formerly Thrilling Crime Cases)
Star Publications: No. 50, Sept, 1952 - No. 60, Oct, 1954 (All crime reprints?)

50-Disbrow "Frankenstein" story 36.00 68.00 270.00
51-Disbrow-a 21.00 62.00 155.00
52-60: 56-Drug use story 19.00 58.00 145.00

NOTE: ***L. B. Cole** covers on all; a-60(2 pgs.). **Hollingsworth** a-52. **Morisi** a-55.*

GD25 FN65 NM94

SHOCKING TALES DIGEST MAGAZINE
Harvey Publications: Oct, 1981 (95¢)

1-1957-58-r; Powell, Kirby, Nostrand-a 2.00 6.00

SHOCK SUSPENSTORIES
E. C. Comics: Feb-Mar, 1952 - No. 18, Dec-Jan, 1954-55

1-Classic Feldstein electrocution-c 65.00 195.00 625.00
2 38.00 114.00 350.00
3,4: 4-Used in **SOTI**, pg. 387,388 27.00 81.00 230.00
5-Hanging-c 27.00 81.00 230.00
6,7: 6-Classic bondage-c. 7-Classic face melting-c 32.00 96.00 270.00
8-Williamson-a 27.00 81.00 230.00
9-11: 9-Injury to eye panel. 10-Junkie story 22.00 66.00 190.00
12- "The Monkey" classic junkie cover/story; anti-drug propaganda issue 25.00 75.00 230.00
13-Frazetta's only solo story for E.C., 7 pgs. 32.00 96.00 280.00
14-Used in Senate Investigation hearings 16.00 48.00 140.00
15-Used in 1954 Reader's Digest article, "For the Kiddies to Read"; Bill Gaines stars in prose story "The EC Caper" 16.00 48.00 140.00
16- "Red Dupe" editorial; rape story 15.00 45.00 130.00
17,18 15.00 45.00 130.00

NOTE: ***Ray Bradbury** adaptations-1, 7, 9. **Craig** a-11; c-11. **Crandall** a-9-13, 15-18. **Davis** a-1-5. **Evans** a-7, 8, 14-18; c-16-18. **Feldstein** c-1, 7-9, 12. **Ingels** a-1, 2, 6. **Kamen** a-in all; c-10, 13, 15. **Krigstein** a-14, 18. **Orlando** a-1, 3-7, 9, 10, 12, 16, 17. **Wood** a-2-15; c-2-6, 14.*

SHOCK SUSPENSTORIES
Russ Cochran/Gemstone Publishing: Sept, 1992 - No. 18, Dec, 1996 ($1.50/$2.00/$2.50, quarterly)

1-3: Reprints with original-c 1.50
4-16 2.00
17,18: 17-r/HOF #17 2.50

SHOGUN WARRIORS
Marvel Comics Group: Feb, 1979 - No. 20, Sept, 1980 (Based on Mattel toys) (1-3: 35¢; 4-19: 40¢; 20: 50¢)

1-3: Reprints. 1-Raydeen, Combatra, & Dangard Ace begin 3.00
4-20: 11-Austin-c. 12-Simonson-c. 19,20-FF x-over 1.50

SHOOK UP (Magazine) (Satire)
Dodsworth Publ. Co.: Nov, 1958

V1#1 2.80 8.40 28.00

SHORT RIBS
Dell Publishing Co.: No. 1333, Apr - June, 1962

Four Color 1333 4.50 13.50 50.00

SHORT STORY COMICS (See Hello Pal,...)

SHORTY SHINER (The Five-Foot Fighter in the Ten Gallon Hat)
Dandy Magazine (Charles Biro): June, 1956 - No. 3, Oct, 1956

1 5.35 16.00 32.00
2,3 4.00 11.00 22.00

SHOTGUN MARY
Antarctic Press: Sept, 1995 - No. 2; Mar, 1998 - No. 2, May, 1998 ($2.95)

1,2-w/pin-ups 3.00
1-($8.95)-Bagged w/CD 9.00
...Deviltown-(7/96, $2.95) 3.00
...Shooting Gallery-(6/96, $2.95) 3.00
...Son Of The Beast-(10/97, $2.95) Painted-a by Esad Ribic 2.95

SHOTGUN MARY: BLOOD LORE
Antarctic Press: Feb, 1997 - No.4, Aug, 1997 (2.95, mini-series)

1-4 2.95

SHOTGUN SLADE (TV)
Dell Publishing Co.: No. 1111, July-Sept, 1960

Four Color 1111-Photo-c 5.50 16.50 60.00

Showcase #4 © DC

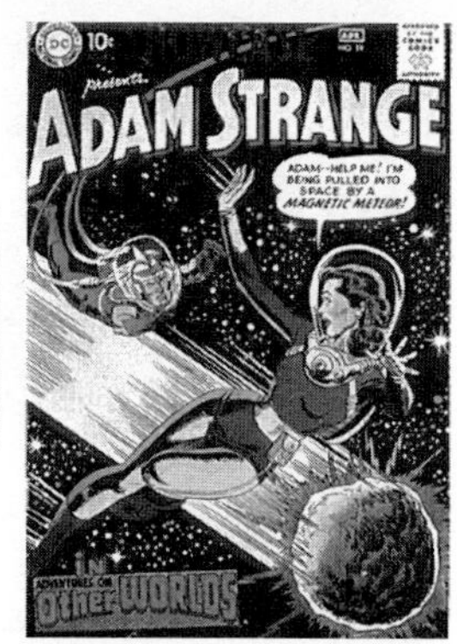

Showcase #19 © DC

Showcase #34 © DC

GD25 FN65 NM94

SHOWCASE (See Cancelled Comic Cavalcade & New Talent...)
National Per. Publ./DC Comics: 3-4/56 - No. 93, 9/70; No. 94, 8-9/77 - No. 104, 9/78

GD25 FN65 VF82 NM94

1-Fire Fighters; w/Fireman Farrell 214.00 642.00 1391.00 3000.00

GD25 FN65 NM94

2-King of the Wild; Kubert-a (animal stories) 69.00 207.00 825.00
3-The Frogmen by Russ Heath; Heath greytone-c (early DC example, 7-8/56) 67.00 200.00 800.00

GD25 FN65 VF82 NM94

4-Origin/1st app. The Flash (1st DC S.A. hero, Sept-Oct, 1956) & The Turtle; Kubert-a; r/in Secret Origins #1 ('61 & '73); Flash shown reading G.A. Flash #13; Infantino/Kubert-c 1100.00 3300.00 11,000.00 25,000.00

GD25 FN65 NM94

5-Manhunters 75.00 225.00 900.00

GD25 FN65 VF82 NM94

6-Origin/1st app. Challengers of the Unknown by Kirby, partly r/in Secret Origins #1 & Challengers #64,65 (1st S.A. hero team & 1st original concept S.A. series)(1-2/56) 243.00 729.00 1575.00 3400.00

GD25 FN65 NM94

7-Challengers of the Unknown by Kirby (2nd app.) reprinted in Challengers of the Unknown #75 123.00 369.00 1600.00

GD25 FN65 VF82 NM94

8-The Flash (5-6/57, 2nd app.); origin & 1st app. Capt. Cold 800.00 2400.00 5600.00 12,000.00
9-Lois Lane (Pre-#1, 7-8/57) (1st Showcase character to win own series) Superman app. on-c 540.00 1620.00 3500.00 6500.00

GD25 FN65 NM94

10-Lois Lane; Jor-el cameo; Superman app. on-c 175.00 525.00 2450.00
11-Challengers of the Unknown by Kirby (3rd) 115.00 345.00 1500.00
12-Challengers of the Unknown by Kirby (4th) 115.00 345.00 1500.00

GD25 FN65 VF82 NM94

13-The Flash (3rd app.); origin Mr. Element 286.00 857.00 1860.00 4000.00
14-The Flash (4th app.); origin Dr. Alchemy, former Mr. Element (rare in NM) 295.00 885.00 2200.00 5000.00
15-Space Ranger (7-8/58, 1st app.) 120.00 360.00 780.00 1700.00

GD25 FN65 NM94

16-Space Ranger (9-10/58, 2nd app.) 75.00 225.00 900.00

GD25 FN65 VF82 NM94

17-(11-12/58)-Adventures on Other Worlds; origin/1st app. Adam Strange by Gardner Fox & Mike Sekowsky. 150.00 450.00 975.00 2100.00
18-Adventures on Other Worlds (2nd A. Strange) 85.00 255.00 1100.00
19-Adam Strange; 1st Adam Strange logo 92.00 276.00 1200.00
20-Rip Hunter; origin & 1st app. (5-6/59); Moriera-a 69.00 207.00 825.00
21-Rip Hunter (7-8/59, 2nd app.); Sekowsky-c/a 42.00 126.00 460.00

GD25 FN65 VF82 NM94

22-Origin & 1st app. Silver Age Green Lantern by Gil Kane (9-10/59); reprinted in Secret Origins #2 293.00 880.00 2050.00 4400.00
23-Green Lantern (3-4.60, 2nd app.); nuclear explosion-c 113.00 339.00 735.00 1475.00
24-Green Lantern (1-2/60, 3rd app.) 113.00 339.00 735.00 1475.00

GD25 FN65 NM94

25,26-Rip Hunter by Kubert. 25-Grey tone-c 29.00 87.00 290.00
27-Sea Devils (7-8/60, 1st app.); Heath-c/a 61.00 182.00 720.00
28-Sea Devils (9-10/60, 2nd app.); Heath-c/a 34.00 102.00 375.00
29-Sea Devils; Heath-c/a; grey tone c-27-29 33.00 100.00 370.00
30-Origin Silver Age Aquaman (1-2/61) (see Adventure #260 for 1st S.A. origin) 58.00 174.00 690.00
31,32-Aquaman 34.00 102.00 375.00
33-Aquaman 38.00 114.00 420.00

GD25 FN65 VF82 NM94

34-Origin & 1st app. Silver Age Atom by Kane & Anderson (9-10/61); reprinted in Secret Origins #2 92.00 276.00 600.00 1200.00

GD25 FN65 NM94

35-The Atom by Gil Kane (2nd); last 10¢ issue 60.00 180.00 725.00
36-The Atom by Gil Kane (1-2/62, 3rd app.) 43.00 129.00 545.00
37-Metal Men (3-4/62, 1st app.) 45.00 135.00 550.00
38-Metal Men (5-6/62, 2nd app.) 38.00 114.00 420.00
39-Metal Men (7-8/62, 3rd app.) 31.00 93.00 320.00
40-Metal Men (9-10/62, 4th app.) 29.00 87.00 290.00
41,42-Tommy Tomorrow (parts 1 & 2). 42-Origin 16.00 48.00 160.00
43-Dr. No (James Bond); Nodel-a; originally published as British Classics Illustrated #158A & as #6 in a European Detective series, all with diff. painted-c. This Showcase #43 version is actually censored, deleting all racial skin color and dialogue thought to be racially demeaning (1st DC S.A. movie adaptation)(based on Ian Fleming novel & movie) 40.00 120.00 450.00
44-Tommy Tomorrow 11.00 33.00 110.00
45-Sgt. Rock (7-8/63); pre-dates B&B #52; origin retold; Heath-c 24.00 72.00 240.00
46,47-Tommy Tomorrow 9.00 27.00 90.00
48,49-Cave Carson (3rd tryout series; see B&B) 7.00 21.00 70.00
50,51-I Spy (Danger Trail-r by Infantino), King Farady story (#50 has new 4 pg. story) 7.00 21.00 70.00
52-Cave Carson 5.50 16.50 55.00
53,54-G.I. Joe (11-12/64, 1-2/65); Heath-a 10.00 30.00 100.00
55-Dr. Fate & Hourman (3-4/65); origin of each in text; 1st solo app. G.A. Green Lantern in Silver Age (pre-dates Gr. Lantern #40); 1st S.A. app. Solomon Grundy 22.50 68.00 225.00
56-Dr. Fate & Hourman 12.00 36.00 120.00
57-Enemy Ace by Kubert (7-8/65, 4th app. after Our Army at War #155) 17.00 51.00 170.00
58-Enemy Ace by Kubert (5th app.) 15.00 45.00 150.00
59-Teen Titans (11-12/65, 3rd app.) 9.50 28.50 95.00
60-1st S. A. app. The Spectre; Anderson-a (1-2/66); origin in text 24.00 72.00 240.00
61-The Spectre by Anderson (2nd app.) 13.00 39.00 130.00
62-Origin & 1st app. Inferior Five (5-6/66) 8.50 25.50 85.00
63,65-Inferior Five. 65-X-Men parody (11-12/66) 4.50 13.50 45.00
64-The Spectre by Anderson (5th app.) 12.50 38.00 125.00
66,67-B'wana Beast 2.80 8.40 28.00
68,69,71-Maniaks 2.80 8.40 28.00
70-Binky (9-10/67)-Tryout issue 2.80 8.40 28.00
72-Top Gun (Johnny Thunder-r)-Toth-a 2.80 8.40 28.00
73-Origin/1st app. Creeper; Ditko-c/a (3-4/68) 10.50 32.00 105.00
74-Intro/1st app. Anthro; Post-c/a (5/68) 7.00 21.00 70.00
75-Origin/1st app. Hawk & the Dove; Ditko-c/a 9.00 27.00 90.00
76-1st app. Bat Lash (8/68) 5.00 15.00 50.00
77-1st app. Angel & The Ape (9/68) 5.00 15.00 50.00
78-1st app. Jonny Double (11/68) 2.80 8.40 28.00
79-1st app. Dolphin (12/68); Aqualad origin-r 4.50 13.50 45.00
80-1st S.A. app. Phantom Stranger (1/69); Neal Adams-c 3.00 9.00 30.00
81-Windy & Willy 2.50 7.50 25.00
82-1st app. Nightmaster (5/69) by Grandenetti & Giordano; Kubert-c 5.50 16.50 55.00
83,84-Nightmaster by Wrightson w/Jones/Kaluta ink assist in each; Kubert-c. 83-Last 12¢ issue 84-Origin retold; begin 15¢ 5.00 15.00 50.00
85-87-Firehair; Kubert-a 2.50 7.50 20.00
88-90-Jason's Quest: 90-Manhunter 2070 app. 1.75 5.25 14.00
91-93-Manhunter 2070: 92-Origin 1.75 5.25 14.00
94-Intro/origin new Doom Patrol & Robotman(8-9/77) .90 2.70 9.00
95,96-The Doom Patrol. 95-Origin Celsius .90 2.70 8.00
97-99-Power Girl; origin-97,98; JSA cameos .90 2.70 8.00
100-(52 pgs.)-Most Showcase characters featured 1.20 3.60 12.00
101-103-Hawkman; Adam Strange x-over .90 2.70 8.00
104-(52 pgs.)-O.S.S. Spies at War .90 2.70 8.00

NOTE: ***Anderson** a-22-24i, 34-36i, 55, 56, 60, 61, 64, 101-103i; c-50i, 51i, 55, 56, 60, 61, 64. **Aparo** c-94-96. **Boring** c-10. **Estrada** a-104. **Fraden** c(p)-30, 31, 33. **Heath** c-3, 27-29. **Infantino** c/a(p)-4, 8, 13, 14; c-50p, 51p. **Gil Kane** a-22-24p, 34-36p; c-17-19, 22-24p(w/*

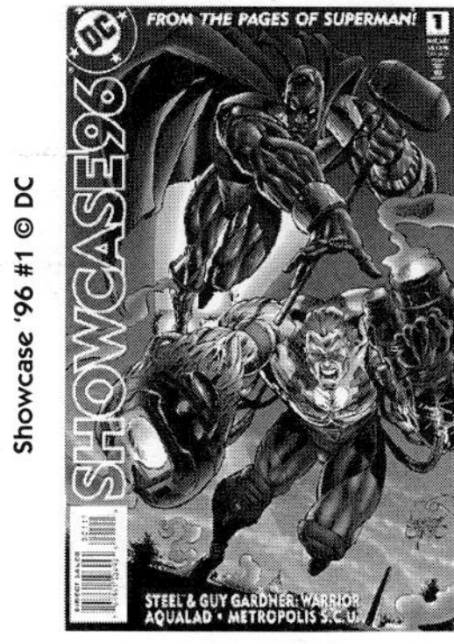

Showcase '96 #1 © DC

Shut Up and Die #1 © James D. Hudnall

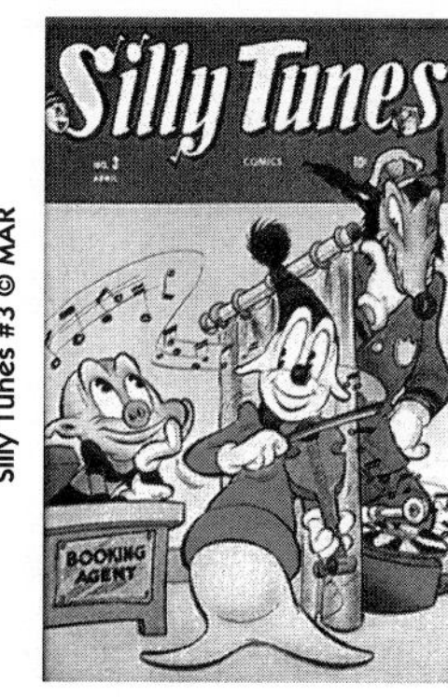

Silly Tunes #3 © MAR

GD25 FN65 NM94

Giella), 31. ***Kane/Anderson*** *c-34-36.* ***Kirby*** *c-11, 12.* ***Kirby/Stein*** *c-6, 7.* ***Kubert*** *a-2, 4i, 25, 26, 45, 53, 54, 72; c-25, 26, 53, 54, 57, 58, 82-87, 101-104; c-2, 4i.* ***Moriera*** *c-5.* ***Orlando*** *a-62p, 63p, 97i; c-62, 63, 97i.* ***Sekowsky*** *a-65p.* ***Sparling*** *a-78.* ***Staton*** *a-94, 95-99p, 100; c-97-100p.*

SHOWCASE '93
DC Comics: Jan, 1993 - No. 12, Dec, 1993 ($1.95, limited series, 52 pgs.)

1-12: 1-Begin 4 part Catwoman story & 6 part Blue Devil story; begin Cyborg story; Art Adams/Austin-c. 3-Flash by Travis Charest (p) 6-Azrael in Bat-costume (2 pgs.). 7,8-Knightfall parts 13 & 14. 6-10-Deathstroke app. (6,10-cameo). 9,10-Austin-i. 10-Azrael as Batman in new costume app.; Gulacy-c. 11-Perez-c. 12-Creeper app.; Alan Grant scripts. 2.00

NOTE: ***Chaykin*** *c-9.* ***Fabry*** *c-8.* ***Giffen*** *a-12.* ***Golden*** *c-3.* ***Zeck*** *c-6.*

SHOWCASE '94
DC Comics: Jan, 1994 - No. 12, Dec, 1994 ($1.95, limited series, 52 pgs.)

1-12: 1,2-Joker & Gunfire stories. 1-New Gods. 4-Riddler story. 5-Huntress-c/story w/app. new Batman. 6-Huntress-c/story w/app. Robin; Atom story. 7-Penguin story.by Peter David, P. Craig Russell, & Michael T. Gilbert; Penguin-c by Jae Lee. 8,9-Scarface origin story by Alan Grant, John Wagner,& Teddy Kristiansen; Prelude to Zero Hour. 10-Zero Hour tie-in story. 11-Man-Bat. 2.00

NOTE: ***Alan Grant*** *scripts-3, 4.* ***Kelley Jones*** *c-12.* ***Mignola*** *c-3.* ***Nebres*** *a(i)-2.* ***Quesada*** *c-10.* ***Russell*** *a-7p.* ***Simonson*** *c-5.*

SHOWCASE '95
DC Comics: Jan, 1995 - No. 12, Dec, 1995 ($2.50/$2.95, limited series)

1-4-Supergirl story. 3-Eradicator-c.; The Question story. 4-Thorn c/story 2.50
5-12: 5-Thorn-c/story; begin $2.95-c. 8-Spectre story. 12-The Shade story by James Robinson & Wade Von Grawbadger; Maitresse story by Chris Claremont & Alan Davis. 3.00

SHOWCASE '96
DC Comics: Jan, 1996 - No. 12, Dec, 1996 ($2.95, limited series)

1-12: 1-Steve Geppi cameo. 3-Black Canary & Lois Lane-c/story; Deadman story by Jamie Delano & Wade Von Grawbadger, Gary Frank-c. 4-Firebrand & Guardian-c/story; The Shade & Dr. Fate "Times Past" story by James Robinson & Matt Smith begins, ends #5. 6-Superboy-c/app.; Atom app.; Capt. Marvel (Mary Marvel)-c/app. 8-Supergirl by David & Dodson. 11-Scare Tactics app. 11,12-Legion of Super-Heroes vs. Brainiac. 12-Jesse Quick app. 3.00

SHOWGIRLS (Formerly Sherry the Showgirl #3)
Atlas Comics (MPC No. 2): No. 4, 2/57; June, 1957 - No. 2, Aug, 1957

4-Dan DeCarlo-c/a begins 7.15 21.50 50.00
1-Millie, Sherry, Chili, Pearl & Hazel begin 9.30 28.00 70.00
2 7.15 21.50 50.00

SHROUD, THE (See Super-Villain Team-Up #5)
Marvel Comics: Mar, 1994 - No. 4, June, 1994 ($1.75, mini-series)

1-4: 1,2,4-Spider-Man & Scorpion app. 1.75

SHROUD OF MYSTERY
Whitman Publications: June, 1982

1 4.00

SHUT UP AND DIE
Image Comics/Halloween: 1998 - Present ($2.95,B&W, bi-monthly)

1-3: Hudnall-s 3.00

SICK (Sick Special #131) (Magazine) (Satire)
Feature Publ./Headline Publ./Crestwood Publ. Co./Hewfred Publ./ Pyramid Comm./Charlton Publ. No. 109 (4/76) on: Aug, 1960 - No. 134, Fall, 1980

V1#1-Jack Paar photo on-c; Torres-a 13.00 39.00 130.00
2-5-Torres-a in all 7.00 21.00 70.00
6 5.00 15.00 50.00
V2#1-8(#7-14) 5.00 15.00 50.00
V3#1-8(#15-22) 3.00 9.00 30.00
V4#1-5(#23-27) 2.50 7.50 25.00
28,30-32,34-40 1.80 5.40 18.00
29-Beatles-c by Jack Davis 2.50 7.50 25.00
33-Ringo Starr photo-c & spoof on "A Hard Day's Night"; inside-c has Beatles photos 3.50 10.50 35.00
41-60: 45 has #44 on-c & #45 on inside 1.60 4.80 16.00
61-80,100: 70-John & Yoko-c 1.40 4.20 14.00
81-99 1.00 3.00 10.00
101-120 .90 2.70 8.00
121-130: 128-Superman-c/movie parody 1.20 3.60 12.00
131-133: 131-Superman parody 1.80 5.40 18.00
134 (scarce) 2.70 8.00 30.00
Annual 1969, 1970, 1971 2.20 6.25 22.00
Annual 2-4(1980) .90 2.70 9.00
Big Sick Laff-in (1968)-w/psychedelic posters 2.50 7.50 25.00
Birthday Annual (1967)-3 pg. Huckleberry Fink fold out 3.00 9.00 30.00
7th Annual Yearbook (1967)-Davis-c, 2 pg. glossy poster insert 2.50 7.50 25.00
Special 2 (1978) .90 2.70 9.00
Yearbook 14(1974), 15(1975, 84 pgs.) 1.20 3.60 12.00

NOTE: ***Davis*** *a-42, 87; c-22, 23, 25, 29, 31, 32.* ***Powell*** *a-7, 31, 57.* ***Simon*** *a-1-3, 10, 41, 42, 87, 99; c-1, 47, 57, 59, 69, 91, 95-97, 99, 100, 102, 107, 112.* ***Torres*** *a-1-3, 29, 31, 47, 49.* ***Tuska*** *a-14, 41-43. Civil War Blackouts-23, 24. #42 has biography of Bob Powell.*

SIDESHOW
Avon Periodicals: 1949 (one-shot)

1-(Rare)-Similar to Bachelor's Diary 27.00 82.00 205.00

SIEGE
Image Comics (WildStorm Prod.): Jan, 1997 - No. 4, Apr, 1997 ($2.50)

1-4 2.50

SIEGEL AND SHUSTER: DATELINE 1930s
Eclipse Comics: Nov, 1984 - No. 2, Sept, 1985 ($1.50/$1.75, Baxter paper #1)

1-Unpublished samples of strips from the '30s; includes 'Interplanetary Police'; Shuster-c 1.50
2 ($1.75, B&W)-unpublished strips; Shuster-c 1.75

SIGMA
Image Comics (WildStorm Productions): March, 1996 - No. 3, June, 1996 ($2.50, limited series)

1-3: 1-"Fire From Heaven" prelude #2; Coker-a
2-"Fire From Heaven" pt. 6. 3-"Fire From Heaven" pt. 14. 2.50

SILENT INVASION, THE
Rengade Press: Apr, 1986 - No.12, Mar, 1988 ($1.70/$2.00, B&W)

1-12-UFO sightings of the '50's 2.00
Book 1- reprints ($7.95) 8.00

SILENT MOBIUS
Viz Select Comics: 1991 - No. 5, 1992 ($4.95, color, squarebound, 44 pgs.)

1-5: Japanese stories translated to English 5.00

SILENT RAPTURE
Avatar Press: Jan, 1997 - No.2, Apr, 1997 ($3.00, B&W, limited series)

1,2 3.00

SILLY PILLY (See Frank Luther's...)

SILLY SYMPHONIES (See Dell Giants)

SILLY TUNES
Timely Comics: Fall, 1945 - No. 7, June, 1947

1-Silly Seal, Ziggy Pig begin 17.00 50.00 125.00
2-(2/46) 9.30 28.00 65.00
3-7: 6-New logo 7.15 21.50 50.00

SILVER (See Lone Ranger's Famous Horse...)

Silver Sable and the Wild Pack #25 © MAR

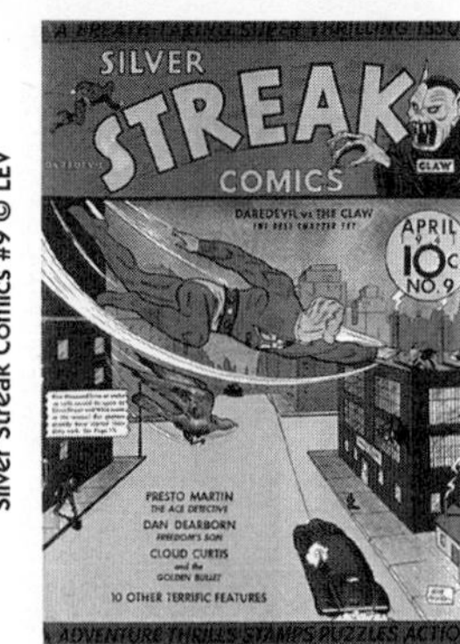

Silver Streak Comics #9 © LEV

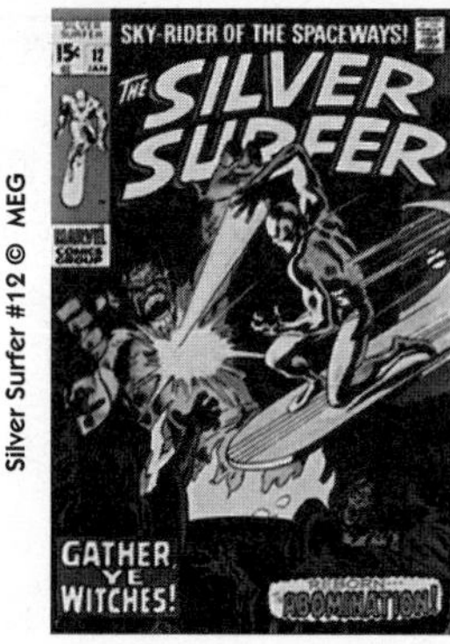

Silver Surfer #12 © MEG

GD25 FN65 NM94

SILVERBACK
Comico: 1989 - No. 3, 1990 ($2.50, color, limited series, mature readers)

1-3: Character from Grendel: Matt Wagner-a — 3.00

SILVERBLADE
DC Comics: Sept, 1987 - No. 12, Sept, 1988

1-12: Colan -c/a in all — 1.50

SILVER CROSS (See Warrior Nun series)
Antarctic Press: Nov, 1997 - No. 3, Mar, 1998 ($2.95)

1-3-Ben Dunn-s/a — 2.95

SILVERHAWKS
Star Comics/Marvel Comics #6: Aug, 1987 - No. 6, June, 1988 ($1.00)

1-6 — 1.00

SILVERHEELS
Pacific Comics: Dec, 1983 - No. 3, May, 1984 ($1.50)

1-3 — 1.50

SILVER KID WESTERN
Key/Stanmor Publications: Oct, 1954 - No. 5, July?, 1955

	GD25	FN65	NM94
1	8.50	26.00	60.00
2	5.00	15.00	30.00
3-5	4.25	13.00	28.00
I.W. Reprint #1,2-Severin-c: 1-r/#? 2-r/#1	1.25	3.75	10.00

SILVER SABLE AND THE WILD PACK (See Amazing Spider-Man #265)
Marvel Comics: June, 1992 - No. 35, Apr, 1995 ($1.25/$1.50

1-($2.00)-Embossed & foil stamped-c; Spider-Man app. — 2.50
2-4: 4,5-Dr. Doom-c/story — 1.75
5-23: 6,7-Deathlok-c/story. 9-Origin Silver Sable. 10-Punisher-c/s. 15-Capt. America-c/s. 16,17-Intruders app. 18,19-Venom-c/s. 19-Siege of Darkness x-over. 23-Daredevil (in new costume) & Deadpool app. — 1.25
24,26-35: 24-Begin $1.50-c; bound-in card sheet. Li'l Sylvie backup story — 1.50
25-($2.00, 52 pgs.)-Li'l Sylvie backup story — 2.00

SILVER STAR (Also see Jack Kirby's...)
Pacific Comics: Feb, 1983 - No. Jan, 1984 ($1.00)

1-6: 1-1st app. Last of the Viking Heroes. 1-5-Kirby-c/a. 2-Ditko-a — 1.00

SILVER STREAK COMICS (Crime Does Not Pay #22 on)
Your Guide Publs. No. 1-7/New Friday Publs. No. 8-17/Comic House Publ./Newsbook Publ.: Dec, 1939 - No. 21, May, 1942; No. 22-24, 1946 (Silver logo-#1-5)

	GD25	FN65	VF82	NM94
1-(Scarce)-Intro The Claw by Cole (r-/in Daredevil #21), Red Reeves, Boy Magician, & Captain Fearless; The Wasp, Mister Midnight begin; Spirit Man app. Silver metallic-c begin, end #5; Claw c-1,2,6-8	910.00	2730.00	5460.00	10,500.00

	GD25	FN65	NM94
2-The Claw by Cole; Simon-c/a	347.00	1041.00	3300.00
3-1st app. & origin Silver Streak (2nd with lightning speed); Dickie Dean the Boy Inventor, Lance Hale, Ace Powers, Bill Wayne, & The Planet Patrol begin	295.00	885.00	2800.00
4-Sky Wolf begins; Silver Streak by Jack Cole (new costume); 1st app. Jackie, Lance Hale's sidekick	147.00	441.00	1250.00
5-Jack Cole c/a(2)	176.00	528.00	1500.00

	GD25	FN65	VF82	NM94
6-(Scarce, 9/40)-Origin & 1st app. Daredevil (blue & yellow costume) by Jack Binder; The Claw returns; classic Cole Claw-c	1000.00	3000.00	6000.00	12,000.00
7-Claw vs. Daredevil (new costume-blue & red) by Jack Cole & 3 other Cole stories (38 pgs.)	700.00	2100.00	4200.00	7200.00

	GD25	FN65	NM94
8-Claw vs. Daredevil by Cole; last Cole Silver Streak	253.00	760.00	2400.00
9-Claw vs. Daredevil by Cole	171.00	513.00	1450.00
10-Origin & 1st app. Captain Battle (5/41); Claw vs. Daredevil by Cole; Robot-c	147.00	441.00	1250.00
11-Intro. Mercury by Bob Wood, Silver Streak's sidekick; conclusion Claw vs. Daredevil by Rico; in 'Presto Martin,' 2nd pg., newspaper says 'Roussos does it again'	100.00	300.00	850.00
12-14: 13-Origin Thun-Dohr	76.00	228.00	650.00
15, 17-Last Daredevil issue.	71.00	213.00	600.00
16-Hitler-c	76.00	228.00	650.00
18-The Saint begins (2/42, 1st app.) by Leslie Charteris (see Movie Comics #2 by DC); The Saint-c	59.00	177.00	500.00
19-21(1942): 20,21 have Wolverton's Scoop Scuttle. 21-Hitler app. in strip on cover	46.00	138.00	390.00
22,24(1946)-Reprints	28.00	84.00	210.00
23-Reprints?; bondage-c	28.00	84.00	210.00
nn(11/46)(Newsbook Publ.)-R-/S.S. story from #4-7 plus 2 Captain Fearless stories, all in color; bondage/torture-c	42.00	127.00	340.00

NOTE: ***Binder*** *c-3, 4, 13-15, 17.* ***Jack Cole*** *a-(Daredevil)-#6-10, (Dickie Dean)-#3-10, (Pirate Prince)-#7, (Silver Streak)-#4-8, nn; c-5 (Silver Streak), 6 (Claw), 7, 8 (Daredevil).* ***Everett*** *Red Reed begins #20.* ***Guardineer*** *a-#8-13.* ***Don Rico*** *a-11-17 (Daredevil); c-11, 12, 16.* ***Simon*** *a-3 (Silver Streak).* ***Bob Wood*** *a-9 (Silver Streak); c-9, 10. Captain Battle c-11, 13-15, 17. Claw c-#1, 2, 6-8. Daredevil c-7, 8, 12. Dickie Dean c-19. Ned of the Navy c-20 (war). The Saint c-18. Silver Streak c-5, 9, 10, 16, 23.*

SILVER SURFER (See Fantastic Four, Fantasy Masterpieces V2#1, Fireside Book Series, Marvel Graphic Novel, Marvel Presents #8, Marvel's Greatest Comics & Tales To Astonish #92)

SILVER SURFER, THE
Marvel Comics Group: Aug, 1968 - No. 18, Sept, 1970; June, 1982

	GD25	FN65	NM94
1-More detailed origin by John Buscema (p); The Watcher back-up stories begin (origin), end #7; (No. 1-7: 25¢, 68 pgs.)	39.00	117.00	435.00
2	17.50	52.00	175.00
3-1st app. Mephisto	13.50	41.00	135.00
4-Low distribution; Thor & Loki app.	36.00	108.00	400.00
5-7-Last giant size. 5-The Stranger app.; Fantastic Four app. 6-Brunner inks. 7-(8/69)-1st app. Frankenstein's monster (cameo)	8.50	25.50	85.00
8-10: 8-18-(15¢ issues)	6.50	19.50	65.00
11-13,15-18: 15-Silver Surfer vs. Human Torch; Fantastic Four app. 17-Nick Fury app. 18-Vs. The Inhumans; Kirby-c/a	5.00	15.00	50.00
14-Spider-Man x-over	7.00	21.00	70.00
V2#1 (6/82, 52 pgs.)-Byrne-c/a	1.10	3.30	9.00

NOTE: ***Adkins*** *a-8-15i.* ***Brunner*** *a-6i.* ***J. Buscema*** *a-1-17p.* ***Colan*** *a-1-3p.* ***Reinman*** *a-1-4i. #1-14 were reprinted in Fantasy Masterpieces V2#1-14.*

SILVER SURFER (Volume 3) (See Marvel Graphic Novel #38)
Marvel Comics Group: V3#1, July, 1987 - No. 146, Nov, 1998

	GD25	FN65	NM94
1-Double size ($1.25)	.90	2.70	8.00
2			4.00
3-17: 15-Ron Lim-c/a begins (9/88)			4.00
18-20			3.00
21-33,39-43: 25,31 ($1.50, 52 pgs.). 25-Skrulls app. 32,39-No Ron Lim-c/a. 39-Alan Grant scripts			2.00
34-Thanos returns (cameo); Starlin scripts begin			4.00
35-1st full Thanos app. in Silver Surfer (3/90); reintro Drax the Destroyer on last pg. (cameo)		2.00	6.00
36-38: 36-Recaps history of Thanos; Capt. Marvel & Warlock app. in recap. 37-1st full app. Drax the Destroyer; Drax-c. 38-Silver Surfer battles Thanos			5.00
44,45,49-Thanos stories (c-44,45)			2.50
46,47: 46-Return of Adam Warlock (2/91); re-intro Gamora & Pip the Troll. 47-Warlock battles Drax			4.00
48-Last Starlin scripts (also #50)			2.00
50-($1.50, 52 pgs.)-Embossed & silver foil-c; Silver Surfer has brief battle w/Thanos; story cont'd in Infinity Gauntlet #1	.85	2.60	7.00
50-2nd & 3rd printings			2.00
51-53: Infinity Gauntlet x-over			2.50

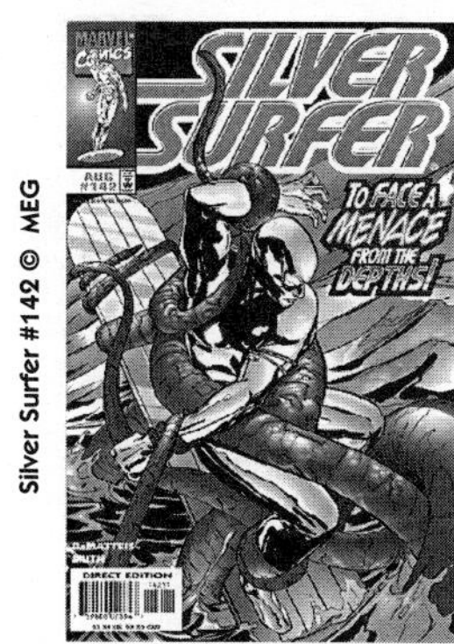

Silver Surfer #142 © MEG

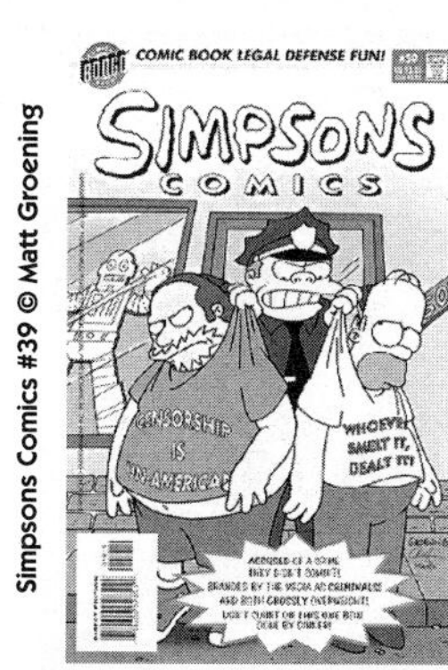

Simpsons Comics #39 © Matt Groening

Sin City: Just Another Saturday Night © Frank Miller

54-57: Infinity Gauntlet x-overs. 54-Rhino app. 55,56-Thanos-c & app. 57-Thanos-c & cameo 2.00
58,59-Infinity Guantlet x-overs; 58-Ron Lim-c only. 59-Thanos battles Silver Surfer-c/story; Thanos joins 3.00
60-66: 61-Last $1.00-c. 63-Capt. Marvel app. 1.50
67-69-Infinity War x-overs 2.00
70-74,76-81,83-91: 76-78-Jack of Hearts-c/s. 83-85-Infinity Crusade x-over; 83,84-Thanos cameo. 85-Storm, Wonder Man x-over. 86-Thor-c/s. 87-Dr. Strange & Warlock app. 88-Thanos-c/s 1.25
75-($2.50, 52 pgs.)-Embossed foil-c; Lim-c/a 3.50
82-($1.75, 52 pgs.) 1.75
92-99; 101-109: 92-Begin $1.50-c; bound-in card sheet. 95-FF app. 96-Hulk & FF app. 97-Terrax & Nova app. 106-Doc Doom app. 1.50
100 ($2.25, 52 pgs.)-Wraparound-c 2.25
100 ($3.95, 52 pgs.)-Enhanced-c 4.00
110-117: 110-Begin $1.95-c 2.00
118-124,126: 118-Begin $1.50-c. 121-Quasar & Beta Ray Bill app. 123-w/card insert; begin Garney-a. 126-Dr. Strange-c/app. 1.50
125 ($2.95)-Wraparound-c; Vs. Hulk-c/app. 3.00
127-129, -1(7/97)-($1.95): 128-Spider-Man & Daredevil-c/app. 2.00
130-139: 130-Begin $1.99-c. 138-Thing-c. 2.00
140-142,144,145-Muth-c/a 2.50
143,146-Cowan-a. 146-Last issue 2.00
Annual 1 (1988, $1.75)-Evolutionary War app.; 1st Ron Lim-a on Silver Surfer (20 pg. back-up story & pin-ups) 5.00
Annual 2-4 (1989-91, $2.00, 68 pgs.): 2-Atlantis Attacks. 4-3 pg. origin story; Silver Surfer battles Guardians of the Galaxy 2.50
Annual 5 (1992, $2.25, 68 pgs.)-Return of the Defenders, part 3; Lim-c/a (3 pgs. of pin-ups only) 2.50
Annual 6 (1993, $2.95, 68 pgs.)-Polybagged w/trading card; 1st app. Legacy; card is by Lim/Austin 3.00
Annual 7 (1994, $2.95) 3.00
Annual '97 ($2.99) 3.00
.../Thor Annual '98 ($2.99) 3.00
...Dangerous Artifacts-(1996, $3.95)-Ron Marz scripts; Galactus-c/app. 4.00
Essential Silver Surfer Vol. 1 ('98, $12.99) B&W reprint of material from SS#1-18 and Fantastic Four Annual #5 12.99
Graphic Novel (Hardcover, $14.95) 15.00
The Enslavers Graphic Novel (1990, $16.95) 17.00
Inner Demons TPB (4/98, $3.50)r/#123,125,126 3.50
...: The First Coming of Galactus nn (11/92, $5.95, 68 pgs.)-Reprints Fantastic Four #48-50 with new Lim-c 2.00 6.00

NOTE: *Austin c(i)-71, 73, 74, 76, 79.* ***Cully Hamner*** *a-83p.* ***Ron Lim*** *a(p)-15-31, 33-38, 40-55, (56, 57-part-p), 60-65, 73-82; c(p)-15-31, 32-38, 40-84, 86-92, Annual 5, 6.* ***M. Rogers*** *a-1-10, 12, 19, 21; c-1-12, 21.*

SILVER SURFER, THE
Marvel Comics (Epic): Dec, 1988 - No. 2, Jan, 1989 ($1.00, lim. series)
1,2: By Stan Lee scripts & Moebius-c/a 4.00
...: Parable ('98, $5.99) r/#1&2 6.00

SILVER SURFER/SUPERMAN
Marvel Comics: 1996 ($5.95,one-shot)
1-Perez-s/Lim-c/a(p) 2.00 6.00

SILVER SURFER VS. DRACULA
Marvel Comics: Feb, 1994 ($1.75, one-shot)
1-r/Tomb of Dracula #50; Everett Vampire-r/Venus #19; Howard the Duck back-up by Brunner; Lim-c(p) 1.75

SILVER SURFER/WARLOCK: RESURRECTION
Marvel Comics: Mar, 1993 - No. 4, June, 1993 ($2.50, limited series)
1-4: Starlin-c/a & scripts 2.50

SILVER SURFER/WEAPON ZERO
Marvel Comics: Apr, 1997 ($2.95,one-shot)
1-"Devil's Reign" pt. 8 2.95

SILVERTIP (Max Brand)
Dell Publishing Co.: No. 491, Aug, 1953 - No. 898, May, 1958
Four Color 491 (#1); all painted-c 7.00 22.00 80.00
Four Color 572,608,637,667,731,789,898-Kinstler-a 3.60 11.00 40.00
Four Color 835 3.60 11.00 40.00

SIMPSONS COMICS (See Bartman, Itchy & Scratchy & Radioactive Man)
Bongo Comics Group: 1993 - Present ($1.95, color)
1-($2.25)-FF#1-c swipe; pull-out poster; flip book 3.00
2,3-($1.95): 2-Patty & Selma on flip side. 3-Krusty, Agent of K.L.O.W.N. flip-c/story 2.50
4-($2.25)-Infinity-c; flip-c of Busman #1; w/trading card 2.25
5-Wraparound-c w/trading card 2.25
6-39: All Flip books. 6-w/Chief Wiggum's "Crime Comics". 7-w/"McBain Comics". 8-w/"Edna, Queen of the Congo". 9-w/"Barney Gumble". 10-w/"Apu". 11-w/"Homer". 12-w/"White Knuckled War Stories". 13-w/"Jimbo Jones' Wedgie Comics". 14-w/"Grampa". 15-w/"Itchy & Scratchy". 16-w/"Bongo Grab Bag". 17-w/"Headlight Comics". 18-w/"Milhouse". 19-22-w/"Roswell". 23-w/"Hellfire Comics". 24-w/"Lil' Homey" 36-39-Flip book w/Radioactive Man 2.25
...Extravaganza (1994, $10.00)-r/#1-4; infinity-c 10.00
...On Parade (1998, $11.95)-r/#24-27 12.00
...Simpsorama (1996, $10.95)-r/#11-14 11.00

SIMPSONS COMICS AND STORIES
Welsh Publishing Group: 1993 ($2.95, one-shot)
1-(Direct Sale)-Polybagged w/Bartman poster 4.00
1-(Newsstand Edition)-Without poster 3.50

SIMULATORS, THE
Neatly Chiseled Features: 1991 ($2.50, stiff-c)
1-Super hero group 2.50

SINBAD, JR (TV Cartoon)
Dell Publishing Co.: Sept-Nov, 1965 - No. 3, May, 1966
1 1.80 5.40 20.00
2,3 1.50 4.50 16.00

SIN CITY (See Dark Horse Presents, Decade of Dark Horse, A & San Diego Comic Con Comics #2,4)
Dark Horse Comics (Legend)
TPB ($15.00) Reprints early DHP stories 15.00

SIN CITY: A DAME TO KILL FOR
Dark Horse Comics (Legend): Nov, 1993 - No. 6, May, 1994 ($2.95, B&W, limited series)
1-6: Frank Miller-c/a & story in all. 1-1st app. Dwight. 5.00
Limited Edition Hardcover 100.00
Hardcover 25.00
TPB ($15.00) 15.00

SIN CITY: FAMILY VALUES
Dark Horse Comics (Legend): Oct, 1997 ($10.00, B&W, squarebound, one-shot)
nn-Miller-c/a & story 10.00

SIN CITY: JUST ANOTHER SATURDAY NIGHT
Dark Horse Comics (Legend): Aug, 1997 (Wizard 1/2 offer, B&W, one-shot)
1/2-Miller-c/a & story 1.20 3.60 12.00
nn (10/98, $2.50) r/#1/2 2.50

SIN CITY: LOST, LONELY & LETHAL
Dark Horse Comics (Legend): Dec, 1996 ($2.95, B&W and blue, one-shot)
nn-Miller-c/s/a; w/pin-ups 4.00

SIN CITY: SEX AND VIOLENCE
Dark Horse Comics (Legend): Mar, 1997 ($2.95, B&W and blue, one-shot)

Siren Special #1 © MAL

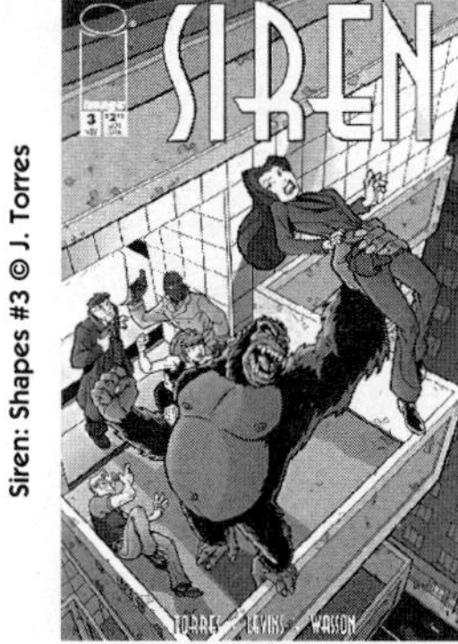

Siren: Shapes #3 © J. Torres

Sisters of Mercy #2 © Rikki Rockett & Mark Williams

	GD25	FN65	NM94

nn-Miller-c/a & story 4.00

SIN CITY: SILENT NIGHT
Dark Horse Comics (Legend): Dec, 1995 ($2.95, B&W, one-shot)

1-Miller-c/a & story; Marv app. 4.00

SIN CITY: THAT YELLOW BASTARD
Dark Horse Comics (Legend): Feb, 1996 - No. 6, July, 1996 ($2.95/$3.50, B&W and yellow, limited series)

1-5: Miller-c/a & story in all. 1-1st app. Hartigan. 5.00
6-($3.50) Error & corrected 4.00
Limited Edition Hardcover 25.00
TPB ($15.00) 15.00

SIN CITY: THE BABE WORE RED AND OTHER STORIES
Dark Horse Comics (Legend): Nov, 1994 ($2.95, B&W and red, one-shot)

1-r/serial run in Previews as well as other stories; Miller-c/a & scripts; Dwight app. 3.00

SIN CITY: THE BIG FAT KILL
Dark Horse Comics (Legend): Nov, 1994 - No. 5, Mar, 1995 ($2.95, B&W, limited series)

1-4-Miller story & art in all; Dwight app. 4.00
5 ($3.50)-Dwight app. 4.00
Hardcover 25.00
TPB ($15.00) 15.00

SINDBAD (See Capt. Sindbad under Movie Comics, and Fantastic Voyages of Sindbad)

SINGING GUNS (See Fawcett Movie Comics)

SINGLE SERIES (Comics on Parade #30 on)(Also see John Hix...)
United Features Syndicate: 1938 - No. 28, 1942 (All 68 pgs.)

Note: See Individual Alphabetical Listings for prices

1-Captain and the Kids (#1)
2-Broncho Bill (1939) (#1)
3-Ella Cinders (1939)
4-Li'l Abner (1939) (#1)
5-Fritzi Ritz (#1)
6-Jim Hardy by Dick Moores (#1)
7-Frankie Doodle
8-Peter Pat (On sale 7/14/39)
9-Strange As It Seems
10-Little Mary Mixup
11-Mr. and Mrs. Beans
12-Joe Jinks
13-Looy Dot Dope
14-Billy Make Believe
15-How It Began (1939)
16-Illustrated Gags (1940)-Has ad for Captain and the Kids #1 reprint listed below
17-Danny Dingle
18-Li'l Abner (#2 on-c)
19-Broncho Bill (#2 on-c)
20-Tarzan by Hal Foster
21-Ella Cinders (#2 on-c; on sale 3/19/40)
22-Iron Vic
23-Tailspin Tommy by Hal Forrest (#1)
24-Alice in Wonderland (#1)
25-Abbie and Slats
26-Little Mary Mixup (#2 on-c, 1940)
27-Jim Hardy by Dick Moores (1942)
28-Ella Cinders & Abbie and Slats (1942)
1-Captain and the Kids (1939 reprint)-2nd Edition
1-Fritzi Ritz (1939 reprint)-2nd ed.

NOTE: *Some issues given away at the 1939-40 New York World's Fair (#6).*

SINISTER HOUSE OF SECRET LOVE, THE (Becomes Secrets of Sinister House No. 5 on)
National Periodical Publ.: Oct-Nov, 1971 - No. 4, Apr-May, 1972

1 (52 pgs.) 11.00 32.00 115.00
2-4: (52 pgs.). 2-Jeff Jones-c. 3-Toth-a 3.25 10.00 35.00

SINJA
Lightning Comics: June, 1996 ($3.00, one-shot)

1,1b-Cleary-c 3.00
1-($9.95) "Nude" Edition; polybagged 10.00
1-($5.95)Commemorative Edition; polybagged 6.00
1-American Entertainment Exclusive Ed.; polybagged w/certificate 5.00

SINJA: RESURRECTION
Lightning Comics: Aug, 1996 ($3.00, one-shot)

1-Flip book w/Kunichi #1 3.00
1-($5.95) Platinum Edition 6.00
1-($9.95) "Nude" Edition 10.00

SIR CHARLES BARKLEY AND THE REFEREE MURDERS
Hamilton Comics: 1993 ($9.95, 8-1/2" x 11", 52 pgs.)

nn-Photo-c; Sports fantasy comic book fiction (uses real names of NBA super stars). Script by Alan Dean Foster, art by Joe Staton. Comes with bound-in sheet of 35 gummed "Moods of Charles Barkley" stamps. Photo/story on Barkley 1.00 3.00 10.00
Special Edition of 100 copies for charity signed on an affixed book plate by Barkley, Foster & Staton 150.00
Ashcan edition given away to dealers, distributors & promoters (low distribution). Four pages in color, balance of story in b&w 1.00 3.00 10.00

SIREN (Also see Eliminator & Ultraforce)
Malibu Comics (Ultraverse): Sept, 1995 - No. 3, Dec, 1995 ($1.50)

Infinity, 1-3: Infinity-Black-c & painted-c exists. 1-Regular-c & painted-c; War Machine app. 2-Flip book w/Phoenix Resurrection Pt. 3 1.50
Special 1-(2/96, $1.95, 28 pgs.)-Origin Siren; Marvel Comic's Juggernaut-c/app. 2.00

SIREN: SHAPES
Image Comics: May, 1998 - No. 3, Nov, 1998 ($2.95, B&W, limited series)

1-3-J. Torres -s 2.95

SIR LANCELOT (TV)
Dell Publishing Co.: No. 606, Dec, 1954 - No. 775, Mar, 1957

Four Color 606 (not TV) 6.40 19.00 70.00
Four Color 775(...and Brian)-Buscema-a; photo-c 7.00 22.00 80.00

SIR WALTER RALEIGH (Movie)
Dell Publishing Co.: May, 1955 (Based on movie "The Virgin Queen")

Four Color 644-Photo-c 5.50 16.50 60.00

SISTERHOOD OF STEEL (See Eclipse Graphic Adventure Novel #13)
Marvel Comics (Epic Comics): Dec, 1984 -No. 8, Feb, 1986 ($1.50, Baxter paper, mature)

1-8 1.50

SISTERS OF MERCY
Maximum Press/No Mercy Comics #3 on: Dec, 1995 - No. 5, Oct, 1996 ($2.50)

1-5: 1-Liefeld variant-c exists 2.50
V2#0-(3/97, $1.50) Liefeld-c 1.50

SISTERS OF MERCY: PARADISE LOST
London Night Studios/No Mercy Comics: Apr, 1997 - No. 4 ($2.50)

1-4 2.50

SISTERS OF MERCY: WHEN RAZORS CRY CRIMSON TEARS
No Mercy Comics: Oct, 1996 ($2.50, one-shot)

1 2.50

6, THE
Virtual Comics (Byron Preiss Multimedia): Oct, 1996 - No. 3, Dec, 1996 ($2.50, limited series)

1-3: L. Simonson-s 2.50

6 BLACK HORSES (See Movie Classics)

SIX FROM SIRIUS
Marvel Comics (Epic Comics): July, 1984 - No. 4, Oct, 1984 ($1.50, limited series, mature)

1-4: Moench scripts; Gulacy-c/a in all 1.50

SIX FROM SIRIUS II
Marvel Comics (Epic Comics): Feb, 1986 - No. 4, May, 1986 ($1.50, limited series, mature)

1-4: Moench scripts; Gulacy-c/a in all 1.50

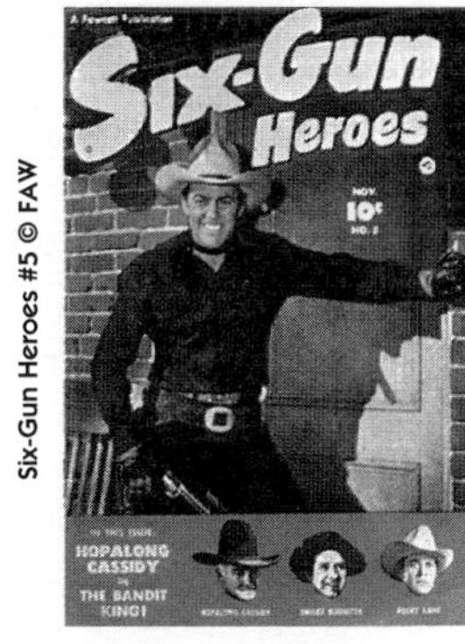

Six-Gun Heroes #5 © FAW

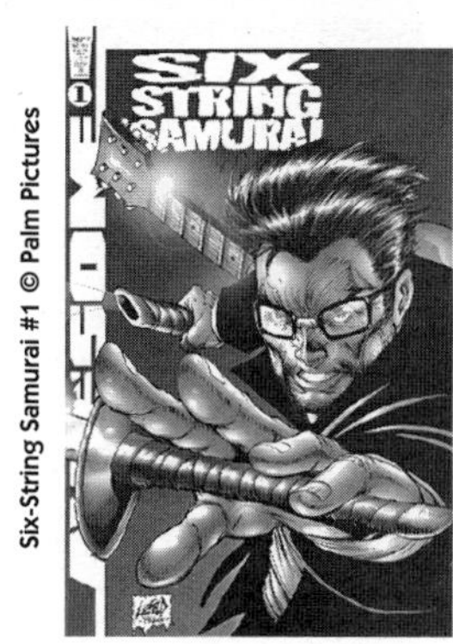

Six-String Samurai #1 © Palm Pictures

Skeleton Key #30 © Andrew Watson

SIX-GUN HEROES
Fawcett Publications: March, 1950 - No. 23, Nov, 1953 (Photo-c #1-23)

	GD25	FN65	NM94
1-Rocky Lane, Hopalong Cassidy, Smiley Burnette begin (same date as Smiley Burnette #1)	42.00	127.00	340.00
2	24.00	72.00	180.00
3-5: 5-Lash LaRue begins	16.00	48.00	120.00
6-15	13.00	38.00	95.00
16-22: 17-Last Smiley Burnette. 18-Monte Hale begins	11.00	32.00	80.00
23-Last Fawcett issue	12.00	36.00	90.00

NOTE: *Hopalong Cassidy photo c-1-3. Monte Hale photo c-18. Rocky Lane photo c-4, 5, 7, 9, 11, 13, 15, 17, 20, 21, 23. Lash LaRue photo c-6, 8, 10, 12, 14, 16, 19, 22.*

SIX-GUN HEROES (Cont'd from Fawcett; Gunmasters #84 on) (See Blue Bird)
Charlton Comics: No. 24, Jan, 1954 - No. 83, Mar-Apr, 1965 (All Vol. 4)

	GD25	FN65	NM94
24-Lash LaRue, Hopalong Cassidy, Rocky Lane & Tex Ritter begin; photo-c	18.00	54.00	135.00
25	8.50	26.00	60.00
26-30: 26-Rod Cameron story. 28-Tom Mix begins?	7.15	21.50	50.00
31-40: 38-Jingles & Wild Bill Hickok (TV)	6.50	19.50	45.00
41-46,48,50	5.70	17.00	40.00
47-Williamson-a, 2 pgs; Torres-a	6.50	19.50	45.00
49-Williamson-a (5 pgs.)	7.15	21.50	50.00
51-56,58-60: 58-Gunmaster app.	2.80	8.40	28.00
57-Origin & 1st app. Gunmaster	3.20	9.60	32.00
61-70: 62-Origin Gunmaster	2.50	7.50	22.00
71-83: 76-Gunmaster begins. 79-1st app. & origin of Bullet, the Gun-Boy	2.00	6.00	16.00

SIXGUN RANCH (See Luke Short & Four Color #580)

SIX-GUN WESTERN
Atlas Comics (CDS): Jan, 1957 - No. 4, July, 1957

	GD25	FN65	NM94
1-Crandall-a; two Williamson text illos	17.00	50.00	125.00
2,3-Williamson-a in both	13.00	38.00	95.00
4-Woodbridge-a	7.85	23.50	55.00

NOTE: ***Ayers** a-2, 3. **Maneely** a-1; c-2, 3. **Orlando** a-2. **Pakula** a-2. **Powell** a-3. **Romita** a-1, 4. **Severin** c-1, 4. **Shores** a-2.*

SIX MILLION DOLLAR MAN, THE (TV)
Charlton Comics: 6/76 - No. 4, 12/76; No. 5, 10/77; No. 6, 2/78 - No. 9, 6/78

	GD25	FN65	NM94
1-Staton-c/a; Lee Majors photo on-c	.90	2.70	8.00
2-9: 2-Neal Adams-c; Staton-a		2.00	6.00

SIX MILLION DOLLAR MAN, THE (TV)(Magazine)
Charlton Comics: July, 1976 - No. 7, Nov, 1977 (B&W)

	GD25	FN65	NM94
1-Neal Adams-c/a	1.20	3.60	12.00
2-Neal Adams-c	1.00	3.00	10.00
3-N. Adams part inks; Chaykin-a	1.00	3.00	10.00
4-7	.85	2.60	7.00

SIX STRING SAMURAI
Awesome-Hyperwerks: Sept, 1998 ($2.95)

	GD25	FN65	NM94
1-Stinsman & Fraga-a			3.00

67 SECONDS
Marvel Comics (Epic Comics): 1992 ($15.95, 54 pgs., graphic novel)

	GD25	FN65	NM94
nn-James Robinson scripts; Steve Yeowell-c/a	1.80	5.40	18.00

SKATEMAN
Pacific Comics: Nov, 1983 (Baxter paper, one-shot)

	GD25	FN65	NM94
1-Adams-c/a			2.00

SKATING SKILLS
Custom Comics, Inc./Chicago Roller Skates: 1957 (36 & 12 pgs.; 5x7", two versions) (10¢)

	GD25	FN65	NM94
nn-Resembles old ACG cover plus interior art	3.20	8.00	16.00

SKELETON HAND (...In Secrets of the Supernatural)
American Comics Gr. (B&M Dist. Co.): Sept-Oct, 1952 - No. 6, Jul-Aug, 1953

	GD25	FN65	NM94
1	39.00	116.00	290.00
2	26.00	78.00	195.00
3-6	22.00	66.00	165.00

SKELETON KEY
Amaze Ink: July, 1995 - No. 30, Jan, 1998 ($1.25/$1.50/$1.75, B&W)

	GD25	FN65	NM94
1			1.25
2-9: 2-Begin $1.50			1.50
10-30: 10-Begin $1.75			1.75
Special #1 (2/98, $4.95) Unpublished short stories			4.95
Sugar Kat Special (10/98, $2.95) Halloween stories			2.95
Beyond The Threshold TPB (6/96. $11.95)-r/#1-6			12.00
The Celestial Calendar TPB ($19.95)-r/#7-18			20.00
Telling Tales TPB (6/96. $12.95)-r/#19-24			13.00

SKELETON WARRIORS
Marvel Comics: Apr, 1995 - No. 4, July, 1995 ($1.50)

	GD25	FN65	NM94
1-4: Based on animated series.			1.50

SKIN GRAFT: THE ADVENTURES OF A TATTOOED MAN
DC Comics (Vertigo): July, 1993 - No. 4, Oct, 1993 ($2.50, lim. series, mature)

	GD25	FN65	NM94
1-4			2.50

SKI PARTY (See Movie Classics)

SKIPPY'S OWN BOOK OF COMICS (See Popular Comics)
No publisher listed: 1934 (Giveaway, 52 pgs., strip reprints)

	GD25	FN65	NM94
nn-(Scarce)-By Percy Crosby	450.00	1350.00	4500.00

Published by Max C. Gaines for Phillip's Dental Magnesia to be advertised on the Skippy Radio Show and given away with the purchase of a tube of Phillip's Tooth Paste. This is the first four-color comic book of reprints about one character.

SKREEMER
DC Comics: May, 1989 - No. 6, Oct, 1989 ($2.00, limited series, mature)

	GD25	FN65	NM94
1-6: Contains graphic violence			2.00

SKRULL KILL KREW
Marvel Comics: Sept, 1995 - No. 5, Dec, 1995 ($2.95, limited series)

	GD25	FN65	NM94
1-5: Grant Morrison scripts. 2,3-Cap America app.			3.00

SKUL, THE
Virtual Comics (Byron Preiss Multimedia): Oct, 1996 - No. 3, Dec, 1996 ($2.50, limited series)

	GD25	FN65	NM94
1-3: Ron Lim & Jimmy Palmiotti-a			2.50

SKULL & BONES
DC Comics: 1992 - No. 3, 1992 ($4.95, limited series, 52 pgs.)

	GD25	FN65	NM94
Book 1-3: 1-1st app.			5.00

SKULL, THE SLAYER
Marvel Comics Group: Aug, 1975 - No. 8, Nov, 1976 (20¢/25¢)

	GD25	FN65	NM94
1-Origin & 1st app.; Gil Kane-c			5.00
2-8: 2-Gil Kane-c. 8-Kirby-c			3.00

SKY BLAZERS (CBS Radio)
Hawley Publications: Sept, 1940 - No. 2, Nov, 1940

	GD25	FN65	NM94
1-Sky Pirates, Ace Archer, Flying Aces begin	53.00	159.00	450.00
2-WWII aerial battle-c	37.00	110.00	275.00

SKY KING "RUNAWAY TRAIN" (TV)
National Biscuit Co.: 1964 (Regular size, 16 pgs.)

	GD25	FN65	NM94
nn	2.25	6.75	18.00

SKYMAN (See Big Shot Comics & Sparky Watts)
Columbia Comics Gr.: Fall?, 1941 - No. 2, Fall?, 1942; No. 3, 1948 - No. 4, 1948

	GD25	FN65	NM94
1-Origin Skyman, The Face, Sparky Watts app.; Whitney-c/a; 3rd story-r from Big Shot #1; Whitney c-1-4	94.00	282.00	800.00
2 (1942)-Yankee Doodle	49.00	147.00	420.00

Slacker Comics #17 © Doug Slack

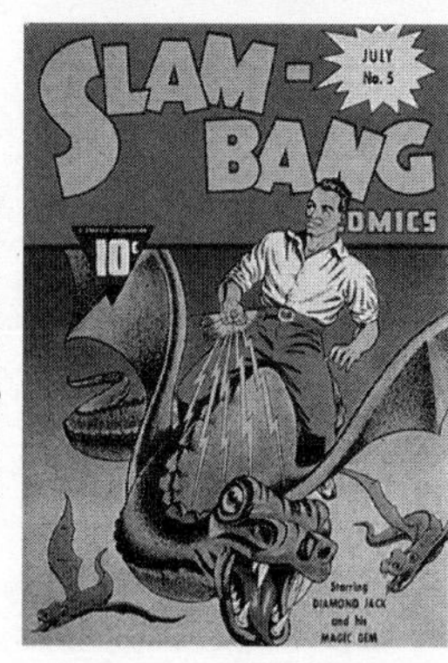

Slam Bang Comics #5 © FAW

Slingers #1 (Hornet edition) © MAR

GD25 FN65 NM94

3,4 (1948) 35.00 104.00 260.00

SKYPILOT
Ziff-Davis Publ. Co.: No. 10, 1950(nd) - No. 11, Apr-May, 1951

10,11-Frank Borth-a; Saunders painted-c 11.00 34.00 85.00

SKY RANGER (See Johnny Law...)

SKYROCKET
Harry 'A' Chesler: 1944

nn-Alias the Dragon, Dr. Vampire, Skyrocket & The Desperado app.; WWII Jap zero-c 24.00 72.00 180.00

SKY SHERIFF (Breeze Lawson...) (Also see Exposed & Outlaws)
D. S. Publishing Co.: Summer, 1948

1-Edmond Good-c/a 11.00 34.00 80.00

SKY WOLF (Also see Airboy)
Eclipse Comics: Mar, 1988 - No. 3, Oct, 1988 ($1.25/$1.50/$1.95, lim. series)

1,2-($1.75) 1.75
3-($1.95) 1.95

SLACKER COMICS
Slave Labor Graphics: Aug, 1994 - Present ($2.95, B&W, quarterly)

1-18 3.00
1 (2nd printing)-Reads "2nd print" in indicia 3.00

SLAINE, THE BERSERKER (Slaine the King #21 on)
Quality: July, 1987 - No. 28, 1989 ($1.25/$1.50)

1-12 1.25
13-28: 13-Begin $1.50-c 1.50

SLAINE, THE HORNED GOD
Fleetway: 1998 - No. 3 ($6.99)

1-Reprints series from 2000 A.D.; Bisley-a 6.99

SLAM BANG COMICS (Western Desperado #8)
Fawcett Publications: Mar, 1940 - No. 7, Sept, 1940 (Combined with Master Comics #7)

1-Diamond Jack, Mark Swift & The Time Retarder, Lee Granger, Jungle King begin & continue in Master 176.00 528.00 1500.00
2 76.00 229.00 650.00
3-Classic-c 106.00 318.00 900.00
4-7: 6-Intro Zoro, the Mystery Man (also in #7) 62.00 186.00 525.00

SLAM BANG COMICS
Post Cereal Giveaway: No. 9, No date

9-Dynamic Man, Echo, Mr. E, Yankee Boy app. 5.00 15.00 30.00

SLAPSTICK
Marvel Comics: Nov, 1992 - No. 4, Feb, 1993 ($1.25, limited series)

1-4: Fry/Austin-c/a. 4-Ghost Rider, D.D., F.F. app. 1.25

SLAPSTICK COMICS
Comic Magazines Distributors: nd (1946?) (36 pgs.)

nn-Firetop feature; Post-a(2) 20.00 60.00 150.00

SLASH-D DOUBLECROSS
St. John Publishing Co.: 1950 (Pocket-size, 132 pgs.)

nn-Western comics 19.00 56.00 140.00

SLASH MARAUD
DC Comics: Nov, 1987 - No. 6, Apr, 1988 ($1.75, limited series)

1-6 1.75

SLAUGHTERMAN
Comico: Feb, 1983 - No. 2, 1983 ($1.50, B&W)

1,2 1.50

SLAVE GIRL COMICS (See Malu... & White Princess of the Jungle #2)
Avon Periodicals/Eternity Comics (1989): Feb, 1949 - No. 2, Apr, 1949 (52 pgs.); Mar, 1989 (B&W, 44 pgs)

1-Larsen-c/a 76.00 229.00 650.00
2-Larsen-a 57.00 171.00 485.00
1-(3/89, $2.25, B&W, 44 pgs.)-r/#1 2.25

SLEDGE HAMMER (TV)
Marvel Comics: Feb, 1988 - No. 2, Mar,1988 ($1.00, limited series)

1,2 1.00

SLEEPING BEAUTY (See Dell Giants & Movie Comics)
Dell Publishing Co.: No. 973, May, 1959 - No. 984, June, 1959 (Disney)

Four Color 973 (...and the Prince) 11.00 33.00 120.00
Four Color 984 (...Fairy Godmother's) 8.00 25.00 90.00

SLEEPWALKER
Marvel Comics: June, 1991 - No. 33, Feb, 1994 ($1.00/$1.25)

1-1st app. Sleepwalker 1.50
2-5: 4-Williamson-i. 5-Spider-Man-c/story 1.50
6-10: 7-Infinity Gauntlet x-over. 8-Vs. Deathlok-c/story 1.50
11-18,20-24,26-33: 11-Ghost Rider-c/story. 12-Quesada-c/a(p) 14-Intro Spectra. 15-F.F.-c/story. 17-Darkhawk & Spider-Man x-over. 18-Infinity War x-over; Quesada/Williamson-c. 21,22-Hobgoblin app. 1.25
19-($2.00)-Die-cut Sleepwalker mask cover 2.00
25-($2.95, 52 pgs.)-Holo-grafx foil-c; origin 3.00
Holiday Special 1 (1/93, $2.00, 52 pgs.)-Quesada-c(p) 2.00

SLEEPWALKING
Hall of Heroes: Jan, 1996 ($2.50, B&W)

1-Kelley Jones-c 2.50

SLEEZE BROTHERS, THE
Marvel Comics (Epic Comics): Aug, 1989 - No. 6, Jan, 1990 ($1.75, mature)

1-6: 4-6 (9/89 - 11/89 indicia dates) 1.80
nn-(1991, $3.95, 52 pgs.) 4.00

SLICK CHICK COMICS
Leader Enterprises: 1947(nd) - No. 3, 1947(nd)

1-Teenage humor 9.30 28.00 70.00
2,3 7.15 21.50 50.00

SLIDERS (TV)
Acclaim Comics (Armada): June, 1996 - No. 2, July, 1996 ($2.50, lim. series)

1,2: D.G. Chichester scripts; Dick Giordano-a. 2.50

SLIDERS: DARKEST HOUR (TV)
Acclaim Comics (Armada): Oct, 1996 - No. 3, Dec, 1996 ($2.50, limited series)

1-3 2.50

SLIDERS SPECIAL
Acclaim Comics (Armada): Nov, 1996 - No 3, Mar, 1997 ($3.95, limited series)

1-Narcotica-Jerry O'Connell-s 4.00
2-Blood and Splendor 4.00
3-Deadly Secrets 4.00

SLIDERS: ULTIMATUM (TV)
Acclaim Comics (Armada): Sept, 1996 - No. 2, Sept, 1996 ($2.50, lim. series)

1,2 2.50

SLIMER! (TV cartoon) (Also see the Real Ghostbusters)
Now Comics: 1989 - No. 19, Feb?, 1991 ($1.75)

1-19: Based on animated cartoon 1.75

SLIM MORGAN (See Wisco)

SLINGERS (See Spider-Man: Identity Crisis issues)
Marvel Comics: Dec, 1998 - Present ($2.99/$1.99)

0-(Wizard #88 supplement) Prelude story .50
1-($2.99) Four editions w/different covers for each hero, 16 pages common to

Smash Comics #31 © QUA

Smiley #1 © Chaos!

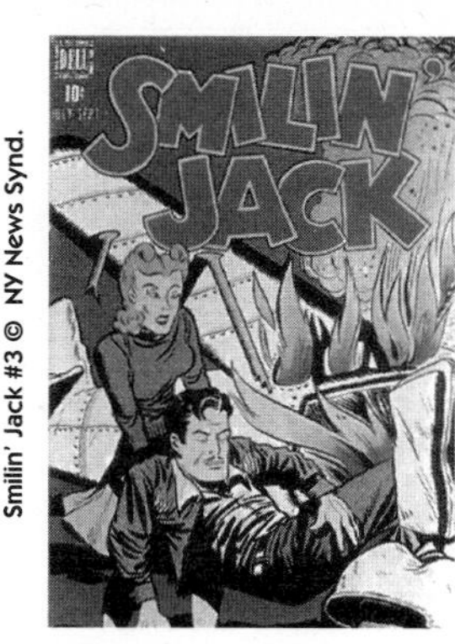

Smilin' Jack #3 © NY News Synd.

	GD25	FN65	NM94
all, the other pages from each hero's perspective			3.00
2-($1.99) Two covers			2.00

SLUDGE
Malibu Comics (Ultraverse): Oct, 1993 - No. 12, Dec, 1994 ($2.50/$1.95)

	GD25	FN65	NM94
1-($2.50, 48 pgs.)-Intro/1st app. Sludge; Rune flip-c/story Pt. 1 (1st app., 3 pgs.) by Barry Smith; The Night Man app. (3 pg. preview); The Mighty Magnor 1 pg strip begins by Aragones (cont. in other titles)			2.50
1-Ultra 5000 Limited silver foil			5.00
2-11: 3-Break-Thru x-over. 4-2 pg. Mantra origin. 8-Bloodstorm app.			2.00
12 ($3.50)-Ultraverse Premiere #8 flip book; Alex Ross poster			3.50
...:Red Xmas (12/94, $2.50, 44 pgs.)			2.50

SLUGGER (Little Wise Guys Starring...)(Also see Daredevil Comics)
Lev Gleason Publications: April, 1956

	GD25	FN65	NM94
1-Biro-c	5.70	17.00	35.00

SMASH COMICS (Becomes Lady Luck #86 on)
Quality Comics Group: Aug, 1939 - No. 85, Oct, 1949

	GD25	FN65	NM94
1-Origin Hugh Hazard & His Iron Man, Bozo the Robot, Espionage, Starring Black X by Eisner, & Hooded Justice (Invisible Justice #2 on); Chic Carter & Wings Wendall begin; 1st Robot on the cover of a comic book (Bozo)	224.00	672.00	1900.00
2-The Lone Star Rider app; Invisible Hood gains power of invisibility	85.00	255.00	725.00
3-Captain Cook & Eisner's John Law begin	55.00	165.00	470.00
4,5: 4-Flash Fulton begins	49.00	147.00	420.00
6-12: 12-One pg. Fine-a	43.00	129.00	360.00
13-Magno begins (8/40); last Eisner issue; The Ray app. in full page ad; The Purple Trio begins	44.00	132.00	375.00
14-Intro. The Ray (9/40) by Lou Fine & others	233.00	700.00	2100.00
15,16: 16-The Scarlet Seal begins	109.00	327.00	925.00
17-Wun Cloo becomes plastic super-hero by Jack Cole (9-months before Plastic Man)	115.00	345.00	975.00
18-Midnight by Jack Cole begins (origin & 1st app., 1/41)	135.00	405.00	1150.00
19-22: Last Ray by Fine; The Jester begins-#22	74.00	222.00	625.00
23,24: 24-The Sword app.; last Chic Carter; Wings Wendall dons new costume #24,25	58.00	174.00	490.00
25-Origin/1st app. Wildfire; Rookie Rankin begins	67.00	200.00	570.00
26-30: 28-Midnight-c begin, end #85	55.00	165.00	470.00
31,32,34: Ray by Rudy Palais; also #33	43.00	129.00	360.00
33-Origin The Marksman	54.00	162.00	460.00
35-37	43.00	129.00	360.00
38-The Yankee Eagle begins; last Midnight by Jack Cole	53.00	159.00	450.00
39,40-Last Ray issue	42.00	127.00	340.00
41,44-50	29.00	88.00	220.00
42-Lady Luck begins by Klaus Nordling	68.00	204.00	575.00
43-Lady Luck-c (1st & only in Smash)	24.00	72.00	180.00
51-60	21.00	64.00	160.00
61-70	18.00	54.00	135.00
71-85: 79-Midnight battles the Men from Mars-c/s	17.00	50.00	125.00

NOTE: ***Al Bryant** c-54, 63-68. **Cole** a-17-38, 68, 69, 72, 73, 78, 80, 83, 85; c-38, 60-62, 69-84. **Crandall** a-(Ray)-23-29, 35-38; c-36, 39, 40, 42-44, 46. **Fine** a(Ray)-14, 15, 16(w/**Tuska**), 17-22. **Fox** c-24-35. **Fuje** Ray-30. **Gil Fox** a-6-7, 9, 11-13. **Guardineer** a-(The Marksman)-39-?, 49, 52. **Gustavson** a-4-7, 9, 11-13 (The Jester)-22-46; (Magno)-13-21; (Midnight)-39(Cole inks), 49, 52, 63-65. **Kotzky** a-(Espionage)-33-38; c-45, 47-53. **Nordling** a-49, 52, 63-65. **Powell** a-11, 12, (Abdul the Arab)-13-24.Black X c-2, 6, 9, 11, 13, 16. Bozo the Robot c-1, 3, 5, 8, 10, 12, 14, 18, 20, 22, 24, 26. Midnight c-28-85. The Ray c-15, 17, 19, 21, 23, 25, 27. Wings Wendall c-4, 7.*

SMASH HIT SPORTS COMICS
Essankay Publications: V2#1, Jan, 1949

	GD25	FN65	NM94
V2#1-L.B. Cole-c/a	27.00	80.00	200.00

SMILE COMICS (Also see Gay Comics, Tickle, & Whee)
Modern Store Publ.: 1955 (52 pgs.; 5x7-1/4") (7¢)

	GD25	FN65	NM94
1	1.20	3.00	6.00

SMILEY BURNETTE WESTERN (Also see Patches #8 & Six-Gun Heroes)
Fawcett Publ.: March, 1950 - No. 4, Oct, 1950 (All photo front & back-c)

	GD25	FN65	NM94
1-Red Eagle begins	42.00	127.00	340.00
2-4	30.00	90.00	225.00

SMILEY (THE PSYCHOTIC BUTTON) (See Evil Ernie)
Chaos! Comics: July, 1998 ($2.95, one-shot)

	GD25	FN65	NM94
1-Ivan Reis-a			3.00
... Holiday Special (1/99)			2.95

SMILIN' JACK (See Famous Feature Stories, Popular Comics, Super Book #1, 2, 7, 19 & Super Comics)
Dell Publishing Co.: No. 5, 1940 - No. 8, Oct-Dec, 1949

	GD25	FN65	NM94
Four Color 5	54.00	162.00	595.00
Four Color 10 (1940)	49.00	146.00	535.00
Large Feature Comic 12,14,25 (1941)	47.00	140.00	515.00
Four Color 4 (1942)	40.00	121.00	445.00
Four Color 14 (1943)	32.00	97.00	355.00
Four Color 36,58 (1943-44)	21.00	64.00	235.00
Four Color 80 (1945)	14.00	42.00	155.00
Four Color 149 (1947)	9.00	27.00	100.00
1 (1-3/48)	9.00	27.00	100.00
2	5.00	15.00	54.00
3-8 (10-12/49)	3.00	10.00	36.00
Popped Wheat Giveaway (1947)-1938 strip reprints; 16 pgs. in full color	1.00	2.00	5.00
Shoe Store Giveaway-1938 strip reprints; 16 pgs.	4.25	13.00	28.00
Sparked Wheat Giveaway (1942)-16 pgs. in full color	4.25	13.00	28.00

SMILING SPOOK SPUNKY (See Spunky)

SMITTY (See Popular Comics, Super Book #2, 4 & Super Comics)
Dell Publishing Co.: No. 11, 1940 - No. 7, Aug-Oct, 1949; No. 909, Apr, 1958

	GD25	FN65	NM94
Four Color 11 (1940)	34.00	101.00	370.00
Large Feature Comic 26 (1941)	24.00	71.00	260.00
Four Color 6 (1942)	20.00	60.00	220.00
Four Color 32 (1943)	14.00	44.00	160.00
Four Color 65 (1945)	11.00	34.00	125.00
Four Color 99 (1946)	9.00	29.00	105.00
Four Color 138 (1947)	8.00	25.00	90.00
1 (2-4/48)	8.00	25.00	90.00
2-(5-7/48)	4.00	12.00	45.00
3,4: 3-(8-10/48), 4-(11-1/48-49)	3.00	10.00	36.00
5-7, Four Color 909 (4/58)	1.80	5.50	20.00

SMOKEY BEAR (TV) (See March Of Comics #234, 362, 372, 383, 407)
Gold Key: Feb, 1970 - No. 13, Mar, 1973

	GD25	FN65	NM94
1	2.00	6.00	22.00
2-5	.90	2.70	8.00
6-13			5.00

SMOKEY STOVER (See Popular Comics, Super Book #5,17,29 & Super Comics)
Dell Publishing Co.: No. 7, 1942 - No. 827, Aug, 1957

	GD25	FN65	NM94
Four Color 7 (1942)-Reprints	30.00	90.00	330.00
Four Color 35 (1943)	16.00	47.00	170.00
Four Color 64 (1944)	11.00	34.00	125.00
Four Color 229 (1949)	4.50	13.50	50.00
Four Color 730,827	3.50	11.00	38.00
General Motors giveaway (1953)	2.75	8.00	30.00
National Fire Protection giveaway(1953 & 1954)-16 pgs., paper-c	2.75	8.00	30.00

SMOKEY THE BEAR (See Forest Fire for 1st app.)
Dell Publ. Co.: No. 653, 10/55 - No. 1214, 8/61 (See March of Comics #234)

	GD25	FN65	NM94
Four Color 653 (#1)	9.00	27.00	100.00

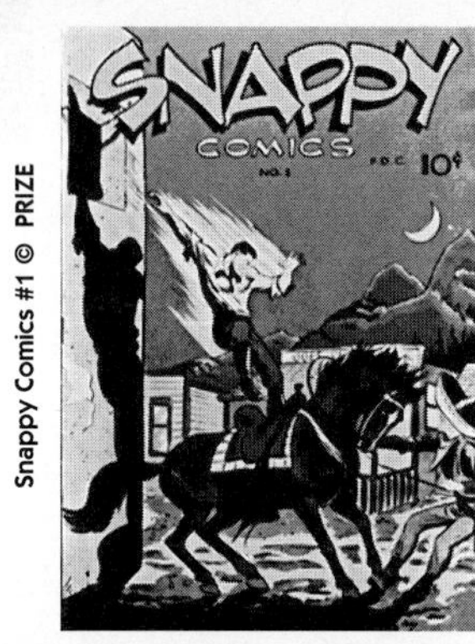

Snappy Comics #1 © PRIZE

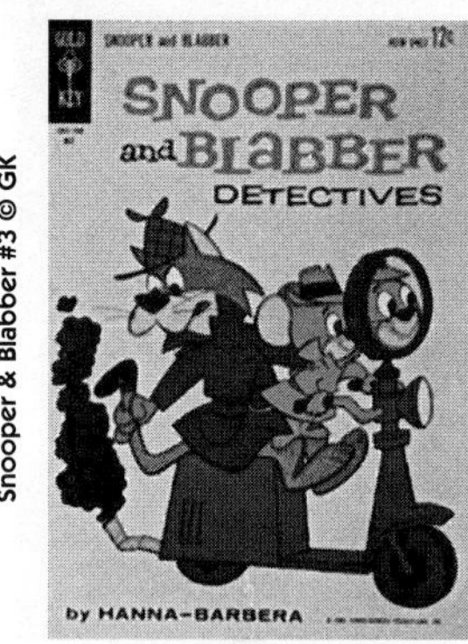

Snooper & Blabber #3 © GK

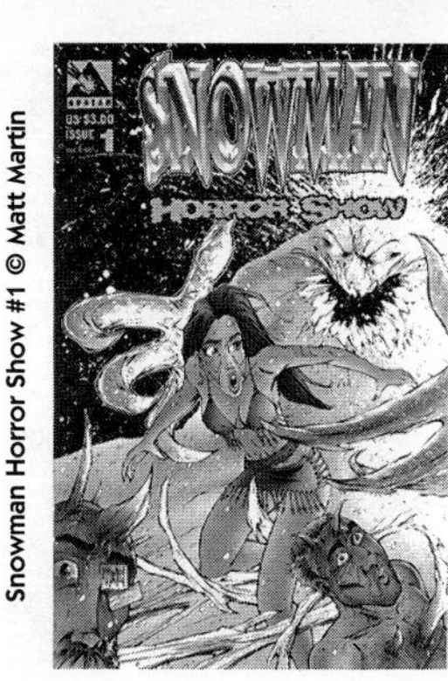

Snowman Horror Show #1 © Matt Martin

	GD25	FN65	NM94
Four Color 708,754,818,932	4.50	13.50	50.00
Four Color 1016,1119,1214	2.75	8.00	30.00
True Story of..., The('59)-U.S. Forest Service giveaway-Publ. by Western Printing Co. (reprinted in 1964 & 1969)-Reprints 1st 16 pgs. of Four Color 932	3.20	8.00	16.00

SMOKY (See Movie Classics)

SMURFS (TV)
Marvel Comics: 1982 (Dec) - No. 3, 1983

	GD25	FN65	NM94
1-3			3.50
...Treasury Edition 1 (64 pgs.)-r/#1-3	2.20	6.25	22.00

SNAFU (Magazine)
Atlas Comics (RCM): Nov, 1955 - V2#2, Mar, 1956 (B&W)

	GD25	FN65	NM94
V1#1-Heath/Severin-a; Everett, Maneely-a	11.00	32.00	80.00
V2#1,2-Severin-a	8.50	26.00	60.00

SNAGGLEPUSS (TV)(See Hanna-Barbera Band Wagon #3, Quick-Draw McGraw #5 & Spotlight #4)
Gold Key: Oct, 1962 - No. 4, Sept, 1963 (Hanna-Barbera)

	GD25	FN65	NM94
1	7.25	22.00	80.00
2-4	5.00	15.00	55.00

SNAP (Formerly Scoop #8; becomes Jest #10,11 & Komik Pages #10)
Harry 'A' Chesler: No. 9, 1944

	GD25	FN65	NM94
9-Manhunter, The Voice	16.00	48.00	120.00

SNAPPY COMICS
Cima Publ. Co. (Prize Publ.): 1945

	GD25	FN65	NM94
1-Airmale app.; 9 pg. Sorcerer's Apprentice adapt; Kiefer-a	26.00	78.00	195.00

SNARKY PARKER (See Life With...)

SNIFFY THE PUP
Standard Publ. (Animated Cartoons): No. 5, Nov, 1949 - No. 18, Sept, 1953

	GD25	FN65	NM94
5-Two Frazetta text illos	9.30	28.00	65.00
6-10	4.00	12.00	24.00
11-18	3.60	9.00	18.00

SNOOPER AND BLABBER DETECTIVES (TV) (See Whitman Comic Books)
Gold Key: Nov, 1962 - No. 3, May, 1963 (Hanna-Barbera)

	GD25	FN65	NM94
1	7.25	22.00	80.00
2,3	5.50	16.50	60.00

SNOW FOR CHRISTMAS
W. T. Grant Co.: 1957 (16 pgs.) (Giveaway)

	GD25	FN65	NM94
nn	3.60	9.00	18.00

SNOWMAN
Hall of Heroes/Avatar Press: 1996 - Present ($2.50, B&W)

	GD25	FN65	NM94
1	1.50	4.50	15.00
1-Ltd. Ed.	2.25	6.80	25.00
2,3			4.00
2,3-Ltd. Ed.	1.20	3.60	12.00
3-Chromium-c			4.00
0-(Avatar Press)			5.00
0-Alternate-c			4.50
0-Gold			12.00
0-Silver Foil			15.00
0-Black Leather			25.00
0-Blue Foil-c			45.00

SNOWMAN DEAD AND DYING
Avatar Press: Nov,1997 - No. 3, Apr, 1998 ($3.00, B&W, limited series)

	GD25	FN65	NM94
1			3.00
1-($4.95) Ltd. Edition			5.00
2,3-($3.50)			3.50
3-($4.95) variant-c			5.00
3-($25.00) White velvet variant-c			25.00

SNOWMAN HORROR SHOW
Avatar Press: Mar, 1998 ($3.00, B&W, one-shot)

	GD25	FN65	NM94
1-Pin-ups by Matt Martin			3.00
1-($4.95) Frozen Fear Edition			5.00
1-Leather-c			30.00

SNOWMAN 1944
Entity Comics: Oct, 1996 - No. 4 ($2.75, B&W)

	GD25	FN65	NM94
1			4.00
1-Ltd. Ed.	.90	2.70	8.00
2			4.00
3,4			2.75
3-Ltd. Ed.			3.00
...Special 1 (10/97, $3.95)			4.00

SNOWMAN SQUARED
Avatar Press: Sept, 1998 - No. 2 ($3.00, B&W, limited series)

	GD25	FN65	NM94
1-Matt Martin-s/a; Snowman vs. Snowman 1944			3.00
1-Commemorative Edition			5.00

SNOW WHITE (See Christmas With..., Mickey Mouse Mag., Movie Comics & Seven Dwarfs)
Dell Publishing Co.: No. 49, July, 1944 - No. 382, Mar, 1952 (Disney-Movie)

	GD25	FN65	NM94
Four Color 49 (...& the Seven Dwarfs)	56.00	169.00	620.00
Four Color 382 (1952)-origin; partial reprint of Four Color 49	10.00	30.00	110.00

SNOW WHITE
Marvel Comics: Jan, 1995 ($1.95, one-shot)

	GD25	FN65	NM94
1-r/1937 Sunday newspaper pages			2.00

SNOW WHITE AND THE SEVEN DWARFS
Bendix Washing Machines: 1952 (32 pgs., 5x7-1/4", soft-c) (Disney)

	GD25	FN65	NM94
nn	10.00	30.00	75.00

SNOW WHITE AND THE SEVEN DWARFS
Promotional Publ. Co.: 1957 (Small size)

	GD25	FN65	NM94
nn	4.00	10.50	21.00

SNOW WHITE AND THE SEVEN DWARFS
Western Printing Co.: 1958 (16 pgs, 5x7-1/4", soft-c) (Disney premium)

	GD25	FN65	NM94
nn- "Mystery of the Missing Magic"	5.70	17.00	40.00

SNOW WHITE AND THE SEVEN DWARFS
Whitman Publications: April, 1982 (60¢)

	GD25	FN65	NM94
nn-r/Four Color 49			4.00

SNOW WHITE AND THE SEVEN DWARFS GOLDEN ANNIVERSARY
Gladstone: Fall, 1987 ($2.95, magazine size, 52 pgs.)

	GD25	FN65	NM94
1-Contains poster	.90	2.70	8.00

SNOW WHITE AND THE 7 DWARFS IN "MILKY WAY"
American Dairy Assoc.: 1955 (16 pgs., soft-c, 5x7-1/4") (Disney premium)

	GD25	FN65	NM94
nn	10.00	30.00	75.00

SOAP OPERA LOVE
Charlton Comics: Feb, 1983 - No. 3, June, 1983

	GD25	FN65	NM94
1-3			2.00

SOAP OPERA ROMANCES
Charlton Comics: July, 1982 - No. 5, March, 1983

	GD25	FN65	NM94
1-5-Nurse Betsy Crane-r			2.00

SOCK MONKEY
Dark Horse Comics: Sept, 1998 - Present ($2.95, B&W)

	GD25	FN65	NM94
1,2-Tony Millionaire-s/a			2.95

Solar #33 © Voyager Comm.

Solitaire #5 © MAL

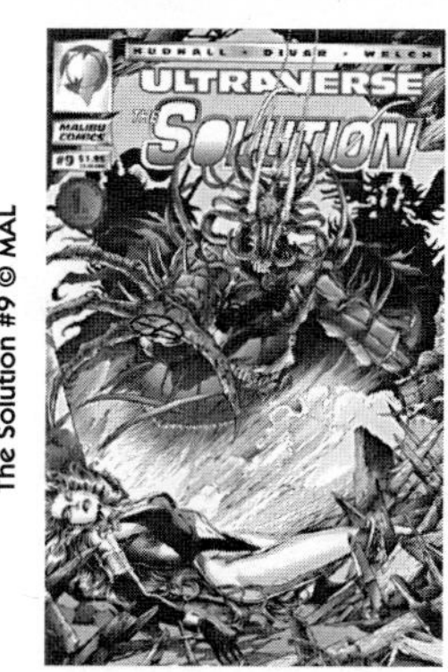

The Solution #9 © MAL

GD25 FN65 NM94

SO DARK THE ROSE
CFD Productions: Oct, 1995 ($2.95)

1-Wrightson-c 3.00

SOJOURN
White Cliffs Publ. Co.: Sept, 1977 - No. 2, 1978 ($1.50, B&W & color, full tabloid size)

1,2: 1-Tor by Kubert, Eagle by Severin, E. V. Race, Private Investigator by Doug Wildey, T. C. Mars by Aragones begin plus other strips 2.00 6.00

NOTE: Most copies came folded. Unfolded copies are worth 50% more.

SOLAR (...Man of the Atom) (Also see Doctor Solar)
Valiant/Acclaim Comics (Valiant): Sept, 1991 - No. 60, Apr, 1996 ($1.75/$1.95/$2.50, 44 pgs.)

1-Layton-a(i) on Solar; Barry Windsor-Smith-c/a 3.00
2,3: 2-Layton-a(i) on Solar, B. Smith-a. 3-1st app. Harada (11/91) 2.00
4-9: 7-vs. X-O Armor; last $1.95-c. 8-$2.25-c begins 2.00
10-(6/92, $3.95)-1st app. Eternal Warrior (6 pgs.); black embossed-c; origin & 1st app. Geoff McHenry (Geomancer) 4.00
10-($3.95)-2nd printing 4.00
11-15: 11-1st full app. Eternal Warrior. 12,13-Unity x-overs. 14-1st app. Fred Bender (becomes Dr. Eclipse). 15-2nd Dr. Eclipse 3.00
16-45: 17-X-O Manowar app. 23-Solar splits. 29-1st Valiant Vision book. 33-Valiant Vision; bound-in trading card. 38-Chaos Effect Epsilon Pt.1 2.25
46-60: 46-$2.50-c begins. 46-52-Dan Jurgens-a(p)/scripts w/Giordano-i. 53,54-Jurgens scripts only. 60-Giffen scripts; Jeff Johnson-a(p) 2.50
0-($9.95, trade paperback)-r/Alpha and Omega origin story; polybagged w/poster 10.00
...:Second Death (1994, $9.95)-r/issues #1-4. 10.00

NOTE: *#1-10 all have free 8 pg. insert "Alpha and Omega" which is a 10 chapter Solar origin story. All 10 centerfolds can pieced together to show climax of story.* ***Ditko*** *a-11p, 14p.* ***Giordano*** *a-46, 47, 48, 49, 50, 51, 52i.* ***Johnson*** *a-60p.* ***Jurgens*** *a-46, 47, 48, 49, 50 , 51, 52p.* ***Layton*** *a-1-3i; c-2i, 11i, 17i, 25i.* ***Miller*** *c-12.* ***Quesada*** *c-17p, 20-23p, 29p.* ***Simonson*** *c-13.* ***B. Smith*** *a-1-10; c-1, 3, 5, 7, 19i.* ***Thibert*** *c-22i, 23i.*

SOLARMAN (See Pendulum Ill. Originals)
Marvel Comics: Jan, 1989 - No. 2, May, 1990 ($1.00, limited series)

1,2 1.00

SOLAR, MAN OF THE ATOM (Man of the Atom on cover)
Acclaim Comics (Valiant Heroes): Vol. 2, May, 1997 ($3.95, one-shot, 46 pgs) (1st Valiant Heroes Special Event)

Vol. 2-Reintro Solar; Ninjak cameo; Warren Ellis scripts; Darick Robertson-a 4.00

SOLAR, MAN OF THE ATOM: HELL ON EARTH
Acclaim Comics (Valiant Heroes): Jan, 1998 - No. 4 ($2.50, limited series)

1-4-Priest-s/ Zircher-a(p) 2.50

SOLAR, MAN OF THE ATOM: REVELATIONS
Acclaim Comics (Valiant Heroes): Nov, 1997 ($3.95, one-shot, 46 pgs.)

1-Krueger-s/ Zircher-a(p) 4.00

SOLDIER & MARINE COMICS (Fightin' Army #16 on)
Charlton Comics (Toby Press of Conn. V1#11): No. 11, Dec, 1954 - No. 15, Aug, 1955; V2#9, Dec, 1956

V1#11 (12/54)-Bob Powell-a 5.70 17.00 35.00
V1#12(2/55)-15: 12-Photo-c 4.00 11.00 22.00
V2#9(Formerly Never Again; Jerry Drummer V2#10 on) 4.00 11.00 22.00

SOLDIER COMICS
Fawcett Publications: Jan, 1952 - No. 11, Sept, 1953

1 9.50 28.75 72.00
2 5.70 17.00 35.00
3-5 4.25 13.00 28.00
6-11: 8-Illo. in **POP** 4.00 12.00 24.00

SOLDIERS OF FORTUNE
American Comics Group (Creston Publ. Corp.): Mar-Apr, 1951 - No. 13, Feb-Mar, 1953

1-Capt. Crossbones by Shelly, Ace Carter, Lance Larson begin 20.00 60.00 150.00
2 11.50 34.00 85.00
3-10: 6-Bondage-c 10.00 30.00 75.00
11-13 (War format) 5.70 17.00 35.00

NOTE: ***Shelly*** *a-1-3, 5.* ***Whitney*** *a-6, 8-11, 13; c-1-3, 5, 6.*

SOLDIERS OF FREEDOM
Americomics: 1987 - No. 2, 1987 ($1.75)

1,2 1.80

SOLITAIRE (Also See Prime V2#6-8)
Malibu Comics (Ultraverse): Nov, 1993 - No. 12, Dec, 1994 ($1.95)

1-($2.50)-Collector's edition bagged w/playing card 2.50
1-12: 1-Regular edition w/o playing card. 2,4-Break-Thru x-over. 3-2 pg. origin The Night Man. 4-Gatefold-c. 5-Two pg. origin the Strangers 2.00

SOLO
Marvel Comics: Sept, 1994 - No. 4, Dec, 1994 ($1.75, limited series)

1-4: Spider-Man app. 1.75

SOLO (Movie)
Dark Horse Comics: July, 1996 - No. 2, Aug, 1996 ($2.50, limited series)

1,2: Adaptation of film; photo-c 1.00 2.50

SOLO AVENGERS (Becomes Avenger Spotlight #21 on)
Marvel Comics: Dec, 1987 - No. 20, July, 1989 (75¢/$1.00)

1-Jim Lee-a on back-up story 2.50
2-5 1.50
6-20: 11-Intro Bobcat 1.00

SOLOMON AND SHEBA (Movie)
Dell Publishing Co.: No. 1070, Jan-Mar, 1960

Four Color 1070-Sekowsky-a; photo-c 9.00 27.00 100.00

SOLOMON KANE (Also see Blackthorne 3-D Series #60 & Marvel Premiere)
Marvel Comics: Sept, 1985 - No. 6, July, 1986 (Limited series)

1-6: 1-Double size. 3-6-Williamson-a(i) 1.00

SOLUTION, THE
Malibu Comics (Ultraverse): Sept, 1993 - No. 17, Feb, 1995 ($1.95)

1,3-13: 1-Intro Meathook, Deathdance, Black Tiger, Tech. 4-Break-Thru x-over; gatefold-c. 5-2 pg. origin The Strangers. 11-Brereton-c 2.00
1-($2.50)-Newsstand ed. polybagged w/trading card 2.50
1-Ultra 5000 Limited silver foil 5.00
0-Obtained w/Rune #0 by sending coupons from 11 comics 3.00
2-($2.50, 48 pgs.)-Rune flip-c/story by B. Smith; The Mighty Magnor 1 pg. strip by Aragones 2.50
11-15: 11-Brereton-c 2.00
16 ($3.50)-Flip-c Ultraverse Premiere #10 3.50
17 ($2.50) 2.50

SOMERSET HOLMES (See Eclipse Graphic Novel Series)
Pacific Comics/ Eclipse Comics No. 5, 6: Sept, 1983 - No. 6, Dec, 1984 ($1.50, Baxter paper)

1-Brent Anderson-c/a. Cliff Hanger by Williamson begins, ends #6 1.50
2-6 1.50

SONG OF THE SOUTH (See Brer Rabbit)

SONIC & KNUCKLES
Archie Comics: Aug, 1995 ($2.00)

1 3.00

SONIC DISRUPTORS

Sonic Super Special #7 © SEGA

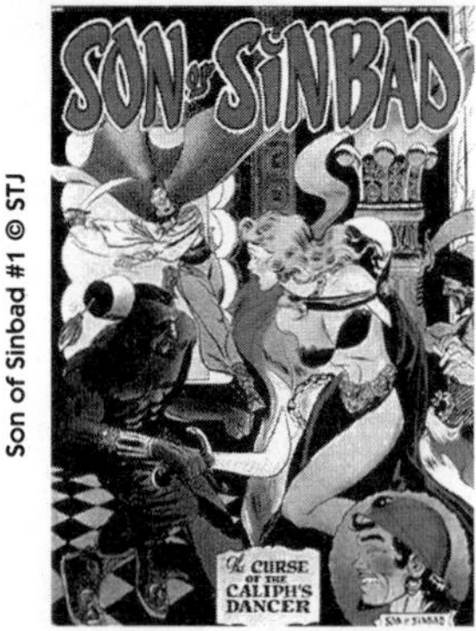

Son of Sinbad #1 © STJ

Sovereign Seven #36 © Chris Claremont

DC Comics: Dec, 1987 - No. 7, July, 1988 ($1.75, limited series, mature)

	GD25	FN65	NM94
1-7		.70	1.75

SONIC THE HEDGEHOG (TV, video game)
Feb, 1993 - No. 3, May, 1993 ($1.25, mini-series)
Archie Comics: July, 1993 - Present ($1.25/$1.50/$1.75)

	GD25	FN65	NM94
0(2/93),1-3: Shaw-a(p) & covers		2.00	6.00
1		2.00	6.00
2-10: 8-Neon ink-c.			4.00
11-20			3.00
21-50 ($1.50): 25-Silver ink-c			2.50
51-63: 54-Begin $1.75-c			2.00
64-67			1.75
Triple Trouble Special (10/95, $2.00, 48 pgs.)			2.00

SONIC'S FRIENDLY NEMESIS KNUCKLES
Archie Publications: July, 1996 - No. 3, Sept, 1996 ($1.50, limited series)

	GD25	FN65	NM94
1-3			2.00

SONIC SUPER SPECIAL
Archie Publications: 1997 - Present ($2.00/$2.25, 48 pgs)

	GD25	FN65	NM94
1-3			2.00
4-6			2.25
7-(w/Image) Spawn, Maxx, Savage Dragon-c/app.; Valentino-a			2.25

SONIC VS. KNUCKLES "BATTLE ROYAL" SPECIAL
Archie Publications: 1997 ($2.00, one-shot)

	GD25	FN65	NM94
1			2.00

SON OF AMBUSH BUG (See Ambush Bug)
DC Comics: July, 1986 - No. 6, Dec, 1986 (75¢)

	GD25	FN65	NM94
1-6: Giffen-c/a in all. 5-Bissette-a.			.75

SON OF BLACK BEAUTY (Also see Black Beauty)
Dell Publishing Co.: No. 510, Oct, 1953 - No. 566, June, 1954

	GD25	FN65	NM94
Four Color 510, 566	2.75	8.00	30.00

SON OF FLUBBER (See Movie Comics)

SON OF MUTANT WORLD
Fantagor Press: 1990 - No. 5, 1990? ($2.00, bi-monthly)

	GD25	FN65	NM94
1-3: Corben-c/a			2.00
4,5 ($1.75, B&W)			1.75

SON OF ORIGINS OF MARVEL COMICS (See Fireside Book Series)

SON OF SATAN (Also see Ghost Rider #1 & Marvel Spotlight #12)
Marvel Comics Group: Dec, 1975 - No. 8, Feb, 1977 (25¢)

	GD25	FN65	NM94
1-Mooney-a; Kane-c(p), Starlin splash(p)	1.50	4.50	15.00
2,4,6-8: 2-Origin The Possessor. 8-Heath-a	.90	2.70	9.00
3,5-(Regular 25¢ edition)(4,8/76): 5-Russell-p	.90	2.70	9.00
3,5-(30¢-c, limited distribution)	2.70	8.00	30.00

SON OF SINBAD (Also see Abbott & Costello & Daring Adventures)
St. John Publishing Co.: Feb, 1950

	GD25	FN65	NM94
1-Kubert-c/a	38.00	114.00	285.00

SON OF TOMAHAWK (See Tomahawk)

SON OF VULCAN (Formerly Mysteries of Unexplored Worlds #1-48; Thunderbolt V3#51 on)
Charlton Comics: V2#49, Nov, 1965 - V2#50, Jan, 1966

	GD25	FN65	NM94
V2#49,50: 50-Roy Thomas scripts (1st pro work)	2.25	6.75	18.00

SON OF YUPPIES FROM HELL (See Yuppies From Hell)
Marvel Comics: 1990 ($3.50, B&W, squarebound, 52 pgs.)

	GD25	FN65	NM94
nn			3.50

SONS OF KATIE ELDER (See Movie Classics)

SORCERY (See Chilling Adventures in... & Red Circle...)

SORORITY SECRETS
Toby Press: July, 1954

	GD25	FN65	NM94
1	6.50	19.50	45.00

SOULSEARCHERS AND COMPANY
Claypool Comics: June, 1995 - Present ($2.50, B&W)

	GD25	FN65	NM94
1-10: Peter David scripts			3.00
11-32			2.50

SOULQUEST
Innovation: Apr, 1989 ($3.95, squarebound, 52 pgs.)

	GD25	FN65	NM94
1-Blackshard app.			4.00

SOULWIND
Image Comics: Mar, 1997 - Present ($2.95, B&W, limited series)

	GD25	FN65	NM94
1-8: 5-"The Day I Tried To Live" pt. 1			3.00
...The Kid From Planet Earth (1997, $9.95, TPB)			9.95

SOUPY SALES COMIC BOOK (TV)(The Official...)
Archie Publications: 1965

	GD25	FN65	NM94
1	8.00	24.00	80.00

SOUTHERN KNIGHTS, THE (See Crusaders #1)
Guild Publ/Fictioneer Books: 1983 - No. 34? (B&W)

	GD25	FN65	NM94
2-Magazine size			3.00
3-34			1.50
Dread Halloween Special 1			2.25
Special 1 (Spring, 1989, $2.25)			2.25
Graphic Novels #1-4			4.00

SOVEREIGN SEVEN (Also see Showcase '95 #12)
DC Comics: July, 1995 - No. 36, July, 1998 ($1.95) (1st creator-owned mainstream DC comic)

	GD25	FN65	NM94
1-1st app. Sovereign Seven (Reflex, Indigo, Cascade, Finale, Cruiser, Network & Rampart); 1st app. Maitresse; Darkseid app.; Chris Claremont scripts & Dwayne Turner-c/a begins.			3.00
1-Gold			8.00
2-25: 2-Wolverine cameo. 4-Neil Gaiman cameo. 5,8-Batman app. 7-Ramirez cameo (from the movie Highlander). 9-Humphrey Bogart cameo from Casablanca. 10-Impulse app; Manoli Wetherell & Neal Conan cameo from Uncanny X-Men #226. 11-Robin app. 16-Final Night. 24-Superman app. 25-Power Girl app.			2.00
26-36: 26-Begin $2.25-c. 28-Impulse-c/app.			2.25
Annual 1 (1995, $3.95)-Year One story; Big Barda & Lobo app.; Jeff Johnson-c/a.			4.00
Annual 2 (1996, $2.95)-Legends of the Dead Earth; Leonardi-c/a			3.00
...Plus 1(2/97, $2.95)-Legion-c/app.			3.00
TPB-($12.95) r/#1-5, Annual #1 & Showcase '95 #12			13.00

SPACE: ABOVE AND BEYOND (TV)
Topps Comics: Jan, 1996 - No. 3, Mar, 1996 ($2.95, limited series)

	GD25	FN65	NM94
1-3: Adaptation of pilot episode; Steacy-c.			3.00

SPACE: ABOVE AND BEYOND--THE GAUNTLET (TV)
Topps Comics: May, 1996 -No. 2, June, 1996 ($2.95, limited series)

	GD25	FN65	NM94
1,2			3.00

SPACE ACE (Also see Manhunt!)
Magazine Enterprises: No. 5, 1952

	GD25	FN65	NM94
5(A-1 #61)-Guardineer-a	43.00	129.00	360.00

SPACE ACTION
Ace Magazines (Junior Books): June, 1952 - No. 3, Oct, 1952

	GD25	FN65	NM94
1-Cameron-a in all (1 story)	61.00	183.00	520.00
2,3	48.00	144.00	410.00

SPACE ADVENTURES (War At Sea #22 on)
Capitol Stories/Charlton Comics: 7/52 - No. 21, 8/56; No. 23, 5/58 - No. 59,

Space Adventures V3 #29 © CC

Space Comics #4 © AVON

Spaceman #5 © MAR

11/64; V3#60, 10/67; V1#2, 7/68 - V1#8, 7/69; No. 9, 5/78 - No. 13, 3/79

	GD25	FN65	NM94
1	41.00	123.00	325.00
2	21.00	64.00	160.00
3-5: 4,6-Flying saucer-c/stories	17.00	50.00	125.00
6-9: 7-Sex change story "Transformation". 8-Robot-c. 9-A-Bomb panel	15.00	44.00	110.00
10,11-Ditko-c/a. 10-Robot-c. 11-Two Ditko stories	40.00	120.00	320.00
12-Ditko-c (classic)	44.00	132.00	370.00
13-(Fox-r, 10-11/54); Blue Beetle-c/story	17.00	50.00	125.00
14-Blue Beetle-c/story; Fox-r (12-1/54-55, last pre-code)	15.00	45.00	115.00
15,17,18-Rocky Jones-c/s.(TV); 15-Part photo-c	16.00	47.00	120.00
16-Krigstein-a; Rocky Jones-c/story (TV)	18.00	54.00	135.00
19	11.00	33.00	80.00
20-Reprints Fawcett's "Destination Moon"	24.00	71.00	175.00
21-(8/56) (no #22)(Becomes War At Sea)	11.00	33.00	80.00
23-(5/58; formerly Nyoka, The Jungle Girl)-Reprints Fawcett's "Destination Moon"	19.00	56.00	140.00
24,25,31,32-Ditko-a. 24-Severin-a(signed "LePoer")	16.00	47.00	120.00
26,27-Ditko-a(4) each. 26,28-Flying saucer-c	17.00	51.00	130.00
28-30	6.50	19.50	45.00
33-Origin/1st app. Capt. Atom by Ditko (3/60)	32.00	96.00	360.00
34-40,42-All Captain Atom by Ditko	13.00	39.00	135.00
41,43-59: 44-1st app. Mercury Man; also in #45	2.50	7.50	25.00
V3#60(#1, 10/67)-Origin & 1st app. Paul Mann & The Saucers From the Future	3.00	9.00	30.00
2,5,6,8 (1968-69)-Ditko-a: 2-Aparo-c/a	2.25	6.75	18.00
3,4,7: 4-Aparo-c/a	1.85	5.50	15.00
9-13(1978-79)-Capt. Atom-r/Space Adventures by Ditko; 9-Reprints origin/1st app. Capt. Atom from #33			4.00

NOTE: ***Aparo** a-V3#60. c-V3#8. **Ditko** c-12, 31-42. **Giordano** c-3, 4, 7-9, 18p. **Krigstein** c-15. **Shuster** a-11. Issues 13 & 14 have Blue Beetle logos; #15-18 have Rocky Jones logos.*

SPACE ARK
Americomics (AC Comics)/ Apple Comics #3 on: June, 1985 - No. 5, Sept, 1987 ($1.75)

	GD25	FN65	NM94
1-5: Funny animal (#1,2-color; #3-5-B&W)			1.80

SPACE BUSTERS
Ziff-Davis Publ. Co.: Spring, 1952 - No. 2, Fall, 1952

	GD25	FN65	NM94
1-Krigstein-a(3); Painted-c by Norman Saunders	71.00	212.00	600.00
2-Kinstler-a(2 pgs.); Saunders painted-c	55.00	165.00	470.00

NOTE: ***Anderson** a-2. Bondage c-2.*

SPACE CADET (See Tom Corbett,...)

SPACE COMICS (Formerly Funny Tunes)
Avon Periodicals: No. 4, Mar-Apr, 1954 - No. 5, May-June, 1954

	GD25	FN65	NM94
4,5-Space Mouse, Peter Rabbit, Super Pup (formerly Spotty the Pup), & Merry Mouse continue from Funny Tunes	5.35	16.00	32.00
I.W. Reprint #8 (nd)-Space Mouse-r	1.10	3.30	9.00

SPACED
Anthony Smith Publ. #1,2/Unbridled Ambition/Eclipse Comics #10 on: 1982 - No. 13, 1988 ($1.25/$1.50, B&W, quarterly)

	GD25	FN65	NM94
1-($1.25-c)			4.00
2-($1.25-c)			3.00
3-13: 3-Begin $1.50-c			1.50
Special Edition (1983, Mimeo)			3.00

SPACE DETECTIVE
Avon Periodicals: July, 1951 - No. 4, July, 1952

	GD25	FN65	NM94
1-Rod Hathway, Space Detective begins, ends #4; Wood-c/a(3)-23 pgs.; "Opium Smugglers of Venus" drug story; Lucky Dale-r/Saint #4	90.00	270.00	765.00
2-Tales from the Shadow Squad story; Wood/Orlando-c; Wood inside layouts; "Slave Ship of Saturn" story	60.00	180.00	510.00
3,4: 3-Kinstler-c. 4-Kinstlerish-a by McCann	36.00	108.00	270.00
I.W. Reprint #1(Reprints #2), 8(Reprints cover #1 & part Famous Funnies #191)	3.00	9.00	30.00
I.W. Reprint #9-Exist?	3.00	9.00	30.00

SPACE EXPLORER (See March of Comics #202)

SPACE FAMILY ROBINSON (TV)(...Lost in Space #15-37, ...Lost in Space On Space Station One #38 on)(See Gold Key Champion)
Gold Key: Dec, 1962 - No. 36, Oct, 1969; No. 37, 10/73 - No. 54, 11/78; No. 55, 3/81 - No. 59, 5/82 (All painted covers)

	GD25	FN65	NM94
1-(Low distribution); Spiegle-a in all	22.00	66.00	245.00
2(3/63)-Family becomes lost in space	10.00	31.00	115.00
3-10: 6-Captain Venture back-up stories begin	5.25	16.00	58.00
11-20: 14-(10/65). 15-Title change (1/66)	3.50	10.50	38.00
21-36: 28-Last 12¢ issue. 36-Captain Venture ends	2.20	6.50	24.00
37-48: 37-Origin retold	.90	2.70	8.00
49-59: Reprints #49,50,55-59			4.00

NOTE: *The TV show first aired on 9/15/65. Title changed after TV show debuted.*

SPACE FAMILY ROBINSON (See March of Comics #320, 328, 352, 404, 414)

SPACE GHOST (TV) (Also see Golden Comics Digest #2 & Hanna-Barbera Super TV Heroes #3-7)
Gold Key: March, 1967 (Hanna-Barbera) (TV debut was 9/10/66)

	GD25	FN65	NM94
1 (10199-703)-Spiegle-a	31.00	93.00	340.00

SPACE GHOST (TV cartoon)
Comico: Mar, 1987 ($3.50, deluxe format, one-shot) (Hanna-Barbera)

	GD25	FN65	NM94
1-Steve Rude-c/a		2.00	6.00

SPACE GHOST COAST TO COAST
Cartoon Network: Apr, 1994 (giveaway to Turner Broadcasting employees)

	GD25	FN65	NM94
1-8 pgs.; origin of Space Ghost			4.00

SPACE GIANTS, THE (TV cartoon)
FBN Publications: 1979 ($1.00, B&W, one-shots)

	GD25	FN65	NM94
1-Based on Japanese TV series			5.00

SPACEHAWK
Dark Horse Comics: 1989 - No. 3, 1990 ($2.00, B&W)

	GD25	FN65	NM94
1-3-Wolverton-c/a(r) plus new stories by others.			2.00

SPACE JAM
DC Comics: 1996 ($5.95, one-shot)

	GD25	FN65	NM94
1-Wraparound photo cover of Michael Jordan; movie adaption			5.95

SPACE KAT-ETS (...in 3-D)
Power Publishing Co.: Dec, 1953 (25¢, came w/glasses)

	GD25	FN65	NM94
1	31.00	92.00	225.00

SPACEMAN (Speed Carter...)
Atlas Comics (CnPC): Sept, 1953 - No. 6, July, 1954

	GD25	FN65	NM94
1-Grey tone-c	55.00	165.00	470.00
2	39.00	116.00	290.00
3-6: 4-A-Bomb explosion-c	35.00	104.00	260.00

NOTE: ***Everett** c-1, 3. **Heath** a-1. **Maneely** a-1(3), 2(4), 3(3), 4-6; c-5, 6. **Romita** a-1. **Sekowsky** c-4. **Sekowsky/Abel** a-4(3). **Tuska** a-5(3).*

SPACE MAN
Dell Publ. Co.: No. 1253, 1-3/62 - No. 8, 3-5/64; No. 9, 7/72 - No. 10, 10/72

	GD25	FN65	NM94
Four Color 1253 (#1)(1-3/62)	6.40	19.00	70.00
2,3	3.00	10.00	36.00
4-8	2.50	7.50	27.00
9,10: 9-Reprints #1253. 10-Reprints #2		2.40	6.00

SPACE MOUSE (Also see Funny Tunes & Space Comics)
Avon Periodicals: April, 1953 - No. 5, Apr-May, 1954

	GD25	FN65	NM94
1	7.15	21.50	50.00
2	5.35	16.00	32.00

Space Squadron #5 © MAR

Space Worlds #6 © MAR

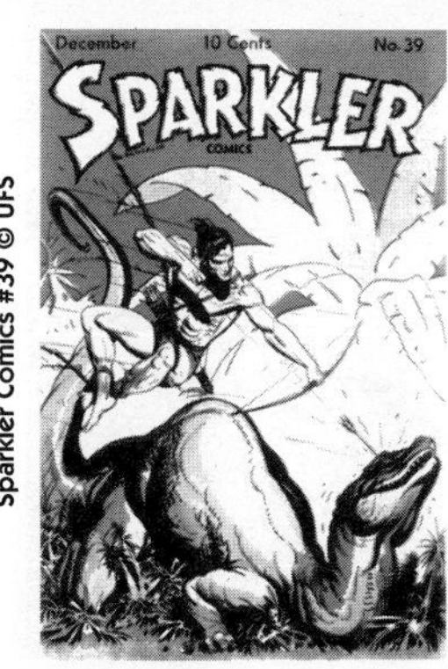

Sparkler Comics #39 © UFS

	GD25	FN65	NM94
3-5	4.00	11.00	22.00

SPACE MOUSE (Walter Lantz...#1; see Comic Album #17)
Dell Publishing Co./Gold Key: No. 1132, Aug-Oct, 1960 - No. 5, Nov, 1963 (Walter Lantz)

	GD25	FN65	NM94
Four Color 1132,1244	3.60	11.00	40.00
1(11/62)(G.K.)	3.60	11.00	40.00
2-5	2.75	8.00	30.00

SPACE MYSTERIES
I.W. Enterprises: 1964 (Reprints)

	GD25	FN65	NM94
1-r/Journey Into Unknown Worlds #4 w/new-c	1.75	5.25	14.00
8,9: 9-r/Planet Comics #73	2.00	6.00	16.00

SPACE: 1999 (TV) (Also see Power Record Comics)
Charlton Comics: Nov, 1975 - No. 7, Nov, 1976

	GD25	FN65	NM94
1-Origin Moonbase Alpha; Staton-c/a	.85	2.60	7.00
2,7: 2-Staton-a			5.00
3-6: All Byrne-a; c-3,5,6	.90	2.70	8.00

SPACE: 1999 (TV)(Magazine)
Charlton Comics: Nov, 1975 - No. 8, Nov, 1976 (B&W) (#7 shows #6 inside)

	GD25	FN65	NM94
1-Origin Moonbase Alpha; Morrow-c/a	1.00	3.00	10.00
2-8: 2,3-Morrow-c/a. 4-6-Morrow-c. 5,8-Morrow-a		2.00	6.00

SPACE PATROL (TV)
Ziff-Davis Publishing Co. (Approved Comics): Summer, 1952 - No. 2, Oct-Nov, 1952 (Painted-c by Norman Saunders)

	GD25	FN65	NM94
1-Krigstein-a	76.00	229.00	650.00
2-Krigstein-a(3)	55.00	165.00	465.00
...'s Special Mission (8 pgs., B&W, Giveaway)	56.00	168.00	475.00

SPACE PIRATES (See Archie Giant Series #533)

SPACE RANGER (See Mystery in Space #92, Showcase #15 & Tales of the Unexpected)

SPACE SQUADRON (In the Days of the Rockets)(Becomes Space Worlds #6)
Marvel/Atlas Comics (ACI): June, 1951 - No. 5, Feb, 1952

	GD25	FN65	NM94
1-Space team; Brodsky c-1,5	55.00	165.00	470.00
2: Tuska c-2-4	47.00	142.00	400.00
3-5: 3-Capt. Jet Dixon by Tuska(3). 4-Weird advs. begin	41.00	122.00	325.00

SPACE THRILLERS
Avon Periodicals: 1954 (25¢ Giant)

	GD25	FN65	NM94
nn-(Scarce)-Robotmen of the Lost Planet; contains 3 rebound comics of The Saint & Strange Worlds. Contents could vary	94.00	282.00	800.00

SPACE TRIP TO THE MOON (See Space Adventures #23)

SPACE USAGI
Mirage Studios: June, 1992 - No. 3, 1992 ($2.00, B&W, mini-series)
V2#1, Nov, 1993 - V2#3, Jan, 1994 ($2.75)

	GD25	FN65	NM94
1-3: Stan Sakai-c/a/scripts			2.00
V2#1-3			2.75

SPACE USAGI
Dark Horse Comics: Jan, 1996 - No. 3, Mar, 1996 ($2.00, B&W, limited series)

	GD25	FN65	NM94
1-3: Stan Sakai-c/a/scripts			2.00

SPACE WAR (Fightin' Five #28 on)
Charlton Comics: Oct, 1959 - No. 27, Mar, 1964; No. 28, Mar, 1978 - No. 34, 3/79

	GD25	FN65	NM94
V1#1-Giordano-c begin, end #3	12.00	36.00	120.00
2,3	6.00	18.00	60.00
4-6,8,10-Ditko-c/a	12.00	36.00	120.00
7,9,11-15: Last 10¢ issue?	3.00	9.00	30.00
16-27 (3/64): 18,19-Robot-c	2.80	8.40	28.00
28(3/78),29,33,34-Ditko-c/a(r)			5.00
30-Ditko-c/a(r); Staton, Sutton/Wood-a			5.00
31-Ditko-c/a(3); same-c as Strange Suspense Stories #2 (1968); atom blast-c		2.00	6.00
32-r/Charlton Premiere V2#2; Sutton-a			3.00

SPACE WESTERN (Formerly Cowboy Western Comics; becomes Cowboy Western Comics #46 on)
Charlton Comics (Capitol Stories): No. 40, Oct, 1952 - No. 45, Aug, 1953

	GD25	FN65	NM94
40-Intro Spurs Jackson & His Space Vigilantes; flying saucer story	49.00	148.00	420.00
41,43-45: 41-Flying saucer-c. 45-Hitler app.	39.00	117.00	295.00
42-Atom bomb explosion-c	41.00	122.00	325.00

SPACE WORLDS (Formerly Space Squadron #1-5)
Atlas Comics (Male): No. 6, April, 1952

	GD25	FN65	NM94
6-Sol Brodsky-c	39.00	117.00	295.00

SPANKY & ALFALFA & THE LITTLE RASCALS (See The Little Rascals)

SPANNER'S GALAXY
DC Comics: Dec, 1984 - No. 6, May, 1985 (limited series)

	GD25	FN65	NM94
1-6: Mandrake-c/a in all.			1.00

SPARKIE, RADIO PIXIE (Radio)(Becomes Big Jon & Sparkie #4)
Ziff-Davis Publ. Co.: Winter, 1951 - No. 3, July-Aug, 1952 (Painted-c)(Sparkie #2,3; #1?)

	GD25	FN65	NM94
1-Based on children's radio program	19.00	56.00	140.00
2,3: 3-Big Jon and Sparkie on-c only	13.00	40.00	100.00

SPARKLE COMICS
United Features Synd.: Oct-Nov, 1948 - No. 33, Dec-Jan, 1953-54

	GD25	FN65	NM94
1-Li'l Abner, Nancy, Captain & the Kids, Ella Cinders (#1-3: 52 pgs.)	12.00	36.00	90.00
2	6.50	19.50	45.00
3-10	5.70	17.00	35.00
11-20	5.00	15.00	30.00
21-33	4.00	12.00	24.00

SPARKLE PLENTY (See Harvey Comics Library #2 & Dick Tracy)

SPARKLER COMICS (1st series)
United Feature Comic Group: July, 1940 - No. 2, 1940

	GD25	FN65	NM94
1-Jim Hardy	36.00	108.00	270.00
2-Frankie Doodle	28.00	84.00	210.00

SPARKLER COMICS (2nd series)(Nancy & Sluggo #121 on)(Cover title becomes Nancy and Sluggo #101? on)
United Features Syndicate: July, 1941 - No. 120, Jan, 1955

	GD25	FN65	NM94
1-Origin 1st app. Sparkman; Tarzan (by Hogarth in all issues), Captain & the Kids, Ella Cinders, Danny Dingle, Dynamite Dunn, Nancy, Abbie & Slats, Broncho Bill, Frankie Doodle, begin; Spark Man c-1-9,11,12; Hap Hopper c-10,13	200.00	600.00	1700.00
2	71.00	212.00	600.00
3,4	55.00	166.00	470.00
5-9: 9-Spark Man's new costume	49.00	148.00	420.00
10-Origin Spark Man?	53.00	159.00	450.00
11,12-Spark Man war-c. 12-Spark Man's new costume (color change)	43.00	129.00	350.00
13-Hap Hopper war-c	40.00	120.00	320.00
14-Tarzan-c by Hogarth	46.00	138.00	390.00
15,17: 15-Capt & Kids-c. 17-Nancy & Sluggo-c	39.00	117.00	300.00
16,18-Spark Man war-c	41.00	124.00	330.00
19-1st Race Riley and the Commandos-c/s	40.00	120.00	320.00
20-Nancy war-c	39.00	117.00	310.00
21,25,28,31,34,37,39-Tarzan-c by Hogarth	40.00	120.00	320.00
22-24,26,27,29,30: 22-Race Riley & the Commandos strips begin, ends #44	31.00	94.00	235.00
32,33,35,36,38,40	17.00	52.00	125.00
41,43,45,46,48,49	13.00	38.00	95.00

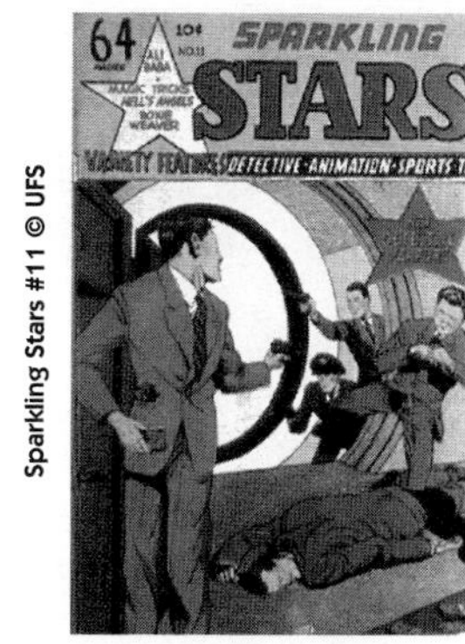

Sparkling Stars #11 © UFS

Spawn #6 © Todd McFarlane Prod.

Spawn #77 © Todd McFarlane Prod.

GD25 FN65 NM94

42,44,47,50-Tarzan-c (42,47,50 by Hogarth) 24.00 72.00 180.00
51,52,54-70: 57-Li'l Abner begins (not in #58); Fearless Fosdick app. in #58 11.00 32.00 80.00
53-Tarzan-c by Hogarth 20.00 60.00 150.00
71-80 7.15 21.50 50.00
81,82,84-86: 86 Last Tarzan; lingerie panels 6.50 19.50 45.00
83-Tarzan-c; Li'l Abner ends 9.30 28.00 70.00
87-96,98-99 5.70 17.00 40.00
97-Origin Casey Ruggles by Warren Tufts 11.00 32.00 80.00
100 7.15 21.50 50.00
101-107,109-112,114-120 4.25 13.00 28.00
108,113-Toth-a 7.15 21.50 50.00

SPARKLING LOVE
Avon Periodicals/Realistic (1953): June, 1950; 1953

1(Avon)-Kubert-a; photo-c 19.00 56.00 140.00
nn(1953)-Reprint; Kubert-a 7.50 22.50 45.00

SPARKLING STARS
Holyoke Publishing Co.: June, 1944 - No. 33, March, 1948

1-Hell's Angels, FBI, Boxie Weaver, Petey & Pop, & Ali Baba begin 14.00 42.00 105.00
2-Speed Spaulding story 9.30 28.00 65.00
3-Actual FBI case photos & war photos 6.85 21.00 48.00
4-10: 7-X-Mas-c 5.70 17.00 40.00
11-19: 13-Origin/1st app. Jungo the Man-Beast-c/s 5.70 17.00 35.00
20-Intro Fangs the Wolf Boy 5.70 17.00 40.00
21-29,32,33: 29-Bondage-c 5.70 17.00 35.00
31-Sid Greene-a 5.70 17.00 40.00

SPARK MAN (See Sparkler Comics)
Frances M. McQueeny: 1945 (36 pgs., one-shot)

1-Origin Spark Man r/Sparkler #1-3; female torture story; cover redrawn from Sparkler #1 28.00 84.00 210.00

SPARKY WATTS (Also see Big Shot Comics & Columbia Comics)
Columbia Comic Corp.: Nov?, 1942 - No. 10, 1949

1(1942)-Skyman & The Face app; Hitler-c 42.00 127.00 340.00
2(1943) 23.00 68.00 170.00
3(1944) 16.00 48.00 120.00
4(1944)-Origin 15.00 44.00 110.00
5(1947)-Skyman app.; Boody Rogers-c/a 12.00 36.00 90.00
6,7,9,10: 6(1947),10(1949) 7.85 23.50 55.00
8(1948)-Surrealistic-c 11.00 34.00 85.00

NOTE: *Boody Rogers c-1-8.*

SPARTACUS (Movie)
Dell Publishing Co.: No. 1139, Nov, 1960 (Kirk Douglas photo-c)

Four Color 1139-Buscema-a 12.00 35.00 130.00

SPARTAN: WARRIOR SPIRIT (Also see WildC.A.T.S: Covert Action Teams)
Image Comics (WildStorm Productions): July, 1995 - No. 4, Nov, 1995 ($2.50, limited series)

1-4: Kurt Busiek scripts; Mike McKone-c/a 2.50

SPAWN (Also see Curse of the Spawn)
Image Comics (Todd McFarlane Productions): May, 1992 - Present ($1.95)

1-1st app. Spawn; McFarlane-c/a begins; McFarlane/Steacy-c; 1st Todd McFarlane Productions title. 1.50 4.50 15.00
2,3: 2-1st app. Violator; McFarlane/Steacy-c 1.20 3.60 12.00
4-Contains coupon for Image Comics #0 1.20 3.60 12.00
4-With coupon missing 4.00
4-Newstand edition w/o poster or coupon 5.00
5-Cerebus cameo (1 pg.) as stuffed animal; Spawn mobile poster #1 .85 2.60 7.00
6-8,10: 7-Spawn Mobile poster #2. 8-Alan Moore scripts; Miller poster. 10-Cerebus app.; Dave Sim scripts; 1 pg. cameo app. by Superman. 2.00 6.00
9-Neil Gaiman scripts; Jim Lee poster; 1st Angela. .90 2.70 8.00
11-17,19,20,22-30: 11-Miller script; Darrow poster. 12-Bloodwulf poster by Liefeld. 14,15-Violator app. 16,17-Grant Morrison scripts; Capullo-c/a(p). 23,24-McFarlane-a/stories. 25-(10/94). 19-(10/94). 20-(11/94) 5.00
18-Grant Morrison script, Capullo-c/a(p); low distribution. 1.20 3.60 12.00
21-low distribution 1.20 3.60 12.00
31-49, 51-60: 31-1st app. The Redeemer; new costume cameo. 32-1st full app new costume. 38-40,42,44,46,48-Tony Daniel-c/a(p). 38-1st app. Cy-Gor. 40,41-Cy-Gor & Curse app. 52-Savage Dragon app. 56-w/ Darkchylde preview. 57-Cy-Gor-c/app. 3.00
50-($3.95, 48 pgs.) 4.00
61-66: 64-Polybagged w/McFarlane Toys catalog. 65-Photo-c of movie Spawn and McFarlane 3.00
67-74 2.00
75-77: 75-Spawn goes to the Greenworld 1.95
...Bible-(8/96, $1.95)-Character bios 3.50
Book 1 TPB ($9.95) r/#1-5 9.95
Book 2 TPB ($9.95) r/#6-9,11 9.95
Book 3 TPB ($9.95) r/#12-15 9.95
Book 4 TPB ($9.95) r/#16-20 9.95
Book 5 TPB ($9.95) r/#21-25 9.95
Book 6 TPB ($9.95) r/#26-30 9.95
Book 7 TPB ($9.95) r/#31-34 9.95

NOTE: ***Capullo** a-16p-18p; c-16p-18p. **Daniel** a-38-40, 42, 44, 46. **McFarlane** a-1-15; c-1-15p. **Thibert** a-16i(part). Posters come with issues 1, 4, 7-9, 11, 12. #25 was released before #19 & 20.*

SPAWN-BATMAN (Also see Batman/Spawn: War Devil under Batman: One-Shots)
Image Comics (Todd McFarlane Productions): 1994 ($3.95, one-shot)

1-Miller scripts; McFarlane-c/a 2.00 6.00

SPAWN: BLOOD FEUD
Image Comics (Todd McFarlane Productions): June, 1995 - No. 4, Sept, 1995 ($2.25, limited series)

1-4-Alan Moore scripts, Tony Daniel-a 3.50

SPAWN FAN EDITION
Image Comics (Todd McFarlane Productions): Aug, 1996 - No. 3, Oct, 1996 (Giveaway, 12 pgs.) (Polybagged w/Overstreet's FAN)

1-3: Beau Smith scripts; Brad Gorby-a(p). 1-1st app. Nordik, the Norse Hellspawn. 2-1st app. McFallon, the Dragon Master. 3-1st app. Mercy .90 2.70 7.50
1-3-(Gold): All retailer incentives 16.00
1-3-Variant-c 2.00 6.00
2-(Platinum)-Retailer incentive 25.00

SPAWN THE IMPALER
Image Comics (Todd McFarlane Productions): Oct, 1996 - No. 3, Dec, 1996 ($2.95, limited series)

1-3-Mike Grell scripts, painted-a 3.50

SPAWN/WILDC.A.T.S
Image Comics (WildStorm Productions): Jan, 1996 - No. 4, Apr, 1996 ($2.50, limited series)

1-4: Alan Moore scripts in all. 3.50

SPECIAL AGENT (Steve Saunders...)(Also see True Comics #68)
Parents' Magazine Institute (Commended Comics No. 2): Dec, 1947 - No. 8, Sept, 1949 (Based on true FBI cases)

1-J. Edgar Hoover photo on-c 9.30 28.00 70.00
2 5.70 17.00 40.00
3-8 5.00 15.00 30.00

SPECIAL COLLECTORS' EDITION (See Savage Fists of Kung-Fu)

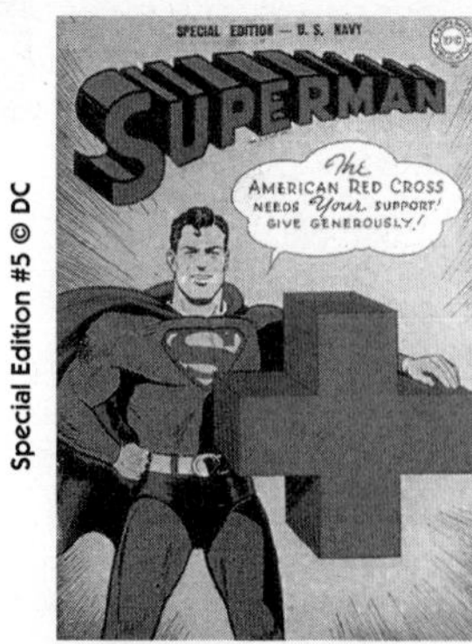

Special Edition #5 © DC

Species #4 © MGM

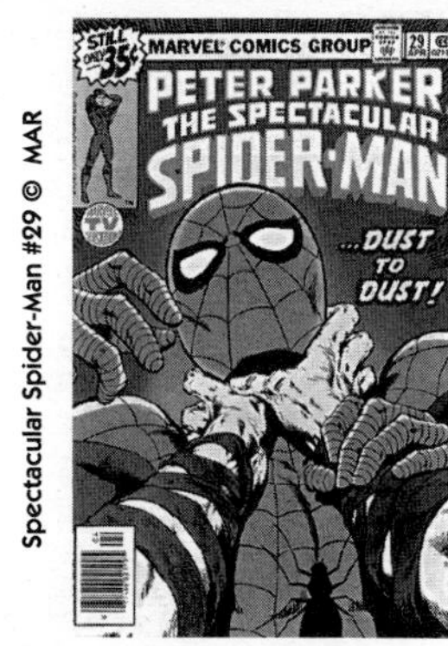

Spectacular Spider-Man #29 © MAR

GD25 FN65 NM94

SPECIAL COMICS (Becomes Hangman #2 on)
MLJ Magazines: Winter, 1941-42

1-Origin The Boy Buddies (Shield & Wizard x-over); death of The Comet; origin The Hangman retold; Hangman-c 235.00 706.00 2000.00

SPECIAL DELIVERY
Post Hall Synd.: 1951 (32 pgs.; B&W) (Giveaway)

nn-Origin of Pogo, Swamp, etc.; 2 pg. biog. on Walt Kelly (One copy sold in 1980 for $150.00)

SPECIAL EDITION (See Gorgo and Reptisaurus)

SPECIAL EDITION (U. S. Navy Giveaways)
National Periodical Publications: 1944 - 1945 (Regular comic format with wording simplified, 52 pgs.)

	GD25	FN65	NM94
1-Action (1944)-Reprints Action #80	59.00	177.00	500.00
2-Action (1944)-Reprints Action #81	59.00	177.00	500.00
3-Superman (1944)-Reprints Superman #33	59.00	177.00	500.00
4-Detective (1944)-Reprints Detective #97	62.00	185.00	525.00
5-Superman (1945)-Reprints Superman #34	59.00	177.00	500.00
6-Action (1945)-Reprints Action #84	59.00	177.00	500.00

NOTE: ***Wayne Boring** c-1, 2, 6. **Dick Sprang** c-4.*

SPECIAL EDITION COMICS
Fawcett Publications: 1940 (August) (68 pgs., one-shot)

	GD25	FN65	VF82	NM94
1-1st book devoted entirely to Captain Marvel; C.C. Beck-c/a; only app. of Capt. Marvel with belt buckle; Capt. Marvel appears with button-down flap; 1st story (came out before Captain Marvel #1)	800.00	2400.00	4800.00	8000.00

NOTE: *Prices vary widely on this book. Since this book is all Captain Marvel stories, it is actually a pre-Captain Marvel #1. There is speculation that this book almost became **Captain Marvel** #1. After **Special Edition** was published, there was an editor change at Fawcett. The new editor commissioned Kirby to do a nn **Captain Marvel** book early in 1941. This book was followed by a 2nd book several months later. This 2nd book was advertised as a #3 (making Special Edition the #1, & the nn issue the #2). However, the 2nd book did come out as a #2.*

SPECIAL EDITION: SPIDER-MAN VS. THE HULK (See listing under The Amazing Spider-Man)

SPECIAL EDITION X-MEN
Marvel Comics Group: Feb, 1983 ($2.00, one-shot, Baxter paper)

	GD25	FN65	NM94
1-r/Giant-Size X-Men #1 plus one new story	1.00	3.00	10.00

SPECIAL MARVEL EDITION (Master of Kung Fu #17 on)
Marvel Comics Group: Jan, 1971 - No. 16, Feb, 1974 (#1-4: 25¢, 68 pgs.; #5-16: 20¢, regular ed.)

	GD25	FN65	NM94
1-Thor-r by Kirby; 68 pgs.	1.80	5.40	18.00
2-4: Thor-r by Kirby; 68 pg. Giant	1.20	3.60	12.00
5-14: Sgt. Fury-r; 11-r/Sgt. Fury #13 (Capt. America)	.85	2.60	7.00
15-Master of Kung Fu (Shang-Chi) begins (1st app., 12/73); Starlin-a; origin/1st app. Nayland Smith & Dr. Petric	3.80	11.50	42.00
16-1st app. Midnight; Starlin-a (2nd Shang-Chi)	1.60	4.80	16.00

SPECIAL MISSIONS (See G.I. Joe...)

SPECIAL WAR SERIES (Attack V4#3 on?)
Charlton Comics: Aug, 1965 - No. 4, Nov, 1965

	GD25	FN65	NM94
V4#1-D-Day (also see D-Day listing)	2.50	7.50	22.00
2-Attack!	1.75	5.25	14.00
3-War & Attack (also see War & Attack)	1.75	5.25	14.00
4-Judomaster (intro/1st app.; see Sarge Steel)	4.20	12.60	42.00

SPECIES (Movie)
Dark Horse Comics: June, 1995 - No. 4, Sept, 1995 ($2.50, limited series)

1-4: Adaptation of film 2.50

SPECIES: HUMAN RACE (Movie)
Dark Horse Comics: Nov, 1996 - No. 4, Feb, 1997 ($2.95, limited series)

1-4 2.95

SPECTACULAR ADVENTURES (See Adventures)

SPECTACULAR FEATURE MAGAZINE, A (Formerly My Confessions) (Spectacular Features Magazine #12)
Fox Feature Syndicate: No. 11, April, 1950

	GD25	FN65	NM94
11 (#1)-Samson and Delilah	27.00	80.00	200.00

SPECTACULAR FEATURES MAGAZINE (Formerly A Spectacular Feature Magazine)
Fox Feature Syndicate: No. 12, June, 1950 - No. 3, Aug, 1950

	GD25	FN65	NM94
12 (#2)-Iwo Jima; photo flag-c	27.00	80.00	200.00
3-True Crime Cases From Police Files	20.00	60.00	150.00

SPECTACULAR SCARLET SPIDER
Marvel Comics: Nov, 1995 - No. 2, Dec, 1995 ($1.95, limited series)

1,2: Replaces Spectacular Spider-Man 2.00

SPECTACULAR SPIDER-MAN, THE (See Marvel Special Edition and Marvel Treasury Edition)

SPECTACULAR SPIDER-MAN, THE (Magazine)
Marvel Comics Group: July, 1968 - No. 2, Nov, 1968 (35¢)

	GD25	FN65	NM94
1-(B&W)-Romita/Mooney 52 pg. story plus updated origin story with Everett-a(i)	7.00	21.00	70.00
1-Variation w/single c-price of 40¢	8.50	25.50	85.00
2-(Color)-Green Goblin-c & 58 pg. story; Romita painted-c (story reprinted in King Size Spider-Man #9); Romita/Mooney-a	9.00	27.00	90.00

SPECTACULAR SPIDER-MAN, THE (Peter Parker...#54-132, 134)
Marvel Comics Group: Dec, 1976 - No. 263, Nov, 1998

	GD25	FN65	NM94
1-Origin recap in text; return of Tarantula	2.25	6.80	25.00
2-Kraven the Hunter app.	1.10	3.30	11.00
3-5: 3-Intro Lightmaster. 4-Vulture app.	.90	2.70	8.00
6-8-Morbius app.; 6-r/Marvel Team-Up #3 w/Morbius	1.10	3.30	11.00
9-20: 9,10-White Tiger app. 11-Last 30¢-c. 17,18-Angel & Iceman app. (from Champions); Ghost Rider cameo in flashback		2.00	6.00
21,24-26: 21-Scorpion app. 26-Daredevil app.			5.00
22,23-Moon Knight app.	.85	2.60	7.00
27-Miller's 1st art on Daredevil (2/79); also see Captain America #235	1.20	3.60	12.00
28-Miller Daredevil (p)	.90	2.70	9.00
29-55,57,59: 33-Origin Iguana. 38-Morbius app.			5.00
56-2nd app. Jack O'Lantern (Macendale) & 1st Spidey/Jack O'Lantern battle (7/81)		2.00	6.00
58-Byrne-a(p)			5.00
60-Double size; origin retold with new facts revealed		2.00	6.00
61-63,65-68,71-74: 65-Kraven the Hunter app.			4.00
64-1st app. Cloak & Dagger (3/82)	.85	2.60	7.00
69,70-Cloak & Dagger app.			5.00
75-Double size			5.00
76-80: 78,79-Punisher cameo			4.00
81,82-Punisher, Cloak & Dagger app.			4.00
83-Origin Punisher retold (10/83)	.85	2.60	7.00
84,86-99: 90-Spider-man's new black costume, last panel(ties w/Amazing Spider-Man #252 & Marvel Team-Up #141 for 1st app.). 94-96-Cloak & Dagger app. 98-Intro The Spot			3.00
85-Hobgoblin (Ned Leeds) app. (12/83); gains powers of original Green Goblin (see Amazing Spider-Man #238)	.85	2.60	7.00
100-(3/85)-Double size			5.00
101-115,117,118,120-129: 107-110-Death of Jean DeWolff. 111-Secret Wars II tie-in. 128-Black Cat new costume			2.50
116,119-Sabretooth-c/story			4.50
130-Hobgoblin app.			5.00
131-Six part Kraven tie-in			5.00
132-Kraven tie-in			5.00

Spectacular Spider-Man #214 © MAR

Spectacular Spider-Man #263 © MEG

The Spectre #62 (3rd Series) © DC

GD25 FN65 NM94

133-139: 138-1st full app. Tombstone (origin #139) 2.00
140-Punisher cameo app. 2.00
141-Punisher app. 3.00
142,143-Punisher app. 3.00
144-146,148-157: 151-Tombstone returns 2.25
147-1st app. new Hobgoblin (Macendale) in 1 pg. cameo; continued in Web of Spider-Man #48 1.00 3.00 10.00
158-Spider-Man gets new powers (1st Cosmic Spidey, cont'd in Web of Spider-Man #59) 5.00
159-Cosmic Spider-Man app. 4.00
160-170: 161-163-Hobgoblin app. 168-170-Avengers x-over. 169-1st app. The Outlaws 2.00
171-184: 180,181,183,184-Green Goblin app. 1.50
185-188,190-199: 197-199-Original X-Men-c/story 1.50
189-($2.95, 52 pgs.)-Silver hologram on-c; battles Green Goblin; origin Spidey retold; Vess poster w/Spidey & Hobgoblin 4.00
189-(2nd printing)-Gold hologram on-c 3.00
195-(Deluxe ed.)-Polybagged w/audio cassette 3.00
200-($2.95)-Holo-grafx foil-c; Green Goblin-c/story 3.00
201-211: 203-Maximum Carnage x-over. 204-Begin 4 part death of Tombstone story. 207,208-The Shroud-c/story. 208-Siege of Darkness x-over (#207 is a tie-in). 209-Black Cat back-up 1.50
212-219,221,222,224,226-228,230-247,-1(7/97): 212-Begin $1.50-c; w/card sheet. 215,216-Scorpion app. 217-Power & Responsibility Pt. 4. 231-Return of Kaine; Spider-Man corpse discovered. 232-New Doc Octopus app. 233-Carnage-c/app. 235-Dragon Man cameo. 236-Dragon Man-c/app; Lizard app.; Peter Parker regains powers. 238,239-Lizard app. 239-w/card insert. 240-Revelations storyline begins. -1-Flashback 1.50
213-Collectors ed. polybagged w/16 pg. preview & animation cel; foil-c; 1st meeting Spidey & Typhoid Mary 3.00
213-Version polybagged w/Gamepro #7; no-c date, price 1.50
217 ($2.95)-Deluxe edition foil-c: flip book 3.00
219-($2.95)-Deluxe edition foil-c; flip book 3.00
220 ($2.25, 52 pgs.)-Flip book, Mary Jane reveals pregnancy 3.00
223 ($2.50) 2.50
223 ($2.95)-Die Cut-c 3.00
225 ($3.95)-Direct Market Holodisk-c (Green Goblin) 4.00
225 ($2.95)-Newsstand-Green Goblin 3.00
229 ($3.95)-Acetate-c, Spidey quits 4.00
229 ($2.50)-Spidey quits 2.50
240-Variant-c 3.00
248,249,251-254,256: 248-Begin $1.99-c. 249-Return of Norman Osborne 256-1st app. Prodigy 2.00
250-($3.25) Double gatefold-c 3.25
255-($2.99) Spiderhunt pt. 4 3.00
257-262: 257-Double cover with "Spectacular Prodigy #1"; battles Jack O'Lantern. 258-Spidey is cleared. 259,260-Green Goblin & Hobgoblin app. 262-Byrne-s 2.00
263-Final issue; Byrne-c; Aunt May returns 2.00
Annual 1 (1979)-Doc Octopus-c & 46 pg. story .85 2.60 7.00
Annual 2 (1980)-Origin/1st app. Rapier 4.00
Annual 3-7: 3(1981)-Last Man-Wolf. 4(1984). 5(1985). 6(10/86). 7(1987) 3.00
Annual 8 (1988,$ 1.75)-Evolutionary War x-over; Daydreamer returns Gwen Stacy "clone" back to real self (not Gwen Stacy) 4.00
Annual 9 (1989, $2.00, 68 pgs.)-Atlantis Attacks 3.00
Annual 10 (1990, $2.00, 68 pgs.)-McFarlane-a 2.50
Annual 11 (1991, $2.00, 68 pgs.)-Iron Man app. 2.00
Annual 12 (1992, $2.25, 68 pgs.)-Venom solo story cont'd from Amazing Spider-Man Annual #26 2.25
Annual 13 (1993, $2.95, 68 pgs.)-Polybagged w/trading card; John Romita, Sr. back-up-a 3.00
Annual 14 (1994, $2.95) 3.00
Special 1 (1995, $3.95)-Flip book 4.00

NOTE: ***Austin*** *c-21i, Annual 11i.* ***Buckler*** *a-103, 107-111, 116, 117, 119, 122, Annual 1, Annual 10; c-103, 107-111, 113, 116-119, 122, Annual 1.* ***Buscema*** *a-121.* ***Byrne*** *c(p)-17, 43, 58, 101, 102.* ***Giffen*** *a-120p.* ***Hembeck*** *c/a-86p.* ***Larsen*** *c-Annual 11p.* ***Miller*** *c-46p, 48p, 50, 51p, 52p, 54p, 55, 56p, 57, 60.* ***Mooney*** *a-7i, 11i, 21p, 23p, 25p, 26p, 29-34p, 36p, 37p, 39i, 41, 42i, 49p, 50i, 51i, 53p, 54-57i, 59-66i, 68i, 71i, 73-79i, 81-83i, 85i, 87-99i, 102i, 125p, Annual 1i, 2p.* ***Nasser*** *c-37p.* ***Perez*** *c-10.* ***Simonson*** *c-54i.* ***Zeck*** *a-118, 131, 132; c-131, 132.*

SPECTACULAR STORIES MAGAZINE (Formerly A Star Presentation)
Fox Feature Syndicate (Hero Books): No. 4, July, 1950 - No. 3, Sept, 1950

4-Sherlock Holmes (true crime stories) 35.00 104.00 260.00
3-The St. Valentine's Day Massacre (true crime) 23.00 68.00 170.00

SPECTRE, THE (1st Series) (See Adventure Comics #431-440, More Fun & Showcase)
National Periodical Publ.: Nov-Dec, 1967 - No. 10, May-June, 1969 (All 12¢)

1-(11-12/67)-Anderson-c/a 9.00 27.00 90.00
2-5-Neal Adams-c/a; 3-Wildcat x-over 6.50 19.50 65.00
6-8,10: 6-8-Anderson inks. 7-Hourman app. 4.00 12.00 40.00
9-Wrightson-a 5.00 15.00 50.00

SPECTRE, THE (2nd Series) (See Saga of the Swamp Thing #58, Showcase '95 #8 & Wrath of the...)
DC Comics: Apr, 1987 - No. 31, Oct, 1989 ($1.00, new format)

1-31: 1-Colan-a begins. 9-Nudity panels. 10-Batman cameo. 10,11-Millenium tie-ins 1.50
Annual 1 (1988, $2.00)-Deadman app. 2.25

NOTE: ***Art Adams*** *c-Annual 1.* ***Colan*** *a-1-6.* ***Kaluta*** *c-1-3.* ***Mignola*** *c-7-9.* ***Morrow*** *a-9-15.* ***Sears*** *c/a-22.* ***Vess*** *c-13-15.*

SPECTRE, THE (3rd Series) (Also see Brave and the Bold #72, 75, 116, 180, 199 & Showcase '95 #8)
DC Comics: Dec, 1992 - No. 62, Feb, 1998 ($1.75/$1.95/$2.25/$2.50)

1-($1.95)-Glow-in-the-dark-c; Mandrake-a begins 4.00
2,3 3.00
4-7,9-12,14-20: 10-Kaluta-c. 11-Hildebrandt painted-c. 16-Aparo/K. Jones-a. 20-Sienkiewicz-c 2.00
8,13-($2.50)-Glow-in-the-dark-c 2.50
21,22: 21-Begin $1.95-c. 22-(9/94)-Superman-c & app. 2.00
0,23-29: 0-(10/94). 23-(11/94) 2.00
30-48: 30-Begin-$2.25-c. 43-Kent Williams-c. 44-Kaluta-c. 47-Final Night x-over 2.25
49-62: 49-Begin-$2.50-c.; Bolton-c. 51-Batman-c/app. 52-Gianni-c. 54-Corben-c. 60-Harris-c 2.50
Annual 1 (1995, $3.95)-Year One story 4.00

NOTE: ***Bisley*** *c-27.* ***Fabry*** *c-2.* ***Kelley Jones*** *c-31.* ***Vess*** *c-5.*

SPEEDBALL (See Amazing Spider-Man Annual #12, Marvel Super-Heroes & The New Warriors)
Marvel Comics: Sept, 1988(10/88-inside) - No. 11, July, 1989 (75¢)

1-11: Ditko/Guice a-1-4, c-1; Ditko a-1-10; c-1-11p 1.00

SPEED BUGGY (TV)(Also see Fun-In #12, 15)
Charlton Comics: July, 1975 - No. 9, Nov, 1976 (Hanna-Barbera)

1 1.80 5.40 18.00
2-9 1.20 3.60 12.00

SPEED CARTER SPACEMAN (See Spaceman)

SPEED COMICS (New Speed)(Also see Double Up)
Brookwood Publ./Speed Publ./Harvey Publications No. 14 on:
10/39 - #11, 8/40; #12, 3/41 - #44, 1-2/47 (#14-16: pocket size, 100 pgs.)

1-Origin & 1st app. Shock Gibson; Ted Parrish, the Man with 1000 Faces begins; Powell-a; becomes Champion #2 on? 267.00 800.00 2400.00
2-Powell-a 91.00 273.00 775.00
3 53.00 159.00 450.00
4,5: 4-Powell-a?5-Dinosaur-c 44.00 132.00 375.00
6-11: 7-Mars Mason begins, ends #11 41.00 122.00 325.00
12 (3/41; shows #11 in indicia)-The Wasp begins; Major Colt app. (Capt. Colt #12) 44.00 132.00 375.00
13-Intro. Captain Freedom & Young Defenders; Girl Commandos, Pat Parker

Speed Force #1 © DC

Spellbound #13 © ACI

Spider-Girl #1 © MAR

GD25 FN65 NM94

(costumed heroine), War Nurse begins; Major Colt app. 50.00 150.00 425.00
14-16 (100 pg. pocket size, 1941): 14-2nd Harvey comic (See Pocket); Shock Gibson dons new costume. 15-Pat Parker dons costume, last in costume #23; no Girl Commandos 53.00 159.00 450.00
17-Black Cat begins (4/42, early app.; see Pocket #1); origin Black Cat-r/ Pocket #1; not in #40,41; S&K-c 62.00 185.00 525.00
18-20-S&K-c 44.00 132.00 375.00
21,22-Kirby-c. 21-Hitler, Tojo-c 44.00 132.00 375.00
23-Origin Girl Commandos; Kirby-c 47.00 141.00 400.00
24-Pat Parker team-up with Girl Commandos; Hitler, Tojo, & Mussolini-c 35.00 104.00 260.00
25-30: 26-Flag-c 36.00 108.00 270.00
31-Schomburg Hitler & Hirohito-c 43.00 129.00 360.00
32-36-Schomburg-c 42.00 127.00 340.00
37,39-42, 44 36.00 108.00 270.00
38-Iwo-Jima Flag-c 39.00 116.00 290.00
43-Robot-c 39.00 117.00 310.00

NOTE: ***Al Avison*** *c-14-16, 30, 43.* ***Briefer*** *a-6, 7.* ***Jon Henri*** *(Kirbyesque) c-17-20.* ***Kubert*** *a-7-11(Mars Mason), 37, 38, 42-44.* ***Kirby/Caseneuve*** *c-21-23.* ***Palais*** *c-37, 39-42.* ***Powell*** *a-1, 2, 4-7, 28, 31, 44.* ***Schomburg*** *c-31-36.* ***Tuska*** *a-3, 6, 7. Bondage c-18, 35. Captain Freedom c-16-24, 25(part), 26-44(w/Black Cat #27, 29, 31, 32-40). Shock Gibson c-1-15.*

SPEED DEMON (Also see Marvel Versus DC #3 & DC Versus Marvel #4)
Marvel Comics (Amalgam): Apr, 1996 ($1.95, one-shot)

1 2.00

SPEED DEMONS (Formerly Frank Merriwell at Yale #1-4?; Submarine Attack #11 on)
Charlton Comics: No. 5, Feb, 1957 - No. 10, 1958

5-10 5.00 15.00 30.00

SPEED FORCE (See The Flash 2nd Series #143-Cobalt Blue)
DC Comics: Nov, 1997 ($3.95, one-shot)

1-Flash & Kid Flash vs. Cobalt Blue; Waid-s/Aparo & Sienkiewicz-a; Flash family stories and pin-ups by various 5.00

SPEED RACER (Also see The New Adventures of...)
Now Comics: July, 1987 - No. 38, Nov, 1990 ($1.75)

1-38, 1-2nd printing 2.00
Special 1 (1988, $2.00) 2.00
Special 2 (1988, $3.50) 3.50

SPEED RACER FEATURING NINJA HIGH SCHOOL
Now Comics: Aug, 1993 - No. 2, 1993 ($2.50, mini-series)

1,2: 1-Polybagged w/card. 2-Exists? 2.50

SPEED RACER: RETURN OF THE GRX
Now Comics: Mar, 1994 - No. 2, Apr, 1994 ($1.95, limited series)

1,2 2.25

SPEED SMITH-THE HOT ROD KING (Also see Hot Rod King)
Ziff-Davis Publishing Co.: Spring, 1952

1-Saunders painted-c 20.00 60.00 150.00

SPEEDY GONZALES
Dell Publishing Co.: No. 1084, Mar, 1960

Four Color 1084 3.65 11.00 40.00

SPEEDY RABBIT (See Television Puppet Show)
Realistic/I. W. Enterprises/Super Comics: nd (1953); 1963

nn (1953)-Realistic Reprint? 2.40 6.00 12.00
I.W. Reprint #1 (2 versions w/diff. c/stories exist)-Peter Cottontail #? 1.00 2.80 7.00
Super Reprint #14(1963) 1.00 2.80 7.00

SPELLBINDERS
Quality: Dec, 1986 - No. 12, Jan, 1988 ($1.25)

1-12: Nemesis the Warlock, Amadeus Wolf 1.25

GD25 FN65 NM94

SPELLBOUND (See The Crusaders)

SPELLBOUND (Tales to Hold You... #1, Stories to Hold You...)
Atlas Comics (ACI 1-15/Male 16-23/BPC 24-34): Mar, 1952 - #23, June, 1954; #24, Oct, 1955 - #34, June, 1957

1-Horror/weird stories in all 53.00 159.00 450.00
2-Edgar A. Poe app. 32.00 96.00 240.00
3-5: 3-Whitney-a; cannibalism story 27.00 80.00 200.00
6-Krigstein-a 27.00 80.00 200.00
7-10: 8-Ayers-a 22.00 66.00 165.00
11-16,18-20: 14-Ed Win-a 18.00 54.00 135.00
17-Krigstein-a 19.00 58.00 145.00
21-23: 23-Last precode (6/54) 16.00 48.00 120.00
24-28,30,31,34: 25-Orlando-a 14.00 42.00 105.00
29-Ditko-a (4 pgs.) 16.00 48.00 120.00
32,33-Torres-a 14.00 42.00 105.00

NOTE: ***Brodsky*** *a-5; c-1, 5-7, 10, 11, 13, 15, 25-27, 32.* ***Colan*** *a-17.* ***Everett*** *a-2, 5, 7, 10, 16, 28, 31; c-2, 8, 9, 14, 17-19, 28, 30.* ***Forgione/Abel*** *a-29.* ***Forte/Fox*** *a-16.* ***Al Hartley*** *a-2.* ***Heath*** *a-2, 4, 8, 9, 12, 14, 16; c-3, 4, 12, 16, 20, 21.* ***Infantino*** *a-15.* ***Keller*** *a-5.* ***Kida*** *a-2, 14.* ***Maneely*** *a-7, 14, 27; c-24, 29, 31.* ***Mooney*** *a-5, 13, 18.* ***Mac Pakula*** *a-22, 32.* ***Post*** *a-8.* ***Powell*** *a-19, 20, 32.* ***Robinson*** *a-1.* ***Romita*** *a-24, 26, 27.* ***R.Q. Sale*** *a-29.* ***Sekowsky*** *a-5.* ***Severin*** *c-29.* ***Sinnott*** *a-8, 16, 17.*

SPELLBOUND
Marvel Comics: Jan, 1988 - Apr, 1988 ($1.50, bi-weekly, Baxter paper)

1-5 1.50
6 ($2.25, 52 pgs.) 2.25

SPELLJAMMER (Also see TSR Worlds Comics Annual)
DC Comics: Sept, 1990 - No. 15, Nov, 1991 ($1.75)

1-15: Based on TSR game. 11-Heck-a. 1.80

SPENCER SPOOK (Formerly Giggle Comics; see Adventures of...)
American Comics Group: No. 100, Mar-Apr, 1955 - No. 101, May-June, 1955

100,101 5.70 17.00 36.00

SPIDER, THE
Eclipse Books: 1991 - Book 3, 1991 ($4.95, 52 pgs., limited series)

Book 1-3-Truman-c/a 5.00

SPIDER-BOY (Also see Marvel Versus DC #3)
Marvel Comics (Amalgam): Apr, 1996 ($1.95)

1-Mike Wieringo-c/a; Karl Kesel story; 1st app. of Bizarnage, Insect Queen, Challengers of the Fantastic, Sue Storm: Agent of S.H.I.E.L. D., & King Lizard. 2.00

SPIDER-BOY TEAM-UP
Marvel Comics (Amalgam): June, 1997 ($1.95, one-shot)

1-Karl Kesel & Roger Stern-s/Jo Ladronn-a(p) 1.95

SPIDER-GIRL (See What If #105)
Marvel Comics: Oct, 1998 - Present ($1.99)

0-($2.99)-r/1st app. Peter Parker's daughter from What If #105; previews reg. series, Avengers-Next and J2 4.00
1-DeFalco-s/Olliffe & Williamson-s 5.00
2-5: 2-Two covers. 3-Fantastic Five-c/app. 1.99

SPIDER-MAN (See Amazing..., Giant-Size..., Marvel Tales, Marvel Team-Up, Spectacular..., Spidey Super Stories, Venom, & Web Of...)

SPIDER-MAN
Marvel Comics: Aug, 1990 - No. 98, Nov, 1998 ($1.75/$1.95/ $1.99)

1-Silver edition, direct sale only (unbagged) 5.00
1-Silver bagged edition; direct sale, no price on comic, but $2.00 on plastic bag (125,000 print run) 15.00
1-Regular edition w/Spidey face in UPC area (unbagged); green-c 5.00
1-Regular bagged edition w/Spidey face in UPC area; green cover (125,000) 10.00
1-Newsstand bagged w/UPC code 8.00

Spider-Man #48 © MAR

Spider-Man #98 © MAR

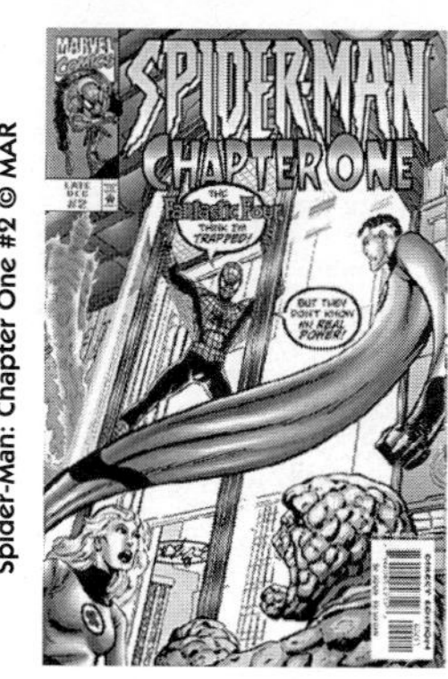

Spider-Man: Chapter One #2 © MAR

GD25 FN65 NM94

1-Gold edition, 2nd printing (unbagged) with Spider-Man in box (400,000-450,000) 5.00
1-Gold 2nd printing w/UPC code; sold in Wal-Mart; not scarce 5.00
1-Platinum ed. mailed to retailers only (10,000 print run); has new McFarlane-a & editorial material instead of ads; stiff-c, no cover price 150.00
2-McFarlane-c/a/scripts continue 4.00
3-5 3.00
6,7-Ghost Rider & Hobgoblin app. 4.00
8-12: 8-Wolverine cameo; Wolverine storyline begins. 12-Wolverine storyline ends 4.00
13-Spidey's black costume returns; Morbius app. 4.00
14,15: 14-Morbius app. 15-Erik Larsen-c/a; Beast c/s 4.00
16,17: 16-X-Force-c/story w/Liefeld assists; continues in X-Force #4; reads sideways; last McFarlane issue. 17-Thanos-c/story; Leonardi/Williamson-c/a 4.00
18-23,25: 13,14-Spidey in black costume. 18-Ghost Rider-c/story. 18-23-Sinister Six storyline w/Erik Larsen-c/a/scripts. 19-Hulk & Hobgoblin-c & app. 20-22-Deathlok app. 22,23-Ghost Rider, Hulk, Hobgoblin app. 23-Wrap-around gatefold-c. 24-Infinity War x-over w/Demogoblin & Hobgoblin-c/story 4.00
24-Demogoblin dons new costume & battles Hobgoblin-c/story 4.00
26-($3.50, 52 pgs.)-Silver hologram on-c w/gatefold poster by Ron Lim; Spidey retells his origin 4.00
26-2nd printing; gold hologram on-c 4.00
27-45: 32-34-Punisher-c/story. 37-Maximum Carnage x-over. 39,40-Electro-c/s (cameo #38). 41-43-Iron Fist-c/stories w/Jae Lee-c/a. 42-Intro Platoon. 44-Hobgoblin app 1.75
46-49,51-53, 55, 56,58-74,76-81 -1(7/97): 46-Begin $1.95-c; bound-in card sheet. 51-Power & Responsibility Pt. 3. 52,53-Venom app. 60-Kaine revealed. 61-Origin Kaine. 65-Mysterio app. 66-Kaine-c/app.; Peter Parker app. 67-Carnage-c/app. 68,69-Hobgoblin-c/app. 72-Onslaught x-over; Spidey vs. Sentinels. 74-Daredevil-c/app. 77-80-Morbius-c/app. 2.25
46-($2.95)-Polybagged; silver ink-c w/16 pg. preview of cartoon series & animation style print; bound-in trading card sheet 3.00
50-($2.50)-Newsstand edition 2.50
50-($3.95)-Collectors edition w/holographic-c 4.00
51-($2.95)-Deluxe edition foil-c; flip book 3.00
54 ($2.75, 52 pgs.)-Flip book 2.75
57 ($2.50) 2.50
57 ($2.95)-Die cut-c 3.00
65-($2.95)-Variant-c; polybagged w/cassette 3.00
75-($2.95)-Wraparound-c; return of the Green Goblin; death of Ben Reilly (who was the clone) 4.00
82-90: 82-Begin $1.99-c. 84-Juggernaut app. 2.00
91-97: 91-Double cover with "Dusk #1"; battles the Shocker. 93-Ghost Rider app. 2.00
98-Double cover; final issue 2.00
Annual '97 ($2.99) 3.00
Annual '98 ($2.99)-Devil Dinosaur-c/app. 3.00
Giant-Sized Spider-Man (12/98, $3.99) r/team-ups 4.00
Super Special (7/95, $3.95)-Planet of the Symbiotes 4.00
...: Carnage nn (6/93, $6.95, TPB)-r/Amazing S-M #344,345,359-363; spot varnish-c 7.00
.../Dr. Strange: "The Way to Dusty Death" nn (1992, $6.95, 68 pgs.) 7.00
.../Elektra '98-($2.99) vs. The Silencer 3.00
...Revelations ('97, $14.99, TPB) r/end of Clone Saga plus 14 new pages by Romita Jr. 14.99
Special Edition 1 (12/92-c, 11/92 inside)-The Trial of Venom; ordered thru mail with $5.00 donation or more to UNICEF; embossed metallic ink; came bagged w/bound-in poster; Daredevil app. 1.00 3.00 10.00
...Vs. Venom nn (1990, $8.95, TPB)-r/Amaz. S-M #300,315-317 w/new McFarlane-c 9.00
NOTE: ***Erik Larsen*** *c/a-15, 18-23.* ***M. Rogers/Keith Williams*** *c/a-27, 28.*

GD25 FN65 NM94

SPIDER-MAN ADVENTURES
Marvel Comics: Dec, 1994 - No. 15, Mar, 1996 ($1.50)
1-15 ($1.50)-Based on animated series 1.50
1-($2.95)-Foil embossed-c 3.00

SPIDER-MAN AND BATMAN
Marvel Comics: 1995 ($5.95, one-shot)
nn-DeMatteis-s; Joker, Carnage app. 2.00 6.00

SPIDER-MAN AND DAREDEVIL
Marvel Comics Group: Mar, 1984 ($2.00, one-shot, deluxe paper)
1-r/Spectacular Spider-Man #26-28 by Miller 3.00

SPIDER-MAN AND HIS AMAZING FRIENDS (See Marvel Action Universe)
Marvel Comics Group: Dec, 1981 (one-shot)
1-Adapted from NBC TV cartoon show; Green Goblin-c/story; 1st Spidey, Firestar, Iceman team-up; Spiegle-p 3.00

SPIDER-MAN AND THE INCREDIBLE HULK (See listing under Amazing...)

SPIDER-MAN AND THE UNCANNY X-MEN
Marvel Comics: Mar, 1996 ($16.95, trade paperback)
nn-r/Uncanny X-Men #27, Uncanny X-men #35, Amazing Spider-Man #92, Marvel Team-Up Annual #1, Marvel Team-Up #150, & Spectacular Spider-Man #197-199 17.00

SPIDER-MAN AND X-FACTOR
Marvel Comics: May, 1994 - No. 3, July, 1994 ($1.95, limited series)
1-3 2.00

SPIDER-MAN /BADROCK
Maximum Press: Mar, 1997 ($2.99, mini-series)
1A, 1B(#2)-Jurgens-s 3.00

SPIDER-MAN: CHAPTER ONE
Marvel Comics: Dec, 1998 - No. 13, ($2.50, limited series)
1-Retelling/updating of origin; John Byrne-s/c/a 2.50
1-($6.95) DF Edition w/variant-c by Jae Lee 6.95
2-4: 2-Two covers (one is swipe of ASM #1); Fantastic Four app. 2.50

SPIDER-MAN CLASSICS
Marvel Comics: Apr, 1993 - No. 16, July, 1994 ($1.25)
1-14,16: 1-r/Amaz. Fantasy #15 & Strange Tales #115. 2-16-r/Amaz. Spider-Man #1-15. 6-Austin-c(i) 1.25
15-($2.95)-Polybagged w/16 pg. insert & animation style print; r/Amazing S-M #14 (1st Green Goblin) 3.00

SPIDER-MAN COLLECTOR'S PREVIEW
Marvel Comics: Dec, 1994 ($1.50, 100 pgs., one-shot)
1-wraparound-c; no comics 1.50

SPIDER-MAN COMICS MAGAZINE
Marvel Comics Group: Jan, 1987 - No. 13, 1988 ($1.50, digest-size)
1-13-Reprints 1.50

SPIDER-MAN: DEAD MAN'S HAND
Marvel Comics: Apr, 1997 ($2.99, one-shot)
1 3.00

SPIDER-MAN: FRIENDS AND ENEMIES
Marvel Comics: Jan, 1995 - No. 4, Apr, 1995 ($1.95, limited series)
1-4-Darkhawk, Nova & Speedball app. 2.00

SPIDER-MAN: FUNERAL FOR AN OCTOPUS
Marvel Comics: Mar, 1995 - No. 3, May, 1995 ($1.50, limited series)
1-3 1.50

SPIDER-MAN/ GEN 13
Marvel Comics: Nov, 1996 ($4.95, one-shot)

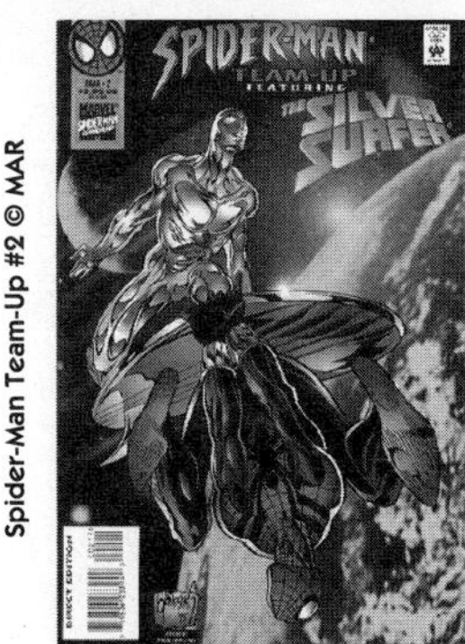

Spider-Man Team-Up #2 © MAR

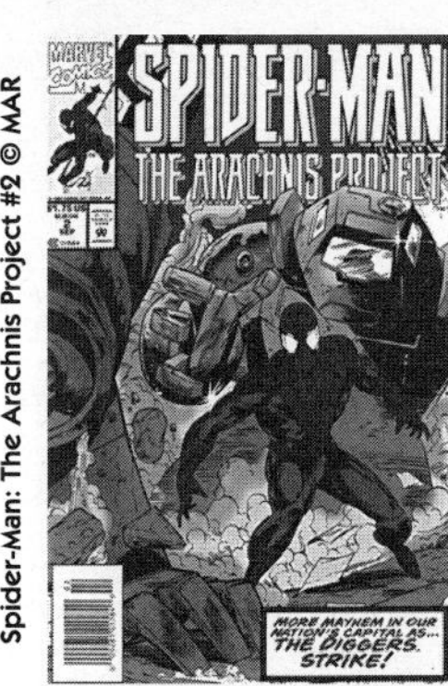

Spider-Man: The Arachnis Project #2 © MAR

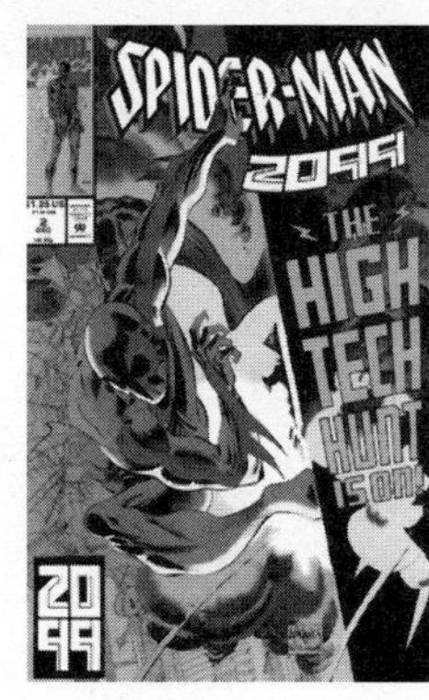

Spider-Man 2099 #2 © MAR

GD25 FN65 NM94

nn-Peter David-s/Stuart Immonen-a 5.00

SPIDER-MAN: HOBGOBLIN LIVES
Marvel Comics: Jan, 1997 - No. 3, Mar, 1997 ($2.50, limited series)

1-3-Wraparound-c 2.50
TPB (1/98, $14.99) r/#1-3 plus timeline 15.00

SPIDER-MAN: HOT SHOTS
Marvel Comics: Jan, 1996 ($2.95, one-shot)

nn-fold out posters by various, inc. Vess and Ross 3.00

SPIDER-MAN: LEGACY OF EVIL
Marvel Comics: June, 1996 ($3.95, one-shot)

1-Kurt Busiek script & Mark Texeira-c/a 4.00

SPIDER-MAN: MADE MEN
Marvel Comics: Aug, 1998 ($5.99, one-shot)

1-Spider-Man & Daredevil vs. Kingpin 6.00

SPIDER-MAN MAGAZINE
Marvel Comics: 1994 - No. 3, 1994 ($1.95, magazine)

1-Contains 4 S-M promo cards & 4 X-Men Ultra Fleer cards; Spider-Man story by Romita, Sr.; X-Men story; puzzles & games 2.00
2,3: 2-Doc Octopus & X-Men stories 2.00

SPIDER-MAN: MAXIMUM CLONAGE
Marvel Comics: 1995 ($4.95)

Alpha #1-Acetate-c. 5.00
Omega #1-Chromium-c. 5.00

SPIDER-MAN MEGAZINE
Marvel Comics: Oct, 1994 - No. 6, Mar, 1995 ($2.95, 100 pgs.)

1-6: 1-r/ASM #16,224,225, Marvel Team-Up #1 3.00

SPIDER-MAN: POWER OF TERROR
Marvel Comics: Jan, 1995 - No. 4, Apr, 1995 ($1.95, limited series)

1-4-Silvermane & Deathlok app. 2.00

SPIDER-MAN/PUNISHER: FAMILY PLOT
Marvel Comics: Feb, 1996 - No. 2, Mar, 1996 ($2.95, limited series)

1,2 3.00

SPIDER-MAN: REDEMPTION
Marvel Comics: Sept, 1996 - No. 4, Dec, 1996 ($1.50, limited series)

1-4: Dematteis scripts; Zeck-a 1.50

SPIDER-MAN SAGA
Marvel Comics: Nov, 1991 - No. 4, Feb, 1992 ($2.95, limited series)

1-4: Gives history of Spider-Man: text & illustrations 3.00

SPIDER-MAN TEAM-UP
Marvel Comics: Dec, 1995 - No. 7, June, 1996 ($2.95)

1-7: 1-w/ X-Men. 2-w/ Silver Surfer. 3-w/Fantastic Four. 4-w/Avengers. 5-Gambit & Howard the Duck-c/app. 7-Thunderbolts-c/app. 3.00

SPIDER-MAN: THE ARACHNIS PROJECT
Marvel Comics: Aug, 1994 - No. 6, Jan, 1995 ($1.75, limited series)

1-6-Venom, Styx, Stone & Jury app. 1.75

SPIDER-MAN: THE CLONE JOURNAL
Marvel Comics: Mar, 1995 ($2.95, one-shot)

1 3.00

SPIDER-MAN: THE FINAL ADVENTURE
Marvel Comics: Nov, 1995 - No. 4, Feb, 1996 ($2.95, limited series)

1-4: 1-Nicieza scripts; foil-c 3.00

SPIDER-MAN: THE JACKAL FILES
Marvel Comics: Aug, 1995 ($1.95, one-shot)

1 2.00

GD25 FN65 NM94

SPIDER-MAN: THE LOST YEARS
Marvel Comics: Aug, 1995-No. 3, Oct, 1995; No. 0, 1996 ($2.95/$3.95,lim. series)

0-(1/96, $3.95)-Reprints. 4.00
1-3-DeMatteis scripts, Romita, Jr.-c/a 3.00
NOTE: ***Romita*** *c-0i.* ***Romita, Jr.*** *a-0r, 1-3p. c-0-3p.* ***Sharp*** *a-0r.*

SPIDER-MAN: THE MANGA
Marvel Comics: Dec, 1997 - Present ($3.99/$2.99, B&W, bi-weekly)

1-($3.99)-English translation of Japanese Spider-Man 4.00
2-24-($2.99) 2.99

SPIDER-MAN: THE MUTANT AGENDA
Marvel Comics: No. 0, Feb, 1994; No. 1, Mar, 1994 - No. 3, May, 1994 ($1.75, limited series)

0-(2/94, $1.25, 52 pgs.)-Crosses over w/newspaper strip; has empty pages to paste in newspaper strips; gives origin of Spidey 1.25
1-3: Beast & Hobgoblin app. 1-X-Men app. 1.75

SPIDER-MAN: THE PARKER YEARS
Marvel Comics: Nov, 1995 ($2.50, one-shot)

1 2.50

SPIDER-MAN 2099 (See Amazing Spider-Man #365)
Marvel Comics: Nov, 1992 - No. 46, Aug, 1996 ($1.25/$1.50/$1.95)

1-($1.75, stiff-c)-Red foil stamped-c; begins origin of Miguel O'Hara (Spider-Man 2099); Leonardi/Williamson-c/a begins 2.00
1-2nd printing ($1.75) 1.50
2-Origin continued, ends #3 1.50
3,4: 4-Doom 2099 app. 1.50
5-18: 13-Extra 16 pg. insert on Midnight Sons 1.25
19-24,26-31: 19-Begin$ 1.50-c; bound-in trading card sheet 1.50
25-($2.25, 52 pgs.)-Newsstand edition 2.25
25-($2.95, 52 pgs.)-Deluxe edition w/embossed foil-c 3.00
32-46: 32-Begin $1.95-c. 35-variant-c. 36-two-c; Jae Lee-a. 37,38-two-c. 46-The Vulture app; Mike McKone-a(p). 2.00
Annual 1 (1994, $2.95, 68 pgs.) 3.00
Special 1 (1995, $3.95) 4.00
NOTE: ***Chaykin*** *c-37.* ***Ron Lim*** *a(p)-18; c(p)-13, 16, 18.* ***Kelley Jones*** *c/a-9.* ***Leonardi/Williamson*** *a-1-8, 10-13, 15-17, 19, 20, 22-25; c-1-13, 15, 17-19, 20, 22-25, 35.*

SPIDER-MAN 2099 MEETS SPIDER-MAN
Marvel Comics: 1995 ($5.95, one-shot)

nn-Peter David script; Leonardi/Williamson-c/a. 2.00 6.00

SPIDER-MAN UNLIMITED
Marvel Comics: May, 1993 - No. 22, Nov, 1998 ($3.95, quarterly, 68 pgs.)

1-Begin Maximum Carnage storyline, ends; Carnage-c/story 5.00
2-12: 2-Venom & Carnage-c/story; Ron Lim-c/a(p) in #2-6. 10-Vulture app., McManus-a 4.00
13-22: 13-Begin $2.99-c; Scorpion-c/app. 15-Daniel-c; Puma-c/app. 19-Lizard-c/app. 20-Hannibal King and Lilith app. 21,22-Deodato-a 3.00

SPIDER-MAN UNMASKED
Marvel Comics: Nov, 1996 ($5.95, one-shot)

nn-Art w/text 6.00

SPIDER-MAN: VENOM AGENDA
Marvel Comics: Jan, 1998 ($2.99, one-shot)

1-Hama-s/Lyle-c/a 3.00

SPIDER-MAN VS. DRACULA
Marvel Comics: Jan, 1994 ($1.75, 52 pgs., one-shot)

1-r/Giant-Size Spider-Man #1 plus new Matt Fox-a 1.75

SPIDER-MAN VS. WOLVERINE
Marvel Comics Group: Feb, 1987; V2#1, 1990 (68 pgs.)

1-Williamson-c/a(i); intro Charlemagne; death of Ned Leeds (old Hobgoblin) 2.00 6.00 20.00

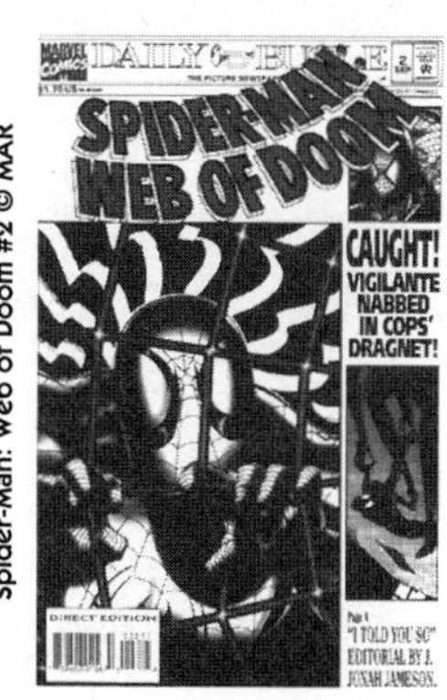

Spider-Man: Web of Doom #2 © MAR

Spider-Woman #1 © MAR

The Spirit 7/7/40 © Will Eisner

	GD25	FN65	NM94

V2#1 (1990, $4.95)-Reprints #1 (2/87) 5.00

SPIDER-MAN: WEB OF DOOM
Marvel Comics: Aug, 1994 - No. 3, Oct, 1994 ($1.75, limited series)

1-3 1.75

SPIDER REIGN OF THE VAMPIRE KING, THE (Also see The Spider)
Eclipse Books: 1992 - No. 3, 1992 ($4.95, limited series, coated stock, 52 pgs.)

Book One - Three: Truman scripts & painted-c 5.00

SPIDER'S WEB, THE (See G-8 and His Battle Aces)

SPIDER-WOMAN (Also see The Avengers #240, Marvel Spotlight #32, Marvel Super Heroes Secret Wars #7 & Marvel Two-In-One #29)
Marvel Comics Group: April, 1978 - No. 50, June, 1983 (New logo #47 on)

1-New complete origin & mask added 5.00
2-5,7-18,21-27,30-36,39-49: 13,15-The Shroud-c/s. 46-Kingpin app. 49-Tigra-c/story 2.00
6,19,20,28,29: 6,19-Werewolf by Night-c/stories. 20,28,29-Spider-Man app. 3.00
37,38-X-Men x-over; 37-1st app. Siryn of X-Force; origin retold 4.00
50-(52 pgs.)-Death of Spider-Woman; photo-c 5.00
NOTE: *Austin a-37i. Byrne c-26p. Layton c-19. Miller c-32p.*

SPIDER-WOMAN
Marvel Comics: Nov, 1993 - No. 4, Feb, 1994 ($1.75, mini-series)

V2#1-4: 1,2-Origin; U.S. Agent app. 1.75

SPIDEY SUPER STORIES (Spider-Man)
Marvel/Children's TV Workshop: Oct, 1974 - No. 57, Mar, 1982 (35¢, no ads)

	GD25	FN65	NM94
1-Origin (stories simplified)	2.00	6.00	20.00
2-12,15: 2-Kraven. 6-Iceman. 15-Storm-c/sty	1.10	3.30	11.00
11-14,16-20	.90	2.70	9.00
21-30	.85	2.60	7.00
31-38,40-44,46-55,57: 31-Moondragon-c/story; Dr. Doom app. 33-Hulk. 34-Sub-Mariner. 38-F.F. 44-Vision.			4.50
39-Thanos-c/story	.90	2.70	9.00
45-Silver Surfer & Dr. Doom app.	.85	2.60	7.00
56-Battles Jack O'Lantern-c/sty (exactly one year after 1st app. in Machine Man #19)	.85	2.60	7.00

SPIKE AND TYKE (See M.G.M.'s...)

SPIN & MARTY (TV) (Walt Disney's)(See Walt Disney Showcase #32)
Dell Publishing Co. (Mickey Mouse Club): No. 714, June, 1956 - No. 1082, Mar-May, 1960 (All photo-c)

	GD25	FN65	NM94
Four Color 714 (#1)	11.00	32.00	120.00
Four Color 767,808 (#2,3)	9.00	27.00	100.00
Four Color 826 (#4)-Annette Funicello photo-c	23.00	68.00	250.00
5(3-5/58) - 9(6-8/59)	7.25	22.00	80.00
Four Color 1026,1082	7.25	22.00	80.00

SPINE-TINGLING TALES (Doctor Spektor Presents...)
Gold Key: May, 1975 - No. 4, Jan, 1976 (All 25¢ issues)

	GD25	FN65	NM94
1-1st Tragg-r/Mystery Comics Digest #3	.85	2.60	7.00
2-4: 2-Origin Ra-Ka-Tep-r/Mystery Comics Digest #1; Dr. Spektor #12. 3-All Durak-r issue; 4-Baron Tibor's 1st app.-r/Mystery Comics Digest #4; painted-c			5.00

SPINWORLD
Amaze Ink (Slave Labor Graphics): July, 1997 - No. 4, Jan, 1998 ($2.95/$3.95, B&W, mini-series)

1-3-Brent Anderson-a(p) 3.00
4-($3.95) 4.00

SPIRAL PATH, THE
Eclipse Comics: July, 1986 - No. 2 ($1.75, Baxter paper, limited series)

1,2 1.80

SPIRAL ZONE
DC Comics: Feb, 1988 - No. 4, May, 1988 ($1.00, mini-series)

1-4-Based on Tonka toys 1.00

SPIRIT, THE (Weekly Comic Book)
Will Eisner: 6/2/40 - 10/5/52 (16 pgs.; 8 pgs.) (no cover) (in color)
(Distributed through various newspapers and other sources)
NOTE: **Eisner** script, pencils/inks for the most part from 6/2/40-4/26/42; a few stories assisted by Jack Cole, Fine, Powell and Kotsky.

	GD25	FN65	NM94
6/2/40(#1)-Origin/1st app. The Spirit; reprinted in Police #11; Lady Luck (Brenda Banks)(1st app.) by Chuck Mazoujian & Mr. Mystic (1st. app.) by S. R. (Bob) Powell begin	65.00	195.00	550.00
6/9/40(#2)	31.00	92.00	225.00
6/16/40(#3)-Black Queen app. in Spirit	18.00	54.00	135.00
6/23/40(#4)-Mr. Mystic receives magical necklace	15.00	45.00	110.00
6/30/40(#5)	15.00	45.00	110.00
7/7/40(#6)-1st app.: Spirit carplane; Black Queen app. in Spirit	15.00	45.00	110.00
7/14/40(#7)-8/4/40(#10): 7/21/40-Spirit becomes fugitive wanted for murder	12.00	36.00	90.00
8/11/40-9/22/40	11.00	33.00	80.00
9/29/40-Ellen drops engagement with Homer Creep	10.00	30.00	70.00
10/6/40-11/3/40	10.00	30.00	70.00
11/10/40-The Black Queen app.	10.00	30.00	70.00
11/17/40, 11/24/40	10.00	30.00	70.00
12/1/40-Ellen spanking by Spirit on cover & inside; Eisner-1st 3 pgs., J. Cole rest	14.00	43.00	110.00
12/8/40-3/9/41	8.35	25.00	55.00
3/16/41-Intro. & 1st app. Silk Satin	13.00	39.00	95.00
3/23/41-6/1/41: 5/11/41-Last Lady Luck by Mazoujian; 5/18/41-Lady Luck by Nick Viscardi begins, ends 2/22/42	8.35	25.00	55.00
6/8/41-2nd app. Satin; Spirit learns Satin is also a British agent	10.00	30.00	75.00
6/15/41-1st app. Twilight	10.00	30.00	65.00
6/22/41-Hitler app. in Spirit	8.35	25.00	55.00
6/29/41-1/25/42,2/8/42	6.00	18.00	45.00
2/1/42-1st app. Duchess	10.00	30.00	65.00
2/15/42-4/26/42-Lady Luck by Klaus Nordling begins 3/1/42	6.70	20.00	50.00
5/3/42-8/16/42-Eisner/Fine/Quality staff assists on Spirit	4.30	13.00	32.00
8/23/42-Satin cover splash; Spirit by Eisner/Fine although signed by Fine	10.00	30.00	70.00
8/30/42,9/27/42-10/11/42,10/25/42-11/8/42-Eisner/Fine/Quality staff assists on Spirit	4.30	13.00	32.00
9/6/42-9/20/42,10/18/42-Fine/Belfi art on Spirit; scripts by Manly Wade Wellman	3.00	9.00	22.00
11/15/42-12/6/42,12/20/42,12/27/42,1/17/43-4/18/43,5/9/43-8/8/43-Wellman/Woolfolk scripts, Fine pencils, Quality staff inks	3.00	9.00	22.00
12/13/42,1/3/43,1/10/43,4/25/43,5/2/43-Eisner scripts/layouts; Fine pencils, Quality staff inks	3.75	11.25	28.00
8/15/43-Eisner script/layout; pencils/inks by Quality staff; Jack Cole-a	2.40	7.20	18.00
8/22/43-12/12/43-Wellman/Woolfolk scripts, Fine pencils, Quality staff inks; Mr. Mystic by Guardineer-10/10/43-10/24/43	2.40	7.20	18.00
12/19/43-8/13/44-Wellman/Woolfolk/Jack Cole scripts; Cole, Fine & Robin King-a; Last Mr. Mystic-5/14/44	2.20	6.50	16.00
8/20/44-12/16/45-Wellman/Woolfolk scripts; Fine art with unknown staff assists	2.20	6.50	16.00

NOTE: *Scripts/layouts by Eisner, or Eisner/Nordling, Eisner/Mercer or Spranger/Eisner; inks by Eisner or Eisner/Spranger in issues 12/23/45-2/2/47.*

	GD25	FN65	NM94
12/23/45-1/6/46: 12/23/45-Christmas-c	4.00	12.00	30.00
1/13/46-Origin Spirit retold	6.40	19.00	48.00
1/20/46-1st postwar Satin app.	5.30	16.00	40.00
1/27/46-3/10/46: 3/3/46-Last Lady Luck by Nordling	4.00	12.00	30.00
3/17/46-Intro. & 1st app. Nylon	5.30	16.00	40.00

The Spirit #7 (Quality) © Will Eisner

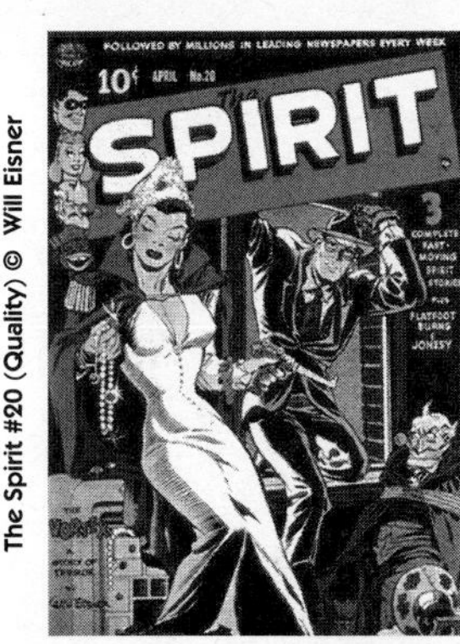

The Spirit #20 (Quality) © Will Eisner

The Spirit #4 (FH) © Will Eisner

	GD25	FN65	NM94
3/24/46,3/31/46,4/14/46	4.00	12.00	30.00
4/7/46-2nd app. Nylon	4.70	14.00	35.00
4/21/46-Intro. & 1st app. Mr. Carrion & His Pet Buzzard Julia	6.40	19.00	48.00
4/28/46-5/12/46,5/26/46-6/30/46: Lady Luck by Fred Schwab in issues 5/5/46-11/3/46	4.00	12.00	30.00
5/19/46-2nd app. Mr. Carrion	4.70	14.00	35.00
7/7/46-Intro. & 1st app. Dulcet Tone & Skinny	5.60	17.00	42.00
7/14/46-9/29/46	4.00	12.00	30.00
10/6/46-Intro. & 1st app. P'Gell	6.40	19.00	48.00
10/13/46-11/3/46,11/16/46-11/24/46	4.00	12.00	30.00
11/10/46-2nd app. P'Gell	5.00	15.00	38.00
12/1/46-3rd app. P'Gell	4.70	14.00	35.00
12/8/46-2/2/47	3.50	10.50	26.00

NOTE: *Scripts, pencils/inks by Eisner except where noted in issues 2/9/47-12/19/48.*

	GD25	FN65	NM94
2/9/47-7/6/47: 6/8/47-Eisner self satire	3.50	10.50	26.00
7/13/47- "Hansel & Gretel" fairy tales	5.30	16.00	40.00
7/20/47-Li'L Abner, Daddy Warbucks, Dick Tracy, Fearless Fosdick parody; A-Bomb blast-c	5.60	17.00	42.00
7/27/47-9/14/47	3.50	10.50	26.00
9/21/47-Pearl Harbor flashback	4.30	13.00	32.00
9/28/47-1st mention of Flying Saucers in comics-3 months after 1st sighting in Idaho on 6/25/47	9.30	28.00	70.00
10/5/47- "Cinderella" fairy tales	5.30	16.00	40.00
10/12/47-11/30/47	3.50	10.50	26.00
12/7/47-Intro. & 1st app. Powder Pouf	6.40	19.00	48.00
12/14/47-12/28/47	3.50	10.50	26.00
1/4/48-2nd app. Powder Pouf	4.70	14.00	35.00
1/11/48-1st app. Sparrow Fallon; Powder Pouf app.	4.70	14.00	35.00
1/18/48-He-Man ad cover; satire issue	4.70	14.00	35.00
1/25/48-Intro. & 1st app. Castanet	5.60	17.00	42.00
2/1/48-2nd app. Castanet	4.00	12.00	30.00
2/8/48-3/7/48	3.50	10.50	26.00
3/14/48-Only app. Kretchma	4.00	12.00	30.00
3/21/48,3/28/48,4/11/48-4/25/48	3.50	10.50	26.00
4/4/48-Only app. Wild Rice	4.00	12.00	30.00
5/2/48-2nd app. Sparrow	3.50	10.50	26.00
5/9/48-6/27/48,7/11/48,7/18/48: 6/13/48-Television issue	3.50	10.50	26.00
7/4/48-Spirit by Andre Le Blanc	2.70	8.00	20.00
7/25/48-Ambrose Bierce's "The Thing" adaptation classic by Eisner/ Grandenetti	9.30	28.00	70.00
8/1/48-8/15/48,8/29/48-9/12/48	3.50	10.50	26.00
8/22/48-Poe's "Fall of the House of Usher" classic by Eisner/Grandenetti	9.30	28.00	70.00
9/19/48-Only app. Lorelei	5.00	15.00	38.00
9/26/48-10/31/48	3.50	10.50	26.00
11/7/48-Only app. Plaster of Paris	5.00	15.00	38.00
11/14/48-12/19/48	3.50	10.50	26.00

NOTE: *Scripts by Eisner or Feiffer or Eisner/Feiffer or Nordling. Art by Eisner with backgrounds by Eisner, Grandenetti, Le Blanc, Stallman, Nordling, Dixon and/or others in issues 12/26/48-4/1/51 except where noted.*

	GD25	FN65	NM94
12/26/48-Reprints some covers of 1948 with flashbacks	3.50	10.50	26.00
1/2/49-1/16/49	3.50	10.50	26.00
1/23/49,1/30/49-1st & 2nd app. Thorne	5.00	15.00	38.00
2/6/49-8/14/49	3.50	10.50	26.00
8/21/49,8/28/49-1st & 2nd app. Monica Veto	5.00	15.00	38.00
9/4/49,9/11/49	3.50	10.50	26.00
9/18/49-Love comic cover; has gag love comic ads on inside	5.00	15.00	38.00
9/25/49-Only app. Ice	4.30	13.00	32.00
10/2/49,10/9/49-Autumn News appears & dies in 10/9 issue	4.30	13.00	32.00
10/16/49-11/27/49,12/18/49,12/25/49	3.50	10.50	26.00
12/4/49,12/11/49-1st & 2nd app. Flaxen	4.00	12.00	30.00
1/1/50-Flashbacks to all of the Spirit girls-Thorne, Ellen, Satin, & Monica	6.70	20.00	50.00
1/8/50-Intro. & 1st app. Sand Saref	9.30	28.00	70.00
1/15/50-2nd app. Saref	6.70	20.00	50.00
1/22/50-2/5/50	3.50	10.50	26.00
2/12/50-Roller Derby issue	4.70	14.00	35.00
2/19/50-Half Dead Mr. Lox - Classic horror	4.70	14.00	35.00
2/26/50-4/23/50,5/14/50,5/28/50,7/23/50-9/3/50	3.50	10.50	26.00
4/30/50-Script/art by Le Blanc with Eisner framing	1.85	5.60	14.00
5/7/50,6/4/50-7/16/50-Abe Kanegson-a	1.85	5.60	14.00
5/21/50-Script by Feiffer/Eisner, art by Blaisdell, Eisner framing	1.85	5.60	14.00
9/10/50-P'Gell returns	5.00	15.00	38.00
9/17/50-1/7/51	3.50	10.50	26.00
1/14/51-Life Magazine cover; brief biography of Comm. Dolan, Sand Saref, Silk Satin, P'Gell, Sammy & Willum, Darling O'Shea, & Mr. Carrion & His Pet Buzzard Julia, with pin-ups by Eisner	5.00	15.00	38.00
1/21/51,2/4/51-4/1/51	3.50	10.50	26.00
1/28/51- "The Meanest Man in the World" classic by Eisner	5.00	15.00	38.00
4/8/51-7/29/51,8/12/51-Last Eisner issue	3.50	10.50	26.00
8/5/51,8/19/51-7/20/52-Not Eisner	1.85	5.60	14.00
7/27/52-(Rare)-Denny Colt in Outer Space by Wally Wood; 7 pg. S/F story of E.C. vintage	32.00	95.00	235.00
8/3/52-(Rare)- "Mission...The Moon" by Wood	32.00	95.00	235.00
8/10/52-(Rare)- "A DP On The Moon" by Wood	32.00	95.00	235.00
8/17/52-(Rare)- "Heart" by Wood/Eisner	27.00	81.00	200.00
8/24/52-(Rare)- "Rescue" by Wood	32.00	95.00	235.00
8/31/52-(Rare)- "The Last Man" by Wood	32.00	95.00	235.00
9/7/52-(Rare)- "The Man in The Moon" by Wood	32.00	95.00	235.00
9/14/52-(Rare)-Eisner/Wenzel-a	8.75	27.00	70.00
9/21/52-(Rare)- "Denny Colt, Alias The Spirit/Space Report" by Eisner/Wenzel	11.50	34.00	85.00
9/28/52-(Rare)- "Return From The Moon" by Wood	32.00	95.00	235.00
10/5/52-(Rare)- "The Last Story" by Eisner	11.50	34.00	85.00

Large Tabloid pages from 1946 on (Eisner) - Price 200 percent over listed prices.
NOTE: *Spirit sections came out in both large and small format. Some newspapers went to the 8-pg. format months before others. Some printed the pages so they cannot be folded into a small comic book section; these are worth less. (Also see Three Comics & Spiritman).*

SPIRIT, THE (1st Series)(Also see Police Comics #11)
Quality Comics Group (Vital): 1944 - No. 22, Aug, 1950

	GD25	FN65	NM94
nn(#1)- "Wanted Dead or Alive"	62.00	186.00	525.00
nn(#2)- "Crime Doesn't Pay"	39.00	117.00	300.00
nn(#3)- "Murder Runs Wild"	30.00	90.00	225.00
4,5: 4-Flatfoot Burns begins, ends #22. 5-Wertham app.	25.00	74.00	185.00
6-10	21.00	62.00	155.00
11	18.00	54.00	135.00
12-17-Eisner-c. 19-Honeybun app.	29.00	88.00	220.00
18-21-Strip-r by Eisner; Eisner-c	39.00	116.00	290.00
22-Used by N.Y. Legis. Comm; classic Eisner-c	47.00	141.00	400.00
Super Reprint #11-r/Quality Spirit #19 by Eisner	2.50	7.50	24.00
Super Reprint #12-r/Spirit #17 by Fine; Sol Brodsky-c	2.50	7.50	22.00

SPIRIT, THE (2nd Series)
Fiction House Magazines: Spring, 1952 - No. 5, 1954

	GD25	FN65	NM94
1-Not Eisner	37.00	112.00	280.00
2-Eisner-c/a(2)	35.00	104.00	260.00
3-Eisner/Grandenetti-c	24.00	72.00	180.00
4-Eisner/Grandenetti-c; Eisner-a	25.00	76.00	190.00
5-Eisner-c/a(4)	31.00	92.00	230.00

The Spirit #1 (Warren) © Will Eisner

The Spirit: The New Adventures #2 © Will Eisner

Spitfire Comics #133 © HARV

GD25 FN65 NM94

SPIRIT, THE
Harvey Publications: Oct, 1966 - No. 2, Mar, 1967 (Giant Size, 25¢, 68 pgs.)
1-Eisner-r plus 9 new pgs.(origin Denny Colt, Take 3, plus 2 filler pgs.)
(#3 was advertised, but never published) 5.50 16.50 55.00
2-Eisner-r plus 9 new pgs.(origin of the Octopus) 5.00 15.00 50.00

SPIRIT, THE (Underground)
Kitchen Sink Enterprises (Krupp Comics): Jan, 1973 - No. 2, Sept, 1973 (Black & White)
1-New Eisner-c & 4 pgs. new Eisner-a plus-r (titled Crime Convention)
1.40 4.20 14.00
2-New Eisner-c & 4 pgs. new Eisner-a plus-r (titled Meets P'Gell)
1.80 5.40 18.00

SPIRIT, THE (Magazine)
Warren Publ. Co./Krupp Comic Works No. 17 on: 4/74 - No. 16, 10/76; No. 17, Winter, 1977 - No. 41, 6/83 (B&W w/color)
1-Eisner-r begin 2.25 6.80 25.00
2-5 1.60 4.80 16.00
6-9,11-15: 7-All Ebony issue. 8-Female Foes issue. 12-X-Mas issue
1.20 3.60 12.00
10-Giant Summer Special ($1.50)-Origin 2.00 6.00 20.00
16-Giant Summer Special ($1.50) 1.60 4.80 16.00
17,18(8/78): 17-Lady Luck-r .90 2.70 8.00
19-21-New Eisner-a. 20,21-Wood-r (#21-r/A DP on the Moon by Wood). 20-Outer Space-r 2.00 6.00
22-41: 22,23-Wood-r (#22-r/Mission the Moon by Wood). 28-r/last story (10/5/52). 30-(7/81)-Special Spirit Jam issue w/Caniff, Corben, Bolland, Byrne, Miller, Kurtzman, Rogers, Sienkiewicz-a & 40 others. 36-Begin Spirit Section-r; r/1st story (6/2/40) in color; new Eisner-c/a(18 pgs.)($2.95). 37-r/2nd story in color plus 18 pgs. new Eisner-a. 38-41: r/3rd - 6th stories in color. 41-Lady Luck Mr. Mystic in color 2.00 6.00
Special 1(1975)-All Eisner-a 3.20 9.50 35.00
NOTE: *Covers pencilled/inked by* ***Eisner*** *only #1-9,12-16; painted by Eisner & Ken Kelly #10 & 11; painted by Eisner #17-up; one color story reprinted in #1-10.* ***Austin*** *a-30i.* ***Byrne*** *a-30p.* ***Miller*** *a-30p.*

SPIRIT, THE (See Will Eisner's 3-D Classics Featuring...)
Kitchen Sink Enterprises: Oct, 1983 - No. 87, Jan, 1992 ($2.00, Baxter paper)
1-4: 1-Origin-r/12/23/45 Spirit Section. 2-r/sections 1/20/46-2/10/46. 3-r/2/17/46-3/10/46. 4-r/3/17/46-4/7/46 2.50
5-11 ($2.95 cover): 11-Last color issue 2.50
12-87 ($1.95/$2.00, B&W): 54-r/section 2/19/50. 85-87-Reprint the Outer Space Spirit stories by Wood. 86-r/A DP on the Moon by Wood from 1952 2.50

SPIRIT JAM
Kitchen Sink Press: Aug, 1998 ($5.95, B&W, oversized, square-bound)
nn-Reprints Spirit (Magazine) #30 by Eisner & 50 others; and "Cerebus Vs. The Spirit" from Cerebus Jam #1 5.95

SPIRIT, THE: THE NEW ADVENTURES
Kitchen Sink Press: 1997 - No. 8, Nov, 1998 ($3.50, anthology)
1-Moore-s/Gibbons-c/a 5.00
2-Gaiman-s/Eisner-c 4.00
3-8: 3-Moore-s/Bolland-c/Moebius back-c. 4-Allred-s/a; Busiek-s/Anderson-a. 5-Chadwick-s/c/a(p); Nyberg-i. 6-S.Hampton & Mandrake-a 3.50

SPIRIT: THE ORIGIN YEARS
Kitchen Sink Press: May, 1992 - No. 10, Dec, 1993 ($2.95, B&W, high quality paper)
1-10: 1-r/sections 6/2/40(origin)-6/23/40 (all 1940s) 3.00

SPIRITMAN (Also see Three Comics)
No publisher listed: No date (1944) (10¢)
(Triangle Sales Co. ad on back cover)
1-Three 16pg. Spirit sections bound together, (1944, 10¢, 52 pgs.)
19.00 56.00 140.00
2-Two Spirit sections (3/26/44, 4/2/44) bound together; by Lou Fine
16.00 48.00 120.00

SPIRIT OF THE BORDER (See Zane Grey & Four Color #197)

SPIRIT OF THE TAO
Image Comics (Top Cow): Jun, 1998 - Present ($2.50)
Preview 1.00 3.00 10.00
1- D-Tron-s/Tan & D-Tron-a 3.00
2-5 2.50

SPIRIT OF WONDER (Manga)
Dark Horse Comics: Apr, 1996 - No. 5, Aug, 1996 ($2.95, B&W, limited series)
1-5 3.00

SPIRIT WORLD (Magazine)
National Periodical Publications: Fall, 1971 (B&W)
1-New Kirby-a; Neal Adams-c; poster inside 5.00 15.00 50.00
(1/2 price without poster)

SPITFIRE
Malverne Herald (Elliot)(J. R. Mahon): No. 132, 1944 (Aug) - No. 133, 1945 (Female undercover agent)
132,133: Both have Classics Gift Box ads on b/c with checklist to #20
21.00 64.00 160.00

SPITFIRE AND THE TROUBLESHOOTERS
Marvel Comics: Oct, 1986 - No. 9, June, 1987 (Codename: Spitfire #10 on)
1-9: 4-McFarlane-a 1.00

SPITFIRE COMICS (Also see Double Up)
Harvey Publications: Aug, 1941 - No. 2, Oct, 1941 (Pocket size; 100 pgs.)
1-Origin The Clown, The Fly-Man, The Spitfire & The Magician From Bagdad
59.00 177.00 500.00
2 50.00 150.00 425.00

SPLITTING IMAGE
Image Comics: Mar, 1993 - No. 2, 1993 ($1.95)
1,2-Simpson-c/a; parody comic 2.00

SPOOF
Marvel Comics Group: Oct, 1970; No. 2, Nov, 1972 - No. 5, May, 1973
1-Infinity-c; Dark Shadows-c & parody 1.40 4.20 14.00
2-5: 3-Beatles, Osmond's, Jackson 5, David Cassidy, Nixon & Agnew-c. 5-Rod Serling, Woody Allen, Ted Kennedy-c .90 2.70 9.00

SPOOK (Formerly Shock Detective Cases)
Star Publications: No. 22, Jan, 1953 - No. 30, Oct, 1954
22-Sgt. Spook-r; acid in face story; hanging-c 31.00 92.00 230.00
23,25,27: 25-Jungle Lil-r. 27-Two Sgt. Spook-r 21.00 62.00 155.00
24-Used in **SOTI**, pgs. 182,183-r/Inside Crime #2; Transvestism story
23.00 70.00 175.00
26-Disbrow-a 21.00 62.00 155.00
28,29-Rulah app. 29-Jo-Jo app. 21.00 62.00 155.00
30-Disbrow-c/a(2); only Star-c 21.00 62.00 155.00
NOTE: ***L. B. Cole*** *covers-all issues; a-28(1 pg.).* ***Disbrow*** *a-26(2), 28, 29(2), 30(2); No. 30 r/Blue Bolt Weird Tales #114.*

SPOOK COMICS
Baily Publications/Star: 1946
1-Mr. Lucifer story 24.00 71.00 175.00

SPOOKY (The Tuff Little Ghost; see Casper The Friendly Ghost)
Harvey Publications: 11/55 - 139, 11/73; No. 140, 7/74 - No. 155, 3/77; No. 156, 12/77 - No. 158, 4/78; No. 159, 9/78; No. 160, 10/79; No. 161, 9/80
1-Nightmare begins (see Casper #19) 30.00 90.00 300.00
2 15.00 45.00 150.00
3-10(1956-57) 9.00 27.00 90.00

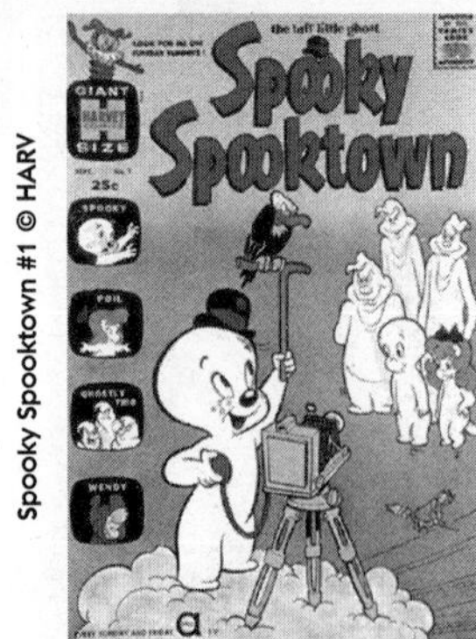

Spooky Spooktown #1 © HARV

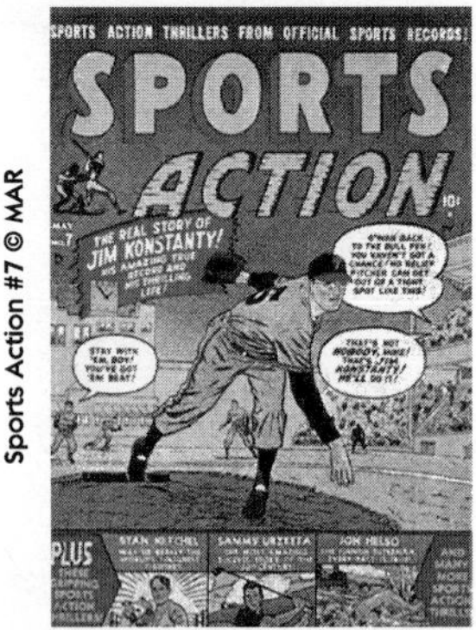

Sports Action #7 © MAR

Spy Cases #14 © MAR

	GD25	FN65	NM94
11-20(1957-58)	4.50	13.50	45.00
21-40(1958-59)	3.00	9.00	30.00
41-60	2.00	6.00	20.00
61-80	1.60	4.80	16.00
81-99	1.40	4.20	14.00
100	1.60	4.80	16.00
101-120	1.00	3.00	10.00
121-126,133-140	.90	2.70	8.00
127-132: All 52 pg. Giants	1.20	3.60	12.00
141-161			5.00

SPOOKY
Harvey Comics: Nov, 1991 - No. 4, Sept, 1992 ($1.00/$1.25)

	GD25	FN65	NM94
1			3.00
2-4: 3-Begin $1.25-c			2.00
...Digest 1-3 (10/92, 6/93, 10/93, $1.75, 100 pgs.)-Casper, Wendy, etc.			3.00

SPOOKY HAUNTED HOUSE
Harvey Publications: Oct, 1972 - No. 15, Feb, 1975

	GD25	FN65	NM94
1	2.60	7.80	26.00
2-5	1.20	3.60	12.00
6-10	.90	2.70	8.00
11-15		2.00	6.00

SPOOKY MYSTERIES
Your Guide Publ. Co.: No date (1946) (10¢)

	GD25	FN65	NM94
1-Mr. Spooky, Super Snooper, Pinky, Girl Detective app.	16.00	48.00	120.00

SPOOKY SPOOKTOWN
Harvey Publ.: 9/61; No. 2, 9/62 - No. 52, 12/73; No. 53, 10/74 - No. 66, 12/76

	GD25	FN65	NM94
1-Casper, Spooky; 68 pgs. begin	14.00	42.00	140.00
2	7.50	22.50	75.00
3-5	5.00	15.00	50.00
6-10	3.50	10.50	35.00
11-20	2.50	7.50	25.00
21-39: 39-Last 68 pg. issue	1.80	5.40	18.00
40-45: All 52 pgs.	1.20	3.60	12.00
46-66: 61-Hot Stuff/Spooky team-up story		2.00	6.00

SPORT COMICS (Becomes True Sport Picture Stories #5 on)
Street & Smith Publications: Oct, 1940 (No mo.) - No. 4, Nov, 1941

	GD25	FN65	NM94
1-Life story of Lou Gehrig	46.00	138.00	390.00
2	27.00	80.00	200.00
3,4	23.00	68.00	170.00

SPORT LIBRARY (See Charlton Sport Library)

SPORTS ACTION (Formerly Sport Stars)
Marvel/Atlas Comics (ACI No. 2,3/SAI No. 4-14): No. 2, Feb, 1950 - No. 14, Sept, 1952

	GD25	FN65	NM94
2-Powell painted-c; George Gipp life story	31.00	92.00	230.00
3-Everett-a	19.00	58.00	145.00
4-11,14: Weiss-a	17.00	52.00	130.00
12,13: 12-Everett-c. 13-Krigstein-a	19.00	58.00	145.00

NOTE: *Title may have changed after No. 3, to Crime Must Lose No. 4 on, due to publisher change.* ***Sol Brodsky*** *c-4-7, 13, 14.* ***Maneely*** *c-3, 8-11.*

SPORT STARS
Parents' Magazine Institute (Sport Stars): Feb-Mar, 1946 - No. 4, Aug-Sept, 1946 (Half comic, half photo magazine)

	GD25	FN65	NM94
1- "How Tarzan Got That Way" story of Johnny Weissmuller	35.00	104.00	260.00
2-Baseball greats	22.00	66.00	165.00
3,4	19.00	58.00	145.00

SPORT STARS (Becomes Sports Action #2 on)
Marvel Comics (ACI): Nov, 1949 (52 pgs.)

	GD25	FN65	NM94
1-Knute Rockne; painted-c	31.00	92.00	230.00

SPORT THRILLS (Formerly Dick Cole; becomes Jungle Thrills #16)
Star Publications: No. 11, Nov, 1950 - No. 15, Nov, 1951

	GD25	FN65	NM94
11-Dick Cole begins, ends #13?; Ted Williams & Ty Cobb life stories	25.00	76.00	190.00
12-Joe DiMaggio, Phil Rizzuto stories & photos on-c; L.B. Cole-c/a	20.00	60.00	150.00
13-15-All L. B. Cole-c. 13-Jackie Robinson, Pee Wee Reese stories & photo on-c. 14-Johnny Weissmuler life story	20.00	60.00	150.00
Accepted Reprint #11 (#15 on-c, nd); L.B. Cole-c	5.70	17.00	40.00
Accepted Reprint #12 (nd); L.B. Cole-c; Joe DiMaggio & Phil Rizzuto life stories-r/#12	5.70	17.00	40.00

SPOTLIGHT (TV) (newsstand sales only)
Marvel Comics Group: Sept, 1978 - No. 4, Mar, 1979 (Hanna-Barbera)

	GD25	FN65	NM94
1-Huckleberry Hound, Yogi Bear; Shaw-a	1.80	5.40	18.00
2,4: 2-Quick Draw McGraw, Augie Doggie, Snooper & Blabber. 4-Magilla Gorilla, Snagglepuss	1.20	3.60	12.00
3-The Jetsons; Yakky Doodle	1.80	5.40	18.00

SPOTLIGHT COMICS (Becomes Red Seal Comics #14 on?)
Harry 'A' Chesler (Our Army, Inc.): Nov, 1944 - No. 3, 1945

	GD25	FN65	NM94
1-The Black Dwarf (cont'd in Red Seal?), The Veiled Avenger, & Barry Kuda begin; Tuska-c	53.00	159.00	450.00
2	44.00	132.00	375.00
3-Injury to eye story (reprinted from Scoop #3)	46.00	138.00	390.00

SPOTTY THE PUP (Becomes Super Pup #4, see Television Puppet Show)
Avon Periodicals/Realistic Comics: No. 2, Oct-Nov, 1953 - No. 3, Dec-Jan, 1953-54 (Also see Funny Tunes)

	GD25	FN65	NM94
2,3	4.00	12.00	24.00
nn (1953, Realistic-r)	2.80	7.00	14.00

SPUNKY (...Junior Cowboy)(...Comics #2 on)
Standard Comics: April, 1949 - No. 7, Nov, 1951

	GD25	FN65	NM94
1,2-Text illos by Frazetta	6.85	21.00	48.00
3-7	4.00	11.00	22.00

SPUNKY THE SMILING SPOOK
Ajax/Farrell (World Famous Comics/Four Star Comic Corp.): Aug, 1957 - No. 4, May, 1958

	GD25	FN65	NM94
1-Reprints from Frisky Fables	7.15	21.50	50.00
2-4	5.00	15.00	30.00

SPY AND COUNTERSPY (Becomes Spy Hunters #3 on)
American Comics Group: Aug-Sept, 1949 - No. 2, Oct-Nov, 1949 (52 pgs.)

	GD25	FN65	NM94
1-Origin, 1st app. Jonathan Kent, Counterspy	20.00	60.00	150.00
2	13.00	40.00	100.00

SPY CASES (Formerly The Kellys)
Marvel/Atlas Comics (Hercules Publ.): No. 26, Sept, 1950 - No. 19, Oct, 1953

	GD25	FN65	NM94
26 (#1)	19.00	56.00	140.00
27(#2),28(#3, 2/51): 27-Everett-a; bondage-c	11.00	34.00	85.00
4(4/51) - 7,9,10	9.30	28.00	70.00
8-A-Bomb-c/story	11.00	32.00	80.00
11-19: 10-14-War format	7.85	23.50	55.00

NOTE: ***Sol Brodsky*** *c-1-5, 8, 9, 11-14, 17, 18.* ***Maneely*** *a-8; c-7, 10.* ***Tuska*** *a-7.*

SPY FIGHTERS
Marvel/Atlas Comics (CSI): March, 1951 - No. 15, July, 1953 (Cases from official records)

	GD25	FN65	NM94
1-Clark Mason begins; Tuska-a; Brodsky-c	20.00	60.00	150.00
2-Tuska-a	11.00	33.00	80.00
3-13: 3-5-Brodsky-c. 7-Heath-c	9.30	28.00	70.00
14,15-Pakula-a(3), Ed Win-a. 15-Brodsky-c	10.00	30.00	75.00

SPY-HUNTERS (Formerly Spy & Counterspy)

Spy Smasher #2 © FAW

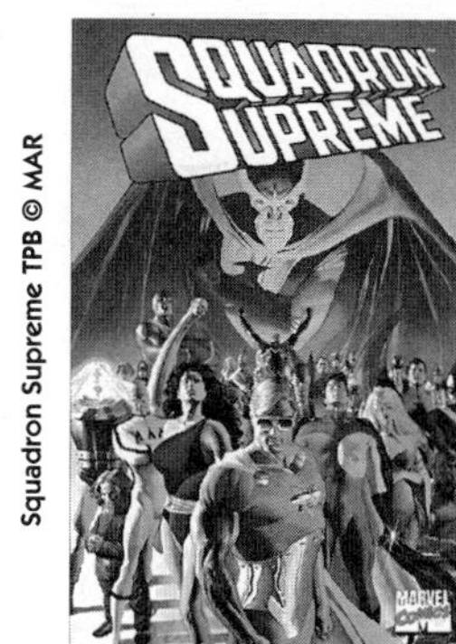

Squadron Supreme TPB © MAR

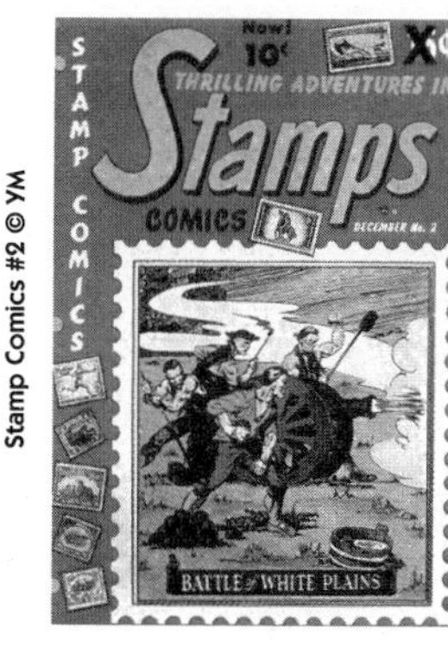

Stamp Comics #2 © YM

GD25 FN65 NM94

American Comics Group: No. 3, Dec-Jan, 1949-50 - No. 24, June-July, 1953 (#3-14: 52 pgs.)

	GD25	FN65	NM94
3-Jonathan Kent continues, ends #10	20.00	60.00	150.00
4-10: 4,8,10-Starr-a	11.00	34.00	85.00
11-15,17-22,24: 18-War-c begin. 21-War-c/stories begin	9.30	28.00	65.00
16-Williamson-a (9 pgs.)	14.00	42.00	105.00
23-Graphic torture, injury to eye panel	19.00	56.00	140.00

NOTE: ***Drucker** a-12. **Whitney** a-many issues; c-7, 8, 10-12, 15, 16.*

SPYMAN (Top Secret Adventures on cover)
Harvey Publications (Illustrated Humor): Sept, 1966 - No. 3, Feb, 1967 (12¢)

	GD25	FN65	NM94
1-Origin and 1st app. of Spyman. Steranko-a(p)-1st pro work; 1 pg. Neal Adams ad; Tuska-c/a, Crandall-a(i)	4.50	13.50	45.00
2,3: Simon-c. 2-Steranko-a(p)	2.80	8.40	28.00

SPY SMASHER (See Mighty Midget, Whiz & Xmas Comics) (Also see Crime Smasher)
Fawcett Publications: Fall, 1941 - No. 11, Feb, 1943

	GD25	FN65	NM94
1-Spy Smasher begins; silver metallic-c	295.00	884.00	2800.00
2-Raboy-c	147.00	441.00	1250.00
3,4: 3-Bondage-c	97.00	291.00	825.00
5-7: Raboy-a; 6-Raboy-c/a. 7-Part photo-c (movie).	88.00	265.00	750.00
8,11	71.00	212.00	600.00
9-Hitler, Tojo, Mussolini-c.	79.00	238.00	675.00
10-Hitler-c	77.00	229.00	650.00
Well Known Comics (1944, 12 pgs., 8-1/2x10-1/2"), paper-c, glued binding, printed in green; Bestmaid/Samuel Lowe giveaway	14.00	42.00	105.00

SPY THRILLERS (Police Badge No. 479 #5)
Atlas Comics (PrPI): Nov, 1954 - No. 4, May, 1955

	GD25	FN65	NM94
1-Brodsky c-1,2	17.00	52.00	130.00
2-Last precode (1/55)	10.00	30.00	75.00
3,4	8.50	26.00	60.00

SQUADRON SUPREME
Marvel Comics Group: Aug, 1985 - No. 12, Aug, 1986 (Maxi-series)

	GD25	FN65	NM94
1-Double size			1.50
2-12			1.00
TPB ($24.99) r/#1-12; Alex Ross painted-c; printing inks contain some of the cremated remains of late writer Mark Gruenwald			25.00
TPB-2nd printing ($24.99): Inks contain no ashes			25.00

SQUADRON SUPREME: NEW WORLD ORDER
Marvel Comics: Sept, 1998 ($5.99, one-shot)

	GD25	FN65	NM94
1-Wraparound-c; Kaminski-s		2.40	6.00

SQUALOR
First Comics: Dec, 1989 - Aug, 1990 ($2.75, limited series)

	GD25	FN65	NM94
1-4: Sutton-a			2.75

SQUEE
Slave Labor Graphics: Apr, 1997 - Present ($2.95, B&W)

	GD25	FN65	NM94
1-3-Jhonen Vasquez-s/a			3.00
4-(5/98)			3.00

SQUEEKS (Also see Boy Comics)
Lev Gleason Publications: Oct, 1953 - No. 5, June, 1954

	GD25	FN65	NM94
1-Funny animal; Biro-c; Crimebuster's pet monkey "Squeeks" begins	5.70	17.00	40.00
2-Biro-c	4.00	11.00	22.00
3-5: 3-Biro-c	3.60	9.00	18.00

S.R. BISSETTE'S SPIDERBABY COMIX
SpiderBaby Grafix: Aug, 1996 - No. 2 ($3.95, B&W, magazine size)

	GD25	FN65	NM94
Preview-(8/96, $3.95)-Graphic violence & nudity; Laurel & Hardy app.			4.00
1,2			3.95

S.R. BISSETTE'S TYRANT
SpiderBaby Grafix: Sept, 1994 - No. 4 ($2.95, B&W)

	GD25	FN65	NM94
1-4			5.00

STAINLESS STEEL RAT
Eagle Comics: Oct, 1985 - No. 6, Mar, 1986 (Limited series)

	GD25	FN65	NM94
1 (52 pgs.; $2.25-c)			2.25
2-6 ($1.50)			1.50

STALKER
National Periodical Publications: June-July, 1975 - No. 4, Dec-Jan, 1975-76

	GD25	FN65	NM94
1-Origin & 1st app; Ditko/Wood-c/a			5.00
2-4-Ditko/Wood-c/a			3.00

STALKERS
Marvel Comics (Epic Comics): Apr, 1990 - No. 12, Mar, 1991 ($1.50)

	GD25	FN65	NM94
1-12: 1-Chadwick-c			1.50

STAMP COMICS (Stamps... on-c; Thrilling Adventures In...#8)
Youthful Magazines/Stamp Comics, Inc.: Oct, 1951 - No. 7, Oct, 1952

	GD25	FN65	NM94
1-(15¢) ('Stamps' on indicia No. 1-3,5,7)	27.00	80.00	200.00
2	15.00	44.00	110.00
3-6: 3,4-Kiefer, Wildey-a	13.00	40.00	100.00
7-Roy Krenkel (4 pgs.)	16.00	48.00	120.00

NOTE: *Promotes stamp collecting; gives stories behind various commemorative stamps. No. 2, 10¢ printed over 15¢ c-price. **Kiefer** a-1-7. **Kirkel** a-1-6. **Napoli** a-2-7. **Palais** a-2-4, 7.*

STANLEY & HIS MONSTER (Formerly The Fox & the Crow)
National Periodical Publ.: No. 109, Apr-May, 1968 - No. 112, Oct-Nov, 1968

	GD25	FN65	NM94
109-112	2.50	7.50	20.00

STANLEY & HIS MONSTER
DC Comics: Feb, 1993 - No. 4, May, 1993 ($1.50, limited series)

	GD25	FN65	NM94
1-4			1.50

STAN SHAW'S BEAUTY & THE BEAST
Dark Horse Comics: Nov, 1993 ($4.95, one-shot)

	GD25	FN65	NM94
1			5.00

STAR
Image Comics (Highbrow Entertainment): June, 1995 - No. 4, Oct, 1995 ($2.50, limited series)

	GD25	FN65	NM94
1-4			2.50

STARBLAST
Marvel Comics: Jan, 1994 - No. 4, Apr, 1994 ($1.75, limited series)

	GD25	FN65	NM94
1-($2.00, 52 pgs.)-Nova, Quasar, Black Bolt; painted-c			2.00
2-4			1.75

STAR BLAZERS
Comico: Apr, 1987 - No. 4, July, 1987 ($1.75, limited series)

	GD25	FN65	NM94
1-4			1.75

STAR BLAZERS
Comico: 1989 ($1.95/$2.50, limited series)

	GD25	FN65	NM94
1 ($1.95)- Steacy wraparound painted-c on all			2.00
2-5 ($2.50)			2.50

STAR BLAZERS (The Magazine of Space Battleship Yamato)
Argo Press: No. 0, Aug, 1995 - No. 3, Dec, 1995 ($2.95)

	GD25	FN65	NM94
0-3			3.00

STAR BRAND
Marvel Comics (New Universe): Oct, 1986 - No. 19, May, 1989 (75¢/$1.25)

	GD25	FN65	NM94
1-19: 14-begin $1.25-c. 16-19-Byrne story & art.			1.00
Annual 1 (10/87)			1.25

Star Comics V2 #2 © CEN

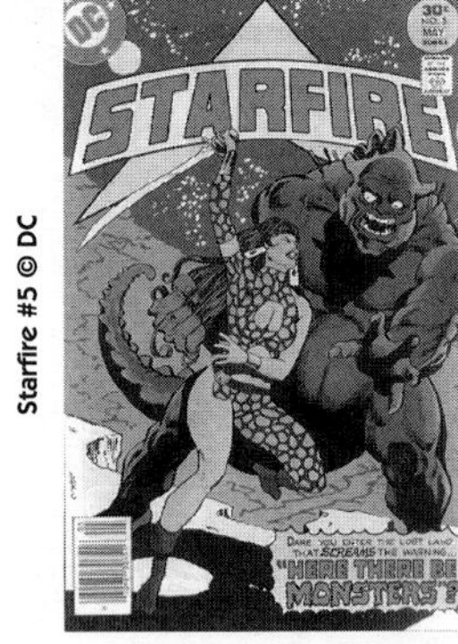

Starfire #5 © DC

Starman #34 (1st Series) © DC

GD25 FN65 NM94

STARCHILD
Tailspin Press: 1992 - No. 12($2.25/$2.50, B&W)

1,2-(1992) 4.00
0-(4/93)-Illos by Chadwick, Eisner, Sim, M. Wagner; $2.50-c begins 4.00
3-12: 3-(7/93). 4-(11/93). 6-(2/94) 4.00

STARCHILD: MYTHOPOLIS
Image Comics: July, 1997 - Present ($2.95, B&W, limited series)

0-2-James Owen-s/a 2.95

STAR COMICS
Ultem Publ. (Harry `A' Chesler)/Centaur Publications: Feb, 1937 - V2#7 (No. 23), Aug, 1939 (#1-6: large size)

V1#1-Dan Hastings (s/f) begins 129.00 388.00 1100.00
2 62.00 185.00 525.00
3-6 (#6, 9/37): 4,5-Little Nemo-c/stories 58.00 173.00 490.00
7-9: 8-Severed head centerspread; Impy & Little Nemo by Winsor McCay Jr, Popeye app. by Bob Wood; Mickey Mouse & Popeye app. as toys in Santa's bag on-c; X-Mas-c 50.00 150.00 425.00
10 (1st Centaur; 3/38)-Impy by Winsor McCay Jr; Don Marlow by Guardineer begins 71.00 212.00 600.00
11-1st Jack Cole comic-a, 1 pg. (4/38) 50.00 150.00 425.00
12-15: 12-Riders of the Golden West begins; Little Nemo app. 15-Speed Silvers by Gustavson & The Last Pirate by Burgos begins 44.00 132.00 375.00
16 (12/38)-The Phantom Rider & his horse Thunder begins, ends V2#6 44.00 132.00 375.00
V2#1(#17, 2/39)-Phantom Rider-c (only non-funny-c) 44.00 132.00 375.00
2-7(#18-23): 2-Diana Deane by Tarpe Mills app. 3-Drama of Hollywood by Mills begins. 7-Jungle Queen app. 41.00 122.00 325.00

NOTE: ***Biro*** *c-6, 9, 10.* ***Burgos*** *a-15, 16, V2#1-7.* ***Ken Ernst*** *a-10, 12, 14.* ***Filchock*** *c-15, 18, 22.* ***Gill Fox*** *c-14, 19.* ***Guardineer*** *a-6, 8-14.* ***Gustavson*** *a-13-16, V2#1-7.* ***Winsor McCay*** *c-4, 5.* ***Tarpe Mills*** *a-15, V2#1-7.* ***Schwab*** *c-20, 23.* ***Bob Wood*** *a-10, 12, 13; c-7, 8.*

STAR COMICS MAGAZINE
Marvel Comics (Star Comics): Dec, 1986 - No. 13, 1988 ($1.50, digest-size)

1,9-Spider-Man-c/s .85 2.60 7.00
2-8-Heathcliff, Ewoks, Top Dog, Madballs-r in #1-13 5.00
10-13 2.00 6.00

S.T.A.R. CORPS
DC Comics: Nov, 1993 - No. 6, Apr, 1994 ($1.50, limited series)

1-6: 1,2-Austin-c(i). 1-Superman app. 1.50

STAR CROSSED
DC Comics (Helix): June, 1997 - No. 3, Aug, 1997 ($2.50, limited series)

1-3-Matt Howarth-s/a 2.50

STARDUST (See Neil Gaiman and Charles Vess' Stardust)

STAR FEATURE COMICS
I. W. Enterprises: 1963

Reprint #9-Stunt-Man Stetson-r/Feat. Comics #141 1.00 2.80 7.00

STARFIRE (Not the Teen Titans character)
National Periodical Publ./DC Comics: Aug-Sept, 1976 - No. 8, Oct-Nov, 1977

1-Origin (CCA stamp fell off cover art; so it was approved by code) .85 2.60 7.00
2-8 5.00

STARGATE (Movie)
Entity Comics: July, 1996 - No. 4, Oct, 1996 ($2.95, limited series)

1-4: Based on film 3.00
1-4-($3.50): Special Edition foil-c 3.50

STARGATE: DOOMSDAY WORLD (Movie)
Entity Comics: Nov, 1996 - No. 3, Jan, 1997 ($2.95, limited series)

1-3 3.00
1-3-($3.50)-Foil-c 3.50

STARGATE: ONE NATION UNDER RA (Movie)
Entity Comics: Apr, 1997 ($2.75, B&W, one-shot)

1-($2.75) 2.75
1-($3.50)-Foil-c 3.50

STARGATE: REBELLION (Movie)
Entity Comics: May/June, 1997 - No. 3, Nov, 1997 ($2.75, B&W, limited series)

1-3 2.75
1-3-($3.50)-Gold foil-c 3.50

STARGATE: THE NEW ADVENTURES COLLECTION (Movie)
Entity Comics: Dec, 1997 ($5.95, B&W)

1-Regular and photo-c 5.95

STARGATE: UNDERWORLD (Movie)
Entity Comics: May, 1997 ($2.75, B&W, one-shot)

1 2.75

STAR HUNTERS (See DC Super Stars #16)
National Periodical Publ./DC Comics: Oct-Nov, 1977 - No. 7, Oct-Nov, 1978

1,7: 1-Newton-a(p). 7-44 pgs. 4.00
2-6 3.00

NOTE: ***Buckler*** *a-4-7p; c-1-7p.* ***Layton*** *a-1-5i; c-1-6i.* ***Nasser*** *a-3p.* ***Sutton*** *a-6i.*

STARJAMMERS (See X-Men Spotlight on Starjammers)

STARJAMMERS (Also see Uncanny X-Men)
Marvel Comics: Oct, 1995 - No. 4, Jan, 1996 ($2.95, limited series)

1-4: Foil-c; Ellis scripts 3.00

STARK TERROR
Stanley Publications: Dec, 1970 - No. 5, Aug, 1971 (B&W, magazine, 52 pgs.)

1-Bondage, torture-c 3.80 11.50 40.00
2-4 (Gillmor/Aragon-r) 2.20 6.25 22.00
5 (ACG-r) 1.80 5.40 18.00

STARLET O'HARA IN HOLLYWOOD (Teen-age) (Also see Cookie)
Standard Comics: Dec, 1948 - No. 4, Sept, 1949

1-Owen Fitzgerald-a in all 16.00 48.00 120.00
2 11.00 32.00 80.00
3,4 9.30 28.00 70.00

STAR-LORD THE SPECIAL EDITION (Also see Marvel Comics Super Special #10, Marvel Premiere & Preview & Marvel Spotlight V2#6,7)
Marvel Comics Group: Feb, 1982 (one-shot, direct sales)
(1st Baxter paper comic)

1-Byrne/Austin-a; Austin-c; 8 pgs. of new-a by Golden (p); Dr. Who story by Dave Gibbons; 1st deluxe format comic 3.00

STARLORD
Marvel Comics: Dec, 1996 - No. 3, Feb, 1997 ($2.50, limited series)

1-3-Timothy Zahn-s 2.50

STARLORD MEGAZINE
Marvel Comics: Nov, 1996 ($2.95, one-shot)

1-Reprints w/preview of new series 3.00

STARMAN (1st Series) (Also see Justice League & War of the Gods)
DC Comics: Oct, 1988 - No. 45, Apr, 1992 ($1.00)

1-25,27-45: 1-Origin. 4-Intro The Power Elite. 9,10,34-Batman app. 14-Superman app. 17-Power Girl app. 27-Starman (David Knight) app. 28-Starman disguised as Superman; leads into Superman #50. 38-War of the Gods x-over. 42-Lobo cameo.42-45-Eclipso-c/stories (#43,44 with Lobo) 2.00
26-Ist app. David Knight (G.A.Starman's son). 3.00

STARMAN (2nd Series) (Also see The Golden Age, Showcase 95 #12,

Starman #44 (2nd Series) © DC

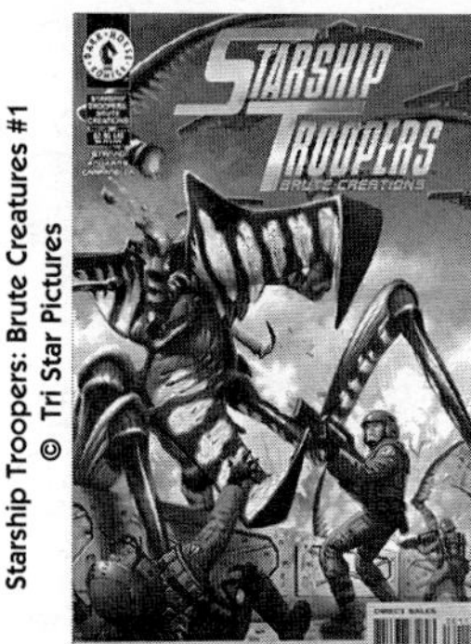

Starship Troopers: Brute Creatures #1 © Tri Star Pictures

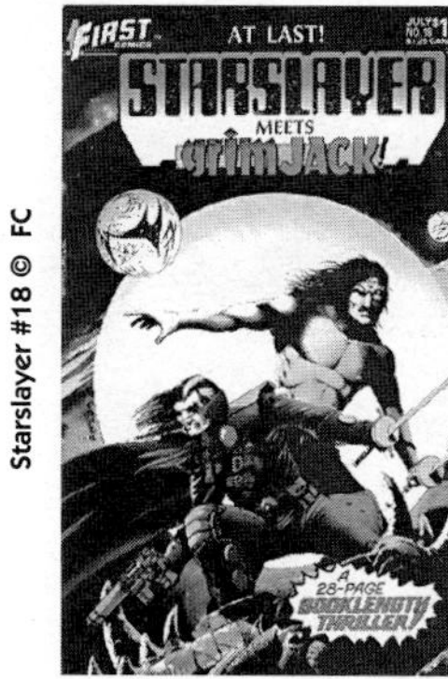

Starslayer #18 © FC

GD25 FN65 NM94

Showcase 96 #4,5)
DC Comics : No. 0, Oct, 1994 - Present ($1.95/$2.25/$2.50)

0,1: 0-James Robinson scripts, Tony Harris-c/a(p) & Wade Von Grawbadger-a(i) begins; Sins of the Father storyline begins, ends #3; 1st app. new Starman (Jack Knight); reintro of the G.A. Mist & G.A. Shade; 1st app. Nash; David Knight dies 1.00 3.00 10.00
2-7: 2-Reintro Charity from Forbidden Tales of Dark Mansion. 3-Reintro/2nd app "Blue" Starman (1st app. in 1st Issue Special #12); Will Payton app. (both cameos). 5-David Knight app. 6-The Shade "Times Past" story; Teddy Kristiansen-a. 7-The Black Pirate cameo .90 2.70 8.00
8-17: 8-Begin $2.25-c. 10-1st app. new Mist.(Nash) 11-JSA "Times Past" story; Matt Smith-a. 12-Sins of the Child storyline begins, ends #16. 17-The Black Pirate app. 5.00
18-32: 18-G.A. Starman "Times Past" story; Watkiss-a. 19-David Knight app. 20-23-G.A. Sandman app. 24-26-Demon Quest; all 3 covers make-up triptych. 3.50
33-37: 33-36-Batman-c/app. 37-David Knight and deceased JSA members app. 3.00
38-46: 38-Nash vs. Justice League Europe. 39,40-Crossover w/ Power of Shazam! #35,36; Bulletman app. 42-Demon-c/app. 43-JLA-c/app. 44-Phantom Lady-c/app. 46-Gena Ha-a 2.25
47-49: 47-Begin $2.50-c 2.50
50-($3.95) Gold foil logo on-c; Star Boy (LSH) app. 4.00
#1,000,000 (11/98) 853rd Century x-over; Snejbjerg-a 2.50
Annual 1 (1996, $3.50)-Legends of the Dead Earth story; Prince Gavyn & G.A. Starman stories; J.H. Williams III, Bret Blevins, Craig Hamilton-c/a(p) 4.00
Annual 2 (1997, $3.95)-Pulp Heroes story; 4.00
...80 Page Giant (1/99, $4.95) Harris-c 4.95
...Secret Files 1 (4/98, $4.95)-Origin stories and profile pages 5.00
...The Mist (6/98, $1.95) Girlfrenzy; Mary Marvel app. 2.00
Night and Day-($14.95, trade paperback)-r/#7-10,12-16 15.00
Sins of the Father-($12.95, trade paperback)-r/#0-5 13.00

STARMASTERS
Americomics: Mar, 1984 ($1.50, one-shot)

1-Origin The Women of W.O.S.P. & Breed 1.50

STAR PRESENTATION, A (Formerly My Secret Romance #1,2; Spectacular Stories #4 on) (Also see This Is Suspense)
Fox Features Syndicate (Hero Books): No. 3, May, 1950

3-Dr. Jekyll & Mr. Hyde by Wood & Harrison (reprinted in Startling Terror Tales #10); "The Repulsing Dwarf" by Wood; Wood-c 46.00 138.00 390.00

STAR QUEST COMIX (Warren Presents... on cover)
Warren Publications: Oct, 1978

1-Corben, Maroto, Neary-a; Ken Kelly-c 1.00 3.00 10.00

STAR RAIDERS (See DC Graphic Novel #1)

STAR RANGER (Cowboy Comics #13 on)
Ultem Publ./Centaur Publ.: Feb, 1937 - No. 12, May, 1938 (Large size: No. 1-6)

1-(1st Western comic)-Ace & Deuce, Air Plunder; Creig Flessel-a 141.00 424.00 1200.00
2 62.00 185.00 525.00
3-6 53.00 159.00 450.00
7-9: 8-Christmas-c 43.00 129.00 360.00
V2#10 (1st Centaur; 3/38) 71.00 212.00 600.00
11,12 54.00 162.00 460.00

NOTE: ***J. Cole** a-10, 12; c-12. **Ken Ernst** a-11. **Gill Fox** a-8(illo), 9, 10. **Guardineer** a-1, 3, 6, 7, 8(illos), 9, 10, 12. **Gustavson** a-8-10, 12. **Fred Schwab** c-2-11. **Bob Wood** a-8-10.*

STAR RANGER FUNNIES (Formerly Cowboy Comics)
Centaur Publications: V1#15, Oct, 1938 - V2#5, Oct, 1939

V1#15-Eisner, Gustavson-a 87.00 261.00 740.00
V2#1 (1/39) 62.00 185.00 525.00
2-5: 2-Night Hawk by Gustavson. 4-Kit Carson app. 53.00 159.00 450.00

NOTE: ***Jack Cole** a-V2#1, 3; c-V2#1. **Filchock** c-V2#2, 3. **Guardineer** a-V2#3. **Gustavson** a-V2#2. **Pinajian** c/a-V2#5.*

GD25 FN65 NM94

STAR REACH CLASSICS
Eclipse Comics: Mar, 1984 - No. 6, Aug, 1984 ($1.50, Baxter paper)

1-6: Neal Adams-r/Star Reach #1 1.50

NOTE: ***Dave Sim** a-1. **Starlin** a-1.*

STARR FLAGG, UNDERCOVER GIRL (See Undercover...)

STARRIORS
Marvel Comics: Aug, 1984 - Feb, 1985 (Limited series) (Based on Tomy toys)

1-4 1.00

STARS AND STRIPES COMICS
Centaur Publications: No. 2, May, 1941 - No. 6, Dec, 1941

2(#1)-The Shark, The Iron Skull, A-Man, The Amazing Man, Mighty Man, Minimidget begin; The Voice & Dash Dartwell, the Human Meteor, Reef Kinkaid app.; Gustavson Flag-c 194.00 582.00 1650.00
3-Origin Dr. Synthe; The Black Panther app. 112.00 335.00 950.00
4-Origin/1st app. The Stars and Stripes; injury to eye-c 100.00 300.00 850.00
5(#5 on cover & inside) 69.00 208.00 590.00
5(#6)-(#5 on cover, #6 on inside) 69.00 208.00 590.00

NOTE: ***Gustavson** c/a-3. **Myron Strauss** c-4, 5(#5), 5(#6).*

STAR SEED (Formerly Powers That Be)
Broadway Comics: No. 7, 1996 - Present ($2.95)

7-9 3.00

STARSHIP TROOPERS
Dark Horse Comics: 1997 - No. 2, 1997 ($2.95, limited series)

1,2-Movie adaption 2.95

STARSHIP TROOPERS: BRUTE CREATIONS
Dark Horse Comics: 1997 ($2.95, one-shot)

1 2.95

STARSHIP TROOPERS: DOMINANT SPECIES
Dark Horse Comics: Aug, 1998 - No. 4, Nov, 1998 ($2.95, limited series)

1-4-Strnad-s/Bolton-c 2.95

STARSHIP TROOPERS: INSECT TOUCH
Dark Horse Comics: 1997 - No. 3, 1997 ($2.95, limited series)

1-3 2.95

STAR SLAMMERS (See Marvel Graphic Novel #6)
Malibu Comics (Bravura): May, 1994 - No. 4, Aug, 1994 ($2.50, unfinished limited series)

1-4: W. Simonson-a/stories; contain Bravura stamps 2.50

STAR SLAMMERS SPECIAL
Dark Horse Comics (Legend): June, 1996 ($2.95, one-shot)

nn-Simonson-c/a/scripts; concludes Bravura limited series. 3.00

STARSLAYER
Pacific Comics/First Comics No. 7 on: Feb, 1982 - No. 6, Apr, 1983; No. 7, Aug, 1983 - No. 34, Nov, 1985

1-Origin & 1st app.; excessive blood & gore; 1 pg. Rocketeer cameo which continues in #2 3.00
2-Origin/1st full app. the Rocketeer (4/82) by Dave Stevens (Chapter 1 of Rocketeer saga; see Pacific Presents #1,2) .90 2.70 8.00
3-Chapter 2 of Rocketeer saga by Stevens 5.00
4,6,7: 7-Grell-a ends 2.00
5-2nd app. Groo the Wanderer by Aragones 2.00 6.00
8-34: 10-1st app. Grimjack (11/83, ends #17). 18-Starslayer meets Grimjack. 20-The Black Flame begins (9/84, 1st app.), ends #33. 27-Book length Black Flame story 1.00

NOTE: ***Grell** a-1-7; c-1-8. **Stevens** back c-2, 3. **Sutton** a-17p, 20-22p, 24-27p, 29-33p.*

Star Spangled Comics #98 © DC

Star Spangled War Stories #73 © DC

Star Spangled War Stories #151 © DC

GD25 FN65 NM94

STARSLAYER (The Director's Cut)
Acclaim Comics (Windjammer): June, 1994 - No. 8, Dec, 1995 ($2.50)

1-8: Mike Grell-c/a/scripts 2.50

STAR SPANGLED COMICS (Star Spangled War Stories #131 on)
National Periodical Publications: Oct, 1941 - No. 130, July, 1952

1-Origin/1st app. Tarantula; Captain X of the R.A.F., Star Spangled Kid (see Action #40), Armstrong of the Army begin; Robot-c 400.00 1200.00 3800.00
2 147.00 441.00 1250.00
3-5 91.00 273.00 775.00
6-Last Armstrong/Army; Penniless Palmer begins 58.00 174.00 490.00

GD25 FN65 VF82 NM94

7-(4/42)-Origin/1st app. The Guardian by S&K, & Robotman (by Paul Cassidy & created by Siegel);The Newsboy Legion (1st app.), Robotman & TNT begin; last Captain X 600.00 1800.00 3600.00 6300.00

GD25 FN65 NM94

8-Origin TNT & Dan the Dyna-Mite 200.00 600.00 1700.00
9,10 153.00 459.00 1300.00
11-17 112.00 336.00 950.00
18-Origin Star Spangled Kid 141.00 423.00 1200.00
19-Last Tarantula 110.00 330.00 935.00
20-Liberty Belle begins (5/43) 110.00 330.00 935.00
21-29-Last S&K issue; 23-Last TNT. 25-Robotman by Jimmy Thompson begins. 29-Intro Robbie the Robotdog 91.00 273.00 775.00
30-40: 31-S&K-c 47.00 141.00 400.00
41-50: 41,49,-Kirby-c. 50-1st S.A. issue 43.00 129.00 360.00
51-64: Last Newsboy Legion & The Guardian; last Liberty Belle? 51-Robot-c by Kirby. 53 by S&K 43.00 129.00 360.00
65-Robin begins with c/app. (2/47); Batman cameo in 1 panel; Robin-c begins, end #95 129.00 387.00 1100.00
66-Batman cameo in Robin story 77.00 229.00 650.00
67,68,70-80: 72-Burnley Robin-c 62.00 185.00 525.00
69-Origin/1st app. Tomahawk by F. Ray; atom bomb story & splash (6/47) 94.00 282.00 800.00
81-Origin Merry, Girl of 1000 Gimmicks in Star Spangled Kid story 47.00 141.00 400.00
82,85: 82-Last Robotman? 47.00 141.00 400.00
83-Tomahawk enters the lost valley, a land of dinosaurs; Capt. Compass begins, ends #130 47.00 141.00 400.00
84,87 (Rare): 87-Batman cameo in Robin 74.00 221.00 625.00
86-Batman cameo in Robin story; last Star Spangled Kid 53.00 159.00 450.00
88(1/49)-94: Batman-c/stories in all. 91-Federal Men begin, end #93. 94-Manhunters Around the World begin, end #121 56.00 168.00 475.00
95-Batman story; last Robin-c 52.00 156.00 440.00
96,98-Batman cameo in Robin stories. 96-1st Tomahawk-c (also #97-121) 37.00 112.00 280.00
97,99 31.00 94.00 235.00
100 (1/50)-Pre-Bat-Hound tryout in Robin story (pre-dates Batman #92). 39.00 116.00 290.00
101-109,118,119,121: 121-Last Tomahawk-c 29.00 86.00 215.00
110,111,120-Batman cameo in Robin stories. 120-Last 52 pg. issue 30.00 90.00 225.00
112-Batman & Robin story 32.00 96.00 240.00
113-Frazetta-a (10 pgs.) 39.00 117.00 310.00
114-Retells Robin's origin (3/51); Batman & Robin story 42.00 126.00 335.00
115,117-Batman app. in Robin stories 31.00 94.00 235.00
116-Flag-c 31.00 92.00 230.00
122-(11/51)-Ghost Breaker-c/stories begin (origin/1st app.), ends #130 (Ghost Breaker covers #122-130) 35.00 104.00 260.00
123-126,128,129 25.00 74.00 185.00
127-Batman cameo 26.00 78.00 195.00
130-Batman cameo in Robin story 27.00 82.00 205.00

NOTE: *Most all issues after #29 signed by Simon & Kirby are not by them.* ***Bill Ely*** *c-122-130.* ***Mortimer*** *c-65-74(most), 76-95(most).* ***Fred Ray*** *c-96-106, 109, 110, 112, 113, 115-120.* ***S&K*** *c-7-31, 33, 34, 36, 37, 39, 40, 48, 49, 50-54, 56-58.* ***Hal Sherman*** *c-1-6.* ***Dick Sprang*** *c-75.*

STAR SPANGLED KID (See Action #40, Leading Comics & Star Spangled Comics)

STAR SPANGLED WAR STORIES (Formerly Star Spangled Comics #1-130; Becomes The Unknown Soldier #205 on) (See Showcase)
National Periodical Publications: No. 131, 8/52 - No. 133, 10/52; No. 3, 11/52 - No. 204, 2-3/77

131(#1) 80.00 240.00 850.00
132 58.00 174.00 600.00
133-Used in **POP**, pg. 94 50.00 150.00 490.00
3-6: 4-Devil Dog Dugan app. 6-Evans-a 29.00 87.00 270.00
7-10 23.00 69.00 215.00
11-20 20.00 60.00 190.00
21-30: 30-Last precode (2/55) 17.00 51.00 160.00
31-33,35-40 11.50 34.00 115.00
34-Krigstein-a 11.00 33.00 110.00
41-50: 45-1st DC grey tone-c (5/56) 11.00 33.00 110.00
51,52,54-63,65,66, 68-83 7.50 22.50 75.00
53-"Rock Sergeant," 3rd Sgt. Rock prototype; inspired "P.I. & The Sand Fleas" in G.I. Combat #56 (1/57) 11.00 33.00 110.00
64-Pre-Sgt. Rock Easy Co. story (12/57) 9.00 27.00 90.00
67-2 Easy Co. stories without Sgt. Rock 9.50 28.50 95.00
84-Origin Mlle. Marie 16.00 48.00 160.00
85-89-Mlle. Marie in all 9.00 27.00 90.00
90-1st app. "War That Time Forgot" series; dinosaur issue-c/story (4-5/60) 31.00 93.00 350.00
91,93-No dinosaur stories 7.00 21.00 70.00
92,95-99: All dinosaur-c/s. 11.00 33.00 110.00
94 (12/60)- "Ghost Ace" story; Baron Von Richter as The Enemy Ace (pre-dates Our Army... #151) 15.00 45.00 150.00
100-Dinosaur-c/story. 13.00 39.00 130.00
101-115: All dinosaur issues 9.00 27.00 90.00
116-125,127-133,135-137-Last dinosaur story; Heath Birdman-#129,131 8.00 24.00 80.00
126-No dinosaur story 5.50 16.50 55.00
134-Dinosaur story; Neal Adams-a 8.00 24.00 80.00
138-New Enemy Ace-c/stories begin by Joe Kubert (4-5/68), end #150 (also see Our Army at War #151 and Showcase #57) 10.00 30.00 100.00
139-Origin Enemy Ace (7/68) 8.00 24.00 80.00
140-143,145: 145-Last 12¢ issue (6-7/69) 5.00 15.00 50.00
144-Neal Adams/Kubert-a 6.50 19.50 65.00
146-Enemy Ace-c only 3.30 9.90 33.00
147,148-New Enemy Ace stories 4.00 12.00 40.00
149,150-Last new Enemy Ace by Kubert. Viking Prince by Kubert 3.50 10.50 35.00
151-1st solo app. Unknown Soldier (6-7/70); Enemy Ace-r begin (from Our Army at War, Showcase & SSWS); end #161 12.00 36.00 130.00
152,153,155-Enemy Ace reprints 2.00 6.00 20.00
154-Origin Unknown Soldier 9.00 27.00 100.00
156-1st Battle Album; Unknown Soldier story; Kubert-c/a 2.00 6.00 20.00
157-Sgt. Rock x-over in Unknown Soldier story. 1.40 4.20 14.00
158-163-(52 pgs.): New Unknown Soldier storys; Kubert-c/a. 161-Last Enemy Ace-r .90 2.70 8.00
164-183,200: 181-183-Enemy Ace vs. Balloon Buster serial app; Frank Thorne-a. 200-Enemy Ace back-up 1.00 3.00 10.00
184-199,201-204 .90 2.70 8.00

NOTE: ***Anderson*** *a-28.* ***Chaykin*** *a-167.* ***Drucker*** *a-59, 61, 64, 66, 67, 73-84.* ***Estrada*** *a-149.* ***John Giunta*** *a-72.* ***Glanzman*** *a-167, 171, 172, 174.* ***Heath*** *a-122, 132, 133; c-67, 122, 132-134.* ***Kaluta*** *a-197i; c-167.* ***G. Kane*** *a-169.* ***Kubert*** *a-6-163(most later issues), 200.* ***Maurer*** *a-160, 165.* ***Severin*** *a-65, 162.* ***S&K*** *c-7-31, 33, 34, 37, 40.* ***Simonson*** *a-170, 172, 174, 180.* ***Sutton*** *a-168.* ***Thorne*** *a-183.* ***Toth*** *a-164.* ***Wildey*** *a-161. Suicide Squad in 110, 116-118, 120, 121, 127.*

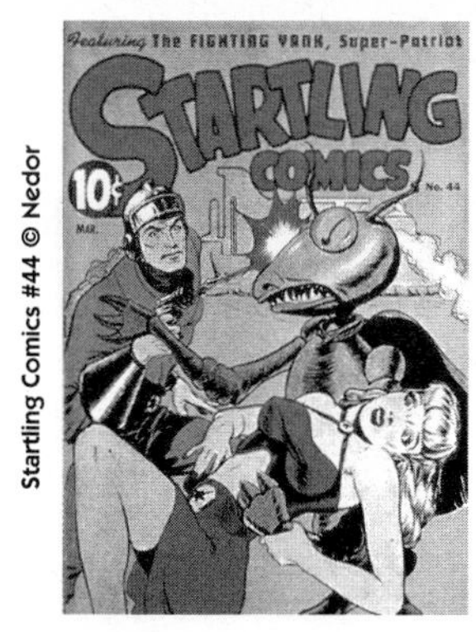

Startling Comics #44 © Nedor

Startling Terror Tales #13 © STAR

Star Trek #6 (1st DC Series) © Paramount

GD25 FN65 NM94

STARSTREAM (Adventures in Science Fiction)(See Questar illustrated)
Whitman/Western Publishing Co.: 1976 (79¢, 68 pgs, cardboard-c)

1-4: 1-Bolle-a. 2-4-McWilliams & Bolle-a .90 2.70 8.00

STARSTRUCK
Marvel Comics (Epic Comics): Feb, 1985 - No. 6, Feb, 1986 ($1.50, mature)

1-6: Kaluta-a. 3.00

STARSTRUCK
Dark Horse Comics: Aug, 1990 - No. 4, Nov?, 1990 ($2.95, B&W, limited series, 52pgs.)

1-3:Kaluta-r/Epic series plus new-c/a in all 3.00
4 (68, pgs.)-contains 2 trading cards 3.00

STAR STUDDED
Cambridge House/Superior Publishers: 1945 (25¢, 132 pgs.); 1945 (196 pgs.)

nn-Captain Combat by Giunta, Ghost Woman, Commandette, & Red Rogue app.; Infantino-a 27.00 80.00 200.00
nn-The Cadet, Edison Bell, Hoot Gibson, Jungle Lil (196 pgs.); copies vary; Blue Beetle in some 22.00 66.00 165.00

STAR TEAM
Marvel Comics Group: 1977 (6-1/2x5", 20 pgs.) (Ideal Toy Giveaway)

nn .90 2.70 8.00

STARTLING COMICS
Better Publications (Nedor): June, 1940 - No. 53, May, 1948

1-Origin Captain Future-Man Of Tomorrow, Mystico (By Eisner/Fine), The Wonder Man; The Masked Rider & his horse Pinto begins; Masked Rider formerly in pulps; drug use story 200.00 600.00 1700.00
2 -Don Davis, Espionage Ace begins 79.00 238.00 675.00
3 65.00 194.00 550.00
4 49.00 148.00 420.00
5-9 42.00 127.00 340.00
10-The Fighting Yank begins (9/41, origin/1st app.) 274.00 821.00 2600.00
11-2nd app. Fighting Yank 91.00 274.00 775.00
12-Hitler, Hirohito, Mussolini-c 65.00 194.00 550.00
13-15 48.00 145.00 410.00
16-Origin The Four Comrades; not in #32,35 54.00 162.00 460.00
17-Last Masked Rider & Mystico 40.00 120.00 320.00
18-Pyroman begins (12/42, origin)(also see America's Best Comics #3 for 1st app., 11/42) 82.00 247.00 700.00
19 40.00 120.00 320.00
20-The Oracle begins (3/43); not in issues 26,28,33,34 41.00 122.00 325.00
21-Origin The Ape, Oracle's enemy 42.00 127.00 340.00
22-33 40.00 120.00 315.00
34-Origin The Scarab & only app. 40.00 120.00 315.00
35-Hypodermic syringe attacks Fighting Yank in drug story 40.00 120.00 315.00
36-43: 36-Last Four Comrades. 38-Bondage/torture-c. 40-Last Capt. Future & Oracle. 41-Front Page Peggy begins; A-Bomb-c. 43-Last Pyroman 36.00 108.00 270.00
44-Lance Lewis, Space Detective begins; Ingels-c; sci/fi-c begin 49.00 148.00 420.00
45-Tygra begins (intro/origin, 5/47); Ingels-c/a (splash pg. & inside f/c B&W ad 49.00 148.00 420.00
46-Ingels-c/a 49.00 148.00 420.00
47,48,50-53: 50,51-Sea-Eagle app. 46.00 138.00 390.00
49-Classic Schomburg Robot-c; last Fighting Yank 253.00 758.00 2400.00

NOTE: ***Ingels** a-44, 45; c-44, 45, 46(wash). **Schomburg (Xela)** c-21-43; 47-53 (airbrush). **Tuska** c-45? Bondage c-16, 21, 37, 46-49. Captain Future c-1-9, 13, 14. Fighting Yank c-10-12, 15-17, 21, 22, 24, 26, 28, 30, 32, 34, 36, 38, 40, 42. Pyroman c-18-20, 23, 25, 27, 29, 31, 33, 35, 37, 39, 41, 43.*

STARTLING TERROR TALES
Star Publications: No. 10, May, 1952 - No. 14, Feb, 1953; No. 4, Apr, 1953 - No. 11, 1954

10-(1st Series)-Wood/Harrison-a (r/A Star Presentation #3) Disbrow/Cole-c; becomes 4 different titles after #10; becomes Confessions of Love #11 on, The Horrors #11 on, Terrifying Tales #11 on, Terrors of the Jungle #11 on & continues w/Startling Terror #11 56.00 168.00 475.00
11-(8/52)-L. B. Cole Spider-c; r-Fox's "A Feature Presentation" #5 (blue-c) 53.00 159.00 450.00
11-Black-c (variant; believed to be a pressrun change) (Unique) 76.00 229.00 650.00
12,14 21.00 64.00 160.00
13-Jo-Jo-r; Disbrow-a 23.00 68.00 170.00
4-9,11(1953-54) (2nd Series): 11-New logo 19.00 56.00 140.00
10-Disbrow-a 21.00 64.00 160.00

NOTE: ***L. B. Cole** covers-all issues. **Palais** a-V2#8r, V2#11r.*

STAR TREK (TV) (See Dan Curtis Giveaways, Dynabrite Comics & Power Record Comics)
Gold Key: 7/67; No. 2, 6/68; No. 3, 12/68; No. 4, 6/69 - No. 61, 3/79

1-Photo-c begin, end #9 36.00 109.00 400.00
2 22.00 66.00 240.00
2 (rare variation w/photo back-c) 33.00 99.00 360.00
3-5 15.00 44.00 160.00
3 (rare variation w/photo back-c) 23.00 68.00 250.00
6-9 12.00 36.00 130.00
10-20 7.00 21.00 75.00
21-30 5.00 15.00 55.00
31-40 3.20 9.50 35.00
41-61: 52-Drug propaganda story 2.25 6.75 25.00
...the Enterprise Logs nn (8/76)-Golden Press, ($1.95, 224 pgs.)-r/#1-8 plus 7 pgs. by McWilliams (#11185)-Photo-c 2.50 7.50 24.00
...the Enterprise Logs Vol. 2 ('76)-r/#9-17 (#11187)-Photo-c 2.50 7.50 24.00
...the Enterprise Logs Vol. 3 ('77)-r/#18-26 (#11188); McWilliams-a (4 pgs.)-Photo-c 2.50 7.50 28.00
Star Trek Vol. 4 (Winter '77)-Reprints #27,28,30-34,36,38 (#11189) plus 3 pgs. new art 2.50 7.50 28.00

NOTE: ***McWilliams** a-38, 40-44, 46-61. #29 reprints #1; #35 reprints #4; #37 reprints #5; #45 reprints #7. The tabloids all have photo covers and blank inside covers. Painted covers #10-44, 46-59.*

STAR TREK
Marvel Comics Group: April, 1980 - No. 18, Feb, 1982

1: 1-3-r/Marvel Super Special; movie adapt. 2.00 6.00
2-16: 5-Miller-c 5.00
17 (scarce) .90 2.70 8.00
18-Last issue 1.50 4.50 15.00

NOTE: ***Austin** c-18i. **Buscema** a-13. **Gil Kane** a-15. **Nasser** c/a-7. **Simonson** c-17.*

STAR TREK (Also see Who's Who In Star Trek)
DC Comics: Feb, 1984 - No. 56, Nov, 1988 (75¢, Mando paper)

1-Sutton-a(p) begins .90 2.70 9.00
2-5 5.00
6-10: 7-Origin Saavik 4.00
11-20: 19-Walter Koenig story 3.00
21-32 2.50
33-($1.25, 52 pgs.)-20th anniversary issue 3.00
34-49: 37-Painted-c. 49-Begin $1.00-c 2.00
50-($1.50, 52 pgs.) 2.00
51-56 1.75
Annual 1-3: 1(1985). 2(1986). 3(1988, $1.50) 2.50

NOTE: ***Morrow** a-28, 35, 36, 56. **Orlando** c-8i. **Perez** c-1-3. **Spiegle** a-19. **Starlin** c-24, 25. **Sutton** a-1-6p, 8-18p, 20-27p, 29p, 31-34p, 39-52p, 55p; c-4-6p, 8-22p, 46p.*

STAR TREK
DC Comics: Oct, 1989 - No. 80, Jan, 1996 ($1.50/$1.75/$1.95/$2.50)

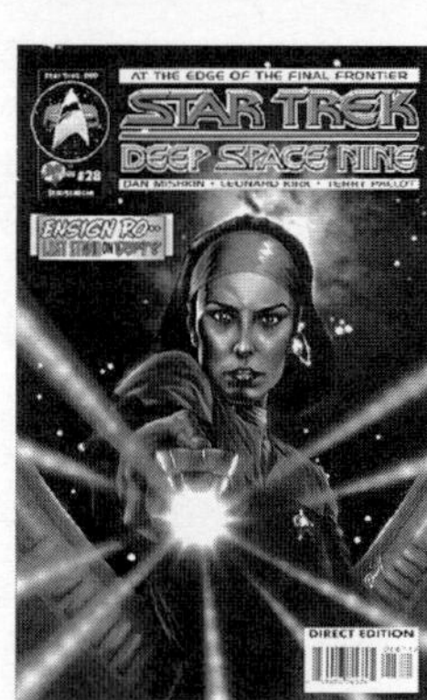

AT THE EDGE OF THE FINAL FRONTIER
STAR TREK
DEEP SPACE NINE
DIRECT EDITION

Star Trek: Deep Space Nine #28 © Paramount

Star Trek: Star Fleet Academy #18 (Klingon edition) © Paramount

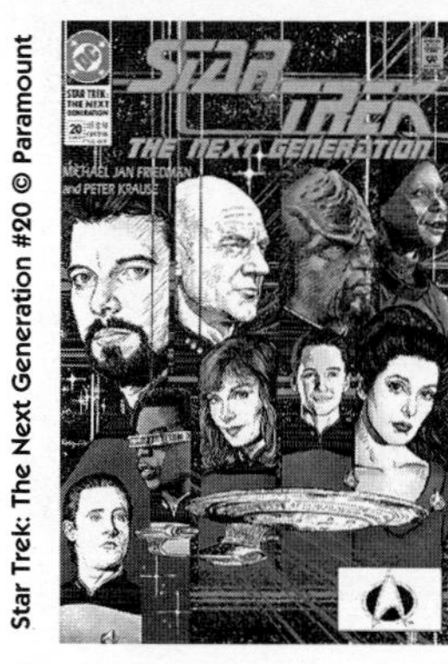

Star Trek: The Next Generation #20 © Paramount

GD25 FN65 NM94

1-Capt. Kirk and crew 5.00
2,3 3.00
4-23,25-30: 10-12-The Trial of James T. Kirk. 21-Begin $1.75-c 2.00
24-($2.95, 68 pgs.)-40 pg. epic w/pin-ups 3.50
31-49,51-60 2.00
50-($3.50, 68 pgs.)-Painted-c 3.50
61-70: 61-Begin $1.95-c 2.25
71-74, 76-80: 71-begin $2.50-c 2.50
75 ($3.95) 4.00
Annual 1,2('90, '91, $2.95, 68 pgs.): 1-Morrow-a 3.50
Annual 3,4 ('92,93, $3.50, 68 pgs.): 3-Painted-c 4.00
Annual 5 (1994, $3.95) 4.00
Annual 6 (1995, $3.95) 4.00
Special 1 (1994, $3.50, 68 pgs.)-Sutton-a. 3.50
Special 2 (1995, $3.50, 68 pgs.) 3.50
Special 3 (1995, $3.95) 4.00
...: The Ashes of Eden (1995, $14.95, 100 pgs.)-Shatner story 1.50 4.50 15.00
...Generations (1994, $3.95, 68 pgs.)-Movie adaptation 4.00
...Generations (1994, $5.95, 68 pgs.)-Squarebound 2.00 6.00

STAR TREK: DEEP SPACE NINE (TV)
Malibu Comics: Aug, 1993 - No. 32, Jan, 1996 ($2.50)

1-Direct Sale Edition w/line drawn-c 2.50
1-Newsstand Edition with photo-c 2.50
0 (1/95, $2.95)-Terok Nor 3.00
2-30: 2-Polybagged w/trading card. 9-4 pg. prelude to Hearts & Minds 2.50
31-($3.95) 4.00
32-($3.50) 3.50
Annual 1 (1/95, $3.95, 68 pgs.) 4.00
Special 1 (1995, $3.50) 3.50
Ultimate Annual 1 (12/95, $5.95) 2.00 6.00
...:Lightstorm (12/94, $3.50) 3.50

STAR TREK: DEEP SPACE NINE (TV)
Marvel Comics (Paramount Comics): Nov, 1996 - No. 15, Mar, 1998 ($1.95/$1.99)

1-3 2.00
4-15: 4-Begin $1.99-c. 12,13-"Telepathy War" pt. 2,3 2.00

STAR TREK DEEP SPACE NINE-THE CELEBRITY SERIES
Malibu Comics: May, 1995 ($2.95)

1-Blood and Honor; Mark Lenard script 3.00
1-Rules of Diplomacy; Aron Eisenberg script 3.00

STAR TREK: DEEP SPACE NINE HEARTS AND MINDS
Malibu Comics: June, 1994 - No. 4, Sept, 1994 ($2.50, limited series)

1-4 2.50
1-Holographic-c 4.00

STAR TREK: DEEP SPACE NINE, THE MAQUIS
Malibu Comics: Feb, 1995 - No. 3, Apr, 1995 ($2.50, limited series)

1-3-Newstand-c, 1-Photo-c 2.50

STAR TREK: DEEP SPACE NINE/THE NEXT GENERATION
Malibu Comics: Oct, 1994 - No. 2, Nov, 1994 ($2.50, limited series)

1,2: Parts 2 & 4 of "Prophet & Losses." 2.50

STAR TREK: DEEP SPACE NINE WORF SPECIAL
Malibu Comics: Dec, 1995 ($3.95, one-shot)

1-Includes pinups 4.00

STAR TREK EARLY VOYAGES(TV)
Marvel Comics (Paramount Comics): Feb, 1997 - No. 17, Jun, 1998 ($2.95/$1.95/$1.99)

1-($2.95) 3.00
2-6-($1.95) 2.00
7-17: 7-Begin- $1.99-c 2.00

STAR TREK: FIRST CONTACT (Movie)
Marvel Comics (Paramount Comics): Nov, 1996 ($5.95, one-shot)

nn-Movie adaption 2.00 6.00

STAR TREK: MIRROR MIRROR
Marvel Comics (Paramount Comics): Feb, 1997 ($3.95, one-shot)

1-DeFalco-s 4.00

STAR TREK MOVIE SPECIAL
DC Comics: 1984 (June) - No. 2, 1987 ($1.50); No. 1, 1989 ($2.00, 52 pgs)

nn-(#1)-Adapts Star Trek III; Sutton-p (68 pgs.) 1.75
2-Adapts Star Trek IV; Sutton-a; Chaykin-c. (68 pgs.) 1.75
1 (1989)-Adapts Star Trek V; painted-c 2.25

STAR TREK: OPERATION ASSIMILATION
Marvel Comics (Paramount Comics): Dec, 1996 ($2.95, one-shot)

1 3.00

STAR TREK VI: THE UNDISCOVERED COUNTRY (Movie)
DC Comics: 1992

1-($2.95, regular edition, 68 pgs.)-Adaptation of film 3.00
nn-($5.95, prestige edition)-Has photos of movie not included in regular edition; painted-c by Palmer; photo back-c 2.00 6.00

STAR TREK: STARFLEET ACADEMY
Marvel Comics (Paramount Comics): Dec, 1996 - No. 19, Jun, 1998 ($1.95/$1.99)

1-8-Begin new series 2.00
9-19: 9-Begin $1.99-c. 12-"Telepathy War" pt. 1. 18-English and Klingon language editions 2.00

STAR TREK: TELEPATHY WAR
Marvel Comics (Paramount Comics): Nov, 1997 ($2.99, 48 pgs., one-shot)

1-"Telepathy War" x-over pt. 6 3.00

STAR TREK - THE ASHES OF EDEN
DC Comics: 1995 ($14.95, 100 pgs., one-shot)

nn-Shatner scripts 1.50 4.50 15.00

STAR TREK - THE MODALA IMPERATIVE
DC Comics: Late July, 1991 - No. 4, Late Sept, 1991 ($1.75, limited series)

1 2.50
2-4 2.00

STAR TREK: THE NEXT GENERATION (TV)
DC Comics: Feb, 1988 - No. 6, July, 1988 (limited series)

1 ($1.50, 52 pgs.)-Sienkiewicz painted-c 5.00
2-6 ($1.00) 3.00

STAR TREK: THE NEXT GENERATION (TV)
DC Comics: Oct, 1989 -No. 80, 1995 ($1.50/$1.75/$1.95)

1-Capt. Picard and crew from TV show 5.00
2,3 3.00
4,5 2.50
6-10 2.50
11-23,25-30: 21-Begin $1.75-c 2.00
24-($2.50, 52 pgs.) 3.00
31-49,51-60 2.00
50-($3.50, 68 pgs.)-Painted-c 4.00
61-70: 61-Begins $1.95-c 2.25
71-74,76-80: 71-begin $2.50-c 2.50
75-($3.95, 50 pgs.) 4.00
Annual 1 (1990, $2.95, 68 pgs.) 4.00
Annual 2-4 (1991-93, $3.50, 68 pgs.) 4.50
Annual 5 (1994, $3.95, 68 pgs.) 4.00

Star Trek Voyager Splashdown #1 © Paramount

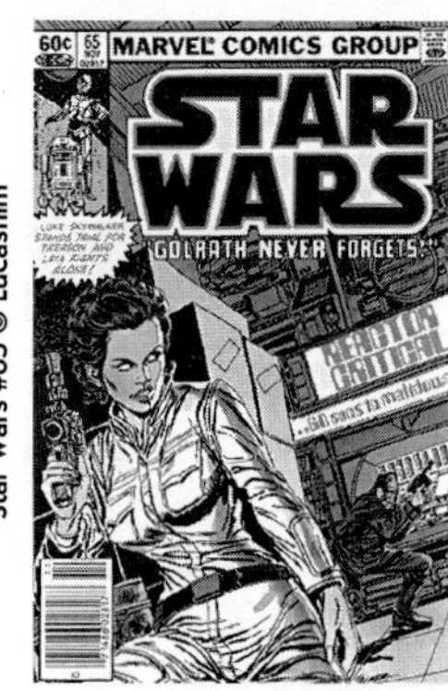

Star Wars #65 © Lucasfilm

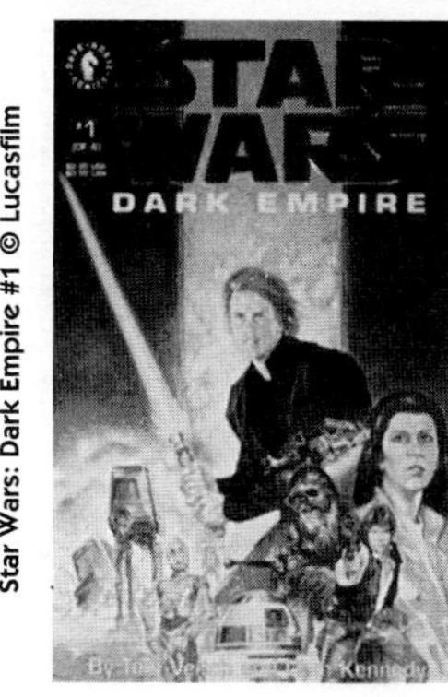

Star Wars: Dark Empire #1 © Lucasfilm

GD25 FN65 NM94

Annual 6 (1995, $3.95) 4.00
Special 1 (1993, $3.50, 68 pgs.)-Contains 3 stories 4.00
Special 2 (Sum/94, $3.95, 68 pgs.) 4.00
Special 3 ('95, $3.95) 4.00
...-The Series Finale (1994, $3.95, 68 pgs.) 4.00

STAR TREK: THE NEXT GENERATION/DEEP SPACE NINE (TV)
DC Comics: Dec, 1994 - No. 2, Jan, 1995 ($2.50, limited series)
1,2-Parts 1 & 3 of "Prophets & Losses" 2.50

STAR TREK: THE NEXT GENERATION - ILL WIND
DC Comics: Nov, 1995 - No. 3, Feb, 1996 ($2.50, limited series)
1-3 2.50

STAR TREK: THE NEXT GENERATION - RIKER
Marvel Comics (Paramount Comics): July, 1998 ($3.50, one-shot)
1-Riker joins the Maquis 3.50

STAR TREK: THE NEXT GENERATION - SHADOWHEART
DC Comics: Dec, 1994 - No. 4, Mar, 1995 ($1.95, limited series)
1-4 2.00

STAR TREK: THE NEXT GENERATION - THE MODALA IMPERATIVE
DC Comics: Early Sept, 1991 - No. 4, Late Oct, 1991 ($1.75, limited series)
1 2.50
2-4 2.00

STAR TREK UNLIMITED
Marvel Comics (Paramount Comics): Nov, 1996 - No. 10, July, 1998 ($2.95/$2.99)
1,2-Stories from original series and Next Generation 3.00
3-10: 3-Begin $2.99-c. 6-"Telepathy War" pt. 4. 7-Q & Trelane swap Kirk & Picard 3.00

STAR TREK: VOYAGER
Marvel Comics (Paramount Comics): Nov, 1996 - No. 15, Mar, 1998 ($1.95/$1.99)
1-4 2.00
5-15: 5-Begin $1.99-c. 13-"Telepathy War" pt. 5. 14-Seven of Nine joins crew 2.00

STAR TREK: VOYAGER SPLASHDOWN
Marvel Comics (Paramount Comics): Apr, 1998 - No. 4, July, 1998 ($2.50, limited series)
1-4-Voyager crashes on a water planet 2.50

STAR TREK/ X-MEN: 2ND CONTACT
Marvel Comics (Paramount Comics): May, 1998 ($4.99, 64 pgs., one-shot)
1-Next Gen. crew & X-Men battle Kang, Sentinels & Borg following First Contact movie 5.00
1-Painted wraparound variant cover 5.00

STAR WARS (Movie) (See Classic..., Contemporary Motivators, Dark Horse Comics, The Droids, The Ewoks, Marvel Movie Showcase, Marvel Special Ed.)
Marvel Comics Group: July, 1977 - No. 107, Sept, 1986
1-(Regular 30¢ edition)-Price in square w/UPC code; #1-6 adapt first movie 2.70 8.00 30.00
1-(35¢-c; limited distribution - 1500 copies?)- Price in square w/UPC code (see note below) 41.00 123.00 510.00
2-6: 2-4-30¢ issues. 4-Battle with Darth Vader. 6-Dave Stevens-a(i). 1.50 4.50 15.00
2-4-35¢ with UPC code; not reprints 6.50 19.00 72.00
7-20 1.00 3.00 10.00
21-91, 93-99: 39-44-The Empire Strikes Back-r by Al Williamson in all. 68,81-Reintro Boba Fett. 98-Williamson-a. .85 2.60 7.00
92,100-106: 92,100-($1.00, 52 pgs.). 1.10 3.30 11.00
107 (scarce); Portacio-a(i) 3.80 11.50 40.00
1-9: Reprints; has "reprint" in upper lefthand corner of cover or on inside or price and number inside a diamond with no date or UPC on cover; 30¢ and 35¢ issues published 3.00
Annual 1 (12/79, 52 pgs.)-Simonson-c .85 2.60 7.00
Annual 2 (11/82, 52 pgs.), 3(12/83, 52 pgs.) 2.00 6.00

NOTE: *The rare 35¢ edition has the cover price in a square box, and the UPC box in the lower left hand corner has the UPC code lines running through it.* ***Austin*** *c-11-15i, 21i, 38; c-12-15i, 21i.* ***Byrne*** *c-13p.* ***Chaykin*** *a-1-10p; c-1.* ***Golden*** *c/a-38.* ***Miller*** *c-47p; pin-up-43.* ***Nebres*** *c/a-Annual 2i.* ***Portacio*** *a-107i.* ***Sienkiewicz*** *c-92i, 98.* ***Simonson*** *a-16p, 49p, 51-63p, 65p, 66p; c-16, 49-51, 52p, 53-62, Annual 1.* ***Steacy*** *painted a-105i, 106i; c-105.* ***Williamson*** *a-39-44p, 50p, 98; c-39, 40, 41-44p. Painted c-81, 87, 92, 95, 98, 100, 105.*

STAR WARS: A NEW HOPE- THE SPECIAL EDITION
Dark Horse Comics: Jan, 1997 - No. 4, Apr, 1997 ($2.95, limited series)
1-4-Dorman-c 5.00

STAR WARS: BOBA FETT
Dark Horse Comics: Dec, 1995 - No. 3 ($3.95) (Originally intended as a one-shot)
1-Kennedy-c/a .90 2.70 8.00
2,3 2.00 6.00
Death, Lies, & Treachery TPB (1/98, $12.95) r/#1-3 12.95
Twin Engines of Destruction (1/97, $2.95) 3.00

STAR WARS: CRIMSON EMPIRE
Dark Horse Comics: Dec, 1997 - No. 6, May, 1998 ($2.95, limited series)
1-Richardson-s/Gulacy-a 2.00 6.00
2-6 4.00

STAR WARS: DARK EMPIRE
Dark Horse Comics: Dec, 1991 - No. 6, Oct, 1992 ($2.95, limited series)
Preview-(99¢) 1.00
1-All have Dorman painted-c 1.50 4.50 15.00
1-2nd printing 5.00
2-Low print run 2.00 6.00 20.00
2,3-2nd printings 5.00
3 .90 2.70 8.00
4-6 4.00
Gold Embossed Set (#1-6)-With gold embossed foil logo (price is for set) 80.00
Platinum Embossed Set (#1-6) 150.00
Trade paperback (4/93, 16.95) 17.00
Ltd. Ed. Hardcover ($99.95) Signed & numbered 125.00

STAR WARS: DARK EMPIRE II
Dark Horse Comics: Dec, 1994 - No. 6, May, 1995 ($2.95, limited series)
1-Dave Dorman painted-c 2.00 6.00
2-6: Dorman-c in all. 5.00
Platinum Embossed Set (#1-6) 35.00
Trade paperback ($17.95) 18.00

STAR WARS: DARK FORCE RISING
Dark Horse Comics: May, 1997 - No. 6, Oct, 1997 ($2.95, limited series)
1-6 5.00
TPB (2/98, $17.95) r/#1-6 17.95

STAR WARS: DROIDS (See Dark Horse Comics #17-19)
Dark Horse Comics: Apr, 1994 - #6, Sept, 1994; V2#1, Apr, 1995 - V2#8, Dec, 1995 ($2.50, limited series)
1-($2.95)-Embossed-c 3.00
2-6 ($2.25) 2.50
Special 1 (1/95, $2.50) 2.50
V2#1-8 2.50

STAR WARS: EMPIRE'S END
Dark Horse Comics: Oct, 1995 - No. 2, Nov, 1995 ($2.95, limited series)
1,2-Dorman-c 3.00

STAR WARS HANDBOOK: X-WING ROGUE SQUADRON
Dark Horse Comics: July, 1998 ($2.95, one-shot)

Star Wars: Mara Jade #1 © Lucasfilm

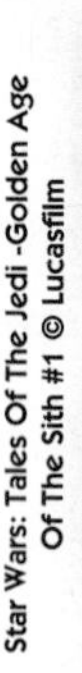

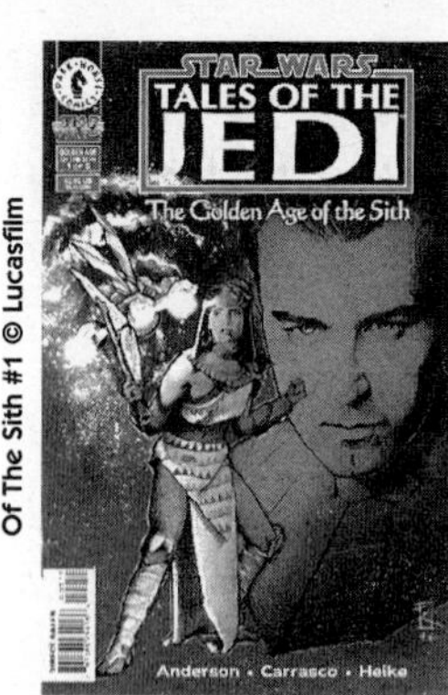

Star Wars: Tales Of The Jedi -Golden Age Of The Sith #1 © Lucasfilm

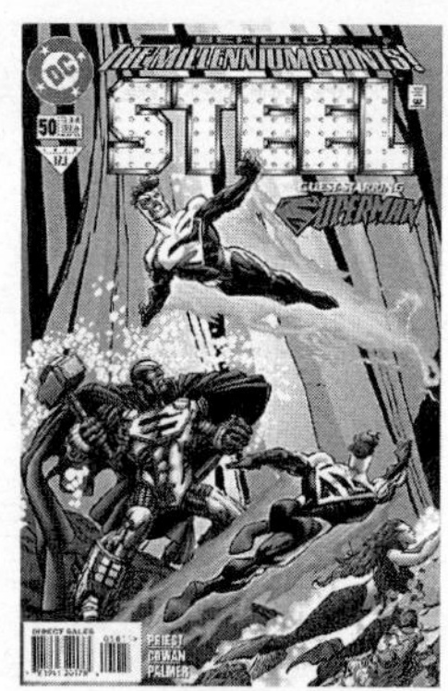

Steel #50 © DC

GD25 FN65 NM94

1-Guidebook to characters and spacecraft 3.00

STAR WARS : HEIR TO THE EMPIRE
Dark Horse Comics: Oct, 1995 - No.6, Apr, 1996 ($2.95, limited series)

1-6: Adaptation of Zahn novel 3.00

STAR WARS: JABBA THE HUTT
Dark Horse Comics: Apr, 1995 ($2.50, one-shots)

nn 2.50
...The Betrayal 2.50
...The Dynasty Trap 2.50
...The Hunger of Princess Nampi 2.50

STAR WARS: JEDI ACADEMY - LEVIATHAN
Dark Horse Comics: Oct, 1998 - No. 4, Jan, 1999 ($2.95, limited series)

1-4-Lago-c 3.00

STAR WARS: MARA JADE
Dark Horse Comics: Aug, 1998 - No. 6, Jan, 1999 ($2.95, limited series)

1-3-Ezquerra-a 3.00

STAR WARS: RETURN OF THE JEDI (Movie)
Marvel Comics Group: Oct, 1983 - No. 4, Jan, 1984 (limited series)

1-4-Williamson-p in all; r/Marvel Super Special #27 5.00
Oversized issue (1983, $2.95, 10-3/4x8-1/4", 68 pgs., cardboard-c)-r/#1-4 .90 2.70 9.00

STAR WARS: RIVER OF CHAOS
Dark Horse Comics: June, 1995 - No. 4, Sept, 1995 ($2.95, limited series)

1-4: Louise Simonson scripts 2.50

STAR WARS: SHADOWS OF THE EMPIRE
Dark Horse Comics: May, 1996 - No. 6, Oct, 1996 ($2.95, limited series)

1-6: Story details events between The Empire Strikes Back & Return of the Jedi; Russell-a(i). 3.00

STAR WARS: SHADOWS OF THE EMPIRE - EVOLUTION
Dark Horse Comics: Feb, 1998 - No. 5, June, 1998 ($2.95, limited series)

1-5: Perry-s/Fegredo-c. 3.00

STAR WARS: SHADOW STALKER
Dark Horse Comics: Sept, 1997 ($2.95, one-shot)

nn-Windham-a. 3.00

STAR WARS: SPLINTER OF THE MIND'S EYE
Dark Horse Comics: Dec, 1995 - No. 4, June, 1996 ($2.50, limited series)

1-4: Adaption of Alan Dean Foster novel 2.50

STAR WARS: TALES FROM MOS EISLEY
Dark Horse Comics: Mar, 1996 ($2.95, one-shot)

nn-Bret Blevins-a. 3.00

STAR WARS: TALES OF THE JEDI (See Dark Horse Comics #7)
Dark Horse Comics: Oct, 1993 - No. 5, Feb, 1994 ($2.50, limited series)

1-5: All have Dave Dorman painted-c. 3-r/Dark Horse Comics #7-9 w/new coloring & some panels redrawn 3.00
1-5-Gold foil embossed logo; limited # printed-7500 50.00

STAR WARS: TALES OF THE JEDI-DARK LORDS OF THE SITH
Dark Horse Comics: Oct, 1994 - No. 6, Mar, 1995 ($2.50, limited series)

1-6: 1-Polybagged w/trading card 3.00

STAR WARS: TALES OF THE JEDI-REDEMPTION
Dark Horse Comics: July, 1998 - No. 5, Nov, 1998 ($2.95, limited series)

1-5: 1-Kevin J. Anderson-s/Kordey-c 3.00

STAR WARS: TALES OF THE JEDI-THE FALL OF THE SITH
Dark Horse Comics: June, 1997 - No. 5, Oct, 1997 ($2.95, limited series)

1-5 3.00

GD25 FN65 NM94

STAR WARS: TALES OF THE JEDI-THE FREEDON NADD UPRISING
Dark Horse Comics: Aug, 1994 - No. 2, Nov, 1994 ($2.50, limited series)

1,2 2.50

STAR WARS: TALES OF THE JEDI-THE GOLDEN AGE OF THE SITH
Dark Horse Comics: July, 1996 - No. 5, Feb, 1997 (99¢/$2.95, limited series)

0-(99¢)-Anderson-s 1.00
1-5-Anderson-s 3.00

STAR WARS: TALES OF THE JEDI-THE SITH WAR
Dark Horse Comics: Aug, 1995 - No. 6, Jan, 1996 ($2.50, limited series)

1-6: Anderson scripts 2.50

STAR WARS: THE LAST COMMAND
Dark Horse Comics: Nov, 1997 - No. 6, July, 1998 ($2.95, limited series)

1-6:Based on the Timothy Zaun novel 5.00

STAR WARS: THE PROTOCOL OFFENSIVE
Dark Horse Comics: Sept, 1997 ($4.95, one-shot)

nn-Anthony Daniels & Ryder Windham-s 5.00

STAR WARS: X-WING ROGUE SQUADRON (Star Wars: X-Wing Rogue Squadron-The Phantom Affair #5-8 appears on cover only))
Dark Horse Comics: July, 1995 - Present ($2.95)

1/2 5.00
1-24: 1-4-Baron scripts. 5-20-Stackpole scripts 3.00
25-($3.95) 4.00
26-34 3.00
The Phantom Affair TPB ($12.95) r/#5-8 12.95

S.T.A.T.
Majestic Entertainment: Dec, 1993 ($2.25)

1 2.25

STATIC (Also see Eclipse Monthly)
Charlton Comics: No, 11, Oct, 1985 - No. 12, Dec, 1985

11,12-Ditko-c/a 1.00

STATIC (See Heroes)
DC Comics (Milestone): June, 1993 - No. 45, Mar, 1997 ($1.50/$1.75/$2.50)

1-($2.95)-Collector's Edition; polybagged w/poster & trading card & backing board (direct sales only) 3.00
1-13: 2-Origin. 8-Shadow War; Simonson silver ink-c 1.50
14-($2.50, 52 pgs.)-Worlds Collide Pt. 14 2.50
15-24: 15-Begin $1.75-c 1.75
25 ($3.95) 4.00
26-30,32-45: 26-Begin $2.50-c. 27-Kent Williams-c 2.50
31-(99¢) 1.00

STEALTH SQUAD
Petra Comics: Sept, 1993 ($2.50, unfinished limited series)

1-Super hero team 2.50

STEED AND MRS. PEEL (TV)(Also see The Avengers)
Eclipse Books/ ACME Press: 1990 - No. 3, 1991 ($4.95, limited series)

Books One - Three: Grant Morrison scripts 5.00

STEEL (Also see JLA)
DC Comics: Feb, 1994 - No. 52, July, 1998 ($1.50/$1.95/$2.50)

1-8: 1-From Reign of the Supermen storyline. 6,7-Worlds Collide Pt. 5 & 12. 8-(9/94) 1.50
0,9-15: 0-(10/94). 9-(11/94) 1.50
16-46: 16-Begin $1.95-c. 46-Superboy-c/app. 2.00
47-52-($2.50). 50-Millennium Giants x-over 2.50
Annual 1 (1994, $2.95)-Elseworlds story 3.00
Annual 2 (1995, $3.95)-Year One story 4.00
...Forging of a Hero TPB (1997, $19.95) r/ early app. 20.00

Steel, The Indestructible Man #4 © DC

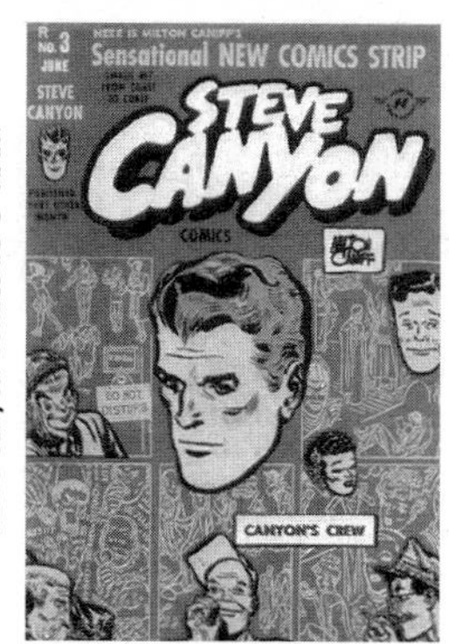

Steve Canyon Comics #3 © HARV

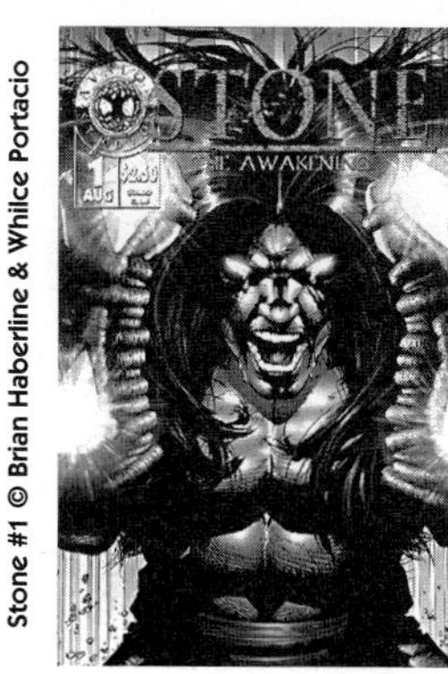

Stone #1 © Brian Haberline & Whilce Portacio

	GD25	FN65	NM94

STEEL: THE OFFICIAL COMIC ADAPTION OF THE WARNER BROS. MOTION PICTURE
DC Comics: 1997 ($4.95, Prestige format, one-shot)

nn-Movie adaption; Bogdanove & Giordano-a			5.00

STEELGRIP STARKEY
Marvel Comics (Epic Comics): June, 1986 - No. 6, July, 1987 ($1.50, limited series, Baxter paper)

1-6			1.50

STEEL STERLING (Formerly Shield-Steel Sterling; see Blue Ribbon, Jackpot, Mighty Comics, Mighty Crusaders, Roly Poly & Zip Comics)
Archie Enterprises, Inc.: No. 4, Jan, 1984 - No. 7, July, 1984

4-7: 6-McWilliams-a			1.00

STEEL, THE INDESTRUCTIBLE MAN (See All-Star Squadron #8)
DC Comics: Mar, 1978 - No. 5, Oct-Nov, 1978

1,5: 5-44 pgs.			4.00
2-4			3.00

STEELTOWN ROCKERS
Marvel Comics: Apr, 1987 - No. 6, Sept, 1990 ($1.00, limited series)

1-6: Small town teens form rock band			1.00

STEVE CANYON (See Harvey Comics Hits #52)
Dell Publishing Co.: No. 519, 11/53 - No. No. 1033, 9/59 (All Milton Caniff-a except #519, 939, 1033)

Four Color 519 (1, '53)	8.00	25.00	90.00
Four Color 578 (8/54), 641 (7/55), 737 (10/56), 804 (5/57), 939 (10/58), 1033 (9/59) (photo-c)	4.50	13.50	50.00

STEVE CANYON
Grosset & Dunlap: 1959 (6-3/4x9", 96 pgs., B&W, no text, hardcover)

100100-Reprints 2 stories from strip (1953, 1957)	4.15	12.50	25.00
100100 (softcover edition)	4.00	10.00	20.00

STEVE CANYON COMICS
Harvey Publ.: Feb, 1948 - No. 6, Dec, 1948 (Strip reprints, No. 4,5: 52pgs.)

1-Origin; has biography of Milton Caniff; Powell-a, 2 pgs.; Caniff-a	19.00	56.00	140.00
2-Caniff, Powell-a in #2-6	12.00	36.00	90.00
3-6: 6-Intro Madame Lynx-c/story	11.00	32.00	80.00
Dept. Store giveaway #3(6/48, 36pp)	9.30	28.00	70.00
...'s Secret Mission (1951, 16 pgs., Armed Forces giveaway); Caniff-a	9.30	28.00	65.00
Strictly for the Smart Birds (1951, 16 pgs.)-Information Comics Div. (Harvey) Premium	8.00	24.00	56.00

STEVE CANYON IN 3-D
Kitchen Sink Press: June, 1986 ($2.25, one-shot)

1-Contains unpublished story from 1954			4.00

STEVE DITKO'S STRANGE AVENGING TALES
Fantagraphics Books: Feb, 1997 ($2.95, B&W)

1-Ditko-c/s/a			3.00

STEVE DONOVAN, WESTERN MARSHAL (TV)
Dell Publishing Co.: No. 675, Feb, 1956 - No. 880, Feb, 1958 (All photo-c)

Four Color 675-Kinstler-a	7.00	22.00	80.00
Four Color 768-Kinstler-a	5.50	16.50	60.00
Four Color 880	3.60	11.00	40.00

STEVE ROPER
Famous Funnies: Apr, 1948 - No. 5, Dec, 1948

1-Contains 1944 daily newspaper-r	10.00	30.00	75.00
2	5.70	17.00	40.00
3-5	5.35	16.00	32.00

STEVE SAUNDERS SPECIAL AGENT (See Special Agent)

STEVE SAVAGE (See Captain...)

STEVE ZODIAC & THE FIRE BALL XL-5 (TV)
Gold Key: Jan, 1964

10108-401 (#1)	7.30	22.00	80.00

STEVIE (Mazie's boy friend)(Also see Flat-Top, Mazie & Mortie)
Mazie (Magazine Publ.): Nov, 1952 - No. 6, Apr, 1954

1-Teenage humor; Stevie, Mortie & Mazie begin	5.70	17.00	40.00
2-6	4.15	12.50	25.00

STEVIE MAZIE'S BOY FRIEND (See Harvey Hits #5)

STEWART THE RAT (See Eclipse Graphic Album Series)

ST. GEORGE (See listing under Saint...)

STIGG'S INFERNO
Vortex/Eclipse: 1985 - No. 7, Mar, 1987 ($1.95, B&W)

1-7 ($1.95)			2.00
Graphic Album (1988, $6.95, B&W, 100 pgs.)			7.00

STING OF THE GREEN HORNET (See The Green Hornet)
Now Comics: June, 1992 - No. 4, 1992 ($2.50, limited series)

1-4: Butler-c/a			2.50
1-4 ($2.75)-Collectors Ed.; polybagged w/poster			2.75

STONE
Avalon Studios: Aug, 1998 - Present ($2.50)

1-Portacio-a/Haberlin-s			2.50
1-Alternate-c			10.00
2,3			2.50
2-($14.95) DF Stonechrome Edition			14.95

STONEY BURKE (TV)
Dell Publishing Co.: June-Aug, 1963 - No. 2, Sept-Nov, 1963

1,2: Jack Lord photo-c	1.85	5.50	15.00

STONY CRAIG
Pentagon Publishing Co.: 1946 (No #)

nn-Reprints Bell Syndicate's "Sgt. Stony Craig" newspaper strips	5.70	17.00	40.00

STORIES BY FAMOUS AUTHORS ILLUSTRATED (Fast Fiction #1-5)
Seaboard Publ./Famous Authors Ill.: No. 6, Aug, 1950 - No. 13, Mar, 1951

1-Scarlet Pimpernel-Baroness Orczy	32.00	96.00	240.00
2-Capt. Blood-Raphael Sabatini	32.00	96.00	240.00
3-She, by Haggard	39.00	117.00	295.00
4-The 39 Steps-John Buchan	21.00	64.00	160.00
5-Beau Geste-P. C. Wren	21.00	64.00	160.00

NOTE: *The above five issues are exact reprints of Fast Fiction #1-5 except for the title change and new Kiefer covers on #1 and 2. Kiefer c(r)-3-5. The above 5 issues were released before Famous Authors #6.*

6-Macbeth, by Shakespeare; Kiefer art (8/50); used in **SOTI**, pg. 22,143; Kiefer-c; 36 pgs.	28.00	84.00	210.00
7-The Window; Kiefer-c/a; 52 pgs.	20.00	60.00	150.00
8-Hamlet, by Shakespeare; Kiefer-c/a; 36 pgs.	25.00	76.00	190.00
9-Nicholas Nickleby, by Dickens; G. Schrotter-a; 52 pgs.	21.00	64.00	160.00
10-Romeo & Juliet, by Shakespeare; Kiefer-c/a; 36 pgs.	21.00	64.00	160.00
11-Ben-Hur; Schrotter-a; 52 pgs.	20.00	60.00	150.00
12-La Svengali; Schrotter-a; 36 pgs.	20.00	60.00	150.00
13-Scaramouche; Kiefer-c/a; 36 pgs.	20.00	60.00	150.00

NOTE: *Artwork was prepared/advertised for #14, The Red Badge Of Courage. Gilberton bought out Famous Authors, Ltd. and used that story as C.I. #98. Famous Authors, Ltd. then published the Classics Junior series. The Famous Authors titles were published as part of the regular Classics Ill. Series in Brazil starting in 1952.*

STORIES OF CHRISTMAS
K. K. Publications: 1942 (Giveaway, 32 pgs., paper cover)

StormWatch #25 © WildStorm Prod.

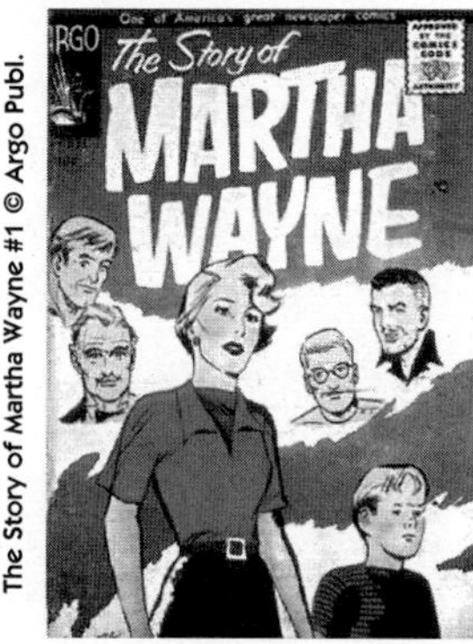

The Story of Martha Wayne #1 © Argo Publ.

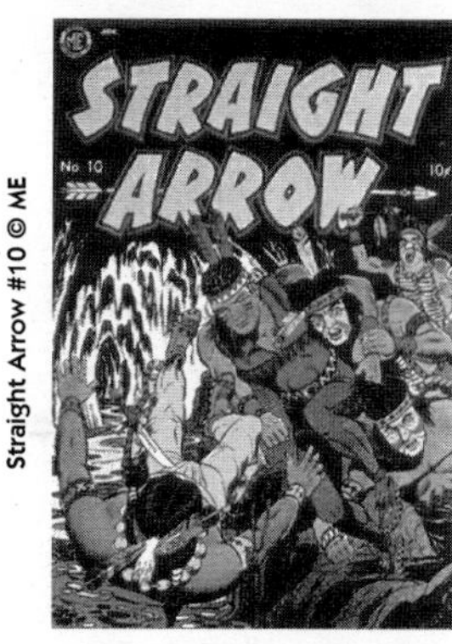

Straight Arrow #10 © ME

	GD25	FN65	NM94
nn-Adaptation of "A Christmas Carol"; Kelly story "The Fir Tree"; Infinity-c	35.00	104.00	260.00

STORIES OF ROMANCE (Formerly Meet Miss Bliss)
Atlas Comics (LMC): No. 5, Mar, 1956 - No. 13, Aug, 1957

	GD25	FN65	NM94
5-Baker-a?	7.85	23.50	55.00
6-10,12,13	5.35	16.00	32.00
11-Baker, Romita-a; Colletta-c/a	5.70	17.00	38.00

NOTE: ***Ann Brewster** a-13. **Colletta** a-9(2), 11; c-5, 11.*

STORM
Marvel Comics: Feb, 1996 - No. 4, May, 1996 ($2.95, limited series)

1-4-Foil-c; Dodson-a(p); Ellis-s: 2-4-Callisto; 3.00

STORMQUEST
Caliber Press (Sky Universe): Nov, 1994 - No. 6, Apr, 1995 ($1.95)

1-6 2.00

STORMWATCH
Image Comics (WildStorm Prod.): May, 1993 - No. 50, Jul, 1997 ($1.95/$2.50)

	GD25	FN65	NM94
1-8: 1-Intro StormWatch (Battalion, Diva, Winter, Fuji, & Hellstrike); 1st app. Weatherman; Jim Lee-c & part scripts; Lee plots in all. 1-Gold edition. 1-3-Includes coupon for limited edition StormWatch trading card #00 by Lee. 3-1st app. Backlash (cameo).			2.00
0-($2.50)-Polybagged w/card; 1st full app. Backlash			2.50
9-(4/94, $2.50)-Intro Defile			2.50
10-17: 10-(6/94), 11,12-Both (8/94). 13,14-(9/94). 15-(10/94)			2.00
10-Alternate Portacio-c, see Deathblow #5		2.00	6.00
18-21: 18-$2.50-c begins. 21-Reads #1 on-c.			2.50
22-36: 22-Direct Market; Wildstorm Rising Pt. 9, bound-in card. 23-Spartan joins team. 25-(6/94, June 1995 on-c, $2.50). 35-Fire From Heaven Pt. 5. 36-Fire From Heaven Pt. 12			2.50
22-($1.95)-Newsstand, Wildstorm Rising Pt. 9			2.00
37-(7/96, $3.50, 38 pgs.)-Weatherman forms new team; 1st app. Jenny Sparks, Jack Hawksmoor & Rose Tattoo; Warren Ellis scripts begin; Justice League #1-c/swipe			3.50
38-49: 38-Begin $2.50-c. 44-Three covers.			2.50
50-($4.50)			4.50
Special 1 (1/94, $3.50, 52 pgs.)			3.50
Special 2 (5/95, $3.50, 52 pgs.)			3.50
Sourcebook 1 (1/94, $2.50)			2.50

STORMWATCH
Image Comics (WildStorm): Oct, 1997 - No. 11, Sept, 1998 ($2.50)

	GD25	FN65	NM94
1-Ellis-s/Jimenez-a(p); two covers by Bennett			2.50
1-($3.50)-Voyager Pack bagged w/Gen 13 preview			3.50
2-11: 7,8-Freefall app. 9-Gen13 & DV8 app.			2.50

STORMWATCHER
Eclipse Comics (Acme Press): Apr, 1989 - No. 4, Dec, 1989 ($2.00, B&W, limited series)

1-4 2.00

STORMY (Disney) (Movie)
Dell Publishing Co.: No. 537, Feb, 1954

	GD25	FN65	NM94
Four Color 537 (...the Thoroughbred)-on top 2/3 of each page; Pluto story on bottom 1/3	2.75	8.00	30.00

STORY HOUR SERIES (Disney)
Whitman Publ. Co.: 1948, 1949; 1951-1953 (36 pgs., paper-c) (4-3/4x6-1/2")
Given away with subscription to Walt Disney's Comics & Stories

	GD25	FN65	NM94
nn(1948)-Mickey Mouse and the Boy Thursday	11.00	34.00	85.00
nn(1948)-Mickey Mouse the Miracle Master	11.00	34.00	85.00
nn(1948)-Minnie Mouse and Antique Chair	11.00	34.00	85.00
nn(1949)-The Three Orphan Kittens(B&W & color)	6.50	19.50	45.00
nn(1949)-Danny-The Little Black Lamb	6.50	19.50	45.00
800(1948)-Donald Duck in "Bringing Up the Boys"	13.00	40.00	100.00
1953 edition	7.85	23.50	55.00
801(1948)-Mickey Mouse's Summer Vacation	9.30	28.00	65.00
1951, 1952 editions	4.25	13.00	28.00
802(1948)-Bugs Bunny's Adventures	7.15	21.50	50.00
803(1948)-Bongo	5.70	17.00	35.00
804(1948)-Mickey and the Beanstalk	7.15	21.50	50.00
805-15(1949)-Andy Panda and His Friends	5.70	17.00	40.00
806-15(1949)-Tom and Jerry	6.50	19.50	45.00
808-15(1949)-Johnny Appleseed	5.70	17.00	35.00
1948, 1949 Hard Cover Edition of each....	$3.00 - $5.00 more.		

STORY OF EDISON, THE
Educational Comics: 1956 (16 pgs.) (Reddy Killowatt)

	GD25	FN65	NM94
nn-Reprint of Reddy Kilowatt #2(1947)	5.00	15.00	30.00

STORY OF HARRY S. TRUMAN, THE
Democratic National Committee: 1948 (Giveaway, regular size, soft-c, 16 pg.)

	GD25	FN65	NM94
nn-Gives biography on career of Truman; used in **SOTI**, pg. 311	9.30	28.00	70.00

STORY OF JESUS (See Classics Illustrated Special Issue)

STORY OF MANKIND, THE (Movie)
Dell Publishing Co.: No. 851, Jan, 1958

	GD25	FN65	NM94
Four Color 851-Vincent Price/Hedy Lamarr photo-c	6.40	19.00	70.00

STORY OF MARTHA WAYNE, THE
Argo Publ.: April, 1956

	GD25	FN65	NM94
1-Newspaper strip-r	4.25	13.00	28.00

STORY OF RUTH, THE
Dell Publishing Co.: No. 1144, Nov-Jan, 1961 (Movie)

	GD25	FN65	NM94
Four Color #1144-Photo-c	9.00	27.00	100.00

STORY OF THE COMMANDOS, THE (Combined Operations)
Long Island Independent: 1943 (15¢, B&W, 68 pgs.) (Distr. by Gilberton)

	GD25	FN65	NM94
nn-All text (no comics); photos & illustrations; ad for Classic Comics on back cover (Rare)	27.00	80.00	200.00

STORY OF THE GLOOMY BUNNY, THE (See March of Comics #9)

STRAIGHT ARROW (Radio)(See Best of the West & Great Western)
Magazine Enterprises: Feb-Mar, 1950 - No. 55, Mar, 1956 (All 36 pgs.)

	GD25	FN65	NM94
1-Straight Arrow (alias Steve Adams) & his palomino Fury begin; 1st mention of Sundown Valley & the Secret Cave	39.00	117.00	300.00
2-Red Hawk begins (1st app?) by Powell (origin), ends #55	19.00	56.00	140.00
3-Frazetta-c	27.00	80.00	200.00
4,5: 4-Secret Cave-c	17.00	52.00	130.00
6-10	16.00	48.00	120.00
11-Classic story "The Valley of Time", with an ancient civilization made of gold	17.00	52.00	130.00
12-19	13.00	38.00	95.00
20-Origin Straight Arrow's Shield	15.00	44.00	110.00
21-Origin Fury	17.00	52.00	130.00
22-Frazetta-c	18.00	54.00	135.00
23,25-30: 25-Secret Cave-c. 28-Red Hawk meets The Vikings	7.85	23.50	55.00
24-Classic story "The Dragons of Doom!" with prehistoric pteradactyls	9.30	28.00	70.00
31-38: 36-Red Hawk drug story by Powell	5.70	17.00	40.00
39-Classic story "The Canyon Beast", with a dinosaur egg hatching a Tyranosaurus Rex	9.30	28.00	65.00
40-Classic story "Secret of The Spanish Specters", with Conquistadors' lost treasure	8.50	26.00	60.00
41,42,44-54: 45-Secret Cave-c	5.70	17.00	35.00
43-Intro & 1st app. Blaze, S. Arrow's Warrior dog	7.15	21.50	50.00
55-Last issue	8.50	26.00	60.00

NOTE: ***Fred Meagher** a 1-55; c-1, 2, 4-21, 23-55. **Powell** a 2-55. **Whitney** a-1. Many issues*

Strange Adventures #8 © DC

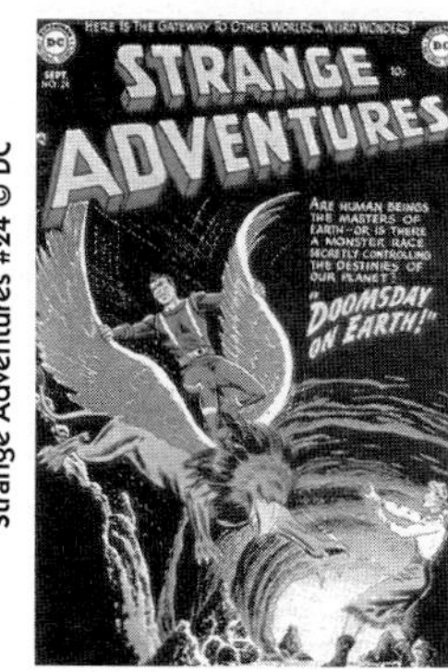

Strange Adventures #24 © DC

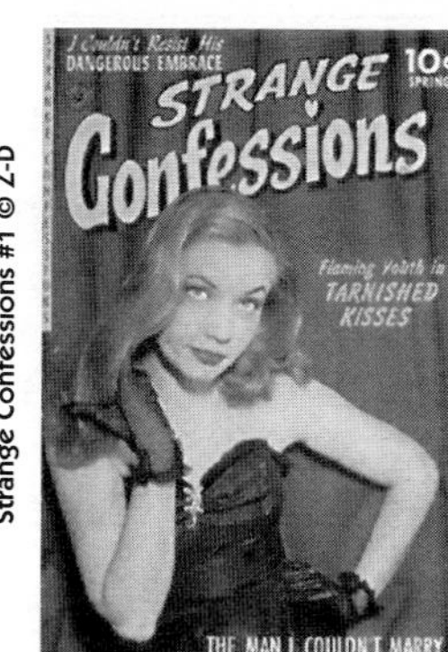

Strange Confessions #1 © Z-D

GD25 FN65 NM94

advertise the radio premiums associated with Straight Arrow.

STRAIGHT ARROW'S FURY (Also see A-1 Comics)
Magazine Enterprises: No. 119, 1954 (one-shot)

	GD25	FN65	NM94
A-1 119-Origin; Fred Meagher-c/a	12.00	36.00	90.00

STRANGE (Tales You'll Never Forget)
Ajax-Farrell Publ. (Four Star Comic Corp.): March, 1957 - No. 6, May, 1958

	GD25	FN65	NM94
1	16.00	48.00	120.00
2-Censored r/Haunted Thrills	8.50	26.00	60.00
3-6	7.15	21.50	50.00

STRANGE ADVENTURES
National Periodical Publications: Aug-Sept, 1950 - No. 244, Oct-Nov, 1973 (No. 1-12: 52 pgs.)

	GD25	FN65	NM94
1-Adaptation of "Destination Moon"; preview of movie w/photo-c from movie (also see Fawcett Movie Comic #2); adapt. of Edmond Hamilton's "Chris KL-99" in #1-3; Darwin Jones begins	250.00	750.00	2500.00
2	110.00	330.00	1150.00
3,4	70.00	210.00	770.00
5-8,10: 7-Origin Kris KL-99	64.00	192.00	650.00
9-(6/51)-Origin/1st app. Captain Comet (c/story).	150.00	450.00	1500.00
11-20: 12,13,17,18-Toth-a. 14-Robot-c	44.00	132.00	450.00
21-30: 28-Atomic explosion panel. 30-Robot-c	35.00	105.00	360.00
31,34-38	34.00	102.00	320.00
32,33-Krigstein-a	34.00	102.00	325.00
39-Ill. in **SOTI** "Treating police contemptuously" (top right)	38.00	114.00	375.00
40-49-Last Capt. Comet; not in 45,47,48	32.00	96.00	290.00
50-53-Last precode issue (2/55)	24.00	72.00	220.00
54-70	16.00	48.00	160.00
71-99	11.50	34.00	115.00
100	13.00	39.00	130.00
101-110: 104-Space Museum begins by Sekowsky.	9.00	27.00	90.00
111-116,118,119: 114-Star Hawkins begins, ends #185; Heath-a in Wood E.C. style	8.00	24.00	80.00
117-(6/60)-Origin/1st app. Atomic Knights.	47.00	141.00	570.00
120-2nd app. Atomic Knights	23.00	69.00	230.00
121,122,125,127,128,130,131,133,134: 134-Last 10¢ issue	7.00	21.00	70.00
123,126-3rd & 4th app. Atomic Knights	13.50	40.00	135.00
124-Intro/origin Faceless Creature	7.50	22.50	75.00
129,132,135,138,141,147-Atomic Knights app.	8.50	25.50	85.00
136,137,139,140,143,145,146,148,149,151,152,154,155,157-159: 159-Star Rovers app.; Gil Kane/Anderson-a.	4.80	14.40	48.00
142-2nd app. Faceless Creature	5.20	15.60	52.00
144-Only Atomic Knights-c (by M. Anderson)	9.50	28.50	95.00
150,153,156,160: Atomic Knights in each. 153-(6/63)-3rd app. Faceless Creature; atomic explosion-c. 160-Last Atomic Knights	6.50	19.50	65.00
161-179: 161-Last Space Museum. 163-Star Rovers app. 170-Infinity-c. 177-Intro/origin Immortal Man	3.50	10.50	35.00
180-Origin/1st app. Animal Man	19.00	51.00	190.00
181-183,185-189: 187-Intro/origin The Enchantress	2.50	7.50	20.00
184-2nd app. Animal Man by Gil Kane	11.50	34.00	115.00
190-1st app. Animal Man in costume	14.00	42.00	140.00
191-194,196-200,202-204	2.00	6.00	16.00
195-1st full app. Animal Man	7.50	22.50	75.00
201-Last Animal Man; 2nd full app.	3.50	10.50	35.00
205-(10/67)-Intro/origin Deadman by Infantino & begin series, ends #216	9.50	28.50	95.00
206-Neal Adams-a begins	6.00	18.00	60.00
207-210	4.80	14.40	48.00
211-216: 211-Space Museum-r. 216-(1-2/69)-Deadman story finally concludes in Brave & the Bold #86 (10-11/69); secret message panel by Neal Adams (pg. 13); tribute to Steranko	3.60	10.80	36.00
217-221,223-225: 217-r/origin & 1st app. Adam Strange from Showcase #17, begin-r; Atomic Knights-r begin. 218-Last 12¢ issue. 225-Last 15¢ issue	1.25	3.75	10.00
222-New Adam Strange story; Kane/Anderson-a	2.50	7.50	24.00
226,227,230-236-(68-52 pgs.): 226, 227-New Adam Strange text story w/illos by Anderson (8,6 pgs.) 231-Last Atomic Knights-r. 235-JLA-c/s	1.50	4.50	12.00
228,229 (68 pgs.)	1.85	5.50	15.00
237-243	1.00	3.00	8.00
244-Last issue	1.25	3.75	10.00

NOTE: ***Neal Adams** a-206-216; c-207-216, 228, 235. **Anderson** a-8-52, 94, 96, 99, 115, 117, 119-163, 217r, 218r, 222, 223-225r, 226, 229r, 242i(r); c-18, 19, 21, 23, 24, 27, 30, 32-44(most); c/r-157i, 190i, 217-224, 228-231, 233, 235-239, 241-243. **Ditko** a-188, 189. **Drucker** a-42, 43, 45. **Elias** a-212. **Finlay** a-2, 3, 6, 7, 210r, 229r. **Giunta** a-237r. **Heath** a-116. **Infantino** a-10-101, 106-151, 154, 157-163, 180, 190, 218-221r, 223-244p(r); c-50; c(r)-190p, 197, 199-211, 218-221, 223-244. **Kaluta** c-238, 240. **Gil Kane** a-8-116, 124, 125, 130, 138, 146-157, 173-186, 204r, 222r, 227-231r; c(p)-11-17, 25, 154, 157. **Kubert** a-55(2 pgs.), 226; c-219, 220, 225-227, 232, 234. **Moriera** c-26, 28, 29, 71. **Morrow** c-230. **Mortimer** c-8. **Powell** a-4. **Sekowsky** a-71p, 97-162p, 217p(r), 218p(r); c-206, 217-219r. **Simon & Kirby** a-2r (2 pgs) **Sparling** a-201. **Toth** a-8, 12, 13, 17-19. **Wood** a-154i. Atomic Knights in #117, 120, 123, 126, 129, 132, 135, 138, 141, 144, 147, 150, 153, 156, 160. Atomic Knights reprints by **Anderson** in 217-221, 223-231. Chris KL99 in 1-3, 5, 7, 9, 11, 15. Capt. Comet covers-9-14, 17-19, 24, 26, 27, 32-44.*

STRANGE AS IT SEEMS (See Famous Funnies-A Carnival of Comics, Feature Funnies #1, The John Hix Scrap Book & Peanuts)

STRANGE AS IT SEEMS
McNaught Syndicate: 1936 (B&W, 5x7", 24 pgs.)

	GD25	FN65	NM94
nn-Ex-Lax giveaway	3.60	9.00	18.00

STRANGE AS IT SEEMS
United Features Syndicate: 1939

	GD25	FN65	NM94
Single Series 9, 1, 2	31.00	92.00	230.00

STRANGE ATTRACTORS
RetroGraphix: 1993 - No. 15, Feb, 1997 ($2.50, B&W)

	GD25	FN65	NM94
1-15: 1-(5/93), 2-(8/93), 3-(11/93), 4-(2/94)			2.50
Volume One-($14.95, trade paperback)-r/#1-7			15.00

STRANGE ATTRACTORS: MOON FEVER
Caliber Comics: Feb, 1997 - No. 3, June, 1997 ($2.95, B&W, mini-series)

	GD25	FN65	NM94
1-3			3.00

STRANGE COMBAT TALES
Marvel Comics (Epic Comics): Oct, 1993 - No. 4, Jan, 1994 ($2.50, limited series)

	GD25	FN65	NM94
1-4			2.50

STRANGE CONFESSIONS
Ziff-Davis Publ. Co.: Jan-Mar (Spring on-c), 1952 - No. 4, Fall, 1952 (All have photo-c) (Approved)

	GD25	FN65	NM94
1(Scarce)-Kinstler-a	41.00	122.00	325.00
2(Scarce, 7-8/52)	28.00	84.00	210.00
3(Scarce, 9-10/52)-#3 on-c, #2 on inside; Reformatory girl story; photo-c	28.00	84.00	210.00
4(Scarce)	28.00	84.00	210.00

STRANGE DAYS
Eclipse Comics: Oct, 1984 - No. 3, Apr, 1985 ($1.75, Baxter paper)

	GD25	FN65	NM94
1-3: Freakwave, Johnny Nemo, & Paradax from Vanguard Illustrated; nudity, violence & strong language			1.80

STRANGE DAYS (Movie)
Marvel Comics: Dec, 1995 ($5.95, squarebound, one-shot)

	GD25	FN65	NM94
1-Adaptation of film		2.00	6.00

STRANGE FANTASY (Eerie Tales of Suspense!)(Formerly Rocketman #1)
Ajax-Farrell: Aug, 1952 - No. 14, Oct-Nov, 1954

2(#1, 8/52)-Jungle Princess story; Kamenish-a; reprinted from Ellery Queen #1

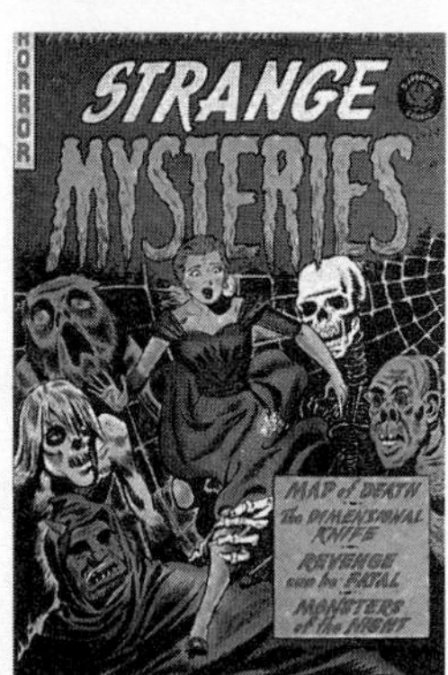

Strange Mysteries #10 © SUPR

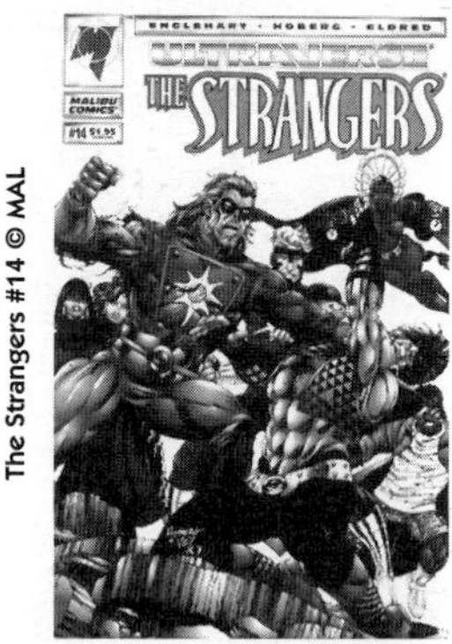

The Strangers #14 © MAL

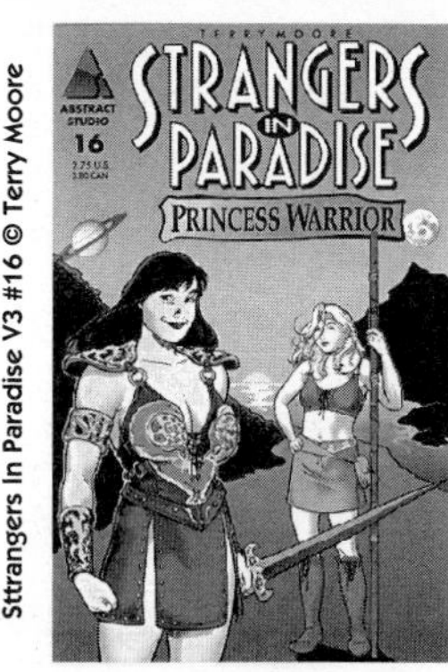

Sttrangers In Paradise V3 #16 © Terry Moore

GD25 FN65 NM94

37.00 112.00 280.00
2(10/52)-No Black Cat or Rulah; Bakerish, Kamenish-a; hypo/meathook-c 29.00 88.00 220.00
3-Rulah story, called Pulah 28.00 84.00 210.00
4-Rocket Man app. (2/53) 25.00 76.00 190.00
5,6,8,10,12,14 19.00 56.00 140.00
7-Madam Satan/Slave story 25.00 76.00 190.00
9(w/Black Cat), 9(w/Boy's Ranch; S&K-a)(A rebinding of Harvey interiors; not publ. by Ajax) 23.00 70.00 175.00
9-Regular issue; Steve Ditko's 3rd published work (tied with Captain 3D) 37.00 110.00 275.00
11-Jungle story 25.00 76.00 190.00
13-Bondage-c; Rulah (Kolah) story 25.00 76.00 190.00

STRANGE GALAXY
Eerie Publications: V1#8, Feb, 1971 - No. 11, Aug, 1971 (B&W, magazine)
V1#8-Reprints-c/Fantastic V19#3 (2/70) (a pulp) 2.40 7.00 26.00
9-11 1.80 5.40 18.00

STRANGEHAVEN
Abiogenesis Press: June, 1995 - Present ($2.95, B&W)
1-9 3.00

STRANGE JOURNEY
America's Best (Steinway Publ.) (Ajax/Farrell): Sept, 1957 - No. 4, Jun, 1958 (Farrell reprints)
1 15.00 45.00 115.00
2-4: 2-Flying saucer-c 11.00 32.00 80.00

STRANGE LOVE (See Fox Giants)

STRANGELOVE
Entity Comics: 1995 ($2.50)
1 2.50

STRANGE MYSTERIES
Superior/Dynamic Publications: Sept, 1951 - No. 21, Jan, 1955
1-Kamenish-a & horror stories begin 47.00 141.00 400.00
2 27.00 80.00 200.00
3-5 23.00 70.00 175.00
6-8 19.00 58.00 145.00
9-Bondage 3-D effect-c 25.00 76.00 190.00
10-Used in **SOTI**, pg. 181 18.00 54.00 135.00
11-18 15.00 46.00 115.00
19-r/Journey Into Fear #1; cover is a splash from one story; Baker-r(2) 18.00 54.00 135.00
20,21-Reprints; 20-r/#1 with new-c 11.00 32.00 80.00

STRANGE MYSTERIES
I. W. Enterprises/Super Comics: 1963 - 1964
I.W. Reprint #9; Rulah-r/Spook #28; Disbrow-a 2.50 7.50 24.00
Super Reprint #10-12,15-17(1963-64): 10,11-r/Strange #2,1. 12-r/Tales of Horror #5 (3/53) less-c. 15-r/Dark Mysteries #23. 16-r/The Dead Who Walk. 17-r/Dark Mysteries #22 2.50 7.50 24.00
Super Reprint #18-r/Witchcraft #1; Kubert-a 2.50 7.50 24.00

STRANGE PLANETS
I. W. Enterprises/Super Comics: 1958; 1963-64
I.W. Reprint #1(nd)-Reprints E. C. Incredible S/F #30 plus-c/Strange Worlds #3 5.50 16.50 55.00
I.W. Reprint #9-Orlando/Wood-r/Strange Worlds #4; cover-r from Flying Saucers #1 7.50 22.50 75.00
Super Reprint #10-Wood-r (22 pg.) from Space Detective #1; cover-r/Attack on Planet Mars 7.00 21.00 70.00
Super Reprint #11-Wood-r (25 pg.) from An Earthman on Venus 8.50 25.50 85.00
Super Reprint #12-Orlando-r/Rocket to the Moon 7.00 21.00 70.00

GD25 FN65 NM94

Super Reprint #15-Reprints Journey Into Unknown Worlds #8; Heath, Colan-r 3.00 9.00 30.00
Super Reprint #16-Reprints Avon's Strange Worlds #6; Kinstler, Check-a 3.50 10.50 35.00
Super Reprint #18-r/Great Exploits #1 (Daring Adventures #6); Space Busters, Explorer Joe, The Son of Robin Hood; Krigstein-a 2.50 7.50 25.00

STRANGERS, THE
Malibu Comics (Ultraverse): June, 1993 - No. 24, May, 1995 ($1.95/$2.50)
1-4,6-12,14-20: 1-1st app. The Strangers; has coupon for Ultraverse Premiere #0; 1st app. the Night Man (not in costume). 2-Polybagged w/trading card. 7-Break-Thru x-over. 8-2 pg. origin Solution. 12-Silver foil logo; wraparound-c. 17-Rafferty app. 2.00
1-With coupon missing 1.50
1-Full cover holographic edition, 1st of kind w/Hardcase #1 & Prime #1 5.00
1-Ultra 5000 limited silver foil 4.00
4-($2.50)-Newsstand edition bagged w/card 2.50
5-($2.50, 52 pgs.)-Rune flip-c/story by B. Smith (3 pgs.); The Mighty Magnor 1 pg. strip by Aragones; 3-pg. Night Man preview 2.50
13-($3.50, 68 pgs.)-Mantra app.; flip book w/Ultraverse Premiere #4 3.50
21-24 ($2.50) 2.50
...:The Pilgrim Conundrum Saga (1/95, $3.95, 68pgs.) 4.00

STRANGERS IN PARADISE
Antarctic Press: Nov, 1993 - No. 3, Feb, 1994 ($2.75, B&W, limited series)
1 6.00 17.50 65.00
1-2nd/3rd prints .85 2.60 7.00
2 (2300 printed) 4.50 13.50 50.00
3 2.70 8.00 30.00
Trade paperback (Antarctic Press, $6.95)-Red -c (5000 print run) 15.00
Trade paperback (Abstract Studios, $6.95)-Red-c (2000 print run) 20.00
Trade paperback (Abstract Studios, $6.95, 1st-4th printing)-Blue- 7.00
Hardcover ('98, $29.95) includes first draft pages 29.95
Gold Reprint Series ($2.75) 1-3-r/#1-3 2.75

STRANGERS IN PARADISE
Abstract Studios: Sept, 1994 - No. 14, July, 1996 ($2.75, B&W)
1 2.00 6.00 20.00
1,3- 2nd printings 5.00
2,3: 2-Color dream sequence. 1.00 3.00 10.00
4-10 5.00
4-6-2nd printings 2.75
11-14: 14-The Letters of Molly & Poo 3.00
Gold Reprint Series ($2.75) 1-13-r/#1-13 2.75
I Dream Of You ($16.95, TPB) r/#1-9 17.00
It's a Good Life ($8.95, TPB) r/#10-13 9.00

STRANGERS IN PARADISE (Volume Three)
Homage Comics #1-8/Abstract Studios #9-on: Oct, 1996 - Present ($2.75, color #1-5, B&W #6-on)
1-Terry Moore-c/s/a in all; dream seq. by Jim Lee-a 2.00 6.00
1-Jim Lee variant-c .95 2.70 8.00
2-5 4.00
6-15: 6-Return to B&W. 13-15-High school flashback 3.00
16-Xena Warrior Princess parody; two covers 3.00
17-19 2.75
Immortal TPB ('98, $14.95) r/#6-12 14.95
Love Me Tender ($12.95, TPB) r/#1-5 in B&W w/ color Lee seq. 12.95

STRANGE SPORTS STORIES (See Brave & the Bold #45-49, DC Special, and DC Super Stars #10)
National Periodical Publications: Sept-Oct, 1973 - No. 6, July-Aug, 1974
1 2.20 6.25 22.00
2-6: 2-Swan/Anderson-a 1.40 4.20 14.00

STRANGE STORIES FROM ANOTHER WORLD (Unknown World #1)
Fawcett Publications: No. 2, Aug, 1952 - No. 5, Feb, 1953

Strange Suspense Stories #62 © CC

Strange Tales #35 © MAR

Strange Tales #108 © MAR

	GD25	FN65	NM94
2-Saunders painted-c	43.00	129.00	345.00
3-5-Saunders painted-c	33.00	100.00	250.00

STRANGE STORIES OF SUSPENSE (Rugged Action #1-4)
Atlas Comics (CSI): No. 5, Oct, 1955 - No. 16, Aug, 1957

	GD25	FN65	NM94
5(#1)	31.00	94.00	235.00
6,9	19.00	56.00	140.00
7-E. C. swipe cover/Vault of Horror #32	19.00	58.00	145.00
8-Morrow/Williamson-a; Pakula-a	19.00	58.00	145.00
10-Crandall, Torres, Meskin-a	19.00	58.00	145.00
11-13: 12-Torres, Pakula-a. 13-E.C. art swipes	15.00	46.00	115.00
14-16: 14-Williamson/Mayo-a. 15-Krigstein-a. 16-Fox, Powell-a	16.00	48.00	120.00

NOTE: ***Everett** a-6, 7, 13; c-8, 9, 11-14. **Heath** a-5. **Maneely** c-5. **Morisi** a-11. **Morrow** a-13. **Powell** a-8. **Severin** c-7. **Wildey** a-14.*

STRANGE STORY (Also see Front Page)
Harvey Publications: June-July, 1946 (52 pgs.)

	GD25	FN65	NM94
1-The Man in Black Called Fate by Powell	25.00	74.00	185.00

STRANGE SUSPENSE STORIES (Lawbreakers Suspense Stories #10-15; This Is Suspense #23-26; Captain Atom V1#78 on)
Fawcett Publications/Charlton Comics No. 16 on: 6/52 - No. 5, 2/53; No. 16, 1/54 - No. 22, 11/54; No. 27, 10/55 - No. 77, 10/65; V3#1, 10/67 - V1#9, 9/69

	GD25	FN65	NM94
1-(Fawcett)-Powell, Sekowsky-a	61.00	184.00	520.00
2-George Evans horror story	41.00	122.00	325.00
3-5 (2/53)-George Evans horror stories	37.00	112.00	280.00
16(1-2/54)-Formerly Lawbreakers S.S.	23.00	70.00	175.00
17,21: 21-Shuster-a	19.00	56.00	140.00
18-E.C. swipe/HOF 7; Ditko-c/a(2)	32.00	96.00	240.00
19-Ditko electric chair-c; Ditko-a	42.00	126.00	335.00
20-Ditko-c/a(2)	32.00	96.00	240.00
22(11/54)-Ditko-c, Shuster-a; last pre-code issue; becomes This Is Suspense	27.00	80.00	200.00
27(10/55)-(Formerly This Is Suspense #26)	11.00	32.00	80.00
28-30,38	7.15	21.50	50.00
31-33,35,37,40-Ditko-c/a(2-3 each)	17.00	50.00	125.00
34-Story of ruthless business man, Wm. B. Gaines; Ditko-c/a	35.00	104.00	260.00
36-(15¢, 68 pgs.); Ditko-a(4)	18.00	54.00	135.00
39,41,52,53-Ditko-a	14.00	42.00	105.00
42-44,46,49,54-60	3.20	9.60	32.00
45,47,48,50,51-Ditko-c/a	8.50	25.50	85.00
61-74	1.85	5.50	15.00
75(6/65)-Reprints origin/1st app. Captain Atom by Ditko from Space Advs. #33; r/Severin-a/Space Advs. #24 (75-77: 12¢ issues)	10.00	30.00	100.00
76,77-Captain Atom-r by Ditko/Space Advs.	4.50	13.50	45.00
V3#1(10/67): 12¢ issues begin	2.50	7.50	20.00
V1#2-Ditko-c/a; atom bomb-c	1.85	5.50	15.00
V1#3-9: All 12¢ issues	1.25	3.75	10.00

NOTE: ***Alascia** a-19. **Aparo** a-60, V3#1, 2, 4; c-V1#4, 8. **Baily** a-1-3; c-2, 5. **Evans** c-3, 4. **Giordana** c-16, 17p, 24p, 25p. **Montes/Bache** c-66. **Powell** a-4. **Shuster** a-19, 21. **Marcus Swayze** a-27.*

STRANGE TALES (...Featuring Warlock #178-181; Doctor Strange #169 on)
Atlas (CCPC #1-67/ZPC #68-79/VPI #80-85)/Marvel #86(7/61) on: June, 1951 - #168, May, 1968; #169, Sept, 1973 - #188, Nov, 1976

	GD25	FN65	NM94
1-Horror/weird stories begin	255.00	766.00	2500.00
2	95.00	286.00	825.00
3,5: 3-Atom bomb panels	70.00	211.00	600.00
4-Cosmic eyeball story "The Evil Eye"	76.00	230.00	650.00
6-9: 6-Heath-c/a. 7-Colan-a	53.00	159.00	460.00
10-Krigstein-a	58.00	172.00	490.00
11-14,16-20	38.00	114.00	290.00
15-Krigstein-a	39.00	116.00	295.00
21,23-27,29-34: 27-Atom bomb panels. 33-Davis-a. 34-Last pre-code issue (2/55)	30.00	90.00	225.00
22-Krigstein, Forte/Fox-a	31.00	92.00	230.00
28-Jack Katz story used in Senate Investigation report, pgs. 7 & 169	31.00	94.00	235.00
35-41,43,44: 37-Vampire story by Colan	18.50	55.00	185.00
42,45,59,61-Krigstein-a; #61 (2/58)	19.00	57.00	190.00
46-57,60: 51-1st S.A. issue. 53,56-Crandall-a. 60-(8/57)	16.50	50.00	165.00
58,64-Williamson-a in each, with Mayo-#58	16.50	50.00	165.00
62,63,65,66: 62-Torres-a. 66-Crandall-a	15.50	47.00	155.00
67-Prototype ish. (Quicksilver)	18.00	54.00	180.00
68,71,72,74,77,80: Ditko/Kirby-a in #67-80	16.00	48.00	160.00
69-Prototype ish. (Prof. X)	22.00	66.00	220.00
70-Prototype ish. (Giant Man)	22.00	66.00	220.00
73-Prototype ish. (Ant-Man)	22.00	66.00	220.00
75-Prototype ish. (Iron Man)	22.00	66.00	220.00
76-Prototype ish. (Human Torch)	22.00	66.00	220.00
78-Prototype ish. (Ant-Man)	22.00	66.00	220.00
79-Prototype ish. (Dr. Strange) (12/60)	22.00	66.00	220.00
81-83,85-88,90,91-Ditko/Kirby-a in all: 86-Robot-c. 90-(11/61)-Atom bomb blast panel	14.00	42.00	140.00
84-Prototype ish. (Magneto)(5/61); has powers like Magneto of X-Men, but two years earlier; Ditko/Kirby-a	18.00	54.00	180.00
89-1st app. Fin Fang Foom (10/61) by Kirby	38.00	114.00	420.00
92-Prototype ish. (Ancient One); last 10¢ issue	15.00	45.00	150.00
93,95,96,98-100: Kirby-a	13.00	39.00	130.00
94-Prototype ish. (The Thing); Kirby-a	15.00	45.00	150.00
97-1st app. Aunt May & Uncle Ben by Ditko (6/62), before Amazing Fantasy #15; (see Tales Of Suspense #7); Kirby-a	31.00	93.00	325.00

	GD25	FN65	VF82	NM94
101-Human Torch begins by Kirby (10/62); origin recap Fantastic Four & Human Torch; H. Torch-c begin	73.00	219.00	438.00	875.00

	GD25	FN65	NM94
102-1st app. Wizard; robot-c	29.00	87.00	290.00
103-105: 104-1st app. Trapster. 105-2nd Wizard	24.00	72.00	240.00
106,108,109: 106-Fantastic Four guests (3/63)	15.50	47.00	155.00
107-(4/63)-Human Torch/Sub-Mariner battle; 4th S.A. Sub-Mariner app. & 1st x-over outside of Fantastic Four	18.50	55.00	185.00

	GD25	FN65	VF82	NM94
110-(7/63)-Intro Doctor Strange, Ancient One & Wong by Ditko	82.00	246.00	492.00	990.00

	GD25	FN65	NM94
111-2nd Dr. Strange	29.00	87.00	290.00
112,113	10.50	32.00	105.00
114-Acrobat disguised as Captain America, 1st app. since the G.A.; intro. & 1st app. Victoria Bentley; 3rd Dr. Strange app. & begin series (11/63)	31.00	93.00	325.00
115-Origin Dr. Strange; Human Torch vs. Sandman (Spidey villain; 2nd app. & brief origin); early Spider-Man x-over, 12/63	38.00	114.00	425.00
116-(1/64)-Human Torch battles The Thing; 1st Thing x-over	10.00	30.00	100.00
117,118,120: 120-1st Iceman x-over (from X-Men)	6.50	19.50	65.00
119-Spider-Man x-over (2 panel cameo)	9.00	27.00	90.00
121,122,124,126-134: Thing/Torch team-up in 121-134. 126-Intro Clea. 128-Quicksilver & Scarlet Witch app. (1/65). 130-The Beatles cameo. 134-Last Human Torch; The Watcher-c/story; Wood-a(i)	4.50	13.50	45.00
123-1st app. The Beetle (see Amazing Spider-Man #21 for next app.); 1st Thor x-over (8/64); Loki app.	5.00	15.00	50.00
125-Torch & Thing battle Sub-Mariner (10/64)	4.50	13.50	45.00
135-Col. (formerly Sgt.) Nick Fury becomes Nick Fury Agent of Shield (origin/1st app.) by Kirby (8/65); series begins	8.00	24.00	80.00

136-147,149: 138-Intro Eternity. 145-Begins alternating-c features w/Nick Fury (odd #'s) & Dr. Strange (even #'s). 146-Last Ditko Dr. Strange who is in consecutive stories since #113. 146-Only Ditko Dr. Strange-c this title. 147-Dr. Strange (by Everett #147-152) continues thru #168, then Dr.

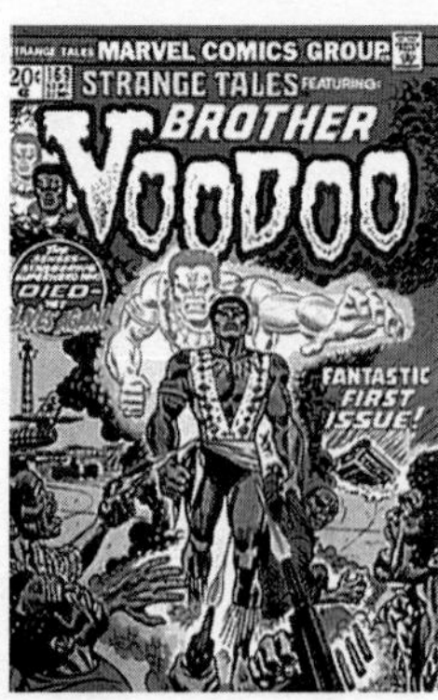

Strange Tales #169 © MAR

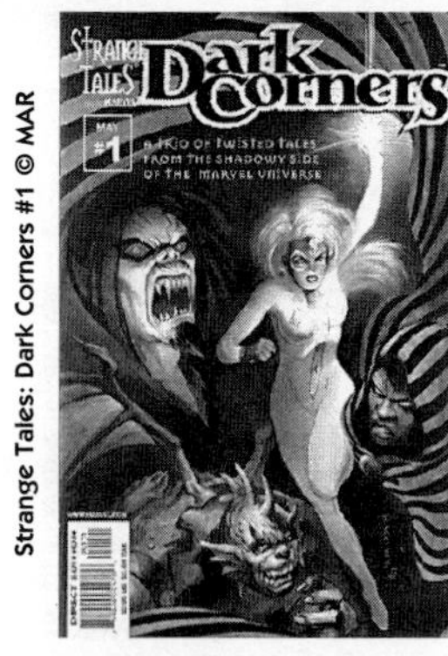

Strange Tales: Dark Corners #1 © MAR

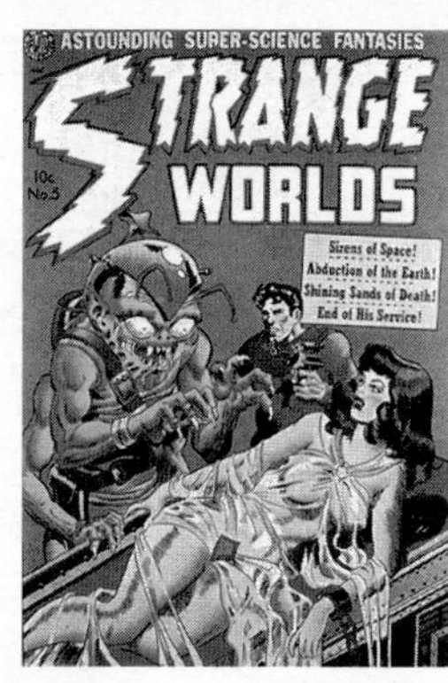

Strange Worlds #5 © AVON

	GD25	FN65	NM94
Strange #169	3.00	9.00	30.00
148-Origin Ancient One	5.50	16.50	55.00
150(11/66)-John Buscema's 1st work at Marvel	3.00	9.00	30.00
151-Kirby/Steranko-c/a; 1st Marvel work by Steranko	4.00	12.00	40.00
152,153-Kirby/Steranko-a	3.00	9.00	30.00
154-158-Steranko-a/script	3.00	9.00	30.00
159-Origin Nick Fury retold; Intro Val; Captain America-c/story; Steranko-a	3.20	9.60	32.00
160-162-Steranko-a/scripts; Capt. America app.	2.50	7.50	25.00
163-166,168-Steranko-a(p). 168-Last Nick Fury (gets own book next month) & last Dr. Strange who also gets own book	2.50	7.50	25.00
167-Steranko pen/script; classic flag-c	3.00	12.00	30.00
169-1st app. Brother Voodoo(origin in #169,170) & begin series, ends #173.	1.00	3.00	10.00
170-173	.90	2.70	8.00
174-Origin Golem		2.00	6.00
175-177: 177-Brunner-c			4.00
178-(2/75)-Warlock by Starlin begins; origin Warlock & Him retold; 1st app. Magus; Starlin-c/a/scripts in 178-181 (all before Warlock #9)	1.30	3.90	13.00
179-181-All Warlock. 179-Intro/1st app. Pip the Troll. 180-Intro Gamora. 181-(8/75)-Warlock story continued in Warlock #9	.90	2.70	8.00
182-188			3.50
Annual 1(1962)-Reprints from Strange Tales #73,76,78, Tales of Suspense #7,9, Tales to Astonish #1,6,7, & Journey Into Mystery #53,55,59; (1st Marvel annual?)	40.00	120.00	450.00
Annual 2(7/63)-Reprints from Strange Tales #67, Strange Worlds (Atlas) #1-3, World of Fantasy #16; new Human Torch vs. Spider-Man story by Kirby/Ditko (1st Spidey x-over; 4th app.); Kirby-c	41.00	123.00	490.00

NOTE: **Briefer** *a-17.* **Burgos** *a-123p.* **J. Buscema** *a-174p.* **Colan** *a-7, 11, 20, 37, 53, 169-173p, 188p.* **Davis** *c-71.* **Ditko** *a-46, 50, 67-122, 123-125p, 126-146, 175r, 182-188r; c-51, 93, 115, 121, 146.* **Everett** *a-4, 21, 40-42, 73, 147-152, 164i; c-8, 10, 11, 13, 15, 24, 45, 49-54, 56, 58, 60, 61, 63, 148, 150, 152, 158i.* **Forte** *a-27, 43, 50, 53, 54, 60.* **Heath** *a-6; c-6, 18-20.* **Kamen** *a-45.* **G. Kane** *c-170-173, 182p.* **Kirby** *Human Torch-101-105, 108, 109, 114, 120; Nick Fury-135p, 141-143p; (Layouts)-135-153; other* **Kirby** *a-67-100p; c-68-70, 72-74, 76-92, 94, 95, 101-114, 116-123, 125-130, 132-135, 136p, 138-145, 147, 149, 151p.* **Kirby/Ayers** *c-101-106, 108-110.* **Kirby/Ditko** *a-80, 88, 121; c-75, 93, 97, 100. .* **Lawrence** *a-29.* **Leiber/ Fox** *a-110, 111, 113.* **Maneely** *a-3, 7, 37, 42; c-33, 40.* **Moldoff** *a-20.* **Mooney** *a-174i.* **Morisi** *a-53, 56.* **Morrow** *a-54.* **Orlando** *a-41, 44, 46, 49, 52.* **Powell** *a-42, 44, 49, 54, 130-134p; c-131p.* **Reinman** *a-11, 50, 74, 88, 91, 95, 104, 106, 112i, 124-127i.* **Robinson** *a-17.* **Romita** *c-169.* **Roussos** *c-201i.* **R.Q. Sale** *a-56; c-16.* **Sekowski** *a-3, 11.* **Severin** *a(i)-136-138; c-137.* **Starlin** *a-178, 179, 180p, 181p; c-178-180, 181p.* **Steranko** *a-151-161, 162-168p; c-151i, 153, 155, 157, 159, 161, 163, 165, 167.* **Torres** *a-53, 62.* **Tuska** *a-14, 166p.* **Whitney** *a-149.* **Wildey** *a-42, 56.* **Woodbridge** *a-59. Fantastic Four cameos #101-134. Jack Katz app.-26.*

STRANGE TALES
Marvel Comics Group: Apr, 1987 - No. 19, Oct, 1988

	GD25	FN65	NM94
V2#1-19			1.00

STRANGE TALES
Marvel Comics: Nov, 1994 ($6.95, one-shot)

	GD25	FN65	NM94
V3#1-acetate-c	.85	2.60	7.00

STRANGE TALES (Anthology; continues stories from Man-Thing #8 and Werewolf By Night #6)
Marvel Comics: Sept, 1998 - No. 2, Oct, 1998 ($4.99)

	GD25	FN65	NM94
1,2: 1-Silver Surfer app. 2-Two covers			5.00

STRANGE TALES: DARK CORNERS
Marvel Comics: May, 1998 ($3.99, one-shot)

	GD25	FN65	NM94
1-Anthology; stories by Baron & Maleev, McGregor & Dringenberg, DeMatteis & Badger; Estes painted-c			4.00

STRANGE TALES OF THE UNUSUAL
Atlas Comics (ACI No. 1-4/WPI No. 5-11): Dec, 1955 - No. 11, Aug, 1957

	GD25	FN65	NM94
1-Powell-a	39.00	117.00	295.00
2	22.00	66.00	165.00
3-Williamson-a (4 pgs.)	23.00	68.00	170.00
4,6,8,11	15.00	46.00	115.00
5-Crandall, Ditko-a	20.00	60.00	150.00
7,9: 7-Kirby, Orlando-a. 9-Krigstein-a	17.00	50.00	125.00
10-Torres, Morrow-a	15.00	46.00	115.00

NOTE: **Baily** *a-6.* **Brodsky** *c-2-4.* **Everett** *a-2, 6; c-6, 9, 11.* **Heck** *a-1.* **Maneely** *c-1.* **Orlando** *a-7.* **Pakula** *a-10.* **Romita** *a-1.* **R.Q. Sale** *a-3.* **Wildey** *a-3.*

STRANGE TERRORS
St. John Publishing Co.: June, 1952 - No. 7, Mar, 1953

	GD25	FN65	NM94
1-Bondage-c; Zombies spelled Zoombies on-c; Fine-*esque* -a	42.00	127.00	340.00
2	24.00	72.00	180.00
3-Kubert-a; painted-c	32.00	96.00	240.00
4-Kubert-a (reprinted in Mystery Tales #18); Ekgren painted-c; Fine-*esque* -a; Jerry Iger caricature	40.00	120.00	320.00
5-Kubert-a; painted-c	32.00	96.00	240.00
6-Giant (25¢, 100 pgs.)(1/53); bondage-c	40.00	120.00	320.00
7-Giant (25¢, 100 pgs.); Kubert-c/a	43.00	129.00	350.00

NOTE: **Cameron** *a-6, 7.* **Morisi** *a-6.*

STRANGE WORLD OF YOUR DREAMS
Prize Publications: Aug, 1952 - No. 4, Jan-Feb, 1953

	GD25	FN65	NM94
1-Simon & Kirby-a	54.00	162.00	460.00
2,3-Simon & Kirby-c/a. 2-Meskin-a	43.00	129.00	360.00
4-S&K-c; Meskin-a	39.00	117.00	300.00

STRANGE WORLDS (#18 continued from Avon's Eerie #1-17)
Avon Periodicals: 11/50 - No. 9, 11/52; No. 18, 10-11/54 - No. 22, 9-10/55 (No #11-17)

	GD25	FN65	NM94
1-Kenton of the Star Patrol by Kubert (r/Eerie #1 from 1947); Crom the Barbarian by John Giunta	76.00	229.00	650.00
2-Wood-a; Crom the Barbarian by Giunta; Dara of the Vikings app.; used in **SOTI**, pg. 112; injury to eye panel	74.00	221.00	625.00
3-Wood/Orlando-a (Kenton), Wood/Williamson/Frazetta/Krenkel/Orlando-a (7 pgs.); Malu Slave Girl Princess app.; Kinstler-c	147.00	441.00	1250.00
4-Wood-c/a (Kenton); Orlando-a; origin The Enchanted Daggar; Sultan-a	71.00	212.00	600.00
5-Orlando/Wood-a (Kenton); Wood-c	46.00	138.00	390.00
6-Kinstler-a(2); Orlando/Wood-c; Check-a	36.00	108.00	270.00
7-Fawcette & Becker/Alascia-a	29.00	88.00	220.00
8-Kubert, Kinstler, Hollingsworth & Lazarus-a; Lazarus Robot-c	29.00	88.00	220.00
9-Kinstler, Fawcette, Alascia-a	28.00	84.00	210.00
18-(Formerly Eerie #17)-Reprints "Attack on Planet Mars" by Kubert	27.00	80.00	200.00
19-r/Avon's "Robotmen of the Lost Planet"; last pre-code issue; Robot-c	27.00	80.00	200.00
20-War-c/story; Wood-c(r)/U.S. Paratroops #1	7.50	22.50	50.00
21,22-War-c/stories. 22-New logo	5.70	17.00	38.00
I.W. Reprint #5-Kinstler-a(r)/Avon's #9	2.25	6.75	18.00

STRANGE WORLDS
Marvel Comics (MPI No. 1,2/Male No. 3,5): Dec, 1958 - No. 5, Aug, 1959

	GD25	FN65	NM94
1-Kirby & Ditko-a; flying saucer issue	71.00	212.00	600.00
2-Ditko-c/a	42.00	127.00	340.00
3-Kirby-a(2)	35.00	104.00	260.00
4-Williamson-a	32.00	96.00	240.00
5-Ditko-a	27.00	80.00	200.00

NOTE: **Buscema** *a-3, 4.* **Ditko** *a-1-5; c-2..* **Heck** *a-2.* **Kirby** *a-1, 3.* **Kirby/Brodsky** *c-1, 3-5.*

STRAWBERRY SHORTCAKE
Marvel Comics (Star Comics): Jun, 1985 - No. 7, Apr, 1986 (Children's comic)

	GD25	FN65	NM94
1-7: Howie Post-a			2.00

STRAY BULLETS
El Capitan Books: 1995 - Present ($2.95, B&W, mature readers)

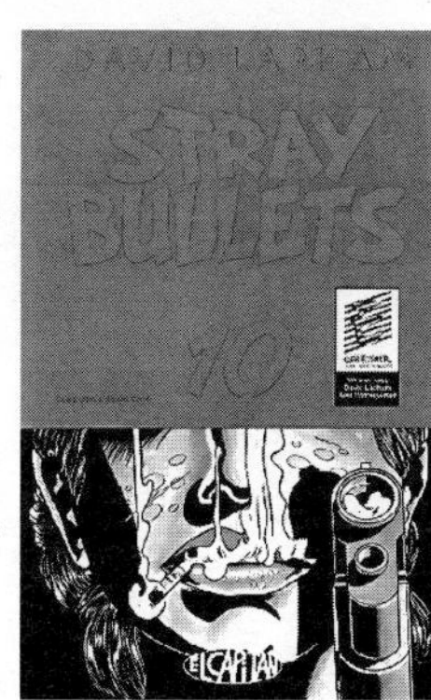

Stray Bullets #10 © David Lapham

Strikeback! #3 © Jonathan Peterson & Kevin Maguire

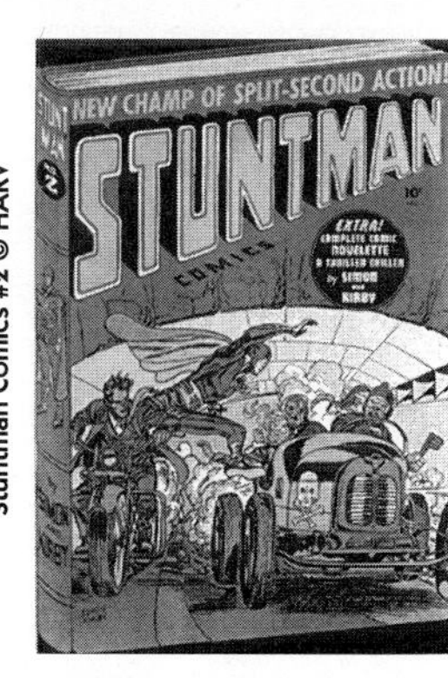

Stuntman Comics #2 © HARV

	GD25	FN65	NM94
1-David Lapham-c/a/scripts	1.50	4.50	15.00
2,3	1.00	3.00	10.00
4,6-8	.90	2.70	8.00
5 ($3.50)		2.00	6.00
9-13			5.00
14-($3.50)			3.50
15,16-(2.95)			2.95
Volume 1 ($29.95, hardcover)			30.00

NOTE: *Multiple issues of all issues exist & are worth cover price.*

STRAY TOASTERS
Marvel Comics (Epic Comics): Jan, 1988 - No. 4, April, 1989 ($3.50, squarebound, limited series)

	GD25	FN65	NM94
1-4: Sienkiewicz-c/a/scripts			3.50

STREET COMIX
Street Enterprises/King Features: 1973 (50¢, B&W, 36 pgs.)(20,000 print run)

	GD25	FN65	NM94
1,2: 1-Rip Kirby. 2-Flash Gordon	.90	2.70	8.00

STREETFIGHTER
Ocean Comics: Aug, 1986 - No. 4, Spr, 1987 ($1.75, limited series)

	GD25	FN65	NM94
1-4: 2-Origin begins			1.80

STREET FIGHTER
Malibu Comics: Sept, 1993 - No. 3, Nov, 1993 ($2.95)

	GD25	FN65	NM94
1-3: 3-Includes poster; Ferret x-over			3.00

STREET FIGHTER: THE BATTLE FOR SHADALOO
DC Comics/CAP Co. Ltd.: 1995 ($3.95, one-shot)

	GD25	FN65	NM94
1-polybagged w/trading card & Tattoo			4.00

STREET FIGHTER II
Tokuma Comics (Viz): Apr, 1994 - No. 8, Nov, 1994 ($2.95, limited series)

	GD25	FN65	NM94
1-8			3.00

STREET POET RAY
Blackthorne Publ./Marvel Comics: Spring, 1989; 1990 - No. 4, 1990 ($2.95, B&W, squarebound)

	GD25	FN65	NM94
1 (Blackthorne, $2.00)			2.00
1-4 (Marvel, $2.95, thick-c & paper)			3.00

STREETS
DC Comics: 1993 - No. 3, 1993 ($4.95, limited series, 52 pgs.)

	GD25	FN65	NM94
Book 1-3-Estes painted-c			5.00

STREET SHARKS
Archie Publications: Jan, 1996 - No. 3, Mar, 1996 ($1.50, limited series)

	GD25	FN65	NM94
1-3			1.50

STREET SHARKS
Archie Publications: May, 1996 - Present ($1.50, published 8 times a year)

	GD25	FN65	NM94
1-6			1.50

STRICTLY PRIVATE (You're in the Army Now)
Eastern Color Printing Co.: July, 1942 (#1 on sale 6/15/42)

	GD25	FN65	NM94
1,2: Private Peter Plink. 2-Says 128 pgs. on-c	21.00	62.00	155.00

STRIKE!
Eclipse Comics: Aug, 1987 - No. 6, Jan, 1988 ($1.75)

	GD25	FN65	NM94
1-6			1.80
...Vs. Sgt. Strike Special 1 (5/88, $1.95)			2.00

STRIKEBACK! (The Hunt For Nikita)
Malibu Comics (Bravura): Oct, 1994 - No. 3, Jan, 1995 ($2.95, unfinished limited series)

	GD25	FN65	NM94
1-3: Jonathon Peterson script, Kevin Maguire-c/a			3.00
1-Gold foil embossed-c			8.00

STRIKEBACK!
Image Comics (WildStorm Productions): Jan, 1996 - No. 5, May, 1996 ($2.50, limited series)

	GD25	FN65	NM94
1-5: Reprints original Bravura series w/additional story & art by Kevin Maguire & Jonathon Peterson; new Maguire-c in all. 4,5-New story & art.			2.50

STRIKEFORCE: AMERICA
Comico: Dec, 1995 ($2.95)

	GD25	FN65	NM94
V2#1-Polybagged w/gaming card; S. Clark-a(p)			3.00

STRIKEFORCE: MORITURI
Marvel Comics Group: Dec, 1986 - No. 31, July, 1989

	GD25	FN65	NM94
1-12, 14: 14-Williamson-i			1.00
13-Double size			1.50
15-23 ($1.00-$1.25)			1.25
24-31 ($1.50): 25-Heath-c			1.50

STRIKEFORCE MORITURI: ELECTRIC UNDERTOW
Marvel Comics: Dec, 1989 - No. 5, Mar, 1990 ($3.95, 52 pgs., limited series)

	GD25	FN65	NM94
1-5 Squarebound			4.00

STRONG GUY REBORN (See X-Factor)
Marvel Comics: Sept, 1997 ($2.99, one-shot)

	GD25	FN65	NM94
1-Dezago-s/Andy Smith, Art Thibert-a			3.00

STRONG MAN (Also see Complimentary Comics & Power of...)
Magazine Enterprises: Mar-Apr, 1955 - No. 4, Sept-Oct, 1955

	GD25	FN65	NM94
1(A-1 #130)-Powell-c/a	19.00	56.00	140.00
2-4: (A-1 #132,134,139)-Powell-a. 2-Powell-c	15.00	46.00	115.00

STRONTIUM DOG
Eagle Comics: Dec, 1985 - No. 4, Mar, 1986 ($1.25, limited series)

	GD25	FN65	NM94
1-4: 4-Moore scripts.			1.30
Special 1 (1986)-Moore scripts			1.50

STRYFE'S STRIKE FILE
Marvel Comics: Jan, 1993 ($1.75, one-shot, no ads)

	GD25	FN65	NM94
1-Stroman, Capullo, Andy Kubert, Brandon Peterson-a; silver metallic ink-c; X-Men tie-in to X-Cutioner's Song			1.75
1-Gold metallic ink 2nd printing			1.75

STRYKE
London Night Studios: 1995 ($3.00)

	GD25	FN65	NM94
0			3.00
0-Alternate-c			5.00

STUMBO THE GIANT (See Harvey Hits #49, 54, 57, 60, 63, 66, 69, 72, 78, 88 & Hot Stuff #2)

STUMBO TINYTOWN
Harvey Publications: Oct, 1963 - No. 13, Nov, 1966 (All 25¢ giants)

	GD25	FN65	NM94
1-Stumbo, Hot Stuff & others begin	13.00	39.00	130.00
2	7.50	22.50	75.00
3-5	5.00	15.00	50.00
6-13	4.00	12.00	40.00

STUNT DAWGS
Harvey Comics: Mar, 1993 ($1.25, one-shot)

	GD25	FN65	NM94
1			1.25

STUNTMAN COMICS (Also see Thrills Of Tomorrow)
Harvey Publ.: Apr-May, 1946 - No. 2, June-July, 1946; No. 3, Oct-Nov, 1946

	GD25	FN65	NM94
1-Origin Stuntman by S&K reprinted in Black Cat #9; S&K-c	91.00	274.00	775.00
2-S&K-c/a; The Duke of Broadway story	59.00	176.00	500.00
3-Small size (5-1/2x8-1/2"; B&W; 32 pgs.); distributed to mail subscribers only; S&K-a; Kid Adonis by S&K reprinted in Green Hornet #37 Estimated value...			$250.00-$400.00

(Also see All-New #15, Boy Explorers #2, Flash Gordon #5 & Thrills of Tomorrow)

The Sub-Mariner #6 © MAR

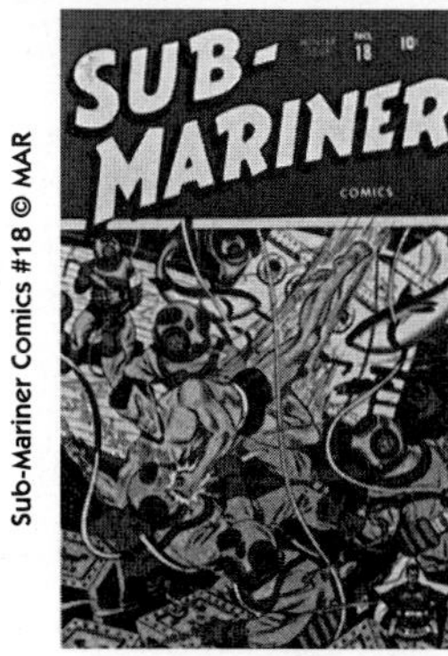

Sub-Mariner Comics #18 © MAR

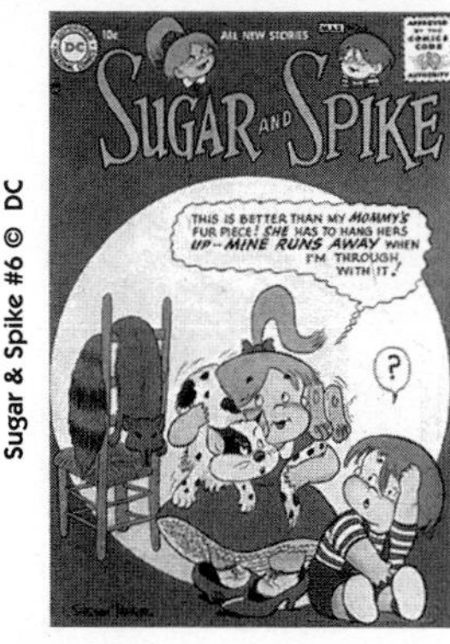

Sugar & Spike #6 © DC

STUPID HEROES
Mirage Studios: Sept, 1993 - No. 3, Dec, 1994 ($2.75, unfinished limited series)

	GD25	FN65	NM94
1-3-Laird-c/a & scripts; 2 trading cards bound in			2.75

STYGMATA
Entity Comics: No. 0, July, 1994 - No. 3, Oct, 1994 ($2.95, B&W, limited series)

	GD25	FN65	NM94
0, 1-3: 0,1-Foil-c. 3-Silver foil logo			3.00
Yearbook 1 (1995, $2.95)			3.00

SUBMARINE ATTACK (Formerly Speed Demons)
Charlton Comics: No. 11, May, 1958 - No. 54, Feb-Mar, 1966

	GD25	FN65	NM94
11	2.60	7.80	26.00
12-20	2.50	7.50	22.00
21-30	2.25	6.75	18.00
31-54	1.85	5.50	15.00

NOTE: ***Glanzman** c/a-25. **Montes/Bache** a-38, 40, 41.*

SUB-MARINER (See All-Select, All-Winners, Blonde Phantom, Daring, The Defenders, Fantastic Four #4, Human Torch, The Invaders, Iron Man &..., Marvel Mystery, Marvel Spotlight #27, Men's Adventures, Motion Picture Funnies Weekly, Namora, Namor, The..., Prince Namor, The Sub-Mariner, Saga Of The..., Tales to Astonish #70 & 2nd series, USA & Young Men)

SUB-MARINER, THE (2nd Series)(Sub-Mariner #31 on)
Marvel Comics Group: May, 1968 - No. 72, Sept, 1974 (No. 43: 52 pgs.)

	GD25	FN65	NM94
1-Origin Sub-Mariner; story continued from Iron Man & Sub-Mariner #1	8.00	24.00	100.00
2-Triton app.	4.00	12.00	40.00
3-10: 5-1st Tiger Shark (9/68). 6-Tiger Shark-c & 2nd app., cont'd from #5. 7-Photo-c. (1968). 8-Sub-Mariner vs. Thing. 9-1st app. Serpent Crown (origin in #10 & 12)	2.80	8.40	28.00
11-13,15: 15-Last 12¢ issue	2.50	7.50	20.00
14-Sub-Mariner vs. G.A. Human Torch; death of Toro (1st modern app. & only app. Toro, 6/69)	2.80	8.40	28.00
16-20: 19-1st Sting Ray (11/69); Stan Lee, Romita, Heck, Thomas, Everett & Kirby cameos. 20-Dr. Doom app.	1.25	3.75	10.00
21-33,36-40: 22-Dr. Strange x-over. 25-Origin Atlantis. 30-Capt. Marvel x-over. 37-Death of Lady Dorma. 38-Origin retold. 40-Spider-Man x-over	.85	2.60	7.00
34,35-Prelude to 1st Defenders story. 34-Hulk & Silver Surfer x-over. 35-Namor/Hulk/Silver Surfer team-up to battle The Avengers-c/story (3/71); hints at teaming up again	1.20	3.60	12.00
41-49,56,62,64-72: 42-Last 15¢ issue. 43-King Size Special (52 pgs.). 44,45-Sub-Mariner vs. H. Torch. 47,48-Dr. Doom app. 49-Cosmic Cube story. 62-1st Tales of Atlantis, ends #66. 64-Hitler cameo. 67-New costume; F.F. x-over. 69-Spider-Man x-over (6 panels)			4.00
50-1st app. Nita, Namor's niece (later Namorita in New Warriors)	.80	2.40	6.50
51-55,57-61,63-Everett issues: 59-1st battle with Thor. 61-Last artwork by Everett; 1st 4 pgs. completed by Mortimer; pgs. 5-20 by Mooney.			4.00
Special 1 (1/71)-r/Tales to Astonish #70-73	.90	2.70	7.50
Special 2 (1/72)-r/T.T.A. #74-76; Everett-a	.80	2.40	6.50

NOTE: ***Bolle** a-67i. **Buscema** a(p)-1-8, 20, 24. **Colan** a(p)-10, 11, 40, 43, 46-49, Special 1, 2; c(p)-10, 11, 40. **Craig** a-17i, 19-23i. **Everett** a-45r, 50-55, 57, 58, 59-61(plot), 63(plot); c-47, 48i, 55, 57-59i, 61, Spec. 2. **G. Kane** c(p)-42-52, 58, 66, 70, 71. **Mooney** a-24i, 25i, 32-35i, 39i, 42i, 44i, 45i, 60i, 61i, 65p, 66p, 68i. Severin c/a-38i. **Starlin** c-59p. **Tuska** a-41p, 42p, 69-71p. **Wrightson** a-36i. #53, 54-r/stories Sub-Mariner Comics #41 & 39.*

SUB-MARINER COMICS (1st Series) (The Sub-Mariner #1, 2, 33-42)(Official True Crime Cases #24 on; Amazing Mysteries #32 on; Best Love #33 on)
Timely/Marvel Comics (TCI 1-7/SePI 8/MPI 9-32/Atlas Comics (CCC 33-42)): Spring, 1941 - No. 23, Sum, 1947; No. 24, Wint, 1947 - No. 31, 4/49; No. 32, 7/49; No. 33, 4/54 - No. 42, 10/55

	GD25	FN65	VF82	NM94
1-The Sub-Mariner by Everett & The Angel begin	1818.00	5455.00	10,910.00	20,000.00

	GD25	FN65	NM94
2-Everett-a	430.00	1290.00	4300.00
3-Churchill assassination-c; 40 pg. Sub-Mariner story	316.00	947.00	3000.00
4-Everett-a, 40 pgs.; 1 pg. Wolverton-a	263.00	790.00	2500.00
5: 5,8-Gabrielle/Klein-c	200.00	600.00	1700.00
6-10: 9-Wolverton-a, 3 pgs.; flag-c	165.00	494.00	1400.00
11-15	118.00	353.00	1000.00
16-20	106.00	318.00	900.00
21-Last Angel; Everett-a	88.00	265.00	750.00
22-Young Allies app.	88.00	265.00	750.00
23-The Human Torch, Namora x-over (Sum/47); 2nd app. Namora after Marvel Mystery #82	88.00	265.00	750.00
24-Namora x-over (3rd app.)	88.00	265.00	750.00
25-The Blonde Phantom begins (Spr/48), ends No. 31; Kurtzman-a; Namora x-over; last quarterly issue	106.00	318.00	900.00
26-28: 28-Namora cover; Everett-a	88.00	265.00	750.00
29-31 (4/49): 29-The Human Torch app. 31-Capt. America app.	88.00	265.00	750.00
32 (7/49, Scarce)-Origin Sub-Mariner	141.00	424.00	1200.00
33 (4/54)-Origin Sub-Mariner; The Human Torch app.; Namora x-over in Sub-Mariner #33-42	82.00	245.00	695.00
34,35-Human Torch in each	66.00	198.00	560.00
36,37,39-41: 36,39-41-Namora app.	66.00	198.00	560.00
38-Origin Sub-Mariner's wings; Namora app.; last pre-code (2/55)	75.00	225.00	635.00
42-Last issue	78.00	233.00	660.00

NOTE: *Angel by **Gustavson**-#1, 8. **Brodsky** c-34-36, 42. **Everett** a-1-4, 22-24, 26-42; c-32, 33, 40. **Maneely** a-38; c-37, 39-41. **Rico** c-27-31. **Schomburg** c-1-4, 6, 8-18, 20. **Sekowsky** c-24. 25, 26(w/**Rico**). **Shores** c-21-23, 38. Bondage c-13, 22, 24, 25, 34.*

SUBSPECIES
Eternity Comics: May, 1991 - No. 4, Aug, 1991 ($2.50, limited series)

	GD25	FN65	NM94
1-4: New stories based on horror movie			2.50

SUBTLE VIOLENTS
CFD Productions: 1991 ($2.50, B&W, mature)

	GD25	FN65	NM94
1-Linsner-c & story	2.25	6.80	25.00
San Diego Limited Edition	10.00	30.00	110.00

SUE & SALLY SMITH (Formerly My Secret Life)
Charlton Comics: V2#48, Nov, 1962 - No. 54, Nov, 1963 (Flying Nurses)

	GD25	FN65	NM94
V2#48	2.25	6.75	18.00
49-54	1.50	4.50	12.00

SUGAR & SPIKE (Also see The Best of DC & DC Silver Age Classics)
National Periodical Publications: Apr-May, 1956 - No. 98, Oct-Nov, 1971

	GD25	FN65	NM94
1 (Scarce)	177.00	531.00	1500.00
2	65.00	195.00	550.00
3-5: 3-Letter column begins	53.00	159.00	450.00
6-10	36.00	108.00	270.00
11-20	31.00	93.00	230.00
21-29: 26-Christmas-c	20.00	60.00	150.00
30-Scribbly & Scribbly, Jr. x-over	20.00	60.00	150.00
31-40	14.00	42.00	140.00
41-60	8.00	24.00	80.00
61-80: 69-1st app. Tornado-Tot-c/story. 72-Origin & 1st app. Bernie the Brain	5.50	16.50	55.00
81-84,86-95: 84-Bernie the Brain apps. as Superman in 1 panel (9/69)	3.80	11.40	38.00
85 (68 pgs.)-r/#72	5.00	15.00	50.00
96 (68 pgs.)	6.00	18.00	60.00
97,98 (52 pgs.)	4.50	13.50	45.00

NOTE: *All written and drawn by **Sheldon Mayer.***

SUGAR BEAR
Post Cereal Giveaway: No date, circa 1975? (2-1/2x4-1/2", 16 pgs.)
"The Almost Take Over of the Post Office", "The Race Across the Atlantic",

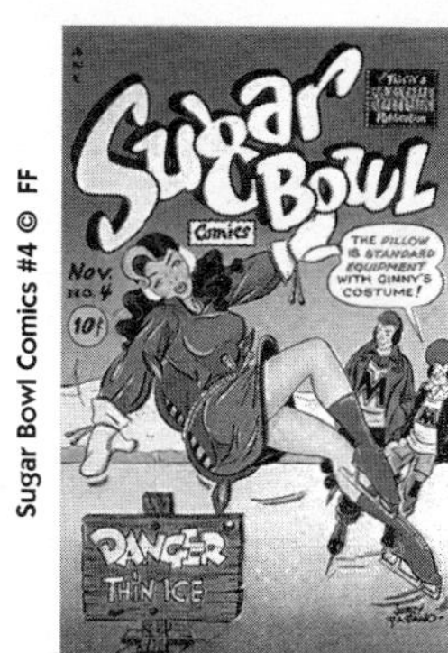

Sugar Bowl Comics #4 © FF

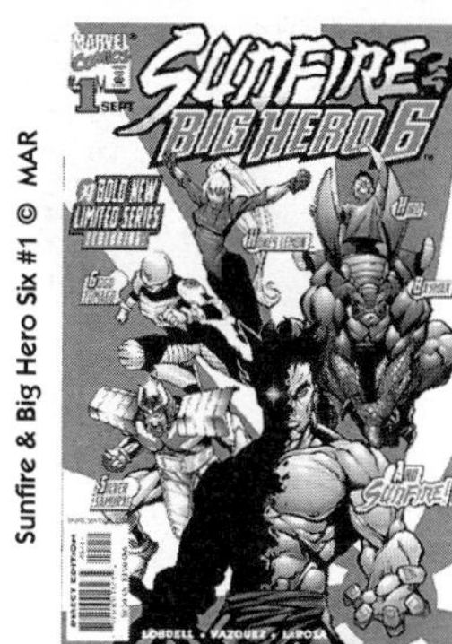

Sunfire & Big Hero Six #1 © MAR

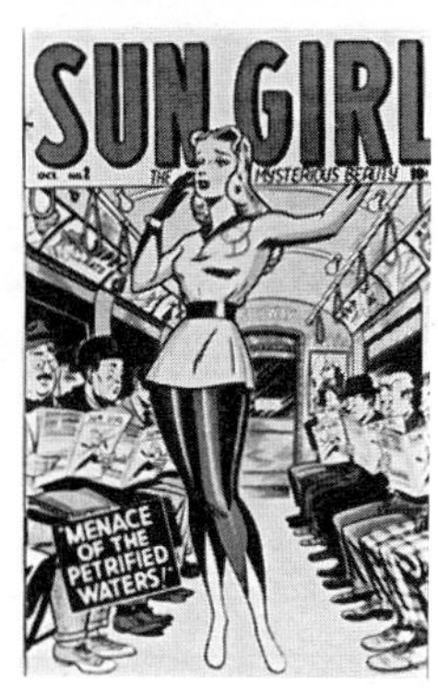

Sun Girl #2 © MAR

GD25 FN65 NM94

"The Zoo Goes Wild" each... 1.00

SUGAR BOWL COMICS (Teen-age)
Famous Funnies: May, 1948 - No. 5, Jan, 1949

	GD25	FN65	NM94
1-Toth-c/a	13.00	38.00	95.00
2,4,5	5.70	17.00	40.00
3-Toth-a	9.30	28.00	65.00

SUGARFOOT (TV)
Dell Publishing Co.: No. 907, May, 1958 - No. 1209, Oct-Dec, 1961

	GD25	FN65	NM94
Four Color 907 (#1)-Toth-a, photo-c	12.00	37.00	135.00
Four Color 992 (5-7/59), Toth-a, photo-c	11.00	34.00	125.00
Four Color 1059 (11-1/60), 1098 (5-7/60), 1147 (11-1/61), 1209-all photo-c	8.00	25.00	90.00

SUICIDE SQUAD (See Brave & the Bold and Doom Patrol & Suicide Squad Spec., Legends #3 & note under Star Spangled War stories)
DC Comics: May, 1987 - No. 66, June, 1992 (Direct sales only #32 on)

1-66: 9-Millennium x-over. 10-Batman-c/story. 13-JLI app. (Batman). 16-Re-intro Shade The Changing Man. 27-34-Snyder-a. 36,37-Snyder-a. 40-43-"The Phoenix Gambit" Batman storyline. 40-Free Batman/Suicide Squad poster 1.00
Annual 1 (1988, $1.50)-Manhunter x-over 1.50
NOTE: ***Chaykin** c-1.*

SUIT, THE
Virtual Comics (Byron Preiss Multimedia): Oct, 1996 - No. 3, Dec, 1996 ($2.50, limited series)

1-3 2.50

SUMMER FUN (See Dell Giants)

SUMMER FUN (Formerly Li'l Genius; Holiday Surprise #55)
Charlton Comics: No. 54, Oct, 1966 (Giant)

54 2.80 8.40 28.00

SUMMER FUN (Walt Disney's...)
Disney Comics: Summer, 1991 ($2.95, annual, 68 pgs.)

1-D. Duck, M. Mouse, Brer Rabbit, Chip 'n' Dale & Pluto, Li'l Bad Wolf, Super Goof, Scamp stories 3.00

SUMMER LOVE (Formerly Brides in Love?)
Charlton Comics: V2#46, Oct, 1965; V2#47, Oct, 1966; V2#48, Nov, 1968

	GD25	FN65	NM94
V2#46-Beatles-c/story	10.00	30.00	100.00
47-Beatles story	9.00	27.00	90.00
48			5.00

SUMMER MAGIC (See Movie Comics)

SUNDANCE (See Hotel Deparee...)

SUNDANCE KID (Also see Blazing Six-Guns)
Skywald Publications: June, 1971 - No. 3, Sept, 1971 (52 pgs.)

	GD25	FN65	NM94
1-Durango Kid; Two Kirby Bullseye-r	1.00	3.00	10.00
2,3: 2-Swift Arrow, Durango Kid, Bullseye by S&K; Meskin plus 1 pg. origin. 3-Durango Kid, Billy the Kid, Red Hawk-r	.85	2.60	7.00

SUNDAY FUNNIES
Harvey Publications: 1950

1 5.00 15.00 30.00

SUN DEVILS
DC Comics: July, 1984 - No. 12, June, 1985 ($1.25, maxi series)

1-12: 6-Death of Sun Devil 1.25

SUN FUN KOMIKS
Sun Publications: 1939 (15¢, B&W & red)

1-Satire on comics 25.00 76.00 190.00

SUNFIRE & BIG HERO SIX (See Alpha Flight)
Marvel Comics: Sept, 1998 - No. 3, Nov, 1998 ($2.50, limited series)

1-3-Lobdell-s 2.50

SUN GIRL (See The Human Torch & Marvel Mystery Comics #88)
Marvel Comics (CCC): Aug, 1948 - No. 3, Dec, 1948

	GD25	FN65	NM94
1-Sun Girl begins; Miss America app.	129.00	388.00	1100.00
2,3: 2-The Blonde Phantom begins	97.00	291.00	825.00

SUNGLASSES
Verotik: Nov, 1995 - No. 6, Nov, 1996 ($2.95, limited series, mature)

1-5: Nancy Collins scripts; adapt. of "Sunglasses after Dark" 3.00
6-($3.95) 4.00

SUNNY, AMERICA'S SWEETHEART (Formerly Cosmo Cat #1-10)
Fox Features Syndicate: No. 11, Dec, 1947 - No. 14, June, 1948

	GD25	FN65	NM94
11-Feldstein-c/a	62.00	185.00	525.00
12-14-Feldstein-c/a; 14-Lingerie panels	49.00	147.00	415.00
I.W. Reprint #8-Feldstein-a; r/Fox issue	10.00	30.00	100.00

SUN-RUNNERS (Also see Tales of the...)
Pacific Comics/Eclipse Comics/Amazing Comics: 2/84 - No. 3, 5/84; No. 4, 11/84 - No. 7, 1986 (Baxter paper)

1-7: P. Smith-a in #2-4 1.60
Christmas Special 1 (1987, $1.95)-By Amazing 2.00

SUNSET CARSON (Also see Cowboy Western)
Charlton Comics: Feb, 1951 - No. 4, 1951 (No month) (Photo-c on each)

	GD25	FN65	NM94
1-Photo/retouched-c (Scarce, all issues)	77.00	230.00	650.00
2-Kit Carson story; adapts "Kansas Raiders" w/Brian Donlevy, Audie Murphy & Margaret Chapman	56.00	168.00	475.00
3,4	43.00	129.00	360.00

SUNSET PASS (See Zane Grey & 4-Color #230)

SUPER ANIMALS PRESENTS PIDGY & THE MAGIC GLASSES
Star Publications: Dec, 1953 (25¢, came w/glasses)

1-(3-D Comics)-L. B. Cole-c 40.00 120.00 320.00

SUPER BOOK OF COMICS
Western Publishing Co.: nd (1943?) (Soft-c, 32 pgs.) (Pan-Am/Gilmore Oil/Kelloggs premiums)

	GD25	FN65	NM94
nn-Dick Tracy (Gilmore)-Magic Morro app.	39.00	117.00	295.00
1-Dick Tracy & The Smuggling Ring; Stratosphere Jim app. (Rare) (Pan-Am)	33.00	98.00	245.00
1-Smilin' Jack, Magic Morro (Pan-Am)	10.00	30.00	75.00
2-Smilin' Jack, Stratosphere Jim (Pan-Am)	10.00	30.00	75.00
2-Smitty, Magic Morro (Pan-Am)	10.00	30.00	75.00
3-Captain Midnight, Magic Morro (Pan-Am)	16.00	48.00	120.00
3-Moon Mullins?	9.30	28.00	65.00
4-Red Ryder, Magic Morro (Pan-Am)	9.30	28.00	65.00
4-Smitty, Stratosphere Jim (Pan-Am)	9.30	28.00	65.00
5-Don Winslow, Magic Morro (Gilmore)	9.30	28.00	70.00
5-Don Winslow, Stratosphere Jim (Pan-Am)	9.30	28.00	70.00
5-Terry & the Pirates	15.00	44.00	110.00
6-Don Winslow, Stratosphere Jim (Pan-Am)-McWilliams-a	11.00	32.00	80.00
6-King of the Royal Mounted, Magic Morro (Pan-Am)	10.00	30.00	75.00
7-Dick Tracy, Magic Morro (Pan-Am)	16.00	48.00	120.00
7-Little Orphan Annie	10.00	30.00	75.00
8-Dick Tracy, Stratosphere Jim (Pan-Am)	16.00	48.00	120.00
8-Dan Dunn, Magic Morro (Pan-Am)	10.00	30.00	75.00
9-Terry & the Pirates, Magic Morro (Pan-Am)	13.00	40.00	100.00
10-Red Ryder, Magic Morro (Pan-Am)	9.30	28.00	65.00

SUPER-BOOK OF COMICS
Western Publishing Co.: (Omar Bread & Hancock Oil Co. giveaways) 1944 - No. 30, 1947 (Omar); 1947 - 1948 (Hancock) (16 pgs.)

Note: The Hancock issues are all exact reprints of the earlier Omar issues.

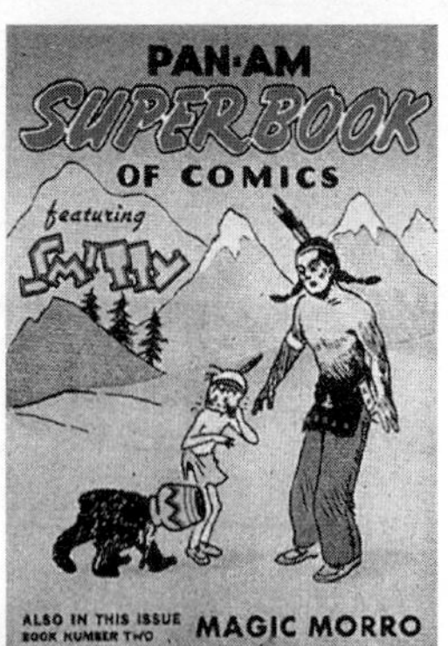

Super-Book Of Comics #2 © WEST

Superboy #21 © DC

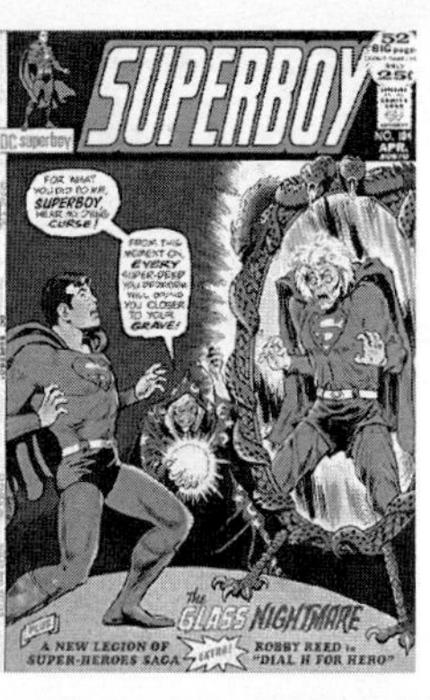

Superboy #184 © DC

The issue numbers were removed in some of the reprints.

	GD25	FN65	NM94
1-Dick Tracy (Omar, 1944)	20.00	60.00	150.00
1-Dick Tracy (Hancock, 1947)	15.00	44.00	110.00
2-Bugs Bunny (Omar, 1944)	6.50	19.50	45.00
2-Bugs Bunny (Hancock, 1947)	5.70	17.00	35.00
3-Terry & the Pirates (Omar, 1944)	11.00	34.00	85.00
3-Terry & the Pirates (Hancock, 1947)	10.00	30.00	75.00
4-Andy Panda (Omar, 1944)	6.50	19.50	45.00
4-Andy Panda (Hancock, 1947)	5.70	17.00	35.00
5-Smokey Stover (Omar, 1945)	5.70	17.00	35.00
5-Smokey Stover (Hancock, 1947)	4.15	12.50	25.00
6-Porky Pig (Omar, 1945)	6.50	19.50	45.00
6-Porky Pig (Hancock, 1947)	5.70	17.00	35.00
7-Smilin' Jack (Omar, 1945)	6.50	19.50	45.00
7-Smilin' Jack (Hancock, 1947)	5.70	17.00	35.00
8-Oswald the Rabbit (Omar, 1945)	5.70	17.00	35.00
8-Oswald the Rabbit (Hancock, 1947)	4.15	12.50	25.00
9-Alley Oop (Omar, 1945)	12.00	36.00	90.00
9-Alley Oop (Hancock, 1947)	11.00	32.00	80.00
10-Elmer Fudd (Omar, 1945)	5.70	17.00	35.00
10-Elmer Fudd (Hancock, 1947)	4.15	12.50	25.00
11-Little Orphan Annie (Omar, 1945)	7.15	21.50	50.00
11-Little Orphan Annie (Hancock, 1947)	5.70	17.00	38.00
12-Woody Woodpecker (Omar, 1945)	5.70	17.00	35.00
12-Woody Woodpecker (Hancock, 1947)	4.15	12.50	25.00
13-Dick Tracy (Omar, 1945)	12.00	36.00	90.00
13-Dick Tracy (Hancock, 1947)	11.00	32.00	80.00
14-Bugs Bunny (Omar, 1945)	5.70	17.00	35.00
14-Bugs Bunny (Hancock, 1947)	4.15	12.50	25.00
15-Andy Panda (Omar, 1945)	5.00	15.00	30.00
15-Andy Panda (Hancock, 1947)	4.15	12.50	25.00
16-Terry & the Pirates (Omar, 1945)	11.00	32.00	80.00
16-Terry & the Pirates (Hancock, 1947)	9.30	28.00	65.00
17-Smokey Stover (Omar, 1946)	5.70	17.00	35.00
17-Smokey Stover (Hancock, 1948?)	4.15	12.50	25.00
18-Porky Pig (Omar, 1946)	5.00	15.00	30.00
18-Porky Pig (Hancock, 1948?)	4.15	12.50	25.00
19-Smilin' Jack (Omar, 1946)	5.70	17.00	35.00
nn-Smilin' Jack (Hancock, 1948)	4.15	12.50	25.00
20-Oswald the Rabbit (Omar, 1946)	5.00	15.00	30.00
nn-Oswald the Rabbit (Hancock, 1948)	4.00	12.00	24.00
21-Gasoline Alley (Omar, 1946)	7.15	21.50	50.00
nn-Gasoline Alley (Hancock, 1948)	5.70	17.00	38.00
22-Elmer Fudd (Omar, 1946)	5.00	15.00	30.00
nn-Elmer Fudd (Hancock, 1948)	4.00	12.00	24.00
23-Little Orphan Annie (Omar, 1946)	6.50	19.50	45.00
nn-Little Orphan Annie (Hancock, 1948)	5.70	17.00	35.00
24-Woody Woodpecker (Omar, 1946)	5.00	15.00	30.00
nn-Woody Woodpecker (Hancock, 1948)	4.00	12.00	24.00
25-Dick Tracy (Omar, 1946)	11.00	32.00	80.00
nn-Dick Tracy (Hancock, 1948)	8.50	26.00	60.00
26-Bugs Bunny (Omar, 1946))	5.00	15.00	30.00
nn-Bugs Bunny (Hancock, 1948)	4.00	12.00	24.00
27-Andy Panda (Omar, 1946)	5.00	15.00	30.00
27-Andy Panda (Hancock, 1948)	4.00	12.00	24.00
28-Terry & the Pirates (Omar, 1946)	11.00	32.00	80.00
28-Terry & the Pirates (Hancock, 1948)	8.50	26.00	60.00
29-Smokey Stover (Omar, 1947)	5.00	15.00	30.00
29-Smokey Stover (Hancock, 1948)	4.00	12.00	24.00
30-Porky Pig (Omar, 1947)	5.00	15.00	30.00
30-Porky Pig (Hancock, 1948)	4.00	12.00	24.00
nn-Bugs Bunny (Hancock, 1948)-Does not match any Omar book	4.00	12.00	24.00

SUPERBOY (See Adventure, Aurora, DC Comics Presents, DC 100 Page Super Spectacular #15, DC Super Stars, 80 Page Giant #10, More Fun Comics, The New Advs. of... & Superman Family #191)

SUPERBOY (1st Series)(...& the Legion of Super-Heroes with #231)(Becomes The Legion of Super-Heroes No. 259 on)
National Periodical Publications/DC Comics: Mar-Apr, 1949 - No. 258, Dec, 1979 (#1-16: 52 pgs.)

	GD25	FN65	VF82	NM94
1-Superman cover; intro in More Fun #10 (1-2/45)	650.00	1950.00	3900.00	6500.00

	GD25	FN65	NM94
2-Used in **SOTI**, pg. 35-36,226	171.00	512.00	1450.00
3	129.00	388.00	1100.00
4,5: 5-1st pre-Supergirl tryout (c/story, 11-12/49)	88.00	265.00	750.00
6-10: 8-1st Superbaby. 10-1st app. Lana Lang	77.00	230.00	650.00
11-15	59.00	177.00	500.00
16-20	41.00	122.00	325.00
21-26,28-30: 21-Lana Lang app.	35.00	104.00	260.00
27-Low distribution	36.00	108.00	270.00
31-38: 38-Last pre-code issue (1/55)	25.00	76.00	190.00
39-48,50 (7/56)	17.00	51.00	170.00
49 (6/56)-1st app. Metallo (Jor-El's robot)	20.00	60.00	200.00
51-60: 52-1st S.A. issue	13.50	41.00	135.00
61-67	11.00	33.00	110.00
68-Origin/1st app. original Bizarro (10-11/58)	42.00	125.00	460.00
69-77,79: 75-Spanking-c. 76-1st Supermonkey	8.50	25.50	85.00
78-Origin Mr. Mxyzptlk & Superboy's costume	15.00	45.00	150.00
80-1st meeting Superboy/Supergirl (4/60)	12.50	38.00	125.00
81,83-85,87,88: 83-Origin/1st app. Kryptonite Kid	7.00	21.00	70.00
82-1st Bizarro Krypto	7.50	22.50	75.00
86-(1/61)-4th Legion app; Intro Pete Ross	12.50	38.00	125.00
89-(6/61)-1st app. Mon-el; 2nd Phantom Zone	23.00	69.00	230.00
90-92: 90-Pete Ross learns Superboy's I.D. 92-Last 10¢ issue	7.00	21.00	70.00
93-10th Legion app.(12/61); Chameleon Boy app.	8.00	24.00	80.00
94-97,99	4.50	13.50	45.00
98-(7/62)-18th Legion app; origin & 1st app. Ultra Boy; Pete Ross joins Legion	9.00	27.00	90.00
100-(10/62)-Ultra Boy app; 1st app. Phantom Zone villains, Dr. Xadu & Erndine. 2 pg. map of Krypton; origin Superboy retold; r-cover of Superman #1	17.00	51.00	170.00
101-120: 104-Origin Phantom Zone. 115-Atomic bomb-c. 117-Legion app.	3.50	10.50	35.00
121-128: 124-(10/65)-1st app. Insect Queen (Lana Lang). 125-Legion cameo. 126-Origin Krypto the Super Dog retold with new facts	3.20	9.60	32.00
129-(80-pg. Giant G-22)-Reprints origin Mon-el	4.00	12.00	40.00
130-137,139,140: 131-Legion statues cameo in Dog Legionnaires story. 132-1st app. Supremo. 133-Superboy meets Robin	2.50	7.50	20.00
138 (80-pg. Giant G-35)	4.00	12.00	40.00
141-146,148-155: 145-Superboy's parents regain their youth. 148-Legion app.	1.50	4.50	15.00
147(6/68)-Giant G-47; 1st origin of L.S.H. (Saturn Girl, Lightning Lad, Cosmic Boy); origin Legion of Super-Pets-r/Adv. #293	2.50	7.50	27.00
156,165,174 (Giants G-59,71,83): 165-r/1st app. Krypto the Superdog from Adventure Comics #210	2.00	6.00	20.00
157-164,166-173,175,176: 171-1st app. Aquaboy? 172,173,176-Legion app. 172-Origin Yango (Super Ape). 176-Partial photo-c	1.50	4.50	12.00
177-184,186,187 (All 52 pgs.): 182-All new origin of the classic World's Finest team (Superman & Batman) as teenagers (2/72, 22pgs). 184-Origin Dial H for Hero-r.	1.40	4.20	14.00

185-Also listed as DC 100 Pg. Super Spectacular #12; Legion-c/story; Teen Titans, Kid Eternity(r/Hit #46), Star Spangled Kid-r(S.S. #55)
(see DC 100 Pg. Super Spectacular #12 for price)

Superboy #215 © DC

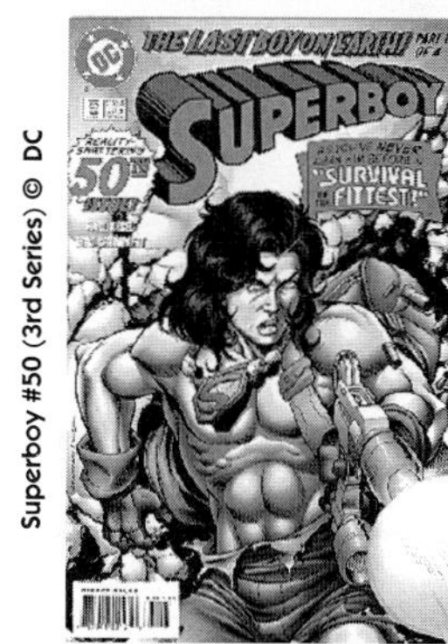

Superboy #50 (3rd Series) © DC

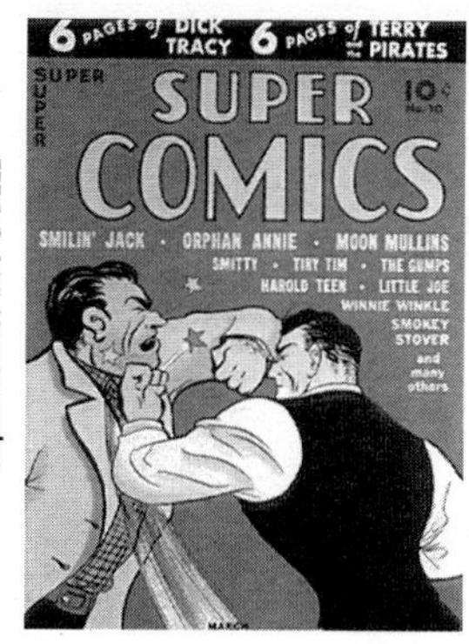

Super Comics #10 © DELL

GD25 FN65 NM94

188-190,192,194,196: 188-Origin Karkan. 196-Last Superboy solo story 2.00 6.00
191,193,195: 191-Origin Sunboy retold; Legion app. 193-Chameleon Boy & Shrinking Violet get new costumes. 195-1st app. Erg-1/Wildfire; Phantom Girl gets new costume. .90 2.70 8.00
197-Legion series begins; Lightning Lad's new costume 1.40 4.20 14.00
198,199: 198-Element Lad & Princess Projectra get new costumes 1.00 3.00 10.00
200-Bouncing Boy & Duo Damsel marry; J'onn J'onzz cameo 1.40 4.20 14.00
201,204,206,207,209: 201-Re-intro Erg-1 as Wildfire. 204-Supergirl resigns from Legion. 206-Ferro Lad & Invisible Kid app. 209-Karate Kid gets new costume 1.00 3.00 10.00
202,205-(100 pgs.): 202-Light Lass gets new costume; Mike Grell's 1st comic work-i (5-6/74) 2.60 8.00 29.00
203-Invisible Kid dies 1.40 4.20 14.00
208,210: 208-(68 pgs.). 208-Legion of Super-Villains app. 210-Origin Karate Kid 1.00 3.00 10.00
211-220: 212-Matter-Eater Lad resigns. 216-1st app. Tyroc who joins the Legion in #218 5.00
221-230,246-249: 226-Intro. Dawnstar. 228-Death of Chemical King 3.00
231-245: (Giants). 240-Origin Dawnstar. 242-(52 pgs.). 243-Legion of Substitute Heroes app. 243-245-(44 pgs.). 2.00 6.00
250-258: 253-Intro Blok. 257-Return of Bouncing Boy & Duo Damsel by Ditko 2.00
Annual 1 (Sum/64, 84 pgs.)-Origin Krypto-r 16.50 50.00 165.00
Spectacular 1 (1980, Giant)-Distr. through comic stores; mostly-r 4.00

NOTE: ***Neal Adams*** *c-143, 145, 146, 148-155, 157-161, 163, 164, 166-168, 172, 173, 175, 176, 178.* ***M. Anderson*** *a-245i.* ***Ditko*** *a-257p.* ***Grell*** *a-202i, 203-219, 220-224p, 235p; c-207-232, 235, 236p, 237, 239p, 240p, 243p, 246, 258.* ***Nasser*** *a(p)-222, 225, 226, 230, 231, 233, 236.* ***Simonson*** *a-237p.* ***Starlin*** *a(p)-239, 250, 251; c-238.* ***Staton*** *a-227p, 243-249p, 252-258p; c-247-251p.* ***Swan/Moldoff*** *c-109.* ***Tuska*** *a-172, 173, 176, 183, 235p.* ***Wood*** *inks-153-155, 157-161. Legion app.-172, 173, 176, 177, 183, 184, 188, 190, 191, 193, 195.*

SUPERBOY (TV)(2nd Series)(The Adventures of...#19 on)
DC Comics: Feb, 1990 - No. 22, Dec, 1991 ($1.00/$1.25)

1-15: Mooney-a(p) in 1-8,18-20; 1-Photo-c from TV show. 8-Bizarro-c/story; Arthur Adams-a(i). 9-12,14-17-Swan-p 1.00
16-22: 16-Begin $1.25-c 1.30
...Special 1 (1992, $1.75) Swan-a 1.75

SUPERBOY (3rd Series)
DC Comics: Feb, 1994 - Present ($1.50/$1.95/$1.99)

1-5-Metropolis Kid from Reign of the Supermen 1.50
6-8: 6,7-Worlds Collide Pts. 3 & 8. 8-(9/94)-Zero Hour x-over 1.50
0, 9-15: 0-(10/94). 9-(11/94)-King Shark app. 1.50
16-24: 16-$1.95-c begins. 21-Legion app. 2.00
25-($2.95)-New Gods & Female Furies app.; w/pin-ups 3.00
26-41: 28-Supergirl-c/app. 33-Final Night. 38-41-"Meltdown" 2.00
42-54: 45-Legion-c/app. 47-Green Lantern-c/app. 50-Last Boy on Earth begins. 1.95
55-58: 55-Begin $1.99-c 1.99
#1,000,000 (11/98) 853rd Century x-over 2.00
Annual 1 (1994, $2.95, 68 pgs.)-Elseworlds story, Pt. 2 of The Super Seven (see Adventures Of Superman Annual #6) 3.00
Annual 2 (1995, $3.95)-Year One story 4.00
Annual 3 (1996, $2.95)-Legends of the Dead Earth 3.00
Annual 4 (1997, $3.95)-Pulp Heroes story 4.00
...Plus 1 (Jan, 1997, $2.95) w/Capt. Marvel Jr. 2.95
...Plus 2 (Fall, 1997, $2.95) w/Slither (Scare Tactics) 2.95
.../Risk Double-Shot 1 (Feb, 1998, $1.95) w/Risk (Teen Titans) 1.95

SUPERBOY & THE RAVERS
DC Comics: Sept, 1996 - No. 19, March, 1998 ($1.95)

1-19: 4-Adam Strange app. 7-Impulse-c/app. 9-Superman-c/app. 2.00

GD25 FN65 NM94

SUPERBOY/ROBIN: WORLD'S FINEST THREE
DC Comics: 1996 - No. 2, 1996 ($4.95, squarebound, limited series)

1,2: Superboy & Robin vs. Metallo & Poison Ivy; Karl Kesel & Chuck Dixon scripts; Tom Grummett-c(p)/a(p) 5.00

SUPER BRAT
Toby Press: Jan, 1954 - No. 4, July, 1954

1 5.70 17.00 35.00
2-4: 4-Li'l Teevy by Mel Lazarus 4.00 11.00 22.00
I.W. Reprint #1,2,3,7,8('58): 1-r/#1 1.00 2.80 7.00
I.W. (Super) Reprint #10('63) 1.00 2.80 7.00

SUPERCAR (TV)
Gold Key: Nov, 1962 - No. 4, Aug, 1963 (All painted-c)

1 22.00 65.00 235.00
2,3 10.00 30.00 110.00
4-Last issue 14.00 44.00 160.00

SUPER CAT (Formerly Frisky Animals; also see Animal Crackers)
Star Publications #56-58/Ajax/Farrell Publ. (Four Star Comic Corp.): No. 56, Nov, 1953 - No. 58, May, 1954; Aug, 1957 - No. 4, May, 1958

56-58-L.B. Cole-c on all 17.00 52.00 130.00
1(1957-Ajax)- "The Adventures of..." c-only 7.15 21.50 50.00
2-4 5.00 15.00 30.00

SUPER CIRCUS (TV)
Cross Publishing Co.: Jan, 1951 - No. 5, Sept, 1951 (Mary Hartline)

1-(52 pgs.)-Cast photos on-c 10.00 30.00 75.00
2-Cast photos on-c 7.15 21.50 50.00
3-5 5.70 17.00 40.00
1-(1951, Weather Bird Shoes giveaway) 5.00 15.00 30.00

SUPER CIRCUS (TV)
Dell Publ. Co.: No. 542, Mar, 1954 - No. 694, Mar, 1956 (Mary Hartline)

Four Color 542: Mary Hartline photo-c 6.40 19.00 70.00
Four Color 592,694: Mary Hartline photo-c 5.50 16.50 60.00

SUPER COMICS
Dell Publishing Co.: May, 1938 - No. 121, Feb-Mar, 1949

1-Terry & The Pirates, The Gumps, Dick Tracy, Little Orphan Annie, Little Joe, Gasoline Alley, Smilin' Jack, Smokey Stover, Smitty, Tiny Tim, Moon Mullins, Harold Teen, Winnie Winkle begin 266.00 800.00 1900.00
2 100.00 300.00 675.00
3 91.00 275.00 625.00
4,5: 4-Dick Tracy-c; also #8-10,17,26(part),31 73.00 219.00 490.00
6-10 58.00 174.00 390.00
11-20: 20-Smilin' Jack-c (also #29,32) 45.00 137.00 310.00
21-29: 21-Magic Morro begins (origin & 1st app., 2/40). 22,27-Ken Ernst-c (also #25?); Magic Morro c-22,25,27,34 34.00 101.00 280.00
30- "Sea Hawk" movie adaptation-c/story with Errol Flynn 34.00 101.00 280.00
31-40: 31-1st Dick Tracy-c. 34-Ken Ernst-c 28.00 84.00 210.00
41-50: 41-Intro Lightning Jim. 43-Terry & The Pirates ends 23.00 68.00 170.00
51-60 17.00 50.00 125.00
61-70: 62-Flag-c. 65-Brenda Starr-r begin? 67-X-Mas-c 15.00 44.00 110.00
71-80 11.00 34.00 85.00
81-99 9.30 28.00 70.00
100 11.00 32.00 80.00
101-115-Last Dick Tracy (moves to own title) 6.50 19.50 45.00
116-121: 116,118-All Smokey Stover. 117-All Gasoline Alley. 119-121-Terry & The Pirates app. in all 5.70 17.00 38.00

SUPER COPS, THE
Red Circle Productions (Archie): July, 1974 (one-shot)

Super Duck Comics #18 © AP

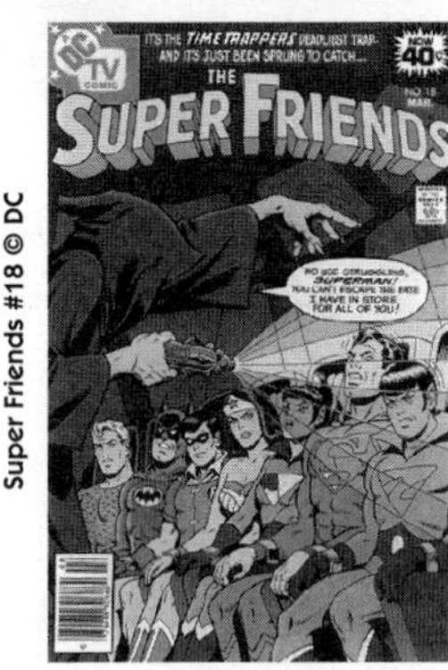

Super Friends #18 © DC

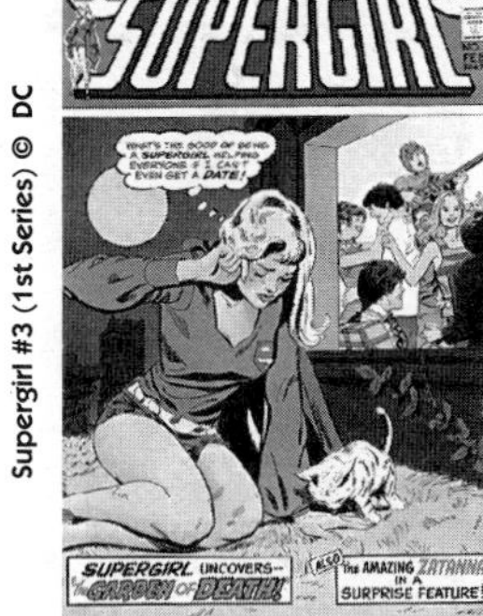

Supergirl #3 (1st Series) © DC

GD25 FN65 NM94

1-Morrow-c/a 4.00

SUPER COPS
Now Comics: Sept, 1990 - No. 4, Dec?, 1990 ($1.75)

1-($2.75, 52 pgs.)-Dave Dorman painted-c 2.80
1-2nd printing ($2.75) 2.80
2-4 1.80

SUPER CRACKED (See Cracked)

SUPER DC GIANT (25-50¢, all 68-52 pg. Giants)
National Periodical Publications: No. 13, 9-10/70 - No. 26, 7-8/71; V3#27, Summer, 1976 (No #1-12)

S-13-Binky 8.00 23.00 85.00
S-14-Top Guns of the West; Kubert-c; Trigger Twins, Johnny Thunder, Wyoming Kid-r; Moreira-r (9-10/70) 2.40 7.00 26.00
S-15-Western Comics; Kubert-c; Pow Wow Smith, Vigilante, Buffalo Bill-r; new Gil Kane-a (9-10/70) 2.40 7.00 26.00
S-16-Best of the Brave & the Bold; Batman-r & Metamorpho origin-r from Brave & the Bold; Spectre pin-up. 2.40 7.00 26.00
S-17-Love 1970 (scarce) 17.00 52.00 190.00
S-18-Three Mouseketeers; Dizzy Dog, Doodles Duck, Bo Bunny-r; Sheldon Mayer-a 7.00 21.00 75.00
S-19-Jerry Lewis; Neal Adams pin-up 6.50 19.50 70.00
S-20-House of Mystery; N. Adams-c; Kirby-r(3) 3.80 11.50 40.00
S-21-Love 1971 (scarce) 21.00 61.00 225.00
S-22-Top Guns of the West; Kubert-c 1.80 5.40 18.00
S-23-The Unexpected 2.20 6.50 24.00
S-24-Supergirl 2.20 6.50 24.00
S-25-Challengers of the Unknown; all Kirby/Wood-r 1.80 5.40 18.00
S-26-Aquaman (1971)-r/S.A. Aquaman origin story from Showcase #30 1.80 5.40 18.00
27-Strange Flying Saucers Adventures (Sum, 1976) .90 2.70 8.00

NOTE: ***Sid Greene** r-27p(2), **Heath** r-27. **G. Kane** a-14r(2), 15, 27r(p). **Kubert** r-16.*

SUPER-DOOPER COMICS
Able Manufacturing Co.:1946 - No. 8, 1946 (10¢, 32 pgs., paper-c, #1-4 exist?)

1-The Clock, Gangbuster app. 15.00 44.00 110.00
2 9.30 28.00 70.00
3,4,6 8.50 26.00 60.00
5,7-Capt. Freedom & Shock Gibson 10.00 30.00 75.00
8-Shock Gibson, Sam Hill 10.00 30.00 75.00

SUPER DUCK COMICS (The Cockeyed Wonder) (See Jolly Jingles)
MLJ Mag. No. 1-4(9/45)/Close-Up No. 5 on (Archie): Fall, 1944 - No. 94, Dec, 1960 (Also see Laugh #24)(#1-5 are quarterly)

1-Origin; Hitler & Hirohito-c 42.00 127.00 340.00
2-Bill Vigoda-c 19.00 58.00 145.00
3-5: 4-20-Al Fagaly-c (most) 13.00 40.00 100.00
6-10 11.00 32.00 80.00
11-20(6/48) 8.50 26.00 60.00
21,23-40 (10/51) 5.70 17.00 50.00
22-Used in **SOTI**, pg. 35,307,308 7.85 23.50 55.00
41-60 (2/55) 5.70 17.00 35.00
61-94 4.00 12.00 24.00

SUPER DUPER (Formerly Pocket Comics #1-4?)
Harvey Publications: No. 5, 1941 - No. 11, 1941

5-Captain Freedom & Shock Gibson app. 26.00 78.00 195.00
8,11 16.00 48.00 120.00

SUPER DUPER COMICS (Formerly Latest Comics?)
F. E. Howard Publ.: No. 3, May-June, 1947

3-1st app. Mr. Monster 9.30 28.00 65.00

SUPER FRIENDS (TV) (Also see Best of DC & Limited Collectors' Edition)
National Periodical Publications/DC Comics: Nov, 1976 - No. 47, Aug, 1981 (#14 is 44 pgs.)

GD25 FN65 NM94

1-Superman, Batman, Robin, Wonder Woman, Aquaman, Atom, Wendy, Marvin & Wonder Dog begin (1st Super Friends) 1.50 4.50 15.00
2-Penquin-c/sty .90 2.70 8.00
3-5 2.00 6.00
6-10,14:7-1st app. Wonder Twins & The Seraph. 8-1st app. Jack O'Lantern. 9-1st app. Icemaiden. 14-Origin Wonder Twins 5.00
11-13,15-20: 13-1st app. Dr. Mist. 4.00
21-30,32-46: 25-1st app. Fire as Green Fury. 28-Bizarro app. 36,43-Plastic Man app. 3.00
31,47: 31-Black Orchid app. 47-Origin Fire & Green Fury 4.00
...Special 1 (1981, giveaway, no ads, no code or price)-r/Super Friends #19 & 36 2.00

NOTE: ***Estrada** a-1p, 2p. **Orlando** a-1p. **Staton** a-43, 45.*

SUPER FUN
Gillmor Magazines: Jan, 1956 (By A.W. Nugent)

1-Comics, puzzles, cut-outs by A.W. Nugent 3.20 8.00 16.00

SUPER FUNNIES (...Western Funnies #3,4)
Superior Comics Publishers Ltd. (Canada): Dec, 1953 - No. 4, Sept, 1954

1-(3-D, 10¢)-...Presents Dopey Duck; make your own 3-D glasses cut-out inside front-c; did not come w/glasses 36.00 108.00 270.00
2-Horror & crime satire 10.00 30.00 75.00
3-Phantom Ranger-c/s; Geronimo, Billy the Kid app. 5.70 17.00 35.00
4-Phantom Ranger-c/story 5.70 17.00 35.00

SUPERGEAR COMICS
Jacobs Corp.: 1976 (Giveaway, 4 pgs. in color, slick paper)

nn-(Rare)-Superman, Lois Lane; Steve Lombard app. (500 copies printed, over half destroyed?) 2.00 6.00

SUPERGIRL (See Action, Adventure #281, Brave & the Bold, Crisis on Infinite Earths #7, Daring New Advs. of..., Super DC Giant, Superman Family, & Super-Team Family)

SUPERGIRL
National Periodical Publ.: Nov, 1972 - No. 9, Dec-Jan, 1973-74; No. 10, Sept-Oct, 1974 (1st solo title)(20¢)

1-Zatanna back-up stories begin, end #5 2.20 6.50 24.00
2-4,6,7,9 .90 2.70 9.00
5,8,10: 5-Zatanna origin-r. 8-JLA x-over; Batman cameo. 10-Prez 1.20 3.60 12.00

NOTE: *Zatanna in #1-5, 7(Guest); Prez app. in #10. #1-10 are 20¢ issues.*

SUPERGIRL (Formerly Daring New Adventures of...)
DC Comics: No. 14, Dec, 1983 - No. 23, Sept, 1984

14-23: 16-Ambush Bug app. 20-JLA & New Teen Titans app. 1.00
...Movie Special (1985)-Adapts movie; Morrow-a; photo back-c 1.25
Giveaway ('84, '86 Baxter, nn)(American Honda/U.S. Dept. Transportation)-Torres-c/a 1.25

SUPERGIRL
DC Comics: Feb, 1994 - No. 4, May, 1994 ($1.50, limited series)

1-4: Guice-a(i) 1.50

SUPERGIRL (See Showcase '96 #8)
DC Comics: Sept, 1996 - Present ($1.95/$1.99)

1: Peter David scripts & Gary Frank-c/a; DC cover logo in upper left is blue 1.00 3.00 10.00
1-2nd printing-DC cover logo in upper left is red 4.00
2 2.00 6.00
3-Final Night, Gorilla Grodd app. 4.00
4-9: 4-Gorilla Grodd-c/app. 6-Superman-c/app. 9-Last Frank-a 3.50
10-19: 14-Genesis x-over. 16-Power Girl app. 2.50
20-24: 20-Millennium Giants x-over; Superman app. 23-Steel-c/app. 24-Resurrection Man x-over. 2.00
25-28: 25-Comet ID revealed; begin $1.99-c 2.00
#1,000,000 (11/98) 853rd Century x-over 2.00
Annual 1 (1996, $2.95)-Legends of the Dead Earth 3.00

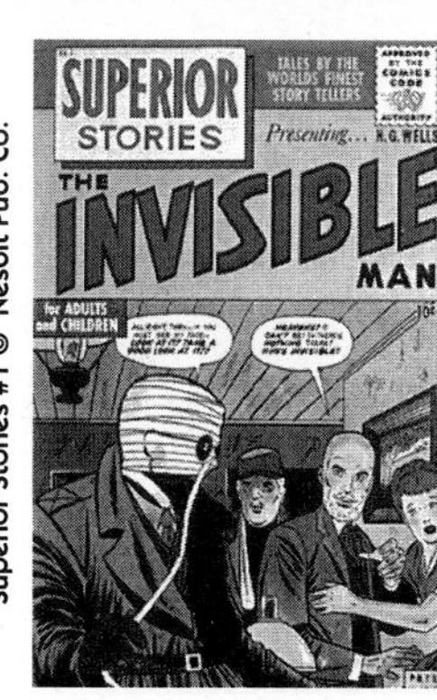

Superior Stories #1 © Nesbit Pub. Co.

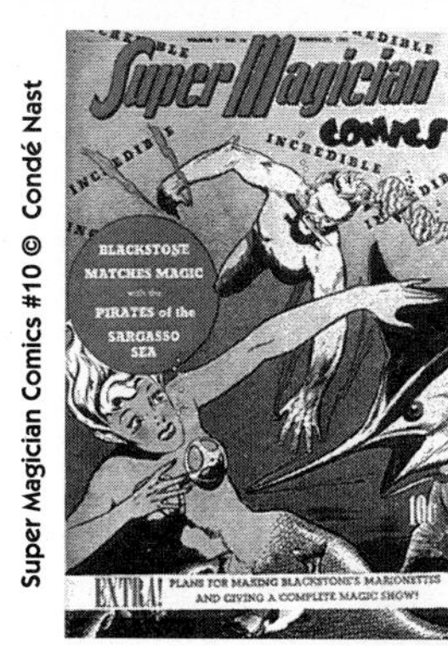

Super Magician Comics #10 © Condé Nast

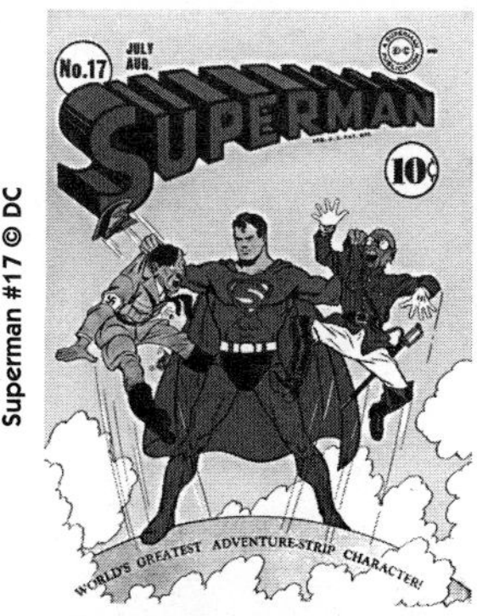

Superman #17 © DC

GD25 FN65 NM94

Annual 2 (1997, $3.95)-Pulp Heroes; LSH app.; Chiodo-c 4.50
...Plus (2/97, $2.95) Capt.(Mary) Marvel-c/app.; David-s/Frank-a 3.00
.../Prysm Double-Shot 1 (Feb, 1998, $1.95) w/Prysm (Teen Titans) 1.95
TPB-('98, $14.95) r/Showcase '96 #8 & Supergirl #1-9 14.95

SUPERGIRL/LEX LUTHOR SPECIAL (Supergirl and Team Luthor on-c)
DC Comics: 1993 ($2.50, 68 pgs., one-shot)

1-Pin-ups by Byrne & Thibert 2.50

SUPER GOOF (Walt Disney) (See Dynabrite & The Phantom Blot)
Gold Key No. 1-57/Whitman No. 58 on: Oct, 1965 - No. 74, 1982

1 2.40 7.20 24.00
2-5 1.20 3.60 12.00
6-10 1.00 3.00 10.00
11-20 .80 2.40 8.00
21-30 5.00
31-50 4.00
51-57 3.00
58,59 (Whitman) 4.00
60-62 (8/80-12/80, 3-pack?) .80 2.40 8.00
63-66('81) 5.00
67-69 3.00
70-74 (#90180 on-c; pre-pack? nd, nd code) .70 2.10 7.00
NOTE: *Reprints in #16, 24, 28, 29, 37, 38, 43, 45, 46, 54(1/2), 56-58, 65(1/2), 72(r-#2).*

SUPER GREEN BERET (Tod Holton...)
Lightning Comics (Milson Publ. Co.): Apr, 1967 - No. 2, Jun, 1967

1,2-(25¢, 68 pgs) 3.00 9.00 30.00

SUPER HEROES (See Giant-Size... & Marvel...)

SUPER HEROES
Dell Publishing Co.: Jan, 1967 - No. 4, June, 1967

1-Origin & 1st app. Fab 4 2.80 8.40 28.00
2-4 1.80 5.40 18.00

SUPER-HEROES BATTLE SUPER-GORILLAS (See DC Special #16)
National Periodical Publications: Winter, 1976 (52 pgs., all reprints, one-shot)

1-Superman, Batman, Flash stories; Infantino-a(p) 2.00 6.00

SUPER HEROES PUZZLES AND GAMES
General Mills Giveaway (Marvel Comics Group): 1979 (32 pgs., regular size)

nn-Four 2-pg. origin stories of Spider-Man, Captain America, The Hulk, & Spider-Woman 1.00 3.00 10.00

SUPER HEROES VERSUS SUPER VILLAINS
Archie Publications (Radio Comics): July, 1966 (no month given)(68 pgs.)

1-Flyman, Black Hood, Web, Shield-r; Reinman-a 4.50 13.50 45.00

SUPERHERO WOMEN, THE - FEATURING THE FABULOUS FEMALES OF MARVEL COMICS (See Fireside Book Series)

SUPERICHIE (Formerly Super Richie)
Harvey Publications: No. 5, Oct, 1976 - No. 18, Jan, 1979 (52 pgs. giants)

5-Origin/1st app. new costumes for Rippy & Crashman .90 2.70 8.00
6-18 2.00 6.00

SUPERIOR STORIES
Nesbit Publishers, Inc.: May-June, 1955 - No. 4, Nov-Dec, 1955

1-The Invisible Man by H.G. Wells 17.00 52.00 130.00
2-The Pirate of the Gulf by J.H. Ingrahams 9.30 28.00 65.00
3-Wreck of the Grosvenor by William Clark Russell 9.30 28.00 65.00
4-The Texas Rangers by O'Henry 9.30 28.00 65.00
NOTE: ***Morisi** c/a in all. Kiwanis stories in #3 & 4. #4 has photo of Gene Autry on-c.*

SUPER MAGIC (Super Magician Comics #2 on)
Street & Smith Publications: May, 1941

V1#1-Blackstone the Magician-c/story; origin/1st app. Rex King (Black Fury); Charles Sultan-c; Blackstone-c begin 112.00 335.00 950.00

GD25 FN65 NM94

SUPER MAGICIAN COMICS (Super Magic #1)
Street & Smith Publications: No. 2, Sept, 1941 - V5#8, Feb-Mar, 1947

V1#2-Blackstone the Magician continues; Rex King, Man of Adventure app. 47.00 141.00 400.00
3-Tao-Anwar, Boy Magician begins 32.00 96.00 240.00
4-Origin Transo 29.00 88.00 220.00
5-7,9-12: 11-Supersnipe app. 29.00 88.00 220.00
8-Abbott & Costello story (1st app?, 11/42) 32.00 96.00 240.00
V2#1-The Shadow app. 35.00 104.00 260.00
2-12: 5-Origin Tigerman. 8-Red Dragon begins 15.00 44.00 110.00
V3#1-12: 5-Origin Mr. Twilight 15.00 44.00 110.00
V4#1-12: 11-Nigel Elliman Ace of Magic begins (3/46) 12.00 36.00 90.00
V5#1-6 12.00 36.00 90.00
7,8-Red Dragon by Edd Cartier-c/a 31.00 92.00 230.00
NOTE: ***Jack Binder** c-1-14(most). Red Dragon c-V5#7, 8.*

SUPERMAN (See Action Comics, Advs. of..., All-New Coll. Ed., All-Star Comics, Best of DC, Brave & the Bold, Cosmic Odyssey, DC Comics Presents, Heroes Against Hunger, The Kents, Krypton Chronicles, Limited Coll. Ed., Man of Steel, Phantom Zone, Power Record Comics, Special Edition, Steel, Super Friends, Superman: The Man of Steel, Superman: The Man of Tomorrow, Taylor's Christmas Tabloid, Three-Dimension Advs., World Of Krypton, World Of Metropolis, World Of Smallville & World's Finest)

SUPERMAN (Becomes Adventures of...#424 on)
National Periodical Publ./DC Comics: Summer, 1939 - No. 423, Sept, 1986 (#1-5 are quarterly)

GD25 FN65 VF82 NM94

1(nn)-1st four Action stories reprinted; origin Superman by Siegel & Shuster; has a new 2 pg. origin plus 4 pgs. omitted in Action story; see The Comics Magazine #1 & More Fun #14-17 for Superman proto-type app.; cover r/splash page from Action #10; 1st pin-up Superman on back-c - 1st pin-up in comics 12,500.00 37,500.00 75,000.00 130,000.00

1-Reprint, Oversize 13-1/2x10". **WARNING**: This comic is an exact duplicate reprint of the original except for its size. DC published it in 1978 with a second cover titling it as a Famous First Edition. There have been many reported cases of the outer cover being removed and the interior sold as the original edition. The reprint with the new outer cover removed is practically worthless. See Famous First Edition for value.

GD25 FN65 NM94

2-All daily strip-r; full pg. ad for N.Y. World's Fair 970.00 2910.00 9700.00
3-2nd story-r from Action #5; 3rd story-r from Action #6 640.00 1920.00 6400.00
4-2nd mention of Daily Planet (Spr/40); also see Action #23; 2nd & 3rd app. Luthor (red-headed; also see Action #23) 480.00 1440.00 4800.00
5-4th Luthor app. (red hair); classic-c 347.00 1041.00 3300.00
6,7: 6-1st splash pg. in a Superman comic. 7-1st Perry White? (11-12/40) 282.00 846.00 2400.00
8-10: 10-5th app. Luthor (1st bald Luthor, 5-6/41) 247.00 741.00 2100.00
11-13,15: 13-Jimmy Olsen & Luthor app. 177.00 531.00 1500.00
14-Patriotic Shield-c classic by Fred Ray 294.00 882.00 2500.00
16,18-20: 16-1st Lois Lane-c this title (5-6/42); 2nd Lois-c after Action #29 147.00 441.00 1250.00
17-Hitler, Hirohito-c 165.00 495.00 1400.00
21-23,25: 25-Clark Kent's only military service; Fred Ray's only super-hero story 112.00 336.00 950.00
24-Jack Burnley flag-c 147.00 441.00 1250.00
26-29: 27,29-31-Lois Lane-c. 28-Lois Lane Girl Reporter series begins, ends #40,42 103.00 309.00 875.00
28-Overseas edition for Armed Forces; same as reg. #28 103.00 309.00 875.00
30-Origin & 1st app. Mr. Mxyztplk (9-10/44)(pronounced "Mix-it-plk") in comic books; name later became Mxyzptlk ("Mix-yez-pit-l-ick"); the character was inspired by a combination of the name of Al Capp's Joe Blyfstyk (the little man with the black cloud over his head) & the devilish antics of Bugs Bunny; he 1st app. in newspapers 3/7/44 165.00 495.00 1400.00
31-40: 33-(3-4/45)-3rd app. Mxyztplk. 35,36-Lois Lane-c. 38-Atomic bomb story (1-2/46); delayed because of gov't censorship; Superman shown reading Batman #32 on cover. 40-Mxyztplk-c 88.00 264.00 750.00

Superman #147 © DC

Superman #208 © DC

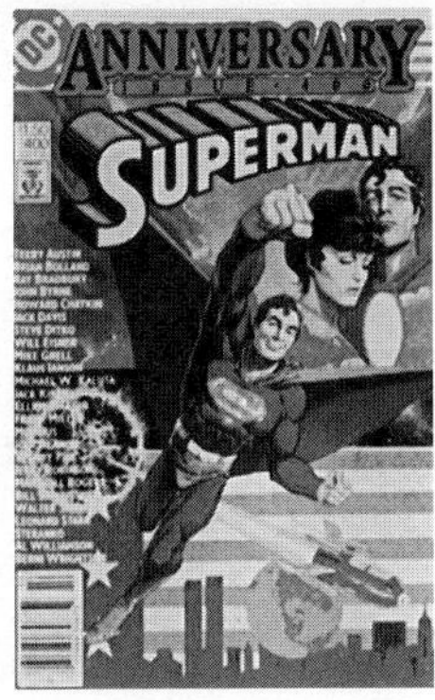

Superman #400 © DC

GD25 FN65 NM94

41-50: 42-Lois Lane-c. 45-Lois Lane as Superwoman (see Action #60 for 1st app.). 46-(5-6/47)-1st app. Superboy this title? 48-1st time Superman travels thru time 67.00 200.00 570.00
51,52: 51-Lois Lane-c 55.00 165.00 470.00
53-Origin Superman retold; 10th anniversary ('48) 235.00 705.00 2000.00
54,56-60: 57-Lois Lane as Superwoman-c. 58-Intro Tiny Trix 55.00 165.00 470.00
55-Used in **SOTI**, pg. 33 59.00 177.00 500.00
61-Origin Superman retold; origin Green Kryptonite (1st Kryptonite story); Superman returns to Krypton for 1st time & sees his parents for 1st time since infancy, discovers he's not an Earth man 111.00 332.00 940.00
62-65,67-70: 62-Orson Welles-c/story. 65-1st Krypton Foes: Mala, K120, & U-Ban. 67-Perry Como-c/story. 68-1st Luthor-c this title (see Action Comics) 53.00 159.00 450.00
66-2nd Superbaby story 53.00 159.00 450.00
71-75: 74-2nd Luthor-c this title. 75-Some have #74 on-c 50.00 150.00 425.00
72-Giveaway(9-10/51)-(Rare)-Price blackened out; came with banner wrapped around book; without banner 62.00 186.00 525.00
72-Giveaway with banner 88.00 264.00 750.00
76-Batman x-over; Superman & Batman learn each other's I.D. for the 1st time (5-6/52)(also see World's Finest #71) 147.00 441.00 1250.00
77-81: 78-Last 52 pg. issue. 81-Used in **POP**, pg. 88 47.00 141.00 400.00
82-87,89,90 44.00 132.00 375.00
88-Prankster, Toyman & Luthor team-up 47.00 141.00 400.00
91-95: 95-Last precode issue (2/55) 41.00 122.00 325.00
96-99: 96-Mr. Mxyztplk-c/story 29.00 87.00 290.00

GD25 FN65 VF82 NM94

100 (9-10/55)-Shows cover to #1 on-c 150.00 450.00 900.00 1600.00

GD25 FN65 NM94

101-105,107-110: 109-1st S.A. issue 27.00 82.00 275.00
106 (7/56)-Retells origin 30.00 90.00 300.00
111-120 23.00 69.00 230.00
121,122,124-127,129: 127-Origin/1st app. Titano. 129-Intro/origin Lori Lemaris, The Mermaid 19.00 57.00 190.00
123-Pre-Supergirl tryout-c/story (8/58). 20.00 60.00 200.00
128-(4/59)-Red Kryptonite used. Bruce Wayne x-over who protects Superman's i.d. (3rd story) 20.00 60.00 200.00
130-(7/59)-1st app, Krypto, the Superdog with Superman (all previous app. w/Superboy 19.00 57.00 190.00
131-139: 139-Lori Lemaris app.; "Untold Story of Red Kryptonite" back-up story 15.00 45.00 150.00
140-1st Blue Kryptonite & Bizarro Supergirl; origin Bizarro Jr. #1 16.50 50.00 165.00
141-145,148: 142-2nd Batman x-over 12.00 36.00 120.00
146-(7/61)-Superman's life story; back-up hints at Earth II. Classic-c 15.00 45.00 150.00
147(8/61)-7th Legion app; 1st app. Legion of Super-Villains; 1st app. Adult Legion; swipes-c to Adv. #247 14.00 42.00 140.00
149(11/61)-8th Legion app. (cameo); "The Death of Superman" imaginary story; last 10¢ issue 12.50 38.00 125.00
150-162: 152(4/62)-15th Legion app. 155-(8/62)-19th Legion app; Lightning Man & Cosmic Man, & Adult Legion app. 156,162-Legion app. 157-Gold Kryptonite used (see Adv. 299); Mon-el app.; Lightning Lad cameo (11/62). 158-1st app. Flamebird & Nightwing & Nor-Kan of Kandor (12/62). 161-1st told death of Ma and Pa Kent 7.00 21.00 70.00
161-2nd printing (1987, $1.25)-New DC logo; sold thru So Much Fun Toy Stores (cover title: Superman Classic) .90 2.25
163-166,168-180: 166-XMas-c. 168-All Luthor issue; JFK tribute/memorial. 169-Bizarro Invasion of Earth-c/story; last Sally Selwyn. 170-Pres. Kennedy story is finally published after delay from #169 due to assassination. 172,173-Legion cameos. 174-Super-Mxyzptlk; Bizarro app. 5.50 16.50 55.00
167-New origin Brainiac & Brainiac 5; intro Tixarla (later Luthor's wife) 8.50 25.50 85.00
181,182,184-186,188-192,194-196,198,200: 181-1st 2965 story/series. 182-1st S.A. app. of The Toyman (1/66). 189-Origin/destruction of Krypton II. 4.50 13.50 45.00
183,187,193,197 (Giants G-18,G-23,G-31,G-36) 5.50 16.50 55.00
199-1st Superman/Flash race (8/67): also see Flash #175 & World's Finest #198,199 (r-in Limited Coll. Ed. #48) 21.00 63.00 210.00
201,203-206,208-211,213-216: 213-Brainiac-5 app. 2.80 8.40 31.00
202 (80-pg. Giant G-42)-All Bizarro issue 3.80 11.50 40.00
207,212,217,222,239 (Giants G-48,G-54,G-60,G-66,G-84): 207-30th anniversary Superman (6/68) 3.50 10.50 38.00
218-221,223-226,228-231 2.40 7.00 26.00
227,232(Giants, G-72,G-78)-All Krypton issues 3.25 10.00 36.00
233-2nd app. Morgan Edge; Clark Kent switches from newspaper reporter to TV newscaster; all Kryptonite on earth destroyed; classic Adams-c 3.50 10.50 38.00
234-238 2.00 6.00 20.00
240-Kaluta-a 1.00 3.00 10.00
241-244 (All 52 pgs.): 243-G.A.-r/#38 1.40 4.20 14.00
245-Also listed as DC 100 Pg. Super Spectacular #7; Air Wave, Kid Eternity, Hawkman-r; Atom-r/Atom #3
(see DC 100 Pg. Super Spectacular #7 for price)
246-248,250,251,253 (All 52 pgs.): 246-G.A.-r/#40. 248-World of Krypton story. 251-G.A.-r/#45. 253-Finlay-a, 2 pgs., G.A.-r/#1 1.40 4.20 14.00
249,254-Neal Adams-a. 249-(52 pgs.); origin & 1st app. Terra-Man by Neal Adams (inks) 1.80 5.40 18.00
252-Also listed as DC 100 Pg. Super Spectacular #13; Ray(r/Smash #17), Black Condor, (r/Crack #18), Hawkman(r/Flash #24); Starman-r/Adv. #67; Dr. Fate & Spectre-r/More Fun #57; N. Adams-c
(see DC 100 Pg. Super Spectacular #13 for price)
255-271,273-277,279-283: 263-Photo-c. 264-1st app. Steve Lombard. 276-Intro Capt. Thunder. 279-Batman, Batgirl app. 2.00 6.00
272,278,284-All 100 pgs. G.A.-r in all. 272-r/2nd app. Mr. Mxyztplk from Action #80 2.20 6.50 24.00
285-299: 289-Partial photo-c. 292-Origin Lex Luthor retold 5.00
300-Retells origin (6/76) 1.80 5.40 18.00
301-399: 301,320-Solomon Grundy app. 323-Intro. Atomic Skull. 327-329-(44 pgs.). 330-More facts revealed about I. D. 338-The bottled city of Kandor enlarged. 344-Frankenstein & Dracula app. 353-Brief origin. 354,355,357-Superman 2020 stories (354-Debut of Superman III). 356-World of Krypton story (also #360,367,375). 366-Fan letter by Todd McFarlane. 372-Superman 2021 story. 376-Free 16 pg. preview Daring New Advs. of Supergirl. 377-Free 16 pg. preview Masters of the Universe 2.50
400 (10/84, $1.50, 68 pgs.)-Many top artists featured; Chaykin painted cover, Miller back-c 5.00
401-422: 405-Super-Batman story. 408-Nuclear Holocaust-c/story. 411-Special Julius Schwartz tribute issue. 414,415-Crisis x-over. 422-Horror-c 2.50
423-Alan Moore scripts; Perez-a(i); last Earth I Superman story, cont'd in Action #583 .85 2.60 7.00
Annual 1(10/60, 84 pgs.)-Reprints 1st Supergirl story/Action #252; r/Lois Lane #1; Krypto-r (1st Silver Age DC annual) 75.00 225.00 900.00
Annual 2(Win, 1960-61)-Super-villain issue; Brainiac, Titano, Metallo, Bizarro origin-r 36.00 108.00 400.00
Annual 3(Sum, 1961)-Strange Lives of Superman 27.00 82.00 275.00
Annual 4(Win, 1961-62)-11th Legion app; 1st Legion origins (text & pictures); advs. in time, space & on alien worlds 22.50 68.00 225.00
Annual 5(Sum, 1962)-All Krypton issue 18.00 54.00 180.00
Annual 6(Win, 1962-63)-Legion-r/Adv. #247 16.50 50.00 165.00
Annual 7(Sum, 1963)-Origin-r/Superman-Batman team/Adv. 275; r/1955 Superman dailies 12.00 36.00 120.00
Annual 8(Win, 1963-64)-All origins issue 10.50 32.00 105.00
Annual 9(8/64)-Was advertised but came out as 80 Page Giant #1 instead
Annual 9(1983)-Toth/Austin-a 5.00

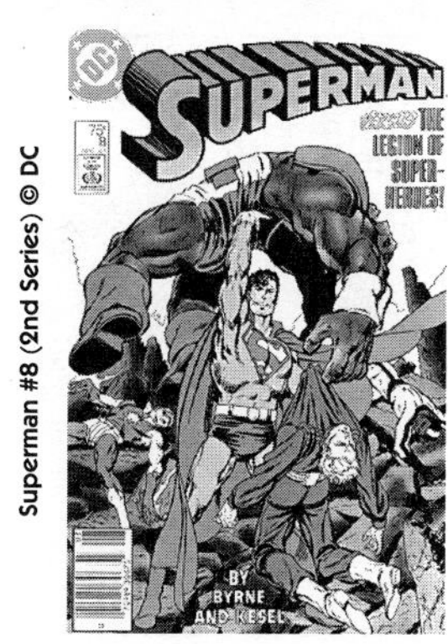

Superman #8 (2nd Series) © DC

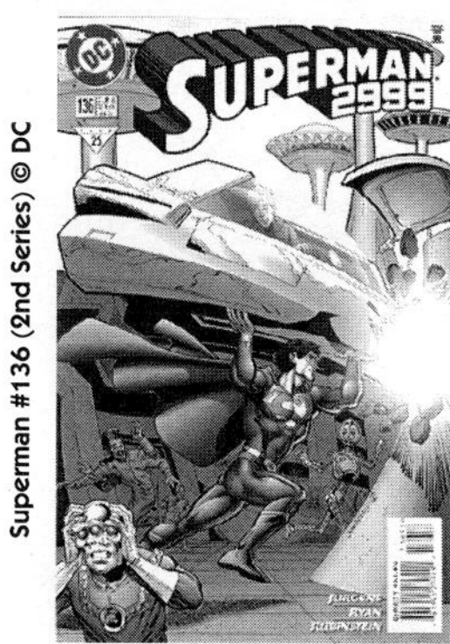

Superman #136 (2nd Series) © DC

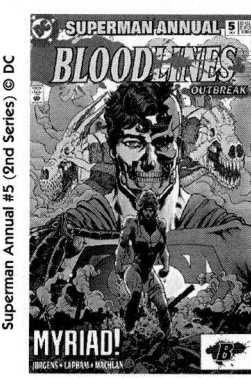

Superman Annual #5 (2nd Series) © DC

GD25 FN65 NM94

Annuals 10-12: 10(1984, $1.25)-M. Anderson inks. 11(1985)-Moore scripts. 12(1986)-Bolland-c 4.00
Special 1(1983)-G. Kane-c/a; contains German-r 4.00
Special 2,3(1984, 1985, $1.25, 52 pgs.) 4.00
The Amazing World of Superman "Official Metropolis Edition" (1973, $2.00, 14x10-1/2")-Origin retold; Wood-r(i) from Superboy #153,161 2.00 6.00 20.00
Kelloggs Giveaway-(2/3 normal size, 1954)-r-two stories/Superman #55 32.00 96.00 240.00
...Meets the Quik Bunny (1987, Nestles Quik premium, 36 pgs.) 1.50
Pizza Hut Premiums (12/77)-Exact reprints of 1950s comics except for paid ads (set of 6 exist?); Vol. 1-r#97 (#113-r also known) 2.00
Radio Shack Giveaway-36 pgs. (7/80) "The Computers That Saved Metropolis", Starlin/Giordano-a; advertising insert in Action #509, New Advs. of Superboy #7, Legion of Super-Heroes #265, & House of Mystery #282. (All comics were 68 pgs.) Cover of inserts printed on newsprint. Giveaway contains 4 extra pgs. of Radio Shack advertising that inserts do not 2.00
Radio Shack Giveaway-(7/81) "Victory by Computer" 2.00
Radio Shack Giveaway-(7/82) "Computer Masters of Metropolis" 2.00
11195 (2/79, $1.95, 224 pgs.)-Golden Press 2.50

NOTE: ***N. Adams** a-249i, 254p; c-204-206, 210, 212-215, 219, 231i, 233-237, 240-243, 249-252, 254, 263, 307, 308, 313, 314, 317. **Adkins** a-323i. **Austin** c-368i. **Wayne Boring** art-late 1940's to early 1960's. **Buckler** a(p)-352, 363, 364, 369; c(p)-324-327, 356, 363, 368, 369, 373, 376, 378. **Burnley** a-252r; c-19-25, 30, 33, 34, 35p, 38p, 39p, 45p. **Fine** a-252r. **Kaluta** a-400. **Gil Kane** a-272r, 367, 372, 375, Special 2; c-374p, 375p, 377, 381, 382, 384-390, 392, Annual 9, Special 2. **Joe Kubert** c-216. **Miller**-pin-up. **Morrow** a-238. **Mortimer** a-250r. **Perez** c-364p. **Fred Ray** a-25; c-6, 8-18. **Starlin** c-355. **Staton** a-354i, 355i. **Swan/Moldoff** c-149. **Williamson** a(i)-408-410, 412-416; c-408i, 409i. **Wrightson** a-400, 416.*

SUPERMAN (2nd Series)
DC Comics: Jan, 1987 - Present (75¢/$1.00/$1.25/$1.50/$1.95/$1.99)

1-Byrne-c/a begins; intro new Metallo 4.00
2-8,10: 3-Legends x-over; Darkseid-c & app. 7-Origin/1st app. Rampage. 8-Legion app. 2.00
9-Joker-c 4.00
11-49,51,52,54-56,58-67: 11-1st new Mr. Mxyzptlk. 12-Lori Lemaris revived. 13-1st app. new Toyman. 13,14-Millennium x-over. 16-1st app. new Supergirl (4/88). 20-Doom Patrol app.; Supergirl cameo. 21-Supergirl-c/story; 1st app. Matrix who becomes new Supergirl. 31-Mr. Mxyzptlk app. 37-Newsboy Legion app. 41-Lobo app. 44-Batman storyline, part 1. 45-Free extra 8 pgs. 54-Newsboy Legion story. 63-Aquaman x-over. 67-Last $1.00-c 2.00
50-($1.50, 52 pgs.)-Clark Kent proposes to Lois 4.50
50-2nd printing 1.75
53-Clark reveals i.d. to Lois (Cont'd from Action #662) 3.00
53-2nd printing 1.50
57-($1.75, 52 pgs.) 1.75
68-72: 65,66,68-Deathstroke-c/stories. 70-Superman & Robin team-up 1.50
73-Doomsday cameo 3.00
74-Doomsday Pt. 2 (Cont'd from Justice League #69); Superman battles Doomsday 4.00
73,74-2nd printings 2.00
75-($2.50)-Collector's Ed.; Doomsday Pt. 6; Superman dies; polybagged w/poster of funeral, obituary from Daily Planet, postage stamp & armband premiums (direct sales only) 1.00 3.00 10.00
75-Direct sales copy (no upc code, 1st print) 3.00
75-Direct sales copy (no upc code, 2nd print) 1.25
75-Direct sales copy (no upc code, 3rd, 4th prints) 1.25
75-Newsstand copy w/upc code 3.50
75-Platinum Edition; given away to retailers 30.00
76,77-Funeral For a Friend parts 4 & 8 2.25
78-($1.95)-Collector's Edition with die-cut outer-c & bound-in mini poster; Doomsday cameo 2.25
78-($1.50)-Newsstand Edition w/poster and different-c; Doomsday-c & cameo 2.00
79-81,83-89: 83-Funeral for a Friend epilogue; new Batman (Azrael) cameo. 87,88-Bizarro-c/story 2.00
82-($3.50)-Collector's Edition w/all chromium-c; real Superman revealed; Green Lantern x-over from G.L. #46; no ads 3.50
82-($2.00, 44 pgs.)-Regular Edition w/different-c 2.00
90-93: 93-(9/94)-Zero Hour 1.50
0, 94-99: 0-(10/94). 94-(11/94). 95-Atom app. 96-Return of Brainiac 1.50
100-Death of Clark Kent foil-c 4.00
100-Newsstand 3.00
101-122: 101-Begin $1.95-c; Black Adam app. 105-Green Lantern app. 110-Plastic Man-c/app. 114-Brainiac app; Dwyer-c. 115-Lois leaves Metropolis. 116-(10/96)-1st app. Teen Titans by Dan Jurgens & George Perez in 8 pg. preview. 117-Final Night. 118-Wonder Woman app. 119-Legion app. 122-New powers 2.00
123-Collector's Edition w/glow in the dark-c, new costume 4.00
123-Standard ed., new costume 3.00
124-137: 128-Cyborg-c/app. 131-Birth of Lena Luthor. 132-Superman Red/ Superman Blue. 134-Millenium Giants. 136,137-Superman 2999 2.00
138-140: 138-Begin $1.99-c. 139-Starlin-a. 140-Grindberg-a 1.99
#1,000,000 (11/98) 853rd Century x-over; Gene Ha-c 2.00
Annual 1,2: 1 (1987)-No Byrne-a. 2 (1988)-Byrne-a; Newsboy Legion; return of the Guardian 4.00
Annual 3 (1991, $2.00, 68 pgs.)-Armageddon 2001 x-over; Batman app.; Austin-c(i) & part inks 2.25
Annual 3-2nd & 3rd printings; 3rd has silver ink 2.00
Annual 4 (1992, $2.50, 68 pgs.)-Eclipso app. 2.50
Annual 5 (1993, $2.50, 68 pgs.) 2.50
Annual 6 (1994, $2.95, 68 pgs.)-Elseworlds story 3.00
Annual 7 (1995, $3.95, 69 pgs.)-Year One story 4.00
Annual 8 (1996, $2.95)-Legends of the Dead Earth story 3.00
Annual 9 (1997, $3.95)-Pulp Heroes story 4.00
Annual 10 (1998, $2.95)-Ghosts; Wrightson-c 2.95
...Plus 1(2/97, $2.95)-Legion of Super-Heroes-c/app. 3.00
Special 1 (1992, $3.50, 68 pgs.)-Simonson-c/a 3.50
...: EXILE (1998, $14.95)-Reprints space exile following execution of Kryptonian criminals; 1st Eradicator 15.00
...: TIME AND TIME AGAIN (1994, $7.50)-Reprints 7.50
THE DEATH OF CLARK KENT TPB nn (1997, $19.95)-Reprints Man of Steel #43 (1 page), Superman #99 (1 page),#100-102, Action #709 (1 page), #710,711, Advs. of Superman #523-525, Superman:The Man of Tomorrow #1 20.00
THE DEATH OF SUPERMAN TPB nn (1993, $4.95)-Reprints Man of Steel #17-19, Superman #73-75, Advs. of Superman #496,497, Action #683,684 & Justice League #69 6.00
THE DEATH OF SUPERMAN, 2nd & 3rd printings 5.00
THE DEATH OF SUPERMAN Platinum Edition 15.00
THE TRIAL OF SUPERMAN TPB ('97, $14.95) r/ 15.00
TIME AND TIME AGAIN TPB ('94, $7.50) r/ 7.50
TRANSFORMED TPB ('98, $12.95) r/post Final Night powerless Superman to Electric Superman 13.00

NOTE: ***Austin** a(i)-1-3. **Byrne** a-1-16p, 17, 19-21p, 22; c-1-17, 20-22; scripts-1-22. **Guice** c/a-64. **Kirby** c-37p. **Joe Quesada** c-Annual 4. **Russell** c/a-23i. **Simonson** c-69i. #19-21 2nd printings sold in multi-packs.*

SUPERMAN (one-shots)
DAILY NEWS MAGAZINE PRESENTS DC COMICS' SUPERMAN
nn-(1987, 8 pgs.)-Supplement to New York Daily News; Perez-c/a 4.00
...: A NATION DIVIDED (1999, $4.95)-Elseworlds Civil War story 4.95
...: AT EARTH'S END (1995, $4.95)-Elseworlds story 5.00
...: DISTANT FIRES (1998, $5.95)-Elseworlds; Chaykin-s 6.00
... FOR EARTH (1991, $4.95, 52 pgs, printed on recycled paper)-Ordway wraparound-c. 5.00
...IV MOVIE SPECIAL (1987, $2.00)-Movie adaptation; Heck-a 2.00
...GALLERY, THE 1 (1993, $2.95)-Poster-a 3.00
...: KAL (1995, $5.95)-Elseworlds story 2.00 6.00
...MOVIE SPECIAL-(9/83)-Adaptation of Superman III; other versions exist with

The Superman Adventures #21 © DC

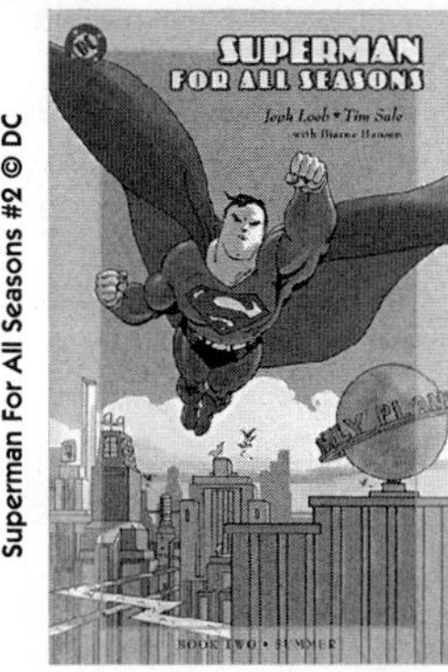

Superman For All Seasons #2 © DC

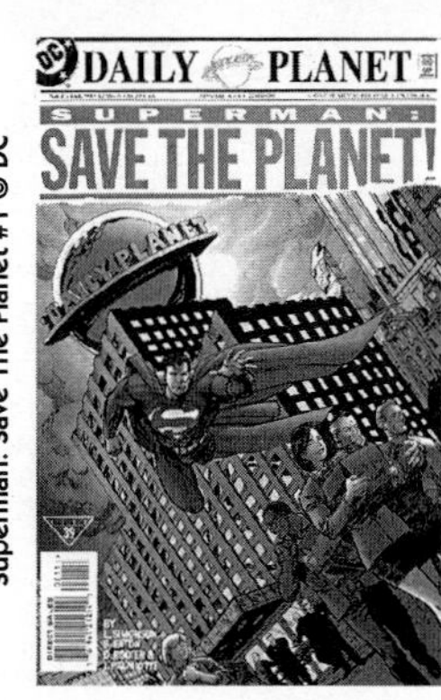

Superman: Save The Planet #1 © DC

GD25 FN65 NM94

store logos on bottom 1/3 of-c 3.00
...'S METROPOLIS-(1996, $5.95, prestige format)-Elseworlds
Ted McKeever-c/a 2.00 6.00
...: SPEEDING BULLETS-(1993, $4.95, 52 pgs.)-Elseworlds 5.00
.../SPIDER-MAN-(1995, $3.95)-r/DC and Marvel Presents...
...: THE EARTH STEALERS 1-(1988, $2.95, 52 pgs, prestige format)
1-Byrne script; painted-c 3.50
...: THE EARTH STEALERS 1-2nd printing 3.00
...: THE LEGACY OF SUPERMAN #1 (3/93, $2.50, 68 pgs.)-Art Adams-c;
Simonson-a 2.50
.../TOYMAN-(1996, $1.95) 2.00
...: 3-D (12/98, $3.95)-with glasses 3.95
...: UNDER A YELLOW SUN nn (1994, $5.95, 68 pgs.)-A Novel by Clark Kent;
embossed-c 2.00 6.00
...: WAR OF THE WORLDS (1999, $5.95)-Battles Martians 5.95

SUPERMAN ADVENTURES, THE (TV)
DC Comics: Oct, 1996 - Present ($1.75/$1.95/$1.99)(Based on animated series)

1-Rick Burchett-c/a begins; Paul Dini script; Lex Luthor app.; silver ink,
wraparound-c. 2.00
1-Preview issue distributed at Warner Bros. stores 2.00
2-13: 2-Scott McCloud scripts begin; Metallo-c/app. 3-Brainiac-c/app.
6-Mxyzptlk-c/app. 1.75
14-20,22: 14-Begin $1.95-c 2.00
21-($3.95) 1st animated Supergirl 4.00
23-28: 23-Begin $1.99-c; Livewire app. 25-Batgirl-c/app. 28-Manley-a 1.99
Annual 1 (1997, $3.95)-Zatanna and Bruce Wayne app. 4.00
Special 1 (2/98, $2.95) Superman vs. Lobo 3.00
TPB (1998, $7.95) r/#1-6 8.00

SUPERMAN & BATMAN: GENERATIONS (Elseworlds)
DC Comics: 1999 - No. 4, 1999 ($4.95, limited series)

1-4-Superman & Batman team-up from 1939 to the future; Byrne-c/s/a 4.95

SUPERMAN AND THE GREAT CLEVELAND FIRE
National Periodical Publ.: 1948 (Giveaway, 4 pgs., no cover) (Hospital Fund)

nn-In full color 58.00 174.00 490.00

SUPERMAN/BATMAN: ALTERNATE HISTORIES
DC Comics: 1996 ($14.95, trade paperback)

nn-Reprints Detective Comics Annual #7, Action Comics Annual #6, Steel
Annual #1, Legends of the Dark Knight Annual #4 15.00

SUPERMAN/DOOMSDAY: HUNTER/PREY
DC Comics: 1994 - No. 3, 1994 ($4.95, limited series, 52 pgs.)

1-3 5.00

SUPERMAN FAMILY, THE (Formerly Superman's Pal Jimmy Olsen)
National Per. Publ./DC Comics: No. 164, Apr-May, 1974 - No. 222, Sept, 1982

164-(100 pgs.) Jimmy Olsen, Supergirl, Lois Lane begin
2.70 8.00 30.00
165-169 (100 pgs.) 2.00 6.00 20.00
170-176 (68 pgs.) 1.40 4.20 14.00
177-181 (52 pgs.) .85 2.60 7.00
182-Marshall Rogers-a; $1.00 issues begin; Krypto begins, ends #192
.85 2.60 7.00
183-190: 183-Nightwing-Flamebird begins, ends #194. 189-Brainiac 5,
Mon-el app. .85 2.60 7.00
191-193,195-199: 191-Superboy begins, ends #198 5.00
194,200: 194-Rogers-a. 200-Book length sty .85 2.60 7.00
201-222: 211-Earth II Batman & Catwoman marry 4.00
NOTE: ***N. Adams*** *c-182-185.* ***Anderson*** *a-186i.* ***Buckler*** *c(p)-190, 191, 209, 210, 215, 217, 220.* ***Jones*** *a-191-193.* ***Gil Kane*** *c(p)-221, 222.* ***Mortimer*** *a(p)-191-193, 199, 201-222.* ***Orlando*** *a(i)-186, 187.* ***Rogers*** *a-182, 194.* ***Staton*** *a-191-194, 196p.* ***Tuska*** *a(p)-203, 207-209.*

SUPERMAN FOR ALL SEASONS
DC Comics: 1998 - No, 4, 1998 ($4.95, limited series, prestige format)

GD25 FN65 NM94

1-Loeb-s/Sale-a/c; Superman's first year in Metropolis 7.00
2-4 5.00

SUPERMAN FOR EARTH (See Superman one-shots)

SUPERMAN FOREVER
DC Comics: Jun, 1998 ($5.95, one-shot)

1-($5.95)-Collector's Edition with a 7-image lenticular-c by Alex Ross;
Superman returns to normal; s/a by various .85 2.60 7.00
1-($4.95) Standard Edition with single image Ross-c 5.00

SUPERMAN: LOIS LANE (Girlfrenzy)
DC Comics: Jun, 1998 ($1.95, one shot)

1-Connor & Palmiotti-a 2.00

SUPERMAN/MADMAN HULLABALOO!
Dark Horse Comics: June, 1997 - No. 3, Aug, 1997 ($2.95, limited series)

1-3-Mike Allred-c/s/a 3.00
TPB (1997, $8.95) 8.95

SUPERMAN (Miniature)
National Periodical Publ.: 1942; 1955 - 1956 (3 issues, no #'s, 32 pgs.)
The pages are numbered in the 1st issue: 1-32; 2nd: 1A-32A, and 3rd: 1B-32B

No date-Py-Co-Pay Tooth Powder giveaway (8 pgs.; circa 1942)
74.00 221.00 625.00
1-The Superman Time Capsule (Kellogg's Sugar Smacks)(1955)
50.00 150.00 425.00
1A-Duel in Space (1955) 44.00 132.00 375.00
1B-The Super Show of Metropolis (also #1-32, no B)(1955)
44.00 132.00 375.00
NOTE: *Numbering variations exist. Each title could have any combination-#1, 1A, or 1B.*

SUPERMAN: PEACE ON EARTH
DC Comics: Jan, 1999 ($9.95, Treasury-sized, one-shot)

1-Alex Ross painted-c/a; Paul Dini-s 10.00

SUPERMAN RECORD COMIC
National Periodical Publications: 1966 (Golden Records)

(With record)-Record reads origin of Superman from comic; came with iron-on
patch, decoder, membership card & button; comic-r/Superman #125,146
18.00 54.00 135.00
Comic only 11.50 34.00 85.00

SUPERMAN RED/ SUPERMAN BLUE
DC Comics: Feb, 1998 ($4.95, one shot)

1-Polybagged w/3-D glasses and reprint of Superman 3-D (1955); Jurgens-
plot/3-D cover; script and art by various 5.00
1-($3.95)-Standard Ed.; comic only, non 3-D cover 4.00

SUPERMAN: SAVE THE PLANET
DC Comics: Oct, 1998 ($2.95, one-shot)

1-($2.95) Regular Ed.; Luthor buys the Daily Planet 3.00
1-($3.95) Collector's Ed. with acetate cover 4.00

SUPERMAN'S BUDDY (Costume Comic)
National Periodical Publications: 1954 (4 pgs., slick paper-c; one-shot)
(Came in box w/costume)

1-w/box & costume 118.00 353.00 1000.00
Comic only 53.00 159.00 450.00
1-(1958 edition)-Printed in 2 colors 15.00 44.00 110.00

SUPERMAN'S CHRISTMAS ADVENTURE
National Periodical Publications: 1940, 1944 (Giveaway, 16 pgs.)
Distributed by Nehi drinks, Bailey Store, Ivey-Keith Co., Kennedy's Boys Shop,
Macy's Store, Boston Store

1(1940)-Burnley-a; F. Ray-c/r from Superman #6 (Scarce)-Superman saves
Santa Claus. Santa makes real Superman Toys offered in 1940. 1st
merchandising story 500.00 1500.00 4200.00
nn(1944) w/Santa Claus & X-mas tree-c 100.00 300.00 850.00

Superman's Girlfriend Lois Lane #136 © DC

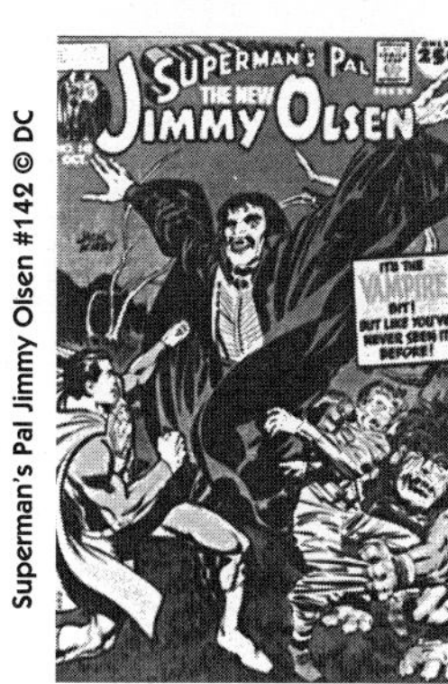

Superman's Pal Jimmy Olsen #142 © DC

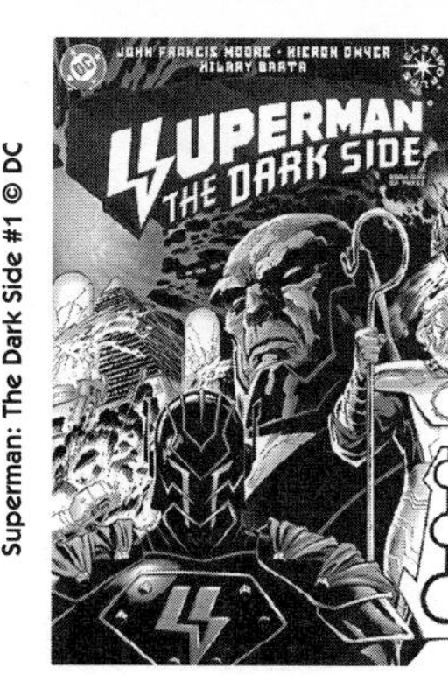

Superman: The Dark Side #1 © DC

GD25 FN65 NM94

nn(1944) w/Candy cane & Superman-c 88.00 265.00 750.00

SUPERMAN SCRAPBOOK (Has blank pages; contains no comics)

SUPERMAN: SECRET FILES
DC Comics: Jan, 1998 ($4.95, one shot)

1-Retold origin story, "lost" pages & pin-ups 5.00

SUPERMAN'S GIRLFRIEND LOIS LANE (See Action Comics #1, 80 Page Giant #3, 14, Lois Lane, Showcase #9, 10, Superman #28 & Superman Family)

SUPERMAN'S GIRLFRIEND LOIS LANE (See Showcase #9,10)
National Periodical Publ.: Mar-Apr, 1958 - No. 136, Jan-Feb, 1974; No. 137, Sept-Oct, 1974

	GD25	FN65	VF82	NM94
1-(3-4/58)	230.00	690.00	1500.00	3000.00

	GD25	FN65	NM94
2	65.00	195.00	775.00
3	41.00	123.00	500.00
4,5	36.00	108.00	400.00
6,7	31.00	93.00	310.00
8-10: 9-Pat Boone-c/story	26.00	78.00	260.00
11-20: 12-(10/59)-Aquaman app. 14-Supergirl x-over; Batman app? 20-Supergirl-c/sty	15.00	45.00	150.00
21-28: 23-1st app. Lena Thorul, Lex Luthor's sister. 27-Bizarro-c/story	11.50	34.00	115.00
29-Aquaman, Batman, Green Arrow cover app. and cameo; last 10¢ issue	12.50	38.00	125.00
30-32,34-46,48,49	6.00	18.00	60.00
33(5/62)-Mon-el app.	7.00	21.00	70.00
47-Legion app.	7.00	21.00	70.00
50(7/64)-Triplicate Girl, Phantom Girl & Shrinking Violet app.	5.50	16.50	55.00
51-55,57-67,69: 59-Jor-el app.; Batman back-up sty	4.50	13.50	45.00
56-Saturn Girl app.	4.50	13.50	45.00
68-(Giant G-26)	5.50	16.50	55.00
70-Penguin & Catwoman app. (1st S.A. Catwoman, 11/66; also see Detective #369 for 3rd app.); Batman & Robin cameo	22.00	66.00	220.00
71-Batman & Robin cameos (3 panels); Catwoman story cont'd from #70 (2nd app.); see Detective #369 for 3rd app	12.50	38.00	125.00
72,73,75,76,78	2.50	7.50	24.00
74-1st Bizarro Flash (5/67); JLA cameo	3.40	10.20	34.00
77-(Giant G-39)	4.50	13.50	45.00
79-Neal Adams-c or c(i) begin, end #95,108	1.60	4.80	16.00
80-85,87,88,90-92,94	1.60	4.80	16.00
86,95: (Giants G-51,G-63)-Both have Neal Adams-c	3.25	10.00	36.00
89,93: 89-Batman x-over; all N. Adams-c. 93-Wonder Woman-c/story	1.60	4.80	16.00
96-103,106-110	1.40	4.20	14.00
104,113-(Giants G-75,87): 113-Kubert-a (previously unpublished G.A. story)	3.25	10.00	36.00
105-Origin/1st app. The Rose & the Thorn.	3.20	9.50	34.00
111-Justice League-c/s; Morrow-a	1.80	5.40	18.00
112,114-123 (52 pgs.): 122-G.A. Lois Lane-r/Superman #30. 123-G.A. Batman-r/Batman #35 (w/Catwoman)	1.60	4.80	16.00
124-135: 130-Last Rose & the Thorn. 132-New Zatanna story		2.00	6.00
136,137: 136-Wonder Woman x-over	1.00	3.00	10.00
Annual 1(Sum, 1962)-r/L. Lane #12; Aquaman app.	18.00	54.00	180.00
Annual 2(Sum, 1963)	12.00	36.00	120.00

NOTE: ***Buckler*** *a-117-121p.* ***Curt Swan or Kurt Schaffenberger*** *a-1-50(most); c(p)-1-15.*

SUPERMAN: SILVER BANSHEE
DC Comics: Dec, 1998 - No. 2, Jan, 1999 ($2.25, mini-series)

1,2-Brereton-s/c; Chin-a 2.25

SUPERMAN'S PAL JIMMY OLSEN (Superman Family #164 on)
(See Action Comics #6 for 1st app. & 80 Page Giant)
National Periodical Publ.: Sept-Oct, 1954 - No. 163, Feb-Mar, 1974 (Fourth World #133-148)

	GD25	FN65	VF82	NM94
1	300.00	900.00	2150.00	4500.00

	GD25	FN65	NM94
2	104.00	312.00	1250.00
3-Last pre-code issue	56.00	168.00	675.00
4,5	43.00	129.00	475.00
6-10	31.00	93.00	320.00
11-20: 15-1st S.A. issue	21.00	63.00	210.00
21-30: 29-1st app. Krypto in Jimmy Olsen	14.00	42.00	140.00
31-Origin & 1st app.Elastic Lad (Jimmy Olsen)	11.00	33.00	110.00
32-40: 33-One pg. biography of Jack Larson (TV Jimmy Olsen). 36-Intro Lucy Lane. 37-2nd app. Elastic Lad & 1st cover app.	9.50	28.50	95.00
41-50: 41-1st J.O. Robot. 48-Intro/origin Superman Emergency Squad	7.50	22.50	75.00
51-56: 56-Last 10¢ issue	6.00	18.00	60.00
57-62,64-70: 57-Olsen marries Supergirl. 62-Mon-el & Elastic Lad app. but not as Legionnaires. 70-Element Boy (Lad) app.	3.50	10.50	35.00
63(9/62)-Legion of Super-Villains app.	4.00	12.00	40.00
71,74,75,78,80-84,86,89,90: 86-Jimmy Olsen Robot becomes Congorilla	3.00	9.00	30.00
72(10/63)-Legion app; Elastic Lad (Olsen) joins	3.20	9.50	32.00
73-Ultra Boy app.	3.20	9.50	32.00
76,85-Legion app.	3.20	9.50	32.00
77,79: 77-Olsen with Colossal Boy's powers & costume; origin Titano retold. 79-(9/64)-Titled The Red-headed Beatle of 1000 B.C.	3.20	9.50	32.00
87-Legion of Super-Villains app.	3.20	9.50	32.00
88-Star Boy app.	3.20	9.50	32.00
91-94,96-98	2.50	7.50	22.00
95,104 (Giants G-25,G-38)	4.00	12.00	40.00
99-Olsen w/powers & costumes of Lightning Lad, Sun Boy & Element Lad	2.50	7.50	24.00
100-Legion cameo	3.40	10.20	34.00
101-103,105-112,114-121,123-130,132: 106-Legion app. 110-Infinity-c. 117-Batman & Legion cameo	1.60	4.80	16.00
113,122,131,140 (Giants G-50,G-62,G-74,G-86)	3.00	9.00	33.00
133-(10/70)-Re-intro Newsboy Legion; Kirby story & art begins; 1st app. Morgan Edge.	4.00	12.25	45.00
134-1st app. Darkseid (1 panel, 12/70)	6.00	18.00	65.00
135-2nd app. Darkseid (1 pg. cameo; see New Gods & Forever People); G.A. Guardian app.	2.20	6.50	24.00
136-139: 136-Origin new Guardian. 138-Partial photo-c. 139-Last 15¢ issue	1.80	5.40	18.00
141-150: (25¢,52 pgs.). 141-Photo-c; Newsboy Legion-r by S&K begin; full pg. self-portrait Kirby; Don Rickles cameo. 149,150-G.A. Plastic Man-r in both; 150-Newsboy Legion app.	1.80	5.40	18.00
151-163:	1.10	3.30	11.00

NOTE: *Issues #141-148 contain* ***Simon & Kirby*** *Newsboy Legion reprints from Star Spangled #7, 8, 9, 10, 11, 12, 13, 14 in that order.* ***N. Adams*** *c-109-112, 115, 117, 118, 120, 121, 132, 134-136, 147, 148.* ***Kirby*** *a-133-139p, 141-148p; c-133, 137, 139, 142, 145p.* ***Kirby/N. Adams*** *c-137, 138, 141-144, 146.* ***Curt Swan*** *c-1-14(most)., 140.*

SUPERMAN SPECTACULAR (Also see DC Special Series #5)
DC Comics: 1982 (Magazine size, square binding)

1-Saga of Superman Red/ Superman Blue 2.00 6.00

SUPERMAN: THE DARK SIDE
DC Comics: 1998 - No. 3, 1998 ($4.95, squarebound, mini-series)

1-3: Elseworlds; Kal-El lands on Apokolips 4.95

SUPERMAN: THE DOOMSDAY WARS
DC Comics: 1998 - No. 3, 1999 ($4.95, squarebound, mini-series)

1-3: Superman & JLA vs. Doomsday; Jurgens-s/a(p) 4.95

SUPERMAN: THE MAN OF STEEL (Also see Man of Steel, The)

Superman: The Man of Steel #81 © DC

Superman: The Secret Years #2 © DC

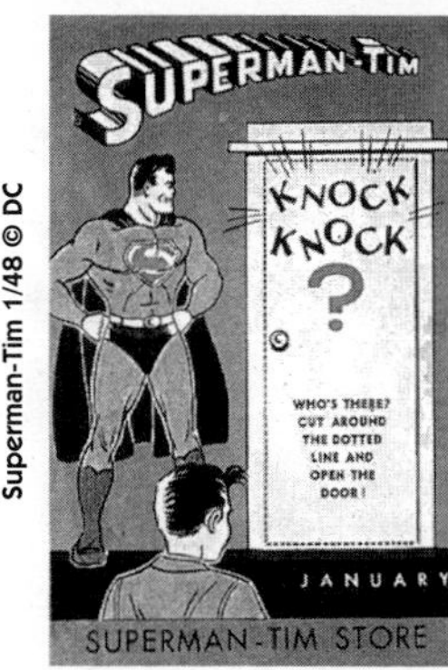

Superman-Tim 1/48 © DC

	GD25	FN65	NM94
DC Comics: July, 1991 - Present ($1.00/$1.25/$1.50/$1.95)			
1-($1.75, 52 pgs.)-Painted-c			3.00
2-16: 3-War of the Gods x-over. 5-Reads sideways. 10-Last $1.00-c. 14-Superman & Robin team-up			1.25
17-1st app. Doomsday (cameo)			5.00
17-2nd printing			1.25
18-1st full app. Doomsday	.85	2.60	7.00
18-2nd & 3rd printings			1.25
19-Doomsday battle issue (c/story)			3.00
20,21-Funeral for a Friend			2.00
22-($1.95)-Collector's Edition w/die-cut outer-c & bound-in poster; Steel-c/story			2.00
22-($1.50)-Newsstand Ed. w/poster & different-c			1.50
23-37: 23-$1.50-c begins. 30-Regular edition. 32-Bizarro-c/story. 35,36-Worlds Collide Pt. 1 & 10. 37-(9/94)-Zero Hour x-over			1.50
30-($2.50)-Collector's Edition; polybagged with Superman & Lobo vinyl clings that stick to wraparound-c; Lobo-c/story			2.50
0, 38-44-(10/94). 38-(11/94)			1.50
45-49,51-77: 45-$1.95-c begins. 48-Aquaman app. 54-Spectre-c/app; Lex Luthor app. 56-Mxyzptlk-c/app. 57-G.A. Flash app. 58-Supergirl app. 59-Parasite-c/app.; Steel app. 60-Reintro Bottled City of Kandor 62-Final Night. 64-New Gods app. 67-New powers. 75-"Death" of Mxyzptlk			1.95
50 ($2.95)-The Trial of Superman			3.00
78-82: 78,79-Millennium Giants. 80-Golden Age style			2.00
83-85: 83-Begin $1.99-c			1.99
#1,000,000 (11/98) 853rd Century x-over; Gene Ha-c			2.00
Annual 1,2 (1992-93, $2.50, 68 pgs.): 1-Eclipso app.; Joe Quesada-c(p). 2-Intro Edge			2.50
Annual 3 (1994, $2.95, 68 pgs.)-Elseworlds story; Mignola-c; Batman app.			3.00
Annual 4 (1995, $2.95)-Year One story			3.00
Annual 5 (1996, $2.95)-Legends of the Dead Earth story			3.00
Annual 6 (1997, $3.95)-Pulp Heroes story			4.00
...Gallery (1995, $3.50) Pin-ups by various			3.50

SUPERMAN: THE MAN OF TOMORROW
DC Comics: 1995 - Present ($1.95, quarterly)

	GD25	FN65	NM94
1-10: 1-Lex Luthor app. 3-Lex Luthor-c/app; Joker app. 4-Shazam! app. 5-Wedding of Lex Luthor. 10-Maxima-c/app.			2.00
11,12: 11-Begin $1.99-c			1.99
#1,000,000 (11/98) 853rd Century x-over; Gene Ha-c			2.00

SUPERMAN: THE SECRET YEARS
DC Comics: Feb, 1985 - No. 4, May, 1985 (limited series)

	GD25	FN65	NM94
1-Miller-c on all			1.50
2-4			1.00

SUPERMAN: THE WEDDING ALBUM
DC Comics: Dec, 1996 ($4.95, 96 pgs, one-shot)

	GD25	FN65	NM94
1-Standard Edition-Story & art by past and present Superman creators; gatefold back-c. Byrne-c			5.00
1-Collector's Edition-Embossed cardstock variant-c w/ metallic silver ink and matte and gloss varnishes			5.00

SUPERMAN 3-D (See Three-Dimension Adventures)

SUPERMAN-TIM (Becomes Tim)
Superman-Tim Stores/National Periodical Publ.: Aug, 1942 - May, 1950 (Half size) (B&W Giveaway w/2 color covers)

	GD25	FN65	NM94
8/42(#1)-All have Superman illos.	82.00	246.00	700.00
3/43(#2)	39.00	117.00	300.00
5/43, 6/43, 7/43, 8/43	33.00	100.00	250.00
9/43, 10/43, 12/43	29.00	88.00	220.00
2/44, 3/44, 4/44-12/44	23.00	68.00	170.00
1/45, 2/45, 3/45, 4/45, 5/45, 8/45, 9/45, 10/45-12/45, 1/46-4/46, 5/46, 6/46, 7/46, 8/46	20.00	60.00	150.00
6/45-Classic Superman-c	22.00	66.00	165.00
7/45-Classic Superman flag-c	22.00	66.00	165.00
9/46-1st stamp album issue (worth more if complete with Superman stamps)	39.00	117.00	300.00
10/46-1st Superman story	29.00	88.00	220.00
11/46, 12/46, 1/47, 2/47, 3/47, 4/47, 5/47,6/47, 7/47, 8/47 issues-Superman story in each; 2/47-Infinity-c. All 36 pgs.	29.00	88.00	220.00
9/47-Stamp album issue & Superman story	37.00	112.00	280.00
10/47, 11/47, 12/47-Superman stories (24 pgs.)	29.00	88.00	220.00
1/48, 2/48, 3/48, 4/48, 5/48, 6/48, 7/48,10/48, 11/48, 2/49, 4/49-11/49	23.00	68.00	170.00
8/48-Contains full page ad for Superman-Tim watch giveaway	23.00	70.00	175.00
9/48-Stamp album issue	24.00	72.00	180.00
1/49-Full page Superman bank cut-out	23.00	70.00	175.00
3/49-Full page Superman boxing game cut-out	23.00	70.00	175.00
12/49-3/50, 5/50-Superman stories	26.00	78.00	195.00
4/50-Superman story, baseball stories; photo-c without Superman	24.00	72.00	180.00

NOTE: *All issues have Superman illustrations throughout. The page count varies depending on whether a Superman-Tim comic story is inserted. If it is, the page count is either 36 or 24 pages. Otherwise all issues are 16 pages. Each issue has a special place for inserting a full color Superman stamp. The stamp album issues had spaces for the stamps given away the past year. The books were mailed as a subscription premium. The stamps were given away free (or when you made a purchase) only when you physically came into the store.*

SUPERMAN VILLAINS SECRET FILES
DC Comics: Jun, 1998 ($4.95, one shot)

	GD25	FN65	NM94
1-Origin stories, "lost" pages & pin-ups			5.00

SUPERMAN VS. ALIENS
DC Comics/Dark Horse Comics: July, 1995 - No. 3, Sept, 1995 ($4.95, limited series)

	GD25	FN65	NM94
1-3: Jurgens/Nowlan-a			5.00

SUPERMAN VS. THE AMAZING SPIDER-MAN (Also see Marvel Treasury Edition No. 28)
National Periodical Publications/Marvel Comics Group: 1976 ($2.00, Treasury sized, 100 pgs.)

	GD25	FN65	NM94
1-Andru/Giordano-a; 1st Marvel/DC x-over.	5.50	16.50	60.00
1-2nd printing; 5000 numbered copies signed by Stan Lee & Carmine Infantino on front cover & sold through mail	11.00	33.00	120.00
nn-(1995, $5.95)-r/#1		2.00	6.00

SUPERMAN/WONDER WOMAN: WHOM GODS DESTROY
DC Comics: 1997 ($4.95, prestige format, limited series)

	GD25	FN65	NM94
1-4-Elseworlds; Claremont-s			5.00

SUPERMAN WORKBOOK
National Periodical Publ./Juvenile Group Foundation: 1945 (B&W, one-shot, reprints, 68 pgs)

	GD25	FN65	NM94
nn-Cover-r/Superman #14	129.00	388.00	1100.00

SUPER MARIO BROS. (Also see Adventures of the..., Blip, Gameboy, and Nintendo Comics System)
Valiant Comics: 1990 - No. 5?, 1991 ($1.95, slick-c) V2#1, 1991 - No. 5, 1991

	GD25	FN65	NM94
1-Wildman-a		2.00	6.00
2-5			5.00
V2#1-5-($1.50)			3.00
Special Edition 1 (1990, $1.95)-Wildman-a		2.00	6.00

SUPERMODELS IN THE RAINFOREST
Sirius: 1998 - No. 3, 1999 ($2.95, B&W, limited series)

	GD25	FN65	NM94
1-Photo-c: Dark One-a			2.95

SUPERMOUSE (...the Big Cheese; see Coo Coo Comics)
Standard Comics/Pines No. 35 on (Literary Ent.): Dec, 1948 - No. 34, Sept,

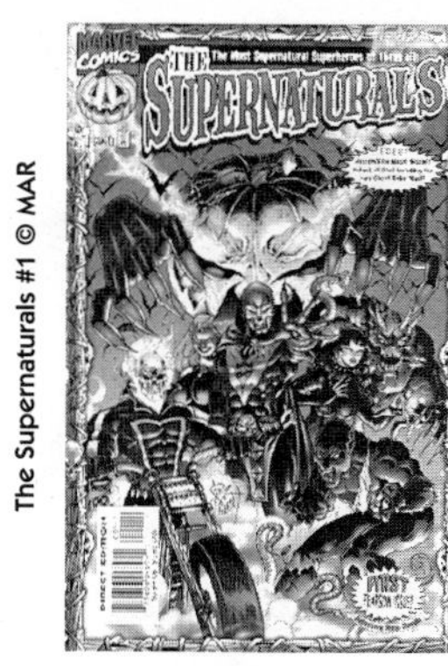

The Supernaturals #1 © MAR

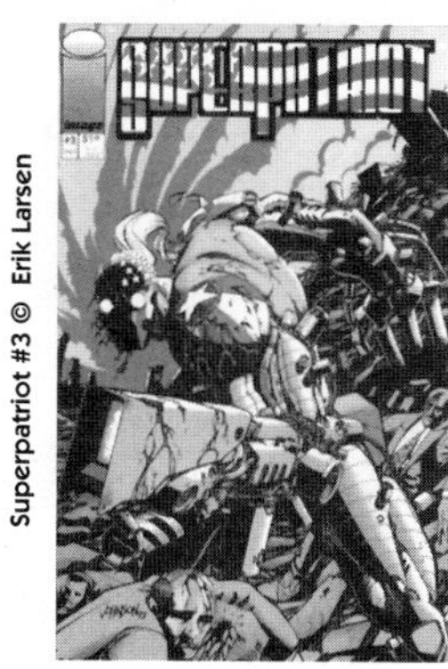

Superpatriot #3 © Erik Larsen

Supersnipe #15 © S&S

GD25 FN65 NM94

1955; No. 35, Apr, 1956 - No. 45, Fall, 1958
1-Frazetta text illos (3) 27.00 80.00 200.00
2-Frazetta text illos 13.00 40.00 100.00
3,5,6-Text illos by Frazetta in all 11.00 32.00 80.00
4-Two pg. text illos by Frazetta 11.00 34.00 85.00
7-10 5.00 15.00 30.00
11-20: 13-Racist humor (Indians) 4.00 12.00 24.00
21-45 3.60 9.00 18.00
1-Summer Holiday issue (Summer, 1957, 25¢, 100 pgs.)-Pines 11.00 32.00 80.00
2-Giant Summer issue (Summer, 1958, 25¢, 100 pgs.)-Pines; has games, puzzles & stories 8.50 26.00 60.00

SUPER-MYSTERY COMICS
Ace Magazines (Periodical House): July, 1940 - V8#6, July, 1949
V1#1-Magno, the Magnetic Man & Vulcan begins (1st app.); Q-13, Corp. Flint, & Sky Smith begin 153.00 460.00 1300.00
2 74.00 222.00 625.00
3-The Black Spider begins (1st app.) 64.00 192.00 540.00
4-Origin Davy 49.00 148.00 420.00
5-Intro. The Clown & begin series (12/40) 49.00 148.00 420.00
6(2/41) 42.00 127.00 340.00
V2#1(4/41)-Origin Buckskin 42.00 127.00 340.00
2-6(2/42): 6-Vulcan begins again 39.00 117.00 310.00
V3#1(4/42),2: 1-Black Ace begins 36.00 108.00 270.00
3-Intro. The Lancer; Dr. Nemesis & The Sword begin; Kurtzman-c/a(2) (Mr. Risk & Paul Revere Jr.); Robot-c 43.00 129.00 360.00
4-Kurtzman-c/a 39.00 117.00 310.00
5-Kurtzman-a(2); L.B. Cole-a; Mr. Risk app. 43.00 129.00 360.00
6(10/43)-Mr. Risk app.; Kurtzman's Paul Revere Jr.; L.B. Cole-a 43.00 129.00 360.00
V4#1(1/44)-L.B. Cole-a 39.00 117.00 300.00
2-6(4/45): 2,5,6-Mr. Risk app. 25.00 76.00 190.00
V5#1(7/45)-6 27.00 80.00 200.00
V6#1-6: 3-Torture story. 4-Last Magno. Mr. Risk app. in #2,4-6. 6-New logo 21.00 62.00 155.00
V7#1-6, V8#1-4,6 21.00 62.00 155.00
V8#5-Meskin, Tuska, Sid Greene-a 21.00 62.00 155.00
NOTE: ***Sid Greene** a-V7#4. **Mooney** c-V1#5, 6, V2#1-6. **Palais** a-V5#3, 4; c-V4#6-V5#4, V6#2, V8#4. Bondage c-V2#5, 6, V3#2, 5. Magno c-V1#1-V3#6, V4#2-V5#5, V6#2. The Sword c-V4#1, 6(w/Magno).*

SUPERNATURALS
Marvel Comics: Dec, 1998 - No. 4, Dec, 1998 ($3.99, weekly limited series)
1-4-Pulido-s/Balent-c; bound-in Halloween masks 4.00
1-4-With bound-in Ghost Rider mask (1 in 10) 4.00

SUPERNATURAL THRILLERS
Marvel Comics Group: Dec, 1972 - No. 6, Nov, 1973; No. 7, Jul, 1974 - No. 15, Oct, 1975
1-It!; Sturgeon adap. (see Astonishing Tales #21). 1.50 4.50 15.00
2-4: 2-The Invisible Man; H.G. Wells adapt. 3-The Valley of the Worm; R.E. Howard adapt. 4-Dr. Jekyll & Mr. Hyde; R.L. Stevenson adapt. 1.00 3.00 10.00
5-1st app. The Living Mummy 2.70 8.00 30.00
6-15: 6-The Headless Horseman; last 20¢ issue. 7-The Living Mummy begins .85 2.60 7.00
NOTE: ***Brunner** c-11. **Buckler** a-5p. **Ditko** a-8r, 9r. **G. Kane** a-3p; c-3, 9p, 15p. **Mayerik** a-2p, 7, 8, 9p, 10p, 11. **McWilliams** a-14i. **Mortimer** a-4. **Steranko** c-1, 2. **Sutton** a-15. **Tuska** a-6p.*

SUPERPATRIOT (Also see Freak Force & Savage Dragon #2)
Image Comics (Highbrow Entertainment): July, 1993 - No. 4, Dec, 1993 ($1.95, limited series)
1-4: Dave Johnson-c/a; Larsen scripts; Giffen plots 2.00

SUPERPATRIOT: LIBERTY & JUSTICE
Image Comics (Highbrow Entertainment): July, 1995 - No. 4, Oct, 1995 ($2.50, limited series)
1-4: Dave Johnson-c/a. 1-1st app. Liberty & Justice 2.50

SUPER POWERS (1st Series)
DC Comics: July, 1984 - No. 5, Nov, 1984
1-Joker/Penguin-c/story; Batman app. 2.00
2-5: 1-5-Kirby-c; 5-Kirby-c/a 2.00

SUPER POWERS (2nd Series)
DC Comics: Sept, 1985 - No. 6, Feb, 1986
1-Kirby-c/a in all; Capt. Marvel & Firestorm join; Batman cameo; Darkseid storyline in #1-6 2.00
2-6: 4-Batman cameo. 5,6-Batman app. 2.00

SUPER POWERS (3rd Series)
DC Comics: Sept, 1986 - No. 4, Dec, 1986
1-4: 1-Cyborg joins; 1st app. Samurai from Super Friends TV show. 1-4-Batman cameos; Darkseid storyline in #1-4 2.00

SUPER PUP (Formerly Spotty The Pup) (See Space Comics)
Avon Periodicals: No. 4, Mar-Apr, 1954 - No. 5, 1954
4,5: 5-Robot-c 4.25 13.00 28.00

SUPER RABBIT (See All Surprise, Animated Movie Tunes, Comedy Comics, Comic Capers, Ideal Comics, It's A Duck's Life, Movie Tunes & Wisco)
Timely Comics (CmPI): Fall, 1944 - No. 14, Nov, 1948
1-Hitler & Hirohito-c; war effort paper recycling PSA by S&K; Ziggy Pig & Silly begin? 58.00 173.00 490.00
2 31.00 94.00 235.00
3-5 20.00 60.00 150.00
6-Origin 21.00 64.00 160.00
7-10: 9-Infinity-c 12.00 36.00 90.00
11-Kurtzman's "Hey Look" 13.00 38.00 95.00
12-14 11.00 34.00 85.00
I.W. Reprint #1,2('58),7,10('63): 1-r/#13. 2-r/#10. 2.00 6.00 16.00

SUPER RICHIE (Superichie #5 on) (See Richie Rich Millions #68)
Harvey Publications: Sept, 1975 - No. 4, Mar, 1976 (All 52 pg. Giants)
1 1.40 4.20 14.00
2-4 .90 2.70 9.00

SUPERSNIPE COMICS (Formerly Army & Navy #1-5)
Street & Smith Publications: V1#6, Oct, 1942 - V5#1, Aug-Sept, 1949 (See Shadow Comics V2#3)
V1#6-Rex King - Man of Adventure (costumed hero, see Super Magic/ Magician) by Jack Binder begins; Supersnipe by George Marcoux continues from Army & Navy #5; Bill Ward-a 71.00 212.00 600.00
7,10-12: 10,11-Little Nemo app. 43.00 129.00 365.00
8-Hitler, Tojo, Mussolini in Hell with Devil-c 46.00 138.00 390.00
9-Doc Savage x-over in Supersnipe; Hitler-c 57.00 171.00 485.00
V2#1-12: Both V2#1(2/44) & V2#2(4/44) has V2#1 on outside-c. 1-Huck Finn by Clare Dwiggins begins, ends V3#5; V2#2 shows V2#1 on cover 33.00 100.00 250.00
V3#1-12: 8-Bobby Crusoe by Dwiggins begins, ends V3#12. 9-X-Mas-c 29.00 88.00 220.00
V4#1-12, V5#1: V4#10-X-Mas-c 21.00 62.00 155.00
NOTE: ***George Marcoux** c-V1#6-V3#4. Doc Savage app. in some issues.*

SUPER SOLDIER (See Marvel Versus DC #3)
DC Comics (Amalgam): Apr, 1996 ($1.95, one-shot)
1-Mark Waid script & Dave Gibbons-c/a. 2.00

SUPER SOLDIER: MAN OF WAR
DC Comics (Amalgam): June, 1997 ($1.95, one-shot)
1-Waid & Gibbons-s/Gibbons & Palmiotti-c/a. 2.00

SUPER SOLDIERS
Marvel Comics UK: Apr, 1993 - No. 8, Nov, 1993 ($1.75)

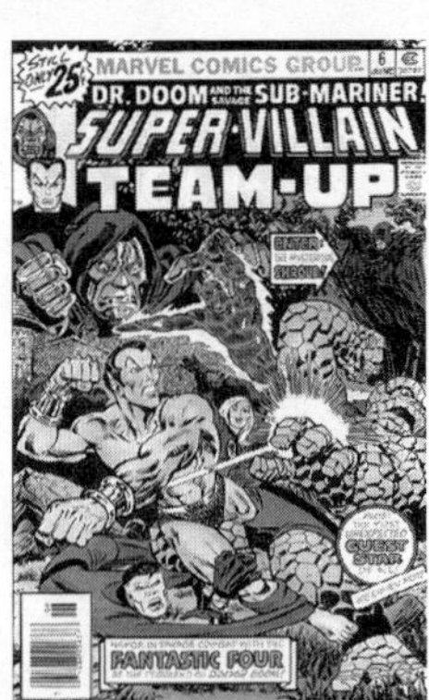

Super-Villain Team-Up #6 © MAR

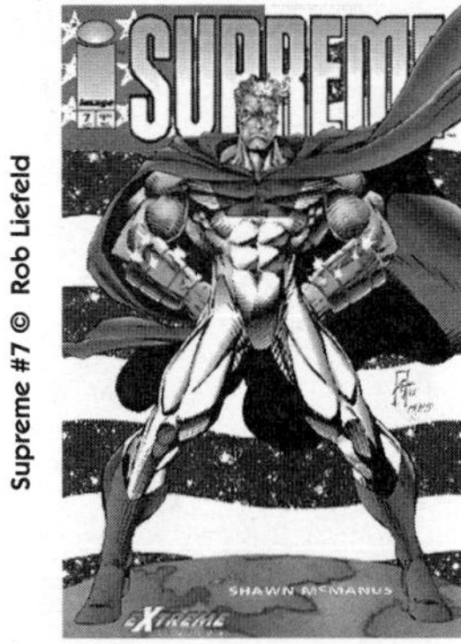

Supreme #7 © Rob Liefeld

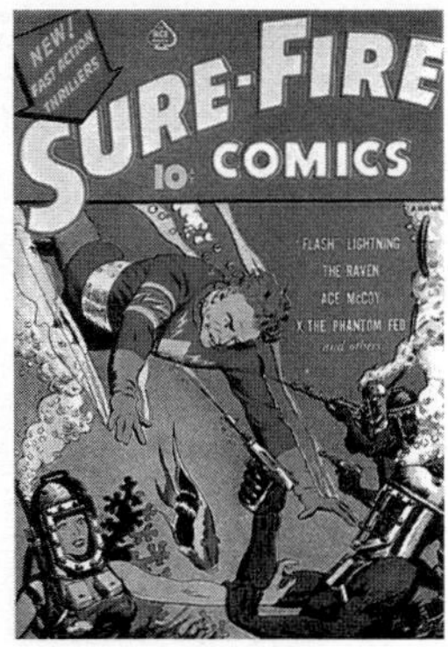

Sure-Fire Comics #2 © ACE

1-($2.50)-Embossed silver foil logo 2.50
2-8: 5-Capt. America app. 6-Origin; Nick Fury app.; neon ink-c 1.75

SUPERSPOOK (Formerly Frisky Animals on Parade)
Ajax/Farrell Publications: No. 4, June, 1958

4 6.00 18.00 42.00

SUPER SPY (See Wham Comics)
Centaur Publications: Oct, 1940 - No. 2, Nov, 1940 (Reprints)

1-Origin The Sparkler 100.00 300.00 850.00
2-The Inner Circle, Dean Denton, Tim Blain, The Drew Ghost, The Night Hawk by Gustavson, & S.S. Swanson by Glanz app. 62.00 185.00 525.00

SUPER STAR HOLIDAY SPECIAL (See DC Special Series #21)

SUPER-TEAM FAMILY
National Periodical Publ./DC Comics: Oct-Nov, 1975 - No. 15, Mar-Apr, 1978

1-Reprints by Neal Adams & Kane/Wood; 68 pgs. begin, ends #4. New Gods app. 1.20 3.60 12.00
2,3: New stories 2.00 6.00
4-7: Reprints. 4-G.A. JSA-r & Superman/Batman/Robin-r from World's Finest. 5-52 pgs. begin .85 2.60 7.00
8-10: New Challengers of the Unknown stories .90 2.70 8.00
11-14: New stories .90 2.70 8.00
15-New Gods app. New stories 1.00 3.00 10.00

NOTE: ***Neal Adams*** *r-1-3.* ***Brunner*** *c-3.* ***Buckler*** *c-8p.* ***Tuska*** *a-7r.* ***Wood*** *a-1i(r), 3.*

SUPER TV HEROES (See Hanna-Barbera...)

SUPER-VILLAIN CLASSICS
Marvel Comics Group: May, 1983

1-Galactus - The Origin 3.00

SUPER-VILLAIN TEAM-UP (See Fantastic Four #6 & Giant-Size...)
Marvel Comics Group: 8/75 - No. 14, 10/77; No. 15, 11/78; No. 16, 5/79; No. 17, 6/80

1-Giant-Size Super-Villian Team-Up #2; Sub-Mariner & Dr. Doom begin, end #10 1.00 3.00 10.00
2 2.00 6.00
3-5,7-17: 5-1st app. The Shroud. 7-Origin Shroud. 9-Avengers app. 11-15-Dr. Doom & Red Skull app. 3.00
6-(Regular 25¢ edition)(6/76)-F.F., Shroud app. 3.00
6-(30¢-c, limited distribution) 1.20 3.60 12.00

NOTE: ***Buckler*** *c-4p, 5p, 7p.* ***Buscema*** *c-1.* ***Byrne/Austin*** *c-14.* ***Evans*** *a-1p, 3p.* ***Everett*** *a-1p.* ***Giffen*** *a-8p, 13p; c-13p.* ***Kane*** *c-2p, 9p.* ***Mooney*** *a-4i.* ***Starlin*** *c-6.* ***Tuska*** *r-1p, 15p.* ***Wood*** *r-15p.*

SUPER WESTERN COMICS (Also see Buffalo Bill)
Youthful Magazines: Aug, 1950 - No. 4, Mar, 1951

1-Buffalo Bill begins; Wyatt Earp, Calamity Jane & Sam Slade app; Powell-c/a 11.00 34.00 85.00
2-4 7.15 21.50 50.00

SUPER WESTERN FUNNIES (See Super Funnies)

SUPERWORLD COMICS
Hugo Gernsback (Komos Publ.): Apr, 1940 - No. 3, Aug, 1940 (68 pgs.)

1-Origin & 1st app. Hip Knox, Super Hypnotist; Mitey Powers & Buzz Allen, the Invisible Avenger, Little Nemo begin; cover by Frank R. Paul (all have sci/fi-c)(Scarce) 450.00 1350.00 4500.00
2-Marvo 1-2 Go+, the Super Boy of the Year 2680 (1st app.); Paul-c (Scarce) 295.00 885.00 2800.00
3 (Scarce) 224.00 672.00 1900.00

SUPREME (Becomes ...The New Adventures #43-48)(See Youngblood #3) (Also see Bloodwulf Special, Legend of Supreme, & Trencher #3)
Image Comics (Extreme Studios)/ Awesome Entertainment #49 on: V2#1, Nov, 1992 - V2#42, Sept, 1996; V3#49 - Present ($1.95/$2.50/$2.99)

V2#1-Liefeld-a(i) & scripts; embossed foil logo 3.00
1-Gold Edition 6.00
2-(3/93)-Liefeld co-plots & inks; 1st app. Grizlock 2.00
3-12,25: 3-Intro Bloodstrike; 1st app. Khrome. 5-1st app. Thor. 6-The Starguard cameo. 7-1st full app. The Starguard. 10-Black and White Pt 1 (1st app.) by Art Thibert (2 pgs. ea. installment). 25-(5/94)-Platt-c 2.00
13-24, 26-40: 11-Coupon #4 for Extreme Prejudice #0; Black and White Pt. 7 by Thibert. 12-(4/94)-Platt-c. 13,14-(6/94). 15 (7/94). 16 (7/94)-Stormwatch app. 18-Kid Supreme Sneak Preview; Pitt app. 19,20-Polybagged w/trading card. 20-1st app. Woden & Loki (as a dog); Overtkill app. 21-1st app. Loki (in true form). 21-23-Polybagged trading card. 32-Lady Supreme cameo. 33-Origin & 1st full app. of Lady Supreme (Probe from the Starguard); Babewatch! tie-in. 37-Intro Loki; Fraga-c. 40-Retells Supreme's past advs. 2.50
28-Variant-c by Quesada & Palmiotti 3.00
41-Alan Moore scripts begin; Supreme revised; intro The Supremacy; Jerry Ordway-c (Joe Bennett variant-c exists). 2.00 6.00
42-New origin w/Rick Veitch-a; intro Radar, The Hound Supreme & The League of Infinity 4.00
(#43-48-See Supreme: The New Adventures)
V3#49,51: 49-Begin $2.99-c 3.00
50-($3.95)-Double sized, 2 covers, pin-up gallery 4.00
52a,52b-($3.50) 3.50
53-($2.50)-Sprouse-a begins 2.50
54-56-($2.99): 56-McGuinness-c 3.00
Annual 1-(1995, $2.95) 3.00

NOTE: ***Rob Liefeld*** *a(i)-1, 2; co-plots-2-4; scripts-1, 5, 6.* ***Ordway*** *c-41.* ***Platt*** *c-12, 25.* ***Thibert*** *c(i)-7-9.*

SUPREME: GLORY DAYS
Image Comics (Extreme Studios): Oct, 1994 - No. 2, Dec, 1994 ($2.95/$2.50, limited series)

1 3.00
2-Diehard, Roman, Superpatriot, & Glory app. 2.50

SUPREME: THE NEW ADVENTURES (Formerly Supreme)
Maximum Press: V3#43, Oct, 1996 - V3#48, May, 1997 ($2.50)

V3#43-48: 43-Alan Moore scripts begin; Joe Bennett-a; Rick Veitch-a (8 pgs.); Dan Jurgens-a (1 pg.); intro Citadel Supreme & Suprematons; 1st app. Allied Supermen of America 3.00

SURE-FIRE COMICS (Lightning Comics #4 on)
Ace Magazines: June, 1940 - No. 4, Oct, 1940 (Two No. 3's)

V1#1-Origin Flash Lightning & begins; X-The Phantom Fed, Ace McCoy, Buck Steele, Marvo the Magician, The Raven, Whiz Wilson (Time Traveler) begin (all 1st app.); Flash Lightning c-1-4 135.00 405.00 1150.00
2 71.00 212.00 600.00
3(9/40), 3(#4)(10/40)-nn on-c, #3 on inside 53.00 159.00 450.00

SURF 'N' WHEELS
Charlton Comics: Nov, 1969 - No. 6, Sept, 1970

1 2.50 7.50 22.00
2-6 2.00 6.00 16.00

SURGE
Eclipse Comics: July, 1984 - No. 4, Jan, 1985 ($1.50, lim. series, Baxter paper)

1-4 Ties into DNAgents series 1.50

SURPRISE ADVENTURES (Formerly Tormented)
Sterling Comic Group: No. 3, Mar, 1955 - No. 5, July, 1955

3-5: 3,5-Sekowsky-a 5.35 16.00 32.00

SUSIE Q. SMITH
Dell Publishing Co.: No. 323, Mar, 1951 - No. 553, Apr, 1954

Four Color 323 (#1) 3.00 9.00 35.00
Four Color 377, 453 (2/53), 553 2.75 8.00 30.00

Suspense Comics #7 © Continental Magazines

Suzie Comics #76 © AP

Swamp Thing #146 © DC

GD25 FN65 NM94

SUSPENSE (Radio/TV issues #1-11; Real Life Tales of... #1-4) (Amazing Detective Cases #3 on?)
Marvel/Atlas Comics (CnPC No. 1-10/BFP No. 11-29): Dec, 1949 - No. 29, Apr, 1953 (#1-8,17-23: 52 pgs.)

1-Powell-a; Peter Lorre, Sidney Greenstreet photo-c from Hammett's "The Verdict" 49.00 148.00 420.00
2-Crime stories; Dennis O'Keefe & Gale Storm photo-c from Universal movie "Abandoned" 28.00 84.00 210.00
3-Change to horror 29.00 88.00 220.00
4,7-10: 7-Dracula-sty 23.00 68.00 170.00
5-Krigstein, Tuska, Everett-a 24.00 72.00 180.00
6-Tuska, Everett, Morisi-a 23.00 70.00 175.00
11-17,19,20: 14-Hypo-c; A-Bomb panels 17.00 52.00 130.00
18,22-Krigstein-a 19.00 58.00 145.00
21,23,24,26-29: 24-Tuska-a 16.00 48.00 120.00
25-Electric chair-c/story 21.00 64.00 160.00

NOTE: ***Ayers** a-20. **Briefer** a-5, 7, 27. **Brodsky** c-4, 6-9, 11, 16, 17, 25. **Colan** a-8(2), 9. **Everett** a-5, 6(2), 19, 23, 28; c-21-23, 26. **Fuje** a-29. **Heath** a-5, 6, 8, 10, 12, 14; c-14, 19, 24. **Maneely** a-12, 23, 24, 28, 29; c-5, 6p, 10, 13, 15, 18. **Mooney** a-24, 28. **Morisi** a-6, 12. **Palais** a-10. **Rico** a-7-9. **Robinson** a-29. **Romita** a-20(2), 25. **Sekowsky** a-11, 13, 14. **Sinnott** a-23, 25. **Tuska** a-5, 6(2), 12; c-12. **Whitney** a-15, 16, 22. **Ed Win** a-27.*

SUSPENSE COMICS
Continental Magazines: Dec, 1943 - No. 12, Sept, 1946

1-The Grey Mask begins; bondage/torture-c; L. B. Cole-a (7 pgs.) 300.00 900.00 3000.00
2-Intro. The Mask; Rico, Giunta, L. B. Cole-a (7 pgs.) 259.00 777.00 2200.00
3-L.B. Cole-a; classic Schomburg-c (Scarce) 1250.00 3750.00 10,000.00
4-6: 5-L. B. Cole-c begin 188.00 565.00 1600.00
7,9,10,12: 9-L.B. Cole eyeball-c 147.00 441.00 1250.00
8-Classic L. B. Cole spider-c 320.00 960.00 3200.00
11-Classic Devil-c 260.00 780.00 2600.00

NOTE: ***L. B. Cole** c-5-12. **Fuje** a-8. **Larsen** a-11. **Palais** a-10, 11. Bondage c-1, 3, 4.*

SUSPENSE DETECTIVE
Fawcett Publications: June, 1952 - No. 5, Mar, 1953

1-Evans-a (11 pgs); Baily-c/a 37.00 112.00 280.00
2-Evans-a (10 pgs.) 22.00 66.00 165.00
3-5 18.00 54.00 135.00

NOTE: ***Baily** a-4, 5; c-1-3. **Sekowsky** a-2, 4, 5; c-5.*

SUSPENSE STORIES (See Strange Suspense Stories)

SUSPIRA: THE GREAT WORKING
Chaos! Comics: Apr, 1997 - No. 4, Aug, 1997 ($2.95, limited series)

1-4 3.00

SUSSEX VAMPIRE, THE (Sherlock Holmes)
Caliber Comics: 1996 ($2.95, 32 pgs., B&W, one-shot)

nn-Adapts Sir Arthur Conan Doyle's story; Warren Ellis scripts 3.00

SUZIE COMICS (Formerly Laugh Comix; see Laugh Comics, Liberty Comics #10, Pep Comics & Top-Notch Comics #28)
Close-Up No. 49,50/MLJ Mag./Archie No. 51 on: No. 49, Spring, 1945 - No. 100, Aug, 1954

49-Ginger begins 21.00 64.00 160.00
50-55: 54-Transvestism story 13.00 40.00 100.00
56-Katy Keene begins by Woggon 12.00 36.00 90.00
57-65 9.30 28.00 65.00
66-80 8.50 26.00 60.00
81-87,89-100: 100-Last Katy Keene 7.85 23.50 55.00
88-Used in **POP**, pgs. 76,77; Bill Woggon draws himself in story 8.50 26.00 60.00

NOTE: ***Al Fagaly** c-49-67. Katy Keene app. in 53-82, 85-100.*

SWAMP FOX, THE (TV, Disney)(See Walt Disney Presents #2)
Dell Publishing Co.: No. 1179, Dec, 1960

Four Color 1179-Leslie Nielson photo-c 8.00 25.00 90.00

SWAMP FOX, THE
Walt Disney Productions: 1960 (14 pgs, small size) (Canada Dry Premiums)

Titles: (A)-Tory Masquerade, (B)-Rindau Rampage, (C)-Turnabout Tactics; each came in paper sleeve, books 1,2 & 3;
Set with sleeves 4.00 12.00 40.00
Comic only 1.85 5.50 15.00

SWAMP THING (See Brave & the Bold, Challengers of the Unknown #82, DC Comics Presents #8 & 85, DC Special Series #2, 14, 17, 20, House of Secrets #92, Limited Collectors' Edition C-59, & Roots of the...)

SWAMP THING
National Per. Publ./DC Comics: Oct-Nov, 1972 - No. 24, Aug-Sept, 1976

1-Wrightson-c/a begins; origin 6.50 19.00 70.00
2-1st app. Patchwork Man (1 panel cameo) 3.20 9.50 35.00
3-1st full app. Patchwork Man (see House of Secrets #140) 2.20 6.25 22.00
4-6,8-10: 10-Last Wrightson issue 2.00 6.00 20.00
7-Batman-c/story 2.25 6.80 25.00
11-24: 11-19-Redondo-a. 13-Origin retold (1 pg.) 23,24-Swamp Thing reverts back to Dr. Holland. 23-New logo .85 2.60 7.00

NOTE: ***J. Jones** a-9i(assist). **Kaluta** a-9i. **Redondo** c-12-19, 21. **Wrightson** issues (#1-10) reprinted in DC Special Series #2, 14, 17, 20 & Roots of the Swampthing.*

SWAMP THING (Saga Of The... #1-38,42-45) (See Essential Vertigo:...)
DC Comics (Vertigo imprint #129 on): May, 1982 - No. 171, Oct, 1996 (Direct sales #65 on)

1-Origin retold; Phantom Stranger series begins; ends #13; Yeates-c/a begins 3.00
2-15: 2-Photo-c from movie. 13-Last Yeates-a 1.75
16-19: Bissette-a. 3.00
20-1st Alan Moore issue 1.60 4.80 16.00
21-New origin 1.30 3.90 13.00
22,23,25: 25-John Constantine 1-panel cameo .85 2.60 7.00
24-JLA x-over; Last Yeates-c. 1.00 3.00 10.00
26-30 4.50
31-33,35,36: 33-r/1st app. from House of Secrets #92 3.50
34 .85 2.60 7.00
37-1st app. John Constantine (Hellblazer) (6/85) 1.30 3.90 13.00
38-40: John Constantine app. 2.00 6.00
41-51: 44-Batman cameo. 44-51-John Constantine app. 46-Crisis x-over; Batman cameo. 49-Spectre app. 50-($1.25, 52 pgs.)-Deadman, Dr. Fate, Demon 2.00
52-Arkham Asylum-c/story; Joker-c/cameo 3.00
53-($1.25, 52 pgs.)-Arkham Asylum; Batman-c/story 4.00
54-64: 58-Spectre preview. 64-Last Moore issue 2.00
65-83,85-99,101-124,126-130: 65-Direct sales only begins. 66-Batman & Arkham Asylum story. 70,76-John Constantine x-over; 76-X-over w/Hellblazer #9. 79-Superman-c/story. 85-Jonah Hex app. 102-Preview of World Without End. 116-Photo-c. 129-Metallic ink on-c 2.00
84-Sandman (Morpheus) cameo. 5.00
100 ($2.50, 52 pgs.) 2.50
125-($2.95, 52 pgs.)-20th anniversary issue 3.50
131-149, 151-153: 131-$1.95-c begins. 140-Millar scripts begin, end #171 3.00
150 ($2.95, 52 pgs.)-Anniversary issue 3.00
154-171: 154-$2.25-c begins. 165-Curt Swan-a(p). 166,169,171-John Constantine & Phantom Stranger app. 168-Arcane returns 2.25
Annual 1(1982, $1.00)-Movie Adaptation; painted-c 1.50
Annual 2(1985)-Alan Moore scripts; Bissette-a(p); Spectre app. 3.00
Annual 3(1987, $2.00)-New format; Bolland-c 2.00
Annual 4(1988, $2.00)-Batman-c/story 3.00
Annual 5(1989, $2.95, 68 pgs.)-Batman cameo; re-intro Brother Power (Geek),

Sweethearts #119 © FAW

Sweet Love #3 © HARV

Sweet Sixteen #2 © PMI

	GD25	FN65	NM94
1st app. since 1968			3.00
Annual 6(1991, $2.95, 68 pgs.)			3.00
Annual 7(1993, $3.95)-Children's Crusade			4.00
...: Roots (1998, $7.95) Jon J Muth-s/painted-a/c			8.00
Saga of the Swamp Thing (1987, $10.95)-r/#21-27			11.00
Saga of the Swamp Thing (1989, $12.95, 2nd Printing)			13.00
...Love and Death (1990, $17.95)-r/#28-34 & Annual #2; Totleben painted-c			18.00

NOTE: ***Bissette*** *a(p)-16-19, 21-27, 29, 30, 34-36, 39-42, 44, 46, 50, 64; c-17i, 24-32p, 35-37p, 40p, 44p, 46-50p, 51-58, 61, 62, 63p.* ***Kaluta*** *c/a-74.* ***Spiegle*** *a-1-3, 6.* ***Sutton*** *a-98p.* ***Totleben*** *a(i)-10, 16-27, 29, 31, 34-40, 42, 44, 46, 48, 50, 53, 55i; c-25-32i, 33, 35-40i, 42i, 44i, 46-50i, 53, 55i, 59p, 64, 65, 68, 73, 76, 80, 82, 84, 89, 91-100, Annual 4, 5.* ***Vess*** *painted c-121, 129-139, Annual 7.* ***Williamson*** *86i.* ***Wrightson*** *a-18i(r), 33r. John Constantine appears in #37-40, 44-51, 65-67, 70-77, 80-90, 99, 114, 115, 130, 134-138.*

SWARM (See Futuretech)
Mushroom Comics: Jan, 1996 - Present ($2.50, limited series)

	GD25	FN65	NM94
1-Flip book w/Futuretech #1			2.50

SWAT MALONE (America's Home Run King)
Swat Malone Enterprises: Sept, 1955

	GD25	FN65	NM94
V1#1-Hy Fleishman-a	9.30	28.00	65.00

SWEENEY (Formerly Buz Sawyer)
Standard Comics: No. 4, June, 1949 - No. 5, Sept, 1949

	GD25	FN65	NM94
4,5: 5-Crane-a	7.15	21.50	50.00

SWEE'PEA (Also see Popeye #46)
Dell Publishing Co.: No. 219, Mar, 1949

	GD25	FN65	NM94
Four Color 219	8.00	25.00	90.00

SWEET CHILDE
Advantage Graphics Press: 1995 - No. 2, 1995 ($2.95, B&W, mature)

	GD25	FN65	NM94
1,2			3.00

SWEETHEART DIARY (Cynthia Doyle #66-on)
Fawcett Publications/Charlton Comics No. 32 on: Wint, 1949; #2, Spr, 1950; #3, 6/50 - #5, 10/50; #6, 1951(nd); #7, 9/51 - #14, 1/53; #32, 10/55; #33, 4/56 - #65, 8/62 (#1-14: photo-c)

	GD25	FN65	NM94
1	13.00	38.00	95.00
2	7.50	22.50	48.00
3,4-Wood-a	13.00	39.00	95.00
5-10: 8-Bailey-a	6.35	19.00	40.00
11-14: 13-Swayze-a. 14-Last Fawcett issue	4.25	13.00	26.00
32 (10/55; 1st Charlton issue)(Formerly Cowboy Love #31)	5.35	16.00	32.00
33-40: 34-Swayze-a	3.60	9.00	18.00
41-(68 pgs.)	4.00	10.00	20.00
42-60	1.75	5.25	14.00
61-65	1.50	4.50	12.00

SWEETHEARTS (Formerly Captain Midnight)
Fawcett Publications/Charlton No. 122 on: #68, 10/48 - #121, 5/53; #122, 3/54; V2#23, 5/54 - #137, 12/73

	GD25	FN65	NM94
68-Photo-c begin	13.00	38.00	95.00
69-80	5.35	16.00	32.00
81-84,86-93,95-99,105	4.00	12.00	24.00
85,94,103,110,117-George Evans-a	5.70	17.00	38.00
100	4.25	13.00	28.00
101,107-Powell-a	4.25	13.00	26.00
102,104,106,108,109,112-116,118	3.60	9.00	18.00
111-1 pg. Ronald Reagan biography	5.70	17.00	38.00
119-Marilyn Monroe & Richard Widmark photo-c (1/54?); also appears in story; part Wood-a	29.00	86.00	230.00
120-Atom Bomb story	7.15	21.50	50.00
121-Liz Taylor/Fernanado Lamas photo-c	5.70	17.00	38.00
122-(1st Charlton? 3/54)-Marijuana story	6.85	21.00	48.00
V2#23 (5/54)-28: 28-Last precode issue (2/55)	4.00	10.00	20.00
29-39,41,43-45,47-50	1.50	4.50	12.00
40-Photo-c; Tommy Sands story	2.50	7.50	20.00
42-Ricky Nelson photo-c/story	5.50	16.50	55.00
46-Jimmy Rodgers photo-c/story	2.50	7.50	20.00
51-60	2.25	6.75	18.00
61-80,100	1.75	5.25	14.00
81-99	1.50	4.50	12.00
101-110	.90	2.70	9.00
111-137	.85	2.60	7.00

NOTE: *Photo c-68-121(Fawcett), 40, 42, 46(Charlton).* ***Swayze*** *a(Fawcett)-70-118(most).*

SWEETHEART SCANDALS (See Fox Giants)

SWEETIE PIE
Dell Publishing Co.: No. 1185, May-July, 1961 - No. 1241, Nov-Jan, 1961/62

	GD25	FN65	NM94
Four Color 1185 (#1), 1241	2.75	8.00	30.00

SWEETIE PIE
Ajax-Farrell/Pines (Literary Ent.): Dec, 1955 - No. 15, Fall, 1957

	GD25	FN65	NM94
1-By Nadine Seltzer	5.70	17.00	35.00
2 (5/56; last Ajax?)	4.00	11.00	22.00
3-15 (#3-10, exist?)	2.60	6.50	13.00

SWEET LOVE
Home Comics (Harvey): Sept, 1949 - No. 5, May, 1950 (All photo-c)

	GD25	FN65	NM94
1	7.85	23.50	55.00
2	5.00	15.00	30.00
3,4: 3-Powell-a	4.00	12.00	24.00
5-Kamen, Powell-a	5.70	17.00	40.00

SWEET ROMANCE
Charlton Comics: Oct, 1968

	GD25	FN65	NM94
1			4.00

SWEET SIXTEEN (...Comics and Stories for Girls)
Parents' Magazine Institute: Aug-Sept, 1946 - No. 13, Jan, 1948 (All have movie stars photos on covers)

	GD25	FN65	NM94
1-Van Johnson's life story; Dorothy Dare, Queen of Hollywood Stunt Artists begins (in all issues); part photo-c	15.00	46.00	115.00
2-Jane Powell, Roddy McDowall "Holiday in Mexico" photo on-c; Alan Ladd story	11.00	32.00	80.00
3,5,6,8-11: 5-Ann Francis photo on-c; Gregory Peck story. 6-Dick Haymes story. 8-Shirley Jones photo on-c. 10-Jean Simmons photo on-c; James Stewart story	7.85	23.50	55.00
4-Elizabeth Taylor photo on-c	9.30	28.00	65.00
7-Ronald Reagan's life story	15.00	46.00	115.00
12-Bob Cummings, Vic Damone story	7.85	23.50	55.00
13-Robert Mitchum's life story	8.50	26.00	60.00

SWEET XVI
Marvel Comics: May, 1991 - No. 5, Sept, 1991($1.00, color)

	GD25	FN65	NM94
..1-5: Barbara Slate story & art			1.00

SWIFT ARROW (Also see Lone Rider & The Rider)
Ajax/Farrell Publications: Feb-Mar, 1954 - No. 5, Oct-Nov, 1954; Apr, 1957 - No. 3, Sept, 1957

	GD25	FN65	NM94
1(1954) (1st Series)	12.00	36.00	90.00
2	6.50	19.50	45.00
3-5: 5-Lone Rider story	5.70	17.00	35.00
1 (2nd Series) (Swift Arrow's Gunfighters #4)	5.70	17.00	40.00
2,3: 2-Lone Rider begins	5.00	15.00	30.00

SWIFT ARROW'S GUNFIGHTERS (Formerly Swift Arrow)
Ajax/Farrell Publ. (Four Star Comic Corp.): No. 4, Nov, 1957

	GD25	FN65	NM94
4	5.00	15.00	30.00

SWING WITH SCOOTER
National Periodical Publications: June-July, 1966 - No. 35, Aug-Sept, 1971; No. 36, Oct-Nov, 1972

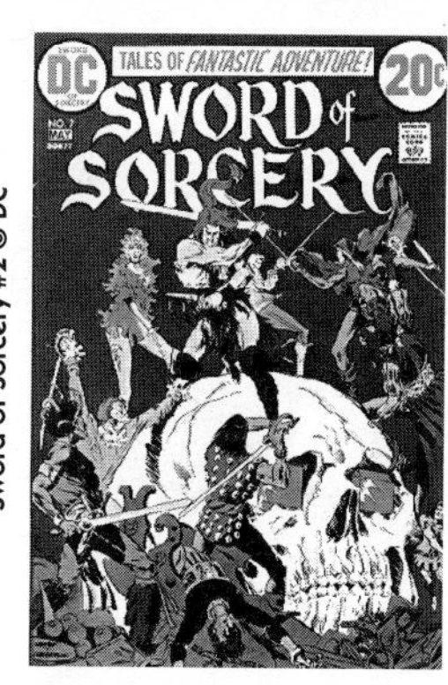

Sword of Sorcery #2 © DC

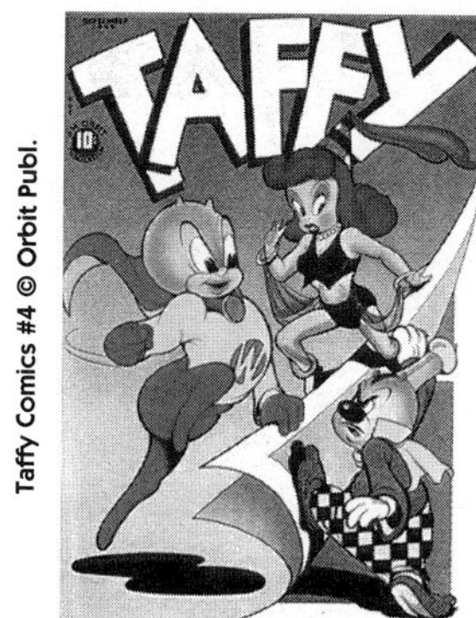

Taffy Comics #4 © Orbit Publ.

Takion #2 © DC

GD25 FN65 NM94

1 5.50 16.50 55.00
2,6-10: 9-Alfred E. Newman swipe in last panel 2.50 7.50 22.00
3-5: 3-Batman cameo on-c. 4-Batman cameo inside. 5-JLA cameo
2.50 7.50 25.00
11-13,15-19: 18-Wildcat of JSA 1pg. text 2.00 6.00 16.00
14-Alfred E. Neuman cameo 2.50 7.50 20.00
20 (68 pgs.) 3.00 9.00 30.00
21-31: 24-Frankenstein-c. 1.50 4.50 12.00
32-34 (68 pgs.). 33-Interview with David Cassidy. 34-Interview with Ron Ely (Doc Savage) 2.50 7.60 28.00
35-(52 pgs.). 1 pg. app. Clark Kent and 4 full pgs. of Superman
6.00 17.50 65.00
36-Bat-signal refererence to Batman 1.80 5.40 18.00
NOTE: ***Aragones*** *a-13 (1pg.), 18(1pg.), 30(2pgs.)* ***Orlando*** *a-1-11; c-1-11, 13. #20, 33, 34: 68 pgs.; #35: 52 pgs.*

SWISS FAMILY ROBINSON (Walt Disney's..; see King Classics & Movie Comics)
Dell Publishing Co.: No. 1156, Dec, 1960
Four Color 1156-Movie-photo-c 6.40 19.00 70.00

SWORD & THE DRAGON, THE
Dell Publishing Co.: No. 1118, June, 1960
Four Color 1118-Movie, photo-c 7.00 22.00 80.00

SWORD & THE ROSE, THE (Disney)
Dell Publishing Co.: No. 505, Oct, 1953 - No. 682, Feb, 1956
Four Color 505-Movie, photo-c 8.00 25.00 90.00
Four Color 682-When Knighthood Was in Flower-Movie, reprint of #505; Renamed the Sword & the Rose for the novel; photo-c
6.40 19.00 70.00

SWORD IN THE STONE, THE (See March of Comics #258 & Movie Comics & Wart and the Wizard)

SWORD OF DAMOCLES
Image Comics (WildStorm Productions): Mar, 1996 - No. 2, Apr, 1996 ($2.50, limited series)
1,2: Warren Ellis scripts. 1-Prelude to "Fire From Heaven" x-over; 1st app. Sword 2.50

SWORD OF SORCERY
National Periodical Publications: Feb-Mar, 1973 - No. 5, Nov-Dec, 1973 (20¢)
1-Leiber Fafhrd & The Grey Mouser; Chaykin/Neal Adams (Crusty Bunkers) art; Kaluta-c 1.20 3.60 12.00
2,3: 2-Wrightson-c(i); Adams-a(i). 3-Wrightson-i(5 pgs.) .90 2.70 8.00
4,5: . 5-Starlin-a(p); Conan cameo 2.00 6.00
NOTE: ***Chaykin*** *a-1-4p; c-2p, 3-5.* ***Kaluta*** *a-3i.* ***Simonson*** *a-3i, 4i, 5p; c-5.*

SWORD OF THE ATOM
DC Comics: Sept, 1983 - No. 4, Dec, 1983 (Limited series)
1-4: Kane-c/a in all 1.50
Special 1(1984), 2(1985): Kane-c/a each 1.50
Special 3(1988, $1.50) 1.50

SWORDS OF TEXAS (See Scout #15)
Eclipse Comics: Oct, 1987 - No. 4, Jan, 1988 ($1.75, color, Baxter paper)
1-4: Scout app. 1.80

SWORDS OF THE SWASHBUCKLERS (See Marvel Graphic Novel)
Marvel Comics (Epic Comics): May, 1985 - No. 12, Jun, 1987 ($1.50; mature)
1-12-Butch Guice-c/a (Cont'd from Marvel G.N.) 1.60

SWORN TO PROTECT
Marvel Comics: Sept, 1995 ($1.95) (Based on card game)
nn-Overpower Game Guide; Jubilee story 2.00

SYNDICATE FEATURES (Sci/fi)
Harry A. Chesler Syndicate: V1#3, 11/15/37 (Tabloid size, 3 colors, 4 pgs.)

GD25 FN65 NM94

(Editors premium)
V1#3-Dan Hastings daily strips-Guardineer-a 259.00 777.00 2200.00

SYPHONS
Now Comics: V2#1, May, 1994 - V2#3, 1994 ($2.50, limited series)
V2#1-3: 1-Stardancer, Knightfire, Raze & Brigade begin 2.50

SYSTEM, THE
DC Comics (Vertigo Verite): May, 1996 - No. 3, July, 1996 ($2.95, lim. series)
1-3: Kuper-c/a 3.00
TPB (1997, $12.95) r/#1-3 12.95

TAFFY COMICS
Rural Home/Orbit Publ.: Mar-Apr, 1945 - No. 12, 1948
1-L.B. Cole-c; origin & 1st app. of Wiggles The Wonderworm plus 7 chapter WWII funny animal adventures 43.00 129.00 350.00
2-L.B. Cole-c; Wiggles-c/stories in #1-4 21.00 64.00 160.00
3,4,6-12: 6-Perry Como-c/story. 7-Duke Ellington, 2 pgs. 8-Glenn Ford-c/story. 9-Lon McCallister part photo-c & story. 10-Mort Leav-c. 11-Mickey Rooney-c/story 10.00 30.00 75.00
5-L.B. Cole-c; Van Johnson-c/story 16.00 48.00 120.00

TAILGUNNER JO
DC Comics: Sept, 1988 - No. 6, Jan, 1989 ($1.25)
1-6 1.25

TAILS
Archie Publications; Dec, 1995 - No. 3, Feb, 1996 ($1.50, limited series)
1-3: Based on Sonic, the Hedgehog video game 2.00

TAILSPIN
Spotlight Publishers: November, 1944
nn-Firebird app.; L.B. Cole-c 23.00 68.00 170.00

TAILSPIN TOMMY (Also see Popular Comics)
United Features Syndicate/Service Publ. Co.: 1940; 1946
Single Series 23(1940) 36.00 108.00 270.00
Best Seller (nd, 1946)-Service Publ. Co. 12.00 36.00 90.00

TAINTED
DC Comics (Vertigo): Jan, 1995 ($4.95, one-shot)
1-Jamie Delano scripts; Al Davison-c/a; reads February '95 on-c 5.00

TAKION
DC Comics: June, 1996 - No. 7, Dec, 1996 ($1.75)
1-7: Aaron Lopresti-c/a(p). 1-Origin; Green Lantern app. 6-Final Night x-over
1.75

TALENT SHOWCASE (See New Talent Showcase)

TALE OF ONE BAD RAT, THE
Dark Horse Comics: Oct, 1994 - No. 4, Jan, 1995 ($2.95, limited series)
1-4: Bryan Talbot-c/a/scripts 3.00
HC ($69.95, signed and numbered) R/#1-4 70.00

TALES CALCULATED TO DRIVE YOU BATS
Archie Publications: Nov, 1961 - No. 7, Nov, 1962; 1966 (Satire)
1-Only 10¢ issue; has cut-out Werewolf mask (price includes mask)
9.00 27.00 90.00
2-Begin 12¢ issues 4.80 14.40 48.00
3-6: 3-UFO cover 3.80 11.40 38.00
7-Storyline change 3.20 9.60 32.00
1(1966, 25¢, 44 pg. Giant)-r/#1; UFO cover 4.00 12.00 40.00

TALES CALCULATED TO DRIVE YOU MAD
E.C. Publications: Summer, 1997 - Present ($3.99, satire)
1-6-Full color reprints of Mad: 1-(#1-3), 2-(#4-6), 3-(#7-9), 4-(#10-12) 5-(#13-15), 6-(#16-18) 4.00

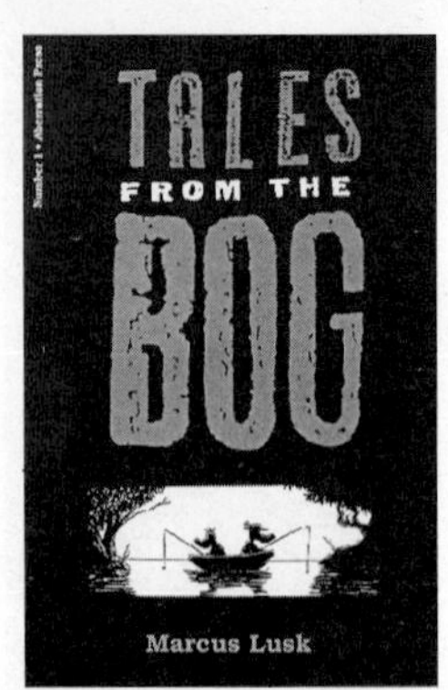

Tales From The Bog #1 © Markus Lusk

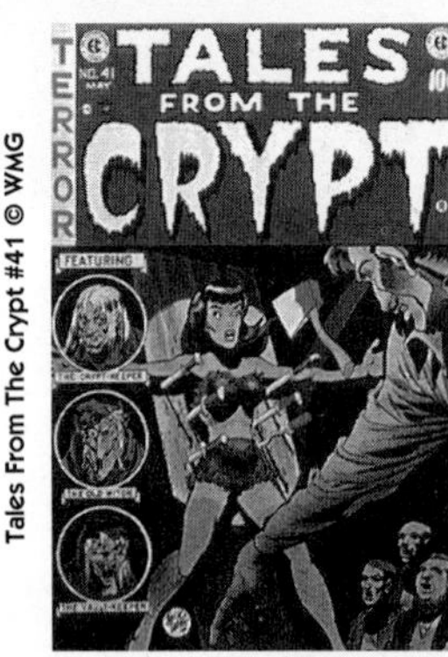

Tales From The Crypt #41 © WMG

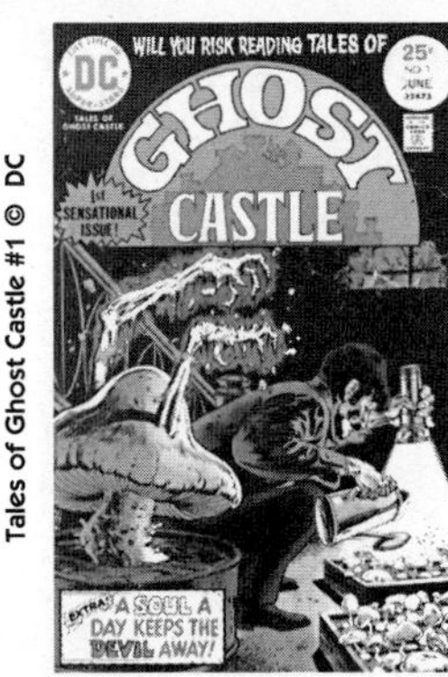

Tales of Ghost Castle #1 © DC

TALES FROM THE AGE OF APOCALYPSE
Marvel Comics: 1996 ($5.95, prestige format, one-shots)

	GD25	FN65	NM94
1			6.00
...: Sinister Bloodlines (1997, $5.95)			6.00

TALES FROM THE BOG
Aberration Press: Nov, 1995 - Present ($2.95/$3.95, B&W)

	GD25	FN65	NM94
1-4			3.00
5-7-($3.95)			4.00

TALES FROM THE CRYPT (Formerly The Crypt Of Terror; see Three Dimensional...)
E.C. Comics: No. 20, Oct-Nov, 1950 - No. 46, Feb-Mar, 1955

	GD25	FN65	NM94
20-See Crime Patrol #15 for 1st Crypt Keeper	100.00	300.00	950.00
21-Kurtzman-r/Haunt of Fear #15(#1)	84.00	252.00	750.00
22-Moon Girl costume at costume party, one panel	65.00	195.00	600.00
23-25: 24-E. A. Poe adaptation	49.00	147.00	450.00
26-30	38.00	114.00	350.00
31-Williamson-a(1st at E.C.); B&W and color illos. in **POP**; Kamen draws himself, Gaines & Feldstein; Ingels, Craig & Davis draw themselves in his story	40.00	120.00	375.00
32,35-39: 38-Censored-c	34.00	102.00	290.00
33-Origin The Crypt Keeper	56.00	168.00	500.00
34-Used in **POP**, pg. 83; lingerie panels	34.00	102.00	290.00
40-Used in Senate hearings & in Hartford Cournat anti-comics editorials-1954	34.00	102.00	290.00
41-45: 45-2 pgs. showing E.C. staff	34.00	102.00	290.00
46-Low distribution; pre-advertised cover for unpublished 4th horror title "Crypt of Terror" used on this book	37.00	111.00	340.00

NOTE: ***Ray Bradbury*** *adaptations-34, 36.* ***Craig*** *a-20, 22-24; c-20.* ***Crandall*** *a-38, 44.* ***Davis*** *a-24-46; c-29-46.* ***Elder*** *a-37, 38.* ***Evans*** *a-32-34, 36, 40, 41, 43, 46.* ***Feldstein*** *a-20-23; c-21-25, 28. Ingels a-in all.* ***Kamen*** *a-20, 22, 25, 27-31, 33-36, 39, 41-45.* ***Krigstein*** *a-40, 42, 45.* ***Kurtzman*** *a-21.* ***Orlando*** *a-27-30, 35, 37, 39, 41-45.* ***Wood*** *a-21, 24, 25; c-26, 27. Canadian reprints known; see Table of Contents.*

TALES FROM THE CRYPT (Magazine)
Eerie Publications: No. 10, July, 1968 (35¢, B&W)

	GD25	FN65	NM94
10-Contains Farrell reprints from 1950s	2.60	7.80	26.00

TALES FROM THE CRYPT
Gladstone Publishing: July, 1990 - No. 6, May, 1991 ($1.95/$2.00, 68 pgs.)

	GD25	FN65	NM94
1-r/TFTC #33 & Crime S.S. #17; Davis-c(r)			2.00
2-6: 2,3,5,6-Davis-c(r). 4-Begin $2.00-c; Craig-c(r)			2.00

TALES FROM THE CRYPT
Extra-Large Comics (Russ Cochran)/Gemstone Publishing: Jul, 1991 - No. 6 ($3.95, 10 1/4 x13 1/4", 68 pgs.)

	GD25	FN65	NM94
1-Davis-c(r); Craig back-c(r); E.C. reprints			4.00
2-6 ($2.00, comic sized)			2.00

TALES FROM THE CRYPT
Russ Cochran: Sept, 1991 - No. 7, July, 1992 ($2.00, 64 pgs.)

	GD25	FN65	NM94
1-7			2.00

TALES FROM THE CRYPT
Russ Cochran/Gemstone Publishing: Sept, 1992 - Present ($1.50, quarterly)

	GD25	FN65	NM94
1-4-r/Crypt of Terror #17-19, TFTC #20 w/original-c			1.50
5-15 ($2.00)-r/TFTC #21-23 w/original-c			2.00
16-26 ($2.50)			2.50
Annual 1 (1993, $8.95) r/#1-5			8.95
Annual 2 (1995, $9.95) r/#6-10			9.95
Annual 3 (1996, $10.95) r/#11-15			10.95
Annual 4 (1997, $12.95) r/#16-20			12.95
Annual 5 (1998, $13.50) r/#21-25			13.50

TALES FROM THE GREAT BOOK
Famous Funnies: Feb, 1955 - No. 4, Jan, 1956

	GD25	FN65	NM94
1-Story of Samson; John Lehti-a in all	6.50	19.50	45.00
2-4: 2-Joshua. 3-Joash the Boy King. 4-David	4.15	12.50	25.00

TALES FROM THE HEART OF AFRICA (The Temporary Natives)
Marvel Comics (Epic Comics): Aug, 1990 ($3.95, 52 pgs.)

	GD25	FN65	NM94
1			4.00

TALES FROM THE TOMB (Also see Dell Giants)
Dell Publishing Co.: Oct, 1962 (25¢ giant)

	GD25	FN65	VF82	NM94
1(02-810-210)-All stories written by John Stanley	9.75	29.00	68.00	175.00

TALES FROM THE TOMB (Magazine)
Eerie Publications: V1#6, July, 1969 - V7#3, 1975 (52 pgs.)

	GD25	FN65	NM94
V1#6-8	5.00	15.00	50.00
V2#1-6: 4-LSD story-r/Weird V3#5. 6-Rulah-r	3.50	10.50	35.00
V3#1-Rulah-r	3.50	10.50	35.00
2-6('70),V4#1-5('72),V5#1-6('73),V6#1-6('74),V7#1-3('75)	3.00	9.00	30.00

TALES OF ASGARD
Marvel Comics Group: Oct, 1968 (25¢, 68 pgs.); Feb, 1984 ($1.25, 52 pgs.)

	GD25	FN65	NM94
1-Reprints Tales of Asgard (Thor) back-up stories from Journey into Mystery #97-106; new Kirby-c	3.00	9.00	30.00
V2#1 (2/84)-Thor-r; Simonson-c			2.00

TALES OF DEMON DICK & BUNKER BILL
Whitman Publishing Co.: 1934 (B&W, 5x10-1/2", hardcover, 78 pgs.)

	GD25	FN65	NM94
793-By Dick Spencer	24.00	72.00	180.00

TALES OF EVIL
Atlas/Seaboard Publ.: Feb, 1975 - No. 3, July, 1975 (All 25¢ issues)

	GD25	FN65	NM94
1-3: 2-Intro. The Bog Beast; Sparling-a. 3-Origin The Man-Monster; Buckler-a(p)		1.20	4.00

NOTE: ***Grandenetti*** *a-1, 2.* ***Lieber*** *c-1.* ***Sekowsky*** *a-1.* ***Sutton*** *a-2.* ***Thorne*** *c-2.*

TALES OF GHOST CASTLE
National Periodical Publications: May-June, 1975 - No. 3, Sept-Oct, 1975 (All 25¢ issues)

	GD25	FN65	NM94
1-3: 1,3-Redondo-a. 2-Nino-a	1.00	3.00	10.00

TALES OF G.I. JOE
Marvel Comics: Jan, 1988 - No. 15, Mar, 1989

	GD25	FN65	NM94
1 ($2.25, 52 pgs.)			2.25
2-15 ($1.50): 1-15-r/G.I. Joe #1-15			1.50

TALES OF HORROR
Toby Press/Minoan Publ. Corp.: June, 1952 - No. 13, Oct, 1954

	GD25	FN65	NM94
1	32.00	96.00	240.00
2-Torture scenes	26.00	78.00	195.00
3-8,13	16.00	48.00	120.00
9-11-Reprints Purple Claw #1-3	16.00	48.00	120.00
12-Myron Fass-c/a; torture scenes	17.00	52.00	130.00

NOTE: ***Andru*** *a-5.* ***Baily*** *a-5.* ***Myron Fass*** *a-2, 3, 12; c-1-3, 12.* ***Hollingsworth*** *a-2.* ***Sparling*** *a-6, 9; c-9.*

TALES OF JUSTICE
Atlas Comics(MjMC No. 53-66/Male No. 67): No. 53, May, 1955 - No. 67, Aug, 1957

	GD25	FN65	NM94
53	13.00	38.00	95.00
54-57: 54-Powell-a	9.30	28.00	65.00
58,59-Krigstein-a	10.00	30.00	70.00
60-63,65: 60-Powell-a	7.85	23.50	55.00
64,67-Crandall-a	9.30	28.00	65.00
66-Torres, Orlando-a	9.30	28.00	65.00

NOTE: ***Everett*** *a-53, 60.* ***Orlando*** *a-65, 66.* ***Severin*** *a-64; c-58, 60, 65.* ***Wildey*** *a-64, 67.*

TALES OF SUSPENSE (Becomes Captain America #100 on)
Atlas (WPI No. 1,2/Male No. 3-12/VPI No. 13-18)/Marvel No. 19 on:

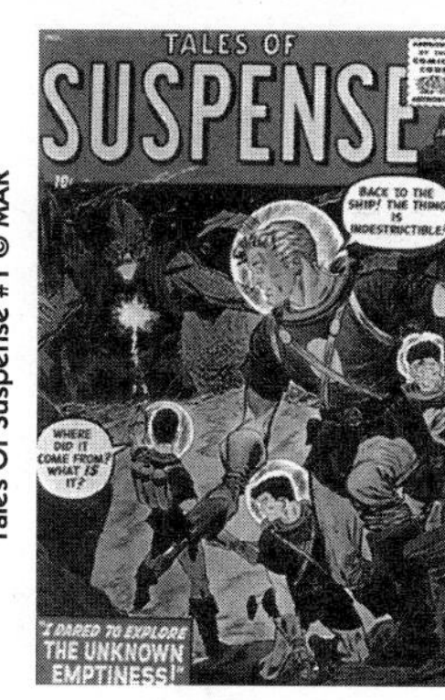

Tales Of Suspense #1 © MAR

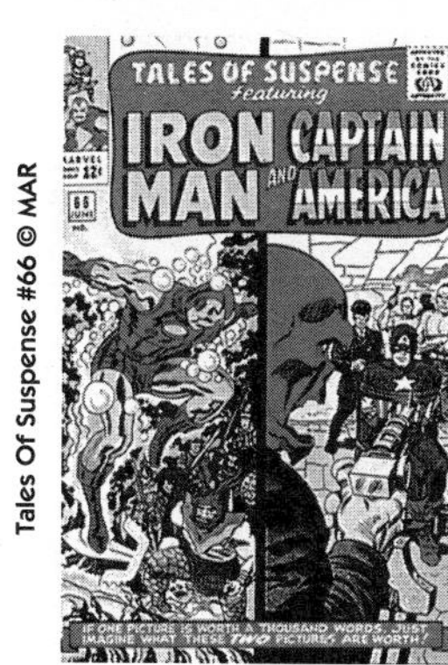

Tales Of Suspense #66 © MAR

Tales Of The Darkness #1 © Top Cow

GD25 FN65 NM94

Jan, 1959 - No. 99, Mar, 1968

1-Williamson-a (5 pgs.); Heck-c; #1-4 have sci/fi-c 121.00 363.00 1450.00
2,3: 2-Robot-c. 3-Flying saucer-c/story 45.00 135.00 550.00
4-Williamson-a (4 pgs.); Kirby/Everett-c/a 40.00 120.00 480.00
5,6,8,10: 5-Kirby monster-c begin 31.00 93.00 320.00
7-Prototype ish. (Lava Man); 1 panel app. Aunt May (see Str. Tales #97) 32.00 96.00 360.00
9-Prototype ish. (Iron Man) 35.00 105.00 390.00
11,12,15,17-19: 12-Crandall-a. 25.00 75.00 250.00
13-Elektro-c/story 26.00 78.00 260.00
14-Intro/1st app. Colossus-c/sty 31.00 93.00 310.00
16-1st Metallo-c/story (4/61, Iron Man prototype) 31.00 93.00 310.00
20-Colossus-c/story (2nd app.) 26.00 78.00 260.00
21-25: 25-Last 10¢ issue 19.00 57.00 190.00
26,27,29,30,33,34,36-38: 33-(9/62)-Hulk 1st x-over cameo (picture on wall) 16.50 50.00 165.00
28-Prototype ish. (Stone Men) 17.00 51.00 170.00
31-Prototype ish. (Dr. Doom) 21.00 63.00 210.00
32-Prototype ish. (Dr. Strange)(8/62)-Sazzik The Sorcerer app.; "The Man and the Beehive" story, 1 month before TTA #35 (2nd Antman), came out after "The Man in the Ant Hill" in TTA #27 (1/62) (1st Antman)-Characters from both stories were tested to see which got best fan response 31.00 93.00 320.00
35-Prototype issue (The Watcher) 21.00 63.00 210.00

GD25 FN65 VF82 NM94

39 (3/63)-Origin/1st app. Iron Man & begin series; 1st Iron Man story has Kirby layouts 267.00 800.00 1870.00 4000.00

GD25 FN65 NM94

40-2nd app. Iron Man (in new armor) 100.00 300.00 1200.00
41-3rd app. Iron Man; Dr. Strange (villain) app. 54.00 162.00 650.00
42-45: 45-Intro. & 1st app. Happy & Pepper 31.00 93.00 320.00
46,47: 46-1st app. Crimson Dynamo 19.50 58.00 195.00
48-New Iron Man armor by Ditko 24.00 72.00 240.00
49-1st X-Men x-over (same date as X-Men #3, 1/64); also 1st Avengers x-over (w/o Captain America); 1st Tales of the Watcher back-up story & begins (2nd app. Watcher; see F.F. #13) 17.00 51.00 170.00
50-1st app. Mandarin 12.50 38.00 125.00
51-1st Scarecrow 10.00 30.00 100.00
52-1st app. The Black Widow (4/64) 13.50 41.00 135.00
53-Origin The Watcher; 2nd Black Widow app. 12.00 36.00 120.00
54-56: 56-1st app. Unicorn; 4th Avengers x-over 7.00 21.00 70.00
57-Origin/1st app. Hawkeye (9/64) 15.50 47.00 155.00
58-Captain America battles Iron Man (10/64)-Classic-c; 2nd Kraven app. (Cap's 1st app. in this title) 26.00 80.00 265.00
59-Iron Man plus Captain America double feature begins (11/64); 1st S.A. Captain America solo story; intro Jarvis, Avenger's butler; classic-c 26.00 80.00 265.00
60-2nd app. Hawkeye (#64 is 3rd app.) 12.00 36.00 120.00
61,62,64: 62-Origin Mandarin (2/65) 7.00 21.00 70.00
63-1st Silver Age origin Captain America (3/65) 20.00 60.00 200.00
65,66-G.A. Red Skull in WWII stories: 65-1st Silver-Age Red Skull (5/65). 66-Origin Red Skull 13.50 41.00 135.00
67-78,81-98: 69-1st app. Titanium Man. 70-Begin alternating-c features w/Capt. America (even #'s) & Iron Man (odd #'s). 75-1st app. Agent 13 later named Sharon Carter. 76-Intro Batroc & Sharon Carter, Agent 13 of Shield. 78-Col. Nick Fury app. 81-Intro the Adaptoid by Kirby (also in #82-84). 88-Mole Man app. in Iron Man story. 92-1st Nick Fury x-over (cameo, as Agent of Shield, 8/67). 94-Intro Modok. 95-Capt. America's i.d. revealed. 98-1st app. new Zemo (son?) in cameo (#99 is 1st full app.) 4.00 12.00 40.00
79-Begin 3 part Iron Man Sub-Mariner battle story; Sub-Mariner-c & cameo; 1st app. Cosmic Cube; 1st modern Red Skull 5.50 16.50 55.00
80-Iron Man battles Sub-Mariner story cont'd in Tales to Astonish #82; classic Red Skull-c 5.00 15.00 50.00
99-Captain America story cont'd in Captain America #100; Iron Man story cont'd in Iron Man & Sub-Mariner #1 5.50 16.50 55.00

NOTE: ***Abel*** *a-73-81i(as Gary Michaels),* ***J. Buscema*** *a-1; c-3.* ***Colan*** *a-39, 73-99p; c(p)-73, 75, 77, 79, 81, 83, 85-87, 89, 91, 93, 95, 97, 99.* ***Crandall*** *a-12.* ***Davis*** *a-38.* ***Ditko*** *a-1-15, 17-44, 46, 47-49p; c-2, 10i, 13i, 23i.* ***Kirby/Ditko*** *a-7; c-10, 13, 22, 28, 34.* ***Everett*** *a-8.* ***Forte*** *a-5, 9.* ***Giacoia*** *a-82.* ***Heath*** *a-2, 10.* ***Gil Kane*** *a-88p, 89-91; c-88, 89-91p.* ***Kirby*** *a(p)-2-4, 6-35, 40, 41, 43, 59-75, 77-86, 92-99; layouts-69-75, 77; c(p)4-28(most), 29-56, 58-72, 74, 76, 78, 80, 82, 84, 86, 92, 94, 96, 98.* ***Leiber/Fox*** *a-42, 43, 45, 51.* ***Reinman*** *a-26, 44i, 49i, 52i, 53i.* ***Tuska*** *a-58, 70-74.* ***Wood*** *c/a-71i.*

TALES OF SUSPENSE
Marvel Comics: V2#1, Jan, 1995 ($6.95, one-shot)

V2#1-James Robinson script; acetate-c. 7.00

TALES OF SWORD & SORCERY (See Dagar)

TALES OF TERROR
Toby Press Publications: 1952 (no month)

1-Fawcette-c; Ravielli-a 20.00 60.00 150.00
NOTE: *This title was cancelled due to similarity to the E.C. title.*

TALES OF TERROR (See Movie Classics)

TALES OF TERROR (Magazine)
Eerie Publications: Summer, 1964

1 3.00 9.00 30.00

TALES OF TERROR
Eclipse Comics: July, 1985 - No. 13, July, 1987 ($2.00, Baxter paper, mature)

1-8 ($1.75-c): 5-1st Lee Weeks-a. 7-Sam Kieth-a. 1.80
9-13 ($2.00-c): 10-Snyder-a. 12-Vampire story 2.00

TALES OF TERROR ANNUAL
E.C. Comics: 1951 - No. 3, 1953 (25¢, 132 pgs., 16 stories each)

GD25 FN65 VF82

nn(1951)(Scarce)-Feldstein infinity-c 371.00 1115.00 3200.00

GD25 FN65 NM94

2(1952)-Feldstein-c 156.00 468.00 1400.00
3(1953)-Feldstein bondage/torture-c 122.00 366.00 1100.00
NOTE: *No. 1 contains three horror and one science fiction comic which came out in 1950. No. 2 contains a horror, crime, and science fiction book which generally had cover dates in 1951, and No. 3 had horror, crime, and shock books that generally appeared in 1952. All E.C. annuals contain four complete books that did not sell on the stands which were rebound in the annual format, minus the covers, and sold from the E.C. office and on the stands in key cities. The contents of each annual may vary in the same year. Crypt Keeper, Vault Keeper, Old Witch app. on all-c.*

TALES OF TERROR ILLUSTRATED (See Terror Illustrated)

TALES OF TEXAS JOHN SLAUGHTER (See Walt Disney Presents, 4-Color #997)

TALES OF THE BEANWORLD
Beanworld Press/Eclipse Comics: Feb, 1985 - No. 19, 1991; No. 20, 1993 - No. 21, 1993 ($1.50/$2.00, B&W)

1 3.00
2-19 2.00
20 ($2.50) 2.50
21 ($2.95) 3.00

TALES OF THE DARKNESS
Image Comics (Top Cow): Apr, 1998 - Present ($2.95)

1,2-Portacio-c/a(p) 3.00
1-American Entertainment Ed. 3.50
3,4-Lansing & Nocon-a(p) 2.95

TALES OF THE GREEN BERET
Dell Publishing Co.: Jan, 1967 - No. 5, Oct, 1969

1-Glanzman-a in 1-4 & 5r 2.00 6.00 22.00
2-5: 5-Reprints #1 1.60 4.80 16.00

TALES OF THE GREEN HORNET
Now Comics: Sept, 1990 - No. 2, 1990; V3#1, Sept, 1992 - No. 3, Nov, 1992

1,2 1.75
V3#1 ($2.75)-Polybagged w/hologram trading card 2.75

Tales of the Legion #325 © DC

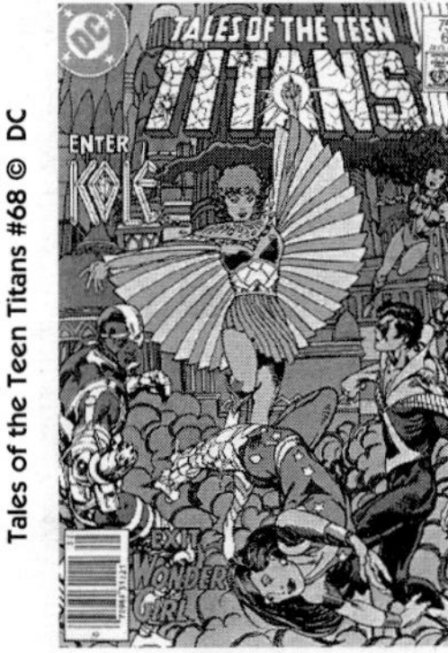

Tales of the Teen Titans #68 © DC

Tales of the Unexpected #13 © DC

	GD25	FN65	NM94
V3#2,3 ($2.50)			2.50

TALES OF THE GREEN LANTERN CORPS (See Green Lantern #107)
DC Comics: May, 1981 - No. 3, July, 1981 (Limited series)

	GD25	FN65	NM94
1-3: 1-Origin of G.L. & the Guardians			1.50
Annual 1 (1/85)-Gil Kane-c/a			1.75

TALES OF THE INVISIBLE SCARLET O'NEIL (See Harvey Comics Hits #59)

TALES OF THE KILLERS (Magazine)
World Famous Periodicals: V1#10, Dec, 1970 - V1#11, Feb, 1971 (B&W, 52 pg)

	GD25	FN65	NM94
V1#10-One pg. Frazetta; contains r/Crime Does Not Pay	2.40	7.00	26.00
11-similar cover to Crime Does Not Pay #47; contains r/Crime Does Not Pay	2.00	6.00	20.00

TALES OF THE LEGION (Formerly Legion of Super-Heroes)
DC Comics: No. 314, Aug, 1984 - No. 354, Dec, 1987

	GD25	FN65	NM94
314-354: 326-Reprints begin			1.25
Annual 4,5 (1986, 1987)-Formerly LSH Annual			1.40

TALES OF THE MARINES (Formerly Devil-Dog Dugan #1-3)
Atlas Comics (OPI): No. 4, Feb, 1957 (Marines At War #5 on)

	GD25	FN65	NM94
4-Powell-a; Severin-c	5.70	17.00	35.00

TALES OF THE MARVELS
Marvel Comics: 1995/1996 (all acetate, painted-c)

	GD25	FN65	NM94
...BLOCKBUSTER 1 (1995, $5.95, one-shot			6.00
...INNER DEMONS 1 (1996, $5.95, one shot)			6.00
...WONDER YEARS 1,2 (1995, $4.95, limited series			5.00

TALES OF THE MARVEL UNIVERSE
Marvel Comics: Feb, 1997 ($2.95, one-shot)

	GD25	FN65	NM94
1-Anthology; wraparound-c; Thunderbolts, Ka-Zar app.			3.00

TALES OF THE MYSTERIOUS TRAVELER (See Mysterious...)
Charlton Comics: Aug, 1956 - No. 13, June, 1959; V2#14, Oct, 1985 - No. 15, Dec, 1985

	GD25	FN65	NM94
1-No Ditko-a; Giordano/Alascia-c	39.00	117.00	300.00
2-Ditko-a(1)	35.00	104.00	260.00
3-Ditko-c/a(1)	35.00	104.00	260.00
4-6-Ditko-c/a(3-4 stories each)	39.00	117.00	300.00
7-9-Ditko-a(1-2 each). 8-Rocke-c	33.00	98.00	245.00
10,11-Ditko-c/a(3-4 each)	36.00	108.00	270.00
12	13.00	38.00	95.00
13-Baker-a (r?)	15.00	44.00	110.00
V2#14,15 (1985)-Ditko-c/a			3.00

TALES OF THE NEW TEEN TITANS
DC Comics: June, 1982 - No. 4, Sept, 1982 (Limited series)

	GD25	FN65	NM94
1-4			1.00

TALES OF THE PONY EXPRESS (TV)
Dell Publishing Co.: No. 829, Aug, 1957 - No. 942, Oct, 1958

	GD25	FN65	NM94
Four Color 829 (#1)--Painted-c	3.60	11.00	40.00
Four Color 942-Title -Pony Express	3.60	11.00	40.00

TALES OF THE SUN RUNNERS
Sirius Comics/Amazing Comics No. 3: V2#1, July, 1986 - V2#3, 1986? ($1.50)

	GD25	FN65	NM94
V2#1			1.50
V2#2,3 ($1.95)			2.00
Christmas Special 1(12/86)			1.50

TALES OF THE TEENAGE MUTANT NINJA TURTLES
Mirage Studios: May, 1987 - No. 7, Aug (Apr-c), 1989 (B&W, $1.50) (See Teenage Mutant...)

	GD25	FN65	NM94
1			2.00
2-7: Title merges w/Teenage Mutant Ninja...			1.50

TALES OF THE TEEN TITANS (Formerly The New Teen Titans)
DC Comics: No. 41, Apr, 1984 - No. 91, July, 1988 (75¢)

	GD25	FN65	NM94
41,45-59: 46-Aqualad & Aquagirl join. 50-Double size; app. Betty Kane (Bat-Girl) out of costume. 52-1st app. Azrael in cameo (not same as newer character). 53-1st full app. Azrael; Deathstroke cameo (1 panel). 54,55-Deathstroke-c/stories. 56-Intro Jinx. 57-Neutron app. 59-r/DC Comics Presents #26			1.00
42-44: The Judas Contract part 1-3 with Deathstroke the Terminator in all; concludes in Annual #3. 44-Dick Grayson becomes Nightwing (3rd to be Nightwing) & joins Titans; Jericho (Deathstroke's son) joins; origin Deathstroke			3.00
60-91-r/New Teen Titans Baxter series. 68-B. Smith-c. 70-Origin Kole. 83-91 are $1.00 cover			1.00
Annual 3(1984, $1.25)-Part 4 of The Judas Contract; Deathstroke-c/story; Death of Terra; indicia says Teen Titans Annual; formerly New Teen Titans Annual #1,2			3.00
Annual 4,5: 4-(1986, $1.25)-Reprints. 5-(1987)			1.25

TALES OF THE TEXAS RANGERS (See Jace Pearson...)

TALES OF THE UNEXPECTED (Becomes The Unexpected #105 on)(See Adventure #75, Super DC Giant)
National Periodical Publications: Feb-Mar, 1956 - No. 104, Dec-Jan, 1967-68

	GD25	FN65	NM94
1	83.00	250.00	1000.00
2	40.00	120.00	485.00
3-5	31.00	93.00	330.00
6-10: 6-1st Silver Age issue	25.00	75.00	250.00
11,14,19,20	15.50	47.00	155.00
12,13,15-18,21-24: All have Kirby-a. 15,17-Grey tone-c. 16-Character named 'Thor' with a magic hammer by Kirby (8/57, not like later Thor)	19.00	57.00	190.00
25-30	15.00	45.00	150.00
31-39	12.00	36.00	120.00
40-Space Ranger begins (8/59, 3rd ap.), ends #82	73.00	219.00	875.00
41,42-Space Ranger stories	28.00	85.00	285.00
43-1st Space Ranger-c this title; grey tone-c	56.00	168.00	670.00
44-46	21.00	63.00	210.00
47-50	15.00	45.00	150.00
51-60: 54-Dinosaur-c/story	13.00	39.00	130.00
61-67: 67-Last 10¢ issue	10.50	32.00	105.00
68-82: 82-Last Space Ranger	6.00	18.00	60.00
83-90,92-99	3.60	10.80	36.00
91,100: 91-1st Automan (also in #94,97)	4.00	12.00	40.00
101-104	3.20	9.60	32.00

NOTE: ***Neal Adams** c-104. **Anderson** a-50. **Brown** a-50-82(Space Ranger); c-19, 40, & many Space Ranger-c. **Cameron** a-24, 27, 29; c-24. **Heath** a-49. **Bob Kane** a-24, 48. **Kirby** a-12, 13, 15-18, 21-24; c-13, 18, 22. **Meskin** a-15, 18, 26, 27, 35, 66. **Moreira** a-16, 20, 29, 38, 44, 62, 71; c-38. **Roussos** c-10. **Wildey** a-31.*

TALES OF THE WEST (See 3-D...)

TALES OF THE WITCHBLADE
Image Comics (Top Cow Productions): Nov, 1996 - Present ($2.95)

	GD25	FN65	NM94
1-Daniel-c/a(p)	1.00	3.00	10.00
1-Variant-c by Turner	1.20	3.60	12.00
1-Platinum Edition			20.00
2,3		2.00	6.00
4-6			2.95
1/2	.90	2.70	9.00
1/2 Gold			15.00

TALES OF THE WITCHBLADE COLLECTION EDITION
Image Comics (Top Cow): May, 1998 - Present ($4.95, square-bound)

	GD25	FN65	NM94
1-r/#1,2			5.00

TALES OF THE WIZARD OF OZ (See Wizard of OZ, 4-Color #1308)

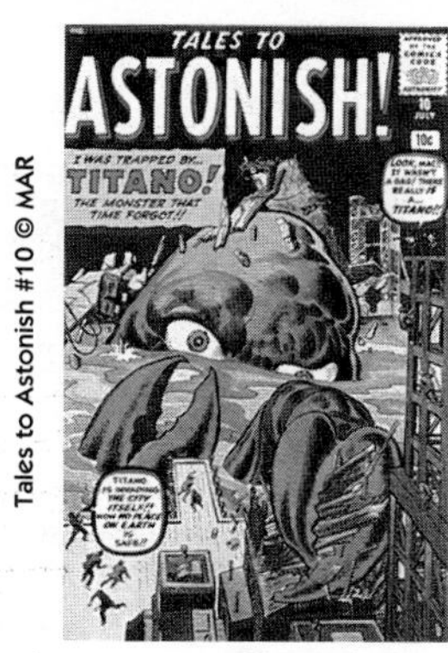

Tales to Astonish #10 © MAR

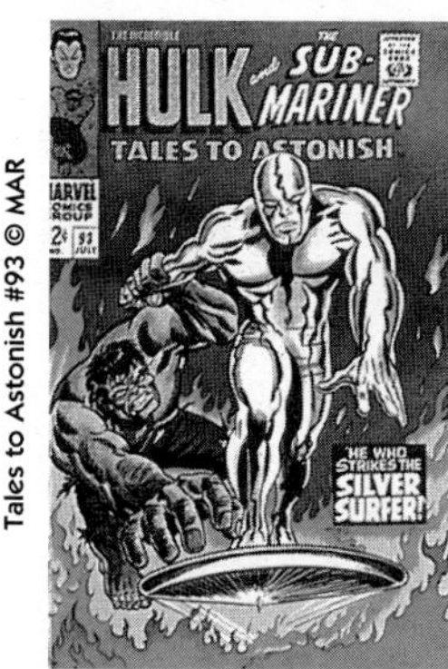

Tales to Astonish #93 © MAR

Tales to Offend #1 © Frank Miller

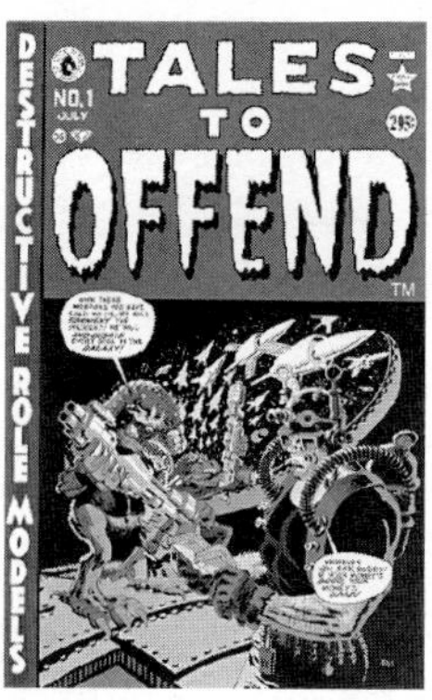

GD25 FN65 NM94

TALES OF THE ZOMBIE (Magazine)
Marvel Comics Group: Aug, 1973 - No. 10, Mar, 1975 (75¢, B&W)

V1#1-Reprint/Menace #5; origin 2.00 6.00 20.00
2,3: 2-Everett biog. & memorial 1.20 3.60 12.00
V2#1(#4)-Photos & text of James Bond movie "Live & Let Die" 1.20 3.60 12.00
5-10: 8-Kaluta-a 1.20 3.60 12.00
Annual 1(Summer,'75)(#11)-B&W; Everett, Buscema-a 1.20 3.60 12.00

NOTE: Brother Voodoo app. 2, 5, 6, 10. ***Alcala** a-7-9.* ***Boris** c-1-4.* ***Colan** a-2r, 6.* ***Heath** a-5r.* ***Reese** a-2.* ***Tuska** a-2r.*

TALES OF THUNDER
Deluxe Comics: Mar, 1985

1-Dynamo, Iron Maiden, Menthor app.; Giffen-a 2.00

TALES OF VOODOO
Eerie Publications: V1#11, Nov, 1968 - V7#6, Nov, 1974 (Magazine)

V1#11 4.00 12.00 40.00
V2#1(3/69)-V2#4(9/69) 3.00 9.00 30.00
V3#1-6('70): 4- "Claws of the Cat" redrawn from Climax #1 2.50 7.50 24.00
V4#1-6('71), V5#1-7('72), V6#1-6('73), V7#1-6('74) 2.50 7.50 24.00
Annual 1 2.50 7.50 24.00

NOTE: *Bondage-c-V1#10, V2#4, V3#4.*

TALES OF WELLS FARGO (TV)(See Western Roundup under Dell Giants)
Dell Publishing Co.: No. 876, Feb, 1958 - No. 1215, Oct-Dec, 1961

Four Color 876 (#1)-Photo-c 9.00 27.00 100.00
Four Color 968 (2/59), 1023, 1075 (3/60), 1113 (7-9/60)-All photo-c 8.00 25.00 90.00
Four Color 1167 (3-5/61), 1215-Photo-c 7.00 22.00 80.00

TALESPIN (Also see Cartoon Tales & Disney's Talespin Limited Series)
Disney Comics: June, 1991 - No. 7, Dec, 1991 ($1.50)

1-7 1.50

TALES TO ASTONISH (Becomes The Incredible Hulk #102 on)
Atlas (MAP No. 1/ZPC No. 2-14/VPI No. 15-21/Marvel No. 22 on: Jan, 1959 - No. 101, Mar, 1968

1-Jack Davis-a; monster-c. 125.00 375.00 1500.00
2-Ditko flying saucer-c (Martians); #2-4 have sci/fi-c. 52.00 155.00 620.00
3,4 37.00 112.00 410.00
5-Prototype issue (Stone Men); Williamson-a (4 pgs.); Kirby monster-c begin 40.00 120.00 440.00
6-Prototype issue (Stone Men) 32.00 96.00 360.00
7-Prototype issue (Toad Men) 31.00 93.00 350.00
8-10 31.00 93.00 320.00
11-14,17-20: 13-Swipes story from Menace #8 24.00 72.00 240.00
15-Prototype issue (Electro) 32.00 96.00 360.00
16-Prototype issue (Stone Men) 27.00 81.00 270.00
21-(7/61)-Hulk prototype 27.00 81.00 270.00
22-26,28-34 17.50 52.00 175.00

GD25 FN65 VF82 NM94

27-1st Ant-Man app. (1/62); last 10¢ issue (see Strange Tales #73,78 & Tales of Suspense #32) 242.00 726.00 1575.00 3200.00
35-(9/62)-2nd app. Ant-Man, 1st in costume; begin series & Ant-Man-c 100.00 300.00 650.00 1400.00

GD25 FN65 NM94

36-3rd app. Ant-Man 47.00 141.00 570.00
37-40: 38-1st app. Egghead 32.00 96.00 360.00
41-43 22.00 66.00 220.00
44-Origin & 1st app. The Wasp (6/63) 25.00 75.00 250.00
45-48: Origin & 1st app. The Porcupine. 14.00 42.00 140.00
49-Ant-Man becomes Giant Man (11/63) 17.00 51.00 170.00
50-56,58: 50-Origin/1st app. Human Top (alias Whirlwind). 52-Origin/1st app. Black Knight (2/64). 53-Origin Colossus 9.50 28.50 95.00
57-Early Spider-Man app. (7/64) 13.00 39.00 130.00
59-Giant Man vs. Hulk feature story (9/64); Hulk's 1st app. this title 15.00 45.00 150.00
60-Giant Man & Hulk double feature begins 17.00 51.00 170.00
61-69: 61-All Ditko issue; 1st mailbag. 62-1st app./origin The Leader; new Wasp costume. 63-Origin Leader; 65-New Giant Man costume. 68-New Human Top costume. 69-Last Giant Man. 5.00 15.00 50.00
70-Sub-Mariner & Incredible Hulk begins (8/65) 6.00 18.00 60.00
71-81,83-91,94-99: 72-Begin alternating-c features w/Sub-Mariner (even #'s) & Hulk (odd #'s). 79-Hulk vs. Hercules-c/story. 81-1st app. Boomerang. 90-1st app. The Abomination. 97-X-Men cameo (brief) 4.00 12.00 40.00
82-Iron Man battles Sub-Mariner (1st Iron Man x-over outside The Avengers & TOS); story cont'd from Tales of Suspense #80 4.50 13.50 45.00
92-1st Silver Surfer x-over (outside of Fantastic Four, 6/67); 1 panel cameo only 5.00 15.00 50.00
93-Hulk battles Silver Surfer-c/story (1st full x-over) 5.00 15.00 50.00
100-Hulk battles Sub-Mariner full-length story 5.00 15.00 50.00
101-Hulk story cont'd in Incredible Hulk #102; Sub-Mariner story continued in Iron Man & Sub-Mariner #1 6.00 18.00 60.00

NOTE: ***Ayers** c(i)-9-12, 16, 18, 19.* ***Berg** a-1.* ***Burgos** a-62-64p.* ***Buscema** a-85-87p.* ***Colan** a(p)-70-76, 78-82, 84, 85, 101; c(p)-71-76, 78, 80, 82, 84, 86, 88, 90.* ***Ditko** a-1, 3-48, 50i, 60-67p; c-2, 7i, 8i, 14i, 17i.* ***Everett** a-78, 79i, 80-84, 85-90i, 94i, 95, 96; c(i)-79-81, 83, 86, 88.* ***Forte** a-6.* ***Kane** a-76, 88-91; c-89, 91.* ***Kirby** a(p)-1, 5-34-40, 44, 49-51, 68-70, 82, 83; layouts-71-84; c(p)-1, 3-48, 50-70, 72, 73, 75, 77, 78, 79, 81, 85, 90.* ***Kirby/Ditko** a-7, 8, 12, 13, 50; c-7, 8, 10, 13.* ***Leiber/Fox** a-47, 48, 50, 51.* ***Powell** a-65-69p, 73, 74.* ***Reinman** a-6, 36, 45, 46, 54i, 56-60i.*

TALES TO ASTONISH (2nd Series)
Marvel Comics Group: Dec, 1979 - No. 14, Jan, 1981

V1#1-Reprints Sub-Mariner #1 by Buscema 2.00
2-14: Reprints Sub-Mariner #2-14 1.50

TALES TO ASTONISH
Marvel Comics: V3#1, Oct, 1994 ($6.95, one-shot)

V3#1-Peter David scripts; acetate, painted-c .85 2.60 7.00

TALES TO HOLD YOU SPELLBOUND (See Spellbound)

TALES TO OFFEND
Dark Horse Comics: July, 1997 ($2.95, one-shot)

1-Frank Miller-s/a, EC-style cover 3.50

TALKING KOMICS
Belda Record & Publ. Co.: 1947 (20 pgs, slick-c)

Each comic contained a record that followed the story - much like the Golden Record sets. Known titles: Chirpy Cricket, Lonesome Octopus, Sleepy Santa, Grumpy Shark, Flying Turtle, Happy Grasshopper with records... 2.00 5.00 10.00

TALLY-HO COMICS
Swappers Quarterly (Baily Publ. Co.): Dec, 1944

nn-Frazetta's 1st work as Giunta's assistant; Man in Black horror story; violence; Giunta-c 35.00 105.00 260.00

TALOS OF THE WILDERNESS SEA
DC Comics: Aug, 1987 ($2.00, one-shot)

1 2.00

TALULLAH (See Comic Books Series I)

TAMMY, TELL ME TRUE
Dell Publishing Co.: No. 1233, 1961

Four Color 1233-Movie 5.50 16.50 60.00

TANGENT COMICS
.../ THE ATOM, DC Comics: Dec, 1997 ($2.95, one-shot)
1-Dan Jurgens-s/Jurgens & Paul Ryan-a 3.00
.../ THE BATMAN, DC Comics: Sept, 1998 ($1.95, one-shot)

Tangent Comics/ JLA #1 © DC

Tank Girl 2 #2 © Deadline Publ.

Target Comics #11 © NOVP

GD25 FN65 NM94

1-Dan Jurgens-s/Klaus Janson-a 1.95

.../ DOOM PATROL, DC Comics: Dec, 1997 ($2.95, one-shot)
1- Dan Jurgens-s/Sean Chen & Kevin Conrad-a 3.00

.../ THE FLASH, DC Comics: Dec, 1997 ($2.95, one-shot)
1-Todd Dezago-s/Gary Frank & Cam Smith-a 3.00

.../ GREEN LANTERN, DC Comics: Dec, '97 ($2.95, one-shot)
1-James Robinson-s/J.H. Williams III & Mick Gray-a 3.00

.../ JLA, DC Comics: Sept, 1998 ($1.95, one-shot)
1-Dan Jurgens-s/Banks & Rapmund-a 1.95

.../ THE JOKER, DC Comics: Dec, 1997 ($2.95, one-shot)
1-Karl Kesel-s/Matt Haley & Tom Simmons-a 3.00

.../ THE JOKER'S WILD, DC Comics: Sept, 1998 ($1.95, one-shot)
1-Kesel & Simmons-s/Phillips & Rodriguez-a 1.95

.../ METAL MEN, DC Comics: Dec, 1997 ($2.95, one-shot)
1-Ron Marz-s/Mike McKone & Mark McKenna-a 3.00

.../ NIGHTWING, DC Comics: Dec, 1997 ($2.95, one-shot)
1-John Ostrander-s/Jan Duursema-a 3.00

.../ NIGHTWING: NIGHTFORCE, DC Comics: Sept, 1998 ($1.95, one-shot)
1-John Ostrander-s/Jan Duursema-a 1.95

.../ POWERGIRL, DC Comics: Sept, 1998 ($1.95, one-shot)
1-Marz-s/Abell & Vines-a 1.95

.../ SEA DEVILS, DC Comics: Dec, 1997 ($2.95, one-shot)
1-Kurt Busiek-s/Vince Giarrano & Tom Palmer-a 3.00

.../ SECRET SIX, DC Comics: Dec, 1997 ($2.95, one-shot)
1-Chuck Dixon-s/Tom Grummett & Lary Stucker-a 3.00

.../ THE SUPERMAN, DC Comics: Sept, 1998 ($1.95, one-shot)
1-Millar-s/Guice-a 1.95

.../ TALES OF THE GREEN LANTERN, DC Comics: Sept, 1998 ($1.95, one-shot)
1-Story & art by various 1.95

.../ THE TRIALS OF THE FLASH, DC Comics: Sept, 1998 ($1.95, one-shot)
1-Dezago-s/Pelletier & Lanning-a 1.95

.../ WONDER WOMAN DC Comics: Sept, 1998 ($1.95, one-shot),
1-Peter David-s/Unzueta & Mendoza-a 1.95

TANK GIRL
Dark Horse Comics: May, 1991 - No. 4, Aug, 1991 ($2.25, B&W, mini-series)

1-4: 1-Contains Dark Horse trading cards 4.00

TANK GIRL: APOCALYPSE
DC Comics: Nov, 1995 - No. 4, Feb, 1996 ($2.25, limited series)

1-4 2.25

TANK GIRL: MOVIE ADAPTATION
DC Comics: 1995 ($5.95, 68 pgs., one-shot)

nn-Peter Milligan scripts 6.00

TANK GIRL: THE ODYSSEY
DC Comics: May, 1995 - No.4, Oct, 1995 ($2.25, limited series)

1-4: Peter Milligan scripts; Hewlett-a 2.25

TANK GIRL 2
Dark Horse Comics: June, 1993 - No. 4, Sept, 1993 ($2.50, lim. series, mature)

1-4: Jamie Hewlett & Alan Martin-s/a 2.50
TPB (2/95, $17.95) r/#1-4 18.00

TAPPAN'S BURRO (See Zane Grey & 4-Color #449)

TAPPING THE VEIN (Clive Barker's...)
Eclipse Comics: 1989 - No. 5, 1992 ($6.95, squarebound, mature, 68 pgs.)

Book 1-5: 1-Russell-a, Bolton-c. 2-Bolton-a. 4-Die-cut-c 7.00

TARANTULA (See Weird Suspense)

GD25 FN65 NM94

TARGET: AIRBOY
Eclipse Comics: Mar, 1988 ($1.95)

1 2.00

TARGET COMICS (...Western Romances #106 on)
Funnies, Inc./Novelty Publications/Star Publications: Feb, 1940 - V10#3 (#105), Aug-Sept, 1949

	GD25	FN65	NM94
V1#1-Origin & 1st app. Manowar, The White Streak by Burgos, & Bulls-Eye Bill by Everett; City Editor (ends #5), High Grass Twins by Jack Cole (ends #4), T-Men by Joe Simon(ends #9), Rip Rory (ends #4), Fantastic Feature Films by Tarpe Mills (ends #39), & Calling 2-R (ends #14) begin; marijuana use story	379.00	1137.00	3600.00
2	212.00	636.00	1800.00
3,4	118.00	354.00	1000.00
5-Origin The White Streak in text; Space Hawk by Wolverton begins (6/40) (see Blue Bolt & Circus)	347.00	1041.00	3300.00
6-The Chameleon by Everett begins (7/40, 1st app.); White Streak origin cont'd. in text; early mention of comic collecting in letter column; 1st letter column in comics? (7/40)	147.00	441.00	1250.00
7-Wolverton Spacehawk-c/story (Scarce)	380.00	1140.00	3800.00
8,9,12: 12-(1/41)	115.00	345.00	975.00
10-Intro/1st app. The Target (11/40); Simon-c	147.00	441.00	1250.00
11-Origin The Target & The Targeteers	135.00	406.00	1150.00
V2#1-Target by Bob Wood; Uncle Sam flag-c	71.00	212.00	600.00
2-Ten part Treasure Island serial begins; Harold Delay-a; reprinted in Catholic Comics V3#1-10 (see Key Comics #5)	64.00	191.00	540.00
3-5: 4-Kit Carter, The Cadet begins	47.00	141.00	400.00
6-9: Red Seal with White Streak in #6-10	47.00	141.00	400.00
10-Classic-c	82.00	247.00	700.00
11,12: 12-10-part Last of the Mohicans serial begins; Delay-a	46.00	138.00	390.00
V3#1-7,9,10: 10-Last Wolverton issue	46.00	138.00	390.00
8-Hitler, Tojo, Flag-c; 6-part Gulliver Travels serial begins; Delay-a.	53.00	160.00	450.00
11,12	11.00	34.00	85.00
V4#1-12: 6-Targetoons by Wolverton. 8-X-Mas-c	9.30	28.00	65.00
V5#1-8	8.50	26.00	60.00
V6#1-10, V7#1-12	7.85	23.50	55.00
V8#1,3-5,8,9,11,12	7.15	21.50	50.00
2,6,7-Krigstein-a	7.85	23.50	55.00
10-L.B. Cole-c	27.00	80.00	200.00
V9#1,4,6,8,10,12, V10#2,3-L.B. Cole-c	27.00	80.00	200.00
V9#2,3,5,7,9,11, V10#1	7.15	21.50	50.00

NOTE: *Certa c-V8#9, 11, 12, V9#5, 9, 11, V10#1.* ***Jack Cole*** *a-1-8.* ***Everett*** *a-1-9; c(signed Blake)-1, 2.* ***Al Fago*** *c-V6#8.* ***Sid Greene*** *c-V2#9, 12, V3#3.* ***Walter Johnson*** *c-V5#6, V6#4.* ***Tarpe Mills*** *a-1-4, 6, 8, 11, V3#1.* ***Rico*** *a-V7#4, 10, V8#5, 6, V9#3; c-V7#6, 8, 10, V8#2, 4, 6, 7.* ***Simon*** *a-1, 2.* ***Bob Wood*** *c-V2#2, 3, 5, 6.*

TARGET: THE CORRUPTORS (TV)
Dell Publishing Co.: No. 1306, Mar-May, 1962 - No. 3, Oct-Dec, 1962 (All have photo-c)

Four Color 1306(#1), #2,3 5.00 15.00 55.00

TARGET WESTERN ROMANCES (Formerly Target Comics; becomes Flaming Western Romances #3)
Star Publications: No. 106, Oct-Nov, 1949 - No. 107, Dec-Jan, 1949-50

	GD25	FN65	NM94
106(#1)-Silhouette nudity panel; L.B. Cole-c	32.00	96.00	240.00
107(#2)-L.B. Cole-c; lingerie panels	27.00	80.00	200.00

TARGITT
Atlas/Seaboard Publ.: March, 1975 - No. 3, July, 1975

1-3: 1-Origin; Nostrand-a in all. 2-1st in costume 3.00

TARZAN (See Aurora, Comics on Parade, Crackajack, DC 100-Page Super Spec., Famous Feature Stories #1, Golden Comics Digest #4, 9, Jeep Comics #1-29, Jungle Tales of..., Limited Collectors' Edition, Popular, Sparkler, Sport Stars #1, Tip Top & Top Comics)

TARZAN

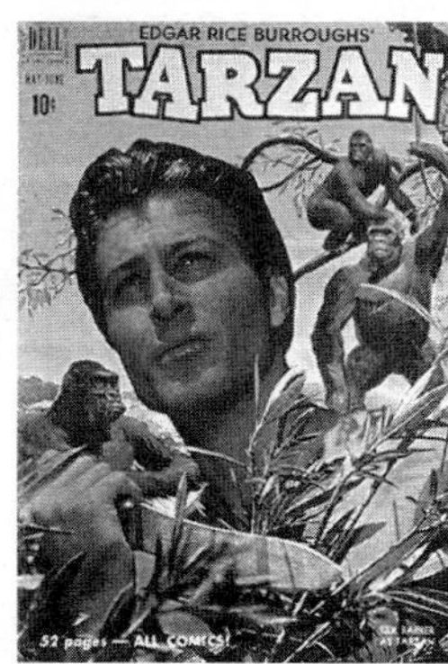

Tarzan #21 (Dell) © ERB

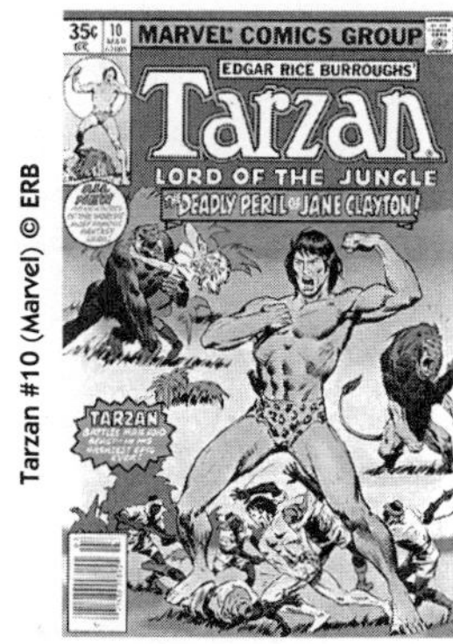

Tarzan #10 (Marvel) © ERB

Tarzan/ Carson of Venus #3 © ERB

GD25 FN65 NM94

Dell Publishing Co./United Features Synd.: No. 5, 1939 - No. 161, Aug, 1947

Large Feature Comic 5('39)-(Scarce)-By Hal Foster; reprints 1st dailies from 1929 118.00 355.00 1300.00
Single Series 20(:40)-By Hal Foster 91.00 273.00 1000.00
Four Color 134(2/47)-Marsh-c/a 59.00 177.00 650.00
Four Color 161(8/47)-Marsh-c/a 50.00 150.00 550.00

TARZAN (...of the Apes #138 on)
Dell Publishing Co./Gold Key No. 132 on: 1-2/48 - No. 131, 7-8/62; No. 132, 11/62 - No. 206, 2/72

1-Jesse Marsh-a begins 86.00 258.00 950.00
2 46.00 137.00 500.00
3-5 32.00 95.00 350.00
6-10: 6-1st Tantor the Elephant. 7-1st Valley of the Monsters 26.00 77.00 280.00
11-15: 11-Two Against the Jungle begins, ends #24. 13-Lex Barker photo-c begin 21.00 63.00 230.00
16-20 16.00 49.00 180.00
21-24,26-30 13.00 38.00 140.00
25-1st "Brothers of the Spear" episode; series ends #156,160,161,196-206 15.00 45.00 165.00
31-40 8.00 25.00 90.00
41-54: Last Barker photo-c 5.50 16.50 60.00
55-60: 56-Eight pg. Boy story 3.60 11.00 40.00
61,62,64-70 3.00 9.00 32.00
63-Two Tarzan stories, 1 by Manning 3.00 9.00 35.00
71-79 2.40 7.00 26.00
80-99: 80-Gordon Scott photo-c begin 2.50 7.60 28.00
100 3.20 9.50 35.00
101-109 2.25 6.75 24.00
110 (Scarce)-Last photo-c 2.70 8.00 30.00
111-120 1.80 5.50 20.00
121-131: Last Dell issue 1.45 4.35 16.00
132-1st Gold Key issue 3.20 9.50 35.00
133-154: 139-(12/63)-1st app. Korak (Boy); leaves Tarzan & gets own book 1/64 2.50 7.50 28.00
155-Origin Tarzan 2.90 8.70 32.00
156-161: 157-Banlu, Dog of the Arande begins, ends #159, 195. 169-Leopard Girl app. 1.80 5.50 20.00
162,165,168,171 (TV)-Ron Ely photo covers 2.40 7.00 26.00
163,164,166,167,169,170: 169-Leopard Girl app. 1.65 5.00 18.00
172-199,201-206: 178-Tarzan origin-r/#155; Leopard Girl app., also in #179, 190-193 1.50 4.60 17.00
200 (Scarce) 1.80 5.50 20.00
Story Digest 1-(6/70, G.K.)(scarce) 6.50 19.50 65.00

NOTE: *#162, 165, 168, 171 are TV issues. #1-153 all have* ***Marsh*** *art on Tarzan. #154-161, 163, 164, 166, 167, 172-177 all have* ***Manning*** *art on Tarzan. #178, 202 have* ***Manning*** *Tarzan reprints. No "Brothers of the Spear" in #1-24, 157-159, 162-195. #39-126, 128-156 all have* ***Russ Manning*** *art on "Brothers of the Spear". #196-201, 203-205 all have* ***Manning*** *B.O.T.S. reprints; #25-38, 127 all have Jesse* ***Marsh*** *art on B.O.T.S. #206 has a Marsh B.O.T.S. reprint.* ***Gollub*** *c-8-12.* ***Marsh*** *c-1-7.* ***Doug Wildey*** *a-162, 179-187. Many issues have front and back photo covers.*

TARZAN (Continuation of Gold Key series)
National Periodical Publications: No. 207, Apr, 1972 - No. 258, Feb, 1977

207-Origin Tarzan by Joe Kubert, part 1; John Carter begins (origin); 52 pg. issues thru #209 2.20 6.25 22.00
208,209: 208-210-Parts 2-4 of origin. 209-Last John Carter 1.20 3.60 12.00
210-229,236,237,239-258: 210-Kubert-a. 211-Hogarth, Kubert-a. 212-214: Adaptations from "Jungle Tales of Tarzan". 213-Beyond the Farthest Star begins, ends #218. 215-218,224,225-All by Kubert. 215-part Foster-r. 219-223: Adapts "The Return of Tarzan" by Kubert. 226-Manning-a. 240-243 adapts "Tarzan & the Castaways". 250-256 adapts "Tarzan the Untamed." 252,253-r/#213 1.00 3.00 10.00
230-DC 100 Page Super Spectacular; Kubert, Kaluta-a(p); Korak begins, ends #234; Carson of Venus app. 2.00 6.00 20.00
231-235-New Kubert-a.: 231-234-(All 100 pgs.)-Adapts "Tarzan and the Lion Man"; Rex, the Wonder Dog r-#232, 233. 235-(100 pgs.)-Last Kubert issue. 1.80 5.40 18.00
238-(68 pgs.) 1.40 4.20 14.00
Comic Digest 1-(Fall, 1972, 50¢, 164 pgs.)(DC)-Digest size; Kubert-c; Manning-a 4.00 12.25 45.00

NOTE: ***Anderson*** *a-207, 209, 217, 218.* ***Chaykin*** *a-216.* ***Finlay*** *a(r)-212.* ***Foster*** *strip-r #207-209, 211, 212, 221.* ***Heath*** *a-230i.* ***G. Kane*** *a(r)-232p, 233p.* ***Kubert*** *a-207-225, 227-235, 257r, 258r; c-207-249, 253.* ***Lopez*** *a-250-255p; c-250p, 251, 252, 254.* ***Manning*** *strip-r 230-235, 238.* ***Morrow*** *a-208.* ***Nino*** *a-231-234.* ***Sparling*** *a-230, 231.* ***Starr*** *a-233r.*

TARZAN (Lord of the Jungle)
Marvel Comics Group: June, 1977 - No. 29, Oct, 1979

1 4.00
2-29: 2-Origin by John Buscema 2.50
Annual 1-3: 1-(1977). 2-(1978). 3-(1979) 3.00

NOTE: ***N. Adams*** *c-11i, 12i.* ***Alcala*** *a-9i, 10i; c-8i, 9i.* ***Buckler*** *c-25-27p, Annual 3p.* ***John Buscema*** *a-1-3, 4-18p, Annual 1; c-1-7, 8p, 9p, 10, 11p, 12p, 13, 14-19p, 21p, 22, 23p, 24p, 28p, Annual 1.* ***Mooney*** *a-22i.* ***Nebres*** *a-22i.* ***Russell*** *a-29i.*

TARZAN
Dark Horse Comics: July, 1996 - No. 20, Mar, 1998 ($2.95)

1-20: 1-6-Suydam-c 3.00

TARZAN / CARTER OF VENUS
Dark Horse Comics: May, 1998 - No. 4, Aug, 1998 ($2.95, limited series)

1-4-Darko Macan-s/Igor Korday-a 2.95

TARZAN FAMILY, THE (Formerly Korak, Son of Tarzan)
National Periodical Publications: No. 60, Nov-Dec, 1975 - No. 66, Nov-Dec, 1976

60-62-(68 pgs.): 60-Korak begins; Kaluta-r .90 2.70 9.00
63-66 (52 pgs.) .85 2.60 7.00

NOTE: *Carson of Venus-r 60-65. New John Carter-62-64, 65r, 66r. New Korak-60-66. Pellucidar feature-66. Foster strip r-60(9/4/32-10/16/32), 62(6/29/32-7/31/32), 63(10/11/31-12/13/31).* ***Kaluta*** *Carson of Venus-60-65.* ***Kubert*** *a-61, 64; c-60-64.* ***Manning*** *strip-r 60-62, 64.* ***Morrow*** *a-66r.*

TARZAN/JOHN CARTER: WARLORDS OF MARS
Dark Horse Comics: Jan, 1996 - No. 4, June, 1996 ($2.50, limited series)

1-4: Bruce Jones scripts in all. 1,2,4-Bret Blevins-c/a. 2-(4/96)-Indicia reads #3 2.50

TARZAN KING OF THE JUNGLE (See Dell Giant #37, 51)

TARZAN, LORD OF THE JUNGLE
Gold Key: Sept, 1965 (Giant) (25¢, soft paper-c)

1-Marsh-r 7.00 21.00 75.00

TARZAN: LOVE, LIES AND THE LOST CITY (See Tarzan the Warrior)
Malibu Comics: Aug. 10, 1992 - No. 3, Sept, 1992 ($2.50, limited series)

1-($3.95, 68 pgs.)-Flip book format; Simonson & Wagner scripts 4.00
2,3-No Simonson or Wagner scripts 2.50

TARZAN MARCH OF COMICS (See March of Comics #82, 98, 114, 125, 144, 155, 172, 185, 204, 223, 240, 252, 262, 272, 286, 300, 332, 342, 354, 366)

TARZAN OF THE APES
Metropolitan Newspaper Service: 1934? (Hardcover, 4x12", 68 pgs.)

1-Strip reprints 19.00 56.00 140.00

TARZAN OF THE APES
Marvel Comics Group: July, 1984 - No. 2, Aug, 1984 (Movie adaptation)

1,2: Origin-r/Marvel Super Spec. 1.50

TARZAN'S JUNGLE ANNUAL (See Dell Giants)

TARZAN'S JUNGLE WORLD (See Dell Giant #25)

TARZAN: THE LOST ADVENTURE (See Edgar Rice Burroughs' ...)

TARZAN THE WARRIOR (Also see Tarzan: Love, Lies and the Lost City)
Malibu Comics: Mar, 19, 1992 - No. 5, 1992 ($2.50, limited series)

Tattered Banners #1 © Alan Grant & Keith Giffen

Team 7 #1 © WildStorm Prod.

Team Youngblood #14 © Rob Liefeld

	GD25	FN65	NM94
1-5: 1-Bisley painted pack-c (flip book format-c)			3.00
1-2nd printing w/o flip-c by Bisley			2.50

TARZAN VS. PREDATOR AT THE EARTH'S CORE
Dark Horse Comics: Jan, 1996 - No. 4, June, 1996 ($2.50, limited series)

1-4: Lee Weeks-c/a; Walt Simonson scripts			2.50

TASMANIAN DEVIL & HIS TASTY FRIENDS
Gold Key: Nov, 1962 (12¢)

1-Bugs Bunny & Elmer Fudd x-over	11.00	32.00	120.00

TASTEE-FREEZ COMICS
Harvey Comics: 1957 (10¢, 36 pgs.)(6 different issues given away)

1,3: 1-Little Dot. 3-Casper	3.80	11.40	38.00
2,4,5: 2-Rags Rabbit. 4-Sad Sack. 5-Mazie	2.40	7.20	24.00
6-Dick Tracy	3.50	10.50	35.00

TATTERED BANNERS
DC Comics (Vertigo): Nov, 1998 - No. 4, Feb, 1999 ($2.95, limited series)

1-4-Grant & Giffen-s/McMahon-a			2.95

TAYLOR'S CHRISTMAS TABLOID
Dept. Store Giveaway: Mid 1930s, Cleveland, Ohio (Tabloid size; in color)

nn-(Very Rare)-Among the earliest pro work of Siegel & Shuster; one full color page called "The Battle in the Stratosphere", with a pre-Superman look; Shuster art thoughout. (Only 1 known copy)
Estimated value... 3000.00

TEAM AMERICA (See Captain America #269)
Marvel Comics Group: June, 1982 - No. 12, May, 1983

1-Origin; Ideal Toy motorcycle characters			1.00
2-10: 9-Iron man app.			1.00
11-Ghost Rider app.			3.00
12-Double size			2.00

TEAM ANARCHY
Dagger Comics: Oct, 1993 - No.8, 1994? ($2.50)

1-($2.75)-Red foil logo; intro Team Anarchy			2.75
1-Platinum			2.75
2,3,3-Bronze,3-Gold,3-Silver,4-8			2.75

TEAM HELIX
Marvel Comics: Jan, 1993 - No. 4, Apr, 1993 ($1.75, limited series)

1-4: Teen Super Group. 1,2-Wolverine app.			1.75

TEAM ONE: STORMWATCH (Also see StormWatch)
Image Comics (WildStorm Productions): June, 1995 - No. 2, Aug, 1995 ($2.50, limited series)

1,2: Steven T. Seagle scripts			2.50

TEAM ONE: WILDC.A.T.S (Also see WildC.A.T.S)
Image Comics (WildStorm Productions): July, 1995 - No. 2, Aug, 1995 ($2.50, limited series)

1,2: James Robinson scripts			2.50

TEAM 7
Image Comics (WildStorm Productions): Oct, 1994 - No.4, Feb, 1995 ($2.50, limited series)

1-Dixon scripts in all			4.00
1-Portacio variant-c		2.00	6.00
2-4			2.50

TEAM 7-DEAD RECKONING
Image Comics (WildStorm Productions): Jan, 1996 - No. 4, Apr, 1996 ($2.50, limited series)

1-4: Dixon scripts in all			2.50

TEAM 7-OBJECTIVE HELL
Image Comics (WildStorm Productions): May, 1995 - No. 3, July, 1995 ($1.95/$2.50, limited series)

	GD25	FN65	NM94
1-($1.95)-Newstand; Dixon scripts in all; Barry Smith-c			2.00
1-($2.50)-Direct Market; Barry Smith-c, bound-in card			2.50
2,3-($2.50)			2.50

TEAM SUPERMAN
DC Comics: May, 1998 ($4.95, one-shot)

1-Origin-s and pin-ups of Superboy, Supergirl and Steel			5.00

TEAM TITANS (See Deathstroke & New Titans Annual #7)
DC Comics: Sept, 1992 - No. 24, Sept, 1994 ($1.75/$1.95)

1-Five different #1s exist w/origins in 1st half & the same 2nd story in each: Kilowat, Mirage, Nightrider w/Netzer/Perez-a, Redwing, & Terra w/part Perez-p; Total Chaos Pt. 3			2.25
2-Total Chaos Pt 6			2.00
3-21: 11-Metallik app.			1.75
22-24: 22-$1.95-c begins. 24-Zero Hour x-over			2.00
Annual 1 (1993, $3.50, 68 pgs.)			3.50
Annual 2 (1994, $3.50, 68 pgs.)-Elseworlds story			3.50

TEAM X/TEAM 7
Marvel Comics: Nov, 1996 ($4.95, one-shot)

1			5.00

TEAM YANKEE
First Comics: Jan, 1989 - No. 6, Feb, 1989 ($1.95, weekly limited series)

1-6			2.00

TEAM YOUNGBLOOD (Also see Youngblood)
Image Comics (Extreme Studios): Sept, 1993 - No. 22, Sept, 1995 ($1.95/$2.50)

1-9-Liefeld scripts in all: 1,2,4-6,8-Thibert-c(i). 1-1st app. Dutch & Masada. 3-Spawn cameo. 5-1st app. Lynx. 7,8-Coupons 1 & 4 for Extreme Prejudice #0; Black and White Pt. 4 & 8 by Thibert. 8-Coupon #4 for E. P. #0. 9-Liefeld wraparound-c(p)/a(p) on Pt. I			2.00
10-22: 10-$2.50-c begin; Liefeld-c(p). 16-Polybagged w/trading card 17-Polybagged w/trading card. 18-Extreme 3000 Prelude. 19-Cruz-a. 21-Angela & Glory-app. 22-Shadowhawk-c/app			2.50

TEDDY ROOSEVELT & HIS ROUGH RIDERS (See Real Heroes #1)
Avon Periodicals: 1950

1-Kinstler-c; Palais-a; Flag-c	15.00	46.00	115.00

TEDDY ROOSEVELT ROUGH RIDER (See Battlefield #22 & Classics Illustrated Special Issue)

TED MCKEEVER'S METROPOL
Marvel Comics (Epic Comics): Mar, 1991 - No. 12, Mar, 1992 ($2.95, limited series)

V1#1-12: Ted McKeever-c/a/scripts			3.00

TED MCKEEVER'S METROPOL A.D.
Marvel Comics (Epic Comics): Oct, 1992 - No. 3, Dec, 1992 ($3.50, limited series)

V2#1-3: Ted McKeever-c/a/scripts			3.50

TEE AND VEE CROSLEY IN TELEVISION LAND COMICS
(Also see Crosley's House of Fun)
Crosley Division, Avco Mfg. Corp. : 1951 (52 pgs.; 8x11"; paper cover; in color) (Giveaway)

Many stories, puzzles, cut-outs, games, etc.	5.00	15.00	30.00

TEENA
Magazine Enterprises/Standard Comics No. 20 on: No. 11, 1948 - No. 15, 1948; No. 20, Aug, 1949 - No. 22, Oct, 1950

A-1 #11-Teen-age; Ogden Whitney-c	6.50	19.50	45.00
A-1 #12, 15	5.70	17.00	40.00
20-22 (Standard)	4.00	12.00	24.00

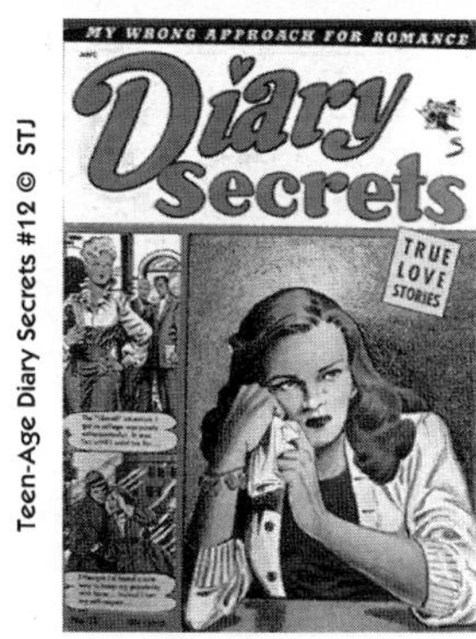

Teen-Age Diary Secrets #12 © STJ

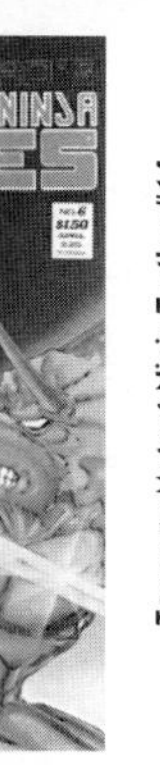

Teenage Mutant Ninja Turtles #6 © Mirage Studios

Teenage Mutant Ninja Turtles #14 © Mirage Studios

TEEN-AGE BRIDES (True Bride's Experiences #8 on)
Harvey/Home Comics: Aug, 1953 - No. 7, Aug, 1954

	GD25	FN65	NM94
1-Powell-a	9.30	28.00	65.00
2-Powell-a	6.00	18.00	42.00
3-7: 3,6-Powell-a	5.35	16.00	32.00

TEEN-AGE CONFESSIONS (See Teen Confessions)

TEEN-AGE CONFIDENTIAL CONFESSIONS
Charlton Comics: July, 1960 - No. 22, 1964

	GD25	FN65	NM94
1	2.80	8.40	28.00
2-10	2.25	6.75	18.00
11-22	1.50	4.50	12.00

TEEN-AGE DIARY SECRETS (Formerly Blue Ribbon Comics; becomes Diary Secrets #10 on)
St. John Publishing Co.: No. 4, 9/49; nn (#5), 9/49 - No. 7, 11/49; No. 8, 2/50; No. 9, 8/50

	GD25	FN65	NM94
4(9/49)-Oversized; part mag., part comic	22.00	66.00	165.00
nn(#5),6,8: 6,8-Photo-c; Baker-a(2-3) in each	18.00	54.00	135.00
7,9-Digest size	20.00	60.00	150.00

TEEN-AGE DOPE SLAVES (See Harvey Comics Library #1)

TEENAGE HOTRODDERS (Top Eliminator #25 on; see Blue Bird)
Charlton Comics: Apr, 1963 - No. 24, July, 1967

	GD25	FN65	NM94
1	4.00	12.00	40.00
2-10	2.50	7.50	22.00
11-24	2.25	6.75	18.00

TEEN-AGE LOVE (See Fox Giants)

TEEN-AGE LOVE (Formerly Intimate)
Charlton Comics: V2#4, July, 1958 - No. 96, Dec, 1973

	GD25	FN65	NM94
V2#4	3.00	9.00	30.00
5-9	2.50	7.50	22.00
10(9/59)-20	2.00	6.00	16.00
21-35	1.75	5.25	14.00
36-70	1.25	3.75	10.00
71-96: 61&62-Jonnie Love begins (origin)	.85	2.60	7.00

TEENAGE MUTANT NINJA TURTLES (Also see Anything Goes, Donatello, First Comics Graphic Novel, Gobbledygook, Grimjack #26, Leonardo, Michaelangelo, Raphael & Tales Of The...)
Mirage Studios: 1984 - No. 62, Aug, 1993 ($1.50/$1.75, B&W; all 44-52 pgs.)

	GD25	FN65	NM94
1-1st printing (3000 copies)-Only printing to have ad for Gobbledygook #1 & 2; Shredder app. (#1-4: 7-1/2x11")	10.50	31.00	115.00
1-2nd printing (6/84)(15,000 copies)	1.00	3.00	10.00
1-3rd printing (2/85)(36,000 copies)			5.00
1-4th printing, new-c (50,000 copies)			4.00
1-5th printing, new-c (8/88-c, 11/88 inside)			2.00
1-Counterfeit. **Note**: Most counterfeit copies have a half inch wide white streak or scratch marks across the center of back cover. Black part of cover is a bluish black instead of a deep black. Inside paper is very white & inside cover is bright white. These counterfeit the 1st printings (no value).			
2-1st printing (1984; 15,000 copies)	2.70	8.00	30.00
2-2nd printing		2.00	6.00
2-3rd printing; new Corben-c/a (2/85)			2.75
2-Counterfeit with glossy cover stock (no value).			
3-1st printing (1985, 44 pgs.)	1.50	4.50	15.00
3-Variant, 500 copies, given away in NYC. Has 'Laird's Photo' in white rather than light blue	4.50	13.50	50.00
3-2nd printing; contains new back-up story			2.75
4-1st printing (1985, 44 pgs.)	1.00	3.00	10.00
4-2nd printing (5/87)			1.75
5-Fugitoid begins, ends #7; 1st full color-c (1985)	.85	2.60	7.50
5-2nd printing (11/87)			1.75
6-1st printing (1986)			5.00
6-2nd printing (4/88-c, 5/88 inside)			1.75
7-4 pg. Eastman/Corben color insert; 1st color TMNT (1986, $1.75-c); Bade Biker back-up story			5.00
7-2nd printing (1/89) w/o color insert			1.75
8-Cerebus-c/story with Dave Sim-a (1986)			4.50
9,10: 9 (9/86)-Rip In Time by Corben			4.00
11-15			3.00
16-18: 18-Mark Bode'-a			2.50
18-2nd printing ($2.25, color, 44 pgs.)-New-c			2.25
19-34: 19-Begin $1.75-c. 24-26-Veitch-c/a.			1.80
32-2nd printing ($2.75, 52 pgs., full color)			2.75
35-49,51: 35-Begin $2.00-c.			2.00
50-Features pin-ups by Larsen, McFarlane, Simonson, etc.			2.50
52-62: 52-Begin $2.25-c			2.25
Book 1,2($1.50, B&W): 2-Corben-c			1.50
...Christmas Special 1 (12/90, $1.75, B&W, 52 pgs.)-Cover title: Michaelangelo Christmas Special; r/Michaelangelo one-shot plus new Raphael story			1.75
...Special (The Maltese Turtle) nn (1/93, $2.95, color, 44 pgs.)			3.00
...Special: "Times" Pipeline nn (9/92, $2.95, color, 44 pgs.)-Mark Bode-c/a			3.00
Hardcover ($100)-r/#1-10 plus one-shots w/dust jackets - limited to 1000 w/letter of authenticity			100.00
Softcover ($40)-r/#1-10			40.00

TEENAGE MUTANT NINJA TURTLES
Mirage Studios: V2#1, Oct, 1993 - V2#13, Oct, 1995 ($2.75)

	GD25	FN65	NM94
V2#1-13: 1-Wraparound-c			2.75

TEENAGE MUTANT NINJA TURTLES ADVENTURES (TV)
Archie Comics: 8/88 - No. 3, 12/88; 3/89 - No. 62, 1995? ($1.00/$1.25/$1.50/$1.75)

	GD25	FN65	NM94
1-Adapts TV cartoon; not by Eastman/Laird			2.00
2,3 (Mini-series)			1.50
1 (2nd on going series)			2.00
2-5: 5-Begins original stories not based on TV			1.50
1-11: 2nd printings			1.00
6-49,51-58: 14-Simpson-a(p). 19-1st Mighty Mutanimals (also in #20, 51-54). 20-Begin $1.25-c. 22-Gene Colan-c/a			1.25
50-($1.50)-Poster by Eastman/Laird			1.50
59-61,63-73: 59-Begin $1.50-c			1.50
62-($1.75)-w/poster			1.75
nn (1990, $5.95)-Movie adaptation		2.00	6.00
nn (Spring, 1991, $2.50, 68 pgs.)-(Meet Archie)			2.50
nn (Sum, 1991, $2.50, 68 pgs.)-(Movie II)-Adapts movie sequel			2.50
...Meet the Conservation Corps 1 (1992, $2.50, 68 pgs.)			2.50
...III The Movie: The Turtles are Back...In Time (1993, $2.50, 68 pgs.)			2.50
Special 1 (Sum/92, $2.50, 68 pgs.)-Bill Wray-c			2.50
Special 4 (Spr/93, $2.50, 68 pgs.)			2.50
Special 5 (Sum/93, $2.50, 68 pgs.)			2.50
Giant Size Special 6 (Fall/93, $1.95, 52 pgs.)			2.00
Special 7,8 (Win/93, Spr/94, $1.95, 52 pgs.)			2.00
Special 9 (Sum/94, $1.95, 52 pgs.)-Jeff Smith-c			2.00
Special 10 (Fall/94, $2.00, 52 pgs.)			2.00

NOTE: *There are 2nd printings of #1-11 w/B&W inside covers. Originals are color.*

TEENAGE MUTANT NINJA TURTLES (Adventures)
Archie Publications: Jan, 1996 - No. 3, Mar, 1996 ($1.50, limited series)

	GD25	FN65	NM94
1-3			1.50

TEENAGE MUTANT NINJA TURTLES
Image Comics (Highbrow Entertainment): June, 1996 - Present ($1.95)

	GD25	FN65	NM94
1-8: Eric Larsen-c(i) on all			2.00
9-18-($2.95) 10-Savage Dragon-c/app.			3.00

TEENAGE MUTANT NINJA TURTLES CLASSICS DIGEST (TV)

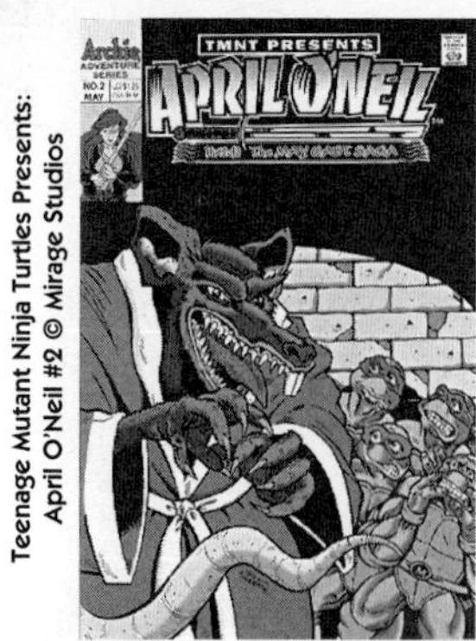

Teenage Mutant Ninja Turtles Presents: April O'Neil #2 © Mirage Studios

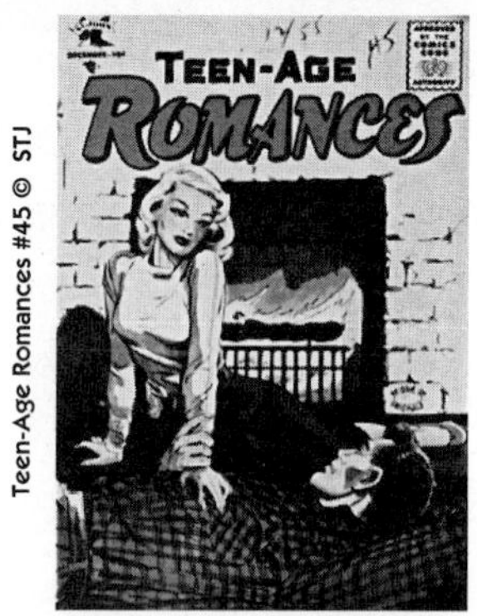

Teen-Age Romances #45 © STJ

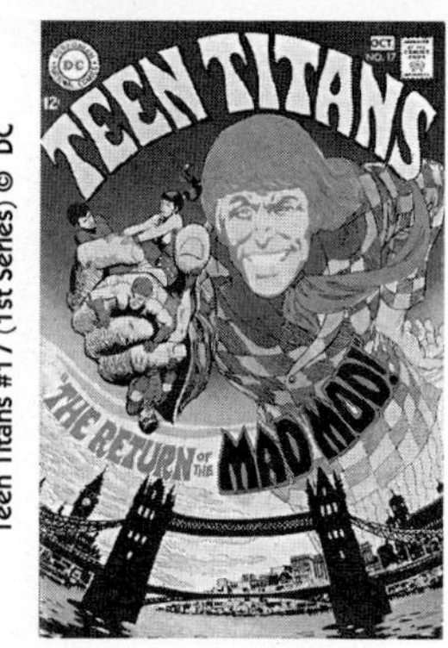

Teen Titans #17 (1st Series) © DC

Archie Comics: Aug, 1993 - No. 8, Mar, 1995? ($1.75)

	GD25	FN65	NM94
1-8: Reprints TMNT Advs.			1.75

TEENAGE MUTANT NINJA TURTLES/FLAMING CARROT CROSSOVER
Mirage Publishing: Nov, 1993 - No. 4, Feb, 1994 ($2.75, limited series)

	GD25	FN65	NM94
1-4: Bob Burden story			2.75

TEENAGE MUTANT NINJA TURTLES PRESENTS: APRIL O'NEIL
Archie Comics: Mar, 1993 - No. 3, June, 1993 ($1.25, limited series)

	GD25	FN65	NM94
1-3			1.25

TEENAGE MUTANT NINJA TURTLES PRESENTS: DONATELLO AND LEATHERHEAD
Archie Comics: July, 1993 - No. 3, Sept, 1993 ($1.25, limited series)

	GD25	FN65	NM94
1-3			1.25

TEENAGE MUTANT NINJA TURTLES PRESENTS: MERDUDE
Archie Comics: Oct, 1993 - No. 3, Dec, 1993 ($1.25, limited series)

	GD25	FN65	NM94
1-3-See Mighty Mutanimals #7 for 1st app. Merdude			1.25

TEENAGE MUTANT NINJA TURTLES/SAVAGE DRAGON CROSSOVER
Mirage Studios: Aug, 1995 ($2.75, one-shot)

	GD25	FN65	NM94
1			2.75

TEEN-AGE ROMANCE (Formerly My Own Romance)
Marvel Comics (ZPC): No. 77, Sept, 1960 - No. 86, Mar, 1962

	GD25	FN65	NM94
77-86	2.25	6.75	18.00

TEEN-AGE ROMANCES
St. John Publ. Co. (Approved Comics): Jan, 1949 - No. 45, Dec, 1955

	GD25	FN65	NM94
1-Baker-c/a(1)	33.00	100.00	250.00
2-Baker-c/a	19.00	56.00	140.00
3-Baker-c/a(3); spanking panel	19.00	56.00	140.00
4,5,7,8-Photo-c; Baker-a(2-3) each	16.00	48.00	120.00
6-Slightly large size; photo-c; part magazine; Baker-a (10/49)	17.00	52.00	130.00
9-Baker-c/a; Kubert-a	20.00	60.00	150.00
10-12,20-Baker-c/a(2-3) each	14.00	42.00	105.00
13-19,21,22-Complete issues by Baker	20.00	60.00	150.00
23-25-Baker-c/a(2-3) each	13.00	38.00	95.00
26,27,33,34,36-40,42: Baker-a. 33-Signed story by Estrada. 38-Suggestive-c. 42-r/Cinderella Love #9; Last pre-code (3/55)	9.30	28.00	65.00
28-30-No Baker-a	4.15	12.50	25.00
31,32-Baker-c	7.15	21.50	50.00
35-Baker-c/a (16 pgs.)	9.30	28.00	65.00
41-Baker-c; Infantino-a(r); all stories are Ziff-Davis-r	7.15	21.50	50.00
43-45-Baker-a	7.15	21.50	50.00

TEEN-AGE TALK
I.W. Enterprises: 1964

	GD25	FN65	NM94
Reprint #1	1.85	5.50	15.00
Reprint #5,8,9: 5-r/Hector #? 9-Punch Comics #?; L.B. Cole-c reprint from School Day Romances #1	1.25	3.75	10.00

TEEN-AGE TEMPTATIONS (Going Steady #10 on)(See True Love Pictorial)
St. John Publishing Co.: Oct, 1952 - No. 9, Aug, 1954

	GD25	FN65	NM94
1-Baker-c/a; has story "Reform School Girl" by Estrada	39.00	117.00	300.00
2,4-Baker-c	13.00	40.00	100.00
3,5-7,9-Baker-c/a	19.00	58.00	145.00
8-Teenagers smoke reefers; Baker-c/a	19.00	58.00	145.00

NOTE: ***Estrada** a-1, 3-5.*

TEEN BEAM (Formerly Teen Beat #1)
National Periodical Publications: No. 2, Jan-Feb, 1968

	GD25	FN65	NM94
2-Orlando, Drucker-a(r); Monkees photo-c	5.50	16.50	55.00

TEEN BEAT (Becomes Teen Beam #2)
National Periodical Publications: Nov-Dec, 1967

	GD25	FN65	NM94
1-Photos & text only; Monkees photo-c	6.50	19.50	65.00

TEEN COMICS (Formerly All Teen; Journey Into Unknown Worlds #36 on)
Marvel Comics (WFP): No. 21, Apr, 1947 - No. 35, May, 1950

	GD25	FN65	NM94
21-Kurtzman's "Hey Look"; Patsy Walker, Cindy (1st app.?), Georgie, Margie app.; Syd Shores-a begins, end #23	11.00	34.00	85.00
22,23,25,27,29,31-35: 22-(6/47)-Becomes Hedy Devine #22 (8/47) on?	7.85	23.50	55.00
24,26,28,30-Kurtzman's "Hey Look"	10.00	30.00	75.00

TEEN CONFESSIONS
Charlton Comics: Aug, 1959 - No. 97, Nov, 1976

	GD25	FN65	NM94
1	6.00	18.00	60.00
2	3.00	9.00	30.00
3-10	2.50	7.50	20.00
11-30	1.75	5.25	14.00
31-Beatles-c	9.50	28.50	95.00
32-36,38-55	1.50	4.50	12.00
37 (1/66)-Beatles Fan Club story; Beatles-c	9.50	28.50	95.00
56-58,60-97: 89,90-Newton-c		2.00	6.00
59-Kaluta's 1st pro work? (12/69)	1.60	4.80	16.00

TEENIE WEENIES, THE (America's Favorite Kiddie Comic)
Ziff-Davis Publishing Co.: No. 10, 1950 - No. 11, Apr-May, 1951 (Newspaper reprints)

	GD25	FN65	NM94
10,11-Painted-c	17.00	50.00	125.00

TEEN-IN (Tippy Teen)
Tower Comics: Summer, 1968 - No. 4, Fall, 1969

	GD25	FN65	NM94
nn(#1, Summer, 1968)	4.20	12.60	42.00
nn(#2, Spring, 1969),3,4	3.00	9.00	30.00

TEEN LIFE (Formerly Young Life)
New Age/Quality Comics Group: No. 3, Winter, 1945 - No. 5, Fall, 1945 (Teenage magazine)

	GD25	FN65	NM94
3-June Allyson photo on-c & story	9.30	28.00	70.00
4-Duke Ellington photo on-c & story	7.15	21.50	50.00
5-Van Johnson, Woody Herman & Jackie Robinson articles; Van Johnson & Woody Herman photos on-c	10.00	30.00	75.00

TEEN ROMANCES
Super Comics: 1964

	GD25	FN65	NM94
10,11,15-17-Reprints			5.00

TEEN SECRET DIARY (Nurse Betsy Crane #12 on)
Charlton Comics: Oct, 1959 - No. 11, June, 1961; No. 1, 1972

	GD25	FN65	NM94
1	2.60	7.80	26.00
2	2.25	6.75	18.00
3-11	1.75	5.25	14.00
1 (1972)	1.20	3.60	12.00

TEEN TALK (See Teen)

TEEN TITANS(See Brave & the Bold #54,60, DC Super-Stars #1, Marvel & DC Present, New Teen Titans, New Titans, Official...Index and Showcase #59)
National Periodical Publications/DC Comics: 1-2/66 - No. 43, 1-2/73; No. 44, 11/76 - No. 53, 2/78

	GD25	FN65	NM94
1-(1-2/66)-Titans join Peace Corps; Batman, Flash, Aquaman, Wonder Woman cameos	23.00	69.00	185.00
2	8.50	25.50	85.00
3-5: 4-Speedy app.	5.00	15.00	50.00
6-10: 6-Doom Patrol app.; Beast Boy x-over; readers polled on him joining Titans	4.00	12.00	40.00
11-19: 11-Speedy app. 13-X-Mas-c. 18-1st app. Starfire (11-12/68). 19-Wood-i; Speedy begins as regular	3.50	10.50	35.00

20-22: All Neal Adams-a. 21-Hawk & Dove app.; last 12¢ issue. 22-Origin

Teen Titans Annual #1 (2nd Series) © DC

Tek World #24 © William Shatner

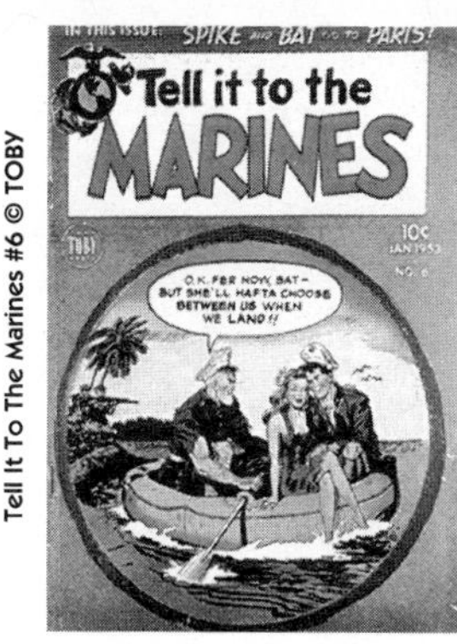

Tell It To The Marines #6 © TOBY

GD25 FN65 NM94

Wonder Girl 3.80 11.40 38.00
23-30: 23-Wonder Girl dons new costume. 25-Flash, Aquaman, Batman, Green Arrow, Green Lantern, Superman, & Hawk & Dove guests; 1st app. Lilith who joins T.T. West in #50. 29-Hawk & Dove & Ocean Master app. 30-Aquagirl app. 2.25 6.75 18.00
31-35,40-43: 31-Hawk & Dove app. 1.00 3.00 10.00
36-39-52 pgs.: 36,37-Superboy-r. 38-Green Arrow/Speedy-r; Aquaman/ Aqualad story. 39-Hawk & Dove-r. 1.20 3.60 12.00
44,45,47,49,51,52: 44-Mal becomes the Guardian 2.00 6.00
46-Joker's daughter begins (see Batman Family) 1.10 3.30 11.00
48-Intro Bumblebee; Joker's daughter becomes Harlequin 1.10 3.30 11.00
50-1st revival original Bat-Girl; intro. Teen Titans West 2.40 7.00 26.00
53-Origin retold .90 2.70 8.00

NOTE: ***Aparo** a-36. **Buckler** c-46-53. **Cardy** c-1-16. **Kane** a(p)-19, 22-24, 39r. **Tuska** a(p)-31, 36, 38, 39. DC Super-Stars #1 (3/76) was released before #44.*

TEEN TITANS (Also see JLA/Titans)
DC Comics: Oct, 1995 - No. 24, Sept, 1998 ($1.95)

1-Dan Jurgens-c/a(p)/scripts & George Perez-c/a(i) begin; Atom forms new team (Risk, Argent, Prysm, & Joto); 1st app.Loren Jupiter & Omen; no indicia. 1-3-Origin. 2.00
2-11: 4,5-Robin, Nightwing, Supergirl, Capt. Marvel Jr. app. 2.00
12-($2.95)"Then and Now" begins w/original Teen Titans-c/app. 3.00
13-24: 15-Death of Joto. 17-Capt. Marvel Jr. and Fringe join. 19-Millennium Giants x-over. 23,24-Superman app. 1.95
Annual 1 (1997, $3.95)-Pulp Heroes story 4.00

TEEN TITANS SPOTLIGHT
DC Comics: Aug, 1986 - No. 21, Apr, 1988

1-21: 7-Guice's 1st work at DC. 14-Nightwing; Batman app. 15-Austin-c(i). 18,19-Millenium x-over. 21-($1.00-c)-Original Teen Titans; Spiegle-a 1.00

*Note: **Guice** a-7p, 8p; c-7,8. **Orlando** c/a-11p. **Perez** c-1, 17i, 19. **Sienkiewicz** c-10*

TEEPEE TIM (...Heap Funny Indian Boy)(Formerly Ha Ha Comics)
American Comics Group: No. 100, Feb-Mar, 1955 - No. 102, June-July, 1955

100-102 4.00 11.00 22.00

TEGRA JUNGLE EMPRESS (Zegra Jungle Empress #2 on)
Fox Features Syndicate: August, 1948

1-Blue Beetle, Rocket Kelly app.; used in **SOTI**, pg. 31 45.00 134.00 380.00

TEKNO COMIX HANDBOOK
Tekno Comix: May, 1996 ($3.95, one-shot)

1-Guide to the Tekno Universe 4.00

TEKNOPHAGE (See Neil Gaiman's...)

TEKNOPHAGE VERSUS ZEERUS
BIG Entertainment: July, 1996 ($3.25, one-shot)

1-Paul Jenkins script 3.25

TEKWORLD (William Shatner's... on-c only)
Epic Comics (Marvel): Sept, 1992 - Aug, 1994 ($1.75)

1-Based on Shatner's novel, TekWar, set in L.A. in the year 2120 2.50
2-24 1.75

TELEVISION (See TV)

TELEVISION COMICS
Standard Comics (Animated Cartoons): No. 5, Feb, 1950 - No. 8, Nov, 1950

5-1st app. Willy Nilly 8.50 26.00 60.00
6-8: 6 has #2 on inside 6.50 19.50 45.00

TELEVISION PUPPET SHOW (See Spotty the Pup)
Avon Periodicals: 1950 - No. 2, Nov, 1950

GD25 FN65 NM94

1-1st app. Speedy Rabbit, Spotty The Pup 16.00 48.00 120.00
2 12.00 36.00 90.00

TELEVISION TEENS MOPSY (See TV Teens)

TELL IT TO THE MARINES
Toby Press Publications: Mar, 1952 - No. 15, July, 1955

1-Lover O'Leary and His Liberty Belles (with pin-ups), ends #6; Spike & Bat begin, end #6 17.00 50.00 125.00
2-Madame Cobra-c/story 9.30 28.00 70.00
3-5 6.50 19.50 45.00
6-12,14,15: 7-9,14,15-Photo-c 5.35 16.00 32.00
13-John Wayne photo-c 10.00 30.00 75.00
I.W. Reprint #9-r/#1 above 1.10 3.30 9.00
Super Reprint #16(1964)-r/#4 above 1.10 3.30 9.00

TEMPEST (See Aquaman, 3rd Series)
DC Comics: Nov, 1996 - No. 4, Feb, 1997 ($1.75, limited series)

1-4: Formerly Aqualad; Phil Jimenez-c/a/scripts in all 1.75

TEMPUS FUGITIVE
DC Comics: 1990 - No. 4, 1991 ($4.95, squarebound, 52 pgs.)

Book 1,2: Ken Steacy painted-c/a & scripts 5.00
Book 3,4-($5.95-c) 6.00
TPB (Dark Horse Comics, 1/97, $17.95) 18.00

TEN COMMANDMENTS (See Moses & the... and Classics Illustrated Special)

TENDER LOVE STORIES
Skywald Publ. Corp.: Feb, 1971 - No. 4, July, 1971

1 (All 25¢, 52 pgs.) 1.20 3.60 12.00
2-4 .90 2.70 8.00

TENDER ROMANCE (Ideal Romance #3 on)
Key Publications (Gilmour Magazines): Dec, 1953 - No. 2, Feb, 1954

1-Headlight & lingerie panels; B. Baily-c 13.00 40.00 100.00
2-Bernard Baily-c 7.85 23.50 55.00

TENNESSEE JED (Radio)
Fox Syndicate? (Wm. C. Popper & Co.): nd (1945) (16 pgs.; paper cover; regular size; giveaway)

nn 16.00 48.00 120.00

TENNIS (...For Speed, Stamina, Strength, Skill)
Tennis Educational Foundation: 1956 (16 pgs.; soft cover; 10¢)

Book 1-Endorsed by Gene Tunney, Ralph Kiner, etc. showing how tennis has helped them 4.00 12.00 24.00

TENSE SUSPENSE
Fago Publications: Dec, 1958 - No. 2, Feb, 1959

1,2 6.70 20.00 45.00

TEN STORY LOVE (Formerly a pulp magazine with same title)
Ace Periodicals: V29#3, June-July, 1951 - V36#5(#209), Sept, 1956 (#3-6: 52 pgs.)

V29#3(#177)-Part comic, part text; painted-c 9.30 28.00 65.00
4-6(1/52) 5.00 15.00 30.00
V30#1(3/52)-6(1/53) 4.25 13.00 26.00
V31#1(2/53),V32#2(4/53)-6(12/53) 4.00 10.00 20.00
V33#1(1/54)-3(5#54, #195), V34#4(7/54, #196)-6(10/54, #198) 4.00 10.00 20.00
V35#1(12/54, #199)-3(4/55, #201)-Last precode 3.20 8.00 16.00
V35#4-6(9/55, #201-204), V36#1(11/55, #205)-3, 5(9/56, #209) 2.80 7.00 14.00
V36#4-L.B. Cole-a 6.50 19.50 45.00

TENTH, THE
Image Comics: Jan, 1997 - No. 4, June, 1997 ($2.50, limited series)

1-4-Tony Daniel-c/a, Beau Smith-s 2.00 6.00

The Tenth #8 (2nd Series) © Tony Daniel

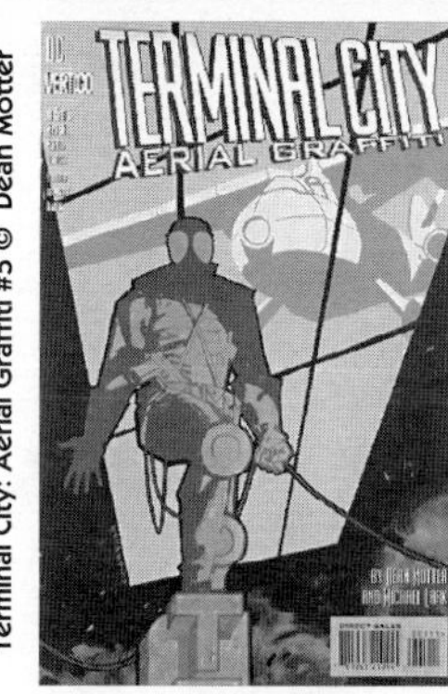

Terminal City: Aerial Graffiti #5 © Dean Motter

Terrarists #3 © MAR

GD25 FN65 NM94

Abuse of Humanity TPB ($10.95) r/#1-4 10.95

TENTH, THE
Image Comics: Sept, 1997 - Present ($2.50)

0-(8/97, $5.00) American Ent. Ed. 5.00
1-Tony Daniel-c/a, Beau Smith-s 5.00
2-9 4.00
3,7- Variant-c 4.00
10-13 2.50
...Configuration (8/98) Re-cap and pin-ups 2.50
...Collected Edition 1 ('98, $4.95, square-bound) r/#1,2 5.00

TEN WHO DARED (Disney)
Dell Publishing Co.: No. 1178, Dec, 1960

Four Color 1178-Movie, painted-c; cast member photo on back-c 6.40 19.00 70.00

TERMINAL CITY
DC Comics (Vertigo): July, 1996 - No. 9, Mar, 1997 ($2.50, limited series)

1-9: Dean Motter scripts, 7,8-Matt Wagner-c 2.50
TPB ('97, $19.95) r/series 19.95

TERMINAL CITY: AERIAL GRAFFITI
DC Comics (Vertigo): Nov, 1997 - No. 5, Mar, 1998 ($2.50, limited series)

1-5: Dean Motter-s/Lark-a/Chiarello-c 2.50

TERMINATOR, THE (See Robocop vs. ... & Rust #12 for 1st app.)
Now Comics: Sept, 1988 - No. 17, 1989 ($1.75, Baxter paper)

1-Based on movie 2.00 6.00
2-10,12: 12-($2.95, 52 pgs.)-Intro. John Connor 3.00
11,13-17 2.00
Trade paperback (1989, $9.95) 10.00

TERMINATOR, THE
Dark Horse Comics: Aug, 1990 - No. 4, Nov, 1990 ($2.50, limited series)

1-Set 39 years later than the movie 4.00
2-4 2.50

TERMINATOR, THE
Dark Horse Comics: 1998 - No. 4, 1999 ($2.95, limited series)

1-4-Alan Grant-s/Steve Pugh-a/c 2.95
...Special (1998, $2.95) Darrow-c/Grant-s 3.00

TERMINATOR, THE: ALL MY FUTURES PAST
Now Comics: V3#1, Aug, 1990 - V3#2, Sept, 1990 ($1.75, limited series)

V3#1,2 1.75

TERMINATOR, THE: ENDGAME
Dark Horse Comics: Sept, 1992 - No. 3, Nov, 1992 ($2.50, limited series)

1-3: Guice-a(p); painted-c 2.50

TERMINATOR, THE: HUNTERS AND KILLERS
Dark Horse Comics: Mar, 1992 - No. 3, May, 1992 ($2.50, limited series)

1-3 2.50

TERMINATOR, THE: ONE SHOT
Dark Horse Comics: July, 1991 ($5.95, 56 pgs.)

nn-Matt Wagner-a; contains stiff pop-up inside 2.00 6.00

TERMINATOR, THE: SECONDARY OBJECTIVES
Dark Horse Comics: July, 1991 - No. 4, Oct, 1991 ($2.50, limited series)

1-Gulacy-c/a(p) in all 2.50
2-4 2.50

TERMINATOR, THE: THE BURNING EARTH
Now Comics: V2#1, Mar, 1990 - V2#5, July, 1990 ($1.75, limited series)

V2#1-5 1.75
Trade paperback (1990, $9.95)-Reprints V2#1-5 10.00

GD25 FN65 NM94

TERMINATOR: THE ENEMY FROM WITHIN, THE
Dark Horse Comics: Nov, 1991 - No. 4, Feb, 1992 ($2.50, limited series)

1-4: All have Simon Bisley painted-c 2.50

TERMINATOR 2: CYBERNETIC DAWN
Malibu: Nov, 1995 - No.4, Feb, 1996; No. 0. Apr, 1996 ($2.50, lim. series)

0 (4/96, $2.95)-Gary Erskine-c/a; flip book w/Terminator 2:Nuclear Twilight. 3.00
1-4: Continuation of film. 2.50

TERMINATOR 2: JUDGEMENT DAY
Marvel Comics: Early Sept, 1991 - No. 3, Early Oct, 1991 ($1.00, lim. series)

1-3: Based on movie sequel; 1-3-Same as nn issues 1.00
nn (1991, $4.95, squarebound, 68 pgs.)-Photo-c 5.00
nn (1991, $2.25, B&W, magazine, 68 pgs.) 2.25

TERMINATOR 2: NUCLEAR TWILIGHT
Malibu: Nov, 1995 - No.4, Feb, 1996; No. 0, Apr, 1996 ($2.50, lim. series)

0 (4/96, $2.95)-Gary Erskine-c/a; flip book w/Terminator 2:Cybernetic Dawn. 3.00
1-4:Continuation of film. 2.50

TERRAFORMERS
Wonder Color Comics: April, 1987 - No. 2, 1987 ($1.95, limited series)

1,2-Kelley Jones-a 2.00

TERRANAUTS
Fantasy General Comics: Aug, 1986 - No. 2, 1986 ($1.75, limited series)

1,2 1.80

TERRARISTS
Marvel Comics (Epic): Nov, 1993 - No. 4, Feb, 1994 ($2.50, lim. series)

1-4-Bound-in trading cards in all 2.50

TERRIFIC COMICS (Also see Suspense Comics)
Continental Magazines: Jan, 1944 - No. 6, Nov, 1944

1-Kid Terrific; opium story 294.00 882.00 2500.00
2-1st app. The Boomerang by L.B. Cole & Ed Wheelan's "Comics" McCormick, called the world's #1 comic book fan begins 218.00 653.00 1850.00
3-Diana becomes Boomerang's costumed aide; L.B. Cole-c 218.00 653.00 1850.00
4-Classic war-c (Scarce) 336.00 1011.00 3200.00
5-The Reckoner begins; Boomerang & Diana by L.B. Cole; Schomburg bondage-c (Scarce) 550.00 1650.00 4500.00
6-L.B. Cole-c/a 194.00 582.00 1650.00
NOTE: ***L.B. Cole*** *a-1, 2(2), 3-6.* ***Fuje*** *a-5, 6.* ***Rico*** *a-2; c-1.* ***Schomburg*** *c-2, 5.*

TERRIFIC COMICS (Formerly Horrific; Wonder Boy #17 on)
Mystery Publ.(Comic Media)/(Ajax/Farrell): No. 14, Dec, 1954; No. 16, Mar, 1955 (No #15)

14-Art swipe/Advs. into the Unknown #37; injury-to-eye-c; pg. 2, panel 5 swiped from Phantom Stranger #4; surrealistic Palais-a; Human Cross story 23.00 68.00 170.00
16-Wonder Boy-c/story (last pre-code) 15.00 46.00 115.00

TERRIFYING TALES (Formerly Startling Terror Tales #10)
Star Publications: No. 11, Jan, 1953 - No. 15, Apr, 1954

11-Used in **POP**, pgs. 99,100; all Jo-Jo-r 42.00 126.00 335.00
12-Reprints Jo-Jo #19 entirely; L.B. Cole splash 39.00 117.00 295.00
13-All Rulah-r; classic devil-c 43.00 129.00 350.00
14-All Rulah reprints 39.00 117.00 300.00
15-Rulah, Zago-r; used in **SOTI**-r/Rulah #22 39.00 117.00 300.00
NOTE: *All issues have* ***L.B. Cole*** *covers; bondage covers-No. 12-14.*

TERROR ILLUSTRATED (Adult Tales of...)
E.C. Comics: Nov-Dec, 1955 - No. 2, Spring (April on-c), 1956 (Magazine, 25¢)

1-Adult Entertainment on-c 12.00 36.00 90.00
2-Charles Sultan-a 10.00 30.00 75.00

Terrors of the Jungle #21 © STAR

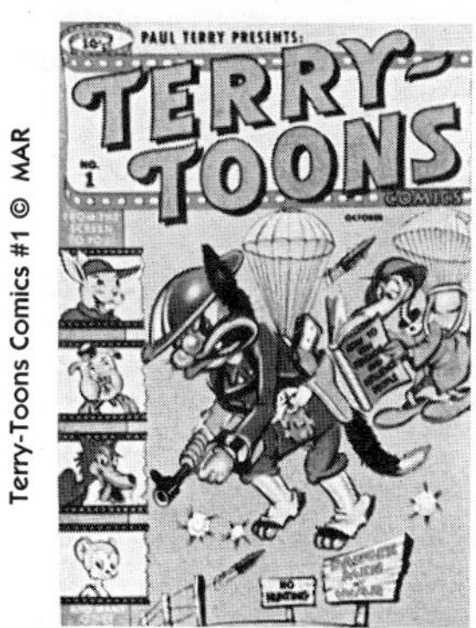

Terry-Toons Comics #1 © MAR

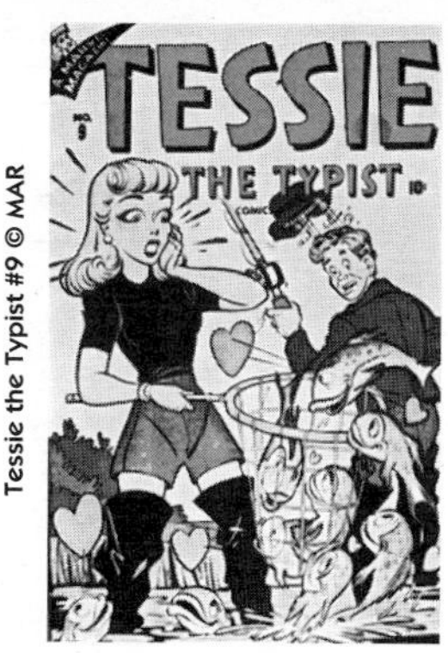

Tessie the Typist #9 © MAR

GD25 FN65 NM94

NOTE: *Craig, Evans, Ingels, Orlando art in each. Crandall c-1, 2.*

TERROR INC. (See A Shadowline Saga #3)
Marvel Comics: July, 1992 - No. 13, July, 1993 ($1.75)

1-13: 6,7-Punisher-c/story. 9,10-Wolverine-c/story. 13-Ghost Rider app. 1.75

TERRORS OF THE JUNGLE (Formerly Jungle Thrills)
Star Publications: No. 17, 5/52 - No. 21, 2/53; No. 4, 4/53 - No. 10, 9/54

17-Reprints Rulah #21, used in **SOTI**; L.B. Cole bondage-c 42.00 127.00 340.00
18-Jo-Jo-r 29.00 88.00 220.00
19,20(1952)-Jo-Jo-r; Disbrow-a 28.00 84.00 210.00
21-Jungle Jo, Tangi-r; used in **POP**, pg. 100 & color illos.; shrunken heads on-c 31.00 92.00 230.00
4-10: All Disbrow-a. 5-Jo-Jo-r. 8-Rulah, Jo-Jo-r. 9-Jo-Jo-r; Disbrow-a; Tangi by Orlando10-Rulah-r 28.00 84.00 210.00
NOTE: *L.B. Cole c-all; bondage c-17, 19, 21, 5, 7.*

TERROR TALES (See Beware Terror Tales)

TERROR TALES (Magazine)
Eerie Publications: V1#7, 1969 - V6#6, Dec, 1974; V7#1, Apr, 1976 - V10, 1979? (V1-V6: 52 pgs.; V7 on: 68 pgs.)

V1#7 4.20 12.60 42.00
V1#8-11('69): 9-Bondage-c 3.20 9.60 32.00
V2#1-6('70), V3#1-6('71), V4#1-7('72), V5#1-6('73), V6#1-6('74) 2.40 7.00 26.00
V7#1,4(no V7#2), V8#1-3('77) 2.40 7.00 26.00
V7#3-LSD story-r/Weird V3#5 2.40 7.00 26.00
V9#2-4, V10 2.50 7.60 28.00

TERRY AND THE PIRATES (See Famous Feature Stories, Merry Christmas From Sears Toyland, Popular Comics, Super Book #3,5,9,16,28, & Super Comics)

TERRY AND THE PIRATES
Dell Publishing Co.: 1939 - 1953 (By Milton Caniff)

Large Feature Comic 2(1939) 57.00 172.00 630.00
Large Feature Comic 6(1938)-r/1936 dailies 57.00 172.00 630.00
Four Color 9(1940) 54.00 161.00 590.00
Large Feature Comic 27('41), 6('42) 47.00 142.00 520.00
Four Color 44('43) 37.00 112.00 410.00
Four Color 101('45) 25.00 74.00 270.00
Buster Brown Shoes giveaway(1938)-32 pgs.; in color 27.00 80.00 200.00
Canada Dry Premiums-Books #1-3(1953, 36 pgs.; 2x5")-Harvey; #1-Hot Shot Charlie Flies Again; 2-In Forced Landing; 3-Dragon Lady in Distress) 13.00 38.00 95.00
Family Album(1942) 17.00 52.00 130.00
Gambles Giveaway (1938, 16 pgs.) 7.85 23.50 55.00
Gillmore Giveaway (1938, 24 pgs.) 8.50 26.00 60.00
Popped Wheat Giveaway(1938)-Strip reprints in full color; Caniff-a 1.00 2.00 5.00
Shoe Store giveaway (Weatherbird)(1938, 16 pgs., soft-c)(2-diff.) 7.85 23.50 55.00
Sparked Wheat Giveaway(1942, 16 pgs.)-In color 7.85 23.50 55.00

TERRY AND THE PIRATES
Libby's Radio Premium: 1941 (16 pgs.; reg. size)(shipped folded in the mail)

GD25 FN65 VF82

"Adventure of the Ruby of Genghis Khan" - Each pg. is a puzzle that must be completed to read the story 200.00 600.00 1700.00

TERRY AND THE PIRATES (Formerly Boy Explorers; Long John Silver & the Pirates #30 on) (Daily strip-r) (Two #26's)
Harvey Publications/Charlton No. 26-28: No. 3, 4/47 - No. 26, 4/51; No. 26, 6/55 - No. 28, 10/55

GD25 FN65 NM94

3(#1)-Boy Explorers by S&K; Terry & the Pirates begin by Caniff; 1st app. The Dragon Lady 35.00 104.00 260.00
4-S&K Boy Explorers 19.00 56.00 140.00
5-11: 11-Man in Black app. by Powell 9.30 28.00 65.00
12-20: 16-Girl threatened with red hot poker 7.15 21.50 50.00
21-26(4/51)-Last Caniff issue & last pre-code issue 6.50 19.50 45.00
26-28('55)(Formerly This Is Suspense)-No Caniff-a 5.70 17.00 35.00
NOTE: *Powell a (Tommy Tween)-5-10, 12, 14; 15-17(1/2 to 2 pgs. each).*

TERRY BEARS COMICS (TerryToons, The... #4)
St. John Publishing Co.: June, 1952 - No. 3, Mar, 1953

1-By Paul Terry 5.70 17.50 40.00
2,3 5.00 15.00 30.00

TERRY-TOONS ALBUM (See Giant Comics Edition)

TERRY-TOONS COMICS (1st Series) (Becomes Paul Terry's Comics #85 on; later issues titled "Paul Terry's...")
Timely/Marvel No. 1-59 (8/47)(Becomes Best Western No. 58 on?, Marvel)/ St. John No. 60 (9/47) on: Oct, 1942 - No. 86, May, 1951

1 (Scarce)-Features characters that 1st app. on movie screen; Gandy Goose & Sourpuss begin; war-c; Gandy Goose c-1-37 141.00 424.00 1200.00
2 55.00 164.00 465.00
3-5 40.00 120.00 315.00
6,8-10 29.00 88.00 220.00
7-Hitler, Hirohito, Mussolini-c 36.00 108.00 270.00
11-20 18.00 54.00 135.00
21-37 13.00 38.00 95.00
38-Mighty Mouse begins (1st app., 11/45); Mighty Mouse-c begin, end #86; Gandy, Sourpuss welcome Mighty Mouse on-c 94.00 282.00 800.00
39-2nd app. Mighty Mouse 31.00 92.00 230.00
40-49: 43-Infinity-c 14.00 42.00 105.00
50-1st app. Heckle & Jeckle (11/46) 31.00 94.00 235.00
51-60: 55-Infinity-c. 60-(9/47)-Atomic explosion panel; 1st St. John issue 9.30 28.00 70.00
61-84 7.85 23.50 55.00
85,86-Same book as Paul Terry's Comics #85,86 with only a title change; published at same time? 7.85 23.50 55.00

TERRY-TOONS COMICS (2nd Series)
St. John Publishing Co./Pines: June, 1952 - No. 9, Nov, 1953; 1957; 1958

1-Gandy Goose & Sourpuss begin by Paul Terry 15.00 44.00 110.00
2 7.15 21.50 50.00
3-9 6.50 19.50 45.00
Giant Summer Fun Book 101,102-(Sum, 1957, Sum, 1958, 25¢, Pines)(TV) CBS Television Presents...; Tom Terrific, Mighty Mouse, Heckle & Jeckle Gandy Goose app. 11.00 34.00 85.00

TERRYTOONS, THE TERRY BEARS (Formerly Terry Bears Comics)
Pines Comics: No. 4, Summer, 1958 (CBS Television Presents...)

4 4.25 13.00 28.00

TESSIE THE TYPIST (Tiny Tessie #24; see Comedy Comics, Gay Comics & Joker Comics)
Timely/Marvel Comics (20CC): Summer, 1944 - No. 23, Aug, 1949

1-Doc Rockblock & others by Wolverton 52.00 155.00 440.00
2-Wolverton's Powerhouse Pepper 32.00 96.00 240.00
3-(3/45)-No Wolverton 10.00 30.00 75.00
4,5,7,8-Wolverton-a. 4-(Fall/45) 21.00 62.00 155.00
6-Kurtzman's "Hey Look", 2 pgs. Wolverton-a 21.00 62.00 155.00
9-Wolverton's Powerhouse Pepper (8 pgs.) & 1 pg. Kurtzman's "Hey Look" 24.00 72.00 180.00
10-Wolverton's Powerhouse Pepper (4 pgs.) 22.00 66.00 165.00
11-Wolverton's Powerhouse Pepper (8 pgs.) 24.00 72.00 180.00
12-Wolverton's Powerhouse Pepper (4 pgs.) & 1 pg. Kurtzman's "Hey Look" 22.00 66.00 165.00
13-Wolverton's Powerhouse Pepper (4 pgs.) 22.00 66.00 165.00
14-Wolverton's Dr. Whackyhack (1 pg.); 1-1/2 pgs. Kurtzman's "Hey Look"

Texas Kid #10 © MAR

Tex Ritter Western #1 © FAW

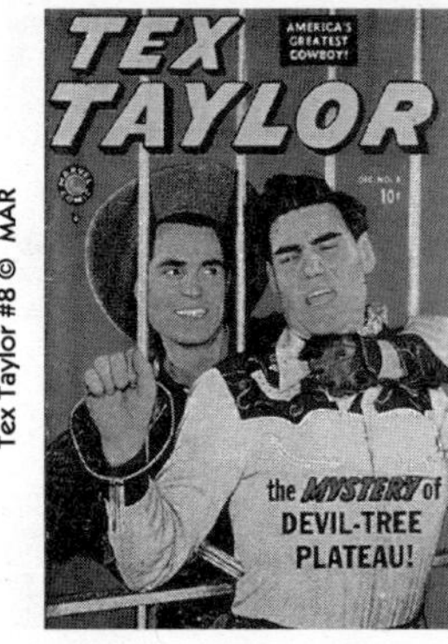

Tex Taylor #8 © MAR

GD25 FN65 NM94 GD25 FN65 NM94

17.00 50.00 125.00
15-Kurtzman's "Hey Look" (3 pgs.) & 3 pgs. Giggles 'n' Grins 17.00 50.00 125.00
16-18-Kurtzman's "Hey Look" (?, 2 & 1 pg.) 11.00 34.00 85.00
19-Annie Oakley story (8 pgs.) 8.50 26.00 60.00
20-23: 20-Anti-Wertham editorial (2/49) 7.15 21.50 50.00
NOTE: *Lana app.-21. Millie The Model app.-13, 15, 17, 21. Rusty app.-10, 11, 13, 15, 17.*

TEXAN, THE (Fightin' Marines #15 on; Fightin' Texan #16 on)
St. John Publishing Co.: Aug, 1948 - No. 15, Oct, 1951
1-Buckskin Belle 13.00 39.00 95.00
2 7.50 22.50 50.00
3,10: 10-Oversized issue 7.00 21.00 45.00
4,5,7,15-Baker-c/a 13.00 38.00 95.00
6,9-Baker-c 9.30 28.00 65.00
8,11,13,14-Baker-c/a(2-3) each 13.00 38.00 95.00
12-All Matt Baker-c/a; Peyote story 17.00 52.00 130.00
NOTE: ***Matt Baker** c-4-9, 11-15. **Larsen** a-4-6, 8-10, 15. **Tuska** a-1, 2, 7-9.*

TEXAN, THE (TV)
Dell Publishing Co.: No. 1027, Sept-Nov, 1959 - No. 1096, May-July, 1960
Four Color 1027 (#1)-Photo-c 8.00 25.00 90.00
Four Color 1096-Rory Calhoun photo-c 7.00 22.00 80.00

TEXAS JOHN SLAUGHTER (See Walt Disney Presents, 4-Color #997, 1181 & #2)

TEXAS KID (See Two-Gun Western, Wild Western)
Marvel/Atlas Comics (LMC): Jan, 1951 - No. 10, July, 1952
1-Origin; Texas Kid (alias Lance Temple) & his horse Thunder begin; Tuska-a 20.00 60.00 150.00
2 10.00 30.00 75.00
3-10 8.50 26.00 60.00
NOTE: ***Maneely** a-1-4; c-1, 3, 5-10.*

TEXAS RANGERS, THE (See Jace Pearson of... and Superior Stories #4)

TEXAS RANGERS IN ACTION (Formerly Captain Gallant or Scotland Yard?)
Charlton Comics: No. 5, Jul, 1956 - No. 79, Aug, 1970 (See Blue Bird Comics)
5 6.50 19.50 45.00
6,7,9,10 4.25 13.00 26.00
8-Ditko-a (signed) 7.15 21.50 50.00
11-Williamson-a(5&8 pgs.); Torres/Williamson-a (5 pgs.) 7.85 23.50 55.00
12,14-20 4.00 10.00 20.00
13-Williamson-a (5 pgs); Torres, Morisi-a 5.70 17.00 40.00
21-30: 31-Last 10¢ issue? 2.25 6.75 18.00
31-59 1.75 5.25 14.00
60-Riley's Rangers begin 1.50 4.50 12.00
61-65,68-70 1.10 3.30 9.00
66,67: 66-1st app. The Man Called Loco. 67-Origin 1.50 4.50 12.00
71-79 1.00 2.80 7.00
76(Modern Comics-r, 1977) 4.00

TEXAS SLIM (Also see A-1 Comics)
Magazine Enterprises: No. 2, 1947 - No.10, 1948
A-1 2-8,10: Texas Slim & Dirty Dalton, The corsair, Teddy Rich, Dotty Dripple, Inca Inca, Tommy Tinker, Little Mexico & Tugboat Tim, The Masqu'rader & others. 7-Corsair-c/s. 8-Intro Rodeo Ryan 4.25 13.00 28.00
A-1 9-All Texas Slim 5.00 15.00 30.00

TEX DAWSON, GUN-SLINGER (Gunslinger #2 on)
Marvel Comics Group: Jan, 1973 (20¢)(Also see Western Kid, 1st series)
1-Steranko-c; Williamson-r (4 pgs.); Tex Dawson-r by Romita(3) from 1955; Tuska-r 1.40 4.20 14.00

TEX FARNUM (See Wisco)

TEX FARRELL (...Pride of the Wild West)
D. S. Publishing Co.: Mar-Apr, 1948
1-Tex Farrell & his horse Lightning; Shelly-c 11.00 32.00 80.00

TEX GRANGER (Formerly Calling All Boys; see True Comics)
Parents' Magazine Inst./Commended: No. 18, Jun, 1948 - No. 24, Sept, 1949
18-Tex Granger & his horse Bullet begin 9.30 28.00 70.00
19 7.15 21.50 50.00
20-24: 22-Wild Bill Hickok story. 23-Vs. Billy the Kid; Tim Holt app. 5.70 17.00 40.00

TEX MORGAN (See Blaze Carson and Wild Western)
Marvel Comics (CCC): Aug, 1948 - No. 9, Feb, 1950
1-Tex Morgan, his horse Lightning & sidekick Lobo begin 24.00 72.00 180.00
2 16.00 48.00 120.00
3-6: 3,4-Arizona Annie app. 10.00 30.00 75.00
7-9: All photo-c. 7-Captain Tootsie by Beck. 8-18 pg. story "The Terror of Rimrock Valley"; Diablo app. 16.00 48.00 120.00
NOTE: *Tex Taylor app.-6, 7, 9. **Brodsky** c-6. **Syd Shores** c-2, 5.*

TEX RITTER WESTERN (Movie star; singing cowboy; see Six-Gun Heroes and Western Hero)
Fawcett No. 1-20 (1/54)/Charlton No. 21 on: Oct, 1950 - No. 46, May, 1959 (Photo-c: 1-21)
1-Tex Ritter, his stallion White Flash & dog Fury begin; photo front/back-c begin 61.00 184.00 520.00
2 28.00 84.00 210.00
3-5: 5-Last photo back-c 21.00 64.00 160.00
6-10 17.00 50.00 125.00
11-19 11.00 34.00 85.00
20-Last Fawcett issue (1/54) 13.00 38.00 95.00
21-1st Charlton issue; photo-c (3/54) 15.00 44.00 110.00
22-B&W photo back-c begin, end #32 9.30 28.00 65.00
23-30: 23-25-Young Falcon app. 7.85 23.50 55.00
31-38,40-45 6.50 19.50 45.00
39-Williamson-a; Whitman-c (1/58) 8.50 26.00 60.00
46-Last issue 7.85 23.50 55.00

TEX TAYLOR (...The Fighting Cowboy on-c #1, 2)(See Blaze Carson, Kid Colt, Tex Morgan, Wild West, Wild Western, & Wisco)
Marvel Comics (HPC): Sept, 1948 - No. 9, March, 1950
1-Tex Taylor & his horse Fury begin 25.00 76.00 190.00
2 14.00 42.00 105.00
3 13.00 38.00 95.00
4-6: All photo-c. 4-Anti-Wertham editorial. 5,6-Blaze Carson app. 15.00 44.00 110.00
7-Photo-c; 18 pg. Movie-Length Thriller "Trapped in Time's Lost Land!" with sabre toothed tigers, dinosaurs; Diablo app. 17.00 50.00 125.00
8-Photo-c; 18 pg. Movie-Length Thriller "The Mystery of Devil-Tree Plateau!" with dwarf horses, dwarf people & a lost miniature Inca type village; Diablo app. 17.00 50.00 125.00
9-Photo-c; 18 pg. Movie-Length Thriller "Guns Along the Border!" Captain Tootsie by Schreiber; Nimo the Mountain Lion app. 17.00 50.00 125.00
NOTE: ***Syd Shores** c-1-3.*

THANE OF BAGARTH (Also see Hercules, 1967 series)
Charlton Comics: No. 24, Oct, 1985 - No. 25, Dec, 1985
24,25 1.00

THANOS QUEST, THE (See Capt. Marvel #25, Infinity Gauntlet, Iron Man #55, Logan's Run, Marvel Feature #12, Silver Surfer #34 & Warlock #9)
Marvel Comics: 1990 - No. 2, 1990 ($4.95, squarebound, 52 pgs.)
1,2-Both have Starlin scripts & covers 5.00
1,2-($4.95, 2nd printings) 5.00

THAT CHEMICAL REFLEX
CFD Productions: 1994 - No. 3 ($2.50, B&W, mature)

THB #1 © Paul Pope

The Thing #36 © MAR

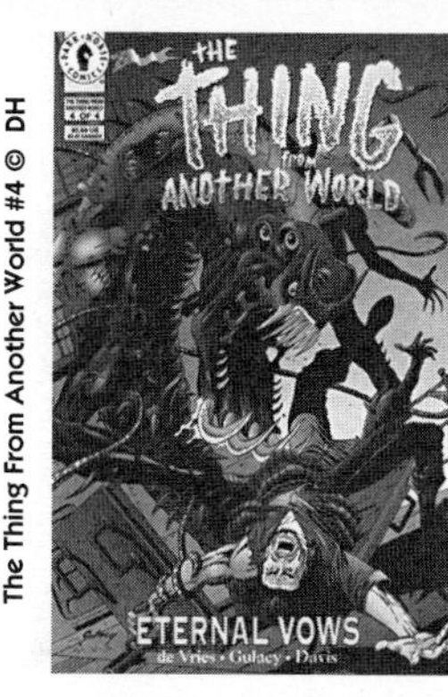

The Thing From Another World #4 © DH

	GD25	FN65	NM94
1-3: 1-Dan Brereton-c/a			2.50

THAT DARN CAT (See Movie Comics & Walt Disney Showcase #19)

THAT'S MY POP! GOES NUTS FOR FAIR
Bystander Press: 1939 (76 pgs., B&W)

nn-by Milt Gross	23.00	70.00	175.00

THAT THE WORLD MAY BELIEVE
Catechetical Guild Giveaway: No date (16 pgs.) (Graymoor Friars distr.)

nn	1.60	4.00	8.00

THAT WILKIN BOY (Meet Bingo...)
Archie Publications: Jan, 1969 - No. 52, Oct, 1982

1-1st app. Bingo's Band, Samantha &Tough Teddy	2.50	7.50	24.00
2-11	.90	2.70	9.00
12-26-Giants. 12-No # on-c	1.20	3.60	12.00
27-40(1/77)			4.00
41-52			2.00

THB
Horse Press: Oct, 1994 - Present ($5.50/$2.50/$2.95, B&W)

1 ($5.50)	1.20	3.60	12.00
1 (2nd Printing)-r/#1 w/new material			2.50
2 ($2.50)	1.00	3.00	10.00
3-5			4.00
69 (1995, no price, low distribution, 12 pgs.)-story reprinted in #1 (2nd Printing).			3.00
Giant THB-($4.95)			5.00

T.H.E. CAT (TV)
Dell Publishing Co.: Mar, 1967 - No. 4, Oct, 1967 (All have photo-c)

1	2.50	7.50	24.00
2-4	2.25	6.75	18.00

THERE'S A NEW WORLD COMING
Spire Christian Comics/Fleming H. Revell Co.: 1973 (35/49¢)

nn			3.00

THEY ALL KISSED THE BRIDE (See Cinema Comics Herald)

THEY RING THE BELL
Fox Feature Syndicate: 1946

1	10.00	30.00	75.00

THIEF OF BAGHDAD
Dell Publishing Co.: No. 1229, Oct-Dec, 1961 (one-shot)

Four Color 1229-Movie, Crandall/Evans-a, photo-c	6.00	18.00	65.00

THIEVES & KINGS
I Box: 1994 - Present ($2.35, B&W, bi-monthly)

1		2.00	6.00
1-(2nd printing), 2-16			3.00
17-24			2.35

THIMK (Magazine) (Satire)
Counterpoint: May, 1958 - No. 6, May, 1959

1	6.50	19.50	45.00
2-6	5.00	15.00	30.00

THING!, THE (Blue Beetle #18 on)
Song Hits No. 1,2/Capitol Stories/Charlton: Feb, 1952 - No. 17, Nov, 1954

1-Weird/horror stories in all; shrunken head-c	67.00	201.00	570.00
2,3	46.00	139.00	395.00
4-6,8,10: 5-Severed head-c; headlights	41.00	124.00	330.00
7-Injury to eye-c & inside panel	57.00	171.00	485.00
9-Used in **SOTI**, pg. 388 & illo "Stomping on the face is a form of brutality which modern children learn early"	64.00	191.00	540.00
11-Necronomicon story; Hansel & Gretel parody; Injury-to-eye panel; Check-a	51.00	152.00	430.00
12-1st published Ditko-c; "Cinderella" parody; lingerie panels. Ditko-a	68.00	203.00	575.00
13,15-Ditko-c/a(3 & 5)	68.00	203.00	575.00
14-Extreme violence/torture; Rumpelstiltskin story; Ditko-c/a(4)	67.00	199.00	565.00
16-Injury to eye panel	43.00	129.00	345.00
17-Ditko-c; classic parody "Through the Looking Glass"; Powell-r/Beware Terror Tales #1 & recolored	61.00	183.00	530.00

NOTE: *Excessive violence, severed heads, injury to eye are common No. 5 on.* ***Al Fago*** *c-4.* ***Forgione*** *c-1i, 2, 6, 8, 9. All* ***Ditko*** *issues #14, 15.*

THING, THE (See Fantastic Four, Marvel Fanfare, Marvel Feature #11, 12 & Marvel Two-In-One)
Marvel Comics Group: July, 1983 - No. 36, June, 1986

1-Life story of Ben Grimm; Byrne scripts begin			2.25
2-36: 5-Spider-Man, She-Hulk app.			1.30

NOTE: ***Byrne*** *a-2i, 7; c-1, 7, 36i; scripts-1-13, 19-22.* ***Sienkiewicz*** *c-13i.*

THING, THE (From Another World)
Dark Horse Comics: 1991 - No. 2, 1992 ($2.95, mini-series, stiff-c)

1,2-Based on Universal movie; painted-c/a			3.00

THING FROM ANOTHER WORLD: CLIMATE OF FEAR, THE
Dark Horse Comics: July, 1992 - No. 4, Dec, 1992 ($2.50, mini-series)

1-4: Painted-c			2.50

THING FROM ANOTHER WORLD: ETERNAL VOWS
Dark Horse Comics: Dec, 1993 - No. 4, 1994 ($2.50, mini-series)

1-4-Gulacy-c/a			2.50

THIRD WORLD WAR
Fleetway Publ. (Quality): 1990 - No. 6, 1991 ($2.50, thick-c, mature)

1-6			2.50

THIRTEEN (...Going on 18)
Dell Publishing Co.: 11-1/61-62 - No. 25, 12/67; No. 26, 7/69 - No. 29, 1/71

1	5.00	15.00	50.00
2-10	4.00	12.00	40.00
11-29: 26-29-r	3.00	9.00	30.00

NOTE: ***John Stanley*** *script-No. 3-29; art?*

13: ASSASSIN
TSR, Inc.: 1990 - No. 8, 1991 ($2.95, 44 pgs.)

1-8: Agent 13; Alcala-a(i); Springer back-up-a			3.00

THIRTY SECONDS OVER TOKYO (See American Library)

THIS IS SUSPENSE! (Formerly Strange Suspense Stories; Strange Suspense Stories #27 on)
Charlton Comics: No. 23, Feb, 1955 - No. 26, Aug, 1955

23-Wood-a(r)/A Star Presentation #3 "Dr. Jekyll & Mr. Hyde"; last pre-code issue	22.00	66.00	165.00
24-Censored Fawcett-r; Evans-a (r/Suspense Detective #1)	12.00	36.00	85.00
25,26: 26-Marcus Swayze-a	8.35	25.00	50.00

THIS IS THE PAYOFF (See Pay-Off)

THIS IS WAR
Standard Comics: No. 5, July, 1952 - No. 9, May, 1953

5-Toth-a	11.50	34.00	80.00
6,9-Toth-a	10.00	30.00	65.00
7,8: 8-Ross Andru-c	5.00	15.00	30.00

THIS IS YOUR LIFE, DONALD DUCK (See Donald Duck..., Four Color #1109)

THIS MAGAZINE IS CRAZY (Crazy #? on)
Charlton Publ. (Humor Magazines): V3#2, July, 1957 - V4#8, Feb, 1959 (25¢, magazine, 68 pgs.)

This Magazine is Haunted #9 © FAW

Thor #277 © MAR

Thor #342 © MAR

GD25 FN65 NM94

V3#2-V4#7: V4#5-Russian Sputnik-c parody 5.70 17.00 40.00
V4#8-Davis-a (8 pgs.) 7.15 21.50 50.00

THIS MAGAZINE IS HAUNTED (Danger and Adventure #22 on)
Fawcett Publications/Charlton No. 15(2/54) on: Oct, 1951 - No. 14, 12/53; No. 15, 2/54 - V3#21, Nov, 1954

1-Evans-a; Dr. Death as host begins 50.00 150.00 425.00
2,5-Evans-a 39.00 116.00 290.00
3,4: 3-Vampire-c/story 25.00 74.00 185.00
6-9,11,12,14 17.00 52.00 130.00
10-Severed head-c 27.00 82.00 205.00
13-Severed head-c/story 26.00 78.00 195.00
15,20: 15-Dick Giordano-c. 20-Cover is swiped from panel in The Thing #16 15.00 45.00 110.00
16,19-Ditko-c. 19-Injury-to-eye panel; story-r/#1 31.00 93.00 235.00
17-Ditko-c/a(4); blood drainage story 39.00 117.00 290.00
18-Ditko-c/a(1 story); E.C. swipe/Haunt of Fear #5; injury-to-eye panel; reprints "Caretaker of the Dead" from Beware Terror Tales & recolored 33.00 100.00 250.00
21-Ditko-c, Evans-r/This Magazine Is Haunted #1 30.00 90.00 225.00

NOTE: ***Baily*** *a-1, 3, 4, 21r/#1.* ***Moldoff*** *c/a-1-13.* ***Powell*** *a-3-5, 11, 12, 17.* ***Shuster*** *a-18-20. Issues 19-21 have reprints which have been recolored from This Magazine is Haunted #1.*

THIS MAGAZINE IS HAUNTED (2nd Series) (Formerly Zaza the Mystic; Outer Space #17 on)
Charlton Comics: V2#12, July, 1957 - V2#16, May, 1958

V2#12-14-Ditko-c/a in all 33.00 100.00 250.00
15-No Ditko-c/a 5.70 17.00 40.00
16-Ditko-a 21.00 62.00 155.00

THIS MAGAZINE IS WILD (See Wild)

THIS WAS YOUR LIFE (Religious)
Jack T. Chick Publ.: 1964 (3 1/2 x 5 1/2", 40 pgs., B&W and red)

nn 4.00
Another version (5x2 3/4", 26 pgs.) 4.00

THOR (See Avengers #1, Giant-Size..., Marvel Collectors Item Classics, Marvel Graphic Novel #33, Marvel Preview, Marvel Spectacular, Marvel Treasury Edition, Special Marvel Edition & Tales of Asgard)

THOR (Journey Into Mystery #1-125, 503-on)(The Mighty Thor #413-490)
Marvel Comics Group: No. 126, Mar, 1966 - No. 502, Sept, 1996

126-Thor continues (#125-130 Thor vs. Hercules) 12.50 38.00 125.00
127-133,135-140: 127-1st app. Pluto 4.50 13.50 45.00
134-Intro High Evolutionary 5.65 17.00 56.00
141-157,159,160: 146-Inhumans begin (early app.), end #151 (see Fantastic Four #45 for 1st app.). 146,147-Origin The Inhumans. 148,149-Origin Black Bolt in each. 149-Origin Medusa, Crystal, Maximus, Gorgon, Kornak 3.00 9.00 30.00
158-Origin-r/#83; 158,159-Origin Dr. Blake (Thor) 6.25 18.75 62.00
161,167,170-179: 179-Last Kirby issue 2.50 7.50 20.00
162,168,169-Origin Galactus; Kirby-a 3.20 9.60 32.00
163,164-2nd & 3th brief cameo Warlock (Him) 2.50 7.50 20.00
165-1st full app. Warlock (Him) (6/69, see Fantastic Four #67); last 12¢ issue; Kirby-a 5.50 16.50 55.00
166-2nd full app. Warlock (Him); battles Thor 4.20 12.60 42.00
180,181-Neal Adams-a 1.60 4.80 16.00
182-192,194-200 .90 2.70 9.00
193-(25¢, 52 pgs.); Silver Surfer x-over 3.80 11.50 40.00
201-247,249: 225-Intro. Firelord 5.00
248,250-(Regular 25¢ edition)(6,8/76) 5.00
248,250-(30¢-c, limited distribution) 2.00 6.00 20.00
251-280: 271-Iron Man x-over. 274-Death of Balder the Brave 3.25
281-299: 294-Origin Asgard & Odin 2.75
300-(12/80)-End of Asgard; origin of Odin & The Destroyer 2.00 6.00
301-336,338-340: 316-Iron Man x-over. 340-Donald Blake returns as Thor 2.00
337-Simonson-c/a begins, ends #382; Beta Ray Bill becomes new Thor 2.00 6.00
341-373,375-381,383: 341-Clark Kent & Lois Lane cameo. 373-X-Factor tie-in 1.50
374-Mutant Massacre; X-Factor app. 3.00
382-($1.25)-Anniversary issue; last Simonson-a 2.50
384-Intro. new Thor 2.00
385-399,401-410,413-428: 385-Hulk x-over. 391-Spider-Man x-over; 1st Eric Masterson. 395-Intro Earth Force. 408-Eric Masterson becomes Thor. 427, 428-Excalibur x-over 1.25
400-($1.75, 68 pgs.)-Origin Loki 2.50
411-Intro New Warriors (appears in costume in last panel); Juggernaut-c/story 3.00
412-1st full app. New Warriors (Marvel Boy, Kid Nova, Namorita, Night Thrasher, Firestar & Speedball) 4.00
429,430-Ghost Rider x-over 2.00
431,434-443: 434-Capt. America x-over. 437-Thor vs. Quasar; Hercules app.; Tales of Asgard back-up stories begin. 443-Dr. Strange & Silver Surfer x-over; last $1.00-c 1.50
432-($1.50, 52 pgs.)-Thor's 300th app. (vs. Loki); reprints origin & 1st app. from Journey into Mystery #83 3.25
433-Intro new Thor 4.00
444-449,451-473: 448-Spider-Man-c/story. 455,456-Dr. Strange back-up. 457-Old Thor returns (3 pgs.). 459-Intro Thunderstrike. 460-Starlin scripts begin. 465-Super Skrull app. 466-Drax app. 469,470-Infinity Watch x-over. 472-Intro the Godlings 1.50
450-($2.50, 68 pgs.)-Flip-book format; r/story JIM #87 (1st Loki) plus-c plus a gallery of past-c; gatefold-c 3.00
474,476-481,483-499,501,502: 474-Begin $1.50-c; bound-in trading card sheet. 459-Intro Thunderstrike, 460-Starlin scripts begin. 472-Intro the Godlings. 49The Absorbing Man app. 491-Warren Ellis scripts begins, ends #494; Deodato-c/a begins. 492-Reintro The Enchantress; Beta Ray Bill dies. 495-Wm. Messner-Loebs scripts begin; Isherwood-c/a. 501-Reintro Red Norvell. 502-Onslaught tie-in; Red Norvell, Jane Foster & Hela app. 1.50
475 ($2.00, 52 pgs.)-Regular edition 2.00
475 ($2.50, 52 pgs.)-Collectors edition w/foil embossed-c 2.50
482 ($2.95, 84 pgs.)-400th issue 3.00
500 ($2.50)-Double-size; wraparound-c; Deodato-c/a; Dr. Strange app. 5.00
Special 2(9/66)-See Journey Into Mystery for 1st annual 5.00 15.00 50.00
King Size Special 3(1/71) 1.20 3.60 12.00
Special 4(12/71)-r/Thor #131,132 & JIM #113 1.00 3.00 10.00
Annual 5-8: 5(11/76). 6(10/77)-Guardians of the Galaxy app. 7(1978). 8(1979)-Thor vs. Zeus-c/story .85 2.60 7.00
Annual 9-12: 9('81). 10('82). 11('83). 12('84) 3.50
Annual 13-16: 13(1985). 14('89, $2.00, 68 pgs.)-Atlantis Attacks. 15('90, $2.00, 68 pgs.). 16('91, $2.00, 68 pgs.)-3 pg. origin; Guardians of the Galaxy x-over 2.00
Annual 17 (1992, $2.25, 68 pgs.) 2.25
Annual 18 (1993, $2.95, 68 pgs.)-Polybagged w/card 3.00
Annual 19 (1994, $2.95, 68 pgs.) 3.00
...Alone Against the Celestials nn (6/92, $5.95)-r/Thor #387-389 6.00
...: Worldengine (8/96, $9.95)-r/#491-494; Deodato-c/a; story & new intermission by Warren Ellis 10.00

NOTE: ***Neal Adams*** *a-180,181; c-179-181.* ***Austin*** *a-342i, 346i; c-312i.* ***Buscema*** *a(p)-178, 182-213, 215-226, 231-238, 241-253, 254r, 256-259, 272-278, 283-285, 370, Annual 6, 8, 11i; c(p)-175, 182-196, 198-200, 202-204, 206, 211, 212, 215, 219, 221, 226, 256, 259, 261, 262, 272-278, 283, 289, 370, Annual 6.* ***Everett*** *a(i)-143, 170-175; c(i)-171, 172, 174, 176, 241.* ***Gil Kane*** *a-318p; c(p)-201, 205, 207-210, 216, 220, 222, 223, 231, 233-240, 242, 243, 318.* ***Kirby*** *a(p)-126-177, 179, 194r, 254r; c(p)-126-169, 171-174, 176-178, 249-253, 255, 257, 258, Annual 5, Special 1-4.* ***Mooney*** *a(i)-201, 204, 214-216, 218, 322i, 324i, 325i, 327i.* ***Sienkiewicz*** *c-332, 333, 335.* ***Simonson*** *a-260-271p, 337-354, 357-367, 380, Annual 7p; c-260, 263-271, 337-355, 357-369, 371, 373-382, Annual 7.* ***Starlin*** *c-213.*

THOR (Volume 2)

Thor V2 #2 © MAR

3-D-ELL #1 © DELL

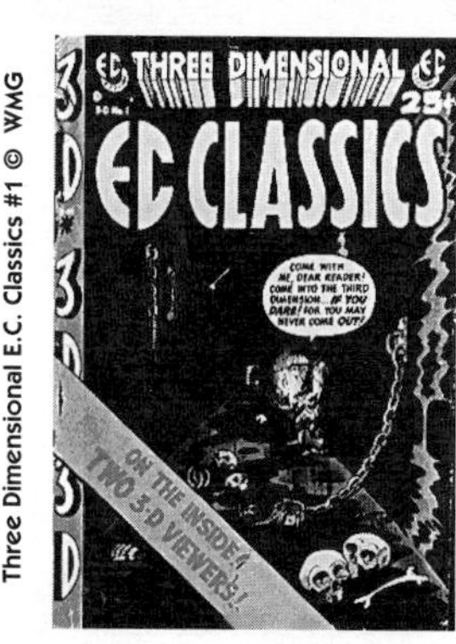

Three Dimensional E.C. Classics #1 © WMG

GD25 FN65 NM94

Marvel Comics: July, 1998 - Present ($2.99/$1.99)

1-($2.99)-Follows Heroes Return; Jurgens-s/Romita Jr. & Janson-a; wraparound-c; battles the Destroyer 5.00
1-Variant-c .90 2.70 8.00
1-Rough Cut-($2.99) Features original script and pencil pages 3.00
2-($1.99) Two covers; Avengers app. 3.00
3-8: 3-Assumes Jake Olson ID. 4-Namor-c/app. 8-Spider-Man-c/app. 1.99

THOR CORPS
Marvel Comics: Sept, 1993 - No. 4, Jan, 1994 ($1.75, limited series)

1-4: 1-Invaders cameo. 2-Invaders app. 3-Spider-Man 2099, Rawhide Kid, Two-Gun Kid & Kid Colt app. 4-Painted-c 1.75

THORION OF THE NEW ASGODS
Marvel Comics (Amalgam): June, 1997 ($1.95, one-shot)

1-Keith Giffen-s/John Romita Jr.-c/a 2.00

THOR: THE LEGEND
Marvel Comics: Sept, 1996 ($3.95, one-shot)

nn-Tribute issue 4.00

THOSE MAGNIFICENT MEN IN THEIR FLYING MACHINES (See Movie Comics)

THRAX
Event Comics: Nov, 1996 ($2.95, one-shot)

1 3.00

THREE CABALLEROS (Walt Disney's...)
Dell Publishing Co.: No. 71, 1945

Four Color 71-by Walt Kelly, c/a 75.00 225.00 825.00

THREE CHIPMUNKS, THE (TV)
Dell Publishing Co.: No. 1042, Oct-Dec, 1959

Four Color 1042 (#1)-(Alvin, Simon & Theodore) 5.00 15.00 55.00

THREE COMICS (Also see Spiritman)
The Penny King Co.: 1944 (10¢, 52 pgs.) (2 different covers exist)

1,3,4-Lady Luck, Mr. Mystic, The Spirit app. (3 Spirit sections bound together); Lou Fine-a 21.00 64.00 160.00
NOTE: *No. 1 contains Spirit Sections 4/9/44 - 4/23/44, and No. 4 is also from 4/44.*

3-D (NOTE: The prices of all the 3-D comics listed include glasses. Deduct 40-50 percent if glasses are missing, and reduce slightly if glasses are loose.)

3-D ACTION
Atlas Comics (ACI): Jan, 1954 (Oversized, 15¢)(2 pairs of glasses included)

1-Battle Brady; Sol Brodsky-c 35.00 106.00 265.00

3-D ADVENTURE COMICS
Stats, Etc.: Aug, 1986 (one shot)

1-Promo material 3.00

3-D ALIEN TERROR
Eclipse Comics: June, 1986 ($2.50)

1-Old Witch, Crypt-Keeper, Vault Keeper cameo; Morrow, John Pound-a, Yeates-c 4.00
...in 2-D: 100 copies signed, numbered(B&W) 2.00 6.00

3-D ANIMAL FUN (See Animal Fun)

3-D BATMAN (Also see Batman 3-D)
National Periodical Publications: 1953 (Reprinted in 1966)

1953-(25¢)-Reprints Batman #42 & 48 (Penguin-c/story); Tommy Tomorrow app.; came with pair of 3-D Bat glasses 100.00 300.00 850.00
1966-Tommy Tomorrow app.; Penguin-c/story(r); has inside-c photos of Batman & Robin from TV show (50¢) 33.00 100.00 250.00

3-D CIRCUS
Fiction House Magazines (Real Adventures Publ.): 1953 (25¢, w/glasses)

1 37.00 110.00 275.00

GD25 FN65 NM94

3-D COMICS (See Mighty Mouse, Tor and Western Fighters)

3-D DOLLY
Harvey Publications: December, 1953 (25¢, came with 2 pairs of glasses)

1-Richie Rich story redrawn from his 1st app. in Little Dot #1; shows cover in 3-D on inside 22.00 66.00 165.00

3-D-ELL
Dell Publishing Co.: No. 1, 1953; No. 3, 1953 (3-D comics) (25¢, came w/glasses)

1-Rootie Kazootie (#2 does not exist) 39.00 116.00 290.00
3-Flukey Luke 35.00 104.00 260.00

3-D EXOTIC BEAUTIES
The 3-D Zone: Nov, 1990 ($2.95, 28 pgs.)

1-L.B. Cole-c 3.00

3-D FEATURES PRESENTS JET PUP
Dimensions Publications: Oct-Dec (Winter on-c), 1953 (25¢, came w/glasses)

1-Irving Spector-a(2) 37.00 110.00 275.00

3-D FUNNY MOVIES
Comic Media: 1953 (25¢, came w/glasses)

1-Bugsey Bear & Paddy Pelican 37.00 110.00 275.00

THREE-DIMENSION ADVENTURES (Superman)
National Periodical Publications: 1953 (25¢, large size, came w/glasses)

nn-Origin Superman (new art) 100.00 300.00 850.00

THREE DIMENSIONAL ALIEN WORLDS (See Alien Worlds)
Pacific Comics: July, 1984 (1st Ray Zone 3-D book)(one-shot)

1-Bolton-a(p); Stevens-a(i); Art Adams 1st published-a(p) 4.00

THREE DIMENSIONAL DNAGENTS (See New DNAgents)

THREE DIMENSIONAL E. C. CLASSICS (Three Dimensional Tales From the Crypt No. 2)
E. C. Comics: Spring, 1954 (Prices include glasses; came with 2 pair)

1-Stories by Wood (Mad #3), Krigstein (W.S. #7), Evans (F.C. #13), & Ingels (CSS #5); Kurtzman-c (rare in high grade due to unstable paper) 77.00 229.00 650.00
NOTE: *Stories redrawn to 3-D format. Original stories not necessarily by artists listed. CSS: Crime SuspenStories; F.C.: Frontline Combat; W.S.: Weird Science.*

THREE DIMENSIONAL TALES FROM THE CRYPT (Formerly Three Dimensional E. C. Classics)(Cover title: ...From the Crypt of Terror)
E. C. Comics: No. 2, Spring, 1954 (Prices include glasses; came with 2 pair)

2-Davis (TFTC #25), Elder (VOH #14), Craig (TFTC #24), & Orlando (TFTC #22) stories; Feldstein-c (rare in high grade due to unstable paper) 79.00 238.00 675.00
NOTE: *Stories redrawn to 3-D format. Original stories not necessarily by artists listed. TFTC: Tales From the Crypt; VOH: Vault of Horror.*

3-D LOVE
Steriographic Publ. (Mikeross Publ.): Dec, 1953 (25¢, came w/glasses)

1 37.00 110.00 275.00

3-D NOODNICK (See Noodnick)

3-D ROMANCE
Steriographic Publ. (Mikeross Publ.): Jan, 1954 (25¢, came w/glasses)

1 37.00 110.00 275.00

3-D SHEENA, JUNGLE QUEEN (Also see Sheena 3-D)
Fiction House Magazines: 1953 (25¢, came w/glasses)

1-Maurice Whitman-c 65.00 194.00 550.00

3-D SUBSTANCE
The 3-D Zone: July, 1990 ($2.95, 28 pgs.)

1-Ditko-c/a(r) 4.00

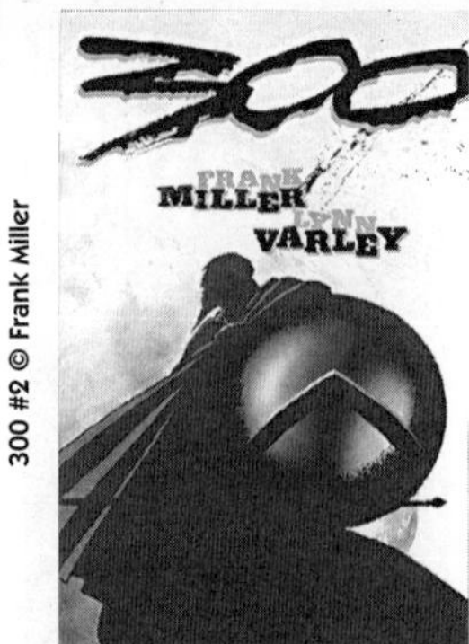

300 #2 © Frank Miller

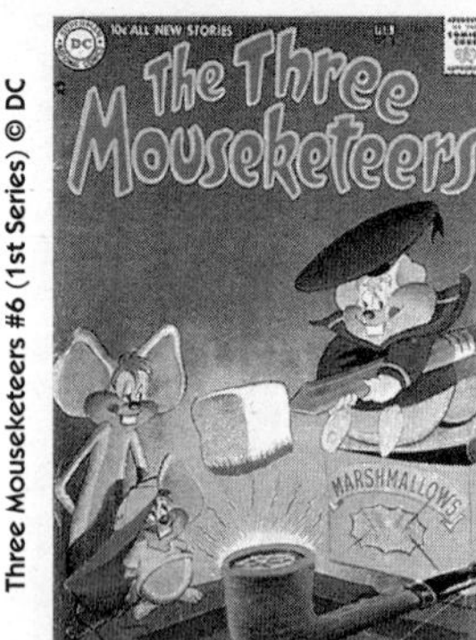

Three Mouseketeers #6 (1st Series) © DC

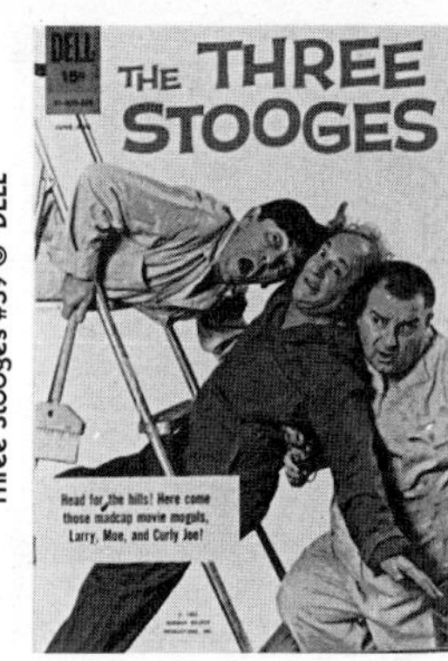

Three Stooges #39 © DELL

GD25 FN65 NM94

3-D TALES OF THE WEST
Atlas Comics (CPS): Jan, 1954 (Oversized) (15¢, came with 2 pair of glasses)

1 (3-D)-Sol Brodsky-c 37.00 112.00 280.00

3-D THREE STOOGES (Also see Three Stooges)
Eclipse Comics: Sept, 1986 - No. 2, Nov, 1986; No. 3, Oct, 1987; No. 4, 1989 ($2.50)

1-3 (10/87)-Maurer-r 4.00
4 (1989, $3.50)-Reprints "Three Missing Links" 4.00
1-3 (2-D) 4.00

3-D WHACK (See Whack)

3-D ZONE, THE
The 3-D Zone (Renegade Press)/Ray Zone: Feb, 1987 - No. 20, 1989 ($2.50)

1-10: 1-r/A Star Presentation, 2-Wolverton-r, 3-Picture Scope Jungle Advs., 4-Electric Fear, 5-Krazy Kat-r, 6-Ratfink, 7-Hollywood 3-D Jayne Mansfield photo-c, 8-High Seas 3-D, 9-Redmask-r, 10-Jet 3-D; Powell & Williamson-r 4.00
11-20: 11-Danse MAcabre; Matt Fox c/a(r). 12-3-D Presidents. 13-Flash Gordon. 14-Tyranostar. 15-3-Dementia Comics; Kurtzman-c, Kubert, Maurer-a. 16-Space Vixens; Dave Stevens-c/a. 17-Thrilling Love. 18-Spacehawk; Wolverton-r. 19-Cracked Classics. 20-Commander Battle and His Atomic Submarine 4.00

NOTE: *Davis r-19. Ditko r-19. Elder r-19. Everett r-19. Feldstein r-17. Frazetta r-17. Heath r-19. Kamen r-17. Severin r-19. Ward r-17,19. Wolverton r-2,18,19. Wood r-1,17. Photo c-12*

300
Dark Horse Comics: May, 1998 - No. 5 ($2.95, limited series)

1-Frank Miller-s/c/a; Spartans vs. Persians war 4.00
1-Second printing 3.00
2-4 3.00
5-($3.95) 4.00

3 LITTLE PIGS (Disney)(...and the Wonderful Magic Lamp)
Dell Publishing Co.: No. 218, Mar, 1949

Four Color 218 (#1) 11.00 33.00 120.00

3 LITTLE PIGS, THE (See Walt Disney Showcase #15 & 21)
Gold Key: May, 1964; No. 2, Sept, 1968 (Walt Disney)

1-Reprints Four Color #218 2.20 6.50 24.00
2 1.40 4.20 14.00

THREE MOUSEKETEERS, THE (1st Series)(See Funny Stuff #1)
National Per. Publ.: 3-4/56 - No. 24, 9-10/59; No. 25, 8-9/60 - No. 26, 10-12/60

1 17.50 52.00 175.00
2 9.00 27.00 90.00
3-10: 6,8-Grey tone-c 7.00 21.00 70.00
11-26: 24-Cover says 11/59, inside says 9-10/59 5.50 16.50 55.00

NOTE: *Rube Grossman a-1-26. Sheldon Mayer a-1-8; c-1-7.*

THREE MOUSEKETEERS, THE (2nd Series) (See Super DC Giant)
National Periodical Publications: May-June, 1970 - No. 7, May-June, 1971 (#5-7: 68 pgs.)

1-Mayer-r in all 3.20 9.50 34.00
2-4 2.00 6.00 20.00
5-7: (68 pgs.). 5-Dodo & the Frog, Bo Bunny & Doodles Duck begin 3.20 9.50 35.00

THREE MUSKETEERS, THE (See Disney's The Three Musketeers)

THREE NURSES (Confidential Diary #12-17; Career Girl Romances #24 on)
Charlton Comics: V3#18, May, 1963 - V3#23, Mar, 1964

V3#18-23 1.75 5.25 14.00

THREE RASCALS
I. W. Enterprises: 1958; 1963

I.W. Reprint #1,2,10: 1-(Says Super Comics on inside)-(M.E.'s Clubhouse Rascals). #2-(1958). 10-(1963)-r/#1 1.00 3.00 8.00

GD25 FN65 NM94

THREE RING COMICS
Spotlight Publishers: March, 1945

1-Funny animal 12.00 36.00 90.00

THREE RING COMICS (Also see Captain Wizard & Meteor Comics)
Century Publications: April, 1946

1-Prankster-c; Captain Wizard, Impossible Man, Race Wilkins, King O'Leary, & Dr. Mercy app. 29.00 88.00 220.00

THREE ROCKETEERS (See Blast-Off)

THREE STOOGES (See Comic Album #18, Top Comics, The Little Stooges, March of Comics #232, 248, 268, 280, 292, 304, 316, 336, 373, Movie Classics & Comics & 3-D Three Stooges)

THREE STOOGES
Jubilee No. 1/St. John No. 1 (9/53) on: Feb, 1949 - No. 2, May, 1949; Sept, 1953 - No. 7, Oct, 1954

1-(Scarce, 1949)-Kubert-a; infinity-c 94.00 282.00 800.00
2-(Scarce)-Kubert, Maurer-a 68.00 203.00 575.00
1(9/53)-Hollywood Stunt Girl by Kubert (7 pgs.) 59.00 177.00 500.00
2(3-D, 10/53, 25¢)-Came w/glasses; Stunt Girl story by Kubert 42.00 127.00 340.00
3(3-D, 10/53, 25¢)-Came w/glasses; has 3-D-c 42.00 127.00 340.00
4(3/54)-7(10/54): 4-1st app. Li'l Stooge? 35.00 104.00 260.00

NOTE: *All issues have **Kubert-Maurer** art & **Maurer** covers. 6, 7-Partial photo-c.*

THREE STOOGES
Dell Publishing Co./Gold Key No. 10 (10/62) on: No. 1043, Oct-Dec, 1959 - No. 55, June, 1972

Four Color 1043 (#1) 18.00 55.00 200.00
Four Color 1078,1127,1170,1187 10.00 30.00 110.00
6(9-11/61) - 10: 6-Professor Putter begins; ends #16 8.00 25.00 90.00
11-14,16,18-20 6.40 19.00 70.00
15-Go Around the World in a Daze (movie scenes) 7.00 22.00 80.00
17-The Little Monsters begin (5/64)(1st app.?) 7.00 22.00 80.00
21,23-30 5.50 16.50 60.00
22-Movie scenes from "The Outlaws Is Coming" 6.40 19.00 70.00
31-55 4.50 13.50 50.00

NOTE: *All Four Colors, 6-50, 52-55 have photo-c.*

THREE STOOGES IN 3-D, THE
Eternity Comics: 1991 ($3.95, high quality paper, w/glasses)

1-Reprints Three Stooges by Gold Key; photo-c 4.00

3 WORLDS OF GULLIVER
Dell Publishing Co.: No. 1158, July, 1961 (2 issues exist with diff. covers)

Four Color 1158-Movie, photo-c 5.50 16.50 65.00

THRILL COMICS (See Flash Comics, Fawcett)

THRILLER
DC Comics: Nov, 1983 - No. 12, Nov, 1984 ($1.25, Baxter paper)

1-9,11,12: 1-Intro Seven Seconds; Von Eeden-c/a begins. 2-Origin. 5,6-Elvis satire. 1.30
10-($2.00) 2.00

THRILLING ADVENTURES IN STAMPS COMICS (Formerly Stamp Comics)
Stamp Comics, Inc. (Very Rare): V1#8, Jan, 1953 (25¢, 100 pgs.)

V1#8-Harrison, Wildey, Kiefer, Napoli-a 65.00 194.00 550.00

THRILLING ADVENTURE STORIES (See Tigerman)
Atlas/Seaboard Publ.: Feb, 1975 - No. 2, Aug, 1975 (B&W, 68 pgs.)

1-Tigerman, Kromag the Killer begin; Heath, Thorne-a. 1.00 3.00 10.00
2-Heath, Toth, Severin, Simonson-a; Adams-c 1.60 4.80 16.00

THRILLING COMICS
Better Publ./Nedor/Standard Comics: Feb, 1940 - No. 80, April, 1951

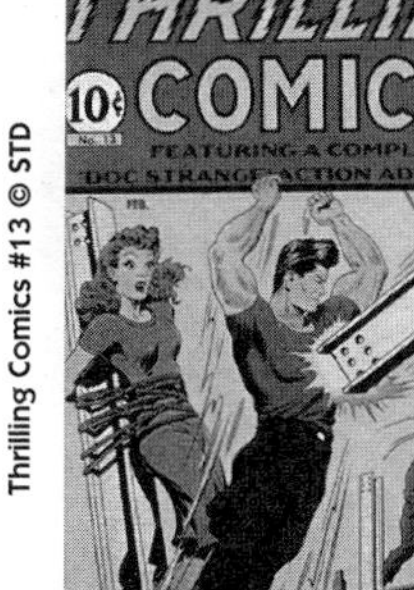

Thrilling Comics #13 © STD

Thrillkiller '62 © DC

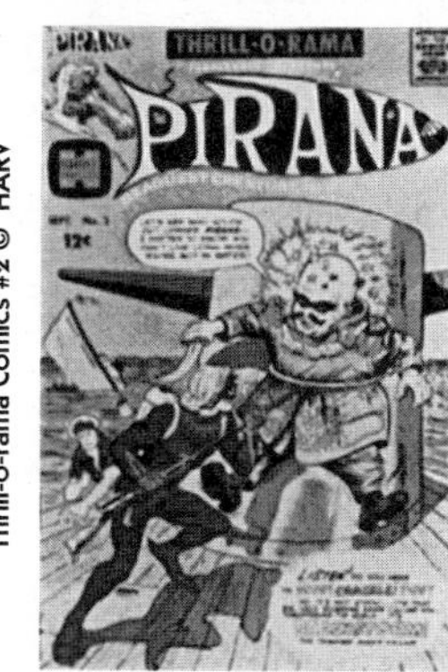

Thrill-o-rama Comics #2 © HARV

GD25 FN65 NM94

1-Origin & 1st app. Dr. Strange (37 pgs.), ends #?; Nickie Norton of the Secret Service begins 235.00 706.00 2000.00
2-The Rio Kid, The Woman in Red, Pinocchio begins 112.00 335.00 950.00
3-The Ghost & Lone Eagle begin 71.00 212.00 600.00
4-10: 5-Dr. Strange changed to Doc Strange 54.00 162.00 460.00
11-18,20 45.00 134.00 380.00
19-Origin & 1st app. The American Crusader (8/41), ends #39,41 54.00 162.00 460.00
21-30: 24-Intro. Mike, Doc Strange's sidekick (1/42). 27-Robot-c. 29-Last Rio Kid 40.00 120.00 315.00
31-40: 36-Commando Cubs begin (7/43, 1st app.) 33.00 100.00 250.00
41-Hitler & Mussolini-c 35.00 106.00 265.00
42,43,45-52: 52-The Ghost ends. 45-Hitler pict. on-c 26.00 78.00 195.00
44-Hitler-c 39.00 117.00 300.00
53-The Phantom Detective begins; The Cavalier app.; no Commando Cubs 24.00 72.00 180.00
54-The Cavalier app.; no Commando Cubs 24.00 72.00 180.00
55-Lone Eagle ends 24.00 72.00 180.00
56-Princess Pantha begins (10/46, 1st app.) 40.00 120.00 315.00
57-66: 61-Ingels-a; The Lone Eagle app. 65-Last Phantom Detective & Commando Cubs. 66-Frazetta text illo 33.00 100.00 250.00
67,70-73: Frazetta-a(5-7 pgs.) in each. 72-Sea Eagle app.; Buck Ranger, Cowboy Detective begins 40.00 120.00 315.00
68,69-Frazetta-a(2), 8 & 6 pgs.; 9 & 7 pgs. 42.00 127.00 340.00
74-Last Princess Pantha; Tara app. 25.00 76.00 190.00
75-78: 75-All western format begins 12.00 36.00 90.00
79-Krigstein-a 13.00 38.00 95.00
80-Severin & Elder, Celardo, Moreira-a 13.00 38.00 95.00

NOTE: *Bondage c-5, 9, 13, 20, 22, 27-30, 38, 41, 52, 54, 70.* ***Kinstler*** *a-45.* ***Leo Morey*** *a-7.* ***Schomburg (Xela)*** *c-7, 9-19, 36-80 (airbrush 62-71).* ***Tuska*** *a-62, 63. Woman in Red not in #19, 23, 31-33, 39-45. No. 45 exists as a Canadian reprint but numbered #48. No. 72 exists as a Canadian reprint with no* ***Frazetta*** *story.American Crusader c-20-24. Buck Ranger c-72-80. Commando Cubs c-37, 39, 41, 43, 45, 47, 49, 51. Doc Strange c-1-19, 25-36, 38, 40, 42, 44, 46, 48, 50, 52-57, 59. Princess Pantha c-58, 60-71.*

THRILLING CRIME CASES (Formerly 4Most; becomes Shocking Mystery Cases #50 on)
Star Publications: No. 41, June-July, 1950 - No. 49, July, 1952

41 23.00 68.00 170.00
42-45: 42-L. B. Cole-c/a (1); Chameleon story (Fox-r) 20.00 60.00 150.00
46-48: 47-Used in **POP**, pg. 84 19.00 56.00 140.00
49-(7/52)-Classic L. B. Cole-c 37.00 110.00 275.00

NOTE: ***L. B. Cole*** *c-all; a-43p, 45p, 46p, 49(2 pgs.).* ***Disbrow*** *a-48.* ***Hollingsworth*** *a-48.*

THRILLING ROMANCES
Standard Comics: No. 5, Dec, 1949 - No. 26, June, 1954

5 9.30 28.00 70.00
6,8 5.35 16.00 32.00
7-Severin/Elder-a (7 pgs.) 7.50 22.50 52.00
9,10-Severin/Elder-a; photo-c 6.00 18.00 42.00
11,14-21,26: 12-Tyrone Power/ Susan Hayward photo-c.14-Gene Tierney & Danny Kaye photo-c from movie "On the Riviera". 15-Tony Martin/Janet Leigh photo-c 4.25 13.00 26.00
12-Wood-a (2 pgs.) 8.50 26.00 60.00
13-Severin-a 5.70 17.00 35.00
22-25-Toth-a 6.50 19.50 45.00

NOTE: *All photo-c.* ***Celardo*** *a-9, 16.* ***Colletta*** *a-23, 24(2).* ***Toth*** *text illos-19.* ***Tuska*** *a-9.*

THRILLING SCIENCE TALES
AC Comics: 1989 - No. 2 ($3.50, 2/3 color, 52 pgs.)

1-r/Bob Colt #6(saucer); Frazetta, Guardineer (Space Ace), Wood, Krenkel, Orlando, WIlliamson-r; Kaluta-c 3.50
2-Capt. Video-r by Evans, Capt. Science-r by Wood, Star Pirate-r by Whitman & Mysta of the Moon-r by Moreira 3.50

GD25 FN65 NM94

THRILLING TRUE STORY OF THE BASEBALL...
Fawcett Publications: 1952 (Photo-c, each)

...Giants-photo-c; has Willie Mays rookie photo-biography; Willie Mays, Eddie Stanky & others photos on-c 59.00 177.00 500.00
...Yankees-photo-c; Yogi Berra, Joe DiMaggio, Mickey Mantle & others photos on-c 54.00 162.00 460.00

THRILLING WONDER TALES
AC Comics : 1991 ($2.95, B&W)

1-Includes a Bob Powell Thun'da story 3.00

THRILLKILLER
DC Comics : Jan, 1997 - No. 3, Mar, 1997($2.50, limited series)

1-3-Elseworlds Robin & Batgirl; Chaykin-s/Brereton-c/a 3.00
...'62 ('98, $4.95, one-shot) Sequel; Chaykin-s/Brereton-c/a 5.00
TPB-(See Batman: Thrillkiller)

THRILLOGY
Pacific Comics: Jan, 1984 (One-shot, color)

1-Conrad-c/a 1.00

THRILL-O-RAMA
Harvey Publications (Fun Films): Oct, 1965 - No. 3, Dec, 1966

1-Fate (Man in Black) by Powell app.; Doug Wildey-a(2); Simon-c 3.50 10.50 35.00
2-Pirana begins (see Phantom #46); Williamson 2 pgs.; Fate (Man in Black) app.; Tuska/Simon-c 2.50 7.50 24.00
3-Fate (Man in Black) app.; Sparling-c 2.25 6.75 18.00

THRILLS OF TOMORROW (Formerly Tomb of Terror)
Harvey Publications: No. 17, Oct, 1954 - No. 20, April, 1955

17-Powell-a (horror); r/Witches Tales #7 10.00 30.00 75.00
18-Powell-a (horror); r/Tomb of Terror #1 8.50 26.00 60.00
19,20-Stuntman-c/stories by S&K (r/from Stuntman #1 & 2); 19 has origin & is last pre-code (2/55) 26.00 78.00 195.00

NOTE: ***Kirby*** *c-19, 20.* ***Palais*** *a-17.* ***Simon*** *c-18?*

THROBBING LOVE (See Fox Giants)

THROUGH GATES OF SPLENDOR
Spire Christian Comics (Flemming H. Revell Co.): 1973, 1974 (36 pages) (39-49 cents)

nn 4.00

THUMPER (Disney)
Dell Publishing Co.: No, 19, 1942 - No. 243, Sept, 1949

Four Color 19-Walt Disney's...Meets the Seven Dwarfs; reprinted in Silly Symphonies 51.00 153.00 560.00
Four Color 243-...Follows His Nose 9.00 27.00 100.00

THUMPER (Disney)
Grosset & Dunlap: 1942 (50 cents, 32pgs., hardcover book, 7"x8-1/2" w/dust jacket)

nn-Given away (along with a copy of Bambi) for a $2.00, 2-year subscription to WDC&S in 1942. (Xmas offer). Book only 15.00 44.00 110.00
Dust jacket only 7.85 23.50 55.00

THUN'DA (...King of the Congo)
Magazine Enterprises: 1952 - No. 6, 1953

1(A-1 #47)-Origin; Frazetta c/a; only comic done entirely by Frazetta; all Thun'da stories, no Cave Girl 94.00 282.00 800.00
2(A-1 #56)-Powell-c/a begins, ends #6; Intro/1st app. Cave Girl in filler strip (also app. in 3-6) 17.00 52.00 130.00
3(A-1 #73), 4(A-1 #78) 12.00 36.00 90.00
5(A-1 #83), 6(A-1 #86) 11.00 32.00 80.00

THUN'DA TALES (See Frank Frazetta's...)

THUNDER AGENTS (See Dynamo, Noman & Tales Of Thunder)

Thunderbolts #12 © MAR

Thunderstrike #5 © MAR

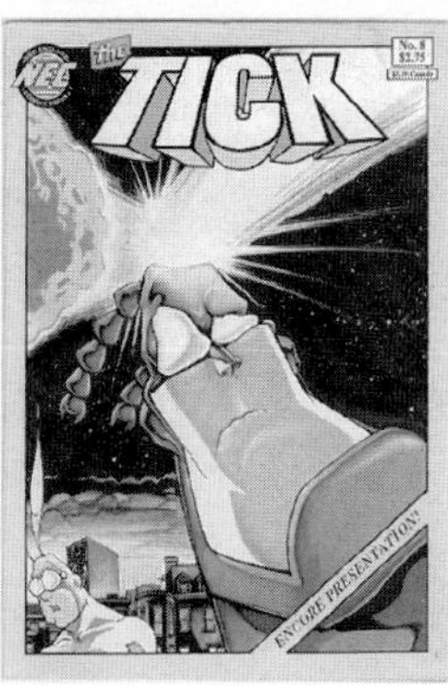

The Tick #8 (2nd prinitng) © Ben Edlund

GD25 FN65 NM94

Tower Comics: 11/65 - No. 17, 12/67; No. 18, 9/68, No. 19, 11/68, No. 20, 11/69 (No. 1-16: 68 pgs.; No. 17 on: 52 pgs.)(All are 25¢)

1-Origin & 1st app. Dynamo, Noman, Menthor, & The Thunder Squad; 1st app. The Iron Maiden 14.00 42.00 140.00
2-Death of Egghead; A-bomb blast panel 8.00 24.00 80.00
3-5: 4-Guy Gilbert becomes Lightning who joins Thunder Squad; Iron Maiden app. 5.00 15.00 50.00
6-10: 7-Death of Menthor. 8-Origin & 1st app. The Raven 3.80 11.40 38.00
11-15: 13-Undersea Agent app.; no Raven story 2.60 7.80 26.00
16-19 2.80 8.40 28.00
20-Special Collectors Edition; all reprints 2.00 6.00 16.00

NOTE: ***Crandall** a-1, 4p, 5p, 18, 20r; c-18. **Ditko** a-6, 7p, 12p, 13?, 14p, 16, 18. **Giunta** a-6. **Kane** a-1, 5p, 6p?, 14, 16p; c-14, 15. **Reinman** a-13. **Sekowsky** a-6. **Tuska** a-1p, 7, 8, 10, 13-17, 19. **Whitney** a-9p, 10, 13, 15, 17, 18; c-17. **Wood** a-1-11, 15(w/**Ditko**-12, 18), (inks-#9, 13, 14, 16, 17), 19i, 20r; c-1-8, 9i, 10-13(#10 w/**Williamson**(p)), 16.*

T.H.U.N.D.E.R. AGENTS (See Blue Ribbon Comics, Hall of Fame Featuring the…, JCP Features & Wally Wood's…)
JC Comics (Archie Publications): May, 1983 - No. 2, Jan, 1984

1,2: 1-New Manna/Blyberg-c/a. 2-Wood-r; new Kane/Tuska-a; Ditko-c 3.00

THUNDER BIRDS (See Cinema Comics Herald)

THUNDERBOLT (See The Atomic…)

THUNDERBOLT (Peter Cannon…; see Crisis on Infinite Earths & Peter…)
Charlton Comics: Jan, 1966; No. 51, Mar-Apr, 1966 - No. 60, Nov, 1967

1-Origin & 1st app. Thunderbolt 2.50 7.50 22.00
51-(Formerly Son of Vulcan #50) 2.00 6.00 16.00
52-59: 54-Sentinels begin. 59-Last Thunderbolt & Sentinels (back-up story) 1.40 4.15 11.00
60-Prankster app. 1.60 4.85 13.00
57,58 ('77)-Modern Comics-r 4.00

NOTE: ***Aparo** a-60. **Morisi** a-1, 51-56, 58; c-1, 51-56, 58, 59.*

THUNDERBOLTS (Also see Incredible Hulk #449)
Marvel Comics: Apr, 1997 - Present ($1.95/$1.99)

1-($2.99)-Busiek-s/Bagley-c/a .90 2.70 8.00
1-2nd printing; new cover colors 2.50
2-4: 2-Two covers. 4-Intro. Jolt 5.00
5-11: 5-Begin $1.99-c. 9-Avengers app. 3.00
12-($2.99)-Avengers and Fantastic Four-c/app. 3.00
13-22: 14-Thunderbolts return to Earth. 21-Hawkeye app. 1.99
Annual '97 ($2.99)-Wraparound-c 3.00
First Strikes (1997, $4.99,TPB) r/#1,2 5.00
…: Marvel's Most Wanted TPB ('98, $16.99) r/origin stories of original Masters of Evil 16.99

THUNDERBOLTS: DISTANT RUMBLINGS
Marvel Comics: July, 1997 ($1.95, one-shot)

minus 1-Flashback; Busiek-s 4.00

THUNDERBUNNY (Also see Blue Ribbon Comics #13,Charlton Bullseye & Pep Comics #393)
Red Circle Comics: Jan, 1984 (Direct sale only)

1-Origin 3.00

THUNDERCATS (TV)
Marvel Comics (Star Comics)/Marvel #22 on: Dec, 1985 - No. 24, June, 1988 (75¢)

1-Mooney-c/a begins 4.00
2-24: 2-(65¢ & 75¢ cover exists). 12-Begin $1.00-c. 18-20-Williamson-i. 23-Williamson-c(i) 3.00

THUNDERGOD
Crusade Entertainment: July, 1996 - No. 3 ($2.95, B&W)

1-3: Christopher Golden scripts; painted-c 3.00

GD25 FN65 NM94

THUNDERGOD
Caliber Comics: 1997 ($2.95, B&W, one-shot)

1 3.00

THUNDER MOUNTAIN (See Zane Grey, Four Color #246)

THUNDERSTRIKE (See Thor #459)
Marvel Comics: June, 1993 - No. 24, July, 1995 ($1.25)

1-($2.95, 52 pgs.)-Holo-grafx lightning patterned foil-c; Bloodaxe returns 3.00
2-7: 2-Juggernaut-c/s. 4-Capt. America app. 4-6-Spider-Man app. 1.25
8-24: 8-Begin $1.50-c; bound-in trading card sheet. 18-Bloodaxe app. 24-Death of Thunderstrike. 1.50
Marvel Double Feature…Thunderstrike/Code Blue #13 ($2.50)-Same as Thunderstrike #13 w/Code Blue flip book 2.50

TICK, THE (Also see The Chroma-Tick)
New England Comics Press: Jun, 1988 - No. 12, May, 1993 ($1.75/$1.95/$2.25; B&W, over-sized)

Special Edition 1-1st comic book app. serially numbered & limited to 5,000 copies 3.80 11.50 40.00
Special Edition 1-(5/96, $5.95)-Double-c; foil-c; serially numbered (5,001 thru 14,000) & limited to 9,000 copies 2.00 6.00
Special Edition 2-Serially numbered and limited to 3000 copies 3.80 11.50 40.00
Special Edition 2-(8/96, $5.95)-Double-c; foil-c; serially numbered (5,001 thru 14,000) & limited to 9,000 copies 2.00 6.00
1-Reprints Special Ed. 1 w/minor changes 2.70 8.00 30.00
1-2nd printing 5.00
1-3rd printing ($1.95, 6/89) 3.00
1-4th printing ($2.25) 2.50
1-5th printing ($2.75) 3.00
2-Reprints Special Ed. 2 w/minor changes 2.00 6.00 20.00
2-2nd printing ($1.95) 5.00
2-3rd & 4th printings ($2.25) 2.50
2-5th printing ($2.75) 3.00
3-5 ($1.95): 4-1st app. Paul the Samurai 5.00
3-2nd & 3rd printings ($2.25) 2.50
3-4th printing ($2.75) 3.00
4-2nd printing ($2.25) 2.50
4-3rd - 5th printings ($2.75) 3.00
6-8 ($2.25): 7-1st app. Man-Eating Cow. 4.00
5-8-2nd printings ($2.75) 3.00
6-3rd printing ($2.75) 3.00
8-Variant with no logo, price, issue number or company logos. 1.50 4.50 15.00
9-12 ($2.75) 3.00
12-Special Edition; card-stock, virgin foil-c; numbered edition 2.00 6.00 20.00
Promo Sampler-(1990)-Tick-c/story 1.00 3.00 10.00

TICK BIG BACK TO SCHOOL SPECIAL, THE
New England Comics: Oct, 1998 ($3.50, B&W)

1-Tick and Arthur undercover in high school 3.50

TICK BIG BLUE DESTINY, THE
New England Comics: Oct, 1997 - Present ($2.95)

1-4: 1-"Keen" Ed. 2-Two covers 3.00
1-($4.95) "Wicked Keen" Ed. w/die cut-c 5.00
5-($3.50) 3.50
6-Luny Bin Trilogy Preview #0 (7/98, $1.50) 1.50
7,8: 7-Luny Bin Trilogy begins 3.50

TICK BIG BLUE YULE LOG SPECIAL, THE
New England Comics: Dec, 1997 ($2.95, B&W)

1-"Jolly" and "Traditional" covers; flip book w/"Arthur Teaches the Tick

The Tick Karma Tornado #5 © Ben Edlund

Timber Wolf #5 © DC

Timeslip Collection #1 © MAR

GD25 FN65 NM94

About Hanukkah" 2.95
...1999 ($3.50) 3.50

TICK BIG SUMMER FUN SPECIAL, THE
New England Comics: Aug, 1998 ($3.50, B&W, one-shot)
1-Tick and Arthur at summer camp 3.50

TICK'S BACK, THE
New England Comics: Aug, 1997 ($2.95, B&W, one-shot)
0 3.00

TICK'S BIG ROMANTIC ADVENTURE, THE
New England Comics: Feb, 1998 ($2.95, B&W, one-shot)
1-Candy box cover with candy map on back 3.00

TICK'S GIANT CIRCUS OF THE MIGHTY, THE
New England Comics: Summer, 1992 - No. 3, Fall, 1993 ($2.75, B&W, magazine size)
1-(A-O). 2-(P-Z). 3-1993 Update 3.50

TICK KARMA TORNADO (The...)
New England Comics Press: Oct, 1993 - No. 9, Mar, 1995 ($2.75, B&W)
1-($3.25) 3.50
2-9: 2-$2.75-c begins 3.00

TICKLE COMICS (Also see Gay, Smile, & Whee Comics)
Modern Store Publ.: 1955 (7¢, 5x7-1/4", 52 pgs)
1 1.20 3.00 6.00

TICK TOCK TALES
Magazine Enterprises: Jan, 1946 - V3#33, Jan-Feb, 1951
1-Koko & Kola begin 11.00 32.00 80.00
2 5.70 17.00 40.00
3-10 5.35 16.00 32.00
11-33: 19-Flag-c. 23-Muggsy Mouse, The Pixies & Tom-Tom the Jungle Boy app. 25-The Pixies & Tom-Tom app. 4.15 12.50 25.00

TIGER (Also see Comics Reading Libraries)
Charlton Press (King Features): Mar, 1970 - No. 6, Jan, 1971 (15¢)
1 1.40 4.20 14.00
2-6 .90 2.70 8.00

TIGER BOY (See Unearthly Spectaculars)

TIGER GIRL
Gold Key: Sept, 1968 (15¢)
1(10227-809)-Sparling-c/a; Jerry Siegel scripts 2.50 7.60 28.00

TIGERMAN (Also see Thrilling Adventure Stories)
Seaboard Periodicals (Atlas): Apr, 1975 - No. 3, Sept, 1975 (All 25¢ issues)
1-3: 2,3-Ditko-p in each 3.00

TIGER WALKS, A (See Movie Comics)

TIGRESS, THE
Hero Graphics: Aug, 1992 - No. 6?, July, 1993 ($3.95/$2.95/$3.95, B&W)
1-Tigress vs. Flare 3.50
2-5: 2-$2.95-c begins 3.00
6-(6/93, $3.95, 44 pgs.) 4.00

TILLIE THE TOILER (See Comic Monthly)
Dell Publishing Co.: No. 15, 1941 - No. 237, July, 1949
Four Color 15(1941) 32.00 95.00 360.00
Large Feature Comic 30(1941) 21.00 63.00 230.00
Four Color 8(1942) 21.00 63.00 230.00
Four Color 22(1943) 16.00 49.00 180.00
Four Color 55(1944), 89(1945) 12.00 37.00 135.00
Four Color 106('45),132('46): 132-New stories begin 9.00 27.00 100.00
Four Color 150,176,184 8.00 25.00 90.00
Four Color 195,213,237 5.50 16.50 60.00

GD25 FN65 NM94

TILLY AND TED-TINKERTOTLAND
W. T. Grant Co.: 1945 (Giveaway, 20 pgs.)
nn-Christmas comic 5.70 17.00 38.00

TIM (Formerly Superman-Tim; becomes Gene Autry-Tim)
Tim Stores: June, 1950 - Oct, 1950 (B&W, half-size)
4 issues; 6/50, 9/50, 10/50 known 6.00 18.00 42.00

TIMBER WOLF (See Action Comics #372, & Legion of Super-Heroes)
DC Comics: Nov, 1992 - No. 5, Mar, 1993 ($1.25, limited series)
1-5 1.25

TIME BANDITS
Marvel Comics Group: Feb, 1982 (one-shot)
1-Movie adaptation 2.00

TIME BEAVERS (See First Comics Graphic Novel #2)

TIME BREAKERS
DC Comics (Helix): Jan, 1997 - No. 5, May, 1997 ($2.25, limited series)
1-5-Pollack-s 2.25

TIMECOP (Movie)
Dark Horse Comics: Sept, 1994 - No. 2, Nov, 1994 ($2.50, limited series)
1,2-Adaptation of film 2.50

TIME FOR LOVE (Formerly Romantic Secrets)
Charlton Comics: V2#53, Oct, 1966; Oct, 1967 - No. 47, May, 1976
V2#53(10/66) 1.25 3.75 10.00
1(10/67) 2.50 7.50 25.00
2(12/67)-10 1.85 5.50 15.00
11-20 1.50 4.50 12.00
21-29 .90 2.70 8.00
30-(10/72)-Full-length portrait of David Cassidy 1.40 4.20 14.00
31-47 .85 2.60 7.00

TIMELESS TOPIX (See Topix)

TIME MACHINE, THE
Dell Publishing Co.: No. 1085, Mar, 1960 (H.G. Wells)
Four Color 1085-Movie, Alex Toth-a; Rod Taylor photo-c 14.00 44.00 160.00

TIME MASTERS
DC Comics: Feb, 1990 - No. 8, Sept, 1990 ($1.75, mini-series)
1-8: New Rip Hunter series. 5-Cave Carson, Viking Prince app. 6-Dr. Fate app. 1.80

TIMESLIP COLLECTION
Marvel Comics: Nov, 1998 ($2.99, one-shot)
1-Pin-ups reprinted from Marvel Vision magazine 3.00

TIMESLIP SPECIAL (The Coming of the Avengers)
Marvel Comics: Oct, 1998 ($5.99, one-shot)
1-Alternate world Avengers vs. Odin 2.00 6.00

TIMESPIRITS
Marvel Comics (Epic Comics): Oct, 1984 - No. 8, Mar, 1986 ($1.50, Baxter paper, direct sales)
1-8: 4-Williamson-a 1.50

TIME TUNNEL, THE (TV)
Gold Key: Feb, 1967 - No. 2, July, 1967 (12¢)
1,2-Photo back-c 4.00 12.25 45.00

TIME TWISTERS
Quality Comics: Sept, 1987 - No. 21, 1989 ($1.25/$1.50)
1-10: Alan Moore scripts in 1-4, 6-9, 14 (2 pg.) 1.25
11-21 ($1.50): 14-Bolland-a (2 pg.). 15,16 Guice-c 1.50

VALIANT PRESENTS
TIMEWALKER
TIME FOR A NEW KIND OF HERO!

Timewalker #1 © VAL

Tim Holt #4 © ME

Tiny Tim Four Color #235 © News Synd.

GD25 FN65 NM94

TIME 2: THE EPIPHANY (See First Comics Graphic Novel #9)

TIMEWALKER (Also see Archer & Armstrong)
Valiant: Jan, 1994 - No. 15, Oct, 1995 ($2.50)

	GD25	FN65	NM94
1-15: 2-"JAN" on-c, February, 1995 in indicia.			2.50
0-(3/96)			2.50
Yearbook 1 (5/95, $2.95)			3.00

TIME WARP (See The Unexpected #210)
DC Comics, Inc.: Oct-Nov, 1979 - No. 5, June-July, 1980 ($1.00, 68 pgs.)

	GD25	FN65	NM94
1-5		2.00	6.00

NOTE: ***Aparo** a-1. **Buckler** a-1p. **Chaykin** a-2. **Ditko** a-1-4. **Kaluta** c-1-5. **G. Kane** a-2. **Nasser** a-4. **Newton** a-1-5p. **Orlando** a-2. **Sutton** a-1-3.*

TIME WARRIORS THE BEGINNING
Fantasy General Comics: 1986 (Aug) - No. 2, 1986? ($1.50)

	GD25	FN65	NM94
1,2-Alpha Track/Skellon Empire			1.50

TIM HOLT (Movie star) (Becomes Red Mask #42 on; also see Crack Western #72, & Great Western)
Magazine Enterprises: 1948 - No. 41, April-May, 1954 (All 36 pgs.)

	GD25	FN65	NM94
1-(A-1 #14)-Line drawn-c w/Tim Holt photo on-c; Tim Holt, His horse Lightning & sidekick Chito begin	56.00	168.00	475.00
2-(A-1 #17)(9-10/48)-Photo-c begin, end #18	32.00	96.00	240.00
3-(A-1 #19)-Photo back-c	24.00	72.00	180.00
4(1-2/49),5: 5-Photo front/back-c	18.00	54.00	135.00
6-(5/49)-1st app. The Calico Kid (alias Rex Fury), his horse Ebony & Sidekick Sing-Song (begin series); photo back-c	31.00	92.00	230.00
7-10: 7-Calico Kid by Ayers. 8-Calico Kid by Guardineer (r-in/Great Western #10). 9-Map of Tim's Home Range	15.00	44.00	110.00
11-The Calico Kid becomes The Ghost Rider (origin & 1st app.) by Dick Ayers (r-in/Great Western I.W. #8); his horse Spectre & sidekick Sing-Song begin series	39.00	117.00	310.00
12-16,18-Last photo-c	11.00	34.00	85.00
17-Frazetta Ghost Rider-c	31.00	94.00	235.00
19,22,24: 19-Last Tim Holt-c; Bolle line-drawn-c begin; Tim Holt photo on covers #19-28,30-41. 22-interior photo-c	9.30	28.00	70.00
20-Tim Holt becomes Redmask (origin); begin series; Redmask-c #20-on	15.00	44.00	110.00
21-Frazetta Ghost Rider/Redmask-c	28.00	84.00	210.00
23-Frazetta Redmask-c	24.00	72.00	180.00
25-1st app. Black Phantom	18.00	54.00	135.00
26-30: 28-Wild Bill Hickok, Bat Masterson team up with Redmask. 29-B&W photo-c	8.50	26.00	60.00
31-33-Ghost Rider ends	7.85	23.50	55.00
34-Tales of the Ghost Rider begins (horror)-Classic "The Flower Women" & "Hard Boiled Harry!"	10.00	30.00	75.00
35-Last Tales of the Ghost Rider	8.50	26.00	60.00
36-The Ghost Rider returns, ends #41; liquid hallucinogenic drug story	9.30	28.00	70.00
37-Ghost Rider classic "To Touch Is to Die!", about Inca treasure	9.30	28.00	70.00
38-The Black Phantom begins (not in #39); classic Ghost Rider "The Phantom Guns of Feather Gap!"	9.30	28.00	70.00
39-41: All 3-D effect c/stories	13.00	38.00	95.00

NOTE: ***Dick Ayers** a-7, 9-41. **Bolle** a-1-41; c-19, 20, 22, 24-28, 30-41.*

TIM IN SPACE (Formerly Gene Autry Tim; becomes Tim Tomorrow)
Tim Stores: 1950 (1/2 size giveaway) (B&W)

	GD25	FN65	NM94
nn	4.00	11.00	22.00

TIM McCOY (Formerly Zoo Funnies; Pictorial Love Stories #22 on)
Charlton Comics: No. 16, Oct, 1948 - No. 21, Aug, 1949 (Western Movie Stories)

	GD25	FN65	NM94
16-John Wayne, Montgomery Clift app. in "Red River"; photo back-c	40.00	120.00	320.00
17-21: 17-Allan "Rocky" Lane guest stars. 18-Rod Cameron guest stars. 19-Whip Wilson, Andy Clyde guest star; Jesse James story. 20-Jimmy Wakely guest stars. 21-Johnny Mack Brown guest stars	37.00	112.00	280.00

TIM McCOY, POLICE CAR 17
Whitman Publishing Co.: No. 674, 1934 (32 pgs.) (11x14-3/4") (B&W) (Like Feature Books)

	GD25	FN65	NM94
674-1933 movie ill.; first Whitman comic book; 1st movie adaption in comic books	27.00	80.00	200.00

TIMMY
Dell Publishing Co.: No. 715, Aug, 1956 - No. 1022, Aug-Oct, 1959

	GD25	FN65	NM94
Four Color 715 (#1)	2.75	8.00	30.00
Four Color 823 (8/57), 923 (8/58), 1022	1.80	5.50	20.00

TIMMY THE TIMID GHOST (Formerly Win-A-Prize?; see Blue Bird)
Charlton Comics: No. 3, 2/56 - No. 44, 10/64; No. 45, 9/66; 10/67 - No. 23, 7/71; V4#24, 9/85 - No. 26, 1/86

	GD25	FN65	NM94
3(1956) (1st Series)	7.15	21.50	50.00
4,5	4.15	12.50	25.00
6-10	2.00	6.00	16.00
11,12(4/58,10/58)(100 pgs.)	5.00	15.00	50.00
13-20	1.75	5.25	14.00
21-45(1966)	1.25	3.75	10.00
1(10/67, 2nd series)	1.75	5.25	14.00
2-10	1.10	3.30	9.00
11-23	.85	2.60	7.00
24-26 (1985-86): Fago-r			3.00

TIM TOMORROW (Formerly Tim In Space)
Tim Stores: 8/51, 9/51, 10/51, Christmas, 1951 (5x7-3/4")

	GD25	FN65	NM94
nn-Prof. Fumble & Captain Kit Comet in all	4.25	13.00	26.00

TIM TYLER (See Harvey Comics Hits #54)

TIM TYLER (Also see Comics Reading Libraries)
Better Publications: 1942

	GD25	FN65	NM94
1	11.00	32.00	80.00

TIM TYLER COWBOY
Standard Comics (King Features Synd.): No. 11, Nov, 1948 - No. 18, 1950

	GD25	FN65	NM94
11-By Lyman Young	7.15	21.50	50.00
12-18: 13-15-Full length western adventures	5.70	17.00	35.00

TINKER BELL (Disney, TV)(See Walt Disney Showcase #37)
Dell Publishing Co.: No. 896, Mar, 1958 - No. 982, Apr-June, 1959

	GD25	FN65	NM94
Four Color 896 (#1)-The Adventures of...	8.00	23.00	85.00
Four Color 982-The New Advs. of...	7.00	22.00	80.00

TINY FOLKS FUNNIES
Dell Publishing Co.: No. 60, 1944

	GD25	FN65	NM94
Four Color 60	13.00	40.00	145.00

TINY TESSIE (Tessie #1-23; Real Experiences #25)
Marvel Comics (20CC): No. 24, Oct, 1949 (52 pgs.)

	GD25	FN65	NM94
24	7.15	21.50	50.00

TINY TIM (Also see Super Comics)
Dell Publishing Co.: No. 4, 1941 - No. 235, July, 1949

	GD25	FN65	NM94
Large Feature Comic 4('41)	29.00	87.00	320.00
Four Color 20(1941)	27.00	80.00	295.00
Four Color 42(1943)	16.00	47.00	170.00
Four Color 235	3.60	11.00	40.00

TINY TOT COMICS
E. C. Comics: Mar, 1946 - No. 10, Nov-Dec, 1947 (For younger readers)

	GD25	FN65	NM94
1(nn)-52 pg. issues begin, end #4	29.00	88.00	220.00
2 (5/46)	17.00	52.00	130.00
3-10: 10-Christmas-c	15.00	46.00	115.00

Tiny Tots Comics #10 © EC

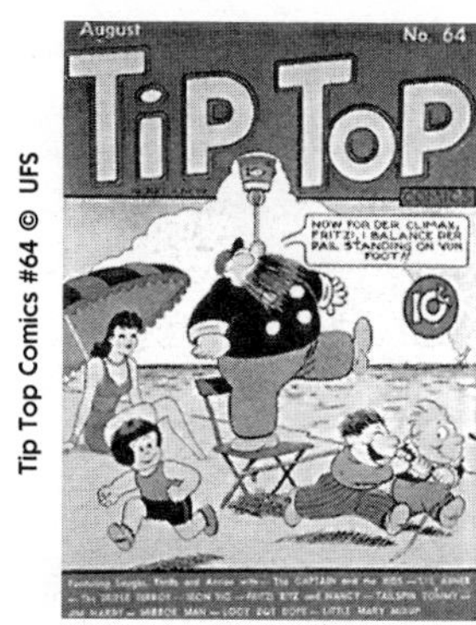

Tip Top Comics #64 © UFS

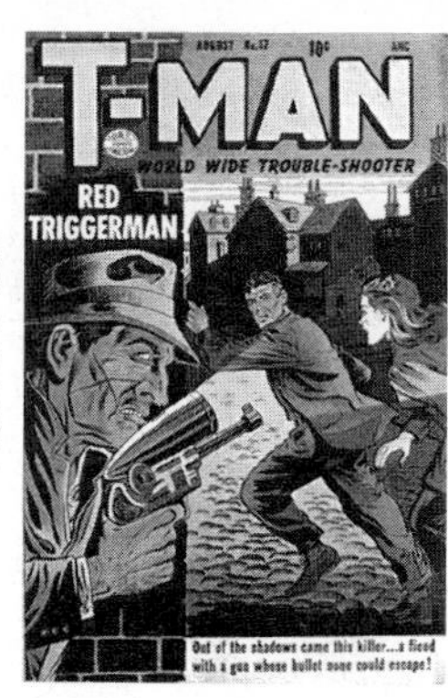

T-Man #17 © QUA

	GD25	FN65	NM94

TINY TOT FUNNIES (Formerly Family Funnies; becomes Junior Funnies)
Harvey Publ. (King Features Synd.): No. 9, June, 1951

	GD25	FN65	NM94
9-Flash Gordon, Mandrake, Dagwood, Daisy, etc.	5.00	15.00	30.00

TINY TOTS COMICS
Dell Publishing Co.: 1943 (Not reprints)

	GD25	FN65	NM94
1-Kelly-a(2); fairy tales	39.00	117.00	300.00

TIPPY & CAP STUBBS (See Popular Comics)
Dell Publishing Co.: No. 210, Jan, 1949 - No. 242, Aug, 1949

	GD25	FN65	NM94
Four Color 210 (#1)	3.60	11.00	40.00
Four Color 242	2.75	8.00	30.00

TIPPY'S FRIENDS GO-GO & ANIMAL
Tower Comics: July, 1966 - No. 15, Oct, 1969 (25¢)

	GD25	FN65	NM94
1	4.50	13.50	45.00
2-5,7,9-15: 12-15 titled "Tippy's Friend Go-Go"	2.50	7.50	22.00
6-The Monkees photo-c	4.50	13.50	45.00
8-Beatles app. on front/back-c	7.50	22.50	75.00

TIPPY TEEN (See Vicki)
Tower Comics: Nov, 1965 - No. 27, Feb, 1970 (25¢)

	GD25	FN65	NM94
1	4.50	13.50	45.00
2-4,6-10	2.80	8.40	28.00
5-1 pg. Beatles pin-up	3.20	9.60	32.00
11-20: 16-Twiggy photo-c	2.50	7.50	22.00
21-27	2.00	6.00	16.00
Special Collectors' Editions nn-(1969, 25¢)	2.60	7.80	26.00

TIPPY TERRY
Super/I. W. Enterprises: 1963

	GD25	FN65	NM94
Super Reprint #14('63)-r/Little Groucho #1	1.10	3.30	9.00
I.W. Reprint #1 (nd)-r/Little Groucho #1	1.10	3.30	9.00

TIP TOP COMICS
United Features #1-187/St. John #188-210/Dell Publishing Co. #211 on:
4/36 - No. 210, 1957; No. 211, 11-1/57-58 - No. 225, 5-7/61

	GD25	FN65	VF82	NM94
1-Tarzan by Hal Foster, Li'l Abner, Broncho Bill, Fritzi Ritz, Ella Cinders, Capt. & The Kids begin; strip-r (1st comic book app. of each)	900.00	2700.00	4400.00	6400.00

	GD25	FN65	NM94
2	200.00	600.00	1500.00
3-Tarzan-c	186.00	560.00	1400.00
4	110.00	330.00	825.00
5-8,10: 7-Photo & biography of Edgar Rice Burroughs. 8-Christmas-c	80.00	240.00	600.00
9-Tarzan-c	100.00	300.00	750.00
11,13,16,18-Tarzan-c: 11-Has Tarzan pin-up	79.00	237.00	550.00
12,14,15,17,19,20: 20-Christmas-c	64.00	192.00	410.00
21,24,27,30-(10/38)-Tarzan-c	64.00	192.00	420.00
22,23,25,26,28,29	40.00	120.00	320.00
31,35,38,40	39.00	117.00	295.00
32,36-Tarzan-c: 32-1st published Jack Davis-a (cartoon). 36-Kurtzman panel (1st published comic work)	48.00	145.00	410.00
33,34,37,39-Tarzan-c	46.00	138.00	390.00
41-Reprints 1st Tarzan Sunday; Tarzan-c	48.00	145.00	410.00
42-50: 43-Mort Walker panel	37.00	110.00	275.00
51,53	31.00	92.00	230.00
52-Tarzan-c	39.00	117.00	300.00
54-Origin Mirror Man & Triple Terror, also featured on cover	38.00	114.00	285.00
55,56,58,60: Last Tarzan by Foster	25.00	74.00	185.00
57,59,61,62-Tarzan by Hogarth	31.00	92.00	230.00
63-80: 65,67-70,72-74,77,78-No Tarzan	15.00	44.00	110.00
81-90	13.00	38.00	95.00
91-99	11.00	32.00	80.00
100	12.00	36.00	90.00
101-140: 110-Gordo story. 111-Li'l Abner app. 118, 132-No Tarzan. 137-Sadie Hawkins Day story	7.15	21.50	50.00
141-170: 145,151-Gordo stories. 157-Last Li'l Abner; lingerie panels	5.70	17.00	35.00
171-188-Tarzan reprints by B. Lubbers in all. 177-Peanuts by Schulz begins?; no Peanuts in #178,179,181-183	5.70	17.00	38.00
189-225	4.15	12.50	25.00
Bound Volumes (Very Rare) sold at 1939 World's Fair; bound by publisher in pictorial comic boards (also see Comics on Parade)			
Bound issues 1-12	194.00	582.00	1650.00
Bound issues 13-24	129.00	387.00	1100.00
Bound issues 25-36	112.00	335.00	950.00

NOTE: *Tarzan covers-#1(part), 2(part), 3, 9, 11, 13, 16, 18, 21, 24, 27, 30, 32-34, 36, 37, 39, 41, 43, 45, 47, 50, 52 (all worth 10-20 percent more). Tarzan by* ***Foster****-#1-40, 44-50; by* ***Rex Maxon****-#41-43; by* ***Burne Hogarth****-#57, 59, 62.*

TIP TOPPER COMICS
United Features Syndicate: Oct-Nov, 1949 - No. 28, 1954

	GD25	FN65	NM94
1-Li'l Abner, Abbie & Slats	8.50	26.00	60.00
2	5.70	17.00	35.00
3-5: 5-Fearless Fosdick app.	5.00	15.00	30.00
6-10: 6-Fearless Fosdick app.	4.15	12.50	25.00
11-25: 17-22,24,26-Peanuts app. (2 pgs.)	4.00	10.00	20.00
26-28-Twin Earths	5.00	15.00	30.00

NOTE: *Many lingerie panels in Fritzi Ritz stories.*

TITAN SPECIAL
Dark Horse Comics: June, 1994 ($3.95, one-shot)

	GD25	FN65	NM94
1-($3.95, 52 pgs.)			4.00

TITANS: SCISSORS, PAPER, STONE
DC Comics: 1997 ($4.95, one-shot)

	GD25	FN65	NM94
1-Manga style Elseworlds; Adam Warren-s/a(p)			5.00

TITANS SELL-OUT SPECIAL
DC Comics: Nov, 1992 ($3.50, 52 pgs., one-shot)

	GD25	FN65	NM94
1-Fold-out Nightwing poster; 1st Teeny Titans			3.50

T-MAN (Also see Police Comics #103)
Quality Comics Group: Sept, 1951 - No. 38, Dec, 1956

	GD25	FN65	NM94
1-Pete Trask, T-Man begins; Jack Cole-a	35.00	104.00	260.00
2-Crandall-c	19.00	56.00	140.00
3,7,8: All Crandall-c	16.00	48.00	120.00
4,5-Crandall-c/a each	17.00	52.00	130.00
6-"The Man Who Could Be Hitler" c/story; Crandall-c.	19.00	56.00	140.00
9,10-Crandall-c	14.00	42.00	105.00
11-Used in **POP**, pg. 95 & color illo.	10.00	30.00	75.00
12,13,15-19,21,22-26: 21- "The Return of Mussolini" c/story. 23-H-Bomb panel. 24-Last pre-code issue (4/55). 25-Not Crandall-a	8.35	25.00	60.00
14-Hitler-c	9.30	28.00	70.00
20-H-Bomb explosion-c/story	11.00	34.00	85.00
27-38	7.85	23.50	55.00

NOTE: *Anti-communist stories common.* ***Crandall*** *c-2-10p.* ***Cuidera*** *c(i)-1-38. Bondage c-15.*

TMNT MUTANT UNIVERSE SOURCEBOOK
Archie Comics: 1992 - No. 3, 1992? ($1.95, 52 pgs.)(Lists characters from A-Z)

	GD25	FN65	NM94
1-3: 3-New characters; fold-out poster			2.00

TNT COMICS
Charles Publishing Co.: Feb, 1946 (36 pgs.)

	GD25	FN65	NM94
1-Yellowjacket app.	23.00	70.00	175.00

TOBY TYLER (Disney, see Movie Comics)
Dell Publishing Co.: No. 1092, Apr-June, 1960

	GD25	FN65	NM94
Four Color 1092-Movie, photo-c	5.50	16.50	60.00

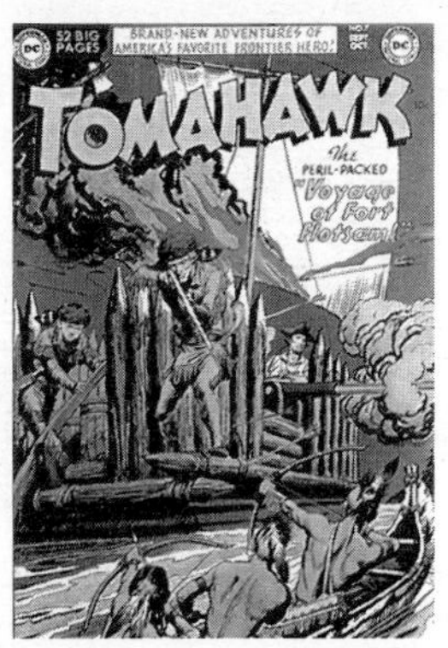

Tomahawk #7 © DC

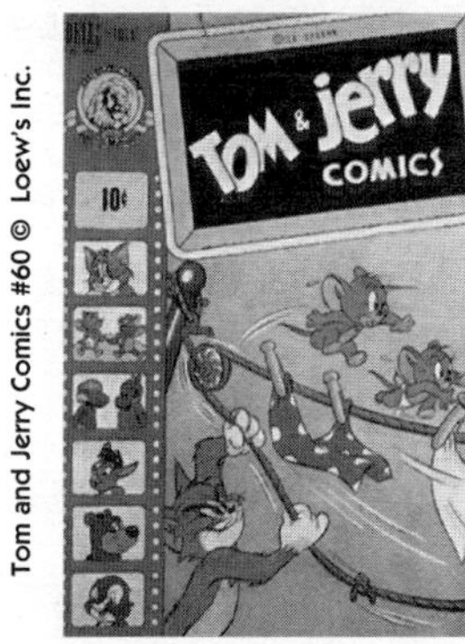

Tom and Jerry Comics #60 © Loew's Inc.

Tomb of Dracula #11 © MAR

TODAY'S BRIDES
Ajax/Farrell Publishing Co.: Nov, 1955; No. 2, Feb, 1956; No. 3, Sept, 1956; No. 4, Nov, 1956

	GD25	FN65	NM94
1	6.00	18.00	42.00
2-4	4.25	13.00	28.00

TODAY'S ROMANCE
Standard Comics: No. 5, March, 1952 - No. 8, Sept, 1952 (All photo-c?)

	GD25	FN65	NM94
5-Photo-c	6.00	18.00	42.00
6-Photo-c; Toth-a	6.85	21.00	48.00
7,8	4.25	13.00	28.00

TOKA (Jungle King)
Dell Publishing Co.: Aug-Oct, 1964 - No. 10, Jan, 1967 (Painted-c #1,2)

	GD25	FN65	NM94
1	2.80	8.40	28.00
2	2.25	6.75	18.00
3-10	1.75	5.25	14.00

TOMAHAWK (Son of... on-c of #131-140; see Star Spangled Comics #69 & World's Finest Comics #65)
National Periodical Publications: Sept-Oct, 1950 - No. 140, May-June, 1972

	GD25	FN65	NM94
1-Tomahawk & boy sidekick Dan Hunter begin by Fred Ray	141.00	424.00	1200.00
2-Frazetta/Williamson-a (4 pgs.)	56.00	168.00	475.00
3-5	39.00	117.00	300.00
6-10: 7-Last 52 pg. issue	28.00	84.00	210.00
11-20	20.00	60.00	150.00
21-27,30: 30-Last precode (2/55)	16.00	48.00	120.00
28-1st app. Lord Shilling (arch-foe)	17.00	52.00	130.00
29-Frazetta-r/Jimmy Wakely #3 (3 pgs.)	21.00	64.00	160.00
31-40	10.00	30.00	100.00
41-50	8.00	24.00	80.00
51-56,58-60	5.50	16.50	55.00
57-Frazetta-r/Jimmy Wakely #6 (3 pgs.)	8.50	25.50	85.00
61-77: 77-Last 10¢ issue	4.50	13.50	45.00
78-85: 81-1st app. Miss Liberty. 83-Origin Tomahawk's Rangers	3.00	9.00	30.00
86-99: 96-Origin/1st app. The Hood, alias Lady Shilling	2.25	6.75	18.00
100	2.50	7.50	25.00
101-110: 107-Origin/1st app. Thunder-Man	2.00	6.00	16.00
111-130	1.50	4.50	15.00
131-Frazetta-r/Jimmy Wakely #7 (3 pgs.); origin Firehair retold	1.80	5.40	18.00
132-135,140	1.10	3.30	11.00
136-138,140 (52 pg. Giants)	1.50	4.50	15.00
139-Frazetta-r/Star Spangled #113	1.80	5.40	18.00

NOTE: ***Neal Adams*** *c-116-119, 121, 123-130.* ***Fred Ray*** *c-1, 2, 8, 11, 30, 34, 35, 40-43, 45, 46, 82. Firehair by* ***Kubert****-131-134, 136.* ***Maurer*** *a-138.* ***Severin*** *a-135.* ***Starr*** *a-5.* ***Thorne*** *a-137, 140.*

TOM AND JERRY (See Comic Album #4, 8, 12, Dell Giant #21, Dell Giants, Golden Comics Digest #1, 5, 8, 13, 15, 18, 22, 25, 28, 35, Kite fun Book & March of Comics #21, 46, 61, 70, 88, 103, 119, 128, 145, 154, 173, 190, 207, 224, 281, 295, 305, 321,333, 345, 361, 365, 388, 400, 444, 451, 463, 480)

TOM AND JERRY (...Comics, early issues) (M.G.M.)
(Formerly Our Gang No. 1-59) (See Dell Giants for annuals)
Dell Publishing Co./Gold Key No. 213-327/Whitman No. 328 on:
No. 193, 6/48; No. 60, 7/49 - No. 212, 7-9/62; No. 213, 11/62 - No. 291, 2/75; No. 292, 3/77 - No. 342, 5/82 - No. 344, 4/83

	GD25	FN65	NM94
Four Color 193 (#1)-Titled "M.G.M. Presents..."	13.00	38.00	140.00
60-Barney Bear, Benny Burro cont. from Our Gang; Droopy begins	7.00	22.00	80.00
61	6.40	19.00	70.00
62-70: 66-X-Mas-c	4.50	13.50	50.00
71-80: 77,90-X-Mas-c. 79-Spike & Tyke begin	3.60	11.00	40.00
81-99	2.90	8.70	32.00
100	3.20	9.50	35.00
101-120	2.40	7.00	26.00
121-140: 126-X-Mas-c	2.20	6.50	24.00
141-160	1.80	5.40	18.00
161-200	1.50	4.50	15.00
201-212(7-9/62)(Last Dell issue)	1.00	3.00	10.00
213,214-(84 pgs.)-Titled "...Funhouse"	4.00	12.25	45.00
215-240: 215-Titled "...Funhouse"	1.80	5.40	18.00
241-270	1.20	3.60	12.00
271-300: 286- "Tom & Jerry"	.90	2.70	8.00
301-327 (Gold Key)			3.00
328,329 (Whitman)			4.00
330(8/80),331(10/80), 332-(3-pack?)	.90	2.70	8.00
333-341			5.00
342-344-All #90058, no date or date code (3-pack?)	.85	2.60	7.00
Mouse From T.R.A.P. 1(7/66)-Giant, G. K.	2.50	7.60	28.00
Summer Fun 1(7/67, 68 pgs.)(Gold Key)-Reprints Barks' Droopy from Summer Fun #1	2.50	7.60	28.00

NOTE: *#60-87, 98-121, 268, 277, 289, 302 are 52 pgs.. Reprints-#225, 241, 245, 247, 252, 254, 266, 268, 270, 292-327, 329-342, 344.*

TOM & JERRY
Harvey Comics: Sept, 1991 - No. 4, 1992 ($1.25)

	GD25	FN65	NM94
1-4: 1-Tom & Jerry, Barney Bear-r by Barks			1.30
50th Anniversary Special 1 (10/91, $2.50, 68 pgs.)-Benny the Lonesome Burro-r by Barks (story/a)/Our Gang #9			2.50

TOMB OF DARKNESS (Formerly Beware)
Marvel Comics Group: No. 9, July, 1974 - No. 23, Nov, 1976

	GD25	FN65	NM94
9	1.40	4.20	14.00
10-23: 15,19-Ditko-r. 17-Woodbridge-r/Astonishing #62; Powell-r. 20-Everett Venus-r/Venus #19. 22-r/Tales To Astonish #27; 1st Hank Pym. 23-Everett-r	.90	2.70	9.00

TOMB OF DRACULA (See Giant-Size Dracula, Dracula Lives, Nightstalkers, Power Record Comics & Requiem for Dracula)
Marvel Comics Group: Apr, 1972 - No. 70, Aug, 1979

	GD25	FN65	NM94
1-1st app. Dracula & Frank Drake; Colan-p in all	8.00	24.00	90.00
2	4.00	12.25	45.00
3-5: 3-Intro. Dr. Rachel Van Helsing & Inspector Chelm	2.70	8.00	30.00
6-9	2.25	6.80	25.00
10-1st app. Blade the Vampire Slayer	3.50	10.50	38.00
11,12,14-20: 12-Brunner-c(p)	1.50	4.50	15.00
13-Origin Blade	2.00	6.00	20.00
21-40: 25-1st app. & origin Hannibal King	1.20	3.60	12.00
41-45,48,49,51-60		2.00	6.00
46,47-(Regular 25¢ edition)(7-8/76)		2.00	6.00
46,47-(30¢-c, limited distribution)	2.20	6.50	24.00
50-Silver Surfer app.	1.00	3.00	10.00
61-69		2.00	6.00
70-Double size	.85	2.60	7.00

NOTE: ***N. Adams*** *c-1, 6.* ***Colan*** *a-1-70p; c(p)-8, 38-42, 44-56, 58-70.* ***Wrightson*** *c-43.*

TOMB OF DRACULA, THE (Magazine)
Marvel Comics Group: Oct, 1979 - No. 6, Aug, 1980 (B&W)

	GD25	FN65	NM94
1,4-6			5.00
2,3: 2-Ditko-a (36 pgs.). 3-Miller-a(2 pg. sketch)			5.00

NOTE: ***Buscema*** *a-4p, 5p.* ***Chaykin*** *c-5, 6.* ***Colan*** *a(p)-1, 3-6.* ***Miller*** *a-3.* ***Romita*** *a-2p.*

TOMB OF DRACULA
Marvel Comics (Epic Comics): 1991 - No. 4, 1992 ($4.95, 52 pgs., squarebound, mini-series)

	GD25	FN65	NM94
Book 1-4: Colan/Williamson-a; Colan painted-c			5.00

TOMB OF LEGEIA (See Movie Classics)

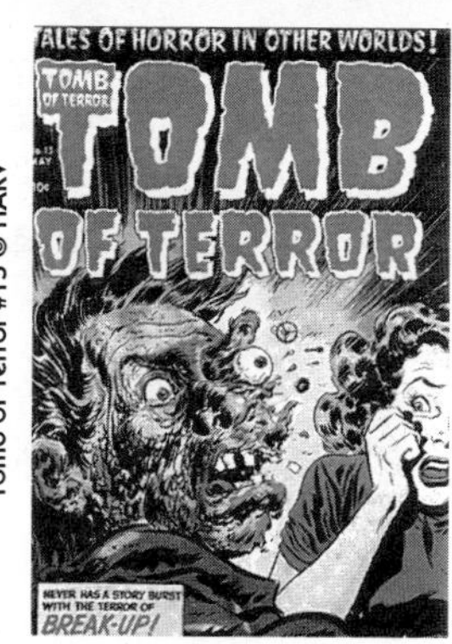

Tomb of Terror #15 © HARV

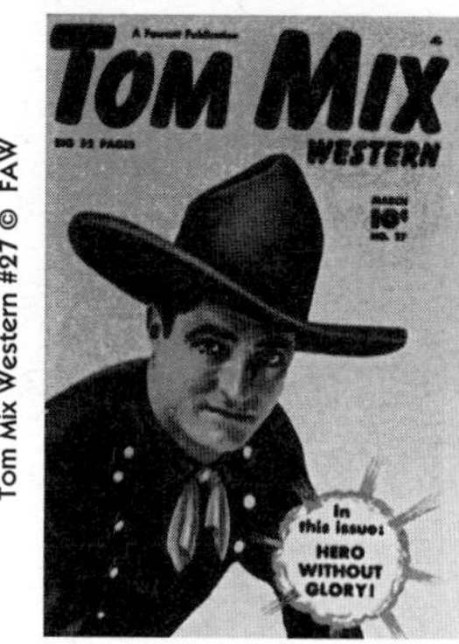

Tom Mix Western #27 © FAW

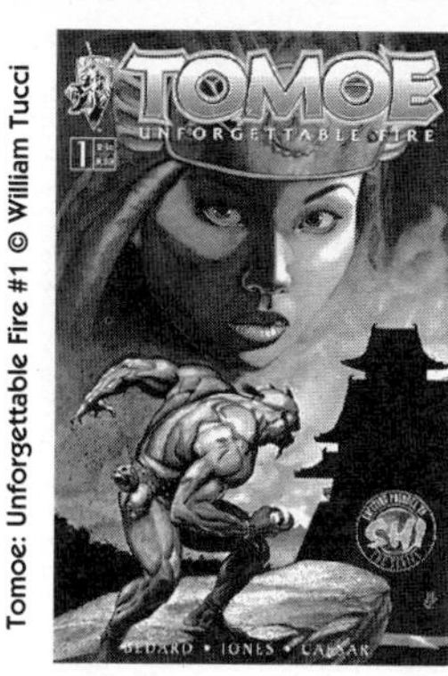

Tomoe: Unforgettable Fire #1 © William Tucci

TOMB OF TERROR (Thrills of Tomorrow #17 on)
Harvey Publications: June, 1952 - No. 16, July, 1954

	GD25	FN65	NM94
1	35.00	104.00	260.00
2	19.00	56.00	140.00
3-Bondage-c; atomic disaster story	19.00	58.00	145.00
4-12: 4-Heart ripped out. 8-12-Nostrand-a	18.00	54.00	135.00
13,14-Special S/F issues. 14-Check-a	22.00	66.00	165.00
15-S/F issue; c-shows head exploding	26.00	78.00	195.00
16-Special S/F issue; Nostrand-a	22.00	66.00	165.00

NOTE: ***Edd Cartier** a-13? **Elias** c-2, 5-16. **Kremer** a-1, 7; c-1. **Nostrand** a-8-12, 15r 16. **Palais** a-2, 3, 5-7. **Powell** a-1, 3, 5, 9-16. **Sparling** a-12, 13, 15.*

TOMB RAIDER/WITCHBLADE SPECIAL (Also see Witchblade/Tomb Raider)
Top Cow Prod.: Dec, 1997 (mail-in offer, one-shot)

	GD25	FN65	NM94
1-Turner-s/a(p); green background cover	1.00	3.00	10.00
1-Variant-c with orange sun background	.90	2.70	8.00
1-Variant-c with black sides	1.00	3.00	10.00
1-Revisited (12/98, $2.95) reprints #1, Turner-c			2.95

TOMBSTONE TERRITORY (See Four Color #1123)

TOM CAT (Formerly Bo; Atom The Cat #9 on)
Charlton Comics: No. 4, Apr, 1956 - No. 8, July, 1957

	GD25	FN65	NM94
4-Al Fago-c/a	5.70	17.00	40.00
5-8	4.25	13.00	28.00

TOM CORBETT, SPACE CADET (TV)
Dell Publishing Co.: No. 378, Jan-Feb, 1952 - No. 11, Sept-Nov, 1954
(All painted covers)

	GD25	FN65	NM94
Four Color 378 (#1)-McWilliams-a	16.00	48.00	175.00
Four Color 400,421-McWilliams-a	9.00	27.00	100.00
4(11-1/53) - 11	6.40	19.00	70.00

TOM CORBETT SPACE CADET (See March of Comics #102)

TOM CORBETT SPACE CADET (TV)
Prize Publications: V2#1, May-June, 1955 - V2#3, Sept-Oct, 1955

	GD25	FN65	NM94
V2#1-Robot-c	25.00	74.00	185.00
2,3-Meskin-c	21.00	64.00	160.00

TOM, DICK & HARRIET (See Gold Key Spotlight)

TOM LANDRY AND THE DALLAS COWBOYS
Spire Christian Comics/Fleming H. Revell Co.: 1973 (35/49¢)

	GD25	FN65	NM94
nn			4.00

TOMMI GUNN
London Night Studios: May, 1996 - No. 3, Aug, 1996 ($3.00, lim. series, mature)

	GD25	FN65	NM94
1/2,1-3: W/J.J. North centerfold			3.00
1/2-($10.00)-Naughty Edition; photo-c			10.00
1-Naughty Platinum; embossed nude-c w/nude J.J. North centerfold inside			10.00
2-Variant nude-c			5.00
Annual 1(1997, $3.00)			3.00
Annual 1(1997, $6.00)"Naughty Ed."; photo-c			6.00

TOMMI GUNN: KILLER'S LUST
London Night Studios: Feb, 1997 - No. 3($3.00, mature)

	GD25	FN65	NM94
0,1,2,3			3.00
0,1,2,3-($6.00)-"Naughty Ed."; photo-c (Elizabeth Parkhurst)			6.00

TOM MIX (...Commandos Comics #10-12)
Ralston-Purina Co.: Sept, 1940 - No. 12, Nov, 1942 (36 pgs.); 1983 (one-shot)
Given away for two Ralston box-tops; 1983 came in cereal box

	GD25	FN65	NM94
1-Origin (life) Tom Mix; Fred Meagher-a	284.00	853.00	2700.00
2	94.00	282.00	800.00
3-9	59.00	176.00	500.00
10-12: 10-Origin Tom Mix Commando Unit; Speed O'Dare begins; Japanese sub-c. 12-Sci/fi-c	47.00	141.00	400.00
1983- "Taking of Grizzly Grebb", Toth-a; 16 pg. miniature		2.00	6.00

TOM MIX WESTERN (Movie, radio star) (Also see The Comics, Crackajack Funnies, Master Comics, 100 Pages Of Comics, Popular Comics, Real Western Hero, Six Gun Heroes, Western Hero & XMas Comics)
Fawcett Publications: Jan, 1948 - No. 61, May, 1953 (1-17: 52 pgs.)

	GD25	FN65	NM94
1 (Photo-c, 52 pgs.)-Tom Mix & his horse Tony begin; Tumbleweed Jr. begins, ends #52,54,55	88.00	265.00	750.00
2 (Photo-c)	40.00	120.00	320.00
3-5 (Painted/photo-c): 5-Billy the Kid & Oscar app.	31.00	92.00	230.00
6,7 (Painted/photo-c)	25.00	76.00	190.00
8-Kinstler tempera-c	25.00	76.00	190.00
9,10 (Painted/photo-c)-Used in **SOTI**, pgs. 323-325	23.00	70.00	175.00
11-Kinstler oil-c	21.00	64.00	160.00
12 (Painted/photo-c)	19.00	56.00	140.00
13-17 (Painted-c, 52 pgs.)	19.00	56.00	140.00
18,22 (Painted-c, 36 pgs.)	16.00	48.00	120.00
19 (Photo-c, 52 pgs.)	17.00	50.00	125.00
20,21,23 (Painted-c, 52 pgs.)	13.00	40.00	100.00
24,25,27-29 (52 pgs.): 24-Photo-c begin, end #61. 29-Slim Pickens app.	13.00	40.00	100.00
26,30 (36 pgs.)	12.00	36.00	90.00
31-33,35-37,39,40,42 (52 pgs.): 39-Red Eagle app.	11.00	34.00	85.00
34,38 (36 pgs. begin)	10.00	30.00	75.00
41,43-60: 57-(9/52)-Dope smuggling story	7.85	23.50	55.00
61-Last issue	9.30	28.00	70.00

NOTE: *Photo-c from 1930s Tom Mix movies (he died in 1940). Many issues contain ads for Tom Mix, Rocky Lane, Space Patrol and other premiums. Captain Tootsie by **C.C. Beck** in #6-11, 20.*

TOM MIX WESTERN
AC Comics: 1988 - No. 2, 1989? ($2.95, B&W w/16 pgs. color, 44 pgs.)

	GD25	FN65	NM94
1-Tom Mix-r/Master #124,128,131,102 plus Billy the Kid-r by Severin; photo front/back/inside-c			3.00
2-($2.50, B&W)-Gabby Hayes-r; photo covers			2.50
...Holiday Album 1 (1990, $3.50, B&W, one-shot, 44 pgs.)-Contains photos & 1950s Tom Mix-r; photo inside-c			3.50

TOMMY OF THE BIG TOP (Thrilling Circus Adventures)
King Features Synd./Standard Comics: No. 10, Sep, 1948 - No. 12, Mar, 1949

	GD25	FN65	NM94
10-By John Lehti	5.70	17.00	38.00
11,12	4.00	12.00	24.00

TOMMY TOMORROW (See Action Comics #127, Real Fact #6, Showcase #41,42,44,46,47 & World's Finest #102)

TOMOE (Also see Shi: The Way Of the Warrior #6)
Crusade Comics: July, 1995 - No. 3, June, 1996($2.95)

	GD25	FN65	NM94
0-3: 2-B&W Dogs o' War preview. 3-B&W Demon Gun preview			3.00
0 (3/96, $2.95)-variant-c.			3.00
0-Commemorative edition (5,000)	1.70	5.10	17.00
1-Commemorative edition (5,000)	2.00	6.00	20.00
1-($2.95)-FAN Appreciation edition			3.00
TPB (1997, $14.95) r/#0-3			15.00

TOMOE: UNFORGETTABLE FIRE
Crusade Comics: June, 1997 ($2.95, one-shot)

	GD25	FN65	NM94
1-Prequel to Shi: The Series			3.00

TOMOE-WITCHBLADE/FIRE SERMON
Crusade Comics: Sept, 1996 ($3.95, one-shot)

	GD25	FN65	NM94
1-Tucci-c			4.00
1-($9.95)-Avalon Ed. w/gold foil-c			10.00

TOMOE-WITCHBLADE/MANGA SHI PREVIEW EDITION
Crusade Comics: July, 1996 ($5.00, B&W)

	GD25	FN65	NM94
nn-San Diego Preview Edition			5.00

TOMORROW KNIGHTS
Marvel Comics (Epic Comics): June, 1990 - No. 6, Mar, 1991 ($1.50)

Tom Terrific #4 © Terry Toons

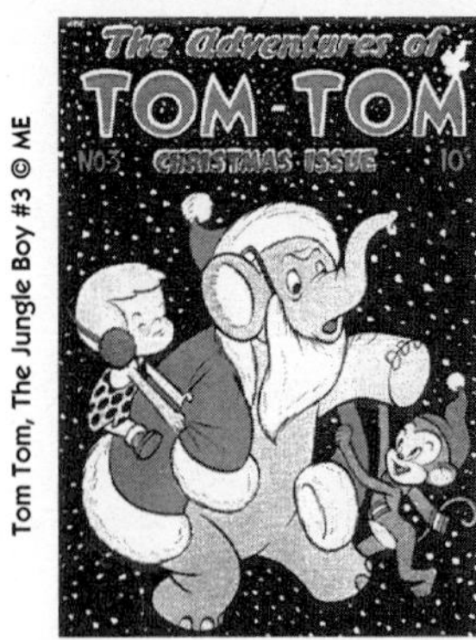

Tom Tom, The Jungle Boy #3 © ME

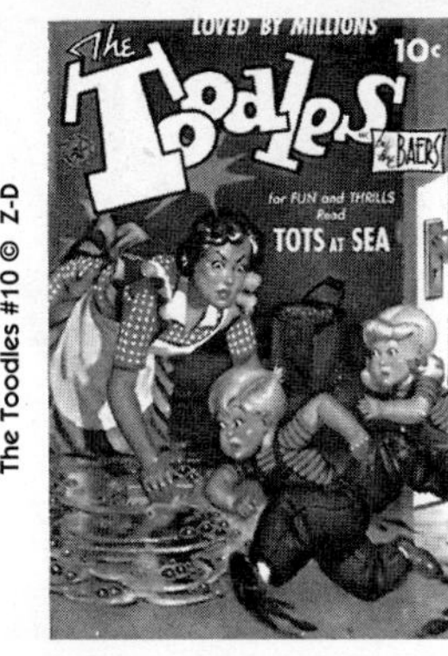

The Toodles #10 © Z-D

GD25 FN65 NM94

1-($1.95, 52 pgs.) 2.00
2-6 1.50

TOM SAWYER (See Adventures of... & Famous Stories)

TOM SAWYER COMICS
Giveaway: 1951? (Paper cover)
nn-Contains a coverless Hopalong Cassidy from 1951; other combinations known 2.00 5.00 10.00

TOM SKINNER-UP FROM HARLEM (See Up From Harlem)

TOM TERRIFIC! (TV)(See Mighty Mouse Fun Club Magazine #1)
Pines Comics (Paul Terry): Summer, 1957 - No. 6, Fall, 1958
(See Terry Toons Giant Summer Fun Book)
1-1st app.?; CBS Television Presents... 20.00 60.00 150.00
2-6-(scarce) 15.00 44.00 110.00

TOM THUMB
Dell Publishing Co.: No. 972, Jan, 1959
Four Color 972-Movie, George Pal 9.00 27.00 100.00

TOM-TOM, THE JUNGLE BOY (See A-1 Comics & Tick Tock Tales)
Magazine Enterprises: 1947 - No. 3, 1947; Nov, 1957 - No. 3, Mar, 1958
1-Funny animal 7.85 23.50 55.00
2,3(1947): 3-Christmas issue 5.70 17.00 35.00
Tom-Tom & Itchi the Monk 1(11/57) - 3(3/58) 1.75 5.25 14.00
I.W. Reprint No. 1,2,8,10: 1,2,8-r/Koko & Kola #? 2.40 6.00

TONGUE LASH
Dark Horse Comics: Aug, 1996 - No. 2, Sept, 1996 ($2.95, limited series, mature)
1,2: Taylor-c/a 3.00

TONKA (Disney)
Dell Publishing Co.: No. 966, Jan, 1959
Four Color 966-Movie (Starring Sal Mineo)-photo-c 7.00 22.00 80.00

TONTO (See The Lone Ranger's Companion...)

TONY TRENT (The Face #1,2)
Big Shot/Columbia Comics Group: No. 3, 1948 - No. 4, 1949
3,4: 3-The Face app. by Mart Bailey 15.00 44.00 110.00

TOODLES, THE (The Toodle Twins with #1)
Ziff-Davis (Approved Comics)/Argo: No. 10, July-Aug, 1951; Mar, 1956 (Newspaper-r)
10-Painted-c, some newspaper-r by The Baers 7.85 23.50 55.00
...Twins 1(Argo, 3/56)-Reprints by The Baers 5.70 17.00 35.00

TOO MUCH COFFEE MAN
Adhesive Comics: July, 1993 - Present ($2.50, B&W)
1-Shannon Wheeler story & art 1.60 4.80 16.00
2,3 1.10 3.30 11.00
4,5 .90 2.70 8.00
6-8 2.95
Full Color Special-($2.95) 3.25
Full Color Special 2-(7/97, $3.95) 4.00

TOO MUCH COFFEE MAN SPECIAL
Dark Horse Comics: July, 1997 ($2.95, B&W)
nn-Reprints Dark Horse Presents #92-95 3.00

TOOTS & CASPER
Dell Publishing Co.: No. 5, 1942
Large Feature Comic 5 10.00 30.00 110.00

TOP ADVENTURE COMICS
I. W. Enterprises: 1964 (Reprints)
1-r/High Adv. (Explorer Joe #2); Krigstein-r 2.00 6.00 16.00
2-Black Dwarf-r/Red Seal #22; Kinstler-c 2.00 6.00 16.00

TOP CAT (TV) (Hanna-Barbera)(See Kite Fun Book)
Dell Publishing Co./Gold Key No. 4 on: 12-2/61-62 - No. 3, 6-8/62; No. 4, 10/62 - No. 31, 9/70
1 (TV show debuted 9/27/61) 13.00 40.00 145.00
2-Augie Doggie back-ups in #1-4 7.00 22.00 80.00
3-5: 3-Last 15¢ issue. 4-Begin 12¢ issues; 1st app. Yakky Doodle in 1 pg. strip. 5-1st app. Touche' Turtle 5.50 16.50 60.00
6-10 3.60 11.00 40.00
11-20 2.75 8.00 30.00
21-31: 21,24,25,29-Reprints 1.80 5.50 20.00

TOP CAT (TV) (Hanna-Barbera)(See TV Stars #4)
Charlton Comics: Nov, 1970 - No. 20, Nov, 1973
1 4.00 12.00 40.00
2-10 2.50 7.50 22.00
11-20 2.00 6.00 16.00
NOTE: *#8 (1/72) went on sale late in 1972 between #14 and #15 with the 1/73 issues.*

TOP COMICS
K. K. Publications/Gold Key: July, 1967 (All reprints)
nn-The Gnome-Mobile (Disney-movie) 1.25 3.75 10.00
1-Beagle Boys (#7), Beep Beep the Road Runner (#5), Bugs Bunny, Chip 'n' Dale, Daffy Duck (#50), Flipper, Huckleberry Hound, Huey, Dewey & Louie, Junior Woodchucks, Lassie, The Little Monsters (#71), Moby Duck, Porky Pig (has Gold Key label - says Top Comics on inside), Scamp, Super Goof, Tarzan of the Apes (#169), Three Stooges (#35), Tom & Jerry Top Cat (#21), Tweety & Sylvester (#7), Walt Disney C&S (#322), Woody Woodpecker, Yogi Bear, Zorro (r/G.K. Zorro #7 w/Toth-a; says 2nd printing) known; each character given own book 1.00 3.00 8.00
1-Uncle Scrooge (#70) 1.75 5.25 14.00
1-Donald Duck (not Barks), Mickey Mouse 1.50 4.50 12.00
1-Flintstones 2.50 7.50 25.00
1-The Jetsons 3.50 10.50 35.00
2-Bugs Bunny, Daffy Duck, Donald Duck (not Barks), Mickey Mouse (#114), Porky Pig, Super Goof, Three Stooges, Tom & Jerry, Tweety & Sylvester, Uncle Scrooge (#71)-Barks-c, Walt Disney's C&S (r/#325), Woody Woodpecker, Yogi Bear (#30), Zorro (r/#8; Toth-a) 1.00 3.00 8.00
2-Snow White & 7 Dwarfs(6/67)(1944-r) 1.25 3.75 10.00
3-Donald Duck 1.10 3.30 9.00
3-Uncle Scrooge (#72) 1.50 4.50 12.00
3,4-The Flintstones 2.50 7.50 25.00
3-Mickey Mouse (r/#115), Tom & Jerry, Woody Woodpecker, Yogi Bear 1.00 3.00 8.00
4-Mickey Mouse, Woody Woodpecker 1.00 3.00 8.00
NOTE: *Each book in this series is identical to its counterpart except for cover, and came out at same time. The number in parentheses is the original issue it contains.*

TOP COW PRODUCTIONS, INC./BALLISTIC STUDIOS SWIMSUIT SPECIAL
Image Comics (Top Cow Productions): May, 1995 ($2.95, one-shot)
1 5.00

TOP COW SECRETS:SPECIAL WINTER LINGERIE EDITION
Image Comics (Top Cow Productions): Jan, 1996 ($2.95, one-shot)
1-Pin-ups 3.00

TOP DETECTIVE COMICS
I. W. Enterprises: 1964 (Reprints)
9-r/Young King Cole #14; Dr. Drew (not Grandenetti) 1.50 4.50 12.00

TOP DOG (See Star Comics Magazine, 75¢)
Star Comics (Marvel): Apr, 1985 - No. 14, June, 1987 (Children's book)
1-14: 10-Peter Parker & J. Jonah Jameson cameo 1.00

TOP ELIMINATOR (Teenage Hotrodders #1-24; Drag 'n' Wheels #30 on)
Charlton Comics: No. 25, Sept, 1967 - No. 29, July, 1968
25-29 1.75 5.25 14.00

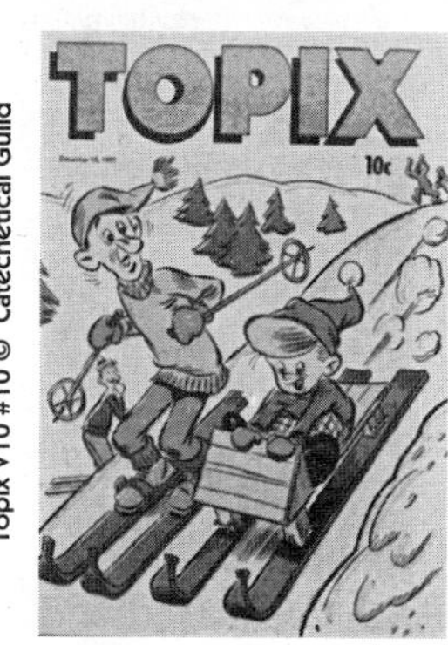

Topix V10 #10 © Catechetical Guild

Top Love Stories #9 © STAR

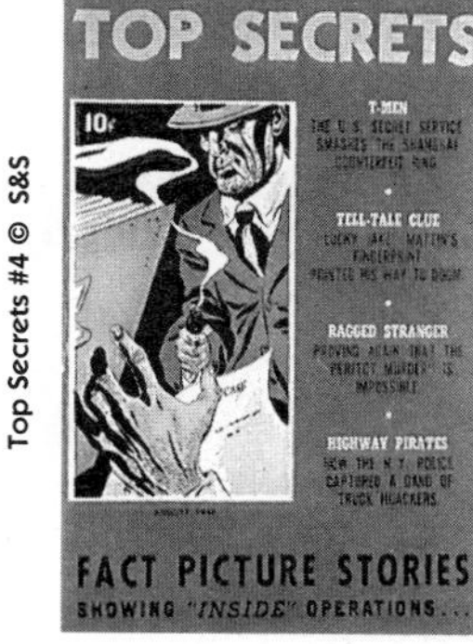

Top Secrets #4 © S&S

GD25 FN65 NM94

TOP FLIGHT COMICS
Four Star Publications/St. John Publishing Co.: 1947; July, 1949
1(1947) 10.00 30.00 75.00
1(7/49, St. John)-Hector the Inspector; funny animal 7.00 21.00 45.00

TOP GUN (See Luke Short, 4-Color #927 & Showcase #72)

TOP GUNS OF THE WEST (See Super DC Giant)

TOPIX (...Comics) (Timeless Topix-early issues) (Also see Men of Battle, Men of Courage & Treasure Chest)(V1-V5#1,V7#1-20-paper-c)
Catechetical Guild Educational Society: 11/42 - V10#15, 1/28/52 (Weekly - later issues)
V1#1(8 pgs.,8x11") 20.00 60.00 150.00
2,3(8 pgs.,8x11") 11.00 34.00 85.00
4-8(16 pgs.,8x11") 9.30 28.00 65.00
V2#1-10(16 pgs.,8x11"): V2#8-Pope Pius XII 7.85 23.50 55.00
V3#1-10(16 pgs.,8x11") 7.85 23.50 55.00
V4#1-10 5.70 17.00 40.00
V5#1(10/46,52 pgs.)-9,12-15(12/47): 13-Lists V5#4 5.00 15.00 30.00
10,11-Life of Christ editions 7.15 21.50 50.00
V6#1-14 4.00 11.00 22.00
V7#1(9/1/48)-20(6/15/49), 32 pgs. 4.00 11.00 22.00
V8#1(9/19/49)-3,5-11,13-30(5/15/50) 4.00 11.00 22.00
4-Dagwood Splits the Atom(10/10/49)-Magazine format
4.25 13.00 28.00
12-Ingels-a 7.15 21.50 50.00
V9#1(9/25/50)-11,13-30(5/14/51) 4.00 10.00 20.00
12-Special 36 pg. Xmas issue, text illos format 4.00 11.00 22.00
V10#1(10/1/51)-15: 14-Hollingsworth-a 4.00 10.00 20.00

TOP JUNGLE COMICS
I. W. Enterprises: 1964 (Reprint)
1(nd)-Reprints White Princess of the Jungle #3, minus cover; Kintsler-a
2.50 7.50 22.00

TOP LOVE STORIES (Formerly Gasoline Alley #2)
Star Publications: No. 3, 5/51 - No. 19, 3/54
3(#1) 19.00 56.00 140.00
4,5,7-9: 8-Wood story 15.00 44.00 110.00
6-Wood-a 20.00 60.00 150.00
10-16,18,19-Disbrow-a 15.00 44.00 110.00
17-Wood art (Fox-r) 16.00 48.00 120.00
NOTE: *All have **L. B. Cole** covers.*

TOP-NOTCH COMICS (...Laugh #28-45; Laugh Comix #46 on)
MLJ Magazines: Dec, 1939 - No. 45, June, 1944
1-Origin/1st app. The Wizard; Kardak the Mystic Magician, Swift of the Secret Service (ends #3), Air Patrol, The Westpointer, Manhunters (by J. Cole), Mystic (ends #2) & Scott Rand (ends #3) begin; Wizard covers begin, end #8
480.00 1440.00 4800.00
2-Dick Storm (ends #8), Stacy Knight M.D. (ends #4) begin; Jack Cole-a
200.00 600.00 1700.00
3-Bob Phantom, Scott Rand on Mars begin; J. Cole-a
135.00 405.00 1150.00
4-Origin/1st app. Streak Chandler on Mars; Moore of the Mounted only app.; J. Cole-a 112.00 336.00 950.00
5-Flag-c; origin/1st app. Galahad; Shanghai Sheridan begins (ends #8); Shield cameo; Novick-a; classic-c 124.00 372.00 1050.00
6-Meskin-a 89.00 267.00 760.00
7-The Shield x-over in Wizard; The Wizard dons new costume
109.00 327.00 925.00
8-Origin/1st app. The Firefly & Roy, the Super Boy (9/40, 2nd costumed boy hero after Robin?; also see Toro in Human Torch #1 (Fall/40)
124.00 372.00 1050.00
9-Origin & 1st app. The Black Hood; 1st Black Hood-c & logo (10/40); Fran Frazier begins (Scarce) 450.00 1350.00 4500.00
10-2nd app. Black Hood 141.00 423.00 1200.00
11-15 85.00 255.00 725.00
16-20 76.00 229.00 650.00
21-30: 23-26-Roy app. 24-No Wizard. 25-Last Bob Phantom. 27-Last Firefly. 28-Suzie, Pokey Oakey begin. 29-Last Kardak 59.00 177.00 500.00
31-44: 33-Dotty & Ditto by Woggon begins (2/43, 1st app.). 44-Black Hood series ends 37.00 112.00 280.00
45-Last issue 39.00 117.00 310.00
NOTE: ***J. Binder** a-1-3. **Meskin** a-2, 3, 6, 15. **Bob Montana** a-30; c-28-31. **Harry Sahle** c-42-45. **Woggon** a-33-40, 42. Bondage c-17, 19. Black Hood also appeared on radio in 1944. Black Hood app. on c-9-34, 41-44. Roy the Super Boy app. on c-8, 9, 11-27. The Wizard app. on c-1-8, 11-13, 15-22, 24, 25, 27. Pokey Oakey app. on c-28-43. Suzie app. on c-44-on.*

TOPPER & NEIL (TV)
Dell Publishing Co.: No. 859, Nov, 1957
Four Color 859 3.60 11.00 40.00

TOPPS COMICS
Four Star Publications: 1947
1-L. B. Cole-c 20.00 60.00 150.00

TOPPS COMICS PRESENTS
Topps Comics: No. 0, 1993 (Giveaway, B&W, 36 pgs.)
0-Dracula vs. Zorro, Teenagents, Silver Star, & Bill the Galactic Hero stories
1.00

TOPS
July, 1949 - No. 2, Sept, 1949 (25¢, 10-1/4x13-1/4", 68 pgs.)
Tops Magazine, Inc. (Lev Gleason): (Large size-magazine format; for the adult reader)
1 (Rare)-Story by Dashiell Hammett; Crandall/Lubbers, Tuska, Dan Barry, Fuje-a; Biro painted-c 94.00 282.00 800.00
2 (Rare)-Crandall/Lubbers, Biro, Kida, Fuje, Guardineer-a
88.00 265.00 750.00

TOPS COMICS
Consolidated Book Publishers: 1944 (10¢, 132 pgs.)
2000-(Color-c, inside in red shade & some in full color)-Ace Kelly by Rick Yager, Black Orchid, Don on the Farm, Dinky Dinkerton (Rare)
24.00 72.00 180.00
NOTE: *This book is printed in such a way that when the staple is removed, the strips on the left side of the book correspond with the same strips on the right side. Therefore, if strips are removed from the book, each strip can be folded into a complete comic section of its own.*

TOPS COMICS (See Tops in Humor)
Consolidated Book (Lev Gleason): 1944 (7-1/4x5", 32 pgs.)
2001-The Jack of Spades (costumed hero) 13.00 38.00 95.00
2002-Rip Raider 7.50 22.50 52.00
2003-Red Birch (gag cartoons) 2.00 5.00 10.00

TOP SECRET
Hillman Publ.: Jan, 1952
1 18.00 54.00 135.00

TOP SECRET ADVENTURES (See Spyman)

TOP SECRETS (...of the F.B.I.)
Street & Smith Publications: Nov, 1947 - No. 10, July-Aug, 1949
1-Powell-c/a 30.00 90.00 225.00
2-Powell-c/a 22.00 66.00 165.00
3-6,8,10-Powell-a 19.00 56.00 140.00
9-Powell-c/a 20.00 60.00 150.00
7-Used in **SOTI**, pg. 90 & illo. "How to hurt people"; used by N.Y. Legis. Comm.; Powell-c/a 29.00 88.00 220.00
NOTE: ***Powell** c-1-3, 5-10.*

TOPS IN ADVENTURE
Ziff-Davis Publishing Co.: Fall, 1952 (25¢, 132 pgs.)
1-Crusader from Mars, The Hawk, Football Thrills, He-Man; Powell-a;

Torchy #3 © QUA

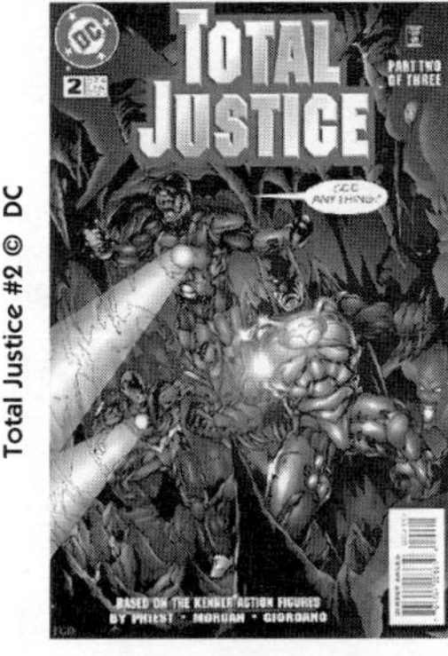

Total Justice #2 © DC

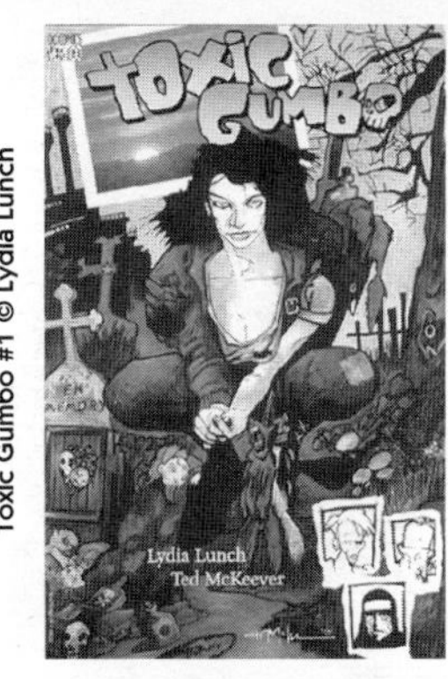

Toxic Gumbo #1 © Lydia Lunch

GD25 FN65 NM94

painted-c 40.00 120.00 320.00

TOPS IN HUMOR (See Tops Comics?)
Consolidated Book Publ. (Lev Gleason): 1944 (7-1/4x5")

2001(#1)-Origin The Jack of Spades, Ace Kelly by Rick Yager, Black Orchid (female crime fighter) app. 14.00 42.00 105.00
2 9.30 28.00 65.00

TOP SPOT COMICS
Top Spot Publ. Co.: 1945

1-The Menace, Duke of Darkness app. 28.00 84.00 210.00

TOPSY-TURVY
R. B. Leffingwell Publ.: Apr, 1945

1-1st app. Cookie 9.30 28.00 65.00

TOR (Prehistoric Life on Earth) (Formerly One Million Years Ago)
St. John Publ. Co.: No. 2, Oct, 1953; No. 3, May, 1954 - No. 5, Oct, 1954

3-D 2(10/53)-Kubert-c/a 11.00 34.00 85.00
3-D 2(10/53)-Oversized, otherwise same contents 10.00 30.00 75.00
3-D 2(11/53)-Kubert-c/a; has 3-D cover 10.00 30.00 75.00
3-5-Kubert-c/a: 3-Danny Dreams by Toth; Kubert 1 pg. story (w/self portrait) 11.00 34.00 85.00
NOTE: *The two October 3-D's have same contents and* ***Powell*** *art; the October & November issues are titled 3-D Comics. All 3-D issues are 25¢ and came with 3-D glasses.*

TOR (See Sojourn)
National Periodical Publications: May-June, 1975 - No. 6, Mar-Apr, 1976

1-6: 1-New origin by Kubert. 2-Origin-r/St. John #1 4.00
NOTE: ***Kubert*** *a-1, 2-6r; c-1-6.* ***Toth*** *a(p)-3r.*

TOR (3-D)
Eclipse Comics: July, 1986 - No. 2, Aug, 1987 ($2.50)

1,2: 1-r/One Million Years Ago. 2-r/Tor 3-D #2 4.00
...2-D: 1,2-Limited signed & numbered editions 4.00

TOR
Marvel Comics (Epic Comics/Heavy Hitters): June, 1993 - No. 4, 1993 ($5.95, limited series)

1-4: Joe Kubert-c/a/scripts 2.00 6.00

TORCH OF LIBERTY SPECIAL
Dark Horse Comics (Legend): Jan, 1995 ($2.50, one-shot)

1-Byrne scripts 2.50

TORCHY (...Blonde Bombshell) (See Dollman, Military, & Modern)
Quality Comics Group: Nov, 1949 - No. 6, Sept, 1950

1-Bill Ward-c, Gil Fox-a 115.00 344.00 975.00
2,3-Fox-c/a 56.00 168.00 475.00
4-Fox-c/a(3), Ward-a (9 pgs.) 71.00 212.00 600.00
5,6-Ward-c/a, 9 pgs; Fox-a(3) each 91.00 274.00 775.00
Super Reprint #16(1964)-r/#4 with new-c 7.50 22.50 75.00

TO RIVERDALE AND BACK AGAIN (Archie Comics Presents...)
Archie Comics: 1990 ($2.50, 68 pgs.)

nn-Byrne-c, Colan-a(p); adapts NBC TV movie 4.00

TORMENTED, THE (Becomes Surprise Adventures #3 on)
Sterling Comics: July, 1954 - No. 2, Sept, 1954

1,2: Weird/horror stories 19.00 56.00 140.00

TORNADO TOM (See Mighty Midget Comics)

TORSO (See Jinx: Torso)

TOTAL ECLIPSE
Eclipse Comics: May, 1988 - No. 5, Apr, 1989 ($3.95, 52 pgs., deluxe size)

Book 1-5: 3-Intro/1st app. new Black Terror 4.00

TOTAL ECLIPSE: THE SERAPHIM OBJECTIVE
Eclipse Comics: Nov, 1988 ($1.95, one-shot, Baxter paper)

GD25 FN65 NM94

1-Airboy, Valkyrie, The Heap app. 2.00

TOTAL JUSTICE
DC Comics: Oct, 1996 - No. 3, Nov, 1996 ($2.25, bi-weekly limited series) (Based on toyline)

1-3 2.25

TOTAL RECALL (Movie)
DC Comics: 1990 ($2.95, 68 pgs., movie adaptation, one-shot)

1-Arnold Schwarzenegger photo-c 3.00

TOTAL WAR (M.A.R.S. Patrol #3 on)
Gold Key: July, 1965 - No. 2, Oct, 1965 (Painted-c)

1,2: Wood-a in each 4.00 12.25 45.00

TO THE LAST MAN (See Zane Grey Four Color #616)

TOUCH OF SILVER, A
Image Comics: Jan, 1997 - Present ($2.95, B&W, bi-monthly)

1-7-Valentino-s/a; photo-c: 5-color pgs. w/Round Table 3.00

TOUGH KID SQUAD COMICS
Timely Comics (TCI): Mar, 1942

GD25 FN65 VF82 NM94

1-(Scarce)-Origin & 1st app.The Human Top & The Tough Kid Squad; The Flying Flame app. 800.00 2400.00 4800.00 8000.00

TOUR OF TORTURE
London Night Studios: June, 1996 ($10.00, one-shot)

GD25 FN65 NM94

nn-Photo-c 1.00 3.00 10.00

TOWER OF SHADOWS (Creatures on the Loose #10 on)
Marvel Comics Group: Sept, 1969 - No. 9, Jan, 1971

1-Steranko, Craig-a(p) 3.80 11.40 38.00
2,3: 2-Neal Adams-a. 3-Barry Smith, Tuska-a 2.50 7.50 22.00
4-6: 4-Marie Severin-c. 5-B. Smith-a(p), Wood-a. 5-Wood draws himself (1st pg., 1st panel). 6-Wood-a 1.50 4.50 15.00
7-9: 7-B. Smith-a(p), Wood-a.. 8-Wood-a; 8-Wrightson-c. 9-Wrightson-c; Roy Thomas app. 2.20 6.50 24.00
Special 1(12/71)-Neal Adams-a 1.20 3.60 12.00
NOTE: ***J. Buscema*** *a-1p, 2p, Special 1r.* ***Colan*** *a-3p, 6p, Special 1.* ***J. Craig*** *a(r)-1p.* ***Ditko*** *a-6, 8, 9r, Special 1.* ***Everett*** *a-9(i)r; c-5i.* ***Kirby*** *a-9(p)r.* ***Severin*** *c-5p, 6.* ***Steranko*** *a-1p.* ***Tuska*** *a-3.* ***Wood*** *a-5-8. Issues 1-9 contain new stories with some pre-Marvel age reprints in 6-9.* ***H. P. Lovecraft*** *adaptation-9.*

TOWN & COUNTRY
Publisher?: May, 1940

nn-Origin The Falcon 42.00 127.00 340.00

TOWN THAT FORGOT SANTA, THE
W. T. Grant Co.: 1961 (Giveaway, 24 pgs.)

nn 2.00 6.00 16.00

TOXIC AVENGER (Movie)
Marvel Comics: Apr, 1991 - No. 11, Feb, 1992 ($1.50)

1-10: Based on movie character. 3,10-Photo-c 1.50
11-($1.75) 1.80

TOXIC CRUSADERS (TV)
Marvel Comics: May, 1992 - No. 8, Dec, 1992 ($1.25)

1-3-Sam Kieth-c; based on USA network cartoon 1.50
4-8: 8-Kieth-c(i) 1.25

TOXIC GUMBO
DC Comics (Vertigo): 1998 ($5.95, one-shot, mature)

1-McKeever-a/Lydia Lunch-s 2.00 6.00

TOYBOY
Continuity Comics: Oct, 1986 - No. 7, 1991 ($2.00, Baxter paper)

1-7 2.00

Transformers #63 © Hasbro

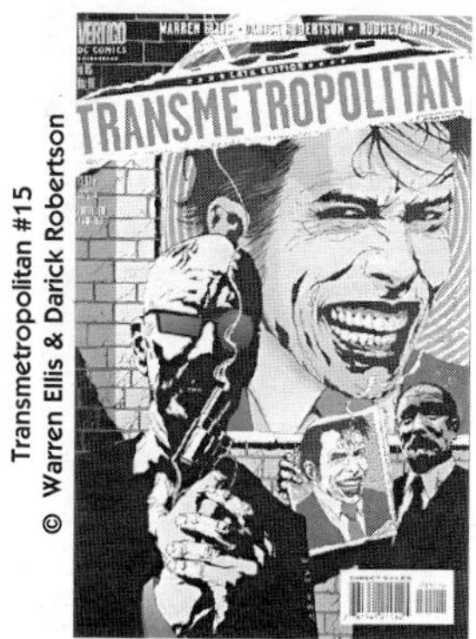

Transmetropolitan #15 © Warren Ellis & Darick Robertson

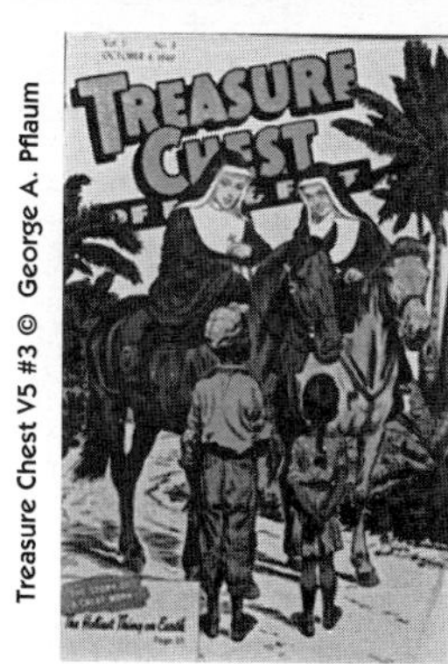

Treasure Chest V5 #3 © George A. Pflaum

GD25 FN65 NM94

*NOTE: **N. Adams** a-1; c-1, 2,5. **Golden** a-7p; c-6,7. **Nebres** a(i)-1,2.*

TOYLAND COMICS
Fiction House Magazines: Jan, 1947 - No. 2, Mar, 1947; No. 3, July, 1947 - No. 4, 1947

1-Wizard of the Moon begins 23.00 68.00 170.00
2-4: 2,3-Bob Lubbers-c. 3-Tuska-a 14.00 42.00 105.00
148 pg. issue 25.00 74.00 185.00
*NOTE: All above contain strips by **Al Walker.***

TOY TOWN COMICS
Toytown/Orbit Publ./B. Antin/Swapper Quarterly: 1945 - No. 7, May, 1947

1-Mertie Mouse; L. B. Cole-c/a; funny animal 29.00 88.00 220.00
2-L. B. Cole-a 19.00 56.00 140.00
3-7-L. B. Cole-a. 5-Wiggles the Wonderworm-c 16.00 48.00 120.00

TRAGG AND THE SKY GODS (See Gold Key Spotlight, Mystery Comics Digest #3,9 & Spine Tingling Tales)
Gold Key/Whitman No. 9: June, 1975 - No. 8, Feb, 1977; No. 9, May, 1982 (Painted-c #3-8)

1-Origin 5.00
2-9: 4-Sabre-Fang app. 8-Ostellon app.; 9-r/#1 3.00
*NOTE: **Santos** a-1, 2, 9r; c-3-7. **Spiegel** a-3-8.*

TRAIL BLAZERS (Red Dragon #5 on)
Street & Smith Publications: 1941; No. 2, Apr, 1942 - No. 4, Oct, 1942 (True stories of American heroes)

1-Life story of Jack Dempsey & Wright Brothers 31.00 92.00 230.00
2-Brooklyn Dodgers-c/story; Ben Franklin story 19.00 56.00 140.00
3,4: 3-Fred Allen, Red Barber, Yankees stories 17.00 52.00 130.00

TRAIL COLT (Also see Extra Comics & Manhunt!)
Magazine Enterprises: 1949 - No. 2, 1949

nn(A-1 #24)-7 pg. Frazetta-a r-in Manhunt #13; Undercover Girl app.; The Red Fox by L. B. Cole; Ingels-c; Whitney-a (Scarce) 35.00 104.00 260.00
2(A-1 #26)-Undercover Girl; Ingels-c; L. B. Cole-a (6 pgs.) 29.00 88.00 220.00

TRANSFORMERS, THE (TV)(See G.I. Joe and...)
Marvel Comics Group: Sept, 1984 - No. 80, July, 1991 (75¢/$1.00)

1-Based on Hasbro Toys 5.00
2,3 3.00
4-10 2.50
11-49: 21-Intro Aerialbots 1.00
50-60: 54-Intro Micromasters 1.50
61-80: 75-($1.50, 52 pgs.) 3.00
*NOTE: Second and third printings of all issues exist and are worth less than originals. Was originally planned as a four issue mini-series. **Wrightson** a-64i(4 pgs.).*

TRANSFORMERS DIGEST
Marvel Comics: Jan, 1987 - No. 9, May, 1988

1,2-Spider-Man-c/s 2.00 6.00
3-9 4.00

TRANSFORMERS: GENERATION 2
Marvel Comics: Nov, 1993 - No. 12, Oct, 1994 ($1.75)

1-($2.95, 68 pgs.)-Collector's ed. w/bi-fold metallic-c 3.00
1-11: 1-Newsstand edition (68 pgs.) 1.75
12-($2.25, 52 pgs.) 2.25

TRANSMETROPOLITAN
DC Comics (Vertigo): Sept, 1997 - Present ($2.50)

1-Warren Ellis-s/Darick Robertson-a(p) 2.00 6.00
2 5.00
3,4 4.00
5-8 4.00
9-14, 16-18 2.50
15-Jae Lee-c 2.50

GD25 FN65 NM94

Back on the Street ('97, $7.95) r/#1-3 7.95

TRANSMUTATION OF IKE GARUDA, THE
Marvel Comics (Epic Comics): July, 1991 - No. 2, 1991 ($3.95, 52 pgs.)

1,2 4.00

TRAPMAN
Phantom Comics: June, 1994 - No. 2, 1994? ($2.95, quarterly, unfinished limited series)

1,2 3.00

TRAPPED
Harvey Publications (Columbia Univ. Press): 1951 (Giveaway, soft-c, 16 pgs)

nn-Drug education comic (30,000 printed?) distributed to schools.; mentioned in **SOTI**, pgs. 256,350 1.60 4.00 8.00
NOTE: Many copies surfaced in 1979 causing a setback in price; beware of trimmed edges, because many copies have a brittle edge.

TRAPPED!
Periodical House Magazines (Ace): Oct, 1954 - No. 5, June?, 1955

1 (All reprints) 8.70 26.00 55.00
2-5: 4-r/Men Against Crime #4 in its entirety 5.70 17.00 35.00
*NOTE: **Colan** a-1, 4. **Sekowsky** a-1.*

TRASH
Trash Publ. Co.: Mar, 1978 - No. 4, Oct, 1978 (B&W, magazine, 52 pgs.)

1,2: 1-Star Wars parody. 2-UFO-c 1.20 3.60 12.00
3-Parodies of KISS, the Beatles, and monsters 1.80 5.40 18.00
4-(84 pgs.)-Parodies of Happy Days, Rocky movies 2.20 6.50 22.00

TRAVELS OF JAIMIE McPHEETERS, THE (TV)
Gold Key: Dec, 1963

1-Kurt Russell photo on-c plus photo back-c 2.70 8.00 30.00

TREASURE CHEST (Catholic Guild; also see Topix)
George A. Pflaum: 3/12/46 - V27#8, July, 1972 (Educational comics) (Not published during Summer)

V1#1 21.00 64.00 160.00
2-6 (5/21/46): 5-Dr. Styx app. by Baily 9.30 28.00 70.00
V2#1-20 (9/3/46-5/27/47) 7.85 23.50 55.00
V3#1-5,7-20 (1st slick cover) 6.50 19.50 45.00
V3#6-Jules Verne's "Voyage to the Moon" 9.30 28.00 65.00
V4#1-20 (9/9/48-5/31/49) 5.70 17.00 35.00
V5#1-20 (9/6/49-5/31/50) 5.00 15.00 30.00
V6#1-20 (9/14/50-5/31/51) 5.00 15.00 30.00
V7#1-20 (9/13/51-6/5/52) 4.00 12.00 24.00
V8#1-20 (9/11/52-6/4/53) 4.00 11.00 22.00
V9#1-20 ('53-'54) 4.00 10.00 20.00
V10#1-20 ('54-'55) 4.00 10.00 20.00
V11('55-'56), V12('56-'57) 3.60 9.00 18.00
V13#1,3-5,7,9-V17#1 ('57-'63) 3.20 8.00 16.00
V13#2,6,8-Ingels-a 5.00 15.00 50.00
V17#2- "This Godless Communism" series begins(not in odd #'d issues); cover shows hammer & sickle over Statue of Liberty; 8 pg. Crandall-a of family life under communism 15.00 45.00 150.00
V17#3,5,7,9,11,13,15,17,19 1.10 3.30 9.00
V17#4,6,14- "This Godless Communism" stories 9.50 28.50 95.00
V17#8-Shows red octopus encompassing Earth, firing squad; 8 pgs. Crandall-a 12.50 38.00 125.00
V17#10- "This Godless Communism" - how Stalin came to power, part I; Crandall-a 11.00 33.00 110.00
V17#12-Stalin in WWII, forced labor, death by exhaustion; Crandall-a 11.00 33.00 110.00
V17#16-Kruschev takes over; de-Stalinization 11.00 33.00 110.00
V17#18-Kruschev's control; murder of revolters, brainwash, space race by Crandall 11.00 33.00 110.00
V17#20-End of series; Kruschev-people are puppets, firing squads hammer &

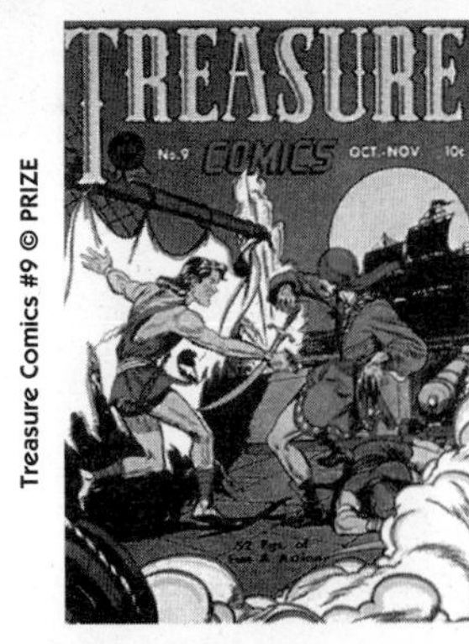

Treasure Comics #9 © PRIZE

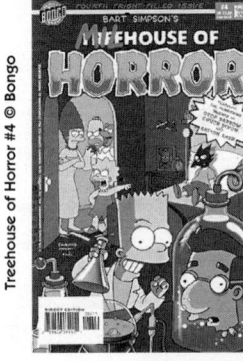

Treehouse of Horror #4 © Bongo

Trinity Angels #5 © Acclaim

GD25 FN65 NM94

sickle over Statue of Liberty, snake around communist manifesto by Crandall 12.50 38.00 125.00
V18#1-20, V19#11-20, V20#1-20(1964-65): V18#11-Crandall draws himself & 13 other artists on cover 1.50 4.50 12.00
V18#5- "What About Red China?" - describes how communists took over China 4.50 13.50 45.00
V19#1-10- "Red Victim" anti-communist series in all 4.50 13.50 45.00
V21-V25(1965-70)-(two V24#5's 11/7/68 & 11/21/68) (no V24#6) 1.25 3.75 10.00
V26, V27#1-8 (V26,27-68 pgs.) 1.50 4.50 12.00
Summer Edition V1#1-6('66), V2#1-6('67) 1.85 5.50 15.00

NOTE: ***Anderson*** *a-V18#13.* ***Borth*** *a-V7#10-19 (serial), V8#8-17 (serial), V9#1-10 (serial), V13#2, 6, 11, V14-V25 (except V22#1-3, 11-13), Summer Ed. V1#3-6.* ***Crandall*** *a-V16#7, 9, 12, 14, 16-18, 20; V17#1, 2, 4-6, 10, 12, 14, 16-18, 20; V18#1, 2, 3(2 pg.), 7, 9-20; V19#4, 11, 13, 16, 19, 20; V20#1, 2, 4, 6, 8-10, 12, 14-16, 18, 20; V21#1-5, 8-11, 13, 16-18; V22#3, 7, 9-11, 14; V23#3, 6, 9, 16, 18; V24#7, 8, 10, 13, 16; V25#8, 16; V27#1-7r, 8r(2 pg.), Summer Ed. V1#3-5, V2#3; c-V16#7, V18#2(part), 7, 11, V19#4, 19, 20, V20#15, V21#5, 9, V22#3, 7, 9, 11, V23#9, 16, V24#13, 16, V25#8, Summer Ed. V1#2 (back c-V1#2-5).* ***Powell*** *a-V10#11. V19#11, 15, V10#13, V13#6, 8 all have wraparound covers. All the above Crandall issues should be priced by condition from $4-8.00 in mint unless already priced.*

TREASURE CHEST OF THE WORLD'S BEST COMICS
Superior, Toronto, Canada: 1945 (500 pgs., hard-c)

Contains Blue Beetle, Captain Combat, John Wayne, Dynamic Man, Nemo, Li'l Abner; contents can vary - represents random binding of extra books; Capt. America on-c 77.00 229.00 650.00

TREASURE COMICS
Prize Publications? (no publisher listed): No date (1943) (50¢, 324 pgs., cardboard-c)

1-(Rare)-Contains rebound Prize Comics #7-11 from 1942 (blank inside-c) 177.00 529.00 1500.00

TREASURE COMICS
Prize Publ. (American Boys' Comics): June-July, 1945 - No. 12, Fall, 1947

1-Paul Bunyan & Marco Polo begin; Highwayman & Carrot Topp only app.; Kiefer-a 27.00 80.00 200.00
2-Arabian Knight, Gorilla King, Dr. Styx begin 13.00 40.00 100.00
3,4,9,12: 9-Kiefer-a 10.00 30.00 75.00
5-Marco Polo-c; Krigstein-a 17.00 50.00 125.00
6,11-Krigstein-a; 11-Krigstein-c 15.00 44.00 110.00
7,8-Frazetta-a (5 pgs. each). 7-Capt. Kidd Jr. app. 31.00 92.00 230.00
10-Simon & Kirby-c/a 25.00 76.00 190.00

NOTE: ***Barry*** *a-9-11; c-12.* ***Kiefer*** *a-3, 5, 7; c-2, 6, 7.* ***Roussos*** *a-11.*

TREASURE ISLAND (See Classics Illustrated #64, Doc Savage Comics #1, King Classics, Movie Classics & Movie Comics)
Dell Publishing Co.: No. 624, Apr, 1955 (Disney)

Four Color 624-Movie, photo-c 8.00 25.00 90.00

TREASURY OF COMICS
St. John Publishing Co.: 1947; No. 2, July, 1947 - No. 4, Sept, 1947; No. 5, Jan, 1948

nn(#1)-Abbie an' Slats (nn on-c, #1 on inside) 13.00 40.00 100.00
2-Jim Hardy Comics; featuring Windy & Paddles 9.30 28.00 70.00
3-Bill Bumlin 7.15 21.50 50.00
4-Abbie an' Slats 9.30 28.00 70.00
5-Jim Hardy Comics #1 9.30 28.00 70.00

TREASURY OF COMICS
St. John Publishing Co.: Mar, 1948 - No. 5, 1948 (Reg. size); 1948-1950 (Over 500 pgs., $1.00)

1 17.00 52.00 130.00
2(#2 on-c, #1 on inside) 9.30 28.00 70.00
3-5 8.50 26.00 60.00
1-(1948, 500 pgs., hard-c)-Abbie & Slats, Abbott & Costello, Casper, Little Annie Rooney, Little Audrey, Jim Hardy, Ella Cinders (16 books bound together) (Rare) 94.00 282.00 800.00

GD25 FN65 NM94

1(1949, 500 pgs.)-Same format as above 94.00 282.00 800.00
1(1950, 500 pgs.)-Same format as above; different-c; (also see Little Audrey Yearbook) (Rare) 94.00 282.00 800.00

TREASURY OF DOGS, A (See Dell Giants)

TREASURY OF HORSES, A (See Dell Giants)

TREEHOUSE OF HORROR (Bart Simpson's...)
Bongo Comics: 1995 -Present ($2.95/$2.50, annual)

1-(1995, $2.95)-Groening-c; Allred, Robinson & Smith stories. 4.00
2-(1996, $2.50)-Stories by Dini & Bagge; infinity-c by Groening 3.00
3-(1997, $2.50)-Dorkin-s/Groening-c 2.50
4-(1998, $2.50)-Lash & Dixon-s/Groening-c 2.50

TREKKER (See Dark Horse Presents #6)
Dark Horse Comics: May, 1987 - No. 6, Mar,1988 ($1.50, B&W)

1-6: Sci/Fi stories 1.50
Color Special 1 (1989, $2.95, 52 pgs.) 3.00
Collection ($5.95, B&W) 6.00

TRENCHER (See Blackball Comics)
Image Comics: May, 1993 - No. 4, Oct, 1993 ($1.95, unfinished limited series)

1-4: Keith Giffen-c/a/scripts. 3-Supreme-c/story 2.00

TRIBAL FORCE
Mystic Comics: Aug, 1996 ($2.50)

1-Reads "Special Edition" on-c 2.50

TRIB COMIC BOOK, THE
Winnipeg Tribune: Sept. 24, 1977 - Vol.4, #36, 1980 (8-1/2"x11", 24 pgs., weekly) (155 total issues)

V1# 1-Color pages (Sunday strips)-Spiderman, Asterix, Disney's Scamp, Wizard of Id, Doonesbury, Inside Woody Allen, Mary Worth, & others (similar to Spirit sections) 1.40 4.20 14.00
V1#2-15, V3#1-52, V4#1-33 1.00 3.00 10.00
V2#1-52, V4#34-36 (not distributed) 2.00 6.00 20.00

Note: All issues have Spider-Man. Later issues contain Star Trek and Star Wars. 20 strips in ea. The first newspaper to put Sunday pages into a comic book format.

TRIBE (See WildC.A.T.S #4)
Image Comics/Axis Comics No. 2 on: Apr, 1993; No. 2, Sept, 1993 - No. 3, 1994 ($2.50/$1.95)

1-By Johnson & Stroman; gold foil & embossed on black-c 2.50
1-($2.50)-Ivory Edition; gold foil & embossed on white-c; available only through the creators 2.50
2,3: 2-1st Axis Comics issue. 3-Savage Dragon app. 2.00

TRIGGER (See Roy Rogers'...)

TRIGGER TWINS
National Periodical Publications: Mar-Apr, 1973 (20¢, one-shot)

1-Trigger Twins & Pow Wow Smith-r/All-Star Western #94,103 & Western Comics #81; Infantino-r(p) 1.80 5.40 18.00

TRINITY (See DC Universe: Trinity)

TRINITY ANGELS
Acclaim Comics (Valiant Heroes): July, 1997 - No. 12, June, 1998 ($2.50)

1-12-Maguire-s/a(p):4-Copycat-c 2.50

TRIPLE GIANT COMICS (See Archie All-Star Specials under Archie Comics)

TRIPLE THREAT
Special Action/Holyoke/Gerona Publ.: Winter, 1945

1-Duke of Darkness, King O'Leary 20.00 60.00 150.00

TRIPLE-X
Dark Horse Comics: Dec, 1994 - No. 7, June, 1995 ($3.95, B&W, limited series)

1-7 4.00

Triumph #2 © DC

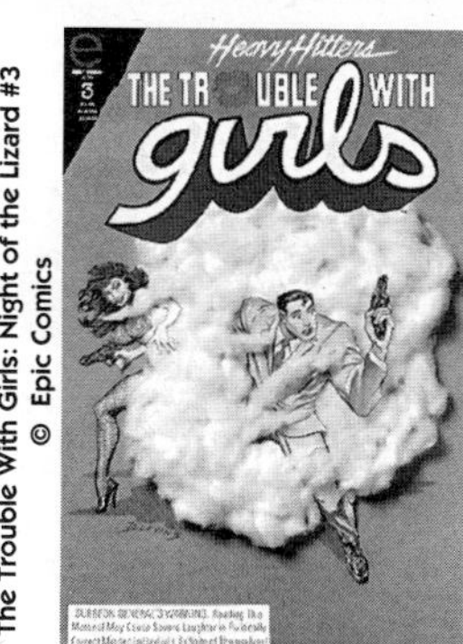

The Trouble With Girls: Night of the Lizard #3 © Epic Comics

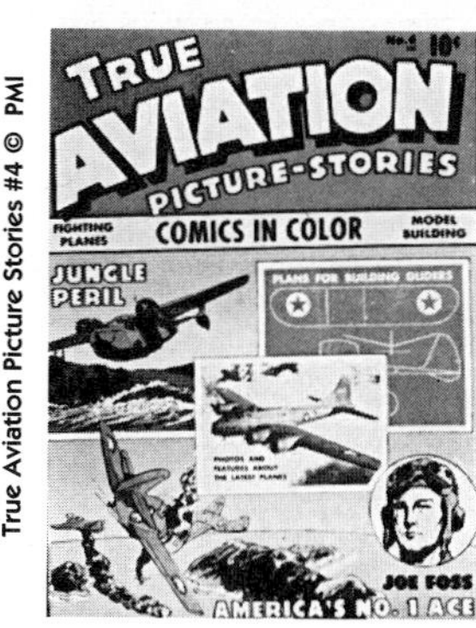

True Aviation Picture Stories #4 © PMI

GD25 FN65 NM94

TRIP TO OUTER SPACE WITH SANTA
Sales Promotions, Inc/Peoria Dry Goods: 1950s (self-c)
nn-Comics, games & puzzles 4.00 10.00 20.00

TRIP WITH SANTA ON CHRISTMAS EVE, A
Rockford Dry Goods Co.: No date (Early 1950s) (Giveaway, 16 pgs., paper-c)
nn 4.00 10.00 20.00

TRIUMPH (Also see Justice League Task Force & Zero Hour)
DC Comics: June, 1995 - No. 4, Sept, 1995 ($1.75, limited series)
1-4: 3-Hourman, JLA app. 1.75

TRIUMPHANT UNLEASHED
Triumphant Comics: No. 0, Nov, 1993 - No. 1, Nov, 1993 ($2.50, lim. series)
0-Serially numbered, 0-Red logo 2.50
0-White logo (no cover price; giveaway) 2.50
1-Cover is negative & reverse of #0-c 2.50

TROLL (Also see Brigade)
Image Comics (Extreme Studios): Dec, 1993 ($2.50, one-shot, 44 pgs.)
1-1st app. Troll; Liefeld scripts; Matsuda-c/a(p) 2.50
Halloween Special (1994, $2.95)-Maxx app. 3.00
...Once A Hero (8/94, $2.50) 2.50

TROLLORDS
Tru Studios/Comico V2#1 on: 2/86 - No. 15, 1988; V2#1, 11/88 - V2#4, 1989 (1-15: $1.50, B&W)
1-1st & 2nd printings 1.50
2-15: 6-Christmas issue; silver logo 1.50
V2#1 ($1.75, color, Comico) 1.80
V2#2,3 ($1.95, color) 2.00
4 ($2.50, color) 2.50
Special 1 ($1.75, 2/87, color)-Jerry's Big Fun Bk. 1.80

TROLLORDS
Apple Comics: July, 1989 - No. 6, 1990 ($2.25, B&W, limited series)
1-6: 1-"The Big Batman Movie Parody" 2.30

TROLL PATROL
Harvey Comics: Jan, 1993 ($1.95, 52 pgs.)
1 2.00

TROLL II (Also see Brigade)
Image Comics (Extreme Studios): July, 1994 ($3.95, one-shot)
1 4.00

TROUBLED SOULS
Fleetway: 1990 ($9.95, trade paperback)
nn-Garth Ennis scripts & John McCrea painted-c/a. 10.00

TROUBLEMAKERS
Acclaim Comics (Valiant Heroes): Apr, 1997 - No. 19, June, 1998 ($2.50)
1-19: Fabian Nicieza scripts in all. 1-1st app. XL, Rebound & Blur. 8-Copycat-c. 12-Shooting of Parker 2.50

TROUBLEMAN
Image Comics (Motown Machineworks): June, 1996 - No. 3, Aug, 1996 ($2.25, limited series)
1-3 2.25

TROUBLE SHOOTERS, THE (TV)
Dell Publishing Co.: No. 1108, Jun-Aug, 1960
Four Color 1108-Keenan Wynn photo-c 4.50 13.50 50.00

TROUBLE WITH GIRLS, THE
Malibu Comics (Eternity Comics) #7-14/Comico V2#1-4/Eternity V2#5 on: 8/87 - #14, 1988; V2#1, 2/89 - V2#10, 1990? ($1.95, B&W/color)
1-14 ($1.95, B&W, Eternity)-Gerard Jones scripts & Tim Hamilton-c/a in all. 2.00
V2#1-10-Jones scripts, Hamilton-c/a. 2.00
Annual 1 (1988, $2.95) 3.00
Christmas Special 1 (12/91, $2.95, B&W, Eternity)-Jones scripts, Hamilton-c/a. 3.00
Graphic Novel 1 (7/88, $6.95, B&W)-r/#1-3 7.00
Graphic Novel 2 (1989, $7.95, B&W)-r/#4-6 8.00

TROUBLE WITH GIRLS, THE: NIGHT OF THE LIZARD
Marvel Comics (Epic Comics/Heavy Hitters): 1993 - No. 4, 1993 ($2.50/$1.95, limited series)
1-Embossed-c; Gerard Jones scripts & Bret Blevins-c/a in all 2.50
2-4: 2-Begin $1.95-c. 2.00

TRUE ADVENTURES (Formerly True Western)(Men's Adventures #4 on)
Marvel Comics (CCC): No. 3, May, 1950 (52 pgs.)
3-Powell, Sekowsky-a; Brodsky-c 13.00 40.00 100.00

TRUE ANIMAL PICTURE STORIES
True Comics Press: Winter, 1947 - No. 2, Spring-Summer, 1947
1,2 7.85 23.50 55.00

TRUE AVIATION PICTURE STORIES (Becomes Aviation Adventures & Model Building #16 on)
Parents' Mag. Institute: 1942; No. 2, Jan-Feb, 1943 - No. 15, Sept-Oct, 1946
1-(#1 & 2 titled ...Aviation Comics Digest)(not digest size) 12.00 36.00 90.00
2 7.15 21.50 50.00
3-14: 3-10-Plane photos on-c. 11,13-Photo-c 6.50 19.50 45.00
15-(Titled "True Aviation Adventures & Model Building") 5.70 17.00 40.00

TRUE BRIDE'S EXPERIENCES (Formerly Teen-Age Brides)
(True Bride-To-Be Romances No. 17 on)
True Love (Harvey Publications): No. 8, Oct, 1954 - No. 16, Feb, 1956
8 5.70 17.00 40.00
9,10: 10-Last pre-code (2/55) 4.25 13.00 26.00
11-15 4.00 11.00 22.00
16-Spanking panels (3) 5.85 17.50 35.00
NOTE: *Powell* a-8-10, 12, 13.

TRUE BRIDE-TO-BE ROMANCES (Formerly True Bride's Experiences)
Home Comics/True Love (Harvey): No. 17, Apr, 1956 - No. 30, Nov, 1958
17-S&K-c, Powell-a 8.30 25.00 58.00
18-20,22,25-28,30 4.00 11.00 22.00
21,23,24,29-Powell-a. 29-Baker-a (1 pg.) 4.25 13.00 26.00

TRUE COMICS (Also see Outstanding American War Heroes)
True Comics/Parents' Magazine Press: April, 1941 - No. 84, Aug, 1950
1-Marathon run story; life story Winston Churchill 29.00 86.00 215.00
2-Red Cross story; Everett-a 13.00 40.00 100.00
3-Baseball Hall of Fame story 15.00 46.00 115.00
4,5: 4-Story of American flag "Old Glory". 5-Life story of Joe Louis 11.00 32.00 80.00
6-Baseball World Series story 15.00 44.00 110.00
7-10: 7-Buffalo Bill story. 10,11-Teddy Roosevelt 7.85 23.50 55.00
11-14,16,18-20: 11-Thomas Edison, Douglas MacArthur stories. 13-Harry Houdini story. 14-Charlie McCarthy story. 18-Story of America begins, ends #26. 19-Eisenhower-c/s 7.15 21.50 50.00
15-Flag-c; Bob Feller story 8.50 26.00 60.00
17-Brooklyn Dodgers story 9.30 28.00 70.00
21-30: 24-Marco Polo story 6.00 18.00 42.00
31-Red Grange "Galloping Ghost" story 5.00 15.00 30.00
32-46: 33-Origin/1st app. Steve Saunders, Special Agent. 39-FDR story. 46-George Gershwin story 4.25 13.00 26.00
47-Atomic bomb issue (c/story, 3/46) 7.85 23.50 55.00
48-54,56-65: 58-Jim Jeffries (boxer) story; Harry Houdini story. 59-Bob Hope

True Comics #48 © PMI

True Crime Comics #5 © Magazine Village

True Love Pictorial #6 © STJ

GD25 FN65 NM94

story. 60-Speedway Speed Demon-c/story. 4.00 12.00 24.00
55-(12/46)-1st app. Sad Sack by Baker (1/2 pg.) 5.35 16.00 32.00
66-Will Rogers-c/story 4.25 13.00 28.00
67-1st oversized issue (12/47); Steve Saunders, Special Agent begins 5.70 17.00 35.00
68-70,74-77,79: 68-70,74-77-Features True FBI advs. 69-Jack Benny story. 74-Amos 'n' Andy story 4.00 12.00 24.00
71-Joe DiMaggio-c/story. 5.70 17.00 40.00
72-Jackie Robinson story; True FBI advs. 5.00 15.00 30.00
73-Walt Disney's life story 5.70 17.00 40.00
78-Stan Musial-c/story; True FBI advs. 5.00 15.00 30.00
80-84 (Scarce)-All distr. to subscribers through mail only; paper-c. 80-Rocket trip to the moon story. 81-Red Grange story 15.00 44.00 110.00
(Prices vary widely on issues 80-84)

NOTE: ***Bob Kane** a-7. **Palais** a-80. **Powell** c/a-80. #80-84 have soft covers and combined with Tex Granger, Jack Armstrong, and Calling All Kids. #68-78 featured true FBI adventures.*

TRUE COMICS AND ADVENTURE STORIES
Parents' Magazine Institute: 1965 (Giant) (25¢)

1,2: 1-Fighting Hero of Viet Nam; LBJ on-c 1.25 3.75 10.00

TRUE COMPLETE MYSTERY (Formerly Complete Mystery)
Marvel Comics (PrPl): No. 5, Apr, 1949 - No. 8, Oct, 1949

5 21.00 64.00 160.00
6-8: 6-8-Photo-c 17.00 50.00 125.00

TRUE CONFIDENCES
Fawcett Publications: 1949 (Fall) - No. 4, June, 1950 (All photo-c)

1-Has ad for Fawcett Love Adventures #1, but publ. as Love Memoirs #1 as Marvel published the title first; Swayze-a 14.00 42.00 105.00
2-4: 3-Swayze-a. 4-Powell-a 9.30 28.00 65.00

TRUE CRIME CASES (...From Official Police Files)
St. John Publishing Co.: 1944 (25¢, 100 pg. Giant)

nn-Matt Baker-c 39.00 117.00 300.00

TRUE CRIME COMICS (Also see Complete Book of...)
Magazine Village: No. 2, May, 1947; No. 3, July-Aug, 1948 - No. 6, June-July, 1949; V2#1, Aug-Sept, 1949 (52 pgs.)

2-Jack Cole-c/a; used in **SOTI**, pgs. 81,82 plus illo. "A sample of the injury-to-eye motif" & illo. "Dragging living people to death"; used in **POP**, pg. 105; "Murder, Morphine and Me" classic drug propaganda story used by N.Y. Legis. Comm. 120.00 360.00 1020.00
3-Classic Cole-c/a; drug story with hypo, opium den & with drawing addict 88.00 264.00 750.00
4-Jack Cole-c/a; c-taken from a story panel in #3 (r-(2) **SOTI** & **POP** stories/#2?) 80.00 240.00 680.00
5-Jack Cole-c, Marijuana racket story (Canadian ed. w/cover similar to #3 exists w/out drug story) 52.00 156.00 440.00
6-Not a reprint, original story (Canadian ed. reprints #4 w/different coloring on-c) 42.00 126.00 340.00
V2#1-Used in **SOTI**, pgs. 81,82 & illo. "Dragging living people to death"; Toth, Wood (3 pgs.), Roussos-a; Cole-r from #2 70.00 210.00 600.00

NOTE: *V2#1 was reprinted in Canada as V2#9 (12/49); same-c & contents minus Wood-a.*

TRUE FAITH
Fleetway: 1990 ($9.95, graphic novel)

nn-Garth Ennis scripts 2.25 6.80 25.00
Reprinted by DC/Vertigo ('97, $12.95) 13.00

TRUE GHOST STORIES (See Ripley's...)

TRUE LIFE ROMANCES (...Romance on cover)
Ajax/Farrell Publications: Dec, 1955 - No. 3, Aug, 1956

1 8.30 25.00 58.00
2 5.35 16.00 32.00
3-Disbrow-a 5.70 17.00 38.00

TRUE LIFE SECRETS
Romantic Love Stories/Charlton: Mar-April, 1951 - No. 28, Sept, 1955; No. 29, Jan, 1956

1-Photo-c begin, end #3? 9.30 28.00 70.00
2 5.70 17.00 35.00
3-19: 12-"I Was An Escort Girl" story 4.25 13.00 26.00
20-29: 25-Last precode(3/55) 4.00 11.00 22.00

TRUE LIFE TALES (Formerly Mitzi's Romances #8?)
Marvel Comics (CCC): No. 8, Oct, 1949 - No. 2, Jan, 1950 (52 pgs.)

8(#1, 10/49), 2-Both have photo-c 8.30 25.00 58.00

TRUE LOVE
Eclipse Comics: Jan, 1986 - No. 2, Jan, 1986 ($2.00, Baxter paper)

1,2-Love stories reprinted from pre-code Standard Comics; Toth-a(p) in both; 1-Dave Stevens-c. 2-Mayo-a 2.00

TRUE LOVE CONFESSIONS
Premier Magazines: May, 1954 - No. 11, Jan, 1956

1-Marijuana story 8.50 26.00 60.00
2 4.25 13.00 28.00
3-11 4.00 12.00 24.00

TRUE LOVE PICTORIAL
St. John Publishing Co.: 1952 - No. 11, Aug, 1954

1-Only photo-c 13.00 40.00 100.00
2-Baker-c/a 15.00 46.00 115.00
3-5(All 25¢, 100 pgs.): 4-Signed story by Estrada. 5-(4/53)-Formerly Teen-Age Temptations; Kubert-a in #3; Baker-a in #3-5 28.00 84.00 210.00
6,7: Baker-c/a. 7-Signed story by Estrada 14.00 42.00 105.00
8,10,11-Baker-c/a 13.00 40.00 100.00
9-Baker-c 11.00 32.00 80.00

TRUE LOVE PROBLEMS AND ADVICE ILLUSTRATED (Becomes Romance Stories of True Love No. 45 on)
McCombs/Harvey Publ./Home Comics: June, 1949 - No. 6, Apr, 1950; No. 7, Jan, 1951 - No. 44, Mar, 1957

V1#1 13.00 38.00 95.00
2 6.85 21.00 48.00
3-10: 7-9-Elias-c 5.35 16.00 32.00
11-13,15-23,25-31: 31-Last pre-code (1/55) 4.00 11.00 22.00
14,24-Rape scene 4.25 13.00 28.00
32-37,39-44 3.60 9.00 18.00
38-S&K-c 6.00 18.00 42.00

NOTE: ***Powell** a-1, 2, 7-14, 17-25, 28, 29, 33, 40, 41. #3 has True Love... on inside.*

TRUE MOVIE AND TELEVISION (Part teenage magazine)
Toby Press: Aug, 1950 - No. 3, Nov, 1950; No. 4, Mar, 1951 (52 pgs.)(1-3: 10¢)

1-Elizabeth Taylor photo-c; Gene Autry, Shirley Temple, Li'l Abner app. 38.00 114.00 285.00
2-(9/50)-Janet Leigh/Liz Taylor/Ava Gardner & others photo-c; Frazetta John Wayne illo from J.Wayne Adv. Comics #2 (4/50) 28.00 84.00 210.00
3-June Allyson photo-c; Montgomery Cliff, Esther Williams, Andrews Sisters app; Li'l Abner featured; Sadie Hawkins' Day 25.00 74.00 185.00
4-Jane Powell photo-c (15¢) 12.00 36.00 90.00

NOTE: *16 pgs. in color, rest movie material in black & white.*

TRUE SECRETS (Formerly Our Love?)
Marvel (IPS)/Atlas Comics (MPI) #4 on: No. 3, Mar, 1950; No. 4, Feb, 1951 - No. 40, Sept, 1956

3 (52 pgs.)(IPS one-shot) 10.00 30.00 75.00
4,5,7-10 5.70 17.00 40.00
6,22-Everett-a 7.15 21.50 50.00
11-20 5.35 16.00 32.00
21,23-28: 24-Colletta-c. 28-Last pre-code (2/55) 4.00 12.00 24.00
29-40: 34,36-Colletta-a 4.00 11.00 22.00

TRUE SPORT PICTURE STORIES (Formerly Sport Comics)

True Sport Picture Stories V2 #7 © S&S

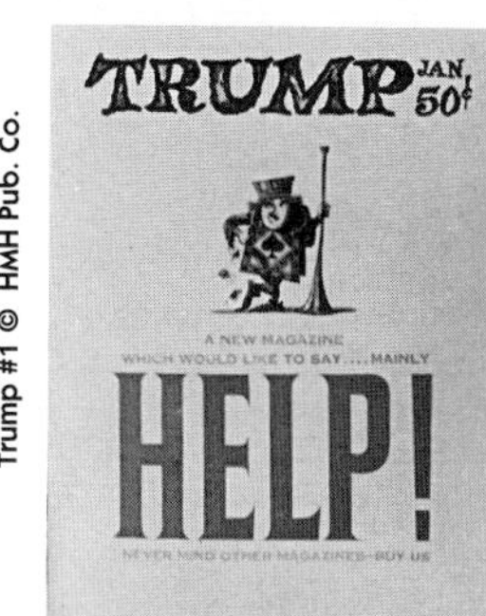

Trump #1 © HMH Pub. Co.

Tug & Buster #7 © Marc Hempel

Street & Smith Publications: V1#5, Feb, 1942 - V5#2, July-Aug, 1949

	GD25	FN65	NM94
V1#5-Joe DiMaggio-c/story	31.00	92.00	230.00
6-12 (1942-43): 12-Jack Dempsey story	17.00	52.00	130.00
V2#1-12 (1944-45): 7-Stan Musial-c/story; photo story of the New York Yankees	15.00	46.00	115.00
V3#1-12 (1946-47): 7-Joe DiMaggio, Stan Musial, Bob Feller & others back from the armed service story. 8-Billy Conn vs. Joe Louis-c/story	13.00	40.00	100.00
V4#1-12 (1948-49), V5#1,2	12.00	36.00	90.00

NOTE: ***Powell** a-V3#10, V4#1-4, 6-8, 10-12; V5#1, 2; c-V3#11, V4#3-7, 9-12. **Ravielli** c-V5#2.*

TRUE STORIES OF ROMANCE
Fawcett Publications: Jan, 1950 - No. 3, May, 1950 (All photo-c)

	GD25	FN65	NM94
1	10.00	30.00	75.00
2,3: 3-Marcus Swayze-a	7.15	21.50	50.00

TRUE STORY OF JESSE JAMES, THE (See Jesse James, Four Color 757)

TRUE SWEETHEART SECRETS
Fawcett Publications: 5/50; No. 2, 7/50; No. 3, 1951(nd); No. 4, 9/51 - No. 11, 1/53 (All photo-c)

	GD25	FN65	NM94
1-Photo-c; Debbie Reynolds?	11.00	32.00	80.00
2-Wood-a (11 pgs.)	15.00	44.00	110.00
3-11: 4,5-Powell-a. 8-Marcus Swayze-a. 11-Evans-a	7.85	23.50	55.00

TRUE TALES OF LOVE (Formerly Secret Story Romances)
Atlas Comics (TCI): No. 22, April, 1956 - No. 31, Sept, 1957

	GD25	FN65	NM94
22	6.00	18.00	42.00
23-24,26-31-Colletta-a in most:	4.00	12.00	24.00
25-Everett-a; Colletta-a	5.00	15.00	30.00

TRUE TALES OF ROMANCE
Fawcett Publications: No. 4, June, 1950

	GD25	FN65	NM94
4-Photo-c	6.50	19.50	45.00

TRUE 3-D
Harvey Publications: Dec, 1953 - No. 2, Feb, 1954 (25¢)(Both came with 2 pair of glasses)

	GD25	FN65	NM94
1-Nostrand, Powell-a	5.00	15.00	50.00
2-Powell-a	5.50	16.50	55.00

NOTE: *Many copies of #1 surfaced in 1984.*

TRUE-TO-LIFE ROMANCES (Formerly Guns Against Gangsters)
Star Publ.: #8, 11-12/49; #9, 1-2/50; #3, 4/50 - #5, 9/50; #6, 1/51 - #23, 10/54

	GD25	FN65	NM94
8(#1, 1949)	19.00	58.00	145.00
9(#2),4-10	14.00	42.00	105.00
3-Janet Leigh/Glenn Ford photo on-c plus true life story of each	16.00	48.00	120.00
11,22,23	12.00	36.00	90.00
12-14,17-21-Disbrow-a	14.00	42.00	105.00
15,16-Wood & Disbrow-a in each	16.00	48.00	120.00

NOTE: ***Kamen** a-13. **Kamen/Feldstein** a-14. All have **L.B. Cole** covers.*

TRUE WAR EXPERIENCES
Harvey Publications: Aug, 1952 - No. 4, Dec, 1952

	GD25	FN65	NM94
1	7.50	22.50	75.00
2-4	4.00	12.00	40.00

TRUE WAR ROMANCES (Becomes Exotic Romances #22 on)
Quality Comics Group: Sept, 1952 - No. 21, June, 1955

	GD25	FN65	NM94
1-Photo-c	11.00	32.00	80.00
2	5.70	17.00	38.00
3-10: 9-Whitney-a	4.25	13.00	28.00
11-21: 20-Last precode (4/55). 14-Whitney-a	4.00	12.00	24.00

TRUE WAR STORIES (See Ripley's...)

TRUE WESTERN (True Adventures #3)
Marvel Comics (MMC): Dec, 1949 - No. 2, March, 1950

	GD25	FN65	NM94
1-Photo-c; Billy The Kid story	13.00	40.00	100.00
2: Alan Ladd photo-c	17.00	52.00	130.00

TRUMP
HMH Publishing Co.: Jan, 1957 - No. 2, Mar, 1957 (50¢, magazine)

	GD25	FN65	NM94
1-Harvey Kurtzman satire	21.00	62.00	155.00
2-Harvey Kurtzman satire	17.00	50.00	125.00

NOTE: ***Davis, Elder, Heath, Jaffee** art-#1,2; **Wood** a-1. Article by Mel Brooks in #2.*

TRUMPETS WEST (See Luke Short, Four Color #875)

TRUTH ABOUT CRIME (See Fox Giants)

TRUTH ABOUT MOTHER GOOSE (See Mother Goose, Four Color #862)

TRUTH BEHIND THE TRIAL OF CARDINAL MINDSZENTY, THE (See Cardinal Mindszenty)

TRUTHFUL LOVE (Formerly Youthful Love)
Youthful Magazines: No. 2, July, 1950

	GD25	FN65	NM94
2-Ingrid Bergman's true life story	7.85	23.50	55.00

TRY-OUT WINNER BOOK
Marvel Comics: Mar, 1988

	GD25	FN65	NM94
1-Spider-Man vs. Doc Octopus			1.25

TSR WORLD (...Annual on cover only)
DC Comics: 1990 ($3.95, 84 pgs.)

	GD25	FN65	NM94
1-Advanced D&D, ForgottenRealms, Dragonlance & 1st app. Spelljammer			4.00

TUBBY (See Marge's...)

TUFF GHOSTS STARRING SPOOKY
Harvey Publications: July, 1962 - No. 39, Nov, 1970; No. 40, Sept, 1971 - No. 43, Oct, 1972

	GD25	FN65	NM94
1-12¢ issues begin	10.00	30.00	100.00
2-5	5.00	15.00	50.00
6-10	3.00	9.00	30.00
11-20	2.40	7.00	24.00
21-30: 29-Hot Stuff/Spooky team-up story	1.50	4.50	15.00
31-39,43	1.00	3.00	10.00
40-42: 52 pg. Giants	1.40	4.20	14.00

TUFFY
Standard Comics: No. 5, July, 1949 - No. 9, Oct, 1950

	GD25	FN65	NM94
5-All by Sid Hoff	4.25	13.00	26.00
6-9	3.20	8.00	16.00

TUFFY TURTLE
I. W. Enterprises: No date

	GD25	FN65	NM94
1-Reprint	1.10	3.60	9.00

TUG & BUSTER
Art & Soul Comics: Nov, 1995 - No. 7, Feb, 1998 ($2.95, B&W, bi-monthly)

	GD25	FN65	NM94
1-7: Marc Hempel-c/a/scripts			3.00

TUG & BUSTER
Image Comics: Aug, 1998 - Present ($2.95, B&W)

	GD25	FN65	NM94
1-Marc Hempel-s/a			3.00

TUROK, CHILD OF BLOOD
Acclaim Comics (Valiant): Jan, 1998 ($3.95, one-shot)

	GD25	FN65	NM94
1-Nicieza-s/Kayanan-a			3.95

TUROK, DINOSAUR HUNTER (See Magnus Robot Fighter #12 & Archer & Armstrong #2)
Valiant/Acclaim Comics: June, 1993 - No. 47, Aug, 1996 ($2.50)

	GD25	FN65	NM94
1-($3.50)-Chromium & foil-c			3.50
1-Gold foil-c variant			5.00

0, 2-47: 4-Andar app. 5-Death of Andar. 7-9-Truman/Glanzman-a. 11-Bound-in

Turok, Dinosaur Hunter #18 © WEST

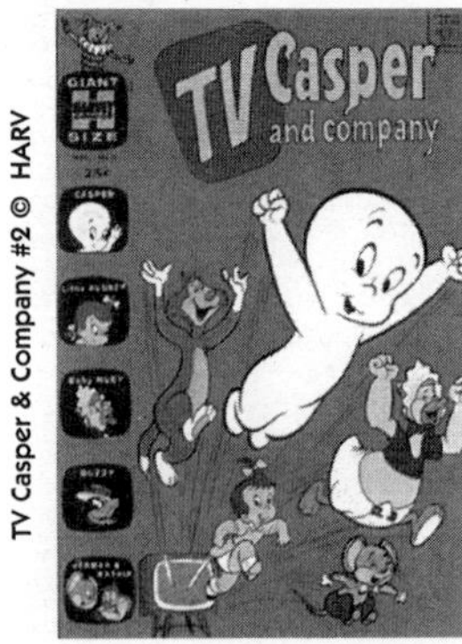

TV Casper & Company #2 © HARV

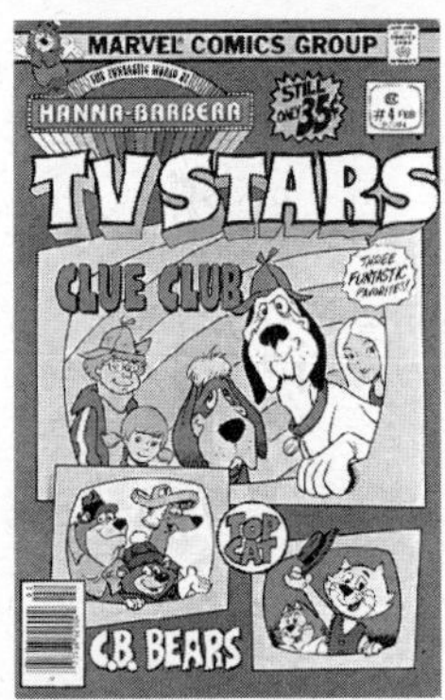

TV Stars #4 © H-B

	GD25	FN65	NM94
trading card. 16-Chaos Effect			2.50
Yearbook 1 (1994, $3.95, 52 pgs.)			4.00

TUROK, REDPATH
Acclaim Comics (Valiant): Oct, 1997 ($3.95, one-shot)

	GD25	FN65	NM94
1-Nicieza-s/Kayanan-a			4.00

TUROK, SON OF STONE (See Dan Curtis, Golden Comics Digest #31 & March of Comics #378, 399, 408)
Dell Publ. Co. #1-29(9/62)/Gold Key #30(12/62)-85(7/73)/Gold Key or Whitman #86(9/73)-125(1/80)/Whitman #126(3/81) on: No. 596, 12/54 - No. 29, 9/62; No. 30, 12/62 - No. 91, 7/74; No. 92, 9/74 - No. 125, 1/80; No. 126, 3/81 - No. 130, 4/82

	GD25	FN65	NM94
Four Color 596 (12/54)(#1)-1st app./origin Turok & Andar; dinosaur-c. Created by Matthew H. Murphy; written by Alberto Giolitti	55.00	165.00	600.00
Four Color 656 (10/55)(#2)-1st mention of Lanok	32.00	96.00	350.00
3(3-5/56)-5: 3-Cave men	18.00	55.00	200.00
6-10: 8-Dinosaur of the deep; Turok enters Lost Valley; series begins. 9-Paul S. Newman-s (most issues thru end)	12.00	35.00	130.00
11-20: 17-Prehistoric Pygmies	8.00	23.00	85.00
21-30: 30-33-Painted back-c pin-ups	5.50	16.50	60.00
31-Drug use story	5.50	16.50	60.00
32-40	3.60	11.00	40.00
41-50	2.75	8.00	30.00
51-60: 58-Flying Saucer c/story	2.25	6.75	25.00
61-70: 62-12 & 15¢-c. 63-Only line drawn-c	1.80	5.40	18.00
71-84: 84-Origin & 1st app. Hutec	1.20	3.60	12.00
85-99: 93-r-c/#19 w/changes. 94-r-c/#28 w/changes. 97-r-c/#31 w/changes. 98-r/#58 w/o spaceship & spacemen on-c. 99-r-c/#52 w/changes.		2.00	6.00
100	1.50	4.50	15.00
101-129: 114,115-(52 pgs.)	1.20	3.60	12.00
130-Last issue	1.50	4.50	15.00
Giant 1(30031-611) (11/66)-Slick-c; r/#10-12 & 16 plus cover to #11	8.00	25.00	90.00
Giant 1-Same as above but with paper-c	9.00	27.00	100.00

NOTE: *Most painted-c; line-drawn #63 & 130.* ***Alberto Gioletti*** *a-24-27, 30-119, 123; painted-c No. 30-129.* ***Sparling*** *a-117, 120-130. Reprints-#36, 54, 57, 75, 112, 114(1/3), 115(1/3), 118, 121, 125, 127(1/3), 128, 129(1/3), 130(1/3), Giant 1. Cover r-93, 94, 97-99, 126(all different from original covers.*

TUROK: SPRING BREAK IN THE LOST LAND
Acclaim Comics (Valiant): July, 1997 ($3.95, one-shot)

	GD25	FN65	NM94
1-Nicieza-s/Kayanan-a			4.00

TUROK: THE EMPTY SOULS
Acclaim Comics (Valiant): Apr, 1997 ($3.95, one-shot)

	GD25	FN65	NM94
1-Nicieza-s/Kayanan-a; variant-c			4.00

TUROK THE HUNTED
Valiant/Acclaim Comics: Mar, 1995 - No. 2, Apr, 1995 ($2.50, limited series)

	GD25	FN65	NM94
1,2-Mike Deodato-a(p); price omitted on #1			2.50

TUROK THE HUNTED
Acclaim Comics (Valiant): Feb, 1996 - No. 2, Mar, 1996 ($2.50, limited series)

	GD25	FN65	NM94
1,2-Mike Grell story			2.50

TUROK, TIMEWALKER
Acclaim Comics (Valiant): Aug, 1997 - No. 2, Sept, 1997 ($2.50, limited series)

	GD25	FN65	NM94
1,2-Nicieza story			2.50

TURTLE SOUP
Mirage Studios: Sept, 1987 ($2.00, 76 pgs., B&W, one-shot)

	GD25	FN65	NM94
1-Featuring Teenage Mutant Ninja Turtles			2.00

TURTLE SOUP
Mirage Studios: Nov, 1991 - No. 4, 1992 ($2.50, limited series, coated paper)

	GD25	FN65	NM94
1-4: Features the Teenage Mutant Ninja Turtles			2.50

TV CASPER & COMPANY
Harvey Publications: Aug, 1963 - No. 46, April, 1974 (25¢ Giants)

	GD25	FN65	NM94
1: 68 pg. Giants begin; Casper, Little Audrey, Baby Huey, Herman & Catnip, Buzzy the Crow begin	10.00	30.00	100.00
2-5	4.50	13.50	45.00
6-10	3.50	10.50	35.00
11-20	2.25	6.75	18.00
21-31: 31-Last 68 pg. issue	1.40	4.20	14.00
32-46: All 52 pgs.	1.00	3.00	10.00

NOTE: *Many issues contain reprints.*

TV FUNDAY FUNNIES (See Famous TV...)

TV FUNNIES (See New Funnies)

TV FUNTIME (See Little Audrey)

TV LAUGHOUT (See Archie's...)

TV SCREEN CARTOONS (Formerly Real Screen)
National Periodical Publ.: No. 129, July-Aug, 1959 - No. 138, Jan-Feb, 1961

	GD25	FN65	NM94
129-138 (Scarce)	7.00	21.00	70.00

TV STARS (TV) (Newsstand sales only)
Marvel Comics Group: Aug, 1978 - No. 4, Feb, 1979 (Hanna-Barbera)

	GD25	FN65	NM94
1-Great Grape Ape app.	1.80	5.40	18.00
2,4: 4-Top Cat app.	1.50	4.50	15.00
3-Toth-c/a; Dave Stevens inks	1.80	5.40	18.00

TV TEENS (Formerly Ozzie & Babs; Rock and Rollo #14 on)
Charlton Comics: V1#14, Feb, 1954 - V2#13, July, 1956

	GD25	FN65	NM94
V1#14 (#1)-Ozzie & Babs	6.85	21.00	48.00
15 (#2)	4.25	13.00	26.00
V2#3(6/54) - 6-Don Winslow	4.25	13.00	28.00
7-13-Mopsy. 8(7/55)	4.25	13.00	26.00

TWEETY AND SYLVESTER (1st Series) (TV)
Dell Publishing Co.: No. 406, June, 1952 - No. 37, June-Aug, 1962

	GD25	FN65	NM94
Four Color 406 (#1)-1st app.?	7.00	22.00	80.00
Four Color 489,524	3.50	10.50	38.00
4 (3-5/54) - 20	1.80	5.50	20.00
21-37	1.20	3.60	12.00

(See March of Comics #421, 433, 445, 457, 469, 481)

TWEETY AND SYLVESTER (2nd Series)(See Kite Fun Book)
Gold Key No. 1-102/Whitman No. 103 on: Nov, 1963; No. 2, Nov, 1965 - No. 121, July, 1984

	GD25	FN65	NM94
1	2.00	6.00	20.00
2-10	1.40	4.20	14.00
11-30	1.00	3.00	10.00
31-50		2.00	6.00
51-70			4.00
71-102			2.00
103,104 (Whitman)			3.00
105(9/80),106(10/80),107(12/80) 3-pack?	.90	2.70	8.00
108-116			5.00
117-121: (All # 90094 on-c; nd, nd code). 119-r(1/3)	.85	2.60	7.00
Mini Comic No. 1(1976, 3-1/4x6-1/2")		1.60	4.00

12 O'CLOCK HIGH (TV)
Dell Publishing Co.: Jan-Mar, 1965 - No. 2, Apr-June, 1965 (Photo-c)

	GD25	FN65	NM94
1	4.50	13.50	50.00
2	3.60	11.00	40.00

24 PAGES OF COMICS (No title) (Also see Pure Oil Comics, Salerno Carnival of Comics, & Vicks Comics)
Giveaway by various outlets including Sears: Late 1930s

	GD25	FN65	NM94
nn-Contains strip reprints-Buck Rogers, Napoleon, Sky Roads, War on Crime	33.00	100.00	250.00

2099 A.D.

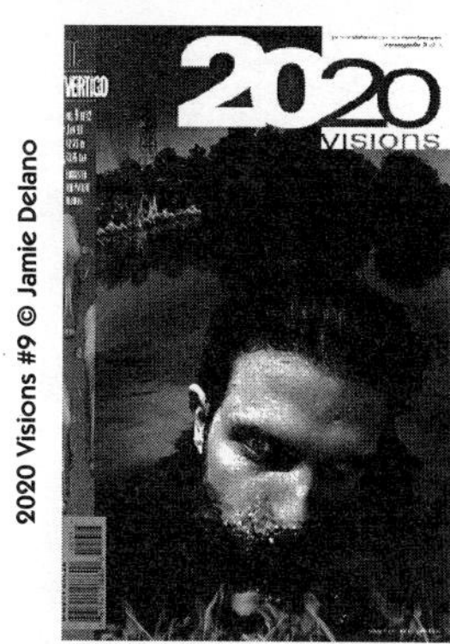

2020 Visions #9 © Jamie Delano

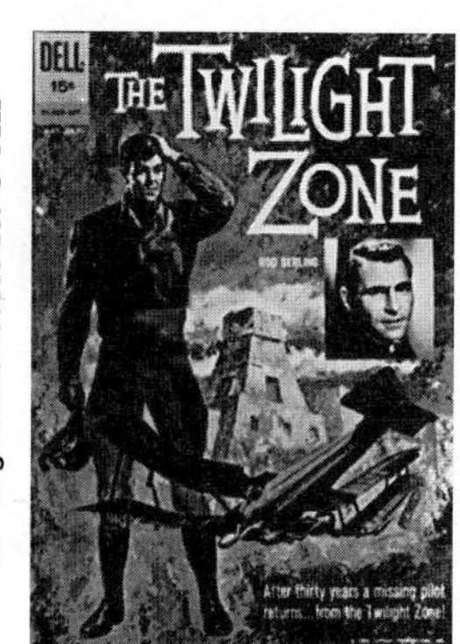

The Twilight Zone #01860-207 © DELL

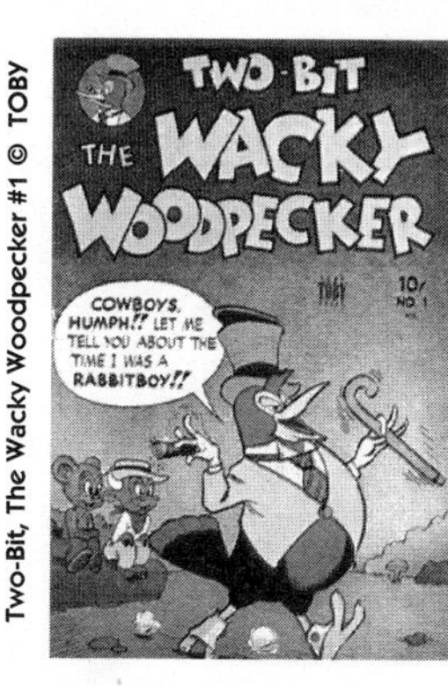

Two-Bit, The Wacky Woodpecker #1 © TOBY

GD25 FN65 NM94

Marvel Comics: May, 1995 ($3.95, one-shot)
1-Acetate-c by Quesada & Palmiotti. 4.00

2099 APOCALYPSE
Marvel Comics: Dec, 1995 ($4.95, one-shot)
1-Chromium wraparound-c; Ellis script 5.00

2099 GENESIS
Marvel Comics: Jan, 1996 ($4.95, one-shot)
1-Chromium wraparound-c; Ellis script 5.00

2099 MANIFEST DESTINY
Marvel Comics: Mar, 1998 ($5.99, one-shot)
1-Origin of Fantastic Four 2099; intro Moon Knight 2099 6.00

2099 UNLIMITED
Marvel Comics: Sept, 1993 - No. 10, 1996 ($3.95, 68 pgs.)
1-10: 1-1st app. Hulk 2099 & begins. 1-3-Spider-Man 2099 app. 9-Joe Kubert-c; Len Wein & Nancy Collins scripts 4.00

2099 WORLD OF DOOM SPECIAL
Marvel Comics: May, 1995 ($2.25, one-shot)
1-Doom's "Contract w/America" 2.25

2099 WORLD OF TOMORROW
Marvel Comics: Sept, 1996 - No. 8, Apr, 1997 ($2.50) (Replaces 2099 titles)
1-8: 1-Wraparound-c. 2-w/bound-in card. 4,5-Phalanx 2.50

21
Image Comics (Top Cow Productions): Feb, 1996 - No. 3, Apr, 1996 ($2.50)
1-3: Len Wein scripts 2.50
1-Variant-c 5.00

2020 VISIONS
DC Comics (Vertigo): May, 1997 - No. 12, Apr, 1998 ($2.25, limited series)
1-12-Delano-s: 1-3-Quitely-a. 4-"la tormenta"-Pleece-a 2.25

20,000 LEAGUES UNDER THE SEA (Movie)(See King Classics, Movie Comics & Power Record Comics)
Dell Publishing Co.: No. 614, Feb, 1955 (Disney)
Four Color 614-Movie, painted-c 9.00 27.00 100.00

22 BRIDES (See Ash/)
Event Comics: Mar, 1996 - No. 4, Jan, 1997 ($2.95)
1-4: Fabian Nicieza scripts 3.00
2,3-Variant-c 4.50

TWICE TOLD TALES (See Movie Classics)

TWILIGHT
DC Comics: 1990 - No. 3, 1991 ($4.95, 52 pgs, lim. series, squarebound, mature)
1-3: Tommy Tomorrow app; Chaykin scripts, Garcia-Lopez-c/a. 5.00

TWILIGHT AVENGER, THE
Elite Comics: July, 1986 - No. 4, 1987 ($1.75, 28 pgs, limited series)
1-4 1.80

TWILIGHT MAN
First Publishing: June, 1989 - No. 4, Sept, 1989 ($2.75, limited series)
1-4 2.80

TWILIGHT ZONE, THE (TV) (See Dan Curtis)
Dell Publishing Co./Gold Key/Whitman No. 92: No. 1173, 3-5/61 - No. 91, 4/79; No. 92, 5/82
Four Color 1173 (#1)-Crandall-c/a 18.00 55.00 200.00
Four Color 1288-Crandall/Evans-c/a 11.00 32.00 115.00
01-860-207 (5-7/62-Dell, 15¢) 7.00 22.00 80.00
12-860-210 on-c; 01-860-210 on inside(8-10/62-Dell)-Evans-c/a (3 stories) 7.00 22.00 80.00
1(11/62-Gold Key)-Crandall/Frazetta-a (10 & 11 pgs.); Evans-a 9.50 29.00 105.00
2 6.00 18.00 65.00
3-11: 3(11 pgs.),4(10 pgs.),9-Toth-a 4.00 12.00 45.00
12-15: 12-Williamson-a. 13,15-Crandall-a. 14-Orlando/Crandall/Torres-a 3.00 9.00 32.00
16-20 2.00 6.00 22.00
21-27: 21-Crandall-a(r). 25-Evans/Crandall-a(r); Toth-r/#4. 26-Flying Saucer-c/story; Crandall, Evans-a(r). 27-Evans-r(2) 1.60 4.80 16.00
28-32: 32-Evans-a(r) 1.20 3.60 12.00
33-51: 43-Celardo-a. 51-Williamson-a .90 2.70 9.00
52-70 2.00 6.00
71-82,85-91: 71-Reprint 3.00
83,84-(52 pgs.). 84-Frank Miller's 1st comic book work 1.00 3.00 10.00
92-Last issue; r/#1. 4.00
Mini Comic #1(1976, 3-1/4x6-1/2") 2.00 6.00
NOTE: ***Bolle** a-13(w/**McWilliams**), 50, 55, 57, 59, 77, 78, 80, 83, 84. **McWilliams** a-59, 78, 80, 82, 84. **Miller** a-84, 85. **Orlando** a-15, 19, 20, 22, 23. **Sekowsky** a-3. **Simonson** a-50, 54, 55, 83r. **Weiss** a-39, 79r(#39). (See Mystery Comics Digest 3, 6, 9, 12, 15, 18, 21, 24). Reprints-26(1/3), 71, 73, 79, 83, 84, 86, 92. Painted c-1-91.*

TWILIGHT ZONE, THE (TV)
Now Comics: Nov, 1990 ($2.95); Oct, 1991; V2#1, Nov, 1991 - No. 14? 1992 ($1.95); V3#1, 1993 - No. 4, 1993 ($2.50)
1-(11/90, $2.95, 52 pgs.)-Direct sale edition; Neal Adams-a, Sienkiewicz-c; Harlan Ellison scripts 3.00
1-(11/90, $1.75)-Newsstand ed. w/N. Adams-c 2.00
1-Prestige Format (10/91, $4.95)-Reprints above with extra Harlan Ellison short story 5.00
1-Collector's Edition (10/91, $2.50)-Non-code approved and polybagged; reprints 11/90 issue; gold logo 2.50
1-Reprint ($2.50)-r/direct sale 11/90 version 2.50
1-Reprint ($2.50)-r/newsstand 11/90 version 2.50
V2#1-Direct sale & newsstand ed. w/different-c 2.00
V2#2-8,10-14 2.00
V2#9-($2.95)-3-D Special; polybagged w/glasses & hologram on-c 3.00
V2#9-($4.95)-Prestige Edition; contains 2 extra stories & a different hologram on-c; polybagged w/glasses 5.00
V3#1-4 2.50
Anniversary Special 1 (1992, $2.50) 2.50
Annual 1 (4/93, $2.50)-No ads 2.50

TWINKLE COMICS
Spotlight Publishers: May, 1945
1 20.00 60.00 150.00

TWIST, THE
Dell Publishing Co.: July-Sept, 1962
01-864-209-Painted-c 2.90 8.70 32.00

TWISTED TALES (See Eclipse Graphic Album Series #15)
Pacific Comics/Independent Comics Group (Eclipse) #9,10: 11/82 - No. 8, 5/84; No. 9, 11/84; No. 10, 12/84 (Baxter paper)
1-B. Jones/Corben-c; nudity/violence in all 2.00
2-10 1.50
NOTE: ***Alcala** a-1. **Bolton** painted c-4, 6, 7; a-7. **Conrad** a-1, 3, 5; c-1i, 3, 5. **Guice** a-8. **Morrow** a-10. **Ploog** a-2. **Wildey** a-3. **Wrightson** a(Painted)-10; c-2.*

TWO BIT THE WACKY WOODPECKER (See Wacky...)
Toby Press: 1951 - No. 3, May, 1953
1 7.15 21.50 50.00
2,3 4.25 13.00 28.00

TWO FACES OF COMMUNISM (Also see Double Talk)
Christian Anti-Communism Crusade, Houston, Texas: 1961 (Giveaway, paper-c, 36 pgs.)
nn 12.00 36.00 90.00

Two-Fisted Tales #19 © WMG

Two-Gun Kid #62 © MAR

2001, A Space Odyssey #5 © MAR

	GD25	FN65	NM94

TWO FACES OF TOMORROW, THE
Dark Horse: Aug, 1997 - No. 13, Aug, 1998 ($2.95/$3.95, B&W, lim. series)

1-Manga			3.00
2-13-($3.95)			4.00

TWO-FISTED TALES (Formerly Haunt of Fear #15-17)
E. C. Comics: No. 18, Nov-Dec, 1950 - No. 41, Feb-Mar, 1955

18(#1)-Kurtzman-c	75.00	225.00	725.00
19-Kurtzman-c	54.00	162.00	525.00
20-Kurtzman-c	35.00	105.00	300.00
21,22-Kurtzman-c	26.00	78.00	230.00
23-25-Kurtzman-c	20.00	60.00	175.00
26-35: 33- "Atom Bomb" by Wood	14.00	42.00	125.00
36-41	10.00	30.00	95.00
Two-Fisted Annual (1952, 25¢, 132 pgs.)	65.00	195.00	600.00
Two-Fisted Annual (1953, 25¢, 132 pgs.)	48.00	144.00	420.00

NOTE: ***Berg*** *a-29.* ***Colan*** *a-39p.* ***Craig*** *a-18, 19, 32.* ***Crandall*** *a-35, 36.* ***Davis*** *a-20-36, 40; c-30, 34, 35, 41, Annual 2.* ***Evans*** *a-34, 40, 41; c-40.* ***Feldstein*** *a-18.* ***Krigstein*** *a-41.* ***Kubert*** *a-32, 33.* ***Kurtzman*** *a-18-25; c-18-29, 31, Annual 1.* ***Severin*** *a-26, 28, 29, 31, 34-41 (No. 37-39 are all-Severin issues); c-36-39.* ***Severin/Elder*** *a-19-29, 31, 33, 36.* ***Wood*** *a-18-28, 30-35, 41; c-32, 33. Special issues: #26 (ChanJin Reservoir), 31 (Civil War), 35 (Civil War). Canadian reprints known; see Table of Contents. #25-Davis biog. #27-Wood biog. #28-Kurtzman biog.*

TWO-FISTED TALES
Russ Cochran/Gemstone Publishing: Oct, 1992 - No. 24, May, 1998 ($1.50/$2.00/$2.50)

1-15: 1-4r/Two-Fisted Tales #18-21 w/original-c			2.00
16-24			2.50

TWO-GUN KID (Also see All Western Winners, Best Western, Black Rider, Blaze Carson, Kid Colt, Western Winners, Wild West, & Wild Western)
Marvel/Atlas (MCI No. 1-10/HPC No. 11-59/Marvel No. 60 on): 3/48(No mo.) - No. 10, 11/49; No. 11, 12/53 - No. 59, 4/61; No. 60, 11/62 - No. 92, 3/68; No. 93, 7/70 - No. 136, 4/77

1-Two-Gun Kid & his horse Cyclone begin; The Sheriff begins	88.00	265.00	750.00
2	39.00	117.00	300.00
3,4: 3-Annie Oakley app.	30.00	90.00	225.00
5-Pre-Black Rider app. (Wint. 48/49); spanking panel; Anti-Wertham editorial (1st?)	36.00	108.00	270.00
6-10(11/49): 8-Blaze Carson app. 9-Black Rider app.	23.00	70.00	175.00
11(12/53)-Black Rider app.; 1st to have Atlas globe on-c; explains how Kid Colt became an outlaw	18.00	54.00	135.00
12-Black Rider app.	18.00	54.00	135.00
13-20: 14-Opium story	13.00	38.00	95.00
21-24,26-29	11.00	34.00	85.00
25,30: 25-Williamson-a (5 pgs.). 30-Williamson/Torres-a (4 pgs.)	12.00	36.00	90.00
31-33,35,37-40	6.00	18.00	60.00
34-Crandall-a	6.50	19.50	65.00
36,41,42,48-Origin in all	6.50	19.50	65.00
43,44,47	4.50	13.50	45.00
45,46-Davis-a	5.00	15.00	50.00
49,50,52,53-Severin-a(2/3) in each	4.00	12.00	40.00
51-Williamson-a (5 pgs.)	5.00	15.00	50.00
54,55,57,59-Severin-a(3) in each. 59-Kirby-a; last 10¢ issue (4/61)	3.60	10.80	36.00
56	2.50	7.50	22.00
58,60-New origin. 58-Kirby/Ayers-c/a "The Monster of Hidden Valley" cover/story (Kirby monster-c)	3.00	9.00	30.00
61,62-Kirby-a	2.50	7.50	25.00
63-74: 64-Intro. Boom-Boom	2.00	6.00	16.00
75-77-Kirby-a	2.50	7.50	20.00
78-89	2.25	6.75	18.00
90,95-Kirby-a	2.00	6.00	16.00
91,92: 92-Last new story; last 12¢ issue	1.75	5.25	14.00
93,94,96-99	1.20	3.60	12.00
100,101: 101-Origin retold/#58; Kirby-a	1.40	4.20	14.00
102-120-reprints	.90	2.70	9.00
121-136-reprints	.85	2.60	7.00

NOTE: ***Ayers*** *a-26, 27.* ***Davis*** *c-45-47.* ***Drucker*** *a-23.* ***Everett*** *a-82, 91.* ***Fuje*** *a-13.* ***Heath*** *a-3(2), 4(3), 5(2), 7; c-13, 21, 23, 53.* ***Keller*** *a-16, 19, 28.* ***Kirby*** *a-54, 55, 57-62, 75-77, 90, 95, 101, 119, 120, 129; c-10, 52, 54-65, 67-72, 74-76, 116.* ***Maneely*** *a-20; c-11, 12, 16, 19, 20, 25-28, 35, 49.* ***Powell*** *a-38, 102, 104.* ***Severin*** *a-9, 29, 51, 55, 57, 99r(3); c-9, 51, 99.* ***Shores*** *c-1-8, 11.* ***Tuska*** *a-11, 12.* ***Whitney*** *a-87, 89-91, 98-113, 124, 129; c-87, 89, 91, 113.* ***Wildey*** *a-21.* ***Williamson*** *a-110r. Kid Colt in #13, 14, 16-21.*

TWO GUN KID:SUNSET RIDERS
Marvel Comics: Nov, 1995 - No. 2, Dec, 1995 ($6.95, squarebound, lim. series)

1,2: Fabian Nicieza scripts in all. 1-painted-c.			7.00

TWO GUN WESTERN (1st Series) (Formerly Casey Crime Photographer #1-4? or My Love #1-4?)
Marvel/Atlas Comics (MPC): No. 5, Nov, 1950 - No. 14, June, 1952

5-The Apache Kid (Intro & origin) & his horse Nightwind begin by Buscema	23.00	68.00	170.00
6-10: 8-Kid Colt, The Texas Kid & his horse Thunder begin?	15.00	46.00	115.00
11-14: 13-Black Rider app.	11.00	32.00	80.00

NOTE: ***Maneely*** *a-6, 7, 9; c-6, 11-13.* ***Morrow*** *a-9.* ***Romita*** *a-8.* ***Wildey*** *a-8.*

2-GUN WESTERN (2nd Series) (Formerly Billy Buckskin #1-3; Two-Gun Western #5 on)
Atlas Comics (MgPC): No. 4, May, 1956

4-Colan, Ditko, Severin, Sinnott-a; Maneely-c	15.00	44.00	110.00

TWO-GUN WESTERN (Formerly 2-Gun Western)
Atlas Comics (MgPC): No. 5, July, 1956 - No. 12, Sept, 1957

5-Return of the Gun-Hawk-c/story; Black Rider app.	11.00	34.00	85.00
6,7	8.50	26.00	60.00
8,10,12-Crandall-a	9.30	28.00	70.00
9,11-Williamson-a in both (5 pgs. each)	9.30	28.00	70.00

NOTE: ***Ayers*** *a-9.* ***Colan*** *a-5.* ***Everett*** *c-12.* ***Forgione*** *a-5, 6.* ***Kirby*** *a-12.* ***Maneely*** *a-6, 8, 12; c-5, 6, 8, 11.* ***Morrow*** *a-9, 10.* ***Powell*** *a-7, 11.* ***Severin*** *c-10.* ***Sinnott*** *a-5.* ***Wildey*** *a-9.*

TWO MOUSEKETEERS, THE (See 4-Color #475, 603, 642 under M.G.M.'s...;

TWO ON A GUILLOTINE (See Movie Classics)

2000 A.D. MONTHLY/PRESENTS (Showcase #25 on)
Eagle Comics/Quality Comics No. 5 on: 4/85 - #6, 9/85; 4/86 - #54, 1991 ($1.25-$1.50, Mando paper)

1-6 ($1.25): 1-4 r/British series featuring Judge Dredd; Alan Moore scripts begin			1.25
1-25 ($1.25)-Reprints from British 2000 AD			1.25
26,27/28, 29/30, 31-44: 27/28, 29/30,31-Guice-c			1.25
45-54: 45-Begin $1.75-c			1.75

2001, A SPACE ODYSSEY (Movie)
Marvel Comics Group: Dec, 1976 - No. 10, Sept, 1977 (30¢)

1-Adaptation of film; Kirby-c/a in all			4.00
2-10: 8-Original/1st app. Machine Man (called Mr. Machine)			3.00
Howard Johnson giveaway (1968, 8pp); 6 pg. movie adaptation, 2 pg. games, puzzles; McWilliams-a			2.00
...Treasury 1 ('76, 84 pgs.)-All new Kirby-a	1.20	3.60	12.00

2001 NIGHTS
Viz Premiere Comics: 1990 - No. 10, 1991 ($3.75, B&W, limited series, mature readers, 84 pgs.)

1-5: Japanese sci-fi. 1-Wraparound-c			3.75
6-10: 6-Begin $4.25-c			4.25

2010 (Movie)
Marvel Comics Group: Apr, 1985 - No. 2, May, 1985

1,2-r/Marvel Super Special movie adaptation.			1.00

Ultimate Strike #6 © Everette Hartsoe

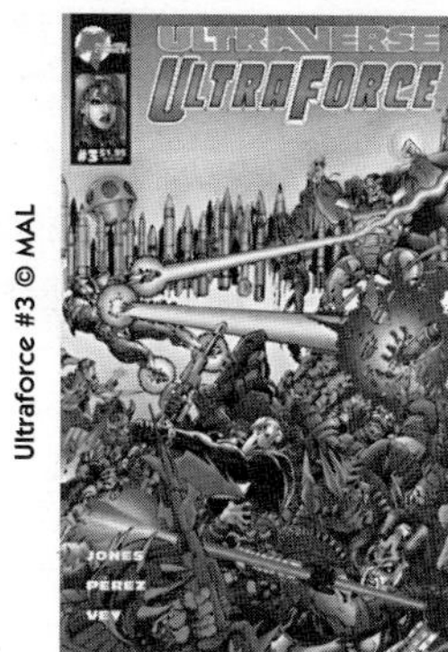

Ultraforce #3 © MAL

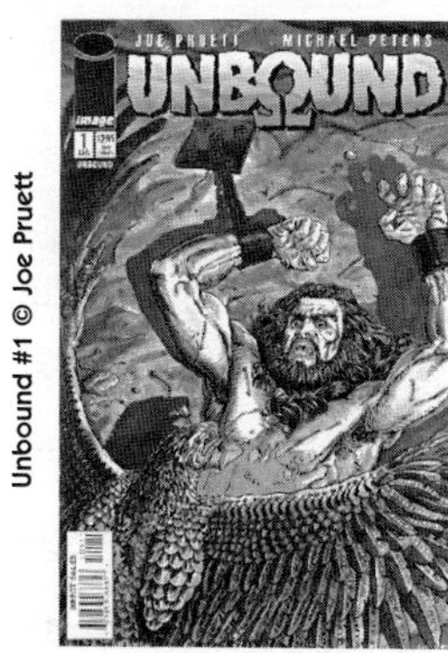

Unbound #1 © Joe Pruett

GD25 FN65 NM94

TYPHOID (Also see Daredevil)
Marvel Comics: Nov, 1995 - No. 4, Feb, 1996 ($3.95, squarebound, lim. series)
1-4: Van Fleet-c/a 4.00

UFO & ALIEN COMIX
Warren Publishing Co.: Jan, 1978 (one-shot)
nn-Toth, Severin-a(r) 1.00 3.00 10.00

UFO & OUTER SPACE (Formerly UFO Flying Saucers)
Gold Key: No. 14, June, 1978 - No. 25, Feb, 1980 (All painted covers)
14-Reprints UFO Flying Saucers #3 2.00 6.00
15,16-Reprints 4.00
17-20-New material 5.00
21-25: 23-McWilliams-a. 24-(3 pg.-r). 25-Reprints UFO Flying Saucers #2 w/cover 4.00

UFO ENCOUNTERS
Western Publishing Co.: May, 1978 ($1.95, 228 pgs.)
11192-Reprints UFO Flying Saucers 2.20 6.50 24.00
11404-Vol.1 (128 pgs.)-See UFO Mysteries for Vol.2 1.80 5.40 18.00

UFO FLYING SAUCERS (UFO & Outer Space #14 on)
Gold Key: Oct, 1968 - No. 13, Jan, 1977 (No. 2 on, 36 pgs.)
1(30035-810) (68 pgs.) 2.25 6.75 25.00
2(11/70), 3(11/72), 4(11/74) 1.50 4.50 12.00
5(2/75)-13: Bolle-a #4 on 1.10 3.30 9.00

UFO MYSTERIES
Western Publishing Co.: 1978 ($1.00, reprints, 96 pgs.)
11400, 11404(Vol.2)-Cont'd from UFO Encounters, pgs. 129-224 1.50 4.50 15.00

ULTIMATE STRIKE (See Razor, Stryke)
London Night Studios: Dec, 1996 - Present ($3.95/$3.00, B&W)
1-($3.95)-Wraparound chromium-c 4.00
1-12-($6.00) Nude Edition 6.00
2-12-($3.00) 3.00

ULTRACYBERNETIC DOLPHINDROIDS, THE
Polestar Comics: Dec, 1993 ($2.50, unfinished limited series)
1 2.50

ULTRAFORCE (1st Series) (Also see Avengers/Ultraforce #1)
Malibu Comics (Ultraverse): Aug, 1994 - No. 10, Aug, 1995 ($1.95/$2.50)
0 (9/94, $2.50)-Perez-c/a. 2.50
1-($2.50, 44 pgs.)-Bound-in trading card; team consisting of Prime, Prototype, Hardcase, Pixx, Ghoul, Contrary & Topaz; Gerard Jones scripts begin, ends #6; Perez-c/a begins. 2.50
1-Ultra 5000 Limited Silver Foil Edition 4.00
1-Holographic-c, no price 5.00
2-5: Perez-c/a in all. 2 (10/94, $1.95)-Prime quits, Strangers cameo. 3-Origin of Topaz; Prime rejoins. 5-Pixx dies. 2.00
2 ($2.50)-Flourescent logo; limited edition stamp on-c 2.50
6-10: 6-Begin $2.50-c, Perez-c/a. 7-Ghoul story, Steve Erwin-a. 8-Marvel's Black Knight enters the Ultraverse (last seen in Avengers #375); Perez-c/a. 9,10-Black Knight app.; Perez-c. 10-Leads into Ultraforce/Avengers Prelude. 2.50
Malibu "Ashcan ": Ultraforce (6/94) .75
.../Avengers Prelude 1 (8/95, $2.50)-Perez-c. 2.50
.../Avengers 1 (8/95, $3.95)-Warren Ellis script; Perez-c/a; foil-c 4.00

ULTRAFORCE (2nd Series)(Also see Black September)
Malibu Comics (Ultraverse): Infinity, Sept, 1995 - V2#15, Dec, 1996 ($1.50)
Infinity, V2#1-15: Infinity-Team consists of Marvel's Black Knight, Ghoul, Topaz, Prime & redesigned Prototype; Warren Ellis scripts begin, ends #3; variant-c exists. 1-1st app.Cromwell, Lament & Wreckage. 2-Contains free encore presentation of Ultraforce #1; flip book "Phoenix Resurrection" Pt. 7. 7-Darick Robertson, Jeff Johnson & others-a. 8,9-Intro. Future Ultraforce (Prime, Hellblade, Angel of Destruction, Painkiller & Whipslash); Gary Erskine-c/a. 9-Foxfire app. 10-Len Wein scripts & Deodato Studios-c/a begin. 10-Lament back-up story. 11-Ghoul back-up story by Pander Bros. 12-Ultraforce vs. Maxis (cont'd in Ultraverse Unlimited #2); Exiles & Iron Clad app. 13-Prime leaves; Hardcase returns 1.50
Infinity (2000 signed) 4.00
.../Spider-Man ($3.95)-Marv Wolfman script; Green Goblin app; 2 covers exist. 4.00

GD25 FN65 NM94

ULTRAGIRL
Marvel Comics: Nov, 1996 - No. 3 Mar, 1997($1.50, limited series)
1-3: 1-1st app. 1.50

ULTRA KLUTZ
Onward Comics: 1981; 6/86 - #27, 1/89, #28, 4/90 - #31, 1990? ($1.50/$1.75/$2.00, B&W)
1 (1981)-Re-released after 2nd #1 1.50
1-22: 1-(6/86) 1.50
23-30: 23-$2.00-c begins. 27-Photo back-c 2.00
31-($2.95, 52 pgs.) 3.00

ULTRAMAN
Nemesis Comics: Mar, 1994 - No. 4, 1995? ($1.75/$1.95)
1-($2.25)-Collector's edition; foil-c; special 3/4 wraparound-c 2.25
1-($1.75)-Newsstand edition 1.75
2-4: 3-$1.95-c begins 2.00

ULTRAVERSE DOUBLE FEATURE
Malibu Comics (Ultraverse): Jan, 1995 ($3.95, one-shot, 68 pgs.)
1-Flip-c featuring Prime & Solitaire. 4.00

ULTRAVERSE ORIGINS
Malibu Comics (Ultraverse): Jan, 1994 (99¢, one-shot)
1-Gatefold-c; 2 pg. origins all characters 1.00
1-Newsstand edition; different-c, no gatefold 1.00

ULTRAVERSE PREMIERE
Malibu Comics (Ultraverse): 1994 (one-shot)
0-Ordered thru mail w/coupons 5.00

ULTRAVERSE UNLIMITED
Malibu Comics (Ultraverse): June, 1996; No. 2, Sept, 1996 ($2.50)
1,2: 1-Adam Warlock returns to the Marvel Universe; Rune-c/app. 2-Black Knight, Reaper & Sierra Blaze return to the Marvel Universe 2.50

ULTRAVERSE YEAR ONE
Malibu Comics (Ultraverse): 1994 ($4.95, one-shot)
nn-In-depth synopsis of the first year's titles & stories. 5.00

ULTRAVERSE YEAR TWO
Malibu Comics (Ultraverse): Aug, 1995 ($4.95, one-shot)
nn-In-depth synopsis of second year's titles & stories 5.00

ULTRAVERSE YEAR ZERO: THE DEATH OF THE SQUAD
Malibu Comics (Ultraverse): Apr, 1995 - No. 4, July, 1995 ($2.95, lim. series)
1-4: 3-Codename: Firearm back-up story. 3.00

UNBIRTHDAY PARTY WITH ALICE IN WONDERLAND (See Alice In Wonderland, Four Color #341)

UNBOUND
Image Comics (Desperado): Jan, 1998 - Present ($2.95, B&W)
1-Pruett-s/Peters-a 3.00

UNCANNY ORIGINS
Marvel Comics: Sept, 1996 - No. 14, Oct, 1997 (99¢)
1-14: 1-Cyclops. 2-Quicksilver. 3-Archangel. 4-Firelord. 5-Hulk. 6-Beast

Uncanny Tales #2 © MAR

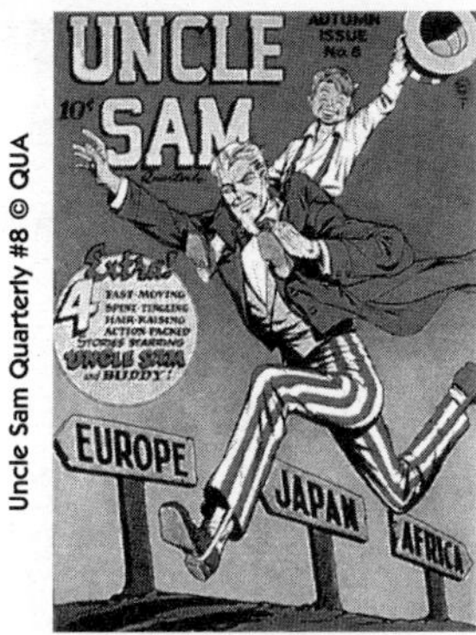

Uncle Sam Quarterly #8 © QUA

Uncle Scrooge #30 © WDC

GD25 FN65 NM94 GD25 FN65 NM94

7-Venom. 8-Nightcrawler. 9-Storm. 10-Black Cat. 11-Black Knight.
12-Dr. Strange. 13-Daredevil. 14-Iron Fist 1.00

UNCANNY TALES
Atlas Comics (PrPl/PPI): June, 1952 - No. 56, Sept, 1957

	GD25	FN65	NM94
1-Heath-a; horror/weird stories begin	71.00	212.00	600.00
2	41.00	122.00	325.00
3-5	36.00	108.00	270.00
6-Wolvertonish-a by Matt Fox	36.00	108.00	270.00
7-10: 8-Atom bomb story; Tothish-a (by Sekowsky?). 9-Crandall-a	31.00	92.00	230.00
11-20: 17-Atom bomb panels; anti-communist story; Hitler story. 19-Krenkel-a	23.00	70.00	175.00
21-25,27: 25-Nostrand-a?	19.00	58.00	145.00
26-Spider-Man prototype c/story	28.00	84.00	210.00
28-Last precode issue (1/55); Kubert-a; #1-28 contain 2-3 sci/fi stories each	21.00	62.00	155.00
29-41,43-49,51,52: 52-Oldest? Iron Man prototype (2/57)	13.00	38.00	95.00
42,54,56-Krigstein-a	13.50	41.00	100.00
50,53,55-Torres-a	13.00	38.00	95.00

NOTE: ***Andru** a-15, 27. **Ayers** a-22. **Bailey** a-51. **Briefer** a-19, 20. **Brodsky** c-1, 3, 4, 6, 8, 12-16, 19. **Brodsky/Everett** c-9. **Cameron** a-47. **Colan** a-11, 16, 17, 52. **Drucker** a-37, 42, 45. **Everett** a-2, 9, 12, 32, 36, 39, 48; c-7, 11, 17, 39, 41, 50, 52, 53. **Fass** a-9, 10, 15, 24. **Forte** a-18, 27, 34, 52, 53. **Heath** a-13, 14; c-5, 10, 18. **Keller** a-3. **Lawrence** a-14, 17, 19, 23, 27, 28, 35. **Maneely** a-4, 8, 10, 16, 29, 35; c-2, 22, 26, 33, 38. **Moldoff** a-23. **Morisi** a-48, 52. **Morrow** a-46, 51. **Orlando** a-49, 50, 53. **Powell** a-12, 18, 34, 36, 38, 43, 50, 56. **Robinson** a-3, 13. **Reinman** a-12. **Romita** a-10. **Roussos** a-8. **Sale** a-47, 53; c-20. **Sekowsky** a-25. **Sinnott** a-15, 52. **Torres** a-53. **Tothish**-a by **Andru**-27. **Wildey** a-22, 48.*

UNCANNY TALES
Marvel Comics Group: Dec, 1973 - No. 12, Oct, 1975

	GD25	FN65	NM94
1-Crandall-r/Uncanny Tales #9('50s)	1.50	4.50	15.00
2-12	.90	2.70	9.00

NOTE: ***Ditko** reprints-#4, 6-8, 10-12.*

UNCANNY X-MEN, THE (See **X-Men, The**, 1st series)

UNCANNY X-MEN AND THE NEW TEEN TITANS (See Marvel and DC Present...)

UNCENSORED MOUSE, THE
Eternity Comics: Apr, 1989 - No. 2, Apr, 1989 ($1.95, B&W)(Came sealed in plastic bag)

	GD25	FN65	NM94
1-Early Gottfredson strip-r in each	.90	2.70	8.00
2-Both contain racial stereotyping & violence		2.00	6.00

NOTE: *Both issues contain unauthorized reprints. Series was cancelled. **Win Smith** r-1, 2.*

UNCLE CHARLIE'S FABLES
Lev Gleason Publ.: Jan, 1952 - No. 5, Sept, 1952 (All have Biro painted-c)

	GD25	FN65	NM94
1-Norman Maurer-a; has Biro's picture	11.00	34.00	85.00
2-Fuje-a; Biro photo	7.15	21.50	50.00
3-5	5.70	17.00	40.00

UNCLE DONALD & HIS NEPHEWS DUDE RANCH (See Dell Giant #52)

UNCLE DONALD & HIS NEPHEWS FAMILY FUN (See Dell Giant #38)

UNCLE JOE'S FUNNIES
Centaur Publications: 1938 (B&W)

	GD25	FN65	NM94
1-Games, puzzles & magic tricks, some interior art; Bill Everett-c	42.00	127.00	340.00

UNCLE MILTY (TV)
Victoria Publications/True Cross: Dec, 1950 - No. 4, July, 1951 (52 pgs.)-(Early TV comic)

	GD25	FN65	NM94
1-Milton Berle photo on-c of #1,2	44.00	132.00	375.00
2	28.00	84.00	210.00
3,4	23.00	70.00	175.00

UNCLE REMUS & HIS TALES OF BRER RABBIT (See Brer Rabbit, 4-Color #129, 208, 693)

UNCLE SAM
DC Comics (Vertigo): 1997 - No. 2, 1997 ($4.95, limited series)

	GD25	FN65	NM94
1,2-Alex Ross painted c/a. Story by Ross and Steve Darnell			5.00

UNCLE SAM QUARTERLY (Blackhawk #9 on)(See Freedom Fighters)
Quality Comics Group: Autumn, 1941 - No. 8, Fall, 1943 (see National Comics)

	GD25	FN65	NM94
1-Origin Uncle Sam; Fine/Eisner-c, chapter headings, 2 pgs. by Eisner; (2 versions: dark cover, no price; light cover with price sticker); Jack Cole-a	295.00	884.00	2800.00
2-Cameos by The Ray, Black Condor, Quicksilver, The Red Bee, Alias the Spider, Hercules & Neon the Unknown; Eisner, Fine-c/a	115.00	344.00	975.00
3-Tuska-c/a; Eisner-a(2)	85.00	256.00	725.00
4	77.00	229.00	650.00
5,7-Hitler, Mussolini & Tojo-c	79.00	238.00	675.00
6,8	59.00	176.00	500.00

NOTE: ***Kotzky** (or **Tuska**) a-3-8.*

UNCLE SAM'S CHRISTMAS STORY
Promotional Publ. Co.: 1958 (Giveaway)

	GD25	FN65	NM94
nn-Reprints 1956 Christmas USA	1.50	4.50	12.00

UNCLE SCROOGE (Disney) (Becomes Walt Disney's... #210 on) (See Cartoon Tales, Dell Giants #33, 55, Disney Comic Album, Donald and Scrooge, Dynabrite, Four Color #178, Gladstone Comic Album, Walt Disney's Comics & Stories #98, Walt Disney's ...)
Dell #1-39/Gold Key #40-173/Whitman #174-209: No. 386, 3/52 - No. 39, 8-10/62; No. 40, 12/62 - No. 209, 1984

	GD25	FN65	NM94
Four Color 386(#1)-in "Only a Poor Old Man" by Carl Barks; r-in Uncle Scrooge & Donald Duck #1('65) & The Best of Walt Disney Comics (1974). The very 1st cover app. of Uncle Scrooge	86.00	259.00	950.00
1-(1986)-Reprints F.C. #386; given away with lithograph "Dam Disaster at Money Lake" & as a subscription offer giveaway to Gladstone subscribers	2.25	6.75	18.00
Four Color 456(#2)-in "Back to the Klondike" by Carl Barks; r-in Best of U.S. & D.D. #1('66) & Gladstone C.A. #4	57.00	170.00	625.00
Four Color 495(#3)-r-in #105	43.00	130.00	475.00
4(12-2/53-54)-r-in Gladstone Comic Album #11	32.00	95.00	350.00
5-r-in Gladstone Special #2 & Walt Disney Digest #1	26.00	79.00	290.00
6-r-in U.S. #106,165,233 & Best of U.S. & D.D. #1('66)	20.00	60.00	220.00
7-The Seven Cities of Cibola by Barks; r-in #217 & Best of D.D. & U.S. #2 ('67)	18.00	55.00	200.00
8-10: 8-r-in #111,222. 9-r-in #104,214. 10-r-in #67	15.00	45.00	165.00
11-20: 11-r-in #237. 17-r-in #215. 19-r-in Gladstone C.A. #1. 20-r-in #213	14.00	41.00	150.00
21-30: 24-X-Mas-c. 26-r-in #211	11.00	34.00	125.00
31-35,37-40: 34-r-in #228. 40-X-Mas-c	9.00	29.00	105.00
36-1st app. Magica De Spell; Number one dime 1st identified by name	11.00	32. 00	115.00
41-60: 48-Magica De Spell-c/story (3/64). 49-Sci/fi-c. 51-Beagle Boys-c/story (8/64)	8.00	23.00	85.00
61-63,65,66,68-71:71-Last Barks issue w/original story (#71-he only storyboarded the script)	6.40	19.00	70.00
64-Barks Vietnam War story "Treasure of Marco Polo" banned for reprints by Disney since the 1970s because of its third world revolutionary war theme	9.00	27.00	100.00
67,72,73: 67,72,73-Barks-r	6.40	19.00	70.00
74-84: 74-Barks-r(1pg.). 75-81,83-Not by Barks. 82,84-Barks-r begin	4.00	12.00	45.00
85-110	3.00	10.00	36.00
111-141,143-152,154-157	1.65	5.00	18.00

Uncle Wiggly Four Color #349 © Howard R. Garis

Underworld #1 © D. S. Pub.

Underworld Unleashed: Batman-Devil's Asylum #1 © DC

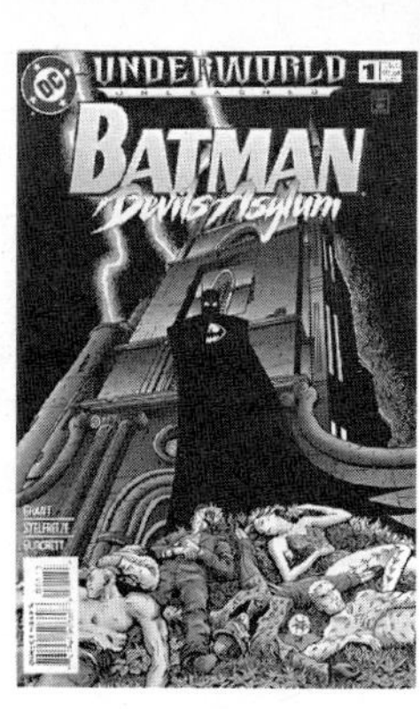

GD25 FN65 NM94

142-Reprints Four Color #456 with-c 2.00 6.00 22.00
153,158,162-164,166,168-170,178,180: No Barks 1.00 2.80 7.00
159-160,165,167 1.25 3.75 10.00
161(r/#14), 171(r/#11), 177(r/#16),183(r/#6)-Barks-r 1.25 3.75 10.00
172(1/80),173(2/80)-Gold Key. Barks-a 1.30 3.90 13.00
174(3/80),175(4/80),176(5/80)-Whitman. Barks-a 1.50 4.50 15.00
177(6/80),178(7/80) 1.80 5.40 18.00
179(4/#9)-Distr. only in Whitman 3-pack 7.00 20.00 75.00
180(11/80),181(12/80, r/4-Color #495) pre-pack? 2.00 6.00 20.00
182-195: 184,185,187,188-Barks-a. 182,186,191-194-No Barks. 189(r/#5), 190(r/#4), 195(r/4-Color #386) .90 2.70 9.00
196(4/82),197(5/82): 196(r/#13) 1.20 3.60 12.00
198-209 (All #90038 on-c; pre-pack?; no date or date code)
198-202,204-206: No Barks. 203(r/#12), 207(r/#93,92), 208(r/U.S. #18), 209(r/U.S. #21)-Barks-r 1.40 4.20 14.00
Uncle Scrooge & Money(G.K.)-Barks-r/from WDC&S #130 (3/67) 3.00 9.00 35.00
Mini Comic #1(1976)(3-1/4x6-1/2")-r/U.S. #115; Barks-c 2.40 6.00
NOTE: *Barks c-Four Color 386, 456, 495, #4-37, 39, 40, 43-71.*

UNCLE SCROOGE & DONALD DUCK
Gold Key: June, 1965 (25¢, paper cover)
1-Reprint of Four Color #386(#1) & lead story from Four Color #29 6.40 19.00 70.00

UNCLE SCROOGE COMICS DIGEST
Gladstone Publishing: Dec, 1986 - No. 5, Aug, 1987 ($1.25, Digest-size)
1,3 2.00 6.00
2,4 4.00
5 (scarce) .85 2.60 7.00

UNCLE SCROOGE GOES TO DISNEYLAND (See Dell Giants)
Gladstone Publishing Ltd.: Aug, 1985 ($2.50)
1-Reprints Dell Giant w/new-c by Mel Crawford, based on old cover 1.00 3.00 10.00
...Comics Digest 1 ($1.50, digest size) 1.20 3.60 12.00

UNCLE SCROOGE IN COLOR
Gladstone Publishing: 1987 ($29.95, Hardcover, 9-1/4"X12-1/4", 96 Pgs.)
nn-Reprints "Christmas on Bear Mountain" from Four Color 178 by Barks; Uncle Scrooge's Christmas Carol (published as Donald Duck & the Christmas Carol, A Little Golden Book), reproduced from the original art as adapted by Norman McGary from pencils by Barks; and Uncle Scrooge the Lemonade King, reproduced from the original art, plus Barks' original pencils 4.50 13.50 50.00
nn-Slipcase edition of 750, signed by Barks, issued at $79.95 90.00 300.00

UNCLE SCROOGE THE LEMONADE KING
Whitman Publishing Co.: 1960 (A Top Top Tales Book, 6-3/8"x7-5/8", 32 pgs.)
2465-Storybook pencilled by Carl Barks, finished art adapted by Norman McGary 36.00 108.00 400.00

UNCLE WIGGILY (See March of Comics #19)
Dell Publishing Co.: No. 179, Dec, 1947 - No. 543, Mar, 1954
Four Color 179 (#1)-Walt Kelly-c 14.00 44.00 160.00
Four Color 221 (3/49)-Part Kelly-c 9.00 27.00 100.00
Four Color 276 (5/50), 320 (#1, 3/51) 7.00 22.00 80.00
Four Color 349 (9-10/51), 391 (4-5/52) 5.50 16.50 60.00
Four Color 428 (10/52), 503 (10/53), 543 3.60 11.00 40.00

UNDERCOVER GIRL (Starr Flagg) (See Extra Comics & Manhunt!)
Magazine Enterprises: No. 5, 1952 - No. 7, 1954
5(#1)(A-1 #62)-Fallon of the F.B.I. in all 37.00 110.00 275.00
6(A-1 #98), 7(A-1 #118)-All have Starr Flagg 34.00 102.00 255.00
NOTE: ***Powell** c-6, 7. **Whitney** a-5-7.*

UNDERDOG (TV)(See Kite Fun Book, March of Comics #426, 438, 467, 479)
Charlton Comics/Gold Key: July, 1970 - No. 10, Jan, 1972; Mar, 1975 - No. 23, Feb, 1979
1 (1st series, Charlton)-1st app. Underdog 5.50 16.50 60.00
2-10 3.20 9.50 35.00
1 (2nd series, Gold Key) 4.00 12.25 45.00
2-10 2.25 6.80 25.00
11-20: 13-1st app. Shack of Solitude 1.50 4.50 15.00
21-23 2.00 6.00 20.00

UNDERDOG
Spotlight Comics: 1987 - No. 3?, 1987 ($1.50)
1-3 1.50

UNDERDOG SUMMER SPECIAL (TV)
Harvey Comics: Oct, 1993 ($2.25, 68 pgs.)
1 3.00

UNDERSEA AGENT
Tower Comics: Jan, 1966 - No. 6, Mar, 1967 (25¢, 68 pgs.)
1-Davy Jones, Undersea Agent begins 5.50 16.50 55.00
2-6: 2-Jones gains magnetic powers. 5-Origin & 1st app. of Merman. 6-Kane/Wood-c(r) 3.50 10.50 35.00
NOTE: ***Gil Kane** a-3-6; c-4, 5. **Moldoff** a-2i.*

UNDERSEA FIGHTING COMMANDOS (See Fighting Undersea...)
I.W. Enterprises: 1964
I.W. Reprint #1,2('64): 1-r/#? 2-r/#1; Severin-c 1.25 3.75 10.00

UNDERWATER CITY, THE
Dell Publishing Co.: No. 1328, 1961
Four Color 1328-Movie, Evans-a 6.40 19.00 70.00

UNDERWORLD (...True Crime Stories)
D. S. Publishing Co.: Feb-Mar, 1948 - No. 9, June-July, 1949 (52 pgs.)
1-Moldoff (Shelly)-c; excessive violence 39.00 117.00 300.00
2-Moldoff (Shelly)-c; Ma Barker story used in **SOTI**, pg. 95; female electrocution panel; lingerie art 39.00 117.00 300.00
3-McWilliams-c/a; extreme violence, mutilation 33.00 100.00 250.00
4-Used in Love and Death by Legman; Ingels-a 25.00 76.00 190.00
5-Ingels-a 19.00 58.00 145.00
6-9: 8-Ravielli-a 14.00 42.00 105.00

UNDERWORLD
DC Comics: Dec, 1987 - No. 4, Mar, 1988 ($1.00, limited series, mature)
1-4 1.00

UNDERWORLD CRIME
Fawcett Publications: June, 1952 - No. 9, Oct, 1953
1 25.00 76.00 190.00
2 17.00 50.00 125.00
3-6,8,9 (8,9-exist?) 14.00 42.00 105.00
7-(6/53)-Bondage/torture-c 23.00 68.00 170.00

UNDERWORLD STORY, THE (Movie)
Avon Periodicals: 1950
nn-(Scarce)-Ravielli-c 25.00 74.00 185.00

UNDERWORLD UNLEASHED
DC Comics: Nov, 1995 - No. 3, Jan, 1996 ($2.95, limited series)
1-3: Mark Waid scripts & Howard Porter-c/a(p) 4.00
...: Abyss: Hell's Sentinel 1-($2.95)-Alan Scott, Phantom Stranger, Zatanna app. 3.00
...: Apokolips-Dark Uprising 1 ($1.95) 2.00
...: Batman-Devil's Asylum 1-($2.95)-Batman app. 3.00
...: Patterns of Fear-($2.95) 3.00
TPB (1998, $17.95) r/#1-3 & Abyss-Hell's Sentinel 17.95

UNEARTHLY SPECTACULARS

Unexpected #186 © DC

Union #4 © Aegis Entertainment

Union Jack #1 © MAR

GD25 FN65 NM94

Harvey Publications: Oct, 1965 - No. 3, Mar, 1967

1-(12¢)-Tiger Boy; Simon-c 2.50 7.50 24.00
2-(25¢ giants)-Jack Q. Frost, Tiger Boy & Three Rocketeers app.; Williamson, Wood, Kane-a; r-1 story/Thrill-O-Rama #2 3.00 9.00 30.00
3-(25¢ giants)-Jack Q. Frost app.; Williamson/Crandall-a; r-from Alarming Advs. #1,1962 3.00 9.00 30.00
NOTE: ***Crandall** a-3r. **G. Kane** a-2. **Orlando** a-3. **Simon, Sparling, Wood** c-2. **Simon/Kirby** a-3r. **Torres** a-1?. **Wildey** a-1(3). **Williamson** a-2, 3r. **Wood** a-2(2).*

UNEXPECTED, THE (Formerly Tales of the...)
National Per. Publ./DC Comics: No. 105, Feb-Mar, 1968 - No. 222, May, 1982

105-Begin 12¢ cover price 3.50 10.50 35.00
106-113: 113-Last 12¢ issue (6-7/69) 2.50 7.50 20.00
114,115,117,118,120,122-125 1.75 5.25 15.00
116,119,121 (36 pgs.) 2.20 6.60 22.00
126,127,129-136-(52 pgs.) 1.50 4.50 15.00
128(52 pgs.)-Wrightson-a 2.20 6.25 22.00
137-156 1.00 3.00 10.00
157-162-(100 pgs.) 2.00 6.00 20.00
163-188: 187,188-(44 pgs.) 2.00 6.00
189,190,192-195 ($1.00, 68 pgs.): 189 on are combined with House of Secrets & The Witching Hour .85 2.60 7.00
191-Rogers-a(p) ($1.00, 68 pgs.) .90 2.70 8.00
196-221: 200-Return of Johnny Peril by Tuska. 205-213-Johnny Peril app. 210-Time Warp story 3.00
NOTE: ***Neal Adams** c-110, 112-115, 118, 121, 124. **J. Craig** a-195. **Ditko** a-189, 221p, 222p; c-222. **Drucker** a-107r, 132r. **Giffen** a-219, 222. **Kaluta** c-203, 212. **Kirby** a-127r, 162. **Kubert** c-204, 214-216, 219-221. **Mayer** a-217p, 220, 221p. **Moldoff** a-136r. **Moreira** a-133. **Mortimer** a-212p. **Newton** a-204p. **Orlando** a-202; c-191. **Perez** a-217p. **Redondo** a-155, 166, 195. **Reese** a-145. **Sparling** a-107, 205-209p, 212p. **Spiegle** a-217. **Starlin** c-198. **Toth** a-126r, 127r. **Tuska** a-127, 132, 134, 136, 139, 152, 180, 200p. **Wildey** a-128r, 193. **Wood** a-122i, 133i, 137i, 138i. **Wrightson** a-161r(2 pgs.). Johnny Peril in #106-114, 116, 117, 200, 205-213.*

UNEXPECTED ANNUAL, THE (See DC Special Series #4)

UNIDENTIFIED FLYING ODDBALL (See Walt Disney Showcase #52)

UNION
Image Comics (WildStorm Productions): June, 1993 - No. 0, July, 1994 ($1.95, limited series)

0-(7/94, $2.50) 2.50
0-Alternate Portacio-c (See Deathblow #5) 5.00
1-($2.50)-Embossed foil-c; Texeira-c/a in all 2.50
1-($1.95)-Newsstand edition w/o foil-c 2.00
2-4: 4-(7/94) 2.00

UNION
Image Comics (WildStorm Prod.): Feb, 1995 - No. 9, Dec, 1995 ($2.50)

1-3,5-9: 3-Savage Dragon app. 6-Fairchild from Gen 13 app. 2.50
4-($1.95, Newsstand)-Wildstorm Rising Pt. 3 2.00
4-($2.50, Direct Market)-Wildstorm Rising Pt. 3, bound-in card 2.50

UNION: FINAL VENGEANCE
Image Comics (WildStorm Productions): Oct, 1997 - Present ($2.50)

1-Golden-c/Heisler-s 2.50

UNION JACK
Marvel Comics: Dec, 1998 - No. 3, Feb, 1999 ($2.99, limited series)

1-3-Raab-s/Cassaday-s/a 3.00

UNITED COMICS (Formerly Fritzi Ritz #7; has Fritzi Ritz logo)
United Features Syndicate: Aug, 1940; No. 8, 1950 - No. 26, Jan-Feb, 1953

1(68 pgs.)-Fritzi Ritz & Phil Fumble 20.00 60.00 150.00
8-Fritzi Ritz, Abbie & Slats 4.25 13.00 28.00
9-26: 20-Strange As It Seems; Russell Patterson Cheesecake-a. 22,25-Peanuts app. 4.00 12.00 24.00
NOTE: *Abbie & Slats reprinted from Tip Top.*

UNITED NATIONS, THE (See Classics Illustrated Special Issue)

UNITED STATES AIR FORCE PRESENTS: THE HIDDEN CREW
U.S. Air Force: 1964 (36 pgs.)

nn-Schaffenberger-a 4.00

UNITED STATES FIGHTING AIR FORCE (Also see U.S. Fighting Air Force)
Superior Comics Ltd.: Sept, 1952 - No. 29, Oct, 1956

1 7.85 23.50 55.00
2 4.25 13.00 28.00
3-10 3.60 9.00 18.00
11-29 3.00 7.50 15.00

UNITED STATES MARINES
William H. Wise/Life's Romances Publ. Co./Magazine Ent. #5-8/Toby Press #7-11: 1943 - No. 4, 1944; No. 5, 1952 - No. 8, 1952; No. 7 - No. 11, 1953

nn-Mart Bailey-a 11.00 32.00 80.00
2-Bailey-a; Tojo classic-c 17.00 52.00 130.00
3-Tojo-c 12.00 36.00 90.00
4 7.15 21.50 50.00
5(A-1 #55)-Bailey-a, 6(A-1 #60), 7(A-1 #68), 8(A-1 #72) 5.70 17.00 35.00
7-11 (Toby) 4.00 10.00 20.00
NOTE: ***Powell** a-5-7.*

UNITY
Valiant: No. 0, Aug, 1992 - No. 1, 1992 (Free comics w/limited dist., 20 pgs.)

0 (Blue)-Prequel to Unity x-overs in all Valiant titles; B. Smith-c/a. (Free to everyone that bought all 8 titles that month.) 2.00
0 (Red)-Same as above, but w/red logo (5,000). 4.00
0 (Gold)-Promotional copy. 3.00
1-Epilogue to Unity x-overs; B. Smith-c/a. (1 copy available for every 8 Valiant books ordered by dealers.) 2.00
1 (Gold)-Promotional copy. 3.00
1 (Platinum)-Promotional copy. 4.00
Yearbook 1 (2/95, $3.95)-"1994" in indicia. 4.00

UNIVERSAL MONSTERS
Dark Horse Comics: 1993 ($4.95/$5.95, 52 pgs.)(All adapt original movies)

Frankenstein nn-($3.95)-Painted-c/a 5.00
Dracula nn-($4.95) 2.00 6.00
The Mummy nn-($4.95)-Painted-c 2.00 6.00
Creature From the Black Lagoon nn-($4.95)-Art Adams/Austin-c/a 2.00 6.00

UNIVERSAL PRESENTS DRACULA-THE MUMMY& OTHER STORIES
Dell Publishing Co.: Sept-Nov, 1963 (one-shot, 84 pgs.) (Also see Dell Giants)

GD25 FN65 VF82 NM94
02-530-311-r/Dracula 12-231-212, The Mummy 12-437-211 & part of Ghost Stories No. 1 12.00 37.00 85.00 220.00

UNIVERSAL SOLDIER (Movie)
Now Comics: Sept, 1992 - No. 3, Nov, 1992 (Limited series, polybagged, mature)

1-3 ($2.50, Direct Sales) 1-Movie adapatation; hologram on-c (all direct sales editions have painted-c) 2.50
1-3 ($1.95, Newsstand)-Rewritten & redrawn code approved version; all newsstand editions have photo-c 2.00

UNKEPT PROMISE
Legion of Truth: 1949 (Giveaway, 24 pgs.)

nn-Anti-alcohol 7.85 23.50 55.00

UNKNOWN MAN, THE (Movie)
Avon Periodicals: 1951

nn-Kinstler-c 25.00 75.00 185.00

UNKNOWN SOLDIER (Formerly Star-Spangled War Stories)
National Periodical Publications/DC Comics: No. 205, Apr-May, 1977 - No. 268, Oct, 1982 (See Our Army at War #168 for 1st app.)

Unknown Soldier #3 (mini-series) © DC

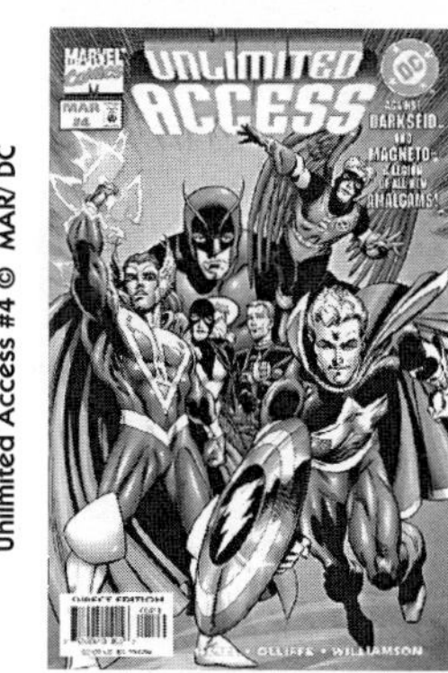

Unlimited Access #4 © MAR/ DC

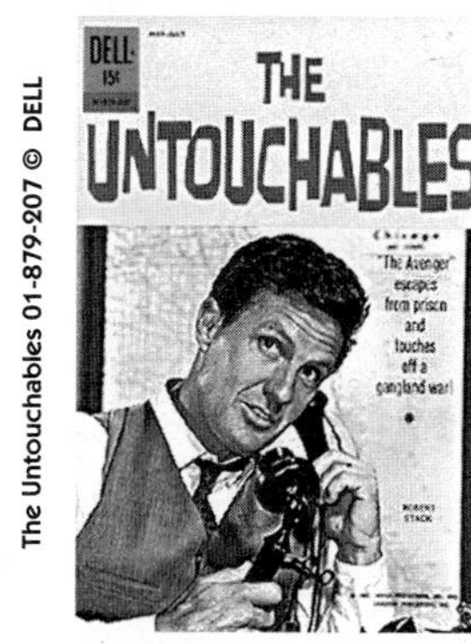

The Untouchables 01-879-207 © DELL

GD25 FN65 NM94

205 1.00 3.00 10.00
206-210,220,221,251: 220,221 (44pgs.). 251-Enemy Ace begins .85 2.60 7.00
211-218,222-247,250,252-264 5.00
219-Miller-a (44 pgs.) 1.00 3.00 10.00
248,249,265-267: 248,249-Origin. 265-267-Enemy Ace vs. Balloon Buster. 2.00 6.00
268-Death of Unknown Soldier 1.00 3.00 10.00
NOTE: *Chaykin a-234. Evans a-265-267; c-235. Kubert c-Most. Miller a-219p. Severin a-251-253, 260, 261, 265-267. Simonson a-254-256. Spiegle a-258, 259, 262-264.*

UNKNOWN SOLDIER, THE (Also see Brave &the Bold #146)
DC Comics: Winter, 1988-'89 - No. 12, Dec, 1989 ($1.50, maxi-series, mature)
1-12: 8-Begin $1.75-c 1.50

UNKNOWN SOLDIER
DC Comics (Vertigo): Apr, 1997 - No 4, July, 1997 ($2.50, mini-series)
1-Ennis-s/Plunkett-a/Bradstreet-c in all 1.00 2.00 6.00
2 5.00
3,4 3.50
TPB (1998, $12.95) r/#1-4 12.95

UNKNOWN WORLD (Strange Stories From Another World #2 on)
Fawcett Publications: June, 1952
1-Norman Saunders painted-c 36.00 107.00 260.00

UNKNOWN WORLDS (See Journey Into...)

UNKNOWN WORLDS
American Comics Group/Best Synd. Features: Aug, 1960 - No. 57, Aug, 1967
1-Schaffenberger-c 17.00 51.00 170.00
2-Dinosaur-c/story 10.50 32.00 105.00
3-5 9.50 28.50 95.00
6-11: 9-Dinosaur-c/story. 11-Last 10¢ issue 7.00 21.00 70.00
12-19: 12-Begin 12¢ issues?; ends #57 6.00 18.00 60.00
20-Herbie cameo (12-1/62-63) 6.50 19.50 65.00
21-35 3.50 10.50 35.00
36- "The People vs. Hendricks" by Craig; most popular ACG story ever 4.00 12.00 40.00
37-46 3.00 9.00 30.00
47-Williamson-a r-from Adventures Into the Unknown #96, 3 pgs.; Craig-a 3.20 9.60 32.00
48-57: 53-Frankenstein app. 2.80 8.40 28.00
NOTE: *Ditko a-49, 50p, 54. Forte a-3, 6, 11. Landau a-56(2). Reinman a-3, 9, 13, 20, 22, 23, 36, 38, 54. Whitney c/a-most issues. John Force, Magic Agent app.-35, 36, 48, 50, 52, 54, 56.*

UNKNOWN WORLDS OF FRANK BRUNNER
Eclipse Comics: Aug, 1985 - No. 2, Aug, 1985 ($1.75)
1,2-B&W-r in color 1.80

UNKNOWN WORLDS OF SCIENCE FICTION
Marvel Comics: Jan, 1975 - No. 6, Nov, 1975; 1976 ($1.00, B&W Magazine)
1-Williamson/Krenkel/Torres/Frazetta-r/Witzend #1, Neal Adams-r/Phase 1; Brunner & Kaluta-r; Freas/Romita-c .85 2.60 7.00
2-6: 5-Kaluta text illos 2.00 6.00
Special 1(1976,100 pgs.)-Newton painted-c .85 2.60 7.00
NOTE: *Brunner a-2; c-4, 6. Buscema a-Special 1p. Chaykin a-5. Colan a(p)-1, 3, 5, 6. Corben a-4. Kaluta a-2, Special 1(ext illos); c-2. Morrow a-3, 5. Nino a-3, 6, Special 1. Perez a-2, 3. Ray Bradbury interview in #1.*

UNLIMITED ACCESS (Also see Marvel Vs. DC))
Marvel Comics: Dec, 1997 - No. 4, Mar, 1998 ($2.99/$1.99, limited series)
1-Spider-Man, Wonder Woman, Green Lantern & Hulk app. 3.50
2,3-($1.99): 2-X-Men, Legion of Super-Heroes app. 3-Original Avengers vs. original Justice League 2.00
4-($2.99) Amalgam Legion vs. Darkseid & Magneto 3.00

UNSANE (Formerly Mighty Bear #13, 14? or The Outlaws #10-14?)
Star Publications: No. 15, June, 1954
15-Disbrow-a(2); L. B. Cole-c 32.00 96.00 240.00

UNSEEN, THE
Visual Editions/Standard Comics: No. 5, 1952 - No. 15, July, 1954
5-Horror stories in all; Toth-a 32.00 96.00 240.00
6,7,9,10-Jack Katz-a 23.00 68.00 170.00
8,11,13,14 15.00 46.00 115.00
12,15-Toth-a. 12-Tuska-a 23.00 68.00 170.00
NOTE: *Nick Cardy c-12. Fawcette a-13, 14. Sekowsky a-7, 8(2), 10, 13, 15.*

UNTAMED
Marvel Comics (Epic Comics/Heavy Hitters): June, 1993 - No. 3, Aug, 1993 ($1.95, limited series)
1-($2.50)-Embossed-c 2.50
2,3 2.00

UNTAMED LOVE (Also see Frank Frazetta's Untamed Love)
Quality Comics Group (Comic Magazines): Jan, 1950 - No. 5, Sept, 1950
1-Ward-c, Gustavson-a 22.00 66.00 165.00
2,4: 2-5-Photo-c 13.00 38.00 95.00
3,5-Gustavson-a 14.00 42.00 105.00

UNTOLD LEGEND OF CAPTAIN MARVEL, THE
Marvel Comics: Apr, 1997 - No. 3, June, 1997 ($2.50, limited series)
1-3 2.50

UNTOLD LEGEND OF THE BATMAN, THE
DC Comics: July, 1980 - No. 3, Sept, 1980 (Limited series)
1-Origin; Joker-c; Byrne's 1st work at DC 4.00
2,3 3.00
1-3: Batman cereal premiums (1989, 28 pgs., 6X9"); 1st & 2nd printings known 3.00
NOTE: *Aparo a-1i, 2, 3. Byrne a-1p.*

UNTOLD ORIGIN OF THE FEMFORCE, THE (Also see Femforce)
AC Comics: 1989 ($4.95, 68 pgs.)
1-Origin Femforce; Bill Black-a(i) & scripts 5.00

UNTOLD TALES OF SPIDER-MAN (Also see Amazing Fantasy #16-18)
Marvel Comics: Sept, 1995 - No. 25, Sept, 1997 (99¢)
1-Kurt Busiek scripts begin; Pat Olliffe-c/a in all (except #9). 2.00
2-22, -1(7/97), 23-25: 2-1st app. Batwing. 4-1st app. The Spacemen (Gantry, Orbit, Satellite & Vacuum). 8-1st app. The Headsman; The Enforcers (The Big Man, Montana, The Ox & Fancy Dan) app. 9-Ron Frenz-a. 10-1st app. Commanda. 16-Reintro Mary Jane Watson. 21-X-Men-c/app. 25-Green Goblin 1.50
...'96-(1996, $1.95, 46 pgs.)-Kurt Busiek scripts; Mike Allred-c/a; Kurt Busiek & Pat Olliffe app. in back-up story; contains pin-ups 2.00
...'97-(1997, $1.95)-Wraparound-c 2.00
...: Strange Encounters ('98, $5.99) Dr. Strange app. 2.00 6.00

UNTOUCHABLES, THE (TV)
Dell Publishing Co.: No. 1237, 10-12/61 - No. 4, 8-10/62
(All have Robert Stack photo-c)
Four Color 1237(#1) 22.00 65.00 240.00
Four Color 1286 16.00 47.00 170.00
01-879-207, 12-879-210(01879-210 on inside) 8.00 25.00 90.00
Topps Bubblegum premiums produced by Leaf Brands, Inc.-2-1/2x4-1/2", 8 pgs. (3 diff. issues) "The Organization, Jamaica Ginger, The Otto Frick Story (drug), 3000 Suspects, The Antidote, Mexican Stakeout, Little Egypt, Purple Gang, Bugs Moran Story, & Lily Dallas Story" 2.00 6.00 16.00

UNTOUCHABLES
Caliber Comics: Aug, 1997 - Present ($2.95, B&W)
1-4: 1-Pruett-s; variant covers by Kaluta & Showman 2.95

UNUSUAL TALES (Blue Beetle & Shadows From Beyond #50 on)

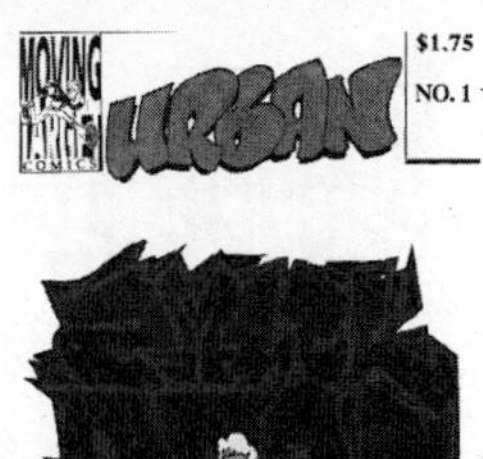

Urban #1 © Moving Target Ent.

U.S. Agent #1 © MAR

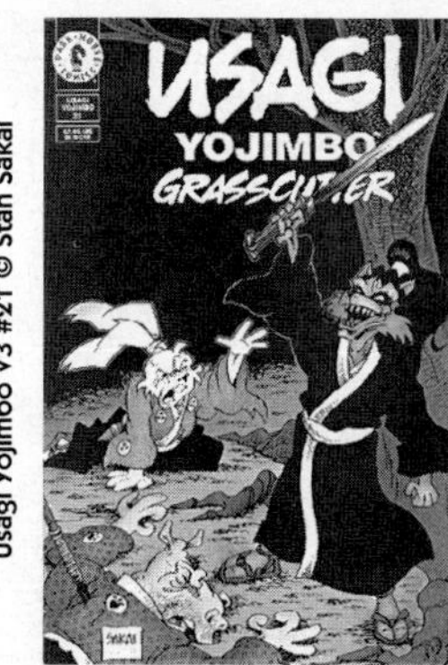

Usagi Yojimbo V3 #21 © Stan Sakai

	GD25	FN65	NM94

Charlton Comics: Nov, 1955 - No. 49, Mar-Apr, 1965

	GD25	FN65	NM94
1	21.00	64.00	160.00
2	11.00	32.00	80.00
3-5	7.85	23.50	55.00
6-Ditko-c only	9.30	28.00	65.00
7,8-Ditko-c/a. 8-Robot-c	20.00	60.00	150.00
9-Ditko-c/a (20 pgs.)	21.00	64.00	160.00
10-Ditko-c/a(4)	24.00	72.00	180.00
11-(3/58, 68 pgs.)-Ditko-a(4)	23.00	68.00	170.00
12,14-Ditko-a	14.00	42.00	105.00
13,16-20	3.80	11.40	38.00
15-Ditko-c/a	12.00	36.00	120.00
21,24,28	2.80	8.40	28.00
22,23,25-27,29-Ditko-a	7.50	22.50	75.00
30-49	2.50	7.50	22.00

NOTE: *Colan a-11. Ditko c-22, 23, 25-27, 31(part).*

UP FROM HARLEM (Tom Skinner...)
Spire Christian Comics (Fleming H. Revell Co.): 1973 (35/49¢)

nn 4.00

UP-TO-DATE COMICS
King Features Syndicate: No date (1938) (36 pgs.; B&W cover) (10¢)

nn-Popeye & Henry cover; The Phantom, Jungle Jim & Flash Gordon by Raymond, The Katzenjammer Kids, Curley Harper & others. Note: Variations in content exist. 21.00 64.00 160.00

UP YOUR NOSE AND OUT YOUR EAR (Satire)
Klevart Enterprises: Apr, 1972 - No. 2, June, 1972 (52 pgs., magazine)

V1#1,2 .90 2.70 8.00

URBAN
Moving Target Entertainment: 1994 ($1.75, B&W)

1 1.75

URTH 4
Continuity Comics: 1990 - No. 4, 1990 ($2.00, deluxe format)

1-4: Ms. Mystic characters. 2-Neal Adams-c(i) 2.00

URZA-MISHRA WAR ON THE WORLD OF MAGIC THE GATHERING
Acclaim Comics (Armada): 1996 - No. 2, 1996 ($5.95, limited series)

1,2 6.00

U.S. (See Uncle Sam)

USA COMICS
Timely Comics (USA): Aug, 1941 - No. 17, Fall, 1945

	GD25	FN65	VF82	NM94
1-Origin Major Liberty (called Mr. Liberty #1), Rockman by Wolverton, & The Whizzer by Avison; The Defender with sidekick Rusty & Jack Frost begin; The Young Avenger only app.; S&K-c plus 1 pg. art	950.00	2850.00	5700.00	9500.00

	GD25	FN65	NM94
2-Origin Captain Terror & The Vagabond; last Wolverton Rockman; Hitler-c	300.00	900.00	2700.00
3-No Whizzer	235.00	705.00	2000.00
4-Last Rockman, Major Liberty, Defender, Jack Frost, & Capt. Terror; Corporal Dix app.	200.00	600.00	1700.00
5-Origin American Avenger & Roko the Amazing; The Blue Blade, The Black Widow & Victory Boys, Gypo the Gypsy Giant & Hills of Horror only app.; Sergeant Dix begins; no Whizzer; Hitler, Mussolini & Tojo-c	176.00	529.00	1500.00
6-Captain America (ends #17), The Destroyer, Jap Buster Johnson, Jeep Jones begin; Terror Squad only app.	235.00	706.00	2000.00
7-Captain Daring, Disk-Eyes the Detective by Wolverton app.; origin & only app. Marvel Boy (3/43); Secret Stamp begins; no Whizzer, Sergeant Dix	200.00	600.00	1700.00
8-10: 9-Last Secret Stamp; Hitler-c. 10-The Thunderbird only app.	159.00	477.00	1350.00
11,12: 11-No Jeep Jones	129.00	388.00	1100.00
13-17: 13-No Whizzer; Jeep Jones ends. 15-No Destroyer; Jap Buster Johnson ends	94.00	282.00	800.00

NOTE: *Brodsky c-14. Gabrielle c-4, 8. Schomburg c-6-8, 10, 12, 13, 15-17. Shores a-1, 4; c-9, 11. Ed Win a-4. Cover features: 1-The Defender; 2, 3-Captain Terror; 4-Major Liberty; 5-Victory Boys; 6-17-Captain America & Bucky.*

U.S. AGENT (See Jeff Jordan...)

U.S. AGENT (See Captain America #354)
Marvel Comics: June, 1993 - No. 4, Sept, 1993 ($1.75, limited series)

1-4 1.75

USAGI YOJIMBO (See Albedo, Doomsday Squad #3 & Space Usagi)
Fantagraphics Books: July, 1987 - No. 38 ($2.00/$2.25, B&W)

	NM94
1	4.00
1,8,10-2nd printings	2.00
2-9,11-29: 11-Aragonés-a	2.50
10-Leonardo app. (TMNT)	2.50
30-38: 30-Begin $2.25-c	2.25
Color Special 1 (11/89, $2.95, 68 pgs.)-new & r	3.00
Color Special 2 (10/91, $3.50)	3.50
Color Special #3 (10/92, $3.50)-Jeff Smith's Bone promo on inside-c	3.50
Summer Special 1 (1986, B&W, $2.75)-r/early Albedo issues	3.00

USAGI YOJIMBO
Mirage Studios: V2#1, Mar, 1993 - No. 16, 1994 ($2.75)

V2#1-16: 1-Teenage Mutant Ninja Turtles app. 2.75

USAGI YOJIMBO
Dark Horse Comics: V3#1, Apr, 1996 - Present ($2.95, B&W)

	NM94
V3#1-24: Stan Sakai-c/a	3.00
Color Special #4 (7/97, $2.95) "Green Persimmon"	3.00

U.S. AIR FORCE COMICS (Army Attack #38 on)
Charlton Comics: Oct, 1958 - No. 37, Mar-Apr, 1965

	GD25	FN65	NM94
1	3.80	11.40	38.00
2	2.50	7.50	22.00
3-10	2.00	6.00	16.00
11-20	1.75	5.25	14.00
21-37	1.25	3.75	10.00

NOTE: *Glanzman c/a-9, 10, 12. Montes/Bache a-33.*

USA IS READY
Dell Publishing Co.: 1941 (68 pgs., one-shot)

1-War propaganda 37.00 112.00 280.00

U.S. BORDER PATROL COMICS (Sgt. Dick Carter of the...) (See Holyoke One Shot)

U.S. FIGHTING AIR FORCE (Also see United States Fighting Air Force)
I. W. Enterprises: No date (1960s?)

1,9(nd): 1-r/United States Fighting...#?. 9-r/#1 1.40 3.50 7.00

U.S. FIGHTING MEN
Super Comics: 1963 - 1964 (Reprints)

	GD25	FN65	NM94
10-r/With the U.S. Paratroops #4(Avon)	1.80	4.50	9.00
11,12,15-18: 11-r/Monty Hall #10. 12,16,17,18-r/U.S. Fighting Air Force #10,3,?&? 15-r/Man Comics #11	1.60	4.00	8.00

U.S. JONES (Also see Wonderworld Comics #28)
Fox Features Syndicate: Nov, 1941 - No. 2, Jan, 1942

	GD25	FN65	NM94
1-U.S. Jones & The Topper begin; Nazi-c	110.00	330.00	935.00
2-Nazi-c	75.00	225.00	660.00

U.S. MARINES
Charlton Comics: Fall, 1964 (12¢, one-shot)

1-1st app. Capt. Dude; Glanzman-a 2.25 6.75 18.00

V #3 © DC

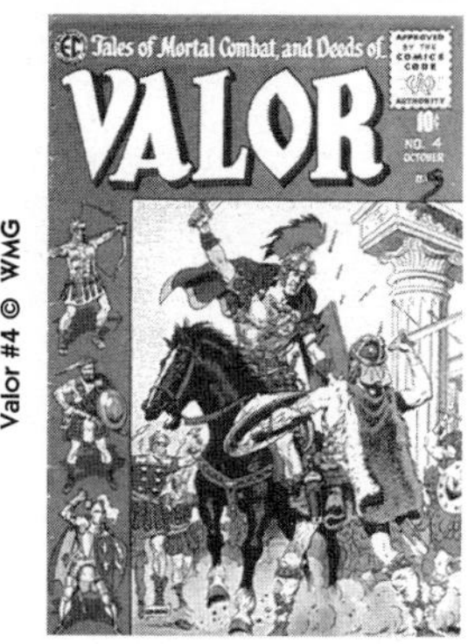

Valor #4 © WMG

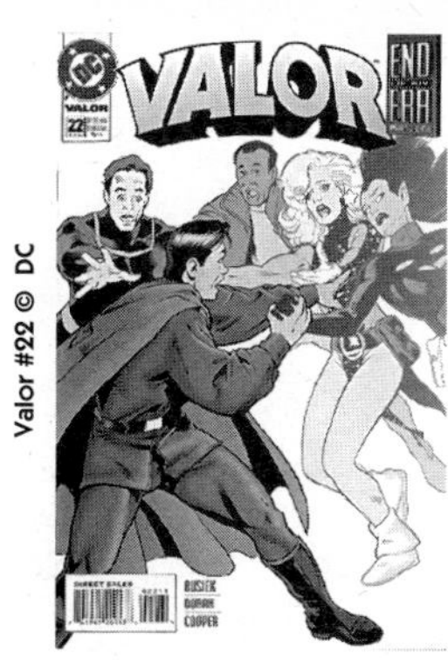

Valor #22 © DC

	GD25	FN65	NM94

U.S. MARINES IN ACTION
Avon Periodicals: Aug, 1952 - No. 3, Dec, 1952

1-Louis Ravielli-c/a	6.85	21.00	48.00
2,3: 3-Kinstler-c	4.25	13.00	28.00

U.S. 1
Marvel Comics Group: May, 1983 - No. 12, Oct, 1984 (7,8: painted-c)

1-12: 2-Sienkiewicz-c. 3-12-Michael Golden-c — 1.00

U.S. PARATROOPS (See With the...)

U.S. PARATROOPS
I. W. Enterprises: 1964?

1,8: 1-r/With the U.S. Paratroops #1; Wood-c. 8-r/With the U.S. Paratroops #6; Kinstler-c	1.25	3.75	10.00

U.S. TANK COMMANDOS
Avon Periodicals: June, 1952 - No. 4, Mar, 1953

1-Kinstler-c	7.50	22.50	52.00
2-4: Kinstler-c	5.70	17.00	36.00
I.W. Reprint #1,8: 1-r/#1. 8-r/#3	1.25	3.75	10.00

NOTE: ***Kinstler** a-I.W. #1; c-1-4, I.W. #1, 8.*

"V" (TV)
DC Comics: Feb, 1985 - No. 18, July, 1986

1-Based on TV movie & series (Sci/Fi) — 2.00
2-18: 17,18-Denys Cowan-c/a — 1.50

VACATION COMICS (Also see A-1 Comics)
Magazine Enterprises: No. 16, 1948 (one-shot)

A-1 16-The Pixies, Tom Tom, Flying Fredd & Koko & Kola	4.00	12.00	24.00

VACATION DIGEST
Harvey Comics: Sept, 1987 ($1.25, digest size)

1 — 4.00

VACATION IN DISNEYLAND (Also see Dell Giants)
Dell Publishing Co./Gold Key (1965): Aug-Oct, 1959; May, 1965 (Walt Disney)

Four Color 1025-Barks-a	18.00	55.00	200.00
1(30024-508)(G.K., 5/65, 25¢)-r/Dell Giant #30 & cover to #1 ('58); celebrates Disneyland's 10th anniversary	3.60	11.00	40.00

VACATION PARADE (See Dell Giants)

VALERIA THE SHE BAT
Continuity Comics: May, 1993 - No. 5, Nov, 1993

1-Premium; acetate-c; N. Adams-a/scripts; given as gift to retailers — 5.00
5 (11/93)-Embossed-c; N. Adams-a/scripts — 2.50

NOTE: *Due to lack of continuity, #2-4 do not exist.*

VALERIA THE SHE BAT
Acclaim Comics (Windjammer): Sept, 1995 - No.2, Oct, 1995 ($2.50, limited series)

1,2 — 2.50

VALKYRIE (See Airboy)
Eclipse Comics: May,1987 - No. 3, July, 1987 ($1.75, limited series)

1-3: 2-Holly becomes new Black Angel — 2.50

VALKYRIE
Marvel Comics: Jan, 1997 ($2.95, one-shot)

1-w/pin-ups — 3.00

VALKYRIE!
Eclipse Comics: July, 1988 - No. 3, Sept, 1988 ($1.95, limited series)

1-3 — 2.00

VALLEY OF THE DINOSAURS (TV)
Charlton Comics: Apr, 1975 - No. 11, Dec, 1976 (Hanna-Barbara)

1,3: 3-Byrne text illos (early work, 7/75)	1.00	3.00	10.00
2,4-11: 1,2-W. Howard-i	.85	2.60	7.00

VALLEY OF THE DINOSAURS (TV)
Harvey Comics: Oct, 1992 ($1.50, giant-sized)

1-Reprints — 2.00 — 5.00

VALLEY OF GWANGI (See Movie Classics)

VALOR
E. C. Comics: Mar-Apr, 1955 - No. 5, Nov-Dec, 1955

1-Williamson/Torres-a; Wood-c/a	23.00	69.00	220.00
2-Williamson-c/a; Wood-a	20.00	60.00	180.00
3,4: 3-Williamson, Crandall-a. 4-Wood-c	13.00	39.00	125.00
5-Wood-c/a; Williamson/Evans-a	12.00	36.00	115.00

NOTE: ***Crandall** a-3, 4. **Ingels** a-1, 2, 4, 5. **Krigstein** a-1-5. **Orlando** a-3, 4; c-3. **Wood** a-1, 2, 5; c-1, 4, 5.*

VALOR
Gemstone Publishing: Oct, 1998 - No. 5, Feb, 1999 ($2.50)

1-5-Reprints — 2.50

VALOR (Also see Legion of Super-Heroes & Legionnaires)
DC Comics: Nov, 1992 - No. 23, Sept, 1994 ($1.25/$1.50)

1-12: 1-Eclipso The Darkness Within aftermath. 2-Vs. Supergirl. 4-Vs. Lobo. 12-Lobo cameo — 1.25
13-22: 13-Begin $1.50-c. 14-Legionnaires, JLA app. 17-Austin-c(i); death of Valor. 18-22-Build-up to Zero Hour — 1.50
23-Zero Hour tie-in — 1.75

VALOR THUNDERSTAR AND HIS FIREFLIES
Now Comics: Dec, 1986 ($1.50)

1-Ordway-c(p) — 1.50

VAMPIRE BITES
Brainstorm Comics: May, 1995 - No. 2, Sept, 1996 ($2.95, B&W)

1,2:1-Color pin-up — 1.20 — 3.00

VAMPIRE LESTAT, THE
Innovation Publishing: Jan, 1990 - No. 12, 1991 ($2.50, painted limited series)

1-Adapts novel; Bolton painted-c on all	2.25	6.80	25.00
1-2nd printing (has UPC code, 1st prints don't)			4.00
1-3rd & 4th printings			2.50
2-1st printing	1.20	3.60	12.00
2-2nd & 3rd printings			2.50
3-5	.90	2.70	8.00
3-6,9-2nd printings			2.50
6-12			4.00

VAMPIRELLA (Magazine)(See Warren Presents)
Warren Publishing Co./Harris Publications #113: Sept, 1969 - No. 112, Feb, 1983; No. 113, Jan, 1988? (B&W)

1-Intro. Vampirella	32.00	96.00	385.00
2-Amazonia series begins, ends #12	11.00	34.00	125.00
3 (Low distribution)	29.00	88.00	330.00
4-7	7.25	22.00	80.00
8-Vampi begins by Tom Sutton as serious strip (early issues-gag line)	8.00	24.00	90.00
9-Barry Smith-a; Boris-c	7.25	22.00	80.00
10-No Vampi story	2.90	8.70	32.00
11-15: 11-Origin & 1st app. Pendragon. 12-Vampi by Gonzales begins	4.50	13.50	50.00
16-18,20-25: 17-Tomb of the Gods begins, ends #22. 25-Begin partial color issues	3.50	10.50	38.00
19 (1973 Annual)	5.00	15.00	55.00
26,28-36,38-40: 30-Intro. Pantha; Corben-a(color). 31-Origin Luana, the Beast Girl. 33-Pantha ends	2.20	6.50	24.00
27 (1974 Annual)	2.90	8.70	32.00

Vampirella (The New Monthly) #7 © Harris

Vampirella/Painkiller Jane #1 © Harris

Vampirella Retro #1 © Harris

GD25 FN65 NM94

37 (1975 Annual) 2.70 8.00 30.00
41-45,47-50: 49-1st app. The Blood Red Queen of Hearts. 50-Spirit cameo by Eisner 1.80 5.40 18.00
46-Origin retold (10/75) 2.25 6.80 25.00
51-66,68,70,72,73,75,79-99: 60-62,65,66-The Blood Red Queen of Hearts app. 93-Cassandra St. Knight begins, ends #103; new Pantha series begins, ends #108 1.50 4.50 15.00
67,69,71,74,76-78-photo-c 2.20 6.25 22.00
100 (96 pg. r-special)-Origin reprinted; Vampirella appears topless 5.00 15.00 55.00
101-110,112: 101,102-The Blood Red Queen of Hearts app. 108-Torpedo series by Toth begins 3.00 9.00 33.00
111-Giant Collector's Edition ($2.50) 4.00 12.00 44.00
113 (1988)-1st Harris Issue 23.00 68.00 250.00
Annual 1(1972)-New origin Vampirella by Gonzales; reprints by Neal Adams (from #1), Wood (from #9) 23.00 68.00 250.00
Special 1 (1977; large-square bound)(soft-c) 6.50 19.50 70.00
Special 1 (color, 1977; large-square bound)-Only available through mail order (scarce)(hard-c) 18.00 55.00 200.00

NOTE: ***Neal Adams*** *a-1, 10p, 19p(r/#10).* ***Alcala*** *a-90, 93i.* ***Bode'/Todd*** *c-3.* ***Bode'/Jones*** *c-4.* ***Boris*** *c-9.* ***Brunner*** *a-10, 12(1 pg.).* ***Corben*** *a-30, 31, 33, 54.* ***Crandall*** *a-1, 19(r/#1).* ***Frazetta*** *c-1, 5, 7, 11, 31.* ***Heath*** *a-76-78, 83.* ***Jones*** *a-5, 9, 12, 27, 32, 33(2 pg.), 34, 50i, 83r.* ***Nino*** *a-59i, 61i, 67, 76, 85, 90.* ***Ploog*** *a-14.* ***Barry Smith*** *a-9.* ***Starlin*** *a-78.* ***Sutton*** *a-11.* ***Toth*** *a-90i, 108, 110.* ***Wood*** *a-9, 10, 12, 19(r/#12), 27r; c-9.* ***Wrightson*** *a-33(w/****Jones****), 63r. All reprint issues-37, 74, 83, 87, 91, 105, 107, 109, 111. Annuals from 1973 on are included in regular numbering. Later annuals are same format as regular issues.*

VAMPIRELLA (Also see Cain/... & Vengeance of...)
Harris Publications: Nov, 1992 - No. 5, Nov, 1993 ($2.95)

0 3.00
0-Gold 2.25 6.80 25.00
1-Jim Balent inks in #1-3; Adam Hughes c-1-3 2.00 6.00 20.00
1-2nd printing 2.00 6.00
1-(11/97) Commemorative Edition 3.00
2 1.00 3.00 10.00
3-5: 4-Snyder III-c. 5-Brereton painted-c 2.00 6.00
Trade paperback nn (10/93, $5.95)-r/#1-4; Jusko-c 6.00

NOTE: *Issues 1-5 contain certificates for free* ***Dave Stevens*** *Vampirella poster.*

VAMPIRELLA (THE NEW MONTHLY)
Harris Publications: Nov, 1997 - Present ($2.95)

1-3-"Ascending Evil" -Morrison & Millar-s/Conner &Palmiotti-a. 1-Three covers by Quesada/Palmiotti, Conner, andConner/Palmiotti 3.00
1-3-($9.95) Jae Lee variant covers 10.00
1-($24.95) Platinum Ed.w/Quesada-c 25.00
4-6-"Holy War"-Small & Stull-a 3.00
4-Linsner variant-c 5.00
7-9-"Queen's Gambit"-Shi app. 7-Two covers. 8-Pantha-c/app. 2.95
7-($9.95) Conner variant-c 10.00
10-12-"Hell on Earth"; Small-a/Coney-s. 12-New costume 2.95
TPB ($7.50) r/#1-3 "Ascending Evil" 7.50
Hell on Earth Ashcan (7/98, $1.00) 1.00

VAMPIRELLA & PANTHA SHOWCASE
Harris Publications: Jan, 1997 ($1.50, one-shot)

1-Millar-s/Texeira-c/a; flip book w/"Blood Lust"; Robinson-s/Jusko-c/a 1.50

VAMPIRELLA & THE BLOOD RED QUEEN OF HEARTS
Harris Publications: Sept, 1996 ($9.95, 96 pgs., B&W, squarebound, one-shot)

nn-r/Vampirella #49,60-62,65,66,101,102; John Bolton-c; Michael Bair back-c 1.00 3.00 10.00

VAMPIRELLA: BLOODLUST
Harris Publications: July, 1997 - No. 2, Aug, 1997 ($4.95, limited series)

1,2-Robinson-s/Jusko-painted c/a 5.00

VAMPIRELLA CLASSICS
Harris Publications: Feb, 1995 - No. 5, Nov, 1995 ($2.95, limited series)

1-5: Reprints Archie Goodwin stories. 3.00

VAMPIRELLA: CROSSOVER GALLERY
Harris Publications: Sept, 1997 ($2.95, one-shot)

1-Wraparound-c by Campbell, pinups by Jae Lee, Mack, Allred, Art Adams, Quesada & Palmiotti and others 2.95

VAMPIRELLA: DEATH & DESTRUCTION
Harris Publications: July, 1996 - No. 3, Sept, 1996 ($2.95, limited series)

1-3: Amanda Conner-a(p) in all. 1-Tucci-c. 2-Hughes-c. 3-Jusko-c 3.00
1-($9.95)-Limited Edition; Beachum-c 10.00

VAMPIRELLA/DRACULA & PANTHA SHOWCASE
Harris Publications: Aug, 1997 ($1.50, one-shot)

1-Ellis, Robinson, and Moore-s; flip book w/"Pantha" 1.50

VAMPIRELLA/DRACULA: THE CENTENNIAL
Harris Publications: Oct, 1997 ($5.95, one-shot)

1-Ellis, Robinson, and Moore-s; Beachum, Frank/Smith, and Mack/Mays-a Bolton-painted-c 5.95

VAMPIRELLA LIVES
Harris Publications: Dec, 1996 - No. 3, Feb, 1997 ($3.50/$2.95, limited series)

1-Die cut-c; Quesada & Palmiotti-c, Ellis-s/Conner-a 3.50
1-Deluxe Ed.-photo-c 3.50
2,3-($2.95)-Two editions (1 photo-c): 3-J. Scott Campbell-c 3.00

VAMPIRELLA: MORNING IN AMERICA
Harris Publications/Dark Horse Comics: 1991 - No. 4, 1992 ($3.95, B&W, limited series, 52 pgs.)

1-All have Kaluta painted-c .85 2.60 7.00
2-4 5.00

VAMPIRELLA OF DRAKULON
Harris Publications: Jan, 1996 - No. 5, Sept, 1996 ($2.95)

0-5: All reprints. 0-Jim Silke-c. 3-Polybagged w/card. 4-Texiera-c 3.00

VAMPIRELLA/PAINKILLER JANE
Harris Publications: May, 1998 ($3.50, one-shot)

1-Waid & Augustyn-s/Leonardi & Palmiotti-a 3.50
1-($9.95) Variant-c 10.00

VAMPIRELLA PIN-UP SPECIAL
Harris Publications: Oct, 1995 ($2.95, one-shot)

1-Hughes-c, pin-ups by various 3.00
1-Variant-c 3.00

VAMPIRELLA: RETRO
Harris Publications: Mar, 1998 - No. 3, May, 1998 ($2.50, B&W, limited series)

1-3: Reprints; Silke painted covers 2.50

VAMPIRELLA: SAD WINGS OF DESTINY
Harris Publications: Sept, 1996 ($3.95, one-shot)

1-Jusko-c 4.00

VAMPIRELLA/SHADOWHAWK: CREATURES OF THE NIGHT (Also see Shadowhawk)
Harris Publications: 1995 ($4.95, one-shot)

1 5.00

VAMPIRELLA/SHI (SeeShi/Vampirella)
Harris Publications: Oct, 1997 ($2.95, one-shot)

1-Ellis-s 2.95
..1-Chromium-c 8.00

VAMPIRELLA: SILVER ANNIVERSARY COLLECTION
Harris Publications: Jan, 1997 - No. 4 Apr, 1997($2.50, limited series)

1-4: Two editions: Bad Girl by Beachum, Good Girl by Silke 2.50

VAMPIRELLA'S SUMMER NIGHTS

Vanguard #6 © Image

Vault of Evil #2 © MAR

Vault of Horror #15 © WMG

	GD25	FN65	NM94
Harris Publications: 1992 (one-shot)			
1-Art Adams infinity cover; centerfold by Stelfreeze	2.70	8.00	30.00

VAMPIRELLA STRIKES
Sept, 1995 - No. 8, Dec, 1996 ($2.95, limited series)
Harris Publications

	GD25	FN65	NM94
1-8: 1-Photo-c. 2-Deodato-c; polybagged w/card. 5-Eudaemon-c/app; wraparound-c; alternate-c exists. 6-(6/96)-Mark Millar script; Texeira-c; alternate-c exists. 7-Flip book			3.00
1-Newsstand Edition; different photo-c.			3.00
1-Limited Edition; different photo-c.			3.00
Annual 1-(12/96, $2.95) Delano-s; two covers			3.00

VAMPIRELLA: 25TH ANNIVERSARY SPECIAL
Harris Publications: Oct, 1996 ($5.95, squarebound, one-shot)

	GD25	FN65	NM94
nn-Reintro The Blood Red Queen of Hearts; James Robinson, Grant Morrison & Warren Ellis scripts; Mark Texeira, Michael Bair & Amanda Conner-a(p); Frank Frazetta-c			6.00
nn-($6.95)-Silver Edition			7.00

VAMPIRELLA VS. HEMORRHAGE
Harris Publications: Apr, 1997($3.50)

	GD25	FN65	NM94
1			3.50

VAMPIRELLA VS. PANTHA
Harris Publications: Mar, 1997 ($3.50)

	GD25	FN65	NM94
1-Two covers; Millar-s/Texiera-c/a			3.50

VAMPIRELLA/WETWORKS (See Wetworks/Vampirella)
Harris Publications: June, 1997 ($2.95, one-shot)

	GD25	FN65	NM94
1			2.95
1-($9.95) Alternate Edition; cardstock-c			10.00

VAMPIRE TALES
Marvel Comics Group: Aug, 1973 - No. 11, June, 1975 (75¢, B&W, magazine)

	GD25	FN65	NM94
1-Morbius, the Living Vampire begins by Pablo Marcos (1st solo Morbius series & 5th Morbius app.)	3.20	9.50	35.00
2-Intro. Satana; Steranko-r	2.70	8.00	30.00
3,5,6,8: 3-Satana app. 5-Origin Morbius. 6-1st Lilith app. 8-Blade app. (see Tomb of Dracula)	2.00	6.00	20.00
4,7,9-11: 9-Blade app.	1.50	4.50	15.00
Annual 1(10/75)-Heath-r/#9	1.40	4.20	14.00

NOTE: ***Alcala*** *a-6, 8, 9i.* ***Boris*** *c-4, 6.* ***Chaykin*** *a-7.* ***Everett*** *a-1r.* ***Gulacy*** *a-7p.* ***Heath*** *a-9.* ***Infantino*** *a-3r.* ***Gil Kane*** *a-4, 5r.*

VAMPIRE VERSES, THE
CFD Productions: Aug, 1995 - No. 4, 1995 ($2.95, B&W, mature)

	GD25	FN65	NM94
1-4			3.00

VAMPRESS LUXURA, THE
Brainstorm Comics: Feb, 1996 ($2.95)

	GD25	FN65	NM94
1-Lindo-c/a/scripts			3.00
1-($10.00, Gold edition)-Gold foil logo			10.00
Leather Special-(3/96, $2.95)			3.00

VAMPS
DC Comics (Vertigo): Aug, 1994 - No. 6, Jan, 1995 ($1.95, lim. series, mature)

	GD25	FN65	NM94
1-Bolland-c			3.00
2-6: Bolland-c in all			3.00
Trade paperback ($9.95)-r/#1-6			10.00

VAMPS: HOLLYWOOD & VEIN
DC Comics (Vertigo): Feb, 1996 - No. 6, July, 1996 ($2.25, lim. series, mature)

	GD25	FN65	NM94
1-6: Winslade-c			2.25

VAMPS: PUMPKIN TIME
DC Comics (Vertigo): Dec, 1998 - No. 3, Feb, 1999 ($2.50, lim. series, mature)

	GD25	FN65	NM94
1-3: Quitely-c			2.50

VANGUARD (...Outpost: Earth) (See Megaton)
Megaton Comics: 1987 ($1.50)

	GD25	FN65	NM94
1-Erik Larsen-c(p)			3.00

VANGUARD (See Savage Dragon #2)
Image Comics (Highbrow Entertainment): Oct, 1993 - No.6, 1994 ($1.95)

	GD25	FN65	NM94
1-6: 1-Wraparound gatefold-c; Erik Larsen back-up-a; Supreme x-over. 3-(12/93)-Indicia says December 1994. 4-Berzerker back-up. 5-Angel Medina-a(p).			2.00

VANGUARD (See Savage Dragon #2)
Image Comics: Aug, 1996 - No.4, Feb, 1997 ($2.95, B&W, limited series)

	GD25	FN65	NM94
1-4			3.00

VANGUARD ILLUSTRATED
Pacific Comics: Nov, 1983 - No. 11, Oct, 1984 (Baxter paper)(Direct sales only)

	GD25	FN65	NM94
1-6,8-11: 1,7-Nudity scenes. 2-1st app. Stargrazers (see Legends of the Stargrazers; Dave Stevens-c			1.50
7-1st app. Mr. Monster (r-in Mr. Monster #1)			5.00

NOTE: ***Evans*** *a-7.* ***Kaluta*** *c-5, 7p.* ***Perez*** *a-6; c-6.* ***Rude*** *a-1-4; c-4.* ***Williamson*** *c-3.*

VANGUARD: STRANGE VISITORS
Image Comics: Oct, 1996 - No.4, Feb, 1997 ($2.95, B&W, limited series)

	GD25	FN65	NM94
1-4: 3-Supreme-c/app.			3.00

VANITY (See Pacific Presents #3)
Pacific Comics: Jun, 1984 - No. 2, Aug, 1984 ($1.50, direct sales)

	GD25	FN65	NM94
1,2: Origin			1.50

VARIETY COMICS (The Spice of Comics)
Rural Home Publ./Croyden Publ. Co.: 1944 - No. 2, 1945; No. 3, 1946

	GD25	FN65	NM94
1-Origin Captain Valiant	18.00	54.00	135.00
2-Captain Valiant	10.00	30.00	75.00
3(1946-Croyden)-Captain Valiant	9.30	28.00	65.00

VARIETY COMICS (See Fox Giants)

VARIOGENESIS
Dagger Comics Group: June, 1994 ($3.50)

	GD25	FN65	NM94
0			3.50

VARSITY
Parents' Magazine Institute: 1945

	GD25	FN65	NM94
1	6.50	19.50	40.00

VAULT OF EVIL
Marvel Comics Group: Feb, 1973 - No. 23, Nov, 1975

	GD25	FN65	NM94
1 (1950s reprints begin)	1.20	3.60	12.00
2-23: 3,4-Brunner-c	.90	2.70	8.00

NOTE: ***Ditko*** *a-14r, 15r, 20-22r.* ***Drucker*** *a-10r(Mystic #52), 13r(Uncanny Tales #42).* ***Everett*** *a-11r(Menace #2), 13r(Menace #4); c-10.* ***Heath*** *a-5r.* ***Gil Kane*** *c-1, 6.* ***Krigstein*** *a-20r(Uncanny Tales #54).* ***Reinman*** *r-1.* ***Tuska*** *a-6r.*

VAULT OF HORROR (Formerly War Against Crime #1-11)
E. C. Comics: No. 12, Apr-May, 1950 - No. 40, Dec-Jan, 1954-55

	GD25	FN65	NM94
12 (Scarce)	380.00	1140.00	3800.00
13-Morphine story	84.00	252.00	800.00
14	77.00	231.00	700.00
15- "Terror in the Swamp" is same story w/minor changes as "The Thing in the Swamp" from Haunt of Fear #15	63.00	189.00	600.00
16	45.00	135.00	450.00
17-19	38.00	114.00	325.00
20-25: 22-Frankenstein-c & adaptation. 23-Used in **POP**, pg. 84; Davis-a(2). 24-Craig biography	31.00	93.00	260.00
26-B&W & color illos in **POP**	31.00	93.00	260.00
27-35: 30-Dismemberment-c. 31-Ray Bradbury biog. 32-Censored-c. 35-X-Mas-c	22.00	66.00	200.00
36- "Pipe Dream" classic opium addict story by Krigstein; "Twin Bill" cited in articles by T.E. Murphy, Wertham	22.00	66.00	200.00

ALSO IN THIS ISSUE: WEIRD FANTASY!
THE VAULT OF HORROR

Vault of Horror (Gladstone) #6 © WMC

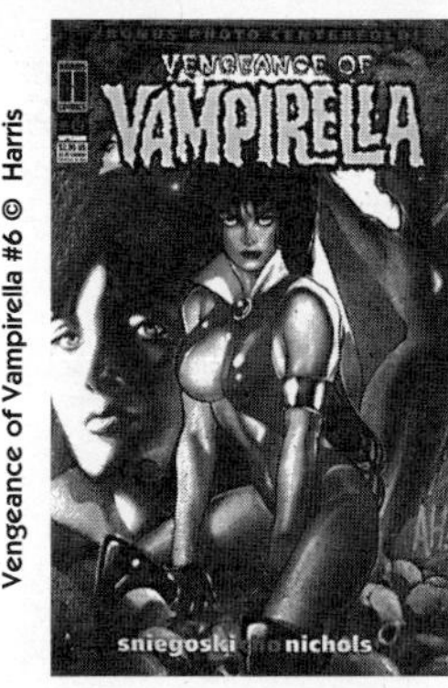

Vengeance of Vampirella #6 © Harris

Venom: The Mace #1 © MAR

	GD25	FN65	NM94
37-1st app. Drusilla, a Vampirella look alike; Williamson-a	22.00	66.00	200.00
38-39: 39-Bondage-c	18.00	54.00	170.00
40-Low distribution	22.00	66.00	220.00

NOTE: ***Craig** art in all but No. 13 & 33; c-12-40. **Crandall** a-33, 34, 39. **Davis** a-17-38. **Evans** a-27, 28, 30, 32, 33. **Feldstein** a-12-16. **Ingels** a-13-20, 22-40. **Kamen** a-15-22, 25, 29, 35. **Krigstein** a-36, 38-40. **Kurtzman** a-12, 13. **Orlando** a-24, 31, 40. **Wood** a-12-14. #22, 29 & 31 have Ray Bradbury adaptations. #16 & 17 have H. P. Lovecraft adaptations.*

VAULT OF HORROR, THE
Gladstone Publ.: Aug, 1990 - No. 6, June, 1991 ($1.95, 68 pgs.)(#4 on: $2.00)

	GD25	FN65	NM94
1-Craig-c(r); all contain EC reprints			4.00
2-6: 2,4-6-Craig-c(r). 3-Ingels-c(r)			2.00

VAULT OF HORROR
Russ Cochran/Gemstone Publishing: Sept, 1991 - No. 5, May, 1992? ($2.00); Oct, 1992 - Present ($1.50/$2.00/$2.50)

	GD25	FN65	NM94
1-5: E.C reprints			2.00
1-15: 1-4r/VOH #12-15 w/original-c			2.00
16-25			2.50

V...-COMICS (Morse code for "V" - 3 dots, 1 dash)
Fox Features Syndicate: Jan, 1942 - No. 2, Mar-Apr, 1942

	GD25	FN65	NM94
1-Origin V-Man & the Boys; The Banshee & The Black Fury, The Queen of Evil, & V-Agents begin; Nazi-c	112.00	335.00	950.00
2-Nazi bondage/torture-c	81.00	244.00	690.00

VECTOR
Now Comics: 1986 - No. 4, 1986? ($1.50, 1st color comic by Now Comics)

	GD25	FN65	NM94
1-4: Computer-generated art			1.50

VEGAS KNIGHTS
Pioneer Comics: 1989 ($1.95, one-shot)

	GD25	FN65	NM94
1			2.00

VELOCITY (Also see Cyberforce)
Image Comics (Top Cow Productions): Nov, 1995 - No. 3, Jan, 1996 ($2.50, limited series)

	GD25	FN65	NM94
1-3: Kurt Busiek scripts in all. 2-Savage Dragon-c/app.			2.50

VENGEANCE OF VAMPIRELLA (Becomes Vampirella: Death & Destruction)
Harris Comics: Apr, 1994 - No. 25, Apr, 1996 ($2.95)

	GD25	FN65	NM94
1-($3.50)-Quesada/Palmiotti "bloodfoil" wraparound-c		2.00	6.00
1-2nd printing; blue foil-c			4.00
1-Gold			20.00
2			5.00
3,4			3.00
5-25: 8-Polybagged w/trading card; 10-w/coupon for Hyde -25 poster. 11, 19-Polybagged w/ trading card. 25-Quesada & Palmiotti red foil-c.			3.00
...: Bloodshed (1995, $6.95)			7.00

VENGEANCE OF VAMPIRELLA: THE MYSTERY WALK
Harris Comics: Nov, 1995 ($2.95, one-shot)

	GD25	FN65	NM94
0			3.00

VENGEANCE SQUAD
Charlton Comics: July, 1975 - No. 6, May, 1976 (#1-3 are 25¢ issues)

	GD25	FN65	NM94
1-Mike Mauser, Private Eye begins by Staton		2.00	6.00
2-6: Morisi-a in all			4.00
5,6(Modern Comics-r, 1977)			3.00

VENOM: ALONG CAME A SPIDER (See Amazing Spider-Man #298 & Marvel Comics Presents)
Marvel Comics: Jan, 1996 - No. 4, Apr, 1996 ($2.95, limited series)

	GD25	FN65	NM94
1-4:Spider-Man & Carnage app.			3.00

VENOM: CARNAGE UNLEASHED, Marvel Comics: 4/95 - No. 4, 7/95 ($2.95)

	GD25	FN65	NM94
1-4			3.00

VENOM: FINALE, Marvel Comics: 11/97 - No. 3, 1/98 ($1.99)

	GD25	FN65	NM94
1-3: Hama-s			2.00

VENOM: FUNERAL PYRE, Marvel Comics: 8/93- No. 3, 10/93 ($2.95)

	GD25	FN65	NM94
1-3: 1-Holo-grafx foil-c; Punisher app. in all			3.00

VENOM: LETHAL PROTECTOR
Marvel Comics: Feb, 1993 - No. 6, July, 1993 ($2.95, limited series)

	GD25	FN65	NM94
1-Red holo-grafx foil-c; Bagley-c/a in all			5.00
1-Gold variant sold to retailers			20.00
1-Black-c	14.00	41.00	150.00
2-6: Spider-Man app. in all			3.00

VENOM: LICENSE TO KILL, Marvel Comics: 6/97 - No. 3, 8/97 ($1.95)

	GD25	FN65	NM94
1-3			2.00

VENOM: NIGHTS OF VENGEANCE, Marvel Comics:8/94 - No. 4, 11/94($2.95)

	GD25	FN65	NM94
1-4: 1-Red foil-c			3.00

VENOM ON TRIAL, Marvel Comics: 3/97 - No. 3, 5/97 ($1.95)

	GD25	FN65	NM94
1-3			2.00

VENOM: SEED OF DARKNESS, Marvel Comics: 7/97 ($1.95, one-shot)

	GD25	FN65	NM94
-1-Flashback story			2.00

VENOM: SEPARATION ANXIETY, Marvel Comics: 12/94- No. 4, 3/95 ($2.95)

	GD25	FN65	NM94
1-4: 1-Embossed-c			3.00

VENOM: SIGN OF THE BOSS, Marvel Comics: 3/97 - No. 2, 10/97 ($1.99)

	GD25	FN65	NM94
1,2			2.00

VENOM: SINNER TAKES ALL, Marvel Comics: 8/95 - No. 5, 10/95 ($2.95)

	GD25	FN65	NM94
1-5			3.00

VENOM: SUPER SPECIAL, Marvel Comics: 8/95($3.95, one-shot)

	GD25	FN65	NM94
1-Flip book			4.00

VENOM: THE ENEMY WITHIN, Marvel Comics: 2/94 - No. 3, 4/94 ($2.95)

	GD25	FN65	NM94
1-3: Demogoblin & Morbius app. 1-Glow-in-the-dark-c.			3.00

VENOM: THE HUNGER, Marvel Comics: 8/96- No. 4, 11/96 ($1.95)

	GD25	FN65	NM94
1-4			2.00

VENOM: THE HUNTED, Marvel Comics: 5/96-No. 3, 7/96($2.95)

	GD25	FN65	NM94
1-3			3.00

VENOM: THE MACE, Marvel Comics: 5/94 - No. 3, 7/94 ($2.95)

	GD25	FN65	NM94
1-3: 1-Embossed-c			3.00

VENOM: THE MADNESS, Marvel Comics: 11/93- No. 3, 1/94($2.95)

	GD25	FN65	NM94
1-3: Kelley Jones-c/a(p). 1-Embossed-c; Juggernaut app.			3.00

VENOM: TOOTH AND CLAW, Marvel Comics: 12/96 - No. 3, 2/97($1.95)

	GD25	FN65	NM94
1-3: Wolverine-c/app.			2.00

VENTURE
AC Comics (Americomics): Aug, 1986 - No. 3, 1986? ($1.75)

	GD25	FN65	NM94
1-3: 1-3-Bolt. 1-Astron. 2-Femforce. 3-Fazers			1.80

VENUS (See Marvel Spotlight #2 & Weird Wonder Tales)
Marvel/Atlas Comics (CMC 1-9/LCC 10-19): Aug, 1948 - No. 19, Apr, 1952 (Also see Marvel Mystery #91)

	GD25	FN65	NM94
1-Venus & Hedy Devine begin; 1st app. Venus; Kurtzman's "Hey Look"	106.00	318.00	900.00
2	62.00	185.00	525.00
3,5	52.00	157.00	440.00
4-Kurtzman's "Hey Look"	53.00	161.00	450.00
6-9: 6-Loki app. 7,8-Painted-c. 9-Begin 52 pgs.; book-length feature "Whom the Gods Destroy!"	47.00	142.00	400.00
10-S/F-horror issues begin (7/50)	56.00	168.00	475.00
11-S/F end of the world (11/50)	71.00	212.00	600.00
12-Colan-a	43.00	129.00	360.00
13-19-Venus by Everett, 2-3 stories each; covers-#13,15-19; 14-Everett part cover (Venus). 17-Bondage-c	65.00	195.00	550.00

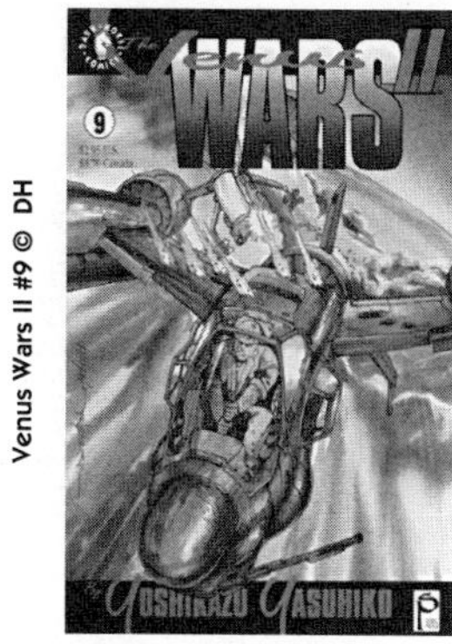

Venus Wars II #9 © DH

Veronica #81 © AP

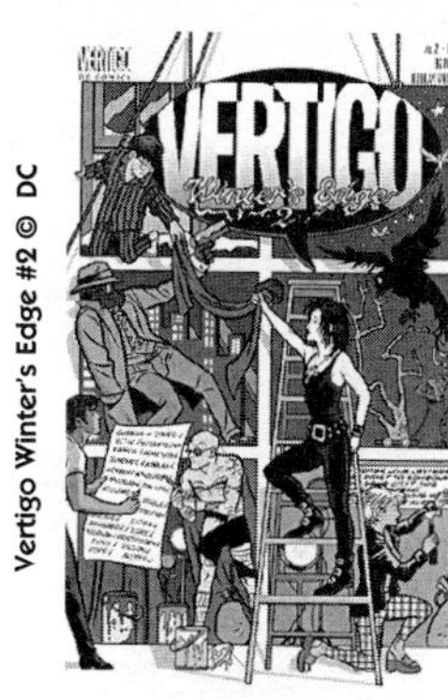

Vertigo Winter's Edge #2 © DC

GD25 FN65 NM94

NOTE: *Berg s/f story-13.* ***Everett*** *c-13, 14(part; Venus only), 15-19.* ***Heath*** *s/f story-11.* ***Maneely*** *s/f story-10(3pg.), 16.* ***Morisi*** *a-19.* ***Syd Shores*** *c-6.*

VENUS DOMINA
Verotik: July, 1996 - No. 3 ($2.95/$4.95, mature)

1-($4.95)-Embossed-c w/nudity by Dave Stevens 5.00
1-($2.95, San Diego Edition)-Wing Bird-c/a 3.00
2,3-($4.95) 5.00
Candlemass Eve Special Ed.-($4.95) 5.00

VENUS WARS, THE (Manga)
Dark Horse Comics: Apr, 1991 - No.14, May, 1992 ($2.25, B&W)

1-6,8,9,11-14: 1-3 Contain 2 Dark Horse trading cards 2.25
7,10 ($2.50): 1,3,7,10-(44 pgs.) 2.50

VERI BEST SURE FIRE COMICS
Holyoke Publishing Co.: No date (circa 1945) (Reprints Holyoke one-shots)

1-Captain Aero, Alias X, Miss Victory, Commandos of the Devil Dogs, Red Cross, Hammerhead Hawley, Capt. Aero's Sky Scouts, Flagman app.; same-c as Veri Best Sure Shot #1 33.00 100.00 250.00

VERI BEST SURE SHOT COMICS
Holyoke Publishing Co.: No date (circa 1945) (Reprints Holyoke one-shots)

1-Capt. Aero, Miss Victory by Quinlan, Alias X, The Red Cross, Flagman, Commandos of the Devil Dogs, Hammerhead Hawley, Capt. Aero's Sky Scouts; same-c as Veri Best Sure Fire #1 33.00 100.00 250.00

VERMILLION
DC Comics (Helix): Oct, 1996 - No. 12, Sept, 1997 ($2.25/$2.50)

1-4: Lucius Shepard scripts. 4-Kaluta-c 2.25
5-12: 5-Begin $2.50-c. 12-Kaluta-c 2.50

VERONICA (Also see Archie's Girls, Betty &...)
Archie Comics: Apr, 1989 - Present

1-21: 1,2-(75¢). 3-30-(95¢-$1.00) 1.00
21-36: 21-Begin $1.25-c. 34-Neon ink-c 1.25
36-70 1.50
71-85: 71-Begin $1.75-c 1.75

VERONICA'S PASSPORT DIGEST MAGAZINE (Becomes Veronica's Digest Magazine #3 on)
Archie Comics: Nov, 1992 - Present ($1.50/$1.79, digest size)

1-5 1.50
6-($1.79) 1.79

VERONICA'S SUMMER SPECIAL (See Archie Giant Series Magazine #615, 625)

VEROTIKA
Verotik: Mar, 1995 - Present ($2.95, mature) (1st Verotik title)

1,2 .90 2.70 8.00
3-6 4.00
7-14: 9-Adam Pollina-a. 10,13-Nudity-c 3.00
15-($3.95) 4.00

VEROTIK EAST
Verotik: Jan, 1997 ($11.95, mature)

nn,2-Manga style 12.00

VEROTIK ILLUSTRATED
Verotik: Aug, 1997 - Present ($6.95, mature)

1,2:1-Bisley-c. 2-Dave Stevens-c 7.00

VERTIGO GALLERY, THE: DREAMS AND NIGHTMARES
DC Comics (Vertgo): 1995 ($3.50, one-shot)

1-Pin-ups of Vertigo characters by Sienkiewicz, Toth, Van Fleet & others; Dave McKean-c 4.00

VERTIGO JAM
DC Comics (Vertigo): Aug, 1993 ($3.95, one-shot, 68 pgs.)(Painted-c by Fabry)

1-Sandman by Neil Gaiman, Hellblazer, Animal Man, Doom Patrol, Swamp Thing, Kid Eternity & Shade the Changing Man 5.00

VERTIGO PREVIEW
DC Comics (Vertigo): 1992 (75¢, one-shot, 36 pgs.)

1-Vertigo previews; Sandman story by Neil Gaiman 2.00

VERTIGO RAVE
DC Comics (Vertigo): Fall, 1994 (99¢, one-shot)

1-Vertigo previews 2.00

VERTIGO VERITE: THE UNSEEN HAND
DC Comics (Vertigo): Sept, 1996 - No. 4, Dec, 1996 ($2.50, limited series)

1-4: Terry LaBan scripts in all 2.50

VERTIGO VISIONS
DC Comics (Vertigo): June, 1993 - Present (one-shots)

Dr. Occult 1 (7/94, $3.95) 4.00
Dr. Thirteen 1 (9/98, $5.95) Howarth-s 6.00
Prez 1 (7/95, $3.95) 4.00
The Geek 1 (6/93, $3.95) 4.00
The Eaters ($4.95, 1995)-Milligan story. 5.00
The Phantom Stranger 1 (10/93, $3.50) 3.50
Tomahawk 1 (7/98, $4.95) Pollack-s 5.00

VERTIGO WINTER'S EDGE
DC Comics (Vertigo): 1998, 1999 ($7.95/$6.95, square-bound, annual)

1-Winter stories by Vertigo creators; Desire story by Gaiman/Bolton; Bolland wraparound-c 8.00
2-($6.95)-Winter stories; Allred-c 6.95

VERY BEST OF DENNIS THE MENACE, THE
Fawcett Publ.: July, 1979 - No. 2, Apr, 1980 (95¢/$1.00, digest-size, 132 pgs.)

1,2-Reprints 4.00

VERY BEST OF DENNIS THE MENACE, THE
Marvel Comics Group: Apr, 1982 - No. 3, Aug, 1982 ($1.25, digest-size)

1-3: Reprints 2.00 6.00
NOTE: ***Hank Ketcham*** *c-all. A few thousand of #1 & 2 were printed with DC emblem.*

VERY VICKY
Meet Danny Ocean: 1993? - No. 8, 1995 ($2.50, B&W)

1-8 2.50
...:Calling All Hillbillies (1995, $2.50) 2.50

V FOR VENDETTA
DC Comics: Sept, 1988 - No. 10, May, 1989 ($2.00, maxi-series)

1-10: Alan Moore scripts in all 2.00
Trade paperback (1990, $14.95) 15.00

VIC BRIDGES FAZERS SKETCHBOOK AND FACT FILE
AC Comics: Nov, 1986 ($1.75)

1 1.80

VIC FLINT(Crime Buster...)(See Authentic Police Cases #10-14 & Fugitives From Justice #2)
St. John Publ. Co.: Aug, 1948 - No. 5, Apr, 1949 (Newspaper reprints; NEA Service)

1 11.00 32.00 80.00
2 7.85 23.50 55.00
3-5 6.00 18.00 42.00

VIC FLINT (Crime Buster...)
Argo Publ.: Feb, 1956 - No. 2, May, 1956 (Newspaper reprints)

1,2 6.85 21.00 48.00

VIC JORDAN (Also see Big Shot Comics #32)
Civil Service Publ.: April, 1945

1-1944 daily newspaper-r 11.50 34.00 80.00

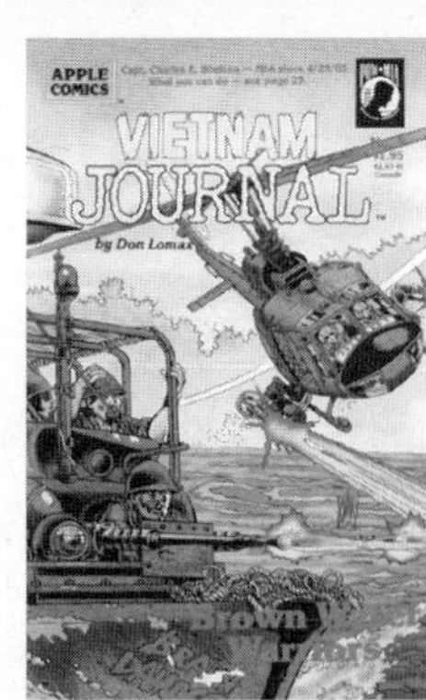

Vietnam Journal #9 © Don Lomax

Vigilante #23 © DC

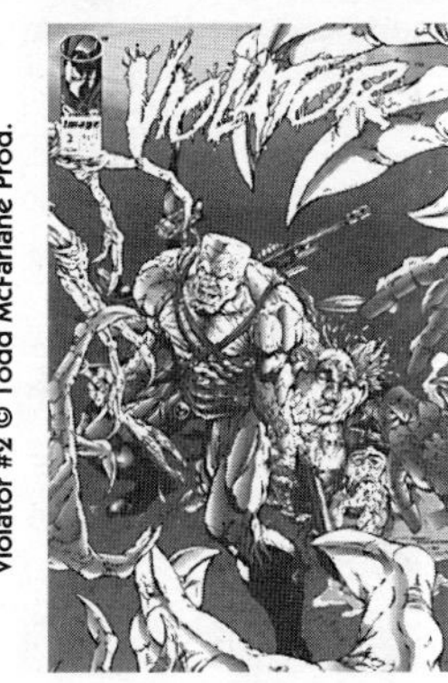

Violator #2 © Todd McFarlane Prod.

VICKI (Humor)
Atlas/Seaboard Publ.: Feb, 1975 - No. 4, Aug, 1975 (No. 1,2: 68 pgs.)

	GD25	FN65	NM94
1-(68 pgs.)-Reprints Tippy Teen	1.80	5.40	18.00
2-4: 2-(68pgs.)	1.20	3.60	12.00

VICKI VALENTINE (...Summer Special #1)
Renegade Press: July, 1985 - No. 4, July, 1986 ($1.70, B&W)

1-4: Woggon, Rausch-a; all have paper dolls. 2-Christmas issue 1.70

VICKS COMICS (See Pure Oil Comics, Salerno Carnival of Comics & 24 Pages of Comics)
Eastern Color Printing Co. (Vicks Chemical Co.): nd (circa 1938) (Giveaway, 68 pgs. in color)

	GD25	FN65	NM94
nn-Famous Funnies-r (before #40); contains 5 pgs. Buck Rogers (4 pgs. from F.F. #15, & 1 pg. from #16) Joe Palooka, Napoleon, etc. app.	65.00	194.00	550.00
nn-16 loose, untrimmed page giveaway; paper-c; r/Famous Funnies #14; Buck Rogers, Joe Palooka app.	25.00	74.00	185.00

VICKY
Ace Magazine: Oct, 1948 - No. 5, June, 1949

	GD25	FN65	NM94
nn(10/48)-Teenage humor	5.35	16.00	32.00
4(12/48), nn(2/49), 4(4/49), 5(6/49): 5-Dotty app.	4.25	13.00	26.00

VIC TORRY & HIS FLYING SAUCER (Also see Mr. Monster's...#5)
Fawcett Publications: 1950 (one-shot)

	GD25	FN65	NM94
nn-Book-length saucer story by Powell; photo/painted-c	52.00	155.00	440.00

VICTORY
Topps Comics: June, 1994 ($2.50, unfinished limited series)

1-Kurt Busiek script; Giffen-c/a; Rob Liefeld variant-c exists 2.50

VICTORY COMICS
Hillman Periodicals: Aug, 1941 - No. 4, Dec, 1941 (#1 by Funnies, Inc.)

	GD25	FN65	NM94
1-The Conqueror by Bill Everett, The Crusader, & Bomber Burns begin; Conqueror's origin in text; Everett-c	259.00	777.00	2200.00
2-Everett-c/a	109.00	327.00	925.00
3,4	74.00	221.00	625.00

VIC VERITY MAGAZINE
Vic Verity Publ: 1945; No. 2, Jan?, 1947 - No. 7, Sept, 1946 (A comic book)

	GD25	FN65	NM94
1-C. C. Beck-c/a	16.00	48.00	120.00
2-Beck-c	9.30	28.00	65.00
3-7: 6-Beck-a. 7-Beck-c	7.85	23.50	55.00

VIDEO JACK
Marvel Comics (Epic Comics): Nov, 1987 - No. 6, Nov, 1988 ($1.25)

1-6: 6-Neal Adams, Keith Giffen, Wrightson, others-a 1.30

VIETNAM JOURNAL
Apple Comics: Nov, 1987 - No. 16, Apr, 1991 ($1.75/$1.95, B&W)

1-Don Lomax-c/a/scripts in all 2.00
1-2nd print 2.00
2-16: 10,11-$2.00/$2.25-c 2.00
...: Indian Country Vol. 1 (1990, $12.95)-r/#1-4 plus one new story 13.00

VIETNAM JOURNAL: VALLEY OF DEATH
Apple Comics: June, 1994 - No. 2, Aug, 1994 ($2.75, B&W, limited series)

1,2: By Don Lomax 2.75

VIGILANTE, THE (Also see New Teen Titans #23 & Annual V2#2)
DC Comics: Oct, 1983 - No. 50, Feb, 1988 ($1.25, Baxter paper)

1-Origin 3.00
2-10: 3-Cyborg app. 4-1st app. The Exterminator; Newton-a(p). 6,7-Origin 1.50
11-50: 17,18-Alan Moore scripts. 20,21-Nightwing app. 35-Origin Mad Bomber. 47-Batman-c/story. 50-Ken Steacy painted-c 1.25
Annual (1985) 2.50
Annual 2 (1986) 2.00

VIGILANTE: CITY LIGHTS, PRAIRIE JUSTICE (Also see Action Comics #42, Justice League of America #78, Leading Comics & World's Finest #244)
DC Comics: Nov, 1995 - No. 4, Feb, 1995 ($2.50, limited series)

1-4: James Robinson scripts in all 2.50

VIGILANTES, THE
Dell Publishing Co.: No. 839, Sept, 1957

	GD25	FN65	NM94
Four Color 839-Movie	6.40	19.00	70.00

VIKINGS, THE (Movie)
Dell Publishing Co.: No. 910, May, 1958

	GD25	FN65	NM94
Four Color 910-Buscema-a, Kirk Douglas photo-c	8.00	25.00	90.00

VILLAINS AND VIGILANTES
Eclipse Comics: Dec, 1986 - No. 4, May, 1987 ($1.50/$1.75, limited series, Baxter paper)

1-4: Based on role-playing game. 2-4 ($1.75-c) 1.75

VINTAGE MAGNUS (...Robot Fighter)
Valiant: Jan, 1992 - No. 4, Apr, 1992 ($2.25, limited series)

1-4: 1-Layton-c; r/origin from Magnus R.F. #22 2.25

VIOLATOR (Also see Spawn #2)
Image Comics (Todd McFarlane Productions): May, 1994 - No. 3, Aug, 1994 ($1.95, limited series)

1-Alan Moore scripts in all 5.00
2,3: Bart Sears-c(p)/a(p) 4.00

VIOLATOR VS. BADROCK
Image Comics (Extreme Studios): May, 1995 - No. 4, Aug, 1995 ($2.50, limited series)

1-4: Alan Moore scripts in all. 1-1st app Celestine; variant-c (3?) 2.50

VIPER (TV)
DC Comics: Aug, 1994 - No. 4, Nov, 1994 ($1.95, limited series)

1-4-Adaptation of television show 2.00

VIRGINIAN, THE (TV)
Gold Key: June, 1963

	GD25	FN65	NM94
1(10060-306)-Part photo-c of James Drury plus photo back-c	3.20	9.50	35.00

VIRTUA FIGHTER (Video Game)
Marvel Comics: Aug, 1995 (2.95, one-shot)

1-Sega Saturn game 3.00

VIRUS
Dark Horse Comics: 1993 - No. 4, 1993 ($2.50, limited series)

1-4: Ploog-c 2.50

VISION, THE
Marvel Comics: Nov, 1994 - No. 4, Feb, 1995 ($1.75, limited series)

1-4 1.75

VISION AND THE SCARLET WITCH, THE (See Marvel Fanfare)
Marvel Comics Group: Nov, 1982 - No. 4, Feb, 1983 (Limited series)

1 1.80
2-4: 2-Nuklo & Future Man app. 1.25

VISION AND THE SCARLET WITCH, THE
Marvel Comics Group: Oct, 1985 - No. 12, Sept, 1986 (Maxi-series)

V2#1-Origin; 1st app. in Avengers #57 1.80
2-5: 2-West Coast Avengers x-over 1.50
6-12 1.30

VISIONARIES
Marvel Comics (Star)/Marvel Comics #3 on: Nov, 1987 - No. 6, Sept, 1988

Voodoo #17 © AJAX

Voodoo #4 © DC

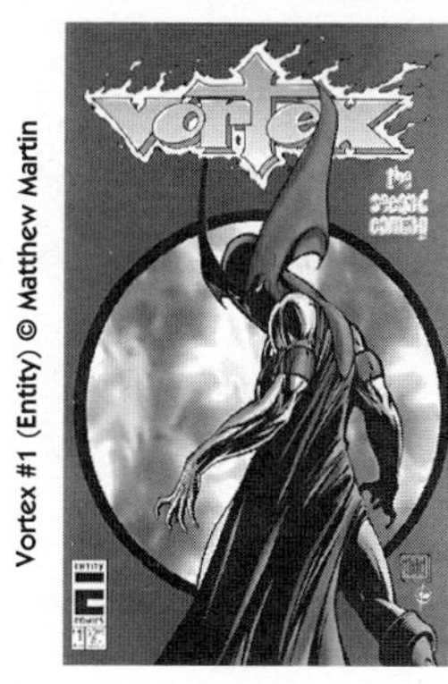

Vortex #1 (Entity) © Matthew Martin

GD25 FN65 NM94

1-6 1.00

VISIONS
Vision Publications: 1979 - No. 5, 1983 (B&W, fanzine)

1-Flaming Carrot begins(1st app?); N. Adams-c 2.25 6.80 25.00
2-N. Adams, Rogers-a; Gulacy back-c; signed & numbered to 2000 2.00 6.00 20.00
3-Williamson-c(p); Steranko back-c 1.00 3.00 10.00
4-Flaming Carrot-c & info. 1.00 3.00 10.00
5-1 pg. Flaming Carrot 5.00

NOTE: ***Eisner*** *a-4.* ***Miller*** *a-4.* ***Starlin*** *a-3.* ***Williamson*** *a-5. After #4, Visions became an annual publication of The Atlanta Fantasy Fair.*

VISITOR, THE
Valiant/Acclaim Comics (Valiant): Apr, 1995 - No. 13, Nov, 1995 ($2.50)

1-13: 8-Harbinger revealed. 13-Visitor revealed to be Sting from Harbinger. 2.50

VISITOR, VS. THE VALIANT UNIVERSE, THE
Valiant: Feb, 1995 - No. 2, Mar, 1995 ($2.95, limited series)

1,2 3.00

VOGUE (Also see Youngblood)
Image Comics (Extreme Studios): Oct, 1995 - No.3, Jan, 1996 ($2.50, limited series)

1-3: 1-Liefeld-c 2.50
1-Variant-c 3.00

VOID INDIGO (Also see Marvel Graphic Novel)
Marvel Comics (Epic Comics): 11/84 - No. 2, 3/85 ($1.50, direct sales, unfinished series, mature)

1,2: Cont'd from Marvel G.N.; graphic sex & violence 1.50

VOLTRON (TV)
Modern Publishing: 1985 - No. 3, 1985 (75¢, limited series)

1-3: Ayers-a in all 1.00

VOODA (Jungle Princess) (Formerly Voodoo)
Ajax-Farrell (Four Star Publications): No. 20, April, 1955 - No. 22, Aug, 1955

20-Baker-c/a (r/Seven Seas #6) 31.00 92.00 230.00
21,22-Baker-a plus Kamen/Baker story, Kimbo Boy of Jungle, & Baker-c (p) in all. 22-Censored Jo-Jo-r (name Powaa) 27.00 80.00 200.00

NOTE: *#20-22 each contain one heavily censored-r of South Sea Girl by* ***Baker*** *from Seven Seas Comics with name changed to Vooda. #20-r/Seven Seas #6; #21-r/#4; #22-4/#3.*

VOODOO (Weird Fantastic Tales) (Vooda #20 on)
Ajax-Farrell (Four Star Publ.): May, 1952 - No. 19, Jan-Feb, 1955

1-South Sea Girl-r by Baker 45.00 134.00 380.00
2-Rulah story-r plus South Sea Girl from Seven Seas #2 by Baker (name changed from Alani to El'nee) 39.00 117.00 300.00
3-Bakerish-a; man stabbed in face 28.00 84.00 210.00
4,8-Baker-r. 8-Severed head panels 28.00 84.00 210.00
5-7,9,10: 5-Nazi death camp story (flaying alive). 6-Severed head panels 23.00 68.00 170.00
11-18: 14-Zombies take over America. 15-Opium drug story-r/Ellery Queen #3. 16-Post nuclear world story.17-Electric chair panels 19.00 58.00 145.00
19-Bondage-c; Baker-r(2)/Seven Seas #5 w/minor changes & #1, heavily modified; last pre-code; contents & covers chane to jungle theme 25.00 76.00 190.00
Annual 1(1952, 25¢, 100 pgs.)-Baker-a (scarce) 59.00 176.00 500.00

VOODOO
Image Comics (WildStorm): Nov, 1997 - No. 4, Mar, 1998 ($2.50, lim. series)

1-4:Alan Moore-s in all; Hughes-c 2.50
1-Platinum Ed 15.00

VOODOO (See Tales of...)

GD25 FN65 NM94

VOODOO-ZEALOT: SKIN TRADE (See WildC.A.T.S: Covert Action Teams)
Image Comics (WildStorm Productions): Aug, 1995 ($4.95, one-shot)

1 5.00

VORTEX
Vortex Publs.: Nov, 1982 - No. 15, 1988 (No month) ($1.50/$1.75, B&W)

1 ($1.95)-Peter Hsu-a; Ken Steacy-c; nudity 2.00 6.00
2-1st app. Mister X (on-c only) 3.00
3 2.00
4-15: 12-Sam Kieth-a 1.75

VORTEX
Comico: 1991 - No. 2? ($2.50, limited series)

1,2: Heroes from The Elementals 2.50

VORTEX
Entity Comics: 1996 ($2.95)

1,1b: 1b-Kaniuga-c 3.00

VOYAGE TO THE BOTTOM OF THE SEA (Movie, TV)
Dell Publishing Co./Gold Key: No. 1230, Sept-Nov, 1961; Dec, 1964 - #16, Apr, 1970 (Painted-c)

Four Color 1230 (1961) 9.00 27.00 100.00
10133-412(#1, 12/64)(Gold Key) 6.00 17.50 65.00
2(7/65) - 5: Photo back-c, 1-5 4.00 12.25 45.00
6-14 2.90 8.70 32.00
15,16-Reprints 2.00 6.00 18.00

VOYAGE TO THE DEEP
Dell Publishing Co.: Sept-Nov, 1962 - No. 4, Nov-Jan, 1964 (Painted-c)

1 3.80 11.40 38.00
2-4 2.80 8.40 28.00

VR VIXEN
London Night Studios: July, 1997 ($3.00, B&W)

0 3.00
0-($6.00) Nude Edition 6.00

WACKO
Ideal Publ. Corp.: Sept, 1980 - No. 3, Oct, 1981 (84 pgs., B&W, magazine)

1-3 4.00

WACKY ADVENTURES OF CRACKY (Also see Gold Key Spotlight)
Gold Key: Dec, 1972 - No. 12, Sept, 1975

1 1.20 3.60 12.00
2 .85 2.60 7.00
3-12 5.00

(See March of Comics #405, 424, 436, 448)

WACKY DUCK (...Comics #3-6; formerly Dopey Duck; Justice Comics #7 on) (See Film Funnies)
Marvel Comics (NPP): No. 3, Fall, 1946 - No. 6, Summer, 1947; Aug, 1948 - No. 2, Oct, 1948

3 16.00 48.00 120.00
4-Infinity-c 16.00 48.00 120.00
5,6(1947)-Becomes Justice comics 13.00 38.00 95.00
1,2(1948) 9.30 28.00 65.00
I.W. Reprint #1,2,7('58): 1-r/Wacky Duck #6 1.25 3.75 10.00
Super Reprint #10(I.W. on-c, Super-inside) 1.25 3.75 10.00

WACKY QUACKY (See Wisco)

WACKY RACES (TV)
Gold Key: Aug, 1969 - No. 7, Apr, 1972 (Hanna-Barbera)

1 3.20 9.50 35.00
2-7 1.85 5.50 20.00

WACKY SQUIRREL (Also see Dark Horse Presents)
Dark Horse Comics: Oct, 1987 - No. 4, 1988 ($1.75, B&W)

The Waiting Place #6 © Sean Kelly McKeever

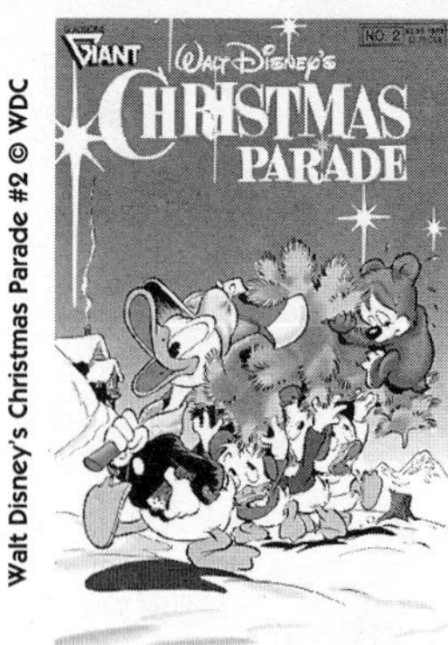

Walt Disney's Christmas Parade #2 © WDC

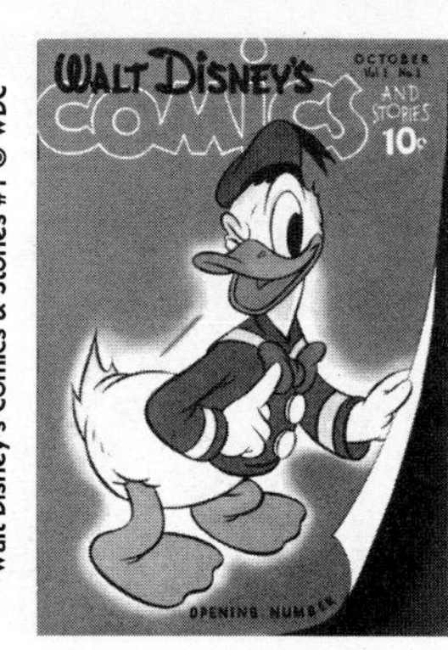

Walt Disney's Comics & Stories #1 © WDC

GD25 FN65 NM94

1-4: 4-Superman parody 1.75
Halloween Adventure Special 1 (1987, $2.00) 2.00
Summer Fun Special 1 (1988, $2.00) 2.00

WACKY WITCH (Also see Gold Key Spotlight)
Gold Key: March, 1971 - No. 21, Dec, 1975

1 2.20 6.50 24.00
2 1.20 3.60 12.00
3-10 1.00 3.00 10.00
11-21 5.00
(See March of Comics #374, 398, 410, 422, 434, 446, 458, 470, 482)

WACKY WOODPECKER (See Two Bit the...)
I. W. Enterprises/Super Comics: 1958; 1963
I.W. Reprint #1,2,7 (nd-reprints Two Bit...): 7-r/Two-Bit, the Wacky Woodpecker #1. 1.10 3.30 9.00
Super Reprint #10('63): 10-r/Two-Bit, The Wacky Woodpecker #? 1.10 3.30 9.00

WAGON TRAIN (1st Series) (TV) (See Western Roundup under Dell Giants)
Dell Publishing Co.: No. 895, Mar, 1958 - No. 13, Apr-June, 1962 (All photo-c)
Four Color 895 (#1) 11.00 33.00 120.00
Four Color 971(#2),1019(#3) 6.00 18.00 65.00
4(1-3/60),6-13 5.00 15.00 55.00
5-Toth-a 5.50 16.50 60.00

WAGON TRAIN (2nd Series)(TV)
Gold Key: Jan, 1964 - No. 4, Oct, 1964 (All front & back photo-c)
1-Tufts-a in all 4.50 13.50 50.00
2-4 3.20 9.50 35.00

WAITING PLACE, THE
Slave Labor Graphics: Apr, 1997 - No. 6, Sept, 1997 ($2.95)
1-6-Sean McKeever-s 3.00

WAITING ROOM WILLIE (See Sad Case of...)

WALLY (Teen-age)
Gold Key: Dec, 1962 - No. 4, Sept, 1963
1 2.50 7.50 26.00
2-4 2.00 6.00 18.00

WALLY THE WIZARD
Marvel Comics (Star Comics): Apr, 1985 - No. 12, Mar, 1986 (Children's comic)
1-12: Bob Bolling a-1,3; c-1,9,11,12 1.00

WALLY WOOD'S T.H.U.N.D.E.R. AGENTS (See Thunder Agents)
Deluxe Comics: Nov, 1984 - No. 5, Oct, 1986 ($2.00, 52 pgs.)
1-5: 5-Jerry Ordway-c/a in Wood style 3.00
NOTE: ***Anderson** a-2i, 3i. **Buckler** a-4. **Ditko** a-3, 4. **Giffen** a-1p-4p. **Perez** a-1p, 2, 4; c-1-4.*

WALT DISNEY CHRISTMAS PARADE (Also see Christmas Parade)
Whitman Publ. Co. (Golden Press): Wint, 1977 ($1.95, cardboard-c, 224 pgs.)
11191-Barks-r/Christmas in Disneyland #1, Dell Christmas Parade #9 & Dell Giant #53 1.50 4.50 15.00

WALT DISNEY COMICS DIGEST
Gold Key: June, 1968 - No. 57, Feb, 1976 (50¢, digest size)
1-Reprints Uncle Scrooge #5; 192 pgs. 7.00 21.00 75.00
2-4-Barks-r 4.00 12.25 45.00
5-Daisy Duck by Barks (8 pgs.); last published story by Barks (art only) plus 21 pg. Scrooge-r by Barks 8.00 23.00 85.00
6-13-All Barks-r 2.90 8.70 32.00
14,15 1.80 5.40 18.00
16-Reprints Donald Duck #26 by Barks 2.90 8.70 32.00
17-20-Barks-r 2.40 7.00 26.00
21-31,33,35-37-Barks-r; 24-Toth Zorro 2.00 6.00 22.00
32,41,45,47-49 1.40 4.20 14.00
34-Reprints 4-Color #318 2.00 6.00 22.00
38-Reprints Christmas in Disneyland #1 2.00 6.00 22.00
39-Two Barks-r/WDC&S #272, 4-Color #1073 plus Toth Zorro-r 2.00 6.00 22.00
40-Mickey Mouse-r by Gottfredson 1.60 4.80 16.00
42,43-Barks-r 1.60 4.80 16.00
44-(Has Gold Key emblem, 50¢)-Reprints 1st story of 4-Color #29,256,275,282 4.00 12.25 45.00
44-Republished in 1976 by Whitman; not identical to original; a bit smaller, blank back-c, 69¢ 1.80 5.50 20.00
46,50,52-Barks-r. 52-Barks-r/WDC&S #161,132 1.40 4.20 14.00
51-Reprints 4-Color #71 2.00 6.00 22.00
53-55: 53-Reprints Dell Giant #30. 54-Reprints Donald Duck Beach Party #2. 55-Reprints Dell Giant #49 1.20 3.60 12.00
56-r/Uncle Scrooge #32 (Barks) 1.60 4.80 16.00
57-r/Mickey Mouse Almanac('57) & two Barks stories 1.40 4.20 14.00
NOTE: ***Toth** a-52r. #1-10, 196 pgs.; #11-41, 164 pgs.; #42 on, 132 pgs. Old issues were being reprinted & distributed by Whitman in 1976.*

WALT DISNEY GIANT (Disney)
Bruce Hamilton Company (Gladstone): Sept, 1995 - No. 7, Sept, 1996 ($2.25, bi-monthly, 48 pgs.)
1-7: 1-Scrooge McDuck in the Yukon; Rosa-c/a/scripts plus r/F.C. #218. 2-Uncle Scrooge-r by Barks plus 17 pg. text story. 3-Donald the Mighty Duck; Rosa-c; Barks & Rosa-r. 4-Mickey and Goofy; new-a (story actually stars Goofy. Mickey Mouse by Caesar Ferioli; Donald Duck by Giorgio Cavazzano (1st in U.S.). 6-Uncle Scrooge & the Jr. Woodchucks; new-a and Barks-r. 7-Uncle Scrooge-r by Barks plus new-a 2.25
NOTE: *Series was initially solicited as Uncle Walt's Collectory. Issue #8 was advertised, but later cancelled.*

WALT DISNEY PAINT BOOK SERIES
Whitman Publ. Co.: No dates; circa 1975 (Beware! Has 1930s copyright dates) (79¢-c, 52pgs. B&W, 10 3/4 x 14 3/4") (Coloring books, text stories & comics-r)
#2052 (Whitman #886-r) Mickey Mouse & Donald Duck Gag Book 2.25 6.80 25.00
#2053 (Whitman #677-r) 2.25 6.80 25.00
#2054 (Whitman #670-r) Donald-c 2.70 8.00 30.00
#2055 (Whitman #627-r) Mickey-c 2.25 6.80 25.00
#2056 (Whitman #660-r) Buckey Bug-c 2.00 6.00 20.00
#2057 (Whitman #887-r) Mickey & Donald-c 2.25 6.80 25.00

WALT DISNEY PRESENTS (TV)(Disney)
Dell Publishing Co.: No. 997, 6-8/59 - No. 6, 12-2/1960-61; No. 1181, 4-5/61 (All photo-c)
Four Color 997 (#1) 6.40 19.00 70.00
2(12-2/60)-The Swamp Fox(origin), Elfego Baca, Texas John Slaughter (Disney TV show) begin 4.00 12.00 45.00
3-6: 5-Swamp Fox by Warren Tufts 3.60 11.00 40.00
Four Color 1181-Texas John Slaughter 6.40 19.00 70.00

WALT DISNEY'S CHRISTMAS PARADE (Also see Christmas Parade)
Gladstone: Winter, 1988; No. 2, Winter, 1989 ($2.95, 100 pgs.)
1-Barks-r/painted-c 1.00 3.00 10.00
2-Barks-r .90 2.70 8.00

WALT DISNEY'S COMICS AND STORIES (Cont. of Mickey Mouse Magazine) (#1-30 contain Donald Duck newspaper reprints) (Titled "Comics And Stories" #264 to #?; titled "Walt Disney's Comics And Stories" #511 on)
Dell Publishing Co./Gold Key #264-473/Whitman #474-510/Gladstone #511-547(4/90)/Disney Comics #548(6/90)-#585/Gladstone #586(8/93) on: 10/40 - #263, 8/62; #264, 10/62 - #510, 1984; #511, 10/86 - Present

NOTE: The whole number can always be found at the bottom of the title page in the lower left-hand or right hand panel.

GD25 FN65 VF82 NM94
1(V1#1-c; V2#1-indicia)-Donald Duck strip-r by Al Taliaferro & Gottfredson's Mickey Mouse begin 1454.00 4360.00 8725.00 16,000.00

Walt Disney's Comics & Stories #69 © WDC

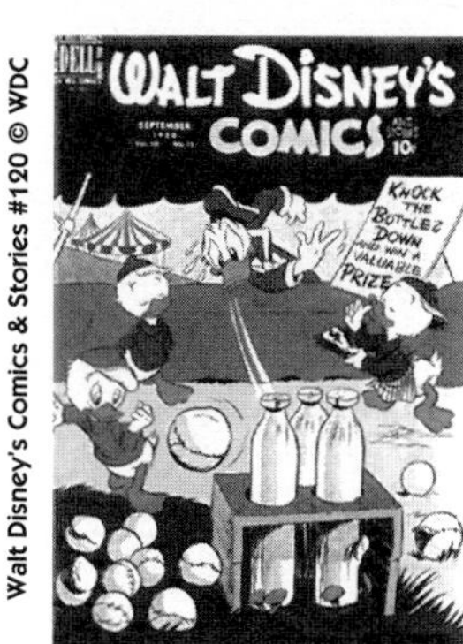

Walt Disney's Comics & Stories #120 © WDC

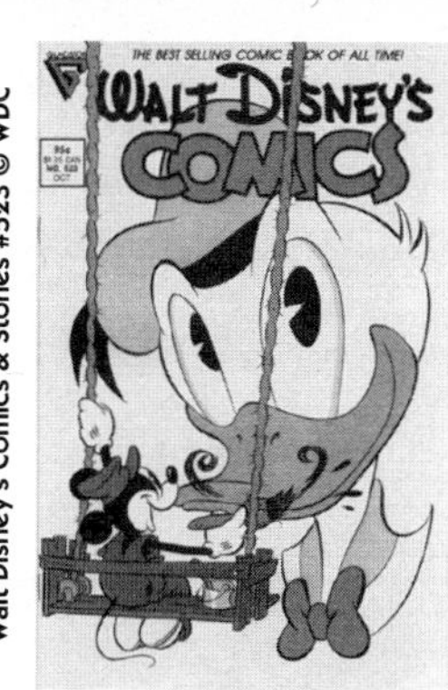

Walt Disney's Comics & Stories #523 © WDC

	GD25	FN65	NM94
2	550.00	1650.00	6000.00
3	185.00	555.00	1850.00
4-X-Mas-c; 1st Huey, Dewey & Louie-c this title (See Mickey Mouse Magazine V4#2 for 1st-c ever)	130.00	390.00	1300.00
4-Special promotional, complimentary issue; cover same except one corner was blanked out & boxed in to identify the giveaway (not a paste-over). This special pressing was probably sent out to former subscribers to Mickey Mouse Mag. whose subscriptions had expired. (Very rare-5 known copies)	220.00	660.00	2200.00
5-Goofy-c	100.00	300.00	1000.00
6-10: 8-Only Clarabelle Cow-c. 9-Taliaferro-c (1st)	85.00	255.00	850.00
11-14: 11-Huey, Dewey & Louie-c/app.	70.00	210.00	700.00
15-17: 15-The 3 Little Kittens (17 pgs.). 16-The 3 Little Pigs (29 pgs.); X-Mas-c. 17-The Ugly Duckling (4 pgs.)	64.00	192.00	640.00
18-21	52.00	156.00	525.00
22-30: 22-Flag-c. 24-The Flying Gauchito (1st original comic book story done for WDC&S). 27-Jose Carioca by Carl Buettner (2nd original story in WDC&S)	45.00	135.00	450.00
31-New Donald Duck stories by Carl Barks begin (See F.C. #9 for 1st Barks Donald Duck)	290.00	870.00	2900.00
32-Barks-a	125.00	375.00	1250.00
33-Barks-a; infinity-c	90.00	270.00	900.00
34-Gremlins by Walt Kelly begin, end #41; Barks-a	75.00	225.00	750.00
35,36-Barks-a	67.00	202.00	675.00
37-Donald Duck by Jack Hannah	34.00	102.00	340.00
38-40-Barks-a. 39-X-Mas-c. 40,41-Gremlins by Kelly	45.00	135.00	450.00
41-50-Barks-a. 43-Seven Dwarfs-c app. (4/44). 45-50-Nazis in Gottfredson's Mickey Mouse Stories	36.00	108.00	360.00
51-60-Barks-a. 51-X-Mas-c. 52-Li'l Bad Wolf begins, ends #203 (not in #55). 58-Kelly flag-c	25.00	75.00	250.00
61-70: Barks-a. 61-Dumbo story. 63,64-Pinocchio stories. 63-Cover swipe from New Funnies #94. 64-X-Mas-c. 65-Pluto story. 66-Infinity-c. 67,68-Mickey Mouse Sunday-r by Bill Wright	21.00	63.00	210.00
71-80: Barks-a. 75-77-Brer Rabbit stories, no Mickey Mouse. 76-X-Mas-c	16.00	48.00	155.00
81-87,89,90: Barks-a. 82-Goofy-c. 82-84-Bongo stories. 86-90-Goofy & Agnes app. 89-Chip 'n' Dale story	14.00	42.00	140.00
88-1st app. Gladstone Gander by Barks (1/48)	19.00	57.00	185.00
91-97,99: Barks-a. 95-1st WDC&S Barks-c. 96-No Mickey Mouse; Little Toot begins, ends #97. 99-X-Mas-c	12.00	36.00	120.00
98-1st Uncle Scrooge app. in WDC&S (11/48)	24.00	72.00	240.00
100-(1/49)-Barks-a	15.00	45.00	150.00
101-110-Barks-a. 107-Taliaferro-c; Donald acquires super powers	11.00	33.00	110.00
111,114,117-All Barks	8.50	25.50	85.00
112-Drug (ether) issue (Donald Duck)	8.50	25.50	85.00
113,115,116,118-123: No Barks. 116-Dumbo x-over. 121-Grandma Duck begins, ends #168; not in #135,142,146,155	3.80	11.40	38.00
124,126-130-All Barks. 124-X-Mas-c	7.00	21.00	70.00
125-1st app. Junior Woodchucks (2/51); Barks-a	10.50	32.00	105.00
131,133,135-137,139-All Barks	7.00	21.00	70.00
132-Barks-a(2) (D. Duck & Grandma Duck)	7.50	22.50	75.00
134-Intro. & 1st app. The Beagle Boys (11/51)	16.00	48.00	160.00
138-Classic Scrooge money story	12.00	36.00	120.00
140-(5/52)-1st app. Gyro Gearloose by Barks; 2nd Barks Uncle Scrooge-c; 3rd Uncle Scrooge-c app.	16.00	48.00	160.00
141-150-All Barks. 143-Little Hiawatha begins, ends #151,159	5.00	15.00	50.00
151-170-All Barks	4.00	12.00	40.00
171-199-All Barks	3.50	10.50	35.00
200	4.50	13.50	45.00
201-240: All Barks. 204-Chip 'n' Dale & Scamp begin	3.50	10.50	35.00

	GD25	FN65	NM94
241-283: Barks-a. 241-Dumbo x-over. 247-Gyro Gearloose begins, ends #274. 256-Ludwig Von Drake begins, ends #274	2.60	7.80	26.00
284,285,287,290,295,296,309-311-Not by Barks	1.50	4.50	12.00
286,288,289,291-294,297,298,308-All Barks stories; 293-Grandma Duck's Farm Friends. 297-Gyro Gearloose. 298-Daisy Duck's Diary-r	2.00	6.00	16.00
299-307-All contain early Barks-r (#43-117). 305-Gyro Gearloose	2.25	6.75	18.00
312-Last Barks issue with original story	2.25	6.75	18.00
313-315,317-327,329-334,336-341	1.50	4.50	12.00
316-Last issue published during life of Walt Disney	1.50	4.50	12.00
328,335,342-350-Barks-r	1.50	4.50	12.00
351-360-With posters inside; Barks reprints (2 versions of each with & without posters)-without posters...	1.50	4.50	12.00
351-360-With posters...	2.25	6.75	18.00
361-400-Barks-r	1.20	3.60	12.00
401-429-Barks-r	1.20	3.60	12.00
430,433,437,438,441,444,445,466-No Barks		2.00	6.00
431,432,434-436,439,440,442,443-Barks-r		2.00	6.00
446-465,467-473-Barks-r		2.00	5.00
474(3/80),475-478 (Whitman)	.85	2.60	7.00
479(8/80),481(10/80)-484(1/81) pre-pack?	1.40	4.20	14.00
480 (8-12/80)-Distr. only in Whitman 3-pack	3.20	9.50	35.00
485-499: 494-r/WDC&S #98	.90	2.70	8.00
500-510 (All #90011 on-c; pre-packs?): 506-No Barks	1.00	3.00	10.00
511-Donald Duck by Daan Jippes (1st in U.S.; in all through #518); Gyro Gearloose Barks-r begins (in most through #547); Wuzzles by Disney studio (1st by Gladstone)	2.00	6.00	20.00
512,513	1.20	3.60	12.00
514-516,520,523: 523-1st Rosa 10 pager	.85	2.60	7.00
517-519,521,522,524-547: 518-Infinity-c. 522-r/1st app. Huey, Dewey & Louie from D. Duck Sunday. 535-546-Barks-r. 537-1st Donald Duck by William Van Horn in WDC&S. 541-545-52 pgs. 546,547-68 pgs. 546-Kelly-r. 547-Rosa-a			3.00
548-($1.50, 6/90)-1st Disney issue; new-a; no M. Mouse			1.75
549,551-570,572,573,577-579,581,584 ($1.50): 549-Barks-r begin, ends #585, not in #555, 556, & 564. 551-r/1 story from F.C. #29. 556,578-r/Mickey Mouse Cheerios Premium by Dick Moores. 562,563,568-570, 572, 581-Gottfredson strip-r. 570-Valentine issue; has Mickey/Minnie centerfold. 584-Taliaferro strip-r			1.60
550 ($2.25, 52 pgs.)-Donald Duck by Barks; previously only printed in The Netherlands (1st time in U.S.); also r/Chip 'n Dale & Scamp from #204			2.50
571-($2.95, 68 pgs)-r/Donald Duck's Atomic Bomb by Barks from 1947 Cheerios premium			4.00
574-576,580,582,583 ($2.95, 68 pgs.): 574-r/1st Pinocchio Sunday strip (1939-40). 575-Gottfredson-r, Pinocchio-r/WDC&S #64. 580-r/Donald Duck's 1st app. from Silly Symphony strip 12/16/34 by Taliaferro; Gottfredson strip-r begin; not in #584 & 600. 582,583-r/Mickey Mouse on Sky Island from WDC&S #1,2			3.25
585 ($2.50, 52 pgs.)-r/#140; Barks-r/WDC&S #140			3.25
586,587: 586-Gladstone issues begin again; begin $1.50-c; Gottfredson-r begins (not in #600). 587-Donald Duck by William Van Horn begins			2.00
588-597: 588,591-599-Donald Duck by William Van Horn			1.50
598,599 ($1.95, 36 pgs.): 598-r/1st drawings of Mickey Mouse by Ub Iwerks			2.00
600 ($2.95, 48 pgs.)-L.B. Cole-c(r)/WDC&S #1; Barks-r/WDC&S #32 plus Rosa, Jippes, Van Horn-r and new Rosa centerspread			3.00
601-611 ($5.95, 64 pgs., squarebound, bi-monthly): 601-Barks-c, r/Mickey Mouse V1#1, Rosa-a/scripts. 602-Rosa-c. 604-Taliaferro strip-r/1st Silly Symphony Sundays from 1932. 604,605-Jippes-a. 605-Walt Kelly-c; Gottfredson "Mickey Mouse Outwits the Phantom Blot" r/F.C. #16			6.00
612-634 ($6.95)			7.00

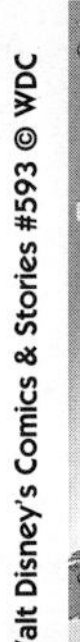

Walt Disney's Comics & Stories #593 © WDC

Walt Disney's Comics Digest #2 © WDC

Walt Disney's Donald and Mickey #30 © WDC

GD25 FN65 NM94

NOTE: *(#1-38, 68 pgs.; #39-42, 60 pgs.; #43-57, 61-134, 143-168, 446, 447, 52 pgs.; #58-60, 135-142, 169-540, 36 pgs.)*

NOTE: ***Barks** art in all issues #31 on, except where noted; c-95, 96, 104, 108, 109, 130-172, 174-178, 183, 198-200, 204, 206-209, 212-216, 218, 220, 226, 228-233, 235-238, 240-243, 247, 250, 253, 256, 260, 261, 276-283, 288-292, 295-298, 301, 303, 304, 306, 307, 309, 310, 313-316, 319, 321, 322, 324, 326, 328, 329, 331, 332, 334, 341, 342, 350, 351, 527r, 530r, 540(never before published), 546r, 557-586r(most), 596p, 601p.* **Kelly** *a-24p, 34-41, 43; r-522-524, 546, 547, 582, 583; covers(most)-34-118, 531r, 537r, 541r-543r, 562r, 571r, 605r. Walt Disney's Comics & Stories featured Mickey Mouse serials which were in practically every issue from #1 through #394 and #511 to date. The titles of the serials, along with the issues they are in, are listed in previous editions of this price guide.* **Floyd Gottfredson** *Mickey Mouse serials in issues #1-14, 18-66, 69-74, 78-100, 128, 562, 563, 568-572, 582, 583, 586-599 , 601-603 , 605-present , plus "Service with a Smile" in #13; "Mickey Mouse in a Warplant" (3 pgs.), and "Pluto Catches a Nazi Spy" (4 pgs.) in #62; "Mystery Next Door", #93; "Sunken Treasure", #94; "Aunt Marissa", #95 (r in #575); "Gangland", #98 (r in #562); "Thanksgiving Dinner", #99 (r in #567); and "The Talking Dog", #100 (r in #563); "Morty's Escapade," #128. "The Brave Little Tailor", #580; "Introducing Mickey Mouse Movies ", #581; Circus Roustabout, #585; "Rumplewatt the Giant", #604. Mickey Mouse by* **Paul Murry** *#152-547 except 155-57 (***Dick Moore***), 327-29 (***Tony Strobl***), 348-50 (***Jack Manning***), 533 (***Bill Wright***).* **Don Rosa** *story/a-523, 524, 526, 528, 531, 547, 601-present.* **Al Taliaferro** *Silly Symphonies in #5-"Three Little Pigs"; #13-"Birds of a Feather"; #14-"The Boarding School Mystery"; #15-"Cookieland" and "Three Little Kittens"; #16-"The Practical Pig"; #17-"The Ugly Duckling"; "The Wise Little Hen" in #580; and "Ambrose the Robber Kitten"; #19-"Penguin Isle"; and "Bucky Bug" in #20-23, 25, 26, 28 (one continuous story from 1932-34; first 2 pgs. not Taliaferro).* **Gottfredson** *strip r-562, 563, 568-572, 581, 585, 586, 590.* **Taliaferro** *strip r-584, 580.* **Van Horn** *a-537, 545, 561, 574, 587, 588, 591-present.*

WALT DISNEY'S COMICS & STORIES
Walt Disney Productions: 1943 (36 pgs.) (Dept. store Xmas giveaway)

nn-X-Mas-c with Donald & the Boys; Donald Duck by Jack Hannah; Thumper by Ken Hultgren 39.00 117.00 390.00

WALT DISNEY'S COMICS & STORIES
K.K. Publications: 1942-1963 known (7-1/3"x10-1/4", 4 pgs. in color, slick paper) (folded horizontally once or twice as mailers) (Xmas subscription offer)

1942 mailer-r/Kelly cover to WDC&S 25; 2-year subscription + two Grosset & Dunlap hardcover books (32-pages each), of Bambi and of Thumper, offered for $2.00; came in an illustrated C&S envelope with an enclosed postage paid envelope (Rare) Mailer only 16.00 48.00 165.00
with envelopes 23.00 69.00 230.00
1947,1948 mailer 11.00 33.00 115.00
1949 mailer-A rare Barks item: Same WDC&S cover as 1942 mailer, but with art changed so that newphew is handing teacher Donald a comic book rather than an apple, as originally drawn by Kelly. The tiny, 7/8"x1-1/4" cover shown was a rejected cover by Barks that was intended for C&S 110, but was redrawn by Kelly for C&S 111. The original art has been lost and this is its only app. (Rare) 32.00 96.00 320.00
1950 mailer-P.1 r/Kelly cover to Dell Xmas Parade 1 (without title); p.2 r/Kelly cover to C&S 101 (w/o title), but with the art altered to show Donald reading C&S 122 (by Kelly); hardcover book, "Donald Duck in Bringing Up the Boys" given with a $1.00 one-year subscription; P.4 r/full Kelly Xmas cover to C&S 99 (Rare) 11.00 33.00 115.00
1953 mailer-P.1 r/cover Dell Xmas Parade 4 (w/o title); insides offer "Donald Duck Full Speed Ahead," a 28-page, color, 5-5/8"x6-5/8" book, not of the Story Hour series; P.4 r/full Barks C&S 148 cover (Rare) 7.00 21.00 70.00
1963 mailer-Pgs. 1,2 & 4 r/GK Xmas art; P.3 r/a 1963 C&S cover (Scarce) 4.00 12.00 40.00

NOTE: *It is assumed a different mailer was printed each Xmas for at least twenty years. A 1952 mailer is known.*

WALT DISNEY'S COMICS DIGEST
Gladstone: Dec, 1986 - No. 7, Sept, 1987

1 .85 2.60 7.00
2-7 5.00

WALT DISNEY'S COMICS PENNY PINCHER
Gladstone: May, 1997 - No. 4, Aug, 1997 (99¢, limited series)

1-4 1.00

WALT DISNEY'S DONALD AND MICKEY (Formerly Walt Disney's Mickey and Donald)
Gladstone (Bruce Hamilton Company): No. 19, Sept, 1993 - No. 30, 1995 ($1.50, 36 & 68 pgs.)

19,21-24,26-30: New & reprints. 19,21,23,24-Barks-r. 19,26-Murry-r. 22-Barks "Omelet" story r/WDC&S #146. 27-Mickey Mouse story by Caesar Ferioli (1st U.S work). 29-Rosa-c; Mickey Mouse story actually starring Goofy (does not include Mickey except on title page. 4.00
20,25-($2.95, 68 pgs.): 20-Barks, Gottfredson-r 5.00

NOTE: *Donald Duck stories were all reprints.*

WALT DISNEY'S DONALD DUCK ADVENTURES (D.D. Adv. #1-3)
Gladstone: 11/87-No. 20, 4/90 (1st Series); No. 21, 8/93-Present (3rd Series)

1 .85 2.60 7.00
2-r/F.C. #308 3.00
3,4,6,7,9-11,13,15-18: 3-r/F.C. #223. 4-r/F.C. #62. 9-r/F.C. #159, "Ghost of the Grotto". 11-r/F.C. #159, "Adventure Down Under." 16-r/F.C. #291; Rosa-c. 18-r/FC #318; Rosa-c 2.50
5,8-Don Rosa-c/a 4.00
12($1.50, 52pgs)-Rosa-c/a w/Barks poster 4.00
14-r/F.C. #29, "Mummy's Ring" 3.00
19($1.95, 68 pgs.)-Barks-r/F.C. #199 (1 pg.) 3.00
20($1.95, 68 pgs.)-Barks-r/F.C. #189 & cover-r; William Van Horn-a 3.00
21,22: 21-r/D.D. #46. 22-r/F.C. #282 2.25
23-25,27,29,31,32-($1.50, 36 pgs.): 21,23,29-Rosa-c. 23-Intro/1st app. Andold Wild Duck by Marco Rota. 24-Van Horn-a. 27-1st Pat Block-a, "Mystery of Widow's Gap." 31,32-Block-c. 2.00
26,28,33($2.95, 68 pgs.): 26-Barks-r/F.C. #108, "Terror of the River". 28-Barks-r/F.C. #199, "Sheriff of Bullet Valley" 4.00
30($2.95, 68 pgs.)-r/F.C. #367, Barks' "Christmas for Shacktown" 4.00
34-44: 34-Resume $1.50-c. 34,35,37-Block-a/scripts. 38-Van Horn-c/a 1.50
45-49 1.95

NOTE: ***Barks** a-1-22r, 26r, 28r, 33r, 36r; c-10r, 14r, 20r.* **Block** *a-27, 30, 34, 35, 37; c-27, 30-32, 34, 35, 37; c-27, 30, 31, 32, 34, 35, 37.* **Rosa** *a-5, 8, 12; c-13, 16-18, 21, 23.*

WALT DISNEY'S DONALD DUCK ADVENTURES (2nd Series)
Disney Comics: June, 1990 - No. 38, July, 1993 ($1.50)

1-Rosa-a & scripts 3.00
2-38: 2-Barks-r/WDC&S #35; William Van Horn-a begins, ends #20. 9-Barks-r/F.C. #178. 9,11,14,17-No Van Horn-a. 11-Mad #1 cover parody. 14-Barks-r. 17-Barks-r. 21-r/FC #203 by Barks. 22-Rosa-a (10 pgs.) & scripts. 24-Rosa-a & scripts. 26-r/March of Comics #41 by Barks. 29-r/MOC #20 by Barks. 34-Rosa-c/a. 37-Rosa-a; Barks-r 2.00

NOTE: ***Barks** r-2, 4, 9(F.C. #178), 14(D.D. #45), 17, 21, 26, 27, 29 , 35, 36(D.D #60)-38.* **Taliaferro** *a-34r, 36r.*

WALT DISNEY'S DONALD DUCK AND MICKEY MOUSE (Formerly Walt Disney's Donald and Mickey)
Gladstone (Bruce Hamilton Company): Sept, 1995 - No. 7, Sept, 1996 ($1.50, 32 pgs.)

1-7: 1-Barks-r and new Mickey Mouse stories in all. 5,6-Mickey Mouse stories by Caesar Ferioli. 7-New Donald Duck and Mickey Mouse x-over story; Barks-r/WDC&S #51 1.50

NOTE: *Issue #8 was advertised, but cancelled.*

WALT DISNEY SHOWCASE
Gold Key: Oct, 1970 - No. 54, Jan, 1980 (No. 44-48: 68pgs., 49-54: 52pgs.)

	GD25	FN65	NM94
1-Boatniks (Movie)-Photo-c	2.40	7.00	26.00
2-Moby Duck	1.60	4.80	16.00
3,4,7: 3-Bongo & Lumpjaw-r. 4,7-Pluto-r	1.20	3.60	12.00
5-$1,000,000 Duck (Movie)-Photo-c	1.80	5.40	18.00
6-Bedknobs & Broomsticks (Movie)	1.80	5.40	18.00
8-Daisy & Donald	1.20	3.60	12.00
9-101 Dalmatians (cartoon feat.); r/F.C. #1183	1.60	4.80	16.00
10-Napoleon & Samantha (Movie)-Photo-c	1.80	5.40	18.00
11-Moby Duck-r	1.00	3.00	10.00

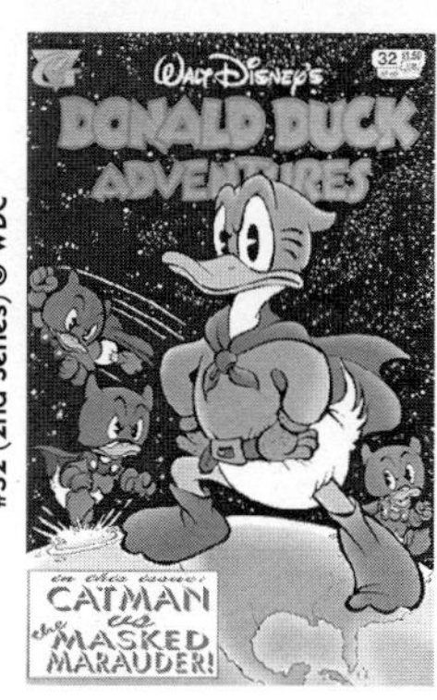

Walt Disney's Donald Duck Adventures #32 (2nd Series) © WDC

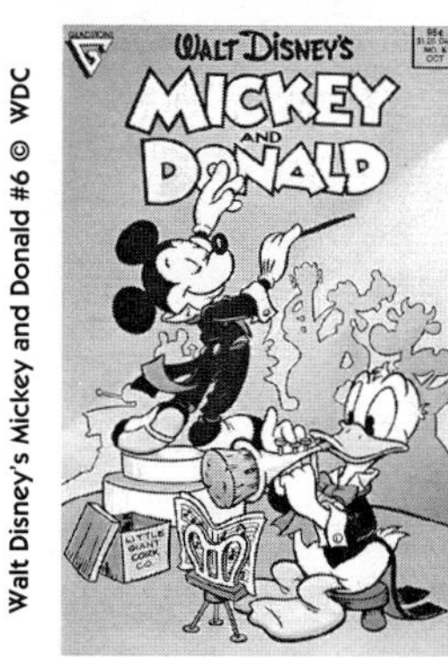

Walt Disney's Mickey and Donald #6 © WDC

Walt Disney's Uncle Scrooge #238 © WDC

GD25 FN65 NM94

12-Dumbo-r/Four Color #668 1.20 3.60 12.00
13-Pluto-r 1.00 3.00 10.00
14-World's Greatest Athlete (Movie)-Photo-c 1.80 5.40 18.00
15-3 Little Pigs-r 1.20 3.60 12.00
16-Aristocats (cartoon feature); r/Aristocats #1 1.80 5.40 18.00
17-Mary Poppins; r/M.P. #10136-501-Photo-c 1.80 5.40 18.00
18-Gyro Gearloose; Barks-r/F.C. #1047,1184 2.20 6.50 24.00
19-That Darn Cat; r/That Darn Cat #10171-602-Hayley Mills photo-c
1.80 5.40 18.00
20,23-Pluto-r 1.20 3.60 12.00
21-Li'l Bad Wolf & The Three Little Pigs 1.00 3.00 10.00
22-Unbirthday Party with Alice in Wonderland; r/Four Color #341
1.60 4.80 16.00
24-26: 24-Herbie Rides Again (Movie); sequel to "The Love Bug"; photo-c. 25-Old Yeller (Movie); r/F.C. #869; Photo-c. 26-Lt. Robin Crusoe USN (Movie); r/Lt. Robin Crusoe USN #10191-601; photo-c
1.20 3.60 12.00
27-Island at the Top of the World (Movie)-Photo-c 1.60 4.80 16.00
28-Brer Rabbit, Bucky Bug-r/WDC&S #58 1.20 3.60 12.00
29-Escape to Witch Mountain (Movie)-Photo-c 1.60 4.80 16.00
30-Magica De Spell; Barks-r/Uncle Scrooge #36 & WDC&S #258
2.50 7.60 28.00
31-Bambi (cartoon feature); r/Four Color #186 1.60 4.80 16.00
32-Spin & Marty-r/F.C. #1026; Mickey Mouse Club (TV)-Photo-c
1.80 5.40 18.00
33-39: 33-Pluto-r/F.C. #1143. 34-Paul Revere's Ride with Johnny Tremain (TV); r/F.C. #822. 35-Goofy-r/F.C. #952. 36-Peter Pan-r/F.C. #442. 37-Tinker Bell & Jiminy Cricket-r/F.C. #982,989. 38,39-Mickey & the Sleuth, Parts 1 & 2 1.00 3.00 10.00
40-The Rescuers (cartoon feature) 1.00 3.00 10.00
41-Herbie Goes to Monte Carlo (Movie); sequel to "Herbie Rides Again"; photo-c 1.20 3.60 12.00
42-Mickey & the Sleuth 1.00 3.00 10.00
43-Pete's Dragon (Movie)-Photo-c 1.60 4.80 16.00
44-Return From Witch Mountain (new) & In Search of the Castaways-r (Movies)-Photo-c; 68 pg. giants begin 1.60 4.80 16.00
45-The Jungle Book (Movie); r/#30033-803 1.60 4.80 16.00
46-The Cat From Outer Space (Movie)(new), & The Shaggy Dog (Movie)-r/F.C. #985; photo-c 1.00 3.00 10.00
47-Mickey Mouse Surprise Party-r 1.00 3.00 10.00
48-The Wonderful Advs. of Pinocchio-r/F.C. #1203; last 68 pg. issue
1.00 3.00 10.00
49-54: 49-North Avenue Irregulars (Movie); Zorro-r/Zorro #11; 52 pgs. begin; photo-c. 50-Bedknobs & Broomsticks-r/#6; Mooncussers-r/World of Adv. #1; photo-c. 51-101 Dalmatians-r. 52-Unidentified Flying Oddball (Movie); r/Picnic Party #8; photo-c. 53-The Scarecrow-r (TV). 54-The Black Hole (Movie)-Photo-c (predates Black Hole #1) .90 2.70 8.00

WALT DISNEY'S MAGAZINE (TV)(Formerly Walt Disney's Mickey Mouse Club Magazine) (50¢, bi-monthly)
Western Publishing Co.: V2#4, June, 1957 - V4#6, Oct, 1959

V2#4-Stories & articles on the Mouseketeers, Zorro, & Goofy and other Disney characters & people 4.50 13.50 45.00
V2#5, V2#6(10/57) 3.50 10.50 35.00
V3#1(12/57), V3#3-5 2.80 8.40 28.00
V3#2-Annette Funicello photo-c 9.00 27.00 90.00
V3#6(10/58)-TV Zorro photo-c 6.00 18.00 60.00
V4#1(12/58) - V4#2-4,6(10/59) 2.80 8.40 28.00
V4#5-Annette Funicello photo-c, w/ 2-photo articles 9.00 27.00 90.00
NOTE: *V2#4-V3#6 were 11-1/2x8-1/2", 48 pgs.; V4#1 on were 10x8", 52 pgs. (Peak circulation of 400,000).*

WALT DISNEY'S MERRY CHRISTMAS (See Dell Giant #39)

WALT DISNEY'S MICKEY AND DONALD(M & D #1,2)(Becomes Walt Disney's Donald & Mickey #19 on)
Gladstone: Mar, 1988 - No. 18, May, 1990 (95¢)

1-Don Rosa-a; r/1949 Firestone giveaway 2.00 6.00
2-8: 3-Infinity-c. 4-8-Barks-r 3.00
9-15: 9-r/1948 Firestone giveaway; X-Mas-c 3.00
16($1.50, 52 pgs.)-r/FC #157 5.00
17,18($1.95, 68 pgs.): 17-Barks M.M.-r/FC #79 plus Barks D.D.-r; Rosa-a; X-Mas-c. 18-Gottfredson-r/WDC&S #13,72-74; Kelly-c(r); Barks-r
5.00
NOTE: ***Barks** reprints in 1-15, 17, 18. **Kelly** c-13r, 14 (r/Walt Disney's C&S #58), 18r.*

WALT DISNEY'S MICKEY MOUSE CLUB MAGAZINE (TV)(Becomes Walt Disney's Magazine)
Western Publishing Co.: Winter, 1956 - V2#3, Apr, 1957 (11-1/2x8-1/2", quarterly, 48 pgs.)

V1#1 12.00 36.00 120.00
2-4 6.00 18.00 60.00
V2#1,2 4.50 13.50 45.00
3-Annette photo-c 10.00 30.00 100.00
Annual(1956)-Two different issues; ($1.50-Whitman); 120 pgs., cardboard covers, 11-3/4x8-3/4"; reprints 13.00 39.00 130.00
Annual(1957)-Same as above 11.00 33.00 115.00

WALT DISNEY'S PINOCCHIO SPECIAL
Gladstone: Spring, 1990 ($1.00)

1-50th anniversary edition; Kelly-r/F.C. #92 3.00

WALT DISNEY'S THE JUNGLE BOOK
W.D. Publications (Disney Comics): 1990 ($5.95, graphic novel, 68 pgs.)

nn-Movie adaptation; movie rereleased in 1990 2.00 6.00
nn-($2.95, 68 pgs.)-Comic edition; wraparound-c 3.00

WALT DISNEY'S UNCLE SCROOGE (Formerly Uncle Scrooge #1-209)
Gladstone #210-242/Disney Comics #243-280/Gladstone #281 on: No. 210, 10/86 - No. 242, 4/90; No. 243, 6/90 - Present

210-1st Gladstone issue; r/WDC&S #134 (1st Beagle Boys)
1.50 4.50 15.00
211-218: 216-New story ("Go Slowly Sands of Time") plotted and partly scripted by Barks. 217-r/U.S. #7, "Seven Cities of Cibola" 1.50 4.50 15.00
219-"Son Of The Sun" by Rosa 2.25 6.80 25.00
220-Don Rosa-a/scripts 5.00
221-230: 224-Rosa-c/a. 226,227-Rosa-a 3.00
231-240: 235-Rosa-a/scripts 3.00
241-($1.95, 68 pgs.)-Rosa finishes over Barks-r 3.00
242-($1.95, 68 pgs.)-Barks-r; Rosa-a(1 pg.) 3.00
243-249,251-280,282-284-($1.50): 243-1st by Disney Comics. 261-263, 276-Don Rosa-c/a. 274-All Barks issue. 275-Contains poster by Rosa. 283-r/WDC&S #98 2.25
250-($2.25, 52 pgs.)-Barks-r; wraparound-c 3.00
281-Gladstone issues start again; Rosa-c 5.00
285-The Life and Times of Scrooge McDuck Pt. 1; Rosa-c/a/scripts
1.00 3.00 10.00
286-292: The Life and Times of Scrooge McDuck Pt. 2-8; Rosa-c/a/scripts
5.00
293-($1.95, 36 pgs.)-The Life and Times of Scrooge McDuck Pt. 9
294-299, 301-308-($1.50, 32 pgs.): 294-296-The Life and Times of Scrooge McDuck Pt. 10-12. 297-The Life and Times of Uncle Scrooge Pt. 0; Rosa-c/a/scripts 1.50
300-($2.25, 48 pgs.)-Rosa-c; Barks-r/WDC&S #104 and U.S. #216; r/U.S. #220; includes new centerfold. .90 2.25
309-318-($6.95) 6.95
NOTE: ***Barks** r-210-218, 220-223, 224(2pg.), 225-234, 236-242, 245, 246, 250-253, 255, 256, 258, 261(2 pg.), 265, 267, 268, 270(2), 272-284, 299-present; c(r)-210, 212, 221, 228, 229, 232, 233, 284. scripts-287, 293. **Rosa** a-219, 220, 224, 226, 227, 235, 261-263, 268, 275-277, 285-289; c-219, 224, 231, 261-263, 276, 278-281, 285-289; scripts-219, 220, 224, 235, 261-263, 268, 276, 285-289.*

WALT DISNEY'S UNCLE SCROOGE ADVENTURES (U. Scrooge Advs. #1-3)

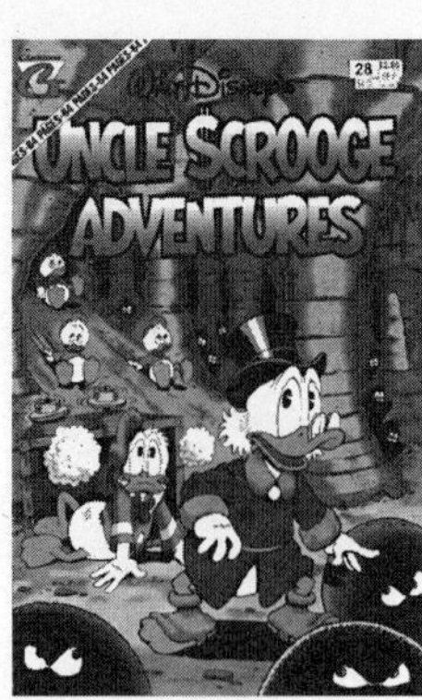

Walt Disney's Uncle Scrooge Adventures #28 © WDC

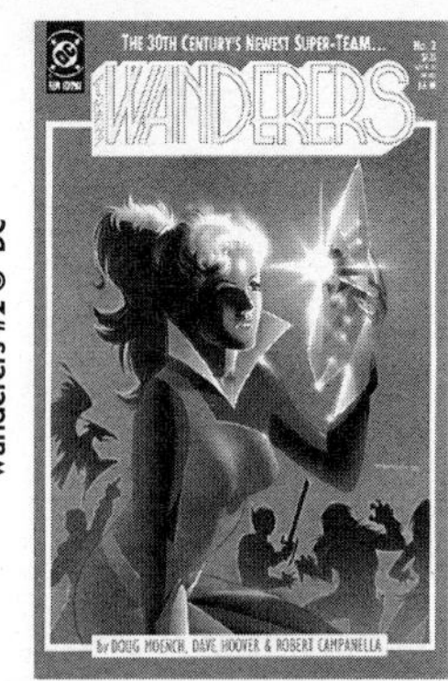

Wanderers #2 © DC

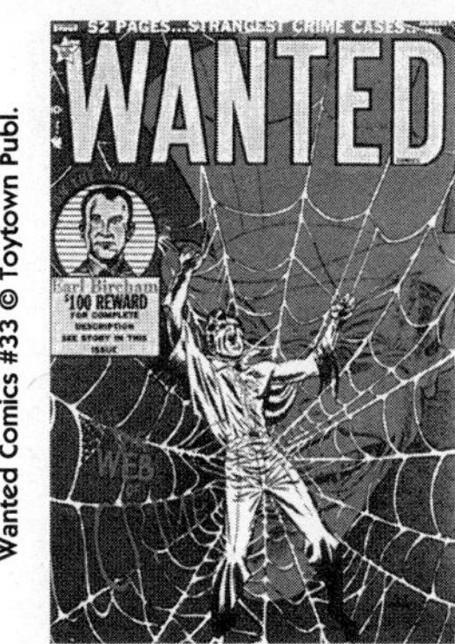

Wanted Comics #33 © Toytown Publ.

	GD25	FN65	NM94

Gladstone Publishing: Nov, 1987 - No. 21, May, 1990; No. 22, Sept, 1993 - Present

1-Barks-r begin, ends #26	.90	2.70	8.00
2-5: 5-Rosa-c/a; no Barks-r			4.00
6-19: 9,14-Rosa-a. 10-r/U.S. #18(all Barks)			3.00
20,21 ($1.95, 68 pgs.) 20-Rosa-c/a. 21-Rosa-a			3.00
22 ($1.50)-Rosa-c; r/U.S. #26			5.00
23-($2.95, 68 pgs.)-Vs. The Phantom Blot-r/P.B. #3; Barks-r			4.00
24-26,29,31,32,34-36: 24,25,29,31,32-Rosa-c. 25-r/U.S. #21			2.00
27-Guardians of the Lost Library - Rosa-c/a/story; origin of Junior Woodchuck Guidebook			3.00
28-($2.95, 68 pgs.)-r/U.S. #13 w/restored missing panels			4.00
30-($2.95, 68 pgs.)-r/U.S. #12; Rosa-c			4.00
33-($2.95, 64 pgs.)-New Barks story			3.00
37-45: 37-Begin $1.50-c			1.50
46-55: 46-Begin-$1.95-c			1.95

NOTE: ***Barks** r-1-4, 6-8, 10-13, 15-21, 23, 22, 24; c(r)-15, 16, 17, 21. **Rosa** a-5, 9, 14, 20, 21, 27; c-5, 13, 14, 17(finishes), 20, 22, 24, 25, 27, 28; scripts-5, 9, 14, 27.*

WALT DISNEY'S UNCLE SCROOGE ADVENTURES IN COLOR
Gladstone Publ.: Dec, 1995 - Present ($8.95/$9.95, squarebound, 56 issue limited series) (Polybagged w/card) (Series chronologically reprints all the stories written & drawn by Carl Barks)

1-38: 1-(12/95)-r/FC #386. 15-(12/96)-r/US #15. 16-(12/96)-r/US #16. 18-(1/97)-r/US #18			9.00
39-56: 39-Begin $9.95-c			9.95

WALT DISNEY'S WHEATIES PREMIUMS (See Wheaties)

WALTER (Campaign of Terror) (Also see The Mask)
Dark Horse Comics: Feb, 1996 - No. 4, May, 1996 ($2.50, limited series)

1-4			2.50

WALTER LANTZ ANDY PANDA (Also see Andy Panda)
Gold Key: Aug, 1973 - No. 23, Jan, 1978 (Walter Lantz)

1-Reprints	1.20	3.60	12.00
2-10-All reprints	.85	2.60	7.00
11-23: 15,17-19,22-Reprints			4.00

WALT KELLY'S...
Eclipse Comics: Dec, 1987; Apr, 1988 ($1.75/$2.50, Baxter paper)

...Christmas Classics 1 (12/87, $1.75)-Kelly-r/Peter Wheat & Santa Claus Funnies			1.75
...Springtime Tales 1 (4/88, $2.50)-Kelly-r			2.50

WALTONS, THE (See Kite Fun Book)

WALT SCOTT (See Little People)

WALT SCOTT'S CHRISTMAS STORIES (See Christmas Stories, 4-Color #959, 1062)

WAMBI, JUNGLE BOY (See Jungle Comics)
Fiction House Magazines: Spr, 1942; No. 2, Win, 1942-43; No. 3, Spr, 1943; No. 4, Fall, 1948; No. 5, Sum, 1949; No. 6, Spr, 1950; No. 7-10, 1950(nd); No. 11, Spr, 1951 - No. 18, Win, 1952-53 (#1-3: 68 pgs.)

1-Wambi, the Jungle Boy begins	79.00	238.00	675.00
2 (1942)-Kiefer-c	44.00	132.00	375.00
3 (1943)-Kiefer-c/a	31.00	92.00	230.00
4 (1948)-Origin in text	19.00	56.00	140.00
5 (Fall, 1949, 36 pgs.)-Kiefer-c/a	16.00	48.00	120.00
6-10: 7-(52 pgs.)-New logo	15.00	44.00	110.00
11-18	10.00	30.00	75.00
I.W. Reprint #8('64)-r/#12 with new-c	2.25	6.75	18.00

NOTE: ***Alex Blum** c-8. **Kiefer** c-1-5. **Whitman** c-11-18.*

WANDERERS (See Adventure Comics #375, 376)
DC Comics: June, 1988 - No. 13, Apr, 1989 ($1.25) (Legion of Super-Heroes spin off)

1-13: 1,2-Steacy-c. 3-Legion app.			1.30

WANDERING STAR
Pen & Ink Comics/Sirius Entertainment No. 12 on: 1993 - No. 21, Mar, 1997 ($2.50/$2.75, B&W)

1-1st printing; Teri Sue Wood c/a/scripts in all	1.00	3.00	10.00
1-2nd and 3rd printings			2.50
2-1st printing			5.00
2-2nd printing			2.50
3-9: 1st and 2nd printings exist			3.00
10-11: 10-$2.75-c begins			2.75
12-21: 12-(1/96)-1st Sirius issue; $2.50-c begins			2.50
Trade paperback ($11.95)-r/1-7; 1st printing of 1000, signed and numbered			15.00
Trade paperback-2nd printing, 2000 signed			12.00
TPB Volume 2 (11/98, $14.95) r/#8-14			14.95

WANTED COMICS
Toytown Publications/Patches/Orbit Publ.: No. 9, Sept-Oct, 1947 - No. 53, April, 1953 (#9-33: 52 pgs.)

9-True crime cases; radio's Mr. D. A. app.	16.00	48.00	120.00
10,11: 10-Giunta-a; radio's Mr. D. A. app.	11.00	32.00	80.00
12-Used in **SOTI**, pg. 277	11.00	34.00	85.00
13-Heroin drug propaganda story	10.00	30.00	75.00
14-Marijuana drug mention story (2 pgs.)	8.00	24.00	56.00
15-17,19,20	6.50	19.50	45.00
18-Marijuana story, "Satan's Cigarettes"; r-in #45 & retitled	19.00	56.00	140.00
21,22: 21-Krigstein-a. 22-Extreme violence	7.85	23.50	55.00
23,25-34,36-38,40-44,46-48,53	5.00	15.00	30.00
24-Krigstein-a; "The Dope King", marijuana mention story	7.85	23.50	55.00
35-Used in **SOTI**, pg. 160	7.85	23.50	55.00
39-Drug propaganda story "The Horror Weed"	11.00	34.00	85.00
45-Marijuana story from #18	6.50	19.50	45.00
49-Has unstable pink-c that fades easily; rare in mint condition	5.70	17.00	35.00
50-Has unstable pink-c like #49; surrealist-c by Buscema; horror stories	11.00	32.00	80.00
51- "Holiday of Horror" junkie story; drug-c	7.85	23.50	55.00
52-Classic "Cult of Killers" opium use story	7.85	23.50	55.00

NOTE: ***Buscema** c-50, 51. **Lawrence** and **Leav** c/a most issues. **Syd Shores** c/a-48; c-37. Issues 9-46 have wanted criminals with their descriptions & drawn picture on cover.*

WANTED: DEAD OR ALIVE (TV)
Dell Publishing Co.: No. 1102, May-July, 1960 - No. 1164, Mar-May, 1961

Four Color 1102 (#1)-Steve McQueen photo-c	12.00	37.00	125.00
Four Color 1164-Steve McQueen photo-c	9.00	27.00	100.00

WANTED, THE WORLD'S MOST DANGEROUS VILLAINS (See DC Special)
National Periodical Publications: July-Aug, 1972 - No. 9, Aug-Sept, 1973 (All reprints & 20¢ issues)

1-Batman, Green Lantern (story r-from G.L. #1), & Green Arrow	2.00	6.00	20.00
2-Batman/Joker/Penguin-c/story r-from Batman #25; plus Flash story (r-from Flash #121)	1.80	5.40	18.00
3-9: 3-Dr. Fate(r/More Fun #65), Hawkman(r/Flash #100), & Vigilante(r/Action #69). 4-Gr. Lantern(r/All-American #61) & Kid Eternity(r/Kid Eternity #15). 5-Dollman/Green Lantern. 6-Burnley Starman; Wildcat/Sargon. 7-Johnny Quick(r/More fun #76), Hawkman(r/Flash #90), Hourman by Baily(r/Adv. #72). 8-Dr. Fate/Flash(r/Flash #114). 9-S&K Sandman/Superman	1.20	3.60	12.00

NOTE: ***B. Bailey** a-7r. **Infantino** a-2r. **Kane** r-1, 5. **Kubert** r-3i, 6, 7. **Meskin** r-3, 7. **Reinman** r-4, 6.*

WAR (See Fightin' Marines #122)
Charlton Comics: Jul, 1975 - No. 9, Nov, 1976; No. 10, Sept, 1978 - No. 49, 1984

1-Boyette painted-c	.90	2.70	9.00

War Action #4 © ATL

Warchild #1 © Rob Liefeld

War Comics #2 © DELL

	GD25	FN65	NM94
2-10			6.00
11-49: 47-Reprints			3.00
7,9 (Modern Comics-r, 1977)			3.00

WAR, THE (See The Draft & The Pitt)
Marvel Comics: 1989 - No. 4, 1990 ($3.50, squarebound, 52 pgs.)

1-4: Characters from New Universe			3.50

WAR ACTION (Korean War)
Atlas Comics (CPS): April, 1952 - No. 14, June, 1953

1	16.00	48.00	120.00
2	10.00	30.00	60.00
3-10,14: 7-Pakula-a	6.70	20.00	45.00
11-13-Krigstein-a	8.35	25.00	55.00

NOTE: ***Brodsky** c-1-4. **Heath** a-1; c-7, 14. **Keller** a-6. **Maneely** a-1. **Tuska** a-2, 8.*

WAR ADVENTURES
Atlas Comics (HPC): Jan, 1952 - No. 13, Feb, 1953

1-Tuska-a	13.00	40.00	100.00
2	7.50	22.50	50.00
3-7,9-13: 3-Pakula-a. 7-Maneely-c	5.70	17.00	38.00
8-Krigstein-a	8.35	25.00	55.00

NOTE: ***Brodsky** c-1-3, 6, 8, 11, 12. **Heath** a-5, 7, 10; c-4, 5, 9, 13. **Robinson** a-3; c-10.*

WAR ADVENTURES ON THE BATTLEFIELD (See Battlefield)

WAR AGAINST CRIME! (Becomes Vault of Horror #12 on)
E. C. Comics: Spring, 1948 - No. 11, Feb-Mar, 1950

1-Real Stories From Police Records on-c #1-9	53.00	159.00	525.00
2,3	30.00	90.00	260.00
4-9	28.00	84.00	240.00
10-1st Vault Keeper app. & 1st Vault of Horror	160.00	480.00	1500.00
11-2nd Vault Keeper app.; 1st horror-c	92.00	276.00	850.00

NOTE: *All have **Johnny Craig** covers. **Feldstein** a-4, 7-9. **Harrison/Wood** a-11. **Ingels** a-1, 2, 8. **Palais** a-8. Changes to horror with #10.*

WAR AND ATTACK (Also see Special War Series #3)
Charlton Comics: Fall, 1964; V2#54, June, 1966 - V2#63, Dec, 1967

1-Wood-a (25 pgs.)	3.00	9.00	30.00
V2#54(6/66)-#63 (Formerly Fightin' Air Force)	1.50	4.50	12.00

NOTE: ***Montes/Bache** a-55, 56, 60, 63.*

WAR AT SEA (Formerly Space Adventures)
Charlton Comics: No. 22, Nov, 1957 - No. 42, June, 1961

22	4.00	12.00	24.00
23-30	3.00	9.00	18.00
31-42	1.75	5.25	14.00

WAR BATTLES
Harvey Publications: Feb, 1952 - No. 9, Dec, 1953

1-Powell-a; Elias-c	9.00	27.00	90.00
2-Powell-a	4.50	13.50	45.00
3-5,7-9: 3,7-Powell-a	4.00	12.00	40.00
6-Nostrand-a	5.00	15.00	50.00

WAR BIRDS
Fiction House Magazines: 1952(nd) - No. 3, Winter, 1952-53

1	12.00	36.00	90.00
2,3	8.35	25.00	50.00

WARBLADE: ENDANGERED SPECIES (Also see WildC.A.T.S: Covert Action Teams)
Image Comics (WildStorm Productions): Jan, 1995 - No. 4, Apr, 1995 ($2.50, limited series)

1-4: 1-Gatefold wraparound-c			2.50

WARCHILD
Maximum Press: Jan. 1995 - No. 4, Aug, 1995 ($2.50)

1-4-Rob Liefeld-c/a/scripts			2.50
1-4: Variant-c			3.00
Trade paperback (1/96, $12.95)-r/#1-4.			13.00

WAR COMBAT (Becomes Combat Casey #6 on)
Atlas Comics (LBI No. 1/SAI No. 2-5): March, 1952 - No. 5, Nov, 1952

	GD25	FN65	NM94
1	11.00	34.00	85.00
2	6.70	20.00	45.00
3-5	5.35	16.00	32.00

NOTE: ***Berg** a-2, 4, 5. **Brodsky** c-1, 2, 4, 5. **Henkel** a-5. **Maneely** a-1, 4; c-3.*

WAR COMICS (War Stories #5 on)(See Key Ring Comics)
Dell Publishing Co.: May, 1940 (No month given) - No. 4, Sept, 1941?

1-Sikandur the Robot Master, Sky Hawk, Scoop Mason, War Correspondent begin; McWilliams-c; 1st war comic	49.00	148.00	420.00
2-Origin Greg Gilday (5/41)	31.00	92.00	230.00
3-Joan becomes Greg Gilday's aide	19.00	58.00	145.00
4-Origin Night Devils	22.00	66.00	165.00

WAR COMICS
Marvel/Atlas (USA No. 1-41/JPI No. 42-49): Dec, 1950 - No. 49, Sept, 1957

1	21.00	64.00	160.00
2	11.00	32.00	80.00
3-10	9.30	28.00	65.00
11-Flame thrower w/burning bodies on-c	10.00	30.00	70.00
12-20	7.85	23.50	55.00
21,23-32: 26-Valley Forge story. 32-Last precode issue (2/55)	5.70	17.00	38.00
22-Krigstein-a	7.85	23.50	55.00
33-37,39-42,44,45,47,48	5.70	17.00	38.00
38-Kubert/Moskowitz-a	7.50	22.50	50.00
43,49-Torres-a. 43-Severin/Elder E.C. swipe from Two-Fisted Tales #31	7.50	22.50	50.00
46-Crandall-a	7.50	22.50	50.00

NOTE: ***Colan** a-4, 36, 48, 49. **Drucker** a-37, 43, 48. **Everett** a-17. **Heath** a-7-9, 16, 19, 25, 36; c-11, 16, 19, 25, 26, 29-31, 36. **G. Kane** a-19. **Lawrence** a-36. **Maneely** a-7, 9; c-6, 27, 37. **Orlando** a-42, 48. **Pakula** a-26. **Ravielli** a-27. **Reinman** a-26. **Robinson** a-15; c-13. **Severin** a-26, 27; c-48.*

WAR DANCER (Also see Charlemagne, Doctor Chaos #2 & Warriors of Plasm)
Defiant: Feb, 1994 - No. 6, July, 1994 ($2.50)

1-3,5,6: 1-Intro War Dancer; Weiss-c/a begins. 1-3-Weiss-a(p). 6-Pre-Schism issue			2.50
4-($3.25, 52 pgs.)-Charlemagne app.			3.25

WAR DOGS OF THE U.S. ARMY
Avon Periodicals: 1952

1-Kinstler-c/a	12.00	36.00	90.00

WARFRONT
Harvey Publications: 9/51 - #35, 11/58; #36, 10/65; #39, 2/67

1-Korean War	9.00	27.00	90.00
2	5.00	15.00	50.00
3-10	3.50	10.50	35.00
11,12,14,16-20	2.50	7.50	25.00
13,15,22-Nostrand-a	5.00	15.00	50.00
21,23-27,29,31-33,35	2.50	7.50	25.00
28,30,34-Kirby-c	5.00	15.00	50.00
36-(12/66)-Dynamite Joe begins, ends #39; Williamson-a	3.50	10.50	35.00
37-Wood-a (17 pgs.)	3.20	9.60	32.00
38,39-Wood-a, 2-3 pgs.; Lone Tiger app.	2.20	6.60	22.00

NOTE: ***Powell** a-1-6, 9-11, 14, 17, 20, 23, 25-28, 30, 31, 34, 36. **Powell/Nostrand** a-12, 13, 15. **Simon** c-36?, 38.*

WAR FURY
Comic Media/Harwell (Allen Hardy Assoc.): Sept, 1952 - No. 4, Mar, 1953

1-Heck-c/a in all; Palais-a; bullet hole in forehead-c; all issues are very violent	11.00	32.00	80.00

War Heroes #10 © DELL

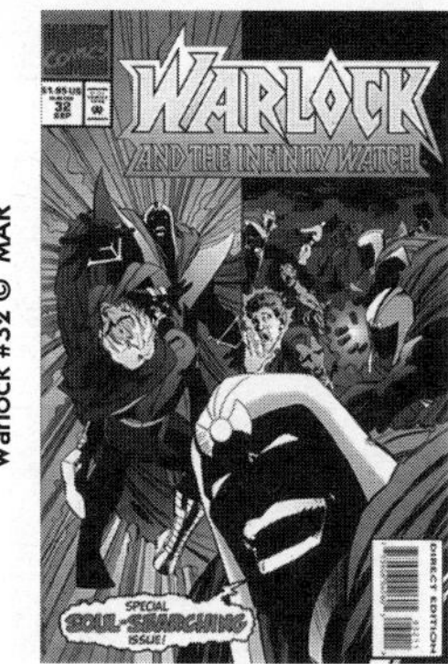

Warlock #32 © MAR

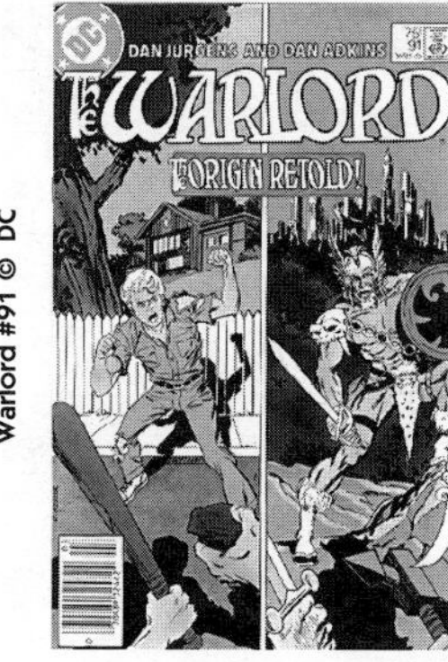

Warlord #91 © DC

GD25 FN65 NM94

2-4: 4-Morisi-a 6.50 19.50 45.00

WAR GODS OF THE DEEP (See Movie Classics)

WARHAWKS
TSR, Inc.: 1990 - No. 10, 1991 ($2.95, 44 pgs.)

1-10-Based on TSR game, Spiegle a-1-6 3.00

WARHEADS
Marvel Comics UK: June, 1992 - No. 14, Aug, 1993 ($1.75)

1-Wolverine-c/story; indicia says #2 by mistake 2.00
2-14: 2-Nick Fury app. 3-Iron Man-c/story. 4,5-X-Force. 5-Liger vs. Cable. 6,7-Death's Head II app. (#6 is cameo) 1.75

WAR HEROES (See Marine War Heroes)

WAR HEROES
Dell Publishing Co.: 7-9/42 (no month); No. 2, 10-12/42 - No. 11, 3/45 (Published quarterly)

	GD25	FN65	NM94
1-General Douglas MacArthur-c	21.00	64.00	160.00
2	11.00	34.00	85.00
3,5: 3-Pro-Russian back-c	9.30	28.00	65.00
4-Disney's Gremlins app.	15.00	46.00	115.00
6-11: 6-Tothish-a by Discount	7.50	22.50	52.00

NOTE: *No. 1 was to be released in July, but was delayed. Painted c-4, 6-9.*

WAR HEROES
Ace Magazines: May, 1952 - No. 8, Apr, 1953

	GD25	FN65	NM94
1	9.00	27.00	60.00
2-Lou Cameron-a	5.70	17.00	35.00
3-8: 6,7-Cameron-a	4.15	12.50	25.00

WAR HEROES (Also see Blue Bird Comics)
Charlton Comics: Feb, 1963 - No. 27, Nov, 1967

	GD25	FN65	NM94
1,2: 2-John F. Kennedy story	2.50	7.50	22.00
3-10	1.75	5.25	14.00
11-27	1.25	3.75	10.00
27-1st Devils Brigade by Glanzman	1.75	5.25	14.00

NOTE: ***Montes/Bache*** *a-3-7, 21, 25, 27; c-3-7.*

WAR IS HELL
Marvel Comics Group: Jan, 1973 - No. 15, Oct, 1975

	GD25	FN65	NM94
1-Williamson-a(r), 5 pgs.; Ayers-a	1.50	4.50	15.00
2-8-Reprints	.90	2.70	9.00
9-Intro Death	2.50	7.60	28.00
10-15-Death app.	1.20	3.60	12.00

NOTE: ***Bolle*** *a-3r.* ***Powell*** *a-1.* ***Woodbridge*** *a-1. Sgt. Fury reprints-7, 8.*

WARLOCK (The Power of...)(Also see Fantastic Four #66, 67, Incredible Hulk #178, Infinity Crusade, Infinity Gauntlet, Infinity War, Marvel Premiere #1, Silver Surfer V3#46, Strange Tales #178-181 & Thor #165)
Marvel Comics Group: Aug, 1972 - No. 8, Oct, 1973; No. 9, Oct, 1975 - No. 15, Nov, 1976

	GD25	FN65	NM94
1-Origin by Kane	1.00	3.00	10.00
2,3			5.00
4-8: 4-Death of Eddie Roberts			4.00
9-Starlin's 2nd Thanos saga begins, ends #15; new costume Warlock; Thanos cameo only; story cont'd from Strange Tales #178-181; Starlin-c/a in #9-15			5.00
10-Origin Thanos & Gamora; recaps events from Capt. Marvel #25-34. Thanos vs.The Magus-c/story	1.20	3.60	12.00
11-Thanos app.; Warlock dies	.90	2.70	8.00
12,14: 14-Origin Star Thief; last 25¢ issue			4.00
13-(Regular 25¢ edition)(6/76)			5.00
13-(30¢-c, limited distribution)	2.00	6.00	20.00
15-Thanos-c/story	.85	2.60	7.00

NOTE: ***Buscema*** *a-2p; c-8p.* ***G. Kane*** *a-1p, 3-5p; c-1p, 2, 3, 4p, 5p, 7p.* ***Starlin*** *a-9-14p, 15; c-9, 10, 11p, 12p, 13-15.* ***Sutton*** *a-1-8i.*

WARLOCK (...Special Edition on-c)
Marvel Comics Group: Dec, 1982 - No. 6, May, 1983 ($2.00, slick paper, 52 pgs.)

1-Warlock-r/Strange Tales #178-180. 3.00
2-6: 2-r/Str. Tales #180,181 & Warlock #9. 3-r/Warlock #10-12(Thanos origin recap). 4-r/Warlock #12-15. 5-r/Warlock #15, Marvel Team-Up #55 & Avengers Ann. #7. 6-r/2nd half Avengers Annual #7 & Marvel Two-in-One Annual #2 2.00
Special Edition #1(12/83) 2.25

NOTE: ***Byrne*** *a-5r.* ***Starlin*** *a-1-6r; c-1-6(new). Direct sale only.*

WARLOCK
Marvel Comics: V2#1, May, 1992 - No. 6, Oct, 1992 ($2.50, limited series)

V2#1-6: 1-Reprints 1982 reprint series w/Thanos 2.50

WARLOCK
Marvel Comics: Nov, 1998 - No. 4, Feb, 1999 ($2.99, limited series)

1-4-Warlock vs. Drax 3.00

WARLOCK AND THE INFINITY WATCH (Also see Infinity Gauntlet)
Marvel Comics: Feb, 1992 - No. 42, July, 1995 ($1.75) (Sequel to Infinity Gauntlet)

1-Starlin scripts begin; brief origin recap Warlock; sequel to Infinity Gauntlet 2.50
2,3: 2-Reintro Moondragon 2.00
4-24,26: 7-Reintro The Magus; Moondragon app.; Thanos cameo on last 2 pgs. 8,9-Thanos battles Gamora-c/story. 8-Magus & Moondragon app. 10-Thanos-c/story; Magus app. 13-Hulk x-over. 21-Drax vs. Thor 1.75
25-($2.95, 52 pgs.)-Die-cut & embossed double-c; Thor & Thanos app. 3.00
28-42: 28-$1.95-c begins; bound-in card sheet 2.00

NOTE: ***Austin*** *c/a-1-4i, 7i.* ***Leonardi*** *a(p)-3, 4.* ***Medina*** *c/a(p)-1, 2, 5; 6, 9, 10, 14, 15, 20.* ***Williams*** *a(i)-8, 12, 13, 16-19.*

WARLOCK CHRONICLES
Marvel Comics: June, 1993 - No. 8, Feb, 1994 ($2.00, limited series)

1-($2.95)-Holo-grafx foil & embossed-c; origin retold; Starlin scripts begin; Keith Williams-a(i) in all 3.00
2-8: 3-Thanos & Mephisto-c/story. 4-Vs. Magus-c/s. 8-Contains free 16 pg. Razorline insert 2.00

WARLOCK 5
Aircel Pub.: 11/86 - No. 22, 5/89; V2#1, June, 1989 - V2#5?, 1989 ($1.70, B&W)

1-9-All issues by Barry Blair. 5-Green Cyborg on-c. 6-Misnumbered; Blue Girl on-c. 1.70
10-22: 18-$1.95-c begins 2.00
V2#1-5 ($2.00, B&W) 2.00
Compilation 1-r/#1-5 (1988, $5.95) 6.00
Compilation 2-r/#6-9 ($5.95) 6.00

WARLORD (See 1st Issue Special #8)
National Periodical Publications/DC Comics #123 on: 1-2/76; No.2, 3-4/76; No.3, 10-11/76 - No. 133, Win, 1988-89

	GD25	FN65	NM94
1-Story cont'd. from 1st Issue Special #8	1.00	3.00	10.00
2-Intro. Machiste			5.00
3-5			3.50
6-10: 6-Intro Mariah. 7-Origin Machiste. 9-Dons new costume			3.00
11-20: 11-Origin-r. 12-Intro Aton. 15-Tara returns; Warlord has son			3.00
21-36,40: 27-New facts about origin. 28-1st app. Wizard World. 32-Intro Shakira. 40-Warlord gets new costume			2.00
37-39: 37,38-Origin Omac by Starlin. 38-Intro Jennifer Morgan, Warlord's daughter. 39-Omac ends.			3.00
41,49-52: 49-Claw The Unconquered app. 50-Death of Aton. 51-Reprints #1			1.50
42-47-Omac back-up series			2.00
48-(52 pgs.)-1st app. Arak; contains free 14 pg. Arak Son of Thunder; Claw The Unconquered app.			2.00

53-130,132: 55-Arion Lord of Atlantis begins, ends #62. 63-The Barren Earth

War Machine #3 © MAR

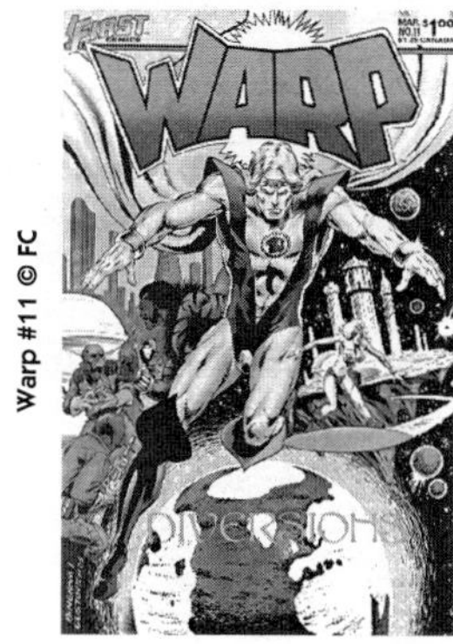

Warp #11 © FC

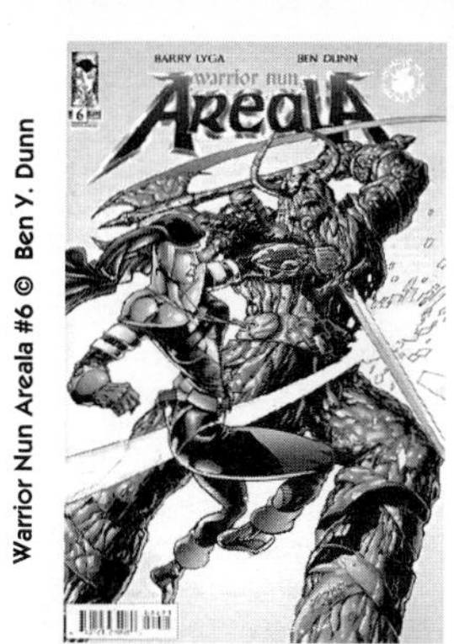

Warrior Nun Areala #6 © Ben Y. Dunn

	GD25	FN65	NM94
begins; free 16pg. Masters of the Universe preview. 91-Origin w/new facts. 114,115-Legends x-over. 100-($1.25, 52 pgs.). 125-Death of Tara			1.50
131-1st DC work by Rob Liefeld (9/88)		2.00	6.00
133-($1.50, 52 pgs.)			4.00
Remco Toy Giveaway (2-3/4x4")			1.00
Annual 1(1982)-Grell-c,/a(p)			2.00
Annual 2-6: 2(1983). 3(1984). 4(1985). 5(1986). 6(1987, $1.25)-New Gods app.			1.00

NOTE: ***Grell*** *a-1-15, 16-50p, 51r, 52p, 59p, Annual 1p; c-1-70, 100-104, 112, 116, 117, Annual 1, 5.* ***Wayne Howard*** *a-64i.* ***Starlin*** *a-37-39p.*

WARLORD
DC Comics: Jan, 1992 - No. 6, June, 1992 ($1.75, limited series)

	GD25	FN65	NM94
1-6: Grell-c & scripts in all			1.75

WARLORDS (See DC Graphic Novel #2)

WAR MAN
Marvel Comics (Epic Comics): Nov, 1993 - No. 2, Dec, 1993 ($2.50, lim. series)

	GD25	FN65	NM94
1,2			2.50

WAR MACHINE (Also see Iron Man #281,282 & Marvel Comics Presents #152)
Marvel Comics: Apr, 1994 - No. 25, Apr, 1996 ($1.50)

	GD25	FN65	NM94
"Ashcan" edition (nd, 75¢, B&W, 16 pgs.)			.75
1-($2.00, 52 pgs.)-Newsstand edition; Cable app.			2.00
1-($2.95, 52 pgs.)-Collectors ed.; embossed foil-c			3.00
2-14, 16-25: 2-Bound-in trading card sheet; Cable app. 2,3-Deathlok app. 8-red logo			1.50
8-($2.95)-Polybagged w/16 pg. Marvel Action Hour preview & acetate print; yellow logo			3.00
15 ($2.50)-Flip book			2.50

WAR OF THE GODS
DC Comics: Sept, 1991 - No. 4, Dec, 1991 ($1.75, limited series)

	GD25	FN65	NM94
1-4: Perez layouts, scripts & covers. 1-Contains free mini posters (Robin, Deathstroke). 2-4-Direct sale versions include 4 pin-ups printed on cover stock plus different-c			1.80

WAR OF THE WORLDS, THE
Caliber: 1996 - Present ($2.95, B&W, 32 pgs.)(Based on H. G. Wells novel)

	GD25	FN65	NM94
1-Randy Zimmerman scripts begin			3.00

WARP
First Comics: Mar, 1983 - No. 19, Feb, 1985 ($1.00/$1.25, Mando paper)

	GD25	FN65	NM94
1-Sargon-Mistress of War app.			1.00
2-19: 2-Faceless Ones begin. 10-New Warp advs., & Outrider begin			1.25
Special 1-3: 1(7/83, 36 pgs.)-Origin Chaos-Prince of Madness; origin of Warp Universe begins, ends #3. 2(1/84)-Lord Cumulus vs. Sargon Mistress of War ($1.00). 3(6/84)-Chaos-Prince of Madness			1.00

WAR PARTY
Lightning Comics: Oct, 1994 (2.95, B&W)

	GD25	FN65	NM94
1-1st app. Deathmark			3.00

WARPED
Empire Entertainment (Solson): Jun, 1990 - No. 2, Oct-Nov, 1990 (B&W mag)

	GD25	FN65	NM94
1,2			2.00

WARPATH (Indians on the...)
Key Publications/Stanmor: Nov, 1954 - No. 3, Apr, 1955

	GD25	FN65	NM94
1	8.50	26.00	60.00
2,3	5.70	17.00	35.00

WARP GRAPHICS ANNUAL
WaRP Graphics: Dec, 1985; 1988 ($2.50)

	GD25	FN65	NM94
1-Elfquest, Blood of the Innocent, Thunderbunny & Myth Adventures app.			2.50
1 (1988)			2.50

WARREN PRESENTS
Warren Publications: Jan, 1979 - No. 14, Nov, 1981

	GD25	FN65	NM94
1-Eerie, Creepy, & Vampirella-r	1.50	4.50	15.00
2-6 10/79): 2-The Rook	1.00	3.00	10.00
8(10/80)-1st app. Pantha	1.50	4.50	15.00
9(11/80)	1.20	3.60	12.00
13(10/81),14(11/81)	1.80	5.40	18.00
(#7,10,11,12 may not exist, or may be a Special below)			
Special-Alien Collectors Edition (1979)	1.80	5.40	18.00
Special-Close Encounters of the Third Kind (1978)	1.20	3.60	12.00
Special-Lord of the Rings (6/79)	1.80	5.40	18.00
Special-Meteor (1/80)	1.20	3.60	12.00
Special-Moonraker (10/79)	1.20	3.60	12.00
Special-Star Wars (1977)	2.20	6.60	22.00

WAR REPORT
Ajax/Farrell Publications (Excellent Publ.): Sept, 1952 - No. 5, May, 1953

	GD25	FN65	NM94
1	8.50	26.00	60.00
2	5.70	17.00	35.00
3-5: 4-Used in **POP**, pg. 94	5.00	15.00	30.00

WARRIOR (Wrestling star)
Ultimate Creations: May, 1996 - No. 4, 1997 ($2.95)

	GD25	FN65	NM94
1-4: Warrior scripts; Callahan-c/a. 3-Wraparound-c. 4-Warrior #3 in indicia; pin-ups			3.00
1-Variant-c.	.85	2.60	7.00

WARRIOR COMICS
H.C. Blackerby: 1945 (1930s DC reprints)

	GD25	FN65	NM94
1-Wing Brady, The Iron Man, Mark Markon	17.00	52.00	130.00

WARRIOR NUN AREALA
Antarctic Press: Dec, 1994 - No. 3, Apr, 1995 ($2.95, limited series)

	GD25	FN65	NM94
1	1.00	3.00	10.00
1-Special Edition (5000)	1.50	4.50	15.00
2-3	.85	2.60	7.00
3-Bagged w/CD	.85	2.60	7.00

WARRIOR NUN AREALA,
Antarctic Press: July, 1997 - No. 6, May, 1998 ($2.95)

	GD25	FN65	NM94
1-6-Lyga-s			2.95

WARRIOR NUN AREALA AND AVENGELYNE 1996 (See Avengelyne/...)
Antarctic Press: Dec, 1996 ($2.95)

	GD25	FN65	NM94
1			3.00

WARRIOR NUN AREALA AND GLORY,
Antarctic Press: Sept, 1997

	GD25	FN65	NM94
1-Ben Dunn-s/a ($2.95, color)			2.95
1-($5.95) Ltd. Poster Edition w/pin-ups			5.95

WARRIOR NUN AREALA: HAMMER AND THE HOLOCAUST
Antarctic Press: June, 1997- Present ($2.95)

	GD25	FN65	NM94
1,2			3.00

WARRIOR NUN AREALA: PORTRAITS,
Antarctic Press: Mar, 1996 ($3.95, one-shot)

	GD25	FN65	NM94
1-Pin-ups			4.00

WARRIOR NUN AREALA: RITUALS,
Antarctic Press: July, 1995 - No. 6, June, 1996 ($2.95/$3.50)

	GD25	FN65	NM94
1-5			3.00
6-($3.50)			3.50

WARRIOR NUN AREALA: SCORPIO ROSE
Antarctic Press: Sept, 1996 - No. 4, Mar, 1997 ($2.95, color)

	GD25	FN65	NM94
1-4			3.00

WARRIOR NUN AREALA VS. RAZOR (See Razor/...)

Warrior Nun Frenzy #2 © Antarctic Press

Warstrike #1 © MAL

Watchmen #12 © DC

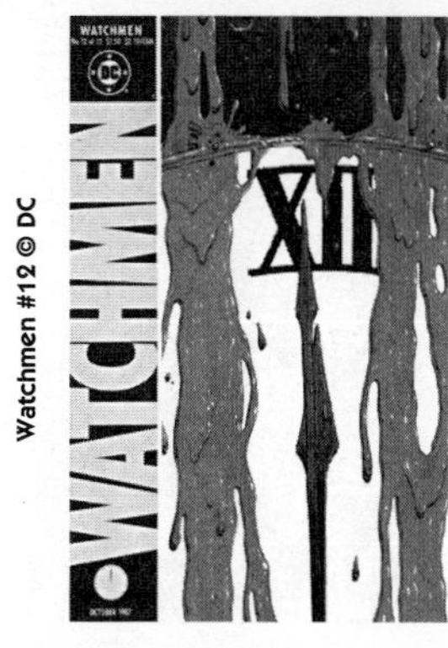

	GD25	FN65	NM94
Antarctic Press: May, 1996 ($3.95, one-shot)			
1-Dunn-c/a			4.00
1-($9.95)-Comic polybagged w/CD			10.00

WARRIOR NUN: BLACK AND WHITE,
Antarctic Press: Feb, 1997 - Present ($2.95, B&W)

1-17 — 3.00

WARRIOR NUN DEI: AFTERTIME
Antarctic Press: Jan, 1997 - No. 2, ($2.95)

1-2-Patrick Thornton-s/a — 3.00

WARRIOR NUN: FRENZY
Antarctic Press: Jan, 1998 - No. 2, Jun, 1998 ($2.95)

1,2: 1-Ribic painted-c/a. 2-Horvatic-s/a — 3.00

WARRIOR NUN: RHEINTÖCHTER
Antarctic Press: Dec, 1997 - No. 2, Apr, 1998 ($2.95, B&W, limited series)

1,2-Set in medieval Europe; Paquette & Lacombe-s/a — 3.00

WARRIOR OF WAVERLY STREET, THE
Dark Horse Comics: Nov, 1996 - No. 2, Dec, 1996 ($2.95, mini-series)

1,2-Darrow-c — 3.00

WARRIORS
CFD Productions: 1993 (B&W, one-shot)

	GD25	FN65	NM94
1-Linsner, Dark One-a	2.25	6.80	25.00

WARRIORS OF PLASM (Also see Plasm)
Defiant: Aug, 1993 - No. 13, Aug, 1995 ($2.95/$2.50)

	GD25	FN65	NM94
1-4: Shooter-scripts; Lapham-c/a: 1-1st app. Glory. 4-Bound-in fold-out poster			3.00
5-7,10-13: 5-Begin $2.50-c. 13-Schism issue			2.50
8,9-($2.75, 44 pgs.)			2.75
The Collected Edition (2/94, $9.95)-r/Plasm #0, WOP #1-4 & Splatterball			10.00

WAR ROMANCES (See True...)

WAR SHIPS
Dell Publishing Co.: 1942 (36 pgs.)(Similar to Large Feature Comics)

	GD25	FN65	NM94
nn-Cover by McWilliams; contains photos & drawings of U.S. war ships	14.00	42.00	105.00

WAR STORIES (Formerly War Comics)
Dell Publ. Co.: No. 5, 1942(nd); No. 6, Aug-Oct, 1942 - No. 8, Feb-Apr, 1943

	GD25	FN65	NM94
5-Origin The Whistler	23.00	68.00	170.00
6-8: 6-8-Night Devils app. 8-Painted-c	17.00	50.00	125.00

WAR STORIES (Korea)
Ajax/Farrell Publications (Excellent Publ.): Sept, 1952 - No. 5, May, 1953

	GD25	FN65	NM94
1	9.00	27.00	55.00
2	4.25	13.00	28.00
3-5	4.00	12.00	24.00

WAR STORIES (See Star Spangled...)

WARSTRIKE
Malibu Comics (Ultraverse): May, 1994 - No. 7, Nov, 1995 ($1.95)

	GD25	FN65	NM94
1-7: 1-Simonson-c			2.00
1-Ultra 5000 Limited silver foil			4.00
Giant Size 1 (12/94, 2.50, 44pgs.)-Prelude to Godwheel			2.50

WART AND THE WIZARD (See The Sword & the Stone under Movie Comics)
Gold Key: Feb, 1964 (Walt Disney)(Characters from Sword in the Stone movie)

	GD25	FN65	NM94
1 (10102-402)	3.20	9.50	35.00

WARTIME ROMANCES
St. John Publishing Co.: July, 1951 - No. 18, Nov, 1953

	GD25	FN65	NM94
1-All Baker-c/a	27.00	80.00	200.00
2-All Baker-c/a	19.00	56.00	140.00
3,4-All Baker-c/a	16.00	48.00	120.00
5-8-Baker-c/a(2-3) each	14.00	42.00	105.00
9,11,12,16,18: Baker-c/a each. 9-Two signed stories by Estrada	11.00	32.00	80.00
10,13-15,17-Baker-c only	6.50	19.50	45.00

WAR VICTORY ADVENTURES (#1 titled War Victory Comics)
U.S. Treasury Dept./War Victory/Harvey Publ.: Summer, 1942 - No. 3, Winter, 1943-44 (5¢)

	GD25	FN65	NM94
1-(Promotion of Savings Bonds)-Featuring America's greatest comic art by top syndicated cartoonists; Blondie, Joe Palooka, Green Hornet, Dick Tracy, Superman, Gumps, etc.; (36 pgs.); all profits were contributed to U.S.O. & Army/Navy relief funds	32.00	96.00	240.00
2-Battle of Stalingrad story; Powell-a (8/43); flag-c	16.00	48.00	120.00
3-Capt. Red Cross-c & text only; Powell-a	15.00	44.00	110.00

WAR WAGON, THE (See Movie Classics)

WAR WINGS
Charlton Comics: Oct, 1968

	GD25	FN65	NM94
1	1.75	5.25	14.00

WARWORLD!
Dark Horse Comics: Feb, 1989 ($1.75, B&W, one-shot)

1-Gary Davis sci/fi art in Moebius style — 1.80

WARZONE
Entity Comics: 1995 ($2.95, B&W)

1-3 — 3.00

WASHABLE JONES AND THE SHMOO (Also see Al Capp's Shmoo)
Toby Press: June, 1953

	GD25	FN65	NM94
1- "Super-Shmoo"	18.00	54.00	135.00

WASH TUBBS (See The Comics, Crackajack Funnies)
Dell Publishing Co.: No. 11, 1942 - No. 53, 1944

	GD25	FN65	NM94
Four Color 11 (#1)	27.00	80.00	295.00
Four Color 28 (1943)	20.00	59.00	215.00
Four Color 53	14.00	44.00	160.00

WASTELAND
DC Comics: Dec, 1987 - No. 18, May, 1989 ($1.75-$2.00 #13 on, mature)

1-5(4/88), 5(5/88), 6(5/88)-18: 13,15-Orlando-a — 2.00

NOTE: *Orlando a-12, 13, 15. Truman a-10; c-13.*

WATCHMEN
DC Comics: Sept, 1986 - No. 12, Oct, 1987 (maxi-series)

	GD25	FN65	NM94
1-Alan Moore scripts & Dave Gibbons-c/a in all			5.00
2-12			3.00
Hardcover Collection-Slip-cased-r/#1-12 w/new material; produced by Graphitti Designs	4.50	13.50	50.00
Trade paperback (1987, $14.95)-r/#1-12			15.00

WATCH OUT FOR BIG TALK
Giveaway: 1950

	GD25	FN65	NM94
nn-Dan Barry-a; about crooked politicians	4.25	13.00	26.00

WATER BIRDS AND THE OLYMPIC ELK (Disney)
Dell Publishing Co.: No. 700, Apr, 1956

	GD25	FN65	NM94
Four Color 700-Movie	4.50	13.50	50.00

WATERWORLD: CHILDREN OF LEVIATHAN
Acclaim Comics: Aug, 1997 - No. 4, Nov, 1997 ($2.50, mini-series)

1-4 — 2.50

WEAPON X
Marvel Comics: Apr, 1994 ($12.95, one-shot)

nn-r/Marvel Comics Presents #72-84 — 13.00

Weasel Guy/Witchblade #1 © Hyperwerks / Top Cow

The Web #14 © DC

Web of Spider-Man #116 © MAR

GD25 FN65 NM94

WEAPON X
Marvel Comics: Mar, 1995 - No. 4, June, 1995 ($1.95)

1-Age of Apocalypse 4.20
2-4 2.00

WEAPON ZERO
Image Comics (Top Cow Productions): No. T-4(#1), June, 1995 - No. T-0(#5), Dec, 1995 ($2.50, limited series)

T-4(#1): Walt Simonson scripts in all. .85 2.60 7.00
T-3(#2) - T-1(#4) 5.00
T-0(#5) 4.00

WEAPON ZERO
Image Comics (Top Cow Productions): V2#1, Mar, 1996 - No. 15, Dec, 1997 ($2.50)

V2#1-Walt Simonson scripts. 4.00
2-10: 8-Begin Top Cow. 10-Devil's Reign 3.00
11-14 2.50
15-($3.50) Benitez-a 3.50

WEAPON ZERO/SILVER SURFER
Image Comics/Marvel Comics: Jan, 1997($2.95, one-shot)

1-Devil's Reign Pt. 1 3.00

WEASELGUY/WITCHBLADE
Hyperwerks: July, 1998($2.95, one-shot)

1-Steve Buccellato-s/a; covers by Matsuda and Altstaetter. 3.00

WEASEL PATROL SPECIAL, THE (Also see Fusion #17)
Eclipse Comics: Apr, 1989 ($2.00, B&W, one-shot)

1-Funny animal 2.00

WEATHER-BIRD (See Comics From..., Dick Tracy, Free Comics to You... Super Circus & Terry and the Pirates)
International Shoe Co./Western Printing Co.: 1958 - No. 16, July, 1962 (Shoe store giveaway)

1 2.50 7.50 22.00
2-16 1.50 4.50 12.00
NOTE: *The numbers are located in the lower bottom panel, pg. 1. All feature a character called Weather-Bird.*

WEATHER BIRD COMICS (See Comics From Weather Bird)
Weather Bird Shoes: 1957 (Giveaway)

nn-Contains a comic bound with new cover. Several combinations possible; contents determines price (40 - 60 percent of contents).

WEAVEWORLD
Marvel Comics (Epic): Dec, 1991 - No. 3, 1992 ($4.95, lim. series, 68 pgs.)

1-3: Clive Barker adaptation 5.00

WEB, THE (Also see Mighty Comics & Mighty Crusaders)
DC Comics (Impact Comics): Sept, 1991 - No. 14, Oct, 1992 ($1.00)

1-14: 5-The Fly x-over 9-Trading card inside 1.00
Annual 1 (1992, $2.50, 68 pgs.)-With Trading card 2.50
NOTE: ***Gil Kane** c-5, 9, 10, 12-14. **Bill Wray** a(i)-1-9, 10(part).*

WEB OF EVIL
Comic Magazines/Quality Comics Group: Nov, 1952 - No. 21, Dec, 1954

1-Used in **SOTI**, pg. 388. Jack Cole-a; morphine use story 47.00 142.00 400.00
2-4,6,7: 2,3-Jack Cole-a. 4,6,7-Jack Cole-c/a 36.00 108.00 270.00
5-Electrocution-c/story; Jack Cole-c/a 39.00 117.00 310.00
8-11-Jack Cole-a 31.00 92.00 230.00
12,13,15,16,19-21 17.00 50.00 125.00
14-Part Crandall-c; Old Witch swipe 18.00 54.00 135.00
17-Opium drug propaganda story 17.00 50.00 125.00
18-Acid-in-face story 19.00 56.00 140.00
NOTE: ***Jack Cole** a(2 each)-2, 6, 8, 9. **Cuidera** c-1-21i. **Ravielli** a-13.*

GD25 FN65 NM94

WEB OF HORROR
Major Magazines: Dec, 1969 - No. 3, Apr, 1970 (Magazine)

1-Jeff Jones painted-c; Wrightson-a, Kaluta-a 8.00 24.00 80.00
2-Jones painted-c; Wrightson-a(2), Kaluta-a 5.50 16.50 55.00
3-Wrightson-c/a (1st published-c); Brunner, Kaluta, Bruce Jones-a 5.00 15.00 50.00

WEB OF MYSTERY
Ace Magazines (A. A. Wyn): Feb, 1951 - No. 29, Sept, 1955

1 43.00 129.00 345.00
2-Bakerish-a 23.00 68.00 170.00
3-10: 4-Colan-a 21.00 64.00 160.00
11-18,20-26: 12-John Chilly's 1st cover art. 13-Surrealistic-c. 20-r/The Beyond #1 19.00 56.00 140.00
19-Reprints Challenge of the Unknown #6 used in N.Y. Legislative Committee 19.00 56.00 140.00
27-Bakerish-a(r/The Beyond #2); last pre-code ish 18.00 54.00 135.00
28,29: 28-All-r 13.00 40.00 100.00
NOTE: *This series was to appear as "Creepy Stories", but title was changed before publication. **Cameron** a-6, 8, 11-13, 17-20, 22, 24, 25, 27; c-8, 13, 17. **Palais** a-28r. **Sekowsky** a-1-3, 7, 8, 11, 14, 21, 29. **Tothish** a-by **Bill Discount** #16. 29-all-r, 19-28-partial-r.*

WEB OF SCARLET SPIDER
Marvel Comics: Oct, 1995 - No. 4, Jan, 1996 ($1.95, limited series)

1-4: Replaces "Web of Spider-Man" 2.00

WEB OF SPIDER-MAN (Replaces Marvel Team-Up)
Marvel Comics Group: Apr, 1985 - No. 129, Sept, 1995

1-Painted-c (5th app. black costume?) 1.00 3.00 10.00
2,3 4.00
4-8: 7-Hulk x-over; Wolverine splash 4.00
9-13: 10-Dominic Fortune guest stars; painted-c 4.00
14-28: 18-1st app. Venom (behind the scenes, 9/86). 19-Intro Humbug & Solo 3.00
29-Wolverine, new Hobgoblin (Macendale) app. 4.00
30-Origin recap The Rose & Hobgoblin I (entire book is flashback story); Punisher & Wolverine cameo 3.00
31,32-Six part Kraven storyline begins 3.00
33-37,39-47,49: 36-1st app. Tombstone (cameo) 2.00
38-Hobgoblin app.; begin $1.00-c 4.00
48-Origin Hobgoblin II(Demogoblin) cont'd from Spectacular Spider-Man #147; Kingpin app. .90 2.70 9.00
50-($1.50, 52 pgs.) 1.50
51-58 1.50
59-Cosmic Spidey cont'd from Spect. Spider-Man 3.00
60-65,68-85,87-89,91-94: 69,70-Hulk x-over. 74-76-Austin-c(i). 76-Fantastic Four x-over. 78-Cloak & Dagger app. 81-Origin/1st app. Bloodshed. 84-Begin 6 part Rose & Hobgoblin II storyline; last $1.00-c. 93-Gives brief history of Hobgoblin. 93,94-Hobgoblin (Macendale) Reborn-c/story, parts 1,2; Moon Knight app. 94-Venom cameo 1.50
66,67-Green Goblin (Norman Osborn) app. as a super-hero 1.50
86-Demon leaves Hobgoblin; 1st Demogoblin 1.50
90-($2.95, 52 pgs.)-Polybagged w/silver hologram-c, gatefold poster showing Spider-Man & Spider-Man 2099 (Williamson-i) 2.00
90-2nd printing; gold hologram-c 1.50
95-Begin 4 part x-over w/Spirits of Venom w/Ghost Rider/Blaze/Spidey vs. Venom & Demogoblin (cont'd in Ghost Rider/Blaze #5,6) 1.50
96-99,101-106: 96-Spirits of Venom part 3; painted-c. 101,103-Maximum Carnage x-over. 103-Venom & Carnage app. 104-106-Nightwatch back-up stories 1.50
100-($2.95, 52 pgs.)-Holo-grafx foil-c; intro new Spider-Armor 4.00
107-111: 107-Intro Sandstorm; Sand & Quicksand app. 1.25
112-116, 118, 119, 121-124, 126-129: 112-Begin $1.50-c; bound-in trading card sheet. 113-Regular Ed.; Gambit & Black Cat app. 118-1st solo clone story; Venom app 1.50
113 ($2.95)-Collector's ed. polybagged w/foil-c; 16 pg. preview of Spider-Man

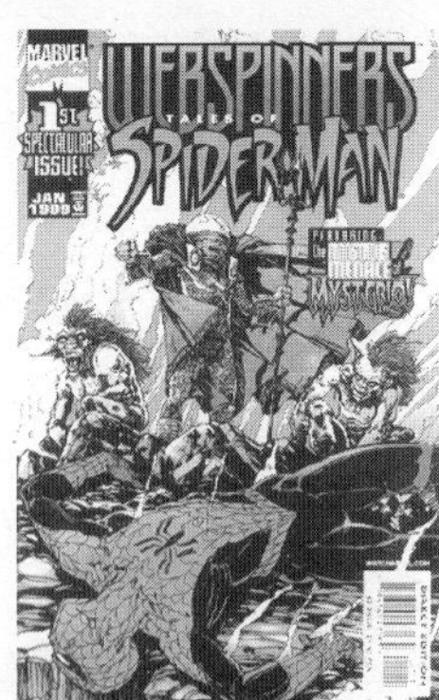

Webspinners: Tales of Spider-Man #1 -MAR

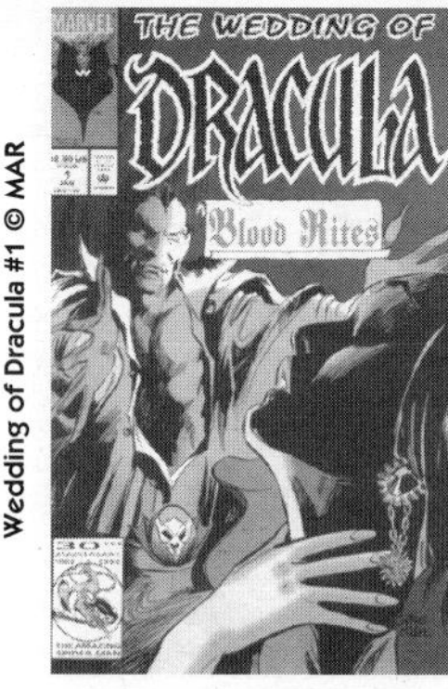

Wedding of Dracula #1 © MAR

Weird Comics #5 © FOX

GD25 FN65 NM94

cartoon & animation cel 2.00
117 ($1.50)-Flip book; Power & Responsibility Pt.1 1.50
117 ($2.95)-Collector's edition; foil-c; flip book 2.00
119 ($6.45)-Direct market edition; polybagged w/ Marvel Milestone Amazing Spider-Man #150 & coupon for Amazing Spider-Man #396, Spider-Man #53, & Spectacular Spider-Man #219. 4.00
120 ($2.25)-Flip book w/ preview of the Ultimate Spider-Man 2.25
125 ($3.95)-Holodisk-c; Gwen Stacy clone 4.00
125 ($2.95)-Newsstand 3.00
Annual 1 (1985) 3.00
Annual 2 (1986)-New Mutants; Art Adams-a .90 2.70 8.00
Annual 3 (1987) 3.00
Annual 4 (1988, $1.75)-Evolutionary War x-over 3.50
Annual 5 (1989, $2.00, 68 pgs.)-Atlantis Attacks; Captain Universe by Ditko (p) & Silver Sable stories; F.F. app. 2.75
Annual 6 ('90, $2.00, 68 pgs.)-Punisher back-up plus Capt. Universe by Ditko; G. Kane-a 2.75
Annual 7 (1991, $2.00, 68 pgs.)-Origins of Hobgoblin I, Hobgoblin II, Green Goblin I & II & Venom; Larsen/Austin-c 2.75
Annual 8 (1992, $2.25, 68 pgs.)-Part 3 of Venom story; New Warriors x-over; Black Cat back-up story 2.75
Annual 9 (1993, $2.95, 68 pgs.)-Bagged w/card 3.00
Annual 10 (1994, $2.95, 68 pgs.) 3.00
Super Special 1 (1995, $3.95)-flip book 4.00
NOTE: ***Art Adams** a-Annual 2. **Byrne** c-3-6. **Chaykin** c-10. **Mignola** a-Annual 2. **Vess** c-1, 8, Annual 1, 2. **Zeck** a-6i, 31, 32; c-31, 32.*

WEBSPINNERS: TALES OF SPIDER-MAN
Marvel Comics: Jan, 1999 - Present ($2.99/$2.50)

1-DeMatteis-s/Zulli-a; back-up story w/Romita Sr. art 3.00

WEDDING BELLS
Quality Comics Group: Feb, 1954 - No. 19, Nov, 1956

1-Whitney-a 12.00 36.00 90.00
2 7.15 21.50 50.00
3-9: 8-Last precode (4/55) 5.00 15.00 30.00
10-Ward-a (9 pgs.) 11.00 32.00 80.00
11-14,17 4.00 12.00 24.00
15-Baker-c 5.00 15.00 30.00
16-Baker-c/a 7.15 21.50 50.00
18,19-Baker-a each 5.70 17.00 40.00

WEDDING OF DRACULA
Marvel Comics: Jan, 1993 ($2.00, 52 pgs.)

1-Reprints Tomb of Dracula #30,45,46 2.00

WEEKENDER, THE (Illustrated...)
Rucker Pub. Co.: V1#3, Sept, 1945 - V1#4, Nov, 1945; V2#1, Jan, 1946 (52 pgs.)

V1#3,4: 3-Super hero-c. 4-Same-c as Punch Comics #10 (9/44); r/Hale the Magician (7 pgs.) & r/Mr. E (8 pgs.-Lou Fine? or Gustavson?) plus 3 humor strips & many B&W photos & r/newspaper articles plus cheesecake photos of Hollywood stars 13.00 40.00 100.00
V2#1-36 pgs. comics, 16 in newspaper format with photos; partial Dynamic Comics reprints; 4 pgs. of cels from the Disney film Pinocchio; Little Nemo story by Winsor McCay, Jr.; Jack Cole-a; same-c as Dynamic #11 16.00 48.00 120.00

WEEKLY COMIC MAGAZINE
Fox Publications: May 12, 1940 (16 pgs.) (Others exist w/o super-heroes)

(1st Version)-8 pg. Blue Beetle story, 7 pg. Patty O'Day story; two copies known to exist. Estimated value... 500.00
(2nd Version)-7 two-pg. adventures of Blue Beetle, Patty O'Day, Yarko, Dr. Fung, Green Mask, Spark Stevens, & Rex Dexter; one copy known to exist. Estimated value... 400.00
Discovered with business papers, letters and exploitation material promoting **Weekly Comic Magazine** for use by newspapers in the same manner of **The Spirit** weeklies. Interesting note: these are dated three weeks before the first Spirit comic. Letters indicate that samples may have been sent to a few newspapers. These sections were actually 15-1/2x22" pages which will fold down to an approximate 8x10" comic booklet. Other various comic sections were found with the above, but were more like the Sunday comic sections in format.

GD25 FN65 NM94

WEEZUL
Lightning Comics: Aug, 1996 ($2.75/$3.00, B&W)

1-($2.75) 2.75
1b-($3.00) 3.00
1-($9.95) Commemorative Edition 1.25 3.75 10.00

WEIRD
Eerie Publications: V1#10, 1/66 - V8#6, 12/74; V9#1, 1/75 - V11#4, Dec, 1978 (Magazine) (V1-V8: 52 pgs.; V9 on: 68 pgs.)

V1#10(#1)-Intro. Morris the Caretaker of Weird (ends V2#10); Burgos-a 5.50 16.50 55.00
11,12 3.20 9.60 32.00
V2#1-4(10/67), V3#1(1/68), V2#6(4/68)-V2#7,9,10(12/68), V3#1(2/69)-V3#4 3.20 9.60 32.00
V2#8-r/Ditko's 1st story/Fantastic Fears #5 4.50 13.50 45.00
5(12/69)-Rulah reprint; "Rulah" changed to "Pulah", LSD story reprinted in Horror Tales V4#4, Tales From the Tomb V2#4, & 20 9.60 32.00
V4#1-6('70), V5#1-6('71), V6#1-7('72), V7#1-7('73), V8#1-6('74), V9#1-4 (1/75-'76), V10#1-3('77), V11#1-4 3.20 9.60 32.00
NOTE: *V9#4 (12/76) has a cover swipe from Horror Tales V5#1 (2/73).*

WEIRD
DC Comics (Paradox Press): Sum, 1997 - Present ($2.99, B&W, magazine)

1 3.00

WEIRD, THE
DC Comics: Apr, 1988 - No. 4, July, 1988 ($1.50, limited series)

1-4: Wrightson-c/a in all 2.00

WEIRD ADVENTURES
P. L. Publishing Co. (Canada): May-June, 1951 - No. 3, Sept-Oct, 1951

1- "The She-Wolf Killer" by Matt Baker (6 pgs.) 43.00 129.00 350.00
2-Bondage/hypodermic panel 37.00 110.00 275.00
3-Male bondage/torture-c; severed head story 33.00 98.00 245.00

WEIRD ADVENTURES
Ziff-Davis Publishing Co.: No. 10, July-Aug, 1951

10-Painted-c 35.00 104.00 260.00

WEIRD CHILLS
Key Publications: July, 1954 - No. 3, Nov, 1954

1-Wolverton-r/Weird Mysteries No. 4; blood transfusion-c by Baily 56.00 168.00 475.00
2-Extremely violent injury to eye-c by Baily; Hitler story 56.00 168.00 475.00
3-Bondage E.C. swipe-c by Baily 39.00 116.00 290.00

WEIRD COMICS
Fox Features Syndicate: Apr, 1940 - No. 20, Jan, 1942

1-The Birdman, Thor, God of Thunder (ends #5), The Sorceress of Zoom, Blast Bennett, Typhon, Voodoo Man, & Dr. Mortal begin; Lou Fine bondage-c 379.00 1137.00 3600.00
2-Lou Fine-c 182.00 547.00 1550.00
3,4: 3-Simon-c. 4-Torture-c 103.00 309.00 875.00
5-Intro. Dart & sidekick Ace (8/40) (ends #20); bondage/hypo-c 106.00 318.00 900.00
6,7-Dynamite Thor app. in each. 6-Super hero covers begin 82.00 247.00 700.00
8-Dynamo, the Eagle (11/40, early app.; see Science #1) & sidekick Buddy & Marga, the Panther Woman begin 82.00 247.00 700.00
9,10: 10-Navy Jones app. 68.00 203.00 575.00
11-19: 16-Flag-c. 17-Origin The Black Rider. 50.00 150.00 425.00
20-Origin The Rapier; Swoop Curtis app; Churchill & Hitler-c

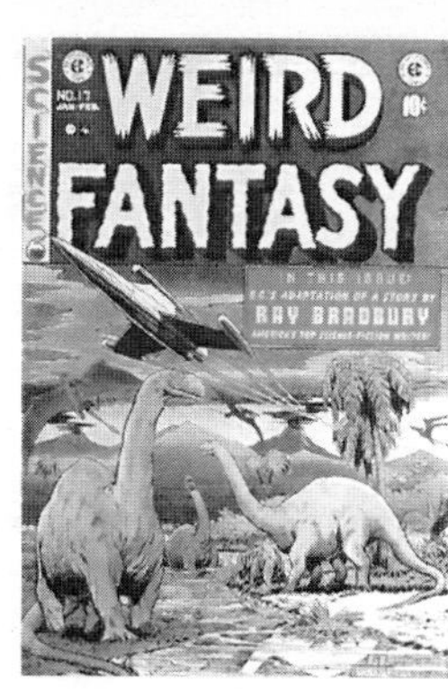

Weird Fantasy #17 © WMG

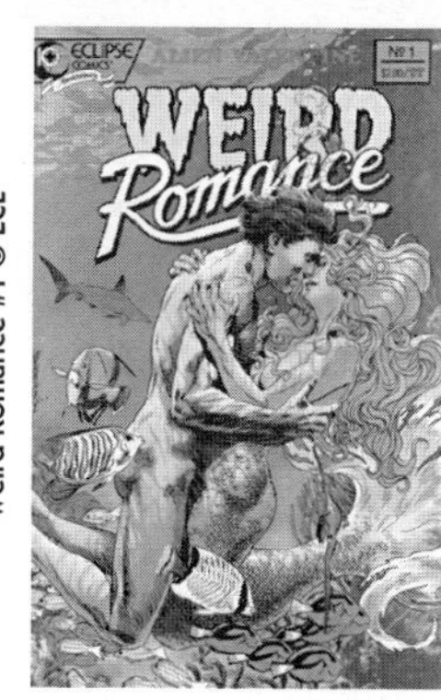

Weird Romance #1 © ECL

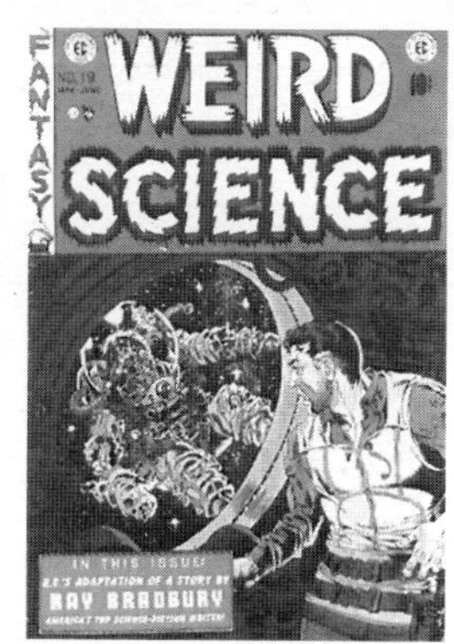

Weird Science #19 © WMG

	GD25	FN65	NM94
	56.00	168.00	475.00

NOTE *Cover features: Sorceress of Zoom-4; Dr. Mortal-5; Dart & Ace-6-13, 15; Eagle-14, 16-20.*

WEIRD FANTASY (Formerly A Moon, A Girl, Romance; becomes Weird Science-Fantasy #23 on)
E. C. Comics: No. 13, May-June, 1950 - No. 22, Nov-Dec, 1953

	GD25	FN65	NM94
13(#1) (1950)	158.00	474.00	1500.00
14-Necronomicon story; cosmic ray bomb explosion-c	58.00	174.00	600.00
15,16: 16-Used in **SOTI**, pg. 144	47.00	141.00	475.00
17 (1951)	41.00	123.00	400.00
6-10: 6-Robot-c	32.00	96.00	290.00
11-13 (1952): 12-E.C. artists cameo. 13-Anti-Wertham "Cosmic Correspondence"	27.00	81.00	230.00
14-Frazetta/Williamson(1st team-up at E.C.)/Krenkel-a (7 pgs.); Orlando draws E.C. staff; "Cosmic Ray Bomb Explosion" by Feldstein stars Gaines & Feldstein	38.00	114.00	340.00
15-Williamson/Evans-a(3), 4,3,&7 pgs.	27.00	81.00	230.00
16-19-Williamson/Krenkel-a in all. 18-Williamson/Feldstein-c	25.00	75.00	220.00
20-Frazetta/Williamson-a (7 pgs.)	27.00	81.00	230.00
21-Frazetta/Williamson-c & Williamson/Krenkel-a	38.00	114.00	340.00
22-Bradbury adaptation	18.00	54.00	160.00

NOTE: ***Ray Bradbury** adaptations-13, 17-20, 22. **Crandall** a-22. **Elder** a-17. **Feldstein** a-13(#1)-8; c-13(#1)-18 (#18 w/**Williamson**), 20. **Harrison/Wood** a-13. **Kamen** a-13(#1)-16, 18-22. **Krigstein** a-22. **Kurtzman** a-13(#1)-17(#5), 6. **Orlando** a-9-22 (2 stories in #16); c-19, 22. **Severin/Elder** a-18-21. **Wood** a-13(#1)-14, 17(2 stories ea. in #10-13). Ray Bradbury adaptations in #17-19, 22. Canadian reprints exist; see Table of Contents.*

WEIRD FANTASY
Russ Cochran/Gemstone Publ.: Oct, 1992 - No. 22, Jan, 1998 ($1.50/$2.00/$2.50)

1,2: 1,2-r/Weird Fantasy #13,14; Feldstein-c			2.00
3-15: 3-5-r/Weird Fantasy #15-17			2.00
16-22			2.50

WEIRD HORRORS (Nightmare #10 on)
St. John Publishing Co.: June, 1952 - No. 9, Oct, 1953

1-Tuska-a	43.00	129.00	350.00
2,3: 3-Hashish story	26.00	78.00	195.00
4,5	22.00	66.00	165.00
6-Ekgren-c; atomic bomb story	39.00	117.00	300.00
7-Ekgren-c; Kubert, Cameron-a	43.00	129.00	345.00
8,9-Kubert-c/a	34.00	102.00	255.00

NOTE: ***Cameron** a-7, 9. **Finesque** a-1-5. **Forgione** a-6. **Morisi** a-3. Bondage c-8.*

WEIRD MYSTERIES
Gillmore Publications: Oct, 1952 - No. 12, Sept, 1954

1-Partial Wolverton-c swiped from splash page "Flight to the Future" in Weird Tales of the Future #2; "Eternity" has an Ingels swipe	60.00	180.00	510.00
2- "Robot Woman" by Wolverton; Bernard Baily-c reprinted in Mister Mystery #18; acid in face panel	82.00	247.00	700.00
3,6: Both have decapitation-c	43.00	129.00	350.00
4- "The Man Who Never Smiled" (3 pgs.) by Wolverton; B. Baily skull-c	75.00	226.00	640.00
5-Wolverton story "Swamp Monster" (6 pgs.)	72.00	217.00	615.00
7-Used in **SOTI**, illo "Indeed", illo "Sex and blood"	62.00	185.00	525.00
8-Wolverton-c panel-r/#5; used in a '54 Readers Digest anti-comics article by T. E. Murphy entitled "For the Kiddies to Read"	43.00	129.00	350.00
9-Excessive violence, gore & torture	42.00	127.00	340.00
10-Silhouetted nudity panel	37.00	112.00	280.00
11,12: 12-r/Mr. Mystery #8(2), Weird Mysteries #3 & Weird Tales of the Future #6	35.00	104.00	260.00

NOTE: ***Baily** c-2-12. Anti-Wertham column in #5. #1-12 all have 'The Ghoul Teacher' (host).*

WEIRD MYSTERIES (Magazine)
Pastime Publications: Mar-Apr, 1959 (35¢, B&W, 68 pgs.)

	GD25	FN65	NM94
1-Torres-a; E. C. swipe from Tales From the Crypt #46 by Tuska "The Ragman"	5.70	17.00	40.00

WEIRD MYSTERY TALES (See DC 100 Page Super Spectacular)

WEIRD MYSTERY TALES (See Cancelled Comic Cavalcade)
National Periodical Publications: July-Aug, 1972 - No. 24, Nov, 1975

1-Kirby-a; Wrightson splash pg.	3.20	9.50	35.00
2,3,21: 21-Wrightson-c	1.60	4.80	16.00
4-10	1.10	3.30	11.00
11-20,22-24	.90	2.70	9.00

NOTE: ***Alcala** a-5, 10, 13, 14. **Aparo** c-4. **Bailey** a-8. **Bolle** a-8?. **Howard** a-4. **Kaluta** a-4, 24; c-1. **G. Kane** a-10. **Kirby** a-1, 2p, 3p. **Nino** a-5, 6, 9, 13, 16, 21. **Redondo** a-9, 17. **Sparling** c-6. **Starlin** a-3?, 4. **Wood** a-23.*

WEIRD ROMANCE (Seduction of the Innocent #9)
Eclipse Comics: Feb, 1988 ($2.00, B&W)

1-Pre-code horror-r; Lou Cameron-r(2)			2.00

WEIRD SCIENCE (Formerly Saddle Romances) (Becomes Weird Science-Fantasy #23 on)
E. C. Comics: No. 12, May-June, 1950 - No. 22, Nov-Dec, 1953

12(#1) (1950)-"Lost in the Microcosm" classic-c/story by Kurtzman	158.00	474.00	1500.00
13-Flying saucers over Washington-c/story, 2 years before the actual event	65.00	195.00	660.00
14-Robot-c/story by Feldstein	65.00	195.00	660.00
15 (1950)	65.00	195.00	660.00
5-10: 5-Atomic explosion-c	38.00	114.00	350.00
11-14 (1952): 12- "Dream of Doom" stars Gaines & E.C. artists	27.00	81.00	230.00
15-18-Williamson/Krenkel-a in each; 15-Williamson-a. 17-Used in **POP**, pgs. 81,82. 18-Bill Gaines doll app. in story	29.00	87.00	250.00
19,20-Williamson/Frazetta-a (7 pgs. each). 19-Used in **SOTI**, illo "A young girl on her wedding night stabs her sleeping husband to death with a hatpin..."	38.00	114.00	325.00
21-Williamson/Frazetta-a (6 pgs.); Wood draws E.C. staff; Gaines & Feldstein app. in story	38.00	114.00	325.00
22-Williamson/Frazetta/Krenkel/Krigstein-a (8 pgs.); Wood draws himself in his story (last pg. & panel)	38.00	114.00	325.00

NOTE: ***Elder** a-14, 19. **Evans** a-22. **Feldstein** a-12(#1)-8; c-12(#1)-8, 11. **Ingels** a-15. **Kamen** a-12(#1)-13, 15-18, 20, 21. **Kurtzman** a-12(#1)-7. **Orlando** a-10-22. **Wood** a-12(#1), 13(#2), 5-22 (#9, 10, 12, 13 all have 2 **Wood** stories); c-9, 10, 12-22. Canadian reprints exist; see Table of Contents. Ray Bradbury adaptations in #17-20.*

WEIRD SCIENCE
Gladstone Publishing: Sept, 1990 - No. 4, Mar, 1991 ($1.95/$2.00, 68 pgs.)

1-4: Wood-c(r); all reprints in each			3.00

WEIRD SCIENCE
Russ Cochran/Gemstone Publishing: Sept, 1992 - No. 22, Dec, 1997 ($1.50/$2.00/$2.50)

1,2: r/Weird Science #12,13 w/original-c			2.00
3-16: 3,4-r/#14,15. 5-7-w/original-c.			2.00
17-22			2.50

WEIRD SCIENCE-FANTASY (Formerly Weird Science & Weird Fantasy) (Becomes Incredible Science Fiction #30)
E. C. Comics: No. 23 Mar, 1954 - No. 29, May-June, 1955 (#23,24: 15¢)

23-Williamson, Wood-a; Bradbury adaptation	27.00	81.00	230.00
24-Williamson & Wood-a; Harlan Ellison's 1st professional story, "Upheaval!", later adapted into a short story as "Mealtime", and then into a TV episode of Voyage to the Bottom of the Sea as "The Price of Doom"	27.00	81.00	230.00
25-Williamson-c; Williamson/Torres/Krenkel-a plus Wood-a; Bradbury adaptation; cover price back to 10¢	30.00	90.00	260.00
26-Flying Saucer Report; Wood, Crandall-a; A-bomb panels	25.00	75.00	220.00

EC
WEIRD
SCIENCE-FANTASY
NO. 29 JUNE
10¢

Weird Science-Fantasy #29 © WMG

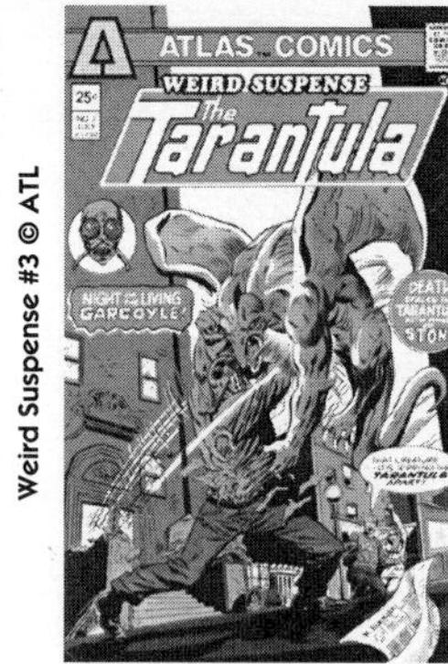

Weird Suspense #3 © ATL

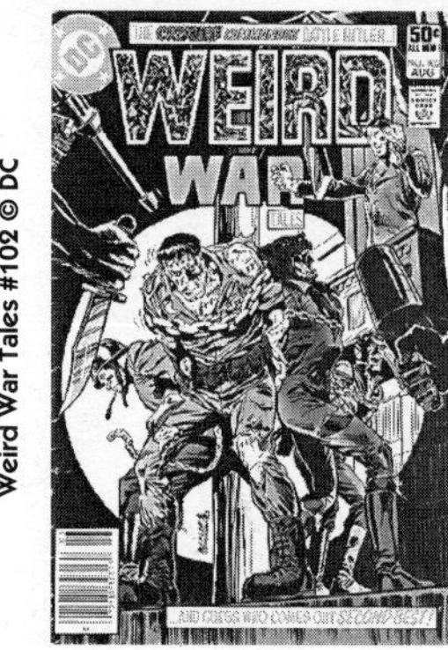

Weird War Tales #102 © DC

	GD25	FN65	NM94
27-Adam Link/I Robot series begins?	27.00	81.00	230.00
28-Williamson/Krenkel/Torres-a; Wood-a	29.00	87.00	250.00
29-Frazetta-c; Williamson/Krenkel & Wood-a; last pre-code issue; new logo	42.00	126.00	450.00

NOTE: ***Crandall*** *a-26, 27, 29.* ***Evans*** *a-26.* ***Feldstein*** *c-24, 26, 28.* ***Kamen*** *a-27, 28.* ***Krigstein*** *a-23-25.* ***Orlando*** *a-in all.* ***Wood*** *a-in all; c-23, 27. The cover to #29 was originally intended for Famous Funnies #217 (Buck Rogers), but was rejected for being "too violent."*

WEIRD SCIENCE-FANTASY
Russ Cochran/Gemstone Publishing: Nov, 1992 - No. 7, May , 1994 ($1.50/$2.00/$2.50)

	GD25	FN65	NM94
1,2: r/Weird Science-Fantasy #23,24			2.00
3-7: r/#25-29			2.50

WEIRD SCIENCE-FANTASY ANNUAL
E. C. Comics: 1952, 1953 (Sold thru the E. C. office & on the stands in some major cities) (25¢, 132 pgs.)

	GD25	FN65	NM94
1952-Feldstein-c	162.00	488.00	1500.00
1953-Feldstein-c	100.00	300.00	950.00

NOTE: *The 1952 annual contains books cover-dated in 1951 & 1952, and the 1953 annual from 1952 & 1953. Contents of each annual may vary in same year.*

WEIRD SUSPENSE
Atlas/Seaboard Publ.: Feb, 1975 - No. 3, July, 1975

	GD25	FN65	NM94
1-3: 1-Tarantula begins.			4.00

NOTE: ***Buckler*** *c-1, 3.*

WEIRD SUSPENSE STORIES (Canadian reprint of Crime SuspenStories #1-3; see Table of Contents)

WEIRD TALES ILLUSTRATED
Millennium Publications: 1992 - No. 2, 1992 ($2.95, high quality paper)

	GD25	FN65	NM94
1,2-Bolton painted-c. 1-Adapts E.A. Poe & Harlan Ellison stories. 2-E.A. Poe & H.P. Lovecraft adaptations			3.50
1-($4.95, 52 pgs.)-Deluxe edition w/Tim Vigil-a not in regular #1; stiff-c; Bolton painted-c			5.00

WEIRD TALES OF THE FUTURE
S.P.M. Publ. No. 1-4/Aragon Publ. No. 5-8: Mar, 1952 - No. 8, July-Aug, 1953

	GD25	FN65	NM94
1-Andru-a(2); Wolverton partial-c	68.00	205.00	580.00
2,3-Wolverton-c/a(3) each. 2- "Jumpin Jupiter" satire by Wolverton begins, ends #5	110.00	330.00	860.00
4- "Jumpin Jupiter" satire & "The Man From the Moon" by Wolverton; partial Wolverton-c	69.00	208.00	590.00
5-Wolverton-c/a(2); "Jumpin Jupiter" satire	101.00	304.00	860.00
6-Bernard Baily-c	43.00	129.00	350.00
7- "The Mind Movers" from the art to Wolverton's "Brain Bats of Venus" from Mr. Mystery #7 which was cut apart, pasted up, partially redrawn, and rewritten by Harry Kantor, the editor; Baily-c	64.00	191.00	540.00
8-Reprints Weird Mysteries #1(10/52) minus cover; gory cover showing heart ripped out by B. Baily	51.00	152.00	430.00

WEIRD TALES OF THE MACABRE (Magazine)
Atlas/Seaboard Publ.: Jan, 1975 - No. 2, Mar, 1975 (75¢, B&W)

	GD25	FN65	NM94
1-Jeff Jones painted-c	1.20	3.60	12.00
2-Boris Vallejo painted-c; Severin-a	1.80	5.40	18.00

WEIRD TERROR (Also see Horrific)
Allen Hardy Associates (Comic Media): Sept, 1952 - No. 13, Sept, 1954

	GD25	FN65	NM94
1- "Portrait of Death", adapted from Lovecraft's "Pickman's Model"; lingerie panels, Hitler story	39.00	118.00	315.00
2-Text on Marquis DeSade, Torture, Demonology, & St. Elmo's Fire	28.00	84.00	210.00
3-Extreme violence, whipping, torture; article on sin eating, dowsing	28.00	84.00	210.00
4-Dismemberment, decapitation, article on human flesh for sale, Devil, whipping	32.00	96.00	240.00
5-Article on body snatching, mutilation; cannibalism story	27.00	80.00	200.00
6-Dismemberment, decapitation, man hit by lightning	31.00	92.00	230.00
7-Body burning in fireplace-c	25.00	76.00	190.00
8-Decapitation story; Ambrose Bierce adapt.	29.00	88.00	220.00
9,10	23.00	70.00	175.00
11-End of the world story with atomic blast panels; Tothish-a by Bill Discount	29.00	88.00	220.00
12-Discount-a	22.00	66.00	165.00
13-Severed head panels	23.00	70.00	175.00

NOTE: ***Don Heck*** *a-most issues; c-1-13.* ***Landau*** *a-6.* ***Morisi*** *a-2-5, 7, 9, 12.* ***Palais*** *a-1, 5, 6, 8(2), 10, 12.* ***Powell*** *a-10.* ***Ravielli*** *a-11, 20.*

WEIRD THRILLERS
Ziff-Davis Publ. Co. (Approved Comics): Sept-Oct, 1951 - No. 5, Oct-Nov, 1952 (#2-5: painted-c)

	GD25	FN65	NM94
1-Rondo Hatton photo-c	62.00	185.00	525.00
2-Toth, Anderson, Colan-a	45.00	136.00	385.00
3-Two Powell, Tuska-a; classic-c	58.00	173.00	490.00
4-Kubert, Tuska-a	43.00	129.00	355.00
5-Powell-a	39.00	117.00	310.00

NOTE: ***M. Anderson*** *a-2, 3.* ***Roussos*** *a-4. #2, 3 reprinted in Nightmare #10 & 13; #4, 5 reprinted in Amazing Ghost Stories #16 & #15.*

WEIRD WAR TALES
National Periodical Publications/DC Comics: Sept-Oct, 1971 - No. 124, June, 1983 (#1-5: 52 pgs.)

	GD25	FN65	NM94
1-Kubert-a in #1-4,7; c-1-7	15.00	44.00	160.00
2,3-Drucker-a: 2-Crandall-a. 3-Heath-a	5.00	15.00	55.00
4,5: 5-Toth-a; Heath-a	4.00	12.25	45.00
6,7,9,10: 6,10-Toth-a. 7-Heath-a	2.20	6.50	24.00
8-Neal Adams-c/a(i)	3.50	10.50	38.00
11-20	1.50	4.50	15.00
21-35	1.00	3.00	10.00
36-(68 pgs.)-Crandall & Kubert-r/#2; Heath-r/#3; Kubert-c	1.40	4.20	14.00
37-63: 38-Kubert-c		2.00	6.00
64,68-Frank Miller-a in both. 64-Miller's 1st DC work	1.30	3.90	13.00
65-67,69-124: 93-Intro/origin Creature Commandos. 101-Intro/origin G.I. Robot			3.00

WEIRD WAR TALES
DC Comics (Vertigo): June, 1997 - No. 4, Sept, 1997 ($2.50)

	GD25	FN65	NM94
1-4-Anthology by various			2.50

WEIRD WESTERN TALES (Formerly All-Star Western)
National Per. Publ./DC Comics: No. 12, June-July, 1972 - No. 70, Aug, 1980

	GD25	FN65	NM94
12-(52 pgs.)-3rd app. Jonah Hex; Bat Lash, Pow Wow Smith reprints; El Diablo by Neal Adams/Wrightson	5.50	16.50	60.00
13-Jonah Hex-c (1st?) & 4th app.; Neal Adams-a	3.80	11.50	40.00
14,15: 14-Toth-a. 15-Adams-c/a; no Jonah Hex	2.20	6.25	22.00
16,17,19,20	1.40	4.20	14.00
18,29: 18-1st all Jonah Hex issue (7-8/73) & begins. 29-Origin Jonah Hex	2.20	6.25	22.00
21-28,30-38: Jonah Hex in all. 38-Last Jonah Hex	.90	2.70	8.00
39-Origin/1st app. Scalphunter & begins	.90	2.70	8.00
40-47,50-69: 64-Bat Lash-c/story			5.00
48,49: (44 pgs.)-1st & 2nd app. Cinnamon		2.00	6.00
70-Last issue		2.00	6.00

NOTE: ***Alcala*** *a-16, 17.* ***Evans*** *inks-39-48; c-39i, 40, 47.* ***G. Kane*** *a-15, 20.* ***Kubert*** *c-12, 33.* ***Starlin*** *c-44, 45.* ***Wildey*** *a-26. 48 & 49 are 44 pgs..*

WEIRD WONDER TALES
Marvel Comics Group: Dec, 1973 - No. 22, May, 1977

	GD25	FN65	NM94
1-Wolverton-r/Mystic #6 (Eye of Doom)	1.40	4.20	14.00
2-10	.90	2.70	9.00
11-22: 16-18-Venus-r by Everett from Venus #19,18 & 17. 19-22-Dr. Druid (Droom)-r	.85	2.60	7.00

Welcome Back Kotter #3 © Wolper Organization

Werewolf by Night V2 #2 © MEG

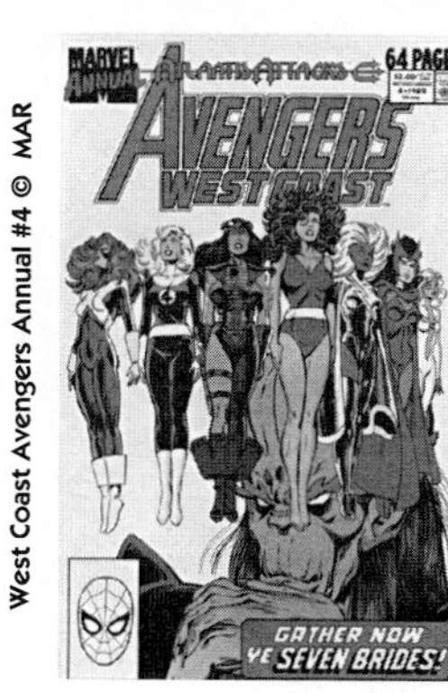

West Coast Avengers Annual #4 © MAR

NOTE: *All 1950s & early 1960s reprints.* ***Check*** *r-1.* ***Colan*** *r-17.* ***Ditko*** *r-4, 5, 10-13, 19-21.* ***Drucker*** *r-12, 20.* ***Everett*** *r-3(Spellbound #16), 6(Astonishing #10), 9(Adv. Into Mystery #5).* ***Heath*** *a-13r.* ***Heck*** *a-1or, 14r.* ***Gil Kane*** *c-1, 2, 10.* ***Kirby*** *r-6, 11, 13, 16-22; c-17, 19, 20.* ***Krigstein*** *r-19.* ***Kubert*** *r-22.* ***Maneely*** *r-8.* ***Mooney*** *r-7p.* ***Powell*** *r-3, 7.* ***Torres*** *r-7.* ***Wildey*** *r-2, 7.*

WEIRD WORLDS (See Adventures Into...)

WEIRD WORLDS (Magazine)
Eerie Publications: V1#10(12/70), V2#1(2/71) - No. 4, Aug, 1971 (52 pgs.)

	GD25	FN65	NM94
V1#10-Sci-fi/horror	2.90	8.70	32.00
V2#1-4	2.25	6.80	25.00

WEIRD WORLDS (Also see Ironwolf: Fires of the Revolution)
National Periodical Publications: Aug-Sept, 1972 - No. 9, Jan-Feb, 1974; No. 10, Oct-Nov, 1974 (All 20¢ issues)

	GD25	FN65	NM94
1-Edgar Rice Burrough's John Carter Warlord of Mars & David Innes begin (1st DC app.); Kubert-c	1.20	3.60	12.00
2-4: 2-Infantino/Orlando-c. 3-Murphy Anderson-c. 4-Kaluta-a	.90	2.70	8.00
5-7: .5-Kaluta-c. 7-Last John Carter.		2.00	6.00
8-10: 8-Iron Wolf begins by Chaykin (1st app.)			5.00

NOTE: ***Neal Adams*** *a-2i, 3i. John Carter by* ***Andersonin*** *#1-3.* ***Chaykin*** *c-7, 8.* ***Kaluta*** *a-4; c-4-6, 10.* ***Orlando*** *a-4i; c-2, 3, 4i.* ***Wrightson*** *a-2i, 4i..*

WELCOME BACK, KOTTER (TV) (See Limited Collectors' Edition #57)
National Periodical Publ./DC Comics: Nov, 1976 - No. 10, Mar-Apr, 1978

	GD25	FN65	NM94
1-Sparling-a(p)	1.40	4.20	14.00
2-10: 3-Estrada-a	.90	2.70	9.00

WELCOME SANTA (See March of Comics #63,183)

WELCOME TO THE LITTLE SHOP OF HORRORS
Roger Corman's Cosmic Comics: May, 1995 -No. 3, July, 1995 ($2.50, limited series)

	GD25	FN65	NM94
1-3			2.50

WELLS FARGO (See Tales of...)

WENDY AND THE NEW KIDS ON THE BLOCK
Harvey Comics: Mar, 1991 - No. 3, July, 1991 ($1.25)

	GD25	FN65	NM94
1-3			1.30

WENDY DIGEST
Harvey Comics: Oct, 1990 - No. 5, Mar, 1992 ($1.75, digest size)

	GD25	FN65	NM94
1-5			3.00

WENDY PARKER COMICS
Atlas Comics (OMC): July, 1953 - No. 8, July, 1954

	GD25	FN65	NM94
1	8.50	26.00	60.00
2	5.70	17.00	35.00
3-8	5.00	15.00	30.00

WENDY, THE GOOD LITTLE WITCH (TV)
Harvey Publ.: 8/60 - #82, 11/73; #83, 8/74 - #93, 4/76; #94, 9/90 - #97, 12/90

	GD25	FN65	NM94
1-Wendy & Casper the Friendly Ghost begin	15.00	45.00	150.00
2	6.50	19.50	65.00
3-5	5.00	15.00	50.00
6-10	4.00	12.00	40.00
11-20	2.50	7.50	25.00
21-30	2.00	6.00	20.00
31-50	1.50	4.50	15.00
51-64,66-69	1.20	3.60	12.00
65 (2/71)-Wendy origin.	1.60	4.80	16.00
70-74: All 52 pg. Giants	1.60	4.80	16.00
75-93	.85	2.60	7.00
94-97 (1990, $1.00-c): 94-Has #194 on-c			3.00

(See Casper the Friendly Ghost #20 & Harvey Hits #7, 16, 21, 23, 27, 30, 33)

WENDY THE GOOD LITTLE WITCH (2nd Series)
Harvey Comics: Apr, 1991 - No. 15, Aug, 1994 ($1.00/$1.25 #7-11/$1.50 #12-15)

	GD25	FN65	NM94
1-15-Reprints Wendy & Casper stories. 12-Bunny app.			2.00

WENDY WITCH WORLD
Harvey Publications: 10/61; No. 2, 9/62 - No. 52, 12/73; No. 53, 9/74

	GD25	FN65	NM94
1-(25¢, 68 pg. Giants begin)	10.00	30.00	100.00
2-5	5.00	15.00	50.00
6-10	3.00	9.00	30.00
11-20	2.60	7.80	26.00
21-30	2.00	6.00	20.00
31-39: 39-Last 68 pg. issue	1.60	4.80	16.00
40-45: 52 pg. issues	1.20	3.60	12.00
46-53		2.00	6.00

WEREWOLF (Super Hero) (Also see Dracula & Frankenstein)
Dell Publishing Co.: Dec, 1966 - No. 3, April, 1967

	GD25	FN65	NM94
1-1st app.	2.50	7.50	20.00
2,3	1.50	4.50	12.00

WEREWOLF BY NIGHT (See Giant-Size..., Marvel Spotlight #2-4 & Power Record Comics)
Marvel Comics Group: Sept, 1972 - No. 43, Mar, 1977

	GD25	FN65	NM94
1-Ploog-a cont'd. from Marvel Spotlight #4	4.50	13.50	50.00
2	2.00	6.00	20.00
3-5	1.60	4.80	16.00
6-10	1.00	3.00	10.00
11-14,16-20	.90	2.70	8.00
15-New origin Werewolf; Dracula-c/story cont'd from Tomb of Dracula #18	1.25	3.75	10.00
21-31			5.00
32-Origin & 1st app. Moon Knight (8/75)	7.00	21.00	75.00
33-2nd app. Moon Knight	2.90	8.70	32.00
34-36,38-43: 35-Starlin/Wrightson-c			5.00
37-Moon Knight app; part Wrightson-c	.90	2.70	8.00

NOTE: ***Bolle*** *a-6i.* ***G. Kane*** *a-11p, 12p; c-21, 22, 24-30, 34p.* ***Mooney*** *a-7i.* ***Ploog*** *1-4p, 5, 6p, 7p, 13-16p; c-5-8, 13-16.* ***Reinman*** *a-8i.* ***Sutton*** *a(i)-9, 11, 16, 35.*

WEREWOLF BY NIGHT (Vol. 2, continues in Strange Tales #1 (9/98))
Marvel Comics Group: Feb, 1998 - No. 6, July, 1998 ($2.99)

	GD25	FN65	NM94
1-6-Manco-a: 2-Two covers. 6-Ghost Rider-c/app.			3.00

WEREWOLVES & VAMPIRES (Magazine)
Charlton Comics: 1962 (One Shot)

	GD25	FN65	NM94
1	6.50	19.50	65.00

WEST COAST AVENGERS
Marvel Comics Group: Sept, 1984 - No. 4, Dec, 1984 (lim. series, Mando paper)

	GD25	FN65	NM94
1-Origin & 1st app. W.C. Avengers (Hawkeye, Iron Man, Mockingbird & Tigra)			2.00
2-4			1.50

WEST COAST AVENGERS (Becomes Avengers West Coast #48 on)
Marvel Comics Group: Oct, 1985 - No. 47, Aug, 1989

	GD25	FN65	NM94
V2#1-20			1.50
21-41			1.00
42-Byrne-a(p)/scripts begin			2.00
43-47: 46-Byrne-c; 1st app. Great Lakes Avengers			1.00
Annual 1-3 (1986-1988): 3-Evolutionary War app.			2.00
Annual 4 (1989, $2.00)-Atlantis Attacks; Byrne/Austin-a			2.00

WESTERN ACTION
I. W. Enterprises: No. 7, 1964

	GD25	FN65	NM94
7-Reprints Cow Puncher #? by Avon	.90	2.70	8.00

WESTERN ACTION
Atlas/Seaboard Publ.: Feb, 1975

	GD25	FN65	NM94
1-Kid Cody by Wildey & The Comanche Kid stories; intro. The Renegade			4.00

WESTERN ACTION THRILLERS

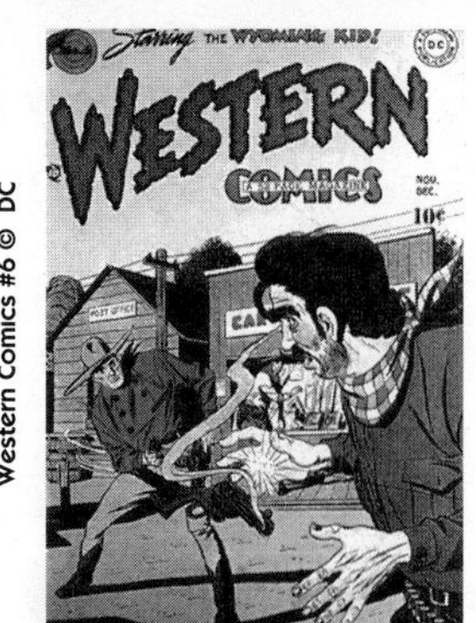

Western Comics #6 © DC

Westerner #16 © Super Comics

Western Gunfighters #5 (2nd series) © MAR

GD25 FN65 NM94

Dell Publishers: Apr, 1937 (10¢, square binding; 100 pgs.)
1-Buffalo Bill, The Texas Kid, Laramie Joe, Two-Gun Thompson, & Wild West Bill app. 74.00 221.00 625.00

WESTERN ADVENTURES COMICS (Western Love Trails #7 on)
Ace Magazines: Oct, 1948 - No. 6, Aug, 1949
nn(#1)-Sheriff Sal, The Cross-Draw Kid, Sam Bass begin 19.00 56.00 140.00
nn(#2)(12/48) 9.30 28.00 70.00
nn(#3)(2/49)-Used in **SOTI**, pgs. 30,31 10.00 30.00 75.00
4-6 8.50 26.00 60.00

WESTERN BANDITS
Avon Periodicals: 1952 (Painted-c)
1-Butch Cassidy, The Daltons by Larsen; Kinstler-a; c-part-r/paperback Avon Western Novel #1 14.00 42.00 105.00

WESTERN BANDIT TRAILS (See Approved Comics)
St. John Publishing Co.: Jan, 1949 - No. 3, July, 1949
1-Tuska-a; Baker-c; Blue Monk, Ventrilo app. 21.00 64.00 160.00
2-Baker-c 17.00 50.00 125.00
3-Baker-c/a; Tuska-a 19.00 58.00 145.00

WESTERN COMICS (See Super DC Giant #15)
National Per. Publ: Jan-Feb, 1948 - No. 85, Jan-Feb, 1961 (1-27: 52pgs.)
1-Wyoming Kid & his horse Racer, The Vigilante in "Jesse James Rides Again" (Meskin-a), Cowboy Marshal, Rodeo Rick begin 71.00 212.00 600.00
2 39.00 117.00 300.00
3,4-Last Vigilante 32.00 96.00 240.00
5-Nighthawk & his horse Nightwind begin (not in #6); Captain Tootsie by Beck 27.00 80.00 200.00
6,7,9,10 20.00 60.00 150.00
8-Origin Wyoming Kid; 2 pg. pin-ups of rodeo queens 29.00 88.00 220.00
11-20 17.00 50.00 125.00
21-40: 24-Starr-a. 27-Last 52 pgs. 28-Flag-c 12.00 36.00 90.00
41-49: Last precode issue (2/55). 43-Pow Wow Smith begins, ends #85 11.00 32.00 80.00
50-60 9.30 28.00 70.00
61-85-Last Wyoming Kid. 77-Origin Matt Savage Trail Boss. 82-1st app. Fleetfoot, Pow Wow's girlfriend 8.50 26.00 60.00
NOTE: ***G. Kane, Infantino*** *art in most.* ***Meskin*** *a-1-4.* ***Moreira*** *a-28-39.* ***Post*** *a-3-5.*

WESTERN CRIME BUSTERS
Trojan Magazines: Sept, 1950 - No. 10, Mar-Apr, 1952
1-Six-Gun Smith, Wilma West, K-Bar-Kate, & Fighting Bob Dale begin; headlight-a 26.00 82.00 205.00
2 15.00 44.00 110.00
3-5: 3-Myron Fass-c 14.00 42.00 105.00
6-Wood-a 28.00 84.00 210.00
7-Six-Gun Smith by Wood 28.00 84.00 210.00
8 14.00 42.00 105.00
9-Tex Gordon & Wilma West by Wood; Lariat Lucy app. 28.00 84.00 210.00
10-Wood-a 27.00 80.00 200.00

WESTERN CRIME CASES (Formerly Indian Warriors #7,8; becomes The Outlaws #10 on)
Star Publications: No. 9, Dec, 1951
9-White Rider & Super Horse; L. B. Cole-c 15.00 44.00 110.00

WESTERN DESPERADO COMICS (Formerly Slam Bang Comics)
Fawcett Publications: No. 8, 1940 (Oct.?)
8-(Rare) 60.00 184.00 520.00

WESTERNER, THE (Wild Bill Pecos)
"Wanted" Comic Group/Toytown/Patches: No. 14, June, 1948 - No. 41, Dec, 1951 (#14-31: 52 pgs.)
14 11.00 32.00 80.00
15-17,19-21: 19-Meskin-a 5.70 17.00 38.00
18,22-25-Krigstein-a 9.30 28.00 65.00
26(4/50)-Origin & 1st app. Calamity Kate, series ends #32; Krigstein-a 11.00 32.00 80.00
27-Krigstein-a(2) 11.00 32.00 80.00
28-41: 33-Quest app. 37-Lobo, the Wolf Boy begins 4.25 13.00 28.00
NOTE: ***Mort Lawrence*** *a-20-27, 29, 37, 39; c-19, 22-24, 26, 27.* ***Leav*** *c-14-18, 20, 31.* ***Syd Shores*** *a-39; c-34, 35, 37-41.*

WESTERNER, THE
Super Comics: 1964
Super Reprint 15-17: 15-r/Oklahoma Kid #? 16-r/Crack West. #65; Severin-c; Crandall-r. 17-r/Blazing Western #2; Severin-c 1.00 3.00 8.00

WESTERN FIGHTERS
Hillman Periodicals/Star Publ.: Apr-May, 1948 - V4#7, Mar-Apr, 1953 (#1-V3#2: 52 pgs.)
V1#1-Simon & Kirby-c 31.00 92.00 230.00
2-Not Kirby-a 7.85 23.50 55.00
3-Fuje-c 7.15 21.50 50.00
4-Krigstein, Ingels, Fuje-a 8.50 26.00 60.00
5,6,8,9,12 5.70 17.00 35.00
7,10-Krigstein-a 8.50 26.00 60.00
11-Williamson/Frazetta-a 26.00 78.00 195.00
V2#1-Krigstein-a 8.50 26.00 60.00
2-12: 4-Berg-a 4.00 12.00 24.00
V3#1-11 4.00 11.00 22.00
12-Krigstein-a 7.85 23.50 55.00
V4#1,4-7 4.00 11.00 22.00
2,3-Krigstein-a 7.85 23.50 55.00
3-D 1(12/53, 25¢, Star Publ.)-Came w/glasses; L. B. Cole-c 33.00 100.00 250.00
NOTE: ***Kinstlerish*** *a-V2#6, 8, 9, 12; V3#2, 5-7, 11, 12; V4#1(plus cover).* ***McWilliams*** *a-11.* ***Powell*** *a-V2#2.* ***Reinman*** *a-1-12, V4#3.* ***Rowich*** *c-5, 6i.* ***Starr*** *a-5.*

WESTERN FRONTIER
P. L. Publishers: Apr-May, 1951 - No. 7, 1952
1 10.00 30.00 75.00
2 5.70 17.00 40.00
3-7 5.00 15.00 30.00

WESTERN GUNFIGHTERS (1st Series) (Apache Kid #11-19)
Atlas Comics (CPS): No. 20, June, 1956 - No. 27, Aug, 1957
20 10.00 30.00 75.00
21-Crandall-a 10.00 30.00 75.00
22-Wood & Powell-a 15.00 46.00 115.00
23,24: 23-Williamson-a. 24-Toth-a 10.00 30.00 75.00
25-27 7.85 23.50 55.00
NOTE: ***Berg*** *a-20.* ***Colan*** *a-20, 26, 27.* ***Crandall*** *a-21.* ***Heath*** *a-25.* ***Maneely*** *a-24, 25; c-22, 23, 25.* ***Morisi*** *a-24.* ***Morrow*** *a-26.* ***Pakula*** *a-23.* ***Severin*** *c-20, 27.* ***Torres*** *a-26.* ***Woodbridge*** *a-27.*

WESTERN GUNFIGHTERS (2nd Series)
Marvel Comics Group: Aug, 1970 - No. 33, Nov, 1975 (#1-6: 25¢, 68 pgs.)
1-Ghost Rider begins; Fort Rango, Renegades & Gunhawk app. 2.50 7.60 28.00
2-6: 2-Origin Nightwind (Apache Kid's horse) 1.80 5.40 18.00
7-(52 pgs) Origin Ghost Rider retold 1.60 4.80 16.00
8-14: 10-Origin Black Rider. 12-Origin Matt Slade 1.10 3.30 11.00
15-20 .90 2.70 8.00
21-33 .85 2.60 7.00
NOTE: ***Baker*** *r-2, 3.* ***Colan*** *r-2.* ***Drucker*** *r-3.* ***Everett*** *a-6i.* ***G. Kane*** *c-29, 31.* ***Kirby*** *a-1p(r), 10, 11.* ***Kubert*** *r-2.* ***Maneely*** *r-2, 10.* ***Morrow*** *r-29.* ***Severin*** *c-10.* ***Shores*** *a-3, 4.* ***Barry Smith*** *a-4.* ***Steranko*** *c-14.* ***Sutton*** *a-1, 2i, 5, 4.* ***Torres*** *r-26('57).* ***Wildey*** *r-8, 9.* ***Williamson*** *r-2, 18.* ***Woodbridge*** *r-27('57). Renegades in #4, 5; Ghost Rider in #1-7.*

WESTERN HEARTS

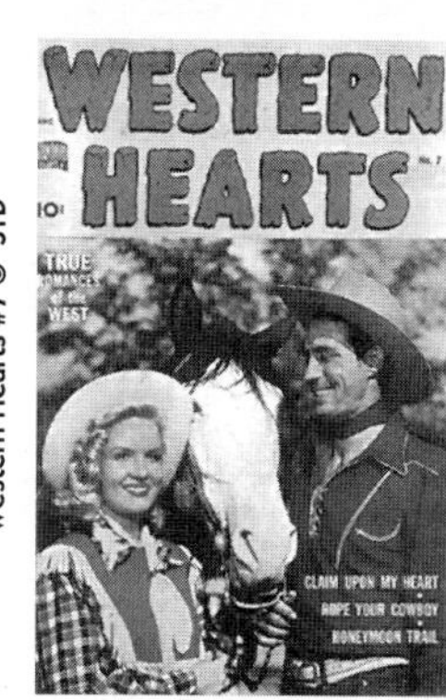

Western Hearts #7 © STD

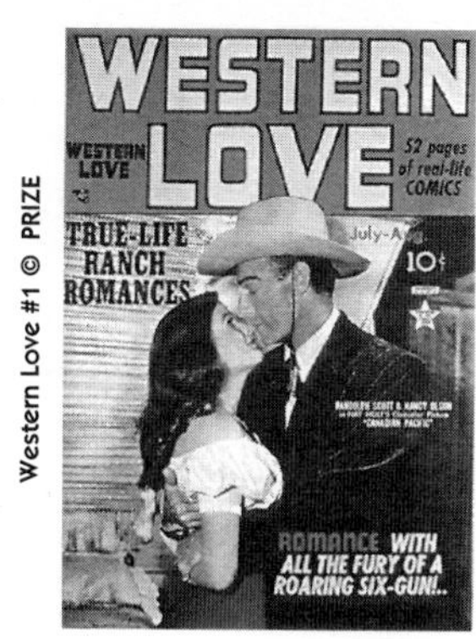

Western Love #1 © PRIZE

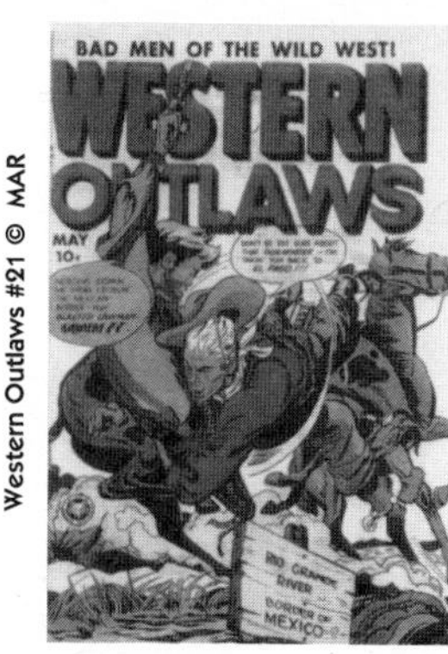

Western Outlaws #21 © MAR

	GD25	FN65	NM94
Standard Comics: Dec, 1949 - No. 10, Mar, 1952 (All photo-c)			
1-Severin-a; Whip Wilson & Reno Browne photo-c	17.00	52.00	130.00
2-Beverly Tyler & Jerome Courtland photo-c from movie "Palomino"; Williamson/Frazetta-a (2 pgs.)	17.00	50.00	125.00
3-Rex Allen photo-c	9.30	28.00	70.00
4-7,10-Severin & Elder, Al Carreno-a. 5-Ray Milland & Hedy Lamarr photo-c from movie "Copper Canyon". 6-Fred MacMurray & Irene Dunn photo-c from movie "Never a Dull Moment". 7-Jock Mahoney photo-c. 10-Bill Williams & Jane Nigh photo-c	9.30	28.00	70.00
8-Randolph Scott & Janis Carter photo-c from "Santa Fe"; Severin & Elder-a	9.50	28.75	72.00
9-Whip Wilson & Reno Browne photo-c; Severin & Elder-a	11.00	34.00	85.00

WESTERN HERO (Wow Comics #1-69; Real Western Hero #70-75)
Fawcett Publications: No. 76, Mar, 1949 - No. 112, Mar, 1952

	GD25	FN65	NM94
76(#1, 52 pgs.)-Tom Mix, Hopalong Cassidy, Monte Hale, Gabby Hayes, Young Falcon (ends #78,80), & Big Bow and Little Arrow (ends #102,105) begin; painted-c begin	27.00	80.00	200.00
77 (52 pgs.)	15.00	44.00	110.00
78,80-82 (52 pgs.): 81-Capt. Tootsie by Beck	15.00	44.00	110.00
79,83 (36 pgs.): 83-Last painted-c	12.00	36.00	90.00
84-86,88-90 (52 pgs.): 84-Photo-c begin, end #112. 86-Last Hopalong Cassidy	13.00	38.00	95.00
87,91,95,99 (36 pgs.): 87-Bill Boyd begins, ends #95	11.00	32.00	80.00
92-94,96-98,101 (52 pgs.): 96-Tex Ritter begins. 101-Red Eagle app.	12.00	36.00	90.00
100 (52 pgs.)	13.00	38.00	95.00
102-111: 102-Begin 36 pg. issues	11.00	32.00	80.00
112-Last issue	12.00	36.00	90.00

NOTE: *1/2 to 1 pg. Rocky Lane (Carnation) in 80-83, 86, 88, 97. Photo covers feature Hopalong Cassidy #84, 86, 89; Tom Mix #85, 87, 90, 92, 94, 97; Monte Hale #88, 91, 93, 95, 98, 100, 104, 107, 110; Tex Ritter #96, 99, 101, 105, 108, 111; Gabby Hayes #103.*

WESTERN KID (1st Series)
Atlas Comics (CPC): Dec, 1954 - No. 17, Aug, 1957

	GD25	FN65	NM94
1-Origin; The Western Kid (Tex Dawson), his stallion Whirlwind & dog Lightning begin	17.00	50.00	125.00
2 (2/55)-Last pre-code	9.30	28.00	65.00
3-8	7.85	23.50	55.00
9,10-Williamson-a in both (4 pgs. each)	8.50	26.00	60.00
11-17	5.70	17.00	40.00

NOTE: ***Ayers** a-6, 7. **Maneely** c-2-7, 10, 14. **Romita** a-1-17; c-1, 12. **Severin** c-17.*

WESTERN KID, THE (2nd Series)
Marvel Comics Group: Dec, 1971 - No. 5, Aug, 1972 (All 20¢ issues)

	GD25	FN65	NM94
1-Reprints; Romita-c/a(3)	1.80	5.40	18.00
2,4,5: 2-Romita-a; Severin-c. 4-Everett-r	1.20	3.60	12.00
3-Williamson-a	1.60	4.80	16.00

WESTERN KILLERS
Fox Features Syndicate: nn, July?, 1948; No. 60, Sept, 1948 - No. 64, May, 1949; No. 6, July, 1949

	GD25	FN65	NM94
nn(#59?)(nd, F&J Trading Co.)-Range Busters; formerly Blue Beetle #57?	21.00	64.00	160.00
60 (#1, 9/48)-Extreme violence; lingerie panel	23.00	70.00	175.00
61-Jack Cole, Starr-a	19.00	56.00	140.00
62-64, 6	17.00	50.00	125.00

WESTERN LIFE ROMANCES (My Friend Irma #3 on?)
Marvel Comics (IPP): Dec, 1949 - No. 2, Mar, 1950 (52 pgs.)

	GD25	FN65	NM94
1-Whip Wilson & Reno Browne photo-c	16.00	48.00	120.00
2-Audie Murphy & Gale Storm photo-c; spanking scene	14.00	42.00	105.00

WESTERN LOVE
Prize Publ.: July-Aug, 1949 - No. 5, Mar-Apr, 1950 (All photo-c & 52 pgs.)

	GD25	FN65	NM94
1-S&K-a; Randolph Scott photo-c from movie "Canadian Pacific" (see Prize Comics #76)	26.00	78.00	195.00
2,5-S&K-a: 2-Whip Wilson & Reno Browne photo-c. 5-Dale Robertson photo-c	21.00	64.00	160.00
3,4: 3-Reno Browne? photo-c	13.00	38.00	95.00

NOTE: ***Meskin** & **Severin/Elder** a-2-5.*

WESTERN LOVE TRAILS (Formerly Western Adventures)
Ace Magazines (A. A. Wyn): No. 7, Nov, 1949 - No. 9, Mar, 1950

	GD25	FN65	NM94
7	9.30	28.00	70.00
8,9	7.85	23.50	55.00

WESTERN MARSHAL (See Steve Donovan...)
Dell Publishing Co.: No. 534, 2-4/54 - No. 640, 7/55 (Based on Ernest Haycox's "Trailtown")

	GD25	FN65	NM94
Four Color 534 (#1)-Kinstler-a	4.50	13.50	50.00
Four Color 591 (10/54), 613 (2/55), 640-All Kinstler-a	4.50	13.50	50.00

WESTERN OUTLAWS (Junior Comics #9-16; My Secret Life #22 on)
Fox Features Syndicate: No. 17, Sept, 1948 - No. 21, May, 1949

	GD25	FN65	NM94
17-Kamen-a; Iger shop-a in all; 1 pg. "Death and the Devil Pills" r-in Ghostly Weird #122	31.00	92.00	230.00
18-21	17.00	52.00	130.00

WESTERN OUTLAWS
Atlas Comics (ACI No. 1-14/WPI No. 15-21): Feb, 1954 - No. 21, Aug, 1957

	GD25	FN65	NM94
1-Heath, Powell-a; Maneely hanging-c	17.00	52.00	130.00
2	9.30	28.00	70.00
3-10: 7-Violent-a by R.Q. Sale	7.50	22.50	52.00
11,14-Williamson-a in both (6 pgs. each)	9.30	28.00	65.00
12,18,20,21: Severin covers	6.85	21.00	48.00
13,15: 13-Baker-a. 15-Torres-a	7.50	22.50	52.00
16-Williamson text illo	6.85	21.00	48.00
17,19-Crandall-a. 17-Williamson text illo	7.50	22.50	52.00

NOTE: ***Ayers** a-7, 10, 18, 20. **Bolle** a-21. **Colan** a-5, 10, 11, 17. **Drucker** a-11. **Everett** a-9, 10. **Heath** a-1; c-3, 4, 8, 16. **Kubert** a-9p. **Maneely** a-13, 16, 17, 19; c-1, 5, 7, 9, 10, 12, 13. **Morisi** a-18. **Powell** a-3, 16. **Romita** a-7, 13. **Severin** a-8, 16, 19; c-17, 18, 20, 21. **Tuska** a-6, 15.*

WESTERN OUTLAWS & SHERIFFS (Formerly Best Western)
Marvel/Atlas Comics (IPC): No. 60, Dec, 1949 - No. 73, June, 1952

	GD25	FN65	NM94
60 (52 pgs.)	19.00	58.00	145.00
61-65: 61-Photo-c	17.00	50.00	125.00
66-Story contains 5 hangings	13.00	40.00	100.00
68-72	12.00	36.00	90.00
67-Cannibalism story	15.00	46.00	115.00
73-Black Rider story; Everett-c	13.00	38.00	95.00

NOTE: ***Maneely** a-62, 67; c-62, 69-73. **Robinson** a-68. **Sinnott** a-70. **Tuska** a-69-71.*

WESTERN PICTURE STORIES (1st Western comic)
Comics Magazine Company: Feb, 1937 - No. 4, June, 1937

	GD25	FN65	NM94
1-Will Eisner-a	147.00	441.00	1250.00
2-Will Eisner-a	88.00	265.00	750.00
3,4: 3-Eisner-a. 4-Caveman Cowboy story	71.00	212.00	600.00

WESTERN PICTURE STORIES (See Giant Comics Edition #6, 11)

WESTERN ROMANCES (See Target...)

WESTERN ROUGH RIDERS
Gillmor Magazines No. 1,4 (Stanmor Publ.): Nov, 1954 - No. 4, May, 1955

	GD25	FN65	NM94
1	6.50	19.50	45.00
2-4	5.00	15.00	30.00

WESTERN ROUNDUP (See Dell Giants & Fox Giants)

WESTERN TALES (Formerly Witches...)
Harvey Publications: No. 31, Oct, 1955 - No. 33, July-Sept, 1956

	GD25	FN65	NM94
31,32-All S&K-a; Davy Crockett app. in each	17.00	50.00	125.00
33-S&K-a; Jim Bowie app.	17.00	50.00	125.00

Western True Crime #16 (#2) © FOX

Wetworks #7 © DC

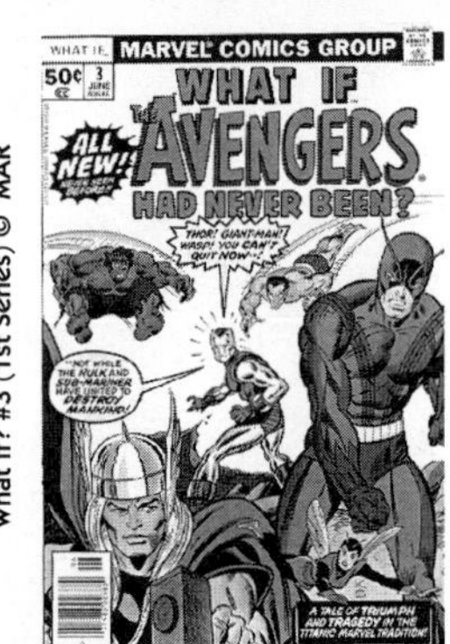

What If? #3 (1st Series) © MAR

	GD25	FN65	NM94

NOTE: *#32 & 33 contain Boy's Ranch reprints.* ***Kirby*** *c-31.*

WESTERN TALES OF BLACK RIDER (Formerly Black Rider; Gunsmoke Western #32 on)
Atlas Comics (CPS): No. 28, May, 1955 - No. 31, Nov, 1955

28 (#1): The Spider (a villain) dies 16.00 48.00 120.00
29-31 11.00 32.00 80.00

NOTE: ***Lawrence*** *a-30.* ***Maneely*** *c-28-30.* ***Severin*** *a-28.* ***Shores*** *c-31.*

WESTERN TEAM-UP
Marvel Comics Group: Nov, 1973 (20¢)

1-Origin & 1st app. The Dakota Kid; Rawhide Kid-r; Gunsmoke Kid-r by Jack Davis 2.00 6.00 20.00

WESTERN THRILLERS (My Past Confessions #7 on)
Fox Features Syndicate/M.S. Distr. No. 52: Aug, 1948 - No. 6, June, 1949; No. 52, 1954?

1- "Velvet Rose" (Kamenish-a); "Two-Gun Sal", "Striker Sisters" (all women outlaws issue); Brodsky-c 42.00 127.00 340.00
2 18.00 54.00 135.00
3,6 16.00 48.00 120.00
4,5-Bakerish-a; 5-Butch Cassidy app. 18.00 54.00 135.00
52-(Reprint, M.S. Dist.)-1954? No date given (becomes My Love Secret #53) 7.00 21.00 42.00

WESTERN THRILLERS (Cowboy Action #5 on)
Atlas Comics (ACI): Nov, 1954 - No. 4, Feb, 1955 (All-r/Western Outlaws & Sheriffs)

1 13.00 38.00 95.00
2-4 7.50 22.50 52.00

NOTE: ***Heath*** *c-3.* ***Maneely*** *a-1; c-2.* ***Powell*** *a-4.* ***Robinson*** *a-4.* ***Romita*** *c-4.* ***Tuska*** *a-2.*

WESTERN TRAILS (Ringo Kid Starring in...)
Atlas Comics (SAI): May, 1957 - No. 2, July, 1957

1-Ringo Kid app.; Severin-c 10.00 30.00 75.00
2-Severin-c 6.85 21.00 48.00

NOTE: ***Bolle*** *a-1, 2.* ***Maneely*** *a-1, 2.* ***Severin*** *c-1, 2.*

WESTERN TRUE CRIME (Becomes My Confessions)
Fox Features Syndicate: No. 15, Aug, 1948 - No. 6, June, 1949

15(#1)-Kamen-a; formerly Zoot #14 (5/48)? 25.00 75.00 185.00
16(#2)-Kamenish-a; headlight panels, violence 19.00 57.00 140.00
3-Kamen-a 20.00 60.00 150.00
4-6: 4-Johnny Craig-a 12.00 36.00 90.00

WESTERN WINNERS (Formerly All-Western Winners; becomes Black Rider #8 on & Romance Tales #7 on?)
Marvel Comics (CDS): No. 5, June, 1949 - No. 7, Dec, 1949

5-Two-Gun Kid, Kid Colt, Black Rider; Shores-c 26.00 78.00 210.00
6-Two-Gun Kid, Black Rider, Heath Kid Colt story; Captain Tootsie by C.C. Beck 22.00 66.00 175.00
7-Randolph Scott Photo-c w/true stories about the West 22.00 66.00 175.00

WEST OF THE PECOS (See Zane Grey, 4-Color #222)

WESTWARD HO, THE WAGONS (Disney)
Dell Publishing Co.: No. 738, Sept, 1956 (Movie)

Four Color 738-Fess Parker photo-c 7.00 22.00 80.00

WETWORKS (See WildC.A.T.S: Covert Action Teams #2)
Image Comics (WildStorm): June, 1994 - No. 43, Aug, 1998 ($1.95/$2.50)

1-"July" on-c; gatefold wraparound-c; Portacio/Williams-c/a 3.00
1-Chicago Comicon edition 2.00 6.00
2-4 2.00
2-Alternate Portacio-c, see Deathblow #5 .90 2.70 8.00
5-7,9-24: 5-($2.50). 13-Portacio-c. 16-Fire From Heaven Pt. 4. 17-Fire From Heaven Pt. 11 2.50
8 ($1.95)-Newstand, Wildstorm Rising Pt. 7 2.00
8 ($2.50)-Direct Market, Wildstorm Rising Pt. 7 2.50
25-($3.95) 3.95
26-43: 32-Variant-c by Pat Lee & Charest. 39,40-Stormwatch app. 42-Gen 13 app. 2.50
Sourcebook 1 (10/94, $2.50)-Text & illustrations (no comics) 2.50
Voyager Pack (8/97, $3.50)- #32 w/Phantom Guard preview 3.50

WETWORKS/VAMPIRELLA (See Vampirella/Wetworks)
Image Comics (WildStorm Productions): July, 1997 ($2.95, one-shot)

1-Gil Kane-c 3.00

WHACK (Satire)
St. John Publishing Co. (Jubilee Publ.): Oct, 1953 - No. 3, May, 1954

1-(3-D, 25¢)-Kubert-a; Maurer-c; came w/glasses 28.00 84.00 210.00
2,3-Kubert-a in each. 2-Bing Crosby on-c; Mighty Mouse & Steve Canyon parodies. 3-Li'l Orphan Annie parody; Maurer-c 15.00 44.00 110.00

WHACKY (See Wacky)

WHAM COMICS (See Super Spy)
Centaur Publications: Nov, 1940 - No. 2, Dec, 1940

1-The Sparkler, The Phantom Rider, Craig Carter and his Magic Ring, Detecto, Copper Slug, Speed Silvers by Gustavson, Speed Centaur & Jon Linton (s/f) begin 141.00 424.00 1200.00
2-Origin Blue Fire & Solarman; The Buzzard app. 94.00 282.00 800.00

WHAM-O GIANT COMICS
Wham-O Mfg. Co. : April, 1967 (98¢, newspaper size, one-shot)(Six issue subscription was advertised)

1-Radian & Goody Bumpkin by Wood; 1 pg. Stanley-a; Fine, Tufts-a; flying saucer reports; wraparound-c 5.50 16.50 55.00

WHAT DO YOU KNOW ABOUT THIS COMICS SEAL OF APPROVAL?
No publisher listed (DC Comics Giveaway): nd (1955) (4 pgs., slick paper-c)

nn-(Rare) 53.00 159.00 450.00

WHAT IF? (1st Series) (What If? Featuring... #13 & #?-33)
Marvel Comics Group: Feb, 1977 - No. 47, Oct, 1984; June, 1988 (All 52 pgs.)

1-Brief origin Spider-Man, Fantastic Four 1.50 4.50 15.00
2-Origin The Hulk retold .85 2.60 7.00
3-5: 3-Avengers. 4-Invaders. 5-Capt. America 4.00
6-12,14-16: 8-Daredevil; Spidey parody. 9-Origins Venus, Marvel Boy, Human Robot, 3-D Man. 11-Marvel Bullpen as F. F. 3.00
13-Conan app.; John Buscema-c/a(p) 4.00
17-Ghost Rider & Son of Satan app. 5.00
18-26,29: 18-Begin 75¢-c; Dr. Strange. 19-Spider-Man. 22-Origin Dr. Doom retold 3.00
27-X-Men app.; Miller-c .90 2.70 8.00
28-Daredevil by Miller; Ghost Rider app. .90 2.70 8.00
30-"What If...Spider-Man's Clone Had Lived?" .90 2.70 8.00
31-Begin $1.00-c; featuring Wolverine & the Hulk; X-Men app.; death of Hulk, Wolverine & Magneto 1.20 3.60 12.00
32-34,36-47: 32,36-Byrne-a. 34-Marvel crew each draw themselves. 37-Old X-Men & Silver Surfer app. 39-Thor battles Conan 3.00
35-What if Elektra had lived?; Miller/Austin-a. 5.00
Special 1 ($1.50, 6/88)-Iron Man, F.F., Thor app. 2.00

NOTE: ***Austin*** *a-27p, 32i, 34, 35i; c-35i, 36i.* ***J. Buscema*** *a-13p, 15p; c-10, 13p, 23p.* ***Byrne*** *a-32i, 36; c-36p.* ***Colan*** *a-21p; c-17p, 18p, 21p.* ***Ditko*** *a-35, Special 1.* ***Golden*** *c-29, 40-42.* ***Guice*** *a-40p.* ***Gil Kane*** *a-3p, 24p; c(p)-2-4, 7, 8.* ***Kirby*** *a-11p; c-9p, 11p.* ***Layton*** *a-32i, 33i; c-30, 32p, 33i, 34.* ***Mignola*** *c-39i.* ***Miller*** *a-28p, 32i, 34(1), 35p; c-27, 28p.* ***Mooney*** *a-8i, 30i.* ***Perez*** *a-15p.* ***Robbins*** *a-4p.* ***Sienkiewicz*** *c-43-46.* ***Simonson*** *a-15p, 32i.* ***Starlin*** *a-32i.* ***Stevens*** *a-8, 16i(part).* ***Sutton*** *a-2i, 18p, 28.* ***Tuska*** *a-5p.* ***Weiss*** *a-37p.*

WHAT IF...? (2nd Series)
Marvel Comics: V2#1, July, 1989 - No. 114, Nov, 1998 ($1.25/$1.50)

V2#1-...The Avengers Had Lost the Evol. War 4.00
2-5: 2-Daredevil, Punisher app. 2.50
6-X-Men app. 3.00

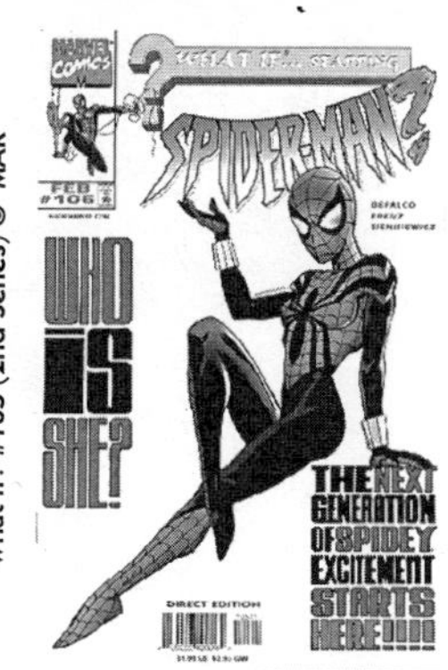

What If? #105 (2nd Series) © MAR

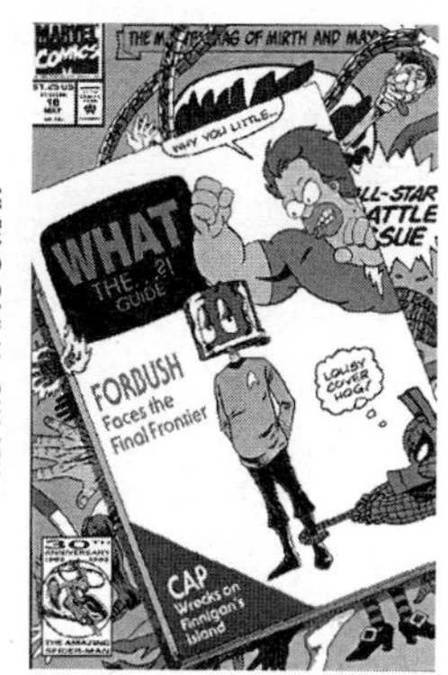

What The--?! #18 © MAR

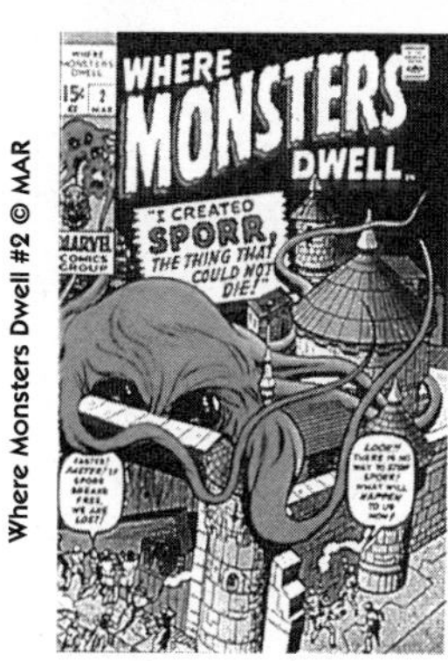

Where Monsters Dwell #2 © MAR

GD25 FN65 NM94

7-Wolverine app.; Liefeld-c/a(1st on Wolvie?) 4.00
8,11: 11-Fantastic Four app.; McFarlane-c(i) 2.00
9,12-X-Men 3.00
10-Punisher 2.50
13-15,17-21,23,27-29: 13-Prof. X; Jim Lee-c. 14-Capt. Marvel; Lim/Austin-c. 15-F.F.; Capullo-c/a(p). 17-Spider-Man/Kraven. 18-F.F. 19-Vision. 20,21-Spider-Man. 23-X-Men. 27-Namor/F.F. 28,29-Capt. America. 29-Swipes cover to Avengers #4 1.50
16-Wolverine battles Conan; Red Sonja app.; X-Men cameo 3.00
22-Silver Surfer by Lim/Austin-c/a 2.00
24-Wolverine; Punisher app. 2.75
25-($1.50, 52 pgs.)-Wolverine app. 3.00
26-Punisher app. 1.50
30-($1.75, 52 pgs.)-Sue Richards/F.F. 1.75
31-40: 31-Cosmic Spider-Man & Venom app.; Hobgoblin cameo. 32,33-Phoenix; X-Men app. 35-Fantastic Five (w/Spidey). 36-Avengers vs. Guardians of the Galaxy. 37-Wolverine; Thibert-c(i). 38-Thor; Rogers-p (part). 40-Storm; X-Men app. 1.50
41-($1.75, 52 pgs.)-Avengers vs. Galactus 1.75
42-49,51-60: 42-Spider-Man. 43-Wolverine. 44-Venom/Punisher. 45-Ghost Rider. 46-Cable. 47-Magneto. 49-Infinity Gauntlet w/Silver Surfer & Thanos. 52-Dr. Doom. 54-Death's Head. 57-Punisher as Shield. 58-"What if Punisher Had Killed Spider-Man" w/cover similar to Amazing S-M #129. 59-...Wolverine led Alpha Flight. 60-X-Men Wedding Album 1.25
50-($2.95, 52 pgs.)-Foil embossed-c; "What If Hulk Had Killed Wolverine" 3.00
61-99: 61-$1.50-c begins; bound-in card sheet. 61,86,88-Spider-Man. 74,77,81,84,85-X-Men. 76-Last app. Watcher in title. 78-Bisley-c. 80-Hulk. 87-Sabretooth. 89-Fantastic Four. 90-Cyclops & Havok. 91-The Hulk. 93-Wolverine. 94-Juggernaut. 95-Ghost Rider 1.50
96-98,-1(7/97)-($1.95): 97-Black Knight 2.00
99,101-104: 99-Begin $1.99-c 2.00
100-($2.99, double-sized) Gambit and Rogue, Fantastic Four 3.00
105-Spider-Girl debut; Sienkiewicz-a .90 2.70 8.00
106-114: 106-Gambit. 108-Avengers. 111-Wolverine. 114-Secret Wars 1.99

WHAT'S BEHIND THESE HEADLINES
William C. Popper Co.: 1948 (16 pgs.)

nn-Comic insert "The Plot to Steal the World" 5.35 16.00 32.00

'WHAT'S NEW? - THE COLLECTED ADVENTURES OF PHIL & DIXIE'
Palliard Press: Oct, 1991 - No. 2, 1991 ($5.95, mostly color, squarebound, 52 pgs.)

1,2-By Phil Foglio 2.00 6.00

WHAT THE- -?!
Marvel Comics: Aug, 1988 - No. 26, 1993 ($1.25/$1.50/$2.50, semi-annual #5 on)

1-All contain parodies 2.50
2,4,5: 5-Punisher/Wolverine parody; Jim Lee-a 1.50
3-X-Men parody; Todd McFarlane-a 2.00
6-24: 6-($1.00)-Punisher, Wolverine, Alpha Flight. 9-Wolverine. 16-EC back-c parody. 17-Wolverine/Punisher parody. 18-Star Trek parody w/Wolverine. 19-Punisher, Wolverine, Ghost Rider. 21-Weapon X parody. 22-Punisher/Wolverine parody 1.25
25-Summer Special 1 (1993, $2.50)-X-Men parody 2.50
26-Fall Special ($2.50, 68 pgs.)-Spider-Ham 2099-c/story; origin Silver Surfer; Hulk & Doomsday parody; indica reads "Winter Special." 2.50

NOTE: *Austin a-6i.* ***Byrne*** *a-2, 6, 10; c-2, 6-8, 10, 12, 13.* ***Golden*** *a-22.* ***Dale Keown*** *a-8p(8 pgs.).* ***McFarlane*** *a-3.* ***Rogers*** *c-15i, 16p.* ***Severin*** *a-2.* ***Staton*** *a-21p.* ***Williamson*** *a-2i.*

WHEATIES (Premiums)
Walt Disney Productions: 1950 & 1951 (32 titles, pocket-size, 32 pgs.)

(Set A-1 to A-8, 1950)

A-1-Mickey Mouse & the Disappearing Island, A-5-Mickey Mouse, Roving Reporter each... 5.00 15.00 30.00
A-2-Grandma Duck, Homespun Detective, A-6-Li'l Bad Wolf, Forest Ranger, A-7-Goofy, Tightrope Acrobat, A-8-Pluto & the Bogus Money each... 4.15 12.50 25.00
A-3-Donald Duck & the Haunted Jewels, A-4-Donald Duck & the Giant Ape each... 5.70 17.00 40.00

(Set B-1 to B-8, 1950)

B-1-Mickey Mouse & the Pharoah's Curse, B-4-Mickey Mouse & the Mystery Sea Monster each... 5.00 15.00 30.00
B-2-Pluto, Canine Cowpoke, B-5-Li'l Bad Wolf in the Hollow Tree Hideout, B-7-Goofy & the Gangsters each... 4.15 12.50 25.00
B-3-Donald Duck & the Buccaneers, B-6-Donald Duck,Trail Blazer, B-8 Donald Duck, Klondike Kid each... 5.70 17.00 40.00

(Set C-1 to C-8, 1951)

C-1-Donald Duck & the Inca Idol, C-5-Donald Duck in the Lost Lakes, C-8-Donald Duck Deep-Sea Diver each... 5.75 17.00 40.00
C-2-Mickey Mouse & the Magic Mountain, C-6-Mickey Mouse & the Stagecoach Bandits each... 5.00 15.00 30.00
C-3-Li'l Bad Wolf, Fire Fighter, C-4-Gus & Jaq Save the Ship, C-7-Goofy, Big Game Hunter each... 4.15 12.50 25.00

(Set D-1 to D-8, 1951)

D-1-Donald Duck in Indian Country, D-5-Donald Duck, Mighty Mystic each... 5.75 17.00 40.00
D-2-Mickey Mouse and the Abandoned Mine, D-6-Mickey Mouse & the Medicine Man each... 5.00 15.00 30.00
D-3-Pluto & the Mysterious Package, D-4-Bre'r Rabbit's Sunken Treasure, D-7-Li'l Bad Wolf and the Secret of the Woods, D-8-Minnie Mouse, Girl Explorer each... 4.15 12.50 25.00

NOTE: *Some copies lack the Wheaties ad.*

WHEE COMICS (Also see Gay, Smile & Tickle Comics)
Modern Store Publications: 1955 (7¢, 5x7-1/4", 52 pgs.)

1-Funny animal 1.20 3.00 6.00

WHEELIE AND THE CHOPPER BUNCH (TV)
Charlton Comics: July, 1975 - No. 7, July, 1976 (Hanna-Barbera)

1-3: 1-Byrne text illo (see Nightmare for 1st art); Staton-a. 2-Byrne-c/a. 2,3-Mike Zeck text illos. 3-Staton-a; Byrne-c/a 1.60 4.80 16.00
4-7-Staton-a 1.00 3.00 10.00

WHEN KNIGHTHOOD WAS IN FLOWER (See The Sword & the Rose, 4-Color #505, 682)

WHEN SCHOOL IS OUT (See Wisco)

WHERE CREATURES ROAM
Marvel Comics Group: July, 1970 - No. 8, Sept, 1971

1-Kirby/Ayers-r 2.20 6.25 22.00
2-8-Kirby-r 1.40 4.20 14.00

NOTE: ***Ditko*** *r-1-6, 7.* ***Heck*** *r-2, 5.* ***Kirby*** *r-2-5. All contain pre super-hero reprints.*

WHERE IN THE WORLD IS CARMEN SANDIEGO (TV)
DC Comics: June, 1996 - No. 4, Dec, 1996 ($1.75)

1-4: Adaptation of TV show 1.75

WHERE MONSTERS DWELL
Marvel Comics Group: Jan, 1970 - No. 38, Oct, 1975

1-Kirby/Ditko-r; all contain pre super-hero-r 2.20 6.25 22.00
2-10,12: 4-Crandall-a(r). 12-Giant issue 1.40 4.20 14.00
11,13-20: 18,20-Starlin-c 1.10 3.30 11.00
21-37 .90 2.70 9.00
38-Williamson-r/World of Suspense #3 1.10 3.30 11.00

NOTE: ***Colan*** *r-12.* ***Ditko*** *a(r)-4, 6, 8, 10, 12, 17-19, 23-25, 37.* ***Kirby*** *r-1-6; c-12?* ***Reinman*** *a-3r, 4r, 12r.* ***Severin*** *c-15.*

WHERE'S HUDDLES? (TV) (See Fun-In #9)
Gold Key: Jan, 1971 - No. 3, Dec, 1971 (Hanna-Barbera)

1 2.25 6.75 24.00
2,3: 3-r/most #1 1.85 5.50 15.00

Whirlwind Comics #2 © Nita Publ.

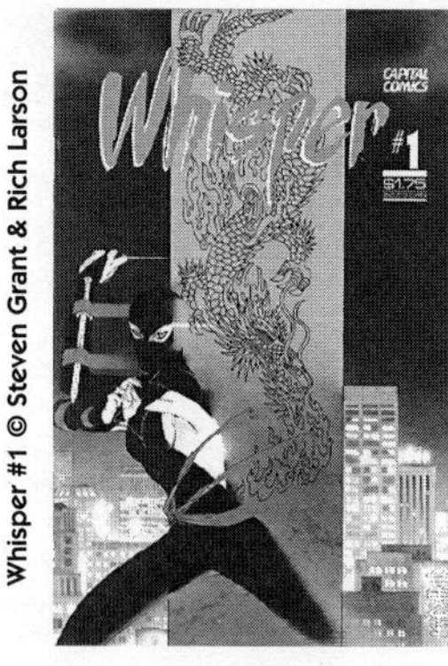

Whisper #1 © Steven Grant & Rich Larson

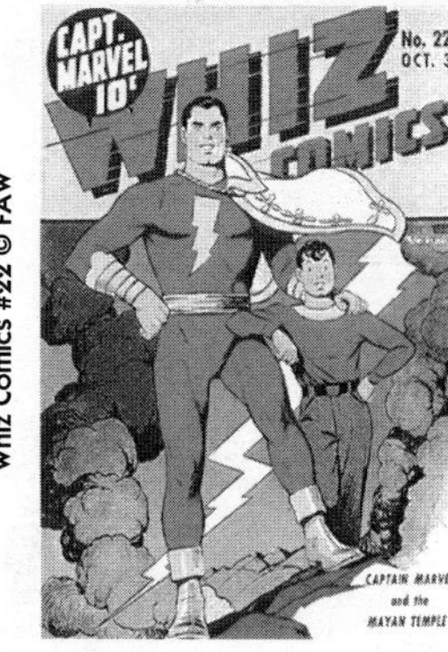

Whiz Comics #22 © FAW

GD25 FN65 NM94

WHIP WILSON (Movie star) (Formerly Rex Hart; Gunhawk #12 on; see Western Hearts, Western Life Romances, Western Love)
Marvel Comics: No. 9, April, 1950 - No. 11, Sept, 1950 (#9,10: 52 pgs.)

9-Photo-c; Whip Wilson & his horse Bullet begin; origin Bullet; issue #23 listed on splash page; cover changed to #9 53.00 159.00 450.00
10,11: Both have photo-c. 11-36 pgs. 32.00 96.00 240.00
I.W. Reprint #1(1964)-Kinstler-c; r-Marvel #11 2.50 7.50 24.00

WHIRLWIND COMICS (Also see Cyclone Comics)
Nita Publication: June, 1940 - No. 3, Sept, 1940

1-Origin & 1st app. Cyclone; Cyclone-c 135.00 406.00 1150.00
2,3: Cyclone-c 88.00 265.00 750.00

WHIRLYBIRDS (TV)
Dell Publishing Co.: No. 1124, Aug, 1960 - No. 1216, Oct-Dec, 1961

Four Color 1124 (#1)-Photo-c 8.00 25.00 90.00
Four Color 1216-Photo-c 7.00 22.00 80.00

WHISPER (Female Ninja)
Capital Comics: Dec, 1983 - No. 2, 1984 ($1.75, Baxter paper)

1,2: 1-Origin; Golden-c 1.75
Special (11/85, $2.50) 2.50

WHISPER (Vol. 2)
Capital Comics: Jun, 1986 - No. 37, June, 1990 ($1.25/$1.75/$1.95)

1-9 1.25
10-17-($1.75) 1.75
18-37-($1.95) 1.95

WHITE CHIEF OF THE PAWNEE INDIANS
Avon Periodicals: 1951

nn-Kit West app.; Kinstler-c 13.00 40.00 100.00

WHITE EAGLE INDIAN CHIEF (See Indian Chief)

WHITE FANG
Disney Comics: 1990 ($5.95, 68 pgs.)

nn-Graphic novel adapting new Disney movie 2.00 6.00

WHITE INDIAN
Magazine Enterprises: No. 11, July, 1953 - No. 15, 1954

11(A-1 94), 12(A-1 101), 13(A-1 104)-Frazetta-r(Dan Brand) in all from Durango Kid. 11-Powell-c 20.00 60.00 150.00
14(A-1 117), 15(A-1 135)-Check-a; Torres-a-#15 9.30 28.00 70.00
NOTE: *#11 contains reprints from Durango Kid #1-4; #12 from #5, 9, 10, 11; #13 from #7, 12, 13, 16. #14 & 15 contain all new stories.*

WHITEOUT
Oni Press: July, 1998 - No. 4, Nov, 1998 ($2.95, B&W, limited series)

1-4: 1-Matt Wagner-c. 2-Mignola-c. 3-Gibbons-c 3.00

WHITE PRINCESS OF THE JUNGLE (Also see Jungle Adventures & Top Jungle Comics)
Avon Periodicals: July, 1951 - No. 5, Nov, 1952

1-Origin of White Princess (Taanda) & Capt'n Courage (r); Kinstler-c 44.00 131.00 370.00
2-Reprints origin of Malu, Slave Girl Princess from Avon's Slave Girl Comics #1 w/Malu changed to Zora; Kinstler-c/a(2) 36.00 108.00 270.00
3-Origin Blue Gorilla; Kinstler-c/a 29.00 88.00 220.00
4-Jack Barnum, White Hunter app.; r/Sheena #9 26.00 78.00 195.00
5-Blue Gorilla by McCann?; Kinstler inside-c; Fawcette/Alascia-a(3) 26.00 78.00 195.00

WHITE RIDER AND SUPER HORSE (Formerly Humdinger V2#2; Indian Warriors #7 on; also see Blue Bolt #1, 4Most & Western Crime Cases)
Novelty-Star Publications/Accepted Publ.: 1950 - No. 6, Mar, 1951

1: 1-3-Exist? 16.00 48.00 120.00
2,3 13.00 40.00 100.00

GD25 FN65 NM94

4-6-Adapts "The Last of the Mohicans". 4-(9/50)-Says #11 on inside 15.00 45.00 110.00
Accepted Reprint #5(r/#5),6 (nd); L.B. Cole-c 6.50 19.50 45.00
NOTE: *All have **L. B. Cole** covers.*

WHITE WILDERNESS (Disney)
Dell Publishing Co.: No. 943, Oct, 1958

Four Color 943-Movie 5.50 16.50 60.00

WHITMAN COMIC BOOK, A
Whitman Publishing Co.: Sept., 1962 (136 pgs.; 7-3/4x5-3/4; hardcover) (B&W)

1-3,5,7: 1-Yogi Bear. 2-Huckleberry Hound. 3-Mr. Jinks and Pixie & Dixie. 5-Augie Doggie & Loopy de Loop. 7-Bugs Bunny-r from #47,51,53,54 & 55 4.00 16.00 40.00
4,6: 4-The Flintstones. 6-Snooper & Blabber Fearless Detectives/ Quick DrawMcGraw of the Wild West 5.00 15.00 50.00
8-Donald Duck-reprints most of WDC&S #209-213. Includes 5 Barks stories, 1 complete Mickey Mouse serial by Paul Murry & 1 Mickey Mouse serial missing the 1st episode 8.00 24.00 80.00
NOTE: *Hanna-Barbera #1-4,6,8(TV), original stories. Dell reprints-#5, 7.*

WHIZ COMICS (Formerly Flash Comics & Thrill Comics #1)
Fawcett Publications: No. 2, Feb, 1940 - No. 155, June, 1953

GD25 FN65 VF82 NM94

1-(nn on cover, #2 inside)-Origin & 1st newsstand app. Captain Marvel (formerly Captain Thunder) by C. C. Beck (created by Bill Parker), Spy Smasher, Golden Arrow, Ibis the Invincible, Dan Dare, Scoop Smith, Sivana, & Lance O'Casey begin 7,000.00 21,000.00 35,000.00 63,000.00
(The only Mint copy sold in 1995 for $176,000 cash)

1-Reprint, oversize 13-1/2x10". **WARNING**: This comic is an exact duplicate reprint (except for dropping "Gangway for Captain Marvel" from-c) of the original except for its size. DC published it in 1974 with a second cover titling it as a Famous First Edition. There have been many reported cases of the outer cover being removed and the interior sold as the original edition. The reprint with the new outer cover removed is practically worthless. See Famous First Edition for value.

GD25 FN65 NM94

2-(3/40, nn on cover, #3 inside); cover to Flash #1 redrawn, pg. 12, panel 4; Spy Smasher reveals I.D. to Eve 421.00 1263.00 4000.00
3-(4/40, #3 on-c, #4 inside)-1st app. Beautia 263.00 790.00 2500.00
4-(5/40, #4 on cover, #5 inside)-Brief origin Capt. Marvel retold 247.00 741.00 2100.00
5-Captain Marvel wears button-down flap on splash page only 200.00 600.00 1700.00
6-10: 7-Dr. Voodoo begins (by Raboy-#9-22) 153.00 459.00 1300.00
11-14: 12-Capt. Marvel does not wear cape 106.00 318.00 900.00
15-Origin Sivana; Dr. Voodoo by Raboy 115.00 344.00 975.00
16-18-Spy Smasher battles Captain Marvel 115.00 344.00 975.00
19,20 74.00 221.00 625.00
21-(9/41)-Origin & 1st cover app. Lt. Marvels, the 1st team in Fawcett comics. In this issue, Capt. Death similar to Dtiko's later Dr. Strange 78.00 235.00 665.00
22-24: 23-Only Dr. Voodoo by Tuska 61.00 182.00 515.00
25-(12/41)-Captain Nazi jumps from Master Comics #21 to take on Capt. Marvel solo after being beaten by Capt. Marvel/Bulletman team, causing the creation of Capt. Marvel Jr.; 1st app./origin of Capt. Marvel Jr. (part II of trilogy origin by CC. Beck & Mac Raboy); Captain Marvel sends Jr. back to Master #22 to aid Bulletman against Capt. Nazi; origin Old Shazam in text. 490.00 1470.00 4900.00
26-30 54.00 162.00 460.00
31,32: 32-1st app. The Trolls; Hitler/Mussolini satire by Beck 45.00 136.00 385.00
33-Spy Smasher, Captain Marvel x-over on cover and inside 54.00 162.00 460.00
34,36-40: 37-The Trolls app. by Swayze 40.00 120.00 315.00
35-Captain Marvel & Spy Smasher-c 43.00 129.00 365.00
41-50: 43-Spy Smasher, Ibis, Golden Arrow x-over in Capt. Marvel. 44-Flag-c.

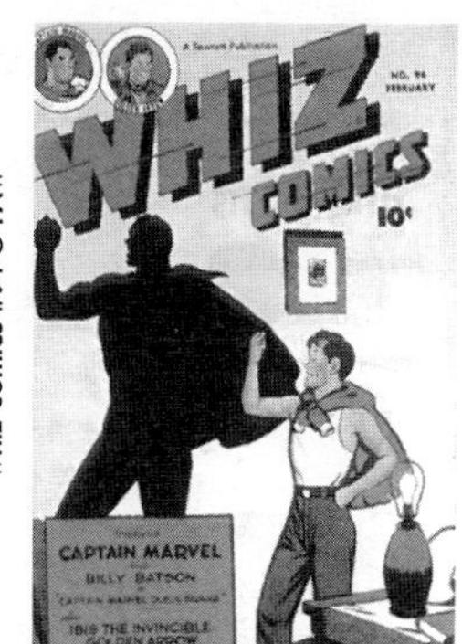

Whiz Comics #94 © FAW

Who's Who in the Legion of Super-Heroes #6 © DC

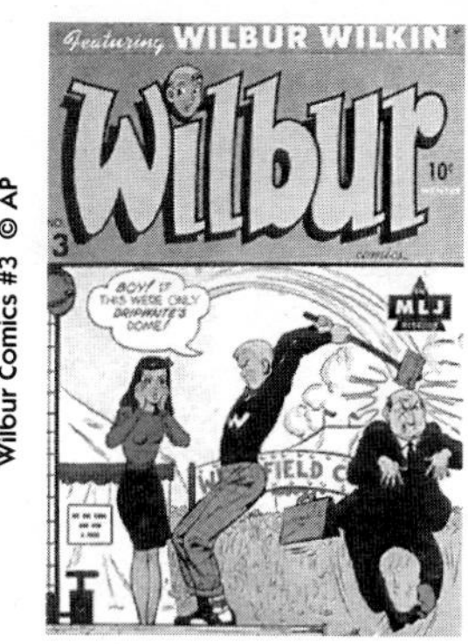

Wilbur Comics #3 © AP

GD25 FN65 NM94

47-Origin recap (1 pg.) 29.00 88.00 220.00
51-60: 52-Capt. Marvel x-over in Ibis. 57-Spy Smasher, Golden Arrow, Ibis cameo 25.00 74.00 185.00
61-70 22.00 66.00 165.00
71,77-80 20.00 60.00 150.00
72-76-Two Captain Marvel stories in each; 76-Spy Smasher becomes Crime Smasher 21.00 62.00 155.00
81-99: 86-Captain Marvel battles Sivana Family; robot-c. 91-Infinity-c 20.00 60.00 150.00
100-(8/48)-Anniversary issue 23.00 70.00 175.00
101-106: 102-Commando Yank app. 106-Bulletman app. 19.00 58.00 145.00
107-152: 107-Capitol Building photo-c. 108-Brooklyn Bridge photo-c. 112-Photo-c. 139-Infinity-c. 140-Flag-c. 142-Used in **POP**, pg. 89 19.00 58.00 145.00
153-155-(Scarce):154,155-1st/2nd Dr. Death stories 25.00 76.00 190.00
Wheaties Giveaway(1946, Miniature, 6-1/2x8-1/4", 32 pgs.); all copies were taped at each corner to a box of Wheaties and are never found in very fine or mint condition; "Capt. Marvel & the Water Thieves", plus Golden Arrow, Ibis, Crime Smasher stories 75.00 300.00 –

NOTE: ***C.C. Beck** Captain Marvel-No. 25(part). **Krigstein** Golden Arrow-No. 75, 78, 91, 95, 96, 98-100. **Mac Raboy** Dr. Voodoo-No. 9-22. Captain Marvel-No. 25(part). **M.Swayze** a-37, 38, 59; c-38. **Schaffenberger** c-138-158(most). **Wolverton** 1/2 pg. "Culture Corner"-No. 65-67, 68(2 1/2 pgs), 70-85, 87-96, 98-100, 102-109, 112-121, 123, 125, 126, 128-131, 133, 134, 136, 142, 143, 146.*

WHOA, NELLIE (Also see Love & Rockets)
Fantagraphics Books: July, 1996 - No. 3, Sept, 1996 ($2.95, B&W, lim. series)
1-3: Jamie Hernandez-c/a/scripts 3.00

WHODUNIT
D.S. Publishing Co.: Aug-Sept, 1948 - No. 3, Dec-Jan, 1948-49 (#1,2: 52 pgs.)
1-Baker-a (7 pgs.) 21.00 63.00 160.00
2,3-Detective mysteries 10.00 30.00 75.00

WHODUNNIT?
Eclipse Comics: June, 1986 - No. 3, Apr, 1987 ($2.00, limited series)
1-3: Spiegle-a. 2-Gulacy-c 2.00

WHO FRAMED ROGER RABBIT (See Marvel Graphic Novel)

WHO IS NEXT?
Standard Comics: No. 5, Jan, 1953
5-Toth, Sekowsky, Andru-a; crime stories 17.00 50.00 125.00

WHO IS THE CROOKED MAN?
Crusade: Sept, 1996 ($3.50, B&W, 40 pgs.)
1-Intro The Martyr, Scarlet 7 & Garrison 3.50

WHO'S MINDING THE MINT? (See Movie Classics)

WHO'S WHO IN STAR TREK
DC Comics: Mar, 1987 - #2, Apr, 1987 ($1.50, limited series)
1,2 5.00
NOTE: ***Byrne** a-1, 2. **Chaykin** c-1, 2. **Morrow** a-1, 2. **McFarlane** a-2. **Perez** a-1, 2. **Sutton** a-1, 2.*

WHO'S WHO IN THE LEGION OF SUPER-HEROES
DC Comics: Apr, 1987 - No. 7, Nov, 1988 ($1.25, limited series)
1-7 1.30

WHO'S WHO: THE DEFINITIVE DIRECTORY OF THE DC UNIVERSE
DC Comics: Mar, 1985 - No. 26, Apr, 1987 (Maxi-series, no ads)
1-DC heroes from A-Z 2.00
2-26: All have 1-2 pgs-a by most DC artists 1.50
NOTE: ***Art Adams** a-4, 11, 18, 20. **Anderson** a-1-5, 7-12, 14, 15, 19, 21, 23-25. **Aparo** a-2, 3, 9, 10, 12, 13, 14, 15, 17, 18, 21, 23. **Byrne** a-4, 7, 14, 16, 18i, 19, 22i, 24; c-22. **Cowan** a-3-5, 8, 10-13, 16-18, 22-25. **Ditko** a-19-22. **Evans** a-20. **Giffen** a-1, 3,-6, 8, 13, 15, 17, 18, 23. **Grell** a-6, 9, 14, 20, 23, 25, 26. **Infantino** a-1-10, 12, 15, 17-22, 24, 25. **Kaluta** a-14, 21. **Gil Kane** a-1-11, 13, 14, 16, 19, 21-23, 25. **Kirby** a-2-6, 8-18, 20, 22, 25. **Kubert** a-2, 3, 7-11, 19, 20, 25. **Erik Larsen** a-24. **McFarlane** a-10-12, 17, 19, 25, 26. **Morrow** a-4, 7, 25, 26. **Orlando** a-1, 4, 10, 11, 21i. **Perez** a-1-5, 8-19, 22-26; c-1-4, 13-18. **Rogers** a-1, 2, 5-7, 11, 12, 15, 24. **Starlin** a-13, 14, 16. **Stevens** a-4, 7, 18.*

WHO'S WHO UPDATE '87
DC Comics: Aug, 1987 - No. 5, Dec, 1987 ($1.25, limited series)
1-5: Contains art by most DC artists 1.50
NOTE: ***Giffen** a-1. **McFarlane** a-1-4; c-4. **Perez** a-1-4.*

WHO'S WHO UPDATE '88
DC Comics: Aug, 1988 - No. 4, Nov, 1988 ($1.25, limited series)
1-4: Contains art by most DC artists 1.25
NOTE: ***Giffen** a-1. **Erik Larsen** a-1.*

WIDOW: BOUND BY BLOOD
Ground Zero Comics: Aug, 1996 - No. 5, 1996 ($3.50/$3.00, B&W/color, limited series, mature)
1-(B&W, $3.50) 3.50
3-5: 2-Begin $3.00-c & color 3.00
Platinum Ed.-(4/96, B&W)-Complete 1st issue prev. 10.00

WIDOW: METAL GYPSIES
London Night Studios: Aug, 1995 - No. 2, 1995 ($3.00)
1,2 3.00
1-Platinum 4.00

WIDOW: THE ORIGIN
Avatar Press: Dec, 1997 - No. 3, Feb, 1998 ($3.95/$3.00, B&W, limited series)
1 3.95
2,3-($3.00) 3.00
1-3-($4.95) Nude cover edition 4.95

WILBUR COMICS (Teen-age) (Also see Laugh Comics, Laugh Comix, Liberty Comics #10 & Zip Comics)
MLJ Magazines/Archie Publ. No. 8, Spring, 1946 on: Sum', 1944 - No. 87, 11/59; No. 88, 9/63; No. 89, 10/64; No. 90, 10/65 (No. 1-46: 52 pgs.) (#1-11 are quarterly)
1 44.00 131.00 370.00
2(Fall, 1944) 25.00 74.00 185.00
3,4(Wint, '44-45; Spr, '45) 18.00 54.00 135.00
5-1st app. Katy Keene (Sum, '45) & begin series; Wilbur story same as Archie story in Archie #1 except Wilbur replaces Archie 53.00 159.00 450.00
6-10: 10-(Fall, 1946) 16.00 48.00 120.00
11-20 9.30 28.00 70.00
21-30: 30-(4/50) 6.50 19.50 45.00
31-50 5.35 16.00 32.00
51-70 4.00 12.00 24.00
71-90: 88-Last 10¢ issue (9/63) 2.00 6.00 16.00
NOTE: *Katy Keene in No. 5-56, 58-69. **Al Fagaly** c-6-9, 12-24 at least. **Vigoda** c-2.*

WILD
Atlas Comics (IPC): Feb, 1954 - No. 5, Aug, 1954
1 23.00 68.00 170.00
2 13.00 40.00 100.00
3-5 11.00 32.00 80.00
NOTE: ***Berg** a-5; c-4. **Burgos** c-3. **Colan** a-4. **Everett** a-1-3. **Heath** a-2, 3, 5. **Maneely** a-1-3, 5; c-1, 5. **Post** a-2, 5. **Ed Win** a-1, 3.*

WILD (This Magazine Is...) (Satire)
Dell Publishing Co.: Jan, 1968 - No. 3, 1968 (Magazine, 52 pgs.)
1-3 1.50 4.50 12.00

WILD ANIMALS
Pacific Comics: Dec, 1982 ($1.00, one-shot, direct sales)
1-Funny animal; Sergio Aragones-a; Shaw-c/a 2.00

WILD BILL ELLIOTT (Also see Western Roundup under Dell Giants)
Dell Publishing Co.: No. 278, 5/50 - No. 643, 7/55 (No #11,12) (All photo-c)
Four Color 278(#1, 52pgs.)-Titled "Bill Elliott"; Bill & his horse Stormy begin; photo front/back-c begin 12.00 35.00 130.00

Wild Bill Hickok #1 © AVON

WildC.A.T.s #16 © WildStorm Prod.

WildC.A.T.s #50 © WildStorm Prod.

GD25 FN65 NM94

2 (11/50), 3 (52 pgs.) 6.40 19.00 70.00
4-10(10-12/52) 4.50 13.50 50.00
Four Color 472(6/53),520(12/53)-Last photo back-c 3.60 11.00 40.00
13(4-6/54) - 17(4-6/55) 3.00 9.00 35.00
Four Color 643 (7/55) 2.75 8.00 30.00

WILD BILL HICKOK (Also see Blazing Sixguns)
Avon Periodicals: Sept-Oct, 1949 - No. 28, May-June, 1956

1-Ingels-c 20.00 60.00 150.00
2-Painted-c; Kit West app. 9.30 28.00 70.00
3-5-Painted-c (4-Cover by Howard Winfield) 5.70 17.00 40.00
6-10,12: 8-10-Painted-c. 12-Kinsler-c? 5.70 17.00 40.00
11,13,14-Kinstler-c/a (#11-c & inside-f/c art only) 6.50 19.50 45.00
15,17,18,20: 18-Kit West story. 20-Kit West by Larsen 5.00 15.00 30.00
16-Kamen-a; r-3 stories/King of the Badmen of Deadwood 5.70 17.00 38.00
19-Meskin-a 5.00 15.00 30.00
21-Reprints 2 stories/Chief Crazy Horse 4.25 13.00 26.00
22-McCann-a?; r/Sheriff Bob Dixon's... 4.25 13.00 26.00
23-27: 23-Kinstler-c. 24-27-Kinstler-c/a(r) (24,25-r?) 5.00 15.00 30.00
28-Kinstler-c/a (new); r-/Last of the Comanches 5.00 15.00 30.00
I.W. Reprint #1-r/#2; Kinstler-c 1.50 4.50 12.00
Super Reprint #10-12: 10-r/#18. 11-r/#?. 12-r/#8 1.50 4.50 12.00

NOTE: *#23, 25 contain numerous editing deletions in both art and script due to code.* ***Kinstler*** *c-6, 7, 11-14, 17, 18, 20-22, 24-28.* ***Howard Larsen*** *a-1, 2, 4, 5, 6(3), 7-9, 11, 12, 17, 18, 20-24, 26.* ***Meskin*** *a-7.* ***Reinman*** *a-6, 17.*

WILD BILL HICKOK AND JINGLES (TV)(Formerly Cowboy Western) (Also see Blue Bird)
Charlton Comics: No. 68, Aug, 1958 - No. 75, Dec, 1959

68,69-Williamson-a (all are 10¢ issues) 8.50 26.00 60.00
70-Two pgs. Williamson-a 5.70 17.00 38.00
71-75 (#76, exist?) 4.00 12.00 24.00

WILD BILL PECOS WESTERN (Also see The Westerner)
AC Comics: 1989 ($3.50, 1/2 color/1/2 B&W, 52 pgs.)

1-Syd Shores-c/a(r)/Westerner; photo back-c 3.50

WILD BOY OF THE CONGO (Also see Approved Comics)
Ziff-Davis No. 10-12,4-8/St. John No. 9 on: No. 10, 2-3/51 - No. 12, 8-9/51; No. 4, 10-11/51 - No. 15, 6/55

10(#1)(2-3/51)-Origin; bondage-c by Saunders (painted); used in **SOTI**, pg. 189; painted-c begin, end #9 19.00 56.00 140.00
11(4-5/51),12(8-9/51)-Norman Saunders painted-c 10.00 30.00 75.00
4(10-11/51)-Saunders painted bondage-c 10.00 30.00 75.00
5(Winter,'51)-Saunders painted-c 9.30 28.00 65.00
6,8,9(10/53),10: 6-Saunders-c. 8,9-Painted-c 9.30 28.00 65.00
7(8-9/52)-Kinstler-a 10.00 30.00 75.00
11-13-Baker-c. 11-r/#7 w/new Baker-c; Kinstler-a (2 pgs.) 11.00 32.00 80.00
14(4/55)-Baker-c; r-#12('51) 11.00 32.00 80.00
15(6/55) 7.85 23.50 55.00

WILD CARDS
Marvel Comics (Epic Comics): Sept, 1990 - No. 4, 1990 ($4.50, limited series, 52 pgs.)

1-4 4.50

NOTE: ***Guice*** *a-1; c-1-4p.* ***Morrow*** *a-4.* ***Rogers*** *a-1, 4.* ***Williamson*** *a-3.*

WILDCAT (See Sensation Comics #1)

WILDC.A.T.S ADVENTURES (TV cartoon)
Image Comics (WildStorm Productions): Sept, 1994 - No. 10, June, 1995 ($1.95/$2.50)

1-5 2.00
6-10: 6-$2.50-c begins 2.50
Sourcebook 1 (1/95, $2.95) 3.00

GD25 FN65 NM94

WILDC.A.T.S: COVERT ACTION TEAMS
Image Comics (WildStorm Productions): Aug, 1992 - No. 4, Mar, 1993; No. 5, Nov, 1993 - No. 50, June, 1998 ($1.95/$2.50)

1-1st app; Jim Lee/Williams-c/a & Lee scripts begin; contains 2 trading cards (Two diff versions of cards inside); 1st WildStorm Productions title. 5.00
1-All gold foil signed edition 12.00
1-All gold foil unsigned edition 8.00
1-Newsstand edition w/o cards 3.00
1-"3-D Special"(8/97, $4.95) w/3-D glasses; variant-c by Jim Lee 5.00
2-($2.50)-Prism foil stamped-c; contains coupon for Image Comics #0 & 4 pg. preview to Portacio's Wetworks (back-up) 2.00 6.00
2-With coupon missing 2.00
2-Direct sale misprint w/o foil-c 3.00
2-Newsstand ed., no prism or coupon 3.00
3-Lee/Liefeld-c (1/93-c, 12/92 inside) 4.00
4-($2.50)-Polybagged w/Topps trading card; 1st app. Tribe by Johnson & Stroman; Youngblood cameo 4.00
4-variant w/red card 2.00 6.00
5-7-Jim Lee/Williams-c/a; Lee script 3.00
8-Begin $2.50-c; X-Men's Jean Grey & Scott Summers cameos 4.00
9-12: 10-1st app. Huntsman & Soldier; Claremont scripts begin, ends #13. 11-1st app. Savant, Tapestry & Mr. Majestic. 3.00
11-Alternate Portacio-c, see Deathblow #5 .85 2.60 7.00
13-19,21-24: 15-James Robinson scripts begin, ends #20. 15,16-Black Razor story. 21-Alan Moore scripts begin, end #34; intro Tao & Ladytron; new WildC.A.T.S team forms (Mr. Majestic, Savant, Condition Red (Max Cash), Tao & Ladytron). 22-Maguire-a 4.00
20-($2.50)-Direct Market, WildStorm Rising Pt. 2 w/bound-in card 2.50
20-($1.95)-Newsstand, WildStorm Rising Part 2 2.00
25-($4.95)-Alan Moore script; wraparound foil-c. 5.00
26-49: 29-(5/96)-Fire From Heaven Pt 7; reads Apr on-c. 30-(6/96)-Fire From Heaven Pt. 13; Spartan revealed to have transplanted personality of John Colt (from Team One: WildC.A.T.S). 31-(9/96)-Grifter rejoins team; Ladytron dies 2.50
40-($3.50)Voyager Pack bagged w/Divine Right preview 8.00
50-($3.50) Stories by Robinson/Lee, Choi & Peterson/Benes, andMoore/Charest Charest sketchbook; Lee wraparound-c 5.00
50-Chromium cover 7.00
Annual 1 (2/98, $2.95) Robinson-s 3.00
Compendium (1993, $9.95)-r/#1-4; bagged w/#0 10.00
Sourcebook 1 (9/93, $2.50)-Foil embossed-c 2.50
Sourcebook 1-($1.95)-Newsstand ed. w/o foil embossed-c 2.00
Sourcebook 2 (11/94, $2.50)-wraparound-c 2.50
Special 1 (11/93, $3.50, 52 pgs.)-1st Travis Charest WildC.A.T.S-a 3.50
...A Gathering of Eagles TPB (5/97, $9.95) r/#10-12 9.95
...Gang War TPB ('98, $16.95) r/#28-34 16.95
...Homecoming TPB (8/98, $19.95) r/#21-27 19.95

WILDC.A.T.S/ ALIENS
Image Comics/Dark Horse: Aug, 1998 ($4.95, one-shot)

1-Ellis-s/Sprouse-a/c; Aliens invade Skywatch 5.00
1-Variant-c by Gil Kane 5.00

WILDC.A.T.S: SAVANT GARDE FAN EDITION
Image Comics/WildStorm Productions: Feb, 1997 - No. 3, Apr, 1997 (Giveaway, 8 pgs.) (Polybagged w/Overstreet's FAN)

1-3: Barbara Kesel-s/Christian Uche-a(p) 4.00
1-3-(Gold): All retailer incentives 16.00

WILDC.A.T.S TRILOGY
Image Comics (WildStorm Productions): June, 1993 - No. 3, Dec, 1993 ($1.95, limited series)

1-($2.50)-1st app. Gen 13 (Fairchild, Burnout, Grunge, Freefall)

Wild Dog #3 © DC

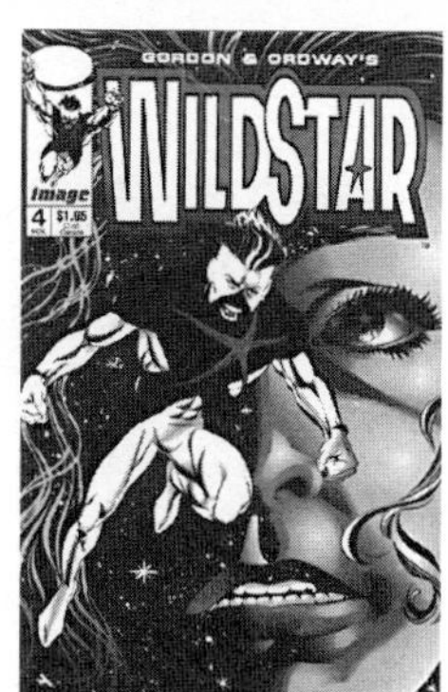

Wildstar #4 © Al Gordon & Jerry Ordway

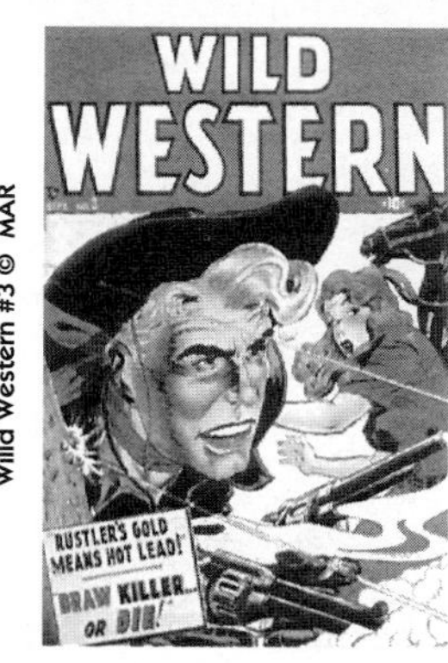

Wild Western #3 © MAR

GD25 FN65 NM94

Multi-color foil-c; Jae Lee-c/a in all 5.00
1-($1.95)-Newsstand ed. w/o foil-c 2.00
2,3-($1.95)-Jae Lee-c/a 2.00

WILDC.A.T.S/ X-MEN: THE GOLDEN AGE
Image Comics (WildStorm Productions): Feb, 1997 ($4.50, one-shot)

1-Lobdell-s/Charest-a; Two covers(Charest, Jim Lee) 4.50
1-"3-D" Edition ($6.50) w/glasses 6.50

WILDC.A.T.S/ X-MEN: THE MODERN AGE
Image Comics (WildStorm Productions): Aug, 1997 ($4.50, one-shot)

1-Robinson-s/Hughes-a; Two covers(Hughes, Paul Smith) 4.50
1-"3-D" Edition ($6.50) w/glasses 6.50

WILDC.A.T.S/ X-MEN: THE SILVER AGE
Image Comics (WildStorm Productions): June, 1997 ($4.50, one-shot)

1-Lobdell-s/Jim Lee-a; Two covers(Neal Adams, Jim Lee) 4.50
1-"3-D" Edition ($6.50) w/glasses 6.50

WILDCORE
Image Comics (WildStorm Prods.): Nov, 1997 - No. 10, Dec, 1998 ($2.50)

1-Two covers (Booth/McWeeney, Charest) 2.50
1-($3.50)-Voyager Pack w/DV8 preview 3.50
1-Chromium-c 10.00
2-10 2.50

WILD DOG
DC Comics: Sept, 1987 - No. 4, Dec, 1987 (75¢, limited series)

1-4 1.00
Special 1 (1989, $2.50, 52 pgs.) 2.50

WILDERNESS TREK (See Zane Grey, Four Color 333)

WILDFIRE (See Zane Grey, FourColor 433)

WILD FRONTIER (Cheyenne Kid #8 on)
Charlton Comics: Oct, 1955 - No. 7, Apr, 1957

	GD25	FN65	NM94
1-Davy Crockett	7.50	22.50	55.00
2-6-Davy Crockett in all	5.35	16.00	32.00
7-Origin & 1st app. Cheyenne Kid	5.70	17.00	38.00

WILD KINGDOM (TV)
Western Printing Co.: 1965 (Giveaway, regular size, slick-c, 16 pgs.)

	GD25	FN65	NM94
nn-Mutual of Omaha's...	1.75	5.25	14.00

WILDSTAR (Also see The Dragon & The Savage Dragon)
Image Comics (Highbrow Entertainment): Sept, 1995 - No. 3, Jan, 1996 ($2.50, limited series)

1-3: Al Gordon scripts; Jerry Ordway-c/a 2.50

WILDSTAR: SKY ZERO
Image Comics (Highbrow Entertainment): Mar, 1993 - No. 4, Nov, 1993 ($1.95, limited series)

1-($2.50)-Embossed-c w/silver ink; Ordway-c/a in all 2.50
1-($1.95)-Newsstand ed. w/silver ink-c, not embossed 2.00
1-Gold variant 8.00
2-4 2.00

WILDSTORM
Image Comics (WildStorm Publishing): 1994/1995 ($2.50/$2.95/$4.95)

...Chamber of Horrors (10/95, $3.50)-Bisley-c 3.50
...Halloween 1 (10/97, $2.50) Warner-c 2.50
...Rarities 1(12/94, $4.95, 52 pgs.)-r/Gen 13 1/2 & other stories .90 2.70 8.00
...Swimsuit Special 1 (12/94, $2.95) 4.00
...Swimsuit Special 2 (1995, $2.50) 3.00
...Swimsuit Special '97 #1 (7/97, $2.50) 2.50
...Ultimate Sports 1 (8/97, $2.50) 2.50
...Universe Sourcebook (5/95, $2.50) 2.50

GD25 FN65 NM94

WILDSTORM!
Image Comics (WildStorm Publishing): Aug, 1995 - No. 4, Nov, 1995 ($2.50, B&W/color, anthology)

1-4: 1-Simonson-a 2.50

WILDSTORM RISING
Image Comics (WildStorm Publishing): May, 1995 - No.2, June, 1995 ($1.95/$2.50)

1 ($2.50)-Direct Market, WildStorm Rising Pt. 1 w/bound-in card 2.50
1 ($1.95)-Newstand, WildStorm Rising Pt. 1 2.00
2 ($2.50)-Direct Market, WildStorm Rising Pt. 10 w/bound-in card; continues in WildC.A.T.S #21. 2.50
2 ($1.95)-Newstand, WildStorm Rising Pt. 10 2.00
Trade paperback (1996, $19.95)-Collects x-over; B. Smith-c 20.00

WILDSTORM SPOTLIGHT
Image Comics (WildStorm Publishing): Feb, 1997 - No. 4 ($2.50)

1-4: 1-Alan Moore-s 2.50

WILDSTORM UNIVERSE '97
Image Comics (WildStorm Publishing): Dec, 1996 - No. 3 ($2.50, limited series)

1-3: 1-Wraparound-c. 3-Gary Frank-c 2.50

WILDTHING
Marvel Comics UK: Apr, 1993 - No. 7, Oct, 1993 ($1.75)

1-($2.50)-Embossed-c; Venom & Carnage cameo 2.50
2-7: 2-Spider-Man & Venom. 6-Mysterio app. 1.75

WILD WEST (Wild Western #3 on)
Marvel Comics (WFP): Spring, 1948 - No. 2, July, 1948

	GD25	FN65	NM94
1-Two-Gun Kid, Arizona Annie, & Tex Taylor begin; Shores-c	30.00	90.00	225.00
2-Captain Tootsie by Beck; Shores-c	21.00	62.00	155.00

WILD WEST (Black Fury #1-57)
Charlton Comics: V2#58, Nov, 1966

	GD25	FN65	NM94
V2#58	1.50	4.50	12.00

WILD WEST C.O.W.-BOYS OF MOO MESA (TV)
Archie Comics: Dec, 1992 - No. 3, Feb, 1993 (limited series)
V2#1, Mar, 1993 - No. 3, July, 1993 ($1.25)

1-3 1.25
V2#1-3 1.25

WILD WESTERN (Formerly Wild West #1,2)
Marvel/Atlas (WFP): No. 3, 9/48 - No. 57, 9/57 (3-11: 52 pgs, 12-on: 36 pgs)

	GD25	FN65	NM94
3(#1)-Tex Morgan begins; Two-Gun Kid, Tex Taylor, & Arizona Annie continue from Wild West	23.00	70.00	175.00
4-Last Arizona Annie; Captain Tootsie by Beck; Kid Colt app.	18.00	54.00	135.00
5-2nd app. Black Rider (1/49); Blaze Carson, Captain Tootsie (by Beck) app.	21.00	62.00	155.00
6-8: 6-Blaze Carson app; anti-Wertham editorial	12.00	36.00	90.00
9-Photo-c; Black Rider begins, ends #19	17.00	50.00	125.00
10-Charles Starrett photo-c	19.00	58.00	145.00
11-(Last 52 pg. issue)	12.00	36.00	90.00
12-14,16-19: All Black Rider-c/stories. 12-14-The Prairie Kid & his horse Fury app.	11.00	32.00	80.00
15-Red Larabee, Gunhawk (origin), his horse Blaze, & Apache Kid begin, end #22; Black Rider-c/story	11.00	34.00	85.00
20-30: 20-Kid Colt-c begin. 24-Has 2 Kid Colt stories. 26-1st app. The Ringo Kid? (2/53); 4 pg. story. 30-Katz-a	9.30	28.00	70.00
31-40	7.15	21.50	50.00
41-47,49-51,53,57	5.70	17.00	40.00
48-Williamson/Torres-a (4 pgs); Drucker-a	8.50	26.00	60.00
52-Crandall-a	8.50	26.00	60.00

Wild Western Action #1 © SKY

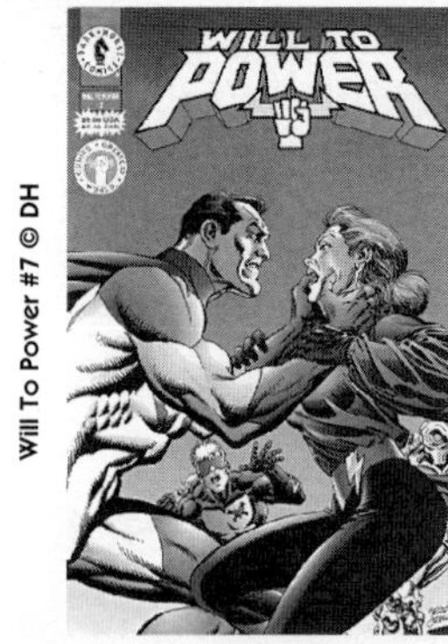

Will To Power #7 © DH

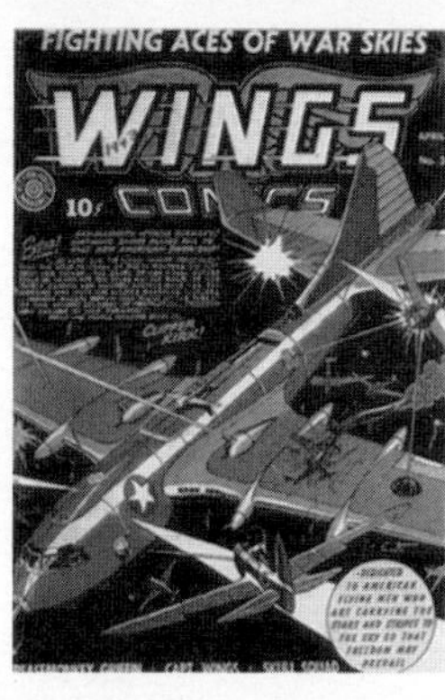

Wings Comics #32 © FH

GD25 FN65 NM94

54,55-Williamson-a in both (5 & 4 pgs.), #54 with Mayo plus 2 text illos
8.50 26.00 60.00
56-Baker-a? 5.70 17.00 40.00
NOTE: *Annie Oakley in #46, 47. Apache Kid in #15-22, 39. Arizona Kid in #21, 23. Arrowhead in #34-39. Black Rider in #5, 9-19, 33-44. Fighting Texan in #17. Kid Colt in #4-6, 9-11, 20-47, 52, 54-56. Outlaw Kid in #43. Red Hawkins in #13, 14. Ringo Kid in #26, 39, 41, 43, 44, 46, 47, 50, 52-56. Tex Morgan in #3, 4, 6, 9, 11. Tex Taylor in #3-6, 9, 11. Texas Kid in #23-25. Two-Gun Kid in #3-6, 9, 11, 12, 33-39, 41. Wyatt Earp in #47.* ***Ayers*** *a-41, 42.* ***Berg*** *a-26; c-24.* ***Colan*** *a-49.* ***Forte*** *a-28, 30.* ***Al Hartley*** *a-16.* ***Heath*** *a-4, 5, 8; c-34, 44.* ***Keller*** *a-24, 26(2), 29-40, 44-46, 48, 52.* ***Maneely*** *a-10, 12, 15, 16, 28, 35, 38, 40-45; c-18-22, 33, 35, 36, 38, 39, 41, 42, 45.* ***Morisi*** *a-23, 52.* ***Pakula*** *a-42, 52.* ***Powell*** *a-51.* ***Romita*** *a-24(2).* ***Severin*** *a-46, 47; c-48.* ***Shores*** *a-3, 5, 30, 31, 33, 35, 36, 38, 41; c-3-5.* ***Sinnott*** *a-34-39.* ***Wildey*** *a-43. Bondage c-19.*

WILD WESTERN ACTION (Also see The Bravados)
Skywald Publ. Corp.: Mar, 1971 - No. 3, June, 1971 (25¢, reprints, 52 pgs.)

1-Durango Kid, Straight Arrow-r; with all references to "Straight" in story relettered to "Swift"; Bravados begin; Shores-a (new)
1.00 3.00 10.00
2,3: 2-Billy Nevada, Durango Kid. 3-Red Mask, Durango Kid
.90 2.70 8.00

WILD WESTERN ROUNDUP
Red Top/Decker Publications/I. W. Enterprises: Oct, 1957; 1960-'61

1(1957)-Kid Cowboy-r 4.00 10.00 20.00
I.W. Reprint #1('60-61)-r/#1 by Red Top 1.25 3.75 10.00

WILD WEST RODEO
Star Publications: 1953 (15¢)

1-A comic book coloring book with regular full color cover & B&W inside
5.35 16.00 32.00

WILD WILD WEST, THE (TV)
Gold Key: June, 1966 - No. 7, Oct, 1969 (Robert Conrad photo-c)

1-McWilliams-a; photo back-c 11.00 34.00 125.00
2-McWilliams-a; photo back-c 9.00 26.00 95.00
3-7 6.40 19.00 70.00

WILD, WILD WEST, THE (TV)
Millennium Publications: Oct, 1990 - No. 4, Jan?, 1991 ($2.95, limited series)

1-4-Based on TV show 3.00

WILKIN BOY (See That...)

WILLIE COMICS (Formerly Ideal #1-4; Crime Cases #24 on; Li'l Willie #20 & 21) (See Gay Comics, Laugh, Millie The Model & Wisco)
Marvel Comics (MgPC): #5, Fall, 1946 - #19, 4/49; #22, 1/50 - #23, 5/50 (No #20 & 21)

5(#1)-George, Margie, Nellie the Nurse & Willie begin
15.00 44.00 110.00
6,8,9 8.50 26.00 60.00
7(1),10,11-Kurtzman's "Hey Look" 10.00 30.00 70.00
12,14-18,22,23 7.15 21.50 50.00
13,19-Kurtzman's "Hey Look" (#19-last by Kurtzman?)
8.50 26.00 60.00
NOTE: *Cindy app. in #17. Jeanie app. in #17. Little Lizzie app. in #22.*

WILLIE MAYS (See The Amazing...)

WILLIE THE PENGUIN
Standard Comics: Apr, 1951 - No. 6, Apr, 1952

1-Funny animal 5.70 17.00 40.00
2-6 4.00 12.00 24.00

WILLIE THE WISE-GUY (Also see Cartoon Kids)
Atlas Comics (NPP): Sept, 1957

1-Kida, Maneely-a 6.50 19.50 45.00

WILLOW
Marvel Comics: Aug, 1988 - No. 3, Oct, 1988 ($1.00)

1-3-R/Marvel Graphic Novel #36 (movie adaptation) 1.00

GD25 FN65 NM94

WILLOW, (A Girl Called)
Angel Entertainment: June, 1996 - No. 2, Spring, 1997 ($2.95, B&W)

0-2 3.00
0-($5.95)-Black Magic Foil 6.00
0-2-($10.00)-Nude Edition 10.00

WILL ROGERS WESTERN (Formerly My Great Love #1-4; see Blazing & True Comics #66)
Fox Features Syndicate: No. 5, June, 1950 - No. 2, Aug, 1950

5(#1) 30.00 90.00 225.00
2: Photo-c 26.00 78.00 195.00

WILL TO POWER (Also see Comic's Greatest World)
Dark Horse Comics: June, 1994 - No. 12, Aug, 1994 ($1.00, weekly limited series, 20 pgs.)

1-12: 12-Vortex kills Titan. 1.25
NOTE: ***Mignola*** *c-10-12.* ***Sears*** *c-1-3.*

WILL-YUM!
Dell Publishing Co.: No. 676, Feb, 1956 - No. 902, May, 1958

Four Color 676 (#1), 765 (1/57), 902 1.80 5.50 20.00

WIN A PRIZE COMICS (Timmy The Timid Ghost #3 on?)
Charlton Comics: Feb, 1955 - No. 2, Apr, 1955

V1#1-S&K-a; Poe adapt; E.C. War swipe 61.00 184.00 520.00
2-S&K-a 44.00 131.00 370.00

WINDY & WILLY
National Periodical Publications: May-June, 1969 - No. 4, Nov-Dec, 1969

1- r/Dobie Gillis with some art changes begin 2.60 7.80 26.00
2-4 2.00 6.00 16.00

WINGS COMICS
Fiction House Mag.: 9/40 - No. 109, 9/49; No. 110, Wint, 1949-50; No. 111, Spring, 1950; No. 112, 1950(nd); No. 113 - No. 115, 1950(nd); No. 116, 1952(nd); No. 117, Fall, 1952 - No. 122, Wint, 1953-54; No. 123 - No. 124, 1954(nd)

1-Skull Squad, Clipper Kirk, Suicide Smith, Jane Martin, War Nurse, Phantom Falcons, Greasemonkey Griffin, Parachute Patrol & Powder Burns begin
206.00 618.00 1750.00
2 82.00 247.00 700.00
3-5 56.00 168.00 475.00
6-10 47.00 141.00 400.00
11-15 42.00 127.00 340.00
16-Origin & 1st app. Captain Wings & begin series 47.00 142.00 400.00
17-20 37.00 112.00 280.00
21-30 33.00 100.00 250.00
31-40 27.00 80.00 200.00
41-50 21.00 64.00 160.00
51-60: 60-Last Skull Squad 19.00 56.00 140.00
61-67: 66-Ghost Patrol begins (becomes Ghost Squadron #71 on), ends #112?
17.00 52.00 130.00
68,69: 68-Clipper Kirk becomes The Phantom Falcon-origin, Part 1; part 2 in #69 17.00 52.00 130.00
70-72: 70-1st app. The Phantom Falcon in costume, origin-Part 3; Capt. Wings battles Col. Kamikaze in all 15.00 46.00 115.00
73-99: 80-Phantom Falcon by Larsen. 99-King of the Congo begins?
15.00 46.00 115.00
100-(12/48) 17.00 50.00 125.00
101-124: 111-Last Jane Martin. 112-Flying Saucer-c/story (1950). 115-Used in **POP**, pg. 89 14.00 42.00 105.00
NOTE: *Bondage covers are common. Captain Wings battles Sky Hag-#75, 76; ...Mr. Atlantis-#85-92; ...Mr. Pupin(Red Agent)-#98-103. Capt. Wings by* ***Elias****-#52-64, 68, 69; by* ***Lubbers****-#29-32, 70-111; by* ***Renee****-#33-46.* ***Evans*** *a-85-106, 108-111(Jane Martin); text illos-72-84.* ***Larsen*** *a-52, 59, 64, 73-77. Jane Martin by* ***Fran Hopper****-#68-84; Suicide Smith by* ***John Celardo****-#72, 74, 76, 80-104; by* ***Hollingsworth****-#68-70, 105-109, 111; Ghost Squadron by* ***Astarita****-#67-79; by* ***Maurice Whitman****-#80-111. King of the Congo by* ***Moreira****-#99, 100. Skull Squad by* ***M. Baker****-#52-60; Clipper Kirk by* ***Baker****-#60, 61; by* ***Colan****-#53; by* ***Ingels****-(some issues?). Phantom Falcon by* ***Larsen****-#73-84.* ***Elias*** *c-58-72.* ***Fawcette*** *c-3-12, 16, 17, 19, 22-33.*

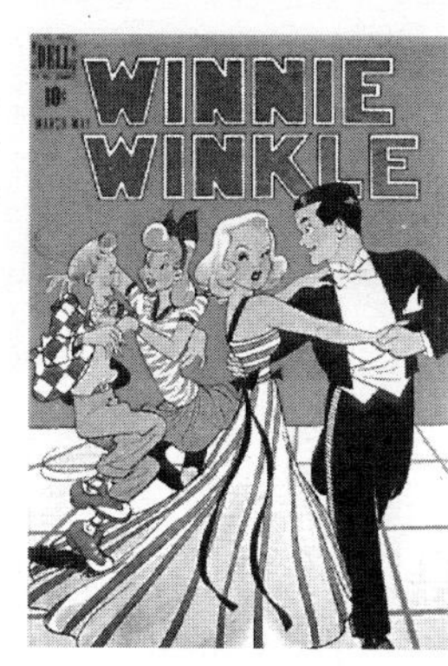
Winnie Winkle #1 © NY News Syndicate

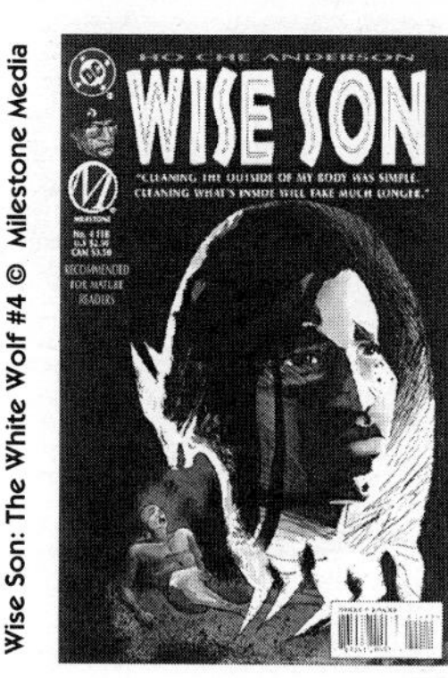

Wise Son: The White Wolf #4 © Milestone Media

Witchblade #25 © Top Cow

GD25 FN65 NM94

Lubbers c-74-109. Tuska a-5. Whitman c-110-124. Zolnerwich c-15, 21.

WINGS OF THE EAGLES, THE
Dell Publishing Co.: No. 790, Apr, 1957 (10¢ & 15¢ editions exist)

Four Color 790-Movie; John Wayne photo-c; Toth-a 14.00 44.00 160.00

WINKY DINK (Adventures of...)
Pines Comics: No. 75, Mar, 1957 (one-shot)

75-Marv Levy-c/a 4.00 12.00 24.00

WINKY DINK (TV)
Dell Publishing Co.: No. 663, Nov, 1955

Four Color 663 (#1) 7.00 22.00 80.00

WINNIE-THE-POOH (Also see Dynabrite Comics)
Gold Key No. 1-17/Whitman No. 18 on: January, 1977 - No. 33, 1984 (Walt Disney) (Winnie-The-Pooh began as Edward Bear in 1926 by Milne)

1-New art .90 2.70 8.00
2-5: 5-New material 5.00
6-17: 12-up-New material 3.00
18,19(Whitman) 4.00
20-22('80) pre-pack? .90 2.70 8.00
23-28 5.00
29-33 (#90299 on-c, no date or date code; pre-pack) .85 2.60 7.00

WINNIE WINKLE (See Popular Comics & Super Comics)
Dell Publishing Co.: 1941 - No. 7, Sept-Nov, 1949

Large Feature Comic 2 (1941) 16.00 49.00 180.00
Four Color 94 (1945) 11.00 33.00 120.00
Four Color 174 6.40 19.00 70.00
1(3-5/48)-Contains daily & Sunday newspaper-r from 1939-1941
5.75 17.00 63.00
2 (6-8/48) 3.00 10.00 36.00
3-7 2.25 6.75 25.00

WINTERWORLD
Eclipse Comics: Sept, 1987 - No. 3, Mar, 1988 ($1.75, limited series)

1-3 1.80

WISCO/KLARER COMIC BOOK (Miniature)
Marvel Comics/Vital Publ./Fawcett Publ.: 1948 - 1964 (3-1/2x6-3/4", 24 pgs.)

Given away by Wisco "99" Service Stations, Carnation Malted Milk, Klarer Health Wieners, Fleers Dubble Bubble Gum, Rodeo All-Meat Wieners, Perfect Potato Chips, & others; see ad in Tom Mix #21

Blackstone & the Gold Medal Mystery (1948) 5.70 17.00 40.00
Blackstone "Solves the Sealed Vault Mystery" (1950) 5.70 17.00 40.00
Blaze Carson in "The Sheriff Shoots It Out" (1950) 5.70 17.00 40.00
Captain Marvel & Billy's Big Game (r/Capt. Marvel Adv. #76)
28.00 84.00 210.00
(Prices vary widely on this book)
China Boy in "A Trip to the Zoo" #10 (1948) 4.00 12.00 24.00
Indoors-Outdoors Game Book 2.00 5.00 10.00
Jim Solar Space Sheriff in "Battle for Mars", "Between Two Worlds", "Conquers Outer Space", "The Creatures on the Comet", "Defeats the Moon Missile Men", "Encounter Creatures on Comet", "Meet the Jupiter Jumpers", "Meets the Man From Mars", "On Traffic Duty", "Outlaws of the Spaceways", "Pirates of the Planet X", "Protects Space Lanes", "Raiders From the Sun", "Ring Around Saturn", "Robots of Rhea", "The Sky Ruby", "Spacetts of the Sky", "Spidermen of Venus", "Trouble on Mercury" 5.70 17.00 35.00
Johnny Starboard & the Underseas Pirates (1948) 3.60 9.00 18.00
Kid Colt in "He Lived by His Guns" (1950) 6.00 18.00 42.00
Little Aspirin as "Crook Catcher" #2 (1950) 2.00 5.00 10.00
Little Aspirin in "Naughty But Nice" #6 (1950) 2.00 5.00 10.00
Return of the Black Phantom (not M.E. character)(Roy Dare)(1948)
4.25 13.00 28.00
Secrets of Magic 2.40 6.00 12.00
Slim Morgan "Brings Justice to Mesa City" #3 2.40 6.00 12.00

GD25 FN65 NM94

Super Rabbit(1950)-Cuts Red Tape, Stops Crime Wave!
8.50 26.00 60.00
Tex Farnum, Frontiersman (1948) 2.80 7.00 14.00
Tex Taylor in "Draw or Die, Cowpoke!" (1950) 4.25 13.00 28.00
Tex Taylor in "An Exciting Adventure at the Gold Mine" (1950)
4.25 13.00 26.00
Wacky Quacky in "All-Aboard" 1.20 3.00 6.00
When School Is Out 1.20 3.00 6.00
Willie in a "Comic-Comic Book Fall" #1 1.60 4.00 8.00
Wonder Duck "An Adventure at the Rodeo of the Fearless Quacker!" (1950)
7.15 21.50 50.00
Rare uncut version of three; includes Capt. Marvel, Tex Farnum, Black Phantom Estimated value... $300.00
Rare uncut version of three; includes China Boy, Blackstone, Johnny Starboard & the Underseas Pirates Estimated value... $82.00

WISE GUYS (See Harvey...)

WISE LITTLE HEN, THE
David McKay Publ./Whitman: 1935 (c.1934)(48 pgs.); 1937 (Story book)

nn-(1935 edition w/dust jacket)(48 pgs. with color, 8-3/4x9-3/4") -Debut of Donald Duck (see Advs. of Mickey Mouse); Donald app. on cover with Wise Little Hen & Practical Pig; painted cover; same artist as the B&W's from Silly Symphony Cartoon, The Wise Little Hen (1934) (McKay)
Book w/dust jacket 133.00 400.00 900.00
Dust jacket only 41.00 125.00 250.00
888(1937)(9-1/2x13", 12 pgs.)(Whitman) Donald Duck app.
24.00 72.00 180.00

WISE SON: THE WHITE WOLF
DC Comics (Milestone): Nov, 1996 - No. 4, Feb, 1997 ($2.50, limited series)

1-4: Ho Che Anderson-c/a 2.50

WITCHBLADE (Also see Cyblade/Shi & Tales Of The...)
Image Comics (Top Cow Productions): Nov, 1995 - Present ($2.50)

0 1.00 3.00 10.00
1/2-Mike Turner/Marc Silvestri-c. 5.00 15.00 55.00
1/2 Gold Ed. 5.50 16.50 60.00
1/2 Chromium-c 5.50 16.50 60.00
1-Mike Turner-a(p) 2.70 12.00 30.00
1-American Ent. Encore Ed. 5.00
2 2.40 7.00 26.00
2-American Ent. Encore Ed. 5.00
3 2.40 7.00 26.00
4,5 1.20 3.60 12.00
6-9: 8-Wraparound-c. 9-Tony Daniel-a(p) .85 2.60 7.00
9-Sunset variant-c 1.00 3.00 10.00
10-Flip book w/Darkness #0, 1st app. the Darkness 1.00 3.00 10.00
10-Variant-c 1.60 4.80 16.00
10-($3.95) Dynamic Forces alternate-c 5.00
11-15 4.00
16-19: 18,19-"Family Ties" Darkness x-over pt. 1,4 3.50
18-Face to face variant-c 5.00
18-American Ent. Ed. 5.00
19-AE Gold Ed. 5.00
20-24, 26-28: 24-Pearson, Green-a 3.00
25-($2.95) Turner-a(p) 3.00
.../Darkness: Family Ties Collected Edition (10/98, $9.95) r/#18,19 and Darkness #9,10 9.95

WITCHBLADE COLLECTED EDITION
Image Comics (Top Cow Productions): July, 1996 - Present ($4.95/$6.95, squarebound, limited series)

1-7-($4.95): Two issues reprinted in each 5.00
8-($6.95) r/#15-17 6.95
...Slipcase (10/96, $10.95)-Packaged w/ Coll. Ed. #1-4 11.00

Witchcraft: La Terreur #2 © DC

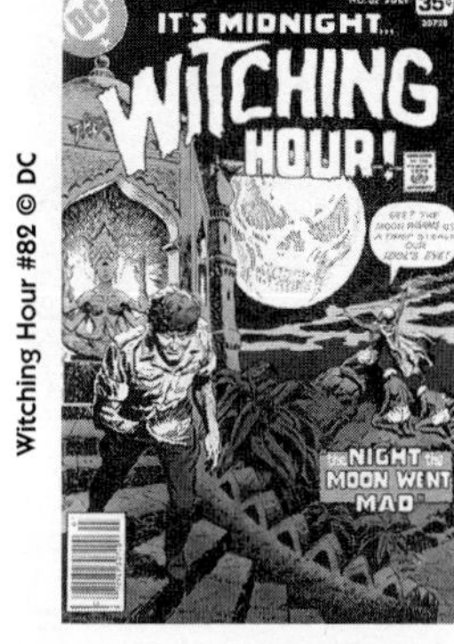

Witching Hour #82 © DC

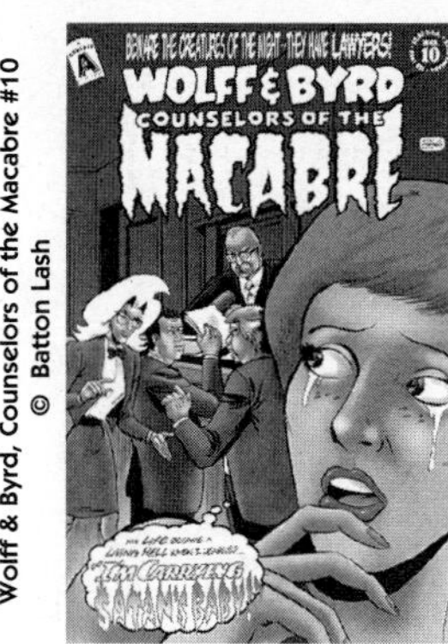

Wolff & Byrd, Counselors of the Macabre #10 © Batton Lash

WITCHBLADE/ ELEKTRA
Image Comics (Top Cow Productions): Mar, 1997 ($2.95)

	GD25	FN65	NM94
1-Devil's Reign Pt. 6			3.00

WITCHBLADE/ TOMB RAIDER SPECIAL (Also see Tomb Raider/...)
Image Comics (Top Cow Productions): Dec, 1998 ($2.95)

	GD25	FN65	NM94
1-Based on video game character; Turner-a(p)			3.00

WITCHCRAFT (See Strange Mysteries, Super Reprint #18)
Avon Periodicals: Mar-Apr, 1952 - No. 6, Mar, 1953

	GD25	FN65	NM94
1-Kubert-a; 1 pg. Check-a	56.00	168.00	475.00
2-Kubert & Check-a	43.00	129.00	350.00
3,6: 3-Lawrence-a; Kinstler inside-c	32.00	96.00	240.00
4-People cooked alive c/story	37.00	110.00	275.00
5-Kelly Freas painted-c	40.00	120.00	320.00

NOTE: ***Hollingsworth*** *a-4-6; c-4, 6.* ***McCann*** *a-3?*

WITCHCRAFT
DC Comics (Vertigo): June, 1994 - No. 3, Aug, 1994 ($2.95, limited series)

	GD25	FN65	NM94
1-3: James Robinson scripts & Kaluta-c in all			5.00
1-Platinum Edition			10.00
Trade paperback-(1996, $14.95)-r/#1-3; Kaluta-c			15.00

WITCHCRAFT: LA TERREUR
DC Comics (Vertigo): Apr, 1998 - No. 3, Jun, 1998 ($2.50, limited series)

	GD25	FN65	NM94
1-3: Robinson-s/Zulli & Locke-a; interlocking cover images			2.50

WITCHES TALES (Witches Western Tales #29,30)
Witches Tales/Harvey Publications: Jan, 1951 - No. 28, Dec, 1954 (date misprinted as 4/55)

	GD25	FN65	NM94
1-Powell-a (1 pg.)	41.00	124.00	330.00
2-Eye injury panel	23.00	68.00	170.00
3-7,9,10	15.00	46.00	115.00
8-Eye injury panels	17.00	50.00	125.00
11-13,15,16: 12-Acid in face story	14.00	42.00	105.00
14,17-Powell/Nostrand-a. 17-Atomic disaster story	17.00	50.00	125.00
18-Nostrand-a; E.C. swipe/Shock S.S.	17.00	50.00	125.00
19-Nostrand-a; E.C. swipe/ "Glutton"; Devil-c	17.00	50.00	125.00
20-24-Nostrand-a. 21-E.C. swipe; rape story. 23-Wood E.C. swipes/Two-Fisted Tales #34	17.00	50.00	125.00
25-Nostrand-a; E.C. swipe/Mad Barber; decapitation-c	17.00	50.00	125.00
26-28: 27-r/#6 with diff.-c. 28-r/#8 with diff.-c	12.00	36.00	90.00

NOTE: ***Check*** *a-24.* ***Elias*** *c-8, 10, 16-27.* ***Kremer*** *a-18; c-25.* ***Nostrand*** *a-17-25; 14, 17(w/****Powell****).* ***Palais*** *a-1, 2, 4(2), 5(2), 7-9, 12, 14, 15, 17.* ***Powell*** *a-3-7, 10, 11, 19-27. Bondage-c 1, 3, 5, 6, 8, 9.*

WITCHES TALES (Magazine)
Eerie Publications: V1#7, July, 1969 - V7#1, Feb, 1975 (B&W, 52 pgs.)

	GD25	FN65	NM94
V1#7(7/69) - 9(11/69)	4.20	12.60	42.00
V2#1-6('70), V3#1-6('71)	3.20	9.60	32.00
V4#1-6('72), V5#1-6('73), V6#1-6('74), V7#1	2.60	7.80	26.00

NOTE: *Ajax/Farrell reprints in early issues.*

WITCHES' WESTERN TALES (Formerly Witches Tales)(Western Tales #31on)
Harvey Publications: No. 29, Feb, 1955 - No. 30, Apr, 1955

	GD25	FN65	NM94
29,30-Featuring Clay Duncan & Boys' Ranch; S&K-r/from Boys' Ranch including-c. 29-Last pre-code	17.00	52.00	130.00

WITCH HUNTER
Malibu Comics (Ultraverse): Apr, 1996 ($2.50, one-shot)

	GD25	FN65	NM94
1			2.50

WITCHING HOUR ("The ..." in later issues)
National Periodical Publ./DC Comics: Feb-Mar, 1969 - No. 85, Oct, 1978

	GD25	FN65	NM94
1-Toth-a, plus Neal Adams-a (2 pgs.)	7.25	22.00	80.00
2,6: 6-Toth-a	2.70	8.00	30.00
3,5-Wrightson-a; Toth-p. 3-Last 12¢ issue	3.20	9.50	35.00
4,7-12: Toth-a in all. 8-Toth, Neal Adams-a	1.80	5.40	18.00
13-Neal Adams-c/a, 2pgs.	2.00	6.00	20.00
14-Williamson/Garzon, Jones-a; N. Adams-c	2.40	7.00	26.00
15-20	1.20	3.60	12.00
21-37,39,40	.90	2.70	8.00
38-(100 pgs.)	2.90	8.70	32.00
41-60		2.00	6.00
61-85: 84-(44 pgs.)			4.00

NOTE: *Combined with The Unexpected with #189.* ***Neal Adams*** *c-7-11, 13, 14.* ***Alcala*** *a-24, 27, 33, 41, 43.* ***Anderson*** *a-9, 38.* ***Cardy*** *c-4, 5.* ***Kaluta*** *a-7.* ***Kane*** *a-12p.* ***Morrow*** *a-10, 13, 15, 16.* ***Nino*** *a-31, 40, 45, 47.* ***Redondo*** *a-20, 23, 24, 34, 65; c-53.* ***Reese*** *a-23.* ***Sparling*** *a-1.* ***Toth*** *a-1, 3-12, 38r.* ***Tuska*** *a-11, 12.* ***Wood*** *a-15.*

WITHIN OUR REACH
Star Reach Productions: 1991 ($7.95, 84 pgs.)

	GD25	FN65	NM94
nn-Spider-Man, Concrete by Chadwick, Gift of the Magi by Russell; X-mas stories; Chadwick-c; Spidey back-c			8.00

WITH THE MARINES ON THE BATTLEFRONTS OF THE WORLD
Toby Press: 1953 (no month) - No. 2, Mar, 1954 (Photo covers)

	GD25	FN65	NM94
1-John Wayne story	27.00	81.00	200.00
2-Monty Hall in #1,2	6.50	19.50	45.00

WITH THE U.S. PARATROOPS BEHIND ENEMY LINES (Also see U.S. Paratroops...; #2-6 titled U.S. Paratroops...)
Avon Periodicals: 1951 - No. 6, Dec, 1952

	GD25	FN65	NM94
1-Wood-c & inside f/c	13.50	41.00	100.00
2-Kinstler-c & inside f/c only	8.00	24.00	50.00
3-6: 6-Kinstler-c & inside f/c only	6.70	20.00	45.00

NOTE: ***Kinstler*** *c-2, 4-6.*

WITNESS, THE (Also see Amazing Mysteries, Captain America #71, Ideal #4, Marvel Mystery #92 & Mystic #7)
Marvel Comics (MjMe): Sept, 1948

	GD25	FN65	NM94
1(Scarce)-Rico-c?	147.00	441.00	1250.00

WITTY COMICS
Irwin H. Rubin Publ./Chicago Nite Life News No. 2: 1945 - No. 7, 1945

	GD25	FN65	NM94
1-The Pioneer, Junior Patrol; war-c	19.00	56.00	140.00
2-The Pioneer, Junior Patrol	9.30	28.00	70.00
3-7-Skyhawk	7.85	23.50	55.00

WIZARD OF FOURTH STREET, THE
Dark Horse Comics: Dec, 1987 - No. 2, 1988 ($1.75, B&W, limited series)

	GD25	FN65	NM94
1,2: Adapts novel by S/F author Simon Hawke			1.80

WIZARD OF OZ (See Classics Illustrated Jr. 535, Dell Jr. Treasury No. 5, First Comics Graphic Novel, Marvelous..., & Marvel Treasury of Oz)
Dell Publishing Co.: No. 1308, Mar-May, 1962 (TV)

	GD25	FN65	NM94
Four Color 1308	11.00	32.00	115.00

WIZARD'S TALE, THE
Image Comics (Homage Comics): 1997 ($19.95, squarebound, one-shot)

	GD25	FN65	NM94
nn-Kurt Busiek-s/David Wenzel-painted-a/c			19.95

WOLF & RED
Dark Horse Comics: Apr, 1995 - No. 3, June, 1995 ($2.50, limited series)

	GD25	FN65	NM94
1-3: Characters created by Tex Avery			2.50

WOLFF & BYRD, COUNSELORS OF THE MACABRE
Exhibit A Press: May, 1994 - Present ($2.50, B&W)

	GD25	FN65	NM94
1-10			2.50

WOLF GAL (See Al Capp's...)

WOLFMAN, THE (See Movie Classics)

WOLFPACK
Marvel Comics: Feb, 1988 ($7.95); Aug, 1988 - No. 12, July, 1989 (Lim. series)

	GD25	FN65	NM94
1-1st app./origin (Marvel Graphic Novel #31)			8.00

Wolverine #131 © MAR

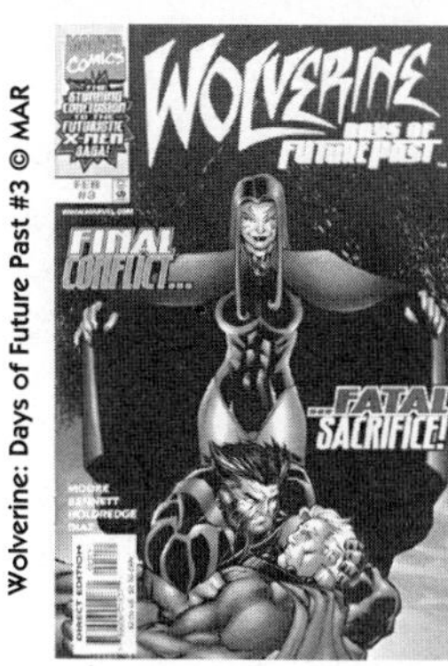

Wolverine: Days of Future Past #3 © MAR

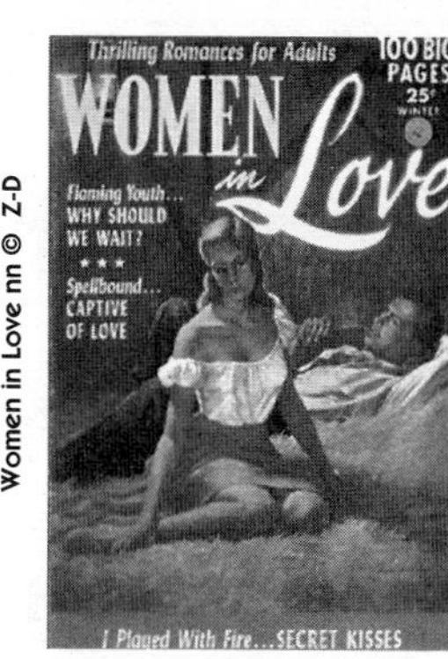

Women in Love nn © Z-D

GD25 FN65 NM94

1-12 1.00

WOLVERINE (See Alpha Flight, Daredevil #196, 249, Ghost Rider; Wolverine; Punisher, Havok &..., Incredible Hulk #180, Incredible Hulk &..., Kitty Pryde And..., Marvel Comics Presents, Power Pack, Punisher and..., Spider-Man vs... & X-Men #94)

WOLVERINE
Marvel Comics Group: Sept, 1982 - No. 4, Dec, 1982 (limited series)

	GD25	FN65	NM94
1-Frank Miller-c/a(p) in all	2.25	6.80	25.00
2,3	1.80	5.40	18.00
4	2.00	6.00	20.00
Trade paperback 1(7/87, $4.95)-Reprints #1-4 with new Miller-c.	1.00	3.00	10.00
Trade paperback nn (2nd printing, $9.95)-r/#1-4	1.20	3.60	12.00

WOLVERINE
Marvel Comics: Nov, 1988 - Present ($1.50/$1.75/$1.95/$1.99, Baxter paper)

	GD25	FN65	NM94
1-Buscema a-1-16, c-1-10; Williamson a(i)-1,4-8	2.20	6.25	22.00
2	1.00	3.00	10.00
3-5: 4-BWS back-c	.90	2.70	9.00
6-9: 6-McFarlane back-c. 7,8-Hulk app.	.85	2.60	7.00
10-1st battle with Sabretooth (before Wolverine had his claws)	1.50	4.50	15.00
11-16: 11-New costume		2.00	6.00
17-20: 17-Byrne-c/a(p) begins, ends #23			4.00
21-30: 24,25,27-Jim Lee-c. 26-Begin $1.75-c			3.00
31-40,44,47			2.00
41-Sabretooth claims to be Wolverine's father; Cable cameo			4.00
41-Gold 2nd printing ($1.75)			2.00
42-Sabretooth, Cable & Nick Fury app.; Sabretooth proven not to be Wolverine's father			4.00
42-Gold ink 2nd printing ($1.75)			2.00
43-Sabretooth cameo (2 panels); saga ends			3.00
45,46-Sabretooth-c/stories			2.50
48,49-Sabretooth app. 48-Begin 3 part Weapon X sequel			2.00
50-($2.50, 64 pgs.)-Die cut-c; Wolverine back to old yellow costume; Forge, Cyclops, Jubilee, Jean Grey & Nick Fury app.			3.00
51-74,76-80: 51-Sabretooth-c & app. 54-Shatterstar (from X-Force) app. 55-Gambit, Jubilee, Sunfire-c/story. 55-57,73-Gambit app. 57-Mariko Yashida dies (Late 7/92). 58,59-Terror, Inc. x-over. 60-64-Sabretooth storyline (60,62,64-c).			2.00
75-($3.95, 68 pgs.)-Wolverine hologram on-c			4.00
81-84,86: 81-Begin $1.95-c; bound-in card sheet			2.25
85-($2.50)-Newsstand edition			2.50
85-($3.50)-Collectors edition			3.50
87-90 ($1.95)-Deluxe edition			2.00
87-90 ($1.50)-Regular edition			1.50
91-99,101-114,-1(7/97): 91-Return from "Age of Apocalypse," 93-Juggernaut app. 94-Gen X app. 101-104-Elektra app. 104-Origin of Onslaught. 105-Onslaught x-over. 110-Shaman-c/app. 114-Alternate-c			2.00
100 ($3.95)-Hologram-c; Wolverine loses humanity.	.90	2.70	8.00
100 ($2.95)-Regular-c.			3.00
115-124: 115-Begin $1.99-c; Operation Zero Tolerance			2.00
125-($2.99) Wraparound-c; Viper secret			3.00
125-($6.95) Jae Lee variant-c			7.00
126-134: 126,127-Sabretooth-c/app. 128-Sabretooth & Shadowcat app.;Platt-a. 129-Wendigo-c/app. 131-Initial printing contained lettering error. 133-Begin Larsen-s/Matsuda-a			2.00
Annual nn (1990, $4.50, squarebound, 52 pgs.)-The Jungle Adventure; Simonson scripts; Mignola-c/a			4.50
Annual 2 (12/90, $4.95, squarebound, 52 pgs.)-Bloodlust			5.00
Annual nn (#3, 8/91, $5.95, 68 pgs.)-Rahne of Terror; Cable & The New Mutants app.; Andy Kubert-c/a (2nd print exists)			6.00
Annual '95 (1995, $3.95)			4.00
Annual '96 (1996, $2.95)- Wraparound-c; Silver Samurai, Yukio, and Red Ronin app.			3.00
Annual '97 (1997, $2.99)- Wraparound-c			2.99
...BATTLES THE INCREDIBLE HULK nn (1989, $4.95, squarebound, 52 pg.) r/Incredible Hulk #180,181			5.00
...BLACK RIO (11/98, $5.99)-Casey-s/Oscar Jimenez-a			6.00
...BLOOD HUNGRY nn (1993, $6.95, 68 pgs.)-Kieth-r/Marvel Comics Presents #85-92 w/ new Kieth-c			7.00
...: BLOODY CHOICES nn (1993, $7.95, 68 pgs.)-r/Graphic Novel; Nick Fury app.			8.00
...EVILUTION (9/94, $5.95)			6.00
...: GLOBAL JEOPARDY 1 (12/93, $2.95, one-shot)-Embossed-c; Sub-Mariner, Zabu, Ka-Zar, Shanna & Wolverine app.; produced in cooperation with World Wildlife Fund			3.00
...:INNER FURY nn (1992, $5.95, 52 pgs.)-Sienkiewicz-c/a			6.00
...: KNIGHT OF TERRA (1995, $6.95)-Ostrander script			7.00
.../ NICK FURY: THE SCORPIO CONNECTION (1989, $16.95)			17.00
...: SAVE THE TIGER 1 (7/92, $2.95, 84 pgs.)-Reprints Wolverine stories from Marvel Comics Presents #1-10 w/new Kieth-c			3.00
...SCORPIO RISING ($5.95, prestige format, one-shot)			6.00
...TRIUMPHS AND TRAGEDIES-(1995, $16.95, trade paperback)-r/Uncanny X-Men #109,172,173, Wolverine limited series #4, & Wolverine #41,42,75			17.00
...TYPHOID'S KISS (6/94, $6.95)-r/Wolverine stories from Marvel Comics Presents #109-116			7.00

NOTE: *Austin c-3i.* ***Bolton*** *c(back)-5.* ***Buscema*** *25, 27p.* ***Byrne*** *a-17-22p, 23; c-1(back), 17-22, 23p.* ***Colan*** *a-24.* ***Andy Kubert*** *c/a-51.* ***Jim Lee*** *c-24, 25, 27.* ***Silvestri*** *a(p)-31-43, 45, 46, 48-50, 52, 53, 55-57; c-31-42p, 43, 45p, 46p, 48, 49p, 50p, 52p, 53p, 55-57p.* ***Stroman*** *a-44p; c-60p.* ***Williamson*** *a-3i; c(i)-1, 3-6.*

WOLVERINE AND THE PUNISHER: DAMAGING EVIDENCE
Marvel Comics: Oct, 1993 - No. 3, Dec, 1993 ($2.00, limited series)

1-3: 2,3-Indicia says "The Punisher and Wolverine..." 2.00

WOLVERINE: DAYS OF FUTURE PAST
Marvel Comics: Dec, 1997 - No. 3, Feb, 1998 ($2.50, limited series)

1-3: J.F. Moore-s/Bennett-a 2.50

WOLVERINE/GAMBIT: VICTIMS
Marvel Comics: Sept, 1995 - No. 4, Dec, 1995 ($2.95, limited series)

1-4: Jeph Loeb scripts & Tim Sale-a; foil-c 4.00

WOLVERINE SAGA
Marvel Comics: Sept, 1989 - No. 4, Mid-Dec, 1989 ($3.95, lim. series, 52 pgs.)

1-Gives history; Liefeld/Austin-c (front & back) 5.00
2-4: 2-Romita, Jr./Austin-c. 4-Kaluta-c 4.00

WOLVERINE VS. SPIDER-MAN
Marvel Comics: Mar, 1995 (2.50, one-shot)

1-r/Marvel Comics Presents #48 - 50 2.50

WOLVERINE/WITCHBLADE
Marvel Comics: Mar, 1997 (2.95, one-shot)

1-Devil's Reign Pt. 5 4.00

WOMAN OF THE PROMISE, THE
Catechetical Guild: 1950 (General Distr.) (Paper cover, 32 pgs.)

	GD25	FN65	NM94
nn	3.60	9.00	18.00

WOMEN IN LOVE (A Feature Presentation #5)
Fox Features Synd./Hero Books: Aug, 1949 - No. 4, Feb, 1950

	GD25	FN65	NM94
1	25.00	76.00	190.00
2-Kamen/Feldstein-c	21.00	64.00	160.00
3	14.00	42.00	105.00
4-Wood-a	17.00	50.00	125.00

WOMEN IN LOVE (Thrilling Romances for Adults)
Ziff-Davis Publishing Co.: Winter, 1952 (25¢, 100 pgs.)

	GD25	FN65	NM94
nn-(Scarce)-Kinstler-a; painted-c	43.00	129.00	365.00

WOMEN OUTLAWS (My Love Memories #9 on)(Also see Red Circle)

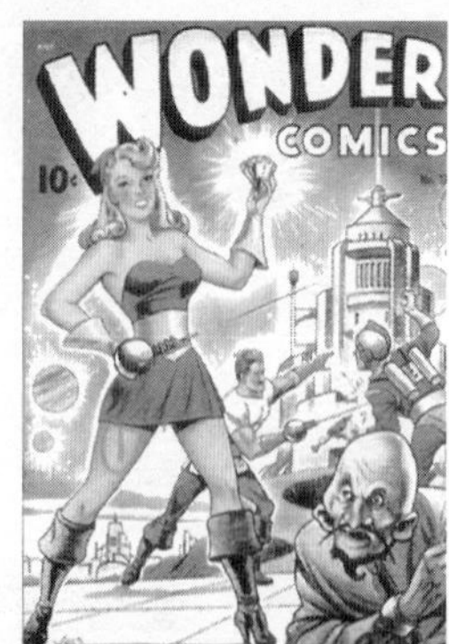

Wonder Comics #17 © BP

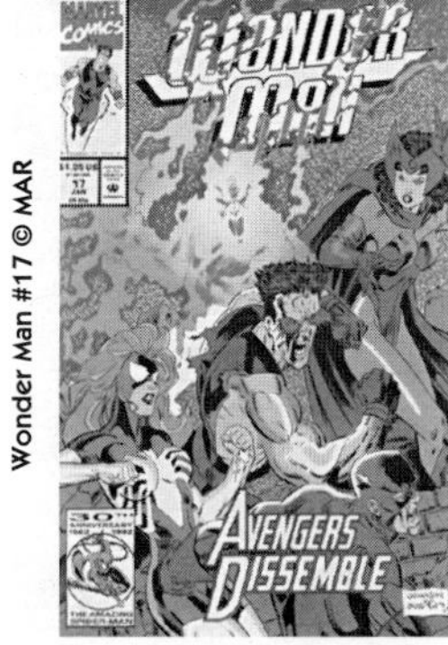

Wonder Man #17 © MAR

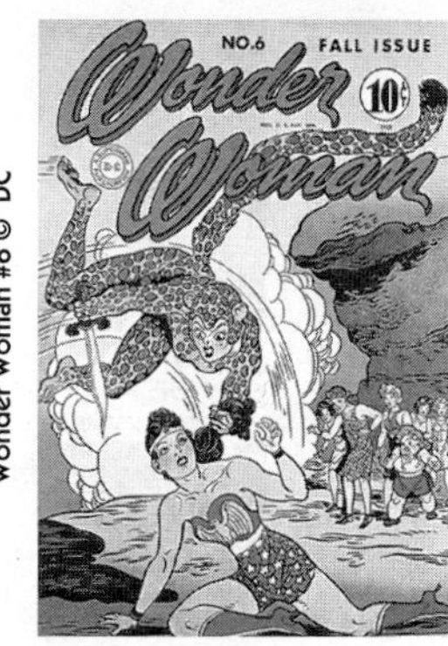

Wonder Woman #6 © DC

GD25 FN65 NM94

Fox Features Syndicate: July, 1948 - No. 8, Sept, 1949

1-Used in **SOTI**, illo "Giving children an image of American womanhood"; negligee panels 62.00 185.00 525.00
2,3: 3-Kamenish-a 50.00 150.00 425.00
4-8 41.00 122.00 325.00
nn(nd)-Contains Cody of the Pony Express; same cover as #7 29.00 86.00 215.00

WOMEN TO LOVE
Realistic: No date (1953)

nn-(Scarce)-Reprints Complete Romance #1; c-/Avon paperback #165 34.00 103.00 255.00

WONDER BOY (Formerly Terrific Comics) (See Blue Bolt, Bomber Comics & Samson)
Ajax/Farrell Publ.: No. 17, May, 1955 - No. 18, July, 1955 (Code approved)

17-Phantom Lady app. Bakerish-c/a 40.00 120.00 320.00
18-Phantom Lady app. 38.00 114.00 285.00
NOTE: *Phantom Lady not by Matt Baker.*

WONDER COMICS (Wonderworld #3 on)
Fox Features Syndicate: May, 1939 - No. 2, June, 1939 (68 pgs.)

GD25 FN65 VF82 NM94
1-(Scarce)-Wonder Man only app. by Will Eisner; Dr. Fung (by Powell), K-51 begins; Bob Kane-a; Eisner-c 1227.00 3680.00 7360.00 13,500.00
GD25 FN65 NM94
2-(Scarce)-Yarko the Great, Master Magician (see Samson) by Eisner begins; 'Spark' Stevens by Bob Kane, Patty O'Day, Tex Mason app. Lou Fine's 1st-c; Fine-a (2 pgs.); Yarko-c (Wonder Man-c #1) 420.00 1260.00 4200.00

WONDER COMICS
Great/Nedor/Better Publications: May, 1944 - No. 20, Oct, 1948

1-The Grim Reaper & Spectro, the Mind Reader begin; Hitler/Hirohito bondage-c 106.00 318.00 900.00
2-Origin The Grim Reaper; Super Sleuths begin, end #8,17 56.00 168.00 475.00
3-5 52.00 155.00 440.00
6-10: 6-Flag-c. 8-Last Spectro. 9-Wonderman begins 42.00 127.00 340.00
11-14: 11-Dick Devens, King of Futuria begins, ends #14. 11,12-Ingels-c & splash pg. 48.00 145.00 410.00
15-Tara begins (origin), ends #20 58.00 173.00 490.00
16,18: 16-Spectro app.; last Grim Reaper. 18-The Silver Knight begins 48.00 145.00 410.00
17-Wonderman with Frazetta panels; Jill Trent with all Frazetta inks 52.00 155.00 440.00
19-Frazetta panels 48.00 145.00 410.00
20-Most of Silver Knight by Frazetta 58.00 173.00 490.00
NOTE: ***Ingels** c-11, 12. **Roussos** a-19. **Schomburg (Xela)** c-1-10; (airbrush)-13-20. Bondage c-12, 13, 15. Cover features: Grim Reaper #1-8; Wonder Man #9-15; Tara #16-20.*

WONDER DUCK (See Wisco)
Marvel Comics (CDS): Sept, 1949 - No. 3, Mar, 1950

1-Funny animal 12.00 36.00 90.00
2,3 8.50 26.00 60.00

WONDERFUL ADVENTURES OF PINOCCHIO, THE (See Movie Comics & Walt Disney Showcase #48)
Whitman Publishing Co.: No. 3, April, 1982 (Walt Disney)

3-(Continuation of Movie Comics?); r/FC #92 3.00

WONDERFUL WORLD OF DISNEY, THE (Walt Disney)
Whitman Publishing Co.: 1978 (Digest, 116 pgs.)

1-Barks-a (reprints) 2.00 6.00 20.00

WONDERFUL WORLD OF DUCKS (See Golden Picture Story Book)
Colgate Palmolive Co.: 1975

1-Mostly-r 2.00

GD25 FN65 NM94

WONDERFUL WORLD OF THE BROTHERS GRIMM (See Movie Comics)

WONDERLAND COMICS
Feature Publications/Prize: Summer, 1945 - No. 9, Feb-Mar, 1947

1-Alex in Wonderland begins; Howard Post-c 11.00 32.00 80.00
2-Howard Post-c/a(2) 6.50 19.50 45.00
3-9: 3,4-Post-c 5.70 17.00 35.00

WONDER MAN (See The Avengers #9, 151)
Marvel Comics Group: Mar, 1986 ($1.25, one-shot, 52 pgs.)

1 1.30

WONDER MAN
Marvel Comics Group: Sept, 1991 - No. 29, Jan, 1994 ($1.00)

1-5: 1-Free fold out poster by Johnson/Austin. 1-3-Johnson/Austin-c/a. 2-Avengers West Coast x-over. 4 Austin-c(i) 1.00
6-29: 6-begin 1.25-c 1.25
Annual 1 (1992, $2.25)-Immonen-a (10 pgs.) 2.25
Annual 2 (1993, $2.25)-Bagged w/trading card 2.25

WONDERS OF ALADDIN, THE
Dell Publishing Co.: No. 1255, Feb-Apr, 1962

Four Color 1255-Movie 5.75 17.00 63.00

WONDER WOMAN (See Adventure Comics #459, All-Star Comics, Brave & the Bold, DC Comics Presents, Justice League of America, Legend of..., Power Record Comics, Sensation Comics, Super Friends and World's Finest Comics #244)

WONDER WOMAN
National Periodical Publications/All-American Publ./DC Comics:
Summer, 1942 - No. 329, Feb, 1986

GD25 FN65 VF82 NM94
1-Origin Wonder Woman retold (more detailed than All-Star #8); H. G. Peter-c/a begins 1545.00 4635.00 9270.00 17,500.00
1-Reprint, Oversize 13-1/2x10". **WARNING:** This comic is an exact reprint of the original except for its size. DC published it in 1974 with a second cover titling it as a Famous First Edition. There have been many reported cases of the outer cover being removed and the interior sold as the original edition. The reprint with the new outer cover removed is practically worthless. See Famous First Edition for value.
GD25 FN65 NM94
2-Origin/1st app. Mars; Duke of Deception app. 271.00 812.00 2300.00
3 171.00 512.00 1450.00
4,5: 5-1st Dr. Psycho app. 141.00 424.00 1200.00
6-10: 6-1st Cheetah app. 10-Invasion from Saturn 115.00 344.00 975.00
11-20 86.00 258.00 730.00
21-30: 23-Story from Wonder Woman's childhood 74.00 221.00 625.00
31-40: 34-Robot-c. 38-Last H.G. Peter-c 52.00 155.00 440.00
41-44,46-49: 49-Used in **SOTI**, pgs. 234,236; last 52 pg. issue 40.00 120.00 320.00
45-Origin retold 77.00 229.00 650.00
50-(44 pgs.)-Used in **POP**, pg. 97 37.00 112.00 280.00
51-60: 60-New logo 27.00 80.00 200.00
61-72: 62-Origin of W.W. i.d. 64-Story about 3-D movies. 70-1st Angle Man app. 72-Last pre-code (2/55) 23.00 68.00 170.00
73-90: 80-Origin The Invisible Plane. 85-1st S.A. issue. 89-Flying saucer-c/story 16.50 50.00 165.00
91-94,96,97,99: 97-Last H. G. Peter-a 12.00 36.00 120.00
95-A-Bomb-c 13.00 39.00 130.00
98-New origin & new art team (Andru & Esposito) begin (5/58); origin W.W. id w/new facts 13.50 41.00 135.00
100-(8/58) 14.00 42.00 140.00
101-104,106,108-110 11.00 33.00 110.00
105-(Scarce, 4/59)-W. W.'s secret origin; W. W. appears as girl (no costume yet) (called Wonder Girl - see DC Super-Stars #1) 45.00 135.00 550.00
107-1st advs. of Wonder Girl; 1st Merboy; tells how Wonder Woman won her costume 12.50 38.00 125.00
111-120 8.00 24.00 80.00
121-126: 122-1st app. Wonder Tot. 124-1st app. Wonder Woman Family. 126-Last 10¢ issue 6.00 18.00 60.00

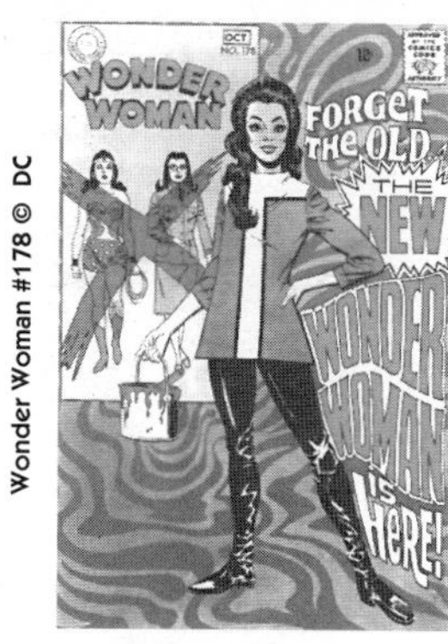

Wonder Woman #178 © DC

Wonder Woman #1,000,000 © DC

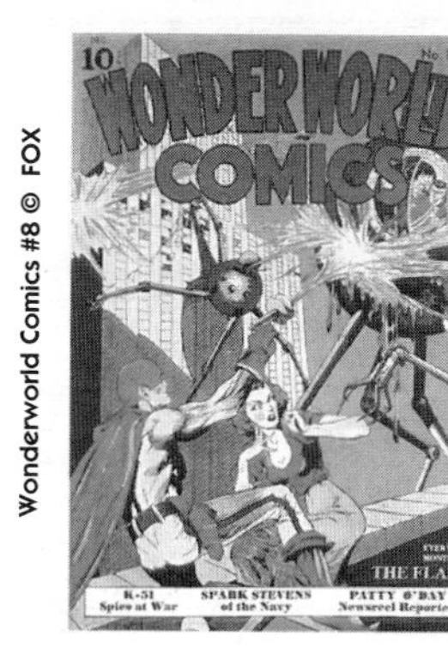

Wonderworld Comics #8 © FOX

GD25 FN65 NM94

127-130: 128-Origin The Invisible Plane retold. 129-2nd app. Wonder Woman Family (#133 is 3rd app.) 4.50 13.50 45.00

131-150: 132-Flying saucer-c 3.50 10.50 35.00

151-155,157,158,160-170 (1967): 151-Wonder Girl solo issue 3.00 9.00 30.00

156-(8/65)-Early mention of a comic book shop & comic collecting; mentions DCs selling for $100 a copy 3.00 9.00 30.00

159-Origin retold (1/66); 1st S.A. origin? 5.00 15.00 50.00

171-176 2.25 6.75 18.00

177-W. Woman/Supergirl battle 2.80 8.40 28.00

178-1st new W. Woman 2.80 8.40 28.00

179-Wears no costume to issue #203. 2.50 7.50 22.00

180-195: 180-Death of Steve Trevor. 195-Wood inks 1.50 4.50 15.00

196 (52 pgs.)-Origin-r/All-Star #8 (6 out of 9 pgs.) 1.80 5.40 18.00

197,198 (52 pgs.)-Reprints 1.80 5.40 18.00

199-Jeff Jones-c; 52 pgs. 2.20 6.25 22.00

200 (5-6/72)-Jeff Jones-c; 52 pgs. 2.90 8.70 32.00

201,202-Catwoman app. 202-Fafhrd & The Grey Mouser debut. 1.20 3.60 12.00

203,205-210,212: 212-The Cavalier app. .90 2.70 9.00

204-Return to old costume; death of I Ching. 1.20 3.60 12.00

211,214-(100 pgs.) 2.50 7.60 28.00

213,215,216,218-220: 220-N. Adams assist 4.50

217: (68 pgs.) 1.60 4.80 16.00

221,222,224-227,229,230,233-236,238-240 3.50

223,228,231,232,237,241,248: 223-Steve Trevor revived as Steve Howard & learns W.W.'s I.D. 228-Both Wonder Women team up & new World War II stories begin, end #243. 231,232: JSA app. 237-Origin retold. 241-Intro Bouncer; Spectre app. 248-Steve Trevor Howard dies (44 pgs.) 4.00

242-246,252-266,269,270: 243-Both W. Women team-up again. 269-Last Wood a(i) for DC? (7/80) 3.00

247,249-251,271: 247,249 (44 pgs.). 249-Hawkgirl app. 250-Origin/1st app. Orana, the new W. Woman. 251-Orana dies. 271-Huntress & 3rd Life of Steve Trevor begin 4.00

267,268-Re-intro Animal Man (5/80 & 6/80) 1.00 3.00 10.00

272-280 2.00

281-283: Joker-c/stories in Huntress back-ups 5.00

284-286,289,290,294-299,301-325 2.00

287,288,291-293: 287-New Teen Titans x-over. 288-New costume & logo. 291-293-Three part epic with Super-Heroines 3.00

300-($1.50, 76 pgs.)-Anniv. issue; Giffen-a; New Teen Titans, Bronze Age Sandman, JLA & G.A. Wonder Woman app.; 1st app. Lyta Trevor who becomes Fury in All-Star Squadron #25; G.A. W.W. & Steve Trevor revealed as married. 3.00

326-328 3.00

329 (Double size)-S.A. W.W. & Steve Trevor wed 5.00

Pizza Hut Giveaways (12/77)-Reprints #60,62 2.00

NOTE: ***Andru/Esposito*** *c-66-160(most).* ***Buckler*** *a-300.* ***Colan*** *a-288-305p; c-288-290p.* ***Giffen*** *a-300p.* ***Grell*** *c-217.* ***Kaluta*** *c-297.* ***Gil Kane*** *c-294p, 303-305, 307, 312, 314.* ***Miller*** *c-298p.* ***Morrow*** *c-233.* ***Nasser*** *a-232p; c-231p, 232p.* ***Bob Oskner*** *c(i)-39-65(most).* ***Perez*** *c-283p, 284p.* ***Spiegle*** *a-312.* ***Staton*** *a(p)-241, 271-287, 289, 290, 294-299; c(p)-241, 245, 246. Huntress back-up stories 271-287, 289, 290, 294-299, 301-321.*

WONDER WOMAN

DC Comics: Feb, 1987 - Present (75¢/$1.00/$1.25/$1.95/$1.99)

1-New origin; Perez-c/a begins 5.00

2-5 3.00

6-20: 9-Origin Cheetah. 12,13-Millennium x-over. 18,26-Free 16 pg. story 2.50

21-49,51-62: 24-Last Perez-a; scripts continue thru #62. 60-Vs. Lobo; last Perez-c. 62-Last $1.00-c 2.00

50-($1.50, 52 pgs.)-New Titans, Justice League 3.00

63-81: 63-New direction & Bolland-c begin; Deathstroke story continued from Wonder Woman Special #1 2.00

82-84: 82-Begin $1.50-c 3.00

GD25 FN65 NM94

85-1st Deodato-a; ends #100 1.40 4.20 14.00

86,87 5.00

88-93: 88-Superman-c & app. 90-(9/94)-1st Artemis. 91-(11/94). 93-Hawkman app. 4.00

0-(10/94) .85 2.60 7.00

94-97: 96-Joker-c 5.00

98,99: 98-Begin $1.75-c 3.00

100 ($2.95, Newsstand)-Death of Artemis; Bolland-c ends. 4.00

100 ($3.95, Direct Market)-Death of Artemis; foil-c. 5.00

101-119, 121-125: 101-Begin $1.95-c; Byrne-c/a/scripts begin. 101-104-Darkseid app. 105-Phantom Stranger cameo. 106-108-Phantom Stranger & Demon app. 107,108-Arion app. 111-1st app. new Wonder Girl. 111,112-Vs.Doomsday. 112-Superman app. 113-Wonder Girl-c/app; Sugar & Spike app. 2.00

120 ($2.95)-Perez-c 3.00

126-136: 128-Hippolyta becomes new W.W. 130-133-Flash (Jay Garrick) & JSA app. 136-Diana returns to W.W. role; last Byrne issue 2.00

137-140: 137-Begin $1.99-c; Priest-s. 139-Luke-s/Paquette-a begin; Hughes-c 1.99

#1,000,000 (11/98) 853rd Century x-over; Deodato-c 2.00

Annual 1,2: 1 ('88, $1.50)-Art Adams-a. 2 ('89, $2.00, 68 pgs.)-All women artists issue; Perez-c(i)/a. 3.00

Annual 3 (1992, $2.50, 68 pgs.)-Quesada-c(p) 2.50

Annual 4 (1995, $3.50)-Year One 3.50

Annual 5 (1996, $2.95)-Legends of the Dead Earth story; Byrne scripts; Cockrum-a 3.00

Annual 6 (1997, $3.95)-Pulp Heroes 4.00

Annual 7 (1998, $2.95)-Ghosts; Wrightson-c 2.95

...Donna Troy (6/98, $1.95) Girlfrenzy; Jimenez-a 2.00

Gallery (1996, $3.50)-Bolland-c; pin-ups by various 4.00

Lifelines TPB ('98, $9.95) r/#106-112; Byrne-c/a 9.95

Plus 1 (1/97, $2.95)-Jesse Quick-c/app. 3.00

Second Genesis TPB (1997, $9.95)-r/#101-105 10.00

Secret Files 1 (3/98, $4.95) 5.00

Special 1 (1992, $1.75, 52 pgs.)-Deathstroke-c/story continued in Wonder Woman #63 2.50

The Challenge Of Artemis TPB (1996, $9.95)-r/#94-100; Deodato-c/a 10.00

NOTE: ***Art Adams*** *a-Annual 1.* ***Byrne*** *c/a 101-107.* ***Bolton*** *a-Annual 1.* ***Deodato*** *a-85-100.* ***Perez*** *a-Annual 1; c-Annual 1(i).* ***Quesada*** *c(p)-Annual 3.*

WONDER WOMAN: AMAZONIA

DC Comics: 1997 ($7.95, Graphic Album format, one shot)

1-Elseworlds; Messner-Loebs-s/Winslade-a 7.95

WONDER WOMAN SPECTACULAR (See DC Special Series #9)

WONDER WOMAN: THE ONCE AND FUTURE STORY

DC Comics: 1998 ($4.95, one-shot)

1-Trina Robbins-s/Doran & Guice-a 5.00

WONDER WORKER OF PERU

Catechetical Guild: No date (5x7", 16 pgs., B&W, giveaway)

nn 4.00 10.00 20.00

WONDERWORLD COMICS (Formerly Wonder Comics)

Fox Features Syndicate: No. 3, July, 1939 - No. 33, Jan, 1942

3-Intro The Flame by Fine; Dr. Fung (Powell-a), K-51 (Powell-a?), & Yarko the Great, Master Magician (Eisner-a) continues; Eisner/Fine-c 600.00 1800.00 6000.00

4-Lou Fine-c 294.00 882.00 2500.00

5,6,9,10: Lou Fine-c 153.00 459.00 1300.00

7,8-Classic Lou Fine-c 212.00 635.00 1800.00

11-Origin The Flame 118.00 353.00 1000.00

12-15:13-Dr. Fung ends; last Fine-c 97.00 291.00 825.00

16-20: 74.00 221.00 625.00

21-Origin The Black Lion & Cub 65.00 194.00 550.00

Wonderworlds #1 © Innovation Publ.

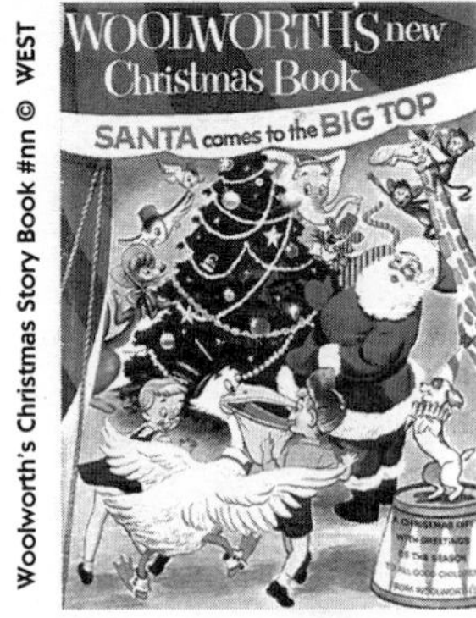

Woolworth's Christmas Story Book #nn © WEST

World Around Us #35 © GIL

22-27: 22,25-Dr. Fung app. 53.00 159.00 450.00
28-Origin & 1st app. U.S. Jones (8/41); Lu-Nar, the Moon Man begins 74.00 221.00 625.00
29,31,33 43.00 129.00 360.00
30-Intro & Origin Flame Girl 79.00 238.00 675.00
32-Hitler-c 53.00 159.00 450.00
NOTE: *Spies at War by* **Eisner** *in #13, 17. Yarko by* **Eisner** *in #3-11.* **Eisner** *text illos-3.* **Lou Fine** *a-3-11; c-3-13, 15; text illos-4.* **Nordling** *a-4-14.* **Powell** *a-3-12.* **Tuska** *a-5-9. Bondage-c 14, 15, 28, 31, 32. Cover features: The Flame-#3, 5-31; U.S. Jones-#32, 33.*

WONDERWORLDS
Innovation Publishing: 1992 ($3.50, squarebound, 100 pgs.)
1-Rebound super-hero comics, contents may vary; Hero Alliance, Terraformers, etc. 3.50

WOODSY OWL (See March of Comics #395)
Gold Key: Nov, 1973 - No. 10, Feb, 1976
1 1.20 3.60 12.00
2-10 .85 2.60 7.00

WOODY WOODPECKER (Walter Lantz... #73 on?)(See Dell Giants for annuals)(Also see The Funnies, Jolly Jingles, Kite Fun Book, New Funnies)
Dell Publishing Co./Gold Key No. 73-187/Whitman No. 188 on:
No. 169, 10/47 - No. 72, 5-7/62; No. 73, 10/62 - No. 201, 4/84 (nn 192)
Four Color 169(#1)-Drug turns Woody into a Mr. Hyde 13.00 40.00 145.00
Four Color 188 9.00 27.00 100.00
Four Color 202,232,249,264,288 5.75 17.00 63.00
Four Color 305,336,350 3.00 10.00 36.00
Four Color 364,374,390,405,416,431('52) 3.00 9.00 34.00
16 (12-1/52-53) - 30('55) 1.80 5.50 20.00
31-50 1.60 4.90 18.00
51-72 (Last Dell) 1.20 3.60 12.00
73-75 (Giants, 84 pgs., Gold Key) 3.60 11.00 40.00
76-80 1.60 4.80 16.00
81-100 1.20 3.60 12.00
101-120 .90 2.70 8.00
121-140 2.00 6.00
141-160 4.00
161-187 3.00
188,189 (Whitman) 4.00
190(9/80),191(11/80)-pre-pack? .90 2.70 8.00
(No #192)
193-197 5.00
198-201 (All #90062 on-c, no date or date code, pre-pack?) 2.00 6.00
Christmas Parade 1(11/68-Giant)(G.K.) 2.25 6.75 25.00
Clover Stamp-Newspaper Boy Contest('56)-9 pg. story-(Giveaway) 1.65 5.00 18.00
In Chevrolet Wonderland(1954-Giveaway)(Western Publ.)-20 pgs., full story line; Chilly Willy app. 15.00 45.00 120.00
...Meets Scotty McTape(1953-Scotch Tape giveaway)-16 pgs., full size 15.00 45.00 120.00
Summer Fun 1(6/66-G.K.)(84 pgs.) 3.30 10.00 36.00
NOTE: *15¢ editions exist. Reprints-No. 92, 102, 103, 105, 106, 124, 125, 152, 153, 157, 162, 165, 194(1/3)-200(1/3).*

WOODY WOODPECKER (See Comic Album #5,9,13, Dell Giant #24, 40, 54, Dell Giants, The Funnies, Golden Comics Digest #1, 3, 5, 8, 15, 16, 20, 24, 32, 37, 44, March of Comics #16, 34, 85, 93, 109, 124, 139, 158, 177, 184, 203, 222, 239, 249, 261, 420, 454, 466, 478, New Funnies & Super Book #12, 24)

WOODY WOODPECKER
Harvey Comics: Sept, 1991 - No. 7, 1993 ($1.25)
1-7: 1-r/W.W. #53 1.30
50th Anniversary Special 1 (10/91, $2.50, 68 pgs.) 2.50

WOODY WOODPECKER AND FRIENDS
Harvey Comics: Dec, 1991 - No. 4, 1992 ($1.25)
1-4 1.30

WOOLWORTH'S CHRISTMAS STORY BOOK
Promotional Publ. Co.(Western Printing Co.): 1952 - 1954 (16 pgs., paper-c) (See Jolly Christmas Book)
nn 4.25 13.00 26.00
NOTE: *1952 issue-Marv Levy c/a.*

WOOLWORTH'S HAPPY TIME CHRISTMAS BOOK
F. W. Woolworth Co.(Whitman Publ. Co.): 1952 (Christmas giveaway, 36 pgs.)
nn 4.25 13.00 26.00

WORDSMITH (1st Series)
Renegade Press: Aug, 1985 - No. 12, Jan, 1988 ($1.70/$2.00, B&W, bi-monthly)
1-6: R. G. Taylor-c/a 1.70
7-12: 7-Begin 2.00-c. R. G. Taylor-c/a in all. 2.00

WORDSMITH (2nd Series)
Caliber: 1996 - No. 6, 1996 ($2.95, B&W, limited series)
1-6: Reprints in all. 1-Contains 3 pg. sketchbook. 6-Flip book w/Raven Chronicles #10 3.00

WORD WARRIORS (Also see Quest for Dreams Lost)
Literacy Volunteers of Chicago: 1987 ($1.50, B&W)(Proceeds donated to help literacy)
1-Jon Sable by Grell, Ms. Tree, Streetwolf; Chaykin-c 1.50

WORLD AROUND US, THE (Illustrated Story of...)
Gilberton Publishers (Classics Illustrated): Sep, 1958 -No. 36, Oct, 1961 (25¢)
1-Dogs; Evans-a 5.70 17.00 40.00
2-4: 2-Indians; Check-a. 3-Horses; L. B. Cole-c. 4-Railroads; L. B. Cole-a (5 pgs.) 5.70 17.00 40.00
5-Space; Ingels-a 7.15 21.50 50.00
6-The F.B.I.; Disbrow, Evans, Ingels-a 7.15 21.50 50.00
7-Pirates; Disbrow, Ingels, Kinstler-a 6.50 19.50 45.00
8-Flight; Evans, Ingels, Crandall-a 6.85 21.00 48.00
9-Army; Disbrow, Ingels, Orlando-a 5.70 17.00 40.00
10-13: 10-Navy; Disbrow, Kinstler-a. 11-Marine Corps. 12-Coast Guard; Ingels-a (9 pgs.). 13-Air Force; L.B. Cole-c 5.70 17.00 40.00
14-French Revolution; Crandall, Evans, Kinstler-a 7.15 21.50 50.00
15-Prehistoric Animals; Al Williamson-a, 6 & 10 pgs. plus Morrow-a 7.85 23.50 55.00
16-18: 16-Crusades; Kinstler-a. 17-Festivals; Evans, Crandall-a. 18-Great Scientists; Crandall, Evans, Torres, Williamson, Morrow-a 6.50 19.50 45.00
19-Jungle; Crandall, Williamson, Morrow-a 7.85 23.50 55.00
20-Communications; Crandall, Evans, Torres-a 7.15 21.50 50.00
21-American Presidents; Crandall/Evans, Morrow-a 7.15 21.50 50.00
22-Boating; Morrow-a 5.70 17.00 35.00
23-Great Explorers; Crandall, Evans-a 6.50 19.50 45.00
24-Ghosts; Morrow, Evans-a 7.15 21.50 50.00
25-Magic; Evans, Morrow-a 7.15 21.50 50.00
26-The Civil War 9.30 28.00 65.00
27-Mountains (High Advs.); Crandall/Evans, Morrow, Torres-a 6.85 21.00 48.00
28-Whaling; Crandall, Evans, Morrow, Torres, Wildey-a; L.B. Cole-c 6.50 19.50 45.00
29-Vikings; Crandall, Evans, Torres, Morrow-a 7.85 23.50 55.00
30-Undersea Adventure; Crandall/Evans, Kirby, Morrow, Torres-a 7.15 21.50 50.00
31-Hunting; Crandall/Evans, Ingels, Kinstler, Kirby-a 6.50 19.50 45.00
32,33: 32-For Gold & Glory; Morrow, Kirby, Crandall, Evans-a. 33-Famous Teens; Torres, Crandall, Evans-a 6.85 21.00 48.00
34-36: 34-Fishing; Crandall/Evans-a. 35-Spies; Kirby, Morrow?, Evans-a.

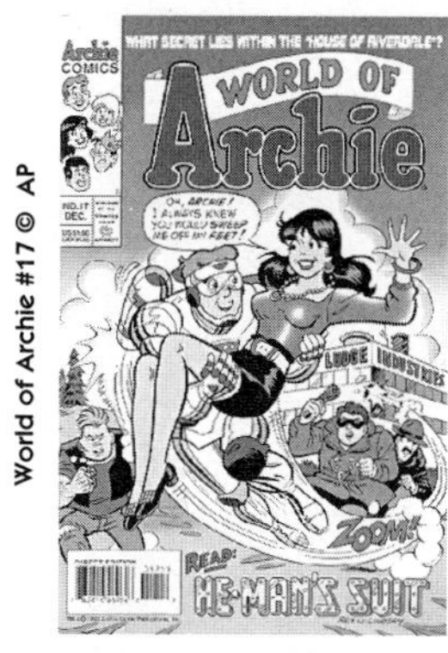

World of Archie #17 © AP

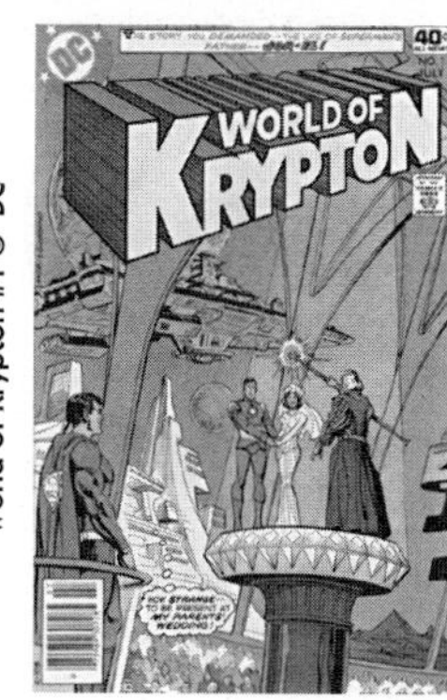

World of Krypton #1 © DC

World's Finest Comics #2 © DC

GD25 FN65 NM94

36-Fight for Life (Medicine); Kirby-a 6.50 19.50 45.00

NOTE: See Classics Illustrated Special Edition. Another *World Around Us* issue entitled *The Sea* had been prepared in 1962 but was never published in the U.S. It was published in the British/European *World Around Us* series. Those series then continued with seven additional WAU titles not in the U.S. series.

WORLD FAMOUS HEROES MAGAZINE
Comic Corp. of America (Centaur): Oct, 1941 - No. 4, Apr, 1942 (comic book)

1-Gustavson-c; Lubbers, Glanzman-a; Davy Crockett, Paul Revere, Lewis & Clark, John Paul Jones stories; Flag-c 106.00 318.00 900.00
2-Lou Gehrig life story; Lubbers-a 47.00 141.00 400.00
3,4-Lubbers-a. 4-Wild Bill Hickok story; 2 pg. Marlene Dietrich story 43.00 129.00 350.00

WORLD FAMOUS STORIES
Croyden Publishers: 1945

1-Ali Baba, Hansel & Gretel, Rip Van Winkle, Mid-Summer Night's Dream 11.00 32.00 80.00

WORLD IS HIS PARISH, THE
George A. Pflaum: 1953 (15¢)

nn-The story of Pope Pius XII 4.15 12.50 25.00

WORLD OF ADVENTURE (Walt Disney's...)(TV)
Gold Key: Apr, 1963 - No. 3, Oct, 1963 (12¢)

1-Disney TV characters; Savage Sam, Johnny Shiloh, Capt. Nemo, The Mooncussers 1.80 5.40 18.00
2,3 1.20 3.60 12.00

WORLD OF ARCHIE, THE (See Archie Giant Series Mag. #148, 151, 156, 160, 165, 171, 177, 182, 188, 193, 200, 208, 213, 225, 232, 237, 244, 249, 456, 461, 468, 473, 480, 485, 492, 497, 504, 509, 516, 521, 532, 543, 554, 565, 574, 587, 599, 612, 627)

WORLD OF ARCHIE
Archie Comics: Aug, 1992 - No. 26 ($1.25/$1.50)

1-11: 9-Neon ink-c 1.25
12-26 1.50

WORLD OF FANTASY
Atlas Comics (CPC No. 1-15/ZPC No. 16-19): May, 1956 - No. 19, Aug, 1959

1 38.00 114.00 300.00
2-Williamson-a (4 pgs.) 24.00 71.00 185.00
3-Sid Check, Roussos-a 21.00 64.00 160.00
4-7 16.00 47.00 125.00
8-Matt Fox, Orlando, Berg-a 17.00 49.00 130.00
9-Krigstein-a 16.00 47.00 125.00
10,12-15 12.00 36.00 95.00
11-Torres-a 13.50 41.00 100.00
16-Williamson-a (4 pgs.); Ditko, Kirby-a 17.00 49.00 135.00
17-19-Ditko, Kirby-a 17.00 49.00 135.00

NOTE: ***Ayers*** *a-3.* ***B. Baily*** *a-4.* ***Berg*** *a-5, 6, 8.* ***Brodsky*** *c-3.* ***Check*** *a-3.* ***Ditko*** *a-17, 19.* ***Everett*** *a-2; c-4-7, 9, 12, 13.* ***Forte*** *a-4.* ***Infantino*** *a-14.* ***Kirby*** *c-15, 17-19.* ***Krigstein*** *a-9.* ***Maneely*** *c-2, 14.* ***Mooney*** *a-14.* ***Morrow*** *a-7.* ***Orlando*** *a-8, 13, 14.* ***Pakula*** *a-9.* ***Powell*** *a-4, 6.* ***R.Q. Sale*** *a-3, 9.* ***Severin*** *c-1.*

WORLD OF GIANT COMICS, THE (See Archie All-Star Specials under Archie Comics)

WORLD OF GINGER FOX, THE (Also see Ginger Fox)
Comico: Nov, 1986 ($6.95, 8 1/2 x 11", 68 pgs., mature)

Graphic Novel ($6.95) 7.00
Hardcover ($27.95) 28.00

WORLD OF JUGHEAD, THE (See Archie Giant Series Mag. #9, 14, 19, 24, 30, 136, 143, 149, 152, 157, 161, 166, 172, 178, 183, 189, 194, 202, 209, 215, 227, 233, 239, 245, 251, 457, 463, 469, 475, 481, 487, 493, 499, 505, 511, 517, 523, 531, 542, 553, 564, 577, 590, 602)

WORLD OF KRYPTON, THE (World of...#3) (See Superman #248)
DC Comics, Inc.: 7/79 - No. 3, 9/79; 12/87 - No. 4, 3/88 (Both are lim. series)

1-3 (1979, 40¢; 1st comic book mini-series): 1-Jor-El marries Lara. 3-Baby Superman sent to Earth; Krypton explodes; Mon-el app. 2.00
1-4 (75¢)-Byrne scripts; Byrne/Simonson-c 1.00

GD25 FN65 NM94

WORLD OF METROPOLIS, THE
DC Comics: Aug, 1988 - No. 4, July, 1988 ($1.00, limited series)

1-4: Byrne scripts 1.00

WORLD OF MYSTERY
Atlas Comics (GPI): June, 1956 - No. 7, July, 1957

1-Torres, Orlando-a; Powell-a? 39.00 117.00 300.00
2-Woodish-a 15.00 44.00 110.00
3-Torres, Davis, Ditko-a 18.00 54.00 135.00
4-Pakula, Powell-a 19.00 56.00 140.00
5,7: 5-Orlando-a 14.00 42.00 105.00
6-Williamson/Mayo-a (4 pgs.); Ditko-a; Crandall text illo 19.00 56.00 140.00

NOTE: ***Brodsky*** *c-2.* ***Colan*** *a-7.* ***Everett*** *c-1, 3.* ***Pakula*** *a-4, 6.* ***Romita*** *a-2.* ***Severin*** *c-7.*

WORLD OF SMALLVILLE
DC Comics: Apr, 1988 - No. 4, July, 1988 (75¢, limited series)

1-4: Byrne scripts 1.00

WORLD OF SUSPENSE
Atlas News Co.: Apr, 1956 - No. 8, July, 1957

1 31.00 92.00 230.00
2-Ditko-a (4 pgs.) 18.00 54.00 135.00
3,7-Williamson-a in both (4 pgs.); #7-with Mayo 18.00 54.00 135.00
4-6,8 14.00 42.00 105.00

NOTE: ***Berg*** *a-6.* ***Cameron*** *a-2.* ***Ditko*** *a-2.* ***Drucker*** *a-1.* ***Everett*** *a-1, 5; c-6.* ***Heck*** *a-5.* ***Maneely*** *a-1; c-1-3.* ***Orlando*** *a-5.* ***Powell*** *a-6.* ***Reinman*** *a-4.* ***Roussos*** *a-6.* ***Shores*** *a-1.*

WORLD OF WHEELS (Formerly Dragstrip Hotrodders)
Charlton Comics: No. 17, Oct, 1967 - No. 32, June, 1970

17-20-Features Ken King 2.25 6.75 18.00
21-32-Features Ken King 1.75 5.25 14.00
Modern Comics Reprint 23(1978) 5.00

WORLD OF WOOD
Eclipse Comics: 1986 - No. 4, 1987; No. 5, 2/89 ($1.75, limited series)

1-4:1-Dave Stevens-c. 2-Wood/Stevens-c 1.80
5 ($2.00, B&W)-r/Avon's Flying Saucers 2.00

WORLD'S BEST COMICS (World's Finest Comics #2 on)
National Per. Publications (100 pgs.): Spring, 1941 (Cardboard-c)(DC's 6th annual format comic)

GD25 FN65 VF82 NM94

1-The Batman, Superman, Crimson Avenger, Johnny Thunder, The King, Young Dr. Davis, Zatara, Lando, Man of Magic, & Red, White & Blue begin; Superman, Batman & Robin covers begin (inside-c is blank); Fred Ray-c; 15¢ cover price 1227.00 3682.00 7360.00 14,000.00

WORLDS BEYOND (Stories of Weird Adventure)(Worlds of Fear #2 on)
Fawcett Publications: Nov, 1951

GD25 FN65 NM94

1-Powell, Bailey-a; Moldoff-c 37.00 112.00 280.00

WORLDS COLLIDE
DC Comics: July, 1994 ($2.50, one-shot)

1-($2.50, 52 pgs.)-Milestone & Superman titles x-over 2.50
1-($3.95, 52 pgs.)-Polybagged w/vinyl clings 4.00

WORLD'S FAIR COMICS (See New York...)

WORLD'S FINEST (Also see Legends of World Finest
DC Comics: 1990 - No. 3, 1990 ($3.95, squarebound, limited series, 52 pgs.)

1-3: Batman & Superman team-up against The Joker and Lex Luthor; Dave Gibbons scripts & Steve Rude-c/a. 2,3-Joker/Luthor painted-c by Steve Rude 5.00
TPB-($19.95) r/#1-3 20.00

WORLD'S FINEST COMICS (Formerly World's Best Comics #1)
National Periodical Publ./DC Comics: No. 2, Sum, 1941 - No. 323, Jan, 1986 (#1-17 have cardboard covers) (#2-9 have 100 pgs.)

2 (100 pgs.)-Superman, Batman & Robin covers continue from World's Best;

NO.41 JULY-AUG
WORLD'S FINEST COMICS
15¢
A 76 PAGE MAGAZINE

World's Finest Comics #41 © DC

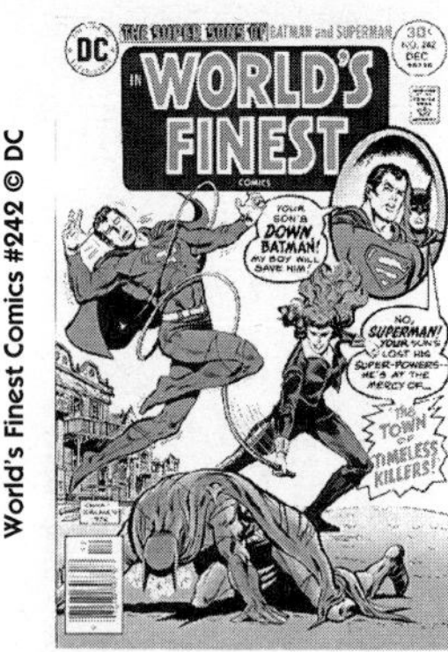

World's Finest Comics #242 © DC

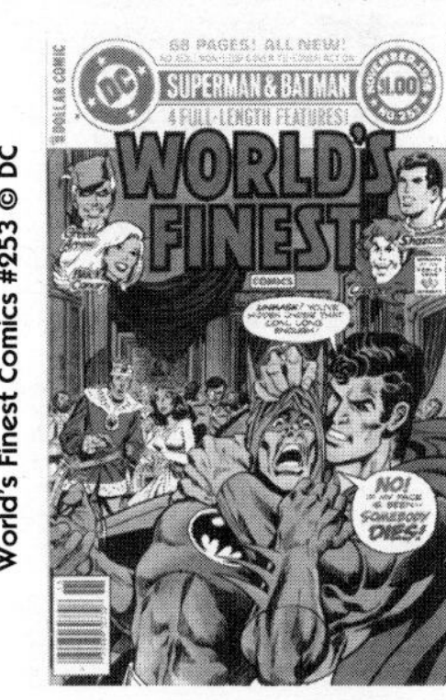

World's Finest Comics #253 © DC

GD25 FN65 NM94

(cover price 15¢ #2-70) 380.00 1140.00 3800.00

3-The Sandman begins; last Johnny Thunder; origin & 1st app. The Scarecrow 306.00 917.00 2750.00

4-Hop Harrigan app.; last Young Dr. Davis 229.00 688.00 1950.00

5-Intro. TNT & Dan the Dyna-Mite; last King & Crimson Avenger 229.00 688.00 1950.00

6-Star Spangled Kid begins (Sum/42); Aquaman app.; S&K Sandman with Sandy in new costume begins, ends #7 171.00 512.00 1450.00

7-Green Arrow begins (Fall/42); last Lando, King, & Red, White & Blue; S&K art 171.00 512.00 1450.00

8-Boy Commandos begin (by Simon(p) #12) 153.00 459.00 1300.00

9-Batman cameo in Star Spangled Kid; S&K-a; last 100 pg. issue; Hitler, Mussolini, Tojo-c 165.00 494.00 1400.00

10-S&K-a; 76 pg. issues begin 135.00 406.00 1150.00

11-17-Last cardboard cover issue 118.00 353.00 1000.00

18-20: 18-Paper covers begin; last Star Spangled Kid. 20-Last quarterly issue 103.00 309.00 875.00

21-30: 21-Begin bi-monthly. 30-Johnny Everyman app. 74.00 221.00 625.00

31-40: 33-35-Tomahawk app. 65.00 194.00 550.00

41-50: 41-Boy Commandos end. 42-Intro The Wyoming Kid & begins (9-10/49), ends #63. 43-Full Steam Foley begins, ends #48. 48-Last square binding. 49-Tom Sparks, Boy Inventor begins; robot-c 49.00 147.00 415.00

51-60: 51-Zatara ends. 54-Last 76 pg. issue. 59-Manhunters Around the World begins (7-8/52), ends #62 49.00 147.00 415.00

61-64: 61-Joker story. 63-Capt. Compass app. 27.00 80.00 200.00

65-Origin Superman; Tomahawk begins (7-8/53), ends #101 65.00 194.00 550.00

66-70-(15¢ issues, scarce)-Last 15¢, 68pg. issue 47.00 141.00 400.00

71-(10¢ issue, scarce)-Superman & Batman begin as team (7-8/54); were in separate stories until now; Superman & Batman exchange identities; 10¢ issues begin 67.00 200.00 800.00

72-(10¢ issue, scarce) 47.00 141.00 565.00

73-(10¢ issue, scarce) 48.00 144.00 580.00

74-Last pre-code issue 40.00 120.00 450.00

75-(1st code approved, 3-4/55) 37.00 111.00 410.00

76-80: 77-Superman loses powers & Batman obtains them this issue only 29.00 87.00 290.00

81-90: 84-1st S.A. issue. 88-1st Joker/Luthor team-up. 89-2nd Batmen of All Nations (aka Club of Heroes). 90-Batwoman's 1st app. in World's Finest (10/57, 3rd app. anywhere) plus-c app. 24.00 72.00 240.00

91-93,95-99: 96-99-Kirby Green Arrow. 99-Robot-c 17.00 51.00 170.00

94-Origin Superman/Batman team retold 43.00 129.00 520.00

100 (3/59) 29.00 87.00 290.00

101-110: 102-Tommy Tomorrow begins, ends #124 12.00 36.00 120.00

111-121: 111-1st app. The Clock King. 113-Intro. Miss Arrowette in Green Arrow; 1st Bat-Mite/Mr. Mxyzptlk team-up (11/60). 121-Last 10¢ issue 9.50 28.50 95.00

122-128,130-142: 123-2nd Bat-Mite/Mr. Mxyzptlk team-up (2/62). 125-Aquaman begins (5/62), ends #139 (Aquaman #1 is dated 1-2/62). 135-Last Dick Sprang story. 140-Last Green Arrow; last Clayface until Action #443. 142-Origin The Composite Superman (villain); Legion app. 5.00 15.00 50.00

129-Joker/Luthor team-up-c/story 6.50 19.50 65.00

143-150: 143-1st Mailbag 4.00 12.00 40.00

151-153,155,157-160: 156-Intro of Bizarro Batman. 157-2nd Super Sons story; last app. Kathy Kane (Bat-woman) until Batman Family #10 3.00 9.00 30.00

154-1st Super Sons story; last Bat-woman in costume until Batman Family #10. 3.00 9.00 30.00

156-1st Bizarro Batman; Joker-c/story 9.00 27.00 90.00

161,170 (80-Pg. Giants G-28,G-40) 3.50 10.50 35.00

162-165,167-169,171,172,174: 168,172-Adult Legion app. 169-3rd app. new Batgirl(9/67)(cover and 1 panel cameo); 3rd Bat-Mite/Mr. Mxyzptlk team-up. 2.50 7.50 22.00

GD25 FN65 NM94

166-Joker-c/story 2.50 7.50 25.00

173-('68)-1st S.A. app. Two-Face as Batman becomes Two-Face in story 7.00 21.00 70.00

175,176-Neal Adams-a; both reprint J'onn J'onzz origin/Detective #225,226 2.00 6.00 20.00

177-Joker/Luthor team-up-c/story 2.00 6.00 20.00

178,180-187: 182-Silent Knight-r/Brave & Bold #6. 186-Johnny Quick-r. 187-Green Arrow origin-r by Kirby (Adv. #256) 1.60 4.80 16.00

179,188 (80-Pg. Giants G-52,G-64): 179-r/#94 2.90 8.70 32.00

189-196: 190-193-Robin-r 1.40 4.20 14.00

197-(80 Pg. Giant G-76) 2.70 8.00 30.00

198,199-3rd Superman/Flash race (see Flash #175 & Superman #199) 5.50 16.50 60.00

200 1.80 5.40 18.00

201-204: 203-Last 15¢ issue. 1.00 3.00 10.00

205-(52 pgs.)-Shining Knight-r (6 pgs.) by Frazetta/Adv. #153; Teen Titans x-over 1.80 5.40 18.00

206 (80-Pg. Giant G-88) 2.50 7.60 28.00

207-212-(25¢, 52 pgs.). 208-Origin Robotman-r/Det. #138. 1.40 4.20 14.00

213,214,216-222,229-248: 217-Metamorpho begins, ends #220; Batman/Superman team-ups begin. 229-r/origin Superman-Batman team. 242-Super Sons. 244-Green Arrow, Black Canary, Wonder Woman, Vigilante begin; $1.00, 84 pg. issues begin. 246-Death of Stuff in Vigilante; origin Vigilante retold. 248-Last Vigilante 1.00 3.00 10.00

215-Intro. Batman Jr. & Superman Jr. 1.80 5.40 18.00

223-228-(100 pgs.). 223-N. Adams-r. 223-Deadman origin. 226-N. Adams, S&K, Toth-r; Manhunter part origin-r/Det. #225,226. 227-Deadman app. 1.70 5.10 17.00

249-The Creeper begins by Ditko, ends #255; 84 pgs .85 2.60 7.00

250-252 (84 pgs.)-250-The Creeper origin retold by Ditko. 252-Last 84 pg. issue .85 2.60 7.00

253-265: 253-Capt. Marvel begins; 68 pgs. begin, end #265. 255-Last Creeper. 256-Hawkman begins. 257-Black Lightning begins. 263-Super Sons 2.00 6.00

266-270,272-299: 266-282-(52 pgs.). 264-Clay Face app. 267-Challengers of the Unknown app. 268-Capt. Marvel Jr. origin retold. 274-Zatanna begins. 279, 280-Capt. Marvel Jr. & Kid Eternity learn they are brothers. 284-Legion app. 4.00

271-Origin Superman/Batman team retold 5.00

300-($1.25, 52pgs.)-Justice League of America, New Teen Titans & The Outsiders app.; Perez-a (3 pgs.) 4.00

301-323: 304-Origin Null and Void. 309,319-Free 16 pg. story in each (309-Flash Force 2000, 319-Mask preview) 2.00

Giveaway (c. 1944-45, 8 pgs., in color, paper-c)-Johnny Everyman-r/World's Finest 19.00 56.00 140.00

Giveaway (c. 1949, 8 pgs., in color, paper-c)- "Make Way For Youth" r/World's Finest; based on film of same name 15.00 44.00 110.00

NOTE: ***Neal Adams** a-230ir; c-174-176, 178-180, 182, 183, 185, 186, 199-205, 208-211, 244-246, 258. **Austin** a-244-246i. **Burnley** a-8, 10; c-7-9, 11-14, 15p?, 16-18p, 20-31p. **Colan** a-274p, 297, 299. **Ditko** a-249-255. **Giffen** a-322; c-284p, 322. **G. Kane** a-38, 174r, 282, 283; c-281, 282, 289. **Kirby** a-187. **Kubert** Zatara-40-44. **Miller** c-285p. **Mooney** c-134. **Morrow** a-245-248. **Mortimer** c-16-21, 26-71. **Nasser** a(p)-244-246, 259, 260. **Newton** a-253-281p. **Orlando** a-224r. **Perez** a-300i; c-271, 276, 277p, 278p. **Fred Ray** c-1-5. **Fred Ray/Robinson** c-13-16. **Robinson** a-2, 9, 13-15; c-6. **Rogers** a-259p. **Roussos** a-212r. **Simonson** c-291. **Spiegle** a-275-278, 284. **Staton** a-262p, 273p. **Swan/Moldoff** c-126. **Swan/Mortimer** c-79-82. **Toth** a-228r. **Tuska** a-230r, 250p, 252p, 254p, 257p, 283p, 284p, 308p. Boy Commandos by **Infantino** #39-41.*

WORLD'S FINEST COMICS DIGEST (See DC Special Series #23)

WORLD'S GREATEST ATHLETE (See Walt Disney Showcase #14)

WORLD'S GREATEST SONGS
Atlas Comics (Male): Sept, 1954

1-(Scarce)-Heath & Harry Anderson-a; Eddie Fisher life story plus-c; gives lyrics to Frank Sinatra song "Young at Heart" 35.00 104.00 260.00

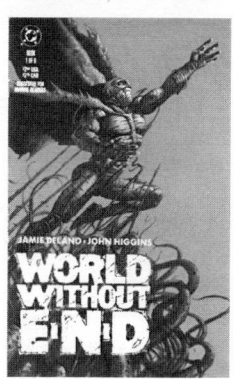

World Without End #1 © DC

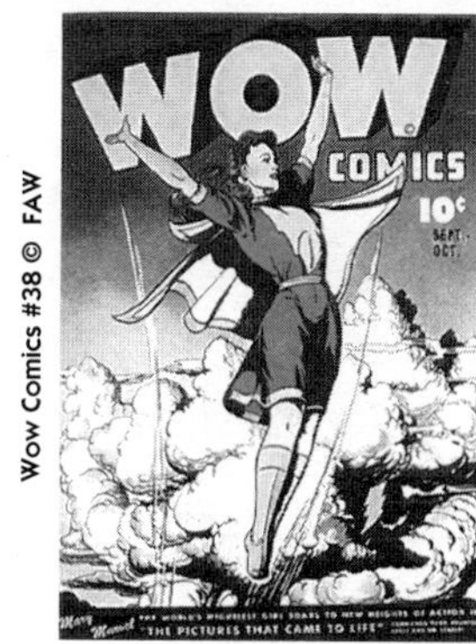

Wow Comics #38 © FAW

Wrath #1 © MAL

GD25 FN65 NM94

WORLD'S GREATEST STORIES
Jubilee Publications: Jan, 1949 - No. 2, May, 1949

	GD25	FN65	NM94
1-Alice in Wonderland; Lewis Carroll adapt.	25.00	76.00	190.00
2-Pinocchio	24.00	72.00	180.00

WORLD'S GREATEST SUPER HEROES
DC Comics (Nutra Comics) (Child Vitamins, Inc.): 1977 (Giveaway, 3-3/4x3-3/4", 24 pgs.)

nn-Batman & Robin app.; health tips 2.00 6.00

WORLDS OF FEAR (Stories of Weird Adventure)(Formerly Worlds Beyond #1)
Fawcett Publications: V1#2, Jan, 1952 - V2#10, June, 1953

	GD25	FN65	NM94
V1#2	37.00	112.00	280.00
3-Evans-a	32.00	96.00	240.00
4-6(9/52)	27.00	80.00	200.00
V2#7-9	23.00	70.00	175.00
10-Saunders painted-c; man with no eyes surrounded by eyeballs-c plus eyes ripped out story	47.00	142.00	400.00

NOTE: ***Moldoff** c-2-8. **Powell** a-2, 4, 5. **Sekowsky** a-4, 5.*

WORLDS UNKNOWN
Marvel Comics Group: May, 1973 - No. 8, Aug, 1974

	GD25	FN65	NM94
1-r/from Astonishing #54; Torres, Reese-a	1.20	3.60	12.00
2-8	.90	2.70	8.00

NOTE: ***Adkins/Mooney** a-5. **Buscema** c/a-4p. W. **Howard** c/a-3i. **Kane** a(p)-1,2; c(p)-5, 6, 8. **Sutton** a-2. **Tuska** a(p)-7, 8; c-7p. No. 7, 8 has Golden Voyage of Sinbad movie adaptation.*

WORLD WAR STORIES
Dell Publishing Co.: Apr-June, 1965 - No. 3, Dec, 1965

	GD25	FN65	NM94
1-Glanzman-a in all	2.50	7.60	28.00
2,3	1.80	5.40	18.00

WORLD WAR II (See Classics Illustrated Special Issue)

WORLD WAR III
Ace Periodicals: Mar, 1953 - No. 2, May, 1953

	GD25	FN65	NM94
1-(Scarce)-Atomic bomb blast-c; Cameron-a	52.00	155.00	440.00
2-Used in **POP**, pg. 78 & B&W & color illos; Cameron-a	49.00	148.00	420.00

WORLD WITHOUT END
DC Comics: 1990 - No. 6, 1991 ($2.50, limited series, mature, stiff-c)

1-6: Horror/fantasy; all painted-c/a 2.50

WORLD WRESTLING FEDERATION BATTLEMANIA
Valiant: 1991 - No. 5?, 1991 ($2.50, magazine size, 68 pgs.)

1-5: 5-Includes 2 free pull-out posters 3.00

WORST FROM MAD, THE (Annual)
E. C. Comics: 1958 - No. 12, 1969 (Each annual cover is reprinted from the cover of the Mad issues being reprinted)

	GD25	FN65	NM94
nn(1958)-Bonus; record labels & travel stickers; 1st Mad annual; r/Mad #29-34	34.00	103.00	275.00
2(1959)-Bonus is small 33-1/3 rpm record entitled "Meet the Staff of Mad"; r/Mad #35-40	40.00	120.00	315.00
3(1960)-Has 20x30" campaign poster "Alfred E. Neuman for President"; r/Mad #41-46	18.50	55.00	185.00
4(1961)-Sunday comics section; r/Mad #47-54	17.00	51.00	170.00
5(1962)-Has 33-1/3 record; r/Mad #55-62	26.50	80.00	265.00
6(1963)-Has 33-1/3 record; r/Mad #63-70	28.00	84.00	280.00
7(1964)-Mad protest signs; r/Mad #71-76	9.50	28.50	95.00
8(1965)-Build a Mad Zeppelin	12.00	36.00	120.00
9(1966)-33-1/3 rpm record	19.00	57.00	190.00
10(1967)-Mad bumper sticker	6.00	18.00	60.00
11(1968)-Mad cover window stickers	5.50	16.50	55.00
12(1969)-Mad picture postcards; Orlando-a	5.50	16.50	55.00

NOTE: *Covers: **Bob Clarke**-#8. **Mingo**-#7, 9-12.*

WOTALIFE COMICS (Formerly Nutty Life #2; Phantom Lady #13 on)
Fox Features Syndicate/Norlen Mag.: No. 3, Aug-Sept, 1946 - No. 12, July, 1947; 1959

	GD25	FN65	NM94
3-Cosmo Cat, Li'l Pan, others begin	8.50	26.00	60.00
4-12-Cosmo Cat, Li'l Pan in all	5.70	17.00	40.00
1(1959-Norlen)-Atomic Rabbit, Atomic Mouse; reprints cover to #6; reprints entire book?	3.50	10.50	35.00

WOTALIFE COMICS
Green Publications: 1957 - No. 5, 1957

	GD25	FN65	NM94
1	4.25	13.00	28.00
2-5	4.00	10.00	20.00

WOW COMICS
Henle Publishing Co.: July, 1936 - No. 4, Nov, 1936 (52 pgs., magazine size)

	GD25	FN65	NM94
1-Buck Jones in "The Phantom Rider" (1st app. in comics), Fu Manchu; Capt. Scott Dalton begins; Eisner-a; Briefer-c	235.00	706.00	2000.00
2-Ken Maynard, Fu Manchu, Popeye by Segar plus article on Popeye; Eisner-a	153.00	459.00	1300.00
3-Eisner-c/a(3); Popeye by Segar, Fu Manchu, Hiram Hick by Bob Kane, Space Limited app.; Jimmy Dempsey talks about Popeye's punch; Bob Ripley Believe it or Not begins; Briefer-a	153.00	459.00	1300.00
4-Flash Gordon by Raymond, Mandrake, Popeye by Segar, Tillie The Toiler, Fu Manchu, Hiram Hick by Bob Kane; Eisner-a(3); Briefer-c/a	188.00	565.00	1600.00

WOW COMICS (Real Western Hero #70 on)(See XMas Comics)
Fawcett Publ.: Winter, 1940-41; No. 2, Summer, 1941 - No. 69, Fall, 1948

	GD25	FN65	VF82	NM94
nn(#1)-Origin Mr. Scarlet by S&K; Atom Blake, Boy Wizard, Jim Dolan, & Rick O'Shay begin; Diamond Jack, The White Rajah, & Shipwreck Roberts, only app.; 1st mention of Gotham City in comics; the cover was printed on unstable paper stock and is rarely found in fine or mint condition; blank inside-c; bondage-c by Beck	1136.00	3410.00	6815.00	12,500.00

	GD25	FN65	NM94
2 (Scarce)-The Hunchback begins	206.00	618.00	1750.00
3 (Fall, 1941)	97.00	291.00	825.00
4-Origin & 1st app. Pinky	100.00	300.00	850.00
5	65.00	194.00	550.00
6-Origin & 1st app. The Phantom Eagle (7/15/42); Commando Yank begins	65.00	194.00	550.00
7,8,10: 10-Swayze-c/a on Mary Marvel	52.00	155.00	440.00
9 (1/6/43)-Capt. Marvel, Capt. Marvel Jr., Shazam app.; Scarlet & Pinky x-over; Mary Marvel-c/stories begin (cameo #9)	112.00	335.00	950.00
11-17,19,20: 15-Flag-c	40.00	120.00	315.00
18-1st app. Uncle Marvel (10/43); infinity-c	41.00	124.00	330.00
21-30: 23-Robot-c. 28-Pinky x-over in Mary Marvel	23.00	68.00	170.00
31-40: 32-68-Phantom Eagle by Swayze	15.00	44.00	110.00
41-50	13.00	40.00	100.00
51-58: Last Mary Marvel	12.00	36.00	90.00
59-69: 59-Ozzie (teenage) begins. 62-Flying Saucer gag-c (1/48). 65-69-Tom Mix stories (cont'd in Real Western Hero)	11.00	32.00	80.00

NOTE: *Cover features: Mr. Scarlet-#1-5; Commando Yank-#6, 7, (w/Mr. Scarlet #8); Mary Marvel-#9-56, (w/Commando Yank-#46-50), (w/Mr. Scarlet & Commando Yank-#51), (w/Mr. Scarlet & Pinky #53), (w/Phantom Eagle #54, 56), (w/Commando Yank & Phantom Eagle #58); Ozzie-#59-69.*

WRATH (Also see Prototype #4)
Malibu Comics: Jan, 1994 - No. 9, Nov, 1995 ($1.95)

	NM94
1-9: 2-Mantra x-over. 3-Intro/1st app. Slayer. 4,5-Freex app. 8-Mantra & Warstrike app. 9-Prime app.	2.00
1-Ultra 5000 Limited silver foil	4.00
Giant Size 1 (2.50, 44 pgs.)	2.50

WRATH OF THE SPECTRE, THE
DC Comics: May, 1988 - No. 4, Aug, 1988 ($2.50, limited series)

	NM94
1-3: Aparo-r/Adventure #431-440	2.50
4-New stories	3.00

Wyatt Earp #3 © MAR

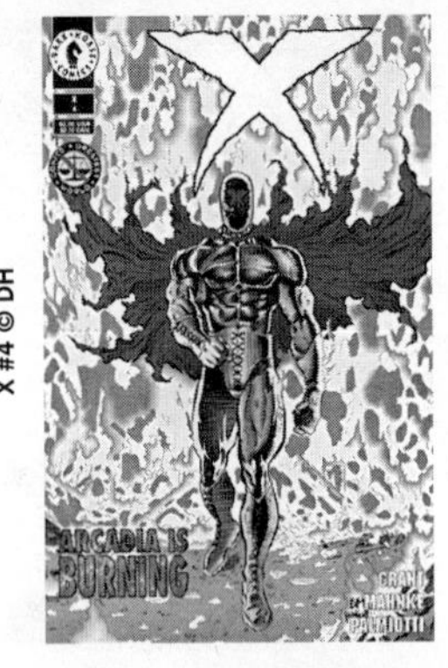

X #4 © DH

Xena: Warrior Princess Vs. Callisto #2 © Universal

WRECK OF GROSVENOR (See Superior Stories #3)

WRETCH, THE
Caliber: 1996 ($2.95, B&W)

1-Phillip Hester-a/scripts 3.00

WRETCH, THE
Amaze Ink: 1997 - Present ($2.95, B&W)

1-4-Phillip Hester-a/scripts 3.00

WRINGLE WRANGLE (Disney)
Dell Publishing Co.: No. 821, July, 1957

Four Color 821-Based on movie "Westward Ho, the Wagons"; Marsh-a; Fess Parker photo-c 7.00 22.00 80.00

WULF THE BARBARIAN
Atlas/Seaboard Publ.: Feb, 1975 - No. 4, Sept, 1975

1,2: 1-Origin. 2-Intro. Berithe the Swordswoman; Neal Adams, Wood, Reese-a assists 4.00
3,4 3.00

WYATT EARP
Atlas Comics/Marvel No. 23 on (IPC): Nov, 1955 - #29, June, 1960; #30, Oct, 1972 - #34, June, 1973

1 19.00 56.00 140.00
2-Williamson-a (4 pgs.) 11.00 32.00 80.00
3-6,8-11: 3-Black Bart app. 8-Wild Bill Hickok app 9.30 28.00 65.00
7,12-Williamson-a, 4 pgs. ea.; #12 with Mayo 9.30 28.00 65.00
13-20: 17-1st app. Wyatt's deputy, Grizzly Grant 7.85 23.50 55.00
21-Davis-c 6.50 19.50 45.00
22-24,26-29: 22-Ringo Kid app. 23-Kid From Texas app. 29-Last 10¢ issue 5.35 16.00 32.00
25-Davis-a 5.70 17.00 35.00
30-Williamson-r (1972) 1.40 4.20 14.00
31-34-Reprints. 32-Torres-a(r) 1.20 3.60 12.00

NOTE: ***Ayers** a-8, 10(2), 17, 20(4). **Berg** a-9. **Everett** c-6. **Kirby** c-25, 29. **Maneely** a-1; c-1-4, 8, 12, 17, 20. **Maurer** a-2(2), 3(4), 4(4), 8(4). **Severin** a-4, 9(4), 10; c-2, 9, 10, 14. **Wildey** a-5, 17, 24, 28.*

WYATT EARP (TV) (Hugh O'Brian Famous Marshal)
Dell Publishing Co.: No. 860, Nov, 1957 - No. 13, Dec-Feb, 1960-61 (Hugh O'Brian photo-c)

Four Color 860 (#1)-Manning-a 10.00 30.00 110.00
Four Color 890,921(6/58)-All Manning-a 7.00 20.00 75.00
4 (9-11/58) - 12-Manning-a. 5-Photo back-c 4.50 13.50 50.00
13-Toth-a 5.00 15.00 55.00

WYATT EARP FRONTIER MARSHAL (Formerly Range Busters) (Also see Blue Bird)
Charlton Comics: No. 12, Jan, 1956 - No. 72, Dec, 1967

12 6.50 19.50 45.00
13-19 4.25 13.00 28.00
20-(68 pgs.)-Williamson-a(4), 8,5,5,& 7 pgs. 8.50 26.00 60.00
21-30 2.25 6.75 18.00
31-50 1.50 4.50 12.00
51-72 1.00 2.80 7.00

WYNONNA EARP
Image Comics (WildStorm Productions): Dec, 1996 - No. 5, Apr, 1997 ($2.50)

1-5-Smith-s/Chin-a 2.50

X (Comics' Greatest World: X #1 only) (Also see Comics' Greatest World & Dark Horse Comics #8)
Feb, 1994 - No. 25, Apr, 1996 ($2.00/$2.50)
Dark Horse Comics

1-7: 3-Pit Bulls x-over 2.00
8-25: 8 ($2.50)-Ghost-c & app. 18-Miller-c.; Predator app. 19-22-Miller-c. 2.50
Hero Illustrated Special #1,2 (1994, $1.00, 20 pgs.) 1.00
One Shot to the Head (1994, $2.50, 36 pgs.)-Miller-c. 2.50

NOTE: ***Miller** c-18-22. **Quesada** c-6. **Russell** a-6.*

XANADU COLOR SPECIAL
Eclipse Comics: Dec, 1988 ($2.00, one-shot)

1-Continued from Thoughts & Images 2.00

XAVIER INSTITUTE ALUMNI YEARBOOK (See X-Men titles)
Marvel Comics: Dec, 1996 ($5.95, square-bound, one-shot)

1-Text w/art by various 6.00

X-BABIES: MURDERAMA
Marvel Comics: Aug, 1998 ($2.99, one-shot)

1-J.J. Kirby-a 3.00

X-CALIBRE
Marvel Comics: Mar, 1995 - No. 4, July, 1995 ($1.95, limited series)

1-4-Age of Apocalypse 2.00

XENA: WARRIOR PRINCESS (TV)
Topps Comics: Aug, 1997 - No. 0, Oct, 1997 ($2.95)

1-Two stories by various; J. Scott Campbell-c .90 2.70 8.00
1,2-Photo-c .90 2.70 8.00
2-Stevens-c 5.00
0-(10/97)-Lopresti-c 2.00 6.00
0-(10/97)-Photo-c 2.00 6.00
...First Appearance Collection ('97, $9.95) r/Hercules the Legendary Journeys #3-5 and 5-page story from TV Guide 10.00

XENA: WARRIOR PRINCESS AND THE ORIGINAL OLYMPICS (TV)
Topps Comics: Jun, 1998 - No. 3, Aug, 1998 ($2.95, limited series)

1-3-Regular and Photo-c; Lim-a/T&M Bierbaum-s 3.00

XENA: WARRIOR PRINCESS-BLOODLINES (TV)
Topps Comics: May, 1998 - No. 2, June, 1998 ($2.95, limited series)

1,2-Lopresti-s/c/a. 2-Reg. and photo-c 4.00
1-Bath photo-c 2.00 6.00
1-American Ent. Ed 5.00

XENA: WARRIOR PRINCESS / JOXER: WARRIOR PRINCE (TV)
Topps Comics: Nov, 1997 - No. 3, Jan, 1998 ($2.95, limited series)

1-3-Regular and Photo-c; Lim-a/T&M Bierbaum-s 4.00

XENA: WARRIOR PRINCESS-THE DRAGON'S TEETH (TV)
Topps Comics: Dec, 1997 - No. 3, Feb, 1998 ($2.95, limited series)

1-3-Regular and Photo-c; Teranishi-a/Thomas-s 4.00

XENA: WARRIOR PRINCESS-THE ORPHEUS TRILOGY (TV)
Topps Comics: Mar, 1998 - No. 3, May, 1998 ($2.95, limited series)

1-3-Regular and Photo-c; Teranishi-a/T&M Bierbaum-s 4.00

XENA: WARRIOR PRINCESS VS. CALLISTO (TV)
Topps Comics: Feb, 1998 - No. 3, Apr, 1998 ($2.95, limited series)

1-3-Regular and Photo-c; Morgan-a/Thomas-s 4.00

XENOBROOD
DC Comics: No. 0, Oct, 1994 - No. 6, Apr, 1995 ($1.50, limited series)

0-6: 0-Indicia says "Xenobroods" 1.50

XENON
Eclipse Comics: Dec, 1987 - No. 23, Nov. 1, 1988 ($1.50, B&W, bi-weekly)

1-23 1.50

XENOTECH
Mirage Studios: Sept, 1993 - No. 3, Dec, 1994 ($2.75)

1-3: Bound with 2 trading cards. 2-(10/94) 2.75

XENOZOIC TALES (Also see Cadillacs & Dinosaurs, Death Rattle #8)
Kitchen Sink Press: Feb, 1986 - No. 14, Oct, 1996

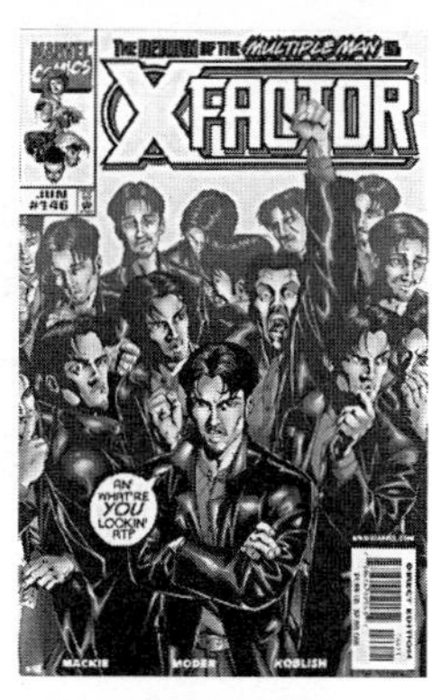
X-Factor #146 © MAR

X-Files: Fight The Future © 20th Century Fox

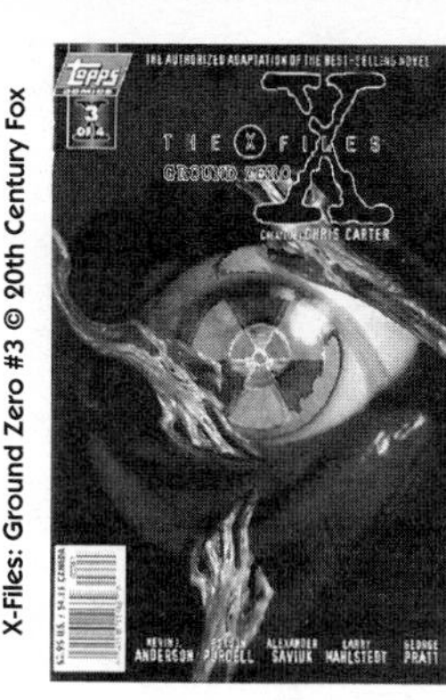
X-Files: Ground Zero #3 © 20th Century Fox

GD25 FN65 NM94

1-7: 1-2nd printing exists (1/89) 3.00
8-14 2.00

XENYA
Sanctuary Press: Apr, 1994 - No. 3 ($2.95)

1-3: 1-Hildebrandt-c; intro Xenya 3.00

XERO
DC Comics: May, 1997 - No. 12, Apr, 1998 ($1.75)

1-7 3.00
8-12: 8-Begin $1.95-c 1.95

X-FACTOR (Also see The Avengers #263, Fantastic Four #286 and Mutant X)
Marvel Comics Group: Feb, 1986 - No. 149, Sept, 1998

1-($1.25, 52 pgs)-Story recaps 1st app. from Avengers #263; story cont'd from F.F. #286; return of original X-Men (now X-Factor); Guice/Layton-a; Baby Nathan app. (2nd after X-Men #201) 2.00 6.00
2-4 3.00
5-1st app. Apocalypse (2-pg. cameo) 3.00
6-1st full app. Apocalypse 1.00 3.00 10.00
7-10: 10-Sabretooth app. (11/86, 3 pgs.) cont'd in X-Men #212; 1st app. in an X-Men comic book 2.00
11-20: 13-Baby Nathan app. in flashback. 14-Cyclops vs. The Master Mold. 15-Intro wingless Angel 1.50
21,22 1.50
23: 23-1st app. Archangel (2 pg. cameo) .85 2.60 7.00
24-1st full app. Archangel (now in Uncanny X-Men); Fall Of The Mutants begins; origin Apocalypse .90 2.70 8.00
25,26: Fall Of The Mutants; 26-New outfits 2.00
27-30 1.00
31-37,39,41-49: 35-Origin Cyclops 1.00
38,50-($1.50, 52 pgs.): 50-Liefeld/McFarlane-c 1.50
40-Rob Liefeld-c/a (4/89, 1st at Marvel?) 2.00
51-53-Sabretooth app. 52-Liefeld-c(p) 1.00
54-59: 54-Intro Crimson; Silvestri-c/a(p) 1.00
60-X-Tinction Agenda x-over; New Mutants (w/Cable) x-over in #60-62; Wolverine in #62 1.00
60-Gold ink 2nd printing 1.00
61,62-X-Tinction Agenda. 62-Jim Lee-c 1.00
63-Portacio/Thibert-c/a(p) begins, ends #69 1.00
64-67,69,70: 65-68-Lee co-plots. 65-The Apocalypse Files begins, ends #68. 66,67-Baby Nathan app. 67-Inhumans app. 69,70-X-Men (w/Wolverine) x-over 1.00
68-Baby Nathan is sent into future to save his life 1.00
71-New team begins (Havok, Polaris, Strong Guy, Wolfsbane & Madrox); Stroman-c/a begins 1.00
71-2nd printing ($1.25) 1.00
72-74: 74-Last $1.00-c 1.00
75-($1.75, 52 pgs.) 1.75
76-83,87-91,93-99,101: 77-Cannonball (of X-Force) app. 87-Quesada-c/a(p) in monthly comic begins, ends #92. 88-1st app. Random. 1.25
84-86 ($1.50)-Polybagged with trading card in each; X-Cutioner's Song x-overs. 84-86-Jae Lee-a(p). 85,86-Jae Lee-c 1.50
92-($3.50, 68 pgs.)-Wraparound-c by Quesada w/Havok hologram on-c; begin X-Men 30th anniversary issues; Quesada-a. 5.00
92-2nd printing 1.50
100-($2.95, 52 pgs.)-Embossed foil-c; Multiple Man dies. 5.00
100-($1.75, 52 pgs.)-Regular edition 2.00
102-105,107: 102-Begin $1.50-c; bound-in card sheet 1.50
106-($2.00)-Newsstand edition 2.00
106-($2.95)-Collectors edition 3.00
108-124,126-135,-1(7/97): 108-Begin $1.95-c. 112-Return from Age of Apocalypse. 115-card insert. 119-123-Sabretooth app. 123-Hound app. 124-w/Onslaught Update. 126-Onslaught x-over; Beast vs. Dark Beast 128-w/card insert; return of Multiple Man. 130-Assassination of Grayson Creed 2.00
125-($2.95)-"Onslaught"; Post app.; return of Havok 3.00
136-149: 136-Begin $1.99-c. 146,148-Moder-a 2.00
Annual 1-3: 1-(10/86). 2-(10/87). 3-(1988, $1.75)-Evolutionary War x-over. 2.50
Annual 4-6: 4-(1989, $2.00, 68 pgs.)-Atlantis Attacks; Byrne/Simonson-a; Byrne-c, 5-(1990, $2.00, 68 pgs.)-Fantastic Four, New Mutants x-over; Keown 2 pg. pin-up. 6-(1991, $2.00, 68 pgs.)-New Warriors app.; 5th app. X-Force cont'd from X-Men Annual #15 2.00
Annual 7 (1992, $2.25, 68 pgs.)-1st Quesada-a(p) on X-Factor plus-c(p) 2.25
Annual 8 (1993, $2.95, 68 pgs.)-Bagged w/trading card 3.00
Annual 9 (1994, $2.95, 68 pgs.)-Austin-a(i) 3.00
...PRISONER OF LOVE nn (1990, $4.95, 52 pgs.)-Starlin scripts; Guice-a 5.00

NOTE: ***Art Adams** a-41p, 42p. **Buckler** a-50p. **Liefeld** a-40; c-40, 50i, 52p. **McFarlane** c-50i. **Mignola** c-70. **Brandon Peterson** a-78p(part). **Whilce Portacio** c/a(p)-63-69. **Quesada** a(p)-87-92, Annual 7. c(p)-78, 79, 82, Annual 7. **Simonson** c/a-10, 11, 13-15, 17-19, 21, 23-31, 33, 34, 36-39; c-12, 16. **Paul Smith** a-44-48; c-43. **Stroman** a(p)-71-75, 77, 78(part), 80, 81; c(p)-71-77, 80, 81, 84. **Zeck** c-2.*

X-FILES, THE (TV)
Topps Comics: Jan, 1995 - No. 40, June, 1998 ($2.50)

-1(9/96)-Silver-c; r/Hero Illustrated Giveaway 1.00 3.00 10.00
0-($3.95)-Adapts pilot episode 4.00
0-"Mulder" variant-c .90 2.70 8.00
0-"Scully" variant-c .90 2.70 8.00
1/2-W/certificate 2.25 6.80 25.00
1-Adaptation of TV show; direct market & newsstand editions; Miran Kim-c on all 3.80 11.50 40.00
2 2.25 6.80 25.00
3,4 1.20 3.60 12.00
5-10 5.00
11-40: 11-Begin $2.95-c. 21-W/bound-in card. 40-Reg. & photo-c 3.00
Annual 1,2 ($3.95) 4.00
Collection 1 TPB ($19.95)-r/#1-6. 20.00
Collection 2 TPB ($19.95)-r/#7-12, Annual #1. 20.00
...Fight the Future ('98, $5.95) Movie adaption 2.00 6.00
Hero Illustrated Giveaway 1.50 4.50 15.00
Special Edition 1 ($4.95)-r/#1-3. 5.00
Special Edition 2 ($4.95)-r/#4-6. 5.00
Special Edition 3 ($4.95)-r/#7-9 5.00
Special Edition 4 ($4.95)-r/#10-12 5.00
Special Edition 5 ($4.95)-r/#13, Annual #1 5.00
Star Wars Galaxy Magazine Giveaway (B&W) 1.00 3.00 10.00
Trade paperback ($19.95) 20.00

X-FILES COMICS DIGEST, THE
Topps Comics: Dec, 1995 - No. 3 ($3.50, quarterly, digest-size)

1,2: New X-Files stories w/Ray Bradbury Comics-r 3.50
3 4.00

NOTE: ***Adlard** a-1, 2. **Jack Davis** a-2r. **Russell** a-1r.*

X-FILES, THE: GROUND ZERO (TV)
Topps Comics: Nov, 1997 - No. 4, March, 1998 ($2.95, limited series)

1-4-Adaption of the Kevin J. Anderson novel 3.00

X-FILES, THE: SEASON ONE (TV)
Topps Comics: July, 1997 - Present ($4.95, adaptions of TV episodes)

1,2,Squeeze, Conduit, Ice, Space, Fire, Beyond the Sea, Shadows 5.00

X-FORCE (Also see The New Mutants #100 & 1992 X-Men Annuals)
Marvel Comics: Aug, 1991 - Present ($1.00/$1.25/$1.50/$1.95/$1.99)

1-($1.50, 52 pgs.)-Polybagged with 1 of 5 diff. Marvel Universe trading cards inside (1 each); 6th app. of X-Force; Liefeld-c/a begins 2.00
1-1st printing with Cable trading card inside 4.00

X-Force #75 © MAR

X-Man #37 © MAR

X-Men #14 (1st Series) © MAR

GD25 FN65 NM94

1-2nd printing; metallic ink-c (no bag or card) 1.50
2-4: 2-Deadpool-c/story. 3-New Brotherhood of Evil Mutants app. 4-Spider-Man x-over; cont'd from Spider-Man #16; reads sideways 2.50
5-10: 6-Last $1.00-c. 7,9-Weapon X back-ups. 8-Intro The Wild Pack (Cable, Kane, Domino, Hammer, G.W. Bridge, & Grizzly); Liefeld-c/a (4); Mignola-a. 10-Weapon X full-length story (part 3). 11-1st Weapon Prime (cameo); Deadpool-c/story. 2.00
11-15,19-24,26-33: 15-Cable leaves X-Force 1.50
16-18-($1.50)-Polybagged w/trading card in each; X-Cutioner's Song x-overs 2.00
25-($3.50, 52 pgs.)-Wraparound-c w/Cable hologram on-c; Cable returns 4.00
34-37,39-45: 34-Begin $1.50-c; bound-in card sheet 1.50
38-($2.00)-Newsstand edition 2.00
38-($2.95)-Collectors edition 5.00
40-43 (1.95)-Deluxe edition 2.00
44-49,51-67,-1(7/97): 44-Return from Age of Apocalypse. 45-Sabretooth app. 49-Sebastian Shaw app. 52-Blob app., Onslaught cameo. 55-Vs. S.H.I.E.L.D. 56-Deadpool app. 57-Mr. Sinister & X-Man-c/app; Onslaught x-over. 58-Onslaught x-over. 59-W/card insert; return of Longshot. 60-Dr. Strange. -1-Flashback 2.00
50 ($3.95)-Gatefold wrap-around foil-c 3.00
50 ($3.95)-Liefeld variant-c 5.00
68-74: 68-Begin $1.99-c; Operation Zero Tolerance 2.00
75-($2.99) Cannonball-c/app. 3.00
76-86: 81-Pollina poster inside 2.00
Annual 1 (1992, $2.25, 68 pgs.)-1st Greg Capullo-a(p) on X-Force 2.25
Annual 2 (1993, $2.95, 68 pgs.)-Polybagged w/trading card; intro X-Treme & Neurtap 3.00
Annual 3 (1994, $2.95) 3.00
...And Cable '95 (12/95, $3.95)-Impossible Man app. 4.00
...And Cable '97 (7/97, $2.99) 3.00
...And Spider-Man: Sabotage nn (11/92, $6.95)-Reprints X-Force #3,4 & Spider-Man #16 7.00
.../ Champions '98 ($3.50) 3.50
...Youngblood (8/96, $4.95)-Platt-c 5.00
NOTE: ***Capullo*** *a(p)-15-25, Annual 1; c(p)-14-27.* ***Rob Liefeld*** *a-1-7, 9p; c-1-9, 11p; plots-1-12.* ***Mignola*** *a-8p.*

X-FORCE MEGAZINE
Marvel Comics: Nov, 1996 ($3.95, one-shot)
1-Reprints 4.00

XIMOS: VIOLENT PAST
Triumphant Comics: Mar, 1994 - No. 2, Mar, 1994 ($2.50, limited series)
1,2 2.50

X-MAN (Also see X-Men Omega & X-Men Prime)
Marvel Comics: Mar, 1995 - Present ($1.95/$1.99)
1-Age of Apocalypse 5.00
1-2nd print 2.00
2-4 3.00
5-24, 26-28,-1(7/97): 5-Post Age of Apocalypse stories begin. 5-7-Madelyne Pryor app. 10-Professor X app. 12-vs. Excalibur. 13-Marauders, Cable app. 14-Vs. Cable; Onslaught app. 15-17-Vs. Holocaust. 17-w/Onslaught Update. 18-Onslaught x-over; X-Force-c/app; Marauders app. 19-Onslaught x-over. 20-Abomination-c/app.; w/card insert. 23-Bishop-c/app. 24-Spider-Man Morbius-c/app. 27-Re-appearance of Aurora(Alpha Flight) 2.00
25-($2.99)-Wraparound-c 3.00
29-47: 29-Begin $1.99-c; Operation Zero Tolerance. 37,38-Spider-Man-c/app. 2.00
...'96-($2.95)-Wraparound-c; Age of Apocalypse 3.00
...'97-($2.99)-Wraparound-c 3.00
...: All Saints' Day ('97, $5.99) Dodson-a 6.00
.../Hulk '98 ($2.99) Wraparound-c; Thanos app. 3.00

XMAS COMICS
Fawcett Publications: 12?/1941 - No. 2, 12?/1942 (50¢, 324 pgs.) No. 3, 12?/1943 - No. 7, 12?/1947 (25¢, 132 pgs.)

	GD25	FN65	VF82	NM94
1-Contains Whiz #21, Capt. Marvel #3, Bulletman #2, Wow #3, & Master #18; Raboy back-c. Not rebound, remaindered comics; printed at same time as originals	320.00	960.00	1920.00	3200.00

	GD25	FN65	NM94
2-Capt. Marvel, Bulletman, Spy Smasher	129.00	388.00	1100.00
3-7-Funny animals (Hoppy, Billy the Kid & Oscar)	50.00	150.00	425.00

XMAS COMICS
Fawcett Publications: No. 4, Dec, 1949 - No. 7, Dec, 1952 (50¢, 196 pgs.)
4-Contains Whiz, Master, Tom Mix, Captain Marvel, Nyoka, Capt. Video, Bob Colt, Monte Hale, Hot Rod Comics, & Battle Stories. Not rebound, remaindered comics; printed at the same time as originals 56.00 168.00 475.00
5-7-Same as above. 7-Bill Boyd app.; stocking on cover is made of green felt (novelty cover) 45.00 134.00 380.00

XMAS FUNNIES
Kinney Shoes: No date (Giveaway, paper cover, 36 pgs.?)
Contains 1933 color strip-r; Mutt & Jeff, etc. 33.00 100.00 250.00

X-MEN, THE (See Adventures of Cyclops and Phoenix, Amazing Adventures, Archangel, Capt. America #172, Classic X-Men, Further Adventures of Cyclops & Phoenix, Gambit, Giant-Size..., Heroes For Hope..., Kitty Pryde & Wolverine, Marvel & DC Present, Marvel Collector's Edition:..., Marvel Fanfare, Marvel Graphic Novel, Marvel Super Heroes, Marvel Team-Up, Marvel Triple Action, The Marvel X-Men Collection, New Mutants, Nightcrawler, Official Marvel Index To..., Rogue, Special Edition..., The Uncanny..., Wolverine, X-Factor, X-Force, X-Terminators)

X-MEN, THE (1st series)(Becomes Uncanny X-Men at #142)(The X-Men #1-93; X-Men #94-141) (The Uncanny X-Men on-c only #114-141)
Marvel Comics Group: Sept, 1963 - No. 66, Mar, 1970; No. 67, Dec, 1970 - No. 141, Jan, 1981

	GD25	FN65	VF82	NM94
1-Origin/1st app. X-Men (Angel, Beast, Cyclops, Iceman & Marvel Girl); 1st app. Magneto & Professor X	400.00	1200.00	2800.00	6000.00

	GD25	FN65	NM94
2-1st app. The Vanisher	142.00	426.00	1700.00
3-1st app. The Blob (1/64)	54.00	163.00	650.00
4-1st Quick Silver & Scarlet Witch & Brotherhood of the Evil Mutants (3/64); 1st app. Toad; 2nd app. Magneto	50.00	150.00	600.00
5-Magneto & Evil Mutants-c/story	38.00	114.00	420.00
6-10: 6-Sub-Mariner app. 7-Magneto app. 8-1st Unus the Untouchable. 9-Early Avengers app. (1/65); 1st Lucifer. 10-1st S.A. app. Ka-Zar & Zabu the sabertooth (3/65)	30.00	90.00	300.00
11,13-15: 11-1st app. The Stranger. 14-1st app. Sentinels. 15-Origin Beast	24.50	74.00	245.00
12-Origin Prof. X; Origin/1st app. Juggernaut	31.00	93.00	315.00
16-20: 19-1st app. The Mimic (4/66)	12.50	38.00	125.00
21-27,29,30: 27-Re-enter The Mimic (r-in #75); Spider-Man cameo	10.00	30.00	100.00
28-1st app. The Banshee (1/67)(r-in #76)	14.50	44.00	145.00
31-34,36,37,39,40: 34-Adkins-c/a. 39-New costumes	7.00	21.00	70.00
35-Spider-Man x-over (8/67)(r-in #83); 1st app. Changeling	11.50	34.00	115.00
38-Origins of the X-Men series begins, ends #57	9.00	27.00	90.00
41-49: 42-Death of Prof. X (Changeling disguised as). 44-1st S.A. app. G.A. Red Raven. 49-Steranko-c; 1st Polaris	6.50	19.50	65.00
50,51-Steranko-c/a	7.00	21.00	70.00
52	4.80	14.40	48.00
53-Barry Smith-c/a (his 1st comic book work)	7.00	21.00	70.00
54,55-B. Smith-c. 54-1st app. Alex Summers who later becomes Havok. 55-Summers discovers he has mutant powers	7.50	22.50	75.00
56,57,59-63,65-Neal Adams-a(p). 56-Intro Havok w/o costume. 60-1st Sauron. 65-Return of Professor X.	6.00	18.00	60.00

X-Men #93 (1st Series) © MAR

X-Men #135 (1st Series) © MAR

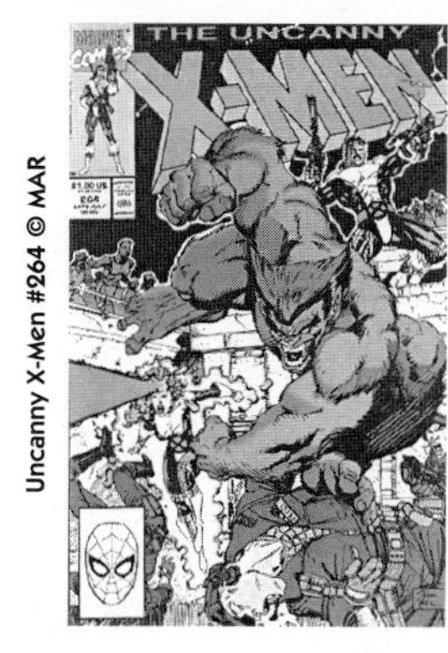

Uncanny X-Men #264 © MAR

	GD25	FN65	NM94
58-1st app. Havok in costume; N. Adams-a(p)	9.00	27.00	90.00
64-1st app. Sunfire	6.50	19.50	65.00
66-Last new story w/original X-Men; battles Hulk	5.50	16.50	55.00
67-70,72: (52 pgs.). 67-Reprints begin, end #93	3.20	9.60	32.00
71,73-93: 71-Last 15¢ issue. 73-86-r/#25-38 w/new-c. 83-Spider-Man-c/story. 87-93-r/#39-45 with covers	2.50	7.50	27.00
94 (8/75)-New X-Men begin (see Giant-Size X-Men for 1st app.); Colossus, Nightcrawler, Thunderbird, Storm, Wolverine, & Banshee join; Angel, Marvel Girl, & Iceman resign	38.00	114.00	440.00
95-Death of Thunderbird	8.50	26.00	95.00
96,97	7.00	21.00	75.00
98,99-(Regular 25¢ edition)(6,8/76)	7.00	21.00	75.00
98,99-(30¢-c, limited distribution)	26.00	76.00	280.00
100-Old vs. New X-Men; part origin Phoenix; last 25¢ issue (8/76)	7.00	21.00	75.00
101-Phoenix origin concludes	6.00	18.00	65.00
102-105,107: 102-Origin Storm. 104-1st app. Starjammers (brief cameo); Magneto-c/story. 107-1st full app. Starjammers; last 30¢ issue	3.00	9.00	33.00
106-(Regular 30¢ edition)(8/77)Old vs. New X-Men	3.00	9.00	33.00
106-(35¢-c, limited distribution)	11.00	34.00	125.00
108-Byrne-a begins (see Marvel Team-Up #53)	6.00	18.00	65.00
109-1st app. Weapon Alpha (becomes Vindicator)	4.50	13.50	50.00
110,111: 110-Phoenix joins	3.00	9.00	33.00
112-119: 117-Origin Professor X	2.50	7.50	28.00
120-1st app. Alpha Flight (cameo), story line begins (4/79); 1st app. Vindicator (formerly Weapon Alpha); last 35¢ issue	4.50	13.50	50.00
121-1st full Alpha Flight story	5.00	15.00	55.00
122-128: 123-Spider-Man x-over. 124-Colossus becomes Proletarian	2.25	6.80	25.00
129-Intro Kitty Pryde (1/80); last Banshee; Dark Phoenix saga begins	2.80	8.40	31.00
130-1st app. The Dazzler by Byrne (2/80)	2.50	7.50	27.00
131-135: 131-Dazzler app. 132-1st White Queen. 133-Wolverine app. 134-Phoenix becomes Dark Phoenix	2.00	6.00	20.00
136,138: 138-Dazzler app.; Cyclops leaves	1.80	5.40	18.00
137-Giant; death of Phoenix	2.00	6.00	20.00
139-Alpha Flight app.; Kitty Pryde joins; new costume for Wolverine	3.00	9.00	33.00
140-Alpha Flight app.	2.80	8.40	31.00
141-Intro Future X-Men & The New Brotherhood of Evil Mutants; 1st app. Rachel (Phoenix II); Death of Franklin Richards	3.00	9.00	33.00

UNCANNY X-MEN, THE (Formerly The X-Men)
Marvel Comics Group: No. 142, Feb, 1981 - Present

	GD25	FN65	NM94
142-Rachel app.; deaths of alt. future Wolverine, Storm & Colossus	1.20	3.60	12.00
143-Last Byrne issue			5.00
144-150: 144-Man-Thing app. 145-Old X-Men app. 148-Spider-Woman, Dazzler app. 150-Double size			4.00
151-157,159-161,163,164: 161-Origin Magneto. 163-Origin Binary. 164-1st app. Binary as Carol Danvers			3.00
158-1st app. Rogue in X-Men (6/82, see Avengers Annual #10)	.90	2.70	8.00
162-Wolverine solo story			5.00
165-Paul Smith-c/a begins, ends #175			4.00
166-Double size; Paul Smith-a			3.00
167-170: 167-New Mutants app. (3/83); same date as New Mutants #1; 1st meeting w/X-Men; ties into N.M. #3,4; Starjammers app.; contains skin "Tattooz" decals. 168-1st app. Madelyne Pryor (last pg. cameo) in X-Men (see Avengers Annual #10)			3.00
171-Rogue joins X-Men; Simonson-c/a	.85	2.60	7.00
172-174: 172,173-Two part Wolverine solo story. 173-Two cover variations, blue & black. 174-Phoenix cameo			4.00
175-(52 pgs.)-Anniversary issue; Phoenix returns			5.00
176-185: 181-Sunfire app. 182-Rogue solo story. 184-1st app. Forge (8/84)			3.00
186-Double-size; Barry Smith/Austin-a			3.00
187-192,194-199: 190,191-Spider-Man & Avengers x-over. 195-Power Pack x-over			2.00
193-Double size; 100th app. New X-Men; 1st app. Warpath in costume (see New Mutants #16)			4.00
200-(12/85, $1.25, 52 pgs.)		2.00	6.00
201-(1/86)-1st app. Cable? (as baby Nathan; see X-Factor #1); 1st Whilce Portacio-c/a(i) on X-Men (guest artist)	1.20	3.60	12.00
202-204,206-209: 204-Nightcrawler solo story; 2nd Portacio-a(i) on X-Men. 207-Wolverine/Phoenix story			3.50
205-Wolverine solo story by Barry Smith	.90	2.70	9.00
210,211-Mutant Massacre begins	1.00	3.00	10.00
212,213-Wolverine vs. Sabretooth (Mutant Mass.)	1.40	4.20	14.00
214-221,223,224: 219-Havok joins (7/87); brief app. Sabretooth			3.25
222-Wolverine battles Sabretooth-c/story	.90	2.70	9.00
225-227: Fall Of The Mutants. 226-Double size			4.50
228-239,241: 229-$1.00 begin			3.50
240-Sabretooth app.			4.00
242-Double size, X-Factor app., Inferno tie-in			3.50
243,245-247: 245-Rob Liefeld-a(p)			3.00
244-1st app. Jubilee	1.40	4.20	14.00
248-1st Jim Lee art on X-Men (1989)	1.40	4.20	14.00
248-2nd printing (1992, $1.25)			1.50
249-252: 252-Lee-c			2.50
253-255: 253-All new X-Men begin. 254-Lee-c			4.50
256,257-Jim Lee-c/a begins		2.00	6.00
258-Wolverine solo story; Lee-c/a		2.00	6.00
259-Silvestri-c/a; no Lee-a			3.50
260-265-No Lee-a. 260,261,264-Lee-c			3.00
266-1st full app. Gambit (see Ann. #14)-No Lee-a	1.80	5.40	18.00
267-Jim Lee-c/a resumes; 2nd full Gambit app.	.85	2.60	7.00
268-Capt. America, Black Widow & Wolverine team-up; Lee-a	1.00	3.00	10.00
268-2nd printing			2.25
269-Lee-a			3.50
270-X-Tinction Agenda begins	.80	2.40	6.50
270-Gold 2nd printing			2.25
271,272-X-Tinction Agenda			4.50
273-New Mutants (Cable) & X-Factor x-over; Golden, Byrne & Lee part pencils			3.25
274			2.75
275-($1.50, 52 pgs.)-Tri-fold-c by Jim Lee (p); Prof. X			3.25
275-Gold 2nd printing			2.75
276-280: 277-Last Lee-c/a. 280-X-Factor x-over			1.60
281-(10/91)-New team begins (Storm, Archangel, Colossus, Iceman & Marvel Girl); Whilce Portacio-c/a begins; Byrne scripts begin; wraparound-c (white logo)			3.25
281-2nd printing with red metallic ink logo w/o UPC box ($1.00-c); does not say 2nd printing inside			1.35
282-1st app. Bishop (cover & 1 pg. cameo)	.90	2.70	7.50
282-Gold ink 2nd printing ($1.00-c)			1.10
283-1st full app. Bishop (12/91)	.90	2.70	7.50
284-293,297-299: 284-Last $1.00-c. 286,287-Lee plots. 287-Bishop joins team. 288-Lee/Portacio plots. 290-Last Portacio-c/a. 294-Brandon Peterson-a(p) begins (#292 is 1st Peterson-c)			1.35
294-296 ($1.50)-Polybagged w/trading card in each; X-Cutioner's Song x-overs; all have Peterson/Austin-c/a			1.65
300-($3.95, 68 pgs.)-Holo-grafx foil-c; Magneto app.		2.00	6.00
301-303,305-309,311			1.35
304-($3.95, 68 pgs.)-Wraparound-c with Magneto hologram on-c; 30th anniversary issue; Jae Lee-a (4 pgs.)		2.00	6.00
307-Gold Edition		2.00	6.00

Uncanny X-Men #360 © MAR

X-Men #46 (2nd Series) © MAR

X-Men #80 DF Ed. (2nd Series) © MAR

GD25 FN65 NM94

310-($1.95)-Bound-in trading card sheet 2.25
312-$1.50-c begins; bound-in card sheet; 1st Madureira 4.00
313-321 1.65
316,317-($2.95)-Foil enhanced editions 3.25
318-321-($1.95)-Deluxe editions 2.25
322-Onslaught 5.00
323,324,326-345, -1(7/97), 346: 323-Return from Age of Apocalypse. 328-Sabretooth-c. 329,330-Dr. Strange app. 331-White Queen-c/app. 334-Juggernaut app.; w/Onslaught Update. 335-Onslaught, Avengers, Apocalypse, & X-Man app. 336-Onslaught. 338-Archangel's wings return to normal. 339-Havok vs. Cyclops; Spider-Man app. 341-Gladiator-c/app. 342-Deathbird cameo; two covers. 343,344-Phalanx 2.50
325-($3.95)-Anniversary issue; gatefold-c 4.00
342-Variant-c .90 2.70 9.00
347-349:347-Begin $1.99-c. 349-"Operation Zero Tolerance" 2.00
350-($3.99, 48 pgs.) Prismatic etched foil gatefold wraparound-c; Trial of Gambit; Seagle-s begin .90 2.70 8.00
351-359: 353-Bachalo-a begins. 354-Regular-c. 355-Alpha Flight-c/app. 356-Original X-Men-c 2.00
354-Dark Phoenix variant-c 3.00
360-($2.99) 35th Anniv. issue; Pacheco-c 3.00
360-($3.99) Etched Holo-foil enhanced-c 4.00
360-($6.95) DF Edition with Jae Lee variant-c 7.00
361-Gambit returns; Skroce-a 2.00
362-365: 362-Hunt for Xavier pt. 1; Bacheloa-. 364-Yu-a 1.99
Special 1(12/70)-Kirby-c/a; origin The Stranger 6.00 18.00 65.00
Special 2(11/71) 5.00 15.00 55.00
Annual 3(1979, 52 pgs.)-New story; Miller/Austin-c; Wolverine still in old yellow costume 2.20 6.60 22.00
Annual 4(1980, 52 pgs.)-Dr. Strange guest stars .85 2.60 7.50
Annual 5(1981, 52 pgs.) 2.00 6.00
Annual 6(1982, 52 pgs.)-Dracula app. 5.00
Annual 7,8: 7-(1983, 52 pgs.). 8-(1984, 52 pgs.) 5.00
Annual 9(1985)-New Mutants x-over cont'd from New Mutants Special Ed. #1; Art Adams-a 4.00
Annual 10(1986)-Art Adams-a 2.00 6.00
Annual 11(1987) 3.00
Annual 12(1988, $1.75)-Evolutionary War; A.Adams-a(p) 4.00
Annual 13(1989, $2.00, 68 pgs.)-Atlantis Attacks 3.00
Annual 14(1990, $2.00, 68 pgs.)-1st app. Gambit (minor app., 5 pgs.); Fantastic Four, New Mutants (Cable) & X-Factor x-over; Arthur Adams-c/a(p) .90 2.70 8.00
Annual 15 (1991, $2.00, 68 pgs.)-4 pg. origin; New Mutants x-over; 4 pg. Wolverine solo back-up story; 4th app. X-Force cont'd from New Warriors Annual #1 4.00
Annual 16 (1992, $2.25, 68 pgs.)-Jae Lee-c/a(p)(2) 2.50
Annual 17 (1993, $2.95, 68 pgs.)-Bagged w/card 4.00
Annual 18 (1994, $2.95, 68 pgs.) 3.00
...'95-(11/95, $3.95)-Wraparound-c 4.00
...'96-(1996, $2.95)-Wraparound-c 3.00
...'97-(1997, $2.99)-Wraparound-c 3.00
/Fantastic Four Annual '98 ($2.99) Casey-s 3.00
...At The State Fair of Texas (1983, 36 pgs., one-shot); Supplement to the Dallas Times Herald 1.00 3.00 10.00
...: The Dark Phoenix Saga (1990, $12.95, trade paperback) 13.00
...From The Ashes (1990, $14.95, trade paperback) r/#168-176 15.00
...In The Days of Future Past (1989, $3.95, trade paperback, 52 pgs.) 4.00

NOTE: ***Art Adams*** *a-Annual 9, 10p, 12p, 14p; c-218p.* ***Neal Adams*** *a-56-63p, 65p; c-56-63.* ***Adkins*** *a-34, 35p; c-31, 34, 35.* ***Austin*** *a-108i, 109i, 111-117i, 119-143i, 186i, 204i, 228i, 294-297i, Annual 3i, 7i, 9i, 13; c-109-111i, 114-122i, 123, 124-141i, 142, 143, 196i, 204i, 228i, 294-297i, Annual 3i.* ***J. Buscema*** *c-42, 43, 45.* ***Buscema/Tuska*** *a-45.* ***Byrne*** *a(p)-108, 109, 111-143, 273; c(p)-113-116, 127, 129, 131-141.* ***Capullo*** *c-14.* ***Ditko*** *r-86, 89-91, 93.* ***Everett*** *c-73.* ***Golden*** *a-273, Annual 7p.* ***Guice*** *a-216p, 217p.* ***G. Kane*** *c(p)-33, 74-76, 79, 80, 94, 95.* ***Kirby*** *a(p)-1-17 (#12-17, 67r-layouts); c(p)-1-17, 25, 30 (18, 26-parts).* ***Layton*** *a-105i; c-112i, 113i.* ***Jim Lee*** *a(p)-248, 256-258, 267-277; c(p)-252, 254, 256-261, 264, 267, 270, 275-277, 286.* ***Perez*** *a-Annual 3p; c(p)-112, 128, Annual 3.* ***Peterson*** *a(p)-294-300, 304(part); c(p)-294-299.* ***Whilce Portacio*** *a(p)-281-286, 289, 290; a(i)-267; c-281-285p, 289p, 290; c(i)-267.* ***Romita, Jr.*** *a-300; c-300.* ***Roussos*** *a-84i.* ***Simonson*** *a-171p; c-171, 217.* ***B. Smith*** *a-53, 186p, 198p, 205, 214; c-53-55, 186p, 198, 205, 212, 214, 216.* ***Paul Smith*** *a(p)-165-170, 172-175, 278; c-165-170, 172-175, 278.* ***Sparling*** *a-78p.* ***Steranko*** *a-50p, 51p; c-49-51.* ***Sutton*** *a-106i.* ***Art Thibert*** *a(i)-281-286; c(i)-281, 282, 284, 285.* ***Toth*** *a-12p, 67p(r).* ***Tuska*** *a-40-42i, 43-46p, 88i(r); c-39-41, 77p, 78p.* ***Williamson*** *a-202i, 203i, 211i; c-202i, 203i, 206i.* ***Wood*** *c-14i.*

GD25 FN65 NM94

UNCANNY X-MEN AND THE NEW TEEN TITANS (See Marvel and DC Present...)

X-MEN (2nd Series)
Marvel Comics: Oct, 1991 - Present ($1.00/$1.25/$1.95/$1.99)

1 a-d ($1.50, 52 pgs.)-Jim Lee-c/a begins, ends #11; new team begins (Cyclops, Beast, Wolverine, Gambit, Psylocke & Rogue); new Uncanny X-Men & Magneto app.; four different covers exist 3.50
1 e ($3.95)-Double gate-fold-c consisting of all four covers from 1a-d by Jim Lee; contains all pin-ups from #1a-d plus inside-c foldout poster; no ads; printed on coated stock 5.00
2-7: 4-Wolverine back to old yellow costume (same date as Wolverine #50); last $1.00-c. 5-Byrne scripts. 6-Sabretooth-c/story 4.00
8-10: 8-Gambit vs. Bishop-c/story; last Lee-a; Ghost Rider cameo cont'd in Ghost Rider #26. 9-Wolverine vs. Ghost Rider; cont'd/G.R. #26. 10-Return of Longshot 3.00
11-13,17-24,26-29,31: 12,13-Art Thibert-c/a. 28,29-Sabretooth app. 2.00
11-Silver ink 2nd printing; came with X-Men board game 2.00 6.00 20.00
14-16-($1.50)-Polybagged with trading card in each; X-Cutioner's Song x-overs; 14-Andy Kubert-c/a begins 2.00
25-($3.50, 52 pgs.)-Wraparound-c with Gambit hologram on-c; Professor X erases Magneto's mind 1.00 3.00 10.00
25-30th anniversary issue w/B&W-c with Magneto in color & Magneto hologram & no price on-c 1.50 4.50 15.00
25-Gold 30.00
30-($1.95)-Wedding issue w/bound-in trading card sheet 4.00
32-35: 32-Begin $1.50-c; bound-in card sheet. 33-Gambit & Sabretooth-c/story 1.50
36,37-($2.95)-Collectors editions 5.00
38-44,46-49,51-53, 55-65,-1(7/97): 42,43- Paul Smith-a. 46,49,53-56-Onslaught app. 51-Waid scripts begin, end #56. 54-(Regular edition)-Onslaught revealed as Professor X. 55, 56-Onslaught x-over; Avengers, FF & Sentinels app. 56-Dr. Doom app. 57-Xavier taken into custody; Byrne-c/swipe (X-Men, 1st Series #138). 59-Hercules-c/app. 61-Juggernaut-c/app. 62-Re-intro. Shang Chi; two covers. 63-Kingpin cameo. 64- Kingpin app. (-1)-Flashback; origin of Magneto 2.00
45 ($3.95)-Annual issue; gatefold-c 4.00
50 ($2.95)-Vs. Onslaught, wraparound-c. 4.00
50 ($3.95)-Vs. Onslaught, wraparound foil-c. 5.00
50 ($2.95)-Variant-c. .90 2.70 8.00
54-(Limited edition)-Embossed variant-c; Onslaught revealed as Professor X 2.70 8.00 30.00
66-69,71-74: 66-Begin $1.99-c; Operation Zero Tolerance 2.00
70-($2.99, 48 pgs.)-Joe Kelly-s begin, new members join 3.00
71-74, 76-79: 76-Origin of Maggott 2.00
75-($2.99, 48 pgs.) vs. N'Garai; wraparound-c 3.00
80-($3.99) 35th Anniv. issue; holo-foil-c 5.00
80-($2.99) Regular-c 3.00
80-($6.95) Dynamic Forces Ed.; Quesada-c 7.00
81-84: 82-Hunt for Xavier pt. 2 1.99
Annual 1 (1992, $2.25, 68 pgs.)-Lee-c & layouts 4.00
Annual 2 (1993, $2.95, 68 pgs.)-Bagged w/card 4.00
Annual 3 (1994, $2.95) 4.00
Ashcan #1 1.00
Special '95 ($3.95) 4.00
... '96 ($2.95) Wraparound-c 3.00
... '97 ($2.99) Wraparound-c 3.00
.../ Dr. Doom '98 ($2.99) Lopresti-a 3.00
...:Fatal Attractions ('94, $17.95)-r/x-Factor #92, X-Force #25, Uncanny

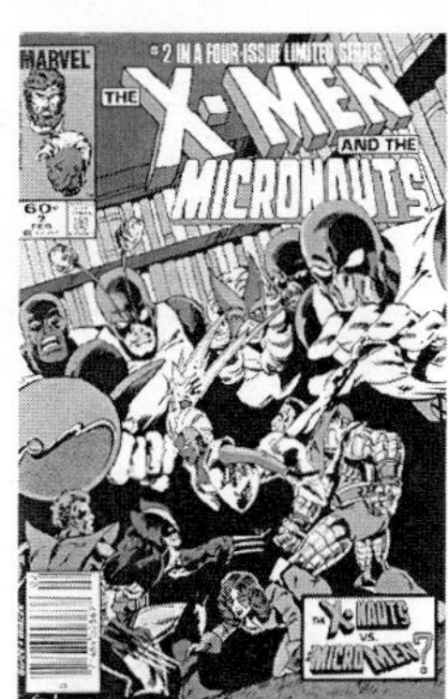

X-Men And The Micronauts #2 © MAR

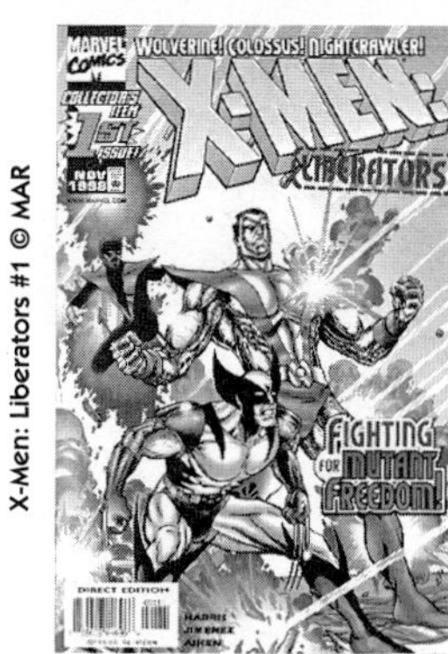

X-Men: Liberators #1 © MAR

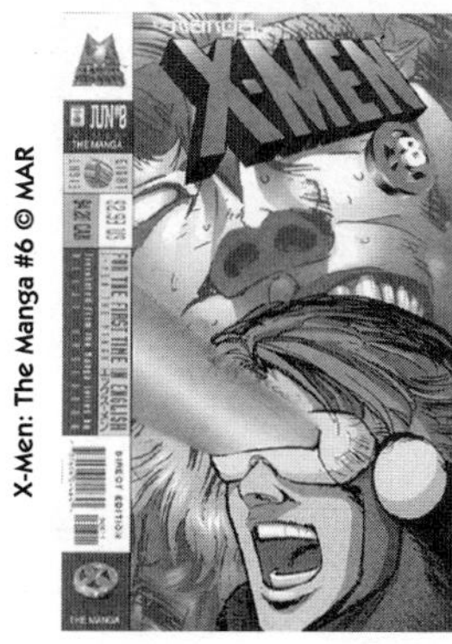

X-Men: The Manga #6 © MAR

	GD25	FN65	NM94
X-Men #304, X-Men #25, Wolverine #75, & Excalibur #71			18.00

...:God Loves, Man Kills (8/94, $6.95)-r/Marvel Graphic Novel #57.00
...Pizza Hut Giveaways-(See Marvel Collector's Edition: X-Men)
...Premium Edition #1 (1993)-Cover says "Toys 'R' Us Limited Edition X-Men" 1.50
...:Rarities (1995, $5.95)-Reprints 6.00
...:The Coming of Bishop ('95, $12.95)-r/Uncanny X-Men #282-285, 287,288 13.00
...:The Rise of Apocalypse ('98, $16.99)-r/Rise Of Apocalypse #1-4, X-Factor #5,6 17.00
... Visionaries : Chris Claremont ('98, $24.95)-r/Claremont-s; art by Byrne, Barry Smith, and Jim Lee 25.00
NOTE: ***Jim Lee** a-1-11p; c-1-6p, 7, 8, 9p, 10, 11p. **Art Thibert** a-6-9i, 12, 13; c-6i, 12, 13.*

X-MEN ADVENTURES (TV)
Marvel Comics: Nov, 1992 - No. 15, Jan, 1994 ($1.25)(Based on animated series)

1-Wolverine, Cyclops, Jubilee, Rogue, Gambit 2.00
2-5: 3-Magneto-c/story 2.00
6-10: 6-Sabretooth-c/story. 7-Cable-c/story. 10-Archangel guest star 2.00
11-14: 11-Cable-c/story 1.25
15-($1.75, 52 pgs.) 1.75

X-MEN ADVENTURES II (TV)
Marvel Comics: Feb, 1994 - No. 13, Feb, 1995 ($1.25/$1.50)(Based on 2nd TV season)

1-8: 4-Bound-in trading card sheet. 5-Alpha Flight app. 1.25
9-13: 9-Begin $1.50-c 1.50
...Captive Hearts/Slave Island (TPB, $4.95)-r/X-Men Adventures #5-8 5.00
...The Irresistible Force, The Muir Island Saga (5.95, 10/94, TPB) r/X-Men Adventures #9-12 6.00

X-MEN ADVENTURES III (TV)(See Adventures of the X-Men)
Marvel Comics: Mar, 1995 - No. 13, Mar, 1996 ($1.50) (Based on 3rd TV season)

1-13 1.50

X-MEN ALPHA
Marvel Comics: 1994 ($3.95, one-shot)

	GD25	FN65	NM94
nn-Age of Apocalypse; wraparound chromium-c	.90	2.70	8.00
nn ($49.95)-Gold logo			50.00

X-MEN/ALPHA FLIGHT
Marvel Comics Group: Dec, 1985 - No. 2, Dec, 1985 ($1.50, limited series)

1,2: 1-Intro The Berserkers; Paul Smith-a 5.00

X-MEN/ALPHA FLIGHT
Marvel Comics Group: May, 1998 - No. 2, June, 1998 ($2.99, limited series)

1,2-Flashback to early meeting; Raab-s/Cassaday-s/a 3.00

X-MEN AND THE MICRONAUTS, THE
Marvel Comics Group: Jan, 1984 - No. 4, Apr, 1984 (Limited series)

1-4: Guice-c/a(p) in all 3.00

X-MEN ARCHIVES
Marvel Comics: Jan, 1995 - No. 4, Apr, 1995 ($2.25, limited series)

1-4: Reprints Legion stories from New Mutants. 4-Magneto app. 2.25

X-MEN ARCHIVES FEATURING CAPTAIN BRITAIN
Marvel Comics: July, 1995 - No. 7, 1996 ($2.95, limited series)

1-7: Reprints early Capt. Britain stories 3.00

X-MEN BOOKS OF ASKANI
Marvel Comics: 1995 ($2.95, one-shot)

1-Painted pin-ups w/text 3.00

X-MEN CHRONICLES
Marvel Comics: Mar, 1995 - No. 2, June, 1995 ($3.95, limited series)

1,2: Age of Apocalypse x-over. 1-wraparound-c 5.00

X-MEN: CLANDESTINE
Marvel Comics: Oct, 1996 - No. 2, Nov, 1996 ($2.95, limited series, 48 pgs.)

1,2: Alan Davis-c(p)/a(p)/scripts & Mark Farmer-c(i)/a(i) in all; wraparound-c 3.00

X-MEN CLASSIC (Formerly Classic X-Men)
Marvel Comics: No. 46, Apr, 1990 - No. 110, Aug, 1995 ($1.25/$1.50)

46-69,71-78,80-89,91-96,98,99: Reprints from X-Men. 54-($1.25, 52 pgs.). 57, 60-63,65-Russell-c(i); 62-r/X-Men #158(Rogue). 66-r/#162(Wolverine). 69-Begins-r of Paul Smith issues (#165 on) 1.50
70,79,90,97-($1.75, 52 pgs.): 70-r/X-Men #166. 90-r/#186 2.00
100-110: 100-($1.50). 104-r/X-Men #200. 1.75

X-MEN CLASSICS
Marvel Comics Group: Dec, 1983 - No. 3, Feb, 1984 ($2.00, Baxter paper)

1-3: X-Men-r by Neal Adams 4.00
NOTE: ***Zeck** c-1-3.*

X-MEN: EARTHFALL
Marvel Comics: Sept, 1996 ($2.95, one-shot)

1-r/Uncanny X-Men #232-234; wraparound-c 3.00

X-MEN FIRSTS
Marvel Comics: Feb, 1996 ($4.95, one-shot)

1-r/Avengers Annual #10, Uncanny X-Men #266, #221; Incredible Hulk #181 5.00

X-MEN: LIBERATORS
Marvel Comics: Nov, 1998 - No. 4, Feb, 1999 ($2.99, limited series)

1-4-Wolverine, Nightcrawler & Colossus; P. Jimenez 3.00

X-MEN LOST TALES
Marvel Comics: 1997 ($2.99)

1,2-r/Classic X-Men back-up stories 3.00

X-MEN OMEGA
Marvel Comics: June, 1995 ($3.95, one-shot)

nn-Age of Apocalyse finale 5.00
nn-($49.95)-Gold edition 50.00

X-MEN PRIME
Marvel Comics: July, 1995 ($4.95, one-shot)

nn-Post Age of Apocalyse begins 5.00

X-MEN RARITIES
Marvel Comics: 1995 ($5.95, one-shot)

nn-Reprints hard-to-find stories 6.00

X-MEN ROAD TO ONSLAUGHT
Marvel Comics: Oct, 1996 ($2.50, one-shot)

nn-Retells Onslaught Saga 2.50

X-MEN SPOTLIGHT ON... STARJAMMERS (Also see X-Men #104)
Marvel Comics: 1990 - No. 2, 1990 ($4.50, 52 pgs.)

1,2: Features Starjammers 4.50

X-MEN SURVIVAL GUIDE TO THE MANSION
Marvel Comics: Aug, 1993 ($6.95, spiralbound)

1 7.00

X-MEN: THE EARLY YEARS
Marvel Comics: May, 1994 - No. 17, Sept, 1995 ($1.50/$2.50)

1-16: r/X-Men #1-8 w/new-c 1.50
17-$2.50-c; r/X-Men #17,18 2.50

X-MEN: THE MANGA
Marvel Comics: Mar, 1998 - Present ($2.99, B&W)

1-19-English version of Japanese X-Men comics 3.00

X-Men 2099 #12 © MAR

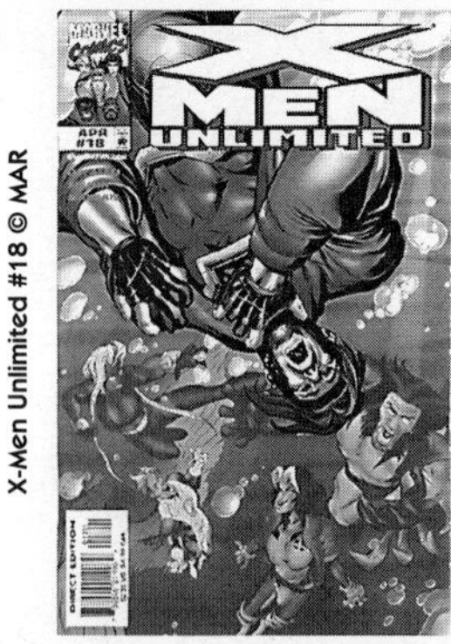

X-Men Unlimited #18 © MAR

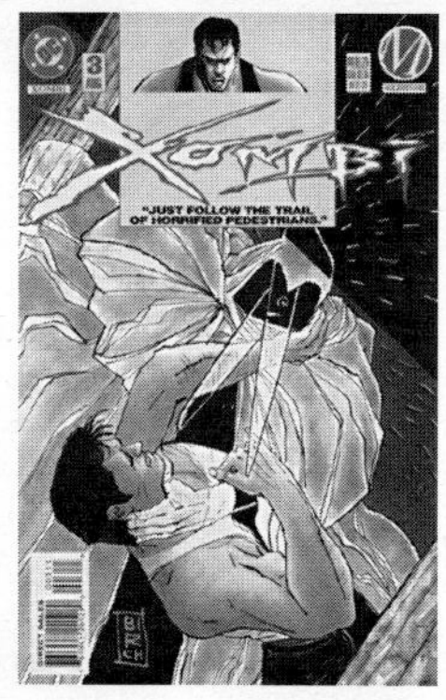

Xombi #3 © DC

GD25 FN65 NM94

X-MEN: THE ULTRA COLLECTION
Marvel Comics: Dec, 1994 - No. 5, Apr, 1995 ($2.95, limited series)

1-5: Pin-ups; no scripts 3.00

X-MEN: THE WEDDING ALBUM
Marvel Comics: 1994 ($2.95, magazine size, one-shot)

1-Wedding of Scott Summers & Jean Grey 3.00

X-MEN 2099 (Also see 2099: World of Tomorrow)
Marvel Comics: Oct, 1993 - No. 35, Aug, 1996 ($1.25/$1.50/$1.95)

1-($1.75)-Foil-c; Ron Lim/Adam Kubert-a begins 2.00
1-2nd printing ($1.75) 1.75
1-Gold edition (15,000 made); sold thru Diamond for $19.40 20.00
2-7: 3-Death of Tina; Lim-c/a(p) in #1-8 1.25
8-19: 8-Begin $1.50-c; bound-in trading card sheet 1.50
20-24,26-35: 20-$1.95-c begins. 35-Nostromo (from X-Nation) app; storyline cont'd in 2099: World of Tomorrow. 2.00
25 ($2.50)-Double sized 2.50
Special 1 ($3.95) 4.00
...: Oasis ($5.95, one-shot) -Hildebrandt Bros.-c/a 6.00

X-MEN ULTRA III PREVIEW
Marvel Comics: 1995 ($2.95)

nn-Kubert-a 3.00

X-MEN UNLIMITED
Marvel Comics: 1993 - Present ($3.95/$2.99, 68 pgs.)

1-Chris Bachalo-c/a; Quesada-a. 4.00
2,4-9: 2-Origin of Magneto script. 4.00
3-Sabretooth-c/story 4.00
10-Dark Beast vs. Beast; Mark Waid script 4.00
11-Magneto & Rogue 4.00
12-21: 12-Begin $2.99-c; Onslaught x-over; Juggernaut-c/app. 19-Caliafore-a 20-Generation X app. 3.00
NOTE: ***Bachalo*** *c/a-1.* ***Quesada*** *a-1.* ***Waid*** *scripts-10*

X-MEN VS. DRACULA
Marvel Comics: Dec, 1993 ($1.75)

1-r/X-Men Annual #6; Austin-c(i) 1.75

X-MEN VS. THE AVENGERS, THE
Marvel Comics Group: Apr, 1987 - No. 4, July, 1987 ($1.50, limited series, Baxter paper)

1 4.00
2-4 3.00

X-MEN VS. THE BROOD, THE
Marvel Comics Group: Sept, 1996 - No. 2, Oct, 1996 ($2.95, limited series)

1,2-Wraparound-c; Ostrander-s/Hitch-a(p) 3.00
TPB('97, $16.99) reprints X-Men/Brood: Day of Wrath #1,2 & Uncanny X-Men #232-234 16.99

X-MEN VISIONARIES
Marvel Comics: 1995 ($8.95, trade paperback)

nn-Reprints X-Men stories; Adam & Andy Kubert-a 9.00

X-MEN/WILDC.A.T.S.: THE DARK AGE (See also WildC.A.T.S./X-Men...)
Marvel Comics: 1998 ($4.50, one-shot)

1-Two covers (Broome & Golden); Ellis-s 4.50

X-NATION 2099
Marvel Comics: Mar, 1996 - No. 6, Aug, 1996 ($1.95)

1-($3.95)-Humberto Ramos-a(p); wraparound, foil-c 4.00
2-6: 2,3-Ramos-a. 4-Exodus-c/app. 5-Exodus cameo. 6-Reed Richards app 2.00

X-O MANOWAR (1st Series)
Valiant/Acclaim Comics (Valiant) No. 43 on: Feb, 1992 - No. 68, Sept, 1996 ($1.95/$2.25/$2.50, high quality)

0-(8/93, $3.50)-Wraparound embossed chromium-c by Quesada; Solar app.; origin Aric (X-O Manowar) 3.50
0-Gold variant 4.00
1-Intro/1st app. & partial origin of Aric (X-O Manowar); Barry Smith/Layton-a 2.00
2-4: 2-B. Smith/Layton-c; Layton part inks. 3-Layton-c(i). 4-1st app. Shadowman (cameo) 2.00
5-8: 5-B. Smith-c. 6-Begin $2.25-c; Ditko-a(p). 7,8-Unity x-overs. 7-Miller-c. 8-Simonson-c 2.00
9-13: 12-1st app. Randy Calder 2.00
14,15-Turok-c/stories 2.00
15-Hot pink logo variant; came with Ultra Pro Rigid Comic Sleeves box; no price on cover 3.00
16-24,26-43: 20-Serial number contest insert. 27-29-Turok x-over. 28-Bound-in trading card. 30-1st app. new "good skin"; Solar app. 33-Chaos Effect Delta Pt. 3. 42-Shadowman app.; includes X-O Manowar Birthquake! Prequel 2.25
25-($3.50)-Has 16 pg. Armorines #0 bound-in w/origin 3.50
44-68: 44-Begin $2.50-c. 50-X, 50-O, 51, 52, 63-Bart Sears-c/a/scripts. 68-Revealed that Aric's past stories were premonitions of his future 2.50
Trade paperback nn (1993, $9.95)-Polybagged with copy of X-O Database #1 inside 10.00
Yearbook 1 (4/95, $2.95) 3.00
NOTE: ***Layton*** *a-1i, 2i(part); c-1, 2i, 3i, 6i, 21i.* ***Reese*** *a-4i(part); c-26i.*

X-O MANOWAR (2nd Series)(Also see Iron Man/X-O Manowar: Heavy Metal)
Acclaim Comics (Valiant Heroes): V2#1, Oct, 1996 - Present ($2.50)

V2#1-14: 1-Mark Waid & Brian Augustyn scripts begin; 1st app. Donavon Wylie; Rand Banion dies; painted variant-c exists. 2-Donavon Wylie becomes new X-O Manowar. 7-9-Augustyn-s. 10-Copycat-c 2.50

X-O MANOWAR FAN EDITION
Acclaim Comics (Valiant Heroes): Feb, 1997 (Overstreet's FAN giveaway)

1-Reintro the Armorines & the Hard Corps; 1st app. Citadel; Augustyn scripts; McKone-c/a 4.00

X-O MANOWAR/IRON MAN: IN HEAVY METAL (See Iron Man/X-O Manowar: Heavy Metal)
Acclaim Comics (Valiant Heroes): Sept, 1996 ($2.50, one-shot)
(1st Marvel/Valiant x-over)

1-Pt 1 of X-O Manowar/Iron Man x-over; Arnim Zola app.; Fabian Nicieza scripts; Andy Smith-a 2.50

XOMBI
DC Comics (Milestone): Jan, 1994 - No. 21, Feb, 1996 ($1.75/$2.50)

0-($1.95)-Shadow War x-over; Simonson silver ink varnish-c 2.00
1-13: 1-John Byrne-c 1.75
1-Platinum 15.00
14-21: 14-Begin $2.50-c 2.50

X-PATROL
Marvel Comics (Amalgam): Apr, 1996 ($1.95, one-shot)

1-Cruz-a(p) 2.00

XSE
Marvel Comics: Nov, 1996 - No. 4, Feb, 1997 ($1.95, limited series)

1-4: 1-Bishop & Shard app. 2.00
1-Variant-c 3.00

X-TERMINATORS
Marvel Comics: Oct, 1988 - No. 4, Jan, 1989 ($1.00, limited series)

1-1st app.; X-Men/X-Factor tie-in; Williamson-i 3.00
2 1.75
3,4 1.25

X-Venture #2 © Victory Magazine

Yellowjacket Comics #3 © Frank Communale

Yogi Bear Giant Size V2#1 © H-B

GD25 FN65 NM94   GD25 FN65 NM94

X, THE MAN WITH THE X-RAY EYES (See Movie Comics)

X-UNIVERSE
Marvel Comics: May, 1995 - No. 2, June, 1995 ($3.50, limited series)

1,2: Age of Apocalypse 5.00

X-VENTURE (Super Heroes)
Victory Magazines Corp.: July, 1947 - No. 2, Nov, 1947

1-Atom Wizard, Mystery Shadow, Lester Trumble begin 74.00 221.00 625.00
2 43.00 129.00 360.00

XYR (See Eclipse Graphic Album Series #21)

YAK YAK
Dell Publishing Co.: No. 1186, May-July, 1961 - No. 1348, Apr-June, 1962

Four Color 1186 (#1)- Jack Davis-c/a; 2 versions, one minus 3pgs. 7.00 22.00 80.00
Four Color 1348 (#2)-Davis c/a 7.00 22.00 80.00

YAKKY DOODLE & CHOPPER (TV) (Also see Spotlight #3 & Top Cat #4)
Gold Key: Dec, 1962 (Hanna-Barbera)

1 5.50 16.50 60.00

YALTA TO KOREA (Also see Korea My Home)
M. Phillip Corp. (Republican National Committee): 1952 (Giveaway, paper-c)

nn-(8 pgs.)-Anti-communist propaganda book 19.00 56.00 140.00

YANG (See House of Yang)
Charlton Comics: Nov, 1973 - No. 13, May, 1976; V14#14, Sept, 1985 - No. 17, Jan, 1986

1-Origin; Sattler-a begins .90 2.70 9.00
2-13(1976) 5.00
14-17(1986): 15-Reprints #1 3.00
3,10,11(Modern Comics-r, 1977) 3.00

YANKEE COMICS
Harry 'A' Chesler: Sept, 1941 - No. 7, 1942?

1-Origin The Echo, The Enchanted Dagger, Yankee Doodle Jones, The Firebrand, & The Scarlet Sentry; Black Satan app.; Yankee Doodle Jones app. on all covers 129.00 387.00 1100.00
2-Origin Johnny Rebel; Major Victory app.; Barry Kuda begins 65.00 194.00 550.00
3,4: 4-(3/42) 50.00 150.00 425.00
4 (nd, 1940s; 7-1/4x5", 68 pgs, distr. to the service)-Foxy Grandpa, Tom, Dick & Harry, Impy, Ace & Deuce, Dot & Dash, Ima Slooth by Jack Cole (Remington Morse publ.) 2.40 6.00 12.00
5-7 (nd; 10¢, 7-1/4x5", 68 pgs.)(Remington Morse publ.)-urges readers to send their copies to servicemen. 2.40 6.00 12.00

YANKS IN BATTLE
Quality Comics Group: Sept, 1956 - No. 4, Dec, 1956; 1963

1-Cuidera-c(i) 8.00 24.00 50.00
2-4: Cuidera-c(i) 5.00 15.00 30.00
I.W. Reprint #3(1963)-r/#?; exist? 1.10 3.30 9.00

YARDBIRDS, THE (G. I. Joe's Sidekicks)
Ziff-Davis Publishing Co.: Summer, 1952

1-By Bob Oskner 8.50 26.00 60.00

YARN MAN (See Megaton Man)
Kitchen Sink : Oct, 1989 ($2.00, B&W, one-shot)

1-Donald Simpson-c/a/scripts 2.00

YARNS OF YELLOWSTONE
World Color Press: 1972 (50¢, 36 pgs.)

nn-Illustrated by Bill Chapman 2.00 6.00

YELLOW CLAW (Also see Giant Size Master of Kung Fu)
Atlas Comics (MjMC): Oct, 1956 - No. 4, Apr, 1957

1-Origin by Joe Maneely 79.00 238.00 675.00
2-Kirby-a 64.00 192.00 545.00
3,4-Kirby-a; 4-Kirby/Severin-a 61.00 182.00 515.00

NOTE: ***Everett*** *c-3.* ***Maneely*** *c-1.* ***Reinman*** *a-2i, 3.* ***Severin*** *c-2, 4.*

YELLOWJACKET COMICS (Jack in the Box #11 on)(See TNT Comics)
E. Levy/Frank Comunale/Charlton: Sept, 1944 - No. 10, June, 1946

1-Intro & origin Yellowjacket; Diana, the Huntress begins; E.A. Poe's "The Black Cat" adaptation 50.00 150.00 425.00
2-Yellowjacket-c begin, end #10 31.00 92.00 230.00
3,5 29.00 88.00 220.00
4-E.A. Poe's "Fall of the House Of Usher" adaptation; Palais-a 31.00 92.00 230.00
6-10: 1,3,4,6-10-Have stories narrated by old witch in "Tales of Terror" (1st horror series?) 28.00 84.00 210.00

YELLOWSTONE KELLY (Movie)
Dell Publishing Co.: No. 1056, Nov-Jan, 1959/60

Four Color 1056-Clint Walker photo-c 5.00 15.00 54.00

YELLOW SUBMARINE (See Movie Comics)

YIN FEI THE CHINESE NINJA
Leung's Publications: 1988 - No. 8, 1990 ($1.80/$2.00, 52 pgs.)

1-6: 1-Begin $1.80-c 1.80
7,8: 7-Begin $2.00-c 2.00

YOGI BEAR (See Dell Giant #41, Golden Comics Digest, Kite Fun Book, March of Comics #253, 265, 279, 291, 309, 319, 337, 344, Movie Comics under "Hey There It's..." & Whitman Comic Books)

YOGI BEAR (TV) (Hanna-Barbera) (See Four Color #990)
Dell Publishing Co./Gold Key No. 10 on: No. 1067, 12-2/59-60 - No. 9, 7-9/62; No. 10, 10/62 - No. 42, 10/70

Four Color 1067 (#1)-TV show debuted 1/30/61 10.50 31.00 115.00
Four Color 1104,1162 (5-7/61) 7.00 20.00 75.00
4(8-9/61) - 6(12-1/61-62) 4.50 13.50 50.00
Four Color 1271(11/61) 4.50 13.50 50.00
Four Color 1349(1/62)-Photo-c 9.00 27.00 100.00
7(2-3/62) - 9(7-9/62)-Last Dell 4.50 13.50 50.00
10(10/62-G.K.), 11(1/63)-titled "Yogi Bear Jellystone Jollies" (80 pgs.); 11-X-Mas-c 6.25 18.50 70.00
12(4/63), 14-20 3.20 9.50 35.00
13(7/63, 68 pgs.)-Surprise Party 6.25 18.50 70.00
21-30 2.00 6.00 22.00
31-42 1.80 5.40 18.00
Giveaway ('84, '86)-City of Los Angeles, "Creative First Aid" & "Earthquake Preparedness for Children" 4.00

YOGI BEAR (TV)
Charlton Comics: Nov, 1970 - No. 35, Jan, 1976 (Hanna-Barbera)

1 3.00 9.00 33.00
2-6,8-10 2.00 6.00 20.00
7-Summer Fun (Giant, 52 pgs.) 3.80 11.50 40.00
11-20 1.60 4.80 16.00
21-35: 28-31-partial-r 1.20 3.60 12.00

YOGI BEAR (TV)(See The Flintstones, 3rd series & Spotlight #1)
Marvel Comics Group: Nov, 1977 - No. 9, Mar, 1979 (Hanna-Barbera)

1,7-9: 1-Flintstones begin (Newsstand sales only) 1.20 3.60 12.00
2-6 .90 2.70 9.00

YOGI BEAR (TV)
Harvey Comics: Sept, 1992 - No. 6, Mar, 1994 ($1.25/$1.50) (Hanna-Barbera)

V2#1-4 1.25
5,6: 5-Begin $1.50-c 1.50
...Big Book V2#1,2 ($1.95, 52 pgs): 1-(11/92). 2-(3/93) 2.00

Young Allies Comics #13 © MAR

Youngblood V3#2 © Awesome Ent.

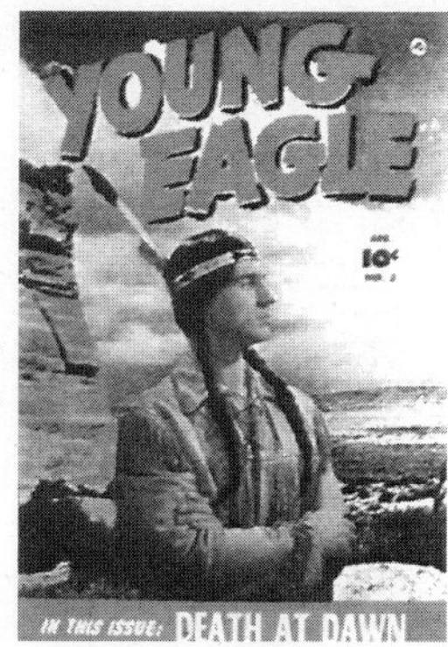

YOUNG EAGLE
IN THIS ISSUE: DEATH AT DAWN

Young Eagle #3 © FAW

GD25 FN65 NM94

...Giant Size V2#1,2 ($2.25, 68 pgs.): 1-(10/92). 2-(4/93) 2.25

YOGI BEAR'S EASTER PARADE (See The Funtastic World of Hanna-Barbera #2)

YOGI BERRA (Baseball hero)
Fawcett Publications: 1951 (Yankee catcher)

	GD25	FN65	NM94
nn-Photo-c	56.00	168.00	475.00

YOSEMITE SAM (...& Bugs Bunny) (TV)
Gold Key/Whitman: Dec, 1970 - No. 81, Feb, 1984

	GD25	FN65	NM94
1	2.20	6.50	24.00
2-10	1.20	3.60	12.00
11-20	.90	2.70	9.00
21-30	.85	2.60	7.00
31-50			5.00
51-65 (Gold Key)			3.00
66,67 (Whitman)			4.00
68(9/80), 69(10/80), 70(12/80) 3-pack?	1.00	3.00	10.00
71-78		2.00	6.00
79-81 (All #90263 on-c, no date or date code; 3-pack?): 81-(1/3-r)	.90	2.80	8.00

(See March of Comics #363, 380, 392)

YOUNG ALLIES COMICS (All-Winners #21; see Kid Komics #2)
Timely Comics (USA 1-7/NPI 8,9/YAI 10-20): Sum, 1941 - No. 20, Oct, 1946

	GD25	FN65	VF82	NM94
1-Origin/1st app. The Young Allies (Bucky, Toro, others); 1st meeting of Captain America & Human Torch; Red Skull-c & app.; S&K-c/splash; Hitler-c	950.00	2850.00	5700.00	9500.00

	GD25	FN65	NM94
2-(Winter, 1941)-Captain America & Human Torch app.; Simon & Kirby-c	263.00	790.00	2500.00
3-Fathertime, Captain America & Human Torch app.; Remember Pearl Harbor issue (Spring, 1942); Stan Lee scripts; Vs. Japs-c/full-length story	212.00	635.00	1800.00
4-The Vagabond & Red Skull, Capt. America, Human Torch app. Classic Red Skull-c	295.00	884.00	2800.00
5-Captain America & Human Torch app.	135.00	406.00	1150.00
6-8,10: 10-Origin Tommy Tyme & Clock of Ages; ends #19	91.00	274.00	775.00
9-Hitler, Tojo, Mussolini-c.	103.00	309.00	875.00
11-20: 12-Classic decapitation story	77.00	229.00	650.00

NOTE: ***Brodsky** c-15. **Gabrielle** a-3; c-3, 4. **S&K** c-1, 2. **Schomburg** c-5-14, 16-19. **Shores** c-20.*

YOUNG ALL-STARS
DC Comics: June, 1987 - No. 31, Nov, 1989 ($1.00, deluxe format)

1-31: 1-1st app. Iron Munro & The Flying Fox. 7-18-$1.25. 8,9-Millennium tie-ins. 19-23-$1.50. 24-Begin $1.75-c 2.00
Annual 1 (1988, $2.00) 2.00

YOUNGBLOOD (See Brigade #4, Megaton Explosion & Team Youngblood)
Image Comics (Extreme Studios): Apr, 1992 - No. 4, Feb, 1993 ($2.50, lim. series); No. 6, June, 1994 (No #5) - No. 10, Dec, 1994 ($1.95/$2.50)

1-Liefeld-c/a/scripts in all; flip book format with 2 trading cards; 1st Image/Extreme Studios title. 5.00
1-2nd printing 2.00
2-(JUN-c, July 1992 indicia)-1st app. Shadowhawk in solo back-up story; 2 trading cards inside; flip book format; 1st app. Prophet, Kirby, Berzerkers, Darkthorn 2.00
2-2nd printing (1.95) 2.00
3-(OCT-c, August 1992 indicia)-Contains 2 trading cards inside (flip book); 1st app. Supreme in back-up story; 1st app. Showdown 2.50
0-(12/92, $1.95)-Contains 2 trading cards; 2 cover variations exist, green or beige logo; w/Image #0 coupon 2.00
4,5: 4-(2/93)-Glow-in-the-dark-c w/2 trading cards; 2nd app. Dale Keown's The Pitt; Bloodstrike app. 5-Flip book w/Brigade #4 2.50
6-($3.50, 52 pgs.)-Wraparound-c 3.50
7-10: 7, 8-Liefeld-c(p)/a(p)/story. 8,9-(9/94) 9-Valentino story & art 2.50
Battlezone 1 (MAY-c, 4/93 inside, $1.95)-Arsenal book; Liefeld-c(p) 2.00
Battlezone 2 (7/94, $2.95)-Wraparound-c 3.00
Yearbook 1 (7/93, $2.50)-Fold out panel; 1st app. Tyrax & Kanan 2.50
...Super Special (Winter '97, $2.99) Sprouse -a 3.00
TPB (1996, $16.95)-r/Team Youngblood #8-10 & Youngblood #6-8,10 17.00

YOUNGBLOOD
Image Comics (Extreme Studios)/Maximum Press No. 14: V2#1, Sept, 1995 - No. 14, Dec, 1996 ($2.50)

V2#1-10,14: Roger Cruz-a in all. 4-Extreme Destroyer Pt. 4 w/gaming card. 5-Variant-c exists. 6-Angela & Glory. 7-Shadowhunt Pt. 3; Shadowhawk app. 8,10-Thor (from Supreme) app. 10-(7/96). 14-(12/96)-1st Maximum Press issue 2.50

YOUNGBLOOD (Volume 3)
Awesome/ Awesome-Hyperwerks #2 on: Feb, 1998 - Present ($2.50)

1-Alan Moore-s/Skroce & Stucker-a; 12 diff. covers 2.50
1-Gold foil-c 9.00
1-Blue foil-c Orlando Con Ed. 15.00
1+ Alter Ego Gold Foil 9.00
2-(8/98) Skroce & Liefeld covers 2.50

YOUNGBLOOD: STRIKEFILE
Image Comics (Extreme Studios): Apr, 1993 - No. 11, Feb, 1995 ($1.95/$2.50/$2.95)

1-($1.95)-Flip book w/Jae Lee-c/a & Liefeld-c/a in #1-3; 1st app. The Allies, Giger, & Glory 2.00
2-4,11: 2-Begin $2.50. 3-Thibert-i asisst. 4-Liefeld-c(p); no Lee-a 2.50
5-10: 5-Begin $2.95-c; Liefeld-c(p). 8-Platt-c 3.00

NOTE: *Youngblood: Strikefile began as a four issue limited series.*

YOUNGBLOOD/X-FORCE
Image Comics (Extreme Studios): July, 1996 ($4.95, one-shot)

1-Cruz-a(p); two covers exist 5.00

YOUNG BRIDES (True Love Secrets)
Feature/Prize Publ.: Sept-Oct, 1952 - No. 30, Nov-Dec, 1956 (Photo-c: 1-4)

	GD25	FN65	NM94
V1#1-Simon & Kirby-a	25.00	76.00	190.00
2-S&K-a	13.00	38.00	95.00
3-6-S&K-a	11.00	34.00	85.00
V2#1,3-7,10-12 (#7-18)-S&K-a	11.00	32.00	80.00
2,8,9-No S&K-a	4.00	12.00	24.00
V3#1-3(#19-21)-Last precode (3-4/55)	4.00	10.00	20.00
4,6(#22,24), V4#1,3(#25,27)	3.00	7.50	15.00
V3#5(#23)-Meskin-c	4.00	11.00	22.00
V4#2(#26)-All S&K issue	9.30	28.00	65.00
V4#4(#28)-S&K-a	7.85	23.50	55.00
V4#5,6(#29,30)	4.25	13.00	26.00

YOUNG DR. MASTERS (See The Adventures of Young Dr. Masters)

YOUNG DOCTORS, THE
Charlton Comics: Jan, 1963 - No. 6, Nov, 1963

	GD25	FN65	NM94
V1#1	2.50	7.50	22.00
2-6	1.75	5.25	14.00

YOUNG EAGLE
Fawcett Publications/Charlton: 12/50 - No. 10, 6/52; No. 3, 7/56 - No. 5, 4/57 (Photo-c: 1-10)

	GD25	FN65	NM94
1-Intro Young Eagle	15.00	44.00	110.00
2-Complete picture novelette "The Mystery of Thunder Canyon"	7.85	23.50	55.00
3-9	7.15	21.50	50.00
10-Origin Thunder, Young Eagle's Horse	5.70	17.00	35.00
3-5(Charlton)-Formerly Sherlock Holmes?	4.00	12.00	24.00

Young Heroes in Love #16 © Dan Raspler & Dev Madan

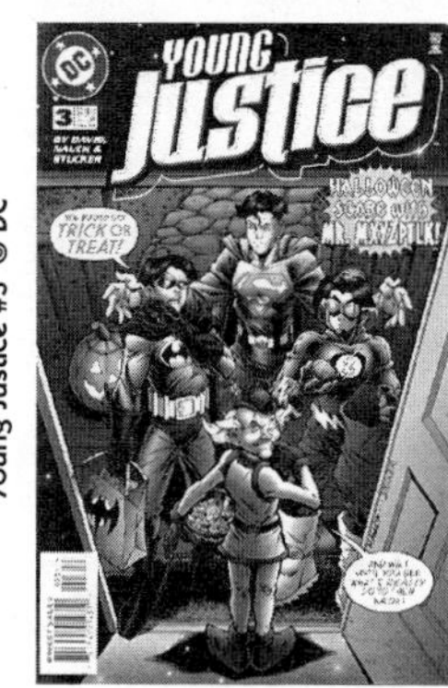

Young Justice #3 © DC

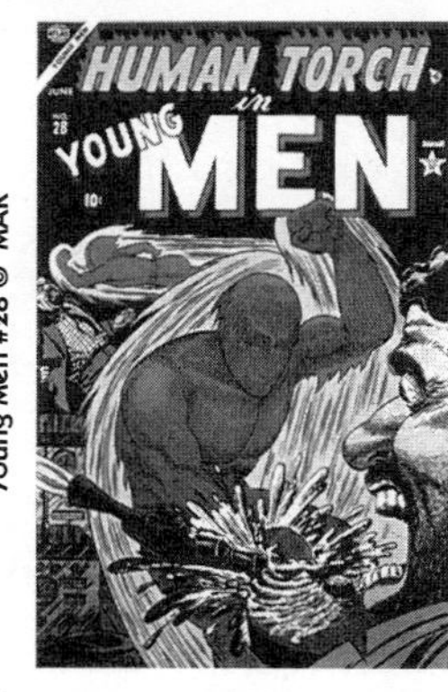

Young Men #28 © MAR

YOUNG HEARTS
Marvel Comics (SPC): Nov, 1949 - No. 2, Feb, 1950

	GD25	FN65	NM94
1-Photo-c	9.30	28.00	70.00
2-Colleen Townsend photo-c from movie	6.35	19.00	42.00

YOUNG HEARTS IN LOVE
Super Comics: 1964

	GD25	FN65	NM94
17,18: 17-r/Young Love V5#6 (4-5/62)	1.25	3.75	10.00

YOUNG HEROES (Formerly Forbidden Worlds #34)
American Comics Group (Titan): No. 35, Feb-Mar, 1955 - No. 37, Jun-Jul, 1955

	GD25	FN65	NM94
35-37-Frontier Scout	8.50	26.00	60.00

YOUNG HEROES IN LOVE
DC Comics: June, 1997 - No. 17; #1,000,000, Nov, 1998 ($1.75/$1.95/$2.50)

	GD25	FN65	NM94
1-1st app. Young Heroes; Madan-a			3.00
2-17: 3-Superman-c/app. 7-Begin $1.95-c			2.00
#1,000,000 (11/98, $2.50) 853 Century x-over			2.50

YOUNG INDIANA JONES CHRONICLES, THE
Dark Horse Comics: Feb, 1992 - No. 12, Feb, 1993 ($2.50)

	GD25	FN65	NM94
1-12: Dan Barry scripts in all			2.50

NOTE: ***Dan Barry** a(p)-1, 2, 5, 6, 10; c-1-10. **Morrow** a-3, 4, 5p, 6p. **Springer** a-1i, 2i.*

YOUNG INDIANA JONES CHRONICLES, THE
Hollywood Comics (Disney): 1992 ($3.95, squarebound, 68 pgs.)

	GD25	FN65	NM94
1-3: 1-r/YIJC #1,2 by D. Horse. 2-r/#3,4. 3-r/#5,6			4.00

YOUNG JUSTICE
DC Comics: Sept, 1998 - Present ($2.50)

	GD25	FN65	NM94
1-Robin, Superboy & Impulse team-up; David-s			3.00
2-5: 3-Mxyzptlk app. 4-Wonder Girl, Arrowette and the Secret join			2.50
#1,000,000 (11/98) 853 Century x-over			2.50
...: Secret Files (1/99, $4.95) Origin-s & pin-ups			5.00
...: The Secret (6/98, $1.95) Girlfrenzy; Nauck-a		.80	2.00

YOUNG KING COLE (...Detective Tales)(Becomes Criminals on the Run)
Premium Group/Novelty Press: Fall, 1945 - V3#12, July, 1948

	GD25	FN65	NM94
V1#1-Toni Gayle begins	25.00	76.00	190.00
2	11.00	34.00	85.00
3-4	10.00	30.00	75.00
V2#1-7(8-9/46-7/47): 6,7-Certa-c	7.85	23.50	55.00
V3#1,3-6,8,9,12: 3-Certa-c. 5-McWilliams-c/a. 8,9-Harmon-c	7.15	21.50	50.00
2-L.B. Cole-a; Certa-c	13.00	38.00	95.00
7-L.B. Cole-c/a	17.00	52.00	130.00
10,11-L.B. Cole-c	15.00	44.00	110.00

YOUNG LAWYERS, THE (TV)
Dell Publishing Co.: Jan, 1971 - No. 2, Apr, 1971

	GD25	FN65	NM94
1,2	1.40	4.20	14.00

YOUNG LIFE (Teen Life #3 on)
New Age Publ./Quality Comics Group: Summer, 1945 - No. 2, Fall, 1945

	GD25	FN65	NM94
1-Skip Homeier, Louis Prima stories	11.00	34.00	85.00
2-Frank Sinatra photo on-c plus story	11.00	34.00	85.00

YOUNG LOVE (Sister title to Young Romance)
Prize(Feature)Publ.(Crestwood): 2-3/49 - No. 73, 12-1/56-57; V3#5, 2-3/60 - V7#1, 6-7/63

	GD25	FN65	NM94
V1#1-S&K-c/a(2)	39.00	116.00	290.00
2-Photo-c begin; S&K-a	20.00	60.00	150.00
3-S&K-a	15.00	46.00	115.00
4-5-Minor S&K-a	9.30	28.00	65.00
V2#1(#7)-S&K-a(2)	15.00	46.00	115.00
2-5(#8-11)-Minor S&K-a	7.15	21.50	50.00
6,8(#12,14)-S&K-c only. 14-S&K 1 pg. art	9.30	28.00	65.00
7,9-12(#13,15-18)-S&K-c/a	13.00	40.00	100.00
V3#1-4(#19-22)-S&K-c/a	12.00	36.00	90.00
5-7,9-12(#23-25,27-30)-Photo-c resume; S&K-a	11.00	32.00	80.00
8(#26)-No S&K-a	4.00	12.00	24.00
V4#1,6(#31,36)-S&K-a	10.00	30.00	75.00
2-5,7-12(#32-35,37-42)-Minor S&K-a	7.15	21.50	50.00
V5#1-12(#43-54), V6#1-9(#55-63)-Last precode; S&K-a in some	4.25	13.00	26.00
V6#10-12(#64-66)	2.25	6.75	18.00
V7#1-7(#67-73)	2.00	6.00	16.00
V3#5(2-3/60),6(4-5/60)(Formerly All For Love)	1.75	5.25	14.00
V4#1(6-7/60)-6(4-5/61)	1.50	4.50	12.00
V5#1(6-7/61)-6(4-5/62)	1.50	4.50	12.00
V6#1(6-7/62)-6(4-5/63), V7#1	1.00	3.00	8.00

NOTE: ***Meskin** a-14(2), 27, 42. **Powell** a-V4#6. **Severin/Elder** a-V1#3. S&K art not in #53, 57, 58, 61, 63-65. Photo c-V3#5-V5#11.*

YOUNG LOVE
National Periodical Publ.(Arleigh Publ. Corp #49-61)/DC Comics: #39, 9-10/63 - #120, Wint./75-76; #121, 10/76 - #126, 7/77

	GD25	FN65	NM94
39	3.50	10.50	35.00
40-50	2.50	7.50	22.00
51-70	2.50	7.50	20.00
71-80: 73,78,79-Toth-a	1.80	5.40	18.00
81-99	1.40	4.20	14.00
100	1.80	5.40	18.00
101-106,115-122	.90	2.70	9.00
107 (100 pgs.): 107-DC 100 Pg. Super Spect.	9.00	27.00	100.00
108-114 (100 pgs.)	7.00	21.00	75.00
123-126 (52 pgs.)	2.25	6.80	25.00

NOTE: ***Bolle** a-117. **Colan** a-107r. **Nasser** a-123, 124. **Orlando** a-122. **Simonson** c-125. **Toth** a-73, 78, 79, 122-125r. **Wood** a-109r(4 pgs.).*

YOUNG LOVER ROMANCES (Formerly & becomes Great Lover...)
Toby Press: No. 4, June, 1952 - No. 5, Aug, 1952

	GD25	FN65	NM94
4,5-Photo-c	5.00	15.00	30.00

YOUNG LOVERS (My Secret Life #19 on)(Formerly Brenda Starr?)
Charlton Comics: No. 16, July, 1956 - No. 18, May, 1957

	GD25	FN65	NM94
16,17('56): 16-Marcus Swayze-a	5.35	16.00	32.00
18-Elvis Presley picture-c, text story (biography)(Scarce)	49.00	148.00	420.00

YOUNG MARRIAGE
Fawcett Publications: June, 1950

	GD25	FN65	NM94
1-Powell-a; photo-c	10.00	30.00	70.00

YOUNG MEN (Formerly Cowboy Romances)(...on the Battlefield #12-20 (4/53); ...In Action #21)
Marvel/Atlas Comics (IPC): No. 4, 6/50 - No. 11, 10/51; No. 12, 12/51 - No. 28, 6/54

	GD25	FN65	NM94
4-(52 pgs.)	15.00	44.00	110.00
5-11	9.30	28.00	65.00
12-23: 12-20-War format. 21-23-Hot Rod issues starring Flash Foster	8.50	26.00	60.00
24-(12/53)-Origin Captain America, Human Torch, & Sub-Mariner which are revived thru #28; Red Skull app.	200.00	600.00	1700.00
25-28: 25-Romita-c/a (see Men's Advs.)	97.00	291.00	825.00

NOTE: ***Berg** a-7, 14, 17, 18, 20; c-17? **Brodsky** c-4-9, 13, 14, 16, 17, 21-25. **Burgos** c-26-28. **Colan** a-14, 15. **Everett** a-18-20. **Heath** a-13, 14. **Maneely** c-10, 12, 15. **Pakula** a-14, 15. **Robinson** c-18. Captain America by **Romita**-#24?, 25, 26?, 27, 28. Human Torch by **Burgos**-#25, 27, 28. Sub-Mariner by **Everett**-#24-28.*

YOUNG REBELS, THE (TV)
Dell Publishing Co.: Jan, 1971

	GD25	FN65	NM94
1-Photo-c	1.20	3.60	12.00

YOUNG ROMANCE COMICS (The 1st romance comic)
Prize/Headline (Feature Publ.) (Crestwood): Sept-Oct, 1947 - V16#4, June-

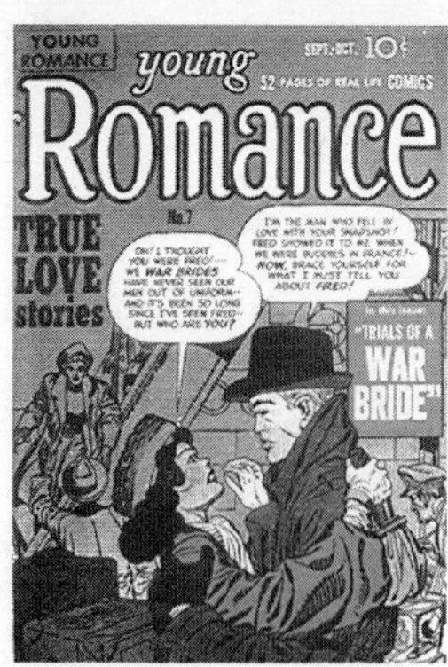

Young Romance #7 © PRIZE

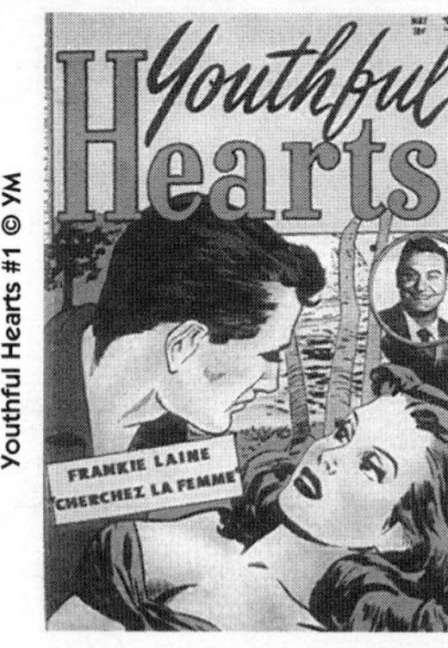

Youthful Hearts #1 © YM

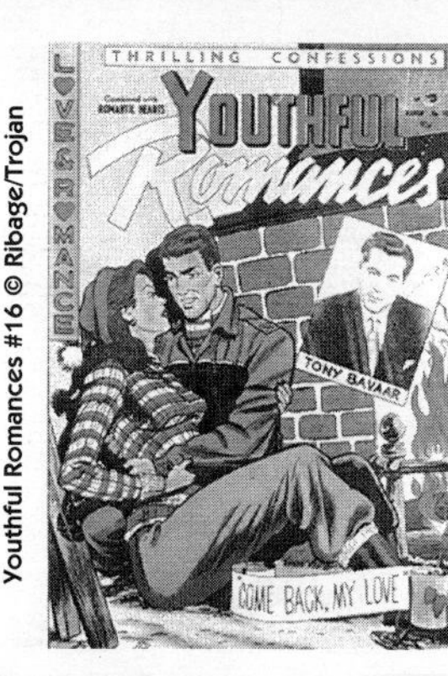

Youthful Romances #16 © Ribage/Trojan

	GD25	FN65	NM94
July, 1963 (#1-33: 52 pgs.)			
V1#1-S&K-c/a(2)	40.00	120.00	315.00
2-S&K-c/a(2-3)	25.00	74.00	185.00
3-6-S&K-c/a(2-3) each	22.00	66.00	165.00
V2#1-6(#7-12)-S&K-c/a(2-3) each	19.00	58.00	145.00
V3#1-3(#13-15): V3#1-Photo-c begin; S&K-a	13.00	38.00	95.00
4-12(#16-24)-Photo-c; S&K-a	13.00	38.00	95.00
V4#1-11(#25-35)-S&K-a	12.00	36.00	90.00
12(#36)-S&K, Toth-a	14.00	42.00	105.00
V5#1-12(#37-48), V6#4-12(#52-60)-S&K-a	12.00	36.00	90.00
V6#1-3(#49-51)-No S&K-a	5.35	16.00	32.00
V7#1-11(#61-71)-S&K-a in most	10.00	30.00	70.00
V7#12(#72), V8#1-3(#73-75)-Last precode (12-1/54-55)-No S&K-a	4.00	10.00	20.00
V8#4(#76, 4-5/55), 5(#77)-No S&K-a	3.60	9.00	18.00
V8#6-8(#78-80, 12-1/55-56)-S&K-a	7.15	21.50	50.00
V9#3,5,6(#81, 2-3/56, 83,84)-S&K-a	7.15	21.50	50.00
4, V10#1(#82,85)-All S&K-a	8.50	26.00	60.00
V10#2-6(#86-90, 10-11/57)-S&K-a	5.00	15.00	50.00
V11#1,2,5,6(#91,92,95,96)-S&K-a	5.00	15.00	50.00
3,4(#93,94), V12#2,4,5(#98,100,101)-No S&K	1.75	5.25	14.00
V12#1,3,6(#97,99,102)-S&K-a	5.00	15.00	50.00
V13#1(#103)-Powell-a; S&K's last-a for Crestwood	5.00	15.00	50.00
2,4-6(#104-108)	1.10	3.30	9.00
V13#3(, #105, 4-5/60)-Elvis Presley-c app. only	2.50	7.50	22.00
V14#1-6, V15#1-6, V16#1-4(#109-124)	1.00	2.80	7.00

NOTE: ***Meskin** a-16, 24(2), 33, 47, 50. **Robinson/Meskin** a-6. **Leonard Starr** a-11. Photo c-13-32, 34-65. Issues 1-3 say "Designed for the More **Adult** Readers of **Comics**" on cover.*

YOUNG ROMANCE COMICS (Continued from Prize series)
National Periodical Publ.(Arleigh Publ. Corp. No. 127): No. 125, Aug-Sept, 1963 - No. 208, Nov-Dec, 1975

	GD25	FN65	NM94
125	6.00	18.00	60.00
126-140	3.00	9.00	30.00
141-153,155-162	2.50	7.50	24.00
154-Neal Adams-c	3.20	9.60	32.00
163,164-Toth-a	2.50	7.50	24.00
165-177: 170-Michell from Young Love ends; Lily Martin, the Swinger begins	1.80	5.40	18.00
178-183 (52 pgs.)	2.25	6.80	25.00
184-196	1.40	4.20	14.00
197-204-(100 pgs.)	7.00	21.00	75.00
205-208	1.00	3.00	10.00

YOUNG ZEN: CITY OF DEATH
Entity Comics: Late 1994 ($3.25, B&W)

	GD25	FN65	NM94
1			3.25

YOUNG ZEN INTERGALACTIC NINJA (Also see Zen...)
Entity Comics: 1993 - No. 3, 1994 ($3.50/$2.95, B&W)

	GD25	FN65	NM94
1-($3.50)-Polybagged w/Sam Kieth chromium trading card; gold foil logo			3.50
2,3-($2.95)-Gold foil logo			3.00

YOUR DREAMS (See Strange World of...)

YOU'RE UNDER ARREST (Manga)
Dark Horse Comics: Dec, 1995 - No. 8, July, 1996 ($2.95, limited series)

	GD25	FN65	NM94
1-8			3.00

YOUR TRIP TO NEWSPAPERLAND
Philadelphia Evening Bulletin (Printed by Harvey Press): June, 1955 (14x11-1/2", 12 pgs.)

	GD25	FN65	NM94
nn-Joe Palooka takes kids on newspaper tour	4.00	12.00	24.00

YOUR UNITED STATES
Lloyd Jacquet Studios: 1946

	GD25	FN65	NM94
nn-Used in **SOTI**, pg. 309,310; Sid Greene-a	21.00	62.00	155.00

YOUTHFUL HEARTS (Daring Confessions #4 on)
Youthful Magazines: May, 1952 - No. 3, Sept, 1952

	GD25	FN65	NM94
1- "Monkey on Her Back" swipes E.C. drug story/Shock SuspenStories #12; Frankie Laine photo on-c; Doug Wildey-a in all	23.00	68.00	170.00
2,3: 2-Vic Damone photo on-c. 3-Johnny Raye photo on-c	16.00	48.00	120.00

YOUTHFUL LOVE (Truthful Love #2)
Youthful Magazines: May, 1950

	GD25	FN65	NM94
1	9.30	28.00	65.00

YOUTHFUL ROMANCES
Pix-Parade #1-14/Ribage #15 on: 8-9/49 - No. 5, 4/50; No. 6, 2/51; No. 7, 5/51 - #14, 10/52; #15, 1/53 - #18, 7/53; No. 5, 9/53 - No. 9, 8/54

	GD25	FN65	NM94
1-(1st series)-Titled Youthful Love-Romances	20.00	60.00	150.00
2-Walter Johnson c-1-4	11.00	34.00	85.00
3-5	9.30	28.00	65.00
6,7,9-14(10/52, Pix-Parade; becomes Daring Love #15); 7-Tony Martin photo-c. 10(1/52)-Mel Torme photo-c/story. 13-Richard Hayes (singer) photo-c/story; Bob & Ray photo/text story.	7.85	23.50	55.00
8-Wood-c	14.00	42.00	105.00
15-18 (Ribage)-All have photos on-c. 12-Tony Bennett photo-c, 8pg. story & text bio.15-Spike Jones photo-c/story	6.50	19.50	45.00
5(9/53, Ribage)-Les Paul & Mary Ford photo-c/story; Charlton Heston photo/text story	5.70	17.00	40.00
6-9: 6-Bobby Wayne (singer) photo-c/story; Debbie Reynolds photo/text story 7(2/54)-Tony Martin photo-c/story; Cyd Charise photo/text story. 8(5/54)-Gordon McCrae photo-c/story. 9(8/54)-Ralph Flanagan (band leader) photo-c/story; Audrey Hepburn photo/text story.	5.00	15.00	30.00

YUPPIES FROM HELL (Also see Son of...)
Marvel Comics: 1989 ($2.95, B&W, one-shot, direct sales, 52 pgs.)

	GD25	FN65	NM94
1-Satire			3.00

ZAGO, JUNGLE PRINCE (My Story #5 on)
Fox Features Syndicate: Sept, 1948 - No. 4, Mar, 1949

	GD25	FN65	NM94
1-Blue Beetle app.; partial-r/Atomic #4 (Toni Luck)	52.00	155.00	440.00
2,3-Kamen-a	40.00	120.00	320.00
4-Baker-c	35.00	104.00	260.00

ZANE GREY'S STORIES OF THE WEST
Dell Publishing Co./Gold Key 11/64: No. 197, 9/48 - No. 996, 5-7/59; 11/64 (All painted-c)

	GD25	FN65	NM94
Four Color 197(#1)(9/48)	11.00	32.00	115.00
Four Color 222,230,236('49)	5.50	16.50	60.00
Four Color 246,255,270,301,314,333,346	3.60	11.00	40.00
Four Color 357,372,395,412,433,449,467,484	2.75	8.00	30.00
Four Color 511-Kinstler-a; Kubert-a	3.60	11.00	40.00
Four Color 532,555,583,604,616,632(5/55)	2.75	8.00	30.00
27(9-11/55) - 39(9-11/58)	3.00	9.00	32.00
Four Color 996(5-7/59)	2.75	8.00	30.00
10131-411-(11/64-G.K.)-Nevada; r/4-Color #996	1.65	5.00	18.00

ZANY (Magazine)(Satire)(See Frantic & Ratfink)
Candor Publ. Co.: Sept, 1958 - No. 4, May, 1959

	GD25	FN65	NM94
1-Bill Everett-c	7.85	23.50	55.00
2-4: 4-Everett-c	5.70	17.00	40.00

ZATANNA (See Adv. Comics #413, JLA #161, Supergirl #1, World's Finest Comics #274)
DC Comics: July, 1993 - No. 4, Oct, 1993 ($1.95, limited series)

	GD25	FN65	NM94
1-4			2.00
Special 1(1987, $2.00)-Gray Morrow-c/a			2.00

ZAZA, THE MYSTIC (Formerly Charlie Chan; This Magazine Is Haunted V2#12 on)

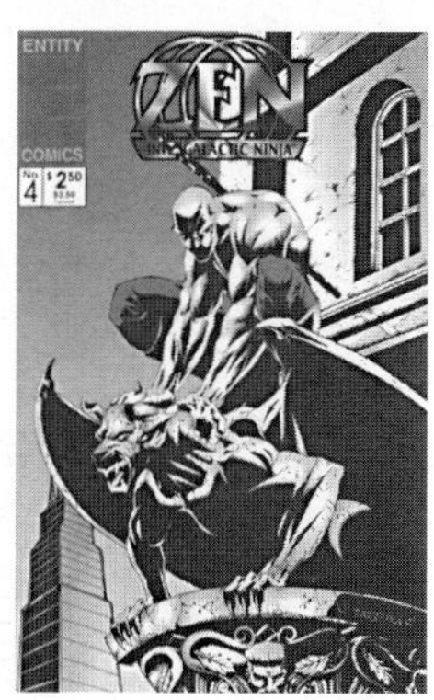

Zen Intergalactic Ninja #4 © Entity

Zero Hour #2 © DC

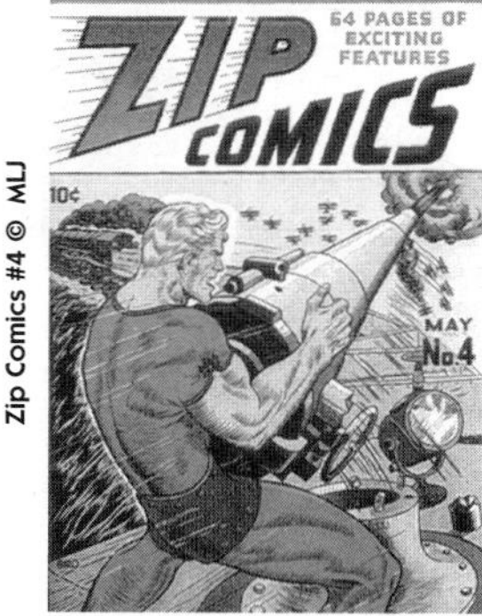

Zip Comics #4 © MLJ

	GD25	FN65	NM94
Charlton Comics: No. 10, Apr, 1956 - No. 11, Sept, 1956			
10,11	10.00	30.00	70.00

ZEALOT (Also see WildC.A.T.S: Covert Action Teams)
Image Comics: Aug, 1995 - No. 3, Nov, 1995 ($2.50, limited series)

	GD25	FN65	NM94
1-3		1.00	2.50

ZEGRA JUNGLE EMPRESS (Formerly Tegra)(My Love Life #6 on)
Fox Features Syndicate: No. 2, Oct, 1948 - No. 5, April, 1949

	GD25	FN65	NM94
2	53.00	159.00	450.00
3-5	41.00	122.00	325.00

ZEN INTERGALACTIC NINJA
No Publisher: 1987 -1993 ($1.75/$2.00, B&W)

	NM94
1-6: Copyright-Stern & Cote	4.00
V2#1-4-($2.00)	3.00
V3#1-5-($2.95)	3.00
... :Christmas Special 1 (1992, $2.95)	3.00
... :Earth Day Special 1 (1993, $2.95)	3.00

ZEN, INTERGALACTIC NINJA (mini-series)
Zen Comics/Archie Comics: Sept, 1992 - No. 3, 1992 ($1.25)(Formerly a B&W comic by Zen Comics)

	NM94
1-3: 1-Origin Zen; contains mini-poster	1.25

ZEN, INTERGALACTIC NINJA
Zen Comics/Archie Comics: 1992 - No. 3, 1992 ($1.25)

	NM94
1-3	1.25

ZEN INTERGALACTIC NINJA
Entity Comics: No. 0, June-July, 1993 - No. 3, 1994 ($2.95, B&W, limited series)

	NM94
0-Gold foil stamped-c; photo-c of Zen model	3.00
1-3: Gold foil stamped-c; Bill Maus-c/a	3.00
0-(1993, $3.50, color)-Chromium-c by Jae Lee	3.50
...Sourcebook 1-(1993, $3.50)	3.50
...Sourcebook '94-(1994, $3.50)	3.50

ZEN INTERGALACTIC NINJA: APRIL FOOL'S SPECIAL
Parody Press: 1994 ($2.50, B&W)

	NM94
1-w/flip story of Renn Intergalactic Chihuahua	2.50

ZEN INTERGALACTIC NINJA COLOR
Entity Comics: 1994 - No. 7, 1995 ($2.25)

	NM94
1-($3.95)-Chromium die cut-c	4.00
1-($2.25)	2.25
0-($2.25)-Newsstand; Jae Lee-c; r/...All New Color Special #0	2.25
2-($2.50)-Flip book	2.50
2-($3.50)-Flip book, polybagged w/chromium trading card	3.50
3-5: 3-Begin $2.50-c	2.50
6,7: 6-Begin $2.95-c	3.00
Summer Special (1994, $2.95)	3.00
Yearbook: Hazardous Duty 1 (1995)	3.00
Zen-isms 1 (1995, 2.95)	3.00
Ashcan-Tour of the Universe-(no price) w/flip cover	1.00

ZEN INTERGALACTIC NINJA COMMEMORATIVE EDITION
Zen Comics Publishing: 1997 ($5.95, color)

	NM94
1-Stern-s/Cote-a	5.95

ZEN INTERGALACTIC NINJA MILESTONE
Entity Comics: 1994 - No. 3, 1994 ($2.95, limited series)

	NM94
1-3: Gold foil logo; r/Defend the Earth	3.00

ZEN INTERGALATIC NINJA SPRING SPECTACULAR
Entity Comics: 1994 ($2.95, B&W, one-shot)

	NM94
1-Gold foil logo	3.00

ZEN INTERGALACTIC NINJA STARQUEST
Entity Comics: 1994 - No. 6, 1995 ($2.95, B&W)

	NM94
1-6: Gold foil logo	3.00

ZEN, INTERGALACTIC NINJA: THE HUNTED
Entity Comics: 1993 - No. 3, 1994 ($2.95, B&W, limited series)

	NM94
1-3: Newsstand Edition; foil logo	3.00
1-($3.50)-Polybagged w/chromium card by Kieth; foil logo	3.50

ZERO HOUR: CRISIS IN TIME (Also see Showcase '94 #8-10)
DC Comics: No. 4(#1), Sept, 1994 - No. 0(#5), Oct, 1994 ($1.50, limited series)

	NM94
4(#1)-0(#5)	4.00
"Ashcan"-(1994, free, B&W, 8 pgs.)	1.00
TPB ('94, $9.95)	10.00

ZERO PATROL, THE
Continuity Comics: Nov, 1984 - No. 2; 1987 - No. 5, 1989? ($2.00)

	NM94
1,2: Neal Adams-c/a; Megalith begins	2.00
1-5 (#1,2-reprints above, 1987)	2.00

ZERO TOLERANCE
First Comics: Oct, 1990 - No. 4, Jan, 1991 ($2.25, limited series)

	NM94
1-4: Tim Vigil-c/a(p) (his 1st color limited series)	2.25

ZERO ZERO
Fantagraphics: Mar, 1995 - Present ($3.95, B&W, anthology, mature)

	NM94
1-24	4.00

ZIGGY PIG-SILLY SEAL COMICS (See Animal Fun, Animated Movie-Tunes, Comic Capers, Krazy Komics, Silly Tunes & Super Rabbit)
Timely Comics (CmPL): Fall, 1944 - No. 6, Fall, 1946

	GD25	FN65	NM94
1-Vs. the Japs	20.00	60.00	150.00
2	10.00	30.00	75.00
3-5	9.30	28.00	65.00
6-Infinity-c	11.00	32.00	80.00
I.W. Reprint #1(1958)-r/Krazy Komics	1.25	3.75	10.00
I.W. Reprint #2,7,8	1.10	3.30	9.00

ZIP COMICS
MLJ Magazines: Feb, 1940 - No. 47, Summer, 1944 (#1-7?: 68 pgs.)

	GD25	FN65	NM94
1-Origin Kalathar the Giant Man, The Scarlet Avenger, & Steel Sterling; Mr. Satan (by Edd Ashe), Nevada Jones (masked hero) & Zambini, the Miracle Man, War Eagle, Captain Valor begins	379.00	1137.00	3600.00
2-Nevada Jones adds mask & horse Blaze	176.00	529.00	1500.00
3	124.00	371.00	1050.00
4,5	103.00	309.00	875.00
6-8	88.00	265.00	750.00
9-Last Kalathar & Mr. Satan; classic-c	106.00	318.00	900.00
10-Inferno, the Flame Breather begins, ends #13	97.00	291.00	825.00
11,12: 11-Inferno without costume	76.00	229.00	650.00
13-17,19: 17-Last Scarlet Avenger	76.00	229.00	650.00
18-Wilbur begins (9/41, 1st app.)	79.00	238.00	675.00
20-Origin & 1st app. Black Jack (11/41); Hitler-c	115.00	344.00	975.00
21,23-26: 25-Last Nevada Jones. 26-Black Witch begins; last Captain Valor	68.00	203.00	575.00
22-Classic-c	79.00	238.00	675.00
27-Intro. Web (7/42) plus-c app.	112.00	335.00	950.00
28-Origin Web	103.00	309.00	875.00
29,30: 29-The Hyena app.	49.00	148.00	420.00
31-38: 34-1st Applejack app. 35-Last Zambini, Black Jack. 38-Last Web issue	40.00	120.00	320.00
39-Red Rube begins (origin, 8/43)	40.00	120.00	320.00
40-47: 45-Wilbur ends	33.00	100.00	250.00

*NOTE: **Biro** a-5, 9, 17; c-3-17. **Meskin** a-1-3, 5-7, 9, 10, 12, 13, 15, 16 at least. **Montana** c-29, 30, 32-35. **Novick** c-18-28, 31. **Sahle** c-37, 38, 40-46. Bondage c-8, 9, 33, 34. Cover features: Steel Sterling-1-43, 47; (w/Blackjack-20-27 & Web-27-35), 28-39; (w/Red Rube-40-43); Red Rube-44-47.*

Zombie World: Home For The Holidays © DH

Zoot #12 © FOX

Zorro #10 © Johnston McCulley

GD25 FN65 NM94

ZIP-JET (Hero)
St. John Publishing Co.: Feb, 1953 - No. 2, Apr-May, 1953

1-Rocketman-r from Punch Comics; #1-c from splash in Punch #10 56.00 168.00 475.00
2 43.00 129.00 350.00

ZIPPY THE CHIMP (CBS TV Presents...)
Pines (Literary Ent.): No. 50, March, 1957; No. 51, Aug, 1957

50,51 5.35 16.00 32.00

ZODY, THE MOD ROB
Gold Key: July, 1970

1 1.60 4.80 16.00

ZOMBIE WORLD (one-shots)
Dark Horse Comics

... :Eat Your Heart Out (4/98, $2.95) Kelley Jones-c/s/a 3.00
... :Home For The Holidays (12/97, $2.95) 3.00

ZOMBIE WORLD: CHAMPION OF THE WORMS
Dark Horse Comics: Sept, 1997 - No. 3, Nov, 1997 ($2.95, limited series)

1-3-Mignola & McEown-c/s/a 2.95

ZOMBIE WORLD: DEAD END
Dark Horse Comics: Jan, 1998 - No. 2, Feb, 1998 ($2.95, limited series)

1,2-Stephen Blue-c/s/a 3.00

ZOMBIE WORLD: WINTER'S DREGS
Dark Horse Comics: May, 1998 - No. 4, Aug, 1998 ($2.95, limited series)

1-4-Fingerman-s/Edwards-a 3.00

ZONE (Also see Dark Horse Presents)
Dark Horse Comics: 1990 ($1.95, B&W)

1-Character from Dark Horse Presents 2.00

ZONE CONTINUUM, THE
Caliber Press: 1994 ($2.95, B&W)

1 3.00

ZOO ANIMALS
Star Publications: No. 8, 1954 (15¢, 36 pgs.)

8-(B&W for coloring) 4.00 12.00 24.00

ZOO FUNNIES (Tim McCoy #16 on)
Charlton Comics/Children Comics Publ.: Nov, 1945 - No. 15, 1947

101(#1)(11/45, 1st Charlton comic book)-Funny animal; Al Fago-c 16.00 48.00 120.00
2(12/45, 52 pgs.) 8.50 26.00 60.00
3-5 7.15 21.50 50.00
6-15: 8-Diana the Huntress app. 5.70 17.00 35.00

ZOO FUNNIES (Becomes Nyoka, The Jungle Girl #14 on?)
Capitol Stories/Charlton Comics: July, 1953 - No. 13, Sept, 1955; Dec, 1984

1-1st app.? Timothy The Ghost; Fago-c/a 8.50 26.00 60.00
2 5.70 17.00 35.00
3-7 (8/46) 4.25 13.00 28.00
8-13-Nyoka app. 6.50 19.50 45.00
1(1984) 2.00

ZOONIVERSE
Eclipse Comics: 8/86 - No. 6, 6/87 ($1.25/$1.75, limited series, Mando paper)

1-5 ($1.25) 1.30
6 ($1.75) 1.80

ZOO PARADE (TV)
Dell Publishing Co.: #662, 1955 (Marlin Perkins)

Four Color 662 4.00 12.00 45.00

ZOOM COMICS
Carlton Publishing Co.: Dec, 1945 (one-shot)

GD25 FN65 NM94

nn-Dr. Mercy, Satannas, from Red Band Comics; Capt. Milksop origin retold 39.00 116.00 290.00

ZOOT (Rulah Jungle Goddess #17 on)
Fox Features Syndicate: nd (1946) - No. 16, July, 1948 (Two #13s & 14s)

nn-Funny animal only 16.00 48.00 120.00
2-The Jaguar app. 15.00 44.00 110.00
3(Fall, 1946) - 6-Funny animals & teen-age 8.50 26.00 60.00
7-(6/47)-Rulah, Jungle Goddess (origin/1st app.) 82.00 247.00 700.00
8-10 56.00 168.00 475.00
11-Kamen bondage-c 59.00 176.00 500.00
12-Injury-to-eye panels, torture scene 41.00 122.00 325.00
13(2/48) 41.00 122.00 325.00
14(3/48)-Used in **SOTI**, pg. 104, "One picture showing a girl nailed by her wrists to trees with blood flowing from the wounds, might be taken straight from an ill. ed. of the Marquis deSade" 50.00 150.00 425.00
13(4/48),14(5/48)-Western True Crime #15 on? 41.00 122.00 325.00
15,16 41.00 122.00 325.00

ZORRO (Walt Disney with #882)(TV)(See Eclipse Graphic Album)
Dell Publishing Co.: May, 1949 - No. 15, Sept-Nov, 1961 (Photo-c 882 on)
(Zorro first appeared in a pulp story Aug 19, 1919 - 1994 was 75th anniversary)

Four Color 228 (#1) 20.00 60.00 220.00
Four Color 425,617,732 11.00 34.00 125.00
Four Color 497,538,574-Kinstler-a 12.00 37.00 135.00
Four Color 882-Photo-c begin; Toth-a 16.00 49.00 180.00
Four Color 920,933,960,976-Toth-a in all 11.00 34.00 125.00
Four Color 1003('59)-Toth-a 11.00 34.00 125.00
Four Color 1037-Annette Funicello photo-c 14.00 44.00 160.00
8(12-2/59-60) 7.00 22.00 80.00
9-Toth-a 8.00 23.00 85.00
10,11,13-15-Last photo-c 6.40 19.00 70.00
12-Toth-a; last 10¢ issue 8.00 23.00 85.00

NOTE: ***Warren Tufts*** *a-4-Color 1037, 8, 9, 10, 13.*

ZORRO (Walt Disney)(TV)
Gold Key: Jan, 1966 - No. 9, Mar, 1968 (All photo-c)

1-Toth-a 6.40 19.00 70.00
2,4,5,7-9-Toth-a. 5-r/F.C. #1003 by Toth 3.60 11.00 40.00
3,6-Tufts-a 3.00 9.00 35.00

NOTE: *#1-9 are reprinted from Dell issues.* ***Tufts*** *a-3, 4. #1-r/F.C. #882. #2-r/F.C. #960. #3-r/#12-c & #8 inside. #4-r/#9-c & insides. #6-r/#11(all); #7-r/#14-c. #8-r/F.C. #933 inside & back-c & #976-c. #9-r/F.C. #920.*

ZORRO (TV)
Marvel Comics: Dec, 1990 - No. 12, Nov, 1991 ($1.00)

1-12: Based on TV show. 12-Toth-c 1.00

ZORRO (Also see Mask of Zorro)
Topps Comics: Nov, 1993 - No. 11, Nov, 1994 ($2.50/$2.95)

0-(11/93, $1.00, 20 pgs.)-Painted-c; collector's ed. 1.00
1,4,6-9,11: 1-Miller-c. . 4-Mike Grell-c. 6-Mignola-c. 7-Lady Rawhide-c by Gulacy. 8-Perez-c. 10-Julie Bell-c. 11-Lady Rawhide-c. 3.00
2-Lady Rawhide-app. (not in costume) 2.00 6.00
3-1st app. Lady Rawhide in costume, 3-Lady Rawhide-c by Adam Hughes .90 2.70 8.00
5-Lady Rawhide app. 4.00
10 ($2.95)-Lady Rawhide-c/app. 3.00

ZOT! (Also see Adventures of Zot)
Eclipse Comics: 4/84 - No. 10, 7/85; No. 11, 1/87 - No. 35 3/91 ($1.50, Baxter-p)

1 4.00
2,3 3.00
4-10: 4-Origin. 10-Last color issue 2.00
11-35: 11-Begin $2.00-c, B&W issues 2.00

Z-2 COMICS (Secret Agent...)(See Holyoke One-Shot #7)

ZULU (See Movie Classics)

CONTINUED ON NEXT PAGE

CONTINUED FROM PREVIOUS PAGE

CONTINUED ON SECOND PAGE FOLLOWING

CONTINUED FROM TWO PAGES PREVIOUS

THIRD PLANET
POUNDING
the competition
since 1975!
comics, toys, cards, games,
videos, anime, posters, statues,
art prints, models, magazines,
novels, pulps, imports, pre-orders,
world wide mail orders & subscription
service , lay-aways and much more!
2718 SW FWY
Houston, TX 77098
(713) 528-1067
www.third-planet.com
3planet@third-planet.com
over 8,000
sq.ft. of
merchandise
in one
location!

John M. Hauser
The Best from the Midwest!
Do you want to sell your comics?
Call, write, or e-mail me TODAY! I will travel to view collections. I am very active in comics and am always looking for fresh stock. I have purchased some of the largest collections in the Midwest. I have and will continue to PAY TOP PRICES!
I WANT TO BUY YOUR COMICS!
Senior Advisor to Overstreet Comic Book Price Guide
8 consecutive CBG Customer Service Awards
Are you looking to buy comics?
Call, write, or e-mail me TODAY! I offer you a dependable and reputable source for your comic book needs. Featuring accurate and knowledgeable grading, I have a large selection of books in all grades. I publish a large catalog every 6 weeks. Send $1 for a copy of my latest. Prices start at $1 and there is no minimum order! I also present a full booth at most major national conventions, and many local and regional shows here in the Midwest! C'mon by and say hello!
20 years in the comic business!
Past member of Sotheby's Grading Commitee
John M. Hauser
(414) 789-1863
jmhcomics@aol.com
P.O.Box 510673, New Berlin, WI 53151-0673
BUY-SELL-TRADE
COMIC BOOKS
GOLDEN AGE
SILVER AGE
PRE-CODE HORROR
PULPS
Ad design & production by Herman Shilts EMAIL herman@marcus-online.net

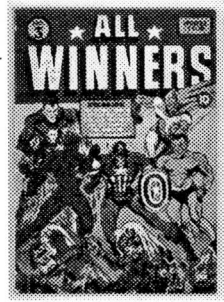

IN HIS SPECIAL DOGHOUSE OF EPHEMERA BUILT IN THE IDEAL COLLECTING ENVIRONS OF SPACE, ECLECTO "HEARS" A FAMILIAR SOUND...
WHEEETT!
COMIC KENNEL
NEAT STUFF'S IN!
YES, IT'S THE SPECIAL WHISTLE DARK ADVENTURE USES TO SUMMON THE ESOTERIC COLLECTOR...
COMIC KENNEL
I HAVE TO GET INTO COSTUME AND FLY! WHAT DO THEY HAVE THIS TIME... SO MANY THINGS...
DARK ADVENTURE
COMICS
2785 Buford Hwy. Ste 102-B
Duluth, GA 30096
[770] 232-1931
THEY BUY AND SELL GOLD, SILVER, AND BRONZE COMICS IN ALL GRADES! PAY TOP DOLLAR FOR THE RAREST DC, MARVEL AND COMICS MEMORABILIA! WAREHOUSES-STORE STOCKS-THEY BUY AND SELL THE MOST ESOTERIC ITEMS IN THE UNIVERSE! WHETHER IT'S WANT LISTS, COLLECTIONS, ANOTHER AUCTION OR GREAT CATALOG, THEY ARE ALWAYS FAIR AND FUN! DARK ADVENTURE IS THE PLACE FOR ECLECTO THE COMIC HOUND!
JEFF

SPECIALIZING IN GOLDEN & SILVER AGE COMICS

We Buy & Sell!!

Golden & Silver Age
Gaming
Comic & Card Supplies

New & Old Figures
All Collectables
Movie & Comic Posters

and more!!

Full Want List Services • Accurate Grading •
No Collection Too Big or Small • Competitive Pricing •
Many Comics Priced Below Guide

New Catalogue Available - Send $1.00 - Refundable With First Order

---

Come Visit Us In The Heart Of Toronto

PARADISE COMICS

VISA

(416) 487-9807

3278 YONGE STREET TORONTO, CANADA M4N 2L6

COMICS BOUGHT & SOLD

BUYING: 1940's to 1975

- Paying up to 50% Of Overstreet prices for comics in Fine or better condition

SELLING: Gold and Silver Age plus back issues

- Marvel, DC, Dell, Gold Key, Classics, EC, ACG, Timely, Fawcett, Archies, Fiction House, Disney, Others
- Thousands of titles available
- Satisfaction guaranteed
- Send your want list and SASE for immediate reply

FOREIGN ORDERS ACCEPTED

PHOENIX ENTERPRISES
223 Fairview Rd. Dept. PG
Erin, N. Y. 14838
Tel (607) 796-2547

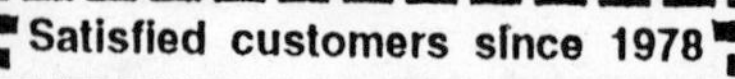

COMIC BOOK

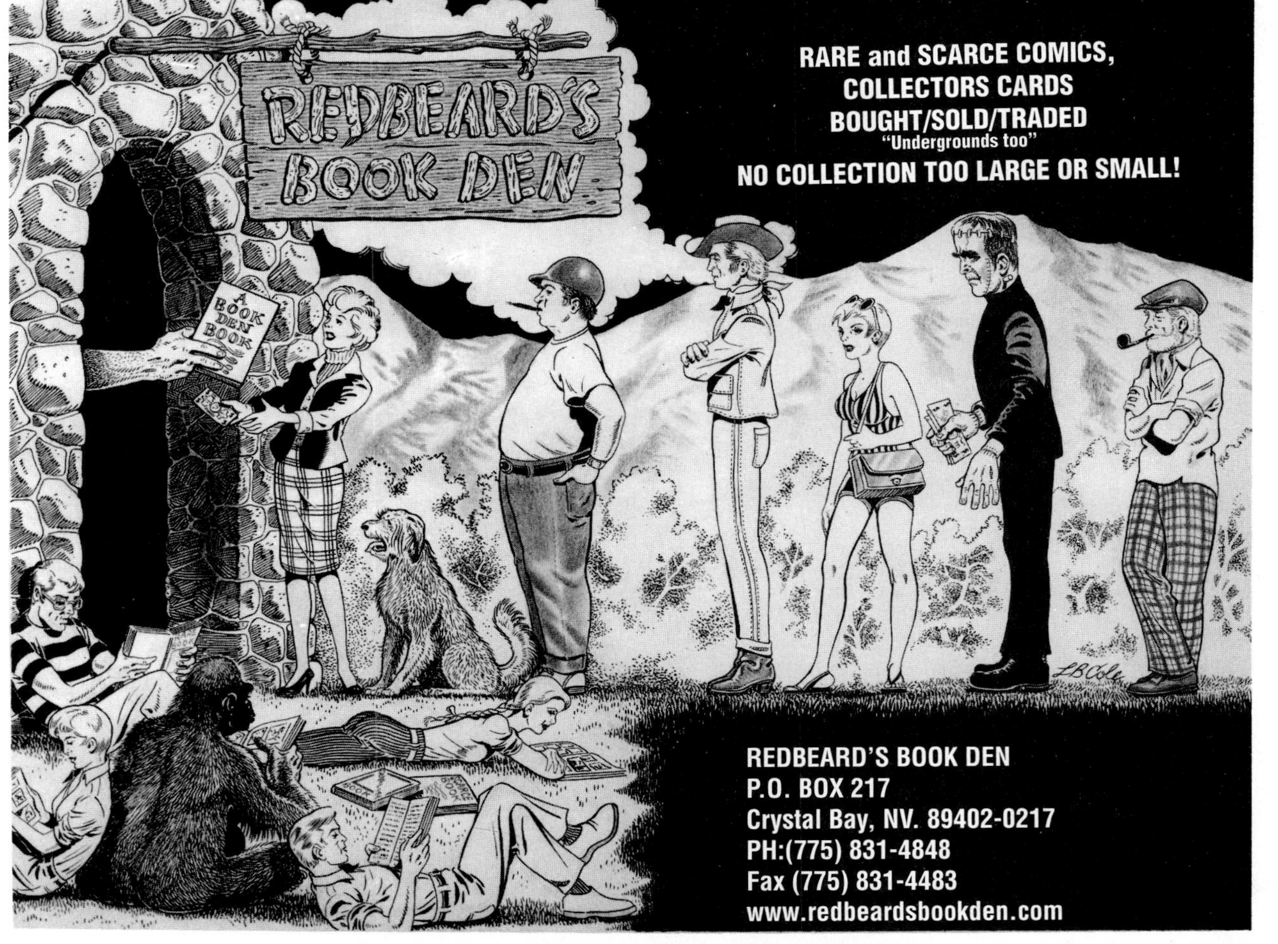
REDBEARD'S BOOK DEN
A BOOK DEN BOOK
RARE and SCARCE COMICS,
COLLECTORS CARDS
BOUGHT/SOLD/TRADED
"Undergrounds too"
NO COLLECTION TOO LARGE OR SMALL!
REDBEARD'S BOOK DEN
P.O. BOX 217
Crystal Bay, NV. 89402-0217
PH:(775) 831-4848
Fax (775) 831-4483
www.redbeardsbookden.com

Follow the Leader in Golden and Silver Age Comics with
BEDROCK CITY
COMIC COMPANY
TM
6517 Westheimer
(at Hillcroft)
Houston, Texas 77057
(713) 780-0675
2204-D FM 1960 W.
(at Kuykendahl)
Houston, Texas 77090
(281) 444-9763
fax (713) 780-2366
www.bedrockcity.com
Captain America © 1997 Marvel Entertainment Group

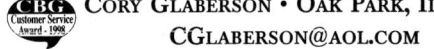

the GOBLIN'S DEN
3437 Pinesmoke Cr.
Mississauga, Ontario, Canada
L4Y 3L4
Ph#(905)848-0559 Fax#(416)622-0574
email:GOBLINS@ionsys.com
ALWAYS
Buying & Selling
Pre-1977
Comics
(AFTER ROMITA)
*We also buy: Action Figures, Model Kits & Memorabilia
*Highest Prices Paid for quality pre-code Horror, Crime & Good Girl

BUSINESS CARD ADS

THE OVERSTREET COMIC BOOK PRICE GUIDE BUSINESS CARD ADS are a whole new way to advertise in the Guide! Simply send us your business card and we'll reduce it and run it as is. Have your ad seen by thousands of serious comic book collectors for an entire year! If you are a comic book or collectible dealer, retail establishment, mail-order house, etc., you can reach potential customers throughout the United States and around the world in our **BUSINESS CARD ADS**!

For more information, contact our Advertising Dept.
Call Toll Free (888) 375-9800 or fax (410) 560-6107.

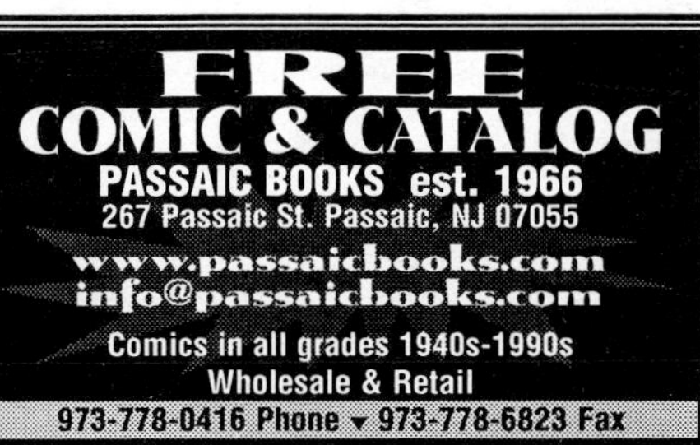

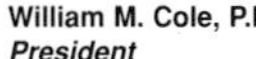

TEL: 781-986-2653
FAX: 781-986-2656

Bill Cole Enterprises, Inc.

P.O. Box 60 • Randolph, MA 02368-0060
e-mail: bcemylar@internetmci.com
web site: http://www.neponset.com/bcemylar

Manufacturers and Distributors of Preservation Supplies-
for the Collector and the Archivist

THE ULTIMATE BACK-ISSUE SERVICE

P.O. BOX 3855
SCOTTSDALE, AZ 85271
Phone: (602) 949-8499
Fax: (602) 947-3244

STRICT GRADING, FAIR PRICING, AND PROMPT SHIPPING ON POPULAR ISSUES FROM THE '40'S TO PRESENT

ROBERT M. LETSCHER II OWNER

James F. Payette
Rare Books & Comics

P.O. Box 750
Bethlehem, NH 03574

Dealing in Old & New
Rare Comic Books

Big Little Books • 1st Ed. Books • Pulp Magazines
Sci-Fi Fantasy Material • Old Coins • Baseball Cards
TELEPHONE: (603) 869-2097

Order your new comics in advance.

Get **Big Discounts!**
Never miss an issue!
CBG Customer
Service Award
14 years in a row!

13617 Southwest Hwy. Orland Park, IL 60462
888-MM-COMICS (888-662-6642)
www.mmcomics.com

° COMICS
° ACTION FIGURES
° TRADING CARDS
° STATUES
° MORE!

since 1989

Online Store - Easy Checkout
Search Option - Fast Service
Updated Daily - LOTS of Pictures

www.alteredstatecomics.com

phone (800) 278-9691, (718) 721-9691 fax (718) 728-9691
22-55 31ST STREET, ASTORIA, N.Y. 11105

SPECIALIZING IN PRE-1970'S COMICS

www.silveragecomics.com e-mail gus@silveragecomics.com

TRILOGY COMICS

Comics Cards Games
Anime SF Memorabilia

5773 Princess Anne Rd.
Va. Beach, VA 23462
Ph: 757-490-2205
Fax: 757-671-7721

700 E. Little Creek Rd.
Norfolk, VA 23518
Ph: 757-587-2540
Fax: 757-587-5637

e-mail: trilogy@nfx.net

the
GUIDE
THE OVERSTREET COMIC BOOK PRICE UPDATE
JUSTICE LEAGUE OF AMERICA
FRANK MILLER DAVE GIBBONS
GIVE ME LIBERTY
AN AMERICAN DREAM
1: HOMES & GARDENS
SPAWN
THE STRANGEST SUPER-HEROES OF ALL!
the X-MEN
DIRECT SALES
$2.95/$3.95 CAN

#2
Edition
the
GUIDE
THE OVERSTREET® COMIC BOOK PRICE UPDATE
JAY & SILENT BOB
FATHOM
FRANK MILLER
SIN CITY
JLA
AVENGERS
CAPTAIN AMERICA LIVES AGAIN!

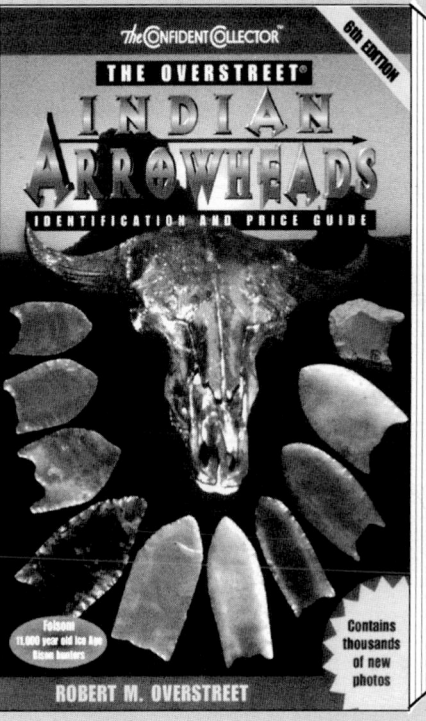

CREATOR LISTINGS

THE OVERSTREET COMIC BOOK PRICE GUIDE CREATOR LISTINGS is accepting business card ads from comic book writers, artists, editors, colorists, letterers--any and all comic book creators! This is your chance to reach out to editors, publishers, and even other creators throughout the United States and around the world. Our **CREATOR LISTINGS** will help you publicize your artwork, writing, web site, self-published series--the choice is yours!

For more information, contact our Advertising Dept.
Call Toll Free (888) 375-9800 or fax (410) 560-6107.

TODD McFARLANE
PRODUCTIONS

Beau Smith

TODD McFARLANE PRODUCTIONS, INC.
740 SECOND STREET WEST, P.O. BOX 706
CEREDO, WV 25507 USA

EMAIL_beausmith@aol.com
PAGER_800.804.8714

TEL_304.453.1050
FAX_304.453.6853
http://www.spawn.com

SHELDON MOLDOFF (954) 485-8551
3710 Inverrary Dr. Lauderhill, FL 33319

Jamal Y.Igle
Hyperactive Illustration

"Be AFRAID, be very Afraid..."

ph/fax (718) 788- 5747

Halloween Comics
James D. Hudnall
Writer/Publisher/Producer

Creator of Harsh Realm,
ESPers,
The Age of Heroes

www.thehud.com/home
e-mail: hud@thehud.com

CREATORS!
JOIN US FOR OUR EXPANDED CREATOR LISTINGS IN THE 30TH EDITION OF
THE OVERSTREET COMIC BOOK PRICE GUIDE!
E-MAIL: ads@gemstonepub.com
FOR DETAILS!
DON'T BE LEFT OUT!

CLASSIFIED ADS

(PAID ADVERTISING - STORE LISTINGS)

You can have your store listed here for very reasonable rates. Send for details for next year's Guide. The following list of stores have paid to be included in this list. We cannot assume any responsibility in your dealings with these shops. This list is provided for your information only. When planning trips, it would be advisable to make appointments in advance. Remember, to get your shop included in the next edition, call, fax or write us for rates. **Gemstone Publishing, Inc., 1966 Greenspring Dr., Suite LL3, Timonium, MD 21093. PH 888-375-9800 or 410-560-5806, FAX 410-560-6107**.

Items stocked by these shops are listed just after the telephone number and are coded as follows:

(a) Golden Age Comics
(b) Silver Age Comics
(c) New Comics, Magazines
(d) Pulps
(e) Paperbacks
(f) Big Little Books
(g) Magazines
(h) Books (old)
(i) Movie Posters
(j) Original Art
(k) Toys
(l) Records/CDs, Video Tapes
(m) Trading Cards
(n) Underground Comics
(o) Premiums
(p) Comic Related Posters
(q) Comic Supplies
(r) Role Playing Games
(s) Star Trek Items
(t) Doctor Who Items
(u) Japanimation Items

ALABAMA

Campbell's Collectibles
1221 Littlebrook Ln.
Birmingham, AL 35235
PH: (205) 853-8227
FX: (205) 853-9951
E-Mail: billanne@bellsouth.net
(a,d-h,k,m,o)

Wizard's Comics
324 North Ct.
Florence, AL 35630
PH: (256) 766-6821
(a-c,g,i,k,l,p-u)

Sincere Comics
4667 Airport Blvd.
Mobile, AL 36608
PH: (334) 342-2603
E-Mail: sincerecomics@mindspring.com
(a-c,e,m,p-s,u)

ALASKA

Bosco's
2606 Spenard Rd.
Anchorage, AK 99503
PH: (907) 274-4112
E-Mail: info@boscos.com
Web: www.boscos.com
(a-c,g,i,k,m,n,p-s,u-v)

ARIZONA

Atomic Comics III
5965 West Ray Rd. #19
Chandler, AZ 85226
PH: (602) 940-6061
(b,c,g,i-k,m-u)

Atomic Comics
1310 West Southern #3
Mesa, AZ 85202
PH: (602) 649-0807
(a-c,f,g,j,k,m,n,p-u)

Atomic Comics
Direct Mail Order
1310 West Southern #3
Mesa, AZ 85202
PH: (800) 332-9027
E-Mail: mail@atomiccomics.com
Web: www.atomiccomics.com
(a-c,g,j-u)

Greg's Comics
2722 South Alma School Rd. #8
Mesa, AZ 85210
PH: (602) 752-1881
(a-c,k,m,q-s)

All About Books & Comics
517 E. Camelback Rd.
Phoenix, AZ 85012
PH: (602) 277-0757
Web: www.all-about-comics.com
(a-v)

Atomic Comics II
3029 West Peoria #CC
Phoenix, AZ 85021
PH: (602) 395-1066
(a-c,f,g,j,k,m,n,p-u)

Key Comics: Discount Back-Issues
P.O. Box 3855
Scottsdale, AZ 85271
PH: (602) 949-8499
FX: (602) 947-3244
(a-c,j)

Dirt Cheap Collectibles
P.O. Box 13971
Scottsdale, AZ 85267
PH: (602) 515-0150
(a-c,g,k,m)

ARKANSAS

Alternate Worlds
3812 Central Ave. Suite G
Hot Springs, AR 71913
PH: (501) 525-8999
(b,c,g,k,m,q-v)

The Comic Book Store
9307 Treasure Hill
Little Rock, AR 72227
PH: (501) 227-9777
(a-c,g,k,m,p,q,s,u,v)

Collector's Edition Comics
3217 John F. Kennedy Blvd.
North Little Rock, AR 72116
PH: (501) 791-4222
(a-c,g,k,m,p,q,s,u,v)

CALIFORNIA

Terry's Comics
P.O. Box 471
Atwood, CA 92811
PH: (800) 938-0325
FX: (714) 288-8992
E-Mail: terryscomics@webtv.net
(a,b,d-i,k,q)

Comic Relief Berkeley
2138 University Avenue
Berkeley, CA 94704
PH: (510) 843-5002
E-Mail: email@comicrelief.net
(a-d,f-h,j,n,p,q,u,v)

Crush Comics
2869 Castro Valley Blvd.
Castro Valley, CA 94546
PH: (510) 581-4779
FX: (510)-581-4779
(b,c,g,k,m,p,q,s,v)

Collectors Ink
932-A West 8th Ave.
Chico, CA 95926
PH: (530) 345-0958
E-Mail: collink@cmc.net
Web: www.cmc.net/~collink
(a-c,e,g,k-n,p-u)

Comic Bookie
415 West Foothill Blvd. #318
Claremont, CA 91711
PH: (909) 399-0228
E-mail: nlcs29a@prodigy.com
(b,c,g,k,i,m,n,p,q,s,u,v)

Flying Colors Comics
& Other Cool Stuff
2980 Treat Blvd.,
Oak Grove Plaza
Concord, CA 94518
PH: (925) 825-5410
(a-c,j,k,m,p,q,u,v)

Superior Comics
1970 Newport Blvd.
Costa Mesa, CA 92627
PH: (949) 631-3933
(a-c,f,g,j,k,m,n,p-r,u)

High Quality Comics
(Mail Order Only)
1106 2nd St. Ste. #110
Encinitas, CA 92024
PH: (800) 682-3936
E-Mail:
mbxstation@aol.com
Web:
www.publiconline.com/
=highqualitycom
(a-c,g,j,n)

Comic Gallery
322-J West El Norte Pkwy.
Escondido, CA 92026
PH: (760) 745-5660
(b,c,j,k,m,q-s,u)

Comicmania!
124 W. Commonwealth
Fullerton, CA 92832
PH: (714) 992-6649
(a-c,f,g,i-k,m-q,s,u)

Mile High Comics
Mega-Cal
12591 Harbor Blvd.
Garden Grove, CA 92840
PH: (714) 741-2096
Web: www.milehigh-
comics.com
(a-c,e,g-v)

Geoffrey's Comics
15530 Crenshaw Blvd.
Gardena, CA 90249
PH: (888) 538-3198
(a-c,l,n,q,u)

Shooting Star Comics
618 E. Colorado Blvd.
Glendale, CA 91205
PH: (818) 502-1535
(b,c,g,m,p,q,u)

Treasures Of Youth
1201 C St.
Hayward, CA 94541
PH: (510) 888-9675
E-Mail:
smcatoyguy@aol.com
(a,b,d-k,m-o)

Amazing Comics & Cards
5555 Stearns St., Suite 103
Long Beach, CA 90815
PH: (562) 493-4427
E-Mail: amazingcomic
scards@worldnet.att.net
(b,c,e,g,k,l,m,p,q,s-v)

Ambrosia Books,
Comics & Collectibles
10679 West Pico Blvd.
Los Angeles, CA 90064
PH: (310) 475-5825
PH: (888) 47-DRWHO
Web: www.concentric.net/
~jslyon
(b,c,e,g,h,k,l-n,p-u)

Another World Comics
& Books
1615 Colorado Blvd.
Los Angeles, CA 90041
PH: (323) 257-7757
E-Mail: bob
@anotherworld.com
Web: www.
anotherworld.com
(a-g,i,m,p,t,u)

Golden Apple Comics
7711 Melrose Ave.
Los Angeles, CA 90046
PH: (213) 658-6047
Web: www.
goldenapplecomics.com
(a-c,l-n,p,q,t)

Meltdown Comics
& Collectibles
7529 Sunset Blvd.
Los Angeles, CA 90046
PH: (323) 851-7223
E-mail: meltdown
@primenet.com
Web:
www.meltcomics.com
(b,c,e,g,j,k-q,s,u,v)

Pacific Comic
Exchange, Inc.
(By Appointment Only)
P. O. Box 34849
Los Angeles, CA 90034
PH: (310) 836-7234 (PCEI)
FX: (310) 836-7127
E-Mail: sales@pcei.com
Web: www.pcei.com/
(a, b)

Century Comic Center
193 Terry Cr.
Marina, CA 93933
PH: (800) 817-3353
FX: (408) 883-4257
E-mail: bill@centu-
rycomiccenter.com
Web: www.
centurycomiccenter.com
(a,b,f,k,s)

Brian's Books
73 North Milpitas Blvd.
Milpitas, CA 95035
PH: (408) 942-6903
(a-c,g,m,p,q,s,u)

Pegasus Hobbies
5505 Moreno Blvd.
Montclair, CA 91763
PH: (909) 931-4872
(a-c,g,k,m,q-s,u)

The Big Guy's Comics
167 El Camino East
Mountain View, CA 94040
PH: (650) 965-8272
(a-d,f,k,n,p,q,v)

Golden Apple Comics
8962 Reseda Blvd.
Northridge, CA 91324
PH: (818) 993-7804
Web: www.
goldenapplecomics.com
(a-c,e,l-n,p,q,u)

Lee's Comics, Inc.
3783 El Camino Real
Palo Alto, CA 94306
PH: (650) 493-3957
E-Mail: lee@lcomics.com
Web: www.lcomics.com
(a-g,k-n,p-s,u)

A-1 Comics
5800 Madison Ave.
Sacramento, CA 95841
PH: (916) 331-9203
FX: (916) 331-2141
(a-m,p-s,u,v)

Comic Gallery
4224 Balboa Ave.
San Diego, CA 92117
PH: (619) 483-4853
(b,c,j,k,m,q-s,u)

Comic Gallery
9460-G Mira Mesa Blvd.
San Diego, CA 92126
PH: (619) 578-9444
(b,c,j,k,m,q-s,u)

San Diego Comics
& Collectibles
6937 El Cajon Blvd.
San Diego, CA 92115
PH: (619) 698-1177
(a-c,g,k,s)

Southern
California Comics
8280 Clairemont Mesa Bl.
#124, San Diego, CA 92117
PH: (619) 715-8669
FX: (619) 715-8669#
E-Mail:
socalcomix@aol.com
Web:web18.topchoice.
com/~socalcom
(a-c,g,k,q)

Cards and
Comics Central
5522 Geary Blvd.
San Francisco, CA 94121
PH: (415) 668-3544
Web:
www.candccentral.com
(c,e,g,k-n,p,q,s,u)

Captain Nemo
Comics & Games
797 Marsh St.
San Luis Obispo, CA 93401
PH: (805) 544-6366
FX: (805) 543-3938
E-Mail: nemoslo@aol.com
(a-c,e,g,i,k-v)

Lee's Comics, Inc.
2222 S. El Camino Real
San Mateo, CA 94402
PH: (650) 571-1489
(a-g,k-n,p-s,u)

Metro Comics & Games
6 West Anapamu
Santa Barbara, CA 93101
PH: (805) 963-2168
E-Mail: metrocomix
@aol.com
(a-c,g,k,m,n,p-s,u-v)

Brian's Books
2767 El Camino
Santa Clara, CA 95051
PH: (408) 985-7481
(a-c,g,m,p,q,s,u)

Atlantis Fantasyworld
1020 Cedar St.
Santa Cruz, CA 95060
PH: (831) 426-0158
(a-c,g,i,k-m,p,q,s,u,v)

Hi De Ho Comics
& Books With Pictures
525 Santa Monica Blvd.
Santa Monica, CA
90401-2409
PH: (310) 394-2820
Web: www.hideho.com
(a-v)

Mega City Comics & Toys
2955 B-201 Cochran St.
Simi Valley, CA 93065
PH: (805) 583-3027
(b,c,e,g,i-k,m,n,p-s,u)

Ralph's Comic Corner
2379 E. Main St.
Ventura, CA 93003
PH: (805) 653-2732
E-Mail: ralphs@fishnet.net
Web: www.ralphscomic-
corner.com
(a-c,f,k,m,n,p-s,u,v)

Pegasus Hobbies
6554 Greenleaf Ave.
Whittier, CA 90601
PH: (562) 907-4663
(a-c,g,k,m,q-s,u)

A Collector's Dream
21222 Venture Blvd.
Woodland Hills, CA 91364
PH: (818) 992-1636
(a-c,g,j,k,m-s)

Bonanza Books & Comics
2308 McHenry Avenue
Modesto, CA 95350-3216
PH: (209) 529-0415
(a-c,e,g,h,k,m,o-s,v)

Comic Detectives/ Collectors' Corner
959 El Camino Real
Menlo Park, CA 94025
PH: (650) 327-1085
(a,b,g,j,k,m,n,q,s)

Back Issue Comics
695 E. Lewelling
Hayward, CA 94541
PH: (510) 276-5262
(b,e,g,k,l,m)

COLORADO

All C's Collectibles, Inc.
1113 So. Abilene St. #104
Aurora, CO 80012
PH: (303) 751-6882
(a-e,g,j,k,m-s,v)

Time Warp Comics & Cards, Inc.
1631 28th St.
Boulder, CO 80301
PH: (303) 443-4500
E-Mail: timewarp@earthlink.net
Web: www.time-warp.com
(a-c,g,n,q-s)

Bargain Comics
21 1/2 E. Bijou St.
Colorado Springs, CO 80903
PH: (719) 578-8847
E-Mail: bargaincom@aol.com
(a-c,g,k,n,q,v)

Comic Vault
929 N. Murray
Colorado Springs, CO 80915
PH: (719) 596-2155
E-Mail: cvault@pcisys.net
(a-c,h,k,o-s,v)

Mile High Comics Glendale
760 S. Colorado Blvd., Unit J
Glendale, CO 80246
PH: (303) 691-2212
Web: www.milehigh-comics.com
(b-c,k-m,p,q,s,u,v)

Mile High Comics
Tabor Center
16th & Lawrence
Denver, CO 80202
PH: (303) 446-8250
Web: www.milehighcomics.com
(a-c,f-u)

Blue Coyote Comics
P. O. Box 2163
Evergreen, CO 80439
PH: (303) 670-8386
(a,b,n)

J. R. R. Comix
P. O. Box 2163
3869 Evergreen Pkwy.
Evergreen, CO 80437-2163
PH: (303) 670-8386
(a-e,g,k-n,p-u)

Mile High Comics
Lakewood
98 Wadsworth #123
Lakewood, CO 80226
PH: (303) 238-8125
Web: www.milehighcomics.com
(b,c,k,m,p,q,s,u,v)

RTS Unlimited Inc.
P. O. Box 150412
Lakewood, CO 80215-0412
PH: (303) 403-1840
(a,b,q)

Moulton's Comics & Collectibles
60 W. Littleton Blvd., Unit #105
Littleton, CO 80120
(b,c,g,l,k-m,o-q,u,v)

Mile High Comics
Mega-Thornton
9201 N. Washington
Thornton, CO 80229
PH: (303) 457-2612
(b-v)

Mile High Comics
Corporate Headquarters
2151 W. 56th Ave.
Denver, CO 80221
PH: (303) 455-2659
FX: (303) 477-5315
E-Mail: backissue@milehighcomics.com
Web: www.milehighcomics.com
(b-g,i,k,m-v)

Mile High Comics
Buckingham Square
1388 S. Havana
Aurora, CO 80012
PH: (303) 695-9664
Web: www.milehigh-comics.com
(b,c,l,k,m,p-s,u,v)

CONNECTICUT

The Bookie
206 Burnside Ave.
E. Hartford, CT 06108
PH: (860) 289-1208
(a-h,j,k,m,n,p,q-s,u,v)

D.J.'s Comics, Cards, Games
303 East Main St.
Meriden, CT 06450
PH: (203) 235-7300
(a-c,g,k,m,q,r,u)

D.J.'s Comics & Cards
166 Washington Ave.
N. Haven, CT 06473
PH: (203) 234-2989
(b,c,e,j,k,m,q-s)

Sarge's Comics Etc.
124 State Street
New London, CT 06320
PH: (860) 443-2004
E-Mail: sarges@uconect.net
Web: www.uconect.net/~sarges
(a-c,e,g,k-n,p,q-v)

Legends of Superheros
1269 W. Main St.
Waterbury, CT 06708
PH: (203) 756-2440
Web: www.legendsofsuperheros.com
(b,c,k-m,o-s,u,v)

DELAWARE

Captain Blue Hen Comics & Cards
280 E. Main St. #1
Newark, DE 19711
PH: (302) 737-3434
Web: www.captainbluehen.com
(a-c,g,j,k,m-q,u,v)

FLORIDA

Lost Realms, Inc.
23066 Sandlefoot Plaza Dr.
Boca Raton, FL 33428
PH: (561) 470-5700
(b,c,e,g,j,k,m,n,p-s,u)

Emerald City Too Comics & Collectables, Inc.
2475-L McMullen Booth Rd.
Clearwater, FL 33759
PH: (727) 797-0664
E-Mail: CowardlyLion@emeraldcitycomics.com
Web: www.emeraldcitycomics.com
(a-c,g,j-u,v)

SMRC Comics
6927 Red Road
Coral Gables, FL 33143
PH: (800) 826-3089
(a,b)

World of Comics
2133 S. Ridgewood Ave.
South Daytona, FL 32119
PH: (904) 760-0555
(a-c,e,g-i,k-n,p-u)

Borderlands Comics & Games
10230-10 Atlantic Blvd.
Jacksonville, FL 32225
PH: (904) 720-0774
(b,c,g,k,m,p,q,r,u)

Phil's Comic Shoppe
6512 W. Atlantic Blvd.
Margate, FL 33063
PH: (954) 977-6947
(a-c,i,k,m,q)

Tropic Comics South, Inc.
1870 N.E. 163 St.
N. Miami Beach, FL 33162
PH: (305) 940-8700
FX: (305) 940-1551
E-Mail: abcsales@a-bombcomics.com
Web: www.a-bombcomics.com
(a-g,i-q,s-u)

Tropic Comics, Inc.
313 S. State R. 7
Plantation, FL 33317
PH: (954) 587-8878
FX: (954) 587-0409
E-Mail: trcsale@tropiccomics.com
Web: www.tropiccomics.com
(a-g,i-k,m-q,s,u)

Emerald City Comics & Collectibles, Inc.
9249 Seminole Blvd.
Seminole, FL 33772
PH: (813) 398-2665
E-Mail: CowardlyLion@emeraldcitycomics.com
Web: www.emeraldcitycomics.com
(a-c,e,g,j-v)

Past Present Future Superstore-Sunrise
8432 W. Oakland Park Blvd.
Sunrise, FL 33351
PH: (954) 742-0777
(b,c,e,g,j,k,m,n,p-u)

The Comics Club, Inc.
8126 N. University Dr.
Tamarac, FL 33321
PH: (954) 726-2121
(a-c,e,g,i,k,m,q-s)

Past Present Future Superstore-West Palm Beach
1387 N. Military Trail
West Palm Beach, FL 33409
PH: (561) 697-2554
(b,c-g,j,k,m,n,p-u)

GEORGIA

Oxford Comics, Inc.
2855 Piedmont Rd. N.E.
Atlanta, GA 30305
Ph: (404) 233-8682
(a-u)

Titan Games & Comics
5436 Riverdale Rd.
College Park, GA 30349
PH: (770) 996-9129
(a-c,e,g,k-m,p-u)

Comic Company
1058 Mistletoe Rd.
Decatur, GA 30033
PH: (404) 248-9846
FX: (404) 325-2334
E-Mail: mail@comiccompany.com
Web: www.comiccompany.com
(a-c,g,k,m,p,q,v)

Titan Games & Comics IV
2131 Pleasant Hill Rd.
Duluth, GA 30136
PH: (770) 497-0202
(a-c,e,g,k-m,p-u)

Heroes Ink
2500 Cobb Pkwy. NW
Kennesaw, GA 30152
Ph: (770) 428-3033
(b,c,e,g,k,m,q,s,v)

Odin's Cosmic Bookshelf
Killian Hill Crossing
4760 Hwy. 29, Suite A-1
Lilburn, GA 30047
PH: (770) 923-8223
E-Mail: odins@aol.com
(a-c,e,g,h,m,o-s,u)

Titan Games & Comics III
2585 Spring Rd.
Smyrna, GA 30080
PH: (770) 433-8223
(a-c,e,g,k-m,p-u)

Odin's Cosmic Bookshelf
Stone Mountain Festival
1825 Rockbridge Rd. S.W.
Stone Mountain, GA 30087
PH: (770) 413-0123
(a-c,g,k,m,o-s,u)

HAWAII

Compleat Comics Company
1728-E Kaahumanu Ave.
Wailuku, HI 96793
PH: (808) 242-5875
(c,k,m,n,p-s,u,v

ILLINOIS

Graham Crackers Comics, Ltd.
2047 Bloomingdale Rd.
Glendale Heights, IL 60108
PH: (630) 894-8810
E-Mail: info@grahamcrackers.com
(b,c,g,k,m,p-s,u,v)

Graham Crackers Comics, Ltd.
120 North Bolingbrook Dr. (Rt.53)
Bolingbrook, IL 60440
PH: (630) 739-6810
(b,c,g,k,m,o,p,r-v)

Chicago Comics
3244 North Clark St.
Chicago, IL 60657
PH: (773) 528-1983
Web: www.chicago-comics.com
(a-c,g,k,m,n,p,q,u)

Independence Comics & Cards
3955 West Irving Park Rd.
Chicago, IL 60618
PH: (773) 539-6720
FX: (773) 588-1628
(a-c,i,k,m,o-s,u,v)

Joe Sarno's Comic Kingdom
5941 W. Irving Park Rd.
Chicago, IL 60634
PH: (773) 545-2231
Web: home.earthlink.net/~joesarno/
(a-d)

Larry's Comic Book Store
1219 W. Devon Ave.
Chicago, IL 60660
PH: (773) 274-1832
(a-c,q,t,u)

Yesterday
1143 West Addison
Chicago, IL 60613
PH: (773) 248-8087
(a,b,d-h,l-n,q,s)

The Paper Escape
205 West First St.
Dixon, IL 61021
PH: (815) 284-7567
(c,e,m,p,r,s,v)

Graham Crackers Comics, Ltd.
5223 South Main St.
Downers Grove, IL 60515
PH: (630) 852-1810
(b,c,g,k,m,p-r,t-v)

GEM Comics
156 N. York Rd.
Elmhurst, IL 60126
PH: (630) 833-8787
(b,c,g,k,m,p-r,v)

The Comix Revolution
999 N. Elmhurst Road
Mt. Prospect, IL 60056
PH: (847) 506-8948
(c,e,g,k-n,p,q,u,v)

Graham Crackers Comics, Ltd.
1271 Rickert Dr.
Naperville, IL 60540
PH: (630) 355-4310
(a-c,g,j-n,p-v)

M & M Comic Service
13617 Southwest Hwy.
Orland Park, IL 60462
PH: (888) 662-6642
Web: www.mmcomics.com
(b,c,g,i,k,o,p,q,u)

Tomorrow is Yesterday, Inc.
5600 N. 2nd St.
Rockford, IL 61111
PH: (815) 633-0330
(a-n,p-v)

Graham Crackers Comics, Ltd.
108 East Main St. (Rt.64)
St. Charles, IL 60174
PH: (630) 584-0610
(b,c,g,k,m,o,p,r,s,u,v)

Unicorn Comics & Cards
216 S. Villa Ave.
Villa Park, IL 60181
PH: (630) 279-5777
(a-g,k-m,p,q,s,v)

Graham Crackers Comics, Ltd.
1207 East Butterfield Rd.
Wheaton, IL 60187
PH: (630) 668-1350
(b,c,g,k,m,o,p,r,v)

INDIANA

Comic Cave
3221 E. 17th Street
Columbus, IN 47201
PH: (812) 372-8430
E-Mail: comiccave@surf-ici.com
(b,c,g,i,k,m,o,p,q,s,u,v)

The Book Broker
2717 Covert Avenue
Evansville, IN 47714
PH: (812) 479-5647
(a-h,l-n,p-v)

Matthew Hawes' Comics Unlimited
654-B E. Diamond Avenue
Evansville, IN 47711
PH: (812) 423-6952
(b,c,e,m,p-s)

Books Comics and Things
2212 Maplecrest Rd.
Fort Wayne, IN 46815-7628
PH: (219) 446-0025
FX: (219) 446-0030
E-mail: bct@bctcomics.com
Web: www.bctcomics.com
(a-c,f,g,i,k,m,p-u,v)

Books Comics & Things #2
5936 West Jefferson Blvd.
Fort Wayne, IN 46804
PH: (219) 431-4999
E-mail: Judy@bctcomics.com
Web: www.bctcomics.com
(a-c,f,g,i,k,m,p-v)

Comic Carnival
6265 North Carrollton Ave.
Indianapolis, IN 46220
PH: (317) 253-8882
(a-j,l-t)

Comic Carnival
7311 U.S. 31 South
Indianapolis, IN 46227
PH: (317) 889-8899
(a-j,l-t)

Comic Carnival
3837 N. High School Rd.
Indianapolis, IN 46254
PH: (317) 293-4386
(a-j,l-t)

Comic Carnival
9729 E. Washington St.
Indianapolis, IN 46229
PH: (317) 898-5010
(a-j,l-t)

Downtown Comics
111 N. Pennsylvania St.
Indianapolis, IN 46204
PH: (317) 237-0397
(a-u)

Downtown Comics - Carmel
13682 N. Meridian St.
Indianapolis, IN 46032
PH: (317) 848-2305
(a-u)

Downtown Comics - Castleton
5767 E. 86th St.
Indianapolis, IN 46258
PH: (317) 845-9991
(a-u)

Downtown Comics - Greenwood
8925 S. Meridian St.
Indianapolis, IN 46227
PH: (317) 885-6395
(a-u)

Downtown Comics - West
8336 W. 10th St.
Indianapolis, IN 46234
PH: (317) 271-7610
(a-u)

Galactic Greg's
1407 E. Lincolnway
Valparaiso, IN 46383
PH: (219) 464-0119
(b,c,k,p-r,u,v)

IOWA

Oak Leaf Comics
23-5th St. S.W.
Mason City, IA 50401
PH: (515) 424-0333
(a-c,f,i,k-s,u)

KANSAS

Prairie Dog Comics
Main Store
7130 W. Maple, Suite 150
Wichita, KS 67209
PH: (316) 942-3456
(a-v)

KENTUCKY

Pac-Rat's
1051 Bryant Way
Bowling Green, KY 42103
PH: (502) 782-8092
(a-c,e,g,h,k,l,m,p,q,r,v)

Comic Book World
7130 Turfway Rd.
Florence, KY 41042
PH: (606) 371-9562
(a-c,m,n,p-u)

Red Rock Collectables
929 Liberty Rd.
Lexington, KY 40505
PH: (606) 225-5452
(c,e,g,j,k,m,n,p-s,u,v)

Comic Book World
6905 Shepherdsville Rd.
Louisville, KY 40219
PH: (502) 964-5500
(a-c,m,n,p-u)

The Great Escape
2433 Bardstown Road
Louisville, KY 40205
PH: (502) 456-2216
(a-c,e,g,i,k,l-n,p-v)

LOUISIANA

B.T. & W.D. Giles
P. O. Box 271
Keithville, LA 71047
PH: (318) 925-6654
(a,b,d-f,h,l)

MAINE

Top Shelf Comics
34 Main St.
Bangor, ME 04401
PH: (207) 947-4939
FX: (207) 947-4939
E-Mail: topshelf
@tcomics.com
Web: www.tcomics.com
(a-c,m,p,r,v)

Moonshadow Comics
251 US Route 1
Falmouth, ME 04105
PH: (207) 781-8902
E-Mail: moonshadow
@ime.net
Web: www.
moonshadowcomics.com
(a-c,g,i,m,n,q-v)

MARYLAND

Another Universe.com Annapolis Mall
191 Annapolis Mall
Annapolis, MD 21401
PH: (410) 224-0007
(c,e,i,k,m,p-s,u)

Geppi's Comic World
Security
1722 N. Rolling Road
Baltimore, MD 21244
PH: (410) 298-1758
(a-c,k-m,q,s,t,v)

Big Planet Comics
4908 Fairmont Ave.
Bethesda, MD 20814
PH: (301) 654-6856
Web: www.erols.com/
big.planet.comics
(b,c,n,p,q)

Alternate Worlds
72 Cranbrook Rd.
Yorktowne Plaza
Cockeysville, MD 21030
PH: (410) 666-3290
(b,c,g,k-n,p-u)

The Closet of Comics
7315 Baltimore Ave. (US.1)
College Park, MD 20740
PH: (301) 699-0498
(a-e,g,h,m,n,p,q)

Another Universe.com Columbia Mall
2076 Columbia Mall
Columbia, MD 21044
PH: (410) 715-4444
(c,e,i,k,m,p-s,u)

Comics To Astonish
9400 Snowden River Pkwy.
Columbia, MD 21045
PH: (410) 381-2732
Web: www.comicsto
astonish.com
(a-c,j,k,m,p-r)

Comic Classics
203 East Main St.
Frostburg, MD 21532
PH: (301) 689-1823
(a-c,m,n,p,q,s)

Beyond Comics
701 Russell Ave.,
Lakeforest Mall
Gaithersburg, MD 20877
PH: (301) 216-0007
E-Mail: burntig
r@erols.com
Web: www.
beyondcomics.com
(a-d,g,j,k,n,p,q-s,u,v)

Comic Classics
365 Main St.
Laurel, MD 20707
PH: (301) 490-9811
(410) 792-4744
(a-c,k,m,n,p,q,s-u)

Adventure Comics
1063 Rockville Pike
Rockville, MD 20852
PH: (301) 251-2888
Web: www.erols.com/
advcomix/
(a-c,j,p,q)

Geppi's Comic World
Silver Spring
8317 Fenton St.
Silver Spring, MD 20910
PH: (301) 588-2546
(a-c,k-m,q,s,t,v)

Another Universe.com White Marsh Mall
2110 White Marsh Mall
8200 Perry Hall Blvd.
White Marsh, MD 21236
PH: (410) 931-2900
(c,e,i,k,m,p-s,u)

Another Universe.com Georgetown
3231 P. Street, NW
Washington, DC 20007
PH: (202) 333-8651
(c,e,i,k,m,p-s,u)

MASSACHUSETTS

New England Comics
131 Harvard Avenue
Allston, MA 02134
PH: (617) 783-1848
Web: www.necomics.com
(a-c,e,g,k-n,p-v)

New England Comics
744 Crescent St.
East Crossing Plaza
Brockton, MA 02402
PH: (508) 559-5068
Web: www.necomics.com
(a-c,e,g,k-n,p-v)

New England Comics
316 Harvard St.
Coolidge Corner
Brookline, MA 02146
PH: (617) 566-0115
Web: www.necomics.com
(a-c,e,g,k-n,p-v)

New England Comics
14A Eliot Street
Harvard Square
Cambridge, MA 02138
PH: (617) 354-5352
Web: www.necomics.com
(a-c,e,g,k-n,p-v)

That's Entertainment
371 John Fitch Hwy.
Fitchburg, MA 01420
PH: (978) 342-8607
Web: www.thatse.com
(a-u)

Bedrock Comics
Framingham Mall
371 Worchester Rd. (Rt. 9)
Framingham, MA 01701
PH: (508) 872-2317
Web: www.
bedrockcomics.com
(a-u)

New England Comics
18 Pleasant St.
Malden Center
Malden, MA 02148
PH: (781) 322-2404
Web: www.necomics.com
(a-c,e,g,k-n,p-v)

New England Comics
732 Washington Street
Norwood Center
Norwood, MA 02062
PH: (781) 769-4552
Web: www.necomics.com
(a-c,e,g,k-n,p-v)

New England Comics
1511 Hancock St.
Quincy Center
Quincy, MA 02169
PH: (617) 770-1848
Web: www.necomics.com
(a-c,e,g,k-n,p-v)

New England Comics
FFAST New Comic Service
(Mail Order Only)
P.O. Box 690346
Quincy, MA 02269
PH: (617) 774-1745
Web: www.necomics.com
(a-c,e,g,k-n,p-v)

The Outer Limits
463 Moody St.
Waltham, MA 02453
PH: (781) 891-0444
(a-v)

That's Entertainment
244 Park Ave.
Worcester, MA 01609
PH: (508) 755-4207
FX: (508) 754-3882
Web: www.thatse.com
(a-u)

MICHIGAN

Cashman's Comics
1018 S. Madison Ave.
Bay City, MI 48708-7261
PH: (517) 895-1113
E-Mail: jcash1111
@aol.com
(a-c,f,g,j,k-v)

Curious Comic Shop
307 East Grand River
East Lansing, MI 48823
PH: (517) 332-0112
E-Mail: cbsmail
@curiousbooks.com
Web:
www.curiousbooks.com
(d-k,m,s)

Curious Comic Shop
210 M.A.C. Ave.
East Lansing, MI 48823
PH: (517) 332-0222
(a-c,m,n,p-u)

Amazing Book Store, Inc.
3718 Richfield Rd.
Flint, MI 48506
PH: (810) 736-3025
(a-c,n,q)

Argos Book Shop
1405 Robinson Rd. S.E.
Grand Rapids, MI 49506
PH: (616) 454-0111
(a-k,p-u)

Tardy's Collector's Corner, Inc.
2009 Eastern Ave. S.E.
Grand Rapids, MI 49507
Ph: (616) 247-7828
(a-d,g,j,n,p,q)

Galaxy Comics II
1319 S. Mission
Mt. Pleasant, MI 48858
PH: (517) 775-7838
(b,c,g,k,m,p,q,s)

Galaxy Comics
3089 Bay Plaza Dr.
Saginaw, MI 48604
PH: (517) 799-6334
(a-c,g,k,m,n,p-s,u)

MINNESOTA

Nostalgia Zone
3149 1/2 Hennepin Ave. S.
Minneapolis, MN 55408
PH: (612) 822-2806
E-Mail: nostzone
@spacestar.net
(a,b,d-n,p,q,u)

Midway Book & Comic
1579 University Ave.
St Paul, MN 55104
PH: (612) 644-7605
(a-h,n,q)

MISSOURI

Antiquarium Books & Collectibles
504 East High St.
Jefferson City, MO 65101
PH: (573) 636-8995
(a-h,k-m,p-t)

The Book Barn
3128 S. Main
Joplin, MO 64804
PH: (417) 782-2778
FX: (417) 782-0024
E-Mail: BOOKBARN
@prodigy.net
(a-c,e,k,i,m,n,q,s,v)

Friendly Frank's Comic Cavern
5404 N.W. 64th St.
Kansas City, MO 64151
PH: (816) 746-4569
(a-d,f,g,j-n,p-u)

MO's Comics & Stories
4573 Gravois
St. Louis, MO 63116
PH: (314) 353-9500
(a-d, f, g, k, o-q)

MONTANA

The Book Exchange
Butte Plaza Mall
3100 Harrison Ave.
Butte, MT 59701
PH: (406) 494-7788
(a-c, e, h, q-s)

The Book Exchange
Tremper's Shopping Ctr.
2335 Brooks St.
Missoula, MT 59801
PH: (406) 728-6342
(a-c,e,h,q-s)

NEVADA

Silver Cactus Comics
480 N. Nellis Blvd. #C1A
Las Vegas, NV 89110
PH: (702) 438-4408
FX: (702) 438-5208
(b,c,e,g,k,l,m,p-s,u)

NEW HAMPSHIRE

Rare Books & Comics
James F. Payette
P.O. Box 750
Bethlehem, NH 03574
PH: (603) 869-2097
(a,b,d-h)

Collectibles Unlimited
30A Warren St.
Concord, NH 03301
PH: (603) 228-3712
(b,c,m,q-s)

NEW JERSEY

The Hobby Shop
1077C Route 34
Aberdeen, NJ 07747
PH: (732) 583-0505
Web: www.
hobbyshopnj.com
(c,k,q-s,v)

Pegasus Enterprises
607 Main St.
Boonton, NJ 07005
PH: (973) 335-3428
(a-c,g,k,l,m,p,q)

Altered State Comics & Cards
234 Main St.
Chatham, NJ 07928
PH: (973) 927-3895
E-Mail: comix973
@aol.com
(b,c,g,k,m,q,s,u)

Comics and More
Cherry Hill Mall
Upper Level
Cherry Hill, NJ 08002
PH: (609) 663-7550
(b,c,g,k,m,p-u)

Eldorado Comics
2110 E. Rt. 70
P.O. Box 3630
Cherry Hill, NJ 08034
PH: (609) 489-1199
(a-g,i-k,m,n,p-v)

Thunder Road Sportscards & Comics
1973 North Olden Ave.
Ewing, NJ 08618
PH: (609) 771-1055
(a,b,k,m,q)

A Time Lost...And Found
310 East Evesham Rd.
Glendora, NJ 08029
PH: (609) 939-1909
(a-c,k,m,n,p,s,t)

Thunder Road Sportscards & Comics
1637 Route 33
Hamilton Sq., NJ 08690
PH: (609) 587-5353
(a,b,k,m,q)

One Flight Up Books
63 Main St.
Millburn, NJ 07041
PH: (973) 467-9288
(b,c,g,i,k-r,s,u,v)

Comic Explosion
339 Franklin Ave.
Nutley, NJ 07110
PH: (973) 235-1336
(c,g,m,n,p,q,u)

Fat Jack's Comicrypt
521 White Horse Pike
Oaklyn, NJ 08107
PH: (609) 858-3877
(a-c,g,m,n,p,q,u)

MC Comics Inc.
54 Old Matawan Rd.
Old Bridge, NJ 08857
PH: (732) 238-5969
FX: (732) 238-8435
Web: www.mccomics.com
(b,c,g,k,m,n,p-t)

Excellent Adventures
72 Hanover St.
Pemberton, NJ 08068
PH: (609) 894-0255
(a-c,f,g,k,m,o-s,u,v)

Zapp! Comics, Cards & Toys
574 Valley Rd.
Wayne, NJ 07470
PH: (973) 628-4500
FX: (973) 628-1771
E-mail: zappcomics @aol.com
(a-c,g,k,m,n,p-u)

Frankenstein Comics
845 Mantua Pike, Rt. 45
Woodbury, NJ 08096
PH: (609) 848-6347
(b,c,g,k)

JHV Associates
By Appointment Only
P. O. Box 317
Woodbury Hghts, NJ 08097
PH: (609) 845-4010
(a,b,d)

Retroactive Comics
P.O. Box 181
Haddon Heights, NJ 08035
PH: (609) 547-1469
E-Mail: retroactive @snip.net
(a-c,k)

J.C. Comics
187 Somerset St.
North Plainfield, NJ 07060
PH: (908) 756-1212
FX: (908) 756-5606
E-Mail: JoeConzolo @msn.com
(b,c,g,h,k-m,o-q,s,u)

NEW YORK

Silver Age Comics
22-55 31 St.
Astoria, NY 11105
PH: (718) 721-9691
PH: (800) 278-9691
FX: (718) 728-9691
E-Mail: gus @silveragecomics.com
Web: www. silveragecomics.com
(a-c,f,g,k,m,n,p-s,u)

Long Island Comics
672 Sunrise Hwy.
West Babylon, NY 11704
PH: (516) 321-4822
(12-6 p.m. only)
E-Mail: licomics@aol.com
(a-c,g,q,s)

Wow Comics
2395 West Chester Ave.
Bronx, NY 10461
PH: (718) 829-0461
FX: (718) 828-1700
E-Mail: wowcomics @aol.com
Web: www. wowcomics.com
(a-c,e,k,m,o-s,u)

Pinocchio Comic Shop
1814 McDonald Ave.
Brooklyn, NY 11223
PH: (718) 645-2573
(b,c,g,k,m,q)

Comic Quest
57-10 Hoffman Drive
Elmhurst, NY 11373
PH: (718) 205-8174
(a-e,g,k,m,n,q,r,v)

Golden Memories
250 Broadway
Hicksville, NY 11801
PH: (516) 932-8581
E-Mail: stryke222 @aol.com
(a-c,k,m,q)

Comic Box Productions
74-05 Metropolitan
Middle Village, NY 11379-2636
PH/FX: (718) 326-2248
E-Mail: comicbox @hotmail.com
(a-m)

Action Comics
1551 Second Ave., 2nd Flr.
New York, NY 10028
PH: (212) 639-1976
(a-c,g,k,m,p-s,u)

Alex's MVP Cards & Comics
256 East 89th St.
New York, NY 10128
PH: (212) 831-2273
FX: (212) 831-4825
(a-c,g,j,k,m,n,p-s,v)

Four Color Comics
115 West 27th St.
New York, NY 10007
PH: (212) 675-6990
E-Mail: keybooks@aol.com
Web: www. fourcolorcomics.com

Gotham City Comics
800 Lexington Ave.
New York, NY 10021
PH: (212) 980-0009
E-Mail: GothamCT @aol.com
(b-c-e-g-u)

Jerry Ohlinger's Movie Material Store, Inc.
242 West 14 Street
New York, NY 10011
PH: (212) 989-0869
(i)

Jim Hanley's Universe
4 West 33rd St.
(Opposite the Empire State Building)
New York, NY 10001
PH: (212) 268-7088
(a-c,g,m,n,p-u)

Manhattan Comics & Cards
228 West 23rd. St.
New York, NY 10011
PH: (212) 243-9349
(a-c,g,j-n,q,u)

Metropolis Collectibles
873 Broadway, Ste. 201
New York, NY 10003
PH: (212) 260-4147
(a,b,k,i,j)

Village Comics
214 Sullivan St.
New York, NY 10012
PH: (212) 777-2770
FX: (212) 475-9727
E-Mail: infosales @villagecomics.com
Web: www. villagecomics.com
(b,c,e,g,h,k,m,n,p,q,s,u,v)

Fantastic Planet
24 Oak St.
Plattsburgh, NY 12901
PH: (518) 563-2946
(c,e,g,k,m,p-v)

Dragon's Den
Poughkeepsie Plaza
Poughkeepsie, NY 12601
PH: (914) 471-1401
Web: www.dragons-den.com
(b,c,e,g,k,m,p-r,u)

Empire® Comics
1176 Mt. Hope Ave.
Rochester, NY 14620
PH: (716) 442-0371
E-Mail: empireco @frontiernet.net
(a-c,f,h,k,m,q-s,u)

Empire® Comics
375 Stone Rd.
Rochester, NY 14616
PH: (716) 663-6877
E-Mail: empireco @frontiernet.net
(a-c,f,h,k,m,q-s,u)

Amazing Comics
12 Gillette Ave.
Sayville, NY 11782
PH: (516) 567-8069
(a-c,g,j,k,m,q,v)

One if by Cards, Two if by Comics
1107 Central Ave.
Scarsdale, NY 10583
PH: (914) 725-2225
Web: www.1ifbycards.com

Electric City Comics
1704 Van Vranken Ave.
Schenectady, NY 12308
(518) 377-1500
(a-d,g,k,l,n,p,q,u)

Jim Hanley's Universe
325 New Dorp Ln.
Staten Island, NY 10306
PH: (718) 351-6299
(a-c,g,m,n,p-u)

Krypton Comics of Staten Island, Inc.
604 Midland Ave.
Staten Island, NY 10306
PH: (718) 667-7695
Web: members. aol.com/KRYPTON604/ kryptoncomics.html
(b,c,g,k,m,q)

Twilight Book & Game
1401 North Salina St.
Syracuse, NY 13208
PH: (315) 471-3139
E-Mail: bgray @pipeline.com
Web: www. twilightonline.com
(a-c,e,g,k,m,n,p-v)

Ravenswood, Inc.
8451 Seneca Turnpike
New Hartford, NY 13413
PH: (315) 735-3699
(a-c,g,k,m,p-t)

Excellent Adventures
(Rte. 50)
110 Milton Avenue
Ballston SPA, NY 12020
PH: (518) 884-9498
(a-c,f,g,k,m,o-s,u)

NORTH CAROLINA

Super Giant Comics
697 Brevard Rd.
Asheville, NC 28806
PH: (828) 665-2800
(a-c,j,l,n,q)

Heroes Aren't Hard To Find
Corner Central Ave.
& The Plaza
P. O. Box 9181
Charlotte, NC 28299
PH: (704) 375-7462
(a-c,g,j-n,p,s,u)

Acme Comics
3808-C High Point Rd.
Greensboro, NC 27405
PH: (336) 855-0217
(a-c,g,k,m,n,p,q,s,u,v)

Acme Comics
2150 Lawndale Dr.
Greensboro, NC 27408
PH: (336) 574-2263
(a-c,g,k,m,n,p,q,s,u,v)

Capitol Comics of Raleigh
3027-A Hillsborough St.
Raleigh, NC 27607
PH: (919) 832-4600
E-Mail: capitol.comics2@juno.com
(a-c,m,p,q)

Capitol Comics II
5212 Hollyridge Dr.
Raleigh, NC 27612
PH: (919) 781-9500
E-Mail: capitol.comics2@juno.com
(a-c,k,m,p,q,s)

Tales Resold
3936 Atlantic Avenue
Raleigh, NC 27604
PH: (919) 878-8551
(a-c,e,g,h,j,k,m,q)

Comics & Cards Unlimited
506 Waynesville Plaza
Waynesville, NC 28786
PH: (828) 456-8787
(a-c,g,k,l,m,q,r)

The Nostalgia Newsstand
919 Dickinsen Ave.
Greenville, NC 27834
PH: (252) 758-6909
(b,c,e,g,m,n,p,q,u)

NORTH DAKOTA

Tom's Coin Stamp Gem Baseball & Comic Shop
#2 1st Street S.W.
Minot, ND 58701
PH: (701) 852-4522
Web: www.minot.com/~tomscoin
(a-q,s,u)

OHIO

Dark Star III
Fairfield Plaza
1273 North Fairfield Rd.
Beavercreek, OH 45432
PH: (937) 427-3213
(b-e,g,k,m,p-v)

Comic Book World, Inc.
4016 Harrison Avenue
Cincinnati, OH 45211
PH: (513) 661-6300
(a-c,m,n,p-u)

British Papermill
5733 Brice Outlet Mall
Columbus, OH 43232
PH: (614) 577-0220
(b,g,k)

Bookery Fantasy & Comics
16 W. Main St.
Fairborn, OH 45324
PH: (937) 879-1408
FX: (937) 879-9327
E-Mail: bookeryfan@aol.com
Web: www.bookeryfantasy.com
(a-u)

Parker's Records & Comics
1222 Ste. C Route 28
Milford, OH 45150
PH: (513) 575-3665
FX: (513) 575-3665
(a-c,g,k-m,p-s,u-v)

Funnie Farm Bookstore
328 N. Dixie Drive
Vandalia, OH 45377
PH: (937) 898-2794
(a-c,f,k,m,p-r,v)

Dark Star Books & Comics
237 Xenia Ave.
Yellow Springs, OH 45387
PH: (937) 767-9400
E-Mail: ysdrkstr@aol.com
(b-h,k-m,p-v)

OKLAHOMA

New World Comics & Games
6219 N. Meridian
Oklahoma City, OK 73112
PH: (405) 721-7634
(a-c,g,i,k,m-v)

New World Comics & Games
4420 SE 44th St.
Oklahoma City, OK 73135
PH: (405) 677-2559
(c,g,k,m,p-v)

Comic Empire of Tulsa
3122 S. Mingo Rd.
Tulsa, OK 74146
PH: (918) 664-5808
(a-c,n,p,q)

Starbase 21
2130 S. Sheridan Rd.
Tulsa, OK 74129
PH: (918) 838-3388
(a-c,e,g,i,k-m,p-v)

Want List Comics
(Appointment Only)
P. O. Box 701932
Tulsa, OK 74170-1932
PH: (918) 299-0440
(a,b,f,h-k,m)

OREGON

Emerald City Comics
770 E. 13th
Eugene, OR 97401
PH: (541) 345-2568
(c,e,g,k-n,q,r,u,v)

Westside Comics and Cards
3133 W. 11th-G-1
Eugene, OR 97402
PH: (541) 342-5243
(c,g,k,m,q,r,v)

Nostalgia Collectibles
527 Willamette
Eugene, OR 97401
PH: (541) 484-9202
(a-i,k-n,p,q,s,v)

Beyond Comics
322 E. Main
Medford, OR 97501
PH: (541) 779-9543
(a,b,m,p-r,v)

Future Dream East Burnside
1800 E. Burnside
Portland, OR 97214-1599
PH: (503) 231-8311
E-Mail: fdb@hevanet.com
(a-c,e-j,m,n,p-u)

Heroes Haven
635 S.E. Jackson St.
Roseburg, OR 97470
PH: (541) 673-5004
E-Mail: grendel@rosenet.net
(a-c,e,g,k,m,p-s,u,v)

Ancient Wonders
19060 S.W. Boones Ferry Rd.
Tualatin, OR 97062
PH: (503) 692-0753
(a-c,g,k-n,p-s,v)

PENNSYLVANIA

Cap's Comic Cavalcade
1894 Catasauqua Rd.
Allentown, PA 18103
PH: (610) 264-5540
(a-c,e,g,k,m,n,p-v)

Dreamscape Comics
310 W. Broad St.
Bethlehem, PA 18018
PH: (610) 867-1178
(a-c,m,n,p-r)

Comix Connection - Camp Hill
604 Camp Hill Mall
Camp Hill, PA 17011
PH: (800) 730-0994
(a-c,k,m,n,q-s,u)

New Dimension Comics
20550 Route 19,
Piazza Plaza
Cranberry Township, PA 16066-7520
PH: (724) 776-0433
Web: www.ndcomics.com
(a-c,k,i,m-s,u,v)

Dreamscape Comics
25th St. Shopping Ctr.
Easton, PA 18045
PH: (610) 250-9818
(a-c,m,n,p-r)

New Dimension Comics
508 Lawrence Ave.
Ellwood City, PA 16117
PH: (724) 758-2324
(a-c,k,i,m-s,u-v)

Comic Collection, Toys & Compact Discs
931 Bustleton Pike
at Street Rd.
Feasterville, PA 19053
PH: (215) 357-3332
Web: members.aol.com/comicdeity/index.html
(a-c,g,j-n,p,r-u)

Comics and More
King of Prussia Plaza
Upper Level
King of Prussia, PA 19406
PH: (610) 337-1555
(b,c,g,k,m,p-u)

The Comic Store
28 McGovern Ave.
Lancaster, PA 17602
PH: (717) 397-8737
(a-c,e,g,m,n,p-s,u)

Comics and More
2550 Cottman Ave.
Philadelphia, PA 19149
PH: (215) 333-6869
(b,c,g,k,m,p-u)

Fat Jack's Comicrypt
2006 Sansom St.
Philadelphia, PA 19103
PH: (215) 963-0788
(a-c,g,m,n,p,q,u)

Fat Jack's Comicrypt
7596 Haverford Ave.
Philadelphia, PA 19151
PH: (215) 473-6333
(a-c,g,m,n,p,q,u)

Duncan Comics, Books, and Accessories
1047 Perry Highway
Pittsburgh (North Hills), PA 15237
PH: (412) 635-0886
(a-e,g,h,k-m,p-s,v)

Eide's Entertainment
1111 Penn Ave.
Pittsburgh, PA 15222
PH: (412) 261-0900
FX: (412) 261-3102
E-Mail: eides@eides.com
Web: www.eides.com
(a-q,s-v)

Comic Store West
351 Loucks Rd.
York, PA 17474
PH: (717) 845-9198
(c,m,q,r)

Comix Connection - York
1201 Carlisle Rd.
York, PA 17404
PH: (717) 843-6516
(a-c,k,m,n,q-s,u)

Comic Swap
110 South Fraser Street
State College, PA 16801
PH: (814) 234-6005
E-Mail: kboose6474@aol.com
(b,c,g,k,n,p-r,v)

RHODE ISLAND

The Annex
314 Broadway
Newport, RI 02840
PH: (401) 847-4607
(b,c,g,m,q,s,u,v)

SOUTH CAROLINA

Planet Comics
3448 Cinema Ctr.
Anderson, SC 29621
PH: (864) 261-3578
Web: www.planetcomics.net
(a-c,k,m,n,p-r,u-v)

Heroes & Dragons Mega-Store
Boozer Shopping Ctr.
1563-B Broad River Rd.
Columbia, SC 29210
PH: (803) 731-4376
FX: (803) 772-5010
E-Mail: hdcomics@aol.com
Web: www.heroesanddragons.com
(b,c,k,p-s,u)

SOUTH DAKOTA

Storyteller
520 Sixth St.
Rapid City, SD 57701
PH: (605) 348-7242
E-mail: story@rapidcity.com
(a-c,e,k,m,p-s,u)

TENNESSEE

The Great Escape
111-B Gallatin Rd. North
Madison, TN 37115
PH: (615) 865-8052
(a-c, e-h, k-n, p-u)

The Great Escape
1925 Broadway
Nashville, TN 37203
PH: (615) 327-0646
(a-v)

Funny Pages #2
2218 North Roan Street
Johnson City, TN 37601
PH: (423) 282-3164
(a-c,g,i-m,p,q,s,v)

TEXAS

Lone Star Comics Books & Games
511 East Abram St.
Arlington, TX 76010
PH: (817) 860-7827
FX: (817) 860-2769
E-Mail: lonestar@lonestarcomics.com
Web: www.lonestarcomics.com
(a-c,e,g,k,m,p-v)

Lone Star Comics Books & Games
504 East Abram St.
Arlington, TX 76010
PH: (817) Metro 265-0491
(a-c,e,g,k,m,p-v)

Lone Star Comics Books & Games
5720 Forest Bend Dr., Suite 101
Arlington, TX 76017
PH: (817) 563-2550
(b,c,e,g,k,m,p-v)

Austin Books & Sports Cards
5002 N. Lamar
Austin, TX 78751
PH: (512) 454-4197
(a-e,g-i,k,m,p,q,s-u)

Lone Star Comics Books & Games
11661 Preston Rd. #151
Dallas, TX 75230
PH: (214) 373-0934
(a-c,e,g,k,m,p-v)

Remember When
2431 Valwood Pkwy.
Dallas, TX 75234
PH: (972) 243-3439
(a-c,g,i,j,m,p,q,s,t)

All Star Comixs & Games
4406 Dyer St.
El Paso, TX 79930
PH: (915) 562-0443
(b,c,e,g,i,k,m,q-s,v)

Lone Star Comics Books & Games
6312 Hulen Bend Blvd.
Ft. Worth, TX 76132
PH: (817) 346-7773
(b,c,e,g,k,m,p-v)

Bedrock City Comic Co.
6521 Westheimer
Houston, TX 77057
PH: (713) 780-0675
FX: (713) 780-2366
E-Mail: bedrock@flash.net
Web: www.bedrockcity.com
(a-h,j,k,mq,s,u)

Bedrock City Comic Co.
2204-D FM 1960 W.
Houston, TX 77090
PH: (281) 444-9763
E-Mail: bedrock2@flash.net
Web: www.bedrockcity.com
(a-h,,j,k,m-q,s,u)

Phoenix Comics & Games
2424 Montrose
Houston, TX 77006
PH: (713) 524-1150
(c,e,g,p-r,v)

Third Planet
2718 S.W. FWY.
Houston, TX 77098
PH: (713) 528-1067
E-Mail: 3planet@third-planet.com
Web: www.third-planet.com
(a-u)

Lone Star Comics Books & Games
931 Melbourne
Hurst, TX 76053
PH: (817) 595-4375
(b,c,e,g,k,m,p-v)

Lone Star Comics Books & Games
2550 N. Beltine Rd.
Irving, TX 75062
PH: (972) 659-0317
(b,c,e,g,k,m,p-v)

Lone Star Comics Books & Games
3600 Gus Thomasson, Suite 107
Mesquite, TX 75150
PH: (972) 681-2040
(b,c,e,g,k,m,p-v)

Lone Star Comics Books & Games
3100 Independence Pkwy., Suite 219
Plano, TX 75075
PH: (972) 985-1953
(b,c,e,g,k,m,p-v)

Ground Zero Comics
1700 SSE Loop 323 Ste. 302
Tyler, TX 75701
PH: (903) 566-1185
(c,e,g,l,m,p-s,u,v)

Bankstons Used Books
1321 Southgate Shopping Ctr
Waco, TX 76711
PH: (254) 755-0070
(a-d,g,i,k,m,p,q,s,v)

VIRGINIA

Comic and Card Collectorama
2008 Mt. Vernon Ave.
Alexandria, VA 22301
(Greater D.C. area)
PH: (703) 548-3466
(a-c,f,h,m,p,q,s,t)

Geppi's Comic World Crystal City
1606 Crystal
Square Arcade
Arlington, VA 22202
PH: (703) 413-0618
(a-c,k-m,q,s,t,v)

Atlas Comics
1669 Seminole Trail
Charlottesville, VA 22901
PH: (804) 974-7512
(b,c,p-r,v)

Zeno's Books
1112 Sparrow Rd.
Chesapeake, VA 23325
PH: (757) 420-2344
(a-j,m,r,t,v)

Another Universe.com Fair Oaks Mall
11737L Fair Oaks Mall
Fairfax, VA 22033
PH: (703) 273-3355
(c,e,i,k,m,p-s,u)

Hole in the Wall Books
905 West Broad St.
Falls Church, VA 22046
PH: (703) 536-2511
(b-e,g,h,l,n,q,s,t,u)

Marie's Books & Things
1701 Princess Anne St.
Fredericksburg, VA 22401
PH: (540) 373-5196
(a-c,e-h,k,l,p,q,s)

Bender's Books & Cards
22 South Mallory St.
Hampton, VA 23663
PH: (757) 723-3741
(a-j,m-u,v)

World's Best
9817 Jefferson Ave.
Newport News, VA 23605
PH: (757) 595-9005
(b,c,g,i,k-n,p-s,u,v)

Trilogy Shop #2
700 E. Little Creek Rd.
Norfolk, VA 23518
PH: (757) 587-2540
FX: (757) 587-5637
E-Mail: trilogy2
@trilogycomics.com
Web: www.
trilogycomics.com
(c,m,q,r-v)

Nostalgia Plus
1601 Willow Lawn Dr.
Richmond, VA 23230
PH: (804) 282-5532
E-Mail: funnybuk@aol.com
(a-c,g,k,m,p,q)

B & D Comic Shop
802 Elm Avenue S.W.
Roanoke, VA 24016
PH: (540) 342-6642
(c,g,m,p-s,v)

Another Universe.com Springfield Mall
6383 Springfield Mall
Springfield, VA 22150
PH: (703) 313-0404
(c,e,i,k,m,p-s,u)

Big Planet Comics
426 Maple Ave. East
Vienna, VA 22180
PH: (703) 242-9412
Web: www.erols.com
/big.planet.comics
(b,c,p,q)

Trilogy Shop #1
5773 Princess Anne Rd.
Virginia Beach, VA 23462
PH: (757) 490-2205
FX: (757) 671-7721
E-Mail: trilogy1
@trilogycomics.com
Web: www.
trilogycomics.com
(a-i,k-o,p-v)

WASHINGTON

Christopher's Comics & Books
P.O. Box 3072
Bellevue, WA 98009-3072
PH: (206) 940-7119
E-Mail: fur@silver-age.com
Web: www.silver-age.com
(a-c,f,k,m)

Comics Dungeon
1622 N. 45th
Seattle, WA 98103
PH: (206) 545-8373
(a-c,f,g,k,m,n,q,s,v)

Golden Age Collectables LTD
1501 Pike Place Market
401 Lower Level
Seattle, WA 98101
PH: (206) 622-9799
(a-g,l-n,p-q,s,u,v)

Rocket Comics
8408 Greenwood Ave. N.
Seattle, WA 98103
PH: (206) 784-7300
E-Mail: rocket@jetcity.com
(a-h,p,q)

O'Leary's Books
3828 100th St. S.W.
Tacoma, WA 98499
PH: (253) 588-2503
PH: (800) 542-1791
FX: (253) 589-9115
(a-c,e-h,j-m,p-s,u,v)

WEST VIRGINIA

Comic Castle
233 Second St.
Beckley, WV 25801
PH: (304) 253-1974
(b,c,k,p,q)

WISCONSIN

Clairemont Comics
2543 E. Clairemont Pkwy.
Eau Claire, WI 54701
PH: (715) 831-2112
(a-c,g,m,q,r)

Capital City Comics
1910 Monroe St.
Madison, WI 53711
PH: (608) 251-8445
(a-d,f,j,m,n,o,q,u)

CANADA

ALBERTA

Another Dimension Comics
324-10 S. NW
Calgary, AB T2NIV8
PH: (403) 283-7078
(a-c,e,g,k,m,n,p-s,u)

Redd Skull Comics & CD's
720 A Edmonton Trail N. E.
Calgary, AB T2E 3J4
PH: (403) 230-2716 (+ fax)
Web: www.cadvision.com/
reddskul
(a-c,k-r,u,v)

Comic Fever
11338-132 Ave.
Edmonton, AB T5EIAI
PH: (403) 452-6324
(b,c,g,l-k,m,p-s)

BRITISH COLUMBIA

Golden Age Collectables
830 Granville St.
Vancouver, BC V6Z 1K3
PH: (604) 683-2819
(a-d,g,i,j,k,m,p,q-s,u,v)

MANITOBA

The Collector's Slave
156 Imperial Ave.
WPG., MB., R2M 0K8
PH: (204) 237-4428
(a-c,e-g,k-n,p-q,s)

ONTARIO

The Comic Cave
25 Perth Street
Brockville, ONT K6V 5C3
613-345-4349
PH: (613-345-4349
(a-c,e,i-k,q,p)

B.A.'s Comics & Nostalgia
121 Oxford St. East
London, Ontario N6A 1T4
PH: (519) 439-9636
(b,c,g,m,n,p,q,u)

3RD Quadrant
226 Queen St. W. UPR
Toronto, ON M5V 1Z6
PH: (416) 974-9211
(b,c,k,m,p-s)

The Final Stop...
381 McArthur Avenue
Vanier, ON K1L 6N5
PH: (613) 749-1247
E-Mail: comics
@thefinalstop.com
(c,g,k,m,n,p,q)

Heroes Comics
1116 Cure La Belle
Laval, QC H7V 2V5
PH: (450) 686-9155
(a-c,e,g,k,m,o,p-s,u,v)

Komico Inc.
4210 Decarie
Montreal, QC H4A 3K3
PH: (514) 489-4009
E-Mail: MEGAH@total.net
(b,c,g,k,n,p,q)

SILVER & MODERN AGE INDEX

Below is a comprehensive listing of titles published by the nine most popular comic book companies today. Where several titles exist by the same name, we have listed the title once for space considerations.

ACCLAIM COMICS
Armed & Dangerous
Armed & Dangerous: Hell's Slaughterhouse
Bad Eggs, The
Baywatch Comic Stories
Grackle, The
Master Darque
Sliders: Darkest Hour
Sliders: Ultimatum
Waterworld: Children of Leviathan
Armada
Dakkon Blackblade on the World of Magic The Gathering
Gravediggers
Ice Age on the World of Magic The Gathering
Killer Instinct
Magic The Gathering
: Antiquities War
...: Arabian Nights
...: Collection
...: Convocations
...: Elder Dragons
...: Fallen Angel
...: Fallen Empires
...: Homelands
...: Legend of Jedit Ojanen
...: Nightmare
...: Shandalar
...: The Shadow Mage
...: Wayfarer
Mutant Chronicles
Serra Angel on the World of Magic The Gathering
Urza-Mishra War on the World of Magic The Gathering
Valiant
Bloodshot
Eternal Warrior
Eternal Warrior: Fist & Steel
Ninjak
Punx
Shadowman
Solar
Turok, Dinosaur Hunter
Turok, the Hunted
X-O Manowar
Valiant Heroes
Acclaim Adventure Zone
Dr. Tomorrow
Quantum & Woody
Solar, Man of the Atom: Hell on Earth
Solar, Man of the Atom: Revelations
Trinity Angels
Troublemakers
X-O Manowar (2nd Series)
Windjammer
Bar Sinister
Knighthawk
Starslayer: The Director's Cut
Valeria, The She-Bat

AWESOME ENTERTAINMENT/ MAXIMUM PRESS
Avengelyne
...: Armegeddon
.../Glory
.../Power
Battlestar Galactica
...: Apollo's Journey
...: Journey's End
...: Special Edition
...: Starbuck
...: The Enemy Within
Black Flag
Coven
Cybrid
Darkchylde
Devlin
Fighting American
Judgment Day
Kaboom
Law and Order
Menace
Re: Gex
Supreme
Warchild

CHAOS! COMICS
Brinke of Eternity
Chaos Bible
Chaos Gallery
Chaos Quarterly
Chastity: Theater of Pain
Cremator
Dead King
Detonator
Evil Ernie
...: Destroyer
...: Revenge
...: Straight to Hell
...: The Resurrection
...Vs. the Movie Monsters
...Vs. the Super Heroes
Lady Death
...: The Crucible
...: The Odyssey
...: The Reckoning
...II: Between Heaven and Hell
Lynch Mob
Nightmare Theater
Purgatori
Rack & Pain: Killers
Smiley

DARK HORSE COMICS
Abyss, The
Adventures of Luther Arkwright, The
Adventures of the Mask
Agents of Law
Age of Reptiles
Alien Resurrection
Aliens
...: Alchemy
...: Berserkers
...: Colonial Marines
...: Earth Angel
...: Earth War
...: Genocide
...: Glass Corridor
...: Havoc
...: Hive
...: Kidnapped
...: Labyrinth
...: Lovesick
...: Mondo Heat
...: Mondo Pest
...: Music of the Spears
...: Pig
.../Predator: The Deadliest of the Species
...: Purge
...: Rogue
...: Sacrifice
...: Salvation
...: Special
...: Stalker
...: Stronghold
...: Survival
...: Wraith
Aliens Vs. Predator
...: Booty
...: Duel
...: Eternal
...: War
Alien3
American, The
American: Lost in America
American Splendor
...: Comic-Con Comics
...: Music Comics
...: On the Job
... Special: A Step Out of the Nest
...: Windfall
Appleseed Databook
Army of Darkness
Atlas
Badger: Shattered Mirror
...: Zen Pop Funny-Animal Version
Badlands
Barb Wire
...: Ace of Spades
Basil Wolverton's Fantastic Fables
...Gateway to Horror
...Planet of Terror
Bettie Page Comics
Big
Billi 99
Black Cross: Dirty Work
Black Cross Special
Black Pearl
Blade of the Immortal
Body Bags
Book of Night, The
Bubblegum Crisis: Grand Mal
Buffy The Vampire Slayer
By Bizarre Hands
Catalyst: Agents of Change
Cheval Noir
Classic Star Wars
...: A New Hope
...: Han Solo at Star's End
...: Return of the Jedi
...: The Early Adventures
...: The Empire Strikes Back
Clonezone Special
Colors in Black
Columbus
Comics & Stories
Comics' Greatest World
Concrete
...: A New Life
...: Celebrates Earth Day
...: Color Special
...: Eclectica
...: Fragil Creature
...: Land and Sea
...: Odd Jobs
Cormac Mac Art
Cross
Cud Comics
Dark Horse Classics
...Comics
...Down Under
...Presents
Deadface: Doing the Islands with Bacchus
...: Earth, Water, Air, and Fire
Dead in the West
Deadline USA
Decade of Dark Horse, A
Dirty Pair: Fatal but Not Serious
...: Sim Hell
...II
...III, The
Division 13
Doc Savage: Curse of the Fire God
Dr. Giggles
Dominion: Conflict 1
Drakuun
Edgar Rice Burroughs' Tarzan: A Tale of Mugambi
... In The Land That Time Forgot And The Pool Of Time
...: The Lost Adventure
Elric: Stormbringer
Enemy
Eudaemon, The
Flaming Carrot
Floaters
Foot Soldiers, The
Ghost
...and the Shadow
.../Hellboy
Ghost in the Shell
G.I. Joe
Girl Crazy
Give Me Liberty
Godzilla
Grendel Classics
...Cycle
...: Devil by the Deed
...: Devil Quest
Grendel Tales: Devils and Deaths
...: Devil's Choices
...: Four Devils, One Hell
...: Homecoming
...: The Devil in Our Midst
...: The Devil May Care
...: The Devil's Apprentice
...: The Devil's Hammer
Grendel: War Child
Hammer, The
Hammer of God: Butch
...: Pentathlon
Happy Birthday Martha Washington
Hard Boiled
Harlan Ellison's Dream Corridor
Harlan Ellison's Dream Corridor Quarterly
Heartbreakers
Hellhounds
Herbie
Hermes Vs. the Eyeball Kid
Hero Zero
Homicide
Hypersonic
Indiana Jones and the Arms of Gold
...and the Fate of Atlantis
...and the Golden Fleece
...and the Iron Phoenix
...and the Sargasso Pirates
...and the Shrine of the She Devil
...and the Spear of Destiny
...: Thunder in the Orient
Insane
Instant Piano
Ironhand of Almuric
Jam, The
James Bond 007: A Silent Armageddon
...: Serpent's Tooth
...: Shattered Helix
...: The Quasimodo Gambit
Johnny Dynamite
Jonny Demon
Junior Carrot Patrol
Kings of the Night
Land of Nod, The
Legend of Mother Sarah
...: City of the Angels
...: City of the Children
Lords of Misrue, The
Lost in Space
Machine, The
Magnus Robot Fighter/ Nexus (w/**Valiant**)
Mark, The
Mask, The
...: Hunt for Green October
...: Official Movie Adaptation
...Returns
...Southern Discomfort
...Strikes Back
...Summer Vacation
...Virtual Surreality
Mayhem
Mecha
...Special
Medal of Honor Special
Mezz: Galactic Tour 2494
Mr. Monster
Moebius: The Man From Cigur
Motorhead
New Two-Fisted Tales, The
Nexus: Alien Justice
...: Executioner's Song
...Meets Madman
...: The Wages of Sin
Night Before Christmas
Oh My Goddess!
...Part II
...Part III
Oktane
Otis Goes to Hollywood
Outlanders
Out of the Vortex
Predator

...: Bad Blood
...: Big Game
...: Bloody Sands of Time
...: Captive
...: Cold War
...: Dark River
...: Hell and Hot Water
...: Hell Come A Walkin'
...: Invaders from the Fourth Dimension
...: Jungle Tales
...: Kindred
...: Nemesis
...: Primal
...: Race War
...:Strange Roux
...2
...Vs. Judge Dredd
...Vs. Magnus Robot Fighter (w/**Valiant**)
Propellerman
Pumpkinhead: The Rites of Exorcism
Race of Scorpions
Rack & Pain
Rascals in Paradise
Rebel Sword
Redblade
Rick Geary's Wonders and Oddities
Rio at Bay
Roachmill
Robocop
...: Mortal Coils
...: Prime Suspect
...: Roulette
...3
...Versus the Terminator
Rocketeer Adventure Magazine, The
Safest Place in the World
Scatterbrain
Screwball Squirrel
Sergio Aragonés
...Boogeyman
...Louder Than Words
Shadow, The
...and Doc Savage
Shadow Empires: Faith Conquers
Shadow: Hell's Heat Wave
...: In the Coils of the Leviathan
Spacehawk
Space Usagi
Species
Stan Shaw's Beauty & the Beast
Starship Troopers
Starstruck
Star Wars
...: Boba Fett
...: Crimson Empire
...: Dark Empire
...: Dark Empire II
...: Dark Force Rising
...: Droids
...: Empire's End
...: Heir to the Empire
...: Jabba the Hutt
...: Mara Jade
...: River of Chaos
...: Shadows of the Empire
...-Evolution
...: Shadow Stalker
...:Splinter of the Mind's Eye
...: Tales From Mos Eisley
Star Wars: Tales of the Jedi
...-Dark Lords of the Sith
...-Fall of the Sith Empire
...-Golden Age of the Sith
...-Redemption
...-The Freedon Nadd Uprising
...-The Sith War
Star Wars: The Last Command
...: The Protocol Offensive
...: X-Wing Rogue Squadron
Tale of One Bad Rat, The
Tank Girl
...2
Tarzan
.../John Carter: Warlord of Mars
...Vs. Predator at the Earth's Core
Terminator, The
...: Endgame, The
...: Hunters and Killers, The
...: One Shot, The
...: Secondary Objectives
...: The Enemy Within, The
Thing, The
Thing from Another World: Climate of Fear
...: Eternal Vows
Timecop
Titan Special
Trekker
Triple-X
Universal Monsters
Usagi Yojimbo
Venus Wars, The
Virus
Wacky Squirrel
Walter
Warworld!
Will to Power
Wizard of Fourth Street
Wolf & Red
X
Young Indiana Jones Chronicles, The
You're Under Arrest
Zombie World
Zone

Legend

Babe
...2
Big Guy and Rusty the Boy Robot, The
Concrete
...: Eclectica
...: Killer Smile
...: Think Like A Mountain
Danger Unlimited
Hellboy
...: Almost Colossus
...: Seed of Destruction
...: The Corpse and the Iron Shoes
...: The Wolves of St. August
...: Wake The Devil
John Byrne's Next Men
Martha Washington Goes to War
...Stranded in Space
Madman Comics
Monkeyman and O'Brien
Red Rocket 7
Sin City
...: A Dame to Kill For
...: Family Values
...: Just Another Saturday Night
...: Sex and Violence
...: Silent Night
...: That Yellow Bastard
...: The Babe Wore Red
...: The Big Fat Kill
Superman/ Madman Hullabaloo! **(w/DC)**
300
Torch of Liberty Special

DC COMICS

Action Comics
Adam Strange
Advanced Dungeons & Dragons
Adventure Comics
Adventures in the DC Universe
Adventures of Bob Hope
...of Ford Fairlane
...of Jerry Lewis
...of Superman
...of the Outsiders
Agent Liberty Special
Alien Nation
All American Men of War
All-New Collectors' Edition
All-Out War
All-Star Comics
All-Star Squadron
All-Star Western
Ambush Bug
America Vs. The Justice Society
Amethyst
..., Princess of Gemworld
Anarky
Angel and the Ape
Angel Love
Anima
Animaniacs
Animal Man
Animaniacs
Anthro
Aquaman
...: Time & Tide
Arak/Son of Thunder
Argus
Arion, Lord of Atlantis
...the Immortal
Armageddon: Alien Agenda
Armageddon: Inferno
Armageddon 2001
Army at War
Arsenal
...Special
Artemis: Requiem
Atari Force
Atlantis Chronicles, The
Atom, The
...and the Hawkman
Avatar
Azrael
Azrael/Ash (w/**Event**)
Aztek, The Ultimate Man
Babylon 5
Batgirl Adventures
Batgirl Special
Batlash
Batman
... Adventures, The
... Adventures, The: The Lost Years
.../Aliens **(w/Dark Horse)**
...and Robin Adventures
...and Superman Adventures :World's Finest
..:and the Outsiders
...Black And White
...Chronicles, The
...Darknight Dynasty, The
...Darknight Gallery, The
...Family, The
...Forever
...: Gordon's Law
...: Gotham Adventures
...: Gotham Nights II
.../Grendel **(w/Comico)**
...Grendel **(w/Dark Horse)**
...: Knightgallery
...: Legends of the Dark Knight
...: Legends of the Dark Knight-Jazz
...: Manbat
.../Predator **(DC w/Dark Horse Comics)**
...Record Comic
...: Run, Riddler, Run
...: Shadow of the Bat
...: Sword of Azrael
...: The Cult
...: The Dark Knight Returns
...: The Killing Joke
...: The Long Halloween
...: The Official Comic Adaptation of the Warner Bros. Motion Picture
...: The Ultimate Evil
...3-D
...: Two-Face Strikes Twice
...: Versus Predator
...II: Bloodmatch
.../Wildcat
Battle Classics
Beowulf
Best of DC, The
Best of the Brave and the Bold, The
Beware the Creeper
Bill & Ted's Excellent Adventure Movie Adaptation
Binky
Birds of Prey
...: Batgirl
...: Manhunt
...: Revolution
...: Wolves
Black Canary
.../Oracle: Birds of Prey
Black Condor
Blackhawk
Black Lightning
Black Magic
Black Mask
Black Orchid
Blasters Special
Blind Justice
Blitzkrieg
Bloodbath
Bloodpack
Blue Beetle
Blue Devil
Bob, The Galactic Bum
Bomba, The Jungle Boy
Book of Fate
Booster Gold
Brave and the Bold, The
Breathtaker
Brother Power, The Geek
Bugs Bunny
Butcher, The
Camelot 3000
Cancelled Comic Cavalcade
Captain Action
Captain Atom
Captain Carrot and His Amazing Zoo Crew
Captain Storm
Catwoman
.../Vampirella: The Furies **(DC w/Harris)**
Centurions
Chain Gang War
Challengers of the Unknown
Chase
Checkmate
Christmas with the Super-Heroes
Chronos
Cinder and Ashe
Clash
Claw the Unconquered
Congorilla
Conqueror of the Barren Earth
Cool World
Cops
Cosmic Boy
Cosmic Odyssey
Creeper The
Crimson Avenger, The
Crisis on Infinite Earths
Crucible
Damage
Danger Trail
Daring New Adventures of Supergirl
Dark Mansion of Forbidden Love
Darkseid Vs. Galactus: The Hunger (w/ **Marvel**)
Darkstars, The
DC Challenge
DC Comics Presents
DC Graphic Novel
DC 100 Page Super Spectacular
DC One Million
DC Science Fiction Graphic Novel
DC Silver Age Classics
DC Special
DC Special Blue-Ribbon Digest
DC Special Series
DC Spotlight
DC Super-Stars
DC Universe Holiday Bash
DC Universe: Trinity
Deadman
...: Exorcism
...: Love After Death
Deadshot
Deathstroke: The Terminator
Demolition Man
Demon, The
Detective Comics
Detention Comics
Doc Savage
Doctor Fate
Doom Force Special
Doom Patrol
Doomsday
Doorway to Nightmare
Dragonlance
Duckman
Dynamic Classics
Eclipso
...: The Darkness Within
80 Page Giant
El Diablo
Electric Warrior
Elongated Man
Elseworld's Finest
Elson's Presents
Elvira's House of Mystery
Emerald Dawn
Enemy Ace Special
Epicurus the Sage
Eradicator
Etc
Extreme Justice
Famous First Edition
Fast Forward
Fate
Fighting American
Final Night
Firebrand
Firestorm
..., the Nuclear Man
1st Issue Special
Flash
Flash Gordon
Flintstones and the Jetsons
Forever People

Forgotten Realms
Freedom Fighters
From Beyond the Unknown
Funny Stuff Stocking Stuffer
Fury of Firestorm, The
Gammarauders
Genesis
Ghostdancing
Ghosts
G. I. Combat
Gilgamesh II
Golden Age, The
Gotham by Gaslight
...Nights
Green Arrow
...: The Long Bow Hunters
...: The Wonder Year
Green Lantern
...Corps, The
...Corps Quarterly
...: Emerald Dawn
...: Emerald Dawn II
.../Green Arrow
...: Mosaic
Griffin, The
Gross Point
Guardians of Metropolis
Gunfire
Guy Gardner
...Reborn
Hacker Files, The
Hammerlocke
Hardcore Station
Hawk and Dove
Hawkman
Hawkworld
Haywire
Heart of the Beast, The
Hercules Unbound
Heroes Against Hunger
Hero Hotline
Hex
History of the DC Universe
Hitchhiker's Guide to the Galaxy
Hitman
Hot Wheels
House of Mystery, The
House of Secrets, The
Human Target Special
Huntress, The
Immortal Doctor Fate, The
Impulse
Inferior Five, The
Inferno
Infinity, Inc.
Invasion
Ironwolf
...: Fires of the Revolution
Isis
Jack Kirby's Fourth World
Jemm, Son of Saturn
JLA
...: Paradise Lost
...: Secret Files
...: The Nail
...: World Without Grown-ups
...: Year One
Joker, The
Jonah Hex
...and Other Western Tales
Jonni Thunder
Judge Dredd
...: Legends of the Law
Justice, Inc.
Justice League
...Europe
...International
...of America
...Quarterly
...Task Force
Justice Society of America
Kamandi: At Earth's End
..., the Last Boy on Earth
Karate Kid
Kents, The
Kid Eternity
Kingdom Come
Kissyfur
Kobra
Kong the Untamed
Korak
Krypton Chronicles
Last Days of the Justice Society
Legend of Wonder Woman, The
Legends
...of the DC Universe
...of the Legion
...of the World's Finest
L. E. G. I. O. N.
Legionnaires
...Three
Legion of Substitute Heroes Special
Legion of Super-Heroes
Legion: Science Police
Lex Luthor: The Unauthorized Biography
Limited Collectors' Edition
Little Shop of Horrors Special
Lobo
...: A Contract on Gawd
.../Deadman: The Brave and the Bald
...: Death and Taxes
...Gallery
...: Infanticide
.../Judge Dredd
.../Mask
...'s Back
...'s Big Babe Spring Break Special
...Unamerican Gladiators
Lois & Clark, the New Adventures of Superman
Lois Lane
Long Hot Summer, The
Looney Tunes
Loose Cannon
Lords of the Ultra-Realm
Losers Special
Madame Xanadu
Major Bummer
Man-Bat
Manhunter
Man of Steel, The
Many Loves of Dobie Gillis
Martian Manhunter
...: American Secrets
Marvel and DC Present (w/**Marvel Comics**)
Mask
Masters of the Universe
'Mazing Man
Men of War
Metal Men
Metamorpho
Metropolis S. C. U.
Millenium
Mister E
Mister Miracle
Ms. Tree Quarterly/Special
My Greatest Adventure
My Name is Chaos
Mystery in Space
Nathaniel Dusk
...II
Nazz, The
New Adventures of Superboy, The
New Gods
New Guardians, The
New Talent Showcase
New Teen Titans, The
New Titans, The
Night Force, The
Nightwing
...: Alfred's Return
...And Huntress
Nine Princes In Amber
Omac: One Man Army Corps
Omega Men, The
Our Army at War
...Fighting Forces
Outcasts
Outsiders
Oz-Wonderland Wars, The
Parallax: Emerald Night
Peacemaker
Peter Cannon-Thunderbolt
Phantom, The
Phantom Stranger, The
Phantom Zone, The
Pinky and The Brain
Plastic Man
Plop
Power Girl
Power Lords
Power of Shazam, The
Power of the Atom
Prez
Primal Force
Prisoner, The
Psyba-Rats
Question, The
...Quarterly, The
Ragman
...: Cry of the Dead
Rainbow Brite and the Star Stealer
Ray, The
R. E. B. E. L. S.
Red Tornado
Restaurant at the End of the Universe
Resurrection Man
Richard Dragon, Kung-Fu Fighter
Rima, The Jungle Girl
Ring of the Nibelung, The
Rip Hunter Time Master
Robin
...: A Hero Reborn
...II
...III: Cry of the Huntress
...3000
Robotech Defenders
Rogue's Gallery
Ronin
Roots of the Swamp Thing
Sandman, The
Saga of Ra's Al Ghul, The
Scare Tactics
Scarlett
Scooby Doo
Secret Origins
...of the World's Greatest Super-Heroes
Secret Society of Super-Villains
Secrets of Haunted House
Secrets of Sinister House
...of the Legion of Super-Heroes
Sergio Aragonés Destroys DC
Sgt. Rock
...Special
...Prize Battle Tales
Shade, The
Shade, The Changing Man
Shado: Song of the Dragon
Shadow, The
Shadowdragon
Shadow of the Batman
Shadow Strikes!, The
Shadow War of Hawkman
Shazam!
...: The New Beginning
Showcase
...'93
...'94
...'95
...'96
Silverblade
Sinister House of Secret Love, The
Skreemer
Skull & Bones
Slash Maraud
Sonic Disruptors
Son of Ambush Bug
Sovereign Seven
Spanner's Galaxy
Spectre, The
Speed Force
Spelljammer
Spider-Man and Batman (w/**Marvel Comics**)
Spiral Zone
Stalker
Stanley & His Monster
S. T. A. R. Corps
Starfire
Star Hunters
Starman
Star Spangled War Tales
Star Trek
...Movie Special
...VI: The Undiscovered Country
...-The Modala Imperative
Star Trek.: The Next Generation
.../Deep Space Nine
...-Ill Wind
...-The Modala Imperative
...-Shadowheart
Steel
..., the Indestructible Man
Strange Adventures
...Sports Stories
Street Fighter: The Battle for Shadaloo
Streets
Sugar & Spike
Suicide Squad
Sun Devils
Superboy
...And The Ravers
Super DC Giant
Super Friends
Supergirl
.../Lex Luthor Special
Superman
And Spider-Man (w/**Marvel Comics**)
.../Batman: Alternate Realities
.../Doomsday: Hunter/Prey
...Family, The
...For All Seasons
...For Earth
...Forever
...Record Comic
...Red/ Superman Blue
...'s Girlfriend Lois Lane
...'s Pal Jimmy Olsen
...Spectacular
...: Speeding Bullets
...: The Earth Stealers
...: The Man of Steel
...: The Man of Tomorrow
...: The Secret Years
...: The Wedding Album
.../Toyman
...Vs. Aliens
...Vs. the Amazing Spider-Man (w/**Marvel Comics**)
Super Powers
Super-Team Family
Swamp Thing
Sword of Sorcery
Sword of the Atom
Tailgunner Jo
Takion
Tales of the Green Lantern Corps
...of the Legion
...of the New Teen Titans
...of the Teen Titans
...of the Unexpected
Talos of the Wilderness Sea
Tank Girl
Tarzan
...Family, The
Team Titans
Teen Titans
...Spotlight
Tempus Fugitive
Thriller
Thrillkiller
Timber Wolf
Time Masters
...Warp
Titans Sell-Out Special
Tor
Total Recall
Triumph
TSR World
Twilight
Underworld
Underworld Unleashed
...: Abyss-Hell's Sentinel
...: Apokolips-Dark Uprising
...: Batman-Devil's Asylum
...: Patterns of Fear
Unexpected, The
Unknown Soldier, The
Untold Legend of the Batman, The
"V"
Valor
V for Vendetta
Vigilante, The
...: City Lights, Prairie Justice
Viper
Wanderers
Wanted, the World's Most Dangerous Villains
Warlord
War of the Gods
Wasteland
Watchmen
Weird, The
Weird Mystery Tales
...War Tales
...Western Tales
...Worlds
Welcome Back, Kotter
Where in the World is Carmen Sandiego?
Who's Who in Star Trek
...in the Legion of Super-Heroes
...: The Definitive Directory of the DC Universe
...Update '87
...Update '88
Wild Dog
Witching Hour
Wonder Woman
World of Krypton, The
...of Metropolis, The

Marvel Action Hour, Featuring...
...Action Universe
...Adventures Starring Daredevil
...and DC Present (w/**DC Comics**)
...Chillers
...Classics Comics Series Featuring...
...Collector's Edition
...Collector's Edition: X-Men
...Collectors' Item Classics
...Comics Presents
...Comics Super Special
...Double Feature
...Fanfare
...Feature
...Fumetti Book
...Graphic Novel
...Holiday Special
...Illustrated: Swimsuit Issue
...Masterpieces Collection
...Masterpieces 2 Collection, The
...Milestone Edition
...Mini-Books
...Movie Premiere
...Movie Showcase Featuring Star Wars
...Movie Spotlight Featuring Raiders of the Lost Ark
...No-Prize Book, The
...Premiere
...Presents
...Preview
...Riot
Marvels
Marvel Saga, The
...'s Greatest Comics
...Special Edition Featuring...
...Spectacular
Marvels: Portraits
Marvel Spotlight
...Super Action
...Super Hero Contest of Champions
...Super-Heroes
...Super-Heroes Megazine
...Super-Heroes Secret Wars
...Swimsuit Special
...Tails Starring Peter Porker the Spectacular Spider-Ham
...Tales
...Team-Up
...Treasury Edition
...Treasury of Oz
...Treasury Special
...Triple Action
...Two-in-One
...Universe
...Versus DC
...X-Men Collection, The
Master of Kung Fu
...: Bleeding Black
Masters of Terror
Maverick
Men in Black: Retribution
...: The Movie
Mephisto Vs...
Meteor Man
MGM's Marvelous Wizard of Oz
Micronauts
...Special Edition
Midnight Sons Unlimited
Mighty Marvel Western
Mighty Morphin' Power Rangers: The Movie
Mighty Mouse
Millie the Model
Monster Menace
Monsters on the Prowl
Monsters Unleashed
Moon Knight
...: Divided We Fall
...Special
...Special Edition
Morbius Revisited
...: The Living Vampire
Mort the Dead Teenager
Ms. Marvel
Mutant Misadventures of Cloak and Dagger, The
Mutant X
My Love
'Nam, The
...Magazine, The
Namor, the Sub-Mariner
New Mutants, The
...Warriors, The
Nick Fury, Agent of S. H. I. E. L. D.
...Vs. S. H. I. E. L. D.
Nightcrawler
Nightmare
Nightmask
Night Nurse
NightRider
Nightstalkers
Night Thrasher
...: Four Control
Nightwatch
Nocturne
No Escape
Nomad
Northstar
Not Brand Echh
Nothing Can Stop the Juggernaut
Nova
Nth Man the Ultimate Ninja
Obnoxio the Clown
Official Handbook of the Marvel Universe, The
Official Marvel Index to Marvel Team-Up
...to the Amazing Spider-Man
...to the Avengers, The
...to the Fantastic Four
...to the X-Men, The
Omega the Unknown
101 Ways to End the Clone Saga
Open Space
Original Ghost Rider, The
...Rides Again, The
Our Love Story
Outlaw Kid, The
Over the Edge
Peter, The Little Pest
Phantom: The Ghost Who Walks
...2040
Phoenix
Pitt, The
Planet of the Apes
Police Academy
Power Man
...Pachyderms
...Pack
...Record Comics
Prince Namor, the Sub-Mariner
Prince Valiant
Professor Xavier and the X-Men
Prowler, The
Psi-Force
Psylocke & Archangel: Crimson Dawn
Punisher
...Armory, The
... Kills The Marvel Universe
...Magazine, The
...Movie Comic
...: Origin of Micro Chip
...: P.O.V.
...: The Ghosts of Innocents
...2099
...War Journal, The
...: War Zone, The
...: Year One
Quasar
Questprobe
Quicksilver
Raiders of the Lost Ark
Rampaging Hulk
Ravage 2099
Rawhide Kid
Razorline
Red Sonja
...: Scavenger Hunt
...: The Movie
Red Wolf
Ren & Stimpy Show, The
Requiem for Dracula
Ringo Kid, The
Rise of Apocalypse
Robert E. Howard's Conan
Robocop
...2
Robotix
Rocket Raccoon
Rocko's Modern Life
Rogue
Rom
Ruins
Saban's Mighty Morphin' Power Rangers
Sabretooth
...Classic
Saga of Crystar, Crystal Warrior, The
...of the Original Human Torch
...of the Sub-Mariner
Saint Sinner
Savage Return of Dracula
...She-Hulk, The
...Sword of Conan
...Tales
Scarlet Spider
...Unlimited
Scarlet Witch
Scooby-Doo
Secret Defenders
...Wars II
Sectaurs
Seeker 3000
Semper Fi
Sensational She-Hulk, The
...in Ceremony
Sensational Spider-Man
Sgt. Fury
Shadowmasters
Shadows & Light
Shanna, the She-Devil
Sheena
S. H. I. E. L. D.
Shogun Warriors
Shroud, The
Silver Sable and the Wild Pack
Silver Surfer, The
...Vs. Dracula
.../Warlock: Resurrection
.../Weapon Zero
Skeleton Warriors
Skrull Kill Krew
Skull, the Slayer
Slapstick
Sledge Hammer
Sleepwalker
Slingers
Smurfs
Snow White
Solarman
Solo
...Avengers
Solomon Kane
Son of Satan
...of Yuppies From Hell
Special Collectors' Edition
...Edition X-Men
...Marvel Edition
Spectacular Scarlet Spider
...Spider-Man, The
Speedball
Spellbound
Spider-Girl
Spider-Man
...Adventures
...and Batman (w/**DC Comics**)
...and Daredevil
...and His Amazing Friends
...and X-Factor
...: Chapter One
...Classics
...Collector's Preview
...Comics Magazine
...: Friends and Enemies
...: Funeral for an Octopus
...: Hobgoblin Lives
...: Hot Shots
...Magazine
...: Maximum Clonage
...Megazine
...: Power of Terror
...Saga
...: Super Special
...Team-Up
...: The Arachnis Project
...: The Clone Journal
...: The Final Adventure
...: The Jackal Files
...: The Lost Years
...: The Manga
...: The Mutant Agenda
...: The Parker Years
...2099
...2099 Meets Spider-Man
...Unlimited
...: Venom Agenda
...Vs. Dracula
...Vs. Wolverine
...: Web of Doom
Spider-Woman
Spidey Super Stories
Spitfire and the Troubleshooters
Spoof
Spotlight
Squadron Supreme
Starblast
Star Brand
Starjammers
Star-Lord the Special Edition
Starriors
Star Team
Star Trek
...Deep Space Nine
...Early Voyages
...Starfleet Academy
...Voyager
Star Wars
...: Return of the Jedi
Steeltown Rockers
Strange Days
Strange Tales
Street Poet Ray
Strikeforce: Morituri
...: Electric Undertow
Stryfe's Strike File
Sub-Mariner, The
Supernaturals
Supernatural Thrillers
Super-Villain Classics
...Team-Up
Sweet XVI
Sworn to Protect
Tales of Asgard
...of G. I. Joe
...of Suspense
...of the Marvels
...of the Zombie
...to Astonish
Tarzan
...of the Apes
Team America
...Helix
Terminator 2: Judgment Day
Terror Inc.
Tex Dawson, Gun-Slinger
Thanos Quest, The
Thing, The
Thor
...Corps
Thunderstrike
Time Bandits
Timespirits
Tomb of Darkness
...of Dracula
Tower of Shadows
Toxic Avenger
...Crusaders
Transformers, The
...: Generation 2
Try-Out Winner Book
TV Stars
2099 A. D.
...Apocalypse
...Genesis
...Unlimited
...World of Doom Special
Two-Gun Kid
...: Sunset Riders
2001, A Space Odyssey
2010
Typhoid
Ultragirl
Uncanny Tales
Uncanny X-Men, The
...at the State Fair of Texas
...in Days of Future Past
Union Jack
Unknown Worlds of Science Fiction
Unlimited Access
Untold Legend of Captain Marvel
Untold Tales of Spider-Man
U. S. Agent
U. S. 1
Vampire Tales
Vault of Evil
Venom: Along Came a Spider
...: Carnage Unleashed
...: Finale
...: Funeral Pyre
...: Lethal Protector
...: License to Kill
...: Nights of Vengeance
...: On Trial
...: Seed of Darkness
...: Separation Anxiety
...: Sign of the Boss
...: Sinner Takes All
...: Super Special
...: The Enemy Within
...: The Mace

...: The Madness
...: Tooth and Claw
Very Best of Dennis the Menace, The
Virtua Fighter
Vision, The
...and the Scarlet Witch
War, The
War is Hell
Warlock
...and the Infinity Watch
...Chronicles
War Machine
Weapon X
Web of Scarlet Spider
Web of Spider-Man
Webspinners: Tales of Spider-Man
Wedding of Dracula
Weird Wonder Tales
Werewolf by Night
West Coast Avengers
Western Gunfighters
...Kid, The
...Team-Up
What If?
What The--?!
Where Creatures Roam
...Monsters Dwell
Willow
Wolfpack
Wolverine
...and the Punisher: Damaging Evidence
...: Days of Future Past
.../Gambit: Victims
...Saga
...Vs. Spider-Man
Wonder Man
Worlds Unknown
X-Calibre
X-Factor
X-Force
...Megazine
X-Man
X-Men
...Adventures
...Adventures II
...Adventures III
...Alpha
.../Alpha Flight
...and the Micronauts, The
...Archives
...Archives Featuring Captain Britain
...Chronicles
.../Clandestine
...Classic
...Classics
...Liberators
...Omega
...Prime
...Spotlight on Starjammers
...Survival Guide to the Mansion
...: The Early Years
...The Manga
...: The Ultra Collection
...: The Wedding Album
...2099
...Ultra III Preview
...Unlimited
...Vs. Dracula
...Vs. the Avengers, The
X-Terminators
X-Universe
Yogi Bear
Yuppies from Hell
Zorro

Amalgam

Bruce Wayne, Agent of S.H.I.E.L.D.
Bullets and Bracelets
Challengers of the Fantastic
Exciting X-Patrol
Iron Lantern
Magnetic Men Featuring Magneto
Magneto and the Magnetic Men
Speed Demon
Spider-Boy
...Team-Up
Thorion of the New Asgods
X-Patrol

Epic

Abraham Stone
Airtight Garage, The
Akira
Alien Legion
...: Binary Deep
...: Jugger Grimrod
...: One Planet at a Time
...: On the Edge
...: Tennants of Hell
A-1
Atomic Age
Black Dragon, The
Blood
Bloodlines: A Tale from the Heart of Africa
Blueberry
Bozz Chronicles, The
Brats Bizarre
Cadillacs & Dinosaurs
Captain Confederacy
Car Warriors
Chiller
Clive Barker's Book of the Damned
...Hellraiser
...Nightbreed
...The Harrowers
Coyote
Crash Ryan
Crime and Punishment: Marshall Law Takes Manhattan
Dinosaurs, a Celebration
Doctor Zero
Dragon Lines
...: Way of the Warrior
Dreadlands
Dreadstar
...and Company
Elfquest
Elsewhere Prince, The
Epic
...Illustrated
...Lite
Everyman, The
Feud
Groo Carnival, The
...Chronicles, The
...the Wanderer
Havok & Wolverine - Meltdown
Heavy Hitters
Hellhound, The Redemption Quest
Hellraiser Nightbreed - Jihad
Hollywood Superstars
Idol
Incal, The
Interface
Last American, The
Lawdog/Grimrod: Terror at the Crossroads
Lieutenant Blueberry
Light and Darkness War, The
Marshal Blueberry
Marshal Law
Midnight Men
Moebius
Moonshadow
Mutatis
Necromancer: The Graphic Novel
One, The
Onyx Overlord
Pinhead
...Vs. Marshal Law
Plastic Forks
Power Line
Psychonauts
Sachs & Violens
St. George
Samurai Cat
Seven Block
Shadowline Saga: Critical Mass, A
Sisterhood of Steel
Six From Sirius
...II
Sleeze Brothers, The
Stalkers
Starstruck
Steelgrip Starkey
Strange Combat Tales
Stray Toasters
Swords of the Swashbucklers
Tales from the Heart of Africa
Ted McKeever's Metropol
Tekworld
Terrarists
Tomb of Dracula
Tomorrow Knights
Tor
Transmutation of Ike Garuda
Untamed
Video Jack
Void Indigo
War Man
Weaveworld
Wild Cards

Malibu

Angels of Destruction
Battletech
...Fallout
Black September
Bravura
Break-Thru
Breed
...II
Bruce Lee
Codename: Firearm
Curse of Rune
Dinosaurs for Hire
Dreadstar
Dream Team
Edge
Eliminator
Elven
Exiles
Ex-Mutants
Ferret
Firearm
Flood Relief
Freex
Godwheel
Gravestone
Hardcase
Lord Pumpkin
.../Necromantra
Malibu Ashcan: Rafferty
Man Called A-X, The
Man of War
Mantra
Metaphysique
Mortal Kombat
...: Baraka
...: Battlewave
...: Goro, Prince of Pain
...: Kitana and Mileena
...: Kung Lao
...: Raydon & Kano
...: U. S. Special Forces
Mutants Vs. Ultras
Night Man, The
Nocturnals, The
Power & Glory
Power of Prime
Prime
Project A-KO
Protectors
Prototype
Ripfire
Rune
.../Silver Surfer
Siren
Sludge
Solitaire
Solution, The
Star Slammers
Star Trek: Deep Space Nine
...-The Celebrity Series: Blood and Honor
...Hearts and Minds
..., The Maquis
.../The Next Generation
Strangers, The
Street Fighter
Strikeback!
Tarzan: Love, Lies and the Lost City
...the Warrior
Terminator 2: Cybernetic Dawn
...: Nuclear Twilight
Ultraforce
Ultraverse Double Feature
...Origins
...Premiere
...Year One
...Year Two
...Year Zero: The Death of the Squad
Warstrike
Wrath

Marvel UK

Action Force
Battletide
...II
Captain Britain
Codename: Genetix
Dark Angel
...Guard
Death Metal
...Vs. Genetix
Death's Head
...II
...II & the Origin of Die-Cut
Death 3
...Wreck
Die-Cut
...Vs. G-Force
Digitek
Dragon's Claws
Gene Dogs
Genetix
Gun Runner
Hell's Angel
Incomplete Death's Head
Killpower: The Early Years
King Arthur and the Knights of Justice
Knights of Pendragon, The
Motormouth
Mys-Tech Wars
Nightraven: The Collected Stories
Pendragon
Plasmer
Shadow Riders
Super Soldiers
Warheads
Wildthing

Star Comics

Air Raiders
Animax
Bullwinkle and Rocky
Care Bears
Chuck Norris
Defenders of the Earth
Droids
Ewoks
Flintstone Kids, The
Flintstones, The
Foofur
Fraggle Rock
Getalong Gang, The
Heathcliff
...'s Funhouse
Hugga Bunch
Inhumanoids, The
Madballs
Masters of the Universe
Misty
Muppet Babies, The
Muppets Take Manhattan, The
Peter Porker the Spectacular Spider-Ham
Planet Terry
Popples
Royal Roy
Silverhawks
Star Comics Magazine
Strawberry Shortcake
Thundercats
Top Dog
Visionaries
Wally the Wizard

TOPPS COMICS

Barbi Twins, The
Bombast
Bram Stoker's Dracula
Cadillacs and Dinosaurs
Captain Glory
Dracula Chronicles
...Versus Zorro
...: Vlad the Impaler
Duckman
...: The Mob Frog Saga
Exosquad
Frankenstein/Dracula War
Jackie Chan's Spartan X
Jack Kirby's Secret City Saga
...Silver Star
...Teenagents
Jason Goes to Hell: The Final Friday
...Vs. Leatherface
Jurassic Park
...: Raptor
...: Raptors Attack
...: Raptors Hijack
Lady Rawhide
Lone Ranger and Tonto
Lost World, The
Mars Attacks
...High School
...Image
...The Savage Dragon
Mary Shelley's Frankenstein
Night Glider
Ray Bradbury Comics
Return to Jurassic Park
Satan's Six
...: Hellspawn
Topps Comics Presents
Victory
Xena: Warrior Princess
X-Files, The
...: Ground Zero
...: Season One
Zorro

FIRST APPEARANCES

A-Man the Amazing Man - Amazing-Man Comics #5, 9/39
Adam Strange - Showcase #17, 11-12/58
Adult Legion - Superman #147, 8/61
Agent Liberty - Superman #60 (2nd Series), 10/91
Air Man - (Hawkman imitator) Keen Detective Funnies #23, 8/40
Air Wave - Detective Comics #60, 2/42
Air Wave II - Green Lantern #100, 1/78
Airboy - Air Fighters Comics V1#2, 11/42
Airwave I - Detective Comics #60, 2/42
Alex Summers - (becomes Havok) X-Men #54, 3/69
Alfred - Batman #16 4-5/43; (1st skinny Alfred) Detective Comics #83, 1/44
Alice Cooper - Marvel Premiere #50, 10/79
Alicia Masters - Fantastic Four #8, 11/62
Aliens - Aliens #1 May '88; Magnus, Robot Fighter #1, 2/63
Alley Oop - Funnies #1, 10/36
Alpha Flight - X-Men #120, 4/78
Amazing Man - All Star Squadron #23, 7/83
American Ace - (1st newsstand app.) Marvel Mystery Comics #2, 12/39
American Crusader - Thrilling Comics #19, 8/41
American Eagle - Marvel Two-In-One Annual #6, 1981; (1st pub lished app.) Motion Picture Funnies Weekly #1, 1939
Ancient One - Strange Tales #110, 7/63
Andy Panda - Crackajack Funnies #39, 9/41
Angel - Marvel Comics #1, 10-11/39
Angel (now Archangel) - X-Men #1, 9/63
Angel & the Ape - Showcase #77, 9/68
Animal Man - (in costume) Strange Adventures #190, 7/66; (no cos tume) Strange Adventures #180, 9/65; (re-intro) Wonder Woman #267, 5/80
Ant-Man - (costume) Tales to Astonish #35, 9/62; (new) Marvel Premiere #47, 4/79; (no costume) Tales to Astonish #27, 1/62; (re-intro) Avengers #46, 11/67
Anthro - Showcase #74, 5/68
Apache Kid - Two Gun Western #5, 11/50
Ape, The - Startling Comics #21, 5/43
Aqua-Girl - Aquaman #33, 5-6/67
Aquababy - Aquaman #23, 9-10/65
Aquaboy - Superboy #171
Aquagirl - (try out, not same as other) Adventure Comics #266, 11/59
Aquagirl - Aquaman #33, 5-6/67
Aqualad - Adventure Comics #269, 2/60
Aquarian (Wundarr) - Adventure Into Fear #17, '73
Aquaman - More Fun Comics #73, 11/41
Arak - Warlord #48, 8/81
Archangel - (cameo) (formerly Angel) X-Factor #23, 12/87; (full app.) X-Factor #24, 1/88
Archie Andrews - Pep Comics #22, 12/41
Arion - Warlord #55
Arrow - Funny Pages V2#10, 9/38
Arthur Stacy - Amazing Spider-Man #93, 2/71
Asbestos Lady - Captain America Comics #63, 7/47
Astro Boy - Astro Boy #1, 8/65
Atom - All-American Comics #19, 10/40; (S.A.) Showcase #34, 9-10/61
Atoman - Atoman #1, 2/46
Atomaster - Comic Books #1, 1950
Atomic Mouse - Atomic Mouse #1, 3/53
Atomic Rabbit - Atomic Rabbit #1, 8/55
Atomic Thunderbolt - Atomic Thunderbolt #1, 2/46
Aunt May - Amazing Fantasy #15, 8-9/62; (prototype) Strange Tales #92, 6/62
Aurora - X-Men #120
Avenger - Shadow Comics #2, 4/40
Azrael - (cameo) Tales of the Teen Titans #52, 4/85; (full app.) Tales of the Teen Titans #53, 5/85
Baby Huey - Casper, the Friendly Ghost #1, 9/49; (1st Harvey app.) Harvey Comics Hits #60, 9/52
Badger - Badger #1, 12/83
Balbo, the Boy Magician - Master Comics #32, 11/42
Bamm Bamm - (Flintstones) Flintstones #16, 1/64
Barker - National Comics #42, 5/44
Barney Bear - Our Gang Comics #1, 9-10/42
Baron Strucker - Sgt. Fury #5, 1/64
Bat Lash - Showcase #76, 8/68
Bat-Girl - Batman #139, 4/61; (new) Detective #359, 1/67
Batgirl - Detective Comics #359, 1/67
Batman - Detective Comics #27, May '39; (new look w/new costume) Detective Comics #327, 5/64
Batman, Jr. - World's Finest Comics #215, 10/72
Batmite - Detective Comics #267, 5/59
Batwoman - Detective Comics #233, 7/56; (1st modern app. G.A. Batwoman) Brave and the Bold #182, 1/82; (new) Detective Comics #624, 12/90; (re-intro) Batman Family #10, 3-4/77
Beast - X-Men #1, 9/63; (new) (1st in mutated form) Amazing Adventures #11, 3/72
Beast Boy - (becomes Changeling) Doom Patrol #99, 11/65
Belit - Giant-Size Conan #1, 9/74
Bennett Brant - Amazing Spider-Man #11, 4/64
Bernie the Brain - Sugar & Spike #72, ?, '68
Berserkers, The - X-Men/Alpha Flight #1, 12/85
Betty - Pep Comics #22, 12/41
Betty Brant - Amazing Spider-Man #4, 9/63
Bill Barnes - (Air Ace) Shadow Comics #1, 3/40
Binary - (formerly Ms. Marvel) X-Men #164, 12/82
Birdman, The - Weird Comics #1, 4/40
Bishop - (cameo) X-Men #282, 11/91; (full app.) X-Men #283, 12/91
Bizarro Jimmy Olsen - Adventure Comics #287, 8/61
Bizarro Lana Lang - Adventure Comics #292, 1/62
Bizarro Lois Lane - Action Comics #255, 8/59
Bizarro Lucy Lane - Adventure Comics #292, 1/62
Bizarro Marilyn Monroe - Adventure Comics #294, 3/62
Bizarro Perry White - Adventure Comics #287, 8/61
Bizarro President Kennedy - Adventure Comics #294, 3/62
Black Bolt - (1st full app.) Fantastic Four #46, 1/66 (cameo) (from Inhumans) Fantastic Four #45, 12/65
Black Canary - Flash Comics #86, 8/47; (Silver Age) Justice League of America #73; (1st modern app.) Detective Comics #554, 9/85; (1st solo story) Flash Comics #92, 2/48
Black Cat - Pocket Comics #1, 8/41
Black Cobra - Captain Flight Comics #8 ?, '46
Black Condor - Crack Comics #1, 5/40
Black Dwarf - Spotlight Comics #1, 11/44
Black Flame - Starslayer #20 9/84; Action Comics #304, 9/63
Black Fury - Fantastic Comics #18, 5/41
Black Goliath - Black Goliath #1, 2/76
BlackHawk - Military Comics #1, 8/41
Black Hood - Top-Notch Comics #9, 10/40; (S.A.) Adventures of the Fly #7, 7/60
Black Jack - Zip Comics #20, 11/41
Black Knight - Black Knight #1, 5/55
Black Knight - Tales to Astonish #52, 2/64
Black Knight II - Avengers #48, 1/68
Black Lightning - Black Lightning #1, 4/77
Black Marvel - Mystic Comics #5, 3/41
Black Orchid - Adventure Comics #428, 6-7/73; (new) Black Orchid #1, 12/88
Black Owl - Prize Comics #2, 4/40
Black Panther - Stars & Stripes #3, 7/41
Black Panther - Fantastic Four #52, 7/66
Black Phantom - Tim Holt #25, 9/51
Black Pirate - Sensation Comics #1, 1/42
Black Rider - All Western Winners #2, Win '48-49
Black Spider - Super-Mystery Comics V1#3, 10/40
Black Terror - Exciting Comics #9, 5/41
Black Widow - Mystic Comics #4, 7-8/40
Black Widow - Tales of Suspense #52, 4/64
Blackie the Hawk - Blackhawk #75, 4/54
Blackie the Hawk - (re-intro) Blackhawk #108, 1/57
Blade the Vampire Slayer - Tomb of Dracula #10, ?/73?
Blok - (Legion) Superboy #253, 7/79
Blonde Phantom - All-Select Comics #11, Fall '46; (re-intro) Sensational She-Hulk #4, 8/89
Blondie - Ace Comics #1, 4/37
Bloodshot - (cameo) Eternal Warrior #4, 11/92; (1st full app.) Rai #0, 11/92
Bloodstone - Marvel Presents #1, 10/75
Blue Beetle - (G.A.) Mystery Men Comics #1, 8/39; (Charlton) Blue Beetle #18, 2/55; (Ted Kord) Captain Atom #83, 11/66; (1st DC app.) Crisis on Infinite Earths #1, 4/85
Blue Blade - USA Comics #5, Sum '42
Blue Blaze - Mystic Comics #1, 3/40
Blue Bolt - Blue Bolt #1, 6/40
Blue Circle - Blue Circle Comics #1, 6/44
Blue Devil - Fury of Firestorm #24, 6/84
Blue Streak - Crash Comics #1, 5/40
Bo Bunny - Funny Stuff #70, 1-2?/53
Bobby Benson - Bobby Benson's B-Bar-B Riders #1, 5-6/50
Boboes - Marvel Mystery Comics #32, 6/42
Bomba - Bomba, the Jungle Boy #1, 9-10/67
Bombshell - Boy Comics #3, 4/42
Booster Gold - Booster Gold #1, 2/86
Bouncer - Bouncer nn, 1944
Bouncing Boy - (Legion) Action Comics #276, 5/61
Boy Commandos - Detective Comics #64, 6/42
Bozo the Robot - Smash Comics #1, 8/39
Brainiac 5 - Action Comics #276, 5/61
Brick Bradford - King Comics #1, 4/36
Broncho Bill - Tip Top Comics #1, 4/36
Brother Power - Brother Power, the Geek #1, 9-10/68; (re-intro) Saga of Swamp Thing Annual #5, 1989
Buck Rogers - (in comics) Famous Funnies #3, 9/34
Buckskin - Super Mystery V2#1, 4/41
Bucky - (Captain America's sidekick) Captain America Comics #1, 3/41; (Silver Age) Avengers #4, 3/64
Bugs Bunny - Looney Tunes & Merrie Melodies #1, 1941
Bullet - Amazing Mystery Funnies V3#1, 1/40
Bulletboy - Master Comics #48, 3/44
Bulletman - Nickel Comics #1, 5/40
Bumblebee - Teen Titans (1st series) #48, 1977
Buzzy - All Funny Comics #1, Win '43-44
Buzzy the Crow - Harvey Comics Hits #60, 9/52
B'Wanna Beast - Showcase #66
Cable - (1st full app.) New Mutants #87, 3/90; (cameo) New Mutants #86, 2/90
Cain - (House of Mystery host) House of Mystery #176, 10/67
Calico Kid - (becomes Ghost Rider) Tim Holt #6, 5/49
Camilla - Jungle Comics #1, 1/40
Candy - Police Comics #37, 12/44
Captain & the Kids - Famous Comics Cartoon Books #1200, 1934; Tip Top Comics #1, 4/36
Captain Action - Captain Action & Action Boy nn, 1967
Captain Aero - Captain Aero Comics V1#7, 12/41
Captain America - Captain America Comics #1, 3/41; (Silver Age) Strange Tales #114, 11/63; (Acrobat disguised as) Avengers #4, 3/64; (fomerly Super Patriot) Captain America #333, 9/87; (new) Captain America #181, 1/75; (new) (formerly Nomad) Captain America #183, 3/75
Captain Atom - (1st DC app.) Crisis on Infinite Earths #6, 9/85; (new) Captain Atom #84, 1/67; (new) Captain Atom #1 3/87; (S.A.) Space Adventures #33, 3/60
Captain Battle - Silver Streak

Comics #10, 5/41

Captain Britain - Captain Britain #1, 3/87; (1st U.S. app.) Marvel Team-Up #65, 1/78

Captain Comet - Strange Adventures #9, 6/51; (re-intro) Secret Society of Super-Villains #2, 7-8/76

Captain Commando - Pep Comics #30, 8/42

Captain Courageous - Banner Comics #3, 9/41

Captain Daring - Buccaneers #19, 1/50; Daring Mystery Comics #7, 4/41

Captain Desmo - Adventure Comics #32, 11/38

Captain Easy - Funnies #1, 10/36; Famous Comics Cartoon Books #1202, 1934

Captain Fearless - Silver Streak Comics #1, 12/39

Captain Fight - Fight Comics #16, 12/41

Captain Flag - Blue Ribbon Comics #16, 9/41

Captain Flash - Captain Flash #1, 11/54

Captain Freedom - Speed Comics #13, 5/41

Captain Future - Man of Tomorrow - Startling Comics #1, 6/40

Captain George Stacy - Amazing Spider-Man #56, 1/68

Captain Marvel (Shazam) - Whiz Comics #1, 2/40; (M.F.Enterprises) Captain Marvel #1, 4/66; (modern) Shazam: the New Beginning #1, 4/87; (new) Legends #1, 11/86; (re-intro) Shazam! #1, 2/73

Captain Marvel (female) - Amazing Spider-Man Annual #16, 1982

Captain Marvel of the Kree - Marvel Super-Heroes #12, 12/67

Captain Marvel, Jr. - Whiz Comics #25, 12/41

Captain Midnight - Funnies #57, 7/41

Captain Savage - Mystery Men Comics #4, 11/39

Captain Storm - Captain Storm #1, 5-6/64

Captain Strong - Action Comics #421, 3/73

Captain Terror - U.S.A. #2, 11/41

Captain Terry Thunder - Jungle Comics #1, 1/40

Captain Thunder - Flash Comics (Fawcett) #1, 1/40

Captain Thunder - Superman #276, ?'74

Captain Triumph - Crack Comics #27, 1/43

Captain Universe - Micronauts #8, 8/79

Captain Victory - Our Flag Comics #1, 8/41

Captain Wizard - Red Band Comics #3, ?'45

Captain Wonder - Kid Komics #1, 2/43

Captain Yank - Big Shot Comics #29, 11/42

Casper the Friendly Ghost - (1st Harvey app.) Harvey Comics Hits #60, 9/52; Casper #1, 9/49

Cat - The Cat #1, 11/72

Cat Girl - Adventures of the Fly #9, 11/60

Catman - Crash Comics #5, 11/40

Cave Carson - Brave and the Bold #31, 8-9/60

Cerebus - Cerebus the Aardvark #1, 12/77

Challenger - Mystic Comics #6, 10/41

Chameleon - Target Comics V1#6, 7/40

Chameleon Boy - (Legion) Action Comics #267, 8/60

Champ - Champion Comics #2, 12/39

Changeling - (formerly Beast Boy) New Teen Titans #1, 11/80; (X-Men) X-Men #35, 8/67

Charlie Chan - Feature Comics #23, 8/39

Charlie-27 - Marvel Super Heroes #18, 1/69

Checkmate - Action Comics #598, 3/88

Chemical King - (Legion) Adventure Comics #371, 8/68

Chlorophyll Kid - (Legion) Adventure Comics #306, 2/63

Chop Chop - (Blackhawk's sidekick) Military Comics #3, 10/41

Chuck - (Black Fury's aide) Fantastic Comics #18, 5/41

Cisco Kid - Cisco Kid Comics #1, Win '44

Claw the Unconquered - Claw the Unconquered #1, 5-6/75

Clea - Strange Tales #126, 11/64

Cletus Kasady - (1st full app.) Amazing Spider-Man #345, 3/91; (cameo; becomes Carnage) Amazing Spider-Man #344, 2/91

Clip Carson - Action Comics #14, 7/39

Cloak - (Spy Master) Big Shot Comics #1, 5/40

Cloak & Dagger - Spec. Spider-Man #64, 3/82

Clock - Crack Comics #1, 5/40

Clock - Funny Pages V1#6, 11/36

Clown - Super-Mystery Comics V1#5, 12/40

Clown - Spitfire Comics #1, 8/41

Cobra Kid - (Black Cobra's sidekick) Captain Flight Comics #8, ?'46

Colossal Boy - (Legion) Action Comics #267, 8/60

Colossus - Tales of Suspense #14, 2/61; Giant-Size X-Men #1, Sum '75

Combat Kelly - Combat Kelly #1, 11/51; (new) Combat Kelly #1, 6/72

Comet - Pep Comics #1, 1/40; (re-intro) Comet #1, 10/83; (S.A.) Advent. of the Fly #30, 10/64

Commando Yank - Wow Comics #6, 7/15/42

Commissioner Gordon - Detective Comics #27, 5/39

Conan, the Barbarian - (1st in comics) Conan, the Barbarian #1, 10/70

Concrete - Dark Horse Presents #1, 7/86

Congo Bill - More Fun Comics #56, 6/40

Congorilla - Action Comics #248, 1/59

Conqueror, The - Victory Comics #1, 8/41

Cookie - Topsy-Turvy #1, 4/45

Corporal Collins - Blue Ribbon Comics #2, 12/39

Cosmic Boy - (Legion) Adventure Comics #247, 4/58

Cosmo Cat - All Top Comics #1, 1945

Cosmo Mann - Bang-Up Comics #1, 12/41

Cosmo, the Phantom of Disguise - Detective Comics #1, 3/37

Cotton Carver - Adventure Comics #50, 5/40

Cougar - The Cougar #1, 4/75

Creeper - Showcase #73, 3-4/67

Crimebuster - Boy Comics #3, 4/42

Crimson Avenger - Detective Comics #20, 10/38

Crusader - Aquaman #56, 3-4/71; (formerly old Marvel Boy) Fantastic Four #164, 11/75

Crypt Keeper - Crime Patrol #15, 12-1/49-50

Crystal - Fantastic Four #45, 12/65

Cyborg - (New Teen Titans) DC Comics Presents #26, 10/80

Cyclone - Whirlwind Comics #1, 6/40

Cyclops - X-Men #1, 9/63

Cyclotronic Man - Black Lightning #4, 7/77

D-Man - Captain America #328, 4/86

Daffy Duck - Looney Tunes & Merrie Melodies #1, 1941

Daimon Hellstrom - (1st full app.) Ghost Rider #2, 10/73; (cameo) (Son of Satan) Ghost Rider #1, 9/73

Daisy Duck - (back cover only) Large Feature Comic #16, 6/41

Dale Daring - Adventure Comics #32, 11/38

Dan Hastings - Star Comics #1, 2/37

Danny Chase - New Teen Titans Annual #3, 1987

Daredevil - Silver Streak Comics #6, 9/40 (blue & yellow costume)

Daredevil - Daredevil #1, 4/64

Darkhawk - Darkhawk #1, 3/91

Darklon the Mystic - Eerie #79, 11/76

Dart & sidekick Ace - Weird Comics #5, 8/40

David - (Samson's aide) Fantastic Comics #10, 9/40

Dawnstar - (Legion) Superboy #226, 4/77

Dazzler - X-Men #130, 2/80

Deadman - Strange Adventures #205, 10/67

Deadpool - New Mutants #98, 2/91

Death - Sandman #8, 1990

Death's Head - (new) (1 pg. strip on back-c) Dragon's Claws #3, 9/88; (new) (1st full app.) Dragon's Claws #5, 11?/88

Deathlok the Demolisher - Astonishing Tales #25, 8/74

Deathstroke the Terminator - New Teen Titans #2, 12/80; (1st solo story) New Titans #70, 10/90

Demon - Demon #1, 8-9/72

Dennis the Menace - Dennis the Menace #1, 8/53

Deputy Dawg - New Terrytoons #1, 6-8/60

Destroyer, The - USA Comics #6, 12/42

Destroyer - Invaders #16, 5/77; Mystic Comics #6, 10/41

Destroyer Duck - Destroyer Duck #1, 1982

Destructor - The Destructor #1, 2/75

Devil-Slayer - Marvel Spotlight #33, 4/77

Dial "H" for Hero - (Robby Reed) House of Mystery #156, 11-12/65

Dick Cole - Blue Bolt #1, 6/40

Dick Tracy - (1st comic book app.) Popular Comics #1, 2/36

Dixie Dugan - Feature Funnies #1, 10/37

Doc Samson - Incredible Hulk #141, 7/71

Doc Savage - (1st in comics) Shadow Comics #1, 3/40; (pulp-1st app.) 3/33

Doc Strong - Blue Ribbon Comics #4, 6/40

Doctor Fate - (female) Doctor Fate #25, 2/91

Doctor Midnight - (new) Infinity, Inc. #21, 12/85

Doctor Solar - Doctor Solar #1, 10/62; (1st in costume) Doctor Solar #5, ?'63

Doctor Strange - Strange Tales #110, 7/63

Dodo & the Frog - Funny Stuff #18, 2/47

Doiby Dickles - (Green Lantern's side-kick) All-American Comics #27, 6/41

Doll Man - Feature Comics #27, 12/39

Dolphin - (of Forgotten Heroes) Showcase #79, 12/68

Dominic Fortune - Marvel Preview #2, 1975; (1st color app.) Marvel Premiere #56, 10/80; (new) Iron Man #213, 12/86

Domino - New Mutants #98, 2/91

Donald Duck - The Wise Little Hen, 1934

Don Winslow - Popular Comics #1, 2/36

Doodles Duck - Dodo & the Frog #80, 9-10/54

Dotty & Ditto - Top-Notch Comics #33, 2/43

Dr. Fate - More Fun Comics #55, 5/40; (Silver Age) Justice League of America #21

Dr. Hypno - Amazing-Man Comics #14, 7/40

Dr. Mid-Nite - (1st story app.) All-American Comics #25, 4/41; (text only) All-American Comics #24, 3/41

Dr. Mystic - (Superman prototype) Comics Magazine #1, 5/36

Dr. Neff, Ghost Breaker - Red Dragon Comics #3, 5/48

Dr. Occult - New Fun Comics #6, 10/35; (1st in color & 1st DC app.) More Fun Comics #14, 10/36

Dr. Specktor - Mystery Comics Digest #5, 7/72

Dr. Strange - Thrilling Comics #1, 2/40

Dr. Strange - Strange Tales #110, 7/63

Dr. Who - Marvel Premiere #57, 12/80

Dracula - Tomb of Dracula #1, 4/72; Dracula #2, 11/66

Dragon - (1st full app.) Megaton #3, 2/86; (cameo)(later Savage Dragon) Megaton #2, 10/85

Drax the Destroyer - Iron Man #55, 2/73

Dreadstar - Epic Illustrated #15, 12/82

Dream Girl - (Legion) Adventure Comics #317, 2/64

Duo Damsel - (Legion)(formerly Triplicate Girl) Adventure Comics #341, 2/66

Duplicate Boy - Adventure Comics #324

Dusty - (Shield's sidekick) Pep Comics #11, 1/41

Dynamic Man - Mystic Comics #1, 3/40

Dynamite Thor - Blue Beetle #6, 3-4/41

Dynamo - Thunder Agents #1, 11/65; (Electro #1 only) Science Comics #1, 2/40

Dynamo, The Eagle - Weird Comics #8, 11/40

Eagle - Science Comics #1, 2/40

Ebony - Police Comics #12, 10/42

Echo, The - All-New Comics #1, 1/43

Eclipso - House of Secrets #61, 7-8/63

Eddie Brock - (becomes Venom) Amazing Spider-Man #298, 3/88

Egbert - Egbert #1, Spr '46

El Diablo - All Star Western #2, 10-11/70

Elasti-Girl - My Greatest Adventure #80, 6/63

Elastic Lad - (Jimmy Olsen) Superman's Pal Jimmy Olsen #31, ?/62

Electro, the Marvel of the Age - Marvel Mystery Comics #4, 2/40

Elektra - Daredevil #168, ? /81?

Element Girl - Metamorpho #10, 1-2/67

Element Lad - (Legion) Adventure Comics #307, 4/63
Elfquest - Fantasty Quarterly #1, Spr '78
Ella Cinders - Famous Comics Cartoon Books #1203, 1934; Tip Top Comics #1, 4/36
Ellery Queen - (1st app. in comics) Crackajack Funnies #23, 5/40
Elmer Fudd - Looney Tunes & Merrie Melodies #1, 1941
Elongated Man - Flash #112, 4-5/60
E-Man - E-Man #1, 10/73
Enchantress - Journey Into Mystery #103, 4/64
Enemy Ace - Our Army at War #151, 2/65
Erg -1 (becomes Wildfire) Superboy #195,6/73
Eternal Warrior - (cameo) Solar #10, 6/92; (full app.) Solar #11, 7/92
Evangeline - Primer #6, 2/84
Everyman - Captain America #267, 3/82
Face - (Tony Trent) Big Shot Comics #1, 5/40
Faceless Creature - Strange Adv. #124, 1/61
Falcon - Pep Comics #1, 1/40
Falcon - Captain America #117, 9/69; Daring Mystery Comics #5, 6/40
Fantomah, Mystery Woman - Jungle Comics #1, 1/40
Fatman - Fatman the Human Flying Saucer #1, 4/67
Fearless Flint, the Flint Man - Famous Funnies #89, 12/42
Feral - (of X-Force) New Mutants #99, 3/91
Ferret - Man of War #2, 1/42
Ferret, Mystery Detective - Marvel Mystery Comics #4, 2/40
Ferris - (becomes Star Sapphire) Showcase #22, 9-10/59
Ferro Lad - (Legion) Adventure Comics #346, 7/66
Fiery Mask - Daring Mystery Comics #1, 1/40
Fighting American - Fighting American #1, 4-5/54
Fighting Yank - Startling Comics #10, 9/41
Fin - Daring Mystery Comics #7, 4/41
Fin Fang Foom - Strange Tales #89, 10/61
Fire - Super Friends #25
Fireball - Pep Comics #12, 2/41; (S.A.) Mighty Crusaders #4, 5?/66
Firebrand - Police Comics #1, 8/41
Firefist - Blue Beetle #1, 6/86
Firefly - Top-Notch Comics #8, 9/40
Firehair - Rangers Comics #21, 2/45
Firehawk - Fury of Firestorm #17, 10/83
Fire Lad - Adventure Comics #306, 2/63
Firelord - Thor #225, 7/74
FireStar - X-Men #193, 4/85
Firestorm - Firestorm, the Nuclear Man #1, 3/78; (new) Firestorm, the Nuclear Man Annual #5, 10/87
Flag, The - Our Flag Comics #2, 10/41
Flame, The - Wonderworld Comics #3, 7/39
Flamebird - (Jimmy Olsen as) Superman #158, 12/62; (new) Secret Origins Annual #3, 1989
Flaming Carrot - Visions #1, 1979
Flash (Jay Garrick)- Flash Comics #1, 1/40; (1st app. in S.A.) Flash #123, 9/61
Flash (Barry Allen)- Showcase #4, 9-10/56
Flash (Wally West) (former Kid Flash) Flash #110, 12-1/59-60; (as Flash) Crisis on Infinite Earths #12, 3/86
Flash Gordon - King Comics #1, 4/36
Flash Lightning - (becomes Lash Lightning) Sure-Fire Comics #1, 6/40
Flash Rabbit - All Top Comics #1, 1945
Flexo the Rubber Man - Mystic Comics #1, 3/40
Flintstones - Dell Giant #48, 7/61
Fly - Double Life of Private Strong #1, 6/59
Fly Girl - (1st in costume) Adventures of the Fly #14, 9?/61; (w/o costume) Adventures of the Fly #13, 7?/61
Fly-Man, The - Spitfire Comics #1, 8/41
Forbush Man - Not Brand Echh #5, 12/67
Forge - (X-Force) X-Men #184, 8/84
Fox - Blue Ribbon Comics #4, 6/40; (new) Black Hood #11, 11/92
Frankenstein - Prize Comics #7, 12/40; Frankenstein #2, 9/66
Frankenstein's monster - (cameo) Silver Surfer #7, 8/69
Freckles & His Friends - Famous Comics Cartoon Books #1204, 1934
Fred Bender - (becomes Dr. Eclipse) Solar #14, 10/92
Freezum - Blue Bolt V2#5, 10/41
Fritzi Ritz - Tip Top Comics #1, 4/36
Fu Manchu - (1st in Detective) Detective Comics #17, 7/38; (1st cvr.) Det. #1, 3/37
G. I. Robot - Weird War Tales #101, 7/81
Gambit - (cameo) X-Men Annual #14, 1990; (full app.) X-Men #266, 8/90
Gandy Goose - Terry-Toons Comics #1, 10/42
Gangbuster - Adventures of Superman #434, 11/87
Gargoyle - Defenders #94, 4/80
Gary Concord - (Ultra Man) All-American Comics #8, 11/39
Gay Ghost - Sensation Comics #1, 1/42
Genius Jones - All Funny Comics #1, Win '43-44
Gentleman Ghost - Atom & Hawkman #43, 6-7/69
Ghost Breaker - Star Spangled Comics #122, 11/51
Ghost Patrol - Flash Comics #29, 5/42
Ghost Patrol - Wings #66, 2/46
Ghost Rider - (formerly Calico Kid) Tim Holt #11, ?/49
Ghost Rider - (western) Ghost Rider #1, 2/67; (Johnny Blaze) Marvel Spotlight #5, 8/72; (new-Daniel Ketch) Ghost Rider V2#1, 5/90
Giant-Man - (formerly Ant-Man) Tales to Astonish #49, 11/63
Gideon - New Mutants #98, 2/91
Gladstone Gander - Walt Disney's Comics and Stories #88, 1/48
Glory Grant - Amazing Spider-Man #140, 1/75
Gnort - Justice League International #10
God Of Thunder, The - Weird Comics #1, 4/40
Godiva - New Teen Titans Annual #3, 11/87
Golden Arrow - Whiz Comics #1, 2/40
Golden Dragon - Adventure Comics #32, 11/38
Golden Girl - Golden Lad #5, 6/46
Golden Gladiator - Brave and the Bold #1, 8-9/55
Golden Gorilla - Action Comics #224, 1/57
Golden Lad - Golden Lad #1, 7/45
Golem - Strange Tales #174, 2/74
Goliath - (formerly Giant-Man) Avengers #28, 5/66 (formerly Hawkeye) Avengers #63, 4/69
Grandma Duck - Donald and Mickey Merry Christmas nn, 1945
Great Gazoo - (Flintstones) Flintstones #34
Green Arrow - More Fun Comics #73, 11/41
Green Falcon - Blue Ribbon Comics #4, 6/40
Green Flame - Super Friends #42, 3/81
Green Fury - (formerly Green Flame) Infinity, Inc. #32, 11/86
Green Hornet - (1st in comics) Green Hornet Comics #1, 12/40; (Silver Age) Green Hornet #1, 2/67
Green Lama - Prize Comics #7, 12/40
Green Lantern (Alan Scott)- (G.A) All-American Comics #16, 7/40
Green Lantern (Hal Jordan)- (S.A.) Showcase #22, 9-10/59
Green Lantern (Kyle Rayner)- (Mod.) Green Lantern #50 (3rd series), 3/94
Green Mask - Mystery Men Comics #1, 8/39
Green Turtle - Blazing Comics #1, 6/44
Grendel - Primer #2, 2/83
Grey Mask - Suspense Comics #1, 12/43
Grimjack - Starslayer #10, 11/83
Grim Reaper, The - Wonder Comics #1, 5/44
Groo the Wanderer - Destroyer Duck #1, 1982
Gruesomes - (Flintstones) Flintstones #24
Guardian - Star Spangled Comics #7, 4/42; (formerly Vindicator) Alpha Flight #2, 9/83
Guardian Angel - (formerly Hop Harrigan) All-American Comics #25, 4/41
Guardsman I - Iron Man #43, 11?/71?
Guardsman II - Iron Man #96, 3/77
Gunner & Sarge - All-American Men of War #57, ? '58?; Our Fighting Forces #45, 5/59
Guy Gardner - (later a Green Lantern)Green Lantern #59, 3/68; (1st app. as a Green Lantern) Green Lantern #116, 5/79
Gwen Stacy - Amazing Spider-Man #31, 12/65
Gyro Gearloose - Walt Disney's Comics and Stories #140, 5/52
Halo - Blue Beetle #24, 8/43
Hangman - Pep Comics #17, 7/41
Hangman - (re-intro) Comet #6, 12/91; (S.A.) Fly Man #33, 9/65
Happy Houlihans - Blackstone, the Magician Detective #1, Fall '47
Harada - Solar #3, 11/91
Harbinger - Harbinger #1, 1/92
Harlequin - (Joker's Daughter) Teen Titans #48, '77
Harry Osborn - (later becomes Green Goblin II) Amazing Spider-Man #31, 12/65
Harvey Bullock - Batman #361, 7/83
Havok - (no costume) X-Men #56, 5/69; (with costume) X-Men #58, 7/69
Hawk & Dove - Showcase #75, 7-8/67
Hawkeye - Tales of Suspense #57, 9/64; (formerly Goliath) Avengers #98, 4/72
Hawkgirl - (formerly Shiera Sanders) All Star Comics #5, 6-7/41; (Silver Age) Brave & the Bold #34, 2-3/61
Hawkman - Flash Comics #1, 1/40; (S.A.) Brave and the Bold #34, 2-3/61; (modern) Hawkworld: Book #1, 1989
Heap - Air Fighters Comics V1#3, 12/42
Heckle & Jeckle - Terry-Toons Comics #50, 11/46
Hedy Devine - Hedy Devine Comics #22, 8/47
Hedy Wolfe - Miss America Magazine #2, 11/44
Heimdall - Journey Into Mystery #85, 10/62
Hellblazer - (John Constantine) Saga of Swamp Thing #37, 6/85
Hellboy - John Byrne's Next Men #21
Hellcat - Avengers #144, 2/76
Her - (formerly Paragon) Marvel Two-In-One #61, 3/80
Herbie - Forbidden Worlds #73, '59?
Hercules - Blue Ribbon Comics #4, 6/40; Incredible Hulk #3, 9/62; Hit Comics #1 7/40; Mystic Comics #3, 6/40
Herman & Catnip - Harvey Comics Hits #60, 9/52
High Evolutionary - Thor #134, 11/66
Him - (Warlock) (cameo) Fantastic Four #67, 10/67 (Warlock) (full app.) Thor #165, 6/69
Hocus & Pocus - Action Comics #83, 4/45
Hooded Horseman - Blazing West #14, 11-12/50
Hooded Wasp - Shadow Comics #7, 11/40
Hop Harrigan - All-American Comics #1, 4/39
Hoppy the Marvel Bunny - Fawcett's Funny Animals #1, 12/42
Hourman - Adventure Comics #48, 3/40; (1st app. in S.A.) Justice League of America #21, 8/63
Hourman -(new) Infinity, Inc. #21, 12/85
Hourman - (future) JLA #12, 11/97
Howard the Duck - Fear #19, 12/73
Huey, Dewey and Louie - Donald Duck nn (bubble pipe cover)
Hulk - (green skin) Incredible Hulk #2, 7/62; (grey skin) Incredible Hulk #1, 5/62; (new) Incredible Hulk #377, 1/91; (re-intro with grey skin) Incredible Hulk #324, 10/86
Hulk 2099 - 2099 Unlimited #1, 9/93
Human Target - Action Comics #419, 1/73
Human Top - Red Raven Comics #1, 8/40; Tough Kid Squad #1, 3/42
Human Torch - Marvel Comics #1, 10-11/39; (Johnny Storm) Fantastic Four #1, 11/61; (re-intro G.A.) Avengers West Coast #50, 9?/89
Humphrey - Joe Palooka #15, 12/47
Hunchback, The - Wow Comics #2, Spr, 1941
Huntress - (G.A.) Sensation Comics #68, 8/47; (1st S.A. app. of G.A. Huntress) Brave and the Bold #62, 10-11/65; (modern) All Star Comics #69, 11-12/77
Hurricane - Captain America Comics #1, 3/41
Hydroman - Heroic Comics #1, 8/40
Hyper, the Phenomenal - Hyper Mystery Comics #1, 5/40
Ibis the Invincible - Whiz Comics #1, 2/40
Ice - Super Friends #9
Ice Cream Soldier - Our Army at War #85, 8/59
Iceman - X-Men #1, 9/63
Imp - Captain America Comics #12, 3/42
Impossible Man - Fantastic Four #11, 2/63; (re-intro) Fantastic Four #176, 11/76
Impossible Woman - Marvel Two-In-One #60, 2/80
Impulse - Flash #92 (2nd series), 7/94

Inferno - (S.A.) Mighty Crusaders #4, 5?/66
Inferno, the Flame Breather - Zip Comics #10, 1/41
Insect Queen - (Lana Lang) (Legion) Superboy #124, 10/65
Invisible Girl - (Sue Storm) Fantastic Four #1, 11/61
Invisible Kid - (Legion) Action Comics #267, 8/60 (new) Legion of Super-Heroes Annual #1, 1982
Invisible Scarlett O'Neil - Famous Funnies #81, 4/42
Iron Fist - Marvel Premiere #15, 5/74; (re-intro, cameo) Namor, the Sub-Mariner #8, 11/90; (re-intro, full app.) Namor, the Sub-Mariner #10, 1/91
Iron Major - Our Army at War #158, 9/65
Iron Man - (Tony Starks) Tales of Suspense #39, 3/63; (new armor) Tales of Suspense #40, 4/63; (new) (Jim Rhodes) Iron Man #231, 6/88
Iron Wolf - Weird Worlds #8, 11-12/73
Isis - Shazam! #25, ?'76
Jack Monroe - (1st full app.) Captain America #154, 10/72; (cameo) Captain America #153, 9/72
Jack of Hearts - Deadly Hands of Kung-Fu #22, 4?/76; (1st solo book) Marvel Premiere #44, 10/78
Jack Q. Frost - Unearthly Spectaculars #1, 10/65
Jack Woods - Adventure Comics #39, 1/39
Jaguar - Adventures of the Jaguar #1, 9/61
Jarella (Hulk's love) - The Incredible Hulk #140, 6/71
Jason Bard - (becomes Robin) Detective Comics #392, 10/69
Jason Todd - Batman #357, 3/83; (1st in Robin costume) Batman #366, 12/83
Jean DeWolf - Marvel Team Up #48, 8/76
Jester - Smash Comics #22, 5/41
Jigsaw - Jigsaw #1, 9/66
Jiminy Cricket - Mickey Mouse Magazine V5#3, 12/39
Jimmy "Minuteman" Martin - Adventure Comics #53, 8/40
Jimmy Martin as Hourman's aide - Adventure Comics #71, 2/42
Jimmy Olsen - Action Comics #6, 11/38; (new) Man of Steel #2, 10/86
Jo-Jo, Congo King - Jo-Jo Comics #7, 7/47
Joe Palooka - Joe Palooka nn, 1933; (1st in comic book format) Feature Funnies #1, 10/37
Joe Robertson - Amazing Spider-Man #52, 9/67
John Carter of Mars - Funnies #30, 4/39
John Carter, Warlord of Mars - Weird Worlds #1, 8-9/72
John Connor - Terminator #12, ?/89
John Constantine - (Hellblazer) Saga of Swamp Thing #37, 6/85
John Force - (Magic Agent) Magic Agent #1, 1-2/62
John Jameson - Amazing Spider-Man #1, 3/63
John Law - Smash Comics #3, 10/39
John Stewart - (later a Green Lantern) Green Lantern #87, 12-1/71-72
Johnny Blaze - (re-intro) Ghost Rider V2#10, 2/91; (Ghost Rider) Marvel Spotlight #5, 8/72
Johnny Cloud - All-American Men of War #82
Johnny Dynamite - Dynamite #3, 9/53
Johnny Peril - Comic Cavalcade #15, 6-7/46
Johnny Quick - More Fun Comics #71, 9/41
Johnny Thunder - All-American Comics #100, 8/48; Flash Comics #1, 1/40; (1st S.A. app.) Flash #137, ?/63
Jon Linton - Amazing Mystery Funnies V2#11, 11/39
Jonah Hex - All Star Western #10, 2-3/72
J'onn J'onzz (See Martian Manhunter)
Jonni Thunder - (Thunderbolt) Jonni Thunder #1, 2/85
Jonny Double - Showcase #78, 11/68
Jordan Brothers - Green Lantern #9, 11-12/61
Jose Delgado - (becomes Gangbuster) Adventures of Superman #432, 9/87
Jubilee - X-Men #244, 2?/89
Judomaster - Special War Series V4#4, 11/65; (1st DC app.) Crisis on Infinite Earths #6, 9/85
Jughead Jones - Pep Comics #22, 12/41
Julie Madison - Detective Comics #31, 9/39
Jungle Jim - Ace Comics #1, 4/37
Junior Woodchucks - Walt Disney's Comics and Stories #125, 2/51
Kaanga, Lord of the Jungle - Jungle Comics #1, 1/40
Kamandi - Kamandi, the Last Boy on Earth #1, 10-11/72
Karate Kid - (Legion) Adventure Comics #346, 7/66
Karma - (New Mutants) Marvel Team-Up #100, 12/80
Katy Keene - Wilbur Comics #5, Sum '45
Kazar the Great - Marvel Comics #1, 10-11/39; (Silver Age) X-Men #10, 6/64
Ken Shannon - Police Comics #103, 12/50
Kid Eternity - Hit Comics #25, 12/42
Kid Flash - (later becomes Flash) Flash #110, 12-1/59-60
Killer Frost - Firestorm, the Nuclear Man #3, 6-7/78
King Kull - Creatures on the Loose #10, 3/71
Kit - (Black Cat's sidekick) Black Cat Comics #28, 4/51
Kitty Pryde - (Ariel) (X-Men) X-Men #129, 1/80
Kobra - Kobra #1, 2-3/76
Kole - (New Teen Titan) New Teen Titans #8, 5?/85
Kong the Untamed - Kong the Untamed #1, 6-7/75
Kraven - (War of the Worlds) Amazing Adventures #18, 5/73
Krazy Kat - Ace Comics #1, 4/37
Krypto - Adventure Comics #210, 3/55
Kryptonite (Blue) - Superman #128, 4/59
Kryptonite (Gold) - Superman #140, 4/60
Kryptonite (Red) - Adventure #299, 8/62
Kryptonite Kid - Superboy #83, ?/60
Lady Blackhawk - Blackhawk #133, 2/58
Lady Luck - Spirit nn, 6/2/40
Lana Lang - (becomes Insect Queen) Superboy #10, 9-10/50
Lance Hale - Silver Streak Comics #3, 3/40
Lance O'Casey - Whiz Comics #1, 2/40
Lancer - Super-Mystery Comics V3#3, 1/43
Lash Lightning - (formerly Flash Lightning) Lightning Comics V2#2, 8/41
Lassie - Adventures of Lassie nn, ?/49
Lemonade Kid - Bobby Benson's B-Bar-B Riders #15, 6/50
Leopard Girl - Jungle Action #1, 10/54
Li'l Abner - Tip Top Comics #1, 4/36
Li'l Jinx - Pep Comics #62, 7/47
Liberator - Exciting Comics #15, 12/41
Liberty Belle - Star Spangled #20, 5/43
Light Lass - (formerly Lightning Lass) Adventure Comics #317, 2/64
Lightning - Thunder Agents #4, 4/66
Lightning - (cover only) Jumbo Comics #14, 4/40; (1st story app.) Jumbo Comics #15, 5/40
Lightning Boy - (Legion) Adventure Comics #247, 4/58
Lightning Girl - Lightning Comics V3#1, 6/42
Lightning Lad - (formerly Lightning Boy) Adventure Comics #267, 12/59
Lightning Lass - (Legion) Adventure Comics #308, 5/63
Lilith - Vampire Tales #6, ?/74; (Dracula's daughter) Giant-Size Chillers #1, 6/74; (re-intro) New Teen Titans #2, 9/84; (Teen Titans) Teen Titans #25, 1-2/70
Little Audrey - LIttle Audrey #1, 4/48
Little Dot - Sad Sack Comics #1, 9/49
Little Dynamite - Boy Comics #6, 10/42
Little Lotta - LIttle Dot #1, 9/53
Little Lulu - Marge's Little Lulu 4-Color #74, 6/45; (as text illo) King Comics #46, 2/40
Little Max - Joe Palooka #27, 12/48
Little Orphan Annie - Popular Comics #1, 2/36
Little Wise Guys - Daredevil Comics #13, 10/42
LIving Mummy - Supernatural Thrillers #5, 8/73
Liz Allen - Amazing Spider-Man #4, 9/63
Lobo - (1st full story) Omega Men #10, 1/84; (1st solo story, back-up) Omega Men #37, 4/86; (cameo) Omega Men #3, 6/83
Lockheed - X-Men #166, 2/83
Lois Lane - Action Comics #1, 6/38; (new) Man of Steel #2, 10/86
Lois Lane as Superwoman - Action Comics #60, 5/43
Lone Warrior - Banner Comics #3, 9/41
Longshot - Longshot #1, 9/85
Lori Lemaris the Mermaid - Superman #129, 5/59
Lt. Marvels - Whiz Comics #21, 9/41
Lucy Lane - Superman's Pal Jimmy Olsen #36, ?/62
Luke Cage - (Hero for Hire) Hero For Hire #1, 6/72
Lynx & sidekick Blackie - Mystery Men Comics #13, 8/40
Mad Hatter - Mad Hatter #1, 1-2/46
Madame Satan - Pep Comics #16, 6/41
Madame Web - Amazing Spider-Man #210, 11/80
Madelyne Pryor - (of X-Men) Avengers Annual #10, 1981
Madrox - Giant-Size Fantastic Four #4, 2/75
Mage - (re-intro) Grendel #16, 1/88
Magic Morro - Super Comics #21, 2/40
Magician from Mars - Amazing-Man Comics #7, 11/39
Magicman - Forbidden Worlds #125
Magma - New Mutants #10, 12/83
Magno the Magnetic Man & Davey - Super-Mystery Comics V1#1, 7/40
Magnus, Robot Fighter - Magnus, Robot Fighter #1, 2/63
Major Mynah - Atom #37, 6-7/68
Man Bat - Detective #400, 6/70
Man in Black - Front Page Comic Book #1, 1945
Man of War - Man of War #1, 11/41
Manowar - Target Comics #1, 2/40
Man-Thing - Savage Tales #1, 5/71; (1st full story) Fear #15, 8/73
Mandrake the Magician - King Comics #1, 4/36
Manhunter - Police Comics #8, 3/42; (1st in new costume) Detective Comics #437, 10-11/73; (Paul Kirk) Adventure Comics #58, 1/41; (new) Adventure Comics #73, 4/42
Mantis - Avengers #112, 6/73
Margie - Comedy Comics #34, Fall '46
Mark Merlin - House of Secrets #23, 8/59
Marshal Law - Marshal Law #1, 10/87
Martan, the Marvel Man - Popular Comics #46, 12/39
Martian Manhunter - (J'onn J'onzz) Detective Comics #225, 11/55; (re-intro) Justice League of America #228, 7/84
Marvel Boy - (1st & only app.) Daring Mystery Comics #6, 9/40
Marvel Girl - (becomes Phoenix) X-Men #1, 9/63
Marvel Man - (later Quasar) Captain America #217, 1/78
Mary Jane & Sniffles - Looney Tunes & Merrie Melodies #1, 1941
Mary Jane Watson - (1st mention) Amazing Spider-Man #15, 8/64; (cameo, face not shown) Amazing Spider-Man #25, 6/65; (cameo, face shown) Amazing Spider-Man #42, 11/66; (cameo, not shown) Amazing Spider-Man #38, 7/66; (re-intro) Amazing Spider-Man #243, 8/83
Mary Marvel - Captain Marvel Adventures #18, 12/42
Mask, The - Exciting Comics #1, 4/40
Mask, The - Suspense Comics #2, 1944
Masked Marvel - Keen Detective Funnies V2#7, 7/39
Masked Raider - Marvel Comics #1, 10-11/39
Master Key - Scoop Comics #1, 11/41
Master Man - Master Comics #1, 3/40
Master of Kung-Fu - (Shang-Chi) Special Marvel Edition #15, 12/73
Matter-Eater Lad - (Legion) Adventure Comics #303, 12/62
Maximillian O'Leary - (Sargon's aide) All-American Comics #70, 1-2/46
Maya - Atom #1, 6-7/62
Megaton - Megaton #1, 11/83
Menthor - Thunder Agents #1, 11/65
Mento - (non-member) Doom Patrol #91, 11/64
Mentor - Iron Man #55, 2/73
Mera - Aquaman #11, 9-10/63
Merboy - Wonder Woman #107
Mercury - (Silver Streak's sidekick) Silver Streak Comics #11, 6/41
Mercury Man - Space Adventures #44, ?/61?
Metal Men - Showcase #37, 3-4/62
Metallo - (Jor-El's robot) Superboy #49, 6/56
Metamorpho - Brave and the Bold #57, 12-1/64-65
Mickey Finn - (1st comic book app.) Feature Funnies #1, 10/37
Mickey Mouse - Mickey Mouse Book

nn, '30
Midnight - Smash Comics #18, 1/41
Mighty Girl - Adventure Comics #453, 9-10/77
Mighty Mouse - Terry-Toons Comics #38, 11/45
Mighty Samson - Mighty Samson #1, 7/64
Millie the Model - Gay Comics #1, 3/44
Milton Berle - Uncle Milty #1, 12/50
Minnie Mouse - Mickey Mouse Book nn, 1930
Minute Man - Master Comics #11, 2/41
Minuteman - (re-intro) Shazam! #31, 9-10/77
Miss Arrowette - World's Finest #113, 4/60
Miss America - (modern) Giant-Size Avengers #1, 8/74
Miss Masque - Exciting Comics #51, 9/46; America's Best Comics #23, 9/47
Miss Patriot - Marvel Mystery Comics #50, 12/43
Miss Victory - Captain Fearless Comics #1, 8/41
Mister Miracle - Mister Miracle #1, 3-4/71
Mister X - (on cover only) Vortex #2
Moby Duck - Donald Duck #112
Mockingbird - Marvel Team-Up #95, 7/80
Modred the Mystic - Marvel Chillers #1, 10/75
Molly O'Day - Molly O'Day #1, 2/45
Mon-El - (Legion) Superboy #89, 6/61
Monarch Starstalker - Marvel Premiere #32, 10/76
Moon Girl - Happy Houlihans #1, Fall '47; Moon Girl and the Prince #1, Fall '47
Moon Knight - Werewolf by Night #32, 8/75; (1st solo book) Marvel Spotlight #28, 6/76
Moondragon - Iron Man #54, 1/73; (re-intro) Warlock and the Infinity Watch #2, 3/92
Morbius - Amaz. Spider-Man #101, 10/71
Morgan Edge - (cameo) Superman's Pal Jimmy Olsen #133, 10/70
Morlock 2001 - Morlock 2001 #1, 2/75
Morty and Ferdie - (Mickey Mouse's nephews) Mickey Mouse #3, 1933
Moth Man - Mystery Men Comics #9, 4/40
Mr. America - (formerly Tex Thompson) Action Comics #33, 2/41
Mr. Fantastic - (Reed Richards) Fantastic Four #1, 11/61
Mr. Justice - Blue Ribbon Comics #9, 2/41
Mr. Miracle - Captain Fearless Comics #1, 8/41
Mr. Monster - Super Duper Comics #3, 5-6/47; (new) Vanguard Illustrated #7, 5/84
Mr. Mystic - Spirit nn, 6/2/40
Mr. Satan - Zip Comics #1, 2/40
Mr. Scarlet - Wow Comics #1, Win '40-41
Mr. Tawny - Captain Marvel #79, 12/47; (Silver Age) Shazam! #2, 4/73
Mr. Terrific - Sensation Comics #1, 1/42; (1st app. in S.A.) Justice League of America #37, 8?/65
Ms. Marvel - (becomes Binary) Ms. Marvel #1, 1/77
Ms. Victory - Femforce Special #1, Fall '84; (new) Femforce #25
Mutt & Jeff - (1st in comic book for mat) Funnies #1, 10/36
Mutt & Jeff - Mutt & Jeff #1, 1910
Mystery Men of Mars - All-American Comics #1, 4/39
Nam - Savage Tales #1, 11/85
Namora - Marvel Mystery Comics #82, 5/47
Ned Leeds - (later becomes Hobgoblin) Amazing Spider-Man #18, 11/64
Negative Man - My Greatest Adventure #80, 6/63
Neil the Horse - Charlton Bullseye #2, 8?/81
Nemesis - Adventures into the Unknown #154, ?/66?
Nemesis Kid - (Legion) Adventure Comics #346, 7/66
Neon the Unknown - Hit Comics #1, 7/40
Neuman, Alfred E. - (cover only, fake ad) Mad #21, 3/55
Nevada Jones - Zip Comics #1, 2/40
New Gods - New Gods #1, 2-3/71
Nick Fury - (formerly Sgt. Fury) Strange Tales #135, 8/65
Night Hawk - All-New Comics #1, 1/43
Nightcrawler - Giant-Size X-Men #1, Sum '75
Nightgirl - Adventure Comics #306, 11/63
Nighthawk - Avengers #71, 12/69
Nightmare - (Casper's horse) Casper, the Friendly Ghost #19, 4/54
Nightmaster - Showcase #82, 5/69
Nightshade - Amazing-Man Comics #24, 10/41; Captain Atom #82, 9/66; (1st DC app.) Crisis on Infinite Earths #6, 9/85
Night Thrasher - Thor #412
Nightwing - (Dick Grayson) Tales of the Teen Titans #44, 7/84; (Superman as) Superman #158, 12/62; (Van-Zee) Superman Family #183, 5-6/77
Nita - (later Namorita in New Warriors) Sub-Mariner #50
Nomad - (formerly Steve Rogers) Captain America #180, 12/74
Noman - Thunder Agents #1, 11/65
Norman Osborn - (Green Goblin I) Amazing Spider-Man #37, 6/66
Nova - E-Man #8, 1975
Nth Man - Marvel Comics Presents #25, ?/89
Nukla - Nukla #1, 10-12/65
Nutsy Squirrel - Funny Folks #1, 4-5/46
Nyoka, the Jungle Girl - Jungle Girl #1, Fall/42 (movie serial adaption)
Ocean Master - Aquaman #25, 1-2/66
Odin - (1st full app.) Journey Into Myst. #86, 11/62; (cameo) Journey Into Mystery #85, 10/62
Omac - Omac #1, 9-10/74
Omega - Omega the Unknown #1, 3/76
Oracle, The - Startling Comics #20, 2/43
Orion - (New Gods) New Gods #1, 2-3/71; (of New Gods) (1st new costume) First Issue Special #13, 4/76
Oswald the Rabbit - New Fun Comics #1, 2/35
Outlaw Kid - Outlaw Kid #1, 9/54
Owl - Crackajack Funnies #25, 7/40
Pantha - (New Titan) New Titans #74, 3/91
Paragon - (becomes Her) Incredible Hulk Annual #6, 1977
Pat Parker - (in costume) Speed Comics #15, 11/41; (no costume) Speed Comics #13, 5/41
Pat, Patsy & Pete - Looney Tunes & Merrie Melodies #1, 1941
Patchwork Man - (cameo) Swamp Thing #2, 12-1/72-73; (full app.) Swamp Thing #3, 2-3/73
Patriot - Marvel Mystery Comics #21, 7/41; (modern age) Marvel Premiere #29, 4/76
Patsy Walker - Miss America Magazine #2, 11/44
Peacemaker - Fightin' Five V2#40, ?/66; (1st DC app.) Crisis on Infinite Earths #6, 9/85
Pebbles - (Flintstones) Flintstones #11, 6/63
Perry White - Superman #7, 11-12/40
Pete Ross - (Legion) Superboy #86, 1/61; (tryout only) Superboy #77, 9?/59
Peter Parker's parents - Amazing Spider-Man Special #5, 11/68; (re-intro) Amazing Spider-Man #365, 8/92
Peter Porkchops - Leading Comics #23, 2-3/47
Phantasmo, Master of the World - Funnies #45, 7/40
Phantom - Ace Comics #11, 2/38
Phantom Eagle - (S.A.) Marvel Super-Heroes #16, 9/68; (G.A.) Wow Comics #6, 7/42
Phantom Falcon - Wings #68, 4/46
Phantom Girl - (Legion) Action Comics #276, 5/61
Phantom Lady - Police Comics #1, 8/41
Phantom Lady - Phantom Lady #13, 8/47
Phantom of the Fair - Amazing Mystery Funnies V2#7, 7/39
Phantom Rider - Star Comics #16, 12/38
Phantom Stranger - Phantom Stranger #1, 5-6/69
Phoenix - (formerly Marvel Girl) X-Men #101, 10/76
Phoenix II - (Rachel) X-Men #141, 1/81
Pinocchio - (cameo) Mickey Mouse Mag. V5#2, 11/39; (full app.) Mickey Mouse Magazine V5#3, 12/39
Pip the Troll - Strange Tales #179, 4/75
Plastic Man - Police Comics #1, 8/41; (S.A. tryout) House of Mystery #160, 7/66; (S.A.) Plastic Man #1, 11-12/66
Pluto - Thor #127, 4/66
Pluto - (Disney) Mickey Mouse #2, 1932
Pogo - Animal Comics #1, 12-1/41-42
Polar Boy - Adventure #306, 11/63
Polaris - (X-Men) X-Men #44, 5/68
Popsicle Pete - All-American Comics #6, 9/39
Porky Pig - Looney Tunes & Merrie Melodies #1, '41
Pow Wow Smith - Detective Comics #151, 9/49
Power Girl - All Star Comics #58, 1-2/76
Power Man - (Rip Regan) Fight Comics #3, 3/40
Power Nelson the Future Man - Prize Comics #1, 3/40
Powerhouse Pepper - Joker Comics #1, 4/42
Predator - Predator #1, 6/89
Presto Kid - Red Mask #51, 9/55
Prince Ra-Man - (formerly Mark Merlin) House of Secrets #73, 7-8/65
Prince Valiant - Ace Comics #26, 5/39
Princess Pantha - Thrilling Comics #56, 10/46
Princess Projectra - (Legion) Adventure Comics #346, 7/66
Professor Supermind & Son - Popular Comics #60, 2/41
Professor Warren - Amazing Spider-Man #31, 12/65
Professor X - X-Men #1, 9/63
Psylocke - New Mutants Annual #2, 10/86
Punisher - Amaz. Spider-Man #129, 2/74
Punisher 2099 - Punisher War Journal #50, 1/93
Pureheart the Powerful - Archie as Pureheart the Powerful #1, 9/66
Purple Mask - Daring Mystery Comics #3, 4/40
Pyroman - America's Best Comics #3, 11/42; Startling Comics #18, 12/42
Quantum Queen - Adventure Comics #375, 12/68
Quasar - (formerly Marvel Man) Incredible Hulk #234, Apr '79; (re-intro) Avengers #302, 4/89
Question - Captain Atom #83, 11/66; (1st DC app.) Crisis on Infinite Earths #6, 9/85
Quicksilver - National Comics #5, 11/40; X-Men #4, 3/64
Quislet - (Legion) Legion of Super-Heroes #14, 9/85
Quisp - Aquaman #1, 1-2/62
Rachel - (Pheonix II) X-Men #141, 1/81
Radar - Captain Marvel Adventures #35, 5/44; Master Comics #50, 5/44
Rage - Avengers #326, 11/90
Ragman - Ragman #1, 8-9/76
Rags Rabbit - Nutty Comics #5, ?/46
Rai - Magnus Robot Fighter #5, 10/91; (new) Rai #0, 11/92
Rainbow Boy - Heroic Comics #14, 9/42
Randy Robertson - Amazing Spider-Man #67, 12/68
Ravage 2099 - Marvel Comics Presents #117, '92
Raven, The - Sure-Fire Comics #1, 6/40
Raven - Thunder Agents #8, 9?/66; (New Teen Titans) DC Comics Presents #26, 10/80
Rawhide Kid - Rawhide Kid #1, 3/55
Ray - Smash Comics #14, 9/40
Ray O'Light - All-New Comics #1, 1/43
Red Bee - Hit Comics #1, 7/40
Red Blazer - Pocket Comics #1, 8/41; All-New Comics #6, 1/44
Red Demon - Black Cat Comics #4, 2-3/47
Red Dragon - (1st story app.) Red Dragon Comics #6, 3/43; (text app. only) Red Dragon Comics #5, 1/43
Red Guardian - Avengers #43, 8/67; (new) Defenders #3, 5/76
Red Hawk - Blazing Comics #1, 6/44
Red Hawk - Straight Arrow #2, 4-5/50
Red Mask - Best Comics #1, 11/39
Red Raven - Red Raven Comics #1, 8/40; (1st modern app. G.A. Red Raven) X-Men #44, 5/69
Red Rocket - Captain Flight Comics #5, 11/44
Red Rube - Zip Comics #39, 8/43
Red Ryder - (1st app. in comics, strip-r) Crackajack Funnies #9, 3/39
Red Sonja - (1st full app.) Conan, the Barbarian #24, 3/73; (cameo) Conan #23, 2/73
Red Tornado - (formerly Ma Hunkle) All-American Comics #20, 11/40; (S.A.) Justice League of America #64, 8/68
Red White & Blue - All-American Comics #1, 4/39
Red Wolf - Avengers #80, 9/70; (1st solo book) Marvel Spotlight #1, 11/71

Reflecto - (Legion) Legion of Super-Heroes #277, 7/81
Rex Dexter of Mars - Mystery Men Comics #1, 8/39
Rex King - Supersnipe #6, 10/42
Rex The Wonder Dog - Rex the Wonder Dog #1, 1-2/52
Richie Rich - LIttle Dot #1, 9/53
Richy the Amazing Boy - Blue Ribbon Comics #1, 11/39
Rip Hunter - Showcase #20, 5-6/59
Robby Reed - (Dial "H" for Hero) House of Mystery #156, 11-12/65
Robin - (1st app. in S.A.) Justice League of America #55, ?/67; (Batman's sidekick) Detective Comics #38, 4/40; (Jason Todd) Batman #368, 2/84; (Carrie Kelly) Batman: The Dark Knight #2, 4/86; (Timothy Drake) Batman #442 (1st), #457 (official) 12/90
Robin Hood - (DC) Brave and the Bold #5, 4-4/56
Robocop - Robocop #1, 10/87
Robotman - Star Spangled Comics #7,4/42; (new) Showcase #94, Aug-Sept '77; (S.A.) My Greatest Adventure #80, 6/63
Rocket Girl - Hello Pal Comics #1, 1/43
Rocket Man - Hello Pal Comics #1, 1/43
Rocketeer - (cameo) Starslayer #1, 2/82; (full app.) Starslayer #2, 4/82
Rocketgirl - Scoop Comics #1, 11/41
Rocketman - Scoop Comics #1, 11/41
Rocky X of the Rocketeers - Boy Comics #80
Rogue - (of X-Men) Avengers Annual #10, 1981 (see X-Men #158)
Roh Kar, the Man Hunter from Mars - Batman #78, 8-9/53
Rom - Rom #1, 12/79
Rond Vidar - (Universo's son, Legion) Adventure Comics #349, 10/66
Rose And The Thorn - Superman's Girlfriend Lois Lane #105, 1968
Roy Raymond - Detective Comics #153, 11/49
Roy the Super Boy - Top-Notch Comics #8, 9/40
Rudolph the Red Nosed Reindeer - Rudolph the Red Nosed Reindeer nn, 1939
Ruff and Reddy - Four Color #937, 9/58
Rulah, Jungle Goddess - Zoot #7, 6/47
Rusty & His Pals - Adventure Comics #32, 11/38
Sabre - Eclipse Graphic Album Series #1, 10/78
Sabrina the Teen-age Witch - Archie's Madhouse #22, 10/62
Sad Sack - True Comics #55, 12/46
Saint, The - Silver Streak Comics #18, 2/42
Samson - Fantastic Comics #1, 12/39
Sandman - (1st published app.) New York World's Fair nn, 1939; (1st app. in S.A.) Justice League of America #46, 8/66; (1st conceived story) Adventure Comics #40, 7/39; (modern) Sandman (2nd Series) #1, 1/89
Sandy the Golden Boy - Adventure Comics #69, 12/41
Sarge Steel - Sarge Steel #1, 12/64
Sargon The Sorcerer - All American Comics #26, 5/41
Sasquatch - X-Men #120
Satana - Vampire Tales #2, ?/73
Saturn Girl - Adventure Comics #247, 4/58
Scalphunter - Weird Western Tales #39, 3-4/77
Scarlet Avenger - Zip Comics #1, 2/40
Scarlet Witch - X-Men #4, 3/64
Scorpion - Scorpion #1, 2/75
Scribbly - Funnies #2, 11/36
Sensor Girl - (Legion) Legion of Super-Heroes #14, 9/85
Sergeant Spook - Blue Bolt #1, 6/40
Sgt. Bilko - Sgt. Bilko #1, 5-6/57
Sgt. Fury - (becomes Nick Fury of Shield) Sgt. Fury #1, 5/63
Sgt. Rock - Our Army at War #81, 4/59
Sgt. Rock (by Kubert & Kanigher) - Our Army at War #83, 6/59
Shade the Changing Man - Shade #1, 6-7/77
Shadow - (1st in comics) Shadow Comics #1, 3/40; (DC) The Shadow #1,10-11/73
Shadowcat - X-Men #129
Shadow Lass - (Legion) Adventure Comics #365, 2/68
Shadow, Jr. - Shadow Comics V6#9, 12/46
Shadowhawk - Youngblood #2, 6/92
Shadowman - Shadowman #1, 5/92; (cameo) X-O Manowar #4, 5/92
Shang-Chi - (Master of Kung-Fu) Special Marvel Edition #15, 12/73
Shanna, the She-Devil - Shanna, the She-Devil #1, 12/72
Shakira - Warlord #32
Sharon Carter - Tales of Suspense #76 (formerly Agent 13), 1966
Shatterstar - (of X-Force) (cameo) New Mutants Annual #6, 1990
Shazam (Captain Marvel) - Shazam #1, 2/73
She-Bat - Detective Comics #424, 6?/72
She-Hulk - Savage She-Hulk #1, 2/80
Sheena - Jumbo Comics #1, 9/38
Sherlock Holmes - Classic Comics #33, 1/47
Shield - Pep Comics #1, 1/40; (S.A.) Adventures of the Fly #8, 9/60
Shiera Sanders - (later becomes Hawkgirl) Flash Comics #1, 1/40
Shining Knight - Adventure Comics #66, 9/41
Shock Gibson - Speed Comics #1, 10/39
Shrinking Violet - (Legion) Action Comics #276, 5/61
Sif - Journey Into Mystery #102, 3/64
Silent Knight - Brave and the Bold #1, 8-9/55
Silly Seal - Krazy Komics #1, 7/42
Silver Fox - Blue Ribbon Comics #2, 12/39
Silver Knight - Wonder Comics #18, 6/48
Silver Sable - Amazing Spider-Man #265, 6/85
Silver Streak - Silver Streak Comics #3, 3/40
Silver Surfer - Fantastic Four #48, 3/66
Siryn - (of X-Force) Spider-Woman #37, 4/81
Skippy - Skippy's Own Book Of Comics, 1934
Skull the Slayer - Skull, the Slayer #1, 8/75
Sky Wizard - Miracle Comics #1, 2/40
Skyman - Big Shot Comics #1, 5/40; (formerly Star Spangled Kid) Infinity, Inc. #31, 10/86
Skywolf - Air Fighters Comics V1#2, 11/42
Slam Bradley - Detective Comics #1, 3/37
Sleepwalker - Sleepwalker #1, 6/91
Snapper Carr - Brave and the Bold #28,2-3/60
Snow White & the Seven Dwarfs - Mickey Mouse Magazine V3#3, 12/37
Socko Strong - Adventure Comics #40, 7/39
Solomon Kane - (1st color app.) Marvel Premiere #33, 12/76
Son Of Satan (Daimon Hellstrom) - (cameo) Ghost Rider #1, 9/73; (full app.) #2, 10/73
Son of Vulcan - Mysteries of Unexplored Worlds #46, 5/65
Space Ace - Manhunt! #1, 10/47
Space Cabbie - Mystery In Space #21, 8-9/54
Space Museum - Strange Adventures #104, 5/59
Space Ranger - Showcase #15, 7-8/58
Sparkler, The - Super Spy #1, 10/40
Sparkman - Sparkler Comics #1, 7/41
Sparky - (Blue Beetle's sidekick) Blue Beetle #14, 9/42; (Red Blazer's sidekick) All-New Comics #6, 1/44
Sparky Watts - Big Shot Comics #14, 6/41
Spawn - Spawn #1, 5/92
Spectre - (1st full app. in costume) More Fun Comics #54, 4/40; (in costume splash panel) More Fun Comics #52, 2/40; (S.A.) Showcase #60, 1-2/66; (in costume in one panel ad) More Fun Comics #51, 1/40
Speed Centaur - Amazing Mystery Funnies V2#8, 8/39
Speed Saunders - Detective Comics #1, 3/37
Speed Spaulding - Famous Funnies #72, 7/40
Speedball - Amazing Spider-Man Annual #22, '88
Speedboy - (Fighting America's side kick) Fighting American #1, 4-5/54
Speedy - (Green Arrow's sidekick) More Fun Comics #73, 11/41
Spencer Smythe - Amazing Spider-Man #25, 6/65
Spider-Girl - What If...? #105, 2/98
Spider-Man - Amazing Fantasy #15, 8-9/62; (cosmic) Spectacular Spider-Man #158, 12/89
Spider-Man - (black costume) Amazing Spider-Man #252, 5/84
Spider-Man 2099 - Amazing Spider-Man #365, 8/92
Spider-Woman - Marvel Spotlight #32, 2/77; (new) Marvel Super Heroes Secret Wars #7, 11/84
Spirit - Spirit nn, 6/40; (1st comic book app.) Police Comics #11, 9/42
Spooky - Casper, the Friendly Ghost #10, 6/53
Spy Smasher - Whiz Comics #1, 2/40
Stalker - Stalker #1, 6-7/75
Stanley & His Monster - Fox and the Crow #95, 12-1?/65-66
Star Boy - (Legion) Adventure Comics #282, 3/61
Starfire - (Teen Titans) Teen Titans #18, 11-12/68; (new) (New Teen Titans) DC Comics Presents #26, 10/80
Starfox - Iron Man #55, 2/73
Starhawk - (1st full app.) Defenders #28, 10/75; (cameo) Defenders #27, 9/75; (re-intro) Guardians of the Galaxy #22, 3/92
Star-Lord - Marvel Preview #4, 11/75
Starman - Adventure Comics #61, 4/41; (1st app. in S.A.) Justice League of America #29, 8/64; (new) First Issue Special #12, 3/76
Star Sapphire - All-Flash #32, 12-1/47-48; (formerly Ferris) Green Lantern #16, 10/62; (re-intro, 1st full app.) Green Lantern #191, 8/85; (re-intro, cameo) Green Lantern #191, 8/85
Starslayer - Starslayer #1, 2/82
Star Spangled Kid - Action Comics #40, 9/41
Stars and Stripes - Stars and Stripes Comics #4, 9/41
Star Spangled Kid - Star Spangled Comics #1, 10/41
Steel Fist - Blue Circle Comics #1, 6/44
Steel Sterling - Zip Comics #1, 2/40; (Silver Age) Fly Man #39, 9/66
Steel the Indestructable Man - Steel #1, 3/78; (re-intro) All Star Squadron #8, 4/82
Steve Conrad Adventurer - Adventure Comics #47, 2/40
Stone Boy - Adventure Comics #306, 2/63
Storm - Giant-Size X-Men #1, Sum '75
Stormy Foster, the Great Defender - Hit Comics #18, 12/41
Straight Arrow - Straight Arrow #1, 2-3/50
Stranger - X-Men #11, 5/65
Stratosphere Jim - Crackajack Funnies #18, 12/39
Stripesy - Action Comics #40, 9/41
Strongman - Crash Comics #1, 5/40
Stuff - (Vigilante sidekick) Action Comics #45, 2/42
Stumbo the Giant - Hot Stuff, the Little Devil #2, 12/57
Stuntman - Stuntman #1, 4-5/46
Stuntman Stetson - Feature Comics #140, 11/49
Sub-Mariner - (1st newsstand app.) Marvel Comics #1, 10-11/39; (1st published app.?) Motion Pic.Funnies Weekly #1, 1939; (Silver Age) FantasticFour #4, 5/62; (new) Namor, the Sub-Mariner #26, 5/92
Sub-Zero Man - Blue Bolt #1, 6/40
Sun Boy - (Legion) Action Comics #276, 5/61
Sunfire - (X-Men) X-Men #64, 1/70
Super American - Fight Comics #15, 10/41
Superbaby - Superboy #8, 5-6/50
Superboy - More Fun Comics #101, 1-2/45
Super Cat - Animal Crackers #1, 1946
Super Duck - Jolly Jingles #10, Sum '43; (re-intro) Laugh #24, ?/90
Supergirl - Action Comics #252, 5/59; (re-intro) Action Comics #674, 2/92; (tryout only) Superboy #5, 11-12/49
Super Goof - Phantom Blot #2, ?/65
Super Mouse - Coo Coo Comics #1, 10/42
Super Patriot - Nick Fury Agent of Shield #13, 6?/69; (new) Captain America #323, 11/86
Super Rabbit - Comedy Comics #14, 3/43
Super Richie - Richie Rich Millions #68, 11/74
Superichie - Superichie #5, 10/76
Superkatt - Giggle #9, 6/44
Superman - Action Comics #1, 6/38
Superman, Jr. - World's Finest Comics #215, 10/72
Supersnipe - Shadow Comics V2#3, 3/42
Superwoman - DC Comics Presents Annual #2, 7/83
Supreme - Youngblood #3, 10/92
Swamp Thing - House of Secrets #92, 6-7/71
Swift Deer - (J. Thunder's sidekick) All-American Western #113, 4-

5/50
Sword - Captain Courageous Comics #6, 3/42; Super-Mystery Comics V3#3, 1/43
T-Man - Police Comics #103, 12/50
Tailspin Tommy - Tailspin Tommy Story & Picture Book #266, 1931; (1st in comic book format) Funnies #1, 10/36
Tank Killer - G. I. Combat #67, 12?/58
Tarantula - All-Star Comics #1, 10/41
Target - Target Comics V1#10, 11/40
Targitt - (in costume) Targitt #2, 6/75; (no costume) Targitt #1, 3/75
Tarzan - Tarzan Book #1, 1929; (1st comic book app.) Tip Top Comics #1, 4/36
Teenage Mutant Ninja Turtles - Teenage Mutant Ninja Turtles #1, 1984
Tellus - (Legion) Legion of Super-Heroes #14, 9/85
Terminator - Rust #12, 8/88
Terra - (New Teen Titan) New Teen Titans #26, 12/82
Terra-Man - Superman #249, 12/71
Terry & The Pirates - Popular Comics #1, 2/36
Tessie the Typist - Joker Comics #2, 6/42
Tex Thompson - (becomes Mr. America) Action Comics #1, 6/38
Thing - (Ben Grimm) Fantastic Four #1, 11/61
Thongor - Creatures On The Loose #22, 1973
Thor - (Beta Ray Bill) Thor #337, 11/83; (Dargo) Thor #384, 10/87; (Donald Blake) Journey Into Mystery #83, 8/62; (Eric Masterson) Thor #433, 6/91
Thorndike - (becomes Hourman's aide)Adventure Comics #74, 5/42
Three Lt. Marvels - Whiz # 21, 9/41; (re-intro) Shazam! #30, 7-8/77
Three-D Man - Marvel Premiere #35, 4/77
Thunderbird - Giant-Size X-Men #1, Sum '75
Thunderbolt - Power Man #41, 10/76; (1st DC app.) Crisis on Infinite Earths #6, 9/85; (Jonni Thunder) Jonni Thunder #1, 2/85; (Peter Cannon) Thunderbolt #1, 1/66
Thunderbunny - Charlton Bullseye #6, 12?/81
Thunderstrike - (Eric Masterson) Thor #459, 2/93
Tick - Tick #1, 6/88
Tiger Girl - Fight Comics #32, 6/44
Tigra - Startling Comics #45, 5/47
Tigra - (formerly The Cat) Giant-Size Creatures #1, 5/75
Tim - (Black Terror's sidekick) Exciting Comics #9, 5/41
Timber Wolf - (Legion) Adventure Comics #327, 12/64
Timecop -Dark Horse Comics #1, 8/82
Timothy Drake - Batman #436, 8/89; (1st in Robin costume) Batman #442, 1990
Timothy the Ghost - Zoo Funnies #1, 7/53
TNT & Dan the Dyna-Mite - World's Finest Comics #5, Spr '42
Todd Hunter - Adventure Comics #32, 11/38
Tom & Jerry - Our Gang Comics #1, 9-10/42
Tom Brent - Adventure Comics #32, 11/38
Tom Mix - The Comics #1, 3/37
Tomahawk - Star Spangled Comics #69, 6/47
Tommy the Amazing Kid - Amazing-Man Comics #23, 8/41
Tommy Tomorrow - Real Fact Comics #6, 1-2/47
Tony Trent - (The Face) Big Shot Comics #1, 5/40
Tor - One Million Years Ago #1, 9/53
Torchy - Doll Man Quarterly #8, Spr '46
Toro - (Human Torch's sidekick) Human Torch #2(#1), Fall '40; (modern) Sub-Mariner #14, 6/69
Torpedo - (new) Daredevil #126, 9/75
Tragg - Mystery Comics Digest #3, ?/72
Trail Colt - Manhunt! #8, 5/48
Triplicate Girl - (Legion) Action Comics #276, 5/61
Tubby - King Comics #46, 2/40; Marge's Little Lulu Four Color #74, ? '45
Tuk the Cave Boy - Captain America Comics #1, 3/41
Turbo - New Warriors #28, 10/92
Turok - Turok Four Color #596, 12/54; (re-intro in Valiant Universe) Magnus Robot Fighter #12, 5/92
Two Gun Kid - Two Gun Kid #1, 3/48
Ty-Gor, Son of the Tiger - Blue Ribbon Comics #4, 6/40
Tygra - Startling Comics #45, 5/47
Tyroc - (Legion) Superboy #216
U.S. Agent - Captain America #354, 6/89
Ultra Boy - (Legion) Superboy #98, 7/62
Ultra Man - (Gary Concord) All-American Comics #8, 11/9
Uncle Ben - Amazing Fantasy #15, 8-9/62
Uncle Marvel - Captain Marvel Adventures #43, 2/45, Wow Comics #18, 10/43
Uncle Sam - National Comics #1, 7/40
Uncle Scrooge - Donald Duck 4-Color #178, 12/47
Underdog - Underdog #1, 7/70
Union Jack I - Invaders #7, 7/76
Union Jack II - Invaders #20, 9/77
Union Jack III - Captain America #254, 2/81
Unknown Soldier - Star Spangled War Stories #151, 6-7/70
Untouchables - Four Color 1237, 10-12/61
Usagi Yojimbo - Albedo #1, 4/85
U.S. Jones - Wonderworld #28, 8/41
Val - Strange Tales #159, 8/67
V-Man - Big-3 #7, 1/42; V...- Comics #1, 1/42
Valkyrie - Air Fighters Comics V2#2, 11/43
Vampirella - Vampirella #1, 9/69
Vanessa - (Kingpin's wife) Amazing Spider-Man #83, 4/70
Vanguard - New Teen Titans Annual #1, 1985; Iron Man #109, Apr '78; Megaton #1, 11/83
Vault Keeper - War Against Crime #10, 12-1/49-50
Veiled Avenger - Spotlight Comics #1, 11/44
Venus - Venus #1, 8/48
Veronica Lodge - Pep Comics #26, 4/42
Vicki Vale - Batman #45, 2-3/48
Victoria Bentley - Strange Tales #114, 11/63
Victory Boys - USA Comics #5, Sum '42
Vigilante - Action Comics #42, 11/41; (female) (1st full app.) Deathstroke: the Terminator #10, 5/92; (female) (cameo) Deathstroke: the Terminator #9, 4/92; (modern, in costume) New Teen Titans Annual #2, 1985; (modern, not in costume) New Teen Titans #23, 9/82; (S.A.) Justice League of America #78, 2/70
Viking Prince - Brave and the Bold #1, 8-9/55
Vindicator - (formerly Weapon Alpha) (becomes Guardian) X-Men #120, 4/79
Vision - (G.A.) Marvel Mystery Comics #13, 11/40; (S.A.) Avengers #57, 10/68
Vixen - Action Comics #521, 7/81
Voice, The - Popular Comics #51, 5/40
Voltage, Man of Lightning - Fat & Slat #1, Sum '47
Vulcan - Super-Mystery Comics V1#1, 7/40
Wagon Train - Four Color #895, 3/58
Wambi, Jungle Boy - Jungle Comics #1, 1/40
Warlock - (Him) (cameo) Fantastic Four #67, 10/67; (Him) (full app.) Thor #165, 6/69; (new) New Mutants #18, 8/84; (re-intro) Silver Surfer #46, 2/91
Warlord - First Issue Special #8, 11/75
Warpath - (with costume) X-Men #193, 5/85; (without costume) New Mutants #16, 6/84
Wash Tubbs - Famous Comics Cartoon Books #1202, 1934
Wasp, The - Speed Comics #12, 3/41
Wasp - Tales to Astonish #44, 6/63
Wasplet - (Hooded Wasp's sidekick) Shadow Comics #7, 11/40
Watcher - Fantastic Four #13, 4/63
Waverider - Armageddon 2001 #1, 5/91
Weapon Alpha - (becomes Vindicator) X-Men #109, 2/78
Web - Zip Comics #27, 7/42; (S.A.) Fly Man #36, 3/66
Wendigo - Incredible Hulk #162, 4/73
Wendy the Good Little Witch - Casper, the Friendly Ghost #20, ?/54
Werewolf - Werewolf #1, 12/66
Werewolf by Night - Marvel Spotlight #2, 1?/72
Whirlybats - Detective Comics #257, 7/58
White Rider & Super Horse - Blue Bolt #1, 6/40
White Streak - Target Comics V1#1, 2/40
White Tiger - Deadly Hands of Kung-Fu #19, 1?/76
White Witch - (Legion) Adventure Comics #351, 12/66
Whizzer, The - USA Comics #1, 8/41; (modern) Giant-Size Avengers #1, 8/74
Whizzer McGee - (Phantasmo's side kick) Funnies #45, 7/40
Wiggles the Wonderworm - Taffy Comics #1, 3/45
Wilbur - Zip Comics #18, 9/41
Wild Bill Elliott - Four Color #278, 5/50
Wildcat - Sensation Comics #1, 1/42; (S.A.) Brave and the Bold #62, 10-11/65
Wildfire - (formerly Erg-1) Superboy #201, 4/74
Will O' the Wisp - Amazing Spider-Man #167, 4/77
Willie - Gay Comics #1, Mar '44
Winky, Blinky & Noddy - All-Flash #5, Sum '42
Witchblade - Cyblade/ Shi #1, 1995
Witch Hazel - Marge's Little Lulu #39, 9/51
Witness - Mystic Comics #7, 12/40
Wizard - Top-Notch Comics #1, 12/39; (S.A.) Fly Man #33, 9/65
Wizard - Strange Tales #102, 11/62
Wolverine - (1st full app.) Incredible Hulk #181, 11/74; (cameo) Incredible Hulk #180, 10/74
Wonder Boy - Blue Bolt #1, 6/40; National Comics #1, 7/40
Wonder Boy - Bomber Comics #1, 3/44
Wonder Duck - Wonder Duck #1, 9/49
Wonder Girl - Wonder Woman #107, 7/61; (new) (Teen Titan) Brave and the Bold #60, 6-7/65
Wonder Man - Startling Comics #1, 6/40
Wonderman - Wonder Comics #9, 1945
Wonder Man - Avengers #9, 10/64; Wonder Comics #1, 5/39; (re-intro) Avengers #151, 9/76
Wonder Tot - Wonder Woman #122
Wonder Woman - All Star Comics #8, 12-1/41-42; (Orana) Wonder Woman #250, 12/78
Wonder Woman Family - Wonder Woman #124, 12/62
Wonderman - (Brad Spencer) Mystery Comics #1, 1944
Wong - Strange Tales #110, 7/63
Woodgod - Marvel Premiere #31, 8/76
Woody Woodpecker - Funnies #64, 5/42
Woozy Winks - Police Comics #13, 11/42
X-O Manowar - X-O Manowar #1, 2/92
XS - (Legion) Legionnaires #0, 10/94
X-Terminators - X-Terminators #1, 10/88
Yank and Doodle - Prize Comics #13, 8/41
Yankee Doodle Jones - Yankee Comics #1, 9/41
Yarko the Great, Master Magician - Wonder Comics #2, 6/39
Yellow Claw - Yellow Claw #1, 10/56
Yellowjacket - Yellowjacket #1, 9/44
Yellowjacket - Avengers #59, 12/68; (formerly Goliath) Avengers #63, 4/69
Yogi Bear - Four Color #1067, 12-2/59-60
Yosemite Sam - Yosemite Sam #1, 12/70
Zanzibar - Mystery Men Comics #1, 8/39
Zardi, the Eternal Man - Amazing-Man Comics #11, 4/40
Zatanna - Hawkman #4, 10-11/64
Zatara - Action Comics #1, 6/38
Zebra - All-New Comics #7, 3/44; Pocket Comics #1, 8/41
Zegra, Jungle Empress - Zegra #2, 10/48
Ziggy Pig - Krazy Komics #1, 7/42
Zombie - Menace #5, 7/53
Zorro - Zorro Four Color #228, 5/49

FIRST APPEARANCES: VILLAINS

Abomination - Tales to Astonish #90, 4/67
Abra Kadabra - Flash #128, 2?/62
Absorbing Man - Journey Into Mystery #114, 3/65
Amazo The Android - Brave & The Bold #30, 6-7/60
Angle Man - Wonder Woman #70, 11/54
Annihilus - Fantastic Four Annual #6, 11/68
Apocalypse - (cameo) X-Factor #5, 6/86; (full app.) X-Factor #6, 7/86
Arcade - Marvel Team-Up #66, 2/78
Atomic Skull - Superman #323, 5/78; (modern) Action Comics #670, 10/91
Attuma - Fantastic Four #33, 12/64
Bane - Batman: Vengeance of Bane Special #1, '92
Banshee - X-Men #28, 1/67
Baron Blood - Invaders #7, 7/76
Baron Mordo - Strange Tales #111, 8/63
Baron Strucker - Sgt. Fury #5, 1963
Baron Zemo - Captain America #276
Batmite - Detective #267, 5/59
Batroc - Tales of Suspense #76, 4/66
Beetle - Strange Tales #123, 8/64
Bengal - Daredevil #258, 9/88
Beyonder - Marvel Two-In-One #63, 1986
Big Man - Amazing Spider-Man #10, 3/64
Bizarro - Superboy #68, 10-11/56
Bizarro Batman - World's Finest Comics #156
Bizarro Flash - Superman's Girlfriend Lois Lane #74, 5/67
Bizarro Krypto - Superboy #82, ?/60
Bizarro Lana Lang - Adventure Comics #292, 1/62
Bizarro Lucy Lane -Adventure Comics #292, 1/62
Bizarro Lex Luthor - Adventure Comics #293, 2/62
Bizarro Lois Lane - Action Comics #255, 8/59
Bizarro Mxyzptlk - Adventure Comics #286, 7/61
Bizarro Supergirl - Superman #140, 10/60
Bizarro Titano - Adventure Comics #295, 4/62
Black Cat - Amazing Spider-Man #194, 7/79
Black Mask - Batman #386, 8/85
Blackout - Ghost Rider #2, 6/90
Black Racer - New Gods #3, 6-7/71
Black Spider - Detective Comics #463
Blastarr - Fantastic Four #62, 5/67
Blizzard - Iron Man #86, ?/76?
Blob - X-Men #3, 1/64
Blockbuster - Detective Comics #345, 11/65
Boomerang - Tales to Astonish #81, 7/66
Brain Storm - Justice League of America #32, 12/64
Brain Wave - All Star Comics #15, 2-3/43
Brainiac - Action Comics #242, 7/58; (modern) Adventures of Superman #438, 2/88
Brainwasher - (Kingpin) Amazing Spider-Man #59, 4/68
Brother Blood - New Teen Titans #21, 7/82
Brother Voodoo - Strange Tales #169, 9/73
Bullet - Daredevil #250, 12/88
Bullseye - Nick Fury Agent of Shield #15, 11/69
Calypso - Amazing Spider-Man #209, 10/80
Captain Boomerang - Flash #117, 12/60
Captain Cold - Showcase #8, 5-6/57
Captain Fear - Adventure Comics #425, 12-1/72-73
Captain Nazi - Master Comics #21, 12/41
Cardinal - New Warriors #28, 10/92
Carnage - (1st full app.) Amazing Spider-Man #361, 4/92; (cameo) Amazing Spider-Man #360, 3/92
Carrion - Spectacular Spider-Man #25, 12/78
Cat-Man - Detective Comics #311, 1/63
Catwoman - (1st in costume) Batman #3, Fall '40; (1st time called Catwoman) Batman #2, Sum '40; (modern, Selina Kyle) Batman #404, 2/87; (new costume w/o cat-head mask) Batman #35, 5-6/46; (new) Detective Comics #624, 12/90; (S.A.) Superman's Girlfriend Lois Lane #70, 11/66; (The Cat) Batman #1, Spr '40
Cavalier - Detective Comics #81, 11/43
Chameleon - Amazing Spider-Man #1, 3/63
Changeling - X-Men #35, 8/67
Cheetah - Wonder Woman #6, Fall '43; (new) (cameo) Wonder Woman #274, 12/80; (new) (full app.) Wonder Woman #275, 1/81
Chronos - Atom #3, 10-11/62
Chunk - Flash #9, 2/88
Claw - Silver Streak Comics #1, 12/39
Clayface I - (Basil Karlo) Detective Comics #40, 6/40
Clayface II - (Matt Hagen) Detective Comics #298, 12/61
Clayface III - (Preston Payne) Detective Comics #478, 7-8/78
Clock King - World's Finest Comics #111, 8/60
Clown - Flash #270, 2/79
Cobra (see Human Cobra)
Colonel Computron - Flash #304, 12/81
Composite Superman - World's Finest #142
Computo - Adventure Comics #340, 1/66
Constrictor - Incredible Hulk #212, 6/77
Copperhead - Daredevil #124, 6?/75
Crime Master - Amazing Spider-Man #26, 7/65
Crimson Dynamo - (Anton Vanko) Tales of Suspense #46, 10/63
Crimson Dynamo II - (Boris Turgenov) Tales of Suspense #52, 4/64
Crimson Dynamo III - (Alex Nevsky) Iron Man #21, 3/78
Crimson Dynamo IV - (Yuri Petrovich) Champions #8, 10/76
Crimson Dynamo V - (Dimitri Bukharin) Iron Man #109, 4/78
Cyborg - (Superman impersonator) Adventures of Superman #466, 5/90
Cyclone - Amazing Spider-Man #143, 4/75
Dark Phoenix - X-Men #134
Darkseid - (1st full app.) Forever People #1, 2-3/71; (cameo) Superman's Pal Jimmy Olsen #134, 12/70
Deadshot - Batman #59, 6-7/50; (1st modern app.) Detective Comics #474, 11-12/77
Death's Head - Daredevil #56, 9/69
Deathstalker - (formerly Death's Head) Daredevil #114, 7/?/74
Demogoblin - Web of Spider-Man #86, 3/92
Despero - Justice League of America #1, 10-11/60
Destroyer - Journey Into Mystery #118, 7/65
Dev-Em, the Knave from Krypton - Adventure Comics #287, 8/61
Diablo - Fantastic Four #30, 9/64
Doctor Destiny - Justice League of America #5, 6-7/61
Doctor Doom - Fantastic Four #5, 6/62
Doctor Light I - Justice League of America #12, 6/62
Doctor Light II - Crisis on Infinite Earths #4, 6/85
Doctor Octopus - Amazing Spider-Man #3, 6/63
Doctor Polaris - Green Lantern #21, 6/63
Doctor Regulus - Adventure Comics #348, 9/66
Doom 2099 - Marvel Comics Presents #118, '92
Doomsday - (cameo) Superman: The Man of Steel #17, 11/92; (full app.) Superman: The Man of Steel #18, 12/92
Dormammu - Strange Tales #126, 11/64
Dr. Death - (modern) Batman #345, 3/82
Dr. Doom - Fantastic Four #5, 6/62
Dr. Double X - Detective Comics #261, 11/58
Dr Light - Justice League of America #12, '62
Dr. Octopus - Amazing Spider-Man #3, 5/63
Dr. Phosphorous - Detective Comics #469
Dr. Psycho - Wonder Woman #5, 6-7/43
Dr. Spectro - Captain Atom #78, 12/65; (new) Captain Atom #6, 8/87; (1st DC app.) Crisis on Infinite Earths #9, 12/85
Dragon Man - Fantastic Four #35, 2/65
Drax the Destroyer - (re-intro) (cameo) Silver Surfer #35, 3/90; (re-intro) (full app.) Silver Surfer #37, 5/90
Dreadknight - Iron Man #101, 8/77
Dragon Man - Fantastic Four #35, 2/65
Dummy - (Vigilante villain) Leading Comics #1, Win '41-42
Electro - Amazing Spider-Man #9, 2/64
Enchantress - Journey Into Mystery #103, 4/64
Enchantress - Strange Adventures #187
Enforcer - Ghost Rider #22, ?/77
Evil Star - Green Lantern #37, 7/65
Exterminator - (becomes Death-Stalker) Daredevil #39, 4/68
Fatal Five - Adventure Comics #352, 1/67
Fatman - Batman #113, 2/58
Felix Faust - Justice League of America #10, 3/62
Fiddler - All-Flash #32, 12-1/47-48
Fin Fang Foom - Strange Tales #89, 10/61
Firelord - Thor #225
Foolkiller - (1st) Man-Thing #3, 3/74
Foolkiller II - (Greg Salinger) (cameo) Omega the Unknown #8, 5/77; (Greg Salinger) (full app.) Omega the Unknown #9, 7/77
Galactus - Fantastic Four #48, 3/66
Gambler - Green Lantern #12, Sum '44
Gamora - Strange Tales #180, 6/75; (re-intro) Silver Surfer #46, 2/91
Gentleman Ghost - (modern) Batman #310, 4/79
Gibbon - Amazing Spider-Man #110, 7/72
Gladiator - Daredevil #18, 7/66
Golden Glider - Flash #250, 6/77
Gorgon - Fantastic Four #44, 11/65
Gorilla Grodd, the Super Gorilla - Flash #106, 4-5/59
Green Goblin I - (Norman Osborn) Amazing Spider-Man #14, 7/64
Green Goblin II - (Harry Osborn) Amazing Spider-Man #136, 9/74
Grey Gargoyle - Journey Into Mystery #107, 8/64
Grim Reaper - Avengers #52, 5/68
Grizzly - Amazing Spider-Man #139, 12/74
Hammerhead - Amazing Spider-Man #113, 10/72
Harlequin - All-American Comics #89, 9/47
Hate Monger - Fantastic Four #21, 12/63
Havoc - (not in costume) X-Men #56; (in costume) #58
Heat Wave - Flash #140, 6/63
Hector Hammond - Green Lantern #5, 3-4/61
Hela - Journey Into Mystery #102, 3/64
High Evolutionary - Thor #134, 11/66
Hobgoblin - (new) (Macendale) Spectacular Spider-Man #147, 2/89
Hobgoblin I - (Ned Leeds) Amazing Spider-Man #238, 3/83
Hobgoblin II - (Macendale/Jack O'Lantern) Amazing Spider-Man #289, 6/87
Hugo Strange - (1st modern app.) Detective Comics #470, 3-4/77
Human Cobra - Journey Into Mystery #98, 11/63
Human Top - (Whirlwind) Tales to Astonish #50, 12/63
Humbug - Web of Spider-Man #19, 10/86
Hydro Man - Amazing Spider-Man #212, 12/81
Hyena - Firestorm #4, 8-9/78
Icicle - All-American Comics #90, 10/47
Insect Queen - (Lana Lang) Superboy #124, 10/65
Iron Jaw - Boy Comics #3, 4/42
Jack O'Lantern - (Macendale) Machine Man #19, 2/81; (new) Captain America #396, 1/92
Jackal - Amazing Spider-Man #129,

2/74
Jester - Daredevil #42 ,7/68
Jigsaw - Amazing Spider-Man #188, 1/79
Joker - Batman #1, Spr '40
Joker's Daughter - Batman Family #6, 7-8/76
Juggernaut - X-Men #12, 7/65
Kang - Avengers #8, 9/64
Kanjar Ro - Justice League of America #3, 2-3/61
Key, The - Justice League of America #41, 12/65
Killer Croc - Batman #357, 3/83
Killer Shark - Blackhawk #50, 3/52
Kingpin - Amazing Spider-Man #50, 7/67
Klaw - Fantastic Four #53, 8/66
Kraven the Hunter - Amazing Spider-Man #15, 8/64
Kurgo - Fantastic Four #7, 10/62
Leader - Tales to Astonish #62, 12/64
Legion of Super Villains - Superman #147, 8/61
Lex Luthor - (bald) Superman #10, 5-6/41; (new) Man of Steel #4, 12/86; (red hair) Action Comics #23, 5/40; (Silver Age) Adventure Comics #271, 4/60
Lightmaster - Spectacular Spider-Man #3, 2/77
Living Monolith - X-Men #56
Lizard - Amazing Spider-Man #6, 11/63
Loki - Journey Into Mystery #85, 10/62
Looter - Amazing Spider-Man #36, 5/66
Lord Shilling - (Tomahawk foe) Tomahawk #28, 11/54
Lunatik - (1st full app.) Defenders #56, 2/78; (cameo) Defenders #53, 11/77
Mad Hatter - Batman #49, 10-11/48; Detective Comics #230, 4/56
Mad Thinker - Fantastic Four #15, 6/63
Madame Medusa - Fantastic Four #36, 3/65
Maelstrom - Marvel Two-In-One #71, 1/81
Magica de Spell-Uncle Scrooge #36, 12/62
Magneto - X-Men #1, 9/63
Magpie - (new) Man of Steel #3, 11/86
Magus - Strange Tales #178, 2/75; (re-intro) Warlock and the Infinity Watch #7, 8/92
Malevolence - (Mephisto's daugh ter) Guardians of the Galaxy #7, 12/90
Man-Ape - Avengers #62
Man-Bat - Detective Comics #400, 6/70
Man-Wolf - Amazing Spider-Man #124, 9/73
Mandarin - Tales of Suspense #50, 2/64
Manhunters - 1st Issue Special #5, 8/75
Mephisto - Silver Surfer #3, 12/68
Metallo (Jor-El's robot) - (1st app.) Superboy #49, 6/56; (new) Superman #310, 4/77; (new) Superman #1, 1/87; (re-intro) Action Comics #252, 5/59; (re-intro, 3rd app.) Adventure Comics #276, 9/60
Microwave Man - Action Comics #487, 9/78
Mime - Batman #412, 10/87
Mimic - X-Men #19, 4/66
Mirror Master - Flash #105, 2-3/59
Mist - Adventure Comics #67, 10/41
Mister Element - Showcase #13, 3-4/58
Mister Sinister - X-Men #221
Modok - Tales of Suspense #94, 10/67
Modred the Mystic - (re-intro) Darkhold #3, 12/92
Mole Man- Fantastic Four #1, 11/61
Molecule Man - Fantastic Four #20, 11/63
Molten Man - Amazing Spider-Man #28, 9/65
Morbius the Living Vampire - Amazing Spider-Man #101, 10/71
Mordru - Adventure Comics #369, 6/68
Mortan - (Adam Strange foe) Mystery In Space #62
Mr. Atom - Captain Marvel Adventures #78, 11/47
Mr. Baffle - Detective Comics #63, 5/42
Mr. Freeze - Batman #121, 2/59
Mr. Hyde - Journey Into Mystery #99,12/63
Mr. Mind - Captain Marvel Adventures #22, 3/43; (re-intro) Shazam! #2, 4/73
Mr. Mxyzptlk - Superman #131, 8/59; (new) Superman #11, 11/87; Superman #30, 10/44
Mr. Tawny - Captain Marvel Adventures #79, 12/47
Multi-Man - Challengers of the Unknown #14, 12-1/59-60
Mysterio - Amazing Spider-Man #13, 6/64
Nightmare - Strange Tales #110, 7/63
Nightshade - Captain America #164, 8/73
Nitro - Captain Marvel #34, 9/74
Ocean Master - Aquaman #29
Outsider - Detective Comics #334, 12/64
Owl - Daredevil #3, 8/64
Paladin - Daredevil #150, 2/78
Parasite - Action Comics #340, 8/66; Fury of Firestorm #58, 4/87
Peg-leg Pete - Mickey Mouse #3, 1933
Penguin - Detective Comics #58, 12/41; (S.A.) Batman #155, 4/63
Pied Piper - Flash #106, 4-5/59
Pieface - Green Lantern #2, 9-10/60
Plant-Master - Atom #1, 6-7/62
Plunderer - Daredevil #12, 1/66
Poison Ivy - Batman #181, 6/66
Porcupine - Tales To Astonish #48, 10/63
Prankster - Action Comics #51, 8/42
Princess Python - Amazing Spider-Man #22, 3/65
Professor Amos Fortune - Justice League of America #6, 8-9/61
Professor Zoom - Flash #139, ?/63
Prowler - Amazing Spider-Man #78, 11/69
Psycho Pirate - All Star Comics #23, Win '44-45
Psycho-Man - Fantastic Four Annual #5, 11/67
Puma - Amazing Spider-Man #256, 9/84
Punisher - Amazing Spider-Man #129, 2/74
Puppet Master - Batman #3, Fall '40; Fantastic Four #8, 11/62
Rainbow Raider - Flash #286, 6/80
Rama-Tut - Fantastic Four #19, 10/63
Rampage - Superman #7, 7/87
Rancor - (1st full app.) Guardians of the Galaxy #9, 2/91; (cameo) (descendant of Wolverine) Guardians of the Galaxy #8, 1/91
Ras Al Ghul - Batman #232, 7/71
Reaper - Batman #237, 12/71
Red Ghost - Fantastic Four #13, 4/63
Red Skull - Captain America Comics #1, 3/41; (S.A.) Tales of Suspense #65, 5/65
Rhino - Amazing Spider-Man #41, 10/66
Riddler - Detective Comics #140, 10/48; (S.A.) Batman #171, 5/65
Ringmaster - Incredible Hulk #3, 9/62
Rose - Amazing Spider-Man #253, 6/84
Rose and the Thorn - Flash Comics #89, 11/47; (new) Superman's Girlfriend Lois Lane #105
Saber-Tooth - Flash #291, 11/80
Sabretooth - Iron Fist #14, 8/77
Sandman - Amazing Spider-Man #4, 9/63
Sandstorm - Web of Spider-Man #107, 12/93
Sargon - (re-intro) Flash #186, 8?/69
Sargon the Sorcerer - (1st story app.) All-American Comics #26, 5/41; (text only) All-American Comics #24, 3/41
Sauron - X-Men #60
Scarecrow - Tales of Suspense #51, 3/64; World's Finest Comics #3, Fall '41; Dead of Night #11, 8/75; (S.A.) Batman #189, ? '67?
Schemer - Amazing Spider-Man #83, 4/70
Scorpion - Amazing Spider-Man #20, 1/65
Serpent Crown - Sub-Mariner #9, 1/69
Sha-Shan - Amazing Spider-Man #108, 5/72
Shade - (modern) Flash #298, 6/81
Shadow Thief - Brave and the Bold #36,6-7/61
Shaper - Incredible Hulk #155, 9/72
Shark - Amazing-Man Comics #6, 10/39; Green Lantern #24, 10/63
Shocker - Amazing Spider-Man #46, 3/67
Shotgun - Daredevil #272, 9?/89
Shroud - Super-Villain Team-Up #5, 4/76
Signalman - Batman #112, 12/57; (S.A.) Detective Comics #466
Silver Banshee - Action Comics #495, 12/87
Silvermane - Amazing Spider-Man #73, 6/69
Silver Samurai - Daredevil #111, 6/74
Sinestro - Green Lantern #7, 7-8/61
Sivana - Whiz Comics #1, 2/40
Sivana, Jr. - Captain Marvel Adventures #52, 1/46
Sky Pirate - Green Lantern #27, 8-9/47
Solarr - Captain America #160, 4/73
Solo - Web of Spider-Man #19, 10/86
Solomon Grundy - All-American Comics #61, 11/44; (S.A.) Showcase #55, 3-4/65
Sonar - Green Lantern #14, 7/62
Sorcerer - Alpha Flight #71, 5/89
Speed McGee - Flash #5, 10/87
Spirit of Vengeance - (futuristic Ghost Rider) Guardians of the Galaxy #13, 6/91
Spyder - New Mutants #68, 10/88
Star Thief - Warlock #14, 10/76
Stilt-Man - Daredevil #8, 6/65
Sting Ray - Sub-Mariner #19, 11/69
Stranger - X-Men #11, 5/65
Sub-Mariner - (S.A) Fantastic Four #4, 5/62
Sunburst - New Adventures of Superboy #45, 9/83
Super Skrull - Fantastic Four #18, 9/63
Supremo - Superboy #132, ?/66
Swordsman - Avengers #19, 8/65
Tantrum - Night Thrasher: Four Control #2, 11/92
Tarantula - Amazing Spider-Man #134, 7/74
Taskmaster - Avengers #119, 1/80
Tattooed Man - Green Lantern #23, 9?/63
Terra-Man - Superman #249, 4/72
Terrax - Fantastic Four #211, 10/79
Terrible Tinkerer - Amazing Spider-Man #2, 5/63
Thanos - Iron Man #55, 2/73; (re-intro) (cameo) Silver Surfer #34, 2/90; (re-intro) (full app.) Silver Surfer #35, 3/90
Thinker - All-Flash #12, Fall '43
Thundra - Fantastic Four #129, 12/72
Tiger Shark - (new) Namor, the Sub-Mariner #35, 2/93; (S.A.) Sub-Mariner #5, 9/68
Time Trapper - Adventure Comics #321, 6/64
Titanium Man - Tales of Suspense #69, 9/65
Titano - Superman #127, 2/59
Toad - X-Men #4, 3/64
Tombstone - Web of Spider-Man #36, 3/88; (full app.) Spectacular Spider-Man #138, 5/88
Top - Flash #122, 6-7?/61
Torpedo - Daredevil #126, 8?/75
Toyman - Action Comics #64, 9/43; (new) Superman #13, 1/88; (S.A.) Action Comics #432, 2/74
Trapster - Strange Tales #104, 1/63
Trauma - Incredible Hulk #394, 6/92
Trickster - Flash #113, 6-7/60
Turtle - Showcase #4, 9-10/56
Tweedledum & Tweedledee - Detective Comics #74, 4/43
Two-Face - Detective Comics #66, 8/42; (S.A) World's Finest #173, 1/68
Typhoid Mary - Daredevil #254, 5/88
Ulik - Thor #137
Ultron - Avengers #54
Ulthoon - (Adam Strange foe) Mystery In Space #61,
Umar - Strange Tales #150, 11/66
Unicorn - Tales of Suspense #56, 8/64
Universo - Adventure Comics #349, 10/66
Unus the Untouchable - X-Men #8, 11/64
U. S. Jones - Wonderworld Comics #28, 8/41
Vandall Savage - Green Lantern #10 ,Win '43; (S.A.) Flash #137, ?/63
Vanisher - X-Men #2, 11/63
Venom - (1st full app.) Amazing Spider-Man #300, 5/88; (cameo w/costume) Amazing Spider-Man #298; (cameo, no costume), #299, 4/88
Vindicator - X-Men #109, 5/78
Viper - Captain America #110, 2/69
Vulture - Amazing Spider-Man #2, 5/63
Warpath - X-Men #193, 5/85
Watcher - Fantastic Four #13, 4/63
Weapon Omega - Alpha Flight #102, 11/81
Weather Wizard - Flash #110, 12-1/59-60
Whirlwind - (Human Top) Tales to Astonish #50, 12/63
White Queen - X-Men #132, 4/80
Wizard - Strange Tales #102, 11/62
Zemo - Avengers #6, 7/64
Zzzax - Incredible Hulk #166, 8/73

FIRST APPEARANCES: GROUPS

Adult Legion - Superman #147, 8/61
All Star Squadron - Justice League of America #193, 8/81
All Winners Squad - All Winners Comics #19, Fall, 1946
Alpha Flight -(cameo) X-Men #120, 4/79; (full app.) X-Men #121, 5/79
Atari Force - New Teen Titans #27, 1/83
Atomic Knights - Strange Adventures #117, 6/60
Avengers - Avengers #1, 9/63
Avengers new line up - Avengers #16, 5/65; Avengers #150, 8/76; Avengers #181, 3/79; Avengers #211, 9/81
Avengers West Coast - West Coast Avengers #1, 9/84
Big-3 - (Blue Beetle/Flame/ Samson) Big-3 #1, Fall, 1940
Bizarro Legionnaires - Adventure Comics #329, 2/65
Boy Commandos - Detective Comics #64, 6/42
Challengers of the Unknown - Showcase #6, 1-2/57
Champions - Champions #1, 10/75
Creature Commandos - Weird War Tales #93, 11/80
Damage Control - Marvel Comics Presents #19, 5/89
Darkstars - Dark Stars #1, 10/92
Defenders - Marvel Feature #1, 12/71; (new) Defenders #125, 11/83; (pre-lude) Sub-Mariner #34, 2/71
Doom Patrol - My Greatest Adventure #80, 6/63; (new) Showcase #94, 8-9/77
Easy Company - Our Army At War #81, 4/59
Elementals, The - Justice Machine Annual #1, 1/84
Eternals - Eternals #1, 7/76
Excalibur - Excalibur Special Edition nn, 1987
Explorers - Boy Explorers #1, 5-6/46
Fab 4 - Super Heroes #1, 1/67
Fantastic Four - Fantastic Four #1, 11/61; (1st in costumes) Fantastic Four #3, 3/62; (new team) Fantastic Four #306, 9/87
Federal Men - New Comics #2, 1/36
Femforce - Femforce Special #1, Fall, 1984
Fightin' Five - Fightin' Five V2#28, 7/64
Forever People - Forever People #1, 2-3/71
Freedom Fighters - Justice League of America #107, 1975
Frightful Four - Fantastic Four #36, 10/64
Future X-Men - X-Men #141, 1/81
Gen13 - WildC.A.T.S Trilogy #1, 6/93
Ghost Patrol - Flash Comics #29, 5/42
Girl Commandos - Speed Comics #13, 4/41
Great Lakes Avengers - West Coast Avengers #46, 7/89
Green Lantern Corp. - Green Lantern #130
Guardians of the Galaxy - Marvel Super-Heroes #18, 1/69; (1st solo book) Marvel Presents #3, 2/76
Guardians of the Universe - Green Lantern #1, 7-8/60
H.A.R.D. Corps - Harbinger #10, 10/92
Inferior Five - Showcase #62, 5-6/66
Infinity, Inc. - All Star Squadron #25, 9/83
Inhumans - Fantastic Four #45, 12/65
Injustice Society Of The World - All Star Comics #37, 10-11/47
Intergalactic Vigilante Squadron - Adventure Comics #237, 6/57
International Sea Devils - Sea Devils #22, 3-4/66
Invaders - Avengers #71, 12/69; (re-intro) Namor, the Sub-Mariner #12, 3/91
Justice League Europe - Justice League International #24, 2/89; (new) Justice League Spectacular #1, 1992
Justice League International - (new) Justice League Spectacular #1, 1992
Justice League of America - Brave and the Bold #28, 2-3/60; Legends #6, 4/87; (new team) Justice Leagueof America Annual #2, 1984
Justice Legion A - JLA #23, 10/98
Justice Society of America - All Star Comics #3, Win, '40-41; (1st S.A. cameo) Flash #137, ?/63
Kiss - (1st full app.) Howard the Duck #13, 6/77; (cameo) Howard the Duck #12, 3/77
Knights of the Galaxy - Mystery In Space #1, 4-5/51
Legion of Monsters - (Ghost Rider, Man-Thing, Morbius, Werewolf) Marvel Premiere #28, 1975
Legion of Substitute Heroes - Adventure Comics #306, 3/63
Legion of Super Heroes - Adventure Comics #247, 4/58
Legion Of Super Pets - Adventure Comics #293, 2/62
Liberators - Avengers #83, 12/70
Liberty Legion - Marvel Premiere #29, 1975
Losers - (Storm/Gunner/Sarge/J. Cloud) G. I. Combat #138, 10-11/69
Lt. Marvels - Whiz Comics #21, 9/41
Marvel Family - Captain Marvel Adventures #18, 12/42
Masters Of Evil - Avengers #6, 2/64
Masters of the Universe - New Teen Titans #25, 11/82
Mercenaries - G.I. Combat #244, 1982
Metal Men - Showcase #37, 3-4/62
Mighty Crusaders - Mighty Crusaders #1, 11/65
New Gods - New Gods #1, 2-3/71
New Mutants - Marvel Graphic Novel #4, 1982
New Teen Titans - DC Comics Presents #26, 10/80
New Warriors - (cameo) Thor #411, 12/89; (full app.) Thor #412, 12/89
Newsboy Legion - Star Spangled Comics #7, 4/42; (re-intro) Superman's Pal Jimmy Olsen #133, 10/70
Next Men - Dark Horse Presents #54, 9/91
Night Force - New Teen Titans #21, 7/82
Omega Men - Green Lantern #141, 6/81
Our Gang - Our Gang Comics #1, 9-10/42
Outsiders - Brave and the Bold #200, 7/83
Planeteers - Real Fact Comics #16, 9-10/48
Power Elite - Starman #4, Win '88
Power Pack - Power Pack #1, 8/84
Sea Devils - Showcase #27, 7-8/60
Secret Six - Secret Six #1, 4-5/68; (re-intro) Action Comics #601, 6/88
Sentinels - X-Men #14, 11/65
Seven Soldiers of Victory - Leading Comics #1, Wint, '41-42
Shadowmaster - Punisher #24, ?/89
S.H.I.E.L.D. - Nick Fury Agent of Shield #1, 6/68
Stargazers - Vanguard Ill. #2, 12/83
Starjammers - (cameo) X-Men #104, 4/77; (full app.) X-Men #107, 10/77
Star Rovers - Mystery In Space #66, 1961
Stargrazers - Vanguard Illustrated #2, 12/83
Suicide Squad - Brave and the Bold #25, 8-9/59; (new) Legends #3, 1/87
Super Friends - Super Friends #1, 11/76
Team America - Captain America #269, 5/82
Team Titans - (Teen Titans) New Titans Annual #7, 1991
Teenage Mutant Ninja Turtles - Gobbledygook #1, 1984
Teen Titans - Brave and the Bold #54, 6-7/64
Terrific Three - (Jaguar, Mr. Justice, Steel Sterling) Mighty Crusaders #5, 9/66
Three Mouseketeers - Funny Stuff #1, Sum '44
Thunder Agents - Thunder Agents #1, 11/65
Tiger Squadron - Blue Beetle #20, 4/43
Toxic Crusaders - Toxic Crusaders #1, 5/92
Tough Kid Squad - Tough Kid Squad #1, 3/42
Transformers - Transformers #1, 9/84
Tribe - WILDC.A.T.s: Covert Action Teams #4, 3/93
Ultra-Men - (Fox, Web, Capt. Flag) Mighty Crusaders #5, 9/66
Wanderers - Adventure Comics #375, 12/68
West Coast Avengers - West Coast Avengers #1, 9/84
Wildcats - WILDC.A.T.s: Covert Action Teams #1, 8/92
X-Factor - Avengers #263, 1/86; (new team) X-Factor #71, 10/91
X-Force - (cameo) New Mutants #100, 4/91
X-Men - X-Men #1, 9/63; X-Men #1, 10/91; (new team) X-Men #253, 1989; (new team) X-Men #281, 10/91; (new) Giant-Size X-Men #1, Sum, '75
X-Terminators - X-Terminators #1, 10/88
Young Allies - Young Allies #1, Sum '41
Youngblood - (1 pg. ad) Megaton #8, 8/87; (2pgs.) Megaton Explosion nn, 6/87
Young Justice - Young Justice: The Secret #1, 6/98

FIRST APPEARANCES: VILLAIN GROUPS

Beagle Boys - Walt Disney's Comics and Stories #134, 11/51
Blue Trinity - Flash #7, 12/87
Brotherhood of Evil - (new) New Teen Titans #15, 1/82
Brotherhood of Evil Mutants - X-Men #4, 3/64; (new) X-Men #141, 1/81
Citadel - Green Lantern #136, 1/81
Enforcers - Amazing Spider-Man #10, 3/64
Fearsome Five - New Teen Titans #3, 1/81
Frightful Four - (Sandman/Wizard/P.P. Pete) Fantastic Four #36, 3/65
Injustice Society - All Star Comics #37, 10-11/47
Krypton Foes - Superman #65, 7-8/50
Legion of Super-Villains - Superman #147, 8/61
Masters of Evil - Avengers #6, 7/64; (new) Avengers #54, 7/68
Phantom Zone Villains (Dr. Zadu & Emdine) - Superboy #100, 10/62
Royal Flush Gang - Justice League of America #43, ?/66; (new) Justice League of America #203, 6/82
Secret Society of Super-Villains - Secret Society of Super-Villains #1, 5-6/76
Sinister Six - Amazing Spider-Man Annual #1, 1964
Skrulls - Fantastic Four #2, 1/62
Toad Men - Incredible Hulk #2, 7/62

FIRST CROSSOVERS

Ant-Man - Fantastic Four #16, 7/63
Avengers - Tales of Suspense #49, 1/64
Capt. America - (outside of Avengers) Sgt. Fury #13
Conan - Savage Tales #1, 5/71
Daredevil - Amazing Spider-Man #16, 9/64
Doctor Strange - Fantastic Four #27, 6/64
Fantastic Four - Amazing Spider-Man #1, 3/63
Hulk - Fantastic Four #12, 3/63
G.A. Green Lantern x-over in S.A. - Showcase #55, 3-4/65
Iceman - Strange Tales #120, 5/64
Iron Man - (x-over outside Avengers) Tales to Astonish #82, 8/66
Magneto - Journey Into Mystery #109, 10/64
Nick Fury - (as agent of Shield) Tales of Suspense #92, 8/67
S.A. Captain America - Sgt. Fury #13, 12/64
Sgt. Fury - Fantastic Four #21, 12/63
Silver Surfer - (cameo) Tales to Astonish #92, 6/67; (full app.) Tales to Astonish #93, 7/67
Spider-Man - Strange Tales Annual #2, 7/63
Sub-Mariner - (outside Fantastic Four) Strange Tales #107, (4/63)
Thing - Strange Tales #116, 1/64
Thor - Strange Tales #123, 8/64
X-Men - Tales of Suspense #49, 1/64

FIRST SUPERPETS

Ace the Bat-Hound - Batman #92, 6/55
Beppo the Supermonkey - Superboy #76, 8/59
Captain Carrot - New Teen Titans #16, 2/82
Comet the Superhorse - Adventure Comics #293, 2/62
Cosmo - (Challengers Spacepet) Challengers of the Unknown #18, 9-10/60
Krypto the Super Dog - Adventure Comics #210, 3/55
Legion of Super Pets - Adventure Comics #293, 2/62
Proty II - Adventure Comics #316 , 1/64
Rang-A-Tang the Wonder Dog - Blue Ribbon Comics #1, 11/39
Streak the Wonder Dog - Green Lantern #30, 2-3/48
Streaky the Super Cat - Action Comics #261, 2/60
Wolf - (Boy Commandos mascot) Boy Commandos #34, 7-8/49

FIRST PROTOTYPES

Some of today's popular super hero characters were developed from or after earlier forms or prototypes. These prototype characters sometimes were introduced to test new ideas and concepts which later developed into full fledged super heroes, or old material sometimes would inspire new characters. Below is a list of all known prototypes. The Marvel/Atlas issues have been verified by Stan Lee, Steve Ditko and Jack Kirby.

Ancient One - Strange Tales #92, 1/62
Ant-Man - Strange Tales #73, 2/60; Strange Tales #78, 11/60
Aunt May - Strange Tales #97, 6/62
Doctor Doom - Tales of Suspense #31, 7/62
Doctor Strange - Journey Into Mystery #78, 3/62; Strange Tales #79, 12/60; Tales of Suspense #32, 8/62
Electro - Tales To Astonish #15, 1/61
Giant-Man - Strange Tales #70, 8/59
Hulk - Journey Into Mystery #62, 11/60; Journey Into Mystery #66, 3/61
Human Torch - Strange Tales #76, 8/60
Iron Man - Strange Tales #75, 6/60; Tales of Suspense #9, 5/60; Tales of Suspense #16, 4/61
Kamandi - Alarming Tales #1, 9/57
Lava Men - Tales of Suspense #7, 1/60
Magneto - Strange Tales #84, 5/61
Mr. Hyde - Journey Into Mystery #79, 4/62
Professor X - Amazing Adult Fantasy #14, 7/62; Strange Tales #69, 6/59
Quicksilver - Strange Tales #67, 2/59
Red Tornado - House Of Mystery #155, 9-10/65
Sandman - Journey Into Mystery #70, 7/61
Savage Dragon - Marvel Comics Presents #50, 1990
Spider-Man - Journey Into Mystery #73, 10/61
Stone Men - Tales of Suspense #28, 4/62; Tales to Astonish #5, 9/59; Tales to Astonish #16, 2/61
Superman - (Dr. Mystic) Comics Magazine #1, 5/36; More Fun Comics #14, 10/36; New Book of Comics #2, Spr '38
Toad Men - Tales to Astonish #7, 1/60
Uncle Ben - Strange Tales #97, 6/62
Watcher - Tales of Suspense #35, 11/62

FIRST OF A PUBLISHER

Ace Magazines - Sure-Fire #1, 6/40
American Comics Group - Giggle #1 & Ha Ha #1, 10/43
Atlas Comics - All Winners #11, Wint.'43/44
Avon Comics -Molly O'Day #1, 2/45
Better Publications (Standard) - Best Comics #1, 11/39
Bilbara Publishing Co. - Cyclone #1, 6/40
Brookwood Publications - Speed Comics #1, 10/39
Carlton Publishing Co. - Zoom Comics #1, 12/45
Catechetical Guild - Topix #1, 11/42
Centaur Publications -Funny Pages V2#6, 3/38; Funny Picture Stories V2#6, 3/38; Star Comics #10, 3/38; Star Ranger V2#10, 3/38
Charlton Comics -Zoo Funnies #1, 11/45
Columbia Comics Group - Big Shot #1, 5/40
Comico - Primer #1, 10/82
Comics Magazine - Comics Magazine #1, 5/36
Dark Horse - Dark Horse Presents #1, 7/86
David McKay Publ. - King Comics #1, 4/36
DC Comics - New Fun Comics #1, 2/35
Defiant Comics - Warriors Of Plasm #1, 8/93
Dell Publishing Co. - Popular Comics #1, 2/36
Eastern Color - Funnies On Parade nn, 1933
Elliot Publications - Double Comics, 1940
Fawcett Publications - Whiz Comics #2 (#1), 2/40
Fiction House - Jumbo Comics #1, 9/38
Flying Cadet - Flying Cadet #1, 1/43
Fox Features Syndicate - Wonder Comics #1, 5/39
Funnies, Inc. - Motion Picture Funnies Weekly #1, 1939
Gilberton Publ. - Classic Comics #1, 10/41
Gladstone - Disneyland Birthday Party, 8/85; Uncle Scrooge Goes To Disneyland, 8/85
Globe Syndicate - Circus Comics #1, 6/38
Great Publications - Great Comics #1, 11/41
Harry 'A' Chesler - Star Comics #1, 2/37
Harvey Comics - Pocket Comics #1, 8/41
Hawley Publications - Captain Easy nn, 1939
Hillman Periodicals - Miracle Comics #1, 2/40
Holyoke (Continental) - Crash Comics #1, 5/40
Hugo Gernsback - Superworld #1, 4/40
Hyper Publications - Hyper Mystery #1, 5/40
Image Comics - Youngblood #1, 4/92
K.K. Publications - Mickey Mouse Magazine #1, Sum, 1935
Lev Gleason - Silver Streak #1, 12/39
Mirage Studios - Gobbledygook #1, no month '84
MLJ Magazines - Blue Ribbon Comics #1, 11/39
Nita Publications - Whirlwind Comics #1, 6/40
Novelty Publications - Target Comics #1, 6/40
Parents' Magazine Institute - True Comics #1, 4/41
Prize Publications - Prize Comics #1, 3/40
Progressive Publishers - Feature Comics #21, 6/39
Quality Comics Group - Feature Comics #21, 6/39
Ralston-Purina Co. - Tom Mix #1, 9/40
Standard Comics (Better Publ.) - Best Comics #1, 11/39
Street and Smith Publications - Shadow Comics #1, 3/40
Sun Publications - Colossus Comics #1, 3/40
Timely Comics - Marvel Mystery #1, 11/39
United Features Syndicate - Tip Top Comics #1, 4/36
Valiant Comics - (hero) Magnus Robot Fighter, 5/91
Warren all comics magazine - Creepy #1, no month '64
Whitman Publishing Co. - Mammoth Comics #1, 1937
Will Eisner - Spirit #1, 6/2/40
William H. Wise - Columbia Comics #1, 1943

OVERSTREET COMIC BOOK PRICE GUIDE BACK ISSUES

The Overstreet® Comic Book Price Guide has held the record for being the longest running annual comic book publication. We are now celebrating our 29th anniversary and comic book collectors are as interested in putting together complete sets of these books as they are in collecting the old comics. The demand for the Overstreet® price guides is very strong and the collectors have created a legitimate market for them. They continue to bring record prices each year. Besides the price consideration, collectors also have a record of comic book prices going back further than any other source in comic fandom. The prices listed below are for near mint condition only. The other grades can be determined as follows: Good - 25% and Fine - 50% of the near mint value. Canadian editions exist for a couple of the early issues. Special thanks is given to Robert Rogovin of Four Color Comics for his assistance in researching the prices listed in this section.

Abbreviations used: SC = soft cover; HC = hard cover, L = leather bound.

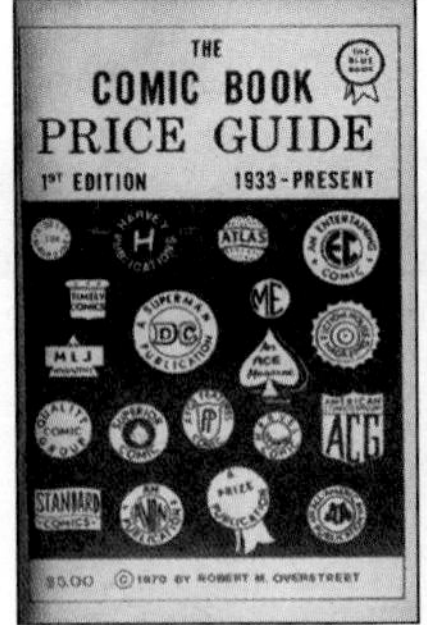

#1 White Soft Cover
$1700.00

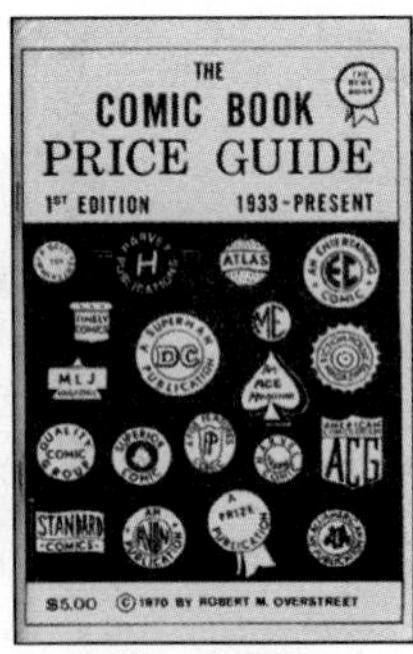

printed 1970

#1 Blue Soft Cover
(2nd Printing)
$1400.00

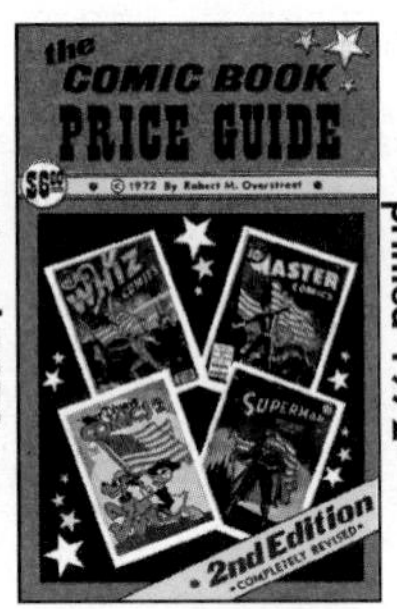

printed 1972

#2 SC $600.00
#2 HC $1000.00

printed 1973

#3 SC $275.00
#3 HC $900.00

printed 1974

#4 SC $150.00
#4 HC $450.00

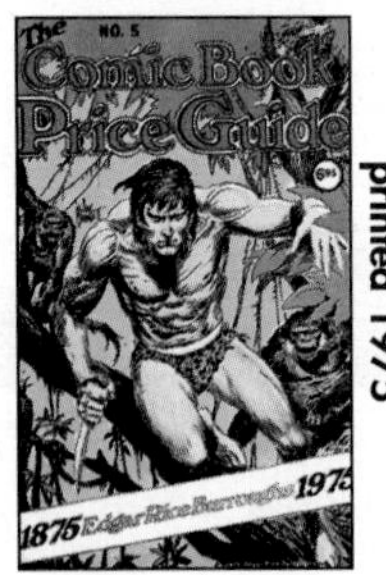

printed 1975

#5 SC $150.00
#5 HC $250.00

printed 1976

#6 SC $100.00
#6 HC $150.00

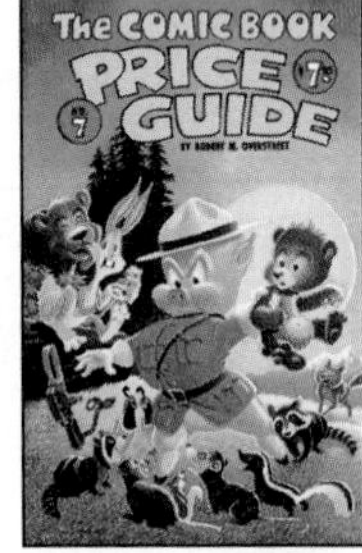

printed 1977

#7 SC $140.00
#7 HC $225.00

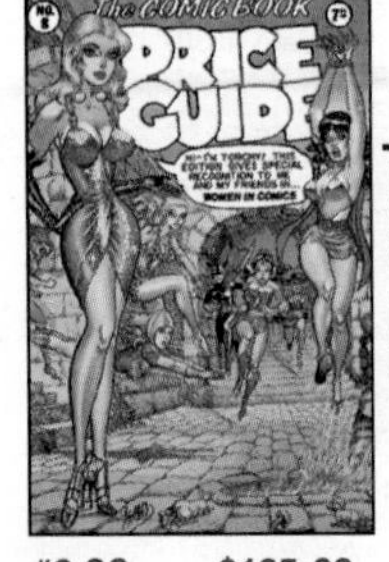

printed 1978

#8 SC $125.00
#8 HC $175.00

printed 1979

#9 SC $125.00
#9 HC $175.00

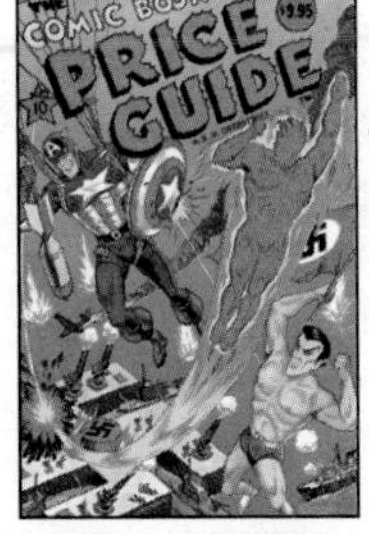

printed 1980

#10 SC $125.00
#10 HC $175.00

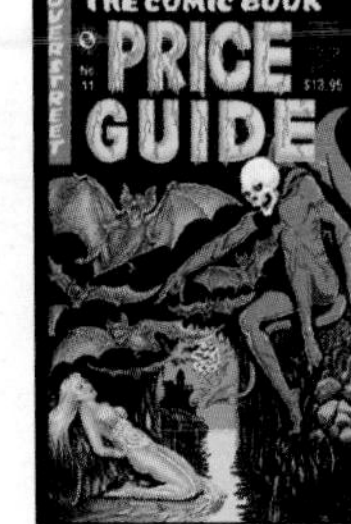

printed 1981

#11 SC $80.00
#11 HC $110.00

printed 1982

#12 SC $80.00
#12 HC $110.00

printed 1983

#13 SC $80.00
#13 HC $110.00

printed 1984

#14 SC $55.00
#14 HC $110.00
#14 L $170.00

printed 1985

#15 SC $55.00
#15 HC $80.00
#15 L $160.00

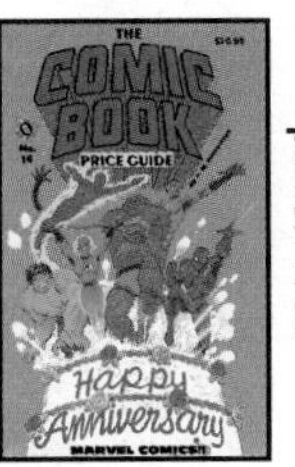

printed 1986

#16 SC $55.00
#16 HC $80.00
#16 L $160.00

printed 1987

#17 SC $55.00
#17 HC $110.00
#17 L $160.00

printed 1988

#18 SC $45.00
#18 HC $65.00
#18 L $160.00

printed 1989

#19 SC $45.00
#19 HC $55.00
#19 L $160.00

printed 1990

#20 SC $32.00
#20 HC $50.00
#20 L $135.00

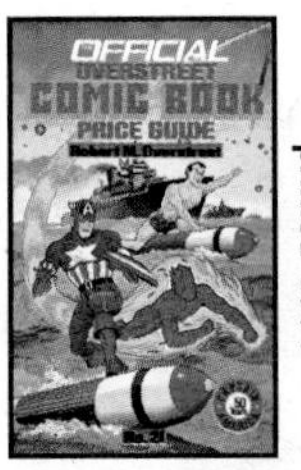

printed 1991

#21 SC $32.00
#21 HC $50.00
#21 L $135.00

printed 1992

#22 SC $32.00
#22 HC $50.00

printed 1993

#23 SC $32.00
#23 HC $50.00

printed 1994

#24 SC $24.00
#24 HC $34.00

printed 1995

#25 SC $24.00
#25 HC $34.00
#25 L $100.00

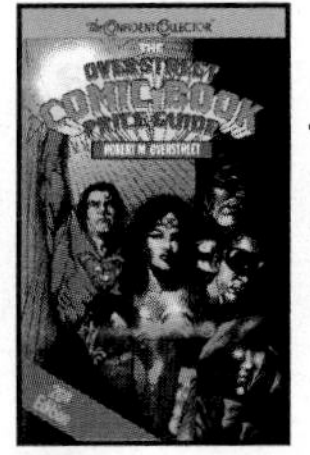

printed 1996

#26 SC $20.00
#26 HC $30.00
#26 L $100.00

printed 1997

#27 SC $22.00
#27 HC $32.00
#27 L $125.00

printed 1997

#27 SC $22.00
#27 HC $32.00
#27 L $125.00

printed 1998

#28 SC $20.00
#28 HC $30.00

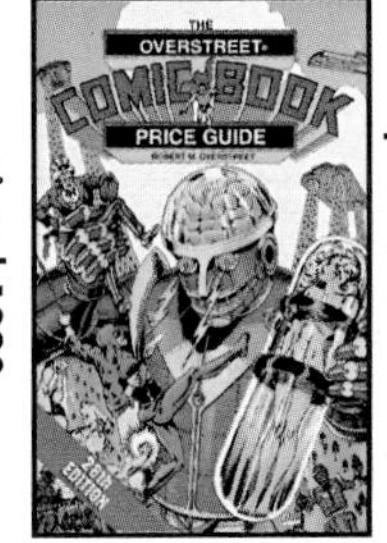

printed 1998

#28 SC $20.00
#28 HC $30.00

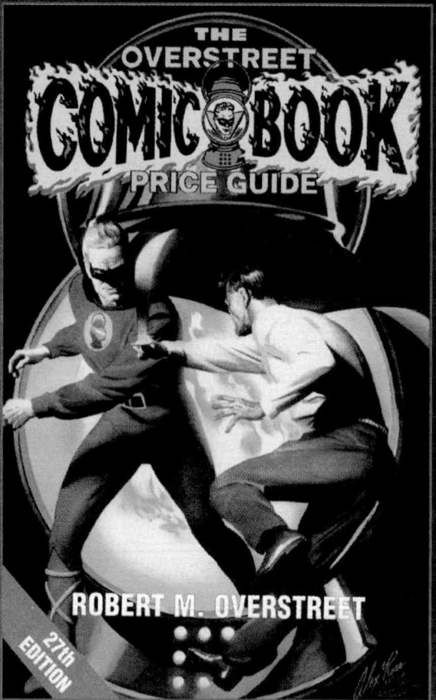

PRESENTING THE COVE
COMIC BOOK PRICE
ORIGINAL ART

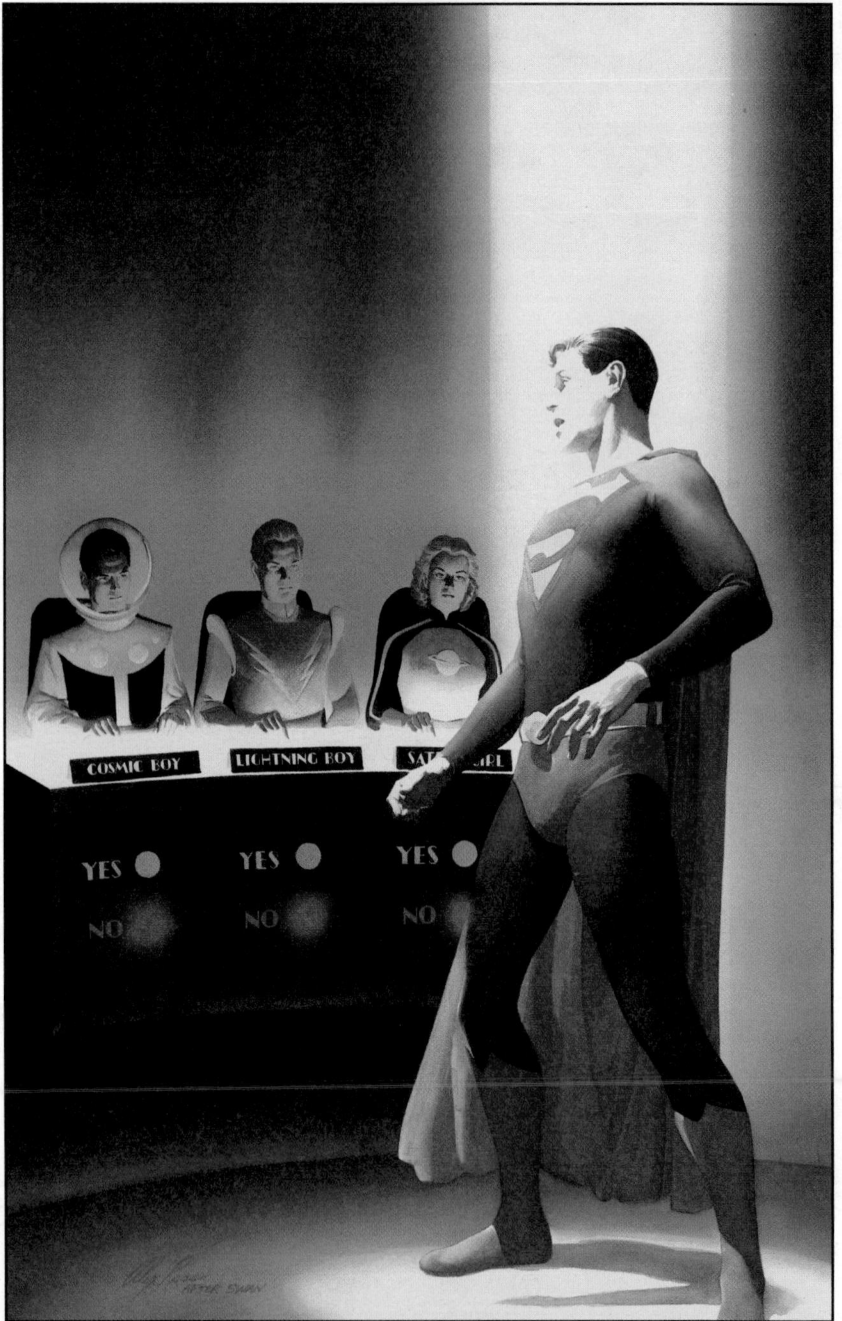

Re-creation of Cover Art for ADVENTURE COMICS #247 (original by Curt Swan)

RS TO THE OVERSTREET
GUIDE, 29th EDITION
BY ALEX ROSS

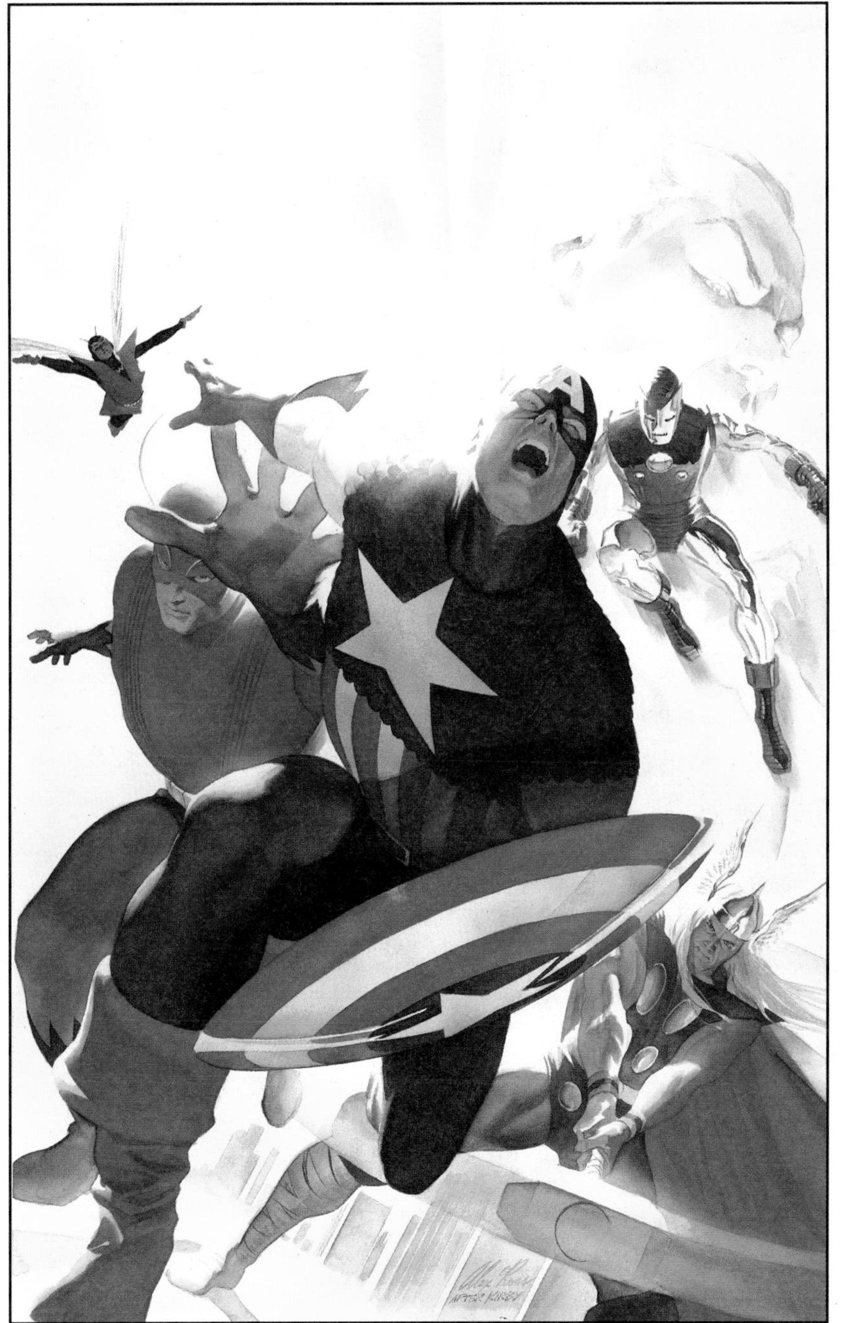

Re-creation of Cover Art for AVENGERS #4 (original by Jack Kirby)

COVER

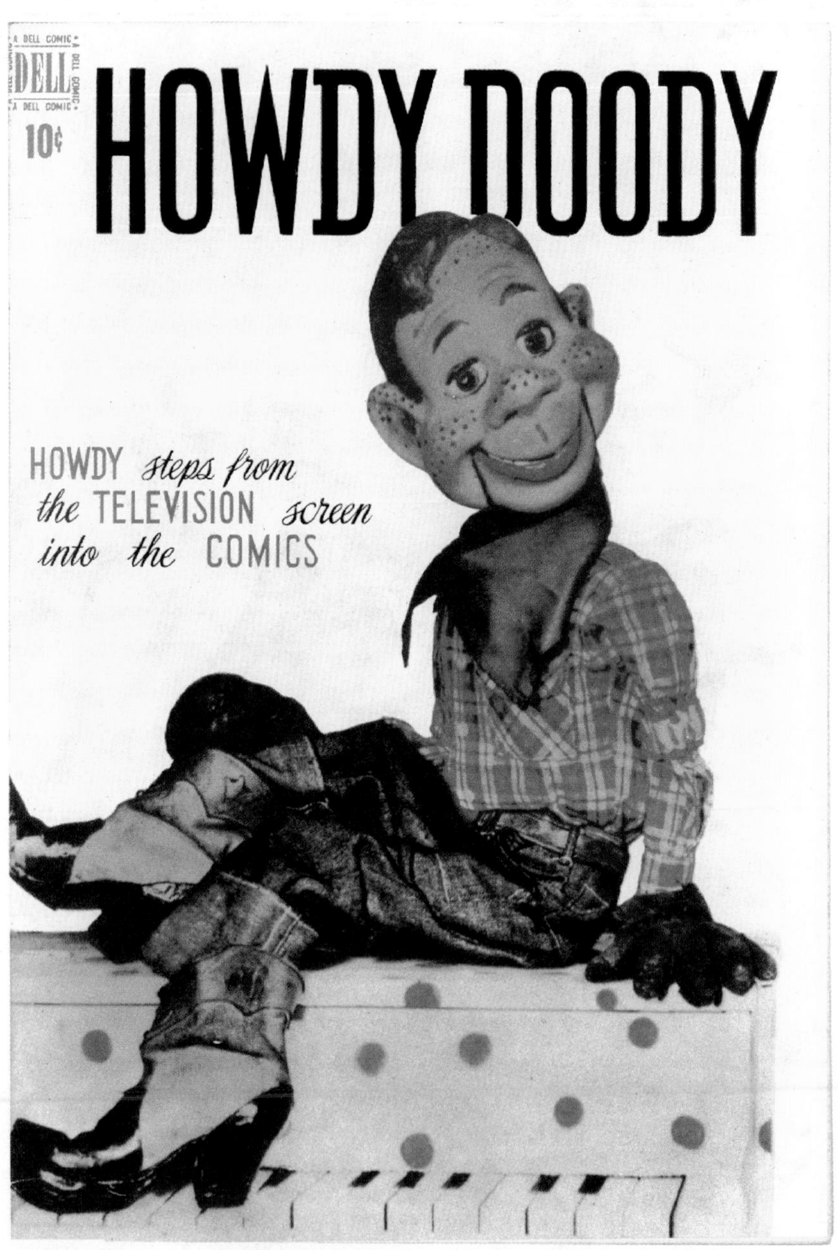

HOWDY DOODY #1, January 1950 © DELL
In memory of Buffalo Bob who passed away July 29, 1998, 80 years old.

GALLERY

ROY ROGERS COMICS #3, March 1948 © DELL
In memory of our hero, who passed away July 6, 1998, 86 years old.

C O V E R

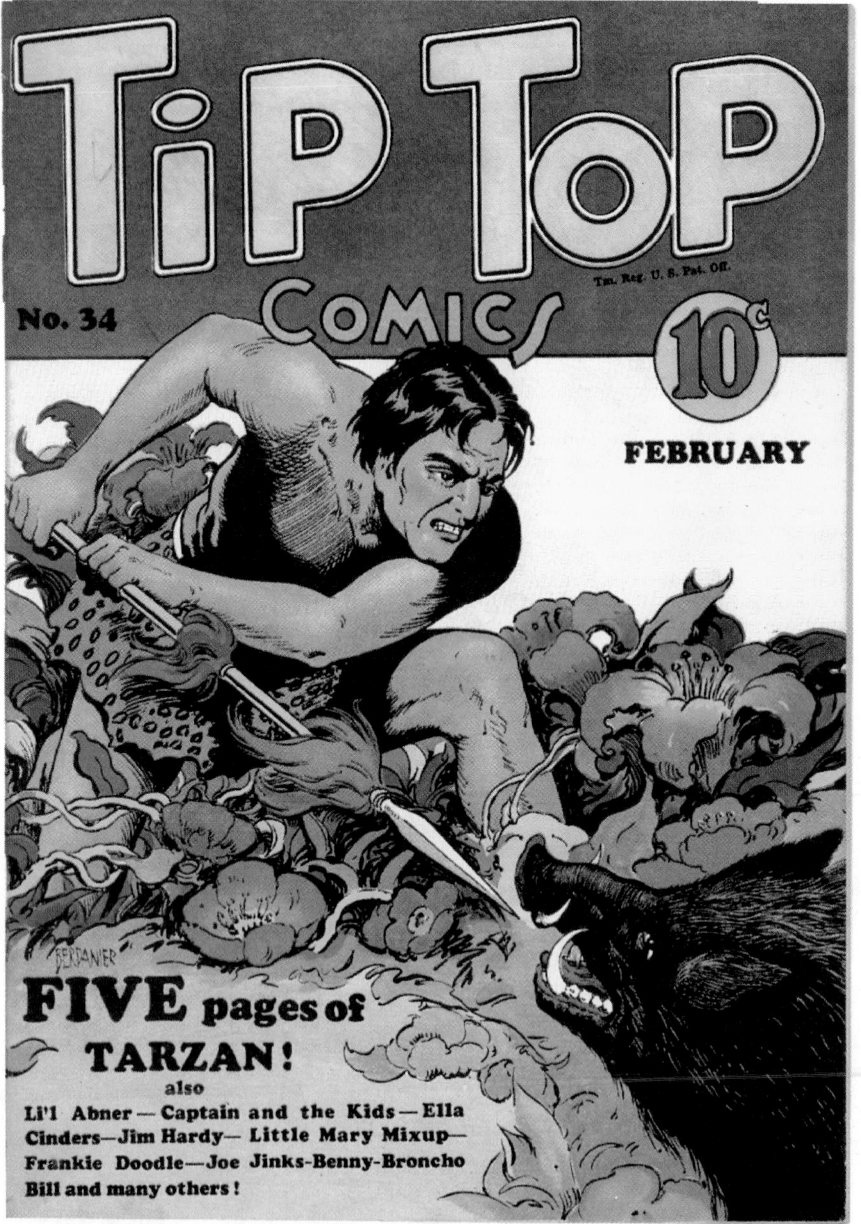

TIP TOP COMICS #34
February 1939 © UFS

GALLERY

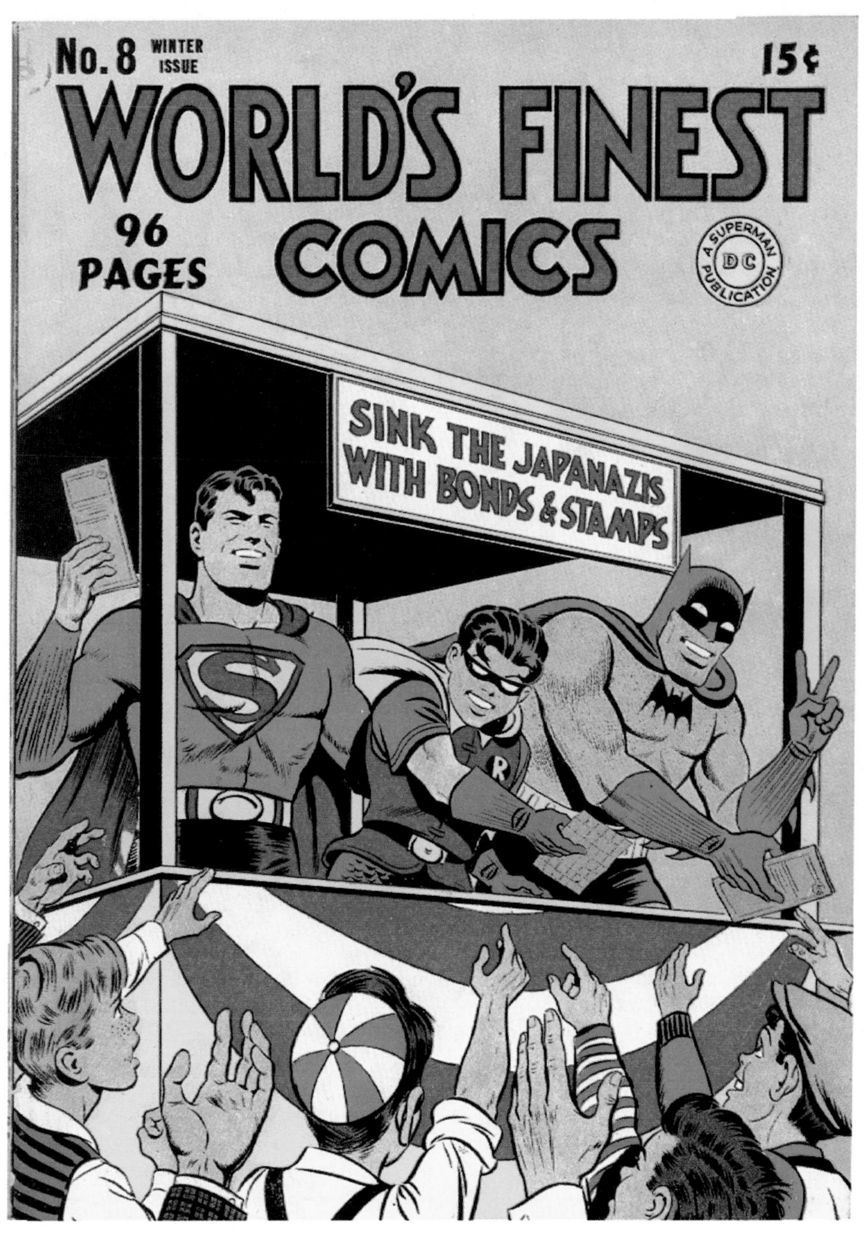

WORLD'S FINEST COMICS #8
Winter 1942 © DC

COVER

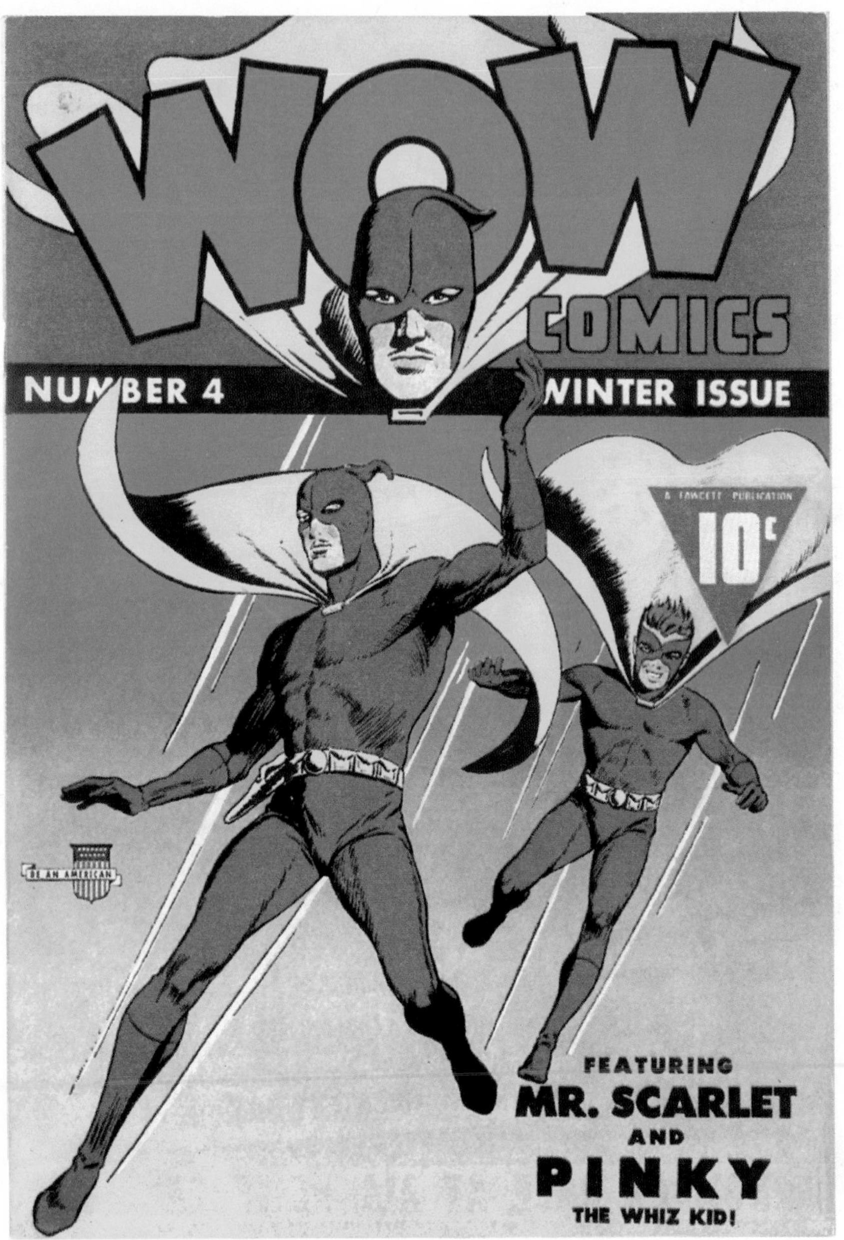

WOW COMICS #4
Winter 1941-42 © FAW

GALLERY

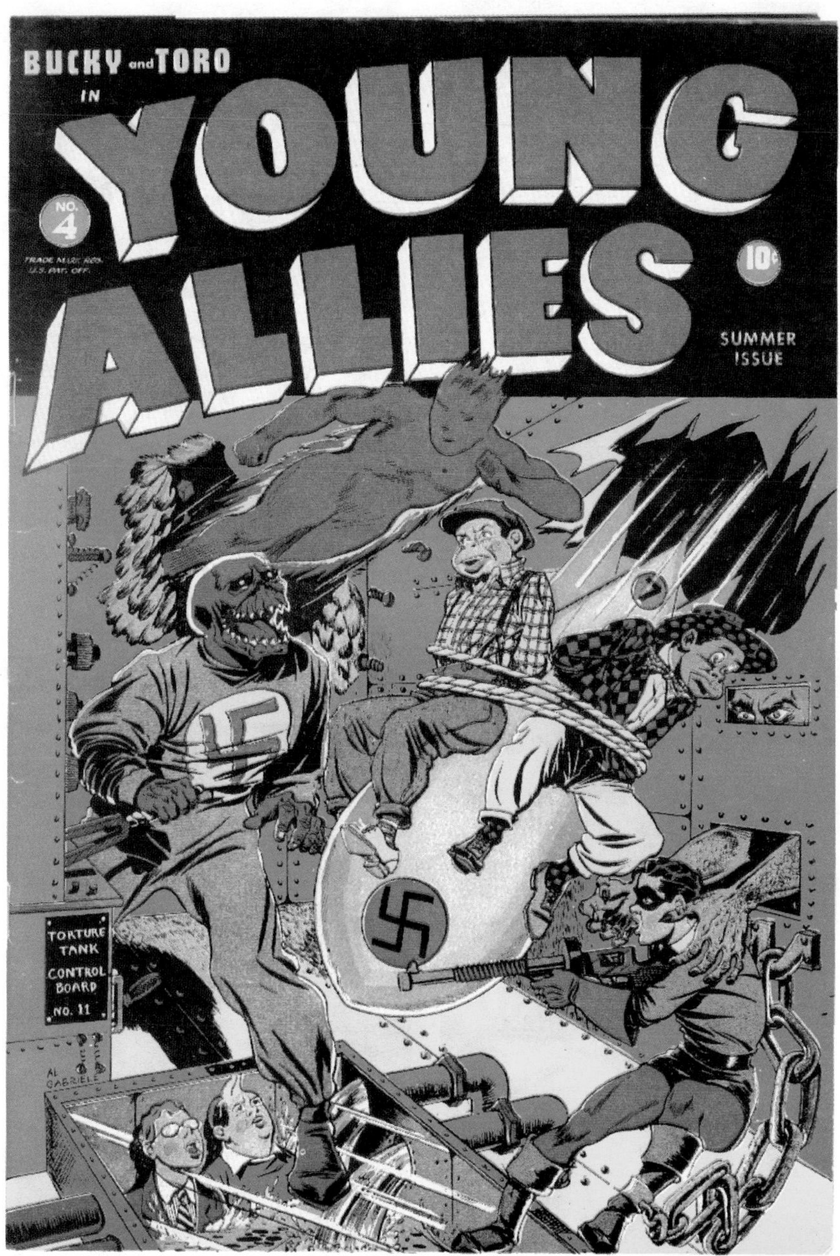

YOUNG ALLIES COMICS #4
Summer 1942 © MAR

C O V E R

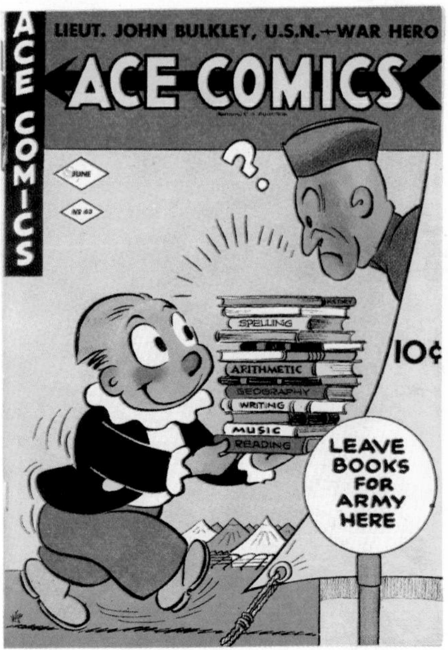

ACE COMICS #63
June 1942 © DMP

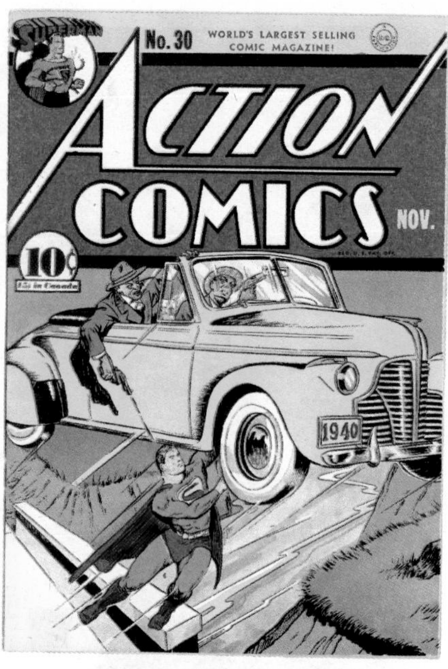

ACTION COMICS #30
November 1940 © DC

ADVENTURES #1
November 1949 © STJ

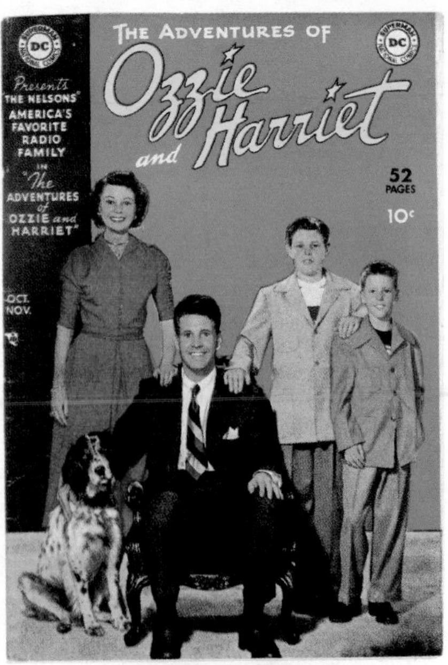

THE ADVENTURES OF
OZZIE AND HARRIET #1
October-November 1949 © DC

GALLERY

AL CAPP'S WOLF GAL #1
1951 © TOBY

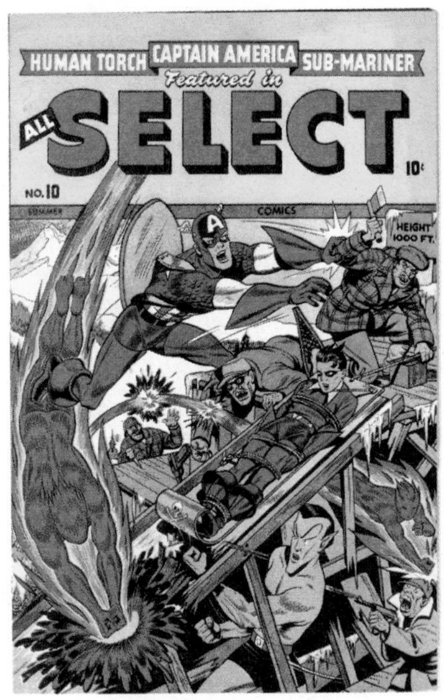

ALL SELECT COMICS #10
Summer 1946 © MAR

ALL STAR COMICS #38
January 1948 © DC

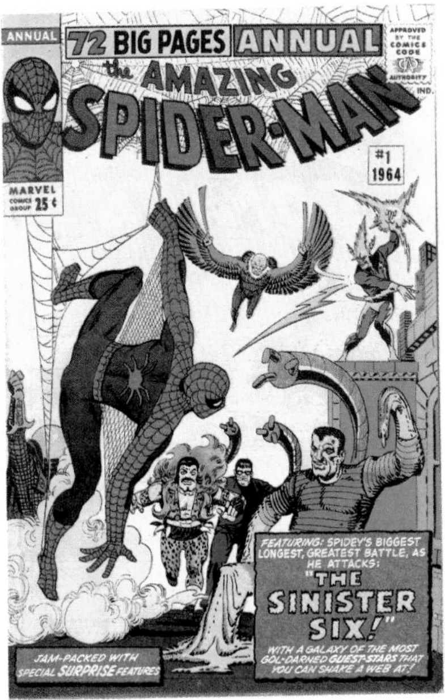

AMAZING SPIDER-MAN ANNUAL #1
1964 © MAR

C O V E R

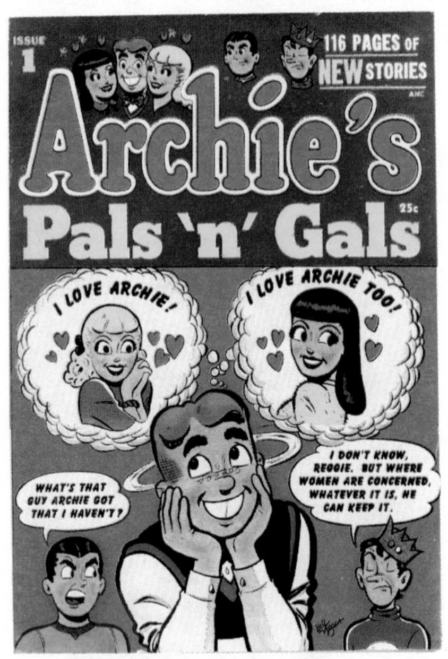

ARCHIE'S PALS 'N' GALS #1
1952-1953 © AP

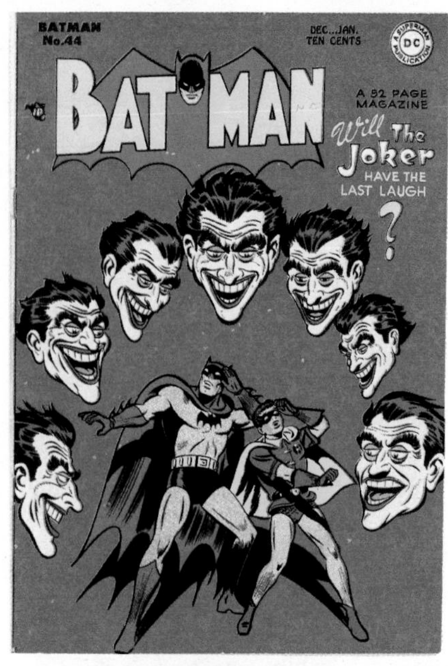

BATMAN #44
January 1948 © DC

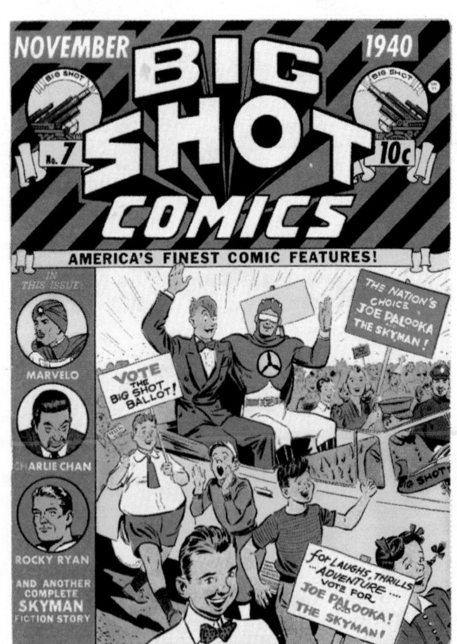

BIG SHOT COMICS #7
November 1940 © CCG

BLUE BOLT V2 #6
November 1941 © NOVP

GALLERY

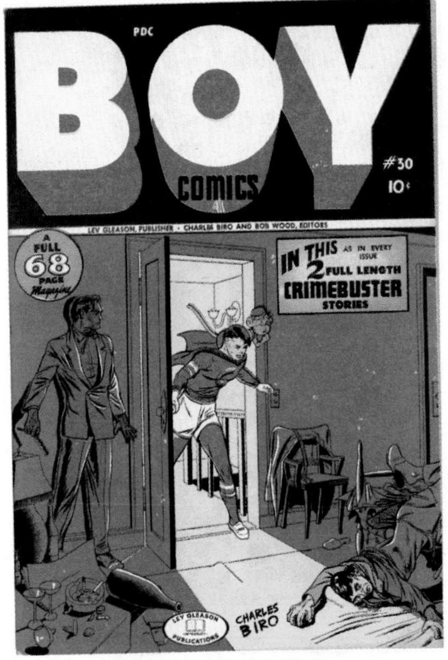

BOY COMICS #30
October 1946 © LEV

CAPTAIN AMERICA COMICS #62
May 1947 © MAR

CAPTAIN MARVEL #27
September 1943 © FAW

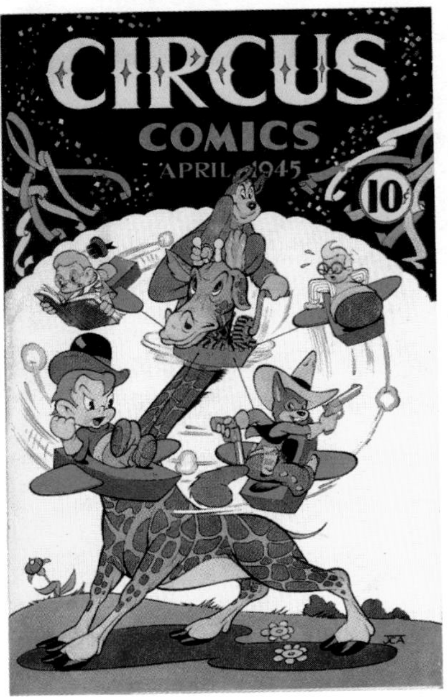

CIRCUS COMICS #1
April 1945 © Farm Woman's Publ.

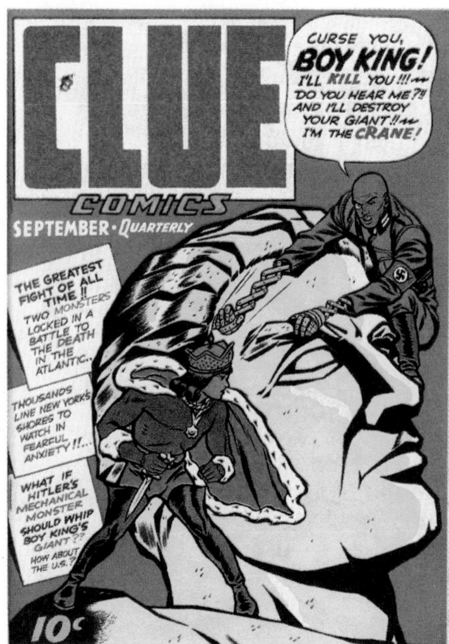

CLUE COMICS #5
September 1943 © HILL

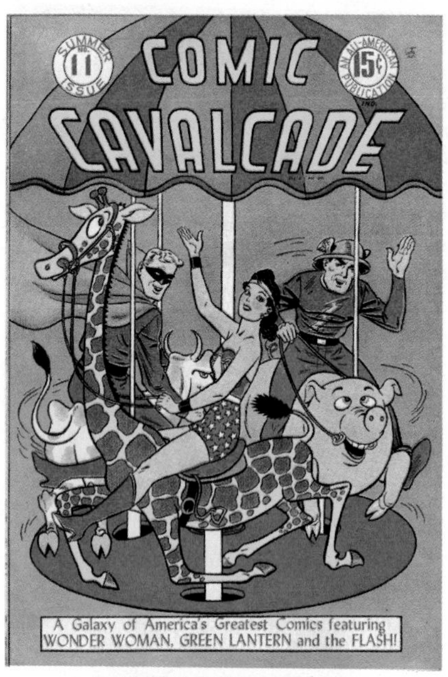

COMIC CAVALCADE #11
Summer 1945 © DC

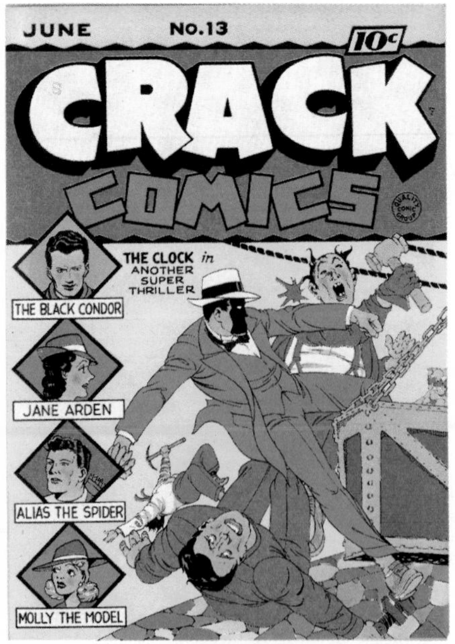

CRACK COMICS #13
June 1941 © QUA

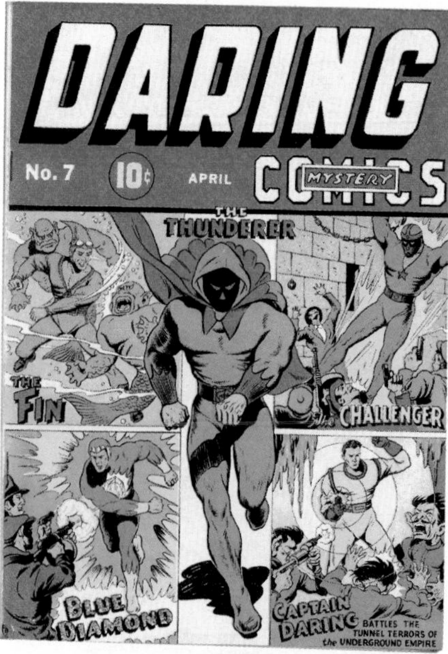

DARING MYSTERY COMICS #7
April 1941 © MEG

GALLERY

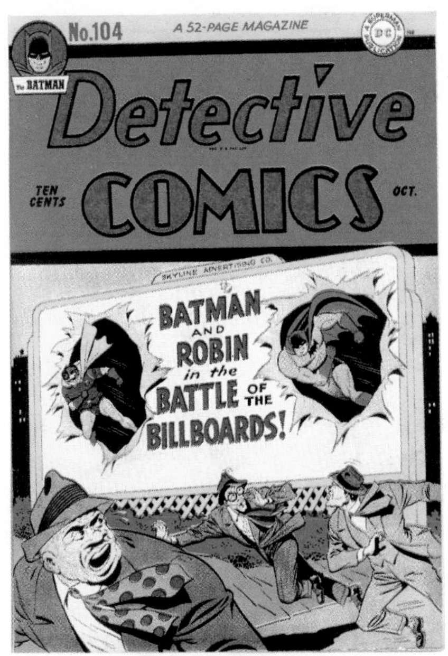

DETECTIVE COMICS #104
October 1945 © DC

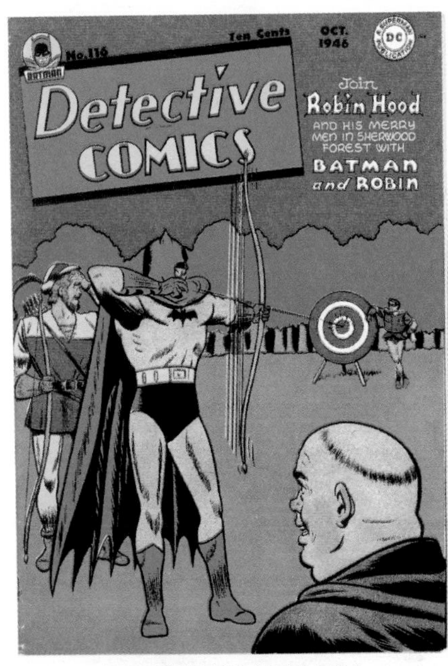

DETECTIVE COMICS #116
October 1946 © DC

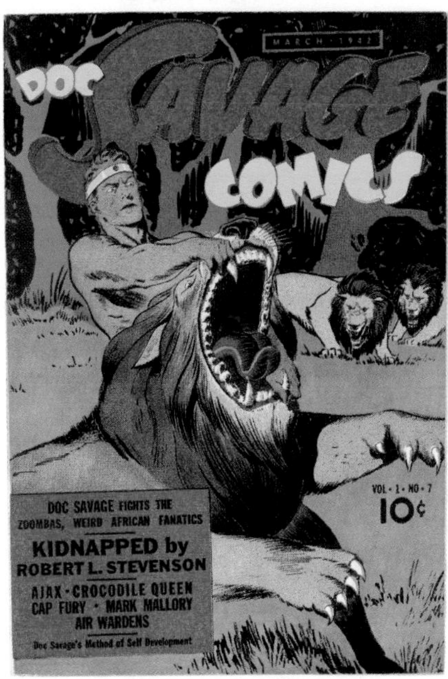

DOC SAVAGE COMICS #7
March 1942 © S&S

DON WINSLOW OF THE NAVY #25
April 1945 © FAW

COVER

FANTASTIC FOUR #4
May 1962 © MAR

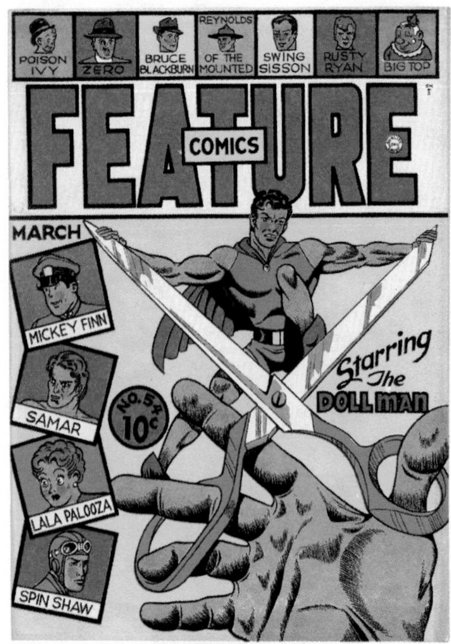

FEATURE COMICS #54
March 1942 © QUA

FLASH COMICS #83
May 1947 © DC

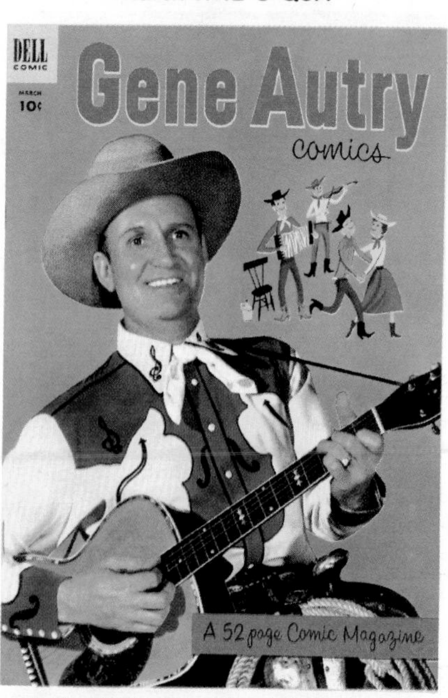

GENE AUTRY #73, March 1953 © DELL
In memory of our hero who passed away October 2, 1998, 91 years old.

GALLERY

GREEN LANTERN #10
Winter 1943 © DC

HIT COMICS #24
October 1942 © QUA

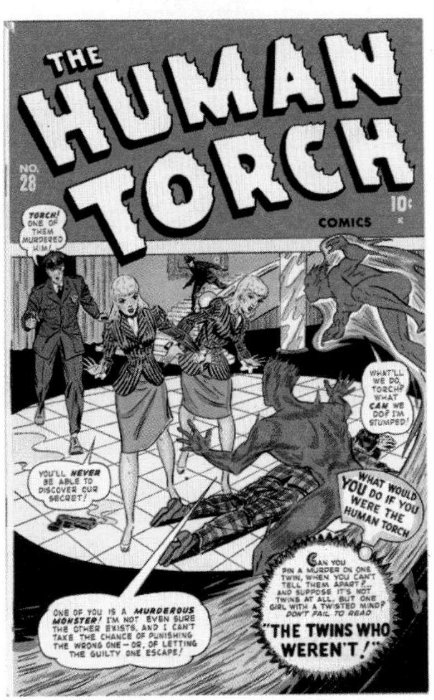

THE HUMAN TORCH #28
Fall 1947 © MAR

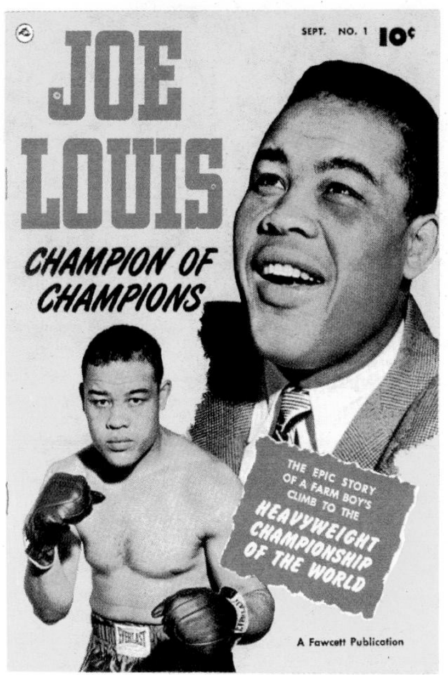

JOE LOUIS #1
September 1950 © FAW

C O V E R

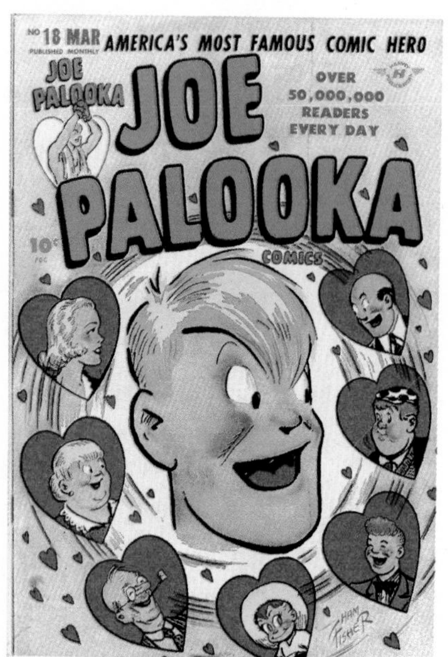

JOE PALOOKA #18
March 1948 © HARV

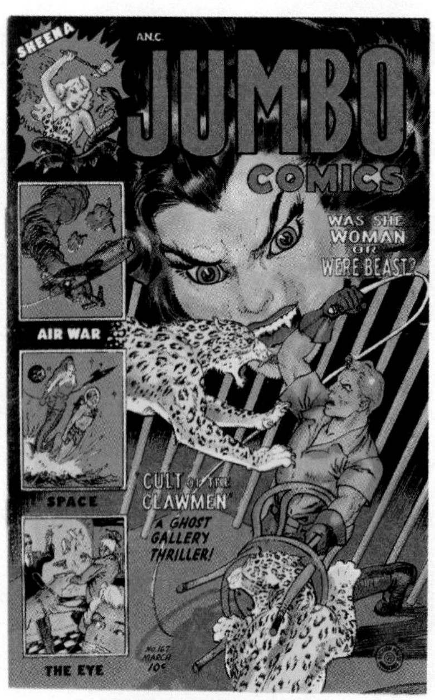

JUMBO COMICS #167
March 1953 © FH

JUNGLE COMICS #25
January 1942 © FH

KING COMICS #26
May 1938 © DMP

GALLERY

KING COMICS #47
March 1940 © DMP

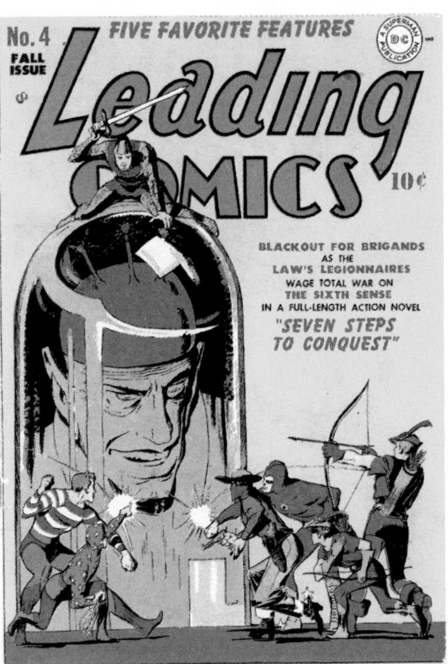

LEADING COMICS #4
Fall 1942 © DC

LOONEY TUNES AND MERRY
MELODIES COMICS #8
June 1942 © DELL

MANHUNT! #4
January 1948 © ME

C O V E R

MARVEL BOY #1
December 1950 © MAR

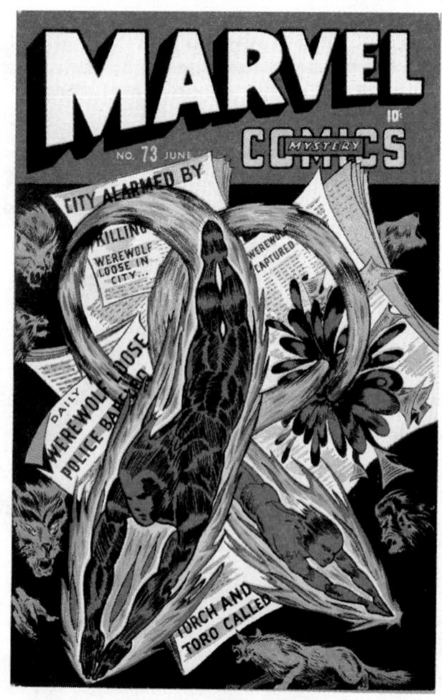

MARVEL MYSTERY COMICS #73
June 1946 © MAR

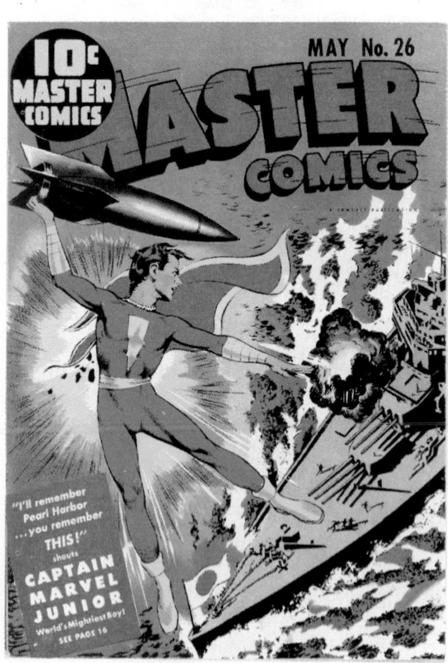

MASTER COMICS #26
May 1942 © FAW

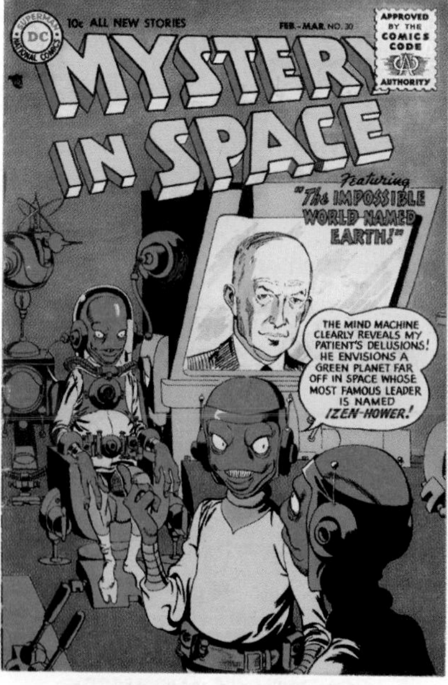

MYSTERY IN SPACE #30
March 1956 © DC

GALLERY

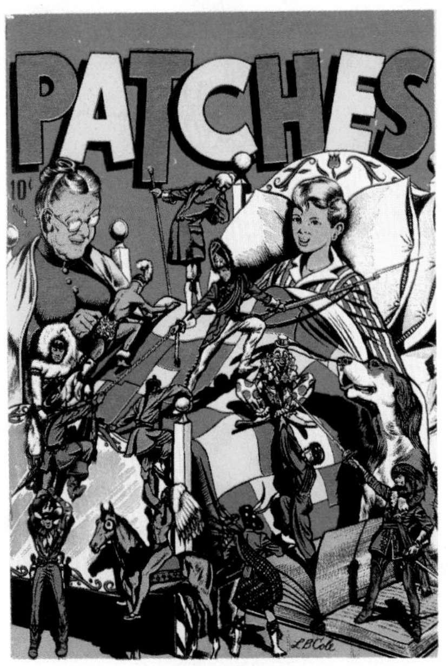

PATCHES #1
March-April 1945 © RH

PEP COMICS #31
September 1942 © MLJ

PLANET COMICS #59
March 1949 © FH

PLASTIC MAN #33
January 1952 © QUA

C O V E R

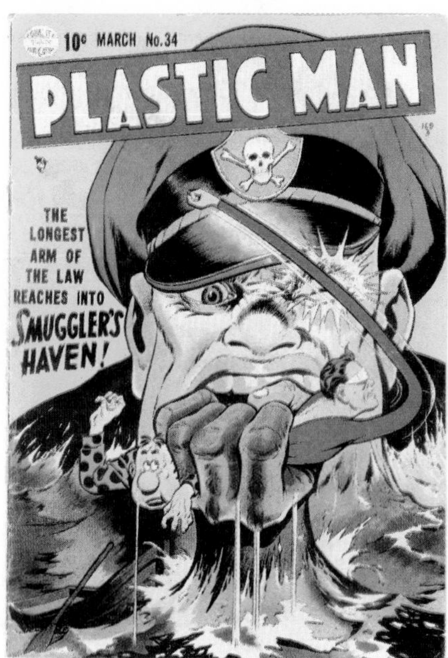

PLASTIC MAN #34
March 1952 © QUA

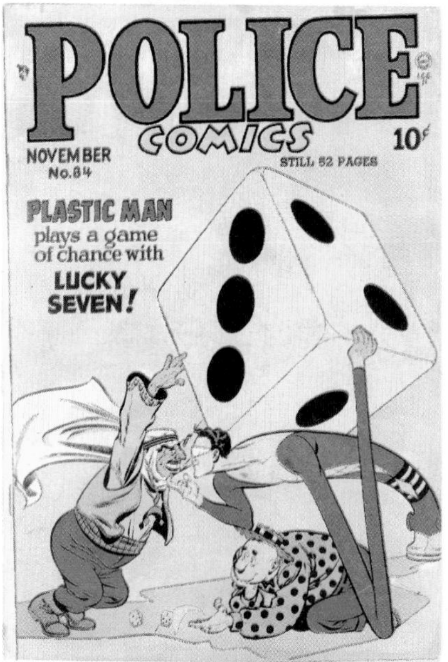

POLICE COMICS #84
November 1948 © QUA

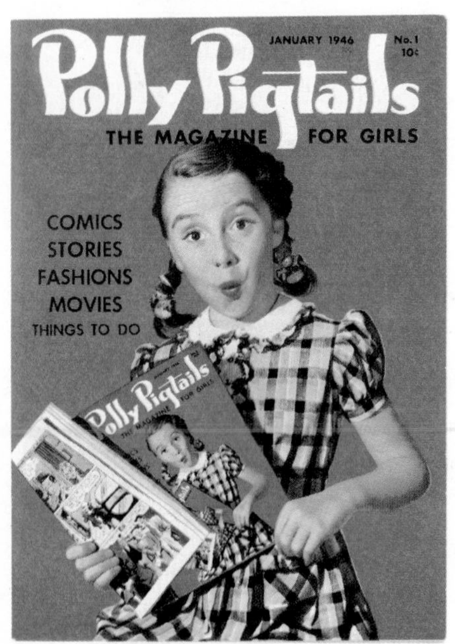

POLLY PIGTAILS #1
January 1946 © PMI

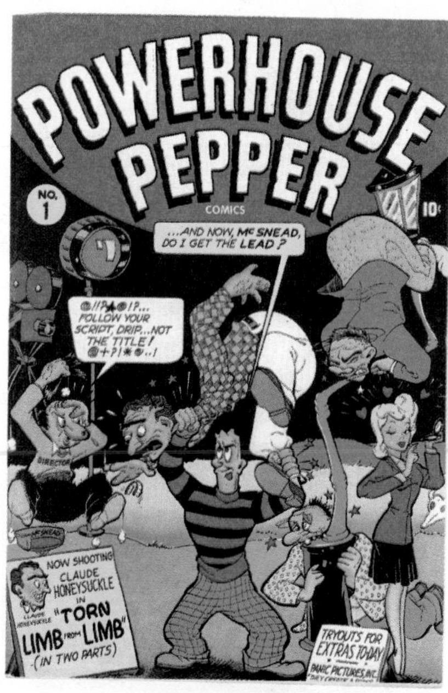

POWERHOUSE PEPPER #1
1943 © MAR

GALLERY

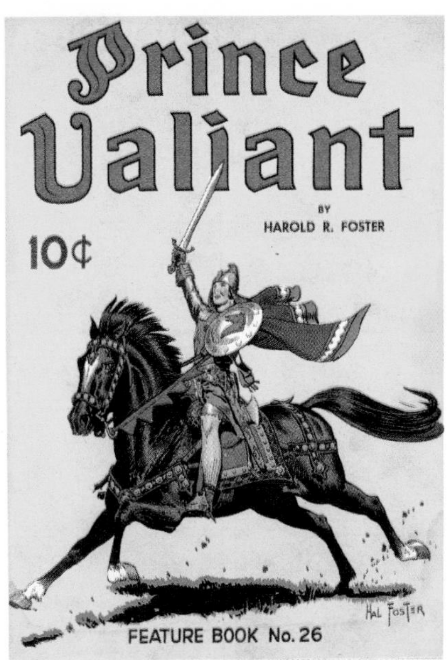

PRINCE VALIANT FEATURE BOOKS #26
1941 © KFS

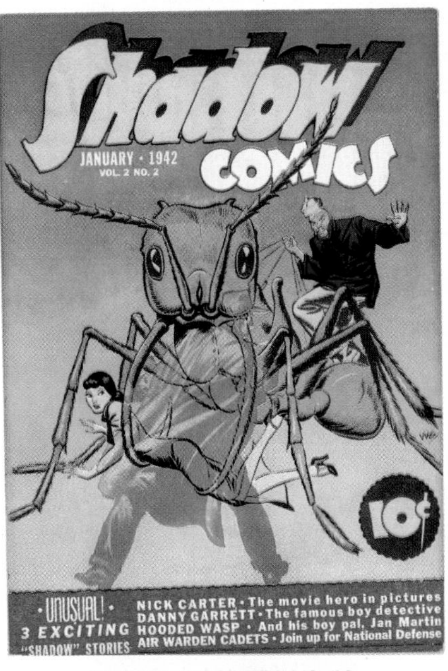

SHADOW COMICS V2 #2
January 1942 © S&S

SHOWCASE #10
October 1957 © DC

SHOWCASE #17
December 1958 © DC

C O V E R

SPELLBOUND #14
April 1953 © MEG

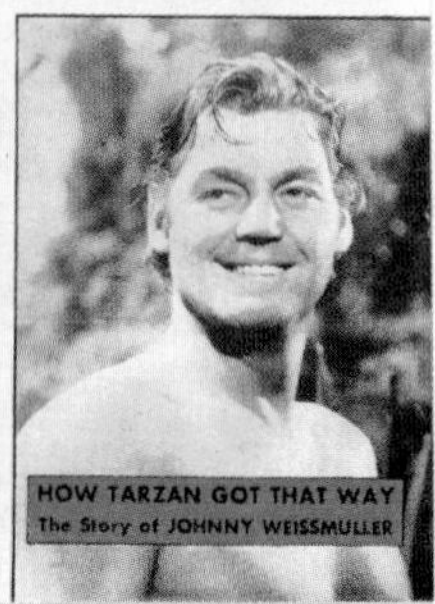

SPORT STARS #1
February-March 1946 © PMI

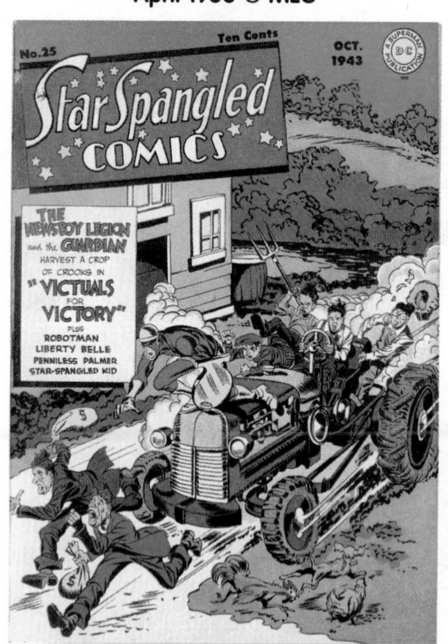

STAR SPANGLED COMICS #25
October 1943 © DC

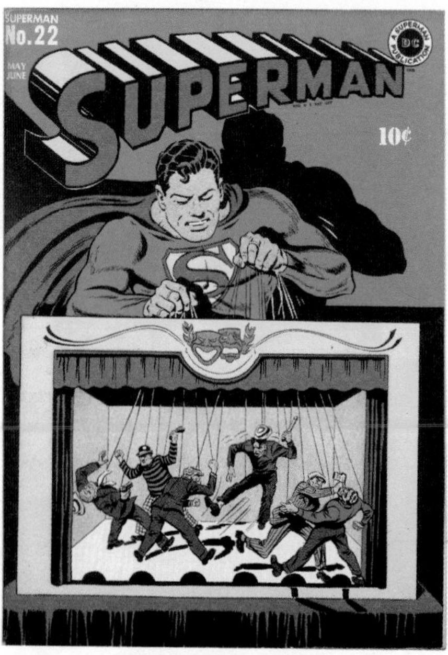

SUPERMAN #22
May-June 1943 © DC

GALLERY

SUPER RABBIT COMICS #1
1944 © MAR

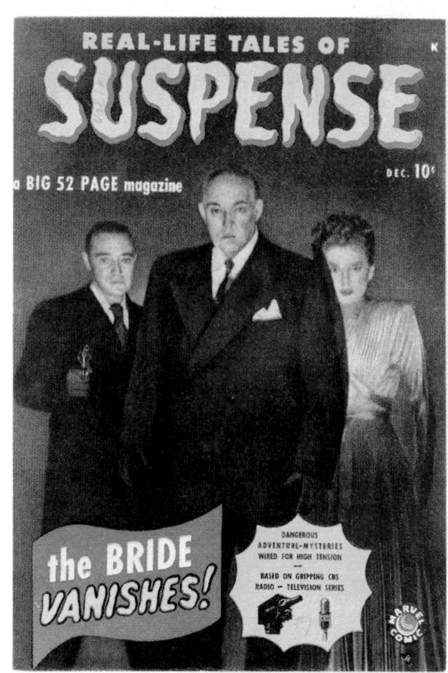

SUSPENSE #1
December 1949 © MAR

TARZAN #17
September-October 1950 © DELL

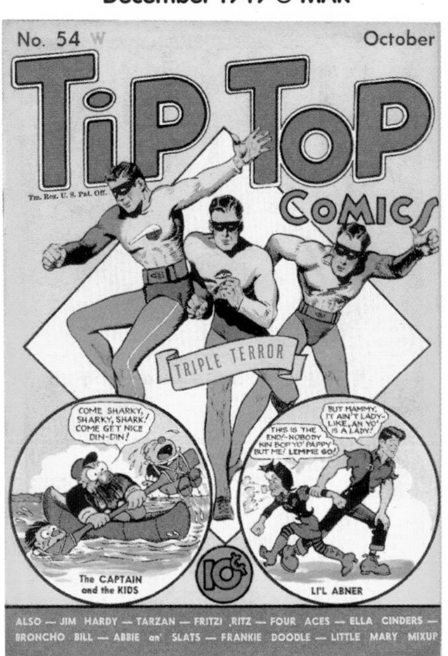

TIP TOP COMICS #54
October 1940 © UFS

C O V E R

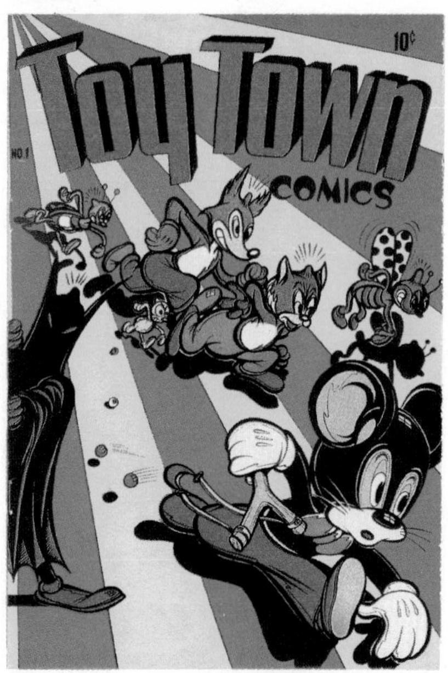

TOY TOWN COMICS #1
1945 © Swappers Quarterly

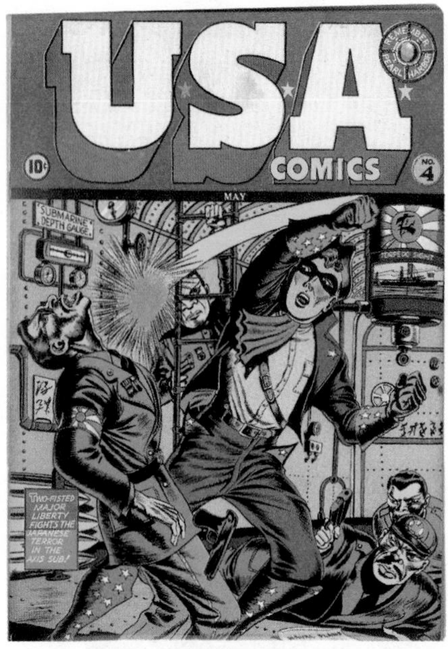

USA COMICS #4
1942 © MAR

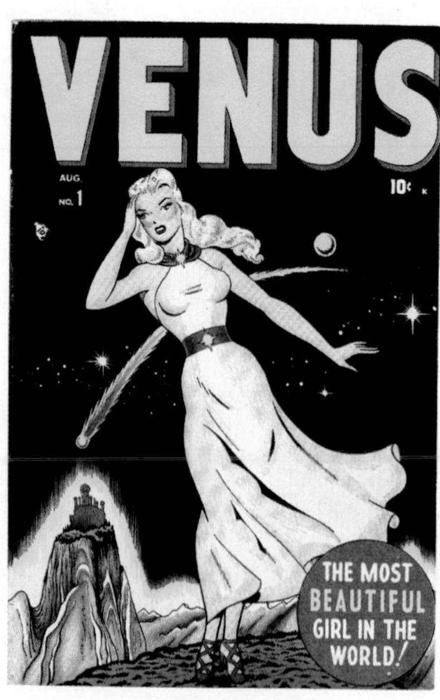

VENUS #1
August 1948 © MAR

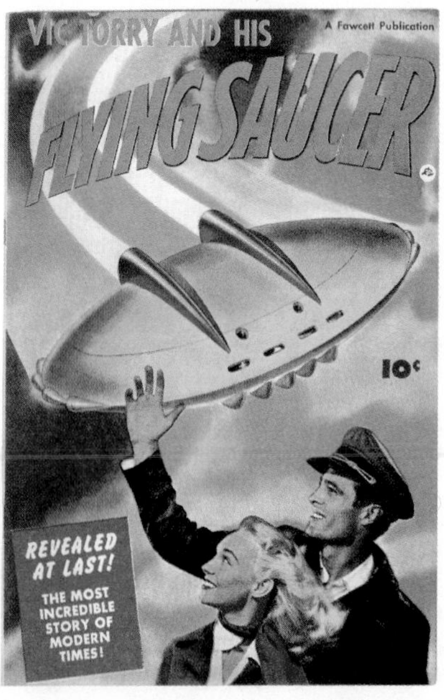

VIC TORRY AND HIS FLYING SAUCER NN
1950 © FAW

GALLERY

WALT DISNEY'S COMICS AND STORIES #22
July 1942 © WDC

WILD WEST #1
Spring 1948 © MAR

WINGS COMICS #79
March 1947 © FH

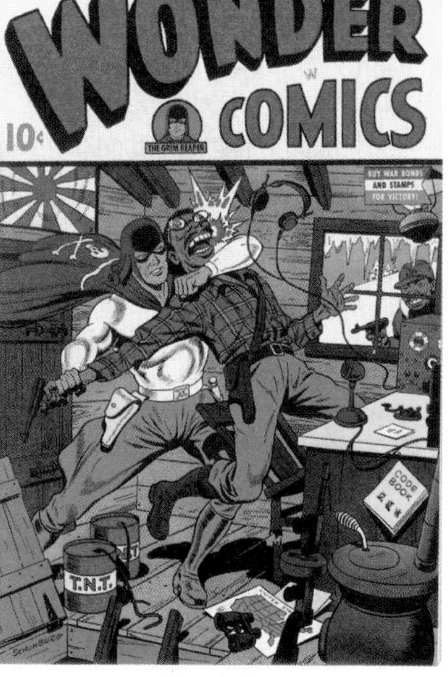

WONDER COMICS #4
February 1945 © BP

COVER GALLERY

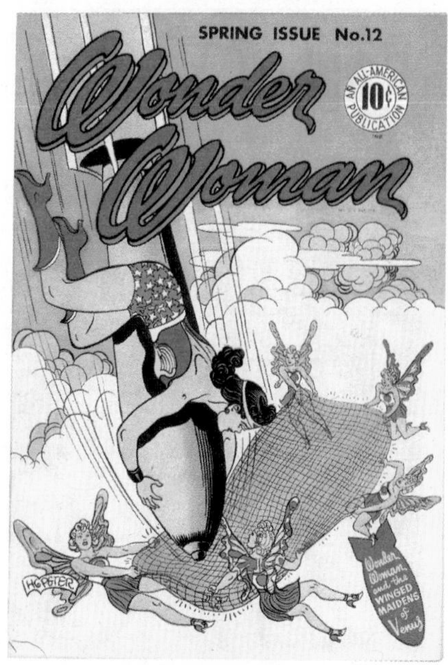

WONDER WOMAN #12
Spring 1945 © DC

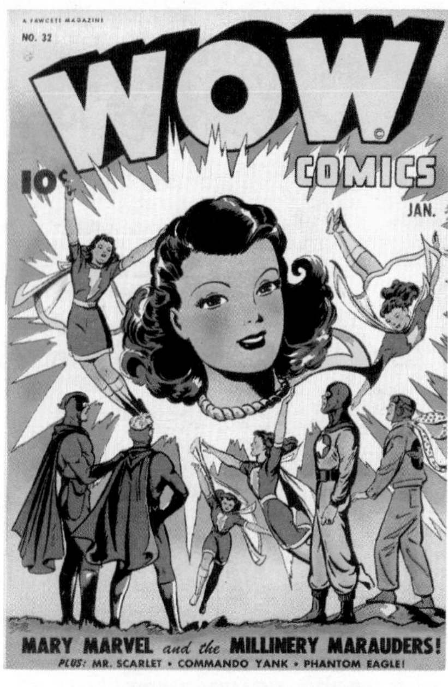

WOW COMICS #32
January 1945 © FAW

X-MEN #7
September 1964 © MAR

ZIP COMICS #20
November 1941 © MLJ

TOYS
The Confident Collector
2nd Edition
Overstreet Presents
Hake's Price Guide to
Character
Toys
OKs
REWARD
BETTER
BREAKFAST
SUPERMAN
MAKE
MINE
MARVEL
Buck Rogers
25th CENTURY
CHEMICAL LABORATORY

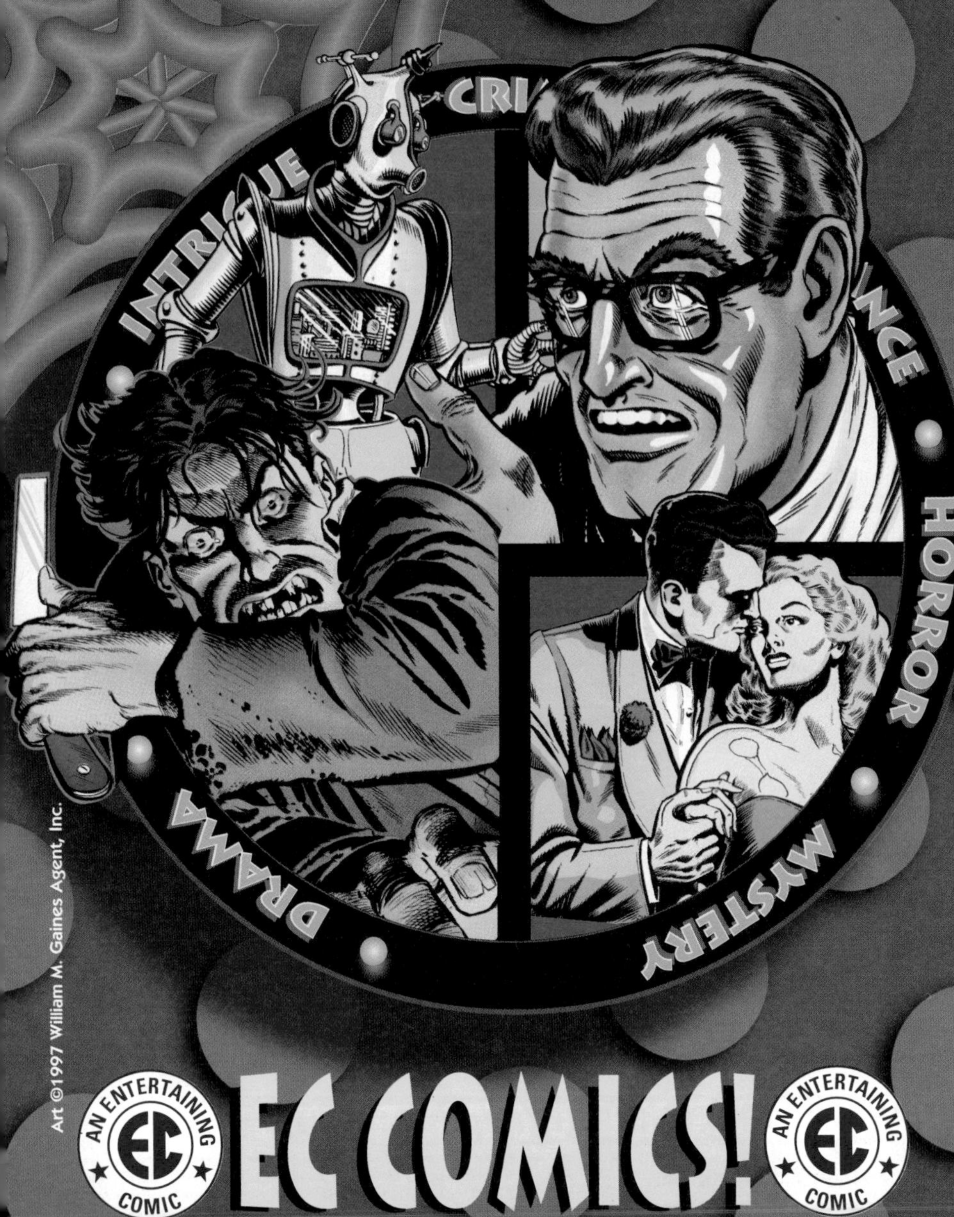
HORROR
MYSTERY
DRAMA

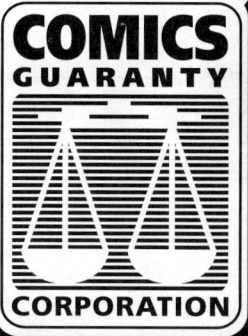

FAN WEBSITE DIRECTORY

New websites are springing up all the time, providing more and more information on various publishers, creators, titles and characters. The following list is a collection of fan-based websites.
If you have a website you'd like to see listed in our directory, visit the Gemstone Publishing website at www.gemstonepub.com and go to The FAN Universe. You will find a submit form; simply fill it out, and e-mail it directly to us. Maybe next time, you'll see YOUR site listed here in the Overstreet Fan Website Directory!

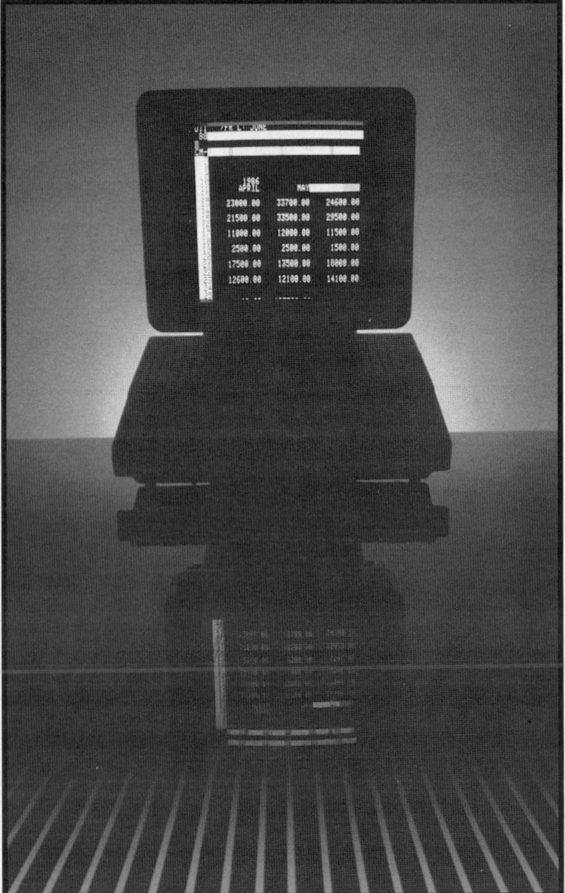

ALEN YEN'S TOYBOXDX
www.ToyboxDX.com
Fan-powered site celebrating the coolness of Japanese comic and animation-related character collectibles. Featuring open-access BBS and Cafe Chogokin weekly chats. Massive link resource list, and over 40 MB of images and AVIs.

ALEX HORLEY
members.xoom.com/horley_art
The Alex Horley website.

ALPHA ZONE
www.geocities.com/Hollywood/Lot/2267/
A huge source of information of **Alpha Flight** by Marvel. Everything from character guides to interactive games

ARTFUL ONLINE
www.geocities.com/SoHo/Studios/3125
Online home to cult 1970s comic strip character Octobriana. Features information on this fascinating character's current appearances in mainstream comics.

THE ATTACK OF THE SECOND STRINGERS
www.flash.net/~jeanneb
Bios of those obscure good guys who turn up in trivia contests.

AVENGERS ASSEMBLE!
www.lads.com/~plexiva/avengers
The first and greatest Avengers site on the Web—news, files, art, bios, chat room, and the infamous Avengers Mailing List!

BATMAN: FOREVER KNIGHT
batman.techv.net
Comprehensive site covering all things related to Batman and Batman-related comic books.

THE BATTLE CHASERS REALM
www.geocities.com/~bladeshadow
This site has everything for your **Battle Chasers** needs. Images, reviews, games, you name it and it's here

BEEK'S BOOKS
www.RZero.com/books/
A guide to many favorite graphic novels and comicbook series, including in-depth reviews of a diverse variety of genres.

BIGBOT.COM - TRANSFORMERS/ BEAST WARS/ BEASTIES
www.bigbot.com/
Your gateway to BeastWars/Transformers info on the Web!

BIRDWATCHING: BLACK CANARY & ORACLE: BIRDS OF PREY
members.tripod.com/~Norya
Perhaps the first and only site devoted to DC's Birds of Prey.

THE BLACK ZONE
http://www.hiprofile.com/blackzone
The Black Zone is "The Official Black Comics Hall of Fame." This is not an EXCLUSIVE BLACK SITE. However, the content of the site will feature contemporary works of African Americans, African Canadians and Blacks alike. The Black Zone will have articles, reviews, and promotion for the works of African American artists, writers, books, publications, and titles dealing with topics of minority comic book themes, characters, titles, writers, and artists.

BRING ON THE BAD GUYS: THE VILLAINS OF MARVEL COMICS
www.sigma.net/burch
A salute to the villains—if not for them, the heroes wouldn't have anything to do!

BUG ZAPPER— THE BLUE BEETLE FAN PAGE
student-www.uchicago.edu/users/smhenry/Beetle/
A fan page dedicated to the Blue Beetle, star of DC and Charlton comics.

CAPTAIN ULTRA!
www.sigma.net/4free-doms/captultra
A tribute to one of Marvel's most under-used, under-appreciated heroes: Captain "I Like Color" Ultra!

CAPTAMER1'S HOME PAGE
http://members.aol.com/CaptAmer1/Capindex.html
For more Captain America information than you can shake a stick at, check out my web page.

THE CATWOMAN CENTER
www.infinet.com/~jsulliva/catwoman/
All things regarding the DC Comic character Catwoman: reviews, essays, pictures and fun.

CBC WEB-MAG
www.sfcentral.com/cbc/
A FREE online web magazine for comic book collectors and readers including reviews, news, interviews, fan art, links, a FREE ad section, and much much more!

CHAOS MOM'S NEXUS
members.xoom.com/chaosmom/
The Nexus is "dead"-icated to Chaos! Comics—where darkness dwells! Mythology, bios and checklists, personalities, 50+ working fan-site links, reviews, and more...Evil Ernie and Lady Death await you in the Nexus.

CHECKER COMICS
www.checkercomics.com
The online presence of Checker Comics Publishing, where you can browse the latest releases and back issues.

CHRONOS: THE HOMEPAGE
www.geocities.com/Area51/Labyrinth/6198/CHRONOSSA.html
The net's first web site dedicated to Chronos II, Walker Gabriel. Includes: Complete list of Appearances, Cover Gallery, the home of the Chronos Index, and much more.

CLARK'S BAR ONLINE
members.xoom.com/apala/clark
It's the online version of the comic fanzine created by some Italian comic fans and containing some interesting reviews, interviews, news, comics, original images. Work in progress

COLLECTING COMICS.COM
www.collecting-comics.com
For everyone that loves comic books. We have everything from creator interviews, comic news, comic reviews, message boards, and a Comic Book Museum showcasing the best comics ever made.

COMIC ART
members.tripod.com/~GILLENTOONS/index-7.html
Comic art and animated gifs.

COMIC ART
www.geocities.com/soho/cafe/6707
Original comic art, including Neal Adams, Carl Barks, John Byrne, Bruce Timm, etc.

THE COMIC BOOK
www.sigma.net/marvel/
One of the most informative, detailed, and resourceful comic sites online, filled with bios, summaries, images, newsletters, games, and tons more.

COMIC BOOK AWARDS ALMANAC
www.enteract.com/~aardy/comics/awards/
An attempt to list, in one place, all awards ever given to comic books.

COMIC BOOK DEBATING CLUB
members.xoom.com/4HorsemenWar/~alancole.html
This site is dedicated to arguing certain aspects of the comic book industry (fights, characters, methods, selling tactics, etc.).

COMIC BOOK NETWORK
members.aol.com/ComicBkNet
Home of the weekly **Comic Book Net Electronic Magazine**—cutting edge news, reviews, opinions, and a trivia contest—free online or by e-mail. PLUS links, convention lists and more!

COMIC BOOK RESOURCES
www.comicbookresources.com/
The resource for comic fans on the web. Industry news, message boards, interviews, huge links database, calendars and much more.

THE COMIC PAGE— YOUR GUIDE TO THE HISTORY OF COMICS
www.dereksantos.com/comicpage/

Dedicated to the history and details of the 100+ year American comic book medium. Also features message boards, polls, free giveaways, and a giant link directory.

COMICFAN
www.colba.net/~minhta
A comic book information center featuring news, reviews, previews, interviews, and a monthly drawing contest with prizes!

COMICPOINT.COM
www.comicpoint.com
Featuring an online database of comics and a directory of comic-related web sites.

COMICS PARAGON
www.comicsparagon.org
Comics Paragon is devoted to bringing you the coolest comic book industry news and the best images.

COMICS 2 FILM
www.comics2film.com
Comics 2 Film tracks the development of comics into movies. Updated with news several times a week. Free e-mail newsletter!

CRAWLSPACE
www.crawlspace.com/
News and info on WildStorm books, links to WildStorm & CliffHanger fansites.

THE CREEPING FLESH
members.tripod.com/~creepingflesh
A personal 'zine site containing reviews of comics, CDs, books, etc.

DANGER GIRL BY CRAWLSPACE
www.dangergirl.com/
Hands down the most comprehensive Danger Girl website on the 'net!

DANGER GIRL ONLINE
dangergirl.simplenet.com
A fan-site dedicated to the action packed comic from Andy Hartnell and J. Scott Campbell. Featuring up to the minute news and all the best images. Updated daily

DAREDEVIL:THE MAN WITHOUT FEAR
www.interlog.com/~mithra/daredevil.html
Site devoted to the Marvel Comics superhero, with news, interviews and much more.

DAVID MACK'S KABUKI
http://www.geocities.com/SoHo/Studios/6561/
The first exhaustive Kabuki web site! Kabuki (c) David Mack

DC COMICS' STARMAN: A COMPENDIUM
users.aol.com/nachro2/starhome.htm
The most complete online source of information on the cult favorite DC series Starman, this site features plot summaries, character profiles, interviews with James Robinson, David Goyer, Tony Harris, and more.

DCU: NEXT GENERATION
members.aol.com/teensdc
For all the latest news and info on DC's teen heroes! Featuring: live creator chats, creator interviews, pro art, newsroom, character bios, fan fic, fan art, discussion board, reviews, upcoming comics, free classifieds, DC teens quiz, and more!

DE LONG'S COMIC PAGE
members.aol.com/tydelong/comic.htm
Typical fan site. I review one book a week, always my favorite. I also have a listing of my favorite comic stories of all time, links, what I buy, etc.

DEADPOOL: MARVEL'S MERC WITH A MOUTH!
www.geocities.com/Area51/Dimension/4062/main.html
A website featuring a comprehensive look at Marvel's favorite Mercenary!

DEADPOOL: THE MERC WITH A MOUTH
www.frontiernet.net/~jrvp/dp/
The best Deadpool fan site out there, and the most comprehensive, t'boot

DISABLED COMIC COLLECTOR'S CLUB
www.airnet.net/kenj/dclub.html
Free Pen-Pal Club for Disabled/Challenged People who collect comicbooks and want to meet new friends who are just like them, and understand about being disabled.

DISCIPLES OF THE BLADE
www.iinet.net.au/~ratty/witchblade
The DOTB is dedicated to quality coverage of this quality comic book. We're also a vibrant and fun web community, so come on over to the DOTB to find other like-minded comics fans like yourself!

DITKO LOOKED UP
www.interlog.com/~ditko37/ditko.html
Unofficial site for Steve Ditko, including three-tiered checklist, scans and original articles.

DIVINE RIGHT BY CRAWLSPACE
www.maxfaraday.com/
A huge fan site for Jim Lee's **Divine Right**—and he's even on the mailing list!

DR. STRANGE: SANCTUM SANCTORUM
www.strange1.chicagonet.net
Dedicated to Marvel's Master of the Mystic Arts. Featuring the latest news on Dr. Strange appearances, series chronologies, character profiles, discussion forum, and mystical links.

DV8 BY CRAWLSPACE
dv8.crawlspace.com/
DV8 images, message board, mad libs and reader reviews!

EC COMICS FROM THE FIFTIES
www.sci.fi/~karielk/eccomics.htm
EC titles, issues, genres and reprints. Lists of selected readings about EC Comics and EC artists.

THE ELDER GODS' RAVE
members.tripod.com/~eldergodsrave
A personal 'zine site covering such topics as comics, movies, books, television, games and whatever else strikes the author's fancy.

EVERYTHING'S ARCHIE
www.sigma.net/archie
Everything's Archie is THE coolest website on the 'net dedicated to that crazy gang from Riverdale. Currently, it features reviews, historical information (concering **Archie Comics**), links, trivia, a message

board, and more. In fact, it even contains a section dedicated to The Mighty Crusaders!

THE FACETED SKELETON
members.aol.com/ aliens25

The Faceted Skeleton - The fan may grow up to one day transition into working on writing, drawing, inking, lettering, coloring, printing, distributing, and/or retailing; wherefore, contributing to a finished product that ends up back in the hands of a fan. This site is a rapport and reflective touchstone for fans within this metaphorical framework.

FANDOM DIRECTORY
www.fandata.com

Your on-line link to Fandom around the world! Science Fiction, Star Trek, Comics, Trading Cards, Gaming and More! Point and click access to thousands of fan, collector, dealer, store, publisher, club and convention email addresses and web sites. Listings are FREE!

FANS OF TERI SUE WOOD
www.sentex.net/ ~jnorthey/TSW/

Dedicated to the great Teri Sue Wood, creator of **Wandering Star**.

FANZING: THE INDEPENDENT ONLINE DC COMICS FAN MAGAZINE
www.fanzing.com

An independent online DC comics fan magazine that features monthly columns and articles, interviews, reviews, original fan artwork and fiction stories devoted to DC comics characters and comic books.

FATHOM ONE
come.to/fathomone

Fathom One is the first site ever dedicated to Michael Turner's **Fathom**. This award winning database features everything you need to know about the comic and then some, and is updated almost everyday.

FIN WORLD— THE UNOFFICIAL SAVAGE DRAGON PAGE
www.neudesign.com/ savagedragon/

The original Savage Dragon page on the Web, still going strong! Constantly updated, a Fin Addict's heaven online!

FLASH: THOSE WHO RIDE THE LIGHTNING
www.pobox.com/ ~kelson/flash/

A "Who's Who" of DC's speedsters, plus supporting characters, allies, and enemies.

4-COLOR REVIEW
4colorreview. simplenet.com

Regularly updated reviews, news, previews of and columns on comic books, from the biggest publishers to the smallest indies.

4 FREEDOMS PLAZA
www.sigma.net/ 4freedoms

Dedicated to the **Fantastic Four**, this site covers all aspects of the "World's Greatest Comic Magazine!"

GEN13 BY CRAWLSPACE
www.gen13.com/

A comprehensive Gen13 site with daily image additions—over 800 images in the gallery.

GHENT'S STAR WARS COMICS REPORT
theforce.net/comics

Up-to-date news and reviews of all **Star Wars** comics, new and old.

THE GHOST RIDER PROTECTION FRONT
members.tripod.com/ ~Ghostrider2/index.html

This site is devoted to the return of Ghost Rider to the pages of a monthly comic. It contains news, downloads, and a poll.

GOLD KEY RESEARCH DATABASE
www.oz.net/~fur/ comics/gk.htm

A complete list of all Gold Key Comics in a searchable page formatted for IE 4+ browsers. Text-only, also available.

GOLDEN AGE BATMAN SITE
www.ocsonline.com/ ~bjourdain

Devoted to the Golden Age Batman and contains cover reprints, index of stories, reprint index and other helpful information.

THE GOOD GUYS & GALS OF THE GOLDEN-AGE
members.tripod.com/ ~mysterymen

Come explore the past with us on this exciting journey into the Who's Who of the Golden Age of Comics. See the way it really was, with concise biographies of heroes and heroines as they truly happened. See pictures of those great Good Guys and Gals from the Glorious Golden Age of Comics.

GOTHIK APA
members.tripod.com/ ~gothikapa

An Amateur Press Association devoted to comics which push the boundaries of what comics can be. Such as: **Bone**, **Castle Waiting**, **Hate**, **Love & Rockets**, **Preacher**, **Sandman**, etc.

GREEN LANTERN CORPS WEB PAGE
www.glcorps.org/

Huge resource site with profiles and pictures of nearly every Green Lantern ever known.

HI PROFILE
http://www.hiprofile.com

One of the highest quality and most comprehensive web sites on the net, focusing on the creative talents of the comic book industry. Hi Profile is dedicated to the uplifting of those creative talents that make the comic industry function.

THE HIGHLY UNOFFICIAL, UNAUTHORIZED PIRATE PAGE OF MARVEL COMICS IMAGES
members.aol.com/ Marvel2Day/MC.html

For those who still believe Kirby is king, Ditko dazzles, and Stan the Man began the plan.

THE HISTORY OF SUPERHERO COMIC BOOKS!
www.geocities.com/ Athens/8580/

100+ years of comic book history! Cover scans, character and creator biographies, fun and educational! Used by schools, teachers and students.

HOUSE OF PARADOX
www.geocities.com/ Area51/Chamber/6234

Comic reviews in the "Dox Report," Dox's Cool Thing of the Week Award, artwork, and CeleBabes of the Week.

THE HOUSE OF VERTIGO
members.xoom.com/ Vertigo_page

A central guide to DC's Mature Readers imprint, featuring the Vertigo Discussion List, fan fiction, and fan art.

HOWARD THE DUCK FAN PAGE
hjem.get2net.dk/d_archer/HTD_Fan.htm

Cover pages and movie items to the History of Howard the Duck—Marvel's only Hero without super powers; hatched By Steve Gerber.

IMAGES UNPLUGGED
welcome.to/imagesunplugged

Large site of over 55MB of images from Wildstorm, Top Cow, Cliffhanger and Image. Wizard TGTC Top10 and BuzzBin, and more.

INCOMPLETE COMICBOOK ARTIST CHECKLIST
www.casema.net/~pafrankn/

This site contains checklists of some of the greatest artists in world of comics.

INCREDIBLE HULK—EARTH'S MIGHTIEST MORTAL
www.netside.com/~chl3/index.html

An incredible resource for information about the Hulk's powers history, various incarnations, merchandise, friends, foes and much more.

INVISIBLES - THE BOMB
www.btinternet.com/~orlando/bomb/

Readers' resource for Grant Morrison's DC Vertigo subversive epic.

JAYCE'S TOO KEWL FOR YOU GEN13 WEBSITE
www.se.mediaone.net/~jbacani/gen_13.html

One of the oldest, yet one of the most original Gen13 websites out on the net!!! A must visit for the complete Gen13 fan!!!

JAZMA UNIVERSE ONLINE!
www.twmgrafix.com/jazma

We promote amateur and professional comic book artwork, scripts, storylines and unpublished comic books! We have reviews, interviews, a message board, hot links and the online comic book, The Legendary Dark Silhouette!

JLA HEADQUARTERS
members.aol.com/MSR77/headquarters.html

A website dedicated to the modern incarnation of the greatest team of heroes on the face of the Earth, the Justice League of America. The site also includes a section on **Young Justice**.

JOE ACEVEDO'S CUSTOM ACTION FIGURES
members.aol.com/JoeAce

Custom action figures of DC Comics and AC Comics characters.

THE JUSTICE LEAGUE GALLERY
members.xoom.com/can3boy

A gallery dedicated to the JLA. Witness the Justice League of America at their best.

KABUKI TOUCH THE SUN
members.xoom.com/red_branch/shi

Description of Kabuki story. Images of books, art, and links to other Kabuki sites.

KEITH GIFFEN'S FAN BITE BACK
www.es.co.nz/~darrens/giffen.html

All the stuff you ever wanted to know about the creative force behind Lobo, Ambush Bug, The Heckler and lots more besides.

THE LEGION OF SUPER-RESOURCES
www.idyllmtn.com/rac/dc/lsh/lsh_res.htm

A comprehensive listing of resources on and off the internet, dedicated to **The Legion of Super-Heroes** in all their incarnations.

MARVEL ATLAS PROJECT
www.sigma.net/4freedoms/MAP

Ever wonder where Latveria or Wakanda really is? Use the M.A.P. to find anyplace in the Marvel Universe.

MARVEL CHRONOLOGY PROJECT
www.geocities.com/Hollywood/7735/mcp.htm

Listing every appearance of every Marvel character...in chronological order.

THE MARVEL FAMILY WEB
shazam.imginc.com

The Marvel Family Web is devoted to the original Captain Marvel and members of his family as well as all the other great Fawcett characters!

METAL RE:GEX'S AWESOME DOMAIN
welcome.to/MetalREGEX

The best Awesome Comic database on the entire internet at your finger tips.

MICHAEL TOMIAK'S COMIC PAGES
www.ping.de/sites/wolverine/index.html

A great jumping-on-point for new readers and people who want to learn about the different series. A short synopsis is given to each series that is presented, inlcuding the reasons why they are worth reading.

MORBIUS: TALES OF THE LIVING VAMPIRE
www.wild.net/~gkaiser/morbius2.phtml

A comprehensive site devoted to Marvel's living vampire, featuring complete appearances listing, art, reference guide, and an ongoing fan fiction series.

THE MUTANT PAGE
www.santarosa.edu/~sthoemke/x/x.html

Marvel's Merry Mutant X-Men Universe

THE NEXT MEN REFERENCE
members.aol.com/tsmith1544/jbnm.html

The most comprehensive site of **John Byrne's Next Men** information.

THE OFFICIAL BRYAN TALBOT FANPAGE
www.bryan-talbot.com/

The definitive place for all information on Bryan Talbot (author of **One Bad Rat** and **The Adventures of Luther Arkwright**), including biographies, stripographies, image galleries and more.

PAUL MICHAEL KANE'S IMAGINATION
www.epix.net/~pmkane

A nifty site all around, but comic fans will find the Nightwing Art Gallery of special interest. Represented here are over 30 interpretations of the former Boy Wonder drawn by commissioned professional and amateur artists...and it keeps getting bigger!

PHOENIX APA WEB SITE
www.eaze.net/~oz/phoenix
This is the official site of Phoenix APA, which is dedicated to comics, science fiction, writing and art.

PIPELINE COMMENTARY AND REVIEW
www.nic.com/~augie/pipeline
Weekly commentary on the comic book industry and reviews of recent and not-so-recent comic books.

PLANET OF THE APES INTERNATIONAL FAN CLUB
www.dlcwest.com/~comicsape/ape.htm
Website devoted to the movies, memorabilia, and Marvel & Adventure Comics products!

POST MORTEM
www.redhillsonline.com
A dark comedy about zombies, acid, seventies super-flies, mad scientists, and the concentration camp known as Post Mortem (which used to be the state of North Dakota).

PSYCHIC DONUT PRODUCTIONS
www.crackbaby.com
Home of Crackbaby—the world's most loveable drug addict!!!

THE PUNISHER ONLINE
webhome.idirect.com/~jasantan
The definitive resource for all things Punisher, drawing from the past 24 years of comics, media, and merchandise.

RIBMAN: THE SITE HAT BITES
www.ribman.net
A low-level superhero strives to be amongst the ranks of the legends. It is a comedic approach to the entire genre.

ROLAND: DAYS OF WRATH
www.rolandcomic.com
The official website of the roland comic!

SABRE'S EDGE
www.sabresedge.com
The official site for indi comic company Sabre's Edge. Inside info on Cancer: The Crab Boy, Darkside Daydreams, and ANDI:RAGGEDY NATION. Also on the site: original freefonts, a comic "primer" and lotsa' pretty pictures!

SDTV COMIC BOOK PUBLISHERS CHANNEL LIST
www.SmartDigitalTelevision.com/comicbooks.html
A complete guide to comic book publisher websites on the World Wide Web.

SEQUENTIAL ELLISON: THE HARLAN ELLISON COMIC BOOK BIBLIOGRAPHY
www.enteract.com/~chrisday/Ellison/
Sequential Ellison is a disgustingly detailed listing, organization, and bibliographic reference exploring the comic book and comic book related work of the award-winning writer Harlan Ellison.

SEQUENTIAL TART
www.sequentialtart.com
sequential tart (si-kwen'shel tart) n.— 1. a Web Zine about the comics industry published by an eclectic band of women; 2. a publication dedicated to providing exclusive interviews, in-depth articles and news, while working towards raising the awareness of women's influence in the comics industry and other realms.

SNAP JUDGMENTS ONLINE REVIEWS
www.snapjudgments.com
Weekly reviews of new comics, with additional reviews added daily.

THE SOURCE
www.geocities.com/Area51/Stargate/3999/
Dedicated to the **Fourth World** works of Jack Kirby.

SPLAT GRAPHICS
home1.gte.net/clarknt1/index.htm
Home of Splat Graphics and Owner of Comics Index.com...just you wait!

SQUADRON SUPREME: OTHER-EARTH'S MIGHTIEST HEROES
www.geocities.com/Area51/Stargate/4489/main.html
A database dedicated to the Squadron Supreme.

STORM XPRESS
www.geocities.com/TelevisionCity/Studio/2542/
It was the #1 site dedicated to Storm! The only windrider in Marvel comics! Lots of information and stuff that you can feast your eyes on! Storm Xpress was voted by Storm's fans as the best site dedicated to Storm!

SUPERGIRL'S WALLY: FACT OR FICTION?
members.xoom.com/rip_hunter/
Ever meet God? Ever meet Wally? In-depth annotations of all appearances made by the supporting character, Wally. Wally's List of Appearances, and the Wally Who's Who entry.

THE SUPER-RUBBER-CATS FREE ON-LINE COMICS
pages.citenet.net/users/ctmx3276
3 techno-soldiers must stop 4 deadly aliens running loose on earth. LOTS of action and FX.

THE SWAMP
www.es.co.nz/~darrens/mtmain.html
Information and links regarding Man-Thing as well as some of the other Muck Monsters.

TRUCKSTOP
www.trukstop.com
Online portfolio and gallery featuring freelance work for DC Comics and also my concert poster design work.

TWILIGHT OF THE DAWN
members.aol.com/evildoodah/twilight/
Fan site devoted to the works of Joseph Michael Linsner with an emphasis on Dawn.

THE ULTIMATE HELLBLAZER INDEX
members.tripod.com/~hellblazer666
A site which catalogs all the appearances of John Constantine both in his own comic, **Hellblazer**, and in other titles.

THE UNCANNY X-PAGE HOTLIST
x-page.com/hotlist/
More links to X-Men related sites and information than anyone else on the web. Updated regularly, and featuring an "X-Page of the Week" to spotlight the best new X-Men sites out there.

THE UNOFFICIAL AQUAMAN WEBSITE
www.eskimo.com/~tegan/aqua/index.html
A page that covers Aquaman in all his incarnations.

UNOFFICIAL CHARLES VESS PAGE
www.mindspring.com/~elixia/bizarre/vess.html
A fan site dedicated to comics artist and illustrator Charles Vess, known from **Sandman**, **Stardust**, and **The Book of Ballads and Sagas** among other projects.

THE UNOFFICIAL CHUCK TAINE WEBSITE
members.tripod.com/~Bouncing_Boy/CTaine/
A website dedicated to Chuck Taine, who appears in the **Legion of Super-Heroes** titles.

THE UNOFFICIAL CYCLOPS HOME PAGE
www.best.com/~cgriffen/cyclops/
Dedicated to the fearless leader of Marvel Comics' X-Men!

THE UNOFFICIAL DC COMICS BIG EVENTS HOMEPAGE
www.geocities.com/Area51/Labyrinth/6198/events.html
From Pre-Crisis to Crisis and Kingdom and beyond. Includes: Complete Checklist, Core Issue Cover Galleries, series bios, complete Annual checklist, and much more.

THE UNOFFICIAL GUIDE TO THE DC UNIVERSE
welcome.to/the.DC.Guide/
A web-based encyclopedia of the DC Universe, including **Who's Who** profiles, issue-by-issue indexes, and a history of the DC Universe.

THE UNOFFICIAL IMPULSE WEBSITE
www/geocities.com/Athens/Troy/7023
One of the best fan sites about Impulse, the coolest of DC characters. Here you will find a lot about our little friend and his world.

UNOFFICIAL INDEX TO SGT. FURY & HIS HOWLING COMMANDOS
members.aol.com/FuryHowler/index.html
Information on every **Sgt. Fury** issue plus a cover gallery.

THE UNOFFICIAL JAE LEE HOME PAGE
members.tripod.com/~jae_lee
This page feature Jae Lee's spectacular comic book art. It also includes previews, a comic list, a gallery and links.

THE UNOFFICIAL METAL MEN PAGE
www.rpi.edu/~foutzl
A site dedicated to the DC Comics' super-hero team Metal Men.

THE UNOFFICIAL RIP HUNTER... TIME MASTER HOMEPAGE
www.geocities.com/Area51/Labyrinth/6198/
In-depth annotations of Time Masters, complete Rip Hunter and The Linear Men appearences, Who's Who, cover galleries, and much more.

THE UNOFFICIAL SPIDER-MAN SITE
www.sigma.net/spiderman
The most complete Spider-Man reference site on the Internet, incorporating Peter Parker's Pad, a monthly e-zine featuring reviews of the latest **Spider-Man** comics, plus news and editorials on everything in the Spider-Verse. Reviews, Quizzes, Images, Icons, Sounds, Themes, History, Profiles, Games, Books, Fan Fiction—has to be seen to be believed.

THE UNOFFICIAL SUPERBOY WEBSITE!
fly.to/superboy
Everything you need to know about Superboy, from past to present and beyond. Lots of exclusives, shocking interviews, breaking news, comprehensive bios, and much, much, more!!!!!

THE UNOFFICIAL TEEN TITANS HOMEPAGE
titans.simplenet.com/titan.htm
A detailed listing of the Titans past and present including synopsis of every book they've appeared in along with character bios, cover scans, and much, much more.

WAHOO! LINKS DIRECTORY - YOUR GUIDE TO COMICS ON THE INTERNET
www.dereksantos.com/wahoo/
Contains hundreds of quality links to comic-related websites, organized into dozens of easy-to-use categories

THE WOMEN OF MARVEL COMICS
www.geocities.com/Hollywood/2855
A salute to the oft-overlooked heroines of Marvel Comics

X-FAN
www.wvinter.net/~phlipcat/xfan/x-fan.htm
X-Fan is the most complete X-Men reference site! Features, reviews, cover scans, character bios, title overviews, charts price guides and heaps more!

THE XENA COMIC BOOKS WEBSITE
www.eskimo.com/~tegan/xena/index.html
A website that hopes to clear up any confusion surrounding the various Xena comic books and her other appearances as a comic book character.

YOUNG JUSTICE: THE HANGOUT
www.geocities.com/Area51/Nebula/9376/
This site is dedicated to Young Justice, DC Comics' newest superhero team. The site is also home, to the Young Justice Experience Webring.

YOUNG JUSTICE HOME PAGE
welcome.to/YoungJustice
A website dedicated to the young heroes Robin, Superboy, Impulse, Arrowette, Wondergirl, Secret, and their mentor Red Tornado, who make up DC's newest team, Young Justice.

Mile High Money!

After 25 years in the business, I've come to the conclusion that there's never going to be a find of any type of collectibles as incredible as the late Edgar Church's collection of comics.

In fact, it's my goal to reunite that collection. That's why we're publishing an exclusive "Buy List" for comics from the Mile High Collection and paying instant cash in multiples of Guide for the right comics.

This is going to be an on-going project. You can find the latest edition of the Buy List on-line at www.diamondgalleries.com.. This list quotes the prices we're offering in addition to the titles we're looking for.

If you've got one or more comics from the Mile High Collection (particularly those NM to NM+), I urge you to review our Buy List at once.

Stephen A. Geppi

Chief Executive Officer
and Owner
Diamond International Galleries

DAVID T. ALEXANDER
David Alexander Comics
Tampa, FL

DAVE ANDERSON
Want List Comics
Tulsa, OK

ROBERT BEERBOHM
Robert Beerbohm
Comic Art
Fremont, NE

JON BERK
Collector
Hartford, CT

GARY CARTER
Editor, CBM
Coronado, CA

JOHN CHRUSCINSKI
Tropic Comics
Plantation, FL

GARY COLABUONO
Classics International Ent.
Elk Grove Village, IL

BILL COLE
Bill Cole Enterprises, Inc.
Archival Preservation Supplies
Randolph, MA

LARRY CURCIO
Avalon Comics
Boston, MA

GARY DOLGOFF
Gary Dolgoff Comics
Easthampton, MA

CONRAD ESCHENBERG
Comic & Original Art
Collector/Dealer
Cold Spring, NY

RICHARD EVANS
President AACBC
Bedrock City Comics
Houston, TX

STEPHEN FISHLER
Metropolis Collectibles
New York, NY

STEVEN GENTNER
Golden Age Specialist
Portland, OR

MICHAEL GOLDMAN
Motor City Comics
Southfield, MI

JAMIE GRAHAM
Graham Crackers
Chicago, IL

DANIEL GREENHALGH
Showcase New England
Northford, CT

ERIC J. GROVES
Dealer/Collector
Oklahoma City, OK

ROBERT HALL
Collector
Harrisburg, PA

BRUCE HAMILTON
Hamilton Comics
Prescott, AZ

JOHN HAUSER
Dealer/Collector
New Berlin, WI

BILL HOWARD
Collector
San Francisco, CA

BILL HUGHES
Executive Collectibles
Roanoke, TX

ROB HUGHES
Arch Angels
Manhattan Beach, CA

JOSEPH KOCH
Dealer/Collector
Brooklyn, NY

PHIL LEVINE
Dealer/Collector
Three Bridges, NJ

SENIOR ADVISORS

HARRY MATETSKY
Collector
Middletown, NJ

JON McCLURE
Dealer/Collector
Newport, OR

PETER MEROLO
Collector
Sedona, AZ

MICHAEL NAIMAN
Silver Age Specialist
San Diego, CA

MATT NELSON
Classic Conservations
New Orleans, LA

RICHARD OLSON
Dealer/Collector
Slidell, LA

JIM PAYETTE
Golden Age Specialist
Bethlehem, NH

CHRIS PEDRIN
Pedrin Conservatory
Redwood City, CA

RON PUSSELL
Redbeard's Book Den
Crystal Bay, NV

TODD REZNIK
Pacific Comic Exchange
Los Angeles, CA

ROBERT ROGOVIN
Four Color Comics
New York, NY

RORY ROOT
Comic Relief
Berkeley, CA

ROBERT ROTER
Pacific Comic Exchange
Los Angeles, CA

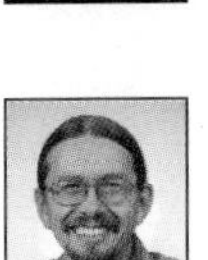

CHUCK ROZANSKI
Mile High Comics
Denver, CO

MATT SCHIFFMAN
Bronze Age Specialist
Aloha, OR

DAVID SMITH
Fantasy Illustrated
Rocket Comics
Seattle, WA

JOHN SNYDER
Diamond Int. Galleries
Timonium, MD

CRAIG SOIFER
Comic Shop Owner
Bronx, NY

TONY STARKS
Silver Age Specialist
Evansville, IN

TERRY STROUD
Dealer/Collector
Santa Monica, CA

DOUG SULIPA
"Everything 1960-1996"
Manitoba, Canada

JOE VERENEAULT
JHV Associates
Woodbury Heights, NJ

JERRY WEIST
Sotheby's
New York, NY

MARK WILSON
World's Finest Comics
Castle Rock, WA

HARLEY YEE
Dealer/Collector
Detroit, MI

VINCENT ZURZOLO, JR.
Vincent's Collectibles
Belle Harbor, NY

A-1 Comics
Brian Peets
5800 Madison Ave.
Sacramento, CA 95841
916.331.9203
a1comics@a-1comics.com

All About Books & Comics
Brian Johnson
517 East Camelback Road
Phoenix, AZ 85012
602.277.0757
mike@all-about-comics.com

Amazing Comics
Bob Nastasi
12 Gillette Ave
Sayville, NY 11782-3123
516.567.8069
mooch@pb.net

The American Comic Book Co.
Terry Stroud
P.O.Box 23
Santa Monica, CA 90406
818.505.1462

Arch Angels
Rob Hughes
1116 8th Street #106
Manhattan, CA 90266
310.335.1359
rhughes@archangels.com

Avalon Comics
Larry Curcio
P.O. Box 821
Medford, MA 02155
617.262.5544

Bedrock City Comic Co.
Richard Evans
6521 Westheimer
Houston, TX 77057
713.780.0675
bedrock@flash.net

CB Comics Plus
Brian and Carol Morris
P.O. Box 3792
Champaign, IL 61826-3792
217.398.0155
bkmorris@prairienet.org

Clarence Road Productions
Dale & Sheri Moore
631 N. Trafton #2
Tacoma, WA 98403
253.274.8274
crinc6@webtv.net

Classic Conservations
Matt Nelson
P.O. Box 2335
Slidell, LA 70459
504.639.0621

The Comic Art Foundation
Eric Groves
P.O. Box 1414
Oklahoma City, OK 73101
405.236.5303

The Comic Book Store
Michael Tierney
9307 Treasure Hill
Little Rock, AR 72227
501.227.9777

Comic Detectives
Dan & Kim Fogel/Jim Pitts/Rick Calou
P.O. Box 629
Menlo Park, CA 94026-0629
510.758.0688
tgfogel@aol.com

Comic Heaven
John Verzyl
P.O. Box 900
Big Sandy, TX 75755
903.636.5555

Comics Ina Flash!
Tony Starks
P.O. Box 3611
Evansville, IN 47735
812.867.1149
comicflash@aol.com

Compleat Comics Company
Perry Margolin
1728-E Kaahumanu Ave.
Wailuku, HI 96793
808.242.5875

David T. Alexander's Comics
David T. Alexander
P. O. Box 273086
Tampa, FL 33618
813.968.1805
dtacoll@tampa.mindspring.com

Doc Robinson's Comics
Doc Robinson
687 N. High St.; Suite 3A
Columbus, OH 43215
888.266.9362

Doug Sulipa's Comic World
Doug Sulipa
Box #21986
Steinbach, Manitoba
Canada R5G 1B5
204.346.3674

Eldorado Comics
Austin Flinn
2110 E. Rt. 70
Cherry Hill, NJ 08034
609.489.1199
eldorado@uscom.com

Emerald City
Chad Rivard
2475-L McMullen Booth Rd
Clearwater, FL 33759
727.797.0664
Cowardlylion@emeraldcitycomics.com

Conrad Eschenberg
Route 1, Box 204-A
Cold Spring, NY 10516
914.265.2649
comicart@pcrealm.net

Fantasy Illustrated
David Smith
P.O. Box 30183
Seattle, WA 98103
206.784.7300
rocket@jetcity.com

Flying Color Comics
Joe Field
2980 Treat Blvd.
Concord, CA 94518
925.825.5410
flyingcolorscomics@compuserve.com

Four Color Comics
Robert Rogovin
115 W. 27th St.
New York, NY 10001
212.675.6990
Keybooks@aol.com

Funny Business Comics Ltd.
Dr. Roger Smyth
660B Amsterdam Ave.
New York, NY 10025
212.799.9477

Gary Dolgoff Comics
Gary Dolgoff
116 Pleasant St.
Easthampton, MA 01027
413.529.0326
gdcomics@javanet.com

Steven Gentner
2430 SW 83rd Avenue
Portland, OR 97225
503.228.7221

Geoffrey's Comics
Geoffrey Patterson
15530 Crenshaw Blvd.
Gardena, CA 90249
888.538.3198

Golden Age Collectables Ltd.
Rod B. Dyke
1501 Pike Place Marketplace #401
Seattle, WA 98101
206.622.9799

Graham Crackers
Jamie Graham
1271 Rickert Dr., Suite 135
Naperville, IL 60540
630.778.0700

ADVISORS

John M. Hauser
P.O. Box 510673
New Berlin, WI 53151-0673
414.789.8227
JMHComics@aol.com

JHV Associates
Joe Vereneault
P.O. Box 317
Woodbury Hts., NJ 08097
609.845.4010

L.E.B. Enterprise
Lauren Becker
3411 Heron Point Ct.
Waterford, MI 48328
248.706.0886
Comiclord@aol.com

Lee's Comics
Mark Crane
Lee Hester
3783 El Camino Real
Palo Alto, CA 94306
650.493.3957
lee@lcomics.com

Jon McClure
P.O. Box 2406
Newport, OR 97365
541.574.9376
MCCL@newportnet.com

Metro Comics
Chris Bonham
6 W. Anapamu
Santa Barbara, CA 93101
805.963.2168
metrocomix@aol.com

Metropolis Comics
Stephen Fishler
873 Broadway #201
New York, NY 10003
212.260.4147
comicbooks@earthlink.net

Mile High Comics
Chuck Rozanski
2151 West 56th Avenue
Denver, CO 80221
303.455.2659
chuck@milehighcomics.com

John Mlachnik
P.O. Box 69
Chisolm, MN 55719
218.254.3763

Motor City Comics
Michael Goldman
Gary Bishop
19785 W. 12 Mile Rd, Ste. 231
Southfield, MI 48076
248.426.8059

Michael Naiman
P.O. Box 151029
San Diego, CA 92175-1029
619.465.2669

New Dimension Comics
Todd McDevitt
20550 Route 19
Cranberry Township, PA 16066-7520
724.776.0433
NDC@SGI.NET

Pacific Comic Exchange
Robert Roter & Todd Reznik
P.O. Box 34849
Los Angeles, CA 90034
310.836.7234
sales@pcei.com

Pegasus Hobbies
John Franco
6554 Greenleaf Ave.
Whittier, CA 90601
562.907.4663

Phil's Classics
Phil Gaudino
49 Park Ave.
Port Washington, NY 11050
516.883.5659
prospect19@aol.com

Quantum Comics/ Marketing
Kevin J. Cleary
2490 Black Rock Tpk #290
Fairfield, CT 06430
203.336.9511
quantumcomics@juno.com

Rare Books & Comics
Jim Payette
P.O. Box 750
Bethlehem, NH 03574-0750
603.869.2097

Redbeard's Book Den
Ron Pussell
P.O. Box 217
Crystal Bay, NV 89402-0217
775.831.4848
redbeard@comic-art.com

Robert Beerbohm Comic Art
Robert Beerbohm
P.O. Box 507
Fremont, NE 68026
402.727.4071
beerbohm@teknetwork.com

RTS Unlimited Inc.
Tim Collins
P.O. Box 150412
Lakewood, CO 80215-0412
303.403.1840

San Diego Comics & Collectibles
Greg Pharis
6937 El Cajon
San Diego, CA 92115
619.698.1177

Matt Schiffman
4475 S.W. Scottie Pl.
Aloha, OR 97007
503.356.1124

Showcase New England
Dan Greenhalgh
67 Gail Dr.
Northford, CT 06472
203.484.4579

Sincere Comics
David Sincere
4667 Airport Blvd.
Regency Square
Mobile, AL 36608
334.342.2603
sincerecomics@pen.net

Terry's Comics
Terry O'Neill
P.O. Box 471
Atwood, CA 92811
714.288.8993

Tropic Comics
John Chruscinski
313 S. State Rd. #7
Plantation, FL 33317
954.587.8878

Vincent's Collectibles
Vincent Zurzolo, Jr.
424 Beach 134th Street
Belle Harbor, NY 11694
718.318.2423
vincentcoll@earthlink.net

Want List Comics
Dave Anderson
P.O. Box 701932
Tulsa, OK 74170-1932
918.299.0440

World's Finest Comics
Mark Wilson
P.O. Box 340
Castle Rock WA 98611
360.274.9163
Mark.Wilson@worldsfinestcomics.com

WOW Comics
Craig Soifer
2395 West Chester Avenue
Bronx, NY 10461
718.829.0461

Harley Yee
P.O. Box 51758
Livonia, MI 48151-5758
800.731.1029

ADVERTISERS' DIRECTORY

A

B

C

D

E

F

G

H

I

J

K

L

M